2011

NEW YORK LAWYERS DIARY

AND

MANUAL®

Bar Directory of the State of New York

ONE HUNDREDTH TWELFTH YEAR OF PUBLICATION

LAWYERS DIARY and MANUAL®

NEW YORK LAWYERS DIARY AND MANUAL®

240 Mulberry Street, P.O. Box 50

Newark, N.J. 07101-0050

(973) 642-1440

(800) 444-4041

FAX: (973) 642-4280

E-mail: mail@lawdiary.com

Visit our web site at http://www.lawdiary.com

PREFACE

We proudly present the one hundred twelfth edition of the *New York Lawyers Diary and Manual*® including the Bar Directory of New York. We are also very pleased to continue as your reference of choice for and about the communities of law and government.

At press time, the Governor, Attorney General, Comptroller, and many of the judges and officials listed in this edition were subject to election. We are pleased to offer our post-election supplement to this edition, detailing changes in these listings resulting from the November 2, 2010 election and other post-press changes to this volume, free on our web site at http://www.lawdiary.com.

We acknowledge with thanks the cooperation of the judges and clerks of the various courts, federal, state and city officials, and local bar associations, without whose kind assistance this book would not be possible.

The New York Lawyers Diary and Manual® is also available on the Web or installed on servers. Lawyers Diary Online—For and About Law—offers all of the information found in the New York Lawyers Diary and Manual® in a robust electronic search engine. This electronic version also includes practice calculators, calendaring options and extensive federal and state rules/reference materials too cumbersome to fit between our printed covers. Visit www.lawdiary.com for a demonstration or call us at (800) 444-4041, Ext. 2 for further details on this invaluable time saver.

Your comments and suggestions are welcome and appreciated. Please let us know how we can continue to improve your *Lawyers Diary* and serve you better.

Mailing address:	P.O. Box 50, Newark, NJ 07101
Telephone:	(800) 444-4041
Fax:	(973) 642-4280
E-mail:	mail@lawdiary.com
Web site:	http://www.lawdiary.com

Now search New York Supreme Court civil cases for FREE from anywhere at anytime! Imagine having us monitor case status for you as they navigate through the twists and turns of the judicial system. Imagine one calendar where all upcoming appearances reside—automatically synchronized with the docket—just a few mouse clicks and you are viewing potential schedule conflicts, multiple appearances grouped on the same date, and associate commitments. Well, imagine no more—discover http://www.e-law.com, introduced and sponsored by Lawyers Diary and Manual®.

We wish you a successful and productive year.

NEW YORK LAWYERS DIARY AND MANUAL®

Classic Edition: ISBN 1-57741-363-6

Special Edition: ISBN 1-57741-364-4

CALENDAR

2011

JANUARY 2011

S	M	T	W	T	F	S
						1
2	3	4	5	6	7	8
9	10	11	12	13	14	15
16	17	18	19	20	21	22
23	24	25	26	27	28	29
30	31					

FEBRUARY 2011

S	M	T	W	T	F	S
		1	2	3	4	5
6	7	8	9	10	11	12
13	14	15	16	17	18	19
20	21	22	23	24	25	26
27	28					

MARCH 2011

S	M	T	W	T	F	S
		1	2	3	4	5
6	7	8	9	10	11	12
13	14	15	16	17	18	19
20	21	22	23	24	25	26
27	28	29	30	31		

APRIL 2011

S	M	T	W	T	F	S
					1	2
3	4	5	6	7	8	9
10	11	12	13	14	15	16
17	18	19	20	21	22	23
24	25	26	27	28	29	30

MAY 2011

S	M	T	W	T	F	S
1	2	3	4	5	6	7
8	9	10	11	12	13	14
15	16	17	18	19	20	21
22	23	24	25	26	27	28
29	30	31				

JUNE 2011

S	M	T	W	T	F	S
			1	2	3	4
5	6	7	8	9	10	11
12	13	14	15	16	17	18
19	20	21	22	23	24	25
26	27	28	29	30		

JULY 2011

S	M	T	W	T	F	S
					1	2
3	4	5	6	7	8	9
10	11	12	13	14	15	16
17	18	19	20	21	22	23
24	25	26	27	28	29	30
31						

AUGUST 2011

S	M	T	W	T	F	S
	1	2	3	4	5	6
7	8	9	10	11	12	13
14	15	16	17	18	19	20
21	22	23	24	25	26	27
28	29	30	31			

SEPTEMBER 2011

S	M	T	W	T	F	S
				1	2	3
4	5	6	7	8	9	10
11	12	13	14	15	16	17
18	19	20	21	22	23	24
25	26	27	28	29	30	

OCTOBER 2011

S	M	T	W	T	F	S
						1
2	3	4	5	6	7	8
9	10	11	12	13	14	15
16	17	18	19	20	21	22
23	24	25	26	27	28	29
30	31					

NOVEMBER 2011

S	M	T	W	T	F	S
		1	2	3	4	5
6	7	8	9	10	11	12
13	14	15	16	17	18	19
20	21	22	23	24	25	26
27	28	29	30			

DECEMBER 2011

S	M	T	W	T	F	S
				1	2	3
4	5	6	7	8	9	10
11	12	13	14	15	16	17
18	19	20	21	22	23	24
25	26	27	28	29	30	31

2012

JANUARY 2012

S	M	T	W	T	F	S
1	2	3	4	5	6	7
8	9	10	11	12	13	14
15	16	17	18	19	20	21
22	23	24	25	26	27	28
29	30	31				

FEBRUARY 2012

S	M	T	W	T	F	S
			1	2	3	4
5	6	7	8	9	10	11
12	13	14	15	16	17	18
19	20	21	22	23	24	25
26	27	28	29			

MARCH 2012

S	M	T	W	T	F	S
				1	2	3
4	5	6	7	8	9	10
11	12	13	14	15	16	17
18	19	20	21	22	23	24
25	26	27	28	29	30	31

APRIL 2012

S	M	T	W	T	F	S
1	2	3	4	5	6	7
8	9	10	11	12	13	14
15	16	17	18	19	20	21
22	23	24	25	26	27	28
29	30					

MAY 2012

S	M	T	W	T	F	S
		1	2	3	4	5
6	7	8	9	10	11	12
13	14	15	16	17	18	19
20	21	22	23	24	25	26
27	28	29	30	31		

JUNE 2012

S	M	T	W	T	F	S
					1	2
3	4	5	6	7	8	9
10	11	12	13	14	15	16
17	18	19	20	21	22	23
24	25	26	27	28	29	30

JULY 2012

S	M	T	W	T	F	S
1	2	3	4	5	6	7
8	9	10	11	12	13	14
15	16	17	18	19	20	21
22	23	24	25	26	27	28
29	30	31				

AUGUST 2012

S	M	T	W	T	F	S
			1	2	3	4
5	6	7	8	9	10	11
12	13	14	15	16	17	18
19	20	21	22	23	24	25
26	27	28	29	30	31	

SEPTEMBER 2012

S	M	T	W	T	F	S
						1
2	3	4	5	6	7	8
9	10	11	12	13	14	15
16	17	18	19	20	21	22
23	24	25	26	27	28	29
30						

OCTOBER 2012

S	M	T	W	T	F	S
	1	2	3	4	5	6
7	8	9	10	11	12	13
14	15	16	17	18	19	20
21	22	23	24	25	26	27
28	29	30	31			

NOVEMBER 2012

S	M	T	W	T	F	S
				1	2	3
4	5	6	7	8	9	10
11	12	13	14	15	16	17
18	19	20	21	22	23	24
25	26	27	28	29	30	

DECEMBER 2012

S	M	T	W	T	F	S
						1
2	3	4	5	6	7	8
9	10	11	12	13	14	15
16	17	18	19	20	21	22
23	24	25	26	27	28	29
30	31					

2013

JANUARY 2013

S	M	T	W	T	F	S
		1	2	3	4	5
6	7	8	9	10	11	12
13	14	15	16	17	18	19
20	21	22	23	24	25	26
27	28	29	30	31		

FEBRUARY 2013

S	M	T	W	T	F	S
					1	2
3	4	5	6	7	8	9
10	11	12	13	14	15	16
17	18	19	20	21	22	23
24	25	26	27	28		

MARCH 2013

S	M	T	W	T	F	S
					1	2
3	4	5	6	7	8	9
10	11	12	13	14	15	16
17	18	19	20	21	22	23
24	25	26	27	28	29	30
31						

APRIL 2013

S	M	T	W	T	F	S
	1	2	3	4	5	6
7	8	9	10	11	12	13
14	15	16	17	18	19	20
21	22	23	24	25	26	27
28	29	30				

MAY 2013

S	M	T	W	T	F	S
			1	2	3	4
5	6	7	8	9	10	11
12	13	14	15	16	17	18
19	20	21	22	23	24	25
26	27	28	29	30	31	

JUNE 2013

S	M	T	W	T	F	S
						1
2	3	4	5	6	7	8
9	10	11	12	13	14	15
16	17	18	19	20	21	22
23	24	25	26	27	28	29
30						

JULY 2013

S	M	T	W	T	F	S
	1	2	3	4	5	6
7	8	9	10	11	12	13
14	15	16	17	18	19	20
21	22	23	24	25	26	27
28	29	30	31			

AUGUST 2013

S	M	T	W	T	F	S
				1	2	3
4	5	6	7	8	9	10
11	12	13	14	15	16	17
18	19	20	21	22	23	24
25	26	27	28	29	30	31

SEPTEMBER 2013

S	M	T	W	T	F	S
1	2	3	4	5	6	7
8	9	10	11	12	13	14
15	16	17	18	19	20	21
22	23	24	25	26	27	28
29	30					

OCTOBER 2013

S	M	T	W	T	F	S
		1	2	3	4	5
6	7	8	9	10	11	12
13	14	15	16	17	18	19
20	21	22	23	24	25	26
27	28	29	30	31		

NOVEMBER 2013

S	M	T	W	T	F	S
					1	2
3	4	5	6	7	8	9
10	11	12	13	14	15	16
17	18	19	20	21	22	23
24	25	26	27	28	29	30

DECEMBER 2013

S	M	T	W	T	F	S
1	2	3	4	5	6	7
8	9	10	11	12	13	14
15	16	17	18	19	20	21
22	23	24	25	26	27	28
29	30	31				

2014

JANUARY 2014

S	M	T	W	T	F	S
			1	2	3	4
5	6	7	8	9	10	11
12	13	14	15	16	17	18
19	20	21	22	23	24	25
26	27	28	29	30	31	

FEBRUARY 2014

S	M	T	W	T	F	S
						1
2	3	4	5	6	7	8
9	10	11	12	13	14	15
16	17	18	19	20	21	22
23	24	25	26	27	28	

MARCH 2014

S	M	T	W	T	F	S
						1
2	3	4	5	6	7	8
9	10	11	12	13	14	15
16	17	18	19	20	21	22
23	24	25	26	27	28	29
30	31					

APRIL 2014

S	M	T	W	T	F	S
		1	2	3	4	5
6	7	8	9	10	11	12
13	14	15	16	17	18	19
20	21	22	23	24	25	26
27	28	29	30			

MAY 2014

S	M	T	W	T	F	S
				1	2	3
4	5	6	7	8	9	10
11	12	13	14	15	16	17
18	19	20	21	22	23	24
25	26	27	28	29	30	31

JUNE 2014

S	M	T	W	T	F	S
1	2	3	4	5	6	7
8	9	10	11	12	13	14
15	16	17	18	19	20	21
22	23	24	25	26	27	28
29	30					

JULY 2014

S	M	T	W	T	F	S
		1	2	3	4	5
6	7	8	9	10	11	12
13	14	15	16	17	18	19
20	21	22	23	24	25	26
27	28	29	30	31		

AUGUST 2014

S	M	T	W	T	F	S
					1	2
3	4	5	6	7	8	9
10	11	12	13	14	15	16
17	18	19	20	21	22	23
24	25	26	27	28	29	30
31						

SEPTEMBER 2014

S	M	T	W	T	F	S
	1	2	3	4	5	6
7	8	9	10	11	12	13
14	15	16	17	18	19	20
21	22	23	24	25	26	27
28	29	30				

OCTOBER 2014

S	M	T	W	T	F	S
			1	2	3	4
5	6	7	8	9	10	11
12	13	14	15	16	17	18
19	20	21	22	23	24	25
26	27	28	29	30	31	

NOVEMBER 2014

S	M	T	W	T	F	S
						1
2	3	4	5	6	7	8
9	10	11	12	13	14	15
16	17	18	19	20	21	22
23	24	25	26	27	28	29
30						

DECEMBER 2014

S	M	T	W	T	F	S
	1	2	3	4	5	6
7	8	9	10	11	12	13
14	15	16	17	18	19	20
21	22	23	24	25	26	27
28	29	30	31			

2015

JANUARY 2015

S	M	T	W	T	F	S
				1	2	3
4	5	6	7	8	9	10
11	12	13	14	15	16	17
18	19	20	21	22	23	24
25	26	27	28	29	30	31

FEBRUARY 2015

S	M	T	W	T	F	S
1	2	3	4	5	6	7
8	9	10	11	12	13	14
15	16	17	18	19	20	21
22	23	24	25	26	27	28

MARCH 2015

S	M	T	W	T	F	S
1	2	3	4	5	6	7
8	9	10	11	12	13	14
15	16	17	18	19	20	21
22	23	24	25	26	27	28
29	30	31				

APRIL 2015

S	M	T	W	T	F	S
			1	2	3	4
5	6	7	8	9	10	11
12	13	14	15	16	17	18
19	20	21	22	23	24	25
26	27	28	29	30		

MAY 2015

S	M	T	W	T	F	S
					1	2
3	4	5	6	7	8	9
10	11	12	13	14	15	16
17	18	19	20	21	22	23
24	25	26	27	28	29	30
31						

JUNE 2015

S	M	T	W	T	F	S
	1	2	3	4	5	6
7	8	9	10	11	12	13
14	15	16	17	18	19	20
21	22	23	24	25	26	27
28	29	30				

JULY 2015

S	M	T	W	T	F	S
			1	2	3	4
5	6	7	8	9	10	11
12	13	14	15	16	17	18
19	20	21	22	23	24	25
26	27	28	29	30	31	

AUGUST 2015

S	M	T	W	T	F	S
						1
2	3	4	5	6	7	8
9	10	11	12	13	14	15
16	17	18	19	20	21	22
23	24	25	26	27	28	29
30	31					

SEPTEMBER 2015

S	M	T	W	T	F	S
		1	2	3	4	5
6	7	8	9	10	11	12
13	14	15	16	17	18	19
20	21	22	23	24	25	26
27	28	29	30			

OCTOBER 2015

S	M	T	W	T	F	S
				1	2	3
4	5	6	7	8	9	10
11	12	13	14	15	16	17
18	19	20	21	22	23	24
25	26	27	28	29	30	31

NOVEMBER 2015

S	M	T	W	T	F	S
1	2	3	4	5	6	7
8	9	10	11	12	13	14
15	16	17	18	19	20	21
22	23	24	25	26	27	28
29	30					

DECEMBER 2015

S	M	T	W	T	F	S
		1	2	3	4	5
6	7	8	9	10	11	12
13	14	15	16	17	18	19
20	21	22	23	24	25	26
27	28	29	30	31		

2016

JANUARY 2016

S	M	T	W	T	F	S
					1	2
3	4	5	6	7	8	9
10	11	12	13	14	15	16
17	18	19	20	21	22	23
24	25	26	27	28	29	30
31						

FEBRUARY 2016

S	M	T	W	T	F	S
	1	2	3	4	5	6
7	8	9	10	11	12	13
14	15	16	17	18	19	20
21	22	23	24	25	26	27
28	29					

MARCH 2016

S	M	T	W	T	F	S
		1	2	3	4	5
6	7	8	9	10	11	12
13	14	15	16	17	18	19
20	21	22	23	24	25	26
27	28	29	30	31		

APRIL 2016

S	M	T	W	T	F	S
					1	2
3	4	5	6	7	8	9
10	11	12	13	14	15	16
17	18	19	20	21	22	23
24	25	26	27	28	29	30

MAY 2016

S	M	T	W	T	F	S
1	2	3	4	5	6	7
8	9	10	11	12	13	14
15	16	17	18	19	20	21
22	23	24	25	26	27	28
29	30	31				

JUNE 2016

S	M	T	W	T	F	S
			1	2	3	4
5	6	7	8	9	10	11
12	13	14	15	16	17	18
19	20	21	22	23	24	25
26	27	28	29	30		

JULY 2016

S	M	T	W	T	F	S
					1	2
3	4	5	6	7	8	9
10	11	12	13	14	15	16
17	18	19	20	21	22	23
24	25	26	27	28	29	30
31						

AUGUST 2016

S	M	T	W	T	F	S
	1	2	3	4	5	6
7	8	9	10	11	12	13
14	15	16	17	18	19	20
21	22	23	24	25	26	27
28	29	30	31			

SEPTEMBER 2016

S	M	T	W	T	F	S
				1	2	3
4	5	6	7	8	9	10
11	12	13	14	15	16	17
18	19	20	21	22	23	24
25	26	27	28	29	30	

OCTOBER 2016

S	M	T	W	T	F	S
						1
2	3	4	5	6	7	8
9	10	11	12	13	14	15
16	17	18	19	20	21	22
23	24	25	26	27	28	29
30	31					

NOVEMBER 2016

S	M	T	W	T	F	S
		1	2	3	4	5
6	7	8	9	10	11	12
13	14	15	16	17	18	19
20	21	22	23	24	25	26
27	28	29	30			

DECEMBER 2016

S	M	T	W	T	F	S
				1	2	3
4	5	6	7	8	9	10
11	12	13	14	15	16	17
18	19	20	21	22	23	24
25	26	27	28	29	30	31

CURRENT YEAR (2011)

THE NEXT FIVE YEARS (2012–2016)

FIVE-YEAR CALENDAR OF IMPORTANT DATES

	2011	2012	2013	2014	2015
NEW YEAR'S DAY	Saturday January 1	Sunday January 1	Tuesday January 1	Wednesday January 1	Thursday January 1
BIRTHDAY OF MARTIN L. KING, JR.	Monday January 17	Monday January 16	Monday January 21	Monday January 20	Monday January 19
LINCOLN'S BIRTHDAY	Saturday February 12	Sunday February 12	Tuesday February 12	Wednesday February 12	Thursday February 12
VALENTINE'S DAY	Monday February 14	Tuesday February 14	Thursday February 14	Friday February 14	Saturday February 14
†WASHINGTON'S BIRTHDAY	Monday February 21	Monday February 20	Monday February 18	Monday February 17	Monday February 16
ASH WEDNESDAY	Wednesday March 9	Wednesday February 22	Wednesday February 13	Wednesday March 5	Wednesday February 18
ST. PATRICK'S DAY	Thursday March 17	Saturday March 17	Sunday March 17	Monday March 17	Tuesday March 17
PALM SUNDAY	Sunday April 17	Sunday April 1	Sunday March 24	Sunday April 13	Sunday March 29
PASSOVER** (First Day)	Tuesday April 19	Saturday April 7	Tuesday March 26	Tuesday April 15	Saturday April 4
GOOD FRIDAY	Friday April 22	Friday April 6	Friday March 29	Friday April 18	Friday April 3
EASTER	Sunday April 24	Sunday April 8	Sunday March 31	Sunday April 20	Sunday April 5
EASTER (ORTHODOX)	Sunday April 24	Sunday April 15	Sunday May 5	Sunday April 20	Sunday April 12
MOTHER'S DAY	Sunday May 8	Sunday May 13	Sunday May 12	Sunday May 11	Sunday May 10
VICTORIA DAY (Canada)	Monday May 23	Monday May 21	Monday May 20	Monday May 19	Monday May 18
MEMORIAL DAY NAT'L OBS.	Monday May 30	Monday May 28	Monday May 27	Monday May 26	Monday May 25
TRADITIONAL MEMORIAL DAY	Monday May 30	Wednesday May 30	Thursday May 30	Friday May 30	Saturday May 30
PENTECOST	Sunday June 12	Sunday May 27	Sunday May 19	Sunday June 8	Sunday May 24
SHAVUOT**	Wednesday June 8	Sunday May 27	Wednesday May 15	Wednesday June 4	Sunday May 24
FLAG DAY*	Tuesday June 14	Thursday June 14	Friday June 14	Saturday June 14	Sunday June 14
FATHER'S DAY	Sunday June 19	Sunday June 17	Sunday June 16	Sunday June 15	Sunday June 21
CANADA DAY	Friday July 1	Sunday July 1	Monday July 1	Tuesday July 1	Wednesday July 1
INDEPENDENCE DAY	Monday July 4	Wednesday July 4	Thursday July 4	Friday July 4	Saturday July 4
LABOR DAY	Monday September 5	Monday September 3	Monday September 2	Monday September 1	Monday September 7
JEWISH** NEW YEAR	Thurs.-Fri. September 29-30	Mon.-Tues. September 17-18	Thurs.-Fri. September 5-6	Thurs.-Fri. September 25-26	Mon.-Tues. September 14-15
YOM KIPPUR**	Saturday October 8	Wednesday September 26	Saturday September 14	Saturday October 4	Wednesday September 23
SUKKOT** (First Day)	Thursday October 13	Monday October 1	Thursday September 19	Thursday October 9	Monday September 28
COLUMBUS DAY CELEBRATION	Monday October 10	Monday October 8	Monday October 14	Monday October 13	Monday October 12
CANADIAN THANKSGIVING	Monday October 10	Monday October 8	Monday October 14	Monday October 13	Monday October 12
ELECTION DAY	Tuesday November 8	Tuesday November 6	Tuesday November 5	Tuesday November 4	Tuesday November 3
VETERANS' DAY	Friday November 11	Sunday November 11	Monday November 11	Tuesday November 11	Wednesday November 11
THANKSGIVING	Thursday November 24	Thursday November 22	Thursday November 28	Thursday November 27	Thursday November 26
HANUKAH** (First Day)	Wednesday December 21	Sunday December 9	Thursday November 28	Wednesday December 17	Monday December 7
CHRISTMAS	Sunday December 25	Tuesday December 25	Wednesday December 25	Thursday December 25	Friday December 25
KWANZAA (First Day)	Monday December 26	Wednesday December 26	Thursday December 26	Friday December 26	Saturday December 26

†Called President's Day in most states

***Note: N.Y. State celebrates Flag Day on the 2nd Sunday of June**

****Special note concerning Jewish Holidays:**
In addition to dates noted, observant Jews celebrate the second, seventh and eighth days of Passover; the second, eighth and ninth days of Sukkot; and two days of Shavuot. All Jewish holidays begin at sundown, the evening prior to the day of the holiday.

TABLE OF CONTENTS

INDEX

INDEX

* **Available in Classic Edition only**

C

* Available in Classic Edition only

D

*** Available in Classic Edition only**

INDEX

E

F

G

INDEX

*** Available in Classic Edition only**

P

INDEX

INDEX

* **Available in Classic Edition only**

T

INDEX

*** Available in Classic Edition only**

UNITED STATES COURTS AND OFFICES

SUPREME COURT OF THE UNITED STATES

U.S. Supreme Court Bldg., 1 First St. N.E., Washington, DC 20543
(202) 479-3000; Attorney Admissions: (202) 479-3387; (202) 479-3018

Chief Justice: John G. Roberts, Jr., New York

Justices:
Antonin Scalia, Virginia
Anthony M. Kennedy, California
Clarence Thomas, Georgia
Ruth Bader Ginsburg, New York
Stephen G. Breyer, Massachusetts
Samuel A. Alito, Jr., New Jersey
Sonia Sotomayor, New York
Elena Kagan, New York

Clerk: William K. Suter (202) 479-3011

Reporter of Decisions: Frank D. Wagner (202) 479-3390

Marshal: Pamela Talkin (202) 479-3333

Librarian: Judith Gaskell (202) 479-3175

Public Information Officer: Kathy Arberg (202) 479-3211

Court Schedule: The Court holds one term annually, commencing on the first Mon. in October.

UNITED STATES COURT OF FEDERAL CLAIMS

717 Madison Place NW, Washington, DC 20005
(202) 357-6400; Fax: (202) 357-6401

Chief Judge: Emily C. Hewitt (202) 357-6564

Judges:
Francis Allegra (202) 357-6492
Lawrence M. Baskir (202) 357-6500
Lawrence J. Block (202) 357-6508
Susan G. Braden (202) 357-6516
Lynn J. Bush (202) 357-6532
Edward J. Damich (202) 357-6483
Nancy B. Firestone (202) 357-6540
Marian Blank Horn (202) 357-6580
Charles F. Lettow (202) 357-6588
Christine Odell Cook Miller (202) 357-6620
George W. Miller (202) 357-6628
Margaret M. Sweeney (202) 357-6644
Thomas C. Wheeler (202) 357-6596
Mary Ellen Coster Williams (202) 357-6660
Victor J. Wolski (202) 357-6668

Senior Judges:
Eric G. Bruggink (202) 357-6524
Bohdan A. Futey (202) 357-6548
Robert H. Hodges, Jr. (202) 357-6572
Lawrence S. Margolis (202) 357-6604
James F. Merow (202) 357-6612
Loren A. Smith (202) 357-6636
John P. Wiese (202) 357-6652
Robert J. Yock (202) 357-6676

UNITED STATES COURT OF INTERNATIONAL TRADE

One Federal Plaza, New York, NY 10278-0001
(212) 264-2800; Fax: (212) 264-1085
Internet: www.cit.uscourts.gov

Chief Judge: Jane A. Restani (212) 264-2018
Case Mgr.: Stephen Swindell

Judges:
Judith M. Barzilay (212) 264-2018
Case Mgr.: Stephen Swindell
Gregory W. Carman (212) 264-1625
Case Mgr.: Carolyn Washington
Richard K. Eaton (212) 264-1615
Case Mgr.: Casey Cheevers
Leo M. Gordon (212) 264-2018
Case Mgr.: Stephen Swindell
Donald C. Pogue (212) 264-1628
Case Mgr.: Rebecca Ricci
Delissa A. Ridgway (212) 264-1615
Case Mgr.: Casey Cheevers
Timothy C. Stanceu (212) 264-2923
Case Mgr.: Cynthia Love
Evan J. Wallach (212) 264-1628
Case Mgr.: Rebecca Ricci

Senior Judges:
Thomas J. Aquilino, Jr. (212) 264-1625
Case Mgr.: Carolyn Washington
Richard W. Goldberg (212) 264-1615
Case Mgr.: Casey Cheevers
R. Kenton Musgrave (212) 264-1628
Case Mgr.: Rebecca Ricci
Nicholas Tsoucalas (212) 264-2923
Case Mgr.: Cynthia Love

Clerk: Tina Potuto Kimble
(212) 264-2814; Fax: (212) 264-4138

Librarian: Daniel R. Campbell (212) 264-2816

UNITED STATES COURT OF APPEALS SECOND CIRCUIT

(Connecticut, New York, Vermont)

Chief Judge: Dennis Jacobs
U.S. Courthouse, 40 Foley Sq., New York, NY 10007
(212) 857-2150

Judges:
José A. Cabranes
U.S. Courthouse, 141 Church St., New Haven, CT 06510
(203) 867-8782
Peter W. Hall
P.O. Box 885, Rutland, VT 05702 (802) 775-3712
Robert A. Katzmann
U.S. Courthouse, 40 Foley Sq., New York, NY 10007
(212) 857-2180
Debra Ann Livingston
U.S. Courthouse, 40 Foley Sq., New York, NY 10007
(212) 857-2230
Gerard E. Lynch
500 Pearl St., Room 910, New York, NY 10007-1312
(212) 805-0427
Rosemary S. Pooler
U.S. Courthouse, 100 S. Clinton St., P.O. Box 7395, Syracuse, NY 13261-7395 (315) 448-0420
Reena Raggi
U.S. Courthouse, 225 Cadman Plaza E., Brooklyn, NY 11201 (718) 613-2490
Richard C. Wesley
Livingston County Govt. Center, 6 Court St., Geneseo, NY 14454-1030 (585) 243-7910

Senior Judges:
Guido Calabresi
Connecticut Financial Center, 157 Church St., New Haven, CT 06510 (203) 773-2291
Wilfred Feinberg
U.S. Courthouse, 40 Foley Sq., New York, NY 10007
(212) 857-2100
Amalya L. Kearse
U.S. Courthouse, 40 Foley Sq., New York, NY 10007
(212) 857-2250
Pierre N. Leval
U.S. Courthouse, 40 Foley Sq., New York, NY 10007
(212) 857-2310
Joseph M. McLaughlin
U.S. Courthouse, 40 Foley Sq., New York, NY 10007
(212) 857-2200
Roger J. Miner
414 James T. Foley U.S. Cthse., 445 Broadway, Albany, NY 12207-2928 (518) 431-0401
Jon O. Newman
U.S. Courthouse, 450 Main St., Hartford, CT 06103
(860) 240-3260
Barrington D. Parker, Jr.
U.S. Courthouse, 40 Foley Sq., New York, NY 10007
(212) 857-2211

Senior Judges, U.S. Court of Appeals, Second Circuit—Cont'd

Robert D. Sack
U.S. Courthouse, 40 Foley Sq., New York, NY 10007
(212) 857-2140

Chester J. Straub
2530 U.S. Courthouse, 500 Pearl St., New York, NY 10007
(212) 857-2130

John M. Walker, Jr.
Connecticut Financial Center, 157 Church St., New Haven, CT 06510 (203) 773-2181

Ralph K. Winter
U.S. Courthouse, 141 Church St., New Haven, CT 06510
(203) 782-3682

Circuit Executive: Karen Greve Milton
2904 U.S. Courthouse, 40 Foley Sq., New York, NY 10007
(212) 857-8700; Fax: (212) 857-8680

Clerk: Catherine O'Hagan Wolfe
U.S. Courthouse, 40 Foley Sq., New York, NY 10007
(212) 857-8500; ABBS: (212) 857-8650;
AVIS: (212) 857-8656; Fax: (212) 857-8710
Internet: www.ca2.uscourts.gov

UNITED STATES TAX COURT

N.Y.C. Courtroom
Jacob K. Javits Federal Bldg., Room 206, 26 Federal Plaza, N.Y.C. 10278
Courtroom 206: (202) 521-0860;
Courtroom 208: (202) 521-0865
Internet: www.ustaxcourt.gov

New York office staffed only when court is in session in N.Y.

Washington Office
400 Second St. N.W., Washington, DC 20217
(202) 521-0700

Chief Judge: John O. Colvin (202) 521-0777

Judges:
Mary Ann Cohen (202) 521-0655
Maurice B. Foley (202) 521-0681
Joseph H. Gale (202) 521-0688
Joseph R. Goeke (202) 521-0690
David Gustafson (202) 521-0850
James S. Halpern (202) 521-0707
Mark V. Holmes (202) 521-0714
Diane L. Kroupa (202) 521-0725
L. Paige Marvel (202) 521-0740
Richard T. Morrison (202) 521-0853
Elizabeth Crewson Paris (202) 521-0839
Michael B. Thornton (202) 521-0766
Juan F. Vasquez (202) 521-0778
Thomas B. Wells (202) 521-0790
Robert A. Wherry, Jr. (202) 521-0800

Senior Judges:
Renato Beghe (202) 521-0638
Herbert L. Chabot (202) 521-0644
Carolyn P. Chiechi (202) 521-0650
Howard A. Dawson, Jr. (202) 521-0670
Joel Gerber (202) 521-0774
Harry A. Haines (202) 521-0699
Julian I. Jacobs (202) 521-0720
David Laro (202) 521-0738
Arthur L. Nims III (202) 521-0750
Robert P. Ruwe (202) 521-0751
Stephen J. Swift (202) 521-0760
Laurence J. Whalen (202) 521-0792

Chief Special Trial Judge: Peter J. Panuthos
(202) 521-4707

Special Trial Judges:
Robert N. Armen, Jr. (202) 521-4711
Lewis R. Carluzzo (202) 521-3339
John F. Dean (202) 521-3366
Stanley J. Goldberg (202) 521-3370

Clerk of the Court: Robert R. Di Trolio (202) 521-4600

U.S. DISTRICT COURT

SOUTHERN DISTRICT OF NEW YORK
Daniel Patrick Moynihan U.S. Courthouse, 500 Pearl St., N.Y.C. 10007-1312
(212) 805-0136
Internet: www.nysd.uscourts.gov
U.S. Courthouse, 300 Quarropas St., White Plains 10601
(914) 390-4100

Jurisdiction—Counties of Bronx, Dutchess, New York, Orange, Putnam, Rockland, Sullivan, Westchester

Chief Judge: Loretta A. Preska, Room 1320 (212) 805-0240

Judges:
Deborah A. Batts, Room 2510 (212) 805-0186
John G. Koeltl, Room 1030 (212) 805-0222
Denise L. Cote, Room 1040 (212) 805-0202
Lewis A. Kaplan, Room 1310 (212) 805-0216
Shira Scheindlin, Room 1620
(212) 805-0246; Fax: (212) 805-7920
Barbara S. Jones, Room 1920 (212) 805-6185
Sidney H. Stein, Room 1010 (212) 805-0192
Jed S. Rakoff, Room 1340 (212) 805-0401
Richard M. Berman (212) 805-6715
Colleen McMahon, Chambers 1350 (212) 805-6325
Alvin K. Hellerstein, Room 1050 (212) 805-0152
William H. Pauley III, Room 2210 (212) 805-6387
Naomi Reice Buchwald, Room 2270
(212) 805-0194; Fax: (212) 805-7927
Victor Marrero, Room 660
(212) 805-6374; Fax: (212) 805-6382
George B. Daniels, Room 630 (212) 805-6735
Laura Taylor Swain, Room 755
(212) 805-0417; Fax: (212) 805-0426
Kenneth M. Karas, Room 533, White Plains
(914) 390-4145
P. Kevin Castel, Room 2260 (212) 805-0262
Richard J. Holwell, Room 1950 (212) 805-0256
Paul A. Crotty, Room 735
(212) 805-6309; Fax: (212) 805-6304
Richard J. Sullivan, Room 640 (212) 805-0264
Cathy Seibel, Room 275 (914) 390-4271
Paul G. Gardephe, Room 920 (212) 805-0224

Senior Judges:
Thomas P. Griesa, Room 1630 (212) 805-0210
Lawrence M. McKenna, Room 1640 (212) 805-0230
Robert L. Carter, Room 2220
(212) 805-0196; Fax: (212) 805-7904
Richard Owen, Room 2240
(212) 805-6155; Fax: (212) 805-6161
Robert W. Sweet, Room 1940 (212) 805-0254
Leonard B. Sand, Room 1650 (212) 805-0244
Charles S. Haight, Jr.
U.S. Courthouse, Chambers 17C, 141 Church St., New Haven, CT 06510 (203) 773-2052
Louis L. Stanton, Room 2250 (212) 805-0252
John F. Keenan, Room 1930 (212) 805-0220, 21
Peter K. Leisure, Room 1910 (212) 805-0226
Miriam Goldman Cedarbaum, Room 1330 (212) 805-0198
Robert P. Patterson, Jr., Room 2550
(212) 805-0238; Fax: (212) 805-7917
Kevin Thomas Duffy, Room 2540 (212) 805-6125
Harold Baer, Jr., Room 2230 (212) 805-0184
Kimba M. Wood, Room 1610
(212) 805-0258; Fax: (212) 805-7900

U.S. Magistrate Judges:
Henry Pitman (Chief), Room 750 (212) 805-6105
Theodore H. Katz, Room 1660 (212) 805-0218
Andrew J. Peck, Room 1370
(212) 805-0036; Fax: (212) 805-7933
James C. Francis IV, Room 1960 (212) 805-0206
Michael H. Dolinger, Room 1670
(212) 805-0204; Fax: (212) 805-7928

U.S. Magistrate Judges, U.S. Dist. Court, So. Dist. of N.Y.—Cont'd
Martin R. Goldberg
225 Dolson Ave., Suite 206, P.O. Box 2083, Middletown 10940 (845) 343-1130; Fax: (845) 344-5547
Courtroom Address, 25 South St., Middletown 10940 (845) 343-1130
Ronald L. Ellis, Room 1970 (212) 805-0242
Lisa Margaret Smith, Room 530, White Plains (914) 390-4130; Fax (call first): (914) 390-4135
Douglas F. Eaton, Room 1360 (212) 805-6175; Fax: (212) 805-6181
George A. Yanthis, Room 118, White Plains (914) 390-4088
Kevin Nathaniel Fox, Room 530 (212) 805-6705; Fax: (212) 805-6712
Frank Maas, Room 740 (212) 805-6727; Fax: (212) 805-6724
Debra Freeman, Room 525 (212) 805-4250
Gabriel W. Gorenstein, Room 510 (212) 805-4260
Paul E. Davison, Room 421 (914) 390-4250
James L. Cott, Room 1360 (212) 805-0250

District Exec.: Clifford P. Kirsch, Room 820 (212) 805-0500
Clerk: Ruby J. Krajick
New York City: (212) 805-0136; Fax: (212) 805-0389; White Plains Office: (914) 390-4100
Chief Deputy Clerk: Richard Wilson
Deputy-in-Charge: Robert Rogers (914) 390-4100
Operations Mgr.: John Gencarello (212) 805-0725
Facilities Mgr.: Eleanor Harrold
Room 264, White Plains (914) 390-4075
Senior Staff Atty.: Sarah Netburn, Room 230 (212) 805-0175
Staff Attys.: (212) 805-0175
Kelly Benson
Jonathan Giovanni
Dawnmarie Goins
Ariadne Green
Barbara Lerner
Kathleen Sanders
Emmanuella Souffrant

U.S. ATTORNEY'S OFFICE

SOUTHERN DISTRICT OF NEW YORK
The Silvio J. Mollo Bldg., One Saint Andrew's Plaza, N.Y.C. 10007
(212) 637-2200; Fax: (212) 637-2611

U.S. Atty.: Preet Bharara (212) 637-1025
Deputy U.S. Atty.: Boyd M. Johnson III (212) 637-2276
Associate U.S. Atty.: John M. McEnany (212) 637-2571
Exec. Asst. U.S. Atty.: Federico E. Virella, Jr. (212) 637-2568
Chief Counsel to U.S. Atty.: Shirah Neiman (212) 637-2576
Administrative Officer: Edward Tyrrell (212) 637-2269
Public Affairs Officer: Yusill Scribner (212) 637-2464
Intelligence Research Specialist: Sharon Garvey (212) 637-1083
Coordinator, Victim Witness: Wendy Olsen-Clancy (212) 637-1028

Civil Division
86 Chambers St., N.Y.C. 10007
(212) 637-2800

Chief, Civil Division: Andrew W. Schilling (212) 637-2695
Chief Appellate Atty.: Sarah Normand (212) 637-2709
Deputy Chief Appellate Atty. for Immigration:
Elizabeth Wolstein (212) 637-2743
Chief, Civil Rights Unit: David Kennedy (212) 637-2733
Chief, Environmental Protection Unit: Sarah E. Light (212) 637-2774
Chief, Financial Litigation Unit: Kathleen A. Zebrowski (212) 637-2710
Chief, Immigration Unit: Patricia L. Buchanan (212) 637-3274
Chief, Tax & Bankruptcy Unit: Jeanette Vargas (212) 637-2737
Health Care Fraud Coordinator: Rebecca C. Martin (212) 637-2714
Office Mgr.: Carmen Sepulveda (212) 637-2767

Criminal Division

Chief, Criminal Division: Richard B. Zabel (212) 637-2519
Chief Appellate Atty.: Katherine P. Failla (212) 637-2324
Deputy Chief Appellate Attys.:
Daniel Braun (212) 637-2215
Andrew Fish (212) 637-2548
Jessie Furman (212) 637-2475
Michael Levy (212) 637-2346
Chief, Complex Frauds Unit: Jonathan Kolodner (212) 637-2561
Chief, Asset Forfeiture Unit: Sharon Levin (212) 637-1060
Chief, Civil Frauds: Heidi A. Wendel
Chiefs, General Crimes:
Joan M. Loughnane
Stephen Ritchin (212) 637-2503
Chief, Intl. Narcotics Trafficking: Guruanjan Sahni (212) 637-2491
Chief, Narcotics: Karl Metzner (212) 637-2476
Deputy Chief, Narcotics: Glen McGorty (212) 637-2505
Chief, Organized Crime: Miriam E. Rocah
Deputy Chiefs, Organized Crime:
Jennifer Rodgers (212) 637-2513
Jocelyn E. Strauber
Chief, Public Corruption Unit: Daniel L. Stein
Chief, Securities & Commodities Fraud:
Christopher J Garcia
Chief, Terrorism & National Security: David A. Raskin (212) 637-2635
Deputy Chief, Terrorism & National Security:
Leslie Brown (212) 637-2638
Chief, Violent Crimes: David M. Rody (212) 637-2304
Chief, Securities & Commodities Fraud: Raymond Lohier (212) 637-2235

White Plains Office
300 Quarropas St., 3rd Floor, White Plains 10601
(914) 993-1946

Chief: Diane Gujarati (914) 993-1941

U.S. MARSHALS SERVICE

SOUTHERN DISTRICT OF NEW YORK
500 Pearl St., Suite 400, N.Y.C. 10007
(212) 331-7200; Fax: (212) 637-6130
White Plains Sub-Office, U.S. Courthouse, 300 Quarropas St., White Plains 10601
(914) 682-6175

U.S. Marshal: Hon. Joseph R. Guccione

U.S. PROBATION OFFICE

SOUTHERN DISTRICT OF NEW YORK
Woolworth Bldg., 14th Floor, 233 Broadway, N.Y.C. 10279-1312
Mailing Address: 500 Pearl St., N.Y.C. 10007-1312
(212) 805-0040; Fax: (212) 805-0047
25 South St., Middletown 10940-6435
(845) 344-2789; Fax: (845) 344-2722
300 Quarropas St., White Plains 10601-1901
(914) 390-4040; Fax: (914) 390-4055

Chief Probation Officer: Michael J. Fitzpatrick

FEDERAL DEFENDERS OF NEW YORK, INC.

SOUTHERN DISTRICT OF NEW YORK
52 Duane St., 10th Floor, N.Y.C. 10007-1207
(212) 417-8700; Fax: (212) 571-0392

300 Quarropas St., Suite 260, White Plains 10601
(914) 428-7124; Fax: (914) 997-6872

Federal Community Defender: Leonard F. Joy

Attys.-in-Charge:
Susanne Brody (White Plains) (914) 428-7124
John J. Byrnes (Trials) (212) 417-8735
Formerly affiliated with the Legal Aid Society

U.S. DISTRICT COURT

EASTERN DISTRICT OF NEW YORK
U.S. Courthouse, 225 Cadman Plaza East, Brooklyn 11201
General Information and Intake: (718) 613-2285;
Clerk of the Court: (718) 613-2600;
Chief Deputy Clerk: (718) 613-2600;
Attorney Admissions: (718) 613-2285;
Alternative Dispute Resolution: (718) 613-2577;
Appeals: (718) 613-2310; Arbitration: (718) 613-2325;
Docketing (Judges): (718) 613-2610;
Docketing (Magistrates): (718) 613-2620;
Interpreters: (718) 613-2390;
Interpreters Fax: (718) 613-2330;
Appeals: (718) 613-2310; Arbitration: (718) 613-2325;
Docketing: (718) 613-2610
Internet: www.nyed.uscourts.gov

Alfonse M. D'Amato U.S. Courthouse,
100 Federal Plaza, Central Islip 11722-4449
(631) 712-6000

Jurisdiction—Counties of Kings, Nassau, Queens, Richmond, Suffolk

Chief Judge: Raymond J. Dearie, Room 912S
(718) 613-2430; Fax: (718) 613-2437
Law Clerks:
Brian Alexander, Robert Polemeni
Eric Del Pozo, John Quinn
Linda Mischel-Eisner
Courtroom Deputy: Ellen Mulqueen (718) 613-2435

Judges:

Carol B. Amon, Room 908S
(718) 613-2410; Fax: (718) 613-2416
Law Clerks:
Kevin Angle, Colin Watson
Secretary: Marie Liberatore (718) 613-2412
Courtroom Deputy: Vanessa Holley (718) 613-2415

Joseph F. Bianco, Room 924, Central Islip
(631) 712-5670; Fax: (631) 712-5677
Law Clerks:
John Cooney, Svetlana Nagiel
Kelly Graves
Courtroom Deputy: Michele Dasaro-Savona (631) 712-5676

Brian Cogan, Room 717S
(718) 613-2230; Fax: (718) 613-2236
Law Clerks:
Jane Dattilo, Audrey Spektor
Secretary: Peggy Weisberg (718) 613-2232
Courtroom Deputy: Gaby Batista (718) 613-2235

Sandra J. Feuerstein, Room 1014, Central Islip
(631) 712-5630; Fax: (631) 712-5636
Law Clerks:
April Adell (631) 712-5633
Benjamin R. Fliegel (631) 712-5634
Secretary: Maryanne Cerny (631) 712-5630
Courtroom Deputy: Bryan Morabito (631) 712-5635

Nicholas G. Garaufis, Room 1416S (718) 613-2540
Law Clerks:
Emily Chapuis, Jacob Sherkow
Ian Richardson
Courtroom Deputy: John Fitzpatrick

John Gleeson, Room 727S
(718) 613-2450; Fax: (718) 613-2456
Law Clerks:
Alicyn Cooley (718) 613-2453
Miriam Glaser (718) 613-2454
Hayley Horowitz (718) 613-2452
Courtroom Deputy: Ilene Lee (718) 613-2455

Dora L. Irizarry, Room 928S
(718) 613-2150; Fax: (718) 613-2156
Law Clerks:
Aleah Borghard, Adam Rodriguez
Joyce Chen
Courtroom Deputy: Christy Carosella (718) 613-2155

Kiyo A. Matsumoto, Room N406
(718) 613-2180; Fax: (718) 613-2185
Law Clerks:
Anna Hershenberg, Rachel Zeehandelaar
Law Clerk/Clerical Asst.: Carmen Iquina
Courtroom Deputy: Sandra Jackson

Roslynn R. Mauskopf, Room N626
(718) 613-2210; Fax: (718) 613-2216
Law Clerks:
Danielle Kantor, Gerald Moody
Brian Ketcham, Stephen Wallant
Courtroom Deputy: Winnethka Toribio (718) 613-2215

Allyne R. Ross, Room 915S
(718) 613-2380; Fax: (718) 613-2386
Law Clerks:
Clay Kaminsky (718) 260-2384
Michael Robotti (718) 613-2380
Secretary: Pamela Warren (718) 613-2382
Courtroom Deputy: Dennis Lasalle (718) 613-2385

Joanna Seybert, Room 1034
Mailing Address: P.O. Box 9014, Central Islip 11722-9014
(631) 712-5610; Fax: (631) 712-5611
Law Clerks:
John Curley, Jacob Oslick
Secretary: Bonnie Nohs (613) 712-5612
Courtroom Deputy: Charles Baran (631) 712-5615

Sandra L. Townes, Room 905S (718) 613-2160
Law Clerks:
Laura Berman, Heather Dietrick
Alexander P. Caspari
Courtroom Deputy: Veronica Frullo (718) 613-2165

Eric N. Vitaliano, Room 714S
(718) 613-2130; Fax: (718) 613-2136
Law Clerks:
Sparkle Alexander, Tristan Snell
Sean Nuttall
Courtroom Deputy: William Villanueva (718) 613-2135

Senior Judges:

Frederic Block, Room 925S
(718) 613-2420; Fax: (718) 613-2426
Law Clerks:
Hawa Allan, Alexander Zolan
Charles T. Cone
Courtroom Deputy: Michael Innelli (718) 613-2425

Nina Gershon, Room 1429S
(718) 613-2650; Fax: (718) 613-2656
Law Clerks:
Dina Chelst, Ryan Wilson
Susan Lawless
Courtroom Deputy: Victor Joe (718) 613-2655

I. Leo Glasser, Room 921S
(718) 613-2440; Fax: (718) 613-2446
Law Clerks:
Alexander Ibrahim, Judd R. Rothstein
Secretary: Marie Chiodo (718) 613-2442
Courtroom Deputy: Ogoro Francis (718) 613-2445

Denis R. Hurley, Sr., Room 934
Mailing Address: P.O. Box 1094, Central Islip 11722-1094
(631) 712-5650
Law Clerks:
Michele Gapinski
Debbie Lanin (631) 712-5653
Laura Monaco
Judicial Asst.: Karen Costantini (631) 712-5650
Courtroom Deputy: Trish Best (631) 712-5652

Senior Judges, U.S. Dist. Court, Eastern Dist of N.Y.—Cont'd

Sterling Johnson, Jr., Room 720S
(718) 613-2460; Fax: (718) 613-2466
Law Clerks:
Marcia Henry — Dana Vincent
Secretary: Sharon Taylor (718) 613-2462
Courtroom Deputy: Ana Rodriguez (718) 613-2465

Edward R. Korman, Room 918S
(718) 613-2470; Fax: (718) 613-2477
Law Clerks:
Alexee D. Conroy — Brian D. Mogck
James M. Hays II
Case Mgr.: Paula Marie Susi (718) 613-2476

Thomas C. Platt, Room 1044
Mailing Address: P.O. Box 9014, Central Islip 11722-9014
(631) 712-5600; Fax: (631) 712-5606
Law Clerks:
Joshua Paster — Denise Shanley
Secretary: Toni Pressimone
Courtroom Deputy: Karen McMorrow (631) 712-5605

Arthur D. Spatt, Room 1024, Central Islip
(631) 712-5620; Fax: (631) 712-5626
Law Clerks:
Jared Marx — Amanda Sue Nichols
Judicial Asst.: Valerie Cohen
Courtroom Deputy: Mary Ellen Schaffner (631) 712-5625

David G. Trager, Room 707S
(718) 613-2510; Fax: (718) 613-2518
Law Clerks:
Jeremy Adler (718) 613-2514
Brian Morris (718) 613-2513
Robert Terranova (718) 613-2512
Courtroom Deputy: Ezra Spilke (718) 613-2515

Jack B. Weinstein, Room 1420S
(718) 613-2520; Fax: (718) 613-2527
Law Clerks:
Jack Figuera — Anita Nabah
Secretary: Jean Capobianco
Courtroom Deputy: June Lowe (718) 613-2525

Leonard D. Wexler, Room 944, Central Islip
(631) 712-5640
Law Clerks:
Peter Ausili (631) 712-5643
Anne Y. Shields (631) 712-5644
Secretary: Mary Ellen Muse
Courtroom Deputy: Josiah Kharjie (631) 712-5645

U.S. Magistrate Judges:

Steven M. Gold (Chief), Room 1217S
(718) 613-2560; Fax: (718) 613-2565
Law Clerks:
Erin O'Connor — Ben Welikson
Secretary: Lea Vasquez

Joan M. Azrack, Room N605
(718) 613-2530; Fax: (718) 613-2535
Law Clerks:
Tina Bhatt — Jacqlyn Rovine
Kerry Docherty

Lois Bloom, Room 1210S
(718) 613-2170; Fax: (718) 613-2175
Law Clerk/Deputy: Michael Turilli
Law Clerks:
Sean Malley — Amelia Toledo (Part-time)
Lara Rablee (Part-time)

E. Thomas Boyle, Room 834, Central Islip
(631) 712-5710
Law Clerk: Deanna Minerva
Secretary/Judicial Asst.: Dolores P. Joy
Courtroom Deputy: Lisa Lundy (631) 712-5714

Andrew L. Carter, Room N505 (718) 613-2220
Law Clerks:
Kruti Dharia — Davina Figeroux
Courtroom Deputy: Tara Hunter-Hicks

Marilyn Dolan Go, Room 1214S
(718) 613-2550; Fax: (718) 613-2555
Law Clerk: Joshua Proujansky (718) 613-2553
Law Clerk/Clerical Asst.: Motria Kuzycz (718) 613-2554
Secretary: Yvonne DeVeaux

Robert M. Levy, Room 1223S
(718) 613-2340; Fax: (718) 613-2345
Law Clerk: Leslie Rubin (718) 613-2343
Law Clerk/Clerical Asst.: Benjamin Geffen (718) 613-2344
Secretary: Janine Marino (718) 613-2342

Arlene R. Lindsay, Room 814 (631) 712-5730
Law Clerks:
Dina Miller — Aaron Warshaw
Courtroom Deputy: Eric Horbey (631) 712-5734

Roanne L. Mann, Room 1220S
(718) 613-2350; Fax: (718) 613-2355
Law Clerks:
Jeannie Rose Field (718) 613-2354
Nathan Treadwell (718) 613-2353
Secretary: Pat Maynard (718) 613-2352

James Orenstein
(718) 613-2110; Fax: (718) 613-2115
Law Clerks:
Melissa Lardo — Christine Scott-Hayward
Courtroom Deputy: Alicia Guy (718) 613-2114

Michael L. Orenstein, Room 844, Central Islip
(631) 712-5700; Fax: (631) 712-5705
Law Clerk: Linda Johnston (631) 712-5701
Courtroom Deputy: Robert Imrie (631) 712-5704
Secretary: Cristine Danisi

Viktor V. Pohorelsky, Room 1207S
(718) 613-2400; Fax: (718) 613-2405
Law Clerk: Jeremy Sporn
Secretary/Judicial Asst.: Joan Newton
Courtroom Deputy/Law Clerk: James Toritto (718) 613-2400

Cheryl L. Pollak, Room 1230S
(718) 613-2360; Fax: (718) 613-2365
Law Clerk: Melissa Berger
Law Clerk/Clerical Asst.: Ben Sedrish
Secretary: Diana Caggiano (718) 613-2362
Clerical Asst.: Ishai Mooreville

Ramon Reyes, Jr., Room N208
(718) 613-2120; Fax: (718) 613-2125
Law Clerk: Victoria Lee
Secretary: Marta Rivera (718) 613-2122
Courtroom Deputy: Miriam Vertus (718) 613-2123

A. Kathleen Tomlinson, Room 914 (631) 712-5760
Law Clerks:
Richard Spatola — Ellen Tobin
Magistrate Clerical: Edher Montero

William D. Wall, Room 824, Central Islip
(631) 712-5720; Fax: (631) 712-5725
Law Clerks:
Sandra Disbrow — F. Judith Hepworth
Clerical Asst.: Thomas Talbot

District Exec.: James E. Ward, Jr. (718) 613-2260

Clerk: Robert C. Heinemann (718) 613-2600

Chief Deputy Clerk, Automated Services:
Douglas Palmer (718) 613-2291

Chief Deputy Clerk, Courtroom Operations:
Terry Vaughn (718) 613-2331

Pro Se Staff Attys.:
Catherine Wolff Gilodsky (718) 613-2671
Jill Hanekamp (718) 613-2667
I. Alexei Martinez (718) 613-2668
Mary Ellen Moule (718) 613-2666
Aliza Silber-Weiss (718) 613-2670

U.S. ATTORNEY'S OFFICE

EASTERN DISTRICT OF NEW YORK
271 Cadman Plaza E., Brooklyn 11201
(718) 254-7000; Fax: (718) 254-6550
Long Island Federal Plaza, 610 Federal Plaza, Central Islip 11722-4454
(631) 715-7900; Fax (Civil): (631) 715-7920; Fax (Criminal): (631) 715-7922

U.S. Atty.: Loretta Lynch
Exec. Asst. U.S. Atty.: William J. Muller
Admin. Officer: Pete M. Kurtin

U.S. Attorney's Office, Eastern Dist of N.Y.—Cont'd
Public Affairs: Robert Nardoza
Branch Asst. U.S. Atty. In Charge, Central Islip: Vacancy at Press Time
Chief, Appeals Division: Peter A. Norling
Chief, Asset Forfeiture: Kathleen Nandan
Chief, Civil Division: Susan Riley
Chief, Criminal Division: Richard P. Donoghue
Chief, Criminal Litigation: Jack Smith
Chief, Criminal Div., Central Islip Branch: Nicole Boeckmann
Chief, Financial Litigation: Beth P. Schwartz
Chief, General Crimes: Margo Brodie
Chief, Narcotics: Carolyn Pokorny
Coordinator, Anti-Terrorism Advisory Council (ATAC): Kellie T. Currie
Intelligence Research Specialist: Michael Zeller
Coordinator, Law Enforcement Coordinating Committee (LECC): Richard Capobianco
Coordinator, Victim Witness: Lisa Forster

U.S. MARSHALS SERVICE

EASTERN DISTRICT OF NEW YORK
U.S. Courthouse, Room G-20,
225 Cadman Plaza East, Brooklyn 11201-1818
(718) 260-0400; Operations: (718) 260-0450
100 Federal Plaza, Central Islip 11722
(631) 712-6000

U.S. Marshal: Charles G. Dunne

U.S. PROBATION OFFICE

EASTERN DISTRICT OF NEW YORK
147 Pierrepont St., Brooklyn 11201
(347) 534-3400; Fax: (347) 534-3509
Long Island Federal Courthouse, 2nd Floor,
202 Federal Plaza, Central Islip 11722
(631) 712-6300; Fax: (631) 712-6395

Chief Probation Officer: Eileen Kelly

U.S. PRETRIAL SERVICES AGENCY

EASTERN DISTRICT OF NEW YORK
225 Cadman Plaza East, Room 219, Brooklyn 11201
(718) 613-2570; Fax: (718) 613-2568
Internet: www.nyept.uscourts.gov
Long Island Federal Courthouse, Room 200,
200 Federal Plaza, West Wing, Central Islip 11722
(631) 712-6400; Fax: (631) 712-6415

Chief: Cynthia Lawyer (718) 613-2678
E-mail: cynthia_lawyer@nyept.uscourts.gov

FEDERAL DEFENDERS OF NEW YORK, INC.

EASTERN DISTRICT OF NEW YORK
One Pierrepont Plz., 16th Floor, Brooklyn 11201
(718) 330-1200; Fax: (718) 855-0760
Long Island Federal Courthouse, 770 Federal Plz., Central Islip 11722-4422
(631) 712-6500; Fax: (631) 712-6505

Exec. Dir.: Leonard F. Joy
52 Duane St., 10th Floor, N.Y.C. 10007-1226
(212) 417-8700; Fax: (212) 571-0392

Attys.-in-Charge:
Randi L. Chavis (Central Islip)
Peter R. Kirchheimer (Brooklyn)

Formerly affiliated with the Legal Aid Society

U.S. DISTRICT COURT

NORTHERN DISTRICT OF NEW YORK
James Hanley Federal Bldg. U.S. Cthse., 100 S. Clinton St., P.O. Box 7367, Syracuse 13261-7367
Clerk's Office: (315) 234-8500
Internet: www.nynd.uscourts.gov
14 Durkee St., Suite 350, Plattsburgh 12901
Clerk's Office: (518) 247-1501
James T. Foley U.S. Courthouse, 445 Broadway, Albany 12207-2974
Clerk's Office: (518) 257-1800
Alexander Pirnie Federal Bldg., 10 Broad St., Utica 13501
Clerk's Office: (315) 793-8151
Federal Building & U.S. Courthouse, 15 Henry St., Binghamton 13901
Clerk's Office: (607) 773-2893

Jurisdiction—Counties of Albany, Broome, Cayuga, Chenango, Clinton, Columbia, Cortland, Delaware, Essex, Franklin, Fulton, Greene, Hamilton, Herkimer, Jefferson, Lewis, Madison, Montgomery, Oneida, Onondaga, Oswego, Otsego, Rensselaer, Saint Lawrence, Saratoga, Schenectady, Schoharie, Tioga, Tompkins, Ulster, Warren, Washington

Chief Judge: Norman A. Mordue
P.O. Box 7336, Syracuse 13261-7336
(315) 234-8570; Fax: (315) 234-8571
Law Clerks:
Karen Guyder Felter, Stephanie Reagan
Annelle McCullough, Melissa Romano
Judicial Asst.: Jeanne M. Linsday

Judges:
David N. Hurd, Room 300, Utica
(315) 793-9571; Fax: (315) 793-8034
Law Clerks:
Donna J. Case, Chelsea L. Selby
Judicial Asst.: Charlene E. Rouillier

Gary L. Sharpe, Albany (518) 257-1870
Law Clerks:
Jason Hughes, Cela Delgado Webster
R. James Madigan III

Glenn T. Suddaby (315) 234-8580; Fax: (315) 234-8581
Law Clerks:
Jason Halpin, Michael Langan
Judicial Asst.: Kelly Easton

Senior Judges:
Lawrence E. Kahn, Room 424, Albany
(518) 257-1830; Fax: (518) 257-1831
Law Clerks:
Jeremy Benjamin, Aaron Hall
Judicial Asst.: Scott J. Barnes

Thomas J. McAvoy, Binghamton (607) 773-2892
Law Clerks:
James Connor (518) 257-1885
Seth Eisenberg
Judicial Asst.: Marlene Price

Neal P. McCurn, Syracuse 13261-7365
(315) 234-8590; Fax: (315) 234-8591
Law Clerks:
Linda L. Illingworth, Catherine Shamlian
Courtroom Deputy: Philip McBrearty

Frederick J. Scullin, Jr., Syracuse 13261-7255
(315) 234-8560; Fax: (315) 234-8561
Law Clerks:
Deborah E. Moore, Brian T. Onofry

U.S. Magistrate Judges:
Andrew T. Baxter, P.O. Box 7396, Syracuse 13261-7396
(315) 234-8600; Fax: (315) 234-8601
Law Clerks:
Gioia A. Gensini, Casey Johnson

David R. Homer, Albany
(518) 257-1850; Fax: (518) 257-1851
Law Clerk: Adrienne Foederer
Judicial Asst.: Lynda Hennessy

U.S. Magistrate Judges, U.S. Dist. Court, Northern Dist of N.Y.—Cont'd
George H. Lowe, P.O. Box 7346, Syracuse 13261-7346
(315) 234-8610; Fax: (315) 234-8611
Law Clerks:
Courtenay McKeon Karen Southwick
David E. Peebles, P.O. Box 7367, Syracuse 13261-7367
(315) 234-8620; Fax: (315) 234-8621
Law Clerk: Lisa DiPoala-Haber
Judicial Asst.: Cindy McNulty
Randolph F. Treece, Albany
(518) 257-1840; Fax: (518) 257-1841
Law Clerks:
Benjamin Hill Robyn L. Hoffman

Clerk: Lawrence K. Baerman (315) 234-8500
Chief Deputy Clerk: John Domurad (518) 257-1809
Admin. Asst.: Robin Smith (315) 234-8513
Sr. Pro Se Staff Atty.: Thomas Smith
Pro Se Staff Attys.:
Sharon Broton Marguerite Conan

U.S. ATTORNEY'S OFFICE

NORTHERN DISTRICT OF NEW YORK
James F. Hanley Federal Bldg., 9th Floor, 100 S. Clinton St., P.O. Box 7198, Syracuse 13261-7198
(315) 448-0672; Fax: (315) 448-0689
Internet: www.usaondny.org

U.S. Atty.: Richard S. Hartunian
First Asst. U.S. Atty.: Grant C. Jaquith
James Foley Bldg., Room 218, 445 Broadway, Albany 12207
Chief Asst. U.S. Atty., Civil: William H. Pease, 8th Floor
Chief, Appellate Division: Brenda K. Sannes
Chief, Criminal Division: Steven D. Clymer
Assoc. Criminal Chief, Chief Organized Crime Unit, ATAC Coordinator: Gregory A. West
Executive Asst. U.S. Atty.: John G. Duncan
Asst. U.S. Attys.:
Craig A. Benedict John M. Katko
Edward R. Broton, S.L.C. William F. Larkin
Paula Ryan Conan Ransom P. Reynolds
Carl G. Eurenius Elizabeth S. Riker
Lisa M. Fletcher Charles E. Roberts
Carla Freedman Richard R. Southwick
Stephen C. Green Tamara B. Thompson

James T. Foley U.S. Courthouse, Room 218, 445 Broadway, Albany 12207-2924
(518) 431-0247; Fax: (518) 431-0249

Supervisory Asst. U.S. Atty.: William C. Pericak
E-mail: william.pericak@usdoj.gov
Chief, Narcotics: Richard S. Hartunian
E-mail: richard.hartunian@usdoj.gov
Deputy Chief, Civil Section: Barbara D. Cottrell
E-mail: barbara.cottrell@usdoj.gov
Asst. U.S. Attys.:
Diane J. Cagino; E-mail: diane.cagino@usdoj.gov
Thomas A. Capezza; E-mail: thomas.capezza@usdoj.gov
Elizabeth C. Coombe; E-mail: elizabeth.c.coombe@usdoj.gov
Nathaniel J. Dorfman; E-mail: nathaniel.dorfman@usdoj.gov
Edward P. Grogan; E-mail: edward.grogan@usdoj.gov
Terrence E. Kelly; E-mail: terrence.kelly@usdoj.gov
Carlos A. Moreno; E-mail: carlos.moreno2@usdoj.gov
Robert A. Sharpe; E-mail: robert.sharpe@usdoj.gov
Paul D. Silver; E-mail: paul.silver@usdoj.gov
Thomas Spina, Jr.; E-mail: thomas.spina@usdoj.gov
Robert P. Storch; E-mail: robert.storch@usdoj.gov
Joshua S. Vinciguerra; E-mail: joshua.vinciguerra@usdoj.gov

Federal Bldg. & U.S. Courthouse, Suite 304, 15 Henry St., Binghamton 13901
(607) 773-2887; Fax: (607) 773-2901

Supervising Asst. U.S. Atty.: Thomas P. Walsh
Asst. U.S. Attys.:
Kevin P. Dooley Miroslav Lovric

U.S. MARSHALS SERVICE

NORTHERN DISTRICT OF NEW YORK
James Hanley Federal Bldg., 100 S. Clinton St., Syracuse 13261
(315) 473-7601
445 Broadway, Albany 12207
(518) 431-0101

U.S. Marshal: James Parmley

U.S. PROBATION OFFICE

NORTHERN DISTRICT OF NEW YORK
Atrium Bldg., 2 Clinton Sq., Suite 370, 100 S. Salina St., Syracuse 13202
Mailing Address: P.O. Box 7035, Syracuse 13261-7035
(315) 234-8700; Fax: (315) 234-8701
445 Broadway, Room 347, Albany 12207
(518) 257-1700; Fax: (518) 257-1701
Mezzanine Level, 15 Henry St., Binghamton 13901
(607) 773-3202; Fax: (607) 773-3140
14 Durkee St., Suite 110, Plattsburgh 12901
(518) 247-4510; Fax: (518) 247-4516

Chief Probation Officer: Matthew L. Brown

OFFICE OF THE FEDERAL PUBLIC DEFENDER

NORTHERN DISTRICT OF NEW YORK
39 N. Pearl St., Albany 12207
(518) 436-1850; Fax: (518) 436-1780
4 Clinton Exchange Bldg., Syracuse 13202
(315) 701-0080; Fax: (315) 701-0081

Federal Public Defender: Alexander Bunin

U.S. DISTRICT COURT

WESTERN DISTRICT OF NEW YORK
U.S. Courthouse, 68 Court St., Buffalo 14202-3406
Clerk's Office: (716) 332-1700; Fax: (716) 551-4850
Internet: www.nywd.uscourts.gov
U.S. Courthouse, 100 State St., Rochester 14614-1387
(585) 613-4000; Fax: (585) 613-4035

Jurisdiction—Counties of Allegany, Cattaraugus, Chautauqua, Chemung, Erie, Genesee, Livingston, Monroe, Niagara, Ontario, Orleans, Schuyler, Seneca, Steuben, Wayne, Wyoming, Yates

Chief Judge: William M. Skretny, Room 507
(716) 332-7820; Fax: (716) 332-7825
Law Clerks:
Amanda Goun Andrew W. Moeller
Staff Atty.: Judy S. Hernandez

Judges:
Richard J. Arcara, Room 609 (716) 332-7810
Law Clerks:
Giuseppe A. Ippolito Monica Piga Wallace
Charles J. Siragusa, Room 1380
(585) 613-4050; Fax: (585) 613-4055
Law Clerks:
J. Michael Kehoe
E-mail: michael_kehoe@nywd.uscourts.gov
Mark W. Pedersen
E-mail: mark_pedersen@nywd.uscourts.gov
Judicial Asst.: Kelly A. Pruden
E-mail: kelly_pruden@nywd.uscourts.gov

Senior Judges:
John T. Curtin, Room 624 (716) 332-7830
E-mail: john_curtin@nywd.uscourts.gov
Law Clerks:
William C. Schoellkopf Karen M. McMahon
David G. Larimer, Room 2500
(585) 613-4040; Fax: (585) 613-4045
Law Clerks:
Rayne Hammond Benz David P. Chapus
Michael A. Telesca, Room 2720
(585) 613-4060; Fax: (585) 613-4065
Law Clerks:
Bryce M. Baird Maria M. Herrero-Jaarsma

U.S. Dist. Court, Western Dist of N.Y.—Cont'd

U.S. Magistrate Judges:

Jonathan W. Feldman, Room 2330
(585) 613-4070; Fax: (585) 613-4075
Law Clerk: Carey Ann Denefrio

Leslie G. Foschio (On Recall), Room 310
(716) 332-7850; Fax: (716) 332-7855
Law Clerks:
Therésè A. Hopkins, Rebecca McCauley
Judicial Asst.: Sandra D. Wilson

Jeremiah J. McCarthy, Room 424
(716) 362-9350; Fax: (716) 362-9355
Law Clerk: Matthew D. Yusick (716) 362-9352

Marian W. Payson, Suite 2310
(585) 613-4080; Fax: (585) 613-4085
Law Clerk: Karen M. Phillips
Secretary: Kimberly A. Hardies

H. Kenneth Schroeder, Jr., Room 418
(716) 332-7870; Fax: (716) 332-7875
Law Clerks:
Allison P. Gioia, Karen E. Richardson

Hugh B. Scott, Room 414
(716) 332-7860; Fax: (716) 332-7865
Law Clerks:
James R. Arnone, David R. Hayes, Sr.

Clerk: Michael J. Roemer
(716) 332-1700; Fax: (716) 551-3288

Admin. Asst.: Rosalie A. Zavarella, Room 304
(716) 332-1752

Chief Deputy: Jeanne M. Spampata (716) 332-1756

Deputy-in-Charge: Jean Marie McCarthy
Room 2120, Rochester (585) 613-4010; Fax: (585) 613-4035

304 U.S. Courthouse, 68 Court St., Buffalo 14202-3406
(716) 332-1711; Fax: (716) 551-4850

Pro Se Law Clerk: Charles S. Carra, Room 508
(716) 332-1761

Court Reporters:

Christi A. Macri (Judge Larimer), Room 2500 (585) 613-4310
Michelle L. McLaughlin (Judge Skretny) (716) 332-3560
Yvonne M. Garrison (Judge Arcara) (716) 847-2477
Karen J. Bush (Judge Siragusa and Judge Telesca)
(585) 613-4312

U.S. ATTORNEY'S OFFICE

WESTERN DISTRICT OF NEW YORK
138 Delaware Ave., Buffalo 14202
(716) 843-5700; Fax: (716) 551-3052

U.S. Atty.: William J. Hochul, Jr.

First Asst. U.S. Atty.: James P. Kennedy

Chief Asst. U.S. Atty., Appellate Division:
Joseph J. Karaszewski

Chief Asst. U.S. Atty., Civil Division: Mary Pat Fleming

Chief Asst. U.S. Atty., Criminal Prosecutions:
Joseph M. Guerra III

Chief Asst. U.S. Atty., Narcotics Division: Timothy C. Lynch

Chief Asst. U.S. Atty., National Security Division:
Brett Harvey

Senior Litigation Counsel: Anthony M. Bruce

Chief, White Collar Div.: Trini E. Ross

Asst. U.S. Attys.:

Stephan J. Baczynski
Mary C. Baumgarten
Gregory L. Brown
George C. Burgasser
Paul J. Campana
Michael S. Cerrone
Michael DiGiacomo
Thomas S. Duszkiewicz
Lynn S. Edelman
William J. Gillmeister
Marie P. Grisanti
Mary C. Kane
Richard D. Kaufman
William J. Knapp
Mary Ellen Kresse
Kathleen A. Lynch
Richard P. Maigret
Aaron J. Mango
Micheal L. McCabe
Gail Y. Mitchell
Robert C. Moscati
Maura K. O'Donnell
Monica Richards
Molly Roach
Kevin D. Robinson
John E. Rogowski
Joseph M. Tripi
Robert G. Trusiak
Joel L. Violanti
Edward H. White
Jane B. Wolfe
Charles B. Wydysh
Gretchen L. Wylegala

620 Federal Bldg., 100 State St.,
Rochester 14614-1387
(585) 263-6760; Fax: (585) 263-6226

Supervisory Asst. U.S. Atty.: Bret A. Puscheck

Special Asst. U.S. Atty.: Grace M. Carducci

Asst. U.S. Attys.:

John J. Field
Craig R. Gestring
Douglas E. Gregory
Tiffany H. Lee
Robert Marangola
Marissa J. Miller
Charles E. Moynihan
Jennifer M. Noto
Richard A. Resnick
Everardo (Andy) Rodriguez
Frank H. Sherman
Kathryn Smith
Bradley E. Tyler

U.S. MARSHALS SERVICE

WESTERN DISTRICT OF NEW YORK
129 U.S. Courthouse, 68 Court St., Buffalo 14202
(716) 551-4851; Fax: (716) 551-5505

2120 U.S. Courthouse, 100 State St., Rochester 14614

U.S. Marshal: Bryan Matthews (Acting)

U.S. PROBATION OFFICE

WESTERN DISTRICT OF NEW YORK
234 U.S. Courthouse, 68 Court St., Buffalo 14202-3495
(716) 551-4241; Fax: (716) 551-4988

111 Federal Bldg., 100 State St.,
Rochester 14614-1366
(585) 263-6810; Fax: (585) 263-5766

Chief Probation Officer: Anthony M. San Giacomo

OFFICE OF THE FEDERAL PUBLIC DEFENDER

WESTERN DISTRICT OF NEW YORK
300 Pearl St., Suite 200, Buffalo 14202
(716) 551-3341; Fax: (716) 551-3346

400 First Federal Plaza, 28 E. Main St.,
Rochester 14614
(585) 263-6201; Fax: (585) 263-5871

Federal Public Defender: Marianne Mariano

Administrative Officer: Lisa Raetz

U.S. BANKRUPTCY COURT

SOUTHERN DISTRICT OF NEW YORK
Alexander Hamilton Custom House,
One Bowling Green, N.Y.C. 10004-1408
(212) 668-2870
Internet: www.nysb.uscourts.gov

300 Quarropas St., White Plains 10601
(914) 390-4060

355 Main St., Poughkeepsie 12601
(845) 452-4200

Jurisdiction—Counties of Bronx, New York

Chief Judge: Arthur J. Gonzalez (212) 668-2894
Law Clerks:
Lorraine Echevarria, Christine F. Pirro
Courtroom Deputy: Jacqueline DePierola

Judges:

Stuart M. Bernstein (212) 668-2304
Law Clerks:
Konstantina Mitsis, Carl Wedoff
Courtroom Deputy: Maria Parks

Shelley C. Chapman (212) 668-2301
Law Clerks:
Jamie Eisen, Mark Schneiderman
Courtroom Deputy: Dorothy Li

Judges, U.S. Bankruptcy Court, Southern Dist of N.Y.—Cont'd

Robert D. Drain, White Plains (914) 390-4155
E-mail: rdd.chambers@nysb.uscourts.gov
Law Clerks:
Rosemary DiSalvo   John J. Ramirez
William Hibbold
Chapter 13 Specialist: Lisa O'Shea
Courtroom Deputy: Eddie Andino
Robert E. Gerber (212) 668-5660
Law Clerks:
Adi Habbu   Isely Markman
Courtroom Deputy: Helene Blum
Martin Glenn (212) 284-4551
Law Clerks:
Peter Amend   Claire James
Daniel Harris
Courtroom Deputy: Deanna Tetzlaff
Allan L. Gropper (212) 668-5629
Law Clerks:
Matthew Bruckner   Matthew Hutchins
Courtroom Deputy: Marguerite Porter
Sean H. Lane (212) 668-5637
Courtroom Deputy: Liza Ebanks
Burton R. Lifland (On Recall) (212) 668-5663
Law Clerks:
Lara J. Fogel   Stephanie Tumbiolo
Courtroom Deputy: Monica L. Saenz de Viteri
Cecelia G. Morris
(For Dutchess, Putnam, Orange and Sullivan Counties)
355 Main St., Poughkeepsie 12601
(845) 452-4200; Fax: (845) 452-8375
Law Clerks:
Brenda Giuliano   Mary Kate Guccion
Courtroom Deputy: Frances Fredericks
James M. Peck (212) 668-5632
Law Clerks:
Harrison Denman   David Meshkov
Stacy Lutkus
Courtroom Deputy: Lynda Calderon

Clerk of Court: Vito Genna (212) 668-2870

Chief Deputy Clerk: Una O'Boyle (212) 668-2870

Admin. Analyst to Clerk: Dexter Gillies (212) 668-2870

Deputies in Charge:
Marlene Guercy, White Plains (914) 390-4060
Mary Leary, Poughkeepsie (845) 452-4200

U.S. BANKRUPTCY COURT

EASTERN DISTRICT OF NEW YORK

271 Cadman Plaza E., Suite 1595, Brooklyn 11201-1800
(347) 394-1700
Internet: www.nyeb.uscourts.gov

Jurisdiction—Counties of Kings, Queens, Richmond

Chief Judge: Carla E. Craig, Suite 1595 (347) 394-1840
Law Clerks:
Natacha Carbajal (347) 394-1875
Martin Goldstein (631) 712-6272
Elise Kanter (347) 394-1874
Sharon Weiss (347) 394-1843
Judicial Asst.: Vivian Moser Greene (347) 394-1841
Courtroom Deputy: Tracie Leonard (347) 394-1844

Judges:
Jerome Feller (347) 394-1830; Fax: (347) 394-1835
Judicial Asst.: Mildred Santiago-Amador (347) 394-1831
Law Clerk: Evan Zucker (347) 394-1833
Courtroom Deputy Clerk: Veronica Anemone (347) 394-1834
Elizabeth S. Stong (347) 394-1862
Law Clerks:
Natacha Carbajal (347) 394-1875
Hillary Comb (347) 394-1863
Joan Gottesman (347) 394-1861
Courtroom Deputy Clerk: Sheree Jackson (347) 394-1864

Clerk: Robert A. Gavin, Jr. (347) 394-1741

Chief Deputy Clerk: Paul Dickson (347) 394-1753

Admin. Asst.: Shermaine Y. Sanders (347) 394-1748

290 Federal Plaza, P.O. Box 9013, Central Islip 11722
(631) 712-6200; Fax: (631) 712-6298

Jurisdiction—Counties of Nassau, Suffolk

Judges:
Dorothy T. Eisenberg (631) 712-5690
Law Clerks:
Michael Sabella (631) 712-5687
Winnie Tsang-Louie (631) 712-5694
Judicial Asst.: Dawn Marie Rizzi (631) 712-5692
Courtroom Deputy: Christine Moffett (631) 712-6278
Robert E. Grossman (631) 712-5740
Law Clerks:
Catherine Cozette (631) 712-5691
Elena Gonzalez (631) 712-5752
Lynn Ryan (631) 712-5683
Courtroom Deputy: Madrie Tagle (631) 712-6276
Alan S. Trust (631) 712-5680
Judicial Asst.: Ruth Anziano (631) 712-5682
Law Clerk: Nicole Mignone (631) 712-5742
Courtroom Deputy: Yvette Mills (631) 712-6277

Clerk: Robert A. Gavin, Jr. (631) 712-6281

Operations Mgr.: Jennifer Jolly (631) 712-6202

Court Services Mgr.: Nancy Profit (631) 712-6204

U.S. BANKRUPTCY COURT

NORTHERN DISTRICT OF NEW YORK

330 James T. Foley U.S. Courthouse, 445 Broadway, Albany 12207
(518) 257-1661; Fax: (518) 257-1648
Internet: www.nynb.uscourts.gov

10 Broad St., Room 230, Utica 13502
(315) 793-8101; Fax: (315) 793-8128

James M. Hanley Federal Bldg., Room 315, 100 S. Clinton St., Syracuse 13261
(315) 295-1600

Jurisdiction—Counties of Albany, Broome, Cayuga, Chenango, Clinton, Columbia, Cortland, Delaware, Essex, Franklin, Fulton, Greene, Hamilton, Herkimer, Jefferson, Lewis, Madison, Montgomery, Oneida, Onondaga, Oswego, Otsego, Rensselaer, Saint Lawrence, Saratoga, Schenectady, Schoharie, Tioga, Tompkins, Ulster, Warren, Washington

Chief Judge: Robert E. Littlefield, Jr. (518) 257-1661
Law Clerk: Cynthia A. Platt (518) 257-1620
Judicial Asst.: Sue Skinner

Judges:
Margaret M. Cangilos-Ruiz (315) 295-1683
Law Clerks:
Jessica Indingaro   Dawn Simmons-Norris
Diane Davis (315) 793-8111
Law Clerk: Jill Novak Dalrymple
Judicial Asst.: Diana Roy

Clerk: Kim F. Lefebvre

Chief Deputy Clerk: Diann M. Freeman (Utica)

U.S. BANKRUPTCY COURT

WESTERN DISTRICT OF NEW YORK

Olympic Towers, Suite 250, 300 Pearl St., Buffalo 14202-2501
(716) 362-3200; Fax: (716) 362-3232
Internet: www.nywb.uscourts.gov

1220 U.S. Courthouse, 100 State St., Rochester 14614-1367
(585) 613-4200; Fax: (585) 613-4242

Chief Judge: Carl L. Bucki (For Allegany, Cattaraugus, Chautauqua and Erie Counties)
Suite 350 (716) 362-3281
Law Clerk: Adolph C. Iannaccone (716) 362-3282
Judicial Asst.: Marcia Bannister

U.S. Bankruptcy Court, Western Dist of N.Y.—Cont'd

Judges:

Michael J. Kaplan (For Genesee, Orleans, Wyoming, Niagara & Erie Counties)
Suite 350 (716) 362-3271
Law Clerk: Christopher K. Reed (716) 362-3272
Judicial Asst.: Christine Klimko

John C. Ninfo II (For Chemung, Livingston, Monroe, Ontario, Seneca, Schuyler, Steuben, Wayne & Yates Counties), 1400 U.S. Courthouse, Rochester (585) 613-4200
Law Clerk: Timothy J. Lyster
Judicial Asst.: Andrea M. Siderakis

Clerk: Paul R. Warren
(585) 613-4200, (716) 362-3200

Chief Deputy Clerk: Lisa Bertino Beaser (716) 362-3200

Operations Supervisor: Michelle Wood (Buffalo)
(716) 362-3215

UNITED STATES ADMINISTRATIVE LAW JUDGES

SOCIAL SECURITY ADMINISTRATION OFFICE OF DISABILITY ADJUDICATION AND REVIEW

Regional Office
26 Federal Plaza, Room 34-116, N.Y.C. 10278-0004
(212) 264-4036; Fax: (212) 264-1519

Regional Chief Admin. Law Judge:
Mark Sochaczewsky
E-mail: mark.sochaczewsky@ssa.gov

Regional Management Officer: Thomas Harper
E-mail: thomas.harper@ssa.gov

Regional Dir. of Administration: Cristina Grigel
E-mail: cristina.geigel@ssa.gov

Regional Dir. of Operations: Robert O'Connor
E-mail: robert.oconnor@ssa.gov

Regional Atty.: Jeanne Salidar
E-mail: jeanne.salidar@ssa.gov

For more Administrative Law Judges, see Federal Departments and Agencies

26 Federal Plaza, Room 33-118, N.Y.C. 10278-0035
(212) 264-8819; Fax: (212) 264-8633

Hearing Office Chief Admin. Law Judge:
Newton Greenberg

Admin. Law Judges:
Robin J. Arzt
Robert C. Dorf
David Ettinger
Michael Friedman
Mark Hecht
Jerome Hornblass
Kenneth Levin
Joseph K. Rowe
Mark Shapiro
Mark Solomon
Wallace Tannenbaum

Concourse Plaza Mall, 2nd Floor,
226 E. 161st St., Suite 4, Bronx 10451
(866) 563-9573; Fax: (718) 590-1673

Hearing Office Chief Admin. Law Judge: John W. Noonan

Admin. Law Judges:
William C. Berg
Paul A. Heyman
Kenneth Scheer
Sean Walsh
Leonard Olarsch, SSA ODAR, 1100 Raymond Blvd., 3rd Floor, Newark, NJ 07102

111 Livingston St., 18th Floor, Brooklyn 11201
(866) 964-9971; Fax: (718) 330-2009

Hearing Office Chief Admin. Law Judge:
Lucian A. Vecchio

Admin. Law Judges:
Ronald Bosch
Harvey Feldmeier
Robert J. Lazarus
Jane Polisar
Lori Ann Romeo
Leonard Ryan
Miriam Shire
Linda A. Stagno
Robert Ward
Maryellen Weinberg
Leonard E. Yoswein

375 N. Broadway, 3rd Floor, Jericho 11753-2008
(866) 931-4494; Fax: (516) 942-0353

Hearing Office Chief Admin. Law Judge: Jay L. Cohen

Admin. Law Judges:
Brian Crawley
Joseph Faraguna
Seymour Raynor
Ronald Waldman
Andrew Weiss

155-10 Jamaica Ave., P.O. Box 319300, Jamaica 11431
(866) 931-6092; Fax: (718) 557-6575

Hearing Office Chief Admin. Law Judge:
David Z. Nisnewitz

Admin. Law Judges:
Manuel Cofresi
Seymour Fier
Marilyn Hoppenfeld
Gal Lahat
Margaret Pecoraro
Hazel C. Strauss
Sol Wieselthier

75 S. Broadway, 2nd Floor, White Plains 10601
(914) 761-7190; Fax: (914) 682-7006

Hearing Office Chief Admin. Law Judge:
Brian Lemoine

Admin. Law Judges:
Katherine C. Edgell
Robert Gonzalez
Dennis G. Katz
Michael Rodriguez
Neil R. Ross

74 N. Pearl St., 6th Floor, Albany 12207
(866) 643-3035; Fax: (518) 462-1524

Hearing Office Chief Admin. Law Judge: Carl Stephan

Admin. Law Judges:
Dale Black-Pennington
Terence Farrell
Thomas Grabeel
Michelle Marcus
Arthur Patane
John J. Pickett
Robert Ringler
Robert Wright

Senior Admin. Law Judge: Gordon Mahley

Buffalo Hearing Office
Key Center, Suite 200, 50 Fountain Plz., Buffalo 14202
(866) 348-5819; Fax: (716) 551-4078

Admin. Law Judges:
Eric L. Glazer
Nancy Gregg Pasiecznik
Grenville W. Harrop, Jr.
Robert T. Harvey
Bruce R. Mazzarella
Timothy M. McGuan
Stanley A. Moskal, Jr.
William R. Pietz
William E. Straub
Timothy J. Trost
William M. Weir
Marilyn D. Zahm

300 S. State St., 5th Floor, Syracuse 13202-2520
(888) 655-6477; Fax: (315) 479-3933

Hearing Office Chief Admin. Law Judge: Robert Gale

Admin. Law Judges:
F. Patrick Flanagan
Marie D. Greener
Elizabeth Koenecke
John M. Lischak
Gordon Mahley
Barry Ryan

U.S. IMMIGRATION COURT

New York Office
26 Federal Plaza, Room 1237, N.Y.C. 10278
(917) 454-1040; Fax: (212) 264-1070

Chief Immigration Judge: Brian M. O'Leary
(703) 305-1554; Fax: (703) 305-1448

Immigration Judges:
Terry A. Bain
Javier E. Balasquide
Noël A. Brennan
Joanna M. Bukszpan
Sarah M. Burr
Mary Cheng
George T. Chew
Annette S. Elstein
Noel Anne Ferris
Vivienne E. Gordon-Uruakpa
Sandy K. Hom
Brigitte Laforest
Elizabeth A. Lamb
Margaret McManus
Philip L. Morace
Thomas J. Mulligan
Barbara A. Nelson
Patricia A. Rohan
Douglas B. Schoppert
Helen J. Sichel
William Van Wyke
Gabriel C. Videla
Alan A. Vomacka
Robert D. Weisel
Randa Zagzoug

Court Administrator: Star B. Pacitto

Deputy Court Administrator: Regina Rau

For more Administrative Law Judges, see Federal Departments and Agencies

U.S. Immigration Court—Cont'd

New York—Varick Office
201 Varick St., Room 1140, N.Y.C. 10014
(212) 620-6279

Immigration Judges:
Steven R. Abrams
Alan L. Page
Alan A. Vomacka

Court Administrator: Thomas J. Bonita III

Buffalo Office
Federal Center, Suite 410, 130 Delaware Ave., Buffalo 14202
(716) 551-3442
Internet: www.usdoj.gov/eoir
4250 Federal Dr., Batavia 14020
(585) 345-4300

Immigration Judges:
Philip J. Montante, Jr.
Michaelangelo Rocco
John B. Reid (Batavia)

Court Administrator: Gary Somerville

Fishkill Office
Downstate Correctional Facility,
121 Red Schoolhouse Road, Fishkill 12524
(845) 831-3657

Immigration Judge: Roger F. Sagerman
Court Administrator: Thomas J. Bonita III

Napanoch Office
Ulster Correctional Facility, Berme Road,
P.O. Box 800, Napanoch 12458
(845) 647-5506

Immigration Judge: Roger F. Sagerman

Court Administrator: Thomas J. Bonita III

UNITED STATES DEPARTMENT OF LABOR

Office of Administrative Law Judges
2 Executive Campus, Suite 450,
Cherry Hill, NJ 08002
(856) 486-3800; Fax: (856) 486-3806
Internet: www.oalj.dol.gov

District Chief Judge: Adele H. Odegard
E-mail: odegard.adele@dol.gov

Admin. Law Judges:
Janice K. Bullard; E-mail: bullard.janice@dol.gov
Ralph A. Romano; E-mail: romano.ralph@dol.gov
Theresa C. Timlin; E-mail: timlin.theresa@dol.gov
For more Administrative Law Judges, see Federal Departments and Agencies

NEW YORK STATE COURTS

JUDICIAL DEPARTMENTS OF THE STATE OF NEW YORK
(§ 70, Judiciary Law)

1st Dept. 1st and 12th Judicial Districts
2nd Dept. 2nd, 9th, 10th and 11th Judicial Districts
3rd Dept. 3rd, 4th and 6th Judicial Districts
4th Dept. 5th, 7th and 8th Judicial Districts

(Also see chart at page 56 and map at page 57)

JUDICIAL DISTRICTS OF THE STATE OF NEW YORK
(§ 140, Judiciary Law)

I. County of New York.
II. Counties of Kings and Richmond.
III. Counties of Albany, Columbia, Greene, Rensselaer, Schoharie, Sullivan and Ulster.
IV. Counties of Clinton, Essex, Franklin, Fulton, Hamilton, Montgomery, St. Lawrence, Saratoga, Schenectady, Warren and Washington.
V. Counties of Herkimer, Jefferson, Lewis, Oneida, Onondaga and Oswego.
VI. Counties of Broome, Chemung, Chenango, Cortland, Delaware, Madison, Otsego, Schuyler, Tioga and Tompkins.
VII. Counties of Cayuga, Livingston, Monroe, Ontario, Seneca, Steuben, Wayne and Yates.
VIII. Counties of Allegany, Cattaraugus, Chautauqua, Erie, Genesee, Niagara, Orleans and Wyoming.
IX. Counties of Dutchess, Orange, Putnam, Rockland and Westchester.
X. Counties of Nassau and Suffolk.
XI. County of Queens.
XII. County of Bronx.

COURTS OF RECORD AND NOT OF RECORD
(§ 2, Judiciary Law)

Each of the following courts of the state is a court of record:

1. The court for the trial of impeachments.
2. A court on the judiciary.
3. The court of appeals.
4. The appellate division of the supreme court in each department.
5. The supreme court.
6. The court of claims.
7. A county court in each county, except the counties of New York, Bronx, Kings, Queens & Richmond.
8. The family court.
9. A surrogate's court in each county.
10. Each city court outside the City of New York.
11. The district court in each county where established.
12. The civil court of the City of New York and the criminal court of the City of New York.

All courts other than those specified in this section are courts not of record.

OFFICE OF COURT ADMINISTRATION
25 Beaver St., N.Y.C. 10004
(212) 428-2700
Internet: www.nycourts.gov
Agency Bldg. 4, Suite 2001,
4 E.S.P., Empire State Plaza, Albany 12223-1450
(518) 473-6087; Fax: (518) 473-5514

Chief Administrative Judge: Ann T. Pfau
(212) 428-2100; Fax: (212) 428-2188
E-mail: apfau@courts.state.ny.us

Administrative Dir. of the Office of Court Administration: Lawrence K. Marks (212) 428-2884

Chief of Operations of the Office of Court Administration: Ronald P. Younkins (212) 428-2126

Deputy Chief Admin. Judges:
Fern A. Fisher (N.Y.C. Courts)
111 Centre St., N.Y.C. 10013
(646) 386-4200; Fax: (212) 374-5709
E-mail: dcaj@courts.state.ny.us

Michael V. Coccoma (Outside N.Y.C.)
Empire State Plaza, Suite 2001, 4 E.S.P.,
Albany 12223-1450 (518) 474-3828; Fax: (518) 473-5514

Judy Harris Kluger (Chief, Office of Policy & Planning; Dir., Office of Drug Treatment Programs)
25 Beaver St., N.Y.C. 10004
(212) 428-2130; Fax: (212) 428-2192
E-mail: jkluger@courts.state.ny.us

Statewide Judicial Director of Ethics Education and Counsel: George D. Marlow
Courthouse, 10 Market St., Poughkeepsie 12601
(845) 486-2200; Fax: (845) 473-5403

Dean, New York State Judicial Institute:
Juanita Bing Newton, 84 N. Broadway, White Plains 10603
(914) 824-5800

Vice Dean, New York State Judicial Institute:
Sharon S. Townsend (Family and Matrimonial Law)
84 N. Broadway, White Plains 10603 (914) 824-5800

Dir., Appellate Education, New York State Judicial Institute: John T. Buckley
84 N. Broadway, White Plains 10603 (914) 824-5800

Dir., New York State Access to Justice Programs:
Fern A. Fisher, 111 Centre St., N.Y.C. 10013
(646) 386-4200; Fax: (212) 374-5709

Counsel: John W. McConnell
(212) 428-2150; Fax: (212) 428-2155

First Deputy Counsel: Marc Bloustein (Albany)
(518) 474-7469

Deputy Counsel: (212) 428-2150
John Eiseman Raymond Hack
Janet Fink Paul McDonnell

First Asst. Deputy Counsel: Kenneth Falk
(212) 428-2150

Asst. Deputy Counsel:
Eugene Colon (212) 428-2150
Lisa M. Evans (212) 428-2150
Shawn Kerby (212) 428-2172
Pedro Morales (212) 428-2150
Virginia Neary (212) 428-2150
John Sullivan (Albany) (518) 474-7469

Assoc. Counsel: Ellen Smithberg (212) 428-2150

Public Affairs Dir.: Greg Murray
(212) 428-2116; Fax: (212) 428-2117

Communications Dir.: David Bookstaver
(212) 428-2500; Fax: (212) 428-2508

Inspector General: Sherrill Spatz
(646) 386-3500; Fax: (212) 514-7158

Atty. Registration: Samuel Younger
(212) 428-2800; Fax: (212) 428-2819

Retainer and Closing Statements: Samuel Younger
(212) 428-2807; Fax: (212) 428-2804

Criminal History Search: Michael Andujar
(212) 428-2950; Fax: (212) 428-2949

Div. of Legal Resources: Ellen Robinson (Albany)
(518) 238-4373; Fax: (518) 238-2894

Section 28 of Article VI of the Constitution, as amended November 8, 1977, effective April 1, 1978, provides that the Chief Judge of the Court of Appeals is the Chief Judge of the state and its chief judicial officer. The Chief Judge appoints a Chief Administrator of the Courts (who is called the Chief Administrative Judge of the Courts if the incumbent is a judge) with the advice and consent of the Administrative Board of the Courts. The Administrative Board consists of the Chief Judge as chair and the Presiding Justices of the four Appellate Divisions of Supreme Court.

The Chief Administrator, on behalf of the Chief Judge, is responsible for supervising the administration and operation of the trial courts and for the establishment and direction of an administrative office of the courts.

The Chief Judge establishes statewide administrative standards and policies after consultation with the Administrative Board and promulgates them after approval by the Court of Appeals.

Art. 78 of the Judiciary Law implements these constitutional provisions.

For court emergencies, call (800) COURT-NY or see Internet website www.nycourts.gov; in N.Y.C., closings also noted on radio on WINS (1010) and WCBS (880)

OFFICE OF THE DEPUTY CHIEF ADMINISTRATIVE JUDGE NEW YORK CITY COURTS

Deputy Chief Administrative Judge, N.Y.C. Courts: Fern A. Fisher, 111 Centre St., N.Y.C. 10013
(646) 386-4200; E-mail: dcaj@courts.state.ny.us

Administrative Judge of the Family Court of the City of New York: Edwina Richardson-Mendelson
60 Lafayette St., N.Y.C. 10013
(646) 386-5190; Fax: (212) 374-2127

Administrative Judge, Supreme Court, Civil Term, New York County: Sherry Klein Heitler
60 Centre St., N.Y.C. 10007 (646) 386-3211

Administrative Judge, Supreme Court, Criminal Term, New York County: Michael J. Obus
100 Centre St., N.Y.C. 10013
(646) 386-3947; Fax: (212) 401-9264

Administrative Judge, Supreme Court, Criminal Div., Bronx County: Efrain Alvarado
Bronx Hall of Justice, 265 E. 161st St., Bronx 10451
(718) 618-3700

Administrative Judge, Supreme Court, Kings County, Civil Term: Sylvia O. Hinds-Radix
360 Adams St., Brooklyn 11201
(347) 296-1200; Fax: (718) 643-2095

Administrative Judge, Supreme Court, Kings County, Criminal Term: Barry Kamins
320 Jay St., Brooklyn 11201
(347) 296-1000; Fax: (347) 296-1327

Administrative Judge, Supreme Court, Richmond County Criminal and Civil Terms: Philip G. Minardo
18 Richmond Terr., Staten Island 10301
(718) 675-8600; Fax: (718) 815-2775

Administrative Judge, Supreme Court, Queens County, Civil Term: Jeremy S. Weinstein
88-11 Sutphin Blvd., Jamaica 11435
(718) 298-1100; Fax: (718) 520-2499

Administrative Judge, Supreme Court, Queens County, Criminal Term: Fernando M. Camacho
125-01 Queens Blvd., Kew Gardens 11415 (718) 298-1440

COMMISSION ON JUDICIAL CONDUCT

61 Broadway, Suite 1200, N.Y.C. 10006
(646) 386-4800; Fax: (646) 458-0037
Internet: www.scjc.state.ny.us

Corning Tower, Suite 2301, Empire State Plz., Albany 12223
(518) 453-4600; Fax: (518) 486-1850

400 Andrews St., Suite 700, Rochester 14604
(585) 784-4141; Fax: (585) 232-7839

Chairperson: Hon. Thomas A. Klonick

Vice Chair: Stephen R. Coffey

Administrator and Counsel: Robert H. Tembeckjian
E-mail: tembeckjian@cjc.ny.gov

Clerk: Jean M. Savanyu; E-mail: savanyu@cjc.ny.gov

Deputy, Litigation: Edward Lindner
E-mail: lindner@cjc.ny.gov

Deputy, Albany: Cathleen S. Cenci; E-mail: cenci@cjc.ny.gov

Deputy, Rochester: John J. Postel; E-mail: postel@cjc.ny.gov

Deputy, New York City: Jorge Dopico
E-mail: dopico@cjc.ny.gov

Investigates complaints against judges of the unified court system and, where appropriate, may admonish, censure or remove a judge from office, subject to review by the Court of Appeals.

LAWYERS FUND FOR CLIENT PROTECTION

119 Washington Ave., Albany 12210
(518) 434-1935, (800) 442-3863; Fax: (518) 434-5641
Internet: www.nylawfund.org

Trustees:
Eleanor Breitel Alter (Chairman)
Eric A. Seiff (Vice Chairman)
Theresa B. Mazzullo (Treasurer)
Peter A. Bellacosa
Nancy Burner
Patricia L. Gatling
Charlotte G. Holstein

Exec. Dir. & Counsel: Timothy O'Sullivan

Pursuant to section 468-b of the Judiciary Law, the Lawyers' Fund for Client Protection reimburses misappropriations by attorneys in the practice of law. The Fund is administered by a Board of Trustees appointed by the Judges of the Court of Appeals. The Trustees' regulations and procedures are contained in 22 NYCRR Part 7200.

COURT OF APPEALS

Court of Appeals Hall, 20 Eagle St., Albany 12207-1095
(518) 455-7700
Internet: www.courts.state.ny.us/ctapps

Chief Judge: Jonathan Lippman
Court of Appeals Hall, 20 Eagle St., Albany 12207-1095
(518) 455-7700

Associate Judges:
Carmen Beauchamp Ciparick
3700 Chanin Bldg., 122 E. 42nd St., N.Y.C. 10168-0002
(212) 661-2144
Victoria A. Graffeo
Court of Appeals Hall, 20 Eagle St., Albany 12207
(518) 285-5050
Susan Phillips Read
Court of Appeals Hall, 20 Eagle St., Albany 12207-1095
(518) 455-7721
Robert S. Smith
780 Third Ave., N.Y.C. 10017 (646) 386-3824
Eugene F. Pigott, Jr.
438 Main St., Suite 900, Buffalo 14202 (716) 845-2101
Theodore T. Jones, Jr.
140 Grand St., Suite 900, White Plains 10601
(914) 824-5780

Clerk: Andrew W. Klein
Court of Appeals Hall, 20 Eagle St., Albany 12207-1095
(518) 455-7707

Deputy Clerk: Richard Reed
Court of Appeals Hall, 20 Eagle St., Albany 12207-1095
(518) 455-7707

Chief Court Atty.: Paul J. McGrath
Court of Appeals Hall, 20 Eagle St., Albany 12207-1095
(518) 488-7757

Public Information Officer: Gary Spencer
Court of Appeals Hall, 20 Eagle St., Albany 12207-1095
(518) 455-7711

PRACTICE TIME TABLE FOR APPEALS TO COURT OF APPEALS

As amended to September 2010.

1. Notice of Appeal.

Where appeal is of right notice of appeal must be served and filed with the clerk with whom the judgment or order appealed from is entered within 30 days after service of copy of judgment or order appealed from with notice of entry thereof; or if appellant's attorney enters judgment or order, within 30 days thereafter. If judgment or order is served by mail or overnight service, additional time shall be added to the prescribed period. Where appellant erroneously attempts to appeal by permission instead of by right, or as of right instead of by permission, the time to appeal or to move for leave to appeal is extended for 30 days after the entry of the order dismissing the appeal or denying the application. (C.P.L.R. 5513, 5514, 5515)

Court of Appeals—Cont'd

2. Preliminary Appeal Statement.

Within 10 days after appeal is taken by 1) a notice of appeal as requried by C.P.L.R. 5515; 2) an order granting a motion for leave to appeal in a civil case; or 3) issuance of a certificate granting leave to appeal in a non-capital criminal case, appellant must file with the clerk of the Court of Appeals an original and one copy of a Preliminary Appeal Statement on a form prescribed by the Court, with required attachments and proof of service of one copy to each other party. (Ct. App., Rule 500.9)

3. Stay of Execution

If judgment appealed from does not come within C.P.L.R., 5519(a) or (b), motion is made in proper court pursuant to C.P.L.R. 5519(c).

4. Exceptions to and Justification of Sureties.

Same as in Appellate Division.

5. Record on Appeal.

Record material shall be supplied to the Court by 1) subpeona of the original file from the clerk of the court of original instance, with original exhibits to be relied upon, supplemented with an original and 24 copies of an appendix as prescribed in Ct. App. Rule 500.14(b); 2) one copy of the reproduced record used at the court below, supplemented with an original and 24 copies of an appendix as prescribed in Ct. App. Rule 500.14(b); or 3) an original and 24 copies of a new and full record to include the record used at the court below, notice of appeal or order granting leave to appeal, the decision and order appealed from, and any other decision and order brought up for review with proof of service of three copies of the new record on each other party. (Ct. App., Rule 500.14)

6. Service and Filing of Record and Briefs.

The clerk generally issues a scheduling letter after filing of Preliminary Appeal Statement. If no scheduling letter is issued, Appellant serves three copies on respondent and files 24 copies with clerk within 60 days after the service of the notice of appeal, or, in the alternative files the original record and 24 copies of the brief and appendix and serves 3 copies of the brief and appendix on each party. Respondent must serve three and file 24 copies of his brief within 45 days thereafter. A reply brief may be served and filed within 15 days after receipt of respondent's brief. (Ct. App., Rule 500.12)

7. Notice of Argument.

Calendar–The clerk will advise counsel of the date assigned for argument. (Ct. App., Rule 500.17)

8. Motion for Reargument.

Notice of motion for reargument must be served not later than 30 days after the appeal or motion sought to be reargued has been decided, unless otherwise permitted by the Court. Movant shall file original and six copies of its papers with proof of service of two copies on each other party An original and one copy of a motion for reargument of a motion may be served and filed if filing of an original and one copy of papers was allowed on the underlying motion. (Ct. App., Rules 500.24(a), (b))

9. Motions in Court of Appeals.

Motions shall be returnable on Mondays, or if Monday is a legal holiday, the next business day. Motions shall be submitted without oral argument unless otherwise directed. (Ct. App., Rule 500.21)

MATERIALS TO BE FILED INITIALLY ON APPEAL

Preliminary Appeal Statement

Copy of the filed notice of appeal, order granting leave to appeal (civil case) or certificated granting leave to appeal (noncapital criminal case), whichever is applicable

Order, judgment or determination appealed from to the Court of Appeals

Any order, judgment or determination which is the subject of the order appealed from, or which is otherwise brought up for review

All decisions or opinions relating to the orders appealed from to the Court of Appeals

If required a copy of the notice sent to the Attorney General pursuant to Ct. App. Rule 500.9

COURT OF CLAIMS

Justice Bldg., 7th Floor, Empire State Plaza, Albany 12223
Mailing Address: Capitol Station, P.O. Box 7344, Albany 12224
Filing Unit: (518) 432-3411;
Motion Unit: (518) 432-3416;
Fax Filing: (866) 413-1069
E-mail: rdecatal@courts.state.ny.us
Internet: www.nyscourtofclaims.state.ny.us

26 Broadway, 10th Floor, N.Y.C. 10004-1824
(212) 361-8100; Fax: (212) 361-8103

Presiding Judge: Richard E. Sise
P.O. Box 7344, Capitol Station, Albany 12224
(518) 432-3435; Fax: (518) 432-3428

Judges:

Francis T. Collins
65 S. Broadway, Room 220, Saratoga Springs 12866
(518) 583-5340; Fax: (518) 583-5345

W. Brooks DeBow
Capitol Station, P.O. Box 7344, Albany 12224
(518) 242-3701

James H. Ferreira
Capitol Station, P.O. Box 7344, Albany 12224
(518) 242-3710

Diane L. Fitzpatrick
Salina Place, 2nd Floor, 205 S. Salina St.,
Syracuse 13202 (315) 466-7161; Fax: (315) 466-7164

Judith A. Hard
Capitol Station, P.O. Box 7344, Albany 12224
(518) 432-3907; Fax: (518) 432-3908

Michael E. Hudson
130 S. Elmwood Ave., Buffalo 14202
(716) 515-4810; Fax: (716) 515-4813

James J. Lack
State Office Bldg., 3rd Floor, Veterans Memorial Hwy.,
Hauppauge 11788 (631) 952-6542; Fax: (631) 952-6727

Alan C. Marin
26 Broadway, 10th Floor, N.Y.C. 10004
(212) 361-8130; Fax: (212) 361-8133

Christopher J. McCarthy
Capitol Station, P.O. Box 7344, Albany 12224
(518) 242-3730

Thomas J. McNamara
65 S. Broadway, Room 210, Saratoga Springs 12866
(518) 583-5330; Fax: (518) 583-5335

Nicholas V. Midey, Jr.
Salina Place, 2nd Floor, 205 S. Salina St.,
Syracuse 13202 (315) 466-7151; Fax: (315) 466-7154

Stephen J. Mignano
140 Grand St., Suite 910, White Plains 10601
(914) 289-2320; Fax: (914) 289-2323

Frank P. Milano
Capitol Station, P.O. Box 7344, Albany 12224
(518) 242-3720

Renée Forgensi Minarik
500 Court Exchange Bldg., 144 Exchange Blvd.,
Rochester 14614 (585) 987-4212; Fax: (585) 262-3019

Jeremiah J. Moriarty III
130 S. Elmwood Ave., Suite 300, Buffalo 14202
(716) 515-4820; Fax: (716) 515-4823

Philip J. Patti
500 Court Exchange Bldg., 144 Exchange Blvd.,
Rochester 14614-2108
(585) 325-4500; Fax: (585) 262-5715

Richard Platkin
Capitol Station, P.O. Box 7344, Albany 12224
(518) 242-3740; Fax: (518) 242-3735
Acting Supreme Court Justice

Terry Jane Ruderman
140 Grand St., 5th Floor, White Plains 10601
(914) 289-2310; Fax: (914) 289-2313

Catherine C. Schaewe
State Office Bldg., 18th Floor, 44 Hawley St.,
Binghamton 13901-4418
(607) 721-8623; Fax: (607) 721-8590

Judges, Court of Claims—Cont'd

Melvin L. Schweitzer
26 Broadway, 10th Floor, N.Y.C. 10004
(212) 361-8170; Fax: (212) 361-8173
Acting Supreme Court Justice

Thomas H. Scuccimarra
140 Grand St., 9th Floor, White Plains 10601
(914) 289-2330; Fax: (914) 289-2333

O. Peter Sherwood
60 Centre St., Room 615, N.Y.C. 10007
(646) 386-3807; Fax: (212) 748-7793
Acting Supreme Court Justice

Norman I. Siegel
State Office Bldg., 207 Genesee St., Utica 13501
(315) 793-2184; Fax: (315) 793-2217

Faviola A. Soto
26 Broadway, 10th Floor, N.Y.C. 10004
(212) 361-8160; Fax: (212) 361-8165

Gina M. Lopez Summa
State Office Bldg., 3rd Floor, Veterans Memorial Pkwy., Hauppauge 11788 (631) 952-4955; Fax: (631) 952-2070

Clerk: Robert T. DeCataldo
Capitol Station, P.O. Box 7344, Albany 12224
(518) 432-3463

Deputy Clerk: Joan M. Fontana
Capitol Station, P.O. Box 7344, Albany 12224
(518) 432-3914

EMERGENCY DANGEROUS DRUG CONTROL PROGRAM

Acting Supreme Court Justices, Emergency Dangerous Drug Control Program:

M. William Boller
Erie County Court Bldg., 25 Delaware Ave., Buffalo 14202 (718) 845-9357; Fax: (718) 851-3327

John J. Brunetti
Criminal Courts Bldg., Suite 380, 505 S. State St., Syracuse 13202 (315) 671-1058; Fax: (315) 671-1178

Mark D. Cohen
Arthur M. Cromarty Court Complex, 210 Center Dr., Riverhead 11901 (631) 852-2168; Fax: (631) 852-2156

William C. Donnino
262 Old Country Rd., Mineola 11501
(516) 571-2797; Fax: (516) 571-1485

Philip M. Grella
Nassau County Court, 262 Old Country Rd., Mineola 11501 (516) 571-1488; Fax: (516) 571-2642

Robert K. Holdman
Richard J. Daronco Courthouse,
111 Dr. Martin Luther King, Jr. Blvd.,
White Plains 10601 (914) 824-5379

James M. Kindler
Bronx Hall of Justice, Room 953, 265 E. 161st St., Bronx 10451 (718) 618-3680

Albert Lorenzo
Richard J. Daronco Courthouse,
111 Dr. Martin Luther King, Jr. Blvd.,
White Plains 10601 (914) 824-5403

Guy J. Mangano, Jr.
320 Jay St., Brooklyn 11201 (347) 296-1046

Roger D. McDonough
Albany County Judicial Center, Room 309, 6 Lodge St., Albany 12207 (518) 285-8776; Fax: (518) 436-3986

Juan M. Merchan
100 Centre St., N.Y.C. 10013 (646) 386-3934

John L. Michalski
Erie County Court Bldg., 3rd Floor, 25 Delaware Ave., Buffalo 14202 (716) 845-9462; Fax: (716) 851-3314

Joseph C. Pastoressa
Arthur M. Cromarty Court Complex, 210 Center Dr., Riverhead 11901 (631) 852-2163; Fax: (631) 852-3043

Maxwell Wiley
100 Centre St., N.Y.C. 10013 (646) 386-4433

Ronald Zweibel
100 Centre St., Room 1731, N.Y.C. 10013
(646) 386-3987; Fax: (212) 748-5920

Acting Supreme Court Justices, Pursuant to Chapter 906, Laws of 1986:

Catherine M. Bartlett, 275 Main St., Goshen 10924
(845) 291-3137; Fax: (845) 291-2106

Antonio I. Brandveen, 100 Supreme Court Dr., Mineola 11501 (516) 571-3360; Fax: (516) 571-1283

Fernando M. Camacho
(Administrative Judge, Criminal Term, Queens County)
125-01 Queens Blvd., Kew Gardens 11415
(718) 298-1440; Fax: (718) 520-6426

Gregory Carro, 100 Centre St., Room 1702, N.Y.C. 10013
(646) 386-4424; Fax: (212) 401-9263

Thomas J. Carroll, 320 Jay St., Brooklyn 11201
(347) 296-1848; Fax: (347) 296-1351

Margaret Clancy, Hall of Justice, 265 E. 161st St., Bronx 10451 (718) 618-3638; Fax: (212) 884-8910

Robert J. Collini
18 Richmond Terr., Staten Island 10301 (718) 675-8650

Lawrence V. Cullen, 88-11 Sutphin Blvd., Room 44A, Jamaica 11435 (718) 298-1083; Fax: (718) 298-1005

Vincent M. Del Giudice, 320 Jay St., Brooklyn 11201
(347) 296-1851; Fax: (347) 296-1349

Matthew J. D'Emic, 320 Jay St., Room 25-007, Brooklyn 11201 (347) 296-1031; Fax: (347) 296-1337

Mark R. Dwyer
320 Jay St., Brooklyn 11201 (347) 401-9096

Marcia P. Hirsch
125-01 Queens Blvd., Kew Gardens 11415 (718) 298-1435

Alan L. Honorof, 262 Old Country Rd., Mineola 11501
(516) 571-3423; Fax: (516) 571-1849

John G. Ingram
320 Jay St., Brooklyn 11201 (347) 296-1489

Richard C. Kloch, Sr.
Niagara County Courthouse, 175 Hawley St., Lockport 14094 (716) 439-7055; Fax: (716) 439-7039

Dan Lamont
County Courthouse, 290 Main St., P.O. Box 369, Schoharie 12157 (518) 295-8640; Fax: (518) 295-8638

Joseph J. Maltese
130 Stuyvesant Pl., Staten Island 10301 (718) 675-7860

Lawrence K. Marks
25 Beaver St., N.Y.C. 10004 (212) 428-2884

Daniel Martin, John P. Cohalan Jr. Courthouse, 400 Carleton Ave., Central Islip 11722 (631) 853-4523

Juanita Bing Newton (Dean, N.Y. State Judicial Institute)
84 N. Broadway, White Plains 10603 (914) 824-5800

Stephen J. Rooney
18 Richmond Terr., Staten Island 10301 (718) 675-8640

Denise L. Sher
100 Supreme Court Dr., Mineola 11501 (516) 571-2883

Acting Supreme Court Justices, Pursuant to Chapter 209, Laws of 1990:

Russell P. Buscaglia
Erie County Court Bldg., Suite 504, 25 Delaware Ave., Buffalo 14202 (716) 845-9435; Fax: (716) 851-3316

Donald F. Cerio, Jr.
Madison County Courthouse, P.O. Box 545, Wampsville 13163 (315) 366-2321; Fax: (315) 366-2539

Ann M. Donnelly
265 E. 161st St., Bronx 10451 (718) 618-3650

Jill Konviser, 100 Centre St., N.Y.C. 10013
(646) 386-4411; Fax: (347) 296-1375

Jeffrey D. Lebowitz
88-11 Sutphin Blvd., Jamaica 11435 (718) 298-1219

Martin Marcus
Hall of Justice, 265 E. 161st St., Bronx 10451
(718) 618-3678; Fax: (718) 618-3571

Michael H. Melkonian, 80 Second St., Troy 12180
(518) 285-6132; Fax: (518) 274-1367

Richard A. Molea, Richard J. Daronco Courthouse, 111 Dr. M. Luther King, Jr. Blvd., White Plains 10601
(914) 824-5454; Fax: (914) 995-8654

Robert A. Neary, Bronx Hall of Justice, 265 E. 161st St., Bronx 10451 (718) 618-3610

Wayne M. Ozzi, Hall of Justice, 265 E. 161st St., Bronx 10461 (718) 618-3717

Court of Claims—Cont'd

Acting Supreme Court Justices, Pursuant to Chapter 240, Laws of 2006:

Thomas A. Adams, 100 Supreme Court Dr., Mineola 11501 (516) 571-2961; Fax: (516) 571-1704
John C. Cherundolo, Onondaga County Cthse., Room 404, 401 Montgomery St., Syracuse 13202 (315) 671-1090; Fax: (315) 671-1180
Gerald W. Connolly, 112 State St., Room 1350, Albany 12207 (518) 285-8592; Fax: (518) 487-5378
Daniel P. Conviser 111 Centre St., N.Y.C. 10013 (646) 386-3977
Richard A. Dollinger, 207 Hall of Justice, 99 Exchange Blvd., Rochester 14614 (585) 428-2879
Elizabeth A. Foley, 320 Jay St., Brooklyn 11201 (347) 296-1616; Fax: (347) 296-1362
Cassandra Mullen 111 Centre St., N.Y.C. 10013 (646) 386-5710
Kimberly A. O'Connor, 112 State St., Room 1360, Albany 12207 (518) 285-8597
Dineen A. Riviezzo 320 Jay St., Brooklyn 11201 (347) 296-1113
Timothy J. Walker Erie County Court Bldg., 3rd Floor, 25 Delaware Ave., Buffalo 14202 (718) 845-7479; Fax: (716) 851-3440
Henry F. Zwack, 80 Second St., Troy 12180 (518) 285-6170; Fax: (518) 270-5435

Judges sit at assignments, subject to constant change, throughout New York State. Consult Judges' Directory for Judges' addresses and telephone numbers at press time.

APPELLATE DIVISION

APPELLATE DIVISION FIRST DEPARTMENT
27 Madison Ave., N.Y.C. 10010
(212) 340-0400

Presiding Justice: Luis A. Gonzalez (212) 340-0400; Fax: (212) 340-0547

Associate Justices:

Sheila Abdus-Salaam	James M. McGuire
Rolando T. Acosta	Karla Moskowitz
Richard T. Andrias	*Eugene L. Nardelli
*John T. Buckley	Dianne T. Renwick
James M. Catterson	Rosalyn H. Richter
Leland G. DeGrasse	Nelson S. Roman
Helen E. Freedman	David B. Saxe
David Friedman	John W. Sweeny, Jr.
Sallie Manzanet-Daniels	Peter Tom
Angela M. Mazzarelli	

Clerk: Vacancy at Press Time

Deputy Clerks:
Elba I. Castro — Eric B. Schumacher

Deputy Chief Law Asst.: Mariann Sullivan

Chief Law Asst.: Susanna Rojas

Librarian: Eugene A. Preudhomme

Law Clerks to Justices:

(Abdus-Salaam) . . . . . Deborah Woll
(Acosta) . . . . . Rosalí Vázquez
(Andrias) . . . . . Neil Friedkin
(Catterson) . . . . . Joanna Elm
(DeGrasse) . . . . . Margaret Georges
(Freedman) . . . . . David S. Cohen
(Friedman) . . . . . Daniel J. Fish
(Gonzalez) . . . . . Linda M. Byrne
(Manzanet-Daniels) . . . . . Carol Polizzi
(Mazzarelli) . . . . . Robert Patchen
(McGuire) . . . . . Melissa Ringel
(Moskowitz) . . . . . Melissa Crane
(Nardelli) . . . . . Gregg Snigur
(Renwick) . . . . . William Ramos
(Richter) . . . . . Thomas Hickey, Pamela Walitt
(Roman) . . . . . Fidel E. Gomez
(Saxe) . . . . . Lauren A. Foodim
(Sweeny) . . . . . Joseph D. Cerreto
(Tom) . . . . . Robert F. Peake

*Justice Serving under Certification

First Department Committee on Character and Fitness of Applicants for Admission to the Bar
41 Madison Ave., 26th Floor, N.Y.C. 10010
(646) 386-5893; Fax: (212) 779-1889

Chairman: Peter J. Johnson, Jr. 120 Wall St., N.Y.C. 10005

Executive Secretary: Vacancy at Press Time

First Department Disciplinary Committee
61 Broadway, 2nd Floor, N.Y.C. 10006
(212) 401-0800; Fax: (212) 287-1045

Chief Counsel: Vacancy at Press Time

APPELLATE DIVISION SECOND DEPARTMENT
45 Monroe Pl., Brooklyn 11201
(718) 875-1300
Internet: www.nycourts.gov/courts/ad2/

Presiding Justice: A. Gail Prudenti 45 Monroe Pl., Brooklyn 11201 (718) 722-6400; Fax: (718) 855-2884

Associate Justices:

Daniel D. Angiolillo Courthouse Sq., Room 644, 140 Grand St., White Plains 10601 (914) 824-5390; Fax: (914) 946-1026
Leonard B. Austin Supreme Court Bldg., 100 Supreme Court Dr., Mineola 11501 (516) 571-2683; Fax: (516) 571-0131
Ruth C. Balkin 100 Supreme Court Dr., Room 419, Mineola 11501 (516) 571-2323; Fax: (516) 571-0180
Ariel E. Belen (718) 722-6384
Cheryl E. Chambers, 320 Jay St., Room 25.49, Brooklyn 11201 (347) 296-1040; Fax: (347) 296-1331
Joseph Covello, 100 Supreme Court Dr., Mineola 11501 (516) 571-2073; Fax: (516) 571-0135
Thomas A. Dickerson, Courthouse Sq., 140 Grand St., White Plains 10601 (914) 824-5405; Fax: (718) 946-1026
Mark C. Dillon, Courthouse Square, 6th Floor, 140 Grand St., White Plains 10601 (914) 824-5409; Fax: (212) 401-9170
Randall T. Eng, 125-01 Queens Blvd., Kew Gardens 11415 (718) 298-1555; Fax: (718) 520-3557
Steven W. Fisher, 88-11 Sutphin Blvd., Jamaica 11435 (718) 298-1175; Fax: (718) 298-1098
Anita R. Florio Courthouse Square, 6th Floor, 140 Grand St., White Plains 10601 (914) 824-5877; Fax: (914) 328-5743
L. Priscilla Hall (347) 296-1061; Fax: (347) 296-1372
John M. Leventhal (718) 875-1300
Plummer E. Lott (347) 296-1028
William F. Mastro, 60 Bay St., 5th Floor, Staten Island 10301 (718) 675-8680; Fax: (718) 816-4587
Reinaldo E. Rivera (718) 722-6486; Fax: (718) 722-6492
Sheri S. Roman, 125-01 Queens Blvd., Room 851, Kew Gardens 11415 (718) 298-1441; Fax: (718) 520-8247
Fred T. Santucci, 88-11 Sutphin Blvd., Jamaica 11435 (718) 298-1087; Fax: (718) 520-1464
Sandra L. Sgroi, John P. Cohalan, Jr. Court Complex, 400 Carleton Ave., P.O. Box 9075, Central Islip 11722-9075 (631) 853-5138; Fax: (631) 853-5798
Peter B. Skelos Supreme Court Bldg., 100 Supreme Court Dr., Mineola 11501 (516) 571-2727; Fax: (516) 571-1281

Clerk: Matthew Kiernan (718) 722-6307

Deputy Clerks:
April Agostino (718) 722-6314
Mel Harris (718) 722-6304
Mary-Ellen Skenyon (718) 722-6305

Associate Deputy Clerks:
Maria Fasulo (718) 722-6472
Karen Hochberg Tommer (718) 722-6365

Chief Court Atty.: Alan Chevat (718) 722-6466

Law Librarian: Bruce Bosso (718) 722-6356; Fax: (718) 722-6302 E-mail: bbosso@nysad2d.org

Appellate Division Second Department—Cont'd

Law Clerks to Justices:

(Angiolillo) . . . . . Vija K. Stamey
(Austin) . . . . . Nancy Nicotra
(Balkin) . . . . . Javier Vargas
(Belen) . . . . . Rossiya Fajardo
(Chambers) . . . . . Michael Scarinci
(Covello) . . . . . Daniel Ray
(Dickerson) . . . . . Jonathan Glenn
(Dillon) . . . . . Mary Chapyak Pernicone
(Eng) . . . . . Wendy Cohen
(Fisher) . . . . . Jay Weiner
(Florio) . . . . . Vacancy at Press Time
(Hall) . . . . . J. Machelle Sweeting
(Leventhal) . . . . . Ben Darvil, Jr.
(Lott) . . . . . Daniel Leventhal
(Mastro) . . . . . Terence Henchey
(Prudenti) . . . . . Karl Pflanz
(Rivera) . . . . . Maria E. Marti
(Roman) . . . . . James A. Dollin
(Santucci) . . . . . Richard DeRose
(Sgroi) . . . . . Barbara Gonzo
(Skelos) . . . . . Lisa Stone

Second Department
Committees on Character and Fitness
335 Adams St., Room 2404, Brooklyn 11201
(718) 923-6360

Chairman, Second, Tenth, Eleventh & Thirteenth Districts: Vincent G. Berger, Jr.
133 E. Main St., Suite 3G, Babylon 11702 (631) 422-2130

Chairman, Ninth Judicial District: Lawrence A. Mandelker
Kantor, Davidoff, Wolfe, Mandelker, Toomey and Gallanty, P.C., 51 E. 42nd St., N.Y.C. 10017 (212) 682-8383

Executive Secretary: Vacancy at Press Time

Deputy Executive Secretary: Patricia D. Collins

Second Department Grievance Committee
Second, Eleventh and Thirteenth Judicial Districts
Renaissance Plaza, Suite 2400, 335 Adams St., Brooklyn 11201-3745
(718) 923-6300

Jurisdiction—Counties of Kings, Queens, Richmond

Chief Counsel: Diana Maxfield Kearse

Deputy Counsel: Robert J. Saltzman

Second Department Grievance Committee
Ninth Judicial District Office
399 Knollwood Rd., Suite 200, White Plains 10603
(914) 824-5070; Fax: (914) 949-0997

Jurisdiction—Counties of Dutchess, Orange, Putnam, Rockland, Westchester

Chief Counsel: Gary L. Casella

Second Department Grievance Committee
Tenth Judicial District
150 Motor Pkwy., Suite 102, Hauppauge 11788
(631) 231-3775

Jurisdiction—Counties of Nassau, Suffolk

Chief Counsel: Robert A. Green

APPELLATE DIVISION THIRD DEPARTMENT
Justice Bldg., 5th Floor, Empire State Plaza, Albany 12223
Mailing Address: Capitol Station, P.O. Box 7288, Albany 12224
(518) 471-4777
Internet: www.nycourts.gov/ad3

Presiding Justice: Anthony V. Cardona
Albany County Courthouse, Room 412, Eagle St., Albany 12207 (518) 285-8301; Fax: (518) 487-5042

Associate Justices:

John C. Egan, Jr., Chambers, 1st Floor, 50 Chapel St., Albany 12207 (518) 285-8999
Elizabeth A. Garry, 6 E. Main St., Suite 201, Norwich 13815 (607) 337-1724; Fax: (607) 337-1722
E. Michael Kavanagh
Supreme Court Chambers, 1 Pearl St., Kingston 12401 (845) 340-3888; Fax: (845) 340-3893
John A. Lahtinen, 36 Oak St., P.O. Box 38, Plattsburgh 12901 (518) 562-1446; Fax: (518) 562-1792
Bernard J. Malone, Jr.
Courthouse, Room 269, 16 Eagle St., Albany 12207 (518) 285-8919; Fax: (518) 487-5137
William E. McCarthy
Courthouse, Room 118, 16 Eagle St., Albany 12207 (518) 285-8986; Fax: (518) 487-5155
Thomas E. Mercure, 383 Broadway, Ft. Edward 12828-0346 (518) 746-2540; Fax: (518) 746-2551
Karen K. Peters, Courthouse, 281 Wall St., Kingston 12401-3817 (845) 340-3757; Fax: (845) 340-3760
Robert S. Rose, Broome County Courthouse, 92 Court St., P.O. Box 1766, Binghamton 13902-1766 (607) 778-2473; Fax: (607) 778-2405
Edward O. Spain
Courthouse, Congress and Second Sts., Troy 12180 (518) 285-6159; Fax: (518) 270-0066
Leslie E. Stein, 50 Chapel St., 1st Floor, Albany 12207 (518) 285-8939; Fax: (518) 434-5980

Clerk: Michael J. Novack (518) 471-4777; Fax: (518) 471-4750
E-mail: mnovack@courts.state.ny.us

Deputy Clerk: Robert D. Mayberger
(518) 471-4801; Fax: (518) 471-4756
E-mail: rmayberg@courts.state.ny.us

Chief Appellate Court Atty.: Sean M. Morton
(518) 471-4801

Law Clerks to Justices:

(Cardona) . . . . . Lisa Connelly, Michele A. McKay, Katie Rotello
(Egan) . . . . . Jessica R. Wilcox
(Garry) . . . . . Catherine F. Murphy
(Kavanagh) . . . . . Beth A. Lifshin-Clark
(Lahtinen) . . . . . Dana Peck
(Malone) . . . . . Erika L. Bergen
(McCarthy) . . . . . Matthew P. Side
(Mercure) . . . . . Leah Amyot
(Peters) . . . . . Anthony Beccari
(Rose) . . . . . Michael T. Snyder
(Spain) Julia S. Bielawski, Jacqueline M. Guidarelli-Wu
(Stein) . . . . . Jessie A. Aitcheson

Committee on Character and Fitness, Third Judicial District
Appellate Div. Admission Office, Third Dept., P.O. Box 7350, Capitol Station, Albany 12224-0350
(518) 471-4778

Chairman: Michael L. Costello
Tobin & Dempf, 33 Elk St., Albany 12207 (518) 463-1177

Third Department Committee on Character and Fitness of Applicants for Admission to the Bar
Fourth Judicial District
Appellate Div. Admission Office, Third Dept., P.O. Box 7350, Capitol Station, Albany 12224
(518) 471-4778

Chairman: Lawrence Paltrowitz
Bartlett, Pontiff, Stewart & Rhodes, P.C., 1 Washington St., P.O. Box 2168, Glens Falls 12801 (518) 792-2117

Third Department Committee on Character and Fitness of Applicants for Admission to the Bar
Sixth Judicial District
Appellate Div. Admission Office, Capitol Station, P.O. Box 7350, Capitol Station, Albany 12224
(518) 471-4778

Chair: Jon S. Blechman
Hinman, Howard & Kattell, L.L.P., 700 Security Mutual Bldg., 80 Exchange St., P.O. Box 5250, Binghamton 13902-5250 (607) 723-5341

Third Department Committee on Professional Standards
40 Steuben St., Suite 502, Albany 12207
(518) 285-8350; Fax: (518) 474-0389
E-mail: ad3cops@courts.state.ny.us
Internet: www.courts.state.ny.us/ad3/cops/

Chief Atty.: Mark S. Ochs

APPELLATE DIVISION, FOURTH DEPARTMENT
M. Dolores Denman Cthse., 50 East Ave., Rochester 14604
(585) 530-3100; Fax: (585) 530-3247;
Library: (585) 530-3250
Internet: www.courts.state.ny.us/ad4

Presiding Justice: **Henry J. Scudder
19 E. Pulteney Sq., Bath 14810-1575
(607) 776-9623; Fax: (607) 776-7168

Associate Justices:

Edward D. Carni, Onondaga County Courthouse, Room 409, 401 Montgomery St., Syracuse 13202
(315) 671-1108; Fax: (315) 671-1177

John V. Centra, Onondaga County Courthouse, Room 401, 401 Montgomery St., Syracuse 13202
(315) 671-1105; Fax: (315) 671-1182

**Eugene M. Fahey, 50 Delaware Ave., Buffalo 14202
(716) 845-9444; Fax: (716) 852-6367

*Jerome C. Gorski, 50 Delaware Ave., Buffalo 14202
(716) 845-2107; Fax: (716) 852-6367

*Samuel L. Green, 50 Delaware Ave., Buffalo 14202
(716) 845-2104; Fax: (716) 852-6367

Stephen K. Lindley, 50 East Ave., Rochester 14604
(585) 530-3227; Fax: (585) 530-3243

Salvatore R. Martoche, 50 Delaware Ave., 10th Floor, Buffalo 14202 (716) 845-2111; Fax: (716) 852-6367

Erin M. Peradotto, 50 Delaware Ave., Buffalo 14202-2721
(716) 845-9360; Fax: (716) 852-6367

Rose H. Sconiers, 50 Delaware Ave., Buffalo 14202
(716) 845-9495; Fax: (716) 851-3328

Nancy E. Smith, 50 East Ave., Rochester 14604
(585) 530-3282; Fax: (585) 530-3193

Clerk: Patricia L. Morgan
(585) 530-3100; Fax: (585) 530-3246

Deputy Clerk: Francis E. Cafarell (585) 530-3100

Consultation Clerk: Joan P. Brimlow
(585) 530-3100; Fax: (585) 530-3248

Law Clerks to Justices:

(Carni) .... John E. Short
(Centra) .... Colleen M. Farrell
(Fahey) .... Michael Pastrick
(Gorski) .... Jennifer Phillips
(Green) .... Susan Von Arx
(Lindley) .... Michael Nolan
(Martoche) .... Donald Stefanski
(Peradotto) .... Elizabeth Fox-Solomon
(Sconiers) .... John A. Ziegler
(Scudder) ...... Mary Hope Benedict, Glenda Brayman
James P. Mulley
(Smith) .... James D. Stevenson

Fourth Department Committee on Character and Fitness of Applicants for Admission to the Bar
Fifth Judicial District

Chair: Doreen A. Simmons
Hancock & Estabrook, L.L.P., 1500 AXA Tower I,
100 Madison St., Syracuse 13202
(315) 471-3151; Fax: (315) 471-3167

Fourth Department Attorney Grievance Committee
Fifth Judicial District Office
224 Harrison St., Suite 408, Syracuse 13202-3066
(315) 471-1835; Fax: (315) 479-0123
Internet: www.courts.state.ny.us/ad4

Chief Counsel: Gregory J. Huether

Fourth Department Committee on Character and Fitness of Applicants for Admission to the Bar
Seventh Judicial District

Chairperson: John F. Speranza
28 E. Main St., Suite 1800, Rochester 14614
(585) 454-1500

Fourth Department Attorney Grievance Committee
Seventh Judicial District Office
M. Dolores Denman Cthse., Suite 404, 50 East Ave., Rochester 14604-2206
(585) 530-3180; Fax: (585) 530-3191

Chief Counsel: Gregory J. Huether

Fourth Department Committee on Character and Fitness of Applicants for Admission to the Bar
Eighth Judicial District

Chair: Cheryl Smith Fisher
Magavern Magavern & Grimm, 1100 Rand Bldg.,
14 Lafayette Sq., Buffalo 14203-1414
(716) 856-3500, Ext. 204; Fax: (716) 856-3390

Fourth Department Attorney Grievance Committee
Eighth Judicial District Office
438 Main St., Suite 800, Buffalo 14202-3212
(716) 845-3630; Fax: (716) 856-2701
Internet: www.nycourts.gov/ad4

Chief Counsel: Gregory J. Huether

PRACTICE TIME TABLE IN APPELLATE DIVISION ON APPEALS FROM SUPREME COURT

As amended to September 2010.

1. Time to Appeal.

Within thirty days after service of copy of judgment or order appealed from with notice of entry thereof, or if entered by appellant within thirty days from entry of judgment or order, or service of notice of its entry. (CPLR 5513)

2. Notice of Appeal–Service.

Must be served on adverse party and filed in the office where judgment or order appealed from is entered. (CPLR 5515)

3. Stay of Enforcement.

Security is not required to perfect appeal, but merely to stay execution. Thirty days' stay of execution may be granted by trial court where judgment is for money only. For further stay, undertaking must be filed with Clerk, and copy thereof with notice of filing must be served on respondent's attorney. In lieu of undertaking money may be deposited with Clerk. If judgment or order appealed from does not come within CPLR 5519(a) or (b), motion must be made for stay. (CPLR 5519)

4. Exception to and Justification of Sureties.

Within ten days after service of copy of undertaking, notice of exception to sufficiency of sureties may be served. Within ten days thereafter sureties must move to justify on notice. (CPLR 2506, 2507)

5. Transcript.

Must be ordered from Court Stenographer.

6. Settlement of Proposed Transcript.

Within 15 days after receipt of the transcript, appellant shall serve a copy with proposed amendments upon respondent who shall have 15 days to make and serve objections and proposed amendments. If the parties can agree on the correctness or amendments to the transcript they may certify the same. If they cannot agree the proposed amendments and objections shall be submitted for settlement to the judge or referee before whom the proceedings were had on at least 4 days' notice. (CPLR 5525(c))

7. Statement in Lieu of Transcript.

Where no stenographic record is made the appellant shall serve a statement of the proceedings within 10 days after taking the appeal and the respondent shall have 10 days thereafter to serve objections or proposed amendments. (CPLR 5525(d))

8. Statement in Lieu of Record.

Shall be presented to the court for approval within 20 days after appeal taken where questions presented can be determined without examination of all of the proceedings. (CPLR 5527)

9. Filing Record, Briefs, and Serving Briefs.

By appellant within twenty days after settlement of transcript or statement in lieu thereof. By respondent within 15 days thereafter. (CPLR 5530)

Note: The Appellate Division in each department may, by rule, prescribe different time limitations. Check specific department rules.

***Justice Serving under Certification**
****Pending November 2010 Election Results**

SUPREME COURT APPELLATE TERM

First Judicial Department Appellate Term, Supreme Court
60 Centre St., N.Y.C. 10007
(646) 386-3040

Presiding Justice: Douglas E. McKeon (646) 386-3241

Justices:
Alexander W. Hunter, Jr. (718) 618-1423
Martin Schoenfeld (646) 386-3232
Martin Shulman (646) 386-5687

Chief Clerk: Peter Diskint, Room 401 (646) 386-3040

Second Judicial Department Appellate Term, Supreme Court
Clerk's Office, 141 Livingston St., Brooklyn 11201-5133
(347) 401-9580; Fax: (718) 643-7889

Chief Clerk: Paul Kenny (347) 401-9580

Deputy Chief Clerk: Vacancy at Press Time
Note: All briefs and motions are to be filed at Clerk's office, 141 Livingston St., 15th Floor, Brooklyn 11201. Orders to Show Cause and applications pursuant to CPLR 5704(b) may be filed via the Appellate Term coordinators, located in the Supreme Court in each county except Kings and Richmond Counties. All motions returnable Mon.-Fri. at 10 A.M. All papers in support or opposition are to be filed on or before the return date. All motions are submitted only.
Courtrooms (9:30 A.M.) for Appellate Term, 2nd, 11th and 13th Judicial Districts are located at
Kings County—141 Livingston St., Rm. 1504, Brooklyn 11201-5133
Queens Supreme—88-11 Sutphin Blvd., Jamaica 11435
Courtrooms (9:30 A.M.) for Appellate Term, 9th and 10th Judicial Districts, are located at:
Nassau Supreme—100 Supreme Ct. Dr., Mineola 11501.
Westchester Supreme—140 Grand St., White Plains 10601
Suffolk Supreme—Supreme Court Bldg., Cohalan Ctr., 400 Carleton Ave., Central Islip 11722
Orange Supreme—County Govt. Center, 255 Main St., Goshen 10924
Dutchess County—Poughkeepsie Courthouse, 10 Market St., Poughkeepsie, NY 12601

2nd, 11th and 13th Judicial Districts, Appellate Term, Supreme Court

Presiding Justice: Michael L. Pesce (347) 296-1007

Associate Justices:
Michelle Weston (347) 296-1480; Fax: (718) 643-7325
Joseph G. Golia (718) 298-1190
Jaime A. Rios (718) 298-1079; Fax: (718) 298-1122
Marsha L. Steinhardt (347) 296-1545

9th and 10th Judicial Districts, Appellate Term, Supreme Court

Presiding Justice: Francis A. Nicolai
Richard J. Daronco Courthouse,
111 Dr. Martin Luther King, Jr. Blvd.,
White Plains 10601 (914) 824-5100

Associate Justices:
Angela G. Iannacci
100 Supreme Court Dr., Mineola 11501 (516) 571-2484
John R. LaCava
Richard J. Daronco Courthouse, 17th Floor,
111 Dr. Martin Luther King, Jr. Blvd., White Plains 10601
(914) 824-5417
Denise F. Molia
One Court St., Ctrm. 201A, Riverhead 11901
(631) 852-3750
Melvyn Tanenbaum
400 Carleton Ave., Central Islip 11722 (631) 853-6323

***Justice Serving under Certification**
****Pending November 2010 Election Results**

SUPREME COURT, FIRST DEPARTMENT

FIRST JUDICIAL DISTRICT, SUPREME COURT
Jurisdiction—County of New York
60 Centre St., N.Y.C. 10007
(646) 386-3600; County Clerk: (646) 386-5956; Chief Clerk: (646) 386-3001; Deputy Chief Clerk: (646) 386-3005
100 Centre St., N.Y.C. 10013
(646) 386-4000
111 Centre St., N.Y.C. 10013
(646) 386-4646
80 Centre St., N.Y.C. 10013
(646) 386-3685
71 Thomas St., N.Y.C. 10013
(646) 386-3770
Harlem Community Court, 170 E. 121st St., N.Y.C. 10035
(212) 360-4100

Justices:
Sherry Klein Heitler (Admin. Judge, Civil Div.) (646) 386-3211
Michael J. Obus (Admin. Judge, Criminal Div.; Acting Justice, from Criminal Court) (646) 386-3947; Fax: (212) 401-9264
Eileen Bransten (646) 386-3184; Fax: (212) 374-1475
Richard F. Braun (646) 386-3755
Carol Edmead (646) 386-3250; Fax: (212) 374-8355
Paul G. Feinman (646) 386-3375
Fern A. Fisher (Deputy Admin. Judge, N.Y.C. Courts) (646) 386-4200; Fax: (212) 374-5709
Bernard J. Fried (646) 386-3359
Judith J. Gische (646) 386-3723
Emily Jane Goodman (646) 386-3235; Fax: (212) 401-9045
Carol E. Huff (646) 386-3217
Marcy L. Kahn (646) 386-3986
Barbara R. Kapnick (Commercial Division) (646) 386-3226
Shirley Werner Kornreich (646) 386-3363
Doris Ling-Cohan (646) 386-3733
Joan B. Lobis (646) 386-3247
Richard B. Lowe III (646) 386-3259
Joan A. Madden (646) 386-3190
Douglas E. McKeon (From 12th District) (646) 386-3241
Donna M. Mills (From 12th District) (646) 386-3348
Eduardo Padro (646) 386-3980
Richard Lee Price (Sitting in the Bronx) (718) 618-3646; Fax: (718) 618-3565
Charles E. Ramos (646) 386-3229
Alice Schlesinger (646) 386-3253
Martin Schoenfeld (646) 386-3232
Martin Shulman (646) 386-5687
*Lewis Bart Stone (646) 386-3984; Fax: (212) 608-7566
Milton A. Tingling, Jr. (646) 386-3178, 386-3370; Fax: (212) 374-3326
Laura Visitacion-Lewis (646) 386-3196
Lottie E. Wilkins (646) 386-3813; Fax: (212) 374-8417
Paul Wooten (From 2nd District) (646) 386-3604
James A. Yates (646) 386-3985; Fax: (212) 374-0607
Louis B. York (646) 386-3810

Acting Justices:
Bruce Allen (Criminal Court) (646) 386-4408
A. Kirke Bartley, Jr. (Criminal Court) (646) 386-4623; Fax: (212) 374-2579
Carol Berkman (Criminal Court) (646) 386-3968
Gregory Carro (Court of Claims) (646) 386-4424; Fax: (212) 401-9263
Richard D. Carruthers (Criminal Court) (646) 386-3978
Ellen M. Coin (Criminal Court) (646) 386-4615; Fax: (212) 374-2579
Daniel P. Conviser (Court of Claims) (646) 386-3977
**Matthew F. Cooper (Civil Court) (646) 386-5696
Tandra L. Dawson (Family Court) (646) 386-5701
Marylin G. Diamond (Civil Court) (646) 386-3255
Laura E. Drager (Criminal Court) (646) 386-3356

Acting Justices, Supreme Court, 1st Jud Dist.—Cont'd

Saralee E. Evans (Civil Court) (646) 386-3819
Thomas A. Farber (Criminal Court) (646) 386-3892
Daniel P. FitzGerald (Criminal Court) (646) 386-3967
Marcy S. Friedman (Civil Court) (646) 386-3760
Ellen Gesmer (Civil Court) (646) 386-3730; Fax: (212) 884-8986
Arlene D. Goldberg (Criminal Court) (646) 386-4417
Shlomo S. Hagler (Civil Court) (646) 386-5691; Fax: (212) 374-2594
Roger S. Hayes (Criminal Court) (646) 386-4405
Barbara Jaffe (Civil Court) (646) 386-3724
Debra A. James (Civil Court) (646) 386-3352; Fax: (212) 374-0402
Deborah A. Kaplan (Civil Court) (646) 386-5567; Fax: (212) 401-9037
Joan M. Kenney (Civil Court) (646) 386-3816
**Cynthia S. Kern (Civil Court) (646) 386-3729
Judy Harris Kluger (Criminal Court; Chief, Office of Policy & Planning, Office of Ct. Admin.; Dir., Office of Drug Treatment Programs) (212) 428-2130; Fax: (212) 428-2192
Jill Konviser (Court of Claims) (646) 386-4411
Lawrence K. Marks (Court of Claims) 25 Beaver St., N.Y.C. 10004 (212) 428-2884
Edward J. McLaughlin (Criminal Court) (646) 386-3972
Manuel J. Mendez (Civil Court) (646) 386-5705
Juan M. Merchan (Court of Claims) (646) 386-3934
Peter Moulton (Civil Court) (646) 386-5712
Cassandra Mullen (Court of Claims) (646) 386-5710
Juanita Bing Newton (Court of Claims; Dean, N.Y. State Judicial Institute) 84 N. Broadway, White Plains 10603 (914) 824-5800
Patricia M. Nunez (Criminal Court) (646) 386-4971
Kibbie F. Payne (Civil Court) (646) 386-3336
Ruth Pickholz (Criminal Court) (646) 386-4402; Fax: (212) 374-2579
Eileen A. Rakower (Civil Court) (646) 386-5749
Clark V. Richardson (Family Court) (646) 386-5101
Saliann Scarpulla (Civil Court) (646) 386-5716
Melvin L. Schweitzer (Court of Claims) (212) 361-8170
O. Peter Sherwood (Court of Claims) (646) 386-3807; Fax: (212) 748-7793
George J. Silver (Civil Court) (646) 286-3271
Anil C. Singh (Civil Court) (646) 386-5692
Charles H. Solomon (Criminal Court) (646) 386-3976
Jane S. Solomon (Civil Court) (646) 386-3181
Michael R. Sonberg (Criminal Court) (646) 386-4503
Michael D. Stallman (Civil Court) (646) 386-3342
Robert M. Stolz (Criminal Court) (646) 386-3991
Analisa Torres (Civil Court) (646) 386-5219
Laura A. Ward (Criminal Court) (646) 386-4653; Fax: (212) 295-4891
Richard Weinberg (Criminal Court) Midtown Community Court, 314 W. 54th St., N.Y.C. 10019 (646) 264-1318
Renee Allyn White (Criminal Court) (646) 386-3970
Maxwell Wiley (Court of Claims) (646) 386-4433
Bonnie G. Wittner (Criminal Court) (646) 386-4427
Ronald Zweibel (Court of Claims) (646) 386-3987; Fax: (212) 748-5920

Special Referees:

Louis Crespo (646) 386-3794; Fax: (212) 374-8417
Marilyn Dershowitz (646) 386-3657
Nicholas Doyle (646) 386-3653
Lancelot B. Hewitt (646) 386-3680
Sue Ann Hoahng (646) 386-3676
Howard Leventhal (646) 386-3630
Steve Liebman (646) 386-3662
Leslie S. Lowenstein (646) 386-3792

Judicial Hearing Officers:

Herbert J. Adlerberg (646) 386-3974
Herbert I. Altman (646) 386-4282
John A.K. Bradley (646) 386-5977
Beverly S. Cohen (646) 386-3719
Nicholas Figueroa
Ira Gammerman (646) 386-3265
Phyllis Gangel-Jacob (646) 386-3205
Edward H. Lehner (646) 386-3258
William Leibovitz (646) 386-3717
Robert D. Lippmann (646) 386-3338
William P. McCooe (646) 386-3223
Norman C. Ryp (212) 595-0232
Stanley L. Sklar (646) 386-3165
Robert H. Straus (646) 386-4429

For Supreme Court Clerk's offices for all counties, see listings under specific county, pp. 58-96

Law Clerks to Justices:

(Allen) . . . . . Jean-Paul Mayer
(Bartley) . . . . . Jennifer Arons
(Berkman) . . . . . Janice Wieder
(Bransten) . . . . . Robert S. Hardman, Angela Higgins, Jeff K. Leung
(Braun) . . . . . Miriam A. Boggio, Gary Eckstein
(Carro) . . . . . Marjorie Liss
(Carruthers) . . . . . Katherine McHale
(Coin) . . . . . Niya Bryant
(Conviser) . . . . . Joseph DiFlumeri
(Cooper) . . . . . Joshua H. Pike, Joanne D. Quinones
(Dawson) . . . . . Linda Capitti
(Diamond) . . . . . Harvey Berman, Nicholas Moyne
(Drager) . . . . . Anne P. Bryant, Lindsay N. Feinberg
(Edmead) . . . . . Elenor C. Reid, Jay A. Thompson
(Evans) . . . . . Nancy Hobbs
(Farber) . . . . . Susan Miller
(Feinman) . . . . . Julia Herd, Gennaro Savastano
(Fisher) . . . . . Maria Logus
(FitzGerald) . . . . . James McGevna
(Fried) . . . . . Janel Alania, Alexandra Harris, Lisa M. Mahowald
(Friedman) . . . . . Harvard D. Gregory, Jared Paioff
(Gesmer) . . . . . Kristin Bebelaar, Ashley J. McDowell
(Gische) . . . . . Eileen Kaspar, Beth M. Kaufman
(Goldberg) . . . . . Sharon Glazer
(Goodman) . . . . . Andrea S. Field
(Hagler) . . . . . Meshulom Buls, Aaron Hauptman
(Hayes) . . . . . Elizabeth Gazay
(Heitler) . . . . . Roberta McClintock, Kelly O'Neill Levy
(Huff) . . . . . Guy Owen
(Jaffe) . . . . . Catherine Paszkowska
(James) . . . . . Jon Mark McGowan, Stacy Osborne
(Kahn) . . . . . Christopher Benbow
(Kaplan) . . . . . Deanna J. Lucci, Hemalee J. Patel
(Kapnick) . . . . . Michael L. Katz
(Kenney) . . . . . Ingrid Ayber, John Wang
(Kern) . . . . . Rachel Fremmer, Aeri Pang
(Kluger) . . . . . Bruna L. DiBiase
(Konviser) . . . . . Mark H. Levine
(Kornreich) . . . . . Fiona Dutta, Julie A. Ebenstein, Deborah Porder, Tracy Young Wells
(Ling-Cohan) . . . . . Donna Albano, Anna Fontana
(Lobis) . . . . . Sean A. McConnell, Elizabeth Osborne
(Lowe) . . . . . Michael Freedman, Megan McHugh
(Madden) . . . . . Julia Cort, Karen Schwartz
(McKeon) . . . . . Rori Kelly, Sophia Rackman
(McLaughlin) . . . . . Frank J. Loss
(Mendez) . . . . . Martha Tessler
(Merchan) . . . . . Janet Poppoly
(Mills) . . . . . Adrian Armstrong
(Moulton) . . . . . W. Frank Perry
(Mullen) . . . . . Sara R. Litman
(Nunez) . . . . . Pamela Faison
(Obus) . . . . . Daniel Rosen
(Padro) . . . . . Michelle Smith
(Payne) . . . . . Christopher Polizano
(Pickholz) . . . . . Myles Baer
(Price) . . . . . David J. Kirschner
(Rakower) . . . . . Iris Roberts, Ryan Singer
(Ramos) . . . . . Orna Artal, Timothy Corbo, Edward Liu
(Scarpulla) . . . . . Danielle Schweilach, Mikhail Sheynker, Ariella Zarfati
(Schlesinger) . . . . . Rose Ann Magaldi
(Schoenfeld) . . . . . Laura Jacobs, Michael Macrides, Monica Senter
(Schweitzer) . . . . . Joseph Hansen, P. Jay Wilker
(Shulman) . . . . . Melinda P. Lisanti
(Solomon, C.) . . . . . Helen Dames

**Pending November 2010 Election Results

Law Clerks to Justices, Supreme Court, First Judicial District—Cont'd

(Solomon, J.)............ Joseph Burke, Stefano Costa
(Sonberg) .... Oma Deonarine
(Stallman)............. Lyris Rodriguez, Richard Tsai
(Stolz)............................... Wendy Eaton
(Stone) .... Nina G. Keller
(Tingling).......................... Manuel Tavarez
(Torres).............................. Elba Galvan
(Visitacion-Lewis) . Steven N. Atchison, Lissett C. Ferreira
(Ward)............................... Peter Merker
(Weinberg)........................ Daniel Kenneally
(White)........................... Judith McMahon
(Wiley).............................. Ellen Schutz
(Wilkins) .... Anthony Cannataro
(Wittner) .... Carol Gerstman
(Wooten) .... Maiysha Rashad, Lyssa Sampson
(Yates)..... Tammy Chang, Alma Gomez, Berton Kraus
(York) .... Beth L. Herstein
(Zweibel)............................. Lisa Rubin

TWELFTH JUDICIAL DISTRICT, SUPREME COURT

Jurisdiction—County of Bronx
851 Grand Concourse, Bronx 10451
Civil Branch: (718) 618-1400

Bronx Hall of Justice, 265 E. 161st St., Bronx 10451
Criminal Branch: (718) 618-3100; Fax: (718) 618-3584

Administrative Judge, Criminal Term:
Efrain Alvarado (Acting Justice from Criminal Court) Bronx Hall of Justice (718) 618-3700

Administrative Judge, Civil Term: Subject to Appointment

Justices, Civil Term:
John A. Barone (718) 618-1401
Laura G. Douglas (718) 618-1410
Mark Friedlander (718) 618-1411
Yvonne Gonzalez (718) 618-1417
Wilma Guzman (718) 618-1421
Alexander W. Hunter, Jr. (718) 618-1423; Fax: (718) 618-3531
LaTia W. Martin (718) 618-1586
Douglas E. McKeon (718) 618-1427; Fax: (718) 618-3557
Donna M. Mills (Sitting in Manhattan) (646) 386-3348
Norma Ruiz (718) 618-1435
Robert A. Sackett (Sitting in Sullivan County) 414 Broadway, Monticello 12701 (845) 794-9776
Howard H. Sherman (718) 618-1451
Howard R. Silver (718) 618-1480
Betty Owen Stinson (718) 618-1455; Fax: (718) 590-3776
Lucindo Suarez (718) 618-1456; Fax: (718) 537-5076
Kenneth L. Thompson, Jr. (718) 618-1459; Fax: (718) 618-3543
Robert E. Torres (718) 618-1773
Alison Y. Tuitt (718) 618-1461; Fax: (718) 618-3590

Justices, Criminal Term:
Sharon A.M. Aarons, Bronx Hall of Justice (718) 618-3643
*John N. Byrne, Bronx Hall of Justice (718) 618-3689
Caesar D. Cirigliano, Bronx Hall of Justice (718) 618-3648; Fax: (718) 618-3571
Darcel D. Clark, Bronx Hall of Justice (718) 618-3626
*Dominic R. Massaro, Bronx Hall of Justice (718) 618-3664; Fax: (212) 457-2881
Richard Lee Price (From 1st District), Bronx Hall of Justice (718) 618-3646; Fax: (718) 618-3565
*David Stadtmauer, Bronx Hall of Justice (718) 618-3666
George R. Villegas, Bronx Hall of Justice (718) 618-3653; Fax: (718) 618-3571
Troy K. Webber, Bronx Hall of Justice (718) 618-3620

Acting Justices, Civil Term:
Stanley B. Green (Civil Court) (718) 618-1420
Diane A. Lebedeff (Civil Court) (718) 618-1557
Nelida Malave-Gonzalez (Civil Court) (718) 618-2542
Larry Schachner (Civil Court) (718) 618-1449
Fernando Tapia (Civil Court) (718) 618-2550
Geoffrey D. Wright (Civil Court) (718) 618-1432; Fax: (718) 618-3511
Julia I. Rodriguez (Civil Court) (718) 618-1416
**Edgar G. Walker (Civil Court) (718) 618-1465; Fax: (212) 419-8494

Acting Justices, Criminal Term:
Harold A. Adler (Civil Court), Bronx Hall of Justice (718) 618-3619
Allen G. Alpert (Criminal Court) 900 Sheridan Ave., Bronx 10451 (718) 618-2200
Steven L. Barrett (Criminal Court), Bronx Hall of Justice (718) 618-3659
Peter J. Benitez (Criminal Court), Bronx Hall of Justice (718) 618-3631
Miriam Best (Criminal Court), Bronx Hall of Justice (718) 618-3690
Denis John Boyle (Criminal Court), Bronx Hall of Justice (718) 618-3677
Raymond L. Bruce (Civil Court), Bronx Hall of Justice (718) 618-3661
John W. Carter (Criminal Court), Bronx Hall of Justice (718) 618-3635
Margaret Clancy (Court of Claims), Bronx Hall of Justice (718) 618-3638; Fax: (212) 884-8910
Joseph J. Dawson (Criminal Court), Bronx Hall of Justice (718) 618-3625
Ann M. Donnelly (Court of Claims), Bronx Hall of Justice (718) 618-3650
Ralph A. Fabrizio (Criminal Court), Bronx Hall of Justice (718) 618-3623
Doris M. Gonzalez (Civil Court), Bronx Hall of Justice (718) 618-3682
Ethan R. Greenberg (Criminal Court), Bronx Hall of Justice (718) 618-3616
Michael A. Gross (Criminal Court), Bronx Hall of Justice (718) 618-3668
Nicholas J. Iacovetta (Criminal Court), Bronx Hall of Justice (718) 618-3673
Diane R. Kiesel (Criminal Court), Bronx Hall of Justice (718) 618-3640; Fax: (212) 457-2663
James M. Kindler (Court of Claims), Bronx Hall of Justice (718) 618-3680
Judith S. Lieb (Criminal Court), Bronx Hall of Justice (718) 618-3645
Martin Marcus (Court of Claims), Bronx Hall of Justice (718) 618-3678; Fax: (718) 618-3571
Please call before sending a Fax
Seth L. Marvin (Criminal Court), Bronx Hall of Justice (718) 618-3784
William I. Mogulescu (Criminal Court), Bronx Hall of Justice (718) 618-3685
John S. Moore (Criminal Court), Bronx Hall of Justice (718) 618-3686
Robert A. Neary (Court of Claims), Bronx Hall of Justice (718) 618-3610
Barbara F. Newman (Criminal Court), Bronx Hall of Justice (718) 618-3657
Eugene Oliver, Jr. (Dep. Admin. Judge, Criminal Div.; Acting Justice, from Criminal Court) Bronx Hall of Justice (718) 618-3600
Wayne M. Ozzi (Court of Claims), Bronx Hall of Justice (718) 618-3717
Jane Pearl (Family Court), 900 Sheridan Ave. (718) 618-2200
Robert G. Seewald (Criminal Court), Bronx Hall of Justice (718) 618-3675
Ruth E. Smith (Criminal Court), Bronx Hall of Justice (718) 618-1016
Megan Tallmer (Criminal Court), Bronx Hall of Justice (718) 618-3615
Patricia Anne Williams (Criminal Court) (718) 618-1467; Fax: (718) 618-3575
Alvin M. Yearwood (Criminal Court), Bronx Hall of Justice (718) 618-1034

Judicial Hearing Officers:
Lawrence H. Bernstein, Bronx Hall of Justice (718) 618-3654
Robert Cohen, Bronx Hall of Justice (718) 618-3689
Edward M. Davidowitz, Bronx Hall of Justice (718) 618-3655
Eileen Koretz, Bronx Hall of Justice (718) 618-3725

For Supreme Court Clerk's offices for all counties, see listings under specific county, pp. 58-96

***Justice Serving under Certification**
****Pending November 2010 Election Results**

Supreme Court, Twelfth Judicial Dist.—Cont'd

Law Clerks to Justices:

(Aarons) .... Carol Sharpe
(Adler) .... Jeffrey Silverbush
(Alvarado).......... David Demar
(Barone) .... Jonathan Jacobs
(Barrett).......... Hillard Wiese
(Benitez) .... Patricia Avery
(Best) .... Carly Stapelton
(Boyle).......... Robert E. Epstein
(Bruce) .... Cynthia Parache-Brito
(Byrne) .... Kathryn Salensky
(Carter).......... Belkis Alonso-Ortiz
(Cirigliano).......... Glenda M. Hernandez
(Clancy).......... Jeffrey Garcia
(Clark) .... Julian O'Connor
(Dawson).......... Matthew White
(Donnelly) .... Victoria Vossen
(Douglas) .... Anthony Nuñez
(Fabrizio) .... Joseph Doherty
(Friedlander) .... Alan Gross
(Gonzalez).......... Jack Lehnert
(Gonzalez) .... Mary Yamagata
(Green) .... Anne Chabot
(Greenberg) .... Fred Gilbert
(Gross).......... Ann Marie Modica-Schaffer
(Guzman).......... Bahaati Pitt
(Hunter).......... Lorraine Ross
(Iacovetta).......... Eleanor Pesce-Fusto
(Kiesel) .... Caroline Oppenheim
(Kindler).......... Yael Levy
(Lebedeff) .... Howard Liker
(Lieb) .... Beth Beller
(Malave-Gonzalez).......... Magdalena Porrata
(Marcus) .... Denise Parillo
(Martin).......... Dafina Cobinah, Chinyelu Udoh
(Marvin) .... Charles A. Goldsmith
(Massaro).......... Kevin C. Reilly
(McKeon) .... Rori Kelly, Sophia Rackman
(Mills).......... Adrian Armstrong
(Mogulescu).......... Amy Cohen
(Moore) .... Rosemary Martinez-Borges
(Neary).......... Michael White
(Newman) .... Albert Degatano
(Oliver) .... Charlene Williams-Pulakos
(Price) .... David J. Kirschner
(Rodriguez).......... Brenda Torres
(Ruiz) .... Marcia Tricoche
(Sackett).......... Mary Grace Conneely
(Schachner) .... Monique Carro
(Seewald).......... Bruce Goldstock
(Sherman) .... Patricia Broderick
(Silver) .... Stewart Davis
(Stadtmauer) .... A.S. Ben-Merre
(Stinson).......... Patricia A. Fernandez
(Suarez) .... Rebecca Chan, Deborah Rubino
(Tallmer).......... Catherine Daly
(Thompson).......... Kevin Castillo, Erious Johnson
(Torres).......... Llinet Beltre-Rosado
(Tuitt).......... Alicea M. Gerez
(Villegas).......... Connie Morales
(Walker).......... Mary Ann Amodeo
(Webber) .... Sandra Lespinasse
(Williams).......... Heather Russell-Loux
(Wright).......... Vivienne White
(Yearwood).......... Michael Hughes

SUPREME COURT SECOND DEPARTMENT

SECOND JUDICIAL DISTRICT, SUPREME COURT

Jurisdiction—County of Kings

360 Adams St., Brooklyn 11201
(718) 675-7699

320 Jay St., Brooklyn 11201
(347) 296-1100

Administrative Judge, Civil Term:
Sylvia O. Hinds-Radix (347) 296-1200

Administrative Judge, Criminal Term: Barry Kamins (Acting Justice, from Criminal Court) (347) 296-1000

Supervising Judge, Matrimonial Matters:
**Jeffrey Sunshine (Acting Justice, from Family Court) (347) 296-1527

Justices:

Bruce M. Balter (347) 296-1842; Fax: (347) 296-1352
Betsy Barros (347) 296-1507
Jack M. Battaglia (347) 401-9244
Bernadette F. Bayne (347) 296-1551
Michael J. Brennan (347) 296-1827
*Bert A. Bunyan (347) 296-1504
*Anthony J. Cutrona (347) 296-1498
Gloria M. Dabiri (347) 296-1563
Carolyn E. Demarest (347) 296-1458
Patricia M. DiMango (347) 296-1857
Deborah A. Dowling (347) 296-1025
*Abraham G. Gerges (347) 296-1013
Raymond Guzman (347) 296-1037
Allen Z. Hurkin-Torres (347) 296-1560
M. Randolph Jackson (347) 296-1470
Laura L. Jacobson (347) 296-1554
Lawrence S. Knipel (347) 296-1548
*Herbert Kramer (347) 296-1476
Donald Scott Kurtz (347) 401-9047
Yvonne Lewis (347) 296-1473
Larry D. Martin (347) 296-1461
Robert J. Miller (347) 296-1836; Fax: (718) 643-5406
Esther M. (Micky) Morgenstern (347) 401-9208
Mark I. Partnow (347) 296-1542
Michael L. Pesce (347) 296-1007
Eric I. Prus (347) 296-1486
Gustin L. Reichbach (347) 296-1845
**Francois A. Rivera (347) 296-1524
*Gerard H. Rosenberg (347) 296-1513
Karen B. Rothenberg (347) 296-1533
Leon Ruchelsman (347) 296-1521
Wayne P. Saitta (347) 296-1492
Arthur M. Schack (347) 296-1518
David I. Schmidt (347) 296-1501
Martin M. Solomon (347) 296-1495
Ellen Spodek (347) 401-9312
Marsha L. Steinhardt (347) 296-1545
James P. Sullivan (347) 296-1049
Delores J. Thomas (347) 296-1539
Albert Tomei (347) 296-1010
David B. Vaughan (347) 296-1455
Richard Velasquez (347) 296-1600
Michelle Weston (347) 296-1480

Acting Justices:

**Rachel Amy Adams (Civil Court) (347) 401-9260; Fax: (212) 401-9232
Michael A. Ambrosio (Family Court) (347) 296-1854
Loren Baily-Schiffman (Civil Court) (347) 401-9015
Johnny Lee Baynes (Civil Court) (718) 404-9093
Alex M. Calabrese (Criminal Court) Red Hook Community Justice Center, 88-94 Visitation Pl., Brooklyn 11231 (718) 923-8225; Fax: (718) 923-8223
Thomas J. Carroll (Court of Claims) (347) 296-1848
Danny K. Chun (Criminal Court) (347) 296-1067; Fax: (347) 296-1346
Noach Dear (Civil Court) (718) 404-9071
Vincent M. Del Giudice (Court of Claims) (347) 296-1851; Fax: (347) 296-1349
Matthew J. D'Emic (Court of Claims) (347) 296-1031; Fax: (347) 296-1337
Mark R. Dwyer (Court of Claims) (347) 401-9096
JoAnn Ferdinand (Criminal Court) (347) 296-1052; Fax: (347) 296-1367
Neil Jon Firetog (Criminal Court) (347) 296-1840; Fax: (347) 296-1348
Elizabeth A. Foley (Court of Claims) (347) 296-1616
William E. Garnett (Criminal Court) (347) 401-9381

***Justice Serving under Certification**
****Pending November 2010 Election Results**

Acting Justices, Supreme Court, Second Judicial District—Cont'd
Michael A. Gary (Criminal Court) (347) 296-1058
Joel M. Goldberg (Criminal Court) (347) 296-1860
Joseph Gubbay (Criminal Court)
(347) 404-9435; Fax: (718) 643-3538
Patricia E. Henry (Criminal Court) (347) 296-1366
John G. Ingram (Court of Claims) (347) 296-1489
Kathy J. King (Civil Court) (347) 401-9186
Sarah L. Krauss (Family Court) (347) 401-9883
Guy J. Mangano, Jr. (Court of Claims) (347) 296-1046
Alan D. Marrus (Criminal Court) (347) 296-1830
Joseph K. McKay (Criminal Court) (347) 296-1824
William Miller (Criminal Court)
(347) 404-9600; Fax: (718) 643-3538
Suzanne M. Mondo (Criminal Court)
(347) 404-9470; Fax: (718) 643-3538
Martin P. Murphy (Family Court) (347) 401-9061
Ann E. O'Shea (Civil Court) (347) 401-9894
Sheryl L. Parker (Criminal Court) (347) 296-1833
Dineen A. Riviezzo (Court of Claims) (347) 296-1113
Kenneth P. Sherman (Civil Court) (347) 296-1134
Debra Silber (Civil Court) (347) 296-1043
Wavny Toussaint (Civil Court) (347) 404-9870
John P. Walsh (Criminal Court) (347) 296-1055
Betty J. Williams (Civil Court)
(347) 404-9472; Fax: (718) 643-7733

Judicial Hearing Officers:
Gloria Aronin (347) 296-1566
Leon Deutsch (347) 401-9360
Lewis Douglass (347) 401-9252
Louise Gans (347) 296-1571
Ira Harkavy (347) 401-9303
Ira B. Harkavy (347) 401-9303
Muriel Hubsher (347) 401-9342
Luigi Marano (347) 296-1569
Milton Platt (347) 296-1071

Principal Court Reporter: Keith Olarnick
(347) 296-1938

For Supreme Court Clerk's offices for all counties, see listings under specific county, pp. 58-96

Law Clerks to Justices:
(Adams) . . . . Alex S. Rosenblum
(Ambrosio) . . . . Fernando H. Silva
(Baily-Schiffman) . . . . Dakota Ramsuer
(Balter) . . . . Meira C. Mednick
(Barros) . . . . Debra A. Gandler
(Battaglia) . . . . Robert A. Markoff
(Bayne) . . . . Adam C. Zucker
(Baynes) . . . . Jill Epstein
(Brennan) . . . . Thomas R. Quinlan III
(Bunyan) . . . . Joanne M. Cohen
(Calabrese) . . . . Karen Gopee
(Carroll) . . . . Ellen J. Shapiro
(Chun) . . . . Jean Chung Choi
(Cutrona) . . . . Charles Siegel
(Dabiri) . . . . Yvonne R. Marin
(Dear) . . . . Stephen Gurfinkel
(Del Giudice) . . . . Kevin Quinn
(Demarest) . . . . Sarah Izfar, Carl Regelmann
(D'Emic) . . . . Karen Kleinberg
(DiMango) . . . . Doris A. Bergemann
(Dowling) . . . . Marsha Michael
(Dwyer) . . . . Christine Silber
(Ferdinand) . . . . Christine Edwards
(Firetog) . . . . Marcia Margolin
(Foley) . . . . Christina Curry
(Garnett) . . . . Fredric Stetson
(Gary) . . . . Lisa R. Rosenzweig
(Gerges) . . . . Kerry J. Ward
(Goldberg) . . . . Ernest M. Hambrock
(Gubbay) . . . . Christina Bionda, Jacqui Sclasani
(Guzman) . . . . John McPadden
(Henry) . . . . Valerie A. Pels
(Hinds-Radix) . . . . Derefim B. Neckles
(Hurkin-Torres) . . . . David MacDonald
(Ingram) . . . . Elizabeth M. Mignone
(Jackson) . . . . Inga O'Neale
(Jacobson) . . . . Debbie I. Humphrey
(Kamins) . . . . John T. Hecht, Charles M. Troia
(King) . . . . Craig S. Walker
(Knipel) . . . . Aaron I. Blinder
(Kramer) . . . . Abby Shvartsman
(Krauss) . . . . H.J. Joseph
(Kurtz) . . . . Gina Abadi
(Lewis) . . . . Kimberly Detherage
(Mangano) . . . . Steven A. Pilewski
(Marrus) . . . . Marvin K. Scharf
(Martin) . . . . Linda Atlas
(McKay) . . . . James J. Fox
(Miller, R.) . . . . Carolyn M. Genovesi
(Miller, W.) . . . . Hiram L. Bell III
(Mondo) . . . . Eric Fieldman
(Morgenstern) . . . . Brian Kieran
(Murphy) . . . . Rosemarie A. Wyman
(Parker) . . . . Gabriela Lukas
(Partnow) . . . . Cherise Hewitt
(Pesce) . . . . Louis M. Reale
(Prus) . . . . Marilyn L. Rothstein
(Reichbach) . . . . Ellen C. Mishkin
(Rivera) . . . . Darren Guez
(Riviezzo) . . . . Alfred C. Tartaglia
(Rosenberg) . . . . Kenneth P. Starace
(Rothenberg) . . . . Jennifer R. Rapaport
(Ruchelsman) . . . . Mark M. Kagan
(Saitta) . . . . Pamela K. Allred
(Schack) . . . . Ronald D. Bratt
(Schmidt) . . . . Felicia A. Feinberg
(Sherman) . . . . Lizette Colon, Talia Koss
(Silber) . . . . Howard J. Graubard
(Solomon) . . . . David C. Pepper
(Spodek) . . . . Kristen Borruso, Monique Holaman
(Steinhardt) . . . . Consuelo Mallafre
(Sullivan) . . . . Robyn Hederman
(Sunshine) . . . . Lara J. Genovesi
(Thomas) . . . . Jeffrey Chery, Susan A. Liebman
(Tomei) . . . . Carol Teague Schwartzkopf
(Toussaint) . . . . William Bowman
(Vaughan) . . . . Joy Campanelli
(Velasquez) . . . . Carol Horwitz
(Walsh) . . . . Elliot J. Cook
(Weston) . . . . Iris Cross Bugliosi, Cristina B. Martinez

NINTH JUDICIAL DISTRICT, SUPREME COURT

Jurisdiction—Counties of Dutchess, Orange, Putnam, Rockland, Westchester

Admin. Judge: Alan D. Scheinkman
111 Dr. Martin Luther King Jr. Blvd., White Plains 10601
(914) 824-5100; Fax: (212) 884-8939

Justices:
Richard A. Molea (Supervising Judge of the Criminal Cts., 9th Jud. Dist.; Acting Justice, from Court of Claims)
Richard J. Daronco Courthouse,
111 Dr. M. Luther King, Jr. Blvd., White Plains 10601
(914) 824-5454; Fax: (914) 995-8654
Lester B. Adler, Richard J. Daronco Courthouse,
111 Dr. Martin Luther King, Jr. Blvd.,
White Plains 10601 (914) 824-5386; Fax: (914) 995-8653
Orazio R. Bellantoni, Richard J. Daronco Courthouse,
111 Dr. Martin Luther King, Jr. Blvd.,
White Plains 10601 (914) 824-5394; Fax: (914) 995-4010
Robert M. Berliner, Courthouse, 1 S. Main St.,
New City 10956 (845) 708-7218; Fax: (845) 638-5055
James V. Brands, Courthouse, 10 Market St.,
Poughkeepsie 12601 (845) 486-2531; Fax: (845) 486-6497
Jeffrey A. Cohen, 255-275 Main St., Goshen 10924
(845) 291-3130; Fax: (845) 291-3045
Nicholas Colabella, Richard J. Daronco Courthouse,
111 Dr. Martin Luther King, Jr. Blvd.,
White Plains 10601 (914) 824-5398; Fax: (914) 995-4182
Francesca E. Connolly, Richard J. Daronco Courthouse,
111 Dr. Martin Luther King, Jr. Blvd.,
White Plains 10601 (914) 824-5411
Margaret Garvey, Courthouse, 1 S. Main St.,
New City 10956 (845) 638-5982

Justices, Supreme Court, 9th Judicial Dist.—Cont'd

William J. Giacomo, Richard J. Daronco Courthouse, 111 Dr. Martin Luther King, Jr. Blvd., White Plains 10601 (914) 824-5429

Linda S. Jamieson, Courthouse, 1 S. Main St., New City 10956 (845) 638-5340

William A. Kelly, Courthouse, 1 S. Main St., New City 10956 (845) 638-5386; Fax: (845) 708-7236

John R. LaCava, Richard J. Daronco Courthouse, 111 Dr. Martin Luther King, Jr. Blvd., White Plains 10601 (914) 824-5417

Joan B. Lefkowitz, Richard J. Daronco Courthouse, 111 Dr. Martin Luther King, Jr. Blvd., White Plains 10601 (914) 824-5421; Fax: (914) 995-4184

Richard B. Liebowitz, Richard J. Daronco Courthouse, 111 Dr. Martin Luther King, Jr. Blvd., White Plains 10601 (914) 824-5451; Fax: (914) 995-4182

Lewis J. Lubell, 255 Main St., Goshen 10924 (845) 291-3126

John K. McGuirk, 255 Main St., Goshen 10924 (845) 291-3140

**J. Emmett Murphy, Richard J. Daronco Courthouse,15th Fl., 111 Dr. Martin Luther King, Jr. Blvd.,White Plains 10601 (914) 824-5733; Fax: (914) 995-4396

Francis A. Nicolai, 20 County Center, Carmel 10512 (845) 268-7890

Andrew P. O'Rourke, 20 County Center, Carmel 10512 (845) 208-7890; Fax: (845) 228-9617

Elaine Slobod, Courthouse, 285 Main St., Goshen 10924 (845) 291-2107

Mary H. Smith, 111 Dr. Martin Luther King Jr. Blvd., White Plains 10601 (914) 824-5431

Christine A. Sproat, Courthouse, 10 Market St., Poughkeepsie 12601 (845) 486-2220; Fax: (845) 486-2014

Bruce E. Tolbert, 111 Dr. Martin Luther King, Jr. Blvd., White Plains 10601 (914) 824-5435; Fax: (914) 995-4010

Sam D. Walker, Richard J. Daronco Courthouse, Ctrm. 1001, 111 Dr. Martin Luther King, Jr. Blvd., White Plains 10601 (914) 824-5427; Fax: (212) 401-9165

Alfred J. Weiner, Courthouse, 1 S. Main St., New City 10956 (845) 638-5355; Fax: (845) 638-5834

Charles D. Wood, Courthouse, 10 Market St., Poughkeepsie 12601 (845) 486-6444

Acting Justices:

Charles Apotheker (Rockland County Court) Courthouse, Suite 200, 1 S. Main St., New City 10956 (845) 638-5239

Catherine M. Bartlett (Court of Claims) 275 Main St., Goshen 10924 (845) 291-3137; Fax: (845) 291-2106

Jeffrey G. Berry (Orange County Court; Supervising Judge, City Courts, Ninth Judicial District) Courthouse, 285 Main St., Goshen 10924 (845) 291-3120

Andrew P. Bivona (Orange County Family Court) Orange Cty. Courthouse, 285 Main St., Goshen 10924 (845) 291-3020; Fax: (845) 291-3051

Nicholas DeRosa (Orange County Court) Orange Cty. Govt. Ctr., 255-275 Main St., Goshen 10924 (845) 291-3115

Robert M. DiBella (County Court), Richard J. Daronco Cthse., 111 Dr. Martin Luther King, Jr. Blvd., White Plains 10601 (914) 824-5407; Fax: (914) 995-8654

Peter M. Forman (Dutchess County, Family Court) 50 Market St., Poughkeepsie 12602-3204 (845) 486-2526

Robert H. Freehill (Orange County Court) County Courthouse, 285 Main St., Goshen 10924 (845) 291-3110; Fax: (845) 291-2103

Robert K. Holdman (Court of Claims) Richard J. Daronco Cthse., 111 Dr. M. Luther King, Jr. Blvd., White Plains 10601 (914) 824-5379

Debra J. Kiedaisch (Orange County Family Court; Presiding Judge, Integrated Domestic Violence Part) Orange Cty. Courthouse, 285 Main St., Goshen 10924 (845) 291-3050; Fax: (845) 291-4520

Carol S. Klein (Orange County Family Court and Presiding Judge, Family Treatment and Juv. Drug Treatment Courts) Orange Cty. Courthouse, 285 Main St., Goshen 10924 (845) 291-3040; Fax: (845) 291-4405

Gerald E. Loehr (Westchester County Courts) 111 Dr. Martin Luther King, Jr. Blvd., White Plains 10601 (914) 824-5413; Fax: (914) 995-8651

Albert Lorenzo (Court of Claims) Richard J. Daronco Courthouse, 111 Dr. Martin Luther King, Jr. Blvd., White Plains 10601 (914) 824-5403

William K. Nelson (Rockland County Court) Courthouse, 1 S. Main St., New City 10956 (845) 638-5336

Robert A. Onofry (Orange County Surrogate) 30 Park Pl., Goshen 10924 (845) 291-2300; Fax: (845) 291-2543

Joan S. Posner (Dutchess County Family Court) 50 Market St., Poughkeepsie 12601-3204 (845) 486-2521

James F. Reitz (Putnam County Court) Courthouse, 20 County Ctr., Carmel 10512 (845) 208-7875

Valentino T. Sammarco (Dutchess County, Family Court) 50 Market St., Poughkeepsie 12601-3204 (845) 486-2230; Fax: (845) 486-2510

Barbara Gunther Zambelli (Westchester County Court) Richard J. Daronco Courthouse, 111 Dr. Martin Luther King, Jr. Blvd., White Plains 10601 (914) 824-5439; Fax: (914) 995-8653

For Supreme Court Clerk's offices for all counties, see listings under specific county, pp. 58-96

Law Clerks to Justices:

(Adler) . . . . . Lee Spaulding
(Apotheker) . . . . . Arielle Schoenberger
(Bartlett) . . . . . Adam Garth
(Bellantoni) . . . . . Eric Conroy
(Berliner) . . . . . Alan E. Goldstein
(Berry) . . . . . Richard Clarino
(Bivona) . . . . . Rebecca E. Stage
(Brands) . . . . . Maria G. Rosa
(Cohen) . . . . . Joanne Matthews-Forbes
(Colabella) . . . . . Raymond Powers
(Connolly) . . . . . Stephane Martin, Denise O'Connor
(DeRosa) . . . . . Janet Haislip
(DiBella) . . . . . Lisa Citarella
(Forman) . . . . . Denise Watson
(Freehill) . . . . . John Goldsmith
(Garvey) . . . . . Edward Gaffney
(Giacomo) . . . . . Tara Monteleone-Mansfield
(Holdman) . . . . . Maureen Gorman-Phelan
(Jamieson) . . . . . Judith M. Shampanier
(Kelly) . . . . . Brian P. Coffey
(Kiedaisch) . . . . . Martin Schaffer
(Klein) . . . . . Lisa Noroian
(LaCava) . . . . . John R. Mechmann
(Lefkowitz) . . . . . James G. Fine
(Liebowitz) . . . . . Lillian Krusz Welby
(Loehr) . . . . . Bruce Pearl
(Lorenzo) . . . . . Pamela Goldsmith
(Lubell) . . . . . Alfred Farella
(McGuirk) . . . . . Joseph P. Fogarty
(Molea) . . . . . George Hlapatsos, Jr.
(Murphy) . . . . . Susan Pianforini
(Nelson) . . . . . Bruce A. Muldoon
(Nicolai) . . . . . Amelia Del Vecchio
(Onofry) . . . . . Amanda Brady
(Posner) . . . . . Susan L. Flynn
(Reitz) . . . . . Cari S. Young
(Sammarco) . . . . . Lisa Rubenstein
(Scheinkman) . . . . . Gretchen Walsh
(Slobod) . . . . . Gregory C. Grasselena
(Smith) . . . . . Deborah Cohen
(Sproat) . . . . . Jude T. Martini
(Tolbert) . . . . . Renee Motola
(Walker) . . . . . Keri A. Fiore, Julie Mills-Worthey
(Weiner) . . . . . Edward Kallen
(Wood) . . . . . Michael Curti
(Zambelli) . . . . . Barbara Sheridan

****Pending November 2010 Election Results**

TENTH JUDICIAL DISTRICT, SUPREME COURT
Jurisdiction—Counties of Nassau, Suffolk

Administrative Judges:
H. Patrick Leis III (Suffolk)
John P. Cohalan, Jr. Court Complex, Ctrm. S-24,
400 Carleton Ave., P.O. Box 9070, Central Islip 11722-9070
(631) 853-5368; Fax: (631) 853-7741
Anthony F. Marano (Nassau)
100 Supreme Court Dr., Mineola 11501
(516) 571-2684; Fax: (516) 571-3713
E-mail: amarano@courts.state.ny.us

Supervising Judge, Matrimonial: Robert A. Ross (Nassau)
Matrimonial Center, 400 County Seat Dr.,
Mineola 11501 (516) 571-0021

Justices:
Joel K. Asarch (Nassau), Supreme Court Bldg.,
100 Supreme Court Dr., Mineola 11501 (516) 571-2870
Paul J. Baisley, Jr. (Suffolk), Supreme Court Bldg.,
Room A-301, 1 Court St., Riverhead 11901
(631) 852-3888; Fax: (631) 852-3745
John C. Bivona (Suffolk)
John P. Cohalan, Jr. Court Complex, Ctrm. S31,
400 Carleton Ave., P.O. Box 9070, Central Islip 11722
(631) 853-5155; Fax: (631) 853-3288
**Donald R. Blydenburgh (Suffolk)
John P. Cohalan, Jr. Court Complex, Room S22,
400 Carleton Ave., Central Islip 11722
(631) 853-6162; Fax: (631) 853-6326
Jeffrey S. Brown (Nassau), Matrimonial Center,
400 County Seat Dr., Mineola 11501 (516) 571-0766
Robert A. Bruno (Nassau), Matrimonial Center,
400 County Seat Dr., Mineola 11501 (516) 571-5810
Stephen A. Bucaria (Nassau), Supreme Court Bldg.,
100 Supreme Ct. Dr., Mineola 11501 (516) 571-3320
*Peter Fox Cohalan (Suffolk), Supreme Court Bldg.,
Ctrm. 6, 1 Court St., Riverhead 11901
(631) 852-2395; Fax: (631) 852-2719
William J. Condon (Suffolk)
Arthur M. Cromarty Court Complex, Chambers 4188,
210 Center Dr., Riverhead 11901
(631) 852-2670; Fax: (631) 852-2925
**Ralph F. Costello (Suffolk), Supreme Court Bldg.,
Room A-257, 1 Court St., Riverhead 11901
(631) 852-2422; Fax: (631) 852-2834
R. Bruce Cozzens, Jr. (Nassau), Supreme Court Bldg.,
100 Supreme Ct. Dr., Mineola 11501 (516) 571-3716
Vito M. DeStefano (Nassau), Matrimonial Center,
400 County Seat Dr., Mineola 11501 (516) 571-2475
Arthur M. Diamond (Nassau)
100 Supreme Court Dr., Mineola 11501
(516) 571-2874; Fax: (516) 571-3623
*Robert W. Doyle (Suffolk)
Arthur M. Cromarty Court Complex, Room 15 & 3,
210 Center Dr., Riverhead 11901
(631) 852-2169; Fax: (631) 852-2855
Timothy S. Driscoll (Nassau)
100 Supreme Court Dr., Mineola 11501 (516) 571-3891
Elizabeth H. Emerson (Suffolk)
Arthur M. Cromarty Court Complex, Ctrm. 7,
210 Center Dr., Riverhead 11901
(631) 852-2781; Fax: (631) 852-3732
Anthony J. Falanga (Nassau), Matrimonial Center,
400 County Seat Dr., Mineola 11501
(516) 571-0017; Fax: (516) 571-0029
Thomas Feinman (Nassau), Supreme Court Bldg.,
100 Supreme Court Dr., Mineola 11501 (516) 571-2952
Jerry Garguilo (Suffolk)
John P. Cohalan, Jr. Courthouse, 400 Carleton Ave.,
Central Islip 11722 (631) 853-4302
C. Randall Hinrichs (Suffolk)
Arthur M. Cromarty Court Complex, 210 Center Dr.,
Riverhead 11901 (631) 852-2586
Angela G. Iannacci (Nassau)
100 Supreme Court Dr., Mineola 11501 (516) 571-2484
John J.J. Jones, Jr. (Suffolk)
Arthur M. Cromarty Court Complex, Room 6,
210 Center Dr., Riverhead 11901
(631) 852-1429; Fax: (631) 852-2730
*William J. Kent III (Suffolk)
John P. Cohalan, Jr. Courthouse, Ctrm. S-34,
400 Carleton St., P.O. Box 9070, Central Islip 11722-9070
(631) 853-5471; Fax: (631) 853-3281
Ute Wolff Lally (Nassau), Supreme Court Bldg.,
100 Supreme Ct. Dr., Mineola 11501 (516) 571-2949
Hector D. LaSalle (Suffolk)
John P. Cohalan, Jr. Court Complex, 400 Carleton Ave.,
Central Islip 11722 (631) 853-7703; Fax: (631) 853-7542
Carol MacKenzie (Suffolk)
John P. Cohalan, Jr. Court Complex, Ctrm. D63,
400 Carleton Ave., P.O. Box 9075, Central Islip 11722-9075
(631) 853-7750; Fax: (631) 853-6431
Roy S. Mahon (Nassau), Supreme Court Bldg.,
100 Supreme Ct. Dr., Mineola 11501 (516) 571-3337
Randy Sue Marber (Nassau), Supreme Court Bldg.,
100 Supreme Court Dr., Mineola 11501
(516) 571-3310; Fax: (516) 571-1316
Edward A. Maron (Nassau), Matrimonial Center,
400 County Seat Dr., Mineola 11501
(516) 571-5908; Fax: (516) 571-5970
Peter H. Mayer (Suffolk), Supreme Court Bldg.,
Room A-259, 1 Court St., Riverhead 11901
(631) 852-1760; Fax: (631) 852-2102
Edward W. McCarty III (Nassau), Supreme Court Bldg.,
100 Supreme Ct. Dr., Mineola 11501
(516) 571-2154; Fax: (516) 571-2966
Marion T. McNulty (Suffolk)
John P. Cohalan, Jr. Court Complex, Ctrm. S-21,
400 Carleton Ave., P.O. Box 9070, Central Islip 11722-9070
(631) 853-4332, 33; Fax: (631) 853-7412
Denise F. Molia (Suffolk), Supreme Court Bldg.,
Room A-201, 1 Court St., Riverhead 11901
(631) 852-3750; Fax: (631) 852-2867
Karen V. Murphy (Nassau), Supreme Court Bldg.,
100 Supreme Court Dr., Mineola 11501 (516) 571-2325
Anthony L. Parga (Nassau), Supreme Court Bldg.,
100 Supreme Ct. Dr., Mineola 11501 (516) 571-2373
Thomas P. Phelan (Nassau), Supreme Court Bldg.,
100 Supreme Ct. Dr., Mineola 11501 (516) 571-2427
Emily Pines (Suffolk), Supreme Court Bldg., 1 Court St.,
Riverhead 11901 (631) 852-3117; Fax: (631) 852-3120
Arthur G. Pitts (Suffolk)
Arthur M. Cromarty Court Complex, Ctrm. 5,
210 Center Dr., Riverhead 11901
(631) 852-2174; Fax: (631) 852-2769
William B. Rebolini (Suffolk), Supreme Court Bldg.,
Room A-260, 1 Court St., Riverhead 11901
(631) 852-3166; Fax: (631) 852-3188
*Melvyn Tanenbaum (Suffolk)
John P. Cohalan, Jr. Courthouse, Ctrm. S-32,
400 Carleton Ave., Central Islip 11722
Mailing Address: 400 Carleton Ave., Central Islip 11722
(631) 853-6323
Ira B. Warshawsky (Nassau), Supreme Court Bldg.,
100 Supreme Ct. Dr., Mineola 11501
(516) 571-3351; Fax: (516) 571-0163
Thomas F. Whelan (Suffolk), Supreme Court Bldg.,
Room A-258, 1 Court St., Riverhead 11901
(631) 852-2365; Fax: (631) 852-1961
F. Dana Winslow (Nassau), Supreme Court Bldg.,
100 Supreme Ct. Dr., Mineola 11501
(516) 571-2480; Fax: (516) 571-0213
Michele M. Woodard (Nassau), Supreme Court Bldg.,
100 Supreme Ct. Dr., Mineola 11501
(516) 571-2736; Fax: (516) 571-2170

Acting Justices:
Thomas A. Adams (Nassau; Court of Claims)
Supreme Court Bldg., 100 Supreme Ct. Dr.,
Mineola 11501 (516) 571-2961
David J. Ayres (Nassau; County Court)
West Wing, 252 Old Country Rd., Mineola 11501
(516) 571-3833; Fax: (516) 571-2137
Meryl J. Berkowitz (Nassau; County Court)
262 Old Country Rd., Mineola 11501
(516) 571-2241; Fax: (516) 571-2078

***Justice Serving under Certification**
****Pending November 2010 Election Results**

Acting Justices, Supreme Court, Tenth Judicial Dist.—Cont'd

Antonio I. Brandveen (Nassau; Court of Claims)
100 Supreme Court Dr., Mineola 11501
(516) 571-3360; Fax: (516) 571-1283

Joseph C. Calabrese (Nassau; County Court)
262 Old Country Rd., Mineola 11501
(516) 571-2065; Fax: (516) 571-0566

Jerald S. Carter (Nassau; County Court)
262 Old Country Rd., Mineola 11501
(561) 571-3563; Fax: (561) 571-0565

Mark D. Cohen (Suffolk; Court of Claims)
Arthur M. Cromarty Court Complex, Room 2,
210 Center Dr., Riverhead 11901
(631) 852-2168; Fax: (631) 852-2156

**Andrew A. Crecca (Suffolk; County Court)
John P. Cohalan Court Complex, 400 Carleton Ave.,
Central Islip 11722 (631) 853-6092; Fax: (631) 853-3289

William C. Donnino (Nassau; Court of Claims)
262 Old Country Rd., Mineola 11501
(516) 571-2797; Fax: (516) 571-1485

James F.X. Doyle (Suffolk; County Court)
Arthur M. Cromarty Court Complex, 210 Center Dr.,
Riverhead 11901-3310 (631) 852-1640; Fax: (631) 852-3547

Joseph Farneti (Suffolk; County Court)
Arthur M. Cromarty Court Complex, 210 Center Dr.,
Riverhead 11901 (631) 852-3160; Fax: (631) 852-3161

David Freundlich (Suffolk; Family Court)
John P. Cohalan, Jr. Court Complex, Ctrm. F26,
400 Carleton Ave., Central Islip 11722
(631) 853-4318; Fax: (631) 853-6218

John Michael Galasso (Nassau; County Court)
100 Supreme Court Dr., Mineola 11501
(516) 571-2613; Fax: (516) 571-2164

Ralph T. Gazzillo (Suffolk; County Court)
Arthur M. Cromarty Court Complex, 210 Center Dr.,
Riverhead 11901-3310 (631) 852-2584; Fax: (631) 852-3854

Philip M. Grella (Nassau; Court of Claims)
262 Old Country Rd., Mineola 11501
(516) 571-1488; Fax: (516) 571-2642
Assigned to County Court

Alan L. Honorof (Nassau; Court of Claims)
262 Old Country Rd., Mineola 11501
(516) 571-3423; Fax: (516) 571-1849

James C. Hudson (Suffolk; County Court)
Arthur M. Cromarty Court Complex, 210 Center Dr.,
Riverhead 11901 (631) 852-3850; Fax: (631) 852-3225

Steven M. Jaeger (Nassau; County Court)
262 Old Country Rd., Mineola 11501
(516) 571-3378; Fax: (516) 571-3220

John L. Kase (Nassau; County Court)
262 Old Country Rd., Mineola 11501
(516) 571-2628; Fax: (516) 571-6300

John Kelly (Suffolk; Family Court)
John P. Cohalan, Jr. Court Complex, 400 Carleton Ave.,
Central Islip 11722 (631) 853-4286; Fax: (631) 853-4288

Martha Luft (Suffolk; Family Court)
John P. Cohalan, Jr. Court Complex, 400 Carleton Ave.,
Central Islip 11722 (631) 853-4537; Fax: (631) 853-5427

Daniel Martin (Suffolk; Court of Claims)
John P. Cohalan Jr. Courthouse, 400 Carleton Ave.,
Central Islip 11722 (631) 853-4523

James P. McCormack (Nassau; County Court)
West Wing, 252 Old Country Rd., Mineola 11501
(516) 571-2768; Fax: (516) 571-1093

**Daniel R. Palmieri (Nassau; County Court)
Supreme Court Bldg., 100 Supreme Court Dr.,
Mineola 11501 (516) 571-2878; Fax: (516) 571-0129

Joseph C. Pastoressa (Suffolk; Court of Claims)
Arthur M. Cromarty Court Complex, Ctrm. 14,
210 Center Dr., 3rd Fl., Riverhead 11901
(631) 852-2163; Fax: (631) 852-3043

George R. Peck (Nassau; County Court)
262 Old Country Rd., Mineola 11501
(516) 571-3765; Fax: (516) 571-3256

Christopher G. Quinn (Nassau; County Court)
99 Main St., Hempstead 11550
(516) 572-2166; Fax: (516) 572-2457

Tammy S. Robbins (Nassau; County Court)
West Wing, 252 Old Country Rd., Mineola 11501
(516) 571-2768; Fax: (516) 571-2758

Norman St. George (Nassau; County Court)
262 Old Country Rd., Mineola 11501
(516) 571-3560; Fax: (516) 571-1600

Denise L. Sher (Nassau; Court of Claims)
100 Supreme Court Dr., Mineola 11501 (516) 571-2883

Jeffrey Arlen Spinner (Suffolk; County Court)
Supreme Court Bldg., 1 Court St., Riverhead 11901
(631) 852-2309; Fax: (631) 852-3226

David P. Sullivan (Nassau; County Court;
Supervising Judge, Village Courts, Nassau County)
West Wing, 252 Old Country Rd., Mineola 11501
(516) 571-2408; Fax: (516) 571-1491

Patrick A. Sweeney (Suffolk; Family Court)
John P. Cohalan, Jr. Court Complex, 400 Carleton Ave.,
Central Islip 11722 (631) 853-2207; Fax: (631) 853-8407

Gary J. Weber (Suffolk, County Court)
Arthur M. Cromarty Court Complex, 210 Center Dr.,
Riverhead 11901-3310 (631) 852-2176; Fax: (631) 852-3857

Hope S. Zimmerman (Nassau; Family Court)
Matrimonial Center, 400 County Seat Dr.,
Mineola 11501 (516) 571-9005; Fax: (516) 571-9205

Judicial Hearing Officers:

Stanley Gartenstein, Matrimonal Center,
44 County Seat Dr., Mineola 11501 (516) 571-5893

Geoffrey J. O'Connell, Matrimonial Center,
400 County Seat Dr., Mineola 11501 (516) 571-0760

For Supreme Court Clerk's offices for all counties, see listings under specific county, pp. 58-96

Law Clerks to Justices:

(Adams) . . . . Michael T. Langan
(Asarch) . . . . Lisa Petrocelli
(Ayres) . . . . Judith Gann
(Baisley) . . . . Carol L. Moore
(Berkowitz) . . . . Jennifer Feingold
(Bivona) . . . . Catherine S. Kash
(Blydenburgh) . . . . Susan Pierini
(Brandveen) . . . . Ronald Travis
(Brown) . . . . Helene Gugerty
(Bruno) . . . . Tricia Morites
(Bucaria) . . . . Charles Goldburg
(Calabrese) . . . . Charles J. Weinschrider
(Carter) . . . . Patricia Harrington
(Cohalan) . . . . Daniel J. Murphy
(Cohen) . . . . James Fagan
(Condon) . . . . Robert Caccese
(Costello) . . . . Athena Voorhees
(Cozzens) . . . . William J. Riccio
(Crecca) . . . . Vincent Zambito
(DeStefano) . . . . Walter J. Kraker
(Diamond) . . . . Kurt S. Holmes
(Donnino) . . . Patricia Harrington, Susan Katz-Richman
Michael Tarbutton
(Doyle, J.) . . . . Edward J. Fox
(Doyle, R.) . . . . Robert T. Lee
(Driscoll) . . . . Madeline Pomerantz
(Emerson) . . . . Joan L. Hannon
(Falanga) . . . . Charlene Malone
(Farneti) . . . . Evan Zuckerman
(Feinman) . . . . Catherine Rizzo
(Freundlich) . . . . Christine Czajkowski
(Galasso) . . . . Joyce M. Andren
(Garguilo) . . . . Stephanie C. Galteri
(Gazzillo) . . . . Gabrielle Weglein
(Grella) . . . . Thomas A. Rademaker
(Hinrichs) . . . . Stewart Krupin
(Honorof) . . . . Howard Sturim
(Hudson) . . . . Bernard Cheng
(Iannacci) . . . . David W. Wright
(Jaeger) . . . . Helen Voutsinas
(Jones) . . . . Anne Molloy Boucher
(Kase) . . . . James Tini
(Kelly) . . . . John Kilgallon
(Kent) . . . . Matthew Deedy
(Lally) . . . . Else Goddard
(LaSalle) . . . . Rosamaria Abbate
(Leis) . . . . Colleen Fondulis

****Pending November 2010 Election Results**

Law Clerks to Justices, Supreme Court, Tenth Judicial Dist.—Cont'd

(Luft) . . . . . Bert Zweroff
(MacKenzie) . . . . . Mary Buetow
(Mahon) . . . . . Peter S. Williams
(Marano) . . . . . Jeffrey Goodstein
(Marber) . . . . . Joseph Lorintz, Mili Makhijani
(Maron) . . . . . Linda K. Mejias
(Martin) . . . . . Robert A. Lifson
(Mayer) . . . . . Oliver Raymond Voorhees III
(McCarty) . . . . . Alice J. Hollmuller
(McCormack) . . . . . Cheryl Bartow
(McNulty) . . . . . Gregory Ostermann
(Molia) . . . . . Gary Brunjes
(Murphy) . . . . . Mary Louise Biunno
(Palmieri) . . . . . Philip C. Weis
(Parga) . . . . . Elizabeth Pessala
(Pastoressa) . . . . . Matthew G. Hughes
(Peck) . . . . . Frank O'Regan
(Phelan) . . . . . Kathleen Wright
(Pines) . . . . . Caren Loguerico
(Pitts) . . . . . Glenn Mikalsen
(Quinn) . . . . . Virginia Clavin
(Rebolini) . . . . . Stephen J. Lynch
(Robbins) . . . . . Amy Marion
(Ross) . . . . . Linda Kevins
(St. George) . . . . . Eileen Daly-Sapraicone
(Sher) . . . . . Cara Patton
(Spinner) . . . . . Robert DeGregorio
(Sullivan) . . . . . Lawrence Schaeffer
(Sweeney) . . . . . Leonard Lozito
(Tanenbaum) . . . . . Howard Heckman, Jr.
(Warshawsky) . . . . . Daniel J. Dillon
(Weber) . . . . . Thomas F. Moore
(Whelan) . . . . . Susan Tobey
(Winslow) . . . . . Christine Conlon, Rachel S. Zampino
(Woodard) . . . . . Victoria R. Gumbs Moore
(Zimmerman) . . . . . Martha Haesloop

ELEVENTH JUDICIAL DISTRICT, SUPREME COURT
Jurisdiction—County of Queens

Administrative Judge, Civil Term: Jeremy S. Weinstein
88-11 Sutphin Blvd., Jamaica 11435
(718) 298-1100; Fax: (718) 298-1099

Administrative Judge, Criminal Term:
Fernando M. Camacho (Acting Justice, Court of Claims)
125-01 Queens Blvd., Kew Gardens 11415
(718) 298-1440; Fax: (718) 520-6426

Justices:

Augustus C. Agate, 88-11 Sutphin Blvd., Jamaica 11435 (718) 298-1186; Fax: (718) 298-1158
Michael B. Aloise, 125-01 Queens Blvd., Kew Gardens 11415 (718) 298-1373; Fax: (718) 520-2494
Evelyn L. Braun, 125-01 Queens Blvd., Kew Gardens 11415 (718) 298-1442; Fax: (718) 520-2236
Richard L. Buchter, 125-01 Queens Blvd., Kew Gardens 11415 (718) 298-1336; Fax: (718) 520-2494
Denis J. Butler, 88-11 Sutphin Blvd., Jamaica 11435 (718) 298-1216; Fax: (718) 298-1149
David Elliot, 88-11 Sutphin Blvd., Jamaica 11435 (718) 298-1119; Fax: (718) 298-1130
William M. Erlbaum, 125-01 Queens Blvd., Kew Gardens 11415 (718) 298-1401
Phyllis Orlikoff Flug, 88-11 Sutphin Blvd., Jamaica 11435 (718) 298-1192; Fax: (718) 298-1810
Darrell Lori Gavrin, 125-01 Queens Blvd., Kew Gardens 11415 (718) 298-1416
James J. Golia, 25-10 Court Sq., Long Island City 11101 (718) 298-1604; Fax: (718) 520-6707
Joseph G. Golia, 88-11 Sutphin Blvd., Jamaica 11435 (718) 298-1190
Marguerite A. Grays, 88-11 Sutphin Blvd., Jamaica 11435 (718) 298-1212; Fax: (718) 298-1107
Duane A. Hart, 88-11 Sutphin Blvd., Jamaica 11435 (718) 298-1144
Kenneth C. Holder, 125-01 Queens Blvd., Kew Gardens 11415 (718) 298-1328
Ronald D. Hollie, 125-01 Queens Blvd., Kew Gardens 11415 (718) 298-1438; Fax: (718) 520-6474
Peter J. Kelly, 88-11 Sutphin Blvd., Jamaica 11435 (718) 298-1114
Kevin J. Kerrigan, 88-11 Sutphin Blvd., Jamaica 11435 (718) 298-0013; Fax: (718) 298-0088
Orin R. Kitzes, 88-11 Sutphin Blvd., Jamaica 11435 (718) 298-1003
Stephen A. Knopf, 125-01 Queens Blvd., Kew Gardens 11415 (718) 298-1443; Fax: (718) 520-7732
Robert C. Kohm, 125-01 Queens Blvd., Kew Gardens 11415 (718) 298-1375
Howard G. Lane, 88-11 Sutphin Blvd., Jamaica 11435 (718) 298-0674; Fax: (718) 298-1154
Gregory L. Lasak, 125-01 Queens Blvd., Kew Gardens 11415 (718) 298-1387; Fax: (718) 520-2494
Daniel Lewis, 125-01 Queens Blvd., Kew Gardens 11415 (718) 298-1359; Fax: (212) 419-8424
Charles J. Markey, 25-10 Court Sq., Long Island City 11101 (718) 298-1615; Fax: (718) 520-7379
Lee Mayersohn, 88-11 Sutphin Blvd., Jamaica 11435 (718) 298-1626; Fax: (718) 298-1149
Robert J. McDonald, 25-10 Court Sq., Long Island City 11101 (718) 298-1661; Fax: (718) 520-8577
Valerie Brathwaite Nelson, 88-11 Sutphin Blvd., Jamaica 11425 (718) 298-1170; Fax: (718) 298-1101
Peter J. O'Donoghue, 88-11 Sutphin Blvd., Jamaica 11435 (718) 298-1124; Fax: (718) 298-1129
Steven W. Paynter, 125-01 Queens Blvd., Kew Gardens 11415 (718) 298-1376
Diccia Pineda-Kirwan, 25-10 Court Sq., Long Island City 11101 (718) 298-0083; Fax: (718) 520-2571
Thomas D. Raffaele, 88-11 Sutphin Blvd., Jamaica 11435 (718) 298-1670; Fax: (718) 298-1090
Jaime A. Rios, 88-11 Sutphin Blvd., Jamaica 11435 (718) 298-1079; Fax: (718) 298-1122
Martin E. Ritholtz, 88-11 Sutphin Blvd., Jamaica 11435 (718) 298-1089
Roger N. Rosengarten, 88-11 Sutphin Blvd., Jamaica 11435 (718) 298-1097
Frederick D.R. Sampson, 25-10 Court Sq., Long Island City 11101 (718) 298-1671
Patricia P. Satterfield, 88-11 Sutphin Blvd., Jamaica 11435 (718) 298-1095
Martin J. Schulman, 88-11 Sutphin Blvd., Jamaica 11435 (718) 298-1006
Bernice D. Siegal, 88-11 Sutphin Blvd., Jamaica 11435 (718) 298-1080; Fax: (718) 298-1090
Sidney F. Strauss, 88-11 Sutphin Blvd., Jamaica 11435 (718) 298-1081
Janice A. Taylor, 88-11 Sutphin Blvd., Jamaica 11435 (718) 298-1194
Allan B. Weiss, 88-11 Sutphin Blvd., Jamaica 11435 (718) 298-1184

Acting Justices:

Joel L. Blumenfeld (Criminal Court) 125-01 Queens Blvd., Kew Gardens 11415 (718) 298-1363; Fax: (212) 419-8400
Dorothy K. Chin-Brandt (Civil Court) 125-01 Queens Blvd., Kew Gardens 11415 (718) 298-0922; Fax: (718) 520-3992
Lawrence V. Cullen (Court of Claims) 88-11 Sutphin Blvd., Room 44A, Jamaica 11435 (718) 298-1083
Anna Culley (Civil Court) 89-17 Sutphin Blvd., Jamaica 11435 (718) 262-7357
Timothy J. Dufficy (Civil Court) 89-17 Sutphin Blvd., Jamaica 11435 (718) 262-7354
Joseph J. Esposito (Civil Court) 89-17 Sutphin Blvd., Jamaica 11435 (718) 262-7379
Mary Ellen Fitzmaurice (Family Court) 151-20 Jamaica Ave., Jamaica 11432 (718) 298-0222
James P. Griffin (Criminal Court) 125-01 Queens Blvd., Kew Gardens 11415 (718) 298-1434; Fax: (718) 520-2263
Joseph A. Grosso (Criminal Court) 125-01 Queens Blvd., Kew Gardens 11415 (718) 298-1418
William M. Harrington (Criminal Court) 125-01 Queens Blvd., Kew Gardens 11415 (718) 298-1204

***Justice Serving under Certification**

Acting Justices, Supreme Court, Eleventh Judicial District—Cont'd

Marcia P. Hirsch (Court of Claims)
125-01 Queens Blvd., Kew Gardens 11415 (718) 298-1435
Pam B. Jackman-Brown (Civil Court)
88-11 Sutphin Blvd., Jamaica 11435 (718) 298-1653
Barry Kron (Criminal Court)
125-01 Queens Blvd., Kew Gardens 11415 (718) 298-1358
John B. Latella, Jr. (Criminal Court)
125-01 Queens Blvd., Kew Gardens 11415
(718) 298-1357; Fax: (718) 520-2494
Jeffrey D. Lebowitz (Court of Claims)
88-11 Sutphin Blvd., Jamaica 11435 (718) 298-1219
Charles S. Lopresto (Civil Court)
89-17 Sutphin Blvd., Jamaica 11435 (718) 262-7333
Robert C. McGann (Criminal Court)
125-01 Queens Blvd., Kew Gardens 11415
(718) 298-1385; Fax: (718) 520-2539
Deborah Stevens Modica (Criminal Court; Supervising Judge)
125-01 Queens Blvd., Kew Gardens 11415
(718) 286-0839; Fax: (718) 520-3992
Salvatore J. Modica (Criminal Court)
125-10 Queens Blvd., Kew Gardens 11415 (718) 298-1055
Pauline A. Mullings (Criminal Court)
125-01 Queens Blvd., Kew Gardens 11415 (718) 298-0930
Robert M. Raciti (Criminal Court)
125-01 Queens Blvd., Kew Gardens 11415 (718) 298-0981
Douglas S. Wong (Criminal Court)
125-01 Queens Blvd., Kew Gardens 11415 (718) 298-1408

For Supreme Court Clerk's offices for all counties, see listings under specific county, pp. 58-96

Law Clerks to Justices:

(Agate) .... Richard Chase
(Aloise) .... Miriam McEnroe
(Blumenfeld) .... Brian H. Lowy
(Braun) .... Marian B. Morris
(Buchter) .... Kathleen Ward
(Butler) .... Andrew Axler
(Camacho) .... Jeneen Wunder
(Chin-Brandt) .... Jill Posner
(Cullen) .... Candace Hesse
(Culley) .... Eric Conroy
(Dufficy) .... June Briese
(Elliot) .... Myra J. Doyle
(Erlbaum) .... Elise Rucker
(Esposito) .... Richard Goldman
(Fitzmaurice) .... Joan Piccirillo, Traci Woods
(Flug) .... Abby C. Goldstein
(Gavrin) .... Margaret Crowley
(Golia, James) .... Laurentina McKetney-Butler
(Golia, Joseph) .... Mitchell Kaufman
(Grays) .... Nicole McGregor
(Griffin) .... Paul DuBois
(Grosso) .... William Sarro
(Harrington) .... William Kane
(Hart) .... T. Anthony Hayles
(Hirsch) .... Francis Consigli
(Holder) .... Traci Wilkerson
(Hollie) .... Arlene A. Hamilton
(Jackman-Brown) . Cassandra Johnson, Denetra Thompson
(Kelly) .... Francis Kahn III
(Kerrigan) .... Nicholas Bais
(Kitzes) .... Robert Caloras
(Knopf) .... Ilene Reichman
(Kohm) .... Ira Hofher
(Kron) ..... Elizabeth Fox-McDonough, Karen Moroney
(Lane) .... Kimberly Tivin
(Lasak) .... Rosemarie Montalbano
(Latella) .... Jaewon Chung
(Lebowitz) .... Kerian Finnegan, Anna Grimaldi
(Lewis) .... Richard Johnson
(Lopresto) .... Maura Curtin
(Markey) .... Howard Wieder
(Mayersohn) .... Leigh Cheng
(McDonald) .... Dennis Lebwohl
(McGann) .... Peter Dunne
(Modica) .... John Zoll
(Mullings) .... Paul Gamble
(Nelson) .... Karen Richardson
(O'Donoghue) .... Joseph Hand, Elizabeth MacEwen
(Paynter) .... Lorraine O'Donoghue
(Pineda-Kirwan) .... Matthew Wagoner
(Raciti) .... Thomas King
(Raffaele) .... Sally Maiolo
(Rios) .... Sharon Kapusta, Alexandra Zervopoulos
(Ritholtz) .... Debra Edwards
(Rosengarten) .... Morgan Lancman
(Sampson) .... Edward Schacter
(Satterfield) .... Deirdre A. Finley
(Schulman) .... Ilene P. Fern
(Siegal) .... Alan Schiff
(Strauss) .... Maria Bradley
(Taylor) .... Denise Johnson
(Weinstein) .... Tracy Catapano-Fox
(Weiss) .... Agnes Kirschner
(Wong) .... David Heller

THIRTEENTH JUDICIAL DISTRICT, SUPREME COURT
Jurisdiction—County of Richmond
County Courthouse, 18 Richmond Terr., Staten Island 10301
(718) 675-8600
Homeport (Civil Term), 355 Front St., Staten Island 10304
(718) 876-6411

Administrative Judge: Philip G. Minardo
(718) 675-8600; Fax: (718) 815-2775

Justices:
Thomas P. Aliotta (718) 675-8620; Fax: (718) 876-8129
*John A. Fusco (718) 876-6444
*Anthony I. Giacobbe (718) 876-6433
Judith N. McMahon (718) 675-8630

Acting Justices:
Robert J. Collini (Court of Claims) (718) 675-8650
Kim Dollard (Civil Court) (718) 675-8438
Joseph J. Maltese (Court of Claims) (718) 675-7860
Alan J. Meyer (Criminal Court) (718) 675-8550
Barbara I. Panepinto (Civil Court) (718) 876-6424
Leonard P. Rienzi (Criminal Court) (718) 675-8610
Stephen J. Rooney (Court of Claims) (718) 675-8640

Judicial Hearing Officers:
Michael V. Ajello (718) 876-6439; Fax: (718) 876-6416
Vincent Pizzuto (718) 675-8678
Lester Sacks (718) 876-6411, 20

For Supreme Court Clerk's offices for all counties, see listings under specific county, pp. 58-96

Law Clerks to Justices:

(Aliotta) .... Elyse von Egloffstein
(Collini) .... Michael Pulizotto
(Fusco) .... Eva-Marie Cusack
(Giacobbe) .... Michael K. Degree
(Maltese) .... Jeffrey Alfano
(McMahon) .... Carol Wojtowicz
(Minardo) .... Ralph P. Marra
(Panepinto) .... Marjorie Steinberg
(Rienzi) .... Nechama Sokolow
(Rooney) .... Michael Dwyer

SUPREME COURT THIRD DEPARTMENT

THIRD JUDICIAL DISTRICT, SUPREME COURT
Jurisdiction—Counties of Albany, Columbia, Greene, Rensselaer, Schoharie, Sullivan, Ulster

Administrative Judge: George B. Ceresia, Jr.
Courthouse, 80 Second St., Troy 12180 (518) 285-6152
Admin. Office, 40 Steuben St., 6th Floor, Albany 12207
(518) 285-8300; Fax: (518) 426-1604

Supervising Judge, Third District Criminal Courts:
Thomas A. Breslin (Albany County Court)
Judicial Center, Room 320, 6 Lodge St.,
Albany 12207-1019 (518) 285-8769; Fax: (518) 436-3982

Supervising Judge, Third District Family Courts:
Gerard E. Maney (Albany County Family Court)
30 Clinton Ave., Albany 12207
(518) 285-8661; Fax: (518) 462-4157

***Justice Serving under Certification**

Supreme Court, Third Judicial District—Cont'd

Justices:

Christopher E. Cahill
Courthouse, 285 Wall St., Kingston 12401-3817
(845) 340-3225; Fax: (845) 340-3228

Eugene P. Devine
Albany Co. Courthouse, Room 342, 16 Eagle St., Albany 12207 (518) 285-8959; Fax: (518) 487-5864

James P. Gilpatric
Courthouse, 285 Wall St., Kingston 12401 (845) 334-8277

Michael C. Lynch
112 State St., Suite 1212, Albany 12207 (518) 447-2510

Patrick J. McGrath, County Courthouse, 80 Second St., Troy 12180 (518) 285-6140

Robert A. Sackett (From 12th District)
414 Broadway, Monticello 12701 (845) 794-9776

Joseph C. Teresi, Courthouse, Room 256, 16 Eagle St., Albany 12207 (518) 285-8949

Acting Justices:

George R. Bartlett III (County Court, Schoharie Co.)
Courthouse, 290 Main St., P.O. Box 669, Schoharie 12157
(518) 295-8740

Catherine Cholakis (Family Court, Rensselaer Co.)
1504 Fifth Ave., Troy 12180-4107
(518) 270-3761, Ext. 329; Fax: (518) 272-6573

Gerald W. Connolly (Court of Claims)
112 State St., Room 1350, Albany 12207
(518) 285-8592; Fax: (518) 487-5378

Paul Czajka (County Court, Columbia Co.)
Courthouse, 401 Union St., Hudson 12534 (518) 822-0453

Stephen W. Herrick (County Court, Albany Co.)
Judicial Center, Room 218, 6 Lodge St., Albany 12207
(518) 285-8759

Christian F. Hummel (Surrogate's Court, Rensselaer Co.)
County Courthouse, 80 Second St., Troy 12180
(518) 285-6100; Fax: (518) 272-5452

Dan Lamont (Court of Claims)
County Courthouse, 290 Main St., P.O. Box 369, Schoharie 12157 (518) 295-8640; Fax: (518) 295-8638

Judicial Center, Room 210, 6 Lodge St., Albany 12207
(518) 285-8749; Fax: (518) 436-3981

Roger D. McDonough (Court of Claims)
Albany County Judicial Center, Room 309, 6 Lodge St., Albany 12207 (518) 285-8776; Fax: (518) 436-3986

Thomas J. McNamara (Court of Claims)
65 S. Broadway, Room 210, Saratoga Springs 12866
(518) 583-5330; Fax: (518) 583-5335

Mark M. Meddaugh (Family Court, Sullivan Co.)
Govt. Center, 100 North St., Monticello 12701
(845) 807-0654; Fax: (845) 794-8300

Michael H. Melkonian (Court of Claims)
Couinty Courthouse, 80 Second St., Troy 12180
(518) 285-6132; Fax: (518) 274-1367

Jonathan D. Nichols (County Court, Columbia Co.)
Courthouse, 401 Union St., Hudson 12534 (518) 828-7909

Kimberly A. O'Connor (Court of Claims)
112 State St., Room 1360, Albany 12207
(518) 285-8597; Fax: (518) 487-5823

Richard Platkin (Court of Claims)
Justice Bldg., 7th Floor, Empire State Plz., Capitol Station, P.O. Box 7344, Albany 12224
(518) 242-3740; Fax: (518) 242-3735

George J. Pulver, Jr. (County Court, Greene Co.)
County Courthouse, 320 Main St., Catskill 12414
(518) 444-8760

Henry F. Zwack (Court of Claims)
County Courthouse, 3rd Floor, 80 Second St., Troy 12180
(518) 285-6170

Court Reporters:

Cindy Affinati (Glenmont) (518) 285-8765
Judith C. Battisti-DeSilva (Kingston) (845) 340-3364
Terri Boccio (Albany) (518) 285-8765
Sharon Cherny (Kingston) (845) 340-3379
Judy Del Cogliano (Troy) (518) 285-6118
Tracie Hilton (Clifton Park) (518) 285-8765
John Koletas (Melrose) (518) 285-6194
Theresa Marino (Waterford) (518) 285-8765
David Mayo (Latham) (518) 285-8739
Amy McKenzie (Delmar) (518) 285-8765
Judy McMahon (Voorheesville) (518) 285-8765
Deborah Mehm (Albany) (518) 285-8743
Donna Meo (Leeds) (845) 340-3361
Cheryl Moore (Schenectady) (518) 285-6195
Doris Russell (North Branch) (845) 796-2255
Georgette Sayers (Middletown) (845) 794-8885
Melvyn Tapper (Kerhonkson) (845) 340-3382
Cindy West (Schoharie) (518) 828-6410

For Supreme Court Clerk's offices for all counties, see listings under specific county, pp. 58-96

Law Clerks to Justices:

(Bartlett) . . . . . William J. Minkel
(Breslin) . . . . . Laura Beebe
(Cahill) . . . . . Shari S. Gold
(Ceresia) . . . . . William Aram
(Cholakis) . . . . . Joanne Dean
(Connolly) . . . . . Tara Kersey
(Czajka) . . . . . William Cranna
(Devine) . . . . . Rebecca Clancy
(Gilpatric) . . . . . Kerri L. Wilks
(Herrick) . . . . . Mary C. O'Neill
(Hummel) . . . . . Loretta Branigan Tobin
(Lamont) . . . . . Darrin Dietz
(Lynch) . . . . . Amy Joyce
(Maney) . . . . . Catherine Sliwinski
(McDonough) . . . . . Steven Connolly
(McGrath) . . . . . Jennifer Shatz
(McNamara) . . . . . Robert Foley
(Meddaugh) . . . . . Sandra Heck
(Melkonian) . . . . . Jaime C. Louridas
(Nichols) . . . . . John Clark
(O'Connor) . . . . . Justina Cintron-Perino
(Platkin) . . . . . Scott Lieberman
(Pulver) . . . . . Kelly Ann Nagle-Zaik
(Sackett) . . . . . Mary Grace Conneely
(Teresi) . . . . . Joshua L. Farrell
(Zwack) . . . . . Rebecca M. Vaccariello

FOURTH JUDICIAL DISTRICT, SUPREME COURT

Jurisdiction—Counties of Clinton, Essex, Franklin, Fulton, Hamilton, Montgomery, Saint Lawrence, Saratoga, Schenectady, Warren, Washington

Administrative Judge: Vito C. Caruso
Courthouse, 612 State St., Schenectady 12305
(518) 285-8415; Fax: (518) 346-5919

Admin. Office, 65 S. Broadway, Suite 101, Saratoga Springs 12866 (518) 285-5099

Justices:

Richard T. Aulisi, County Bldg., 223 W. Main St., Johnstown 12095 (518) 736-5533; Fax: (518) 762-1158

David R. Demarest, Courthouse, 48 Court St., Canton 13617-1169 (315) 379-0326; Fax: (315) 379-2311

Stephen A. Ferradino, P.O. Box 2380, Malta 12020-2380
(518) 581-1006; Fax: (518) 581-0825

Barry D. Kramer, Courthouse, 4th Floor, 612 State St., Schenectady 12305-2113
(518) 285-8460; Fax: (518) 347-1972

David B. Krogmann, Warren County Municipal Center, 1340 State Route 9, Lake George 12845
(518) 761-6547; Fax: (518) 761-6465

Robert J. Muller, Warren Co. Munic. Center, 1340 State Rt. 9, Lake George 12845 (518) 824-6696

Essex County Govt. Center, 7552 Court St., Elizabethtown 12932 (518) 873-3375

Thomas D. Nolan, Jr., Saratoga County Munic. Center, 30 McMaster St., Ballston Spa 12020
(518) 451-8820; Fax: (518) 884-4761

Vincent J. Reilly, Jr., Schenectady County Courthouse, 612 State St., Schenectady 12305
(518) 285-8422; Fax: (518) 377-5897

Joseph M. Sise, Courthouse, 58 Broadway, P.O. Box 1500, Fonda 12068-1500
(518) 853-4432; Fax: (518) 853-8378

Frank B. Williams, Supreme Court Chambers, Suite 201, 433 Broadway, Saratoga Springs 12866
(518) 581-9454; Fax: (518) 581-9458

Supreme Court, Fourth Judicial District—Cont'd

Acting Justice: Patrick R. McGill (Clinton County Court)
County Government Center, Suite 317,
137 Margaret St., Plattsburgh 12901-2933
(518) 565-4657; Fax: (518) 565-4887

Sr. Court Reporters:
Kimberly L. Duskas (Fort Edward) (518) 746-2521
Mary Lou Frazier (Johnstown) (518) 736-5834
Rose E. Gardner (Canton) (315) 379-2481
Karen E. Hand (Ballston Spa) (518) 834-4750
Dianne M. Hardy (Plattsburgh) (518) 565-4530
Melissa A. Matthews (Schenectady) (518) 285-8401
Joseph J. Mondella (Lake George) (518) 761-6232
Kim K. Nethaway (Fonda) (518) 853-8161
Lisa M. Reale (Ballston Spa) (518) 884-4748
Mary Ann Roemer (Lake George) (518) 761-6530
Lisa Stadtlander (Schenectady) (518) 285-8401
Malcolm R. Thatcher, Jr. (Schenectady) (518) 285-5016

For Supreme Court Clerk's offices for all counties, see listings under specific county, pp. 58-96

Law Clerks to Justices:
(Aulisi) .... Kris Singh
(Caruso) .... Joanne B. Haelen
(Demarest) .... Mary M. Farley
(Ferradino) .... Ann Cummings Crowell
(Krogmann) .... Tatiana Coffinger, E. Guy Roemer
(Muller) .... Jenifer Purcell
(Nolan) .... Mark F. Cacozza
(Reilly) .... Regina C. Puma-Ries
(Sise) .... Charles M. Clark
(Williams) .... Karla B. Conway

SIXTH JUDICIAL DISTRICT, SUPREME COURT

Jurisdiction—Counties of Broome, Chemung, Chenango, Cortland, Delaware, Madison, Otsego, Schuyler, Tioga, Tompkins

Administrative Judge: Robert C. Mulvey
Tompkins County Courthouse, 320 N. Tioga St.,
P.O. Box 70, Ithaca 14851-0070
(607) 272-0674; Fax: (607) 272-0691

Admin. Office, The Kilmer Bldg., 31 Lewis St.,
Binghamton 13901 (607) 240-5350; Fax: (607) 722-1629

Justices:
Michael V. Coccoma (Deputy Chief Admin. Judge)
Otsego County Office Bldg., 197 Main St.,
Cooperstown 13326 (607) 547-4212

Admin. Office, 4 Empire State Plaza, Suite 2001,
Albany 12223-1450 (518) 474-3828

Kevin M. Dowd
Chenango County Courthouse, West Park Pl.,
Norwich 13815 (607) 337-1740; Fax: (607) 336-3648

Molly R. Fitzgerald, Broome County Courthouse,
92 Court St., P.O. Box 1766, Binghamton 13902
(607) 778-1027; Fax: (607) 778-3866

Ferris D. Lebous, Broome County Courthouse,
92 Court St., P.O. Box 1766, Binghamton 13902
(607) 778-2428; Fax: (607) 778-2065

Judith F. O'Shea, Hazlett Bldg., 203-205 Lake St.,
P.O. Box 588, Elmira 14902
(607) 737-3560; Fax: (607) 737-3562

Phillip R. Rumsey, 46 Greenbush St., Suite 301,
Cortland 13045-2772 (607) 756-3480; Fax: (607) 753-0854

Jeffrey A. Tait, Broome County Courthouse,
92 Court St., P.O. Box 1766, Binghamton 13902
(607) 778-2201; Fax: (607) 778-2398

Acting Justices:
J. C. Argetsinger, Schuyler County Cthse., Unit 35,
105 9th St., Watkins Glen 14891
(607) 535-7015; Fax: (607) 535-4718

David M. Brockway (Chemung County, Family Court)
203-209 William St., P.O. Box 588, Elmira 14902-0588
(607) 737-2901; Fax: (607) 737-2961

Donald F. Cerio, Jr. (Court of Claims)
Madison County Cthse., N. Court St., P.O. Box 545,
Wampsville 13163 (315) 366-2321; Fax: (315) 366-2539

Court Reporters:
Aaron Alweis (Binghamton) (607) 778-2409
Catherine Andrews (Binghamton) (607) 778-2216
Althea Beagen (Otsego) (607) 547-4263
Rena Bonczek (Binghamton) (607) 778-2408
Brenda Boyce (Binghamton) (607) 778-2068
Jeannette M. Franzese (Ithaca) (607) 272-0571
Brenda Friedel (Norwich) (607) 336-6706
Helen F. Hagen (Norwich) (607) 337-1831
Tammy E. Huckabone (Wampsville) (315) 366-2703
Janice L. Kulikowsky (Cortland) (607) 756-3470
Lenore Raymond (Binghamton) (607) 778-2068
Linda Schlosser (Owego) (607) 687-6021
Deborah Thiel-Stalker (Binghamton) (607) 778-2078

For Supreme Court Clerk's offices for all counties, see listings under specific county, pp. 58-96

Law Clerks to Justices:
(Argetsinger) .... William C. Elkins
(Brockway) .... Richard J. Brink
(Cerio) .... Melissa C. Stearns
(Coccoma) .... Stephen H. Judd
(Dowd) .... Claudette Y. Newman
(Fitzgerald) .... Stephanie G. Beck
(Lebous) .... Joan C. Long
(Mulvey) .... Timothy C. Eckel
(O'Shea) .... Christopher P. Baker
(Rumsey) .... Mark G. Masler
(Tait) .... Andrea B. Sarra, Lisa D. Smith

SUPREME COURT, FOURTH DEPARTMENT

FIFTH JUDICIAL DISTRICT, SUPREME COURT

Jurisdiction—Counties of Herkimer, Jefferson, Lewis, Oneida, Onondaga, Oswego

Administrative Judge: James C. Tormey III
Onondaga County Courthouse, 401 Montgomery St.,
Syracuse 13202 (315) 671-1100;
Admin. Office: (315) 671-2111; Fax: (315) 671-1183

Justices:
Bernadette T. Clark, Oneida County Courthouse,
200 Elizabeth St., Utica 13501
(315) 798-5860; Fax: (315) 798-5861

Michael E. Daley, County Office and Courts Facility,
5th Floor, 301 N. Washington St., Herkimer 13350
(315) 867-1185; Fax: (315) 867-1531

Brian F. DeJoseph, 401 Montgomery St., 403 Floor,
Syracuse 13202 (315) 671-1107; Fax: (315) 671-1181

Hugh A. Gilbert (Supervising Judge, Family Courts)
317 Washington St., 10th Floor, Watertown 13601
(315) 785-7918; Fax: (315) 785-7909

Donald A. Greenwood, Onondaga County Courthouse,
401 Montgomery St., Syracuse 13202
(315) 671-1103; Fax: (315) 671-1187

Samuel D. Hester, Oneida County Courthouse,
302 N. James St., Rome 13440
(315) 266-4300; Fax: (315) 356-0603

Deborah H. Karalunas, Onondaga County Courthouse,
Room 401, 401 Montgomery St., Syracuse 13202
(315) 671-1106; Fax: (315) 671-1184

James W. McCarthy, Courthouse, 25 E. Oneida St.,
Oswego 13126 (315) 349-3286

Joseph D. McGuire, Courthouse, 7660 State St.,
Lowville 13367-1396 (315) 376-5347; Fax: (315) 376-5398

David A. Murad, Oneida County Office Bldg., 8th Floor,
800 Park Ave., Utica 13501
(315) 798-5877; Fax: (315) 798-6457

James P. Murphy, Onondaga County Courthouse,
Room 411, 401 Montgomery St., Syracuse 13202
(315) 671-1109; Fax: (315) 671-1186

Anthony J. Paris, Onondaga County Courthouse,
401 Montgomery St., Syracuse 13202
(315) 671-1104; Fax: (315) 671-1179

Norman W. Seiter, Jr., Oswego County Courthouse,
25 E. Oneida St., Oswego 13126
(315) 349-3270; Fax: (315) 349-3299

Justices, Supreme Court, Fifth Judicial Dist.—Cont'd

*Anthony F. Shaheen, Oneida County Courthouse, 200 Elizabeth St., Utica 13501 (315) 266-4297; Fax: (315) 798-6431

Kevin G. Young, State Office Bldg., 8th Floor, 333 E. Washington St., Syracuse 13202 (315) 428-3215

Acting Justices:

John J. Brunetti (Court of Claims) Criminal Courts Bldg., Suite 380, 505 S. State St., Syracuse 13202 (315) 671-1058; Fax: (315) 671-1178

John C. Cherundolo (Court of Claims) Onondaga County Courthouse, 401 Montgomery St., Syracuse 13202 (315) 671-1090; Fax: (315) 671-1180

Michael L. Hanuszczak (Onondaga County Family Court) Onondaga County Courthouse, 401 Montgomery St., Syracuse 13202 (315) 671-2010; Fax: (315) 671-1166

Martha E. Mulroy (Onondaga County Family Court) 401 Montgomery St., Syracuse 13202 (315) 671-2050; Fax: (315) 671-1170

Norman I. Siegel (Court of Claims) State Office Bldg., 207 Genesee St., Utica 13501 (315) 793-2184; Fax: (315) 793-2217

**Martha Walsh Hood (Onondaga County Family Court) State Office Bldg., 333 E. Washington St., Syracuse 13202 (315) 428-3256

Court Reporters:

Jennifer Adydan (Syracuse) (315) 671-2799
Patricia A. Alexander (Syracuse) (315) 671-1078
Adam Alweis (Syracuse) (315) 671-1081
Susan L. Andrews (Syracuse) (315) 671-1084
Terri L. Austin (Watertown) (315) 785-7914
Wendy Barnett (Watertown) (315) 785-3026
Elizabeth Black (Syracuse) (315) 671-1083
Regina Dewhurst (Utica) (315) 798-6424
Deborah Dlugolecki (Syracuse) (315) 671-1073
Nicola Fanelli (Utica) (315) 798-5998
Bridget Hernon (Utica) (315) 798-5932
Donna Jackson-Kempt (Utica) (315) 798-5407
Therese Jalonack (Utica) (315) 798-5625
Valerie A. Jones (Utica) (315) 798-5547
Erin Keniston (Syracuse) (315) 671-4275
Pamela King (Oswego) (315) 349-8583
Donald Lynskey (Utica) (315) 798-5895
Ann A. Makowiec (Syracuse) (315) 671-1080
Janice Marozzi-Brown (Syracuse) (315) 671-1074
Anne Messineo (Syracuse) (315) 671-1080
Carol S. Moore (Herkimer) (315) 867-1188
Jamie Pacheco (Syracuse) (315) 671-1085
Patrick J. Reagan (Syracuse) (315) 671-1086
Colleen H. Reed (Syracuse) (315) 671-1077
Tracy Rommel (Utica) (315) 798-5246
Amy Rosato (Herkimer) (315) 867-1424
Deborah Rose (Utica) (315) 798-5999
Marie Schmidt (Syracuse) (315) 671-1074
Carrie Sorensen (Watertown) (315) 785-7915
Shelley J. Strader (Syracuse) (315) 671-1076
Judy Tracy (Syracuse) (315) 671-1072
Merrill Turner (Oswego) (315) 349-3418
Amy J. Van Alstyne (Oswego) (315) 349-3367
Lori Vayo (Oswego) (315) 349-8584
Valerie Waite (Syracuse) (315) 671-1085

For Supreme Court Clerk's offices for all counties, see listings under specific county, pp. 58-96

Law Clerks to Justices:

(Brunetti) .... Yvette Velasco
(Cherundolo) .... Robin Zimpel-Fontaine
(Clark) .... Peter Angelini
(Daley) .... John Brennan
(DeJoseph) .... John W. Brandt
(Gilbert) .... Mary D. Caughlin
(Greenwood) .... Loretta Kilpatrick
(Hanuszczak) .... Janet J. Dougherty
(Hester) .... Linda A. Hughes
(Karalunas) .... Tania Anderson
(McCarthy) .... Andrew T. Wolfe
(McGuire) .... Kathlene Loconti
(Mulroy) .... Kimberly A. Pedone
(Murad) .... Margaret Murphy Peterson
(Murphy) .... John G. Stone
(Paris) .... Sandra L. Holihan
(Seiter) .... Kathryn Greene Wolfe
(Shaheen) .... Gail N. Uebelhoer
(Siegel) .... Andrea Lynch
(Tormey) .... David Gideon, Gerard J. Neri
(Walsh Hood) .... Kurt Sherman
(Young) .... Joanne Hunt Piersma

***Justice Serving under Certification**
****Pending November 2010 Election Results**

SEVENTH JUDICIAL DISTRICT, SUPREME COURT

Jurisdiction—Counties of Cayuga, Livingston, Monroe, Ontario, Seneca, Steuben, Wayne, Yates

Administrative Judge: Thomas M. Van Strydonck (Supervising), 545 Hall of Justice, 99 Exchange Blvd., Rochester 14614-2184 (585) 428-2885; Fax: (585) 784-4225

Supervising Judge, 7th District Criminal Courts: Patricia D. Marks (County Court), 545 Hall of Justice, 99 Exchange Blvd., Rochester 14614-2184 (585) 428-5276; Fax: (585) 784-4226

Justices:

Francis A. Affronti, 545 Hall of Justice, 99 Exchange Blvd., Rochester 14614-2184 (585) 428-5397; Fax: (585) 784-4219

John J. Ark, 545 Hall of Justice, 99 Exchange Blvd., Rochester 14614-2184 (585) 428-3547; Fax: (585) 784-4218

David Michael Barry, 545 Hall of Justice, 99 Exchange Blvd., Rochester 14614-2184 (585) 428-2929; Fax: (585) 428-2513

Elma A. Bellini, 545 Hall of Justice, 99 Exchange Blvd., Rochester 14614-2184 (585) 428-2616; Fax: (585) 428-1848

Daniel J. Doyle, 545 Hall of Justice, 99 Exchange Blvd., Rochester 14614-2184 (545) 428-4372; Fax: (545) 428-2987

David D. Egan, 545 Hall of Justice, 99 Exchange Blvd., Rochester 14614-2184 (585) 428-2008; Fax: (585) 784-4221

Kenneth R. Fisher, 545 Hall of Justice, 99 Exchange Blvd., Rochester 14614-2184 (585) 428-2888; Fax: (585) 428-2983

Evelyn Frazee, 545 Hall of Justice, 99 Exchange Blvd., Rochester 14614-2184 (585) 428-2486; Fax: (585) 784-4227

Harold L. Galloway, 545 Hall of Justice, 99 Exchange Blvd., Rochester 14614-2184 (585) 428-2011; Fax: (585) 428-5887

John M. Owens, 545 Hall of Justice, 99 Exchange Blvd., Rochester 14614-2184 (585) 428-4338; Fax: (585) 428-4517

William P. Polito, 545 Hall of Justice, 99 Exchange Blvd., Rochester 14614-2184 (585) 428-5271; Fax: (585) 428-3554

Alexander R. Renzi, 545 Hall of Justice, 99 Exchange Blvd., Rochester 14614 (585) 428-4369; Fax: (585) 428-4371

Matthew A. Rosenbaum, 545 Hall of Justice, 99 Exchange Blvd., Rochester 14614-2184 (585) 428-5288; Fax: (585) 428-2995

Thomas A. Stander, 421 Hall of Justice, 99 Exchange Blvd., Rochester 14614-2184 (585) 428-2082; Fax: (585) 428-2994

Ann Marie Taddeo, 545 Hall of Justice, 99 Exchange Blvd., Rochester 14614-2184 (585) 428-5541; Fax: (585) 428-4122

Joseph D. Valentino, 545 Hall of Justice, 99 Exchange Blvd., Rochester 14614-2184 (585) 428-2034; Fax: (585) 428-1885

Joanne M. Winslow, 545 Hall of Justice, 99 Exchange Blvd., Rochester 14614-2184 (585) 428-1891; Fax: (585) 428-1889

Acting Justices:

Richard A. Dollinger, 545 Hall of Justice, 99 Exchange Blvd., Rochester 14614 (585) 428-2879; Fax: (585) 428-4346

William F. Kocher (Ontario County Court) Courthouse, 27 N. Main St., Canandaigua 14424 (585) 396-4260; Fax: (585) 396-4087

Supreme Court, Seventh Judicial Dist.—Cont'd

Judicial Hearing Officers:

Gerard J. Alonzo, Livingston County Cthse., 2 Court St., Geneseo 14454 (585) 243-7060

David H. Brind, 37 Seneca St., Geneva 14456 (315) 789-9191

Arnold F. Ciaccio, 30 W. Broad St., Suite 400, Rochester 14614 (585) 262-6413; Fax: (585) 325-4696

Sidney T. Farber, Monroe County Family Court, Hall of Justice, 3rd Floor, 99 Exchange Blvd., Rochester 14614 (585) 428-5787; Fax: (585) 784-4224

L. Paul Kehoe
Harris, Chesworth, O'Brien et al., 300 Linden Oaks, Suite 100, Rochester 14625 (585) 899-1414

Roy W. King, 545 Hall of Justice, 99 Exchange Blvd., Rochester 14614 (585) 428-5001

Charles T. Maloy, Monroe County Family Court, Hall of Justice, 3rd Floor, 99 Exchange Blvd., Rochester 14614 (585) 428-5787

Donald J. Mark, 545 Hall of Justice, 99 Exchange Blvd., Rochester 14614 (585) 428-5001

Timothy K. Mattison, 150 Lake St., Suite 102, Elmira 14901 (607) 734-5204

Glenn R. Morton, Hall of Justice, 3rd Floor, 99 Exchange Blvd., Rochester 14614 (585) 428-5787; Fax: (585) 784-4224

Ann E. Pfeiffer, Hall of Justice, 3rd Floor, 99 Exchange Blvd., Rochester 14614 (585) 428-2000; Fax: (585) 784-4224

Andrew V. Siracuse, 2 State St., Suite 1600, Rochester 14614 (585) 232-3730

Gary Smith, 6 Hall of Justice, Rochester 14614 (585) 428-2444

Maurice E. Strobridge, 605 Mason St., Newark 14513 (315) 331-0730

Herman Walz, 6 Hall of Justice, Rochester 14614 (585) 428-2444

Principal Management Analyst: Michael J. DeVito
161-B Hall of Justice, Rochester 14614
(585) 428-5069; Fax: (585) 428-5189
All court reporters in Seventh Judicial District may be reached at this address

Asst. Administrative Reporter: Patricia A. Harding (Rochester) (585) 428-2473

Sr. Court Reporters:

Debbie Bernstein (Rochester) (585) 428-2465
Meredith Bonn (Rochester) (585) 428-2430
Susan Bozzelli (Rochester) (585) 428-5026
Margaret Coppa (Rochester) (585) 428-5854
Anthony DiMartino (Rochester) (585) 428-4320
Valerie Doyle (Rochester) (585) 428-5508
Sue Furgiuele (Rochester) (585) 428-5528
Cyndi Germuga (Rochester) (585) 428-5023
Robin Gifford (Rochester) (585) 428-2433
Judith Ging (Rochester) (585) 428-2479
Lori Healy (Rochester) (585) 428-2499
Lori Henderson (585) 428-2494
Lori G. Keenan (Rochester) (585) 428-2402
Barbara Liberti (Rochester) (585) 428-5626
Cathy Pietak (Rochester) (585) 428-2497
Carol Raes (Rochester) (585) 428-4115
Laurie Reed (Rochester) (585) 428-2496
Diana Rinck (Rochester) (585) 428-5025
Deborah F. Romano (Rochester) (585) 428-5020
Carol Ann Scorza (Rochester) (585) 428-2429
Patricia N. Stuver (Rochester) (585) 428-2466
Janet Taddeo (Rochester) (585) 428-5021
Kelly J. Taddeo (Rochester) (585) 428-2081
Lisa S. Thyne (Rochester) (585) 428-2498
Janine Vascukynas (Rochester) (585) 428-2491
Shari Vitalone (Rochester) (585) 428-5725
Judith Warner (Rochester) (585) 428-2421

For Supreme Court Clerk's offices for all counties, see listings under specific county, pp. 58-96

Law Clerks to Justices:

(Affronti) . . . . . Walter Kohl
(Ark) . . . . . Fred J. Infantino
(Barry) . . . . . Sharon L. Higginbotham
(Bellini) . . . . . Lori Fioravanti
(Dollinger) . . . . . James V. D'Anza
(Doyle) . . . . . Hilary Merkel McMillan
(Egan) . . . . . Daniel P. Majchrzak, Jr.
(Fisher) . . . . . Aimee Allen, Michael Mazzullo
(Frazee) . . . . . Edward J. Usinger
(Galloway) . . . . . Jennifer Snyder-Haas
(Kocher) . . . . . Nicole Botti
(Marks) . . . . . Joseph J. Valentino
(Owens) . . . . . Kevin Nasca
(Polito) . . . . . Edward W. White
(Renzi) . . . . . Thomas Brilbeck
(Rosenbaum) . . . . . Maryanne Townsend
(Stander) . . . . . Sherry E. Vile
(Taddeo) . . . . . Donald Scardino
(Valentino) . . . . . Valerie Milonas
(Van Strydonck) . . . . . Peter A. Jacobson
(Winslow) . . . . . Jessica Birkahn Housel

EIGHTH JUDICIAL DISTRICT, SUPREME COURT

Jurisdiction—Counties of Allegany, Cattaraugus, Chautauqua, Erie, Genesee, Niagara, Orleans, Wyoming

Administrative Judge: Paula L. Feroleto (Part 12)
Erie County Court Bldg., 2nd Floor, 25 Delaware Ave., Buffalo 14202 (716) 845-9438; Fax: (716) 851-4696

Supervising Justices:

Richard C. Kloch, Sr. (Criminal Courts; Acting Justice, from Court of Claims)
Niagara County Courthouse, 175 Hawley St., Lockport 14094 (716) 439-7055; Fax: (716) 439-7039

Janice M. Rosa (Matrimonial Matters)
Erie County Court Bldg., 2nd Floor, 25 Delaware Ave., Buffalo 14202 (716) 845-9490; Fax: (716) 851-3225

Donna M. Siwek (Civil Matters)
Buffalo City Court Bldg., 8th Floor, 50 Delaware Ave., Buffalo 14202 (716) 845-9354; Fax: (716) 851-3318

Justices:

Tracey A. Bannister
Buffalo City Court Bldg., 8th Floor, 50 Delaware Ave., Buffalo 14202 (716) 845-9492; Fax: (716) 851-3357

Ralph A. Boniello III
Angelo DelSignore Civic Bldg., 775 Third St., Niagara Falls 14302-1710
(716) 278-1840; Fax: (716) 278-1827

Christopher J. Burns
Erie County Court Bldg., 3rd Floor, 25 Delaware Ave., Buffalo 14202 (716) 845-9381; Fax: (716) 851-3321

Frank Caruso, Angelo DelSignore Civic Bldg., 775 Third St., Niagara Falls 14302-1710
(716) 278-1815; Fax: (716) 278-1822

John M. Curran, Erie County Courthouse, 3rd Floor, 92 Franklin St., Buffalo 14202
(716) 845-9471; Fax: (716) 851-3227

Diane Y. Devlin, Buffalo City Court Bldg., 9th Floor, 50 Delaware Ave., Buffalo 14202
(716) 845-9483; Fax: (716) 851-3325

James H. Dillon, Erie County Court Bldg., 4th Floor, 25 Delaware Ave., Buffalo 14202
(716) 845-1800; Fax: (716) 851-3317

**Kevin M. Dillon, Erie County Courthouse, 3rd Floor, 92 Franklin St., Buffalo 14202
(716) 845-9441; Fax: (716) 851-3223

Timothy J. Drury, Erie County Court Bldg., 1st Floor, 25 Delaware Ave., Buffalo 14202
(716) 845-9372; Fax: (716) 851-3335

Joseph R. Glownia, Erie County Courthouse, 3rd Floor, 92 Franklin St., Buffalo 14202
(716) 845-9450; Fax: (716) 851-3320

Deborah A. Haendiges, Erie County Court Bldg., 1st Floor, 25 Delaware Ave., Buffalo 14202
(716) 845-9762; Fax: (716) 851-3222

Frederick J. Marshall, Buffalo City Court Bldg., 9th Floor, 50 Delaware Ave., Buffalo 14202
(716) 845-9468; Fax: (716) 851-3315

**Pending November 2010 Election Results

Justices, Supreme Court, 8th Judicial Dist.—Cont'd

John A. Michalek, Erie County Court Bldg., 4th Floor, 25 Delaware Ave., Buffalo 14202 (716) 845-9474; Fax: (716) 851-3323

Patrick H. NeMoyer, Buffalo City Court Bldg., 10th Floor, 50 Delaware Ave., Buffalo 14202 (716) 845-9480; Fax: (716) 851-3345

John F. O'Donnell, Erie County Court Bldg., 25 Delaware Ave., Buffalo 14202 (716) 845-9486; Fax: (716) 851-3326

Frank A. Sedita, Jr., Buffalo City Court Bldg., 9th Floor, 50 Delaware Ave., Buffalo 14202 (716) 845-9351; Fax: (716) 851-3329

Sharon S. Townsend (Vice Dean for Family and Matrimonial Law, N.Y. State Judicial Institute) Erie County Courthouse, 3rd Floor, 92 Franklin St., Buffalo 14202-2721 (716) 845-2502; Fax: (716) 845-7503

84 N. Broadway, White Plains 10603 (914) 824-5800

Shirley Troutman, Erie County Court Bldg., 25 Delaware Ave., Buffalo 14202 (716) 845-9378; Fax: (716) 845-3224

Gerald J. Whalen, Erie County Court Bldg., 4th Floor, 25 Delaware Ave., Buffalo 14202 (716) 845-2750; Fax: (716) 851-3221

Penny M. Wolfgang, Erie County Court Bldg., 4th Floor, 25 Delaware Ave., Buffalo 14202 (716) 845-9363; Fax: (716) 851-3331

Acting Justices:

M. William Boller (Court of Claims) Erie County Court Bldg., 2nd Floor, 25 Delaware Ave., Buffalo 14202 (716) 845-9357; Fax: (716) 851-3327

Russell P. Buscaglia (Court of Claims) Erie County Court Bldg., 25 Delaware Ave., Buffalo 14202 (716) 845-9435; Fax: (716) 851-3316

John L. Michalski (Court of Claims) Erie County Court Bldg., 3rd Floor, 25 Delaware Ave., Buffalo 14202 (716) 845-9462; Fax: (716) 851-3314

Timothy J. Walker (Court of Claims) Erie County Court Bldg., 3rd Floor, 25 Delaware Ave., Buffalo 14202 (716) 845-7479; Fax: (716) 851-3440

Principal Court Reporter: Carolyn A. Vario (716) 845-2126

Court Reporters:

Valerie Antos (718) 845-2146
Kathleen R. Arent (716) 845-3601
Sherri Bailey (716) 439-7143
Linda Cancilla (716) 845-2141
Liliana G. Cirulli (716) 845-3618
Virginia Cobti (716) 845-2134
Amy Coghlan (716) 278-1818
Barbara Cultrara (716) 845-2140
Danielle G. Daigler (716) 845-2137
Mary Jo Dean (716) 845-2147
Lynn S. Dulak (716) 845-2139
Sally Frizzell (716) 845-3624
Nancy Jo Hutch (716) 845-2129
Michelle Jacob (716) 845-3619
Lorianne Jasinski (716) 845-3607
Karen A. Kristich (716) 845-3611
Marcia M. Langer (716) 845-3620
Sandra Lelito (716) 845-3622
Barbara Louisos (716) 845-2135
Brigit Marszalkowski (716) 845-3615
Michael Martin (716) 845-2144
Kerry Meegan (718) 845-3623
Michelle Moore (716) 845-3610
Lisa Mullane (716) 436-7056
Donna Nowaczyk (716) 845-2130
Lisa Pazderski (716) 845-3625
Charles Pizzolanti (716) 845-2136
Sally M. Schneider (716) 845-2133
Sandra Scruggs (716) 845-3603
Phyllis Senick (716) 845-3604
Colleen Shea (716) 845-3605
Marilyn L. Shimskey (716) 845-2142
Philip A. Sterlace (716) 845-3616
Lori Strong (716) 845-2131
Sheila O. Thie (716) 845-2145
Cynthia Williams (716) 278-1819
Linda Wolniewicz (716) 845-2143
Joanne Wratny (716) 845-3621
Deborah Zito (716) 845-2148

For Supreme Court Clerk's offices for all counties, see listings under specific county, pp. 58-96

Law Clerks to Justices:

(Bannister) . . . . Catherine Nugent Panepinto
(Boller) . . . . Frederick J. Platek
(Boniello) . . . . John Fiorella
(Burns) . . . . David C. Caywood
(Buscaglia) . . . . Paul B. Wojtaszek
(Caruso) . . . . Robert Richardson
(Curran) . . . . Melissa Nickson
(Devlin) . . . . Timothy Kane
(Dillon, J.) . . . . Michael Nowak
(Dillon, K.) . . . . Therese Wincott
(Drury) . . . . Peter J. Crotty
(Feroleto) . . . . Daniel Marren
(Glownia) . . . . Kurt T. Sajda
(Haendiges) . . . . Ann Boland
(Kloch) . . . . Ronald J. Winter
(Marshall) . . . . Amy Ziegler
(Michalek) . . . . Lynn A. Clarke
(Michalski) . . . . Michael McHale
(NeMoyer) . . . . Daniel C. Murphy
(O'Donnell) . . . . Kevin J. Maley
(Rosa) . . . . Christine Saturnino
(Sedita) . . . . Michael P. Daumen
(Siwek) . . . . Katherine B. Roach
(Townsend) . . . . Diana M. Boccio
(Troutman) . . . . Regan Ihde
(Walker) . . . . Darryl J. Colosi
(Whalen) . . . . Jonathan Gorman
(Wolfgang) . . . . Daniel Weinstein

PRACTICE TIME TABLE FOR THE SUPREME COURT

As amended to September 2010.

Admission of Facts.

Anytime after service of answer or 20 days after service of summons whichever is sooner, but not later than 20 days before trial, any party may serve on the other a notice to admit certain facts and/or documents. Matters requesting admission will be deemed admitted unless the opposing party specifically denies those matters within 20 days after service of notice. (CPLR 3123)

Admission to Practice.

See CPLR 9401-9407.

Amendments of Pleadings.

Service of amended pleading may be made once without leave of court within 20 days after (1) Service of the pleading amended; (2) before period for responding to it expires; or (3) service of responsive pleading. (CPLR 3025)

Answer.

Time to answer.– Within 20 days after complaint served if personally served in state. If not personally served or served outside state then within 30 days after service is complete. (CPLR 3012)

After motion addressed to pleading.– Answer or reply must be served within 10 days after service of order disposing of motion with notice of entry. (CPLR 3211f)

Motion to Correct Pleading.– Motion for a more definite statement or to strike unnecessary scandalous or prejudicial matter may be made within 20 days after service of the challenged pleading. (CPLR 3024)

Practice Time Table for the Supreme Court—Cont'd

Motion to Dismiss Pleading.– At any time before service of a responsive pleading is required a party may move to dismiss a cause of action on the grounds of (1) defense founded on documentary evidence; (2) lack of subject matter jurisdiction; (3) no legal capacity to sue; (4) another action pending; (5) arbitration and award, collateral estoppel, bankruptcy, infancy or other disability of the moving party, payment, release, res judicata, or statute of limitations or statute of frauds; (7) failure to state a cause of action; (8) lack of personal jurisdiction; (9) absence of necessary party; (10) the court has no personal jurisdiction where service made under CPLR 314 or 315; (11) immunity from liability pursuant to §720-a of the not-for-profit corporation law. These objections or defenses are waived unless raised by such motion or in the responsive pleading, except that (2), (7) or (10) may be made by motion at any subsequent time. An objection for improper service is waived unless objecting party moves for judgment within 60 days of service, unless the court extends the time due to hardship. This does not apply in proceedings under § 711, subdivisions 1 or 2 of the Real Property Actions and Proceedings Law. A motion based on improper service shall include a copy of the proof of service. (CPLR 3211)

Motion to Dismiss a Defense.– May be made on ground that no defense is stated. (CPLR 3211b)

When Motion to Dismiss to be Treated as one for Summary Judgment.– Where evidence is submitted which could properly be considered on a motion for a summary judgment, the court may treat the motion as one for summary judgment. (CPLR 3211c)

Leave to Plead Again.– Where motion made under (7) or to dismiss a defense and the opposing party desires leave to plead again if motion is granted he shall so state in opposing papers and set forth evidence in support of new pleading. (CPLR 3211)

Appearance.

Defendant must appear within 20 days after personal service of Summons within the state, and within 30 days after any other kind of service. (CPLR 320)

Arbitration.

See (CPLR 7501-7514)

Application to Compel or Stay Arbitration.– A party aggrieved by failure of another to arbitrate may apply for an order compelling arbitration. An application to stay arbitration must be within 20 days after service of the notice of intention to arbitrate. (CPLR 7503)

Motion to confirm award.– Must be made within 1 year after the delivery of an award unless vacated or modified. (CPLR 7510)

Motion to vacate, modify or correct award.– Must be made within 90 days after delivery of award. (CPLR 7511)

Arrest as Provisional Remedy–Repealed as a provisional remedy, effective June 29, 1972.

Attachment.

See (CPLR 6201-6226)

Bill of Particulars.

Must be served within 30 days after demand, except any item to which the party objects; reasons for objection must be stated with reasonable particularity. (CPLR 3042)

The court may make such orders as are just, in the event of willful failure to comply, or in case of improper or unduly burdensome demand. (CPLR 3042)

Certiorari Proceedings.

See Infra Proceedings vs. a Body or Officer.

Change of Venue.

See Venue, infra.

Commencement of Action.

Action is commenced by filing a summons and complaint (or summons with notice) with the clerk of the court in the county of venue or other person designated by the clerk. (CPLR 304). A special proceeding is commenced by filing a petition. (CPLR 304) Such filings shall not be accepted unless required fees have been paid. (CPLR 304)

Where demand necessary.– Time to commence action is computed from time when right to make demand is complete, except (1) where right arose out of receipt or detention of money or property by person in fiduciary capacity, time begins to run when party entitled to make demand discovered the facts, and (2) where money is not to be repaid or property not to be returned except on special demand time is computed from demand and (3) except as provided in Article 3 of the Uniform Commercial Code. (CPLR 206)

Effect of death of claimant.– If cause of action survives, action may be brought after expiration of time for commencement of action and within one year after his death. (CPLR 210)

Effect of death of defendant.– The period of 18 months after death is not part of the time within which the action must be commenced. (CPLR 210)

Effect of stay.– Period of stay is not part of time limited. (CPLR 204)

Disabilities excluded from time to commence action.– If a person is, when his cause of action first accrues, either under a disability due to infancy, or insane, and the statute of limitations is 3 or more years and expires no later than 3 years after the disability ceases, or the person under the disability dies, the statute of limitations shall be extended to 3 years after the disability ceases or the person dies, whichever occurs first. If the statue of limitations is less than 3 years, it will be extended by the period of the disability. In no event shall the statute of limitations be extended more than 10 years after the cause of action accrues, in any action other than for medical, dental or podiatric malpractice, where the person was under a disability due to infancy. (CPLR 208)

Complaints.

Service of complaint must be made within 20 days after demand. (CPLR 3012)

Certificate of Merit to accompany complaint in all medical, dental or podiatric malpractice actions as provided by CPLR 2013-a.

Decision of Court.

Filing.– Decision by court without jury shall be rendered within 60 days after cause or matter is finally submitted or within 60 days after a motion under R. 4403, whichever is later. (CPLR 4213)

Default Judgment.

Application for Default without Appearance.– Prior to entry of a default judgment against a natural person based upon nonpayment of a contractual debt where the defaulting defendant has made no appearance, plaintiff must provide additional notice by mailing a copy of the summons and complaint by first class mail to defendant's place of residence in an envelope bearing the legend "personal and confidential" and without indicating that it is from an attorney or concerns an alleged debt. The additional notice may be mailed simultaneously with original service, but must be sent at least 20 days prior to entry of a default judgment. (CPLR 3215(f))

Relief against.– Within one year after notice of default judgment, application may be made for relief. (CPLR 5015)

Leave to defend after substituted service.– Except when personal service is made on defendant or his agent, within or outside state, he may apply to defend action within 1 year after he obtains knowledge of entry of judgment, or where he did not personally receive notice of the summons not more than 5 years after such entry. (CPLR 317)

Default Order.

Application for relief may be made within 1 year after notice served. (CPLR 5015)

Depositions and Interrogatories.

Notice of taking an oral examination.– Notice of taking must be served at least 20 days before time specified. The other party may serve notice for examination of any other party, to be held at the same time and place, upon 10 days notice. (CPLR 3107)

Practice Time Table for the Supreme Court—Cont'd

Notice of Taking Upon Written Questions.– Where testimony is to be taken without the state or where examining party and deponent stipulate to take deposition on written questions, within 15 days after service of the written questions, the party so served may serve written cross-questions. Within 7 days thereafter the original party may serve written redirect questions and within 5 days thereafter recross questions may be served. (CPLR 3109)

Divorce.

Co-respondent, appearance by.— May appear within 20 days after service pleading. (Dom. Rel., 172)

Co-respondent, demand for complaint– Co-respondent may, at any time before entry of judgment, demand a copy of pleadings. Complaint must be served within 10 days thereafter. (Dom. Rel., 172)

Examinations Before Trial.

See Depositions, supra.

Excusable Delay or Default.

Law Office Failure.– Upon an application satisfying the requirements of subdivision (d) of § 3012 or subdivision (a) of Rule 5015, the court shall not, as a matter of law, be precluded from exercising its discretion in the interest of justice to excuse, delay or default resulting from law office failure. (CPRL 2005)

Execution.

Issuance.– An execution may be issued by the clerk of the court or the attorney for the judgment creditor at any time before a judgment is satisfied or vacated. (CPLR 5320)

Return by Sheriff.– Must be made within 60 days after issuance of execution, unless extended in writing. (CPLR 5230)

Notice of sale of personal property.– At least 6 days' notice must be given by posting conspicuously written or printed notices in at least 3 public places or city or town where sale is made. Publication in lieu of posting is available in New York City. (CPLR 5233)

Notice of Sale of Real Property.– (1) For at least 56 days before sale, printed notice must be conspicuously posted in 3 public places in city or town where sale is to take place, and also in 3 public places in city or town where property is situated, and (2) copy of notice must be published at least once in each of four periods of 14 successive days during the 63 days immediately preceding the original date fixed for sale in a newspaper published in the county. The owner, and judgment debtor and judgment creditors and mortgagees shall be served by the Sheriff with a copy of the notice in the same manner as provided for service of a summons, at least 30 days before the time fixed for sale. Sale shall take place on any day on or after the 56th day and on or before the 63rd day of the first publication. Notice of postponement need be given only to those who request it at least 5 days before the sale and to those who appear at the time and place previously appointed for the sale. (CPLR 5236)

Expert Witnesses.

Upon request and except for good cause shown each party shall identify each expert witness together with such expert's qualifications and expected testimony prior to trial. (CPLR 3101(d))

Foreclosure.

Lis Pendens shall be filed before or after service of summons and at anytime prior to judgment. (CPLR 6511)

Where Lis Pendens filed with complaint prior to service of summons.– Summons must be served within 30 days after filing Lis Pendens. (CPLR 6512)

Report of officer making sale.– Report must be filed within 30 days after completing sale and execution of proper conveyance to purchaser. (R.P.A. & P., 1355)

Motion for deficiency judgment.– Motion may be made on notice simultaneously with motion for order confirming sale or within 90 days after consummation of sale by delivery of proper conveyance to purchaser. (R.P.A. & P., 1371)

Guardian Ad Litem.

Appointment of.– (1) Application may be made by an infant party over 14 years or a relative, friend or guardian or conservator of the property at any stage of the action.

(2) Application may be made by any other party to action at any time after expiration of 10 days after completion of service on defendant. (CPLR 1202)

Habeas Corpus.

Notice before order of discharge.– 8 days' notice of hearing must be given. (CPLR 7009)

Infants.

Default judgment.– Cannot be taken against an infant defendant until 20 days after appointment of guardian ad litem. (CPLR 1203)

Settlement of Actions.– Infants' actions, whether joined with parents' claims or not, cannot be settled without court approval. (CPLR 1207).

Interpleader.

A stakeholder may require adverse claimants to litigate their claims in one action with or without stakeholder. See (CPLR 1006)

Temporary restraining order may be granted without notice, except in a labor dispute or against a public officer or body, where it is shown that immediate and irreparable injury, loss or damages will result. (CPLR 6313)

Interrogatories.

Except in a matrimonial action, a party may not serve written interrogatories and also demand a bill of particulars of the same party. Nor, in a case to recover damages for injury to person, property or wrongful death based solely upon negligence or wrongful death, may a party serve interrogatories and also request a deposition of the same party without leave of court. (CPLR 3130)

Judgment.

Application for Default without Appearance.– Prior to entry of a default judgment against a natural person based upon nonpayment of a contractual debt where the defaulting defendant has made no appearance, plaintiff must provide additional notice by mailing a copy of the summons and complaint by first class mail to defendant's place of residence in an envelope bearing the legend "personal and confidential" and without indicating that it is from an attorney or concerns an alleged debt. The additional notice may be mailed simultaneously with original service, but must be sent at least 20 days prior to entry of a default judgment. (CPLR 3215(f))

Application for Default with Appearance.– Except where judgment may be entered by the clerk, or on a stipulation of settlement, any defendant appearing is entitled to at least 5 days notice of application for judgment. The court may dispense with notice where defendant who has appeared defaults at trial. (CPLR 3215)

Confession of Judgment.– Statement must be filed and judgment entered within 3 years after affidavit is executed. (CPLR 3218)

Setting aside for excusable default.– Motion must be made within 1 year after service of a copy of the judgment with notice of entry. (CPLR 5015(a)(1))

Action upon judgment.– Action may be maintained between original parties (1) where 10 years have elapsed since docketing of judgment; or (2) where judgment obtained by default and summons was not served personally; or (3) where order is obtained granting leave to bring action. (CPLR 5014)

Lien on real property.– Judgment is a lien on real property for 10 years from filing of judgment in County Clerk's office of county where real property is located. (CPLR 5203)

Satisfaction.– Satisfaction-piece may be executed by attorney of record within 10 years after entry of judgment. (CPLR 5020)

Jury Demand.

Any party may demand a trial by jury by serving and filing a note of issue demanding the same. Any party served with a note of issue not containing such demand may demand a jury within 15 days thereafter. (CPLR 4102)

Practice Time Table for the Supreme Court—Cont'd

Lis Pendens.
See Pendency of Action, Notice of, infra.

Matrimonial Actions.
(See Divorce)

Dissolution.– Unexplained absence for 5 years is ground for dissolution. Publication of notice to be once a week for 3 successive weeks. Hearing to be at least 40 days after completion of publication. (Domestic Relations Law, Sec. 221)

Residence Requirements.– 1 year for either party where they were married in state, or they have lived in state as husband and wife or the cause occurred in state; no requirement where the cause occurred in state and both parties reside here when the action commenced; 2 years for either party in all other cases. (Dom. Rel. L. 230)

Remarriage.– Either party may marry again without conditions. (Dom. Rel. L. 8)

Motions.

Notice.– Generally 8 days' notice must be given in which case answering affidavits must be served at least 2 days before the return date. (CPLR 2214)

Notice where answering affidavits required.– Where notice is served 16 days before return day, it may contain a requirement that answering affidavits and any notice of cross-motion, with supporting papers, be served at least 7 days before hearing. (CPLR 2214)

Notice demanding relief by other than moving party.– Must be served at least 3 days prior to the return of the motion, or 7 days prior to return if demand is made pursuant to subdivision (b) of CPLR 2214; however if served by mailing, they must be served 3 days earlier than prescribed in the rule, and if served by overnight delivery, they must be delivered 1 day earlier than prescribed in the rule. (CPLR 2215)

Motions to dismiss:

Failure to prosecute.– Motion may be made where a party unreasonably neglects to proceed in the action. No such motion shall be granted until at least 1 year after joinder of issue and a written demand by Registered or Certified mail requiring plaintiff to serve and file a note of issue within 90 days. (CPLR 3216)

Notice of taxation.– Costs may be taxed upon at least 5 days notice, or without notice in which event any party may re-tax costs upon 5 days notice to the party who has taxed the costs. (CPLR 8402, 8403)

Security for costs.– May be demanded any time during pendency of action. (CPLR 8501-8503)

New Trial.
Motion for new trial must be made within 15 days after verdict is received, or after jury is discharged, or after decision rendered in non-jury actions. (CPLR 4404, 4405)

Note of Issue.
See (CPLR 3402)

Service and filing.– May be served and filed at any time after issue first joined or subsequent to forty days after service of summons irrespective of joinder of issue. Must be filed within 10 days after service thereof. (CPLR 3402)

Partition.

Notice of reference.– Referee must publish, once a week for 4 successive weeks in newspaper published in county of place of trial and in county where property is situated, a notice to appear before referee to establish a lien. (R. Prop. A. & P. 913)

Notice of application for money paid into Court.– Notice must be served as follows: (1) if served within state, personally or by leaving with person of suitable age, at least 14 days prior to application; or (2) if personal service outside state at least 20 days prior to application or (3) if service by publication, by publication in newspapers directed by Court once each week for 4 weeks immediately preceding application. (R. Prop. A. & P., 963)

Pendency of Action, Notice of.

Filing.– May be filed at time of filing verified complaint or any time after commencement of action. (CPLR 6511). In foreclosure action must be filed at least 20 days before entry of final judgment. (R. Prop. A. & P., 1331)

Service of summons where Lis Pendens filed before service of summons.– Summons must be served within 30 days after filing of Lis Pendens. (CPLR 6512)

Duration.– Lis Pendens shall be effective as notice for 3 years from date of filing. (CPLR 6513)

Pleadings.

Motion to correct pleading must be made within 20 days after service of pleading to which motion is addresed. If motion denied the responsive pleading must be served within 10 days after service of order with notice of entry. (CPLR 3024)

Objections not waived by failure to move or raise in responsive pleading.

See Motion to Dismiss Pleadings, supra.

Preliminary Injunction.

Time.– Application may accompany summons, or be made at any time after commencement of action and prior to judgment. (CPLR 6311)

Proceedings Against a Body or Officer.

Limitation of time.– Proceedings must be instituted within 4 months after the determination to be reviewed becomes final and binding, or if petitioner was under age of 21 years or under legal disability within 2 years with court's permission after determination became final and binding. (CPLR 217)

Notice of application.– 8 days' notice must be given respondent unless shorter time is prescribed by order to show cause (CPLR 403)

Answer.– Respondent shall serve and file verified answer at least 1 day prior to return day unless 10 days notice is given by petitioner with a demand that an answer be served at least 5 days before the return date. (CPLR 403)

Reply.– May be served and filed on or before return day except where 10 days notice is given and answer served 5 days before return date, reply must be served at least 1 day before the return date. (CPLR 403)

Publication.

Service of summons.– Order for service by publication must direct publication in 2 newspapers specified in order, not less than once in each of 4 successive weeks. Copies of papers must be mailed to defendant on or before first day of publication in matrimonial actions. (CPLR 316)

When service complete.– Service by publication is complete on twenty-eighth day after first publication. (CPLR 316)

Referee's Report.

Filing.– Referee's report must be filed with Clerk or delivered to attorney for one of the parties within 30 days from time case is finally submitted to him. Failure to comply entitles party to new trial. (CPLR 4319)

Replevin.

Exception to and justification of plaintiff's sureties. – Within 10 days after replevin by Sheriff, defendant may serve notice of exception to plaintiff's sureties on Sheriff and upon plaintiff's counsel. Within 10 days thereafter plaintiff must serve notice of justification. (CPLR 7102f, 2507a)

Demands for return of chattel.– Defendant may make demand within 10 days after chattel is replevied. (CPLR 7102f)

Claim of third person.– May be made pursuant to CPLR 1012.

Return by Sheriff.– Must be made within 20 days after delivery of chattel to party. (CPLR 7107)

Compelling return.– If Sheriff fails to make return he may be punished for contempt on 10 days notice of motion. (CPLR 7107)

Practice Time Table for the Supreme Court—Cont'd

Service.

Filings.– Prior to service, the summons must be filed, to commence an action and an index number obtained from the County Clerk. The summons served upon the defendant must bear the index number assigned. (CPLR 305(a) and 306(a))

Personal Service.– Original service may be made by mail pursuant to CPLR 312-a.

Substituted service on resident defendant.– Service is complete 10 days after filing of proof of such service,which proof must be filed within 20 days after such service. (CPLR 308(2))

Service by mail.– Adverse party has 5 days additional time. (CPLR 2103(b)(2))

Service on Prisoner.– Officer having custody of prisoner must deliver papers served within 2 days after receipt by him. (Cor. L. 620)

Service upon State Officer in Official Capacity or State Agency.– May be made by personal service or by mail. (CPLR 307)

Service by leaving at office of attorney or residence of party.– See CPLR 2103.

Service upon Attorney via Telefacsimile Device or Overnight Delivery Service.– See CPLR 2103.

Time to serve.– Generally, proof of service of the summons and complaint (or notice) must be filed within 120 days of the date of filing of the summons and complaint (or notice), but time for service may be extended by the court for good cause shown. (CPLR 306(b))

Simplified Procedure For Court Determination of Disputes.

Commencement of civil actions without summons.– A civil action may be commenced within the service of a summons, or may be continued after the service of a summons, without pleadings, by the filing of a statement, signed and acknowledged by all the parties to the action, specifying the claims and defenses between the parties and the relief requested. Such a filing, together with a note of issue, to be filed at the same time, shall constitute the joinder of issues in the action. A submission of controversy under this procedure shall constitute a waiver of right to trial by jury. (CPLR 3031)

Contracts for Submission of Disputes Under this Procedure.– If the parties to a dispute arising under a contract to submit a controversy to the court under section 3031 are unable to agree on a statement of claims and defenses and relief sought, the court, on 8 days' notice of motion or such notice as the court deems appropriate, shall settle the terms of the statement. In deciding the motion the court shall consider and determine any questions as to the existence of the contract or its validity or the failure of any party to perform. If the court shall find that a substantial issue of fact has been raised as to the making of the contract or submission or the failure to comply therewith, and the motion shall not have been denied as a matter of law, the court shall proceed with the trial thereof without a jury, unless a jury trial is demanded in writing as to the issue of making the contract or submission. (CPLR 3033, 3034)

Evidence.– Except on a trial under Rule 3034(3), the rules of procedure and admissibility of evidence, except as to privileged communications, shall be dispensed with unless the court otherwise directs. (CPLR 3036(1))

Pre-Trial Procedure.– At a pre-trial conference, or at any other time on motion of any party or on its own motion, on notice, the court may (a) order or allow any party to serve an additional or amended statement of facts; (b) direct pretrial disclosure of evidence and discovery and inspection of books, records and documents; (c) permit the taking of depositions for use at the hearing; (d) limit or restrict the number of experts to be heard as witnesses; (e) clarify and define the issues to be tried; (f) stay or transfer and consolidate with the action any other civil action or proceeding pending in any court between the parties to the action; (g) grant summary judgment in favor of any party as in Rule 3212 provided. Completion of preliminary procedures required by local court rules prior to placing of a case on the calendar for trial shall not be required. (CPLR 3036(5))

Judgment Roll.– Consists of the submission or contract; statement of claims and defenses; each paper submitted to the court upon a motion and each other thereon; a copy of the judgment and each paper necessarily affecting it. (CPLR 3036(7))

Costs and Disbursements.– May be awarded in the court's discretion. (CPLR 3036(9))

Statute of Limitations.

Action where limitation not specifically prescribed must be commenced within 6 years. (CPLR 213)

Annulment of marriage for fraud.– Within 3 years after discovery of fraud. (CPLR 214)

Annulment of marriage for incapacity.– Within 5 years after marriage. (Dom. Rel., 140d)

Architects, Engineers and Land Surveyors.– A claim against an architect, engineer, land surveyor or firm based on professional performance more than 10 years prior to the date of the claim must be commenced by notice to the architect, engineer, land surveyor or firm at least 90 days before commencement of the action. Service of such notice shall toll the applicable statute of limitations to 120 days following such servioe. (CPLR 214-d)

Assault and Battery.– Within 1 year. (CPLR 215)

Bonds secured by real property.– Within 6 years. (CPLR 213)

Chattel, recovery of.– Within 3 years. (CPLR 214)

Civil Rights Law.– Action for violation of rights of privacy.–Within 1 year. (CPLR 215)

Common informer, action by.– Within 1 year. (CPLR 215)

Constable.– Action against constable for act or omission in official capacity except nonpayment of money collected on execution.–Within 1 year. (CPLR 215)

Contract.– (except judgment, or where otherwise provided in Art. 2 of the Uniform Commercial Code.) Within 6 years. (CPLR 213)

Corporation (moneyed) or banking association.— Action for penalty, forfeiture or liability of director or stockholder. Within 6 years. (CPLR 213)

Crime Victims.– Action by a crime victim or representative to recover damages from defendant convicted of crime which is subject of action. Within 7 years; for certain specified crimes, within 10 years. (CPLR 213-b)

Divorce.– Within 5 years after discovery of adultery. (Dom. Rel., 210)

Engineers.– See Architects, Engineers and Land Surveyors.

Escape.– Action against officer having custody. Within 1 year. (CPLR 215)

False imprisonment.– Within 1 year. (CPLR 215)

Fraud.– Within the greater of 6 years from when the cause of action accrued or two years from the time when the fraud was discovered or could have been discovered by reasonable diligence. (CPLR 213)

Money Judgment.– Within 20 years after plaintiff was first entitled to mandate to enforce judgment. (CPLR 211)

Libel.– Within 1 year. (CPLR 215)

Labor Union.– Within 4 months of the union's alleged breach of duty of fair representation. (CPLR 217)

Malicious prosecution.– Within 1 year. (CPLR 215)

Malpractice.– Within 3 years except for medical, dental or podiatric malpractice, which is within 2 years 6 months, and discovery of a foreign object in the body, which is within 1 year of discovery of the object or the facts which would reasonably lead to such discovery, regardless of whether action is based in contract or tort. (CPLR 214, 214-a)

Mortgage.– Action to redeem real property from mortgage. Within 10 years. (CPLR 212)

Mortgage, action on.– Within 6 years. (CPLR 213)

Municipal Corporations, Acts Against– Within 1 year and 90 days from accrual; In "Ground Zero" rescue and recovery actions, a special extension was created, to no later than Sept. 16, 2010. (Gen. Mun. Law § 50-i)

Negligence resulting in personal injury.– Within 3 years. (CPLR 214)

Overcharge of Interest.– 1 year. (CPLR 215)

Practice Time Table for the Supreme Court—Cont'd

Penalty for Interest Overcharge or Failure to Disclose Information.– 1 year. (CPLR 215)

Personal injury, except as otherwise provided.– Within 3 years, except for those caused by phenoxy herbicides while serving in the military during the Vietnam War, then within 2 years of discovery or prior to June 16, 2012. (CPLR 214, 214-b)

Property damage, except where different period is prescribed.– Within 3 years. (CPLR 214)

Real property, action by state or grantee of state to recover.– Within 20 years. (CPLR 211)

Real Property, action by state to recover after annulment of letters patent.– Within 10 years. (CPLR 212)

Real property, where adversely possessed.– Within 10 years. (CPLR 212)

Sealed instrument.– Within 6 years. (CPLR 213)

Sheriff, coroner, or other officers.– For nonpayment of money collected on execution. Within 3 years. (CPLR 214)

Sheriff or coroner.– Action against for act or omission other than non-payment of money collected on execution. Within 1 year. (CPLR 215)

Slander.– Within 1 year. (CPLR 215)

Statutory liability.– Within 3 years. (CPLR 215)

Support or maintenance– Within 20 years of the date of default in payment of an order or judgment awarding same. (CPLR 211)

Tax Appeal of N.Y.C. Tax Tribunal.– Within 4 months from notice of determination. (CPLR 506(b))

Tenants' action against landlord for retaliation.– Within 1 year of the retaliation. (R. Prop. Law 223-b, CPLR 215)

Tenants' action against landlord for overcharge.– Within 4 years of the first alleged overcharge. (CPLR 213-a)

Toxic Torts.– Within 3 years of the time of discovery. (CPLR 214-c)

Where no other time prescribed by law.– Within 6 years. (CPLR 213)

Subpoena Duces Tecum.

Production of hospital records.– Must be served at least 3 days before production required. (CPLR 2306)

Production of records of any department or bureau of a municipal corporation or of the state.– Must be issued by supreme court judge on motion with at least 1 day's notice. (CPLR 2307)

Production of books and papers of libraries, public departments and officers.– Must be issued by justice of Supreme Court on 1 day's notice. (CPLR 2307)

Summary Judgment.– Motion for Summary Judgment shall be after notice of issue, but no later than 120 days after notice of issue, except with leave of the court on good cause shown. (CPLR 3212)

Proceeding to recover possession of real property, Notice of petition, service.– Must be served at least 5 and not more than 12 days before the return, unless show cause order specified otherwise. (R. Prop. A. & P., 733)

Discretionary stay where premises occupied for dwelling purposes. In New York City.– Judge may stay issuance of warrant for not more than 6 months. (R. Prop. A. & P., 753)

Redemption by lessee.– Lessee has 1 year to redeem where unexpired term of lease exceeds 5 years. (R. Prop. A. & P., 761)

Redemption by creditor of lessee.– Judgment-creditor of lessee may redeem before 2 P.M. of day following expiration of lessee's right to redeem. (R. Prop. A. & P., 763)

Supplementary Proceedings.

Examination by subpoena.– May be issued by creditor's attorney addressed to any person at any time before judgment is satisfied or vacated. (CPLR 5221)

Subsequent Examinations.– Must be had on order if sought within 1 year from last examination. (CPLR 5224)

Service of Order or Subpoena.– Not less than 10 days before return day unless otherwise provided. (CPLR 5224)

Appointment of Receiver.– Receiver may be appointed upon such notice as the court may require. (CPLR 5228)

Sureties.

Exceptions to and justification of.– If a certificate of qualification is not filed notice of exceptions to be served within 10 days after receipt of copy of undertaking. Sureties must justify within 10 days thereafter. (CPLR 2506, 2507)

Tender.

Tender must be made by payment into Court not later than 10 days before trial. (CPLR 3219)

Offer by defendant to liquidate damage.– In action for breach of contract defendant may serve an offer that damages be assessed against him for a specified sum. If he fails in his defense, not later than 10 days before trial. Claimant has 10 days thereafter to accept. (CPLR 3220)

Defendant's offer to compromise.– May be served any time not later than 10 days before trial. Notice of acceptance of such offer must be served within 10 days after receipt of offer. (CPLR 3221)

Venue.

Demand for change on ground that county designated is not proper.– Must be served with or before answer. Within 5 days thereafter plaintiff may consent to change of venue or serve affidavit setting forth reason. Motion must be made within 15 days after service of demand. (CPLR 511)

JUDICIAL DEPARTMENTS, THEIR APPELLATE DIVISIONS DISTRICTS WITHIN, COUNTIES WITHIN THE DISTRICTS AND PLACE WHERE SUPREME COURT TERMS ARE HELD.

Department	District	Counties
FIRST DEPARTMENT **Appellate Division at New York City**	**1st District**	New York County at New York City
	12th District	Bronx County at Bronx
SECOND DEPARTMENT	**2nd District**	Kings County at Brooklyn
Appellate Division at Brooklyn	**9th District**	Dutchess County at Poughkeepsie Orange County at Goshen Putnam County at Carmel Rockland County at New City Westchester County at White Plains
	10th District	Nassau County at Mineola Suffolk County at Central Islip and Riverhead
	11th District	Queens County at Jamaica, Kew Gardens and Long Island City
	13th District	Richmond County at St. George, Staten Island
THIRD DEPARTMENT **Appellate Division at Albany**	**3rd District**	Albany County at Albany Columbia County at Hudson Greene County at Catskill Rensselaer County at Troy Schoharie County at Schoharie Sullivan County at Monticello Ulster County at Kingston
	4th District	Clinton County at Plattsburgh Essex County at Elizabethtown Franklin County at Malone Fulton County at Johnstown Hamilton County at Lake Pleasant Montgomery County at Fonda St. Lawrence County at Canton Saratoga County at Ballston Spa Schenectady County at Schenectady Warren County at Lake George Washington County at Fort Edward
	6th District	Broome County at Binghamton Chemung County at Elmira Chenango County at Norwich Cortland County at Cortland Delaware County at Delhi Madison County at Wampsville Otsego County at Cooperstown Schuyler County at Watkins Glen Tioga County at Owego Tompkins County at Ithaca
FOURTH DEPARTMENT **Appellate Division at Rochester**	**5th District**	Herkimer County at Herkimer Jefferson County at Watertown Lewis County at Lowville Oneida County at Utica and Rome Onondaga County at Syracuse Oswego County at Oswego and Pulaski
	7th District	Cayuga County at Auburn Livingston County at Geneseo Monroe County at Rochester Ontario County at Canandaigua Seneca County at Waterloo and Ovid Steuben County at Bath, Hornell and Corning Wayne County at Lyons Yates County at Penn Yan
	8th District	Allegany County at Belmont Cattaraugas County at Little Valley and Olean Chatauqua County at Mayville Erie County at Buffalo Genesee County at Batavia Niagara County at Lockport and Niagara Falls Orleans County at Albion Wyoming County at Warsaw and Batavia

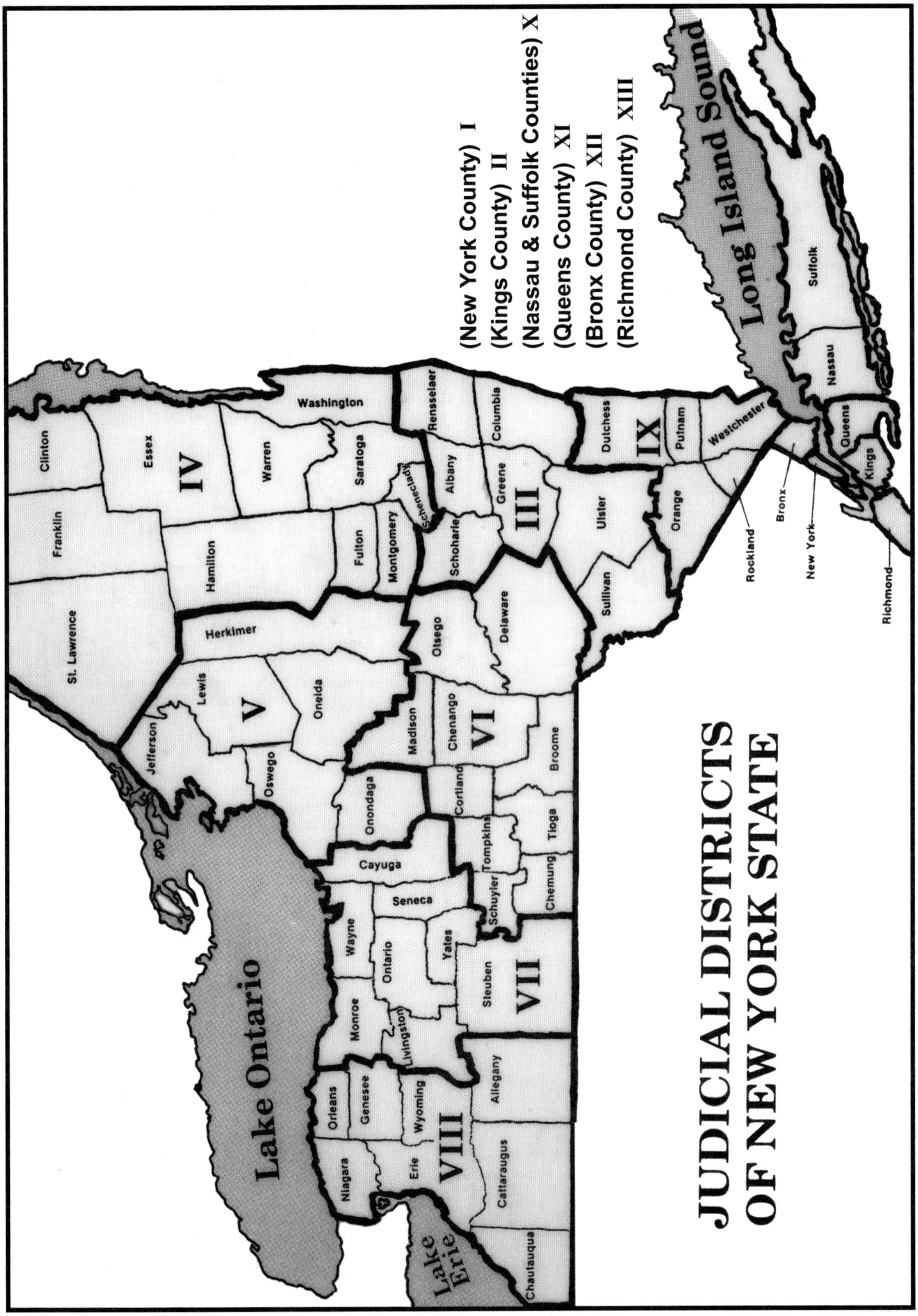
JUDICIAL DISTRICTS
OF NEW YORK STATE
(New York County) I
(Kings County) II
(Nassau & Suffolk Counties) X
(Queens County) XI
(Bronx County) XII
(Richmond County) XIII
Lake Ontario
Lake Erie
Long Island Sound
I
II
III
IV
V
VI
VII
VIII
IX
Clinton
Franklin
St. Lawrence
Essex
Hamilton
Herkimer
Lewis
Jefferson
Oswego
Oneida
Warren
Washington
Saratoga
Schenectady
Fulton
Montgomery
Rensselaer
Albany
Columbia
Greene
Schoharie
Otsego
Delaware
Madison
Chenango
Onondaga
Cortland
Broome
Tioga
Tompkins
Cayuga
Seneca
Wayne
Ontario
Yates
Schuyler
Chemung
Steuben
Monroe
Livingston
Orleans
Genesee
Wyoming
Allegany
Niagara
Erie
Cattaraugus
Chautauqua
Dutchess
Putnam
Westchester
Ulster
Orange
Sullivan
Rockland
Bronx
New York
Richmond
Kings
Queens
Nassau
Suffolk

COUNTY DIRECTORY

SUPREME, COUNTY AND FAMILY COURTS AND COUNTY OFFICIALS
All judicial positions and County Officials whose position will be decided by election have been marked accordingly*

ALBANY COUNTY

Albany, County Seat

SUPREME COURT
Albany County Cthse., Room 128, 16 Eagle St., Albany 12207
(518) 285-8989; Fax: (518) 487-5020
Judicial Center, 6 Lodge St., Albany 12207

Chief Clerk: Charles E. Diamond, Room 128
Deputy Chief Clerk: Vacancy at Press Time, Judicial Center, 6 Lodge St., Albany 12207
(518) 285-8777; Fax: (518) 436-3986
Assoc. Court Clerks:
Dawn D. Donnelly
Maureen A. Hartmann

SURROGATE'S COURT
30 Clinton Ave., Albany 12207
(518) 285-8585

Surrogate:
* Cathryn M. Doyle (518) 285-8581
Chief Clerk: Stacy L. Pettit
Deputy Chief Clerk: Vacancy at Press Time
Law Clerk: Lisa M. Buccini (518) 285-8581

COUNTY COURT
Judicial Center, Room 113, 6 Lodge St., Albany 12207
(518) 285-8777; Fax: (518) 436-3986

Judges:
Thomas A. Breslin
(Supervising Judge of the Criminal Courts, 3rd Judicial District & Acting Supreme Court Justice)
Room 320 (518) 285-8769; Fax: (518) 436-3982
Stephen W. Herrick, Room 218 (518) 285-8759
Acting Supreme Court Justice
Dan Lamont, Room 210 (518) 285-8749
Judge, Court of Claims and Acting Supreme Court Justice
Chief Clerk: Charles E. Diamond, Room 113
Deputy Chief Clerk: Vacancy at Press Time, Room 113
(518) 285-8777

FAMILY COURT
30 Clinton Ave., Albany 12207
(518) 285-8600; Fax: (518) 462-4248

Judges:
W. Dennis Duggan
(518) 285-8681; Fax: (518) 462-4164
E-mail: wddfcj@yahoo.com; wduggan@courts.state.ny.us
Law Clerk: Brenda K. Eckstein
E-mail: beckstei@courts.state.ny.us
Gerard E. Maney
(Supervising Judge of the Family Courts, 3rd Jud. Dist.)
(518) 285-8661; Fax: (518) 462-4157
E-mail: gmaney@courts.state.ny.us
Acting Supreme Court Justice
Law Clerk: Catherine A. Sliwinski
Margaret T. Walsh
(518) 285-8671; Fax: (518) 462-4236
E-mail: mtwalsh@courts.state.ny.us
Law Clerk: Marne Onderdonk
Chief Clerk: David B. Cardona
(518) 285-8600; Fax: (518) 462-4248
Deputy Chief Clerk: Daniel Pekrol
(518) 285-8600; Fax: (518) 462-4248

COUNTY OFFICIALS

County Atty.: Craig A. Denning
112 State St., Room 900, Albany 12207
(518) 447-7110; Fax: (518) 447-5564
D.A.: P. David Soares, 6 Lodge St., Albany 12207
(518) 487-5460; Fax: (518) 487-5093

***Pending November 2010 Election Results**

County Clerk: Thomas G. Clingan
32 N. Russell Rd., Albany 12206
(518) 487-5100; Fax: (518) 487-5099
E-mail: countyclerk@albanycounty.com
County Executive: Michael G. Breslin
112 State St., Room 200, Albany 12207
(518) 447-7040; Fax: (518) 447-5589
County Comptroller: Michael F. Conners II
112 State St., Room 930, Albany 12207
(518) 447-7130; Fax: (518) 433-1554
Reference Librarian: Bob Emery
Schaffer Law Library, 80 New Scotland Ave., Albany 12208 (518) 445-2340
Sheriff: James L. Campbell, 16 Eagle St., Albany 12207
(518) 487-5440; Civil Div.: (518) 487-5400;
Fax: (518) 487-5037; Civil Fax: (518) 487-5352
Daily, 9 A.M.-5 P.M.
Correctional Facility:
840 Albany Shaker Rd., Albany 12211-1088
(518) 869-2724; Fax: (518) 869-3923;
Inmate Services: (518) 869-2643, 45
Atty. Visitation: Daily, 8-11 A.M.; Noon-2:15 P.M.; 3:30-5 P.M.; 6-9:30 P.M.

ALLEGANY COUNTY

Belmont, County Seat

SUPREME COURT
Courthouse, 7 Court St., Belmont 14813-1084
(585) 268-5813; Fax: (585) 268-7090

Chief Clerk I: Laura H. Gabler
Deputy Chief Clerk: Jose Cruzado

SURROGATE'S COURT
Courthouse, 7 Court St., Belmont 14813
(585) 268-5815; Fax: (585) 268-7090

Surrogates:
Thomas P. Brown (585) 268-5800
*Subject to Election
(585) 268-5800, Ext. 13; Fax: (585) 266-7090
Chief Clerk: Dawn A. Wildrick-Cole
E-mail: dwildric@courts.state.ny.us
Principal Court Atty.: Warren M. Emerson
E-mail: wemerson@courts.state.ny.us
Court Atty.: Michael J. Regan
E-mail: mregan@courts.state.ny.us

COUNTY COURT
Courthouse, 7 Court St., Belmont 14813-1084
(585) 268-5813; Fax: (585) 268-7090

Judges:
Thomas P. Brown (Acting Supreme Court Justice)
(585) 268-5800
Acting Supreme Court Justice
*Vacancy at Press Time
(585) 268-5800, Ext. 13; Fax: (585) 268-7090
Chief Clerk I: Laura H. Gabler
Deputy Chief Clerk: Jose Crusado

FAMILY COURT
Courthouse, 7 Court St., Belmont 14813
(585) 268-5816; Fax: (585) 268-7090

Judges:
Thomas P. Brown (585) 268-5800
E-mail: tbrown@courts.state.ny.us
*Vacancy at Press Time
(585) 268-5800, Ext. 13; Fax: (585) 268-7090
Chief Clerk I: Kathryn Q. Brownell (585) 268-5814, 16
E-mail: kbrownel@courts.state.ny.us
Principal Court Atty.: Warren M. Emerson
Court Atty.: Michael J. Regan
Support Magistrate: Beth E. Farwell
Judicial Hearing Officer: Lynn L. Hartley

Allegany County—Cont'd

COUNTY OFFICIALS

County Atty.: Thomas A. Miner
7 Court St., Belmont 14813-1039
(585) 268-9410; Fax: (585) 268-9651

D.A.: Terrence M. Parker (585) 268-9225

County Clerk: Robert L. Christman
Courthouse, 7 Court St., Belmont 14813
(585) 268-9270; Fax: (585) 268-9569

County Treasurer: Terri L. Ross
7 Court St., Belmont 14813
(585) 268-9289; Fax: (585) 268-7506
E-mail: rosstl@alleganyco.com

Law Library: Courthouse, Belmont 14813 (585) 268-5813

Sheriff: *William R. Tompkins
4884 Rt. 19 S., Belmont 14813
(585) 268-9200; Fax: (585) 268-9484
Internet: www.alleganyco.com
Hours: Weekdays, closed 11:30 A.M.-12:30 P.M.

Jail: 4884 Rt. 19 S., Belmont 14813-1082
(585) 268-9200; Fax: (585) 268-9301
Atty. Visitation: Daily, except Lock down:
6:30-8 A.M.,11:30 AM.-1 P.M. & 3:30-5 P.M.

BRONX COUNTY

Bronx, County Seat

SUPREME COURT

Civil Division, 851 Grand Concourse, Bronx 10451
(718) 618-1300

Criminal Division, Hall of Justice, 265 E. 161st St., Bronx 10451
(718) 618-3100

County Clerk: Luis M. Diaz
851 Grand Concourse, Room 118, Bronx 10451
(718) 618-3300; Fax: (718) 590-8122

Chief Clerk, Civil Term: Tracy Pardo
851 Grand Concourse, Room 610, Bronx 10451
(718) 618-1200

Chief Clerk, Criminal Division: Steven B. Clark
265 E. 161st St., Bronx 10451 (718) 618-3100

Deputy Chief Clerk, Administration: Walter Nicholson
851 Grand Concourse (718) 618-1264

First Deputy Chief Clerk, Criminal Div.: John Murray
265 E. 161st St. (718) 618-3715

First Deputy Chief Clerk, Civil Term: Helen Corporan
851 Grand Concourse, Room 611 (718) 618-1400

Bureau Chief, Legal Support Bur.: John C. James
851 Grand Concourse, Room 217 (718) 618-1380

Bureau Chief, Matrimonial Bur.: Esther Kelly
851 Grand Concourse, Room 217 (718) 618-1340

Bureau Chief, Motion Support Bur.: Michael Golden
851 Grand Concourse, Room 217 (718) 618-1310

Guardianship Referee: Edward V. Corrigan (Civil Division)
851 Grand Concourse, Room 530 (718) 618-1306

Bureau Chief, Guardianship/Fiduciary Department:
Phil Conran, 851 Grand Concourse, Room 212
(718) 618-1330; Fax: (718) 993-3116

Chief Clerk Jury Div.: Vacancy at Press Time, Room 212
(718) 618-3360

Deputy County Clerk, Jury Div.: Kay Amer,
851 Grand Concourse, Room 313 (718) 618-3360

Librarian: Margaret Beirne,
851 Grand Concourse, Room 817 (718) 618-3192
Internet: www.courts.state.ny.us/library/bronx.shtml

Criminal Court in Bronx County has been consolidated with Supreme Court, Twelfth Judicial District, Criminal Division

***Pending November 2010 Election Results**

SURROGATE'S COURT

851 Grand Concourse, Bronx 10451
(718) 618-2300; Fax: (718) 537-5158

Surrogate: Lee L. Holzman (718) 618-2350
Chief Clerk: Michael P. Hausler (718) 618-2310
Deputy Chief Clerk: Earnestine Glover (718) 618-2310
Supervising Court Atty.: Kate E. Scooler (718) 618-2329
Court Atty. Referees:
Laura Anne Adams (718) 618-2326
Louise C. Conway (718) 618-2324
Martin L. Popovic (718) 618-2325
John Raniolo (718) 618-2327
Evette Soto-Maldonado (718) 618-2331
Secretary to Surrogate: Rose Marie Tocci (718) 618-2350
Principal Law Clerk to Surrogate: Matthew J. Scooler (718) 618-2330
Probate Clerk: Wilson Kenney, Room 317-318 (718) 618-2365
Administration Clerk: Ling T. Li, Room 320 (718) 618-2370
Accounting Clerk: Rosanne DeSalvo, Room 319 (718) 618-2375
Guardian Clerk: Yvette Star-Reid, Room 321 (718) 618-2380
Cashier: Robert Muniz, Room 325 (718) 618-2396
Certification Dept.: Jean Pierre Ithier, Record Room (718) 618-2395
Computer/Data Entry: Virginia Berger, Room 322 (718) 618-2323

FAMILY COURT

See Family Court, N.Y.C., pp. 98-99

COUNTY OFFICIALS

D.A.: Robert T. Johnson, 198 E. 161st St., Bronx 10451
(718) 590-2000
County Clerk: Luis M. Diaz
851 Grand Concourse, Room 118, Bronx 10451
(718) 618-3300; Fax: (718) 590-8122
Comptroller: John Liu
530 Municipal Bldg., 1 Centre St., N.Y.C. 10007
(212) 669-3500; Fax: (212) 669-2707
Commissioner of Finance: David M. Frankel,
1 Centre St., Suite 500, N.Y.C. 10007 (212) 669-4855
Public Administrator: Bonnie Gould
851 Grand Concourse, Room 336, Bronx 10451
(718) 293-7660
Law Librarian: Margaret Beirne
Supreme Court Law Library, Room 817,
851 Grand Concourse, Bronx 10451 (718) 618-3192
Sheriff's Office
3030 Third Ave., 2nd Floor, Bronx 10455
(718) 993-3880; Fax: (718) 993-3116
Under Sheriff: Joseph Fucito
Commanding Officer: Lt. P. Mulqueen

BROOME COUNTY

Binghamton, County Seat

SUPREME COURT

Broome County Courthouse, Room 204, 92 Court St., P.O. Box 1766, Binghamton 13902-1766
(607) 778-2448; Fax: (607) 778-6426

Chief Clerk: Karen K. Stephens
Deputy Chief Clerk: Vacancy at Press Time

SURROGATE'S COURT

Broome County Courthouse, Binghamton 13901
(607) 778-2111; Fax: (607) 778-2308

Surrogate: *Eugene E. Peckham
Suite 104, P.O. Box 1766, Binghamton 13902-1766
(607) 778-2118; Fax: (607) 778-6155
E-mail: epeckham@courts.state.ny.us
Acting Supreme Court Justice
Principal Court Atty.: Frances C. Bowen (607) 778-2062
E-mail: fbowen@courts.state.ny.us
Secretary: Lisa Sokol; E-mail: lsokol@courts.state.ny.us
Chief Clerk: Rebecca A. Malmquist
(607) 778-2111; Fax: (607) 778-2308
Deputy Chief Clerk: Tracy A. Allen
(607) 778-2111; Fax: (607) 778-2308

Broome County—Cont'd

COUNTY COURT
Broome County Family and County Courts Bldg., 65 Hawley St., P.O. Box 1766, Binghamton 13902-1766
(607) 778-2448; Fax: (607) 778-6426

Judges:
Joseph F. Cawley
65 Hawley St., P.O. Box 1766, Binghamton 13902-1766
(607) 778-2431; Fax: (607) 778-6133
Law Clerk: Sandra Garufi (607) 778-2015
*Martin E. Smith
65 Hawley St., P.O. Box 1766, Binghamton 13902-1766
(607) 778-2418; Fax: (607) 778-6135
Law Clerk: Marjory Kirkaldy

Chief Clerk: Karen K. Stephens
Broome County Courthouse, Room 204,
(607) 778-2448; Fax: (607) 778-6246

Deputy Chief Clerk: Vacancy at Press Time
Broome County Courthouse, Room 204,

FAMILY COURT
65 Hawley St., Binghamton 13901
Mailing Address: P.O. Box 1766, Binghamton 13902
(607) 778-2156; Fax: (607) 778-2439

Judges:
Peter P. Charnetsky (607) 778-2181; Fax: (607) 778-2439
Court Atty.: Kenneth P. Craig
Secretary: Jean C. Keibel
Mary Rita Connerton (607) 778-2156
Secretary: Jane Sbarra
Court Atty.: Jacinta M. Testa
Spero Pines (607) 778-2156
Secretary: Teri Smith
Court Atty.: Margaret M. Fries

Chief Clerk: Debbi D. Singer
(607) 778-2156; Fax: (607) 778-2439

Deputy Clerk: Margaret Raftis

Support Magistrates:
Robert J. Eberz (607) 778-6101; Fax: (607) 778-2439
Eileen Kane (607) 778-2039; Fax: (607) 778-2439

COUNTY OFFICIALS

County Atty.: Joseph Sluzar
County Office Bldg., Government Plaza, P.O. Box 1766, Binghamton 13902 (607) 778-2117
E-mail: bclaw@co.broome.ny.us

D.A.: Gerald F. Mollen
George Harvey Justice Bldg., 4th Floor, 45 Hawley St., Binghamton 13901 (607) 778-2423; Fax: (607) 778-8870
E-mail: gmollen@co.broome.ny.us

County Clerk: Richard R. Blythe
County Office Bldg., Government Plaza, P.O. Box 2062, Binghamton 13902 (607) 778-2255; Fax: (607) 778-2243
E-mail: rblythe@co.broome.ny.us

Comptroller: Alex J. McLaughlin
County Office Bldg., Government Plaza, P.O. Box 1766, Binghamton 13902 (607) 778-2178
E-mail: amclaughlin@co.broome.ny.us

Commissioner of Finance: Jerome Z. Knebel
County Office Bldg., Government Plaza, P.O. Box 1766, Binghamton 13902 (607) 778-2162
E-mail: jknebel@co.broome.ny.us

County Executive: Barbara Fiala
County Office Bldg., Government Plaza, P.O. Box 1766, Binghamton 13902 (607) 778-2109
E-mail: bfiala@co.broome.ny.us

Senior Law Librarian: Judy A. Lauer
NYS Supreme Court Law Library,
Courthouse, 1st Floor, 92 Court St., Binghamton 13901
(607) 778-2119; Fax: (607) 772-8331
E-mail: jlauer@courts.state.ny.us

Sheriff: *David E. Harder
155 Lt. VanWinkle Dr., Binghamton 13905-1555
(607) 778-1911; Fax: (607) 778-2100
E-mail: dharder@co.broome.ny.us
Internet: www.glbroomecounty.com/departments/sheriff

Sheriff's Correctional Facility
155 Lt. VanWinkle Dr., Binghamton 13905
(607) 778-2105; Fax: (607) 778-1942
Atty. Visitation: Weekdays, 8:30-11:30 A.M.; 12:30-2:30 P.M.; 3:15-4:45 P.M.; 6-10 P.M.; Weekends By appointment only

Administrator: Mark W. Smolinsky (607) 778-8865
E-mail: dharder@co.broome.ny.us
Internet: www.gobroomecounty.com

CATTARAUGUS COUNTY

Little Valley, County Seat

SUPREME COURT
County Center, 303 Court St., Little Valley 14755
(716) 938-9111, Ext. 2388; Fax: (716) 938-6413

Chief Clerk: Verna R. Dry; E-mail: vdry@courts.state.ny.us

SURROGATE'S COURT
Courthouse, 303 Court St., Little Valley 14755-1096
(716) 938-2327; Fax: (716) 938-6983
One Leo Moss Dr., Olean 14760-1151
(716) 373-8043

Surrogates:
Larry M. Himelein, Little Valley (716) 938-2381
Law Clerk: Jennifer Widger (716) 938-2381
Michael L. Nenno, Olean (716) 373-8043
Law Clerk: Frederick Gram (716) 373-3043

Chief Clerk: Christine M. Wrona, Little Valley
(716) 938-2327; Fax: (716) 938-6983

Direct all Documents, Inquiries and telephone calls to Little Valley Office

COUNTY COURT
Courthouse, 303 Court St., Little Valley 14755
(716) 938-9111, Ext. 2387, Ext. 2388;
Fax: (716) 938-6413
County Office Bldg., 1 Leo Moss Dr., Olean 14760
(716) 373-8035; Fax: (716) 701-3761

Judges:
Larry M. Himelein, Little Valley (716) 938-9111, Ext. 2381
Law Clerk: Jennifer Widger
Michael L. Nenno, Olean (716) 373-8035, Ext. 3253
Law Clerk: Fritz Gram

Chief Clerk: Verna R. Dry
(716) 938-2388; Fax: (716) 938-6413
E-mail: vdry@courts.state.ny.us

FAMILY COURT
1 Leo Moss Dr., Suite 1140, Olean 14760-1152
(716) 373-8035; Fax: (716) 373-0449

Judges:
Larry M. Himelein, Little Valley (716) 938-9111, Ext. 2381
Law Clerk: Jennifer Widger Ext. 2301
Michael L. Nenno, Olean (716) 938-9111, Ext. 3253
Law Clerk: Fritz Gram (716) 373-8035, Ext. 3248

Chief Clerk: Ruth Dickerson, Olean
(716) 938-9111, Ext. 3242
E-mail: rdickers@courts.state.ny.us

Support Magistrate: William J. Gabler
(716) 938-9111, Ext. 3245
E-mail: wgable@courts.state.ny.us

COUNTY OFFICIALS

County Atty.: Dennis V. Tobolski,
County Office Bldg., 303 Court St., Little Valley 14755
(716) 938-9111, Ext. 2391; Fax: (716) 938-2763

D.A.: Lori Rieman,
County Office Bldg., 303 Court St., Little Valley 14755
(716) 938-9111, Ext. 2222; Fax: (716) 938-2771

County Clerk: James K. Griffith,
County Office Bldg., 303 Court St., Little Valley 14755
(716) 938-9111, Ext. 2297; Fax: (716) 938-2773

County Administrator/Auditor: Jack Searles,
County Office Bldg., 303 Court St., Little Valley 14755
(716) 938-9111, Ext. 2577; Fax: (716) 938-2760

***Pending November 2010 Election Results**

Cattaraugus County Officials—Cont'd

Jury Commissioner: Verna Dry
Fax: (716) 938-9111, Ext. 2383

County Treasurer: Joseph E. Keller
County Office Bldg., 303 Court St., Little Valley 14755
(716) 938-9111, Ext. 2286; Fax: (716) 938-2762

Law Librarian: Barbara Phelan
Courthouse, 303 Court St., Little Valley 14755-1028
(716) 938-9111, Ext. 2326; Fax: (716) 938-6953

Jury Analyst: Mary Reynolds
Courthouse, 303 Court St., Little Valley 14755-1028
(716) 938-9111, Ext. 2250

Sheriff: Timothy S. Whitcomb
301 Court St., Little Valley 14755
(716) 938-9191; Sheriff: Ext. 2216; Fax: (716) 938-6552
Internet: www.sheriff.cattco.org

Jail: 301 Court St., Little Valley 14755
(716) 938-9194; Fax: (716) 938-6235
Atty. Visitation: Any time except 7-8:30 A.M., 11 A.M.-12:30 P.M. & 4-5:30 P.M.

CAYUGA COUNTY

Auburn, County Seat

SUPREME COURT
Courthouse, 152 Genesee St., Auburn 13021-3474
(315) 255-4320; Fax: (315) 255-4322

Chief Clerk: Kelly J. Wejko
E-mail: kwejko@courts.state.ny.us

SURROGATE'S COURT
Courthouse, 3rd Floor, 152 Genesee St., Auburn 13021-3471
(315) 255-4316; Fax: (315) 255-4324

Surrogate: Mark H. Fandrich
(315) 255-4316; Fax: (315) 255-4324

Chief Clerk: MaryAnne Marr

COUNTY COURT
Courthouse, 152 Genesee St., Auburn 13021-3474
(315) 255-4320; Fax: (315) 255-4322

Judge: Thomas G. Leone
Historic Post Office Bldg., 157 Genesee St.

Chief Clerk: Kelly J. Wejko

FAMILY COURT
Historic Old Post Office Bldg., 2nd Floor, 157 Genesee St., Auburn 13021-3476
(315) 255-4306; Fax: (315) 255-4312

Judges:
Mark H. Fandrich (315) 255-4306; Fax: (315) 255-4312
Surrogate Court Judge Assigned to Family Court
Thomas G. Leone (315) 255-4306; Fax: (315) 255-4312
Law Clerk: Nancy Hussey (315) 255-4336

Chief Clerk: L. D. Serafino

Support Magistrate: George J. Shamon

Judicial Hearing Officer: Robert A. Contiguglia

COUNTY OFFICIALS

County Atty.: Frederick Westphal
160 Genesee St., 6th Floor, Auburn 13021
(315) 253-1274; Fax: (315) 253-1098

D.A.: Jon Budelmann
95 Genesee St., 1st Floor, Auburn 13021
(315) 253-1391; Fax: (315) 253-1521

County Clerk: Susan M. Dwyer
Cayuga Cty. Ofc. Bldg., 1st Floor, 160 Genesee St., Auburn 13021-3424 (315) 253-1271; Fax: (315) 253-1653

County Treasurer: *James H. Orman
160 Genesee St., 5th Floor, Auburn 13021
(315) 253-1211; Fax: (315) 253-1369

Law Librarian: Jill Fandrich,
NYS Supreme Court Law Library, Courthouse, 154 Genesee St., Auburn 13021 (315) 255-4310

Sheriff: *David S. Gould
7445 County House Rd., Auburn 13021-8297
(315) 253-1222; Admin. Fax: (315) 253-4575;
Records Fax: (315) 253-3022; Jail: (315) 253-2911
E-mail: sheriff@co.cayuga.ny.us
Internet: www.co.cayuga.ny.us/sheriff

Jail: 7445 County House Rd., Auburn 13021
(315) 253-2911; Fax: (315) 253-6731
Atty. Visitation: Tues.-Wed. & Fri.-Sun., 8 A.M.-1 P.M. & 2:30-9:30 P.M.; Call for Appt.

CHAUTAUQUA COUNTY

Mayville, County Seat

SUPREME COURT
Courthouse, 1 N. Erie St., P.O. Box 292, Mayville 14757-0292
(716) 753-4266

Chief Clerk & Commissioner of Jurors:
Kathleen D. Krauza, Gerace Office Bldg., 3 N. Erie St.
(716) 753-4266; Fax: (716) 753-4993

Deputy Chief Clerk: Judith Helman
Gerace Office Bldg., 3 N. Erie St.

SURROGATE'S COURT
Gerace Office Bldg., 3 N. Erie St., P.O. Box C, Mayville 14757-0299
(716) 753-4339; Fax: (716) 753-4600

Surrogate: Stephen W. Cass
(716) 753-4337; Fax: (716) 753-4730
E-mail: scass@courts.state.ny.us

Chief Clerk: Lydia Romer; E-mail: lromer@courts.state.ny.us

COUNTY COURT
Courthouse, 1 N. Erie St., P.O. Box 292, Mayville 14757-0292
(716) 753-4266; Fax: (716) 753-4993

Judge: John T. Ward (716) 753-4188

Chief Clerk and Commissioner of Jurors:
Kathleen D. Krauza, Gerace Office Blvd., 3 N. Erie St.
Fax: (716) 753-4993; E-mail: kkrauza@courts.state.ny.us

FAMILY COURT
2 Academy St., Suite 5, Mayville 14757
(716) 753-4351; Fax: (716) 753-4350

Judge: Judith S. Claire

Chief Clerk: Frank B. Baggiano

Law Clerk: Beverly D. Ungerer

County Atty./Referee: Margaret Logan

Support Magistrate: David L. Turnbull

COUNTY OFFICIALS

County Atty.: Stephen M. Abdella
Gerace Office Bldg., 3 N. Erie St., Mayville 14757
(716) 753-4247; Fax: (716) 753-4129

D.A.: David W. Foley, Courthouse, 1 N. Erie St., Mayville 14757 (716) 753-4241; Fax: (716) 753-4628

County Clerk: Sandra K. Sopak
Courthouse, 1 N. Erie St., P.O. Box 170, Mayville 14757
(716) 753-4331; Fax: (716) 753-4293

County Executive: Gregory J. Edwards
Gerace Office Bldg., 3 N. Erie St., Mayville 14757
(716) 753-4211

Dir. of Finance: Darin R. Schulz, Gerace Office Bldg., 3 N. Erie St., Mayville 14757 (716) 753-4223

Law Library: Courthouse, 1 N. Erie St., Mayville 14757-0292 (716) 753-7111

Sheriff: Joseph A. Gerace
15 E. Chautauqua St., P.O. Box 128, Mayville 14757
(716) 753-4231; Civil: (716) 753-4371;
Sheriff: (716) 753-4900; Fax: (716) 753-4987
Internet: www.sheriff.us

Jail: 15 E. Chautauqua St., P.O. Box 128, Mayville 14757
(716) 753-4935; Fax: (716) 753-4778
Internet: www.sheriff.us
Atty. Visitation: Daily, 8 A.M.-8 P.M., or by Appt.

***Pending November 2010 Election Results**

CHEMUNG COUNTY

Elmira, County Seat

SUPREME COURT
203 Lake St., 6th Floor, P.O. Box 588, Elmira 14902-0588
(607) 737-2847; Fax: (607) 732-8879

Chief Clerk, Combined Courts: Nancy Y. Kreisler (607) 737-2084

Deputy Chief Clerk, Supreme Court: Vacancy at Press Time

SURROGATE'S COURT
Courthouse, 224 Lake St., P.O. Box 588, Elmira 14902-0588
(607) 737-2946, 737-2819; Fax: (607) 737-2874

Surrogates:
Peter C. Buckley (607) 737-2940
Law Clerk: Brian Dovi; E-mail: bdovi@courts.state.ny.us
Secretary: Clare E. Williams
E-mail: cewillia@courts.state.ny.us
James T. Hayden
Justice Bldg., 2nd Floor, 203 William St., P.O. Box 588, Elmira 14902-0588 (607) 737-2923
Law Clerk: Louise Herzl-Betz

Chief Clerk: Patricia A. Kreitzer (607) 737-2873

Deputy Chief Clerk: Laurie A. Hubbard (607) 737-2819

COUNTY COURT
Courthouse, 224 Lake St., P.O. Box 588, Elmira 14902
(607) 737-2084; Fax: (607) 732-8879

Judges:
Peter C. Buckley (607) 737-2940; Fax: (607) 732-3343
Law Clerks:
Brian Dovi; E-mail: bdovi@courts.state.ny.us
Clare E. Williams; E-mail: cewilla@courts.state.ny.us
James T. Hayden
Justice Bldg., 2nd Floor, 203 William St., P.O. Box 588, Elmira 14902 (607) 737-2923; Fax: (607) 737-2913
Law Clerk: Louise Herzl-Betz (607) 737-2923
E-mail: lherzl@courts.state.ny.us

Chief Clerk: Nancy Y. Kreisler
203-205 Lake St., 6th Floor, P.O. Box 588, Elmira 14902
(607) 737-2084; Fax: (607) 732-8879

Deputy Chief Clerk III: Vacancy at Press Time,
203-205 Lake St., 6th Floor, P.O. Box 588, Elmira 14902
(607) 737-2847

FAMILY COURT
203-209 William St., P.O. Box 588, Elmira 14902-0588
(607) 737-2902, 03; Fax: (607) 737-2898

Judges:
David M. Brockway (607) 737-2901; Fax: (607) 737-2961
E-mail: dbrockwa@courts.state.ny.us
Acting Supreme Court Justice
Court Atty.: Richard J. Brink
E-mail: rbrink@courts.state.ny.us
Secretary: Maureen R. Gubbins
E-mail: mgubbins@courts.state.ny.us
Peter C. Buckley (607) 737-2940; Fax: (607) 732-3343
Court Atty.: Brian Dovi
E-mail: bdovi@courts.state.ny.us
Secretary: Clare E. Williams
E-mail: cewillia@courts.state.ny.us
James T. Hayden (607) 737-2923; Fax: (607) 737-2913
Court Atty.: Louise Herzl-Betz
E-mail: lherzl@courts.state.ny.us
Secretary: Greta C. Malone
E-mail: gcmalone@courts.state.ny.us

Chief Clerk: Rebecca L. Walp

Deputy Chief: Vacancy at Press Time

Support Magistrate: Elizabeth A. Corley

COUNTY OFFICIALS

County Atty.: Bryan Maggs, 203 Lake St., 1st Floor, Elmira 14902-0588 (607) 737-2982; Fax: (607) 737-0351

D.A.: Weeden A. Wetmore, 226 Lake St., Elmira 14902-0588 (607) 737-2944; Fax: (607) 737-2965

County Clerk: Catherine K. Hughes, 210 Lake St., Elmira 14902-0588 (607) 737-2920; Fax: (607) 737-2897

County Treasurer: Joseph J. Sartori III, 320 Market St., Elmira 14902-0588 (607) 737-2927; Fax: (607) 737-2846

County Executive: Thomas J. Santulli
203 Lake St., 2nd Floor, Elmira 14902-0588
(607) 737-2912; Fax: (607) 737-0351

Law Librarian: Jean Paul Vivian
Charles B. Swartwood Supreme Court Library,
203 Lake St., 1st Floor, Elmira 14902-0588
(607) 737-2983; Fax: (607) 733-9863

Commissioner of Jurors: Marilyn E. Patno
203 Lake St., 6th Floor, Elmira 14902-0588
(607) 737-2838

Sheriff: Christopher J. Moss
203 William St., P.O. Box 588, Elmira 14902-0588
(607) 737-2987; Fax: (607) 737-2930;
Jail: (607) 737-2934; Jail Fax: (607) 732-5734
Internet: www.chemungsheriff.com

Jail: 211 William St., P.O. Box 588, Elmira 14902-0588
(607) 737-2934; Fax: (607) 732-5734
Atty. Visitation: Weekdays, 6 A.M.-4 P.M.

CHENANGO COUNTY

Norwich, County Seat

SUPREME COURT
County Office Bldg., 5 Court St., Norwich 13815
(607) 337-1457

Court Clerk: Catherine Schell
County Office Bldg., 5 Court St., Norwich 13815
(607) 337-1457; Fax: (607) 337-1835
E-mail: cschell@courts.state.ny.us

SURROGATE'S COURT
County Office Bldg., 5 Court St., Norwich 13815-1676
(607) 337-1827, 22; Fax: (607) 337-1834

Surrogate: W. Howard Sullivan
(607) 337-1827; Fax: (607) 337-1834

Chief Clerk: Linda J. Wiley (607) 337-1827
E-mail: lwiley@courts.state.ny.us

COUNTY COURT
County Office Bldg., 5 Court St., Norwich 13815-1676
(607) 337-1457; Fax: (607) 337-1835

Judge: W. Howard Sullivan
(607) 337-1825; Fax: (607) 337-1834
Principal Court Atty.: Thomas Kelly (607) 337-1825
E-mail: tekelly@courts.state.ny.us
Secretary: Maria Matott
E-mail: mmatott@courts.state.ny.us

Court Clerk: Catherine Schell
(607) 337-1457; Fax: (607) 337-1835
E-mail: cschell@courts.state.ny.us

FAMILY COURT
County Office Bldg., 5 Court St., Norwich 13815-1676
(607) 337-1824; Fax: (607) 337-1835

Judge: W. Howard Sullivan
(607) 337-1825; Fax: (607) 337-1834

Clerk: Carole S. Dunham
(607) 337-1824; Fax: (607) 337-1835
E-mail: cdunham@courts.state.ny.us

Associate Court Atty.: Thomas E. Kelly
(607) 337-1828; Fax: (607) 337-1834
E-mail: tekelly@courts.state.ny.us

Support Magistrate: Robert E. Cuffney (607) 337-1833

COUNTY OFFICIALS

County Atty.: Richard W. Breslin, County Office Bldg., 5 Court St., Norwich 13815 (607) 337-1405

D.A.: Joseph McBride, County Office Bldg., 5 Court St., Norwich 13815 (607) 337-1745; Fax: (607) 337-1746
E-mail: districtattorney@co.chenango.ny.us

County Clerk: Mary C. Weidman, County Office Bldg., 5 Court St., Norwich 13815 (607) 337-1450

*Pending November 2010 Election Results

Chenango County Officials—Cont'd

County Treasurer: *William E. Evans, County Office Bldg., 5 Court St., Norwich 13815 (607) 337-1414

Chairman, Bd. of Supervisors: Richard B. Decker
County Office Bldg., 5 Court St., Norwich 13815
(607) 337-1400

Law Library:
David L. Follett Memorial Supreme Court Library,
5-9 W. Main St., 1st Floor, Norwich 13815 (607) 334-9463

Sheriff: Ernest R. Cutting, Jr.
279 County Rd. 46, Norwich 13815
(607) 334-2000; Civil Division: (607) 334-1849;
Sheriff: (607) 337-1857; Fax: (607) 336-1568
Internet: www.chenangosheriff.us

Correctional Facility:
279 County Rd. 46, Norwich 13815
(607) 336-1402, 337-1851; Fax: (607) 336-8015
E-mail: chenangosheriff.us
Atty. Visitation: Daily, 8:30-11:30 A.M.

CLINTON COUNTY

Plattsburgh, County Seat

SUPREME COURT

**Clinton County Government Center,
137 Margaret St., Plattsburgh 12901
(518) 565-4715; Fax: (518) 565-4708**

Chief Clerk II: Jan Lavigne
E-mail: jlavigne@courts.state.ny.us

SURROGATE'S COURT

**County Government Center, Suite 315,
137 Margaret St., Plattsburgh 12901-2933
(518) 565-4630; Fax: (518) 565-4769**

Surrogate: Kevin K. Ryan

Law Clerk: Catherine M. Paul

Chief Clerk I: Patricia A. Leclerc

COUNTY COURT

**County Government Center, 137 Margaret St.,
Plattsburgh 12901-2933
Court: (518) 565-4715; Fax: (518) 565-4708**

Judge: Patrick R. McGill, Suite 317
(518) 565-4657; Fax: (518) 565-4887
Acting Supreme Court Justice

County Clerk: John H. Zurlo
(518) 565-4700; Fax: (518) 565-4718

Chief Clerk II: Jan Lavigne

FAMILY COURT

**County Government Center, Suite 311,
137 Margaret St., Plattsburgh 12901-2933
(518) 565-4658; Fax: (518) 565-4688**

Judge: Timothy J. Lawliss, Suite 311
(518) 565-4404; Fax: (518) 565-4692
Secretary: Tara A. Lawrence
E-mail: talawren@courts.state.ny.us
Principal Court Atty.: Amy Asadourian
E-mail: aasadour@courts.state.ny.us

Chief Clerk: Cathy Williams (518) 565-4715

COUNTY OFFICIALS

County Atty.: William A. Favreau
206 W. Bay Plz., Plattsburgh 12901 (518) 562-0600

D.A.: Andrew J. Wylie, County Government Center, 137 Margaret St., Plattsburgh 12901-2933 (518) 565-4770

County Clerk: John H. Zurlo, County Government Center, 137 Margaret St., Plattsburgh 12901 (518) 565-4700

County Treasurer: Joseph Giroux
County Government Center, 137 Margaret St.,
Plattsburgh 12901 (518) 565-4730

Law Librarian: Lynn Bezio
Supreme Court Library, 72 Clinton St.,
Plattsburgh 12901 (518) 565-4808

Sheriff: *David N. Favro
25 McCarthy Dr., Plattsburgh 12901
(518) 565-4300; Fax: (518) 565-4333
E-mail: sheriff@co.clinton.ny.us
Hours: Weekdays, 8 A.M.-5 P.M.

Jail: 25 McCarthy Dr., Plattsburgh 12901
(518) 565-4330; Fax: (518) 565-4343
Atty. Visitation: Any time, except lockdown

COLUMBIA COUNTY

Hudson, County Seat

SUPREME COURT

**Courthouse, 401 Union St., Hudson 12534
(518) 828-7858; Fax: (518) 828-1603**

Chief Clerk: Diana Morelock

SURROGATE'S COURT

**Courthouse, 401 Union St., Hudson 12534
(518) 828-0414; Fax: (518) 828-1603**

Surrogates:
Paul Czajka (518) 822-0453; Fax: (518) 822-0514
E-mail: pczajka@courts.state.ny.us
Acting Supreme Court Justice
Legal Asst.: William F. Cranna (518) 822-0453
Jonathan D. Nichols (518) 828-7909
Acting Supreme Court Justice

Legal Asst.: John H. Clark III (518) 828-7909

Chief Clerk: Lee A. Norton (518) 828-0414

Court Reporters:
Barbara Bennett Calkins (518) 671-6740
Theresa Vining (518) 828-0429
Cyndi West (518) 828-6410

COUNTY COURT

**Courthouse, 401 Union St., Hudson 12534
(518) 828-7858**

Judges:
Paul Czajka (518) 822-0453; Fax: (518) 822-0514
E-mail: pczajka@courts.state.ny.us
Acting Supreme Court Justice
Jonathan D. Nichols (518) 828-7909; Fax: (518) 828-1603
E-mail: jnichols@courts.state.ny.us
Acting Supreme Court Justice

Chief Clerk: Diana Morelock
(518) 828-7858; Fax: (518) 828-1603
E-mail: dmoreloc@courts.state.ny.us

Law Assts.:
John H. Clark III (518) 828-7909; Fax: (518) 828-1603
E-mail: jhclark@courts.state.ny.us
William F. Cranna (518) 822-0453; Fax: (518) 828-0514

FAMILY COURT

**Courthouse, 401 Union St., Hudson 12534
(518) 828-0315; Fax: (518) 828-1603**

Judges:
Paul Czajka (518) 822-0453; Fax: (518) 822-0514
Acting Supreme Court Justice
Jonathan D. Nichols (518) 828-7909; Fax: (518) 828-1603
Acting Supreme Court Justice

Chief Clerk: Diana Morelock

Support Magistrate: John Stegmayer (518) 828-7858

COUNTY OFFICIALS

County Atty.: Rob Fitzsimmons, 401 State St., Suite 2B, Hudson 12534 (518) 828-3303; Fax: (518) 828-9535

D.A.: Beth G. Cozzolino, Courthouse Annex, 410 Union St., Hudson 12534 (518) 828-3414

County Clerk: Holly Tanner, 560 Warren St.,
Hudson 12534 (518) 828-3339; Fax: (518) 828-5299
E-mail: htanner@govt.co.columbia.ny.us
Internet: www.columbiacountyny.com-countyclerk

Public Defender: Arlene Levinson, 610 State St., Hudson 12534 (518) 828-3410; Fax: (518) 828-4076

County Treasurer: Kenneth Wilber, 560 Warren St., Hudson 12534 (518) 828-0513; Fax: (518) 822-1110

***Pending November 2010 Election Results**

Columbia County Officials—Cont'd

Law Librarian: Emily M. Wildey
Supreme Court Law Library, Courthouse,
401 Union St., Hudson 12534
(518) 828-3206; Fax: (518) 822-1110

Sheriff: David W. Harrison, Jr.
85 Industrial Tract, Hudson 12534
(518) 828-0601; Fax: (518) 828-9088
Internet: www.columbiacountysheriff.us

Jail: 85 Industrial Tract, Hudson 12534
(518) 828-3324; Fax: (518) 828-2032
Atty. Visitation: Any time except Noon-12:30 P.M. & 5-6 P.M.

CORTLAND COUNTY

Cortland, County Seat

SUPREME COURT
Courthouse, Suite 301, 46 Greenbush St., Cortland 13045-2772
(607) 753-5013; Fax: (607) 756-3409

Chief Clerk: Christina E. DeMass
E-mail: cdemass@courts.state.ny.us

SURROGATE'S COURT
Courthouse, Suite 301, 46 Greenbush St., Cortland 13045-2725
(607) 753-5355
Internet: www.nycourts.gov/courts/6jd/cortland/surrogate

Surrogates:
William F. Ames (607) 758-5556; Fax: (607) 753-1899
Law Clerk: Lorraine Seager (607) 758-5557
Julie A. Campbell (607) 753-5001; Fax: (607) 758-5531
Law Clerk: MaryBeth Mathey (607) 756-3453

Chief Clerk: Maxine B. Ripley
(607) 753-5355; Fax: (607) 756-3409
E-mail: mripley@courts.state.ny.us

COUNTY COURT
Courthouse, Suite 301, 46 Greenbush St., Cortland 13045-2772
(607) 753-5013; Fax: (607) 756-3409

Judges:
William F. Ames (607) 758-5556; Fax: (607) 753-1899
Law Clerk: Lorraine Seager (607) 758-5557
Julie A. Campbell (607) 753-5001; Fax: (607) 758-5531
Law Clerk: MaryBeth Mathey (607) 756-3453

Chief Clerk: Christina E. DeMass
(607) 753-5013; Fax: (607) 756-3409
E-mail: cdemass@courts.state.ny.us

FAMILY COURT
46 Greenbush St., Suite 301, Cortland 13045
(607) 753-5353; Fax: (607) 756-3409
E-mail: lcase@courts.state.ny.us

Judges:
William F. Ames (607) 758-5556; Fax: (607) 753-1899
Law Clerk: Lorraine Seager
(607) 758-5556; Fax: (607) 753-1899
Julie A. Campbell (607) 753-5001; Fax: (607) 758-5531
Law Clerk: MaryBeth Mathey (607) 756-3453

Chief Clerk: Laurie L. Case
E-mail: lcase@courts.state.ny.us

Support Magistrate: Sarah A. Hinchcliff,

COUNTY OFFICIALS

County Atty.: Edward R. Purser
County Office Bldg., 80 Central Ave., Cortland 13045
(607) 753-5095; Fax: (607) 753-3489

D.A.: Mark D. Suben, Courthouse, Room 101,
46 Greenbush St., Cortland 13045-5590
(607) 753-5008; Fax: (607) 756-3477

County Clerk: Elizabeth P. Larkin, Courthouse,
Suite 105, 46 Greenbush St., Cortland 13045-5590
(607) 753-5021; Fax: (607) 753-5378

County Administrator: Martin D. Murphy
County Office Bldg., 60 Central Ave.,
Cortland 13045-5590 (607) 753-5048

Treasurer: Patrick O'Mara, County Office Bldg.,
60 Central Ave., Cortland 13045-5590 (607) 753-5070

Chairman, County Legislature: Robert Jack Williams
County Office Bldg., 60 Central Ave., Cortland 13045-5590
(607) 753-5048

Law Librarian: Elizabeth M. Wenz
Louis H. Folmer Supreme Court Library,
Courthouse, Room 301, 46 Greenbush St.,
Cortland 13045-5590 (607) 753-5011

Sheriff: Lee A. Price, Public Safety Bldg., 54 Greenbush St.,
Cortland 13045 (607) 758-5599; Fax: (607) 753-7815

Jail: 54 Greenbush St., Cortland 13045
(607) 756-4275; Fax: (607) 756-3405
Atty. Visitation: Any time

DELAWARE COUNTY

Delhi, County Seat

SUPREME COURT
Courthouse, 3 Court St., Delhi 13753
(607) 746-2131; Fax: (607) 746-3253

Chief Clerk III: Kelly Sanfilippo

SURROGATE'S COURT
Courthouse, 3 Court St., Delhi 13753
(607) 746-2126; Fax: (607) 746-2288

Surrogate: Carl F. Becker

Chief Clerk: Lisa M. Loucks

COUNTY COURT
Courthouse, 3 Court St., Delhi 13753
(607) 746-2131; Fax: (607) 746-3253

Judge: Carl F. Becker

Chief Clerk: Kelly Sanfilippo

FAMILY COURT
Courthouse, 3 Court St., Delhi 13753
(607) 746-2298; Fax: (607) 746-2288

Judge: Carl F. Becker

Chief Clerk: Lori L. Metzko

COUNTY OFFICIALS

County Atty.: Richard B. Spinney
P.O. Box 219, Stamford 12167 (607) 652-3443

D.A.: Richard D. Northrup, Jr., Courthouse, Suite 5,
1 Court St., P.O. Box 148, Delhi 13753 (607) 746-3557

County Clerk: *Sharon A. O'Dell, P.O. Box 426,
Delhi 13753 (607) 746-2123

County Treasurer: Beverly J. Shields
P.O. Box 431, Delhi 13753 (607) 832-5070

Chairman, Bd. of Supervisors: James E. Eisel, Sr.
111 Main St., Delhi 13753 (607) 832-5113

Law Librarian: Vacancy at Press Time
Delhi Supreme Court Library, Courthouse, 3 Court St.,
Delhi 13753 (607) 746-3959

Sheriff: *Thomas E. Mills
280 Phoebe Ln., Suite 1, Delhi 13753
(607) 746-2336; Fax: (607) 746-2632
E-mail: tom.mills@co.delaware.ny.us

Correctional Facility: 280 Phoebe Ln., Suite 6, Delhi 13753
(607) 746-2336; Fax: (607) 746-9549
Atty. Visitation: Any time

***Pending November 2010 Election Results**

DUTCHESS COUNTY

Poughkeepsie, County Seat

SUPREME COURT

Courthouse, 10 Market St., Poughkeepsie 12601-3203
(845) 486-2260; Fax: (845) 473-5403

Chief Clerk: Ronald Varricchio

Deputy Chief Clerk: Michael Thompson (845) 486-2260

Associate Court Clerks:
Jennifer Ladue (845) 486-2260
John J. Nelson (845) 486-6445

Court Clerks:
Linda Dorrer (845) 486-2208
Victoria Gallante (845) 486-2219
Derek Hogg (845) 486-2258
Richard Kiggins (845) 486-2231
Deloris Sherman (845) 486-2240

SURROGATE'S COURT

Courthouse, 10 Market St., Poughkeepsie 12601-3203
(845) 486-2235; Fax: (845) 486-2234

Surrogate: James D. Pagones
(845) 486-2242; Fax: (845) 486-2245
Secretary: Nancy S. Tang (845) 486-2242

Chief Clerk: John J. Atherton (845) 486-2236

Deputy Chief Clerk: Karen A. Johnson (845) 486-2237

Principal Court Atty.: Kenneth M. Bernstein
(845) 486-2244

COUNTY COURT

Courthouse, 10 Market St., Poughkeepsie 12601-3203
(845) 486-2260; Fax: (845) 473-5403

Judges:
Thomas J. Dolan (Acting Supreme Court Justice)
(845) 486-2210
Law Clerk: Richard C. Schisler
Gerald V. Hayes (845) 486-2225
Law Clerk: Wayne R. Witherwax

Chief Clerk: Ronald Varricchio (845) 486-2260

FAMILY COURT

50 Market St., Poughkeepsie 12601-3204
(845) 486-2500;
Fax (Family Court Papers): (845) 486-2510;
Fax (Supreme Court Papers): (845) 486-6485

Judges:
Peter M. Forman (845) 486-2526
E-mail: pforman@courts.state.ny.us
Acting Supreme Court Justice
Law Clerk: Denise Watson
Secretary: Viola Cummings
Joan S. Posner (845) 486-2521
Acting Supreme Court Justice
Law Clerk: Susan L. Flynn
Secretary: Denise E. Jackson
Valentino T. Sammarco (845) 486-2230; Fax: (845) 486-2510
E-mail: vsammarc@courts.state.ny.us
Acting Supreme Court Justice
Law Clerk: Lisa E. Rubenstein
Secretary: Nancy Habinowski

Court Atty. Referee: Adina Gilbert (845) 486-2699

Support Magistrate:
Elaine Greenblatt (845) 486-2519
E-mail: ewinslow@courts.state.ny.us
Steven R. Kaufman (845) 486-2518
E-mail: skaufman@courts.state.ny.us

Chief Clerk/Court Administrator: Peter A. Palladino
(845) 486-2505; E-mail: ppalladino@courts.state.ny.us

Deputy Chief Clerk: Lisa D. Mack (845) 486-2506
E-mail: lmack@courts.state.ny.us

***Pending November 2010 Election Results**

COUNTY OFFICIALS

County Atty.: James M. Fedorchak, County Office Bldg., 22 Market St., Poughkeepsie 12601
(845) 486-2110; Fax: (845) 486-2002

D.A.: William V. Grady, 236 Main St., Poughkeepsie 12601
(845) 486-2300; Fax: (845) 486-2324

County Clerk: Bradford Kendall, County Office Bldg., 22 Market St., Poughkeepsie 12601
(845) 486-2120; Fax: (845) 486-2138

Controller: James L. Coughlan, County Office Bldg., 22 Market St., Poughkeepsie 12601
(845) 486-2050; Fax: (546) 486-2055

Commissioner of Finance: Pamela Barrack
County Office Bldg., 22 Market St., Poughkeepsie 12601
(845) 486-2025; Fax: (845) 486-2198

County Executive: William R. Steinhaus
County Office Bldg., 22 Market St., Poughkeepsie 12601
(845) 486-2000; Fax: (845) 486-2198

Law Librarian: Mary Boback
Joseph F. Barnard Memorial Law Library,
50 Market St., Poughkeepsie 12601 (845) 486-2215

Sheriff: Adrian H. (Butch) Anderson
150 N. Hamilton St., Poughkeepsie 12601
(845) 486-3800; Fax: (845) 452-2987

Jail: 150 N. Hamilton St., Poughkeepsie 12601
Mailing Address: Inmates only, P.O. Box 1389, Poughkeepsie 12602-1390
(845) 486-3900; Fax: (845) 486-3913
Atty. Visitation: Daily, 8:30-11 A.M.; 12:30-3 P.M.; 5:30-8 P.M.

ERIE COUNTY

Buffalo, County Seat

SUPREME COURT

Erie County Court Bldg., 25 Delaware Ave., Buffalo 14202
(716) 845-9301; Fax: (716) 851-3293

Chief Clerk: Ellis W. Bozzolo

Deputy Chief Clerk: Kevin Kelley

Secretary: Amy E. Oliver

Assoc. Court Clerks:
Deborah Drake
Billie Jo Zakia

Senior Court Analyst: Robert Pazik

Court Clerks:
Robert Adamski
Patricia Aiello
Joan Aquila
Madonna Barber
Lynne Borrelli
Richard Brown
Michelle Carter
Judy Connors
Mary Louise Enser
Karen Falzone
Denise Filosofos
Rosemarie Garbo
Patricia Hall
Edward Holmes
Judith Insalaco
Nancy Jeski
Gregory Joseph
James Kasprzak
Sally Lemley
Janet Marchinda
Celeste Marino
Margaret McMahon
Susan Monan
Margaret Morgan
Kevin O'Connor
Mary Pazik
Joan Penders
Mollie Redmond
Amanda Rice
Laura L. Rodgers
Brigitte Roestel
Melanie Ruszaj
Christine Ryder
Diane Smith
Carol Williams
Elaine Xenos

SURROGATE'S COURT

Erie County Hall, 92 Franklin St., Buffalo 14202
(716) 845-2560; Fax: (716) 853-3741

Surrogate: Barbara Howe (716) 845-9453
E-mail: bhowe@courts.state.ny.us
Law Clerk: Rebecca D. LaCivita (716) 845-2564
E-mail: rlacivit@courts.state.ny.us
Secretary: Martha Howe (716) 845-9453
E-mail: mhowe@courts.state.ny.us
Chief Court Atty.: Joseph A. Shifflett (716) 845-9454

Chief Clerk: Mary Dee Martoche (716) 845-2568
E-mail: mmartoch@courts.state.ny.us

Erie County—Cont'd

COUNTY COURT
Erie County Court Bldg., 25 Delaware Ave., Buffalo 14202
(716) 845-9301; Fax: (716) 851-3293

Judges:
Michael L. D'Amico (716) 845-9366; Fax: (716) 851-3251
Law Clerk: Lawrence Cataldi (716) 845-9367
Secretary: Cindy Pietz
Sheila A. DiTullio (716) 845-9369; Fax: (716) 851-3334
Law Clerk: Evelyn Gawronski (716) 845-9370
Secretary: Karen Piegzik
Thomas P. Franczyk (716) 845-9447; Fax: (716) 851-3319
E-mail: tfranczyk@courts.state.ny.us
Law Clerk: Jennifer Runfola (716) 845-9448
Secretary: Kathleen Schroeder
Michael F. Pietruszka (716) 845-9375; Fax: (716) 851-3332
Law Clerk: Ann Demopoulos (716) 845-9376
Secretary: Laura Kane
Vacancy at Press Time

Chief Clerk: Ellis Bozzolo (716) 845-9301

Deputy Chief Clerk: Kevin M. Kelley (716) 845-9301

Secretary: Amy E. Oliver (716) 845-9301

FAMILY COURT
One Niagara Plaza, Buffalo 14202
(716) 845-7400; Fax: (716) 858-8432

Judges:
Rosalie S. Bailey, Room 700
(716) 845-7475; Fax: (716) 858-7789
Law Clerk: Thomas Smith (716) 845-7476
Paul G. Buchanan, Room 610
(716) 845-7496; Fax: (716) 858-7788
Law Clerk: Daniel Scott (716) 845-7497
Kevin M. Carter, Room 710
(716) 845-7484; Fax: (716) 858-7794
Law Clerk: Brandon Portis (716) 845-7485
Debra L. Givens (Acting)
(716) 845-1804; Fax: (716) 858-7901
E-mail: dgivens@courts.state.ny.us
Craig D. Hannah (Acting)
(716) 845-1804; Fax: (716) 858-7901
E-mail: cdhannah@courts.state.ny.us
Sharon M. LoVallo (Acting), Room 702
(716) 845-7453; Fax: (716) 858-7899
E-mail: slovallo@courts.state.ny.us
Law Clerk: Vacancy at Press Time
Patricia A. Maxwell, Room 606
(716) 845-7493; Fax: (716) 858-7757
Law Clerk: Frank Longo (716) 845-7494
E. Jeannette Ogden (Acting), Room 602
(716) 845-1804; Fax: (716) 858-7901
E-mail: eogden@courts.state.ny.us
Law Clerks:
Joseph Deren
Karen McCaferty
Mary Kosmerl
Tearah Mullins
Alice Patterson (716) 845-1805
Lisa Bloch Rodwin, Room 600
(716) 845-7487; Fax: (716) 858-7756
Law Clerks:
Jackie Gurney (716) 845-7488
Lynn Keane
Margaret Olszewski Szczur, Room 706
(716) 845-7481; Fax: (716) 858-7792
Law Clerk: Theresa Guenther (716) 845-7482

Chief Clerk: Frank J. Boccio, Room 408
(716) 845-7444; Fax: (716) 858-8432

Deputy Chief Clerk: Daniel S. Johnston, Room 404
(716) 845-7440; Fax: (716) 858-8432

Support Magistrates:
John J. Aman, Room 312
(716) 845-7465; Fax: (716) 858-6293
Neil J. Bernholz, Room 310
(716) 845-7465; Fax: (716) 858-6293
Julie A. Dee, Room 308
(716) 845-7465; Fax: (716) 845-6293
Lenora B. Foote-Beavers, Room 304
(716) 845-7465; Fax: (716) 858-6293
Mary Jo Lattimore Young, Room 400
(716) 845-7465; Fax: (716) 858-6293
Catherine E. Marra, Room 302
(716) 845-7465; Fax: (716) 858-6293
John S. Wiencek, Room 300
(716) 845-7465; Fax: (716) 858-6293

COUNTY OFFICIALS

County Atty.: Cheryl A. Green, 69 Delaware Ave., Buffalo 14202 (716) 858-2200; Fax: (716) 858-2281

D.A.: Frank A. Sedita III, 25 Delaware Ave., Buffalo 14202 (716) 858-2424; Fax: (716) 858-7425

County Clerk: Kathy Hochul, 92 Franklin St., Buffalo 14202 (716) 858-8865; Fax: (716) 858-6550

Comptroller: Mark C. Poloncarz
Edward A. Rath County Ofc. Bldg., Suite 1100,
95 Franklin St., Buffalo 14202
(716) 858-8400; Fax: (716) 858-8507

Dir. of Budget and Mgmt.: Greg Gach
Edward A. Rath County Ofc. Bldg., 95 Franklin St.,
Buffalo 14202 (716) 858-8515

County Executive: Christopher C. Collins
Edward A. Rath County Office Bldg., 95 Franklin St.,
Buffalo 14202 (716) 858-8500

Sheriff: Timothy B. Howard
10 Delaware Ave., Buffalo 14202
(716) 858-7618; Sheriff: (716) 858-7608; Fax: (716) 858-7680
E-mail: howardt@erie.gov
Internet: www.erie.gov/sheriff

Under Sheriff: Richard T. Donovan
(716) 858-6168; Fax: (716) 858-7962
E-mail: donovanr@erie.gov

Civil Process: John Anthony, 134 W. Eagle, Buffalo 14202
(716) 858-7606

Correctional Facility: 11581 Walden Ave., Alden 14004
(716) 937-9101; Main Lobby: (716) 858-7642;
Fax: (716) 937-5595; E-mail: kochr@erie.gov
Atty. Visitation: Daily, 7:30-11:30 A.M.; 1-2:30 P.M.,
3:30-5:30 P.M. & 6:30-9 P.M.

Superintendent: Robert Koch
(716) 858-7635; Fax: (716) 858-8645
E-mail: kochr@erie.gov

Deputy Superintendent: Donald J. Livingston
(Correctional Facility) (716) 937-5501
E-mail: livingsd@erie.gov

ESSEX COUNTY

Elizabethtown, County Seat

SUPREME COURT
Essex County Courthouse, 7559 Court St.,
P.O. Box 217, Elizabethtown 12932
(518) 873-3370, 71; Fax: (518) 873-3376

Chief Clerk I: Terry A. Stoddard (518) 873-3375

Deputy Chief Clerk: Lise M. Johnson (518) 873-3701

SURROGATE'S COURT
Courthouse, 7559 Court St., P.O. Box 217,
Elizabethtown 12932
(518) 873-3384; Fax: (518) 873-3731
Internet: www.courts.state.ny.us

Surrogate: Richard B. Meyer
Must have permission to use Fax
Court Atty.: Amy N. Quinn
Secretary: Jill H. Drummond (518) 873-3326

Chief Clerk: Mary Ann Badger (518) 873-3385

Sr. Court Office Asst.: Christina Bigelow

COUNTY COURT
Courthouse, 7559 Court St., P.O. Box 217,
Elizabethtown 12932
(518) 873-3370, 71; Fax: (518) 873-3376

Judge: Richard B. Meyer (518) 873-3326; Fax: (518) 873-3732
Court Atty.: Amy N. Quinn
Secretary: Jill H. Drummond (518) 873-3326

Chief Clerk I: Terry A. Stoddard (518) 873-3375

***Pending November 2010 Election Results**

Essex County—Cont'd

FAMILY COURT
Courthouse, 7559 Court St., P.O. Box 217, Elizabethtown 12932
(518) 873-3320; Fax: (518) 873-3626

Judge: Richard B. Meyer
Court Atty.: Amy N. Quinn
Secretary: Jill H. Drummond (518) 873-3326

Chief Clerk: Terry Stoddard (Acting)
(518) 873-3324; Fax: (518) 873-3626

COUNTY OFFICIALS

County Atty.: Daniel T. Manning III
7551 Court St., P.O. Box 217, Elizabethtown 12932
(518) 873-3380; Fax: (518) 873-3894

D.A.: Kristy L. Sprauge
7559 Court St., P.O. Box 217, Elizabethtown 12932
(518) 873-3335; Fax: (518) 873-3788

County Clerk: Joseph A. Provoncha
7559 Court St., P.O. Box 247, Elizabethtown 12932
(518) 873-3600; Fax: (518) 873-3548

County Treasurer: *Michael Diskin
7551 Court St., P.O. Box 217, Elizabethtown 12932
(518) 873-3310; Fax: (518) 873-3318

Law Library: Joseph A. Provoncha, 7559 Court St., P.O. Box 247, Elizabethtown 12932 (518) 573-3707

Sheriff: Richard C. Cutting, 702 Stowersville Rd., P.O. Box 68, Elizabethtown 12932
(518) 873-6321; Fax: (518) 873-3340

Correctional Facility:
702 Stowersville Rd., P.O. Box 68, Lewis 12950
(518) 873-6321; Civil: (518) 873-6907;
Civil Fax: (518) 873-6992; Jail Fax: (518) 873-6944, 49;
Booking: (518) 873-6974; Shift Supervisors: (518) 873-6950
Atty. Visitation: Daily, 7:30 A.M.-9:30 P.M.

FRANKLIN COUNTY

Malone, County Seat

SUPREME COURT
Courthouse, Suite 405, 355 W. Main St., Malone 12953-1826
(518) 481-1748; Fax: (518) 481-5456

Chief Clerk: Bruce J. Cox (518) 481-1817
E-mail: bcox@courts.state.ny.us

SURROGATE'S COURT
Courthouse, Suite 3223, 355 W. Main St., Malone 12953-1826
(518) 481-1737; Fax: (518) 481-1443

Surrogate: Robert G. Main, Jr.
(518) 481-1732; Fax: (518) 481-1443
E-mail: rgmain@courts.state.ny.us
Law Clerk: Shannon A. Bessette (518) 481-1732
Secretary: Karen A. Coughlin

Chief Clerk: Martha A. LaBarge (518) 481-1736
E-mail: mlabarge@courts.state.ny.us

COUNTY COURT
Courthouse, Suite 3223, 355 W. Main St., Malone 12953-1826
(518) 481-1748; Fax: (518) 481-5456

Judge: Robert G. Main, Jr. (518) 481-1732
E-mail: rgmain@courts.state.ny.us
Law Clerk: Shannon A. Bessette
Secretary: Karen A. Coughlin

Chief Clerk: Bruce J. Cox (518) 481-1817; Fax: (518) 481-5456
E-mail: bcox@courts.state.ny.us

FAMILY COURT
Courthouse, Suite 3223, 355 W. Main St., Malone 12953-1826
(518) 481-1742; Fax: (518) 481-5453

Judge: Robert G. Main, Jr.
(518) 481-1732; Fax: (518) 481-5453
E-mail: rgmain@courts.state.ny.us
Court Atty.: Shannon A. Bessette
Secretary: Karen A. Coughlin

Chief Clerk: Janice F. Mock (518) 481-1742

COUNTY OFFICIALS

County Atty.: Jonathan J. Miller
355 W. Main St., Suite 409, Malone 12953
(518) 481-1641, 483-8400; Fax: (518) 483-2054

D.A.: Derek Champagne, 355 W. Main St., Suite 466, Malone 12953-1826 (518) 481-1544

County Clerk: Wanda D. Murtagh, Courthouse, Suite 248, 355 W. Main St., P.O. Box 70, Malone 12953-1871
(518) 481-1681; Fax: (518) 483-9143

Public Defender: Thomas G. Soucia
355 W. Main St., Suite 237, Malone 12953-1826
(518) 481-1624; Fax: (518) 483-4690

Conflict Defender: Lorelei B. Smith Miller
355 W. Main St., Suite 252, Malone 12953 (518) 481-1593

County Treasurer: *Bryon A. Varin
Courthouse, Suite 140, 355 W. Main St., Malone 12953-1826
(518) 481-1511, 18

Chairman, Bd. of Legislators: *Guy (Tim) Smith
659 County Route 3, Fort Covington 12937
(518) 358-2592

Law Library: ,
Courthouse, Suite 3223, 355 W. Main St., Malone 12953-1826 (518) 481-1732

Commissioner of Jurors: Kathleen M. Monette
Courthouse, Suite 4332, 355 W. Main St., Malone 12953-1826
(518) 481-1756; Fax: (518) 481-6204

Sheriff: *Jack Pelkey
45 Bare Hill Rd., Malone 12953
(518) 483-6795, 96; Fax: (518) 483-3205;
Civil: (518) 483-3349, 483-3529;
Sheriff: (518) 483-3304, 05; Jail Fax: (518) 483-3139
E-mail: jpelkey@co.franklin.ny.us

Jail: 45 Bare Hill Rd., Malone 12953
(518) 483-6795, 96; Fax: (518) 483-3139
E-mail: jpelkey@co.franklin.ny.us
Atty. Visitation: Any time

FULTON COUNTY

Johnstown, County Seat

SUPREME COURT
County Bldg., 223 W. Main St., Johnstown 12095
(518) 736-5539; Fax: (518) 762-5078

County Clerk: William E. Eschler
(518) 736-5555; Fax: (518) 762-9214

Chief Clerk: Patricia M. Eschler
(518) 736-5539; Fax: (518) 762-5078

Court Assts.:
Christine Chrzanowski (518) 736-5539
Ingrid Edwards (518) 736-5537

SURROGATE'S COURT
County Bldg., 223 W. Main St., Johnstown 12095
(518) 736-5685; Fax: (518) 762-6372

Surrogates:
Richard C. Giardino (518) 736-5695
Polly A. Hoye (518) 736-5691

Chief Clerk: Barbara E. Shattuck (518) 736-5685

COUNTY COURT
County Bldg., 223 W. Main St., Johnstown 12095
(518) 736-5539; Fax: (518) 762-5078

Judges:
Richard C. Giardino (518) 736-5695; Fax: (518) 762-8776
Law Clerk: Thomas Bell (518) 736-5694
Polly A. Hoye (518) 736-5691
Law Clerk: Mark Hallenbeck (518) 736-5693

County Clerk: William E. Eschler
(518) 736-5555; Fax: (518) 762-9214

Chief Clerk: Patricia Eschler
(518) 736-5539; Fax: (518) 762-5078

Court Assts.:
Christine Chrzanowski
Ingrid Edwards (518) 736-5539

***Pending November 2010 Election Results**

Fulton County—Cont'd

FAMILY COURT
11 N. William St., Johnstown 12095
(518) 762-3840; Fax: (518) 762-9540

Judge: Edward F. Skoda
Chief Clerk: Geraldine A. Bastolla
Court Atty.: Beth V. Kelly-May
Support Magistrate: Richard A. DiMatteo

COUNTY OFFICIALS

County Atty.: Arthur C. Spring
County Office Bldg., 223 W. Main St., Johnstown 12095
(518) 762-4503; Fax: (518) 762-4504
Asst. County Atty.: Allen Day, 289 N. Main St., Gloversville 12078 (518) 773-8225; Fax: (518) 725-7731
D.A.: *Louise K. Sira, County Office Bldg., 223 W. Main St., Johnstown 12095 (518) 736-5511; Fax: (518) 762-2042
County Clerk: William E. Eschler, County Office Bldg., 223 W. Main, P.O. Box 485, Johnstown 12095
(518) 736-5555; Fax: (518) 762-3839
Deputy Clerk: Anne L. Nickloy, County Office Bldg., 223 W. Main, P.O. Box 485, Johnstown 12095
(518) 736-5555; Fax: (518) 762-3839
County Treasurer: Edgar Blodgett, County Office Bldg., 223 W. Main St., Johnstown 12095
(518) 762-5580; Fax: (518) 762-0224
Law Library: Barbara E. Shattuck, County Bldg., Johnstown 12095 (518) 762-5697
Sheriff: Thomas J. Lorey
2712 State Hwy. 29, P.O. Box 29, Johnstown 12095
(518) 736-2100; Fax: (518) 736-2126
E-mail: tlorey@co.fulton.ny.us
Correctional Facility:
2710 State Hwy. 29, P.O. Box 20, Johnstown 12095
(518) 736-2118; Fax: (518) 736-2191
E-mail: rbenedict@co.fulton.ny.us
Atty. Visitation: Must call for appointment

GENESEE COUNTY

Batavia, County Seat

SUPREME COURT
Genesee County Courts Facility, 1 W. Main St., Batavia 14020
(585) 344-2550, Ext. 2239; Fax: (585) 344-8517

Chief Clerk: Mary Lou Strathearn, Ext. 2238
E-mail: mstrathe@courts.state.ny.us

SURROGATE'S COURT
Genesee County Courts Facility, 1 W. Main St., Batavia 14020
(585) 344-2550, Ext. 2237; Fax: (585) 344-8517

Surrogate: Robert C. Noonan
(585) 344-2550, Ext. 2236; Fax: (585) 344-3108
Law Clerk: Stephen D. Wieczorek, Ext. 2427
Secretary: Shelley M. DeVinney, Ext. 2236
Chief Clerk: Michele A. Westfall-Owens, Ext. 2237
E-mail: mawestfa@courts.state.ny.us

COUNTY COURT
Genesee County Courts Facility, 1 W. Main St., Batavia 14020
(585) 344-2550, Ext. 2298; Fax: (585) 344-8517

Judge: Robert C. Noonan
(585) 344-2550, Ext. 2236; Fax: (585) 344-3108
Law Clerk: Stephen D. Wieczorek
(585) 344-2550, Ext. 2427
Chief Clerk: Mary Lou Strathearn
E-mail: mstrathe@courts.state.ny.us

FAMILY COURT
Genesee County Courts Facility, 1 W. Main St., Batavia 14020
(585) 344-2550, Ext. 2228; Fax: (585) 344-8520

Judge: *Eric R. Adams, Ext. 2233
E-mail: eradams@courts.state.ny.us

***Pending November 2010 Election Results**

Court Atty.: Robert Croyle, Ext. 2475
E-mail: rcroyle@courts.state.ny.us
Chief Clerk Admin.: Kathleen D. Blake, Ext. 2231
E-mail: kblake@courts.state.ny.us
Support Magistrate: Kathleen J. Gray, Ext. 2430

COUNTY OFFICIALS

County Atty.: Charles N. Zambito, 7 W. Main St., Batavia 14020 (585) 344-2550, Ext. 2206
D.A.: Lawrence Friedman
Genesee County Courts Facility, 1 W. Main St., Batavia 14020 (585) 344-2550, Ext. 2250;
Fax: (585) 344-8544
E-mail: lfriedman@co.genesee.ny.us
County Clerk: Don M. Read, County Office Bldg. No. 1, 15 Main St., P.O. Box 379, Batavia 14021-0379
(585) 344-2550, Ext. 2244; Fax: (585) 344-8521
E-mail: dread@co.genesee.ny.us
County Treasurer: Scott D. German
County Office Bldg. No. 1, 15 Main St.,
Batavia 14020-3199
(585) 344-2550, Ext. 2210; Fax: (585) 344-2442
E-mail: sgerman@co.genesee.ny.us
Law Library: Genesee County Courts Facility, 1 W. Main St., Batavia 14020 (585) 344-2550, Ext. 2224
Sheriff: Gary T. Maha
165 Park Rd., Batavia 14020
(585) 345-3000; Fax: (585) 344-3102
E-mail: gmaha@co.genesee.ny.us
Internet: www.co.genesee.ny.us
Jail: 14 W. Main St., P.O. Box 151, Batavia 14020-0151
(585) 343-0838; Fax: (585) 344-0236
E-mail: rgreer@co.genesee.ny.us
Atty. Visitation: Daily, 9 A.M.-9 P.M.

GREENE COUNTY

Catskill, County Seat

SUPREME COURT
320 Main St., Catskill 12414
(518) 444-8760; Fax: (518) 943-0247

Chief Clerk: Kathleen Barry Gorczyca
Deputy Chief Clerk: Michelle L. Carroll

SURROGATE'S COURT
320 Main St., Catskill 12414
(518) 444-8750; Fax: (518) 943-5811

Surrogates:
George J. Pulver, Jr. (518) 444-8750
Law Clerk: Kelly Ann Nagle-Zaik
*Subject to Election
Chief Clerk: Eric Maurer

COUNTY COURT
320 Main St., Catskill 12414
(518) 444-8760; Fax: (518) 943-0247

Judges:
George J. Pulver, Jr. (518) 444-8760; Fax: (518) 943-3014
Acting Supreme Court Justice
Law Clerk: Kelly Ann Nagle-Zaik Fax: (518) 943-3014
*Subject to Election (518) 444-8770
Chief Clerk: Kathleen Barry Gorczyca
(518) 444-8760; Fax: (518) 943-0247
Deputy Chief Clerk: Michelle L. Carroll
(518) 444-8760; Fax: (518) 943-0247

FAMILY COURT
320 Main St., Catskill 12414
(518) 444-8780; Fax: (518) 943-1864

Judges:
George J. Pulver, Jr. (518) 444-8780
*Subject to Election (518) 444-8770
Chief Clerk: Brenda VanDermark
E-mail: bvanderm@courts.state.ny.us
Deputy Chief Clerk: Carol A. Peters
E-mail: cpeters@courts.state.ny.us

Greene County—Cont'd

COUNTY OFFICIALS

County Atty.: Carol Stevens, 411 Main St., Catskill 12414 (518) 719-3540; Fax: (518) 719-3790

D.A.: Terry J. Wilhelm, County Office Bldg., 411 Main St., Catskill 12414 (518) 719-3590; Fax: (518) 719-3792

County Clerk: Michael T. Flynn, County Office Bldg., Suite 212, 411 Main St., Catskill 12414 (518) 719-3255

County Treasurer: Willis Vermilyea, County Office Bldg., 411 Main St., P.O. Box 191, Catskill 12414 (518) 719-3530; Fax: (518) 719-3794

Law Librarian: Angelina Knott
Emory A. Chase Memorial Library, Courthouse, 320 Main St., Catskill 12414
(518) 444-8797; Fax: (518) 943-7763

Sheriff: Gregory R. Seeley, 80 Bridge St., Catskill 12414 (518) 943-3300; Fax: (518) 943-6832
E-mail: sheriff@discovergreene.com

Jail: 80 Bridge St., Catskill 12414
(518) 943-3527; Fax (Jail): (518) 943-5710
Atty. Visitation: Daily, 9 A.M.-10 P.M.; call for appt.

HAMILTON COUNTY

Lake Pleasant, County Seat

SUPREME COURT
County Clerk's Office, 102 County View Dr., P.O. Box 204, Lake Pleasant 12108
(514) 548-7111
E-mail: countyclerk@hamiltoncountyny.gov

NO SESSIONS HELD IN HAMILTON COUNTY; SESSIONS HELD IN FULTON COUNTY—Send all papers and Index Number Application to County Clerk's Office for assignment. Separate Checks Required

SURROGATE'S COURT
Offices and Chambers, 79 White Birch Lane, Indian Lake 12842
Mailing Address: P.O. Box 780, Indian Lake 12842-0780
(518) 648-5411; Fax: (518) 648-6286
Court House, 102 County View Dr., Lake Pleasant 12108

Surrogate: S. Peter Feldstein
Law Clerk: Brendan J. Hanley

Chief Clerk: Araina C. Eldridge

Send all correspondence to mailing address

COUNTY COURT
Offices and Chambers, 79 White Birch Ln., Indian Lake 12842
Mailing Address: P.O. Box 780, Indian Lake 12842-0780
(518) 648-5411; Fax: (518) 648-6286
Court House, 102 County View Dr., Lake Pleasant 12108

Judge: S. Peter Feldstein
Law Clerk: Brendan J. Hanley

County Clerk: Jane S. Zarecki
102 County View Dr., P.O. Box 204, Lake Pleasant 12108 (518) 548-7111

Chief Clerk: Araina C. Eldridge

Send all correspondence to the mailing addresses

FAMILY COURT
Offices and Chambers, 79 White Birch Ln., Indian Lake 12842
Mailing Address: P.O. Box 780, Indian Lake 12842-0780
(518) 648-5411; Fax: (518) 648-6286
Courthouse, Route 102 County View Dr., Lake Pleasant 12108

Judge: S. Peter Feldstein
Law Clerk: Brendan J. Hanley

Chief Clerk: Araina C. Eldridge

Send all correspondence to the mailing address

***Pending November 2010 Election Results**

COUNTY OFFICIALS
P.O. Box 205, Lake Pleasant 12108
(518) 548-6385

County Atty.: Charles R. Getty, Jr.
503 N. George St., P.O. Box 950, Rome 13442-0950
(315) 336-3900; Fax: (315) 336-3902

D.A.: James T. Curry
P.O. Box 277, Indian Lake 12842 (518) 648-5113

County Clerk: Jane S. Zarecki
102 County View Dr., P.O. Box 204, Lake Pleasant 12108 (518) 548-7111
E-mail: countyclerk@hamiltoncountyny.gov

County Treasurer: Beth Hunt
Courthouse, 102 County View Dr., P.O. Box 206, Lake Pleasant 12108 (518) 548-7911

Law Library: Courthouse, 102 County View Dr., Lake Pleasant 12108 (518) 548-3211

Sheriff: Karl Abrams, 102 County View Dr., P.O. Box 210, Lake Pleasant 12108 (518) 548-3113

Jail: 102 County View Dr., P.O. Box 210, Lake Pleasant 12108 (518) 548-3113; Fax: (518) 548-3113
Atty. Visitation: Daily, 9 A.M.-5 P.M.

HERKIMER COUNTY

Herkimer, County Seat

SUPREME COURT
County Office and Courts Facility, Suite 5509, 301 N. Washington St., Herkimer 13350-0749
(315) 867-1209; Fax: (315) 866-1802

Chief Clerk: Paul B. Heintz
(315) 867-1346; Fax: (315) 866-1802

SURROGATE'S COURT
County Office and Courts Facility, Suite 5550, 301 N. Washington St., Herkimer 13350-0749
(315) 867-1170; Fax: (315) 866-1722

Surrogate: Patrick L. Kirk
(315) 867-1171; Fax: (315) 867-1344

Chief Clerk: Mary T. Grogan
(315) 867-1170; Fax: (315) 866-1722

COUNTY COURT
Herkimer County Office and Court Facility, Suite 55 50, 301 N. Washington St., Herkimer 13350-0749
(315) 867-1282; Fax: (315) 866-1802

Judge: Patrick L. Kirk
(315) 867-1171; Fax: (315) 867-1344

Chief Clerk: Mary T. Grogan
(315) 867-1170; Fax: (315) 866-1722

FAMILY COURT
Herkimer County Office and Court Facility, 4th Floor, 301 N. Washington St., P.O. Box 749, Herkimer 13350-0749
(315) 867-1139; Fax: (315) 867-1369

Judge: Subject to Election (315) 867-1334

Clerk: Lynn Kohl (315) 867-1197
E-mail: lkohl@courts.state.ny.us

Support Magistrate: G. Stephen Getman (315) 867-1284
E-mail: gsgetman@courts.state.ny.us

COUNTY OFFICIALS

County Atty.: Robert J. Malone
County Office Bldg., Suite 1320, 109 Mary St., Herkimer 13350 (315) 867-1123; Fax: (315) 867-1109

D.A.: *John H. Crandall, Sr.
301 N. Washington St., Suite 2401, Herkimer 13350
(315) 867-1155; Fax: (315) 867-1348

County Clerk: Sylvia M. Rowan
County Office Bldg., Suite 1111, 109 Mary St., Herkimer 13350 (315) 867-1129; Fax: (315) 866-4396

Treasurer: Kimberlee Enea
Treasurer's Bldg., Suite 3100, 108 Court St., Herkimer 13350 (315) 867-1145; Fax: (315) 867-1315

Herkimer County Officials—Cont'd

Law Library Asst.: Lisa Liskiewicz
Herkimer County Law Library, 301 N. Washington St., Suite 5551, Herkimer 13350-0749
(315) 867-1172; Fax: (315) 866-7991

Sheriff: Christopher P. Farber
320 N. Main St., Suite 2900, Herkimer 13350
(315) 867-1167; Fax: (315) 867-1354

Correctional Facility: 126 Court St., Herkimer 13350
Mailing Address: 320 N. Main St., Suite 2900, Herkimer 13350
(315) 867-1252; Fax: (315) 867-1354;
Fax (Jail): (315) 867-1263
Atty. Visitation: Any time

JEFFERSON COUNTY

Watertown, County Seat

SUPREME COURT
State Office Bldg., 10th Floor, 317 Washington St., Watertown 13601-3783
(315) 785-7906; Fax: (315) 785-7909

Chief Clerk: Vacancy at Press Time

Deputy Chief Clerk: Deanna L. Morse
163 Arsenal St., 2nd Floor, Watertown 13601
(315) 785-3044; Fax: (315) 186-7409

SURROGATE'S COURT
Jefferson County Court Complex, 3rd Floor, 163 Arsenal St., Watertown 13601-2562
Office: (315) 785-3019; Fax: (315) 785-5194

Surrogate: *Peter A. Schwerzmann (315) 785-3019

Chief Clerk: Benjamin J. Cobb

Law Clerk: Timothy L. Virkler

COUNTY COURT
Jefferson County Court Complex, 2nd Floor, 163 Arsenal St., Watertown 13601
(315) 785-3044; Fax: (315) 786-7409

Judge: Kim H. Martusewicz
(315) 785-3010; Fax: (315) 786-6931
E-mail: kmartuse@courts.state.ny.us
Law Clerk: Susan Drake Jenne
(315) 785-3010; Fax: (315) 781-6931

Chief Clerk: Vacancy at Press Time
State Office Bldg., 10th Floor, 317 Washington St., Watertown 13601 (315) 785-7906; Fax: (315) 785-7909

Deputy Chief Clerk: Deanna L. Morse
Jefferson County Court Complex, 2nd Floor, 163 Arsenal St., Watertown 13601
(315) 786-7417; Fax: (315) 786-7409
E-mail: dmorse@courts.state.ny.us

FAMILY COURT
Jefferson County Court Complex, 1st Floor, 163 Arsenal St., Watertown 13601-2560
(315) 785-3001; Fax: (315) 785-3198

Judge: Richard V. Hunt
Law Clerk: Erica L. Cohen

Chief Clerk: Tanice A. Gebo

Support Magistrate: Paul V. Frank

COUNTY OFFICIALS

County Atty.: David J. Paulsen
175 Arsenal St., Watertown 13601 (315) 785-3088

D.A.: Cindy Intschert, 175 Arsenal St., Watertown 13601
(315) 785-3053; Fax: (315) 785-3371

County Clerk: Cheryl D. Lane
175 Arsenal St., Watertown 13601-2555
(315) 785-3312; Fax: (315) 785-5145

Deputy County Clerk: Jo Ann Wilder
175 Arsenal St., Watertown 13601
(315) 785-3312; Fax: (315) 785-5145

County Treasurer: Nancy D. Brown
175 Arsenal St., Watertown 13601-2569 (315) 785-3055

***Pending November 2010 Election Results**

Law Librarian: Catherine Miller
Supreme Court Law Library, Courthouse, 163 Arsenal St., Watertown 13601
(315) 785-3064; Fax: (315) 785-3330

Sheriff: *John P. Burns
753 Waterman Dr., Watertown 13601
(315) 788-2700; Fax: (315) 786-2743;
Civil: (315) 786-2714; Fax: (315) 786-2721
Sheriff: (315) 786-2660; Fax: (315) 786-2684

Jail: 753 Waterman Dr., Watertown 13601 (315) 786-2688
Atty. Visitation: Any time

KINGS COUNTY

Brooklyn, County Seat

SUPREME COURT
Civil Term, 360 Adams St., Brooklyn 11201
(718) 675-7699
Internet: www.nycourts.gov/kingscivil
Criminal Term, 320 Jay St., Brooklyn 11201
(347) 296-1076

County Chief Clerk for Civil Matters: Thomas R. Kilfoyle
(347) 296-1800

Chief Clerk: James F. Imperatrice (Criminal Term)
320 Jay St. (347) 296-1100

Chief Court Atty.: Ellen Leventhal (347) 296-1682

Deputy Chief Court Atty.: John Fiumara (347) 296-1680

Principal Court Attys.:
Robert Rood, 320 Jay St. (347) 296-1257
Kenneth Schiffrin (347) 401-9183

Court Attys.:
Kwaku Agyeman (347) 296-1677
Neal S. Barkan (347) 296-1678
Dale Berson (347) 296-1677
Georgia Coffinas (347) 401-9353
Carol H. Hauge (347) 296-1672
Paula Havener (347) 296-1671
Hildy Herzfeld (347) 296-1670
Linda J. Horn (347) 296-1669
Myra Jette (347) 296-1628
Cynthia L. Johnson (347) 296-1663
Eileen McKenna (347) 296-1667
Jeanette Mercedes (347) 296-1723
Janice Purvis (347) 296-1673
Marcello Romanelli (347) 296-1662
Alexander Simon (347) 401-9184
Noreen Soto-Fier (347) 296-1743
Charles M. Sporn (347) 296-1751
Jeffrey Stichinsky (347) 296-1658
Christina Tener (347) 401-9403

Court Atty. Referees:
Richard Allman (347) 296-1424
Jeffrey Amster (347) 401-9288
Maxine L. Archer (347) 296-1689
William P. DiMaria (347) 296-1674
Deborah Goldstein (347) 296-1629
Charmaine E. Henderson (347) 401-9127
Nina L. Kurtz (347) 401-9025
Clare Laurino (347) 296-1668
Andrea W.M. Louie (347) 296-1530
Paul Nuccio (347) 296-1681
Stephen Rossini (347) 401-9287
Marlene Schwarz (347) 296-1081
Steven J. Skrzypczak (347) 296-1659
Miriam Sunshine (347) 401-9259

Court Examiner Specialist: Laura Messiana
(347) 296-1075

Guardianship Referees:
Janice Chen (347) 401-9075
Alix Mondesir (347) 296-1474
Carol Stark Tiernan (347) 401-9116

First Deputy Chief Clerk, Civil Term: Donna J. Farrell
(347) 296-1802

Kings County Supreme Court—Cont'd

Deputy Chief Clerk, Criminal Term: Joseph F. Canella
320 Jay St. (347) 296-1278

Clerks of IAS Parts:
Rod Randall (Order Dept.) (347) 296-1721
Felix Ferretti (Tax Certiorari/ Bldg. Condemnation Proceedings) (347) 296-1262
John Yackel (Matrimonial Part) (347) 296-1714
Theresa Busti-O'Leary (Guardianship Proceedings) (347) 296-1757
Rod Randall (ExParte Motions) (347) 296-1721
Felix Ferretti (Mental Hygiene IAS Part 77) (347) 296-1262

Civil Term Motion Support Service/Trial Support: George King (347) 296-1694

Civil Term—Foreclosure Dept.: Grace A. Christie (347) 401-9169

Civil Term—Up Front Parts: Ralph Palma (347) 296-1165

Civil Term—Office for the Self Represented: Patrick M. McConnell (347) 296-1740

Civil Term—Subpoenaed Records: Lucille Franco (347) 296-1755

Criminal Term—General Information: ,320 Jay St. (347) 296-1076

Juror's Division: Loretta Argiro (347) 404-9798

Justice Library: Grace Crawford (347) 296-1688

Law Library: Paul Henrich (347) 296-1144

SURROGATE'S COURT
2 Johnson St., Brooklyn 11201
(347) 404-9700; Fax: (718) 643-6237

Surrogates:
Diana A. Johnson (347) 404-9653
Law Clerk: Ronald Rossi
Margarita López Torres (347) 404-9744
Law Secretary: Olga Statz

Chief Clerk/Clerk of Court: Vacancy at Press Time (347) 404-9720

Deputy Chief Clerk: Mary Egan Dunbar (347) 404-9725

Probate Clerk: Kevin McTernan (347) 404-9671

Administration Clerk: Lisa Mathis (347) 404-9691

Miscellaneous Clerk: Vacancy at Press Time (347) 404-9681

Accounting Clerk: Vacancy at Press Time (347) 404-9685

Adoption Clerk/Guardianship Clerk: Tina Davis (347) 404-9665

Cashier/Certification: Michael Nocera
Cashier and Index: (347) 404-9730

Calendar Clerk: Vacancy at Press Time (347) 404-9718

Guardian Accounts Clerk: Vacancy at Press Time (347) 404-0973

Records: James Dillon (347) 404-9710

FAMILY COURT
See Family Court, N.Y.C., pp. 98-99

COUNTY OFFICIALS

D.A.: Charles J. Hynes, Renaissance Plaza, 350 Jay St., Brooklyn 11201-2908 (718) 250-2000

County Clerk: Nancy T. Sunshine
Supreme Court Bldg., Room 189, 360 Adams St., Brooklyn 11201 (347) 404-9772

Deputy County Clerk: Louis D. Fiorillo

Comptroller: John Liu, Municipal Bldg., Room 530, 1 Centre St., N.Y.C. 10007
(212) 669-3500; Fax: (212) 669-2707

Commissioner of Finance: David M. Frankel
1 Centre St., Suite 500, N.Y.C. 10007 (212) 669-4855

Public Administrator: Bruce L. Stein
360 Adams St., Room 144, Brooklyn 11201
(718) 643-3032; Fax: (718) 552-4475

Law Librarian: Paul Henrich
Supreme Court Law Library, 360 Adams St., Room 349, Brooklyn 11201 (347) 296-1144

Sheriff: Vacancy at Press Time
210 Joralemon St., 9th Floor, Brooklyn 11201
(718) 802-3545, 41; Fax: (718) 802-3715

Under Sheriff: Frank Shor

LEWIS COUNTY
Lowville, County Seat

SUPREME COURT
Courthouse, 7660 N. State St., Lowville 13367-1396
(315) 376-5380; Fax: (315) 376-1656

County Clerk: Douglas P. Hanno
(315) 376-5333; Fax: (315) 376-3768
E-mail: dhanno@lewiscountyny.org

Clerk of Courts: Bart R. Pleskach (Chief Clerk I)
(315) 376-5380; E-mail: bpleskach@courts.state.ny.us

Principal Law Clerk: Kathlene Loconti (315) 376-5347

SURROGATE'S COURT
Courthouse, 7660 State St., Lowville 13367-1396
(315) 376-5344; Fax: (315) 376-1647
Internet: www.nycourts.gov/courts/5jd/lewis

Surrogate: Charles C. Merrell (315) 376-5366
Law Clerk: Kevin M. McArdle (315) 376-5366

Chief Clerk: Lori K. Pfendler

COUNTY COURT
Courthouse, 7660 N. State St., Lowville 13367-1396
(315) 376-5366; Fax: (315) 376-4145

Judge: Charles C. Merrell
E-mail: cmerrell@courts.state.ny.us

Clerk of Courts: Bart R. Pleskach (315) 376-5380
E-mail: bpleskach@courts.state.ny.us

FAMILY COURT
Courthouse, 7660 N. State St., Lowville 13367-1396
(315) 376-5345; Fax: (315) 376-5189

Judge: Charles C. Merrell (315) 376-5366
E-mail: cmerrell@courts.state.ny.us

Support Magistrate: Todd W. McIntyre

Chief Clerk: Judy Meekins

Law Clerk: Kevin McArdle (315) 376-5412

COUNTY OFFICIALS

County Atty.: Richard Graham
Cthse., 7660 N. State St., Lowville 13367
(315) 376-5282; Fax: (315) 376-3857

D.A.: Leanne K. Moser, Cthse., 7660 N. State St., Lowville 13367 (315) 376-5390; Fax: (315) 376-5873

County Clerk: Douglas P. Hanno
Cthse., 7660 N. State St., Lowville 13367
(315) 376-5333; Fax: (315) 376-3768

County Treasurer: Vicki Roy
Cthse., 7660 N. State St., Lowville 13367
(315) 376-5325; Fax: (315) 376-8552

Law Librarian: Ann Marie Hill, Cthse., 7660 N. State St., Lowville 13367-1396 (315) 376-5317

Sheriff: L. Michael Tabolt
Public Safety Bldg., Outer Stowe St., P.O. Box 233, Lowville 13367 (315) 376-3511; Fax: (315) 376-5232

Jail: Public Safety Bldg., 5252 Outer Stowe St., P.O. Box 233, Lowville 13367
(315) 376-3511; Fax: (315) 376-5657
Atty. Visitation: Upon request 7 A.M.-11 P.M.

LIVINGSTON COUNTY
Geneseo, County Seat

SUPREME COURT
Courthouse, 2 Court St., Geneseo 14454-1030
(585) 243-7060; Fax: (585) 243-7067

Chief Clerk: Diane C. Murphy
E-mail: dmurphy@courts.state.ny.us

Livingston County—Cont'd

SURROGATE'S COURT
Courthouse, 2 Court St., Geneseo 14454-1030
(585) 243-7095; Fax: (585) 243-7583

Surrogates:
Dennis S. Cohen (585) 243-7078; Fax: (585) 243-7076
Court Atty.: Marjorie Byrnes
Robert B. Wiggins (585) 243-7088; Fax: (585) 243-7583
Court Atty.: Gordon Lawrence
Chief Clerk: Toni A. Moore
(585) 243-7095; Fax: (585) 243-7583
E-mail: tmoore@courts.state.ny.us

COUNTY COURT
Courthouse, 2 Court St., Geneseo 14454-1030
(585) 243-7060; Fax: (585) 243-7067

Judges:
Dennis S. Cohen (585) 243-7078; Fax: (585) 243-7076
Robert B. Wiggins (585) 243-7088; Fax: (585) 243-7067
County Clerk: *James A. Culbertson
Government Center, Room 201, 6 Court St.,
Geneseo 14454-1030 (585) 243-7010; Fax: (585) 243-7928
Chief Clerk: Diane C. Murphy
(585) 243-7060; Fax: (585) 243-7067
E-mail: dmurphy@courts.state.ny.us

FAMILY COURT
Courthouse, 2 Court St., Geneseo 14454-1030
(585) 243-7070; Fax: (585) 243-7076

Judges:
Dennis S. Cohen (585) 243-7078; Fax: (585) 243-7076
Robert B. Wiggins (585) 243-7088; Fax: (585) 243-7076
Chief Clerk: Robert M. Lewis (585) 243-7070
Law Clerks:
Marjorie Byrnes (585) 243-7119
Gordon Lawrence (585) 243-7590
Support Magistrate: Michael T. Allen (585) 243-7070

COUNTY OFFICIALS

County Atty.: David J. Morris,
Cty. Govt. Center, Room 302, 6 Court St., Geneseo 14454
(585) 243-7033; Fax: (585) 243-7045
D.A.: Thomas E. Moran, Courthouse, 2 Court St.,
Geneseo 14454 (585) 243-7020; Fax: (585) 243-7199
County Clerk: *James A. Culbertson
Cty. Govt. Center, Room 201, 6 Court St.,
Geneseo 14454 (585) 243-7010; Fax: (585) 243-7928
County Treasurer: Carolyn D. Taylor
Cty. Govt. Center, Room 203, 6 Court St.,
Geneseo 14454 (585) 243-7050; Fax: (585) 243-7597
Sheriff: John M. York, 4 Court St., Geneseo 14454
(585) 243-7120; Fax: (585) 243-7104
E-mail: sheriffyork@co.livingston.ny.us
Jail: 4 Court St., Geneseo 14454
(585) 243-7180; Fax: (585) 243-7925
Atty. Visitation: Any time

MADISON COUNTY

Wampsville, County Seat

SUPREME COURT
Courthouse, Bldg. 3, 138 N. Court St., P.O. Box 545,
Wampsville 13163-0545
(315) 366-2267

Chief Clerk: Marianne Kincaid
(315) 366-2267; Fax: (315) 366-2539

SURROGATE'S COURT
Cthse., 138 N. Court St., Bldg. 3, P.O. Box 607,
Wampsville 13163-0607
(315) 366-2392; Fax: (315) 366-2539

Surrogates:
Biagio J. DiStefano (315) 366-2381; Fax: (315) 366-2739
Law Clerk: Edward M. Kane (315) 366-2393
Secretary: Linda Mulford
Dennis K. McDermott (315) 366-2360; Fax: (315) 366-2722
Law Clerk: Elizabeth J. Worth (315) 366-2437
Secretary: Judith A. Blair
Chief Clerk: Deborah A. Samoyedny (315) 366-2392

COUNTY COURT
Courthouse, Bldg. 3, 138 N. Court St., P.O. Box 545,
Wampsville 13163-0545
(315) 366-2266; Fax: (315) 366-2539

Judges:
Biagio J. DiStefano (315) 366-2381; Fax: (315) 366-2828
Law Clerk: Edward M. Kane (315) 366-2393
Secretary: Linda Mulford
Dennis K. McDermott (315) 366-2360; Fax: (315) 366-2539
Law Clerk: Elizabeth J. Worth (315) 366-2437
Secretary: Judith A. Blair
Chief Clerk: Marianne Kincaid (315) 366-2267

FAMILY COURT
Courthouse, Bldg. 3, 138 N. Court St., P.O. Box 607,
Wampsville 13163-0607
(315) 366-2291; Fax: (315) 366-2828

Judges:
Biagio J. DiStefano (315) 366-2381; Fax: (315) 366-2828
Law Clerk: Edward M. Kane (315) 366-2393
Secretary: Linda Mulford
Dennis K. McDermott (315) 366-2360; Fax: (315) 366-2722
Law Clerk: Elizabeth J. Worth (315) 366-2437
Secretary: Judith A. Blair (315) 366-2360
Chief Clerk: Cheryl A. Collins (315) 366-2391
Deputy Chief Clerk: Karen N. McKie (315) 366-2563
Support Magistrate: Todd Dexter
(315) 366-2411; Fax: (315) 366-2828

COUNTY OFFICIALS

County Atty.: S. John Campanie
P.O. Box 635, Wampsville 13163-0635 (315) 366-2203
E-mail: john.campanie@co.madison.ny.us
D.A.: William G. Gabor
138 N. Court St., Bldg. 2, P.O. Box 578,
Wampsville 13163-0578 (315) 366-2236
E-mail: william.gabor@co.madison.ny.us
County Clerk: Kenneth J. Kunkel, Jr.
138 N. Court St., Bldg. 4, P.O. Box 668,
Wampsville 13163-0668 (315) 366-2261
E-mail: ken.kunkel@co.madison.ny.us
Internet:
www.madisoncounty.org/county_clerks/ccmain.htm
Chairman, Bd. of Supervisors: John Becker
138 N. Court St., Bldg. 4, P.O. Box 635,
Wampsville 13163-0063 (315) 366-2201
E-mail: john.becker@co.madison.ny.us
County Treasurer: *Cindy J. Edick
138 N. Court St., Bldg. 4, P.O. Box 665,
Wampsville 13163-0665 (315) 366-2371
Sheriff: Allen Riley
County Correctional Facility, Bldg. 7, P.O. Box 16,
Wampsville 13163-0016
(315) 366-2318; Sheriff: (315) 366-2318, Ext. 7;
Fax: (315) 366-2590
Internet: www.madisoncountysheriff.us
Jail: 138 North Court St., Bldg. 7, P.O. Box 16,
Wampsville 13163 (315) 366-2289; Fax: (315) 366-2590
E-mail: timothy.flynn@co.madison.ny.us
Atty. Visitation: Daily, 24 hrs., except
11 A.M.-12:30 P.M. & 3:30-5 P.M.

MONROE COUNTY

Rochester, County Seat

SUPREME COURT
545 Hall of Justice, 99 Exchange Blvd.,
Rochester 14614-2184
(585) 428-2020; Fax: (585) 428-2190

Chief Clerk: James L. Hendricks (585) 428-5001
E-mail: jhendric@courts.state.ny.us
Deputy Chief Clerk: Connie R. Roselli
(585) 428-2781; Fax: (585) 428-2190

***Pending November 2010 Election Results**

Monroe County—Cont'd

SURROGATE'S COURT
Hall of Justice, Room 541, Rochester 14614-2186
(585) 428-5200

Surrogate: Edmund A. Calvaruso
(585) 428-2482; Fax: (585) 428-2791
E-mail: ecalvaru@courts.state.ny.us

Chief Court Clerk: Mark L. Annunziata (585) 428-3491

Deputy Chief Clerk: Sarah T. Sennett
(585) 428-1779; Fax: (212) 295-4922
E-mail: ssennett@courts.state.ny.us

Court Attys.:
Christopher T. Krutell (585) 428-1803
E-mail: ckrutell@courts.state.ny.us
Margaret J. Lavery (585) 428-5202
E-mail: mlavery@courts.state.ny.us

Principal Law Clerk: Vincent Dinolfo (585) 428-3490
E-mail: vdinolfo@courts.state.ny.us

COUNTY COURT
545 Hall of Justice, 99 Exchange Blvd.,
Rochester 14614-2184
(585) 428-2331; Fax: (585) 428-2190

Judges:
Patricia D. Marks (Supervising), 213 Hall of Justice
(585) 428-5276; Fax: (585) 784-4226
John L. DeMarco, 209 Hall of Justice
(585) 425-2452; Fax: (585) 784-4217
Frank P. Geraci, Jr., 224 Hall of Justice
(585) 428-4315; Fax: (585) 784-4210
Teresa D. Johnson (Acting), 106 Hall of Justice
(585) 428-2096; Fax: (585) 428-4265
*Richard A. Keenan, 214 Hall of Justice
(585) 428-1912; Fax: (585) 784-4212
Stephen T. Miller (Acting), 113 Hall of Justice
(585) 428-2470; Fax: (585) 428-2730
E-mail: stmiller@courts.state.ny.us
John R. Schwartz (Acting)
(585) 428-2450; Fax: (585) 428-2737
E-mail: jschwart@courts.state.ny.us
*Kelly C. Wolford, 414 Hall of Justice
(585) 428-4483; Fax: (585) 428-4482

Chief Clerk: James L. Hendricks
(585) 428-1903; Fax: (585) 428-2190
E-mail: jhendric@courts.state.ny.us

Deputy Chief Court Clerk: Connie Roselli
(585) 428-2781; Fax: (585) 428-2190

FAMILY COURT
Hall of Justice, 3rd Floor, 99 Exchange Blvd.,
Rochester 14614-2187
(585) 428-5429; Fax: (585) 428-2597
Internet: www.nycourts.gov

Supervising Judge: Craig J. Doran
Ontario County Courthouse, 27 N. Main St.,
Canandaigua 14424 (585) 396-4479; Fax: (585) 396-4580
E-mail: cdoran @courts.state.ny.us

Judges:
Gail A. Donofrio (585) 428-5597; Fax: (585) 428-2597
Patricia E. Gallaher (585) 428-2049; Fax: (585) 428-2597
E-mail: pgallahe@courts.state.ny.us
Joan S. Kohout (585) 428-5486; Fax: (585) 784-4230
Joseph G. Nesser (585) 428-1904; Fax: (585) 784-4228
*John J. Rivoli (585) 428-2227; Fax: (585) 428-2597
Dandrea Lynn Ruhlmann
(585) 428-5488; Fax: (585) 428-1807
Kelly C. Wolford (Acting)
(585) 428-4483; Fax: (585) 428-4482

Court Atty. Referee: Julie Anne Gordon
(585) 428-1791; Fax: (585) 784-4223

Court Atty.: Thomas W. Polito
(585) 428-1791; Fax: (585) 784-4223

Chief Clerk: Ronald W. Pawelczak
(585) 428-2002; Fax: (585) 530-3285
E-mail: rpawelcz@courts.state.ny.us

***Pending November 2010 Election Results**

Deputy Chief Clerk: Loreen Nash
(585) 428-2001; Fax: (585) 530-3285
E-mail: lnash@courts.state.ny.us

Support Magistrates:
Margaret M. Boldt (585) 428-3512; Fax: (585) 428-1953
Diana M. Irizarry (585) 428-4515; Fax: (585) 428-1953
Linda Lohner-Pilato (585) 428-2663; Fax: (585) 428-1953
Deborah K. Owlett (585) 428-1838; Fax: (585) 428-1953
Michael G. Rao (585) 428-4516; Fax: (585) 428-1953

Judicial Hearing Officers:
Sidney T. Farber (585) 428-5787; Fax: (585) 784-4224
Ann E. Pfeiffer (585) 428-5787; Fax: (585) 784-4224

COUNTY OFFICIALS

County Atty.: William K. Taylor, 307 County Office Bldg., 39 W. Main St., Rochester 14614 (585) 753-1401

D.A.: Michael C. Green, 47 S. Fitzhugh St., Rochester 14614 (585) 753-4780; Fax: (585) 753-4692

County Clerk: Cheryl Dinolfo, 101 County Office Bldg., 39 W. Main St., Rochester 14614
(585) 753-1600; Fax: (585) 753-1624

Controller: Anthony Feroce, 402 County Office Bldg., 36 W. Main St., Rochester 14614
(585) 753-1170; Fax: (585) 753-1196

County Executive: Maggie Brooks, 110 County Office Bldg., 39 W. Main St., Rochester 14614
(585) 753-1000; Fax: (585) 753-1014

Law Librarians:
David Voisinet, Appellate Div. Law Library, 50 East Ave., Suite 100, Rochester 14604 (585) 530-3250
Timothy Hunt, 525 Hall of Justice, 99 Exchange Blvd., Rochester 14614 (585) 428-1854

Sheriff: Patrick M. O'Flynn
130 S. Plymouth Ave., Rochester 14614
(585) 753-4178; Fax: (585) 753-4524
Sheriff: (585) 753-4178; Fax: (585) 753-4049
E-mail: sheriff@monroesheriffny.org
Internet: www.monroecountysheriff.info

Jail: 130 Plymouth Ave., S., Rochester 14614
(585) 753-4055; Fax: (585) 753-4051
Internet: htt/://monroecountysheriff.info
Atty. Visitation: Any time

MONTGOMERY COUNTY

Fonda, County Seat

SUPREME COURT
Courthouse, Rte. 30A, 58 Broadway, P.O. Box 1500,
Fonda 12068
(518) 853-4516; Fax: (518) 853-3596

Chief Clerk: Timothy J. Riley

Law Clerk: Charles M. Clark (518) 853-8102

SURROGATE'S COURT
New Courthouse, Room 50, 58 Broadway,
P.O. Box 1500, Fonda 12068-1500
(518) 853-8108; Fax: (518) 853-8230

Surrogate: Guy P. Tomlinson
(518) 853-8108; Fax: (518) 853-8230

Chief Clerk: Ella L. Bowerman (518) 853-8204
E-mail: ebowerma@courts.state.ny.us

Law Asst.: Donna M. Ross (518) 853-8107

COUNTY COURT
Courthouse, Rte. 30A, 58 Broadway, P.O. Box 1500,
Fonda 12068-1500
(518) 853-3834; Fax: (518) 853-8396

Judge: Felix J. Catena (518) 853-3834; Fax: (518) 853-8396

Chief Clerk: Timothy J. Riley
(518) 853-4516; Fax: (518) 853-3596

FAMILY COURT
Courthouse, 58 Broadway, Rt. 30A, P.O. Box 1500,
Fonda 12068-1500
(518) 853-8133; Fax: (518) 853-8148

Judge: Philip V. Cortese (518) 853-8135; Fax: (518) 853-8148

Chief Clerk: Donna Caravella

Support Magistrate: Kathleen Jennings

Court Atty.: Rebecca A. Slezak

Montgomery County—Cont'd

COUNTY OFFICIALS

County Atty.: Douglas E. Landon, 3 Market St., Amsterdam 12010 (518) 843-1300; Fax: (518) 842-5331

D.A.: James E. Conboy, Courthouse, 58 Broadway, P.O. Box 1500, Fonda 12068-1500 (518) 853-8250; Fax: (518) 853-8212

County Clerk: *Helen A. Bartone, County Office Bldg., 64 Broadway , Rt. 30A, P.O. Box 1500, Fonda 12068 (518) 853-8111; Fax: (518) 853-8171

Treasurer: Shawn J. Bowerman, County Annex, 20 Park St., P.O. Box 1500, Fonda 12068-1500 (518) 853-8175; Fax: (518) 853-8344

Law Library: ,Courthouse, 58 Broadway, Rt. 30A, P.O. Box 1500, Fonda 12068-1500 (518) 853-8518

Sheriff: *Michael J. Amato, Sheriff's Office, 200 Clark Dr., P.O. Box 432, Fultonville 12072
Switchboard: (518) 853-5500; Civil: (518) 853-5515;
Sheriff: (518) 853-5533; Fax: (518) 853-4096

Jail: 200 Clark Dr., P.O. Box 432, Fultonville 12072 (518) 853-5555; Fax: (518) 853-4685
Atty. Visitation: Daily, 8:30-11 A.M.; 12:30-3:30 P.M.; 5-10 P.M.

NASSAU COUNTY

Mineola, County Seat

SUPREME COURT
Supreme Court Bldg., 100 Supreme Court Dr., Mineola 11501
(516) 571-2903; Calendar: (516) 571-3511;
Ex-Parte: (516) 571-3252; Matrimonial: (516) 571-0025;
Fax: (516) 571-1575

Matrimonial Center—Supreme Court, 400 County Seat Dr., Mineola 11501

Chief Clerk, Supreme Ct.: Kathryn D. Hopkins (516) 571-2904; Fax: (516) 571-1575

Deputy Chief Clerk: Cheryl Davis (516) 571-3895

Court Clerk Specialist: William B. Harkins (516) 571-2906; Fax: (516) 571-1427

Chief Court Atty.: John L. Hiller (516) 571-2777

SURROGATE'S COURT
262 Old Country Rd., Mineola 11501
(516) 571-2082; Fax: (516) 571-2997

Surrogate: *John B. Riordan
(516) 571-2040; Fax: (516) 571-2997
E-mail: jriordan@courts.state.ny.us
Secretary: Karen E. Serkes

Chief Clerk: Vacancy at Press Time (516) 571-2082

Principal Court Atty.-Referee: Vacancy at Press Time (516) 571-2042

Deputy Chief Clerk IV: Michael J. Murphy (516) 571-2045

Court Clerk Specialist: Vacancy at Press Time (516) 571-2082

Court Atty.-Referees: (516) 571-2042
Sally Donohue
Gail B. Singer
Lori Sullivan
Anne E. Tozier
Nomi Zomick

Chief Court Atty.: Andrew L. Martin (516) 571-2042

Accounting:
Susan Terrano (516) 571-2222
Grace Witte (516) 571-2223

Small Estates: Andrea Rothstein (516) 571-3492

Administration: Vacancy at Press Time (516) 571-3493

Adoption: Deborah Vintaloro (516) 571-3487

Calendar:
Jillian Howard (516) 571-2224
Kathy Moran (516) 571-2709

Certificates:
Tammar Goodwin (516) 571-3482
Vacancy at Press Time (516) 571-2084

Computer: William Callaghan (516) 571-2984

Document Room: Gladys Taylor (516) 571-2086

Indexing: Vacancy at Press Time (516) 571-2085

Guardianship:
Louise Kuchynskas (516) 571-2293
Ellen Mauro (516) 571-1866

Probate:
Rosemarie Hacsi (516) 571-3490
Yolanda Mulholland (516) 571-3486
Denise Pipolo (516) 571-5072

Probate Clerk: James McDerby (516) 571-2220

Miscellaneous: Vacancy at Press Time (516) 571-2221

Index: Lisa Moore (516) 571-2262

Microfilm: Doris Merchant (516) 571-2263

COUNTY COURT
County Courthouse, 262 Old Country Rd., Mineola 11501
(516) 571-2801; Fax: (516) 571-2160

West Wing, 252 Old Country Rd., Mineola 11501

Supervising Judge, Criminal Term: William C. Donnino (Court of Claims and Acting Justice, Supreme Court)
(516) 571-2797; Fax: (516) 571-1485
E-mail: wdonnino@courts.state.ny.us
Law Clerks:
Susan Katz Richman
E-mail: srichman@courts.state.ny.us
Michael Tarbutton
E-mail: mtarbutt@courts.state.ny.us
Secretary: Renee Nash
E-mail: rnash@courts.state.ny.us

Judges:

David J. Ayres (Acting Supreme Court Justice)
West Wing, 252 Old Country Rd.,
(516) 571-3833; Fax: (516) 571-2137
E-mail: dayres@courts.state.ny.us
Law Clerk: Judith Gann; E-mail: jgann@courts.state.ny.us
Secretary: Jane Volz; E-mail: jvolz@courts.state.ny.us

Meryl J. Berkowitz (Acting Supreme Court Justice)
(516) 571-2241; Fax: (516) 571-2078
E-mail: mberkowi@courts.state.ny.us
Law Clerk: Jennifer Feingold
E-mail: jfeingol@courts.state.ny.us
Secretary: Jacqueline Parise
E-mail: jparise@courts.state.ny.us

Joseph C. Calabrese (Acting Supreme Court Justice)
(516) 571-2065; Fax: (516) 571-0566
E-mail: jcalabre@courts.state.ny.us
Law Clerk: Charles J. Weinschreider
E-mail: cweinsch@courts.state.ny.us
Secretary: Joan Laserna
E-mail: jlaserna@courts.state.ny.us

Jerald S. Carter (Acting Supreme Court Justice)
(516) 571-3563; Fax: (516) 571-0565
E-mail: jscarter@courts.state.ny.us
Law Secretary: Patricia Harrington
E-mail: pharring@courts.state.ny.us
Secretary: Charmaine Cooper
E-mail: ccooper@courts.state.ny.us

John Michael Galasso (Acting Supreme Court Justice)
100 Supreme Court Dr., Mineola 11501
(516) 571-2613; Fax: (516) 571-2164
E-mail: jgalasso@courts.state.ny.us
Law Clerk: Joyce M. Andren
E-mail: jandren@courts.state.ny.us
Secretary: Nicole T. Troncone
E-mail: ntroncone@courts.state.ny.us

Philip M. Grella
(Court of Claims and Acting Justice, Supreme Court)
(516) 571-1488; Fax: (516) 571-2642

Alan L. Honorof (Acting Judge; Court of Claims Judge and Acting Sup. Ct. Justice)
(516) 571-3423; Fax: (516) 571-1849
E-mail: ahonorof@courts.state.ny.us
Law Clerk: Howard Sturim
E-mail: hsturim@courts.state.ny.us
Secretary: Patricia Riehl; E-mail: priehl@courts.state.ny.us

*Pending November 2010 Election Results

Judges, Nassau County Court—Cont'd
Steven M. Jaeger (Acting Justice, Supreme Court)
(516) 571-3378; Fax: (516) 571-3220
E-mail: sjaeger@courts.state.ny.us
Law Clerk: Helen Voutsinas
E-mail: hvoutsin@courts.state.ny.us
Secretary: Luisa Lezaja
E-mail: llezaja@courts.state.ny.us
John L. Kase (Acting Supreme Court Justice)
(516) 571-2628; Fax: (516) 571-6300
E-mail: jkase@courts.state.ny.us
Law Clerk: James Tini; E-mail: jtini@courts.state.ny.us
Secretary: Laureen DeLay
E-mail: ldelay@courts.state.ny.us
James P. McCormack (Acting Supreme Court Justice)
(516) 571-2768; Fax: (516) 571-1093
E-mail: jmccorma@courts.state.ny.us
Law Clerk: Cheryl Bartow
E-mail: cbartow@courts.state.ny.us
Secretary: Melissa Lopez
E-mail: mklopez@courts.state.ny.us
*Daniel R. Palmieri (Acting Supreme Court Justice)
100 Supreme Court Dr., Mineola 11501
(516) 571-2878; Fax: (516) 571-0129
E-mail: dpalmier@courts.state.ny.us
Law Clerk: Philip C. Weis
E-mail: pweis@courts.state.ny.us
Secretary: Carol Peluso
E-mail: cpeluso@courts.state.ny.us
George R. Peck (Acting Supreme Court Justice)
(516) 571-3765; Fax: (516) 571-3256
E-mail: gpeck@courts.state.ny.us
Law Clerk: Frank O'Regan
E-mail: foregan@courts.state.ny.us
Secretary: Sharron Horod
E-mail: shorod@courts.state.ny.us
Christopher G. Quinn (Acting Supreme Court Justice & Supervising Judge, Nassau County District Court)
99 Main St., Hempstead 11550
(516) 572-2166; Fax: (516) 572-2457
E-mail: cgquinn@courts.state.ny.us
Law Clerk: Virginia Clavin
E-mail: vclavin@courts.state.ny.us
Secretary: Carmen Culhane
E-mail: cculhane@courts.state.ny.us
Tammy S. Robbins (Acting Supreme Court Justice)
West Wing, 252 Old Country Rd.
(516) 571-3259; Fax: (516) 571-1349
E-mail: trobbins@courts.state.ny.us
Law Clerk: Vacancy at Press Time
Secretary: Gladiz DiGangi
E-mail: gdigangi@courts.state.ny.us
Norman St. George (Acting Supreme Court Justice)
(516) 571-3560; Fax: (516) 571-1600
E-mail: nstgeorg@courts.state.ny.us
Law Clerk: Eileen Daly-Sapraicone
E-mail: edalysap@courts.state.ny.us
Secretary: Jeanette Milone
E-mail: jmilone@courts.state.ny.us
David P. Sullivan (Acting Supreme Court Justice & Supervising Judge, Village Courts, Nassau County)
West Wing (516) 571-2408; Fax: (516) 571-1491
E-mail: dpsulliv@courts.state.ny.us
Law Clerk: Lawrence Schaeffer
E-mail: lschaeff@courts.state.ny.us
Secretary: Lorraine Ciesinski
E-mail: lciesins@courts.state.ny.us

Chief Clerk: Kathryn A. Cunningham
(516) 571-2801; Fax: (516) 571-2160
E-mail: kacunning@courts.state.ny.us

Deputy Chief Clerk: Peter Knoepffler
(516) 571-1826; Fax: (516) 571-2160
E-mail: pknoepff@courts.state.ny.us

Court Clerk Specialist: Donald Vetter
(516) 571-0866; Fax: (516) 571-2160
E-mail: dvetter@courts.state.ny.us

Chief Court Atty.: Robert Bogle
(516) 571-2070; Fax: (516) 571-0416
E-mail: rbogle@courts.state.ny.us

***Pending November 2010 Election Results**

Assoc. Law Attys.:
Bruce Adams (516) 571-2070; Fax: (516) 571-0416
E-mail: badams@courts.state.ny.us
Christopher Hoefenkrieg
(516) 571-2070; Fax: (516) 571-0416
E-mail: choefenk@courts.state.ny.us
Denise Miller (516) 571-2070; Fax: (516) 571-0416
E-mail: dmiller@courts.state.ny.us

FAMILY COURT
1200 Old Country Rd., Westbury 11590
(516) 571-9055; Fax: (516) 571-9599;
Law Department: (516) 571-9038;
Probation Information: (516) 571-9176

Judge: Frank Dikranis (516) 571-9055; Fax: (516) 571-9335

Supervising Judge: Hope S. Zimmerman
Matrimonial Center, 400 County Seat Dr.,
Mineola 11501 (516) 571-9005; Fax: (516) 571-9201
Acting Supreme Court Justice

Judges:
Stacy D. Bennett (516) 571-9362; Fax: (516) 571-9392
Edmund M. Dane (516) 571-9104; Fax: (516) 571-9391
Julianne S. Eisman (516) 571-9015; Fax: (516) 571-9399
Ellen Greenberg (516) 571-9154; Fax: (516) 571-9406
Robin Kent (516) 571-9022; Fax: (516) 571-9393
Conrad D. Singer (516) 571-9010; Fax: (516) 571-9395

Court Attys./Referees:
Patricia E. Doyle (516) 571-9038; Fax: (516) 571-9158
Robert LoPresti (516) 571-9038; Fax: (516) 571-9043
Dorothy A. Phillips (516) 571-9038; Fax: (516) 571-9043
Christopher Pizzolo (516) 571-9038; Fax: (516) 571-9043

Support Magistrates:
Patricia Bannon (516) 571-9048; Fax: (516) 571-9404
Penelope B. Cahn (516) 571-9054; Fax: (516) 571-9366
Diane M. Dwyer (516) 571-9055; Fax: (516) 571-9400
Tejindar S. Kahlon (516) 571-9055; Fax: (516) 571-9403
Neil T. Miller (516) 571-9055; Fax: (516) 571-9402
Kathleen Watson (516) 571-9055; Fax: (516) 571-9409

Chief Clerk: Rosalie Fitzgerald
(516) 571-9030; Fax: (516) 571-9335

Deputy Chief Clerk: John M. Coppola
(516) 571-9035; Fax: (516) 571-9335

Chief Court Atty.: Jeffrey M. Carpenter
(516) 571-9038; Fax: (516) 571-9043

COUNTY OFFICIALS

County Atty.: John Ciampoli, Executive Bldg.,
One West St., Mineola 11501
(516) 571-3056; Fax: (516) 571-6684

D.A.: Kathleen M. Rice, County Courthouse,
262 Old Country Rd., Mineola 11501
(516) 571-2994; Fax: (516) 571-5065

County Clerk: Maureen C. O'Connell, County Office Bldg.,
240 Old Country Rd., Mineola 11501
(516) 571-2664; Fax: (516) 742-4099

County Executive: Edward P. Mangano
County Executive Bldg., 1550 Franklin Ave.,
Mineola 11501 (516) 571-3131; Fax: (516) 571-4000

Comptroller: George Maragos, County Office Bldg.,
240 Old Country Rd., Mineola 11501 (516) 571-2386

County Treasurer: John A. Mastromarino
240 Old Country Rd., Mineola 11501-4248
(516) 571-2090; Fax: (516) 571-1528

Assessor: Thaddeus J. Jankowski, Jr.
County Office Bldg., 4th Floor, 240 Old Country Rd.,
Mineola 11501 (516) 571-2311; Fax: (516) 571-3549

Law Librarian: Jean-Paul Vivian
Supreme Court Law Library, 100 Supreme Court Dr.,
Mineola 11501 (516) 571-3883; Fax: (516) 571-0752

Sheriff: Michael J. Sposato (Acting)
100 Carman Ave., East Meadow 11554
(516) 572-4100; Civil Div.: (516) 571-2113;
Civil Enforcement Div. Fax: (516) 571-5086
Internet: www.nassaucountyny.gov

Correctional Center: 100 Carman Ave., East Meadow 11554
(516) 572-4101; Fax: (516) 572-4300
Atty. Visitation: Mon.,Tues. and Wed., 8 A.M.-4 P.M.;
Thurs., Noon-8 P.M.; Fri., 8 A.M.-8 P.M.

Nassau County Officials—Cont'd

Under Sheriff/Acting Sheriff: Michael J. Sposato (516) 572-4100

Police Headquarters
1490 Franklin Ave., Mineola 11501
(516) 573-7000; Detention Desk: (516) 573-7668; Missing persons: (516) 573-7858

1st Precinct
900 Merrick Rd., Baldwin 11510 (516) 573-6100

2nd Precinct
7700 Jericho Tpke., Woodbury 11797
(516) 573-6200; Accident Clerk: (516) 573-6236

3rd Precinct
214 Hillside Ave., Williston Park 11596 (516) 573-6300

4th Precinct
1699 Broadway, Hewlett 11557 (516) 573-6400

5th Precinct
1655 Dutch Broadway, Elmont 11003 (516) 573-6500

6th Precinct
100 Community Dr., Manhasset 11030 (516) 573-6600

7th Precinct
3636 Merrick Rd., Seaford 11783 (516) 573-6700

8th Precinct
286 Wantagh Ave., Levittown 11756 (516) 573-6800

NEW YORK COUNTY

New York, County Seat

SUPREME COURT

Civil Term
60 Centre St., N.Y.C. 10007-1474
(646) 386-3600; Juror Information: (646) 386-5987
80 Centre St., N.Y.C. 10013
(646) 386-3685
71 Thomas St., N.Y.C. 10013
(646) 386-3770

County Clerk and Clerk of the Supreme Court: Norman Goodman (646) 386-5956

Chief Deputy County Clerk: James A. Rossetti (646) 386-5956

Deputy County Clerk, Jurors Division: Pearl Hampton (646) 386-5991

Counsel to County Clerk: Phyllis M. Mingione (646) 386-5956

Secretary to County Clerk: Linda Arnone (646) 386-5956

Chief Clerk, Jurors Div.: Vincent Homenick (646) 386-5990

Chief Clerk & Executive Officer, Civil Branch: John F. Werner (646) 386-3001

First Dep. Chief Clerk: Robert C. Meade (646) 386-3005

Chief Court Atty.: Lawrence H. Birnbaum (646) 386-3660

Deputy Chief Court Atty.: Linell P. Hunter (646) 386-3645

Principal Court Attys.:
Charles Brieant (646) 386-3043
Roy Bromberg (646) 386-3629
Kathleen Bunyar (646) 386-3646
William Epstein (646) 386-3654
Mary Chris Greene (646) 386-3640
Kathy Kass (646) 386-3655
Nancy Stearns (646) 386-3663
June Turk (646) 386-3612

Prinicipal Law Librarian: Julie Gick (646) 386-3670

Office of Referees: (646) 386-3028

Secretary to Chief Clerk: Doris Benoff (646) 386-3001

IAS Trial Support Office Clerk-In-Charge: Gloria Smyth-Godinger (646) 386-3160, Ext. 63155

Ex Parte Motions Clerk-In-Charge: Kenneth Monahan (646) 386-3125

Clerk-in-Charge, Guardianship & Fiduciary Support Office: Scott Singer (646) 386-3328

Fiduciary Clerk: Steven Flatow (646) 386-3328

Matrimonial Support Office Clerk-In-Charge: James McElligott (646) 386-3010

Annex Office Clerks-In-Charge:
Susan Horowitz (646) 386-3685
Martin McCormack
71 Thomas St., N.Y.C. 10013-3821 (646) 386-3770
Clerks of Special and Trial Term Parts rotate

Principal Court Reporter: Ross Upshaw (646) 386-3052

Deputy Principal Court Reporter: Mary Massa (646) 386-3096

Clerk's Offices Litigated Motions: Jeffrey Carucci
Chief Clerk and Calendar Information: (646) 386-3030

Condemnation Certiorari: Neil Frank
Certiorari Proceedings: (646) 386-3648

Ex Parte: Kenneth Monahan, Room 315 (646) 386-3125

Matrimonial Support Office: James McElligott, Room 311
Motions and Uncontested Matrimonials: (646) 386-3010

Guardianship and Fiduciary Support Office:
Scott Singer, Room 148
Accounting, Guardianships and Conservatorships: (646) 386-3328

IAS Trial Support: Gloria Smith-Godinger
Office and Calendar Information: (646) 386-3155; Interpreters: (646) 386-3155

Law Department:
Lawrence Birnbaum
Chief Court Attorney: (646) 386-3660;
Deputy Chief Court Attorney: (646) 386-3645
Linell Hunter
Chief Court Atty.: (646) 386-3660;
Deputy Chief Court Atty.: (646) 386-3645

Library: Julie Gick, Prin. Law Librarian: (646) 386-3670

Reception Desks:
Main Fl.: (646) 386-3139; 5th Fl., E.: (646) 386-3130; 6th Fl., W.: (646) 386-3137

Court Security: Maj. Gerard Fennell (646) 386-3130

Subpeonaed Records Room: Irene Flahive (646) 386-3161

Supportive Services Court Reporters: Ross Upshaw
Prin. Court Reporter: (646) 386-3050

Public Access Law Library:
80 Centre St., Room 468, N.Y.C. 10007
(800) COURT-NY: (800) 268-7869; (646) 386-3715

Help Center: Nelson Capote (646) 386-3025

Commercial Division Support Office: Pablo Rivera (646) 386-3020

SUPREME COURT

Criminal Term
100 Centre St., N.Y.C. 10013
(646) 386-4000; Fax: (212) 374-3177
111 Centre St., N.Y.C. 10013

Chief Clerk: Barry Clarke
(646) 386-3900; Fax: (212) 374-3177
E-mail: bclarke@courts.state.ny.us

First Deputy Chief Clerk: Conrad Martin (646) 386-3925
E-mail: cmartin@courts.state.ny.us

Court Clerk Specialist: William Hall (646) 386-4300, 02

Chief Law Librarian: David Badertscher (646) 386-3891
E-mail: dbadertscher@courts.state.ny.us

Chief Court Reporter: Frank Rizzo, 111 Centre St.
(646) 386-4400; E-mail: frizzo@courts.state.ny.us

Personnel: Rose Halloran (646) 386-3930
E-mail: rhalloran@courts.state.ny.us

Appeals: James Motylenski (646) 386-3981
E-mail: jmotylenski@courts.state.ny.us

Calendar Information: Annette Gregg-Little
(646) 386-3903; E-mail: agregg-l@courts.state.ny.us

Case Information/General Clerk's Office:
Lawrence Salvato (646) 386-4192

Computer/Network Office: Ted McAlister
(646) 386-3941; E-mail: tmcalister@courts.state.ny.us

Interpreters: Cecilia Solano (646) 386-4141
E-mail: csolano@courts.state.ny.us

Supreme Ct., Crim. Term, New York County—Cont'd

Correspondence/Motion Support: Mary Price
(646) 386-3860; E-mail: mprice@courts.state.ny.us

Court Officer Supervisors:
Maj. Gerard Duffy (646) 386-4100
Robert Garbarino (646) 386-4444
Capt. James Whitehead (646) 386-4111

Supplies/Inventory/ Purchasing: Gary Leigh
(646) 386-3922; E-mail: gleigh@courts.state.ny.us

SURROGATE'S COURT
31 Chambers St., Room 303, N.Y.C. 10007
(646) 386-5000; Fax: (212) 374-3250
Internet:
www.courts.state.ny.us/courts/nyc/surrogates/

Surrogates:
Nora S. Anderson
Principal Law Clerk: Marcia Goffin
Kristin Booth Glen, Room 502 (646) 386-5100
Principal Law Clerk: Janet S. Mishkin
Secretary: Anne R. Neary

Chief Clerk and Clerk of Court: Jane Passenant
(646) 386-5352; General/Personnel Fax: (212) 374-3250

Deputy Chief Clerk of Court: Jana Cohn
(646) 386-5352; General/Personnel Fax: (212) 374-3250

Chief of Law Division: Dorothy F. Henderson, Room 401
(646) 386-5800

Principal Court Attys.: Room 401 (646) 386-5800
Jessica Amelar
Ann Silberman
Gunwani Singh
Del Teague

Senior Court Attys.:
Mary Santamarina, Room 401 (646) 386-5800
Ellen Winner, Room 401 (646) 386-5800

Court Atty.-Referees: Room 401 (646) 386-5800
Janice S. Altizio
Meena I. De
Jay Laubscher
Juliette C. Sears

Accounting Dept. Supervisor: Doreen Quinn, Room 508
(646) 386-5002

Administration Dept. Supervisor: Larry Wolfson
Room 505 (646) 386-5005

Cashier & Certification Supervisor: Patrick Kearney
Room 506 (646) 386-5006

Guardian Dept. & Adoption Supervisor: Anabel Sorrentino
Room 301 (346) 386-5003

Law Dept.—Clerical Staff:
Doris Barlowe, Room 401
(646) 386-5800; Fax (Law Dept. matters): (212) 374-7894
Margaret Chavero, Room 401 (646) 386-5801

Law Library: Richard Parenti, Room 401 (646) 386-5815

Miscellaneous Dept. Supervisor: Alicia Weissmeier
Room 507 (646) 386-5001;
Fax (for calendar matters): (212) 748-5771

Probate Dept. Supervisor: Timothy Ameres, Room 504
(646) 386-5004

Archivist: Kimberly Sulik, Room 402 (646) 386-5090

Records Room Supervisor: Omar Colon, Room 402
(646) 386-5090

FAMILY COURT
See Family Court, N.Y.C., pp. 98-99

COUNTY OFFICIALS

D.A.: Cyrus R. Vance, Jr., 1 Hogan Pl., N.Y.C. 10013
(212) 335-9000

County Clerk: Norman Goodman,
60 Centre St., Room 161, N.Y.C. 10007 (646) 386-5955

Comptroller: John Liu, Municipal Bldg., Room 530,
1 Centre St., N.Y.C. 10007
(212) 669-3500; Fax: (212) 669-2707

Commissioner of Finance: David M. Frankel
1 Centre St., Suite 500, N.Y.C. 10007 (212) 669-4855

Public Administrator: Ethel J. Griffin
31 Chambers St., Room 311, N.Y.C. 10007 (212) 788-8430

Law Librarian: Theodore Pollack
New York Public Access Law Library, 80 Centre St., Room 468, N.Y.C. 10013
(646) 386-3715; 800-COURTNY:

Sheriff: Vacancy at Press Time
66 John St., Room 608, N.Y.C. 10038 (212) 487-8002

Under Sheriff: Joseph Fucito

NIAGARA COUNTY
Lockport, County Seat

SUPREME COURT
775 3rd St., Niagara Falls 14302-1710
(716) 278-1800; Fax: (716) 278-1809

Chief Clerk: Mary Ellen Florian (716) 278-1800
E-mail: mflorian@courts.state.ny.us

Deputy Chief Clerk: Diane Bell (716) 439-7148
E-mail: dbell@courts.state.ny.us

Clerks:
JoAnne Gazy (716) 278-1804
E-mail: jgazy@courts.state.ny.us
Laurie O'Brien (716) 278-1807
E-mail: llobrien@courts.state.ny.us
Nicole Schug (716) 439-7057
E-mail: nschug@courts.state.ny.us
Cynthia Warren (716) 278-1803
E-mail: cwarren@courts.state.ny.us

SURROGATE'S COURT
Courthouse, 175 Hawley St., Lockport 14094-2758
(716) 439-7130; Fax: (716) 439-7319

Surrogates:
Matthew J. Murphy III
(716) 439-7150; Fax: (716) 439-7157
*Sara Sheldon Sperrazza
(716) 439-7140; Fax: (716) 349-7157
E-mail: ssperraz@courts.state.ny.us

Chief Clerk: Ronald A. Sutton, LL.M. (716) 439-7131
E-mail: rsutton@courts.state.ny.us

Deputy Chief Clerk: Michael C. Veruto (716) 439-7131
E-mail: mveruto@courts.state.ny.us

COUNTY COURT
Courthouse, 175 Hawley St., Lockport 14094-2758
(716) 439-7148; Fax: (716) 439-7157

Judges:
Matthew J. Murphy III
(716) 439-7150; Fax: (716) 439-7328
E-mail: mjmurph2@courts.state.ny.us
*Sara Sheldon Sperrazza
(716) 439-7140; Fax: (716) 439-7149
E-mail: ssperraz@courts.state.ny.us
Confidential Law Clerk: Caroline Wojtaszek
(716) 439-7146

Chief Clerk: Mary Ellen Florian
Angelo A. Del Signore Civic Bldg., 775 Third St., Niagara Falls 14302 (716) 278-1800
E-mail: mflorian@courts.state.ny.us

Clerks:
Joanne Sullivan (718) 439-7287
E-mail: jmsulliv@courts.state.ny.us
Judy A. Vacanti (716) 439-7153
E-mail: jvacanti@courts.state.ny.us

Deputy Chief Clerk: Diane Bell (716) 439-7148
E-mail: dbell@courts.state.ny.us

***Pending November 2010 Election Results**

Niagara County—Cont'd

FAMILY COURT
Courthouse, 175 Hawley St., Lockport 14094-2758
(716) 439-7172; Fax: (716) 439-7170
Angelo A. DelSignore Civic Bldg., 775 3rd St., Niagara Falls 14302
(716) 278-1880; Fax: (716) 278-1877

Judges:
John F. Batt (Lockport) (716) 439-7185
E-mail: jbatt@courts.state.ny.us
David E. Seaman (Niagara Falls) (716) 278-1880
E-mail: dseaman@courts.state.ny.us

Chief Clerk: William F. McCarthy (Lockport) (716) 439-7172
E-mail: wmccarth@courts.state.ny.us

Deputy Chief Clerk: Cathy S. Quattrini (Niagara Falls) (716) 278-1880; E-mail: cquattrini@courts.state.ny.us

Clerks:
Patricia Korzelius (Lockport) (716) 439-7172
E-mail: pkorzeli@courts.state.ny.us
Carol McGovern (Niagara Falls) (716) 278-1880
E-mail: cmcover@courts.state.ny.us
Susan M. O'Brien (Lockport) (716) 439-7180
E-mail: sobrien@courts.state.ny.us

Support Magistrates:
Timothy J. Cooper (Niagara Falls and Lockport) (716) 278-1890; E-mail: tcooper@courts.state.ny.us
Judy L. Johnson (Niagara Falls) (716) 278-1890; E-mail: jljohnson@courts.state.ny.us
Kristie T. Kantor (Lockport) (716) 439-7172; E-mail: kkantor@courts.state.ny.us

COUNTY OFFICIALS

County Atty.: Claude A. Joerg
Courthouse, 175 Hawley St., Lockport 14094-2740
(716) 439-7105, 06; Fax: (716) 439-7114

D.A.: Michael J. Violante
Courthouse, 175 Hawley St., Lockport 14094-2740
(716) 439-7085; Fax: (716) 439-7102

County Clerk: Wayne F. Jagow, Courthouse, 175 Hawley St., P.O. Box 461, Lockport 14095-0461
(716) 439-7022; Fax: (716) 439-7035
E-mail: wayne.jagow@niagaracounty.com

County Treasurer: *Kyle R. Andrews
Cty. Office Bldg., 59 Park Ave., Lockport 14094-2740
(716) 439-7018; Fax: (716) 439-7021

Law Library: Courthouse, 175 Hawley St., Lockport 14095-2758 (716) 439-7145

Sheriff: James R. Voutour
5526 Niagara St. Ext., P.O. Box 496, Lockport 14095-0496
(716) 438-3393; Fax: (716) 438-3302
Sheriff: (716) 438-3370; Fax: (716) 438-3357

Jail: 5526 Niagara St. Ext., P.O. Box 496, Lockport 14095-0496
Central Control: (716) 438-3446;
Lobby Control: (716) 438-3436; Fax: (716) 438-3391
Atty. Visitation: Weekdays, 9-11:30 A.M., 12:30-3:30 P.M., 4-5 P.M. & 6-9 P.M.; Weekends and holidays, by appointment

ONEIDA COUNTY

Utica, County Seat

SUPREME COURT
Courthouse, 200 Elizabeth St., Utica 13501
(315) 266-4200; Fax: (315) 798-6436
Rome Courthouse, 302 N. James St., Rome 13323
(315) 266-4300

Chief Clerk IV: Joseph P. Panella

Court Atty./Referee-Matrimonial Dept.: Aneila Carl (315) 266-4215

Court Clerks:
Etta Dontino (315) 266-4257
Valerie Dousharm (315) 266-4229
Patricia Klar (315) 266-4213
Sandra Myers (315) 266-4226
Laurie Noga (Rome) (315) 266-4305
Therese Soules (315) 793-2323

***Pending November 2010 Election Results**

Integrated Domestic Violence Co-Ordination:
Dawn A. Luce, 200 Elizabeth St., Utica 13501
(315) 266-4228; Fax: (315) 798-6423

SURROGATE'S COURT
Oneida County Office Bldg., 8th Floor, 800 Park Ave., Utica 13501
(315) 266-4550; Fax: (315) 797-9237

Surrogate: Louis P. Gigliotti
E-mail: lgigliot@courts.state.ny.us

Chief Clerk: Kristine K. Pecheone

Deputy Chief Clerk: Carra L. Applebee

Law Clerk: Paul M. Lukin

COUNTY COURT
Courthouse, Elizabeth St., Utica 13501
(315) 266-4203; Fax: (315) 798-6047

Judges:
Barry M. Donalty (315) 266-4321; Fax: (315) 731-3416
Michael L. Dwyer (315) 266-4322; Fax: (315) 798-5848

Chief Clerk IV: Joseph P. Panella (315) 266-4200

Deputy Chief Clerk IV: Kathleen Aiello (315) 266-4200

Assoc. Court Clerk: Jeanne Natale (315) 266-4227

Court Clerks:
Susan Careau (315) 266-4242
Maureen Postiglion (315) 266-4248
Terri Bello Vecchio (315) 266-4250

FAMILY COURT
Oneida County Courthouse, 200 Elizabeth St., Utica 13501
(315) 266-4444; Fax: (315) 798-6404
Courthouse, 301 W. Dominick St., Rome 13440-5196
(315) 266-4500; Fax: (315) 336-3828

Judges:
Randal B. Caldwell (315) 266-4455
Law Clerk: Barbara Hughes (315) 266-4458
Secretary: Amy Lawter
James R. Griffith (315) 266-4460
Law Clerk: Steven R. Fortnam (315) 266-4461
Secretary: Pam Falcone (315) 266-4460
Joan E. Shkane (Rome) (315) 266-4512; Fax: (315) 337-0480
Law Clerk: Jeffrey Tompkins (315) 266-4514
Secretary: Ruth Merchant (315) 266-4512

Chief Clerk: Barbara A. Porta (315) 266-4444

Deputy Chief Clerk: Elizabeth A. Gorski (Rome) (315) 266-4500

Support Magistrates:
Christine Barry (315) 266-4471
Steven W. Haggas (315) 266-4463
Jawwaad A. Rasheed (315) 266-4510

County Attorney Referee: Julia Brouillette (315) 266-4465

COUNTY OFFICIALS

County Atty.: Linda Dillon
Oneida Cty. Ofc. Bldg., 800 Park Ave., Utica 13501
(318) 798-5910; Fax: (315) 798-5603

D.A.: Scott D. McNamara
Oneida Cty. Ofc. Bldg., 800 Park Ave., Utica 13501
(315) 798-5766; Fax: (315) 798-5582

County Clerk: *Sandra J. DePerno
Oneida Cty. Ofc. Bldg., 2nd Floor, 800 Park Ave., Utica 13501 (315) 798-5776

Comptroller: Joseph J. Timpano
Oneida Cty. Ofc. Bldg., 800 Park Ave., Utica 13501
(315) 798-5780; Fax: (315) 798-6415

Commissioner of Finance: Anthony R. Carvelli
Oneida Cty. Ofc. Bldg., 800 Park Ave., Utica 13501
(315) 798-5750

County Executive: Anthony J. Picente
Oneida County Office Bldg., 800 Park Ave., Utica 13501
(315) 798-5800; Fax: (315) 798-2390

Law Librarian: Paula J. Eannace
NYS Supreme Court Law Library, Courthouse, 235 Elizabeth St., Utica 13501
(315) 798-5703; Fax: (315) 798-6470

Oneida County Officials—Cont'd

Sheriff: *Subject to Election
Law Enforcement Bldg., 6065 Judd Rd., Oriskany 13424 (315) 765-2222; Fax: (315) 765-2205

Correctional Facility: 6075 Judd Rd., Oriskany 13424 (315) 765-2234; Fax: (315) 765-2205
E-mail: ocsd@borg.com
Atty. Visitation: Daily, 7:30 A.M.- 10 P.M.

ONONDAGA COUNTY

Syracuse, County Seat

SUPREME COURT

Courthouse, Room 302, 401 Montgomery St., Syracuse 13202
(315) 671-1030; Fax: (315) 671-1176;
Court Clerk's Office: (315) 671-1030
State Office Bldg., 5th & 8th Floor, 333 E. Washington St., Syracuse 13202
505 S. State St., Room 110, Syracuse 13202

Chief Clerk: Patricia J. Noll
(315) 671-1020; Fax: (315) 671-1191

Deputy Chief Clerk: James E. Makowiec
(315) 671-1020; Fax: (315) 671-1191

Assoc. Court Clerk: George Panuthos, Room 302
(315) 671-1030

Integrated Domestic Violence (IDV) Part: (315) 671-2038

SURROGATE'S COURT

Courthouse, 401 Montgomery St., Syracuse 13202-2173
(315) 671-2098; Fax: (315) 671-1162
Internet: http://surrogate5th.courts.state.ny.us/public

Surrogate: Ava Shapero Raphael

Chief Clerk: Ellen S. Weinstein, Room 209 (315) 671-2108
E-mail: eweinste@courts.state.ny.us

Deputy Chief: Allyn F. Campbell

Law Asst.: Deborah Barrer

COUNTY COURT

Courthouse, 505 S. State St., Syracuse 13202
(315) 671-1020; Fax: (315) 671-1191

Judges:
Anthony F. Aloi (315) 671-1054
Law Clerk: Bonnie Buccina (315) 671-1055
Secretary: Jean Mumford
Joseph E. Fahey (315) 671-1050
Law Clerk: Lisa Garabedian
Secretary: Catherine DiBiase
*William D. Walsh
Criminal Courts Bldg., Suite 370, 505 S. State St., Syracuse 13202 (315) 671-1056; Fax: (315) 671-1188
Law Clerk: Ben Coffin
Secretary: Kathy Dell

Chief Clerk: Patricia J. Noll, Suite 110
(315) 671-1020; Fax: (315) 671-1191

Deputy Chief Clerk: James E. Makowiec, Suite 110

Assoc. Court Clerk: Virginia Murphy, Suite 110

FAMILY COURT

Onondaga County Courthouse, 401 Montgomery St., Syracuse 13202
Information and Records: (315) 671-2000; Fax: (315) 671-1163

Judges:
Michele Pirro Bailey (315) 671-2030; Fax: (315) 671-1168
E-mail: mbailey@courts.state.ny.us
Court Atty.: Margaret Needham (315) 671-2030
E-mail: mneedham@courts.state.ny.us
*Michael L. Hanuszczak
(315) 671-2010; Fax: (315) 671-1166
E-mail: mhanuszc@courts.state.ny.us
Acting Supreme Court Justice
Court Atty.: Janet J. Dougherty (315) 671-2012
E-mail: jjdoughe@courts.state.ny.us
Bryan R. Hedges (315) 671-2040; Fax: (315) 671-1169
E-mail: bhedges@courts.state.ny.us
Court Atty.: William F. Dowling Fax: (315) 671-2042
E-mail: wdowling@courts.state.ny.us
Martha E. Mulroy (315) 671-2050; Fax: (315) 671-1170
E-mail: mmulroy@courts.state.ny.us
Court Atty.: Kimberly A. Pedone (315) 671-2052
E-mail: kapedone@courts.state.ny.us
Secretary: Heide Newbury-Halliday
E-mail: hhallida@courts.state.ny.us
*Martha Walsh Hood, State Office Bldg., 333 E. Washington St., Syracuse 13202 (315) 428-3256
E-mail: mhood@courts.state.ny.us
Acting Supreme Court Justice
Court Atty.: Kurt Sherman (315) 428-3244

Support Magistrates:
Kathryn Z. Davies (315) 671-2027; Fax: (315) 671-1173
E-mail: kdavies@courts.state.ny.us
Patricia L. DeRue (315) 671-2017; Fax: (315) 671-1171
E-mail: pderue@nycourts.gov
James L. Gorman (315) 671-4249; Fax: (315) 671-1194
E-mail: jlgorman@courts.state.ny.us
Susan Hamlin Nasci (315) 671-2019; Fax: (315) 671-1172
E-mail: shnasci@courts.state.ny.us

Court Attys./Referees:
William F. Dowling (315) 671-2042; Fax: (315) 671-1169
E-mail: wdowling@courts.state.ny.us
Gina M. Glover (315) 671-4243; Fax: (315) 671-1193
E-mail: gglover@courts.state.ny.us
Salvatore Pavone (315) 671-2079; Fax: (315) 671-1197
E-mail: spavone@courts.state.ny.us

Chief Clerk: Sherree A. Jackson
(315) 671-2000; Fax: (315) 671-1163
E-mail: sajackso@courts.state.ny.us

Deputy Chief Clerk: Vacancy at Press Time
(315) 671-2062; Fax: (315) 671-1163

COUNTY OFFICIALS

County Atty.: Gordon C. Cuffy
421 Montgomery St., Syracuse 13202
(315) 435-2170; Fax: (315) 435-5729

D.A.: William J. Fitzpatrick
505 S. State St., Syracuse 13202
(315) 435-2470; Fax: (315) 435-3969

County Clerk: M. Ann Ciarpelli
401 Montgomery St., Syracuse 13202
(315) 435-2226; Fax: (315) 435-3455

Comptroller: Robert E. Antonacci II
421 Montgomery St., Syracuse 13202
(315) 435-2130; Fax: (315) 435-2250

Chief Fiscal Officer: James Rowley
421 Montgomery St., Syracuse 13202
(315) 435-3346; Fax: (315) 435-3439

County Executive: Joanie Mahoney
421 Montgomery St., Syracuse 13202
(315) 435-3516; Fax: (315) 435-8582

Law Librarian: Cynthia Kesler
Supreme Court Law Library, Courthouse, 401 Montgomery St., Syracuse 13202
Circulation: (315) 671-1160; Reference: (315) 671-1151; Fax: (315) 671-1160

Sheriff: *Kevin E. Walsh, 407 S. State St., Syracuse 13202
(315) 435-3044; Civil Process: (315) 435-3060;
Civil Fax: (315) 435-3070; Admin. Fax: (315) 435-2942
E-mail: sheriffwalsh@hotmail.com

Justice Center: Patrick J. Corbert Justice Center, 555 S. State St., Syracuse 13202
(315) 435-1717;
Administrative Unit, Inmate Information:
(315) 435-1770; Fax: (315) 435-1718
Atty. Visitation: Any time

Chief Administrative Officer: Richard E. Carbery
(315) 435-1710

***Pending November 2010 Election Results**

ONTARIO COUNTY

Canandaigua, County Seat

SUPREME COURT

Courthouse, Room 130, 27 N. Main St., Canandaigua 14424-1447
(585) 396-4239; Fax: (585) 396-4576

Chief Clerk: Kathleen D. Sweeney
E-mail: ksweeney@courts.state.ny.us

SURROGATE'S COURT

Courthouse, Room 129, 27 N. Main St., Canandaigua 14424-1447
(585) 396-4055; Fax: (585) 396-4812

Surrogate: Frederick G. Reed
(585) 396-4053; Fax: (585) 396-4086
Law Clerk: Clyde North (585) 396-4056

Clerk: Elizabeth T. Simpson
(585) 396-4054; Fax: (585) 396-4812

COUNTY COURT

Courthouse, Room 130, 27 N. Main St., Canandaigua 14424-1447
(585) 396-4239; Fax: (585) 396-4576

Judges:
Craig J. Doran (585) 396-4479; Fax: (585) 396-4580
E-mail: cdoran@courts.state.ny.us
Law Clerk: Jacqueline Sisson
E-mail: jsisson@courts.state.ny.us
William F. Kocher (585) 396-4260; Fax: (585) 396-4087
E-mail: wkocher@courts.state.ny.us
Acting Supreme Court Justice
Law Clerk: Nicole Botti
E-mail: nbotti@courts.state.ny.us
Frederick G. Reed (585) 396-4053; Fax: (585) 396-4086
E-mail: freed@courts.state.ny.us
Law Clerk: Clyde North (585) 396-4056
E-mail: cnorth@courts.state.ny.us

Chief Clerk: Kathleen D. Sweeney
(585) 396-4239; Fax: (585) 396-4576
E-mail: ksweeney@courts.state.ny.us

FAMILY COURT

Courthouse, Room 130, 27 N. Main St., Canandaigua 14424-1447
(585) 396-4272; Fax: (585) 396-4576
E-mail: ontariofamilycourt@courts.state.ny.us

Judges:
Craig J. Doran (585) 396-4479; Fax: (585) 396-4580
Law Clerk: Jacqueline Sisson (585) 396-4818
Secretary: Ginny Harford
William F. Kocher (585) 396-4260; Fax: (585) 396-4087
Acting Supreme Court Justice
Law Clerk: Nicole Botti
Secretary: Marianne Grambo

Chief Clerk: Barbara E. Abbott (585) 396-4272
E-mail: ontariofamilycourt@courts.state.ny.us

Support Magistrate: John M. Costello (585) 396-8832

COUNTY OFFICIALS

County Atty.: John W. Park,
Courthouse, 27 N. Main St., Canandaigua 14424-1459
(585) 396-4411; Fax: (585) 396-4481

D.A.: R. Michael Tantillo
Courthouse, 27 N. Main St., Canandaigua 14424-1459
(585) 396-4010; Fax: (585) 396-4860

County Clerk: John H. Cooley
Municipal Bldg., 20 Ontario St., Canandaigua 14424
(585) 396-4200; Fax: (585) 393-2951

Treasurer: *Gary G. Baxter
Municipal Bldg., 20 Ontario St., Canandaigua 14424
(585) 396-4432; Fax: (585) 396-4584

Sheriff: *Philip C. Povero (585) 396-4614
Sheriff's Office, 74 Ontario St., Canandaigua 14424
(585) 394-4560; Fax: (585) 396-4844
Internet: www.co.ontario.ny.us

Under Sheriff: David C. Tillman (585) 396-4622

***Pending November 2010 Election Results**

Jail: 3045 County Complex Dr., Canandaigua 14424
(585) 396-1800; Fax: (585) 393-3092
Atty. Visitation: Daily, 8 A.M.-Noon; 1-3 & 3:30-4 P.M.; 5-11 P.M.; Ask about televist availability

Chief Administrative Officer: Alice C. Haskins
(585) 396-4616

ORANGE COUNTY

Goshen, County Seat

SUPREME COURT

Orange County Government Center, 285 Main St., Goshen 10924
(845) 291-3111; Fax: (845) 291-2595

Chief Clerk: Thomas W. Adams (845) 291-3114

Deputy Chief Clerk: Eileen Stanford (845) 291-3113

Senior Court Clerks:
James M. Charette (845) 291-3132
Margaret Ciarimboli (845) 291-3119
Thomas Danielewski (845) 291-3127
Cynthia Forsythe (845) 291-3137
Ellen Guerrera (845) 291-4511
Trisha Rittenhouse (845) 291-3194
Christopher Thomas (845) 291-2301

SURROGATE'S COURT

Surrogate's Courthouse, 30 Park Pl., Goshen 10924
(845) 291-2193; Fax: (845) 291-2196

Surrogate: Robert A. Onofry
(845) 291-2300; Fax: (845) 291-2543
Acting Supreme Court Justice

Chief Clerk: Jeanne M. Smith

Deputy Chief Clerk: Amy J. Miller

Court Atty.-Referee: John Lindstrom (845) 291-2300

Principal Court Atty.: Amanda B. Brady (845) 291-2300

COUNTY COURT

Orange County Courthouse, 285 Main St., Goshen 10924
(845) 291-3100;
Fax (County Court only): (845) 291-2525

Judges:
Jeffrey G. Berry (Acting Supreme Court Justice; Supervising Judge, City Courts, Ninth Judicial District)
(845) 291-3120; Fax: (845) 291-2101
Law Clerk: Richard Clarino (845) 291-3121
Nicholas DeRosa (845) 291-3115; Fax: (845) 291-2102
Acting Supreme Court Justice
Law Clerk: Janet Haislip (845) 291-3134
Robert H. Freehill (845) 291-3110; Fax: (845) 291-2103
Acting Supreme Court Justice
Law Clerk: John Goldsmith (845) 291-3116

Chief Clerk: Thomas W. Adams (845) 291-3114

Deputy Chief Clerk: Eileen Stanford (845) 291-3113

Senior Court Clerks:
Susan Columbus (Judge Berry) (845) 291-3122
Elizabeth Fenlon (845) 291-3102
Stephen Reusch (Judge Freehill) (845) 291-3118
Linda Sicina (Judge DeRosa) (845) 291-3117

Assoc. Court Clerk: Antonia Baez (845) 291-3105

FAMILY COURT

Orange Co. Courthouse, 285 Main St., Goshen 10924
(845) 291-3030; Fax: (845) 291-3054

Judges:
Andrew P. Bivona (845) 291-3020; Fax: (845) 291-3051
Acting Supreme Court Justice
Law Clerk: Rebecca E. Stage (845) 291-3037
E-mail: rstage@courts.state.ny.us
Secretary: Ruth K. Queen (845) 291-3020
E-mail: rqueen@courts.state.ny.us
Debra J. Kiedaisch (845) 291-3050; Fax: (845) 291-4520
Acting Supreme Court Justice; Presiding Justice IDV Part
Law Clerk: Martin B. Schaffer (845) 291-3023
E-mail: mschaffe@courts.state.ny.us
Secretary: Diane Bramich (845) 290-3050
E-mail: dbramich@courts.state.ny.us

Judges, Family Court, Orange County—Cont'd
Carol S. Klein (845) 291-3040; Fax: (845) 291-4405
Acting Supreme Court Justice
Law Clerk: Lisa Noroian (845) 291-3035
E-mail: lnoroian@courts.state.ny.us
Secretary: Diana Lynn Fasano (845) 291-3040
E-mail: dfasano@courts.state.ny.us
Lori J. Currier Woods (845) 291-7640; Fax: (845) 291-7666
Law Clerk: Caryn Markert (845) 291-7661
E-mail: cmarkert@courts.state.ny.us
Secretary: Cheryl Ferguson
E-mail: csfergus@courts.state.ny.us

Support Magistrates:
Gladys Braxton (845) 291-2579; Fax: (845) 291-2519
Christine P. Krahulik (845) 291-2577; Fax: (845) 291-2519
Jeanne Patsalos (845) 291-2578; Fax: (845) 291-2519

Chief Clerk V: Elizabeth C. Holbrook
(845) 291-3031; Fax: (845) 291-3054
E-mail: eholbroo@courts.state.ny.us

Deputy Chief Clerk III: Lynn McKelvey (845) 291-3031

Sr. Court Clerks:
Eileen Baer (Bivona) (845) 291-3022
Darryl Johnson (Kiedaisch) (845) 291-3026
George Laraia (Klein) (845) 291-3024
Elisa Reilly (Currier Woods) (845) 291-7662

COUNTY OFFICIALS

County Atty.: David L. Darwin, Government Center, 255 Main St., Goshen 10924 (845) 291-3150

Legislative Counsel: Antoinette Reed, Government Center, 255 Main St., Goshen 10924 (845) 291-4800

D.A.: Francis D. Phillips II, Government Center, 255 Main St., Goshen 10924 (845) 291-2050

County Clerk: Donna L. Benson
Government Center, 255 Main St., Goshen 10924
(845) 291-2690; Fax: (845) 291-2691

County Executive: Edward A. Diana
Government Center, 255 Main St., Goshen 10924
(845) 291-2700; Fax: (845) 291-2724

Finance Commissioner: Joel Kleiman
Government Center, 255 Main St., Goshen 10924
(845) 291-2488; Fax: (845) 291-2516

Law Librarian: Suparna Barua, Supreme Court Law Library, 255 Main St., Goshen 10924 (845) 291-3138

Sheriff: *Carl E. DuBois, 110 Wells Farm Rd., Goshen 10924
(845) 291-4033; Sheriff: (845) 291-7900; Fax: (845) 294-1590
Internet: www.orangecountygov.com

Correctional Facility: 110 Wells Farm Rd., Goshen 10924
(845) 291-4033; Fax: (845) 294-1590
Internet: www.orangecountygov.com
Atty. Visitation: Any time; call in advance

ORLEANS COUNTY

Albion, County Seat

SUPREME COURT
Courthouse Square, Suite 3, 1 S. Main St., Albion 14411-1497
(585) 589-5458; Fax: (585) 589-0632

Chief Clerk: Barbara A. Hale
E-mail: bhale@courts.state.ny.us

SURROGATE'S COURT
Courthouse Sq., Suite 3, 1 S. Main St., Albion 14411-1497
(585) 589-4457; Fax: (585) 589-0632

Surrogate: *James P. Punch (585) 589-4457

Chief Clerk: Deborah R. Berry
(585) 589-4457; Fax: (585) 589-0632
E-mail: dberry@courts.state.ny.us

COUNTY COURT
Courthouse Sq., Suite 3, 1 S. Main St., Albion 14411-1497
(585) 589-5458; Fax: (585) 589-0632

Judge: *James P. Punch (585) 589-5458

Chief Clerk: Barbara A. Hale
E-mail: bhale@courts.state.ny.us

***Pending November 2010 Election Results**

FAMILY COURT
Courthouse, Suite 3, 1 S. Main St., Albion 14411-1497
(585) 589-4457

Judge: James P. Punch (585) 589-4457, 58

Support Magistrate: Kathleen J. Gray

Chief Clerk: Laurie A. Bower
(585) 589-4457; Fax: (585) 589-0632
E-mail: lbower@courts.state.ny.us

COUNTY OFFICIALS

County Atty.: David C. Schubel, 343 Main St., Medina 14103
(585) 798-2250; Fax: (585) 798-0776
E-mail: occoa@orleansny.com

D.A.: Joseph V. Cardone, 13925 Rt. 31, Suite 300, Albion 14411 (585) 589-4127; Fax: (585) 590-4129
E-mail: da@orleansny.com

County Clerk: Karen Lake-Maynard, 3 S. Main St., Albion 14411-1498 (585) 589-5334; Fax: (585) 589-0181
E-mail: lakemaynard@orleansny.com

County Treasurer: Susan M. Heard, 34 E. Park St., Albion 14411 (585) 589-5353; Fax: (585) 589-9220
E-mail: sheard@orleansny.com

Law Library: Courthouse, 3 S. Main St., Albion 14411
(585) 589-4457

Sheriff: Scott D. Hess
13925 State Route 31, Suite 400, Albion 14411-9386
(585) 590-4142; Fax: (585) 590-4178
E-mail: ocsher@orleansny.com

Jail: 26 Platt St., Albion 14411
(585) 589-4310; Fax: (585) 589-2522
E-mail: ocjail@orleansny.com
Atty. Visitation: Daily, any time not disrupting jail routine

Superintendent: Kevin E. Hale

OSWEGO COUNTY

Oswego, County Seat

SUPREME COURT
Courthouse, 25 E. Oneida St., Oswego 13126-2693
(315) 349-3277; Fax: (315) 349-8513

Chief Clerk: Theresa M. Stephens
E-mail: tstephen@courts.state.ny.us

SURROGATE'S COURT
Courthouse, 25 E. Oneida St., Oswego 13126-2693
(315) 349-3295; Fax: (315) 349-8514

Surrogate: John J. Elliott
Law Clerk: Daryl Wiltsie (315) 349-3295

Chief Clerk: Judy Cooper

COUNTY COURT
Oswego County Courthouse, 25 E. Oneida St., Oswego 13126
(315) 349-3280

Judges:
Walter W. Hafner, Jr.
Public Safety Center, 39 Churchill Rd., Oswego 13126
(315) 349-8666; Fax: (315) 349-8669
*David J. Roman
Public Safety Center, 39 Churchill Rd., Oswego 13126
(315) 349-8741

Case Mgr., Drug Treatment Court: Margo Orton
Courthouse, 25 E. Oneida St., Oswego 13126
(315) 349-3448; Fax: (315) 349-8730
E-mail: morton@courts.state.ny.us

Program Coordinator, Drug Treatment Court:
David Guyer, Courthouse, 25 W. Oneida St., Oswego 13126 (315) 349-8716; Fax: (315) 349-8730
E-mail: dguyer@courts.state.ny.us

Court Clerk: Patricia Cline
Courthouse, 25 E. Oneida St., Oswego 13126
(315) 349-3413; Fax: (315) 349-8513
E-mail: pcline@courts.state.ny.us

Oswego County—Cont'd

FAMILY COURT
Public Safety Center, 39 Churchill Rd., Oswego 13126
(315) 349-3350; Fax: (315) 349-3457

Judge: Kimberly M. Seager
Chief Clerk: Sherryl A. Waldron
E-mail: swaldron@courts.state.ny.us
Confidential Law Asst.: Karen Brandt
E-mail: kbrandt@courts.state.ny.us
Support Magistrates:
James L. Gorman; E-mail: jlgorman@courts.state.ny.us
Eben C. Norfleet

COUNTY OFFICIALS

County Atty.: Richard C. Mitchell, 46 E. Bridge St., Oswego 13126 (315) 349-8296; Fax: (315) 349-8298
D.A.: Donald H. Dodd, Public Safety Center, 39 Churchill Rd., Oswego 13126 (315) 349-3200; Fax: (315) 349-3212
County Clerk: George J. Williams, 46 E. Bridge St., Oswego 13126 (315) 349-8621; Fax: (315) 349-8383
Treasurer: John W. Kruk, 46 E. Bridge St., Oswego 13126 (315) 349-8393; Fax: (315) 349-8255
Law Librarian: Anne M. Thomas (Asst.)
Supreme Court Law Library, Courthouse, 25 E. Oneida St., Oswego 13126
(315) 349-3297; Fax: (315) 349-3273
Sheriff: *Reuel A. Todd
39 Churchill Rd., Oswego 13126
(315) 349-3302; Fax: (315) 349-3303;
Sheriff: (315) 349-3307; Fax: (315) 349-3483
E-mail: sheriff@oswegocounty.com
Internet: www.oswegocounty.com/sheriff
Correctional Facility: 39 Churchill Rd., Oswego 13126
(315) 349-3300; Visitation: (315) 349-3346;
Fax: (315) 349-3349
Atty. Visitation: Daily, 8-11 A.M, Noon-3 P.M. & 5-9 P.M.

OTSEGO COUNTY

Cooperstown, County Seat

SUPREME COURT
County Courthouse, 193 Main St., P.O. Box 710, Cooperstown 13326
(607) 547-4364; Fax: (607) 547-7567

Chief Court Clerk: Gloria L. Chandler
E-mail: gchandle@courts.state.ny.us

SURROGATE'S COURT
Surrogate's Office, 197 Main St., Cooperstown 13326
(607) 547-4338; Fax: (607) 547-7566

Surrogates:
*Brian D. Burns (607) 547-4358
Law Clerk: Nathaniel P. Getman (607) 547-4359
John F. Lambert (607) 547-7573
Law Clerk: Mark Oursler (607) 547-7580
Chief Clerk: Lisa A. Weite
(607) 547-4213; Fax: (607) 547-7566

COUNTY COURT
Court Clerk's Office, Courthouse, 193 Main St., P.O. Box 710, Cooperstown 13326
(607) 547-4364

Judges:
*Brian D. Burns
County Office Bldg., 197 Main St., Cooperstown 13326
(607) 547-4358; Fax: (607) 547-7522
Law Clerk: Nathaniel P. Getman (607) 547-4359
John F. Lambert
County Office Bldg., 197 Main St., Cooperstown 13326
(607) 547-7573; Fax: (607) 547-7566
Law Clerk: Mark Oursler (607) 547-7580
Chief Clerk: Gloria L. Chandler
(607) 547-4364; Fax: (607) 547-7567
E-mail: gchandle@courts.state.ny.us

FAMILY COURT
County Annex Bldg., 32 Chestnut St., Cooperstown 13326
(607) 547-4264; Fax: (212) 457-2956

Judges:
*Brian D. Burns
County Office Bldg., 197 Main St., Cooperstown 13326
(607) 547-4358
Law Clerk: Nathaniel P. Getman
(607) 547-4359; Fax: (607) 547-7522
John F. Lambert
County Office Bldg., 197 Main St., Cooperstown 13326
(607) 547-7573
Law Clerk: Mark N. Oursler (607) 547-7580
Chief Clerk: Karen A. Nichols, County Annex Bldg., 32 Chestnut St., Cooperstown 13326
(607) 547-4288; Fax: (607) 547-6412

COUNTY OFFICIALS

County Atty.: Ellen Coccoma
County Office Bldg., 197 Main St., Cooperstown 13326
(607) 547-4208; Fax: (607) 547-7572
D.A.: John M. Muehl, County Office Bldg., 197 Main St., Cooperstown 13326 (607) 547-4249; Fax: (607) 547-4373
County Clerk: Kathy Sinnott Gardner
County Office Bldg., 197 Main St., Cooperstown 13326
(607) 547-4276; Fax: (607) 547-7544
County Treasurer: Dan Crowell
County Office Bldg., 197 Main St., P.O. Box 265, Cooperstown 13326 (607) 547-4276; Fax: (607) 547-7544
Board of Elections: Meadows Complex, Suite 2, 140 County Hwy. 33W, Cooperstown 13326
(607) 547-4247, 547-4325; Fax: (607) 547-4248
Law Librarian: Carolea Rooney Wilkens
Joseph P. Molinari Supreme Court Library, Courthouse, Cooperstown 13326
(607) 547-5425; Fax: (607) 547-6109
Sheriff: *Richard J. Devlin, Jr.
172 Co. Hwy. 33W, Cooperstown 13326
(607) 547-4271; Fax: (607) 547-6413
Internet: www.sheriffotsegocounty.com
Jail: 172 County Hwy. 33W, Cooperstown 13326
(607) 547-4252; Fax: (607) 547-6494
Atty. Visitation: Any time except 11:30 A.M.-1 P.M. , 4:30-6 P.M. and after 9 P.M.

PUTNAM COUNTY

Carmel, County Seat

SUPREME COURT
County Office Bldg., 40 Gleneida Ave., Carmel 10512
(845) 225-3641, Ext. 49306
Internet: www.putnamcountyny.com
Hearings & Trials, 20 County Center, Carmel 10512
(845) 208-7830

County Clerk: *Dennis J. Sant, Ext. 49301
Deputy County Clerk: Michael C. Bartolotti, Ext. 49303
Calendar Clerk: Leonard A. Pace (845) 208-7854
Asst. Calendar Clerk: Karen Bruns (Criminal)
(845) 208-7853
Address all mailings and filings to 40 Gleneida Ave.

SURROGATE'S COURT
Historic Courthouse, 44 Gleneida Ave., Carmel 10512
(845) 208-7860

Surrogates:
James F. Reitz, County Courthouse, 20 County Ctr., Carmel 10512 (845) 208-7875
Acting Supreme Court Justice
*James T. Rooney, County Courthouse, 20 County Ctr., Carmel 10512 (845) 208-7850
Chief Clerk: Linda M. Schwark (845) 208-7868
Deputy Chief Clerk: Irene Muller (845) 208-7866

***Pending November 2010 Election Results**

Putnam County—Cont'd

COUNTY COURT
Courthouse, 20 County Center, Carmel 10512
(845) 208-7800
Internet: www.courts.state.ny.us/courts/9jd/putnam

Judges:
James F. Reitz (845) 208-7875
Acting Supreme Court Justice
*James T. Rooney (845) 208-7822
Law Clerk: Christi Acker (845) 208-7819

County Clerk: Dennis J. Sant, Putnam County Office Bldg., 40 Gleneida Ave. (845) 225-3641, Ext. 49301

Deputy County Clerk: Michael C. Bartolotti Putnam County Office Bldg., 40 Gleneida Ave. (845) 225-3641, Ext. 49303

Calendar Clerk: Leonard A. Pace (845) 208-7854

Asst. Calendar Clerk: Karen Bruns (845) 208-7853

FAMILY COURT
Putnam County Courthouse, 20 County Center, Carmel 10512
(845) 208-7805; Fax: (845) 228-9614

Judges:
James F. Reitz (845) 208-7875
Acting Supreme Court Justice
*James T. Rooney (845) 208-7818

Chief Clerk: Karen O'Connor (845) 208-7810

Support Magistrate: Rachelle Kaufman (845) 208-7820

COUNTY OFFICIALS
Internet: www.putnamcountyny.com

County Atty.: Jennifer Bumgarner, Cty. Ofc. Bldg., 48 Gleneida Ave., Carmel 10512 (845) 808-1150, Ext. 49405

D.A.: Adam Levy, Cty. Office Bldg., 40 Gleneida Ave., Carmel 10512 (845) 808-1050

County Clerk: *Dennis J. Sant Cty. Ofc. Bldg., Room 100, 40 Gleneida Ave., Carmel 10512 (845) 225-3641, Ext. 49301

Chairman, County Legislature: Vincent Tamagna Cty. Ofc. Bldg., 40 Gleneida Ave., Carmel 10512 (845) 808-1020

County Executive: *Robert J. Bondi Cty. Ofc. Bldg., 3rd Floor, 40 Gleneida Ave., Carmel 10512 (845) 808-1001; Fax: (845) 808-1901

Commissioner of Finance: William J. Carlin, Jr. Cty. Ofc. Bldg., Room 105, 40 Gleneida Ave., Carmel 10512 (845) 808-1075

Law Librarian: Margie O'Loughlin 20 County Center, Carmel 10512 (845) 208-7804

Sheriff: Donald B. Smith, 3 County Center, Carmel 10512 (845) 225-4300; Sheriff: Ext. 42203; Fax: (845) 225-4399 Internet: www.putnamsheriff.com

Correctional Facility: 3 County Ctr., Carmel 10512 (845) 225-5255; Fax: (845) 228-1681 Atty. Visitation: Daily, 9 A.M.-9 P.M.; except 11:30 A.M.-12:30 P.M. & 4:30-5:30 P.M.; Contact corrections administration for approval

---

QUEENS COUNTY
Jamaica, County Seat

SUPREME COURT
Criminal Term, 125-01 Queens Blvd., Kew Gardens 11415
(718) 298-1408
Criminal Term, 25-10 Court Sq., Long Island City 11101
(718) 298-1616
Civil Term, 88-11 Sutphin Blvd., Jamaica 11435
(718) 298-1000

County Clerk and Clerk of the Supreme Court: Gloria D'Amico (718) 298-0601

First Deputy County Clerk: Alexis Cuffee (718) 262-7207

Second Deputy County Clerk: Ruth Deutsch (718) 298-0623

Admin. Asst. to County Clerk: Marie Gentile (718) 298-0601

Counsel to the County Clerk: Donna Furey (718) 298-0604

Administrator to County Clerk: Robert E. Taverni (718) 298-0640

Chief Supreme Court Clerk: Anthony D'Angelis (718) 298-1150

Chief Clerk: Maureen D'Aquila (Criminal Term) (718) 298-1408

First Deputy Chief Clerk: Felix Fernandez (Civil Term) (718) 298-1140

Chief Supreme Court Law Asst.: Jeffrey Ellison (718) 298-1196

Civil Term, Motion Support Office: Gerry Murphy (718) 298-1009

Civil Term, Ex Parte Office: Jeffrey Cohen (718) 298-1018

Civil Term, Motion Office-Matrimonial: Olivia Mathis (718) 298-1012

Civil Term, Motion Office—Bail Rev. & Mental Health: Steven Layton (Civil Term) (718) 298-1021

Civil Term, Motion Office—Tax Cert. & Incompetency: Tamara Kersh (718) 298-1040

Condemnation: Tamara Kersh (718) 298-1040

Civil Term, Jamaica: William Graeper (718) 298-1140; General Information: (718) 298-1000; Court Reporters: (718) 298-1057; Jury Information: (718) 262-7203; Library: (718) 298-1206; Motion Calendar Clerk: (718) 298-1009; Subpoenaed Records: (718) 298-1016; Trial Calendar Clerk: (718) 298-1015

Trial Term, Jamaica: Orestes Rodriguez Clerk's Office: (718) 298-1015

Criminal Term, Kew Gardens: Frances Taylor General Information: (718) 298-1408; Arraignments: (718) 298-1398; Court Reporters: (718) 298-1381; Grand Jury: (718) 298-1725; Jury Service: (718) 298-0621; Library: (718) 298-1327; Record Room: (718) 298-1400; Subpoenaed Records: (718) 298-1400

Criminal Term, Long Island City: Mark Finkelstein General Information: (718) 298-1616

Probation Dept.: General Information: (718) 298-3042

SURROGATE'S COURT
88-11 Sutphin Blvd., Jamaica 11435
(718) 298-0400

Surrogate: Robert L. Nahman

Law Secretary to Surrogate: Donna-Marie Golia

Chief Law Asst.: Lee J. Coulman

Chief Clerk & Clerk of the Court: Margaret M. Gribbon (718) 298-0401

Deputy Chief Clerk & Deputy Clerk of the Court: Vacancy at Press Time (718) 298-0403

Probate Clerk: Mark Chotkowski (718) 298-0436

Accounting Clerk: Giovanna Traugott (718) 298-0432

Adoption & Guardianship Clerk: Eileen Mitchell (718) 298-0426

Administration Clerk: Mona Gill (718) 298-0434

Miscellaneous Clerk: Linda Butrico (718) 298-0438

FAMILY COURT
See Family Court, N.Y.C., pp. 98-99

COUNTY OFFICIALS

D.A.: Richard A. Brown Queens Criminal Court Bldg., 125-01 Queens Blvd., Kew Gardens 11415 (718) 286-6000

County Clerk: Gloria D'Amico 88-11 Sutphin Blvd., Jamaica 11435 (718) 298-0601

Comptroller: John Liu, 1 Centre St., Room 530, N.Y.C. 10007 (212) 669-3500; Fax: (212) 669-2707

Public Administrator: Lois M. Rosenblatt 88-11 Sutphin Blvd., Room 61, Jamaica 11435 (718) 520-3710; Internet: www.queenscountypa.com

Counsel to the Public Administrator: Gerard J. Sweeney 95-25 Queens Blvd., Suite 626, Rego Park 11374 (718) 459-9000; Fax: (718) 459-3163

***Pending November 2010 Election Results**

County Judiciary & Officials

Queens County Officials—Cont'd

Commissioner of Finance: David M. Frankel
1 Centre St., Suite 500, N.Y.C. 10007 (212) 669-8711

Chief Law Librarian: Andrew Tschinkel
NYS Supreme Court Law Library, 11th Judicial Circuit, 88-11 Sutphin Blvd., Room 65, Jamaica 11435
(718) 298-1206

Criminal Term, Law Librarian: Vacancy at Press Time
NYS Supreme Court Law Library Kew Gardens, 125-01 Queens Blvd., Room 722, Kew Gardens 11415
(718) 298-1327

Sheriff: Vacancy at Press Time
30-10 Starr Ave., Long Island City 11101
(718) 610-0491; Fax: (718) 610-0486

Under Sheriff: Joseph Fucito

Jamaica Office: 144-06 94th Ave., Jamaica 11435
(718) 298-7550; Fax: (718) 298-7470

Supervising Deputy Sheriff: Lt. M. Bozymowski,

RENSSELAER COUNTY

Troy, County Seat

SUPREME COURT
Courthouse, Congress & Second St., Troy 12180
(518) 285-5034

Chief Clerk: Richard F. Reilly, Jr.

Deputy Chief Clerk: Lynn M. Laya (518) 285-5033

SURROGATE'S COURT
County Courthouse, 80 Second St., Troy 12180
(518) 285-6100; Fax: (518) 272-5452

Surrogate: Christian F. Hummel
(Acting Supreme Court Justice) (518) 285-6100

Chief Clerk: Paul V. Morgan, Jr.

Court Clerk: Stephen A. Stasack

Principal Court Atty., Trial Part: Loretta Branigan Tobin

COUNTY COURT
Courthouse, Congress & Second St., Troy 12180
(518) 285-5025

Judges:
Andrew G. Ceresia (518) 285-6110
Law Clerk: Olivia Karis-Nix (518) 289-6110
Robert M. Jacon (518) 285-6146
Law Clerk: Jessica Brook Mocerine (518) 285-6146

Chief Clerk: Richard F. Reilly, Jr.

Deputy Chief Clerk: Lynn M. Laya

FAMILY COURT
1504 Fifth Ave., Troy 12180-4107
(518) 270-3761; Fax: (518) 272-6573

Judges:
Catherine Cholakis (Part II), Ext. 329
E-mail: ccholaki@courts.state.ny.us
Acting Supreme Court Justice
Law Clerk/Court Atty.: James Montagnino, Ext. 329
E-mail: jmontagn@courts.state.ny.us
Elizabeth M. Walsh (Part I), Ext. 342
E-mail: emwalsh@courts.state.ny.us
Law Clerk: Leslie Richards Ortiz, Ext. 342
E-mail: lortiz@courts.state.ny.us

Support Magistrates:
William Foley, Ext. 365
E-mail: wfoley@courts.state.ny.us
Thomas Gordon, Ext. 364
E-mail: tgordon@courts.state.ny.us

Chief Clerk: Patricia A. Beeler, Ext. 359
E-mail: pbeeler@courts.state.ny.us

Deputy Chief Clerk: Lee P. Bridenbeck, Ext. 358
E-mail: cbridenb@courts.state.ny.us

Court Clerks:
Robert Brennan (Part II), Ext. 340
E-mail: rbrennan@courts.state.ny.us
Richard Curtin (Part I), Ext. 339
E-mail: rcurtin@courts.state.ny.us

COUNTY OFFICIALS

County Atty.: Stephen A. Pechenik
Cty Ofc. Bldg., 1600 7th Ave., Troy 12180
(518) 270-2950; Fax: (518) 270-2954

County Clerk: Frank J. Merola, 105 3rd St., Troy 12180
(518) 270-4080; Fax: (518) 271-7998

D.A.: Richard J. McNally, Jr., Courthouse, Troy 12180
(518) 270-4040

Chief Fiscal Officer: Michael Slawson
Cty. Ofc. Bldg., 1600 7th Ave., Troy 12180
(518) 270-2750; Fax: (518) 270-2728

County Executive: Kathleen M. Jimino
Cty. Ofc. Bldg., 1600 7th Ave., Troy 12180
(518) 270-2900; Fax: (518) 270-2961

Law Librarian: Laura Barber, Supreme Court Law Library, Courthouse, Second St. Annex, 86 Second St., Troy 12180
(518) 285-6183

Sheriff: Jack Mahar, 4000 Main St., Troy 12180
(518) 266-1900; Fax: (518) 270-5447
E-mail: jmahar@rensco.com

Correctional Facility: 4000 Main St., Troy 12180
(518) 270-5448; Fax: (518) 270-5452
Atty. Visitation: Daily, 9-11 A.M.; 1-3 P.M. & 4-5 P.M. & 6:30-10:30 P.M.

Superintendent: Col. Robert R. Loveridge

RICHMOND COUNTY

Saint George, County Seat

SUPREME COURT
County Courthouse, 18 Richmond Terr., Staten Island 10301
(718) 675-8700

Homeport (Annex), 355 Front St., Staten Island 10304
(718) 876-6411

County Clerk and Clerk of the Supreme Court & Commissioner of Jurors: Stephen J. Fiala
130 Stuyvesant Pl., Staten Island 10301 (718) 675-8910

Chief Clerk: Joseph Como (718) 675-8700

Clerk of Civil Term: John Tenaglia
Civil Term Office, 130 Stuyvesant Pl., Staten Island 10301

Clerk of Criminal Term: Frank J. Mulia

Calendar: Winston Jordan
Civil Term Office, 130 Stuyvesant Pl., Staten Island 10301

Law Library: Philip Klingle
Supreme Court Law Library, 25 Hyatt St., Staten Island 10301 (718) 675-8711

Chief Court Atty.: Jerry A. DiTata, Civil Term Office, 130 Stuyvesant Pl., Staten Island 10301 (718) 390-5383

Court Atty.—Referee: Kenneth McGrail
Civil Term Office, 130 Stuyvesant Pl., Staten Island 10301 (718) 675-8712

Assoc. Court Attys.:
Odette N. Buschmann
Civil Term Office, 130 Stuyvesant Pl., Staten Island 10301 (718) 675-8712
Judith D. Israeli
Civil Term Office, 130 Stuyvesant Pl., Staten Island 10301 (718) 675-8712
Judith F. Moresco
Civil Term Office, 130 Stuyvesant Pl., Staten Island 10301 (718) 675-8712
Maureen A. Reilly
Civil Term Office, 130 Stuyvesant Pl., Staten Island 10301 (718) 675-8712
Eva Tam
Civil Term Office, 130 Stuyvesant Pl., Staten Island 10301 (718) 675-8712

Special Term: Paul Eng
Civil Term Office, 130 Stuyvesant Pl., Staten Island 10301 (718) 675-8575

***Pending November 2010 Election Results**

Richmond County—Cont'd

SURROGATE'S COURT
County Courthouse, St. George, Staten Island 10301
(718) 675-8500

Surrogate: Robert J. Gigante (718) 675-8505
Chief Clerk of the Court: Ronald M. Cerrachio
Deputy Chief Clerk: Jane E. Stilwell
Principal Law Clerk: Vacancy at Press Time
Supervising Court Atty.: Jerry M. Judin
Court Atty.—Referees:
R. Paul Bernhardt
Robert J. Renehan
Court Attys.:
Kevin Michael Elford
Laura Lopez-Keegan

FAMILY COURT
See Family Court, N.Y.C., pp. 98-99

COUNTY OFFICIALS

D.A.: *Daniel M. Donovan, Jr.
130 Stuyvesant Pl., 7th Floor, Staten Island 10301
(718) 876-6300
County Clerk & Commissioner of Jurors: Stephen J. Fiala
Richmond County Clerk, 2nd Floor, 130 Stuyvesant Pl., Staten Island 10301 (718) 675-8910; Fax: (718) 390-3269
Comptroller: John Liu
530 Municipal Bldg., 1 Centre St., N.Y.C. 10007
(212) 669-3500; Fax: (212) 669-2707
Commissioner of Finance: David M. Frankel
1 Centre St., Suite 500, N.Y.C. 10007 (212) 669-4855
Public Administrator: Gary Gotlin
130 Stuyvesant Pl., Suite 402, Staten Island 10301
(718) 876-7228; Fax: (718) 876-8377
Law Librarian: Philip Klingle
NYS Supreme Court Law Library, 25 Hyatt St., Staten Island 10301 (718) 675-8711
Sheriff: Vacancy at Press Time
350 St. Mark's Pl., 4th Floor, Staten Island 10301
(718) 815-8407; Fax: (718) 815-8416
Supervisor: Lt. Steven Burdman

ROCKLAND COUNTY

New City, County Seat

SUPREME COURT
Courthouse, Suite 200, 1 S. Main St., New City 10956
Civil: (845) 638-5393; Criminal: (845) 638-5363;
Fax: (845) 638-5312

Chief Clerk: John F. Hussey (845) 638-5393
Deputy Chief Clerk: Cynthia Salters (845) 638-5373

SURROGATE'S COURT
1 S. Main St., Suite 270, New City 10956
(845) 638-5330; Fax: (845) 638-5632

Surrogates:
Thomas E. Walsh II (845) 638-5365
Secretary: Jean Finan
Chief Clerk: Virginia Athens (845) 638-5330
Deputy Chief Clerk: Eileen Horan (845) 638-5330
Law Clerk: Stephen Lowe (845) 638-5333; Fax: (845) 638-5944

COUNTY COURT
Courthouse, Suite 200, 1 S. Main St., New City 10956
Civil Court: (845) 638-5393;
Criminal Court: (845) 638-5363; Fax: (845) 638-5312

Judges:
Charles Apotheker (845) 638-5239
Acting Supreme Court Justice
Robert Berliner (914) 708-7218
William K. Nelson (Acting Supreme Court Justice)
(845) 638-5336; E-mail: wnelson@courts.state.ny.us
Chief Clerk: John F. Hussey (845) 638-5393
Deputy Chief Clerk: Cynthia Salters (845) 638-5373

***Pending November 2010 Election Results**

FAMILY COURT
1 S. Main St., Suite 300, New City 10956
(845) 638-5300; Fax (Clerks Office): (845) 638-5319;
Chambers: (845) 638-5284

Judges:
*Linda Christopher (845) 638-5328
Law Clerk: Phyllis J. Goldberg (845) 638-5643
Secretary: Susan A. Dizzine
William P. Warren (845) 638-5327; Fax: (845) 638-5284
Law Clerks:
Alden B. Smith (845) 708-7162
Rolf Thorsen (845) 638-5322
Secretary: Sandy Palughi
Support Magistrates:
Rachelle Kaufman (845) 638-5307
Catherine Miklitsch (845) 638-5750
Chief Clerk: Anna Kosovych (845) 638-5311
Deputy Chief Clerk: Diane S. Gould (845) 638-5304

COUNTY OFFICIALS

County Atty.: Patricia Zugibe, County Office Bldg., 11 New Hempstead Rd., New City 10956 (845) 638-5180
D.A.: Thomas P. Zugibe, County Courthouse, Suite 500, 1 S. Main St., New City 10956 (845) 638-5001
County Clerk: Paul Piperato
1 S. Main St., Suite 100, New City 10956 (845) 638-5070
County Executive: C. Scott Vanderhoef
County Office Bldg., 11 New Hempstead Rd., New City 10956 (845) 638-5122
Commissioner of Finance: H. Chris Kopf
Sain Bldg., 18 New Hempstead Rd., New City 10956 (845) 638-5131
Chairman, County Legislature: Harriet Cornell
County Office Bldg., 11 New Hempstead Rd., New City 10956 (845) 638-5100
County Auditor: H. Chris Kopf (Acting)
Dept. of Audit, Sain Bldg., 18 New Hempstead Rd., New City 10956 (845) 638-5131
Law Library Asst.: Frances Nicklus
Supreme Court Law Library, 1 S. Main St., Suite 235, New City 10956 (845) 638-5396
Sheriff: James F. Kralik
55 New Hempstead Rd., New City 10956
(845) 638-5400; Civil Division: (845) 638-5456;
Fax: (845) 638-5460; Jail: (845) 638-5600;
Sheriff: (845) 638-5466; Fax: (845) 638-5035
Jail: 53 New Hempstead Rd., New City 10956
(845) 638-5600; Fax: (845) 638-5399
Atty. Visitation: Daily, call for hours

SAINT LAWRENCE COUNTY

Canton, County Seat

SUPREME COURT
Courthouse, 48 Court St., Canton 13617
(315) 379-2219; Fax: (315) 379-2423

Chief Clerk: Mary B. Curran
Deputy Chief Clerk: Brenda J. Lauer
Law Librarian: Tammy B. Lomaki
(315) 379-2279; Fax: (315) 379-2424

SURROGATE'S COURT
Courthouse, 48 Court St., Canton 13617-1199
(315) 379-2217; Fax: (315) 379-2372

Surrogate: Kathleen M. Rogers
Chief Clerk: Debra A. Dow
Court Atty.: John F. Richey

COUNTY COURT
County Courthouse, 48 Court St., Canton 13617
(315) 379-2219; Fax: (315) 379-2423

Judge: Jerome J. Richards
(315) 379-2214; Fax: (315) 379-9934
County Clerk: Patricia A. Ritchie
(315) 379-2237; Fax: (315) 379-2302
Chief Clerk: Mary B. Curran
Deputy Chief Clerk: Brenda J. Lauer

St. Lawrence County—Cont'd

FAMILY COURT
Courthouse, 48 Court St., Canton 13617-1169
(315) 379-2410; Fax: (315) 386-3197

Judge: Barbara R. Potter
(315) 379-2410; Fax: (315) 386-3197

Chief Clerk: Christy Q. Bass

Deputy Chief Clerk: Deborah L. Darou

Senior Court Atty.: Johanne Sullivan

Court Asst.: Sharon L. Rosenbarker (315) 379-2410

Support Magistrate: Sharon M. W. Lumb

COUNTY OFFICIALS

County Atty.: Mike Crowe
Public Safety Bldg., 48 Court St., Canton 13617
(315) 379-2269; Fax: (315) 379-2254

D.A.: Nicole M. Duve, Courthouse, 48 Court St., Canton 13617 (315) 379-2225; Fax: (315) 379-2301

County Administrator: Karen St. Hilaire
Courthouse, 48 Court St., Canton 13617 (315) 379-2276

County Clerk: Patricia A. Ritchie
Courthouse, 48 Court St., Canton 13617
(315) 379-2237; Fax: (315) 379-2302
E-mail: pritchie@co.st-lawrence.ny.us

County Treasurer: *Robert O. McNeil
Courthouse, 48 Court St., Canton 13617
(315) 379-2234; Fax: (315) 379-5274

Law Librarian: Tammy B. Lomaki
Supreme Court Library, Courthouse, 48 Court St., Canton 13617-1194 (315) 379-2279; Fax: (315) 379-2424

Sheriff: Kevin Wells (315) 379-2365
Public Safety Bldg., 48 Court St., Canton 13617
(315) 379-2222; Sheriff: (315) 379-2365; Fax: (315) 379-2435
E-mail: kwells@stlawco.org

St. Lawrence County Correctional Facility:
17 Commerce Ln., Canton 13617
(315) 379-2367; Fax: (315) 379-2263
Atty. Visitation: Daily, 7:30 A.M.-9 P.M.

SARATOGA COUNTY

Ballston Spa, County Seat

SUPREME COURT
30 McMaster St., Ballston Spa 12020
(518) 451-8840; Fax: (518) 884-4758

Chief Clerk: Carolyn E. Hall
E-mail: cehall@courts.state.ny.us

Deputy Chief Clerk: Timothy J. Doyle

Senior Court Clerk: Mary M. Langley

Assoc. Court Clerk: Norman J. Malenfant

SURROGATE'S COURT
30 McMaster St., Ballston Spa 12020-0600
(518) 451-8830; Fax: (518) 884-4774

Surrogate: Harry W. Seibert, Jr.
Law Clerk: Kathleen D. Kalwa
Secretary: Deborah Scatena (518) 451-8826

Chief Clerk: Debra D. Baker

Deputy Chief Clerk: Catharine A. Ruggles

COUNTY COURT
30 McMaster St., Ballston Spa 12020-0600
(518) 451-8815

Judge: Jerry J. Scarano (518) 451-8815
Principal Law Clerk: Susan M. Fitzsimmons
Secretary: Janette E. Schmitt

Chief Clerk: Carolyn E. Hall (518) 451-8840

Associate Court Clerk: Norman J. Malenfant
(518) 451-8840

Deputy Chief Clerk: Timothy Doyle (518) 451-8840

Senior Court Clerk: Mary M. Langley (518) 451-8840

***Pending November 2010 Election Results**

FAMILY COURT
Saratoga County Municipal Center, 35 W. High St., Ballston Spa 12020-0600
(518) 451-8888

Judges:
*Gil L. Abramson (518) 451-8888
Law Clerk: John Eggleston
Secretary: Silvana Shaughnessy
Courtenay W. Hall (518) 451-8888
Law Clerk: Peter E. Reilly
Secretary: Barbara L. Little

Support Magistrates:
Donald Clark, Jr.
Kathleen Jennings
James H. Densmore

Chief Clerk: Susan P. Samascott

Deputy Chief Clerk: Carianne LaMarche

COUNTY OFFICIALS

County Atty.: Mark M. Rider, 40 McMaster St., Ballston Spa 12020 (518) 884-4770; Fax: (518) 884-4720

D.A.: James A. Murphy III, 25 W. High St., Ballston Spa 12020 (518) 885-2263; Fax: (518) 884-8627

County Clerk: Kathleen Marchione
Saratoga Cty. Munic. Center, 40 McMaster St., Ballston Spa 12020-0600
(518) 885-2213; Fax: (518) 884-4726

County Treasurer: Samuel J. Pitcheralle
40 McMaster St., Bldg. 1, Ballston Spa 12020
(518) 884-4724; Fax: (518) 884-4775

Chairman, Bd. of Assessors: Willard H. Peck
Saratoga County Munic. Center, 40 McMaster St., Ballston Spa 12020 (518) 886-2240; Fax: (518) 886-4771

County Auditor: John D. Murray
Saratoga Cty. Munic. Center, Ballston Spa 12020-0600
(518) 884-4745; Fax: (518) 884-4720

Law Librarian: Vicki Heidelberger
City Hall, Suite 10, 474 Broadway, Saratoga Springs 12866 (518) 451-8777

Sheriff: James D. Bowen
6010 County Farm Rd., Ballston Spa 12020-0600
Civil Division: (518) 885-2469; Sheriff: (518) 885-2450

Jail: 6010 County Farm Rd., Ballston Spa 12020
(518) 885-2480
Atty. Visitation: Daily, 8:30-11:30 A.M.; 12:30-3:45 P.M.; 4:30-10:30 P.M.

SCHENECTADY COUNTY

Schenectady, County Seat

SUPREME COURT
612 State St., Schenectady 12305-2114
(518) 285-8401; Fax: (518) 388-4520

Chief Clerk: Sharon E. Sheffer
E-mail: ssheffer@courts.state.ny.us

Deputy Chief Clerk: Robin Farmer
E-mail: rfarmer@courts.state.ny.us

Sr. Court Clerks:
Mary Adams; E-mail: madams@courts.state.ny.us
Mark DeCaro; E-mail: mdecaro@courts.state.ny.us
Jill Loucks; E-mail: jloucks@courts.state.ny.us
Richard McNally; E-mail: rmcnally@courts.state.ny.us
Peter Pizzurro; E-mail: ppizzurro@courts.state.ny.us

SURROGATE'S COURT
Courthouse, 612 State St., Schenectady 12305-2113
(518) 285-8455; Fax: (518) 377-6378

Chief Clerk: Paula B. Miller

Deputy Chief Clerk: Gisele A. Van Wormer

Law Asst.: Diane D. Enzinna

Schenectady County—Cont'd

COUNTY COURT
Courthouse, 612 State St., Schenectady 12305
(518) 285-8401

Judge: Karen A. Drago (518) 285-8429

Chief Clerk: Sharon E. Sheffer
E-mail: ssheffer@courts.state.ny.us

Deputy Chief Clerk: Robin Farmer
E-mail: rfarmer@courts.state.ny.us

Senior Court Clerk:
Mary Adams; E-mail: madams@courts.state.ny.us
Mark DeCaro; E-mail: mdecaro@courts.state.ny.us
Jill Loucks; E-mail: jloucks@courts.state.ny.us
Richard McNally; E-mail: rmcnally@courts.state.ny.us
Peter Pizzurro; E-mail: ppizzurro@courts.state.ny.us

FAMILY COURT
620 State St., Schenectady 12305-2114
(518) 285-8435; Fax: (518) 393-1565

Judges:
*Jo Anne Assini (518) 285-8435; Fax: (518) 393-1565
E-mail: jassini@courts.state.ny.us
Law Clerk: Eileen B. Kassner
E-mail: ekassner@courts.state.ny.us
Law Secretary: Nicola Stoddard
E-mail: nstoddar@courts.state.ny.us
Mark L. Powers (518) 285-8450; Fax: (518) 393-1565
E-mail: mpowers@court.state.ny.us
Law Clerk: Laura Deitz (518) 255-8452
E-mail: ldeitz@courts.state.ny.us
Secretary: Andrea McConnelee
E-mail: amcconne@court.state.ny.us

Support Magistrate:
Kathleen J. Jennings (518) 285-8435
E-mail: kjennings@courts.state.ny.us
Colleen M. Quirion (518) 285-8435
E-mail: cquirion@courts.state.ny.us

Chief Clerk: Melissa J. Mills (518) 285-8435
E-mail: mjmills@courts.state.ny.us

Deputy Chief Clerk: Denise Riggi (518) 285-8435
E-mail: driggi@courts.state.ny.us

COUNTY OFFICIALS

County Atty.: Christopher H. Gardner
Cty. Ofc. Bldg., 620 State St., Schenectady 12305-2114
(518) 388-4700; Fax: (518) 388-4493

D.A.: Robert M. Carney
Courthouse, 612 State St., Schenectady 12305
(518) 388-4364; Fax: (518) 388-4569

County Clerk: *John J. Woodward
Cty. Ofc. Bldg., 620 State St., Schenectady 12305-2114
(518) 388-4220; Fax: (518) 388-4224

Commissioner of Finance: George Davidson
Cty. Ofc. Bldg., 620 State St., Schenectady 12305-2114
(518) 388-4260; Fax: (518) 388-4248

Law Librarian: Dana E. Wantuch
Joseph F. Egan Memorial Library,
Supreme Court Library, 612 State St.,
Schenectady 12305-2113
(518) 285-8518; Fax: (518) 377-5909

Sheriff: Dominic Dagostino
c/o Schenectady County Jail, 320 Veeder Ave.,
Schenectady 12307
(518) 388-4300; Fax: (518) 388-4593;
Civil: (518) 388-4304; Civil Fax: (518) 374-4873

Correctional Facility:
320 Veeder Ave., Schenectady 12307
(518) 388-4300; Fax: (518) 393-5111
Atty. Visitation: Daily, 7:30 A.M.-2:30 P.M. & 3:30-10 P.M.

***Pending November 2010 Election Results**

SCHOHARIE COUNTY
Schoharie, County Seat

SUPREME COURT
Courthouse, 290 Main St., P.O. Box 669,
Schoharie 12157-0669
(518) 295-8342; Fax: (518) 295-7226

Chief Clerk: F. Christian Spies

SURROGATE'S COURT
290 Main St., P.O. Box 669, Schoharie 12157-0669
(518) 295-8387; Fax: (518) 295-8451

Surrogate: George R. Bartlett III (518) 295-8383, 6098
Chief Clerk: F. Christian Spies

COUNTY COURT
Schoharie County Courthouse, 290 Main St.,
P.O. Box 669, Schoharie 12157-0669
(518) 295-8342; Fax: (518) 295-7226

Judge: George R. Bartlett III (518) 295-8740
Acting Supreme Court Justice
Chief Clerk: F. Christian Spies

FAMILY COURT
290 Main St., P.O. Box 669, Schoharie 12157-0669
(518) 295-8383; Fax: (518) 295-8451

Judge: George R. Bartlett III (518) 295-8740
Chief Clerk: F. Christian Spies

COUNTY OFFICIALS

County Atty.: Michael A. West
2668 State Rt. 7, Suite 12, Cobleskill 12043
(518) 296-8844; Fax: (518) 296-8855

Asst. County Attys.:
Marvin D. Parshall, Jr. Douglas V. Putnam

D.A.: James Sacket
157 Depot Lane, P.O. Box 888, Schoharie 12157
(518) 295-2272; Fax: (518) 295-2273
E-mail: sacketj@co.schoharie.ny.us

County Clerk: M. Indica Jaycox
County Office Bldg., 284 Main St., P.O. Box 549,
Schoharie 12157-0549
(518) 295-8316; Fax: (518) 295-8338
E-mail: indyjaycox@co.schoharie.ny.us

County Treasurer: William E. Cherry
County Office Bldg., 284 Main St., P.O. Box 9,
Schoharie 12157-0009 (518) 295-8386; Fax: (518) 295-8364
E-mail: cherryb@co.schoharie.ny.us

Law Librarian: Timothy Holmes
F. Walter Bliss Memorial Library, Courthouse,
290 Main St., P.O. Box 447, Schoharie 12157-0447
(518) 295-7900; Fax: (518) 295-7901

Sheriff: Anthony F. Desmond
157 Depot Lane, P.O. Box 689, Schoharie 12157-0089
(518) 295-2266; Fax: (518) 295-2267

Jail: 157 Depot Lane, P.O. Box 689, Schoharie 12157
(518) 295-2264; Fax: (518) 295-2284
Atty. Visitation: Weekdays, any time except Noon, 2:30-3:30 P.M., and 5 P.M.

SCHUYLER COUNTY
Watkins Glen, County Seat

SUPREME COURT
105 9th St., Unit 35, Watkins Glen 14891
(607) 535-7760; Fax: (607) 535-4918

Chief Clerk: Rita S. Decker
E-mail: rdecker@courts.state.ny.us

SURROGATE'S COURT
Courthouse, Unit 35, 105 Ninth St.,
Watkins Glen 14891
(607) 535-7144; Fax: (607) 535-4918

Surrogate: J.C. Argetsinger, Unit 35
Law Clerk: William C. Elkins
Chief Clerk: Frances H. Pierce
E-mail: fpierce@courts.state.ny.us

County Judiciary & Officials

Schuyler County—Cont'd

COUNTY COURT
Courthouse, 105 Ninth St., Unit 35, Watkins Glen 14891
(607) 535-7015; Fax: (607) 535-4918

Judge: J.C. Argetsinger
Chief Clerk: Rita Decker (607) 535-7760
E-mail: rdecker@courts.state.ny.us
Law Clerk: William C. Elkins

FAMILY COURT
Courthouse, Unit 35, 105 Ninth St.,
Watkins Glen 14891
(607) 535-7143; Fax: (607) 535-4918
www.courts.state.ny.us/6jf/countymaps/schuyler/fam

Judge: J.C. Argetsinger
Law Clerk: William C. Elkins
Chief Clerk: Lynda L. LoPresti
E-mail: llopresti@courts.state.ny.us

COUNTY OFFICIALS

County Atty.: James P. Coleman, County Office Bldg., Unit 5, 105 Ninth St., Watkins Glen 14891 (607) 535-8121
Asst. County Attys.:
Kristin Hazlitt Dennis J. Morris
D.A.: Joseph G. Fazzary
County Office Bldg., Unit 26, 105 Ninth St., Watkins Glen 14891 (607) 535-8383
County Clerk: Linda M. Compton
County Office Bldg., Unit 8, 105 Ninth St., Watkins Glen 14891 (607) 535-8133; Fax: (607) 535-8130
County Treasurer: Margaret Starbuck
County Office Bldg., Unit 17, 105 Ninth St., Watkins Glen 14891 (607) 535-8181
Chairman, Bd. of Legislators: *Thomas Gifford
County Office Bldg., Unit 6, 105 Ninth St., Watkins Glen 14891 (607) 535-8100
Sheriff: William E. Yessman, Jr.
106 10th St., Unit 2, Watkins Glen 14891
(607) 535-8222; Fax: (607) 535-8216
E-mail: wyessman@co.schuyler.ny.us
Jail: 106 10th St., Unit 2, Watkins Glen 14891
(607) 535-8222; Fax: (607) 535-8216
Atty. Visitation: Daily, 8 A.M.-10 P.M.

SENECA COUNTY

Ovid, County Seat

SUPREME COURT
Courthouse, 48 W. Williams St., Waterloo 13165
(315) 539-7021; Fax: (315) 539-7929

Chief Clerk: Elizabeth C. Young
E-mail: eyoung@courts.state.ny.us

SURROGATE'S COURT
Courthouse, 48 W. Williams St., Waterloo 13165
(315) 539-7531; Fax: (315) 539-3267

Surrogate: Dennis F. Bender
(315) 539-6291; Fax: (315) 539-7850
Law Clerk: Barbara A. Roesch (315) 539-7682
E-mail: broesch@courts.state.ny.us
Secretary: Marjorie Brophy
E-mail: mbrophy@courts.state.ny.us
Chief Clerk: Rosemarie Capozzi
E-mail: rcapozzi@courts.state.ny.us

COUNTY COURT
Courthouse, 48 W. Williams St., Waterloo 13165
(315) 539-7021; Fax: (315) 539-7929

Judge: Dennis F. Bender (315) 539-6291; Fax: (315) 539-7850
E-mail: dbender@courts.state.ny.us
Law Clerk: Barbara A. Roesch (315) 539-7682
E-mail: broesch@courts.state.ny.us
Secretary: Marjorie Brophy (315) 539-6291
E-mail: mbrophy@courts.state.ny.us
Chief Clerk: Elizabeth C. Young
E-mail: eyoung@courts.state.ny.us

FAMILY COURT
Seneca County Courthouse, 48 W. Williams St.,
Waterloo 13165
(315) 539-4917; Fax: (315) 539-4225

Judge: Dennis F. Bender
(315) 539-6291; Fax: (315) 539-7850
E-mail: dbender@courts.state.ny.us
Law Clerk: Barbara A. Roesch (315) 539-7682
E-mail: broesch@courts.state.ny.us
Secretary: Marjorie Brophy (315) 539-6291
E-mail: mbrophy@courts.state.ny.us
Chief Clerk: Conchetta Brown
(315) 539-4917; Fax: (315) 539-4225
E-mail: cbrown@courts.state.ny.us
Support Magistrate: George J. Shamon

COUNTY OFFICIALS
(315) 539-1771

County Atty.: Frank R. Fisher, 1 DiPronio Dr., Waterloo 13165
(315) 539-1833; Fax: (315) 539-1606
D.A.: Barry Porsch, Courthouse, 48 W. Williams St., Waterloo 13165 (315) 539-1300; Fax: (315) 539-0531
County Clerk: Christina L. Lotz
Cty. Office Bldg., 1 DiPronio Dr., Waterloo 13165
(315) 539-1771; Fax: (315) 539-3789
Commissioner of Jurors: Elizabeth C. Young
Courthouse, 48 W. Williams St., Waterloo 13165
(315) 539-7225
Public Defender: Michael J. Mirras
P.O. Box 702, Seneca Falls 13148
(315) 568-4975; Fax: (315) 568-2324
First Asst. Public Defender: John J. Nabinger
P.O. Box 702, Seneca Falls 13148
(315) 568-4975; Fax: (315) 568-2324
Second Asst. Public Defender: Matthew D. Conlon
P.O. Box 702, Seneca Falls 13148
(315) 568-4975; Fax: (315) 568-2324
County Treasurer: Nicholas A. Sciotti
Cty. Office Bldg., 1 DiPronio Dr., Waterloo 13165
(315) 539-1735; Fax: (315) 539-1731
Sheriff: Jack Stenberg
6150 Rt. 96, Romulus 14541
(315) 220-3403; Sheriff: (315) 220-3401;
Fax: (315) 220-3478
E-mail: jstenberg@co.seneca.ny.us
Internet: http://sheriff.co.seneca.ny.us
Under Sheriff: Gary S. Sullivan (315) 220-3402
E-mail: gsullivan@co.seneca.ny.us
Jail: 6150 Rt. 96, Romulus 14541
(315) 220-3469; Fax: (315) 220-3480
Atty. Visitation: Any time

STEUBEN COUNTY

Bath, County Seat

SUPREME COURT
3 E. Pulteney Sq., Bath 14810-1575
(607) 776-7879; Fax: (607) 776-5226
E-mail: steuben_superior@courts.state.ny.us

Chief Clerk: William M. Deninger III
Court Asst.: Kelly Vanskiver

SURROGATE'S COURT
3 E. Pulteney Sq., Bath 14810-1598
(607) 776-7126

Surrogate: Marianne Furfure
3 E. Pulteney Sq., Bldg. 3
(607) 664-2296; Fax: (607) 776-4921
Law Clerk: Danette Miller
Chief Clerk: Peggy Lynn Plank
(607) 776-7126; Fax: (607) 776-4987
E-mail: pplank@courts.state.ny.us
Law Clerk/Court Atty.: Danette Miller
(607) 776-9631, Ext. 3503

***Pending November 2010 Election Results**

Steuben County—Cont'd

COUNTY COURT
Courthouse, 3 E. Pulteney Sq., Bath 14810
(607) 776-7879; Fax: (607) 776-5226

Judges:
Peter C. Bradstreet, County Office Complex, 3rd Floor, 3 E. Pulteney Sq., Bath
(607) 664-2366; Fax: (607) 776-7019
Law Clerk: Mark Schlechter
Marianne Furfure (Acting), 3 E. Pulteney Sq., Bldg. 3
(607) 664-2296; Fax: (607) 776-4921
Law Clerk: Danette Miller
Joseph W. Latham (607) 776-9631, Ext. 2284, 664-2284; Fax: (607) 776-6940
Law Clerk: Craig Snyder
Chief Clerk: William M. Deninger

FAMILY COURT
Courthouse, Bldg. 2, 3 E. Pulteney Sq., Bath 14810
(607) 664-2136; Fax: (607) 776-7857

Judges:
Peter C. Bradstreet, Bldg. 1
(607) 664-2366; Fax: (607) 776-7019
Law Clerk: Mark Schlechter
Marianne Furfure, 3 E. Pulteney Sq., Bldg. 3, Bath 14810 (607) 664-2296; Fax: (607) 776-4921
Law Clerk: Danette Miller
Joseph W. Latham
Courthouse, Bldg. 2, 3 E. Pulteney Sq., Bath 14810
(607) 664-2284; Fax: (607) 776-6940
Law Clerk: Craig Snyder
Support Magistrate: David M. Crosby
(607) 664-2138; Fax: (607) 776-7857
Chief Clerk: Pamela J. Gardner
(607) 664-2136; Fax: (607) 776-7857

COUNTY OFFICIALS
County Atty.: David F. English (Acting)
(607) 664-2355; Fax: (607) 776-4930
D.A.: John C. Tunney, 3 E. Pulteney Sq., Bath 14810-1576
(607) 776-9631, Ext. 2270; Fax: (607) 664-2159
County Clerk: Judith M. Hunter
County Office Bldg., 3 E. Pulteney Sq., Bath 14810
(607) 776-9631, Ext. 3203; Fax: (607) 664-2157
Deputy Clerk: Jennifer L. Bailey
County Office Bldg., 3 E. Pulteney Sq., Bath 14810
(607) 776-9631, Ext. 3214; Fax: (607) 664-2157
County Treasurer: *Carol S. Whitehead
County Office Bldg., 3 E. Pulteney Sq., Bath 14810
(607) 664-2488; Fax: (607) 664-2188
Law Librarian: Kristine Gilbert
Steuben County Supreme Court Library, 3 E. Pultney Sq., Bath 14810-1557 (607) 776-9631, Ext. 2099
Sheriff: Joel R. Ordway, 7007 Rumsey St. Ext., Bath 14810
(607) 776-7009, (800) 724-7777; Fax: (607) 776-7671; Emergency Fax: (607) 776-4271
E-mail: www.steubencony.org
Jail: 7007 Rumsey St. Ext., Bath 14810
(607) 776-4406; Fax: (607) 776-3973
Atty. Visitation: Call ahead to schedule an appointment

SUFFOLK COUNTY

Riverhead, County Seat

SUPREME COURT
Supreme Court Bldg., 1 Court St., Riverhead 11901
(631) 852-2333, 852-2408

John P. Cohalan, Jr. Court Complex,
400 Carleton Ave., P.O. Box 9070, Central Islip 11722
(631) 853-5462

Chief Clerk: Michael Scardino (631) 852-2334
Deputy Chief Clerks:
Theresa Matyszczyk (631) 852-2347
Robert Palmer (631) 853-5462
Principal Court Clerk: Robert Serva
(Individual Assignment Parts) (631) 852-3196
Tax Certiorari: Christina Altomare (631) 853-7441
Special Term: Thomas Clavin (631) 852-2400, 09, 10, 12

***Pending November 2010 Election Results**

SURROGATE'S COURT
320 Center Dr., Riverhead 11901
(631) 852-1745; Fax: (631) 852-1777

Surrogates:
John M. Czygier, Jr.
Stephen L. Braslow (Acting; from County Court)
Arthur M. Cromarty Court Complex, 210 Center Dr., Riverhead 11901-3310
Gary J. Weber (Acting; from County Court)
Arthur M. Cromarty Court Complex, 210 Center Dr., Riverhead 11901-3310 (631) 852-2176
Chief Clerk: Michael Cipollino (631) 852-1746
Deputy Chief Clerk: Vacancy at Press Time
Assoc. Law Clerk to Judge: Brette A. Haefeli
(631) 852-1749
Supervising Court Atty.: Linda Morrone (631) 852-1749
Court Atty. Referees: (631) 852-1749
Mary K. Kane
Frank M. Volz
Scott P. McBride
Probate Clerk: John T. Kluko (631) 852-1725
Accounting Clerk: Sandra Northrup (631) 852-1720
Administration Clerk: Rosalind M. Tamasi
(631) 852-1714
Guardianship Clerk: Cindy Voehl (631) 852-1735
Adoption Clerk: Cindy Voehl (631) 852-1735
Miscellaneous Clerk: Richard Leviness (631) 852-1739
Records Clerk: Catherine Lynch (631) 852-1724

COUNTY COURT
Arthur M. Cromarty Court Complex, 210 Center Dr., Riverhead 11901-3310
Law Department: (631) 852-1613;
Civil Dept.: (631) 852-2129;
Court Reporters: (631) 852-2152;
Criminal Dept. Information: (631) 852-1462

Judges:
Richard Ambro (631) 852-3428
W. Gerard Asher (Acting), Central Islip (631) 852-3415
Stephen L. Braslow (631) 852-1431
*Andrew A. Crecca (Acting Supreme Court Justice)
John P. Cohalan Court Complex, 400 Carleton Ave., Central Islip 11722 (631) 853-6092; Fax: (631) 853-3289
James F.X. Doyle (Acting Supreme Court Justice)
(631) 852-1640; Fax: (631) 852-3547
E-mail: jdoyle@courts.state.ny.us
Martin I. Efman (Acting)
(631) 853-2166; Fax: (631) 852-3161
Joseph Farneti (Acting Justice Supreme Court)
(631) 852-3160; Fax: (631) 852-3161
Ralph T. Gazzillo (Acting Supreme Court Justice)
(631) 852-2584; Fax: (631) 852-3854
Law Clerk: Gabrielle Weglein (631) 852-2583
*James C. Hudson (631) 852-3850; Fax: (631) 852-3225
E-mail: jhudson@courts.state.ny.us
Barbara R. Kahn (631) 852-3040
Gaetan Lozito (Acting), Central Islip (631) 853-4919
Glenn A. Murphy (Acting), Central Islip (631) 853-7418
James F. Quinn (Acting Family Court Judge)
Central Islip (631) 853-3244; Fax: (631) 853-7727
Law Clerk: Anita Prudenti
Secretary: Andrea Bruzik
G. Ann Spelman (Acting), Central Islip (631) 853-7418
Jeffrey Arlen Spinner (Acting Supreme Court Judge)
Supreme Court Bldg., 1 Court St., Riverhead 11901
(631) 852-2309; Fax: (631) 852-3226
E-mail: jspinner@courts.state.ny.us
Principal Law Secretary: Robert DeGregorio
Secretary: Erin M. Kay
Andrew G. Tarantino, Jr. (Acting)
Supreme Court Bldg., 1 Court St., Riverhead 11901
(631) 852-1960; Fax: (631) 852-3351
Gary J. Weber (Acting Supreme Court Justice)
(631) 852-2176; Fax: (631) 852-3857
Chief Clerk: Victor V. Rossomano
(631) 852-2120; Fax: (631) 852-2568
Deputy Chief Clerk: Frank Tropea (631) 852-2120

Suffolk County—Cont'd

FAMILY COURT
John P. Cohalan, Jr. Court Complex,
400 Carleton Ave., Central Islip 11722
(631) 853-4647, 48
Courthouse, Suite 308, 889 E. Main St., Riverhead 11901
(631) 852-3905, 06
WBLI 106.1 FM; WBAB 102.3 FM; WLNG 92.1 FM and on TV, Channel 12 News

Supervising Judge: David Freundlich
(Acting Justice Supreme Court)
(631) 853-4318; Fax: (631) 853-6218

Judges:
Marlene L. Budd (631) 853-7752; Fax: (631) 853-7569
Joan M. Genchi (631) 852-3907; Fax: (631) 852-2851
E-mail: jgenchi@courts.state.ny.us
Richard Hoffmann (631) 853-4268; Fax: (631) 853-4359
John Kelly (631) 853-4286; Fax: (631) 853-4288
Acting Supreme Court Justice
Martha L. Luft (631) 853-4537; Fax: (631) 853-5427
Barbara Lynaugh (631) 852-3845; Fax: (631) 852-2986
E-mail: blynaugh@courts.state.ny.us
James F. Quinn (Acting) (631) 853-3244; Fax: (631) 853-7727
Patrick A. Sweeney (631) 853-2207; Fax: (631) 853-8407
Acting Supreme Court Justice
Andrew G. Tarantino, Jr. (Acting County Court Judge)
Supreme Court Bldg., 1 Court St., Riverhead 11901
(631) 852-1960; Fax: (631) 852-3351
Theresa Whelan (631) 853-4935; Fax: (631) 853-7629
Secretary: Janice Pellicano (631) 853-4935

Chief Clerk: Patricia Herlihy
(631) 853-4280; Fax: (631) 853-5851

Chief Court Atty.: Vacancy at Press Time (Law Dept.)
(631) 853-4311; Fax: (631) 853-7919

Support Magistrates:
Isabel E. Buse (631) 853-6200; Fax: (631) 853-7568
Aletha Fields (631) 853-6200; Fax: (631) 853-7568
David Grier (631) 852-3749; Fax: (631) 852-2877
Cheryl Joseph-Cherry (631) 853-6200; Fax: (631) 853-7568
Denise Livrieri (631) 853-6200; Fax: (631) 853-7568
Rachel Parisi (631) 853-5445
John Raimondi (631) 853-6200; Fax: (631) 853-7568
Melissa Willmott (631) 852-2711; Fax: (631) 852-2877
Vacancy at Press Time (631) 853-6200; Fax: (631) 853-7568

COUNTY OFFICIALS

County Atty.: Christine Malafi, H. Lee Dennison Bldg., 6th Floor, 100 Vet. Mem. Hwy., P.O. Box 6100, Hauppauge 11788 (631) 853-4049; Fax: (631) 853-5169

D.A.: Thomas J. Spota III, North County Complex, Bldg. 77, 725 Veterans Memorial Hwy., Hauppauge 11788 (631) 853-4161; Fax: (631) 853-5820

County Clerk: *Judith A. Pascale
310 Center Dr., Riverhead 11901-3392
(631) 852-2000; Fax: (631) 852-2004

Comptroller: *Joseph Sawicki, Jr.
H. Lee Dennison Bldg., 100 Veterans Memorial Hwy., P.O. Box 6100, Hauppauge 11788-0099
(631) 853-5040; Fax: (631) 853-5057

Dir. of Probation: John K. Desmond, P.O. Box 188, Yaphank 11980 (631) 852-5000; Fax: (631) 852-5103

Public Administrator: Franklyn A. Farris, 300 Center Dr., Riverhead 11901 (631) 852-1753; Fax: (631) 852-2740

County Treasurer: Angie M. Carpenter, 330 Center Dr., Riverhead 11901-3311 (631) 852-1500; Fax: (631) 852-1507

County Executive: Steve Levy, H. Lee Dennison Bldg., 100 Veterans Memorial Hwy., P.O. Box 6100, Hauppauge 11788 (631) 853-4000; Fax: (631) 853-4818

Presiding Officer (Legislature): William J. Lindsay
Wm. H. Rogers Bldg., 725 Veterans Memorial Hwy., Smithtown 11787 (631) 854-9611

Principal Law Librarian: Lynn Fullshire, Supreme Court Law Library, Arthur M. Cromarty Court Complex, 220 Center Dr., Riverhead 11901 (631) 852-2419

***Pending November 2010 Election Results**

Law Librarian: John Hadler
NYS Supreme Court Law Library, John P. Cohalan, Jr. Court Complex, 400 Carleton Ave., Central Islip 11722 (631) 853-7530

Sheriff: Vincent F. DeMarco
100 Center Dr., Riverhead 11901-3389
(631) 852-2200; Sheriff: (631) 852-2205; Fax: (631) 852-1898

Correctional Facility: 100 Center Dr., Riverhead 11901
(631) 852-2200; Fax: (631) 852-1983
Atty. Visitation: Weekdays, 8 A.M.-10 P.M.

SULLIVAN COUNTY

Monticello, County Seat

SUPREME COURT
Lawrence H. Cooke Sullivan County Courthouse,
414 Broadway, Monticello 12701
(845) 794-4066; Fax: (845) 791-6170

Chief Clerk: Earl Lilley

Deputy Clerk: Sarah Katzman

SURROGATE'S COURT
Government Center, Room 250, 100 North St.,
P.O. Box 5012, Monticello 12701
(845) 807-0690; Fax: (845) 794-0310
Courthouse, 414 Broadway, Monticello 12701

Surrogates:
Frank J. LaBuda (845) 794-1248; Fax: (845) 794-6208
Law Clerk: John Diuguid
Secretary: Iva R. Krom Ext. 111
*Subject to Election

Chief Clerk: Lu Ann P. Hering
(845) 807-0690; Fax: (845) 794-0310

COUNTY COURT
Lawrence H. Cooke Sullivan County Courthouse,
414 Broadway, Monticello 12701
(845) 794-4066; Fax: (845) 791-6170

Judges:
Frank J. LaBuda (845) 794-1248; Fax: (845) 794-6208
Law Asst.: John Diuguid
(845) 794-1248; Fax: (845) 794-6208
Secretary: Iva R. Krom
*Subject to Election

Chief Clerk: Earl Lilley

Deputy Chief Clerk: Sarah Katzman

FAMILY COURT
Government Center, 100 North St., Monticello 12701
(845) 807-0650; Fax: (845) 794-0199

Judge: Mark M. Meddaugh
(845) 807-0650; Fax: (845) 794-8300
Acting Supreme Court Judge

Chief Clerk: Christina Benson

Deputy Chief Clerk: Stacey Benton

Law Clerk: Sandra F. Heck

Support Magistrate: Karen L. Linen

COUNTY OFFICIALS

County Atty.: Sam Yasgur
Government Center, 100 North St., P.O. Box 5012, Monticello 12701 (845) 807-0560; Fax: (845) 807-0574

D.A.: James R. Farrell
Lawrence H. Cooke Sullivan County Cthse., 414 Broadway, Monticello 12701
(845) 794-3344; Fax: (845) 794-3646

County Clerk: Daniel L. Briggs
Government Center, 100 North St., P.O. Box 5012, Monticello 12701 (845) 807-0411; Fax: (845) 807-0434

County Treasurer: Ira Cohen, Government Center, 100 North St., P.O. Box 5012, Monticello 12701
(845) 807-0200; Fax: (845) 807-0220

Commissioner of Jurors: Loretta Duarte
Lawrence H. Cooke Sullivan County Courthouse, 414 Broadway, Monticello 12701
(845) 794-4088; Fax: (845) 791-1712

Sullivan County Officials—Cont'd

Law Librarian: Edith Schop
Hamilton O'Dell Library, NYS Supreme Court Library, Lawrence H. Cooke Sullivan County Courthouse, 414 Broadway, Monticello 12701 (845) 794-1547

Sheriff: Michael A. Schiff, 8 Bushnell Ave., Monticello 12701
(845) 794-7100; Fax: (845) 794-7119;
Sheriff's Fax: (845) 794-0810
E-mail: michael.schiff@co.sullivan.ny.us

Jail: 4 Bushnell Ave., Monticello 12701
(845) 794-7102; Fax: (845) 794-4094
E-mail: harold.smith@co.sullivan.ny.us
Atty. Visitation: Any time

TIOGA COUNTY

Owego, County Seat

SUPREME COURT
16 Court St., P.O. Box 307, Owego 13827
(607) 687-0544; Fax: (607) 687-3240

Chief Clerk: JoAnn Peet

SURROGATE'S COURT
Court Annex, 20 Court St., P.O. Box 10, Owego 13827
(607) 687-1303; Fax: (607) 687-3240
Internet:
www.nycourts.gov/courts/6jd/tioga/surrogate/index.

Surrogate: Vincent A. Sgueglia, Courthouse
(607) 687-0338; Fax: (607) 687-1524

Chief Clerk: Deborah A. Stone

COUNTY COURT
Courthouse, 20 Court St., P.O. Box 10, Owego 13827
(607) 687-0338; Fax: (607) 687-5680

Judge: Vincent A. Sgueglia (607) 687-0338; Fax: (607) 687-1524
Law Clerk: Karen Natwick (607) 687-0563

Chief Clerk: JoAnn Peet (607) 687-0544

FAMILY COURT
Court Annex Bldg., 20 Court St., P.O. Box 10, Owego 13827
(607) 687-1730; Fax: (607) 687-3240

Judge: Vincent A. Sgueglia, Courthouse
(607) 687-0338; Fax: (607) 687-1524

Chief Clerk: Denise R. Marsili (607) 687-1730

Deputy Chief Clerk: Deborah Leach (607) 687-1730

Deputy Clerks:
Deborah Simonik
Nancy Whitebird

COUNTY OFFICIALS
56 Main St., Owego 13827

County Atty.: Judith Quigley, 56 Main St., Owego 13827
(607) 687-8253; Fax: (607) 223-7003

D.A.: Gerald A. Keene, 20 Court St., P.O. Box 300, Owego 13827 (607) 687-8650; Fax: (607) 687-1614

County Clerk: Robert L. Woodburn, Jr., 16 Court St., Owego 13827 (607) 687-8660; Fax: (607) 687-8686

County Treasurer: James P. McFadden
56 Main St., 2nd Fl., Room 210, Owego 13827
(607) 687-8670; Fax: (607) 223-7035
Internet: www.tiogacountytreasurer.com

Sheriff: Gary W. Howard, 103 Corporate Dr., Owego 13827
(607) 687-1010; Civil: (607) 687-8461;
Fax: (607) 687-6755

Jail: 103 Corporate Dr., Owego 13827
(607) 687-8463; Fax: (607) 687-8812
Atty. Visitation: Weekdays, any time except meals

***Pending November 2010 Election Results**

TOMPKINS COUNTY

Ithaca, County Seat

SUPREME COURT
Courthouse, 320 N. Tioga St., P.O. Box 70, Ithaca 14851-0070
(607) 272-0466; Fax: (607) 256-0301

Chief Clerk: Paula M. Nichols

SURROGATE'S COURT
Courthouse, 320 N. Tioga St., P.O. Box 70, Ithaca 14851-0070
(607) 277-0622; Fax: (607) 256-2572
Internet: www.nycourts.gov/6jd/countymaps/tompkins/tpksurrog

Surrogates:
John C. Rowley (607) 277-4957; Fax: (212) 457-2938
Law Clerk: Stephen Heller
Secretary: Dianne Valesente
M. John Sherman
Law Clerk: Michael R. Berg
Secretary: Polly White

Chief Clerk: Lori S. Decker

COUNTY COURT
Courthouse, 320 N. Tioga St., P.O. Box 70, Ithaca 14851-0070
(607) 272-0466

Judges:
John C. Rowley (607) 277-4957; Fax: (212) 457-2938
Law Clerk: Stephen Heller
M. John Sherman (607) 277-2355; Fax: (607) 272-0684
Law Clerk: Michael R. Berg
Secretary: Polly White

Chief Clerk: Paula Nichols
(607) 272-0466; Fax: (212) 401-9071

FAMILY COURT
Courthouse, 320 N. Tioga St., P.O. Box 70, Ithaca 14851-0070
(607) 277-1517; Fax: (607) 277-5027

Judges:
John C. Rowley (607) 277-4957; Fax: (212) 457-2938
Law Clerk: Stephen Heller
Secretary: Dianne Valesente
M. John Sherman (607) 277-2355; Fax: (607) 272-0684
Law Clerk: Michael Berg
Secretary: Polly White

Clerk: Cheryl L. Lidell-Obenauer; Fax: (607) 277-5027
E-mail: clidell@courts.state.ny.us

Support Magistrate: Alan D. Scheer (Support Matters)

COUNTY OFFICIALS

County Atty.: Jonathan Wood, 125 E. Court St., Ithaca 14850 (607) 274-5546; Fax: (607) 274-5547

D.A.: Gwen Wilkinson, Courthouse, 320 N. Tioga St., Ithaca 14850 (607) 274-5461; Fax: (607) 274-5429

County Clerk: *Aurora R. Valenti
Courthouse, 320 N. Tioga St., Ithaca 14850
(607) 274-5431; Fax: (607) 274-5445

County Administrator: Joe Mareane, 125 E. Court St., Ithaca 14850 (607) 274-5551; Fax: (607) 274-5558

Law Librarian: Terrie Stewart
Ernest Warren Supreme Court Library, Courthouse, 320 N. Tioga St., Ithaca 14850
(607) 272-0045; Fax: (607) 272-3276

Sheriff: *Peter J. Meskill, 779 Warren Rd., Ithaca 14850
(607) 257-1345; Fax: (607) 266-5436
E-mail: pmeskill@tompkins-co.org

Jail: 779 Warren Rd., Ithaca 14850
(607) 257-5316; Fax: (607) 266-5403
Atty. Visitation: Any time

ULSTER COUNTY

Kingston, County Seat

SUPREME COURT
Courthouse, 285 Wall St., Kingston 12401-0906
(845) 340-3377; Filings only: (845) 340-3288;
Fax: (845) 340-3387

Chief Clerk: Florence R. Brandt (845) 340-3377

Deputy Chief Clerk: Margaret G. Maines (845) 340-3239

Sr. Court Clerk: Beth Cornell (845) 340-3238

Court Clerks:
Joleine Hercules (845) 340-3374
Laura Migliorato (845) 340-3377

Court Asst.: Claudia Jones (845) 340-3775

Court Office Assts.:
Debra Brewster (845) 340-3377
Pam Gudmundsen (845) 340-3377
Nancy Suto (845) 340-3377

SURROGATE'S COURT
244 Fair St., P.O. Box 1800, Kingston 12402-1800
(845) 340-3348; Fax: (845) 340-3352
Internet: www.nycourts.gov

Surrogate: Mary M. Work (845) 340-3348
Law Clerk: Leanora Kovacs (845) 331-1899
E-mail: lkovacs@courts.state.ny.us
Secretary: Linda M. McCluskey (845) 340-3349

Chief Clerk: Mary Ellen Sullivan
(845) 340-3350; Fax: (845) 340-3352

Deputy Chief Clerk: Kathleen T. King
(845) 340-3348; Fax: (845) 340-3352

COUNTY COURT
Courthouse, 285 Wall St., Kingston 12401-0906
(845) 340-3730; Fax: (845) 340-3729

Judge: Donald A. Williams, Jr.
(845) 340-3730; Fax: (845) 340-3739

Chief Clerk: Florence R. Brandt (845) 340-3377

Deputy Clerk: Margaret G. Haines (845) 340-3377

FAMILY COURT
16 Lucas Ave., Kingston 12401-0906
(845) 340-3600; Fax: (845) 340-3626

Judges:
Anthony McGinty (845) 340-3601
E-mail: amcginty@courts.state.ny.us
Law Clerk: Gilda Riccardi (845) 340-3602
Secretary: Donna Weiner (845) 340-3601
Marianne O. Mizel (845) 340-3614
E-mail: mmizel@courts.state.ny.us
Law Clerk: Christine Van Benschoten (845) 340-3610
Secretary: Dawn Mendez Knox (845) 340-3614

Support Magistrate: John K. Beisel (845) 340-3613

Chief Clerk: Kathy Lasko (845) 340-3608
E-mail: klasko@courts.state.ny.us

Deputy Chief Clerk: Elaine Stinemire (845) 340-3606
E-mail: estinemi@courts.state.ny.us

COUNTY OFFICIALS

County Atty.: Beatrice Havranek
County Office Bldg., 244 Fair St., P.O. Box 1800,
Kingston 12402-1800 (845) 340-3685; Fax: (845) 340-3691

D.A.: D. Holley Carnright
County Courthouse, 275 Wall St., Kingston 12401-0906
(845) 340-3280; Fax: (845) 340-3185

County Clerk: Nina A. Postupack, County Office Bldg.,
244 Fair St., P.O. Box 1800, Kingston 12402-1800
(845) 340-3040, 340-3288; Fax: (845) 340-3299

Comptroller: *Elliott Auerbach, County Office Bldg.,
244 Fair St., P.O. Box 1800, Kingston 12402-1800
(845) 340-3526; Fax: (845) 340-3697

Commissioner of Jurors: Richard B. Mathews
285 Wall St., Kingston 12401
(845) 340-3050; Fax: (845) 340-3052

Deputy Commissioner: Terri Johnston
285 Wall St., Kingston 12401 (845) 340-3050

***Pending November 2010 Election Results**

County Executive: Michael P. Hein, County Office Bldg.,
244 Fair St., P.O. Box 1800, Kingston 12402-1800
(845) 340-3636; Fax: (845) 334-5724

Law Librarian: Michael Birzenieks
NYS Supreme Court Library, Courthouse, 285 Wall St.,
Kingston 12401 (845) 340-3053; Fax: (845) 340-3773

Public Defender: Andrew Kossover, 18 Lucas Ave.,
Kingston 12401 (845) 340-3232; Fax: (845) 340-3744
E-mail: akos@co.ulster.ny.us

Commissioner, Dept. of Finance: Paul J. Hewitt
County Office Bldg., 244 Fair St., P.O. Box 1800,
Kingston 12402-1800
(845) 340-3458; Fax: (845) 340-3430

Clerk, County Legislature: Karen L. Binder
County Office Bldg., 244 Fair St., P.O. Box 1800,
Kingston 12402-3800 (845) 340-3646; Fax: (845) 340-3651

Sheriff: *Paul J. VanBlarcum
380 Boulevard, Kingston 12401-2941
(845) 338-3640; Sheriff: (845) 340-3590;
Criminal Fax: (845) 340-3718; Civil Fax: (845) 334-8125
Internet: www.co.ulster.ny.us/sheriff

Law Enforcement Center: 380 Boulevard, Kingston 12401
(845) 340-3644; Fax: (845) 340-3436
Internet: www.co.ulster.ny.us/sheriff
Atty. Visitation: Any time

WARREN COUNTY

Lake George, County Seat

SUPREME COURT
Warren County Municipal Center,
1340 State Route 9, Lake George 12845-9803
(518) 761-6547; Fax: (518) 761-6465

Chief Clerk: Joanne M. Mann
(516) 761-6431; Fax: (518) 761-6253

SURROGATE'S COURT
Warren County Municipal Center,
1340 State Route 9, Lake George 12845-9803
(518) 761-7514; Fax: (518) 761-6511

Surrogate: John S. Hall, Jr. (518) 761-7695
E-mail: jshall@courts.state.ny.us

Confidential Law Clerk: Robert A. Smith (518) 761-7696

Chief Clerk: Deborah K. Ricci (518) 761-6514
E-mail: dkricci@nycourts.gov

COUNTY COURT
Warren County Municipal Center,
1340 State Route 9, Lake George 12845-9803
(518) 761-6430

Judge: John S. Hall, Jr.
(518) 761-7695; Fax: (518) 761-7698
E-mail: jshall@courts.state.ny.us

Law Clerk: Robert A. Smith (518) 761-7696

Chief Clerk: Joanne M. Mann (518) 761-6431

FAMILY COURT
Warren County Municipal Center,
1340 State Route 9, Lake George 12845
(518) 761-6500; Fax: (518) 761-6230

Judge: J. Timothy Breen
E-mail: cbarber@courts.state.ny.us

Support Magistrates:
John T. Ellis II   Jonathan A. Heussi

Law Clerk: Paulette M. Kershko

Chief Clerk: Sally Boivin (518) 761-6500

COUNTY OFFICIALS

County Atty.: Paul B. Dusek, Warren County Munic. Center,
1340 State Route 9, Lake George 12845-9803
(518) 761-6463; Fax: (518) 761-6377
E-mail: dusekp@co.warren.ny.us

D.A.: Kathleen B. Hogan, Warren County Munic. Center,
340 State Route 9, Lake George 12845-9803
(518) 761-6405; Fax: (518) 761-6254

Warren County Officials—Cont'd

County Clerk: Pamela J. Vogel
Warren County Municipal Center, 1340 State Route 9, Lake George 12845-9803
(518) 761-6427; Fax: (518) 761-6551
E-mail: vogelp@co.warren.ny.us
Internet: www.co.warren.ny.us

Clerk, Board of Supervisors: Joan Sady
(518) 761-6563; Fax: (518) 761-7652
E-mail: sadyj@co.warren.ny.us

County Treasurer: Francis X. O'Keefe
Warren County Municipal Center, 1340 State Route 9, Lake George 12845-9803
(518) 761-6375; Fax: (518) 761-6470

Law Librarian: Regina Ellis
Supreme Court Library, Municipal Center, 1340 State Rt. 9, Lake George 12845-9803
(518) 761-6442; Fax: (518) 761-6586

Sheriff: Nathan Bud York
1400 State Rt. 9, Lake George 12845
(518) 743-2500; Fax: (518) 743-2519

Correctional Facility: 1400 State Rt. 9, Lake George 12845
(518) 743-2500; Fax: (518) 743-2589
Atty. Visitation: Daily, Any time except 11:30 A.M.-12:30 P.M. and 4-5:30 P.M.

WASHINGTON COUNTY

Hudson Falls, County Seat

SUPREME COURT
Courthouse, Bldg. C, 383 Broadway, Fort Edward 12828
(518) 746-2521; Fax: (518) 746-2519

County Clerk: Dona J. Crandall, Bldg. A
(518) 746-2170; Fax: (518) 746-2177

Chief Clerk: Kathleen M. LaBelle (518) 746-2520

Deputy Chief Clerk: Tricia M. Robarge (518) 746-2521

SURROGATE'S COURT
Courthouse, Bldg. C, 383 Broadway, Fort Edward 12828
(518) 746-2545; Fax: (518) 746-2547

Surrogates:
Kelly S. McKeighan (518) 746-2515; Fax: (518) 746-2531
Law Clerk: Adam Michelini
Stan L. Pritzker (518) 746-2506; Fax: (518) 746-2505
Law Clerk: Ted Wilson

Chief Clerk: Barbara Z. Smith
(518) 746-2545; Fax: (518) 746-2547

COUNTY COURT
Courthouse, Bldg. C, 383 Broadway, Fort Edward 12828
(518) 746-2521

Judges:
Kelly S. McKeighan (518) 746-2515
Law Clerk: Adam Michelini (518) 746-2511
Stan L. Pritzker (518) 746-2506
Law Clerk: Ted Wilson (518) 746-2510

Chief Clerk: Kathleen M. LaBelle

Deputy Chief Clerk: Tricia M. Robarge (518) 746-2520

FAMILY COURT
Courthouse, 383 Broadway, Fort Edward 12828
(518) 746-2501; Fax: (518) 746-2503

Judges:
Kelly S. McKeighan (518) 746-2515; Fax: (518) 746-2531
Law Clerk: Adam Michelini (518) 746-2515
Stan L. Pritzker (518) 746-2506; Fax: (518) 746-2505
Law Clerk: Ted M. Wilson

Support Magistrate: Donald H. Clark, Jr.

Chief Clerk: Patricia A. Ross

COUNTY OFFICIALS

County Atty.: Roger A. Wickes
383 Broadway, Bldg. B, Fort Edward 12828
(518) 746-2216; Fax: (518) 746-2137

D.A.: Kevin C. Kortright
383 Broadway, Bldg. C, Fort Edward 12828
(518) 746-2525; Fax: (518) 746-2568

Chairman, Bd. of Supervisors: John Rymph
383 Broadway, Bldg. B, Fort Edward 12828
(518) 746-2212; Fax: (518) 746-2219

County Clerk: Dona J. Crandall
383 Broadway, Bldg. A, Fort Edward 12828
(518) 746-2170; Fax: (518) 746-2177

County Treasurer: Phyllis Cooper
383 Broadway, Bldg. B, Fort Edward 12828
(518) 746-2220; Fax: (518) 746-2234

Law Library: Courthouse, Bldg. C, 383 Broadway, Fort Edward 12828 (518) 746-2540

Sheriff: Roger W. Leclaire, 399 Broadway, Ft. Edward 12828
(518) 746-2475; Fax: (518) 746-2483;
Civil: (518) 746-2477; Civil Fax: (518) 746-2385
E-mail: rleclaire@co.washington.ny.us

Jail: 399 Broadway, Fort Edward 12828
(518) 746-2476; Fax: (518) 746-2484
Atty. Visitation: Any time; call in advance

WAYNE COUNTY

Lyons, County Seat

SUPREME COURT
Hall of Justice, 54 Broad St., Lyons 14489-1199
(315) 946-5459; Fax: (315) 946-5456
Internet:
www.nycourts/gov/courts/7jd/wayne/index.shtml

Chief Clerk: Julie R. Brooks
E-mail: jbrooks@courts.state.ny.us

SURROGATE'S COURT
Hall of Justice, 54 Broad St., Lyons 14489-1199
(315) 946-5430; Fax: (315) 946-5433

Surrogates:
Daniel G. Barrett (315) 946-5443; Fax: (315) 946-5428
Dennis M. Kehoe (315) 946-5435; Fax: (315) 946-5434
John B. Nesbitt (315) 946-5441; Fax: (315) 946-5429

Chief Clerk: Nancy L. Secor, Room 106
(315) 946-5430; Fax: (315) 946-5433

COUNTY COURT
Hall of Justice, 54 Broad St., Lyons 14489-1199
(315) 946-5459; Fax: (315) 946-5456

Judges:
Daniel G. Barrett (315) 946-5443; Fax: (315) 946-5428
Law Clerk: Rich Doyle (315) 946-5445
Dennis M. Kehoe (315) 946-5435; Fax: (315) 946-5434
John B. Nesbitt (315) 946-5441; Fax: (315) 946-5429
Law Clerk: Francis Mamuscia
(315) 946-7502; Fax: (315) 946-7411

Chief Clerk: Julie R. Brooks
(315) 946-5459; Fax: (315) 945-5456
E-mail: jbrooks@courts.state.ny.us

FAMILY COURT
Hall of Justice, Suite 106, 54 Broad St., Lyons 14489-1199
(315) 946-5420; Fax: (315) 946-5456
Internet:
www.nycourts.gov/courts/7jd/courts/family/county/w

Judges:
Daniel G. Barrett (315) 946-5443; Fax: (315) 946-5428
Dennis M. Kehoe (315) 946-5435; Fax: (315) 946-5434
Law Clerk: Mary Ellen Walsh (315) 946-5438
John B. Nesbitt, Room 322
(315) 946-5441; Fax: (315) 946-5429
Law Clerk: Francis Mamuscia (315) 946-7502

Chief Clerk: Lorraine T. Fodera, Suite 106
(315) 946-5420; Fax: (315) 946-5456

Support Magistrate: Deborah Gerber Farber (315) 946-7521

Wayne County—Cont'd

COUNTY OFFICIALS

County Atty.: Daniel M. Wyner
Courthouse, 26 Church St., Lyons 14489-1182
(315) 946-7442; Fax: (315) 946-5942

D.A.: Richard M. Healy, Hall of Justice, Suite 202,
54 Broad St., Lyons 14489-1182
(315) 946-5905; Fax: (315) 946-5911

County Clerk: Michael P. Jankowski
9 Pearl St., Box 608, Lyons 14489
(315) 946-7470; Fax: (315) 946-5978
E-mail: mjankowski@co.wayne.ny.us

County Treasurer: Thomas A. Warnick
16 William St., P.O. Box 8, Lyons 14489-0008
(315) 946-5946; Fax: (315) 946-5949

Sheriff: Barry C. Virts, 7368 Rt. 31, Lyons 14489-9107
(315) 946-9711; Fax: (315) 946-5811;
Civil: (315) 946-5793; Records: (315) 946-5790;
Visitation: (315) 946-5714
E-mail: waynecosheriff.org

Jail: 7368 Rt. 31, Lyons 14489
(315) 946-5807; Fax: (315) 946-7065
Internet: www.waynecosheriff.org
Atty. Visitation: 8-11:30 A.M. & 1:15-2:30 P.M. &
3-4:45 P.M. & 6:15-10:15 P.M.

WESTCHESTER COUNTY

White Plains, County Seat

SUPREME COURT
**111 Dr. Martin Luther King, Jr. Blvd.,
White Plains 10601
Civil: (914) 824-5300; Criminal: (914) 824-5400;
Fax: (914) 995-3427**

Chief Clerk: Donna J. Minort

Deputy Chief Clerks:
Ronda Brown (Civil)
Elizabeth Pace (Criminal) (914) 824-5400

SURROGATE'S COURT
**111 Dr. Martin Luther King, Jr. Blvd., 19th Floor,
White Plains 10601
(914) 824-5656;
Records Dept.: (914) 824-5633, 34, 35, 36;
Fax: (914) 995-3728**

Surrogate: Anthony A. Scarpino, Jr.
(914) 824-5654; Fax: (914) 995-7593
Law Clerk: Josephine Trovini (914) 824-5644

Chief Clerk: Charles T. Scott, 19th Floor (914) 824-5646

Deputy Chief Clerk: Johanna K. O'Brien, 19th Floor
(914) 824-5626

Law Assts.:
Joseph M. Accetta (914) 824-5655
Colleen Carew, 19th Floor (914) 824-5571
Jody B. Keltz, 19th Floor (914) 824-5643
Kevin S. Murphy (914) 824-5645

Miscellaneous Clerk: Amy T. Carvelli, 19th Floor
(914) 824-5642

Accountants:
Richard W. Hart, 19th Floor (914) 824-5631
Robin Rodriguez, 19th Floor (914) 824-5630
Mackeema Sullivan (914) 824-5668

Probate/Administration Clerks:
Denise Bennett, 19th Floor (914) 824-5461
John Curtin, 19th Floor (914) 824-5639
Edward J. McGuckin, 19th Floor (914) 824-5628

Guardianship Clerks:
Alfonso D. Rodriguez, 19th Floor (914) 824-5638
Shannon Williams, 19th Floor (914) 824-5637

***Pending November 2010 Election Results**

COUNTY COURT
**111 Dr. Martin Luther King, Jr. Blvd.,
White Plains 10601
(914) 824-5100; Fax: (914) 995-4946**

Judges:
Susan Cacace (914) 824-5401
Law Clerk: Alphonse Naclerio
Secretary: Heather Stradling
Susan Capeci (914) 824-5857; Fax: (914) 995-7470
Law Clerk: Ivy Ozer
Secretary: Donatella Coppa-Runfola
John Colangelo (914) 824-5423; Fax: (914) 995-8653
Law Clerk: Barbara Coleman
Secretary: Lisa Boslow Dorman
Robert M. DiBella (914) 824-5407; Fax: (914) 995-4396
Acting Supreme Court Justice
Law Clerk: Lisa Citarella
Secretary: Brigid McCarney
James W. Hubert (914) 824-5790; Fax: (914) 995-8654
Law Clerk: Jayni Edelstein Alegria
Secretary: Sha-Kee Williams
Gerald E. Loehr (914) 824-5413; Fax: (914) 995-8651
Acting Justice Supreme Justice
Law Clerk: Bruce Pearl (914) 824-5414
Secretary: Jessica Medina
E-mail: jjmedina@courts.state.ny.us
Barry E. Warhit (914) 824-5400
Barbara Gunther Zambelli
(914) 824-5439; Fax: (914) 995-8653
Acting Supreme Court Justice
Law Clerk: Barbara Sheridan
Secretary: Tina Harvey

Chief Clerk: Vacancy at Press Time (914) 824-5300

FAMILY COURT
**111 Dr. Martin Luther King, Jr. Blvd.,
White Plains 10601
(914) 824-5500; Fax: (914) 995-8650;
Fax (Clerk): (914) 995-8647**

**420 North Ave., New Rochelle 10801
(914) 831-6590; Fax (Clerk): (914) 813-5580;
Judges Fax: (914) 813-5634**

**53 S. Broadway, Yonkers 10701
(914) 831-6555; Fax (Clerk): (914) 231-3016;
Judges Fax: (914) 231-2809**

Supervising Judge, Family Cts., 9th Jud. Dist.:
Kathie E. Davidson (914) 824-5479; Fax: (914) 995-4586
Law Clerk: Maria Recine (914) 824-5479
Secretary: Elaine Magnone

Judges:
Sandra B. Edlitz (914) 824-5481; Fax: (914) 995-8645
E-mail: sedlitz@courts.state.ny.us
Law Clerk: Raynette Bernard
Secretary: Janet Hirsch
William Edwards (Acting Judge)
(914) 824-5798; Fax: (914) 995-4490
Law Clerk: Sheila Gabay
Secretary: Gloria Watson
Nilda Morales Horowitz (New Rochelle)
(914) 831-6587; Fax: (914) 813-5634
E-mail: nmhorowi@courts.state.ny.us
Law Clerk: Maritza Fugaro-Norton
Secretary: Gloria Vinelli
David Klein (914) 824-5477; Fax: (914) 995-6565
Law Clerk: Katheryn Ritchie
Secretary: Lawanna Bishop
Janet Malone (Yonkers) (914) 831-6548; Fax: (914) 231-2809
Law Clerk: Sharon Matthie
Secretary: Vacancy at Press Time
Mary Anne Scattaretico-Naber (Yonkers)
(914) 831-6513; Fax: (914) 231-2809
Law Clerk: Michelle D'Ambrosio
Secretary: Catherine Cellini

Chief Clerk: James M. McAllister
(914) 824-5575; Fax: (914) 995-8650

Westchester County Family Court—Cont'd
Deputy Chief Clerks IV:
Sonia Soto (New Rochelle)
(914) 831-6583; Fax: (914) 813-5580
Queenie Anderson (Yonkers)
(914) 831-6510; Fax: (914) 231-3016
Principal Court Clerks:
Omar Cumberbatch (914) 824-5500; Fax: (914) 995-8647
William Curry (914) 824-5500; Fax: (914) 995-8647
Assoc. Court Clerks:
Michael Salcito, 420 North Ave., New Rochelle 10801
(914) 831-6590
James Scully (914) 824-5500; Fax: (914) 995-8647
Kenton Vanzandt (Yonkers)
(914) 831-6555; Fax: (914) 231-3016
Court Atty. Referees:
Stephanie F. Lammers (Yonkers) (914) 831-6555
Michelle I. Schauer (914) 824-5500; Fax: (914) 995-8647

COUNTY OFFICIALS

County Atty.: Robert Meehan
148 Martine Ave., Room 600, White Plains 10601
(914) 995-2690; Fax: (914) 995-5858
D.A.: Janet DiFiore, 111 Dr. Martin Luther King, Jr. Blvd., White Plains 10601 (914) 995-3414; Fax: (914) 995-3363
County Clerk: Timothy C. Idoni
110 Dr. Martin Luther King, Jr. Blvd., Room 350, White Plains 10601 (914) 995-3080; Fax: (914) 995-4030
Commissioner of Finance: Anne Marie Berg
148 Martine Ave., Room 720, White Plains 10601
(914) 995-2757; Fax: (914) 995-3230
County Executive: Rob Astorino, 148 Martine Ave., White Plains 10601 (914) 995-2900; Fax: (914) 995-3372
Commissioner of Jurors: Frances M. Tursi
Courthouse, 111 Dr. Martin Luther King, Jr. Blvd., White Plains 10601 (914) 824-5600; Fax: (914) 995-4945
E-mail: ftursi@courts.state.ny.us
Law Librarian: Sonja Davis
Supreme Court Law Library, Courthouse, 9th Floor, 111 Dr. Martin Luther King, Jr. Blvd., White Plains 10601 (914) 824-5660; Fax: (914) 995-3973
Commissioner of Public Safety (Sheriff):
George Longworth, 110 Dr. Martin Luther King, Jr. Blvd., White Plains 10601
Civil Unit: (914) 995-3053; Jail: (914) 231-1400; Commissioner: (914) 864-7700; Fax: (914) 995-4095
Civil Unit, 110 Dr. M.L.King, Jr. Blvd., Room L217, White Plains 10601 (914) 995-3053; Fax: (914) 995-4095
Internet: www.publicsafety.westchestergov.com
Department of Correction:
10 Woods Rd.- Grasslands Reservation, P.O. Box 389, Valhalla 10595 (914) 231-1400; Fax: (914) 231-1262
Internet: www.westchestergov.com
Atty. Visitation: Daily, 9:30 A.M.-4:30 P.M.
Commissioner: Kevin Cheverko (Acting) (914) 231-1054

WYOMING COUNTY

Warsaw, County Seat

SUPREME COURT
147 N. Main St., Warsaw 14569
(585) 786-2253; Fax: (585) 786-2818

Chief Clerk: Rebecca M. Miller
(585) 786-2253, Ext. 119; Fax: (585) 786-2818

SURROGATE'S COURT
Courthouse, 147 N. Main St., Warsaw 14569-1193
(585) 786-3148; Fax: (585) 786-3800

Surrogates:
Mark H. Dadd (585) 786-3148, Ext. 126
Law Clerk: Mark L. Haynes (585) 786-3148, Ext. 127
Secretary: Shirley J. Ingles (585) 786-3148, Ext. 126
Michael F. Griffith, Ext. 117
Law Clerk: Keith D. Kibler, Ext. 116
Secretary: Janice Eccleston, Ext. 117
Chief Clerk: William C. Beyer, Ext. 106
Deputy Clerk: Susan Scriven, Ext. 103

COUNTY COURT
Courthouse, 147 N. Main St., Warsaw 14569
(585) 786-2253; Fax: (585) 786-2818

Judges:
Mark H. Dadd (585) 786-3148, Ext. 126
Law Clerk: Mark L. Haynes (585) 786-3148, Ext. 127
Secretary: Shirley J. Ingles (585) 786-3148, Ext. 126
Michael F. Griffith (585) 786-3148, Ext. 118
Law Clerk: Keith Kibler (585) 786-3148, Ext. 116
Secretary: Janice Eccleston (585) 786-3148, Ext. 117
Chief Clerk: Rebecca M. Miller, (585) 786-2253, Ext. 119

FAMILY COURT
Courthouse, 147 N. Main St., Warsaw 14569-1193
(585) 786-3148; Fax: (585) 786-3800

Judges:
Mark H. Dadd (585) 786-3148, Ext. 126
Law Clerk: Mark L. Haynes (585) 786-3148, Ext. 127
Secretary: Shirley J. Ingles (585) 786-3148, Ext. 126
Michael F. Griffith
(585) 786-3148, Ext. 117; Fax: (585) 786-2818
Law Clerk: Keith D. Kibler Ext. 116
Secretary: Jan Eccleston Ext. 117
Chief Clerk: Jacqueline Diangelo, Ext. 104
Support Magistrate: Beth Farwell (Support & Paternity) Ext. 134

COUNTY OFFICIALS

County Atty.: Eric T. Dadd, 11 Exchange St., Attica 14011
(585) 591-1724; Fax: (585) 591-1722
D.A.: *Gerald Stout, 147 N. Main St., Warsaw 14569
(585) 786-8822; Fax: (585) 786-8842
E-mail: gstout@wyomingco.net
County Clerk: Rhonda Pierce, 143 Main St., Suite 104, Warsaw 14569 (585) 786-8810; Fax: (585) 786-3703
E-mail: rpierce@wyomingco.net
County Treasurer: Cheryl D. Mayer, 143 N. Main St., Warsaw 14569 (585) 786-8812; Fax: (585) 786-0466
E-mail: cdmayer@wyoming.co.net
Law Library: William C. Beyer, 147 N. Main St., Warsaw 14569 (585) 786-3148, Ext. 105
Sheriff: Farris S. Heimann, 151 N. Main St., Warsaw 14569
(585) 786-8989; Sheriff: (585) 786-2255;
Fax: (585) 786-8961
E-mail: fheimann@wyomingco.net
Internet: www.wyomingco.net
Jail: 151 N. Main St., Warsaw 14569
(585) 786-8808; Fax: (585) 786-8573
Atty. Visitation: Weekdays, 9 A.M.-5 P.M.

YATES COUNTY

Penn Yan, County Seat

SUPREME COURT
Courthouse, 415 Liberty St., Penn Yan 14527-1191
(315) 536-5126; Fax: (315) 536-5190

Chief Clerk: Margaret D. DiMartino
Court Asst.: Robert S. Peelle

SURROGATE'S COURT
Courthouse, 415 Liberty St., Penn Yan 14527-1176
(315) 536-5130; Fax: (315) 536-5190

Surrogate: W. Patrick Falvey
(315) 536-5130; Fax: (315) 536-5190
E-mail: wfalvey@courts.state.ny.us
Chief Clerk: Vanessa V. Smith

COUNTY COURT
Courthouse, 415 Liberty St., Penn Yan 14527-1191
(315) 536-5126; Fax: (315) 536-5190

Judge: W. Patrick Falvey
(315) 536-5128; Fax: (315) 536-5197
E-mail: wfalvey@courts.state.ny.us
Court Atty.: Alice Shoemaker (315) 536-5532
E-mail: ashoemak@courts.state.ny.us
Secretary: Margaret E. Calder
E-mail: mcalder@courts.state.ny.us
Chief Clerk: Margaret D. DiMartino
Court Asst.: Robert S. Peelle
Court Atty.: Alice Shoemaker (315) 536-5532

***Pending November 2010 Election Results**

Yates County—Cont'd

FAMILY COURT
Courthouse, 415 Liberty St., Penn Yan 14527-1182
(315) 536-5127; Fax: (315) 536-5190

Judge: W. Patrick Falvey (315) 536-5127; Fax: (315) 536-5190
E-mail: wfalvey@courts.state.ny.us

Chief Clerk: Roxanne R. Lynn
E-mail: rlynn@courts.state.ny.us

COUNTY OFFICIALS

D.A.: Jason L. Cook
Courthouse, 415 Liberty St., Penn Yan 14527
(315) 536-5550; Fax: (315) 536-5556

County Atty.: Bernetta A. Bourcy
Courthouse, 415 Liberty St., Penn Yan 14527
(315) 531-3233; Fax: (315) 531-3234

Commissioner of Jurors: Margaret D. DiMartino
Courthouse, 415 Liberty St., Penn Yan 14527
(315) 536-5125; Fax: (315) 536-5190

County Clerk: Julie D. Betts, County Office Bldg., Suite 1107, 417 Liberty St., Penn Yan 14527
(315) 536-5120; Fax: (315) 536-5545
E-mail: countyclerk@yatescounty.org
Internet: www.yatescounty.org

County Treasurer: Bonnie L. Percy
417 Liberty St., Suite 1081, Penn Yan 14527-0253
(315) 536-5192; Fax: (315) 536-5527

Sheriff: Ronald G. Spike
Public Safety Bldg., 227 Main St., Penn Yan 14527
(315) 536-4438; Sheriff: (315) 536-5172;
Fax: (315) 536-5191
E-mail: sheriff@yatescounty.org
Internet: www.yatescountysheriff.org

Jail: 227 Main St., Penn Yan 14527
(315) 536-5175; Fax: (315) 536-5121
E-mail: sheriff@yatescounty.org
Internet: www.yatescounty.org
Atty. Visitation: Any time

DISTRICT COURTS

NASSAU COUNTY DISTRICT COURT
99 Main St., Hempstead 11550
(516) 571-2355

Supervising Judge: Christopher G. Quinn
(516) 572-2166; E-mail: cgquinn@courts.state.ny.us
Law Clerk: Virginia Clavin
E-mail: vclavin@courts.state.ny.us
Secretary: Carmen Culhane
E-mail: cculhane@courts.state.ny.us

Judges:
Valerie J. Alexander (516) 572-2103
E-mail: valexand@courts.state.ny.us
Anna R. Anzalone (516) 572-2115
*Bonnie P. Chaikin (516) 572-2111
Michael A. Ciaffa (516) 572-2117
Angelo A. Delligatti (516) 572-2129
Andrew M. Engel (516) 572-2105
Scott Fairgrieve (516) 572-2141
E-mail: sfairgri@courts.state.ny.us
Tricia M. Ferrell (516) 572-2150
Rhonda E. Fischer (516) 572-2133
Sharon M.J. Gianelli (516) 572-2147
David Goodsell (516) 572-2125
Fred J. Hirsh (516) 572-2137
*Norman Janowitz (516) 572-2121
Susan T. Kluewer (President, Board of Judges) (516) 572-2159
Gary F. Knobel (516) 572-2109
Martin J. Massell (516) 572-2161
*David W. McAndrews
Terence P. Murphy (516) 572-2113
William J. O'Brien (516) 572-2101
E-mail: wobrien@courts.state.ny.us
Anthony W. Paradiso (516) 572-2135
*Sondra K. Pardes (516) 572-2153
Andrea Phoenix (516) 572-2143; Fax: (516) 572-2507
Erica L. Prager (516) 572-2131
E-mail: cprager@courts.state.ny.us
*Margaret C. Reilly (516) 572-2107
Francis D. Ricigliano (516) 572-2139
*Robert H. Spergel (516) 572-2123

Assoc. Court Attys.:
Debra Leimback-Keller (516) 572-2376
Melissa Sealy-Franco (516) 572-2554
Charles Givens (516) 572-2384
Maureen McConnell (516) 572-2381
Barbara Solomon (516) 572-2314

Chief Clerk: Kenneth Roll (516) 572-2157

Deputy Chief Clerks:
Michael Beganskas (516) 572-2170
Angela Diliberti (516) 572-2168

First District Civil Court
99 Main St., Hempstead 11550
(516) 572-2226

Clerk: Robert Shimonski (516) 572-2255

First District Court
99 Main St., Hempstead 11550
(516) 572-2355

Clerk: James Sullivan (516) 572-2391

Second District Court
99 Main St., Hempstead 11550
(516) 572-2226
Town of Hempstead

Clerk: Robert Shimonski (516) 572-2255

Third District Court
99 Main St., Hempstead 11550
(516) 572-2226
Town of North Hempstead

Clerk: Robert Shimonski (516) 572-2255

***Pending November 2010 Election Results**

SUFFOLK COUNTY DISTRICT COURT
John P. Cohalan, Jr. Court Complex,
400 Carleton Ave., P.O. Box 9075, Central Islip 11722-9075
(631) 853-7500

Supervising Judge: Madeleine A. Fitzgibbon (631) 853-4917

Judges:
Salvatore A. Alamia (631) 853-4915
*W. Gerard Asher (Acting County Court Judge) (631) 852-3415
Toni A. Bean (631) 853-4916
Stephen M. Behar, Sr. (631) 853-7601
Dennis M. Cohen (1st & 5th Districts)
3105 Veterans Memorial Hwy., Ronkonkoma 11779
(631) 854-9293; Fax: (631) 954-9683
Kevin J. Crowley (Acting County Court Judge) (631) 853-5408
Martin I. Efman (Acting County Court Judge) (631) 852-2166
Patricia M. Filiberto (631) 853-4916
James P. Flanagan (631) 853-4918
William G. Ford (631) 853-4920
C. Stephen Hackeling (Second District) (631) 854-4545
Jennifer A. Henry (631) 853-4915
Paul Hensley (631) 853-5520
Richard I. Horowitz (4th District) (631) 853-4921
John Iliou (631) 853-4921
Chris Ann Kelley (631) 853-7601
Steven A. Lotto (631) 853-4920
Gaetan Lozito (Acting County Court Judge) (631) 853-4919
Glenn A. Murphy (Acting County Court Judge) (631) 853-7418
Joseph A. Santorelli (631) 853-4918
G. Ann Spelman (Acting County Court Judge) (631) 853-7418
John J. Toomey, Jr. (631) 853-4919
Stephen L. Ukeiley (631) 854-1440

Chief Clerk: Warren G. Clark (631) 853-4532

Deputy Chief Clerks:
Frank Incantalupo (631) 853-4530
Michael Paparatto (631) 853-4530

Principal Court Atty.: Steve Miller (631) 853-4545

First District Civil Court
3105 Veterans Mem. Highway, Ronkonkoma 11779
(631) 854-9676
Towns of Babylon, Brookhaven, Huntington, Islip

First District Criminal Court
John P. Cohalan, Jr. Court Complex,
400 Carleton Ave., P.O. Box 9073, Central Islip 11722
(631) 853-7500
Towns of Babylon, Brookhaven, Huntington, Islip

Second District Court
30 E. Hoffman Ave., Lindenhurst 11757
(631) 854-1121
Town of Babylon

Third District Court
1850 New York Ave., Huntington Station 11746
(631) 854-4545
Town of Huntington

Fourth District Court
Veterans' Memorial Highway, Hauppauge 11787
(631) 853-5408
Town of Smithtown

Fifth District Court
3105 Veterans Mem. Highway, Ronkonkoma 11779
(631) 854-9673
Town of Islip

Sixth District Court
150 W. Main St., Patchogue 11772
(631) 854-1440
Town of Brookhaven

Traffic Division
John P. Cohalan, Jr. Court Complex,
400 Carleton Ave., P.O. Box 9074, Central Islip 11722
(631) 853-7500

District Courts—Cont'd

PRACTICE TIME TABLE UNDER THE UNIFORM DISTRICT COURT ACT

As amended to September 2010.

Time to Answer Summons.

If summons is personally delivered to defendent within the county, answer or appearance must be served within 20 days. If service is made by other than personal service within the county, the time to answer or appear is 20 days after proof of service is filed with the clerk. If made outside the county, the time to answer or appear is 30 days after proof of service is filed with the clerk. (U.D.C.A., 402).

Filing Summons.

A copy of the summons with proof of service must be filed with the clerk of the District Court within 20 days of service, if service is made within county. If made outside the county, the summons and proof of service must be filed within 30 days of service. (U.D.C.A., 409).

Personal Service.

Original service may be made by mail pursuant to U.D.C.A. 403.

Provisional Remedies.

May be obtained if it would be available in the Supreme Court in a like case, except that no injunction or restraining order shall issue unless in conjunction with a recovery of chattel or enforcement proceeding. (U.D.C.A., 209)

Bill of Particulars.

Procedure is the same as in the Supreme Court. (U.D.C.A., 1101)

Costs, Taxation of.

Statutory costs: Taxed by clerk forthwith on rendition of judgment. (U.D.C.A., 1907)

Other taxable disbursements: 2 days' notice must be given. (U.D.C.A., 1907)

Review of taxation: Within 10 days after taxation upon 2 days' notice. (U.D.C.A., 1909)

Deposition.

Procedures set forth in C.P.L.R. shall govern except that it may be obtained of a non-party only within the county unless the court orders otherwise. (U.D.C.A., 1101)

Execution.

When issued: See Supreme Court Time Table *supra.* (U.D. C.A., 1501)

Judgment by Default.

May be entered as provided in C.P.L.R. (U.D.C.A., 1402)

Jury Demand.

Service and filing: May be served and filed by any party after joinder of issue or within 10 days after service of a notice of trial without a jury demand. (U.D.C.A., 1303)

Special proceeding: Demand may be made on return of precept by the tenant or at any time before trial by the landlord. (U.D.C.A., 1303)

A jury shall be composed of six persons. (U.D.C.A., 1305)

Motions.

Governed by the C.P.L.R. except that in instances other than where motion to dismiss may be made at any time a motion to dismiss or correct pleadings must be made within the time to respond to such pleading or where no response is required, within 10 days after the service of the challenged pleading. (U.D.C.A., 1001-1003)

Notice of Trial.

Where all parties appear by attorneys: Must be served not less than 15 nor more than 30 days before the day fixed for trial. (U.D.C.A., 1301)

Pleading.

Amendments of: Once without leave of court, at any time before time to respond to pleading has expired or within 10 days after its service or the service of the pleading responding to it. (U.D.C.A., 909)

‡**Acting Supreme Court Justice**

FAMILY COURT OF THE CITY OF NEW YORK

60 Lafayette St., N.Y.C. 10013
(646) 386-5206

Deputy Chief Admin. Judge, N.Y.C. Courts:
Fern A. Fisher, 111 Centre St., N.Y.C. 10013
(646) 386-4200; Fax: (212) 374-5709

Administrative Judge: Edwina Richardson-Mendelson
(646) 386-5190; Fax: (212) 374-2127

Chief Clerk of Family Court: Peter J. Passidomo
(646) 386-5170

First Deputy Chief Clerk: George Cafasso (646) 386-5160

Deputy Chief Clerk: Mary Ellen Keller (Administration)
(646) 386-5163

Judges:

Jody Adams (646) 386-5104
‡Allen G. Alpert (718) 618-2200
Criminal Court Judge Assigned To Family Court
‡Michael A. Ambrosio (347) 296-1854
Maria Arias (718) 298-0204
Nancy N. Bannon (From Civil Court) (718) 618-2204
Alan M. Beckoff (347) 401-9880
Mary E. Bednar (646) 386-5104
Stephen J. Bogacz (718) 298-0204
Rhoda J. Cohen (646) 386-5101
Alma Cordova (718) 618-2200
Criminal Court Judge Assigned to Family Court
James E. d'Auguste (718) 618-2215
Civil Court Judge Assigned to Family Court
Susan S. Danoff (347) 401-9870
‡Tandra L. Dawson (646) 386-3868
Monica Drinane (718) 618-2200
Lee H. Elkins (347) 401-9870
‡Mary Ellen Fitzmaurice (718) 298-0222
Nora L. Freeman (347) 401-9870
Lizbeth Gonzalez (718) 298-0204; Fax: (718) 297-2530
Civil Court Judge Assigned to Family Court
Bernard J. Graham (347) 401-9870
Civil Court Judge Assigned to Family Court
Sidney Gribetz (718) 618-2200; Fax: (718) 590-7305
Paul H. Grosvenor (347) 401-9870
Ilana Gruebel (718) 618-2213
Civil Court Judge Assigned to Family Court
Bryanne Hamill (347) 401-9870
Paula J. Hepner (347) 401-9601
Douglas E. Hoffman (646) 386-5101
John M. Hunt (718) 298-0228, 04
Tanya R. Kennedy (347) 401-9870
Civil Court Judge Assigned to Family Court
Susan K. Knipps (646) 386-5102; Fax: (212) 374-2623, 22
‡Sarah L. Krauss (347) 401-9883
Susan R. Larabee (646) 386-5115
Arnold Lim (347) 401-9870
Fran L. Lubow (718) 298-0204
Karen Lupuloff (718) 618-2200
Criminal Court Judge assigned to Family Court
Myrna M. Martinez-Perez (718) 618-2200
Andrea Masley (718) 618-2209
Civil Court Court Assigned to Family Court
Terrence J. McElrath (718) 675-8800; Fax: (718) 390-8110
Margaret P. McGowan (718) 298-0213
‡Martin P. Murphy (347) 401-9061
‡Ann E. O'Shea (347) 401-9894
Civil Court Judge Assigned to Family Court
Emily Olshansky (347) 401-9870
‡Jane Pearl (718) 618-2200
‡Clark V. Richardson (718) 618-2200
Marybeth Richroath (718) 298-0204
Ronald E. Richter (718) 298-0204
Gayle P. Roberts (718) 618-2200
Jeanette Ruiz (347) 401-9870
Helene Donlan Sacco (718) 675-8800
Barbara Salinitro (718) 298-0204
Lori Sattler (646) 386-5114
Civil Court Judge Assigned to Family Court

Family Court of the City of N.Y.—Cont'd
Carol R. Sherman (718) 618-2200
Gloria Sosa-Lintner (646) 386-5104
Carol A. Stokinger (718) 298-0204
‡*Jeffrey Sunshine (347) 296-1527
Linda Tally (718) 298-0204
Daniel Turbow (347) 401-9870
Stewart H. Weinstein (347) 401-9870
Karen Wolff (718) 675-8800

Family Court, New York County
60 Lafayette St., N.Y.C. 10013
(646) 386-5101, 04

Supervising Judge: Douglas E. Hoffman
Clerk of Court of Family Court: Evelyn Hasanoeddin (646) 386-5206

Family Court, Kings County
330 Jay St., Brooklyn 11201
(347) 401-9870; Fax: (347) 401-9900

Supervising Judge: Paula J. Hepner (347) 401-9601
Clerk of Court of Kings County Family Court: Robert Ratanski (347) 401-9610

Family Court, Bronx County
900 Sheridan Ave., Bronx 10451
(718) 618-2098

Supervising Judge: Monica Drinane (718) 618-2200
Clerk of Court of Family Court: Michael Williams (Acting) (718) 618-2098

Family Court, Queens County
151-20 Jamaica Ave., Jamaica 11432
(718) 298-0204; Fax: (718) 297-2530

Supervising Judge: Carol A. Stokinger
Clerk of Court of Family Court: Vaunda Harris (Acting) (718) 298-0197

Family Court, Richmond County
100 Richmond Terr., Staten Island 10301
(718) 675-8800; Fax: (718) 390-5247
Internet: www.courts.state.ny.us

Supervising Judge: Paula J. Hepner (347) 401-9601
Clerk of Court of Family Court: William J. Quirk

N.Y.C. PROBATION SERVICES, JUVENILE OPERATIONS
33 Beaver St., 23rd Floor, N.Y.C. 10004
(212) 361-8977

Deputy Commissioner, Admin., Planning & Intelligence: Alphonzo Albright
(212) 232-0455; Fax: (212) 361-8969
E-mail: aalbright@probation.nyc.gov

Deputy Commissioner, Adult Operations:
David Muhammad (212) 361-8982; Fax: (212) 361-8987
E-mail: dmuhammad@probation.nyc.gov

General Counsel: Margaret DiGiovanna (Acting)
21st Floor (212) 232-0706; Fax: (212) 361-0718
E-mail: mdigiovanna@probation.nyc.gov

Dir. of Press and Public Information: Ryan Dodge
(212) 361-8957; Fax: (212) 361-8985
E-mail: rdodge@probation.nyc.gov

Deputy Commissioner: Ana Bermudez
33 Beaver St., 23rd Floor, N.Y.C. 10004
(212) 232-0468; Fax: (212) 232-0599
E-mail: abermudez@probation.nyc.gov

Associate Commissioner: Gineen Gray
33 Beaver St., 18th Floor, N.Y.C. 10004
(212) 232-0486; Fax: (212) 232-0499
E-mail: ggray@probation.nyc.gov

Asst. Commissioner: Joseph Dillon
60 Lafayette St., N.Y.C. 10013
(212) 442-6952; Fax: (212) 442-3678
E-mail: jdillon@probation.nyc.gov

Asst. Commissioner for Juvenile Operations:
Audrey Wilson (Acting)
330 Jay St., 11th Floor, Brooklyn 11201
(718) 802-2556; Fax: (718) 802-2569
E-mail: awilson@probation.nyc.gov

Dirs., Family Intake and Services:
Lisa Frost (New York County)
60 Lafayette St., Suite 2C, N.Y.C. 10013
(212) 442-4351; Fax: (212) 442-6978
E-mail: lfrost@porbation.nyc.gov
Olivien Manns-Nelson (Bronx County)
900 Sheridan Ave., Suite 6D1, Bronx 10451
(718) 590-3180; Fax: (718) 590-3217
E-mail: omnelson@probation.nyc.gov
Denise McNeill-Grant (Queens)
151-20 Jamaica Ave., Jamaica 11432
(718) 657-4385; Fax: (718) 657-7508
E-mail: dmcneill@probation.nyc.gov
Myra Radden (Kings County)
330 Jay St., 11th Floor, Staten Island 10301
(718) 802-2563; Fax: (718) 802-2662
E-mail: mradden@probation.nyc.gov
Stacye Spear (Richmond County)
130 Stuyvesant Pl., 4th Floor, Staten Island 10301
(718) 556-4000; Fax: (718) 556-6467
E-mail: sspear@probation.nyc.gov

Probation Officer, Red Hook Community Justice Center: Tasha Holder
88 Visitation Pl., Brooklyn 11231
(718) 923-8205; Fax: (718) 625-3723
E-mail: tholder@probation.nyc.gov

CIVIL COURT OF THE CITY OF NEW YORK
111 Centre St., N.Y.C. 10013
General Information (Civil and Small Claims): (646) 386-5700;
Housing Division matters: (646) 386-5750
Internet: www.nycourts.gov

Deputy Chief Admin. Judge, N.Y.C. Courts: Fern A. Fisher
111 Centre St., 12th Floor, N.Y.C. 10013
(646) 386-5400; Fax: (212) 374-5709

Chief Clerk: Jack Baer (646) 386-5409

First Deputy Chief Clerk: Carol Alt (646) 386-5415

Asst. First Deputy Chief Clerk: Alia Razzaq (646) 386-5416

Deputy Chief Clerks:
Myles McKenna (646) 386-5417
Frank A. Tropea (646) 386-5751

Chief Court Atty.: John Smith (646) 386-5446

Small Claims Arbitrators Assignments & Training:
Debra Brawley (646) 386-5420, 22
Joseph Gebbia (646) 386-3975

The Civil Court has jurisdiction over various types of causes of action, where the value of the subject matter does not exceed $25,000, not including interest and costs (CCA 201). These causes of action include the following:
1) Recovery of money, actions and proceedings for recovery of chattels and foreclosure of liens on personal property, where amount sought or value of property does not exceed $25,000 (CCA 202);
2) Actions involving real property situated in the county where action is brought if: a) partition of property where assessed value at commencement of action is not more than $25,000; b) foreclosure, redemption or satisfaction of mortgage if lien amount does not exceed $25,000; c) specific performance of a sale, if contract price of property does not exceed $25,000; d) establishment, enforcement or foreclosure of mechanics lien, if lien amount does not exceed $25,000; e) action to reform or rescind deed or sales contract, if agreed price in the contract does not exceed $25,000; f) action to reform or rescind mortgage, if unpaid balance does not exceed $25,000; g) action to compel determination of claim to real property under Art. 15, RPAPL, if assessed property value does not exceed $25,000; h) action for civil penalties for violation of housing standards laws, or recovery of costs to City for correction of nuisance or violation, or enforcement of lien for costs, or injunctions or restraining orders; i) actions to vest title to City on abandoned buildings (CCC 203);

City Courts

‡Acting Supreme Court Justice
***Pending November 2010 Election Results**

Civil Court of the City of New York—Cont'd

3) Summary proceedings to recover possession of real property, remove tenants, enter judgment for rent due (regardless of amount), and special proceedings by tenants for judgment directing deposit of rents and their use to remedy dangerous conditions per 7-a RPAPL (CCA 204);

4) Interpleader, where amount does not exceed $25,000 (CCA 205);

5) Determination of arbitrability of questions in controversy under Article 75 of the CPLR; but the court lacks jurisdiction in cases first application arising from arbitrable controversy under 7502(a) CPLR (CCA 206);

6) Small Claims or Commercial Claims not exceeding $5000 (CCA 1801 and 1801-A);

7) Counterclaims, if a) subject matter would be within jurisdiction of court if tried separately; b) for money only, regardless of the amount demanded; c) recission or reformation of transaction on which plaintiffs action is based, if amount does not exceed $25,000; or d) accounting between partners after dissolution of partnership if assets do not exceed $25,000 and plaintiffs action arose out of the partnership (CCA 208);

8) Contempt actions, under similar circumstances as in Supreme Court, except that Civil Court may not punish a judge or justice of any court (CCA 210);

9) Declaratory judgments involving obligation of insurer to defend or indemnify defendant, if amount sought does not exceed $25,000 (CCA 212-a);

10) Recission or reformation of transaction if amount in controversy does not exceed $25,000 (CCA 213);

11) Provisional remedies: an order of attachment or arrest, a warrant to seize chattel per 207 of the Lien Law, or order of seizure of chattel, if such remedy might issue out of supreme court in similar cases (209(a));

12) No injunctions or restraining orders may issue from this court except pursuant to 7102(d), 7103(c) and 7109 CPLR, 211 RPAPL, 1508 CCA or 306 of the Multiple Dwelling Code or Article 53 of the Housing Maintenance Code of the Administrative Code of the City of New York (209(b));

13) No receivers shall be appointed by this court except pursuant to 203(b) or 1508 CCA, or subdivision 5 of 309 of the Multiple Dwelling Code (209(c));

14) Notices of pendency may be filed with the County clerk per Article 65 of the CPLR, in any action within the courts jurisdiction in which similar actions may be filed in Supreme Court; City departments charged with enforcement of housing standards may file notices of pendency per 308 of the Multiple Dwelling Law or D26-50.07 of the Housing Maintenence Code of the Administrative Code of the City of New York (209(d)).

15) Jurisdiction of Housing Part: the Housing Part has jurisdiction over enforcement of state and local laws relating to housing standards in the following areas: a) civil penalties for violation of laws; b) collection of costs to the City to correct nuisances or violations of laws, or removal or demolition of buildings; c) establishment, enforcement or foreclosure of liens for penalties or costs to the City to correct nuisances or violations of laws; d) injunctions or other orders for enforcement of housing standards; e) actions and proceedings under RPAPL 7A; summary proceedings to recover possession of real property, including judgments for rent due without limitation; and cases under RPAPL 755 or MDL 302-a; f) appointment of receiver for rents, issues and building profits to remove nuisances or make repairs; g) actions for removal of violations, or imposition of violation or stay of penalty; and h) special proceedings for the City to gain title to abandoned buildings (110 CCA).

Court Schedule: Calendars are called at 9:30 A.M. All parts shall remain in session until 5 P.M. unless otherwise directed by the Administrative Judge with the approval of the respective Appellate Divisions.
Hours: Weekdays, 9 A.M.-5 P.M.

For the Judges, Clerks and other personnel, see each branch of the Court.

NEW YORK CO. BRANCH, NEW YORK CIVIL COURT
111 Centre St., Room 1240, N.Y.C. 10013
(646) 386-5700; 12th Floor (Chief Clerk): (646) 386-5409;
Fax: (212) 374-5709;
Deputy Chief Admin. Judge: (646) 386-4200
Internet: www.nycourts.gov

Clerk of County: Stewart Feigel
(646) 386-5730; Fax: (212) 374-8053

Deputy Clerk of County: Marcy Hoenig
(646) 386-5730; Fax: (212) 374-8053

Asst. Deputy Chief Clerk Civil Court: Michael Boyle
Room 118 (646) 386-5612

Asst. Dep. Chief Clerk of Housing Court:
Lennox R. Headley, Room 225 (646) 386-5520

Supervising Judge: *Jeffrey K. Oing (646) 386-5722

Supervising Judge, Housing Part: Jean Schneider
(646) 386-5617

Judges:
†‡Harold A. Adler (718) 618-3619
Nancy N. Bannon (718) 618-2204
Assigned to Family Court
‡Lucy Billings (646) 386-3279
Arlene P. Bluth, Room 457 (646) 386-5725
‡Raymond L. Bruce (718) 618-3661
Margaret A. Chan (347) 404-9097
Assigned to Kings County
†‡Dorothy K. Chin-Brandt (718) 298-0922
‡*Matthew F. Cooper (646) 386-5696
James E. D'Auguste (718) 618-2215
Civil Court Judge Assigned to Family Court
‡Marylin G. Diamond (646) 386-3255
Arthur F. Engoron (718) 618-2532
Assigned to Bronx County
‡Saralee E. Evans (646) 386-3819
Kathryn E. Freed (646) 386-5633
‡Marcy S. Friedman (646) 386-3760
‡Ellen Gesmer (646) 386-3730; Fax: (212) 884-8986
†David Godosky (347) 404-9479
Ilana Gruebel (718) 618-2213
Assigned to Family Court
‡Shlomo S. Hagler, Room 623
(646) 386-5691; Fax: (212) 374-2594
‡Barbara Jaffe (646) 386-3724
‡Debra A. James, Room 659
(646) 386-3352; Fax: (212) 374-0402
†Robert D. Kalish (347) 404-9473
‡Deborah A. Kaplan (646) 386-5567; Fax: (212) 401-9037
Tanya R. Kennedy (347) 401-9870
Civil Court Judge Assigned to Family Court
‡Joan M. Kenney (646) 386-3816
‡*Cynthia S. Kern (646) 386-3729
†Lynn R. Kotler (646) 386-5625
‡Diane A. Lebedeff (718) 618-1557
Ruben Martino, Harlem Justice Center,
170 E. 121st St., N.Y.C. 10035 (212) 360-4123
Andrea Masley (718) 618-2209
Assigned to Family Court
†Rita Mella (646) 386-4684
‡Manuel J. Mendez (646) 386-5705
†Shari R. Michels (347) 404-9477
‡Peter Moulton (646) 386-5712
†Frank P. Nervo (646) 386-4333
Jose A. Padilla, Jr. (718) 618-2546
Assigned to Bronx County
‡Kibbie F. Payne (646) 386-3336
‡Eileen A. Rakower, Room 308 (646) 386-5749
Robert R. Reed (718) 618-2530
Assigned to Bronx County
Debra R. Samuels, Room 673 (646) 386-5709
Lori Sattler (646) 386-5114
Civil Court Judge Assigned to Family Court
‡Saliann Scarpulla (646) 386-5716
†Jennifer Schecter (646) 386-4648
‡George J. Silver (646) 386-3271
‡Anil C. Singh (646) 386-5692
‡Jane S. Solomon (646) 386-3181
‡Michael D. Stallman (646) 386-3342
‡Analisa Torres (646) 386-5219
‡Geoffrey D. Wright (718) 618-1432; Fax: (718) 618-3511

†Civil Court Judge assigned to Criminal Court
‡Acting Supreme Court Justice
***Pending November 2010 Election Results**

New York Co. Branch, Civil Court of N.Y.C.—Cont'd
Housing Court Judges:
*Joseph Capella (646) 386-3373
*David B. Cohen (646) 386-5586
Timmie Elsner (646) 386-5591
Arlene H. Hahn (646) 386-5615
Sheldon J. Halprin (646) 386-5620
David Kaplan, Room 439 (646) 386-5582
*Gerald Lebovits (646) 386-5626
Bruce Scheckowitz (646) 386-5584
Michelle D. Schreiber (646) 386-5698
Brenda Spears (646) 386-5589
Peter M. Wendt (646) 386-5622

Appeals: Mary Smyth, Room 118 (646) 386-5606
E-mail: efeehan@courts.state.ny.us

Atty. Counter, Clerk's Office, Landlord & Tenant:
Louis Ruggiero, Room 225 (646) 386-5502
E-mail: lruggiero@courts.state.ny.us

Calendar Clerk/Personal Appearances, Civil Clerk's Office: Room 118 (646) 386-5600

Cashier Section/Fiscal: Che Che Solivan, Room 225 (646) 386-5503, 08

Central Jury Clerk: Doreen Burgess, Room 362 (646) 386-5963, 73; E-mail: dburgess@courts.state.ny.us

Court Reporter Supervisor: Maureen Olivio, Room 1167 (646) 386-5498

Docketing, Civil Clerk's Office: Room 118 (646) 386-5600

Help Center/Pro Se Attys. (Housing):
Lauren Blackman, Room 104 (646) 386-5555
E-mail: lblackman@courts.state.ny.us
Fran Stahl, Room 104 (646) 386-5554
E-mail: fstahl@courts.state.ny.us

Judgments, Civil Clerk's Office: John McCann Room 118 (646) 386-5601

Law & Library Div. Opinion Clerks: John Smith Room 1032 (646) 386-5446
E-mail: jsmith@courts.state.ny.us

Pro Se Proceedings, Clerk's Office, Landlord & Tenant: Steve Goldberg, Room 225 (646) 386-5506; E-mail: srgoldbe@courts.state.ny.us

Record Room & Archives: Femi Oloruntuyi Room 225 (646) 386-5514

Small Claims, Clerk's Office: Florese James Room 322 (646) 386-5481, 84

Special Term, Parts I & II Clerk's Office: James Lopez Room 118 (646) 386-5603, 04
E-mail: jlopez@courts.state.ny.us

Uniformed Court Officers: Room 345 (646) 386-5570, 71

Warrants, Clerk's Office, Landlord & Tenant:
William Smith, Room 225 (646) 386-5513

BRONX CO. BRANCH, NEW YORK CIVIL COURT
851 Grand Concourse, Bronx 10451
(718) 618-2500; Admin. Judge, N.Y.C.: (646) 386-4200

Clerk: Joseph Monastra (718) 466-3000, 618-2500; Fax: (718) 466-3006

Judge-in-Charge: Laura G. Douglas (718) 618-1409

Judges:
Ben R. Barbato (718) 618-2534
Raul Cruz (718) 618-2536
Mitchell J. Danziger (718) 618-2538
Arthur F. Engoron (718) 618-2532
From New York County
†Ruben Franco (718) 618-2463
‡Doris M. Gonzalez (718) 618-3682
Lizbeth Gonzalez (718) 298-0204; Fax: (718) 297-2530
Civil Court Judge Assigned to Family Court
‡Stanley B. Green (718) 618-1420
‡Nelida Malave-Gonzalez (718) 618-2542
Donald A. Miles (718) 618-2544
Jose A. Padilla, Jr. (From New York County) (718) 618-2546
Robert R. Reed (From New York County) (718) 618-2530
‡Julia I. Rodriguez (718) 618-1416
‡Larry Schachner (718) 618-1449
‡Fernando Tapia (718) 618-2550
Elizabeth A. Taylor (718) 618-2549
‡*Edgar G. Walker (718) 618-1465; Fax: (212) 419-8494
†John H. Wilson (347) 404-9464

Housing Court Judges:
Jaya K. Madhavan (Supervising) (718) 466-3117
Paul L. Alpert (718) 466-3126
Ava P. Alterman (718) 466-3171
Marian C. Doherty, Room 904 (718) 466-3161
Jerald R. Klein (718) 466-3191
Sabrina Kraus (718) 466-3131
Lydia C. Lai (718) 466-3165
Andrew Lehrer (718) 466-3135
Kevin C. McClanahan (718) 466-3121
Eardell Rashford (718) 466-3141
Jose Rodriguez (718) 618-2510
Verna Saunders (718) 466-3028
Elizabeth Y. Tao (718) 466-3175
Louis Villella (718) 466-3180
Steven Weissman (718) 466-3151

Housing Court Supervisor: Lydia Grima (718) 466-3025

Administration: Desmond O'Hanlon (Deputy Clerk) (718) 466-3002

Calendar: Emanual Torres (718) 618-2552

Civil Court Clerk: Eddy Valdez (Supervisor) (718) 618-2502

Small Claims: Veronica Wright-Roberts (Supervisor) (718) 618-2518

Special Term, Parts I & II: Susan Rosenthal (Supervisor) (718) 618-2566

KINGS CO. BRANCH, NEW YORK CIVIL COURT
141 Livingston St., Brooklyn 11201
General Information: (347) 404-9000; Fax: (718) 643-3733; Admin. Judge, N.Y.C.: (646) 386-4200

Clerk: Angelo Tropea (Acting) (347) 404-9133

Supervising Judge: Peter P. Sweeney (347) 404-9060

Judges:
‡Rachel Amy Adams (347) 401-9260; Fax: (212) 401-9232
Frederick C. Arriaga (347) 404-9467
*Sylvia G. Ash (347) 404-9096
‡Loren Baily-Schiffman (347) 401-9015
‡Johnny Lee Baynes (718) 404-9093
Reginald A. Boddie (347) 404-9076
Margaret A. Chan (From New York County) (347) 404-9097
Devin P. Cohen (347) 404-9062
‡Noach Dear (718) 404-9071
Dena E. Douglas (347) 404-9483
Genine D. Edwards (718) 262-7252
Assigned to Queens County
Pamela L. Fisher (347) 404-9068
Robin S. Garson (347) 404-9094
†Michael J. Gerstein (646) 386-4658
Bernard J. Graham (347) 401-9870
Civil Court Judge Assigned to Family Court
†Desmond A. Green (347) 404-9468
Dawn M. Jimenez-Salta (347) 404-9070
Ingrid Joseph (347) 404-9063
‡Kathy J. King (347) 401-9186
†Evelyn LaPorte (347) 404-9447; Fax: (718) 643-3538
Katherine A. Levine (347) 404-9066
‡Ann E. O'Shea (347) 401-9894
Civil Court Judge Assigned to Family Court
Lisa S. Otley (347) 401-9889
†Geraldine Pickett (347) 404-9475
Alice Fisher Rubin, Room 606 (347) 404-9061
Robin K. Sheares (347) 404-9077
‡Kenneth P. Sherman (347) 296-1134
‡Debra Silber (347) 296-1043; Fax: (718) 643-3755
†ShawnDya L. Simpson (646) 401-9096
‡Wavny Toussaint (347) 404-9870
Carolyn E. Wade (347) 404-9069
‡Betty J. Williams (347) 404-9472; Fax: (718) 643-7733
Jacqueline D. Williams (347) 404-9133

†Civil Court Judge assigned to Criminal Court
‡Acting Supreme Court Justice
***Pending November 2010 Election Results**

Kings Co. Branch, Civil Court of N.Y.C.—Cont'd

Housing Court Judges:
John Lansden (Supervising) (347) 404-9083
Oymin Chin (347) 404-9086
Marc Finkelstein (347) 404-9092
Anthony J. Fiorella, Jr. (347) 404-9079
Thomas M. Fitzpatrick (347) 404-9081
Cheryl Gonzales (347) 404-9090
George M. Heymann (347) 404-9089
Inez Hoyos (347) 404-9080
Laurie L. Lau (347) 404-9187
Gary Marton (347) 404-9088
Maria Milin (347) 404-9091
Eleanor Ofshtein (347) 404-8092
Marcia Sikowitz (347) 404-9085
John Stanley (347) 404-9084

Clerk of the County: Angelo Tropea (347) 404-9133; Fax: (718) 643-3733

Asst. Deputy Clerk: Vacancy at Press Time (347) 404-9133

Asst. Deputy Chief Clerk—Civil Division: Peter Catella (347) 404-9132

Clerk, General Clerks Office: Kwok Yee Fong (347) 404-9123

Asst. Deputy Chief Clerk, Landlord and Tenant: Kevin McCormack (347) 404-9131; Office: (347) 404-9201

Clerk, Landlord and Tenant: Madeleine Klings (347) 404-9202

Small Claims: Theresa O'Sullivan (347) 404-9021

Clerk, Special Term, Part I and Special Term Part II: Lena Ferrera (347) 404-9030

Captain, Court Officers: Capt. Angelo Torre (347) 404-9222

Court Reporter: Peter Brody (347) 404-9149

QUEENS CO. BRANCH, NEW YORK CIVIL COURT
89-17 Sutphin Blvd., Jamaica 11435
(718) 262-7100; Admin. Judge, N.Y.C.: (646) 386-4200

Clerk: Joseph L. Traynor (718) 262-7300

Deputy Clerk: John S. Barry (718) 262-7300

Supervising Judge: ‡Charles S. Lopresto (718) 262-7333

Supervising Judge, Housing Part: Gilbert Badillo (718) 262-7363

Judges:
Chereé A. Buggs (718) 262-7381
‡Anna Culley (718) 262-7357
‡Timothy J. Dufficy (718) 262-7354
Ginene D. Edwards (From Kings County) (718) 262-7252
‡Joseph J. Esposito (718) 262-7379
Rudolph E. Greco, Jr. (718) 262-7376
Maureen A. Healy (718) 262-7365
‡Pam B. Jackman-Brown (718) 298-1670
Richard G. Latin (718) 262-7391
†Ira H. Margulis (718) 298-0936
Terrence C. O'Connor (718) 262-7368
†Mary R. O'Donoghue (718) 298-0928
Jodi Orlow (718) 262-7394
Leslie J. Purificacion (718) 262-7373
Carmen R. Velasquez (718) 262-7360
William A. Viscovich (718) 262-7385

Housing Court Judges:
Ronni D. Birnbaum (718) 262-7311
Ann Katz (718) 262-7314
Ulysses B. Leverett (718) 262-7388
Michael J. Pinckney (718) 262-7351
Maria Ressos (718) 262-7398
Deighton S. Waithe (718) 262-7121

Judicial Hearing Officers:
Ernest J. Cavallo (718) 262-7133
Stephen S. Gottlieb (718) 262-7330

Calendar Clerk: Irene Kersh (718) 262-7142

Judgment Clerk: Barbara Wraith (718) 262-7290

Law & Library Div.: Anita Postyn (718) 262-7348

Record Room and Index Clerk: Monica Dingle (718) 262-7141

Small Claim Clerk's Office: Francine Amato (718) 262-7135

Cashier: Bibi Ali (718) 262-7183

Central Jury Clerk: (718) 262-7200

Court Officers Security: Maj. Glen J. Lowe (718) 262-7111

Court Reporters: Sharon Cohen (718) 262-7336

Information: (718) 262-7100

Landlord and Tenant: Barbara Oliveri (718) 262-7145

Special Term, Part I & II, Clerk's Office: Wanda Sanchez (718) 262-7180

RICHMOND CO. BRANCH, NEW YORK CIVIL COURT
927 Castleton Ave., West New Brighton, Staten Island 10310
(718) 675-8888; Fax: (718) 390-8108; Admin. Judge, N.Y.C.: (646) 386-4200

Asst. Deputy Chief Clerk IV: Deborah Tortorice (718) 675-8459

Supervising Judge: ‡Philip S. Straniere (718) 675-8437

Judges:
‡Kim Dollard (718) 675-8438
Orlando Marrazzo, Jr. (718) 675-8429
‡Barbara I. Panepinto (718) 876-6424; Fax: (718) 876-6426

Housing Court Judge: Marina C. Mundy (718) 675-8440

CRIMINAL COURT OF THE CITY OF NEW YORK
111 Centre St., N.Y.C. 10013
General Information (City Wide): (646) 386-4500

Deputy Chief Admin. Judge, N.Y.C.: Fern A. Fisher Room 1240 (646) 386-4200

Supervising Judges:
‡Efrain Alvarado (Bronx) (718) 618-3700
Admin. Judge, Bronx County, Criminal Term
Melissa Jackson (Manhattan) (646) 386-4615
‡Alan J. Meyer (Staten Island) (718) 675-8550
‡William Miller (Brooklyn) (347) 404-9600; Fax: (718) 643-3538
‡Deborah Stevens Modica (Queens) (718) 286-0839; Fax: (718) 520-3992

Deputy Supervising Judge: ‡Eugene Oliver, Jr. (Bronx) (718) 618-3600; Fax: (718) 618-3583

Judges:
‡Bruce Allen (646) 386-4408
‡Allen G. Alpert (718) 618-2200
Assigned to Family Court
‡Steven L. Barrett (718) 618-3659
‡A. Kirke Bartley, Jr. (646) 386-4623; Fax: (212) 374-2579
‡Peter J. Benitez (718) 618-3631
‡Carol Berkman (646) 386-3968
‡Miriam Best (718) 618-3690
‡Joel L. Blumenfeld (718) 298-1363
‡Denis John Boyle (718) 618-3677
James M. Burke (646) 386-4665; Fax: (718) 643-7733
‡Alex M. Calabrese, Red Hook Community Justice Ctr., 88-94 Visitation Pl., Brooklyn 11231 (718) 923-8225; Fax: (718) 923-8223
‡Richard D. Carruthers (646) 386-3978
‡John W. Carter (718) 618-3635
†‡Dorothy K. Chin-Brandt (718) 298-0922
‡Danny K. Chun (347) 296-1067; Fax: (347) 296-1346
Abraham L. Clott (646) 386-4654
‡Ellen M. Coin (646) 386-4615; Fax: (212) 374-2579
Alma Cordova (718) 618-2200
Criminal Court Judge Assigned to Family Court
Miriam Cyrulnik (347) 404-9478; Fax: (718) 643-7733
‡Joseph J. Dawson (718) 618-3625
‡Laura E. Drager (646) 386-3356
‡Ralph A. Fabrizio (718) 618-3623
‡Thomas A. Farber (646) 386-3892
‡JoAnn Ferdinand (347) 296-1052
Anthony J. Ferrara (646) 386-4651
‡Neil Jon Firetog (347) 296-1840; Fax: (347) 296-1348
‡Daniel P. FitzGerald (646) 386-3967
†Ruben Franco (718) 618-2463

†Civil Court Judge assigned to Criminal Court
‡Acting Supreme Court Justice

Judges, Criminal Court of the City of N.Y.—Cont'd
‡William E. Garnett (347) 401-9381
‡Michael A. Gary (347) 296-1058
Lenora Gerald (718) 298-0947
†Michael J. Gerstein (646) 386-4658
†David Godosky (347) 404-9479
‡Arlene D. Goldberg (646) 386-4417
‡Joel M. Goldberg (347) 296-1860
†Desmond A. Green (347) 404-9468
‡Ethan R. Greenberg (718) 618-3616
‡James P. Griffin (718) 298-1434
‡Michael A. Gross (718) 618-3668
‡Joseph A. Grosso (718) 298-1418
‡Joseph Gubbay (347) 404-9435; Fax: (718) 643-3538
‡William M. Harrington (718) 298-1204
‡Roger S. Hayes (646) 386-4405
‡Patricia E. Henry (347) 296-1366
Gilbert C. Hong (718) 618-2466
‡Nicholas J. Iacovetta (718) 618-3673
Alexander Jeong (347) 404-9631
†Robert D. Kalish (347) 404-9473
‡Barry Kamins (347) 296-1000; Fax: (347) 296-1327
Admin. Judge, Kings County, Criminal Term
‡Diane R. Kiesel (718) 618-3640; Fax: (212) 457-2663
‡Judy Harris Kluger, 25 Beaver St., N.Y.C. 10004
(212) 428-2130; Fax: (212) 428-2192
Dir., Office of Policy & Planning, and Dir., Court Drug Treatment Programs
Elisa F. Koenderman (646) 386-4678
†Lynn R. Kotler (646) 386-5625
‡Barry Kron (718) 298-1358
†Evelyn LaPorte (347) 404-9447; Fax: (718) 643-3538
‡John B. Latella, Jr. (718) 298-1357
‡Judith S. Lieb (718) 618-3645
Gene R. Lopez (718) 298-0934
†‡Charles S. Lopresto (718) 262-7333
Karen Lupuloff (718) 618-2200
Criminal Court Judge Assigned to Family Court
†Ira H. Margulis (718) 298-0936
‡Alan D. Marrus (347) 296-1830
‡Seth L. Marvin (718) 618-3784
‡Robert C. McGann (718) 298-1385
Kevin McGrath (646) 386-4663
William McGuire (347) 404-9461; Fax: (718) 643-7733
‡Joseph K. McKay (347) 296-1824
‡Edward J. McLaughlin, Room 434 (646) 386-3972
Suzanne Melendez (718) 298-2932; Fax: (718) 520-4712
†Rita Mella (646) 386-4684
†Shari R. Michels (347) 404-9477
‡Salvatore J. Modica (718) 298-1055
‡William I. Mogulescu (718) 618-3685
‡Suzanne M. Mondo (347) 404-9470; Fax: (718) 643-3538
‡John S. Moore (718) 618-3686
‡Pauline A. Mullings (718) 298-0930
†Frank P. Nervo (646) 386-4333
‡Barbara F. Newman (718) 618-3657
‡Patricia M. Nunez (646) 386-4971
†Mary R. O'Donoghue (718) 298-0928
‡Michael J. Obus (646) 386-3947; Fax: (212) 401-9264
Admin. Judge, Criminal Div, Supreme Court
‡Sheryl L. Parker (347) 296-1833
†Geraldine Pickett (347) 404-9475
‡Ruth Pickholz (646) 386-4402; Fax: (212) 374-2579
‡Robert M. Raciti (718) 298-0981; Fax: (718) 520-4712
‡Leonard P. Rienzi (718) 675-8610
Neil E. Ross (646) 386-4666; Fax: (212) 374-2579
†Jennifer Schecter (646) 386-4648
Matthew A. Sciarrino, Jr. (646) 386-4686
‡Robert G. Seewald (718) 618-3675
Toko Serita (718) 298-0925
†ShawnDya L. Simpson (646) 386-4676
‡Ruth E. Smith (718) 618-1016
‡Charles H. Solomon (646) 386-3976
‡Michael R. Sonberg (646) 386-4503

†Civil Court Judge assigned to Criminal Court
‡Acting Supreme Court Justice

Larry R.C. Stephen (646) 386-4661; Fax: (212) 374-2579
‡Robert M. Stolz (646) 386-3991
‡Megan Tallmer (718) 618-3615
‡John P. Walsh (347) 296-1055
‡Laura A. Ward (646) 386-4653; Fax: (212) 295-4891
‡Richard Weinberg, Midtown Community Court, 314 W. 54th St., N.Y.C. 10019 (646) 264-1318
‡Renee Allyn White (646) 386-3970
Marc J. Whiten (646) 386-4655
‡Patricia Anne Williams (718) 618-1467; Fax: (718) 618-3575
†John H. Wilson
(347) 404-9464; Fax: (718) 643-7733
‡Bonnie G. Wittner (646) 386-4427
‡Douglas S. Wong (718) 298-1408
Michael Yavinsky (646) 386-4682
‡Alvin M. Yearwood (718) 618-1034
Stephanie Zaro (718) 298-0926
Joseph Zayas (718) 298-0924

First Deputy Chief Clerk: Vincent Modica (646) 386-4600; Fax: (212) 374-4835

Criminal Court has jurisdiction regarding crimes and offenses committed within New York City to hear, try and determine all misdemeanors, except charges of libel, and all offenses of a grade less than misdemeanor. CCA 31.
Hours: 9 A.M.-5 P.M.

City Courts

NEW YORK CO. BRANCH, NEW YORK CRIMINAL COURT
100 Centre St., N.Y.C. 10013
Judges: (646) 386-4615

Supervising Judge: Melissa Jackson (646) 386-4615
Borough Chief Clerk: Serena Springle (646) 386-4520; Fax: (212) 374-5293
Deputy Borough Chief Clerk: Don Vasti (646) 386-4520
Saturdays, Sundays, Holidays and after 5 P.M.: Vernon Daniels (646) 386-4975
Parts APAR 1, APAR 3, AR4, AR5: Anthony Cuva (646) 386-4585
Part APAR 6: Vacancy at Press Time (646) 264-1320
Part C: Virginia Murray (646) 386-4552
Parts A, B: Deborah Florio (646) 386-4563
Parts SA, D: Mauline Marshall (212) 374-5618, (646) 386-4574
ASC/Cashier Part: Mauline Murrell (646) 386-4541
Part DVC: (646) 386-4578
Part HPI: (646) 386-4580
Parts F, N: Mitchell Primack (646) 386-4559
Jury Parts: Susan Miguel (646) 386-4580
Central Clerk's Office: Michael Lanza (646) 386-4507
Complaint Room (D.A.): Greg Garone (212) 335-9941
Court Stenographers: Howard Goodman (646) 386-4870
District Atty.: (212) 335-9000
Fingerprint: Rudolph Dawson (646) 386-3927
Central Clerks Office: Room 150
General Info.: (646) 386-4511, 12

BRONX CO. BRANCH, NEW YORK CRIMINAL COURT
Bronx Hall of Justice, 265 E. 161st St., Bronx 10451
(718) 618-3010

Deputy Admin. Judge: Eugene Oliver, Jr. (718) 618-3600; Fax: (718) 618-3583
E-mail: eoliver@courts.state.ny.us
Chief Clerk: Steven B. Clark (718) 618-3000
Deputy Chief Clerk: William M. Kalish (718) 618-3250; Fax: (718) 590-2857
Asst. Deputy Chief Clerk, Trial Bureau: Frank Tufano (718) 618-3140
Case Mgmt. Coordinator: Martin Meaney (718) 618-3694
Arraignment Coordinator: Rick Bernstein (718) 618-3008
Bureau Chief, Appeals/Calendar Bureau: Roseann Siegel (718) 618-3050
Part AR1 (Arraignment): (718) 618-2423

Criminal Court, Bronx Cty. Branch—Cont'd
Part AR-2 (Arraignment): (718) 618-2426
Part AR-3 (Night Arraignment): (718) 618-2423
Bronx Couty Branch, N.Y. Criminal Court—Cont'd
Part AR-4 (Holiday, Weekend Arraignment): (718) 618-2423
Part SAP (Summons): (718) 618-2430
Part SAP-2: (718) 618-2434
Part A (Arraignment): (718) 618-1144
Part B (Arraignment): (718) 618-1129
Part DV (Domestic Violence): (718) 618-1088
Part IDV (Integrated Domestic Violence): (718) 618-1067
Part DVC (D.V. Compliance): (718) 618-1082
Part TC (S.C.I): (718) 618-1097
Part MCP (Misdemeanor Conference): (718) 618-1028
Part 7 (Trial): (718) 618-1061
Part 8 (Trial): (718) 618-1013
Part 12 (Trial): (718) 618-1016
Part 15 (Trial): (718) 618-1034
Part 21 (Trial): (718) 618-1022
Part 26 (Trial, D.V.): (718) 618-1085
Part 28 (Trial/Row): (718) 618-1076
Part 29 (Trial): (718) 618-1019
Part 31 (Trial): (718) 618-1031
Grand Jury: (718) 618-1129
Court Reporters Supervisor: Mary Sullivan (718) 618-2450
Criminal Court in Bronx County has been consolidated with Supreme Court, Twelfth Judicial District, Criminal Division

KINGS CO. BRANCH, NEW YORK CRIMINAL COURT
120 Schermerhorn St., Brooklyn 11201
(347) 404-9400, 02

Supervising Judge: ‡William Miller (347) 404-9600; Fax: (718) 643-3538
Borough Chief Clerk: Brian Wynne (347) 404-9500; Fax: (718) 643-7733
Asst. Deputy Chief Clerk: Timothy McGrath (347) 404-9500; Fax: (718) 643-7733
Information—Weekdays—Central Clerk's Office: James Shields (347) 404-9409
Saturdays, Sundays, Holidays and after 5 P.M.: (347) 404-9450, (718) 243-2545
Part APAR1, Arraignment Office (Days): Anthony Colandreo (347) 404-9450, (718) 243-2545; Fax: (718) 643-3303
Summons Arraignment Part: Cheryl Jackson (347) 404-9440
Part APAR3, Arraignment Office (Nights) 6 P.M.-Midnight: James Feeley (347) 404-9450, (718) 243-2545; Fax: (718) 643-3303
Parts AP3, AP4, AP6 (Office): Dino Marrone (347) 404-9515
Parts AP2, AP5 (Office): (347) 404-9525
APIF—STEP—MBTC: Richard Scaturro (347) 404-9530; Fax: (718) 643-4692
Clerk's Office for Jury Parts: Harolyn Baker (347) 404-9548
Jury 1: (347) 404-9370
TP2: (347) 404-9330
TP3: (347) 404-9322
TP4: (347) 404-9350
TP5: (347) 404-9326
Part BTP1: (347) 404-9328
CDRC: Eileen Clancy (347) 404-9565
DAT—Part: (347) 404-9450, (718) 243-2545
Domestic Violence Parts: Jose Colon Clerk's Office: (347) 404-9540
DV1 (Courtroom): (347) 404-9360
DV2 (Courtroom): (347) 404-9362

‡**Acting Supreme Court Justice**

QUEENS CO. BRANCH, NEW YORK CRIMINAL COURT
125-01 Queens Blvd., Kew Gardens 11415
(718) 298-0786; Fax: (718) 520-4712

Supervising Judge: ‡Deborah Stevens Modica (718) 286-0839; Fax: (718) 520-3992
Borough Chief Clerk: Joseph Vitolo (718) 298-0786; Fax: (718) 520-4712
Saturdays, Sundays, Holidays and after 5 P.M.: (718) 298-0736; Fax: (718) 520-7251
Part APAR1: (718) 298-0736; Courtroom: (718) 298-0869; Fax: (718) 520-7251
Part APAR2A (Arraignment Part for Appearance Tickets): (718) 298-0736
Part APAR3: (718) 298-0736; Courtroom: (718) 298-0869; Fax: (718) 520-7251
Part APAR4: (718) 298-0736; Fax: (718) 520-7251
Parts AP1, AP2: (718) 298-0883; Part AP2 Courtroom: (718) 298-0887
QMTC, AP3: (718) 298-0840
Part AR2 (Summons): 120-55 Queens Blvd., Kew Gardens 11424 (718) 298-0700
Part AP4: Domestic Violence Part (718) 298-0891
Part AP5: (718) 298-0874
Part AP6: (718) 298-0859
Trial—2: (718) 298-0855
Jury—1: (718) 298-0851
Hearing Part HP-I/SAP: (718) 298-0847
Narcotics Part (N): (718) 298-0864
Court Dispute Referral Center: (718) 298-0778
D.V. Compliance Part: (718) 298-0847
Central Clerk's Office: (718) 298-0792
Court Officers Bureau: Maj. John D'Amico (718) 298-0729
Court Reporters: Ann Schmidt (718) 298-0751

RICHMOND CO. BRANCH,
NEW YORK CRIMINAL COURT
67 Targee St., Staten Island 10304
(718) 675-8555

Supervising Judge: Alan J. Meyer (718) 675-8550
Borough Chief Clerk: Andrew Hassell (718) 675-8522
Part AP1/General's Clerk's Office: Kenneth Fay (718) 675-8550; Fax: (718) 876-5518
Part AP2/Central Clerk's Office: Stephen Paradiso (718) 675-8520; Fax: (718) 876-5518
Part AP2: Anthony Corvino (718) 675-8520; Fax: (718) 390-8405
General Clerk's Office: Leonard DeTomaso (718) 675-8558; Fax: (718) 876-5518
Supervising Court Reporter: Barbara Veneziano (718) 675-8535
Cashier's Office: William Graff (718) 675-8551

CITY COURTS OUTSIDE OF NEW YORK CITY

ALBANY

Civil Court—Civil Part, 209 City Hall,
Eagle & Corning Pl., Albany 12207
Civil Court: (518) 453-4640; Fax: (518) 434-5034

Criminal Court, Public Safety Bldg.,
1 Morton Ave., Albany 12202
(518) 462-6714

Traffic Court, Basement City Hall,
Eagle & Corning Pl., Albany 12207
(518) 453-4630

Judges:
William A. Carter (Criminal) (518) 462-6714; Fax: (518) 447-8778 E-mail: wcarter@courts.state.ny.us
Helena M. Heath-Roland (Civil, Traffic & Criminal) (518) 453-4640
Thomas K. Keefe (Criminal) (518) 462-6714 E-mail: tkeefe@courts.state.ny.us
Rachel Kretser (Criminal) (518) 462-6714
Gary F. Stiglmeier (Civil, Traffic & Criminal) (518) 453-4640

Albany—Cont'd

Clerks:
Janice Cellucci (Criminal) (518) 462-6714
Linda File (Civil) (518) 453-4640
Anthony Mancino (Traffic) (518) 453-4630

Territorial—City and County of Albany
Civil Monetary—$15,000 exclusive of interest;
Small Claims and Commercial Claims—$5,000.
Court Schedule: Commercial Claims: Wed., 10:30 A.M.; Small Claims, Civil & Summary Proceedings: Mon.- Fri., except holidays, 9 A.M.; Traffic: Mon. and Tues. Criminal: Every day, including weekends and holidays, 9 A.M.

AMSTERDAM
Public Safety Bldg., Room 208,
One Guy Park Ave. Ext., Amsterdam 12010
(518) 842-9510; Fax: (518) 843-8474

Judges:
Howard M. Aison
Lisa W. Lorman

Chief Clerk: Melanie A. Hartman

Territorial—City of Amsterdam
Monetary—$15,000
Court Schedule: Criminal: Tues., 9 A.M.; Civil: Thurs., 9 A.M.; Traffic: Thurs., 10:30 A.M.

AUBURN
157 Genesee St., Auburn 13021-3434
(315) 253-1570; Fax: (315) 253-1085

Judges:
Michael F. McKeon
Thomas J. Shamon

Chief Clerk: Deborah L. Robillard

Territorial—City of Auburn and Cayuga County
Monetary—$15,000; Small Claims—$5,000
Court Schedule: Criminal: Weekdays, 10 A.M.
Civil: Wed., 9 A.M.
Commercial Claims: Thurs., 1:15 P.M.
Small Claims: Tues. and Thurs., 2 & 3 P.M.

BATAVIA
Genesee County Courts Facility, 1 W. Main St., Batavia 14020
(585) 344-2550, Ext. 2415, Ext. 2416, Ext. 2417; Fax: (585) 344-8556; Drug Court: Ext. 2442

Judges:
*Robert J. Balbick, Ext. 2420
E-mail: rbalbick@courts.state.ny.us
Michael A. Del Plato, Ext. 2432
E-mail: mdelplat@courts.state.ny.us

Chief Clerk: Linda M. Giambrone, Ext. 2426
E-mail: lgiambro@courts.state.ny.us

Deputy Chief Clerk: Paula DaBella, Ext. 2418
E-mail: pdabella@courts.state.ny.us

Drug Court Resource Coordinator: Nicole Desmond Ext. 2442; E-mail: ndesmond@courts.state.ny.us

Territorial—Same as Justice of the Peace of the Town
Monetary—$15,000; Small Claims—$5,000
Court Schedule: Civil, Small Claims and Evictions: Weekdays, 10 A.M.-2 P.M.; Traffic: Wed., 9 A.M.; Criminal: Tues., 1 P.M. and Thurs., 10 A.M.; Drug Court: Mon., 1:30 P.M.; Mental Health Court: Thurs., 3 P.M. Hours: Weekdays, 9 A.M.-5 P.M.

BEACON
1 Municipal Plaza, Suite 2, Beacon 12508
(845) 838-5030; Fax: (845) 838-5041

Judges:
Rebecca S. Mensch
Timothy G. Pagones

Chief Clerk: Debra Antonelli

Territorial—City of Beacon; Civil, also Town of Fishkill
Monetary—$15,000
Court Schedule: Civil: Tues.; Criminal: Wed. (Pro Se) and Thurs.; Traffic: Mon.

***Pending November 2010 Election Results**

BINGHAMTON
Governmental Plaza, 38 Hawley St., Binghamton 13901
(607) 772-7006; Fax: (607) 772-7041
Internet: www.courts.state.ny.us/binghamton/city

Judges:
Mary Anne Lehmann
Daniel L. Seiden
William C. Pelella

Chief Clerk: Catherine R. Maloney

Deputy Chief Clerk: Sherry L. Baker

Territorial—Criminal, City of Binghamton; Civil, Binghamton and contiguous towns; Commercial Claims and Small Claims, all of Broome County
Monetary—$15,000; Small Claims—$5,000
Commercial Claims—$5,000
Court Schedule: Weekdays, 9 A.M.-5 P.M.

BUFFALO
50 Delaware Ave., Buffalo 14202
(716) 845-2600; Fax: (716) 847-8257

Chief and Supervising Judge: Thomas P. Amodeo (Part 16), Suite 750
(716) 845-2651; Fax: (716) 845-7568
E-mail: tamodeo@courts.state.ny.us

Judges:
Betty Calvo-Torres (Part 3), Suite 200
(716) 845-2643; Fax: (716) 845-7573
E-mail: bcalvoto@courts.state.ny.us
Patrick M. Carney (Part 13), Suite 600
(716) 845-2642; Fax: (716) 845-7578
E-mail: pcarney@courts.state.ny.us
Joseph A. Fiorella (Part 6), Suite 350
(716) 845-2627; Fax: (716) 845-7575
E-mail: jfiorella@courts.state.ny.us
Debra L. Givens (Part 7), Suite 500
(716) 845-2620; Fax: (716) 845-7576
E-mail: dgivens@courts.state.ny.us
Acting Erie Co. Family Court Judge
Craig D. Hannah (Part 11), Suite 600
(716) 845-2633; Fax: (716) 845-7578
E-mail: channah@courts.state.ny.us
Acting Erie Co. Family Court Judge
Kevin J. Keane (Part 5), Suite 350
(716) 845-2637; Fax: (716) 845-7575
E-mail: kkeane@courts.state.ny.us
Sharon M. LoVallo (Part 10), Suite 550
(716) 845-2628; Fax: (716) 845-7577
E-mail: slovallo@courts.state.ny.us
Acting Erie Co. Family Court Judge
David M. Manz (Part 8), Suite 550
(716) 845-2638; Fax: (716) 845-7577
E-mail: dmanz@courts.state.ny.us
James A.W. McLeod (Part 9), Suite 500
(716) 845-2632; Fax: (716) 845-7576
E-mail: jmcleod@courts.state.ny.us
*Henry J. Nowak (Part 14), Suite 650
(716) 845-2648; Fax: (716) 845-7579
E-mail: hnowak@courts.state.ny.us
E. Jeannette Ogden (Part 12), Suite 650
(716) 845-2647; Fax: (716) 845-7579
Robert T. Russell, Jr. (Part 4), Suite 250
(716) 845-2623; Fax: (716) 845-7574
E-mail: rrussell@courts.state.ny.us

Chief Clerk: Sharon Thomas
(716) 845-2689; Fax: (716) 847-8257
E-mail: sthomas@courts.state.ny.us

Deputy Chief Clerk-Civil: Cina LaGrange
(716) 845-2653; Fax: (716) 845-7570
E-mail: clagrang@courts.state.ny.us

Deputy Chief Clerk-Criminal: Kim Delmont
(716) 845-2654; Fax: (716) 845-7571
E-mail: kdelmont@courts.state.ny.us

Coordinator, Alternative Dispute Resolution:
Michael L. Broderick
(716) 845-2691; Fax: (716) 845-7568

Criminal Records Room:
(716) 845-2661; Fax: (716) 845-7571

City Courts

Buffalo—Cont'd

Civil Judgment Room:
(716) 845-2662; Fax: (716) 845-7570

Small Claims and Commercial Claims: Eileen Taylor
(716) 845-2663; Fax: (716) 845-7572

Housing Court Office:
(716) 845-2673; Fax: (716) 845-7572

C.O.U.R.T.S. Program:
(716) 845-2789; Fax: (716) 845-7580

Landlord and Tenant:
(716) 845-2662; Fax: (716) 845-7570

Territorial—Erie County
Monetary—$15,000

CANANDAIGUA
City Hall, 2 N. Main St., Canandaigua 14424-1448
(585) 396-5011; Fax: (585) 396-5012

Judges:
Stephen D. Aronson; E-mail: saronson@courts.state.ny.us
John A. Schuppenhauer (Part-time)

Clerk: Lisa Schutz

Territorial
Monetary—$15,000
Court Schedule: Tues-Fri., 8:30 A.M.; Finger Lakes Drug Court: Fri., 10 A.M.; Felony Drug Court: Fri., 10 A.M.; Family Court at different time
Hours: Weekdays, 8 A.M.-4 P.M.

COHOES
City Hall, 1st Fl., Room 7, 97 Mohawk St.,
P.O. Box 678, Cohoes 12047-0678
(518) 233-2133; Fax: (518) 233-8202

Judges:
Richard R. Maguire (Criminal & Misdemeanor Traffic) Ext. 7
Stephen J. Van Ullen (Civil & Traffic Infractions)

Clerk: Patricia Pettit

Territorial—City of Cohoes
Monetary—$15,000; Small Claims—$5,000; Commercial Small Claims—$5,000
Court Schedule: Civil & Commercial/Small Claims: Mon., 9 A.M. & Wed., 10 A.M.; Arraignments, Criminal and Code Violations: Tues., 6 P.M..; Criminal & Traffic Misdemeanors: Thurs.; Conference at Noon and D.A. Session at 1 P.M.; Thurs. at 1 P.M.; Traffic: Wed., 8:30 A.M.
Hours: Weekdays 8 A.M.-4 P.M.

CORNING
12 Civic Center Plaza, Corning 14830-2884
(607) 936-4111; Fax: (607) 936-0519

Judge: David B. Kahl

Clerk: Julie L. Machuga

Territorial—Process may be served anywhere in County. One of the parties must be resident of City.
Monetary—$15,000
Criminal—All violations and misdemeanors committed in City
Court Schedule: Weekdays, 8:30 A.M.
Office Hours: Weekdays, 8 A.M.-4 P.M.

CORTLAND
25 Court St., Cortland 13045
(607) 428-5420; Fax: (607) 428-5435

Judge: Thomas A. Meldrim
E-mail: tmeldrim@courts.state.ny.us

Chief Clerk: Kelly L. Preston
E-mail: kpreston@courts.state.ny.us

Territorial—Civil, City of Cortland and contiguous towns; Criminal, City of Cortland; Commercial Claims and Small Claims, all of Cortland County
Monetary—$15,000; Small Claims—$5,000; Commercial Claims—$5,000
Court Schedule: Criminal and Traffic: Mon., Wed. and Fri. at 9 A.M. ; Adult treatment court: Mon., 2 P.M.
Civil Part: Thurs. at 9 A.M.; Small/Com Claims at 1 P.M.

DUNKIRK
City Hall, 342 Central Ave., Dunkirk 14048-2122
(716) 366-2055; Fax: (716) 366-3622

Judges:
Walter F. Drag; E-mail: wdrag@courts.state.ny.us
John M. Kuzdale (Acting)

Clerk: Jean Dill

Territorial—Chautauqua County
Monetary—$15,000; Small Claims—$5,000;
Commercial Claims—$5,000
Court Schedule: Arraignments: Mon.
Trials: Fri., as scheduled
Civil and Small Claims: Wed., as scheduled
Criminal Pretrials Tues., as scheduled
Traffic Pretrials (pro se) Wed., as scheduled

ELMIRA
City Hall, 317 E. Church St., Elmira 14901-2790
(607) 737-5681; Small Claims: (607) 737-5681;
Fax: (212) 401-9240
E-mail: elmiracitycourt@courts.state.ny.us
Internet: www.courts.state.ny.us/6jd

Judges:
Steven W. Forrest; E-mail: sforrest@courts.state.ny.us
Thomas E. Ramich; E-mail: tramich@courts.state.ny.us

Chief Clerk: Teresa B. Seeley
E-mail: tseeley@courts.state.ny.us

Deputy Chief Clerk: Sharon E. Race
E-mail: srace@courts.state.ny.us

Territorial—City of Elmira; Small Claims for all of Chemung County
Monetary Civil—$15,000; Small Claims—$5,000; Commercial Claims—$5,000
Court Schedule: Criminal: Weekdays, 9 A.M.
Arraignments: Weekdays; Emergency arraignments on weekends and holidays as required; Small Claims and Commercial Claims: Tues., Wed. and Fri. at 1:30 P.M.
Small Claims evening session second Mon. of month at 5 P.M.

FULTON
Municipal Bldg., 141 S. 1st St., Fulton 13069
(315) 593-8400; Fax: (315) 592-3415
E-mail: fulton_city@courts.state.ny.us
Internet:
www.nycourts.gov/courts/5jd/oswego/fulton/index.sh

Judges:
Spencer J. Ludington; E-mail: fulton_city@courts.state.ny.us
Jerome A. Mirabito; E-mail: jmirabit@courts.state.ny.us

Chief Clerk: Maureen Ball
E-mail: mball@courts.state.ny.us

Senior Court Assts.:
Sherri Diefenbacher; E-mail: sdiefenb@courts.state.ny.us
Jennifer Cooper; E-mail: jlcooper@courts.state.ny.us
Shelly Fantom; E-mail: sfantom@courts.state.ny.us

Supervising Court Office Asst.: Adolph Eckstein
E-mail: aeckstei@courts.state.ny.us

Territorial—Oswego County—Small Claims / Comm. Claims—$5,000
Monetary—$15,000—City of Fulton—Civil
Court Schedule: Criminal: Wed. and Thurs., 9 A.M.,
Civil and Summary Proceedings: Thurs., 1:30 P.M.

GENEVA
Public Safety Bldg., 255 Exchange St., Geneva 14456
(315) 789-6560; Fax: (315) 781-2802

Supervising Judge: Timothy J. Buckley

Judges:
Bram Lehman
Elisabeth A. Toole

Clerk: Josephine J. Guard

Territorial—Ontario County
Monetary—$15,000
Court Schedule: Mon. and Thurs.

GLEN COVE
13 Glen St., Glen Cove 11542-2776
(516) 676-0109; Fax: (516) 676-1570

Judges:
Joseph D. McCann Richard J. McCord

Chief Clerk: Stacey Newman

Civil—Art. 2 U.C.C.
Monetary—$15,000
Small Claims—$5,000
Commercial Small Claims—$5,000
Criminal—Art. 20 U.C.C.
Court Schedule: Mon. and Tues., 9:30 A.M.

GLENS FALLS
42 Ridge St., 3rd Floor, Glens Falls 12801
(518) 798-4714; Fax: (518) 798-0137

Judges:
Richard P. Tarantino Gary C. Hobbs

Chief Clerk: Philip C. Simms

Territorial—County wide
Monetary—$15,000
Small Claims—$5,000
Court Schedule: Criminal: Tues. and Thurs..; Traffic: Mon., 9 A.M.; Civil and Small Claims: Wed., 9 A.M.; Domestic Violence Court: Alternate Fri.

GLOVERSVILLE
City Hall, 3 Frontage Rd., Gloversville 12078
(518) 773-4527; Fax: (518) 773-4599

Judges:
Joan Antonik Vincent DeSantis

Clerk: Jodi L. Ferguson

Monetary—$15,000—Civil; $5,000—Small Claims & Commercial Claims
Territorial: Civil—City of Gloversville or contiguous town; Small & Commercial Claims—County of Fulton
Court Schedule: Criminal: Mon. and Wed., 9 A.M.; Traffic: Tues., 9 A.M.; Civil: Fri., 9 A.M.

HORNELL
82 Main St., P.O. Box 627, Hornell 14843-0627
(607) 324-7531; Fax: (607) 324-6325

Judge: Joseph E. Damrath (607) 324-7531

Clerk: Love B. Griffin (607) 324-0210

Territorial—According to Uniform City Court Act
Monetary—$15,000
Court Schedule: Tues., 10 A.M.; Thurs., 8:30 A.M.

HUDSON
427-429 Warren St., Hudson 12534
(518) 828-3100; Fax: (518) 828-3628
Internet: www.nycourts.gov/courts/3jd/

Judges:
William F. Cranna Richard M. Koweek

Chief Clerk: Rosemary Zukowski

Territorial—City
Monetary—$15,000
Court Schedule: Criminal: Tues. & Thurs., 8:30 A.M., First & third Wed., 8:30 A.M.; City Code Violation: second Wed., 8:30 A.M.; Small Claims and Commercial Claims: fourth Wed., 8:30 A.M.
Hours: Weekdays, 8 A.M.-3:45 P.M.

ITHACA
118 E. Clinton St., Ithaca 14850
(607) 273-2263; Fax: (607) 277-3702
Internet: www.courts.state.ny.us/ithaca/city

Judges:
James M. Kerrigan Judith A. Rossiter

Chief Clerk: Jim Jecen

Deputy Chief Clerk: Yvonne J. Foote

Civil Jurisdiction
Territorial—County of Tompkins
Monetary—$15,000
Court Schedule: Wed. and Fri., 9:30 A.M.; Civil: Thurs., 9:30 A.M.; Treatment Court: Tues., 1:15 P.M.; Traffic Court: Wed., Noon

JAMESTOWN
City Hall, 200 E. Third St., Jamestown 14701-5433
(716) 483-7561; Fax: (716) 483-7519

Judges:
John L. LaMancuso
George Panebianco (Part-time)

Chief Clerk: Lisa Meacham
E-mail: lmeacham@courts.state.ny.us

Deputy Chief Clerk: Deborah Taft
E-mail: dtaft@courts.state.ny.us

Resource Coordinator II—Drug Court: Catherine Newton
(716) 483-7793; Fax: (716) 483-7647
E-mail: cnewton@courts.state.ny.us

Court Atty.: Robert Nieto (716) 483-7746
E-mail: rnieto@courts.state.ny.us

Court Reporters:
Arlene Anderson (716) 483-7637
Linda Olduni (716) 483-7637

Senior Office Asst.: Heather Eaton
E-mail: heaton@courts.state.ny.us

Case Mgr. I—Drug Court: Vacancy at Press Time

Senior Court Office Assts.:
Lynne Barrett; E-mail: lbarrett@courts.state.ny.us
Holly Garland; E-mail: hgarland@courts.state.ny.us
Bonnie Scranton; E-mail: bscranto@courts.state.ny.us
Jessica Testa (part time)
E-mail: jtesta@courts.state.ny.us

Court Office Asst.: Karen Schultz
E-mail: kschultz@courts.state.ny.us

Territorial—Civil, City of Jamestown and/or areas contiguous to city (under UCCA).
Criminal—misdemeanors, City of Jamestown; felony arraignments; and traffic infractions, city code violations
Monetary—$15,000; Small Claims, Commercial Claims Monetary Limit $5,000
Court Schedule: Weekdays, 9:30 A.M.

JOHNSTOWN
City Hall, 33-41 E. Main St., Johnstown 12095
(518) 762-0007; Fax: (518) 762-2720
Internet: www.nycourts.gov

Judges:
Frederick R. Stortecky Thomas C. Walsh

Chief Clerk: Stephen S. Russo

Territorial—County of Fulton
Monetary—$15,000
Court Schedule: Tues. mornings, last Wed. of each month in afternoon

KINGSTON
1 Garraghan Dr., Kingston 12401
(845) 338-2974; Fax: (845) 338-1443

Judges:
Lawrence E. Ball
Philip W. Kirschner (Part-time)

Chief Clerk: Nicole Murphy

Territorial—Criminal: City of Kingston
Civil: All of Ulster County; Monetary—$15,000;
Court Schedule: Weekdays, 8:30 A.M.-4:30 P.M.
Traffic Court: Wed., 2 P.M.

LACKAWANNA
City Hall, 714 Ridge Rd., Lackawanna 14218-1588
(716) 827-6672; Fax: (716) 825-1874

Chief Judge: Frederic J. Marrano (716) 827-6672

Judge: Louis P. Violanti (Associate) (716) 827-6486

Chief Clerk: Maryann Grzeskowiak (716) 827-6672

Deputy Chief Clerk: Lisa Gauthier (716) 827-6440

Territorial—Civil: Lackawanna and Towns contiguous to City of Lackawanna; Criminal: City of Lackawanna
Monetary—$15,000
Court Schedule: Every day

LITTLE FALLS
City Hall, 659 E. Main St., Little Falls 13365
(315) 823-1690; Fax: (315) 823-1623

Judges:
Bart M. Carrig
Mark Rose

Clerk: Patrice M. Gleim

Territorial—City of Little Falls
Monetary—$15,000
Court Schedule: Traffic: Tues., 9:30 A.M.
Civil/Motions: Tues., 10 A.M.
Criminal: Tues., 10 A.M.
Criminal with D.A.: First, 2nd & 3rd Wed., 1 P.M.
Small Claims: Thurs., 9:30 A.M.

LOCKPORT
Municipal Bldg., One Locks Plaza, Lockport 14094
Civil: (716) 439-6660, Ext. 2;
Criminal: (716) 439-6660, Ext. 1;
Traffic: (716) 439-6660, Ext. 3; Fax: (716) 439-6684;
Treatment Courts: (716) 439-6660, Ext. 4

Judges:
William J. Watson
Thomas M. DiMillo (Part-time)

Chief Clerk: Colleen J. Wagner (716) 439-6660, Ext. 207

Deputy Chief Clerk: Sharon L. Guagliano (716) 439-6660, Ext. 208

Territorial—Niagara County
Monetary—$15,000 limit, except in summary proceedings
Court Schedule: Weekdays, 8:30 A.M.-4:30 P.M.

LONG BEACH
1 West Chester St., Long Beach 11561
(516) 431-1000; Fax: (516) 889-3511

Judge: Roy Teppr, Ext. 7501

Clerk: Robert N. Davis, Ext. 7509

Deputy Chief Clerk: Lynne S. Bianchini, Ext. 7515

Territorial—Process throughout Nassau County, subject to 213 and 404 U.C.C.A.
Monetary—$15,000
Small Claims—$5,000
Court Schedule: Civil: Weekdays
Criminal: Mon., Wed., Thurs. and Fri., 9:30 A.M.

MECHANICVILLE
City Hall, 36 N. Main St., Mechanicville 12118
(518) 664-9876; Fax: (518) 664-8606

Judges:
Keith M. Ferrara; E-mail: kferrara@courts.state.ny.us
Joseph W. Sheehan
Court Schedule: Wed., 9 A.M.

Clerk: Francine Baker

Territorial—Civil—City of Mechanicville or contingent town; Small-Commercial Claims—County of Saratoga
Monetary—$15,000-Civil
$5,000—Small & Commercial Claims
Court Schedule: Tues. and Wed., 8:30 A.M.
Office Hours: Weekdays, 8:30 A.M.

MIDDLETOWN
2 James St., Middletown 10940
(845) 346-4050; Fax: (845) 343-5737

Judges:
Steven W. Brockett
Robert F. Moson

Chief Clerk: Linda F. Padden

Deputy Chief Clerk: Robin L. Siegel

Territorial—City of Middletown;
Commercial & Small Claims for all of Orange County.
Monetary—$15,000; Commercial & Small Claims—$5,000
Court Schedule: Mon.-Fri., 8:30 A.M.-4 P.M.

MOUNT VERNON
Two Roosevelt Sq. N., 2nd Floor,
Mount Vernon 10550-2019
(914) 831-6440; Fax: (914) 699-1230

Judges:
Helen M. Blackwood (914) 831-6440
William Edwards (914) 831-6463
Mark A. Gross (914) 831-6498

Assoc. Judge: Adam Seiden (914) 831-6463

Chief Clerk: Lawrence E. Darden, Jr. (914) 831-6464

Deputy Chief Clerk: Judith M. Hicks (914) 831-6465

Court Attys.:
Andrea Blount (914) 831-6497
Melissa Namba (914) 831-6495

Secretary: Margherite Ciardiello (914) 831-6463

Territorial—Anywhere in Westchester County, if one or more of the parties is a resident or has a place of business in Mount Vernon
Monetary—$15,000
Court Schedule: Weekdays
Hours: Weekdays, 9 A.M.-5 P.M.

NEW ROCHELLE
475 North Ave., New Rochelle 10801-3405
(914) 654-2291

Judges:
Anthony A. Carbone (Acting) (914) 654-2286
Gail B. Rice (914) 654-2287

Clerk: James Generoso (914) 654-2207; Fax: (914) 654-0344

Territorial—City of New Rochelle and Westchester County
Monetary—$15,000; Small Claims—$5,000;
Commercial—$5,000.
Court Schedule: Weekdays, 9:30 A.M.; This court is a court of Special Sessions having Criminal jurisdiction. Felony Arraignments: Weekends, 8 A.M.; Small Claims and Corporate Claims: Wed., 2 & 6:30 P.M. (filing Weekdays, 9 A.M.-3 P.M.)

NEWBURGH
300 Broadway, Newburgh 12550
(845) 483-8100;
Fax, Civil, Traffic, Landlord/Tenant, Housing:
(845) 565-0230; Fax, Criminal: (845) 565-0421

Judges:
B. Harold Ramsey (845) 483-8100
Peter M. Kulkin

Clerk: Sharon Reed

Deputy Chief Clerk: Irene Grant

Territorial—Orange County
Monetary—$15,000
Court Schedule: Weekdays, 8 A.M.-4 P.M.

NIAGARA FALLS
Niagara Falls Municipal Complex, 1925 Main St.,
Niagara Falls 14305
Civil Court: (716) 278-9860;
Criminal Court: (716) 278-9800;
Traffic Court: (716) 278-9840; Fax: (716) 278-9809

Chief Judge: Mark Anthony Violante (716) 278-9820
E-mail: maviolan@courts.state.ny.us

Judges:
Robert P. Merino (716) 278-9821
E-mail: rmerino@courts.state.ny.us
Angelo J. Morinello (716) 278-9822
E-mail: amorinel@courts.state.ny.us
Diane L. Vitello (716) 278-9812

Chief Clerk: Martha J. Farbo-Lincoln (716) 278-9800

Deputy Chief Clerk: Carol M. Glassner (716) 278-9840
Court Schedule: Weekdays

NORTH TONAWANDA
City Hall, 216 Payne Ave.,
North Tonawanda 14120-5446
(716) 693-1010; Fax: (716) 743-1754

Judges:
William R. Lewis
Jeffrey N. Mis

Chief Clerk: Sheila D. Cocco
E-mail: scocco@courts.state.ny.us

Territorial—Niagara County
Monetary—$15,000
Court Schedule: Weekdays

NORWICH
One Court Plaza, Norwich 13815
(607) 334-1224; Fax: (607) 334-8494

Judges:
James G. Cushman James E. Downey
Clerk: Irene R. Williams
E-mail: iwilliam@courts.state.ny.us
Territorial—Chenango County
Small / Commercial Claims—$5,000
Monetary—$15,000-Civil
Court Schedule: Mon., Tues., and Thurs., 9:30 A.M.

OGDENSBURG
330 Ford St., Ogdensburg 13669
(315) 393-3941; Fax: (315) 393-6839

Judges:
George E. Silver
William R. Small (Part-time)
Chief Clerk: Lisa Marie Meyer
Sr. Court Office Assistant: Nancy A. Thompson
Court Office Asst.: Cathy A. Bentley
Mary Jean Mullis
Drug Court Coordinator: Debbie L. Miller
(315) 393-5408
Security: Sgt. Roger Wollman (315) 393-2924
Territorial—St. Lawrence County
(Commercial & Small Claims Only)
Monetary—$15,000
Court Schedule: Weekdays, 8 A.M.-4 P.M.

OLEAN
Municipal Bldg., 101 E. State St., P.O. Box 631, Olean 14760-0631
(716) 376-5621; Fax: (716) 376-5623

Judges:
William H. (Hank) Mountain III
E-mail: wmountai@courts.state.ny.us
Daniel R. Palumbo
Chief Clerk: Stella S. Johnston
Territorial—Either party must reside in Cattaraugus County or have place of business in Cattaraugus County. Process may be served throughout Cattaraugus County and outside county where permitted by Uniform City Court Act.
Monetary—$15,000; Small Claims—$5,000; Commercial Small Claims—$5,000
Court Schedule: Criminal: Tues., 9 A.M.; Criminal Arraignments: Tues., 9 A.M.; Traffic: Thurs., 9 A.M.; Civil filings including small claims: Thur., 10 A.M.

ONEIDA
108 Main St., Oneida 13421
(315) 266-4740; Fax: (315) 363-3230

Judges:
Anthony P. Eppolito
Michael J. Misiaszek (Part-time)
Clerk: Lynne M. Mondrick
Territorial—Madison County
Civil—$15,000
Small Claims—$5,000
Court Schedule: Traffic: Tues., 9 A.M.; Criminal: Fri., 9 A.M.; Civil, Evictions and Commercial Claims: Thurs., 9 A.M.; Small Claims: second Thurs., 6 P.M.; Wed., 3 P.M. as scheduled

ONEONTA
Public Safety Bldg., 81 Main St., Oneonta 13820
(607) 432-4480; Fax: (607) 432-2328
E-mail (not for use in filing papers): oneontacitycourt@courts.state.ny.us

Judges:
Lucy P. Bernier
Richard W. McVinney
Clerk: Catherine Tisenchek
Territorial—Civil: Either party must reside, be employed or have place of business in City or Town of Oneonta; Service must be in Otsego County, or in adjoining counties as permitted by UCCA 404-B.
Criminal and Traffic: City of Oneonta only;
Small / Commercial Claims: Otsego County only
Monetary (Civil)—$15,000; Small Claims / Commercial—$5,000
Court Schedule: Mon.-Fri., 8 A.M.-4 P.M.

OSWEGO
Conway Munic. Center, 20 W. Oneida St., Oswego 13126
(315) 343-0415; Fax: (315) 343-0531

Judges:
James M. Metcalf P. Michael Shanley
Clerk: Cassie Kinney
Territorial—County of Oswego for Small Claims / Comm Claims—$5,000; Civil—City of Oswego
Monetary—$15,000
Court Schedule: Weekdays, 8:30 A.M.-4:30 P.M.
Summer Schedule: Weekdays, 8:30 A.M.-4 P.M.

PEEKSKILL
2 Nelson Ave., Peekskill 10566
(914) 831-6480; Fax: (914) 736-1889

Judges:
Thomas R. Langan William L. Maher
Law Secretary: Linda Gironda
Chief Clerk: Janice Laughlin
Territorial—City of Peekskill
Monetary—$15,000
Small Claims—$5,000
Commercial Claims—$5,000
Westchester County
Court Schedule: Criminal: Mon., 11 A.M., Thurs., 11 A.M.; LL/Tenant: Tues., 9:30 A.M.; Civil, Small Claims and Comm. Claims: Wed., 9:30 A.M.;
Traffic: Mon. and Thurs., 9:30 A.M.

PLATTSBURGH
24 U.S. Oval, Plattsburgh 12903
(518) 563-7870; Fax: (518) 563-3124
Internet:
www.nycourts.gov/courts/4jd/plattsburgh_city/index

Judges:
Penelope D. Clute
Mark J. Rogers (Part-time)
53 Court St., Plattsburgh 12901 (518) 561-3700
Clerk: Kimberly A. Crow
Territorial—City of Plattsburgh / County of Clinton
Monetary—$15,000
Court Schedule: Weekdays, 8 A.M.-4 P.M.

PORT JERVIS
20 Hammond St., Port Jervis 12771-2495
(845) 858-4034; Fax: (845) 858-9883

Judges:
Victoria B. Campbell Matthew D. Witherow
Clerk: Catherine Quinn
Territorial—County of Orange
Monetary—$15,000
Court Schedule: Criminal: Mon., 1 P.M. & Wed., 9 A.M.; Traffic & Civil: Thurs., 9 A.M.

POUGHKEEPSIE
62 Civic Center Plaza, Poughkeepsie 12601
(845) 483-8200; Fax: (845) 485-6795

Judges:
John B. Garrity Katherine A. Moloney
Clerk: Jean Marie Jicha
Territorial—City of Poughkeepsie
Monetary—$15,000
Court Schedule: Criminal: Weekdays, 9 A.M.; Civil and Traffic: Weekdays, 9 A.M.; Drug Treatment Court: Tues., 2:30 P.M.

RENSSELAER
62 Washington St., Rensselaer 12144
(518) 453-4680; Fax: (518) 462-3307

Judges:
Carmelo Laquidara Kathleen Leahey Robichaud

Chief Court Clerk: Patricia L. Wiesmaier

Territorial—Uniform City Court Act
Monetary—$15,000
Court Schedule: Civil: Tues., 8 A.M.; Criminal: Wed., 8:30 A.M.; Traffic: Thurs., 8:30 A.M.
Hours: Weekdays, 8 A.M.-3:30 P.M.

ROCHESTER
Civil Division, 6 Hall of Justice,
99 Exchange Blvd., Rochester 14614
(585) 428-2444; Fax: (585) 428-2588
Internet:
www.nycourts.gov/courts/7jd/rochester/civil.shtml
Criminal Division, 123 Public Safety Bldg., Rochester 14614
(585) 428-2447; Fax: (585) 428-2732

Supervising Judge, City Courts of the Seventh Jud. Dist.:
John R. Schwartz (585) 428-2450; Fax: (585) 428-2737
E-mail: jschwart@courts.state.ny.us
Acting County Court Judge, Monroe County

Supervising Judge: Teresa D. Johnson
(585) 428-2096; Fax: (585) 428-4265
E-mail: tjohnson@courts.state.ny.us
Acting County Court Judge, Monroe County

Judges:
Melchor E. Castro (585) 428-2437; Fax: (585) 428-2731
E-mail: mcastro@courts.state.ny.us
Charles F. Crimi, Jr. (585) 428-4376; Fax: (585) 428-4379
E-mail: ccrimi@courts.state.ny.us
Maija C. Dixon (585) 428-4374; Fax: (585) 428-4379
John E. Elliott (585) 428-2435; Fax: (585) 428-4386
E-mail: jeelliot@courts.state.ny.us
Stephen T. Miller (585) 428-2470; Fax: (585) 428-2741
Acting County Court Judge, Monroe County
Thomas Rainbow Morse
(585) 428-5248; Fax: (585) 428-2731
E-mail: tmorse@courts.state.ny.us
Ellen M. Yacknin (585) 428-1984; Fax: (585) 428-4386
E-mail: eyacknin@courts.state.ny.us

Chief Clerk: Sandra Petrella
6 Hall of Justice, Rochester 14614
(585) 428-3527; Fax: (585) 428-3156
E-mail: spetrell@courts.state.ny.us

Deputy Chief Clerks:
Kim Bostley (Criminal Division)
123 Public Safety Bldg., Rochester 14614
(585) 428-4547; Fax: (585) 428-2935
E-mail: kbostley@courts.state.ny.us
John R. Treusdell (Civil Division)
6 Hall of Justice, Rochester 14614
(585) 428-3526; Fax: (585) 428-2588
E-mail: jtreusde@courts.state.ny.us

Territorial—Monroe County
Monetary—$15,000
Commercial Claims—$5,000
Small Claims—$5,000
Court Schedule: Civil Branch, Part III: Motions, Summary proceedings,Civil Jury trials and hearings: Daily; Small Claims Division hearings: Tues., Wed. & Thurs.; Criminal Branch, Part I: Misdemeanor and Violation arraignments, motions, Mon.-Sat.; Parts II, IV, VI, VII, VIIII: Dispositions, Criminal Trials & Hearings: Weekdays; Part V: Felony arraignments, Preliminary hearings, Mon.-Sat.

ROME
Justice Center, 100 W. Court St., Rome 13440
(315) 337-6440; Fax: (315) 338-0343

Judges:
John C. Gannon (Half time)
Court Schedule: First & third Tues., 6 P.M.; Fifth Tues., 9 A.M.
Daniel C. Wilson (315) 337-6440; Fax: (315) 338-0343
Court Schedule: Second & fourth Mon., 9 A.M.

Chief Clerk: Eleanor T. Coniglio

Deputy Clerk: Susan Exner

Territorial—City of Rome and Oneida County
Civil-Monetary—$15,000;
Small Claims/Commercial Claims—$5,000
Hours: Weekdays, 8:30 A.M.-4:30 P.M.
Criminal & Traffic: Weekdays, 9 A.M.
Small Claims, Commercial and Evictions: Tues. and Thurs., 9 A.M.

RYE
21 McCullough Pl., Rye 10580
(914) 831-6400; Fax: (914) 967-4354

Judges:
Joseph Latwin Richard Runes

Chief Clerk: Antoinette Cipriano

Territorial—Civil: One of parties to action must reside in City of Rye; Service within County of Westchester Small Claims and Commercial: Westchester County
Monetary—$15,000; Small Claims and Commercial—$5,000
Court Schedule: Civil: Mon., Thurs. and Fri., 9 A.M.-5 P.M.; Criminal: Tues., 9 A.M.-5 P.M.; Small Claims and Commercial Claims: Mon., 9 A.M.-5 P.M., and Wed., 5:45 P.M.

SALAMANCA
Municipal Bldg., 225 Wildwood Ave., Salamanca 14779
(716) 945-4153; Fax: (716) 945-2362

Judges:
William J. Gabler Ronald D. Ploetz

Chief Clerk: Stella S. Johnston

Territorial—Summary: City of Salamanca;
Civil: Cattaraugus County
Monetary—$15,000
Court Schedule: Wed. and Fri., 9 A.M.

SARATOGA SPRINGS
City Hall, Suite 3, 474 Broadway,
Saratoga Springs 12866-2295
(518) 451-8780; Fax: (518) 584-3097

Judges:
Jeffrey D. Wait
James E.D. Doern (Part-time)

Chief Clerk: Elizabeth M. Thornhill

Deputy Clerk: Carolyn S. Saxton

Territorial—Civil: Saratoga County; Criminal & Traffic: Saratoga Springs City
Monetary—$15,000
Court Schedule: Civil: Mon. and Wed.; Criminal: Tues., Thurs., and first & third Fri.; Traffic: Wed. and second Fri.

SCHENECTADY
Civil Court, City Hall, Room 215, Jay St., Schenectady 12305
(518) 382-5077; Fax: (518) 382-5080

Criminal Court, 531 Liberty St., Schenectady 12305
(518) 382-5239; Fax: (518) 382-5241

Traffic Court, City Hall, Room 204, Jay St., Schenectady 12305
(518) 382-5041; Fax: (518) 382-5080

Judges:
Mark W. Blanchfield, Room 204 (518) 382-5041
Christine M. Clark
531 Liberty St., Schenectady 12305 (518) 382-5239
Guido A. Loyola (Civil)

Clerk: Patricia A. Jordan

Territorial—Schenectady County
Monetary—$15,000 plus interest and costs—Civil $5,000 Small Claims
Court Schedule: Weekdays, 8 A.M.-4 P.M.

SHERRILL
373 Sherrill Rd., Sherrill 13461
(315) 363-0996; Fax: (315) 363-1176

Judge: Neal P. Rose

Court Clerk: Carol A. Shea

Territorial—City of Sherrill
Monetary—$15,000
Court Schedule: Traffic & Criminal Cases: Thurs., 4 P.M.; Civil & Small Claims: Tues., 1:15 P.M. and as needed

SYRACUSE
505 S. State St., Syracuse 13202-2104

Supervising Judge: Jeffrey R. Merrill
(315) 671-2767; Fax: (315) 671-2740
E-mail: jmerrill@courts.state.ny.us

Judges:
Vanessa E. Bogan (315) 671-2768; Fax: (315) 671-2746
E-mail: vbogan@courts.state.ny.us
James H. Cecile (315) 671-2786; Fax: (315) 671-2748
E-mail: jcecile@courts.state.ny.us
Stephen J. Dougherty (315) 671-2771; Fax: (315) 671-2748
E-mail: sdougher@courts.state.ny.us
Theodore H. Limpert (315) 671-2769; Fax: (315) 671-2746
E-mail: tlimpert@courts.state.ny.us
Langston C. McKinney (315) 671-2766; Fax: (315) 671-2747
E-mail: lmckinne@courts.state.ny.us
Kate Rosenthal (315) 671-2775; Fax: (315) 671-2747
E-mail: krosenth@courts.state.ny.us
Karen M. Uplinger (315) 671-2765; Fax: (315) 671-2740
E-mail: kuplinge@courts.state.ny.us

Chief Clerk: Lucia A. Sander
(315) 671-2776; Fax: (315) 671-2742
E-mail: lsander@courts.state.ny.us

Deputy Chief Clerk: Anthony J. Procopio
(315) 671-2777; Fax: (315) 671-2742
E-mail: tprocopio@courts.state.ny.us

Civil and Small Claims Division
Room 130
Civil Division: (315) 671-2782;
Small Claims: (315) 671-2784; Fax: (315) 671-2741

Court Clerk I: Barbara Tracz
(315) 671-2782; Fax: (315) 671-2741
E-mail: btracz@courts.state.ny.us

Territorial—City of Syracuse, and contiguous towns; Small Claims, all of Onondaga County
Monetary—$15,000; Small Claims—$5,000
Court Schedule: Weekdays; Small Claims: Tues. and Thurs., 1:30 P.M.

Criminal Division
Room 130
(315) 671-2760; Fax: (315) 671-2744

Court Clerk I: Laura M. DelVecchio
(315) 671-2760; Fax: (315) 671-2744
E-mail: ldelvecc@courts.state.ny.us
Court Schedule: Weekdays, 9:30 A.M.; Arraignments also on Weekends & Holidays

Traffic Division
Room 130
(315) 671-2770; Fax: (315) 671-2743

Court Clerk I: Kelly Meacham
(315) 671-2770; Fax: (315) 671-2743
E-mail: kmeacham@courts.state.ny.us
Court Schedule: Weekdays, 9:30 A.M.; Night sessions: Wed., 4:30 P.M.

Community Court
Public Safety Bldg., Room 115, 511 S. State St., Syracuse 13202-2179
(315) 671-2797; Fax: (315) 671-6091

Judge: Langston C. McKinney

Community Court Coordinator: Matthew L. Brown
E-mail: mlbrown@courts.state.ny.us
Court Schedule: Thurs., 9:30 A.M. & 1:45 P.M.; Part 2 at Public Safety Bldg.

Community Treatment Court
Public Safety Bldg., Room 117, 511 S. State St., Syracuse 13202-2179
(315) 671-2795; Fax: (315) 671-2745

Judge: Jeffrey R. Merrill (315) 671-2767

Program Coordinator: Kim Kozlowski
E-mail: kkozlows@courts.state.ny.us
Court Schedule: Tues., and Thurs., 2 P.M.; Part 1 at Public Safety Bldg.

Domestic Violence Court
505 S. State St., Room 130, Syracuse 13202-2104
(315) 671-2815; Fax: (315) 671-4257

Judge: Stephen J. Dougherty (315) 671-2771
Resource Coordinator: Melissa Monroe
E-mail: mamonroe@courts.state.ny.us
Court Schedule: Weekdays, 1:30 P.M.

TONAWANDA
City Hall, 200 Niagara St., Tonawanda 14150
(716) 845-2160; Fax: (716) 693-1612

Judges:
Joseph J. Cassata, Jr.
Mark E. Saltarelli (Acting)

Chief Clerk: Mary A. Strobel

Deputy Chief Clerk: Jennifer Steele

Territorial—All claims can be processed as long as either party resides in Tonawanda or a contiguous town or village contiguous by land. Process may be served anywhere in Tonawanda or a contiguous town or village contiguous by land. Process may be served in any adjoining county in limited Civil cases. Uniform City Court Act 404.
Monetary—Civil $15,000; Small Claims $5,000, for Small Claims the defendant must reside or have place of business in Erie County.
Court Schedule: Weekdays, Criminal; Tues., 9 A.M.; Civil: Wed., 1:30 P.M.; Small Claims: Wed., 9:30 A.M.; also first Wed., 5:30 P.M.; Traffic: Fri., 9:30 A.M.; Domestic Violence Court: Thurs., 9:30 A.M.; Drug Court: Thurs., 1:30 P.M.

TROY
51 State St., Troy 12180
Civil Part: (518) 273-2434; Civil Fax: (518) 271-2360;
Criminal Part: (518) 271-1602;
Criminal Fax: (518) 274-2816
Internet: www.nycourts.gov/courts/3jd/

Judges:
Christopher Maier (Criminal) (518) 271-1602
*Matthew J. Turner (Civil) (518) 273-2434
E-mail: mjturner@courts.state.ny.us

Chief Clerk III: Karen I. DeBenedetto (518) 271-1602

Territorial—See U.C.C.A. 202-213
Monetary—$15,000 exclusive of interest and costs; Small Claims—$5,000
Court Schedule: Civil Tues., Wed. and Thurs.; Criminal: Weekdays, 8:30 A.M.-4 P.M.

UTICA
411 Oriskany St. W., Utica 13502
Civil: (315) 266-4603; Criminal: (315) 266-4602;
Traffic: (315) 266-4601; Civil Fax: (315) 792-8038;
Criminal & Traffic Fax: (315) 724-0762

Judges:
John S. Balzano (315) 266-4607; Fax: (315) 733-7927
Ralph J. Eannace, Jr. (315) 266-4607; Fax: (315) 733-7927
Gerald J. Popeo (315) 266-4607; Fax: (315) 733-7927

Chief Clerk: Steven R. Pecheone (315) 266-4669

Deputy Chief Clerk: Lori E. O'Brien (315) 266-4668

Territorial—Criminal, City of Utica; Civil, throughout Utica and contiguous towns; Small Claims, throughout Oneida County
Monetary—Civil $15,000; Small Claims $5,000; Commercial Claims $5,000
Court Schedule: Weekdays; Criminal Arraignments: also on Saturdays and Holidays

***Pending November 2010 Election Results**

WATERTOWN

Municipal Bldg., 245 Washington St., Watertown 13601
(315) 785-7785; Fax: (315) 785-7856

Judges:
James C. Harberson
Eugene Renzi

Clerk: Julie M. Call

Territorial—City of Watertown
Monetary—$15,000
Small Claims—$5,000
Court Schedule: Jan. 1-June 1—Weekdays, 8:30 A.M.-4:30 P.M.; June 1-Sept. 1—Weekdays, 8:30 A.M.-4 P.M.

WATERVLIET

City Hall, 2 15th St., Watervliet 12189-2894
(518) 270-3803; Fax: (518) 270-3812

Judges:
*Thomas E. Lamb
Susan B. Reinfurt

Clerk: Eugenia R. Robillard

Territorial—City of Watervliet
Monetary—$15,000
Small Claims $5,000
Court Schedule: Daily, 8 A.M.
Traffic: One Thurs. per month, 8 A.M.

WHITE PLAINS

77 S. Lexington Ave., White Plains 10601
(914) 824-5675; Fax: (914) 422-6058

Judges:
Jo Ann Friia (914) 824-5671
Brian Hansbury (914) 824-5673
Barbara A. Leak (914) 824-5672
Eric Press (914) 824-5674

Chief Clerk: Patricia Lupi (914) 824-5686

Deputy Chief Clerk: Eileen Byrne (914) 824-5690

Territorial—Process may be served throughout Westchester County provided one of the parties resides in City of White Plains
Monetary (Civil)—$15,000; (Small Claims and Commercial Claims) (county-wide): $5,000
Court Schedule: Weekdays, 9 A.M.-5 P.M.

YONKERS

Robert W. Cacace Justice Center, 100 S. Broadway, Yonkers 10701
Administration: (914) 831-6940;
City Ordinances: (914) 831-6910; Civil: (914) 831-6920;
Criminal: (914) 831-6930;
Small Claims: (914) 831-6920; Traffic: (914) 831-6910

Chief Judge: Michael A. Martinelli (914) 831-6980

Judges:
Thomas R. Daly (914) 831-6980
Robert C. Cerrato (914) 831-6980
E-mail: rcerrato@courts.state.ny.us
Arthur J. Doran III (914) 831-6980
Mary Anne Scattaretico-Naber (914) 831-6980
Vacancy at Press Time

Chief Clerk: Marisa Garcia
(914) 831-6940; Fax: (914) 377-6395

Deputy Chief Clerks:
Jasmin Reyes-Finch (914) 831-6940; Fax: (914) 377-6395
Sandra Santoro (914) 831-6940; Fax: (914) 377-6395

Territorial—City of Yonkers
Monetary—$15,000
Small Claims—$5,000
Commercial Claims—$5,000
Court Schedule: Weekdays, 9 A.M.-5 P.M;. Criminal arraignment: Saturday morning

PRACTICE TIME TABLE UNDER THE UNIFORM CITY COURT ACT

As Amended to September 2010.

Commencement of Action: Action (or special proceeding) is commenced and jurisdiction is acquired by service of a summons (or petition). (UCCA, 400)

Summons: Must be filed with proof of services within 5 days after personal service within the county and within 10 days if served otherwise. (UCCA, R3000.4)

Personal Service: Original service may be made by mail pursuant to UCCA 403.

Answer: Must be served within 10 days if summons served personally within the county and within 30 days after service is complete if made by any other means (UCCA, 402)

Attachment, Arrest, Seizure of Chattel: Governed by CPLR except may only be executed within the county and the return is made to the clerk of the court. (UCCA, 209, 801)

Counterclaims: A reply is not required. Must be served within 10 days if plaintiff voluntarily elects to serve one. (UCCA, 907a)

Cross-Claims: Shall be answered within 10 days. (UCCA, 907b)

Third party and Interpleader Complaints: Answered same as UCCA 402, depending on method of service. (UCCA, 907c)

Amended and Supplemental Pleadings: Once without leave of court before the period for a response expires or within 10 days after its service or the service of a responsive pleading. An amended pleading must be responded to within 10 days after service or 10 days after the period during which the original pleading could have been responded to, whichever is later. (UCCA, 909)

Motions: Governed by CPLR except:

(a) Time to move to dismiss under CPLR 3211e as to a cause of action in a pleading to which no response is required shall be within 10 days after service. (UCCA, 1002)

(b) Motion for summary judgment in lieu of a complaint shall be returnable as provided by UCCA 402, depending on the method of service. (UCCA, 1004)

Disclosure: Governed by the CPLR. (UCCA, 1101)

Trial: Personal appearance by any party–not less than 5 days nor more than 15 days after issue is joined. Appearance of all parties by attorney–any party may serve a notice of trial fixing a trial date not less than 5 nor more than 8 days after service of such notice. (UCCA, 1301)

Jury: May be demanded by any party after joinder of issue. Must be filed with notice of trial. If party filing notice of trial does not demand jury, any other party may do so within 10 days after service of a copy of the notice of trial by serving a written demand on all parties and filing the same with the clerk within 3 days after service. In summary proceedings, the demand is made by tenant at time of answering and by landlord at any time before day of trial. (UCCA, 1303)

Time for Judgment or Decision where no Jury: 30 days after submission except when further time is granted by consent. (UCCA, 1304)

Judgments and Enforcement: Governed by the CPLR (UCCA, 1401-1509)

Settlement of Case on Appeal: Minutes must be furnished to clerk within 10 days after fees therefor have been paid. Appellant must then settle case on 3 days' notice to clerk and respondent. The judge before whom the case was tried must indorse his settlement within 5 days from its submission to him. Thereupon the clerk must make a return to the appellate court of the settled case. (UCCA, 1704)

Taxation of Costs:

Statutory costs—taxed by clerk forthwith on rendition of judgment.

Other taxable disbursements–2 days' notice must be given. (UCCA, 1907)

Review of taxtion–within 10 days after taxation upon 2 days' notice. (UCCA, 1909)

Small Claims:

Court must hold at least one session per week. Hearing shall be not less than 15 days nor more than 30 days from date the action is recorded. Notice of hearing must be sent to defendant by registered mail within 3 days after action is recorded. A corporation may appear by its attorney, or by any officer, director or employer authorized to appear. Jurisdictional limit is action for money only not in excess of $5,000, or action by party aggrieved by arbitration award in which amount in dispute does not exceed $5,000. (UCCA, 1801)

THE GOVERNMENT OF THE UNITED STATES

THE CONSTITUTION

LEGISLATIVE BRANCH

THE CONGRESS

Senate **House**

Architect of the Capitol
United States Botanic Garden
Government Accountability Office
Government Printing Office
Library of Congress
Congressional Budget Office

EXECUTIVE BRANCH

THE PRESIDENT
THE VICE PRESIDENT
Executive Office of the President

White House Office
Office of the Vice President
Council of Economic Advisers
Council on Environmental Quality
National Security Council
Office of Administration
Office of Management and Budget
Office of National Drug Control Policy
Office of Policy Development
Office of Science and Technology Policy
Office of the U.S. Trade Representative

JUDICIAL BRANCH

The Supreme Court of the United States

United States Courts of Appeals
United States District Courts
Territorial Courts
United States Court of International Trade
United States Court of Federal Claims
United States Court of Appeals for the Armed Forces
United States Tax Court
United States Court of Appeals for Veterans' Claims
Administrative Office of the United States Courts
Federal Judicial Center
United States Sentencing Commission

DEPARTMENT OF AGRICULTURE
DEPARTMENT OF COMMERCE
DEPARTMENT OF DEFENSE
DEPARTMENT OF EDUCATION
DEPARTMENT OF ENERGY
DEPARTMENT OF HEALTH AND HUMAN SERVICES
DEPARTMENT OF HOMELAND SECURITY
DEPARTMENT OF HOUSING AND URBAN DEVELOPMENT
DEPARTMENT OF THE INTERIOR
DEPARTMENT OF JUSTICE
DEPARTMENT OF LABOR
DEPARTMENT OF STATE
DEPARTMENT OF TRANSPORTATION
DEPARTMENT OF THE TREASURY
DEPARTMENT OF VETERANS AFFAIRS

INDEPENDENT ESTABLISHMENTS AND GOVERNMENT CORPORATIONS

African Development Foundation
Broadcasting Board of Governors
Central Intelligence Agency
Commodity Futures Trading Commission
Consumer Product Safety Commission
Corporation for National and Community Service
Defense Nuclear Facilities Safety Board
Environmental Protection Agency
Equal Employment Opportunity Commission
Export-Import Bank of the U.S.
Farm Credit Administration
Federal Communications Commission
Federal Deposit Insurance Corporation
Federal Election Commission
Federal Housing Finance Board
Federal Labor Relations Authority
Federal Maritime Commission
Federal Mediation and Conciliation Service
Federal Mine Safety and Health Review Commission
Federal Reserve System
Federal Retirement Thrift Investment Board
Federal Trade Commission
General Services Administration
Inter-American Foundation
Merit Systems Protection Board
National Aeronautics and Space Administration
National Archives and Records Administration
National Capital Planning Commission
National Credit Union Administration
National Foundation on the Arts and the Humanities
National Labor Relations Board
National Mediation Board
National Railroad Passenger Corporation (Amtrak)
National Science Foundation
National Transportation Safety Board
Nuclear Regulatory Commission
Occupational Safety and Health Review Commission
Office of the Director of National Intelligence
Office of Government Ethics
Office of Personnel Management
Office of Special Counsel
Overseas Private Investment Corporation
Peace Corps
Pension Benefit Guaranty Corporation
Postal Regulatory Commission
Railroad Retirement Board
Securities and Exchange Commission
Selective Service System
Small Business Administration
Social Security Administration
Tennessee Valley Authority
Trade and Development Agency
U.S. Agency for International Development
U.S. Commission on Civil Rights
U.S. International Trade Commission
U.S. Postal Service

See pages 115-144 for detailed listings.

NEW YORK FEDERAL DEPARTMENTS AND AGENCIES

Legislative Branch

THE SENATE
Washington, DC 20510
(202) 224-3622; Internet: www.senate.gov/

Secretary: Nancy Erickson

All legislative power of the United States is vested in the Congress, made of two houses. The Senate has 100 members. The Senate approves all presidential appointments to the Cabinet, the Supreme Court, Ambassadorial positions, tries impeachments, and approves treaties. The Vice President sits as president of the Senate. *U.S. Const. Art. I sec. 1*

THE HOUSE OF REPRESENTATIVES
Office of the Clerk, H-154, The Capitol,
Washington, DC 20515-6601
(202) 225-7000; Internet: clerk.house.gov

Clerk: Lorraine C. Miller (202) 225-7000; Fax: (202) 225-1776

All legislative power of the United States is vested in Congress, made of two houses. The House of Representatives has 435 members. The House originates all legislative provisions raising revenue, and makes all impeachments. *U.S. Const. Art. I sec. 1*

GOVERNMENT ACCOUNTABILITY OFFICE
441 G St. N.W., Washington, DC 20548
(202) 512-3000; Public Affairs: (202) 512-4800
Internet: www.gao.gov

Comptroller General of the United States:
Gene L. Dodaro (Acting) (212) 512-5500

Investigates all matters relating to the receipt and disbursement of public funds including research into the effects of proposed legislative action. Acts as an independent arm of Congress to carry out its public audit duties. *31 U.S.C. 702*

Formerly General Accounting Office

Field Office
575 O'Neill Federal Bldg., 10 Causeway St., Boston, MA 02222
(617) 788-0500; Fax: (617) 788-0505

Manager: Joan Mahagan (617) 788-0521

General Counsel: Lynn Gibson (Acting)
USGAO-OGC, 441 G St. N.W., Rm. 7169,
Washington, DC 20548 (202) 512-5400; Fax: (202) 512-7703

GOVERNMENT PRINTING OFFICE
732 N. Capitol St. N.W., Washington, DC 20401
(202) 512-1800; Public Affairs: (202) 512-1957;
Order Information: (866) 512-1800;
Fax: (202) 512-2104
Internet: www.access.gpo.gov

Public Printer: Robert C. Tapella (Acting)
(202) 512-1000; Fax: (202) 512-1347

General Counsel: Drew Spalding (Acting)
(202) 512-0033; Fax: (202) 512-0076

Superintendent of Documents: Richard G. Davis (Acting)
(202) 512-1991; Fax: (202) 512-1293

Prints, binds, and distributes the publications and printed materials of the Congress and the executive departments of the Federal government. *44 U.S.C. 301 et seq.*

Government Printing Office Bookstore
Superintendent of Documents
732 N. Capital St. N.W., Washington, DC 20401
(866) 512-1800, (202) 512-1800; Fax (Orders): (202) 512-2104
E-mail: contactcenter@gpo.gov
Internet: http://bookstore.gpo.gov; www.gpoaccess.gov/help

Assoc. Director of Marketing: Katherine (Casey) Radican
(202) 465-6640

LIBRARY OF CONGRESS
101 Independence Ave. S.E., Washington, DC 20540
(202) 707-8000; General Information: (202) 707-5000
Internet: www.loc.gov

Librarian of Congress: James H. Billington
(202) 707-5205; Fax: (202) 707-1714

Contains the national library of the United States containing nearly 128 million items and provides such books as may be necessary for the operation and duties of the Congress. Operates the system of copyrights. Operates the largest law library in the world with 2.4 million items. (foreign & domestic) *2 U.S.C. 131.*

Executive Branch

EXECUTIVE OFFICE OF THE PRESIDENT
The White House, 1600 Pennsylvania Ave. N.W.,
Washington, DC 20500
White House Operator: (202) 456-1414;
Comment Line: (202) 456-1111; Fax: (202) 456-2461
E-mail: comments@whitehouse.gov
Internet: www.whitehouse.gov

President: Barack H. Obama

Chief of Staff: Pete Rouse

Deputy Chiefs of Staff:
Jim Messina (Operations)
Mona Sutphen (Policy)

Sr. White House Advisors:
David Axelrod
Valerie B. Jarrett (Office of the Public Liaison and Intergovernmental Affairs)

Counsel to the President: Robert Bauer

Asst. to the President for Natl. Security Affairs:
Thomas Donilon

Press Secretary: Robert Gibbs

Office of Management and Budget
New Executive Office Bldg., 725 17th St. N.W.,
Washington, DC 20503
(202) 395-3080; Fax: (202) 395-3888;
General Counsel: (202) 395-5044
E-mail: ombinfo@eop.gov
Internet: www.whitehouse.gov/OMB

Director: Jacob J. Lew (Pending Confirmation)
(202) 395-4840; Fax: (202) 395-3888

Deputy Dir.: Jeffrey Liebman (Acting)
(202) 395-4742; Fax: (202) 395-3888

Deputy Dir. for Management: Jeffrey Zients
(202) 456-5938, 456-7070

Exec. Assoc. Dir.: Jeffrey Liebman (202) 395-4844

Evaluates, formulates, and coordinates management procedures and program objectives within and among the Federal departments and agencies. Controls the administration of the budget and makes recommendations to the President regarding budget proposals and legislation. *5 U.S.C. app. Reorganization Plan No. 1*

Council of Economic Advisers
1800 G St., N.W., 8th Floor, Washington, DC 20502

Mailing Address: Eisenhower Exec. Ofc. Bldg., Room 468, 17th & Penn Ave. N.W., Washington, DC 20502
(202) 395-5084
Internet: www.whitehouse.gov/administration/eop/cea

Chair: Vacancy at Press Time
(202) 395-5042; Fax: (202) 395-6958

Members:
Austan Goolsbee
Cecilia Rouse

Chief of Staff: Nan Gibson

Analyzes and appraises the national economy to provide policy recommendations to the President. *15 U.S.C. 1023*

National Security Council
Eisenhower Executive Office Bldg., Washington, DC 20504
(202) 456-1414
Internet: www.whitehouse.gov/nsc/

Asst. to the President for Natl. Security Affairs:
Thomas Donilon

Deputy Natl. Security Advisors:
Mike Froman (Intl. Economic Affairs)
Ben Rhodes (Strategic Communications)
Vacancy at Press Time

Advises and assists the President in the formation of an integrated national security policy for the United States in conjunction with the National Economic Council. *50 U.S.C. 402*

Executive Office of the President—Cont'd

Office of the United States Trade Representative
600 17th St. N.W., Washington, DC 20508
(202) 395-7360; Press Office: (202) 395-3230; Fax: (202) 395-4549
E-mail: contactustr@ustr.eop.gov; Internet: www.ustr.gov

U.S. Trade Representative: Ron Kirk

Deputy U.S. Trade Representatives:
Demetrios J. Marantis
Michael Punke
Miriam Sapiro

Chief of Staff: Lisa Garcia (202) 395-6850

General Counsel: Timothy Reif
(202) 395-3150; Fax: (202) 395-3639

Formulates all trade policy and directs all trade negotiations for the United States. *19 U.S.C. 1921*

Council on Environmental Quality
722 Jackson Pl. N.W., Washington, DC 20503
(202) 395-5750; Fax: (202) 456-6546
Internet: www.whitehouse.gov/ceq

Chair: Nancy Sutley

Senior Counsel: Edward Boling (202) 395-3449
E-mail: eboling@ceq.eop.gov

Researches, develops, analyzes, and recommends environmental policy to the President for the preservation and improvement of the quality of the environment. Also oversees federal agencies' implementation of the National Environmental Policy Act. *42 U.S.C. 4341, 42 U.S.C. 4321 et seq., Exec. Order 11991*

Homeland Security Council
Eisenhower Executive Office Bldg., Washington, DC 20504
Internet: www.whitehouse.gov/hsc

Asst. to the President for Homeland Security and Counterterrorism: John O. Brennan

Coordinates homeland security-related activities among executive departments and agencies; promotes development and implementation of homeland security policies. *Exec. Order 13228*

Office of Science and Technology Policy
725 17th St., Room 5228, Washington, DC 20502
(202) 456-7116; Fax: (202) 456-6021
E-mail: ostpinfo@ostp.eop.gov; Internet: www.ostp.gov

Asst. to the President and Dir.: Dr. John P. Holdren
(202) 456-7116; Fax: (202) 456-6021

Assoc. Dir. for Science: Aneesh Chopra

Asst. Dir., Life Sciences and Acting Asst. Dir., Social and Behavioral Sciences: Diane DiEuliis

Assoc. Dir., Energy & Environment Division: Sherburne (Shere) Abbott

General Counsel: Rachael Leonard (Acting)

Chief of Staff: James Kohlenberger

Acts as a source of information and policy recommendations for the President in the fields of science, engineering, and technology. *42 U.S.C. 6611*

Office of National Drug Control Policy
750 17th St. N.W., Washington, DC 20503

Mailing Address: P.O. Box 6000, Rockville, MD 20849-6000
(202) 395-6700; Fax: (202) 395-6680;
General Counsel: (202) 395-6622; Fax: (202) 395-5543
Internet: www.ondcp.gov

Director: R. Gil Kerlikowske

Deputy Dir.: A. Thomas McLellan, Ph.D.

Deputy Dir. of Demand Reduction: David K. Mineta

Deputy Dir. of State, Local and Tribal Affairs: Benjamin B. Tucker

Coordinates and plans national, state, and local efforts to control illegal drug trafficking and drug abuse. *21 U.S.C. 1501*

Office of Administration
725 17th St. N.W., EEOB, Washington, DC 20503
(202) 456-2861; Fax: (202) 456-1655
Internet: www.whitehouse.gov/OA

Director: Cameron Moody

General Counsel: Vacancy at Press Time (202) 395-2237

Provides administrative support services to all units within the Executive Office of the President. *5 U.S.C. app. Reorganization Plan No. 1*

Office of the Vice President of the United States
Eisenhower Executive Office Bldg.,
1600 Pennsylvania Ave. N.W., Washington, DC 20501
(202) 456-7549
E-mail: vice-president@whitehouse.gov
Internet: www.whitehouse.gov/vicepresident

Vice President: Joseph Biden

Chief of Staff: Ron Klain

Counsel to the V.P.: Cynthia Hogan

Participates in the Cabinet meetings, acts as member of the National Security Council, sits on the Board of Regents of the Smithsonian Institution, and is President of the Senate. *U.S. Const. Art. II sec. 1*

DEPARTMENT OF AGRICULTURE
Whitten Bldg., 1400 Independence Ave. S.W., Washington, DC 20250
(202) 720-4623; Employee Locator: (202) 720-8732; Fax: (202) 720-5043
Internet: www.usda.gov

Secretary of Agriculture: Thomas J. Vilsack, Room 200-A
(202) 720-3631; E-mail: agsec@usda.gov

Deputy Secretary: Kathleen Merrigan (202) 720-6052

General Counsel: Steve Silvermann (Acting), Room 107-W
(202) 720-3351

Works to improve and develop agricultural production, income and markets; to stop hunger through food programs; to protect the environment, soil, water and forests; and inspects and grades food products for sale. *7 U.S.C. 2201*

Animal and Plant Health Inspection Services (APHIS), Plant Protection and Quarantine Programs
Eastern Regional Office
920 Main Campus Dr., Suite 200, Raleigh, NC 27606-5202
(919) 855-7300; Fax: (919) 855-7393

Regional Dir.: Victor Harabin

Animal and Plant Health Inspection Services (APHIS), Plant Protection and Quarantine (PPQ)
New York State Office
500 New Karner Rd., 2nd Floor, Albany, NY 12205
(518) 218-7540; Fax: (518) 218-7545

State Dir.: Yvonne DeMarino

Animal and Plant Health Inspection Services (APHIS), Animal Care
Eastern Regional Office
920 Main Campus Dr., Suite 200, Raleigh, NC 27606-5210
(919) 855-7100; Fax: (919) 855-7123
E-mail: aceast@aphis.usda.gov

Regional Dir.: Dr. Elizabeth J. Goldentyer

Animal and Plant Health Inspection Service, Investigative and Enforcement Services
Eastern Regional Office
920 Main Campus Dr., Suite 200, Raleigh, NC 27606
(919) 855-7080; Fax: (919) 855-7090
E-mail: ies@aphis.usda.gov

Regional Dir.: John S. Kinsella

Deputy Regional Dir.: Willie D. Harris

Animal and Plant Health Inspection Services (APHIS), Veterinary Services
500 New Karner Rd., 2nd Floor, Albany, NY 12205
(518) 218-7540; Fax: (518) 218-7545

Veterinarian-in-Charge: Dr. Roxanne Mullaney

Office of the Inspector General/Investigations

Northeast Region Office, 5601 Sunnyside Ave., Suite 2230, Beltsville, MD 20705-5300 (301) 504-2000

Sub-Office, 26 Federal Plz., Room 1409,
New York, NY 10278
(212) 264-8400; Fax: (212) 264-8416

Residency Office, 54 Stiles Rd., Suite 108,
Salem, NH 03079

Residency Office, 421 S. Warren Street, Room 201,
Syracuse, NY 13202
(315) 942-5989

Special Agent in Charge, Investigations: Brian L. Haaser
(301) 504-2000; Fax: (301) 504-2025

Regional Inspecitor General, Audit: Paul Keating
(301) 504-2100; Fax: (301) 504-2437

Department of Agriculture—Cont'd

Rural Development
Washington Office
1400 Independence Ave. S.W., Mailstop 0705,
Washington, DC 20250
(800) 670-6553; Public Affairs: (202) 720-4323;
Fax: (202) 690-4083
Internet: www.rurdev.usda.gov

Under Secretary: Dallas Tonsager
Mailstop 0107, Room 205-W,

Develops sustainable communities by improving the economy and quality of life in rural areas; offers financial programs, technical assistance and educational materials; helps rural Americans build, buy or rent housing; helps rural communities build or expand vital community facilities; offers financial and technical assistance to rural businesses and cooperatives; and ensures that rural communities are served by modern utilities.

Formerly known as Farmer's Home Admin. and Rural Economic & Community Development

Food and Nutrition Service
Northeast Regional Office
501 O'Neill Federal Bldg., 10 Causeway St.,
Boston, MA 02222-1069
(617) 565-6370; Fax: (617) 565-6473

Regional Administrator: James Arena-DeRosa

N.Y.C. Field Office
201 Varick St., Room 609, New York, NY 10014
(212) 620-3691; Fax: (212) 620-6948

Officer in Charge: Denise Thomas

Officer in Charge, Metro 1: Gilda Torres
(Bronx, Nassau, Manhattan, Suffolk & Westchester)
(212) 620-6686

Officer in Charge, Metro 2: Lashon Gilbert
(Brooklyn, Staten Island & Queens) (212) 620-7803

Albany Field Office
O'Brien Fed. Bldg., Room 752, 1 Clinton Ave.,
Albany, NY 12207
(518) 431-4274; Fax: (518) 431-4271

Officer in Charge: Peter S. Conti

Rochester Field Office
100 State St., Room 318, Rochester, NY 14614
(585) 263-6744; Fax: (585) 263-5807

Officer in Charge: Peter S. Conti (Acting)

Milk Market Administration
89 South St., 3rd Floor, Boston, MA 02111

Mailing Address: (Fort Point Station), P.O. Box 51478,
Boston, MA 02205-1478
(617) 737-7199; Fax: (617) 737-8002

Administrator: Erik F. Rasmussen

Food Safety and Inspection Services—Program Enforcement Evaluation & Review (PEER)
701 Market St., Room 4100-C, Philadelphia, PA 19160
(215) 597-4219, Ext. 115; Fax: (215) 597-9099

Regional Dir.: James Borda

United States Forest Service
Eastern Regional Office
626 E. Wisconsin Ave., Suite 800, Milwaukee, WI 53202
(414) 297-3600; Fax: (414) 297-3808; TTY: (414) 297-3507

Regional Forester: Kent Connaughton
(414) 297-3765; Fax: (414) 944-3973

Exec. Asst. to RF: Elizabeth Sporcich
(414) 297-3765; Fax: (414) 944-3973

Deputy Regional Forester: John Phipps (Resources)
(414) 297-3765; Fax: (414) 944-9373
Forrest (Skip) Starke (Operations)
(414) 297-3765; Fax: (414) 944-9373

Eastern Regional Office of the General Counsel
626 E. Wisconsin Ave., Suite 600,
Milwaukee, WI 53202-4616
(414) 297-3774; Fax: (414) 944-3967

Assoc. Regional Atty.: Michael J. Danaher (414) 297-1891

Dep. Assoc. Regional Atty.: Vacancy at Press Time

Northeastern Field Office
271 Mast Rd., P.O. Box 640, Durham, NH 03824
(603) 868-7600; Fax: (603) 868-7604
Internet: www.fs.fed.us/ne/durham

Field Representative: Anne Archie (603) 868-7694

Group Leader, Forest Mgmt.: Robert Clark
(603) 868-7716

Group Leader, Forest Health & Economics:
Bernard Raimo (603) 868-7708

DEPARTMENT OF COMMERCE
Office of the Secretary,
Herbert C. Hoover Bldg., Room 5516,
1401 Constitution Ave. N.W., Washington, DC 20230
(202) 482-2000; Fax: (202) 482-5168;
Legislative and Intergovernmental Affairs:
(202) 482-3663; Public Affairs: (202) 482-4883;
Business Liaison: (202) 482-1360;
Small & Disadvantaged Business Utilization:
(202) 482-1472; OSDBU Fax: (202) 482-0501
Internet: www.doc.gov

Secretary of Commerce: Gary Locke, Room 5516
(202) 482-2112

Deputy Secretary: Dennis F. Hightower, Room 5830
(202) 482-8376; Fax: (202) 501-1262

General Counsel: Cameron Kerry, Room 5870
(202) 482-4772; Fax: (202) 482-0042

Promotes job creation, economic growth, sustainable development and improved living standards for all Americans, by working in partnership with businesses, universities, communities, and workers to: build for the future and promote U.S. competitiveness in the global marketplace, by strengthening and safeguarding the nation's economic infrastructure; keeps America competitive with cutting-edge science and technology; provides effective management and stewardship of our nation's resources and assets.

Bureau of the Census
4600 Silver Hill Rd., Suitland, MD 20746

Mailing Address: 4600 Silver Hill Rd., Bldg. 3,
Washington, DC 20233-0001
(301) 763-2495
Internet: www.census.gov

Director: Robert M. Groves, Room 8H002 (301) 763-2135

Collects and compiles statistical information on the population and economy of the United States. *13 U.S.C. 1*

Regional Office
4 Copley Pl., Suite 301, P.O. Box 9108,
Boston, MA 02117-9108
(617) 424-4501, (800) 562-5721; TDD: (617) 434-0565;
Fax: (617) 424-0547
E-mail: boston.regional.office@census.gov

Regional Dir.: Kathleen Ludgate

New York Regional Office
395 Hudson St., Suite 800, New York, NY 10014-7451
(212) 584-3400; Fax: (212) 478-4800;
Public Information Office: (301) 763-3030
E-mail: new.york.regional.office@census.gov
Internet: www.census.gov/regions/new_york

Regional Dir.: Lester A. Farthing

Asst. Regional Dir.: Ligia Jaquez

Bureau of Economic Analysis
1441 L St. N.W., Room BE-64, Washington, DC 20230
(202) 606-9900
E-mail: customerservice@bea.gov; Internet: www.bea.gov

Director: J. Steven Landefeld

Produces and disseminates economic accounts statistics that provide government, businesses and individuals with a comprehensive, up-to-date picture of economic activity; presents basic information on such key issues as U.S. economic growth, regional economic development, and the Nation's position in the world economy. *Organization Order No. 35-1A*

Department of Commerce—Cont'd

Economic Development Administration
Herbert C. Hoover Bldg., Suite 7800,
1401 Constitution Ave. N.W., Washington, DC 20230
(202) 482-4085; Internet: www.eda.gov

Asst. Secretary: John Fernandez, Room 7804
(202) 482-5081; Fax: (202) 273-4781
E-mail: jfernandez@edu.doc.gov

Chief Counsel: Barry Bird, Room 7005 (202) 482-3085
E-mail: bbird@eda.doc.gov

Works to aid in the creation of new jobs; helps protect existing jobs; and stimulates industrial and commercial growth in distressed areas with low income, high unemployment or in a state of economic dislocation. *42 U.S.C. 3121, et seq.*

Regional Office
The Curtis Center, Suite 140 South,
Independent Sq. W., 601 Walnut St.,
Philadelphia, PA 19106-3821
(215) 597-4603; Fax: (215) 597-1063

Regional Dir.: Willie C. Taylor
E-mail: wtaylor@eda.doc.gov

Regional Counsel: Linda Cruz-Carnall
(215) 597-7896; Fax: (215) 597-1367
E-mail: lcruzcar@eda.doc.gov

Local Office for N.Y.C./New Jersey
The Curtis Center, Suite 140 South, 601 Walnut St.,
Philadelphia, PA 19106-3323
(215) 597-6769; Fax: (215) 597-1367
Economic Development Rep.: Calvin Edghill
E-mail: cedghill@eda.doc.gov

New York State Office
620 Erie Blvd. W., Suite 104, Syracuse, NY 13204-2442
(315) 448-0938; Fax: (315) 448-0939
Economic Development Rep.: Harold John Marshall
E-mail: hmarshal@eda.doc.gov

Economics and Statistics Administration
Herbert C. Hoover Bldg., Room 4848,
14th St. & Constitution Ave. N.W., Washington, DC 20230
(202) 482-3727; Fax: (202) 482-0432;
(800) STAT-USA: (800) 782-8872; (202) 482-2198
E-mail: stat-usa@doc.gov
Internet: www.esa.doc.gov

Under Secretary of Commerce for Economic Affairs:
Rebecca M. Blank; E-mail: rblank@doc.gov

Chief Economist: Mark E. Doms (202) 482-3523

Advises the Secretary and other governmental officials on the economy and economic policy and oversees the Census Bureau, Bureau of Economic Analysis, and STAT-USA.

Bureau of Industry and Security
Herbert C. Hoover Bldg.,
14th St. & Constitution Ave. N.W., Washington, DC 20230
(202) 482-3825; Fax: (202) 482-0751
Internet: www.bis.doc.gov

Under Secretary: Eric L. Hirschhorn
(202) 482-1455; Fax: (202) 482-2387

Chief Counsel: John T. Masterson, Jr.
(202) 482-5301; Fax: (202) 482-0085

Promotes U.S. strategic technology leadership and administers the dual-use export control regime to advance U.S. National Security, Foreign policy, and economic objective.

Formerly called Bureau of Export Administration

International Trade Administration
Herbert C. Hoover Bldg., 1401 Constitution Ave. N.W.,
Washington, DC 20230
1-800-USA-TRADE: (800) 872-8723;
Public Affairs: (202) 482-3809
Internet: http://trade.gov

Under Secretary: Francisco J. Sánchez, Room 3850
(202) 482-2867; Fax: (202) 484-4821

Chief Counsel for Import Administration:
John D. McInerney, Room 3622
(202) 482-5589; Fax: (202) 482-4912

Chief Counsel for Intl. Commerce: John Cobau, Room 5624
(202) 482-2319

Works to promote world trade and strengthen the international trade and investment position of the United States through the following departments: Market Access and Compliance, Import Administration, Trade Development, and U.S. and Foreign Commercial Service.

U.S. and Foreign Commercial Service
3802 Herbert C. Hoover Bldg.,
14th & Constitution Ave. N.W., Washington, DC 20230
(202) 482-0725, (800) 872-8723; Fax: (202) 482-5013
Internet: www.buyusa.gov

Director General: Suresh Kumar (202) 482-5013

Operates 107 U.S. Export Assistance Centers throughout the country, and more than 150 offices overseas, to assist U.S. Companies, particularly small and medium-sized businesses, make sales in international markets; also seeks to protect U.S. business interests abroad.

U.S. Export Assistance Center
New York/Northern New Jersey Regional Office
33 Whitehall St., 22nd Floor, New York, NY 10004
(212) 809-2675; Fax: (212) 809-2687
Internet: www.buyusa.gov/nyc
Director: Carmela Mammas (212) 809-2676
E-mail: carmela.mammas@trade.gov

U.S. Export Assistance Center
Harlem Office
163 W. 125th St., Suite 901, New York, NY 10027
(212) 860-6200; Fax: (212) 860-6203
E-mail: office.harlem@mail.doc.gov
Internet: www.export.gov
Director: K.L. Fredericks
(Serving Upper Manhattan, Bronx, Brooklyn & Queens)

U.S. Export Assistance Center
Westchester Office
707 Westchester Ave., Suite 209, White Plains, NY 10604
(914) 682-6712; Fax: (918) 682-6698
Director: Joan Kanlian
(Hudson Valley, Capital Region and North Country)
E-mail: joan.kanlian@trade.gov

U.S. Export Assistance Center
Rochester Office
400 Andrews St., Suite 300, Rochester, NY 14604
(585) 399-7065; Fax: (585) 423-7570
International Trade Specialist: Timothy McCall
(Chemung, Livingston, Monroe, Ontario, Schuyler, Seneca, Steuben, Wayne and Yates Counties)
E-mail: timothy.mccall@trade.gov

U.S. Export Assistance Center
Buffalo Office
130 S. Elmwood Ave., Suite 530, Buffalo, NY 14202
(716) 551-4191; Fax: (716) 551-5290
Internet: www.buyusa.gov/buffalo
Director: James Mariano
(Allegany, Cattaraugus, Chautauqua, Erie, Genesee, Niagara, Orleans and Wyoming Counties)
E-mail: james.mariano@trade.gov
Intl. Trade Specialist: John Tracy
(Broome, Cayuga, Chenango, Cortland, Jefferson, Lewis, Madison, Oneida, Onondaga, Oswego, Tioga and Tompkins Counties) (315) 453-4070; Fax: (315) 233-1259
E-mail: john.tracy@trade.gov

U.S. Export Assistance Center
Long Island Office
College at Old Westbury, Academic Village,
Marshall Hallam Bldg. 10, 223 Store Hill Rd.,
P.O. Box 210, Old Westbury, NY 11568-0210
(516) 876-3418, (646) 722-0182; Fax: (516) 876-7563
E-mail: office.longisland@mail.doc.gov
Director: Shakir Farsakh (Long Island)
E-mail: shakir.farsakh@trade.gov

Minority Business Development Agency
1401 Constitution Ave. N.W., Room 5053,
Washington, DC 20230
(202) 482-5061, (888) 324-1551
Internet: www.mbda.gov
National Dir.: David Hinson

**Dept. of Commerce,
Minority Business Development Agency—Cont'd**

Develops and coordinates a national program for minority business enterprise investment, participation, and management through technical assistance and granting market opportunities. *Executive Order 11625*

Regional Office
26 Federal Plaza, Room 3720, New York, NY 10278
(212) 264-3262; Fax: (212) 264-0725
E-mail: nyro-info@mbda.gov

Director: Heyward B. Davenport

National Oceanic and Atmospheric Administration
Herbert C. Hoover Bldg., Room 5128,
1401 Constitution Ave. N.W., Washington, DC 20230
(202) 482-6090; Staff Locator: (301) 713-4000;
Fax: (202) 482-3154
Internet: www.noaa.gov

Under Secretary of Commerce for Oceans and Atmosphere: Jane Lubchenco (202) 482-3436; Fax: (202) 408-9674

Deputy Under Secretary for Operations: Mary M. Glackin (202) 482-4569

General Counsel: Lois J. Schiffer
(202) 482-4627; Fax: (202) 482-4893

Responsible for all U.S. weather and climate forecasting, monitoring and archiving of ocean and atmospheric data, management of marine fisheries and mammals, mapping and charting of all U.S. waters, coastal zone management, and research and development in all of these areas. NOAA is the largest agency in the Department of Commerce and manages the U.S. operational weather and environmental satellites, a fleet of ships and aircraft for oceanographic, surveying, fisheries, coastal, and atmospheric studies, twelve environmental research laboratories, and several large supercomputers.

Patent and Trademark Office
401 Dulany St., Arlington, VA 22214
Mailing Address: P.O. Box 1450-GISD, Alexandria, VA 22313-1450
(800) 786-9199, (571) 272-1000
E-mail: usptoinfo@uspto.gov; Internet: www.uspto.gov

Under Secretary of Commerce for Intellectual Property and Dir.: David Kappos (571) 272-8600; Fax: (571) 273-0464

Duputy Under Secretary of Commerce for Intellectual Property and Deputy Dir.: Sharon Barner
(571) 272-8700; Fax: (571) 273-0464

Commissioner for Patents: Robert L. Stoll (571) 272-8752

Commissioner for Trademarks: Lynne Beresford
(571) 272-8901; Fax: (571) 273-8900

General Counsel: Bernard Knight
(571) 272-7000; Fax: (571) 273-0099

Dir., Public Affairs: Richard G. Maulsby
(571) 272-8400; Fax: (571) 273-0340

Examines, researches, and issues design, plant, and utility patents for the protection of innovation, research and invention. Issues, researches, and protects trademarks of symbols, words, devices or any combination thereof. Maintains records of attorneys qualified to practice before the office and patent agents. *35 U.S.C. 1*

National Institute of Standards and Technology
100 Bureau Dr., Mail-Stop 1070,
Gaithersburg, MD 20899-1070
(301) 975-2000; General Inquiries: (301) 975-6478;
Fax: (301) 926-1630
E-mail: inquiries@nist.gov; Internet: www.nist.gov

325 Broadway, MS 107.00, Boulder, CO 80305-3337
(303) 497-3000; Public Inquiries: (303) 497-3444

Director: Patrick D. Gallagher (301) 975-2300

Dir. of Media Relations: Ben Stein (301) 975-3097

Counsel for NIST: Henry Wixon
(301) 975-2803; Fax: (301) 926-8241

Freedom of Information Act Officer: Catherine S. Fletcher
(301) 975-4074; Fax: (301) 926-8091

Promotes U.S. economic growth by working with industry to develop and apply technology, measurements and standards. Oversees the Measurement and Standards Laboratories, Technology Innovation Program, the Manufacturing Extension Partnership and the Malcolm Baldrige National Quality Award.

National Technical Information Service
5301 Shawnee Rd., Alexandria, VA 22312
(703) 605-6040, (800) 553-6847; Fax: (703) 605-6900
E-mail: info@ntis.gov
Internet: www.ntis.gov

Director: Bruce Borzino (703) 605-6405
E-mail: bborzino@ntis.gov

Serves as the nation's clearinghouse for research and development results and other information produced by and for the U.S. Government. 15 U.S.C.§§ 1151-1157.

National Telecommunications and Information Administration
Herbert C. Hoover Bldg., Room 4898,
1401 Constitution Ave. N.W., Washington, DC 20230
Public Affairs: (202) 482-7002
Internet: www.ntia.doc.gov

325 Broadway, Boulder, CO 80505-3328
(303) 497-3500

Asst. Secy. for Communications & Information:
Lawrence E. Strickling
(202) 482-1840; Fax: (202) 501-0536
E-mail: lstrickling@ntia.doc.gov

Chief Counsel: Kathy Smith
(202) 482-1859; Fax: (202) 501-8013
E-mail: ksmith@ntia.doc.gov

Advises the President on telecommunications and information policy, develops and presents plans at international conferences, manages Federal use of the radio frequency spectrum and serves as the principal Federal communications research lab. *47 U.S.C. § 901*

DEPARTMENT OF DEFENSE
Office of the Secretary, 1400 Defense Pentagon, Washington, DC 20301-1000
(703) 571-3343
Internet: www.defense.gov

Secretary of Defense: Robert M. Gates

Deputy Secretary: William J. Lynn III
1010 Defense Pentagon, Washington, DC 20301-1010

General Counsel: Jeh C. Johnson
The Pentagon, Room 3E788 (703) 695-3341

Principal Deputy Asst. Secretary for Public Affairs:
Geoffrey S. Morrell, Room 2E556
(703) 697-9312; Fax: (703) 695-4299

Provides the military forces necessary to deter war and protect the security of the United States through the maintenance of the Army, Navy, Air Force, and Marine Corps consisting of 1.4 million active duty personnel (470,000 overseas) and 67,000 ships at sea. *5 U.S.C. 101*

Department of the Air Force
1690 Air Force Pentagon, Washington, DC 20330
(703) 697-6061; Public Affairs: (703) 695-9664;
Fax: (703) 693-9601
Internet: www.af.mil

Secretary of the Air Force: Michael B. Donley
Room 1670 (703) 697-7376

General Counsel: Charles A. Blanchard
Room 4E856 (703) 697-0941; Fax: (703) 693-9355

Preserves the peace of the United States through the effective control of air and space activities.

Defense Contract Management Agency
General Counsel's Office
6350 Walker Lane, Suite 300, Alexandria, VA 22310-3241
(703) 428-1541; Fax: (703) 428-3580
Internet: www.dcma.mil

Director: Charlie E. Williams, Jr.
(703) 428-1700; Fax: (703) 428-1942
E-mail: charlie.williams@dcma.mil

General Counsel: Nicholas Retson
(703) 428-1824; Fax: (703) 428-1364

East District
495 Summer St., Boston, MA 02210-2184
(617) 753-4006; Contract Integrity Center: (617) 753-4343;
Fax: (617) 753-4005

General Counsel: Bruce Krasker (617) 753-4269

Dept. of Defense, Defense Contract Mgmt. Agency—Cont'd

Defense Contract Management
Long Island
605 Stewart Ave., Garden City, NY 11530-4761
(516) 228-5999; Fax: (516) 228-3647
Counsel: Michael Montefinise

Department of the Army
1400 Defense Pentagon, Washington, DC 20310-1400
(703) 695-6518; Public Affairs: (703) 692-2000;
Fax: (703) 697-8036
Internet: www.army.mil

Secretary of the Army: John M. McHugh

General Counsel: Vacancy at Press Time
104 Army Pentagon, Washington, DC 20310-0104
(703) 697-9235; Fax: (703) 693-9254

Organizes, trains, and equips more than one million men and women on active duty and reserve forces for the preservation of peace, security, and the defense of the nation. Carries out programs for the protection of the environment, improving waterways, flood and erosion control, beach erosion control, and water resource development. *50 U.S.C. 401*

United States Army Corps of Engineers
441 G St. N.W., Washington, DC 20314-1000
(202) 761-0008; General Information: (202) 761-0011
E-mail: hq-publicaffairs@usage.mil
Internet: www.usace.army.mil

Commander: Lt. Gen. Robert L. Van Antwerp
(202) 761-0001

Chief Counsel: Earl H. Stockdale, Room 3A29
(202) 761-0018; Fax: (202) 761-4932
E-mail: ceals@usace.army.mil

Department of the Navy
1000 Navy Pentagon, Washington, DC 20350-1000
(703) 695-3131; Information: (703) 545-6700;
Personnel Command: (866) 827-5672
Internet: www.navy.mil

Secretary of the Navy: Ray Mabus

General Counsel: Paul L. Oostburg Sanz
(202) 685-7000; Fax: (202) 685-6957

Protects the United States by the effective prosecution of war at sea including, with the Marine Corps component, the seizure or defense of advance naval bases, supports all military departments of the United States. Maintains the freedom of the seas. *10 U.S.C. 5011*

DEPARTMENT OF EDUCATION
400 Maryland Ave. S.W., Washington, DC 20202
Information Resource Ctr.: (202) 401-2000;
(800) 872-5327; Fax: (202) 401-0689
Internet: www.ed.gov

Secretary of Education: Arne Duncan, Room 7W301
(202) 401-3000; Fax: (202) 401-0596

General Counsel: Charles P. Rose
(Acting; Deputy General Counsel for Program Service)
Room 6E301 (202) 401-6000

Establishes policy for, administers, and coordinates federal assistance to educational efforts and programs. *20 U.S.C. 3411*

Regional Office
32 Old Slip, 25th Floor, New York, NY 10007
(646) 428-3905; Fax: (646) 428-3904

Office of the Secretary, Regional Representative:
Vacancy at Press Time

Regional Administrator: Vacancy at Press Time

Administrative Officer, Office of Civil Rights:
Diane S. Diggs (646) 428-3811
E-mail: diane.diggs@ed.gov

Regional Dir., Office for Civil Rights: Timothy Blanchard
(646) 428-3805; E-mail: timothy.blanchard@ed.gov

Regional Dir., Guaranteed Eligibility and Oversight:
Robin R. Shinn (646) 428-3774
E-mail: robin.shinn@ed.gov

Regional Dir., Case Mgmt.: Betty Coughlin (646) 428-3750
E-mail: betty.coughlin@ed.gov

Regional Inspector General for Audit: Daniel Schultz
(646) 428-3888; E-mail: daniel.schultz@ed.gov

DEPARTMENT OF ENERGY
Forrestal Bldg., 1000 Independence Ave. S.W.,
Washington, DC 20585
(202) 586-5000; Fax: (202) 586-4403
Internet: www.energy.gov

Secretary of Energy: Dr. Steven Chu, Room 7A-257
(202) 586-6210

General Counsel: Scott Blake Harris, Room 6A-245
(202) 586-5281; Fax: (202) 586-1499

Provides the framework for a coordinated national energy plan. Conducts long-term and high-risk energy research, markets federal power, works for the conservation of energy, oversees the nuclear weapons program, energy regulatory programs, and a central energy data collection and analysis program. *42 U.S.C. 7131*

DEPARTMENT OF HEALTH AND HUMAN SERVICES
200 Independence Ave. S.W., Washington, DC 20201
(202) 619-0257, (877) 696-6775
E-mail: hhsmail@os.dhhs.gov
Internet: www.dhhs.gov

Secretary of Health and Human Services:
Kathleen Sebelius, Room 615F
(202) 690-7000; Fax: (202) 690-7203

General Counsel: Mark B. Childress (Acting), Room 713-F
(202) 690-7741; Fax: (202) 690-7998

Acts as the personal and living services department of government providing assistance and aid in all aspects of life from medical and health care services and aid to addiction and mental health services. *20 U.S.C. 3508*

Regional Office
Jacob Javits Bldg., Room 3835, 26 Federal Plaza,
New York, NY 10278
(212) 264-4600; Fax: (212) 264-3620
Internet: www.hhs.gov/region2

Regional Dir.: Dennis E. Gonzalez (Acting)

Chief Counsel: Joel Lerner, Room 3908 (212) 264-6373

Civil Rights: Michael Carter, Room 3312 (212) 264-3313

Inspector General, Audit: Jim Edert, Room 3900
(212) 264-4620

Inspector General, Investigations: Thomas O'Donnell
Room 13-124 (212) 264-1691

Inspector General, Evaluations & Inspections:
Jodi Nudelman, Room 41-106 (212) 264-2779

Health Resources and Services Administration:
Ronald Moss, Room 3337 (212) 264-4498

National Health Services Corporation:
Lester Theophilakos (212) 264-3999

Aging, Administration: Daniel Quirk, Room 38-102
(212) 264-2976

Children & Families, Adm.: Joyce Thomas, Room 4114
(212) 264-2890, Ext. 103

Centers for Medicare & Medicaid Services: James Kerr
Room 3811 (212) 616-2205

Federal Occupational Health: David Eisenhardt
Room 3337 (212) 264-2607

Office of Public Health and Science: Robert Davidson
Room 3835 (212) 264-2561

Division of Cost Allocation: Robert Aaronson
Room 41-122 (212) 264-1308

Children & Families, Adm.: Mary Ann Higgins
Room 4114 (212) 264-2890, Ext. 103

Inspector General, Audit: Timothy Horgan, Room 3900
(212) 264-4620

Inspector General, Investigations: Gary Heuer,
Room 13-124 (212) 264-1691

Administration on Aging
1 Massachusetts Ave. N.W., Washington, DC 20201
(202) 619-0724; Eldercare Locator: (800) 677-1116;
Public Inquiries: (202) 619-0724; Fax: (202) 357-3555
E-mail: aoainfo@aoa.hhs.gov
Internet: www.aoa.gov

Asst. Secretary for Aging: Kathy Greenlee
(202) 401-4634

Dept. of Health & Human Svces., Admin. on Aging—Cont'd
Established by the Older Americans Act of 1965, this office acts as the leading advocate within the Federal Government for older Americans. Disburses funds for various programs including group and home-delivered meals, in-home assistance for the frail elderly, transportation services, legal assistance, nursing home ombudsman services, employment help and senior center programs. Also funds research, demonstration and training programs.

Regional Office II & III
26 Federal Plaza, Room 38-102, New York, NY 10278
(212) 264-2976; Fax: (212) 264-0114

Regional Administrator: Robert Logan (Acting)

Administration for Children and Families
370 L'Enfant Promenade S.W., Room Aerospace 6th F,
Washington, DC 20447
(202) 401-2337; Fax: (202) 401-4678
Internet: www.acf.hhs.gov

Asst. Secretary: Carmen R. Nazario (202) 401-5383

Coordinates the efforts and programs for the advancement and preservation of the welfare and conditions of children and families.

Regional Office, Region II
Federal Bldg., Room 4114, 26 Federal Plaza,
New York, NY 10278
(212) 264-2890; Fax: (212) 264-4881

Regional Administrator: Joyce A. Thomas, Ext. 103
E-mail: joyce.thomas@acf.hhs.gov

Center for Disease Control and Prevention
1600 Clifton Rd. N.E., Atlanta, GA 30333
(404) 639-3311; Public Inquiries: (404) 448-1515; (800) 232-4636
E-mail: cdcinfo@cdc.gov; Internet: www.cdc.gov
Director: Thomas R. Frieden, M.D., M.P.H.

Food and Drug Administration
10903 New Hampshire Ave., Silver Spring, MD 20993
(888) 463-6332
Internet: www.fda.gov

Commissioner: Margaret A. Hamberg, M.D., Room 1471
(301) 796-5000; Fax: (301) 847-3531

Chief Counsel: Ralph S. Tyler (Acting), Room 605
(301) 796-8535; E-mail: ralph.tyler@fda.hhs.gov

Office of the Administrative Law Judge
10903 New Hampshire Ave., Room 1304,
Silver Spring, MD 20993
(301) 796-4554; Fax: (301) 594-6800

Admin. Law Judge: Daniel J. Davidson
E-mail: daniel.davidson@fda.hhs.gov

Northeast Regional Office
158-15 Liberty Ave., Jamaica, NY 11433
(718) 340-7000; Fax: (718) 662-5434

Regional Dir.: W. Charles Becoat (718) 662-5610

New York District Office
Mail Stop HFR-NE100, 158-15 Liberty Ave.,
Jamaica, NY 11433 (718) 340-7000; Fax: (718) 662-5665
District Dir.: Otto D. Vitillo (718) 662-5447

Buffalo Office
300 Pearl St., Suite 100, Buffalo, NY 14202
(716) 551-4461; Fax: (716) 551-4499
District Dir.: Edward W. Thomas

Centers for Medicare and Medicaid Services
7500 Security Blvd., Baltimore, MD 21244-1850
(410) 786-3000, (877) 267-2323;
Medicare Service Center: (800) 633-4227
Internet: www.cms.hhs.gov

Administrator: Donald M. Berwick (202) 690-6726

Acts mainly as the purchaser of health care services for Medicare and Medicaid beneficiaries; assures proper administration by its contractors and state agencies; establishes policies for the reimbursement of health care providers; conducts research on the effectiveness of various methods of health care management, treatment and financing; and assesses the quality of health care facilities and services. *56 CFR 123474*

Formerly called Health Care Financing Administration

Centers for Medicare & Medicaid Services
Regional Office
Federal Bldg., 38th Floor, 26 Federal Plaza,
New York, NY 10278-0063
(212) 616-2205; Medicaid Division: (212) 264-1121

Regional Administrator: Dr. Jaye Weisman (Acting)
(617) 565-1188; E-mail: robosora@cms.hhs.gov

Deputy Regional Administrator: Dr. Gilbert Kinken
E-mail: ronycora@cms.hhs.gov

Division of Medicaid and Children's Health:
Sue Kelly (Assoc. Regional Administrator)
(212) 616-2400; E-mail: ronydmch@cms.hhs.gov

Division of Medicare Health Plans Operations:
Reginald Slaten (Assoc. Regional Administrator)
(212) 616-2300
E-mail: ronybeneficiary@cms.hhs.gov;
ronyprovider@cms.hhs.gov

Division of Financial Mgmt. And Fee-for-Service:
Peter Reisman (Assoc. Regional Administrator)
(212) 616-2500; E-mail: ronycfm@cms.hhs.gov

Office of Public Health and Science
Hubert H. Humphrey Bldg., Suite 716G,
200 Independence Ave. S.W., Washington, DC 20201
(202) 690-7694; Fax: (202) 690-7425
Internet: www.hhs.gov/ophs

Asst. Secretary for Health: Howard K. Koh, M.P.H.

Principal Deputy Asst. Secretary for Health:
Dr. Wanda K. Jones, P.H.

Chief Counsel, Public Health Service: David Benor
Parklawn Bldg., Room 4A-53, 5600 Fishers Lane,
Rockville, MD 20857
(301) 443-2644; Fax: (301) 443-2639

Coordinates with the states and administers the public health efforts; coordinates and upholds international health-related agreements; conducts medical and biomedical research; develops programs for planning public and private institutional medical programs; and enforces laws for the protection of foods, drugs, and medical apparatus and supplies. *42 U.S.C. 201*

Formerly known as The Office of the Assistant Secretary for Health

Regional Office
3835 Federal Bldg., 26 Federal Plaza,
New York, NY 10278
(212) 264-2560; Fax: (212) 264-1324

Regional Health Administrator: Robert Davidson
(Rear Admiral) (212) 264-2560

Deputy Regional Health Administrator:
April M. Velasco, Ph.D.
(212) 264-2564

Substance Abuse and Mental Health Services Administration
1 Choke Cherry Rd., 8th Floor, Rockville, MD 20857
(240) 276-2000, 276-2130; Fax: (240) 276-2010, 276-2135
Internet: www.samhsa.gov

Administrator: Pamela S. Hyde
(240) 276-2000; Fax: (240) 276-2010

Deputy Admin.: Eric B. Broderick, D.D.S., M.P.H.
(240) 276-2000; Fax: (240) 276-2010

Provides prevention, diagnosis, and treatment services for people at risk for or experiencing substance abuse or mental illnesses. Works in partnership with states, communities and private organizations to address the needs of individuals with substance abuse and mental illnesses, and to identify and respond to the community risk factors that contribute to these illnesses. *P.L. 102-321 and P.L. 106-310.*

If using private courier service use zip code 20850

Office of the Surgeon General
5600 Fishers Ln., Room 1866, Rockville, MD 20857
(301) 443-4000; Fax: (301) 443-3574
Internet: www.surgeongeneral.gov

Surgeon General: Regina Benjamin, M.D.

DEPARTMENT OF HOMELAND SECURITY
Nebraska Ave. Complex, Washington, DC 20528
Mailing Address: U.S. Dept. of Homeland Security, Washington, DC 20528
(202) 282-8000; Comment Line: (202) 282-8495
Internet: www.dhs.gov/dhspublic

Secretary: Janet A. Napolitano
Deputy Secretary: Jane Holl Lute
General Counsel: Ivan K. Fong
Chief Privacy Officer: Mary Ellen Callahan

All correspondence must be sent to mailing address—do not use "Nebraska Ave. Complex" in address.

National Protection and Programs Directorate
(202) 282-8000

Under Secretary, Natl. Protection & Programs Directorate: Rand Beers (202) 282-8400

Responsible for ensuring the nation's preparation for, and ability to recover from, terrorist attacks and natural disasters.

Bureau of Customs and Border Protection
1300 Pennsylvania Ave. N.W., Washington, DC 20229
(202) 344-2001, (877) 227-5511;
Public Affairs: (202) 344-1780;
Commissioner's Fax: (202) 344-1380
Internet: www.cbp.gov

Commissioner: Alan Bersin

Asst. Commissioner, Office of Public Affairs: Maria Luisa O'Connell (202) 344-1770

Chief Counsel: Alfonso Robles, Room 4.4B (202) 344-2990; Fax: (202) 344-2950

Collects duties from imports and enforces customs, immigration and related laws, including the seizure of contraband and narcotics. *19 U.S.C. 2071*

Formerly components of the U.S. Customs Service, Department of the Treasury, Department of Agriculture and Immigration and Naturalization Service, Department of Justice

Executive Office
One Penn Plz., 11th Floor, New York, NY 10119
(646) 733-3100; Fax: (646) 733-3245
Field Operations Dir.: Robert E. Perez

Newark Area Office
1100 Raymond Blvd., Newark, NJ 07102
(973) 368-6100; Fax: (973) 368-6991
Area Dir.: Adele Fasano

Port of Entry
JFK Airport Area Office, Bldg. 77, Jamaica, NY 11430
(718) 487-5164; Fax: (718) 487-5191
Area Dir.: Brian Humphrey

Bureau of Immigration and Customs Enforcement
Buffalo Office
130 Delaware Ave., Room 203, Buffalo, NY 14202
(716) 551-4741; Principal Legal Advisor: (716) 855-7920

Bureau of Immigration and Customs Enforcement
Syracuse Office
412 S. Warren St., Syracuse, NY 13202 (315) 478-1227

Field Office
4455 Genesee St., Buffalo, NY 14225 (716) 626-0400

Border Patrol Sector Headquarters, 201 Lang Blvd., Grand Island, NY 14072 (716) 774-7200
Chief Patrol Agent: Kevin A. Oaks

Border Patrol (Swanton, VT)
155 Grand Ave., Swanton, VT 05488 (800) 247-2434
Chief Patrol Agent: Daniel B. Doty (Acting)

Bureau of Immigration and Customs Enforcement
500 12th St. S.W., Washington, DC 20536
(202) 344-1770; Fax: (202) 307-1918
Internet: www.uscis.gov

Asst. Secretary: John T. Morton

Chief of Staff: Suzie Barr

Principal Legal Advisor: Peter S. Vincent (202) 732-5000

Dir., Office of Public Affairs: Brian P. Hale (202) 732-4242

The primary investigative arm of the Department of Homeland Security, this agency is a law enforcement agency and does not facilitate or provide assistance with immigration issues. Enforces immigration and customs laws and prevents violations by terrorists and other criminals who threaten national security. Combines the investigative, detention & removal, and intelligence functions of the former Immigration and Naturalization Service with the investigative, intelligence, and air & marine functions of the former Customs Service.

Office of the District Counsel—N.Y.C.
26 Federal Plaza, Room 1130, New York, NY 10278
(212) 264-5916
Chief Counsel: Theresa A. Pauling

Intelligence and Analysis
(202) 282-8000

Under Secretary for Intelligence and Analysis: Caryn Wagner (202) 282-8353

Responsible for identifying and assessing intelligence information concerning threats to the homeland, issuing warnings, and taking appropriate preventive and protective action.

Science and Technology Directorate
(202) 254-5601

Under Secretary for Science and Technology: Dr. Tara O'Toole

Coordinates the Department's efforts in research and development, including preparing for and responding to terrorist threats involving weapons of mass destruction.

Office of Health Affairs
(202) 254-6479; E-mail: healthaffairs@dhs.gov

Asst. Secretary for Health Affairs: Dr. Alexander Garza

Management Directorate
(202) 205-4613

Asst. Secretary for Management: Rafael Boras

Responsible for budget, management and personnel issues.

United States Coast Guard
2100 2nd St. S.W., Room 1100,
Washington, DC 20593-0001
Judge Advocate General: (202) 372-3726
Internet: www.uscg.mil

Commandant: Admiral Robert J. Papp, Jr. (202) 372-4411

Judge Advocate General: Calvin Lederer (Acting), Room 1422 (202) 372-3726

Chief Judge, Admin. Law: Joseph N. Ingolia (202) 372-4440

Acts as the Federal Maritime law enforcement agency except when called into service of the United States Navy during times of war or when the President orders. *14 U.S.C. 1*

Formerly a component of the Department of Transportation

District Office
408 Atlantic Ave., Boston, MA 02110-2209
(617) 223-8555, (800) 848-3942; Fax: (617) 223-8501

District Legal Officer: Comdr. Christine Cutter

Legal Office
Legal Service Command, 300 E. Main St., Suite 400, Norfolk, VA 23510-9100
(757) 628-4192, 628-4200; Fax: (757) 628-4217
Internet: www.uscg.mil/lsc

Staff Judge Advocate: Elisabeth Pepper

United States Secret Service
245 Murray Dr., Bldg. 410, Washington, DC 20223
Public Affairs: (202) 406-5708
Internet: www.secretservice.gov

Director: Mark J. Sullivan (202) 406-5700

Chief Counsel: Donna L. Cahill (202) 406-5771; Fax: (202) 406-6544

Protects the President, Vice President, former Presidents, their immediate families, the White House Complex, major Presidential candidates, and foreign dignitaries. Enforces laws regarding counterfeiting, financial institution fraud, telecommunications and computer fraud, false identification, access device fraud, advance fee fraud, electronic funds transfers and money laundering. *Title 3 & 18 U.S.C.*

Formerly a component of the Department of the Treasury

Dept. of Homeland Security, U.S. Secret Service—Cont'd

N.Y. Field Office
335 Adams St., Suite 3200, Brooklyn, NY 11201
(718) 840-1000; Fax: (718) 840-1448

Special Agent in Charge: Brian G. Parr

Deputy Special Agent in Charge: Robert J. Sica

JFK Resident Office
230-59 Rockaway Blvd., Suite 265,
Springfield Gardens, NY 11413
(718) 553-0911; Fax: (718) 553-7626
Resident Agent in Charge: Frederick Sellers

White Plains Resident Office
140 Grand St., Suite 801, White Plains, NY 10601
(914) 682-6300; Fax: (914) 682-6182
Resident Agent in Charge: Rafael Prieto

Buffalo District Office
598 Main St., Suite 300, Buffalo, NY 14202
(716) 551-4401; Fax: (716) 551-5075
Special Agent in Charge: Tracy Gast

Melville Resident Office
145 Pinelawn Rd., Suite 200N, Melville, NY 11747-3154
(631) 293-4028; Fax: (631) 293-4389
Resident Agent in Charge: Michael Seremetis

Rochester Resident Agency
100 Chestnut St., Suite 1820, Rochester, NY 14604
(585) 232-4160
Resident Agent in Charge: Joel Blackerby

Syracuse Resident Office
James M. Hanley Federal Bldg., 100 S. Clinton St.,
P.O. Box 7006, Syracuse, NY 13261
(315) 448-0304; Fax: (315) 448-0302
Resident Agent in Charge: Timothy Kirk

Bureau of Citizenship and Immigration Services
425 Eye St. N.W., Room 7100, Washington, DC 20536
Natl. Customer Service Center: (800) 375-5283;
Fax: (202) 307-9911; Internet: www.uscis.gov

Director: Alejandro (Ali) Mayorkas

Chief, Office of Citizenship: Rebecca S. Carson

Chief Counsel: Roxana Bacon

Facilitates the entry of persons legally admissable as visitors or as immigrants to the United States; grants benefits under the Immigration and Nationality Act, as amended, including providing assistance to those seeking permanent resident status or naturalization; prevents unlawful entry, employment or receipt of benefits by those who are not entitled to them; and apprehends or removes those aliens who enter or remain illegally in the United States and/or whose stay is not in the public interest. *(8 U.S.C. 1551 note) (8 U.S.C. 1101 note)*

Formerly Immigration and Nationalization Service, Department of Justice

Eastern Regional Office
75 Lower Weldon St., Saint Albans, VT 05479-0001
(800) 375-5283; Forms: (800) 870-3676;
Fax (Expedite Requests): (802) 527-4816
Service Center Dir.: Paul Novak

District Office (Buffalo)
Federal Center, 1st Floor, 130 Delaware Ave.,
Buffalo, NY 14202 (716) 843-7900
Special Agent in Charge: Lev J. Kubiak (Acting)

Field Office (Albany)
1086 Troy-Schenectady Rd., Latham, NY 12110
(518) 220-2100, (800) 375-5283
Officer in Charge: Gary L. Hale
Group Supvr.: Roy Tario
(Bureau of Immigration and Customs Enforcement)
Inspector: Michael Lindway
(Bureau of Customs and Border Protection)

District Office (N.Y.C.)
26 Federal Plaza, Room 3-120, New York, NY 10278
(800) 375-5283
District Dir.: Mary Ann Gantner

Field Office (Syracuse)
412 S. Warren St., Syracuse, NY 13202 (315) 478-1227

Office of Inspector General
245 Murray Dr., Bldg. 410, Mailstop 2600,
Washington, DC 20528
(202) 254-4100; Hotline: (800) 323-8603; Fax: (202) 254-4292

Inspector General: Richard L. Skinner

General Counsel to the Inspector General:
Richard N. Reback

Federal Law Enforcement Training Center
1131 Chapel Crossing Rd., Glynco, GA 31524
(912) 267-2100; Fax: (912) 554-4608
Internet: www.fletc.gov

Director: Connie L. Patrick (912) 267-2070

Chief Counsel: David H. Brunjes (912) 267-2441

Atty. Advisors:
Trisha Besselman (912) 267-2441
Diane Buchli (912) 267-2441
Margaret Wright (912) 267-2441

Formerly a component of the Department of the Treasury

Federal Emergency Management Agency
500 C St. S.W., Washington, DC 20472
Mailing Address: P.O. Box 10055,
Hyattsville, MD 20782-7055
Public Affairs: (202) 646-4600; (800) 621-3362;
Contracts and Procurements: (202) 646-4006;
Personnel Locator: (202) 566-1600
Internet: www.fema.gov

Administrator: W. Craig Fugate (202) 646-3900

General Counsel: Brad Kieserman

Assoc. Admin., Mission Support Bureau: David Garratt (Acting)

Assoc. Admin., Response and Recovery:
William L. Carwile III

Asst. Admin., Mitigation: Edward L. Connor (Acting)
(202) 646-2781

Communications Dir., Public Affairs: Pat Philbin
(202) 646-4600

Admin. for the U.S. Fire Administration: Kelvin Cochran
16825 S. Seton Ave., Emmitsburg, MD 21727
(301) 447-1018; Fax: (301) 447-1270

Acts as the Federal focal point of emergency planning, preparedness, mitigation, response, and recovery. Funds emergency programs, provides technical guidance and training, and ensures a broad based program to protect public safety and property. *5 U.S.C. app. Reorganization Plan No. 3 of 1978*

Formerly an independent agency

Regional Office
26 Federal Plaza, Suite 1337, New York, NY 10278
(212) 680-3612; Fax: (212) 680-3681
Internet: www.fema.gov/about/contact/regionii.shtm

Regional Administrator: Michael F. Moriarty (Acting)

DEPARTMENT OF HOUSING AND URBAN DEVELOPMENT
451 7th St. S.W., Washington, DC 20410
(202) 708-1112; Personnel Locator: (202) 708-1422;
TTY: (202) 708-1455
Internet: www.hud.gov

Secretary of Housing and Urban Development:
Shaun Donovan, Room 10000
(202) 708-0417; Fax: (202) 619-8365

General Counsel: Helen R. Kanovsky, Room 10110
(202) 708-2244

Creates and administers programs for the meeting of the nation's housing needs, fair housing opportunity, and improvement and development of the nation's communities. *42 U.S.C. 3532*

Office of Administrative Law Judges
451 7th St., Room B-133, Washington, DC 20410
(202) 254-0000; Fax: (202) 619-7304

Admin. Law Judges:
Alexander Fernendez
Jeremiah J. Mahoney

Department of Housing and Urban Development, Office of Administrative Law Judges—Cont'd

Region II Office
Jacob Javits Federal Bldg., Room 3541, 26 Federal Plaza, New York, NY 10278-0068
(212) 264-8000; Fax: (212) 264-3068
E-mail: ny_webmanger@hud.gov

Regional Dir.: Joanna Aniello (Deputy)

Regional Counsel: John Cahill (212) 542-7200
E-mail: john.j.cahill@hud.gov

Interagency Homelessness Coordinator:
Manuel A. Alvarado (212) 542-7142
E-mail: manuel.a.alvarado@hud.gov

Public Affairs Officer: Adam Glantz (212) 542-7158
E-mail: adam.glantz@hud.gov

Regional Inspector: Rene Febles (212) 542-7950
E-mail: rene.febles@hud.gov

Federal Housing Administration
451 7th St. S.W., Room 9100, Washington, DC 20410-8000
(202) 708-3600, (800) 225-5342; Fax: (202) 708-2580
Internet: www.hud.gov/fha

Federal Housing Commissioner: David H. Stevens
(202) 708-2601

Administers and underwrites housing loans and programs for the elderly, physically challenged, chronically ill, and low income persons. Develops and aids in the development of multi-family housing projects.

Office of Community Planning and Development
451 7th St. S.W., Suite 7100, Washington, DC 20410
(202) 708-2690; Fax: (202) 708-3336
Internet: www.hud.gov/cpd

Asst. Secretary: Mercedes Márquez

Advises the Secretary on development and planning of community programs and projects to meet department goals.

Department of Housing and Urban Development
State Office
Jacob K. Javits Federal Bldg., Room 3513,
26 Federal Plaza, New York, NY 10278-0068
(212) 542-7401; Fax: (212) 264-0993

Dir., Office of Community Planning and Development: Vincent Hom

Deputy Dir.: Kathy Mullins, Ext. 7422

Office of Policy Development and Research
451 7th St. S.W., Room 8100, Washington, DC 20410-6000
(202) 708-3178, (800) 245-2691; Fax: (202) 708-9981
Internet: www.huduser.org

HUD USER, P.O. Box 23268, Washington, DC 20026-3268

Asst. Secy. for Policy Development and Research:
Dr. Raphael Bostic

Evaluates and advises on existing and proposed projects and programs. Operates HUD USER, an information source available to the public with information on urban planning housing policy, building technology and other housing-related topics.

Office of Fair Housing and Equal Opportunity
451 7th St. S.W., Room 5100, Washington, DC 20410
(202) 708-4252; Fax: (202) 708-4483
Internet: www.hud.gov/offices/fheo

Asst. Secretary: John Trasvina

General Deputy Asst. Secy.: Bryan Greene
(202) 708-4211; Fax: (202) 708-4483

Administers laws that prohibit discrimination in housing based on race, color, religion, sex, national origin, familial status or disability (Title VI of The Civil Rights Act of 1964)

Fair Housing and Equal Opportunity
Region II Office
26 Federal Plaza, Room 3532, New York, NY 10278-0068
(212) 542-7519, (800) 496-4294; Fax: (212) 264-9829;
TTY: (212) 264-0927

Director: Jay Golden (212) 542-7500

Senior Intake: Robert Norrington (212) 542-7536

Government National Mortgage Association
550 12th St. S.W., 3rd Floor, Washington, DC 20024
Mailing Address: 451 7th St. S.W., Room B-133, Washington, DC 20410
(202) 708-1535, (888) 446-6434; Fax: (202) 708-0490
Internet: www.ginniemae.gov

President: Theodore W. Tozer

Exec. V.P.: Mary K. Kinney

Supports the government's housing efforts through financing and guarantees for home financing.

DEPARTMENT OF THE INTERIOR
1849 C St. N.W., Washington, DC 20240
Personnel Locator/Information: (202) 208-3100
Internet: www.doi.gov

Secretary of the Interior: Kenneth L. Salazar, Room 6150
(202) 208-7351; Fax: (202) 208-6956

Solicitor: Hilary Tompkins, Room 6352
(202) 208-4423; Fax: (202) 208-5584

Encourages and provides for the management, preservation and operation of the Nation's public lands and natural resources; develops and uses resources in an environmentally sound manner; carries out related scientific research and trust responsibilities of the U.S. government with respect to American and Alaskan natives. The Department also manages more than 441 million acres of Federal lands. *43 U.S.C. 1451*

Office of the Solicitor, Northeast Region
1 Gateway Ctr., Suite 612, Newton, MA 02458-2881
(617) 527-3400; Fax: (617) 527-6848

Regional Solicitor: Anthony R. Conte
E-mail: tony.conte@sol.doi.gov/

Deputy Regional Solicitor: James E. Epstein
E-mail: james.epstein@sol.doi.gov

Asst. Regional Solicitors:
Martha Ansty
Lake Champlain Fish & Wildlife Resource Office,
11 Lincoln St., Essex Junction, VT 05452
(802) 872-0629, Ext. 17; E-mail: martha_ansty@fws.gov
Mark D. Barash; E-mail: mark.barash@sol.doi.gov
Katharine M. Costenbader
Marcia F. Gittes; E-mail: marcia.gittes@sol.doi.gov
Brianna C. Kenny; E-mail: brianna.kenny@sol.doi.gov
Robin Lepore; E-mail: robin.lepore@sol.doi.gov
Joris Naiman; E-mail: joris.naiman@sol.doi.gov
David Rothstein
30 Westgate Center Dr., Hadley, MA 01035-9589
(413) 253-8600; E-mail: dave-s-rothstein@fws.gov
Andrew Tittler; E-mail: andrew.tittler@sol.doi.gov

This office is agency counsel for Dept. of the Interior bureaus in the Northeast Region, principally the National Park Service, Fish and Wildlife Service and U.S. Geological Survey. *43 U.S.C.§1455.*

United States Fish and Wildlife Service
Northeast Regional Office
300 Westgate Center Dr., Hadley, MA 01035-9587
(413) 253-8200; Fax: (413) 253-8308
E-mail: northeast@fws.gov; Internet: www.fws.gov/northeast

Solicitor's Office, 1 Gateway Center, Suite 612, Newton, MA 02458-2881
(617) 527-3400; Fax: (617) 527-6848
Regional Dir.: Marvin Moriarty (413) 253-8300

New York Field Office
3817 Luker Rd., Cortland, NY 13045
(607) 753-9334; Fax: (607) 753-9699

Supervisor: David Stilwell
E-mail: david_stilwell@fws.gov

Asst. Supervisor: Laury Zicari
E-mail: laury_zicari@fws.gov

Pennsylvania Avenue National Historic Park
National Mall & Memorial Parks, 900 Ohio Dr. S.W., Washington, DC 20024; (202) 485-9880

Regional Dir.: Margaret O'Dell

Sidewalks, parks and memorials along Pennsylvania Avenue from 3rd St. to 15th St., including John Marshall Park, Navy Memorial, Freedom Plaza, Pershing Park, Hancock Memorial, GAR Memorial, Mellon Fountain and Temperance Fountain. *40 U.S.C. 871*

Formerly known as Pennsylvania Avenue Development Corp.

DEPARTMENT OF JUSTICE
950 Pennsylvania Ave. N.W., Washington, DC 20530-0001
(202) 514-2000; Fax: (202) 514-4371
E-mail: askdoj@usdoj.gov
Internet: www.justice.gov

Attorney General of the United States:
Eric H. Holder, Jr. (202) 514-2001

Represents the interests of the nation and its citizens in the prosecution of all Federal criminal and civil actions taken to the Supreme Court. Ensures healthy competition in business, protects the nation from illegal immigration and drug trade, and renders legal advice to the President and the heads of the executive departments. *28 U.S.C. 501*

Bureau of Alcohol, Tobacco, Firearms and Explosives
99 New York Ave. N.E., Room 5514,
Washington, DC 20226
(800) 800-3855; Public Information: (202) 927-8500;
Public Information Fax: (202) 927-9750

Deputy Director: Kenneth E. Melson

Chief Counsel: Stephen R. Rubenstein, Room 5E310
(202) 648-7000

Enforces and administers the Federal laws relating to firearms and explosives and the Anti-Arson Act of 1982. Administers the U.S. Criminal Code provisions concerning alcohol and tobacco smuggling and diversion. *18 U.S.C. 2341*

Formerly a component of the Department of Treasury

Division Office
241 37th St., 3rd Floor, Brooklyn, NY 11232
(718) 650-4000; Fax: (718) 650-4001
E-mail: nydiv@atf.gov

Special Agent in Charge: Ronald B. Turk

Division Counsel: Matthew Myerson

Office of the Solicitor General
950 Pennsylvania Ave., N.W., Washington, DC 20530-0001
(202) 514-2201; Case Mgmt.: (202) 514-2217
Internet: www.justice.gov/osg

Solicitor General: Vacancy at Press Time

Supervises and conducts government litigation in the United States Supreme Court. *28 U.S.C. 505*.

Drug Enforcement Administration
8701 Morrissette Dr., Springfield, VA 22152-1080
(202) 307-1000; Public Affairs: (202) 307-7787;
Fax: (202) 307-7965
Internet: www.usdoj.gov/dea/

Administrator: Michele Leonhart (Acting) (202) 307-8000

Chief Counsel: Wendy H. Goggin
(202) 307-7322; Fax: (202) 307-4364

Office of Administrative Law Judges
600 Army-Navy Dr., Arlington, VA 22202
(202) 307-8188; Fax: (202) 307-8198

Chief Admin. Law Judge: Mary Ellen Bittner

Admin. Law Judges:
John J. Mulrooney II
Gail A. Randall

New York Field Division Office
99 10th Ave., New York, NY 10011
(212) 337-3900; Fax: (212) 337-2799
Internet: www.usdoj.gov/dea/deahome.htm

Special Agent in Charge: John P. Gilbride

New York Drug Enforcement Task Force
99 10th Ave., New York, NY 10011
(212) 337-3900; Fax: (212) 620-4377
Special Agent in Charge: John P. Gilbride

Federal Bureau of Investigation
J. Edgar Hoover Bldg., 935 Pennsylvania Ave. N.W.,
Washington, DC 20535-0001
(202) 324-3000; Internet: www.fbi.gov/

Director: Robert S. Mueller III

General Counsel: Valerie E. Caproni

N.Y.C. Office
Federal Bldg., 23rd Floor, 26 Federal Plaza,
New York, NY 10278
(212) 384-1000; Fax: (212) 384-4073;
Secure Fax: (212) 384-4074; E-mail: ny1@ic.fbi.gov

Asst. Dir. in Charge: Janice K. Fedarcyk

Field Office (Albany)
200 McCarty Ave., Albany, NY 12209
(518) 465-7551; Fax: (518) 431-7463

Special Agent in Charge: John F. Pikus

Chief Division Counsel: Paul M. Holstein

Field Office (Buffalo)
One F.B.I. Plaza, Buffalo, NY 14202-2698
(716) 856-7800; Fax: (716) 843-5288
E-mail: buffalo@ic.fbi.gov

Special Agent in Charge: James H. Robertson

Community Relations Service
600 E St. N.W., Suite 6000, Washington, DC 20530
(202) 305-2935; Fax: (202) 305-3009
Internet: www.usdoj.gov/crs/crs.htm

Director: Ondray T. Harris

Deputy Dir.: Diane Mitchum

General Counsel: George E. Henderson
(202) 305-2964; Fax: (202) 305-3005

Provides mediation, conciliation and prevention services for community disputes, disagreements and misunderstandings based on race, color and national origin.

Regional Office
26 Federal Plz., Room 36-118, New York, NY 10278
(212) 264-0700; Fax: (212) 264-2143

Regional Dir.: Reinaldo Rivera, Jr.

Executive Office for U.S. Trustees
20 Massachusetts Ave. N.W., Suite 8000,
Washington, DC 20530
(202) 307-1391; Fax: (202) 307-0672; Internet: www.usdoj.gov/ust

Director: Clifford J. White III

Ensures compliance with the United States Bankruptcy Code. *11 U.S.C. 101, et seq.*

Office of the U.S. Trustee
33 Whitehall St., 21st Floor, New York, NY 10004
(212) 510-0500; Fax: (212) 668-2256

U.S. Trustee: Diana G. Adams

Bureau of Prisons
320 First St. N.W., Washington, DC 20534
(202) 307-3198, (888) 317-8455;
Public Information Office: (202) 514-6551;
Fax: (202) 514-6620
Internet: www.bop.gov

Director: Harley G. Lappin

General Counsel: Kathleen M. Kenney
(202) 307-3062; Fax: (202) 307-2995

Northeast Regional Office
U.S. Customs House, 7th Floor,
2nd and Chestnut Streets, Philadelphia, PA 19106
(215) 521-7301
E-mail: nero/execassistant@bop.gov

Regional Dir.: Joe Norwood
(215) 521-7310; Fax: (215) 597-1893

Community Corrections Regional Administrator:
Edward Hughes
(215) 521-7460; Fax: (215) 521-7476

National Institute of Corrections
500 First St. N.W., Washington, DC 20534
Mailing Address: 320 First St. N.W.,
Washington, DC 20534
Toll Free: (800) 995-6423; (202) 307-3106;
Fax: (202) 307-3361
Internet: www.nicic.org

791 N. Chambers Rd., Aurora, CO 80011
Toll Free: (800) 995-6429; Fax: (303) 365-4455;
Information Center: (800) 877-1461

Director: Morris L. Thigpen

Dept. of Justice, Natl. Institute of Corrections—Cont'd

Academy Chief: Robert M. Brown, Jr.
(800) 995-6429, Ext. 4400

Community Corrections Division Chief:
George Keiser (800) 995-6423, Ext. 34213

Provides leadership and assistance to the field of corrections. Responds directly to the needs identified by those working in state and local corrections agencies. *Public Law 93-415 (1974)*

Parole Commission
5550 Friendship Blvd., Suite 420, Chevy Chase, MD 20815
(301) 492-5990; Legal Fax: (301) 492-5563
Internet: www.usdoj.gov/uspc

Chairman: Isaac Fulwood (301) 492-5933

Vice Chairman: Cranston J. Mitchell (301) 492-5832

Commissioner: Patricia K. Cushwa (301) 492-7014

General Counsel: Rockne Chickinell (301) 492-5959

Exec. Officer: Judy I. Carter (301) 492-5974

Case Operations Administrator: Stephen Husk
(301) 492-5952

Administrator, Case Services: Deirdre M. Jackson
(301) 492-5821

Has sole authority to grant, modify or revoke parole of eligible Federal and District of Columbia prisoners serving sentences of more than one year. Responsible for supervision of parolees and prisoners released upon expiration of their sentences with allowances for statutory good time, and determination of supervisory conditions and terms.

Antitrust Division
950 Pennsylvania Ave. N.W., Washington, DC 20530
(202) 514-2401; Fax: (202) 616-2645
E-mail: antitrust@usdoj.gov
Internet: www.justice.gov/atr/index.html

Asst. Atty. General: Christine A. Varney

New York Regional Office
26 Federal Plaza, Room 3630, New York, NY 10278-0140
(212) 264-0391; Fax: (212) 264-0678
E-mail: newyork.atr@usdoj.gov

Chief: Ralph T. Giordano
E-mail: ralph.giordano@usdoj.gov

Asst. Chief: John W. McReynolds

Civil Division
950 Pennsylvania Ave. N.W., Room 3141,
Washington, DC 20530
(202) 514-3301; Fax: (202) 514-8071
Internet: www.usdoj.gov/civil

Asst. Atty. General: Tony West

Represents the United States, its departments and agencies, members of Congress, cabinet officers, and other Federal employees.

Commercial Litigation Branch
International Trade Field Office
26 Federal Plaza, Room 346, New York, NY 10278
(212) 264-9230; Fax: (212) 264-1916

Atty.-in-Charge: Barbara S. Williams

Civil Rights Division
950 Pennsylvania Ave. N.W., Room 3623,
Washington, DC 20530
(202) 514-4609; Fax: (202) 514-0293
Internet: www.usdoj.gov/crt/crt-home.html

Asst. Atty. General: Thomas E. Perez (202) 514-2151

Secures effective enforcement of Federal civil rights.

Office of Special Counsel for Immigration Related Unfair Employment Practices
950 Pennsylvania Ave., N.W., Washington, DC 20030
(202) 616-5594, (800) 255-7688; Fax: (202) 616-5509;
TDD: (202) 616-5525, (800) 237-2515;
Employer Hotline: (800) 255-8155;
Employer Hotline TDD: (800) 237-2515
E-mail: osccrt@usdoj.gov
Internet: www.justice.gov/crt/osc

Special Counsel: Vacancy at Press Time

Deputy Special Counsel: Katherine A. Baldwin

Enforces the antidiscrimination provisions of the Immigration and Nationality Act, and ensures that proceeded individuals and aliens authorized to work in the United States are not discriminated against with respect to hiring and firing based on their citizenship status or national origin. *8 U.S.C. 1324b*

Criminal Division
950 Pennsylvania Ave. N.W., Room 2107,
Washington, DC 20530-0001
(202) 514-2601; Fax: (202) 514-9412
E-mail: criminal.division@usdoj.gov
Internet: www.usdoj.gov/criminal/

Asst. Atty. General in Charge: Lanny A. Breuer

Formulates criminal law enforcement policy and prosecutes criminal law violations not assigned to other departments.

Environment and Natural Resources Division
950 Pennsylvania Ave. N.W., Room 2143,
Washington, DC 20530
(202) 514-2701; Fax: (202) 514-0557
Internet: www.usdoj.gov/enrd

Asst. Atty. General: Ignacia S. Moreno

Litigates all aspects of environmental law for the government.

Tax Division
950 Pennsylvania Ave. N.W., Room 4141,
Washington, DC 20530
(202) 514-2901; Fax: (202) 514-5479
E-mail: oaag.tax@usdoj.gov
Internet: www.justice.gov/tax/

Asst. Atty. General: John A. DiCicco (Acting)

Investigates and prosecutes all civil and criminal matters arising under the internal revenue laws other than those in the Tax Court of the United States.

Executive Office for Immigration Review
5107 Leesburg Pike, Falls Church, VA 22041
(703) 305-0289; Clerk's Office: (703) 605-1007;
Case Information: (800) 898-7180; TDD: (800) 828-1120;
Fax: (703) 605-0365

Director: Thomas G. Snow (Acting) (703) 305-0169

Deputy Dir.: Vacancy at Press Time (703) 305-0169

Chair, Board of Immigration Appeals: David L. Neal
(Acting) (703) 305-1194

Vice Chair, Board of Immigration Appeals: David L. Neal
(703) 305-1194

General Counsel: Robin Sturman (703) 305-0470

Chief Immigration Judge: Brian M. O'Leary (703) 305-1247

Deputy Chief Immigration Judge: Michael C. McGoings
(703) 205-1247

Chief Admin. Hearing Officer: Michael J. Creppy
(703) 305-0864

Adjudicates immigration cases, including cases involving detained aliens, criminal aliens, and aliens seeking asylum as a form of relief from removal, while ensuring the standards of due process and fair treatment.

DEPARTMENT OF LABOR
200 Constitution Ave. N.W., Washington, DC 20210
(202) 693-5000, (866) 487-2365
Internet: www.dol.gov/

Secretary of Labor: Hilda L. Solis, Room S-2018
(202) 693-6000; Fax: (202) 693-6111

Office of the Solicitor: Vacancy at Press Time
Room S-2002 (202) 693-5261; Fax: (202) 693-5278

Fosters, develops, and promotes the welfare of workers, improves the working conditions of workers, enhances employment opportunities, guarantees worker's rights to safe working conditions, a minimum wage, freedom from discrimination, unemployment compensation, nondiscrimination policies, free collective bargaining, and job training and retraining. *29 U.S.C. 551*

Regional Office
J.F.K Federal Building, Boston, MA 02203
(617) 788-2800; Internet: www.dol.gov

Secretary's Representative: Vacancy at Press Time
(617) 565-2282

Regional Administrator, OASAM: Mark Falk (617) 788-2888

Dept. of Labor, Regional Office—Cont'd

Special Agent in Charge, Investigations, OIG:
Marjorie A. Franzman
201 Varick St., New York, NY 10014 (646) 264-3550
Public Affairs/News Media: John M. Chavez, Room 525-A
(617) 565-2072
Federal Minimum Wage: George Rioux (617) 624-6700
Overtime/Child Labor: (617) 624-6700
Labor Statistics: Denis McSweeney (617) 565-2327
Job Safety and Health: Marthe Kent (617) 565-9860
Pension Rights: Jean Ackerman (617) 565-9600
Federal Workers Compensation: Robert Lotz (617) 624-6600
Veterans' Employment and Training: David Houle
(617) 565-2080
Inspector General, Investigations: Richard A. Alto
(713) 238-7940
Inspector General, Labor Racketeering: Richard A. Alto
(718) 238-7940
Apprenticeship and Training Bureau: Jill Houser
(617) 788-0177

Regional Public Affairs Office
J.F.K. Federal Bldg., Boston, MA 02203
(617) 565-2072; Fax: (617) 565-2076

Director: John M. Chavez

Regional Office
201 Varick St., New York, NY 10014
Regional Representative: Robert Asaro-Angelo, Room 601
(212) 337-2387
Special Agent in Charge, Labor Racketeering & Fraud Investigations: Marjorie A. Franzman, Room 891
(646) 264-3550
Inspector General, Audit Dir.: Mark L. Schwartz
Room 871 (646) 264-3511
Regional Commissioner: Michael L. Dolfman
(N.Y. Bureau of Labor Statistics), Room 808
(212) 337-2500; Fax: (212) 337-2532
E-mail: dolfman.michael@bls.gov
Regional Dir., Office of Workers Comp. Programs:
Robert Sullivan, Room 740
(646) 264-3100; Fax: (646) 264-3004
Solicitor: Patricia M. Rodenhausen, Room 983
(646) 264-3650; Fax: (646) 264-3660
OSHA: Robert Kulick, Room 670
(212) 337-0118; Fax: (212) 337-2371
Regional Dir., Employee Benefits Security Admin.:
Jonathan Kay, 33 Whitehall St., Suite 1200,
New York, NY 10004
(212) 607-8644; Fax: (212) 607-8689
Womens Bureau: Grace Protos, Room 602
(646) 264-3789; Fax: (646) 264-3794
District Dir., Wage & Hour Section: Maria Rosado
26 Federal Plz., Room 3700, New York, NY 10278
(212) 264-8185
Office of Federal Contact Compliance: Michele Hodge
(Acting Regional Dir.), Room 750
(646) 264-3170; Fax: (646) 264-3009
E-mail: ofccp-ne-preaward@dol.gov

Office of Administrative Law Judges
800 K St. N.W., Suite 400 North, Washington, DC 20001-8002
(202) 693-7300; Fax: (202) 693-7365
Chief Judge: Stephan L. Purcell (Acting) (202) 693-7542
Associate Chief Judge for Black Lung: William Colwell
(202) 693-7542
Associate Chief Judge for Longshore: Daniel F. Sutton (Acting)
10 Causeway St., Boston, MA 02222 (617) 223-9355
Judges:
Linda Chapman (202) 693-7500
Paul C. Johnson, Jr.
Christine L. Kirby
Stuart A. Levin (202) 693-7500
Robert B. Rae
Daniel Solomon (202) 693-7500
Richard T. Stansell-Gamm (202) 693-7500
Jeffrey Tureck (202) 693-7500
Pamela Lakes Wood (202) 693-7500
Dir., Office of Program Operations: P.J. Soto (202) 693-7542
Chief Docket Clerk: Yvonne Washington
(202) 693-7300; Fax: (202) 693-7365
Chief, Information Resources Division: Victor V. Soto
(202) 693-7400
FOIA Disclosure Officer: Andrea Thomas (202) 693-7348

Office of the Solicitor of Labor
200 Constitution Ave. N.W., Rm. S-2002, Washington, DC 20210
(202) 693-5260; Fax: (202) 693-5278
E-mail: contact-sol@dol.gov
Solicitor: M. Patricia Smith
Deputy Solicitor: Deborah Greenfield
Provides the Secretary and the departmental officials with legal services as required to accomplish the mission of the department.

Regional Office
201 Varick St., Room 983, New York, NY 10014
(646) 264-3650; Fax: (646) 264-3660

Regional Solicitor: Patricia M. Rodenhausen

Deputy Regional Solicitor: Mark A. Holbert

Employment and Training Administration
200 Constitution Ave. N.W., Rm S-2307, Washington, DC 20210
(202) 693-2700, (877) 872-5627; Fax: (202) 693-7888
Internet: www.doleta.gov/
Asst. Secretary: Jane Oates
Fulfills duties assigned to the Department of Labor relating to job training and retraining, unemployment compensation, and employment services.

Office of Workforce Systems—Region I
JFK Federal Bldg., Room E-350, 15 New Sudbury St.,
Boston, MA 02203
(617) 788-0170; Fax: (617) 788-0101

Regional Administrator: Holly O'Brien (Acting)

Employee Benefits Security Administration
200 Constitution Ave. N.W., Suite S-2524,
Washington, DC 20210
(202) 693-8300; Fax: (202) 219-5526
Internet: www.dol.gov/ebsa/
Asst. Secretary: Phyllis C. Borzi, Suite S-2524
Deputy Asst. Secretary for Program Operations:
Michael L. Davis, Suite S-2524
Alan D. Lebowitz, Suite N-5677
(202) 693-8315; Fax: (202) 219-6531
Protects the economic future and retirement security of working Americans through regulation of private pension and retirement benefits and is guardian of the national workers retirement and welfare system; enforces and provides advice regarding Title I of the Employee Retirement Income Security Act (ERISA) *29 U.S.C. 1001*
Formerly Pension and Welfare Benefits Administration

Employee Benefits Security Administration (EBSA)
Regional Office
J.F.K. Federal Bldg., Room 575, Boston, MA 02203
Pension Rights in the Private Sector: (617) 565-9600;
Fax: (617) 565-9666

Regional Dir.: Jean Ackerman

Employee Benefits Security Administration (EBSA)
Regional Office
33 Whitehall St., Suite 1200, New York, NY 10004
(212) 607-8600; Fax: (212) 607-8681
Internet: www.dol.gov/ebsa

Regional Dir.: Jonathan Kay
(212) 607-8644; Fax: (212) 607-8689

Provide assistance to participants in employee enefit plans and conduct Civil and Criminal investations regarding administration of employee benefit plans.

Office of Workers' Compensation Programs (OWCP)
200 Constitution Ave. N.W., Room S-3524,
Washington, DC 20210
(202) 693-0031; Fax: (202) 693-1378
Internet: www.dol.gov/esa/owcp_org.htm
Director: Shelby Hallmark
Dir. of Federal Employee Compensation:
Douglas C. Fitzgerald (202) 693-0040; Fax: (202) 693-1498

Dept. of Labor, Office of Workers Comp. Programs—Cont'd

Administers the Federal Employees Compensation Act, the Longshore and Harbor Workers' Compensation Act, the Black Lung Benefits Act, and the Energy Employees Occupational Illness Compensation Program Act.

Office of Workers' Compensation Programs
Regional Office
201 Varick St., Room 740, P.O. Box 566,
New York, NY 10014-0566
(646) 264-3100; Fax: (646) 264-3004

Regional Dir.: Robert Sullivan

Occupational Safety and Health Administration
200 Constitution Ave. N.W., Rm. S2315, Washington, DC 20210
(202) 693-2000; Standards: (202) 693-1950, (800) 321-6742;
Public Affairs: (202) 693-1999; TTY: (877) 889-5627
Internet: www.osha.gov

Asst. Secretary: David Michaels (Pending Confirmation)
Room S2315 (202) 693-2000; Fax: (202) 693-1659

Assoc. Solicitor: Joseph M. Woodward (202) 693-5445

Develops and promulgates occupational safety and health standards, develops and issues regulations, and conducts investigations and inspections to enforce compliance. *29 U.S.C. 615*

Occupational Safety and Health Administration
Regional Office
201 Varick St., Room 670, New York, NY 10014
(212) 337-2378; Fax: (212) 337-2371
Internet: www.osha.gov

Regional Administrator: Robert Kulick (212) 337-0118

Albany Area Office
401 New Karner Rd., Suite 300,
Albany, NY 12205-3809
(518) 464-4338; Fax: (518) 464-4337
Area Dir.: Ed Jerome

Buffalo Area Office
130 S. Elmwood Ave., Suite 500,
Buffalo, NY 14202-2465
(716) 551-3053; Fax: (716) 551-3126
Area Dir.: Art Dube

Long Island Area Office
1400 Old Country Rd., Room 208, Westbury, NY 11590
(516) 334-3344; Fax: (516) 334-3326
Area Dir.: Patricia Jones

Manhattan Area Office
201 Varick St., Room 908, New York, NY 10014
(212) 620-3200; Fax: (212) 620-4121
Area Dir.: Kay Gee

Queens Area Office
45-17 Marathon Pkwy., 5th Floor,
Little Neck, NY 11362
(718) 279-9060; Fax: (718) 279-9057
Area Dir.: Kevin Brennan

Syracuse Area Office
3300 Vickery Rd., North Syracuse, NY 13212
(315) 451-0808; Fax: (315) 451-1351
Area Dir.: Christopher Adams

Tarrytown Area Office
660 White Plains Rd., 4th Floor,
Tarrytown, NY 10591-5107
(914) 524-7510; Fax: (914) 524-7515
Area Dir.: Diana Cortez

Mine Safety and Health Administration
1100 Wilson Blvd., Arlington, VA 22209-3939
(202) 693-9400; Fax: (202) 693-9401
Internet: www.msha.gov

Asst. Secretary: Joseph A. Main
(202) 693-9414; Fax: (202) 693-9421
E-mail: zzmsha-asmsha@dol.gov

Dir., Office of Program Education and Outreach Services:
Layne Lathram (202) 693-9400; Fax: (202) 693-9421
E-mail: lathram.layne@dol.gov

Assoc. Solicitor: Heidi W. Strassler (Acting)

Protects miner safety and health through enforcement, education and technical assistance. *30 U.S.C. 801*

Bureau of Labor Statistics
Commissioner's Office
2 Massachusetts Ave. N.E., Room 4040,
Washington, DC 20212-0001
(202) 691-5200; Fax: (202) 691-5899;
Fax-on-demand: (202) 691-7890; Internet: www.bls.gov

Commissioner: Keith Hall (202) 691-7802; Fax: (202) 691-7797

Deputy Commissioner: Philip L. Rones

Collects, processes, and analyzes labor information and statistics.

New York-New Jersey Information Office
201 Varick St., Room 808, New York, NY 10014
(212) 264-2300; Fax: (212) 337-2532;
Hotline: (646) 264-3600
Internet: www.bls.gov/ro2/home.htm

Regional Commissioner: Michael L. Dolfman
(212) 337-2500; E-mail: dolfman.michael@bls.gov

Veterans' Employment and Training Service
200 Constitution Ave. N.W., Room S-1325,
Washington, DC 20210
(202) 693-4700; Fax: (202) 693-4754; Internet: www.dol.gov/vets

Asst. Secretary: Vacancy at Press Time

Administers veterans' training and employment programs. Works with and provides technical assistance to State Employment Security Agencies and Job Training Partnership Act grant recipients to ensure mandated priority services for veterans. Assists federal contractors in compliance with and reporting of veterans affirmative action requirements. Investigates complaints from veterans, reservists and National Guard members regarding their employment and reemployment rights under Uniformed Services Employment and Reemployment Rights Act. *U.S.C. Title 38, Chap. 43*

Women's Bureau
Frances Perkins Bldg., Room S-3002,
200 Constitution Ave. N.W., Washington, DC 20210
(202) 693-6710, (800) 827-5335; Fax: (202) 693-6725
E-mail: wb-wwc@dol.gov; Internet: www.dol.gov/wb

Director: Sara Manzano-Díaz

The Women's Bureau is responsible for formulating standards and policies that promote the welfare of wage-earning women, improve their working conditions, increase their efficiency, and advance their opportunities for profitable employment.

Region 2 Office
201 Varick St., Room 602, New York, NY 10014-4811
(646) 264-3789; Fax: (646) 264-3794
Internet: www.dol.gov/wb

Regional Administrator: Grace Protos
E-mail: protos.grace@dol.gov

DEPARTMENT OF STATE

2201 C St. N.W., Washington, DC 20520
(202) 647-4000; Fax: (202) 261-8577;
TTY: (800) 877-8339
E-mail: secretary@state.gov; Internet: www.state.gov

Secretary of State: Hillary Rodham Clinton
(202) 647-7572

Legal Advisor: Harold Hongju Koh, Room 6541
(202) 647-9598; Fax: (202) 647-1037, 647-7096

Advises the President in the formulation and execution of foreign policy and carries out established foreign policy on behalf of the nation. *1 Stat. 68*

National Passport Center
20 International Dr., Portsmouth, NH 03801
(877) 487-2778; TTY: (888) 874-7793
Internet: http://travel.state.gov/passport

Processing center for applications

Special Issuance Agency
1111 19th St. N.W., Room 200,
Washington, DC 20522-1705
(202) 955-0198;
Dept. of Defense Inquiries: (703) 602-3620, 63; Fax: (703) 602-3605

Director: Barbara M. Chesman

Asst. Dir.: Randall J. Bevins

Applications for Diplomatic, Official and No Fee passports; also Fee passports accompanied by Congressional referrals

Department of State—Cont'd

New York Passport Agency
376 Hudson St., New York, NY 10014-3621
Automated Line: (877) 487-2778
Internet: www.travel.state.gov

Only accepts emergency applications from those leaving within two weeks or who need foreign visas for travel.

By appointment only, Weekdays, 7:30 A.M.-3 P.M.

Connecticut Passport Agency
50 Washington St., 1st Floor, Norwalk, CT 06854-2710
(877) 487-2778

Only accepts emergency applications from those leaving within two weeks or who need foreign visas for travel.

By appointment only, Weekdays, 9 A.M.-4 P.M.

Boston Passport Agency
O'Neill Federal Bldg., Room 247, 10 Causeway St., Boston, MA 02222-1094
(617) 878-0900; Appointments: (877) 487-2778
Internet: http://travel.state.gov

Only accepts emergency applications from those leaving within two weeks or who need foreign visas for travel.

United States Information Agency
Internet: www.usia.gov

See Broadcasting Board of Governors, infra

DEPARTMENT OF TRANSPORTATION

1200 New Jersey Ave., S.E., Washington, DC 20590
(202) 366-2332; Personnel Locator: (202) 366-4000;
Fax: (202) 366-9634
Internet: www.dot.gov

Secretary of Transportation: Raymond L. LaHood
(202) 366-1111; Fax: (202) 366-7202

General Counsel: Robert S. Rivkin
(202) 366-4702; Fax: (222) 366-3388

Establishes the nation's overall transportation policy, administers highway development, restoration, maintenance, mass transit, rail, aviation, and waterway programs. *49 U.S.C. app. 1651 note*

Office of Hearings
M-20, Room E12-320, 1200 New Jersey Ave. S.E., Washington, DC 20590
(202) 366-2142; Fax: (202) 366-7536
Internet: www.dot.govhearings

Chief Admin. Law Judge: Ronnie A. Yoder
E-mail: ronnie.yoder@dot.gov

Admin. Law Judges:
Isaac D. Benkin (202) 366-2144
Richard C. Goodwin (202) 366-5121

Responsible for conduct and initial disposition of formal proceedings falling within the purview of the A.P.A. and instituted under legislation vesting executive authority and responsibility in the Secretary of Transportation, except as prescribed by statute or otherwise ordered by the Secretary.

Federal Aviation Administration
800 Independence Ave. S.W., Washington, DC 20591
(202) 267-3883, (800) 835-5322;
Employee Locator: (202) 366-4000
Internet: www.faa.gov/

Administrator: J. Randolph Babbitt (Acting)
(202) 267-8111; Fax: (202) 267-5047

Chief Counsel: David Grizzle
(202) 267-3222; Fax: (202) 267-3227

Regulates air commerce; controls the use of navigable airspace for both civil and military use; promotes the development of civil aeronautics; conducts research; installs and operates air navigation facilities; and promotes the limitation of environmental effects of aviation. *49 U.S.C. 706*

Eastern Regional Office
159-30 Rockaway Blvd., Jamaica, NY 11434-4848
Mailing Address: 1 Aviation Plaza, Jamaica, NY 11434-4809
(718) 553-3000; Fax: (718) 995-5656

Regional Administrator: Carmine Gallo (718) 553-3001

Regional Counsel: Alfred R. Johnson, Jr. (718) 553-3285

Office of Public Affairs: Arlene Salac (718) 553-3011

Federal Highway Administration
1200 New Jersey Ave. S.E., Washington, DC 20590-9898
(202) 366-0537; Internet: www.fhwa.dot.gov/

Administrator: Victor Mendez (Acting)
(202) 366-0650; Fax: (302) 366-3244

Exec. Dir.: Jeffrey F. Paniati

Chief Counsel: Thomas P. Holian (Acting)
(202) 366-0617; Fax: (202) 366-7499

Coordinates and administers Federal funding for all aspects of highway transportation, construction, maintenance, management, and Federal regulation. *49 U.S.C. app. 1651 note*

Office of Chief Counsel
Leo W. O'Brien Fedl. Bldg., Suite 719, Clinton Ave. & N. Pearl St., Albany, NY 12207
(518) 431-4125, Ext. 224; Fax: (518) 431-4121
Internet: www.fhwa.dot.gov

Division Administrator: Jeffrey W. Kolb
(518) 431-4172; E-mail: jeff.kolb@dot.gov

Senior Atty.: Kenneth Dymond
(518) 431-4125, Ext. 224; E-mail: ken.dymond@dot.gov

Maritime Administration
1200 New Jersey Ave. S.E., Washington, DC 20590
(800) 996-2723; Employee Locator: (202) 366-5812
Internet: www.marad.dot.gov

Administrator: Vacancy at Press Time (202) 366-5823

Deputy Admin.: David T. Matsuda

Chief Counsel: K. Denise Krepp (Acting) (202) 366-5711

Promotes the development and maintenance of the merchant marine, to carry domestic waterborne commerce and a substantial portion of the nation's waterborne commerce, and to serve as a naval and military auxiliary during wartime or national emergency. Also seeks to ensure adequate shipbuilding and repair service, efficient ports, effective intermodal water and land transportation systems, and reserve shipping capacity in time of national emergency.

North Atlantic Gateway Office
1 Bowling Green, Room 418, New York, NY 10004-1415
(212) 668-3330; Fax: (212) 668-3382

Director: Robert F. McKeon; E-mail: robert.mckeon@dot.gov

Federal Railroad Administration
1200 New Jersey Ave., S.E., Washington, DC 20590
(202) 493-6000; Office of Chief Counsel: (202) 493-6052; Fax: (202) 493-6068; Office of Public Affairs: (202) 493-6024;
Internet: www.fra.dot.gov

Administrator: Joseph C. Szabo, Mail Stop 5
(202) 493-6014; Fax: (202) 493-6009

Chief Counsel: Karen J. Hedlund, Mail Stop 10

Promulgates and enforces rail safety regulations, rail assistance programs, research and development in support of improved rail facilities. *49 U.S.C. app. 1652*

Regional Office
55 Broadway, Room 1077, Cambridge, MA 02142
(617) 494-2302; Hotline: (800) 724-5991; Fax: (617) 494-2967

Regional Administrator: Les Fiorenzo

Deputy Regional Administrator: Janet Lee

Deputy Regional Adminstrator: Peter Lapre

Administrative Officer: Robert R. Novak

National Highway Traffic Safety Administration
1200 New Jersey Ave. S.E., Washington, DC 20590
Auto Safety Hotline: (888) 327-4236; TTY: (800) 424-9153
Internet: www.nhtsa.gov

Administrator: David L. Strickland (202) 366-1836

Deputy Admin.: Ronald Medford (Acting)

Chief Counsel: Kevin Vincent (202) 366-5061; Fax: (202) 366-3820

Carries out programs related to driver safety, motor vehicle and related equipment performance. *23 U.S.C. chapter 4; 49 U.S.C. chapter 301.*

Regional Office
222 Mamaroneck Ave., Room 204, White Plains, NY 10605
(914) 682-6162; Fax: (914) 682-6239
E-mail: region2@nhtsa.dot.gov

Regional Administrator: Thomas M. Louizou
E-mail: tom.louizou@dot.gov

Department of Transportation—Cont'd

Federal Transit Administration
1200 New Jersey Ave. S.E., Washington, DC 20590
(800) 877-8339; Public Affairs: (202) 366-4043; Fax: (202) 366-3472
Internet: www.fta.dot.gov/

Administrator: Peter M. Rogoff (202) 366-4040

Deputy Admin.: Therese W. McMillan (202) 366-4041

Chief Counsel: Scott A. Biehl (Acting) Room 9316
(202) 366-4063; Fax: (202) 366-3809

Assists in the development of mass transit facilities; encourages the planning and establishment of urban mass transit systems; and aids state governments in the development and operation of mass transit systems.
5 U.S.C. app. Reorganization Plan No. 2 of 1968

Regional Office
1 Bowling Green, Room 429, New York, NY 10004-1415
(212) 668-2170; Fax: (212) 668-2136

Regional Administrator: Brigid Hynes-Cherin

Chief Counsel: Maisie Grace (212) 668-2178

Pipeline and Hazardous Materials Safety
1200 New Jersey Ave. S.E., Mail Stop E27-303, 2nd Floor, Washington, DC 20590
(202) 366-4433; Fax: (202) 366-3666
Internet: www.phmsa.dot.gov

Administrator: Cynthia L. Quarterman
(202) 366-0656; Fax: (202) 366-5713

Chief Counsel: Bizunesh Scott
(202) 366-4400; Fax: (202) 366-7041

Asst. Chief Counsel for Hazardous Materials Law Div.:
Joseph Solomey (202) 366-4400; Fax: (202) 366-7041

Develops and issues regulations for pipeline and the transportation of hazardous materials, provides training and enforces those regulations. Issues preemption determinations. Provides emergency response support.

Surface Transportation Board
395 E. St., S.W., Washington, DC 20423-0001
(202) 245-0245; Fax: (202) 245-0461
Internet: www.stb.dot.gov

Chair: Daniel R. Elliott III
(202) 245-0220; Fax: (202) 245-0452

Vice Chair: Francis P. Mulrey
(202) 245-0210; Fax: (202) 245-0453

Commissioner: Charles D. Nottingham
(202) 245-0200; Fax: (202) 245-0450

General Counsel: Ellen D. Hanson
(202) 245-0260; Fax: (202) 245-0460

Dir., Office of Public Assistance, Governmental Affairs and Compliance: Matthew T. Wallen
(202) 245-0238

Dir., Ofc. of Economics, Environmental Analysis and Admin.: Leland L. Gardner
(202) 245-0324; Fax: (202) 245-0454

Dir., Office of Proceedings: Rachel D. Campbell
(202) 245-0357; Fax: (202) 245-0464

Adjudicatory body with oversight of railroads; pipeline carriers; intercity bus carriers; household goods carriers; motor carriers involved in collective activities or undercharge claims; and water carriers involved in noncontiguous domestic trade. 49 U.S.C. §§ 701-725, 10101-11908, 15101-16106, and 13101-14914.

Formerly known as Interstate Commerce Commission

Bureau of Transportation Statistics
1200 New Jersey Ave. S.E., Washington, DC 20590
(800) 853-1351;
BTS Products: (202) 366-DATA; (800) 853-1351;
Fax: (202) 366-3759
Internet: www.bts.gov

Director: Steven D. Dillingham (202) 366-6268

Deputy Dir.: Steve K. Smith (202) 493-0145

Atty. Advisor: Robert Monniere
(202) 366-5498; Fax: (202) 366-3671
E-mail: robert.monniere@dot.gov

Compiles, analyzes, and publishes transportation related statistics. Now a division of Research and Innovative Technology Administration (RITA) *49 U.S.C. 111*

Office of Airline Information
1200 New Jersey Ave. S.E., Bldg. E-34, Washington, DC 20590
(800) 853-1351; Fax: (202) 366-3383; Internet: www.bts.gov

Asst. Dir.: Anne Suissa; E-mail: anne.suissa@dot.gov

Volpe National Transportation Systems Center
55 Broadway, Kendall Sq., Cambridge, MA 02142-1093
(617) 494-2224; Internet: www.volpe.dot.gov

Assoc. Administrator: Robert C. Johns
(617) 494-2222; Fax: (617) 494-3731

Chief Counsel: Katie K. Kelly
(617) 494-2731; Fax: (617) 494-3005

Assesses the needs of the transportation community, evaluates research and development activities in the technology, and assists in the application and deployment of state-of-the-art transportation technologies and policies.

DEPARTMENT OF THE TREASURY

1500 Pennsylvania Ave. N.W., Washington, DC 20220
(202) 622-2000; Fax: (202) 622-6415
Internet: www.ustreas.gov

Secretary of the Treasury: Timothy F. Geithner

General Counsel: George W. Madison, Suite 3000
(202) 602-0283; Fax: (202) 622-2882

Formulates and recommends economic, financial, tax, and fiscal policies; serves as financial agent for the U.S. government; enforces the law; and manufactures coin and currency. *31 U.S.C. 1001*

Office of the Comptroller of the Currency
250 E St. S.W., Washington, DC 20219
(202) 874-5000; Internet: www.occ.treas.gov

Comptroller: John C. Dugan (202) 874-4900

Chief Counsel: Julie L. Williams (202) 874-5200

Promulgates rules and regulations for the operation of the national banks and examines the banks for compliance with banking regulations. *12 Stat. 665*

Northeastern District Office
340 Madison Ave., 5th Floor, New York, NY 10173-0002
(212) 790-4000; Fax: (212) 790-4058

Deputy Comptroller: Toney Bland (212) 790-4001

District Counsel: Jonathan H. Rushdoony
(212) 790-4010; Fax: (301) 433-8468
E-mail: jonathan.rushdoony@occ.treas.gov

Senior Counsel: Damon Savoy
(212) 790-4019; Fax: (301) 433-8508
E-mail: damon.savoy@occ.treas.gov

Special Counsel: Jane A. Principe
(215) 245-2606; Fax: (301) 433-8259
E-mail: jane.principe@occ.treas.gov

Counsel:
Helen H. Cha-Choe (212) 790-4014; Fax: (301) 433-6432
E-mail: helen.cha-choe@occ.treas.gov
Jeanne Devine (212) 790-4041; Fax: (301) 433-6665
E-mail: jeanne.devine@occ.treas.gov
Jason D. Redwood (212) 790-4037; Fax: (301) 433-8324
E-mail: jason.redwood@occ.treas.gov

Sr. Attys.:
Ancris Ramdhanie
(212) 790-4039; Fax: (301) 433-7983
E-mail: ancris.munoz@occ.treas.gov
Jeanette Quick (212) 790-4010; Fax: (301) 433-6397
E-mail: jeanette.quick@occ.treas.gov

Atty.: Christian Errico

Bureau of Engraving and Printing
14th & C Sts. S.W., Washington, DC 20228
(202) 874-8888, (877) 874-4114;
External Relations Fax: (202) 874-3177
Internet: www.moneyfactory.gov

9000 Blue Mound Rd., Fort Worth, TX 76131
(817) 847-3800

Director: Larry R. Felix

Chief Counsel: Kevin J. Rice
(202) 874-5363; Fax: (202) 874-5710

The Bureau produces United States obligations and securities. *31 U.S.C. 5114*

Department of the Treasury—Cont'd

Financial Management Service
401 14th St. S.W., Washington, DC 20227
(202) 874-6950; Fax: (202) 874-7016
Internet: www.fms.treas.gov/

Commissioner: David Lebryk
(201) 874-7000; Fax: (202) 874-6743

Dir., Office of Legislative & Public Affairs:
Melody R. Barrett
(202) 874-6557; Fax: (202) 874-7016

Chief Counsel: Margaret Marquette
(202) 874-6681; Fax: (202) 874-6627

The Financial Management Services disburses Federal payments like Social Security, veterans' benefits and income tax refunds, collects Federal revenues, oversees a daily cash flow, provides centralized debt collection services to most Federal agencies and provides government-wide accounting and reporting.

Internal Revenue Service
1111 Constitution Ave. N.W., Washington, DC 20224
(202) 622-5000;
Federal Tax Forms (800) 829-FORM: (800) 829-3676;
Tax Assistance, Information and Problem Resolution:
(800) 829-1040
Internet: www.irs.gov

Commissioner: Douglas Shulman, Room 3000
(202) 622-9511

Chief Counsel: William J. Wilkins, Room 3026
(202) 622-3300; Fax: (202) 622-4277

Administers and enforces all internal revenue laws except those relating to alcohol, tobacco, firearms, and explosives. *26 U.S.C. 7802*

New York/New Jersey Offices

Dir., North Atlantic Area Collection:
Rebecca A. Chiaramida
(Small Business & Self-Employed Div.)
110 W. 44th St., 9th Floor, New York, NY 10036
(212) 719-6792; Fax: (212) 719-6480

Area Counsel, Small Businesses: Linda Dettery
33 Maiden Ln., New York, NY 10038 (917) 421-4737

Industry Dir., Financial Svces.: Paul DeNard
(Large & Mid-Size Business Div.)
290 Broadway, 12th Floor, New York, NY 10007
(212) 298-2130; Fax: (212) 298-2124, 53

Exec. Asst. to Industry Dir., Financial Svces.:
William W. Kingston (Large & Mid-Size Business Div.)
290 Broadway, 12th Floor, New York, NY 10007
(212) 298-2104; Fax: (212) 298-2124

Area Counsel, Large and Mid-Size Business Div.:
Roland Barral
33 Maiden Ln., New York, NY 10038
(917) 421-4667

Dir., Field Operations, Financial Svces. Industry, Northeast: Patricia C. Chaback
(Large & Mid-Size Business Div.)
135 High St., Mail Stop 300, Hartford, CT 06103
(860) 756-4570; Fax: (860) 756-4699

Dir., Field Operations, Financial Svces. Industry, N.Y.C.: Carl Weiss (Large & Mid-Size Business Div.)
290 Broadway, 12th Floor, New York, NY 10007
(212) 298-2112; Fax: (212) 298-2153

Industry Dir., Communications, Technology & Media: Tom Wilson (Large & Mid-Size Business Div.)
1301 Clay St., Suite 1650S, Oakland, CA 94612
(510) 637-4600; Fax: (510) 637-2719

Industry Dir., Heavy Manufacturing & Transportation: John Petrella, Jr.
(Large & Mid-Size Business Div.)
111 Wood Ave. S., 1st Floor, Iselin, NJ 08830
(732) 452-8102; Fax: (732) 452-8140

Dir., Field Operations, Heavy Manufacturing & Transportation Industry (N.J.): Douglas O'Donnell
(Large & Mid-Size Business Div.)
111 Wood Ave. S., 1st Floor, Iselin, NJ 08830
(732) 452-8104; Fax: (732) 452-8140

Industry Dir., Natural Resources & Construction:
Bobby Scott (Large & Mid-Size Business Div.)
1919 Smith St., Mail Stop 1000 HOU, Houston, TX 77002
(713) 209-3704; Fax: (713) 209-3723

Industry Dir., Retailers, Food, Pharmaceuticals & Healthcare: Robert E. Brazzil
(Large & Mid-Size Business Div.)
1901 Butterfield Rd., Suite 310, Downers Grove, IL 60515
(630) 493-5900; Fax: (630) 493-5910

District Office
290 Broadway, Ground Level, New York, NY 10007
Mailing Address: P.O. Box 3000, Church St. Station, New York, NY 10008 (212) 436-1000

Brooklyn Office
10 Metrotech Ctr., 625 Fulton St., Brooklyn, NY 11201
(718) 488-2068
Dir., Taxpayer Education & Communications:
Ellen Murphy (Small Business & Self-Employed Div.)
Taxpayer Advocate: Bernardita Tehrani
(718) 488-2080; Fax: (718) 488-3100

Taxpayer Advocate Service Office
1 Clinton Ave., Room 354, Albany, NY 12207
(518) 427-4250
Taxpayer Advocate: Georgeann Bailey
(518) 427-5413; Fax: (518) 427-5494

Taxpayer Advocate Service Office
130 S. Elmwood Ave., Buffalo, NY 14227-1416
(716) 961-5100
Taxpayer Advocate: William J. Wirth, Jr. P.O. Box 219, Buffalo, NY 14225 (716) 686-4850; Fax: (716) 686-4851

Bureau of the Public Debt
799 9th St. N.W., Washington, DC 20239
(202) 504-3502; Fax: (202) 504-3630
Internet: www.publicdebt.treas.gov

200 Third St., P.O. Box 1328, Parkersburg, WV 26106

Commissioner: Van Zeck (202) 504-3500

Chief Counsel: Paul Wolfteich (202) 504-3520

Borrows money to operate the federal government, accounts for the resulting debt, and provides reimbursable support services to federal agencies 31 U.S.C. §322, note.

Office of Thrift Supervision
1700 G St. N.W., Washington, DC 20552
(202) 906-6000; Consumer Complaints: (800) 842-6929
Internet: www.ots.treas.gov

Director: John E. Bowman (Acting), 5th Floor
(202) 906-6590; Fax: (202) 898-0230
E-mail: john.bowman@ots.treas.gov

Ombudsman: Brian S. Steffey
Harborside Financial Center Plaza Five, Suite 1600, Jersey City, NJ 07311
(877) 781-9044; Fax: (201) 451-5843

Chief Counsel: Deborah Dakin (Acting), 5th Floor
(202) 906-6372; Fax: (202) 906-7606

Regulates and supervises the nation's thrift industry; ensures the safety and soundness of thrift institutions and supports their role as home and mortgage lenders and providers of other community credit and financial services. Regulation of savings associations. *12 U.S.C. 1461* et seq.

Office of Regional Counsel—Northeast
Harborside Financial Center Plaza Five, Suite 1600, Jersey City, NJ 07311
(201) 413-1000; Fax: (201) 413-7543
Internet: www.ots.treas.gov

Regional Enforcement Counsel, Enforcement and Litigation Matters: Margaret Gig Clark
(201) 413-7381; Fax: (201) 413-5863

Regional Counsel, Corporate Matters and Regulatory Advice: James Porreca (201) 413-7304

Northeast Regional Office
Harborside Financial Center Plaza Five, Suite 1600, Jersey City, NJ 07311 (201) 413-1000; Fax: (201) 413-7543

Regional Dir.: Michael E. Finn

Ombudsman: Brian S. Steffey
(877) 781-9044; Fax: (201) 451-5843

Department of the Treasury—Cont'd

United States Mint
801 9th St. N.W., Washington, DC 20220
(202) 354-7200; Fax: (202) 874-6282
Internet: www.usmint.gov

Director: Edward C. Moy, 8th Floor
(202) 354-7200; Fax: (202) 756-6160

Chief Counsel: Daniel Shaver, 8th Floor
(202) 354-7280; Fax: (202) 756-6110

Produces and distributes coins; maintains and protects government's gold and silver reserves.

DEPARTMENT OF VETERANS AFFAIRS
810 Vermont Ave. N.W., Washington, DC 20420
(866) 341-0743
Internet: www.va.gov

Secretary of Veterans Affairs: Eric K. Shinseki
Mailcode 00

General Counsel: Will A. Gunn, Mailcode 02
(202) 461-4995; Fax: (202) 273-6671

Operates programs for the benefit of veterans and their survivors, including disability compensation, pensions, education, rehabilitation, home loan guarantee, medical and hospital program, and death and burial benefits. *38 U.S.C. 201 note*

Regional Office
Norris Cotton Fedl. Bldg., 275 Chestnut St.,
Manchester, NH 03101-2489
(800) 827-1000

Director: Charles W. Woolford
(603) 222-5700; Fax: (603) 222-5766

Manchester Loan Guaranty Officer: William Dallmann
(603) 222-5800

Office of Regional Counsel: Derwood J. Haskell
(603) 222-5850; Fax: (603) 222-5864

Regional Office of Public Affairs
245 W. Houston St., New York, NY 10014
(212) 807-3429; Fax: (212) 807-4030

Regional Counsel: George J. Burns
800 Poly Pl., Bldg. 14, Brooklyn, NY 11209
(718) 630-2900

Independent Establishments and Government Corporations

AFRICAN DEVELOPMENT FOUNDATION
1400 Eye St. N.W., Suite 1000,
Washington, DC 20005-2248
(202) 673-3916; Fax: (202) 673-3810
E-mail: info@adf.gov
Internet: www.adf.gov

President: Lloyd O. Pierson

General Counsel: Doris Mason Martin

Supports the self-help projects and programs of the poor in Africa. Provides economic assistance to African grassroots organizations engaged in development activities. *22 U.S.C. 290*

BROADCASTING BOARD OF GOVERNORS
330 Independence Ave. S.W., Washington, DC 20237
(202) 203-4545; Fax: (202) 203-4568
Internet: www.bbg.gov

Chair: Vacancy at Press Time

Exec. Dir.: Jeffrey N. Trimble

Dir., Office of Strategic Planning and Performance Mgmt.: Bruce Sherman

Dir., Voice of America: Danforth Austin
(202) 203-4500

Deputy Counsel: Paul Kollmer-Dorsey
(202) 203-4545

Responsible for government-sponsored, non-military international broadcasting, including Voice of America, Radio Free Europe, Radio Liberty the Office of Cuba Broadcasting, Radio Free Asia, Middle East Broadcasting Networks, and the International Broadcasting Bureau. *P.L. 105 277.*

CENTRAL INTELLIGENCE AGENCY
Washington, DC 20505
(703) 482-0623;
Public Communications Branch: (703) 482-0623, 24;
Fax (Public Communications): (703) 482-1739
Internet: www.cia.gov

Director: Leon E. Panetta

Deputy Dir.: Michael J. Morell

General Counsel: John A. Rizzo (Acting)

Collects, evaluates, and disseminates valuable information on political, military, economic, scientific, and other developments abroad needed to safeguard national security. *50 U.S.C. 401*

COMMISSION ON CIVIL RIGHTS
624 9th St. N.W., Room 700, Washington, DC 20425
(202) 376-7700; Fax: (202) 376-7672
Internet: www.usccr.gov

Chairman: Gerald A. Reynolds

General Counsel: David Blackwood

Chief, Public Affairs Unit: Lenore Ostrowksy (Acting)
(202) 376-8591

Collects, studies, and evaluates information on discrimination or denials of equal protection of the laws under the Constitution because of race, color, religion, sex, age, disability, or national origin. *42 U.S.C. 1975*

Eastern Regional Office
624 Ninth St. N.W., Suite 740, Washington, DC 20425
(202) 376-7533; TTY: (202) 376-8116; Fax: (202) 376-7548

Director: Ivy L. Davis

COMMODITY FUTURES TRADING COMMISSION
Three Lafayette Centre, 1155 21st St. N.W.,
Washington, DC 20581
(202) 418-5000; Fax: (202) 418-5521
Internet: www.cftc.gov

Chair: Gary Gensler, Room 9060
(202) 418-5014; Fax: (202) 418-5550

General Counsel: Dan Berkowitz
(202) 418-5120; Fax: (202) 418-5524; E-mail: ogc@cftc.gov

Promotes healthy economic growth; protects the rights of customers; and ensures fairness and integrity through the efficient regulation of the trading of futures in commodities. *7 U.S.C. 4a*

Office of Proceedings
Three Lafayette Centre, 4th Floor, 1155 21st St., N.W.,
Washington, DC 20581
(202) 418-5250; Fax: (202) 418-5532

Admin. Law Judges:
Bruce C. Levine (202) 418-5503
E-mail: blevine@cftc.gov
George H. Painter (202) 418-5504
E-mail: gpainter@cftc.gov

Judgment Officer: Philip V. McGuire (202) 418-5500
E-mail: pmcguire@cftc.gov

Hears and decides enforcement and reparations cases arising under the Commodities and Exchange Act as amended. *7 U.S.C. 1-25*

CONSUMER PRODUCT SAFETY COMMISSION
East West Towers, 4330 East West Highway,
Bethesda, MD 20814-4408
Public Affairs: (301) 504-7908;
CPSC Consumer Hotline: (800) 638-2772;
Fax: (301) 504-0124, 504-0025
E-mail: info@cpsc.gov; Internet: www.cpsc.gov

Commissioner: Inez Moore Tenenbaum (301) 504-7896

General Counsel: Cheryl Falvey
(301) 504-7642; Fax: (301) 504-0403
E-mail: cfalvey@cpsc.gov

Protects the public against unreasonable risk of injury from consumer products, develops uniform safety standards for consumer products, negotiates recalls of defective products, and promotes research and investigation into the causes and prevention of product-related illness, death, and injury. *15 U.S.C. 2051*

CORPORATION FOR NATIONAL AND COMMUNITY SERVICE

1201 New York Ave. N.W., Washington, DC 20525
(202) 606-5000; Fax: (202) 565-2796
E-mail: info@cns.gov
Internet: www.cns.gov

C.E.O.: Patrick Corvington (202) 606-6735
General Counsel: Frank R. Trinity (202) 606-6677

Mobilizes Americans for voluntary service throughout the United States through programs that help meet the basic human needs and support self-help efforts of low-income individuals and communities. *42 U.S.C. 4951 and 42 U.S.C. 12501*

Formerly called ACTION

Field Financial Management Center
601 Walnut St., Suite 876E, Philadelphia, PA 19106
(215) 597-9972; Fax: (215) 597-4933
Director: Rocco Gaudio (215) 597-3471

State Office
Leo O'Brien Federal Bldg., Suite 900, One Clinton Sq., Albany, NY 12207
(518) 431-4150; Fax: (518) 431-4154; E-mail: ny@cns.gov
State Program Dir.: Donna M. Smith

DEFENSE NUCLEAR FACILITIES SAFETY BOARD

625 Indiana Ave. N.W., Suite 700, Washington, DC 20004
(202) 694-7000, (800) 788-4016; Fax: (202) 208-6518
Internet: www.dnfsb.gov

Chairman: Dr. Peter S. Winokur
General Counsel: Richard A. Azzaro

Reviews and evaluates the content and implementation of the safety standards relating to the design, construction, operation, and decommissioning of defense nuclear facilities of the Department of Energy. *42 U.S.C. 2286*

ENVIRONMENTAL PROTECTION AGENCY

Ariel Rios Bldg., 1200 Pennsylvania Ave., N.W., Washington, DC 20460
(202) 272-0167
Internet: www.epa.gov

Administrator: Lisa Jackson, Mailbox 1101A
(202) 564-4700
Deputy Admin.: Bob Perciasepe, Mailcode 4101M
(202) 564-4711

Protects and enhances the environment through rigorous enforcement of all environmental legislation, including pesticide, radiation, and toxic substances regulation. Cooperates and coordinates with state and local enforcement efforts. *5 U.S.C. app. Reorganization Plan No. 3 of 1970*

Regional Office
Region II, 290 Broadway, New York, NY 10007-1866
(212) 637-3000; Fax: (212) 637-5046
Internet: www.epa.gov/region2
Regional Administrator: Judith A. Enck (212) 637-5000
E-mail: enck.judith@epa.gov
Regional Counsel: Eric Schaaf (212) 637-3107
E-mail: schaaf.eric@epa.gov

Office of Administrative Law Judges
1099 14th St. N.W., Suite 350, Washington, DC 20005
Mailing Address:
1200 Pennsylvania Ave. N.W., Mailcode 1900L, Washington, DC 20460
(202) 564-6255; Fax: (202) 565-0044
Internet: www.epa.gov/oalj
Chief Admin. Law Judge: Susan L. Biro
Admin. Law Judges:
Barbara Gunning
William B. Moran
Spencer T. Nissen
Dir. of Management: James McDonald

Conduct hearings and render decisions under the Clean Air Act (CAA); the Clean Water Act (CWA); the Comprehensive Environmental Response, Compensation and Liability Act (CERCLA); the Emergency Planning and Community Right-To-Know Act (EPCRA); the Federal Insecticide, Fungicide and Rodenticide Act (FIFRA); the Marine Protection, Research and Sanctuaries Act (MPRSA); the Safe Drinking Water Act (SDWA); the Solid Waste Disposal Act, as amended by the Resource Conservation and Recovery Act (RCRA); the Toxic Substances Control Act (TSCA); and the Asbestos Hazard Emergency Response Act (AHERA). Also serve as mediators in Superfund (CERCLA) cases.

Office of General Counsel
1200 Pennsylvania Ave. N.W., Mailcode 2310A, Washington, DC 20460
(202) 564-8040; Fax: (202) 564-1778
General Counsel: Scott Fulton

Office for Administration and Resources Management (OARM)
1200 Pennsylvania Ave. N.W., Mailcode 3101A, Washington, DC 20460
(202) 564-4600; Fax: (202) 564-0233
Asst. Administrator: Craig Hooks (Acting)

Office of Air and Radiation (OAR)
1200 Pennsylvania Ave. N.W., Mailcode 6101A, Washington, DC 20460
(202) 564-7400; Fax: (202) 501-0986
Internet: www.epa.gov/oar
Asst. Admin.: Gina McCarthy (202) 564-7404
Associate General Counsel: Richard Ossias, Mailcode 2344A
(202) 564-5559

Office of Enforcement and Compliance Assurance (OECA)
1200 Pennsylvania Ave. N.W., Mailcode 2201A, Washington, DC 20460
(202) 564-2440; Fax: (202) 501-3842
Internet: www.epa.gov/compliance
Asst. Admin.: Cynthia Giles

Office of Inspector General (OIG)
1200 Pennsylvania Ave. N.W., Mailcode 2410T, Washington, DC 20460
(202) 566-0847; Hotline: (888) 546-8740;
Fax: (202) 566-0857
Internet: www.epa.gov/oigearth
Inspector General: Arthur A. Elkins, Jr.
(202) 564-5567
Deputy Inspector General: Bill A. Roderick (Acting)
(202) 566-2212
E-mail: roderick.bill@epa.gov
Counsel: Mark Bialek, Mailcode 2411T
(202) 566-0861; Fax: (202) 566-0870
E-mail: bialek.mark@epa.gov

Office of International and Tribal Affairs (OITA)
1200 Pennsylvania Ave. N.W., Mailcode 2610R, Washington, DC 20460
(202) 564-6600; Fax: (202) 565-2411
Internet: www.epa.gov/oia/index.html
Asst. Administrator: Michelle J. DePass
(202) 564-6600

Office of Chief Financial Officer (OCFO)
1200 Pennsylvania Ave. N.W., Mailcode 2710A, Washington, DC 20460
(202) 564-1151; Fax: (202) 501-0771
E-mail: ocfoinfo@epa.gov
Internet: www.epa.gov/ocfopage
Chief Financial Officer: Barbara T. Bennett
E-mail: bennett.barbara@epa.gov

Office of Chemical Safety and Pollution Prevention (OCSPP)
1200 Pennsylvania Ave. N.W., Mailcode 7101M, Washington, DC 20460
(202) 564-2902; Fax: (202) 564-0512
Internet: www.epa.gov/oppts
Asst. Administrator: Steve Owens
Principal Dep. Asst. Administrator: Jim Jones
E-mail: jones.jim@epa.gov

Implementation of Federal Insecticide, Fungicide & Rodenticide Act; Food Quality Protection Act; Toxic Substances Control Act; Emergency Planning and Community Right to Know Act.

Formerly called Office of Prevention, Pesticides and Toxic Substances

Environmental Protection Administration—Cont'd

Office of Research and Development (ORD)
1200 Pennsylvania Ave. N.W., Mailcode 8102R,
Washington, DC 20460
(202) 564-6620; Fax: (202) 565-2431
Internet: www.epa.gov/ord

Asst. Administrator: Paul T. Anastas

Deputy Asst. Administrator for Science: Dr. Kevin Teichman

Office of Solid Waste and Emergency Response (OSWER)
1301 Constitution Ave. N.W., Room 3146,
Washington, DC 20004
Mailing Address:
1200 Pennsylvania Ave. N.W., Mailcode 5101T,
Washington, DC 20460
(202) 566-0200; Fax: (202) 566-0207
Internet: www.epa.gov/osw

Asst. Admin.: Mathy Stanislaus

Assoc. General Counsel: John Michaud (Acting) Mailcode 2366A (202) 564-5518

Office of Water (OW)
1200 Pennsylvania Ave. N.W., Mailcode 4101M,
Washington, DC 20460
(202) 564-5700; Fax: (202) 564-0488

Asst. Administrator: Peter S. Silva

EQUAL EMPLOYMENT OPPORTUNITY COMMISSION

131 M St., N.E., 4th Floor, Washington, DC 20507
(202) 663-4900; TTY: (202) 663-4494;
Outside of Washington, DC: (800) 669-4000;
TTY (Outside of Washington, DC): (800) 669-6820
Internet: www.eeoc.gov

Chair: Jacqueline A. Berrien, Room 10006 (202) 663-4001

Chief Operating Officer: Anthony Kaminski (Acting) Room 10010

General Counsel: P. David Lopez (202) 663-4705

Inspector General: Milton A. Mayo, Jr., Room 3003 (202) 663-4327, (800) 849-4230; Fax: (202) 663-7204

Dir., Office of Communication & Legislative Affairs: Karen Pedrick (202) 663-4900

Eliminates discrimination in employment hiring, promotion, training, apprenticeship, testing, training, and wages. Conducts investigations, files lawsuits, attempts mediation, and assists employers in voluntary program implementation. *42 U.S.C. 2000e; Title VII; Americans with Disabilities Act; Age Discrimination In Employment or Equal Pay Act*

EXPORT-IMPORT BANK OF THE UNITED STATES

811 Vermont Ave. N.W., Washington, DC 20571
(202) 565-3946, (800) 565-3946; Fax: (202) 565-3380
E-mail: info@exim.gov
Internet: www.exim.gov

Chairman and President: Fred P. Hochberg, Room 1215 (202) 565-3337

Sr. V.P. & General Counsel: Jonathan J. Cardone Room 947 (202) 565-3460

Facilitates financing of exports of U.S. goods and services through loans, loan guarantees, and export credit insurance where private sector financing otherwise would not be available. *12 U.S.C. 635*

Export Import Bank of the United States Northeast & Mid-Atlantic Regional Office
33 Whitehall St., Suite B, 22nd Floor, New York, NY 10004
(212) 809-2650; Fax: (212) 809-2687

Regional Dir.: Thomas Cummings (N.Y. & N.J.) (212) 809-2652; E-mail: thomas.cummings@exim.gov

Business Development Officer: Bruce Drossman (212) 809-2651

Business Development Asst.: Jennifer Drakes (General Info. and Forms Requests) (212) 809-2649

FARM CREDIT ADMINISTRATION

1501 Farm Credit Dr., McLean, VA 22102-5090
(703) 883-4000; Fax: (703) 734-5784
E-mail: info-line@fca.gov
Internet: www.fca.gov

Chairperson: Leland A. Strom (703) 883-4005

General Counsel: Charles R. Rawls (703) 883-4020

Ensures safe and sound operation of the banks, associations, affiliated service organizations, and other entities that comprise the Farm Credit System. *12 U.S.C. 2241*

CoBank
5500 S. Quebec St., Greenwood Village, CO 80111
Mailing Address: P.O. Box 5110, Denver, CO 80217
(800) 542-8072
Internet: www.cobank.com

President/C.E.O.: Robert B. Engel (303) 740-6498 E-mail: bengel@cobank.com

C.O.O.: Mary E. McBride (303) 740-4055 E-mail: mcbridem@cobank.com

Chief Financial Officer: David P. Burlage (303) 740-6464; E-mail: dburlage@cobank.com

Chief Legal and Regulatory Officer: Mark W. Yonkman (303) 740-4178; E-mail: myonkman@cobank.com

Board Chairman: Everett Dobrinski

First Vice Chair: Daniel T. Kelley E-mail: dkelley@growmark.com

Cooperative bank serving agricultural and rural needs. Part of the Farm Credit System, a privately owned Federally chartered organization regulated by the Farm Credit Administration.

FEDERAL COMMUNICATIONS COMMISSION

445 12th St. S.W., Washington, DC 20554
Consumer Information:
(202) 418-0260, (888) 225-5322;
Library: (202) 418-0450;
Media Bureau: (202) 418-7200;
Public Affairs: (202) 418-0503;
TDD: (202) 418-2555, (888) 835-5322;
Procurement Branch: (202) 418-0930;
Personnel: (202) 418-0130;
Personnel Locator: (202) 418-0126;
Fax: (202) 418-2830
E-mail: fccinfo@fcc.gov
Internet: www.fcc.gov

Chairman: Julius Genachowski (Acting) (202) 418-1000

General Counsel: Austin Schlick (Acting) (202) 418-1752

Regulates interstate and foreign communication by radio, television, wire, satellite, and cable. Oversees the orderly development and operation of broadcast services, telephone and telegraph services at reasonable rates. *15 U.S.C.; 21 U.S.C.; 47 U.S.C. 35, 151*

District Office
201 Varick St., Room 1151, New York, NY 10014-7046
(888) 225-5322; Fax: (212) 620-3718
E-mail: newyork@fcc.gov
Internet: www.fcc.gov/eb

District Dir.: Daniel W. Noel (212) 337-1865; Fax: (212) 620-3718

Office of Administrative Law Judges
445 12th St. S.W., Washington, DC 20554

Chief Admin. Law Judge: Richard L. Sippel, Room 1-C768 (202) 418-2280

Admin. Law Judge: Vacancy at Press Time (202) 418-2254

Admin. Officer: Mary L. Gosse (202) 418-2299

Media Bureau
445 12th St. S.W., Room 3-C734, Washington, DC 20554
(202) 418-7200, 418-1198; Fax: (202) 418-2376
Internet: www.fcc.gov/mb

Chief: William T. Lake

Administers the regulatory program for AM, FM, low power FM, low power TV, Television; Cable television and post-licensing satellite matters.

Federal Communications Commission—Cont'd

Wireline Competition Bureau
445 12th St. S.W., 5th Floor, Washington, DC 20554
(202) 418-1500; TTY: (202) 418-0484; Fax: (202) 418-2825
Internet: www.fcc.gov/wcb

Chief: Sharon Gillett

Responsible for FCC policies concerning telephone companies that provide interstate telecommunications services to the public through the use of wire-based transmission facilities. These companies, called common carriers, provide voice, data and other transmission services.

Formerly called Common Carrier Bureau

Wireless Telecommunications Bureau
445 12th St. S.W., Washington, DC 20554
(202) 418-0600; Fax: (202) 418-0787
Internet: http://wireless.fcc.gov

Chief: Ruth Milkman

Develops, recommends and administers the Commission's policies, programs and rules governing domestic wireless telecommunications except satellite communications.

Formerly called Private Radio Communications

Office of Engineering and Technology
445 12th St. S.W., Suite 7C155, Washington, DC 20554
(202) 418-2470; Fax: (202) 418-1944
Internet: www.fcc.gov/oet

Chief: Julius P. Knapp

Deputy Chiefs:
Ira Keltz
Alan Stillwell
Ron Repasi

Administers the table of frequency allocations, the Experimental Radio Service, and Equipment Authorization Program.

Consumer and Governmental Affairs Bureau
445 12th St. S.W., Room CYB514, Washington, DC 20554
(888) 225-5322; Fax: (866) 418-0232; TTY: (888) 835-5322
Internet: www.fcc.gov/cgb

Chief: Joel Gurin (202) 418-1400; Fax: (202) 418-2983

FEDERAL DEPOSIT INSURANCE CORPORATION
550 17th St. N.W., Washington, DC 20429-9990
(202) 736-0000, (877) 275-3342
E-mail: publicinfo@fdic.gov
Internet: www.fdic.gov

Chair: Sheila C. Bair (202) 898-6974
General Counsel: Michael Bradfield (202) 898-3645
Dir., Division of Supervision & Consumer Protection: Sandra L. Thompson (202) 898-6636
Dir., Division of Finance: Bret D. Edwards (202) 562-6101
Dir., Division of Information Technology: Russell G. Pittman (703) 516-5781
Dir., Division of Insurance and Research: Arthur J. Murton (202) 898-3938
Inspector General: Jon T. Rymer
3501 N. Fairfax Dr., Room VA-D-9069, Arlington, VA 22226 (800) 964-3342

Promotes and preserves public confidence in the banking system and protects the money supply by providing insurance for bank deposits and periodic examinations of state chartered banks that are not members of the Federal Reserve System. *12 U.S.C. 1811*

Regional Office
350 Fifth Ave., New York, NY 10118-0110
(917) 320-2500; Fax: (800) 334-9593

Regional Dir.: Doreen R. Eberley (917) 320-2575

FEDERAL ELECTION COMMISSION
999 E St. N.W., Washington, DC 20463
(202) 694-1100, (800) 424-9530; TTY: (202) 219-3336
Internet: www.fec.gov

Chairman: Matthew S. Petersen (202) 694-1000
General Counsel: Thomasina Duncan
(202) 694-1650; Fax: (202) 219-3923

Exercises exclusive jurisdiction over the administration and civil enforcement of federal laws pertaining to acquisition and expenditure of funds to influence elections to federal office. *2 U.S.C. §§431-455 and 26 U.S.C. §§9001-9042*

FEDERAL LABOR RELATIONS AUTHORITY
1400 K St. N.W., Washington, DC 20424-0001
(202) 218-7770; Fax: (202) 482-6635
Internet: www.flra.gov

Chairman: Carol Waller Pope (202) 218-7945
Exec. Dir.: Sonna Stampone
(202) 218-7941; Fax: (202) 482-6635
General Counsel: Julia Akins Clark
(202) 218-7910; Fax: (202) 482-6608

Administers the Federal Service Labor-Management Relations Statute, resolving disputes between Federal Agencies and unions. *5 U.S.C. Chapter 71*

Regional Office
10 Causeway St., Suite 472, Boston, MA 02222
(617) 565-5100; Fax: (617) 565-6262

Regional Dir.: Philip Roberts (Acting)

Office of Administrative Law Judges
1400 K St. N.W., Suite 300, Washington, DC 20424
(202) 218-7950; Fax: (202) 482-6629
Internet: www.flra.gov

Chief Admin. Law Judge: Charles Center

Admin. Law Judges:
Susan Jelen
Richard Pearson

FEDERAL MARITIME COMMISSION
800 North Capitol St. N.W., Washington, DC 20573-0001
(202) 523-5725
Internet: www.fmc.gov

Chairman: Richard A. Lidinsky, Jr.
(202) 523-5911; Fax: (202) 523-4224
E-mail: chairman@fmc.gov
Secretary: Karen V. Gregory
(202) 523-5725; Fax: (202) 523-0014
E-mail: secretary@fmc.gov
General Counsel: Vacancy at Press Time
(202) 523-5740; Fax: (202) 523-5738

The Federal Maritime Commission regulates the waterborne foreign commerce of the United States. It ensures that U.S. oceanborne trades are open to all on fair and equitable terms and protects against concerned activities and unlawful practices. *5 U.S.C. app. Reorganization Plan No. 7 of 1961, 75 Stat. 840*

Office of Administrative Law Judges
800 N. Capitol St., N.W., Room 1088,
Washington, DC 20573
(202) 523-5750; Fax: (202) 566-0042
Internet: www.fmc.gov

Admin. Law Judges:
Clay G. Guthridge (Chief)
Erin M. Wirth

The judges act as trial judges presiding over and issuing decisions in formal proceedings involving alleged violation of Federal shipping regulatory law.

FEDERAL MEDIATION AND CONCILIATION SERVICE
2100 K St. N.W., Washington, DC 20427
(202) 606-8100; Arbitration Division: (202) 606-5111;
Fax: (202) 606-4251
Internet: www.fmcs.gov

Director: George H. Cohen
Chief Financial Officer: Frances Leonard
General Counsel: Dawn E. Starr (202) 606-5444

Prevents work stoppages, advocates collective bargaining, and promotes sound labor-management relations through effective mediation and voluntary arbitration programs. *29 U.S.C. 172.*

Northeast Sub-Regional Office
Woodbridge Place Bldg., Suite 3020, 517 U.S. Hwy. 1 S., Iselin, NJ 08830
(732) 726-2181; Fax: (732) 726-2188

Dir. of Mediation Services: John E. Sweeney
(732) 726-3121

Federal Mediation and Conciliation Service, Northeast Sub-Regional Office—Cont'd

Commissioners:
Anthony Bauman (732) 791-1612
Peter W. Donatello (732) 726-2182
James Kinney (732) 726-2183
John J. Muir (516) 338-5964
Kathleen Murray-Cannon (845) 778-0156
Ralph Quattrocchi (631) 960-0141
Guy A. Serota, Suite 2104 (732) 726-2181
Carlos Tatte, Suite 2104 (732) 726-2185
David Thaler, Suite 2104 (732) 726-3123

Local Office
952 Leo O'Brien Federal Bldg., 11A Clinton Sq., Albany, NY 12207 (518) 431-0130; Fax: (518) 431-4327

Mediator: Edward H. Jones (518) 431-0130
E-mail: ejones@fmcs.gov

Federal Mediation and Concilation Service
Local Office
James M. Hanley U.S. Cthse. & Fed. Bldg., Room 840, 100 S. Clinton St., Syracuse, NY 13261-7129
(315) 448-7631; Fax: (315) 448-7632

Mediators:
Edward Garrow (315) 448-7631; E-mail: egarrow@fmcs.gov
Thomas J. Pollard (315) 448-7630; E-mail: tpollard@fmcs.gov

Local Office
100 Corporate Pkwy., Suite 134, Amherst, NY 14226
(716) 838-5097; Fax: (716) 838-5136

Mediators:
Kenneth Armes (716) 838-5097; E-mail: karmes@fmcs.gov
Mary Kluczycki (716) 838-5098
E-mail: mkluczycki@fmcs.gov

Office of the Director of Field Operations
6161 Oak Tree Blvd., Suite 120, Independence, OH 44131
(216) 520-4800; Fax: (216) 520-4815

Dir. of Field Operations: Jack Buettner
E-mail: jbuetter@fmcs.gov

D.M.S's:
D. Scott Blake
(Field Station Responsibility—Albany, NY and Trenton, NJ) (215) 717-7500; E-mail: sblake@fmcs.gov
Jack Sweeney
(Field Station Responsibility—Newark, NJ, Woodbridge, NJ, Boston, MA, New York, NY) (732) 726-3122
E-mail: jsweeney@fmcs.gov

FEDERAL MINE SAFETY AND HEALTH REVIEW COMMISSION

601 New Jersey Ave. N.W., Suite 9500, Washington, DC 20001-2021
(202) 434-9900; Fax: (202) 434-9944
E-mail: fmshrc@fmshrc.gov
Internet: www.fmshrc.gov

1244 Speer Blvd., Room 280, Denver, CO 80204
(303) 844-5267; Fax: (303) 844-5268

Chairperson: Mary Lucille Jordan
(202) 434-9926; Fax: (202) 434-9944

General Counsel: Michael McCord
(202) 434-9935; Fax: (202) 434-9944

Adjudicates disputes regarding compliance with occupational safety and health standards in the Nation's surface and underground metal, coal, and non-metal mines. *30 U.S.C. 801*

FEDERAL RESERVE SYSTEM

Board of Governors of the Federal Reserve System
20th St. & Constitution Ave. N.W., Washington, DC 20551
(202) 452-3000; Publications: (202) 452-3245; Fax: (202) 452-3819
Internet: www.federalreserve.gov

Chairman: Ben S. Bernanke

General Counsel: Scott G. Alvarez, Room B-1046
(202) 452-3583; Fax: (202) 452-3101

Leads the Nation's monetary and credit affairs as the central bank of the United States. Supervises and regulates the banking system to ensure a sound and capable system that can respond to the needs of the Nation. *12 U.S.C. 221*

FEDERAL RETIREMENT THRIFT INVESTMENT BOARD

1250 H St. N.W., Suite 200, Washington, DC 20005
(202) 942-1600; Fax: (202) 942-1676
Internet: www.tsp.gov; www.frtib.gov

Exec. Dir.: Gregory T. Long

General Counsel: Thomas K. Emswiler (202) 942-1660

Administers the Thrift Savings Plan which provides federal employees the same type of savings and tax benefits that many private corporations offer their employees under so-called 401 (k) plans. *5 U.S.C.§§8351 and 8401-8479.*

FEDERAL TRADE COMMISSION

600 Pennsylvania Ave. N.W., Washington, DC 20580
General Information: (202) 326-2222;
Antitrust: (202) 326-3300;
Consumer Protection: (877) 382-4357;
Inspector General: (202) 326-2800;
Procurement: (202) 326-2258;
Personnel (Employee Development & Relations): (202) 326-3633; Press Office: (202) 326-2180;
Phone Mail System: (202) 326-2000
Internet: www.ftc.gov

Chair: Jon Leibowitz, Room H-338
(202) 326-3400; Fax: (202) 326-3442

General Counsel: Willard Tom (202) 326-2424

Maintains the competitive nature of the United States by working to prevent monopolies, unfair trade practices, and restraints to trade, keeping competition free and fair. *15 U.S.C. 41*

Office of Administrative Law Judges
600 Pennsylvania Ave. N.W., Room H, Washington, DC 20580

Chief Admin. Law Judge: D. Michael Chappell (Acting)
Room H-106 (202) 326-3637; Fax: (202) 326-2427

Northeast Regional Office
1 Bowling Green, Suite 318, New York, NY 10004
(212) 607-2829
Internet: www.ftc.gov

Director: Leonard L. Gordon

Asst. Dir.: Deborah Marrone

GENERAL SERVICES ADMINISTRATION

1800 F St. N.W., Washington, DC 20405
(202) 501-0800
Internet: www.gsa.gov

Administrator: Martha N. Johnson
(202) 501-0800; Fax: (202) 219-1243

General Counsel: Kris E. Durmer
(202) 501-2200; Fax: (202) 501-2509

Establishes policy for and administers management of real estate and other property of the U.S. government including construction and operation of buildings; procurement and distribution of supplies, furnishings, and equipment; utilization and disposal of property; and procurement and management of transportation, technology, telecommunications, and other administrative services. *40 U.S.C. 471*

Regional Office
Federal Bldg., Room 18-100, 26 Federal Plaza, New York, NY 10278
General Information: (212) 264-3305;
Small Business Utilization Office: (212) 264-1234
Internet: www.gsa.gov

Regional Administrator: Denise L. Pease (212) 264-2600
E-mail: denise.pease@gsa.gov

Regional Counsel: Carol A. Latterman (212) 264-8308
E-mail: carol.latterman@gsa.gov

Federal Citizen Information Center
Pueblo, CO 81009
(888) 878-3256
Internet: www.pueblo.gsa.gov; www.usa.gov

A clearinghouse for information about the Federal Government. Persons with questions about a Government Program or Agency, and who are unsure of which office can help, may call or write the Center. A specialist will either answer the question or locate an expert who can.

General Services Administration—Cont'd

Chief Information Officer
General Services Bldg., 1800 F St. N.W.,
Washington, DC 20405
(202) 501-1000; Fax: (202) 501-0022

Chief Information Officer: Casey Coleman
E-mail: casey.coleman@gsa.gov

Manages the operation and procurement of government wide automatic data processing equipment, resources, and procedures.

Federal Acquisition Service
2200 Crystal Dr., 11th Floor, Arlington, VA 22202
E-mail: contactfas@gsa.gov

Commissioner: Steven J. Kempf (Acting)
(703) 605-5400

Contracts for and distributes personal property and services for the Federal agencies.

Public Buildings Service
General Services Administration, Room 6340,
1800 F St. N.W., Washington, DC 20405
(202) 501-1100; Fax: (202) 219-2310

Commissioner: Robert A. Peck; E-mail: bob.peck@gsa.gov

Oversees and manages the design, construction, lease, purchase, repair, appraisal, maintenance, and protection of many public buildings comprising 250 million square feet of space.

Human Resources Division
Office of Chief Human Capital Officer
1800 F St. N.W., Room 6242, Washington, DC 20405
(202) 501-0398; Fax: (202) 219-0982

Chief Human Capital Officer: Gail T. Lovelace
E-mail: gail.lovelace@gsa.gov

OFFICE OF GOVERNMENT ETHICS
**1201 New York Ave. N.W., Suite 500,
Washington, DC 20005-3917
(202) 482-9300; TTY: (800) 877-8339;
Fax: (202) 482-9237
Internet: www.usoge.gov**

Director: Robert I. Cusick
(202) 482-9292; Fax: (202) 482-9237

General Counsel: Don W. Fox
(202) 482-9292; Fax: (202) 482-9237

Provides overall direction to the Executive branch in the prevention and management of conflicts of interest. This is the lead agency in the administration and interpretation of the Ethics in Government Act for the Executive branch. *5 U.S.C. app. 401*

INTER-AMERICAN FOUNDATION
**901 Stuart St., 10th Floor, Arlington, VA 22203
(703) 306-4301; Fax: (703) 306-4365
Internet: www.iaf.gov**

Chairperson: John P. Salazar
President: Larry Palmer
General Counsel: Jennifer Hodges

Supports economic and social grassroots development in Latin America and the Caribbean. *22 U.S.C. 290f*

MERIT SYSTEMS PROTECTION BOARD
**1615 M St. N.W., Washington, DC 20419
(202) 653-7200, (800) 209-8960; Fax: (202) 653-7130
E-mail: mspb@mspb.gov
Internet: www.mspb.gov**

Chair: Susan Tsui Grundmann
Clerk of the Board: William D. Spencer
General Counsel: James Eisenmann
(202) 653-7171; Fax: (202) 653-6203

Protects the integrity of the Federal Merit principles and the rights of the workers in the system. Adjudicates Federal employee appeals of removals and other significant employment actions. Conducts studies of the Civil Service and other Federal Merit systems; reviews regulations of the Office of Personnel Management. *5 U.S.C. 1201*

Northeastern Regional Office
1601 Market St., Suite 1700, Philadelphia, PA 19103
(215) 597-9960; Fax: (215) 597-3456

Chief Admin. Judge: William L. Boulden

Field Office (including New York and North and Central Jersey areas)
26 Federal Plaza, Room 3137A,
New York, NY 10278-0022
(212) 264-9372; Fax: (212) 264-1417

Chief Administrative Judge: Arthur S. Joseph

U.S. Office of Special Counsel
1730 M St. N.W., Suite 218, Washington, DC 20036-4505
(202) 254-3600; Fax: (202) 254-3711
Internet: www.osc.gov

Special Counsel: Vacancy at Press Time

Assoc. Special Counsel: William E. Reukauf

The U.S. Office of Special Counsel (OSC) is an independent investigative and prosecutorial agency and operates as a secure channel for disclosures of whistleblower complaints and abuse of authority. Its primary mission is to safeguard the merit system in Federal employment by protecting Federal employees and applicants from prohibited personnel practices, especially retaliation for whistleblowing. OSC also has jurisdiction over the Hatch Act and the Uniformed Services Employment and Reemployment Rights Act. For more information please visit our web site at www.osc.gov or call 1-800-872-9855.

NATIONAL AERONAUTICS AND SPACE ADMINISTRATION
300 E St. S.W., Washington, DC 20024-3210

**Mailing Address: NASA Headquarters, Suite 5K39, Washington, DC 20496-0001
(202) 358-0001; Fax: (202) 358-3469
Internet: www.nasa.gov**

Administrator: Charles E. Bolden, Jr. (202) 358-1010

General Counsel: Michael C. Wholley
(202) 358-2450; Fax: (202) 358-2741

Conducts research for the solution of problems of flights within and outside the Earth's atmosphere and develops, tests, constructs, and operates aeronautical and space vehicles, explores space with manned and unmanned projects, and utilizes the resources of the United States and other nations engaged in space activities for peaceful purposes. *42 U.S.C. 2451*

NATIONAL ARCHIVES AND RECORDS ADMINISTRATION
**8601 Adelphi Rd., College Park, MD 20740-6001
(866) 272-6272; Fax: (301) 837-0483
Internet: www.archives.gov**

Archivist of the United States: David Ferriero
Room 4200

General Counsel: Gary M. Stern, Room 3110
(301) 837-1750; Fax: (301) 837-0293
E-mail: garym.stern@nara.gov

Ensures ready access to essential evidence that documents the rights of American citizens, the actions of Federal officials, and the national experience; establishes policies and procedures for managing U.S. Government records assists Federal agencies in documenting their activities, administering records management programs, scheduling records, and retiring noncurrent records; NARA accessions, arranges, describes, preserves, and provides access to the essential documentation of the three branches of Government; manages the Presidential Libraries system; and publishes the laws, regulations, and Presidential and other public documents; assists the Information Security Oversight Office, which manages Federal classification and declassification policies, and the National Historical Publications and Records Commission. *44 U.S.C. 2101*

Regional Office
201 Varick St., 12th Floor, New York, NY 10014
(212) 401-1620, (866) 840-1752; Fax: (212) 401-1638
E-mail: newyork.archives@nara.gov

Regional Administrator: Diane LeBlanc (781) 663-0133

Asst. Regional Administrator: David Powers (Acting)
(781) 663-0140

Regional Facility Dir.: David Powers (781) 633-0140
E-mail: david.powers@nara.gov

In the Fall of 2011 this office will be moving to Custom House Bldg., 3rd & 4th Flrs., One Bowling Green, New York, NY 10004

National Archives and Records Administration—Cont'd

Office of Regional Records Services
National Archives at College Park, 8601 Adelphi Rd., College Park, MD 20740
(301) 837-1982; Fax: (301) 837-1617

Director: Tom Mills

Office of Records Services—Washington, D.C.
National Archives and Records Administration, 8601 Adelphi Rd., College Park, MD 20740
(301) 837-3110; Fax: (301) 837-3633

Asst. Archivist: Dr. Michael J. Kurtz, Room 3400
E-mail: michael.kurtz@nara.gov

Formerly known as Office of Records Management

Foundation for the National Archives
700 Pennsylvania Ave. N.W., Room G9, Washington, DC 20408 (202) 357-5946
E-mail: museumprograms@nara.gov
Internet: www.archives.gov/nae

Exec. Dir.: Thora S.R. Colot

Counsel: Theodore Segal

Brings the resources of the National Archives to the public through educational workshops and materials, exhibitions, film programs, publications, lectures, genealogy programs, tours, museum shop and other outreach activities.

Office of Special and Regional Archives

All functions now handled by the Office of Regional Records Services, supra

Office of the Federal Register
National Archives and Records Administration, 800 North Capitol St. N.W., Suite 700, Washington, DC 20001
(202) 741-6000; Fax: (202) 741-6012
E-mail: fedreg.info@nara.gov
Internet: www.archives.gov/federal-register; www.gpoaccess.gov/nara

Director: Raymond A. Mosley
E-mail: ray.mosley@nara.gov

Dir., Legal Affairs and Policy: Amy Bunk (202) 741-6030

Provides ready access to the official text of the Public Laws, Presidential documents, Federal administrative regulations and notices, and descriptions of Federal organizations, programs and actitivies. Publishes the daily *Federal Register* and the *Code of Federal Regulations* (CFR) in print and online formats. Administers the constitutional amendment process and coordinates the functions of the Electoral College.*44 U.S.C. Chap. 15.*

Office of Records Administration

All functions now handled by the Office of Records Services, supra

Office of Presidential Libraries
National Archives at College Park, 8601 Adelphi Rd., College Park, MD 20740-6001
(301) 837-3250; Fax: (301) 837-3199

Asst. Archivist for Presidential Libraries: Sharon Fawcett

NATIONAL CAPITAL PLANNING COMMISSION

401 9th St., N.W., North Lobby, Suite 500, Washington, DC 20004
(202) 482-7200; Fax: (202) 482-7272
Internet: www.ncpc.gov

Chairman: L. Preston Bryant, Jr.

Exec. Dir.: Marcel Acosta

General Counsel: Peter D. Coppelman (Acting)

The National Capital Planning Commission is the federal government's central planning agency charged with protecting the federal interest in the National Capital Region. NCPC's jurisdiction covers 2,500 square miles, and includes the District of Columbia and surrounding counties in Maryland and Virginia. The Commission reviews development plans and projects, reviews Federal Capital Improvement Programs, and conducts comprehensive and long-range planning. *See 40 U.S.C.§§ 8701 et seq*

NATIONAL CONSUMER COOPERATIVE BANK

d.b.a. National Cooperative Bank
601 Pennsylvania Ave. N.W., Suite 750, Washington, DC 20004
(202) 349-7444, (800) 955-9622; Fax: (202) 349-7443
Internet: www.ncb.coop

President and Chief Executive Officer:
Charles E. Snyder (202) 336-7610
E-mail: csnyder@ncb.com

Counsel: Chad Oppenheimer (202) 349-7447

A unique financial services company that provides financial products and services to U.S. commercial and real estate ventures governed by certain cooperative principles. Primary lines of business include: real estate lending, commercial lending, small business lending, capital markets capabilities, community development expertise and retail banking through its subsidiary, NCB Savings Bank FSB.

National Cooperative Bank Regional Office
250 Park Ave., Suite 900, New York, NY 10177
(212) 808-0880, (800) 668-9417; Fax: (212) 808-4396

Managing Dir., N.Y. Real Estate Team: Edward Howe III

This office handles two divisions: cooperative housing loans (blanket loans for cooperative housing buildings) team and (loans to individuals who purchase a share a.k.a. unit in a housing cooperative) team.

NATIONAL CREDIT UNION ADMINISTRATION

1775 Duke St., Alexandria, VA 22314-3428
(703) 518-6300; Fax: (703) 518-6319, 518-6660
E-mail: boardmail@ncua.gov
Internet: www.ncua.gov

Chair: Debbie Matz

General Counsel: Robert M. Fenner
(703) 518-6540; Fax: (703) 518-6569, 518-6667
E-mail: ogcmail@ncua.gov

Charters, insures, supervises, and examines Federal Credit Unions and administers the National Credit Union Share Insurance Fund. Manages the Central Liquidity Facility which provides emergency loans to member credit unions. *12 U.S.C. 1752*

Regional Office
9 Washington Square, Washington Ave. Extension, Albany, NY 12205
(518) 862-7400; Fax: (518) 862-7420
E-mail: region1@ncua.gov

Director: Mark A. Treichel

NATIONAL ENDOWMENT FOR THE ARTS

1100 Pennsylvania Ave. N.W., Washington, DC 20506
(202) 682-5400; Fax: (202) 682-5572
E-mail: webmgr@arts.endow.gov
Internet: www.nea.gov

Chairperson: Rocco Landesman
(202) 682-5414; Fax: (202) 682-5639

General Counsel: Karen Elias (Acting)
(202) 682-5418; Fax: (202) 682-5572

Fosters the excellence, diversity and vitality of the arts in the United States; and broadens public access to the arts. *20 U.S.C. 951*

NATIONAL ENDOWMENT FOR THE HUMANITIES

1100 Pennsylvania Ave. N.W., Washington, DC 20506
Public Information Office: (202) 606-8400; (800) 634-1121; Fax: (202) 606-8240;
TDD: (866) 372-2930, (202) 606-8282
E-mail: info@neh.gov
Internet: www.neh.gov

Chair: James A. Leach, Room 503
(202) 606-8310

General Counsel: Michelle Ghim, Room 530
(202) 606-8322

Supports research, education, and public programs in the humanities through a grant-making program. *20 U.S.C. 951*

NATIONAL LABOR RELATIONS BOARD
1099 14th St. N.W., Suite 982,
Washington, DC 20570-0001
(202) 273-1000, (866) 667-6572;
Public Information: (202) 273-1991;
TDD: (202) 273-4300; (866) 315-6572
Internet: www.nlrb.gov

Chairman: Wilma Liebman (202) 273-1700

Executive Secretary: Lester A. Heltzer (202) 273-1067

General Counsel: Ronald E. Meisburg (202) 273-3700

Dir., Division of Administration: Gloria J. Joseph (202) 273-3890

Dir., Officer of Equal Employment Opportunity: Robert J. Poindexter (202) 273-3891

Administers the National Labor Relations Act as the principal labor law of the United States governing relations between unions and employers in the private sector. Prevents and remedies unfair labor practices; determines, through secret-ballot elections, the free democratic choice by employees to be represented by a union and if so, which union. *29 U.S.C. 167*

Division of Judges
1099 14th St. N.W., Suite 5400E,
Washington, DC 20570-0001
(202) 501-8800; Fax: (202) 501-8686

Chief Admin. Law Judge: Robert A. Giannasi

Assoc. Chief Admin. Law Judge: Arthur Amchan

Admin. Law Judges:

George Aleman	Michael Rosas
Paul A. Bogas	Bruce D. Rosenstein
Paul Buxbaum	Mark Rubin
Mark Carissimi	Ira Sandron
John Clark	Earl Shamwell, Jr.
Eric Fine	Jeff Wedekind
David Goldman	

Division of Judges
120 W. 45th St., 11th Floor, New York, NY 10036
(212) 944-2941; Fax: (212) 944-4904

Chief Admin. Law Judge: Joel P. Biblowitz

Admin. Law Judges:

Steven Davis	Mindy Landow
Steven Fish	Eleanor MacDonald
Raymond P. Green	

Region 2 Office
26 Federal Plaza, Room 3614, New York, NY 10278-0104
(212) 264-0300; Fax: (212) 264-2450
Internet: www.nlrb.gov

Regional Dir.: Celeste J. Mattina (212) 264-0330

Regional Atty.: Karen P. Fernbach (212) 264-0332
E-mail: karen.fernbach@nlrb.gov

Asst. to Regional Dir.: Elbert F. Tellem
(212) 264-0334
E-mail: elbert.tellem@nlrb.gov

Region 29 Office
Two Metro Tech Center, 5th Floor, 100 Myrtle Ave.,
Brooklyn, NY 11201-4201
(718) 330-7713; Fax: (718) 330-7579

Regional Dir.: Alvin P. Blyer

Region 3 Office
130 S. Elmwood Ave., Suite 630, Buffalo, NY 14202-2465
(716) 551-4931; Fax: (716) 551-4972

Regional Dir.: Rhonda P. Ley
(716) 651-5514; Fax: (716) 551-4972

Regional Atty.: Michael Israel (716) 551-4947

Asst. to Regional Dir.: Paul J. Murphy (716) 551-4935

Resident Office—Region 3
Leo W. O'Brien Federal Bldg., Room 342,
Clinton Ave. at Pearl St., Albany, NY 12207-2350
(518) 431-4155; Fax: (518) 431-5157

Resident Officer: Barnett Horowitz (518) 431-4156

NATIONAL MEDIATION BOARD
1301 K St. N.W., Suite 250 East,
Washington, DC 20005
(202) 692-5000; Information Hot Line: (202) 692-5050
Internet: www.nmb.gov

Chairman: Harry R. Hoglander
(202) 692-5022; Fax: (202) 692-5082

Members:
Elizabeth Dougherty
(202) 692-5016; Fax: (202) 692-5082
Linda Puchala (202) 692-5019

Dir., Mediation Services: Larry Gibbons
(202) 692-5030; Fax: (202) 692-5084

Dir., ADR Services: Daniel Rainey
(202) 692-5050; Fax: (202) 692-5083

General Counsel: Mary Johnson
(202) 692-5040; Fax: (202) 692-5085

Dir., Arbitration Services: Roland Watkins
(202) 692-5055; Fax: (202) 692-5086

Dir., Office of Administration: June D.W. King
(202) 692-5010; Fax: (202) 692-5081

Resolves disputes in rail and airline management-labor relations in accordance with the Railway Labor Act and provides administrative and financial support in adjusting minor grievances in the railroad industry. *45 U.S.C. 151*

NATIONAL RAILROAD PASSENGER CORPORATION (AMTRAK)
60 Massachusetts Ave. N.E., Washington, DC 20002
(202) 906-3000; Fax: (202) 906-3865
Internet: www.amtrak.com

President & C.E.O.: Joseph Boardman
(202) 906-3960; Fax: (202) 906-2850

General Counsel & Corporate Secy.:
Eleanor D. Acheson
(202) 906-2198; Fax: (202) 906-2821

Develops, operates, and improves a modern inter-city rail transportation system for the nation's transportation needs.

Now a Private Corporation operating passenger rail service.

NATIONAL SCIENCE FOUNDATION
4201 Wilson Blvd., Arlington, VA 22230
(703) 292-5111; TDD: (800) 281-8749
Internet: www.nsf.gov

Director: Dr. Arden L. Bement, Jr.
(703) 292-8000; Fax: (703) 292-9232

General Counsel: Lawrence Rudolph
(703) 292-8060; Fax: (703) 292-9041
E-mail: lrudolph@nsf.gov

Promotes the progress of science and engineering through the support of research and education programs. *42 U.S.C. 1861*

NATIONAL TRANSPORTATION SAFETY BOARD
490 L'Enfant Plaza S.W., Washington, DC 20594
(202) 314-6000; Fax: (202) 314-6110
E-mail: pubinq@ntsb.gov
Internet: www.ntsb.gov

Chair: Deborah Hersman (Acting)

Managing Dir.: David Mayer (202) 314-6060

General Counsel: Gary L. Halbert
(202) 314-6080; Fax: (202) 314-6090

Ensures that all types of transportation are conducted safely by investigating accidents, conducting studies, and making recommendations to government agencies and industry.

Office of Administrative Law Judges
490 L'Enfant Plaza East, S.W., Washington, DC 20594
(202) 314-6150, (800) 854-8758; Fax: (202) 314-6158

4760 Oakland St., Denver, CO 80239
(303) 373-3511; Fax: (303) 373-3507

624 Six Flags Dr., Suite 150, Arlington, TX 76011
(817) 652-7860; Fax: (817) 652-7868

Chief Admin. Law Judge: William E. Fowler, Jr.
(Washington, D.C.); Fax: (202) 314-6158
E-mail: fowlerw@ntsb.gov
Circuit I (Generally the Northeastern States)

National Transportation Safety Board—Cont'd

Admin. Law Judges:
William A. Pope (Washington, D.C.); Fax: (202) 314-6158
E-mail: popew@ntsb.gov
Circuit II (Generally the Southeastern States)
Patrick G. Geraghty (Denver, Col.)
E-mail: geraghp@ntsb.gov
Circuit III (Generally the Western States)
William R. Mullins (Arlington, Tex.)
E-mail: mullinsw@ftwntsb.gov
Circuit IV (Generally the Central States)

NUCLEAR REGULATORY COMMISSION
One White Flint North, 11555 Rockville Pike, Rockville, MD 20852-2738
Mailing Address: Washington, DC 20555-0001
(301) 415-7000, (800) 368-5642
Internet: www.nrc.gov

Chair: Dale E. Klein (301) 415-1750

General Counsel: Karen D. Cyr (301) 415-1743

Licenses and regulates civilian use of nuclear reactors and materials to protect the safety of the public and the environment. *42 U.S.C. 5801*

Region 1 Office
475 Allendale Rd., King Of Prussia, PA 19406-1415
(610) 337-5000, (800) 432-1156; TDD: (301) 415-5575

Regional Administrator: Samuel J. Collins
(610) 337-5299; Fax: (610) 337-5241

Regional Counsel: Karl L. Farrar (610) 337-5301

OCCUPATIONAL SAFETY AND HEALTH REVIEW COMMISSION
One Lafayette Ctr., 9th Floor, 1120 20th St. N.W., Washington, DC 20036-3457
(202) 606-5100; Fax: (202) 606-5050
Internet: www.oshrc.gov

Chairperson: Thomasina V. Rogers
(202) 606-5370; Fax: (202) 606-5396

Dir., Office of Administration: Richard C. Loeb
(202) 606-5380; Fax: (202) 418-3487

Exec. Secy.: Ray H. Darling, Jr.
(202) 606-5400; Fax: (202) 606-5050

General Counsel: Nadine N. Mancini
(202) 606-5410; Fax: (202) 606-8417

Public Affairs Specialist: Melik Abdul
(202) 606-5371; Fax: (202) 606-5417

Issues decisions in disputes between O.S.H.A. and private employers over whether job safety standards were violated. *29 U.S.C. 651-678*

Headquarters Hearing Office
One Lafayette Ctr., 9th Floor, 1120 20th St. N.W.,
Washington, DC 20036-3419
(202) 606-5405

Chief Admin. Law Judge: Irving Sommer

Admin. Law Judges:
G. Marvin Bober
Covette Rooney
Dennis L. Phillips
John Schumacher

Regional Hearing Office
721 19th St., Suite 407, Denver, CO 80202
(303) 844-3409; Fax: (303) 844-3759

Admin. Law Judges:
Patrick B. Augustine
Benjamin R. Loye
Sidney J. Goldstein
James R. Rucker

PEACE CORPS
1111 20th St. N.W., Washington, DC 20526
(800) 424-8580; Fax: (202) 692-2151
Internet: www.peacecorps.gov

Director: Aaron S. Williams (202) 692-2100

General Counsel: Carl Sosebee (202) 692-2150

Promotes world peace and friendship, helps other countries meet their needs for trained individuals, and helps promote understanding between the people of the United States and the people of the rest of the world. *22 U.S.C. 2501*

PENSION BENEFIT GUARANTY CORPORATION
1200 K St. N.W., Washington, DC 20005
(202) 326-4000
E-mail: www.pbgc.gov

Director: Vincent Snowbarger (Acting)
(202) 326-4010; Fax: (202) 326-4016

General Counsel: Judith R. Starr
(202) 326-4000; Fax: (202) 326-4122

Protects the retirement incomes of more than 44 million American workers in more than 30,300 defined benefit pension plans. *29 U.S.C. 1301*

OFFICE OF PERSONNEL MANAGEMENT
1900 E St. N.W., Room 5A09, Washington, DC 20415-1000
(202) 606-1800; TTY: (202) 606-2532;
Fax: (202) 606-2573
Internet: www.opm.gov

Director: John Berry (202) 606-1000; Fax: (202) 606-2183

General Counsel: Elaine Kaplan, Room 7355
(202) 606-1700; Fax: (202) 606-2609

Administers a merit system for federal employment that includes the examination, recruiting, training, and promotion of persons on the basis of their knowledge and skills regardless of their race, color, religion, political influence or other non-merit factors. *5 U.S.C. app Reorganization Plan No. 2 of 1978*

POSTAL REGULATORY COMMISSION
901 New York Ave., Suite 200, Washington, DC 20268-0001
(202) 789-6800; T.T.Y.: (202) 789-6881;
Fax: (202) 789-6886
Internet: www.prc.gov

Chair: Ruth Y. Goldway (203) 789-6810

Chief Admin. Officer: Shoshana Grove (202) 789-6840

General Counsel: Stephen L. Sharfman
(202) 789-6820; Fax: (202) 789-6861

Dir., Public Affairs and Government Relations:
Ann Fisher (202) 789-6880; Fax: (202) 789-6886

Independent agency created by the Postal Reorganization Act. Makes rules and regulations and establishes procedures for postal ratemaking system. Considers formal complaints from interested persons. Acts on appeals of the closing or consolidating of post offices. Makes an annual compliance determination of the operations and finances of the Postal Service.*39 U.S.C. 3601-36040*

RAILROAD RETIREMENT BOARD
844 N. Rush St., Chicago, IL 60611-2092
(312) 751-4500; Fax: (312) 751-7154
Internet: www.rrb.gov

Office of Legislative Affairs, 1310 G St. N.W., Suite 500, Washington, DC 20005-3004
(202) 272-7742; Fax: (202) 272-7728
E-mail: ola@rrb.gov

Chair: Michael S. Schwartz
(312) 751-4900; Fax: (312) 751-7193

Labor Member: V.M. Speakman, Jr.
(312) 751-4905; Fax: (312) 751-7194

Management Member: Jerome F. Kever
(312) 751-4910; Fax: (312) 751-7189

General Counsel: Steven A. Bartholow
(312) 751-4935; Fax: (312) 751-7102

Administers retirement, survivor, unemployment and sickness benefits for railroad workers under the Railroad Retirement Act of 1974 and the Railroad Unemployment Insurance Act. *45 U.S.C. 231-231u, 45 U.S.C. 351-369*

Bureau of Field Services
844 N. Rush St., 9th Floor, Chicago, IL 60611
(312) 751-4952
E-mail: region2@rrb.gov; Internet: http://www.rrb.gov

Deputy Dir.: Martha M. Barringer

District Office
26 Federal Plaza, Room 3404, New York, NY 10278-3499
(877) 772-5772; Fax: (212) 264-1687
E-mail: newyork@rrb.gov

Director: John R. East

Railroad Retirement Board—Cont'd

District Office
264 O'Brien Federal Bldg., Clinton Ave. & Pearl St., P.O. Box 529, Albany, NY 12201-0529
(877) 772-5772; Fax: (518) 431-4000; E-mail: albany@rrb.gov
Director: Daniel M. Layton, Jr.

District Office
186 Exchange St., Suite 110, Buffalo, NY 14204
(877) 772-5772; Fax: (716) 551-3802
E-mail: buffalo@rrb.gov; Internet: www.rrb.gov
District Mgr.: Philip C. Dissek

District Office
1400 Old Country Rd., Suite 202, Westbury, NY 11590-5119
(877) 772-5772; Fax: (516) 334-4763
E-mail: westbury@rrb.gov
District Mgr.: Cathleen Quinn

SECURITIES AND EXCHANGE COMMISSION

100 F St., N.E., Washington, DC 20549
(800) 732-0330;
Filings and Info. (Registered Companies): (202) 551-8090; Human Resources: (202) 551-7500;
Investor Assistance: (202) 551-6551;
Instant Information Recording: (202) 947-8088
Internet: www.sec.gov

Chair: Mary L. Schapiro, Room 10710 (202) 551-2100
General Counsel: David M. Becker, Room 9106 (202) 551-5100

Administers the federal securities laws that seek to provide protection for investors, ensure that markets are fair and honest, and where necessary enforce securities laws with sanctions. *15 U.S.C. 78a-78jj*

Office of Administrative Law Judges
Mail Stop 2557, 100 F St. N.E., Washington, DC 20549-1106
(202) 551-6030; Fax: (202) 777-1031
Chief Admin. Law Judge: Brenda P. Murray
Admin. Law Judges:
Carol Fox Foelak
Robert G. Mahony
James T. Kelly

New York Regional Office
3 World Financial Center, Suite 400, New York, NY 10281
General Information: (212) 336-1100;
Complaint Dept.: (212) 336-0100; Internet: www.sec.gov
Regional Dir.: George Speare Canellos

SELECTIVE SERVICE SYSTEM

1515 Wilson Blvd., Arlington, VA 22209-2425
(703) 605-4100; Fax: (703) 605-4106
E-mail: information@sss.gov
Internet: www.sss.gov

Director: Lawrence G. Romo (703) 605-4010
General Counsel: Rudy Sanchez (703) 605-4012

Prepares to conduct a military draft in a national emergency. Registers virtually all young men and informs them about opportunities to serve America in peace time. *50 App. U.S.C. 451 et seq.*

SMALL BUSINESS ADMINISTRATION

409 3rd St. S.W., Washington, DC 20416
General Information/Personnel Locator: (202) 205-6600;
Answer Desk (800) U-ASK-SBA: (800) 827-5722;
Inspector General: (202) 205-6586;
Office of Financial Assistance: (202) 205-6490;
Office of Disaster Assistance: (202) 205-6734;
Investment Division: (202) 205-6510;
Office of Surety Guarantee: (202) 205-6540;
Office of Business & Community Initiatives: (202) 205-6665; Office of Advocacy: (202) 205-6533;
Office of Women's Business Ownership: (202) 205-6673;
Office of Veterans Business Development: (202) 205-6773;
Office of International Trade: (202) 205-6720;
Office of Small Business Development Centers: (202) 205-6766
Internet: www.sba.gov

Administrator: Karen G. Mills, Suite 7000 (202) 205-6605; Fax: (202) 481-4600
General Counsel: Sara D. Lipscomb, Suite 7200 (202) 205-7425; Fax: (202) 481-0434

Aids, counsels, and protects the interests of small business, ensures that small business concerns receive a fair share of government business, makes loans to small businesses, and licenses, regulates, and makes loans to small business investment companies. *15 U.S.C. 631*

Office of Hearings and Appeals
409 Third St., S.W., 8th Floor, Washington, DC 20416-3212
(202) 401-8200; Fax: (202) 205-7059
E-mail: oha@sba.org
Admin. Law Judge: Vacancy at Press Time
Admin. Judge: Christopher Holleman
Thomas B. Pender
Asst. Administrator for Hearings and Appeals: Delorice P. Ford

Regional Office
26 Federal Plaza, Room 3108, New York, NY 10278
(212) 264-1450; Fax: (212) 264-0038
Regional Administrator: Jorge Silva-Puras

SOCIAL SECURITY ADMINISTRATION

Windsor Park Bldg., 6401 Security Blvd., Baltimore, MD 21235
(410) 965-8882, (800) 772-1213;
Employer Hotline: (800) 772-6270; TTY: (800) 325-0778
Internet: www.ssa.gov

Commissioner: Michael J. Astrue
General Counsel: David F. Black (410) 965-0600; Fax: (410) 966-3146

Administers a national plan of contributory social insurance for retired or disabled persons and their survivors and dependents. *42 U.S.C. 1305, Public Law 103-296, (August 15, 1994)*

Regional Office
26 Federal Plaza, Suite 40-120, New York, NY 10278
(212) 264-2500
Regional Commissioner: Beatrice M. Disman (212) 264-3915
Regional Chief Counsel: Stephen Conte

Field Offices

Federal Bldg., Room 430, 1 Clinton Ave., Albany, NY 12207
(800) 772-1213; TTY: (800) 325-0778;
Fax: (518) 431-4066
Field Mgr.: Walter Herbst

28-18 Steinway St., 4th Floor, Astoria, NY 11103
(800) 772-1213; Fax: (718) 278-7885
Field Mgr.: Mary Jean Baker

571 E. Main St., Batavia, NY 14020
(800) 772-1213; TTY: (800) 325-0778;
Fax: (585) 343-6079
Field Mgr.: Roger Kohler

15 Henry St., Binghamton, NY 13901
(800) 772-1213; TTY: (800) 325-0778;
Fax: (607) 773-2649
Field Mgr.: Michael Soltarnoff

226 E. 161st St., 2nd Floor, Bronx, NY 10451
(800) 772-1213; Fax: (718) 537-2174
Field Mgr.: Ronald Sobel

2770 3rd Ave., 2nd Floor, Bronx, NY 10455
(800) 772-1213

1029 E. 163rd St., 3rd Floor, Bronx, NY 10459
(800) 772-1213; Fax: (718) 589-2129
Field Mgr.: Mary Carroll

1829 Southern Blvd., Bronx, NY 10460
(800) 772-1213; Fax: (718) 542-1477
Field Mgr.: Philip O'Keefe

1380 Parker St., 2nd Floor, Bronx, NY 10462
(800) 772-1213; Fax: (718) 597-4041
Field Mgr.: Diana Valdez

2720 Jerome Ave., Bronx, NY 10468
(800) 772-1213; Fax: (718) 933-3118
Field Mgr.: Bryant Wilder

Social Security Administration, Field Offices—Cont'd

3247 Laconia Ave., Bronx, NY 10469
(800) 772-1213; TTY: (800) 325-0778

195 Montague St., 3rd Floor, Brooklyn, NY 11201
(800) 772-1213; Fax: (718) 330-1783
Field Mgr.: Anthony Perrotti

1111 Myrtle Ave., Brooklyn, NY 11206
(800) 772-1213
Field Mgr.: Louise Cotton

27 Pennsylvania Ave., Brooklyn, NY 11207
(800) 772-1213; Fax: (718) 485-0471
Field Mgr.: Bryant Wilder

3386 Fulton St., Brooklyn, NY 11208
(800) 772-1213; Fax: (718) 235-7681
Field Mgr.: Victor Mirandona

2250 Nostrand Ave., Brooklyn, NY 11210
(800) 772-1213
Field Mgr.: David Pollack

93 N. 9th St., Brooklyn, NY 11211
(800) 772-1213; Fax: (718) 782-6005
Field Mgr.: Paul Cavallaro

1540 Fulton St., Brooklyn, NY 11216
(800) 772-1213
Field Mgr.: Tanya Isler

10 Bouck Ct., Brooklyn, NY 11223
(800) 772-1213; Fax: (718) 627-7385
Field Mgr.: Alyce Furman

1871 Rockaway Pkwy., Brooklyn, NY 11236
(800) 772-1213
Field Mgr.: Steven Beck

186 Exchange St., Suite 100, Buffalo, NY 14204
(800) 772-1213; Fax: (716) 551-4638
Field Mgr.: Vita Casavantes

200 Nasser Civic Center, Corning, NY 14830
(800) 772-1213; TTY: (800) 325-0778;
Fax: (607) 936-3290
Field Mgr.: Michael White

437 Main St., Suite 2, Dunkirk, NY 14048
(716) 366-8211; TTY: (716) 366-0344; Fax: (716) 366-7405
Field Mgr.: James Redmond

100 W. Church St., Suite 201, Elmira, NY 14901
(800) 772-1213; TTY: (607) 734-2882;
Fax: (607) 734-6829
Field Mgr.: Ken Moeller

617 Beach 20th St., Far Rockaway, NY 11691
(800) 772-1213; Fax: (718) 327-9552
Field Mgr.: James Glasser

138-50 Barclay Ave., Flushing, NY 11355
(800) 772-1213; Fax: (718) 661-9617
Field Mgr.: Evelyn Rosario-Martinez

84 N. Main St., Freeport, NY 11520
(800) 772-1213

15 Lewis St., Geneva, NY 14456
(800) 772-1213; TTY: (800) 325-0778; Fax: (315) 789-0150
Field Mgr.: Carol Bryant

67-10 Myrtle Ave., Glendale, NY 11385
(800) 772-1213; Fax: (718) 497-6654
Field Mgr.: Rachele Adler

13 N. Arlington Ave., Gloversville, NY 12078
(888) 528-9446; TTY: (800) 325-0778; Fax: (518) 725-3775
Field Mgr.: Mark Ford

747 Warren St., Hudson, NY 12534
(518) 828-2098; TTY: (800) 325-0778;
Fax: (518) 828-8976
Field Mgr.: Robert Apicello

127 W. State St., 2nd Floor, Ithaca, NY 14850
(800) 772-1213; TTY: (607) 256-7112; Fax: (607) 273-9312
Field Mgr.: David Cook

155-10 Jamaica Ave., 3rd Floor, Jamaica, NY 11432
(800) 772-1213; Fax: (718) 557-6190
Field Mgr.: Ed Hebron

321 Hazeltine Ave., Jamestown, NY 14701
(877) 319-3079; TTY: (716) 487-9055
Field Mgr.: William Struchen

809 Grant Ave., Lake Katrine, NY 12449
(845) 338-2589; TTY: (845) 334-9210
Field Mgr.: Thomas Morris

25-27 E. Park Ave., Long Beach, NY 11561
(800) 772-1213; Fax: (516) 889-0176
Field Mgr.: Joseph D'Orio (516) 889-0731

42-15 Crescent St., 4th Floor,
Long Island City, NY 11101
(800) 772-1213; Fax: (718) 392-3283
Field Mgr.: Ira Shapiro

1121 Walt Whitman Rd., Suite 201, Melville, NY 11747
(800) 772-1213; Fax: (631) 271-2311
Field Mgr.: Elaine Roth

211 Station Rd., 5th Floor, Mineola, NY 11501
(800) 772-1213; Fax: (516) 747-9255
Field Mgr.: Robert Bianchi

60 Jefferson St., Suite 4, Monticello, NY 12701
(845) 794-1293; TTY: (845) 791-4836; Fax: (845) 794-1065
Field Mgr.: Tom Carney

5 Stevens Ave., 3rd Floor, Mount Vernon, NY 10550
(800) 772-1213; Fax: (914) 699-7970
Field Mgr.: Barbara Gentry

85 Harrison St., Street Level, New Rochelle, NY 10801
(800) 772-1213; Fax: (914) 633-4130
Field Mgr.: Roberta Salmas

650 E. 12th St., New York, NY 10009
(800) 772-1213; Fax: (212) 614-1902
Field Mgr.: Robert Baldassano

26 Federal Plaza, Room 120, New York, NY 10278
(800) 772-1213, (212) 264-9417

32 Mercer St., 8th Floor, New York, NY 10013
(800) 772-1213; Fax: (212) 219-3693
Field Mgr.: Reggie Castillo

755 Second Ave., 3rd Floor, New York, NY 10017
(800) 772-1213; Fax: (212) 599-4779
Field Mgr.: Anita Jankowski

55 W. 125th St., 6th Floor, New York, NY 10027
(800) 772-1213; Fax: (914) 633-4130
Field Mgr.: Ed Best

345 E. 102nd St., 4th Floor, New York, NY 10029
(800) 772-1213
Field Mgr.: Debbie Carter

4292 Broadway (Corner of 182nd St.),
New York, NY 10033
(800) 772-1213; Fax: (212) 568-2667
Field Mgr.: Stephen DeLisle

237 W. 48th St., 5th Floor, New York, NY 10036
(800) 772-1213; Fax: (212) 399-5423
Field Mgr.: Richard Heyniger

3 Washington Ctr., Suite 301, Newburgh, NY 12550
(800) 772-1213; TTY: (800) 325-0778; Fax: (845) 561-6507
Field Mgr.: Joseph Dirago

6540 Niagara Falls Blvd., Niagara Falls, NY 14304
(716) 283-1066, (800) 772-1213; TTY: (716) 283-2614;
Fax: (716) 283-1774
Field Mgr.: Gary Witman

Social Security Administration, Field Offices—Cont'd

Industrial Bldg. No. 6, 818 Commerce Park Dr., Ogdensburg, NY 13669
(800) 772-1213; TTY: (315) 394-1210;
Fax: (315) 393-0396
Field Mgr.: Mary Ann James

175 N. Union St., Suite 6, Olean, NY 14760
(877) 319-5773; TTY: (716) 376-8932;
Fax: (716) 372-3045
Field Mgr.: Kenneth Park

31 Main St., Suite 1, Oneonta, NY 13820
(607) 433-0171; TTY: (607) 433-6607;
Fax: (607) 432-0467
Field Mgr.: Kemp Baratier

Hillside Commons, 19 Fourth Ave., Oswego, NY 13126
(800) 772-1213; TTY: (315) 343-8319;
Fax: (315) 343-0068
Field Mgr.: Loretta Fretwell

75 Oak St., Patchogue, NY 11772
(800) 772-1213; Fax: (631) 758-7885
Field Mgr.: Stuart Blau

1 Park Pl., 3rd Floor, Peekskill, NY 10566
(800) 772-1213; Fax: (914) 739-4761
Field Mgr.: Arthur Pollack

14 Durkee St., Plattsburgh, NY 12901
(800) 772-1213; TTY: (800) 325-0778;
Fax: (518) 563-3402
Field Mgr.: Linde Ballentine

332 Main St., Poughkeepsie, NY 12601
(845) 452-3584; TTY: (845) 454-1540;
Fax: (845) 452-7347
Field Mgr.: John Lyons

17 Cronin Rd., Suite 1, Queensbury, NY 12804
(518) 812-0182; TTY: (518) 745-5719;
Fax: (518) 793-6681
Field Mgr.: Paul Brown

6344 Austin St., Rego Park, NY 11374
(800) 772-1213
Field Mgr.: Janice McBean

526 E. Main St., Riverhead, NY 11901
(800) 772-1213; Fax: (631) 369-9470
Field Mgr.: Susan Mack

One HSBC Place, Suite 1400, 100 Chestnut St., Rochester, NY 14604
(800) 772-1213
Field Mgr.: John Orcutt

4050 W. Ridge Rd., 2nd Floor, Rochester, NY 14626
(800) 772-1213; Fax: (585) 225-4079
Field Mgr.: Tom Ragonese

Rosen Bldg., 268 W. Dominick St., Rome, NY 13440
(315) 339-1751; TTY: (315) 334-9007;
Fax: (315) 339-5051
Field Mgr.: Carmel Sullivan

One Broadway Ctr., 8th Floor, Schenectady, NY 12305
(800) 772-1213; TTY: (518) 382-9489;
Fax: (518) 382-7847
Field Mgr.: Paul Thomas

1510 Hylan Blvd., 2nd Floor, Staten Island, NY 10305
(800) 772-1213; Fax: (718) 720-3811
Field Mgr.: Peter Caldone

2389 Richmond Ave., Staten Island, NY 10314
(800) 772-1213; Fax: (718) 698-2005
Field Mgr.: Evelyn Brown

Federal Bldg., 4th Floor, 100 S. Clinton St., Syracuse, NY 13261
(800) 772-1213; Fax: (315) 479-0063
Field Mgr.: Edward Christen

500 Federal St., Suite 101, Troy, NY 12180
(518) 271-1900; TTY: (518) 272-7264;
Fax: (518) 271-8492
Field Mgr.: Randy Rivet

Federal Bldg., 10 Broad St., Utica, NY 13501
(315) 797-7614; TTY: (315) 738-1636; Fax: (315) 797-1173
Field Mgr.: Robert Stanton

156 Bellew Ave. South, Watertown, NY 13601
(866) 627-6995; TTY: (315) 785-3663; Fax: (315) 797-1173
Field Mgr.: James Reichhart

510 Park Ave., West Babylon, NY 11704
(800) 772-1213; Fax: (631) 669-3295
Field Mgr.: Susan Dubinsky

1900 Ridge Rd., Suite 120, West Seneca, NY 14224
(800) 772-1213

297 Knollwood Rd., Suite 4A, White Plains, NY 10607
(800) 772-1213; Fax: (914) 682-6174
Field Mgr.: Hal Golio

20 S. Broadway, Suite 1000, Yonkers, NY 10701
(800) 772-1213; Fax: (914) 963-2546
Field Mgr.: Susan Sobel

TENNESSEE VALLEY AUTHORITY

400 West Summit Hill Dr., Knoxville, TN 37902-1499
(865) 632-2101; Fax: (865) 633-7311
E-mail: tvainfo@tva.gov
Internet: www.tva.gov

One Massachusetts Ave, N.W., Suite 300, Washington, DC 20444-0001
(202) 898-2999

Chairman: Dennis Bottorff, Room ET12A (865) 632-4000
President & C.E.O.: Tom Kilgore
General Counsel: Ralph Rodgers (Acting), Room WT6A (865) 632-4131; Fax: (865) 632-3307

Conducts a unified program of resource development for the advancement of economic growth in the Tennessee Valley region. *16 U.S.C. 831*

U.S. TRADE AND DEVELOPMENT AGENCY

1000 Wilson Blvd., Suite 1600, Arlington, VA 22209
(703) 875-4357; Fax: (703) 875-4009
E-mail: info@ustda.gov
Internet: www.ustda.gov

Director: Leocadia I. Zak (Acting)
General Counsel: James A. Wilderotter

Promotes economic development and market penetration in developing and middle-income countries. *22 U.S.C. 2421*

UNITED STATES AGENCY FOR INTERNATIONAL DEVELOPMENT

1300 Pennsylvania Ave., N.W., Washington, DC 20523-1000
(202) 712-4810;
Information Specialists: (202) 712-4810;
Fax: (202) 216-3524
E-mail: pinquries@usaid.gov
Internet: www.usaid.gov

Administrator: Dr. Rajiv Shah, Room 6-9 (202) 712-4040; Fax: (202) 216-3455
Deputy Administrator: Vacancy at Press Time (202) 712-4070; Fax: (202) 216-3455
Chief Operating Officer: Alonzo L. Fulgham (202) 712-1481

Plans, coordinates, and formulates policy on international issues affecting developing countries. *5 U.S.C. app. Reorganization Plan No. 2 of 1979*

Formerly known as the Agency for International Development

Overseas Private Investment Corporation
1100 New York Ave. N.W., Washington, DC 20527
(202) 336-8400; Information Line: (202) 336-8799;
Fax: (202) 336-7949; Internet: www.opic.gov
President and Chief Executive Officer: Elizabeth L. Littlefield
V.P./General Counsel: Robert O'Sullivan (Acting) (202) 336-8410; Fax: (202) 218-0256

UNITED STATES INTERNATIONAL TRADE COMMISSION
500 E St. S.W., Washington, DC 20436
(202) 205-2000; Fax: (202) 205-2104
Internet: www.usitc.gov

Chair: Deanna Tanner Okun (202) 205-5482

General Counsel: James M. Lyons (202) 205-3101

Furnishes studies, reports, and recommendations involving international trade and tariffs to the president, the Congress, and other governmental agencies. *19 U.S.C. 2231*

UNITED STATES POSTAL SERVICE
475 L'Enfant Plaza S.W., Washington, DC 20260-1100
(800) 275-8777; Internet: www.usps.gov

Postmaster General: John E. Potter (202) 268-2000

Sr. V.P. and General Counsel: Mary Anne Gibbons
Room 6004 (202) 268-2950; Fax: (202) 268-6981

Inspector General: David C. Williams
1735 N. Lynn St., Arlington, VA 22209-2020
(888) 877-7644; Fax: (866) 756-6741

Provides mail processing and delivery services to businesses and individuals in the United States. *39 U.S.C. 101*

Northeast Law Office
8 Griffin Rd. N., Windsor, CT 06006-0170
(860) 285-7090; Fax: (860) 285-7397

Managing Counsel: James Friedman

New York Metro Law Office
90 Church St., Suite 3300, New York, NY 10007-2993
(212) 330-5400; Fax: (212) 330-5470

Managing Counsel: Anne Gallaudet

Quasi-Official Agencies

LEGAL SERVICES CORPORATION
3333 K St., N.W., 3rd Floor, Washington, DC 20007-3522
(202) 295-1500; Fax: (202) 337-6797
E-mail: info@lsc.gov; Internet: www.lsc.gov

President (Acting) and General Counsel:
Victor M. Fortuno; E-mail: vfortuno@lsc.gov

Provides funding for the provision of civil legal assistance to those unable to afford it, and oversees the national legal services program. *42 U.S.C. 2996*

SMITHSONIAN INSTITUTION
1000 Jefferson Dr. S.W., P.O. Box 37012, Washington, DC 20013-7012
(202) 633-1000; T.T.Y.: (202) 633-5285
E-mail: info@si.edu
Internet: http://www.si.edu

Secretary: G. Wayne Clough

General Counsel: Judith Leonard
Room 302, P.O. Box 23286, Washington, DC 20026-3286
(202) 633-5115

Operates as an independent trust instrumentality of the United States that fosters the increase and diffusion of knowledge. *20 U.S.C. 41*

STATE JUSTICE INSTITUTE
1650 King St., Suite 600, Alexandria, VA 22314
(703) 684-6100; Fax: (703) 684-7618
Internet: www.sji.gov

Chair: Hon. Robert A. Miller
(Chief Justice, S.D. Supreme Court, retired)

Exec. Dir.: Jonathan Mattiello, Ext. 210
E-mail: jonathan.mattiello@sji.gov

Awards grants and provides technical support to further the development and adoption of improved judicial administration in the state courts of the United States. *42 U.S.C. 10701*

UNITED STATES INSTITUTE OF PEACE
1200 17th St. N.W., Suite 200, Washington, DC 20036-3011
(202) 457-1700; Fax: (202) 429-6063;
TDD: (202) 457-1719
Internet: www.usip.org

President: Richard H. Solomon
(202) 429-3835

V.P., Education and Training Center, Domestic Programs: Pamela R. Aall (202) 429-3866

V.P., Centers of Innovation Program: Daniel P. Serwer
(202) 429-3840

Dir., Rule of Law Center of Innovation:
Colette Rausch (Acting) (202) 429-3860

An independent, nonpartisan national institution established and funded by Congress. Helps prevent, manage, and resolve violent conflicts by providing knowledge, skills, resources, and direct involvement in peacebuilding efforts.

CONGRESSIONAL DELEGATION

U.S. SENATORS

SENATOR, Kirsten E. Gillibrand
Democrat: Term expires January 2011
478 Russell Senate Office Bldg., Washington, DC 20510
(202) 224-4451; Fax: (202) 228-0282
Internet: http://www.gillibrand.senate.gov
Chief of Staff: Jess Fassler

District Offices:

New York City Office
780 Third Ave., Suite 2601, N.Y.C. 10017
(212) 688-6262; Fax: (212) 688-7444

Albany Office
821 Leo W. O'Brien Federal Bldg., 1 Clinton Sq., Albany 12207 (518) 431-0120; Fax: (518) 431-0128

Buffalo Office
Larkin at Exchange, Suite 511, 726 Exchange St., Buffalo 14201 (716) 854-9725; Fax: (716) 854-9731

Long Island Office
155 Pinelawn Rd., Suite 250 North, Melville 11747
(631) 249-2825; Fax: (631) 249-2847

Rochester Office
4195 Kenneth B. Keating Federal Bldg., 100 State St., Rochester 14614 (585) 263-6250; Fax: (585) 263-6247

Syracuse Office
1470 James M. Hanley Federal Bldg.,
100 S. Clinton St., Syracuse 13261
(315) 448-0470; Fax: (315) 448-0476

North Country Office
P.O. Box 273, Lowville 13367
(315) 376-6118; Fax: (315) 376-6118

Hudson Valley Office
P.O. Box 884, Nyack 10960
(845) 875-4585; Fax: (845) 875-9099

SENATOR, Charles E. Schumer
Democrat: Term expires January 2011
313 Hart Senate Office Bldg., Washington, DC 20510
(202) 224-6542; TDD: (202) 224-0420; Fax: (202) 228-3027
Internet: http://schumer.senate.gov
Chief of Staff: Mike Lynch

District Offices:

Albany Office
420 Leo W. O'Brien Federal Office Bldg., Albany 12207
(518) 431-4070; Fax: (518) 431-4076

Binghamton Office
15 Henry St., Room M103, Binghamton 13901
(607) 772-6792; Fax: (607) 772-8124

Buffalo Office
130 S. Elmwood Ave., Room 660, Buffalo 14202
(716) 846-4111; Fax: (716) 846-4113

Hudson Valley Office
One Park Pl., Suite 100, Peekskill 10566
(914) 734-1532; Fax: (914) 734-1673

Long Island Office
145 Pine Lawn Rd., Suite 300, Melville 11747
(631) 753-0978; Fax: (631) 753-0997

New York Office
757 Third Ave., Suite 17-02, N.Y.C. 10017
(212) 486-4430; TDD: (212) 486-7803;
Fax: (212) 486-7693

Rochester Office
100 State St., Room 3040, Rochester 14614
(585) 263-5866; Fax: (585) 263-3173

Syracuse Office
100 S. Clinton, Room 841, Syracuse 13261-7318
(315) 423-5471; Fax: (315) 423-5185

U.S. REPRESENTATIVES

REPRESENTATIVE, Gary L. Ackerman
5th District, Democrat
2243 Rayburn House Office Bldg., Washington, DC 20515
(202) 225-2601; Fax: (202) 225-1589
Internet: www.ackerman.house.gov
Chief of Staff: Jedd Moskowitz

District Office:

Bayside Office
218-14 Northern Blvd., Bayside 11361
(718) 423-2154; Fax: (718) 423-5053

REPRESENTATIVE, Michael A. Arcuri
24th District, Democrat
127 Cannon House Office Bldg., Washington, DC 20515
(202) 225-3665; Fax: (202) 225-1891
Internet: http://arcuri.house.gov
Chief of Staff: Sam Marchio

District Offices:

Utica Office
10 Broad St., Room 200, Utica 13501
(315) 793-8146, 47; Fax: (315) 798-4099

Auburn Office
17 E. Genesee St., Auburn 13021
(315) 252-2777, 78; Fax: (315) 252-2779

Cortland Office
Carriage House Right, 16 Church St., Cortland 13045
(315) 756-2470; Fax: (315) 756-2472

REPRESENTATIVE, Timothy H. Bishop
1st District, Democrat
306 Cannon House Office Bldg., Washington, DC 20515
(202) 225-3826; Fax: (202) 225-3143
Internet: www.house.gov/timbishop
Chief of Staff: Pete Spiro

District Offices:

Coram Office
3680 Rte. 112, Suite C, Coram 11727
(631) 696-6500; Fax: (631) 696-4520
Dir., Intergovermental Affairs and Community Outreach: Lisa Wieber

Southampton Office
137 Hampton Rd., Southampton 11968
(631) 259-8450; Fax: (631) 259-8451

REPRESENTATIVE, Yvette D. Clarke
11th District, Democrat
1029 Longworth House Office Bldg., Washington, DC 20515
(202) 225-6231; Fax: (202) 226-0112
Internet: http://clarke.house gov
District Dir.: Anita Taylor

District Office:

Brooklyn Office
123 Linden Blvd., 4th Floor, Brooklyn 11226
(718) 287-1142; Fax: (718) 287-1223

REPRESENTATIVE, Joseph Crowley
7th District, Democrat
2404 Rayburn House Office Bldg., Washington, DC 20515
(202) 225-3965; Fax: (202) 225-1909
Internet: http://crowley.house.gov/
Chief of Staff: Kate Winkler

District Offices:

Bronx Office
2800 Bruckner Blvd., Suite 301, Bronx 10465
(718) 931-1400; Fax: (718) 931-1340

Queens Office
74-09 37th Ave., Suite 306-B, Jackson Heights 11372
(718) 779-1400; Fax: (718) 505-0156

Co-Op City Office
177 Dreiser Loop, Room 3, Bronx 10475
(718) 320-2314; Fax: (718) 931-1340

Note: All seats in the House of Representatives subject to November 2010 election results

REPRESENTATIVE, Eliot L. Engel
17th District, Democrat
2161 Rayburn House Office Bldg., Washington, DC 20515
(202) 225-2464; Fax: (202) 225-5513
Internet: www.house.gov/engel

Chief of Staff: Bill Weitz

Admin. Asst.: Ned Michalek

District Offices:

Bronx Office
3655 Johnson Ave., Bronx 10463
(718) 796-9700; Fax: (718) 796-5134

Westchester Office
6 Gramatan Ave., Suite 205, Mount Vernon 10550
(914) 699-4100; Fax: (914) 699-3646

Rockland Office
261 W. Nyack Rd., West Nyack 10994
(845) 735-1000; Fax: (845) 735-1963

REPRESENTATIVE, John Hall
19th District, Democrat
1217 Longworth House Office Bldg., Washington, DC 20515
(202) 225-5441; Fax: (202) 225-3289
Internet: http://johnhall.house.gov

Chief of Staff: Susan Spear

District Offices:

Goshen Office
Orange County Govt. Center, Room 3232G,
255 Main St., Goshen 10924
(845) 291-4100; Fax: (845) 291-4164

Carmel Office
Putnam County Office Bldg., 3rd Floor,
40 Gleneida Ave., Carmel 10512
(845) 225-3641, Ext. 49371; Fax: (845) 228-1480

REPRESENTATIVE, Brian M. Higgins
27th District, Democrat
431 Cannon House Office Bldg., Washington, DC 20515
(202) 225-3306; Fax: (202) 226-0347
Internet: http://higgins.house.gov

Chief of Staff: Andy Tantillo

District Offices:

Buffalo Office
Larkin at Exchange, Suite 601, 726 Exchange St.,
Buffalo 14210 (716) 852-3501; Fax: (716) 852-3929
Chief of Staff: Chuck Eaton

Chautauqua County Office
Fenton Bldg., Suite 300, 2 E. Second St.,
Jamestown 14701
(716) 484-0729; Fax: (716) 484-1049

REPRESENTATIVE, Maurice D. Hinchey
22nd District, Democrat
2431 Rayburn House Office Bldg., Washington, DC 20515
(202) 225-6335; Fax: (202) 226-0774
Internet: www.house.gov/hinchey

Chief of Staff: Jeff Lieberson

District Offices:

Binghamton Office
100A Federal Bldg., Binghamton 13901
(607) 773-2768; Fax: (607) 773-3176

Ithaca Office
123 S. Cayuga St., Suite 201, Ithaca 14850
(607) 273-1388; Fax: (607) 273-8847

Kingston Office
291 Wall St., Kingston 12401
(845) 331-4466; Fax: (845) 331-7456

Middletown Office
City Hall, 3rd Floor, 16 James St., Middletown 10940
(845) 344-3211; Fax: (845) 342-2070

Monticello Office
18 Anawana Lake Rd., Monticello 12776
(845) 791-7116; Fax: (607) 498-5379

REPRESENTATIVE, Steven J. Israel
2nd District, Democrat
2457 Rayburn House Office Bldg., Washington, DC 20515
(202) 225-3335; Fax: (202) 225-4669
Internet: http://israel.house.gov

Chief of Staff: Jack Pratt

District Office:

Long Island Office
150 Motor Pkwy., Suite 108, Hauppauge 11788
(631) 951-2210, (516) 505-1448; Fax: (631) 951-3308

REPRESENTATIVE, Peter T. King
3rd District, Republican
339 Cannon House Office Bldg., Washington, DC 20515
(202) 225-7896; Fax: (202) 226-2279
Internet: http://peteking.house.gov

Chief of Staff: Kevin Fogarty

District Office:

Massapequa Park Office
1003 Park Blvd., Massapequa Park 11762
(516) 541-4225; Suffolk County: (631) 541-4225;
Fax: (516) 541-6602

REPRESENTATIVE, Christopher J. Lee
26th District, Republican
1711 Longworth House Office Bldg.,
Washington, DC 20515
(202) 225-5265; Fax: (202) 225-5910
Internet: http://chrislee.house.gov

Chief of Staff: Brian Schubert

District Offices:

Greece Office
1577 W. Ridge Rd., Rochester 14615
(585) 663-5570; Fax: (585) 663-5711

Williamsville Office
325 Essjay Rd., Suite 405, Williamsville 14221
(716) 634-2324; Fax: (716) 631-7610

REPRESENTATIVE, Nita M. Lowey
18th District, Democrat
2329 Rayburn House Office Bldg., Washington, DC 20515
(202) 225-6506; Fax: (202) 225-0546
Internet: http://lowey.house.gov

Chief of Staff: Elizabeth Stanley

District Office:

White Plains Office
222 Mamaroneck Ave., Suite 310, White Plains 10605
(914) 428-1707; Rockland Area: (845) 639-3485;
Fax: (914) 328-1505

REPRESENTATIVE, Daniel B. Maffei
25th District, Democrat
1630 Longworth House Office Bldg.,
Washington, DC 20515
(202) 225-3701; Fax: (202) 225-4042
Internet: www.maffei.house.gov

Chief of Staff: Jill Allen-Murray

District Offices:

Syracuse Office
1340 Federal Bldg., P.O. Box 7306, Syracuse 13261
(315) 423-5657; Fax: (315) 423-5669
Chief of Staff: Mike Whyland

Irondequiot Office
1280 Titus Ave., Rochester 14617
(585) 336-7291; Fax: (585) 336-7274

Note: All seats in the House of Representatives subject to November 2010 election results

REPRESENTATIVE, Carolyn B. Maloney
14th District, Democrat
2332 Rayburn House Office Bldg., Washington, DC 20515-3214
(202) 225-7944; Fax: (202) 225-4709
Internet: http://maloney.house.gov
Chief of Staff: Ben Chevat

District Offices:

New York Office
1651 Third Ave., Suite 311, N.Y.C. 10128-3679
(212) 860-0606; Fax: (212) 860-0704

Queens Office
28-11 Astoria Blvd., Astoria 11102-1933
(718) 932-1804; Fax: (718) 932-1805

REPRESENTATIVE, Carolyn McCarthy
4th District, Democrat
2346 Rayburn House Office Bldg., Washington, DC 20515
(202) 225-5516; Fax: (202) 225-5758
Internet: http://carolynmccarthy.house.gov
Chief of Staff: Michael Spira

District Office:

Garden City Office
300 Garden City Plz., Suite 200, Garden City 11530
(516) 739-3008; Fax: (516) 739-2973

REPRESENTATIVE, Michael E. McMahon
13th District, Democrat
323 Cannon House Office Bldg., Washington, DC 20515
(202) 225-3371; Fax: (202) 226-1272
Internet: http://mcmahon.house.gov
Chief of Staff: Chris McCannell

District Offices:

Staten Island Office
265 New Dorp Lane, 2nd Floor, Staten Island 10306
(718) 351-1062; Fax: (718) 980-0768

Brooklyn Office
8505 4th Ave., Brooklyn 11209
(718) 630-5277; Fax: (718) 630-5388

REPRESENTATIVE, Gregory W. Meeks
6th District, Democrat
2342 Rayburn House Office Bldg., Washington, DC 20515
(202) 225-3461; Fax: (202) 226-4169
Internet: www.house.gov/meeks
Chief of Staff: Sophia King

District Offices:

Far Rockaway Office
1931 Mott Ave., Room 305, Far Rockaway 11691
(718) 327-9791; Fax: (718) 327-4722

St. Albans Office
153-01 Jamaica Ave., 2nd Floor, Jamaica 11432-3870
(718) 725-6000; Fax: (718) 725-9868

REPRESENTATIVE, Scott Murphy
20th District, Democrat
120 Cannon House Office Bldg., Washington, DC 20515
(202) 225-5614; Fax: (202) 225-1168
Internet: http://scottmurphy.house.gov
Chief of Staff: Todd Schulte

District Offices:

Clifton Park Office
7 Southside Dr., Suite 206, Clifton Park 12065
(518) 280-1791; Fax: (518) 280-2268

Glens Falls Office
136 Glen St., Glens Falls 12801
(518) 743-0964; Fax: (518) 743-1391

Hudson Office
623 Warren St., Hudson 12534
(518) 828-3190; Delaware/Otsego Counties: (607) 746-4889; Fax: (518) 828-3985

Saratoga Springs Office
487 Broadway, Saratoga Springs 12866
(518) 581-8247; Fax: (518) 581-8430

REPRESENTATIVE, Jerrold L. Nadler
8th District, Democrat
2334 Rayburn House Office Bldg., Washington, DC 20515
(202) 225-5635; Fax: (202) 225-6923
Internet: www.house.gov/nadler

District Offices:

New York Office
201 Varick St., Suite 669, N.Y.C. 10014
(212) 367-7350; Fax: (212) 367-7356
Chief of Staff: Amy Rutkin
Director: John Doty

Brooklyn Office
445 Neptune Ave., Brooklyn 11224
(718) 373-3198; Fax: (718) 996-0039

REPRESENTATIVE, William L. Owens
23rd District, Democrat
2366 Rayburn House Office Bldg., Washington, DC 20515-3223
(202) 225-4611; Fax: (202) 226-0621
Chief of Staff: Bradley Katz

District Offices:

Canastota Office
3215 Seneca Tpke., Canastota 13032
(315) 875-5115; Fax: (315) 875-5048

Mayfield Office
28 N. School St., P.O. Box 800, Mayfield 12117-0800
(518) 661-6486; Fax: (518) 661-5704

Plattsburgh Office
14 Durkee St., Suite 320, Plattsburgh 12901
(518) 563-1406; Fax: (518) 561-9723

Watertown Office
120 Washington St., Suite 200, Watertown 13601-3370
(315) 782-3150; Fax: (315) 782-1291

REPRESENTATIVE, Charles B. Rangel
15th District, Democrat
2354 Rayburn House Office Bldg., Washington, DC 20515
(202) 225-4365; Fax: (202) 225-0816
Internet: http://rangel.house.gov
Chief of Staff: George Henry

District Office:

New York Office
163 W. 125th St., Room 737, N.Y.C. 10027
(212) 663-3900; Fax: (212) 663-4277

REPRESENTATIVE, José E. Serrano
16th District, Democrat
2227 Rayburn House Office Bldg., Washington, DC 20515-3216
(202) 225-4361; Fax: (202) 225-6001
Internet: http://serrano.house.gov
Chief of Staff: Paul Lipson

District Office:

Bronx Office
903 Dawson St., Bronx 10455
(718) 620-0084; Fax: (718) 620-0658

REPRESENTATIVE, Louise M. Slaughter
28th District, Democrat
2469 Rayburn House Office Bldg., Washington, DC 20515
(202) 225-3615; Fax: (202) 225-7822
Internet: www.louise.house.gov
Chief of Staff: Greg Regan

District Offices:

Buffalo Office
465 Main St., Suite 105, Buffalo 14203
(716) 853-5813; Fax: (716) 853-6347

Niagara Falls Office
1910 Pine Ave., Niagara Falls 14301
(716) 282-1274; Fax: (716) 282-2479

Rochester Office
3120 Federal Bldg., 100 State St., Rochester 14614
(716) 232-4850; Fax: (716) 232-1954

Note: All seats in the House of Representatives subject to November 2010 election results

REPRESENTATIVE, Paul D. Tonko
21st District, Democrat
128 Cannon House Office Bldg., Washington, DC 20515
(202) 225-5076; Fax: (202) 225-5077
Internet: http://tonko.house.gov
Chief of Staff: Dustin Todd (Acting)

District Offices:

Albany Office
827 O'Brien Federal Bldg., Albany 12207
(518) 465-0700; Fax: (518) 427-5107

Amsterdam Office
61 Church St., Room 309, Amsterdam 12010
(518) 843-3400; Fax: (518) 843-8874

Schenectady Office
105 Jay St., Room 15, Schenectady 12305
(518) 374-4547; Fax: (518) 374-7908

REPRESENTATIVE, Edolphus Towns
10th District, Democrat
2232 Rayburn House Office Bldg., Washington, DC 20515
(202) 225-5936; Fax: (202) 225-1018
Internet: www.house.gov/towns
Chief of Staff: Albert Wiltshire

District Offices:

Brooklyn Office
186 Joralemon St., Suite 1102, Brooklyn 11201
(718) 855-8018; Fax: (718) 858-4542

Brooklyn Office
104-08 Flatlands Ave., Brooklyn 11236
(718) 272-1175; Fax: (718) 272-1178

REPRESENTATIVE, Nydia M. Velazquez
12th District, Democrat
2466 Rayburn House Office Bldg.,
Washington, DC 20515-2104
(202) 225-2361; Fax: (202) 226-0327
Internet: www.house.gov/velazquez
Chief of Staff: Michael Day

District Offices:

Brooklyn Office
266 Broadway, Suite 201, Brooklyn 11211
(718) 599-3658; Fax: (718) 599-4537

Lower East Side Office
173 Avenue B, N.Y.C. 10009
(212) 673-3997; Fax: (212) 473-5242

South West Brooklyn Office
16 Court St., Suite 1006, Brooklyn 11241
(718) 222-5819; Fax: (718) 222-5830

REPRESENTATIVE, Anthony D. Weiner
9th District, Democrat
2104 Rayburn House Office Bldg., Washington, DC 20515
(202) 225-6616; Fax: (202) 226-7253
Internet: http://weiner.house.gov
Chief of Staff: Marie Ternes

District Offices:

Brooklyn Office
1800 Sheepshead Bay Rd., Brooklyn 11235
(718) 743-0441; Fax: (718) 743-7247

Kew Gardens Office
80-02 Kew Gardens Rd., Suite 5000,
Kew Gardens 11415
(718) 520-9001; Fax: (718) 520-9010

Rockaway Office
90-16 Rockaway Beach Blvd., Rockaway 11693
(718) 318-9255

REPRESENTATIVE, Vacancy at Press Time
29th District
1208 Longworth House Office Bldg.,
Washington, DC 20515
(202) 225-3161; Fax: (202) 226-6599

District Offices:

Pittsford Office
101 Grove St., Suite 101, Pittsford 14534
(585) 218-0400; Fax: (585) 218-0053

Corning Office
89 W. Market St., Corning 14830
(607) 654-7566; Fax: (607) 654-7568

Olean Office
317 N. Union St., Olean 14760
(716) 372-2090; Fax: (716) 372-2869

Note: All seats in the House of Representatives subject to November 2010 election results

COSTS AND FEES

NEW YORK STAMP TAXES
Stock Transfer Tax Rates

Sellng Price Per Share	Tax Rate Per 100
$20 and over	$ 5.00
$10 - $19.99	3.75
$5 - $9.99	2.50
Under $5	1.25
Maximum Tax on Sales Transactions	350.00
No Sale Transactions	2.50

***Editors' Note: Effective October 1, 1981, 100% of Stock Transfer Tax is rebatable. Rebate Claims must be made within two years of tax payment date with the State Tax Commission.**

Real Estate Transfer Tax

When consideration for conveyance of real property or an interest therein exceeds $500 the tax is $2.00 for each $500 or fractional part thereof; provided, however, that with respect to (a) a conveyance of a one, two or three-family house and an individual residential condominium unit, or interests therein; and (b) conveyances where the consideration is less than $500,000, the consideration for the interest conveyed shall exclude the value of any lien or encumbrance remaining thereon at the time of conveyances.

In addition, if consideration on conveyance of real property or interest therein is $1,000,000 or more, an additional tax of 1% is imposed, on that portion of the conveyance attributable to residential real property.

FEES OF THE DEPARTMENT OF STATE

Bureau of Corporations

Filing Corporate and Other Certificates (except pursuant to Not-for-Profit Corporation Law)†

Certificate of Incorporation (all corporations)	$125.00
Registration, Domestic Limited Partnership	200.00
Registration, Domestic Limited Liability Partnership	200.00
Registration, Foreign Limited Liability Partnership	250.00
Articles of Organization, Domestic Limited Liability Company or Domestic Professional Limited Liability Company	200.00
Application for Authority,	
Foreign Limited Liability Company	250.00
Foreign Corporation	225.00
Foreign Limited Partnership, Foreign Professional Limited Liability Company or Foreign Professional Corporation	200.00
Amendment, Correction or Restated Certificates	60.00
Consolidation or Merger	60.00
Dissolution	60.00
Certificate of Resignation for Receipt of Process:	
Corporation	60.00
Limited Partnership, Limited Liability Company or Limited Liability Partnership	10.00
Certificate of Resignation of Registered Agent (Corporation)	60.00
Limited Liability Company	20.00
Certificate of Election of Trustees	25.00
Reservation of Name or Extension or Cancellation of Reservation	20.00
Certificate of Change	
§ 121-202-A(a) (Domestic Limited Partnership)	30.00
§ 121-202-A(b) (Domestic Limited Partnership)	5.00
§ 121-903-A(a) (Foreign Limited Partnership)	30.00
§ 121-903-A(b) (Foreign Limited Partnership)	5.00
§ 805-A(a) (Corporation)	30.00
§ 805-A(b) (Corporation)	5.00
§ 211-A(a) (Domestic Limited Liability Company)	$ 30.00
§ 211-A(b) (Domestic Limited Liability Company)	5.00
§ 804-A(a) Foreign Limited Liability Company)	30.00
§ 804-A(b) Foreign Limited Liability Company)	5.00
§ 121-1500 (j-1) Domestic Limited Liability Partnership	5.00
§ 121-1502 (i-1) Foreign Limited Liability Partnership	5.00
Certificate of Joint Stock Association	60.00
Surrender of Authority by Foreign Corporation, Foreign Limited Partnership or Foriegn Limited Liability Company	60.00
Termination of Foreign Corporation, Foreign Limited Partnership or Foriegn Limited Liability Company	60.00
Cancellation, Domestic Limited Partnership	60.00
Certificate of Adoption, Domestic Limited Partnership	200.00
Certificate of Publication, Limited Partnership, Limited Liability Partnership and Limited Liability Company	50.00
Biennial Statement, Corporation or Limited Liability Company	9.00
Biennial Statement Amendment, Corporation...	9.00
Five-Year Statement, Domestic Limited Liability Partnership	20.00
Five-Year Statement, Foreign Limited Liability Partnership	50.00
Judicial Dissolution, Domestic Limited Liability Company	60.00
Certificate of Conversion, Domestic Limited Liability Company	200.00
Withdrawal, Domestic Limited Liability Partnership	60.00
Withdrawal of Notice, Foreign Limited Liability Partnership	60.00
Certificate of Consent, Limited Liability Partnership	50.00

†Organization Tax on share not included

Filing Under the Not-for-Profit Corporation Law

Incorporation	$ 75.00
Amendment or Restated	30.00
Consolidation or Merger	30.00
Certificate of Change	20.00
Dissolution	30.00
Reservation of Name or Extension or Cancellation of Reservation	10.00
Application for Authority	135.00
Termination of Foreign Corporation	30.00
Surrender of Foreign Corporation	30.00
Resignation of Registered Agent	30.00
Type	30.00
Annulment of Dissolution, Reinstatement and Report of Existence	30.00

Serving Process

Corporation, Limited Liability Company, Limited Partnership or Limited Liability Partnership	$ 40.00
Joint Stock Association and Business Trust	40.00
Motor Vehicle, Boats or Aircraft	10.00
Certificate as to Service of Process	25.00

Certificates Issued, Etc.

Certificate as to documents on file, status of corporations, limited liability company, etc.	$ 25.00
Affixing the Great Seal of the State	10.00
Certified copy	10.00
Uncertified photocopy of filed document	5.00

Expedited Handling

Processing within 2 hours	150.00
Processing the same day	75.00
Processing within 24 hours	25.00

Availability of Name

Fee for each corporation, limited partnership or limited liability company name submitted	$ 5.00

UNITED STATES COURT OF APPEALS SCHEDULE OF FEES (Effective January 1, 2009)

The United States should not be charged fees under this schedule, except those specifically prescribed below.
Federal agencies or programs that are funded from judiciary appropriations (agencies, organizations, and individuals providing services authorized by the Criminal Justice Act, 18 U.S.C. § 3006A and bankruptcy administrators) should not be charged any fees under this schedule.

Docket fee, Court of Appeals (a separate fee must be filed by each party filing a notice of appeal, but parties filing a joint notice of appeal are required to pay only one fee)	$450.00
No fee for application for interlocutory appeal under U.S.C. § 1292 (b) or other petition for permission to appear under F.R.A.P. 5 unless the appeal is allowed; also, no fee for direct bankruptcy appeal or direct bankruptcy cross appeal when fee has been collected by the Bankruptcy Court	
Search of Court Records and certification of the results (applies to United States when the information is available through remote electronic access)	26.00
Certifying any document or paper	9.00
Photocopies (from documents or microfilm), per page (applies to United States when the document is available through remote electronic access)	.50
Reproduction of sound recording, including materials (applies to United States when the recording is available through remote electronic access)	26.00
For reproduction of the record in any appeal in which the requirement of an appendix is dispensed with by any court of appeals pursuant to Rule 30(f), F.R.A.P.	71.00
For retrieval of a record from a Federal Records Center, National Archives, or other storage location removed from the place of business of the court	45.00
For a check paid into the court which is returned for lack of funds	45.00
To be paid by appellant or petitioner upon the filing of any separate or joint notice of appeal or application for appeal from the Bankruptcy Appellate Panel, or notice of the allowance of an appeal from the Bankruptcy Appellate Panel	5.00
Admission of attorney to practice (including certificate)	150.00
Duplicate Certificate of Admission or Certificate of Good Standing	15.00

The clerk shall assess a charge for the handling of registry funds, to be assessed from interest earnings and in accordance with the detailed fee schedule issued by the Director of the Administrative Office of the United States Courts.

The court may charge and collect fees, commensurate with the cost of printing, for copies of the local rules of court. The court may also distribute copies of the local rules without charge.

The court may charge and collect a $200.00 per remote location for counsel's requested use of videoconferencing equipment in connection with each oral argument.

For usage of electronic access to court data, $.60 per minute of usage via dialup service, and $.08 per page for public users using a Federal judiciary Internet site [provided the court may, for good cause, exempt persons or classes of persons from the fees, in order to avoid unreasonable burdens and to promote public access to such information]. No fee is owed until an account holder accrues charges of more than $10.00 in a calendar year. All such fees collected shall be deposited to the Judiciary Information Technology Fund.

For printing copies of any record or document accessed electronically at a public terminal in the courthouse, $.10 per page. **This fee shall apply to the United States.**

For every search of court records conducted by the PACER Service Center, $26.00.

FEES OF UNITED STATES DISTRICT COURT

Pursuant to 28 U.S.C. §1914 and the District Court Miscellaneous Fee Schedule (effective Apr. 9, 2006)

Editor's Note: When in doubt of any fees or for fees not specifically mentioned below, inquire of clerk of particular district.

Schedule of Deposits and Fees

Commencing any civil proceeding other than *habeas corpus*	$350.00
Filing application for writ of *habeas corpus*	5.00
Filing notice or petition of appeal in any case—Civil or criminal	455.00
Filing notice of appeal to district judge from a judgment of conviction by a magistrate in a misdemeanor case	32.00
Search of Court Records (each name or item)	26.00
Certifying any document or paper	9.00
Exemplifying any document or paper	$ 18.00
Filing or indexing any paper not in a case or proceeding (i.e., petition to perpetuate testimony, Rule 27(a), Fed.R.Civ.P., the filing of papers by trustees under 28 U.S.C. §754, the filing of papers rogatory or letters of request, and registering of a judgment from another district pursuant to 28 U.S.C. §1963)	39.00
Registration of foreign judgment	30.00
Admission of attorney to practice (including certificate)	
Northern District	150.00
Pro hac vice admission	30.00
Southern District	185.00
Pro hac vice admission	25.00
Eastern District	170.00
Western District	200.00
Duplicate Certificate of Admission or Certificate of Good Standing	15.00
Copies made by Clerk (does not include certification)	
Photographic copies (from documents or microfilm), per page	.50
Reproduction of magnetic tape recording, including materials	26.00
For each microfiche sheet of film or microfilm jacket copy of any court record, where available	5.00
For retrieval of a record from a Federal Records Center, National Archives, or other storage location removed from the place of business of the court	45.00
For a check paid into the court which is returned for lack of funds	45.00
For filing an action brought under Title III of the Cuban Liberty and Democratic Solidarity (LIBERTAD) Act of 1996, P.L. 104-114, 110 Stat. §785 (1996) (in addition to the fee for commencing any civil proceeding other than habeas corpus)	5,431.00

The clerk shall assess a charge for the handling of registry funds, to be assessed from interest earnings and in accordance with the detailed fee schedule issued by the Director of the Administrative Office of the United States Courts.

The court may charge and collect fees, commensurate with the cost of printing, for copies of the local rules of court. The court may also distribute copies of the local rules without charge.

For usage of electronic access to court data, $.60 per minute of usage via dialup service, and $.08 per page for public users using a Federal judiciary Internet site [provided the court may, for good cause, exempt persons or classes of persons from the fees, in order to avoid unreasonable burdens and to promote public access to such information]. No fee is owed until an account holder accrues charges of more than $10.00 in a calendar year.

For printing copies of any record or document accessed electronically at a public terminal in the courthouse, $.10 per page. **This fee shall apply to the United States.**

For every search of court records conducted by the PACER Service Center, $20.00.

Checks and money orders may be made payable to the Clerk, United States District Court.

Fees of the U.S. District Court—Cont'd

Federal Post Judgment Interest Rates

From Oct. 1, 1982 to Dec. 21, 2000, the interest rate on civil money judgments in federal district court was calculated from the date of entry of the judgment at a rate equal to the equivalent coupon issue yield (as determined by the Secretary of the Treasury) of 52-week U.S. Treasury Bills settled immediately prior to the date of the judgment. Effective Dec. 21, 2000, the interest rate is calcuated at a rate equal to the weekly average 1-year constant maturity Treasury yield, as published by the Board of Governors of the Federal Reserve System for the preceding calendar week. 28 U.S. §1961. For the latest yield rate releases, consult the Federal Reserve's website at www.federalreserve.gov/releases/h15.

Jan. 6, 2006	4.37%
Jan. 13, 2006	4.41%
Jan. 20, 2006	4.43%
Jan. 27, 2006	4.50%
Feb. 3, 2006	4.60%
Feb. 10, 2006	4.67%
Feb. 17, 2006	4.70%
Feb. 24, 2006	4.72%
Mar. 3, 2006	4.74%
Mar. 10, 2006	4.77%
Mar. 17, 2006	4.76%
Mar. 24, 2006	4.77%
March 31, 2006	4.82%
April 7, 2006	4.85%
April 14, 2006	4.91%
April 21, 2006	4.90%
April 28, 2006	4.94%
May 5, 2006	4.98%
May 12, 2006	5.01%
May 19, 2006	4.98%
May 26, 2006	4.99%
June 2, 2006	5.03%
June 9, 2006	5.04%
June 16, 2006	5.13%
June 23, 2006	5.24%
June 30, 2006	5.27%
July 7, 2006	5.27%
July 14, 2006	5.24%
July 21, 2006	5.22%
July 28, 2006	5.17%
Aug. 4, 2006	5.10%
Aug. 11, 2006	5.09%
Aug. 18, 2006	5.10%
Aug. 25, 2006	5.07%
Sept. 1, 2006	5.03%
Sept. 8, 2006	5.02%
Sept. 15, 2006	5.02%
Sept. 22, 2006	4.97%
Sept. 29, 2006	4.90%
Oct. 6, 2006	4.90%
Oct. 13, 2006	5.03%
Oct. 20, 2006	5.05%
Oct. 27, 2006	5.07%
Nov. 3, 2006	5.00%
Nov. 10, 2006	5.03%
Nov. 17, 2006	5.03%
Nov. 24, 2006	5.01%
Dec. 1, 2006	4.95%
Dec. 8, 2006	4.90%
Dec. 15, 2006	4.95%
Dec. 22, 2006	4.96%
Dec. 29, 2006	4.99%
Jan. 5, 2007	4.98%
Jan. 12, 2007	5.03%
Jan. 19, 2007	5.08%
Jan. 26, 2007	5.10%
Feb. 2, 2007	5.10%
Feb. 9, 2007	5.07%
Feb. 16, 2007	5.07%
Feb. 23, 2007	5.05%
Mar. 2, 2007	4.96%
Mar. 9, 2007	4.92%
Mar. 16, 2007	4.93%
Mar. 23, 2007	4.93%
Mar. 30, 2007	4.90%
April 6, 2007	4.94%
April 13, 2007	4.97%
April 20, 2007	4.93%
April 27, 2007	4.90%
May 4, 2007	4.90%
May 11, 2007	4.89%
May 18, 2007	4.86%
May 25, 2007	4.95%
June 1, 2007	4.96%
June 8, 2007	4.98%
June 15, 2007	4.98%
June 22, 2007	4.95%
June 29, 2007	4.94%
July 6, 2007	4.99%
July 13, 2007	5.00%
July 20, 2007	4.99%
July 27, 2007	4.91%
Aug. 3, 2007	4.83%
Aug. 10, 2007	4.78%
Aug. 17, 2007	4.44%
Aug. 24, 2007	4.16%
Aug. 31, 2007	4.30%
Sept. 7, 2007	4.27%
Sept 14, 2007	4.15%
Sept. 21, 2007	4.11%
Sept. 28, 2007	4.05%
Oct. 5, 2007	4.12%
Oct. 12, 2007	4.24%
Oct. 19, 2007	4.14%
Oct. 26, 2007	3.97%
Nov. 2, 2007	3.93%
Nov. 9, 2007	3.72%
Nov. 16, 2007	3.58%
Nov. 23, 2007	3.30%
Nov. 30, 2007	3.25%
Dec. 7, 2007	3.17%
Dec. 14, 2007	3.20%
Dec. 21, 2007	3.28%
Dec. 28, 2007	3.42%
Jan. 4, 2008	3.18%
Jan. 11, 2008	3.04%
Jan. 18, 2008	2.83%
Jan. 25, 2008	2.31%
Feb. 1, 2008	2.23%
Feb. 8, 2008	2.08%
Feb. 15, 2008	2.04%
Feb. 22, 2008	2.10%
Feb. 29, 2008	1.98%
Mar. 7, 2008	1.66%
Mar. 14, 2008	1.52%
Mar. 21, 2008	1.35%
Mar. 28, 2008	1.60%
Apr. 4, 2008	1.63%
Apr. 11, 2008	1.63%
Apr. 18, 2088	1.67%
Apr. 25, 2008	1.88%
May 2, 2008	1.93%
May 9, 2008	1.94%
May 16, 2008	2.07%
May 23, 2008	2.09%
May 30, 2008	2.16%
June 6, 2008	2.14%
June 13, 2008	2.51%
June 20, 2008	2.57%
June 27, 2008	2.46%
July 4, 2008	2.35%
July 11, 2008	2.25%
July 18, 2008	2.21%
July 25, 2008	2.33%
Aug. 1, 2008	2.30%
Aug. 8, 2008	2.23%
Aug. 15, 2008	2.18%
Aug. 22, 2008	2.12%
Aug. 29, 2008	2.17%
Sept. 5, 2008	2.08%
Sept. 12, 2008	2.05%
Sept. 19, 2008	1.69%
Sept. 26, 2008	1.95%
Oct. 3, 2008	1.59%
Oct. 10, 2008	1.24%
Oct. 17, 2008	1.25%
Oct. 24, 2008	1.66%
Oct. 31, 2008	1.44%
Nov. 7, 2008	1.24%
Nov. 14, 2008	1.12%
Nov. 21, 2008	0.96%
Nov. 28, 2008	0.93%
Dec. 5, 2008	0.69%
Dec. 12, 2008	0.50%
Dec. 19, 2008	0.45%
Dec. 26, 2008	0.40%
Jan. 2, 2009	0.37%
Jan. 9, 2009	0.44%
Jan. 16, 2009	0.43%
Jan. 23, 2009	0.43%
Jan. 30, 2009	0.49%
Feb. 6, 2009	0.54%
Feb. 13, 2009	0.60%
Feb. 20, 2009	0.64%
Feb. 27, 2009	0.72%
Mar. 6, 2009	0.68%
Mar. 13, 2009	0.70%
Mar. 20, 2009	0.64%
Mar. 27, 2009	0.59%
Apr. 3, 2009	0.58%
Apr. 10, 2009	0.60%
Apr. 17, 2009	0.55%
Apr. 24, 2009	0.52%
May 1, 2009	0.50%
May 8, 2009	0.53%
May 15, 2009	0.52%
May 22, 2009	0.47%
May 29, 2009	0.49%
June 5, 2009	0.50%
June 12, 2009	0.56%
June 19, 2009	0.51%
June 26, 2009	0.48%
July 3, 2009	0.53%
July 10, 2009	0.46%
July 17, 2009	0.48%
July 24, 2009	0.47%
July 31, 2009	0.49%
Aug. 7, 2009	0.49%
Aug. 14, 2009	0.47%
Aug. 21, 2009	0.44%
Aug. 28, 2009	0.45%
Sept. 4, 2009	0.42%
Sept. 11, 2009	0.40%
Sept. 18, 2009	0.40%
Sept. 25, 2009	0.41%
Oct. 2, 2009	0.39%
Oct. 9, 2009	0.36%
Oct. 16, 2009	0.36%
Oct. 23, 2009	0.39%
Oct. 30, 2009	0.39%
Nov. 6, 2009	0.36%
Nov. 13, 2009	0.33%
Nov. 20, 2009	0.29%
Nov. 27, 2009	0.27%
Dec. 4, 2009	0.29%
Dec. 11, 2009	0.32%
Dec. 18, 2009	0.37%
Dec. 25, 2009	0.41%
Jan. 1, 2010	0.47%
Jan. 8, 2010	0.41%
Jan. 15, 2010	0.35%
Jan. 22, 2010	0.31%
Jan. 29, 2010	0.31%
Feb. 5, 2010	0.33%
Feb. 12, 2010	0.35%
Feb. 19, 2010	0.36%
Feb. 26, 2010	0.34%
Mar. 5, 2010	0.34%
Mar. 12, 2010	0.39%
Mar. 19, 2010	0.41%
Mar. 26, 2010	0.42%
Apr. 2, 2010	0.43%
Apr. 9, 2010	0.47%
Apr. 16, 2010	0.44%
Apr. 23, 2010	0.44%
Apr. 30, 2010	0.43%
May 7, 2010	0.39%
May 14, 2010	0.38%
May 21, 2010	0.35%
May 28, 2010	0.36%
June 4, 2010	0.36%
June 11, 2010	0.33%
June 18, 2010	0.30%
June 25, 2010	0.29%
July 2, 2010	0.31%
July 9, 2010	0.31%
July 16, 2010	0.28%
July 23, 2010	0.27%
July 30, 2010	0.30%
Aug. 6, 2010	0.27%
Aug. 13, 2010	0.25%
Aug. 20, 2010	0.25%
Aug. 27, 2010	0.26%
Sept. 3, 2010	0.25%
Sept. 10, 2010	0.26%
Sept. 17, 2010	0.26%
Sept. 25, 2010	0.25%
Oct. 1, 2010	0.26%
Oct. 8, 2010	0.24%
Oct. 15. 2010	0.22%

FEES OF U.S. BANKRUPTCY COURTS
Filing and Conversion Fees

To be collected by the clerk in Bankruptcy Code cases pursuant to 28 U.S.C. §1930 and the Bankruptcy Court Miscellaneous Fee Schedule (effective October 1, 2008)

For a case commenced under Chapter 7 of Title 11 (including $39.00 administrative fee and $15.00 trustee surcharge)	$299.00
For a case commenced under Chapter 13 of Title 11 (including $39.00 administrative fee).	274.00
For a case commenced under Chapter 9 of Title 11 (including $39.00 administrative fee)	1,039.00
For a case commenced under Chapter 12 of Title 11 (including $39.00 administrative fee).	239.00
For a case commenced under Chapter 11 of Title 11 that does not concern a railroad, as defined in section 101 of Title 11 (including $39.00 administrative fee)	1039.00
For filing case under Chapter 15 (formerly a petition ancillary to a foreign proceeding under 11 U.S.C.§304) (including $39.00 administrative fee)	$ 1,039.00
For filing an Adversary proceeding	250.00
For a conversion from Chapter 7 of Title 11 to Chapter 11 on request of debtor	755.00
For a conversion from Chapter 13 of Title 11 to Chapter 11 on request of debtor	765.00
For a conversion from Chapter 7 of Title 11 to Chapter 11 on request of debtor	755.00
For a conversion from Chapter 13 of Title 11 to Chapter 11 on request of debtor	765.00
For a conversion from Chapter 13 of Title 11 to Chapter 7 on request of debtor	25.00
For a conversion from Chapter 12 of Title 11 to Chapter 7 on request of debtor	60.00
For a conversion from Chapter 12 of Title 11 to Chapter 13 on request of debtor	35.00
For splitting of a Joint Chapter 7 case	260.00
For splitting of a Joint Chapter 11 case	1,000.00
For splitting of a Joint Chapter 13 case	235.00
For reopening of a Chapter 7 case	260.00
For reopening of a Chapter 13 case	235.00
For reopening of a Chapter 15 case	1,000.00
For filing Notice of Appeal (including docket fee)	255.00
Addl. fee upon authorization of appeal	200.00
For filing a motion to convert a case to Chapter 7 of Title 11 or a notice of conversion pursuant to Section 1208(a) or Section 1307(a) of Title 11	15.00

Note: Filing fees should also be collected when a case is reopened except in cases of administrative error or actions relating to the discharge.

Miscellaneous Fee Schedule

The fees included in this schedule are to be charged for services provided by the bankruptcy courts.

- The United States should not be charged fees under this schedule, with the exception of those specifically prescribed in Items 1, 3, and 5 when the information requested is available through remote electronic access.
- Federal agencies or programs that are funded from judiciary appropriations (agencies, organizations, and individuals providing services authorized by the Criminal Justice Act, 18 U.S.C. § 3006A and bankruptcy administrators) should not be charged any fees under this schedule.

1. For reproducing any document, $.50 per page. This fee applies to services rendered on behalf of the United States if the document requested is available through electronic access.

2. For certification of any document, $9.00. For exemplification of any document, $18.00.

3. For reproduction of an audio recording of a court proceeding, $26.00. This fee applies to services rendered on behalf of the United States if the recording is available electronically.

4. For filing an amendment to the debtor's schedules, lists of creditors, or mailing lists, $26.00, except:

- The bankruptcy judge may, for good cause, waive the charge in any case.
- The fee must not be charged if:
  - the amendment is to change the address of a creditor or an attorney for a creditor listed on the schedules; or
  - the amendment is to add the name and address of an attorney for a creditor listed on the schedules

5. For conducting a search of the bankruptcy courecords, $26.00 per name or item searched. This fee applies to services rendered on behalf of the United States if the information requested is available through electronic access.

6. For filing a complaint, $250.00, except:

- If a trustee or debtor-in-possession files the complaint, the fee should be paid by the estate, if there is an estate.
- This fee must not be charged if—
  - the debtor is the plaintiff; or
  - a child support creditor or representative files the complaint and submits the form required by § 304(g) of the Bankruptcy Reform Act of 1994.

7. For filing any document that is not related to a pending case or proceeding, $39.00.

8. Administrative fee for filing a case under Title 11 or when a motion to divide the case is filed, $39.00.

9. For payment to trustees pursuant to 11 U.S.C § 330(b)(2), a $15.00 fee applies in the following circumstances:

- For filing a petition under Chapter 7.
- For filing a motion to reopen a Chapter 7 case.
- For filing a motion to divide a joint Chapter 7 case.
- For filing a motion to convert a case to a Chapter 7 case.
- For filing a notice of conversion to a Chapter 7 case.

10. In addition to any fees imposed under Item 9, above, the following fees must be collected:

- For filing a motion to convert a Chapter 12 case to a Chapter 7 case or a notice of conversion pursuant to 11 U.S.C. § 1208(a), $45.
- For filing a motion to convert a Chapter 13 case to a Chapter 7 case or a notice of conversion pursuant to 11 U.S.C. § 1307(a), $10.

The fee amounts in this item are derived from the fees prescribed in 28 U.S.C. § 1930(a).

If the trustee files the motion to convert, the fee is payable only from the estate that exists prior to conversion.

If the filing fee for the chapter to which the case is requested to be converted is less than the fee paid at the commencement of the case, no refund may be provided.

11. For filing a motion to reopen, the following fees apply:

- For filing a motion to reopen a Chapter 7 case, $245.
- For filing a motion to reopen a Chapter 9 case, $1,000.
- For filing a motion to reopen a Chapter 11 case, $1,000.
- For filing a motion to reopen a Chapter 12 case, $200.
- For filing a motion to reopen a Chapter 13 case, $235.
- For filing a motion to reopen a Chapter 15 case, $1,000.

The fee amounts in this item are derived from the fees prescribed in 28 U.S.C. § 1930(a).

The reopening fee must be charged when a case has been closed without a discharge being entered.

The court may waive this fee under appropriate circumstances or may defer payment of the fee from trustees pending discovery of additional assets. If payment is deferred, the fee should be waived if no additional assets are discovered.

The reopening fee must not be charged in the following instances:

- to permit a party to file a complaint to obtain a determination under Rule 4007(b); or
- when a debtor files a motion to reopen a case based upon an alleged violation of the terms of the discharge under 11 U.S.C. § 524; or
- when the reopening is to correct an administrative error.

12. For retrieval of a record from a Federal Records Center, National Archives, or other storage location removed from the place of business of the court, $45.00.

13. For a check paid into the court which is returned for lack of funds, $45.00.

Fees of U.S. Bankruptcy Courts—Cont'd

14. For filing an appeal or cross appeal from a final judgment, $250.00.

- This fee is collected in addition to the statutory fee of $5 that is collected under 28 U.S.C. § 1930 (c) when a notice of appeal is filed.
- Parties filing a joint notice of appeal should pay only one fee.
- If a trustee or debtor in possession is the appellant, the fee must be payable only from the estate and to the extent there is any estate realized.
- Upon notice from the court of appeals that a direct appeal or cross appeal has been authorized, an additional fee of $200 must be collected.

15. For filing a case under Chapter 15 of the Bankruptcy Code, $1,000.

This fee is derived from and equal to the fee prescribed in 28 U.S.C. § 1930 (a)(3) for filing a case commenced under Chapter 11 of Title 11.

16. The court may charge and collect fees commensurate with the cost of providing copies of the local rules of court. The court may also distribute copies of the local rules without charge.

17. The clerk shall assess a charge for the handling of registry funds deposited with the court, to be assessed from interest earnings and in accordance with the detailed fee schedule issued by the Director of the Administrative Office of the United States Courts.

18. For filing a motion to divide a joint case filed under 11 U.S.C. § 302, the following fees apply:

- For filing a motion to divide a Chapter 7 case, $245.
- For filing a motion to divide a Chapter 11 case, $1,000.
- For filing a motion to divide a Chapter 12 case, $200.
- For filing a motion to divide a Chapter 13 case, $235.

These fees are derived from and equal to the filing fees prescribed in 28 U.S.C. § 1930 (a).

19. For filing the following motions, $150:

- To terminate, annul, modify or condition the automatic stay;
- To compel abandonment of property of the estate pursuant to Rule 6007(b) of the Federal Rules of Bankruptcy Procedure; or
- To withdraw the reference of a case or proceeding under 28 U.S.C. § 157(d).

This fee must not be collected in the following situations:

- For a motion for relief from the co-debtor stay;
- For a stipulation for court approval of an agreement for relief from a stay; or

For a motion filed by a child support creditor or its representative, if the form required by § 304(g) of the Bankruptcy Reform Act of 1994 is filed.

FEES OF COUNTY CLERKS AS CLERKS OF COURTS (Sec. 8016-8020, C.P.L.R.)

Note: In some counties, interpretation of statutory fees may vary

Assigning index number	$ 210.00
In Foreclosure matters	400.00
Docketing return of execution	No Fee
Filing, docketing and recording notice of pendency of action or notice of attachment against real property	35.00
each add'l lot	1.00
Cancelling notice of pendency of action	No Fee
Discharging judgment of record by deposit with clerk	No Fee
Placing case on calendar	125.00
Request for Judicial Intervention	95.00
Placing cause on calendar after Request for Judicial Intervention	30.00
Filing of Motion or Cross-Motion	45.00

Where a cause which has been placed on a calendar is transferred before trial to a court for which a larger calendar fee is prescribed, difference in fee is payable when placed on calendar of latter court. No additional fee required when transfer is for consolidation or joint trial with another action.

Filing demand for jury of six:	65.00

Where cause is transferred before trial to a court for which a larger jury fee is prescribed, difference in fee is payable when placed on calendar of latter court. No additional fee when transfer is for consolidation or joint trial with another action in which jury fee was paid.

Filing Notice of Appeal	$ 65.00
Filing Stipulation of Settlement or Voluntary Discontinuance Pursuant to CPLR Rule 3217	35.00

Copies of Records

Preparing copy of any paper or record on file, per page	$.65 minimum $1.30
Certifying prepared copy of any record or paper on file, per page	.65 minimum $5.20
Preparing and certifying copy of any record or paper on file, per page	$ 1.25 minimum $5.00
Preparing and certifying certificate of honorable discharge, except as provided for in the military law (No fee for first copy)	$ 2.50

Certification, exemplification, copies of papers

a. Issuing any certificate, except as otherwise provided in this article:	
In New York City	$8.00
All other counties	4.00
b. Certificate of exemplification, exclusive of certification:	
In New York City	25.00
All other counties	10.00

Searches

Certifying search of court records, per name, for each 2 year period	$5.00

Production of court records

For each day or part thereof in attendance pursuant to a subpoena duces tecum $20.00 plus 12¢ per mile each way and necessary expenses of messenger, but if production is in New York City, then actual transportation costs instead of mileage.

FEES OF COUNTY CLERKS OTHER THAN AS CLERKS OF COURTS (Sec. 8021, C.P.L.R.)

Note: In some counties, interpretation of statutory fees may vary

Instruments Relating to Real Property

Filing and indexing map	$10.00
Affixing and indexing notice of foreclosure of mortgage	10.00

Recording, entering, indexing and endorsing a certificate on any instrument, $45.00, $5.00 per page and 50¢ for each additional town, city, block or other index in which to be indexed, and on assignment of mortgage or release 50¢ extra for each assignment. For each additional mortgage assigned, $3.00.

Note: In addition, state real property transfer tax must be paid on recording deeds, at rate of $2.00 for each $500 or fractional part thereof of consideration in excess of remaining liens. (Sec. 1402, Tax Law). If consideration on conveyance of residential real property exceeds $1,000,000, an additional 1% tax is imposed (Sec. 1402a, Tax Law).

Mortgage Tax (Sec. 253, Tax Law):

On any mortgage to be paid as follows:

By Lender: 25¢ per $100 or every major fraction thereof.

By Borrower:

1. On mortgages of less than $10,000: 50¢ per $100 or major fraction thereof.
2. On mortgages of $10,000 and more: 50¢ per $100 or every major fraction thereof: In transportation districts, add 25¢ per $100 or every major fraction thereof, less $25 credit for 1-or-2-family dwellings only.
3. On mortgage for more-than-2 family dwelling: 75¢ per $100.

Fees of County Clerks—Cont'd

Mortgage Tax—Cont'd

4. In City of New York: See Fees of New York City Register, Pages 159-160.
5. In County of Nassau: Add $1.00 per $100 or major fraction thereof.
6. In counties of Albany, Broome, Cattaraugus, Chautauqua, Cortland, Dutchess, Essex, Genesee, Hamilton, Herkimer, Lewis, Rensselaer, Rockland, Schenectady, Schoharie, Sullivan, Steuben, Warren, Wayne, Westchester, Wyoming and Yates: Add 25¢ per $100 or major fraction thereof.
7. In counties of Columbia and Greene: Add 50¢ per $100 or major fraction thereof.
8. In City of Yonkers: Add 50¢ per $100 or major fraction thereof.

Re-indexing a recorded instrument, for each town, city, block or other index re-indexed.	$2.00
Entering each cross reference of any instrument on margin of record of another instrument	.50
Examining record of assignment of mortgage or other instrument recited in certificate of discharge of mortgage	.50
Filing notice of pendency of action or notice of attachment against real property:	
In New York City	35.00
All other counties	15.00
Cancelling notice of pendency of action	No Fee
Filing any other paper	5.00

plus $3.00 per page, plus 50¢ for each additional surname, plus 50¢ for each index involved.

Combined real property transfer gains tax affidavit	5.00
Filing notice of mechanics lien or notice of lending:	
In New York City	30.00
All other counties	15.00
(No fee for notice or order continuing, amending or cancelling same)	
Filing affidavit of mechanics lien	5.00
Discharge of mechanics lien by deposit with clerk.	3.00
Filing building loan contract:	
In New York City	50.00
All other counties	25.00
Equalization and Assessment	165.00
Qualified Farm or Residential Property as defined in Real Prop. Law § 333 1-e	165.00

Filing Papers Other Than Those Relating To Real Property or the Uniform Commercial Code

Filing any certificate or instrument in relation to a corporation, or pursuant to §49a of the personal property law, or in relation to a joint stock association, limited partnership, continued use of firm name, or registration of hotel name:	
In New York City	$100.00
All other counties	25.00
(No fee for filing proof of publication or cancellation, discontinuance or dissolution certificate)	
Filing certificate pursuant to §130 of the General Business Law	
In New York City	100.00
All other counties	25.00
(No fee for filing proof of publication or cancellation, discontinuance or dissolution certificate)	
Filing assignment of or order for payment of salary or wages:	
In New York City	10.00
All other counties	5.00
(No fee for filing satisfaction, assignment, cancellation or vacation of same)	
Filing and entering any instrument affecting chattels except in New York City	1.50
Filing notice of lien on merchandise or assignment or renewal thereof	1.50
Filing notice of hospital lien	5.00
(No fee for filing satisfaction, amendment, assignment, cancellation or discharge of same)	
Filing transcript of judgment:	
In New York City	$ 25.00
All other counties	10.00
(No fee for filing satisfaction, amendment, cancellation or assignment of same)	
Filing and indexing certificate of appointment of notary public or commissioner of deeds	10.00
Filing assignment of money due on contract, or order on owner	25.00
(No fee for filing notice or order continuing, amending or cancelling same)	
Recording orders of commitment under §384 of the Social Services Law; per instrument or order:	
In New York City	10.00
All other counties	5.00
Filing any other paper or instrument:	
In New York City	10.00
All other counties	5.00

Certifying, Copying and Related Services Other Than In Connection With Real Property Instruments or Instruments Filed Under the Uniform Commercial Code

Issuing execution of a judgment	$ 5.00
Issuing transcript of judgment or other lien:	
In New York City	15.00
All other counties	5.00
Issuing certificate of appointment of notary public	10.00
Issuing certificate authenticating act of notary public, commissioner of deeds, or other public officer	3.00
(No charge on papers required by V.A.)	

Issuing official receipt for instruments affecting personal property

Certificate of exemplification, exclusive of certification	$ 10.00
Preparing and certifying copy of marriage record	5.00
Issuing any other certificate:	
In New York City	10.00
All other counties	5.00

Services Under Part IV, Art. 9, Uniform Commercial Code Note: only applicable to County Clerks if collateral is affixed to Real Property

N.B. Add an additional 75¢ additional party beyond the first named debtor following filings.

1. Filing, indexing, furnishing data for financing or continuation statement (see 19 NYCRR 144.1)	
a) Filing Fee	$ 40.00
b) Search Fee	25.00
c) Certified Copies	10.00
d) Uncertified Copies	5.00
2. Filing assignment or statement of assignment of security interest in or accompanying a termination statement	
a) Filing Fee	40.00
b) Search Fee	25.00
c) Certified Copies	10.00
d) Uncertified Copies	5.00
3. Filing termination statement or statements of assignment or release pertaining thereto of furnishing acknowledgement of filing thereof.	
a) Filing Fee	40.00
b) Search Fee	25.00
c) Certified Copies	10.00
d) Uncertified Copies	5.00
4. Filing, indexing, furnishing data for financing statement indicating assignment of a security interest	
a) Filing Fee	40.00
b) Search Fee	25.00
c) Certified Copies	10.00
d) Uncertified Copies	5.00

Fees of County Clerks—Cont'd

5. Filing, indexing, furnishing data about statement of assignment

a) Filing Fee	$ 40.00
b) Search Fee	25.00
c) Certified Copies	10.00
d) Uncertified Copies	5.00

6. Filing statement and release of collateral

a) Filing Fee	40.00
b) Search Fee	25.00
c) Certified Copies	10.00
d) Uncertified Copies	5.00

7. For noting file number and date and hour of filing on copies of more than 1 page on forms other than Secretary of State, per page ... 1.50

8. For issuing a certificate of a filed financing statement of assignment or release

a) Filing Fee	40.00
b) Search Fee	25.00
c) Certified Copies	10.00
d) Uncertified Copies	5.00

9. For furnishing copies of a filed statement of financing, termination, assignment or release, per page ... 1.50

10. Amendments

a) on U.C.C. forms (one page)	7.00
b) with attachments	12.00
c) Real Estate	.50

Searches

Certifying to search of any records not filed under the U.C.C. and other than in an action or proceeding or relating to real property, per name

1. For each 2 year period	$5.00
2. Census records, in counties in the City of New York, for each 2 year period	1.00
All other counties	5.00

Production of Records

Production in any action or proceeding of any filed or recorded instrument other than those filed with the county clerk as clerk of the court is prohibited unless county clerk consents or judge so orders. Instead, certified copy shall be produced in evidence as provided in §4540, CPLR. In event original is produced on order of judge, or certifed copy is subpoenaed, then fee is $20.00 plus mileage at 12¢ per mile each way and necessary expenses of messenger, but if subpoena is served in and place of attendance is in New York City, then actual transportation costs instead of mileage.

COSTS
§§8201 and 8202, C.P.L.R.

For all proceedings before note of issue is filed	$ 200.00
For proceedings after note of issue is filed and before trial, additional assessment	200.00
	(Total $400.00)
For trial of issue of fact, inquest or assessment of damages, additional assessment	300.00
Motion costs not to exceed	100.00

Upon Appeal to Appellate Division §8203(a), C.P.L.R.

Appeal to Appellate Division before argument (unless a lesser amount is awarded) ... $250.00

Upon Appeal to Appellate Term §8203(b), C.P.L.R.

On appeal from a County Court

1. To appellant on reversal up to	$30.00
2. To respondent on affirmance up to	25.00
3. To either party on modification up to	25.00

On appeal from any other court costs governed by applicable court act.

Upon Appeal to Court of Appeals §Sec. 8204, C.P.L.R.

Appeal to the Court of Appeals (unless a lesser amount is awarded) ... $500.00

Additional Allowances to Plaintiff as of Right §8302, C.P.L.R.

Action for foreclosure of mortgage on real property, partition of real property, or determination of claim to real property, plaintiff is entitled in addition to other costs to recover the following percentages:

1. Upon a sum not exceeding $200	10%
2. Additional sum not exceeding $800	5%
3. Additional sum not exceeding $2,000	2%
4. Additional sum not exceeding $5,000	1%

Settlement of cause, plaintiff is entitled to one-half of the rates.

Additional allowances to plaintiff in foreclosure of mortgage action: §8302, C.P.L.R. $50.00 in foreclosure of real estate mortgage.

§8303, C.P.L.R.

A sum not exceeding 2½% of the sum due or claimed to be due on mortgage, not exceeding $300.00

In partition action or a difficult or extraordinary case where a defense interposed a sum not exceeding 5% of the value of the subject matter, not exceeding $3,000.00

In an action for construction of a will or intervivos trust, or proceeding to dispose of infant's property, reasonable attorney's fees and necessary expenses.

In an action brought by the attorney general a sum not exceeding $2,000.00 against each defendant.

A motion relating to enforcing a judgment, 5% with a minimum of $50.00

Disbursements Which May be Included in Bill of Costs §8301, C.P.L.R.

1. Legal fee of witnesses and of referees or other officers.
2. Reasonable compensation of commissioners taking deposition.
3. Legal fees for publication where publication is directed.
4. Legal fees for certified copy of deposition or other paper used or obtained for use at trial.
5. Copies of opinion and charges of judges.
6. Reasonable expenses of printing of papers for hearing where required.
7. Prospective charges for entering and docketing judgments.
8. Sheriff's fees for receiving and returning one execution.
9. Reasonable costs of taking testimony on an examination before trial and making two transcripts of said testimony but not to exceed $250.00 in any one action.
10. Expenses of searches made by title insurance, abstract or searching companies, or by county clerk or public officer or by attorney for party to whom costs are awarded.
11. Reasonable expenses incurred for undertaking to stay execution of judgment subsequently reversed.
12. Reasonable and necessary expenses as are taxable according to the practice of the court

FEES OF THE COURT OF APPEALS

For filing a civil appeal	$ 315.00
Filing of Motion or Cross-Motion on Appeal	45.00

FEES OF THE APPELLATE DIVISION

Filing fee for the Appellate Division for all civil appeals and special proceedings	$ 315.00
Filing of Motion or Cross-Motion on Appeal	45.00

FEES OF SHERIFFS SUPREME AND COUNTY COURTS

Supreme and County Courts §8011, C.P.L.R.

Pursuant to 1992 N.Y. Laws 55, the fees for sheriff are now uniform statewide. There is no longer a distinction between Fees of New York City Sheriff and Sheriffs in other Counties.

Fees of Sheriffs—Cont'd

Receipt and entry	$ 15.00
Levy upon real and personal property	40.00*
Each additional levy	40.00*
Service of order, per defendant	15.00*
Order of attachment, City of New York (including mileage and surcharges)	80.00
Service of summons (with or without complaint)	15.00
Making and filing description of real property, or inventory of personal property, levied upon by order of attachment, or estimate of value thereof.	15.00

Property Execution

Receipt and entry	$ 15.00
Levy upon property by execution	15.00*
Making inventory of property levied by execution	15.00*

Income Execution; Service Upon Judgment Debtor

Receipt and entry	$ 15.00
Service upon judgment debtor	15.00*

Income Execution; Levy Upon Default or Failure to Serve Judgment Debtor

Receipt and entry	$ 15.00
Levying upon money the judgment debtor is receiving or will receive	15.00*

Recovery of Chattel

Receipt and entry	$ 15.00
Execution of Order of seizure against defendant's chattel	75.00*
Each additional defendant	40.00*
Serving additional copy of required papers	15.00*
Serving summons (with or without complaint)	15.00*

Summary Proceeding

Notice of Petition and Petition

Receiving notice, obtaining index number when required, entry and return (not including cost of index number)	$ 15.00
Serving notice on tenant or person in possession	15.00*
Each additional person to be served	15.00
Affidavit of military or non-military service, each affidavit	15.00

Warrant of Eviction

Requisitioning, receipt, entry and return	15.00
Service of Notice	15.00*
Execution of Warrant	75.00*

Sales

Posting Notice of Sale	$ 15.00
Drawing and Executing Conveyance (paid by grantee)	20.00
Attending Sale	15.00*
Conducting Sale	15.00*

Summons, Subpoenas and other Mandates

Service of summons, with or without complaint or notice, or subpoena or civil process	$ 15.00*
Serving or executing order of arrest, or any other mandate	$ 45.00*

Undertakings; Returns; Copies

Taking an Undertaking	$ 1.50
Plus notary's fees to any affidavit or acknowledgments	
Making copy of description or inventory of property levied upon, or of summons and complaint, or other mandate, or of any other paper served	10.00
Certified copy of execution (and return or satisfaction thereupon), or other certified copy	10.00

Prisoners

Each person committed to or discharged from prison	$ 10.00
Attending before an officer to surrender prisoner, take prisoner into custody, in exoneration of bail	10.00

Jurors; View; Constables' Services

Notifying jurors, per juror notified, including the making and return of inquisition when required	$ 2.50
Attending a jury when required	28.00
Attending a view, per day	10.00

FEES OF CLERK OF SURROGATE'S COURT (All Counties) (SCPA, Art. 24, §2402) (Effective July 1, 2003)

(See Chapter 732, Law of N.Y., 1973, which makes SCPA and EPTL printed below applicable in all counties.)

Value of Estate or Subject Matter	Fee Rate
Less than $10,000	$ 45.00
$10,000 but under $20,000	75.00
$20,000 but under $50,000	215.00
$50,000 but under $100,000	280.00
$100,000 but under $250,000	420.00
$250,000 but under $500,000	625.00
$500,000 and over	1,250.00

For filing a petition to commence the following proceedings, the fee shall be as indicated:

SCPA		Fee Rate
607	To punish respondent for contempt	$ 30.00
711	Suspend, modify, revoke letters or remove a fiduciary other than a custodian or guardian	75.00
711	Suspend, modify, revoke letters or remove a custodian or guardian	30.00
715	Application of fiduciary to resign	30.00
717	Suspend powers - fiduciary in war	30.00
1401	Compel production of will	20.00
1420	Construction of will	75.00
1421	Determination of right of election	75.00
1502	Appointment of trustee	45.00
1508	Release against state	50.00
1703	Appointment of guardian	20.00
2003	Open safe deposit box	20.00
2102	Proceedings against a fiduciary	20.00
2103	Proceedings by fiduciary to discover property	75.00
2107	Advice and directions	75.00
2108	Continue business	45.00
2114	Review corporate trustee compensation	10.00
2205	Petition to compel fiduciary to account	30.00
EPTL		
7-4.6	Appointment of successor custodian	15.00

(b) For filing a petition to commence a proceeding for the appointment of a trustee of a lifetime trust or for the appointment of a conservator, the fee shall be the same as that which is payable in the Supreme Court pursuant to §8018 C.P.L.R.

* Plus mileage; in most instances when two or more services are performed at the same time and place there shall be only one mileage fee. In New York City, mileage is a flat $15.00; elsewhere, mileage is equal to the current I.R.S. reimbursment rate, payable for mile in each direction.

Fees of Clerks of Surrogate's Court—Cont'd

For Filing

(i) a demand for trial by jury in any proceeding, SCPA 502	$ 150.00
(ii) objections to the probate of a will, SCPA 1410	150.00
(iii) a note of issue in any proceeding	45.00
(iv) objection or answer in any action or proceeding other than probate	75.00
(v) a will for safekeeping pursuant to §2507 of this act except that the court in any county may reduce or dispense with such fee	45.00
(vi) a bond, including any additional bond: less than $10,000	20.00
$10,000 and over	30.00
For furnishing a transcript of a decree	20.00
For a certificate of letters evidencing that the appointment of fiduciary is still in full force and effect	6.00
For making and certifying or comparing and certifying a copy of a will or any paper on file or recorded in his office, per page	6.00
Authenticating the same, additional	20.00
For searching and certifying to any record for which search is made:	
For under 25 years	30.00
For over 25 years	90.00
For producing papers, documents, books of record on file in his office under a subpoena duces tecum, for use within the county where the office of the court is situated	$ 30.00
For use in any other county, such fee to be paid for each day or part thereof that the messenger is detailed from the office and to be in addition to mileage fee and the necessary expenses of the messenger. The Clerk of the court shall not be required to make any collection or return of the money so paid for expenses, per mile	.30
For recording:	
Any instrument, decree or other paper which is required by law to be recorded:	
Per page or part	8.00
Minimum	16.00
For filing an authenticated copy of a foreign will:	
Per page	8.00
Minimum	64.00
For taxing bill of costs	15.00

No fee charged:

(a) for filing objections of a guardian ad litem.

(b) for filing the annual account of a guardian.

(c) for any certificate or certified copy of a paper required to be filed with the United States Veterans Administrations.

(d) for filing a petition in a proceeding for filing an additional bond, to reduce the penalty of a bond or substitute a new bond or discharge any bond when no accounting is required.

(e) in respect to the proceedings for the appointment of a fiduciary when the appointment is made solely for the purpose of collecting bounty, arrears of pay, prize money, pension dues or other dues or gratuities due from the federal or state government for services of a minor or of a decedent formerly or now in the military or naval services of the United States or to collect the proceeds of a war risk insurance policy.

(f) to or received from the state of New York or any public agency of the state or any civil subdivision or agency thereof or with respect to a social services official when taking any proceeding with respect to the estate of a person who was a recipient of benefits from social services.

(g) or received for the filing of a petition for an order granting funds for the maintenance or other proper needs of any infant nor for any certificate or any certified copy of the order on such an application.

COMMISSIONS OF EXECUTOR, ADMINISTRATOR, GUARDIAN OR FIDUCIARIES OTHER THAN TRUSTEES (§2307 S.C.P.A.)

For receiving and paying out all sums of money	
Not exceeding $100,000	5%
Additional sums not exceeding $200,000	4%
Additional sums not exceeding $700,000	3%
Additional sums not exceeding $4,000,000	2½%
All sums over $5,000,000	2%

Awards for the September 11 Victim Compensation Act of 2001, established pursuant to Title IV of the Federal Air Transporptation Safety and System Stabilization Act (P.L. 107-42) is exempt from commission. SCPA §2307, subsection 2.

A corporate executor may be paid at a specified rate or commission, if the will provides for that rate or commission, if the executor has agreed to a specific rate or commission, or if the will provides the executor shall be paid according to its published rates, even if the provision, agreement or schedule is not executed in accordance with the provisions required for wills, or is not attested as required for the recording of deeds.

Such commission shall be computed separately for receiving and paying out sums of money, at ½ the statutory rate for receiving and ½ for paying out.

If estate is less than $100,000 with more than one Executor, Administrator or Guardian, only one full commission is appointed among each.

If estate amounts to $100,000 but is less than $300,000 each Executor, Administrator or Guardian is entitled to full compensation as if sole executor, administrator or guardian, but no more than two full commissions are to be paid. If more than two fiduciaries, apportion total commissions among each.

If estate amounts to $300,000 or more each Executor, Administrator or Guardian is entitled to full compensation as if sole Executor, Administrator or Guardian, but no more than three full commissions are to be paid. If more than three fiduciaries, apportion total commission to each.

Note: Effective August 31, 1993, no more than two commissions allowed unless specified by decedent in writing. (§2313 S.C.P.A.)

Collection of Rents: Entitled to 5% of gross rents collected in addition to compensation.

COMMISSIONS OF TESTAMENTARY OR LIFETIME TRUSTEE of Persons Dying or Lifetime Trust Established After August 31, 1956

(§2309 S.C.P.A.)

Annual Commissions on principal	Per Thousand
On first $400,000	$ 10.50
Next $600,000	4.50
Over $1,000,000	3.00

On eleemosynary trusts, annual commissions are paid on income instead of principal at the rate of 6% per annum.

More than one Trustee: If trust amounts to $100,000 or more, but less than $400,000, each Trustee is entitled to full commissions as if sole Trustee unless more than 2 in which case 2 full commissions are to be apportioned according to services rendered. If trust amounts to $400,000 or more each Trustee is entitled to full commissions as if sole trustee unless more than 3 in which case 3 full commissions are to be apportioned according to services rendered.

Note: Effective August 31, 1993, no more than two commissions allowed unless specified by decedent in writing. (§2313 S.C.P.A.)

In trust not measured by a life: If annual income amounts to $4,000.00 or more, each trustee is entitled to full commissions. If more than 2 trustees, 2 full commissions are to be apportioned according to services rendered.

Trustees collecting rent. Entitled to 6% of gross rental collected in addition to other commission.

Trustee authorized to accumulate income entitled to commissions on distribution.

On first $2,500.00	2%
Over $2,500.00	1%

NEW YORK CITY CIVIL COURT COSTS AND FEES

Costs

Where judgment is recovered upon issue joined and after trial or on default in appearance at trial; (C.C.A., §1901)

A. Ordinary Costs.—Except as provided in B or C below, costs shall be:

1. For all proceedings before a notice of trial if filed, $50.00; plus

2. For all proceedings after a notice of trial and before trial, $100.00; plus

3. For each trial, inquest or assessment of damages, $150.00

B. Limited Costs—Where amount of judgment is not more than $6,000, costs shall be:

1. For all proceedings before a notice of trial is filed, $20.00; plus

2. For all proceedings after a notice of trial and before trial, $35.00; plus

3. For each trial, inquest or assessment of damages, $60.00

C. This section does not apply to costs in a summary proceeding or small claims actions (C.C.A. §1906)

Petitioner shall be allowed as additional costs $5.00 for each necessary tenant served with a notice of petition by a person other than a sheriff or marshal, and if there is a default in appearing $5.00 for securing an affidavit that the tenant is not in the military service. (C.C.A., §1906-a)

The court may in its discretion impose costs not exceeding $50.00: (a) upon granting or denying a motion; (b) upon allowing an amendment of a pleading; (c) upon adjournment of a trial. (C.C.A. §1906).

Costs shall not exceed $300.00 except as provided in §1904(b) & (c). (C.C.A., §1904)

Costs, together with fees paid to the clerk and the fee for issuing execution must be taxed by the clerk on the rendition of judgment. Upon issuing a transcript the clerk shall include therein the prospective fees of the county clerk and sheriff. Other taxable disbursements shall be taxed by the clerk on 2 days' notice. (C.C.A., §1907)

Disbursements allowable are fees paid to the clerk, sheriff or marshal, including jury fees, service of process fees, legal fees of witnesses, fees paid for a certified copy of a deposition or other filed paper necessary for the trial, reasonable compensation of commissioners for taking depositions, prospective charges for filing a transcript with the county clerk and sheriff's fees on execution. (C.C.A., §1908)

Fees

Fees payable to the clerk (C.C.A., §1911(a)-(m)) are as follows:

1) Upon issuance of a summons or other process (except in Small Claims)	$ 45.00
2) Upon filing a summons with proof of service, unless there has been a fee paid upon the issuance of the summons	45.00
3) Upon filing an infant's compromise, where no summons has been filed	40.00
4) Upon filing a notice of trial	40.00
5) Upon filing a notice of appeal	30.00
6) Certifying a filed paper	6.00
7) Issuing a notice of petition or an order to show cause in a summary proceeding to recover possession of real property	45.00
8) Exemplification of any filed paper	15.00
9) Issuing certificate of satisfaction of judgment	6.00
10) Issuing any certificate regarding a judgment	6.00
11) Jury fees (6 persons only)	70.00
12) Entry of Judgment on confession	45.00
13) Issuing a petition for change of name	65.00
14) Issuance of transcript of judgment	15.00
15) Subpoena fee	15.00
16) Filing small claims (C.C.A., §1803)	
Claims up to and including $1,000	15.00
Claims over $1,000	20.00
Counterclaims	5.00
17) Filing commercial claim (C.C.A., §1803-A)	25.00
in consumer credit transaction	25.00
Counterclaims	5.00
18) Name Change	65.00

FEES OF CITY MARSHAL, CITY OF NEW YORK

Note: The fees of the City Marshals for services performed in matters in the New York Civil Court are the same as the fees of the Sheriff for like services in the Supreme Court. New York City Civil Court Act §1915.

FEES IN THE JUSTICE COURT

(Uniform Justice Court Act, §1911)

Filing first paper	$ 20.00
Issuing requisition of seizure	20.00
Filing infant's compromise, where no paper was previously filed	20.00
Entry of judgment on confession	20.00
Filing notice of appeal	5.00
Issuing certificate as to judgment	2.00
Jury demand	10.00
Exemplification, not over 3 pages	4.00
($1.00 for each additional page)	
Certification, not over 3 pages	2.00
($1.00 for each additional page)	
Issuing notice of petition on order to show cause in summary proceedings	20.00
Stenographer's fees–as provided in CPLR	

Fees of enforcement officer—same as Sheriff in the Supreme Court

CITY COURT FEES

(Uniform City Court Act, §1911, Subdivision a)

(1) Upon the filing of the first paper in any action or proceeding, $45.00.

(2) For issuing an order of arrest or attachment, or requisition or warrant of seizure, where no paper was previously filed, $45.00.

(3) Upon filing an infant's compromise, where no paper was previously filed, $40.00.

(4) For filing a notice of trial, $40.00.

(5) For entry of judgment upon confession, where no paper was previously filed, $45.00.

(6) On filing notice of appeal, $30.00.

(7) For issuing a satisfaction of judgment, or a certificate regarding the judgment, $6.00.

(8) On a trial by jury, $70.00; to be paid by the party demanding the jury, at the time of the demand.

(9) For exemplification of a copy of a paper on file in the clerk's office not exceeding three pages, $15.00.

(10) For certifying a copy of a paper on file in the clerk's office, except a return on appeal, where such paper does not exceed three pages, $6.00.

(11) For issuing a notice of petition in a summary proceeding to recover possession of real property, $45.00.

(12) For filing small claims:
For claims of $1,000 or less, $15.00.
For claims over $1,000, $20.00.
For counterclaims, $5.00 plus cost of first class mail.

(13) For filing a commercial claim $25.00 plus cost of certified and regular mail.

All fees shall be prepaid before the service shall be performed.

FEES OF THE DISTRICT COURT

(Nassau and Suffolk Counties) U.D.C.A. §1911

(1) Upon issuance of a summons, order of arrest or attachment, requisition or warrant of seizure, or a notice of petition or order to show cause in lieu thereof in a summary proceeding to recover real property	$ 45.00
(2) Upon filing first paper in an action or proceeding, including special proceeding for settlement of a claim of an infant or incompetant (unless fee indicated in (1) has been paid)	45.00
(3) For entry of judgment upon confession (unless fee indicated in (1) or (2) above has been paid)	45.00
(4) On filing notice of appeal	30.00

Fees of the District Court—Cont'd

(5) For issuing a satisfaction of judgment, or a certificate regarding a judgment	$ 6.00
(6) Upon demand for a trial by jury (to be paid by party demanding jury at time of demand)	70.00
(7) Exemplifying a copy of a paper on file	15.00
(8) Certifying a copy of a paper on file	6.00
(9) Filing a notice of trial (to be prepaid before performance of service)	40.00
10) Filing small claims (U.D.C.A. § 1803)	
Claims up to and including $1,000	15.00
Claims over $1,000	20.00
Counterclaims	5.00
11) Filing commercial claim (U.D.C.A. § 1803-A)	25.00
in consumer credit transaction	25.00
Counterclaims	5.00

For fees of enforcement officer (to be paid by party requiring his services), see Fees of Sheriffs.

COSTS IN THE JUSTICE COURT

(Uniform Justice Court Act, §§1901, 1903, 1904, and 1910)

Recovery of money or chattel:	
$100 or less	$ 5.00
For each additional $100 or part thereof	5.00
Appellate costs:	
Appellant upon reversal, not more than	30.00
Respondent upon affirmance, not more than	$ 25.00
Either party upon modification, not more than	25.00
For each party served and each non-military affidavit	1.50
Maximum costs not to exceed $50.00 plus Appellate costs and those allowed under §1102.	

FEES OF COUNTY TREASURER AND COMMISSIONER OF FINANCE THE CITY OF NEW YORK (§8010, C.P.L.R.)

Paying Money out of Court—Upon sum paid out, 2%

Investing Money—Upon the sum invested, ½ of 1%

Assigning and Transferring Investment Out of Court—On par value of investment, 2%

Receiving Securities deposited into Court—on par value of securities, 2%

Issuing certificates certifying as to amount of deposit to the credit of court funds—each certificate, $1.00

FEES OF CONSTABLES (Uniform Justice Court Act, §1911)

Fees of enforcement officer—same as Sheriff in the Supreme Court.

FEES OF THE REGISTER'S OFFICE, CITY OF NEW YORK AND COUNTY CLERK'S OFFICE OF RICHMOND COUNTY

§§7-614 of the Administrative Code of the City of New York

Real Property Fees

Note: Effective July 31, 2002, a $20.00 surcharge imposed on recording of every document.

1. Recording Instruments:

a. $12.00 plus $5.00 per page or part thereof ($22.00 minimum) [in Richmond County, $10.00 plus $2.00 per page or part thereof ($14.00 minimum)]; also $20.00 surcharge, supra.

b. Where the page exceeds 9 x 14 inches and the page is set up in double columns—$29.00 plus $10.00 per page or part thereof [in Richmond County, $10.00 plus $10.00 per page or part thereof]; also $20.00 surcharge, supra.

c. Where the point size is less than 8 points (ordinary news print)—$29.00 plus $10.00 per page or part thereof [in Richmond County, $10.00 plus $4.00 per page or part thereof]; also $20.00 surcharge, supra.

d. Additional Blocks—$2.00 for each block in excess of one.

e. Additional Lots—$3.00 for each lot in excess of one.

2. Assignments of Mortgage—$12.00 plus $5.00 per page or part thereof ($22.00 minimum) [in Richmond County $10.00 plus $2.00 per page or part thereof ($14.00 minimum)]; also $20.00 surcharge, supra.

An additional fee of $3.00 is charged for every mortgage recited in an Assignment of Mortgage in excess of one.

3. Satisfactions of Mortgage—$12.00 plus $5.00 per page or part thereof ($22.00 minimum) [in Richmond County $10.00 plus $2.00 per page or part thereof. ($14.00 minimum)]; also $20.00 surcharge, supra. If the satisfaction is of a consolidated mortgage, the total recording charge must be multiplied by the number of mortgages included in the consolidated mortgage. (A spreader agreement is treated as a separate mortgage.)

4. Affidavit claiming credit against, partial exemption or full exemption from the Mortgage Tax—$8.00

5. Real Property Transfer Tax Filing Fee—$25.00 per form (form can be obtained by fax by calling (718) 935-6114 and selecting document No. 305, or on the Internet at www.nyc.gov/html/dof/html/retaxforms.html).

Note: All instruments to be recorded must be clear and legible. It is suggested that signatures and notarial stamps be in black ink and capable of reproduction on microfilm. Authentication certificates, riders and legal backs are charged for as extra pages.

Note: Effective January 4, 1999 all documents submitted for recording must be accompanied by a Recording and Endorsement page which serves as the last page of every recorded document. The statutory $20.00 per page recording fee applies to this page, and is added to the total cost of recording the document. Richmond County does not have a recording and endorsement page.

Recording Requirements

The following documents must be presented at time of recording:

- New York State Real Estate Transfer Tax Return (Schedule B of TP-584);
- New York City Real Estate Transfer Tax Return (RPT);
- If a multiple dwelling of 3 or more units, a Preliminary Registration Form of the Dept. of Housing Preservation and Development; if property is not a multiple dwelling of 3 or more units, an affidavit to that effect must be filed;
- If a one or two family dwelling, a smoke detector affidavit must be filed with Form NYC-RPT.

New York State Gains Tax Tentative Assessment and Return (TP-582), or a New York State Gains Tax Affidavit are required on transfers occuring prior to June 15, 1996. They are not required for transfers occuring on or after June 15, 1996.

Uniform Commercial Code Fees (effective Sept. 1, 1996; accepted only to perfect interest against cooperative apartments, fixture filings, timber to be cut or mining rights, effective July 1, 2001)

1. Original UCC financing statement, with addendum, first block/lot	$ 40.00
2. Original UCC financing statement, without addendum, first block/lot	40.00
3. Addendum filed susequent to initial filing, first block/lot	40.00
4. Terminations, against filings on or after July 1, 2001, with addendum, first block/lot	40.00
5. Terminations, against filings on or after July 1, 2001, without addendum, first block/lot	40.00
6. Terminations, against filings on or after July 1, 2001, without block/lot	40.00
7. Terminations, against filings on or after July 1, 2001, with block/lot	40.00

Costs & Fees

Fees of N.Y.C. Register & Richmond Co. Clerk—Cont'd

8. Additional fees:
   Each additional block .... $ 2.00
   Each additional lot 3.00
9. Personal Property Search (UCC-11) 25.00
10. Stamping copies of UCC filing, per page....... 5.00
11. Additional charge for filing non-standard form $5.00

Taxes

Note: For information regarding New York State Real Property Transfer Gains Tax and Real Estate Transfer Tax, contact the New York State Dept. of Taxation and Finance at (800) 225-5829. For information regarding Mortgage Tax, call (518) 457-0556.

1. Mortgage Tax:

A. Real property securing a principal debt or obligation of less than $500.000, $2.05 for each $100.00 or major fraction thereof of principal amount secured.* Where property covered is a one or two family dwelling or individual condominium unit (and mortgage so recites) tax rate is $1.75 for each $100.00 on the first $10,000.00 of principal debt.

B. Where the real property is a 1, 2 or 3 family house or individual residential condominium unit securing a principal debt or obligation of $500,000 or more, a tax of $2.175 for each $100.00 or major fraction thereof of principal amount secured.* Where property covered is a 1 or 2 family dwelling or individual residential condominium unit (and mortgage so recites), tax rate is $1.75 for each $100.00 on the first $10,000.00 of principal debt.

C. All other real property, a tax of $2.80 for each $100.00 or major fraction thereof of principal amount secured. If an exemption is claimed, the appropriate tax affidavit must be filed in Duplicate Original.

2. New York State Real Property Transfer Tax (State Stamp Tax):
$2.00 for each $500.00 or any fraction thereof of consideration paid if said consideration is in excess of $500.00.

A Real Estate Transfer Tax Return (TP-584) is required to be filed. Additionally, the scope of this tax has been expanded to include the following: 1) the creation of a lease or sublease for a term exceeding 49 years where substantial capital improvements are or may be made by or for the benefit of the lessee or sublessee and the lease or sublease is for substantially all of the premises constituting the real property; 2) the granting of an option to purchase an interest in real property accompanied with use or occupancy of the property; 3) the assignment of an option or contract for the sale of real property; 4) the transfer of or acquisition of a controlling interest in an entity that owns an interest in real property; and 5) the transfer of an individual cooperative unit.

When there is a transfer of an individual cooperative unit, the TP-584 is required to be filed directly with the N.Y.S. Department of Taxation and Finance.

An additional transfer tax of 1% of the consideration is imposed on each conveyance of residential real property or interest therein where the consideration for the entire conveyance is $1 million or more. Residential real property includes any premises that are or may be used in whole or in part as a personal residence, and: includes a one, two, or three family house, and an individual condominium or cooperative unit. This additional tax is paid by the grantee. However, if the grantee is exempt, it shall be paid by the grantor.

3. New York City Real Property Transfer Tax:

Transfers on or after August 1, 1989, involving nonresidential properties are taxed at the rate of 1.425% where the consideration is $500,000 or less and at the rate of 2.625% if the consideration is greater than $500,000.

Transfers on or after August 1, 1989, for transfers of residential properties, including individual cooperative apartments are taxed at the rate of 1.425%, where the consideration is greater than $500,000. The rate of 1% will apply to transfers of residential properties where the consideration is $500,000 or less. A residential property is a 1, 2, or 3 family house, individual residential condominium or individual cooperative unit.

The new tax law makes the Real Property Transfer Tax applicable to all transfers of shares of stock in a cooperative housing corporation (including transfers of individual cooperative apartments), which occur on or after August 1, 1989, except for transfers made pursuant to a written contract entered into prior to July 25, 1989.

The tax is applicable to any conveyance or transfer of real property or interest therein where the real property is located in New York City, regardless of where transactions, negotiations, transfer of deeds or other actions with regard to the transfer of conveyance take place.

In New York, Bronx, Kings and Queens Counties, filing must be made online using the Automated City Register Information System (ACRIS) which may be accessed at www.nyc.gov/html/dof/html/jump/acris.shtml. In Richmond County, a tax return (Form RPT) must be filed with every conveyance. A $50.00 filing fee is required for each RPT tax return. Checks should be made payable to N.Y.C. Department of Finance. The Register is authorized to reject a return which states that there was no consideration for the deed unless there is attached to such form a statement setting forth the grounds upon which it is claimed that there was no consideration.

In transfers of controlling economic interests in real property or transfers of interests in entities formed for cooperative ownership of real property, returns must be filed, with the applicable filing fee, within 30 days of transfer with the N.Y.C. Dept. of Finance, Real Property Transfer Tax Group, 345 Adams St., 5th Floor, Brooklyn 11201.

Land Title Registration (Torrens System)

Note: Effective Jan. 1, 1997, no new properties may be registered under Torrens System. No voluntary instruments may be registered; only adverse instruments may be registered. See Real Property Law § 463.

1. Filing a mechanics lien or *lis pendens* $35.00

Bad Check Fee

A $20.00 fee will be imposed for processing checks in payment of any tax, recording fee or other charge which are returned unpaid by a bank for any reason other than verified bank error.

Services

1. Issuing a Certified Copy .... $4.00 per page
2. Satisfaction Certificate of Federal Lien.......... 6.00
   in Richmond County 40.00

Note: Costs incurred for private reproduction of map are assumed by requesting party.

Miscellaneous

1. Filing a Federal Lien or a Release................. $40.00
2. Issuing a Certificate of Federal Tax Lien Search 25.00
3. Filing a Map.. 20.00

plus $2.00 for each square foot of map or fraction thereof.

All fees and taxes are due at time of recording or requesting service.

A deed or lease or memorandum thereof cannot be accepted for recording unless a Housing Preservation and Development Preliminary Registration Form (OHPFFORM-515) is filed with the instrument. If the property is not a multiple dwelling, an affidavit to that effect is instead required.

Individuals may photocopy documents on file at the facility; the fee is $.25 per copy. No charge for computer printouts of the index to the UCC or mortgage/deed records from in-house public access computers.

Instruments must be recorded in the county where the property is located.

Fees of N.Y.C. Register & Richmond Co. Clerk—Cont'd

For documents filed in Manhattan, Bronx, Brooklyn or Queens: Checks for Recording Fees, Mortgage Tax, State Stamp Tax and City Real Property Transfer Tax should be made payable to N.Y.C. Department of Finance. Checks for New York State Real Property Transfer Gains Tax should be made payable to New York State Department of Taxation and Finance.

For documents filed in Staten Island: Checks for Recording Fees, Mortgage Recording Tax and State Stamp Tax should be made payable to Richmond County Clerk. Checks for N.Y.C. Real Property Transfer Tax should be made payable to N.Y.C. Department of Finance. Checks for New York State Real Property Transfer Gains Tax should be made payable to New York State Department of Taxation and Finance.

The City Register reserves the right to delay recording and filing until two weeks after and deposit if payment is made by uncertified funds.

INTEREST ON JUDGMENTS IN THE NEW YORK STATE COURTS

Pursuant to CPLR 5004 (effective June 5, 1981), interest on judgments shall be at 9% per annum, except as otherwise provided by statute.

Interest shall be calculated from the date a verdict is rendered or a report or decision is made to the date of entry of final judgment. The interest shall be computed by the clerk of the court and included in the judgment (CPLR 5002). Money judgments shall also bear interest from the date of entry, and every order directing payment of money which has been docketed bears interest from the time of docketing (CPLR 5003).

In some cases prejudgment interest can be recovered. Pursuant to CPRL 5001(a), interest shall be recovered in an action for breach of performance in a contract, or act or omission depriving or interfering with title to, possession or enjoyment of property; however, in an equitable action, interest and the rate and date from which it shall be computed shall be at the court's discretion.

Interest shall be computed from the earliest ascertainable date the cause of action existed; however, interest upon damages incurred thereafter shall be computed from the date incurred. When damages occurred at various times, interest shall be computed upon each item from the date incurred, or upon all damages from an intermediate date (CPLR 5001(b)).

The date from which interest is computed shall be specified in the verdict, report or decision. If the jury is discharged without specifying the date, the court shall fix the date upon motion; however if the date is certain and undisputed, it may be fixed by the clerk of the court upon affidavit. The interest amount shall be computed by the clerk of the court to the date of the verdict, report or decision, and included in the total sum awarded (CPLR 5001(c)).

STATE DEPARTMENTS AND AGENCIES

THE GOVERNOR/EXECUTIVE DEPARTMENT

Executive Chamber, State Capitol, Albany 12224
(518) 474-8390
Internet: www.ny.gov/governor
New York City Office, 633 Third Ave., N.Y.C. 10017
(212) 681-4580

Governor: Subject to Election

Secretary to the Governor: Subject to Appointment (518) 474-4246; Fax: (518) 473-7619

Counsel to the Governor: Subject to Appointment (518) 474-7343; Fax: (518) 474-8099

Appointments Secretary: Subject to Appointment (518) 474-8418

Dir. of Communications: Subject to Appointment (518) 474-8418

OFFICE OF THE STATE COMPTROLLER

110 State St., Albany 12236
(518) 474-4044
Internet: www.osc.state.ny.us
633 3rd Ave., 31st Floor, N.Y.C. 10017
(212) 681-4489

Comptroller: Thomas P. DiNapoli
Subject to Nov. 2010 election

First Deputy Comptroller: Mary Louise Mallick (518) 474-2907

General Counsel: Luke Bierman (518) 474-3444

Supervises, manages, and administers responsibility for the payment into and out of the accounts of the state, including the supervision of autonomous authorities of the state government. *N.Y. Exec. Law § 40 (Consol. 1983)*

OFFICE OF THE ATTORNEY GENERAL

Department of Law
The Capitol, Albany 12224-0341
(518) 474-7330; TDD: (800) 788-9898;
Fax: (518) 473-9909
Internet: www.ag.ny.gov
120 Broadway, N.Y.C. 10271-0332
(212) 416-8000

Atty. General: Subject to Election

Prosecutes and defends all legal actions in which the state is interested; has charge of all legal business of the state for the departments and bureaus; investigates and prosecutes all criminal matters; prepares and drafts contracts, obligations, and other instruments for the use of the state; prosecutes and defends against civil action in which the enforcement of the state laws will be furthered including discrimination and civil rights actions. *N.Y. Exec. Law § 63 (Consol. 1983)*

At press time, some of the positions listed below were subject to change by the incoming Attorney General

Executive Staff

Solicitor General: Barbara D. Underwood (212) 416-8016

Chief of Staff/Counselor to Atty. General: Steven M. Cohen (212) 416-8050

Counsel to Atty. General: Henry M. Greenberg (212) 416-8025

Deputy Counsel to Atty. General: Ben Lawsky (Special Asst. to Atty. General) (212) 416-8050

Dep. Atty. General for Administration: Edna Wells Handy (518) 473-7900, (212) 416-8050

Press Secretary: John Milgrim (518) 473-5525

Division Heads

Dep. Atty. General for Regional Affairs: David Sampson (Buffalo) (716) 852-6274

Exec. Dep. Atty. General, Criminal Justice: Vacancy at Press Time (N.Y.C.) (212) 416-8050

Dep. Atty. General for State Counsel Division: Leslie G. Leach (Albany) (212) 416-8525

Dep. Atty. General, Administration: Edna Wells Handy (Albany) (212) 416-8050, (518) 473-7900

Exec. Dep. Atty General, Economic Justice: Maria T. Vullo (N.Y.C.) (212) 416-8050

Exec. Dep. Atty. General, Social Justice: Mylan Denerstein (N.Y.C.) (212) 416-8050

Chief of Investigations: Joseph D'Amico (N.Y.C.) (212) 416-6328

Division of State Counsel Bureau Chiefs

The Capitol, Albany 12224-7341
(518) 473-0648

120 Broadway, N.Y.C. 10271-0332 (212) 416-8525

Exec. Deputy Atty. General: Leslie G. Leach (N.Y.C.) (212) 416-8525

Deputy Attys. General:
Leonard A. Cohen (N.Y.C.) (212) 416-8579
Megan Levine (Albany) (518) 473-8946

Chief, Civil Recoveries Bureau: Mary E. House (Albany) (518) 474-7131

Chiefs, Claims Bureau:
Katherine Brooks (N.Y.C.) (212) 416-8514
Eileen Bryant (Albany) (518) 474-5209

Chiefs, Litigation Bureau:
June Duffy (N.Y.C.) (212) 416-8610
Jeffrey Dvorkin (Albany; Acting) (518) 474-4367

Chief, Real Property Bureau: Vacancy at Press Time (Albany) (518) 474-5220

Chief, Sex Offender Mgmt. Bureau: Kevin T. Gagan (Albany) (518) 474-9963

Managing Clerk: Stephanie Rosenberg (N.Y.C.) (212) 416-8640

Office of Attorney General
Civil Recoveries Bureau Collections Offices
The Capitol, Albany 12224
(518) 474-7131; Fax: (518) 473-1635

Asst. Attys. General in Charge:

Howard S. Dworkin
(Downstate Medical/Univ. Hosp. Collections Office)
55 Hanson Pl., Suite 732, Brooklyn 11217
(718) 270-3713; Fax: (718) 270-3712

Benjamin Fitt
(Roswell Park Cancer Institute Collections Office)
Elm & Carlton Sts., Buffalo 14263
(716) 845-8682; Fax: (716) 845-8792

Francine Kaplan
(Helen Hayes Hospital Collections Office)
Route 9W, West Haverstraw 10993-1195
(845) 786-4855; Fax: (845) 942-1452

Anne Marie Rago
(Stony Brook University Hospital Collections Office)
2100 Middle Country Rd., 1st Floor, Suite 108, Centereach 11720-3578
(631) 737-6040; Fax: (631) 737-6050

Vacancy at Press Time
(S.U.N.Y. Upstate Medical Univ. Collections Office)
750 E. Adams St., Syracuse 13210
(315) 464-8309; Fax: (315) 464-8327

Criminal Division, Criminal Prosecutions Bureau

The Capitol, Albany 12224-0341
(518) 474-4096; Fax: (518) 474-3364

Deputy Chief: Richard Ernst

Criminal Division, Medicaid Fraud Control Unit

120 Broadway, 13th Floor, N.Y.C. 10271-0007
(212) 417-5300; Fax: (212) 417-4725

Special Dep. Atty. General in Charge: Vacancy at Press Time (212) 417-5250; Fax: (212) 417-4284

First Asst. Atty. General: Monica Hickey-Martin (Legal Affairs) (212) 417-5261; Fax: (212) 417-4215
E-mail: monica.hickeymartin@oag.state.ny.us

Chief Investigator: Vito Spano
(212) 417-5280; Fax: (212) 417-4215
E-mail: vito.spano@oag.state.ny.us

Chief Auditor: Phillip See
(212) 417-5285; Fax: (212) 417-5274
E-mail: phillip.see@ag.ny.gov

***At press time, some of the positions listed above were subject to appointment by the incoming Governor.**

Office of the Atty. Gen., Criminal Div., Medicaid Fraud Control Unit—Cont'd

Regional Dirs.:
Gary A. Baldauf, Statler Towers, 107 Delaware Ave., Buffalo 14202-3473 (716) 853-8507; Fax: (716) 853-8525
E-mail: gary.baldauf@oag.state.ny.us
Alan Buonpastore
300 Motor Pkwy., Suite 210, Hauppauge 11788-5522
(631) 952-6966; Fax: (631) 952-6382
E-mail: alan.buonpastore@oag.state.ny.us
Richard Harrow, The Capitol, Albany 12224-0341
(518) 474-3032; Fax: (518) 474-4519
E-mail: richard.harrow@oag.state.ny.us
Anne Schaible Jardine
1 Blue Hill Plz., P.O. Box 1557, Pearl River 10965-1557
(845) 732-7525; Fax: (845) 732-7555
E-mail: anne.jardine@oag.state.ny.us
Jerry Solomon
144 Exchange Blvd., Suite 600, Rochester 14614-2176
(585) 262-2970; Fax: (585) 262-2866
E-mail: jerry.solomon@oag.state.ny.us
Ralph Tortora III
615 Erie Blvd. W., Suite 301, Syracuse 13204-2465
(315) 423-1121; Fax: (315) 423-1120
E-mail: ralph.tortora@oag.state.ny.us

Deputy Regional Dirs.:
Thomas O'Hanlon
120 Broadway, 13th Floor, N.Y.C. 10271-0332
E-mail: thomas.ohanlon.ag.ny.gov
Christopher Shaw
120 Broadway, 12th Floor, N.Y.C. 10271-0332
(212) 417-5339; Fax: (212) 417-4725
E-mail: christopher.shaw@oag.state.ny.us

Directors:
Paul J. Mahoney (Civil Enforcement Division)
120 Broadway, 13th Floor, N.Y.C. 10271-0332
(212) 417-5254; Fax: (212) 417-5335
E-mail: paul.mahoney@oag.state.ny.us
Jay Speers (Special Projects Division)
1 Blue Hill Plz., 6th Floor, P.O. Box 1747,
Pearl River 10965-1747
(845) 732-7550; Fax: (845) 732-7557

Criminal Justice Div., Organized Crime Task Force
101 E. Post Rd., White Plains 10601-5008
(914) 422-8700; Fax: (914) 422-8835

Albany Office, The Capitol, Albany 12224-0341
(518) 474-1620

Buffalo Office, 350 Main St., Suite 300, Buffalo 14202-3750
(716) 853-8530

Syracuse Office, 615 Erie Blvd. W., Suite 306,
Syracuse 13204-2465 (315) 448-4862

Chief Investigator: Thomas J. Mullen (914) 422-8780

Conducts investigations and prosecutions of organized crime activities between two or more counties of the state or between the state and another jurisdiction; cooperates and assists district attorneys and other local law enforcement officials in their efforts against organized crime. *N.Y. Exec. Law § 70-a (Consol. 1983)*

Criminal Division, Public Integrity Unit
120 Broadway, N.Y.C. 10271-0332
(212) 416-8242; Fax: (212) 416-8026

Special Deputy Atty. General: Ellen Nachtigall Biben (212) 416-8056

Division of Regional Offices
Main Place Tower, 350 Main St., Buffalo 14202
(716) 852-8400; Fax: (716) 853-8464

Deputy Atty. General: David Sampson (716) 852-6274

Binghamton Regional Office
44 Hawley St., 17th Floor, Binghamton 13901-4433
(607) 721-8771; Fax: (607) 721-8789

Asst. Atty. General in Charge: Dennis McCabe

Asst. Attys. General:
Roberto C. Barbosa
Laura M. Barnhill
Carol A. Cocchiola
Michael J. Danaher, Jr.
Joseph F. Romani
Geoffrey B. Rossi
James E. Shoemaker
Mary A. Walsh

Serves counties of Broome, Chemung, Chenango, Delaware, Otsego, Schuyler, Tioga and Tompkins

Brooklyn Regional Office
55 Hanson Pl., Suite 1080, Brooklyn 11217
(718) 722-3949; Fax: (718) 722-3951

Asst. Atty. General in Charge: Lois Booker-Williams

Asst. Atty. General: Matthew Eubank

Serves counties of Kings and Queens

Buffalo Regional Office
Main Place Tower, Suite 300A, 350 Main St., Buffalo 14202
(716) 853-8400; Fax: (716) 853-8571

Asst. Atty. General in Charge: Russell T. Ippolito, Jr.

Asst. Attys. General:
Delia Cadle
Patricia I. Carrington
Jane Coleman-Cameron
Laurie Frank
Richard B. Friedfertig
Timothy L. Hoffman
Kevin Kane
Cydney A. Kelly
Robert J. Lee
William D. Lonergan
Darren Longo
William D. Maldovan
Paul F. McCarthy
Rose McMorrow
Gregory P. Miller
Wendy E. Morcio
James M. Morrissey
Kim S. Murphy
Michael J. Russo
Thomas Schleif
Thomas Schoellkopf
Margot Schoenborn
Michael A. Siragusa
David State
Letizia Tagliefierro
Paul Volcy
Linda E. White
Wendy Whiting
George Zimmermann

Serves Counties of Allegany, Cattaraugus, Chautauqua, Erie, Genesee, Niagra, Orleans and Wyoming

Harlem Regional Office
163 W. 125th St., 13th Floor, N.Y.C. 10027-8201
(212) 961-4475; Fax: (212) 961-4003

Asst. Atty. General in Charge: Guy H. Mitchell

Asst. Attys. General:
Roberto G. Lebron
Judy S. Prosper

Serves Upper Manhattan and the Bronx

Nassau Regional Office
200 Old Country Rd., Suite 240, Mineola 11501
(516) 248-3302; Fax: (516) 747-6432

Asst. Atty. General in Charge: Valerie Singleton

Deputy Asst. Atty. General In Charge: Dorothy Oehler Nese

Asst. Attys. General:
Toni E. Logue
Ralph Pernick
Derrick J. Robinson
Victoria L. Safran

Serves county of Nassau

Plattsburgh Regional Office
43 Durkee St., Plattsburgh 12901
(518) 562-3288; Fax: (518) 562-3294

Asst. Atty. General in Charge: Robert C. Glennon

Asst. Atty. General: Glen Francis Michaels

Serves counties of Clinton, Essex and Franklin

Poughkeepsie Regional Office
235 Main St., 3rd Floor, Poughkeepsie 12601-3194
(845) 485-3900; Fax: (845) 452-3303

Asst. Atty. General in Charge: Vincent Bradley
E-mail: vincent.bradley@ag.ny.gov

Asst. Attys. General:
Nicholas Garin; E-mail: nicholas.garin@ag.ny.gov
Lisa Ghartey; E-mail: lisa.ghartey@ag.ny.gov
Barry Kaufman; E-mail: barry.kaufman@ag.ny.gov
Dewey Lee; E-mail: dewey.lee@ag.ny.gov
J. Gardner Ryan; E-mail: gardner.ryan@ag.ny.gov
Jeane Strickland-Smith; E-mail: jeane.smith@ag.ny.gov
Risa Sugarman; E-mail: risa.sugarman@ag.ny.gov

Serves counties of Dutchess, Orange, Sullivan and Ulster

***At press time, some of the positions listed above were subject to appointment by the incoming Governor.**

Office of the Atty. Gen., Div. of Regional Offices—Cont'd

Rochester Regional Office
Court Exchange Bldg., Suite 200, 144 Exchange Blvd., Rochester 14614-2176
(585) 546-7430; Fax: (585) 546-7514

Asst. Atty. General in Charge: Debra A. Martin

Asst. Attys. General:
J. Richard Benitez
Emil J. Bove, Jr.
Benjamin Bruce
Audrey C. Cooper
Reynolds Hahn
Gary M. Levine
Thomas G. Ramsay

Serves counties of Livingston, Monroe, Ontario, Seneca, Steuben, Wayne and Yates

Suffolk Regional Office
300 Motor Pkwy., Suite 205, Hauppauge 11788-5127
(631) 231-2424; Fax: (631) 435-4757

Asst. Atty. General in Charge: Alan Berkowitz (Acting)

Asst. Attys. General:
John Belford
Susan Connolly
Alan W. Gitter, Suite 125 (631) 231-2412
Patricia M. Hingerton
Kimberly Kinirons
Anne Leahey
Rose F. Lowe, Suite 125 (631) 231-2412
Lori L. Pack
Todd Schall
John M. Shields

Serves county of Suffolk

Syracuse Regional Office
615 Erie Blvd. W., Suite 102, Syracuse 13204
(315) 448-4800; Fax: (315) 448-4853

Asst. Atty. General in Charge: Ed Thompson

Asst. Attys. General:
Patricia M. Bordonaro
Nicholas DeMartino
Andrew Heffner
Bonnie G. Levy
Maureen MacPherson
Judith C. Malkin
Edward F. McArdle
Timothy Mulvey
Michael O'Neill
Heather Rubinstein
Senta Barry Siuda
Christopher Wiles

Serves counties of Cayuga, Cortland, Madison, Onondaga and Oswego

Utica Regional Office
207 Genesee St., Room 508, Utica 13501-2812
(315) 793-2225; Fax: (315) 793-2228

Asst. Atty. General in Charge: Joel L. Marmelstein

Special Deputy Atty. General: Carl J. Boykin (Guns & Gangs)

Asst. Attys. General:
G. Lawrence Dillon
Sean B. Virkler
James J. Williams

Senior Atty.: Thomas Trace

Serves counties of Fulton, Herkimer, Jefferson, Montgomery, Oneida, Otsego and St. Lawrence

Watertown Regional Office
317 Washington St., Watertown 13601-3744
(315) 785-2444; Fax: (315) 785-2294

Asst. Atty. General in Charge: Deanna Nelson

Asst. Atty. General: Matthew A. Goettel

Serves counties of Jefferson, Lewis and St. Lawrence

Westchester Regional Office
101 E. Post Rd., White Plains 10601-5008
(914) 422-8755; Fax: (914) 422-8706

Asst. Atty. General in Charge: Judith C. McCarthy

Asst. Attys. General:
Elyse J. Angelico
Vincent Cascio
Shelley Forde
Jyotsna Gorti
John Healey
Dian Kerr-McCullough
Doris K. Morin
Wanda Perez-Maldonado
Russell Seeman
Elaine Yacyshyn
Rachel Zaffrann

Serves counties of Putnam, Rockland and Westchester

DEPARTMENT OF STATE

One Commerce Plz., 99 Washington Ave., Albany 12231
(518) 474-4750; Fax: (518) 474-4765
E-mail: info@dos.state.ny.us
Internet: www.dos.state.ny.us

123 William St., N.Y.C. 10038-3804
(212) 417-5800, 01, 05

Secretary: Ruth N. Colón (Acting) (518) 474-0050

The Department of State has a wide range of responsibilities, including filing of corporate documents and trademarks; advising the Governor as to local government problems and their solutions; overseeing programs of providing fire safety information; licensing of certain professions, including real estate brokers, cosmetologists and private investigators; supervising administration of cemetery associations; and serving as custodian of the State Seal and official state documents.

Executive Division

First Deputy Secretary of State: Daniel E. Shapiro
(518) 474-0050; Fax: (518) 474-4765

Deputy Secretary of State & Counsel to the Secretary of State: Vacancy at Press Time
(212) 417-5800; Fax: (212) 417-5805

Deputy Secretary of State for Public Affairs: Joel Barkin
(212) 417-5800; Fax: (212) 417-5805

Deputy Secretary of State for Local Government and Community Services: Amanda Hiller
(518) 473-3355; Fax: (518) 474-6572

Chief Counsel to the Secretary: Susan Watson
(518) 474-6740; Fax: (518) 473-9211

Dir. of Public Information: Gabe Roth
(518) 474-4752; Fax: (518) 474-4597

Dir. of Administration & Management: Judith Kenny
(518) 474-4750

Dir. of Intergovernmental & Community Services: Mark Streb (518) 486-9888

Affirmative Action Officer: Antonio Cortes
(518) 474-2752; Fax: (518) 473-3294

Administrative Support Services: Rebecca L. Sebesta
(518) 473-8221; Fax: (518) 473-7182

Division of Administrative Rules
One Commerce Plaza, 99 Washington Ave., Albany 12231
(518) 474-6957; Fax: (518) 473-9055

Director: Deborah A. Ritzko

Responsible for the production of two legislatively mandated publications disseminated statewide: the *New York State Register,* which provides key information on rule making activities of state agencies; and the *Official Compilation of Codes, Rules and Regulations of the State of New York* (NYCRR), a multi-volume, loose-leaf compilation which is supplemented semi-monthly with new and amended pages. In performing these functions, the division serves as the central filing office for the rules and regulations for the state of New York. In addition to fulfilling its statutory responsibility, the division serves the printing and publishing needs of all other divisions within the department. Among other publications produced are: *New York State Constitution,* certain official documents as well as reports, manuals and informational pamphlets for the department's many constituents, including the general public.

State Athletic Commission
123 William St., 20th Floor, N.Y.C. 10038-3804
(212) 417-5700; Fax: (212) 417-4987
E-mail: athletic@dos.state.ny.us
Internet: www.dos.state.ny.us/athletic

Chair: Melvina Lathan

Division of Cemeteries
One Commerce Plaza, 99 Washington Ave., Albany 12231
(518) 474-6226; Fax: (518) 473-0876

123 William St., N.Y.C. 10038-3804
(212) 417-5713; Fax: (212) 417-2322

Director: Richard D. Fishman
(212) 417-5713; Fax: (212) 417-2322

***At press time, some of the positions listed above were subject to appointment by the incoming Governor.**

Dept. of State—Cont'd

Div. of Coastal Resources & Waterfront Revitalization
One Commerce Plaza, 99 Washington Ave., Albany 12231
(518) 474-6000; Fax: (518) 473-2464

Director: George R. Stafford

Division of Code Enforcement and Administration
One Commerce Plaza, 99 Washington Ave., Albany 12231
(518) 486-4487

One Albany Ave., Suite G-5, Kingston 12401
(845) 334-9378; Fax: (845) 334-9373

2 John Walsh Blvd., Peekskill 10566-5323
(914) 734-1342; Fax: (914) 734-1763

Director: Ronald E. Piester (518) 474-4073

The Department of State, Division of Code Enforcement and Administration (Codes Division) performs a broad range of activities related to administration of the state's Uniform Fire Prevention and Building Code (Uniform Code) and State Energy Conservation Construction Code (Energy Code). These are the Codes that must be followed when constructing or renovating a building in New York State (with the exception of New York City). The Codes Division promulgates and maintains the Uniform Code and Energy Code through the statutory authority of the State Fire Prevention and Building Code Council, which is chaired by the Secretary of State. It also provides technical assistance and interpretations of the specific provisions of the Codes as well as their appropriate application to building construction projects. The Codes Division provides training to local fire and code enforcement personnel, elected officials, architects, engineers, manufacturers, contractors, and the general public. Eleven regional field offices, located around the state, provide on-site technical assistance, administrative and regional board of Review variance assistance, direct enforcement, and oversight. The division also administers the state's Manufactured Housing Program.

Division of Corporations, State Records and Uniform Commercial Code
One Commerce Plaza, 99 Washington Ave., Albany 12231
(518) 473-2492; Fax: (518) 474-1418; UCC: (518) 474-5418; Fax: (518) 474-5173; State Records: (518) 474-4770

Director: Sandra Tallman (518) 473-2281

Responsible for the efficient filing of certificates in a secure and readily retrievable manner which will permit the rapid access to and dissemination of corporation and UCC information

Office of Fire Prevention and Control
One Commerce Plaza, 99 Washington Ave., Albany 12231
(518) 474-6746; Fax: (518) 474-3240

600 College Ave., Montour Falls 14865-0811
(607) 535-7136; Fax: (607) 535-4841

State Fire Administrator: Floyd Madison

Legal Services
One Commerce Plaza, 99 Washington Ave., Albany 12231
(518) 474-6740; Fax: (518) 473-9211

123 William St., N.Y.C. 10036-3804
(212) 417-5800; Fax: (212) 417-5805

Chief Counsel to the Secretary: Susan Watson

Division of Licensing Services
Alfred E. Smith Bldg., 10th Floor, 80 S. Swan St., Albany 12231

Mailing Address: P.O. Box 22001, Albany 12201-2001
Clerk's Unit: (518) 474-4429; Examination: (518) 473-2731; Licensing Processing: (518) 474-4429; Fax: (518) 473-6648

123 William St., 19th Floor, N.Y.C. 10038-3804
(212) 417-5747; Fax: (212) 417-5688

Deputy Secretary of State for Business & Licensing: Kathleen M. McCoy
(518) 473-2728; Fax: (518) 473-2730

Division of Local Government & Community Svces.
One Commerce Plaza, 99 Washington Ave., Albany 12231
(518) 473-3355; Fax: (518) 474-6572

c/o Watershed, 2 John Walsh Blvd., Peekskill 10566-5323
(914) 734-1347; Fax: (914) 734-1763

Deputy Secretary of State: Amanda Hiller

Committee on Open Government
One Commerce Plaza, 99 Washington Ave., Albany 12231
(518) 474-2518; Fax: (518) 474-1927

Exec. Dir.: Robert J. Freeman

Provides advice orally and in writing to any person regarding access to government records and meetings in New York.

Office of Public Affairs
One Commerce Plaza, 99 Washington Ave., Albany 12231
(518) 474-4752; Fax: (518) 474-4597

Deputy Secretary of State for Public Affairs: Joel Barkin
(212) 417-5800; Fax: (212) 417-5805

Dir. of Public Information: Gabe Roth

Office of Public Information; oversees the entire public communications effort for the Department of State; charged with responsibility for the Department's World Wide Web site (http://www.dos.state.ny.us) and produces numerous Departmental publications. The Director of Public Information acts as spokesperson for the agency. The Director is responsible for media relations, speech writing and general communications strategy for the Department of State.

Academy of Fire Science
600 College Ave., Montour Falls 14865-9634
(607) 535-7136; Fax: (607) 535-4841

Binghamton Regional Office
State Office Bldg. Annex, 15th Floor, 44 Hawley St., Binghamton 13901-4455
Licensing Services: (607) 721-8757; Fax: (607) 721-8753; Regional Affairs: (607) 721-8367; Fax: (607) 721-8755

Buffalo Regional Office
65 Court St., Buffalo 14202-3471
Cemeteries: (716) 847-7969; Fax: (716) 847-7969; Community Services: (716) 847-7106; Licensing Services: (716) 847-7110; Fax: (716) 847-7109, 847-7969; Code Enforcement and Administration: (716) 847-7611; Fax: (716) 847-7941

Office of Fire Prevention & Control, Electric Tower, Suite 106, 535 Washington St., Buffalo 14203
(716) 847-3320; Fax: (716) 847-3494

Hauppauge Regional Office
Perry B. Duryea Jr. State Office Bldg., 250 Veteran's Memorial Hwy., Hauppauge 11788
Code Enforcement & Administration: (631) 952-4912; Fax: (631) 952-4911; Licensing Services: (631) 952-6579; Fax: (631) 952-7902; Regional Affairs: (631) 952-6583; Fax: (631) 952-7910

Hicksville Regional Office
303 W. Old Country Rd., Hicksville 11801
(516) 934-8572; Fax: (516) 934-8001

Jamestown Regional Office
Municipal Bldg., 4th Floor, 200 E. 3rd St., Jamestown 14701
(716) 483-7517

Kingston Regional Office
One Albany Ave., Suite G-5, Kingston 12401-2946
Code Enforcement & Admin.: (845) 334-9768

New York City Regional Office
123 William St., 19th & 20th Floors, N.Y.C. 10038
Executive & Regional Services: (212) 417-5800; Community Services: (212) 417-5724; Fax: (212) 417-4784; Licensing Services: (212) 417-2063; Fax: (212) 417-5688; State Athletic Commission: (212) 417-5700; Fax: (212) 417-4987; Cemeteries: (212) 417-5713; Fax: (212) 417-2322; Coastal Resources: (212) 417-5005; Fax: (212) 417-5805

Oneonta Regional Office
Homer Folks Bldg., Suite 124, 28 Hill St., Oneonta 13820
Office of Fire Prevention & Control: (607) 433-2872; Fax: (607) 433-2896

Peekskill Regional Office
2 John Walsh Blvd., Suite 206, Peekskill 10566-5323
(914) 734-1347; Fax: (914) 734-1763; Local Government-Watershed: (914) 734-1347; Fax: (914) 734-1763; Code Enforcement & Admin.: (914) 734-1342

***At press time, some of the positions listed above were subject to appointment by the incoming Governor.**

Dept. of State—Cont'd

Plattsburgh Regional Office
22 U.S. Oval, Suite 115, Plattsburgh 12903
Regional Affairs: (518) 562-3640; Fax: (518) 562-3645

Rochester Regional Office/SUNY Brockport
55 St. Paul St., Rochester 14604
Regional Affairs: (585) 395-8100; Fax: (585) 395-8103

Syracuse Regional Office
Hughes State Office Bldg., 5th Floor,
333 E. Washington St., Syracuse 13202-1428
Cemeteries: (315) 428-4258; Fax: (315) 428-4407;
Community Services: (315) 426-2126;
Fax: (315) 426-2124, 428-4407;
Regional Affairs: (315) 428-4337; Fax: (315) 428-4261;
Code Enforcement and Administration: (315) 428-4434;
Fax: (315) 428-4655;
Office of Fire Prevention & Control: (315) 428-3261;
Fax: (315) 428-3293

Utica Regional Office
State Office Bldg., 207 Genesee St., Utica 13501-2812
Code Enforcement and Administration: (315) 793-2526;
Fax: (315) 793-2569; Licensing Services: (315) 793-2533;
Fax: (315) 793-2631; Cemeteries: (315) 793-2567;
Fax: (315) 793-2631; Regional Affairs: (315) 793-2535;
Fax: (315) 793-2635

Watertown Regional Office
Dulles State Office Bldg., 4th Floor, 317 Washington St.,
Watertown 13601-3744
Regional Affairs: (315) 785-2561; Fax: (315) 785-2563;
Licensing Services: (315) 785-2371; Fax: (315) 785-6452

Westchester Regional Office
120 Bloomingdale Rd., White Plains 10605
(914) 997-9538; Fax: (914) 997-9546

DEPARTMENT OF AGRICULTURE AND MARKETS

10B Airline Dr., Albany 12235
(518) 457-3880; Fax: (518) 457-3087;
Toll-Free: (800) 554-4501
E-mail: info@agmkt.state.ny.us
Internet: www.agmkt.state.ny.us

Commissioner: Patrick Hooker (518) 457-8876
First Deputy Commissioner: Robert Haggerty (518) 457-2771
Counsel: Ruth A. Moore (518) 457-1059; Fax: (518) 457-8842
Public Information Officer: Jessica Ziehm (518) 457-3136

Promotes, fosters and encourages the agricultural industry by acting to increase production, efficiency and markets; inspects and regulates all retail food stores, warehouses and processing facilities; regulates and inspects the milk supply; and conducts audit of certain agriculture-related businesses. *N.Y. Agric. & Mkts. Law § 3 (Consol. 1980)*

DIVISION OF ALCOHOLIC BEVERAGE CONTROL

(Executive Department)
80 S. Swan St., Suite 900, Albany 12210-8002
New and Pending Applications: (518) 474-3114;
Fax: (518) 473-2286
Internet: www.abc.state.ny.us

Special Event Permit Applications,
P.O. Box 3796, N.Y.C. 10008-3796

Zone 1, 317 Lenox Ave., N.Y.C. 10027
(212) 961-8385; Fax: (212) 961-8299

Zone 3, Iskalo Electric Tower Bldg., Suite 303,
535 Washingston St., Buffalo 14203
(716) 847-3035; Fax: (716) 847-3435

Responsible for issuing all licenses and permits for the manufacture, wholesale distribution and retail sale of all alcoholic beverages; also monitors compliance with the provisions of the Alcoholic Beverage Control Law. *N.Y. Alco. Bev. Cont. Law § 10 (Consol. 1991)*

State Liquor Authority
Chair: Dennis Rosen (Albany) (518) 473-6559
Commissioners:
Jeanique Greene (N.Y.C.) (212) 961-8300
Noreen Healey (N.Y.C.) (212) 961-8300
C.E.O.: Trina Mead (Albany) (518) 486-4767
Secretary to Chair: Kimberly Ciccone (Albany) (518) 473-6559
Secretary to the Authority: Jacqueline Held (518) 473-6559
Counsel to the Authority: Jean Marie Cho (Albany) (518) 402-4429; N.Y.C.: (212) 961-8385
Deputy Commissioner, Licensing: Kerri O'Brien (Albany) (518) 474-7604
Dir. of Enforcement: Pamela Westlake (Albany) (518) 747-0385
Dir. of Public Affairs: William Crowley (Albany) (518) 486-4767

OFFICE OF ALCOHOLISM AND SUBSTANCE ABUSE SERVICES

1450 Western Ave., Albany 12203-3526
(518) 473-3460
Internet: www.oasas.state.ny.us
New York City Office, 501 7th Ave., N.Y.C. 10018-5903
(646) 728-4533

Commissioner: Karen M. Carpenter-Palumbo (518) 457-2061; Fax: (518) 457-5474
General Counsel: Robert Kent (518) 485-2312; Fax: (518) 485-2335

Provides an administratives framework for the management, licensing and operation of treatment facilities and programs to treat the diseases of alcoholism, drug abuse and gambling; educates, gathers and maintains information for the public and health care providers concerning alcohol and substance abuse; researches chemical addictions. *N.Y. Mental Hyg. Art. 19*

For State operated alcoholism treatment centers and substance abuse services, contact the Helpline: 1-877-846-7369.

BANKING DEPARTMENT

One State St., N.Y.C. 10004
(212) 709-3500; Fax: (212) 709-3520;
Consumer Services: (877) 226-5697;
Complaints: (212) 709-3590
Internet: www.banking.state.ny.us
Albany Office, 80 S. Swan St., Suite 1157, Albany 12210
(518) 473-6160
Upstate Office, 333 E. Washington St., Syracuse 13202
(315) 428-4049

Superintendent: Richard H. Neiman (212) 709-3501
First Deputy Superintendent: Patricia Meadow (212) 709-3502
Chief Operating Officer: Diana Rulon (Albany) (518) 473-6160
Chief Administrative Officer: Cheryl Aini (Albany) (518) 473-6160
Chief Information Officer: William Rachmiel (212) 709-5420
General Counsel: Marjorie Gross (212) 709-1640; Fax: (212) 709-1655
Legislative Counsel: C. Thomas Barletta (Albany) (518) 486-4300
Deputy Superintendent, Community & Regional Banks: Martin Cofsky (212) 709-1610; Fax: (212) 709-1524
Deputy Superintendent, Consumer Services Div.: Dianne E. Dixon (212) 709-3591; Fax: (212) 709-3582
Deputy Superintendent, Foreign and Wholesale Banks Div.: Regina Stone (212) 709-1500; Fax: (212) 709-1586
Deputy Superintendent, Licensed Financial Services Div.: Angelo Sigismondo (212) 709-5500; Fax: (212) 709-5513
Deputy Superintendent, Mortgage Banking Div.: Rholda Ricketts (212) 709-5540; Fax: (212) 709-5555
Dir., Research Applications & Technical Assistance Division: Manzar Sahebjam-Atabaki (212) 709-1530; Fax: (212) 709-1542
Dir., Criminal Investigations Bureau: Ricardo Velez (212) 709-3554; Fax: (212) 709-3555
Press Secretary: Glorimar Perez-Gonzalez (212) 709-1691; Fax: (212) 709-1693
Information Security Officer: Jae Sohn (212) 709-5401
Secy. to Banking Board: Sam L. Abram (212) 709-1658; Fax: (212) 709-1655

***At press time, some of the positions listed above were subject to appointment by the incoming Governor.**

Banking Dept.—Cont'd

Supervises and regulates the business of all banks to ensure the safe and sound conduct of business, to conserve assets, to eliminate unsound banking practices and destructive competition and to maintain public confidence; develops and maintains an infrastructure of information technology and services to enhance the efficiency of the Department's internal business processes. *N.Y. Banking Law § 10 (Consol. 1982)*

Banking Board
One State St., N.Y.C. 10004
(212) 709-5470; Fax: (212) 709-3582

Chair: Richard H. Neiman
(212) 709-3501; Fax: (212) 709-3520

Secretary: Sam L. Abram (212) 709-1658

Board Members:
Wesley Chen, 425 Park Ave., N.Y.C. 10022
(212) 751-7100; Fax: (212) 371-6262
Joseph M. Drayton
Kaye Scholer, L.L.P., 425 Park Ave., N.Y.C. 10022-3598
(212) 836-7177; Fax: (212) 836-8689
Robert M. Fisher
Tioga State Bank, One Main St., P.O. Box 386,
Spencer 14883 (607) 589-7000; Fax: (607) 589-4600
E. Peter Forrestel II
Bank of Akron, 46 Main St., Akron 14001
(716) 542-5401; Fax: (716) 542-5510
Peter G. Humphrey
Financial Institutions, Inc., 220 Liberty St., Warsaw 14569
(585) 786-1100; Fax: (585) 786-1108
Wilbur Klatsky, 10 Tagliabue Rd., Shoreham 11786
(631) 744-0980
P. Nicholas Kourides
Worldwide Life Insur. American International Group,
70 Pine St., 17th Floor, N.Y.C. 10270
(212) 770-6490; Fax: (866) 637-6841
Sara Kovner, 27 W. 67th St., N.Y.C. 10023
(212) 877-3915; Fax: (212) 877-3977
John LaFalce
HoganWillig, One John James Audubon Pkwy.,
Amherst 14228 (716) 636-7600; Fax: (716) 636-7606
Franz S. Leichter, 216 E. 47th St., Apt. 4A, N.Y.C. 10017
(212) 980-0857; Fax: (212) 750-1358
William C. McGarry
Ridgewood Savings Bank, 71-02 Forest Ave.,
Flushing 11385 (718) 240-4973; Fax: (718) 240-4877
Brian D. Obergfell
Emmet, Marvin & Martin, L.L.P.,
120 Broadway, 32nd Floor, N.Y.C. 10271
(212) 238-3032; Fax: (212) 238-3100
Thomas G. Siciliano
Municipal Credit Union, 22 Cortlandt St., 27th Floor,
N.Y.C. 10017-3107 (212) 238-3361; Fax: (212) 416-7050
Florian Strassberger
DZ Bank AG Deutsche Zentral Genossenschaftsbank,
609 Fifth Ave., N.Y.C. 10017-1021
(212) 745-1400; Fax: (212) 745-1405
George Vojta
The Westchester Group, L.L.C.,
420 Lexington Ave., Suite 300, N.Y.C. 10170
(212) 297-6243; Fax: (212) 479-2538

Established by *Sections 13* and *14* of the *N.Y.S. Banking Law,* and is a quasi-legislative body which promulgates regulations of both a general and specific nature for the conduct of banking business in New York.

DEPARTMENT OF CIVIL SERVICE

The State Civil Service Commission
Alfred E. Smith Office Bldg., 80 S. Swan St., Albany 12239
(518) 457-9375
E-mail: pio@cs.state.ny.us
Internet: www.cs.state.ny.us

Civil Service Ourreach, Medgar Evers College, Room M5, 1150 Carroll St., Brooklyn 11238
(718) 804-8278

Outreach & Recruitment Ctr., Adam Clayton Powell, Jr. State Office Bldg., 163 W. 125th St., N.Y.C. 10027
(212) 961-4326

President/Commissioner: Nancy G. Groenwegen (Glenmont) (518) 457-3701

Commissioners:
Caroline Ahl (Loudonville) (518) 473-6598
J. Dennis Hanrahan (Albany) (518) 473-6370

Exec. Deputy Commissioner: Vacancy at Press Time (518) 473-5698

Deputy Commissioner of Operations: Hector Millan (518) 473-5711

Deputy Commissioner of Administration: Deirdre Taylor (518) 473-5698

Dir. of Commission Operations & Municipal Assistance: Nancy B. Kiyonaga (518) 473-5022

Dir. of Public Information: David Ernst (518) 457-9375

Counsel: Judith Ratner (518) 473-2624

The Commission adopts and modifies rules on civil service matters which are subject to the approval of the Governor; hears and determines appeals on examination qualifications and ratings, position classifications, pay grade determinations, disciplinary actions and the use of preferred lists; rules on requests to continue the employment of retired individuals and awards for money-saving ideas submitted to the State Employee Suggestion Program; also oversees municipal civil service commissions and city and county personnel officers. *N.Y. Civ. Serv. Law § 5 (McKinney 1983)*
The Department is the central personnel agency for the Executive Branch of state government which provides technical services to improve the administration of municipal civil service agencies (excluding N.Y.C.). Also administers the State Civil Service Law.

STATE COMMISSION OF CORRECTION

(Executive Department)
80 Wolf Rd., 4th Floor, Albany 12205-2670
(518) 485-2346; Fax: (518) 485-2467
Internet: www.scoc.state.ny.us

Chair: Thomas A. Beilein (518) 485-2330

Commissioners:
Phyllis Harrison-Ross, M.D.
Daniel L. Stewart

Counsel: Michael Donegan

Advises and recommends policy and procedure to the Governor and the administrators of the correctional facilities; visits and inspects correctional facilities; hears and investigates grievances and complaints in the operation of the correctional facilities; promulgates rules and standards for the operation of correctional facilities; approves or rejects plans for the construction or improvement of correctional facilities. *N.Y. Correct. Laws §45 (Consol. 1977)*

DEPARTMENT OF CORRECTIONAL SERVICES

1220 Washington Ave., Bldg. 2, Albany 12226
(518) 457-8126; Inmate Locator: (518) 457-5000
Internet: www.docs.state.ny.us

Commissioner: Brian Fischer (518) 457-8134

Exec. Deputy Commissioner: Anthony J. Annucci (518) 457-1748

Asst. Commissioner/Executive Asst.: Diane J. Van Buren (518) 457-1281

Deputy Commissioner & Chief Medical Officer: Dr. Lester Wright (518) 457-7073

Deputy Commissioner & Counsel: Maureen E. Boll (518) 485-9613

Deputy Commissioner, Administrative Services: Gayle Haponik (518) 457-8188

Deputy Commissioner, Correctional Facilities Operations: Lucien J. Leclaire, Jr. (518) 457-8138

Deputy Commissioner, Correctional Industries/ Accreditation: Osbourne McKay (518) 485-2858

Deputy Commissioner, Program Services: Kenneth S. Perlman (518) 457-5555

Deputy Commissioner/Inspector General: Richard D. Roy (518) 457-2653

Public Information Dir.: Erik Kriss (518) 457-8182

Special Asst. for Labor Relations: Gary Simpson (518) 457-7383

Departments & Agencies

***At press time, some of the positions listed above were subject to appointment by the incoming Governor.**

Dept. of Correctional Services—Cont'd

Administers the state correctional facilities, residential treatment centers, detention centers, correctional camps, diagnostic and treatment centers, general confinement facilities, work release facilities and the system of parole; responsible for the secure confinement of offenders and the preparation of these individuals for successful reintegration in the community upon their release. *N.Y. Correct. Law § 1 (Consol. 1977)*

Adirondack Correctional Facility
196 Ray Brook Rd., P.O. Box 110, Ray Brook 12977-0110
(518) 891-1343; Inmate Records: Ext. 4100;
Fax Inmate Records: Ext. 4199
Superintendent: Leo Bisceglia

Albion Correctional Facility
3595 State School Rd., Albion 14411-9399 (585) 589-5511
Superintendent: William M. Powers

Altona Correctional Facility
555 Devils Den Rd., P.O. Box 3000, Altona 12910-2090
(518) 236-7841
Superintendent: Anthony Boucaud

Arthur Kill Correctional Facility
2911 Arthur Kill Rd., Staten Island 10309-1101
(718) 356-7333
Superintendent: Dennis Breslin

Attica Correctional Facility
639 Exchange St., Attica 14011-0149 (585) 591-2000
Superintendent: James Conway

Auburn Correctional Facility
135 State St., Auburn 13021-1800 (315) 253-8401
Inmate Mail, P.O. Box 618, Auburn 13021
Superintendent: Harold D. Graham

Bare Hill Corrrectional Facility
Caller Box 20, 181 Brand Rd., Malone 12953-0020
(518) 483-8411
Superintendent: Bruce Yelich

Bayview Correctional Facility
550 W. 20th St., N.Y.C. 10011-2678 (212) 255-7590
Superintendent: Wendy Featherstone

Beacon Correctional Facility
50 Camp Beacon Rd., P.O. Box 780, Beacon 12508-0780
(845) 831-4200
Superintendent: Gail Thomas

Bedford Hills Correctional Facility
247 Harris Rd., Bedford Hills 10507-2400 (914) 241-3100
Superintendent: Sabina Kaplan

Buffalo Correctional Facility
3052 Wende Rd., Alden 14004-0300 (716) 937-3786
Superintendent: Maria Tirone

Butler Correctional Facility
14001 Westbury Cutoff Rd., P.O. Box 388,
Red Creek 13143-0388 (315) 754-8001
Butler Alcohol Substance Abuse Comprehensive Treatment Center, P.O. Box 400, Red Creek 13143
Superintendent: Vacancy at Press Time

Camp Georgetown Correctional Facility
3191 Crumb Hill Rd., Georgetown 13072-9307
(315) 837-4446
Superintendent: Randy James

Camp Pharsalia Correctional Facility
496 Center Rd., Rte. 23, South Plymouth 13844-6777
Closed, effective July 1, 2009

Cape Vincent Correctional Facility
36560 State Route 12 E., P.O. Box 599,
Cape Vincent 13618-0599 (315) 654-4100
Superintendent: Patricia LeConey

Cayuga Correctional Facility
2202 State Rt. 38A, P.O. Box 1150, Moravia 13118-1150
(315) 497-1110
Superintendent: David Stallone

Chateaugay Alcohol Substance Abuse Comprehensive Treatment Center
7874 State Rt. 11, P.O. Box 320, Chateaugay 12920-0320
(518) 497-3300
Superintendent: John Demars

Clinton Correctional Facility
1156 Rt. 374, P.O. Box 2000, Dannemora 12929-2000
(518) 492-2511
Inmate Mail, P.O. Box 2001, Dannemora 12929
Superintendent: Thomas LaValley

Collins Correctional Facility
Middle Rd., P.O. Box 490, Collins 14034-0490
(716) 532-4588
Superintendent: Vacancy at Press Time

Coxsackie Correctional Facility
11260 Rt. 9 W., P.O. Box 200, West Coxsackie 12051-0200
(518) 731-2781
Inmate Mail, P.O. Box 999, Coxsackie 12051-0999
Superintendent: Daniel Martuscello

Downstate Correctional Facility
121 Red Schoolhouse Rd., P.O. Box 445, Fishkill 12524-0445
(845) 831-6600
Superintendent: Ada Perez

Eastern N.Y. Correctional Facility
30 Institution Rd., Napanoch 12458-0338 (845) 647-7400
Superintendent: William Brown

Edgecombe Residential Treatment Facility
611 Edgecombe Ave., N.Y.C. 10032-4398 (212) 923-2575
Superintendent: Shelda Washington

Elmira Correctional Facility
1879 Davis St., P.O. Box 500, Elmira 14902-0500
(607) 734-3901
Superintendent: Mark Bradt

Fishkill Correctional Facility
18 Strack Dr., Beacon 12508-0307 (845) 831-4800
Inmate Mail, 271 Matteawan Rd., P.O. Box 1245,
Beacon 12508
Superintendent: William J. Connolly

Five Points Correctional Facility
Caller Box 400, 6600 State Rt. 96, Romulus 14541
(607) 869-5111
Superintendent: John Lempke

Franklin Correctional Facility
62 Bare Hill Rd., P.O. Box 10, Malone 12953-0010
(518) 483-6040
Superintendent: Darwin LaClair

Fulton Correctional Facility
1511 Fulton Ave., Bronx 10457-8398 (718) 583-8000
Superintendent: Elnora Porter

Gouverneur Correctional Facility
112 Scotch Settlement Rd., P.O. Box 370,
Gouverneur 13642-0370 (315) 287-7351
Superintendent: Justin Taylor

Gowanda Correctional Facility
South Rd., P.O. Box 350, Gowanda 14070-0350
(716) 532-0177
Superintendent: Dale Artus

Great Meadow Correctional Facility
11739 State. Rte. 22, P.O. Box 51, Comstock 12821-0051
(518) 639-5516
Superintendent: Norman Bezio

Green Haven Correctional Facility
594 Rte. 216, Stormville 12582-0010 (845) 221-2711
Superintendent: William Lee

Greene Correctional Facility
165 Plank Rd., P.O. Box 8, Coxsackie 12051-0008
(518) 731-2741
Inmate Mail, P.O. Box 975, Eagle Bridge 12057-0975
Superintendent: Jeff McKoy

***At press time, some of the positions listed above were subject to appointment by the incoming Governor.**

Dept. of Correctional Services—Cont'd

Groveland Correctional Facility
7000 Sonyea Rd., Rte. 36, P.O. Box 50, Sonyea 14556-0050
(585) 658-2871
Superintendent: Dawson Brown

Hale Creek Alcohol Substance Abuse Comprehensive Treatment Center
279 Maloney Rd., Johnstown 12095-3769 (518) 736-2094
Superintendent: James Nichols

Hudson Correctional Facility
50 E. Court St., P.O. Box 576, Hudson 12534-0576
(518) 828-4311
Superintendent: Donna Lewin (Acting)

Lakeview Shock Incarceration Facility
9300 Lake Ave., P.O. Box T, Brocton 14716-9798
(716) 792-7100
Superintendent: Ronald Moscicki

Lincoln Correctional Facility
31-33 W. 110th St., N.Y.C. 10026-4398 (212) 860-9400
Superintendent: Joseph Williams

Livingston Correctional Facility
7005 Sonyea Rd., P.O. Box 49, Sonyea 14556-0049
(585) 658-3710
Superintendent: Malcolm R. Cully

Lyon Mountain Correctional Facility
3864 Route 374, Lyon Mountain 12952-0276 (518) 735-4546
Superintendent: Paul Knapp

Marcy Correctional Facility
9000 Old River Rd., P.O. Box 5000, Marcy 13403-5000
(315) 768-1400
Inmate Mail, P.O. Box 3600, Marcy 13403
Superintendent: Joseph Bellnier

Mid-Orange Correctional Facility
900 Kings Highway, Warwick 10990-5000 (845) 986-2291
Superintendent: Theodore Inserra

Mid-State Correctional Facility
9005 Old River Rd., P.O. Box 216, Marcy 13403-0216
(315) 768-8581
Superintendent: William Hulihan

Mohawk Correctional Facility
6514 Route 26, Rome 13440 (315) 339-5232
Superintendent: Vacancy at Press Time

Monterey Shock Incarceration Correctional Facility
2150 Evergreen Hill Rd., Beaver Dams 14812-9718
(607) 962-3184
Superintendent: Paul Gonyea

Moriah Shock Incarceration Facility
78 Burhart Ln., P.O. Box 999, Mineville 12956-0999
(518) 942-7561
Superintendent: Tim Sheehan

Mt. McGregor Correctional Facility
1000 Mt. McGregor Rd., P.O. Box 2071, Wilton 12831-5071
(518) 587-3960
Superintendent: William Haggett
Do not use the P.O. Box for Inmate Mail

Ogdensburg Correctional Facility
1 Correction Way, Ogdensburg 13669-2288 (315) 393-0281
Superintendent: Vacancy at Press Time

Oneida Correctional Facility
6100 School Rd., Rome 13440 (315) 339-6880
Inmate Mail, P.O. Box 4580, Rome 13442-4580
Superintendent: Susan Connell

Orleans Correctional Facility
3595 Gaines Basin Rd., Albion 14411-9199
Mailing Address: 35-31 Gaines Basin Rd., Albion 14411
(585) 589-6820
Superintendent: Sibatu Khahaifa

Otisville Correctional Facility
57 Sanitorium Rd., P.O. Box 8, Otisville 10963-0008
(845) 386-1490
Superintendent: Catherine Cook

Queensboro Correctional Facility
47-04 Van Dam St., Long Island City 11101-3081
(718) 361-8920
Superintendent: Dennis Crowley

Riverview Correctional Facility
1110 Tibbets Dr., P.O. Box 158, Ogdensburg 13669-0158
(315) 393-8400
Superintendent: Calvin Rabsatt

Rochester Correctional Facility
470 Ford St., Rochester 14608-2499 (585) 454-2280
Superintendent: Maria Tirone

Shawangunk Correctional Facility
200 Quick Rd., P.O. Box 750, Wallkill 12589-0750
(845) 895-2081
Superintendent: Joseph Smith

Sing Sing Correctional Facility
354 Hunter St., Ossining 10562-5442 (914) 941-0108
Superintendent: Philip Heath

Southport Correctional Facility
236 Bob Mascia Dr., P.O. Box 2000, Pine City 14871-2000
(607) 737-0850
Superintendent: Patrick Griffin

Sullivan Correctional Facility
325 Riverside Dr., P.O. Box 116, Fallsburg 12733-0116
(845) 434-2080
Superintendent: James Walsh

Summit Shock Incarceration Facility
137 Eagle Heights Rd., R.F.D., P.O. Box 56,
Summit 12175-9608 (518) 287-1721
Superintendent: Patty Nelson

Taconic Correctional Facility
250 Harris Rd., Bedford Hills 10507-2497 (914) 241-3010
Superintendent: Vacancy at Press Time

Ulster Correctional Facility
750 Berme Rd., P.O. Box 800, Napanoch 12458-0800
(845) 647-1670
Superintendent: Scott C. Carlsen

Upstate Correctional Facility
309 Bare Hill Rd., P.O. Box 2000, Malone 12953
(518) 483-6997
Superintendent: David Rock

Wallkill Correctional Facility
50 McKenderick Rd., P.O. Box G, Wallkill 12589-0286
(845) 895-2021
Superintendent: Vacancy at Press Time

Washington Correctional Facility
72 Lock Eleven Ln., P.O. Box 180, Comstock 12821-0180
(518) 639-4486
Superintendent: Jeffrey Tedford

Watertown Correctional Facility
23147 Swan Rd., Watertown 13601-9340 (315) 782-7490
Superintendent: Ekpe Ekpe

Wende Correctional Facility
3040 Wende Rd., P.O. Box 1187, Alden 14004-1187
(716) 937-4000
Superintendent: Robert A. Kirkpatrick

Willard Drug Treatment Campus
7116 County Route 132, P.O. Box 303, Willard 14588-0303
(607) 869-5500
Superintendent: Rickey Bartlett

Woodbourne Correctional Facility
99 Prison Rd., P.O. Box 1000, Woodbourne 12788
(845) 434-7730
Superintendent: Raymond J. Cunningham

Wyoming Correctional Facility
3203 Dunbar Rd., P.O. Box 501, Attica 14011-0501
(585) 591-1010
Superintendent: David Unger

***At press time, some of the positions listed above were subject to appointment by the incoming Governor.**

CRIME VICTIMS BOARD

(Executive Department)
1 Columbia Cir., Suite 200, Albany 12203
(518) 457-8727; Fax: (518) 457-8658;
Toll-free: (800) 247-8035
E-mail: cvbinfo@cvb.state.ny.us
Internet: www.cvb.state.ny.us

55 Hanson Pl., 10th Floor, Brooklyn 11217
(718) 923-4325; Fax: (718) 923-4332

65 Court St., Room 308, Buffalo 14202
(716) 847-7992; Fax: (716) 847-7995

Chair: Tina M. Stanford (Albany) (518) 485-5719

Board Members:
Joan A. Cusack (Brooklyn)
William J. Davis (Brooklyn)
Mary Haviland (Brooklyn)
Jacqueline C. Mattina (Buffalo)

Promulgates and administers rules and regulations for the coordination of victim compensation services, studies the provisions for victim compensation, recommends statutory provisions to the Governor for the improvement of victim services, conducts studies on matters affecting crime victims and makes grants to local crime victim service organizations. *N.Y. Exec. Law § 623 (Consol. 1983)*

DIVISION OF CRIMINAL JUSTICE SERVICES

(Executive Department)
4 Tower Place, 10th Floor, Albany 12203-3764
(518) 457-6113; Fax: (518) 457-3089;
Toll-free: (800) 262-3257
E-mail: infodcjs@dcjs.state.ny.us
Internet: www.criminaljustice.state.ny.us

Commissioner: Sean M. Byrne (Acting) (518) 457-1260

Exec. Deputy Commissioner: Vacancy at Press Time (518) 458-6091

Deputy Commissioner and Counsel: Gina Bianchi (518) 457-8413

Deputy Commissioner, Administration: Donald Capone (518) 457-5046

Deputy Commissioner, Office of Criminal Justice Operations: Joseph Morrissey (518) 486-2995

Deputy Commissioner, Office of Public Safety: Tony Perez (518) 457-6101

Deputy Commissioner, Criminal Justice Programs: Michael Barrett (518) 457-0438

Deputy Commissioner, Office of Justice Research & Performance: Terry Salo (518) 457-3724

Deputy Commissioner, Justice Information Systems: Anne Roest (518) 485-7176

Dir., Public Information: John Caher (518) 457-8828

Advises and assists the Governor and state agencies in developing policies and programs for improving the criminal justice system through statistical analysis and research into the mechanics of the criminal justice system. *N.Y. Exec. Law § 836 (Consol. 1983)*

DEPT. OF ECONOMIC DEVELOPMENT

See New York State Urban Development Corporation

EDUCATION DEPARTMENT

Education Bldg., 89 Washington Ave., Albany 12234
(518) 474-3852
Internet: www.nysed.gov

Commissioner: David M. Steiner (518) 474-5844; Fax: (518) 473-4909

The Commissioner serves as chief executive officer of the Board of Regents which has jurisdiction over the most comprehensive state education system in the nation. The system encompasses every education endeavor in the State, including public and nonpublic elementary, middle and secondary education; public and independent colleges and universities; museums, libraries, historical societies and archives; the vocational rehabilitation system; and responsibility for the licensing, practicing and oversight of 61 professions.

The Board of Regents

Room 110 (518) 474-5889

Chancellor: Merryl H. Tisch
9 E. 79th St., N.Y.C. 10075 (212) 879-9414

Vice Chancellor: Milton L. Cofield
98 Hickory Ridge Rd., Rochester 14625 (585) 200-6284

Board Members:
Charles R. Bendit
111 Eighth Ave., Suite 1500, N.Y.C. 10011 (212) 220-9945
Robert M. Bennett
201 Millwood Lane, Tonawanda 14150 (716) 645-1344
Anthony S. Bottar
AXA Financial Tower II, Suite 1600, 120 Madison St., Syracuse 13202 (315) 422-3466
Joseph E. Bowman, Jr.
ED 124, School of Education, University at Albany, 1400 Washington Ave., Albany 12222 (518) 442-4987
Karen Brooks Hopkins
30 Lafayette Ave., Brooklyn 11217 (718) 636-4135
Christine D. Cea
NYS Institute for Basic Research in Developmental Disabilities, 1050 Forest Hill Rd., Staten Island 10314 (718) 494-5306
Geraldine D. Chapey, 107-10 Shore Front Pkwy., Apt. 9C, Belle Harbor 11694 (718) 634-8471
Saul B. Cohen
82 Taymil Rd., New Rochelle 10804 (914) 633-7889
James C. Dawson
166 U.S. Oval, Plattsburgh 12903 (518) 324-2401
Wade S. Norwood, Finger Lakes Health Systems Agency, 1150 University Ave., Rochester 14607 (585) 461-3520, Ext. 110
Harry Phillips III
71 Hawthorne Way, Hartsdale 10530 (914) 948-2228
Betty A. Rosa
Chambreleng Hall, Fordham University, 441 E. Fordham Rd., Bronx 10458 (718) 817-5053
James R. Tallon, Jr.
United Hospital Fund, 350 Fifth Ave., 23rd Floor, N.Y.C. 10118-2399 (212) 494-0777
Roger Tilles, 100 Crossings Park W., Suite 107, Woodbury 11797 (516) 364-2533
Lester W. Young, Jr.
55 Hanson Pl., Suite 400, Brooklyn 11217 (718) 722-2796

Secretary: Tony Lofrumento

Governs the University of the State of New York and sets education policy for the State Rules established by the Board have the force and effect of law. The Commissioner of Education is appointed by the Regents and serves as President of the University.

Office of Counsel

89 Washington Ave., Room 112 EB, Albany 12234
(518) 474-6400

Counsel and Deputy Commissioner for Legal Affairs:
Erin O'Grady-Parent (Acting)
(518) 474-6400; Fax: (518) 474-1940

Deputy Counsel: Vacancy at Press Time
(518) 474-8864; Fax: (518) 474-1940

Asst. Counsel:
Mary Ellen Clerkin (518) 473-6816; Fax: (518) 473-2925
Joan Gavrilik (518) 474-8806; Fax: (518) 473-2925

Special Counsel for Legislation: Richard J. Trautwein
(518) 473-4921; Fax: (518) 474-4188

Staff Attys.:
Howard Beyer (518) 474-8806; Fax: (518) 474-4188
Alison Bianchi (518) 473-4921; Fax: (518) 473-2925
Patti Boochever (518) 474-8806; Fax: (518) 473-2925
Louise DeCandia (518) 474-8806; Fax: (518) 473-2925
Katherine Gaffney (518) 473-4921; Fax: (518) 474-4188
Seth Gilboord (518) 474-8806; Fax: (518) 474-4188
Victoria Hunter Hay (518) 474-8806; Fax: (518) 473-2925
Melissa Latino (518) 473-6816; Fax: (518) 473-2925
Mary Ellen Lorini (518) 473-6816; Fax: (518) 473-2925
Kathy Marinelli (518) 474-8806; Fax: (518) 474-4188
Richard L. Nabozny (518) 473-4921; Fax: (518) 474-4188
Charles O'Brien (518) 473-6816; Fax: (518) 473-2925
Sara Paupini (518) 473-4921; Fax: (518) 473-2925
Kathyleen Surgalla (518) 473-6816; Fax: (518) 473-2925
Shannon Tahoe (518) 473-4921; Fax: (518) 473-2925

***At press time, some of the positions listed above were subject to appointment by the incoming Governor.**

Education Dept.—Cont'd

The New York State Library
Cultural Education Ctr., Empire State Plaza, Albany 12230
(518) 474-5355; Fax: (518) 474-5786
E-mail: refserv@mail.nysed.gov
Internet: www.nysl.nysed.gov

State Librarian and Asst. Commissioner for Libraries: Bernard Margolis (518) 474-5930; Fax: (518) 486-6880

Dir. of State Library: Loretta Ebert (518) 473-1189

Deputy Commissioner for Cultural Education: Jeffrey Cannell (518) 474-5976; Fax: (518) 474-2718
E-mail: jcannell@mail.nysed.gov

Public Services: Sally Legendre (Principal Librarian) (518) 486-5755

Law Collection consists of over 450,000 titles, ranging from rare editions of early NYS laws to federal statutes, reports, digests; maintains superceded NYS laws and regulations, comprehensive NYS Constitutional material, court of appeals and appellate division records and briefs.

Office of Cultural Education
NYS Education Dept.
Cultural Education Center, Room 10A33, Albany 12230
(518) 474-5976; Fax: (518) 474-2718

Deputy Commissioner: Jeffrey Cannell

Office of Cultural Education
New York State Archives
Cultural Education Center, 11th Floor, Albany 12230
(518) 474-8955; Fax: (518) 408-1940
E-mail: archref@mail.nysed.gov
Internet: www.archives.nysed.gov

Head, Researcher Services: James D. Folts

Asst. Commissioner & State Archivist: Christine Ward
Room 9C49, Albany 12230
(518) 474-6926; Fax: (518) 473-7058

Acquires, preserves, and makes accessible for use records of state government having "sufficient historical value or other value to warrant their continued preservation, as evidence of the government's organization, functions, policies, decisions, procedures, operations or other activities." *N.Y. Arts & Cultural Affairs Law §57.05*

Office of the Professions
Education Bldg., 2nd Floor, Albany 12234
(518) 474-3817; Fax: (518) 474-1449
E-mail: op4info@mail.nysed.gov

Exec. Dir., Div. of Professional Licensing Svces.: Larry Demers (Acting), Ext. 340

Assoc. Commissioner: Frank Munoz, Ext. 470

All correspondence relating to the issue of certificates, details of examinations and admissions to practice.

NEW YORK STATE BOARD OF ELECTIONS
(Executive Department)
40 Steuben St., Albany 12207-2109
(518) 474-6220; Fax: (518) 486-4068;
Voter Information: (800) 367-8683
E-mail: info@elections.state.ny.us
Internet: www.elections.state.ny.us

Co-Executive Dirs.:
Todd Valentine (518) 474-6236
Robert A. Brehm (518) 474-8100

Co-Chairs:
Douglas A. Kellner (518) 474-8100
James A. Walsh (518) 474-6236

Commissioners:
Evelyn J. Aquila (518) 474-8100
Gregory P. Peterson (518) 474-6236

Special Counsel: Kimberly Galvin (518) 474-6367
Enforcement Counsel: Elizabeth C. Hogan (518) 474-2063

EMPIRE STATE DEVELOPMENT CORPORATION
See New York State Urban Development Corporation

STATE EMPLOYMENT RELATIONS BOARD
See Public Employment Relations Board

DEPARTMENT OF ENVIRONMENTAL CONSERVATION
625 Broadway, Albany 12233-1011
(518) 474-2121
Internet: www.dec.ny.gov

Commissioner: Alexander B. Grannis (518) 402-8540; Fax: (518) 402-9016
Exec. Deputy Commissioner: Stuart Gruskin (518) 402-8560; Fax: (518) 402-9016
Deputy Commissioner/General Counsel: Alison Crocker (518) 402-9185; Fax: (518) 402-9018
Deputy Counsel: (518) 402-9509; Fax: (518) 402-9019
Michelle Crew Phillip Lodico
Deputy Commissioner, Administration: Jack McKeon (518) 402-9401; Fax: (518) 402-9016
Asst. Commissioner, Air, Climate Change & Energy: Jared Snyder (518) 402-8537; Fax: (518) 402-9016
Asst. Commissioner, Hearings and Mediation Svces.: Louis A. Alexander (518) 402-8537; Fax: (518) 402-8541
Asst. Commissioner, Natural Resources & Water Quality: Chris Amato (518) 402-8533; Fax: (518) 402-9016
Asst. Commissioner, Public Protection: Henry L. Hamilton (518) 402-8552; Fax: (518) 402-9016
Asst. Commissioner, Water Resources: Jim Tierney (518) 402-2794; Fax: (518) 402-9016
Chief Administrative Law Judge: James McClymonds (Office of Hearings and Mediation Services) (518) 402-9003; Fax: (518) 402-9037
Dir., Div. of Air Resources: David J. Shaw (518) 402-8452; Fax: (518) 402-9035
Dir., Div. of Environmental Permits: Jeff Sama (518) 402-9182; Fax: (518) 402-9168
Dir., Div. of Environmental Remediation: Dale A. Desnoyers (518) 402-9706; Fax: (518) 402-9020
Dir., Div. of Fish, Wildlife, & Marine Resources: Patricia Riexinger (518) 402-8924; Fax: (518) 402-8925
Dir, Div. of Forest Protection & Fire Management: Thomas Rinaldi (518) 402-8839; Fax: (518) 402-8840
Dir., Div. of Information Services: Leslie Brennan (518) 402-9860; Fax: (518) 402-9031
Dir., Div. of Lands and Forests: Robert Davies (518) 402-9405; Fax: (518) 402-9028
Dir., Div. of Law Enforcement: Peter Fanelli (518) 402-8829; Fax: (518) 402-8830
Dir., Legislative Affairs: Chris Ballantyne (518) 402-2797; Fax: (518) 402-9016
Dir., Div. of Management & Budget Services: Nancy W. Lussier (518) 402-9228; Fax: (518) 402-9230
Dir, Div. of Mineral Resources: Bradley J. Field (518) 402-8076; Fax: (518) 402-8060
Dir., Operations: Mark Malinoski (518) 402-9055; Fax: (518) 402-9053
Dir., Div. of Public Affairs & Education: Laurel Remus (518) 402-8049; Fax: (518) 402-8050
Dir., Public Information: Yancey Roy (518) 402-8000; Fax: (518) 402-2209
Dir., Div. of Solid & Hazardous Materials: Ed Dassatti (518) 402-8651; Fax: (518) 402-9024
Dir., Div. of Water: Mark Klotz (518) 402-8233; Fax: (518) 402-8230

The Department is charged with the responsibility for conserving, improving and protecting N.Y.S.'s natural resources and the environment; controls water, land and air pollution; oversees the promulgation and enforcement of regulations pertaining to the protection and conservation of N.Y.S.'s environment under *N.Y.S. Environmental Conservation Law (ECL) § 3-0301 (Consol. 1982)* . Additionally, the Department is responsible for most environmental management conducted by the State. The Department's work includes fish and wildlife protection; open space preservation; management of State lands, campgrounds, and other recreational sites; water quality monitoring, management and improvement; hazardous and contaminated materials monitoring and remediation; enforcement of environmental laws and regulations; fire control and search-and-rescue efforts on State lands; management and permitting of solid and hazardous waste disposal and recycling; enforcement, monitoring, and contrl of air emissions; and oversight of the *State Environmental Quality Review Act (SEQRA)* process.

***At press time, some of the positions listed above were subject to appointment by the incoming Governor.**

Dept. of Environmental Conservation—Cont'd

Region 1 Office
S.U.N.Y. Campus, Bldg. 40, 50 Circle Rd.,
Stony Brook 11790-3409
(631) 444-0345; Fax: (631) 444-0349
Regional Dir.: Peter Scully
Regional Atty.: Vernon G. Rail
(631) 444-0260; Fax: (631) 444-0348

Region 2 Office/Executive Offices (N.Y.C.)
1 Hunter's Point Plaza, 47-40 21st St.,
Long Island City 11101-5407
(718) 482-4900; Fax: (718) 482-4026
Regional Dir.: Suzanne Mattei
Regional Atty.: Louis Oliva
(718) 482-4965; Fax: (718) 482-4962

Region 3 Office
21 S. Putt Corners Rd., New Paltz 12561-1620
(845) 256-3000; Fax: (845) 255-3042
Regional Dir.: William Janeway (845) 250-3033
Regional Atty.: John Parker (845) 256-3037

Region 4 Office
1130 N. Westcott Rd., Schenectady 12306-2014
(518) 357-2068; Fax: (518) 357-2593
Regional Dir.: Eugene Kelly
Regional Atty.: Richard Ostrov
(518) 357-2048; Fax: (518) 357-2087

Region 5 Office
1115 NYS Rt. 86, P.O. Box 296, Ray Brook 12977-0296
(518) 897-1200; Fax: (518) 897-1394
Regional Dir.: Elizabeth Lowe
(518) 897-1211; Fax: (518) 897-1394
Regional Atty.: Chris LaCombe
(518) 897-1227; Fax: (518) 897-1394

Region 6 Office
State Office Bldg., 317 Washington St., Watertown 13601
(315) 785-2239; Fax: (315) 785-2242
Regional Dir.: Judy Drabicki
Regional Atty.: Randall Young (315) 785-2238

Region 7 Office
615 Erie Blvd. W., Syracuse 13204-2400
(315) 426-7403; Fax: (315) 426-7408
Regional Dir.: Kenneth Lynch
Regional Atty.: Vacancy at Press Time (315) 426-7405

Region 8 Office
6274 E. Avon-Lima Rd., Avon 14414-9519
(585) 226-5366; Fax: (585) 226-9485
Regional Dir.: Paul D'Amato
Regional Atty.: Leo Bracci (585) 226-5369

Region 9 Office
270 Michigan Ave., Buffalo 14203-2915
(716) 851-7200; Fax: (716) 851-7211
Regional Dir.: Abby Snyder
Regional Atty.: Maureen Brady (716) 851-7190

STATE ETHICS COMMISSION, DEPT. OF STATE

See Commission on Public Integrity

OFFICE OF GENERAL SERVICES

(Executive Department)
Corning Tower, 41st Floor, Empire State Plaza, Albany 12242
(518) 474-3899; Fax: (518) 486-9179
Internet: www.ogs.state.ny.us

633 Third Ave., 38th Floor, N.Y.C. 10017
(212) 681-4556; Fax: (212) 681-4558

Commissioner: John C. Egan (518) 474-5991
First Deputy Commissioner: Paul W. Larrabee (518) 473-6953
Deputy Commissioner & Counsel: Howard L. Zwickel (518) 474-5988
Deputy Commissioner, Administration: Vacancy at Press Time (518) 473-8550
Deputy Commissioner, Information Technology & Procurement Services: Carla Chiaro (518) 473-3933
Deputy Commissioner, Design & Construction: James M. Davies (518) 474-0337
Deputy Commissioner, Real Property Management & Development: William L. Hill, Jr. (518) 474-5390
Dir., Procurement Services: Jerry Gerard (518) 474-3695
Dir., Public Information: Heather R. Groll (518) 474-5987

Responsible for managing and leasing real property, designing and building State facilities, procuring contracts for goods, services and technology and delivering a wide array of support services including printing, parking, mail services, insurance and surplus property disposition.

STATE DEPARTMENT OF HEALTH

Corning Tower, Empire State Plaza, Albany 12237
Internet: www.nyhealth.gov

Commissioner: Richard F. Daines, M.D.
(518) 474-2011; Fax: (518) 474-5450, 474-6608
Exec. Deputy Commissioner: James W. Clyne, Jr.
(518) 473-0458; Fax: (518) 474-5450, 474-6608

Supervises and controls the registration of births, deaths, marriages and occurrences of disease, conducts research into mortality, health education and diagnostic methods, licenses nursing homes, inspects and operates hospitals and homes, supervises the sanitary aspects of the public water supply, camps, hotels and food service facilities and licenses and regulates the use of ionizing and non-ionizing electromagnetic radiation. *N.Y. Pub. Health Law § 200 (Consol. 1987)*

Division of Administration
Room 1495
(518) 474-8565; Fax: (518) 474-3295
Deputy Commissioner: Robert W. Reed

Center for Environmental Health
Flanigan Square, 547 River St., Troy 12180
(518) 402-7500; Fax: (518) 402-7509
Director: Howard A. Freed, M.D.

Capital Regional Office
Frear Bldg., One Fulton St., Troy 12180-3241
(518) 408-5300; Fax: (518) 408-5280
Regional Director: Geraldine Bunn (518) 408-5268
Asst. Regional Dir.: Robert Welch (518) 408-5268

Central Regional Office
217 S. Salina St., Syracuse 13202-1380
(315) 477-8100; Admin. Fax: (315) 477-8588
Assoc. Dirs.:
Pauline Frazier (315) 477-8485
Ronald Heerkens (315) 477-8484

Metropolitan Area Regional Office
90 Church St., N.Y.C. 10007
(212) 417-5550
Regional Dir.: Celeste M. Johnson
Deputy Regional Dir.: Vacancy at Press Time

Western Regional Office
584 Delaware Ave., Buffalo 14202-1295
(716) 847-4500; Fax (Admin.): (716) 847-4661;
Fax (Disease Control): (716) 847-4333
Assoc. Commissioner: Gregory Young, M.D. (Acting)
(716) 847-4505; Fax: (716) 847-4661

Division of Environmental Health Assessment
Flanigan Square, 547 River St., Troy 12180
(518) 402-7511; Fax: (518) 402-7509
Director: Ed Horn, Ph.D.
Assoc. Dir.: John Wilson

Division of Environmental Health Investigation
Flanigan Sq., 547 River St., Troy 12180
(518) 402-7501; Fax: (518) 402-7509
Director: G. Anders Carlson, Ph.D.
Asst. Dir.: Adela Salame-Alfie

Division of Environmental Health Protection
Flanigan Square, 547 River St., Troy 12180
(518) 402-7510; Fax: (518) 402-7509
Director: Richard Svenson, P.E.

***At press time, some of the positions listed above were subject to appointment by the incoming Governor.**

State Dept. of Health—Cont'd

Division of Epidemiology
Room 503
(518) 474-1055; Fax: (518) 473-2301
Director: Perry Smith, M.D.
Associate Dir.: Marybeth Fader (518) 474-4394

Division of Family Health
Room 890
(518) 473-7922; Fax: (518) 473-2015
Director: Barbara McTague
Associate Dir.: Wendy Shaw

Office of Governmental and External Affairs
Room 1441
(518) 473-1124; Fax: (518) 473-9674
Asst. Commissioner: James Clancy
Deputy Dir. for Government Affairs: Amy Nickson

Health Facilities Management
Room 1683
(518) 474-2772; Fax: (518) 474-0611
Director: Val S. Gray (518) 474-2772

Roswell Park Cancer Institute Corp.
Elm & Carlton Sts., Buffalo 14263-0999
Admin.: (716) 845-5770; (716) 845-2300;
Fax: (716) 845-8261
President & C.E.O.: Donald L. Trump, M.D.
(716) 845-5772; Fax: (716) 845-8261
The Institute is a National Cancer Institute-designated Comprehensive Cancer Center dedicated to patient care, research and education

Helen Hayes Hospital
Route 9-W, West Haverstraw 10993-1195
(845) 786-4000; Fax: (845) 947-0036; TTY: (845) 947-3187
Director & C.E.O.: Val S. Gray
(845) 786-4202; Fax: (845) 947-0036
Deputy Dir.: Edmund Zybert (845) 786-4201
The Hospital is a leading specialty hospital offering treatment and rehabilitation to people with physical disabilities and chronic disabling diseases.

New York State Veterans' Home at Oxford
4211 State Hwy. 220, Oxford 13830
(607) 843-3100; Fax: (607) 843-3199
Administrator: Vathsala Venugopalan (607) 843-3129
Medical Dir.: Philip Dzwonczyk, M.D. (607) 843-3140

New York State Veterans' Home at St. Albans
178-50 Linden Blvd., Jamaica 11434-1467
(718) 990-0300; Fax: (718) 481-6994
Administrator: Neville Goldson (718) 990-0329
Medical Dir.: Thomas Bizarro, M.D. (718) 990-0328

New York State Veterans' Home at Batavia
220 Richmond Ave., Batavia 14020
(585) 345-2000; Fax: (585) 345-9030
Administrator: Joanne I. Hernick
(585) 345-2076; Fax: (585) 345-9030
Medical Dir.: Mary Obear, M.D. (585) 345-2042

New York State Veterans' Home at Montrose
2090 Albany Post Rd., Montrose 10548
(914) 788-6000; Fax: (914) 788-6100
Administrator: Nancy Baa-Danso (914) 788-6003
Medical Dir.: Wellington Liu, M.D. (914) 788-6025

Office of Health Information Technology Transformation
Room 1440
Deputy Commissioner: Rachel Block
(518) 474-5423; Fax: (518) 474-4138
Deputy Dir.: Patricia Hale, M.D., PhD., FACP
(518) 474-4987

Office of Health Insurance Programs (OHIP)
Room 1466
(518) 474-8646; Fax: (518) 486-6852
Deputy Commissioner & State Medicaid Dir.:
Donna Frescatore
Deputy Dir.: Vacancy at Press Time

Division of Coverage & Enrollment
Room 1482
(518) 474-0180; Fax: (518) 474-3295
Director: Judith A. Arnold

Division of Managed Care
Room 2001
(518) 474-5737; Fax: (518) 474-5738
Director: Vallencia Lloyd

Office of Health Systems Management
Room 1408
(518) 474-7028; Fax: (518) 486-2564
Deputy Commissioner: Richard Cook
(518) 474-7028
Deputy Dir.: Lora Lefebvre (518) 474-7028
Dir., Division of Quality & Patient Safety: Lisa McMurdo
(518) 402-1040; Fax: (518) 402-1042
Dir., Division of Health Facility Planning: Thomas Jung
(Acting) (518) 402-0967; Fax: (518) 402-0971
Dir., Division of Certification & Surveillance:
Mary Ellen Hennessy
(518) 402-1004; Fax: (518) 402-1010
Dir., Office of the Medical Director: John N. Morley, M.D.
(518) 408-1828; Fax: (518) 402-5302
Dir., Professional Medical Conduct: Keith Servis
(518) 402-0855; Fax: (518) 402-0866

Division of Legal Affairs
Room 2438
(518) 474-7553; Fax: (518) 473-2802
General Counsel: Thomas Conway
Deputy General Counsel: Janet S. Cohn (518) 473-3818

Office of Long Term Care
Room 1415
Deputy Commissioner: Mark Kissinger
(518) 402-5673; Fax: (518) 486-2564
Deputy Dir.: Carla Williams
(518) 408-1833; Fax: (518) 474-3295

Division of Nutrition
150 Broadway, Menands 12204-2719
(518) 402-7090; Fax: (518) 402-7398
Director: Patricia Hess
Assoc. Dir.: Mary Warr Cowans

Public Affairs Group
Room 1455
(518) 474-7354; Fax: (518) 473-7071
Director: Claudia S. Hutton
Deputy Dir.: Diane Mathis

Office of Public Health
Room 1415
Deputy Commissioner: Guthrie S. Birkhead, M.D., M.P.H.
(518) 402-5302
Deputy Dir.: Phyllis Silver (518) 473-0771

AIDS Institute
Room 412
(518) 474-6399; Fax: (518) 486-1315
Director: Humberto Cruz
Deputy Dir.: Sue Klein (518) 473-8778

Office of Science
Room 2040
Asst. Commissioner: Dale L. Morse, M.D., M.S.
(518) 473-4959; Fax: (518) 486-1455

Division of Chronic Disease and Injury Prevention
Room 515
(518) 474-0512; Fax: (518) 473-2853
Director: Barbara Wallace, M.D.
Associate Dir.: Thomas Blake

Task Force On Life & The Law
90 Church St., N.Y.C. 10007
(212) 417-5444
Exec. Dir.: Beth Roxland
Admin. Asst.: Angela R. Star
Senior Atty.: Carrie Zoubul
Principal Policy Analyst: Susie Han

***At press time, some of the positions listed above were subject to appointment by the incoming Governor.**

State Dept. of Health—Cont'd

Wadsworth Center
Dock J-P1 Level, Room E260, Albany 12237
Mailing Address: P.O. Box 509, Albany 12201-0509
(518) 474-7592; Fax: (518) 474-3439

David Axelrod Institute, 120 New Scotland Ave., Albany 12208
Mailing Address: P.O. Box 22002, Albany 12201-2002
(518) 473-3837

Griffin Laboratory, 5668 State Farm Rd., Slingerlands 12159
Mailing Address: P.O. Box 509, Albany 12201-0509
(518) 485-6770

Director: Lawrence Sturman, M.D.

Deputy Dir.: Jill Taylor (518) 474-3157

DIVISION OF HOUSING AND COMMUNITY RENEWAL
(Executive Department)
25 Beaver St., N.Y.C. 10004
(212) 480-6700; Office of Legal Affairs: (212) 480-7425
Internet: www.nysdhcr.gov

Hampton Plaza, 38-40 State St., Albany 12207
(518) 473-2526; Office of Legal Affairs: (518) 486-6337

Office of Rent Administration, Gertz Plaza,
92-31 Union Hall St., Jamaica 11433
(718) 739-6400

Commissioner: Brian E. Lawlor (518) 473-8384
Exec. Deputy Commissioner: Michael Skrebutenas (518) 473-1829
General Counsel: Gary R. Connor (212) 480-6707
Deputy Commissioner for Rent Administration: Woody Pascal (Acting) (718) 262-4822
Deputy Commissioner for Community Development: Gary Hallock (518) 474-0322
Deputy Commissioner for Housing Operations: Vacancy at Press Time (212) 480-6440
Deputy Commissioner for Intergovernmental Affairs: Lorrie Pizzola (518) 474-9553
Dir., Fair Housing & Equal Opportunity: Cecil Brown (518) 486-5188
Dir., Public Information: James Plastiras (518) 402-3728

Promulgates and administers regulations for apartments subject to rent laws in New York City and counties that have adopted the Emergency Tenant and Protection Act; oversees and regulates the State's publicly assisted rental housing stock; and administers housing and community preservation programs by administering State grants and loans and applying for and administering federal housing grants and loans.

DIVISION OF HUMAN RIGHTS
(Executive Department)
One Fordham Plaza, Bronx 10458
(718) 741-8400; Fax: (718) 741-3214
Internet: www.dhr.state.ny.us

Empire State Plaza, 28th Floor, Corning Twr., Albany 12220
(518) 474-2705

44 Hawley St., Room 603, Binghamton 13901
(607) 721-8467

55 Hanson Pl., Room 304 & 900, Brooklyn 11217
(718) 722-2856, 722-2060

The Walter J. Mahoney State Office Bldg., Suite 506, 65 Court St., Buffalo 14202
(716) 847-7632

N.Y.S. Office Bldg., Room 2B-49, Veterans' Memorial Highway, Hauppauge 11787
(631) 952-6434

175 Fulton Ave., 4th Floor, Hempstead 11550
(516) 538-1360

NYS Office Bldg., 4th Floor, 163 W. 125th St., N.Y.C. 10027
(212) 961-8650

20 Exchange Pl., 2nd Floor, N.Y.C. 10005
(212) 480-2522

8 John Walsh Blvd., Suite 204, Peekskill 10566
(914) 788-8050

1 Monroe Sq., Suite 308, 259 Monroe Ave., Rochester 14607
(585) 238-8250

333 E. Washington St., Room 543, Syracuse 13202
(315) 428-4633

Commissioner: Galen D. Kirkland (718) 741-8326
First Deputy Commissioner: Luis R. Burgos, Jr. (718) 741-8330
Deputy Commissioner for Division-Initiated Investigations: Julian R. Birnbaum (718) 741-8328
Deputy Commissioner for Finance and Administration: Stephen R. Rolandi (718) 741-8360
Deputy Commissioner for Regional Affairs: Jyll D. Townes (718) 741-8334
Deputy Commissioner for Federal Program: Edward A. Watkins (718) 741-8440
Deputy Commissioner for External Affairs: James E. Mulvaney (718) 741-3223
General Counsel: Caroline Downey (718) 741-8402

Promulgates and administers regulations for enforcement of human rights standards including nondiscrimination standards set forth in the statute, holds hearings on the violation of standards, files complaints alleging violation of human rights standards and creates advisory and planning bodies to assist in the research and implementation of standards of conduct. *N.Y. Exec. Law § 293 (Consol. 1983)*

STATE INSURANCE DEPARTMENT
25 Beaver St., N.Y.C. 10004-2319
(212) 480-2289
Internet: www.ins.state.ny.us

One Commerce Plz., Albany 12257
(518) 474-4550

Superintendent: James J. Wrynn (212) 480-2301
First Deputy Superintendent: Martin A. Schwartzman (212) 480-2301
Deputy Supt. & General Counsel: Martha Lees (212) 480-5259
Deputy Supt. & Chief Ethics Officer: Susan Donnellan (Policy & Projects) (212) 480-2296
Deputy Superintendents:
Ivan C. Lafayette (Community Affairs)
Michael Moriarty (Property & Capital Markets)
Steven Nachman (Frauds and Customer Service)
David Neustadt (Public Information)
Troy Oechsner (Health)
Christopher Rulon (Operations)
Asst. Deputy Superintendent: Stacey Rowland (Intergovernmental & Legislative Affairs)
Dir., Public Affairs: Andy Mais (212) 480-5262
Dir., Insurance Fraud Bur.: Frank Orlando (212) 480-5770
Dir., Internal Audit: Phyllis Ann Linker (212) 480-2317

Promulgates and administers regulations for the enforcement of the Insurance Law and supervises and investigates the operation of insurance companies in the state. *N.Y. Ins. Law § 201 (Consol.1985)*

Albany Office
Empire State Plaza, Bldg. 1, Nelson A. Rockefeller Plaza, Albany 12257
(518) 474-4550

Deputy Superintendent, Operations: Christopher Rulon
Chief, Consumer Services Bureau: Mitchell Gennaoui
Supervising Examiner, Consumer Services Bureau: John Chaskey
Chief, Accident & Health Rating Section: James Gutterman
Chief Actuaries, Life: William Carmello
Principal Insurance Examiner: Peter Harkin

Buffalo Office
65 Court St., 1st Floor, Buffalo 14202
(716) 847-7618

Senior Examiner: Joseph Perry

Liquidation Bureau
123 William St., N.Y.C. 10038-3889
(212) 341-6400

Special Deputy Superintendent: Dennis Hayes

Supervises the liquidation of the assets of an insurance company after seizure and upon court order for reasons as set forth in *Ins. Law § 7402. N.Y. Ins. Law § 7405 (Consol. 1985)*

***At press time, some of the positions listed above were subject to appointment by the incoming Governor.**

THE STATE INSURANCE FUND

199 Church St., N.Y.C. 10007
(212) 312-7001
Internet: www.nysif.com

One Watervliet Ave., Albany 12206-1649
(518) 437-5220; Fax: (518) 437-5260

Chair: Robert H. Hurlburt

C.E.O./Exec. Dir.: Vacancy at Press Time
Fax: (212) 385-2073

General Atty.: Gregory Allen
15 Computer Dr. W., Albany 12205 (518) 437-4208

Insures employers against liability for death or injury resulting from employment-related injuries. Collects premiums from employers and pays claims, administers the Disability Benefits Fund. *N.Y. Work. Comp. Law § 76 McKinney 1965 & 1994 Supp.)*

INTERSTATE ENVIRONMENTAL COMMISSION

311 W. 43rd St., Suite 201, N.Y.C. 10036-6413
(212) 582-0380; Fax: (212) 581-5719
E-mail: iecmail@iec-nynjct.org
Internet: www.iec-nynjct.org

IEC Laboratory,
College of Staten Island, Bldg. 6S, Room 106,
2800 Victory Blvd., Staten Island 10314
(718) 982-3792; Fax: (718) 698-8472

Acting Administrator and Counsel: Ross Brady
(Asst. Secretary)

Administers the Tri-State Compact of 1936 by promulgating rules and regulations, monitoring environmental compliance with a particular emphasis on water quality and taking legal action where necessary to enforce the environmental standards set forth in the Compact. *N.Y. Envt'l Conservation Law ECL21-0501 et seq.*

DEPARTMENT OF LABOR

State Campus, Bldg. 12, Albany 12240-0002
(518) 457-9000
E-mail: nysdol@labor.ny.gov
Internet: www.labor.ny.gov

75 Varick St., 7th Floor, N.Y.C. 10013
(212) 775-3670

Commissioner: Colleen Crawford Gardner
(518) 457-2746; Fax: (518) 457-6908

Exec. Deputy Commissioner: Mario Musolino
(518) 457-4318; Fax: (518) 485-6297

Chief Information Officer: Robert J. Vitello
(518) 457-7994; Fax: (518) 485-6297

Deputy Commissioner for Administration & C.F.O.:
Martin Dunbar (518) 457-6662; Fax: (518) 485-6297

Deputy Commissioner for Worker Protection:
Pico Ben-Amotz (518) 457-4317; Fax: (518) 485-6297

Deputy Commissioner for Wage & Immigrant Svces.:
Terri Gerstein (518) 473-3905; Fax: (518) 485-6297

Deputy Commissioner for Federal Affairs:
Bruce Herman (518) 485-6410; Fax: (518) 485-6297

Counsel: Maria Colavito (518) 457-7069; Fax: (518) 457-1164

Dir., Office of Communications: Leo Rosales
(518) 457-5519

Seeks job creation and economic growth through workforce development; administers unemployment insurance system and labor exchange system, oversees state worker protection programs, including enforcement of safety and health regulations in the public sector, state labor laws and federal statues related to working conditions, wages and hours, and laws related to Public Work; serves as the State's principal source for labor market information.

Counsel's Office—Albany
State Campus, Bldg. 12, Room 508, Albany 12240
(518) 457-4380; Fax: (518) 485-1819

Counsel: Maria Colavito (518) 457-7069

Deputy Counsel: Joan A. Connell (518) 457-7069

Senior Attys.:
Kristen L. Broden
John D. Charles
Richard Cucolo
Carolyn D'Antonio
Marshall Day
Benjamin Garry
Tsvi J. Gold
Kevin Jones
Shannon J. Lawlor
Mary E. McManus

Industrial Board of Appeals
Empire State Plaza, 20th Floor, Agency Bldg. 2, Albany 12223
(518) 474-4785; Fax: (518) 473-7533

Chair: Anne P. Stevason

Counsel: Devan A. Rice

Members:
Jean Grumet
LaMarr J. Jackson
J. Christopher Meagher

Counsel: Sandra M. Nathan

Reviews the validity and reasonableness of any rule, regulation or order made by the Commissioner of Labor. *N.Y. Lab. Law § 101 (Consol. 1983)*

Self-Insurance Advisory Committee
20 Park St., Albany 12207
(518) 402-6070; Fax: (518) 402-6078

Chair: John Sweeny
N.Y.C. Law Dept., 350 Jay St., 9th Floor, Brooklyn 11201
(718) 222-2101; Fax: (718) 222-2393

Vice Chair: Steven Scotti
Con Edison, Law Dept., 4 Irving Pl., Room 1815-F, N.Y.C. 10003 (212) 460-3528; Fax: (212) 677-5850

Members:
Colleen Coleman-Russo
395 Flatbush Ave., Ext., Room 700, Brooklyn 11201
(718) 330-8133; Fax: (718) 875-3486
Thomas Howard
Port Authority of N.Y. & N.J., 225 Park Ave. S., 12th Floor, N.Y.C. 10003 (212) 435-5851; Fax: (212) 435-5861
Mark Johnson
Eastman Kodak Co., Corporate Medical, B/28/KP, Rochester 14652-3403 (585) 588-3868; Fax: (585) 722-9856
James O'Bryan
International Paper Company, 568 Shore Airport Rd., Ticonderoga 12883 (518) 585-5354; Fax: (518) 585-5413
Steve Perroots
Marriot International Dept. 924-37, Inc., 1 Marriot Dr., Washington, DC 20058
(301) 820-6341; Fax: (301) 820-6394
Linda Roehner
National Fuel, 6363 Main St., Williamsville 14221
(716) 857-7727; Fax: (716) 857-7195
Greg Saxum
Hamburger & Weiss, One S. Washington St., Suite 500, Rochester 14614
(585) 262-6390; Fax: (585) 262-6399
Mark Stasko
Onondaga County, John H. Mulroy Civic Center, 14th Floor, 421 Montgomery St., Syracuse 13202
(315) 435-3716; Fax: (315) 435-2869

Advises the Chair of the Workers' Compensation Board on all aspects of the regulation of self insurance for workers' compensation by employers. *N.Y. Work. Comp. Law § 50 (McKinney 1994 Supp.)*

Unemployment Insurance Appeal Board
Troy Atrium, Suite 2006, 49 4th St., Troy 12180
Mailing Address: P.O. Box 15126, Albany 12212-5126
(518) 402-0205; Fax: (518) 402-6208

Chair: Leonard D. Polletta

Exec. Secretary: Susan P. Borenstein

Members:
Tanya R. Daniel
Geraldine A. Reilly

Investigates, hears and decides appeals from administrative decisions on the granting of Unemployment Insurance benefits. *N.Y. Lab. Law § 534 (Consol. 1983)*

***At press time, some of the positions listed above were subject to appointment by the incoming Governor.**

Dept. of Labor—Cont'd

Unemployment Insurance Appeal Board (Higher Authority—Troy)
Troy Atrium, Suite 2006, 49 Fourth St., Troy 12180
Mailing Address: P.O. Box 15126, Albany 12212-5126
(518) 402-0205; Fax: (518) 402-6208

Principal Admin. Law Judge: Christopher M. Tate

Sr. Admin. Law Judges:
Deborah Esrick
David H. Kim
William M. Mains
Christine P. Martindale
Diane M. Rafter

Admin. Law Judges:
Catherine Adlerman
Deane Cooke
Anthony Cresho
Peter L. Gautie
Eva Lynn Hayko
Jo Allison Henn
Carol Johnson
E. Yvette Kitchen
John F. Muller
David Novak
William Osta
Mary Beth Philips
Jane E. Scott
Victoria Speciale

Unemployment Insurance Appeal Board (Lower Authority—Albany District)
Troy Atrium, Suite 2005, 49 Fourth St., Troy 12180
Mailing Address: P.O. Box 15125, Albany 12212-5125
(518) 402-0210; Fax: (518) 402-0196
Sr. Admin. Law Judges:
Tracy Myers
Matthew J. Tierney
Admin. Law Judges:
Mary Beth Danner-Conboy
Charles H. Essepian
Holly Matteson
Joyce McAlister
Brian Mohin
Scott Nortz

Syracuse Office
450 S. Salina St., 3rd Floor, Syracuse 13202
(315) 479-3380; Fax: (315) 479-3418
Sr. Admin. Law Judge: Marjorie Z. Olds
Admin. Law Judges:
Michael F. Affleck
Herbert Fowler
Steven Kittleman

Unemployment Insurance Appeal Board (Lower Authority—Buffalo District)
290 Main St., 2nd Floor, Buffalo 14202
(716) 851-2711; Fax: (716) 851-2795
Sr. Admin. Law Judge: Suzanne T. Hagen
Admin. Law Judges:
Catherine M. Agnello
Thomas Feron
Susan Meyer
James S. Parker
Mark R. Sokolowski

Rochester Office
109 S. Union St., Rochester 14607
(585) 258-4538; Fax: (585) 258-4539
Sr. Admin. Law Judge: Marcella Seaburg-Brackett
Admin. Law Judges:
Anette Gaul
Scott Herron
Allan D. Hymes

Unemployment Insurance Appeal Board (Higher Authority—N.Y.C.)
9 Bond St., 4th Floor, Brooklyn 11201
Mailing Address: Admin. Law Judge Section, P.O. Box 29002, Brooklyn 11202-9002
(718) 613-3495; Fax: (718) 613-3507

Chair: Leonard D. Polletta

Members:
Michael T. Greason
Eileen Long-Chelales

Chief Admin. Law Judge: Jayson S. Myers

Principal Admin. Law Judges:
Andrea Addison
Teresa DeMeo

Unemployment Insurance Appeal Board (Lower Authority—N.Y.C. District)
9 Bond St., 4th Floor, Brooklyn 11201
Mailing Address: Admin. Law Judge, Section, P.O. Box 29002, Brooklyn 11202-9002
(718) 613-3500; Fax: (718) 613-3566
Sr. Admin. Law Judges:
Alterio A. Coletti
Beverly Diego
Margaret B. O'Brien
Laurance I. Paver
Paula S. Yorke
Admin. Law Judges:
Nicholas Alimaras
William J. Badillo
Nicole Beason
Joyce Cutler
Diane Dubiac
Stephen J. Giunta
Yolanda Green
Susanna Iafrate
Manuel Marks
Lynn Morrell
Viren Ramanand Pergadia
Wendy Pichardo
Benjamin Reyes
Rachelle Rosenberg
Rebecca S. Schwartz
Henry Sullivan
Dennis Torreggiani
Jacob Weintraub
Joseph Wolfermann

Hauppauge Office
NYS Office Bldg., Room 2B46, 2nd Floor, Hauppauge 11788 (631) 952-6505; Fax: (631) 952-3385
Sr. Admin. Law Judge: Carol Procopio
Admin. Law Judges:
Craig M. Fishkin
Scott E. Mann
Tanya White

Hempstead Office
400 Oak St., Suite 101, Garden City 11530
(516) 228-3908; Fax: (516) 794-1061
Sr. Admin. Law Judge: Leonard R. Shapiro
Admin. Law Judges:
Jean Bell-Jones
Roberta Manda-Flannerty
Richard Ward

White Plains Office
120 Bloomingdale Rd., Room 233, White Plains 10605-1501
(914) 997-9550; Fax: (914) 997-0014
Sr. Admin. Law Judge: Howard Meiseles
Admin. Law Judges:
Adjoa Afriyie
Stephen Ambrecht
James Coffey
Elizabeth Nicolato

DEPARTMENT OF LAW

See Office of the Attorney General

STATE BOARD OF LAW EXAMINERS

Corporate Plaza, Bldg. 3, 254 Washington Ave. Ext., Albany 12203
(518) 452-8700; Fax: (518) 452-5729
Internet: www.nybarexam.org

Exec. Dir.: John J. McAlary

Counsel: Cara J. Brousseau

Chair: Diane F. Bosse
750 Main Seneca Bldg., 237 Main St., Buffalo 14202
(716) 856-3200

Board Members:

David M. Gouldin
450 Plaza Dr., P.O. Box F-1706, Binghamton 13902-0106
(607) 763-9200

Robert S. McMillen
One Washington St., P.O. Box 2168, Glens Falls 12801
(518) 792-2117

E. Leo Milonas
Pillsbury Winthrop, L.L.P., 1540 Broadway, N.Y.C. 10036
(212) 858-1615; Fax: (212) 858-1500

Bryan R. Williams
150 Broadway, Suite 1717, N.Y.C. 10038 (212) 566-2424

Examines, certifies and admits candidates to the State Bar; promulgates rules and regulations for the carrying out of the assigned tasks including measures for re-testing, review of exams and security precautions. *N.Y. Jud. Law § 56 (Consol. 1983)*

LAW REPORTING BUREAU

1 Commerce Plz., Suite 1750, 17th Floor, Albany 12210
(518) 474-8211; Fax: (518) 463-6869
Internet: www.nycourts.gov/reporter

State Reporter: William J. Hooks
E-mail: bhooks@courts.state.ny.us
Appointed by Court of Appeals

Reports every cause determined by the Court of Appeals and the Appellate Division of the Supreme Court, unless otherwise ordered by the court, as well as any cause decided by lower courts determined to be worthy of reporting, basing inclusion on the usefulness to the public as precedent or as an item of public interest. *N.Y. Jud. Law § 431 (Consol. 1983)*

***At press time, some of the positions listed above were subject to appointment by the incoming Governor.**

LEGISLATIVE BILL DRAFTING COMMISSION
(Legislative Branch)
N.Y. State Capitol, Room 308, Albany 12224
(518) 455-7500

Commissioners:
Randall Bluth (518) 455-7506
James E. Long (518) 455-7501

Drafts, aids drafting and examines legislative bills, resolutions and amendments upon request from either house of the Legislature, a legislative committee, an individual member of the Legislature, or a state department, board, commission or officer. Advises as to the constitutionality, consistency and possible effects of proposed legislation and makes any research in its possession available on the subject of legislation. *N.Y. Legis. Law § 24 (Consol. 1979)*

LEGISLATIVE LIBRARY
(Legislative Branch)
N.Y. State Capitol, Room 337, Albany 12224-0345
(518) 455-2468, 455-4000; Fax: (518) 426-6901

Legislative Librarian: James Giliberto
Law Librarian: Kate Balassie

Serves the research and information needs of Senate and Assembly members and staff.

THE NEW YORK STATE LIBRARY
See Education Department supra

OFFICE OF MENTAL HEALTH
44 Holland Ave., Albany 12229
(518) 474-2568; Fax: (518) 474-2149
Internet: www.omh.state.ny.us

Commissioner: Michael F. Hogan, Ph.D.
(518) 474-4403; Fax: (518) 474-2149
Exec. Deputy Commissioner: Bruce E. Feig
(518) 474-7056; Fax: (518) 402-2361
Dir., Office of Diversity Mgmt.: Emy Lopez Murphy
(518) 473-4144; Fax: (518) 486-7988
Medical Dir.: Lloyd I. Sederer, M.D.
(518) 486-4302; Fax: (518) 474-8469
Deputy Commissioner & Chief Counsel: John Tauriello
(518) 474-1331; Fax: (518) 474-7863
Dir., Office of Consumer Affairs: John Allen
(Special Asst. to the Commissioner)
(518) 473-6579; Fax: (518) 474-8998
Dir., Intergovernmental Relations: Leesa Radamacher
(518) 474-4403; Fax: (518) 474-2149
Dir., Office of Planning: Marcia Fazio
(518) 474-8323; Fax: (518) 473-4690
Dir., Public Affairs: Jill Daniels
(518) 474-6540; Fax: (518) 473-3456
Deputy Commissioner & Dir., Office of Financial Mgmt.:
Martha Schaefer-Hayes (518) 474-3631; Fax: (518) 473-4690
Sr. Deputy Commissioner, Div. of Adult Services:
Robert Myers, Ph.D. (518) 486-4327; Fax: (518) 473-4690
Sr. Assoc. Commissioner & Deputy Dir., Div. of Adult Services: Alan Holmes
(518) 474-4447; Fax: (518) 473-7926
Deputy Commissioner & Dir., Div. of Children & Family Services: Kristin Riley
(518) 473-6328; Fax: (518) 473-4690
Assoc. Commissioner, Div. of Forensic Services:
Richard Miraglia (518) 474-8207; Fax: (518) 473-4098
Dir., Office of Quality Mgmt.: Jayne VanBramer
(518) 474-6587; Fax: (518) 474-8998
Deputy Commissioner, Center for Information Technology: Hao Wang, Ph.D.
(518) 474-7359; Fax: (518) 473-2778
Deputy Commissioner, Office of Performance Measurement and Evaluation: Susan M. Essock
(Acting) (212) 543-6950; Fax: (212) 543-5085
Dir., Bureau of Evidence-Based Services and Implementation Science: Molly Finnerty
(212) 543-6180; Fax: (212) 543-6220
Dir., Center for Human Resources Mgmt.:
Deborah Wagoner (518) 474-0171; Fax: (518) 474-7536

Develops and implements comprehensive plans, programs and services in the areas of research, prevention, care, treatment, education and training for people diagnosed with mental illnesses

Psychiatric Centers for Mentally Ill under Jurisdiction of Office of Mental Health

Greater Binghamton Health Center
425 Robinson St., Binghamton 13901
(607) 724-1391; Fax: (607) 773-4387
Exec. Dir.: Margaret Dugan

Bronx Psychiatric Center
1500 Waters Pl., Bronx 10461
(718) 862-3300; Fax: (718) 862-4875
Exec. Dir.: Pamela Turner

Buffalo Psychiatric Center
400 Forest Ave., Buffalo 14213
(716) 885-2261; Fax: (716) 885-4852
Exec. Dir.: Thomas Dodson

Capital District Psychiatric Center
75 New Scotland Ave., Albany 12208
(518) 447-9611; Fax: (518) 434-0041
Exec. Dir.: Lew Campbell

Central New York Psychiatric Center
Old River Rd., Marcy 13403
Mailing Address: P.O. Box 300, Marcy 13404-0300
(315) 765-3600; Fax: (315) 765-3629
Exec. Dir.: Donald Sawyer

Creedmoor Psychiatric Center
79-25 Winchester Blvd., Queens Village 11427
(718) 464-7500; Fax: (718) 264-3636
Exec. Dir.: Kathleen Iverson

Elmira Psychiatric Center
100 Washington St., Elmira 14902-1527
(607) 737-4711; Fax: (607) 737-9080
Exec. Dir.: Mark Stephany

Hudson River Psychiatric Center
10 Ross Circle, Poughkeepsie 12601
(845) 452-8000; Fax: (845) 452-8040
Exec. Dir.: Carol Stevens

Richard H. Hutchings Psychiatric Center
620 Madison St., Syracuse 13210
(315) 426-3600; Fax: (315) 426-3603
Exec. Dir.: Colleen Sawyer

Provides inpatient and outpatient mental health services for 5-county area which includes: Cayuga, Cortland, Madison, Onondaga and Oswego.

Kingsboro Psychiatric Center
681 Clarkson Ave., Brooklyn 11203
(718) 221-7700; Fax: (718) 221-7206
Exec. Dir.: James McCummings

Kirby Forensic Psychiatric Center
600 E. 125th St., Wards Island 10035-6098
(646) 672-5800; Fax: (646) 672-6893
Exec. Dir.: Stephen Rabinowitz

Manhattan Psychiatric Center
Ward Island, 600 E. 125th St., N.Y.C. 10035
(646) 672-6000; Fax: (646) 672-6446
Exec. Dir.: Stephen Rabinowitz

Mid-Hudson Psychiatric Center
2834 Rt. 17M, New Hampton 10958-0158
(845) 374-8700; Fax: (845) 374-8861
Exec. Dir.: Peggi Healy

Mohawk Valley Psychiatric Center
1400 Noyes St. at York, Utica 13502-3852
(315) 738-3800; Fax: (315) 738-4412
Exec. Dir.: Colleen Sawyer

Pilgrim Psychiatric Center
998 Crooked Hill Rd., W. Brentwood 11717-1087
(631) 761-3500; Fax: (631) 761-2600
Exec. Dir.: Dean Weinstock

***At press time, some of the positions listed above were subject to appointment by the incoming Governor.**

Psychiatric Centers for Mentally Ill under Jurisdiction of Office of Mental Health—Cont'd

Rochester Psychiatric Center
1111 Elmwood Ave., Rochester 14620
(585) 241-1200; Fax: (585) 241-1424

Exec. Dir.: Michael P. Zuber, Ph.D.

Rockland Psychiatric Center
140 Old Orangeburg Rd., Orangeburg 10962-1196
(845) 359-1000; Fax: (845) 359-1744

Exec. Dir.: James Bopp

St. Lawrence Psychiatric Center
Station A, 1 Chimney Point Dr., Ogdensburg 13669-2291
(315) 541-2001; Fax: (315) 541-2041

Exec. Dir.: Sam Bastien

South Beach Psychiatric Center
777 Seaview Ave., Staten Island 10305-3499
(718) 667-2300; Fax: (718) 667-2344

Exec. Dir.: William Henri

Children's Psychiatric Centers

Bronx Children's Psychiatric Center
1000 Waters Pl., Bronx 10461
(718) 239-3600; Fax: (718) 239-3669

Exec. Dir.: Christopher Meyers

Brooklyn Children's Psychiatric Center
1819 Bergen St., Brooklyn 11233
(718) 221-4500; Fax: (718) 221-4581

Exec. Dir.: Diane Aman

Queens Children's Psychiatric Center
74-03 Commonwealth Blvd., Bellerose 11426
(718) 264-4500; Fax: (718) 740-0968

Exec. Dir.: Tom McOlvin

Rockland Children's Psychiatric Center
Convent Rd., Orangeburg 10962-1199
(845) 680-4000; Fax: (845) 680-8905

Exec. Dir.: Anita Daniels

Sagamore Children's Psychiatric Center
197 Half Hollow Rd., Dix Hills 11746
(631) 370-1701; Fax: (631) 370-1714

Exec. Dir.: Dennis Dubey, Ph.D.

Western New York Children's Psychiatric Center
1010 East & West Rd., West Seneca 14224
(716) 677-7000; Fax: (716) 675-6455

Exec. Dir.: Kathe Hayes

Research Institutes

New York Psychiatric Institute
1051 Riverside Dr., N.Y.C. 10032
(212) 543-5000; Fax: (212) 542-6012

Exec. Dir.: Jeffrey A. Lieberman, M.D.

Nathan S. Kline Institute for Psychiatric Research
140 Old Orangeburg Rd., Orangeburg 10962
(845) 398-5500; Fax: (845) 398-5510

Director: Harold S. Koplewicz, M.D.

OFFICE OF MENTAL RETARDATION AND DEVELOPMENTAL DISABILITIES

44 Holland Ave., Albany 12229-0001
(518) 474-6601; TTY: (866) 933-4889;
Fax: (518) 474-1335
Internet: www.omr.state.ny.us

Regional Office, 75 Morton St., N.Y.C. 10014
(212) 229-3231

Commissioner: Diana Jones Ritter (518) 473-1997
Exec. Deputy Commissioner: Max E. Chmura (518) 474-8115
Deputy Commissioner & General Counsel:
Patricia Martinelli (518) 474-7700; Fax: (518) 474-7382
Deputy Commissioners:
Gary Lind (Policy & Enterprise Solutions) (518) 473-9697
Sheila McBain, Ph.D. (Quality Management) (518) 474-3625
John Monteiro (Div. of Talent & Workforce Development) (518) 402-4315
James Moran (Fiscal & Administrative Solutions) (518) 473-2747
Dir. of Intergovernmental and Legislative Affairs:
Ceylane Meyers
(518) 474-8080

The State of New York Office of Mental Retardation and Developmental Disabilities has statutory responsibility for the comprehensive planning and provision of supports and services including care, treatment habilitation and rehabilitation of individuals who have mental retardation and developmental disabilities and for the research, prevention and early detection of mental retardation and developmental disabilities. DDSOs, as regional offices of OMRDD, assure individuals with mental retardation and developmental disabilities, in New York State.

Developmental Disabilities Services Offices (DDSO)

DDSO's, as regional offices of OMRDD, assure the development and implementation of comprehensive plans, programs and services for the treatment, training and care of individuals with mental retardation and developmental disabilities in the state. *N.Y. Mental Hyg. Law § 13.07 (Consol. 1989)*

Bernard Fineson Developmental Disabilities Services Office
80-45 Winchester Blvd., Bldg. 12, Queens Village 11427
(718) 217-4242; Fax: (718) 217-4724

Director: Francis Parisi

Brooklyn Developmental Disabilities Services Office
888 Fountain Ave., Brooklyn 11208
Days: (718) 642-6000; Evenings: (718) 642-6151;
Fax: (718) 642-6282

Director: Donna Limiti

Broome Developmental Disabilities Services Office
249 Glenwood Rd., Binghamton 13905
(607) 770-0211; Fax: (607) 770-8037

Director: Carl Letson

Capital District Developmental Disabilities Services Office
Oswald D. Heck Developmental Center,
500 Balltown Rd., Schenectady 12304
(518) 370-7370; Fax: (518) 370-7401

Director: David Slingerland

Central New York Developmental Disabilities Services Office
101 W. Liberty St., Box 550, Rome 13442
(315) 336-2300; Fax: (315) 339-5456

Director: John Gleason

Finger Lakes Developmental Disabilities Services Office
620 Westfall Rd., Rochester 14620
(800) 797-7650, (585) 461-8500; Fax: (585) 461-8576

Director: James Whitehead

Hudson Valley Developmental Disabilities Services Office
9 Wilbur Rd., P.O. Box 470, Thiells 10984
(845) 947-6100; Fax: (845) 947-6004

Director: Jill Gentile

Long Island Developmental Disabilities Services Office
45 Mall Rd., Suite 1, Commack 11725
(631) 493-1704; Fax: (631) 493-1803

Director: Irene (Jill) McGinn

***At press time, some of the positions listed above were subject to appointment by the incoming Governor.**

Developmental Disabilities Services Offices (DDSO), Office of Mental Retardation and Developmental Disabilities—Cont'd

Metro New York Developmental Disabilities Services Office
75 Morton St., N.Y.C. 10014
(212) 229-3000; Fax: (212) 924-0580
Director: Hugh Tarpley, Ph.D.

Staten Island Developmental Disabilities Services Office
1150 Forest Hill Rd., Staten Island 10314
(718) 983-5200; Fax: (718) 983-9768
Director: Richard Monck

Sunmount Developmental Disabilities Services Office
2445 State Rt. 30, Tupper Lake 12986-2502
(518) 359-3311; Fax: (518) 359-2276
Director: Helene DeSanto

Taconic Developmental Disabilities Services Office
26 Center Circle, Wassaic 12592
(845) 877-6821; Fax: (845) 877-9177
Director: John Mizerak

Valley Ridge Developmental Disabilities Services Office
Center for Intensive Treatment, 276 Chiarino Dr., Norwich 13815
(607) 337-7000; Fax: (607) 337-7199
Director: Charles Kearley

Western New York Developmental Disabilities Services Office
1200 East & West Rd., West Seneca 14224
(716) 674-6300; Fax: (716) 674-7488
Director: Bruce Korotkin

NYS Institute for Basic Research in Developmental Disabilities
1050 Forest Hill Rd., Staten Island 10314
(718) 494-0600; Fax: (718) 698-3803
Director: W. Ted Brown, M.D., Ph.D.

DEPARTMENT OF MOTOR VEHICLES
6 Empire State Plaza, Albany 12228
E-mail: nydmv@dmv.state.ny.us
Internet: www.nysdmv.com

Customer Service Inquiries: DMV Call Center
From area code (212, 347, 646, 718, 917): (212) 645-5550, (718) 966-6155;
From area code (631, 516, 914, 845): (718) 477-4820;
From area code (315, 518, 607, 716): (518) 486-9786;
From Outside of N.Y.S.: (518) 473-5595;
Anywhere in N.Y.S. (TDD): (800) 368-1186

Commissioner: David J. Swarts (518) 473-9324
Exec. Deputy Commissioner: Wayne L. Benjamin (518) 474-0846
Deputy Commissioner, Legal Affairs: Neal Schoen (518) 473-1965
Deputy Commissioner, Operations & Customer Svces.: Jack Hope (518) 402-2379
Asst. Commissioner & County Clerk Liaison: Kent Gray (518) 473-1489
Deputy Commissioner, Safety, Consumer Protection & Clean Air: Terri Egan (518) 402-4860
Assoc. Commissioner, Communications: Jackie McGinnis (518) 473-7000
Deputy Commissioner, Administration: Gregory J. Kline (518) 474-6876
Deputy Commissioner, Integrity: Timothy Lennon (518) 474-0846
Legislative Liaison: Meg Murray (518) 474-7726

Albany Central Office Administrative Staff
Safety Hearings, Sr. Administrative Law Judge: Jeffrey Silver (518) 474-0875
Chair, Administrative Appeals Board: Deb Dugan (518) 474-0645
Dir., Audit Services: Edward Wade (518) 474-0881
Dir., Information Technology: Adam Gigandet (518) 474-0605
Dir., Human Resources Management: Tina Zandri (518) 474-7602
Dir., Labor Relations: Steve France (518) 474-2902
Dir. of Personnel: Phil Ruggirello (518) 474-0835
Dir., Fiscal Management: Paul Gauthier (518) 402-2538
Chief Financial Officer and Dir. of Fiscal Management: Kathleen Gilchrist (518) 474-0990
Dir., Agency Program Support Svces.: Kelly Smith-Lawless (518) 474-8328
Exec. Dir., Governor's Traffic Safety Committee: Jim Allen (518) 473-7753
Dir., Field Investigation: Owen McShane (518) 474-8805
Dir., Driver & Vehicle Safety and Clean Air: Jean Rosenthal (518) 473-3347
Dir., Driver Regulation and Insurance Service Bureau: Jerry Clark (518) 408-2232
Dir., Safety Programs: Kevin O'Brien (518) 474-0855
Dir., Data Services and Certified Document Center: Rich Cirino (518) 473-5113
Dir., Operations: Joseph Crisafulli (518) 473-7254
Dir., Field Office Operations: Cheryl Wasley (518) 486-7400
Dir., Central Office Operations, Training and Customer Support Services: Rosanne Kitchner (518) 473-9657
Dir., Central Office Operations and Customer Support Services: William Mogavero (518) 486-5374
Dir., Legal Affairs: Ida Traschen (518) 486-3131
Dir., Bus Driver Unit: Tom Fullington (518) 486-5853

Department of Motor Vehicles Field Operations District Offices
224-260 S. Pearl St., Albany 12202
(518) 486-9786
Director: Vacancy at Press Time
Office Mgr.: Christopher Lynch

Bethpage District Office
4031 Hempstead Tpke., Bethpage 11714-5607
(718) 477-4820
Director: Vacancy at Press Time
Manager: Karen Treder

Massapequa Office
Carmans Plaza Shopping Center, 927 Carmans Rd., Massapequa 11758 (718) 477-4820
Director: George Erker
Manager: Mercedes Little

Hauppauge Office
State Office Bldg., 250 Veterans Memorial Hwy., Hauppauge 11788 (718) 477-4820
Operations Mgr.: Donna Greifenberger
Office Mgr.: Robert Pratt

Garden City Office
801 Axinn Ave., Garden City 11530 (718) 477-4820
Director: Gary Solomon

Huntington Office
813 New York Ave., Big H Shopping Center, Huntington 11743 (718) 477-4820
Director: George Erker
Manager: Joan Amoroso

Medford Office
2799 Rt. 112, Medford 11763 (718) 477-4820
Director: Vacancy at Press Time
Manager: Debbie Boccaccino

Riverhead Office
200 Old Country Rd., Riverhead 11901 (718) 477-4820
Manager: Joanne Colvin

Jamaica Office
168-46 91st Ave., 2nd Floor, Jamaica 11432
(718) 966-6155
Director: Vacancy at Press Time
Manager: Sabin Dennis

Departments & Agencies

***At press time, some of the positions listed above were subject to appointment by the incoming Governor.**

Dept. of Motor Vehicles Field Operations—Cont'd

Bronx District Office
696 E. Fordham Rd., Bronx 10458
(718) 966-6155

Director: Patricia Hatcher

Manager: Raquel Padilla

Buffalo District Office
295 Main St., Suite 219, Buffalo 14203 (716) 851-8222

Director: Douglas L. Drew

New York District Office
11 Greenwich St., N.Y.C. 10004
(718) 966-6155

Regional Dir., Metropolitan N.Y. Offices: Vacancy at Press Time

Manager: William Rath

N.Y. License Express
300 W. 34th St., N.Y.C. 10001 (718) 966-6155
OPS Manager: Wanda Banister

Harlem Office
159 E. 125th St., 3rd Floor, N.Y.C. 10035 (212) 645-5550
Director: Vacancy at Press Time
Manager: Vivian Mitchell

Peekskill Office
1045 Park St., Peekskill 10566 (718) 477-4820

Director: Yvonne Barba

Manager: Barbara Mahoney

Syracuse District Office
4671 Onondaga Blvd., Syracuse 13219 (518) 486-9786

Director: Kay Staley-Smith

Manager: Stephen Jesberger

N. Syracuse District Office
5801 E. Taft Rd., Syracuse 13212 (518) 486-9786

Manager: James Callea

West Haverstraw District Office
50 Samsondale Plaza, West Haverstraw 10993
(718) 477-4820

Director: Yvonne Barba

Manager: Rene Torres

White Plains District Office
200 Hamilton Ave., White Plains 10601 (718) 477-4820

Director: Yvonne Barba

Manager: Sharaine Herron-Muir

Yonkers District Office
1 Larkin Plaza, Yonkers 10701 (718) 477-4820

Director: Patricia Hatcher

Manager: Andy Ng

Richmond District Office
West Shore Shopping Plaza, 1775 South Ave.,
Staten Island 10314 (718) 966-6155

Director: Victoria M. Celardo

Brooklyn District Office
625 Atlantic Ave., Brooklyn 11217
(718) 966-6155

Director: Victoria Celardo

Manager: Timothy Santamour

Coney Island Office
2875 W. 8th St., Brooklyn 11224 (718) 966-6155
Director: Victoria Celardo
Manager: Heidi Burke

Springfield Gardens District Office
168-25 Rockaway Blvd., Jamaica 11434-5233
(718) 966-6155

Director: Vacancy at Press Time

Manager: Caren Eisert

Bronx Licensing Center
1350 Commerce Ave., Bronx 10461
(718) 966-6155

Manager: Miguel M. Jackson

College Point Office
30-56 Whitestone Expwy., Flushing 11354-1946
(718) 966-6155

Director: Vacancy at Press Time

Manager: Barbara Wright

Traffic Violations Bureaus
(718) 488-5710
Adjudicates charges of traffic infractions in New York City, Buffalo, Rochester and the western portion of Suffolk County.

Bronx
696 E. Fordham Rd., Bronx 10458 (718) 488-5710

Supervisiong Admin. Law Judge: Stephen Barkan (Sr. A.L.J.)

Brooklyn North
Atlantic Center Mall, 2nd Floor, 625 Atlantic Ave.,
Brooklyn 11217 (718) 488-5710

Sr. Admin. Law Judge: Laurie Woods

Brooklyn South
2875 W. 8th St., Brooklyn 11224 (718) 488-5710

Sr. Admin. Law Judge: Alan Gelbstein

Buffalo
295 Main St., Room 360, Buffalo 14203 (716) 851-8257

Sr. Admin. Law Judge: Jeff Silver
Sits in Albany

Manhattan North (Harlem)
159 E. 125th St., 3rd Floor, N.Y.C. 10035 (718) 488-5710

Sr. Admin. Law Judge: Robinanne Turiel

Manhattan South
19 Rector St., 2nd Floor, N.Y.C. 10006-2031 (718) 488-5710

Sr. Admin. Law Judge: John Araujo

Queens North
30-56 Whitestone Expwy., Flushing 11354-1947
(718) 488-5710

Sr. Admin. Law Judge: Bushra Vahdat

Queens South
168-35 Rockaway Blvd., Jamaica 11434-5234
(718) 488-5710

Sr. Admin. Law Judge: Della Cohen

Richmond
West Shore Shopping Plaza, 1775 South Ave.,
Staten Island 10314 (718) 488-5710

Sr. Admin. Law Judge: Joel Traube

Rochester
16 E. Main St., 5th Floor, Rochester 14614 (585) 252-2340

Sr. Admin. Law Judge: Jeff Silver
Sits in Albany

Suffolk
NYS Office Bldg., 2nd Floor,
Veterans Memorial Highway, Hauppauge 11788
(718) 488-5710

Sr. Admin. Law Judge: Larry Waldman

Traffic Violations Plea Unit
P.O. Box 2950-ESP, Albany 12220-0950 (518) 474-0941

ORGANIZED CRIME TASK FORCE
See Office of the Attorney General, supra

***At press time, some of the positions listed above were subject to appointment by the incoming Governor.**

DIVISION OF PAROLE
(Executive Department)
97 Central Ave., Albany 12206
(518) 473-9400; Fax: (518) 473-9760
Internet: http://parole.state.ny.us

Region 1, 119 W. 31st St., N.Y.C. 10001
(212) 736-9880, 736-9926; Fax: (212) 736-9846

Region 2, 333 Schermerhorn St., Brooklyn 11217
(718) 254-2007

Region 3, 3 Cottage Pl., New Rochelle 10810
(914) 354-8690

Region 4, 10 N. Russell Rd., Albany 12206
(518) 459-7469

Region 5, 350 South Ave., Rochester 14620
(585) 232-6927

Chairman/C.E.O.: Andrea D. Evans
(518) 473-9548; Fax: (518) 473-6037
Exec. Dir.: Mark Manthei
(518) 473-9672; Fax: (518) 473-6037
Counsel: Terrence X. Tracy
(518) 473-5671; Fax: (518) 473-9760
Dir., Parole Operations: Angela Jimenez
(212) 239-5730; Fax: (212) 239-5725
Dir., Parole Administration: Jeffrey W. Nesich
(518) 473-3901; Fax: (518) 486-5858
Dir., Executive Clemency: Frank Herman
(518) 485-8953; Fax: (518) 485-8950
Dir., Public Relations and Media Affairs: Marc Violette
(518) 486-4631; Fax: (518) 473-6037

Board of Parole
(518) 473-5424; Fax: (518) 473-6037

Chair: Andrea D. Evans

Members:

Joseph Crangle	Christina Hernandez
Lisa Beth Elovich	Henry Lemons, Jr.
James Ferguson	Kevin G. Ludlow
Patrick Gallivan	Mary Ross
Gerald J. Greenan III	W. William Smith, Jr.
Michael A. Hagler	Sally Thompson

5 Vacancies at Press Time

Secretary to the Board: Lester G. Edwards

Admin. Asst.: Lorraine Morse

Determines which prisoners and under what conditions inmates are released on parole from correctional facilities based on investigations, hearings, and the promulgated guidelines and regulations. *N.Y. Exec. Law § 259b (Consol. 1983)*

NEW YORK STATE POLICE
1220 Washington Ave., Bldg. 22, Albany 12226-2252
(518) 457-6811

Superintendent: John P. Melville (Acting)
First Deputy Superintendent: Vacancy at Press Time
Deputy Superintendent, Technology & Communications: Steven F. Cumoletti
Deputy Superintendent, Field: Thomas L. Fazio
Deputy Superintendent, Internal Affairs:
Anthony G. Ellis II
Counsel: Darren S. O'Connor
(518) 457-6137
S.P. Administrative Dir.: William J. Callahan

Detects and prevents crime and apprehends criminals throughout the state. *N.Y. Exec. Law § 210, et seq. (Consol. 1983)*

Troop "A" Headquarters
Batavia Station
4525 W. Saile Dr., Batavia 14020-1095
(585) 344-6200; Fax: (585) 344-2635

Serves Allegany, Cattaraugus, Chatauqua, Erie, Genesee, Niagara, Orleans and Wyoming Counties

Troop A—Zone 1
Albion Station
14122 Rt. 31, Albion 14411 (585) 589-4244

Grand Island Station
2255 Baseline Rd., Grand Island 14072 (716) 773-9651

Le Roy Station
Village Hall, 48 Main St., Le Roy 14482 (585) 768-8070

Lockport Station
6566 Dysinger Rd., Lockport 14094 (716) 434-5588

Niagara Station
3609 Witmer Rd., Niagara Falls 14305 (716) 297-8831

Troop A—Zone 2
Alden Station
12800 W. Main St., Alden 14004 (716) 937-3391

Boston Station
8550 Boston State Rd., Boston 14025 (716) 941-9300

Clarence Station
9825 Main St., Clarence 14031 (716) 759-6831

Elma Station
Town Hall, 1600 Bowen Rd., Elma 14059 (716) 805-1096

Holland Station
Town Hall, 47 Pearl St., Holland 14080 (716) 537-2112

Newstead Station
Town Hall, 5 Clarence Center Rd., Newstead 14001
(716) 542-2245

Warsaw Station
Rt. 19, 5297 Buffalo Rd., Warsaw 14569 (716) 786-5152

Troop A—Zone 3
Collins Station
13670 Rt. 62, P.O. Box 430, Collins 14034 (716) 532-6820

Fredonia Station
10274 Rt. 60, Fredonia 14063 (716) 679-1521

Jamestown Station
3081 N. Main St. Ext., Jamestown 14701 (716) 665-3113

Sherman Station
121 Osbourne St., Sherman 14781 (716) 761-6712

Troop A—Zone 4
Alfred-Almond Station
Hwy. Bldg., 7 Marvin Lane, Almond 14804 (607) 276-6777

Amity Station
5591 State Rt. 19, Amity 14813 (585) 268-9030

Ellicottville Station
1 W. Washington St., Ellicottville 14731 (716) 699-8783

Fillmore Station
20 N. Genesee St., Fillmore 14735 (585) 567-2283

Machias Station
9761 Rt. 16, Machias 14101 (716) 353-8800
Formerly known as Delevan and Franklinville Stations.

Olean Station
722 Homer St., Olean 14760 (716) 373-3968

Troop "B" Headquarters
Ray Brook Station
1097 NYS., Rt. 86, Box 100, Ray Brook 12977-0100
(518) 897-2000

Serves Clinton, Essex, Franklin, Hamilton and St. Lawrence Counties

Troop B—Zone 1
Chazy Station
9774 State Rte. 9, P.O. Box 574, Chazy 12921 (518) 563-3761

Dannemora Station
161 Emmons St., P.O. Box 612, Dannemora 12929
(518) 563-3761

Ellenburg Station
5534 State Rt. 11, P.O. Box 102, Ellenburg 12933
(518) 563-3761

Keeseville Station
1790 State Rt. 22, Keeseville 12944 (518) 834-9040

Malone Station
3909 State Rt. 11, Malone 12953 (518) 483-5000

Plattsburgh Station
4448 State Route 22, Plattsburgh 12901 (518) 563-3761

Valcour Station
P.O. Box 121, Peru 12972 (518) 563-3761

***At press time, some of the positions listed above were subject to appointment by the incoming Governor.**

New York State Police—Cont'd

Troop B—Zone 2
Canton Station
Public Safety Bldg., 49 1/2 Court St., Canton 13617
(315) 379-0012; Fax: (315) 379-0069

Gouverneur Station
45 Murdock St., Gouverneur 13642
(315) 379-0012; Fax: (315) 287-1049

Massena Station
29 Stearns St., Massena 13662
(315) 379-0012; Fax: (315) 769-8360

Norfolk Station
c/o Massena Station, 29 Stearns St., Massena 13662
(315) 379-0012

Ogdensburg Station
410 Cedar St., P.O. Box 236, Ogdensburg 13669
(315) 379-0012

Star Lake Station
5 River Rd., Rt. 3, P.O. Box 152, Star Lake 13690
(315) 379-0012

Winthrop Station
706 S.R. 11C, P.O. Box 102, Winthrop 13697 (315) 379-0012

Troop B—Zone 3
Blue Ridge/High Peaks Station
991 I-87 Northbound, North Hudson 12855 (518) 962-8235

Crown Point Station
43 Potter Mill Rd., Crown Point 12928 (518) 962-8235

Indian Lake Station
Rt. 28, P.O. Box 233, Indian Lake 12842 (518) 897-2000

Ray Brook Station
Rt. 86, Box 100, Ray Brook 12977-0100 (518) 897-2000

Schroon Lake Station
Rt. 9, Box 565, Schroon Lake 12870 (518) 962-8235

Tupper Lake Station
Rt. 30, Box 1266, Tupper Lake 12986 (518) 897-2000

Wilmington Station
Rt. 86, Box 147, Wilmington 12997 (518) 897-2000

Troop "C" Headquarters
Sidney Station
Rt. 7, Box 300, Sidney 13838-0300
(607) 561-7400

Serves Broome, Chenango, Cortland, Delaware, Otsego, Tioga and Tompkins Counties

Troop C—Zone 1
Greene Station
Village Hall, 49 Genesee St., Greene 13778 (607) 656-4275

Margaretville Station
R.D. 2, 450 County Rte. 3, P.O. Box 422,
Margaretville 12455 (845) 586-2681

Norwich Station
5354 State Hwy. 12, Norwich 13815 (607) 334-3296

Oneonta Station
199 Oneida St., Oneonta 13820 (607) 432-3211

Richfield Springs Station
3574 U.S. Hwy. 20, P.O. Box 629,
Richfield Springs 13439 (315) 858-1122

Stamford Station
NYSDEC Region 4, Apt. S-2, Rt. 10, Stamford 12167
(607) 652-3731

Troop C—Zone 2
Binghamton Station
84 Crescent Dr., Kirkwood 13795 (607) 775-1241

Deposit Station
5 Leonard Way, Deposit 13754 (607) 467-3215

Endwell Station
3121 E. Main St., Endwell 13760 (607) 754-3854

Gateway Station
84 Crescent Dr., Kirkwood 13795 (607) 775-1241

Whitney Point Station
2612 Liberty St., Whitney Point 13862 (607) 775-1241

Troop C—Zone 3
Berkshire Station
12478 State Rt. 38, Berkshire 13736 (607) 657-8030

Cortland Station
4-6 Locust Ave., Cortland 13045 (607) 456-5604

Homer Station
2 Technology Pl., Homer 13077 (607) 756-5604

Ithaca Station
1850 Dryden Rd., Freeville 13068 (607) 347-4440

Marathon Station
Corporation Hall, 4 E. Main St., Marathon 13803
(607) 849-3586

Newfield Station
130 Test Rd., Newfield 14867 (607) 564-7270

Owego Station
2356 State Rt. 434, Apalachin 13732 (607) 687-3961

Troop "D" Headquarters
Rt. 5, P.O. Box 30, Oneida 13421-0030
(315) 366-6000

Serves Herkimer, Jefferson, Lewis, Madison, Oneida, Onondaga and Oswego Counties

Troop D—Zone 1
Herkimer Station
126 Gros Blvd., Herkimer 13350 (315) 866-7111

Lee/Rome Station
P.O. Box 175, Lee Center 13363 (315) 337-0036

Marcy Station
9017 River Rd., Marcy 13403 (315) 736-0122

Morrisville Station
P.O. Box 1113, Morrisville 13408 (315) 684-9550

New Woodstock Station
P.O. Box 228, New Woodstock 13122 (315) 662-3111

Old Forge Station
Rt. 28, Main St., P.O. Box 21, Old Forge 13420
(315) 369-3322

Poland Station
Municipal Bldg., Case St., Poland 13431 (315) 826-7276

Remsen Station
9400 State Route 12, Remsen 13438 (315) 831-4177

Sullivan Station
7507 Lakeport Rd., Chittenango 13037 (315) 687-6050

Sylvan Beach Station
P.O. Box 548, Sylvan Beach 13157 (315) 762-4441

Waterville Station
P.O. Box 11, Waterville 13480 (315) 841-8872

West Winfield Station
South St., P.O. Box 308, West Winfield 13491
(315) 822-6755

Troop D—Zone 2
Elbridge Station
Rt. 5, P.O. Box 396, Elbridge 13060 (315) 689-6334

Lafayette Station
2789 Route 11, La Fayette 13084 (315) 677-3124

North Syracuse Station
101 N. Constellation Way, North Syracuse 13212
(315) 455-2826

Lysander Station
3071 Belgium Rd., Rt. 31, Baldwinsville 13027
(315) 638-8200

Troop D—Zone 3
Adams Station
R.R. 4, P.O. Box 29-A, Watertown 13601 (315) 232-2022

Alexandria Bay Station
Rt. 12, P.O. Box 433, Alexandria Bay 13607
(315) 482-2525

Carthage Station
120 S. Mechanic St., Carthage 13619 (315) 493-1331

Fulton Station
6 E. 12th St., Fulton 13069 (315) 598-2335

Grasspoint Station
Grasspoint State Park, Clayton 13624 (315) 686-0054

***At press time, some of the positions listed above were subject to appointment by the incoming Governor.**

New York State Police, Troop D—Zone 3—Cont'd

Hastings Station
Municipal Bldg., R.D. 2, Central Square 13036
(315) 668-2496

Lowville Station
Rt. 26, R.R. 1, Lowville 13367 (315) 376-6513

Orleans Station
39764 1-81 Rest Area, Alexandria Bay 13607
(315) 482-2525

Philadelphia Station
64 Main St., Philadelphia 13673-0068 (315) 642-0032

Pulaski Station
3273 C.R. 2, Pulaski 13142 (315) 298-1444

Watertown Station
25873 State Rt. 37, Watertown 13601 (315) 782-2112

Troop "E" Headquarters
Canandaigua Station
1569 Rochester Rd., P.O. Box 25220, Canandaigua 14425-0220
(585) 398-4100

Serves Cayuga, Chemung, Livingston, Monroe, Ontario, Schuyler, Seneca, Steuben, Wayne and Yates Counties

Troop E—Zone 1

Churchville Station
2 Main St., Churchville 14428 (585) 293-2444

Naples Station
Village Hall, 106 Main St., Naples 14512 (585) 374-2320

Penfield Station
1985 Baird Rd., Penfield 14526 (585) 586-2916

Rochester Station
1155 Scottsville Rd., Suite 400, Rochester 14624
(585) 279-8890

Troop E—Zone 2

Auburn Station
1551 Clark St. Rd., Auburn 13021 (315) 255-2766

Lyons Station
16 Rt. 31 W., Lyons 14489 (315) 946-3039

Moravia Station
General Delivery, Main St., Moravia 13118 (315) 497-2722

Romulus Station
Municipal Bldg., Box 252, Willard 14588 (607) 869-5007

Walworth Station
3600 Lorraine Dr., Walworth 14568 (315) 986-1600

Waterloo Station
853 Waterloo-Geneva Rd., Waterloo 13165 (315) 539-3976

Williamson Station
3957 Rt. 104, Williamson 14589 (315) 589-2046

Wolcott Station
12291 Oswego St., Wolcott 14590 (315) 594-2408

Troop E—Zone 3

Bath Station
7237 Rt. 415, Bath 14810 (607) 776-2182

Canisteo Station
Town Hall, 6 S. Main St., Canisteo 14823 (607) 698-4377

Geneseo Station
5831 Groveland Station Rd., Rt. 63, Mount Morris 14510
(585) 243-4876

Lima Station
P.O. Box 543, Lima 14485 (585) 582-2232

Painted Post Station
3859 Meads Creek Rd., Painted Post 14870
(607) 962-2112

Wayland Station
2634 Rte. 21, Wayland 14572 (585) 728-2200

Troop E—Zone 4

Dundee Station
18 Union St., Dundee 14837 (607) 243-5772

Horseheads Station
3250 Watkins Rd., Horseheads 14845 (607) 739-8796

Montour Falls Station
600 College Ave., Montour Falls 14865 (607) 535-7731

Wellsburg Station
P.O. Box 86, Wellsburg 14894 (607) 732-4253

Troop "F" Headquarters
Middletown Station
55 Crystal Run Rd., Middletown 10941-9755
(845) 344-5300

Serves Greene, Orange, Rockland, Sullivan and Ulster Counties

Troop F—Zone 1

Liberty Station
5754 State Route 55, Liberty 12754 (845) 292-6600

Narrowsburg Station
6509 State Route 97, Narrowsburg 12764 (845) 252-3212

Roscoe Station
c/o Liberty Station, 5754 S.R. 55, Liberty 12754
(607) 498-5300

Wurtsboro Station
2954 SR 209, Wurtsboro 12790 (845) 888-2681

Troop F—Zone 2

Deer Park Station
c/o Middletown Station, 55 Crystal Run Rd.,
Middletown 10941 (845) 856-5911

Florida Station
369 Nininger Rd., Monroe 10950 (845) 651-0019

Greenville Station (Orange County)
1537 U.S. Route 6, Port Jervis 12771 (845) 856-6440

Hamptonsburgh Station
18 Bull Rd., Campbell Hall 10916 (845) 427-7058

Haverstraw Station
8 Thiells Mount Ivy Rd., Pomona 10970 (845) 364-0200

Monroe Station
369 Nininger Rd., Monroe 10950 (845) 782-8311

Newburgh Station
226 Bruenig Rd., New Windsor 12553 (845) 567-1033

Pine Bush Station
Rt. 302, Pine Bush 12566 (845) 744-3891

Troop F—Zone 3

Catskill Station
78 R McLaren Rd. Ext., South Cairo 12482
(518) 622-8600

Coxsackie Station
c/o Catskill State Police, 78R McLaren Rd. Ext.,
South Cairo 12482 (518) 731-2333

Ellenville Station
Rt. 209, P.O. Box 28, Ellenville 12428 (845) 626-2800

Gardiner Station
c/o SP Highland, Box 679, State Rte. 209,
Highland 12528 (845) 255-6166

Greenville Station (Greene County)
P.O. Box 337, Greenville 12083 (518) 966-4441

Hamptonburgh Station
18 Bull Rd., Campbell Hall 10916 (845) 427-7058

Highland Station
State Rte. 209, P.O. Box 679, Highland 12528
(845) 691-2922

Hunter Station
Town of Hunter, Hunter Town Hall, Tannersville 12485
(518) 589-6312

Kingston Station
1791 Route 209, Kingston 12401 (845) 338-1702

Shokan Station
Mountain Rd., Box 26, Shokan 12481 (845) 657-2477

Troop "G" Headquarters
Loudonville Station
504 Loudon Rd., Loudonville 12211-1454
(518) 783-3211

Serves Albany, Fulton, Hamilton, Montgomery, Rensselaer, Saratoga, Schenectady, Schoharie, Warren and Washington Counties

Troop G—Zone 1

Brunswick Station
295 Brickchurch Rd., Troy 12180 (518) 279-3403

Guilderland Station
Willow St., P.O. Box 1309, Guilderland 12084
(518) 456-1118

***At press time, some of the positions listed above were subject to appointment by the incoming Governor.**

New York State Police, Troop G—Zone 1—Cont'd

New Scotland Station
2019 Indian Fields Rd., Feura Bush 12067
(518) 477-9333

Sand Lake Station
Town Hall, Route 66, Box 273, Sand Lake 12153
(518) 674-4440

Schodack Station
1485 S.R. 9, Castleton 12033 (518) 477-9333

Westerlo Station
Town Bldg., C.R. 401, Westerlo 12193 (518) 797-3464

Troop G—Zone 2

Bolton Landing Station
Cross St., P.O. Box 425, Bolton Landing 12814
(518) 644-2555

Charlton Station
4008 Jockey St., Ballston Lake 12019 (518) 399-0947

Chestertown Station
Rt. 9, P.O. Box 402, Chestertown 12817-0402
(518) 494-3201

Clifton Park Station
Public Safety Bldg., 5 Municipal Plaza,
Clifton Park 12065 (518) 371-2287

Granville Station
Rt. 40, P.O. Box 130, North Granville 12854
(518) 642-9776

Greenwich Station
3331 St. 29, Greenwich 12834 (518) 854-7443

Hadley Station
Town Hall, Rts. 1 & 4, Hadley 12835 (518) 696-4117

Northway Station
P.O. Box 706, Clifton Park 12065 (518) 373-8603

Queensbury Station
398 Aviation Rd., Queensbury 12804 (518) 745-7803

Saratoga Station
2455 Rt. 9, Ballston Spa 12020 (518) 899-2224

Schuyerville Station
30 Ferry St., P.O. Box 38, Schuylerville 12871
(518) 695-3626

Wilton Station
Co. Rte. 33, 301 Ballard Rd., Gansevoort 12831
(518) 583-7000

Troop G—Zone 3

Cobleskill Station
950 Mineral Springs Rd., Cobleskill 12043 (518) 234-3131

Fonda Station
3003 State Hwy. 5S, Fultonville 12072-9703
(518) 853-3724

Mayfield Station
Rte. 30, P.O. Box 234, Mayfield 12117 (518) 661-5446

Princetown Station
1370 Duanesburg Rd., Schenectady 12306 (518) 630-1700

Wells Station
c/o Mayfield Station, Route 30, P.O. Box 234,
Mayfield 12117 (518) 661-5446

Troop "K" Headquarters
Poughkeepsie Station
2541 Rte. 44, Salt Point 12578
(845) 677-7300

Serves Columbia, Dutchess, Putnam and Westchester Counties

Troop K—Zone 1

Kinderhook Station
Village Hall, Rt. 9, Kinderhook 12106 (518) 758-7092

Livingston Station
3353 Route 9, Hudson 12534 (518) 851-3111

New Lebanon Station
Rt. 20, P.O. Box 86, New Lebanon 12125 (518) 794-8445

Pine Plains Station
Town Hall, Rte. 199, Pine Plains 12567 (518) 398-0317

Rhinebeck Station
5696 Rte. 9 South, Rhinebeck 12572 (845) 876-4194

Troop K—Zone 2

Brewster Station
1672 Rt. 22, Brewster 10509 (845) 279-6161

Dover Plains Station
Rt. 22, P.O. Box 425, Dover Plains 12522 (845) 877-3669

Lagrangeville Station
120 Stringham Rd., Lagrangeville 12540 (845) 677-7300

Stormville Station
Box 96, Stormville 12582 (845) 223-7898

Wappinger Station
18 Middlebush Rd., Wappingers Falls 12590 (845) 298-0398

Troop K—Zone 3

Cortlandt Station
1 Memorial Dr., Croton On Hudson 10520 (914) 737-7171

Hawthorne Station
200 Bradhurst Ave., Hawthorne 10532 (914) 742-6340

Hudson Valley Traffic Management Center
200 Bradhurst Ave., Hawthorne 10532 (914) 769-2600

Lewisboro Station
81 Spring St., Lewisboro 10590 (914) 763-3900

Mohegan Lake Station
3113 E. Main St., Mohegan Lake 10547 (914) 526-0710

Pound Ridge Station
P.O. Box 45, Pound Ridge 10576 (914) 764-4334

Somers Station
295 Rt. 100, Somers 10589 (914) 277-3651

Troop "L" Headquarters
Farmingdale Station
7140 Republic Airport, East Farmingdale 11735-1597
(631) 756-3300

Serves Nassau and Suffolk Counties

Troop L—Zone 1

Lake Success Station
1022 Marcus Ave., Lake Success 11514 (516) 352-6374

Valley Stream Station
Southern State Pkwy., Valley Stream 11580
(516) 561-8883

Troop L—Zone 2

Brentwood Station
800 Crooked Hill Rd., Brentwood 11717 (631) 231-5962

Fishers Island Station
P.O. Box 271, Fishers Island 06390 (631) 788-7600

Riverside Station
234 Riverleigh Ave., Riverhead 11901 (631) 208-9002

VFW Squad
800 Crooked Hill Rd., Brentwood 11717 (631) 231-5962

Troop "T" Headquarters
Albany Station
P.O. Box 189, Albany 12201-0189 (518) 436-2825

Patrols the NY State Thruway

Troop T—Zone 1

New Rochelle Station
P.O. Box 106, Larchmont 10538 (914) 834-9111

Tarrytown Station
333 S. Broadway, Tarrytown 10591 (914) 524-0223

Troop T—Zone 2

Albany Station
200 Southern Blvd., Albany 12209 (518) 465-7377

Fultonville Station
P.O. Box 121, Fultonville 12072 (518) 853-3261

Kingston Station
50 Rte. 28, Kingston 12401 (845) 331-7017

Troop T—Zone 3

Junius Pond Station
1401 9 Foot Rd., P.O. Box 82, Phelps 14532
(315) 539-9125

Schuyler Station
263 Carder Lane Rd., Frankfort 13340 (315) 894-9000

Syracuse Station
P.O. Box 308, East Syracuse 13057 (315) 437-2831

***At press time, some of the positions listed above were subject to appointment by the incoming Governor.**

New York State Police—Cont'd

Troop T—Zone 4
Buffalo Station
P.O. Box 121, Cheektowaga 14225 (716) 836-0240
Dunkirk Station
3780 Vineyard Dr. Ext., Dunkirk 14048 (716) 366-2862
Henrietta Station
1015 Lehigh Station RD, West Henrietta 14467 (716) 334-5533

Troop T—Zone 5
East Fishkill Station
P.O. Box 41, Stormville 12582 (845) 227-6754
New Hampton Station
P.O. Box 657, New Hampton 10958 (845) 374-6429
Newburgh Station
P.O. Box 7464, Newburgh 12550 (845) 564-6240

Troop NYC Headquarters
New York City
Wards Island, N.Y.C. 10035 (917) 492-7100
Serves New York City

THE PORT AUTHORITY OF NEW YORK AND NEW JERSEY

225 Park Ave. S., 15th Floor, N.Y.C. 10003
(212) 435-7000; Fax: (212) 435-7555
Internet: www.panynj.gov/noc.html

Chairman: David Samson (Pending Confirmation)
Exec. Dir.: Christopher O. Ward
Deputy Exec. Dir.: William E. Baroni, Jr.
General Counsel: Darrell Buchbinder
Deputy General Counsel: James M. Begley (212) 435-3502

Plans, manages, creates, improves and maintains improvements to the ports of New York and New Jersey, including various facilities for the advancement of commerce and transportation in the New York-New Jersey Metropolitan Region such as bridges, tunnels, passenger and freight rail facilities, airports and the World Trade Center site. *N.Y. Unconsol. ch.151 (Consol. 1984)*; *N.J.S.A. 32:1 et seq.*

THE STATE PROBATION COMMISSION

Executive Dept.—Div. of Probation & Correctional Alternatives
80 Wolf Rd., Albany 12205
(518) 485-2395; Fax: (518) 485-5140

Chair & State Dir.: Robert Maccarone (518) 485-7692
Commissioners:
Catherine Abate
Community Healthcare Network, 79 Madison Ave., N.Y.C. 10016 (212) 866-4500, Ext. 2414
Robert Burns (Probation Administrator)
Office of Probation—Community Corrections, 33 N. Fitzhugh St., Suite 2000, Rochester 14614-1233 (585) 753-3765
Wayne P. D'Arcy (Probation Supervisor)
Rensselaer County Probation Dept., Day Reporting Center, 403 Fulton St., Troy 12180 (518) 274-9159
Ann Pfau (Chief Administrative Judge)
Office of Court Administration, Agency Bldg. 4, Empire State Plz., Albany 12223 (518) 473-6087
Rocco A. Pozzi
Westchester County Probation Dept., Judge Duranco Cthse., 3rd Floor, 111 Dr. Martin Luther King Jr. Blvd., White Plains 10601 (914) 995-3502

The Commission members, appointed by the Governor, provide advice and consultation to the State Director on all matters relating to probation in the State, including rules and regulations.

PUBLIC EMPLOYMENT RELATIONS BOARD

80 Wolf Rd., 5th Floor, Albany 12205
(518) 457-2578; Fax: (518) 457-2664
E-mail: perbinfo@perb.state.ny.us
Internet: www.perb.state.ny.us

Chair: Jerome Lefkowitz
Member: Sheila S. Cole
Exec. Dir.: Anthony Zumbolo (518) 457-2676
Deputy Chair and Counsel: William A. Herbert (518) 457-2614
Assoc. Counsel & Dir. of Litigation: David P. Quinn (518) 457-2678
Dir. of Public Employment Practices and Representation: Monte Klein (518) 457-5973
Dir. of Conciliation: Richard A. Curreri (518) 457-2690
Admin. Law Judges: (518) 457-6410
Nancy L. Burritt
Melanie Wlasuk
Kenneth S. Carlson

Administers the *Public Employees' Fair Employment Act*, a state labor relations statute covering public employers and employees and *Article 20* of the *State Employment Relations Act for the Private Sector* for which the NLRB and FMCS do not assert jurisdiction; resolves disputes involving union representation and improperor unfair labor practices; investigates unlawful strike activity; designates managerial/confidential positions; provides mediation, fact-finding and arbitration services.

Brooklyn Office
55 Hanson Pl., Suite 700, Brooklyn 11217
(718) 722-4545; Fax: (718) 722-4550
Regional Dir.: Phillip Maier
Mediators:
Karen R. Kenney
Lori Matles
Admin. Law Judges:
Angela Blassman
Elena Cacavas

Buffalo Office
The Electric Tower, Suite 302, 535 Washington St., Buffalo 14203 (716) 847-3449; Fax: (716) 847-3690
Regional Dir.: Gregory J. Poland
Admin. Law Judges:
Jean Doerr
M. Lynn Fitzgerald

COMMISSION ON PUBLIC INTEGRITY

540 Broadway, Albany 12207
(518) 408-3976; Fax: (518) 408-3975
Internet: www.nyintegrity.org

Exec. Dir.: Barry Ginsberg
Chair: Michael G. Cherkasky

DEPARTMENT OF PUBLIC SERVICE

Public Service Commission
Bldg. 3, Empire State Plaza, Albany 12223-1350
(518) 474-7080; Fax: (518) 474-0421
Internet: www.dps.state.ny.us

90 Church St., N.Y.C. 10007-2919
(212) 417-3168; Fax: (212) 417-2375

295 Main St., Room 814, Buffalo 14203
(716) 847-3400; Fax: (716) 847-3654

Chair: Garry A. Brown (Albany)
(518) 474-2523; Fax: (518) 473-2838
E-mail: garry_brown@dps.state.ny.us
Commissioners:
Patricia L. Acampora (N.Y.C.)
(212) 417-3168; Fax: (212) 417-3169
E-mail: patricia_acampora@dps.state.ny.us
Robert E. Curry, Jr. (N.Y.C.)
(212) 417-3168; Fax: (212) 417-3169
E-mail: robert_curry@dps.state.ny.us
Maureen F. Harris (Albany)
(518) 474-2503; Fax: (518) 473-2838
E-mail: maureen_harris@dps.state.ny.us
James L. Larocca (N.Y.C.)
(212) 417-3168; Fax: (212) 417-3169
E-mail: james_larocca@dps.state.ny.us
Exec. Deputy: Judith Lee
(518) 473-4544; Fax: (518) 473-2838
E-mail: judith_lee@dps.state.ny.us
General Counsel: Peter McGowan
(518) 474-2510; Fax: (518) 486-5710
E-mail: peter_mcgowan@dps.state.ny.us
Secretary to the Commission: Jaclyn A. Brilling
(518) 474-6530; Fax: (518) 486-6081
E-mail: jaclyn_brilling@dps.state.ny.us

Supervises and regulates the provision of public services including gas, electricity, steam, cable, telephone and water.

***At press time, some of the positions listed above were subject to appointment by the incoming Governor.**

COMMISSION ON QUALITY OF CARE AND ADVOCACY FOR PERSONS WITH DISABILITIES

(Executive Department)
401 State St., Schenectady 12305-2397
General Information: (800) 624-4143;
Executive Office: (518) 388-1281; Fax: (518) 388-1275
Internet: www.cqc.state.ny.us

Commissioners:

Bruce Blower — Pat Okoniewski

Chief Operating Officer: Jane Lynch

Counsel: Robert J. Boehlert
(518) 388-1270; Fax: (518) 388-1275

Public Information Officer: Gary W. Masline
(518) 388-1270

Created by the merger of the Commission on Quality of Care for the Mentally Disabled and the State Office of Advocate for Persons with Disabilities; assists the Governor and Legislature in the development of policies to improve the administration of facilities and services for individuals with mental disabilities including the review and inspection of facilities providing care, reviews the costs associated with the administration of mental hygiene facilities and receives and forwards reports of child abuse and maltreatment; also awards and administers state and federal grants promoting the rights of individuals with mental or physical disabilities.

Formerly Commission on Quality of Care for the Mentally Disabled

RACING AND WAGERING BOARD

(Executive Department)
1 Broadway Center, Suite 600, Schenectady 12305
(518) 395-5400; Fax: (518) 347-1250
Internet: www.racing.state.ny.us

86 Chambers St., Suite 201, N.Y.C. 10007
(212) 417-2103

Exec. Dir.: Ronald G. Ochrym

Chair: John D. Sabini

Members:

Charles J. Diamond — Daniel D. Hogan

Secretary: Gail Pronti

Counsel: Robert A. Feuerstein (212) 417-2103

Public Information Officer: Joseph Mahoney

The Board has general jurisdiction over all horse racing and pari-mutuel betting activities, both on-track and off-track, in the state and over the corporations, associations and persons engaged therein; regulates the conduct of bingo and games of chance by authorized non-profit organizations; oversees Indian Gaming pursuant to existing compacts negotiated between the state and the Indian nations. *N.Y. Rac. Pari-Mut. Wag. & Breed. Law § 243 (Consol. 1983)*

DIVISION OF TAX APPEALS/TAX APPEALS TRIBUNAL

Riverfront Professional Tower, 500 Federal St., Troy 12180-2894
Div. of Tax Appeals: (518) 266-3000; Fax: (518) 272-5178;
Tax Appeals Tribunal: (518) 266-3050; Fax: (518) 271-0886
Internet: www.nysdta.org

President/Commissioner: James H. Tully, Jr.
(518) 266-3050

Commissioners: (518) 266-3050

Carroll R. Jenkins — Charles H. Nesbitt

Chief Admin. Law Judge: Andrew F. Marchese

Secretary to the Tribunal: Jean A. McDonnell
(518) 266-3036

Counsel: Donna M. Gardiner (518) 266-3052

Resolves controversies in the application of the tax laws between the Department of Taxation and the taxpayers by processing and reviewing provisions, providing hearings and rendering determinations. *N.Y. Tax Law § 2000 (Consol. 1990)*

DEPARTMENT OF TAXATION AND FINANCE

Bldg. 9, W.A. Harriman Campus, Albany 12227-0125
(518) 457-5181
Internet: www.tax.state.ny.us

Commissioner: Jamie Woodward (Acting)
(518) 457-7358; Fax: (518) 457-8247

Exec. Deputy Commissioner: Vacancy at Press Time

Deputy Commissioner and Counsel: Daniel Smirlock
(518) 457-3746; Fax: (518) 457-8247

Deputy Commissioner of Tax Policy & Analysis:
Robert Plattner (518) 457-4357; Fax: (518) 457-6666

Deputy Commissioner of Tax Enforcement:
William Comiskey (518) 457-9692; Fax: (518) 485-6119

Deputy Commissioner & Treasurer: Aida Brewer
(518) 474-4250; Fax: (518) 402-4118

Deputy Commissioner, Office of Processing and Taxpayer Services: Margaret Sherman
(518) 457-1000; Fax: (518) 485-6119

Chief Financial Officer: Patricia Mitchell
(518) 485-5080; Fax: (518) 457-6666

Chief Information Officer: Brian Digman
(518) 292-7808; Fax: (518) 485-2458

Deputy Inspector General: Marianne Harris
(518) 485-8698; Fax: (518) 457-6703

Dir., Internal Audit and Quality Control: James Brunt
(518) 457-8179; Fax: (518) 457-6514

Dir. of Conciliation & Mediation Services:
Carl Decesare (518) 485-8063; Fax: (518) 485-8070

Dir., Public Information: Brad Maione
(518) 457-4242; Fax: (518) 454-2488

Dir., Information Technology Services: Mike Ventre
(518) 292-7856; Fax: (518) 435-2973

Promulgates and administers rules and regulations for the assessment, determination, readjustment and imposition of state taxes including the corporate tax, tax on transfers of property, tax on transfers of stock, tax on personal income and tax on mortgages. *N.Y. Tax Law § 170 (Consol. 1990)*

For tax appeals, see Division of Tax Appeals / Tax Appeals Tribunal, supra.

Office of Counsel

Bldg. 9, Room 123, W.A. Harriman Campus, Albany 12227-0125

Deputy Counsel:
Deborah Liebman (518) 457-6240; Fax: (518) 485-6607
Mark Volk (518) 457-2070; Fax: (518) 457-8712

Office of Tax Enforcement

Bldg. 9, W.A. Harriman Campus, Albany 12227-0125

Dir., Tax Audit Division: Nonie Manion
(518) 457-8910; Fax: (518) 457-2696

Dir., Collection and Civil Enforcement Division:
Patricia Coneys (518) 591-1980; Fax: (518) 485-8679

Investigations & Criminal Enforcement Division

1740 Broadway, N.Y.C. 10019-4357

Director: Peter Bloch (212) 459-7827; Fax: (212) 459-7950

Dir., Petroleum, Alcohol and Tobacco Bureau:
Thomas Stanton (212) 459-7832; Fax: (212) 459-7950

Dir., Revenue Crimes Bureau: Bruce Kato
(212) 459-8823; Fax: (212) 459-7950

Special Asst.: Emanual Urzi
(212) 459-7831; Fax: (212) 459-7950

Human Resources Management

Director: Kiaran Johnson-Lew
(518) 457-2786; Fax: (518) 457-6653

Dir., Labor Relations Bureau: Todd Wynne
(518) 457-3110; Fax: (518) 457-1070

Dir., Personnel Bureau: Mary Starr
(518) 457-2903; Fax: (518) 457-6653

Dir., Training Bureau: Karen Galarneau
(518) 457-7922; Fax: (518) 457-7806

Office of Tax Policy Analysis

Dir., Taxpayer Guidance Division: William Ryan
(518) 457-1153; Fax: (518) 485-5628

Dir., Legislative Affairs: Maryann Tucker
(518) 457-2398; Fax: (518) 485-0427

Dir., Revenue Reporting: Frans Seastrand
(518) 485-1442; Fax: (518) 485-1365

***At press time, some of the positions listed above were subject to appointment by the incoming Governor.**

Dept. of Taxation and Finance—Cont'd

Capitol Region District Office
Wade Rd., Albany 12227
District Audit Mgr.: Leslie Verde
(518) 389-4702; Fax: (518) 485-5089
Tax Compliance Mgr.: James Breen
(518) 457-0432; Fax: (518) 457-1713

Binghamton District Office
State Office Bldg., 44 Hawley St., Binghamton 13901-4017
Tax Compliance Mgr.: Mary Quinlivan
(607) 721-8492; Fax: (607) 721-8485

Buffalo District Office
State Office Bldg., Suite 112, 77 Broadway, Buffalo 14203-1670
District Audit Mgr.: Roland Sadowski
(716) 855-5330; Fax: (716) 855-5333
Tax Compliance Mgr.: Suzanne McFayden (Acting)
(716) 855-5460; Fax: (716) 855-5462

Manhattan District Office
1740 Broadway, N.Y.C. 10019-4357
District Audit Mgr.: Samuel Cohen
(212) 459-7701; Fax: (212) 459-7921

Metropolitan District Office
55 Hanson Pl., Brooklyn 11217
District Audit Mgr.: Brian Gordon
(718) 722-2427; Fax: (718) 722-2175
Tax Compliance Mgr.: Stan Milstein
(718) 722-2102; Fax: (718) 722-2097

Midwest Regional Office
1011 E. Touhy Ave., Suite 475, Des Plaines, IL 60018
(847) 296-0984; Fax: (847) 296-9109
District Audit Administrator: Robert Cronin

Nassau District Office
400 Oak St., Garden City 11530-6546
District Audit Mgr.: Anthony Vano
(516) 542-5432; Fax: (516) 542-5430
Tax Compliance Mgr.: Richard Buehring
(516) 542-5353; Fax: (516) 542-5430

Queens District Office
8002 Kew Gardens Rd., Kew Gardens 11415
District Audit Mgr.: Robert Santoro
(718) 459-2891; Fax: (718) 459-5992
Tax Compliance Mgr.: Anil Patel
(718) 459-5991; Fax: (718) 459-5397

Rochester District Office
340 E. Main St., Rochester 14604-3686
District Audit Mgr.: Richard Effinger
(585) 530-8414; Fax: (585) 530-2017
Tax Compliance Mgr.: Samuel Mancuso
(585) 530-8470; Fax: (585) 530-2017
District Tax Atty.: Elaine Z. Cole
(585) 530-8465; Fax: (585) 530-2017

Suffolk District Office
State Office Bldg., Room 15,
250 Veterans' Memorial Highway, Hauppauge 11788-5599
District Audit Mgr.: Rosemarie Capozzi
(631) 952-6253; Fax: (631) 952-2071
Tax Compliance Mgr.: Anne Marie Pagano
(631) 952-6235; Fax: (631) 952-6323

Syracuse District Office
State Office Bldg., 333 E. Washington St., Syracuse 13202
District Audit Mgr.: Corrine Buck
(315) 428-4950; Fax: (315) 428-4588
Tax Compliance Mgr.: Margaret Short
(315) 428-4667; Fax: (315) 428-4968

Utica District Office
207 Genesee St., Utica 13501
Tax Compliance Mgr.: Joseph Carey
(315) 793-2506; Fax: (315) 793-2715

Westchester District Office
90 S. Ridge St., Rye Brook 10573
District Audit Mgr.: Michael P. Ryan
(914) 933-2212; Fax: (914) 933-0605
Tax Compliance Mgr.: Stephen Gosik
(914) 933-2302; Fax: (914) 933-0173

OFFICE OF TEMPORARY AND DISABILITY ASSISTANCE

40 North Pearl St., Albany 12243
(518) 474-4152; Fax: (518) 486-6935;
Child Support Enforcement: (888) 208-4485;
HEAP or Food Stamps: (800) 342-3009
Internet: www.otda.state.ny.us
317 Lenox Ave., N.Y.C. 10027
(212) 961-8214

Commissioner: Vacancy at Press Time
General Counsel: Maria Vidal
(518) 474-9502; Fax: (518) 474-9389

Determines the policy, provisions, regulations and basis for the distribution and administration of all public assistance services, care and programs. *N.Y. Soc. Serv. Law § 5 (Consol. 1984)*
Formerly the Department of Social Services

DEPARTMENT OF TRANSPORTATION

50 Wolf Rd., Albany 12232
(518) 457-5100; Fax: (518) 457-5583
Internet: www.nysdot.gov

Commissioner: Stanley Gee (Acting) (518) 457-4422
Chief Counsel: Bruce Feldman (518) 457-2411
Dir. of Audit & Civil Rights Div.: Tina H. Kim
(518) 457-1590
Dir. of Admin. Services Div.: Mike McCarthy
(518) 457-6300
Press Office: Deborah Sturm Rausch (518) 457-6400

Coordinates the overall planning and development of adequate, safe and efficient transportation services and facilities throughout the state at a reasonable cost. *N.Y. Transp. Law § 10 (Consol. 1976)*

Region 1 Office
328 State St., Schenectady 12305
(518) 388-0388; Fax: (518) 388-0347
Regional Dir.: Mary E. Ivey

Region 2 Office
207 Genesee St., Utica 13501
(315) 793-2447; Fax: (315) 793-2182
Regional Dir.: Michael A. Shamma

Region 3 Office
333 E. Washington St., Syracuse 13202
(315) 428-4351; Fax: (315) 428-4834
Regional Dir.: Carl F. Ford, P.E.

Region 4 Office
1530 Jefferson Rd., Rochester 14623
(585) 272-3300
Regional Dir.: Robert Traver

Region 5 Office
100 Seneca St., Buffalo 14203
(716) 847-3238; Fax: (716) 847-3961
Regional Dir.: Alan Taylor

Region 6 Office
107 Broadway, Hornell 14843
(607) 324-8404; Fax: (607) 324-0790
Regional Dir.: Peter E. White

Region 7 Office
317 Washington St., Watertown 13601
(315) 785-2333; Fax: (315) 785-2386
Regional Dir.: Mark Frechette (Acting)

Region 8 Office
Eleanor Roosevelt Bldg., 4 Burnett Blvd., Poughkeepsie 12603
(845) 431-5750; Fax: (845) 431-5703
Regional Dir.: William Gorton (Acting)

Region 9 Office
44 Hawley St., Binghamton 13901
(607) 721-8116; Fax: (607) 721-8119
Regional Dir.: Jack Williams

Region 10 Office
250 Veterans Memorial Hwy., Hauppauge 11788
(631) 952-6632; Fax: (631) 952-6311
Regional Dir.: Subimal Chakraborti

Region 11 Office
47-40 21st St., Room 327, Long Island City 11101
(718) 482-4526; Fax: (718) 482-4525
Regional Dir.: Phillip Eng

***At press time, some of the positions listed above were subject to appointment by the incoming Governor.**

COMMISSION ON UNIFORM STATE LAWS
19 Chenango St., P.O. Box 2039,
Binghamton 13902-2039
(607) 584-4193; Fax: (607) 723-1530

Chair: Richard B. Long; E-mail: rlong@cglawoffices.com
Members:
Norman L. Greene
Schoeman, Updike & Kaufman, L.L.P., 60 E. 42nd St., 39th Floor, N.Y.C. 10165
(212) 661-5030; Fax: (212) 687-2123
E-mail: ngreene@schoeman.com
Sandra S. Stern
Nordquist & Stern, 909 Third Ave., 5th Floor, N.Y.C. 10022 (212) 207-8150
Justin L. Vigdor
Boylan, Brown, Code, Vigdor & Wilson, L.L.P., 2400 Chase Sq., Rochester 14604 (585) 232-5300

Examines, consults and recommends the establishment of uniform legislation throughout the United States by working with similar commissions from other states. Recommends legislation to further its objectives. *N.Y. Exec. Law § 165 (Consol. 1983)*

NEW YORK STATE
URBAN DEVELOPMENT CORPORATION
d/b/a Empire State Development Corporation
633 Third Ave., N.Y.C. 10017
(212) 803-3100
Internet: http://www.empire.state.ny.us
30 S. Pearl St., Albany 12245
(518) 292-5100
420 Main St., Suite 717, Buffalo 14202
(716) 856-8111

Chair/C.E.O.: Dennis M. Mullen
General Counsel: Anita W. Laremont (212) 803-3750
Chief Financial & Administrative Officer:
Frances A. Walton (212) 803-3510

Develops, advocates, and promotes programs and policies that create private-sector jobs and economic growth in New York State; provides business development assistance and services (loans, grants and technical assistance for manufacturing competitiveness improvement, new market devolpment, defense diversification, and skills training); administers business and tourism marketing and advertising programs; and conducts Statewide and regional strategic planning, policy development and economic analysis; delivers its economic development programs and services through ten regional offices located throughout the State and foreign offices in Canada, Europe and Japan, Latin America, Mexico, and South Africa.

WORKERS' COMPENSATION BOARD
20 Park St., Albany 12207
(877) 632-4996; Fax: (518) 473-9166
E-mail: publicinfo@wcb.state.ny.us
Internet: www.wcb.state.ny.us

Chair: Robert Beloten
Vice Chair: Francis Libous (Binghamton) (607) 721-8321
Board Members:
Mona Bargnesi (716) 842-2149
Richard Bell (516) 473-5169
Donna Ferrara (518) 408-0469
Candace K. Finnegan (914) 788-5890
Freida Foster-Tolbert (212) 932-3483
Mark D. Higgins (716) 842-2145
Ellen O. Paprocki (315) 423-1276
Secretary to the Board: Sandra Olson
(518) 402-6070; Fax: (518) 402-6078
Exec. Dir.: Jeffrey Fenster (518) 474-6670
Deputy Exec. Dir. for Regulatory Affairs:
Vacancy at Press Time
(518) 474-6181; Fax: (518) 402-6200
Deputy Exec. Dir. of Administration: Gus Thompson
(518) 474-6671; Fax: (518) 486-6411
General Counsel: Kenneth Munnelly
(518) 486-9564; Fax: (518) 402-0113
Dir. of Public Information: Brian Keegan
(518) 408-0469; Fax: (518) 473-1415
Dir. of Operations: Vacancy at Press Time
(518) 402-0778; Fax: (518) 402-6210
Administrative Review Div.: Madeline Pantzer
(518) 402-0160
Dir. of Human Resources Mgmt.: Gilda Hernandez
(518) 474-2685; Fax: (518) 486-6364
Dir. of Workers Comp. Compliance & Regulatory Services: K. Brian Collins
(518) 474-9598; Fax: (518) 402-6201
Dir. of Finance: Mary Beth Woods
Dir. of Disability Benefits: Vacancy at Press Time
Dir. of Data Processing Services: John A. McDermott
(518) 474-6557; Fax: (518) 474-9367
Advocate for Business: Neil Gilberg (800) 628-3331
Advocate for Injured Workers: Ed Ruff (800) 580-6665

Protects the rights of employees who are injured or ill, and their employers by ensuring the proper delivery of benefits and compliance with the law.

Albany District Office
100 Broadway—Menands, Albany 12241
(866) 750-5157; Fax: (518) 402-6829
Plattsburgh Service Center, 23 Elm St., Plattsburgh 12901
Poughkeepsie Service Center, One Civic Center Plaza, Poughkeepsie 12601
Queensbury Service Center, Northway Plaza, Suite 1323, Queensbury 12804
Saranac Lake Service Ctr., 209 Broadway, Saranac Lake 12983
Hudson Service Gender, 309 Power Ave., Hudson 12534
District Mgr.: Laurie Hart (518) 474-6662

Binghamton District Office
State Office Bldg., 44 Hawley St., Binghamton 13901-4440
(866) 802-3604; Fax: (607) 721-8324
Elmira Service Center, 167 Lake St., Elmira 14901
Monticello Service Ctr., 335 East Broadway, Monticello 12701
Norwich Service Center, Norwich Shopping Plaza, Suite 12, 6142 State Rt. 12, Norwich 13815
Oneonta Service Center, 41-45 Deltz St., Oneonta 13820
District Mgr.: David Gardiner (607) 721-8322

Brooklyn, Manhattan & Queens District Offices
111 Livingston St., Brooklyn 11248
(800) 877-1373; Judges' Fax: (718) 834-2199
New York District Office, 215 W. 125th St., N.Y.C. 10027
(212) 932-2690
Staten Island Service Center, 60 Bay St., Staten Island 10301
(718) 720-5732
Queens Service Center, 168-46 91st Ave., Jamaica 11432
(718) 291-8428
Regional Administrator: Joyce Perry
(718) 802-6644; Fax: (718) 802-6638
District Mgr., Brooklyn District: Tom Agostino (718) 802-6895
District Mgr., Manhattan Dist.: Nance Kaplan (212) 932-8300
District Mgr., Queens Dist.: Brian Pile (718) 291-7428

Buffalo District Office
Cyclorama Building, 369 Franklin St., Buffalo 14202
(716) 842-2148; Fax: (716) 842-2141
Jamestown Service Ctr., 200 East Third St., Jamestown 14701
(716) 484-1592
Lockport Service Center, 81 Walnut St., Lockport 14094
(716) 433-7507
Regional Administrator: Raymond Struzik (716) 842-2170
District Mgr.: Michelle Hirsch (716) 842-2172

Hempstead District Office
175 Fulton Ave., Hempstead 11550
(516) 560-7700; Fax: (516) 560-7799
District Mgr.: Andrea Piecoro (516) 560-7705

Hauppauge District Office
220 Rabro Dr., Suite 100, Hauppauge 11788-4230
(866) 681-5354; Fax: (631) 952-4970
Riverhead Service Center, 211 East Main St., Riverhead 11901
District Mgr.: Robert Williams (631) 952-6358

***At press time, some of the positions listed above were subject to appointment by the incoming Governor.**

Workers' Compensation Board—Cont'd

Peekskill District Office
41 N. Division St., Peekskill 10566
(866) 746-0552; Fax: (914) 788-5793

White Plains Service Ctr., 95 Church St., White Plains 10601

Yonkers Service Center, One Larkin Plaza, Yonkers 10701

Newburgh Service Ctr., 843 Union Ave., Newburgh 12553

District Mgr.: Luis Torres (914) 788-5778

Rochester District Office
130 W. Main St., Rochester 14614
(585) 238-8300; Toll Free: (866) 211-0644;
Fax: (585) 238-8351

Batavia Service Center, 83 Main St., Batavia 14020

Geneva Service Center, 70 Elizabeth Blackwell St., Geneva 14456

Hornell Service Center, State Office Bldg., 107 Broadway, Hornell 14843

District Mgr.: Mary Beth Goodsell

Syracuse District Office
935 James St., Syracuse 13203
(866) 802-3730; Fax: (315) 423-2938

Canton Service Center, 30 Court St., Canton 13617

Oswego Service Center, 73 West 2nd & Seneca Streets, Oswego 13126

Utica Service Center, State Office Bldg., 207 Genesee St., Utica 13501

Watertown Service Center, State Office Bldg., 317 Washington St., Watertown 13601

District Mgr.: Marc J. Johnson (315) 423-1038

***At press time, some of the positions listed above were subject to appointment by the incoming Governor.**

NEW YORK CITY DEPARTMENTS AND AGENCIES

THE EXECUTIVE OFFICE OF THE MAYOR
City Hall, N.Y.C. 10007
(212) 788-3000; Fax: (212) 788-2460
Internet: www.nyc.gov/mayor

Mayor: Michael R. Bloomberg
Deputy Mayor for Legal Affairs & Counsel to the Mayor: Carol A. Robles-Roman (212) 788-3031

Administration for Children's Services
150 William St., 18th Floor, N.Y.C. 10038
(212) 341-0900
Commissioner: John B. Mattingly
General Counsel: Joseph Cardieri (212) 341-0927

The Administration for Children's Services was created in 1996 to make the mission of providing for the safety, care and nurturing of New York City's children the sole objective of one agency.

THE CITY COUNCIL
City Hall, N.Y.C. 10007
(212) 788-7100
Internet: http://council.nyc.gov

Speaker: Christine C. Quinn
(212) 788-7210; District Office: (212) 564-7757
Majority Leader: Joel Rivera
(212) 788-6966; District Office: (718) 542-8100

The City Council is the Legislative Branch of City Government.

City Clerk and Clerk of the Council
Executive Office, 141 Worth St., N.Y.C. 10013
(212) 669-2400; Fax: (212) 669-3300
Internet: www.cityclerk.nyc.gov
City Clerk: Hector L. Diaz

OFFICE OF THE COMPTROLLER
Municipal Bldg., Room 530, 1 Centre St., N.Y.C. 10007
(212) 669-3500; Fax: (212) 669-8878
Internet: www.comptroller.nyc.gov

Comptroller: John C. Liu
First Deputy Comptroller: Eric V. Eve
Deputy Comptroller, Legal Affairs: Ricardo Morales (General Counsel) (212) 669-2048
Deputy Comptroller, Audits: H. Tina Kim (212) 669-8459
Deputy Comptroller, Audits, Accountancy & Contracts: Geneith Turnbull (212) 669-4126
Deputy Comptroller, Public Affairs: Alan Van Capelle (212) 669-3858
Deputy Comptroller, Budget & Accountancy: Simcha Felder (212) 669-2625
Deputy Comptroller, Pensions: Larry Schloss (Chief Investment Officer) (212) 669-8318
Deputy Comptroller, Public Finance: Carol Kostik (212) 669-8334
Press Secretary: Sharon Lee (212) 669-3733

An independently elected official, the Comptroller advises the Mayor, the City Council and the public of the city's financial condition.

PRESIDENT OF THE BOROUGH OF MANHATTAN
Municipal Bldg., 19th Floor,
1 Centre St., N.Y.C. 10007
(212) 669-8300; Fax: (212) 669-3380
Internet: www.mbpo.org
Northern Manhattan Office,
163 W. 125th St., N.Y.C. 10027
(212) 531-1609

Borough President: Scott M. Stringer
E-mail: bp@manhattanbp.org
Deputy Borough President: Rosemonde Pierre-Louis
(212) 669-8299; E-mail: rpierre-louis@manhattanbp.org
General Counsel: Jimmy Yan (212) 669-8157
E-mail: jyan@manhattanbp.org
Press Secretary: Carmen Boon (212) 669-3882
E-mail: cboon@manhattanbp.org

The Borough Presidents work with the Mayor in preparing the annual executive budget submitted to the City Council; review and comment on major land use decisions; propose sites for city facilities; monitor and modify the delivery of city services within their respective boroughs and engage in strategic planning. Each Borough President appoints a member of the Panel for Educational Policy and the City Planning Commission.

PRESIDENT OF THE BOROUGH OF THE BRONX
851 Grand Concourse, Bronx 10451
(718) 590-3500; Fax: (718) 590-3537
Internet: http://bronxboropres.nyc.gov

Borough President: Rubén Díaz, Jr.
Deputy Borough President: Aurelia Greene
President, Bronx Overall Economic Development Corp.: Marlene Cintron
Communications Dir.: John DeSio
General Counsel: Al Rodriguez

The Borough Presidents work with the Mayor in preparing the annual executive budget submitted to the City Council; review and comment on major land use decisions; propose sites for city facilities; monitor and modify the delivery of city services within their respective boroughs and engage in strategic planning. Each Borough President also appoints a member of the Panel for Educational Policy and the City Planning Commission.

PRESIDENT OF THE BOROUGH OF BROOKLYN
209 Joralemon St., Brooklyn 11201
(718) 802-3900; Fax: (718) 802-3959
Internet: www.brooklyn-usa.org

Borough President: Marty Markowitz
Exec. Asst. to the Borough President: Debbie Brill (718) 802-3798
Deputy Borough President: Yvonne J. Graham (718) 802-3842
Chief of Staff: Carlo A. Scissura (718) 802-3757
Counsel: Jason Otano (718) 802-3862
Admin./Human Resources: Melody V. Ruiz (718) 802-4095
Communications: Laura Singara (718) 802-3831
Community Services: Sandra Chapman (718) 802-3884
Facilities/Mgmt. Info. Services: Scott Cotten (718) 802-3759
Public Events/Special Projects & Tourism: Carolyn Greer (718) 802-3803
Topography: Alvin Goodman (Consulting Engineer) (718) 802-3816

The Borough Presidents work with the Mayor in preparing the annual executive budget submitted to the City Council; review and comment on major land use decisions; propose sites for city facilities; monitor and modify the delivery of city services within their respective boroughs and engage in strategic planning. Each Borough President also appoints a member of the Panel for Educational Policy and the City Planning Commission.

PRESIDENT OF THE BOROUGH OF QUEENS
120-55 Queens Blvd., 2nd Floor, Kew Gardens 11424
(718) 286-3000
E-mail: info@queensbp.org
Internet: www.queensbp.org

Borough President: Helen M. Marshall
(718) 286-2870; Fax: (718) 286-2876
E-mail: info@queensbp.org
Deputy Borough President: Barry Grodenchik
(718) 286-2900; Fax: (718) 286-2916
E-mail: bgrodenchik@queensbp.org
Chief of Staff: Alexandra Rosa
(718) 286-2970; Fax: (718) 286-3114
E-mail: arosa@queensbp.org
Consulting Engineer: Vacancy at Press Time
(718) 286-2828; Fax: (718) 286-3116
General Counsel: Hugh Weinberg (718) 286-2881
E-mail: hweinberg@queensbp.org
Press Officer: Daniel Andrews
(718) 286-2640; Fax: (718) 286-2645
E-mail: dandrews@queensbp.org

President of the Borough of Queens—Cont'd

The Borough Presidents work with the Mayor in preparing the annual executive budget submitted to the City Council; review and comment on major land use decisions; propose sites for city facilities; monitor and modify the delivery of city services within their respective boroughs and engage in strategic planning. Each Borough President also appoints a member of the Panel for Educational Policy and the City Planning Commission.

PRESIDENT OF THE BOROUGH OF STATEN ISLAND
Borough Hall, Room 120, 10 Richmond Terr., Staten Island 10301
(718) 816-2200; Fax: (718) 816-2026
Internet: www.statenislandusa.com

Borough President: James P. Molinaro (718) 816-2200

Deputy Borough President: Edward Burke (718) 816-2231

Counsel to the Borough President: John Wm. Zaccone (718) 816-2056

The Borough Presidents work with the Mayor in preparing the annual executive budget submitted to the City Council; review and comment on major land use decisions; propose sites for city facilities and monitor and modify the delivery of city services within their respective boroughs and engage in strategic planning. Each Borough President also appoints a member of the Panel for Educational Policy and the City Planning Commission.

OFFICE OF ADMINISTRATIVE TRIALS AND HEARINGS
40 Rector St., 6th Floor, N.Y.C. 10006
(212) 442-4900; TDD: (212) 442-4939;
Fax: (212) 442-8910, 13
Internet: www.nyc.gov/oath

Chief Admin. Law Judge: Suzanne Beddoe (212) 442-4911

Deputy Chief Admin. Law Judge/Counsel:
Charles D. McFaul (212) 442-4926
E-mail: cmcfaul@oath.nyc.gov

Admin. Law Judges:
Kevin F. Casey (212) 442-8904
E-mail: kcasey@oath.nyc.gov
Raymond E. Kramer (212) 442-4928
E-mail: rkramer@oath.nyc.gov
Faye K. Lewis (212) 442-4933
E-mail: flewis@oath.nyc.gov
Kara J. Miller (212) 442-4934
E-mail: kmiller@oath.nyc.gov
Tynia D. Richard (212) 442-4924
E-mail: trichard@oath.nyc.gov
Julio Rodriguez III (212) 442-2210
E-mail: jrodriguez@oath.nyc.gov
Joan R. Salzman (212) 442-8902
E-mail: jsalzman@oath.nyc.gov
John B. Spooner (212) 442-4922
E-mail: jspooner@oath.nyc.gov
Alessandra F. Zorgniotti (212) 442-4914
E-mail: azorgniotti@oath.nyc.gov

Dir., Center for Mediation Services: Justo A. Sanchez (212) 442-4920; E-mail: jsanchez@oath.nyc.gov

Senior Law Clerk: Martin Rainbow (212) 442-4940
E-mail: mrainbow@oath.nyc.gov

Law Clerks:
Jeremy Freedman (212) 442-1834
E-mail: jfreedman@oath.nyc.gov
Frank Ng (212) 442-4941
E-mail: fng@oath.nyc.gov
Peter Schulman (212) 442-1838
E-mail: pschulman@oath.nyc.gov

Executive Asst.: John M. Stulgaitis (212) 442-4937
E-mail: jstulgaitis@oath.nyc.gov

Created in 1979 by mayoral executive order and established as a charter agency in 1988, OATH is an independent tribunal authorized to conduct adjudicatory hearings for all agencies of the city. The Chief Administrative Law Judge is appointed by the Mayor. Administrative Law Judges are appointed by the Chief Administrative Law Judge to five-year terms.

DEPARTMENT FOR THE AGING
2 Lafayette St., N.Y.C. 10007
(212) 442-1000
Internet: www.nyc.gov/aging

Commissioner: Lilliam Barrios-Paoli (212) 442-1100; Fax: (212) 442-1095

First Deputy Commissioner: Sally Renfro (212) 442-1104; Fax: (212) 442-1095

Deputy Commissioners:
Caryn Resnick (212) 442-1277; Fax: (212) 442-1095
Angeles Pai

The Department plans, coordinates and implements programs for the aging.

DEPARTMENT OF BUILDINGS
280 Broadway, 7th Floor, N.Y.C. 10007
(212) 566-5000; Fax: (212) 566-3784, 566-3859
Internet: www.nyc.gov/buildings

Commissioner: Robert Li Mandri (212) 566-3103

Chief of Staff: Vincent Grippo (212) 566-3506

Deputy Commissioner, Enforcement: Eugene Corcoran (212) 442-7158

Deputy Commissioner, Technical Affairs: Fatma Amer, P.E. (212) 566-3248; Fax: (212) 566-3796

Asst. Commissioner, Administration: Gina Betro (212) 566-3454

Asst. Commissioner, Central Inspections: Laura V. Osorio (212) 566-3394

General Counsel: Mona Sehgal (212) 566-3353

Chief Structural Engineer: Dan Eschenasy (212) 566-3845

Bronx Borough Commissioner: Werner R. deFoe
1932 Arthur Ave., 5th Floor, Bronx 10457
(718) 579-6931

Brooklyn Borough Commissioner: Thomas Farinello, R.A.
Municipal Bldg., 8th Floor, 210 Joralemon St., Brooklyn 11201 (718) 802-3677

Manhattan Borough Commissioner: Derek Lee, R.A.
280 Broadway, 3rd Floor, N.Y.C. 10007 (212) 566-0011

Queens Borough Commissioner: Ira Gluckman, R.A.
120-55 Queens Blvd., Kew Gardens 11424
(718) 286-0601

Staten Island Borough Commissioner:
Marshall Kaminer, P.E.
Borough Hall, 2nd Floor, 10 Richmond Terr., Staten Island 10301 (718) 816-2320

Enforces the Building Code and other laws related to building construction.

DEPARTMENT OF CITYWIDE ADMINISTRATIVE SERVICES
Municipal Bldg., 17th South Floor, 1 Centre St., N.Y.C. 10007
(212) 669-7000
Internet: www.nyc.gov/dcas

Commissioner: Martha K. Hirst (212) 669-7111

General Counsel: Ilene Lees (212) 669-4717; Fax: (212) 669-2139

Dir., Communications: Mark Daly (212) 669-7140; Fax: (212) 313-3111

Deputy Commissioner, Fiscal Mgmt. & Operations: Donald P. Brosen (212) 669-7346; Fax: (212) 313-3050

Deputy Commissioner, Division of Real Estate Services: Lori Fierstein (212) 669-3645; Fax: (212) 313-3450

Deputy Commissioner, Division of Municipal Supply Services: Virginia G. Ross (212) 669-8520; Fax: (212) 669-7723

Deputy Commissioner, Div. of Administration and Security: John Castellaneta (212) 669-3098; Fax: (212) 313-3300

Deputy Commissioner/Chief Engineer, Div. of Facilities Management & Construction: Joseph Wagner, P.E. (212) 669-2670; Fax: (212) 669-2780

Deputy Commissioner, Div. of Citywide Personnel Services: James G. Hein (212) 669-2244; Fax: (212) 669-3101

Dept. of Citywide Administrative Svces.—Cont'd

Deputy Commissioner, Div. of Citywide Equal Employment Opportunity: Diane Crothers (212) 669-4114; Fax: (212) 313-3232

Asst. Commissioner, Agency Chief Contracting Officer (ACCO): Corrine Campbell (212) 669-2777; Fax: (212) 313-3142

Records Access Officer/Senior Counsel: Kenneth Leibowitz (212) 669-7531; Fax: (212) 669-8558

Has all the powers and duties of a municipal civil service commission and administers the provisions of the State Civil Service Law with respect to civil service positions in the city government; establishes and ensures conformity to citywide personnel management standards; fosters equal employment opportunity in New York City government; evaluates Citywide personnel policies and programs; develops and administers examinations for city jobs; and helps agencies manage, train and develop their personnel, with a focus on improving service, reducing cost and increasing revenue. The Department also manages, leases and purchases City real property; operates, manages and repairs courthouses and other City-owned public buildings; administers an energy conservation program; purchases supplies, materials and equipment for use of City agencies; is responsible for Citywide fleet management including operation and maintenance of a motor vehicle pool; publishes and distributes *The City Record, The Green Book,* the *City Charter* and other publications.

DEPARTMENT OF CONSUMER AFFAIRS
42 Broadway, N.Y.C. 10004
Complaints & Licensing: Dial 311 or (212) New York; TTY: (212) 487-2710, 487-3156
Internet: www.nyc.gov/consumers

Commissioner: Jonathan Mintz (212) 487-4401, 02 E-mail: mintzj@dca.nyc.gov

First Deputy Commissioner, Operations: Alba Pico (212) 487-4404; E-mail: picoa@dca.nyc.gov

Deputy Commissioner, External Affairs: Fran Freedman (212) 487-4407; E-mail: freedmanf@dca.nyc.gov

Asst. Commissioner/Chief Information Officer: Christopher Montgomery (212) 487-4478

Deputy Commissioner for Legal Services: Marla Tepper (212) 487-4406 E-mail: tepper@dca.nyc.gov

The Department licenses and regulates designated businesses, mediates consumer complaints, enforces the New York City consumer protection law, and provides education and information on consumer issues.

Legal on 9th Floor; Freedom of Information on 8th Floor

BOARD OF CORRECTION
51 Chambers St., Room 923, N.Y.C. 10007
(212) 788-7840; Fax: (212) 788-7860

Chair: Hildy J. Simmons

Vice Chair: Michael J. Regan

Members:

Catherine M. Abate	Rosemarie Maldonado
Pamela S. Brier, M.P.H.	Alexander Rovt
Robert L. Cohen, M.D.	Milton L. Williams, Jr.
Stanley Kreitman	

Exec. Dir.: Richard T. Wolf (212) 788-7845

Deputy Exec. Dir.: Cathy Potler (212) 788-7849

Dir. of Field Operations: Kennith T. Armstead, Sr. (212) 788-7867

The Board evaluates the performance of the Department of Correction, establishes and ensures compliance with minimum health, mental health and confinement standards, and reviews inmate and employee grievances.

DEPARTMENT OF CORRECTION
75-20 Astoria Blvd., East Elmhurst 11370
(718) 546-0800; Inmate Information: (718) 546-0700
Internet: www.nyc.gov/boldest

Commissioner: Dr. Dora Schriro (718) 546-0890

Senior Deputy Commissioner, Management Services: John Antonelli (718) 546-0995

Deputy Commissioner: Florence Finkle (718) 546-0310

Deputy Commissioner, Public Information & Community Affairs: Sharman Stein (718) 546-0898

Chief of Staff: Archana Jayaram (718) 546-0895

General Counsel/Deputy Commissioner for Legal Matters: Lewis Finkelman (718) 546-0955

Deputy General Counsel: Nadine Pinnock (718) 546-0959

Chief of Department: Larry Davis, Sr. (718) 546-0940

Deputy Chief of Department: Michael Hourihane (718) 546-1900

Supervising Warden: Peter Panagi (Div. I) (718) 546-8331

Supervising Warden: Arthur Olivari (Div. II) (718) 546-8261

Supervising Warden: Jerome Davis (Div. III) (718) 546-8310

Commanding Officer, Criminal Justice Bureau: Michael Fisher (Warden) (212) 487-1097

Asst. Commissioner, Program Admin. & Discharge Planning: Winette Halyard-Saunders (718) 546-0447

Asst. Commissioner, Trials Div.: Robert O'Leary (718) 546-0335, 546-3016

Asst. Commissioner, Health Affairs & Forensic Services: Erik Berliner 360 Mandanici Rd., East Elmhurst 11370 (212) 266-1418

Asst. Commissioner, Financial Mgmt. & Budget Admin.: Sarah Taylor (718) 546-0657

Deputy Commissioner, Discharge Planning: Kathleen Coughlin (718) 546-0455

Asst. Commissioner, Personnel: Alan Vengersky 2 Washington St., 10th Floor, N.Y.C. 10004 (212) 487-6594

Dir., Investigations: Dennis Wall 1755 Hazen St., East Elmhurst 11370 (718) 546-3002

Chief Contracting Officer: Ava Walker 75-20 Astoria Blvd. E., 4th Floor, Elmhurst 11370 (718) 546-0690

Records Access Officer: Rosa Lugo (718) 546-0952

Deputy Warden-in-Command, Employee Assistance Program: Vacancy at Press Time

Supervising Warden, Popultion Mgmt.: Waymon Isaacs (718) 546-1325

Supervising Warden, Special Operations Division: Carmine LaBruzzo (718) 546-5000

Houses of Detention

Brooklyn Detention Complex
275 Atlantic Ave., Brooklyn 11201
Temporarily Closed

Queens Detention Complex
126-02 82nd St., Kew Gardens 11415
Temporarily Closed

Manhattan Detention Complex
125 White St., N.Y.C. 10013 (212) 225-1400
Warden: Rose Agro
Formerly the Bernard B. Kerik Complex

Robert N. Davoren Center
11-11 Hazen St., East Elmhurst 11370 (718) 546-6900
Warden: Emmanuel Bailey
Formerly the N.Y.C. Adolescent Reception & Detention Ctr.

Anna M. Kross Center
18-18 Hazen St., East Elmhurst 11370 (718) 546-3500
Warden: Robert Cripps

Eric M. Taylor Center
10-10 Hazen St., East Elmhurst 11370 (718) 546-5700
Warden: Edmund Duffy

George Motchan Detention Center
15-15 Hazen St., East Elmhurst 11370 (718) 546-4500
Warden: JoAndrea Davis (718) 546-5400

George R. Vierno Center
09-09 Hazen St., East Elmhurst 11370 (718) 546-2000
Warden: Kathleen Mulvey

Dept. of Corrections, Houses of Detention—Cont'd

Otis Bantum Correctional Center
16-00 Hazen St., East Elmhurst 11370 (718) 546-6400

Warden: Joseph Czerniawski

Rose M. Singer Center
19-19 Hazen St., East Elmhurst 11370 (718) 546-7500

Warden: Vanessa Singleton

Rikers Island Security
16-16 Hazen St., East Elmhurst 11370 (718) 546-1560

Deputy Warden-in-Command: Vacancy at Press Time

Transportation Division
17-17 Hazen St., East Elmhurst 11370 (718) 546-1348

Warden: William Clemons (718) 546-1300

West Facility
16-06 Hazen St., East Elmhurst 11370 (718) 546-4100

Warden: Brenda Ross (718) 546-4257

Vernon C. Bain Center
1 Halleck St., Bronx 10474 (718) 579-8300

Warden: Darlene Merritt

North Infirmary Command
1500 Hazen St., East Elmhurst 11370 (718) 546-1100

Warden: Evelyn Mirabal

Hospital Prison Wards

Bellevue Hospital Prison Ward
30th St. & 1st Ave., N.Y.C. 10016 (212) 562-4333

Deputy Warden-in-Command: Luis Rivera
(718) 520-5290

Elmhurst Hospital Prison Ward
79-01 Broadway, East Elmhurst 11373 (718) 334-2110

Deputy Warden-in-Command: Luis Rivera
(718) 520-5290

DEPARTMENT OF CULTURAL AFFAIRS
31 Chambers St., 2nd Floor, N.Y.C. 10007
(212) 513-9300; Fax: (212) 341-3819
Internet: www.nyc.gov/html/dcla

Commissioner: Kate D. Levin (212) 513-9319
Deputy Commissioner: Margaret Morton (212) 513-9321
General Counsel: Tracey Knuckles (212) 513-9327

The Department is responsible for funding and promoting the City not-for- profit cultural organizations.

DEPARTMENT OF DESIGN AND CONSTRUCTION
30-30 Thomson Ave., Long Island City 11101
(718) 391-1000
Internet: www.nyc.gov/buildnyc

Commissioner: David J. Burney, F.A.I.A.
(718) 391-1580; Fax: (718) 391-1893
General Counsel: David J. Varoli
(718) 391-1721; Fax: (718) 391-1894
Deputy General Counsel: Lisa Litera (718) 391-1733
Agency Chief Contracting Officer: Carol DiAgostino
(718) 391-1501
Deputy Commissioner, Administration: Jeff Bonné
(718) 391-1801
Deputy Commissioner, Infrastructure Div.:
Eric Macfarlane, P.E. (718) 391-2251
Deputy Commissioner, Structures Div.:
David Resnick, A.I.A. (718) 391-1214
Asst. Commissioner, Technical Support Div.:
Mark A. Canu (718) 391-1391
Asst. Commissioner, Public Affairs & Records Access Officer: Matthew Monahan
(718) 391-1641; Fax: (718) 391-1892

Responsible for street, sewer, water main and most non-housing building construction funded by the capital budget.

DEPARTMENT OF EDUCATION
52 Chambers St., N.Y.C. 10007
(212) 374-6000
Internet: http://schools.nyc.gov

Chancellor: Joel I. Klein
(212) 374-0200; Fax: (212) 374-5588
E-mail: jklein@schools.nyc.gov
General Counsel: Michael Best
(212) 374-0220; Fax: (212) 374-5584
E-mail: mbest@schools.nyc.gov
Dir. of Communications: Natalie Ravitz
(212) 374-7959; Fax: (212) 374-5588
Press Secretary: David Cantor
(212) 374-5141; Fax: (212) 374-5584
E-mail: dcantor@schools.nyc.gov

The Board of Education was renamed the New York City Department of Education in July 2002.

DEPARTMENT OF ENVIRONMENTAL PROTECTION
59-17 Junction Blvd., Flushing 11373-5108
(718) 595-6579;
Complaints, Services & Permits:
Dial 311 or (212) New York
Internet: www.nyc.gov/dep

Commissioner: Cas Holloway
(718) 595-6565; Fax: (718) 595-3525
General Counsel: Robin M. Levine (718) 595-6586
Dir. of Public Affairs: Michael Saucier
(718) 595-6600; Fax: (718) 595-3477

The Department protects the environmental health, welfare, and natural resources of the City and its residents. It manages the City water supply and waste-water system, carries out Federal Clean Water Act and Clean Air Act regulations, handles hazardous material emergencies and toxic site remediation, oversees asbestos monitoring and removal, enforces the City's noise code, and manages citywide water and energy conservation programs.

DEPARTMENT OF FINANCE

Office of the Commissioner of Finance
1 Centre St., Room 500, N.Y.C. 10007
(212) 669-4855
Internet: www.nyc.gov/finance

Commissioner: David M. Frankel

Deputy Commissioner, Administration and Planning:
Elizabeth Botwin (212) 669-7605

Legal Affairs Division
345 Adams St., Brooklyn 11201
(718) 403-3600; Fax: (718) 403-3650

Deputy Commissioner: Beth Goldman (718) 403-4908

Treasury Division
66 John St., 12th Floor, N.Y.C. 10038 (212) 487-2594

Asst. Commissioner: Elaine A. Kloss

Payment Operations Division
1 Centre St., Room 500, N.Y.C. 10007
(212) 669-4901; Fax: (212) 669-2275

Deputy Commissioner: Andrew Salkin

Property Valuation Division
66 John St., 12th Floor, N.Y.C. 10038
Fax: (212) 361-7100

Asst. Commissioner: Maurice Kellman (212) 361-7120

Asst. Commissioner, Land Records: Annette Hill
(City Register/Surveyor), 13th Floor (212) 361-7130

New York City Sheriff
30-10 Starr Ave., Queens 11101
(718) 610-0491; Fax: (718) 610-0486

Sheriff: Lindsay Eason

First Deputy Sheriff: Oliver Pu-Folkes (718) 610-0489

Chief of Operations/Counsel: Peter Sammarco
(718) 610-7473

The County Offices of Sheriff in the five counties in the City of New York were abolished by a referendum, effective in 1942, but a division is maintained in each county.

Dept. of Finance—Cont'd

Collections
59 Maiden Ln., 28th Floor, N.Y.C. 10038 (212) 232-4222
Asst. Commissioner: Pamela Parker-Cortijo

Bronx Business Center
3030 3rd Ave., Bronx 10455 (718) 993-6003

Brooklyn Business Center
210 Joralemon j?.,m95St., 1st Floor, Brooklyn 11201
(718) 802-4409

Manhattan Business Center
66 John St., 2nd Floor, N.Y.C. 10007 (212) 361-1214

Queens Business Center
144-06 94th Ave., Jamaica 11435 (718) 298-7138

Staten Island Business Center
350 St. Marks Pl., 1st Floor, Staten Island 10301
(718) 815-8400

Audit Division
345 Adams St., 10th Floor, Brooklyn 11201
(718) 403-4539; Fax: (718) 403-4092
Asst. Commissioner: Michael Hyman

Employee Services
66 John St., 9th Floor, N.Y.C. 10038
(212) 361-1800; Fax: (212) 361-1303
Asst. Commissioner: Galia Galansky

FIT
345 Adams St., 12th Floor, Brooklyn 11201
(718) 403-3838; Fax: (718) 403-3744
CIO/Deputy Commissioner: Vacancy at Press Time

Tax Policy Division
253 Broadway, 8th Floor, N.Y.C. 10007
Fax: (212) 788-4114
Asst. Commissioner: Karen Schlain (212) 788-3809

Adjudications
66 John St., 3rd Floor, N.Y.C. 10007 (212) 361-8296
Chief Admin. Law Judge: Mary Gotsopoulis

Communications & Government Affairs
59 Maiden Ln., 22nd Floor, N.Y.C. 10038 (212) 232-1877
Asst. Commissioner: Christopher Browne

FIRE DEPARTMENT
Main Office
9 Metro Tech Ctr., Brooklyn 11201
General Information: (718) 999-2000;
Fax: (718) 999-2582
Internet: www.nyc.gov/fdny

Fire Commissioner: Salvatore J. Cassano
(718) 999-2004
First Deputy Commissioner: Daniel A. Shacknai
(718) 999-2013
Chief of Department: Edward Kilduff (718) 999-2010
Deputy Commissioner, Administration: Douglas White
(718) 999-2007
Deputy Commissioner, Legal/Intergovernmental Affairs: Vacancy at Press Time

DEPARTMENT OF GENERAL SERVICES
See Department of Citywide Administrative Services

DEPARTMENT OF HEALTH AND MENTAL HYGIENE
125 Worth St., N.Y.C. 10013
(212) 788-5261; Fax: (212) 964-0472
Internet: www.nyc.gov/health

Commissioner: Thomas Farley, M.D., M.P.H.
Exec. Deputy Commissioner: Dr. Patsy Yang, C.O.O.
General Counsel: Thomas G. Merrill (212) 788-5025
Secretary to the Department, the Board of Health & Records Access Officer: Rena S. Bryant
(212) 788-5242

The Department of Health and Mental Hygiene's mission is to protect and promote the health and mental health of all New Yorkers, to promote the recovery of those with mental illness and chemical dependencies, and the realization of the full potential of those with mental retardation and developmental disabilities.

DEPARTMENT OF HOMELESS SERVICES
33 Beaver St., 17th Floor, N.Y.C. 10004
(212) 361-8000
Internet: www.nyc.gov/html/dhs

Commissioner: Seth Diamond; Fax: (212) 361-7977
General Counsel: Michele Ovesey (212) 361-7696
Records Access Officer: Aaron Goodman
E-mail: recordsaccess@dsh.nyc.gov

The department works with public and private agencies to provide temporary emergency shelter for homeless people.

DEPARTMENT OF HOUSING PRESERVATION AND DEVELOPMENT
100 Gold St., N.Y.C. 10038
(212) 863-8000; Fax: (212) 863-8071
Internet: www.nyc.gov/hpd

Commissioner: Rafael E. Cestero
(212) 863-6100; Fax: (212) 863-6302
First Deputy Commissioner: Douglas Apple
(212) 863-8566; Fax: (212) 863-8577
Deputy Commissioners:
Kimberly D. Hardy (Community Partnerships)
(212) 863-5128; Fax: (212) 863-8907
Holly Leicht (Development)
(212) 863-6400; Fax: (212) 863-5045
Joseph Rosenberg (Intergovernmental Affairs)
(212) 863-5241; Fax: (212) 863-7450
Bernard Schwarz (Administration) (212) 863-8610
Asst. Commissioner, Communications: Catie Marshall
(212) 863-8076; Fax: (212) 863-8071

The Department promotes quality housing and viable neighborhoods for all New Yorkers by implementing the Mayor's New Housing Marketplace Plan to build and preserve 165,000 units of affordable housing over ten years.

Office of Legal Affairs
(212) 863-8686; Fax: (212) 863-8377
Deputy Commissioner/General Counsel: Matthew Shafit
Provides legal advice and services in the agency's pursuit of housing development and preservation.

COMMISSION ON HUMAN RIGHTS
40 Rector St., 10th Floor, N.Y.C. 10006
(212) 306-5070; Fax: (212) 306-7658
Internet: www.nyc.gov/cchr

Commissioner: Patricia L. Gatling (212) 306-7560
Deputy Commissioner/General Counsel:
Cliff Mulqueen (212) 306-7741
Deputy Commissioner, Public Affairs: Dr. Lee Hudson
(212) 306-7773
Exec. Dir., Law Enforcement Bureau: Carlos Vélez
(212) 306-7764
Dir., Communications: Betsy Herzog (212) 306-7530

Investigates and prosecutes complaints of illegal discrimination and seeks to improve relations among the city's diverse communities. The City Human Rights Law prohibits discrimination based on race, creed, color, age, national origin, alienage or citizenship status, gender (including gender identity), status as a victim of domestic violence, sexual orientation, disability, lawful occupation, arrest or conviction record, marital status, family status, and retaliation. The law prohibits discrimination in employment, housing and public accommodations, as well as bias-related harassment.

DEPARTMENT OF INVESTIGATION
80 Maiden Lane, N.Y.C. 10038
(212) 825-5900; Fax: (212) 825-2823
Internet: www.nyc.gov/html/doi

Commissioner of Investigation: Rose Gill Hearn
(212) 825-5913; Fax: (212) 825-2505
Chief of Staff: Michael Vitiello (212) 825-2870
Deputy Commissioner, Legal Affairs: Marjorie Landa
(212) 825-2404
First Deputy General Counsel: Michael Siller
(212) 825-0646
Deputy Commissioner, Investigations:
Richard Sullivan (212) 825-5619

Dept. of Investigation—Cont'd
Deputy Commissioner for Administration and Operations: Vincent E. Green (212) 825-2468
Asst. Commissioner: Keith Schwam (212) 825-5958
Asst. Commissioner, Background and Auxiliary Investigations Groups: Margaret Tierney (212) 825-2266
Dir., Investigative Audit: Yuval Hibshoosh (212) 825-6819
Press Officer: Diane Struzzi (212) 825-5931
Records Access Officer: Elyse G. Hirschorn (212) 825-5937
City Marshals:
George Airday, 5720 Mosholu Ave. (Rear), Bronx 10471-2234 (718) 601-7320; Fax: (718) 601-7396
Darlene Barone, 42-14 235th St., Douglaston 11363 (718) 224-6732; Fax: (718) 224-6780
Robert Barsch, 3403 Ave. S., 1st Floor, Brooklyn 11234-4825 (718) 382-3571; Fax: (718) 645-9260
Thomas Bia, 181 E. 161st St., Bronx 10451 (718) 681-8878; Fax: (718) 681-8677
Stephen W. Biegel, 109 W. 38th St., Suite 200, N.Y.C. 10018 (212) 627-7425; Fax: (212) 398-2000
Gregg E. Bienstock, 36-35 Bell Blvd., P.O. Box 610600, Bayside 11361 (718) 279-3774; Fax: (718) 423-0014
Martin Bienstock 36-35 Bell Blvd., P.O. Box 610600, Bayside 11361 (718) 279-3660, 279-3774; Fax: (718) 423-0014
Ruth Burko, 38 Westchester Sq., Suite 52, Bronx 10461 (718) 824-5599; Fax: (718) 824-5355
Richard Capuano, 62-59 Woodhaven Blvd., Rego Park 11374 (718) 478-0400; Fax: (718) 478-0020
Maxine Chevlowe, 95-20 63rd Rd., Suite 10, Rego Park 11374 (718) 459-3600; Fax: (718) 459-9563
Henry Daley, 1 Cross Island Plaza, Rosedale 11422 (718) 978-8070; Fax: (718) 978-6719
George Essock, 41-02 Bell Blvd., Suite 1, Bayside 11361 (718) 423-7500; Fax: (718) 423-2244
Alvin Frankenberg, 205-07 Hillside Ave., Room 29, Hollis 11423 (718) 464-3200; Fax: (718) 464-3808
Bruce Frankenberg, 205-07 Hillside Ave., Room 29, Hollis 11423 (718) 464-6500; Fax: (718) 464-3808
Kenneth J. Giachetta, 155 New Dorp Plaza, Staten Island 10306 (718) 351-4515; Fax: (718) 979-7010
Edward F. Guida, 46-15 104th St., Corona 11368 (718) 779-2134, 35; Fax: (718) 779-8123
Roger E. Hammer, 41-02 Bell Blvd., Bayside 11361 (718) 279-4118; Fax: (718) 279-4210
Joseph J. Jacobs, 50 Court St., Room 1006, Brooklyn 11201 (718) 875-6161; Fax: (718) 858-3788
Jerome Janof, 120 Westcheter Sq., Bronx 10461 (718) 904-9200; Fax: (718) 829-1150
Norman Katz, 1800 Kings Hwy., 2nd Floor, Brooklyn 11229 (718) 998-1852; Fax: (718) 336-2738
Bruce Kemp, 39-13 Bell Blvd., P.O. Box 521, Bayside 11361 (718) 224-3434; Fax: (718) 224-3912
Alfred Locascio, 120 Westchester Sq., Bronx 10461 (718) 904-9200; Fax: (718) 829-1150
Charles Marchisotto, 602 20th St., Brooklyn 11218 (718) 853-9815; Fax: (718) 853-9819
John Marchisotto, 602 20th St., Brooklyn 11218 (718) 853-9815; Fax: (718) 853-9819
Richard McCoy, 241-04 Hillside Ave., Bellerose 11426 (718) 347-6844, 52; Fax: (718) 347-6867
Ronald Moses, 116 John St., 15th Floor, N.Y.C. 10038 (212) 349-4303; Fax: (212) 349-4309
Ronald Pazant, One Cross Island Plz., Rosedale 11422 (718) 978-6202; Fax: (718) 978-6183
Diane Pollard, 401 Broadway, Suite 1110, N.Y.C. 10013 (212) 925-2005; Fax: (212) 941-7548
Steven Powell, 774 Manor Rd., Staten Island 10314 (718) 494-7474; Fax: (718) 983-7446
Matthew Regan, 62-59 Woodhaven Blvd., Rego Park 11374 (718) 478-0400; Fax: (718) 478-0020
Ileana Rivera, 6726 11th Ave., Brooklyn 11219 (718) 238-7770; Fax: (718) 238-7773
Gary Rose, 5801 Ave. N., Brooklyn 11234 (718) 645-2100; Fax: (718) 645-5920
Jeffrey Rose, 5801 Ave. N., Brooklyn 11234 (718) 645-2100; Fax: (718) 645-5920
Jacob Sampson, 242-18 Merrick Blvd., Rosedale 11422 (718) 949-4345; Fax: (718) 978-1880
Howard Schain, 370 Atlantic Ave., Brooklyn 11217 (718) 330-0242; Fax: (718) 852-8876
Jerold Shapiro, 1 Cross Island Plz., Rosedale 11422 (718) 978-8070; Fax: (718) 978-6719
Joel Shapiro, 2432 Grand Concourse, Suite 504, Bronx 10458 (718) 295-3333; Fax: (718) 295-8032
Frank Siracusa, 546 Court St., Brooklyn 11231 (718) 855-3434; Fax: (718) 797-4966
Robert Solimine, 9006 5th Ave., Brooklyn 11209 (718) 238-5885; Fax: (718) 238-2965
Linda Swift, 401 Broadway, Suite 1110, N.Y.C. 10013 (212) 925-2005, 08; Fax: (212) 941-7548
Oren Varnai, 144-02 Jewel Ave., Kew Garden Hills 11367 (718) 793-2874; Fax: (718) 793-2875
John Villanueva, 384 E. 149th St., Room 312, Bronx 10455 (718) 402-3100; Fax: (718) 292-9656
Danny Weinheim, 2432 Grand Concourse, Suite 504, Bronx 10458 (718) 295-3333; Fax: (718) 295-8032

The Department of Investigation promotes and maintains integrity and efficiency in government operations. Through its Inspectors General and other investigative staff, the Department investigates and refers for prosecution City employees and contractors engaged in corrupt or fraudulent activities or unethical conduct, and provides the Mayor with recommendations for corrective actions to assist City agencies in the design and implementation of strategies to limit opportunities for criminal misconduct and waste. In addition, the Department oversees the official activities of the independent city marshals.

DEPARTMENT OF JUVENILE JUSTICE

110 William St., 14th Floor, N.Y.C. 10038
(212) 442-8000; TTY/TDD: (212) 442-8578;
Fax: (212) 442-8550
E-mail: nycdjj@djj.nyc.gov
Internet: www.nyc.gov/html/djj

Commissioner: Vacancy at Press Time (212) 442-7630
First Deputy Commissioner: Vacancy at Press Time
Deputy Commissioner, Operations and Detention: Jerome Davis (212) 442-7245
Deputy Commissioner, Administration & Policy: Jacqueline James (212) 442-7840
Deputy Commissioner, Legal Affairs & General Counsel: Herman Dawson (212) 442-7530
Asst. Commissioner, Operations: Josette Nelson-Dabo (212) 442-4956
Asst. Commissioner, Programs Svces.: Nina Aledort (212) 442-7287
Asst. Commissioner, Non-Secure Detention/SEEDS: Stephanie Prussack (212) 442-7164
Asst. Commissioner, Workforce Development: Sandra C. Gordon (212) 442-8462
Asst. Commissioner, Communications and Public: Vacancy at Press Time
Dir., Intergovernmental Affairs: Nicole Halsey (212) 442-4807
Exec. Dir., Crossroads Juvenile Center: Migdalia Aldea 12 Bristol St., Brooklyn 11212 (718) 495-8160; Fax: (718) 495-8254
Exec. Dir., Non-Secure Detention/SEEDS: Marva Chevalier-Barrow (212) 442-7152; Fax: (212) 442-8508
Exec. Dir., Court Services: Kevin Baker (718) 764-2849
Exec. Dir., Horizon Juvenile Center: Eduardo Marcial 560 Brook Ave., Bronx 10456 (718) 292-0065; Fax: (718) 401-8815
Exec. Dir., Bridges Juvenile Center—Intake/Admissions: Donna Locke 1221 Spofford Ave., Bronx 10474 (718) 764-2754; Fax: (718) 589-5406

Responsible for custody of juveniles in detention, aftercare and prevention.

LAW DEPARTMENT
100 Church St., N.Y.C. 10007-2601
(212) 788-0303; Fax: (212) 788-0367
Internet: www.nyc.gov/html/law

Corporation Counsel: Michael A. Cardozo (212) 788-0303
First Asst. Corporation Counsel: Jeffrey D. Friedlander (212) 788-0700
Chief Asst. Corporation Counsel: Leonard Koerner (212) 788-1010
Chief Litigating Asst. Corporation Counsel: Lawrence S. Kahn (212) 788-0600
Managing Atty.: G. Foster Mills (212) 788-0300
Exec. Asst. Corporation Counsel: Paul T. Rephen (212) 788-1200
Exec. Asst. for Public Safety: Celeste Koeleveld (212) 788-0500
E.E.O. Officer: Muriel Goode-Trufant (212) 788-8681
Division Chief, Administrative Law: Gabriel Taussig (212) 788-0813
Division Chief, Administration: Malachy T. Higgins (212) 788-0308
Division Chief, Affirmative Litigation: Gail Rubin (212) 788-0999
Division Chief, Appeals: Leonard Koerner (212) 788-1010
Division Chief, Commercial & Real Estate Litigation: Eric Rundbaken (212) 788-1270
Division Chief, Contracts & Real Estate: Steven Stein Cushman (212) 788-0730
Chief, Disaster Planning & Insurance: Lawrence Martin (212) 788-1009
Division Chief, Economic Development: James W. McSpiritt (212) 788-1333
Division Chief, Environmental Law: Susan Kath (212) 788-1587, 89
Division Chief, Family Court: Angela Albertus
100 Church St., 2nd Floor, N.Y.C. 10007-1207
(212) 442-6803
Division Chief, General Litigation: Thomas Crane (212) 788-0928
Chief Technology Officer, Information Technology: Joseph Merces (212) 788-1116
Inspector General, Dept. of Investigation: Marjorie Landa (General Counsel)
80 Maiden Ln., 19th Floor, N.Y.C. 10038
(212) 825-2403; Fax: (212) 825-2505
Division Chief, Labor & Employment Law: Georgia Pestana (212) 788-0862
Division Chief, Legal Counsel: Stephen Louis (212) 788-1079
Division Chief, Municipal Finance: Albert F. Moncure, Jr. (212) 788-1160
Division Chief, Operations: Kenneth Majerus (212) 788-0373
Division Chief, Pensions: Inga Van Eysden (212) 788-0745
Division Chief, Special Federal Litigation: Muriel Goode-Trufant (212) 788-8681
Division Chief, Tax & Bankruptcy Litigation: Rita D. Dumain (212) 788-0838
Division Chief, Tort: Fay Leoussis (212) 788-0462
Division Chief, Workers Compensation: John Sweeney (718) 222-2101
Chief Information Officer: Jack Hupper (212) 788-0990
Communications Dir.: Kate O'Brien Ahlers (212) 788-0400, 788-0936
Agency Chief Contracting Officer: Samuel Moriber (212) 788-0734
Help Desk: (212) 788-0406

Brooklyn Branch Office, Tort
350 Jay St., 8th Floor, Brooklyn 11201
(718) 222-2000; Fax: (718) 222-2088
Borough Chief: Yolanda Guadagnoli (718) 222-2001

Brooklyn Branch Office, Family Court
350 Jay St., 9th Floor, Brooklyn 11201-2908
(718) 222-2381; Fax: (718) 222-2373
Borough Chief: Patria Frias-Colon (718) 222-2301

Bronx Branch Office, Tort
198 E. 161st St., 3rd Floor, Bronx 10451-3513
(718) 590-3487; Fax: (718) 590-2686
Borough Chief: Betty Lawrence Lewis (718) 590-6017

Bronx Branch Office, Family Court
900 Sheridan Ave., Bronx 10451-3384
(718) 590-3255; Fax: (718) 590-2699
Borough Chief: Melissa Milejov

Manhattan Branch Office, Tort
52 Duane St., 6th Floor, N.Y.C. 10013-4048
(212) 788-0645; fax: (212) 788-8896
Borough Chief: Jenny Montana O'Connor

Manhattan Branch Office, Family Court
60 Lafayette St., (7A9), N.Y.C. 10013-4048
(212) 442-6860; Fax: (212) 442-6865
Borough Chief: Alan Sputz (212) 676-0982

Queens Branch Office, Tort
89-17 Sutphin Blvd., 4th Floor, Jamaica 11435-3710
(718) 206-4731; Fax: (718) 206-4702
Borough Chief: Barbara McLean (718) 206-4733

Queens Branch Office, Family Court
151-20 Jamaica Ave., 2nd Floor, Jamaica 11432
(718) 658-0500; Fax: (718) 658-4025, 523-7855, 523-7378
Borough Chief: Jennifer Gilroy Ruiz

Staten Island Branch Office, Tort
60 Bay St., 4th Floor, Staten Island 10301-2514
(718) 447-5983; Fax: (718) 981-4459
Senior Counsel: Ann Broderick (718) 447-1324

Staten Island Branch Office, Family Court
60 Bay St., 4th Floor, Staten Island 10301-2514
(718) 390-5395; Fax: (718) 390-5338
Atty.-in-Charge: Thea Davis (718) 390-5337

Kingston Office, Environmental Law
71 Smith Ave., Kingston 12401
(845) 340-7508; Fax: (845) 338-0765
Asst. Corporation Counsel: Linda Geary (845) 340-7208

Kingston Office, Tax and Bankruptcy
71 Smith Ave., Kingston 12401 (845) 340-7206
Asst. Corporation Counsel: Joe Kroening

METROPOLITAN TRANSPORTATION AUTHORITY—N.Y.C. TRANSIT
2 Broadway, N.Y.C. 10004
(718) 330-3000; Fax: (718) 243-8501;
Customer Service: (718) 330-3322
Internet: www.mta.info

Chair/C.E.O.: Jay H. Walder
347 Madison Ave., N.Y.C. 10017 (212) 878-7200
Deputy Exec. Dir./Administration: Linda G. Kleinbaum
Deputy Exec. Dir./General Counsel: James B. Henly (718) 694-3900
Auditor General: Michael J. Fucilli
347 Madison Ave., N.Y.C. 10017 (212) 878-0208
President, Business Service: Sebastian L. DeSimone
President, Buses: Joseph J. Smith
President, Bridges & Tunnels: James Ferrara
President, Capital Construction: Michael Horodniceanu
President, Long Island R.R.: Helena E. Williams
President, Metro North R.R.: Howard R. Permut
President, New York City Transit: Thomas F. Prendergast

The MTA is a public-benefit corporation chartered by New York State; it is not part of New York City government. The board of the MTA constitutes the board of New York City Transit, which provides subway service in four New York City counties and bus service in five New York City counties and rail services on Staten Island.

Metropolitan Transportation Authority—Law Dept.
130 Livingston St., Brooklyn 11201
(718) 694-4893; Fax: (718) 694-5727

V.P./General Counsel: Martin B. Schnabel

Exec. Asst. General Counsel, General Law and Contracts: Florence Dean (718) 694-3901

Exec. Asst. General Counsel, Torts: Wallace D. Gossett (718) 694-3860

Dep. Exec. Asst. General Counsel, General Law & Contracts:
Lawrence Eluto (718) 694-3902
Richard I. Dreyfus (Labor Relations & Personnel) (718) 694-3894
Diane Morgenroth (Commercial Litigation) (718) 694-5713

Dep. Exec. Asst. General Counsel, Torts:
David J. Silverberg (Examination & Practice) (718) 694-3872
Danielle Ruttman (Torts/Trial Unit) (718) 694-3835
Lawrence Heisler (Appeals) (718) 694-3851

Dep. Exec. Asst. Gen. Counsel General, Law & Contacts: Denise Fraser (Affirmative Litigation/Foil) (718) 694-3909

Special Counsel: Richard Schoolman (718) 694-4667

Senior Dir., Workers Compensation/No Fault: Paula Ramirez (Acting) (718) 694-1053

Dir., Transit Adjudication Bureau: Dorothy Samuel (347) 643-5810

Senior Dir., Administration & Budget: Brenda Coleman (718) 694-3847

N.Y.C. HEALTH & HOSPITALS CORPORATION
125 Worth St., Suite 510, N.Y.C. 10013
(212) 788-3339; Fax: (212) 788-3348
Internet: www.nyc.gov/hhc

Chairperson of the Board: Michael A. Stocker, M.D. (212) 788-3359; Fax: (212) 385-2644
President & Chief Executive: Alan D. Aviles (212) 788-3321
Exec. V.P., Medical & Professional Affairs: Ramanathan Raju, M.D. (212) 788-3648
Sr. V.P., Finance: Marlene Zurack (212) 788-3494
Sr. V.P., Corporate Planning, Community Health & Intergovernmental Relations: LaRay Brown (212) 788-3448
Sr. V.P./Chief Restructuring Officer: Frank Cirillo (212) 788-3669
Sr. V.P./General Counsel: Salvatore J. Russo (212) 788-3300
Sr. Asst. V.P., Corporate Communications: Ana Marengo (212) 788-3386
Asst. V.P., Workforce Planning & Development: Nancy Doyle (212) 788-9684
Chief of Staff: Joseph Schick (212) 788-3330

The Corporation operates the city's municipal hospitals.

Acute Care Facilities

Bellevue Hospital Center
462 First Ave., N.Y.C. 10016 (212) 562-4141

Coney Island Hospital
2601 Ocean Pkwy., Brooklyn 11235 (718) 616-3000

Elmhurst Hospital Center
79-01 Broadway, Elmhurst 11373 (718) 334-4000

Harlem Hospital Center
506 Lenox Ave., N.Y.C. 10037 (212) 939-1000

Jacobi Medical Center
1400 Pelham Pkwy. S., Bronx 10461 (718) 918-5000

Kings County Hospital Center
451 Clarkson Ave., Brooklyn 11203 (718) 245-3131

Lincoln Medical and Mental Health Center
234 E. 149th St., Bronx 10451 (718) 579-5000

Metropolitan Hospital Center
1901 First Ave., N.Y.C. 10029 (212) 423-6262

North Central Bronx Hospital
3424 Kossuth Ave., Bronx 10467 (718) 519-5000

Queens Hospital Center
82-70 164th St., Jamaica 11432 (718) 883-3000

Woodhull Medical and Mental Health Center
760 Broadway, Brooklyn 11206 (718) 963-8000

Long Term Care Facilities

Coler-Goldwater Specialty Hospital and Nursing Facility
1 Main St. Franklin D. Roosevelt Island, N.Y.C. 10044
Coler Campus: (212) 848-6000;
Goldwater Campus: (212) 318-8000

Sea View Hospital Rehabilitation Center and Home
460 Brielle Ave., Staten Island 10314 (718) 317-3000

Dr. Susan Smith McKinney Nursing and Rehabilitation Center
594 Albany Ave., Brooklyn 11203 (718) 245-7000

Diagnostic and Treatment Centers

Cumberland Diagnostic & Treatment Center
100 N. Portland Ave., Brooklyn 11205 (718) 260-7500

East New York Diagnostic & Treatment Center
2094 Pitkin Ave., Brooklyn 11207 (718) 240-0400

Gouverneur Health Care Services
227 Madison St., N.Y.C. 10002 (212) 238-7000

Morrisania Diagnostic & Treatment Center
1225 Gerard Ave., Bronx 10452 (718) 960-2777

Renaissance Health Care Network Diagnostic & Treatment Center
215 W. 125th St., N.Y.C. 10027 (212) 932-6500

Segundo-Ruiz Belvis Diagnostic & Treatment Center
545 E. 142nd. St., Bronx 10454 (718) 579-4000

OFFICE OF ADMINISTRATIVE TAX APPEALS—N.Y.C. TAX APPEALS TRIBUNAL
1 Centre St., Room 2400, N.Y.C. 10007
(212) 669-2070; Fax: (212) 669-2211;
Admin. Law Judge Div., Rm. 2430: (212) 669-4501;
Fax: (212) 669-4503
Internet: www.nyc.gov/taxtribunal

President and Commissioner: Glenn Newman

Commissioners:

Robert J. Firestone   Ellen E. Hoffman

General Counsel: Mary E. Gallagher

Chief Admin. Law Judge: Steven J. Gombinski (212) 669-4501

Dep. Chief Admin. Law Judge: Warren P. Hauben (212) 669-4501

Admin. Law Judges:

Anne W. Murphy (212) 669-4501

Marlene F. Schwartz (212) 669-4501

Inspector General: Faisal Khan (212) 825-5482

Records Access Officer: Nilda Mendez

The Office of Administrative Tax Appeals is comprised of the N.Y.C. Tax Appeals Tribunal and the N.Y.C. Tax Commission. The Tribunal is a quasi-judicial agency. It consists of the President and two Commissioners (who are appointed by the Mayor to six-year terms) and four Administrative Law Judges. The Tribunal hears and decides cases from notices issued by the Commissioner of Finance (which give the right to petition for a hearing) involving N.Y.C. administered taxes and charges other than Real Property Tax.

OFFICE OF ADMINISTRATIVE TAX APPEALS—N.Y.C. TAX COMMISSION
1 Centre St., Room 936 & 2400, N.Y.C. 10007
(212) 669-4410; Commissioners: (212) 669-2070; Fax: (212) 669-2003
Internet: www.nyc.gov/html/taxcomm

President: Glenn Newman (212) 669-4401
Commissioners: (212) 669-2070

Fadil Brija	Alice Olick
Susan Grossman	Richard Stabile
Aladar Gyimesi	Kirk P. Tzanides

General Counsel: Mary Gallagher (212) 669-2070
Special Counsel: Leonard Picker (212) 669-8559

The Tax Commission consists of the President and six commissioners who are appointed by the Mayor, with advice and consent of the City Council, to staggered six-year terms. The Commission is the City of New York's autonomous administrative review forum with regard to real property tax assessments set by the Dept. of Finance. Determinations rendered by the Tax Commission on annual applications for correction in the formal administrative appeals context are subject to de novo judicial review.

OFFICE OF CHIEF MEDICAL EXAMINER
520 1st Ave., N.Y.C. 10016
Fax: (212) 447-2716

Chief Medical Examiner: Charles S. Hirsch, M.D. (212) 447-2034
First Deputy Chief Medical Examiner: Barbara Sampson, M.D. (212) 447-2335

Bronx Office
Jacobi Medical Center,
1400 Pelham Pkwy. at Eastchester Rd., Bronx 10461
(718) 829-2030
Deputy Chief Medical Examiner: James Gill, M.D. (718) 829-2910

Brooklyn/King's County Office
Kings County Hospital Center, 599 Winthrop St., Brooklyn 11203 (718) 221-0600
Deputy Chief Medical Examiner: Stephen de Roux, M.D. (718) 609-4432

Queens Office
Queens General Hospital, 160-15 82nd Dr., Jamaica 11432
(718) 883-3871
Deputy Chief Medical Examiner: Corine Ambrosi (718) 883-2119

Richmond County/Staten Island Office
Seaview Hospital Center & Home, 460 Brielle Ave., Staten Island 10314 (718) 668-0620
Deputy Chief Medical Examiner: Kristin Roman, M.D.

OFFICE OF CITY WIDE COURT ADMINISTRATION
See Special Listing, p. 30

DEPARTMENT OF PARKS & RECREATION
The Arsenal, Central Park,
830 Fifth Ave., N.Y.C. 10021
(212) 360-8111; Legal Fax: (212) 360-8286
Internet: www.nycparks.org

Commissioner: Adrian Benepe (212) 360-1305; Fax: (212) 360-1345
First Deputy Commissioner, Parks Dept.: Liam Kavanagh (212) 360-1307
Deputy Commissioner, Capital Projects: Therese Braddick (718) 760-6602
Deputy Commissioner, Community Outreach: Larry Scott Blackmon (212) 360-3484
Deputy Commissioner, Management & Budget: Robert L. Garafola (212) 360-1302
Deputy Commissioner, Public Programs: Kevin Jeffrey (212) 360-1382
Asst. Commissioner, Community Relations: Edward J. Lewis (212) 360-1360
Asst. Commissioner, Revenue & Marketing: Elizabeth W. Smith (212) 360-1366
General Counsel/Records Access Appeals Officer: Alessandro G. Olivieri (212) 360-1314
Dir., Public Affairs: Vickie Karp (212) 360-1311

Oversees the parks, beaches, playgrounds, stadia, marines, recreation facilities, gardens, malls, squares and public spaces of the City of New York.

DEPARTMENT OF PERSONNEL
See Department of Citywide Administrative Services

DEPARTMENT OF CITY PLANNING
22 Reade St., N.Y.C. 10007-1216
(212) 720-3300
Internet: www.nyc.gov/planning

Chair: Amanda M. Burden (212) 720-3200; Fax: (212) 720-3219
Exec. Dir.: Richard Barth (212) 720-3500; Fax: (212) 720-3219
Counsel: David Karnovsky (212) 720-3400; Fax: (212) 720-3303
Public Affairs: Rachaele Raynoff (212) 720-3471; Fax: (212) 720-3219

The City Planning Commission has primary responsibility for the conduct of planning in the City. The Chair heads the Department, which serves as her staff.

Manhattan Borough Office
22 Reade St., 6th Floor W., N.Y.C. 10007-1216
(212) 720-3480; Fax: (212) 720-3488
Director: Edith Hsu-Chen (212) 720-3542

Bronx Borough Office
One Fordham Plaza, 5th Floor, Bronx 10458-5891
(718) 220-8500; Fax: (718) 584-8628
Director: Carol Samol (718) 220-8510

Brooklyn Borough Office
16 Court St., 7th Floor, Brooklyn 11241
(718) 780-8290; Fax: (718) 596-2609
Director: Purnima Kapur

Queens Borough Office
120-55 Queens Blvd., Room 201, Kew Gardens 11424
(718) 286-3170; Fax: (718) 286-3183
Director: John Young (718) 286-3168

Staten Island Borough Office
130 Stuyvesant Pl., Room 603, Staten Island 10301-2511
(718) 556-7240; Fax: (718) 556-7305
Director: Leonard Garcia-Duran (718) 556-7241

POLICE DEPARTMENT
Headquarters, 1 Police Plaza, N.Y.C. 10038
(646) 610-5000
Internet: www.nyc.gov/nypd

Commissioner: Raymond W. Kelly (646) 610-5410
First Deputy Commissioner: Rafael Pineiro (646) 610-5420
Deputy Commissioner, Legal Matters: S. Andrew Schaffer (646) 610-5336
Deputy Commissioner, Trials: Martin G. Karopkin (646) 610-5424
Chief of Department: Joseph J. Esposito (646) 610-6710
Chief of Personnel: Thomas V. Dale
Chief of Patrol: James P. Hall (646) 610-6735
Deputy Commissioner, Public Information: Paul J. Browne (646) 610-6700

Freedom of Information Law (F.O.I.L.) Unit
Room 110C (646) 610-5296

DEPARTMENT OF PROBATION
33 Beaver St., N.Y.C. 10004
Internet: www.nyc.gov/html/prob

Commissioner: Vincent Schiraldi, Room 2310 (212) 361-8977; Fax: (212) 361-8985
Chief of Staff: Michael Ognibene (212) 361-8975
First Deputy Commissioner: Vacancy at Press Time (212) 361-8970
Dir. of Public Information: Ryan Dodge (Records Access Officer) (212) 361-8157

The Department of Probation services the New York State Supreme Court and the Family Court in New York City, and the Criminal Court of the City of New York.

Dept. of Probation—Cont'd

Executive Offices

Deputy Commissioner for Administration & Planning: Frank Marchiano (212) 361-8965

Deputy Commissioner for Adult Operations: Vacancy at Press Time (212) 361-8982; Fax: (212) 361-8987

Dir., Division of Staff & Organizational Development: Belinda Teo (212) 361-8868

General Counsel: Florence Hutner (212) 232-0700; Fax: (212) 232-0718

Assoc. Commissioner Operations, Family Court: Pamela Hardy (212) 232-0470; Fax: (212) 232-0499

Deputy Commissioner for Information Technology: Alphonzo Albright (212) 232-0455

Inspector General: Meera Cattafesta 60 Hudson St., Room 714, N.Y.C. 10013 (212) 266-1900

Advocate Dir.: David Vogel (212) 361-8881

Dir. for Management Analysis & Planning: John Corrigan (212) 232-0778

Asst. Commissioner for Budget and Fiscal Svcs.: Leona Braithwaite (212) 232-0676

Assoc. Commissioner for Adult Operations: Lorene Gilmore (212) 232-0410; Fax: (212) 487-3096

Family Services

33 Beaver St., 22nd Floor, N.Y.C. 10004

Deputy Commissioner for Family Court Service: Patricia Brennan (212) 232-0486

Asst. Commissioner: Joseph Dillon (212) 442-6952

Assoc. Commissioner for Family Court Services: Pamela Hardy, Room 2205 (212) 232-0470; Fax: (212) 232-0499

Branch Chief: Jonnie Mae Howard 60 Lafayette St., N.Y.C. 10013 (212) 676-8521

Family Court Services Branch—Manhattan

60 Lafayette St., N.Y.C. 10013

Branch Chief: Jonnie Mae Howard (212) 676-8521; Fax: (212) 442-4310

Family Court Services Branch—Bronx

900 Sheridan Ave., Room 6D1, Bronx 10451
Fax: (718) 590-3217

Branch Chief, Family Intake and Services: Olivien Manns-Nelson (718) 590-3180

Family Court Services Branch—Queens

151-20 Jamaica Ave., Jamaica 11432

Branch Chief, Family Intake and Services: Denise McNeill-Grant (718) 657-4385; Fax: (718) 657-7508

Family Court Services Branch—Brooklyn

330 Jay St., Brooklyn 11201

Asst. Commissioner: Gineen Gray, Room 11.12 (718) 802-2556; Fax: (718) 802-2662

Branch Chief, Family Investigations: Myra Radden (718) 802-2603; Fax: (718) 802-2674

Family Court Services Branch—Staten Island

130 Stuyvesant Pl., 4th Floor, Staten Island 10301

Branch Chief, Family Intake and Services: Evelyn Gonzalez (718) 556-4000; Fax: (718) 556-4042

Citywide Intensive Supervision Program and Kings Juvenile Offender Program

33 Beaver St., 22nd Floor, N.Y.C. 10004 (212) 232-0451

Kings Branch Chief, Intensive Supervision Program/KJOP: Rodney Levy 210 Joralemon St., Brooklyn 11201 (718) 802-4451

Branch Chief, Kings Juvenile Offender Program: Arnold Klein, 345 Adams St., Room 670, Brooklyn 11217 (718) 403-4600

Bronx Branch, Intensive Supervision: Brenda Davis 265 E. 161st St., 4th Floor, Bronx 10451 (718) 410-7268

Manhattan Branch, Intensive Supervision: Monique Begy 346 Broadway, 9th Floor, N.Y.C. 10013 (212) 442-6170; Fax: (212) 442-6200

Staten Island, Intensive Supervision: Richard Eterginoso (Supervising Probation Officer) 340 Bay St., Staten Island 10301 (718) 876-7778

Queens Branch, Intensive Supervision: Karen Armstrong 162-24 Jamaica Ave., Jamaica 11435 (718) 657-7382; Fax: (718) 657-8281

Department of Probation—Adult Services Manhattan Branch Office

100 Centre St., N.Y.C. 10013
(212) 442-9562; Fax: (212) 442-6200

Asst. Commissioner, Manhattan Adult Services: Jane E. Imbasciani, Room 1031B (212) 442-9562

Branch Chief, Adult Investigations-1: Reid Kay Room 1033 (212) 442-9570, 71

Branch Chief, Adult Investigations-2: Sharon Daniel Room 1029 (212) 442-1657

Branch Chief, Special Offenders Unit/Intensive Supervision: Monique Begy 346 Broadway, Rm 9E9, 9th Floor, N.Y.C. 10013 (212) 442-6170; Fax: (212) 442-6200

Branch Chief, High Risk Unit: Elisa Trillo 346 Broadway, 9th Floor, N.Y.C. 10013 (212) 442-6229; Fax: (212) 442-6200

Branch Chief, Adult Supervision Reporting: Jeph Oyeku 346 Broadway, 9th Floor, N.Y.C. 10013 (212) 442-6130; Fax: (212) 442-6180

Coordinator: Doreen Attanasio 346 Broadway, 3rd Floor, N.Y.C. 10013 (212) 442-6902; Fax: (212) 442-5872

Department of Probation—Adult Services Kings Branch Office

210 Joralemon St., Brooklyn 11201
(718) 802-4324; Fax: (718) 802-4108

Asst. Commissioner, Kings Adult Services: Ralph DiFiore 11th Floor

Branch Chief, Adult Supervision Reporting: Chloe Smith 10th Floor, Room 10-152 (718) 802-4351; Fax: (718) 802-4341

Branch Chief, Adult Investigations: Debbie Leon Room 1168 (718) 802-4175; Fax: (718) 802-4191

Branch Chief, Adult High Risk, North: Jay Nechamkin 345 Adams St., Room 601, Brooklyn 11201 (718) 403-3800; Fax: (718) 403-3803

Branch Chief, Adult High Risk, South/JOP: Arnold Klein 345 Adams St., Room 670, Brooklyn 11201 (718) 403-4600; Fax: (718) 403-4636

Branch Chief, Adult Special Offenders Unit/Intensive Supervision: Rodney Levy 10th Floor, Room 10-3-118, (718) 802-4451; Fax: (718) 802-4399

Department of Probation—Adult Services Bronx Branch Office

265 E. 161st St., Bronx 10451
(718) 401-8676; Fax: (718) 401-8427

Asst. Commissioner, Bronx Adult Services: Sharun Goodwin

Branch Chief, Adult High Risk, South: Darryl Williams 198 E. 161st St., Bronx 10451 (718) 537-5196; Fax: (718) 537-5401

Branch Chief, Adult High Risk, North: Nora Santos 198 E. 161st St., Bronx 10451 (718) 537-5190; Fax: (718) 537-6401

Branch Chief, Adult Supervision Reporting: Catrinia Prioleau 198 E. 161st St., Bronx 10451 (718) 537-5195; Fax: (718) 537-5401

Branch Chief, Adult Intensive Supervision: Brenda Davis 265 E. 161st St., 4th Floor, Bronx 10451 (718) 410-7268; Fax: (718) 460-8427

Branch Chief, Adult Special Offenders Unit: Lisa D'Ambrosio, 215 E. 161st St., 5th Floor, Bronx 10451 (718) 590-3077; Fax: (718) 293-3319

Branch Chief, Adult Investigations: Ralph Abreu 215 E. 161st St., 5th Floor, Bronx 10451 (718) 590-3112; Fax: (718) 410-3633

Dept. of Probation—Cont'd

Department of Probation—Adult Services
Queens Branch Office
125-01 Queens Blvd., Kew Gardens 11415
(718) 286-3045; Fax: (218) 286-3063

Asst. Commissioner, Queens Adult Services: Vincent Carrique
Room 294 (718) 286-3045; Fax: (718) 286-3063

Branch Chief, Adult Investigations: Gail Jones
(718) 286-3042; Fax: (718) 286-3018

Branch Chief, Adult Supervision High Risk: Maria Ayda
Room 115 (718) 286-3007, 657-1460;
Fax: (718) 286-2791, 657-8486

Branch Chief, Adult Reporting: Neil Sidenburg
90-02 161st St., Jamaica 11432
(718) 725-0725; Fax: (718) 725-0750

Branch Chief, QSOU/QISP: Karen Armstrong
162-24 Jamaica Ave., Jamaica 11432
(718) 657-7382; Fax: (718) 657-8281

Branch Chief, QASK: Cornell Gibson
162-24 Jamaica Ave., 5th Floor, Jamaica 11432
(718) 658-6845; Fax: (718) 658-8371

Department of Probation—Adult Services
Staten Island Branch Office
340 Bay St., Staten Island 10301
(718) 876-7459; Fax: (718) 876-8799

Director: Annette Carchidi

PUBLIC ADVOCATE FOR THE CITY OF NEW YORK

Municipal Bldg., 15th Floor,
1 Centre St., N.Y.C. 10007
(212) 669-7200; Ombudsman Line: (212) 669-7250;
Ombudsman Fax: (212) 669-4091; TTY: (212) 669-7438;
Public Advocate's Senior Action Line: (212) 669-7670;
General Fax: (212) 669-4701
Internet: www.pubadvocate.nyc.gov

Public Advocate: Bill de Blasio

General Counsel: Jacqueline Sherman
E-mail: jsherman@pubadovace.nyc.gov

Dir. of Integovernmental Affairs: Kirsten J. Foy
E-mail: kjfoy@pubadvocate.nyc.gov

Dir. of Policy: DeNora Getachew
E-mail: dgetachew@pubadvocate.nyc.gov

Chief of Staff: Emma Wolfe
E-mail: ewolfe@pubadvocate.nyc.gov

Press Secretary: Wiley Norvell
E-mail: wnorvell@pubadvocate.nyc.gov

Independently elected to represent the consumers of city services, the Public Advocate reviews and investigates complaints about city services; assesses agencies' response to the public and recommends improvements in agency programs and services; serves as ombudsman for individuals having difficulty receiving city services; and monitors the effectiveness of the city's public information and education efforts.

DEPARTMENT OF RECORDS AND INFORMATION SERVICES

31 Chambers St., Room 305, N.Y.C. 10007-1214
(212) 788-8609; Fax: (212) 788-8614
Internet: www.nyc.gov/records

Commissioner: Brian G. Andersson (212) 788-8607

Deputy Commissioner: Eileen M. Flannelly
(212) 788-8610

Asst. Commissioner: Kenneth R. Cobb (212) 788-8604

Dir., Municipal Archives: Leonora Gidlund
(212) 788-8585

Dir., Municipal Records Management Division:
Pearl Boatswain (212) 788-8550

Supervising Librarian: Christine Bruzzese
City Hall Library (212) 788-8595

Dir., Office of Administration: Naomi Pacheco
(212) 788-8622

Provides municipal reference library, archival and records management services.

CITY REGISTER

66 John St., 13th Floor, N.Y.C. 10038
(212) 361-7130; Fax: (212) 361-7100

Asst. Commissioner: Annette M. Hill
E-mail: hilla@finance.nyc.gov

Responsible for creating and maintaining the records of recorded real property and filed personal property documents. NOTE: For individual filings, contact the appropriate county office listed below

For filing information, see Fees of the Register's Office, Pages 159-161

New York County (Manhattan)
66 John St., 13th Floor, N.Y.C. 10039
(212) 361-7550; Fax: (212) 361-7132

Deputy City Register: Joanne Maya
(212) 361-7690; Fax: (212) 361-7699
E-mail: mayaj@finance.nyc.gov

Bronx Office
3030 Third Ave., Room 280, Bronx 10455 (718) 993-6052

Deputy City Register: Mary Scheman
E-mail: schemanm@finance.nyc.gov

Kings County (Brooklyn)
Municipal Bldg., Room 2, Brooklyn 11201 (718) 802-3590

Deputy City Register: Zena Spence
(718) 802-3588; Fax: (718) 802-3745
E-mail: spencez@finance.nyc.gov

Queens Office
144-06 94th Ave., 1st Floor, Jamaica 11435 (718) 298-7200

Deputy City Register: Wanda Clemons
(718) 298-7150; Fax: (718) 298-7153
E-mail: clemonsw@finance.nyc.gov

DEPARTMENT OF SANITATION

125 Worth St., N.Y.C. 10013-4006
Fax: (212) 385-2560
Internet: www.nyc.gov/sanitation

Commissioner: John J. Doherty (646) 885-4974

First Deputy Commissioner, Operations:
Bernard Sullivan (646) 885-4727

Deputy Commissioner, Financial Management & Administration: Larry Cipollina (646) 885-4793

Deputy Commissioner, Bureau of Long Term Export:
Harry Szarpanski (917) 237-5501

Deputy Commissioner, Legal Affairs: Robert Orlin
(646) 885-5006

Deputy Commissioner, Bureau of Public Information/Community Affairs: Vito A. Turso
(646) 885-5020; Fax: (212) 791-3386

The Department is responsible for keeping New York City clean by collecting and managing solid waste, clearing the streets of litter, snow and ice, and performing other duties such as collecting recyclables.

DEPARTMENT OF SMALL BUSINESS SERVICES

110 William St., 7th Floor, N.Y.C. 10038
(212) 513-6300; Fax: (212) 618-8991
Internet: www.nyc.gov/smallbiz

Commissioner: Robert W. Walsh (212) 513-6350

First Deputy Commissioner: Andrew Schwartz
(212) 513-6428

General Counsel: Deborah Buyer (212) 618-6720

Deputy General Counsel: Michael Owh (212) 513-6432

Provides neighborhood development, small business services, and workforce development services.

BOARD OF STANDARDS AND APPEALS

40 Rector St., 9th Floor, N.Y.C. 10006
(212) 788-8500; Fax: (212) 788-8769
Internet: www.nyc.gov/html/bsa

Chair: Meenakshi Srinivasan (212) 788-8547

Exec. Dir.: Jeff Mulligan (212) 788-8805

Vice Chair: Christopher Collins (212) 788-8661

Commissioners:
Susan M. Hinkson (212) 788-8603
Dara Ottley-Brown (212) 788-8788

Deputy Dir.: Vacancy at Press Time (212) 788-8797

General Counsel: Amy Becca Kelly (212) 788-0296

Board of Standards and Appeals—Cont'd
City Planner: Carlo Costanza (212) 788-8739
Appeals Examiner: Toni Matias (212) 788-8752
Applications: Doretha Whitley (212) 788-8767
Asst. to the Chairman: Anita Lew (212) 788-8773

Hears and decides appeals from property owners whose applications for permits to construct or alter buildings or establish new uses have been denied by the Dept. of Buildings, the Fire Dept. or the Dept. of Business Services.

DEPARTMENT OF TRANSPORTATION

40 Worth St., Room 1015, N.Y.C. 10013
(212) 442-7730; Fax: (212) 442-7733
Internet: www.nyc.gov/dot

Commissioner: Janette Sadik-Khan
(212) 676-0868; Fax: (212) 442-7007
First Deputy Commissioner: Lori Ardito (212) 839-6403
Deputy Commissioner for External Affairs:
David Woloch (212) 839-6410
Deputy Commissioner for Traffic Operations:
Gerard Soffian (718) 433-3370
Deputy Commissioner for Sidewalks & Inspection Mgmt.: Leon W. Heyward (212) 839-4300
Deputy Commissioner, Bridges: Henry D. Perahia
(212) 839-6300
Deputy Commissioner, Staten Island Ferry Operations: Capt. James C. DeSimone
(718) 876-5368; Fax: (718) 875-6644
Asst. Commissioner, Public Information:
Vacancy at Press Time (212) 839-4850
General Counsel: Philip Damashek (212) 839-6503
Bronx Borough Commissioner: Constance Moran
1400 Williamsbridge Rd., Bronx 10461
(212) 748-6680; Fax: (212) 748-6688
Brooklyn Borough Commissioner: Joseph Palmieri
16 Court St., Brooklyn 11241
(718) 222-7259; Fax: (718) 222-7256
Lower Manhattan Borough Commissioner:
Luis Sanchez, 59 Maiden Ln., 37th Floor, N.Y.C. 10038
(212) 839-7250; Fax: (212) 788-8986
Manhattan Borough Commissioner: Margaret Forgione
59 Maiden Ln., 37th Floor, N.Y.C. 10038
(212) 839-6210; Fax: (212) 487-5010
Queens Borough Commissioner: Maura McCarthy
120-55 Queens Blvd., 2nd Floor, Kew Gardens 11424
(718) 286-0826, 391-2705; Fax: (718) 391-2709
Staten Island Borough Commissioner: Tom Cocola
10 Richmond Terr., Room 300, Staten Island 10301
(718) 816-2373; Fax: (718) 816-2385

The Department controls and regulates traffic; builds and maintains streets, sidewalks, bridges and municipal parking facilities; and operates the Staten Island Ferry.

Pothole and Sidewalk Complaints
Prior written notice: Prior Notice Unit,
Dept. of Transportation
40 Worth St., Room 927, N.Y.C. 10013
(212) 442-7864;
Automated Customer Service Line:
(212) or (718) CALL-DOT;
TTY Parking Permits for People with Disabilities:
(718) 433-3111, 00

NEW YORK INSURANCE COMPANIES LOCAL CLAIMS MANAGERS

Ace American RE
See Risk Enterprise Management Limited

ACE USA
National Headquarters
436 Walnut St., Philadelphia, PA 19106
(215) 640-1000; Claims: (800) 433-0385
Internet: www.ace-ina.com
President: Brian E. Dowd (215) 640-5400
Sr. V.P./General Counsel: Kevin M. Rampe (215) 640-1088

Wilmington ESIS Claim Center
One Beaver Valley Rd., 4 West, Wilmington, DE 19803
Mailing Address: ESIS Wilmington Casualty, P.O. Box 31079, Tampa, FL 33631
(302) 476-6200; Casualty Fax: (800) 261-4716; Workers Comp. Fax: (800) 611-7048

Mailing Address: ESIS Workers Comp., P.O. Box 31080, Tampa, FL 33631
V.P., Claims: Linda Williams, Ext. 6003
E-mail: linda.williams@esis.com
Mgr., Claims: Vacancy at Press Time

Workers Compensation Claims Office
33 Dodge Rd., Suite 100, Getzville 14068
Mailing Address: P.O. Box 31121, Tampa, FL 33631
(716) 636-7100; Fax: (800) 914-0956
Regional V.P., Claims Mgr.: Daniel Garrett, Ext. 7147
E-mail: daniel.garrett@esis.com

Adirondack Insurance Exchange
See OneBeacon Insurance Group

AEGON USA
Diversified Investment Advisors, Inc.
4 Manhattanville Rd., Purchase 10577
(877) 342-7253
Internet: www.divinvest.com
Division of AUSA Life Insurance Company

Aetna Casualty & Surety
See Travelers

Affiliated FM Insurance
See FM Global

AIG, Chubb, CAN
See Risk Enterprise Management Limited

All America Insurance Co.
See Central Insurance Companies

Allendale Mutual Insurance Co.
See FM Global

Allstate Insurance Group
Allstate Plaza, 2775 Sanders Rd., Northbrook, IL 60062-6127
(847) 402-5000
Internet: www.allstate.com
Sr. V.P. Property/Casualty Claims: Michael J. Roche

American & Foreign Ins. Co.
See Arrowpoint Capital Corp.

American Casualty Co. of Reading, Pa.
See CNA / Insurance Companies

American European Ins. Co.
See Merchants Insurance Group

American Financial Group
National Headquarters
580 Walnut St., Cincinnati, OH 45202-3180
Mailing Address: P.O. Box 2575, Cincinnati, OH 45201-2575
(513) 369-5000; Fax: (888) 223-1317
Internet: www.afginc.com
C.E.O./Chair: Carl H. Lindner

Great American Ins. Co.
Home Office
Claims Litigation Services, 49 E. 4th St., Suite 800, Cincinnati, OH 45202
(513) 369-5000; Fax: (888) 223-1317
Internet: www.greatmericaninsurance.com
Sr. V.P.: Vito Perrino
Subsidiary of American Financial Group, for Personal Claims, see Infinity Insurance

National Claims Center/Specialty Claims
Alternative Markets Division, 49 E. 4th St., Suite 700, Cincinnati, OH 45202
Mailing Address: Specialty Division, P.O. Box 5432, Cincinnati, OH 45201-5432
(513) 369-5000, (877) 589-6846
Divisional Sr. V.P.: Thomas P. Jabs (513) 287-8132
E-mail: tjabs@gaic.com
Sr. V.P.: Vito Peraino

Alternative Markets Claims
1 Waterside Crossing, Windsor, CT 06095
Mailing Address: P.O. Box 5432, Cincinnati, OH 45201-5432
(800) 824-3052; Fax: (888) 223-1317
Claims Mgr.: Gae Close (Alternative Markets Claims)
E-mail: gclose@gaic.com

Specialty Claims
50 Parsippany Rd., Parsippany, NJ 07054
(800) 222-0305; Fax: (888) 223-1317
D.V.P., Excess Liability: James J. Siessel (973) 952-9888

American Fire & Casualty Co.
See Ohio Casualty Insurance Company

American Guarantee and Liability Insurance Co.
See Zurich North America

American Hardware Mutual Insurance Company
2674 Monroeville Blvd., Monroeville, PA 15146
Mailing Address: P.O. Box 182476, Columbus, OH 43218
(800) 876-8766; Fax: (800) 365-2562
Internet: www.americanhardwareins.com
Claims Mgr.: Judy Palamara
Member of Motorists Mutual-American Hardware Group

American Ins. Co.
See Ohio Casualty Insurance Company

American International Group—Claims Services
National Headquarters
70 Pine St., 38th Floor, N.Y.C. 10270
(212) 770-7000, (877) 638-4244; Fax: (212) 943-1125
Internet: www.aig.com

80 Pine St., N.Y.C. 10005
(212) 770-2000

American Manufacturers Mutual Ins. Co.
See Kemper Insurance Companies

American Motorists Ins. Co.
See Kemper Insurance Companies

American Zurich Insurance Co.
See Zurich North America

Amerisure Companies
National Headquarters
26777 Halsted Rd., Farmington Hills, MI 48331-3586
(800) 257-1900, (248) 615-9000; Claims: (888) 664-2524; Fax: (248) 615-8372, 615-8602
Internet: www.amerisure.com
President: Richard F. Russell
V.P., Claims: Don A. Smith; Fax: (248) 615-8224
E-mail: donsmith@amerisure.com
General Counsel: Susan G. Vincent; Fax: (248) 426-7936
E-mail: svincent@amerisure.com
Formerly known as Michigan Mutual Insurance

Appalachian Insurance
See FM Global

Arkwright Insurance Co.
See FM Global

Arrowpoint Capital Corp.
3600 Arco Corp. Dr., Charlotte, NC 28273
Mailing Address: P.O. Box 1000, Charlotte, NC 28201-1000
(704) 522-2000; Fax: (704) 522-3200
Internet: www.arrowpointcapitalcorp.com
President/C.E.O.: Jim Tighe
General Counsel: James Meehan (704) 522-2073
Chief Claim Officer: Julie Fortune (704) 522-2755
Formerly Royal & Sun Alliance

Assurance Co. of America
See Zurich North America

Atlanta Casualty Insurance Co. Personal Lines
See Infinity Insurance

Atlantic Mutual Companies
Home Offices
100 Wall St., N.Y.C. 10005-3743
(212) 943-1800; Corp. Secy./Legal Fax: (212) 428-6577
Internet: www.atlanticmutual.com
Sr. V.P., Claims: John K. Shea (973) 408-6162

Administrative Center
7 Giralda Farms, Suite 120, Madison, NJ 07940-1027
(973) 408-6000; Fax: (973) 408-6121
President/C.E.O.: Nancy Hahon (973) 408-6030
V.P., Claims: Merreles Schumann (973) 408-6056
National Claims Administrator: Maria Basinski (Workers Compensation) (973) 408-6208

Atlantic Mutual Insurance Company
See Atlantic Mutual Companies

Atlantic Specialty Insurance Company
See OneBeacon Insurance Group

AutoOne Insurance Company
See OneBeacon Insurance Group

AutoOne Select Insurance Company
See OneBeacon Insurance Group

Avomark Insurance Company
See Ohio Casualty Insurance Company

Berkshire Hathaway Insurance Group
3024 Harney St., Omaha, NE 68131
(402) 916-3000; Fax: (402) 536-3030
E-mail: info@nationalindemnity.com
Internet: www.nationalindemnity.com

Claim Dept., 4016 Farnam St., Omaha, NE 68131
(800) 916-3000; Fax: (402) 916-3031
C.E.O.: Donald Wurster

Boston Old Colony Insurance Co.
See Encompass Insurance

Buckeye Union Insurance Co.
See Encompass Insurance

CNA/Insurance Companies
National Headquarters
CNA Plaza, 333 S. Wabash Ave., Chicago, IL 60604
(312) 822-5000, (800) 262-2000; Fax: (312) 822-6419
Internet: www.cna.com
Chair/C.E.O.: Stephen W. Lilienthal
Exec. V.P./General Counsel & Secretary: Jonathan D. Kantor (312) 822-1384; Fax: (312) 817-0511

Commercial Insurance
25 Melville Park Rd., Suite 100, P.O. Box 609, Melville 11747
(631) 756-7300, (800) 953-7389; Fax: (631) 756-7570
Internet: www.cna.com
Corporate V.P.: Kelvin Hazzard
E-mail: kelvin.hazzard@cna.com

Workers Compensation
443 Electronics Pkwy., 1st & 2nd Floor, Liverpool 13088
Mailing Address: P.O. Box 8317, Chicago, IL 60680
(315) 431-6000, (800) 262-6344; Fax: (315) 431-6005
Internet: www.cna.com
Claims Dir.: Kevin M. Culkin (315) 431-6894

California Insurance Co.
See Swiss Re

The Camden Fire Insurance Association
See OneBeacon Insurance Group

Centennial Insurance Company
See Atlantic Mutual Companies

Central Insurance Companies
National Headquarters
800 S. Washington St., Van Wert, OH 45891-2357
Mailing Address: P.O. Box 351, Van Wert, OH 45891-0351
(419) 238-1010, (800) 736-7000; Fax: (800) 736-7026
Internet: www.central-insurance.com

Central Mutual Insurance Companies
404 Wyman St., Suite 360, Waltham, MA 02451-1270
Mailing Address: P.O. Box 9124, Waltham, MA 02454-9124
(781) 890-1752, (800) 359-2233; Fax: (800) 877-2293
Regional Claims Mgr.: Susan E. Sylvester

Central Mutual Insurance Co.
See Central Insurance Companies

Chubb Group of Insurance Companies
World Headquarters
15 Mountain View Rd., Warren, NJ 07059
(908) 903-2000; Fax: (908) 903-2027
Internet: www.chubb.com
President/C.E.O.: John D. Finnegan

333 Earle Ovington Blvd., Suite 800, Uniondale 11553-3644
(516) 745-8423; Fax: (516) 745-8498
Zone Claims Discipline Mgr. (Northeast):
Edward G. Kinzer (516) 745-8423; Fax: (516) 745-8498
E-mail: ekinzer@chubb.com

Parker Corporate Center, Suite 370,
1311 Mamaroneck Ave., White Plains 10605
(914) 989-6500; Fax: (914) 989-6600
Branch Mgr.: Jody Specht (914) 989-6510

700 Clinton Sq., Rochester 14604-1717
(585) 238-8000; Fax: (585) 232-6497
Claims Mgr.: Timothy McGuire (585) 238-8011
E-mail: tmcguire@chubb.com

333 Earle Ovington Blvd., Uniondale 11553-3644
(516) 745-8200; Fax: (516) 745-8498

7 Southwoods Blvd., 3rd Floor, Albany 12211
(518) 433-6200; Fax: (518) 433-6210

CIGNA Companies
Legal Department
Two Liberty Place, 1601 Chestnut St.,
Philadelphia, PA 19192
National Information Center: (215) 761-1000
Internet: www.cigna.com
Exec. V.P. & General Counsel: Carol Ann Petren
Chief Counsel Litigation: Brian Benjet, TL-16H, (215) 761-3623
For Property and Casualty Claims, see ACE USA

CIGNA Insurance Cos.
See ACE USA

Citizens Insurance Co.
See Hanover Insurance Group

Clarendon America Ins. Co.
See Clarendon Insurance Group

Clarendon Insurance Group
Headquarters
466 Lexington Ave., 19th Floor, N.Y.C. 10017-3140
(212) 790-9700; Fax: (212) 790-9800
Internet: www.clarendon.biz
President/C.E.O.: Patrick Fee
General Counsel, Senior V.P. & Secretary: Robert Redpath (212) 790-9862

Clarendon National Ins. Co.
See Clarendon Insurance Group

CNA Casualty of California
See CNA / Insurance Companies

CNA Casualty of Puerto Rico
See CNA / Insurance Companies

Colorado Casualty Insurance Co.
See Liberty Mutual Insurance Co.

Columbia Casualty Company
See CNA / Insurance Companies

Columbia Insurance Company
See Berkshire Hathaway Insurance Group

Commercial Insurance Co. of Newark, N.J.
See Encompass Insurance

Commercial Mutual Insurance Co.
Commercial Auto Claims
15 Joys Lane, Kingston 12401
(845) 331-3288; Fax (Claims): (845) 340-8351

President: John Reiersen, Ext. 366; Fax: (845) 331-8141
E-mail: jreiersen@comutual.com

V.P./Claims Mgr.: William Muller, Ext. 308
E-mail: wmuller@comutual.com

Connecticut General Life Ins. Co.
See CIGNA Companies

Consolidated Rail Corporation
National Headquarters
1717 Arch St., 49th Floor, Philadelphia, PA 19103
(215) 209-2000
Internet: www.conrail.com

President/C.O.O.: Ronald Batory (856) 231-2000

V.P./General Counsel & Corp. Secy.:
Jonathan M. Broder (215) 209-5020
Effective June 1, 1999, Conrail merged with CSXT and Norfolk Southern Railroads

CSX Transportation, Inc.
CSXT Corporation, 1 Bell Crossing Rd., Selkirk 12158-9618
(518) 767-6445; Fax: (518) 767-6446
Internet: www.csx.com
President/C.E.O.: Michael J. Ward
Mgrs., Field Investigations:
Alan Hansen
Patrick Varcasia (518) 767-6349

CSX Transportation, Inc.
CSXT Corporation, Inc., 205 Reiman St., Buffalo 14212
Fax: (716) 891-6022
Mgr., Field Investigations: Daniel Christopher
(716) 891-6011
James R. Hannan (716) 891-6001; Fax: (716) 891-6022

Constitution State Service Co.
See Travelers

Continental Casualty Co.
See Encompass Insurance

Coregis Indemnity Co.
See Swiss Re

Coregis Insurance Co.
See Swiss Re

Coregis Managers Group
See Swiss Re

Countryway Insurance Company
Home Office
224 Harrison St., Suite 800, Syracuse 13214
Mailing Address: P.O. Box 4851, Syracuse 13221-4851
(315) 634-5229; Fax: (315) 634-5321
Internet: www.countryway.com

V.P., Claims: Michael C. Phillips (315) 634-5255

Country-Wide Insurance Company
Home Office
40 Wall St., Suite 13, N.Y.C. 10005
(212) 514-7000; Claims: (212) 344-8700;
Claims Fax: (212) 635-0587; Fax: (212) 514-7291
E-mail: info@cwico.com; Internet: www.cwico.com

V.P., Claims: John M. Stevenson, Ext. 5340

Dir., Special Investigations: Gerry Schlissel, Ext. 5055

Auto Damage Claims Mgr.: Robert Vellozzi, Ext. 5396

Bodily Injury Supervisor: Josephine Braithewait
Ext. 5028

Crum and Forster Indemnity Co.
See Crum and Forster Insurance

Crum and Forster Insurance
Home Office
305 Madison Ave., P.O. Box 1973, Morristown, NJ 07962
(973) 490-6600, (888) 890-1500; Fax: (877) 622-6191
E-mail: information@cfins.com
Internet: www.cfins.com

Chair/C.E.O.: Douglas M. Libby, Ext. 26611

President: Vacancy at Press Time

Sr. V.P., Claims: Paul Kush
(973) 490-6640; Fax: (877) 622-6219

Crum and Forster Underwriters Co. of Ohio
See Crum and Forster Insurance

Dairyland Ins. Co.
See Sentry Claims Service

Discover RE, Old Republic
See Risk Enterprise Management Limited

Empire Insurance Co.
See Empire Insurance Company

Empire Insurance Company
315 Park Ave., 20th Floor, N.Y.C. 10015
(212) 358-6525; Fax: (212) 358-6560
Internet: www.empireinsurancecompany.com

Senior V.P., Claims: Gerald Franzetti (212) 358-6581
Company is no longer writing new business; member of Empire Insurance Group

Encompass Insurance
333 Glen St., Suite 800, P.O. Box 5000, Glens Falls 12801
(518) 761-4000, (800) 262-1145; Fax: (800) 426-3692
Internet: www.encompassinsurance.com

President: Cynthia Young
51 W. Higgins Rd., Suite F2A, Barrington, IL 60010
(847) 844-6110

Regional Claims Mgrs.:
Charles Bothem (New Jersey) (732) 951-6000, Ext. 16033
Michael Mahardy (New York) (518) 761-4217

Auto Express Supervisor: Joanne Weir (New Jersey)
(732) 951-6000, Ext. 16215

Essentia Insurance Company
See OneBeacon Insurance Group

Essex Insurance Cos.
See Markel Corporation

Evanston Insurance Co.
See Markel Corporation

Eveready Ins. Co.
Home Office
59 Maiden Lane, 43rd Floor, N.Y.C. 10038-4502
(212) 412-4700; Fax: (212) 363-1350
Internet: www.evereadyinsurance.com

Claims Mgr.: Richard Smith

Chief Counsel: Wollerstein & Futoran
(212) 412-4750; Fax: (212) 363-1602

Excelsior Insurance Company
See Peerless Insurance Company

Executive Risk Indemnity Inc.
See Chubb Group of Insurance Companies

Executive Risk Specialty Ins. Co.
See Chubb Group of Insurance Companies

FM Global
National Headquarters
270 Central Ave., P.O. Box 7500, Johnston, RI 02919-4923
(401) 275-3000; Fax: (401) 275-3029
E-mail: information@fmglobal.com
Internet: www.fmglobal.com

Chair/C.E.O.: Shivan S. Subramaniam

Sr. V.P./General Counsel: John J. Pomeroy, Ext. 1075

Sr. V.P., Claims Operations: Gerry Alonso, Ext. 1102

NY/NJ Operations
Bldg. D6, 3rd Floor, 400 Interpace Pkwy.,
Parsippany, NJ 07054-1196
(973) 402-2200; Fax: (973) 402-1070
V.P./N.Y. Oper. Claims Mgr.: Jon Ragland

Boston Operations
500 River Ridge Dr., P.O. Box 9102, Norwood, MA 02062
(781) 440-8000; Fax: (781) 440-8748
Operations V.P./Claims Mgr.: Robert F. McGovern (Boston)
E-mail: robert.mcgovern@fmglobal.com
This office covers Upstate New York

Factory Mutual Insurance Co.
See FM Global

Farm Family Casualty Ins. Co.
National Headquarters and Call Center—First Notice of Loss
344 Rt. 9W, Glenmont 12077-2910
Mailing Address: P.O. Box 656, Albany 12201-0656
(518) 431-5000, (800) 843-3276; Fax: (518) 431-5983, 75, 92
Internet: www.farmfamily.com

Exec. V.P., General Counsel and Secy.:
Victoria M. Stanton, J.D., C.P.C.U. (518) 431-5409

Sr. V.P., Casualty Claims:
Richard E. Long, A.I.C., C.P.C.U., A.R.E. (518) 431-5009
E-mail: rick_long@farmfamily.com

V.P., Casualty Claims: Thomas Kelley, C.P.C.U.
124 Grove St., Suite 315, Franklin, MA 02038
(508) 553-9425; Fax: (508) 553-9420
E-mail: tom_kelley@farmfamily.com

Claim Administration Mgr.: Deborah Ptasinski, A.I.M.
E-mail: debbie_ptasinski@farmfamily.com

Claim Counsel: April Elkovitch, J.D., A.I.C., C.P.C.U.
E-mail: april_elkovitch@farmfamily.com.

3249 Route 112, Ste. 3, Bldg. 4, Medford 11763-1411
(631) 732-3301; Fax: (631) 732-3308
District Claims Mgr.: Susan DiScalo
E-mail: sue_discalo@farmfamily.com

41 Liberty St., Suite 2, Batavia 14020-3207
(585) 343-8960; Fax: (585) 343-8962
District Claims Mgr.: John Dollard
E-mail: john_dollard@farmfamily.com

Federal Insurance Company
See Chubb Group of Insurance Companies

Fidelity and Casualty Ins. Co. of N.Y.
See Encompass Insurance

Fireman's Fund Insurance Companies
National Headquarters
777 San Marin Dr., Novato, CA 94998
(415) 899-2000, (800) 227-1700; Fax: (415) 899-3600
E-mail: postmaster@ffic.com
Internet: www.firemansfund.com

President/C.E.O.: Michael LaRocco

General Counsel: Sally Narey

Chief Claims & Risk Services Officer: Paul Stachura

V.P., Field Claims-Auto/Propery/Marine:
Andy Knudsen, 3301 Rider Trail S.,
Earth City, MO 63045 (314) 513-1001

V.P., Field Claims-& GL/wc/Prof. Lines: Frank Sapio
33 W. Monroe St., Chicago, IL 60603 (312) 629-2080
Affiliated with Allianz Insurance Companies

Fireman's Insurance Co. of Newark, N.J.
See Encompass Insurance

First Specialty
See Swiss Re

GEICO Casualty Ins. Co.
See GEICO Companies

GEICO Companies
National Headquarters
5260 Western Ave., Chevy Chase, MD 20815
Mailing Address: 1 GEICO Plaza, Washington, DC 20076
(301) 986-2500, (800) 638-8037; Fax: (301) 986-3054
Internet: www.geico.com

C.E.O./President & Chair: Tony Nicely

General Counsel/V.P.: Dana K. Proulx (301) 986-3479

Regional Office
750 Woodbury Rd., Woodbury 11797-2589
(516) 496-5000
A.V.P., Claims: John Pham

Regional Office
300 Crosspoint Pkwy., Getzville 14068
(800) 418-4625

GEICO General Inc. Co.
See GEICO Companies

GEICO Indemnity Ins. Co.
See GEICO Companies

General Casualty
Northeast Region
82 Hopmeadow St., Simsbury, CT 06089
(860) 651-1065, (800) 961-1121; Claims: (860) 408-3266
Internet: www.generalcasualty.com

Home Office, One General Dr., Sun Prairie, WI 53596
(800) 362-5448, (608) 837-4440;
Claims Fax: (608) 825-5122

President/C.E.O.: Peter Christen

V.P., Claims: Mike Bondura
A Subsidiary of General Casualty Ins. Co.
308 Maltbie St., Suite 104, Syracuse 13204
(315) 451-2246, (888) 865-7756; Fax: (315) 457-4509
Regional V.P.: Richard Van Edsinga (800) 961-1121
Claims handled through Simsbury CT.

General Reinsurance
National Headquarters
Financial Centre, 695 E. Main St., Stamford, CT 06901
Mailing Address: P.O. Box 10350, Stamford, CT 06904-2350
(203) 328-5000; Fax: (203) 328-6423

Senior V.P.: Nicholas S. Canelos (203) 328-5502
E-mail: ncanelos@genre.com

Chief Counsel: Damon N. Vocke (203) 328-6268

Genworth Financial
National Headquarters
6620 W. Broad St., Richmond, VA 23230
(888) 436-9678; Corporate Hdqtrs.: (804) 281-6000;
Directory Assistance: (800) 844-6543
E-mail: contactus@genworth.com; Internet: www.genworth.com

President/C.E.O.: Michael D. Fraizer

The Glens Falls Insurance Co.
See Encompass Insurance

Globe Indemnity Co.
See Arrowpoint Capital Corp.

GMAC Insurance Group
500 W. Fifth St., Winston Salem, NC 27102
Mailing Address: P.O. Box 3199, Winston Salem, NC 27102-3199
(336) 770-2000, (877) 468-3466
Internet: www.gmacpolicy.com

Golden Eagle Insurance Co.
See Liberty Mutual Insurance Co.

Government Employees Insurance Co.
See GEICO Companies

Graphic Arts Mutual Insurance Co.
See Utica National Insurance Group

Great American Ins. Co. Personal Lines
See Infinity Insurance

Great American Insurance Co. Specialty Lines
See American Financial Group

Great Northern Insurance Company
See Chubb Group of Insurance Companies

Greater N.Y. Mutual Ins. Company/Insurance Co. of Greater N.Y.
Home Office
200 Madison Ave., N.Y.C. 10016
(212) 683-9700; Fax: (212) 683-6871

Executive V.P.: Gerard Ragusa, C.P.C.U., A.I.C. (Claims & Liability)

V.P.'s, Claims:
Steve Cangelosi
Larry Cretella

V.P., Property: Ronald Wolfe

377 Summerhill Rd., East Brunswick, NJ 08816-1064
(732) 238-6300; Fax: (732) 238-3781
A.V.P., Claims Mgr., Liability: Lynn Goldberg
Claims Mgr., Initial Action Unit: Joseph McGrath
Claims Mgr., Workers Comp.: James Primamore

180 Glastonbury Blvd., Glastonbury, CT 06033
(860) 652-7090; Fax: (860) 652-7095
A.V.P., Claims: Michael Fuffo

Greater New York Insurance Group
See Greater N.Y. Mutual Ins. Company / Insurance Co. of Greater N.Y.

Group Council Mutual Insurance Company in Liquidation
123 William St., N.Y.C. 10038-3889
(212) 341-6400; Legal Fax: (212) 608-3398

Hanover Insurance Group
National Headquarters
440 Lincoln St., Worcester, MA 01653
(508) 855-7200; Claims Fax: (800) 399-4734
Internet: www.hanover.com

President/C.E.O.: Frederick Eppinger (508) 855-2400

Chief Claims Officer, Property & Casualty Claims: Mark Welzenbach (508) 855-4814

Sr. V.P. & General Counsel: J. Kendall Huber (508) 855-2691

Hanover Insurance Co.
400 Atrium Dr., Somerset, NJ 08873
(732) 805-2000, (800) 257-5720; Fax: (732) 805-2850
Regional Claims Mgr.: Richard Woods Ext. 2200; Fax: (732) 805-2293

Hanover Insurance Co.
103 Commerce Blvd., P.O. Box 4898, Liverpool 13221
(800) 888-4925; Claims: (800) 628-0250;
Workers Comp Claims Fax: (800) 762-7788;
All other Claims Fax: (800) 955-7668
A.V.P. Auto & Property Claims: Dwight H. Lensing (315) 463-4352

Harbor Specialty Ins. Co.
See Clarendon Insurance Group

Healthcare Underwriters Mutual Insurance Co.
See Medical Liability Mutual Insurance Company

Hertz Claim Management Corp.
National Headquarters
225 Brae Blvd., Park Ridge, NJ 07656-0719
(800) 762-0341, (201) 307-5866; Fax: (201) 307-5890
Internet: www.hertzclaimmgt.com; www.hertz.com

V.P., Claims: John P. Fahey (201) 307-2537; Fax: (201) 307-2709

Hertz Rent A Car
See Hertz Claim Management Corp.

Homeland Insurance Company of New York
See OneBeacon Insurance Group

Houston General Insurance Company
See OneBeacon Insurance Group

Houston General Insurance Exchange
See OneBeacon Insurance Group

Hudson Ins. Co.
See The Robert Plan

Hudson Insurance Co.
See Country-Wide Insurance Company

HUM Group of Companies
See Medical Liability Mutual Insurance Company

Indiana Insurance Co.
See Liberty Mutual Insurance Co.

Indiana Insurance Company
See Peerless Insurance Company

Infinity Insurance
Corporate Office
3700 Colonnade Pkwy., Birmingham, AL 35243
(205) 870-4000, (800) 782-2040
Internet: www.infinity-insurance.com

P.O. Box 830693, Birmingham, AL 35283-0693

President: James R. Gober

Insurance Company of Greater New York
See Greater N.Y. Mutual Ins. Company / Insurance Co. of Greater N.Y.

Insurance Company of North America
See ACE USA

Integon Casualty Insurance Corporation
See GMAC Insurance Group

Interboro Ins. Co.
Home Office
155 Mineola Blvd., Mineola 11501
(516) 248-1100; Claims Fax: (516) 248-0211;
Legal Fax: (516) 248-1194

V.P., Claims: Joseph F. Polak, Ext. 219

Legal Counsel: Jerry Cohen
Formerly Interboro Mutual Indemnity Ins. Co.

Investors Insurance Co. of America
See Markel Corporation

Kansas City Fire & Marine Insurance Co.
See Encompass Insurance

Kemper Casualty Ins. Co.
See Kemper Insurance Companies

Kemper Insurance Companies
National Headquarters
1 Kemper Dr., Long Grove, IL 60049
(847) 320-2000, (877) 536-7376; Fax: (847) 320-2228
Internet: www.kemperinsurance.com

President/C.E.O.: Doug Andrews

Claims Mgr.: James Hawkins
Company stopped underwriting commercial insurance policies effective June 1, 2003. Contact customer relations (800) 833-0355 for more information

Kemper Lloyd's Ins. Co.
See Kemper Insurance Companies

Leader National Insurance Co. Personal Lines
See Infinity Insurance

Liberty International Underwriters
Home Office
55 Water St., 18th Floor, N.Y.C. 10041
(212) 208-4100; Fax: (212) 208-4112
Internet: www.libertyiu.com

V.P., Home & Yacht Claims: Alex McCarthy; Fax: (212) 208-4230

Liberty Mutual Insurance Co.
National Headquarters
175 Berkeley St., Boston, MA 02116
(617) 357-9500; Fax: (617) 350-7648
Internet: www.libertymutual.com

President/C.E.O.: Edmund F. Kelly

Sr. V.P.'s & General Claims Mgr.:
Paul Rodliff, Mail Stop 08-B, Ext. 45640
Edward Gramer (Personal Market)
Mail Stop S-2B, Ext. 43519

Sr. V.P. & General Counsel: Christopher C. Mansfield
Mail Stop 07-D, Ext. 45672

Liberty Mutual Insurance Group
Personal, Auto & Homeowners Claims
50 Charles Lindbergh Blvd. CS 500, Uniondale 11553
(516) 222-6060, (800) 225-2467; Fax: (516) 222-0478
Claims Mgrs.:
Joe Schnur (Homeowners), Ext. 81167
Sandra Simon (Bodily Injury), Ext. 81092
Brooklyn, Queens, Staten Island & Nassau County

Liberty Mutual Insurance Group
Personal, Auto & Homeowners Claims
3 Lear Jet Lane, Latham 12110
Mailing Address: P.O. Box 15041, Albany 12212-5041
(518) 782-2541, (800) 252-5730; Fax: (518) 782-2556
Internet: libertymutual.com
Claims Mgr.: Mark Zanta, Ext. 86447

Liberty Mutual Insurance Group
National Market Auto/Liability Claims Office
70 Sunrise Hwy., Suite 618, P.O. Box 9001,
Valley Stream 11582
(516) 593-8200, (800) 441-0122; Fax: (603) 334-8114
V.P. & Claims Mgr., Liability: James E. Thayer
175 Berkeley St., Boston, MA 02116
(617) 357-9500; Fax: (617) 574-6627
Regional Mgr., Liability: Egon W. Brown
Brooklyn, Queens, Staten Island, Nassau and Suffolk Counties

Liberty Mutual Insurance Group
National Market Claims Workers Compensation
520 White Plains Rd., 6th Floor, Tarrytown 10591
(914) 332-9770; Fax: (603) 334-8112
Manhattan, Bronx, Westchester, Rockland

Liberty Mutual Insurance Group
Business & Commercial Claims
5015 Campuswood Dr., Suite 202, Syracuse 13057
Mailing Address: Workers Comp., P.O. Box 4836,
Syracuse 13221
(315) 433-1144, (800) 962-5157; Fax: (315) 433-9850;
Workers Comp.: (800) 762-5026
Team Mgr.: Karen Liscum, Ext. 282
Business Market Claims: James Hall, Ext. 272
All Other New York Areas—Business Claims

Life Ins. Co. of North America
See CIGNA Companies

Lincoln Ins. Co.
See The Robert Plan

Lumbermen's Mutual Cas. Co.
See Kemper Insurance Companies

MGIC (Mortgage Guaranty Insurance Corp.)
National Headquarters
250 E. Kilbourn Ave., Milwaukee, WI 53202
Mailing Address: P.O. Box 488, Milwaukee, WI 53201
(800) 558-9900; Fax: (800) 353-8781

Dir., Claims Mgr. (Administration): Carie Vos
(414) 347-6608

Exec. V.P., General Counsel & Secretary:
Jeffrey H. Lane
250 E. Kilbourn Ave., Milwaukee, WI 53202
E-mail: jeff_lane@mgic.com

Magna Carta Cos.
Home Office
One Park Ave., 15th Floor, N.Y.C. 10016-5807
(212) 591-9500; (888) One-Park:; Fax: (212) 591-9600;
Claims Fax: (212) 591-9647
Internet: www.psmins.com

C.E.O./Chairman of the Bd.: Andrew L. Furgatch

President/C.O.O.: John T. Hill II

Asst. Secretary, Claims Mgr.: Joseph Gallagher
(Fire & Property)

V.P., Home Office Claims: Theodore Smyk

V.P., Claims: Larry Gaddy

Legal Dept.: Law Offices of Milod, Spitz & DeSantis
(212) 869-3200

Manhattan & Bronx Surface Transit Operating
Authority—Law & Claim Dept. (Home Office)
130 Livingston St., Brooklyn 11201
(718) 330-3000
Internet: www.mta.info

Deputy Chief Counsel/Dir. Claims:
Danielle D. Ruttman (718) 694-3835

Chief Counsel: Wallace Gossett (718) 694-3860

Markel Corporation
310 Hwy. 35 S., Red Bank, NJ 07701
(732) 224-0500, (800) 243-6869; Fax: (732) 741-2266
Internet: www.markelcorp.com

Managing Dir.: Alex Sardinia (804) 525-7074

Director: Mike Van Riper (732) 450-8785
Formerly Investors Underwriting Managers; Markel Underwriting Managers

Maryland Casualty Co.
See Zurich North America

Maryland Insurance Group
See Zurich North America

Maryland Lloyd's
See Zurich North America

Massachusetts Bay Insurance Company
See Hanover Insurance Group

Massachusetts Homeland Insurance Company
See OneBeacon Insurance Group

The Mayflower Insurance Co., Ltd.
See Encompass Insurance

Medical Liability Mutual Insurance Company
2 Park Ave., N.Y.C. 10016
(212) 576-9800, (800) 275-6564; Fax: (212) 576-9717;
(212) 686-4060
E-mail: information@mlmic.com; Internet: www.mlmic.com

President: Robert Menotti, M.D.

V.P.'s:
Tim Krieg
James Robb

A.V.P., Claims: Dennis Lee
Effective July 2001 HUM Group merged with Medical Liability Mutual Insurance Company
8 British American Blvd., Latham 12110
(518) 786-2700; Fax: (518) 786-2707
E-mail: information@mlmic.com
Internet: www.humgroup.com; www.mlmic.com
President, MLMIC: Robert Menotti, M.D. (518) 786-2700
Asst. V.P.: Bill Fellner (518) 786-2795

Merchants and Business Men's Insurance Co.
See Liberty Mutual Insurance Co.

Merchants Insurance Group
Home Office
250 Main St., Buffalo 14202
(716) 849-3333; Fax: (716) 849-3105, 849-3200
Internet: www.merchantsgroup.com

Claims Mgr.: Jonathan Perkins (716) 849-3250

Merchant's Mutual Insurance Co.
See Merchants Insurance Group

Merchants National Ins. Co.
See Merchants Insurance Group

Merchants Preferred Insurance Co.
See Merchants Insurance Group

MetLife
Auto & Home
700 Quaker Lane, West Warwick, RI 02893
Mailing Address: P.O. Box 350, Warwick, RI 02887
(401) 885-7300; Fax: (401) 827-2358
Internet: www.metlife.com

1600 Division Rd., West Warwick, RI 02893
(401) 885-7300

C.E.O.: C. Robert Henrikson (401) 827-2000

Exec. V.P./General Counsel: James L. Lipscomb
1 MetLife Plaza, 27-01 Queens Plz. N.,
Long Island City 11101 (212) 578-2211

Michigan Mutual Ins. Co.
See Amerisure Companies

Middlesex Insurance Company
See Sentry Claims Service

Midwestern Insurance Company
See OneBeacon Insurance Group

Montgomery Mutual Insurance Co.
See Liberty Mutual Insurance Co.

Motorists Mutual Insurance Company
See American Hardware Mutual Insurance Company

Mountbatten Surety Co.
See Zurich North America

N.A.S.
See Swiss Re

N.Y.C. Transit Authority—Law Dept.
130 Livingston St., Brooklyn 11201
(718) 694-3860; Fax: (718) 694-1023

V.P. & General Counsel: Martin B. Schnabel
(718) 694-3900

Chief Counsel: Wallace D. Gossett (718) 694-3860

Deputy Chief Counsel/Dir., Claims: Danielle D. Ruttman

National Fire & Marine Insurance Co.
See Berkshire Hathaway Insurance Group

National Fire Insurance Co. of Hartford
See CNA / Insurance Companies

National Indemnity Company
See Berkshire Hathaway Insurance Group

National Indemnity Company of Mid-America
See Berkshire Hathaway Insurance Group

National Indemnity Company of the South
See Berkshire Hathaway Insurance Group

National Liability & Fire Insurance Company
See Berkshire Hathaway Insurance Group

National-Ben Franklin Insurance Co. of Illinois
See Encompass Insurance

Nationwide Insurance Company
National Headquarters
1 Nationwide Plaza, Columbus, OH 43215-2220
(614) 249-7111; Internet: www.nationwide.com

C.E.O.: Steve S. Rasmussen

Exec. V.P./General Counsel: Patricia R. Hatler

State Operations Office
P.O. Box 2069, Syracuse 13220
(315) 451-4660, (800) 992-5358
Claims Mgr.: Peter Arcuri, Ext. 3377;
Fax: (315) 453-3367; (866) 509-7973

The Netherlands Insurance Co.
See Peerless Insurance Company

New York Central Mutual Fire Insurance Co.
1899 Central Plaza E., Edmeston 13335
(607) 965-8321, (888) 234-6926; Fax: (607) 965-2136, 965-2712
Internet: www.nycm.com

Claims Mgr.: Tim Trueworthy

North River Insurance Co.
See Crum and Forster Insurance

Northern Insurance Co. of New York
See Zurich North America

Northwestern Pacific Indemnity Co.
See Chubb Group of Insurance Companies

Ocean Harbor Insurance Company
See Country-Wide Insurance Company

Ohio Casualty Insurance Company
400 Laurel Oak Rd., Suite 3, Voorhees, NJ 08043
Mailing Address: P.O. Box 1951, Voorhees, NJ 08043-9051
(856) 435-2800; Fax: (877) 343-1335

V.P., Claims: Andrew Marquart
E-mail: andy.marquart@ocas.com

Ohio Casualty of New Jersey, Inc.
See Ohio Casualty Insurance Company

Ohio Security Ins. Co.
See Ohio Casualty Insurance Company

OneBeacon America Insurance Company
See OneBeacon Insurance Group

OneBeacon Insurance Company
See OneBeacon Insurance Group

OneBeacon Insurance Group
National Headquarters
One Beacon Ln., Canton, MA 02021
(781) 332-7000; Fax: (781) 332-7969
Internet: www.onebeacon.com

C.E.O.: T. Michael Miller

Chief Counsel: Bradford W. Rich

6400 Sheridan Dr., Suite 300, Williamsville 14221
(716) 932-2000, 932-1500; Fax: (716) 932-9290

Workers Compensation, P.O. Box 302, Buffalo 14240-5155
Workers Comp. Claims Mgr.: David Johnson
Claims Supervisors:
Margaret Attardo (716) 932-2000
Brett Brady (716) 932-9224
Steven Schwagler (716) 932-9255
Claims Mgrs.:
Anthony M. Coia (716) 932-1559
Michael Zimmerman (716) 932-1566

1000 Woodbury Rd., Woodbury 11797
(516) 682-2100
Commercial Claims Mgr.: Kevin Pendergast
E-mail: kpendergast@onebeacon.com

OneBeacon Lloyd's of Texas
See OneBeacon Insurance Group

OneBeacon Midwest Insurance Company
See OneBeacon Insurance Group

Pacific Indemnity Company
See Chubb Group of Insurance Companies

Paramount Insurance Company
See Magna Carta Cos.

Partner Reinsurance Company of the U.S.
1 Greenwich Plz., Greenwich, CT 06830-6352
(203) 485-4200; Fax: (203) 485-4300
Internet: www.partnerre/default.aspx.com
Sr. V.P./Claims Mgr.: CarolAnn O'Dea, J.D.
Asst. V.P.'S, Claims:
Yerger Morehead James Sanchez
V.P.'s:
Gregory Gale Joan Shaw
Kenneth Graham

Patriot General Insurance Co.
See Sentry Claims Service

Peerless Insurance Co.
See Liberty Mutual Insurance Co.

Peerless Insurance Company
National Headquarters
62 Maple Ave., Keene, NH 03431
(603) 352-3221, (800) 542-5385; Legal Fax: (603) 358-4616;
Claims Fax: (603) 352-4363, (800) 526-0675
Internet: www.peerless-ins.com
President/C.E.O.: Michael Christiansen
V.P., General Counsel: Michael John DiRusso
(603) 357-9558; Fax: (603) 358-4616
Regional Mgr., Claims: Bill Davidson (603) 357-9581

Syracuse Regional Office (N.Y. & N.J.)
5062 Brittonfield Pkwy., P.O. Box 4858,
East Syracuse 13057
Mailing Address: P.O. Box 4858, Syracuse 13221-4858
(315) 431-6100, (800) 443-4000;
Fax: (315) 431-6102, (800) 526-0681
Regional V.P.: Joseph Headd
Claims Mgr.: Paul Silva

Southern New England Regional Office (CT & RI)
795 Brook St., Rocky Hill, CT 06067
Mailing Address: P.O. Box 5029, Hartford, CT 06102-5029
(860) 563-2371, (800) 842-3805; CT Fax: (800) 526-1347;
RI Fax: (800) 526-0612

Penn National Insurance
2 N. Second St., Suite 2, Harrisburg, PA 17101
Mailing Address: P.O. Box 2361,
Harrisburg, PA 17105-2361
(717) 234-4941, (800) 388-4764; Fax: (717) 255-6317
Internet: www.pennnationalinsurance.com
President/C.E.O.: Kenneth Shutts
Chairman: Dennis C. Rowe
Claims Mgr.: Joe Holland
Member of Penn National Insurance

Pennsylvania General Insurance Co.
See OneBeacon Insurance Group

Physicians' Reciprocal Insurers
1800 Northern Blvd., P.O. Box 9007, Roslyn 11576
(516) 365-6690, (800) 632-6040, (888) 526-4006;
Fax: (516) 365-5342, 365-5714
E-mail: claims@medmal.com; Internet: www.primedmal.com
C.E.O.: Anthony J. Bonomo

Potomac Insurance Company
See OneBeacon Insurance Group

Progressive Casualty Insurance Company
6300 Wilson Mills Rd., Mayfield Village, OH 44143-2182
(440) 461-5000; Claims: (800) 776-4737; Fax: (440) 446-7168
Internet: www.progressive.com
Member of Progressive Insurance Group

Protection Mutual Insurance Co.
See FM Global

Public Service Mutual Ins. Cos.
See Magna Carta Cos.

QBE Insurance Company
See Country-Wide Insurance Company

Quadrant Indemnity Co.
See Chubb Group of Insurance Companies

Reliance Insurance Companies in Liquidation
National Headquarters
Three Parkway, Philadelphia, PA 19102-1376
(215) 864-4000; Claims Information: (800) 441-1652
Claims Information E-mail:
liquidator@relianceinsurance.com
Internet: www.relianceinsurance.com

Republic Fire & Casualty Ins. Co.
See The Republic Group

The Republic Group
National Headquarters
5525 LBJ Freeway, Dallas, TX 75240
(972) 788-6001, (800) 344-2275; Fax: (972) 788-6099
Internet: www.republicgroup.com
V.P., Claims: Stephen D. Johnson

Republic Lloyd's
See The Republic Group

Republic Underwriters Ins. Co
See The Republic Group

Republic-Franklin Insurance Co.
See Utica National Insurance Group

Republic-Vanguard Ins. Co.
See The Republic Group

Risk Enterprise Management Limited
National Headquarters
2540 Route 130, Suite 109, Cranbury, NJ 08512
(609) 495-0300, 495-0001; Fax: (609) 495-0252
Internet: www.remltd.com
President/C.E.O.: Michael J. Riney
(609) 495-0016; Fax: (609) 495-0250
V.P., General Counsel: Timothy McIntyre
(609) 495-0050; Fax: (609) 495-2030
Senior V.P., Field Claim Operations: Paula Maguire
(609) 495-0018; Fax: (609) 495-0250
V.P., Home Office Claims: John Tobey
(609) 495-0059; Fax: (609) 495-2085

The Robert Plan
999 Stewart Ave., Bethpage 11714
(516) 393-6500; Fax: (516) 393-6592
Internet: www.rpc.com
President/C.E.O.: Robert M. Wallach
General Counsel & Sr. V.P.: Jasper Jackson

Royal Indemnity Co.
See Arrowpoint Capital Corp.

Royal Ins. Co. of America
See Arrowpoint Capital Corp.

Royal Special Risks Ins. Co.
See Arrowpoint Capital Corp.

Royal Surplus Lines Ins. Co.
See Arrowpoint Capital Corp.

Safeguard Ins. Co.
See Arrowpoint Capital Corp.

Safety National Scottsdale
See Risk Enterprise Management Limited

St. Paul Fire and Marine Insurance Co. Personal Lines
See MetLife

Selective Insurance Co. of America
National Headquarters
40 Wantage Ave., Branchville, NJ 07890
(973) 948-3000; Fax: (973) 948-0282
EVP, Chief Claims Officer: Vacancy at Press Time
EV.P., General Counsel & Corporate Secretary:
Michael H. Lanza

Selective Insurance Company of America and its Subsidiaries
See Selective Insurance Co. of America

Sentry Claims Service
National Headquarters
1800 N. Point Dr., Stevens Point, WI 54481
Claims Ctr.: (715) 346-9200, (800) 443-9655;
Fax: (715) 346-9040
Internet: www.sentry.com
C.E.O.: Dale Schuh (715) 346-6000
V.P., General Counsel & Corp. Secy.:
William M. O'Reilly (715) 346-6000

Sentry Claims Service Center
3 Carlisle Rd., P.O. Box 584, Westford, MA 01886-0584
(978) 392-7000; Claims: (800) 225-1390; Fax: (978) 392-7033
Claims Dir.: Kathy Fleming (978) 392-7288

Sentry Insurance Co.
See Sentry Claims Service

Sentry Select Ins. Co.
See Sentry Claims Service

Signet Star Reinsurance Company
National Headquarters
475 Steamboat Rd., P.O. Box 2519, Greenwich, CT 06836
(203) 542-3200; Fax: (203) 542-3290
Internet: www.signetstar.com
President/C.E.O.: Jon Schriber (203) 542-3213
Senior V.P., Claims: Kevin Shea (203) 542-3271
E-mail: kshea@signetstar.com

Southern County Mutual Ins. Co.
See The Republic Group

Southern Ins. Co.
See The Republic Group

Southern Underwriters Ins. Co.
See The Republic Group

Southern Vanguard Ins. Co.
See The Republic Group

Specialty Surplus Ins. Co.
See Kemper Insurance Companies

St. Paul/Travelers, XL Specialty, Zurich
See Risk Enterprise Management Limited

State Farm Mutual Automobile Insurance Co.
National Headquarters
1 State Farm Plaza, Bloomington, IL 61710
(309) 766-2311
Internet: www.statefarm.com
Chair/C.E.O.: Edward B. Rust, Jr.
Chief Counsel: Kim Brunner

State Farm Fire & Casualty
Parsippany Operations Center
300 Kimball Dr., Parsippany, NJ 07054
(973) 739-5000, 739-6321; Fax: (888) 559-2022
Claims Mgr.: David Ziemer (Auto) (973) 739-5141
Section Mgr.: Thad Holman (973) 739-6332

1981 Marcus Ave., Suite 100, Lake Success 11042
(516) 355-3000
Claims Team Mgrs.:
Brianne Dunn (516) 355-3410
Bernie Henao (516) 355-3116
Kelly Malone
Patrick Reilly (516) 355-3433
Linda Sgambati (516) 355-3414
Stephanie Watkins (516) 355-3612
Auto & Homeowners Claims,
1305 Walt Whitman Rd., Suite 300,
Melville 11747-4300
(631) 385-6500

State Farm Insurance
100 State Farm Pl., Ballston Spa 12020
(518) 884-5000, (888) 326-0164; Fax: (800) 868-1456

State Farm Claims Service Information
100 Meridian Centre Blvd., Suite 220, Rochester 14618
(585) 241-7600, (800) 822-4105;
Fax: (800) 868-1456, (888) 863-4565
Claims Mgr.: James M. Radford (585) 241-7644

State-Wide Insurance Co.
Home Office
901 Franklin Ave., Garden City 11530
Mailing Address: P.O. Box 9301, Hempstead 11550-9301
(516) 564-8000; Claims Fax: (516) 564-8017;
Legal Fax: (516) 564-1714
Internet: www.state-wideinsurance.com
Asst. V.P./Claims Mgr.: Don McVeigh
Ext. 26259
E-mail: dmcveigh@state-wideinsurance.com
Asst. Mgr., Claims: Richard Tomlin
Ext. 26270
Chief Counsel: James Hiebler
Ext. 26252

Steadfast Ins. Co.
See Zurich North America

Sterling Insurance Co.
Home Office
182 Barnerville Rd., P.O. Box 9, Cobleskill 12043-0009
(518) 234-2521; Fax: (518) 234-3167
Sr. V.P., Claims: James B. Hogan, Jr.
Fax: (518) 234-8570
E-mail: jhogan@sterlingins.com

Summit Holding Southeast, Inc.
See Liberty Mutual Insurance Co.

SunAlliance
See Arrowpoint Capital Corp.

Swiss Re
5200 Metcalf Ave., Overland Park, KS 66201
(913) 676-5200, (800) 255-6931; Fax: (813) 676-5221
Internet: www.swissre.com
175 King St., Armonk 10504
(914) 828-8050
55 E. 52nd St., N.Y.C. 10055
(212) 317-5400

Texas Pacific Indemnity Co.
See Chubb Group of Insurance Companies

The Employers' Fire Insurance Company
See OneBeacon Insurance Group

The Hartford Financial Services Group, Inc.
National Headquarters
One Hartford Plz., Hartford, CT 06155
(860) 547-5000
Internet: www.thehartford.com
Chairman/C.E.O.: Liam McGee
General Counsel: Alan J. Kreczko

Hartford Insurance Group
Northeast PL Claim Service Center (Key Office 976)
8 Farm Springs Rd., Farmington, CT 06032
Mailing Address: P.O. Box 14268,
Lexington, KY 40512-4268
(800) 280-0555, 409-8000, (859) 422-3378;
Fax: (866) 809-9794
Regional V.P.'s:
Gordon Engstrom, Ext. 28339
James Walz, Ext. 28277

Hartford Insurance Group
Northeast CA&L Claims Service Center (Key Office 408)
8 Farm Springs Rd., Farmington, CT 06032
Mailing Address: P.O. Box 14269,
Lexington, KY 40512-4269
(888) 625-2652, (859) 422-3379; Fax: (866) 809-9795
Director in Charge: Phil Lamb (860) 284-2260

Hartford Financial Services Group, Inc.—Cont'd

Hartford Insurance Group
Northeast WC Claim Center (Key Office 402)
One Park Place, 7th Floor, 300 S. State St.,
Syracuse 13202
Mailing Address: P.O. Box 4771, Syracuse 13221
(315) 385-6000, (877) 469-9222; Fax: (877) 536-3201
Regional V.P.: Mary O'Connor, Ext. 55937

Hartford Insurance Group
Syracuse WC Claim Xchange Center (Key Office 977)
One Park Pl., 300 S. State St., Syracuse 13202
(MedBill): (800) 662-5814; Fax: (315) 478-8999;
(Med only): (888) 235-2304; Fax: (315) 385-5121
Director: Michael Lobevero
Manager: Robin Moleski

The Northern Assurance Company of America
See OneBeacon Insurance Group

The State Insurance Fund
199 Church St., 12th Floor, N.Y.C. 10007
(212) 312-9000; Safety Group Office No. 1: (212) 587-9208;
Safety Group Office No. 1 Fax: (212) 312-7726;
Safety Group Office No. 2: (212) 587-7389;
Safety Group Office No. 2 Fax: (212) 587-4994, 312-7726;
Metro Group 90: (212) 587-2131;
Metro Group 90 Fax: (212) 587-5299
Internet: www.nysif.com

Dir. of Claims: Edward Hiller (212) 312-7880

Deputy Dir. of Claims: Marilyn Carretta (212) 312-7306

Claims Services Mgr., Safety Group Office No. 1: Charles Tedaldi (212) 578-9212

Claims Services Mgr., Safety Group Office No. 2: Louis Vassallo (212) 587-4912

Claims Services Mgrs., Metro 90:
Martha Golden (212) 587-2134
Rita Fenton (212) 312-7379

One Watervliet Ave. Ext., Albany 12206-1649
(518) 437-6400; Fax: (518) 437-8026
Claims Mgr.: Christopher Rattazzi (518) 437-6969

225 Oak St., Buffalo 14203
(716) 851-2000; Fax (Administration): (716) 851-2131
Principal Comp. Claims Examiner: Edward Fries (716) 851-9175

Nassau District Office
8 Corporate Center Dr., 2nd Floor, Melville 11747-3166
(631) 756-4000; Fax: (631) 756-4070
Claims Mgr.: Eric Parsons
(631) 756-4100; Fax: (631) 756-4111

100 Chestnut St., Suite 1000, Rochester 14604-6950
(585) 258-2000; Fax: (585) 258-2065
Claims Services Mgr.: Patty Albert
(585) 258-2134; Fax: (585) 258-8184
E-mail: palbert@nysif.com

1045 7th North St., Liverpool 13088
(315) 453-6500; Fax: (315) 453-8313
Claims Services Mgr.: Sheila Fritz
(315) 453-6639; Fax: (315) 453-6576

105 Corporate Park Dr., Suite 200, White Plains 10604
(914) 701-2120; Fax: (914) 701-2190
Claims Services Mgr.: Trevor Jackson
(914) 701-2194; Fax: (914) 701-2180

Suffolk District Office
8 Corporate Center Dr., 3rd Floor, Melville 11747-3129
(631) 756-4300; Fax (Legal): (631) 756-4273
Claims Mgr.: Tony Hawkins (631) 756-4258

2001 Perimeter Rd. E., Endicott 13760-7390
(607) 741-3900; Fax: (607) 741-5029
Claims Services Mgr.: Joe Pavlovich (607) 741-3928

Traders & General Insurance Company
See OneBeacon Insurance Group

Transcontinental Insurance Company
See CNA / Insurance Companies

Transcontinental Technical Services, Inc.
See CNA / Insurance Companies

Transportation Insurance Company
See CNA / Insurance Companies

Travelers
National Headquarters
385 Washington St., St. Paul, MN 55102-1396
(651) 310-7911, (800) 842-3073;
Fax (Workers Comp.): (877) 389-4682;
Fax (Liability): (877) 288-2793
Internet: www.stpaultravelers.com

Chair/C.E.O.: Jay S. Fishman

Vice Chair/C.F.O.: Jay S. Benet (860) 277-0111

General Counsel/Exec. V.P.: Kenneth F. Spence III (860) 277-0111

Exec. V.P., Claims: Doreen Spadorcia (860) 277-0111
Formerly St. Paul Travelers

Long Island Claims Office
100 Baylis Rd., 3rd Floor, Melville 11747-3931
(800) 987-4735; Fax: (866) 889-8376
Claims Mgr.: Michael Daly, Ext. 7265
Associate Mgr.: Helaine Aledort (Workers Comp) Ext. 7203
Liability Mgr.: Connie O'Hara (631) 577-7249
Regional Property Mgr.: Michael Rashbaum (631) 577-7598

Albany Claims Office
900 Watervliet-Shaker Rd., Albany 12205
(800) 223-4820; Fax: (866) 422-8263

Workers Compensation, P.O. Box 466, Albany 12201-0466

Personal Home & Auto Claims, P.O. Box 22005, Albany 12201-2005

Commercial Liability Claims, P.O. Box 10069, Albany 12201-0069
Claim Center V.P.: Hank McCourt (518) 862-7900

Buffalo Service Ctr.
All Commercial Lines, P.O. Box 4614, Buffalo 14240-4614
(800) 662-2310; Fax: (716) 855-5050;
Claims Fax: (877) 749-0037

Personal Home & Auto Claims, P.O. Box 430, Buffalo 14240-0430

New Jersey Claims Office
343 Thornall St., Edison, NJ 08837
Mailing Address: Liability, P.O. Box 203, Iselin, NJ 08830
(732) 494-3800, (800) 272-1088; Fax: (732) 494-9505

Travelers Property & Casualty Insurance
See Travelers

U.S. Fire Insurance Co.
See Crum and Forster Insurance

Unigard Insurance Company
National Headquarters
15805 N.E. 24th St., Bellevue, WA 98008-2409
Mailing Address: P.O. Box 90701,
Bellevue, WA 98009-0701
(425) 641-4321, (800) 777-1757; Fax: (425) 562-5311
Internet: www.unigard.com

Corporate Secretary: Jennifer Vernon

Chief Corp. Counsel: Jennifer Vernon (608) 825-5827
E-mail: jenifer.vernon@us.gbe.com

Claims V.P.: Mike Bondura

United States Fidelity & Guaranty Co.
See Travelers

Universal Bonding Ins. Co.
See Kemper Insurance Companies

Universal Insurance Company
770 Highland Oaks Dr., Winston Salem, NC 27103
Mailing Address: P.O. Box 25687,
Winston Salem, NC 27114
(336) 771-0400, (800) 288-8050; Fax: (336) 771-0417
Internet: www.seibels-uic.com
Dir., Claims: Kevin T. Roberson, CPCU, AIC
Member of Seibels Bruce Group

Utica Mutual Insurance Co.
See Utica National Insurance Group

Utica National Insurance Group
Home Office
180 Genesee St., New Hartford 13413
Mailing Address: P.O. Box 530, Utica 13503-0530
(315) 734-2000, (800) 274-1914; Fax: (315) 734-2662
Internet: www.uticanational.com
V.P./Sr. Claims Officer/General Counsel:
Richard Creedon, Ext. 2302

N.Y. Metro Regional Office
1 Jericho Plaza, Wing A, 2nd Floor, Jericho 11753-1636
(516) 479-5000, (800) 766-1914; Fax: (516) 479-5001
Regional Claims Mgr.: Paul J. Salvato
E-mail: paul.salvato@uticanational.com

Eastern Regional Office
201 Lafayette St., Utica 13502
(315) 235-6600; Toll-Free: (866) 860-1914;
Toll-Free Fax: (800) 399-4640
E-mail: webcid@uticanational.com
Regional Mgr.: John Griffin

Albany District Claims Office
119 Great Oaks Blvd., Albany 12203
(518) 862-6200; Toll Free: (866) 365-1914;
Fax: (518) 862-6299
Manager: Russell L. Phillips

Amherst Claims Office
130 John Muir Dr., Suite 400, Amherst 14228
(716) 639-2300; Toll Free: (800) 765-1914;
Fax: (716) 639-2301
Manager: Sean McGovern

East Windsor Claims Office
Windsor Corporate Park, 50 Millstone Rd.,
East Windsor, NJ 08520
(609) 308-4500; Toll Free: (800) 759-1914;
Fax: (609) 308-4599
Manager: Joseph Smith

New England Regional Office
201 Edgewater Dr., Suite 295, Wakefield, MA 01880
(781) 224-2600; Toll Free: (800) 695-1914;
Fax: (781) 224-2699
Mgr., Claims: Gary Moran
Regional V.P.: Anthony Sychtysz

Valiant Insurance Co.
See Zurich North America

Vigilant Insurance Co.
See Chubb Group of Insurance Companies

Wausau Insurance Cos.
See Liberty Mutual Insurance Co.

Wesco-Financial Insurance Co.
See Berkshire Hathaway Insurance Group

Western Select Insurance Co.
See Magna Carta Cos.

Westport
See Swiss Re

Windsor Insurance Co. Personal Lines
See Infinity Insurance

York Insurance Company of Maine
See OneBeacon Insurance Group

Zurich Insurance Co.
See Zurich North America

Zurich North America
National Headquarters
Zurich Towers, 1400 American Ln.,
Schaumburg, IL 60196-1056
(847) 605-6000; Fax (Claims): (877) 962-2567
Internet: www.zurichna.com
C.E.O.: Mike Foley (North America)
Exec. V.P., Corporate Law: Dennis Kerrigan
(847) 605-6120
Regional V.P., New York Regional Office:
Vacancy at Press Time
One Liberty Plz., 28th Floor, N.Y.C. 10006
(212) 553-5607; Fax: (212) 553-5300

Workers Comp. & General Liability Claims Office
58 S. Service Rd., Suite 300, Melville 11747-2342
(631) 845-2200; Fax (Claims): (631) 845-2535;
Fax (Policy Admin. & Premium Acctng.: (631) 845-2652
A.V.P., Claims: Joseph Salerno
(631) 845-2341; Fax: (631) 845-2429
E-mail: joseph.salerno@zurichna.com
Covers Claims for Manhattan, Brooklyn, Bronx, Nassau, Queens, Richmond, Suffolk; also counties of Orange, Putnam, Rockland and Westchester

Zurich-American Insurance Co. of Illinois
See Zurich North America

Zurich-American Lloyds
See Zurich North America

INSURANCE COMPANIES AUTHORIZED TO DO BUSINESS IN NEW YORK

LISTED ACCORDING TO THE IDENTIFICATION NUMBERS USED BY POLICE DEPARTMENTS

Source: New York State Department of Insurance

You will find this list convenient to use when you find an Insurance Company identified on a Police Report simply by its number without its name.

001 Travelers Property Casualty Insurance Co.
004 ACE Property & Casualty Insurance Co.
005 Encompass Home & Auto Insurance
007 Great American Alliance Insurance Co.
010 Travelers Indemnity Co. of America
011 Allstate Insurance Co.
012 Allstate Indemnity Co.
013 Protective Insurance Co.
014 American Automobile Insurance Co.
015 American Casualty Co. of Reading, PA
017 Encompass Independent Insurance Co.
018 Union Insurance Co.
019 Response Insurance Co. of America
020 American and Foreign Insurance Co.
021 Ocean Harbor Casualty Insurance Co.
022 SPARTA Insurance Co.
023 Great American Assurance Co.
024 Praetorian Insurance Co.
025 American Guarantee & Liability Insurance Co.
026 American Hardware Mutual Insurance Co.
027 American Home Assurance Co.
028 American Insurance Co.
029 American Protection Insurance Co.
030 American Manufacturers Mutual Insurance Co.
031 American Motorists Insurance Co.
032 Atlantic States Insurance Co.
033 Great American Insurance Co. of NY
034 Villanova Insurance Co.
035 Pacific Specialty Insurance Co.
036 American Transit Insurance Co.
037 Encompass Insurance Co. of America
038 National Continental Insurance Co.
039 Amica Mutual Insurance Co.
040 AMEX Assurance Co.
041 Amerisure Insurance Co.
042 Essentia Insurance Co.
043 Associated Indemnity Corp.
044 Assurance Co. of America
045 Atlantic Mutual Insurance Co.
049 IDS Property & Casualty Insurance Co.
050 Travelers Casualty Co. of Connecticut
051 Travelers Commercial Insurance Co.
052 Balboa Insurance Co.
053 American Economy Insurance Co.
054 American States Insurance Co.
055 Old Republic General Insurance Corp.
056 American International Insurance Co.
057 Bankers Standard Insurance Co.
059 AIG Casualty Co.
061 American Modern Home Insurance Co.
066 Blue Ridge Insurance Co.
067 AXIS Reinsurance Co.
068 Response Indemnity Co. of Delaware
069 Esurance Insurance Co.
070 21st Century Insurance Co.
071 A. Central Insurance Co.
072 Specialty National Insurance Co.
073 Camden Fire Insurance Association
074 Kemper Casualty Insurance Co.
075 Clarendon National Insurance Co.
076 Centennial Insurance Co.
077 Central Mutual Insurance Co.
078 First Central Insurance Co.
079 Drivers Insurance Co.
080 Charter Oak Fire Insurance Co.
082 Carolina Casualty Insurance Co.
083 Response Worldwide Direct Auto Insurance Co.
084 Hartford Casualty Insurance Co.
085 Northeast Mutual Insurance Co.
087 Commerce & Industry Insurance Co.
089 OneBeacon America Insurance Co.
090 Merchants & Business Men's Mutual Ins. Co.
091 Colonial Cooperative Insurance Co.
092 Connecticut Indemnity Co.
093 Encompass Property & Casualty Insurance Co.
095 American Alternative Insurance Corp.
097 Continental Casualty Co.
098 Continental Insurance Co.
099 Response Insurance Co.
100 GEICO Indemnity Co.
101 GEICO Casualty Co.
102 Encompass Indemnity Co.
103 American Reliable Insurance Co.
105 Seneca Insurance Co. Inc.
106 National Merit Insurance Co.
107 Empire Insurance Co.
108 Employers Fire Insurance Co.
110 Employers Mutual Casualty Co.
111 Empire Fire & Marine Insurance Co.
112 Employers Insurance Co. of Wausau
113 Erie Insurance Co.
114 Commercial Guaranty Casualty Insurance Co.
115 Coregis Insurance Co.
116 Excelsior Insurance Co.
117 Selective Insurance Co. of New York
118 Clearwater Insurance Co.
119 Markel Insurance Co.
120 Farm Family Casualty Insurance Co.
122 Federated Mutual Insurance Co.
123 Everest National Insurance Co.
124 Federal Insurance Co.
125 Markel American Insurance Insurance Co.
126 Admiral Indemnity Co.
127 Fidelity and Casualty Co. of New York
128 Dairyland Insurance Co.
129 Fidelity & Guaranty Insurance Underwriters, Inc.
130 Continental Western Insurance Co.
131 Firemen's Fund Insurance Co.
132 Firemen's Insurance Co. of Newark, New Jersey
133 Firemen's Insurance Co. of Washington, D.C.
135 NOVA Casualty Co.
136 Foremost Property & Casualty Insurance Co.
138 Rampart Insurance Co.
139 Seabright Insurance Co.
140 General Insurance Co. of America
142 Hartford Insurance Co. of IL
146 Chubb Indemnity Insurance Co.
147 Globe Indemnity Co.
148 Government Employees Insurance Co.
149 Erie Insurance Co. of NY
151 Granite State Insurance Co.
152 Graphic Arts Mutual Insurance Co.
153 U.S. Surety Co.
154 Great American Insurance Co.
155 Great Northern Insurance Co.
156 Greater New York Mutual Insurance Co.
157 Harco National Insurance Co.
158 Hanover Insurance Co.
159 Blue Ridge Indemnity Co.
160 Sentry Insurance A Mutual Co.
161 Hartford Accident & Indemnity Co.
162 Hartford Fire Insurance Co.
164 Holyoke Mutual Insurance Co. in Salem
166 American Commerce Insurance Co.
169 Nationwide Insurance Co. of America
171 XL Specialty Insurance Co.
172 Indemnity Insurance Co. of North America
173 Insurance Company of North America
174 AXA Re Property & Casualty Insurance Co.
175 Insurance Co. of the State of Pennsylvania
176 Interboro Insurance Co.
178 Interstate Indemnity Co.
181 Kansas City Fire & Marine Insurance Co.
182 Liberty Mutual Fire Insurance Co.
183 Liberty Mutual Insurance Co.
184 Nationwide Agribusiness Insurance Co.
186 York Insurance Co.
187 Lion Insurance Co.
189 Landmark Insurance Co.
190 Lumbermen's Mutual Casualty Co.
191 LMI Insurance Co.
192 LM Insurance Corp.
193 First Liberty Insurance Corp.
195 Victoria Fire & Casualty Co.
196 ALEA North America Insurance Co.
197 Acadia Insurance Co.
198 Maryland Casualty Co.
199 Massachusetts Bay Insurance Co.
200 Victoria Select Insurance Co.
203 American European Insurance Co.
204 Merchants Mutual Insurance Co.
207 Michigan Millers Mutual Insurance Co.
208 American Fuji Fire & Marine Insurance Co.
209 Meritplan Insurance Co.
210 GuideOne Specialty Mutual Insurance Co.
211 Metropolitan Prop. & Casualty Insurance Co.
212 New York Marine & General Insurance Co.
213 North East Insurance Co.
214 Amerisure Mutual Insurance Co.
217 Progressive Preferred Insurance Co.
218 Manufacturers Alliance Insurance Co.
219 Metropolitan Group Property & Casualty Ins. Co.
220 Metropolitan Casualty Insurance Co.
221 Metropolitan General Insurance Co.
224 National Fire Insurance Co. of Hartford
225 National General Insurance Co.
226 NMG Insurance Co.
227 National Surety Corp.
228 National Union Fire Ins. Co. of Pittsburgh, PA
229 Legion Insurance Co.
230 Nationwide Mutual Fire Insurance Co.
231 Nationwide Mutual Insurance Co.
232 Netherlands Insurance Co.
233 National Casualty Co.
234 Nationwide Property & Casualty Insurance Co.
235 New Hampshire Insurance Co.
236 Navigators Insurance Co.
237 Rutgers Casualty Insurance Co.
238 New York Municipal Insurance Reciprocal
239 Harleysville Insurance Co. of New York
240 New York Central Mutual Fire Insurance Co.
242 Hartford Underwriters Insurance Co.
244 Newark Insurance Co.
249 St. Paul Protective Insurance Co.
250 North River Insurance Co.
251 NIPPONKOA Insurance Co., Ltd.
252 Northern Assurance Co. of America
253 Discover Property & Casualty Insurance Co.
254 Northern Insurance Co. of New York
255 Empire State Mutual Insurance Co.
256 Seaton Insurance Co.
258 Sentry Casualty Co.
259 National Interstate Insurance Co.
261 Leader Insurance Co.
262 Infinity Insurance Co.
263 Old Republic Insurance Co.
264 Acceleration National Insurance Co.
265 Infinity Select Insurance Co.
266 Aegis Security Insurance Co.
267 AIU Insurance Co.
268 Pacific Indemnity Co.
269 Regal Insurance Co.
271 Integon Casualty Insurance Co.
272 Westport Insurance Corp.
273 Peerless Insurance Co.
274 National General Assurance Co.
275 Pennsylvania General Insurance Co.
276 Pennsylvania Lumbermens Mut. Insurance Co.
277 StarNet Insurance Co.
278 Penn Millers Insurance Co.
279 Pennsylvania National Mutual Casualty Ins. Co.
280 Philadelphia Indemnity Insurance Co.
282 Phoenix Insurance Co.
283 Cherokee Insurance Co.
284 Atlantic Specialty Insurance Co.
285 Technology Insurance Co., Inc.
286 Deerbrook Insurance Co.
287 Preferred Mutual Insurance Co.
288 GuideOne Mutual Insurance Co.
289 Providence Washington Insurance Co.
290 LM Property & Casualty Insurance Co.
291 Public Service Mutual Insurance Co.
293 Royal Insurance Co. of America
294 Reliance National Indemnity Co.
295 Adirondack Insurance Exchange
297 Insurance Corporation of New York
298 Reliance Insurance Co.
302 Arrowood Indemnity Co.
303 Fiduciary Insurance Co. of America
304 SAFECO Insurance Co. of America
305 Safeguard Insurance Co.
306 SAFECO National Insurance Co.
307 Saint Paul Fire and Marine Insurance Co.
308 Saint Paul Mercury Insurance Co.
309 American Agents Insurance Co.
311 AXIS Insurance Co.

312 Great Divide Insurance Co.
313 Property & Casualty Insurance Co. of Hartford
315 Selective Insurance Co. of America
316 Selective Way Insurance Company
318 SAFECO Insurance Co. of Indiana
319 Reliance Direct Insurance Co.
321 Saint Paul Guardian Insurance Co.
322 Hudson Insurance Co.
323 Valiant Insurance Co.
324 All America Insurance Co.
325 Standard Fire Insurance Co.
326 Hereford Insurance Co.
327 State Farm Fire & Casualty Co.
328 State Farm Mutual Automobile Insurance Co.
329 State Wide Insurance Co.
330 Star Insurance Co.
331 OneBeacon Midwest Insurance Co.
332 Mitsui Sumitomo Insurance Co. of America
334 Nationwide Assurance Co.
335 RLI Insurance Co.
337 Garrison Property & Casualty Insurance Co.
338 Tokio Marine & Nichido Fire Insurance Co., Ltd.
339 Maya Assurance Co.
340 Reliance National Insurance Co.
341 Travelers Property Casualty Co. of America
342 Transcontinental Insurance Co.
343 Transportation Insurance Co.
344 Travelers Indemnity Co.
345 MetLife Insurance Co. of Connecticut
346 Truck Insurance Exchange
347 Twin City Fire Insurance Co.
348 Kingston Insurance Co.
349 USAA General Indemnity Co.
351 TravCo Insurance Co.
352 Travelers Home & Marine Insurance Co.
353 United Pacific Insurance Co.
354 Travelers Indemnity Co. of Connecticut
355 United Services Automobile Assn.
356 USAA Casualty Insurance Co.
357 United States Fidelity & Guaranty Co.
358 United States Fire Insurance Co.
359 Unitrin Preferred Insurance Co.
360 Scottsdale Indemnity Co.
361 Tower Insurance Co. of NY
362 Federated Service Insurance Co.
363 Utica First Insurance Co.
364 Utica Mutual Insurance Co.
365 Universal Underwriters Insurance Co.
366 Valley Forge Insurance Co.
367 XL Insurance America Inc.
368 Vigilant Insurance Co.
369 United Pacific Insurance Co. of New York
370 Wausau Underwriters Insurance Co.
371 Adirondack Indemnity Co.
372 Westchester Fire Insurance Co.
373 Response Worldwide Insurance Co.
374 Wausau Business Insurance Co.
375 Utica National Assurance Co.
376 Regent Insurance Co.
377 Sentinel Insurance Co., Ltd.
378 Sompo Japan Insurance Co. of America
379 Zurich American Insurance Co.
380 Integon Preferred Insurance Co.
381 General Casualty Co. of WI
382 Nationwide General Insurance Co.
383 Integon National Insurance Co.
384 Merastar Insurance Co.
385 Allcity Insurance Co.
386 Main Street America Assurance Co.
389 American Country Insurance Co.
391 Security Indemnity Insurance Co.
392 Foremost Insurance Co.
393 Atlanta Casualty Co.
394 TIG Insurance Corporation of America
395 TIG Insurance Co.
396 TIG Insurance Co. of NY
397 Middlesex Insurance Co.
398 Stonington Insurance Co.
399 Atlanta Specialty Insurance Co.
400 ACE Fire Underwriters Insurance Co.
401 Providence Washington Insurance Co. of NY
402 Fairmont Insurance Co.
404 Lincoln General Insurance Co.
406 American Spirit Insurance Co.
409 Penn-America Insurance Co.
410 Country Wide Insurance Co.
411 Farmers New Century Insurance Co.
412 Trumbull Insurance Co.
413 Progressive Casualty Insurance Group
414 Great American Security Insurance Co.
415 Response Indemnity Co.
416 Eagle Insurance Co.
418 Pennsylvania Manufacturers Indemnity Co.
419 Redland Insurance Co.
421 Mountain Valley Indemnity Co.
422 Pennsylvania Manufacturers' Assn. Insurance Co.
423 Pacific Employers Insurance Co.
424 Fidelity & Deposit Insurance Co. of Maryland
425 Crum & Forster Indemnity Co.
426 New Jersey Manufacturers Insurance Co.
427 First National Insurance Co. of America
428 Long Island Insurance Co.
429 United National Specialty Insurance Co.
430 Eveready Insurance Co.
431 Security Insurance Co. of Hartford
432 New Hampshire Indemnity Co., Inc.
433 Gulf Insurance Co.
435 Lumbermen's Underwriting Alliance
436 Countryway Insurance Co.
438 AIG Advantage Insurance Co.
439 Buckeye Union Insurance Co.
440 American Family Home Insurance Co.
441 TICO Insurance Co.
444 Fairmont Specialty Insurance Co.
446 Unitrin Auto & Home Insurance Co.
447 T.H.E. Insurance Co.
448 CUMIS Insurance Society, Inc.
449 Highlands Insurance Co.
450 Fire & Casualty Insurance Co. of Connecticut
451 General Security National Insurance Co.
453 Insurance Co. of Greater NY
454 Hermitage Insurance Co.
456 United Community Insurance Co.
457 TransGuard Insurance Co. of America, Inc.
458 Horace Mann Insurance Co.
459 Progressive Direct Insurance Co.
460 Utica National Insurance Co. of Texas
461 Victoria National Insurance Co.
462 Unitrin Direct Property & Casualty Co.
463 Electric Insurance Co.
464 American Bankers Insurance Co. of Florida
465 Ohio Casualty Insurance Co.
466 West American Insurance Co.
468 Diamond State Insurance Co.
470 Kemper Independence Insurance Co.
471 American Fire & Casualty Co.
473 WESCO Insurance Co.
474 Great American Contemporary Insurance Co.
475 State National Insurance Co.
476 Century Indemnity Co.
477 AIG Preferred Insurance Co.
478 Allstate Property & Casualty Insurance Co.
479 Mercury Casualty Co.
480 Sentry Select Insurance Co.
481 Gulf Underwriters Insurance Co.
482 AIG Centennial Insurance Co.
483 Warner Insurance Co.
484 New South Insurance Co.
485 Argonaut Insurance Co.
487 ACE American Insurance Co.
489 AIG Indemnity Insurance Co.
490 QBE Insurance Corp.
491 Atlantic Insurance Co.
493 Tower National Insurance Co.
494 ACA Insurance Co.
497 Automobile Insurance Co. of Hartford, CT
498 F&A Casualty Co.
499 Fairfield Insurance Co.
514 Farmers Insurance Exchange
521 Mid Century Insurance Co.
600 Glens Falls Insurance Co.
603 National Ben Franklin Insurance Co. of Illinois
604 Mitsui Sumitomo Insurance USA, Inc.
605 National Union Fire Insurance Co. of PA (NCR)
606 Merchants Preferred Insurance Co.
607 Progressive Northeastern Insurance Co.
608 Economy Premier Assurance Co.
611 Progressive Northwestern Insurance Co.
612 Preferred Professional Insurance Co.
613 Guaranty National Insurance Co.
614 AIG National Insurance Co.
617 Centurion Insurance Co.
618 LM General Insurance Co.
619 Republic Western Insurance Co.
620 Progressive Northern Insurance Co.
621 Patriot General Insurance Co.
622 OneBeacon Insurance Co.
624 Fidelity and Guaranty Insurance Co.
626 Progressive Specialty Insurance Co.
627 Housing Authority Property Ins., A Mutual Co.
628 Illinois National Insurance Co.
629 American Deposit Insurance Co.
631 Lancer Insurance Co.
633 Cincinnati Insurance Co.
635 LM Personal Insurance Co.
637 Northland Insurance Co.
638 Virginia Surety Co., Inc.
639 GEICO General Insurance Co.
641 Paramount Insurance Co.
642 Vanliner Insurance Co.
643 Viking Insurance Co. of Wisconsin
644 Global Liberty Insurance Co. of New York
645 Unitrin Advantage Insurance Co.
646 Allmerica Financial Alliance Insurance Co.
647 Harleysville Worcester Insurance Co.
648 Citizens Insurance Co. of America
649 St. Paul Medical Liability Insurance Co.
650 Greenwich Insurance Co.
651 Athena Assurance Co.
653 Church Mutual Insurance Co.
654 S.U.A. Insurance Co.
655 Hartford Insurance Co. of the Midwest
656 Argonaut Midwest Insurance Co.
657 CIM Insurance Corp.
658 Unitrin Direct Insurance Co.
660 AIG Premier Insurance Co.
661 MIC Property & Casualty Insurance Corp.
663 Florists' Mutual Insurance Co.
665 Washington International Insurance Co.
669 Tri-State Consumer Insurance Co.
670 Frontier Insurance Co.
672 Liberty Insurance Corp.
673 Republic Franklin Insurance Co.
674 United Financial Casualty Co.
675 Pioneer Insurance Company
676 Colonial Indemnity Insurance Co.
678 Progressive Advanced Insurance Co.
679 DaimlerChrysler Insurance Co.
680 ULICO Casualty Co.
681 Genesis Insurance Co.
682 Homeland Insurance Co. of New York
683 AutoOne Select Insurance Co. of NY
684 AutoOne Insurance Co.
686 Sterling Insurance Co.
687 American Zurich Insurance Co.
688 Ironshore Indemnity Co.
689 Farmington Casualty Co.
692 Arch Insurance Co.
693 Progressive Max Insurance Co.
695 Infinity Standard Insurance Co.
696 U.S. Capital Insurance Co.
697 New York Schools Insurance Reciprocal
698 Titan Indemnity Co.
699 North American Specialty Insurance Co.
700 Indiana Lumbermens Mutual Insurance Co.
701 Park Insurance Company
702 Great West Casualty Company
703 Permanent General Assurance Corporation
704 National Liability and Fire Insurance Co.
705 Samsung Fire & Marine Insurance Co., Ltd.
706 Delos Insurance Company
707 National Specialty Insurance Co.
708 Castlepoint Insurance Co.
709 Old Dominion Insurance Co.
710 ICM Insurance Co.
711 Ameriprise Insurance Co.
712 Privilege Underwriters Insurance Exchange
713 Federated Rural Electric Insurance Exchange
714 Liberty Insurance Underwriters, Inc.
715 Chubb National Insurance Co.
716 U.S. Specialty Insurance Co.
717 Brotherhood Mutual Insurance Co.
718 Peerless Indemnity Insurance Co.
719 Victoria Auto Insurance Co.
720 Allmerica Financial Benefit Insurance Co.
721 Riverport Insurance Co.
722 Travelers Casualty Insurance Co. of America
723 WRM America Indemnity Company of America
724 Foremost Signature Insurance Co.
725 Harleysville Insurance Co.
726 Harleysville Preferred Insurance Co.
727 Bituminous Casualty Corporation
728 Safety National Casualty Corporation
989 Out of State Insurance Co.—ITP
990 Department of Transportation
991 Interstate Commerce Commission
992 Farm Vehicle ($1 Registration)
993 For Hire Self-Insurer
994 Government Owned—Political Subdivisions
995 Form FS—113 Filed—Not Valid in U.S. or Canada
996 Financial Security Depositor
997 Self-Insurer
998 Not a Valid Code
999 New York Automobile Insurance Plan

DIRECTORY OF NEW YORK HOSPITALS

Editor's Note: Pursuant to Title II, § 18, Public Health Laws, the statutory fee that a hospital may charge to a patient or the patient's guardian or attorney for copies of hospital records may not exceed $1.00 per page. New York hospitals generally charge this statutory maximum fee for copies of records; however, some facilities charge higher copy fees to other parties, such as insurance companies.

ALBANY Albany County

Albany Medical Center Hospital
43 New Scotland Ave., Albany 12208-3478
(518) 262-3125; Medical Records: (518) 262-3151
Internet: www.amc.edu
President/C.E.O.: James J. Barba
Dir., Health Information Mgmt.: Janis Leonard (518) 262-4470
590 Beds
Fee for Copy of Records: See statutory fee, *supra*

Albany Medical Center—South Clinical Campus
25 Hackett Blvd., Albany 12208
(518) 262-1200
Director: Timothy W. Duffey (518) 262-1461; Fax: (518) 262-1465
Dir., Health Information Mgmt.: Janis Leonard (518) 262-1471, Ext. 4470
20 Beds
Fee for Copy of Records: See statutory fee, *supra*
Formerly Childs Hospital

Albany Memorial Hospital
600 Northern Blvd., Albany 12204
(518) 471-3221; Medical Records: (518) 447-3534
Internet: www.nehealth.com
C.E.O.: Norman E. Dascher, Jr. (518) 271-3202
Administrator/C.O.O.: Karen Tassey (518) 471-3229
General Counsel: Robert Swidler (518) 271-5027
Dir., Health Information Mgmt.: Cindy Richards (518) 471-3223
165 Beds
Fee for Copy of Records: See statutory fee, *supra*
Affiliate of Northeast Health

St. Peter's Hospital
315 S. Manning Blvd., Albany 12208
(518) 525-1550
Internet: www.stpetershealthcare.org
President/C.E.O.: Steven P. Boyle
Dir. of Medical Records: Joanne Hensler
442 Beds
Fee for Copy of Records: See statutory fee, *supra*
Affiliate of Catholic Health East

ALEXANDRIA BAY Jefferson County

River Hospital
4 Fuller St., Alexandria Bay 13607
(315) 482-2511; Fax: (315) 482-4981
Internet: www.riverhospital.org
President/C.E.O.: Ben Moore III (315) 482-1110
Records Administrator: Rhonda Campbell (315) 482-1130
51 Beds
Fee for Copy of Records: See statutory fee, *supra*
Formerly Edward J. Noble Samaritan Hospital of Alexandria Bay

AMITYVILLE Suffolk County

Brunswick Hospital Center, Inc.
81 Louden Ave., Amityville 11701
(631) 789-7431; Fax: (631) 789-7783;
Health Information Mgmt.: (631) 789-7427
President/C.E.O.: Amar Jit Singh, M.D. (631) 789-7225
Dir., Health Information Mgmt.: Betty Bier (631) 789-7427
Internet: www.bbier@brunswickhospital.org
124 Beds
Fee for Copy of Records: See statutory fee, *supra*

AMSTERDAM Montgomery County

St. Mary's Hospital at Amsterdam
427 Guy Park Ave., Amsterdam 12010-1095
(518) 842-1900; Medical Records: (518) 841-7110
Internet: www.smha.org
President/C.E.O.: Victor Giulianelli (518) 841-7102
Records Administrator: Donald O'Niel, Ext. 7434
143 Beds
Fee for Copy of Records: See statutory fee, *supra*
Affiliate of Ascension Health

AUBURN Cayuga County

Auburn Memorial Hospital
17 Lansing St., Auburn 13021
(315) 255-7011; Medical Records: (315) 255-7237
Internet: www.auburnhospital.org
President/C.E.O.: Scott A. Berlucchi (315) 255-7047; Fax: (315) 255-7382
Records Administrator: Vicki Stubbs, R.H.I.A. (Acting) Ext. 7254; Fax: (315) 255-7092
226 Beds
Fee for Copy of Records: See statutory fee, *supra*

BATAVIA Genesee County

United Memorial Medical Center
127 North St., Batavia 14020-2260
(585) 343-6030; Fax: (585) 344-7434;
Medical Records: (585) 344-5271;
Medical Records Fax: (585) 344-7469
Internet: www.ummc.org
President/C.E.O.: Mark C. Schoell (585) 344-5456
Records Administrator: Diane Skelton
131 Beds
Fee for Copy of Records: See statutory fee, *supra*

BATH Steuben County

Ira Davenport Memorial Hospital, Inc.
7571 State Rt. 54, Bath 14810
(607) 776-8500; Fax: (607) 776-8817;
Medical Records: (607) 776-8515;
Medical Records Fax: (607) 776-8835
Internet: www.davenportandtaylor.org
Administrator/C.E.O.: James B. Watson (607) 776-8501; Fax: (607) 776-8808
Chief Legal Counsel: Harter, Secrest & Emery, L.L.P. (585) 232-6500; Fax: (585) 232-2152
Records Administrator: Starlith Farrell (607) 776-8601
66 Beds; 120 Long Term Care Beds
Fee for Copy of Records: See statutory fee, *supra*

BAY SHORE Suffolk County

Southside Hospital
301 E. Main St., Bay Shore 11706
(631) 968-3000; Fax: (631) 968-3315;
Medical Records: (631) 968-3070
Internet: www.northshorelij.com
President/C.E.O.: Winifred Mack (631) 968-3800
Records Administrator: Sandra Murdaugh
371 Beds
Fee for Copy of Records: See statutory fee, *supra*
Affiliate of the North Shore-Long Island Jewish Health System

BAYSIDE **Queens County**

St. Mary's Hospital for Children
29-01 216th Street, Bayside 11360
(718) 281-8800; Medical Records: (718) 281-8798
E-mail: info@stmaryskids.org
Internet: www.stmaryskids.org
President/C.E.O.: Edwin F. Simpser, M.D. (Acting)
General Counsel: Michael Pasternack
Fee for Copy of Records: See statutory fee, *supra*

BETHPAGE **Nassau County**

New Island Hospital
Community Relations Dept., 4295 Hempstead Tpke., Bethpage 11714
(516) 579-6000
Internet: www.newislandhospital.org
President/C.E.O.: Aaron E. Glatt, M.D. (516) 520-2222
Records Administrator: Susan Boch (516) 520-2700
223 Beds
Fee for Copy of Records: See statutory fee, *supra*

BINGHAMTON **Broome County**

Our Lady of Lourdes Memorial Hospital, Inc.
169 Riverside Dr., Binghamton 13905
(607) 798-5111
Internet: www.lourdes.com
President/C.E.O.: David Patak (Acting) (607) 798-5328
Chief Legal Counsel: Hinman, Howard & Kattell
Dir., Health Information Mgmt.: Vacancy at Press Time
165 Beds
Fee for Copy of Records: See statutory fee, *supra*
Affiliate of Ascension Health

United Health Services Hospitals, Inc.
Binghamton General Hospital
10-42 Mitchell Ave., Binghamton 13903
(607) 762-2200
Internet: www.uhs.net
President/C.E.O.: Matthew J. Salanger (607) 762-2263
E-mail: matthew_salanger@uhs.org
General Counsel: Donald P. Carlin (607) 762-3366
E-mail: donald_carlin@uhs.org
Dir., Health Information Mgmt.: Trisha Jewson (607) 763-6202
E-mail: trisha_jewson@uhs.org
516 Beds
Fee for Copy of Records: See statutory fee, *supra*
Affiliate of the United Health Services, Inc.

BROCKPORT **Monroe County**

Lakeside Memorial Hospital
156 West Ave., Brockport 14420
(585) 395-6095; Fax: (585) 395-6036
Internet: www.lakesidehealth.com
President/C.E.O.: Michael Stapleton
Dir., Health Information Mgmt.: Gail Woytek
Fax: (585) 395-6012
61 Beds
Fee for Copy of Records: See statutory fee, *supra*

BRONX **Bronx County**

Bronx-Lebanon Hospital Center
Concourse Division
1650 Grand Concourse, Bronx 10457
(718) 590-1800;
Health Information Mgmt.: (718) 518-5171;
Health Information Mgmt. Fax: (718) 518-5634
Internet: www.bronxcare.org
President/C.E.O.: Miguel A. Fuentes, Jr. (718) 901-8800
Chief Legal Counsel: Fred Miller (516) 393-2250
Dir., Health Information Mgmt.: Karen Lyttle
958 Beds
Fee for Copy of Records: See statutory fee, *supra*

Bronx-Lebanon Hospital Center
Fulton Division
1276 Fulton Ave., 1st Floor, Bronx 10456
(718) 590-1800; Health Information Mgmt.: (718) 518-5171;
Health Information Mgmt. Fax: (718) 518-5634
E-mail: www.bronxcare.org
President/C.E.O.: Miguel A. Fuentes, Jr. (718) 901-8800
Chief Legal Counsel: Fred Miller (516) 393-2250
Dir., Health Information Mgmt.: Karen Lyttle
164 Beds
Fee for Copy of Records: See statutory fee, *supra*

Calvary Hospital, Inc.
1740 Eastchester Rd., Bronx 10461
(718) 863-6900; Fax: (718) 518-2674;
Health Information Mgmt.: (718) 518-2044
Internet: www.calvaryhospital.org
President/C.E.O.: Frank A. Calamari (718) 518-2250
E-mail: fcalamari@calvaryhospital.org
Dir., Health Information Mgmt.: Howard Kaplan (718) 518-2171
225 Beds
Fee for Copy of Records: See statutory fee, *supra*
Affiliate of the Catholic Health Care System

Jacobi Medical Center
1400 Pelham Pkwy. S., Bronx 10461-1197
(718) 918-5000; Medical Records: (718) 918-4736
Senior V.P.: William P. Walsh (718) 918-8141
Dir. of Medical Records: Lisa Moats
774 Beds
Fee for Copy of Records: See statutory fee, *supra*
Affiliate of the North Bronx Healthcare Network

Lincoln Medical & Mental Health Center
234 E. 149th St., Bronx 10451 (718) 579-5000
Senior V.P.: Jose R. Sanchez
(718) 579-5700; Fax: (718) 579-5319
Dir., Health Information Mgmt.: Lebby Delgado, Ext. 5421
340 Beds
Fee for Copy of Records: See statutory fee, *supra*
Member of NYC Health & Hospitals Corporation

Montefiore Medical Center, Weiler Division
1825 Eastchester Rd., Bronx 10467
(718) 920-4321; TTY: (718) 920-5027;
Health Information Mgmt.: (718) 920-5108
Internet: www.montefiore.org
President/C.E.O.: Steven M. Safyer, M.D. (718) 920-2001
Sr. V.P/General Counsel: Christopher S. Panczner (718) 920-7787
Dir., Health Information Mgmt.: Caryl Greaves
381 Beds
Fee for Copy of Records: See statutory fee, *supra*

Montefiore Medical Center, Moses Division
111 E. 210th St., Bronx 10467-2490 (718) 920-4321
Internet: www.montefiore.org
President/C.E.O.: Steven M. Safyer, M.D. (718) 920-2001
Sr. V.P./General Counsel: Christopher S. Panczner (718) 920-7787
Dir., Health Information Mgmt.: Caryl Greaves, Ext. 5108
745 Beds
Fee for Copy of Records: See statutory fee, *supra*

Montefiore Medical Center, North Division
600 E. 233rd St., Bronx 10466-2697
(718) 920-9000; Health Information Mgmt.: (718) 920-9610
Internet: www.montefiore.org
President/C.E.O.: Steven M. Safyer, M.D.
Sr. V.P./General Counsel: Christopher S. Panczner (718) 920-7787
Dir., Health Information Mgmt.: Carol Greaves
429 Beds
Fee for Copy of Records: See statutory fee, *supra*
Formerly Our Lady of Mercy Medical Center, John Cardinal O'Connor Campus

Bronx—Cont'd

New York Westchester Square Medical Center
2475 St. Raymond Ave., Bronx 10461
(718) 430-7300; Fax: (718) 430-7311
Internet: www.nywsmc.org

President/C.E.O.: Alan Kopman (718) 430-7359

Dir. of Medical Records: Gary Albert

205 Beds
Fee for Copy of Records: See statutory fee, *supra*
Affiliate of New York Presbyterian Healthcare Network

North Central Bronx Hospital
3424 Kossuth Ave. & 210th St., Bronx 10467
(718) 519-3500; Fax: (718) 519-4902

Exec. Dir.: Christopher Fugazy

Assoc. Exec. Dir.: Barbara A. Rosado
E-mail: barbara.rosado@nbhn.net

Records Administrator: Lisa Moats
(718) 918-4728
E-mail: lisa.moats@nbhn.net

232 Beds
Fee for Copy of Records: See statutory fee, *supra*
Affiliated with New York City Health and Hospitals Corp.

Our Lady of Mercy Medical Center, John Cardinal O'Connor Campus
See Montefiore Medical Center

St. Barnabas Hospital
4422 Third Ave., Bronx 10457
(718) 960-9000; Medical Records: (718) 960-6111
Internet: www.stbarnabashospital.org

President/C.E.O.: Scott Cooper, M.D.
(718) 960-6100; Fax: (718) 960-6293

Dir. of Medical Records: Phyllis Astorino, Ext. 9219

461 Beds
Fee for Copy of Records: $.75 per page
Affiliate of New York Presbyterian HealthCare System

Union Community Health Center
260 E. 188th St., Bronx 10458
(718) 220-2020
Internet: www.uchcbronx.org

2021 Grand Concourse, Bronx 10453
Admin.: (718) 960-9570

Rehabilitation Center,
4487 3rd Ave. at 182nd St., 7th Floor, Bronx 10457
Admin.: (718) 960-6173

One Fordham Plz., Bronx 10458
(718) 960-6430, 33

C.E.O.: Douglas York

C.O.O.: Anne Spellman, Ext. 8236

V.P., Legal Affairs: Keith Wolf

Records Administrator: Phyllis Asterino

201 Beds
Fee for Copy of Records: See statutory fee, *supra*
Affilate of St. Barnabas Hospital

BRONXVILLE Westchester County

Lawrence Hospital Center
55 Palmer Ave., Bronxville 10708
(914) 787-1000; Medical Records: (914) 787-3272
Internet: www.lawrencehealth.org

President/C.E.O.: Edward M. Dinan
(914) 787-1601

Records Administrator: Ed Levine
(914) 787-3298; Fax: (914) 787-3010

291 Beds
Fee for Copy of Records: See statutory fee, *supra*
Affiliated with N.Y.-Presbyterian Healthcare System

BROOKLYN Kings County

Beth Israel Medical Center, Kings Hwy. Div.
3201 Kings Hwy., Brooklyn 11234
(718) 252-3000; Fax: (718) 951-2726;
Medical Records: (718) 951-2806
Internet: www.wehealny.org

President/C.E.O.: Harris Magler

Records Administrator: Rosalie Kessler

212 Beds
Fee for Copy of Records: $.75 per page
Affiliated with Continuum Health Partners

Brookdale University Hospital and Medical Center
One Brookdale Plz., Suite 346, Brooklyn 11212-3198
(718) 240-5000; Fax: (718) 240-5042;
Medical Records: (718) 240-6022
Internet: www.brookdale.edu

C.E.O./President: David Rosen
(718) 240-5212; Fax: (718) 240-6487

Chief Legal Counsel: Vacancy at Press Time
(718) 240-6163; Fax: (718) 240-6169

Dir. of Medical Records: Mercedes Merchado (718) 240-5566

530 Beds
Fee for Copy of Records: See statutory fee, *supra*

The Brooklyn Hospital Center
121 DeKalb Ave., Brooklyn 11201-5493
(718) 250-8000; Fax: (718) 625-4109
Internet: www.tbh.org

President/C.E.O.: Dr. Richard B. Becker (718) 250-8005

Dir., Health Information Mgmt.: Wade Harless
(718) 250-8691; Fax: (718) 250-6638

464 Beds
Fee for Copy of Records: See statutory fee, *supra*
Affiliate of the New York—Presbyterian Healthcare System

Coney Island Hospital
2601 Ocean Pkwy., Brooklyn 11235
(718) 616-3000; Medical Records: (718) 616-4196

Senior V.P./Exec. Dir.: Arthur Wagner
(718) 616-4100; Fax: (718) 616-4439

Records Administrator: Theresa McGann (718) 616-4222

387 Beds
Fee for Copy of Records: See statutory fee, *supra*
Member of NYC Health & Hospitals Corporation

Interfaith Medical Center
1545 Atlantic Ave., Brooklyn 11213
(718) 613-4000; Fax: (718) 613-4101
Internet: www.interfaithmedical.com

President/C.E.O.: Laurie Gaffney (718) 613-4001

Dir., Health Information Svces.: Myrtle Wilcott

287 Beds
Fee for Copy of Records: See statutory fee, *supra*

Kings County Hospital Center
451 Clarkson Ave., Brooklyn 11203
(718) 245-3131

Exec. Dir.: Antonio D. Martin
(718) 245-3901; Fax: (718) 953-1316

Dir. of Medical Records: Annette Griffith (718) 245-4219

627 Beds
Fee for Copy of Records: See statutory fee, *supra*
Member of NYC Health & Hospitals Corporation

Kingsbrook Jewish Medical Center
585 Schenectady Ave., Brooklyn 11203
(718) 604-5000;
Health Information Mgmt.: (718) 604-5655;
Health Information Mgmt. Fax: (718) 604-5356
E-mail: info@kjmc.org; Internet: www.kingsbrook.org

President: Dr. Linda Brady
(718) 604-5211; Fax: (718) 604-5243

Dir., Health Information Mgmt.:
Andrea Flynn, R.H.I.A. (718) 604-5658

326 Beds
Fee for Copy of Records: See statutory fee, *supra*

Brooklyn—Cont'd

The Long Island College Hospital
339 Hicks St., Brooklyn 11201-5509
(718) 780-1000; Internet: www.lich.org
President/C.E.O.: Dominick Stanzione
V.P./Legal Counsel: Jill Clayton
(212) 523-2162; Fax: (212) 523-3935
Dir., Health Information Mgmt.:
Dawn Maynard, R.R.A. (718) 780-4632
516 Beds
Fee for Copy of Records: See statutory fee, *supra*
Affiliate of the Continuum Health Partners, Inc.

Lutheran Medical Center
150 55th St., Brooklyn 11220
(718) 630-7000; Internet: www.lmcmc.com
President/C.E.O.: Wendy Z. Goldstein
Exec. V.P./General Counsel: Barbara Katz Arky
(718) 630-7345; Fax: (718) 630-6394
Records Administrator: Jeanette Clarke (718) 630-7128
476 Beds
Fee for Copy of Records: See statutory fee, *supra*

Maimonides Medical Center
4802 Tenth Ave., Brooklyn 11219-2916
(718) 283-6000; Health Information Mgmt.: (718) 283-7020
Internet: www.maimonidesmed.org
President/C.E.O.: Pamela S. Brier
V.P., Legal Affairs/General Counsel: Joyce A. Leahy
(718) 283-7441; E-mail: jleahy@maimonidesmed.org
Dir., Health Information Mgmt.: Silvia Sememskaya
705 Beds
Fee for Copy of Records: See statutory fee, *supra*

New York Community Hospital
2525 Kings Hwy., Brooklyn 11229
(718) 692-5300; Medical Records: (718) 692-5377
Internet: www.nych.com
President/C.E.O.: Lin H. Mo (718) 692-5301
Dir., Health Information Mgmt.: Susan Tabickman
(718) 692-5395
134 Beds
Fee for Copy of Records: See statutory fee, *supra*
Affiliated with New York-Presbyterian Healthcare System

New York Methodist Hospital—Main Campus
506 Sixth St., Brooklyn 11215
(718) 780-3000; Fax: (718) 780-3770;
Medical Records: (718) 780-3381
Internet: www.nym.org
President/C.E.O.: Mark J. Mundy (718) 780-3301
Records Administrator: Grethel Marks (718) 780-3385
560 Beds
Fee for Copy of Records: See statutory fee, *supra*
Affiliate of the New York-Presbyterian Healthcare System

**SUNY Downstate Medical Center—
University Hospital of Brooklyn**
450 Clarkson Ave., Brooklyn 11203-2098
(718) 270-1000; Medical Records: (718) 270-1845
Internet: www.downstate.edu
C.E.O.: Debra Carey
(718) 270-6389; Fax: (718) 270-6382
President: John C. LaRosa
Dir., Medical Records: Sonia Davidson
376 Beds
Fee for Copy of Records: See statutory fee, *supra*

Woodhull Medical & Mental Health Center
760 Broadway St., Brooklyn 11206-5383
(718) 963-8000; Health Information Mgmt.: (718) 963-8023
Exec. Dir./V.P.: Iris Jimenez Hernandez
Dir., Health Information Mgmt.: Manickam Rajaram
394 Beds
Fee for Copy of Records: See statutory fee, *supra*
Member of NYC Health & Hospitals Corporation

Wyckoff Heights Medical Center
374 Stockholm St., Brooklyn 11237
(718) 963-7272; Health Information Mgmt.: (718) 963-7151
Internet: www.wyckoffhospital.org
President/C.E.O.: Nirmal K. Mattoo, M.D.
(718) 963-6710; Fax: (718) 963-7196
Dir., Health Information Mgmt.: Glenda Peres
350 Beds
Fee for Copy of Records: See statutory fee, *supra*
Affiliate of New York Presbyterian HealthCare System

BUFFALO Erie County

Buffalo General Hospital
100 High St., Buffalo 14203
(716) 859-5600; Health Information Mgmt.: (716) 859-2759
Internet: www.kaleidahealth.org
President: Larry Zielinski (716) 859-3383
Dir., Health Information Mgmt.: Vicky Trautman
500 Beds
Fee for Copy of Records: See statutory fee, *supra*
Affiliate of Kaleida Health

Erie County Medical Center
462 Grider St., Buffalo 14215-3098
(716) 898-3000; Fax: (716) 898-5178; Internet: www.ecmc.edu
Administrator/C.E.O.: Jody Lomeo (Acting) (716) 898-5568
Chief Legal Counsel: Anthony J. Colucci III (716) 853-4080
Records Administrator: Elizabeth Zivis (716) 898-3190
550 Beds
Fee for Copy of Records: See statutory fee, *supra*
Affiliated with Erie County Medical Center Corp.

Mercy Hospital
565 Abbott Rd., Buffalo 14220
(716) 826-7000; Internet: www.chsbuffalo.org
President/C.E.O.: Charles J. Urlaub (716) 828-2008
Dir., Health Information Mgmt.: Jan Stevens (716) 828-2317
349 Beds
Fee for Copy of Records: See statutory fee, *supra*
Affiliate of Catholic Health System

Millard Fillmore Gates Circle Hospital
3 Gates Circle, Buffalo 14209
(716) 887-4600; Fax: (716) 887-4379;
Health Information Svces.: (716) 887-4720
Internet: http://gates.kaleidahealth.org
President: Tamara Owen (716) 887-4770
General Counsel: Robert J. Nolan (Kaleida Health)
(716) 859-5600
Dir., Health Information Svces.: Vickie Trautman
Fax: (716) 887-4383
189 Beds
Fee for Copy of Records: See statutory fee, *supra*
Affiliate of Kaleida Health

Roswell Park Cancer Institute
Elm and Carlton Sts., Buffalo 14263-0001
(716) 845-2300, (877) 275-7724
Internet: www.roswellpark.org
President/C.E.O.: Donald L. Trump, M.D.
General Counsel: Michael B. Sexton
(716) 845-8717; Fax: (716) 845-8057
E-mail: michael.sexton@roswellpark.org
Dir., Health Information Mgmt.: Karen Battino
(716) 845-5990; Fax: (716) 845-8394
218 Beds
Fee for Copy of Records: See statutory fee, *supra*

Sheehan Memorial Hospital
d/b/a Sheehan Health Newtowk
425 Michigan Ave. at Eagle St., Buffalo 14203
(716) 848-2000; Health Information Mgmt.: (716) 848-2130;
Health Information Mgmt. Fax: (716) 848-2131
Internet: www.sheehanhn.org
President/C.E.O.: Lucille Sheedy
(716) 848-2119; Fax: (716) 848-2125
Dir., Health Information Mgmt.: Gladys Hood
109 Beds
Fee for Copy of Records: See statutory fee, *supra*

Buffalo—Cont'd

Sisters of Charity Hospital
2157 Main St., Buffalo 14214
(716) 862-1000; Fax: (716) 862-1979
Internet: www.chsbuffalo.org

President/C.E.O.: Peter U. Bergmann, F.A.C.H.E. (716) 862-1900

Chief Legal Counsel: Nancy Sheehan (716) 821-4461

General Counsel: Phillips Lytle, L.L.P. (716) 847-8400

Dir., Health Information Mgmt.: Susan Roman (Acting) (716) 862-1979

413 Beds
Fee for Copy of Records: See statutory fee, *supra*
Affiliate of the Catholic Health System

The Women & Children's Hospital of Buffalo
219 Bryant St., Buffalo 14222-2099
(716) 878-7000; Internet: www.wchob.org

C.E.O.: Cheryl Klass (716) 878-7981

Sr. V.P./General Counsel: Robert J. Nolan (Kaleida Health) (716) 859-5600

Dir., Health Information Mgmt.: Vickie Trautman (716) 859-2759

313 Beds
Fee for Copy of Records: See statutory fee, *supra*
Affiliate of Kaleida Health

CALLICOON Sullivan County

Catskill Regional Medical Center—G. Hermann Div.
8881 NYS Rt. 97, Callicoon 12723
(845) 887-5530; Fax: (845) 887-5380; Internet: http://crmcny.org

Administrator: Mark Mendenson

C.E.O.: Steven Ruwoldt

Records Administrator: Carol McCoy

25 Beds
Fee for Copy of Records: See statutory fee, *supra*
Formerly Community General Hospital of Sullivan County G. Hermann Div.

CANANDAIGUA Ontario County

F.F. Thompson Hospital
350 Parrish St., Canandaigua 14424
(585) 396-6000; Fax: (585) 396-6534;
Health Information Mgmt.: (585) 396-6720;
Health Information Mgmt. Fax: (585) 396-6719
Internet: www.thompsonhealth.com

President/C.E.O.: Linda M. Farchione

Dir., Health Information Mgmt.: Judi Kelly (585) 396-6711

113 Beds
Fee for Copy of Records: See statutory fee, *supra*
Affiliate of Thompson Health

CARMEL Putnam County

Putnam Hospital Center
670 Stoneleigh Ave., Carmel 10512-9948
(845) 279-5711; Fax: (845) 279-7482
Internet: www.putnamhospital.org

President/C.E.O.: Donna M. McGregor

Dir., Health Information Mgmt.: Sandra Canivares Ext. 5883

164 Beds
Fee for Copy of Records: See statutory fee, *supra*
Affiliate of Health Quest

CARTHAGE Jefferson County

Carthage Area Hospital
1001 West St., Carthage 13619
(315) 493-1000; Fax: (315) 493-4231
Internet: www.carthagehospital.com

C.E.O.: Walter Becker, Ext. 2318

Records Administrator: Caroline Baker Ext. 2404; Fax: (315) 495-0038

78 Beds
Fee for Copy of Records: See statutory fee, *supra*

CHEEKTOWAGA Erie County

Sisters of Charity Hospital, St. Joseph Campus
2605 Harlem Rd., Cheektowaga 14225
(716) 891-2400; Health Information Mgmt.: (716) 891-2440
Internet: www.chsbuffalo.org

President: Peter U. Bergmann, F.A.C.H.E.

Dir., Health Information Mgmt.: Sue Roman (716) 891-2442

208 Beds
Fee for Copy of Records: See statutory fee, *supra*
Affiliate of Catholic Health System of Western New York

CLIFTON SPRINGS Ontario County

Clifton Springs Hospital and Clinic
2 Coulter Rd., Clifton Springs 14432
(315) 462-9561;
Health Information Mgmt.: (315) 462-1391;
Health Information Mgmt. Fax: (315) 462-6058
Internet: www.cliftonspringshospital.org

President/C.E.O.: John Galati (315) 462-0100; Fax: (315) 462-3492

Dir., Health Information Mgmt.: Sue Fletcher

154 Beds
Fee for Copy of Records: See statutory fee, *supra*

COBLESKILL Schoharie County

Cobleskill Regional Hospital
Bassett Hospital of Schoharie County d.b.a.
178 Grandview Dr., Cobleskill 12043
(518) 254-3456; Fax: (518) 234-4839

President/C.E.O.: Eric H. Stein (518) 254-3270

Dir., Health Information Mgmt.: Mary McKenna (518) 254-3266

40 Beds
Fee for Copy of Records: See statutory fee, *supra*
Affiliate of Bassett HealthCare

COHOES Albany County

Eddy Cohoes Rehabilitation Center
421 W. Columbia St., Cohoes 12047
(518) 237-5630
Internet: www.nehealth.com

C.E.O.: Jo-Ann Constantino, Ext. 4004

94 Beds
Fee for Copy of Records: See statutory fee, *supra*
Affiliate of Northeast Health System

COOPERSTOWN Otsego County

Mary Imogene Bassett Hospital
One Atwell Rd., Cooperstown 13326-1394
(607) 547-3456; Medical Records: Ext. 3770
E-mail: info@bassett.org
Internet: www.bassetthealthcare.org

President/C.E.O.: William F. Streck, M.D. (607) 547-3100

Records Administrator: Pam Ullman-Ferris, Ext. 6971

180 Beds
Fee for Copy of Records: See statutory fee, *supra*
Affiliate of Bassett HealthCare

CORNING Steuben County

Corning Hospital
176 Denison Pkwy E., Corning 14830
(607) 937-7200; Medical Records: (607) 937-7550;
Medical Records Fax: (607) 937-7859
Internet: www.corninghospital.com

President/C.O.O.: Shirley Magana

Records Administrator: Barb Burritt

99 Beds Acute; 120 Skilled Nursing Home
Fee for Copy of Records: See statutory fee, *supra*
Affiliate of Guthrie HealthCare System

CORNWALL **Orange County**

St. Luke's Cornwall Hospital
Cornwall Campus
19 Laurel Ave., Cornwall 12518
(845) 561-7711; Fax: (845) 561-2091
Internet: www.stlukescornwallhospital.org

President/C.E.O.: Allan E. Atzrott

In-House Counsel: Lori E. Masterson (845) 568-2759

Dir., Health Information Mgmt.: Laura Berberich (845) 568-2450

125 Beds
Fee for Copy of Records: See statutory fee, *supra*
Affiliate of Mount Sinai Hospital

CORTLAND **Cortland County**

Cortland Regional Medical Center
134 Homer Ave., P.O. Box 2010, Cortland 13045
(607) 756-3500; Health Information Mgmt.: (607) 756-3685
Internet: www.cortlandregional.org

President/C.E.O.: Brian R. Mitteer, F.A.C.H.E. (607) 756-3501; Fax: (607) 756-3590

Dir., Health Information Mgmt.: Nancy Fuller Ext. 3685

181 Beds
Fee for Copy of Records: See statutory fee, *supra*
Formerly Cortland Memorial Hospital, Inc.

CORTLANDT MANOR **Westchester County**

Hudson Valley Hospital Center
1980 Crompond Rd., Cortlandt Manor 10567-4182
(914) 737-9000; Medical Records: (914) 734-3212
Internet: www.hvhc.org

President: John C. Federspiel

Records Administrator: Thelma Stewart

120 Beds
Fee for Copy of Records: See statutory fee, *supra*
Affiliate of Pinnacle Health System

CUBA **Allegany County**

Cuba Memorial Hospital, Inc.
140 W. Main St., Cuba 14727-1398
(585) 968-2000; Fax: (585) 968-1710
Internet: www.cubamemorialhospital.org

C.E.O.: Andrew Boser III
(585) 968-3877, Ext. 208
E-mail: aboser@cubamemorialhospital.org

Dir., Health Information Mgmt.: Debra Gaeta

20 Acute Beds
Fee for Copy of Records: See statutory fee, *supra*

DANSVILLE **Livingston County**

Nicholas H. Noyes Memorial Hospital
111 Clara Barton St., Dansville 14437
(585) 335-6001; Fax: (585) 335-5044;
Medical Records: (585) 335-4227

President/C.E.O.: James Wissler

Records Administrator: Amy Earner

72 Beds
Fee for Copy of Records: See statutory fee, *supra*

DELHI **Delaware County**

O'Connor Hospital
460 Andes Rd., Rte. 28, Delhi 13753
(607) 746-0300; Fax: (607) 746-0347
Internet: www.oconnorhosp.org

Administrator/C.E.O.: Daniel M. Ayres (607) 746-0326

Records Administrator: Edith Vroman (607) 746-0310; Fax: (607) 746-0312

28 Beds
Fee for Copy of Records: See statutory fee, *supra*
Affiliate of Bassett HealthCare

DOBBS FERRY **Westchester County**

St. Johns Riverside Hospital
Dobbs Ferry Pavilion
128 Ashford Ave., Dobbs Ferry 10522-1896
(914) 693-0700
Internet: www.riversidehealth.org

President/C.E.O.: Ronald J. Corti

Dir., Medical Records: Judy Mendez

50 Beds
Fee for Copy of Records: See statutory fee, *supra*
Formerly Community Hospital at Dobbs Ferry

DUNKIRK **Chautauqua County**

Brooks Memorial Hospital
529 Central Ave., Dunkirk 14048
(716) 366-1111; Fax: (716) 363-7358
Internet: www.brookshospital.org

President: Jonathan I. Lawrence, F.A.C.H.E.

Records Administrator: Cheryll Rogers (716) 363-7283

133 Beds
Fee for Copy of Records: See statutory fee, *supra*

EAST MEADOW **Nassau County**

Nassau University Medical Center
2201 Hempstead Tpke., East Meadow 11554
(516) 572-0123; Fax: (516) 572-5792
Internet: www.numc.edu

President/C.E.O.: Arthur A. Gianelli (516) 572-6011

General Counsel: Reginald Bullock (516) 572-6064

Records Administrator: Petra Freese

1,200 Beds
Fee for Copy of Records: Contact Medical Records Dept. for fee information

EAST PATCHOGUE **Suffolk County**

Brookhaven Memorial Hospital Medical Center, Inc.
101 Hospital Rd., East Patchogue 11772
(631) 654-7100; Fax: (631) 447-3714;
Medical Records: (631) 654-7712
Internet: www.brookhavenhospital.org

President/C.E.O.: Thomas Ockers

Dir. of Medical Records: Sandra Franco, Ext. 7292

306 Beds
Fee for Copy of Records: See statutory fee, *supra*

ELIZABETHTOWN **Essex County**

Elizabethtown Community Hospital
75 Park St., P.O. Box 277, Elizabethtown 12932
(518) 873-6377; Fax: (518) 873-2005
Internet: www.ech.org

Administrator/C.E.O.: Rodney C. Boula, Ext. 3002

Dir. of Medical Records: Charlene Day Fax: (518) 873-3067

25 Beds
Fee for Copy of Records: See statutory fee, *supra*

ELLENVILLE **Ulster County**

Ellenville Regional Hospital
10 Healthy Way, Ellenville 12428
(845) 647-6400; Fax: (845) 647-6450;
Health Information Mgmt.: Ext. 329
Internet: www.ellenvilleregional.org

C.E.O./President: Steven L. Kelley, Ext. 296

Dir., Health Information Mgmt.: Geri Miedreich Ext. 329

51 Beds
Fee for Copy of Records: $.75 per page

ELMHURST Queens County

Elmhurst Hospital Center
79-01 Broadway, Elmhurst 11373
(718) 334-4000
Exec. Dir.: Christopher Constantino
(718) 334-1638 E-mail: constanc@nychhc.org
General Counsel: Salvatore J. Russo (Acting)
(212) 788-3300
Dir., Health Information Mgmt.: Jeanne Papamichail
(718) 334-3127
E-mail: papamicj@nychhc.org
507 Beds
Fee for Copy of Records: See statutory fee, *supra*
Member of the NYC Health & Hospitals Corporation and The Queens Health Network

ELMIRA Chemung County

Arnot Ogden Medical Center
600 Roe Ave., Elmira 14905-1629
(607) 737-4100;
Health Information Mgmt.: (607) 737-4302;
Health Information Mgmt. Fax: (607) 737-4403
Internet: www.arnothealth.org
President/C.E.O.: Anthony J. Cooper (607) 737-4231
Dir., Health Information Mgmt.: Denise Perry
(607) 737-4208
256 Beds
Fee for Copy of Records: See statutory fee, *supra*

St. Joseph's Hospital
555 St. Joseph's Blvd., Elmira 14901
(607) 733-6541; Fax: (607) 737-7837
Internet: www.stjosephs.org
President/C.E.O.: Mr. Donald W. Hartman (Acting)
E-mail: dhartman@stjosephs.org
Records Administrator: Rita Burdick
Fax: (607) 737-7018
224 Beds; 71 Skilled Nursing Facility Beds
Fee for Copy of Records: See statutory fee, *supra*

FAR ROCKAWAY Queens County

Peninsula Hospital Center
51-15 Beach Channel Dr., Far Rockaway 11691-1074
(718) 734-2000; Health Information Mgmt.: (718) 734-2518
Internet: www.peninsulahospital.org
President/C.E.O.: Robert V. Levine
Fax: (718) 734-2993
Dir., Health Information Mgmt.: Diana Waisome
173 Beds
Fee for Copy of Records: See statutory fee, *supra*

St. Johns Episcopal Hospital—South Shore
327 Beach 19th St., Far Rockaway 11691-4424
(718) 869-7000; Medical Records: (718) 869-7796, 97
Internet: www.ehs.org
C.E.O.: John Gupta (718) 869-7320; Fax: (718) 869-7089
E-mail: jgupta@ehs.org
Dir. of Medical Records: Caroline Ware
332 Beds
Fee for Copy of Records: See statutory fee, *supra*
Affiliate of Episcopal Health System

FLUSHING Queens County

Flushing Hospital Medical Center
4500 Parsons Blvd., Flushing 11355
(718) 670-5000; Fax: (718) 670-3077
Internet: www.flushinghospital.org
President/C.E.O.: David P. Rosen
(718) 670-5918
Chief Legal Counsel: Vacancy at Press Time
Records Administrator: Debra Corwin
(718) 670-5424; Fax: (718) 670-4505
282 Beds
Fee for Copy of Records: See statutory fee, *supra*

The New York Hospital Medical Center of Queens
56-45 Main St., Flushing 11355-5000
(718) 670-1231; Health Information Mgmt.: (718) 670-1090
Internet: www.nyhq.org
President/C.E.O.: Stephen S. Mills, F.A.C.H.E.
(718) 670-1025; Fax: (718) 358-1196
S.V.P. & General Counsel: Wm. P. Wissemann
(718) 670-1044; Fax: (718) 358-1196
Dir., Health Information Mgmt.: Karen Tiedemann
457 Beds
Fee for Copy of Records: See statutory fee, *supra*
Affiliate of New York Presbyterian Healthcare System

Parkway Hospital
70-35 113th St., Flushing 11375-4699
(718) 990-4100; Medical Records: (718) 990-4180
President/C.E.O.: Robert J. Aquino, M.D.; Fax: (718) 261-2812
Records Administrator: Marleen Boney, Ext. 44115
251 Beds
Fee for Copy of Records: See statutory fee, *supra*

FOREST HILLS Queens County

Forest Hills Hospital
102-01 66th Rd., Forest Hills 11375-2029
(718) 830-4000; Medical Records: (718) 830-4190
Internet: www.northshorelij.com
Exec. Dir.: Geralyn Randazzo
Sr. V.P./General Counsel: Keith Thompson
(516) 465-8090
Dir., Health Information Mgmt.:
Marlyne Renaudin-Guerrier
302 Beds
Fee for Copy of Records: See statutory fee, *supra*
Formerly North Shore University Hospital at Forest Hills; affiliate of the North Shore-Long Island Jewish Health System

GENEVA Ontario County

Geneva General Hospital
196 North St., Geneva 14456
(315) 787-4000; Medical Records: (315) 787-4120
Internet: www.flhealth.org
President/C.E.O.: Jose Acevedo (Finger Lakes Health)
Dir. of Medical Records: Amy Crowfoot
400 Beds
Fee for Copy of Records: See statutory fee, *supra*
Affiliate of the Finger Lakes Health

GLEN COVE Nassau County

Glen Cove Hospital
101 St. Andrews Lane, Glen Cove 11542
(516) 674-7300; Internet: www.northshorelij.com
Administrator: Dennis Connors
Records Administrator: Jackie Joseph
265 Beds
Fee for Copy of Records: See statutory fee, *supra*

GLEN OAKS Queens County

Zucker Hillside Hospital
7559 263rd St., Glen Oaks 11004
(718) 470-8100; Internet: www.northshorelij.com
Exec. Dir.: Joseph Schulman
223 Beds

GLENS FALLS Warren County

Glens Falls Hospital
100 Park St., Glens Falls 12801
(518) 926-1000
Internet: www.glensfallshospital.org
President/C.E.O.: David Kruczlnicki; Fax: (518) 926-1919
Dir., Medical Data Services: Vacancy at Press Time
(518) 926-5417
442 Beds
Fee for Copy of Records: See statutory fee, *supra*

GLOVERSVILLE Fulton County

Nathan Littauer Hospital and Nursing Home
99 E. State St., Gloversville 12078-1293
(518) 725-8621; Medical Records: (518) 773-5506
E-mail: info@nlh.org
Internet: www.nlh.org

President/C.E.O.: Laurence E. Kelly (518) 773-5500

Chief Legal Counsel: Stan Russell

Records Administrator: Judy Gordon

84 Beds
Fee for Copy of Records: See statutory fee, *supra*

GOSHEN Orange County

Orange Regional Medical Center—Arden Hill Campus
4 Harriman Dr., Goshen 10924-2499
(845) 294-5441; Fax: (845) 294-2105;
Health Information Mgmt.: Ext. 4340
Internet: www.ormc.org

C.E.O.: Scott Batulis
(845) 342-7516

Dir., Health Information Mgmt.: Lisa Newlin

176 Beds
Fee for Copy of Records: See statutory fee, *supra*
Affiliate of New York Presbyterian Healthcare System; formerly Arden Hill Hospital

GOUVERNEUR Saint Lawrence County

Edward John Noble Hospital of Gouverneur
77 W. Barney St., Gouverneur 13642-1090
(315) 287-1000; Fax: (315) 535-9235;
Medical Records: Ext. 336
Internet: www.ejnoble.org

C.E.O.: Charles P. Conole, F.A.C.H.E.

Records Administrator: Tennille Schmidt

47 Beds
Fee for Copy of Records: See statutory fee, *supra*

GOWANDA Cattaraugus County

TLC Health Network
Tri-County Memorial Hospital
100 Memorial Dr., Gowanda 14070
(716) 532-8900; Fax: (716) 532-8901
E-mail: info@tlchealth.org
Internet: www.tlchealth.org

President/C.E.O.: Jonathan I. Lawrence, F.A.C.H.E.

Dir., Health Information Mgmt.: Cheryll Rogers

65 Beds
Fee for Copy of Records: See statutory fee, *supra*

GREENPORT Suffolk County

Eastern Long Island Hospital
201 Manor Pl., Greenport 11944
(631) 477-1000; Medical Records: (631) 477-5232
Internet: www.elih.org

President/C.E.O.: Paul J. Connor III
Ext. 100; Fax: (631) 477-1746

Records Administrator: Heather Romanelli
Ext. 166; Fax: (631) 477-8316

90 Beds
Fee for Copy of Records: See statutory fee, *supra*

HAMILTON Madison County

Community Memorial Hospital
150 Broad St., Hamilton 13346
(315) 824-1100; Health Information Mgmt.: (315) 824-6580
Internet: www.communitymemorial.org

President/C.E.O.: David Felton
(315) 824-6082; Fax: (315) 824-3182

Dir., Medical Records: Vacancy at Press Time

44 Beds
Fee for Copy of Records: See statutory fee, *supra*

HARRIS Sullivan County

Catskill Regional Medical Center
68 Harris Bushville Rd., P.O. Box 800, Harris 12742-0800
(845) 794-3300;
Health Information Mgmt. Fax: (845) 794-3376
Internet: http://crmcny.org

President/C.E.O.: Steven Ruwoldt

C.F.O.: Robert Fisher, Ext. 2105; Fax: (845) 794-3240

Dir., Health Information Mgmt.: Carole McCoy, Ext. 2866

176 Beds
Fee for Copy of Records: See statutory fee, *supra*
Formerly Community General Hospital of Sullivan County

HARRISON Westchester County

St. Vincent Catholic Medical Center
St. Vincent's—Westchester
275 North St., Harrison 10528
(914) 967-6500
Internet: www.svcmc.org/westchester

Exec. Dir.: Bernadette Kingham-Bez

Mgr., Medical Records: Maggie Santoro (914) 925-5260

133 Beds
Fee for Copy of Records: See statutory fee, *supra*

HORNELL Steuben County

St. James Mercy Hospital
411 Canisteo St., Hornell 14843
(607) 324-8000
E-mail: info@stjamesmercy.org
Internet: www.stjamesmercy.org

President/C.E.O.: Mary LaRowe (607) 324-8113

Records Administrator: Denise Becher (607) 324-8018

157 Beds
Fee for Copy of Records: See statutory fee, *supra*
Affiliate of Catholic Health East

HUDSON Columbia County

Columbia Memorial Hospital
71 Prospect Ave., Suite L10, Hudson 12534
(518) 828-7601; Fax: (518) 828-8525
Internet: www.columbiamemorial.com

President/C.E.O.: Jane Ehrlich, Ext. 8039

Dir. of Medical Records: Claudia Overacker
Ext. 8394

192 Beds
Fee for Copy of Records: See statutory fee, *supra*

HUNTINGTON Suffolk County

Huntington Hospital
270 Park Ave., Huntington 11743-9982
(631) 351-2000; Medical Records: (631) 351-2279
E-mail: staff@hunthosp.org; Internet: www.hunthosp.org

President/C.E.O.: Kevin F. Lawlor
(631) 351-2200; Fax: (631) 351-2586

Records Administrator: Robert Coelho

408 Beds
Fee for Copy of Records: See statutory fee, *supra*
Affiliate of North Shore-Long Island Jewish Health System

IRVING Chautauqua County

TLC Health Network, Inc.
Lake Shore Healthcare Center
845 Routes 5 & 20, Irving 14081
(716) 951-7000; Fax: (716) 951-7046;
Health Information Mgmt.: (716) 951-7070
Internet: www.tlchealth.org

President/C.E.O.: Jonathan I. Lawrence, F.A.C.H.E.

Chief Legal Counsel: Vacancy at Press Time

Dir., Health Information Mgmt.: Cheryll Rogers

62 Beds
Fee for Copy of Records: See statutory fee, *supra*
Formerly Lake Shore Healthcare Center

ITHACA Tompkins County

Cayuga Medical Center at Ithaca
101 Dates Dr., Ithaca 14850
(607) 274-4011; Fax: (607) 274-4527
Internet: www.cayugamed.org
President/C.E.O.: Rob MacKenzie, M.D. (607) 274-4443
Chief Legal Counsel: Elena Flash
202 E. State St., Suite 700, Ithaca 14850
(607) 273-4200; Fax: (607) 272-6694
Dir., Health Information Mgmt.: Toni Cornell
(607) 274-4313
204 Beds
Fee for Copy of Records: See statutory fee, *supra*

JAMAICA Queens County

Jamaica Hospital Medical Center
8900 Van Wyck Expressway, Jamaica 11418-2832
(718) 206-6000; Health Information Mgmt.: (718) 206-7909
Internet: www.jamaicahospital.org
President/C.E.O.: David P. Rosen (718) 206-6290
Dir., Health Information Mgmt.: Regina Lieb
365 Beds
Fee for Copy of Records: See statutory fee, *supra*

Queens Hospital Center
82-68 164th St., Jamaica 11432
(718) 883-3000; Fax: (718) 883-6116
Exec. Dir.: Antonio D. Martin (718) 883-2351
Sr. V.P./President: Dr. Ann Sullivan (718) 883-2275
Dir., Health Information Mgmt.: Louis Neville
(718) 883-2437
200 Beds
Fee for Copy of Records: See statutory fee, *supra*

JAMESTOWN Chautauqua County

Jones Memorial Health Center
207 Foote Ave., P.O. Box 840, Jamestown 14702-0840
(716) 487-0141; Medical Records: (716) 664-8147
Internet: www.wcahospital.org
President/C.E.O.: Betsy T. Wright (716) 664-8300
Dir., Health Information Mgmt.: Diane French
(716) 664-8385
88 Beds
Fee for Copy of Records: See statutory fee, *supra*

WCA Hospital
207 Foote Ave., Jamestown 14701
Mailing Address: P.O. Box 840, Jamestown 14702-0840
(716) 487-0141; Fax: (716) 664-8336;
Medical Records: (716) 664-8147
Internet: www.wcahospital.org
President/C.E.O.: Betsy T. Wright (716) 664-8300
Dir., Health Information Mgmt.: Diane French
(716) 664-8385
312 Beds
Fee for Copy of Records: See statutory fee, *supra*
Formerly Woman's Christian Association

JOHNSON CITY Broome County

United Health Services Hospitals, Inc.
Wilson Regional Medical Center
33-57 Harrison St., Johnson City 13790
(607) 763-6000
Internet: www.uhs.net
President/C.E.O.: Matthew Salanger
(607) 763-6130; E-mail: matthew_salanger@uhs.org
General Counsel: Donald P. Carlin
(607) 762-3366; E-mail: donald_carlin@ush.org
Dir., Health Information Mgmt.: Trish Jewson
(607) 762-2112; E-mail: trish_jews@uhs.org
296 Beds
Fee for Copy of Records: See statutory fee, *supra*
Affiliate of the United Health Services

KENMORE Erie County

Kenmore Mercy Hospital
2950 Elmwood Ave., Kenmore 14217-1390
(716) 447-6100; Fax: (716) 447-6090
Internet: www.chsbuffalo.org
President/C.E.O.: James M. Millard
Dir., Health Information Mgmt.: Marise Grosenbaugh
(716) 447-6529
184 Beds
Fee for Copy of Records: See statutory fee, *supra*
Affiliate of Catholic Health System

KINGSTON Ulster County

Benedictine Hospital
105 Mary's Ave., Kingston 12401
(845) 338-2500
Internet: www.benedictine.org
President/C.E.O.: David Lundquist (845) 334-3115
Dir., Health Information Mgmt.: Marcel Pay
(845) 334-4704
Assoc. Dir.: Donna Marshall (845) 334-3075
222 Beds
Fee for Copy of Records: See statutory fee, *supra*

Kingston Hospital
396 Broadway, Kingston 12401-4692
(845) 331-3131
Internet: www.kingstonhospital.org
President/C.E.O.: David W. Lundquist
Dir., Health Information Mgmt.: Marcel Tay
150 Beds
Fee for Copy of Records: See statutory fee, *supra*
Affiliate of the Health Alliance of the Hudson Valley

LAKE PLACID Essex County

Adirondack Medical Center at Lake Placid Site
29 Church St., P.O. Box 790, Lake Placid 12946
(518) 523-3311; Fax: (518) 523-8369
Internet: www.amccares.org
President/C.E.O.: Chandler M. Ralph
Chief Legal Counsel: Robert Iseman (518) 462-3000
Dir., Health Information Mgmt.:
Melody (Starr) Thorton (518) 891-4141, Ext. 2317
2 Beds
Fee for Copy of Records: See statutory fee, *supra*
Affiliate of the Brim HealthCare System

LEWISTON Niagara County

Mount St. Marys Hospital and Health Center
5300 Military Rd., Lewiston 14092
(716) 297-4800; Fax: (716) 298-2333;
Health Information Mgmt.: (716) 298-2230
Internet: www.msmh.org
President/C.E.O.: Judith A. Maness (716) 298-2004
Dir., Health Information Mgmt.: Laurie Merletti
(716) 298-2009
179 Beds
Fee for Copy of Records: See statutory fee, *supra*
Affiliate of Ascension Health, Inc.

LITTLE FALLS Herkimer County

Little Falls Hospital
140 Burwell St., Little Falls 13365
(315) 823-1000; Health Information Mgmt.: (315) 823-5273
Internet: www.lfhny.org
President/C.E.O.: Michael L. Ogden
(315) 823-5262; Fax: (315) 823-5383
Dir., Health Information Mgmt.: Lori Usyk
(315) 823-5362
100 Beds
Fee for Copy of Records: See statutory fee, *supra*
Affiliated with Bassett Healthcare

LONG BEACH **Nassau County**

Long Beach Medical Center
455 E. Bay Dr., Long Beach 11561
(516) 897-1000; Fax: (516) 897-1214;
Medical Records: (516) 897-1414
Internet: www.lbmc.org
C.E.O.: Douglas L. Melzer (516) 897-1208
E-mail: dmelzer@lbmc.org
Records Administrator: Arline Quinteros
Ext. 1416
203 Beds
Fee for Copy of Records: See statutory fee, *supra*

LONG ISLAND CITY **Queens County**

Mount Sinai Hospital of Queens
25-10 30th Ave., Long Island City 11102-2495
(718) 932-1000
Internet: www.mshq.org
Exec. Dir.: Caryn A. Schwab, Ext. 4320
Dir. of Medical Records: Lordy Josama, Ext. 4220
235 Beds
Fee for Copy of Records: See statutory fee, *supra*
Formerly Western Queens Community Hospital

LOWVILLE **Lewis County**

Lewis County General Hospital
7785 N. State St., Lowville 13367
(315) 376-5200; Health Information Mgmt.: (315) 376-5792
Internet: www.lcgh.net
C.E.O.: Eric R. Burch (315) 376-5203
Dir., Health Information Mgmt.: Sally Manning
54 Beds
Fee for Copy of Records: See statutory fee, *supra*

MALONE **Franklin County**

Alice Hyde Medical Center
133 Park St., Malone 12953
(518) 483-3000; Fax: (518) 483-0860;
Health Information Mgmt.: (518) 481-2215
Internet: www.alicehyde.com
President: John W. Johnson (518) 481-2202
Dir., Health Information Mgmt.: Donna Bishop
78 Beds
Fee for Copy of Records: See statutory fee, *supra*

MANHASSET **Nassau County**

North Shore University Hospital
300 Community Dr., Manhasset 11030
(516) 562-0100; Health Information Mgmt.: (516) 465-8920
Internet: www.northshorelij.com
Exec. Dir.: Susan Somerville
(516) 562-4050; Fax: (516) 562-1395
President/C.E.O.: Michael J. Dowling
Chief Legal Counsel: Keith Thompson (516) 465-8090
Dir., Health Information Mgmt.: Elizabeth Heller
(516) 562-4260; Fax: (516) 562-3918
731 Beds
Fee for Copy of Records: See statutory fee, *supra*; plus postage & handling
Affiliate of North Shore-Long Island Jewish Health System

MARGARETVILLE **Delaware County**

Margaretville Memorial Hospital
42084 State Highway 28, Margaretville 12455
(845) 586-2631
Internet: www.margaretvillehospital.org
Administrator/C.E.O.: Edmond Morache
Dir., Health Information Mgmt.: Donna Rutulante
Ext. 3173
15 Beds
Fee for Copy of Records: See statutory fee, *supra*
Affiliate of Kingston Regional Health

MASSENA **Saint Lawrence County**

Massena Memorial Hospital
1 Hospital Dr., Massena 13662
(315) 764-1711; Health Information Mgmt.: (315) 769-4371;
Health Information Mgmt. Fax: (315) 769-4387
Internet: www.massenahospital.org
C.E.O.: Charles F. Fahd II (315) 769-4234
Dir., Health Information Mgmt.: Julie Zyzik
50 Beds
Fee for Copy of Records: See statutory fee, *supra*

MEDINA **Orleans County**

Medina Memorial Hospital
200 Ohio St., Medina 14103
(585) 798-2000; Medical Records: (585) 798-8137, 38;
Medical Records Fax: (585) 798-8144
E-mail: info@medinamemorial.org
Internet: www.medinamemorial.org
President/C.E.O.: Jim Sinner
(585) 798-8103; Fax: (585) 798-8107
General Counsel: Lance J. Mark
(585) 798-5555; Fax: (585) 798-5559
Records Administrator: Theresa Rheinhardt
(585) 798-8140
101 Beds
Fee for Copy of Records: See statutory fee, *supra*

MIDDLETOWN **Orange County**

Orange Regional Medical Center—Horton Campus
60 Prospect Ave., Middletown 10940
(845) 343-2424; Health Information Mgmt.: (845) 342-7565
Internet: www.ormc.org
C.E.O.: Scott Batulis; Fax: (845) 342-7514
Dir., Health Information Mgmt.: Lisa Newlin
374 Beds
Fee for Copy of Records: See statutory fee, *supra*
Affiliate of New York Presbyterian Healthcare System; formerly Horton Medical Center

MINEOLA **Nassau County**

Winthrop-University Hospital
259 First St., Mineola 11501-3987
(516) 663-0333; Fax: (516) 663-2953
Internet: www.winthrop.org
President/C.E.O.: John F. Collins
Dir., Health Information Mgmt.: MaryEllen McGowan
(516) 663-8901
591 Beds
Fee for Copy of Records: See statutory fee, *supra*

MONTOUR FALLS **Schuyler County**

Schuyler Hospital
220 Steuben St., Montour Falls 14865
(607) 535-7121;
Health Information Mgmt. Fax: (607) 535-6210
Internet: www.schuylerhospital.org
President/C.E.O.: Rick Stelzer
Chief Legal Counsel: John Hayes (607) 273-2301
Dir., Health Information Mgmt.: Jeanne Maine
51 Beds
Fee for Copy of Records: See statutory fee, *supra*

MOUNT KISCO **Westchester County**

Northern Westchester Hospital Center
400 E. Main St., Mount Kisco 10549-3477
(914) 666-1200; Medical Records: (914) 666-1859
Internet: www.nwhc.net
President/C.E.O.: Joel Seligman
(914) 666-1301; Fax: (914) 666-1305
Records Administrator: Debbie Pirchio; Fax: (914) 666-1013
233 Beds
Fee for Copy of Records: See statutory fee, *supra*
Affiliate of Stellaris Health Network

MOUNT VERNON **Westchester County**

Mount Vernon Hospital
12 N. 7th Ave., Mount Vernon 10550
(914) 664-8000; Internet: www.ssmc.org

President/C.E.O.: John R. Spicer

Chief Legal Counsel: Clark Walter
(914) 365-4319; Fax: (914) 637-1516

Records Administrator: Robin Artenberry
Fax: (914) 664-8055

196 Beds
Fee for Copy of Records: See statutory fee, *supra*
Affiliate of Sound Shore Health System

NEW HARTFORD **Oneida County**

Faxton St. Luke's HealthCare
1656 Champlain Ave., New Hartford 13413
Mailing Address: P.O. Box 479, Utica 13503
(315) 624-6000

President/C.E.O.: Scott H. Perra (315) 624-6001

Chief Legal Counsel: Thomas Soja (315) 624-5050

Dir., Health Information Mgmt.: S. Michael Marris
(315) 624-6025

346 Beds
Fee for Copy of Records: See statutory fee, *supra*

NEW HYDE PARK **Nassau County**

Long Island Jewish Medical Center
270-05 76th Ave., New Hyde Park 11040
(718) 470-7000; Medical Records: (516) 465-3245
Internet: www.northshorelij.com

President/C.E.O.: Michael J. Dowling

Senior V.P./General Counsel: Keith Thompson
(516) 465-8090

Dir. of Medical Records: Clarence Henry

827 Beds
Fee for Copy of Records: See statutory fee, *supra*

NEW ROCHELLE **Westchester County**

Sound Shore Medical Center of Westchester
16 Guion Pl., New Rochelle 10801-5500
(914) 632-5000; Health Information Mgmt.: (914) 637-1222
Internet: www.ssmc.org

President/C.E.O.: John R. Spicer (914) 365-3700

Chief Legal Counsel: Clark E. Walter
(914) 365-4319; Fax: (914) 632-1976

V.P., Health Information Mgmt.: Rhonda Ruiz
(914) 365-3715

252 Beds
Fee for Copy of Records: See statutory fee, *supra*
Formerly New Rochelle Hospital Medical Center; affiliate of Sound Shore Health System

NEW YORK **New York County**

Bellevue Hospital Center
462 1st Ave. at 27th St., N.Y.C. 10016
(212) 562-4132

Senior V.P.: Lynda D. Curtis

Records Administrator: Debra Wright (212) 562-3105

1242 Beds
Fee for Copy of Records: See statutory fee, *supra*
Member of NYC Health & Hospitals Corporation

Beth Israel Medical Center
Petrie Campus
1st Ave. at 16th St., N.Y.C. 10003
(212) 420-2000; Internet: www.wehealny.org

President: Harris M. Nagler, M.D. (Acting) (212) 420-2873

Exec. V.P./Chief Legal Officer: Kathryn Meyer
(212) 523-2162

Records Administrator: Raymond Cosner, R.H.I.A.
(212) 420-2666

1,106 Beds
Fee for Copy of Records: See statutory fee, *supra*
Affiliate of Continuum Health Partners

Cabrini Medical Center
E-mail: info@cabrininy.org; Internet: www.cabrininy.org
Hospital closed as of March 2008. Call (212) 222-7464 for more information.

Gracie Square Hospital
420 E. 76th Street, N.Y.C. 10021
(212) 988-4400; Fax: (212) 434-5373;
Medical Records: (212) 434-5309
E-mail: info@nygsh.org; Internet: www.nygsh.org

C.E.O.: Frank Bruno

Dir. of Medical Records: Lily Singh

157 Beds (Inpatient Psychiatric Facility)
Fee for Copy of Records: See statutory fee, *supra*
Affiliate of the New York Presbyterian Health System

Harlem Hospital Center
506 Lenox Ave., N.Y.C. 10037-1894
(212) 939-1000; Health Information Mgmt.: (212) 939-2764

Exec. Dir.: John Palmer
(212) 939-1340; Fax: (212) 939-8300

Dir., Health Information Mgmt.: Nelly Valentin

272 Beds
Fee for Copy of Records: See statutory fee, *supra*

Hospital for Special Surgery
535 E. 70th St., N.Y.C. 10021-4898
(212) 606-1000; Health Information Mgmt.: (212) 606-1254
Internet: www.hss.edu

President/C.E.O.: Louis A. Shapiro (212) 606-1236

Dir., Health Information Mgmt.: Glenn Rispaud

160 Beds
Fee for Copy of Records: See statutory fee, *supra*
Affiliate of the New York Presbyterian Healthcare System

Lenox Hill Hospital
100 E. 77th St., N.Y.C. 10021-1883
(212) 434-2000; Medical Records: (212) 434-2420
Internet: www.lenoxhillhospital.org

President/C.E.O.: Gladys George (212) 434-2010

Records Administrator: Francine Fields
(212) 434-2433; E-mail: ffields@lenoxhill.net

652 Beds
Fee for Copy of Records: See statutory fee, *supra*

Manhattan Eye, Ear and Throat Hospital
210 E. 64th St., N.Y.C. 10021-9885
(212) 838-9200; Health Information Mgmt.: (212) 605-3712
Internet: www.nymeeth.org; www.lenoxhillhospital.org

Exec. Dir.: Philip Rosenthal (212) 605-3770

Dir., Health Information Mgmt.: Francine Fields

30 Beds
Fee for Copy of Records: See statutory fee, *supra*
Affiliated with the Lenox Hill Hospital

Memorial Hospital for Cancer and Allied Diseases
Memorial Sloan-Kettering Cancer Center
1275 York Ave., N.Y.C. 10065
(212) 639-2000; Medical Records: (646) 227-2089
Internet: www.mskcc.org/mskcc/html/44.cfm

President/C.E.O.: Dr. Harold Varmus

Sr. V.P./Administrator: Kathryn Martin
(212) 639-2623; Fax: (212) 717-3079

Sr. V.P./General Counsel: Roger Parker
(212) 639-5800; Fax: (212) 717-3079
E-mail: parkerr@mskcc.org

Records Administrator: Kathy Bello (646) 227-2071

565 Beds
Fee for Copy of Records: See statutory fee, *supra*

Metropolitan Hospital Center
1901 First Ave., N.Y.C. 10029 (212) 423-6262

Exec. Dir.: Meryl Weinberg

President: Alan Aviles (212) 788-3300

Dir. of Medical Records: Lebby Delgado
(718) 579-5421; Fax: (718) 579-5412

494 Beds
Fee for Copy of Records: See statutory fee, *supra*
Member of the NYC Health & Hospitals Corporation

New York—Cont'd

Mount Sinai Hospital
One Gustave L. Levy Place,
1190 Fifth Ave., N.Y.C. 10029-6574
(212) 241-6500; Health Information Mgmt.: (212) 241-7601
Internet: www.mountsinaihospital.org

President/C.E.O.: Wayne E. Keathley

General Counsel: Michael MacDonald (212) 659-8105

Dir., Health Information Mgmt.: Susan Cohen

1,171 Beds
Fee for Copy of Records: See statutory fee, *supra*

N.Y.U. Hospital for Joint Diseases
301 E. 17th St., N.Y.C. 10003
(212) 598-6000; Medical Records: (212) 598-6790;
Fax: (212) 260-1203
E-mail: info@hjdhospital.com
Internet: www.jointdiseases.com

Senior V.P. for NYUHJD Hospital Operations & the Musulosketelal Strategic Area:
David A. Dibner, F.A.C.H.E. (212) 598-6534

Chief Legal Counsel: Annette Johnson
(212) 263-7921

Records Administrator: Kristin Keller (212) 598-6781
E-mail: kristin-keller@nyumc.org

220 Beds
Fee for Copy of Records: See statutory fee, *supra*

NY Eye and Ear Infirmary
310 E. 14th St., N.Y.C. 10003
(212) 979-4000
Internet: www.nyee.edu

President/C.E.O.: D. McWilliam S. Kessler
(212) 979-4301; Fax: (212) 228-0664

Records Administrator: Barbara Siegal (212) 979-4344

103 Beds
Fee for Copy of Records: Contact Medical Records Dept. for fee information
Affiliate of the Continuum Health Partners, Inc.

New York Presbyterian Hospital—Weill Cornell Medical Center
525 E. 68th St., N.Y.C. 10021
(212) 746-5454
Internet: www.nyp.org

President/C.E.O.: Dr. Herbert Pardes (212) 305-8000

Sr. V.P./Chief Legal Officer & General Counsel:
Maxine Fass (212) 746-6500

Dir., Health Information Mgmt.: Diana Muscente
(212) 746-0515

920 Beds
Fee for Copy of Records: Contact Chart One representative in Medical Records Dept.

New York Downtown Hospital
170 William St., N.Y.C. 10038-2649
(212) 312-5000; Fax: (212) 312-5977;
Health Information Mgmt.: (212) 312-5122
Internet: www.downtownhospital.org

President/C.E.O.: Jeffrey Menkes
(212) 312-5175; Fax: (212) 312-5741

Dir., Health Information Mgmt.: Diane Chapelle
Fax: (212) 312-5128

300 Beds
Fee for Copy of Records: See statutory fee, *supra*
Formerly NYU Downtown Hospital; affiliate of the New York Presbyterian Healthcare System

New York University Medical Center
550 1st Ave., N.Y.C. 10016
(212) 263-7300; Health Information Mgmt.: (212) 263-7840
Internet: www.nyumedicalcenter.org

President/C.E.O.: Robert I. Grossman
(212) 263-5500; Fax: (212) 263-8460

Sr. V.P./General Counsel: Annette Johnson
(212) 263-8777; Fax: (212) 263-3235

Dir., Health Information Mgmt.: Gabriela Grygus
(212) 263-5495; Fax: (212) 263-7665

879 Beds
Fee for Copy of Records: See statutory fee, *supra*

New York—Presbyterian Hospital
Allen Pavilion
5141 Broadway, N.Y.C. 10034
(212) 932-4000
Internet: www.nyp.org

President/C.E.O.: Dr. Herbert Pardes
(212) 305-8000

Sr. V.P./Chief Legal Officer & General Counsel:
Maxine Fass (212) 746-6500

Dir., Health Information Mgmt.: Diana Muscente
(212) 746-0515

280 Beds
Fee for Copy of Records: Contact Chart One representative in Medical Records Dept.

New York—Presbyterian Hospital
Columbia Presbyterian Medical Center
630 W. 168th St., N.Y.C. 10032
(212) 305-2500; Fax: (212) 305-8012
Internet: www.nyp.org

President/C.E.O.: Dr. Herbert Pardes (212) 305-8000

Sr. V.P./C.O.O.: Robert E. Kelly

Sr. V.P./Chief Legal Officer & General Counsel:
Maxine Fass (212) 746-6500

Dir., Health Information Mgmt.: Diana Muscente
(212) 746-0515

1014 Beds
Fee for Copy of Records: Contact Chart One representative in Medical Records Dept.

North General Hospital
1879 Madison Ave., N.Y.C. 10035
(212) 423-4000; Fax: (212) 423-4204

President/C.E.O.: Dr. Samuel Daniel (212) 423-4111

General Counsel: Lisa Hackett (212) 423-1480

Records Administrator: Peter Micallef (212) 423-4171

240 Beds
Fee for Copy of Records: See statutory fee, *supra*

Rockefeller University Hospital
1230 York Ave., N.Y.C. 10021
(212) 327-8000;
Health Information Systems: (212) 327-8417
Internet: www.rucares.org

Administrator: Maija Williams
(212) 327-8501; Fax: (212) 327-7610

C.E.O.: James Krueger
(212) 327-7441; Fax: (212) 327-8449

Dir., Health Information Svces.: Laurent Laor
(212) 327-7717; Fax: (212) 327-8517

40 Beds
Fee for Copy of Records: See statutory fee, *supra*

St. Luke's Roosevelt Hospital
St. Luke's Hospital Division
1111 Amsterdam Ave., N.Y.C. 10025
(212) 523-4000
Internet: www.wehealny.org

President/C.E.O.: Frank J. Cracolici
(212) 523-8781

Exec. V.P., Corporate Affairs & General Counsel:
Katherine Meyer

Dir., Health Information Mgmt.: Marianne DiMaggio
(212) 523-3264

1,076 Beds
Fee for Copy of Records: See statutory fee, *supra*
Affiliate of Continuum Health Partners

New York—Cont'd

St. Luke's Roosevelt Hospital Center
Roosevelt Hospital Division
1000 Tenth Ave. at 58th St., N.Y.C. 10019
(212) 523-4000; Health Information Mgmt.: (212) 523-7116
Internet: www.wehealny.org

President/C.E.O.: Frank J. Cracolici (212) 523-8781

Exec. V.P., Corporate Affairs & General Counsel: Kathryn Meyer (212) 523-2162

Dir., Health Information Mgmt.: Marianne DiMaggio (212) 523-7097

505 Beds
Fee for Copy of Records: See statutory fee, *supra*
Affiliate of Continuum Health Partners

St. Vincent's Hospital & Medical Center of New York
170 W. 12th St., N.Y.C. 10011
Medical Records: (212) 604-7777
Internet: www.svcmc.org

758 Beds
Fee for Copy of Records: See statutory fee, *supra*
Hospital closed in 2010, See website for more information

St. Vincent's Midtown Hospital
Internet: www.stvincentsmidtown.org

250 Beds
Fee for Copy of Records: See statutory fee, *supra*
Hospital closed in 2007. See website for more information.

NEWARK **Wayne County**

Newark Wayne Community Hospital
1200 Driving Park Ave., P.O. Box 111, Newark 14513-0111
(315) 332-2022
Internet: www.viahealth.org

President: Annette Leahy

Dir., Health Information Mgmt.: Kelly Shay

120 Beds
Fee for Copy of Records: See statutory fee, *supra*
Affiliate of Rochester General Health System

NEWBURGH **Orange County**

St. Lukes Cornwall Hospital
Newburgh Campus
70 Dubois St., Newburgh 12550
(845) 561-4400; Medical Records: (845) 568-2520
Internet: www.stlukescornwallhospital.org

President/C.E.O.: Allan E. Atzrott

Dir., Health Information Mgmt.: Laura Berberich (845) 568-2450

242 Beds
Fee for Copy of Records: See statutory fee, *supra*
Formerly St. Lukes Hospital of Newburgh

NEWFANE **Niagara County**

Eastern Niagara Hospital, Inc.
2600 William St., Newfane 14108
(716) 514-5700

President/C.E.O.: Clare A. Haar (716) 514-5502

Chief Legal Counsel: Francis P. Weimer (716) 854-3015

Records Administrator: Cheryl Quinn (716) 778-5071; Fax: (716) 514-5545

134 Beds
Fee for Copy of Records: Please call Medical Records Dept. for fee schedule
Formerly known as Lockport Memorial Hospital

NIAGARA FALLS **Niagara County**

Niagara Falls Memorial Medical Center
621 Tenth St., Niagara Falls 14302
(716) 278-4000; Internet: www.nfmmc.org

President/C.E.O.: Joseph A. Ruffolo (716) 278-4301

Dir., Health Information Mgmt.: Don Skibniewski

288 Beds
Fee for Copy of Records: See statutory fee, *supra*

NISKAYUNA **Schenectady County**

Bellevue Woman's Hospital, Inc.
Ellis Hospital
2210 Troy-Schenectady Rd., Niskayuna 12309
(518) 346-9400; Medical Records: (518) 346-9519
Internet: www.bellevuewoman.org

President/C.E.O.: James W. Connolly

Dir., Health Information Svces.: Denise Madigan

72 Beds
Fee for Copy of Records: See statutory fee, *supra*
Merged with Ellis Hospital

NORTH TONAWANDA **Niagara County**

DeGraff Memorial Hospital
445 Tremont St., North Tonawanda 14120
(716) 694-4500; Health Information Mgmt.: (716) 859-2734
Internet: http://degraff.kaleidahealth.org

President: Anthony Zito (716) 690-2004; Fax: (716) 690-2300

Dir., Health Information Mgmt.: Vickie Trautman

155 Beds
Fee for Copy of Records: See statutory fee, *supra*
Affiliate of Kaleida Health

NORTHPORT **Suffolk County**

Northport V.A. Medical Center
79 Middleville Rd., Northport 11768-2293
(631) 261-4400; Fax: (631) 754-7933
Internet: www.northport.va.gov

Director: Phillip C. Moschitta
Fee for Copy of Records: $15.00 flat fee

NORWICH **Chenango County**

Chenango Memorial Hospital, Inc.
179 N. Broad St., Norwich 13815-1097
(607) 337-4111; Fax: (607) 337-4284;
Health Information Svces.: (607) 337-4244
Internet: www.uhs.net

President/C.E.O.: Drake Lamen, M.D. (607) 337-4113

V.P., Quality Mgmt.: Wendy Surdoval (607) 337-4138

Mgr., Health Information Svces.: Cheryl Labar

138 Beds
Fee for Copy of Records: See statutory fee, *supra*
Affiliate of United Health Services

NYACK **Rockland County**

Nyack Hospital
160 N. Midland Ave., Nyack 10960-2505
(845) 348-2000
Internet: www.nyackhospital.org

President/C.E.O.: David H. Freed (845) 348-2110; Fax: (845) 348-3040

Dir., Health Information Svces.: Beth Slavis (845) 348-2525; Fax: (845) 348-8433

375 Beds
Fee for Copy of Records: See statutory fee, *supra*
Member of New York Presbyterian Healthcare System

OCEANSIDE **Nassau County**

South Nassau Communities Hospital
One Healthy Way, Oceanside 11572
(516) 632-3000; Fax: (516) 632-3499;
Medical Records: (516) 632-3907;
Medical Records Fax: (516) 336-2951
Internet: www.southnassau.org

President/C.E.O.: Joseph A. Quagliata (516) 632-3939

Records Administrator: Colleen Garvey

429 Beds
Fee for Copy of Records: See statutory fee, *supra*
Affiliate of the Winthrop South Nassau University Health System

OGDENSBURG **Saint Lawrence County**

Claxton-Hepburn Medical Center
214 King St., Ogdensburg 13669
(315) 393-3600
E-mail: info@chmed.org
Internet: www.claxtonhepburn.org
President/C.E.O.: Mark A. Webster
(315) 393-8880, Ext. 5235; Fax: (315) 393-8506
Records Administrator: Joanne Todd, R.R.A.
(315) 393-8880, Ext. 5126
149 Beds
Fee for Copy of Records: See statutory fee, *supra*

OLEAN **Cattaraugus County**

Olean General Hospital
515 Main St., Olean 14760
(716) 373-2600; Medical Records: (716) 375-6205
Internet: www.ogh.org
President/C.E.O.: Timothy J. Finan
E-mail: tfinan@ogh.org
Records Administrator: Kathy Grillo
E-mail: kgrillo@ogh.org
186 Beds
Fee for Copy of Records: See statutory fee, *supra*

ONEIDA **Madison County**

Oneida Healthcare Center
321 Genesee St., Oneida 13421
(315) 363-6000; Health Information Mgmt.: (315) 361-2027
E-mail: info@oneidahealthcare.org
Internet: www.oneidahealthcare.org
C.E.O.: Gene F. Morreale
E-mail: gmorreale@oneidahealthcare.org
Dir., Health Information Mgmt.: JoAnne Nash, R.H.I.A.
E-mail: jnash@oneidahealthcare.org
101 Beds
Fee for Copy of Records: See statutory fee, *supra*

ONEONTA **Otsego County**

Aurelia Osborn Fox Memorial Hospital
One Norton Ave., Oneonta 13820-2697
(607) 432-2000; Medical Records: (607) 431-5456
Internet: www.foxcarenetwork.com
President: John R. Remillard
(607) 431-5900; Fax: (607) 431-5006
Records Administrator: Debra Smith
100 Beds
Fee for Copy of Records: See statutory fee, *supra*
Affiliate of the Bassett Healthcare Network

OSWEGO **Oswego County**

Oswego Hospital
110 W. 6th St., Oswego 13126
(315) 349-5511
Internet: www.oswegohealth.org
President/C.E.O: Ann Gilpin (315) 349-5526
Chief Legal Counsel: Craig Morrissey
(315) 342-7214
Records Administrator: Stephanie Stine
164 Beds
Fee for Copy of Records: See statutory fee, *supra*
Affiliate of Oswego Health

Oswego Hospital
Behavioral Services Division
74 Bunner St., Oswego 13126
(315) 343-8162
Internet: www.oswegohealth.org
Administrator/C.E.O.: Ann C. Gilpin
Dir. Behavioral Svces.: Kimberly Garrow
Dir., Health Information Mgmt.: Stephanie Stine
164 Beds
Fee for Copy of Records: See statutory fee, *supra*

PENN YAN **Yates County**

Soldiers and Sailors Memorial Hospital of Yates County
418 N. Main St., Penn Yan 14527
(315) 531-2000
Internet: www.flhealth.org
President/C.E.O.: Jose Acevedo
Site Administrator: James Hiserodt; Fax: (315) 531-2029
Dir. of Medical Records: Amy Crowfoot
Geneva General Hospital, 196-198 North St.,
Geneva 14456-1651 (315) 787-4122
25 Beds
Fee for Copy of Records: See statutory fee, *supra*
Affiliate of the Finger Lakes Health

PLAINVIEW **Nassau County**

Plainview Hospital
888 Old Country Rd., Plainview 11803-4978
(516) 719-3000; Fax: (516) 719-2719
Internet: www.northshorelij.com
Exec. Dir.: Michael Sener (516) 719-2200
Dir., Health Information Mgmt.: Donna Mei, Ext. 2519
239 Beds
Fee for Copy of Records: See statutory fee, *supra*
Formerly North Shore University Hospital at Plainview; Affiliate of the North Shore-Long Island Health System

PLATTSBURGH **Clinton County**

Champlain Valley Physicians Hospital Medical Center
75 Beekman St., Plattsburgh 12901
(518) 561-2000
Internet: www.cvph.org
President/C.E.O.: Stephens M. Mundy
E-mail: smundy@cvph.org
Records Administrator: Debra Mussen
356 Beds
Fee for Copy of Records: See statutory fee, *supra*

POMONA **Rockland County**

Doctor Robert L. Yeager Health Center
50 Sanatorium Rd., Pomona 10970-3554
(845) 364-2700; Health Information Mgmt.: (845) 364-2782
Commissioner: Richard J. Maloney
Dir., Health Information Mgmt.: Christine Fishberg
Ext. 2770
341 Beds
Fee for Copy of Records: See statutory fee, *supra*
Formerly Summit Park Hospital—Rockland County Infirmary

PORT JEFFERSON **Suffolk County**

John T. Mather Memorial Hospital
75 N. Country Rd., Port Jefferson 11777
(631) 473-1320; Fax: (631) 473-7367
Internet: www.matherhospital.org
President: Kenneth Roberts (631) 476-2837
Dir., Health Information Mgmt.: Debi Santiago
(631) 476-2727
248 Beds
Fee for Copy of Records: See statutory fee, *supra*
Member of the Mather-St. Charles Health Alliance

St. Charles Hospital
200 Belle Terre Rd., Port Jefferson 11777-1968
(631) 474-6000; Fax: (631) 474-6884;
Medical Records: (631) 474-6123
Internet: www.stcharles.org
Exec. Dir.: James O'Connor
(631) 474-6600
Records Administrator: Deborah Lantz (631) 474-6126
231 Beds
Fee for Copy of Records: See statutory fee, *supra*
Affiliate of Catholic Health Services of Long Island

PORT JERVIS **Orange County**

Bon Secours Community Hospital
160 E. Main St., Port Jervis 12771
(845) 858-7000; Fax: (845) 858-7415;
Health Information Mgmt.: (845) 858-7090
Internet: www.bonsecourscommunityhosp.org

Exec. V.P./Administrator: Leah Cerkvenik
(845) 858-7151

Dir., Health Information Mgmt.: Carol Cullinan
(845) 858-7093

187 Beds
Fee for Copy of Records: $.75 per page
Affiliate of the Bon Secours Charity Health System; formerly Mercy Community Hospital

POTSDAM **Saint Lawrence County**

Canton-Potsdam Hospital
50 Leroy St., Potsdam 13676
(315) 265-3300;
Health Information Mgmt.: (315) 261-5270, 71
Internet: www.cphospital.org

C.E.O.: David B. Acker
(315) 261-6001; Fax: (315) 265-4745

General Counsel: Roger Linden
76 Market St., P.O. Box 5153, Potsdam 13676
(315) 265-2747; Fax: (315) 265-2749

Dir., Health Information Mgmt.: Erin O'Connor

94 Beds
Fee for Copy of Records: See statutory fee, *supra*
Affiliated with Fletcher Allen Health Care

POUGHKEEPSIE **Dutchess County**

St. Francis Hospital
241 North Rd., Poughkeepsie 12601-1399
(845) 483-5000; Medical Records: (845) 431-8152;
Medical Records Fax: (845) 483-5099
Internet: www.sfhhc.org

President/C.E.O.: Robert L. Savage

General Counsel: Michael Gartland (845) 454-1110

Records Dir.: Linda Benzie

400 Beds
Fee for Copy of Records: See statutory fee, *supra*

Vassar Brothers Medical Center
45 Reade Place, Poughkeepsie 12601
(845) 454-8500
Internet: www.vassarbrothers.com

President/C.E.O.: Dr. Daniel Aronzon (845) 431-5653

Chief Legal Counsel: Frederick A. Thomas, J.D.,L.L.M.
(845) 483-6920

Dir., Health Information Mgmt.: Roxanne Paraella
(845) 437-3020

365 Beds
Fee for Copy of Records: See statutory fee, *supra*
Formerly Vassar Brothers Hospital

RHINEBECK **Dutchess County**

Northern Dutchess Hospital
6511 Springbrook Ave., P.O. Box 5002, Rhinebeck 12572
(845) 876-3001
E-mail: ndhinfo@health-quest.org
Internet: www.ndhosp.com

President/C.E.O.: Denise George
(845) 871-3100

General Counsel & V.P. for Legal Services:
Frederick Thomas (845) 483-6920

Dir., Health Information Mgmt.: Aleta Jaen
(845) 871-3301

68 Beds
Fee for Copy of Records: See statutory fee, *supra*
Affiliate of Health Quest

RIVERHEAD **Suffolk County**

Peconic Bay Medical Center
1300 Roanoke Ave., Riverhead 11901
(631) 548-6000; Fax: (631) 548-6048;
Medical Records: (631) 548-6377;
Medical Records Fax: (631) 548-6369
Internet: www.pbmedicalcenter.org

President/C.E.O.: Andrew J. Mitchell, F.A.C.H.E.
(631) 548-6060; Fax: (631) 727-8890

Records Administrator: Priscilla Komora; Ext. 6362

182 Beds
Fee for Copy of Records: See statutory fee, *supra*
Formerly Central Suffolk Hospital

ROCHESTER **Monroe County**

Highland Hospital for Rochester
1000 South Ave., Rochester 14620
(585) 473-2200;
Health Information Mgmt.: (585) 341-6766;
Health Information Mgmt. Fax: (585) 341-8493
Internet: www.stronghealth.com

President: Steven Goldstein (585) 275-7685

Dir., Health Information Mgmt.: Donna Barnard
(585) 275-2606

268 Beds
Fee for Copy of Records: See statutory fee, *supra*
Affiliate of University of Rochester

Monroe Community Hospital
435 E. Henrietta Rd., Rochester 14620
(585) 760-6500; Fax: (585) 760-6066
Internet: www.monroehosp.org

Exec. Dir.: Todd C. Spring (585) 760-6304

Chief Legal Counsel: Stefanie Barnes

Dir., Health Information Mgmt.: Cynthia Keller (Acting)
(585) 760-6090

39 Beds; Long-term acute care facility
Fee for Copy of Records: See statutory fee, *supra*

Rochester General Hospital
1425 Portland Ave., Rochester 14621
(585) 922-4000; Health Information Mgmt.: (585) 922-4521;
Health Information Mgmt. Fax: (585) 922-4018
Internet: www.rochestergeneral.org

President/C.E.O.: Mark C. Clement
(585) 922-5070; Fax: (585) 922-5997

Sr. V.P., Corporate Counsel: Hugh R. Thomas
(585) 922-4941; Fax: (585) 922-5997

Dir., Health Information Mgmt.: Barbara Gerringer
(585) 922-5265

528 Beds
Fee for Copy of Records: See statutory fee, *supra*
Affiliate of Rochester General Health System

Strong Memorial Hospital of the University of Rochester
601 Elmwood Ave., Rochester 14642
(585) 275-2100
Internet: www.urmc.rochester.edu

President/C.E.O.: Steven I. Goldstein, Box 612
(585) 275-7685

General Counsel: Christine Burke, Box 278979
(585) 758-7613; Fax: (585) 272-9311

Dir., Health Information Mgmt.: Donna Barnard
(585) 275-2606; Fax: (585) 273-1257

739 Beds
Fee for Copy of Records: See statutory fee, *supra*

Unity Health System—Genesee Street Campus
89 Genesee St., Rochester 14611
(585) 723-7000; Medical Records: (585) 368-3125
Internet: www.unityhealth.org

President/C.E.O.: Warren Hern

Records Administrator: Barbara Tripi

681 Beds
Fee for Copy of Records: See statutory fee, *supra*
Formerly St. Mary's Hospital; affiliate of Unity Health System

Rochester—Cont'd

Unity Hospital
1555 Long Pond Rd., Rochester 14626
(585) 723-7000
Internet: www.unityhealth.org
President/C.E.O.: Warren Hern (585) 368-3295
Records Supervisor: Barbara Tripi, Ext. 7401
259 Beds
Fee for Copy of Records: See statutory fee, *supra*
Formerly Park Ridge Hospital; Affiliate of Unity Health System

ROCKVILLE CENTRE Nassau County

Mercy Medical Center
1000 N. Village Ave., P.O. Box 9024,
Rockville Centre 11570
(516) 705-2525; Fax: (516) 705-1406;
Medical Records: (516) 705-1310
Internet: http://mercymedicalcenter.chsli.org
President/C.E.O.: Alan Guerci, M.D.
(516) 705-1401
Records Administrator: Vacancy at Press Time
375 Beds
Fee for Copy of Records: See statutory fee, *supra*
Member of Catholic Health Services of Long Island

ROME Oneida County

Rome Memorial Hospital, Inc.
1500 N. James St., Rome 13440
(315) 338-7000; Fax: (315) 338-7695
Internet: www.romehospital.org
President/C.E.O.: Darlene A. Burns, Ext. 7031
Records Administrator: JoAnne VanDresar, Ext. 7244
129 Beds
Fee for Copy of Records: See statutory fee, *supra*

ROOSEVELT ISLAND New York County

Coler Goldwater Specialty Hospital & Nursing Facility
Coler Division
One Main St., Roosevelt Island 10044
(212) 848-6000; Fax: (212) 848-6900
Exec. Dir.: Robert Hughes
Dir., Health Information Mgmt.: Jocelyn Izzard
1,025 Beds
Fee for Copy of Records: See statutory fee, *supra*
Component of New York City Health and Hospitals Corporation; formerly Coler Memorial Hospital

Coler Goldwater Specialty Hospital & Nursing Facility
Goldwater Division
1 Main St., Roosevelt Island 10044
(212) 318-8000; Fax: (212) 318-4370
Exec. Dir.: Robert Hughes
Dir., Health Information Mgmt.: Monica Lacassagne
991 Beds
Fee for Copy of Records: See statutory fee, *supra*
Formerly Goldwater Memorial Hospital

ROSLYN Nassau County

St. Francis Hospital
The Heart Center
100 Port Washington Blvd., Roslyn 11576-1348
(516) 562-6000; Health Information Mgmt.: (516) 562-6085
Internet: www.stfrancisheartcenter.com
President/C.E.O.: Alan D. Guerci, M.D.
Chief Legal Counsel: Patricia J. Hajnosz; Fax: (516) 562-6696
Dir., Health Information Mgmt.: Susan Cotter, R.H.I.A.
(516) 562-6078
247 Beds
Fee for Copy of Records: $.75 per page
Affiliate of Catholic Health Services of Long Island

SARANAC LAKE Franklin County

Adirondack Medical Center
Saranac Lake Site
2233 State Rt. 86, P.O. Box 471, Saranac Lake 12983-0471
(518) 891-4141; Fax: (518) 891-1191;
Health Information Mgmt.: (518) 897-2219
Internet: www.amccares.org
President/C.E.O.: Chandler M. Ralph
Chief Legal Counsel: Robert Iseman (518) 462-3000
Dir., Health Information Mgmt.:
Melody (Starr) Thorton, Ext. 2317
98 Beds
Fee for Copy of Records: See statutory fee, *supra*
Affiliate of Brim Healthcare, Inc.

SARATOGA SPRINGS Saratoga County

Saratoga Hospital
211 Church St., Saratoga Springs 12866
(518) 587-3222; Health Information Svces.: (518) 583-8304
Internet: www.saratogacare.org
President/C.E.O.: Angelo G. Calbone (518) 583-8492
Dir., Health Information Svces.: Lorelie Barrett, Ext. 2833
243 Beds
Fee for Copy of Records: See statutory fee, *supra*

SCHENECTADY Schenectady County

Ellis Hopsital
McClellan Campus
600 McClellan St., 2nd Floor, Schenectady 12304
(518) 382-2000; Fax: (518) 347-5409;
Medical Records: (518) 347-5173;
Medical Records Fax: (518) 347-5520
President/C.E.O.: James W. Connolly
Dir. of Medical Records: Debbie Thorington (518) 347-5184
200 Beds
Fee for Copy of Records: See statutory fee, *supra*
Formerly St. Clare's Hospital of Schenectady, N.Y.

Ellis Hospital
1101 Nott St., Schenectady 12308
(518) 243-4000; Health Information Svces.: (518) 243-4076
Internet: www.ellishospital.org
President/C.E.O.: James W. Connolly
(518) 243-4141; Fax: (518) 243-4668
Chief Legal Counsel: Overton, Russell, Doerr & Donovan
(518) 383-4000
Dir., Health Information Svces.: Nancy Binder
Fax: (518) 243-1487
352 Beds
Fee for Copy of Records: See statutory fee, *supra*

St. Clare's Hospital of Schenectady, N.Y.
See Ellis Hopsital

Sunnyview Rehabilitation Hospital
1270 Belmont Ave., Schenectady 12308
(518) 382-4500; Fax: (518) 382-4570
Internet: www.sunnyview.org
Administrator: Edward Eisenman (518) 382-4523
E-mail: eisenmane@nehealth.com
Chief Legal Counsel: Robert Swidler
(Northeast Health Corporate Counsel) (518) 271-5040
Records Administrator: Tammy Breault; Fax: (518) 386-3635
104 Beds
Fee for Copy of Records: See statutory fee, *supra*

SLEEPY HOLLOW Westchester County

Phelps Memorial Hospital Assn.
701 N. Broadway, Sleepy Hollow 10591
(914) 366-3000; Fax: (914) 366-1017
Internet: www.phelpshospital.org
President/C.E.O.: Keith F. Safian, Ext. 1000
Medical Records Administrator: Theresa Silversmith
Ext. 3064
235 Beds
Fee for Copy of Records: See statutory fee, *supra*

SMITHTOWN **Suffolk County**

St. Catherine of Siena Medical Center
50 Route 25A, Smithtown 11787
(631) 862-3000; Fax: (631) 376-4208;
Medical Records: (631) 862-3080
Internet: www.stcatherinemedicalcenter.org

President/C.E.O.: Vacancy at Press Time
(631) 376-4001

Records Administrator: Richard Rosenhagen

240 Beds
Fee for Copy of Records: See statutory fee, *supra*
Affiliate of the Catholic Health Services of Long Island HealthCare System

SOUTHAMPTON **Suffolk County**

Southampton Hospital
240 Meeting House Lane, Southampton 11968
(631) 726-8200; Medical Records: (631) 726-8310
Internet: www.southamptonhospital.org

President/C.E.O.: Robert S. Chaloner

Records Administrator: Tracy D'Errico
(631) 726-8313

168 Beds
Fee for Copy of Records: See statutory fee, *supra*

SPRINGVILLE **Erie County**

Bertrand Chaffee Hospital
224 E. Main St., Springville 14141
(716) 592-2871

President/C.E.O.: Nils J. Gunnersen; Fax: (716) 592-8105

Records Administrator: Linda Lux

49 Beds; Acute and long-term health care facility
Fee for Copy of Records: See statutory fee, *supra*

STAR LAKE **Saint Lawrence County**

Clifton-Fine Hospital
1014 Oswegatchie Trail Rd., P.O. Box 10, Star Lake 13690
(315) 848-3351; Fax: (315) 848-2314

C.E.O.: Rob Kimmes

Records Administrator: Nancy Russell

20 Beds
Fee for Copy of Records: See statutory fee, *supra*

STATEN ISLAND **Richmond County**

Richmond University Medical Center
355 Bard Ave., Staten Island 10310-1699
(718) 818-1234; Health Information Mgmt.: (718) 818-1048
Internet: www.rumcsi.org

President/C.E.O.: Richard J. Murphy

Dir., Health Information Mgmt.: Liza Simanovskaya

510 Beds
Fee for Copy of Records: $.75 per page for patient's attorney; $1.50 per page for Defendant; plus postage & handling
Formerly St. Vincents Catholic Medical Center of NY-Staten Island; Affiliate of Bridge Regional Health System

Richmond University Medical Center
Bayley-Seton
75 Vanderbilt Ave., Staten Island 10304-2605
(718) 818-6000; Medical Records: (718) 818-5780;
Retrieval: (718) 818-2048
Internet: www.rumcsi.org

Director: Debbie Rodriguez (Acting)

Records Administrator: Liza Simanovskaya

198 Beds
Fee for Copy of Records: $.75 per page for patient's attorney; $1.50 per page for Defendant; plus postage & handling
Formerly Saint Vincent Catholic Medical Centers of New York—Bayley-Seton

Staten Island University Hospital—North
475 Seaview Ave., Staten Island 10305-9998
(718) 226-9000; Medical Records: (718) 226-9012
Internet: www.siuh.edu

President/C.E.O.: Anthony C. Ferreri
E-mail: aferreri@siuh.edu

General Counsel: Arthur Fried (718) 226-9990
E-mail: afried@siuh.edu

Records Administrator: Dina Wong
E-mail: dwong@siuh.edu

714 Beds
Fee for Copy of Records: See statutory fee, *supra*
Affiliate of the North Shore-Long Island Jewish Health System

Staten Island University Hospital—South
375 Seguine Ave., Staten Island 10309
(718) 226-1919
Internet: www.siuh.edu

President/C.E.O.: Anthony C. Ferreri
(718) 226-1919; Fax: (718) 226-8966
E-mail: aferreri@siuh.edu

General Counsel: Arthur Fried (718) 226-9990
E-mail: afried@siuh.edu

Records Administrator: Dina Wong (718) 226-9012
E-mail: dwong@siuh.edu

196 Beds
Fee for Copy of Records: See statutory fee, *supra*
Affiliate of the North Shore-Long Island Jewish Health System

STONY BROOK **Suffolk County**

Stony Brook University Medical Center
Nicholls Rd. and Health Sciences Dr. Intersection,
Stony Brook 11794-8430
(631) 689-8333;
Health Information Mgmt.: (631) 444-1300;
Health Information Mgmt. Fax: (631) 444-7738
Internet: www.stonybrookmedicalcenter.org

C.E.O.: Steven L. Strongwater, M.D.
(631) 444-2701; Fax: (631) 444-8925

Dir., Health Information Mgmt.: Christine Edwards

546 Beds
Fee for Copy of Records: See statutory fee, *supra*

SUFFERN **Rockland County**

Good Samaritan Hospital of Suffern
255 Lafayette Ave., Suffern 10901
(845) 368-5000; Medical Records: (845) 368-5126
Internet: www.goodsamhosp.org

President/C.E.O.: Philip A. Patterson
(845) 368-5303; Fax: (845) 368-5430

Dir., Health Information Mgmt.: Nina Gore
(845) 368-5409

370 Beds
Fee for Copy of Records: See statutory fee, *supra*
Affiliate of Bon Secours Health System

SYOSSET **Nassau County**

Syosset Hospital
221 Jericho Tpke., Syosset 11791
(516) 496-6400
Internet: www.northshorelij.com

Exec. Dir.: Michael Fener (516) 496-6401

Dir. of Medical Records: Maryanne Realmuto
(516) 496-6490

204 Beds
Fee for Copy of Records: See statutory fee, *supra*
Affiliate of North Shore—Long Island Jewish Health System

SYRACUSE **Onondaga County**

Community-General Hospital of Greater Syracuse
4900 Broad Rd., Syracuse 13215
(315) 492-5011
Internet: www.cgh.org
President/C.E.O.: Thomas P. Quinn (315) 492-5207
Dir., Health Information Mgmt.: John Connor (315) 492-5090
306 Beds
Fee for Copy of Records: See statutory fee, *supra*

Crouse Hospital
736 Irving Ave., Syracuse 13210
(315) 470-7111; Health Information Mgmt.: (315) 470-7671
Internet: www.crouse.org
President/C.E.O.: Dr. Paul Kronenberg (315) 470-7371; Fax: (315) 470-2993
Dir., Health Information Mgmt.: Carolyn Dupre (315) 470-7543
566 Beds
Fee for Copy of Records: See statutory fee, *supra*

St. Joseph's Hospital Health Center
301 Prospect Ave., Syracuse 13203
(315) 448-5111; Medical Records: (315) 448-5160
Internet: www.sjhsyr.org
President: Theodore M. Pasinski (315) 448-5880
Records Administrator: Sharon Gottel
431 Beds
Fee for Copy of Records: See statutory fee, *supra*

SUNY Upstate Medical University Hospital
750 E. Adams St., Syracuse 13210-2375
(315) 464-5540; Legal Counsel: (315) 464-4700
Internet: www.upstate.edu
C.E.O.: John McCabe, M.D.
Sr. Assoc. Counsel: Regina McGraw
Dir., Clinical Data Services: Virginia Keenan (315) 464-4849
356 Beds
Fee for Copy of Records: See statutory fee, *supra*
Formerly University Hospital SUNY Health Science Center

TICONDEROGA **Essex County**

Inter-Lakes Health
1019 Wicker St., Ticonderoga 12883
(518) 585-2831
Internet: www.interlakeshealth.com
C.E.O.: Kevin P. Haughney (518) 585-3864
Dir., Health Information Mgmt.: Ms. Sue Yaw (518) 585-3793
39 Beds
Fee for Copy of Records: See statutory fee, *supra*

TROY **Rensselaer County**

Samaritan Hospital
2212 Burdett Ave., Troy 12180
(518) 271-3300
Internet: www.nehealth.com
President/C.E.O.: James K. Reed, M.D. (518) 271-5073; Fax: (518) 271-3203
C.O.O.: Karen Tassey (518) 271-3129; Fax: (518) 271-3203 E-mail: tasseyk@nehealth.com
Corporate Counsel: Robert Swidler (Northeast Health) (518) 271-5088; Fax: (518) 273-3307 E-mail: swidlerr@nehealth.com
Records Administrator: Cindy Richards Fax: (518) 271-3605
238 Beds
Fee for Copy of Records: See statutory fee, *supra*

Seton Health System—St. Mary's Hospital
1300 Massachusetts Ave., 2nd Floor, Troy 12180
(518) 268-5000; Medical Records: (518) 268-5504
E-mail: info@setonhealth.org
Internet: www.setonhealth.org
President/C.E.O.: Gino J. Pazzaglini, F.A.C.H.E. (518) 268-5520; E-mail: gpazzaglini@setonhealth.org
Chief Legal Counsel: Marsha Smith
Records Administrator: Julie Bruckner
196 Beds
Fee for Copy of Records: See statutory fee, *supra*
Affiliate of Ascension Health

UTICA **Oneida County**

Faxton St. Luke's Healthcare—Faxton Campus
1676 Sunset Ave., Utica 13502-5475
Mailing Address: P.O. Box 479, Utica 13503-0479
(315) 624-6000;
Health Information Mgmt. Fax: (315) 624-4901
Internet: www.mvnhealth.com
President/C.E.O.: Scott H. Perra (315) 624-6001
Chief Legal Counsel: Thomas Soja (315) 624-5050
Dir., Health Information Mgmt.: S. Michael Marris (315) 624-6025
166 Beds
Fee for Copy of Records: See statutory fee, *supra*
Affiliate of Mohawk Valley Network, Inc.

St. Elizabeth Medical Center
2209 Genesee St., Utica 13501
(315) 798-8100; Fax: (315) 734-3092
E-mail: bgillett@stemc.org; Internet: www.stemc.org
President/C.E.O.: Sister M. Johanna DeLelys
Chief Legal Counsel: Traci A. Boris; Fax: (315) 798-8220 E-mail: tboris@stemc.org
Records Administrator: Elizabeth Kosakowski
201 Beds
Fee for Copy of Records: See statutory fee, *supra*
Formerly St. Elizabeth Hospital

VALHALLA **Westchester County**

Blythedale Children's Hospital
95 Bradhurst Ave., Valhalla 10595-1697
(914) 592-7555; Fax: (914) 592-0407
Internet: www.blythedale.org
President: Larry Levine (914) 592-7138, Ext. 410
Dir., Health Information Mgmt.: Lori Signore, Ext. 403
92 Beds
Fee for Copy of Records: See statutory fee, *supra*

Westchester Medical Center
100 Woods Rd., Valhalla 10595
(914) 493-7000; Medical Records: (914) 493-7600;
Medical Records Fax: (914) 493-1997
Internet: www.worldclassmedicine.com
President/C.E.O.: Michael D. Israel
General Counsel: Julie Switzer (914) 493-2800; Fax: (914) 493-2321
Dir., Health Information Mgmt.: Debbie More
660 Beds
Fee for Copy of Records: See statutory fee, *supra*

VALLEY STREAM **Nassau County**

Franklin Hospital
900 Franklin Ave., Valley Stream 11580
(516) 256-6000; Fax: (516) 256-6503;
Medical Records: (516) 256-6120
Internet: www.fhmc.org
Exec. Dir.: Joseph Manopella, Ext. 6505
Regional Exec. Dir.: Deborah Tascone, Ext. 6506
Dir., Health Information Mgmt.: Colleen Garvey
305 Beds
Fee for Copy of Records: See statutory fee, *supra*
Affiliate of North Shore Long Island Jewish Health System

WALTON **Delaware County**

Delaware Valley Hospital Inc.
1 Titus Place, Walton 13856-1498
(607) 865-2100; Fax: (607) 845-8482;
Medical Records: (607) 865-2181;
Medical Records Fax: (607) 865-4168
Internet: www.uhs.net/dvh

President/C.E.O.: David J. Polge
(607) 865-2160; Fax: (607) 865-8482

Dir., Health Information Mgmt.: Lisa Moffett
(607) 865-2203

25 Beds
Fee for Copy of Records: $.75 per page
Affiliate of United Health Services

WARSAW **Wyoming County**

Wyoming County Community Hospital
400 N. Main St., Warsaw 14569-1025
(585) 786-2233; Fax: (585) 786-1222;
Medical Records Fax: (585) 786-1248
Internet: www.wcchs.net

Administrator/C.E.O.: Ronald J. Krawiec

Chief Legal Counsel: Eric Dadd

Records Administrator: Karen Tallman, Ext. 4429

90 Beds
Fee for Copy of Records: See statutory fee, *supra*

WARWICK **Orange County**

St. Anthony Community Hospital
15 Maple Ave., Warwick 10990-1099
(845) 986-2276; Fax: (845) 986-2687
Internet: www.stanthonycommunityhosp.org

Exec. V.P./Administrator/C.E.O.: Leah Cerkvenik
(845) 987-5317

Records Administrator: Carol Callinan
(845) 987-5202

73 Beds
Fee for Copy of Records: See statutory fee, *supra*
Affiliate of Bon Secours Charity Health System

WATERTOWN **Jefferson County**

Mercy Center for Behavioral Health & Wellness
218 Stone St., Watertown 13601
(315) 782-7400; Fax: (315) 779-8462

C.E.O.: Mike McCoy

Dir. of Medical Records: Mary Fitzsimmons

300 Beds (Nursing Home)
Fee for Copy of Records: See statutory fee, *supra*
Formerly Genesis Healthcare of New York

Samaritan Medical Center
830 Washington St., Watertown 13601
(315) 785-4000
Internet: www.samaritanhealth.com

President/C.E.O.: Thomas H. Carman

Records Administrator: Susan Beausoleil

287 Beds
Fee for Copy of Records: See statutory fee, *supra*
Affiliate of Samaritan Health System

WELLSVILLE **Allegany County**

Jones Memorial Hospital
191 N. Main St., P.O. Box 72, Wellsville 14895-0072
(585) 593-1100; Medical Records: (585) 596-4043
E-mail: we_care@jmhny.org
Internet: www.jmhny.org

President/C.E.O.: Eva Benedict
(585) 596-4002

Records Administrator: Shelly Harris

70 Beds
Fee for Copy of Records: See statutory fee, *supra*

WEST HAVERSTRAW **Rockland County**

Helen Hayes Hospital
Route 9W, West Haverstraw 10993
(845) 786-4000, (888) 707-3422; Fax: (845) 947-0036
Internet: www.helenhayeshospital.org

C.E.O.: Val S. Gray (845) 786-4305

Records Administrator: Jane Cavanagh
(845) 786-4116

155 Beds
Fee for Copy of Records: See statutory fee, *supra*
Physical Rehabilitation Hospital

WEST ISLIP **Suffolk County**

Good Samaritan Hospital Medical Center
1000 Montauk Hwy., West Islip 11795
(631) 376-3000; Fax: (631) 376-4208
Internet: www.good-samaritan-hospital.org

President/C.E.O.: James Caldas (Acting)
(631) 376-4001

Dir., Health Information Svces.: Vacancy at Press Time
(631) 376-4058; Fax: (631) 376-5050

537 Beds
Fee for Copy of Records: See statutory fee, *supra*
Affiliate of Catholic Health Services

WESTFIELD **Chautauqua County**

Westfield Memorial Hospital, Inc.
189 E. Main St., Westfield 14787
(716) 326-4921; Fax: (716) 326-3802;
Medical Records: (716) 793-2241
Internet: www.wmhinc.org

President/C.E.O.: C. Angela Bon Tempo
(716) 793-2200

Records Administrator: Cindy Harper (716) 793-2253

32 Beds
Fee for Copy of Records: See statutory fee, *supra*
Affiliate of the St. Vincent's Healthcare System

WHITE PLAINS **Westchester County**

Burke Rehabilitation Hospital
785 Mamaroneck Avenue, White Plains 10605-2593
(914) 597-2500; Medical Records: (914) 597-2461
E-mail: web@burke.org
Internet: www.burke.org

C.E.O.: Dr. Mary Beth Walsh
(914) 597-2163; Fax: (914) 597-2439

Medical Records Mgr.: Michael Houston
Fee for Copy of Records: Contact Source Corp. representative in Medical Records Dept.

New York Presbyterian Hospital
Westchester Division
21 Bloomingdale Rd., White Plains 10605
(914) 997-5724; Fax: (914) 682-6978

Dir., Health Information Mgmt.: Dana Kerendian
(914) 997-5783
E-mail: daf9021@nyp.org

President/C.E.O.: Dr. Herbert Pardes (212) 305-8000

General Counsel: Maxine Fass (212) 746-6500

297 Beds
Fee for Copy of Records: See statutory fee, *supra*

White Plains Hospital Center
41 E. Post Rd., White Plains 10601
(914) 681-0600; Fax: (914) 681-2902;
Health Information Svces.: (914) 681-1105;
Health Information Svces. Fax: (914) 681-2908
E-mail: wphcmail@wphospital.org
Internet: www.wphospital.org

President/C.E.O.: Jon B. Schandler (914) 681-1200

Dir., Health Information Services: Nicki Pagidas

292 Beds
Fee for Copy of Records: See statutory fee, *supra*
Affiliate of Stellaris Health Network

WILLIAMSVILLE **Erie County**

Millard Fillmore Suburban Hospital
1540 Maple Rd., Williamsville 14221
(716) 568-3600; Fax: (716) 568-3034;
Health Information Mgmt.: (716) 568-6500
Internet: http://suburban.kaleidahealth.org

President: Christopher Lane (716) 568-6700

General Counsel: Robert J. Nolan (Kaleida Health) (716) 859-5600

Dir., Health Information Mgmt.: Vickie Trautman

261 Beds
Fee for Copy of Records: See statutory fee, *supra*
Affiliate of Kaleida Health

YONKERS **Westchester County**

St. Johns Riverside Hospital
Andrus Pavilion
967 N. Broadway, Yonkers 10701-1399
(914) 964-4444; Internet: www.riversidehealth.org

President/C.E.O.: James Foy (914) 964-4221

Dir. of Medical Records: Judy Mendez, Ext. 4396

407 Beds
Fee for Copy of Records: See statutory fee, *supra*
Affiliate of Riverside HealthCare System, Inc.

St. John's Riverside Hospital
Park Care Pavilion
2 Park Ave., Yonkers 10703
(914) 964-7300; Fax: (914) 964-4647;
Medical Records: (914) 964-4344
Internet: www.riversidehealth.org

President/C.E.O.: James Foy (914) 964-4221

Dir. of Medical Records: Judy Mendez

190 Beds
Fee for Copy of Records: See statutory fee, *supra*
Formerly known as Yonkers General Hospital

St. Joseph's Medical Center
127 S. Broadway, Yonkers 10701
(914) 378-7000; Fax: (914) 965-4838;
Health Information Mgmt.: (914) 378-7638
Internet: www.saintjosephs.org

President/C.E.O.: Michael J. Spicer (914) 378-7485

Dir., Health Information Mgmt.: Janice Cordole Ext. 7244

194 Beds / 200 Bed Nursing Home
Fee for Copy of Records: See statutory fee, *supra*

NEW YORK BAR ASSOCIATIONS

American Bar Association
321 N. Clark St., Chicago, IL 60654
(312) 988-5000; Fax: (312) 988-5151
Internet: www.abanet.org

740 15th St. N.W., Washington, DC 20005
(202) 662-1000
Exec. Dir.: Jack L. Rives (312) 988-5225

Annual Meeting: August
Mid-year Meeting: February

Amistad Long Island Black Bar Association
P.O. Box 476, Wheatley Heights 11798
(631) 234-3232; Fax: (631) 234-3341
President: J. Stewart Moore
V.P.: Kevin Satterfield
Secretary: Kimberley M. McLean
Treasurer: AveMaria Thompson

Federal Bar Association
1220 N. Fillmore St., Suite 444, Arlington, VA 22201
(571) 481-9100; Fax: (571) 481-9090
E-mail: fba@fedbar.org
Internet: www.fedbar.org
Exec. Dir.: Jack D. Lockridge
President: Ashley L. Belleau
Annual Convention: September

New York State Bar Association
1 Elk St., Albany 12207
(518) 463-3200; Fax: (518) 487-5564
Internet: www.nysba.org
Exec. Dir.: Patricia K. Bucklin
(518) 487-5555; Fax: (518) 487-5564
President: Stephen P. Younger
Patterson, Belknap, Webb & Tyler, L.L.P.,
1133 Avenue of the Americas, N.Y.C. 10036
(212) 336-2685; Fax: (212) 336-2222
President-Elect: Vincent E. Doyle III
Connors & Vilardo, L.L.P., 1000 Liberty Bldg.,
424 Main St., Buffalo 14202
(716) 852-5533; Fax: (716) 852-5649
Secretary: David P. Miranda
Heslin, Rothenberg, Farley & Mesiti, P.C.,
5 Columbia Cir., Albany 12203
(518) 452-5600; Fax: (518) 452-5579
Treasurer: Seymour W. James, Jr.
The Legal Aid Society, 199 Water St., 6th Floor,
N.Y.C. 10038 (212) 577-3646; Fax: (646) 616-4646
Annual Meeting: Jan. 2011

Albany County Bar Association
The Stedman House, 2nd Floor, 1 Lodge St.,
Albany 12207 (518) 445-7691; Fax: (518) 445-7511
E-mail: acba@albanycountybar.com
Internet: www.albanycountybar.com
Exec. Dir.: Barbara A. Davis (518) 445-7510
E-mail: bdavis@albanycountybar.com
President: Elena DeFio Kean
Towne, Bartkowski & DeFio Kean, P.O. Box 15072,
Albany 12212-5072 (518) 452-1800; Fax: (518) 452-6435
E-mail: elena.defiokean@townelaw.com
President-Elect: Glen P. Doherty
McNamee, Lochner, Titus & Williams, 677 Broadway,
Albany 12201-2503 (518) 447-3200; Fax: (518) 426-4260
E-mail: doherty@mltw.com
V.P.: Robert T. Schofield
Whiteman, Osterman & Hanna, One Commerce Plz.,
Suite 1900, Albany 12260 (518) 487-7777
E-mail: rschofield@who.com; rts@who.com
Treasurer: Michael J. Hutter
Albany Law School, 80 New Scotland Ave., Albany 12208
(518) 445-2311; E-mail: mhutt@albanylaw.edu
Annual Meeting and Election: January
Board and Stated Meetings: Jan., May, Oct. and Dec.
Meetings: Monthly, second Tues.

Allegany County Bar Association
Courthouse, 7 Court St., Belmont 14813
President: Terrence M. Parker
(585) 268-9225; Fax: (585) 268-9727
V.P.: Thomas A. Miner
(585) 268-9410; Fax: (585) 268-9651
E-mail: minerta@alleganyco.com
Secretary: William W. Pulos
(607) 324-7333; Fax: (607) 324-1668
E-mail: wpulos@stny.rr.com
Treasurer: Robert G. Hutter
(585) 593-3341; Fax: (585) 593-3782
E-mail: hutterandfinn@yahoo.com
Meetings: Fourth or fifth Wed. of Jan., Apr., July and Oct.

American Academy of Matrimonial Lawyers
New York Chapter
Internet: www.aaml-ny.org
President: Allan E. Mayefsky
Sheresky, Aaronson, Mayefsky & Sloan, L.L.P.,
485 Lexington Ave., N.Y.C. 10017
(212) 521-3503; Fax: (212) 838-5505
E-mail: mayefsky@samsllp.com
V.P.'s:
Eleanor B. Alter
Kasowitz, Benson, Torres & Friedman, L.L.P.,
1633 Broadway, N.Y.C. 10038
(212) 506-1700; Fax: (212) 506-1800
E-mail: ealter@kasowitz.com
Robert Z. Dobrish
757 Third Ave., N.Y.C. 10017
(212) 532-4000; Fax: (212) 532-3153
E-mail: dobrish@dobrishlaw.com
Nancy Kellman
123 Main St., White Plains 10601
(914) 328-0900; Fax: (914) 328-0916
E-mail: ndkellman@ndkellmanlaw.com
Stephen Schlissel
200 Garden City Plaza, Garden City 11530
(516) 877-1800; Fax: (516) 294-3188
E-mail: profsws@aol.com
Secretary: Robert Arenstein
Law Office of Robert D. Arenstein,
295 Madison Ave., 19th Floor, N.Y.C. 10017-6304
(212) 679-3999; Fax: (212) 370-5822
E-mail: arensteinlaw@aol.com
Treasurer: Christopher S. Mattingly
Lipsitz, Green, et al., 42 Delaware Ave., Suite 120,
Buffalo 14202 (716) 849-1333; Fax: (716) 855-1580
E-mail: cmattingly@lglaw.com
Annual Meeting & Election: January
Meetings: Semi-monthly

American Immigration Lawyers Association
New York Chapter
Internet: www.nyaila.org
Chair: Alexis S. Axelrad
Barst & Mukamal L.L.P.,
Two Park Ave., 19th Floor, N.Y.C. 10016 (212) 686-3838
Vice Chair: David Katona
Katona & Mir, L.L.P.,
49 W. 37th St., 7th Floor, N.Y.C. 10018 (212) 944-1929
Secretary: Elizabeth Barna
305 Broadway, Suite 305, N.Y.C. 10007 (212) 732-0497
Treasurer: Elizabeth Brettschneider
Avirom & Associates, L.L.P.,
42 Broadway, Suite 1220, N.Y.C. 10004
(212) 747-8787; Fax: (212) 747-0857
Annual Meeting and Election: June
Meetings: Monthly, first Mon., except July and Aug.

Assn. of Arbitrators (Small Claims), N.Y.C. Civil Court
111 Centre St., Room 1258, N.Y.C. 10013
(646) 386-5420; Fax: (212) 295-4882
E-mail: jgebbia@courts.state.ny.us
Exec. Dir.: Joseph A.J. Gebbia
President: John P. Bajit
Secretary: Barbara Grcevic
Treasurer: Michael Chung
Annual Election: Bi-annually

Asian American Bar Assn. of New York
Grand Central Station, P.O. Box 3656,
N.Y.C. 10163-3656 (718) 228-7206
E-mail: main@aabany.org
Internet: www.aabany.org
Exec. Dir.: Yang Chen; E-mail: yang.chen@aabany.org
President: Robert W. Leung
Boies, Schiller & Flexner, L.L.P., 575 Lexington Ave.,
N.Y.C. 10022 (212) 754-4208; Fax: (212) 446-2350
E-mail: robert.leung@aabany.org
President-Elect: Linda Lin
Liberty International Underwriters, 55 Water St.,
N.Y.C. 10041-0034 (212) 208-4100; Fax: (212) 208-4112
E-mail: linda.lin@aabany.org
Recording Secretary: Francis Chin
Brooklyn Law School, 250 Joralemon St., Brooklyn 11201
(718) 780-7597; Fax: (718) 228-7206
E-mail: francis.chin@aabany.org
Membership Secretary: William Wang
Paterson, Belknap, Webb & Tyler, L.L.P.,
1133 Ave. of the Americas, N.Y.C. 10036
(212) 336-2000; Fax: (212) 336-2222
E-mail: william.wang@aabany.org
Treasurer: Timothy Wong
Law Offices of Timothy K. Wong, 34 Bowery, N.Y.C. 10002
(212) 966-8638; Fax: (212) 202-3631
E-mail: timothy.wong@aabany.org
Meetings: Monthly, first Tues. except Aug.

The Assn. of the Bar of the City of New York
42 West 44th St., N.Y.C. 10036-6690
(212) 382-6600; Fax: (212) 398-6634
E-mail: www.nycbar.org
Exec. Dir.: Barbara Berger Opotowsky
(212) 382-6620; Fax: (212) 398-6634
E-mail: bopotowsky@nycbar.org
President: Samuel W. Seymour
Sullivan & Cromwell, L.L.P., 125 Broad St.,
N.Y.C. 10004-2498 (212) 558-3156; Fax: (212) 558-3588
E-mail: seymours@sullcrom.com
V.P.'s:
Zachary W. Carter
Dorsey & Whitney, L.L.P., 250 Park Ave., 15th Floor,
N.Y.C. 10177 (212) 415-9345; Fax: (212) 953-7021
E-mail: carter.zachary@dorsey.com
Meilin Kwan-Gett
Willkie, Farr & Gallagher, L.L.P., 787 Seventh Ave.,
N.Y.C. 10019-6099 (212) 728-8503; Fax: (212) 728-8111
E-mail: mkwangett@willkie.com
Robert C. Sheehan
Skadden, Arps, Slate, Meagher & Flom, L.L.P.,
4 Times Sq., N.Y.C. 10036-6522
(212) 735-3350; Fax: (917) 777-3351
E-mail: rsheehan@skadden.com
Secretary: Sheila S. Boston
Kaye Scholer L.L.P., 425 Park Ave., N.Y.C. 10022
(212) 836-7197; Fax: (212) 836-8689
E-mail: sboston@kayescholer.com
Treasurer: Donald S. Bernstein
Davis Polk & Wardwell, 450 Lexington Ave.,
N.Y.C. 10017-3940 (212) 450-4092; Fax: (212) 450-3092
E-mail: donald.bernstein@dpw.com
General Counsel: Alan Rothstein
(212) 382-6623; Fax: (212) 398-6634
E-mail: arothstein@nycbar.org
Communications Dir.: Eric Friedman
(212) 382-6754; Fax: (212) 768-8630
E-mail: efriedman@nycbar.org
Annual Meeting: May

Bath Bar Association
President: Wendy Lee Gould, 3 Robie St., Bath 14810
(607) 776-4164; Fax: (607) 776-9255
Secretary/Treasurer: John K. McCarthy
12 Pulteney Sq., Box 528, Bath 14810
(607) 776-3389; Fax: (607) 776-2876
E-mail: lawmccarthy@verizon.net

Bay Ridge Lawyers Association
Internet: www.bayridgelawyers.org
President: Boris Zivotov, 457 77th St., Brooklyn 11209
(718) 833-7333; Fax: (718) 836-0277
V.P.: Helen Z. Galette, 8212 3rd Ave., Brooklyn 11209
(718) 680-6008; Fax: (718) 238-8212
Secretary: Pasqualino Russo
NYC Dept. of Investigation, 180 Water St., 2nd Floor,
N.Y.C. 10038 (212) 331-3030; Fax: (212) 331-3308
Corresponding Secretary: Lisa M. Becker
1852 W. 10th St., Brooklyn 11223
(718) 420-5636; Fax: (718) 390-1474
Treasurer: Joann Monaco, 1724 86th St., Brooklyn 11214
(718) 259-4500; Fax: (718) 331-4750
Meetings: Monthly, last Wed., except June, July & Aug.
Annual Elections: May

Black Bar Association of Bronx County
P.O. Box 1109, Bronx 10451
President: Bahaati Pitt
851 Grand Concourse, Bronx 10451
(718) 590-3321; Fax: (718) 590-7294
First V.P.: Michelle Smith
NYS Supreme Court, 100 Centre St.,
Room 1710, N.Y.C. 10013 (646) 386-3864
Corresponding Secretary: Deidra Moore
Deidra R. Moore, P.C., 2128 Westchester Ave.,
Bronx 10452 (718) 409-2410; Fax: (718) 409-2411
Treasurer: Eddie J. McShan
Bronx Supreme Court, 851 Grand Concourse,
Bronx 10451 (718) 590-3770; Fax: (718) 590-4514
Annual Election: September
Meetings: Monthly, first Tues.

Association of Black Women Attorneys, Inc.
255 W. 36th St., Suite 800, N.Y.C. 10018
(212) 300-2193
E-mail: abwagroup@yahoo.com
Internet: www.abwanewyork.org
President: S. Jeanine Conley (212) 589-4200
V.P.: B. Shea Owens
Secretary: Yomi Ajaiyeoba (718) 638-3697
Annual Election: Aug.
Installation of Officers: Sept.
Meetings: Monthly

Brandeis Association, Inc.
E-mail: brandeisassociation@yahoo.com
Chair: Hon. Bernice D. Siegal
89-17 Sutphin Blvd., Jamaica 11435 (718) 262-7333
President: Susan Beberfall
N.Y.S. Supreme Ct., 88-11 Sutphin Blvd., Room 610-M,
Jamaica 11435 (718) 298-1202
Corresponding Secretary: Marian Morris
125-01 Queens Blvd., Kew Gardens 11415 (718) 298-1442
Recording Secretary: Warren Hecht
118-21 Queens Blvd., Suite 518, Forest Hills 11375
(718) 575-8721
Treasurer: Martin Olesh, 75-06 192nd St., Flushing 11366
(718) 468-3108; Fax: (718) 740-4599
Financial Secretary: Mona Haas
Epstein, Frankini & Grammatico,
45 Crossways Park Dr., Woodbury 11797 (516) 364-7900
Sergeant-at-Arms: Hon. David I. Weprin
New York City Council, 205-07 Hillside Ave.,
Hollis 11423 (718) 465-8202; Fax: (718) 776-2302
Annual Elections: October
2009-10 Officers

Brehon Law Society

President: Robert Dunne
230 Park Ave., N.Y.C. 10169 (212) 551-1750

First V.P.: Mary E. Bartholomew
693 9th Ave., N.Y.C. 10036 (917) 518-2658

Second V.P.: Patrick W. Doherty
Office of the Comptroller, 1 Centre St., N.Y.C. 10007
(212) 669-2651; Fax: (212) 815-8663

Third V.P.: Niall MacGiollabhui
Law Office of Michael G. Dowd, 112 Madison Ave.,
3rd Floor, N.Y.C. 10016-7416 (212) 751-1640

Secretary & Publicity Dir.: Domhnall O'Cathain
Lesnevich & Marzano-Lesnevich, L.L.C.,
350 5th Ave., Suite 4400, N.Y.C. 10118 (212) 564-2770

Treasurer: Austin P. Murphy, Jr.
MacKay, Wrynn & Brady, L.L.P., 4026 235th St.,
Douglaston 11363-1508 (718) 423-6800

N.G.O. Delegates to the United Nations:
James P. Cullen
Anderson, Kill & Olick, P.C., 1251 Ave. of the Americas,
N.Y.C. 10020-1104 (212) 278-1565
Richard Harvey

Northern Ireland Liaison: Michael P. Carroll
O'Dwyer & Bernstein, 52 Duane St.,
5th Floor, N.Y.C. 10007-1207 (212) 571-7100

Annual Dinner: March
Meetings: As announced

Brehon Law Society of Nassau County, New York
Internet: www.brehonlaw.org

President: Brian O'Keefe
Grey & Grey, L.L.P., 360 Main St., Farmingdale 11735
(516) 249-1342; E-mail: bokeefe@greyandgrey.com

V.P.: Catherine Stanton
Brecher, Fishman, Pasternack, Walsh, Tilker & Ziegler,
P.C., 1325 Franklin Ave., Suite 250, Garden City 11530
(516) 742-3773; Fax: (516) 742-3994
E-mail: cathys@brecherfishman.com

Meetings: Monthly

Bronx County Bar Association
851 Grand Concourse, Bronx 10451
(718) 293-2227; Fax: (718) 681-0098
Internet: www.bronxbar.com

Exec. Dir.: Mary Conlan

Chair: Carlos M. Calderon
6 Gramatan Ave., Mount Vernon 10550
(914) 668-8900; Fax: (914) 668-8949

President: Christopher M. DiLorenzo
944 Gerard Ave., Bronx 10452
(718) 537-9885; Fax: (718) 293-0870

First V.P.: Robert H. Wolff
Rosenberg, Minc, Falkoff & Wolff,
122 E. 42nd St., Suite 3800, N.Y.C. 10168
(212) 697-9280; Fax: (212) 697-9284

Second V.P.: Michael A. Marinaccio
245 Main St., White Plains 10601
(914) 761-0707; Fax: (914) 761-0795

Financial Secretary: Samuel M. Braverman
901 Sheridan Ave., Bronx 10451
(718) 293-1977; Fax: (718) 793-5395

Secretary: Roberto Laracuente
6 King Arthur's Ct., Edison, NJ 08820
(646) 300-3010; Fax: (718) 732-4575

Treasurer: Steven J. Baker
Baker, McEvoy, Morrissey & Moskovits, P.C.,
330 34th St., N.Y.C. 10001
(212) 857-8230; Fax: (212) 857-8238

Annual Meeting: May
Meetings: Monthly, second Wed.

Bronx Women's Bar Association
198 161st St., Bronx 10451

President: Debra Guarnieri (718) 838-7293
E-mail: debguarnesq@aol.com

V.P.: Joshlyn Foreman (718) 838-7263
E-mail: foremanj@bronxda.nyc.gov

Secretary: Eliza Filipowski (718) 838-7231
E-mail: filipowe@bronxda.nyc.gov

Treasurer: Dilia Travieso (718) 838-7250
E-mail: traviesd@bronxda.nyc.gov

Annual Meeting and Election: May

Brooklyn Bar Association
123 Remsen St., Brooklyn 11201-4212
(718) 624-0675; Fax: (718) 797-1713
Internet: www.brooklynbar.org

Exec. Dir.: Avery Eli Okin, C.A.E., Ext. 213
E-mail: aokin@brooklynbar.org

President: Andrea E. Bonina
Bonina and Bonina, P.C., 16 Court St., Suite 1800,
Brooklyn 11241 (718) 522-1786; Fax: (718) 243-2414
E-mail: abonina@medlaw1.com

Secretary: Rebecca Rose Woodland
Lonuzzi & Woodland, L.L.P., 60 Sackett St., Suite 2002,
Brooklyn 11231 (718) 935-1010; Fax: (718) 935-1935

Treasurer: Arthur L. Aidala
8118 13th Ave., Brooklyn 11228
(718) 238-9898; Fax: (718) 921-3292
E-mail: aidalaesq@aidalalaw

Annual Meeting: Second Wed. in May

Brooklyn Women's Bar Association, Inc.
(718) 852-1700; Fax: (718) 852-2468
Internet: www.brooklynwomensbar.org

President: Joanne D. Quiñones
Civil Court, New York Co., c/o Hon. Matthew Cooper,
111 Centre St., Room 668, N.Y.C. 10013
(646) 386-5697; Fax: (212) 374-6321
E-mail: jdqesq@aol.com

V.P.'s:

Carrie Anne D. Cavallo
Fee Schpoont & Cavallo, L.L.P.,
50 Broadway, Suite 1000, N.Y.C. 10004
(212) 792-6070; Fax: (212) 792-6071
E-mail: cav@schpoontcavallo.com

Sue Novick Wasko
N.Y.S.O.C.F.S., Bur. of Special Hearings,
Adam Clayton Powell State Office Bldg., 18th Floor,
163 W. 125th St., N.Y.C. 10027
(212) 961-4408; Fax: (212) 961-5898
E-mail: snwasko@aol.com

Ella Royzman
1101 Avenue U, 2nd Floor, Brooklyn 11223
(718) 645-6030

Corresponding Secretary: Hon. Ellen Spodek
Kings Co. Branch, New York Civil Court,
141 Livingston St., Brooklyn 11201
(347) 404-9060; Fax: (718) 643-3537

Recording Secretary: Joy A. Thompson

Treasurer: John F.K. Coffey
Coffey & Coffey, L.L.P., 142 Joralemon St., 2nd Floor,
Brooklyn 11201-4709 (718) 624-2268

Elections: April/May
Installation of Officers: June

Broome County Bar Association
53 Chenango St., Suite 201, Binghamton 13901
(607) 723-6331; Fax: (607) 724-4085

Exec. Dir.: Sindy L. Garey

President: Michael Baker (607) 778-2403

President-Elect: Greg Catarella (607) 763-9200

V.P.: Carman Garufi (607) 722-5000

Secretary: Paul Battisti (607) 724-8529

Treasurer: Marylynn Reid (607) 798-1521

Annual Meeting: May

Guild of Catholic Lawyers, Inc.
Exec. Dir.: John L. O'Connell
President: Robert E. Crotty
Kelley, Drye & Warren, L.L.P., 101 Park Ave., N.Y.C. 10178 (212) 808-7800; Fax: (212) 808-7897
E-mail: rcrotty@kelleydrye.com
V.P.: Neil Merkl
Kelley, Drye & Warren, L.L.P., 101 Park Ave., N.Y.C. 10178 (212) 808-7811; Fax: (212) 808-7897
E-mail: nmerkl@kelleydrye.com
Treasurer: Christine E. Tormey
Kelley, Drye & Warren, L.L.P., 101 Park Ave., N.Y.C. 10178 (212) 808-7800; Fax: (212) 808-7897
E-mail: ctormey@kelleydrye.com
Meetings: Quarterly

Catholic Lawyers Guild of Brooklyn
President: Sara Gozo
2572 Coyle St., Brooklyn 11235 (718) 743-1407
Treasurer: Frank A. Composto
Composto & Composto, 142 Joralemon St., 2nd Floor, Brooklyn 11201 (718) 875-5199; Fax: (718) 855-6866
Annual Election: May

Cattaraugus County Bar Association
President: Wendy G. Peterson
307 Community Bank Bldg., Olean 14760 (716) 372-8997
E-mail: wendy.pmlaw@yahoo.com
V.P.: Matthew Swenson
Brady & Swenson, 41 Main St., Salamanca 14779 (716) 945-2000; E-mail: mswenson@bradyandswenson.com
Secretary/Treasurer: Michael Morgan
DiCerbo & Palumbo, 201 N. Union St., Olean 14760 (716) 373-2165
Annual Meeting and Election: January 1st
Meetings: Monthly, third Thurs except July and Nov.

Cayuga County Bar Association
144 Genesee St., Suite 102-279, Auburn 13021
President: Charles A. Marangola
141 Main St., P.O. Box 17, Moravia 13118-0017
(315) 497-1190; Fax: (315) 497-1234
E-mail: cam@cayugalaw.com
First V.P.: Hon. Mark H. Fandrich
152 Genesee St., Auburn 13021
Second V.P.: Robert K. Bergan
Boyle & Anderson, P.C., 110 Genesee St., Suite 300, Auburn 13021
Corresponding Secretary: Adam VanBuskirk
3100 S.R. 90, Aurora 13026 (315) 563-5019
Recording Secretary: Timothy Brennan
Treasurer: Ryan Muldoon
11 Court St., Auburn 13021-3713 (315) 253-4050
Annual Meeting and Election: July, third Mon.
Meetings: First Thurs., alternate months

Central New York Women's Bar Association
Downtown Station, P.O. Box 408, Syracuse 13201-0408
Internet: www.cnywba.org
President: Heidi White McCormick
(315) 443-1310; Fax: (315) 443-7278
President-Elect: Deborah Sundquist O'Malley (315) 443-1708
V.P.: Mary C. King
Secretary: Danielle Mikalajunas Fogel
Treasurer: Trista F. O'Hara
Annual Elections: April

Chemung County Bar Association
Internet: www.chemungcountybarassociation.org
President: Kevin Flynn
463 W. Church St., Elmira 14901 (607) 732-8990
First V.P.: Richard W. Rich
219 Madison Ave., Elmira 14902 (607) 737-5681
Second V.P.: Steven W. Forrest
317 E. Church St., Elmira 14901 (607) 737-5681
Secretary: Denice Hamm
523 Church St., Elmira 14901 (607) 734-5004
Treasurer: David P. Pawlak
84 Main St., Suite D, Big Flats 14814
(607) 358-4029; Fax: (607) 358-4042
Annual Meeting: December

Chenango County Bar Association
P.O. Box 671, Norwich 13815
President: Kathleen S. Campbell
V.P.: John D. Cameron
Secretary: Michael D. Ferrarese
Treasurer: Kayphet Mavady
5 N. Main St., P.O. Box 713, Sherburne 13460
(607) 674-2191; Fax: (607) 674-4744
Annual Election: March
2009-10 Officers

Clinton County Bar Association
President: Heidi Dennis
206 W. Bay Plz., Plattsburgh 12901
(518) 562-0600; Fax: (518) 562-0657
First V.P.: Kathleen Insley
187 Margaret St., Suite A, Plattsburgh 12901
(518) 566-0833
Second V.P.: Susan L. Patnode
56 Cornelia St., Plattsburgh 12901
(518) 561-5460; Fax: (518) 561-5468
Secretary: Tina Soloski
14 Durkee St., Suite 420, Plattsburgh 12901
(518) 562-8383; Fax: (518) 562-8384
Treasurer: Kevin L. Peryer
D & H Station, 29 Track Side, P.O. Box 3050, Plattsburgh 12901 (518) 566-0584; Fax: (518) 561-3253
Annual Election: February
2009-10 Officers

Columbia County Bar Association
President: Paul Freeman
437 E. Allen St., P.O. Box 1328, Hudson 12534
(518) 828-2021; Fax: (518) 828-2420
V.P.: Juliette Crill, 19 Rodman Rd., Hillsdale 12529
(518) 325-4100; Fax: (518) 325-5100
Secretary: Anthony Buono
2880 Route 9, P.O. Box 300, Valatie 12184
(518) 758-1979; Fax: (518) 758-1978
Treasurer: Kenneth Esrick, 32 Main St., Chatham 12037
(518) 392-2223; Fax: (518) 392-9650
Annual Election: December

Columbian Lawyers Association, Inc.
c/o Michelle McSweeney,
Law Office of Ann Margaret Carozza,
213-38 40th Ave., Bayside 11361
E-mail: info@columbianlawyers.net
Internet: www.columbianlawyers.net
Chair: Peter Carozzo (718) 359-9700; Fax: (718) 762-9385
E-mail: trumancaro@msn.com
President: Dominic L. Chiariello
(718) 261-5200; Fax: (718) 261-5779
E-mail: dc@chiariello.com
President-Elect: Claudia N. Lanzetta
(718) 224-4746; Fax: (718) 224-4794
E-mail: cnlanzetta@aol.com
First V.P.: Ann Marie Barbagallo
(718) 454-3655; Fax: (718) 454-3657
E-mail: jimebischoff@hotmail.com
Second V.P.: Hon. Joseph Esposito
(718) 262-7379; Fax: (718) 262-7341
E-mail: jesposit@courts.state.ny.us
Third V.P.: James P. Pagano
(212) 732-4740; Fax: (212) 385-2545
E-mail: jpaganoesq@aol.com
Corresponding Secretary: Tracy Catapano-Fox
E-mail: tcfox@courts.state.ny.us
Recording Secretary: Donna Golia
E-mail: dmgolia@courts.state.ny.us
Treasurer: Michelle McSweeney (718) 224-4746
E-mail: michelle1113@nyc.rr.com
Annual Election: June

Columbian Lawyers Association
First Judicial Department
8 E. 69th St., N.Y.C. 10021
Internet: www.columbianlawyers.com
President: Joseph DeMatteo
Bernfeld, DeMatteo & Bernfeld,
600 Third Ave., 15th Floor, N.Y.C. 10016
(212) 661-1661; Fax: (212) 557-9610
First V.P.: Sigismondo F. Renda
Renda & Associates, P.A., 8118 13th Ave., Brooklyn 11228
(718) 921-3344; Fax: (718) 921-3292
Second V.P.: Stephen Savva
250 W. 57th St., Suite 919, N.Y.C. 10107
(212) 245-5820; Fax: (212) 647-0574
Executive Secretary: Victoria A. Lombardi
Silverson, Pareres & Lombardi,
192 Lexington St., 17th Floor, N.Y.C. 10016
(212) 557-1818; Fax: (212) 557-1336
Financial Secretary: Marianne E. Bertuna
Aidala & Bertuna, P.C., 8118 13th Ave., Brooklyn 11228
(718) 238-9898; Fax: (718) 921-3292
Recording Secretary: Hon. Patricia LaFreniere
Kings County Family Court, 330 Jay St., Brooklyn 11201
(347) 401-9600; Fax: (347) 401-9509
Treasurer: Maria Guccione
301 E. 62nd St., N.Y.C. 10021-7746
Annual Election: November
Meetings: Monthly, first Wed. except July and Aug.

Columbian Lawyers Association of Brooklyn
142 Joralemon St., Brooklyn 11201
(718) 875-0158
President: Carl J. Landicino
Borchert, Genovesi, LaSpina & Landicino, P.C.,
19-02 Whitestone Expressway, Suite 302, Whitestone 11357
(718) 767-3333; Fax: (718) 767-3309
E-mail: clandicino@bgllpc.com
First V.P.: Dominic J. Famulari
Law Offices of John D. Famulari, 6741 3rd Ave.,
Brooklyn 11220 (718) 748-3333; Fax: (718) 748-3368
E-mail: domlaw3333@yahoo.com
Second V.P.: Bruno F. Codispoti
111 John St., Room 800, N.Y.C. 10038
(212) 962-6525; Fax: (212) 962-6791
E-mail: bruno@codispotilaw.com
Third V.P.: Robert J. Musso
26 Court St., Suite 2211, Brooklyn 11242
(718) 237-9059; Fax: (718) 625-1966
E-mail: rmwlaw@att.net
Corresponding Secretary: Bartholomew T. Russo
111 John St., N.Y.C. 10038
(212) 608-8840; Fax: (212) 608-8039
E-mail: btr@bzslaw.com
Recording Secretary: Rose Ann C. Branda
7302 13th Ave., Brooklyn 11228
(718) 680-5778; Fax: (718) 680-9671
E-mail: rab.ccb@verizon.net
Treasurer: Mark A. Longo
26 Court St., Suite 1700, Brooklyn 11242
(718) 722-7300; Fax: (718) 802-9495
E-mail: mlongo@markalongo.com
Meetings: Monthly, first Tues., Sept.-May
Annual Election: May

Columbian Lawyers' Assn. of Nassau County, Inc.
Exec. Dir.: Salvatore Spano
370 Old Country Rd., Suite 100, Garden City 11530
(516) 294-7037; Fax: (516) 742-9375
E-mail: clanassau@aol.com
Deputy Exec. Dir.: Hon. Anthony W. Paradiso
99 Main St., Hempstead 11550
(516) 572-2135; Fax: (516) 572-2572
President: Anthony J. Emanuel
Bornstein & Emanuel, 200 Garden City Plaza, Suite 201,
Garden City 11530 (516) 227-3777; Fax: (516) 228-3299
First V.P.: Mary P. Giordano
Franchina & Giordano, P.C., 1100 Franklin Ave.,
Suite 205, Garden City 11530
(516) 877-7743; Fax: (516) 877-7743
Second V.P.: Phillip J. Rizzuto
One Old Country Rd., Suite 285, Carle Place 11514
(516) 622-0606; Fax: (516) 622-2112
Corresponding Secretary: Mark A. Annuziata
229 Seventh St., Suite 201, Garden City 11530
(516) 248-6232; Fax: (516) 248-4785
Recording Secretary: Albert W. Petraglia
Rivkin Radler, L.L.P., 926 RXR Plaza, Uniondale 11556
(516) 357-3000; Fax: (516) 357-3333
Treasurer: Thomas DeMaria
200 W. Poplar St., Floral Park 11001
(516) 352-5544; Fax: (516) 352-3670
Annual Election: Nov.
Meetings: Monthly, last Thurs., except June, July, Aug.

Columbian Lawyers Assn. of Westchester County
President: Michael Amoruso
Amoruso & Amoruso, L.L.P., 800 Westchester Ave.,
Suite S-320, Rye Brook 10573
(914) 253-9255; Fax: (914) 253-9162
First V.P.: Peter E. Tangredi
202 Mamaroneck Ave., Suite 500, White Plains 10601-5318
(914) 328-6900; E-mail: pet@ptangredilaw.com
Second V.P.: John D. Pappalardo, Jr.
700 White Plains Rd., Suite 355, Scarsdale 10583
(914) 725-7000; Fax: (914) 725-1700
E-mail: info@pappalardolaw.com
Third V.P.: Josephine Trovini
111 Dr. Martin Luther King, Jr. Blvd., White Plains 10601
(914) 824-5328
Secretary: Charles A. D'Agostino
427 Bedford Rd., Suite 150, Pleasantville 10570-3035
(914) 747-4455; Fax: (914) 747-3626
E-mail: cad@daglaw.net
Treasurer: Joan Iacono
81 Pondfield Rd., Suite 8, Bronxville 10708
(914) 961-0565; Fax: (914) 961-3333
E-mail: joaniaconlaw@verizon.net
Annual Election: Nov.
Meetings: Monthly, as determined by Board of Directors

Columbian Lawyers of Rockland County
169 S. Main St., P.O. Box 438, New City 10956
(212) 962-6525, Ext. 135
President: Antonio F. Reda
Reda Schwan & Assoc., L.L.P., 20 S.Main St.,
New City 10956 (845) 639-7722; Fax: (845) 639-7744
First V.P.: Fina DelPrincipio
County Office Bldg., New City 10956
(845) 638-5180; Fax: (845) 638-5676
Second V.P.: G. Nicholas Del Pizzi
35 Fourth Ave., Nyack 10960 (845) 358-6091
Secretary: M. Teresa Faherty
20 S. Main St., New City 10956
(845) 638-6495; Fax: (845) 638-3074
Treasurer: Kevin F. Russo
8 Caruso Ct., Thiells 10984
(845) 786-0227; Fax: (845) 947-2900

Commercial Lawyers Conference, Inc.
President: Eric M. Berman
100 Garden City Plz., Suite 500A, Garden City 11530
(631) 486-4900; Fax: (631) 486-4997
E-mail: eberman@ericbermanpc.com
V.P.: Elliott M. Portman
One Corporate Dr., Suite 102, Bohemia 11716
(631) 475-4400; Fax: (631) 475-9882
E-mail: e.portman@rttplaw.com
Secretary: Timothy C. Wan
5036 Jericho Tpke., Commack 11725
(631) 499-5400; Fax: (631) 493-0189
E-mail: twan@smitcarroad.com
Treasurer: Glenn S. Garbus
500 Bi-County Blvd., Farmingdale 11735
(631) 393-9400; Fax: (631) 393-9490
E-mail: ggarbus@fgny.com
Meetings: Monthly, third Tues.

Consumer Credit Assn. of Metropolitan New York
P.O. Box 633, Valley Stream 11582

President: Todd E. Houslanger
Houslanger & Associates, P.L.L.C., 372 New York Ave., Huntington 11743 (631) 427-1140; Fax: (631) 427-1143

V.P.'s:
Joel Leiderman
Forster & Garbus, 500 Bi-County Blvd., Suite 300, Farmingdale 11735 (631) 393-9400
Elliot Phillips
Kirshenbaum & Phillips, P.C., 3000 Hempstead Tpke., 4th Floor, Levittown 11756 (516) 746-1114; Fax: (516) 742-2735
Vincent Zecca; E-mail: papazecca@aol.com

Secretary: Gerard J. Felt
Pressler & Pressler, L.L.P., 15 Wing Dr., Cedar Knolls, NJ 07927 (973) 753-5111

Treasurer: Alan J. Newmark
E-mail: alanjnewmark@gmail.com

Meetings: Quarterly

Cortland County Bar Association
P.O. Box 5381, Cortland 13045
Internet: www.cortlandbar.com

President: Mardis F. Kelsen
The Higgins House, 20 Court St., Cortland 13045
(607) 756-4585; Fax: (607) 756-5329
E-mail: higginshouse98@hotmail.com

V.P.: Randolph V. Kruman
The Higgins House, 20 Court St., Cortland 13045
(607) 756-4585; Fax: (607) 756-5329
E-mail: vankruman@yahoo.com

Secretary/Treasurer: Victoria Monty
Pomeroy, Armstrong Casullo & Monty, 16 Tompkins St., P.O. Box 828, Cortland 13045
(607) 756-7501; Fax: (607) 753-8913
E-mail: vmonty@cortlandattorneys.com

Customs and International Trade Bar Association
Internet: www.citba.org

President: Michael S. O'Rourke
Rode & Qualey, 55 W. 39th St., N.Y.C. 10018
(212) 994-7333; Fax: (212) 719-1828
E-mail: tradelaw@rode-qualey.com

V.P.: James R. Cannon, Jr.
1666 K St. N.W., Suite 1200, Washington, DC 20006
(202) 833-9200; Fax: (202) 293-5939
E-mail: jcannon@williamsmullen.com

Secretary: Joseph W. Dorn
King & Spaulding, 1700 Pennsylvania Ave. N.W., Suite 2000, Washington, DC 20006-4707
(202) 626-5445; Fax: (202) 626-3737
E-mail: jdorn@kslaw.com

Treasurer: M. Page Hall II
Adduci, Mastriani & Schamberg, L.L.P., 1200 Seventeenth St., N.W., 5th Floor, Washington, DC 20036 (202) 467-6300; Fax: (202) 466-2006
E-mail: hall@adduci.com

Annual Election: April
Meetings: As called

The Defense Association of New York, Inc.
P.O. Box 950, N.Y.C. 10274-0950
Internet: www.defenseassociationofnewyork.org
Exec. Dir.: Anthony Celentano (212) 313-3618
E-mail: danyexec@msn.com

President: Julian Ehrlich
Allied North American, 390 N. Broadway, Jericho 11530
(212) 458-1512; Fax: (212) 458-2709

President-Elect: Lawton W. Squires
Herzfeld & Rubin, 40 Wall St., N.Y.C. 10005
(212) 471-8500; Fax: (212) 344-3333

V.P.: James Begley
Port Authority, 225 Park Ave. S., N.Y.C. 10003
(212) 435-3502

Secretary: Brian R. Rayhill
Epstein & Rayhill, 565 Taxter Rd., Elmsford 10523
(516) 364-7900

Treasurer: Patricia Zincke
Cartafalsa, Slattery, Turpin & Metaxas, 165 Broadway, 28th Floor, N.Y.C. 10006
(212) 225-7700; Fax: (212) 225-7745

Delaware County Bar Association

President: Gary A. Rosa
835 Main St., P.O. Box 839, Margaretville 12455
(845) 586-3022; Fax: (845) 586-2815
E-mail: rosa@catskill.net

V.P.: John Hubbard
72 Main St., Stamford 12167
(607) 652-7343; Fax: (607) 652-2812
E-mail: john.hubbard@co.delaware.ny.us

Secretary: Larisa Obolensky
127 Main St., Delhi 13753
(607) 746-7717; Fax: (607) 746-8032
E-mail: obolensky@stny.rr.com

Treasurer: Porter Kirkwood
P.O. Box 66, Delhi 13753
(607) 832-5300; Fax: (607) 832-5372

Annual Meeting/Elections: First Mon., May

Dominican Bar Association
P.O. Box 203, N.Y.C. 10013
Internet: www.dominicanbarassociation.org

President: Peter L. Cedeno
(201) 264-5611; Fax: (212) 643-0237

V.P.: Fiordaliza D. Rodriguez

Corresponding Secretary: Bianka Vega

Recording Secretary: Martha Tessler

Treasurer: Carmen Suardy

Annual Election: November
Meetings: Second Tues., monthly

Dutchess County Bar Association
P.O. Box 4865, Poughkeepsie 12602
(845) 473-2488; Fax: (845) 485-1484
Internet: www.dutchesscountybar.org
Exec. Dir.: Janna Whearty
E-mail: janna@dutchesscountybar.org

President: Hon. Peter M. Forman
Dutchess County Family Court, 50 Market St., Poughkeepsie 12601 (845) 486-2526

President-Elect: Rebecca Valk
VanDeWater & VanDeWater, 40 Garden St., P.O. Box 112, Poughkeepsie 12602
(845) 452-5900; Fax: (845) 452-5848
E-mail: rvalk@vandewaterlaw.com

V.P.: Daniel McCabe
42 Catharine St., Poughkeepsie 12601 (845) 454-3441

Secretary: Richard Greenblatt
Rutberg & Associates, 3390 North Rd., Poughkeepsie 12601 (845) 486-0300

Treasurer: Rebecca M. Blahut
McCabe & Mack, L.L.P., 63 Washington St., P.O. Box 509, Poughkeepsie 12602
(845) 486-6800; Fax: (845) 486-7621
E-mail: rblahut@mccm.com

Eastchester Bar Association

President: Gail M. Boggio
McCarthy Fingar L.L.P., 11 Martine Ave., White Plains 10606 (914) 946-3700; Fax: (914) 946-0134

V.P.: Michael D. Shalhoub
170 Hamilton Ave., Suite 203, White Plains 10601
(914) 798-5400; Fax: (914) 798-5401

Secretary: Michael Servodidio, L.P.A.
279 Main St., Eastchester 10709
(914) 337-0696; Fax: (914) 779-0383

Treasurer: Christopher G. Allocco
8 Roy Pl., Eastchester 10709
(914) 771-8318; Fax: (914) 771-6878

Annual Election: June
Meetings: Monthly, except July and Aug.

Bar Association of Erie County
438 Main St., 6th Floor, Buffalo 14202
(716) 852-8687; Fax: (716) 852-7641
Exec. Dir.: Katherine S. Bifaro
President: Scott M. Schwartz
Lipsitz, Green, Scime & Cambria, L.L.P.,
42 Delaware Ave., Suite 120, Buffalo 14202
(716) 849-1333, Ext. 491
V.P.: Arthur A. Russ, Jr.
Phillips Lytle, L.L.P., 3400 HSBC Center, Buffalo 14202
(716) 504-5703
Annual Meeting and Election: June

Essex County Bar Association
President: William Finucane
P.O. Box D-1, Elizabethtown 12932 (518) 873-6351
V.P.: John T. Wilkins
2461 Main St., Lake Placid 12946 (518) 523-1409
Secretary: Daniel T. Manning
7551 Court St., P.O. Box 217, Elizabethtown 12932
(518) 873-3380
Treasurer: Gregory M. Dennin
Main St., Lake Placid 12946 (518) 523-2595

Federal Bar Assn.,
Southern District of New York Chapter
President: John G. McCarthy
Smith, Gambrell & Russell, L.L.P.,
250 Park Ave., Suite 1900, N.Y.C. 10177
(212) 907-9703; E-mail: jmccarthy@sgrlaw.com
President-Elect: Simeon H. Baum
Resolve Mediation Services, Inc.,
575 Lexington Ave., 10th Floor, N.Y.C. 10022
(212) 355-6527; E-mail: simeonhb@disputeresolve.com
V.P.: Philip R. Schatz
Wrobel & Schatz, 1040 Ave. of the Americas,
11th Floor, N.Y.C. 10018-3703
(212) 421-8100; E-mail: philip.schatz@wandslaw.com
Secretary: Gareth deSantiago-Keene
2 1st Ave., Little Falls, NJ 07424
(973) 689-5638; E-mail: bright324@yahoo.com
Treasurer: William F. Dahill
Wollmuth, Maher & Deutsch, L.L.P.,
500 Fifth Ave., N.Y.C. 10110
(212) 382-3300; E-mail: wdahill@wmd-law.com

Federal Bar Council
123 Main St., Suite L-100, White Plains 10601-3104
(914) 682-8800; Fax: (914) 682-4400
E-mail: federalbar@federalbarcouncil.com
Internet: www.federalbarcouncil.com
Exec. Dir.: Jeanette Redmond
E-mail: jeanette.redmond@federalbarcouncil.com
President: Robert J. Giuffra, Jr.
Sullivan & Cromwell, 125 Broad St., N.Y.C. 10004-2498
(212) 558-3121; Fax: (212) 291-9064
E-mail: giuffrar@sullcrom.com
President-Elect: Robert J. Anello
Morvillo, Abramowitz, Grand, Iason, Anello & Bohrer,
565 5th Ave., N.Y.C. 10017
(212) 880-9520; Fax: (212) 856-9494
E-mail: ranello@maglaw.com
V.P.'s:
William Francis Kuntz II
Baker & Hostetler, L.L.P., 666 5th Ave., 16th Floor,
N.Y.C. 10103-0001 (212) 589-4229; Fax: (212) 589-4201
E-mail: wkuntz@bakerlaw.com
Hon. Elizabeth S. Stong
U.S. Bankruptcy Judge, 271 Cadman Plz.,
Brooklyn 11201-4201 (347) 394-1862; Fax: (347) 394-1865
E-mail: elizabeth_stong@nyeb.uscourts.gov
Audrey Strauss
Fried, Frank, Harris, Shrivers & Jacobson, L.L.P.,
One New York Plz., N.Y.C. 10004
(212) 859-8544; Fax: (212) 859-8584
E-mail: audrey.strauss@fzwz.com
Jay W. Waks
Kaye Scholer, L.L.P., 425 Park Ave., N.Y.C. 10022
(212) 836-8558; Fax: (212) 836-6458
E-mail: jwaks@kayescholer.com
Secretary: Mary Kay Vyskocil
Simpson, Thatcher & Bartlett, L.L.P.,
425 Lexington Ave., N.Y.C. 10017
(212) 455-3093; Fax: (212) 455-2502
E-mail: mvyskocil@stblaw.com
Treasurer: Vilia B. Hayes
Hughes Hubbard & Reed, L.L.P.,
One Battery Park Plz., N.Y.C. 10004-1482
(212) 837-6839; Fax: (212) 299-6839
E-mail: hayes@hugheshubbard.com
Annual Election: October

Federation of the Bar Associations of the Fourth Judicial District
President: Paul Pelagalli
20 Prospect St., Suite 212, Ballston Spa 12020
(518) 889-5000
V.P.: Michelle H. Wildgrube
2310 Nott St. E., Niskayuna 12309 (518) 377-6700
Secretary: Christopher Mills
The Mills Law Firm, 1520 Crescent Rd.,
Clifton Park 12065 (518) 323-9900
Treasurer: Adam Cooper
Carter Conboy et. al., 20 Corporate Woods Blvd.,
Albany 12211-2362 (518) 465-3484
Annual Meeting and Election: April

Franklin County Bar Association
President: John J. Muldowney
Fischer, Bessette, & Muldowney, L.L.P.,
43 Golf Course Rd., Malone 12953
(518) 481-5000; Fax: (518) 481-5203
V.P.: Douglas Wright
Hayes & Wright, 64 Park St., P.O. Box 840,
Tupper Lake 12986 (518) 359-3244; Fax: (518) 359-3432
E-mail: drw12927@verizon.net
Secretary: Virginia Morrow
50 Kiwassa Rd., Saranac Lake 12983
(518) 891-7003; Fax: (518) 891-6943
E-mail: vjmatty@morrowlawfirm.com
Annual Election: October

Fulton County Bar Association
President: Michael W. Smrtic
289 N. Main St., Gloversville 12078
(518) 773-8225; Fax: (518) 725-7731
V.P.: Ellen S. Ross
105 N. Perry St., Johnstown 12095
(518) 736-1146; Fax: (518) 684-9256
Secretary: Brett Preston
Hoyt & Preston, P.O. Box 1119, Broadalbin 12025
(518) 883-4816; Fax: (518) 883-3096
Treasurer: Susan Palmer Johnson
17 W. Main St., Johnstown 12095
(518) 762-3505; Fax: (518) 762-3011
Annual Meeting: Third week, Jan.

Genesee County Bar Association
President: Durin B. Rogers
Genesee County Attorney's Office,
5130 E. Main Rd., Suite 3, Batavia 14020
(585) 344-2580, Ext. 6481; Fax: (585) 343-5548
E-mail: durin.rogers@dfa.state.ny.us
V.P.: Mary Kay Yanik
33 Main St., Mount Morris 14510
(585) 658-9486; Fax: (585) 658-9786
E-mail: marykayyanik@aol.com
Secretary: Benjamin Bonarigo
Bonarigo & McCutcheon, 18 Ellicott St., Batavia 14020
(585) 344-1994
Treasurer: Thomas D. Williams
The Williams Law Firm, L.L.P., 2 Court St. Plz.,
P.O. Box 402, Batavia 14021-0402
(585) 343-1486; Fax: (585) 343-1487
Meetings: Monthly, as scheduled

Greater Rochester Association for Women Attorneys
279 Castlebar Rd., Rochester 14610
(585) 615-0134
E-mail: info@grawa.org
Internet: www.grawa.org

President: Laurie A. Giordano
Leclair, Korona, Giordano & Cole, L.L.P.,
150 State St., Suite 300, Rochester 14614
(585) 327-4101; Fax: (585) 327-4200
E-mail: lgiordano@leclairkorona.com

President-Elect: Kari Ann Smoker
St. John Fisher College, 3690 East Ave., Rochester 14618
(585) 385-7220; E-mail: kariann@rochester.rr.com

Secretary: Dana M. Campbell
The Campbell Law Firm,
First Federal Plaza, Suite 2100, 28 E. Main St.,
Rochester 14614 (585) 730-5551; Fax: (585) 262-3325
E-mail: danalaw@mac.com

Treasurer: Eileen E. Buholtz
Connors & Corcoran, P.L.L.C., 45 Exchange St.,
Suite 250, Rochester 14614
(585) 232-5885; Fax: (585) 546-3631
E-mail: ebuholtz@connorscorcoran.com

Annual Elections: April
Meetings: Monthly, first Tues.

Greene County Bar Association
Greene County Courthouse Library, 320 Main St., Catskill 12414 (518) 943-3130

President: Dominick J. Cornellius
411 Main St., Catskill 12414 (518) 719-3220

V.P.: John Stegmayer
320 Main St., Catskill 12414 (518) 444-8700

Secretary: Jon Perlin

Treasurer: Nuala Woods
P.O. Box 1059, Windham 12496 (518) 734-6992

Meetings: Spring, Sept. and Dec.
Annual Meeting: April

Herkimer County Bar Association

President: Mark Rose
48 N. Ann St., Little Falls 13365 (315) 823-0835

Secretary: Audrey Baron Dunning
47 First St., PMB 368, Ilion 13357
(315) 894-3143; Fax: (315) 894-3238

Annual Meeting and Election: December 31st

Hispanic National Bar Association
National Headquarters
Ben Franklin Station, P.O. Box 14347,
Washington, DC 20044
(202) 223-4777; Fax: (202) 223-2324
E-mail: info@hnba.com
Internet: www.hnba.com

President: Diana Sen
99 Hudson St., 14th Floor, N.Y.C. 10013
(212) 219-3360; Fax: (212) 431-4276

President-Elect: Vacancy at Press Time

N.Y. Region President: Gelvina Rodriguez Stevenson
Weill Medical College of Uiversity,
445 E. 69th St., Room 432, N.Y.C. 10021 (212) 746-0463

Annual Meeting: September
Annual Elections: July

Jamestown Bar Association

President: Peter R. Johnson
Fessenden, Laumer & D'Angelo, 81 Forest Ave.,
P.O. Box 590, Jamestown 14702
(716) 484-7196; Fax: (716) 488-9146

Program Dir.: Kenneth M. Lasker
Burgett & Robbins, P.O. Box 3090,
Jamestown 14702-3090 (716) 488-3090

Annual Meeting: May
Meetings: Monthly, second Thurs., except June, July & Aug.
Officers 2009-10

Jefferson County Bar Association

President: Susan Sovie
800 Washington St., Watertown 13601 (315) 836-1546

V.P.: Eugene J. Langone, Jr.
216 Washington St., Watertown 13601 (315) 788-5900

Secretary: Kathy Quencer
Proven & Quencer, 104 Court St., Watertown 13601
(315) 785-9333

Treasurer: Christina E. Stone
104 Washington St., Watertown 13601
(315) 786-0266; Fax: (315) 786-3488

Annual Meeting: October
Meetings: Varies

Jewish Lawyers Guild, Inc.
Internet: http://jewishlawyersguild.org

Chair: Bruce N. Lederman
Todtman, Nachamie, Spizz & Johns, P.C.,
425 Park Ave., 5th Floor, N.Y.C. 10022
(212) 872-9236; Fax: (866) 832-7205
E-mail: blederman@tnsj-law.com

President: Glenn Jacobson
Abrams, Gorelick, Friedman & Jacobson, P.C.,
One Battery Park Plz., 4th Floor, N.Y.C. 10004
(212) 422-1200; Fax: (212) 968-7573

Corresponding Secretary: David Fiveson
Butler, Fitzgerald, Fiveson & McCarthy, P.C.,
36 W. 44th St., Suite 816, N.Y.C. 10036-8105
(212) 615-2200; Fax: (212) 615-2215
E-mail: dfiveson@bffmlaw.com

John Marshall Lawyers Association, Inc.

President: Thomas J. Adams, Jr.
114-06 Jamaica Ave., Richmond Hill 11418
(718) 847-4572; Fax: (718) 847-5901

V.P.: Joseph T. Santangelo
110-22 Liberty Ave., Richmond Hill 11419
(718) 641-2300; Fax: (718) 641-2302

Treasurer: John F. Scheich
103-42 Lefferts Blvd., Richmond Hill 11419
(718) 843-7200; Fax: (718) 845-0275

Meetings: Bi-monthly

Kings County Criminal Bar Association
Internet: www.kccba.org

President: John B. Stella
305 Broadway, Suite 1400, N.Y.C. 10007
(212) 822-1433; Fax: (212) 822-1497

Executive V.P.: Robert S. Gershon
142 Joralemon St., Suite 5A, Brooklyn 11201
(718) 625-3977; Fax: (718) 855-2507
E-mail: rg@robgershon.com

V.P.'s:

Arthur L. Aidala
8118 13th Ave., Brooklyn 11228
(718) 238-9898; Fax: (718) 921-3292
E-mail: aidalaesq@usa.net

Stanford J. Bandelli
1611 Voorhies Ave., Brooklyn 11235
(212) 338-9898; Fax: (212) 934-4579

Michael O. Hueston
350 5th Ave., Suite 4810, N.Y.C. 10118-4810
(212) 643-2900

Michael A. Millet
32 Court St., Suite 408, Brooklyn 11201
(718) 624-2482; Fax: (718) 625-6837

Estelle Jana Roond
16 Court St., Suite 3601, Brooklyn 11241
(718) 596-4800; Fax: (718) 380-3753
E-mail: ejr@criminal-lawyer.com

Secretary: Jay Schwitzman
26 Court St., Suite 1406, Brooklyn 11242
(718) 797-1000; Fax: (718) 643-0025

Korean American Lawyers Association of Greater New York
Internet: www.kalagny.org

President: Lena Chun
American Transit Ins. Co., 330 W. 34th St., 10th Floor, N.Y.C. 10001 (212) 845-8795
E-mail: lenachun@hotmail.com

Meetings: Monthly, last Thurs.

Lawyers Square Club of New York

President: Martin A. Danoff
230 Park Ave., 23rd Floor, N.Y.C. 10169-0103
(212) 573-6064; Fax: (212) 573-9031
E-mail: legaleagle935@gmail.com

Meetings: Quarterly, last Wed. (Jan., June, Sept. & Nov.)

Lesbian, Gay, Bisexual and Transgender Law Assn. of Greater N.Y.
799 Broadway, Suite 340, N.Y.C. 10003
(212) 353-9118
E-mail: ingo@le-gal.org
Internet: www.le-gal.org

Exec. Dir.: Brad Snyder (Acting)

President: Jaime Piazza

Annual Election: January

Lewis County Bar Association, Inc.

President: Kathlene M. Loconti
Supreme Court Chambers, 7660 N. State St., Lowville 13367 (315) 376-5347; Fax: (315) 376-5398

V.P.: Keith A. Lyndaker
7659 N. State St., Lowville 13367 (315) 376-7543

Secretary: Kevin McArdle
County Court Chambers, 7660 N. State St., Lowville 13367 (315) 376-5366; Fax: (315) 376-4145

Treasurer: Todd W. McIntyre
Lewis County Family Court, 7660 N. State St., Lowville 13367 (315) 376-5535; Fax: (315) 376-1655

Meetings: Alternate months
2009-10 Officers

Livingston County Bar Association

Contact: Kevin Van Allen
Presutti Law Office, P.C., 32 Main St., Geneseo 14454
(585) 243-4320

Annual Election: November

Long Beach Lawyers Association
164 W. Park Ave., Long Beach 11561-0058
(516) 432-6263; Fax: (516) 432-4897

President: Hon. Frank DiKranis
Long Beach City Court, 1 W. Chester St., Long Beach 11561
(516) 431-1000, Ext. 7502; Fax: (516) 889-3511

V.P.'s:

Corey E. Klein
1 Westchester St., Long Beach 11561
(516) 431-1000, Ext. 255; Fax: (516) 431-1016
E-mail: cklein@longbeachny.org

Brian Peknic
Peknic & Peknic, L.L.C., 1005 W. Beech St., Long Beach 11561 (516) 432-9400; Fax: (516) 432-5396

John Petrilli
370 W. Park Ave., Long Beach 11561
(516) 431-6092; Fax: (516) 889-8904

Glenn Sabele
Elovich & Adell, 164 W. Park Ave., Long Beach 11561
(516) 432-6263; Fax: (516) 432-4897

Corresponding Secretary: Gary Muraca
89 Delaware Ave., Long Beach 11561 (516) 739-3322

Treasurer: Mitchell Sommer
Elovich & Adell, 164 W. Park Ave., Long Beach 11561
(516) 432-6263; Fax: (516) 432-4897

Annual Election: January
Meetings: Monthly, third Thurs., Sept.-June

Long Island City Lawyers Club

President: Michael Carlomusto
1065 Old Country Rd., Suite 206, Westbury 11590
(718) 359-2786; Fax: (516) 945-3269
E-mail: mcarlomusto@hotmail.com

V.P.: David L. Cohen
125-10 Queens Blvd., Kew Gardens 11415
(718) 793-1553; Fax: (718) 793-4719

Secretary: Theodore Mavomihalis
34-03 Broadway, Suite 200, Astoria 11106
(718) 777-0400; Fax: (718) 777-0599

Treasurer: Charles A. Forchelli
32-02 30th Ave., Long Island City 11102
(718) 278-6117; Fax: (718) 726-8449

Annual Election: June
Meetings: Monthly, fourth Thurs.

Macon B. Allen Black Bar Association (Queens)
229-19 Merrick Blvd., Jamaica 11413
(718) 217-7146; Internet: www.mbabba.com

President: Fearonce La Lande
207-01 Hillside Ave., Queens Village 11427
(718) 217-7146; Fax: (718) 217-7149
E-mail: fgalande@aol.com

First V.P.: Denise Johnson
88-11 Sutphin Blvd., Queens Village 11435 (718) 298-1194

Second V.P.: Tyrone M. Powell

Corresponding Secretary: Tracey A. Bloodsaw
25-28 Broadway, Astoria 11106
(718) 274-1599; Fax: (718) 274-1598

Recording Secretary: Austin I. Idehen
89-31 161st St., Jamaica 11432
(718) 558-4191; Fax: (718) 504-4430

Treasurer: Zenith Taylor
118-35 Queens Blvd., Suite 1220, Forest Hills 11375
(718) 268-1300; Fax: (718) 268-3343

Annual Election: June
Meetings: Monthly, second Thurs.

Madison County Bar Association
P.O. Box 102, Wampsville 13163

President: Keith R. Wolfe
Baum & Wolfe, 282 Genesee St., Chittenango 13037-1705
(315) 687-7215; Fax: (315) 687-7937
E-mail: kwolfe@verizon.net

V.P.: Elizabeth J. Worth
Courthouse, P.O. Box 607, Wampsville 13163
(315) 366-2437; Fax: (315) 366-2722
E-mail: eworth@courts.state.ny.us

Secretary: Todd D. Dexter
Courthouse, P.O. Box 607, Wampsville 13163
(315) 366-2241; Fax: (315) 366-2828
E-mail: tdexter@twcny.rr.com

Treasurer: Michael J. Miller
Taylor & Miller, L.L.P., 133 Peterboro St., Canastota 13032-1371 (315) 697-2288; Fax: (315) 697-8428
E-mail: miller@taylorandmillerlaw.com

Annual Election: June
Meetings: Bi-monthly

Mamaroneck-Harrison-Larchmont Bar Assn.

President: Denise P. Ward
Green & Ward, 222 Grace Church St., Suite 206B, Port Chester 10573 (914) 937-2800; Fax: (914) 937-7404
E-mail: dpward@dpward.net

V.P.: Jefferson Meighan
100 Mamaroneck Ave., Mamaroneck 10543
(914) 698-0100; Fax: (914) 698-0101
E-mail: meighanfram@aol.com

Secretary: Antonio Vozza
First American Title Co., 633 Third Ave., N.Y.C. 10017
(212) 551-9411; Fax: (646) 487-6932
E-mail: avozza@firstam.com

Treasurer: Martha Sokol McCarty
Law Office of Martha Sokol McCarty, P.C., 910 E. Boston Post Rd., 2nd Floor, Mamaroneck 10543
(914) 698-1110; Fax: (914) 698-9156
E-mail: msmccarty@aol.com
Internet: www.soundshorelaw.com

Metropolitan Black Bar Association
275 Madison Ave., 14th Floor, N.Y.C. 10016
(212) 964-1645; Fax: (212) 964-1668
E-mail: info@mbbanyc.org
Internet: www.mbbanyc.org
President: Joseph Drayton
President-Elect: R. Nadine Fontaine
V.P.'s:
Melnia Cordis-Howell (Programs)
Wayne Melbourne (Finance)
Corresponding Secretary: Francesca Perkins
Recording Secretary: Turquoise Haskins
Treasurer: Emily Jordan
Annual Meeting: May
Meetings: Monthly, third Tues., Sept.-June

Monroe County Bar Association
1 W. Main St., 10th Floor, Rochester 14614-2098
(585) 546-1817; Lawyer Referral Service: (585) 546-2130; Fax: (585) 546-1807
E-mail: reception@mcba.org
Internet: www.mcba.org
Exec. Dir.: Mary Corbitt; E-mail: mcorbitt@mcba.org
President: Susan Schaltz Laluk
Hiscock & Barclay, L.L.P., 2000 HSBC Plaza, 100 Chestnut St., Rochester 14604
(585) 295-4400; Fax: (585) 295-4401
E-mail: slaluk@hblaw.com
President-Elect: Bryan D. Hetherington
Empire Justice Center, Telesca Center For Justice, 1 W. Main St., Rochester 14614 (585) 295-5809
E-mail: bhetherington@empirejustice.org
Secretary: Connie O. Walker
Monroe County Court, 545 Hall of Justice, 99 Exchange Blvd., Rochester 14614 (585) 428-4155
Treasurer: Karla Damico Wilsey
16 W. Main St., Rochester 14614
(585) 232-3680; Fax: (585) 423-8273
Annual Election: June

Nassau County Bar Association
15th & West Sts., Mineola 11501
(516) 747-4070; Fax: (516) 747-4147
Exec. Dir.: Deena R. Ehrlich, Ph.D.
E-mail: dehrlich@nassaubar.org
President: Marc C. Gann
Collins, McDonald & Gann, One Old Country Rd., Suite 250, Carle Place 11514
(516) 294-0300; Fax: (516) 294-0477
President-Elect: Susan Katz Richman
Nassau Cty. Cthse., 262 Old Country Rd., Mineola 11501
(516) 571-2797
First V.P.: Marian C. Rice
L'Abbate Balkan, Golaviat & Contini, 1001 Franklin Ave., Garden City 11530
(516) 294-8844; Fax: (516) 294-8202
Second V.P.: Peter J. Mancuso
272 Old Country Rd., Mineola 11501 (516) 571-2274
Secretary: John L. Kase, 262 Old Country Rd., Mineola 11501
(516) 571-2628; Fax: (516) 571-6300
Treasurer: John P. McEntee
Farrell Fritz, 1320 Rex Corp. Plz., Uniondale 11556-1320
(516) 227-0700; Fax: (516) 336-2270
Meetings: Monthly, second Tues.

Nassau Lawyers' Association of Long Island, Inc.
1 Old Country Rd., Carle Place 11514
Internet: www.nlali.org
Exec. Dir.: Edwin J. Mulhern
(516) 294-8000; Fax: (516) 877-1195
Chair: Henry J. Cernitz
Jacobson & Schwartz, 510 Merrick Rd., Rockville Centre 11571 (516) 536-0900; Fax: (516) 536-2371
E-mail: hcernitz@jandslaw.com
President: Leslie Martin
595 Stewart Ave., Suite 510, Garden City 11530
(516) 222-0900; Fax: (516) 222-2971
E-mail: lmartin532@aol.com
First V.P.: Douglas Mayer
Rogak & Gibbons, L.L.P., 90 Merrick Ave., Suite 520, East Meadow 11554 (516) 620-6360; Fax: (516) 620-6361
E-mail: medmallaw@hotmail.com
Second V.P.: Stephen G. Frommer
Frommer & Cerrato, L.L.P., 42 Nassau Blvd., P.O. Box 8134, Garden City 11530-8134
(516) 742-7900; Fax: (516) 742-7999
E-mail: sgflaw@aol.com
Corresponding Secretary: Myron Jacobson
197 Merrick Rd., Lynbrook 11563 (516) 599-0888
E-mail: mgjacobsonlaw@aol.com
Recording Secretary: David Levine
Treasurer: Chester Greenspan
Annual Election: May
Meetings: Monthly, fourth Wed. except July and Aug.
Send Fed Ex packages to President's address

Nassau-Suffolk Trial Lawyers Association
Chair: Wade T. Dempsey
Hammill, O'Brien, Croutier, Dempsey & Pender, 6851 Jericho Tpke., Syosset 11791
(516) 746-0707; Fax: (516) 677-5475
Vice Chairs:
Joseph S. Bavaro
Salenger, Sack, Schwartz & Kimmel, L.L.P., 233 Broadway, 9th Floor, N.Y.C. 10279
(212) 267-1950; Fax: (212) 385-2170
Thomas Martyn
Martyn, Toher, Martyn, 1983 Marcus Ave., New Hyde Park 11042
Glenn Sabele
Elovich & Adell, 164 W. Park Ave., Long Beach 11561
(516) 432-6263
Secretary: Robert Doyle, Jr.
Lewis, Johs, Avallone, Avilles, L.L.P., 425 Broad Hollow Rd., Suite 400, Melville 11747
(631) 755-0101; Fax: (631) 755-0117
Treasurer: William G. Spratt
Shaub, Ahmuty, Citrin & Spratt, L.L.P., 1983 Marcus Ave., New Hyde Park 11042
(516) 488-3300; Fax: (516) 488-2324
Annual Election: July
Meetings: Monthly

National Employment Lawyers Assn./New York
3 Park Ave., 29th Floor, N.Y.C. 10016
(212) 317-2291; Fax: (212) 977-4005
Internet: www.nelany.com
Exec. Dir.: Shelley Leinheardt
E-mail: shelley@nelany.com
President: Darnley D. Stewart
11 Broadway, Suite 2150, N.Y.C. 10004 (212) 500-5106
E-mail: dstewart@gslawny.com
V.P.'s: J. Patrick DeLince
44 Wall St., 10th Floor, N.Y.C. 10005 (212) 710-9512
E-mail: jpd@delincelaw.com
Joshua Friedman
25 Senate Pl., Larchmont 10538
(212) 308-4338, (914) 484-2531
E-mail: josh@joshuafriedmanesq.com
Secretaries:
Anne Golden, 3 Park Ave., N.Y.C. 10016
(646) 825-9823; E-mail: ag@outtengolden.com
Margaret McIntyre
225 Broadway, Suite 2515, N.Y.C. 10007
(212) 227-9987; E-mail: margmac@earthlink.net
Treasurer: Philip E. Taubman
30 Vesey St., 6th Floor, N.Y.C. 10007 (212) 227-8140
E-mail: ptesquire@aol.com
Meetings: Approximately every six weeks, as announced

National Lawyers Guild (New York City Chap.)
113 University Pl., 8th Floor, N.Y.C. 10003
(212) 679-6018; Fax: (212) 679-6178
E-mail: nlgnyc@igc.org
Internet: www.nlgnyc.org

Chapter Coordinator: Susan Howard
President: Susan V. Tipograph
V.P.'s:
Beth Baltimore
Mark Taylor
Treasurer: Robert Boyle

Network of Bar Leaders
Internet: www.networkofbarleaders.org

President: Taa Grays
MetLife, 1095 Avenue of the Americas, N.Y.C. 10036
(212) 578-1143; E-mail: tgrays@metlife.com
First V.P.: Kathryn Salensky
Bronx Womens Bar Assoc., Hall of Justice,
265 E. 161st St., Bronx 10451
(718) 618-3689; Fax: (718) 618-3577
E-mail: networkofbarleaders@gmail.com
Second V.P.: Sam Braverman
901 Sheridan Ave., Bronx 10451
(718) 293-1977; Fax: (718) 793-5395
Recording Secretary: Mary Lacerenza
N.Y.S. Division of Housing & Community Renewal,
25 Beaver St., 7th Floor, Flushing 11374
(212) 480-7440; E-mail: mlacerenza@dhcr.state.ny.us
Corresponding Secretary: Fiordaliza A. Rodriguez
E-mail: frodriguezesq@aol.com
Treasurer: Gordon Eng
Debevoise & Plimpton, 919 3rd Ave., N.Y.C. 10022
(212) 909-6048; Fax: (212) 521-8848
E-mail: geng@debevoise.com
Annual Election: May
Meetings: Monthly, held at 14 Vesey St., N.Y.C.

New Rochelle Bar Association
P.O. Box 1863, New Rochelle 10802
(914) 633-7900
Internet: www.nrbar.org

President: Julie S. Kattan
271 North Ave., Suite 908, New Rochelle 10801
(914) 355-2955; Fax: (914) 355-2954
E-mail: juliek0601@aol.com
V.P.'s:
Hon. John P. Colangelo
Westchester County Court,
111 Dr. Martin Luther King, Jr. Blvd., White Plains 10601
(914) 824-5423; Fax: (914) 995-8653
E-mail: jcolange@courts.state.ny.us
Marilyn S. Faust
Fourt Country Club Dr., Larchmont 10538
(914) 834-7808; Fax: (914) 834-1437
E-mail: mfaust@mfaustlaw.com
Secretary: Laurie J. Korngold
155 Oxford Rd., New Rochelle 10804
(914) 576-1904; Fax: (914) 576-7249
E-mail: lkorngold@hotmail.com
Treasurer: Frank DiMarco
20 Cedar St., Suite 106, New Rochelle 10801
(914) 633-5330; Fax: (914) 633-5332
E-mail: franknr@aol.com
Annual Meeting: December
Meetings: Monthly, second Thurs.

New York City Trial Lawyers Assn.

President: Paul Fino, Jr.
White, Fleischner & Fino,
61 Broadway, 18th Floor, N.Y.C. 10006
(212) 487-9700; Fax: (212) 487-9777
E-mail: pfino@wff-law.com
V.P.: Maria Del Pilar Ocasio-Douglas
111 John St., Suite 800, N.Y.C. 10038
(212) 719-2821; Fax: (646) 843-4743
E-mail: pilardouglas@aol.com
Secretary: Andrew J. Smiley
Smiley & Smiley, L.L.P., 60 E. 42nd St., N.Y.C. 10165
(212) 986-2022; Fax: (212) 697-4689
E-mail: asmiley@smileylaw.com
Treasurer: Shelly K. Werbel
Werbel, Werbel & Verchick, L.L.P., 1465 Rockaway Plwy., Brooklyn 11236 (718) 485-0400; Fax: (718) 272-3242
E-mail: swerbel4law@aol.com
Annual Election: Bi-Annually in June of odd numbered years
Meetings: Monthly, third Thurs.

New York County Lawyers' Association
14 Vesey St., N.Y.C. 10007
(212) 267-6646; Fax: (212) 406-9252
Internet: www.nycla.org
Exec. Dir.: Sophia J. Gianacoplos, Ext. 220
E-mail: sgianacoplos@nycla.org

President: James B. Kobak, Jr.
Hughes, Hubbard & Reed, L.L.P.,
One Battery Park Plz., N.Y.C. 10004
(212) 837-6757; Fax: (212) 422-4726
E-mail: kobak@hugheshubbard.com
President-Elect: Stewart D. Aaron
Arnold & Porter, L.L.P., 399 Park Ave., N.Y.C. 10022
(212) 715-1114; Fax: (212) 715-1399
E-mail: stewart.aaron@aporter.com
V.P.: Barbara Moses
Morvillo, Abramowitz, Grand, Iason, Anelllo & Bohrer, P.C.,
565 5th Ave., N.Y.C. 10017
(212) 880-9540; Fax: (212) 856-9494
E-mail: bmoses@maglaw.com
Secretary: Susan J. Walsh
Moskowitz, Book & Walsh, L.L.P.,
345 Seventh Ave., 21st Floor, N.Y.C. 10001
(212) 221-7999; Fax: (212) 398-8835
E-mail: swalsh@mbwllp.com
Treasurer: Gail Donoghue
N.Y.C. Law Dept./Corp. Counsel,
100 Church St., N.Y.C. 10007
(212) 788-0500; Fax: (212) 442-8602
E-mail: gdonoghue43@verizon.net
Annual Meeting: May

New York Criminal and Civil Courts Bar Assn., Inc.
30 Vesey St., Suite 1400, N.Y.C. 10007
(212) 766-4030; Fax: (212) 233-3130
Exec. Dir.: Sidney Siller

President: Hon. Francis M. Alessandro (718) 655-2066
V.P.'s:
Joseph S. Alessandro
2244 Esplanade Ave., Bronx 10469
(212) 379-0553; Fax: (718) 379-2229
Hon. Richard Lee Price
851 Grand Concourse, Bronx 10451 (212) 374-8407
Secretary: Sidney Siller
30 Vesey St., 14th Floor, N.Y.C. 10007
(212) 766-4030; Fax: (212) 233-3130
Treasurer: Jeffrey Rich, 30 Vesey St., N.Y.C. 10007
(212) 406-0440; Fax: (212) 233-3130
Annual Meeting and Election: December
Meetings: Bi-annually

New York Criminal Bar Association
Internet: www.nycrimbar.org

President: Genay Ann Leitman
245 E. 44th St., N.Y.C. 10017 (212) 687-4499
V.P.: Michael K. Bachrach
276 5th Ave., Suite 501, N.Y.C. 10001
(212) 929-0592; Fax: (866) 328-1630
E-mail: mbach2000@yahoo.com
Secretary: Frederick Sosinsky
225 Broadway, N.Y.C. 10007 (212) 285-2270
Treasurer: Edward B. Sapone
40 Fulton St., 23rd Floor, N.Y.C. 10038
(212) 349-9000; Fax: (212) 349-9003
E-mail: edward@saponelaw.com
Annual Meeting and Election: February

New York Intellectual Property Law Assn.
2125 Center Ave., Suite 406, Fort Lee, NJ 07024
(201) 461-6603; Fax: (201) 461-6635
E-mail: admin@nyipla.org
Internet: www.nyipla.org

President: Dale L. Carlson
Wiggin & Dana, L.L.P., One Century Twr., P.O. Box 1832, New Haven, CT 06508-1832
(203) 498-4385; Fax: (203) 782-2889
E-mail: dcarlson@wiggin.com

President-Elect: Theresa M. Gillis
Howrey L.L.P., 601 Lexington Ave., N.Y.C. 10022
(212) 896-6631; Fax: (212) 896-6501
E-mail: gillist@howrey.com

First V.P.: Thomas J. Meloro
Willkie, Farr & Gallagher, L.L.P., 787 Seventh Ave., N.Y.C. 10019-6099
(212) 728-8248; Fax: (212) 728-9248
E-mail: tmeloro@willkie.com

Second V.P.: Charles R. Hoffmann
Hoffmann & Baron, L.L.P., 6900 Jericho Tpke., Syosset 11791 (516) 822-3550; Fax: (516) 822-3582
E-mail: choffmann@hoffmannbaron.com

Secretary: Dorothy R. Auth
Cadwalader, Wickersham & Taft, L.L.P., One World Financial Center, N.Y.C. 10281
(212) 504-6018; Fax: (212) 504-6666
E-mail: dorothy.auth@cwt.com

Treasurer: Alice C. Brennan
Verizon Wireless, One Verizon Way, Basking Ridge, NJ 07920
(908) 559-7411; Fax: (908) 559-7111
E-mail: alice.brennan@verizonwireless.com

Meetings: Monthly, as scheduled
Annual Election: May

New York State Academy of Trial Lawyers
39 N. Pearl St., 6th Floor, Albany 12207
(518) 364-4044; Fax: (518) 514-1184
E-mail: info@trialacademy.org
Internet: www.trialacademy.org

Administrator: Michelle Stern
E-mail: mstern@trialacademy.org

President: Anthony Bottar
Bottar Leone, P.L.LC., AXA Tower II, Suite 1600, 120 Madison St., Syracuse 13202
(315) 422-3466; Fax: (315) 422-4621
E-mail: abottar@bottarleone.com

President-Elect: Glenn Verchick
Werbel, Werbel & Verchick, L.L.P., 1465 Rockaway Pkwy., Brooklyn 11236
(718) 485-0400; Fax: (718) 272-3242
E-mail: werbel4law@aol.com

V.P., 1st Dept.: Deborah Truhowsky
Schwartzapfel, Truhowsky & Marcus, P.C., 51 E. 42nd St., Suite 1208, N.Y.C. 10017
(212) 921-4500; Fax: (212) 921-4999
E-mail: dtruhowsky@stmslaw.com

V.P., 2nd Dept.: Michael Kaplen
DeCaro & Kaplen, L.L.P., 427 Bedford Rd., Suite 260, Pleasantville 10570 (914) 747-4410; Fax: (914) 747-4403
E-mail: michael@brainlaw.com

V.P., 3rd Dept.: James Hacker
Hacker & Murphy, L.L.P., 7 Airport Park Blvd., Latham 12110 (518) 783-3843; Fax: (518) 783-8101
E-mail: jhacker@hackermurphy.com

V.P., 4th Dept.: James Reid
Greene & Reid, P.L.L.C., 173 Intrepid Ln., Syracuse 13205 (315) 492-9665; Fax: (315) 492-9741
E-mail: jreid@greenereid.com

New York State Assn. of Criminal Defense Lawyers
2 Wall St., 3rd Floor, N.Y.C. 10005
(212) 532-4434; Fax: (888) 239-4665
Internet: www.nysacdl.org
Exec. Dir.: Margaret Alverson
E-mail: malverson@nysacdc.com

President: George R. Goltzer
200 W. 57th St., 9th Floor, N.Y.C. 10019
(212) 608-1260; Fax: (212) 980-2968
E-mail: george@goltzer.com

President-Elect: Kevin D. O'Connell
New York County Defenders, 225 Broadway, Suite 1100, N.Y.C. 10007 (212) 803-5100; Fax: (212) 571-6035
E-mail: koconnell@nycds.org

Annual Meeting: January

New York State Defenders Assoc., Inc.
194 Washington Ave., Suite 500, Albany 12210
(518) 465-3524; Fax: (518) 465-3249
E-mail: info@nysda.org
Internet: www.nysda.org
Exec. Dir.: Jonathan E. Gradess
E-mail: jgradess@nysda.org

President: Edward J. Nowak

Secretary: Merble H. Reagon

Annual Meeting and Election: July

New York State Trial Lawyers Association
132 Nassau St., 2nd Floor, N.Y.C. 10038
(212) 349-5890; Fax: (212) 608-2310
Internet: www.nystla.org
Exec. Dir.: Lawrence Park; E-mail: lpark@nystla.org

President: Nicholas I. Timko
Kahn, Gordon, Timko & Rodrigues, P.C., 20 Vesey St., Room 300, N.Y.C. 10007 (212) 233-2040; Fax: (212) 732-4666
E-mail: nitimko@kgtrpc.com

President-Elect: Leslie D. Kelmachter
Joseph D. Fuchsberg Law Firm, L.L.P., 500 5th Ave., 45th Floor, N.Y.C. 10110 (212) 869-3500; Fax: (212) 398-1532
E-mail: l.kelmachter@fuchsberg.com

First V.P.: Michael E. Jaffe
Pazer, Epstein & Jaffe, P.C., 20 Vesey St., Suite 700, N.Y.C. 10007 (212) 227-1212; Fax: (212) 374-1778

Second V.P.: Arthur M. Luxenberg
Weitz & Luxenberg, P.C., 180 Maiden Ln., 17th Floor, N.Y.C. 10038-4925 (212) 558-5613; Fax: (212) 344-5461
E-mail: aluxenberg@weitzlux.com

Secretary: Robert F. Danzi
900 Merchants Concourse, Suite 314, Westbury 11590
(516) 228-4226; Fax: (516) 228-6569

Treasurer: Daniel P. O'Toole
Block, O'Toole & Murphy, L.L.P., One Penn Plz., Suite 5315, N.Y.C. 10119 (212) 736-5300; Fax: (212) 971-9840

Annual Meeting: June

New York Women's Bar Association
132 E. 43rd St., Suite 716, N.Y.C. 10017-4019
(212) 490-8202; Fax: (877) 282-1462
E-mail: info@nywba.org
Internet: www.nywba.org

President: Gretchen Beall Schumann
Cohen, Hennessey, et al., 11 W. 42nd St., 19th Floor, N.Y.C. 10036
(212) 512-0814; Fax: (212) 764-3925
E-mail: gschumann@chbrlaw.com

V.P.'s:

Catherine M. Foti
Morvillo, Abramowitz, Grand, Iason, Anello & Bohrer, P.C., 565 Fifth Ave., N.Y.C. 10017
(212) 880-9530; Fax: (212) 856-9494
E-mail: cfoti@maglaw.com

Patricia Ann Grant
Grant & Appelbaum, P.C., 444 Madison Ave., 17th Floor, N.Y.C. 10022
(212) 308-2200; Fax: (212) 308-2223

Jacqueline W. Silbermann
Blank Rome, L.L.P., 405 Lexington Ave., 23rd Floor, N.Y.C. 10174 (212) 885-5000; Fax: (212) 855-5001

New York Women's Bar Assn.—Cont'd
Recording Secretary: Yacine Barry
111 Centre St., N.Y.C. 10013 (646) 386-5700
Corresponding Secretary: Bonnie Cohen-Gallest
45 East End Ave., Room 11H, N.Y.C. 10028 (917) 848-8524
Treasurer: Julie Hyman
Julie Hyman, P.C., 640 W. 237th St., Suite 10D, Bronx 10463 (347) 449-6398
E-mail: juliehymanesq@hotmail.com
Annual Meeting: April

Nigerian Lawyers Association
321 Broadway, 3rd Floor, N.Y.C. 10007
(212) 566-9926; Fax: (212) 571-4309
E-mail: secretariat@nigerianlawyers.org
Internet: www.nigerianlawyers.org
President: Folake Ayoola
V.P.: Abayomi O. Ajaiyeola
Secretary: Oladiran Ajayi
Treasurer: Chisom Ananaba (Acting)
Annual Meeting/Election: November

Northern Westchester Bar Association
President: Alicia Gaudio
Novenstern Fabriani & Gaudio, L.L.P., 69 S. Bedford Rd., Mount Kisco 10549 (914) 241-2400
V.P.: Gregory A. Monteleone
Monteleone & Monteleone, 19 N. Moger Ave., Mount Kisco 10549 (914) 666-2118
Treasurer: Christina Martabano
269 N. Bedford Rd., Mount Kisco 10549
(914) 241-0022; Fax: (914) 241-0187
Membership Chair: Keith Brown
Novenstern, Fabriani & Gaudio, L.L.P., 69 S. Bedford Rd., Mount Kisco 10549 (914) 241-2400
Annual Election: June
Meetings: Monthly, Oct.-June

Oneida County Bar Association
258 Genesee St., Suite 302, Utica 13502-4636
(315) 724-4901; Fax: (315) 724-6010
Internet: www.oneidacountybar.org
Exec. Dir.: Diane M. Godlewski
E-mail: diane@oneidacountybar.org
President: Frank J. Furno
Oneida County Public Defender's Office—Civil Div., 235 Elizabeth St., 2nd Floor, Utica 13501
(315) 266-6100; Fax: (315) 266-6105
E-mail: ffurno@ocgov.net
Annual Meeting: December
Meetings: Monthly

Onondaga County Bar Association
1000 State Tower Bldg., 109 S. Warren St., Syracuse 13202-1860
(315) 471-2667; Fax: (315) 471-0705
E-mail: info@onbar.org
Internet: www.onbar.org
Exec. Dir.: Christine Gray; E-mail: cgray@onbar.org
President: Marion Hancock Fish
Hancock & Estabrook, L.L.P., 1500 AXA Twr. 1, P.O. Box 4976, Syracuse 13221
(315) 471-3151; Fax: (315) 471-3167
E-mail: mfish@hancocklaw.com
President-Elect: Gioia A. Gensini, 100 S. Clinton St., P.O. Box 7367, Syracuse 13261 (315) 234-8600
V.P.: Mary C. John
Frank H. Hiscock Legal Aid Society, 251 S. Warren St., Syracuse 13202 (315) 422-8191, Ext. 124;
Fax: (315) 472-2819; E-mail: mjohn@wnylc.com
Secretary: Nancy L. Pontius
Mackenzie Hughes, L.L.P., 101 S. Salina St., Suite 600, P.O. Box 4967, Syracuse 13221-4967
(315) 474-7571; Fax: (315) 474-6409
E-mail: npontius@mackenziehughes.com
Treasurer: Thomas J. Miller
314 E. Fayette St., Syracuse 13202 (315) 448-0126
Annual Meeting: November
Meetings: Monthly, first and third Thurs.

Ontario County Bar Association
Internet: www.ontariocountybar.org
President: Susan Gray Jones
21 Sly St., Canandaigua 14424 (585) 394-1800
V.P.: Carrie Watkins Bleakley
2 Ontario St., Room G25, Canandaigua 14424
(585) 396-4617
Secretary: David J. Whitcomb
48 N. Main St., Canandaigua 14424 (585) 394-0564
Treasurer: Sonali R. Suvvaru
20 Pleasant St., Suite 300, Canandaigua 14424
(585) 394-1850
Elections: Bi-annually in odd-numbered years during last fiscal quarter

Orange County Bar Association
198 Main St., P.O. Box 88, Goshen 10924
(845) 294-8222; Fax: (845) 294-7480
E-mail: oranglaw@frontiernet.net
Internet: www.orangecountybarassociation.org
Exec. Dir.: Elizabeth Allen
President: Barbara J. Strauss
60 Erie St., Suite 302, Goshen 10924
(845) 294-2616; Fax: (845) 294-3861
E-mail: straussb@frontiernet.net
First V.P.: John S. Selinger
45 Webster Ave., Goshen 10924
(845) 294-2544; Fax: (845) 294-3507
E-mail: newyorklegalteam@yahoo.com
Second V.P.: William A. Medican
46 Sugar Loaf Mountain Rd., Chester 10918
(845) 469-2728; Fax: (845) 469-9670
E-mail: wamlaw@optonline.net
Third V.P.: Patrick S. Owen
P.O. Box 431, Goshen 10924
(845) 294-4499; Fax: (845) 294-4431
E-mail: psowen@frontiernet.net
Secretary: Christine F. Stage
285 Main St., Goshen 10924
(845) 291-2657; Fax: (845) 291-3014
E-mail: cstage@co.orange.ny.us
Treasurer: Kevin F. Preston
34 Grove St., P.O. Box 310, Middletown 10940
(845) 343-3000; Fax: (845) 343-3866
E-mail: kpreston@mlsmlaw.com
Annual Meeting: May
Meetings: Monthly, third Mon.

Ossining Area Bar Association
President: Paul Rosen
130 Marlborough Rd., Briarcliff Manor 10510
(914) 762-0800
Treasurer: Stuart Halper
105 Whitson Rd., Briarcliff Manor 10510 (914) 941-2009
Meetings: Monthly, third Thurs.

Oswego County Bar Association
P.O. Box 5453, Oswego 13126
E-mail: info@oswego.bar.org
Internet: www.oswego-bar.org
President: Mary A. Felasco
163 S. First St., Fulton 13069
(315) 598-8552; Fax: (315) 598-1830
E-mail: mfelasco@oswego-bar.org
First V.P.: Hon. Spencer J. Ludington
141 S. First St., Fulton 13069
(315) 593-8400; Fax: (315) 592-3415
E-mail: spencer@oswego-bar.org
Second V.P.: Craig S. Morrissey
55 W. 2nd St., Oswego 13126 (315) 342-7214
E-mail: cmorrissey@oswego-bar.org
Secretary: Chelsey A. Cole
Oswego County D.A., 39 Churchill Rd., Oswego 13126
(315) 349-3200; Fax: (315) 349-3212
Treasurer: Kristin A. Shanley
283 W. 2nd St., Oswego 13126 (315) 343-2610
E-mail: kshanley@oswego-bar.org
Annual Meeting: January

Otsego County Bar Association
President: Kelley M. Eckmair, 526 Main St., Oneonta 13820 (607) 433-0090; Fax: (607) 433-2828
V.P.: Patricia L. Canner, 22 Dietz St., P.O. Box 945, Oneonta 13820 (607) 432-1521; Fax: (607) 432-1527
Secretary: Bruce Maxson
Otsego Co. Public Defender's Office, 197 Main St., Cooperstown 13326 (607) 547-8772
Treasurer: Robert W. Schlather
192 Main St., P.O. Box 391, Cooperstown 13326
(607) 547-5253; Fax: (607) 547-2420
E-mail: rbs@schlatherbirch.com
Annual Election: July

Peekskill Bar Association
President: Philip Hersh, 1011 Park St., P.O. Box 105, Peekskill 10566 (914) 737-5300; Fax: (914) 737-5739
Treasurer: Thomas R. Langan, 1200 Brown St., Suite 202, Peekskill 10566 (914) 737-0030; Fax: (914) 736-9999
Annual Election: February
Meetings: Monthly, third Wed.

Port Chester-Rye Bar Association
President: Anthony B. Gioffre III
445 Hamilton Ave., 14th Floor, White Plains 10601
(914) 761-1300, 761-5372; E-mail: agioffre@cuddyfeder.com
V.P.: Denise P. Ward
Grean & Ward, 222 Grace Church St., Suite 206B, Port Chester 10573 (914) 937-2800; Fax: (914) 937-7404
E-mail: dpward@dpward.net
Secretary: Lee Wagner
N.Y. Title Research Corp., 550 Mamaroneck Ave., Harrison 10528 (914) 645-7725; Fax: (914) 835-7466
Treasurer: David G. Gallo, 211 S. Ridge St., Port Chester 10573 (914) 939-0002; Fax: (914) 939-4253
Annual Election: Alternate years, Dec.
Meetings: Monthly third Tues., except July and Aug.

Protestant Lawyers Assn. of New York, Inc.
President: Paul Siegert
15 E. 32nd St., 3rd Floor, N.Y.C. 10016
(212) 564-8181; Fax: (212) 564-4414
E-mail: paulsiegert@aol.com
Secretary: Nelson Timken
80-41 230th St., Bellerose 11427 (718) 776-0084
E-mail: ntimken@nyc.rr.com
Treasurer: Robert C. Nielsen, 227 Warren St., Brooklyn 11201
(718) 625-3655; Fax: (718) 625-2303
E-mail: bobbklyn@ix.netcom.com
Annual Election: January
Meetings: Quarterly

Puerto Rican Bar Association, Inc.
Church St. Station, P.O. Box 3494, N.Y.C. 10008-2494
E-mail: prba.ny@gmail.com
Internet: www.prba.net
President: Catherine Torres
895 Broadway, 5th Floor, N.Y.C. 10003 (212) 525-6633
E-mail: ctorres@mirramgroup.com
President-Elect: Rosevelie Marquez Morales
Harris Beach, P.L.L.C., 100 Wall St., N.Y.C. 10005
(212) 687-0100; E-mail: rmarquez@harrisbeach.com
V.P.: Javier E. Vargas
Appellate Div., 2nd Dept., 45 Monroe Pl., Brooklyn 11201
(718) 875-1300; Fax: (718) 858-2446
Corresponding Secretary: Frank Cruz
Motor Vehicle Accident Indemnification Corp., 110 William St., 19th Floor, N.Y.C. 10038-3901
(646) 205-7860
Recording Secretary: Clara Rivera
Wilmer, Cutler, Pickering, Hale and Dorr, L.L.P., 399 Park Ave., 28th Floor, N.Y.C. 10022
(212) 230-8800; Fax: (212) 230-8888
Treasurer: Elena M. Goldberg
Appellate Div., 1st Dept., 27 Madison Ave., N.Y.C. 10010
(212) 340-0400; Fax: (212) 889-4412
Annual Election: Fourth Thurs., April
Meetings: Quarterly

Putnam County Bar Association
P.O. Box 44, Carmel 10512
E-mail: putnamcountybar@yahoo.com
President: Peter J. Reynolds
963 Route 6, Mahopac 10541
(845) 628-8080; Fax: (845) 628-5450
First V.P.: Christopher Rao
Hoffman, Wachtell & Rao, L.L.P., 399 Knollwood Rd., Suite 112, White Plains 10603
(914) 385-4100; Fax: (914) 682-1512
Second V.P.: Bonnie N. Feinzig
Spain & Spain, 671 Route 6, Mahopac 10541
(845) 628-5900; Fax: (845) 628-0694
E-mail: spainlawpc@aol.com
Secretary: William G. Sayegh
65 Gleneida Ave., Carmel 10512 (918) 228-4200
Treasurer: Nina Berry-Gerosa
760 Farmers Mill Rd., Carmel 10512 (845) 225-6686
Annual Election: December
Meetings: Monthly

Queens County Bar Association
90-35 148th St., Jamaica 11435-4097
(718) 291-4500; Fax: (718) 657-1789
E-mail: info@qcba.org
Internet: www.qcba.org
Exec. Dir.: Arthur N. Terranova
President: Chanwoo Lee
35-20 147th St., Suite 1A, Flushing 11354
(718) 961-6355; Fax: (718) 961-6343
E-mail: clee1970@aol.com
President-Elect: Richard M. Gutierrez
118-35 Queens Blvd., Suite 1500, Forest Hills 11375-7205
(718) 520-0663; Fax: (718) 520-8306
E-mail: richlaw101@aol.com
V.P.: Joseph J. Risi, Jr.
35-11 36th St., Suite 404, Long Island City 11106
(718) 278-2600; Fax: (718) 956-4897
E-mail: risi.associates@rcn.com
Secretary: Joseph Carola III
27 Lane Ave., Plainview 11803-5206
(516) 229-6101; Fax: (516) 229-6165
E-mail: joseph.carola.glfu@statefarm.com
Treasurer: Joseph F. DeFelice
125-10 Queens Blvd., Suite 302, Kew Gardens 11415
(718) 261-3358; Fax: (718) 793-5072
E-mail: jdefel4@aol.com
Annual Meeting: First Fri., March

Queens County Criminal Courts Bar Association
President: Steven Zalewski
125-10 Queens Blvd., Suite 10, Kew Gardens 11415
(718) 263-6800; Fax: (718) 261-7164
Secretary: Thomas E. McCullough
37-06 82nd St., Jackson Heights 11372
(718) 898-6969; Fax: (718) 335-4468
Treasurer: Ronald S. Nir
125-10 Queens Blvd., Suite 323, Kew Gardens 11415
(718) 544-3970; Fax: (718) 575-4085

Queens County Women's Bar Association
Borough Hall Station, P.O. Box 585, Kew Gardens 11424
(718) 595-0585; E-mail: qcwbarpresident@gmail.com
Internet: www.qcwba.com
President: Nicole McGregor-Mundy
88-11 Sutphin Blvd., Jamaica 11435 (718) 298-1212
V.P.: Hon. Bernice D. Siegal, 88-11 Sutphin Blvd., Jamaica 11435 (718) 298-1080; Fax: (718) 298-1090
Corresponding Secretary: Donna M. Golia
88-11 Sutphin Blvd., Jamaica 11435
(718) 298-0500; Fax: (718) 520-5048
Recording Secretary: Hon. Margaret Parisi McGowan
151-20 Jamaica Ave., Jamaica 11432 (718) 298-0213
Financial Secretary: Deborah M. Garibaldi
7519 Myrtle Ave., Glendale 11385-7434 (718) 386-4345
Treasurer: Donna Furey
21-83 Steinway St., Astoria 11105 (347) 448-2549
Meetings: Monthly, Oct.-June
Annual Meeting: April

Rensselaer County Bar Association
President: Stephen Pechenik
County Atty., Ned Pattison Govt. Center, 1600 7th Ave., Troy 12180 (518) 270-2950; Fax: (518) 270-2954
First V.P.: Carolyn D'Agostino
21 Everett Rd. Ext., Albany 12205
(518) 489-1098; Fax: (518) 489-3304
Second V.P.: Jonathan Schopf
Pattison, Sampson, Ginsberg & Griffin, P.C., 22 First St., Troy 12180 (518) 266-1025; Fax: (518) 274-6034
Third V.P.: Rachel Kruse
Rensselaer Polytechnic Institute, Rice Bldg., 110 8th St., Troy 12180 (518) 276-8327
Secretary: Kelly Cramer (Deputy County Attorney)
Rensselaer County Attorney Office,
Ned Pattison Govt. Center, 1600 7th Ave., Troy 12180
(518) 270-2950; Fax: (518) 270-2954
Treasurer: William L. Fox, 4 Springhurst Dr., Suite 107, East Greenbush 12061 (518) 477-7553
Annual Meeting: June
Monthly Meeting: Monthly, 2nd Wed.

Richmond County Bar Association
152 Stuyvesant Pl., Suite 203, Staten Island 10301
Mailing Address: P.O. Box 140593,
Staten Island 10314-0593
(718) 442-4500; Fax: (718) 442-2019
Internet: www.richmondcountybar.org
President: John Z. Marangos
Law Office of John Z. Marangos, 1134A Hylan Blvd., Staten Island 10305 (718) 273-8324; Fax: (718) 273-8096
President-Elect: Robert A. Mulhall
Angiuli, Katkin & Gentile, L.L.P., 60 Bay St., Staten Island 10301 (718) 816-0005
V.P.: Thomas A. Sipp
801 Castleton Ave., Staten Island 10310
(718) 273-6000; Fax: (718) 273-6009
Secretary: Thomas J. Hall
Hall & Hall, L.L.P., 57 Beach St., Staten Island 10304
(718) 447-1962; Fax: (718) 447-2761
Treasurer: Christopher J. Fitzpatrick
Jacobi, Sieghardt, Bousanti, Piazza & Fitzpatrick, P.C., 235 Forest Ave., Staten Island 10301
(718) 442-4600; Fax: (718) 442-3148
Annual Meeting: June

Rockland County Bar Association, Inc.
337 N. Main St., Suite 1, New City 10956
(845) 634-2149; Fax: (845) 634-1055
E-mail: office@rocklandbar.org
Internet: www.rocklandbar.org
Exec. Dir.: Sandria Garvin
President: Lynn Hilowitz
DaSilva, Hilowitz & McEvily, L.L.P., 120 N. Main St., New City 10956-3743 (845) 638-1550; Fax: (845) 638-6951
President-Elect: Keith Cornell
82 Maple Ave., New City 10956
(845) 634-7901; Fax: (845) 634-7963
V.P.: Lawrence Codispoti
Mandel, Katz & Brosnan, 210 Route 303, Valley Cottage 10989 (845) 639-7800; Fax: (845) 639-7850
Secretary: Alan G. Rosenblatt
Montalbano, Condon & Frank, P.C.,
67 N. Main St., 3rd Floor, P.O. Box 1070,
New City 10956-8070 (914) 634-7010
Treasurer: Alan E. Goldstein
Courthouse, 1 S. Main St., New City 10956 (846) 708-7219
Annual Meeting: June

Rockland County Women's Bar Association
Internet: www.rcwba.org
President: Kathleen Goodfellow
99 Main Street, Suite 301, Nyack 10960
(845)652-0696; E-mail: kgood1013@aol.com
V.P. Ellen Holtzman
101 N. Middletown Road, Nanuet 10954 (845) 627-0127
Corresponding Secretary: Andrea Osborne
664 Chestnut Ridge Rd., Chestnut Ridge 10977
(845)352-6600; E-mail: aosborneesq@aol.com
Recording Secretary: Phyllis Goldberg
Rockland County Family Court, 1 S. Main St., New City 10956 (845)638-5643
E-mail: pgoldberg@courts.state.ny.us
Treasurer: Bridget Casey
151 South Main Street, New City 10956 (845) 634-3345
E-mail: bcjade@optonline.net
Annual Elections: June

St. Lawrence County Bar Association
President: John F. Richey
Surrogate's Court, 48 Court St., Canton 13617
(315) 379-2217; Fax: (315) 379-2372
Secretary: Cathleen E. O'Horo, 117 Main St., Canton 13617 (315) 386-4595; Fax: (315) 379-1240
Annual Election: May

Saratoga County Bar Association
P.O. Box 994, Saratoga Springs 12866
(518) 280-1974; Fax: (518) 280-1974
Internet: http://saratogacountybar.org
Executive Coordinator: Patricia L. Clute
E-mail: pclute@saratogacountybar.org
V.P.: Matthew L. Chivers
187 Wolf Rd., Albany 12205 (518) 238-4383
President: Marne L. Onderdonk
90 Albany County Family Court, 30 Clinton Ave., Albany 12207 (518) 285-8600; Fax: (518) 462-4236
Secretary: Stephen M. Dorsey, 40 McMaster St., Ballston Spa 12020 (518) 884-4770; Fax: (518) 884-4720
Treasurer: Kyle N. Kordich, P.O. Box 15054, Albany 12212
(518) 464-6770; Fax: (518) 464-6778
Annual Election: June
Meetings: Alternate months

Schenectady County Bar Association, Inc.
P.O. Box 1728, Schenectady 12301-1728
(518) 393-4115; Fax: (518) 377-5450
E-mail: info@schenectadycountybar.org
Internet: http://schenectadycountybar.org
Exec. Dir.: Diane Herrmann
President: Frank M. Putorti, Jr.
1338 Union St., Schenectady 12308
(518) 382-1044; Fax: (518) 372-3686
E-mail: putorti@lawyer.com
V.P.: Michael E. Basile, 1430 Balltown Rd., Schenectady 12309 (518) 374-3399; Fax: (518) 374-9416
Secretary: Jenifer Wharton, 113 Saratoga Rd., Glenville 12302 (518) 399-5400; Fax: (518) 399-5951
E-mail: jwharton@gtdlaw.com
Treasurer: John Fantauzzi
224 State St., P.O. Box 1092, Schenectady 12301-1092
(518) 370-4645; Fax: (518) 370-4979
2009-10 Officers

Schoharie County Bar Association
President: Douglas V. Putnam, P.O. Box 300, Warnerville 12187 (518) 234-7770; Fax: (518) 234-7770
Secretary: Raynor B. Duncombe
283 Main St., P.O. Box 490, Schoharie 12157-0490
(518) 295-7515; Fax: (518) 295-7519
Annual Meeting: May

Schuyler County Bar Association
President: John C.T. Hayes
101 E. Main St., P.O. Box 480, Odessa 14869
(607) 594-4890; Fax: (607) 594-4894
V.P.: Kristin E. Hazlitt
105 9th St., Unit 5, Watkins Glen 14891
(607) 535-8126; Fax: (607) 535-8123
E-mail: khazlitt@co.schuyler.ny.us
Secretary: James P. Coleman
Unit 5, 105 9th. St., Watkins Glen 14891-0271
(607) 535-8121; Fax: (607) 535-8123
Treasurer: Dennis J. Morris
105 9th St., Unit 5, Watkins Glen 14891
(607) 535-8121; Fax: (607) 535-8123
E-mail: dmorris@co.schuyler.ny.us
Meetings: Every Tues., 12:15 P.M., Watkins Glen

Seneca County Bar Asssociation
P.O. Box 6, Seneca Falls 13148

President: David K. Ettman
115 Fall St., P.O. Box 805, Seneca Falls 13148
(315) 568-8199; Fax: (315) 568-8299

V.P.: Stephen R. Ricci
141 Fall St., Seneca Falls 13148 (315) 568-1345

Secretary: Patrick J. Morrell
102 Fall St., 2nd Floor, Seneca Falls 13148 (315) 568-5221

Treasurer: Michael J. Mirras
54 Fall St., P.O. Box 299, Seneca Falls 13148
(315) 568-5861

Staten Island Women's Bar Association

President: Patricia Anne Taylor
Kings County Criminal Court, 120 Schermerhorn St., Brooklyn 11210 (347) 404-9369; Fax: (718) 643-3538
E-mail: annetaylor727@gmail.com

V.P.: Edwina Frances Martin
Legal Services NYC, 350 Broadway, 6th Floor, N.Y.C. 10013 (646) 442-3586; Fax: (646) 442-3586
E-mail: emartin@legalservicesnyc.org
Internet: www.legalservicesnyc.org

Secretary: Brooke T. Skolnik
Sgarlato & Sgarlato, 1444 Clove Rd., Staten Island 10301-4335 (718) 273-7900
E-mail: btskilnik@aol.com

Treasurer: Eve Lynn Newman
900 South Ave., Suite 60, Staten Island 10314
(917) 776-7529; E-mail: enewman27@hotmail.com

Director: Anna E. Vira
1040 Ave. of the Americas, Suite 101, N.Y.C. 10018
(212) 764-0500; Fax: (212) 981-3717
E-mail: avira@viralawfirm.com

Steuben County Bar Association

President: Mat McCarthy
McCarthy Law Offices, 12 W. Pulteney Sq., P.O. Box 528, Bath 14810 (607) 776-3389; Fax: (607) 776-2876

V.P.: Chris Quinlan
2 W. Market St., Suite 201, Corning 14830
(607) 937-9585; Fax: (607) 937-5584

Secretary: Craig A. Patrick
3 E. Pulteney Sq., Bath 14810
(607) 776-9631; Fax: (607) 776-4930

Treasurer: J.M. Bowd

Annual Elections: August

Suffolk County Bar Association
560 Wheeler Rd., Hauppauge 11788-4357
(631) 234-5511; Fax: (631) 234-5899
E-mail: scba@scba.org
Internet: www.scba.org
Exec. Dir.: Sarah Jane LaCova
E-mail: jane@scba.org

President: Sheryl L. Randazzo
Randazzo & Randazzo, L.L.P.,
464 New York Ave., Suite 100, Huntington 11743
(631) 673-4998; Fax: (631) 549-0896
E-mail: srandazzoesq@aol.com

President-Elect: Matthew Pachman
34 Pantigo Rd., Suite 1, East Hampton 11937
(631) 324-3942; Fax: (631) 324-3622

First V.P.: Arthur E. Shulman
1601 Veterans Memorial Hwy., Suite 425, Islandia 11749
(631) 582-9400; Fax: (631) 582-9408

Second V.P.: Dennis R. Chase
The Chase Sensale Law Group, L.L.P.,
64 Smithtown Blvd., Smithtown 11787 (631) 348-7500

Secretary: Donna England
England & England, P.C., 2556 Middle Country Rd., Centereach 11720 (631) 588-0250

Treasurer: William T. Ferris
Bracken & Margolin, L.L.P., 1 Suffolk Sq., Suite 300, Islandia 11749 (631) 234-8585; Fax: (631) 234-8702

Annual Meeting and Election: First Mon., May

Suffolk County Criminal Bar Association

President: Glenn A. Obedin
Law Office of Glenn A. Obedin,
320 Carleton Ave., Suite 4200, Central Islip 11722
(631) 232-3400; Fax: (631) 232-5343
E-mail: gaolaw@optonline.net

First V.P.: Steve Fondulis
503 Main St., Port Jefferson 11777 (631) 878-4847
E-mail: sfondulis@optonline.net

Second V.P.: Ira S. Rosenberg
Law Office of Ira S. Rosenberg, 320 Carleton Ave., Suite 4200, Central Islip 11722
(631) 851-0600; Fax: (631) 232-5343

Secretary: Jason Bassett
320 Carleton Ave., Suite 4200, Central Islip 11722
(631) 234-2511

Treasurer: Ira R. Weissman
Law Offices of Naiburg, Rosenblum & Weismann, 320 Carleton Ave., Suite 2500, Central Islip 11722
(631) 979-7777

Annual Meeting: April
Meetings: Monthly, third Wed., Sept. - May

Suffolk County Matrimonial Bar Association

President: Karen G. Silverman
83 Prospect St., 2nd Floor, Huntington 11743
(631) 385-8600; Fax: (631) 385-8601
E-mail: karen.silverman@gte.net

V.P.: Thomas K. Campagna
4949 Express Dr. N., Ronkonkoma 11779-5510
(631) 737-8200; Fax: (631) 737-8687
E-mail: campagna@optonline.net

Secretary: Howard B. Leff
1055 Franklin Ave., Suite 306, Garden City 11530
(516) 739-7500; Fax: (516) 739-3587

Treasurer: Patricia A. Condon
McGuire & Condon, P.C., 775 Park Ave., Suite 133, Huntington 11743 (631) 421-8600; Fax: (631) 427-5106

Meetings: Second or third Wed., Sept.-May

Suffolk County Women's Bar Association
33 Kings Hwy., Hauppauge 11788
Internet: www.suffolkwomensbar.org

President: Shari Lee Sugarman
900 Route 111, Suite 280, Hauppauge 11788
(631) 406-7600; Fax: (631) 361-9601

Annual Election: April
Meetings: Monthly, third Tues.

Sullivan County Bar Association
P.O. Box 424, Monticello 12701

President: Sam Yasgur
County Attorney's Office, 100 North St., Monticello 12701
(845) 807-0560; Fax: (845) 784-4924
E-mail: samuel.yasgur@scgnet.us

V.P.: Danielle Jose
17 St. John St., Monticello 12701
(845) 791-7800; Fax: (845) 791-5923
E-mail: daniellejose@verizon.net

Secretary: Steven N. Mogel
50 North St., P.O. Box 1320, Monticello 12701
(845) 791-7676; Fax: (845) 791-4660
E-mail: deenasteve@yahoo.com

Treasurer: Scott A. Russell
30 Glen Wild Rd., Rock Hill 12775

Annual Elections: June

Tompkins County Bar Association
P.O. Box 6629, Ithaca 14851
(607) 533-8222; Fax: (607) 533-9218
E-mail: tcba@clarityconnect.com
Internet: www.tcbaweb.com
President: Michael May
Adams, Theisen, May & Miller, 103 W. Seneca St., Ithaca 14850 (607) 272-3442
E-mail: mmay@atmlaw.com
Secretary: Mary J. Schubert
True & Walsh, L.L.P., 950 Danby Rd., Room 310, Ithaca 14850 (607) 273-2301; Fax: (607) 272-1901
E-mail: mjs@truewalshlaw.com
Treasurer: Philip Winn
Tompkins Investment Services, P.O. Box 6437, Ithaca 14851 (607) 273-0037; Fax: (607) 273-0024
E-mail: pwinn@tompkinstrust.com
Annual Election: October
Meetings: Monthly, Third Fri.

Bar Association of the Tonawandas
President: Lori Shawver; E-mail: lorimshawver@aol.com
V.P.: George C. Burgasser
138 Delaware, Buffalo 14202 (716) 843-5811
Secretary/Treasurer: Kendra Vergason
Brick, Brick & Elmer, P.C., 91 Tremont St., P.O. Box 604, North Tonawanda 14120
(716) 693-2335; Fax: (716) 693-4972
E-mail: brickelmer@aol.com
Meetings: Monthly, third Thurs., except July and Aug.
Annual Election: May
2009-10 Officers

Ulster County Bar Association
President: Eric Schneider, 41 Pearl St., P.O. Box 3936, Kingston 12402 (845) 339-6733; Fax: (845) 331-2754
E-mail: ericwrit@aol.com
First V.P.: Derek Spada
Basch & Keegan, L.L.P., 307 Clinton Ave., P.O. Box 4235, Kingston 12401 (845) 338-8884; Fax: (845) 338-2268
E-mail: spadad@baschkeegan.com
Second V.P.: Kerri Savona
Ulster County Dept. of Social Services, 1041 Development Ct., Kingston 12401 (845) 334-5290
E-mail: ksav@co.ulster.ny.us
Secretary: Felicia Raphael, P.O. Box 294, Kerhonkson 12446
E-mail: feliciaraphael@rocketmail.com
Treasurer: Jason Kovacs
Rusk, Wadlin, Heppner & Martuscello, L.L.P., 255 Fair St., P.O. Box 3356, Kingston 12402
(845) 331-4100; E-mail: jkovacs@rwhm.com
Annual Meeting: May
Meetings: Monthly, as announced

Warren County Bar Association, Inc.
107 Bay St., Glens Falls 12801
(518) 792-9239; Fax: (518) 792-3183
E-mail: wcba-ny@verizon.net
Internet: www.wcba-ny.com
Exec. Dir.: Lisa M. Bushman
President: Malcolm O'Hara
Bartlett Pontiff Stewart & Rhodes, 1 Washington Pl., P.O. Box 2168, Glens Falls 12801
(518) 792-2117; Fax: (518) 792-3309
President-Elect: John Silvestri
39 Theriot Ave., P.O. Box 715, Chestertown 12817
(518) 494-3404; Fax: (518) 494-7571
V.P.: Matthew R. Ludemann
Stanclift, Ludeman & McMorris, P.C., 3 Warren St., P.O. Box 358, Glens Falls 12801
(518) 745-4343; E-mail: mrl@stancliftlaw.com
Secretary: Matthew F. Fuller
Fitzgerald, Morris, Baker & Firth, One Broad St. Plz., P.O. Box 2017, Glens Falls 12801
(518) 745-1400; Fax: (518) 745-1575
Treasurer: Kristine K. Flower
Caffry & Flower, 100 Bay St., Glens Falls 12801
(518) 792-1582; Fax: (518) 793-0541
Annual Election/Meeting: May
Meetings: Monthly

Washington County Bar Association
President: Jeffrey E. McMorris
3 Warren St., P.O. Box 358, Glens Falls 12801
(518) 745-4343; Fax: (518) 745-4344
V.P.: Leslie W. Ryan, 136 Broadway, Fort Edward 12828
(518) 747-0338; Fax: (518) 747-0771
Secretary: Christian P. Morris
P.O. Box 1, Schuylerville 12871 (518) 859-5544
Treasurer: Tatiana Coffinger
1340 State Route 9, Lake George 12845 (518) 761-6526
Annual Meeting: May
Annual Election: January

Wayne County Bar Association
54 Broad St., Lyons 14489
President: Douglas M. Jablonski
12061 Main St., Wolcott 14590
(315) 594-1066; Fax: (315) 594-1969
Secretary/Treasurer: Tracey L. Fox
29 W. Main St., Sodus 14551
(315) 483-6733; Fax: (315) 483-2073
Annual Meeting and Election: June
Meetings: Monthly, first Tues., except June, July and Aug.

Westchester Black Bar Association, Inc.
Internet: www.mywbba.com
President: Delores Scott-Brathwaite
333 Mamaroneck Ave., PMB 219, White Plains 10605
(914) 667-8338; Fax: (914) 667-0751
V.P.: Helen Blackwood
Mount Vernon City Court, 2 Roosevelt Sq., Mount Vernon 10550 (914) 665-2366; Fax: (914) 665-9142
Corresponding Secretary: Jacqueline Warner
106 Corporate Park Dr., Suite 317, White Plains 10604
(914) 694-4102; Fax: (914) 694-4510
E-mail: jwarner@hhk.com
Recording Secretary: Linda Morris
111 Dr. Martin Luther King Blvd., White Plains 10601-2509 (914) 995-3941
Treasurer: Julie Mills-Worthy
West County Court, 111 Dr. Martin Luther King Blvd., White Plains 10601 (914) 824-5438
Regular Meetings: As scheduled, alternate months: Jan., Mar., May, July, Sept., and Nov.
Annual Election: January
2009-10 Officers

Westchester County Bar Association
One N. Broadway, Suite 512, White Plains 10601
(914) 761-3707; Fax: (914) 761-9402
Internet: www.wcbany.org
Exec. Dir.: Bill Egan
President: Donald K. Sandford
Law Office of Donald K. Sandford, P.O. Box 6, Briarcliff Manor 10510 (914) 262-6575
E-mail: dks.esq1@yahoo.com
President-Elect: Carol L. Van Scoyoc
White Plains Corporation Counsel, 255 Main St., White Plains 10601 (914) 422-1270
E-mail: cvan@ci.white-plains.ny.us
V.P.'s:
Mayo G. Bartlett
81 Main St., Suite 118, White Plains 10601
(914) 285-1500; Fax: (914) 285-0055
Jerold R. Ruderman
Wilson, Elser, Moskowitz et al, 3 Gannett Dr., White Plains 10604 (914) 323-7000; Fax: (914) 323-7001
E-mail: jerold.ruderman@wilsonelser.com
Secretary: Robert S. Stone
Dorf Law Firm, L.L.P., 740 W. Boston Post Rd., Suite 304, Mamaroneck 10543
(914) 381-7600; Fax: (914) 381-7608
Treasurer: Jody Fay
The Kelsey Company, 199 Main St., Suite 1010, White Plains 10601 (914) 358-9323
E-mail: jody.fay@thekelseycompany.com
Annual Meeting: March

Westchester Women's Bar Association
(914) 347-3662
Internet: www.wwbany.org
President: Dolores Gebhardt
McCarthy Fingar, L.L.P., 11 Martine Ave., 12th Floor, White Plains 10606 (914) 946-3700, Ext. 242;
Fax: (914) 946-0134; E-mail: dgebhardt@mccarthyfingar.com
V.P.'s:
Lonya A. Gilbert
Hyman & Gilbert, 1843 Palmer Ave., Larchmont 10538
(914) 833-5297; Fax: (914) 833-5294
E-mail: nefesh18@hotmail.com
Julie S. Kattan, 271 North Ave., Suite 908, New Rochelle 10801 (914) 355-2955; Fax: (914) 355-2954
E-mail: juliek0601@aol.com
Beth A. Willensky, 225 Overlook Rd., New Rochelle 10804
(914) 576-5874; E-mail: bawesq@optonline.net
Corresponding Secretary: Lisa M. Bluestein
30 Glenn St., Suite 103, White Plains 10606
(914) 948-4320; Fax: (914) 931-2485
E-mail: imbluestein@optonline.net
Recording Secretary: Annette G. Hasapidis
450 Oak Ridge Commons, South Salem 10590
(914) 533-3049; Fax: (914) 533-3051
E-mail: ahasapidis@appellatelaw.biz
Treasurer: Susan D. Edwards
Westchester Community Foundation,
200 N. Central Park Ave., Suite 310, Hartsdale 10550
(914) 948-5166, Ext. 6
E-mail: sedwards@wcf-ny.org
Annual Meeting: June

Western New York Trial Lawyers Association
Niagara Square Station, P.O. Box 14,
Buffalo 14201-0014
President: Brian Sutter
Sugarman Law Firm, L.L.P., 14 Lafayette Sq., Buffalo 14203-1929 (716) 847-2523
Secretary: Kathleen M. Reilly
Damon & Morey, L.L.P., 298 Main St., Buffalo 14202
(716) 858-3861
V.P.: Paul A. Bender, 68 Niagara St., Buffalo 14202-3409
(716) 856-3200; Fax: (716) 556-3270
Treasurer: John P. Danieu
Roach, Brown, McCarthy & Gruber, P.C.,
1920 Liberty Bldg., 424 Main St., Buffalo 14202
(716) 852-0400; Fax: (716) 852-2535
Deputy Treasurer: Robert Viola
770 Main St., P.O. Box 948, Niagara Falls 14302-0948
(716) 285-9555; Fax: (716) 284-0379
Annual Election: January
2010 Officers

White Plains Bar Association
Internet: www.whiteplainsbar.org
President: Andrew K. Brotmann
The Brotmann Law Group, 2 Gannet Dr., Suite 108, White Plains 10604
(914) 694-6200, Ext. 303; Fax: (914) 509-5444
E-mail: akb@brotmannlaw.com
V.P.: Deborah A. Scalise
Scalise & Hamilton, L.L.P., 670 White Plains Rd., Suite 325, Scarsdale 10583
(914) 725-2801; Fax: (914) 931-2112
E-mail: dscalise@scaliseethics.com
Secretary: Hon. Forrest Strauss
Grievance Committee for the Ninth Judicial District,
399 Knollwood Rd., Suite 200, White Plains 10603
(914) 949-4540; E-mail: fstrauss@courts.state.ny.us
Treasurer: Thomas H. Welby
Welby, Brady & Greenblatt, L.L.P.,
Westchester Financial Center,
11 Martine Ave., Penthouse, White Plains 10606
(914) 428-2100, Ext. 302; Fax: (914) 428-2172
E-mail: twelby@wbgllp.com
Meetings: Monthly, third Tues.
Election: June

Women's Bar Assn. of Orange & Sullivan Counties
P.O. Box 911, Warwick 10990
Internet: www.wbaosc.org
President: Kelli M. O'Brien, P.O. Box 562, Goshen 10924
(845) 565-5080; E-mail: kobrien@wbaosc.org
President-Elect/Treasurer: Phaedra Britt
290 Larkin Dr., Suite 103-266, Monroe 10950
(845) 496-1112; E-mail: pbritt@wbaosc.org
V.P.'s:
Julia Goings-Perrot
Tarshis, Catania, Liberth, Mahon & Milligram, P.L.L.C., One Corwin Ct., Newburgh 12550
(845) 565-1100; Fax: (845) 565-1999
Judy Young
P.O. Box 197, Bloomingburg 12721 (845) 888-5802
E-mail: jyoung@wbaosc.org
Corresponding Secretary: Milana Tepermayster
Larkin, Axelrod, Ingrassia & Tetenbaum, L.L.P.,
356 Meadow Ave., Newburgh 12550
(845) 566-5345; Fax: (845) 566-5148
Recording Secretary: Hannah Prall
P.O. Box 188, Bloomingburg 12721
Meetings: Monthly, second Tues.
Annual Elections: June

Women's Bar Association of the State of New York
P.O. Box 936, N.Y.C. 10024-0546
(212) 362-4445; Fax: (212) 721-1620
E-mail: info@wbasny.org
Internet: www.wbasny.org
Exec. Dir.: Linda A. Chiaverini
E-mail: lchiaverini@wbasny.org
President: Deborah W. Estis
Cohen, Estis & Associates, L.L.P.,
40 Matthews St., Suite 203, Goshen 11924
(845) 291-1900; Fax: (845) 291-8601
E-mail: dwe1@frontiernet.net
President-Elect: Karen Richardson
United States District Court, 68 Court St., Room 41B, Buffalo 14202-3405 (716) 332-7872; Fax: (716) 332-7875
E-mail: karen_richardson@nywd.uscourts.gov
V.P.'s:
Linda Kevins
Nassau County Supreme Court, 400 County Seat Dr., Mineola 11501 (516) 571-0022; Fax: (516) 571-0030
E-mail: lkevins@courts.state.ny.us
Maureen E. Maney
Hancock & Estabrook, L.L.P., 1500 AXA Tower 1,
100 Madison St., Syracuse 13221
(315) 471-3151; Fax: (315) 471-3167
E-mail: mmaney@hancocklaw.com
Corresponding Secretary: Irene V. Villacci
Irene V. Villacci, P.L.L.C., 74 N. Village Ave., Rockville Centre 11570 (516) 280-1339; Fax: (516) 764-1446
E-mail: ivlaw@verizon.net
Recording Secretary: Andrea F. Composto
Composto & Composto, 142 Joralemon St., Brooklyn 11201 (718) 875-5199; Fax: (718) 555-6866
E-mail: acomposto@compostolaw.com
Treasurer: Donna E. Frosco
Keane & Beane, P.C., 445 Hamilton Ave., Suite 1500, White Plains 10601 (914) 946-4777; Fax: (914) 946-6868
E-mail: dfrosco@ublaw.com
Annual Convention: May
Meetings: Quarterly in Sept., Nov., Jan., and Mar.

Wyoming County Bar Association
President: Bradley A. Janson
52 N. Main St., Warsaw 14569
(585) 786-3070; Fax: (585) 786-3065
E-mail: bajanson@frontiernet.net
V.P.: Jennifer M. Wilkinson, 11 Exchange St., Attica 14011
(585) 591-1100; Fax: (585) 591-1722
E-mail: jwilkinson@daddandnelson.com
Secretary: Donald G. O'Geen
147 N. Main St., Warsaw 14569
(585) 786-8822; Fax: (585) 786-8842
E-mail: dogeen@wyomingco.net

Wyoming County Bar Assn.—Cont'd
Treasurer: Vincent A. Hemming
147 N. Main St., Warsaw 14569
(585) 786-8822; Fax: (585) 786-8842
E-mail: vhemming@wyomingco.net

Yates County Bar Association
President: Douglas G. Reynolds
312 W. Lake Rd., Penn Yan 14527 (315) 536-3833
V.P.: Allison M. Connor
415 Liberty St., Penn Yan 14527
(315) 536-5350; Fax: (315) 536-5556
Secretary/Treasurer: Susan H. Lindenmuth
415 Liberty St., Penn Yan 14527 (315) 536-5550
Annual Election: December
Meetings: First Mon., May and Dec.
2009-10 Officers

Yonkers Lawyers Association
President: James Dibbini
570 Yonkers Ave., Yonkers 10704 (914) 965-1011
E-mail: jdibbini@dibbinilaw.com
V.P.: Catherine M. Ridgway
700 White Plains Post Rd., Suite 309, Scarsdale 10583-5013
(914) 725-2180; Fax: (914) 725-6160
Secretary: Michelle D'Ambrosio
53 S. Broadway, Yonkers 10701
Treasurer: Carol M. Daly
68 Algonguin Rd., Yonkers 10710 (914) 961-2492
E-mail: daly68@aol.com
Annual Meeting: June
Meetings: Monthly, third Mon., except July and Aug.

Yorktown Bar Association
President: Alfred DePrado
2014 Crompond Rd., Yorktown Heights 10598
(914) 962-4100; Fax: (914) 962-4188
V.P.: Laurence A. Silverman
3270 Curry St., Yorktown Heights 10598 (914) 243-7383
Secretary: Theresa C. Iasiello
1961 Commerce St., Yorktown Heights 10598
(914) 962-5513; Fax: (914) 962-5515
E-mail: tiasiello@juno.com
Treasurer: Barbara R. Diehl
2074 Crompond Rd., Yorktown Heights 10598
(914) 245-7402; Fax: (914) 245-7403
Meetings: Monthly, last Wed., 7:45 A.M.
Annual Meeting: May
Annual Election: June

2011 HOLIDAYS—FEDERAL AND ALL STATES AND TERRITORIES†

Editor's Note: Federal legislation has changed Veterans' Day back to the traditional November 11 but has not changed Memorial Day from the last Monday in May, Washington's Birthday from the 3rd Monday in February or Columbus Day from the 2nd Monday in October. Most States have followed these Federal dates. Local statutes as well as executive orders or proclamations should be checked for possible change during the year after our press time. We have verified the dates listed below but can not be responsible for changes that are pending.

Also, in most States, where a holiday falls on a Sunday it is observed on the following Monday and in some States where a holiday falls on a Saturday it is observed on the preceding Friday. Consult local statutes and case law for specific applications.

2011 Federal Public Holidays observed as Holidays in most States:

January 1—(New Year's Day).

3rd Monday in January—January 17 (Dr. Martin Luther King, Jr.'s Birthday; called Human Rights Day or Civil Rights Day in some states). Now observed in most States.

3rd Monday in February—February 21 (called Washington's Birthday or Presidents Day in most States).

Last Monday in May—May 30 (Memorial Day). Each State celebration is listed below.

July 4—(Independence Day).

1st Monday in September—September 5 (Labor Day).

2nd Monday in October—October 10 (Columbus Day) celebrated by most States.

November 11—(Veterans' Day) celebrated by most States.

4th Thursday in November—November 24. (Thanksgiving Day). Many States close courts and public offices on the day after Thanksgiving.

*December 25—(Christmas Day). Many States close courts and public offices on the day before and after Christmas Day.

2011 State and Territorial Holidays in addition to Federal Public Holidays above.

Alabama—3rd Mon. in Jan.–Jan. 17 (Robert E. Lee's and Dr. Martin Luther King's Birthday); 3rd Mon. in Feb.—Feb. 21 (Thomas Jefferson's Birthday); March 8 (Mardi Gras, Mobile & Baldwin Counties); 4th Mon. in April–April 25 (Confederate Memorial Day); last Mon. in May–May 30 (Memorial Day); 1st Mon. in June–June 6 (Jefferson Davis' Birthday).

Alaska—Last Mon. in March–March 28 (Seward's Day); last Mon. in May—May 30 (Memorial Day); Oct. 18 (Alaska Day).

Arizona—last Mon. in May–May 30 (Memorial Day).

Arkansas—3rd Mon. in Jan.–Jan. 17 (Dr. Martin Luther King's and Robert E. Lee's Birthday); 3rd Mon. in Feb.—Feb. 21 (Washington's Birthday and Daisy Bates Day); last Mon. in May–May 30 (Memorial Day); *Dec. 24 (Christmas Eve Day).

California—*Feb. 12 (Lincoln Day); March 31 (Cesar Chavez Day); April 22 (Good Friday); last Mon. in May–May 30 (Memorial Day); Sept. 9 (Admission Day).

Colorado—last Mon. in May–May 30 (Memorial Day).

Connecticut—*Feb. 12 (Lincoln's Birthday); last Mon. in May–May 30 (Memorial Day).

Delaware—April 22 (Good Friday); last Mon. in May–May 30 (Memorial Day); Thurs. following Election Day–Nov. 10 (Return Day—noon, Sussex County); 4th Fri. in Nov.–Nov. 25 (Day after Thanksgiving); (General Election Day, when applicable).

District of Columbia—Jan. 20 (Presidential Inauguration Day, when Applicable); *April 16 (D.C. Emancipation Day); last Mon. in May–May 30 (Memorial Day).

Florida—Jan. 19 (Robert E. Lee's Birthday); *Feb. 12 (Lincoln's Birthday); Feb. 15 (Susan B. Anthony's Birthday); March 8 (Shrove Tuesday); April 2 (Pascua Florida Day); April 22 (Good Friday); April 26 (Confederate Memorial Day); last Mon. in May–May 30 (Memorial Day); June 3 (Jefferson Davis' Birthday); June 14 (Flag Day); (General Election Day, when applicable).

Georgia—Jan. 19 (Robert E. Lee's Birthday); April 26 (Confederate Memorial Day); last Mon. in May–May 30 (Memorial Day); June 3 (Jefferson Davis' Birthday). Certain holidays require Gubernatorial Proclamation. Statutes must be consulted for particular applications.

Guam—last Mon. in May—May 30 (Memorial Day); July 21 (Liberation Day); Nov. 2 (All Soul's Day); Dec. 8 (Lady of Camarin Day).

Hawaii—*March 26 (Kuhio Day); April 22 (Good Friday); last Mon. in May–May 30 (Memorial Day); *June 11 (Kamehameha Day); 3rd Fri. in Aug.–Aug. 19 (Admission Day); (General Election Day, when applicable).

Idaho—last Mon. in May–May 30 (Memorial Day).

Illinois—*Feb. 12 (Lincoln's Birthday); 1st Mon. in March—March 7 (Casimir Pulaski Day); April 22 (Good Friday); last Mon. in May—May 30 (Memorial Day); General Election Day, when applicable.

Indiana—*Feb. 12 (Lincoln's Birthday); April 22 (Good Friday); last Mon. in May–May 30 (Memorial Day); (Primary and General Election Days, when applicable).

Iowa—*Feb. 12 (Lincoln's Birthday); last Mon. in May–May 30 (Memorial Day).

Kansas—last Mon. in May–May 30 (Memorial Day).

Kentucky—Jan. 19 (Robert E. Lee Day); *Jan. 30 (Franklin D. Roosevelt Day); *Feb. 12 (Lincoln's Birthday); last Mon. in May–May 30 (Memorial Day); June 3 (Confederate Memorial Day and Jefferson Davis Day); (General Election Day, when applicable).

Louisiana—*Jan. 8 (Battle of New Orleans Day); 2nd Mon. in Jan.–Jan. 10 (Inauguration Day, Baton Rouge only); Jan. 19 (Robert E. Lee Day); March 8 (Mardi Gras); April 22 (Good Friday); last Mon. in May–May 30 (Memorial Day); June 3 (Confederate Memorial Day); Aug. 30 (Huey P. Long Day); Nov. 1 (All Saints Day); (General Election Day, when applicable); 4th Fri. in Nov.–Nov. 25 (Acadian Day); Certain holidays require Gubernatorial Proclamation. Statutes must be consulted for particular applications.

Maine—3rd Mon. in April–April 18 (Patriots' Day) last Mon. in May–May 30 (Memorial Day).

Maryland—*Feb. 12 (Lincoln's Birthday); March 25 (Maryland Day); April 22 (Good Friday); last Mon. in May–May 30 (Memorial Day); Sept. 12 (Defender's Day); (General Election Day, when applicable).

Massachusetts—March 17 (Evacuation Day, Suffolk Co.); 3rd Mon. in April–April 18 (Patriots' Day); last Mon. in May–May 30 (Memorial Day); June 17 (Bunker Hill Day, Suffolk Co.).

Michigan—*Feb. 12 (Lincoln's Birthday); last Mon. in May–May 30 (Memorial Day).

Minnesota—last Mon. in May–May 30 (Memorial Day).

Mississippi—3rd Mon. in Jan.–Jan. 17 (Robert E. Lee's and Dr. Martin Luther King, Jr.'s Birthday); March 8 (Mardi Gras, Coastal counties only); last Mon. in April–April 25 (Confederate Memorial Day); last Mon. in May–May 30 (Memorial Day and Jefferson Davis' Birthday);

Missouri—*(Feb. 12 (Lincoln's Birthday); *May 8 (Truman's Birthday); last Mon. in May–May 30 (Memorial Day).

---

† For the legal consequenses of these holidays consult local statutes and case law.
*** Denotes holidays falling on a Saturday or Sunday.**

Montana—last Mon. in May–May 30 (Memorial Day); (General Election Day, when applicable).

Nebraska—Last Fri. in April–April 29 (Arbor Day); last Mon. in May–May 30 (Memorial Day); 4th Fri. in Nov.–Nov. 25 (Day after Thanksgiving).

Nevada—last Mon. in May–May 30 (Memorial Day); last Fri. in Oct.—Oct. 28 (Nevada Day); 4th Fri. in Nov.–Nov. 25 (Family Day).

New Hampshire—last Mon. in May–May 30 (Memorial Day); (General Election Day, when applicable).

New Jersey—*Feb. 12 (Lincoln's Birthday); April 22 (Good Friday); last Mon. in May–May 30 (Memorial Day); (General Election Day, when applicable).

New Mexico—last Mon. in May–May 30 (Memorial Day).

New York—*Feb. 12 (Lincoln's Birthday); last Mon. in May–May 30 (Memorial Day); *2nd Sun. in June–June 12 (Flag Day); (General Election Day, when applicable).

North Carolina—Jan. 19 (Robert E. Lee's Birthday); March 25 (Greek Independence Day); April 12 (Halifax Resolves Anniversary); April 22 (Good Friday); May 10 (Confederate Memorial Day); May 20 (Mechlenberg Declaration of Independence Anniversary); last Mon. in May–May 30 (Memorial Day); Oct. 8 (Yom Kippur); (General Election Day, when applicable).

North Dakota—April 22 (Good Friday); last Mon. in May–May 30 (Memorial Day).

Ohio—last Mon. in May–May 30 (Memorial Day); (General Election Day, when applicable).

Oklahoma—last Mon. in May–May 30 (Memorial Day); 4th Fri. in Nov.–Nov. 25 (Day after Thanksgiving).

Oregon—last Mon. in May–May 30 (Memorial Day).

Pennsylvania—April 22 (Good Friday); last Mon. in May–May 30 (Memorial Day); June 14 (Flag Day); (General Election Day, when applicable).

Puerto Rico—Jan. 6 (Three Kings Day); second Mon. in Jan.–Jan. 10 (De Hostos' Birthday); April 22 (Good Friday); March 22 (Emancipation Day); third Mon. in April–April 18 (de Diego's Birthday and Spanish Only Day); last Mon. in May–May 30 (Memorial Day); third Mon. in July–July 18; July 26 (Commonweath Day); July 27 (Barbosa's Birthday); *Nov. 19 (Discovery of Puerto Rico).

Rhode Island—last Mon. in May–May 30 (Memorial Day); 2nd Mon. in Aug.–Aug. 8 (Victory Day); (General Election Day, when applicable).

South Carolina—May 10 (Confederate Memorial Day); last Mon. in May–May 30 (Memorial Day); 4th Fri. in Nov.–Nov. 25 (Day after Thanksgiving); Dec. 26 (Day after Christmas).

South Dakota—last Mon. in May–May 30 (Memorial Day); 2nd Mon. in Oct.–Oct. 10 (Native Americans' Day).

Tennessee—April 22 (Good Friday); last Mon. in May–May 30 (Memorial Day).

Texas—Jan. 19 (Confederate Heroes Day); March 2 (Texas Independence Day); April 21 (San Jacinto Day); last Mon. in May–May 30 (Memorial Day); *June 19 (Emancipation Day); *Aug. 27 (Lyndon B. Johnson's Birthday); (General Election Day, when applicable).

Utah—last Mon. in May–May 30 (Memorial Day); *July 24 (Pioneer Day).

Vermont—*Feb. 12 (Lincoln's Birthday); 1st Tues. in March–March 1 (Town Meeting Day); last Mon. in May–May 30 (Memorial Day); Aug. 16 (Bennington Battle Day).

Virginia—Fri. preceding 3rd Mon. in Jan–Jan. 14 (Lee-Jackson Day); last Mon. in May–May 30 (Memorial Day); 4th Fri. in Nov.–Nov. 25 (Day after Thanksgiving).

Virgin Islands—Jan. 6 (Three Kings Day); March 31 (Transfer Day); April 21 (Holy Thursday); April 22 (Good Friday); April 25 (Easter Monday); last Mon. in May–May 30 (Memorial Day); *July 3 (Virgin Islands Emancipation Day); 2nd Mon. in Oct–Oct. 10 (Puerto Rico–Virgin Islands Friendship Day); Nov. 1 (D. Hamilton Jackson Day); Dec. 26 (Christmas, second day/Boxing Day); (Primary and General Election Days, when applicable).

Washington—last Mon. in May–May 30 (Memorial Day); 4th Fri. in Nov.–Nov. 25 (Day after Thanksgiving).

West Virginia—June 20 (West Virginia Day); (Primary and General Election Days, when applicable); 4th Fri. in Nov.–Nov. 25 (Day after Thanksgiving).

Wisconsin—April 22 (Good Friday); last Mon. in May–May 30 (Memorial Day); (Primary and General Election Days, when applicable).

Wyoming—last Mon. in May–May 30 (Memorial Day).

*** Denotes holidays falling on a Saturday or Sunday.**

NEW YORK HOLIDAYS 2011

*January 1—New Year's Day
January 17—Dr. Martin Luther King, Jr. Day
*February 12—Lincoln's Birthday
February 21—Washington's Birthday
May 30—Memorial Day
June 12—Flag Day
July 4—Independence Day
September 5—Labor Day
October 10—Columbus Day
November 8—Election Day
November 11—Veterans' Day
November 24—Thanksgiving Day
December 25—Christmas Day
December 25—Christmas Day observed
* Falls on a Saturday in 2011

2011 Tax Deadlines to Remember

January 17—Final Payment on Estimated Federal Income Tax Due Unless Return in Lieu of Final Declaration is Filed by January 31

January 31—New York State Estimated Personal Income and Unincorporated Business Tax Installment Due for Calendar Year Taxpayers

January 31—Quarterly Form 941 Return Due

January 31—Federal Unemployment Form 940 Due for 2010

January 31—Deadline to Furnish Employees Withholding Statements (Forms W-2) and Statements to Recipients of Dividends and Interest Payments (Forms 1099) for the preceding year.

March 15—Federal Corporation Income Tax Returns on Calendar Year Basis Due

March 15—N.Y. State Business Corporation Tax Returns on Calendar Year Basis Due

April 15—Federal Individual Income Tax Returns on Calendar Year Basis Due

April 15—New York State Personal Income Tax and Unincorporated Business Tax Returns Due for Calendar Year Basis Taxpayers

April 15—Quarterly Estimated Federal Income Tax Payment Due

April 15—New York State Quarterly Estimated Personal Income and Unincorporated Business Tax Payment Due for Calendar Year Taxpayers

May 2—Quarterly Form 941 Return Due

May 2—Federal Unemployment Tax Deposit Due

June 15—Quarterly Estimated Federal Income Tax Payment Due

June 15—New York State Estimated Personal Income and Unincorporated Business Tax Payment Due for Calendar Year Taxpayers

August 1—Quarterly Form 941 Return Due

August 1—Federal Unemployment Tax Deposit Due

September 15—Quarterly Estimated Federal Income Tax Payment Due

September 15—New York State Estimated Personal Income and Unincorporated Business Tax Payment Due for Calendar Year Taxpayers

October 31—Quarterly Form 941 Return Due

October 31—Federal Unemployment Tax Deposit Due

If any date falls on a Saturday, Sunday or holiday (national or state-wide) a required act will be timely if performed the following business day. U.S. Postmark controls timely filing. I.R.C. § 7503.

2011 DATES TO REMEMBER

January 1 — New Year's Day
January 17 — Birthday of Martin Luther King, Jr. observed
February 12 — Lincoln's Birthday
February 14 — Valentine's Day
February 15 — Susan B. Anthony's Birthday
February 21 — General observance of Washington's Birthday (called Presidents' Day in most states)
March 13 — Daylight Saving Time Begins
March 17 — St. Patrick's Day
April 22 — Good Friday
April 27 — Administrative Assistants Day
May 1 — Law Day
May 8 — Mother's Day
May 23 — Victoria Day (Canada)
May 30 — Memorial Day observed in most states
June 14 — Flag Day
June 19 — Father's Day
July 1 — Canada Day
July 4 — Independence Day
September 5 — Labor Day
October 10 — Columbus Day
October 10 — Canadian Thanksgiving
November 6 — Daylight Saving Time Ends
November 8 — Election Day
November 11 — Veterans' Day
November 24 — Thanksgiving Day
December 25 — Christmas Day
December 26 — Kwanzaa (An African-American Celebration of Family, Community & Culture)

RELIGIOUS DATES

March 8 — Shrove Tuesday
March 9 — Ash Wednesday
April 17 — Palm Sunday
April 19 — Passover, First Day of
April 22 — Good Friday
April 24 — Easter Sunday
April 24 — Eastern Orthodox Easter
June 8 — Shavuot
June 12 — Whitsunday (Pentecost)
September 29 — Rosh Hashanah (Jewish New Year)
September 30 — Rosh Hashanah (Jewish New Year)
October 8 — Yom Kippur (Jewish Day of Atonement)
October 13 — Sukkot (First Day of Tabernacle)
December 21 — Hanukah, First Day of
December 25 — Christmas Day

Special note concerning Jewish Holidays.
In addition to dates noted, observant Jews celebrate the second, seventh and eighth days of Passover; the second, eighth and ninth days of Sukkot; and two days of Shavuot. All Jewish holidays begin at sundown, the evening prior to the day of the holiday.

JANUARY 2011

JANUARY 2011

Items To Remember This Month

SUNDAY	MONDAY	TUESDAY
DATES TO REMEMBER **January 1** - New Year's Day **January 17** - Birthday of Martin Luther King, Jr. observed **January 18** - Quarterly Estimated Federal Income Tax Payment Due Unless Return in Lieu of Final Declaration is Filed by January 31st. **January 31** - Quarterly Form 941 Return Due - Federal Unemployment Form 940 Due for 2010		
2	**3**	**4**
9	**10**	**11**
16	**17** Birthday of Martin Luther King, Jr. observed	**18** Quarterly Estimated Federal Income Tax Payment Due Unless Return is Filed by January 31st.
23	**24**	**25**
30	**31** Quarterly Form 941 Return Due Federal Unemployment Form 940 Due for 2010	

WEDNESDAY	THURSDAY	FRIDAY	SATURDAY
			1 New Year's Day
5	**6**	**7**	**8**
12	**13**	**14**	**15**
19	**20**	**21**	**22**
26	**27**	**28**	**29**

FEBRUARY 2011

FEBRUARY 2011	SUNDAY	MONDAY	TUESDAY
Items To Remember This Month			**1**
	6	**7**	**8**
	13	**14** Valentine's Day	**15** Susan B. Anthony's Birthday
	20	**21** Washington's Birthday observed (called Presidents' Day in most states)	**22**
	27	**28**	

WEDNESDAY	THURSDAY	FRIDAY	SATURDAY
2	3	4	5
9	10	11	12 Lincoln's Birthday
16	17	18	19
23	24	25	26

DATES TO REMEMBER

February 12 - Lincoln's Birthday
February 14 - Valentine's Day
February 15 - Susan B. Anthony's Birthday
February 21 - Washington's Birthday observed
(called Presidents' Day in most states)

MARCH 2011

MARCH 2011	SUNDAY	MONDAY	TUESDAY
Items To Remember This Month			**1**
	6	**7**	**8** Shrove Tuesday
	13 Daylight Saving Time Begins	**14**	**15**
	20	**21**	**22**
	27	**28**	**29**

WEDNESDAY	THURSDAY	FRIDAY	SATURDAY
2	3	4	5
9 Ash Wednesday	10	11	12
16	17 St. Patrick's Day	18	19
23	24	25	26
30	31		

DATES TO REMEMBER

March 8 - Shrove Tuesday
March 9 - Ash Wednesday
March 13 - Daylight Saving Time Begins
March 17 - St. Patrick's Day

APRIL 2011

Items To Remember This Month	SUNDAY	MONDAY	TUESDAY
	DATES TO REMEMBER **April 15** - Federal Income Tax Return Due - Quarterly Estimated Federal Income Tax Payment Due **April 17** - Palm Sunday **April 19** - First Day of Passover **April 22** - Good Friday **April 24** - Easter Sunday - Eastern Orthodox Easter **April 27** - Administrative Assistants Day		
	3	**4**	**5**
	10	**11**	**12**
	17 Palm Sunday	**18**	**19** First Day of Passover
	24 Easter Sunday Eastern Orthodox Easter	**25**	**26**

WEDNESDAY	THURSDAY	FRIDAY	SATURDAY
		1	2
6	7	8	9
13	14	15 Federal Income Tax Return Due Quarterly Estimated Federal Income Tax Payment Due	16
20	21	22 Good Friday	23
27 Administrative Assistants Day	28	29	30

MAY 2011 Items To Remember This Month	SUNDAY	MONDAY	TUESDAY
	1 Law Day	2 Quarterly Form 941 Return Due Federal Unemployment Tax Deposit Due	3
	8 Mother's Day	9	10
	15	16	17
	22	23 Victoria Day (Canada)	24
	29	30 Memorial Day observed in most states	31

WEDNESDAY	THURSDAY	FRIDAY	SATURDAY
4	5	6	7
11	12	13	14
18	19	20	21
25	26	27	28

DATES TO REMEMBER

May 1 - Law Day
May 2 - Quarterly Form 941 Return Due
- Federal Unemployment Tax Deposit Due

May 8 - Mother's Day
May 23 - Victoria Day (Canada)
May 30 - Memorial Day observed in most states

JUNE 2011

JUNE **2011**	SUNDAY	MONDAY	TUESDAY
Items To Remember This Month	**DATES TO REMEMBER** **June 8** - Shavuot **June 12** - Whitsunday **June 14** - Flag Day **June 15** - Quarterly Estimated Federal Income Tax Payment Due **June 19** - Father's Day		
	5	**6**	**7**
	12 Whitsunday	**13**	**14** Flag Day
	19 Father's Day	**20**	**21**
	26	**27**	**28**

WEDNESDAY	THURSDAY	FRIDAY	SATURDAY
1	2	3	4
8 Shavuot	9	10	11
15 Quarterly Estimated Federal Income Tax Payment Due	16	17	18
22	23	24	25
29	30		

JUNE 2011

JULY 2011

JULY 2011

Items To Remember This Month

SUNDAY	MONDAY	TUESDAY
DATES TO REMEMBER **July 1** - Canada Day **July 4** - Independence Day		
3	**4** Independence Day	**5**
10	**11**	**12**
17	**18**	**19**
24 / **31**	**25**	**26**

WEDNESDAY	THURSDAY	FRIDAY	SATURDAY
		1 Canada Day	2
6	7	8	9
13	14	15	16
20	21	22	23
27	28	29	30

AUGUST 2011

AUGUST 2011	SUNDAY	MONDAY	TUESDAY
Items To Remember This Month		1 Quarterly Form 941 Return Due Federal Unemployment Tax Deposit Due	2
	7	8	9
	14	15	16
	21	22	23
	28	29	30

AUGUST 2011

WEDNESDAY	THURSDAY	FRIDAY	SATURDAY
3	4	5	6
10	11	12	13
17	18	19	20
24	25	26	27
31			

DATES TO REMEMBER

August 1 - Quarterly Form 941 Return Due
- Federal Unemployment Tax Deposit Due

SEPTEMBER 2011

SEPTEMBER 2011	SUNDAY	MONDAY	TUESDAY
Items To Remember This Month			
	4	5 Labor Day	6
	11	12	13
	18	19	20
	25	26	27

DATES TO REMEMBER

September 5 - Labor Day
September 15 - Quarterly Estimated Federal Income Tax Payment Due
September 29 - Rosh Hashanah (Jewish New Year)
September 30 - Rosh Hashanah (Jewish New Year)

SEPTEMBER 2011

WEDNESDAY	THURSDAY	FRIDAY	SATURDAY
	1	**2**	**3**
7	**8**	**9**	**10**
14	**15** Quarterly Estimated Federal Income Tax Payment Due	**16**	**17**
21	**22**	**23**	**24**
28	**29** Rosh Hashanah (Jewish New Year)	**30** Rosh Hashanah (Jewish New Year)	

OCTOBER 2011

OCTOBER 2011	SUNDAY	MONDAY	TUESDAY
Items To Remember This Month			
	2	3	4
	9	10 Columbus Day Canadian Thanksgiving	11
	16	17	18
	23	24	25
	30	31 Quarterly Form 941 Return Due Federal Unemployment Tax Deposit Due	

DATES TO REMEMBER

October 8 - Yom Kippur
October 10 - Columbus Day
- Canadian Thanksgiving

October 13 - Sukkot (First Day of Tabernacle)
October 31 - Quarterly Form 941 Return Due
- Federal Unemployment Tax Deposit Due

WEDNESDAY	THURSDAY	FRIDAY	SATURDAY
			1
5	6	7	8 Yom Kippur
12	13 Sukkot (First Day of Tabernacle)	14	15
19	20	21	22
26	27	28	29

NOVEMBER 2011

NOVEMBER 2011	SUNDAY	MONDAY	TUESDAY
Items To Remember This Month			1
	6 Daylight Saving Time Ends	7	8 Election Day
	13	14	15
	20	21	22
	27	28	29

WEDNESDAY	THURSDAY	FRIDAY	SATURDAY
2	3	4	5
9	10	11 Veterans' Day	12
16	17	18	19
23	24 Thanksgiving Day	25	26
30			

NOVEMBER 2011

DATES TO REMEMBER

November 6 - Daylight Saving Time Ends
November 8 - Election Day
November 11 - Veterans' Day
November 24 - Thanksgiving Day

DECEMBER 2011

DECEMBER 2011	SUNDAY	MONDAY	TUESDAY
Items To Remember This Month			
	4	5	6
	11	12	13
	18	19	20
	25 Christmas Day	26 Kwanzaa (An African-American Celebration of Family, Community & Culture)	27

DATES TO REMEMBER

December 21 - First Day of Hanukah
December 25 - Christmas Day
December 26 - Kwanzaa (An African-American Celebration of Family, Community & Culture)

WEDNESDAY	THURSDAY	FRIDAY	SATURDAY
	1	2	3
7	8	9	10
14	15	16	17
21 First Day of Hanukah	22	23	24
28	29	30	31

TABLE FOR COMPUTATION OF EXPIRATION DATES

Explanation—The following table is designed to indicate the last day on which acts to be done within 10, 15, 20, 30, 35, 45, 60, 90, or 120 days of a given date, must be performed and also to indicate whether the last day falls on a Saturday or Sunday.

To use the table, find the starting date on the left hand column and then move across to the column under the desired time interval. The date thus shown is the expiration date of the given period. Saturdays are designated by an "s" following the date. Sundays are designated by an asterisk (*) following the date.

From	10 Days	15 Days	20 Days	30 Days	35 Days	45 Days	60 Days	90 Days	120 Days
Dec 01 '10	Dec 11 '10 s	Dec 16 '10	Dec 21 '10	Dec 31 '10	Jan 05 '11	Jan 15 '11 s	Jan 30 '11 *	Mar 01 '11	Mar 31 '11
Dec 02 '10	Dec 12 '10 *	Dec 17 '10	Dec 22 '10	Jan 01 '11 s	Jan 06 '11	Jan 16 '11 *	Jan 31 '11	Mar 02 '11	Apr 01 '11
Dec 03 '10	Dec 13 '10	Dec 18 '10 s	Dec 23 '10	Jan 02 '11 *	Jan 07 '11	Jan 17 '11	Feb 01 '11	Mar 03 '11	Apr 02 '11 s
Dec 04 '10 s	Dec 14 '10	Dec 19 '10 *	Dec 24 '10	Jan 03 '11	Jan 08 '11 s	Jan 18 '11	Feb 02 '11	Mar 04 '11	Apr 03 '11 *
Dec 05 '10 *	Dec 15 '10	Dec 20 '10	Dec 25 '10 s	Jan 04 '11	Jan 09 '11 *	Jan 19 '11	Feb 03 '11	Mar 05 '11 s	Apr 04 '11
Dec 06 '10	Dec 16 '10	Dec 21 '10	Dec 26 '10 *	Jan 05 '11	Jan 10 '11	Jan 20 '11	Feb 04 '11	Mar 06 '11 *	Apr 05 '11
Dec 07 '10	Dec 17 '10	Dec 22 '10	Dec 27 '10	Jan 06 '11	Jan 11 '11	Jan 21 '11	Feb 05 '11 s	Mar 07 '11	Apr 06 '11
Dec 08 '10	Dec 18 '10 s	Dec 23 '10	Dec 28 '10	Jan 07 '11	Jan 12 '11	Jan 22 '11 s	Feb 06 '11 *	Mar 08 '11	Apr 07 '11
Dec 09 '10	Dec 19 '10 *	Dec 24 '10	Dec 29 '10	Jan 08 '11 s	Jan 13 '11	Jan 23 '11 *	Feb 07 '11	Mar 09 '11	Apr 08 '11
Dec 10 '10	Dec 20 '10	Dec 25 '10 s	Dec 30 '10	Jan 09 '11 *	Jan 14 '11	Jan 24 '11	Feb 08 '11	Mar 10 '11	Apr 09 '11 s
Dec 11 '10 s	Dec 21 '10	Dec 26 '10 *	Dec 31 '10	Jan 10 '11	Jan 15 '11 s	Jan 25 '11	Feb 09 '11	Mar 11 '11	Apr 10 '11 *
Dec 12 '10 *	Dec 22 '10	Dec 27 '10	Jan 01 '11 s	Jan 11 '11	Jan 16 '11 *	Jan 26 '11	Feb 10 '11	Mar 12 '11 s	Apr 11 '11
Dec 13 '10	Dec 23 '10	Dec 28 '10	Jan 02 '11 *	Jan 12 '11	Jan 17 '11	Jan 27 '11	Feb 11 '11	Mar 13 '11 *	Apr 12 '11
Dec 14 '10	Dec 24 '10	Dec 29 '10	Jan 03 '11	Jan 13 '11	Jan 18 '11	Jan 28 '11	Feb 12 '11 s	Mar 14 '11	Apr 13 '11
Dec 15 '10	Dec 25 '10 s	Dec 30 '10	Jan 04 '11	Jan 14 '11	Jan 19 '11	Jan 29 '11 s	Feb 13 '11 *	Mar 15 '11	Apr 14 '11
Dec 16 '10	Dec 26 '10 *	Dec 31 '10	Jan 05 '11	Jan 15 '11 s	Jan 20 '11	Jan 30 '11 *	Feb 14 '11	Mar 16 '11	Apr 15 '11
Dec 17 '10	Dec 27 '10	Jan 01 '11 s	Jan 06 '11	Jan 16 '11 *	Jan 21 '11	Jan 31 '11	Feb 15 '11	Mar 17 '11	Apr 16 '11 s
Dec 18 '10 s	Dec 28 '10	Jan 02 '11 *	Jan 07 '11	Jan 17 '11	Jan 22 '11 s	Feb 01 '11	Feb 16 '11	Mar 18 '11	Apr 17 '11 *
Dec 19 '10 *	Dec 29 '10	Jan 03 '11	Jan 08 '11 s	Jan 18 '11	Jan 23 '11 *	Feb 02 '11	Feb 17 '11	Mar 19 '11 s	Apr 18 '11
Dec 20 '10	Dec 30 '10	Jan 04 '11	Jan 09 '11 *	Jan 19 '11	Jan 24 '11	Feb 03 '11	Feb 18 '11	Mar 20 '11 *	Apr 19 '11
Dec 21 '10	Dec 31 '10	Jan 05 '11	Jan 10 '11	Jan 20 '11	Jan 25 '11	Feb 04 '11	Feb 19 '11 s	Mar 21 '11	Apr 20 '11
Dec 22 '10	Jan 01 '11 s	Jan 06 '11	Jan 11 '11	Jan 21 '11	Jan 26 '11	Feb 05 '11 s	Feb 20 '11 *	Mar 22 '11	Apr 21 '11
Dec 23 '10	Jan 02 '11 *	Jan 07 '11	Jan 12 '11	Jan 22 '11 s	Jan 27 '11	Feb 06 '11 *	Feb 21 '11	Mar 23 '11	Apr 22 '11
Dec 24 '10	Jan 03 '11	Jan 08 '11 s	Jan 13 '11	Jan 23 '11 *	Jan 28 '11	Feb 07 '11	Feb 22 '11	Mar 24 '11	Apr 23 '11 s
Dec 25 '10 s	Jan 04 '11	Jan 09 '11 *	Jan 14 '11	Jan 24 '11	Jan 29 '11 s	Feb 08 '11	Feb 23 '11	Mar 25 '11	Apr 24 '11 *
Dec 26 '10 *	Jan 05 '11	Jan 10 '11	Jan 15 '11 s	Jan 25 '11	Jan 30 '11 *	Feb 09 '11	Feb 24 '11	Mar 26 '11 s	Apr 25 '11
Dec 27 '10	Jan 06 '11	Jan 11 '11	Jan 16 '11 *	Jan 26 '11	Jan 31 '11	Feb 10 '11	Feb 25 '11	Mar 27 '11 *	Apr 26 '11
Dec 28 '10	Jan 07 '11	Jan 12 '11	Jan 17 '11	Jan 27 '11	Feb 01 '11	Feb 11 '11	Feb 26 '11 s	Mar 28 '11	Apr 27 '11
Dec 29 '10	Jan 08 '11 s	Jan 13 '11	Jan 18 '11	Jan 28 '11	Feb 02 '11	Feb 12 '11 s	Feb 27 '11 *	Mar 29 '11	Apr 28 '11
Dec 30 '10	Jan 09 '11 *	Jan 14 '11	Jan 19 '11	Jan 29 '11 s	Feb 03 '11	Feb 13 '11 *	Feb 28 '11	Mar 30 '11	Apr 29 '11
Dec 31 '10	Jan 10 '11	Jan 15 '11 s	Jan 20 '11	Jan 30 '11 *	Feb 04 '11	Feb 14 '11	Mar 01 '11	Mar 31 '11	Apr 30 '11 s
Jan 01 '11 s	Jan 11 '11	Jan 16 '11 *	Jan 21 '11	Jan 31 '11	Feb 05 '11 s	Feb 15 '11	Mar 02 '11	Apr 01 '11	May 01 '11 *
Jan 02 '11 *	Jan 12 '11	Jan 17 '11	Jan 22 '11 s	Feb 01 '11	Feb 06 '11 *	Feb 16 '11	Mar 03 '11	Apr 02 '11 s	May 02 '11
Jan 03 '11	Jan 13 '11	Jan 18 '11	Jan 23 '11 *	Feb 02 '11	Feb 07 '11	Feb 17 '11	Mar 04 '11	Apr 03 '11 *	May 03 '11
Jan 04 '11	Jan 14 '11	Jan 19 '11	Jan 24 '11	Feb 03 '11	Feb 08 '11	Feb 18 '11	Mar 05 '11 s	Apr 04 '11	May 04 '11
Jan 05 '11	Jan 15 '11 s	Jan 20 '11	Jan 25 '11	Feb 04 '11	Feb 09 '11	Feb 19 '11 s	Mar 06 '11 *	Apr 05 '11	May 05 '11
Jan 06 '11	Jan 16 '11 *	Jan 21 '11	Jan 26 '11	Feb 05 '11 s	Feb 10 '11	Feb 20 '11 *	Mar 07 '11	Apr 06 '11	May 06 '11
Jan 07 '11	Jan 17 '11	Jan 22 '11 s	Jan 27 '11	Feb 06 '11 *	Feb 11 '11	Feb 21 '11	Mar 08 '11	Apr 07 '11	May 07 '11 s
Jan 08 '11 s	Jan 18 '11	Jan 23 '11 *	Jan 28 '11	Feb 07 '11	Feb 12 '11 s	Feb 22 '11	Mar 09 '11	Apr 08 '11	May 08 '11 *
Jan 09 '11 *	Jan 19 '11	Jan 24 '11	Jan 29 '11 s	Feb 08 '11	Feb 13 '11 *	Feb 23 '11	Mar 10 '11	Apr 09 '11 s	May 09 '11
Jan 10 '11	Jan 20 '11	Jan 25 '11	Jan 30 '11 *	Feb 09 '11	Feb 14 '11	Feb 24 '11	Mar 11 '11	Apr 10 '11 *	May 10 '11
Jan 11 '11	Jan 21 '11	Jan 26 '11	Jan 31 '11	Feb 10 '11	Feb 15 '11	Feb 25 '11	Mar 12 '11 s	Apr 11 '11	May 11 '11
Jan 12 '11	Jan 22 '11 s	Jan 27 '11	Feb 01 '11	Feb 11 '11	Feb 16 '11	Feb 26 '11 s	Mar 13 '11 *	Apr 12 '11	May 12 '11
Jan 13 '11	Jan 23 '11 *	Jan 28 '11	Feb 02 '11	Feb 12 '11 s	Feb 17 '11	Feb 27 '11 *	Mar 14 '11	Apr 13 '11	May 13 '11
Jan 14 '11	Jan 24 '11	Jan 29 '11 s	Feb 03 '11	Feb 13 '11 *	Feb 18 '11	Feb 28 '11	Mar 15 '11	Apr 14 '11	May 14 '11 s
Jan 15 '11 s	Jan 25 '11	Jan 30 '11 *	Feb 04 '11	Feb 14 '11	Feb 19 '11 s	Mar 01 '11	Mar 16 '11	Apr 15 '11	May 15 '11 *
Jan 16 '11 *	Jan 26 '11	Jan 31 '11	Feb 05 '11 s	Feb 15 '11	Feb 20 '11 *	Mar 02 '11	Mar 17 '11	Apr 16 '11 s	May 16 '11
Jan 17 '11	Jan 27 '11	Feb 01 '11	Feb 06 '11 *	Feb 16 '11	Feb 21 '11	Mar 03 '11	Mar 18 '11	Apr 17 '11 *	May 17 '11
Jan 18 '11	Jan 28 '11	Feb 02 '11	Feb 07 '11	Feb 17 '11	Feb 22 '11	Mar 04 '11	Mar 19 '11 s	Apr 18 '11	May 18 '11
Jan 19 '11	Jan 29 '11 s	Feb 03 '11	Feb 08 '11	Feb 18 '11	Feb 23 '11	Mar 05 '11 s	Mar 20 '11 *	Apr 19 '11	May 19 '11
Jan 20 '11	Jan 30 '11 *	Feb 04 '11	Feb 09 '11	Feb 19 '11 s	Feb 24 '11	Mar 06 '11 *	Mar 21 '11	Apr 20 '11	May 20 '11
Jan 21 '11	Jan 31 '11	Feb 05 '11 s	Feb 10 '11	Feb 20 '11 *	Feb 25 '11	Mar 07 '11	Mar 22 '11	Apr 21 '11	May 21 '11 s
Jan 22 '11 s	Feb 01 '11	Feb 06 '11 *	Feb 11 '11	Feb 21 '11	Feb 26 '11 s	Mar 08 '11	Mar 23 '11	Apr 22 '11	May 22 '11 *
Jan 23 '11 *	Feb 02 '11	Feb 07 '11	Feb 12 '11 s	Feb 22 '11	Feb 27 '11 *	Mar 09 '11	Mar 24 '11	Apr 23 '11 s	May 23 '11
Jan 24 '11	Feb 03 '11	Feb 08 '11	Feb 13 '11 *	Feb 23 '11	Feb 28 '11	Mar 10 '11	Mar 25 '11	Apr 24 '11 *	May 24 '11
Jan 25 '11	Feb 04 '11	Feb 09 '11	Feb 14 '11	Feb 24 '11	Mar 01 '11	Mar 11 '11	Mar 26 '11 s	Apr 25 '11	May 25 '11
Jan 26 '11	Feb 05 '11 s	Feb 10 '11	Feb 15 '11	Feb 25 '11	Mar 02 '11	Mar 12 '11 s	Mar 27 '11 *	Apr 26 '11	May 26 '11
Jan 27 '11	Feb 06 '11 *	Feb 11 '11	Feb 16 '11	Feb 26 '11 s	Mar 03 '11	Mar 13 '11 *	Mar 28 '11	Apr 27 '11	May 27 '11
Jan 28 '11	Feb 07 '11	Feb 12 '11 s	Feb 17 '11	Feb 27 '11 *	Mar 04 '11	Mar 14 '11	Mar 29 '11	Apr 28 '11	May 28 '11 s
Jan 29 '11 s	Feb 08 '11	Feb 13 '11 *	Feb 18 '11	Feb 28 '11	Mar 05 '11 s	Mar 15 '11	Mar 30 '11	Apr 29 '11	May 29 '11 *
Jan 30 '11 *	Feb 09 '11	Feb 14 '11	Feb 19 '11 s	Mar 01 '11	Mar 06 '11 *	Mar 16 '11	Mar 31 '11	Apr 30 '11 s	May 30 '11

TABLE FOR COMPUTATION OF EXPIRATION DATES

From	10 Days	15 Days	20 Days	30 Days	35 Days	45 Days	60 Days	90 Days	120 Days
Jan 31 '11	Feb 10 '11	Feb 15 '11	Feb 20 '11 *	Mar 02 '11	Mar 07 '11	Mar 17 '11	Apr 01 '11	May 01 '11 *	May 31 '11
Feb 01 '11	Feb 11 '11	Feb 16 '11	Feb 21 '11	Mar 03 '11	Mar 08 '11	Mar 18 '11	Apr 02 '11 s	May 02 '11	Jun 01 '11
Feb 02 '11	Feb 12 '11 s	Feb 17 '11	Feb 22 '11	Mar 04 '11	Mar 09 '11	Mar 19 '11 s	Apr 03 '11 *	May 03 '11	Jun 02 '11
Feb 03 '11	Feb 13 '11 *	Feb 18 '11	Feb 23 '11	Mar 05 '11 s	Mar 10 '11	Mar 20 '11 *	Apr 04 '11	May 04 '11	Jun 03 '11
Feb 04 '11	Feb 14 '11	Feb 19 '11 s	Feb 24 '11	Mar 06 '11 *	Mar 11 '11	Mar 21 '11	Apr 05 '11	May 05 '11	Jun 04 '11 s
Feb 05 '11 s	Feb 15 '11	Feb 20 '11 *	Feb 25 '11	Mar 07 '11	Mar 12 '11 s	Mar 22 '11	Apr 06 '11	May 06 '11	Jun 05 '11 *
Feb 06 '11 *	Feb 16 '11	Feb 21 '11	Feb 26 '11 s	Mar 08 '11	Mar 13 '11 *	Mar 23 '11	Apr 07 '11	May 07 '11 s	Jun 06 '11
Feb 07 '11	Feb 17 '11	Feb 22 '11	Feb 27 '11 *	Mar 09 '11	Mar 14 '11	Mar 24 '11	Apr 08 '11	May 08 '11 *	Jun 07 '11
Feb 08 '11	Feb 18 '11	Feb 23 '11	Feb 28 '11	Mar 10 '11	Mar 15 '11	Mar 25 '11	Apr 09 '11 s	May 09 '11	Jun 08 '11
Feb 09 '11	Feb 19 '11 s	Feb 24 '11	Mar 01 '11	Mar 11 '11	Mar 16 '11	Mar 26 '11 s	Apr 10 '11 *	May 10 '11	Jun 09 '11
Feb 10 '11	Feb 20 '11 *	Feb 25 '11	Mar 02 '11	Mar 12 '11 s	Mar 17 '11	Mar 27 '11 *	Apr 11 '11	May 11 '11	Jun 10 '11
Feb 11 '11	Feb 21 '11	Feb 26 '11 s	Mar 03 '11	Mar 13 '11 *	Mar 18 '11	Mar 28 '11	Apr 12 '11	May 12 '11	Jun 11 '11 s
Feb 12 '11 s	Feb 22 '11	Feb 27 '11 *	Mar 04 '11	Mar 14 '11	Mar 19 '11 s	Mar 29 '11	Apr 13 '11	May 13 '11	Jun 12 '11 *
Feb 13 '11 *	Feb 23 '11	Feb 28 '11	Mar 05 '11 s	Mar 15 '11	Mar 20 '11 *	Mar 30 '11	Apr 14 '11	May 14 '11 s	Jun 13 '11
Feb 14 '11	Feb 24 '11	Mar 01 '11	Mar 06 '11 *	Mar 16 '11	Mar 21 '11	Mar 31 '11	Apr 15 '11	May 15 '11 *	Jun 14 '11
Feb 15 '11	Feb 25 '11	Mar 02 '11	Mar 07 '11	Mar 17 '11	Mar 22 '11	Apr 01 '11	Apr 16 '11 s	May 16 '11	Jun 15 '11
Feb 16 '11	Feb 26 '11 s	Mar 03 '11	Mar 08 '11	Mar 18 '11	Mar 23 '11	Apr 02 '11 s	Apr 17 '11 *	May 17 '11	Jun 16 '11
Feb 17 '11	Feb 27 '11 *	Mar 04 '11	Mar 09 '11	Mar 19 '11 s	Mar 24 '11	Apr 03 '11 *	Apr 18 '11	May 18 '11	Jun 17 '11
Feb 18 '11	Feb 28 '11	Mar 05 '11 s	Mar 10 '11	Mar 20 '11 *	Mar 25 '11	Apr 04 '11	Apr 19 '11	May 19 '11	Jun 18 '11 s
Feb 19 '11 s	Mar 01 '11	Mar 06 '11 *	Mar 11 '11	Mar 21 '11	Mar 26 '11 s	Apr 05 '11	Apr 20 '11	May 20 '11	Jun 19 '11 *
Feb 20 '11 *	Mar 02 '11	Mar 07 '11	Mar 12 '11 s	Mar 22 '11	Mar 27 '11 *	Apr 06 '11	Apr 21 '11	May 21 '11 s	Jun 20 '11
Feb 21 '11	Mar 03 '11	Mar 08 '11	Mar 13 '11 *	Mar 23 '11	Mar 28 '11	Apr 07 '11	Apr 22 '11	May 22 '11 *	Jun 21 '11
Feb 22 '11	Mar 04 '11	Mar 09 '11	Mar 14 '11	Mar 24 '11	Mar 29 '11	Apr 08 '11	Apr 23 '11 s	May 23 '11	Jun 22 '11
Feb 23 '11	Mar 05 '11 s	Mar 10 '11	Mar 15 '11	Mar 25 '11	Mar 30 '11	Apr 09 '11 s	Apr 24 '11 *	May 24 '11	Jun 23 '11
Feb 24 '11	Mar 06 '11 *	Mar 11 '11	Mar 16 '11	Mar 26 '11 s	Mar 31 '11	Apr 10 '11 *	Apr 25 '11	May 25 '11	Jun 24 '11
Feb 25 '11	Mar 07 '11	Mar 12 '11 s	Mar 17 '11	Mar 27 '11 *	Apr 01 '11	Apr 11 '11	Apr 26 '11	May 26 '11	Jun 25 '11 s
Feb 26 '11 s	Mar 08 '11	Mar 13 '11 *	Mar 18 '11	Mar 28 '11	Apr 02 '11 s	Apr 12 '11	Apr 27 '11	May 27 '11	Jun 26 '11 *
Feb 27 '11 *	Mar 09 '11	Mar 14 '11	Mar 19 '11 s	Mar 29 '11	Apr 03 '11 *	Apr 13 '11	Apr 28 '11	May 28 '11 s	Jun 27 '11
Feb 28 '11	Mar 10 '11	Mar 15 '11	Mar 20 '11 *	Mar 30 '11	Apr 04 '11	Apr 14 '11	Apr 29 '11	May 29 '11 *	Jun 28 '11
Mar 01 '11	Mar 11 '11	Mar 16 '11	Mar 21 '11	Mar 31 '11	Apr 05 '11	Apr 15 '11	Apr 30 '11 s	May 30 '11	Jun 29 '11
Mar 02 '11	Mar 12 '11 s	Mar 17 '11	Mar 22 '11	Apr 01 '11	Apr 06 '11	Apr 16 '11 s	May 01 '11 *	May 31 '11	Jun 30 '11
Mar 03 '11	Mar 13 '11 *	Mar 18 '11	Mar 23 '11	Apr 02 '11 s	Apr 07 '11	Apr 17 '11 *	May 02 '11	Jun 01 '11	Jul 01 '11
Mar 04 '11	Mar 14 '11	Mar 19 '11 s	Mar 24 '11	Apr 03 '11 *	Apr 08 '11	Apr 18 '11	May 03 '11	Jun 02 '11	Jul 02 '11 s
Mar 05 '11 s	Mar 15 '11	Mar 20 '11 *	Mar 25 '11	Apr 04 '11	Apr 09 '11 s	Apr 19 '11	May 04 '11	Jun 03 '11	Jul 03 '11 *
Mar 06 '11 *	Mar 16 '11	Mar 21 '11	Mar 26 '11 s	Apr 05 '11	Apr 10 '11 *	Apr 20 '11	May 05 '11	Jun 04 '11 s	Jul 04 '11
Mar 07 '11	Mar 17 '11	Mar 22 '11	Mar 27 '11 *	Apr 06 '11	Apr 11 '11	Apr 21 '11	May 06 '11	Jun 05 '11 *	Jul 05 '11
Mar 08 '11	Mar 18 '11	Mar 23 '11	Mar 28 '11	Apr 07 '11	Apr 12 '11	Apr 22 '11	May 07 '11 s	Jun 06 '11	Jul 06 '11
Mar 09 '11	Mar 19 '11 s	Mar 24 '11	Mar 29 '11	Apr 08 '11	Apr 13 '11	Apr 23 '11 s	May 08 '11 *	Jun 07 '11	Jul 07 '11
Mar 10 '11	Mar 20 '11 *	Mar 25 '11	Mar 30 '11	Apr 09 '11 s	Apr 14 '11	Apr 24 '11 *	May 09 '11	Jun 08 '11	Jul 08 '11
Mar 11 '11	Mar 21 '11	Mar 26 '11 s	Mar 31 '11	Apr 10 '11 *	Apr 15 '11	Apr 25 '11	May 10 '11	Jun 09 '11	Jul 09 '11 s
Mar 12 '11 s	Mar 22 '11	Mar 27 '11 *	Apr 01 '11	Apr 11 '11	Apr 16 '11 s	Apr 26 '11	May 11 '11	Jun 10 '11	Jul 10 '11 *
Mar 13 '11 *	Mar 23 '11	Mar 28 '11	Apr 02 '11 s	Apr 12 '11	Apr 17 '11 *	Apr 27 '11	May 12 '11	Jun 11 '11 s	Jul 11 '11
Mar 14 '11	Mar 24 '11	Mar 29 '11	Apr 03 '11 *	Apr 13 '11	Apr 18 '11	Apr 28 '11	May 13 '11	Jun 12 '11 *	Jul 12 '11
Mar 15 '11	Mar 25 '11	Mar 30 '11	Apr 04 '11	Apr 14 '11	Apr 19 '11	Apr 29 '11	May 14 '11 s	Jun 13 '11	Jul 13 '11
Mar 16 '11	Mar 26 '11 s	Mar 31 '11	Apr 05 '11	Apr 15 '11	Apr 20 '11	Apr 30 '11 s	May 15 '11 *	Jun 14 '11	Jul 14 '11
Mar 17 '11	Mar 27 '11 *	Apr 01 '11	Apr 06 '11	Apr 16 '11 s	Apr 21 '11	May 01 '11 *	May 16 '11	Jun 15 '11	Jul 15 '11
Mar 18 '11	Mar 28 '11	Apr 02 '11 s	Apr 07 '11	Apr 17 '11 *	Apr 22 '11	May 02 '11	May 17 '11	Jun 16 '11	Jul 16 '11 s
Mar 19 '11 s	Mar 29 '11	Apr 03 '11 *	Apr 08 '11	Apr 18 '11	Apr 23 '11 s	May 03 '11	May 18 '11	Jun 17 '11	Jul 17 '11 *
Mar 20 '11 *	Mar 30 '11	Apr 04 '11	Apr 09 '11 s	Apr 19 '11	Apr 24 '11 *	May 04 '11	May 19 '11	Jun 18 '11 s	Jul 18 '11
Mar 21 '11	Mar 31 '11	Apr 05 '11	Apr 10 '11 *	Apr 20 '11	Apr 25 '11	May 05 '11	May 20 '11	Jun 19 '11 *	Jul 19 '11
Mar 22 '11	Apr 01 '11	Apr 06 '11	Apr 11 '11	Apr 21 '11	Apr 26 '11	May 06 '11	May 21 '11 s	Jun 20 '11	Jul 20 '11
Mar 23 '11	Apr 02 '11 s	Apr 07 '11	Apr 12 '11	Apr 22 '11	Apr 27 '11	May 07 '11 s	May 22 '11 *	Jun 21 '11	Jul 21 '11
Mar 24 '11	Apr 03 '11 *	Apr 08 '11	Apr 13 '11	Apr 23 '11 s	Apr 28 '11	May 08 '11 *	May 23 '11	Jun 22 '11	Jul 22 '11
Mar 25 '11	Apr 04 '11	Apr 09 '11 s	Apr 14 '11	Apr 24 '11 *	Apr 29 '11	May 09 '11	May 24 '11	Jun 23 '11	Jul 23 '11 s
Mar 26 '11 s	Apr 05 '11	Apr 10 '11 *	Apr 15 '11	Apr 25 '11	Apr 30 '11 s	May 10 '11	May 25 '11	Jun 24 '11	Jul 24 '11 *
Mar 27 '11 *	Apr 06 '11	Apr 11 '11	Apr 16 '11 s	Apr 26 '11	May 01 '11 *	May 11 '11	May 26 '11	Jun 25 '11 s	Jul 25 '11
Mar 28 '11	Apr 07 '11	Apr 12 '11	Apr 17 '11 *	Apr 27 '11	May 02 '11	May 12 '11	May 27 '11	Jun 26 '11 *	Jul 26 '11
Mar 29 '11	Apr 08 '11	Apr 13 '11	Apr 18 '11	Apr 28 '11	May 03 '11	May 13 '11	May 28 '11 s	Jun 27 '11	Jul 27 '11
Mar 30 '11	Apr 09 '11 s	Apr 14 '11	Apr 19 '11	Apr 29 '11	May 04 '11	May 14 '11 s	May 29 '11 *	Jun 28 '11	Jul 28 '11
Mar 31 '11	Apr 10 '11 *	Apr 15 '11	Apr 20 '11	Apr 30 '11 s	May 05 '11	May 15 '11 *	May 30 '11	Jun 29 '11	Jul 29 '11
Apr 01 '11	Apr 11 '11	Apr 16 '11 s	Apr 21 '11	May 01 '11 *	May 06 '11	May 16 '11	May 31 '11	Jun 30 '11	Jul 30 '11 s
Apr 02 '11 s	Apr 12 '11	Apr 17 '11 *	Apr 22 '11	May 02 '11	May 07 '11 s	May 17 '11	Jun 01 '11	Jul 01 '11	Jul 31 '11 *
Apr 03 '11 *	Apr 13 '11	Apr 18 '11	Apr 23 '11 s	May 03 '11	May 08 '11 *	May 18 '11	Jun 02 '11	Jul 02 '11 s	Aug 01 '11
Apr 04 '11	Apr 14 '11	Apr 19 '11	Apr 24 '11 *	May 04 '11	May 09 '11	May 19 '11	Jun 03 '11	Jul 03 '11 *	Aug 02 '11
Apr 05 '11	Apr 15 '11	Apr 20 '11	Apr 25 '11	May 05 '11	May 10 '11	May 20 '11	Jun 04 '11 s	Jul 04 '11	Aug 03 '11
Apr 06 '11	Apr 16 '11 s	Apr 21 '11	Apr 26 '11	May 06 '11	May 11 '11	May 21 '11 s	Jun 05 '11 *	Jul 05 '11	Aug 04 '11
Apr 07 '11	Apr 17 '11 *	Apr 22 '11	Apr 27 '11	May 07 '11 s	May 12 '11	May 22 '11 *	Jun 06 '11	Jul 06 '11	Aug 05 '11
Apr 08 '11	Apr 18 '11	Apr 23 '11 s	Apr 28 '11	May 08 '11 *	May 13 '11	May 23 '11	Jun 07 '11	Jul 07 '11	Aug 06 '11 s
Apr 09 '11 s	Apr 19 '11	Apr 24 '11 *	Apr 29 '11	May 09 '11	May 14 '11 s	May 24 '11	Jun 08 '11	Jul 08 '11	Aug 07 '11 *
Apr 10 '11 *	Apr 20 '11	Apr 25 '11	Apr 30 '11 s	May 10 '11	May 15 '11 *	May 25 '11	Jun 09 '11	Jul 09 '11 s	Aug 08 '11
Apr 11 '11	Apr 21 '11	Apr 26 '11	May 01 '11 *	May 11 '11	May 16 '11	May 26 '11	Jun 10 '11	Jul 10 '11 *	Aug 09 '11

TABLE FOR COMPUTATION OF EXPIRATION DATES

From	10 Days	15 Days	20 Days	30 Days	35 Days	45 Days	60 Days	90 Days	120 Days
Apr 12 '11	Apr 22 '11	Apr 27 '11	May 02 '11	May 12 '11	May 17 '11	May 27 '11	Jun 11 '11 s	Jul 11 '11	Aug 10 '11
Apr 13 '11	Apr 23 '11 s	Apr 28 '11	May 03 '11	May 13 '11	May 18 '11	May 28 '11 s	Jun 12 '11 *	Jul 12 '11	Aug 11 '11
Apr 14 '11	Apr 24 '11 *	Apr 29 '11	May 04 '11	May 14 '11 s	May 19 '11	May 29 '11 *	Jun 13 '11	Jul 13 '11	Aug 12 '11
Apr 15 '11	Apr 25 '11	Apr 30 '11 s	May 05 '11	May 15 '11 *	May 20 '11	May 30 '11	Jun 14 '11	Jul 14 '11	Aug 13 '11 s
Apr 16 '11 s	Apr 26 '11	May 01 '11 *	May 06 '11	May 16 '11	May 21 '11 s	May 31 '11	Jun 15 '11	Jul 15 '11	Aug 14 '11 *
Apr 17 '11 *	Apr 27 '11	May 02 '11	May 07 '11 s	May 17 '11	May 22 '11 *	Jun 01 '11	Jun 16 '11	Jul 16 '11 s	Aug 15 '11
Apr 18 '11	Apr 28 '11	May 03 '11	May 08 '11 *	May 18 '11	May 23 '11	Jun 02 '11	Jun 17 '11	Jul 17 '11 *	Aug 16 '11
Apr 19 '11	Apr 29 '11	May 04 '11	May 09 '11	May 19 '11	May 24 '11	Jun 03 '11	Jun 18 '11 s	Jul 18 '11	Aug 17 '11
Apr 20 '11	Apr 30 '11 s	May 05 '11	May 10 '11	May 20 '11	May 25 '11	Jun 04 '11 s	Jun 19 '11 *	Jul 19 '11	Aug 18 '11
Apr 21 '11	May 01 '11 *	May 06 '11	May 11 '11	May 21 '11 s	May 26 '11	Jun 05 '11 *	Jun 20 '11	Jul 20 '11	Aug 19 '11
Apr 22 '11	May 02 '11	May 07 '11 s	May 12 '11	May 22 '11 *	May 27 '11	Jun 06 '11	Jun 21 '11	Jul 21 '11	Aug 20 '11 s
Apr 23 '11 s	May 03 '11	May 08 '11 *	May 13 '11	May 23 '11	May 28 '11 s	Jun 07 '11	Jun 22 '11	Jul 22 '11	Aug 21 '11 *
Apr 24 '11 *	May 04 '11	May 09 '11	May 14 '11 s	May 24 '11	May 29 '11 *	Jun 08 '11	Jun 23 '11	Jul 23 '11 s	Aug 22 '11
Apr 25 '11	May 05 '11	May 10 '11	May 15 '11 *	May 25 '11	May 30 '11	Jun 09 '11	Jun 24 '11	Jul 24 '11 *	Aug 23 '11
Apr 26 '11	May 06 '11	May 11 '11	May 16 '11	May 26 '11	May 31 '11	Jun 10 '11	Jun 25 '11 s	Jul 25 '11	Aug 24 '11
Apr 27 '11	May 07 '11 s	May 12 '11	May 17 '11	May 27 '11	Jun 01 '11	Jun 11 '11 s	Jun 26 '11 *	Jul 26 '11	Aug 25 '11
Apr 28 '11	May 08 '11 *	May 13 '11	May 18 '11	May 28 '11 s	Jun 02 '11	Jun 12 '11 *	Jun 27 '11	Jul 27 '11	Aug 26 '11
Apr 29 '11	May 09 '11	May 14 '11 s	May 19 '11	May 29 '11 *	Jun 03 '11	Jun 13 '11	Jun 28 '11	Jul 28 '11	Aug 27 '11 s
Apr 30 '11 s	May 10 '11	May 15 '11 *	May 20 '11	May 30 '11	Jun 04 '11 s	Jun 14 '11	Jun 29 '11	Jul 29 '11	Aug 28 '11 *
May 01 '11 *	May 11 '11	May 16 '11	May 21 '11 s	May 31 '11	Jun 05 '11 *	Jun 15 '11	Jun 30 '11	Jul 30 '11 s	Aug 29 '11
May 02 '11	May 12 '11	May 17 '11	May 22 '11 *	Jun 01 '11	Jun 06 '11	Jun 16 '11	Jul 01 '11	Jul 31 '11 *	Aug 30 '11
May 03 '11	May 13 '11	May 18 '11	May 23 '11	Jun 02 '11	Jun 07 '11	Jun 17 '11	Jul 02 '11 s	Aug 01 '11	Aug 31 '11
May 04 '11	May 14 '11 s	May 19 '11	May 24 '11	Jun 03 '11	Jun 08 '11	Jun 18 '11 s	Jul 03 '11 *	Aug 02 '11	Sep 01 '11
May 05 '11	May 15 '11 *	May 20 '11	May 25 '11	Jun 04 '11 s	Jun 09 '11	Jun 19 '11 *	Jul 04 '11	Aug 03 '11	Sep 02 '11
May 06 '11	May 16 '11	May 21 '11 s	May 26 '11	Jun 05 '11 *	Jun 10 '11	Jun 20 '11	Jul 05 '11	Aug 04 '11	Sep 03 '11 s
May 07 '11 s	May 17 '11	May 22 '11 *	May 27 '11	Jun 06 '11	Jun 11 '11 s	Jun 21 '11	Jul 06 '11	Aug 05 '11	Sep 04 '11 *
May 08 '11 *	May 18 '11	May 23 '11	May 28 '11 s	Jun 07 '11	Jun 12 '11 *	Jun 22 '11	Jul 07 '11	Aug 06 '11 s	Sep 05 '11
May 09 '11	May 19 '11	May 24 '11	May 29 '11 *	Jun 08 '11	Jun 13 '11	Jun 23 '11	Jul 08 '11	Aug 07 '11 *	Sep 06 '11
May 10 '11	May 20 '11	May 25 '11	May 30 '11	Jun 09 '11	Jun 14 '11	Jun 24 '11	Jul 09 '11 s	Aug 08 '11	Sep 07 '11
May 11 '11	May 21 '11 s	May 26 '11	May 31 '11	Jun 10 '11	Jun 15 '11	Jun 25 '11 s	Jul 10 '11 *	Aug 09 '11	Sep 08 '11
May 12 '11	May 22 '11 *	May 27 '11	Jun 01 '11	Jun 11 '11 s	Jun 16 '11	Jun 26 '11 *	Jul 11 '11	Aug 10 '11	Sep 09 '11
May 13 '11	May 23 '11	May 28 '11 s	Jun 02 '11	Jun 12 '11 *	Jun 17 '11	Jun 27 '11	Jul 12 '11	Aug 11 '11	Sep 10 '11 s
May 14 '11 s	May 24 '11	May 29 '11 *	Jun 03 '11	Jun 13 '11	Jun 18 '11 s	Jun 28 '11	Jul 13 '11	Aug 12 '11	Sep 11 '11 *
May 15 '11 *	May 25 '11	May 30 '11	Jun 04 '11 s	Jun 14 '11	Jun 19 '11 *	Jun 29 '11	Jul 14 '11	Aug 13 '11 s	Sep 12 '11
May 16 '11	May 26 '11	May 31 '11	Jun 05 '11 *	Jun 15 '11	Jun 20 '11	Jun 30 '11	Jul 15 '11	Aug 14 '11 *	Sep 13 '11
May 17 '11	May 27 '11	Jun 01 '11	Jun 06 '11	Jun 16 '11	Jun 21 '11	Jul 01 '11	Jul 16 '11 s	Aug 15 '11	Sep 14 '11
May 18 '11	May 28 '11 s	Jun 02 '11	Jun 07 '11	Jun 17 '11	Jun 22 '11	Jul 02 '11 s	Jul 17 '11 *	Aug 16 '11	Sep 15 '11
May 19 '11	May 29 '11 *	Jun 03 '11	Jun 08 '11	Jun 18 '11 s	Jun 23 '11	Jul 03 '11 *	Jul 18 '11	Aug 17 '11	Sep 16 '11
May 20 '11	May 30 '11	Jun 04 '11 s	Jun 09 '11	Jun 19 '11 *	Jun 24 '11	Jul 04 '11	Jul 19 '11	Aug 18 '11	Sep 17 '11 s
May 21 '11 s	May 31 '11	Jun 05 '11 *	Jun 10 '11	Jun 20 '11	Jun 25 '11 s	Jul 05 '11	Jul 20 '11	Aug 19 '11	Sep 18 '11 *
May 22 '11 *	Jun 01 '11	Jun 06 '11	Jun 11 '11 s	Jun 21 '11	Jun 26 '11 *	Jul 06 '11	Jul 21 '11	Aug 20 '11 s	Sep 19 '11
May 23 '11	Jun 02 '11	Jun 07 '11	Jun 12 '11 *	Jun 22 '11	Jun 27 '11	Jul 07 '11	Jul 22 '11	Aug 21 '11 *	Sep 20 '11
May 24 '11	Jun 03 '11	Jun 08 '11	Jun 13 '11	Jun 23 '11	Jun 28 '11	Jul 08 '11	Jul 23 '11 s	Aug 22 '11	Sep 21 '11
May 25 '11	Jun 04 '11 s	Jun 09 '11	Jun 14 '11	Jun 24 '11	Jun 29 '11	Jul 09 '11 s	Jul 24 '11 *	Aug 23 '11	Sep 22 '11
May 26 '11	Jun 05 '11 *	Jun 10 '11	Jun 15 '11	Jun 25 '11 s	Jun 30 '11	Jul 10 '11 *	Jul 25 '11	Aug 24 '11	Sep 23 '11
May 27 '11	Jun 06 '11	Jun 11 '11 s	Jun 16 '11	Jun 26 '11 *	Jul 01 '11	Jul 11 '11	Jul 26 '11	Aug 25 '11	Sep 24 '11 s
May 28 '11 s	Jun 07 '11	Jun 12 '11 *	Jun 17 '11	Jun 27 '11	Jul 02 '11 s	Jul 12 '11	Jul 27 '11	Aug 26 '11	Sep 25 '11 *
May 29 '11 *	Jun 08 '11	Jun 13 '11	Jun 18 '11 s	Jun 28 '11	Jul 03 '11 *	Jul 13 '11	Jul 28 '11	Aug 27 '11 s	Sep 26 '11
May 30 '11	Jun 09 '11	Jun 14 '11	Jun 19 '11 *	Jun 29 '11	Jul 04 '11	Jul 14 '11	Jul 29 '11	Aug 28 '11 *	Sep 27 '11
May 31 '11	Jun 10 '11	Jun 15 '11	Jun 20 '11	Jun 30 '11	Jul 05 '11	Jul 15 '11	Jul 30 '11 s	Aug 29 '11	Sep 28 '11
Jun 01 '11	Jun 11 '11 s	Jun 16 '11	Jun 21 '11	Jul 01 '11	Jul 06 '11	Jul 16 '11 s	Jul 31 '11 *	Aug 30 '11	Sep 29 '11
Jun 02 '11	Jun 12 '11 *	Jun 17 '11	Jun 22 '11	Jul 02 '11 s	Jul 07 '11	Jul 17 '11 *	Aug 01 '11	Aug 31 '11	Sep 30 '11
Jun 03 '11	Jun 13 '11	Jun 18 '11 s	Jun 23 '11	Jul 03 '11 *	Jul 08 '11	Jul 18 '11	Aug 02 '11	Sep 01 '11	Oct 01 '11 s
Jun 04 '11 s	Jun 14 '11	Jun 19 '11 *	Jun 24 '11	Jul 04 '11	Jul 09 '11 s	Jul 19 '11	Aug 03 '11	Sep 02 '11	Oct 02 '11 *
Jun 05 '11 *	Jun 15 '11	Jun 20 '11	Jun 25 '11 s	Jul 05 '11	Jul 10 '11 *	Jul 20 '11	Aug 04 '11	Sep 03 '11 s	Oct 03 '11
Jun 06 '11	Jun 16 '11	Jun 21 '11	Jun 26 '11 *	Jul 06 '11	Jul 11 '11	Jul 21 '11	Aug 05 '11	Sep 04 '11 *	Oct 04 '11
Jun 07 '11	Jun 17 '11	Jun 22 '11	Jun 27 '11	Jul 07 '11	Jul 12 '11	Jul 22 '11	Aug 06 '11 s	Sep 05 '11	Oct 05 '11
Jun 08 '11	Jun 18 '11 s	Jun 23 '11	Jun 28 '11	Jul 08 '11	Jul 13 '11	Jul 23 '11 s	Aug 07 '11 *	Sep 06 '11	Oct 06 '11
Jun 09 '11	Jun 19 '11 *	Jun 24 '11	Jun 29 '11	Jul 09 '11 s	Jul 14 '11	Jul 24 '11 *	Aug 08 '11	Sep 07 '11	Oct 07 '11
Jun 10 '11	Jun 20 '11	Jun 25 '11 s	Jun 30 '11	Jul 10 '11 *	Jul 15 '11	Jul 25 '11	Aug 09 '11	Sep 08 '11	Oct 08 '11 s
Jun 11 '11 s	Jun 21 '11	Jun 26 '11 *	Jul 01 '11	Jul 11 '11	Jul 16 '11 s	Jul 26 '11	Aug 10 '11	Sep 09 '11	Oct 09 '11 *
Jun 12 '11 *	Jun 22 '11	Jun 27 '11	Jul 02 '11 s	Jul 12 '11	Jul 17 '11 *	Jul 27 '11	Aug 11 '11	Sep 10 '11 s	Oct 10 '11
Jun 13 '11	Jun 23 '11	Jun 28 '11	Jul 03 '11 *	Jul 13 '11	Jul 18 '11	Jul 28 '11	Aug 12 '11	Sep 11 '11 *	Oct 11 '11
Jun 14 '11	Jun 24 '11	Jun 29 '11	Jul 04 '11	Jul 14 '11	Jul 19 '11	Jul 29 '11	Aug 13 '11 s	Sep 12 '11	Oct 12 '11
Jun 15 '11	Jun 25 '11 s	Jun 30 '11	Jul 05 '11	Jul 15 '11	Jul 20 '11	Jul 30 '11 s	Aug 14 '11 *	Sep 13 '11	Oct 13 '11
Jun 16 '11	Jun 26 '11 *	Jul 01 '11	Jul 06 '11	Jul 16 '11 s	Jul 21 '11	Jul 31 '11 *	Aug 15 '11	Sep 14 '11	Oct 14 '11
Jun 17 '11	Jun 27 '11	Jul 02 '11 s	Jul 07 '11	Jul 17 '11 *	Jul 22 '11	Aug 01 '11	Aug 16 '11	Sep 15 '11	Oct 15 '11 s
Jun 18 '11 s	Jun 28 '11	Jul 03 '11 *	Jul 08 '11	Jul 18 '11	Jul 23 '11 s	Aug 02 '11	Aug 17 '11	Sep 16 '11	Oct 16 '11 *
Jun 19 '11 *	Jun 29 '11	Jul 04 '11	Jul 09 '11 s	Jul 19 '11	Jul 24 '11 *	Aug 03 '11	Aug 18 '11	Sep 17 '11 s	Oct 17 '11
Jun 20 '11	Jun 30 '11	Jul 05 '11	Jul 10 '11 *	Jul 20 '11	Jul 25 '11	Aug 04 '11	Aug 19 '11	Sep 18 '11 *	Oct 18 '11
Jun 21 '11	Jul 01 '11	Jul 06 '11	Jul 11 '11	Jul 21 '11	Jul 26 '11	Aug 05 '11	Aug 20 '11 s	Sep 19 '11	Oct 19 '11

TABLE FOR COMPUTATION OF EXPIRATION DATES

From	10 Days	15 Days	20 Days	30 Days	35 Days	45 Days	60 Days	90 Days	120 Days
Jun 22 '11	Jul 02 '11 s	Jul 07 '11	Jul 12 '11	Jul 22 '11	Jul 27 '11	Aug 06 '11 s	Aug 21 '11 *	Sep 20 '11	Oct 20 '11
Jun 23 '11	Jul 03 '11 *	Jul 08 '11	Jul 13 '11	Jul 23 '11 s	Jul 28 '11	Aug 07 '11 *	Aug 22 '11	Sep 21 '11	Oct 21 '11
Jun 24 '11	Jul 04 '11	Jul 09 '11 s	Jul 14 '11	Jul 24 '11 *	Jul 29 '11	Aug 08 '11	Aug 23 '11	Sep 22 '11	Oct 22 '11 s
Jun 25 '11 s	Jul 05 '11	Jul 10 '11 *	Jul 15 '11	Jul 25 '11	Jul 30 '11 s	Aug 09 '11	Aug 24 '11	Sep 23 '11	Oct 23 '11 *
Jun 26 '11 *	Jul 06 '11	Jul 11 '11	Jul 16 '11 s	Jul 26 '11	Jul 31 '11 *	Aug 10 '11	Aug 25 '11	Sep 24 '11 s	Oct 24 '11
Jun 27 '11	Jul 07 '11	Jul 12 '11	Jul 17 '11 *	Jul 27 '11	Aug 01 '11	Aug 11 '11	Aug 26 '11	Sep 25 '11 *	Oct 25 '11
Jun 28 '11	Jul 08 '11	Jul 13 '11	Jul 18 '11	Jul 28 '11	Aug 02 '11	Aug 12 '11	Aug 27 '11 s	Sep 26 '11	Oct 26 '11
Jun 29 '11	Jul 09 '11 s	Jul 14 '11	Jul 19 '11	Jul 29 '11	Aug 03 '11	Aug 13 '11 s	Aug 28 '11 *	Sep 27 '11	Oct 27 '11
Jun 30 '11	Jul 10 '11 *	Jul 15 '11	Jul 20 '11	Jul 30 '11 s	Aug 04 '11	Aug 14 '11 *	Aug 29 '11	Sep 28 '11	Oct 28 '11
Jul 01 '11	Jul 11 '11	Jul 16 '11 s	Jul 21 '11	Jul 31 '11 *	Aug 05 '11	Aug 15 '11	Aug 30 '11	Sep 29 '11	Oct 29 '11 s
Jul 02 '11 s	Jul 12 '11	Jul 17 '11 *	Jul 22 '11	Aug 01 '11	Aug 06 '11 s	Aug 16 '11	Aug 31 '11	Sep 30 '11	Oct 30 '11 *
Jul 03 '11 *	Jul 13 '11	Jul 18 '11	Jul 23 '11 s	Aug 02 '11	Aug 07 '11 *	Aug 17 '11	Sep 01 '11	Oct 01 '11 s	Oct 31 '11
Jul 04 '11	Jul 14 '11	Jul 19 '11	Jul 24 '11 *	Aug 03 '11	Aug 08 '11	Aug 18 '11	Sep 02 '11	Oct 02 '11 *	Nov 01 '11
Jul 05 '11	Jul 15 '11	Jul 20 '11	Jul 25 '11	Aug 04 '11	Aug 09 '11	Aug 19 '11	Sep 03 '11 s	Oct 03 '11	Nov 02 '11
Jul 06 '11	Jul 16 '11 s	Jul 21 '11	Jul 26 '11	Aug 05 '11	Aug 10 '11	Aug 20 '11 s	Sep 04 '11 *	Oct 04 '11	Nov 03 '11
Jul 07 '11	Jul 17 '11 *	Jul 22 '11	Jul 27 '11	Aug 06 '11 s	Aug 11 '11	Aug 21 '11 *	Sep 05 '11	Oct 05 '11	Nov 04 '11
Jul 08 '11	Jul 18 '11	Jul 23 '11 s	Jul 28 '11	Aug 07 '11 *	Aug 12 '11	Aug 22 '11	Sep 06 '11	Oct 06 '11	Nov 05 '11 s
Jul 09 '11 s	Jul 19 '11	Jul 24 '11 *	Jul 29 '11	Aug 08 '11	Aug 13 '11 s	Aug 23 '11	Sep 07 '11	Oct 07 '11	Nov 06 '11 *
Jul 10 '11 *	Jul 20 '11	Jul 25 '11	Jul 30 '11 s	Aug 09 '11	Aug 14 '11 *	Aug 24 '11	Sep 08 '11	Oct 08 '11 s	Nov 07 '11
Jul 11 '11	Jul 21 '11	Jul 26 '11	Jul 31 '11 *	Aug 10 '11	Aug 15 '11	Aug 25 '11	Sep 09 '11	Oct 09 '11 *	Nov 08 '11
Jul 12 '11	Jul 22 '11	Jul 27 '11	Aug 01 '11	Aug 11 '11	Aug 16 '11	Aug 26 '11	Sep 10 '11 s	Oct 10 '11	Nov 09 '11
Jul 13 '11	Jul 23 '11 s	Jul 28 '11	Aug 02 '11	Aug 12 '11	Aug 17 '11	Aug 27 '11 s	Sep 11 '11 *	Oct 11 '11	Nov 10 '11
Jul 14 '11	Jul 24 '11 *	Jul 29 '11	Aug 03 '11	Aug 13 '11 s	Aug 18 '11	Aug 28 '11 *	Sep 12 '11	Oct 12 '11	Nov 11 '11
Jul 15 '11	Jul 25 '11	Jul 30 '11 s	Aug 04 '11	Aug 14 '11 *	Aug 19 '11	Aug 29 '11	Sep 13 '11	Oct 13 '11	Nov 12 '11 s
Jul 16 '11 s	Jul 26 '11	Jul 31 '11 *	Aug 05 '11	Aug 15 '11	Aug 20 '11 s	Aug 30 '11	Sep 14 '11	Oct 14 '11	Nov 13 '11 *
Jul 17 '11 *	Jul 27 '11	Aug 01 '11	Aug 06 '11 s	Aug 16 '11	Aug 21 '11 *	Aug 31 '11	Sep 15 '11	Oct 15 '11 s	Nov 14 '11
Jul 18 '11	Jul 28 '11	Aug 02 '11	Aug 07 '11 *	Aug 17 '11	Aug 22 '11	Sep 01 '11	Sep 16 '11	Oct 16 '11 *	Nov 15 '11
Jul 19 '11	Jul 29 '11	Aug 03 '11	Aug 08 '11	Aug 18 '11	Aug 23 '11	Sep 02 '11	Sep 17 '11 s	Oct 17 '11	Nov 16 '11
Jul 20 '11	Jul 30 '11 s	Aug 04 '11	Aug 09 '11	Aug 19 '11	Aug 24 '11	Sep 03 '11 s	Sep 18 '11 *	Oct 18 '11	Nov 17 '11
Jul 21 '11	Jul 31 '11 *	Aug 05 '11	Aug 10 '11	Aug 20 '11 s	Aug 25 '11	Sep 04 '11 *	Sep 19 '11	Oct 19 '11	Nov 18 '11
Jul 22 '11	Aug 01 '11	Aug 06 '11 s	Aug 11 '11	Aug 21 '11 *	Aug 26 '11	Sep 05 '11	Sep 20 '11	Oct 20 '11	Nov 19 '11 s
Jul 23 '11 s	Aug 02 '11	Aug 07 '11 *	Aug 12 '11	Aug 22 '11	Aug 27 '11 s	Sep 06 '11	Sep 21 '11	Oct 21 '11	Nov 20 '11 *
Jul 24 '11 *	Aug 03 '11	Aug 08 '11	Aug 13 '11 s	Aug 23 '11	Aug 28 '11 *	Sep 07 '11	Sep 22 '11	Oct 22 '11 s	Nov 21 '11
Jul 25 '11	Aug 04 '11	Aug 09 '11	Aug 14 '11 *	Aug 24 '11	Aug 29 '11	Sep 08 '11	Sep 23 '11	Oct 23 '11 *	Nov 22 '11
Jul 26 '11	Aug 05 '11	Aug 10 '11	Aug 15 '11	Aug 25 '11	Aug 30 '11	Sep 09 '11	Sep 24 '11 s	Oct 24 '11	Nov 23 '11
Jul 27 '11	Aug 06 '11 s	Aug 11 '11	Aug 16 '11	Aug 26 '11	Aug 31 '11	Sep 10 '11 s	Sep 25 '11 *	Oct 25 '11	Nov 24 '11
Jul 28 '11	Aug 07 '11 *	Aug 12 '11	Aug 17 '11	Aug 27 '11 s	Sep 01 '11	Sep 11 '11 *	Sep 26 '11	Oct 26 '11	Nov 25 '11
Jul 29 '11	Aug 08 '11	Aug 13 '11 s	Aug 18 '11	Aug 28 '11 *	Sep 02 '11	Sep 12 '11	Sep 27 '11	Oct 27 '11	Nov 26 '11 s
Jul 30 '11 s	Aug 09 '11	Aug 14 '11 *	Aug 19 '11	Aug 29 '11	Sep 03 '11 s	Sep 13 '11	Sep 28 '11	Oct 28 '11	Nov 27 '11 *
Jul 31 '11 *	Aug 10 '11	Aug 15 '11	Aug 20 '11 s	Aug 30 '11	Sep 04 '11 *	Sep 14 '11	Sep 29 '11	Oct 29 '11 s	Nov 28 '11
Aug 01 '11	Aug 11 '11	Aug 16 '11	Aug 21 '11 *	Aug 31 '11	Sep 05 '11	Sep 15 '11	Sep 30 '11	Oct 30 '11 *	Nov 29 '11
Aug 02 '11	Aug 12 '11	Aug 17 '11	Aug 22 '11	Sep 01 '11	Sep 06 '11	Sep 16 '11	Oct 01 '11 s	Oct 31 '11	Nov 30 '11
Aug 03 '11	Aug 13 '11 s	Aug 18 '11	Aug 23 '11	Sep 02 '11	Sep 07 '11	Sep 17 '11 s	Oct 02 '11 *	Nov 01 '11	Dec 01 '11
Aug 04 '11	Aug 14 '11 *	Aug 19 '11	Aug 24 '11	Sep 03 '11 s	Sep 08 '11	Sep 18 '11 *	Oct 03 '11	Nov 02 '11	Dec 02 '11
Aug 05 '11	Aug 15 '11	Aug 20 '11 s	Aug 25 '11	Sep 04 '11 *	Sep 09 '11	Sep 19 '11	Oct 04 '11	Nov 03 '11	Dec 03 '11 s
Aug 06 '11 s	Aug 16 '11	Aug 21 '11 *	Aug 26 '11	Sep 05 '11	Sep 10 '11 s	Sep 20 '11	Oct 05 '11	Nov 04 '11	Dec 04 '11 *
Aug 07 '11 *	Aug 17 '11	Aug 22 '11	Aug 27 '11 s	Sep 06 '11	Sep 11 '11 *	Sep 21 '11	Oct 06 '11	Nov 05 '11 s	Dec 05 '11
Aug 08 '11	Aug 18 '11	Aug 23 '11	Aug 28 '11 *	Sep 07 '11	Sep 12 '11	Sep 22 '11	Oct 07 '11	Nov 06 '11 *	Dec 06 '11
Aug 09 '11	Aug 19 '11	Aug 24 '11	Aug 29 '11	Sep 08 '11	Sep 13 '11	Sep 23 '11	Oct 08 '11 s	Nov 07 '11	Dec 07 '11
Aug 10 '11	Aug 20 '11 s	Aug 25 '11	Aug 30 '11	Sep 09 '11	Sep 14 '11	Sep 24 '11 s	Oct 09 '11 *	Nov 08 '11	Dec 08 '11
Aug 11 '11	Aug 21 '11 *	Aug 26 '11	Aug 31 '11	Sep 10 '11 s	Sep 15 '11	Sep 25 '11 *	Oct 10 '11	Nov 09 '11	Dec 09 '11
Aug 12 '11	Aug 22 '11	Aug 27 '11 s	Sep 01 '11	Sep 11 '11 *	Sep 16 '11	Sep 26 '11	Oct 11 '11	Nov 10 '11	Dec 10 '11 s
Aug 13 '11 s	Aug 23 '11	Aug 28 '11 *	Sep 02 '11	Sep 12 '11	Sep 17 '11 s	Sep 27 '11	Oct 12 '11	Nov 11 '11	Dec 11 '11 *
Aug 14 '11 *	Aug 24 '11	Aug 29 '11	Sep 03 '11 s	Sep 13 '11	Sep 18 '11 *	Sep 28 '11	Oct 13 '11	Nov 12 '11 s	Dec 12 '11
Aug 15 '11	Aug 25 '11	Aug 30 '11	Sep 04 '11 *	Sep 14 '11	Sep 19 '11	Sep 29 '11	Oct 14 '11	Nov 13 '11 *	Dec 13 '11
Aug 16 '11	Aug 26 '11	Aug 31 '11	Sep 05 '11	Sep 15 '11	Sep 20 '11	Sep 30 '11	Oct 15 '11 s	Nov 14 '11	Dec 14 '11
Aug 17 '11	Aug 27 '11 s	Sep 01 '11	Sep 06 '11	Sep 16 '11	Sep 21 '11	Oct 01 '11 s	Oct 16 '11 *	Nov 15 '11	Dec 15 '11
Aug 18 '11	Aug 28 '11 *	Sep 02 '11	Sep 07 '11	Sep 17 '11 s	Sep 22 '11	Oct 02 '11 *	Oct 17 '11	Nov 16 '11	Dec 16 '11
Aug 19 '11	Aug 29 '11	Sep 03 '11 s	Sep 08 '11	Sep 18 '11 *	Sep 23 '11	Oct 03 '11	Oct 18 '11	Nov 17 '11	Dec 17 '11 s
Aug 20 '11 s	Aug 30 '11	Sep 04 '11 *	Sep 09 '11	Sep 19 '11	Sep 24 '11 s	Oct 04 '11	Oct 19 '11	Nov 18 '11	Dec 18 '11 *
Aug 21 '11 *	Aug 31 '11	Sep 05 '11	Sep 10 '11 s	Sep 20 '11	Sep 25 '11 *	Oct 05 '11	Oct 20 '11	Nov 19 '11 s	Dec 19 '11
Aug 22 '11	Sep 01 '11	Sep 06 '11	Sep 11 '11 *	Sep 21 '11	Sep 26 '11	Oct 06 '11	Oct 21 '11	Nov 20 '11 *	Dec 20 '11
Aug 23 '11	Sep 02 '11	Sep 07 '11	Sep 12 '11	Sep 22 '11	Sep 27 '11	Oct 07 '11	Oct 22 '11 s	Nov 21 '11	Dec 21 '11
Aug 24 '11	Sep 03 '11 s	Sep 08 '11	Sep 13 '11	Sep 23 '11	Sep 28 '11	Oct 08 '11 s	Oct 23 '11 *	Nov 22 '11	Dec 22 '11
Aug 25 '11	Sep 04 '11 *	Sep 09 '11	Sep 14 '11	Sep 24 '11 s	Sep 29 '11	Oct 09 '11 *	Oct 24 '11	Nov 23 '11	Dec 23 '11
Aug 26 '11	Sep 05 '11	Sep 10 '11 s	Sep 15 '11	Sep 25 '11 *	Sep 30 '11	Oct 10 '11	Oct 25 '11	Nov 24 '11	Dec 24 '11 s
Aug 27 '11 s	Sep 06 '11	Sep 11 '11 *	Sep 16 '11	Sep 26 '11	Oct 01 '11 s	Oct 11 '11	Oct 26 '11	Nov 25 '11	Dec 25 '11 *
Aug 28 '11 *	Sep 07 '11	Sep 12 '11	Sep 17 '11 s	Sep 27 '11	Oct 02 '11 *	Oct 12 '11	Oct 27 '11	Nov 26 '11 s	Dec 26 '11
Aug 29 '11	Sep 08 '11	Sep 13 '11	Sep 18 '11 *	Sep 28 '11	Oct 03 '11	Oct 13 '11	Oct 28 '11	Nov 27 '11 *	Dec 27 '11
Aug 30 '11	Sep 09 '11	Sep 14 '11	Sep 19 '11	Sep 29 '11	Oct 04 '11	Oct 14 '11	Oct 29 '11 s	Nov 28 '11	Dec 28 '11
Aug 31 '11	Sep 10 '11 s	Sep 15 '11	Sep 20 '11	Sep 30 '11	Oct 05 '11	Oct 15 '11 s	Oct 30 '11 *	Nov 29 '11	Dec 29 '11

TABLE FOR COMPUTATION OF EXPIRATION DATES

From	10 Days	15 Days	20 Days	30 Days	35 Days	45 Days	60 Days	90 Days	120 Days
Sep 01 '11	Sep 11 '11 *	Sep 16 '11	Sep 21 '11	Oct 01 '11 s	Oct 06 '11	Oct 16 '11 *	Oct 31 '11	Nov 30 '11	Dec 30 '11
Sep 02 '11	Sep 12 '11	Sep 17 '11 s	Sep 22 '11	Oct 02 '11 *	Oct 07 '11	Oct 17 '11	Nov 01 '11	Dec 01 '11	Dec 31 '11 s
Sep 03 '11 s	Sep 13 '11	Sep 18 '11 *	Sep 23 '11	Oct 03 '11	Oct 08 '11 s	Oct 18 '11	Nov 02 '11	Dec 02 '11	Jan 01 '12 *
Sep 04 '11 *	Sep 14 '11	Sep 19 '11	Sep 24 '11 s	Oct 04 '11	Oct 09 '11 *	Oct 19 '11	Nov 03 '11	Dec 03 '11 s	Jan 02 '12
Sep 05 '11	Sep 15 '11	Sep 20 '11	Sep 25 '11 *	Oct 05 '11	Oct 10 '11	Oct 20 '11	Nov 04 '11	Dec 04 '11 *	Jan 03 '12
Sep 06 '11	Sep 16 '11	Sep 21 '11	Sep 26 '11	Oct 06 '11	Oct 11 '11	Oct 21 '11	Nov 05 '11 s	Dec 05 '11	Jan 04 '12
Sep 07 '11	Sep 17 '11 s	Sep 22 '11	Sep 27 '11	Oct 07 '11	Oct 12 '11	Oct 22 '11 s	Nov 06 '11 *	Dec 06 '11	Jan 05 '12
Sep 08 '11	Sep 18 '11 *	Sep 23 '11	Sep 28 '11	Oct 08 '11 s	Oct 13 '11	Oct 23 '11 *	Nov 07 '11	Dec 07 '11	Jan 06 '12
Sep 09 '11	Sep 19 '11	Sep 24 '11 s	Sep 29 '11	Oct 09 '11 *	Oct 14 '11	Oct 24 '11	Nov 08 '11	Dec 08 '11	Jan 07 '12 s
Sep 10 '11 s	Sep 20 '11	Sep 25 '11 *	Sep 30 '11	Oct 10 '11	Oct 15 '11 s	Oct 25 '11	Nov 09 '11	Dec 09 '11	Jan 08 '12 *
Sep 11 '11 *	Sep 21 '11	Sep 26 '11	Oct 01 '11 s	Oct 11 '11	Oct 16 '11 *	Oct 26 '11	Nov 10 '11	Dec 10 '11 s	Jan 09 '12
Sep 12 '11	Sep 22 '11	Sep 27 '11	Oct 02 '11 *	Oct 12 '11	Oct 17 '11	Oct 27 '11	Nov 11 '11	Dec 11 '11 *	Jan 10 '12
Sep 13 '11	Sep 23 '11	Sep 28 '11	Oct 03 '11	Oct 13 '11	Oct 18 '11	Oct 28 '11	Nov 12 '11 s	Dec 12 '11	Jan 11 '12
Sep 14 '11	Sep 24 '11 s	Sep 29 '11	Oct 04 '11	Oct 14 '11	Oct 19 '11	Oct 29 '11 s	Nov 13 '11 *	Dec 13 '11	Jan 12 '12
Sep 15 '11	Sep 25 '11 *	Sep 30 '11	Oct 05 '11	Oct 15 '11 s	Oct 20 '11	Oct 30 '11 *	Nov 14 '11	Dec 14 '11	Jan 13 '12
Sep 16 '11	Sep 26 '11	Oct 01 '11 s	Oct 06 '11	Oct 16 '11 *	Oct 21 '11	Oct 31 '11	Nov 15 '11	Dec 15 '11	Jan 14 '12 s
Sep 17 '11 s	Sep 27 '11	Oct 02 '11 *	Oct 07 '11	Oct 17 '11	Oct 22 '11 s	Nov 01 '11	Nov 16 '11	Dec 16 '11	Jan 15 '12 *
Sep 18 '11 *	Sep 28 '11	Oct 03 '11	Oct 08 '11 s	Oct 18 '11	Oct 23 '11 *	Nov 02 '11	Nov 17 '11	Dec 17 '11 s	Jan 16 '12
Sep 19 '11	Sep 29 '11	Oct 04 '11	Oct 09 '11 *	Oct 19 '11	Oct 24 '11	Nov 03 '11	Nov 18 '11	Dec 18 '11 *	Jan 17 '12
Sep 20 '11	Sep 30 '11	Oct 05 '11	Oct 10 '11	Oct 20 '11	Oct 25 '11	Nov 04 '11	Nov 19 '11 s	Dec 19 '11	Jan 18 '12
Sep 21 '11	Oct 01 '11 s	Oct 06 '11	Oct 11 '11	Oct 21 '11	Oct 26 '11	Nov 05 '11 s	Nov 20 '11 *	Dec 20 '11	Jan 19 '12
Sep 22 '11	Oct 02 '11 *	Oct 07 '11	Oct 12 '11	Oct 22 '11 s	Oct 27 '11	Nov 06 '11 *	Nov 21 '11	Dec 21 '11	Jan 20 '12
Sep 23 '11	Oct 03 '11	Oct 08 '11 s	Oct 13 '11	Oct 23 '11 *	Oct 28 '11	Nov 07 '11	Nov 22 '11	Dec 22 '11	Jan 21 '12 s
Sep 24 '11 s	Oct 04 '11	Oct 09 '11 *	Oct 14 '11	Oct 24 '11	Oct 29 '11 s	Nov 08 '11	Nov 23 '11	Dec 23 '11	Jan 22 '12 *
Sep 25 '11 *	Oct 05 '11	Oct 10 '11	Oct 15 '11 s	Oct 25 '11	Oct 30 '11 *	Nov 09 '11	Nov 24 '11	Dec 24 '11 s	Jan 23 '12
Sep 26 '11	Oct 06 '11	Oct 11 '11	Oct 16 '11 *	Oct 26 '11	Oct 31 '11	Nov 10 '11	Nov 25 '11	Dec 25 '11 *	Jan 24 '12
Sep 27 '11	Oct 07 '11	Oct 12 '11	Oct 17 '11	Oct 27 '11	Nov 01 '11	Nov 11 '11	Nov 26 '11 s	Dec 26 '11	Jan 25 '12
Sep 28 '11	Oct 08 '11 s	Oct 13 '11	Oct 18 '11	Oct 28 '11	Nov 02 '11	Nov 12 '11 s	Nov 27 '11 *	Dec 27 '11	Jan 26 '12
Sep 29 '11	Oct 09 '11 *	Oct 14 '11	Oct 19 '11	Oct 29 '11 s	Nov 03 '11	Nov 13 '11 *	Nov 28 '11	Dec 28 '11	Jan 27 '12
Sep 30 '11	Oct 10 '11	Oct 15 '11 s	Oct 20 '11	Oct 30 '11 *	Nov 04 '11	Nov 14 '11	Nov 29 '11	Dec 29 '11	Jan 28 '12 s
Oct 01 '11 s	Oct 11 '11	Oct 16 '11 *	Oct 21 '11	Oct 31 '11	Nov 05 '11 s	Nov 15 '11	Nov 30 '11	Dec 30 '11	Jan 29 '12 *
Oct 02 '11 *	Oct 12 '11	Oct 17 '11	Oct 22 '11 s	Nov 01 '11	Nov 06 '11 *	Nov 16 '11	Dec 01 '11	Dec 31 '11 s	Jan 30 '12
Oct 03 '11	Oct 13 '11	Oct 18 '11	Oct 23 '11 *	Nov 02 '11	Nov 07 '11	Nov 17 '11	Dec 02 '11	Jan 01 '12 *	Jan 31 '12
Oct 04 '11	Oct 14 '11	Oct 19 '11	Oct 24 '11	Nov 03 '11	Nov 08 '11	Nov 18 '11	Dec 03 '11 s	Jan 02 '12	Feb 01 '12
Oct 05 '11	Oct 15 '11 s	Oct 20 '11	Oct 25 '11	Nov 04 '11	Nov 09 '11	Nov 19 '11 s	Dec 04 '11 *	Jan 03 '12	Feb 02 '12
Oct 06 '11	Oct 16 '11 *	Oct 21 '11	Oct 26 '11	Nov 05 '11 s	Nov 10 '11	Nov 20 '11 *	Dec 05 '11	Jan 04 '12	Feb 03 '12
Oct 07 '11	Oct 17 '11	Oct 22 '11 s	Oct 27 '11	Nov 06 '11 *	Nov 11 '11	Nov 21 '11	Dec 06 '11	Jan 05 '12	Feb 04 '12 s
Oct 08 '11 s	Oct 18 '11	Oct 23 '11 *	Oct 28 '11	Nov 07 '11	Nov 12 '11 s	Nov 22 '11	Dec 07 '11	Jan 06 '12	Feb 05 '12 *
Oct 09 '11 *	Oct 19 '11	Oct 24 '11	Oct 29 '11 s	Nov 08 '11	Nov 13 '11 *	Nov 23 '11	Dec 08 '11	Jan 07 '12 s	Feb 06 '12
Oct 10 '11	Oct 20 '11	Oct 25 '11	Oct 30 '11 *	Nov 09 '11	Nov 14 '11	Nov 24 '11	Dec 09 '11	Jan 08 '12 *	Feb 07 '12
Oct 11 '11	Oct 21 '11	Oct 26 '11	Oct 31 '11	Nov 10 '11	Nov 15 '11	Nov 25 '11	Dec 10 '11 s	Jan 09 '12	Feb 08 '12
Oct 12 '11	Oct 22 '11 s	Oct 27 '11	Nov 01 '11	Nov 11 '11	Nov 16 '11	Nov 26 '11 s	Dec 11 '11 *	Jan 10 '12	Feb 09 '12
Oct 13 '11	Oct 23 '11 *	Oct 28 '11	Nov 02 '11	Nov 12 '11 s	Nov 17 '11	Nov 27 '11 *	Dec 12 '11	Jan 11 '12	Feb 10 '12
Oct 14 '11	Oct 24 '11	Oct 29 '11 s	Nov 03 '11	Nov 13 '11 *	Nov 18 '11	Nov 28 '11	Dec 13 '11	Jan 12 '12	Feb 11 '12 s
Oct 15 '11 s	Oct 25 '11	Oct 30 '11 *	Nov 04 '11	Nov 14 '11	Nov 19 '11 s	Nov 29 '11	Dec 14 '11	Jan 13 '12	Feb 12 '12 *
Oct 16 '11 *	Oct 26 '11	Oct 31 '11	Nov 05 '11 s	Nov 15 '11	Nov 20 '11 *	Nov 30 '11	Dec 15 '11	Jan 14 '12 s	Feb 13 '12
Oct 17 '11	Oct 27 '11	Nov 01 '11	Nov 06 '11 *	Nov 16 '11	Nov 21 '11	Dec 01 '11	Dec 16 '11	Jan 15 '12 *	Feb 14 '12
Oct 18 '11	Oct 28 '11	Nov 02 '11	Nov 07 '11	Nov 17 '11	Nov 22 '11	Dec 02 '11	Dec 17 '11 s	Jan 16 '12	Feb 15 '12
Oct 19 '11	Oct 29 '11 s	Nov 03 '11	Nov 08 '11	Nov 18 '11	Nov 23 '11	Dec 03 '11 s	Dec 18 '11 *	Jan 17 '12	Feb 16 '12
Oct 20 '11	Oct 30 '11 *	Nov 04 '11	Nov 09 '11	Nov 19 '11 s	Nov 24 '11	Dec 04 '11 *	Dec 19 '11	Jan 18 '12	Feb 17 '12
Oct 21 '11	Oct 31 '11	Nov 05 '11 s	Nov 10 '11	Nov 20 '11 *	Nov 25 '11	Dec 05 '11	Dec 20 '11	Jan 19 '12	Feb 18 '12 s
Oct 22 '11 s	Nov 01 '11	Nov 06 '11 *	Nov 11 '11	Nov 21 '11	Nov 26 '11 s	Dec 06 '11	Dec 21 '11	Jan 20 '12	Feb 19 '12 *
Oct 23 '11 *	Nov 02 '11	Nov 07 '11	Nov 12 '11 s	Nov 22 '11	Nov 27 '11 *	Dec 07 '11	Dec 22 '11	Jan 21 '12 s	Feb 20 '12
Oct 24 '11	Nov 03 '11	Nov 08 '11	Nov 13 '11 *	Nov 23 '11	Nov 28 '11	Dec 08 '11	Dec 23 '11	Jan 22 '12 *	Feb 21 '12
Oct 25 '11	Nov 04 '11	Nov 09 '11	Nov 14 '11	Nov 24 '11	Nov 29 '11	Dec 09 '11	Dec 24 '11 s	Jan 23 '12	Feb 22 '12
Oct 26 '11	Nov 05 '11 s	Nov 10 '11	Nov 15 '11	Nov 25 '11	Nov 30 '11	Dec 10 '11 s	Dec 25 '11 *	Jan 24 '12	Feb 23 '12
Oct 27 '11	Nov 06 '11 *	Nov 11 '11	Nov 16 '11	Nov 26 '11 s	Dec 01 '11	Dec 11 '11 *	Dec 26 '11	Jan 25 '12	Feb 24 '12
Oct 28 '11	Nov 07 '11	Nov 12 '11 s	Nov 17 '11	Nov 27 '11 *	Dec 02 '11	Dec 12 '11	Dec 27 '11	Jan 26 '12	Feb 25 '12 s
Oct 29 '11 s	Nov 08 '11	Nov 13 '11 *	Nov 18 '11	Nov 28 '11	Dec 03 '11 s	Dec 13 '11	Dec 28 '11	Jan 27 '12	Feb 26 '12 *
Oct 30 '11 *	Nov 09 '11	Nov 14 '11	Nov 19 '11 s	Nov 29 '11	Dec 04 '11 *	Dec 14 '11	Dec 29 '11	Jan 28 '12 s	Feb 27 '12
Oct 31 '11	Nov 10 '11	Nov 15 '11	Nov 20 '11 *	Nov 30 '11	Dec 05 '11	Dec 15 '11	Dec 30 '11	Jan 29 '12 *	Feb 28 '12
Nov 01 '11	Nov 11 '11	Nov 16 '11	Nov 21 '11	Dec 01 '11	Dec 06 '11	Dec 16 '11	Dec 31 '11 s	Jan 30 '12	Feb 29 '12
Nov 02 '11	Nov 12 '11 s	Nov 17 '11	Nov 22 '11	Dec 02 '11	Dec 07 '11	Dec 17 '11 s	Jan 01 '12 *	Jan 31 '12	Mar 01 '12
Nov 03 '11	Nov 13 '11 *	Nov 18 '11	Nov 23 '11	Dec 03 '11 s	Dec 08 '11	Dec 18 '11 *	Jan 02 '12	Feb 01 '12	Mar 02 '12
Nov 04 '11	Nov 14 '11	Nov 19 '11 s	Nov 24 '11	Dec 04 '11 *	Dec 09 '11	Dec 19 '11	Jan 03 '12	Feb 02 '12	Mar 03 '12 s
Nov 05 '11 s	Nov 15 '11	Nov 20 '11 *	Nov 25 '11	Dec 05 '11	Dec 10 '11 s	Dec 20 '11	Jan 04 '12	Feb 03 '12	Mar 04 '12 *
Nov 06 '11 *	Nov 16 '11	Nov 21 '11	Nov 26 '11 s	Dec 06 '11	Dec 11 '11 *	Dec 21 '11	Jan 05 '12	Feb 04 '12 s	Mar 05 '12
Nov 07 '11	Nov 17 '11	Nov 22 '11	Nov 27 '11 *	Dec 07 '11	Dec 12 '11	Dec 22 '11	Jan 06 '12	Feb 05 '12 *	Mar 06 '12
Nov 08 '11	Nov 18 '11	Nov 23 '11	Nov 28 '11	Dec 08 '11	Dec 13 '11	Dec 23 '11	Jan 07 '12 s	Feb 06 '12	Mar 07 '12
Nov 09 '11	Nov 19 '11 s	Nov 24 '11	Nov 29 '11	Dec 09 '11	Dec 14 '11	Dec 24 '11 s	Jan 08 '12 *	Feb 07 '12	Mar 08 '12
Nov 10 '11	Nov 20 '11 *	Nov 25 '11	Nov 30 '11	Dec 10 '11 s	Dec 15 '11	Dec 25 '11 *	Jan 09 '12	Feb 08 '12	Mar 09 '12

TABLE FOR COMPUTATION OF EXPIRATION DATES

From	10 Days	15 Days	20 Days	30 Days	35 Days	45 Days	60 Days	90 Days	120 Days
Nov 11 '11	Nov 21 '11	Nov 26 '11 s	Dec 01 '11	Dec 11 '11 *	Dec 16 '11	Dec 26 '11	Jan 10 '12	Feb 09 '12	Mar 10 '12 s
Nov 12 '11 s	Nov 22 '11	Nov 27 '11 *	Dec 02 '11	Dec 12 '11	Dec 17 '11 s	Dec 27 '11	Jan 11 '12	Feb 10 '12	Mar 11 '12 *
Nov 13 '11 *	Nov 23 '11	Nov 28 '11	Dec 03 '11 s	Dec 13 '11	Dec 18 '11 *	Dec 28 '11	Jan 12 '12	Feb 11 '12 s	Mar 12 '12
Nov 14 '11	Nov 24 '11	Nov 29 '11	Dec 04 '11 *	Dec 14 '11	Dec 19 '11	Dec 29 '11	Jan 13 '12	Feb 12 '12 *	Mar 13 '12
Nov 15 '11	Nov 25 '11	Nov 30 '11	Dec 05 '11	Dec 15 '11	Dec 20 '11	Dec 30 '11	Jan 14 '12 s	Feb 13 '12	Mar 14 '12
Nov 16 '11	Nov 26 '11 s	Dec 01 '11	Dec 06 '11	Dec 16 '11	Dec 21 '11	Dec 31 '11 s	Jan 15 '12 *	Feb 14 '12	Mar 15 '12
Nov 17 '11	Nov 27 '11 *	Dec 02 '11	Dec 07 '11	Dec 17 '11 s	Dec 22 '11	Jan 01 '12 *	Jan 16 '12	Feb 15 '12	Mar 16 '12
Nov 18 '11	Nov 28 '11	Dec 03 '11 s	Dec 08 '11	Dec 18 '11 *	Dec 23 '11	Jan 02 '12	Jan 17 '12	Feb 16 '12	Mar 17 '12 s
Nov 19 '11 s	Nov 29 '11	Dec 04 '11 *	Dec 09 '11	Dec 19 '11	Dec 24 '11 s	Jan 03 '12	Jan 18 '12	Feb 17 '12	Mar 18 '12 *
Nov 20 '11 *	Nov 30 '11	Dec 05 '11	Dec 10 '11 s	Dec 20 '11	Dec 25 '11 *	Jan 04 '12	Jan 19 '12	Feb 18 '12 s	Mar 19 '12
Nov 21 '11	Dec 01 '11	Dec 06 '11	Dec 11 '11 *	Dec 21 '11	Dec 26 '11	Jan 05 '12	Jan 20 '12	Feb 19 '12 *	Mar 20 '12
Nov 22 '11	Dec 02 '11	Dec 07 '11	Dec 12 '11	Dec 22 '11	Dec 27 '11	Jan 06 '12	Jan 21 '12 s	Feb 20 '12	Mar 21 '12
Nov 23 '11	Dec 03 '11 s	Dec 08 '11	Dec 13 '11	Dec 23 '11	Dec 28 '11	Jan 07 '12 s	Jan 22 '12 *	Feb 21 '12	Mar 22 '12
Nov 24 '11	Dec 04 '11 *	Dec 09 '11	Dec 14 '11	Dec 24 '11 s	Dec 29 '11	Jan 08 '12 *	Jan 23 '12	Feb 22 '12	Mar 23 '12
Nov 25 '11	Dec 05 '11	Dec 10 '11 s	Dec 15 '11	Dec 25 '11 *	Dec 30 '11	Jan 09 '12	Jan 24 '12	Feb 23 '12	Mar 24 '12 s
Nov 26 '11 s	Dec 06 '11	Dec 11 '11 *	Dec 16 '11	Dec 26 '11	Dec 31 '11 s	Jan 10 '12	Jan 25 '12	Feb 24 '12	Mar 25 '12 *
Nov 27 '11 *	Dec 07 '11	Dec 12 '11	Dec 17 '11 s	Dec 27 '11	Jan 01 '12 *	Jan 11 '12	Jan 26 '12	Feb 25 '12 s	Mar 26 '12
Nov 28 '11	Dec 08 '11	Dec 13 '11	Dec 18 '11 *	Dec 28 '11	Jan 02 '12	Jan 12 '12	Jan 27 '12	Feb 26 '12 *	Mar 27 '12
Nov 29 '11	Dec 09 '11	Dec 14 '11	Dec 19 '11	Dec 29 '11	Jan 03 '12	Jan 13 '12	Jan 28 '12 s	Feb 27 '12	Mar 28 '12
Nov 30 '11	Dec 10 '11 s	Dec 15 '11	Dec 20 '11	Dec 30 '11	Jan 04 '12	Jan 14 '12 s	Jan 29 '12 *	Feb 28 '12	Mar 29 '12
Dec 01 '11	Dec 11 '11 *	Dec 16 '11	Dec 21 '11	Dec 31 '11 s	Jan 05 '12	Jan 15 '12 *	Jan 30 '12	Feb 29 '12	Mar 30 '12
Dec 02 '11	Dec 12 '11	Dec 17 '11 s	Dec 22 '11	Jan 01 '12 *	Jan 06 '12	Jan 16 '12	Jan 31 '12	Mar 01 '12	Mar 31 '12 s
Dec 03 '11 s	Dec 13 '11	Dec 18 '11 *	Dec 23 '11	Jan 02 '12	Jan 07 '12 s	Jan 17 '12	Feb 01 '12	Mar 02 '12	Apr 01 '12 *
Dec 04 '11 *	Dec 14 '11	Dec 19 '11	Dec 24 '11 s	Jan 03 '12	Jan 08 '12 *	Jan 18 '12	Feb 02 '12	Mar 03 '12 s	Apr 02 '12
Dec 05 '11	Dec 15 '11	Dec 20 '11	Dec 25 '11 *	Jan 04 '12	Jan 09 '12	Jan 19 '12	Feb 03 '12	Mar 04 '12 *	Apr 03 '12
Dec 06 '11	Dec 16 '11	Dec 21 '11	Dec 26 '11	Jan 05 '12	Jan 10 '12	Jan 20 '12	Feb 04 '12 s	Mar 05 '12	Apr 04 '12
Dec 07 '11	Dec 17 '11 s	Dec 22 '11	Dec 27 '11	Jan 06 '12	Jan 11 '12	Jan 21 '12 s	Feb 05 '12 *	Mar 06 '12	Apr 05 '12
Dec 08 '11	Dec 18 '11 *	Dec 23 '11	Dec 28 '11	Jan 07 '12 s	Jan 12 '12	Jan 22 '12 *	Feb 06 '12	Mar 07 '12	Apr 06 '12
Dec 09 '11	Dec 19 '11	Dec 24 '11 s	Dec 29 '11	Jan 08 '12 *	Jan 13 '12	Jan 23 '12	Feb 07 '12	Mar 08 '12	Apr 07 '12 s
Dec 10 '11 s	Dec 20 '11	Dec 25 '11 *	Dec 30 '11	Jan 09 '12	Jan 14 '12 s	Jan 24 '12	Feb 08 '12	Mar 09 '12	Apr 08 '12 *
Dec 11 '11 *	Dec 21 '11	Dec 26 '11	Dec 31 '11 s	Jan 10 '12	Jan 15 '12 *	Jan 25 '12	Feb 09 '12	Mar 10 '12 s	Apr 09 '12
Dec 12 '11	Dec 22 '11	Dec 27 '11	Jan 01 '12 *	Jan 11 '12	Jan 16 '12	Jan 26 '12	Feb 10 '12	Mar 11 '12 *	Apr 10 '12
Dec 13 '11	Dec 23 '11	Dec 28 '11	Jan 02 '12	Jan 12 '12	Jan 17 '12	Jan 27 '12	Feb 11 '12 s	Mar 12 '12	Apr 11 '12
Dec 14 '11	Dec 24 '11 s	Dec 29 '11	Jan 03 '12	Jan 13 '12	Jan 18 '12	Jan 28 '12 s	Feb 12 '12 *	Mar 13 '12	Apr 12 '12
Dec 15 '11	Dec 25 '11 *	Dec 30 '11	Jan 04 '12	Jan 14 '12 s	Jan 19 '12	Jan 29 '12 *	Feb 13 '12	Mar 14 '12	Apr 13 '12
Dec 16 '11	Dec 26 '11	Dec 31 '11 s	Jan 05 '12	Jan 15 '12 *	Jan 20 '12	Jan 30 '12	Feb 14 '12	Mar 15 '12	Apr 14 '12 s
Dec 17 '11 s	Dec 27 '11	Jan 01 '12 *	Jan 06 '12	Jan 16 '12	Jan 21 '12 s	Jan 31 '12	Feb 15 '12	Mar 16 '12	Apr 15 '12 *
Dec 18 '11 *	Dec 28 '11	Jan 02 '12	Jan 07 '12 s	Jan 17 '12	Jan 22 '12 *	Feb 01 '12	Feb 16 '12	Mar 17 '12 s	Apr 16 '12
Dec 19 '11	Dec 29 '11	Jan 03 '12	Jan 08 '12 *	Jan 18 '12	Jan 23 '12	Feb 02 '12	Feb 17 '12	Mar 18 '12 *	Apr 17 '12
Dec 20 '11	Dec 30 '11	Jan 04 '12	Jan 09 '12	Jan 19 '12	Jan 24 '12	Feb 03 '12	Feb 18 '12 s	Mar 19 '12	Apr 18 '12
Dec 21 '11	Dec 31 '11 s	Jan 05 '12	Jan 10 '12	Jan 20 '12	Jan 25 '12	Feb 04 '12 s	Feb 19 '12 *	Mar 20 '12	Apr 19 '12
Dec 22 '11	Jan 01 '12 *	Jan 06 '12	Jan 11 '12	Jan 21 '12 s	Jan 26 '12	Feb 05 '12 *	Feb 20 '12	Mar 21 '12	Apr 20 '12
Dec 23 '11	Jan 02 '12	Jan 07 '12 s	Jan 12 '12	Jan 22 '12 *	Jan 27 '12	Feb 06 '12	Feb 21 '12	Mar 22 '12	Apr 21 '12 s
Dec 24 '11 s	Jan 03 '12	Jan 08 '12 *	Jan 13 '12	Jan 23 '12	Jan 28 '12 s	Feb 07 '12	Feb 22 '12	Mar 23 '12	Apr 22 '12 *
Dec 25 '11 *	Jan 04 '12	Jan 09 '12	Jan 14 '12 s	Jan 24 '12	Jan 29 '12 *	Feb 08 '12	Feb 23 '12	Mar 24 '12 s	Apr 23 '12
Dec 26 '11	Jan 05 '12	Jan 10 '12	Jan 15 '12 *	Jan 25 '12	Jan 30 '12	Feb 09 '12	Feb 24 '12	Mar 25 '12 *	Apr 24 '12
Dec 27 '11	Jan 06 '12	Jan 11 '12	Jan 16 '12	Jan 26 '12	Jan 31 '12	Feb 10 '12	Feb 25 '12 s	Mar 26 '12	Apr 25 '12
Dec 28 '11	Jan 07 '12 s	Jan 12 '12	Jan 17 '12	Jan 27 '12	Feb 01 '12	Feb 11 '12 s	Feb 26 '12 *	Mar 27 '12	Apr 26 '12
Dec 29 '11	Jan 08 '12 *	Jan 13 '12	Jan 18 '12	Jan 28 '12 s	Feb 02 '12	Feb 12 '12 *	Feb 27 '12	Mar 28 '12	Apr 27 '12
Dec 30 '11	Jan 09 '12	Jan 14 '12 s	Jan 19 '12	Jan 29 '12 *	Feb 03 '12	Feb 13 '12	Feb 28 '12	Mar 29 '12	Apr 28 '12 s
Dec 31 '11 s	Jan 10 '12	Jan 15 '12 *	Jan 20 '12	Jan 30 '12	Feb 04 '12 s	Feb 14 '12	Feb 29 '12	Mar 30 '12	Apr 29 '12 *

TABLE FOR DETERMINING A FUTURE DATE
FOR ANY GIVEN NUMBER OF DAYS AFTER A STARTING DATE

HOW TO USE THIS TABLE:

Find your starting date. Moving down, a box below your starting date will add 20 days to your starting date. Two boxes down adds 40 days. Three boxes down adds 60 days. Four boxes down adds 80 days.

Each box towards the right adds one more day. Each box towards the left subtracts one less day.

For example, 120 days from January 3, 2011 is May 3, 2011, and 136 days from January 3, 2011 is May 19, 2011, and 139 days from January 3, 2011 is May 22, 2011.

2011	January	1	2	3	4	5	6	7	8	9	10	11	12	13	14	15	16	17	18	19	20
	January/February	21	22	23	24	25	26	27	28	29	30	31	1	2	3	4	5	6	7	8	9
	February/March	10	11	12	13	14	15	16	17	18	19	20	21	22	23	24	25	26	27	28	1
	March	2	3	4	5	6	7	8	9	10	11	12	13	14	15	16	17	18	19	20	21
	March/April	22	23	24	25	26	27	28	29	30	31	1	2	3	4	5	6	7	8	9	10
	April	11	12	13	14	15	16	17	18	19	20	21	22	23	24	25	26	27	28	29	30
	May	1	2	3	4	5	6	7	8	9	10	11	12	13	14	15	16	17	18	19	20
	May/June	21	22	23	24	25	26	27	28	29	30	31	1	2	3	4	5	6	7	8	9
	June	10	11	12	13	14	15	16	17	18	19	20	21	22	23	24	25	26	27	28	29
	June/July	30	1	2	3	4	5	6	7	8	9	10	11	12	13	14	15	16	17	18	19
	July/August	20	21	22	23	24	25	26	27	28	29	30	31	1	2	3	4	5	6	7	8
	August	9	10	11	12	13	14	15	16	17	18	19	20	21	22	23	24	25	26	27	28
	August/September	29	30	31	1	2	3	4	5	6	7	8	9	10	11	12	13	14	15	16	17
	September/October	18	19	20	21	22	23	24	25	26	27	28	29	30	1	2	3	4	5	6	7
	October	8	9	10	11	12	13	14	15	16	17	18	19	20	21	22	23	24	25	26	27
	October/November	28	29	30	31	1	2	3	4	5	6	7	8	9	10	11	12	13	14	15	16
	November/December	17	18	19	20	21	22	23	24	25	26	27	28	29	30	1	2	3	4	5	6
	December	7	8	9	10	11	12	13	14	15	16	17	18	19	20	21	22	23	24	25	26
2012	December/January 2012	27	28	29	30	31	1	2	3	4	5	6	7	8	9	10	11	12	13	14	15
	January/February	16	17	18	19	20	21	22	23	24	25	26	27	28	29	30	31	1	2	3	4
	February	5	6	7	8	9	10	11	12	13	14	15	16	17	18	19	20	21	22	23	24
	February/March	25	26	27	28	29	1	2	3	4	5	6	7	8	9	10	11	12	13	14	15
	March/April	16	17	18	19	20	21	22	23	24	25	26	27	28	29	30	31	1	2	3	4
	April	5	6	7	8	9	10	11	12	13	14	15	16	17	18	19	20	21	22	23	24
	April/May	25	26	27	28	29	30	1	2	3	4	5	6	7	8	9	10	11	12	13	14
	May/June	15	16	17	18	19	20	21	22	23	24	25	26	27	28	29	30	31	1	2	3
	June	4	5	6	7	8	9	10	11	12	13	14	15	16	17	18	19	20	21	22	23
	June/July	24	25	26	27	28	29	30	1	2	3	4	5	6	7	8	9	10	11	12	13
	July/August	14	15	16	17	18	19	20	21	22	23	24	25	26	27	28	29	30	31	1	2
	August	3	4	5	6	7	8	9	10	11	12	13	14	15	16	17	18	19	20	21	22
	August/September	23	24	25	26	27	28	29	30	31	1	2	3	4	5	6	7	8	9	10	11
	September/October	12	13	14	15	16	17	18	19	20	21	22	23	24	25	26	27	28	29	30	1
	October	2	3	4	5	6	7	8	9	10	11	12	13	14	15	16	17	18	19	20	21
	October/November	22	23	24	25	26	27	28	29	30	31	1	2	3	4	5	6	7	8	9	10
	November	11	12	13	14	15	16	17	18	19	20	21	22	23	24	25	26	27	28	29	30
	December	1	2	3	4	5	6	7	8	9	10	11	12	13	14	15	16	17	18	19	20
	December/January 2013	21	22	23	24	25	26	27	28	29	30	31	1	2	3	4	5	6	7	8	9

2010

JANUARY 2010

S	M	T	W	T	F	S
					1	2
3	4	5	6	7	8	9
10	11	12	13	14	15	16
17	18	19	20	21	22	23
24	25	26	27	28	29	30
31						

FEBRUARY 2010

S	M	T	W	T	F	S
	1	2	3	4	5	6
7	8	9	10	11	12	13
14	15	16	17	18	19	20
21	22	23	24	25	26	27
28						

MARCH 2010

S	M	T	W	T	F	S
	1	2	3	4	5	6
7	8	9	10	11	12	13
14	15	16	17	18	19	20
21	22	23	24	25	26	27
28	29	30	31			

APRIL 2010

S	M	T	W	T	F	S
				1	2	3
4	5	6	7	8	9	10
11	12	13	14	15	16	17
18	19	20	21	22	23	24
25	26	27	28	29	30	

MAY 2010

S	M	T	W	T	F	S
						1
2	3	4	5	6	7	8
9	10	11	12	13	14	15
16	17	18	19	20	21	22
23	24	25	26	27	28	29
30	31					

JUNE 2010

S	M	T	W	T	F	S
		1	2	3	4	5
6	7	8	9	10	11	12
13	14	15	16	17	18	19
20	21	22	23	24	25	26
27	28	29	30			

JULY 2010

S	M	T	W	T	F	S
				1	2	3
4	5	6	7	8	9	10
11	12	13	14	15	16	17
18	19	20	21	22	23	24
25	26	27	28	29	30	31

AUGUST 2010

S	M	T	W	T	F	S
1	2	3	4	5	6	7
8	9	10	11	12	13	14
15	16	17	18	19	20	21
22	23	24	25	26	27	28
29	30	31				

SEPTEMBER 2010

S	M	T	W	T	F	S
			1	2	3	4
5	6	7	8	9	10	11
12	13	14	15	16	17	18
19	20	21	22	23	24	25
26	27	28	29	30		

OCTOBER 2010

S	M	T	W	T	F	S
					1	2
3	4	5	6	7	8	9
10	11	12	13	14	15	16
17	18	19	20	21	22	23
24	25	26	27	28	29	30
31						

NOVEMBER 2010

S	M	T	W	T	F	S
	1	2	3	4	5	6
7	8	9	10	11	12	13
14	15	16	17	18	19	20
21	22	23	24	25	26	27
28	29	30				

DECEMBER 2010

S	M	T	W	T	F	S
			1	2	3	4
5	6	7	8	9	10	11
12	13	14	15	16	17	18
19	20	21	22	23	24	25
26	27	28	29	30	31	

2011

JANUARY 2011

S	M	T	W	T	F	S
						1
2	3	4	5	6	7	8
9	10	11	12	13	14	15
16	17	18	19	20	21	22
23	24	25	26	27	28	29
30	31					

FEBRUARY 2011

S	M	T	W	T	F	S
		1	2	3	4	5
6	7	8	9	10	11	12
13	14	15	16	17	18	19
20	21	22	23	24	25	26
27	28					

MARCH 2011

S	M	T	W	T	F	S
		1	2	3	4	5
6	7	8	9	10	11	12
13	14	15	16	17	18	19
20	21	22	23	24	25	26
27	28	29	30	31		

APRIL 2011

S	M	T	W	T	F	S
					1	2
3	4	5	6	7	8	9
10	11	12	13	14	15	16
17	18	19	20	21	22	23
24	25	26	27	28	29	30

MAY 2011

S	M	T	W	T	F	S
1	2	3	4	5	6	7
8	9	10	11	12	13	14
15	16	17	18	19	20	21
22	23	24	25	26	27	28
29	30	31				

JUNE 2011

S	M	T	W	T	F	S
			1	2	3	4
5	6	7	8	9	10	11
12	13	14	15	16	17	18
19	20	21	22	23	24	25
26	27	28	29	30		

JULY 2011

S	M	T	W	T	F	S
					1	2
3	4	5	6	7	8	9
10	11	12	13	14	15	16
17	18	19	20	21	22	23
24	25	26	27	28	29	30
31						

AUGUST 2011

S	M	T	W	T	F	S
	1	2	3	4	5	6
7	8	9	10	11	12	13
14	15	16	17	18	19	20
21	22	23	24	25	26	27
28	29	30	31			

SEPTEMBER 2011

S	M	T	W	T	F	S
				1	2	3
4	5	6	7	8	9	10
11	12	13	14	15	16	17
18	19	20	21	22	23	24
25	26	27	28	29	30	

OCTOBER 2011

S	M	T	W	T	F	S
						1
2	3	4	5	6	7	8
9	10	11	12	13	14	15
16	17	18	19	20	21	22
23	24	25	26	27	28	29
30	31					

NOVEMBER 2011

S	M	T	W	T	F	S
		1	2	3	4	5
6	7	8	9	10	11	12
13	14	15	16	17	18	19
20	21	22	23	24	25	26
27	28	29	30			

DECEMBER 2011

S	M	T	W	T	F	S
				1	2	3
4	5	6	7	8	9	10
11	12	13	14	15	16	17
18	19	20	21	22	23	24
25	26	27	28	29	30	31

2012

JANUARY 2012

S	M	T	W	T	F	S
1	2	3	4	5	6	7
8	9	10	11	12	13	14
15	16	17	18	19	20	21
22	23	24	25	26	27	28
29	30	31				

FEBRUARY 2012

S	M	T	W	T	F	S
			1	2	3	4
5	6	7	8	9	10	11
12	13	14	15	16	17	18
19	20	21	22	23	24	25
26	27	28	29			

MARCH 2012

S	M	T	W	T	F	S
				1	2	3
4	5	6	7	8	9	10
11	12	13	14	15	16	17
18	19	20	21	22	23	24
25	26	27	28	29	30	31

APRIL 2012

S	M	T	W	T	F	S
1	2	3	4	5	6	7
8	9	10	11	12	13	14
15	16	17	18	19	20	21
22	23	24	25	26	27	28
29	30					

MAY 2012

S	M	T	W	T	F	S
		1	2	3	4	5
6	7	8	9	10	11	12
13	14	15	16	17	18	19
20	21	22	23	24	25	26
27	28	29	30	31		

JUNE 2012

S	M	T	W	T	F	S
					1	2
3	4	5	6	7	8	9
10	11	12	13	14	15	16
17	18	19	20	21	22	23
24	25	26	27	28	29	30

JULY 2012

S	M	T	W	T	F	S
1	2	3	4	5	6	7
8	9	10	11	12	13	14
15	16	17	18	19	20	21
22	23	24	25	26	27	28
29	30	31				

AUGUST 2012

S	M	T	W	T	F	S
			1	2	3	4
5	6	7	8	9	10	11
12	13	14	15	16	17	18
19	20	21	22	23	24	25
26	27	28	29	30	31	

SEPTEMBER 2012

S	M	T	W	T	F	S
						1
2	3	4	5	6	7	8
9	10	11	12	13	14	15
16	17	18	19	20	21	22
23	24	25	26	27	28	29
30						

OCTOBER 2012

S	M	T	W	T	F	S
	1	2	3	4	5	6
7	8	9	10	11	12	13
14	15	16	17	18	19	20
21	22	23	24	25	26	27
28	29	30	31			

NOVEMBER 2012

S	M	T	W	T	F	S
				1	2	3
4	5	6	7	8	9	10
11	12	13	14	15	16	17
18	19	20	21	22	23	24
25	26	27	28	29	30	

DECEMBER 2012

S	M	T	W	T	F	S
						1
2	3	4	5	6	7	8
9	10	11	12	13	14	15
16	17	18	19	20	21	22
23	24	25	26	27	28	29
30	31					

1st day
364 days to come

SATURDAY, JANUARY 1, 2011

1st Saturday
of January

New Year's Day

2nd day
363 days to come

SUNDAY, JANUARY 2, 2011

1st Sunday
of January

December 2010

S	M	T	W	T	F	S
			1	2	3	4
5	6	7	8	9	10	11
12	13	14	15	16	17	18
19	20	21	22	23	24	25
26	27	28	29	30	31	

January 2011

S	M	T	W	T	F	S
						1
2	3	4	5	6	7	8
9	10	11	12	13	14	15
16	17	18	19	20	21	22
23	24	25	26	27	28	29
30	31					

February 2011

S	M	T	W	T	F	S
		1	2	3	4	5
6	7	8	9	10	11	12
13	14	15	16	17	18	19
20	21	22	23	24	25	26
27	28					

3rd day
362 days to come

MONDAY, JANUARY 3, 2011

1st Monday
of January

TUESDAY, JANUARY 4, 2011

WEDNESDAY, JANUARY 5, 2011

THURSDAY, JANUARY 6, 2011

FRIDAY, JANUARY 7, 2011

8th day
357 days to come

SATURDAY, JANUARY 8, 2011

2nd Saturday
of January

9th day
356 days to come

SUNDAY, JANUARY 9, 2011

2nd Sunday
of January

December 2010

S	M	T	W	T	F	S
			1	2	3	4
5	6	7	8	9	10	11
12	13	14	15	16	17	18
19	20	21	22	23	24	25
26	27	28	29	30	31	

January 2011

S	M	T	W	T	F	S
						1
2	3	4	5	6	7	8
9	10	11	12	13	14	15
16	17	18	19	20	21	22
23	24	25	26	27	28	29
30	31					

February 2011

S	M	T	W	T	F	S
		1	2	3	4	5
6	7	8	9	10	11	12
13	14	15	16	17	18	19
20	21	22	23	24	25	26
27	28					

MONDAY, JANUARY 10, 2011

TUESDAY, JANUARY 11, 2011

12th day
353 days to come

WEDNESDAY, JANUARY 12, 2011

2nd Wednesday
of January

THURSDAY, JANUARY 13, 2011

FRIDAY, JANUARY 14, 2011

15th day
350 days to come

SATURDAY, JANUARY 15, 2011

3rd Saturday
of January

16th day
349 days to come

SUNDAY, JANUARY 16, 2011

3rd Sunday
of January

December 2010						
S	M	T	W	T	F	S
			1	2	3	4
5	6	7	8	9	10	11
12	13	14	15	16	17	18
19	20	21	22	23	24	25
26	27	28	29	30	31	

January 2011						
S	M	T	W	T	F	S
						1
2	3	4	5	6	7	8
9	10	11	12	13	14	15
16	17	18	19	20	21	22
23	24	25	26	27	28	29
30	31					

February 2011						
S	M	T	W	T	F	S
		1	2	3	4	5
6	7	8	9	10	11	12
13	14	15	16	17	18	19
20	21	22	23	24	25	26
27	28					

MONDAY, JANUARY 17, 2011

Birthday of Martin Luther King Jr., observed

TUESDAY, JANUARY 18, 2011

Final Payment on Estimated Federal Income Tax Due Unless Return in Lieu of Final Declaration is Filed by January 31

WEDNESDAY, JANUARY 19, 2011

Robert E. Lee's Birthday

THURSDAY, JANUARY 20, 2011

FRIDAY, JANUARY 21, 2011

22nd day
343 days to come

SATURDAY, JANUARY 22, 2011

4th Saturday
of January

23rd day
342 days to come

SUNDAY, JANUARY 23, 2011

4th Sunday
of January

December 2010

S	M	T	W	T	F	S
			1	2	3	4
5	6	7	8	9	10	11
12	13	14	15	16	17	18
19	20	21	22	23	24	25
26	27	28	29	30	31	

January 2011

S	M	T	W	T	F	S
						1
2	3	4	5	6	7	8
9	10	11	12	13	14	15
16	17	18	19	20	21	22
23	24	25	26	27	28	29
30	31					

February 2011

S	M	T	W	T	F	S
		1	2	3	4	5
6	7	8	9	10	11	12
13	14	15	16	17	18	19
20	21	22	23	24	25	26
27	28					

MONDAY, JANUARY 24, 2011

TUESDAY, JANUARY 25, 2011

WEDNESDAY, JANUARY 26, 2011

THURSDAY, JANUARY 27, 2011

FRIDAY, JANUARY 28, 2011

29th day
336 days to come

SATURDAY, JANUARY 29, 2011

5th Saturday
of January

30th day
335 days to come

SUNDAY, JANUARY 30, 2011

5th Sunday
of January

December 2010

S	M	T	W	T	F	S
			1	2	3	4
5	6	7	8	9	10	11
12	13	14	15	16	17	18
19	20	21	22	23	24	25
26	27	28	29	30	31	

January 2011

S	M	T	W	T	F	S
						1
2	3	4	5	6	7	8
9	10	11	12	13	14	15
16	17	18	19	20	21	22
23	24	25	26	27	28	29
30	31					

February 2011

S	M	T	W	T	F	S
		1	2	3	4	5
6	7	8	9	10	11	12
13	14	15	16	17	18	19
20	21	22	23	24	25	26
27	28					

31st day
334 days to come

MONDAY, JANUARY 31, 2011

5th Monday
of January

Quarterly Form 941 Return Due

Federal Unemployment Form 940 Due for 2010

TUESDAY, FEBRUARY 1, 2011

WEDNESDAY, FEBRUARY 2, 2011

THURSDAY, FEBRUARY 3, 2011

FRIDAY, FEBRUARY 4, 2011

36th day
329 days to come

SATURDAY, FEBRUARY 5, 2011

1st Saturday
of February

37th day
328 days to come

SUNDAY, FEBRUARY 6, 2011

1st Sunday
of February

January 2011

S	M	T	W	T	F	S
						1
2	3	4	5	6	7	8
9	10	11	12	13	14	15
16	17	18	19	20	21	22
23	24	25	26	27	28	29
30	31					

February 2011

S	M	T	W	T	F	S
		1	2	3	4	5
6	7	8	9	10	11	12
13	14	15	16	17	18	19
20	21	22	23	24	25	26
27	28					

March 2011

S	M	T	W	T	F	S
		1	2	3	4	5
6	7	8	9	10	11	12
13	14	15	16	17	18	19
20	21	22	23	24	25	26
27	28	29	30	31		

MONDAY, FEBRUARY 7, 2011

TUESDAY, FEBRUARY 8, 2011

WEDNESDAY, FEBRUARY 9, 2011

THURSDAY, FEBRUARY 10, 2011

FRIDAY, FEBRUARY 11, 2011

43rd day
322 days to come

SATURDAY, FEBRUARY 12, 2011

2nd Saturday
of February

Lincoln's Birthday

44th day
321 days to come

SUNDAY, FEBRUARY 13, 2011

2nd Sunday
of February

January 2011

S	M	T	W	T	F	S
						1
2	3	4	5	6	7	8
9	10	11	12	13	14	15
16	17	18	19	20	21	22
23	24	25	26	27	28	29
30	31					

February 2011

S	M	T	W	T	F	S
		1	2	3	4	5
6	7	8	9	10	11	12
13	14	15	16	17	18	19
20	21	22	23	24	25	26
27	28					

March 2011

S	M	T	W	T	F	S
		1	2	3	4	5
6	7	8	9	10	11	12
13	14	15	16	17	18	19
20	21	22	23	24	25	26
27	28	29	30	31		

MONDAY, FEBRUARY 14, 2011

Valentine's Day

TUESDAY, FEBRUARY 15, 2011

Susan B. Anthony's Birthday

WEDNESDAY, FEBRUARY 16, 2011

THURSDAY, FEBRUARY 17, 2011

FRIDAY, FEBRUARY 18, 2011

50th day
315 days to come

SATURDAY, FEBRUARY 19, 2011

3rd Saturday
of February

51st day
314 days to come

SUNDAY, FEBRUARY 20, 2011

3rd Sunday
of February

January 2011

S	M	T	W	T	F	S
						1
2	3	4	5	6	7	8
9	10	11	12	13	14	15
16	17	18	19	20	21	22
23	24	25	26	27	28	29
30	31					

February 2011

S	M	T	W	T	F	S
		1	2	3	4	5
6	7	8	9	10	11	12
13	14	15	16	17	18	19
20	21	22	23	24	25	26
27	28					

March 2011

S	M	T	W	T	F	S
		1	2	3	4	5
6	7	8	9	10	11	12
13	14	15	16	17	18	19
20	21	22	23	24	25	26
27	28	29	30	31		

MONDAY, FEBRUARY 21, 2011

Washington's Birthday observed (called Presidents' Day in most states)

TUESDAY, FEBRUARY 22, 2011

WEDNESDAY, FEBRUARY 23, 2011

55th day
310 days to come

THURSDAY, FEBRUARY 24, 2011

4th Thursday
of February

FRIDAY, FEBRUARY 25, 2011

57th day
308 days to come

SATURDAY, FEBRUARY 26, 2011

4th Saturday of February

58th day
307 days to come

SUNDAY, FEBRUARY 27, 2011

4th Sunday of February

January 2011

S	M	T	W	T	F	S
						1
2	3	4	5	6	7	8
9	10	11	12	13	14	15
16	17	18	19	20	21	22
23	24	25	26	27	28	29
30	31					

February 2011

S	M	T	W	T	F	S
		1	2	3	4	5
6	7	8	9	10	11	12
13	14	15	16	17	18	19
20	21	22	23	24	25	26
27	28					

March 2011

S	M	T	W	T	F	S
		1	2	3	4	5
6	7	8	9	10	11	12
13	14	15	16	17	18	19
20	21	22	23	24	25	26
27	28	29	30	31		

MONDAY, FEBRUARY 28, 2011

TUESDAY, MARCH 1, 2011

WEDNESDAY, MARCH 2, 2011

THURSDAY, MARCH 3, 2011

FRIDAY, MARCH 4, 2011

64th day
301 days to come

SATURDAY, MARCH 5, 2011

1st Saturday
of March

65th day
300 days to come

SUNDAY, MARCH 6, 2011

1st Sunday
of March

February 2011

S	M	T	W	T	F	S
		1	2	3	4	5
6	7	8	9	10	11	12
13	14	15	16	17	18	19
20	21	22	23	24	25	26
27	28					

March 2011

S	M	T	W	T	F	S
		1	2	3	4	5
6	7	8	9	10	11	12
13	14	15	16	17	18	19
20	21	22	23	24	25	26
27	28	29	30	31		

April 2011

S	M	T	W	T	F	S
					1	2
3	4	5	6	7	8	9
10	11	12	13	14	15	16
17	18	19	20	21	22	23
24	25	26	27	28	29	30

MONDAY, MARCH 7, 2011

TUESDAY, MARCH 8, 2011

Shrove Tuesday

WEDNESDAY, MARCH 9, 2011

Ash Wednesday

THURSDAY, MARCH 10, 2011

FRIDAY, MARCH 11, 2011

71st day
294 days to come

SATURDAY, MARCH 12, 2011

2nd Saturday
of March

72nd day
293 days to come

SUNDAY, MARCH 13, 2011

2nd Sunday
of March

Daylight Saving Time Begins

February 2011						
S	M	T	W	T	F	S
		1	2	3	4	5
6	7	8	9	10	11	12
13	14	15	16	17	18	19
20	21	22	23	24	25	26
27	28					

March 2011						
S	M	T	W	T	F	S
		1	2	3	4	5
6	7	8	9	10	11	12
13	14	15	16	17	18	19
20	21	22	23	24	25	26
27	28	29	30	31		

April 2011						
S	M	T	W	T	F	S
					1	2
3	4	5	6	7	8	9
10	11	12	13	14	15	16
17	18	19	20	21	22	23
24	25	26	27	28	29	30

WEDNESDAY, MARCH 16, 2011

THURSDAY, MARCH 17, 2011

St. Patrick's Day

Evacuation Day (Suffolk Co., Mass.)

FRIDAY, MARCH 18, 2011

78th day
287 days to come

SATURDAY, MARCH 19, 2011

3rd Saturday
of March

79th day
286 days to come

SUNDAY, MARCH 20, 2011

3rd Sunday
of March

February 2011						
S	M	T	W	T	F	S
		1	2	3	4	5
6	7	8	9	10	11	12
13	14	15	16	17	18	19
20	21	22	23	24	25	26
27	28					

March 2011						
S	M	T	W	T	F	S
		1	2	3	4	5
6	7	8	9	10	11	12
13	14	15	16	17	18	19
20	21	22	23	24	25	26
27	28	29	30	31		

April 2011						
S	M	T	W	T	F	S
					1	2
3	4	5	6	7	8	9
10	11	12	13	14	15	16
17	18	19	20	21	22	23
24	25	26	27	28	29	30

MONDAY, MARCH 21, 2011

TUESDAY, MARCH 22, 2011

WEDNESDAY, MARCH 23, 2011

THURSDAY, MARCH 24, 2011

FRIDAY, MARCH 25, 2011

85th day
280 days to come

SATURDAY, MARCH 26, 2011

4th Saturday
of March

86th day
279 days to come

SUNDAY, MARCH 27, 2011

4th Sunday
of March

February 2011

S	M	T	W	T	F	S
		1	2	3	4	5
6	7	8	9	10	11	12
13	14	15	16	17	18	19
20	21	22	23	24	25	26
27	28					

March 2011

S	M	T	W	T	F	S
		1	2	3	4	5
6	7	8	9	10	11	12
13	14	15	16	17	18	19
20	21	22	23	24	25	26
27	28	29	30	31		

April 2011

S	M	T	W	T	F	S
					1	2
3	4	5	6	7	8	9
10	11	12	13	14	15	16
17	18	19	20	21	22	23
24	25	26	27	28	29	30

MONDAY, MARCH 28, 2011

TUESDAY, MARCH 29, 2011

WEDNESDAY, MARCH 30, 2011

THURSDAY, MARCH 31, 2011

FRIDAY, APRIL 1, 2011

92nd day
273 days to come

SATURDAY, APRIL 2, 2011

1st Saturday of April

Pascua Florida Day

93rd day
272 days to come

SUNDAY, APRIL 3, 2011

1st Sunday of April

March 2011

S	M	T	W	T	F	S
		1	2	3	4	5
6	7	8	9	10	11	12
13	14	15	16	17	18	19
20	21	22	23	24	25	26
27	28	29	30	31		

April 2011

S	M	T	W	T	F	S
					1	2
3	4	5	6	7	8	9
10	11	12	13	14	15	16
17	18	19	20	21	22	23
24	25	26	27	28	29	30

May 2011

S	M	T	W	T	F	S
1	2	3	4	5	6	7
8	9	10	11	12	13	14
15	16	17	18	19	20	21
22	23	24	25	26	27	28
29	30	31				

MONDAY, APRIL 4, 2011

TUESDAY, APRIL 5, 2011

WEDNESDAY, APRIL 6, 2011

THURSDAY, APRIL 7, 2011

FRIDAY, APRIL 8, 2011

99th day
266 days to come

SATURDAY, APRIL 9, 2011

2nd Saturday
of April

100th day
265 days to come

SUNDAY, APRIL 10, 2011

2nd Sunday
of April

March 2011

S	M	T	W	T	F	S
		1	2	3	4	5
6	7	8	9	10	11	12
13	14	15	16	17	18	19
20	21	22	23	24	25	26
27	28	29	30	31		

April 2011

S	M	T	W	T	F	S
					1	2
3	4	5	6	7	8	9
10	11	12	13	14	15	16
17	18	19	20	21	22	23
24	25	26	27	28	29	30

May 2011

S	M	T	W	T	F	S
1	2	3	4	5	6	7
8	9	10	11	12	13	14
15	16	17	18	19	20	21
22	23	24	25	26	27	28
29	30	31				

MONDAY, APRIL 11, 2011

TUESDAY, APRIL 12, 2011

WEDNESDAY, APRIL 13, 2011

THURSDAY, APRIL 14, 2011

105th day
260 days to come

FRIDAY, APRIL 15, 2011

3rd Friday
of April

Federal Income Tax Return Due

First Payment on Estimated Federal Income Tax Due

106th day
259 days to come

SATURDAY, APRIL 16, 2011

3rd Saturday
of April

107th day
258 days to come

SUNDAY, APRIL 17, 2011

3rd Sunday
of April

Palm Sunday

March 2011

S	M	T	W	T	F	S
		1	2	3	4	5
6	7	8	9	10	11	12
13	14	15	16	17	18	19
20	21	22	23	24	25	26
27	28	29	30	31		

April 2011

S	M	T	W	T	F	S
					1	2
3	4	5	6	7	8	9
10	11	12	13	14	15	16
17	18	19	20	21	22	23
24	25	26	27	28	29	30

May 2011

S	M	T	W	T	F	S
1	2	3	4	5	6	7
8	9	10	11	12	13	14
15	16	17	18	19	20	21
22	23	24	25	26	27	28
29	30	31				

MONDAY, APRIL 18, 2011

Passover Begins (Sundown)

Patriots' Day (Mass.)

TUESDAY, APRIL 19, 2011

First Day of Passover

WEDNESDAY, APRIL 20, 2011

THURSDAY, APRIL 21, 2011

FRIDAY, APRIL 22, 2011

Good Friday

113th day
252 days to come

SATURDAY, APRIL 23, 2011

4th Saturday of April

114th day
251 days to come

SUNDAY, APRIL 24, 2011

4th Sunday of April

Easter Sunday

Eastern Orthodox Easter

March 2011

S	M	T	W	T	F	S
		1	2	3	4	5
6	7	8	9	10	11	12
13	14	15	16	17	18	19
20	21	22	23	24	25	26
27	28	29	30	31		

April 2011

S	M	T	W	T	F	S
					1	2
3	4	5	6	7	8	9
10	11	12	13	14	15	16
17	18	19	20	21	22	23
24	25	26	27	28	29	30

May 2011

S	M	T	W	T	F	S
1	2	3	4	5	6	7
8	9	10	11	12	13	14
15	16	17	18	19	20	21
22	23	24	25	26	27	28
29	30	31				

MONDAY, APRIL 25, 2011

TUESDAY, APRIL 26, 2011

Confederate Memorial Day (FL, GA, MS & AL)

WEDNESDAY, APRIL 27, 2011

Administrative Assistants Day

THURSDAY, APRIL 28, 2011

FRIDAY, APRIL 29, 2011

120th day
245 days to come

SATURDAY, APRIL 30, 2011

5th Saturday of April

121st day
244 days to come

SUNDAY, MAY 1, 2011

1st Sunday of May

Law Day

April 2011						
S	M	T	W	T	F	S
					1	2
3	4	5	6	7	8	9
10	11	12	13	14	15	16
17	18	19	20	21	22	23
24	25	26	27	28	29	30

May 2011						
S	M	T	W	T	F	S
1	2	3	4	5	6	7
8	9	10	11	12	13	14
15	16	17	18	19	20	21
22	23	24	25	26	27	28
29	30	31				

June 2011						
S	M	T	W	T	F	S
			1	2	3	4
5	6	7	8	9	10	11
12	13	14	15	16	17	18
19	20	21	22	23	24	25
26	27	28	29	30		

MONDAY, MAY 2, 2011

Quarterly Form 941 Return Due

Federal Unemployment Tax Deposit Due

TUESDAY, MAY 3, 2011

124th day
241 days to come

WEDNESDAY, MAY 4, 2011

1st Wednesday
of May

THURSDAY, MAY 5, 2011

FRIDAY, MAY 6, 2011

127th day
238 days to come

SATURDAY, MAY 7, 2011

1st Saturday
of May

128th day
237 days to come

SUNDAY, MAY 8, 2011

2nd Sunday
of May

Mother's Day

April 2011

S	M	T	W	T	F	S
					1	2
3	4	5	6	7	8	9
10	11	12	13	14	15	16
17	18	19	20	21	22	23
24	25	26	27	28	29	30

May 2011

S	M	T	W	T	F	S
1	2	3	4	5	6	7
8	9	10	11	12	13	14
15	16	17	18	19	20	21
22	23	24	25	26	27	28
29	30	31				

June 2011

S	M	T	W	T	F	S
			1	2	3	4
5	6	7	8	9	10	11
12	13	14	15	16	17	18
19	20	21	22	23	24	25
26	27	28	29	30		

MONDAY, MAY 9, 2011

TUESDAY, MAY 10, 2011

WEDNESDAY, MAY 11, 2011

THURSDAY, MAY 12, 2011

FRIDAY, MAY 13, 2011

134th day
231 days to come

SATURDAY, MAY 14, 2011

2nd Saturday of May

135th day
230 days to come

SUNDAY, MAY 15, 2011

3rd Sunday of May

April 2011

S	M	T	W	T	F	S
					1	2
3	4	5	6	7	8	9
10	11	12	13	14	15	16
17	18	19	20	21	22	23
24	25	26	27	28	29	30

May 2011

S	M	T	W	T	F	S
1	2	3	4	5	6	7
8	9	10	11	12	13	14
15	16	17	18	19	20	21
22	23	24	25	26	27	28
29	30	31				

June 2011

S	M	T	W	T	F	S
			1	2	3	4
5	6	7	8	9	10	11
12	13	14	15	16	17	18
19	20	21	22	23	24	25
26	27	28	29	30		

MONDAY, MAY 16, 2011

TUESDAY, MAY 17, 2011

WEDNESDAY, MAY 18, 2011

THURSDAY, MAY 19, 2011

FRIDAY, MAY 20, 2011

141st day
224 days to come

SATURDAY, MAY 21, 2011

3rd Saturday of May

142nd day
223 days to come

SUNDAY, MAY 22, 2011

4th Sunday of May

April 2011

S	M	T	W	T	F	S
					1	2
3	4	5	6	7	8	9
10	11	12	13	14	15	16
17	18	19	20	21	22	23
24	25	26	27	28	29	30

May 2011

S	M	T	W	T	F	S
1	2	3	4	5	6	7
8	9	10	11	12	13	14
15	16	17	18	19	20	21
22	23	24	25	26	27	28
29	30	31				

June 2011

S	M	T	W	T	F	S
			1	2	3	4
5	6	7	8	9	10	11
12	13	14	15	16	17	18
19	20	21	22	23	24	25
26	27	28	29	30		

MONDAY, MAY 23, 2011

Victoria Day (Canada)

TUESDAY, MAY 24, 2011

WEDNESDAY, MAY 25, 2011

THURSDAY, MAY 26, 2011

FRIDAY, MAY 27, 2011

148th day
217 days to come

SATURDAY, MAY 28, 2011

4th Saturday
of May

149th day
216 days to come

SUNDAY, MAY 29, 2011

5th Sunday
of May

April 2011

S	M	T	W	T	F	S
					1	2
3	4	5	6	7	8	9
10	11	12	13	14	15	16
17	18	19	20	21	22	23
24	25	26	27	28	29	30

May 2011

S	M	T	W	T	F	S
1	2	3	4	5	6	7
8	9	10	11	12	13	14
15	16	17	18	19	20	21
22	23	24	25	26	27	28
29	30	31				

June 2011

S	M	T	W	T	F	S
			1	2	3	4
5	6	7	8	9	10	11
12	13	14	15	16	17	18
19	20	21	22	23	24	25
26	27	28	29	30		

MONDAY, MAY 30, 2011

Memorial Day National Observance

TUESDAY, MAY 31, 2011

WEDNESDAY, JUNE 1, 2011

THURSDAY, JUNE 2, 2011

FRIDAY, JUNE 3, 2011

Jefferson Davis's Birthday

155th day
210 days to come

SATURDAY, JUNE 4, 2011

1st Saturday
of June

156th day
209 days to come

SUNDAY, JUNE 5, 2011

1st Sunday
of June

May 2011

S	M	T	W	T	F	S
1	2	3	4	5	6	7
8	9	10	11	12	13	14
15	16	17	18	19	20	21
22	23	24	25	26	27	28
29	30	31				

June 2011

S	M	T	W	T	F	S
			1	2	3	4
5	6	7	8	9	10	11
12	13	14	15	16	17	18
19	20	21	22	23	24	25
26	27	28	29	30		

July 2011

S	M	T	W	T	F	S
					1	2
3	4	5	6	7	8	9
10	11	12	13	14	15	16
17	18	19	20	21	22	23
24	25	26	27	28	29	30
31						

MONDAY, JUNE 6, 2011

TUESDAY, JUNE 7, 2011

WEDNESDAY, JUNE 8, 2011

Shavuot (first Day of Pentecost-Jewish)

THURSDAY, JUNE 9, 2011

FRIDAY, JUNE 10, 2011

162nd day
203 days to come

SATURDAY, JUNE 11, 2011

2nd Saturday
of June

163rd day
202 days to come

SUNDAY, JUNE 12, 2011

2nd Sunday
of June

Whitsunday (Pentecost)

May 2011

S	M	T	W	T	F	S
1	2	3	4	5	6	7
8	9	10	11	12	13	14
15	16	17	18	19	20	21
22	23	24	25	26	27	28
29	30	31				

June 2011

S	M	T	W	T	F	S
			1	2	3	4
5	6	7	8	9	10	11
12	13	14	15	16	17	18
19	20	21	22	23	24	25
26	27	28	29	30		

July 2011

S	M	T	W	T	F	S
					1	2
3	4	5	6	7	8	9
10	11	12	13	14	15	16
17	18	19	20	21	22	23
24	25	26	27	28	29	30
31						

MONDAY, JUNE 13, 2011

TUESDAY, JUNE 14, 2011

Flag Day

WEDNESDAY, JUNE 15, 2011

Second Payment on Estimated Federal Income Tax Due

THURSDAY, JUNE 16, 2011

FRIDAY, JUNE 17, 2011

Bunker Hill Day (Suffolk Co., Mass.)

169th day
196 days to come

SATURDAY, JUNE 18, 2011

3rd Saturday
of June

170th day
195 days to come

SUNDAY, JUNE 19, 2011

3rd Sunday
of June

Father's Day

May 2011

S	M	T	W	T	F	S
1	2	3	4	5	6	7
8	9	10	11	12	13	14
15	16	17	18	19	20	21
22	23	24	25	26	27	28
29	30	31				

June 2011

S	M	T	W	T	F	S
			1	2	3	4
5	6	7	8	9	10	11
12	13	14	15	16	17	18
19	20	21	22	23	24	25
26	27	28	29	30		

July 2011

S	M	T	W	T	F	S
					1	2
3	4	5	6	7	8	9
10	11	12	13	14	15	16
17	18	19	20	21	22	23
24	25	26	27	28	29	30
31						

MONDAY, JUNE 20, 2011

TUESDAY, JUNE 21, 2011

WEDNESDAY, JUNE 22, 2011

THURSDAY, JUNE 23, 2011

FRIDAY, JUNE 24, 2011

176th day
189 days to come

SATURDAY, JUNE 25, 2011

4th Saturday
of June

177th day
188 days to come

SUNDAY, JUNE 26, 2011

4th Sunday
of June

May 2011

S	M	T	W	T	F	S
1	2	3	4	5	6	7
8	9	10	11	12	13	14
15	16	17	18	19	20	21
22	23	24	25	26	27	28
29	30	31				

June 2011

S	M	T	W	T	F	S
			1	2	3	4
5	6	7	8	9	10	11
12	13	14	15	16	17	18
19	20	21	22	23	24	25
26	27	28	29	30		

July 2011

S	M	T	W	T	F	S
					1	2
3	4	5	6	7	8	9
10	11	12	13	14	15	16
17	18	19	20	21	22	23
24	25	26	27	28	29	30
31						

MONDAY, JUNE 27, 2011

TUESDAY, JUNE 28, 2011

180th day
185 days to come

WEDNESDAY, JUNE 29, 2011

5th Wednesday
of June

THURSDAY, JUNE 30, 2011

FRIDAY, JULY 1, 2011

Canada Day

183rd day
182 days to come

SATURDAY, JULY 2, 2011

1st Saturday of July

184th day
181 days to come

SUNDAY, JULY 3, 2011

1st Sunday of July

June 2011

S	M	T	W	T	F	S
			1	2	3	4
5	6	7	8	9	10	11
12	13	14	15	16	17	18
19	20	21	22	23	24	25
26	27	28	29	30		

July 2011

S	M	T	W	T	F	S
					1	2
3	4	5	6	7	8	9
10	11	12	13	14	15	16
17	18	19	20	21	22	23
24	25	26	27	28	29	30
31						

August 2011

S	M	T	W	T	F	S
	1	2	3	4	5	6
7	8	9	10	11	12	13
14	15	16	17	18	19	20
21	22	23	24	25	26	27
28	29	30	31			

185th day
180 days to come

MONDAY, JULY 4, 2011

1st Monday
of July

Independence Day

TUESDAY, JULY 5, 2011

WEDNESDAY, JULY 6, 2011

THURSDAY, JULY 7, 2011

FRIDAY, JULY 8, 2011

190th day
175 days to come

SATURDAY, JULY 9, 2011

2nd Saturday of July

191st day
174 days to come

SUNDAY, JULY 10, 2011

2nd Sunday of July

June 2011

S	M	T	W	T	F	S
			1	2	3	4
5	6	7	8	9	10	11
12	13	14	15	16	17	18
19	20	21	22	23	24	25
26	27	28	29	30		

July 2011

S	M	T	W	T	F	S
					1	2
3	4	5	6	7	8	9
10	11	12	13	14	15	16
17	18	19	20	21	22	23
24	25	26	27	28	29	30
31						

August 2011

S	M	T	W	T	F	S
	1	2	3	4	5	6
7	8	9	10	11	12	13
14	15	16	17	18	19	20
21	22	23	24	25	26	27
28	29	30	31			

MONDAY, JULY 11, 2011

TUESDAY, JULY 12, 2011

WEDNESDAY, JULY 13, 2011

THURSDAY, JULY 14, 2011

FRIDAY, JULY 15, 2011

197th day
168 days to come

SATURDAY, JULY 16, 2011

3rd Saturday
of July

198th day
167 days to come

SUNDAY, JULY 17, 2011

3rd Sunday
of July

June 2011

S	M	T	W	T	F	S
			1	2	3	4
5	6	7	8	9	10	11
12	13	14	15	16	17	18
19	20	21	22	23	24	25
26	27	28	29	30		

July 2011

S	M	T	W	T	F	S
					1	2
3	4	5	6	7	8	9
10	11	12	13	14	15	16
17	18	19	20	21	22	23
24	25	26	27	28	29	30
31						

August 2011

S	M	T	W	T	F	S
	1	2	3	4	5	6
7	8	9	10	11	12	13
14	15	16	17	18	19	20
21	22	23	24	25	26	27
28	29	30	31			

MONDAY, JULY 18, 2011

TUESDAY, JULY 19, 2011

WEDNESDAY, JULY 20, 2011

THURSDAY, JULY 21, 2011

FRIDAY, JULY 22, 2011

204th day
161 days to come

SATURDAY, JULY 23, 2011

4th Saturday of July

205th day
160 days to come

SUNDAY, JULY 24, 2011

4th Sunday of July

June 2011

S	M	T	W	T	F	S
			1	2	3	4
5	6	7	8	9	10	11
12	13	14	15	16	17	18
19	20	21	22	23	24	25
26	27	28	29	30		

July 2011

S	M	T	W	T	F	S
					1	2
3	4	5	6	7	8	9
10	11	12	13	14	15	16
17	18	19	20	21	22	23
24	25	26	27	28	29	30
31						

August 2011

S	M	T	W	T	F	S
	1	2	3	4	5	6
7	8	9	10	11	12	13
14	15	16	17	18	19	20
21	22	23	24	25	26	27
28	29	30	31			

MONDAY, JULY 25, 2011

TUESDAY, JULY 26, 2011

WEDNESDAY, JULY 27, 2011

THURSDAY, JULY 28, 2011

FRIDAY, JULY 29, 2011

211th day
154 days to come

SATURDAY, JULY 30, 2011

5th Saturday
of July

212th day
153 days to come

SUNDAY, JULY 31, 2011

5th Sunday
of July

July 2011

S	M	T	W	T	F	S
					1	2
3	4	5	6	7	8	9
10	11	12	13	14	15	16
17	18	19	20	21	22	23
24	25	26	27	28	29	30
31						

August 2011

S	M	T	W	T	F	S
	1	2	3	4	5	6
7	8	9	10	11	12	13
14	15	16	17	18	19	20
21	22	23	24	25	26	27
28	29	30	31			

September 2011

S	M	T	W	T	F	S
				1	2	3
4	5	6	7	8	9	10
11	12	13	14	15	16	17
18	19	20	21	22	23	24
25	26	27	28	29	30	

MONDAY, AUGUST 1, 2011

Quarterly Form 941 Return Due

Federal Unemployment Tax Deposit Due

TUESDAY, AUGUST 2, 2011

WEDNESDAY, AUGUST 3, 2011

THURSDAY, AUGUST 4, 2011

FRIDAY, AUGUST 5, 2011

218th day
147 days to come

SATURDAY, AUGUST 6, 2011

1st Saturday
of August

219th day
146 days to come

SUNDAY, AUGUST 7, 2011

1st Sunday
of August

July 2011

S	M	T	W	T	F	S
					1	2
3	4	5	6	7	8	9
10	11	12	13	14	15	16
17	18	19	20	21	22	23
24	25	26	27	28	29	30
31						

August 2011

S	M	T	W	T	F	S
	1	2	3	4	5	6
7	8	9	10	11	12	13
14	15	16	17	18	19	20
21	22	23	24	25	26	27
28	29	30	31			

September 2011

S	M	T	W	T	F	S
				1	2	3
4	5	6	7	8	9	10
11	12	13	14	15	16	17
18	19	20	21	22	23	24
25	26	27	28	29	30	

220th day
145 days to come

MONDAY, AUGUST 8, 2011

2nd Monday
of August

TUESDAY, AUGUST 9, 2011

WEDNESDAY, AUGUST 10, 2011

THURSDAY, AUGUST 11, 2011

FRIDAY, AUGUST 12, 2011

225th day
140 days to come

SATURDAY, AUGUST 13, 2011

2nd Saturday of August

226th day
139 days to come

SUNDAY, AUGUST 14, 2011

2nd Sunday of August

July 2011

S	M	T	W	T	F	S
					1	2
3	4	5	6	7	8	9
10	11	12	13	14	15	16
17	18	19	20	21	22	23
24	25	26	27	28	29	30
31						

August 2011

S	M	T	W	T	F	S
	1	2	3	4	5	6
7	8	9	10	11	12	13
14	15	16	17	18	19	20
21	22	23	24	25	26	27
28	29	30	31			

September 2011

S	M	T	W	T	F	S
				1	2	3
4	5	6	7	8	9	10
11	12	13	14	15	16	17
18	19	20	21	22	23	24
25	26	27	28	29	30	

MONDAY, AUGUST 15, 2011

TUESDAY, AUGUST 16, 2011

WEDNESDAY, AUGUST 17, 2011

THURSDAY, AUGUST 18, 2011

FRIDAY, AUGUST 19, 2011

232nd day
133 days to come

SATURDAY, AUGUST 20, 2011

3rd Saturday
of August

233rd day
132 days to come

SUNDAY, AUGUST 21, 2011

3rd Sunday
of August

July 2011

S	M	T	W	T	F	S
					1	2
3	4	5	6	7	8	9
10	11	12	13	14	15	16
17	18	19	20	21	22	23
24	25	26	27	28	29	30
31						

August 2011

S	M	T	W	T	F	S
	1	2	3	4	5	6
7	8	9	10	11	12	13
14	15	16	17	18	19	20
21	22	23	24	25	26	27
28	29	30	31			

September 2011

S	M	T	W	T	F	S
				1	2	3
4	5	6	7	8	9	10
11	12	13	14	15	16	17
18	19	20	21	22	23	24
25	26	27	28	29	30	

MONDAY, AUGUST 22, 2011

TUESDAY, AUGUST 23, 2011

WEDNESDAY, AUGUST 24, 2011

THURSDAY, AUGUST 25, 2011

FRIDAY, AUGUST 26, 2011

239th day
126 days to come

SATURDAY, AUGUST 27, 2011

4th Saturday of August

240th day
125 days to come

SUNDAY, AUGUST 28, 2011

4th Sunday of August

July 2011

S	M	T	W	T	F	S
					1	2
3	4	5	6	7	8	9
10	11	12	13	14	15	16
17	18	19	20	21	22	23
24	25	26	27	28	29	30
31						

August 2011

S	M	T	W	T	F	S
	1	2	3	4	5	6
7	8	9	10	11	12	13
14	15	16	17	18	19	20
21	22	23	24	25	26	27
28	29	30	31			

September 2011

S	M	T	W	T	F	S
				1	2	3
4	5	6	7	8	9	10
11	12	13	14	15	16	17
18	19	20	21	22	23	24
25	26	27	28	29	30	

MONDAY, AUGUST 29, 2011

TUESDAY, AUGUST 30, 2011

WEDNESDAY, AUGUST 31, 2011

THURSDAY, SEPTEMBER 1, 2011

FRIDAY, SEPTEMBER 2, 2011

246th day
119 days to come

SATURDAY, SEPTEMBER 3, 2011

1st Saturday
of September

247th day
118 days to come

SUNDAY, SEPTEMBER 4, 2011

1st Sunday
of September

August 2011

S	M	T	W	T	F	S
	1	2	3	4	5	6
7	8	9	10	11	12	13
14	15	16	17	18	19	20
21	22	23	24	25	26	27
28	29	30	31			

September 2011

S	M	T	W	T	F	S
				1	2	3
4	5	6	7	8	9	10
11	12	13	14	15	16	17
18	19	20	21	22	23	24
25	26	27	28	29	30	

October 2011

S	M	T	W	T	F	S
						1
2	3	4	5	6	7	8
9	10	11	12	13	14	15
16	17	18	19	20	21	22
23	24	25	26	27	28	29
30	31					

MONDAY, SEPTEMBER 5, 2011

Labor Day

TUESDAY, SEPTEMBER 6, 2011

WEDNESDAY, SEPTEMBER 7, 2011

THURSDAY, SEPTEMBER 8, 2011

FRIDAY, SEPTEMBER 9, 2011

Admission Day (Calif.)

253rd day
112 days to come

SATURDAY, SEPTEMBER 10, 2011

2nd Saturday
of September

254th day
111 days to come

SUNDAY, SEPTEMBER 11, 2011

2nd Sunday
of September

August 2011

S	M	T	W	T	F	S
	1	2	3	4	5	6
7	8	9	10	11	12	13
14	15	16	17	18	19	20
21	22	23	24	25	26	27
28	29	30	31			

September 2011

S	M	T	W	T	F	S
				1	2	3
4	5	6	7	8	9	10
11	12	13	14	15	16	17
18	19	20	21	22	23	24
25	26	27	28	29	30	

October 2011

S	M	T	W	T	F	S
						1
2	3	4	5	6	7	8
9	10	11	12	13	14	15
16	17	18	19	20	21	22
23	24	25	26	27	28	29
30	31					

255th day
110 days to come

MONDAY, SEPTEMBER 12, 2011

2nd Monday
of September

TUESDAY, SEPTEMBER 13, 2011

WEDNESDAY, SEPTEMBER 14, 2011

THURSDAY, SEPTEMBER 15, 2011

Third Payment on Estimated Federal Income Tax Due

FRIDAY, SEPTEMBER 16, 2011

260th day
105 days to come

SATURDAY, SEPTEMBER 17, 2011

3rd Saturday
of September

261st day
104 days to come

SUNDAY, SEPTEMBER 18, 2011

3rd Sunday
of September

August 2011

S	M	T	W	T	F	S
	1	2	3	4	5	6
7	8	9	10	11	12	13
14	15	16	17	18	19	20
21	22	23	24	25	26	27
28	29	30	31			

September 2011

S	M	T	W	T	F	S
				1	2	3
4	5	6	7	8	9	10
11	12	13	14	15	16	17
18	19	20	21	22	23	24
25	26	27	28	29	30	

October 2011

S	M	T	W	T	F	S
						1
2	3	4	5	6	7	8
9	10	11	12	13	14	15
16	17	18	19	20	21	22
23	24	25	26	27	28	29
30	31					

MONDAY, SEPTEMBER 19, 2011

TUESDAY, SEPTEMBER 20, 2011

WEDNESDAY, SEPTEMBER 21, 2011

THURSDAY, SEPTEMBER 22, 2011

FRIDAY, SEPTEMBER 23, 2011

267th day
98 days to come

SATURDAY, SEPTEMBER 24, 2011

4th Saturday
of September

268th day
97 days to come

SUNDAY, SEPTEMBER 25, 2011

4th Sunday
of September

August 2011						
S	M	T	W	T	F	S
	1	2	3	4	5	6
7	8	9	10	11	12	13
14	15	16	17	18	19	20
21	22	23	24	25	26	27
28	29	30	31			

September 2011						
S	M	T	W	T	F	S
				1	2	3
4	5	6	7	8	9	10
11	12	13	14	15	16	17
18	19	20	21	22	23	24
25	26	27	28	29	30	

October 2011						
S	M	T	W	T	F	S
						1
2	3	4	5	6	7	8
9	10	11	12	13	14	15
16	17	18	19	20	21	22
23	24	25	26	27	28	29
30	31					

MONDAY, SEPTEMBER 26, 2011

TUESDAY, SEPTEMBER 27, 2011

WEDNESDAY, SEPTEMBER 28, 2011

Rosh Hashanah Begins (Sundown)

THURSDAY, SEPTEMBER 29, 2011

Rosh Hashanah (Jewish New Year's Day)

FRIDAY, SEPTEMBER 30, 2011

Rosh Hashanah (Jewish New Year's Day)

274th day
91 days to come

SATURDAY, OCTOBER 1, 2011

1st Saturday
of October

275th day
90 days to come

SUNDAY, OCTOBER 2, 2011

1st Sunday
of October

September 2011

S	M	T	W	T	F	S
				1	2	3
4	5	6	7	8	9	10
11	12	13	14	15	16	17
18	19	20	21	22	23	24
25	26	27	28	29	30	

October 2011

S	M	T	W	T	F	S
						1
2	3	4	5	6	7	8
9	10	11	12	13	14	15
16	17	18	19	20	21	22
23	24	25	26	27	28	29
30	31					

November 2011

S	M	T	W	T	F	S
		1	2	3	4	5
6	7	8	9	10	11	12
13	14	15	16	17	18	19
20	21	22	23	24	25	26
27	28	29	30			

MONDAY, OCTOBER 3, 2011

TUESDAY, OCTOBER 4, 2011

WEDNESDAY, OCTOBER 5, 2011

279th day
86 days to come

THURSDAY, OCTOBER 6, 2011

1st Thursday
of October

FRIDAY, OCTOBER 7, 2011

Yom Kippur Begins (Sundown)

281st day
84 days to come

SATURDAY, OCTOBER 8, 2011

2nd Saturday
of October

Yom Kippur (Jewish Day of Atonement)

282nd day
83 days to come

SUNDAY, OCTOBER 9, 2011

2nd Sunday
of October

September 2011

S	M	T	W	T	F	S
				1	2	3
4	5	6	7	8	9	10
11	12	13	14	15	16	17
18	19	20	21	22	23	24
25	26	27	28	29	30	

October 2011

S	M	T	W	T	F	S
						1
2	3	4	5	6	7	8
9	10	11	12	13	14	15
16	17	18	19	20	21	22
23	24	25	26	27	28	29
30	31					

November 2011

S	M	T	W	T	F	S
		1	2	3	4	5
6	7	8	9	10	11	12
13	14	15	16	17	18	19
20	21	22	23	24	25	26
27	28	29	30			

MONDAY, OCTOBER 10, 2011

Columbus Day

Canadian Thanksgiving

TUESDAY, OCTOBER 11, 2011

WEDNESDAY, OCTOBER 12, 2011

THURSDAY, OCTOBER 13, 2011

Sukkot (First Day of Tabernacle)

FRIDAY, OCTOBER 14, 2011

288th day
77 days to come

SATURDAY, OCTOBER 15, 2011

3rd Saturday of October

289th day
76 days to come

SUNDAY, OCTOBER 16, 2011

3rd Sunday of October

September 2011

S	M	T	W	T	F	S
				1	2	3
4	5	6	7	8	9	10
11	12	13	14	15	16	17
18	19	20	21	22	23	24
25	26	27	28	29	30	

October 2011

S	M	T	W	T	F	S
						1
2	3	4	5	6	7	8
9	10	11	12	13	14	15
16	17	18	19	20	21	22
23	24	25	26	27	28	29
30	31					

November 2011

S	M	T	W	T	F	S
		1	2	3	4	5
6	7	8	9	10	11	12
13	14	15	16	17	18	19
20	21	22	23	24	25	26
27	28	29	30			

MONDAY, OCTOBER 17, 2011

TUESDAY, OCTOBER 18, 2011

WEDNESDAY, OCTOBER 19, 2011

THURSDAY, OCTOBER 20, 2011

294th day
71 days to come

FRIDAY, OCTOBER 21, 2011

3rd Friday
of October

295th day
70 days to come

SATURDAY, OCTOBER 22, 2011

4th Saturday
of October

296th day
69 days to come

SUNDAY, OCTOBER 23, 2011

4th Sunday
of October

September 2011

S	M	T	W	T	F	S
				1	2	3
4	5	6	7	8	9	10
11	12	13	14	15	16	17
18	19	20	21	22	23	24
25	26	27	28	29	30	

October 2011

S	M	T	W	T	F	S
						1
2	3	4	5	6	7	8
9	10	11	12	13	14	15
16	17	18	19	20	21	22
23	24	25	26	27	28	29
30	31					

November 2011

S	M	T	W	T	F	S
		1	2	3	4	5
6	7	8	9	10	11	12
13	14	15	16	17	18	19
20	21	22	23	24	25	26
27	28	29	30			

MONDAY, OCTOBER 24, 2011

TUESDAY, OCTOBER 25, 2011

WEDNESDAY, OCTOBER 26, 2011

THURSDAY, OCTOBER 27, 2011

FRIDAY, OCTOBER 28, 2011

302nd day
63 days to come

SATURDAY, OCTOBER 29, 2011

5th Saturday
of October

303rd day
62 days to come

SUNDAY, OCTOBER 30, 2011

5th Sunday
of October

September 2011

S	M	T	W	T	F	S
				1	2	3
4	5	6	7	8	9	10
11	12	13	14	15	16	17
18	19	20	21	22	23	24
25	26	27	28	29	30	

October 2011

S	M	T	W	T	F	S
						1
2	3	4	5	6	7	8
9	10	11	12	13	14	15
16	17	18	19	20	21	22
23	24	25	26	27	28	29
30	31					

November 2011

S	M	T	W	T	F	S
		1	2	3	4	5
6	7	8	9	10	11	12
13	14	15	16	17	18	19
20	21	22	23	24	25	26
27	28	29	30			

MONDAY, OCTOBER 31, 2011

Quarterly Form 941 Return Due

Federal Unemployment Tax Deposit Due

TUESDAY, NOVEMBER 1, 2011

WEDNESDAY, NOVEMBER 2, 2011

THURSDAY, NOVEMBER 3, 2011

FRIDAY, NOVEMBER 4, 2011

309th day
56 days to come

SATURDAY, NOVEMBER 5, 2011

1st Saturday
of November

310th day
55 days to come

SUNDAY, NOVEMBER 6, 2011

1st Sunday
of November

Daylight Saving Time Ends

October 2011

S	M	T	W	T	F	S
						1
2	3	4	5	6	7	8
9	10	11	12	13	14	15
16	17	18	19	20	21	22
23	24	25	26	27	28	29
30	31					

November 2011

S	M	T	W	T	F	S
		1	2	3	4	5
6	7	8	9	10	11	12
13	14	15	16	17	18	19
20	21	22	23	24	25	26
27	28	29	30			

December 2011

S	M	T	W	T	F	S
				1	2	3
4	5	6	7	8	9	10
11	12	13	14	15	16	17
18	19	20	21	22	23	24
25	26	27	28	29	30	31

MONDAY, NOVEMBER 7, 2011

TUESDAY, NOVEMBER 8, 2011

Election Day

WEDNESDAY, NOVEMBER 9, 2011

THURSDAY, NOVEMBER 10, 2011

FRIDAY, NOVEMBER 11, 2011

Veterans' Day

316th day
49 days to come

SATURDAY, NOVEMBER 12, 2011

2nd Saturday
of November

317th day
48 days to come

SUNDAY, NOVEMBER 13, 2011

2nd Sunday
of November

October 2011

S	M	T	W	T	F	S
						1
2	3	4	5	6	7	8
9	10	11	12	13	14	15
16	17	18	19	20	21	22
23	24	25	26	27	28	29
30	31					

November 2011

S	M	T	W	T	F	S
		1	2	3	4	5
6	7	8	9	10	11	12
13	14	15	16	17	18	19
20	21	22	23	24	25	26
27	28	29	30			

December 2011

S	M	T	W	T	F	S
				1	2	3
4	5	6	7	8	9	10
11	12	13	14	15	16	17
18	19	20	21	22	23	24
25	26	27	28	29	30	31

MONDAY, NOVEMBER 14, 2011

TUESDAY, NOVEMBER 15, 2011

WEDNESDAY, NOVEMBER 16, 2011

THURSDAY, NOVEMBER 17, 2011

FRIDAY, NOVEMBER 18, 2011

323rd day
42 days to come

SATURDAY, NOVEMBER 19, 2011

3rd Saturday
of November

324th day
41 days to come

SUNDAY, NOVEMBER 20, 2011

3rd Sunday
of November

October 2011

S	M	T	W	T	F	S
						1
2	3	4	5	6	7	8
9	10	11	12	13	14	15
16	17	18	19	20	21	22
23	24	25	26	27	28	29
30	31					

November 2011

S	M	T	W	T	F	S
		1	2	3	4	5
6	7	8	9	10	11	12
13	14	15	16	17	18	19
20	21	22	23	24	25	26
27	28	29	30			

December 2011

S	M	T	W	T	F	S
				1	2	3
4	5	6	7	8	9	10
11	12	13	14	15	16	17
18	19	20	21	22	23	24
25	26	27	28	29	30	31

MONDAY, NOVEMBER 21, 2011

TUESDAY, NOVEMBER 22, 2011

WEDNESDAY, NOVEMBER 23, 2011

THURSDAY, NOVEMBER 24, 2011

Thanksgiving Day

FRIDAY, NOVEMBER 25, 2011

330th day
35 days to come

SATURDAY, NOVEMBER 26, 2011

4th Saturday
of November

331st day
34 days to come

SUNDAY, NOVEMBER 27, 2011

4th Sunday
of November

October 2011

S	M	T	W	T	F	S
						1
2	3	4	5	6	7	8
9	10	11	12	13	14	15
16	17	18	19	20	21	22
23	24	25	26	27	28	29
30	31					

November 2011

S	M	T	W	T	F	S
		1	2	3	4	5
6	7	8	9	10	11	12
13	14	15	16	17	18	19
20	21	22	23	24	25	26
27	28	29	30			

December 2011

S	M	T	W	T	F	S
				1	2	3
4	5	6	7	8	9	10
11	12	13	14	15	16	17
18	19	20	21	22	23	24
25	26	27	28	29	30	31

MONDAY, NOVEMBER 28, 2011

TUESDAY, NOVEMBER 29, 2011

WEDNESDAY, NOVEMBER 30, 2011

THURSDAY, DECEMBER 1, 2011

FRIDAY, DECEMBER 2, 2011

337th day
28 days to come

SATURDAY, DECEMBER 3, 2011

1st Saturday
of December

338th day
27 days to come

SUNDAY, DECEMBER 4, 2011

1st Sunday
of December

November 2011

S	M	T	W	T	F	S
		1	2	3	4	5
6	7	8	9	10	11	12
13	14	15	16	17	18	19
20	21	22	23	24	25	26
27	28	29	30			

December 2011

S	M	T	W	T	F	S
				1	2	3
4	5	6	7	8	9	10
11	12	13	14	15	16	17
18	19	20	21	22	23	24
25	26	27	28	29	30	31

January 2012

S	M	T	W	T	F	S
1	2	3	4	5	6	7
8	9	10	11	12	13	14
15	16	17	18	19	20	21
22	23	24	25	26	27	28
29	30	31				

MONDAY, DECEMBER 5, 2011

TUESDAY, DECEMBER 6, 2011

WEDNESDAY, DECEMBER 7, 2011

THURSDAY, DECEMBER 8, 2011

FRIDAY, DECEMBER 9, 2011

344th day
21 days to come

SATURDAY, DECEMBER 10, 2011

2nd Saturday
of December

345th day
20 days to come

SUNDAY, DECEMBER 11, 2011

2nd Sunday
of December

November 2011

S	M	T	W	T	F	S
		1	2	3	4	5
6	7	8	9	10	11	12
13	14	15	16	17	18	19
20	21	22	23	24	25	26
27	28	29	30			

December 2011

S	M	T	W	T	F	S
				1	2	3
4	5	6	7	8	9	10
11	12	13	14	15	16	17
18	19	20	21	22	23	24
25	26	27	28	29	30	31

January 2012

S	M	T	W	T	F	S
1	2	3	4	5	6	7
8	9	10	11	12	13	14
15	16	17	18	19	20	21
22	23	24	25	26	27	28
29	30	31				

MONDAY, DECEMBER 12, 2011

TUESDAY, DECEMBER 13, 2011

WEDNESDAY, DECEMBER 14, 2011

THURSDAY, DECEMBER 15, 2011

FRIDAY, DECEMBER 16, 2011

351st day
14 days to come

SATURDAY, DECEMBER 17, 2011

3rd Saturday
of December

352nd day
13 days to come

SUNDAY, DECEMBER 18, 2011

3rd Sunday
of December

November 2011

S	M	T	W	T	F	S
		1	2	3	4	5
6	7	8	9	10	11	12
13	14	15	16	17	18	19
20	21	22	23	24	25	26
27	28	29	30			

December 2011

S	M	T	W	T	F	S
				1	2	3
4	5	6	7	8	9	10
11	12	13	14	15	16	17
18	19	20	21	22	23	24
25	26	27	28	29	30	31

January 2012

S	M	T	W	T	F	S
1	2	3	4	5	6	7
8	9	10	11	12	13	14
15	16	17	18	19	20	21
22	23	24	25	26	27	28
29	30	31				

MONDAY, DECEMBER 19, 2011

TUESDAY, DECEMBER 20, 2011

WEDNESDAY, DECEMBER 21, 2011

First Day of Hanukah

THURSDAY, DECEMBER 22, 2011

FRIDAY, DECEMBER 23, 2011

358th day
7 days to come

SATURDAY, DECEMBER 24, 2011

4th Saturday
of December

359th day
6 days to come

SUNDAY, DECEMBER 25, 2011

4th Sunday
of December

Christmas Day

November 2011						
S	M	T	W	T	F	S
		1	2	3	4	5
6	7	8	9	10	11	12
13	14	15	16	17	18	19
20	21	22	23	24	25	26
27	28	29	30			

December 2011						
S	M	T	W	T	F	S
				1	2	3
4	5	6	7	8	9	10
11	12	13	14	15	16	17
18	19	20	21	22	23	24
25	26	27	28	29	30	31

January 2012						
S	M	T	W	T	F	S
1	2	3	4	5	6	7
8	9	10	11	12	13	14
15	16	17	18	19	20	21
22	23	24	25	26	27	28
29	30	31				

MONDAY, DECEMBER 26, 2011

Kwanzaa (An African-American Celebration of Family, Community & Culture)

TUESDAY, DECEMBER 27, 2011

WEDNESDAY, DECEMBER 28, 2011

THURSDAY, DECEMBER 29, 2011

FRIDAY, DECEMBER 30, 2011

365th day
0 days to come

SATURDAY, DECEMBER 31, 2011

5th Saturday
of December

1st day
365 days to come

SUNDAY, JANUARY 1, 2012

1st Sunday
of January

New Year's Day

December 2011						
S	M	T	W	T	F	S
				1	2	3
4	5	6	7	8	9	10
11	12	13	14	15	16	17
18	19	20	21	22	23	24
25	26	27	28	29	30	31

January 2012						
S	M	T	W	T	F	S
1	2	3	4	5	6	7
8	9	10	11	12	13	14
15	16	17	18	19	20	21
22	23	24	25	26	27	28
29	30	31				

February 2012						
S	M	T	W	T	F	S
			1	2	3	4
5	6	7	8	9	10	11
12	13	14	15	16	17	18
19	20	21	22	23	24	25
26	27	28	29			

JANUARY 2012

FEBRUARY 2012

MARCH 2012

APRIL 2012

MAY 2012

JUNE 2012

JULY 2012

AUGUST 2012

SEPTEMBER 2012

OCTOBER 2012

NOVEMBER 2012

DECEMBER 2012

2012 DATES TO REMEMBER

January 1 — New Year's Day
January 16 — Birthday of Martin Luther King, Jr. observed
February 12 — Lincoln's Birthday
February 14 — Valentine's Day
February 15 — Susan B. Anthony's Birthday
February 20 — General observance of Washington's Birthday (called Presidents' Day in most states)
March 11 — Daylight Saving Time Begins
March 17 — St. Patrick's Day
April 6 — Good Friday
April 25 — Administrative Assistants Day
May 1 — Law Day
May 13 — Mother's Day
May 21 — Victoria Day (Canada)
May 28 — Memorial Day observed in most states
May 30 — Traditional Memorial Day
June 14 — Flag Day
June 17 — Father's Day
July 1 — Canada Day
July 4 — Independence Day
September 3 — Labor Day
October 8 — Columbus Day
October 8 — Canadian Thanksgiving
November 4 — Daylight Saving Time Ends
November 6 — Election Day
November 11 — Veterans' Day
November 22 — Thanksgiving Day
December 25 — Christmas Day
December 26 — Kwanzaa (An African-American Celebration of Family, Community & Culture)

RELIGIOUS DATES

February 21 — Shrove Tuesday
February 22 — Ash Wednesday
April 1 — Palm Sunday
April 6 — Good Friday
April 7 — Passover, First Day of
April 8 — Easter Sunday
April 15 — Eastern Orthodox Easter
May 27 — Shavuot
May 27 — Whitsunday (Pentecost)
September 17 — Rosh Hashanah (Jewish New Year)
September 18 — Rosh Hashanah (Jewish New Year)
September 26 — Yom Kippur (Jewish Day of Atonement)
October 1 — Sukkot (First Day of Tabernacle)
December 9 — Hanukah, First Day of
December 25 — Christmas Day

Special note concerning Jewish Holidays.

In addition to dates noted, observant Jews celebrate the second, seventh and eighth days of Passover; the second, eighth and ninth days of Sukkot; and two days of Shavuot. All Jewish holidays begin at sundown, the evening prior to the day of the holiday.

JANUARY 2012

JANUARY 2012	SUNDAY	MONDAY	TUESDAY
Items To Remember This Month	**1** New Year's Day	**2**	**3**
	8	**9**	**10**
	15	**16** Birthday of Martin Luther King, Jr. observed	**17** Quarterly Estimated Federal Income Tax Payment Due Unless Return is Filed by January 31st
	22	**23**	**24**
	29	**30**	**31** Quarterly Form 941 Return Due Federal Unemployment Form 940 Due for 2011

WEDNESDAY	THURSDAY	FRIDAY	SATURDAY
4	5	6	7
11	12	13	14
18	19	20	21
25	26	27	28

JANUARY 2012

DATES TO REMEMBER

January 1 - New Year's Day
January 16 - Birthday of Martin Luther King, Jr. observed
January 17 - Quarterly Estimated Federal Income Tax Payment Due Unless Return in Lieu of Final Declaration is Filed by January 31st
January 31 - Quarterly Form 941 Return Due
- Federal Unemployment Form 940 Due for 2011

FEBRUARY 2012

Items To Remember This Month

FEBRUARY	SUNDAY	MONDAY	TUESDAY
2012			
	5	6	7
	12 Lincoln's Birthday	13	14 Valentine's Day
	19	20 Washington's Birthday observed (called Presidents' Day in most states)	21 Shrove Tuesday
	26	27	28

DATES TO REMEMBER

February 12 - Lincoln's Birthday
February 14 - Valentine's Day
February 15 - Susan B. Anthony's Birthday
February 20 - Washington's Birthday observed (called Presidents' Day in most states)
February 21 - Shrove Tuesday
February 22 - Ash Wednesday

WEDNESDAY	THURSDAY	FRIDAY	SATURDAY
1	2	3	4
8	9	10	11
15 Susan B. Anthony's Birthday	16	17	18
22 Ash Wednesday	23	24	25
29			

MARCH 2012

MARCH 2012	SUNDAY	MONDAY	TUESDAY
Items To Remember This Month	**DATES TO REMEMBER** **March 11 -** Daylight Saving Time Begins **March 17 -** St. Patrick's Day		
	4	**5**	**6**
	11 Daylight Saving Time Begins	**12**	**13**
	18	**19**	**20**
	25	**26**	**27**

MARCH 2012

WEDNESDAY	THURSDAY	FRIDAY	SATURDAY
	1	2	3
7	8	9	10
14	15	16	17 St. Patrick's Day
21	22	23	24
28	29	30	31

APRIL 2012	SUNDAY	MONDAY	TUESDAY
Items To Remember This Month	**1** Palm Sunday	**2**	**3**
	8 Easter Sunday	**9**	**10**
	15 Eastern Orthodox Easter	**16** Federal Income Tax Return Due Quarterly Estimated Federal Income Tax Payment Due	**17**
	22	**23**	**24**
	29	**30** Quarterly Form 941 Return Due Federal Unemployment Tax Deposit Due	

WEDNESDAY	THURSDAY	FRIDAY	SATURDAY
4	**5**	**6** Good Friday	**7** First Day of Passover
11	**12**	**13**	**14**
18	**19**	**20**	**21**
25 Administrative Assistants Day	**26**	**27**	**28**

APRIL 2012

DATES TO REMEMBER

April 1 - Palm Sunday
April 6 - Good Friday
April 7 - First Day of Passover
April 8 - Easter Sunday
April 15 - Eastern Orthodox Easter
April 16 - Federal Income Tax Return Due
- Quarterly Estimated Federal Income Tax Payment Due

April 25 - Administrative Assistants Day
April 30 - Quarterly Form 941 Return Due
- Federal Unemployment Tax Deposit Due

MAY 2012

MAY 2012	SUNDAY	MONDAY	TUESDAY
Items To Remember This Month	**DATES TO REMEMBER** **May 1** - Law Day **May 13** - Mother's Day **May 21** - Victoria Day **May 27** - Whitsunday **May 27** - Shavuot **May 28** - Memorial Day observed in most states **May 30** - Traditional Memorial Day		**1** Law Day
	6	**7**	**8**
	13 Mother's Day	**14**	**15**
	20	**21** Victoria Day	**22**
	27 Whitsunday Shavuot	**28** Memorial Day observed in most states	**29**

WEDNESDAY	THURSDAY	FRIDAY	SATURDAY
2	3	4	5
9	10	11	12
16	17	18	19
23	24	25	26
30 Traditional Memorial Day	31		

JUNE 2012

JUNE 2012	SUNDAY	MONDAY	TUESDAY
Items To Remember This Month	**DATES TO REMEMBER** **June 14 -** Flag Day **June 15 -** Quarterly Estimated Federal Income Tax Payment Due **June 17 -** Father's Day		
	3	**4**	**5**
	10	**11**	**12**
	17 Father's Day	**18**	**19**
	24	**25**	**26**

WEDNESDAY	THURSDAY	FRIDAY	SATURDAY
		1	2
6	7	8	9
13	14 Flag Day	15 Quarterly Estimated Federal Income Tax Payment Due	16
20	21	22	23
27	28	29	30

JUNE 2012

JULY 2012

JULY 2012	SUNDAY	MONDAY	TUESDAY
Items To Remember This Month	**1** Canada Day	**2**	**3**
	8	**9**	**10**
	15	**16**	**17**
	22	**23**	**24**
	29	**30**	**31** Quarterly Form 941 Return Due Federal Unemployment Tax Deposit Due

JULY 2012

WEDNESDAY	THURSDAY	FRIDAY	SATURDAY
4 Independence Day	**5**	**6**	**7**
11	**12**	**13**	**14**
18	**19**	**20**	**21**
25	**26**	**27**	**28**

DATES TO REMEMBER

July 1 - Canada Day
July 4 - Independence Day
July 31 - Quarterly Form 941 Return Due
- Federal Unemployment Tax Deposit Due

AUGUST 2012

AUGUST **2012**	SUNDAY	MONDAY	TUESDAY
Items To Remember This Month	**DATES TO REMEMBER**		
	5	**6**	**7**
	12	**13**	**14**
	19	**20**	**21**
	26	**27**	**28**

AUGUST 2012

WEDNESDAY	THURSDAY	FRIDAY	SATURDAY
1	2	3	4
8	9	10	11
15	16	17	18
22	23	24	25
29	30	31	

SEPTEMBER 2012

SEPTEMBER 2012	SUNDAY	MONDAY	TUESDAY
Items To Remember This Month			
	2	**3** Labor Day	**4**
	9	**10**	**11**
	16	**17** Quarterly Estimated Federal Income Tax Payment Due Rosh Hashanah (Jewish New Year)	**18** Rosh Hashanah (Jewish New Year)
	23	**24**	**25**
	30		

DATES TO REMEMBER

September 3 - Labor Day
September 17 - Quarterly Estimated Federal Income Tax Payment Due
- Rosh Hashanah (Jewish New Year)
September 18 - Rosh Hashanah (Jewish New Year)
September 26 - Yom Kippur

WEDNESDAY	THURSDAY	FRIDAY	SATURDAY
			1
5	6	7	8
12	13	14	15
19	20	21	22
26 Yom Kippur	27	28	29

OCTOBER 2012

OCTOBER 2012

Items To Remember This Month

SUNDAY	MONDAY	TUESDAY
	1 Sukkot (First Day of Tabernacle)	**2**
7	**8** Columbus Day Canadian Thanksgiving	**9**
14	**15**	**16**
21	**22**	**23**
28	**29**	**30**

OCTOBER 2012

WEDNESDAY	THURSDAY	FRIDAY	SATURDAY
3	4	5	6
10	11	12	13
17	18	19	20
24	25	26	27
31 Quarterly Form 941 Return Due Federal Unemployment Tax Deposit Due			

DATES TO REMEMBER

October 1 - Sukkot (First Day of Tabernacle)
October 8 - Columbus Day
- Canadian Thanksgiving

October 31 - Quarterly Form 941 Return Due
- Federal Unemployment Tax Deposit Due

NOVEMBER 2012

NOVEMBER 2012	SUNDAY	MONDAY	TUESDAY
Items To Remember This Month	**DATES TO REMEMBER** **November 4** - Daylight Saving Time Ends **November 6** - Election Day **November 11** - Veterans' Day **November 22** - Thanksgiving Day		
	4 Daylight Saving Time Ends	**5**	**6** Election Day
	11 Veterans' Day	**12**	**13**
	18	**19**	**20**
	25	**26**	**27**

WEDNESDAY	THURSDAY	FRIDAY	SATURDAY
	1	2	3
7	8	9	10
14	15	16	17
21	22 Thanksgiving Day	23	24
28	29	30	

NOVEMBER 2012

DECEMBER 2012

DECEMBER 2012	SUNDAY	MONDAY	TUESDAY
Items To Remember This Month			
	2	3	4
	9 First Day of Hanukah	10	11
	16	17	18
	23	24	25 Christmas Day
	30	31	

DATES TO REMEMBER

December 9 - First Day of Hanukah
December 25 - Christmas Day
December 26 - Kwanzaa (An African-American Celebration of Family, Community & Culture)

WEDNESDAY	THURSDAY	FRIDAY	SATURDAY
			1
5	6	7	8
12	13	14	15
19	20	21	22
26 Kwanzaa (An African-American Celebration of Family, Community & Culture)	27	28	29

DECEMBER 2012

Anguilla	264	Grenada	473
Antigua	268	Jamaica	876
Bahamas	242	Monserrat	664
Barbados	246	Puerto Rico	787/939
Bermuda	441	St. Kits & Nevis	869
British Virgin Islands	284	St. Lucia	758
Caribbean Islands	809	t. Maarten	721
Cayman Islands	345	St. Vincent & Grenadines	784
Turks and Caicos	649	Trinidad & Tobago	868
Dominica	767	U.S. Virgin Islands	340
Dominican Republic	809/829/849		

Area Code and Time Zone Map

CHART FOR CALCULATING WEEKS IN THE YEAR

*Use the chart to determine the numbered weekday of the year for any week date in 2011 (Saturdays and Sundays excluded)						
Week of 2011	**Mondays in 2011**	**Tuesdays in 2011**	**Wednesdays in 2011**	**Thursdays in 2011**	**Fridays in 2011**	**Week of 2011**
1st	January 3	January 4	January 5	January 6	January 7	1st
2nd	January 10	January 11	January 12	January 13	January 14	2nd
3rd	January 17	January 18	January 19	January 20	January 21	3rd
4th	January 24	January 25	January 26	January 27	January 28	4th
5th	January 31	February 01	February 02	February 03	February 04	5th
6th	February 07	February 08	February 09	February 10	February 11	6th
7th	February 14	February 15	February 16	February 17	February 18	7th
8th	February 21	February 22	February 23	February 24	February 25	8th
9th	February 28	March 01	March 02	March 03	March 04	9th
10th	March 07	March 08	March 09	March 10	March 11	10th
11th	March 14	March 15	March 16	March 17	March 18	11th
12th	March 21	March 22	March 23	March 24	March 25	12th
13th	March 28	March 29	March 30	March 31	April 01	13th
14th	April 04	April 05	April 06	April 07	April 08	14th
15th	April 11	April 12	April 13	April 14	April 15	15th
16th	April 18	April 19	April 20	April 21	April 22	16th
17th	April 25	April 26	April 27	April 28	April 29	17th
18th	May 02	May 03	May 04	May 05	May 06	18th
19th	May 09	May 10	May 11	May 12	May 13	19th
20th	May 16	May 17	May 18	May 19	May 20	20th
21st	May 23	May 24	May 25	May 26	May 27	21st
22nd	May 30	May 31	June 01	June 02	June 03	22nd
23rd	June 06	June 07	June 08	June 09	June 10	23rd
24th	June 13	June 14	June 15	June 16	June 17	24th
25th	June 20	June 21	June 22	June 23	June 24	25th
26th	June 27	June 28	June 29	June 30	July 01	26th
27th	July 04	July 05	July 06	July 07	July 08	27th
28th	July 11	July 12	July 13	July 14	July 15	28th
29th	July 18	July 19	July 20	July 21	July 22	29th
30th	July 25	July 26	July 27	July 28	July 29	30th
31st	August 01	August 02	August 03	August 04	August 05	31st
32nd	August 08	August 09	August 10	August 11	August 12	32nd
33rd	August 15	August 16	August 17	August 18	August 19	33rd
34th	August 22	August 23	August 24	August 25	August 26	34th
35th	August 29	August 30	August 31	September 01	September 02	35th
36th	September 05	September 06	September 07	September 08	September 09	36th
37th	September 12	September 13	September 14	September 15	September 16	37th
38th	September 19	September 20	September 21	September 22	September 23	38th
39th	September 26	September 27	September 28	September 29	September 30	39th
40th	October 03	October 04	October 05	October 06	October 07	40th
41st	October 10	October 11	October 12	October 13	October 14	41st
42nd	October 17	October 18	October 19	October 20	October 21	42nd
43rd	October 24	October 25	October 26	October 27	October 28	43rd
44th	October 31	November 01	November 02	November 03	November 04	44th
45th	November 07	November 08	November 09	November 10	November 11	45th
46th	November 14	November 15	November 16	November 17	November 18	46th
47th	November 21	November 22	November 23	November 24	November 25	47th
48th	November 28	November 29	November 30	December 01	December 02	48th
49th	December 05	December 06	December 07	December 08	December 09	49th
50th	December 12	December 13	December 14	December 15	December 16	50th
51st	December 19	December 20	December 21	December 22	December 23	51st
52nd	December 26	December 27	December 28	December 29	December 30	52nd

***Example of a use:** December 9, 2011 is the 49th Friday of the year 2011.
If Fridays are payroll days, 49 payroll checks for the year 2011 would have been received on December 9, 2011

PAPERS TO BE REFILED

Title	Place of Filing	Date

Frequently-Called Numbers

Area Code	Number	Name & Address

Frequently-Called Numbers

Area Code	Number	Name & Address

Frequently-Called Numbers

Area Code	Number	Name & Address

Frequently-Called Numbers

Area Code	Number	Name & Address

DIRECTORY OF JUDGES IN NEW YORK COURTS

Federal Court

(718) 613-2410 **Amon, Carol B.** (J US Dist Ct East Dist) U.S. Cthse., Rm. 908S, 225 Cadman Plaza East, Bklyn. 11201; **Fax:** (718) 613-2416

(212) 264-1625 **Aquilino, Thomas J., Jr.** (Sr J US Ct of Intl Trade) One Federal Plaza, N.Y.C. 10278-0001; **Fax:** (212) 264-1085

(716) 332-7810 **Arcara, Richard J.** (J US Dist Ct West Dist) U.S. Cthse., Rm. 609, 68 Court St., Buffalo 14202-3406; **Fax:** (716) 551-4850

(718) 613-2530 **Azrack, Joan M.** (US Magis J East Dist) U.S. Cthse., Rm. N605, 225 Cadman Plaza East, Bklyn. 11201; **Fax:** (718) 613-2535

(212) 805-0184 **Baer, Harold, Jr.** (Sr J US Dist Ct South Dist) Daniel Patrick Moynihan U.S. Cthse., Rm. 2230, 500 Pearl St., N.Y.C. 10007-1312

(212) 264-2018 **Barzilay, Judith M.** (J US Ct of Intl Trade) One Federal Plaza, N.Y.C. 10278-0001; **Fax:** (212) 264-1085

(212) 805-0186 **Batts, Deborah A.** (J US Dist Ct South Dist) Daniel Patrick Moynihan U.S. Cthse., Rm. 2510, 500 Pearl St., N.Y.C. 10007-1312

(315) 234-8600 **Baxter, Andrew T.** (US Magis J North Dist) James Hanley Fedl. Bldg. U.S. Cthse., 100 S. Clinton St., P.O. Box 7396, Syracuse 13261-7396; **Fax:** (315) 234-8601

(212) 805-6715 **Berman, Richard M.** (J US Dist Ct South Dist) Daniel Patrick Moynihan U.S. Cthse., 500 Pearl St., N.Y.C. 10007-1312

(212) 668-2304 **Bernstein, Stuart M.** (J US Bank Ct South Dist) Alexander Hamilton Custom House, One Bowling Green, N.Y.C. 10004-1408

(631) 712-5670 **Bianco, Joseph F.** (J US Dist Ct East Dist) Alfonse M. D'Amato U.S. Cthse., Rm. 924, 100 Federal Plaza, Central Islip 11722-4449; **Fax:** (631) 712-5677

(718) 613-2420 **Block, Frederic** (Sr J US Dist Ct East Dist) U.S. Cthse., Rm. 925S, 225 Cadman Plaza East, Bklyn. 11201; **Fax:** (718) 613-2426

(718) 613-2170 **Bloom, Lois** (US Magis J East Dist) U.S. Cthse., Rm. 1210S, 225 Cadman Plaza East, Bklyn. 11201; **Fax:** (718) 613-2175

(631) 712-5710 **Boyle, E. Thomas** (US Magis J East Dist) Alfonse M. D'Amato U.S. Cthse., Rm. 834, 100 Federal Plaza, Central Islip 11722-4449

(212) 805-0194 **Buchwald, Naomi Reice** (J US Dist Ct South Dist) Daniel Patrick Moynihan U.S. Cthse., Rm. 2270, 500 Pearl St., N.Y.C. 10007-1312; **Fax:** (212) 805-7927

(716) 362-3281 **Bucki, Carl L.** (Chief J US Bank Ct West Dist) Olympic Towers, Suite 350, 300 Pearl St., Buffalo 14202-2501; **Fax:** (716) 362-3232

(203) 867-8782 **Cabranes, José A.** (J US Ct of App 2nd Circ) U.S. Cthse., 141 Church St., New Haven, CT 06510

(203) 773-2291 **Calabresi, Guido** (Sr J US Ct of App 2nd Circ) Connecticut Financial Center, 157 Church St., New Haven, CT 06510

(315) 295-1683 **Cangilos-Ruiz, Margaret M.** (J US Bank Ct North Dist) James M. Hanley Fedl. Bldg., Rm. 315, 100 S. Clinton St., Syracuse 13261

(212) 264-1625 **Carman, Gregory W.** (J US Ct of Intl Trade) One Federal Plaza, N.Y.C. 10278-0001; **Fax:** (212) 264-1085

(718) 613-2220 **Carter, Andrew L.** (US Magis J East Dist) U.S. Cthse., Rm. N505, 225 Cadman Plaza East, Bklyn. 11201; **Fax:** (718) 613-2330

(212) 805-0196 **Carter, Robert L.** (Sr J US Dist Ct South Dist) Daniel Patrick Moynihan U.S. Cthse., Rm. 2220, 500 Pearl St., N.Y.C. 10007-1312; **Fax:** (212) 805-7904

(212) 805-0262 **Castel, P. Kevin** (J US Dist Ct South Dist) Daniel Patrick Moynihan U.S. Cthse., Rm. 2260, 500 Pearl St., N.Y.C. 10007-1312

(212) 805-0198 **Cedarbaum, Miriam Goldman** (Sr J US Dist Ct South Dist) Daniel Patrick Moynihan U.S. Cthse., Rm. 1330, 500 Pearl St., N.Y.C. 10007-1312

(212) 668-2301 **Chapman, Shelley C.** (J US Bank Ct South Dist) Alexander Hamilton Custom House, One Bowling Green, N.Y.C. 10004-1408

(860) 240-3659 **Chatigny, Robert N.** (J 2nd Circ US Ct of App Pending Confirmation) 450 Main St., Hartford, CT 06103

(718) 613-2230 **Cogan, Brian** (J US Dist Ct East Dist) U.S. Cthse., Rm. 717S, 225 Cadman Plaza East, Bklyn. 11201; **Fax:** (718) 613-2236

(212) 805-0202 **Cote, Denise L.** (J US Dist Ct South Dist) Daniel Patrick Moynihan U.S. Cthse., Rm. 1040, 500 Pearl St., N.Y.C. 10007-1312

(212) 805-0250 **Cott, James L.** (US Magis J South Dist) Daniel Patrick Moynihan U.S. Cthse., Rm. 1360, 500 Pearl St., N.Y.C. 10007-1312

(347) 394-1840 **Craig, Carla E.** (Chief J US Bank Ct East Dist) 271 Cadman Plaza E., Suite 1595, Bklyn. 11201-1800

(212) 805-6309 **Crotty, Paul A.** (J US Dist Ct South Dist) Daniel Patrick Moynihan U.S. Cthse., Rm. 735, 500 Pearl St., N.Y.C. 10007-1312; **Fax:** (212) 805-6304

(716) 332-7830 **Curtin, John T.** (Sr J US Dist Ct West Dist) U.S. Cthse., Rm. 624, 68 Court St., Buffalo 14202-3406; **Fax:** (716) 551-4850; **E-mail:** john_curtin@nywd.uscourts.gov

(212) 805-6735 **Daniels, George B.** (J US Dist Ct South Dist) Daniel Patrick Moynihan U.S. Cthse., Rm. 630, 500 Pearl St., N.Y.C. 10007-1312

(315) 793-8111 **Davis, Diane** (J US Bank Ct North Dist) 10 Broad St., Rm. 230, Utica 13502; **Fax:** (315) 793-8128

(914) 390-4250 **Davison, Paul E.** (US Magis J South Dist) U.S. Cthse., Rm. 421, 300 Quarropas St., White Plains 10601

(718) 613-2430 **Dearie, Raymond J.** (Chief J US Dist Ct East Dist) U.S. Cthse., Rm. 912S, 225 Cadman Plaza East, Bklyn. 11201; **Fax:** (718) 613-2437

(212) 805-0204 **Dolinger, Michael H.** (US Magis J South Dist) Daniel Patrick Moynihan U.S. Cthse., Rm. 1670, 500 Pearl St., N.Y.C. 10007-1312; **Fax:** (212) 805-7928

(914) 390-4155 **Drain, Robert D.** (J US Bank Ct South Dist) 300 Quarropas St., White Plains 10601; **E-mail:** rdd.chambers@nysb.uscourts.gov

(212) 805-6125 **Duffy, Kevin Thomas** (Sr J US Dist Ct South Dist) Daniel Patrick Moynihan U.S. Cthse., Rm. 2540, 500 Pearl St., N.Y.C. 10007-1312

(212) 805-6175 **Eaton, Douglas F.** (US Magis J South Dist) Daniel Patrick Moynihan U.S. Cthse., Rm. 1360, 500 Pearl St., N.Y.C. 10007-1312; **Fax:** (212) 805-6181

(212) 264-1615 **Eaton, Richard K.** (J US Ct of Intl Trade) One Federal Plaza, N.Y.C. 10278-0001; **Fax:** (212) 264-1085

(631) 712-5690 **Eisenberg, Dorothy T.** (J US Bank Ct East Dist) 290 Federal Plaza, P.O. Box 9013, Central Islip 11722; **Fax:** (631) 712-6298

(212) 805-0242 **Ellis, Ronald L.** (US Magis J South Dist) Daniel Patrick Moynihan U.S. Cthse., Rm. 1970, 500 Pearl St., N.Y.C. 10007-1312

(212) 857-2100 **Feinberg, Wilfred** (Sr J US Ct of App 2nd Circ) U.S. Cthse., 40 Foley Sq., N.Y.C. 10007

(585) 613-4070 **Feldman, Jonathan W.** (US Magis J West Dist) U.S. Cthse., Rm. 2330, 100 State St., Rochester 14614-1387; **Fax:** (585) 613-4075

(347) 394-1830 **Feller, Jerome** (J US Bank Ct East Dist) 271 Cadman Plaza E., Suite 1595, Bklyn. 11201-1800; **Fax:** (347) 394-1835

(631) 712-5630 **Feuerstein, Sandra J.** (J US Dist Ct East Dist) Alfonse M. D'Amato U.S. Cthse., Rm. 1014, 100 Federal Plaza, Central Islip 11722-4449; **Fax:** (631) 712-5636

(716) 332-7850 **Foschio, Leslie G.** (US Magis J West Dist) U.S. Cthse., Rm. 310, 68 Court St., Buffalo 14202-3406; **Fax:** (716) 332-7855

(212) 805-6705 **Fox, Kevin Nathaniel** (US Magis J South Dist) Daniel Patrick Moynihan U.S. Cthse., Rm. 530, 500 Pearl St., N.Y.C. 10007-1312; **Fax:** (212) 805-6712

(212) 805-0206 **Francis, James C., IV** (US Magis J South Dist) Daniel Patrick Moynihan U.S. Cthse., Rm. 1960, 500 Pearl St., N.Y.C. 10007-1312

(212) 805-4250 **Freeman, Debra** (US Magis J South Dist) Daniel Patrick Moynihan U.S. Cthse., Rm. 525, 500 Pearl St., N.Y.C. 10007-1312

(718) 613-2540 **Garaufis, Nicholas G.** (J US Dist Ct East Dist) U.S. Cthse., Rm. 1416S, 225 Cadman Plaza East, Bklyn. 11201; **Fax:** (718) 613-2330

(212) 805-0224 **Gardephe, Paul G.** (J US Dist Ct South Dist) Daniel Patrick Moynihan U.S. Cthse., Rm. 920, 500 Pearl St., N.Y.C. 10007-1312

(212) 668-5660 **Gerber, Robert E.** (J US Bank Ct South Dist) Alexander Hamilton Custom House, One Bowling Green, N.Y.C. 10004-1408

(718) 613-2650 **Gershon, Nina** (Sr J US Dist Ct East Dist) U.S. Cthse., Rm. 1429S, 225 Cadman Plaza East, Bklyn. 11201; **Fax:** (718) 613-2656

(718) 613-2440 **Glasser, I. Leo** (Sr J US Dist Ct East Dist) U.S. Cthse., Rm. 921S, 225 Cadman Plaza East, Bklyn. 11201; **Fax:** (718) 613-2446

(718) 613-2450 **Gleeson, John** (J US Dist Ct East Dist) U.S. Cthse., Rm. 727S, 225 Cadman Plaza East, Bklyn. 11201; **Fax:** (718) 613-2456

(212) 284-4551 **Glenn, Martin** (J US Bank Ct South Dist) Alexander Hamilton Custom House, One Bowling Green, N.Y.C. 10004-1408

(718) 613-2550 **Go, Marilyn Dolan** (US Magis J East Dist) U.S. Cthse., Rm. 1214S, 225 Cadman Plaza East, Bklyn. 11201; **Fax:** (718) 613-2555

(718) 613-2560 **Gold, Steven M.** (Chief US Magis J East Dist) U.S. Cthse., Rm. 1217S, 225 Cadman Plaza East, Bklyn. 11201; **Fax:** (718) 613-2565

(845) 343-1130 **Goldberg, Martin R.** (US Magis J South Dist) 225 Dolson Ave., Suite 206, P.O. Box 2083, Middletown 10940; **Fax:** (845) 344-5547

(845) 343-1130 Courtroom Address, 25 South St., Middletown 10940

(212) 264-1615 **Goldberg, Richard W.** (Sr J US Ct of Intl Trade) One Federal Plaza, N.Y.C. 10278-0001; **Fax:** (212) 264-1085

(212) 668-2894 **Gonzalez, Arthur J.** (Chief J US Bank Ct South Dist) Alexander Hamilton Custom House, One Bowling Green, N.Y.C. 10004-1408

(212) 264-2018 **Gordon, Leo M.** (J US Ct of Intl Trade) One Federal Plaza, N.Y.C. 10278-0001; **Fax:** (212) 264-1085

(212) 805-4260 **Gorenstein, Gabriel W.** (US Magis J South Dist) Daniel Patrick Moynihan U.S. Cthse., Rm. 510, 500 Pearl St., N.Y.C. 10007-1312

(212) 805-0210 **Griesa, Thomas P.** (Sr J US Dist Ct South Dist) Daniel Patrick Moynihan U.S. Cthse., Rm. 1630, 500 Pearl St., N.Y.C. 10007-1312

(212) 668-5629 **Gropper, Allan L.** (J US Bank Ct South Dist) Alexander Hamilton Custom House, One Bowling Green, N.Y.C. 10004-1408

(631) 712-5740 **Grossman, Robert E.** (J US Bank Ct East Dist) 290 Federal Plaza, P.O. Box 9013, Central Islip 11722; **Fax:** (631) 712-6298

(203) 773-2052 **Haight, Charles S., Jr.** (Sr J US Dist Ct South Dist) U.S. Cthse., Chambers 17C, 141 Church St., New Haven, CT 06510

(802) 775-3712 **Hall, Peter W.** (J US Ct of App 2nd Circ) P.O. Box 885, Rutland, VT 05702

(212) 805-0152 **Hellerstein, Alvin K.** (J US Dist Ct South Dist) Daniel Patrick Moynihan U.S. Cthse., Rm. 1050, 500 Pearl St., N.Y.C. 10007-1312

(212) 805-0256 **Holwell, Richard J.** (J US Dist Ct South Dist) Daniel Patrick Moynihan U.S. Cthse., Rm. 1950, 500 Pearl St., N.Y.C. 10007-1312

(518) 257-1850 **Homer, David R.** (US Magis J North Dist) James T. Foley U.S. Cthse., 445 Broadway, Albany 12207-2974; **Fax:** (518) 257-1851

(315) 793-9571 **Hurd, David N.** (J US Dist Ct North Dist) Alexander Pirnie Fedl. Bldg., Rm. 300, 10 Broad St., Utica 13501; **Fax:** (315) 793-8034

(631) 712-5650 **Hurley, Denis R., Sr.** (Sr J US Dist Ct East Dist) Alfonse M. D'Amato U.S. Cthse., Rm. 934, 100 Federal Plaza, Central Islip 11722-4449

(718) 613-2150 **Irizarry, Dora L.** (J US Dist Ct East Dist) U.S. Cthse., Rm. 928S, 225 Cadman Plaza East, Bklyn. 11201; **Fax:** (718) 613-2156

(212) 857-2150 **Jacobs, Dennis** (Chief J US Ct of App 2nd Circ) U.S. Cthse., 40 Foley Sq., N.Y.C. 10007

(718) 613-2460 **Johnson, Sterling, Jr.** (Sr J US Dist Ct East Dist) U.S. Cthse., Rm. 720S, 225 Cadman Plaza East, Bklyn. 11201; **Fax:** (718) 613-2466

(212) 805-6185 **Jones, Barbara S.** (J US Dist Ct South Dist) Daniel Patrick Moynihan U.S. Cthse., Rm. 1920, 500 Pearl St., N.Y.C. 10007-1312

(518) 257-1830 **Kahn, Lawrence E.** (Sr J US Dist Ct North Dist) James T. Foley U.S. Cthse., Rm. 424, 445 Broadway, Albany 12207-2974; **Fax:** (518) 257-1831

(212) 805-0216 **Kaplan, Lewis A.** (J US Dist Ct South Dist) Daniel Patrick Moynihan U.S. Cthse., Rm. 1310, 500 Pearl St., N.Y.C. 10007-1312

(716) 362-3271 **Kaplan, Michael J.** (J US Bank Ct West Dist) Olympic Towers, Suite 350, 300 Pearl St., Buffalo 14202-2501; **Fax:** (716) 362-3232

(914) 390-4145 **Karas, Kenneth M.** (J US Dist Ct South Dist) U.S. Cthse., Rm. 533, 300 Quarropas St., White Plains 10601

(212) 805-0218 **Katz, Theodore H.** (US Magis J South Dist) Daniel Patrick Moynihan U.S. Cthse., Rm. 1660, 500 Pearl St., N.Y.C. 10007-1312

(212) 857-2180 **Katzmann, Robert A.** (J US Ct of App 2nd Circ) U.S. Cthse., 40 Foley Sq., N.Y.C. 10007

(212) 857-2250 **Kearse, Amalya L.** (Sr J US Ct of App 2nd Circ) U.S. Cthse., 40 Foley Sq., N.Y.C. 10007

(212) 805-0220 **Keenan, John F.** (Sr J US Dist Ct South Dist) Daniel Patrick Moynihan U.S. Cthse., Rm. 1930, 500 Pearl St., N.Y.C. 10007-1312

(212) 805-0222 **Koeltl, John G.** (J US Dist Ct South Dist) Daniel Patrick Moynihan U.S. Cthse., Rm. 1030, 500 Pearl St., N.Y.C. 10007-1312

(718) 613-2470 **Korman, Edward R.** (Sr J US Dist Ct East Dist) U.S. Cthse., Rm. 918S, 225 Cadman Plaza East, Bklyn. 11201; **Fax:** (718) 613-2477

(212) 668-5637 **Lane, Sean H.** (J US Bank Ct South Dist) Alexander Hamilton Custom House, One Bowling Green, N.Y.C. 10004-1408

(585) 613-4040 **Larimer, David G.** (Sr J US Dist Ct West Dist) U.S. Cthse., Rm. 2500, 100 State St., Rochester 14614-1387; **Fax:** (585) 613-4045

(212) 805-0226 **Leisure, Peter K.** (Sr J US Dist Ct South Dist) Daniel Patrick Moynihan U.S. Cthse., Rm. 1910, 500 Pearl St., N.Y.C. 10007-1312

(212) 857-2310 **Leval, Pierre N.** (Sr J US Ct of App 2nd Circ) U.S. Cthse., 40 Foley Sq., N.Y.C. 10007

(718) 613-2340 **Levy, Robert M.** (US Magis J East Dist) U.S. Cthse., Rm. 1223S, 225 Cadman Plaza East, Bklyn. 11201; **Fax:** (718) 613-2345

(212) 668-5663 **Lifland, Burton R.** (J US Bank Ct South Dist) Alexander Hamilton Custom House, One Bowling Green, N.Y.C. 10004-1408

(631) 712-5730 **Lindsay, Arlene R.** (US Magis J East Dist) Alfonse M. D'Amato U.S. Cthse., Rm. 814, 100 Federal Plaza, Central Islip 11722-4449

(518) 257-1661 **Littlefield, Robert E., Jr.** (Chief J US Bank Ct North Dist) 330 James T. Foley U.S. Cthse., 445 Broadway, Albany 12207; **Fax:** (518) 257-1648

(212) 857-2230 **Livingston, Debra Ann** (J US Ct of App 2nd Circ) U.S. Cthse., 40 Foley Sq., N.Y.C. 10007

(315) 234-8610 **Lowe, George H.** (US Magis J North Dist) James Hanley Fedl. Bldg. U.S. Cthse., 100 S. Clinton St., P.O. Box 7346, Syracuse 13261-7346; **Fax:** (315) 234-8611

(212) 805-0427 **Lynch, Gerard E.** (J US Ct of App 2nd Circ) 500 Pearl St., Rm. 910, N.Y.C. 10007-1312

(212) 805-6727 **Maas, Frank** (US Magis J South Dist) Daniel Patrick Moynihan U.S. Cthse., Rm. 740, 500 Pearl St., N.Y.C. 10007-1312; **Fax:** (212) 805-6724

(718) 613-2350 **Mann, Roanne L.** (US Magis J East Dist) U.S. Cthse., Rm. 1220S, 225 Cadman Plaza East, Bklyn. 11201; **Fax:** (718) 613-2355

(212) 805-6374 **Marrero, Victor** (J US Dist Ct South Dist) Daniel Patrick Moynihan U.S. Cthse., Rm. 660, 500 Pearl St., N.Y.C. 10007-1312; **Fax:** (212) 805-6382

(718) 613-2180 **Matsumoto, Kiyo A.** (J US Dist Ct East Dist) U.S. Cthse., Rm. N406, 225 Cadman Plaza East, Bklyn. 11201; **Fax:** (718) 613-2185

(718) 613-2210 **Mauskopf, Roslynn R.** (J US Dist Ct East Dist) U.S. Cthse., Rm. N626, 225 Cadman Plaza East, Bklyn. 11201; **Fax:** (718) 613-2216

(607) 773-2892 **McAvoy, Thomas J.** (Sr J US Dist Ct North Dist) Fedl. Bldg. & U.S. Cthse., 15 Henry St., Binghamton 13901

(716) 362-9350 **McCarthy, Jeremiah J.** (US Magis J West Dist) U.S. Cthse., Rm. 424, 68 Court St., Buffalo 14202-3406; **Fax:** (716) 362-9355

(315) 234-8590 **McCurn, Neal P.** (Sr J US Dist Ct North Dist) James Hanley Fedl. Bldg. U.S. Cthse., 100 S. Clinton St., P.O. Box 7367, Syracuse 13261-7365; **Fax:** (315) 234-8591

(212) 805-0230 **McKenna, Lawrence M.** (Sr J US Dist Ct South Dist) Daniel Patrick Moynihan U.S. Cthse., Rm. 1640, 500 Pearl St., N.Y.C. 10007-1312

(212) 857-2200 **McLaughlin, Joseph M.** (Sr J US Ct of App 2nd Circ) U.S. Cthse., 40 Foley Sq., N.Y.C. 10007

(212) 805-6325 **McMahon, Colleen** (J US Dist Ct South Dist) Daniel Patrick Moynihan U.S. Cthse., Chambers 1350, 500 Pearl St., N.Y.C. 10007-1312

(518) 431-0401 **Miner, Roger J.** (Sr J US Ct of App 2nd Circ) 414 James T. Foley U.S. Cthse., 445 Broadway, Albany 12207-2928

(315) 234-8570 **Mordue, Norman A.** (Chief J US Dist Ct North Dist) James Hanley Fedl. Bldg. U.S. Cthse., 100 S. Clinton St., P.O. Box 7336, Syracuse 13261-7336; **Fax:** (315) 234-8571

(845) 452-4200 **Morris, Cecelia G.** (J US Bank Ct South Dist) 355 Main St., Poughkeepsie 12601; **Fax:** (845) 452-8375

(212) 264-1628 **Musgrave, R. Kenton** (Sr J US Ct of Intl Trade) One Federal Plaza, N.Y.C. 10278-0001; **Fax:** (212) 264-1085

(860) 240-3260 **Newman, Jon O.** (Sr J US Ct of App 2nd Circ) U.S. Cthse., 450 Main St., Hartford, CT 06103

(585) 613-4200 **Ninfo, John C., II** (J US Bank Ct West Dist) 1400 U.S. Cthse., 100 State St., Rochester 14614-1367; **Fax:** (585) 613-4242

(718) 613-2110 **Orenstein, James** (US Magis J East Dist) U.S. Cthse., 225 Cadman Plaza East, Bklyn. 11201; **Fax:** (718) 613-2115

(631) 712-5700 **Orenstein, Michael L.** (US Magis J East Dist) Alfonse M. D'Amato U.S. Cthse., Rm. 844, 100 Federal Plaza, Central Islip 11722-4449; **Fax:** (631) 712-5705

(212) 805-6155 **Owen, Richard** (Sr J US Dist Ct South Dist) Daniel Patrick Moynihan U.S. Cthse., Rm. 2240, 500 Pearl St., N.Y.C. 10007-1312; **Fax:** (212) 805-6161

(212) 857-2211 **Parker, Barrington D., Jr.** (Sr J US Ct of App 2nd Circ) U.S. Cthse., 40 Foley Sq., N.Y.C. 10007

(212) 805-0238 **Patterson, Robert P., Jr.** (Sr J US Dist Ct South Dist) Daniel Patrick Moynihan U.S. Cthse., Rm. 2550, 500 Pearl St., N.Y.C. 10007-1312; **Fax:** (212) 805-7917

(212) 805-6387 **Pauley, William H., III** (J US Dist Ct South Dist) Daniel Patrick Moynihan U.S. Cthse., Rm. 2210, 500 Pearl St., N.Y.C. 10007-1312

(585) 613-4080 **Payson, Marian W.** (US Magis J West Dist) U.S. Cthse., Suite 2310, 100 State St., Rochester 14614-1387; **Fax:** (585) 613-4085

(212) 805-0036 **Peck, Andrew J.** (US Magis J South Dist) Daniel Patrick Moynihan U.S. Cthse., Rm. 1370, 500 Pearl St., N.Y.C. 10007-1312; **Fax:** (212) 805-7933

(212) 668-5632 **Peck, James M.** (J US Bank Ct South Dist) Alexander Hamilton Custom House, One Bowling Green, N.Y.C. 10004-1408

(315) 234-8620 **Peebles, David E.** (US Magis J North Dist) James Hanley Fedl. Bldg. U.S. Cthse., 100 S. Clinton St., P.O. Box 7367, Syracuse 13261-7367; **Fax:** (315) 234-8621

(212) 805-6105 **Pitman, Henry** (Chief US Magis J South Dist) Daniel Patrick Moynihan U.S. Cthse., Rm. 750, 500 Pearl St., N.Y.C. 10007-1312

(631) 712-5600 **Platt, Thomas C.** (Sr J US Dist Ct East Dist) Alfonse M. D'Amato U.S. Cthse., Rm. 1044, 100 Federal Plaza, Central Islip 11722-4449; **Fax:** (631) 712-5606

(212) 264-1628 **Pogue, Donald C.** (J US Ct of Intl Trade) One Federal Plaza, N.Y.C. 10278-0001; **Fax:** (212) 264-1085

(718) 613-2400 **Pohorelsky, Viktor V.** (US Magis J East Dist) U.S. Cthse., Rm. 1207S, 225 Cadman Plaza East, Bklyn. 11201; **Fax:** (718) 613-2405

(718) 613-2360 **Pollak, Cheryl L.** (US Magis J East Dist) U.S. Cthse., Rm. 1230S, 225 Cadman Plaza East, Bklyn. 11201; **Fax:** (718) 613-2365

(315) 448-0420 **Pooler, Rosemary S.** (J US Ct of App 2nd Circ) U.S. Cthse., 100 S. Clinton St., P.O. Box 7395, Syracuse 13261-7395

(212) 805-0240 **Preska, Loretta A.** (Chief J US Dist Ct South Dist) Daniel Patrick Moynihan U.S. Cthse., Rm. 1320, 500 Pearl St., N.Y.C. 10007-1312

(718) 613-2490 **Raggi, Reena** (J US Ct of App 2nd Circ) U.S. Cthse., 225 Cadman Plaza E., Brooklyn 11201

(212) 805-0401 **Rakoff, Jed S.** (J US Dist Ct South Dist) Daniel Patrick Moynihan U.S. Cthse., Rm. 1340, 500 Pearl St., N.Y.C. 10007-1312

(212) 264-2018 **Restani, Jane A.** (Chief J US Ct of Intl Trade) One Federal Plaza, N.Y.C. 10278-0001; **Fax:** (212) 264-1085

(718) 613-2120 **Reyes, Ramon, Jr.** (US Magis J East Dist) U.S. Cthse., Rm. N208, 225 Cadman Plaza East, Bklyn. 11201; **Fax:** (718) 613-2125

(212) 264-1615 **Ridgway, Delissa A.** (J US Ct of Intl Trade) One Federal Plaza, N.Y.C. 10278-0001; **Fax:** (212) 264-1085

(718) 613-2380 **Ross, Allyne R.** (J US Dist Ct East Dist) U.S. Cthse., Rm. 915S, 225 Cadman Plaza East, Bklyn. 11201; **Fax:** (718) 613-2386

(212) 857-2140 **Sack, Robert D.** (Sr J US Ct of App 2nd Circ) U.S. Cthse., 40 Foley Sq., N.Y.C. 10007

(212) 805-0244 **Sand, Leonard B.** (Sr J US Dist Ct South Dist) Daniel Patrick Moynihan U.S. Cthse., Rm. 1650, 500 Pearl St., N.Y.C. 10007-1312

(212) 805-0246 **Scheindlin, Shira** (J US Dist Ct South Dist) Daniel Patrick Moynihan U.S. Cthse., Rm. 1620, 500 Pearl St., N.Y.C. 10007-1312; **Fax:** (212) 805-7920

(716) 332-7870 **Schroeder, H. Kenneth, Jr.** (US Magis J West Dist) U.S. Cthse., Rm. 418, 68 Court St., Buffalo 14202-3406; **Fax:** (716) 332-7875

(716) 332-7860 **Scott, Hugh B.** (US Magis J West Dist) U.S. Cthse., Rm. 414, 68 Court St., Buffalo 14202-3406; **Fax:** (716) 332-7865

(315) 234-8560 **Scullin, Frederick J., Jr.** (Sr J US Dist Ct North Dist) James Hanley Fedl. Bldg. U.S. Cthse., 100 S. Clinton St., P.O. Box 7367, Syracuse 13261-7255; **Fax:** (315) 234-8561

(914) 390-4271 **Seibel, Cathy** (J US Dist Ct South Dist) U.S. Cthse., Rm. 275, 300 Quarropas St., White Plains 10601; **Fax:** (914) 390-4271

(631) 712-5610 **Seybert, Joanna** (J US Dist Ct East Dist) Alfonse M. D'Amato U.S. Cthse., Rm. 1034, 100 Federal Plaza, Central Islip 11722-4449; **Fax:** (631) 712-5611

(518) 257-1870 **Sharpe, Gary L.** (J US Dist Ct North Dist) James T. Foley U.S. Cthse., 445 Broadway, Albany 12207-2974

(585) 613-4050 **Siragusa, Charles J.** (J US Dist Ct West Dist) U.S. Cthse., Rm. 1380, 100 State St., Rochester 14614-1387; **Fax:** (585) 613-4055

(716) 332-7820 **Skretny, William M.** (Chief J US Dist Ct West Dist) U.S. Cthse., Rm. 507, 68 Court St., Buffalo 14202-3406; **Fax:** (716) 332-7825

(914) 390-4130 **Smith, Lisa Margaret** (US Magis J South Dist) U.S. Cthse., Rm. 530, 300 Quarropas St., White Plains 10601

(631) 712-5620 **Spatt, Arthur D.** (Sr J US Dist Ct East Dist) Alfonse M. D'Amato U.S. Cthse., Rm. 1024, 100 Federal Plaza, Central Islip 11722-4449; **Fax:** (631) 712-5626

(212) 264-2923 **Stanceu, Timothy C.** (J US Ct of Intl Trade) One Federal Plaza, N.Y.C. 10278-0001; **Fax:** (212) 264-1085

(212) 805-0252 **Stanton, Louis L.** (Sr J US Dist Ct South Dist) Daniel Patrick Moynihan U.S. Cthse., Rm. 2250, 500 Pearl St., N.Y.C. 10007-1312

(212) 805-0192 **Stein, Sidney H.** (J US Dist Ct South Dist) Daniel Patrick Moynihan U.S. Cthse., Rm. 1010, 500 Pearl St., N.Y.C. 10007-1312

(347) 394-1862 **Stong, Elizabeth S.** (J US Bank Ct East Dist) 271 Cadman Plaza E., Suite 1595, Bklyn. 11201-1800

(212) 857-2130 **Straub, Chester J.** (Sr J US Ct of App 2nd Circ) 2530 U.S. Cthse., 500 Pearl St., N.Y.C. 10007

(315) 234-8580 **Suddaby, Glenn T.** (J US Dist Ct North Dist) James Hanley Fedl. Bldg. U.S. Cthse., 100 S. Clinton St., P.O. Box 7367, Syracuse 13261-7367; **Fax:** (315) 234-8581

(212) 805-0264 **Sullivan, Richard J.** (J US Dist Ct South Dist) Daniel Patrick Moynihan U.S. Cthse., Rm. 640, 500 Pearl St., N.Y.C. 10007-1312

(212) 805-0417 **Swain, Laura Taylor** (J US Dist Ct South Dist) Daniel Patrick Moynihan U.S. Cthse., Rm. 755, 500 Pearl St., N.Y.C. 10007-1312; **Fax:** (212) 805-0426

(212) 805-0254 **Sweet, Robert W.** (Sr J US Dist Ct South Dist) Daniel Patrick Moynihan U.S. Cthse., Rm. 1940, 500 Pearl St., N.Y.C. 10007-1312

(585) 613-4060 **Telesca, Michael A.** (Sr J US Dist Ct West Dist) U.S. Cthse., Rm. 2720, 100 State St., Rochester 14614-1387; **Fax:** (585) 613-4065

(631) 712-5760 **Tomlinson, A. Kathleen** (US Magis J East Dist) Alfonse M. D'Amato U.S. Cthse., Rm. 914, 100 Federal Plaza, Central Islip 11722-4449

(718) 613-2160 **Townes, Sandra L.** (J US Dist Ct East Dist) U.S. Cthse., Rm. 905S, 225 Cadman Plaza East, Bklyn. 11201; **Fax:** (718) 613-2330

(718) 613-2510 **Trager, David G.** (Sr J US Dist Ct East Dist) U.S. Cthse., Rm. 707S, 225 Cadman Plaza East, Bklyn. 11201; **Fax:** (718) 613-2518

(518) 257-1840 **Treece, Randolph F.** (US Magis J North Dist) James T. Foley U.S. Cthse., 445 Broadway, Albany 12207-2974; **Fax:** (518) 257-1841

(631) 712-5680 **Trust, Alan S.** (J US Bank Ct East Dist) 290 Federal Plaza, P.O. Box 9013, Central Islip 11722; **Fax:** (631) 712-6298

(212) 264-2923 **Tsoucalas, Nicholas** (Sr J US Ct of Intl Trade) One Federal Plaza, N.Y.C. 10278-0001; **Fax:** (212) 264-1085

(718) 613-2130 **Vitaliano, Eric N.** (J US Dist Ct East Dist) U.S. Cthse., Rm. 714S, 225 Cadman Plaza East, Bklyn. 11201; **Fax:** (718) 613-2136

(203) 773-2181 **Walker, John M., Jr.** (Sr J US Ct of App 2nd Circ) Connecticut Financial Center, 157 Church St., New Haven, CT 06510

(631) 712-5720 **Wall, William D.** (US Magis J East Dist) Alfonse M. D'Amato U.S. Cthse., Rm. 824, 100 Federal Plaza, Central Islip 11722-4449; **Fax:** (631) 712-5725

(212) 264-1628 **Wallach, Evan J.** (J US Ct of Intl Trade) One Federal Plaza, N.Y.C. 10278-0001; **Fax:** (212) 264-1085

(718) 613-2520 **Weinstein, Jack B.** (Sr J US Dist Ct East Dist) U.S. Cthse., Rm. 1420S, 225 Cadman Plaza East, Bklyn. 11201; **Fax:** (718) 613-2527

(585) 243-7910 **Wesley, Richard C.** (J US Ct of App 2nd Circ) Livingston Cty. Govt. Center, 6 Court St., Geneseo 14454-1030

(631) 712-5640 **Wexler, Leonard D.** (Sr J US Dist Ct East Dist) Alfonse M. D'Amato U.S. Cthse., Rm. 944, 100 Federal Plaza, Central Islip 11722-4449

(203) 782-3682 **Winter, Ralph K.** (Sr J US Ct of App 2nd Circ) U.S. Cthse., 141 Church St., New Haven, CT 06510

(212) 805-0258 **Wood, Kimba M.** (Sr J US Dist Ct South Dist) Daniel Patrick Moynihan U.S. Cthse., Rm. 1610, 500 Pearl St., N.Y.C. 10007-1312; **Fax:** (212) 805-7900

(914) 390-4088 **Yanthis, George A.** (US Magis J South Dist) U.S. Cthse., Rm. 118, 300 Quarropas St., White Plains 10601

State, County and City Court Judges

(718) 618-3643 **Aarons, Sharon A.M.** (Justice Sup Ct 12th Jud Dist Crim Term) Bronx Hall of Justice, 265 E. 161st St., Bronx 10451; **Fax:** (718) 618-3584

(212) 340-0561 **Abdus-Salaam, Sheila** (Assoc Justice App Div 1st Dept) 27 Madison Ave., N.Y.C. 10010

(518) 451-8888 **Abramson, Gil L.** (J Saratoga Cty Family Ct) Saratoga Cty. Munic. Ctr., 35 W. High St., Ballston Spa 12020-0600

(212) 340-0400 **Acosta, Rolando T.** (Assoc Justice App Div 1st Dept) 27 Madison Ave., N.Y.C. 10010

(585) 344-2550, Ext. 2233 **Adams, Eric R.** (J Genesee Cty Family Ct) Genesee Cty. Cts. Facility, 1 W. Main St., Batavia 14020; **Fax:** (585) 344-8520; **E-mail:** eradams@courts.state.ny.us

(646) 386-5104 **Adams, Jody** (J Family Ct of NYC) 60 Lafayette St., N.Y.C. 10013

(347) 401-9260 **Adams, Rachel Amy** (J Civil Ct of NYC & Acting Justice Sup Ct 2nd Jud Dist) 360 Adams St., Bklyn. 11201; **Fax:** (212) 401-9232

(516) 571-2961 **Adams, Thomas A.** (J Ct of Claims & Acting Justice Sup Ct 10th Jud Dist) Supreme Ct. Bldg., 100 Supreme Ct. Dr., Mineola 11501; **Fax:** (516) 571-1704

(718) 618-3619 **Adler, Harold A.** (J Civil Ct of NYC & Acting Justice Sup Ct 12th Jud Dist Crim Term) Bronx Hall of Justice, 265 E. 161st St., Bronx 10451; **Fax:** (718) 618-3584

(914) 824-5386 **Adler, Lester B.** (Justice Sup Ct 9th Jud Dist) Richard J. Daronco Cthse., 111 Dr. Martin Luther King, Jr. Blvd., White Plains 10601; **Fax:** (914) 995-8653

(585) 428-5397 **Affronti, Francis A.** (Justice Sup Ct 7th Jud Dist) 545 Hall of Justice, 99 Exchange Blvd., Rochester 14614-2184; **Fax:** (585) 784-4219

(718) 298-1186 **Agate, Augustus C.** (Justice Sup Ct 11th Jud Dist) 88-11 Sutphin Blvd., Jamaica 11435; **Fax:** (718) 298-1158; **E-mail:** agate@courts.state.ny.us

(518) 842-9510 **Aison, Howard M.** (J Amsterdam City Ct) Public Safety Bldg., Rm. 208, One Guy Park Ave. Ext., Amsterdam 12010; **Fax:** (518) 843-8474

(631) 853-4915 **Alamia, Salvatore A.** (J Suffolk Cty Dist Ct) John P. Cohalan, Jr. Ct. Complex, 400 Carleton Ave., P.O. Box 9075, Central Islip 11722-9075

(516) 572-2103 **Alexander, Valerie J.** (J Nassau Cty Dist Ct) 99 Main St., Hempstead 11550; **E-mail:** valexand@courts.state.ny.us

(718) 675-8620 **Aliotta, Thomas P.** (Justice Sup Ct 13th Jud Dist) Cty. Cthse., 18 Richmond Terr., Staten Island 10301; **Fax:** (718) 876-8129

(646) 386-4408 **Allen, Bruce** (J Crim Ct of NYC & Acting Justice Sup Ct 1st Jud Dist) 111 Centre St., N.Y.C. 10013

(315) 671-1054 **Aloi, Anthony F.** (J Onondaga Cty Ct) Cthse., 505 S. State St., Syracuse 13202; **Fax:** (315) 671-1191

(718) 298-1373 **Aloise, Michael B.** (Justice Sup Ct 11th Jud Dist) 125-01 Queens Blvd., Kew Gardens 11415; **Fax:** (718) 520-2494; **E-mail:** maloise@courts.state.ny.us

(718) 618-2200 **Alpert, Allen G.** (J Crim Ct of NYC assigned to Family Ct & Acting Justice Sup Ct 12th Jud Dist Crim Term) 900 Sheridan Ave., Bronx 10451

(718) 466-3126 **Alpert, Paul L.** (J Civil Ct of NYC Housing Part) Housing Ct., 1118 Grand Concourse, Bronx 10456

(718) 466-3171 **Alterman, Ava P.** (J Civil Ct of NYC Housing Part) Housing Ct., 1118 Grand Concourse, Bronx 10456

(718) 618-3700 **Alvarado, Efrain** (J Crim Ct of NYC & Admin J Sup Ct 12th Jud Dist Crim Term) Bronx Hall of Justice, 265 E. 161st St., Bronx 10451; **Fax:** (718) 618-3584**Fax:** (718) 618-3584

(631) 852-3428 **Ambro, Richard** (J Suffolk Cty Ct) Arthur M. Cromarty Ct. Complex, 210 Center Dr., Riverhead 11901-3310

(347) 296-1854 **Ambrosio, Michael A.** (J Family Ct of NYC & Acting Justice Sup Ct 2nd Jud Dist) 360 Adams St., Bklyn. 11201

(607) 758-5556 **Ames, William F.** ((J Cortland Cty Ct Family Ct & Surro) Cthse., Suite 301, 46 Greenbush St., Cortland 13045-2725; **Fax:** (607) 753-1899

(716) 845-2651 **Amodeo, Thomas P.** (Chief & Supv J Buffalo City Ct) 50 Delaware Ave., Suite 750, Buffalo 14202; **Fax:** (716) 845-7568; **E-mail:** tamodeo@courts.state.ny.us

(646) 386-5000 **Anderson, Nora S.** (New York Cty Surro) 31 Chambers St., Rm. 303, N.Y.C. 10007; **Fax:** (212) 374-3250

(212) 340-0400 **Andrias, Richard T.** (Assoc Justice App Div 1st Dept) 27 Madison Ave., N.Y.C. 10010

(914) 824-5390 **Angiolillo, Daniel D.** (Assoc Justice App Div 2nd Dept) Courthouse Sq., Rm. 644, 140 Grand St., White Plains 10601; **Fax:** (914) 946-1026

(718) 875-1300 45 Monroe Pl., Bklyn. 11201

(518) 773-4527 **Antonik, Joan** (J Gloversville City Ct) City Hall, 3 Frontage Rd., Gloversville 12078; **Fax:** (518) 773-4599

(516) 572-2115 **Anzalone, Anna R.** (J Nassau Cty Dist Ct) 99 Main St., Hempstead 11550

(845) 638-5239 **Apotheker, Charles** (J Rockland Cty Ct & Acting Justice Sup Ct 9th Jud Dist) Cthse., Suite 200, 1 S. Main St., New City 10956

(607) 535-7015 **Argetsinger, J.C.** (J Schuyler Cty Ct Family Ct & Surro & Acting Justice Sup Ct 6th Jud Dist) Schuyler County Cthse., Unit 35, 105 9th St., Watkins Glen 14891; **Fax:** (607) 535-4718

(718) 298-0204 **Arias, Maria** (J Family Ct of NYC) 151-20 Jamaica Ave., Jamaica 11432; **Fax:** (718) 297-2530

(585) 428-3547 **Ark, John J.** (Justice Sup Ct 7th Jud Dist) 545 Hall of Justice, 99 Exchange Blvd., Rochester 14614-2184; **Fax:** (585) 784-4218

(585) 396-5011 **Aronson, Stephen D.** (J Canandaigua City Ct) City Hall, 2 N. Main St., Canandaigua 14424-1448; **Fax:** (585) 396-5012; **E-mail:** saronson@courts.state.ny.us

(347) 404-9467 **Arriaga, Frederick C.** (J Civil Ct of NYC) 141 Livingston St., Bklyn. 11201

(516) 571-2870 **Asarch, Joel K.** (Justice Sup Ct 10th Jud Dist) Supreme Ct. Bldg., 100 Supreme Court Dr., Mineola 11501; **E-mail:** asarch@courts.state.ny.us

(347) 404-9096 **Ash, Sylvia G.** (J Civil Ct of NYC) 141 Livingston St., Bklyn. 11201; **E-mail:** sash@courts.state.ny.us

(631) 852-3415 **Asher, W. Gerard** (J Suffolk Cty Dist Ct & Acting J Suffolk Cty Ct) John P. Cohalan, Jr. Ct. Complex, 400 Carleton Ave., P.O. Box 9075, Central Islip 11722-9075

(518) 285-8435 **Assini, Jo Anne** (J Schenectady Cty Family Ct) 620 State St., Schenectady 12305-2114; **Fax:** (518) 393-1565; **E-mail:** jassini@courts.state.ny.us

(518) 736-5533 **Aulisi, Richard T.** (Justice Sup Ct 4th Jud Dist) Cty. Bldg., 223 W. Main St., Johnstown 12095; **Fax:** (518) 762-1158

(516) 571-2683 **Austin, Leonard B.** (Assoc Justice App Div 2nd Dept) Supreme Ct. Bldg., 100 Supreme Court Dr., Mineola 11501; **Fax:** (516) 571-0131; **E-mail:** laustin@courts.state.ny.us

(516) 571-3833 **Ayres, David J.** (J Nassau Cty Ct & Acting Justice Sup Ct 10th Jud Dist) West Wing, 252 Old Country Rd., Mineola 11501; **Fax:** (516) 571-2137; **E-mail:** dayres@courts.state.ny.us

(718) 262-7363 **Badillo, Gilbert** (Supv J Civil Ct of NYC Housing Part) 89-17 Sutphin Blvd., Jamaica 11435

(315) 671-2030 **Bailey, Michele Pirro** (J Onondaga Cty Family Ct) Onondaga Cty. Cthse., 401 Montgomery St., Syracuse 13202; **Fax:** (315) 671-1168; **E-mail:** mbailey@courts.state.ny.us

(716) 845-7475 **Bailey, Rosalie S.** (J Erie Cty Family Ct) One Niagara Plaza, Rm. 700, Buffalo 14202; **Fax:** (716) 858-7789

(347) 401-9015 **Baily-Schiffman, Loren** (J Civil Ct of NYC & Acting Justice Sup Ct 2nd Jud Dist) 320 Jay St., Bklyn. 11201

(631) 852-3888 **Baisley, Paul J., Jr.** (Justice Sup Ct 10th Jud Dist) Supreme Ct. Bldg., Rm. A-301, 1 Court St., Riverhead 11901; **Fax:** (631) 852-3745

(585) 344-2550 Ext. 2420 **Balbick, Robert J.** (J Batavia City Ct) Genesee Cty. Cts. Facility, 1 W. Main St., Batavia 14020; **Fax:** (585) 344-8556; **E-mail:** rbalbick@courts.state.ny.us

(516) 571-2323 **Balkin, Ruth C.** (Assoc Justice App Div 2nd Dept) 100 Supreme Court Dr., Rm. 419, Mineola 11501; **Fax:** (516) 571-0180

(718) 875-1300 45 Monroe Pl., Bklyn. 11201

(845) 338-2974 **Ball, Lawrence E.** (J Kingston City Ct) 1 Garraghan Dr., Kingston 12401; **Fax:** (845) 338-1443

(347) 296-1842 **Balter, Bruce M.** (Justice Sup Ct 2nd Jud Dist) 320 Jay St., Bklyn. 11201; **Fax:** (347) 296-1352

(315) 266-4607 **Balzano, John S.** (J Utica City Ct) 411 Oriskany St. W., Utica 13502; **Fax:** (315) 733-7927

(716) 845-9492 **Bannister, Tracey A.** (Justice Sup Ct 8th Jud Dist) Buffalo City Ct. Bldg., 8th Fl., 50 Delaware Ave., Buffalo 14202; **Fax:** (716) 851-3357

(718) 618-2204 **Bannon, Nancy N.** (J Civil Ct of NYC assigned to Family Ct) 900 Sheridan Ave., Bronx 10451

(718) 618-2534 **Barbato, Ben R.** (J Civil Ct of NYC) 851 Grand Concourse, Bronx 10451

(718) 618-1401 **Barone, John A.** (Justice Sup Ct 12th Jud Dist Civil Term) 851 Grand Concourse, Bronx 10451; **E-mail:** jbarone@courts.state.ny.us

(315) 946-5443 **Barrett, Daniel G.** (J Wayne Cty Ct Family Ct & Surro) Hall of Justice, 54 Broad St., Lyons 14489-1199; **Fax:** (315) 946-5428

(718) 618-3659 **Barrett, Steven L.** (J Crim Ct of NYC & Acting Justice Sup Ct 12th Jud Dist Crim Term) Bronx Hall of Justice, 265 E. 161st St., Bronx 10451

(347) 296-1507 **Barros, Betsy** (Justice Sup Ct 2nd Jud Dist) 360 Adams St., Bklyn. 11201

(585) 428-2929 **Barry, David Michael** (Justice Sup Ct 7th Jud Dist) 545 Hall of Justice, 99 Exchange Blvd., Rochester 14614-2184; **Fax:** (585) 428-2513

(845) 291-3137 **Bartlett, Catherine M.** (J Ct of Claims & Acting Justice Sup Ct 9th Jud Dist) 275 Main St., Goshen 10924; **Fax:** (845) 291-2106

(518) 295-8383 **Bartlett, George R., III** (J Schoharie Cty Ct Family Ct & Surro & Acting Justice Sup Ct 3rd Jud Dist) 290 Main St., P.O. Box 669, Schoharie 12157-0669; **Fax:** (518) 295-8451

(646) 386-4623 **Bartley, A. Kirke, Jr.** (J Crim Ct of NYC & Acting Justice Sup Ct 1st Jud Dist) 100 Centre St., N.Y.C. 10013; **Fax:** (212) 374-2579

(716) 439-7185 **Batt, John F.** (J Niagara Cty Family Ct) Cthse., 175 Hawley St., Lockport 14094-2758; **Fax:** (716) 439-7170; **E-mail:** jbatt@courts.state.ny.us

(347) 401-9244 **Battaglia, Jack M.** (Justice Sup Ct 2nd Jud Dist) 320 Jay St., Bklyn. 11201

(347) 296-1551 **Bayne, Bernadette F.** (Justice Sup Ct 2nd Jud Dist) 360 Adams St., Bklyn. 11201

(718) 404-9093 **Baynes, Johnny Lee** (J Civil Ct of NYC & Acting Justice Sup Ct 2nd Jud Dist) 141 Livingston St., Bklyn. 11201

(631) 853-4916 **Bean, Toni A.** (J Suffolk Cty Dist Ct) John P. Cohalan, Jr. Ct. Complex, 400 Carleton Ave., P.O. Box 9075, Central Islip 11722-9075

(607) 746-2131 **Becker, Carl F.** (J Delaware Cty Ct & Surro) Cthse., 3 Court St., Delhi 13753; **Fax:** (607) 746-3253

(347) 401-9880 **Beckoff, Alan M.** (J Family Ct of NYC) 330 Jay St., Bklyn. 11201; **Fax:** (347) 401-9900

(646) 386-5104 **Bednar, Mary E.** (J Family Ct of NYC) 60 Lafayette St., N.Y.C. 10013

(631) 853-7601 **Behar, Stephen M., Sr.** (J Suffolk Cty Dist Ct) John P. Cohalan, Jr. Ct. Complex, 400 Carleton Ave., P.O. Box 9075, Central Islip 11722-9075

(718) 722-6384 **Belen, Ariel E.** (Assoc Justice App Div 2nd Dept) 45 Monroe Pl., Bklyn. 11201; **E-mail:** abelen@courts.state.ny.us

(914) 824-5394 **Bellantoni, Orazio R.** (Justice Sup Ct 9th Jud Dist) Richard J. Daronco Cthse., 111 Dr. Martin Luther King, Jr. Blvd., White Plains 10601; **Fax:** (914) 995-4010

(585) 428-2616 **Bellini, Elma A.** (Justice Sup Ct 7th Jud Dist) 545 Hall of Justice, 99 Exchange Blvd., Rochester 14614-2184; **Fax:** (585) 428-1848

(315) 539-6291 **Bender, Dennis F.** (J Seneca Cty Ct Family Ct & Surro) Cthse., 48 W. Williams St., Waterloo 13165; **Fax:** (315) 539-7850; **E-mail:** dbender@courts.state.ny.us

(718) 618-3631 **Benitez, Peter J.** (J Crim Ct of NYC & Acting Justice Sup Ct 12th Jud Dist Crim Term) Bronx Hall of Justice, 265 E. 161st St., Bronx 10451

(516) 571-9362 **Bennett, Stacy D.** (J Nassau Cty Family Ct) 1200 Old Country Rd., Westbury 11590; **Fax:** (516) 571-9392

(646) 386-3968 **Berkman, Carol** (J Crim Ct of NYC & Acting Justice Sup Ct 1st Jud Dist) 100 Centre St., N.Y.C. 10013

(516) 571-2241 **Berkowitz, Meryl J.** (J Nassau Cty Ct & Acting Justice Sup Ct 10th Jud Dist) Cty. Cthse., 262 Old Country Rd., Mineola 11501; **Fax:** (516) 571-2078; **E-mail:** mberkowi@courts.state.ny.us

(845) 708-7218 **Berliner, Robert M.** (Justice Sup Ct 9th Jud Dist) Cthse., 1 S. Main St., New City 10956; **Fax:** (845) 638-5055; **E-mail:** rberline@courts.state.ny.us

(607) 432-4480 **Bernier, Lucy P.** (J Oneonta City Ct) Public Safety Bldg., 81 Main St., Oneonta 13820; **Fax:** (607) 432-2328

(845) 291-3120 **Berry, Jeffrey G.** (J Orange Cty Ct & Acting Justice Sup Ct & Supv J City Cts 9th Jud Dist) Orange Cty. Cthse., 285 Main St., Goshen 10924; **Fax:** (845) 291-2101

(718) 618-3690 **Best, Miriam** (J Crim Ct of NYC & Acting Justice Sup Ct 12th Jud Dist Crim Term) Bronx Hall of Justice, 265 E. 161st St., Bronx 10451

(646) 386-3279 **Billings, Lucy** (J Civil Ct of NYC) 71 Thomas St., N.Y.C. 10013

(718) 262-7311 **Birnbaum, Ronni D.** (J Civil Ct of NYC Housing Part) 89-17 Sutphin Blvd., Jamaica 11435

(845) 291-3020 **Bivona, Andrew P.** (J Orange Cty Family Ct & Acting Justice Sup Ct 9th Jud Dist) Orange Cty. Cthse., 285 Main St., Goshen 10924; **Fax:** (845) 291-3051

(631) 853-5155 **Bivona, John C.** (Justice Sup Ct 10th Jud Dist) John P. Cohalan, Jr. Ct. Complex, Ctrm. S31, 400 Carleton Ave., P.O. Box 9070, Central Islip 11722; **Fax:** (631) 853-3288

(914) 831-6440 **Blackwood, Helen M.** (J Mount Vernon City Ct) Two Roosevelt Sq. N., 2nd Fl., Mount Vernon 10550-2019; **Fax:** (914) 699-1230

(518) 382-5041 **Blanchfield, Mark W.** (J Schenectady City Ct) Civil Court, City Hall, Rm. 204, Jay St., Schenectady 12305; **Fax:** (518) 382-5080

(718) 298-1363 **Blumenfeld, Joel L.** (J Crim Ct of NYC & Acting Justice Sup Ct 11th Jud Dist) 125-01 Queens Blvd., Kew Gardens 11415; **Fax:** (212) 419-8400; **E-mail:** jblumenf@courts.state.ny.us

(646) 386-5725 **Bluth, Arlene P.** (J Civil Ct of NYC) 111 Centre St., Rm. 457, N.Y.C. 10013; **Fax:** (212) 374-5709

(631) 853-6162 **Blydenburgh, Donald R.** (Justice Sup Ct 10th Jud Dist) John P. Cohalan, Jr. Ct. Complex, Rm. S22, 400 Carleton Ave., Central Islip 11722; **Fax:** (631) 853-6326

(347) 404-9076 **Boddie, Reginald A.** (J Civil Ct of NYC) 141 Livingston St., Bklyn. 11201

(718) 298-0204 **Bogacz, Stephen J.** (J Family Ct of NYC) 151-20 Jamaica Ave., Jamaica 11432; **Fax:** (718) 297-2530

(315) 671-2768 **Bogan, Vanessa E.** (J Syracuse City Ct) 505 S. State St., Syracuse 13202-2104; **Fax:** (315) 671-2746; **E-mail:** vbogan@courts.state.ny.us

(716) 845-9357 **Boller, M. William** (J Ct of Claims & Acting Justice Sup Ct 8th Jud Dist) Erie Cty. Ct. Bldg., 2nd Fl., 25 Delaware Ave., Buffalo 14202; **Fax:** (716) 851-3327; **E-mail:** wboller@courts.state.ny.us

(716) 278-1840 **Boniello, Ralph A., III** (Justice Sup Ct 8th Jud Dist) Angelo DelSignore Civic Bldg., 775 Third St., Niagara Falls 14302-1710; **Fax:** (716) 278-1827; **E-mail:** rboniell@courts.state.ny.us

(718) 618-3677 **Boyle, Denis John** (J Crim Ct of NYC & Acting Justice Sup Ct 12th Jud Dist Crim Term) Bronx Hall of Justice, 265 E. 161st St., Bronx 10451

(607) 664-2366 **Bradstreet, Peter C.** (J Steuben Cty Ct & Family Ct) Cty. Office Complex, 3rd Fl., 3 E. Pulteney Sq., Bath 14810; **Fax:** (607) 776-7019

(845) 486-2531 **Brands, James V.** (Justice Sup Ct 9th Jud Dist) Cthse., 10 Market St., Poughkeepsie 12601; **Fax:** (845) 486-6497

(516) 571-3360 **Brandveen, Antonio I.** (J Ct of Claims & Acting Justice Sup Ct 10th Jud Dist) 100 Supreme Court Dr., Mineola 11501; **Fax:** (516) 571-1283

(646) 386-3184 **Bransten, Eileen** (Justice Sup Ct 1st Jud Dist) 60 Centre St., Rm. 521, N.Y.C. 10007; **Fax:** (212) 374-1475; **E-mail:** ebranste@courts.state.ny.us

(631) 852-1431 **Braslow, Stephen L.** (J Suffolk Cty Ct & Acting Suffolk Cty Surro) Arthur M. Cromarty Ct. Complex, 210 Center Dr., Riverhead 11901-3310

(718) 298-1442 **Braun, Evelyn L.** (Justice Sup Ct 11th Jud Dist) 125-01 Queens Blvd., Kew Gardens 11415; **Fax:** (718) 520-2236; **E-mail:** ebraun@courts.state.ny.us

(646) 386-3755 **Braun, Richard F.** (Justice Sup Ct 1st Jud Dist) 60 Centre St., Rm. 570, N.Y.C. 10007; **E-mail:** rbraun@courts.state.ny.us

(518) 761-6500 **Breen, J. Timothy** (J Warren Cty Family Ct) Warren Cty. Munic. Center, 1340 State Rt. 9, Lake George 12845; **Fax:** (518) 761-6230; **E-mail:** cbarber@courts.state.ny.us

(347) 296-1827 **Brennan, Michael J.** (Justice Sup Ct 2nd Jud Dist) 320 Jay St., Bklyn. 11201

(518) 285-8769 **Breslin, Thomas A.** (J Albany Cty Ct & Supv J Crim Cts 3rd Jud Dist) Judl. Ctr., Rm. 320, 6 Lodge St., Albany 12207-1019; **Fax:** (518) 436-3982

(845) 346-4050 **Brockett, Steven W.** (J Middletown City Ct) 2 James St., Middletown 10940; **Fax:** (845) 343-5737

(607) 737-2901 **Brockway, David M.** (J Chemung Cty Family Ct & Acting Justice Sup Ct 6th Jud Dist) 203-209 William St., P.O. Box 588, Elmira 14902-0588; **Fax:** (607) 737-2961; **E-mail:** dbrockwa@courts.state.ny.us

(516) 571-0766 **Brown, Jeffrey S.** (Justice Sup Ct 10th Jud Dist) Matrimonial Center, 400 County Seat Dr., Mineola 11501; **E-mail:** jsbrown@courts.state.ny.us

(585) 268-5800 **Brown, Thomas P.** (J Allegany Cty Ct Family Ct & Surro & Acting Justice Sup Ct 8th Jud Dist) Cthse., 7 Court St., Belmont 14813; **Fax:** (585) 268-7090; **E-mail:** tbrown@courts.state.ny.us

(718) 618-3661 **Bruce, Raymond L.** (J Civil Ct of NYC & Acting Justice Sup Ct 12th Jud Dist Crim Term) Bronx Hall of Justice, 265 E. 161st St., Bronx 10451

(315) 671-1058 **Brunetti, John J.** (J Ct of Claims & Acting Justice Sup Ct 5th Jud Dist) Crim. Cts. Bldg., Suite 380, 505 S. State St., Syracuse 13202; **Fax:** (315) 671-1178

(516) 571-5810 **Bruno, Robert A.** (Justice Sup Ct 10th Jud Dist) Matrimonial Center, 400 County Seat Dr., Mineola 11501

(516) 571-3320 **Bucaria, Stephen A.** (Justice Sup Ct 10th Jud Dist) Supreme Ct. Bldg., 100 Supreme Ct. Dr., Mineola 11501

(716) 845-7496 **Buchanan, Paul G.** (J Erie Cty Family Ct) One Niagara Plaza, Rm. 610, Buffalo 14202; **Fax:** (716) 858-7788

(718) 298-1336 **Buchter, Richard L.** (Justice Sup Ct 11th Jud Dist) 125-01 Queens Blvd., Kew Gardens 11415; **Fax:** (718) 520-2494; **E-mail:** rbuchter@courts.state.ny.us

(914) 824-5800 **Buckley, John T.** (Assoc Justice App Div 1st Dept & Dir of App Education NY State Judicial Institute) 84 N. Broadway, White Plains 10603

(315) 798-5858 Oneida County Office Bldg., 800 Park Ave., Utica 13502

(607) 737-2940 **Buckley, Peter C.** (J Chemung Cty Ct Family Ct & Surro) Cthse., 224 Lake St., P.O. Box 588, Elmira 14902-0588; **Fax:** (607) 732-3343

(315) 789-6560 **Buckley, Timothy J.** (Supv J Geneva City Ct) Public Safety Bldg., 255 Exchange St., Geneva 14456; **Fax:** (315) 781-2802

(631) 853-7752 **Budd, Marlene L.** (J Suffolk Cty Family Ct) John P. Cohalan, Jr. Ct. Complex, 400 Carleton Ave., Central Islip 11722; **Fax:** (631) 853-7569

(718) 262-7381 **Buggs, Chereé A.** (J Civil Ct of NYC) 89-17 Sutphin Blvd., Jamaica 11435

(347) 296-1504 **Bunyan, Bert A.** (Justice Sup Ct 2nd Jud Dist) 360 Adams St., Bklyn. 11201

(646) 386-4665 **Burke, James M.** (J Crim Ct of NYC) 120 Schermerhorn St., Bklyn. 11201; **Fax:** (718) 643-7733

(607) 547-4358 **Burns, Brian D.** (J Otsego Cty Ct Family Ct & Surro) Cty. Office Bldg., 197 Main St., Cooperstown 13326; **Fax:** (607) 547-7522

(716) 845-9381 **Burns, Christopher J.** (Justice Sup Ct 8th Jud Dist) Erie Cty. Ct. Bldg., 3rd Fl., 25 Delaware Ave., Buffalo 14202; **Fax:** (716) 851-3321; **E-mail:** cjburns@courts.state.ny.us

(716) 845-9435 **Buscaglia, Russell P.** (J Ct of Claims & Acting Justice Sup Ct 8th Jud Dist) Erie Cty. Ct. Bldg., 25 Delaware Ave., Buffalo 14202; **Fax:** (716) 851-3316; **E-mail:** rbuscagl@courts.state.ny.us

(718) 298-1216 **Butler, Denis J.** (Justice Sup Ct 11th Jud Dist) 88-11 Sutphin Blvd., Jamaica 11435; **Fax:** (718) 298-1149

(718) 618-3689 **Byrne, John N.** (Justice Sup Ct 12th Jud Dist Crim Term) Bronx Hall of Justice, 265 E. 161st St., Bronx 10451; **Fax:** (718) 618-3584

(914) 824-5401 **Cacace, Susan** (J Westchester Cty Ct) 111 Dr. Martin Luther King, Jr. Blvd., White Plains 10601; **Fax:** (914) 995-4946

(845) 340-3225 **Cahill, Christopher E.** (Justice Sup Ct 3rd Jud Dist) Cthse., 285 Wall St., Kingston 12401-3817; **Fax:** (845) 340-3228

(718) 923-8225 **Calabrese, Alex M.** (J Crim Ct of NYC & Acting Justice Sup Ct 2nd Jud Dist) Red Hook Community Justice Center, 88-94 Visitation Pl., Bklyn. 11231; **Fax:** (718) 923-8223

(516) 571-2065 **Calabrese, Joseph C.** (J Nassau Cty Ct & Acting Justice Sup Ct 10th Jud Dist) Cty. Cthse., 262 Old Country Rd., Mineola 11501; **Fax:** (516) 571-0566; **E-mail:** jcalabre@courts.state.ny.us

(315) 266-4455 **Caldwell, Randal B.** (J Oneida Cty Family Ct) Oneida Cty. Cthse., 200 Elizabeth St., Utica 13501; **Fax:** (315) 798-6404

(585) 428-2482 **Calvaruso, Edmund A.** (Monroe Cty Surro) Hall of Justice, Rm. 541, Rochester 14614-2186; **Fax:** (585) 428-2791; **E-mail:** ecalvaru@courts.state.ny.us

(716) 845-2643 **Calvo-Torres, Betty** (J Buffalo City Ct) 50 Delaware Ave., Suite 200, Buffalo 14202; **Fax:** (716) 845-7573; **E-mail:** bcalvoto@courts.state.ny.us

(718) 298-1440 **Camacho, Fernando M.** (J Ct of Claims & Admin J Sup Ct 11th Jud Dist Crim Term) 125-01 Queens Blvd., Kew Gardens 11415; **Fax:** (718) 520-6426

(607) 753-5001 **Campbell, Julie A.** (J Cortland Cty Ct Family Ct & Surro) Cthse., Suite 301, 46 Greenbush St., Cortland 13045-2772; **Fax:** (607) 758-5531

(845) 858-4034 **Campbell, Victoria B.** (J Port Jervis City Ct) 20 Hammond St., Port Jervis 12771-2495; **Fax:** (845) 858-9883

(914) 824-5857 **Capeci, Susan** (J Westchester Cty Ct) 111 Dr. Martin Luther King, Jr. Blvd., White Plains 10601; **Fax:** (914) 995-7470

(646) 386-3373 **Capella, Joseph** (J Civil Ct of NYC Housing Part) 111 Centre St., Rm. 1240, N.Y.C. 10013; **Fax:** (212) 374-5709; **E-mail:** jcapella@courts.state.ny.us

(914) 654-2286 **Carbone, Anthony A.** (Acting J New Rochelle City Ct) 475 North Ave., New Rochelle 10801-3405

(518) 285-8301 **Cardona, Anthony V.** (Pres Justice App Div 3rd Dept) Albany County Cthse., Rm. 412, Eagle St., Albany 12207; **Fax:** (518) 487-5042

(716) 845-2642 **Carney, Patrick M.** (J Buffalo City Ct) 50 Delaware Ave., Suite 600, Buffalo 14202; **Fax:** (716) 845-7578; **E-mail:** pcarney@courts.state.ny.us

(315) 671-1108 **Carni, Edward D.** (Assoc Justice App Div 4th Dept) Onondaga Cty. Cthse., Rm. 409, 401 Montgomery St., Syracuse 13202; **Fax:** (315) 671-1177

(585) 530-3100 M. Dolores Denman Cthse., 50 East Ave., Rochester 14604

(315) 823-1690 **Carrig, Bart M.** (J Little Falls City Ct) City Hall, 659 E. Main St., Little Falls 13365; **Fax:** (315) 823-1623

(646) 386-4424 **Carro, Gregory** (J Ct of Claims & Acting Justice Sup Ct 1st Jud Dist) 100 Centre St., Rm. 1702, N.Y.C. 10013; **Fax:** (212) 401-9263

(347) 296-1848 **Carroll, Thomas J.** (J Ct of Claims & Acting Justice Sup Ct 2nd Jud Dist) 320 Jay St., Bklyn. 11201; **Fax:** (347) 296-1351

(646) 386-3978 **Carruthers, Richard D.** (J Crim Ct of NYC & Acting Justice Sup Ct 1st Jud Dist) 100 Centre St., N.Y.C. 10013

(561) 571-3563 **Carter, Jerald S.** (J Nassau Cty Ct & Acting Justice Sup Ct 10th Jud Dist) Cty. Cthse., 262 Old Country Rd., Mineola 11501; **Fax:** (516) 571-0565; **E-mail:** jscarter@courts.state.ny.us

(718) 618-3635 **Carter, John W.** (J Crim Ct of NYC & Acting Justice Sup Ct 12th Jud Dist Crim Term) Bronx Hall of Justice, 265 E. 161st St., Bronx 10451

(716) 845-7484 **Carter, Kevin M.** (J Erie Cty Family Ct) One Niagara Plaza, Rm. 710, Buffalo 14202; **Fax:** (716) 858-7794

(518) 462-6714 **Carter, William A.** (J Albany City Ct) Crim. Ct., Public Safety Bldg., 1 Morton Ave., Albany 12202; **Fax:** (518) 447-8778; **E-mail:** wcarter@courts.state.ny.us

(716) 278-1815 **Caruso, Frank** (Justice Sup Ct 8th Jud Dist) Angelo DelSignore Civic Bldg., 775 Third St., Niagara Falls 14302-1710; **Fax:** (716) 278-1822; **E-mail:** fcaruso@courts.state.ny.us

(518) 285-8415 **Caruso, Vito C.** (Admin J Sup Ct 4th Jud Dist) Cthse., 612 State St., Schenectady 12305; **Fax:** (518) 346-5919
(518) 285-5099 District Admin. Office, 65 S. Broadway, Suite 101, Saratoga Springs 12866

(716) 753-4337 **Cass, Stephen W.** (Chautauqua Cty Surro) Gerace Office Bldg., 3 N. Erie St., P.O. Box C, Mayville 14757-0299; **Fax:** (716) 753-4730; **E-mail:** scass@courts.state.ny.us

(716) 845-2160 **Cassata, Joseph J., Jr.** (J Tonawanda City Ct) City Hall, 200 Niagara St., Tonawanda 14150; **Fax:** (716) 693-1612

(585) 428-2437 **Castro, Melchor E.** (J Rochester City Ct) 6 Hall of Justice, 99 Exchange Blvd., Rochester 14614; **Fax:** (585) 428-2731; **E-mail:** mcastro@courts.state.ny.us

(518) 853-3834 **Catena, Felix J.** (J Montgomery Cty Ct) Cthse., Rt. 30A, 58 Broadway, P.O. Box 1500, Fonda 12068-1500; **Fax:** (518) 853-8396

(212) 340-0400 **Catterson, James M.** (Assoc Justice App Div 1st Dept) 27 Madison Ave., N.Y.C. 10010
(631) 852-2833 Supreme Court Annex, 235 Griffing Ave., Riverhead 11901; **Fax:** (631) 852-2779

(607) 778-2431 **Cawley, Joseph F.** (J Broome Cty Ct) 65 Hawley St., P.O. Box 1766, Binghamton 13902-1766; **Fax:** (607) 778-6133

(315) 671-2786 **Cecile, James H.** (J Syracuse City Ct) 505 S. State St., Syracuse 13202-2104; **Fax:** (315) 671-2748; **E-mail:** jcecile@courts.state.ny.us

(315) 671-1105 **Centra, John V.** (Assoc Justice App Div 4th Dept) Onondaga Cty. Cthse., Rm. 401, 401 Montgomery St., Syracuse 13202; **Fax:** (315) 671-1182

(518) 285-6110 **Ceresia, Andrew G.** (J Rensselaer Cty Ct) Cthse., Congress & Second St., Troy 12180

(518) 285-6152 **Ceresia, George B., Jr.** (Admin J Sup Ct 3rd Jud Dist) Cthse., 80 Second St., Troy 12180
(518) 285-8300 Admin. Office, 40 Steuben St., 6th Floor, Albany 12207 ; **Fax:** (518) 426-1604

(315) 366-2321 **Cerio, Donald F., Jr.** (J Ct of Claims & Acting Justice Sup Ct 6th Jud Dist) Madison Cty. Cthse., N. Court St., P.O. Box 545, Wampsville 13163; **Fax:** (315) 366-2539

(914) 831-6980 **Cerrato, Robert C.** (J Yonkers City Ct) Robert W. Cacace Justice Center, 100 S. Broadway, Yonkers 10701; **E-mail:** rcerrato@courts.state.ny.us

(516) 572-2111 **Chaikin, Bonnie P.** (J Nassau Cty Dist Ct) 99 Main St., Hempstead 11550

(347) 296-1040 **Chambers, Cheryl E.** (Assoc Justice App Div 2nd Dept) 320 Jay St., Rm. 25.49, Bklyn. 11201; **Fax:** (347) 296-1331

(347) 404-9097 **Chan, Margaret A.** (J Civil Ct of NYC) 141 Livingston St., Bklyn. 11201

(607) 778-2181 **Charnetsky, Peter P.** (J Broome Cty Family Ct) 65 Hawley St., Binghamton 13901 Mailing Address: P.O. Box 1766, Binghamton 13902; **Fax:** (607) 778-2439

(315) 671-1090 **Cherundolo, John C.** (J Ct of Claims & Acting Justice Sup Ct 5th Jud Dist) Onondaga Cty. Cthse., Rm. 404, 401 Montgomery St., Syracuse 13202; **Fax:** (315) 671-1180

(347) 404-9086 **Chin, Oymin** (J Civil Ct of NYC Housing Part) 141 Livingston St., Bklyn. 11201

(718) 298-0922 **Chin-Brandt, Dorothy K.** (J Civil Ct of NYC assigned to Crim Ct & Acting Justice Sup Ct 11th Jud Dist) 125-01 Queens Blvd., Kew Gardens 11415; **Fax:** (718) 520-3992; **E-mail:** dchinbra@courts.state.ny.us

(518) 270-3761 Ext. 329 **Cholakis, Catherine** (J Rensselaer Cty Family Ct & Acting Justice Sup Ct 3rd Jud Dist) 1504 Fifth Ave., Troy 12180-4107; **Fax:** (518) 272-6573;**E-mail:** ccholaki@courts.state.ny.us

(845) 638-5328 **Christopher, Linda** (J Rockland Cty Family Ct) 1 S. Main St., Suite 300, New City 10956

(347) 296-1067 **Chun, Danny K.** (J Crim Ct of NYC & Acting Justice Sup Ct 2nd Jud Dist) 320 Jay St., Bklyn. 11201; **Fax:** (347) 296-1346

(516) 572-2117 **Ciaffa, Michael A.** (J Nassau Cty Dist Ct) 99 Main St., Hempstead 11550

(212) 661-2144 **Ciparick, Carmen Beauchamp** (Assoc J Ct of App) 3700 Chanin Bldg., 122 E. 42nd St., N.Y.C. 10168-0002
(518) 455-7726 Court of Appeals Hall, 20 Eagle St., Albany 12207-1095

(718) 618-3648 **Cirigliano, Caesar D.** (Justice Sup Ct 12th Jud Dist Crim Term) Bronx Hall of Justice, Rm. 935, 265 E. 161st St., Bronx 10451; **Fax:** (718) 618-3571

(716) 753-4351 **Claire, Judith S.** (J Chautauqua Cty Family Ct) 2 Academy St., Suite 5, Mayville 14757; **Fax:** (716) 753-4350

(718) 618-3638 **Clancy, Margaret** (J Ct of Claims & Acting Justice Sup Ct 12th Jud Dist Crim Term) Bronx Hall of Justice, 265 E. 161st St., Bronx 10451; **Fax:** (212) 884-8910

(315) 798-5860 **Clark, Bernadette T.** (Justice Sup Ct 5th Jud Dist) Oneida Cty. Cthse., 200 Elizabeth St., Utica 13501; **Fax:** (315) 798-5861

(518) 382-5239 **Clark, Christine M.** (J Schenectady City Ct) 531 Liberty St., Schenectady 12305; **Fax:** (518) 382-5080

(718) 618-3626 **Clark, Darcel D.** (Justice Sup Ct 12th Jud Dist Crim Term) Bronx Hall of Justice, 265 E. 161st St., Bronx 10451; **Fax:** (718) 618-3584; **E-mail:** ddclark@courts.state.ny.us

(646) 386-4654 **Clott, Abraham L.** (J Crim Ct of NYC) 111 Centre St., N.Y.C. 10013

(518) 563-7870 **Clute, Penelope D.** (J Plattsburgh City Ct) 24 U.S. Oval, Plattsburgh 12903; **Fax:** (518) 563-3124

(607) 547-4212 **Coccoma, Michael V.** (Justice Sup Ct 6th Jud Dist & Deputy Chief Admin J outside NYC) Otsego Cty. Office Bldg., 197 Main St., Cooperstown 13326
(518) 474-3828 Empire State Plaza, Suite 2001, 4 E.S.P., Albany 12223-1450; **Fax:** (518) 473-5514

(631) 852-2395 **Cohalan, Peter Fox** (Justice Sup Ct 10th Jud Dist) Supreme Ct. Bldg., Ctrm. 6, 1 Court St., Riverhead 11901; **Fax:** (631) 852-2719

(646) 386-5586 **Cohen, David B.** (J Civil Ct of NYC Housing Part) 111 Centre St., Rm. 1240, N.Y.C. 10013; **Fax:** (212) 374-5709

(631) 854-9293 **Cohen, Dennis M.** (J Suffolk Cty Dist Ct) 3105 Veterans Memorial Hwy., Ronkonkoma 11779; **Fax:** (631) 954-9683

(585) 243-7078 **Cohen, Dennis S.** (J Livingston Cty Ct Family Ct & Surro) Cthse., 2 Court St., Geneseo 14454-1030; **Fax:** (585) 243-7076

(347) 404-9062 **Cohen, Devin P.** (J Civil Ct of NYC) 141 Livingston St., Bklyn. 11201

(845) 291-3130 **Cohen, Jeffrey A.** (Justice Sup Ct 9th Jud Dist) 255-275 Main St., Goshen 10924; **Fax:** (845) 291-3045; **E-mail:** jecohen@courts.state.ny.us

(631) 852-2168 **Cohen, Mark D.** (J Ct of Claims & Acting Justice Sup Ct 10th Jud Dist) Arthur M. Cromarty Ct. Complex, Rm. 2, 210 Center Dr., Riverhead 11901; **Fax:** (631) 852-2156

(646) 386-5101 **Cohen, Rhoda J.** (J Family Ct of NYC) 60 Lafayette St., N.Y.C. 10013

(646) 386-4615 **Coin, Ellen M.** (J Crim Ct of NYC & Acting Justice Sup Ct 1st Jud Dist) 100 Centre St., N.Y.C. 10013; **Fax:** (212) 374-2579

(914) 824-5398 **Colabella, Nicholas** (Justice Sup Ct 9th Jud Dist) Richard J. Daronco Cthse., 111 Dr. Martin Luther King, Jr. Blvd., White Plains 10601; **Fax:** (914) 995-4182

(914) 824-5423 **Colangelo, John** (J Westchester Cty Ct) 111 Dr. Martin Luther King, Jr. Blvd., White Plains 10601; **Fax:** (914) 995-8653

(718) 675-8650 **Collini, Robert J.** (J Ct of Claims & Acting Justice Sup Ct 13th Jud Dist) Cty. Cthse., 18 Richmond Terr., Staten Island 10301

(518) 583-5340 **Collins, Francis T.** (J Ct of Claims) 65 S. Broadway, Rm. 220, Saratoga Springs 12866; **Fax:** (518) 583-5345

(631) 852-2670 **Condon, William J.** (Justice Sup Ct 10th Jud Dist) Arthur M. Cromarty Ct. Complex, Chambers 4188, 210 Center Dr., Riverhead 11901; **Fax:** (631) 852-2925

(607) 778-2156 **Connerton, Mary Rita** (J Broome Cty Family Ct) 65 Hawley St., Binghamton 13901 Mailing Address: P.O. Box 1766, Binghamton 13902; **Fax:** (607) 778-2439

(914) 824-5411 **Connolly, Francesca E.** (Justice Sup Ct 9th Jud Dist) Richard J. Daronco Cthse., 111 Dr. Martin Luther King, Jr. Blvd., White Plains 10601

(518) 285-8592 **Connolly, Gerald W.** (Ct of Claims & Acting Justice Sup Ct 3rd Jud Dist) 112 State St., Rm. 1350, Albany 12207; **Fax:** (518) 487-5378

(646) 386-3977 **Conviser, Daniel P.** (Ct of Claims & Acting Justice Sup Ct 1st Jud Dist) 111 Centre St., N.Y.C. 10013

(646) 386-5696 **Cooper, Matthew F.** (J Civil Ct of NYC & Acting Justice Sup Ct 1st Jud Dist) 111 Centre St., Rm. 668, N.Y.C. 10013

(718) 618-2200 **Cordova, Alma** (J Crim Ct of NYC assigned to Family Ct) 900 Sheridan Ave., Bronx 10451

(518) 853-8135 **Cortese, Philip V.** (J Montgomery Cty Family Ct) Cthse., 58 Broadway, Rt. 30A, P.O. Box 1500, Fonda 12068-1500; **Fax:** (518) 853-8148

(631) 852-2422 **Costello, Ralph F.** (Justice Sup Ct 10th Jud Dist) Supreme Ct. Bldg., Rm. A-257, 1 Court St., Riverhead 11901; **Fax:** (631) 852-2834

(516) 571-2073 **Covello, Joseph** (Assoc Justice App Div 2nd Dept) 100 Supreme Court Dr., Mineola 11501; **Fax:** (516) 571-0135

(516) 571-3716 **Cozzens, R. Bruce, Jr.** (Justice Sup Ct 10th Jud Dist) Supreme Ct. Bldg., 100 Supreme Ct. Dr., Mineola 11501; **E-mail:** bcozzens@courts.state.ny.us

(518) 828-3100 **Cranna, William F.** (J Hudson City Ct) 427-429 Warren St., Hudson 12534; **Fax:** (518) 828-3628

(631) 853-6092 **Crecca, Andrew A.** (J Suffolk Cty Ct & Acting Justice Sup Ct 10th Jud Dist) John P. Cohalan Court Complex, 400 Carleton Ave., Central Islip 11722; **Fax:** (631) 853-3289

(585) 428-4376 **Crimi, Charles F., Jr.** (J Rochester City Ct) 6 Hall of Justice, 99 Exchange Blvd., Rochester 14614; **Fax:** (585) 428-4379; **E-mail:** ccrimi@courts.state.ny.us

(631) 853-5408 **Crowley, Kevin J.** (Acting J Suffolk Cty Dist Ct) John P. Cohalan, Jr. Ct. Complex, 400 Carleton Ave., P.O. Box 9075, Central Islip 11722-9075

(631) 853-5408 Fourth District Court, Veterans Memorial Hwy., Hauppauge 11788

(718) 618-2536 **Cruz, Raul** (J Civil Ct of NYC) 851 Grand Concourse, Bronx 10451

(718) 298-1083 **Cullen, Lawrence V.** (Ct of Claims & Acting Justice Sup Ct 11th Jud Dist) 88-11 Sutphin Blvd., Rm. 44A, Jamaica 11435; **Fax:** (718) 298-1005

(718) 262-7357 **Culley, Anna** (J Civil Ct of NYC & Acting Justice Sup Ct 11th Jud Dist) 89-17 Sutphin Blvd., Jamaica 11435

(716) 845-9471 **Curran, John M.** (Justice Sup Ct 8th Jud Dist) Erie Cty. Cthse., 3rd Fl., 92 Franklin St., Buffalo 14202; **Fax:** (716) 851-3227; **E-mail:** jmcurran@courts.state.ny.us

(607) 334-1224 **Cushman, James G.** (J Norwich City Ct) One Court Plaza, Norwich 13815; **Fax:** (607) 334-8494

(347) 296-1498 **Cutrona, Anthony J.** (Justice Sup Ct 2nd Jud Dist) 360 Adams St., Bklyn. 11201

(347) 404-9478 **Cyrulnik, Miriam** (J Crim Ct of NYC) 120 Schermerhorn St., Bklyn. 11201; **Fax:** (718) 643-7733

(518) 822-0453 **Czajka, Paul** (J Columbia Cty Ct Family Ct & Surro & Acting Justice Sup Ct 3rd Jud Dist) Cthse., 401 Union St., Hudson 12534; **Fax:** (518) 822-0514; **E-mail:** pczajka@courts.state.ny.us

(631) 852-1745 **Czygier, John M., Jr.** (Suffolk Cty Surro) 320 Center Dr., Riverhead 11901; **Fax:** (631) 852-1777

(347) 296-1563 **Dabiri, Gloria M.** (Justice Sup Ct 2nd Jud Dist) 360 Adams St., Bklyn. 11201

(585) 786-3148 Ext. 126 **Dadd, Mark H.** (J Wyoming Cty Ct Family Ct & Surro) Cthse., 147 N. Main St., Warsaw 14569; **Fax:** (585) 786-2818

(315) 867-1185 **Daley, Michael E.** (Justice Sup Ct 5th Jud Dist) Cty. Office & Cts. Facility, 5th Fl., 301 N. Washington St., Herkimer 13350; **Fax:** (315) 867-1531

(914) 831-6980 **Daly, Thomas R.** (J Yonkers City Ct) Robert W. Cacace Justice Center, 100 S. Broadway, Yonkers 10701

(716) 845-9366 **D'Amico, Michael L.** (J Erie Cty Ct) Erie Cty. Ct. Bldg., 25 Delaware Ave., Buffalo 14202; **Fax:** (716) 851-3251

(607)324-7531 **Damrath, Joseph E.** (J Hornell City Ct) 82 Main St., P.O. Box 627, Hornell 14843-0627; **Fax:** (607) 324-6325

(516) 571-9104 **Dane, Edmund M.** (J Nassau Cty Family Ct) 1200 Old Country Rd., Westbury 11590; **Fax:** (516) 571-9391

(347) 401-9870 **Danoff, Susan S.** (J Family Ct of NYC) 330 Jay St., Bklyn. 11201; **Fax:** (347) 401-9900

(718) 618-2538 **Danziger, Mitchell J.** (J Civil Ct of NYC) 851 Grand Concourse, Bronx 10451

(718) 618-2215 **d'Auguste, James E.** (J Civil Ct of NYC assigned to Family Ct) 900 Sheridan Ave., Bronx 10451

(914) 824-5479 **Davidson, Kathie E.** (Supv J Family Cts 9th Jud Dist) 111 Dr. Martin Luther King, Jr. Blvd., White Plains 10601; **Fax:** (914) 995-4586

(718) 618-3625 **Dawson, Joseph J.** (J Crim Ct of NYC & Acting Justice Sup Ct 12th Jud Dist Crim Term) Bronx Hall of Justice, 265 E. 161st St., Bronx 10451; **Fax:** (718) 618-3584

(646) 386-3868 **Dawson, Tandra L.** (J Family Ct of NYC & Acting Justice Sup Ct 1st Jud Dist) 100 Centre St., N.Y.C. 10013

(718) 404-9071 **Dear, Noach** (J Civil Ct of NYC & Acting Justice Sup Ct 2nd Jud Dist) 141 Livingston St., Bklyn. 11201

(518) 242-3701 **DeBow, W. Brooks** (J Ct of Claims) Capitol Station, P.O. Box 7344, Albany 12224

(212) 340-0400 **DeGrasse, Leland G.** (Assoc Justice App Div 1st Dept) 27 Madison Ave., N.Y.C. 10010

(315) 671-1107 **DeJoseph, Brian F.** (Justice Sup Ct 5th Jud Dist) 401 Montgomery St., 403 Fl., Syracuse 13202; **Fax:** (315) 671-1181

(347) 296-1851 **Del Giudice, Vincent M.** (J Ct of Claims & Acting Justice Sup Ct 2nd Jud Dist) 320 Jay St., Bklyn. 11201; **Fax:** (347) 296-1349

(585) 344-2550 Ext. 2432 **Del Plato, Michael A.** (J Batavia City Ct) Genesee Cty. Cts. Facility, 1 W. Main St., Batavia 14020; **Fax:** (585) 344-8556; **E-mail:** mdelplat@courts.state.ny.us

(516) 572-2129 **Delligatti, Angelo A.** (J Nassau Cty Dist Ct) 99 Main St., Hempstead 11550

(585) 425-2452 **DeMarco, John L.** (J Monroe Cty Ct) 209 Hall of Justice, 99 Exchange Blvd., Rochester 14614-2184; **Fax:** (585) 784-4217

(347) 296-1458 **Demarest, Carolyn E.** (Justice Sup Ct 2nd Jud Dist) 360 Adams St., Bklyn. 11201

(315) 379-0326 **Demarest, David R.** (Justice Sup Ct 4th Jud Dist) Cthse., 48 Court St., Canton 13617-1169; **Fax:** (315) 379-2311; **E-mail:** ddemares@courts.state.ny.us

(347) 296-1031 **D'Emic, Matthew J.** (J Ct of Claims & Acting Justice Sup Ct 2nd Jud Dist) 320 Jay St., Bklyn. 11201; **Fax:** (347) 296-1337

(845) 291-3115 **DeRosa, Nicholas** (J Orange Cty Ct & Acting Justice Sup Ct 9th Jud Dist) Orange Cty. Cthse., 285 Main St., Goshen 10924; **Fax:** (845) 291-2102

(518) 773-4527 **DeSantis, Vincent** (J Gloversville City Ct) City Hall, 3 Frontage Rd., Gloversville 12078; **Fax:** (518) 773-4599

(516) 571-2475 **DeStefano, Vito M.** (Justice Sup Ct 10th Jud Dist) Matrimonial Center, 400 County Seat Dr., Mineola 11501

(518) 285-8959 **Devine, Eugene P.** (Justice Sup Ct 3rd Jud Dist) Albany Co. Cthse., Rm. 342, 16 Eagle St., Albany 12207; **Fax:** (518) 487-5864

(716) 845-9483 **Devlin, Diane Y.** (Justice Sup Ct 8th Jud Dist) Buffalo City Ct. Bldg., 9th Fl., 50 Delaware Ave., Buffalo 14202; **Fax:** (716) 851-3325; **E-mail:** ddevlin@courts.state.ny.us

(516) 571-2874 **Diamond, Arthur M.** (Justice Sup Ct 10th Jud Dist) 100 Supreme Court Dr., Mineola 11501; **Fax:** (516) 571-3623

(646) 386-3255 **Diamond, Marylin G.** (J Civil Ct of NYC & Acting Justice Sup Ct 1st Jud Dist) 60 Centre St., Rm. 566, N.Y.C. 10007

(914) 824-5407 **DiBella, Robert M.** (J Westchester Cty Ct & Acting Justice Sup Ct 9th Jud Dist) Richard J. Daronco Cthse., 111 Dr. Martin Luther King, Jr. Blvd., White Plains 10601; **Fax:** (914) 995-8654

(914) 824-5405 **Dickerson, Thomas A.** (Assoc Justice App Div 2nd Dept) Courthouse Sq., 140 Grand St., White Plains 10601; **Fax:** (718) 946-1026; **E-mail:** tdickers@courts.state.ny.us

(718) 875-1300 45 Monroe Pl., Bklyn. 11201

(516) 571-9055 **Dikranis, Frank** (J Nassau Cty Family Ct) 1200 Old Country Rd., Westbury 11590; **Fax:** (516) 571-9335

(716) 845-1800 **Dillon, James H.** (Justice Sup Ct 8th Jud Dist) Erie Cty. Ct. Bldg., 4th Fl., 25 Delaware Ave., Buffalo 14202; **Fax:** (716) 851-3317; **E-mail:** jdillon@courts.state.ny.us

(716) 845-9441 **Dillon, Kevin M.** (Justice Sup Ct 8th Jud Dist) Erie Cty. Cthse., 3rd Fl., 92 Franklin St., Buffalo 14202; **Fax:** (716) 851-3223; **E-mail:** kdillon@courts.state.ny.us

(914) 824-5409 **Dillon, Mark C.** (Assoc Justice App Div 2nd Dept) Courthouse Sq., 6th Fl., 140 Grand St., White Plains 10601; **Fax:** (212) 401-9170; **E-mail:** mdillon@courts.state.ny.us

(347) 296-1857 **DiMango, Patricia M.** (Justice Sup Ct 2nd Jud Dist) 320 Jay St., Bklyn. 11201

(716) 439-6684 **DiMillo, Thomas M.** (J Lockport City Ct) Munic. Bldg., One Locks Plaza, Lockport 14094; **Fax:** (716) 439-6684

(315) 366-2381 **DiStefano, Biagio J.** (J Madison Cty Ct Family Ct & Surro) Cthse., Bldg. 3, 138 N. Court St., P.O. Box 545, Wampsville 13163-0545; **Fax:** (315) 366-2828

(716) 845-9369 **DiTullio, Sheila A.** (J Erie Cty Ct) Erie Cty. Ct. Bldg., 25 Delaware Ave., Buffalo 14202; **Fax:** (716) 851-3334

(585) 428-4374 **Dixon, Maija C.** (J Rochester City Ct) 6 Hall of Justice, 99 Exchange Blvd., Rochester 14614; **Fax:** (585) 428-4379

(518) 451-8780 **Doern, James E.D.** (J Saratoga Springs City Ct) City Hall, Suite 3, 474 Broadway, Saratoga Springs 12866-2295; **Fax:** (518) 584-3097

(718) 466-3161 **Doherty, Marian C.** (J Civil Ct of NYC Housing Part) Housing Ct., 1118 Grand Concourse, Rm. 904, Bronx 10456

(718) 675-8438 **Dollard, Kim** (J Civil Ct of NYC & Acting Justice Sup Ct 13th Jud Dist) 927 Castleton Ave., West New Brighton, Staten Island 10310; **Fax:** (718) 390-8108

(585) 428-2879 **Dollinger, Richard A.** (J Ct of Claims & Acting Justice Sup Ct 7th Jud Dist) 545 Hall of Justice, 99 Exchange Blvd., Rochester 14614; **Fax:** (585) 428-4346

(315) 266-4321 **Donalty, Barry M.** (J Oneida Cty Ct) Cthse., Elizabeth St., Utica 13501; **Fax:** (315) 731-3416

(718) 618-3650 **Donnelly, Ann M.** (J Ct of Claims & Acting Justice Sup Ct 12th Jud Dist Crim Term) Bronx Hall of Justice, 265 E. 161st St., Bronx 10451; **Fax:** (718) 618-3584

(516) 571-2797 **Donnino, William C.** (J Ct of Claims & Acting Justice Sup Ct 10th Jud Dist & Supv J Nassau Cty Ct Crim Term) 262 Old Country Rd., Mineola 11501; **Fax:** (516) 571-1485; **E-mail:** wdonnino@courts.state.ny.us

(585) 428-5597 **Donofrio, Gail A.** (J Monroe Cty Family Ct) Hall of Justice, 3rd Fl., 99 Exchange Blvd., Rochester 14614-2187; **Fax:** (585) 428-2597

(914) 831-6980 **Doran, Arthur J., III** (J Yonkers City Ct) Robert W. Cacace Justice Center, 100 S. Broadway, Yonkers 10701

(585) 396-4479 **Doran, Craig J.** (J Ontario Cty Ct Family Ct & Surro & Supv J Family Ct 7th Jud Dist) Cthse., Rm. 130, 27 N. Main St., Canandaigua 14424-1447; **Fax:** (585) 396-4580; **E-mail:** cdoran@courts.state.ny.us
(315) 671-2771 **Dougherty, Stephen J.** (J Syracuse City Ct) 505 S. State St., Syracuse 13202-2104; **Fax:** (315) 671-2748; **E-mail:** sdougher@courts.state.ny.us
(347) 404-9483 **Douglas, Dena E.** (J Civil Ct of NYC) 141 Livingston St., Bklyn. 11201
(718) 618-1410 **Douglas, Laura G.** (Justice Sup Ct 12th Jud Dist Civil Term) 851 Grand Concourse, Bronx 10451
(607) 337-1740 **Dowd, Kevin M.** (Justice Sup Ct 6th Jud Dist) Chenango Cty. Cthse., West Park Pl., Norwich 13815; **Fax:** (607) 336-3648
(347) 296-1025 **Dowling, Deborah A.** (Justice Sup Ct 2nd Jud Dist) 320 Jay St., Bklyn. 11201
(607) 334-1224 **Downey, James E.** (J Norwich City Ct) One Court Plaza, Norwich 13815; **Fax:** (607) 334-8494
(518) 285-8581 **Doyle, Cathryn M.** (Albany Cty Surro) 30 Clinton Ave., Albany 12207
(545) 428-4372 **Doyle, Daniel J.** (Justice Sup Ct 7th Jud Dist) 545 Hall of Justice, 99 Exchange Blvd., Rochester 14614-2184; **Fax:** (545) 428-2987
(631) 852-1640 **Doyle, James F.X.** (J Suffolk Cty Ct & Acting Justice Sup Ct 10th Jud Dist) Arthur M. Cromarty Ct. Complex, 210 Center Dr., Riverhead 11901-3310; **Fax:** (631) 852-3547; **E-mail:** jdoyle@courts.state.ny.us
(631) 852-2169 **Doyle, Robert W.** (Justice Sup Ct 10th Jud Dist) Arthur M. Cromarty Ct. Complex, Rm. 15 & 3, 210 Center Dr., Riverhead 11901; **Fax:** (631) 852-2855; **E-mail:** rdoyle@courts.state.ny.us
(716) 366-2055 **Drag, Walter F.** (J Dunkirk City Ct) City Hall, 342 Central Ave., Dunkirk 14048-2122; **Fax:** (716) 366-3622; **E-mail:** wdrag@courts.state.ny.us
(646) 386-3356 **Drager, Laura E.** (J Crim Ct of NYC & Acting Justice Sup Ct 1st Jud Dist) 71 Thomas St., Rm. 310, N.Y.C. 10013
(518) 285-8429 **Drago, Karen A.** (J Schenectady Cty Ct) Cthse., 612 State St., Schenectady 12305
(718) 618-2200 **Drinane, Monica** (Supv J Family Ct of NYC Bronx Cty) 900 Sheridan Ave., Bronx 10451
(516) 571-3891 **Driscoll, Timothy S.** (Justice Sup Ct 10th Jud Dist) 100 Supreme Court Dr., Mineola 11501
(716) 845-9372 **Drury, Timothy J.** (Justice Sup Ct 8th Jud Dist) Erie Cty. Ct. Bldg., 1st Fl., 25 Delaware Ave., Buffalo 14202; **Fax:** (716) 851-3335
(718) 262-7354 **Dufficy, Timothy J.** (J Civil Ct of NYC & Acting Justice Sup Ct 11th Jud Dist) 89-17 Sutphin Blvd., Jamaica 11435
(518) 285-8681 **Duggan, W. Dennis** (J Albany Cty Family Ct) 30 Clinton Ave., Albany 12207; **Fax:** (518) 462-4164; **E-mail:** wddfcj@yahoo.com; wduggan@courts.state.ny.us
(347) 401-9096 **Dwyer, Mark R.** (J Ct of Claims & Acting Justice Sup Ct 2nd Jud Dist) 320 Jay St., Bklyn. 11201
(315) 266-4322 **Dwyer, Michael L.** (J Oneida Cty Ct) Cthse., Elizabeth St., Utica 13501; **Fax:** (315) 798-5848
(315) 266-4607 **Eannace, Ralph J., Jr.** (J Utica City Ct) 411 Oriskany St. W., Utica 13502; **Fax:** (315) 733-7927
(914) 824-5481 **Edlitz, Sandra B.** (J Westchester Cty Family Ct) 111 Dr. Martin Luther King, Jr. Blvd., White Plains 10601; **Fax:** (914) 995-8645; **E-mail:** sedlitz@courts.state.ny.us
(646) 386-3250 **Edmead, Carol** (Justice Sup Ct 1st Jud Dist) 60 Centre St., Rm. 532, N.Y.C. 10007; **Fax:** (212) 374-8355; **E-mail:** cedmead@courts.state.ny.us
(718) 262-7252 **Edwards, Genine D.** (J Civil Ct of NYC) 89-17 Sutphin Blvd., Jamaica 11435
(914) 831-6463 **Edwards, William** (J Mount Vernon City Ct) Two Roosevelt Sq. N., 2nd Fl., Mount Vernon 10550-2019; **Fax:** (914) 699-1230
(914) 824-5798 (Acting J Westchester Cty Family Ct) 111 Dr. Martin Luther King, Jr. Blvd., White Plains 10601; **Fax:** (914) 995-4490
(631) 853-2166 **Efman, Martin I.** (J Suffolk Cty Dist Ct & Acting J Suffolk Cty Ct) Arthur M. Cromarty Ct. Complex, 210 Center Dr., Riverhead 11901-3310; **Fax:** (631) 852-3161
(585) 428-2008 **Egan, David D.** (Justice Sup Ct 7th Jud Dist) 545 Hall of Justice, 99 Exchange Blvd., Rochester 14614-2184; **Fax:** (585) 784-4221
(518) 285-8999 **Egan, John C., Jr.** (Assoc Justice App Div 3rd Dept) 1st Fl., 50 Chapel St., Albany 12207
(516) 571-9015 **Eisman, Julianne S.** (J Nassau Cty Family Ct) 1200 Old Country Rd., Westbury 11590; **Fax:** (516) 571-9399
(347) 401-9870 **Elkins, Lee H.** (J Family Ct of NYC) 330 Jay St., Bklyn. 11201; **Fax:** (347) 401-9900
(718) 298-1119 **Elliot, David** (Justice Sup Ct 11th Jud Dist) 88-11 Sutphin Blvd., Jamaica 11435; **Fax:** (718) 298-1130
(585) 428-2435 **Elliott, John E.** (J Rochester City Ct) 6 Hall of Justice, 99 Exchange Blvd., Rochester 14614; **Fax:** (585) 428-4386; **E-mail:** jeelliot@courts.state.ny.us
(315) 349-3295 **Elliott, John J.** (Oswego Cty Surro) Cthse., 25 E. Oneida St., Oswego 13126-2693; **Fax:** (315) 349-8514
(646) 386-5591 **Elsner, Timmie** (J Civil Ct of NYC Housing Part) 111 Centre St., Rm. 1240, N.Y.C. 10013; **Fax:** (212) 374-5709
(631) 852-2781 **Emerson, Elizabeth H.** (Justice Sup Ct 10th Jud Dist) Arthur M. Cromarty Ct. Complex, Ctrm. 7, 210 Center Dr., Riverhead 11901; **Fax:** (631) 852-3732
(718) 298-1555 **Eng, Randall T.** (Assoc Justice App Div 2nd Dept) 125-01 Queens Blvd., Kew Gardens 11415; **Fax:** (718) 520-3557; **E-mail:** reng@courts.state.ny.us
(516) 572-2105 **Engel, Andrew M.** (J Nassau Cty Dist Ct) 99 Main St., Hempstead 11550
(718) 618-2532 **Engoron, Arthur F.** (J Civil Ct of NYC) 851 Grand Concourse, Bronx 10451; **E-mail:** aengoron@courts.state.ny.us
(315) 266-4740 **Eppolito, Anthony P.** (J Oneida City Ct) 108 Main St., Oneida 13421; **Fax:** (315) 363-3230
(718) 298-1401 **Erlbaum, William M.** (Justice Sup Ct 11th Jud Dist) 125-01 Queens Blvd., Kew Gardens 11415; **E-mail:** werlbaum@courts.state.ny.us
(718) 262-7379 **Esposito, Joseph J.** (J Civil Ct of NYC & Acting Justice Sup Ct 11th Jud Dist) 89-17 Sutphin Blvd., Jamaica 11435
(646) 386-3819 **Evans, Saralee E.** (J Civil Ct of NYC & Acting Justice Sup Ct 1st Jud Dist) 71 Thomas St., Rm. 307, N.Y.C. 10013
(718) 618-3623 **Fabrizio, Ralph A.** (J Crim Ct of NYC & Acting Justice Sup Ct 12th Jud Dist Crim Term) Bronx Hall of Justice, 265 E. 161st St., Bronx 10451
(716) 845-9444 **Fahey, Eugene M.** (Assoc Justice App Div 4th Dept) 50 Delaware Ave., Buffalo 14202; **Fax:** (716) 852-6367; **E-mail:** efahey@courts.state.ny.us
(315) 671-1050 **Fahey, Joseph E.** (J Onondaga Cty Ct) Cthse., 505 S. State St., Syracuse 13202; **Fax:** (315) 671-1191
(516) 572-2141 **Fairgrieve, Scott** (J Nassau Cty Dist Ct) 99 Main St., Hempstead 11550; **E-mail:** sfairgri@courts.state.ny.us
(516) 571-0017 **Falanga, Anthony J.** (Justice Sup Ct 10th Jud Dist) Matrimonial Center, 400 County Seat Dr., Mineola 11501; **Fax:** (516) 571-0029

(315) 536-5128 **Falvey, W. Patrick** (J Yates Cty Ct Family Ct & Surro) Cthse., 415 Liberty St., Penn Yan 14527-1176; **Fax:** (315) 536-5190; **E-mail:** wfalvey@courts.state.ny.us

(315) 255-4316 **Fandrich, Mark H.** (Cayuga Cty Surro) Cthse., 3rd Fl., 152 Genesee St., Auburn 13021-3471; **Fax:** (315) 255-4324
(315) 255-4306 (J Cayuga Cty Family Ct) Historic Old Post Office Bldg., 2nd Fl., 157 Genesee St., Auburn 13021-3476; **Fax:** (315) 255-4312

(646) 386-3892 **Farber, Thomas A.** (J Crim Ct of NYC & Acting Justice Sup Ct 1st Jud Dist) 111 Centre St., N.Y.C. 10013

(631) 852-3160 **Farneti, Joseph** (J Suffolk Cty Ct & Acting Justice Sup Ct 10th Jud Dist) Arthur M. Cromarty Ct. Complex, 210 Center Dr., Riverhead 11901-3310; **Fax:** (631) 852-3161

(646) 386-3375 **Feinman, Paul G.** (Justice Sup Ct 1st Jud Dist) 60 Centre St., Rm. 529, N.Y.C. 10007

(516) 571-2952 **Feinman, Thomas** (Justice Sup Ct 10th Jud Dist) Supreme Ct. Bldg., 100 Supreme Court Dr., Mineola 11501

(518) 648-5411 **Feldstein, S. Peter** (J Hamilton Cty Ct Family Ct & Surro) Chambers, 79 White Birch Ln., Indian Lake 12842 Mailing Address: P.O. Box 780, Indian Lake 12842-0780; **Fax:** (518) 648-6286

(347) 296-1052 **Ferdinand, JoAnn** (J Crim Ct of NYC & Acting Justice Sup Ct 2nd Jud Dist) Bklyn. Treatment Ct., 320 Jay St., Bklyn. 11201; **Fax:** (347) 296-1367

(716) 845-9438 **Feroleto, Paula L.** (Admin J Sup Ct 8th Jud Dist) Erie Cty. Ct. Bldg., 2nd Fl., 25 Delaware Ave., Buffalo 14202; **Fax:** (716) 851-4696; **E-mail:** pferolet@courts.state.ny.us

(518) 581-1006 **Ferradino, Stephen A.** (Justice Sup Ct 4th Jud Dist) P.O. Box 2380, Malta 12020-2380; **Fax:** (518) 581-0825

(646) 386-4651 **Ferrara, Anthony J.** (J Crim Ct of NYC) 111 Centre St., N.Y.C. 10013

(518) 664-9876 **Ferrara, Keith M.** (J Mechanicville City Ct) City Hall, 36 N. Main St., Mechanicville 12118; **Fax:** (518) 664-8606; **E-mail:** kferrara@courts.state.ny.us

(518) 242-3710 **Ferreira, James H.** (J Ct of Claims) Capitol Station, P.O. Box 7344, Albany 12224

(516) 572-2150 **Ferrell, Tricia M.** (J Nassau Cty Dist Ct) 99 Main St., Hempstead 11550

(631) 853-4916 **Filiberto, Patricia M.** (J Suffolk Cty Dist Ct) John P. Cohalan, Jr. Ct. Complex, 400 Carleton Ave., P.O. Box 9075, Central Islip 11722-9075

(347) 404-9092 **Finkelstein, Marc** (J Civil Ct of NYC Housing Part) 141 Livingston St., Bklyn. 11201; **E-mail:** mfinkelstein@courts.state.ny.us

(347) 404-9079 **Fiorella, Anthony J., Jr.** (J Civil Ct of NYC Housing Part) 141 Livingston St., Bklyn. 11201

(716) 845-2627 **Fiorella, Joseph A.** (J Buffalo City Ct) 50 Delaware Ave., Suite 350, Buffalo 14202; **Fax:** (716) 845-7575; **E-mail:** jfiorella@courts.state.ny.us

(347) 296-1840 **Firetog, Neil Jon** (J Crim Ct of NYC & Acting Justice Sup Ct 2nd Jud Dist) 320 Jay St., Bklyn. 11201; **Fax:** (347) 296-1348

(516) 572-2133 **Fischer, Rhonda E.** (J Nassau Cty Dist Ct) 99 Main St., Hempstead 11550

(646) 386-4200 **Fisher, Fern A.** (Justice Sup Ct 1st Jud Dist & Deputy Admin J NYC Cts & Dir NY State Access to Justice Programs) 111 Centre St., N.Y.C. 10013; **Fax:** (212) 374-5709; **E-mail:** dcaj@courts.state.ny.us

(585) 428-2888 **Fisher, Kenneth R.** (Justice Sup Ct 7th Jud Dist) 545 Hall of Justice, 99 Exchange Blvd., Rochester 14614-2184; **Fax:** (585) 428-2983

(347) 404-9068 **Fisher, Pamela L.** (J Civil Ct of NYC) 141 Livingston St., Bklyn. 11201

(718) 298-1175 **Fisher, Steven W.** (Assoc Justice App Div 2nd Dept) 88-11 Sutphin Blvd., Jamaica 11435; **Fax:** (718) 298-1098
(718) 875-1300 45 Monroe Pl., Bklyn. 11201

(646) 386-3967 **FitzGerald, Daniel P.** (J Crim Ct of NYC & Acting Justice Sup Ct 1st Jud Dist) 100 Centre St., N.Y.C. 10013

(607) 778-1027 **Fitzgerald, Molly R.** (Justice Sup Ct 6th Jud Dist) Broome Cty. Cthse., 92 Court St., P.O. Box 1766, Binghamton 13902; **Fax:** (607) 778-3866

(631) 853-4917 **Fitzgibbon, Madeleine A.** (Supv J Suffolk Cty Dist Ct) John P. Cohalan, Jr. Ct. Complex, 400 Carleton Ave., P.O. Box 9075, Central Islip 11722-9075

(718) 298-0222 **Fitzmaurice, Mary Ellen** (J Family Ct of NYC & Acting Justice Sup Ct 11th Jud Dist) 151-20 Jamaica Ave., Jamaica 11432; **E-mail:** mfitzmau@courts.state.ny.us

(315) 466-7161 **Fitzpatrick, Diane L.** (J Ct of Claims) Salina Place, 2nd Fl., 205 S. Salina St., Syracuse 13202; **Fax:** (315) 466-7164

(347) 404-9000 **Fitzpatrick, Thomas M.** (J Civil Ct of NYC Housing Part) 141 Livingston St., Bklyn. 11201

(631) 853-4918 **Flanagan, James P.** (J Suffolk Cty Dist Ct) John P. Cohalan, Jr. Ct. Complex, 400 Carleton Ave., P.O. Box 9075, Central Islip 11722-9075

(914) 824-5877 **Florio, Anita R.** (Assoc Justice App Div 2nd Dept) Courthouse Sq., 6th Fl., 140 Grand St., White Plains 10601; **Fax:** (914) 328-5743

(718) 298-1192 **Flug, Phyllis Orlikoff** (Justice Sup Ct 11th Jud Dist) 88-11 Sutphin Blvd., Jamaica 11435; **Fax:** (718) 298-1810; **E-mail:** poflug@courts.state.ny.us

(347) 296-1616 **Foley, Elizabeth A.** (J Ct of Claims & Acting Justice Sup Ct 2nd Jud Dist) 320 Jay St., Bklyn. 11201; **Fax:** (347) 296-1362

(631) 853-4920 **Ford, William G.** (J Suffolk Cty Dist Ct) John P. Cohalan, Jr. Ct. Complex, 400 Carleton Ave., P.O. Box 9075, Central Islip 11722-9075

(845) 486-2526 **Forman, Peter M.** (J Dutchess Cty Family Ct & Acting Justice Sup Ct 9th Jud Dist) 50 Market St., Poughkeepsie 12601-3204; **E-mail:** pforman@courts.state.ny.us

(607) 737-5681 **Forrest, Steven W.** (J Elmira City Ct) City Hall, 317 E. Church St., Elmira 14901-2790; **Fax:** (212) 401-9240; **E-mail:** sforrest@courts.state.ny.us

(718) 618-2463 **Franco, Ruben** (J Civil Ct of NYC assigned to Crim Ct) Bronx Hall of Justice, 265 E. 161st St., Bronx 10451

(716) 845-9447 **Franczyk, Thomas P.** (J Erie Cty Ct) Erie Cty. Ct. Bldg., 25 Delaware Ave., Buffalo 14202; **Fax:** (716) 851-3319; **E-mail:** tfranczyk@courts.state.ny.us

(585) 428-2486 **Frazee, Evelyn** (Justice Sup Ct 7th Jud Dist) 545 Hall of Justice, 99 Exchange Blvd., Rochester 14614-2184; **Fax:** (585) 784-4227; **E-mail:** efrazee@courts.state.ny.us

(646) 386-5633 **Freed, Kathryn E.** (J Civil Ct of NYC) 111 Centre St., Rm. 1240, N.Y.C. 10013

(212) 340-0524 **Freedman, Helen E.** (Assoc Justice App Div 1st Dept) 27 Madison Ave., N.Y.C. 10010

(845) 291-3110 **Freehill, Robert H.** (J Orange Cty Ct & Acting Justice Sup Ct 9th Jud Dist) Cty. Cthse., 285 Main St., Goshen 10924; **Fax:** (845) 291-2103

(347) 401-9870 **Freeman, Nora L.** (J Family Ct of NYC) 330 Jay St., Bklyn. 11201; **Fax:** (347) 401-9900

(631) 853-4318 **Freundlich, David** (Supv J Suffolk Cty Family Ct & Acting Justice Sup Ct 10th Jud Dist) John P. Cohalan, Jr. Ct. Complex, 400 Carleton Ave., Central Islip 11722; **Fax:** (631) 853-6218

(646) 386-3359 **Fried, Bernard J.** (Justice Sup Ct 1st Jud Dist) 60 Centre St., Rm. 626, N.Y.C. 10007

(718) 618-1411 **Friedlander, Mark** (Justice Sup Ct 12th Jud Dist Civil Term) 851 Grand Concourse, Bronx 10451

(212) 340-0400 **Friedman, David** (Assoc Justice App Div 1st Dept) 27 Madison Ave., N.Y.C. 10010

(646) 386-3760 **Friedman, Marcy S.** (J Civil Ct of NYC & Acting Justice Sup Ct 1st Jud Dist) 60 Centre St., Rm. 663, N.Y.C. 10007

(914) 824-5671 **Friia, Jo Ann** (J White Plains City Ct) 77 S. Lexington Ave., White Plains 10601; **Fax:** (914) 422-6058

(607) 664-2296 **Furfure, Marianne** (J Steuben Cty Ct & Surro & Acting J Steuben Cty Ct) 3 E. Pulteney Sq., Bldg. 3, Bath 14810-1598; **Fax:** (607) 776-4921

(718) 876-6444 **Fusco, John A.** (Justice Sup Ct 13th Jud Dist) Homeport, 355 Front St., Staten Island 10304

(716) 945-4153 **Gabler, William J.** (J Salamanca City Ct) Munic. Bldg., 225 Wildwood Ave., Salamanca 14779; **Fax:** (716) 945-2362

(516) 571-2613 **Galasso, John Michael** (J Nassau Cty Ct & Acting Justice Sup Ct 10th Jud Dist) 100 Supreme Court Dr., Mineola 11501; **Fax:** (516) 571-2164; **E-mail:** jgalasso@courts.state.ny.us

(585) 428-2049 **Gallaher, Patricia E.** (J Monroe Cty Family Ct) Hall of Justice, 3rd Fl., 99 Exchange Blvd., Rochester 14614-2187; **Fax:** (585) 428-2597; **E-mail:** pgallahe@courts.state.ny.us

(585) 428-2011 **Galloway, Harold L.** (Justice Sup Ct 7th Jud Dist) 545 Hall of Justice, 99 Exchange Blvd., Rochester 14614-2184; **Fax:** (585) 428-5887

(315) 337-6440 **Gannon, John C.** (J Rome City Ct) Justice Center, 100 W. Court St., Rome 13440; **Fax:** (315) 338-0343

(631) 853-4302 **Garguilo, Jerry** (Justice Sup Ct 10th Jud Dist) John P. Cohalan, Jr. Cthse., 400 Carleton Ave., Central Islip 11722

(347) 401-9381 **Garnett, William E.** (J Crim Ct of NYC & Acting Justice Sup Ct 2nd Jud Dist) 320 Jay St., Bklyn. 11201

(845) 483-8200 **Garrity, John B.** (J Poughkeepsie City Ct) 62 Civic Center Plaza, Poughkeepsie 12601; **Fax:** (845) 485-6795

(607) 337-1724 **Garry, Elizabeth A.** (Assoc Justice App Div 3rd Dept) 6 E. Main St., Suite 201, Norwich 13815; **Fax:** (607) 337-1722

(347) 404-9094 **Garson, Robin S.** (J Civil Ct of NYC) 141 Livingston St., Bklyn. 11201

(845) 638-5982 **Garvey, Margaret** (Justice Sup Ct 9th Jud Dist) Cthse., 1 S. Main St., New City 10956

(347) 296-1058 **Gary, Michael A.** (J Crim Ct of NYC & Acting Justice Sup Ct 2nd Jud Dist) 320 Jay St., Bklyn. 11201

(718) 298-1416 **Gavrin, Darrell Lori** (Justice Sup Ct 11th Jud Dist) 125-01 Queens Blvd., Kew Gardens 11415; **E-mail:** dgavrin@courts.state.ny.us

(631) 852-2584 **Gazzillo, Ralph T.** (J Suffolk Cty Ct & Acting Justice Sup Ct 10th Jud Dist) Arthur M. Cromarty Ct. Complex, 210 Center Dr., Riverhead 11901-3310; **Fax:** (631) 852-3854

(631) 852-3907 **Genchi, Joan M.** (J Suffolk Cty Family Ct) Cthse., Suite 308, 889 E. Main St., Riverhead 11901; **Fax:** (631) 852-2851; **E-mail:** jgenchi@courts.state.ny.us

(585) 428-4315 **Geraci, Frank P., Jr.** (J Monroe Cty Ct) 224 Hall of Justice, 99 Exchange Blvd., Rochester 14614-2184; **Fax:** (585) 784-4210

(718) 298-0947 **Gerald, Lenora** (J Crim Ct of NYC) 125-01 Queens Blvd., Kew Gardens 11415; **Fax:** (718) 520-4712

(347) 296-1013 **Gerges, Abraham G.** (Justice Sup Ct 2nd Jud Dist) 320 Jay St., Bklyn. 11201; **E-mail:** agerges@courts.state.ny.us

(646) 386-4658 **Gerstein, Michael J.** (J Civil Ct of NYC assigned to Crim Ct) 100 Centre St., N.Y.C. 10013

(646) 386-3730 **Gesmer, Ellen** (J Civil Ct of NYC & Acting Justice Sup Ct 1st Jud Dist) 71 Thomas St., Rm. 209, N.Y.C. 10013; **Fax:** (212) 884-8986; **E-mail:** egesmer@courts.state.ny.us

(718) 876-6433 **Giacobbe, Anthony I.** (Justice Sup Ct 13th Jud Dist) Homeport, 355 Front St., Staten Island 10304

(914) 824-5429 **Giacomo, William J.** (Justice Sup Ct 9th Jud Dist) Richard J. Daronco Cthse., 111 Dr. Martin Luther King, Jr. Blvd., White Plains 10601

(516) 572-2147 **Gianelli, Sharon M.J.** (J Nassau Cty Dist Ct) 99 Main St., Hempstead 11550

(518) 736-5695 **Giardino, Richard C.** (J Fulton Cty Ct & Surro) Cty. Bldg., 223 W. Main St., Johnstown 12095; **Fax:** (518) 762-8776

(718) 675-8505 **Gigante, Robert J.** (Richmond Cty Surro) Cty. Cthse., St. George, Staten Island 10301

(315) 266-4550 **Gigliotti, Louis P.** (Oneida Cty Surro) Oneida County Office Bldg., 8th Fl., 800 Park Ave., Utica 13501; **Fax:** (315) 797-9237; **E-mail:** lgigliot@courts.state.ny.us

(315) 785-7918 **Gilbert, Hugh A.** (Justice Sup Ct & Supv J Family Cts 5th Jud Dist) 317 Washington St., 10th Fl., Watertown 13601; **Fax:** (315) 785-7909

(845) 334-8277 **Gilpatric, James P.** (Justice Sup Ct 3rd Jud Dist) Cthse., 285 Wall St., Kingston 12401

(646) 386-3723 **Gische, Judith J.** (Justice Sup Ct 1st Jud Dist) 60 Centre St., Rm. 232, N.Y.C. 10007; **E-mail:** jgische@courts.state.ny.us

(716) 845-2620 **Givens, Debra L.** (J Buffalo City Ct) 50 Delaware Ave., Suite 500, Buffalo 14202; **Fax:** (716) 845-7576
(716) 845-1804 (Acting J Erie Cty Family Ct) One Niagara Plaza, Buffalo 14202; **Fax:** (716) 858-7901; **E-mail:** dgivens@courts.state.ny.us

(646) 386-5100 **Glen, Kristin Booth** (New York Cty Surro) 31 Chambers St., Rm. 502, N.Y.C. 10007; **Fax:** (212) 374-3250

(716) 845-9450 **Glownia, Joseph R.** (Justice Sup Ct 8th Jud Dist) Erie Cty. Cthse., 3rd Fl., 92 Franklin St., Buffalo 14202; **Fax:** (716) 851-3320; **E-mail:** jglownia@courts.state.ny.us

(347) 404-9479 **Godosky, David** (J Civil Ct of NYC assigned to Crim Ct) 120 Schermerhorn St., Bklyn. 11201

(646) 386-4417 **Goldberg, Arlene D.** (J Crim Ct of NYC & Acting Justice Sup Ct 1st Jud Dist) 111 Centre St., N.Y.C. 10013

(347) 296-1860 **Goldberg, Joel M.** (J Crim Ct of NYC & Acting Justice Sup Ct 2nd Jud Dist) 320 Jay St., Bklyn. 11201

(718) 298-1604 **Golia, James J.** (Justice Sup Ct 11th Jud Dist) 25-10 Court Sq., Long Island City 11101; **Fax:** (718) 520-6707

(718) 298-1190 **Golia, Joseph G.** (Justice Sup Ct 11th Jud Dist & Assoc Justice Sup Ct App Term 2nd 11th & 13th Jud Dists) 88-11 Sutphin Blvd., Jamaica 11435; **E-mail:** jgolia@courts.state.ny.us

(718) 618-3682 **Gonzalez, Doris M.** (J Civil Ct of NYC & Acting Justice Sup Ct 12th Jud Dist Crim Term) Bronx Hall of Justice, 265 E. 161st St., Bronx 10451; **Fax:** (718) 618-3584

(718) 298-0204 **Gonzalez, Lizbeth** (J Civil Ct of NYC assigned to Family Ct) 151-20 Jamaica Ave., Jamaica 11432; **Fax:** (718) 297-2530
(212) 340-0400 **Gonzalez, Luis A.** (Pres Justice App Div 1st Dept) 27 Madison Ave., N.Y.C. 10010; **Fax:** (212) 340-0547
(718) 618-1417 **Gonzalez, Yvonne** (Justice Sup Ct 12th Jud Dist Civil Term) 851 Grand Concourse, Bronx 10451
(646) 386-3235 **Goodman, Emily Jane** (Justice Sup Ct 1st Jud Dist) 60 Centre St., Rm. 551, N.Y.C. 10007; **Fax:** (212) 401-9045; **E-mail:** egoodman@courts.state.ny.us
(516) 572-2125 **Goodsell, David** (J Nassau Cty Dist Ct) 99 Main St., Hempstead 11550
(716) 845-2107 **Gorski, Jerome C.** (Assoc Justice App Div 4th Dept) 50 Delaware Ave., Buffalo 14202; **Fax:** (716) 852-6367; **E-mail:** jcgorski@courts.state.ny.us
(518) 285-5050 **Graffeo, Victoria A.** (Assoc J Ct of App) Court of Appeals Hall, 20 Eagle St., Albany 12207
(347) 401-9870 **Graham, Bernard J.** (J Family Ct of NYC assigned to Family Ct) 330 Jay St., Bklyn. 11201; **Fax:** (347) 401-9900
(718) 298-1212 **Grays, Marguerite A.** (Justice Sup Ct 11th Jud Dist) 88-11 Sutphin Blvd., Jamaica 11435; **Fax:** (718) 298-1107
(718) 262-7376 **Greco, Rudolph E., Jr.** (J Civil Ct of NYC) 89-17 Sutphin Blvd., Jamaica 11435
(347) 404-9468 **Green, Desmond A.** (J Civil Ct of NYC assigned to Crim Ct) 120 Schermerhorn St., Bklyn. 11201
(716) 845-2104 **Green, Samuel L.** (Assoc Justice App Div 4th Dept) 50 Delaware Ave., Buffalo 14202; **Fax:** (716) 852-6367
(718) 618-1420 **Green, Stanley B.** (J Civil Ct of NYC & Acting Justice Sup Ct 12th Jud Dist Civil Term) 851 Grand Concourse, Bronx 10451
(516) 571-9154 **Greenberg, Ellen** (J Nassau Cty Family Ct) 1200 Old Country Rd., Westbury 11590; **Fax:** (516) 571-9406
(718) 618-3616 **Greenberg, Ethan R.** (J Crim Ct of NYC & Acting Justice Sup Ct 12th Jud Dist Crim Term) Bronx Hall of Justice, 265 E. 161st St., Bronx 10451; **Fax:** (718) 618-3584
(315) 671-1103 **Greenwood, Donald A.** (Justice Sup Ct 5th Jud Dist) Onondaga Cty. Cthse., 401 Montgomery St., Syracuse 13202; **Fax:** (315) 671-1187
(516) 571-1488 **Grella, Philip M.** (J Ct of Claims & Acting Justice Sup Ct 10th Jud Dist & Acting J Nassau Cty Ct) Cty. Cthse., 262 Old Country Rd., Mineola 11501; **Fax:** (516) 571-2642
(718) 618-2200 **Gribetz, Sidney** (J Family Ct of NYC) 900 Sheridan Ave., Bronx 10451; **Fax:** (718) 590-7305; **E-mail:** sgribetz@courts.state.ny.us
(718) 298-1434 **Griffin, James P.** (J Crim Ct of NYC & Acting Justice Sup Ct 11th Jud Dist) 125-01 Queens Blvd., Kew Gardens 11415; **Fax:** (718) 520-2263; **E-mail:** jgriffin@courts.state.ny.us
(315) 266-4460 **Griffith, James R.** (J Oneida Cty Family Ct) Oneida Cty. Cthse., 200 Elizabeth St., Utica 13501; **Fax:** (315) 798-6404
(585) 786-3148 Exts. 117, 118 **Griffith, Michael F.** (J Wyoming Cty Ct Family Ct & Surro) Cthse., 147 N. Main St., Warsaw 14569-1193; **Fax:** (585) 786-2818
(914) 831-6498 **Gross, Mark A.** (J Mount Vernon City Ct) Two Roosevelt Sq. N., 2nd Fl., Mount Vernon 10550-2019; **Fax:** (914) 699-1230
(718) 618-3668 **Gross, Michael A.** (J Crim Ct of NYC & Acting Justice Sup Ct 12th Jud Dist Crim Term) Bronx Hall of Justice, 265 E. 161st St., Bronx 10451
(718) 298-1418 **Grosso, Joseph A.** (J Crim Ct of NYC & Acting Justice Sup Ct 11th Jud Dist) 125-01 Queens Blvd., Kew Gardens 11415; **E-mail:** jgrosso@courts.state.ny.us
(347) 401-9870 **Grosvenor, Paul H.** (J Family Ct of NYC) 330 Jay St., Bklyn. 11201; **Fax:** (347) 401-9900
(718) 618-2213 **Gruebel, Ilana** (J Civil Ct of NYC assigned to Family Ct) 900 Sheridan Ave., Bronx 10451
(347) 404-9435 **Gubbay, Joseph** (J Crim Ct of NYC & Acting Justice Sup Ct 2nd Jud Dist) 120 Schermerhorn St., Bklyn. 11201; **Fax:** (718) 643-3538
(347) 296-1037 **Guzman, Raymond** (Justice Sup Ct 2nd Jud Dist) 320 Jay St., Bklyn. 11201
(718) 618-1421 **Guzman, Wilma** (Justice Sup Ct 12th Jud Dist Civil Term) 851 Grand Concourse, Bronx 10451; **E-mail:** wguzman@courts.state.ny.us
(631) 854-4545 **Hackeling, C. Stephen** (J Suffolk Cty Dist Ct) 1850 New York Ave., Huntington Station 11746
(716) 845-2762 **Haendiges, Deborah A.** (Justice Sup Ct 8th Jud Dist) Erie Cty. Ct. Bldg., 1st Fl., 25 Delaware Ave., Buffalo 14202; **Fax:** (716) 851-3222; **E-mail:** dhaendig@courts.state.ny.us
(315) 349-8666 **Hafner, Walter W., Jr.** (J Oswego Cty Ct) Public Safety Center, 39 Churchill Rd., Oswego 13126; **Fax:** (315) 349-8669
(646) 386-5691 **Hagler, Shlomo S.** (J Civil Ct of NYC & Acting Justice Sup Ct 1st Jud Dist) 111 Centre St., Rm. 326, N.Y.C. 10013; **Fax:** (212) 374-2594; **E-mail:** shagler@courts.state.ny.us
(646) 386-5615 **Hahn, Arlene H.** (J Civil Ct of NYC Housing Part) 111 Centre St., Rm. 1240, N.Y.C. 10013; **Fax:** (212) 374-5709
(518) 451-8888 **Hall, Courtenay W.** (J Saratoga Cty Family Ct) Saratoga Cty. Munic. Ctr., 35 W. High St., Ballston Spa 12020-0600
(518) 761-7695 **Hall, John S., Jr.** (J Warren Cty Ct & Surro) Warren Cty. Munic. Center, 1340 State Rt. 9, Lake George 12845-9803; **Fax:** (518) 761-7698; **E-mail:** jshall@courts.state.ny.us
(347) 296-1061 **Hall, L. Priscilla** (Assoc Justice App Div 2nd Dept) 320 Jay St., Rm. 2364, Bklyn. 11201; **Fax:** (347) 296-1372; **E-mail:** phall@courts.state.ny.us
(646) 386-5620 **Halprin, Sheldon J.** (J Civil Ct of NYC Housing Part) 111 Centre St., Rm. 1240, N.Y.C. 10013; **Fax:** (212) 374-5709; **E-mail:** shalprin@courts.state.ny.us
(347) 401-9870 **Hamill, Bryanne** (J Family Ct of NYC) 330 Jay St., Bklyn. 11201; **Fax:** (347) 401-9900
(716) 845-2633 **Hannah, Craig D.** (J Buffalo City Ct) 50 Delaware Ave., Suite 600, Buffalo 14202; **Fax:** (716) 845-7578
(716) 845-1804 (Acting J Erie Cty Family Ct) One Niagara Plaza, Buffalo 14202; **Fax:** (716) 858-7901; **E-mail:** cdhannah@courts.state.ny.us
(914) 824-5673 **Hansbury, Brian** (J White Plains City Ct) 77 S. Lexington Ave., White Plains 10601; **Fax:** (914) 422-6058
(315) 671-2010 **Hanuszczak, Michael L.** (J Onondaga Cty Family Ct & Acting Justice Sup Ct 5th Jud Dist) Onondaga Cty. Cthse., 401 Montgomery St., Syracuse 13202; **Fax:** (315) 671-1166; **E-mail:** mhanuszc@courts.state.ny.us
(315) 785-7785 **Harberson, James C.** (J Watertown City Ct) Munic. Bldg., 245 Washington St., Watertown 13601; **Fax:** (315) 785-7856
(518) 432-3907 **Hard, Judith A.** (J Ct of Claims) Capitol Station, P.O. Box 7344, Albany 12224; **Fax:** (518) 432-3908
(718) 298-1204 **Harrington, William M.** (J Crim Ct of NYC & Acting Justice Sup Ct 11th Jud Dist) 125-01 Queens Blvd., Kew Gardens 11415; **Fax:** (718) 520-4712

(718) 298-1144 **Hart, Duane A.** (Justice Sup Ct 11th Jud Dist) 88-11 Sutphin Blvd., Jamaica 11435; **E-mail:** dhart@courts.state.ny.us

(607) 737-2923 **Hayden, James T.** (J Chemung Cty Ct Family Ct& Surro) 203-209 William St., P.O. Box 588, Elmira 14902-0588; **Fax:** (607) 737-2913

(845) 486-2225 **Hayes, Gerald V.** (J Dutchess Cty Ct) Cthse., 10 Market St., Poughkeepsie 12601-3203; **Fax:** (845) 473-5403

(646) 386-4405 **Hayes, Roger S.** (J Crim Ct of NYC & Acting Justice Sup Ct 1st Jud Dist) 111 Centre St., N.Y.C. 10013

(718) 262-7365 **Healy, Maureen A.** (J Civil Ct of NYC) 89-17 Sutphin Blvd., Jamaica 11435

(518) 453-4640 **Heath-Roland, Helena M.** (J Albany City Ct) 209 City Hall, Eagle & Corning Pl., Albany 12207; **Fax:** (518) 434-5034

(315) 671-2040 **Hedges, Bryan R.** (J Onondaga Cty Family Ct) Onondaga Cty. Cthse., 401 Montgomery St., Syracuse 13202; **Fax:** (315) 671-1169; **E-mail:** bhedges@courts.state.ny.us

(646) 386-3211 **Heitler, Sherry Klein** (Admin J Sup Ct 1st Jud Dist Civil Div) 60 Centre St., Rm. 620, N.Y.C. 10007

(646) 386-3211 (Admin J Sup Ct 1st Jud Dist Civil Term) 60 Centre St., N.Y.C. 10007

(631) 853-4915 **Henry, Jennifer A.** (J Suffolk Cty Dist Ct) John P. Cohalan, Jr. Ct. Complex, 400 Carleton Ave., P.O. Box 9075, Central Islip 11722-9075

(347) 296-1366 **Henry, Patricia E.** (J Crim Ct of NYC & Acting Justice Sup Ct 2nd Jud Dist) 320 Jay St., Bklyn. 11201

(631) 853-5520 **Hensley, Paul** (J Suffolk Cty Dist Ct) John P. Cohalan, Jr. Ct. Complex, 400 Carleton Ave., P.O. Box 9075, Central Islip 11722-9075

(347) 401-9601 **Hepner, Paula J.** (Supv J Family Ct of NYC Kings & Richmond Cty) 330 Jay St., Bklyn. 11201; **Fax:** (347) 401-9900

(518) 285-8759 **Herrick, Stephen W.** (J Albany Cty Ct & Acting Justice Sup Ct 3rd Jud Dist) Judl. Ctr., Rm. 218, 6 Lodge St., Albany 12207

(315) 266-4300 **Hester, Samuel D.** (Justice Sup Ct 5th Jud Dist) Oneida Cty. Cthse., 302 N. James St., Rome 13440; **Fax:** (315) 356-0603

(347) 404-9089 **Heymann, George M.** (J Civil Ct of NYC Housing Part) 141 Livingston St., Bklyn. 11201

(716) 938-9111 Ext. 2381 **Himelein, Larry M.** (J Cattaraugus Cty Ct Family Ct & Surro) Cthse., 303 Court St., Little Valley 14755; **Fax:** (716) 938-6413

(347) 296-1200 **Hinds-Radix, Sylvia O.** (Admin J Sup Ct 2nd Jud Dist Civil Term) 360 Adams St., Bklyn. 11201; **Fax:** (718) 643-2095

(631) 852-2586 **Hinrichs, C. Randall** (Justice Sup Ct 10th Jud Dist) Arthur M. Cromarty Ct. Complex, 210 Center Dr., Riverhead 11901

(718) 298-1435 **Hirsch, Marcia P.** (J Ct of Claims & Acting Justice Sup Ct 11th Jud Dist) 125-01 Queens Blvd., Kew Gardens 11415; **E-mail:** mhirsch@courts.state.ny.us

(516) 572-2137 **Hirsh, Fred J.** (J Nassau Cty Dist Ct) 99 Main St., Hempstead 11550

(518) 798-4714 **Hobbs, Gary C.** (J Glens Falls City Ct) 42 Ridge St., 3rd Fl., Glens Falls 12801; **Fax:** (518) 798-0137

(646) 386-5101 **Hoffman, Douglas E.** (Supv J Family Ct of NYC New York Cty) 60 Lafayette St., N.Y.C. 10013

(631) 853-4268 **Hoffmann, Richard** (J Suffolk Cty Family Ct) John P. Cohalan, Jr. Ct. Complex, 400 Carleton Ave., Central Islip 11722; **Fax:** (631) 853-4359

(718) 298-1328 **Holder, Kenneth C.** (Justice Sup Ct 11th Jud Dist) 125-01 Queens Blvd., Kew Gardens 11415

(914) 824-5379 **Holdman, Robert K.** (J Ct of Claims & Acting Justice Sup Ct 9th Jud Dist) Richard J. Daronco Cthse., 111 Dr. Martin Luther King, Jr. Blvd., White Plains 10601

(718) 298-1438 **Hollie, Ronald D.** (Justice Sup Ct 11th Jud Dist) 125-01 Queens Blvd., Kew Gardens 11415; **Fax:** (718) 520-6474; **E-mail:** rhollie@courts.state.ny.us

(718) 618-2350 **Holzman, Lee L.** (Bronx Cty Surro) 851 Grand Concourse, Bronx 10451; **Fax:** (718) 537-5158

(718) 618-2466 **Hong, Gilbert C.** (J Crim Ct of NYC) Bronx Hall of Justice, 265 E. 161st St., Bronx 10451

(516) 571-3423 **Honorof, Alan L.** (J Ct of Claims & Acting Justice Sup Ct 10th Jud Dist & and Acting J Nassau Cty Ct) Cty. Cthse., 262 Old Country Rd., Mineola 11501; **Fax:** (516) 571-1849; **E-mail:** ahonorof@courts.state.ny.us

(914) 831-6587 **Horowitz, Nilda Morales** (J Westchester Cty Family Ct) 420 North Ave., New Rochelle 10801; **Fax:** (914) 813-5634; **E-mail:** nmhorowi@courts.state.ny.us

(631) 853-4921 **Horowitz, Richard I.** (J Suffolk Cty Dist Ct) John P. Cohalan, Jr. Ct. Complex, 400 Carleton Ave., P.O. Box 9075, Central Islip 11722-9075

(716) 845-9453 **Howe, Barbara** (Erie Cty Surro) Erie Cty. Hall, 92 Franklin St., Buffalo 14202; **Fax:** (716) 853-3741; **E-mail:** bhowe@courts.state.ny.us

(518) 736-5691 **Hoye, Polly A.** (J Fulton Cty Ct & Surro) Cty. Bldg., 223 W. Main St., Johnstown 12095; **Fax:** (518) 762-5078

(347) 404-9080 **Hoyos, Inez** (J Civil Ct of NYC Housing Part) 141 Livingston St., Bklyn. 11201

(914) 824-5790 **Hubert, James W.** (J Westchester Cty Ct) 111 Dr. Martin Luther King, Jr. Blvd., White Plains 10601; **Fax:** (914) 995-8654

(631) 852-3850 **Hudson, James C.** (J Suffolk Cty Ct & Acting Justice Sup Ct 10th Jud Dist) Arthur M. Cromarty Ct. Complex, 210 Center Dr., Riverhead 11901-3310; **Fax:** (631) 852-3225; **E-mail:** jhudson@courts.state.ny.us

(716) 515-4810 **Hudson, Michael E.** (J Ct of Claims) 130 S. Elmwood Ave., Buffalo 14202; **Fax:** (716) 515-4813

(646) 386-3217 **Huff, Carol E.** (Justice Sup Ct 1st Jud Dist) 60 Centre St., Rm. 624, N.Y.C. 10007

(518) 285-6100 **Hummel, Christian F.** (Rensselaer Cty Surro & Acting Justice Sup Ct 3rd Jud Dist) Cty. Cthse., 80 Second St., Troy 12180; **Fax:** (518) 272-5452

(718) 298-0228 **Hunt, John M.** (J Family Ct of NYC) 151-20 Jamaica Ave., Jamaica 11432; **Fax:** (718) 297-2530

(315) 785-3001 **Hunt, Richard V.** (J Jefferson Cty Family Ct) Jefferson Cty. Ct. Complex, 1st Fl., 163 Arsenal St., Watertown 13601-2560; **Fax:** (315) 785-3198

(718) 618-1423 **Hunter, Alexander W., Jr.** (Justice Sup Ct 12th Jud Dist & Justice Sup Ct App Term 1st Jud Dept) 851 Grand Concourse, Bronx 10451; **Fax:** (718) 618-3531

(347) 296-1560 **Hurkin-Torres, Allen Z.** (Justice Sup Ct 2nd Jud Dist) 360 Adams St., Bklyn. 11201

(718) 618-3673 **Iacovetta, Nicholas J.** (J Crim Ct of NYC & Acting Justice Sup Ct 12th Jud Dist Crim Term) Bronx Hall of Justice, 265 E. 161st St., Bronx 10451

(516) 571-2484 **Iannacci, Angela G.** (Justice Sup Ct 10th Jud Dist & Assoc Justice Sup Ct App Term 9th and 10th Jud Dists) 100 Supreme Court Dr., Mineola 11501

(631) 853-4921 **Iliou, John** (J Suffolk Cty Dist Ct) John P. Cohalan, Jr. Ct. Complex, 400 Carleton Ave., P.O. Box 9075, Central Islip 11722-9075

(347) 296-1489 **Ingram, John G.** (J Ct of Claims & Acting Justice Sup Ct 2nd Jud Dist) 320 Jay St., Bklyn. 11201

(718) 298-1653 **Jackman-Brown, Pam B.** (J Civil Ct of NYC & Acting Justice Sup Ct 11th Jud Dist) 88-11 Sutphin Blvd., Jamaica 11435

(347) 296-1470 **Jackson, M. Randolph** (Justice Sup Ct 2nd Jud Dist) 360 Adams St., Bklyn. 11201

(646) 386-4615 **Jackson, Melissa** (Supv J Crim Ct of NYC New York Cty) 100 Centre St., N.Y.C. 10013 Midtown Community Court, 314 W. 54th St., N.Y.C. 10019

(347) 296-1554 **Jacobson, Laura L.** (Justice Sup Ct 2nd Jud Dist) 360 Adams St., Bklyn. 11201

(518) 285-6146 **Jacon, Robert M.** (J Rensselaer Cty Ct) Cthse., Congress & Second St., Troy 12180

(516) 571-3378 **Jaeger, Steven M.** (J Nassau Cty Ct & Acting Justice Sup Ct 10th Jud Dist) 262 Old Country Rd., Mineola 11501; **Fax:** (516) 571-3220; **E-mail:** sjaeger@courts.state.ny.us

(646) 386-3724 **Jaffe, Barbara** (J Civil Ct of NYC & Acting Justice Sup Ct 1st Jud Dist) 80 Centre St., N.Y.C. 10013; **E-mail:** bjaffe@courts.state.ny.us

(646) 386-3352 **James, Debra A.** (J Civil Ct of NYC & Acting Justice Sup Ct 1st Jud Dist) 111 Centre St., Rm. 632, N.Y.C. 10013; **Fax:** (212) 374-0402; **E-mail:** djames@courts.state.ny.us

(845) 638-5340 **Jamieson, Linda S.** (Justice Sup Ct 9th Jud Dist) Cthse., 1 S. Main St., New City 10956; **E-mail:** ljamieso@courts.state.ny.us

(516) 572-2121 **Janowitz, Norman** (J Nassau Cty Dist Ct) 99 Main St., Hempstead 11550

(347) 404-9631 **Jeong, Alexander** (J Crim Ct of NYC) 120 Schermerhorn St., Bklyn. 11201

(347) 404-9070 **Jimenez-Salta, Dawn M.** (J Civil Ct of NYC) 141 Livingston St., Bklyn. 11201

(347) 404-9653 **Johnson, Diana A.** (Kings Cty Surro) 2 Johnson St., Bklyn. 11201; **Fax:** (718) 643-6237

(585) 428-2096 **Johnson, Teresa D.** (Supv J Rochester City Ct & Acting J Monroe Cty Ct) Hall of Justice, 99 Exchange Blvd., Rochester 14614; **Fax:** (585) 428-4265; **E-mail:** tjohnson@courts.state.ny.us

(631) 852-1429 **Jones, John J.J., Jr.** (Justice Sup Ct 10th Jud Dist) Arthur M. Cromarty Ct. Complex, Rm. 6, 210 Center Dr., Riverhead 11901; **Fax:** (631) 852-2730

(914) 824-5780 **Jones, Theodore T., Jr.** (Assoc J Ct of App) 140 Grand St., Suite 900, White Plains 10601

(347) 404-9063 **Joseph, Ingrid** (J Civil Ct of NYC) 141 Livingston St., Bklyn. 11201

(607) 936-4111 **Kahl, David B.** (J Corning City Ct) 12 Civic Center Plaza, Corning 14830-2884; **Fax:** (607) 936-0519

(631) 852-3040 **Kahn, Barbara R.** (J Suffolk Cty Ct) Arthur M. Cromarty Ct. Complex, 210 Center Dr., Riverhead 11901-3310

(646) 386-3986 **Kahn, Marcy L.** (Justice Sup Ct 1st Jud Dist) 100 Centre St., N.Y.C. 10013

(347) 404-9473 **Kalish, Robert D.** (J Civil Ct of NYC assigned to Crim Ct) 120 Schermerhorn St., Bklyn. 11201

(347) 296-1000 **Kamins, Barry** (J Crim Ct of NYC & Admin J Sup Ct 2nd Jud Dist Crim Term) 320 Jay St., Bklyn. 11201; **Fax:** (347) 296-1327

(646) 386-5582 **Kaplan, David** (J Civil Ct of NYC Housing Part) 111 Centre St., Rm. 439, N.Y.C. 10013; **Fax:** (212) 374-5709

(646) 386-5567 **Kaplan, Deborah A.** (J Civil Ct of NYC & Acting Justice Sup Ct 1st Jud Dist) 60 Centre St., Rm. 660, N.Y.C. 10007; **Fax:** (212) 401-9037; **E-mail:** dkaplan@courts.state.ny.us

(646) 386-3226 **Kapnick, Barbara R.** (Justice Sup Ct 1st Jud Dist) 60 Centre St., Rm. 555, N.Y.C. 10007; **E-mail:** bkapnick@courts.state.ny.us

(315) 671-1106 **Karalunas, Deborah H.** (Justice Sup Ct 5th Jud Dist) Onondaga Cty. Cthse., Rm. 401, 401 Montgomery St., Syracuse 13202; **Fax:** (315) 671-1184

(516) 571-2628 **Kase, John L.** (J Nassau Cty Ct & Acting Justice Sup Ct 10th Jud Dist) West Wing, 252 Old Country Rd., Mineola 11501; **Fax:** (516) 571-6300; **E-mail:** jkase@courts.state.ny.us

(718) 262-7314 **Katz, Ann** (J Civil Ct of NYC Housing Part) 89-17 Sutphin Blvd., Jamaica 11435

(845) 340-3888 **Kavanagh, E. Michael** (Assoc Justice App Div 3rd Dept) Supreme Ct. Chambers, 1 Pearl St., Kingston 12401; **Fax:** (845) 340-3893

(716) 845-2637 **Keane, Kevin J.** (J Buffalo City Ct) 50 Delaware Ave., Suite 350, Buffalo 14202; **Fax:** (716) 845-7575; **E-mail:** kkeane@courts.state.ny.us

(518) 462-6714 **Keefe, Thomas K.** (J Albany City Ct) Crim. Ct., Public Safety Bldg., 1 Morton Ave., Albany 12202; **E-mail:** tkeefe@courts.state.ny.us

(585) 428-1912 **Keenan, Richard A.** (J Monroe Cty Ct) 214 Hall of Justice, 99 Exchange Blvd., Rochester 14614-2184; **Fax:** (585) 784-4212

(315) 946-5435 **Kehoe, Dennis M.** (J Wayne Cty Ct Family Ct & Surro) Hall of Justice, Suite 106, 54 Broad St., Lyons 14489-1199; **Fax:** (315) 946-5434

(631) 853-7601 **Kelley, Chris Ann** (J Suffolk Cty Dist Ct) John P. Cohalan, Jr. Ct. Complex, 400 Carleton Ave., P.O. Box 9075, Central Islip 11722-9075

(631) 853-4286 **Kelly, John** (J Suffolk Cty Family Ct) John P. Cohalan, Jr. Ct. Complex, 400 Carleton Ave., Central Islip 11722; **Fax:** (631) 853-4288

(718) 298-1114 **Kelly, Peter J.** (Justice Sup Ct 11th Jud Dist) 88-11 Sutphin Blvd., Jamaica 11435; **E-mail:** pkelly@courts.state.ny.us

(845) 638-5386 **Kelly, William A.** (Justice Sup Ct 9th Jud Dist) Cthse., 1 S. Main St., New City 10956; **Fax:** (845) 708-7236; **E-mail:** wkelly@courts.state.ny.us

(347) 401-9870 **Kennedy, Tanya R.** (J Civil Ct of NYC assigned to Family Ct) 330 Jay St., Bklyn. 11201; **Fax:** (347) 401-9900; **E-mail:** tkennedy@courts.state.ny.us

(646) 386-3816 **Kenney, Joan M.** (J Civil Ct of NYC & Acting Justice Sup Ct 1st Jud Dist) 71 Thomas St., N.Y.C. 10013; **E-mail:** jkenney@courts.state.ny.us

(516) 571-9022 **Kent, Robin** (J Nassau Cty Family Ct) 1200 Old Country Rd., Westbury 11590; **Fax:** (516) 571-9393

(631) 853-5471 **Kent, William J., III** (Justice Sup Ct 10th Jud Dist) John P. Cohalan, Jr. Ct. Complex, Ctrm. S-34, 400 Carleton St., P.O. Box 9070, Central Islip 11722-9070; **Fax:** (631) 853-3281

(646) 386-3729 **Kern, Cynthia S.** (J Civil Ct of NYC & Acting Justice Sup Ct 1st Jud Dist) 80 Centre St., N.Y.C. 10013; **E-mail:** cskern@courts.state.ny.us

(607) 273-2263 **Kerrigan, James M.** (J Ithaca City Ct) 118 E. Clinton St., Ithaca 14850; **Fax:** (607) 277-3702

(718) 298-0013 **Kerrigan, Kevin J.** (Justice Sup Ct 11th Jud Dist) 88-11 Sutphin Blvd., Jamaica 11435; **Fax:** (718) 298-0088

(845) 291-3050 **Kiedaisch, Debra J.** (J Orange Cty Family Ct & Acting Justice Sup Ct & Pres J Integrated Domestic Violence Part 9th Jud Dist) Orange Cty. Cthse., 285 Main St., Goshen 10924; **Fax:** (845) 291-4520

(718) 618-3640 **Kiesel, Diane R.** (J Crim Ct of NYC & Acting Justice Sup Ct 12th Jud Dist Crim Term) Bronx Hall of Justice, 265 E. 161st St., Bronx 10451; **Fax:** (212) 457-2663

(718) 618-3680 **Kindler, James M.** (J Ct of Claims & Acting Justice Sup Ct) Bronx Hall of Justice, Rm. 953, 265 E. 161st St., Bronx 10451

(347) 401-9186 **King, Kathy J.** (J Civil Ct of NYC & Acting Justice Sup Ct 2nd Jud Dist) 320 Jay St., Bklyn. 11201; **E-mail:** kjking@courts.state.ny.us

(315) 867-1171 **Kirk, Patrick L.** (J Herkimer Cty Ct & Surro) Herkimer Cty. Office & Ct. Facility, Suite 5550, 301 N. Washington St., Herkimer 13350-0749; **Fax:** (315) 867-1344

(845) 338-2974 **Kirschner, Philip W.** (J Kingston City Ct) 1 Garraghan Dr., Kingston 12401; **Fax:** (845) 338-1443

(718) 298-1003 **Kitzes, Orin R.** (Justice Sup Ct 11th Jud Dist) 88-11 Sutphin Blvd., Jamaica 11435; **E-mail:** okitzes@courts.state.ny.us

(845) 291-3040 **Klein, Carol S.** (J Orange Cty Family Ct & Acting Justice Sup Ct & Pres J Family Treatment & Juv Drug Treatment Cts 9th Jud Dist) Orange Cty. Cthse., 285 Main St., Goshen 10924; **Fax:** (845) 291-4405

(914) 824-5477 **Klein, David** (J Westchester Cty Family Ct) 111 Dr. Martin Luther King, Jr. Blvd., White Plains 10601; **Fax:** (914) 995-6565

(718) 466-3191 **Klein, Jerald R.** (J Civil Ct of NYC Housing Part) Housing Ct., 1118 Grand Concourse, Bronx 10456; **E-mail:** jklein@courts.state.ny.us

(716) 439-7055 **Kloch, Richard C., Sr.** (J Ct of Claims & Acting Justice & Supv J Crim Cts 8th Jud Dist) Niagara Cty. Cthse., 175 Hawley St., Lockport 14094; **Fax:** (716) 439-7039

(516) 572-2159 **Kluewer, Susan T.** (J Nassau Cty Dist Ct & Pres Bd of Judges) 99 Main St., Hempstead 11550

(212) 428-2130 **Kluger, Judy Harris** (J Crim Ct of NYC & Acting Justice Sup Ct 1st Jud Dist & Chief Office of Policy & Planning & Dir Office of Drug Treatment Programs) 25 Beaver St., N.Y.C. 10004; **Fax:** (212) 428-2192; **E-mail:** jkluger@courts.state.ny.us

(347) 296-1548 **Knipel, Lawrence S.** (Justice Sup Ct 2nd Jud Dist) 360 Adams St., Bklyn. 11201

(646) 386-5102 **Knipps, Susan K.** (J Family Ct of NYC) 60 Lafayette St., N.Y.C. 10013; **Fax:** (212) 374-2623

(516) 572-2109 **Knobel, Gary F.** (J Nassau Cty Dist Ct) 99 Main St., Hempstead 11550

(718) 298-1443 **Knopf, Stephen A.** (Justice Sup Ct 11th Jud Dist) 125-01 Queens Blvd., Kew Gardens 11415; **Fax:** (718) 520-7732

(585) 396-4260 **Kocher, William F.** (J Ontario Cty Ct & Family Ct & Acting Justice Sup Ct 7th Jud Dist) Cthse., 27 N. Main St., Canandaigua 14424; **Fax:** (585) 396-4087; **E-mail:** wkocher@courts.state.ny.us

(646) 386-4678 **Koenderman, Elisa F.** (J Crim Ct of NYC) 100 Centre St., N.Y.C. 10013

(718) 298-1375 **Kohm, Robert C.** (Justice Sup Ct 11th Jud Dist) 125-01 Queens Blvd., Kew Gardens 11415; **E-mail:** rkohm@courts.state.ny.us

(585) 428-5486 **Kohout, Joan S.** (J Monroe Cty Family Ct) Hall of Justice, 3rd Fl., 99 Exchange Blvd., Rochester 14614-2187; **Fax:** (585) 784-4230

(646) 386-4411 **Konviser, Jill** (J Ct of Claims & Acting Justice Sup Ct 1st Jud Dist) 100 Centre St., N.Y.C. 10013; **Fax:** (347) 296-1375

(646) 386-3363 **Kornreich, Shirley Werner** (Justice Sup Ct 1st Jud Dist) 60 Centre St., Rm. 649, N.Y.C. 10007

(646) 386-5625 **Kotler, Lynn R.** (J Civil Ct of NYC assigned to Crim Ct) 100 Centre St., N.Y.C. 10013

(518) 828-3100 **Koweek, Richard M.** (J Hudson City Ct) 427-429 Warren St., Hudson 12534; **Fax:** (518) 828-3628

(518) 285-8460 **Kramer, Barry D.** (Justice Sup Ct 4th Jud Dist) Cthse., 4th Fl., 612 State St., Schenectady 12305-2113; **Fax:** (518) 347-1972

(347) 296-1476 **Kramer, Herbert** (Justice Sup Ct 2nd Jud Dist) 360 Adams St., Bklyn. 11201

(718) 466-3131 **Kraus, Sabrina** (J Civil Ct of NYC Housing Part) 851 Grand Concourse, Bronx 10451

(347) 401-9883 **Krauss, Sarah L.** (J Fasmily Ct of NYC Acting Justice Sup Ct 2nd Jud Dist) 330 Jay St., Bklyn. 11201; **Fax:** (347) 401-9900

(518) 462-6714 **Kretser, Rachel** (J Albany City Ct) Crim. Ct., Public Safety Bldg., 1 Morton Ave., Albany 12202

(518) 761-6547 **Krogmann, David B.** (Justice Sup Ct 4th Jud Dist) Warren Cty. Munic. Center, 1340 State Rt. 9, Lake George 12845; **Fax:** (518) 761-6465; **E-mail:** dkrogman@courts.state.ny.us

(718) 298-1358 **Kron, Barry** (J Crim Ct of NYC & Acting Justice Sup Ct 11th Jud Dist) 125-01 Queens Blvd., Kew Gardens 11415; **E-mail:** bkron@courts.state.ny.us

(845) 483-8100 **Kulkin, Peter M.** (J Newburgh City Ct) 300 Broadway, Newburgh 12550

(347) 401-9047 **Kurtz, Donald Scott** (Justice Sup Ct 2nd Jud Dist) 360 Adams St., Bklyn. 11201

(716) 366-2055 **Kuzdale, John M.** (J Dunkirk City Ct) City Hall, 342 Central Ave., Dunkirk 14048-2122; **Fax:** (716) 366-3622

(845) 794-1248 **LaBuda, Frank J.** (J Sullivan Cty Ct & Surro) Lawrence H. Cooke Sullivan Cty. Cthse., 414 Broadway, Monticello 12701; **Fax:** (845) 794-6208

(914) 824-5417 **LaCava, John R.** (Justice Sup Ct 9th Jud Dist & Assoc Justice Sup Ct App Term 9th and 10th Jud Dists) Richard J. Daronco Cthse., 17th Fl., 111 Dr. Martin Luther King, Jr. Blvd., White Plains 10601

(631) 952-6542 **Lack, James J.** (J Ct of Claims) State Office Bldg., 3rd Fl., Veterans Memorial Hwy., Hauppauge 11788; **Fax:** (631) 952-6727

(518) 562-1446 **Lahtinen, John A.** (Assoc Justice App Div 3rd Dept) 36 Oak St., P.O. Box 38, Plattsburgh 12901; **Fax:** (518) 562-1792

(718) 466-3165 **Lai, Lydia C.** (J Civil Ct of NYC Housing Part) Housing Ct., 1118 Grand Concourse, Bronx 10456

(516) 571-2949 **Lally, Ute Wolff** (Justice Sup Ct 10th Jud Dist) Supreme Ct. Bldg., 100 Supreme Ct. Dr., Mineola 11501

(716) 483-7561 **LaMancuso, John L.** (J Jamestown City Ct) City Hall, 200 E. Third St., Jamestown 14701-5433; **Fax:** (716) 483-7519

(518) 270-3803 **Lamb, Thomas E.** (J Watervliet City Ct) City Hall, 2 15th St., Watervliet 12189-2894; **Fax:** (518) 270-3812

(607) 547-7573 **Lambert, John F.** (J Otsego Cty Ct Family Ct & Surro) Cty. Office Bldg., 197 Main St., Cooperstown 13326; **Fax:** (607) 547-7566

(518) 295-8640 **Lamont, Dan** (J Ct of Claims & Acting Justice Sup Ct 3rd Jud Dist & Acting J Albany Cty Ct) Cty. Cthse., 290 Main St., P.O. Box 369, Schoharie 12157; **Fax:** (518) 295-8638
(518) 285-8749 Judl. Ctr., Rm. 210, 6 Lodge St., Albany 12207; **Fax:** (518) 436-3986
(718) 298-0674 **Lane, Howard G.** (Justice Sup Ct 11th Jud Dist) 88-11 Sutphin Blvd., Jamaica 11435; **Fax:** (718) 298-1154
(914) 831-6480 **Langan, Thomas R.** (J Peekskill City Ct) 2 Nelson Ave., Peekskill 10566; **Fax:** (914) 736-1889
(347) 404-9083 **Lansden, John** (Supv Civil Ct of NYC Housing Part Kings Cty Branch) 141 Livingston St., Bklyn. 11201
(347) 404-9447 **LaPorte, Evelyn** (J Civil Ct of NYC assigned to Crim Ct) 120 Schermerhorn St., Bklyn. 11201; **Fax:** (718) 643-3538
(518) 453-4680 **Laquidara, Carmelo** (J Rensselaer City Ct) 62 Washington St., Rensselaer 12144; **Fax:** (518) 462-3307
(646) 386-5115 **Larabee, Susan R.** (J Family Ct of NYC) 60 Lafayette St., N.Y.C. 10013
(718) 298-1387 **Lasak, Gregory L.** (Justice Sup Ct 11th Jud Dist) 125-01 Queens Blvd., Kew Gardens 11415; **Fax:** (718) 520-2494; **E-mail:** glasak@courts.state.ny.us
(631) 853-7703 **LaSalle, Hector D.** (Justice Sup Ct 10th Jud Dist) John P. Cohalan, Jr. Ct. Complex, 400 Carleton Ave., Central Islip 11722; **Fax:** (631) 853-7542
(718) 298-1357 **Latella, John B., Jr.** (J Crim Ct of NYC & Acting Justice Sup Ct 11th Jud Dist) 125-01 Queens Blvd., Kew Gardens 11415; **Fax:** (718) 520-2494; **E-mail:** jlatella@courts.state.ny.us
(607) 776-9631 Ext. 2284 **Latham, Joseph W.** (J Steuben Cty Ct & Family Ct) Cthse., 3 E. Pulteney Sq., Bath 14810; **Fax:** (607) 776-6940
(718) 262-7391 **Latin, Richard G.** (J Civil Ct of NYC) 89-17 Sutphin Blvd., Jamaica 11435
(914) 831-6400 **Latwin, Joseph** (J Rye City Ct) 21 McCullough Pl., Rye 10580; **Fax:** (914) 967-4354
(347) 404-9187 **Lau, Laurie L.** (J Civil Ct of NYC Housing Part) 141 Livingston St., Bklyn. 11201; **E-mail:** llau@courts.state.ny.us
(518) 565-4404 **Lawliss, Timothy J.** (J Clinton Cty Family Ct) Cty. Govt. Ctr., Suite 311, 137 Margaret St., Plattsburgh 12901-2933; **Fax:** (518) 565-4692
(914) 824-5672 **Leak, Barbara A.** (J White Plains City Ct) 77 S. Lexington Ave., White Plains 10601; **Fax:** (914) 422-6058
(718) 618-1557 **Lebedeff, Diane A.** (J Civil Ct of NYC & Acting Justice Sup Ct 12th Jud Dist Civil Term) 851 Grand Concourse, Bronx 10451; **E-mail:** dlebedeff@courts.state.ny.us
(607) 778-2428 **Lebous, Ferris D.** (Justice Sup Ct 6th Jud Dist) Broome Cty. Cthse., 92 Court St., P.O. Box 1766, Binghamton 13902; **Fax:** (607) 778-2065
(646) 386-5626 **Lebovits, Gerald** (J Civil Ct of NYC Housing Part) 111 Centre St., Rm. 1240, N.Y.C. 10013; **Fax:** (212) 374-5709; **E-mail:** glebovit@courts.state.ny.us
(718) 298-1219 **Lebowitz, Jeffrey D.** (Ct of Claims & Acting Justice Sup Ct 11th Jud Dist) 88-11 Sutphin Blvd., Jamaica 11435
(914) 824-5421 **Lefkowitz, Joan B.** (Justice Sup Ct 9th Jud Dist) Richard J. Daronco Cthse., 111 Dr. Martin Luther King, Jr. Blvd., White Plains 10601; **Fax:** (914) 995-4184
(315) 789-6560 **Lehman, Bram** (J Geneva City Ct) Public Safety Bldg., 255 Exchange St., Geneva 14456; **Fax:** (315) 781-2802
(607) 772-7006 **Lehmann, Mary Anne** (J Binghamton City Ct) Governmental Plaza, 38 Hawley St., Binghamton 13901; **Fax:** (607) 772-7041
(718) 466-3135 **Lehrer, Andrew** (J Civil Ct of NYC Housing Part) Housing Ct., 1118 Grand Concourse, Bronx 10456
(631) 853-5368 **Leis, H. Patrick, III** (Admin J Sup Ct 10th Jud Dist Suffolk Cty) John P. Cohalan, Jr. Ct. Complex, Ctrm. S-24, 400 Carleton Ave., P.O. Box 9070, Central Islip 11722-9070; **Fax:** (631) 853-7741
(315) 255-4306 **Leone, Thomas G.** (J Cayuga Cty Ct & Family Ct) Historic Old Post Office Bldg., 2nd Fl., 157 Genesee St., Auburn 13021-3476; **Fax:** (315) 255-4312
(718) 875-1300 **Leventhal, John M.** (Assoc Justice App Div 2nd Dept) 45 Monroe Pl., Bklyn. 11201
(718) 262-7388 **Leverett, Ulysses B.** (J Civil Ct of NYC Housing Part) 89-17 Sutphin Blvd., Jamaica 11435
(347) 404-9066 **Levine, Katherine A.** (J Civil Ct of NYC) 141 Livingston St., Bklyn. 11201
(718) 298-1359 **Lewis, Daniel** (Justice Sup Ct 11th Jud Dist) 125-01 Queens Blvd., Kew Gardens 11415; **Fax:** (212) 419-8424; **E-mail:** dlewis@courts.state.ny.us
(716) 693-1010 **Lewis, William R.** (J North Tonawanda City Ct) City Hall, 216 Payne Ave., North Tonawanda 14120-5446; **Fax:** (716) 743-1754
(347) 296-1473 **Lewis, Yvonne** (Justice Sup Ct 2nd Jud Dist) 360 Adams St., Bklyn. 11201
(718) 618-3645 **Lieb, Judith S.** (J Crim Ct of NYC & Acting Justice Sup Ct 12th Jud Dist Crim Term) Bronx Hall of Justice, 265 E. 161st St., Bronx 10451
(914) 824-5451 **Liebowitz, Richard B.** (Justice Sup Ct 9th Jud Dist) Richard J. Daronco Cthse., 111 Dr. Martin Luther King, Jr. Blvd., White Plains 10601; **Fax:** (914) 995-4182
(347) 401-9870 **Lim, Arnold** (J Family Ct of NYC) 330 Jay St., Bklyn. 11201; **Fax:** (347) 401-9900
(315) 671-2769 **Limpert, Theodore H.** (J Syracuse City Ct) 505 S. State St., Syracuse 13202-2104; **Fax:** (315) 671-2746; **E-mail:** tlimpert@courts.state.ny.us
(585) 530-3227 **Lindley, Stephen K.** (Assoc Justice App Div 4th Dept) 50 East Ave., Rochester 14604; **Fax:** (585) 530-3243; **E-mail:** slindley@courts.state.ny.us
(646) 386-3733 **Ling-Cohan, Doris** (Justice Sup Ct 1st Jud Dist) 60 Centre St., Rm. 629, N.Y.C. 10007
(518) 455-7700 **Lippman, Jonathan** (Chief J Ct of App) Court of Appeals Hall, 20 Eagle St., Albany 12207-1095; **E-mail:** jlippman@courts.state.ny.us
(212) 661-6787 230 Park Ave., Suite 826, N.Y.C. 10169
(646) 386-3247 **Lobis, Joan B.** (Justice Sup Ct 1st Jud Dist) 60 Centre St., N.Y.C. 10007
(914) 824-5413 **Loehr, Gerald E.** (J Westchester Cty Ct & Acting Justice Sup Ct 9th Jud Dist) 111 Dr. Martin Luther King, Jr. Blvd., White Plains 10601; **Fax:** (914) 995-8651
(718) 298-0934 **Lopez, Gene R.** (J Crim Ct of NYC) 125-01 Queens Blvd., Kew Gardens 11415; **Fax:** (718) 520-4712

(718) 262-7333 **Lopresto, Charles S.** (Supv J Civil Ct of NYC Queens Cty Branch assigned to Crim Ct & Acting Justice Sup Ct 11th Jud Dist) 89-17 Sutphin Blvd., Jamaica 11435

(914) 824-5403 **Lorenzo, Albert** (J Ct of Claims & Acting Justice Sup Ct 9th Jud Dist) Richard J. Daronco Cthse., 111 Dr. Martin Luther King, Jr. Blvd., White Plains 10601

(518) 842-9510 **Lorman, Lisa W.** (J Amsterdam City Ct) Public Safety Bldg., Rm. 208, One Guy Park Ave. Ext., Amsterdam 12010; **Fax:** (518) 843-8474

(347) 296-1028 **Lott, Plummer E.** (Assoc Justice App Div 2nd Dept) 320 Jay St., Rm. 2555, Bklyn. 11201

(631) 853-4920 **Lotto, Steven A.** (J Suffolk Cty Dist Ct) John P. Cohalan, Jr. Ct. Complex, 400 Carleton Ave., P.O. Box 9075, Central Islip 11722-9075

(716) 845-2628 **LoVallo, Sharon M.** (J Buffalo City Ct) 50 Delaware Ave., Suite 550, Buffalo 14202; **Fax:** (716) 845-7577; **E-mail:** slovallo@courts.state.ny.us

(716) 845-7453 (Acting J Erie Cty Family Ct) One Niagara Plaza, Rm. 702, Buffalo 14202; **Fax:** (716) 858-7899

(646) 386-3259 **Lowe, Richard B., III** (Justice Sup Ct 1st Jud Dist) 100 Centre St., N.Y.C. 10013

(518) 382-5077 **Loyola, Guido A.** (J Schenectady City Ct) Civil Court, City Hall, Rm. 215, Jay St., Schenectady 12305; **Fax:** (518) 382-5080

(631) 853-4919 **Lozito, Gaetan** (J Suffolk Cty Dist Ct & Acting J Suffolk Cty Ct) John P. Cohalan, Jr. Ct. Complex, 400 Carleton Ave., P.O. Box 9075, Central Islip 11722-9075

(845) 291-3126 **Lubell, Lewis J.** (Justice Sup Ct 9th Jud Dist) 255 Main St., Goshen 10924

(718) 298-0204 **Lubow, Fran L.** (J Family Ct of NYC) 151-20 Jamaica Ave., Jamaica 11432; **Fax:** (718) 297-2530

(315) 593-8400 **Ludington, Spencer J.** (J Fulton City Ct) Munic. Bldg., 141 S. 1st St., Fulton 13069; **Fax:** (315) 592-3415; **E-mail:** fulton_city@courts.state.ny.us

(631) 853-4537 **Luft, Martha L.** (J Suffolk Cty Family Ct & Acting Justice Sup Ct 10th Jud Dist) John P. Cohalan, Jr. Ct. Complex, 400 Carleton Ave., Central Islip 11722; **Fax:** (631) 853-5427

(718) 618-2200 **Lupuloff, Karen** (J Crim Ct of NYC assigned to Family Ct) 900 Sheridan Ave., Bronx 10451

(631) 852-3845 **Lynaugh, Barbara** (J Suffolk Cty Family Ct) Cthse., Suite 308, 889 E. Main St., Riverhead 11901; **Fax:** (631) 852-2986; **E-mail:** blynaugh@courts.state.ny.us

(518) 447-2510 **Lynch, Michael C.** (Justice Sup Ct 3rd Jud Dist) 112 State St., Suite 1212, Albany 12207

(631) 853-7750 **MacKenzie, Carol** (Justice Sup Ct 10th Jud Dist) John P. Cohalan, Jr. Ct. Complex, Ctrm. D63, 400 Carleton Ave., P.O. Box 9075, Central Islip 11722-9075; **Fax:** (631) 853-6431

(646) 386-3190 **Madden, Joan A.** (Justice Sup Ct 1st Jud Dist) 60 Centre St., Rm. 611, N.Y.C. 10007

(718) 466-3117 **Madhavan, Jaya K.** (Supv J Civil Ct of NYC Housing Part Bronx Cty Branch) Housing Ct., 1118 Grand Concourse, Bronx 10456

(518) 233-2133 Ext. 7 **Maguire, Richard R.** (J Cohoes City Ct) City Hall, 1st Fl., Rm. 7, 97 Mohawk St., P.O. Box 678, Cohoes 12047-0678; **Fax:** (518) 233-8202

(914) 831-6480 **Maher, William L.** (J Peekskill City Ct) 2 Nelson Ave., Peekskill 10566; **Fax:** (914) 736-1889

(516) 571-3337 **Mahon, Roy S.** (Justice Sup Ct 10th Jud Dist) Supreme Ct. Bldg., 100 Supreme Ct. Dr., Mineola 11501

(518) 271-1602 **Maier, Christopher** (J Troy City Ct) 51 State St., Troy 12180; **Fax:** (518) 271-2360

(518) 481-1732 **Main, Robert G., Jr.** (J Franklin Cty Ct Family Ct & Surro) Cthse., Suite 3223, 355 W. Main St., Malone 12953-1826; **Fax:** (518) 481-5456; **E-mail:** rgmain@courts.state.ny.us

(718) 618-2542 **Malave-Gonzalez, Nelida** (J Civil Ct of NYC & Acting Justice Sup Ct 12th Jud Dist Civil Term) 851 Grand Concourse, Bronx 10451

(518) 285-8919 **Malone, Bernard J., Jr.** (Assoc Justice App Div 3rd Dept) Cthse., Rm. 269, 16 Eagle St., Albany 12207; **Fax:** (518) 487-5137

(914) 831-6548 **Malone, Janet** (J Westchester Cty Family Ct) 53 S. Broadway, Yonkers 10701; **Fax:** (914) 231-2809

(718) 675-7860 **Maltese, Joseph J.** (J Ct of Claims & Acting Justice Sup Ct 13th Jud Dist) 130 Stuyvesant Pl., Staten Island 10304

(518) 285-8661 **Maney, Gerard E.** (J Albany Cty Family Ct & Supv J of Family Cts 3rd Jud Dist) 30 Clinton Ave., Albany 12207; **Fax:** (518) 462-4157; **E-mail:** gmaney@courts.state.ny.us

(347) 296-1046 **Mangano, Guy J., Jr.** (J Ct of Claims & Acting Justice Sup Ct 2nd Jud Dist) 320 Jay St., Bklyn. 11201

(716) 845-2638 **Manz, David M.** (J Buffalo City Ct) 50 Delaware Ave., Suite 550, Buffalo 14202; **Fax:** (716) 845-7577; **E-mail:** dmanz@courts.state.ny.us

(718) 618-1425 **Manzanet-Daniels, Sallie** (Assoc Justice App Div 1st Dept) 851 Grand Concourse, Bronx 10451; **Fax:** (718) 618-3552

(516) 571-2684 **Marano, Anthony F.** (Admin J Sup Ct 10th Jud Dist Nassau Cty) 100 Supreme Court Dr., Mineola 11501; **Fax:** (516) 571-3713; **E-mail:** amarano@courts.state.ny.us

(516) 571-3310 **Marber, Randy Sue** (Justice Sup Ct 10th Jud Dist) Supreme Ct. Bldg., 100 Supreme Court Dr., Mineola 11501; **Fax:** (516) 571-1316; **E-mail:** rmarber@courts.state.ny.us

(718) 618-3678 **Marcus, Martin** (J Ct of Claims & Acting Justice Sup Ct 12th Jud Dist Crim Term) Bronx Hall of Justice, 265 E. 161st St., Bronx 10451; **Fax:** (718) 618-3571

(718) 298-0936 **Margulis, Ira H.** (J Civil Ct of NYC assigned to Crim Ct) 125-01 Queens Blvd., Kew Gardens 11415; **Fax:** (718) 520-4712

(212) 361-8130 **Marin, Alan C.** (J Ct of Claims) 26 Broadway, 10th Floor, N.Y.C. 10004; **Fax:** (212) 361-8133

(718) 298-1615 **Markey, Charles J.** (Justice Sup Ct 11th Jud Dist) 25-10 Court Sq., Long Island City 11101; **Fax:** (718) 520-7379; **E-mail:** cmarkey@courts.state.ny.us

(212) 428-2884 **Marks, Lawrence K.** (Ct of Claims & Acting Justice Sup Ct 1st Jud Dist) 25 Beaver St., N.Y.C. 10004

(585) 428-5276 **Marks, Patricia D.** (Supv J Monroe Cty Ct & Supv J Crim Cts 7th Jud Dist) 545 Hall of Justice, 99 Exchange Blvd., Rochester 14614-2184; **Fax:** (585) 784-4226

(845) 486-2200 **Marlow, George D.** (Statewide Judicial Dir of Ethics Education & Counsel) Cthse., 10 Market St., Poughkeepsie 12601; **Fax:** (845) 473-5403

(516) 571-5908 **Maron, Edward A.** (Justice Sup Ct 10th Jud Dist) Matrimonial Center, 400 County Seat Dr., Mineola 11501; **Fax:** (516) 571-5970; **E-mail:** emaron@courts.state.ny.us

(716) 827-6672 **Marrano, Frederic J.** (Chief J Lackawanna City Ct) City Hall, 714 Ridge Rd., Lackawanna 14218-1588; **Fax:** (716) 825-1874

(718) 675-8429 **Marrazzo, Orlando, Jr.** (J Civil Ct of NYC) 927 Castleton Ave., West New Brighton, Staten Island 10310; **Fax:** (718) 390-8108

(347) 296-1830 **Marrus, Alan D.** (J Crim Ct of NYC & Acting Justice Sup Ct 2nd Jud Dist) 320 Jay St., Bklyn. 11201

(716) 845-9468 **Marshall, Frederick J.** (Justice Sup Ct 8th Jud Dist) Buffalo City Ct. Bldg., 9th Fl., 50 Delaware Ave., Buffalo 14202; **Fax:** (716) 851-3315; **E-mail:** fmarshall@courts.state.ny.us

(631) 853-4523 **Martin, Daniel** (J Ct of Claims & Admin J Sup Ct 10th Jud Dist) John P. Cohalan Jr. Cthse., 400 Carleton Ave., Central Islip 11722

(347) 296-1461 **Martin, Larry D.** (Justice Sup Ct 2nd Jud Dist) 360 Adams St., Bklyn. 11201

(718) 618-1586 **Martin, LaTia W.** (Justice Sup Ct 12th Jud Dist Civil Term) 851 Grand Concourse, Bronx 10451

(914) 831-6980 **Martinelli, Michael A.** (Chief J Yonkers City Ct) Robert W. Cacace Justice Center, 100 S. Broadway, Yonkers 10701

(718) 618-2200 **Martinez-Perez, Myrna M.** (J Family Ct of NYC) 900 Sheridan Ave., Bronx 10451

(212) 360-4123 **Martino, Ruben** (J Civil Ct of NYC) Harlem Justice Center, 170 E. 121st St., N.Y.C. 10035; **Fax:** (212) 374-5709

(716) 845-2111 **Martoche, Salvatore R.** (Assoc Justice App Div 4th Dept) 50 Delaware Ave., 10th Fl., Buffalo 14202; **Fax:** (716) 852-6367

(347) 404-9088 **Marton, Gary** (J Civil Ct of NYC Housing Part) 141 Livingston Ave., Bklyn. 11201

(315) 785-3010 **Martusewicz, Kim H.** (J Jefferson Cty Ct) Jefferson Cty. Ct. Complex, 2nd Fl., 163 Arsenal St., Watertown 13601; **Fax:** (315) 786-6931; **E-mail:** kmartuse@courts.state.ny.us

(718) 618-3784 **Marvin, Seth L.** (J Crim Ct of NYC & Acting Justice Sup Ct 12th Jud Dist Crim Term) Bronx Hall of Justice, Rm. 9-24, 265 E. 161st St., Bronx 10451; **Fax:** (718) 618-3584; **E-mail:** smarvin@courts.state.ny.us

(718) 618-2209 **Masley, Andrea** (J Civil Ct of NYC assigned to Family Ct) 900 Sheridan Ave., Bronx 10451

(718) 618-3664 **Massaro, Dominic R.** (Justice Sup Ct 12th Jud Dist Crim Term) Bronx Hall of Justice, 265 E. 161st St., Bronx 10451; **Fax:** (212) 457-2881

(516) 572-2161 **Massell, Martin J.** (J Nassau Cty Dist Ct) 99 Main St., Hempstead 11550

(718) 675-8680 **Mastro, William F.** (Assoc Justice App Div 2nd Dept) 60 Bay St., 5th Fl., Staten Island 10301; **Fax:** (718) 816-4587; **E-mail:** wmastro@courts.state.ny.us

(718) 722-6483 45 Monroe Pl., Bklyn. 11201

(716) 845-7493 **Maxwell, Patricia A.** (J Erie Cty Family Ct) One Niagara Plaza, Rm. 606, Buffalo 14202; **Fax:** (716) 858-7757

(631) 852-1760 **Mayer, Peter H.** (Justice Sup Ct 10th Jud Dist) Supreme Ct. Bldg., Rm. A-259, 1 Court St., Riverhead 11901; **Fax:** (631) 852-2102

(718) 298-1626 **Mayersohn, Lee** (Justice Sup Ct 11th Jud Dist) 88-11 Sutphin Blvd., Jamaica 11435; **Fax:** (718) 298-1149

(212) 340-0400 **Mazzarelli, Angela M.** (Assoc Justice App Div 1st Dept) 27 Madison Ave., N.Y.C. 10010

(516) 571-2355 **McAndrews, David W.** (J Nassau Cty Dist Ct) 99 Main St., Hempstead 11550

(516) 676-0109 **McCann, Joseph D.** (J Glen Cove City Ct) 13 Glen St., Glen Cove 11542-2776; **Fax:** (516) 676-1570

(518) 242-3730 **McCarthy, Christopher J.** (J Ct of Claims) Capitol Station, P.O. Box 7344, Albany 12224

(315) 349-3286 **McCarthy, James W.** (Justice Sup Ct 5th Jud Dist) Cthse., 25 E. Oneida St., Oswego 13126; **E-mail:** jmccarthy@courts.state.ny.us

(518) 285-8986 **McCarthy, William E.** (Assoc Justice App Div 3rd Dept) Cthse., Rm. 118, 16 Eagle St., Albany 12207; **Fax:** (518) 487-5155

(516) 571-2154 **McCarty, Edward W., III** (Justice Sup Ct 10th Jud Dist) Supreme Ct. Bldg., 100 Supreme Ct. Dr., Mineola 11501; **Fax:** (516) 571-2966

(718) 466-3121 **McClanahan, Kevin C.** (J Civil Ct of NYC Housing Part) Housing Ct., 1118 Grand Concourse, Bronx 10456; **E-mail:** kmcclanahan@courts.state.ny.us

(516) 676-0109 **McCord, Richard J.** (J Glen Cove City Ct) 13 Glen St., Glen Cove 11542-2776; **Fax:** (516) 676-1570

(516) 571-2768 **McCormack, James P.** (J Nassau Cty Ct & Acting Justice Sup Ct 10th Jud Dist) West Wing, 252 Old Country Rd., Mineola 11501; **Fax:** (516) 571-1093; **E-mail:** jmccorma@courts.state.ny.us

(315) 366-2360 **McDermott, Dennis K.** (J Madison Cty Ct Family Ct & Surro) Cthse., Bldg. 3, 138 N. Court St., P.O. Box 545, Wampsville 13163-0545; **Fax:** (315) 366-2539

(718) 298-1661 **McDonald, Robert J.** (Justice Sup Ct 11th Jud Dist) 25-10 Court Sq., Long Island City 11101; **Fax:** (718) 520-8577; **E-mail:** rjmcdona@courts.state.ny.us

(518) 285-8776 **McDonough, Roger D.** (J Ct of Claims & Acting Justice Sup Ct 3rd Jud Dist) Albany County Judl. Ctr., Rm. 309, 6 Lodge St., Albany 12207; **Fax:** (518) 436-3986

(718) 675-8800 **McElrath, Terrence J.** (J Family Ct of NYC) 100 Richmond Terr., Staten Island 10301; **Fax:** (718) 390-8110

(718) 298-1385 **McGann, Robert C.** (J Crim Ct of NYC & Acting Justice Sup Ct 11th Jud Dist) 125-01 Queens Blvd., Kew Gardens 11415; **Fax:** (718) 520-2539; **E-mail:** rmcgann@courts.state.ny.us

(518) 565-4657 **McGill, Patrick R.** (J Clinton Cty Ct & Acting Justice Sup Ct 4th Jud Dist) Cty. Govt. Ctr., Suite 317, 137 Margaret St., Plattsburgh 12901-2933; **Fax:** (518) 565-4887

(845) 340-3601 **McGinty, Anthony** (J Ulster Cty Family Ct) 16 Lucas Ave., Kingston 12401-0906; **Fax:** (845) 340-3626; **E-mail:** amcginty@courts.state.ny.us

(718) 298-0213 **McGowan, Margaret P.** (J Family Ct of NYC) 151-20 Jamaica Ave., Jamaica 11432; **Fax:** (718) 297-2530

(646) 386-4663 **McGrath, Kevin** (J Crim Ct of NYC) 100 Centre St., N.Y.C. 10013

(518) 285-6140 **McGrath, Patrick J.** (Justice Sup Ct 3rd Jud Dist) Cty. Cthse., 80 Second St., Troy 12180

(212) 340-0400 **McGuire, James M.** (Assoc Justice App Div 1st Dept) 27 Madison Ave., N.Y.C. 10010

(315) 376-5347 **McGuire, Joseph D.** (Justice Sup Ct 5th Jud Dist) Cthse., 7660 State St., Lowville 13367-1396; **Fax:** (315) 376-5398

(347) 404-9461 **McGuire, William** (J Crim Ct of NYC) 120 Schermerhorn St., Bklyn. 11201; **Fax:** (718) 643-7733

(845) 291-3140 **McGuirk, John K.** (Justice Sup Ct 9th Jud Dist) 255 Main St., Goshen 10924; **E-mail:** jmcguirk@courts.state.ny.us

(347) 296-1824 **McKay, Joseph K.** (J Crim Ct of NYC & Acting Justice Sup Ct 2nd Jud Dist) 320 Jay St., Bklyn. 11201

(518) 746-2515 **McKeighan, Kelly S.** (J Washington Cty Ct Family Ct & Surro) Cthse., Bldg. C, 383 Broadway, Fort Edward 12828; **Fax:** (518) 746-2531

(718) 618-1427 **McKeon, Douglas E.** (Justice Sup Ct 12th Jud Dist Civil Term & Pres Justice Sup Ct App Term 1st Jud Dept) 851 Grand Concourse, Bronx 10451; **Fax:** (718) 618-3557

(646) 386-3241 60 Centre St., N.Y.C. 10007

(315) 253-1570 **McKeon, Michael F.** (J Auburn City Ct) 157 Genesee St., Auburn 13021-3434; **Fax:** (315) 253-1085

(315) 671-2766 **McKinney, Langston C.** (J Syracuse City Ct) 505 S. State St., Syracuse 13202-2104; **Fax:** (315) 671-2747; **E-mail:** lmckinne@courts.state.ny.us

(646) 386-3972 **McLaughlin, Edward J.** (J Crim Ct of NYC & Acting Justice Sup Ct 1st Jud Dist) 100 Centre St., N.Y.C. 10013; **E-mail:** emclaugh@courts.state.ny.us

(716) 845-2632 **McLeod, James A.W.** (J Buffalo City Ct) 50 Delaware Ave., Suite 500, Buffalo 14202; **Fax:** (716) 845-7576; **E-mail:** jmcleod@courts.state.ny.us

(718) 675-8630 **McMahon, Judith N.** (Justice Sup Ct 13th Jud Dist) Cty. Cthse., 18 Richmond Terr., Staten Island 10301

(518) 583-5330 **McNamara, Thomas J.** (J Ct of Claims & Acting Justice Sup Ct 3rd Jud Dist) 65 S. Broadway, Rm. 210, Saratoga Springs 12866; **Fax:** (518) 583-5335

(631) 853-4332 **McNulty, Marion T.** (Justice Sup Ct 10th Jud Dist) John P. Cohalan, Jr. Ct. Complex, Ctrm. S-21, 400 Carleton Ave., P.O. Box 9070, Central Islip 11722-9070; **Fax:** (631) 853-7412; **E-mail:** mmcnulty@courts.state.ny.us

(607) 432-4480 **McVinney, Richard W.** (J Oneonta City Ct) Public Safety Bldg., 81 Main St., Oneonta 13820; **Fax:** (607) 432-2328

(845) 807-0654 **Meddaugh, Mark M.** (J Family Ct Sullivan Cty & Acting Justice Sup Ct 3rd Jud Dist) Govt. Center, 100 North St., Monticello 12701; **Fax:** (845) 794-8300

(607) 428-5420 **Meldrim, Thomas A.** (J Cortland City Ct) 25 Court St., Cortland 13045; **Fax:** (607) 428-5435; **E-mail:** tmeldrim@courts.state.ny.us

(718) 298-2932 **Melendez, Suzanne** (J Crim Ct of NYC) 125-01 Queens Blvd., Kew Gardens 11415; **Fax:** (718) 520-4712

(518) 285-6132 **Melkonian, Michael H.** (Ct of Claims & Acting Justice Sup Ct 3rd Jud Dist) Cty. Cthse., 80 Second St., Troy 12180; **Fax:** (518) 274-1367

(646) 386-4684 **Mella, Rita** (J Civil Ct of NYC assigned to Crim Ct) 100 Centre St., N.Y.C. 10013

(646) 386-5705 **Mendez, Manuel J.** (J Civil Ct of NYC & Acting Justice Sup Ct 1st Jud Dist) 111 Centre St., Rm. 1240, N.Y.C. 10013; **Fax:** (212) 374-5709; **E-mail:** mmendez@courts.state.ny.us

(845) 838-5030 **Mensch, Rebecca S.** (J Beacon City Ct) 1 Municipal Plaza, Suite 2, Beacon 12508; **Fax:** (845) 838-5041

(646) 386-3934 **Merchan, Juan M.** (Ct of Claims & Acting Justice Sup Ct 1st Jud Dist) 100 Centre St., N.Y.C. 10013

(518) 746-2540 **Mercure, Thomas E.** (Assoc Justice App Div 3rd Dept) 383 Broadway, Fort Edward 12828-0346; **Fax:** (518) 746-2551

(716) 278-9821 **Merino, Robert P.** (J Niagara Falls City Ct) Niagara Falls Munic. Complex, 1925 Main St., Niagara Falls 14305; **Fax:** (716) 278-9809; **E-mail:** rmerino@courts.state.ny.us

(315) 376-5366 **Merrell, Charles C.** (J Lewis Cty Ct Family Ct & Surro) Cthse., 7660 N. State St., Lowville 13367-1396; **Fax:** (315) 376-4145; **E-mail:** cmerrell@courts.state.ny.us

(315) 671-2767 **Merrill, Jeffrey R.** (Supv J Syracuse City Ct) 505 S. State St., Syracuse 13202-2104; **Fax:** (315) 671-2740; **E-mail:** jmerrill@courts.state.ny.us

(315) 343-0415 **Metcalf, James M.** (J Oswego City Ct) Conway Munic. Center, 20 W. Oneida St., Oswego 13126; **Fax:** (315) 343-0531

(718) 675-8550 **Meyer, Alan J.** (Supv J Crim Ct of NYC & Acting Justice Sup Ct 13th Jud Dist) 67 Targee St., Staten Island 10304

(518) 873-3326 **Meyer, Richard B.** (J Essex Cty Ct Family Ct & Surro) Cthse., 7559 Court St., P.O. Box 217, Elizabethtown 12932; **Fax:** (518) 873-3732

(716) 845-9474 **Michalek, John A.** (Justice Sup Ct 8th Jud Dist) Erie Cty. Ct. Bldg., 4th Fl., 25 Delaware Ave., Buffalo 14202; **Fax:** (716) 851-3323; **E-mail:** jmichale@courts.state.ny.us

(716) 845-9462 **Michalski, John L.** (J Ct of Claims & Acting Justice Sup Ct 8th Jud Dist) Erie Cty. Ct. Bldg., 3rd Fl., 25 Delaware Ave., Buffalo 14202; **Fax:** (716) 851-3314; **E-mail:** jmichals@courts.state.ny.us

(347) 404-9477 **Michels, Shari R.** (J Civil Ct of NYC assigned to Crim Ct) 120 Schermerhorn St., Bklyn. 11201

(315) 466-7151 **Midey, Nicholas V., Jr.** (J Ct of Claims) Salina Place, 2nd Fl., 205 S. Salina St., Syracuse 13202; **Fax:** (315) 466-7154

(914) 289-2320 **Mignano, Stephen J.** (J Ct of Claims) 140 Grand St., Suite 910, White Plains 10601; **Fax:** (914) 289-2323

(518) 242-3720 **Milano, Frank P.** (J Ct of Claims) Capitol Station, P.O. Box 7344, Albany 12224

(718) 618-2544 **Miles, Donald A.** (J Civil Ct of NYC) 851 Grand Concourse, Bronx 10451

(347) 404-9091 **Milin, Maria** (J Civil Ct of NYC Housing Part) 141 Livingston St., Bklyn. 11201; **E-mail:** mmilin@courts.state.ny.us

(347) 296-1836 **Miller, Robert J.** (Justice Sup Ct 2nd Jud Dist) 360 Adams St., Bklyn. 11201; **Fax:** (718) 643-5406; **E-mail:** rjmiller@courts.state.ny.us

(585) 428-2470 **Miller, Stephen T.** (J Rochester City Ct & Acting J Monroe Cty Ct) 6 Hall of Justice, 99 Exchange Blvd., Rochester 14614; **Fax:** (585) 428-2730; **E-mail:** stmiller@courts.state.ny.us

(347) 404-9600 **Miller, William** (Supv J Crim Ct of NYC & Acting Justice Sup Ct 2nd Jud Dist) 120 Schermerhorn St., Bklyn. 11201; **Fax:** (718) 643-3538

(646) 386-3348 **Mills, Donna M.** (Justice Sup Ct 1st Jud Dist) 111 Centre St., Rm. 545, N.Y.C. 10013; **Fax:** (212) 374-5709

(718) 675-8600 **Minardo, Philip G.** (Admin J Sup Ct 13th Jud Dist) Cty. Cthse., 18 Richmond Terr., Staten Island 10301; **Fax:** (718) 815-2775

(585) 987-4212 **Minarik, Renée Forgensi** (J Ct of Claims) 500 Court Exchange Bldg., 144 Exchange Blvd., Rochester 14614; **Fax:** (585) 262-3019

(315) 593-8400 **Mirabito, Jerome A.** (J Fulton City Ct) Munic. Bldg., 141 S. 1st St., Fulton 13069; **Fax:** (315) 592-3415; **E-mail:** jmirabit@courts.state.ny.us

(716) 693-1010 **Mis, Jeffrey N.** (J North Tonawanda City Ct) City Hall, 216 Payne Ave., North Tonawanda 14120-5446; **Fax:** (716) 743-1754

(315) 266-4740 **Misiaszek, Michael J.** (J Oneida City Ct) 108 Main St., Oneida 13421; **Fax:** (315) 363-3230

(845) 340-3614 **Mizel, Marianne O.** (J Ulster Cty Family Ct) 16 Lucas Ave., Kingston 12401-0906; **Fax:** (845) 340-3626; **E-mail:** mmizel@courts.state.ny.us

(718) 286-0839 **Modica, Deborah Stevens** (Supv J Crim Ct of NYC & Acting Justice Sup Ct 11th Jud Dist) 125-01 Queens Blvd., Kew Gardens 11415; **Fax:** (718) 520-3992

(718) 298-1055 **Modica, Salvatore J.** (J Crim Ct of NYC & Acting Justice Sup Ct 11th Jud Dist) 125-10 Queens Blvd., Kew Gardens 11415; **E-mail:** smodica@courts.state.ny.us

(718) 618-3685 **Mogulescu, William I.** (J Crim Ct of NYC & Acting Justice Sup Ct 12th Jud Dist Crim Term) Bronx Hall of Justice, 265 E. 161st St., Bronx 10451; **Fax:** (718) 618-3584

(914) 824-5454 **Molea, Richard A.** (J Ct of Claims & Acting Justice Sup Ct & Supv J of the Crim Cts 9th Jud Dist) Richard J. Daronco Cthse., 111 Dr. Martin Luther King, Jr. Blvd., White Plains 10601; **Fax:** (914) 995-8654; **E-mail:** rmolea@courts.state.ny.us

(631) 852-3750 **Molia, Denise F.** (Justice Sup Ct 10th Jud Dist & Assoc Justice Sup Ct App Term 9th and 10th Jud Dists) Supreme Ct. Bldg., Rm. A-201, 1 Court St., Riverhead 11901; **Fax:** (631) 852-2867

(845) 483-8200 **Moloney, Katherine A.** (J Poughkeepsie City Ct) 62 Civic Center Plaza, Poughkeepsie 12601; **Fax:** (845) 485-6795

(347) 404-9470 **Mondo, Suzanne M.** (J Crim Ct of NYC & Acting Justice Sup Ct 2nd Jud Dist) 120 Schermerhorn St., Bklyn. 11201; **Fax:** (718) 643-3538

(718) 618-3686 **Moore, John S.** (J Crim Ct of NYC & Acting Justice Sup Ct 12th Jud Dist Crim Term) Bronx Hall of Justice, 265 E. 161st St., Bronx 10451; **Fax:** (718) 618-3584

(347) 401-9208 **Morgenstern, Esther M. (Micky)** (Justice Sup Ct 2nd Jud Dist) 320 Jay St., Bklyn. 11201

(716) 515-4820 **Moriarty, Jeremiah J., III** (J Ct of Claims) 130 S. Elmwood Ave., Suite 300, Buffalo 14202; **Fax:** (716) 515-4823

(716) 278-9822 **Morinello, Angelo J.** (J Niagara Falls City Ct) Niagara Falls Munic. Complex, 1925 Main St., Niagara Falls 14305; **Fax:** (716) 278-9809; **E-mail:** amorinel@courts.state.ny.us

(585) 428-5248 **Morse, Thomas Rainbow** (J Rochester City Ct) 6 Hall of Justice, 99 Exchange Blvd., Rochester 14614; **Fax:** (585) 428-2731; **E-mail:** tmorse@courts.state.ny.us

(212) 340-0515 **Moskowitz, Karla** (Assoc Justice App Div 1st Dept) 27 Madison Ave., N.Y.C. 10010; **Fax:** (212) 340-0511; **E-mail:** kmoskowi@courts.state.ny.us

(845) 346-4050 **Moson, Robert F.** (J Middletown City Ct) 2 James St., Middletown 10940; **Fax:** (845) 343-5737

(646) 386-5712 **Moulton, Peter** (J Civil Ct of NYC & Acting Justice Sup Ct 1st Jud Dist) 111 Centre St., Rm. 1240, N.Y.C. 10013; **E-mail:** pmoulton@courts.state.ny.us

(716) 376-5621 **Mountain, William H. (Hank), III** (J Olean City Ct) Munic. Bldg., 101 E. State St., P.O. Box 631, Olean 14760-0631; **Fax:** (716) 376-5623; **E-mail:** wmountai@courts.state.ny.us

(646) 386-5710 **Mullen, Cassandra** (Ct of Claims & Acting Justice Sup Ct 1st Jud Dist) 111 Centre St., N.Y.C. 10013

(518) 824-6696 **Muller, Robert J.** (Justice Sup Ct 4th Jud Dist) Warren Cty. Munic. Center, 1340 State Rt. 9, Lake George 12845

(518) 873-3375 Essex County Govt. Center, 7551 Court St., Elizabethtown, NY 12932

(718) 298-0930 **Mullings, Pauline A.** (J Crim Ct of NYC & Acting Justice Sup Ct 11th Jud Dist) 125-01 Queens Blvd., Kew Gardens 11415

(315) 671-2050 **Mulroy, Martha E.** (J Onondaga Cty Family Ct & Acting Justice Sup Ct 5th Jud Dist) 401 Montgomery St., Syracuse 13202; **Fax:** (315) 671-1170; **E-mail:** mmulroy@courts.state.ny.us

(607) 272-0674 **Mulvey, Robert C.** (Admin J Sup Ct 6th Jud Dist) Tompkins Cty. Cthse., 320 N. Tioga St., P.O. Box 70, Ithaca 14851-0070; **Fax:** (607) 272-0691

(607) 240-5350 Admin. Office, The Kilmer Bldg., 31 Lewis St., Binghamton, NY 13901; **Fax:** (607) 722-1629

(718) 675-8440 **Mundy, Marina C.** (Housing Ct J Civil Ct of NYC) 927 Castleton Ave., West New Brighton, Staten Island 10310; **Fax:** (718) 390-8108

(315) 798-5877 **Murad, David A.** (Justice Sup Ct 5th Jud Dist) Oneida Cty. Office Bldg., 8th Fl., 800 Park Ave., Utica 13501; **Fax:** (315) 798-6457

(631) 853-7418 **Murphy, Glenn A.** (J Suffolk Cty Dist Ct & Acting J Suffolk Cty Ct) John P. Cohalan, Jr. Ct. Complex, 400 Carleton Ave., P.O. Box 9075, Central Islip 11722-9075

(914) 824-5733 **Murphy, J. Emmett** (Justice Sup Ct 9th Jud Dist) Richard J. Daronco Cthse., 15th Fl., 111 Dr. Martin Luther King, Jr. Blvd., White Plains 10601; **Fax:** (914) 995-4396

(315) 671-1109 **Murphy, James P.** (Justice Sup Ct 5th Jud Dist) Onondaga Cty. Cthse., Rm. 411, 401 Montgomery St., Syracuse 13202; **Fax:** (315) 671-1186

(516) 571-2325 **Murphy, Karen V.** (Justice Sup Ct 10th Jud Dist) Supreme Ct. Bldg., 100 Supreme Court Dr., Mineola 11501

(347) 401-9061 **Murphy, Martin P.** (J Family Ct of NYC & Acting Justice Sup Ct 2nd Jud Dist) 320 Jay St., Bklyn. 11201

(716) 439-7150 **Murphy, Matthew J., III** (J Niagara Cty Ct & Surro) Cthse., 175 Hawley St., Lockport 14094-2758; **Fax:** (716) 439-7328; **E-mail:** mjmurph2@courts.state.ny.us

(516) 572-2113 **Murphy, Terence P.** (J Nassau Cty Dist Ct) 99 Main St., Hempstead 11550

(718) 298-0400 **Nahman, Robert L.** (Queens Cty Surro) 88-11 Sutphin Blvd., Jamaica 11435

(212) 340-0400 **Nardelli, Eugene L.** (Assoc Justice App Div 1st Dept) 27 Madison Ave., N.Y.C. 10010

(718) 618-3610 **Neary, Robert A.** (J Ct of Claims & Acting Justice Sup Ct 12th Jud Dist Crim Term) Bronx Hall of Justice, 265 E. 161st St., Bronx 10451; **Fax:** (718) 618-3584

(718) 298-1170 **Nelson, Valerie Brathwaite** (Justice Sup Ct 11th Jud Dist) 88-11 Sutphin Blvd., Jamaica 11425; **Fax:** (718) 298-1101

(845) 638-5336 **Nelson, William K.** (J Rockland Cty Ct & Acting Justice Sup Ct 9th Jud Dist) Cthse., Suite 200, 1 S. Main St., New City 10956; **Fax:** (845) 638-5312; **E-mail:** wnelson@courts.state.ny.us

(716) 845-9480 **NeMoyer, Patrick H.** (Justice Sup Ct 8th Jud Dist) Buffalo City Ct. Bldg., 10th Fl., 50 Delaware Ave., Buffalo 14202; **Fax:** (716) 851-3345; ; **E-mail:** pnemoyer@courts.state.ny.us

(716) 938-9111 Ext. 3253 **Nenno, Michael L.** (J Cattaraugus Cty Ct Family Ct & Surro) 1 Leo Moss Dr., Suite 1140, Olean 14760-1152; **Fax:** (716) 373-0449

(646) 386-4333 **Nervo, Frank P.** (J Civil Ct of NYC assigned to Crim Ct) 100 Centre St., N.Y.C. 10013; **E-mail:** fnervo@courts.state.ny.us

(315) 946-5441 **Nesbitt, John B.** (J Wayne Cty Ct Famil;y Ct & Surro) Hall of Justice, 54 Broad St., Lyons 14489-1199; **Fax:** (315) 946-5429

(585) 428-1904 **Nesser, Joseph G.** (J Monroe Cty Family Ct) Hall of Justice, 3rd Fl., 99 Exchange Blvd., Rochester 14614-2187; **Fax:** (585) 784-4228

(718) 618-3657 **Newman, Barbara F.** (718) 618-3657 (J Crim Ct of NYC & Acting Justice Sup Ct 12th Jud Dist Crim Term) Bronx Hall of Justice, 265 E. 161st St., Bronx 10451

(914) 824-5800 **Newton, Juanita Bing** (J Ct of Claims & Acting Justice Sup Ct 1st Jud Dist & Dean NY State Judicial Institute) 84 N. Broadway, White Plains 10603

(518) 828-7909 **Nichols, Jonathan D.** (J Columbia Cty Ct Family Ct & Surro & Acting Justice Sup Ct 3rd Jud Dist) Cthse., 401 Union St., Hudson 12534; **Fax:** (518) 828-1603; **E-mail:** jnichols@courts.state.ny.us

(845) 268-7890 **Nicolai, Francis A.** (Justice Sup Ct 9th Jud Dist) 20 County Center, Carmel 10512

(914) 824-5100 (Pres Justice Sup Ct App Term 9th & 10th Jud Dists) Richard J. Daronco Cthse., 111 Dr. Martin Luther King, Jr. Blvd., White Plains 10601

(518) 451-8820 **Nolan, Thomas D., Jr.** (Justice Sup Ct 4th Jud Dist) Saratoga Cty. Munic. Center, 30 McMaster St., Ballston Spa 12020; **Fax:** (518) 884-4761

(585) 344-2550 Ext. 2236 **Noonan, Robert C.** (J Genesee Cty & Surro) Genesee Cty. Cts. Facility, 1 W. Main St., Batavia 14020; **Fax:** (585) 344-3108

(716) 845-2648 **Nowak, Henry J.** (J Buffalo City Ct) 50 Delaware Ave., Suite 650, Buffalo 14202; **Fax:** (716) 845-7579; **E-mail:** hnowak@courts.state.ny.us

(646) 386-4971 **Nunez, Patricia M.** (J Crim Ct of NYC & Acting Justice Sup Ct 1st Jud Dist) 111 Centre St., N.Y.C. 10013

(516) 572-2101 **O'Brien, William J.** (J Nassau Cty Dist Ct) 99 Main St., Hempstead 11550; **E-mail:** wobrien@courts.state.ny.us

(646) 386-3947 **Obus, Michael J.** (J Crim Ct of NYC & Admin J Sup Ct 1st Jud Dist Crim Div) 100 Centre St., N.Y.C. 10013; **Fax:** (212) 401-9264; **E-mail:** mobus@courts.state.ny.us

(518) 285-8597 **O'Connor, Kimberly A.** (Ct of Claims & Acting Justice Sup Ct 3rd Jud Dist) 112 State St., Rm. 1360, Albany 12207; **Fax:** (518) 487-5823

(718) 262-7368 **O'Connor, Terrence C.** (J Civil Ct of NYC) 89-17 Sutphin Blvd., Jamaica 11435

(716) 845-9486 **O'Donnell, John F.** (Justice Sup Ct 8th Jud Dist) Erie Cty. Ct. Bldg., 25 Delaware Ave., Buffalo 14202; **Fax:** (716) 851-3326; **E-mail:** jodonnel@courts.state.ny.us

(718) 298-0928 **O'Donoghue, Mary R.** (J Civil Ct of NYC assigned to Crim Ct) 125-01 Queens Blvd., Kew Gardens 11415; **Fax:** (718) 520-4712

(718) 298-1124 **O'Donoghue, Peter J.** (Justice Sup Ct 11th Jud Dist) 88-11 Sutphin Blvd., Jamaica 11435; **Fax:** (718) 298-1129; **E-mail:** podonogh@courts.state.ny.us

(347) 404-8092 **Ofshtein, Eleanor** (J Civil Ct of NYC Housing Part) 141 Livingston St., Bklyn. 11201

(716) 845-2647 **Ogden, E. Jeannette** (J Buffalo City Ct) 50 Delaware Ave., Suite 650, Buffalo 14202; **Fax:** (716) 845-7579; **E-mail:** eogden@courts.state.ny.us

(716) 845-1804 (Acting J Erie Cty Family Ct) One Niagara Plaza, Rm. 602, Buffalo 14202; **Fax:** (716) 858-7901

(646) 386-5722 **Oing, Jeffrey K.** (Supv J Civil Ct of NYC) 111 Centre St., Rm. 1240, N.Y.C. 10013; **Fax:** (212) 374-5709; **E-mail:** joing@courts.state.ny.us

(718) 618-3600 **Oliver, Eugene, Jr.** (J Crim Ct of NYC & Acting Justice & Dep Admin J 12th Jud Dist Crim Term) Bronx Hall of Justice, 265 E. 161st St., Bronx 10451; **Fax:** (718) 618-3584; **E-mail:** eoliver@courts.state.ny.us

(347) 401-9870 **Olshansky, Emily** (J Family Ct of NYC) 330 Jay St., Bklyn. 11201; **Fax:** (347) 401-9900

(845) 291-2300 **Onofry, Robert A.** (Orange Cty Surro & Acting Justice Sup Ct 9th Jud Dist) 30 Park Pl., Goshen 10924; **Fax:** (845) 291-2543

(718) 262-7394 **Orlow, Jodi** (J Civil Ct of NYC) 89-17 Sutphin Blvd., Jamaica 11435

(845) 208-7890 **O'Rourke, Andrew P.** (Justice Sup Ct 9th Jud Dist) 20 County Center, Carmel 10512; **Fax:** (845) 228-9617

(347) 401-9894 **O'Shea, Ann E.** (J Civil Ct of NYC assigned to Family Ct & Acting Justice Sup Ct 2nd Jud Dist) 330 Jay St., Bklyn. 11201; **Fax:** (347) 401-9900

(607) 737-3560 **O'Shea, Judith F.** (Justice Sup Ct 6th Jud Dist) Hazlett Bldg., 203-205 Lake St., P.O. Box 588, Elmira 14902; **Fax:** (607) 737-3562

(347) 401-9889 **Otley, Lisa S.** (J Civil Ct of NYC) 141 Livingston St., Bklyn. 11201

(585) 428-4338 **Owens, John M.** (Justice Sup Ct 7th Jud Dist) 545 Hall of Justice, 99 Exchange Blvd., Rochester 14614-2184; **Fax:** (585) 428-4517

(718) 618-3717 **Ozzi, Wayne M.** (J Ct of Claims & Acting Justice Sup Ct 12th Jud Dist Crim Term) Bronx Hall of Justice, 265 E. 161st St., Bronx 10451

(718) 618-2546 **Padilla, Jose A., Jr.** (J Civil Ct of NYC) 851 Grand Concourse, Bronx 10451; **E-mail:** jpadilla@courts.state.ny.us

(646) 386-3980 **Padro, Eduardo** (Justice Sup Ct 1st Jud Dist) 100 Centre St., N.Y.C. 10013

(845) 486-2242 **Pagones, James D.** (Dutchess Cty Surro) Cthse., 10 Market St., Poughkeepsie 12601-3203; **Fax:** (845) 486-2245

(845) 838-5030 **Pagones, Timothy G.** (J Beacon City Ct) 1 Municipal Plaza, Suite 2, Beacon 12508; **Fax:** (845) 838-5041

(516) 571-2878 **Palmieri, Daniel R.** (J Nassau Cty Ct & Acting Justice Sup Ct 10th Jud Dist) 100 Supreme Court Dr., Mineola 11501; **Fax:** (516) 571-0129; **E-mail:** dpalmier@courts.state.ny.us

(716) 376-5621 **Palumbo, Daniel R.** (J Olean City Ct) Munic. Bldg., 101 E. State St., P.O. Box 631, Olean 14760-0631; **Fax:** (716) 376-5623

(716) 483-7561 **Panebianco, George** (J Jamestown City Ct) City Hall, 200 E. Third St., Jamestown 14701-5433; **Fax:** (716) 483-7519

(718) 876-6424 **Panepinto, Barbara I.** (J Civil Ct of NYC & Acting Justice Sup Ct 13th Jud Dist) Homeport, 355 Front St., Staten Island 10304; **Fax:** (718) 876-6426

(516) 572-2135 **Paradiso, Anthony W.** (J Nassau Cty Dist Ct) 99 Main St., Hempstead 11550

(516) 572-2153 **Pardes, Sondra K.** (J Nassau Cty Dist Ct) 99 Main St., Hempstead 11550

(516) 571-2373 **Parga, Anthony L.** (Justice Sup Ct 10th Jud Dist) Supreme Ct. Bldg., 100 Supreme Ct. Dr., Mineola 11501

(315) 671-1104 **Paris, Anthony J.** (Justice Sup Ct 5th Jud Dist) Onondaga Cty. Cthse., 401 Montgomery St., Syracuse 13202; **Fax:** (315) 671-1179

(347) 296-1833 **Parker, Sheryl L.** (J Crim Ct of NYC & Acting Justice Sup Ct 2nd Jud Dist) 320 Jay St., Bklyn. 11201

(347) 296-1542 **Partnow, Mark I.** (Justice Sup Ct 2nd Jud Dist) 360 Adams St., Bklyn. 11201

(631) 852-2163 **Pastoressa, Joseph C.** (J Ct of Claims & Acting Justice Sup Ct 10th Jud Dist) Arthur M. Cromarty Ct. Complex, Ctrm. 14, 210 Center Dr., 3rd Fl., Riverhead 11901; **Fax:** (631) 852-3043

(585) 325-4500 **Patti, Philip J.** (J Ct of Claims) 500 Court Exchange Bldg., 144 Exchange Blvd., Rochester 14614-2108; **Fax:** (585) 262-5715

(646) 386-3336 **Payne, Kibbie F.** (J Civil Ct of NYC & Acting Justice Sup Ct 1st Jud Dist) 111 Centre St., N.Y.C. 10013; **E-mail:** kpayne@courts.state.ny.us

(718) 298-1376 **Paynter, Steven W.** (Justice Sup Ct 11th Jud Dist) 125-01 Queens Blvd., Kew Gardens 11415

(718) 618-2200 **Pearl, Jane** (J Family Ct of NYC & Acting Justice Sup Ct 12th Jud Dist Crim Term) 900 Sheridan Ave., Bronx 10451

(516) 571-3765 **Peck, George R.** (J Nassau Cty Ct & Acting Justice Sup Ct 10th Jud Dist) Cty. Cthse., 262 Old Country Rd., Mineola 11501; **Fax:** (516) 571-3256; **E-mail:** gpeck@courts.state.ny.us

(607) 778-2118 **Peckham, Eugene E.** (Broome Cty Surro) Broome Cty. Cthse., Suite 104, P.O. Box 1766, Binghamton 13902-1766; **Fax:** (607) 778-6155; **E-mail:** epeckham@courts.state.ny.us

(607) 772-7006 **Pelella, William C.** (J Binghamton City Ct) Governmental Plaza, 38 Hawley St., Binghamton 13901; **Fax:** (607) 772-7041

(716) 845-9360 **Peradotto, Erin M.** (Assoc Justice App Div 4th Dept) 50 Delaware Ave., Buffalo 14202-2721; **Fax:** (716) 852-6367; **E-mail:** eperadot@courts.state.ny.us

(347) 296-1007 **Pesce, Michael L.** (Justice Sup Ct 2nd Jud Dist & Pres Justice Sup Ct App Term 2nd 11th & 13th Jud Dists) 360 Adams St., Bklyn. 11201

(845) 340-3757 **Peters, Karen K.** (Assoc Justice App Div 3rd Dept) Cthse., 281 Wall St., Kingston 12401-3817; **Fax:** (845) 340-3760

(212) 428-2100 **Pfau, Ann T.** (Chief Admin J) 25 Beaver St., N.Y.C. 10004; **Fax:** (212) 428-2188; **E-mail:** apfau@courts.state.ny.us

(516) 571-2427 **Phelan, Thomas P.** (Justice Sup Ct 10th Jud Dist) Supreme Ct. Bldg., 100 Supreme Ct. Dr., Mineola 11501

(516) 572-2143 **Phoenix, Andrea** (J Nassau Cty Dist Ct) 99 Main St., Hempstead 11550; **Fax:** (516) 572-2507

(347) 404-9475 **Pickett, Geraldine** (J Civil Ct of NYC assigned to Crim Ct) 120 Schermerhorn St., Bklyn. 11201

(646) 386-4402 **Pickholz, Ruth** (J Crim Ct of NYC & Acting Justice Sup Ct 1st Jud Dist) 111 Centre St., N.Y.C. 10013; **Fax:** (212) 374-2579

(716) 845-9375 **Pietruszka, Michael F.** (J Erie Cty Ct) Erie Cty. Ct. Bldg., 25 Delaware Ave., Buffalo 14202; **Fax:** (716) 851-3332

(716) 845-2101 **Pigott, Eugene F., Jr.** (Assoc J Ct of App) 438 Main St., Suite 900, Buffalo 14202

(718) 262-7351 **Pinckney, Michael J.** (J Civil Ct of NYC Housing Part) 89-17 Sutphin Blvd., Jamaica 11435

(718) 298-0083 **Pineda-Kirwan, Diccia** (Justice Sup Ct 11th Jud Dist) 25-10 Court Sq., Long Island City 11101; **Fax:** (718) 520-2571

(631) 852-3117 **Pines, Emily** (Justice Sup Ct 10th Jud Dist) Supreme Ct. Bldg., 1 Court St., Riverhead 11901; **Fax:** (631) 852-3120

(607) 778-2156 **Pines, Spero** (J Broome Cty Family Ct) 65 Hawley St., Binghamton 13901 Mailing Address: P.O. Box 1766, Binghamton 13902; **Fax:** (607) 778-2439

(631) 852-2174 **Pitts, Arthur G.** (Justice Sup Ct 10th Jud Dist) Arthur M. Cromarty Ct. Complex, Ctrm. 5, 210 Center Dr., Riverhead 11901; **Fax:** (631) 852-2769; **E-mail:** apitts@courts.state.ny.us

(518) 242-3740 **Platkin, Richard** (J Ct of Claims & Acting Justice Sup Ct 3rd Jud Dist) Justice Bldg., 7th Fl., Empire State Plz., Capitol Station, P.O. Box 7344, Albany 12224; **Fax:** (518) 242-3735

(716) 945-4153 **Ploetz, Ronald D.** (J Salamanca City Ct) Munic. Bldg., 225 Wildwood Ave., Salamanca 14779; **Fax:** (716) 945-2362

(585) 428-5271 **Polito, William P.** (Justice Sup Ct 7th Jud Dist) 545 Hall of Justice, 99 Exchange Blvd., Rochester 14614-2184; **Fax:** (585) 428-3554

(315) 266-4607 **Popeo, Gerald J.** (J Utica City Ct) 411 Oriskany St. W., Utica 13502; **Fax:** (315) 733-7927

(845) 486-2521 **Posner, Joan S.** (J Dutchess Cty Family Ct & Acting Justice Sup Ct 9th Jud Dist) 50 Market St., Poughkeepsie 12601-3204

(315) 379-2410 **Potter, Barbara R.** (J St Lawrence Cty Family Ct) Cthse., 48 Court St., Canton 13617-1169; **Fax:** (315) 386-3197

(518) 285-8450 **Powers, Mark L.** (J Schenectady Cty Family Ct) 620 State St., Schenectady 12305-2114; **Fax:** (518) 393-1565; **E-mail:** mpowers@court.state.ny.us

(516) 572-2131 **Prager, Erica L.** (J Nassau Cty Dist Ct) 99 Main St., Hempstead 11550; **E-mail:** cprager@courts.state.ny.us

(914) 824-5674 **Press, Eric** (J White Plains City Ct) 77 S. Lexington Ave., White Plains 10601; **Fax:** (914) 422-6058

(718) 618-3646 **Price, Richard Lee** (Justice Sup Ct 12th Jud Dist Crim Term)) Bronx Hall of Justice, 265 E. 161st St., Bronx 10451; **Fax:** (718) 618-3565; **E-mail:** rprice@courts.state.ny.us

(518) 746-2506 **Pritzker, Stan L.** (J Washington Cty Ct Family Ct & Surro) Cthse., 383 Broadway, Fort Edward 12828; **Fax:** (518) 746-2505

(718) 722-6400 **Prudenti, A. Gail** (Pres Justice App Div 2nd Dept) 45 Monroe Pl., Bklyn. 11201; **Fax:** (718) 855-2884

(347) 296-1486 **Prus, Eric I.** (Justice Sup Ct 2nd Jud Dist) 360 Adams St., Bklyn. 11201

(518) 444-8750 **Pulver, George J., Jr.** (J Greene Cty Ct Family Ct & Surro & Acting Justice Sup Ct 3rd Jud Dist) 320 Main St., Catskill 12414; **Fax:** (518) 943-3014

(585) 589-4457 **Punch, James P.** (J Orleans Cty Ct Family Ct & Surro) Cthse., Suite 3, 1 S. Main St., Albion 14411-1497; **Fax:** (585) 589-0632
(718) 262-7373 **Purificacion, Leslie J.** (J Civil Ct of NYC) 89-17 Sutphin Blvd., Jamaica 11435
(516) 572-2166 **Quinn, Christopher G.** (J Nassau Cty Ct & Supv J Nassau Cty Dist Ct & Acting Justice Sup Ct 10th Jud Dist) 99 Main St., Hempstead 11550; **Fax:** (516) 572-2457; **E-mail:** cgquinn@courts.state.ny.us
(631) 853-3244 **Quinn, James F.** (J Suffolk Cty Ct & Acting J Suffolk Cty Family Ct) 400 Carleton Ave., Rm. F-32, Central Islip 11722; **Fax:** (631) 853-7727
(718) 298-0981 **Raciti, Robert M.** (J Crim Ct of NYC & Acting Justice Sup Ct 11th Jud Dist) 125-01 Queens Blvd., Kew Gardens 11415; **Fax:** (718) 520-4712
(718) 298-1670 **Raffaele, Thomas D.** (Justice Sup Ct 11th Jud Dist) 88-11 Sutphin Blvd., Jamaica 11435; **Fax:** (718) 298-1090
(646) 386-5749 **Rakower, Eileen A.** (J Civil Ct of NYC & Acting Justice Sup Ct 1st Jud Dist) 80 Centre St., Rm. 308, N.Y.C. 10013; **E-mail:** erakower@courts.state.ny.us
(607) 737-5681 **Ramich, Thomas E.** (J Elmira City Ct) City Hall, 317 E. Church St., Elmira 14901-2790; **Fax:** (212) 401-9240; **E-mail:** tramich@courts.state.ny.us
(646) 386-3229 **Ramos, Charles E.** (Justice Sup Ct 1st Jud Dist) 60 Centre St., Rm. 691, N.Y.C. 10007
(845) 483-8100 **Ramsey, B. Harold** (J Newburgh City Ct) 300 Broadway, Newburgh 12550
(315) 671-2098 **Raphael, Ava Shapero** (Onondaga Cty Surro) Cthse., 401 Montgomery St., Syracuse 13202-2173; **Fax:** (315) 671-1162
(718) 466-3141 **Rashford, Eardell** (J Civil Ct of NYC Housing Part) 851 Grand Concourse, Bronx 10451
(518) 455-7721 **Read, Susan Phillips** (Assoc J Ct of App) Court of Appeals Hall, 20 Eagle St., Albany 12207-1095
(631) 852-3166 **Rebolini, William B.** (Justice Sup Ct 10th Jud Dist) Supreme Ct. Bldg., Rm. A-260, 1 Court St., Riverhead 11901; **Fax:** (631) 852-3188
(585) 396-4053 **Reed, Frederick G.** (J Ontario Cty Ct & Surro) Cthse., Rm. 130, 27 N. Main St., Canandaigua 14424-1447; **Fax:** (585) 396-4086; **E-mail:** freed@courts.state.ny.us
(718) 618-2530 **Reed, Robert R.** (J Civil Ct of NYC) 851 Grand Concourse, Bronx 10451
(347) 296-1845 **Reichbach, Gustin L.** (Justice Sup Ct 2nd Jud Dist) 320 Jay St., Bklyn. 11201
(516) 572-2107 **Reilly, Margaret C.** (J Nassau Cty Dist Ct) 99 Main St., Hempstead 11550
(518) 285-8422 **Reilly, Vincent J., Jr.** (Justice Sup Ct 4th Jud Dist) Schenectady Cty. Cthse., 612 State St., Schenectady 12305; **Fax:** (518) 377-5897
(518) 270-3803 **Reinfurt, Susan B.** (J Watervliet City Ct) City Hall, 2 15th St., Watervliet 12189-2894; **Fax:** (518) 270-3812
(845) 208-7875 **Reitz, James F.** J Putnam Cty Ct Family Ct & Surro & Acting Justice Sup Ct 9th Jud Dist) Cthse., 20 County Ctr., Carmel 10512
(212) 340-0400 **Renwick, Dianne T.** (Assoc Justice App Div 1st Dept) 27 Madison Ave., N.Y.C. 10010; **Fax:** (212) 779-0305; **E-mail:** drenwick@courts.state.ny.us
(585) 428-4369 **Renzi, Alexander R.** (Justice Sup Ct 7th Jud Dist) 545 Hall of Justice, 99 Exchange Blvd., Rochester 14614; **Fax:** (585) 428-4371; **E-mail:** arenzi@courts.state.ny.us
(315) 785-7785 **Renzi, Eugene** (J Watertown City Ct) Munic. Bldg., 245 Washington St., Watertown 13601; **Fax:** (315) 785-7856
(718) 262-7398 **Ressos, Maria** (J Civil Ct of NYC Housing Part) 89-17 Sutphin Blvd., Jamaica 11435
(914) 654-2287 **Rice, Gail B.** (J New Rochelle City Ct) 475 North Ave., New Rochelle 10801-3405
(315) 379-2214 **Richards, Jerome J.** (J St Lawrence Cty Ct) Cty. Cthse., 48 Court St., Canton 13617; **Fax:** (315) 379-9934
(646) 386-5101 **Richardson, Clark V.** (J Family Ct of NYC & Acting Justice Sup Ct 1st Jud Dist) 60 Lafayette St., N.Y.C. 10013
(646) 386-5190 **Richardson-Mendelson, Edwina** (Admin J Family Ct of NYC) 60 Lafayette St., N.Y.C. 10013; **Fax:** (212) 374-2127
(718) 298-0204 **Richroath, Marybeth** (J Family Ct of NYC) 151-20 Jamaica Ave., Jamaica 11432; **Fax:** (718) 297-2530
(718) 298-0204 **Richter, Ronald E.** (J Family Ct of NYC) 151-20 Jamaica Ave., Jamaica 11432; **Fax:** (718) 297-2530
(212) 340-0567 **Richter, Rosalyn H.** (Assoc Justice App Div 1st Dept) 27 Madison Ave., N.Y.C. 10010; **E-mail:** rrichter@courts.state.ny.us
(516) 572-2139 **Ricigliano, Francis D.** (J Nassau Cty Dist Ct) 99 Main St., Hempstead 11550
(718) 675-8610 **Rienzi, Leonard P.** (J Crim Ct of NYC & Acting Justice Sup Ct 13th Jud Dist) Cty. Cthse., 18 Richmond Terr., Staten Island 10301
(516) 571-2040 **Riordan, John B.** (Nassau Cty Surro) 262 Old Country Rd., Mineola 11501; **Fax:** (516) 571-2997; **E-mail:** jriordan@courts.state.ny.us
(718) 298-1079 **Rios, Jaime A.** (Justice Sup Ct 11th Jud Dist & Assoc Justice Sup Ct App Term 2nd 11th & 13th Jud Dists) 88-11 Sutphin Blvd., Jamaica 11435; **Fax:** (718) 298-1122
(718) 298-1089 **Ritholtz, Martin E.** (Justice Sup Ct 11th Jud Dist) 88-11 Sutphin Blvd., Jamaica 11435; **E-mail:** mritholtz@courts.state.ny.us
(347) 296-1524 **Rivera, Francois A.** (Justice Sup Ct 2nd Jud Dist) 360 Adams St., Bklyn. 11201
(718) 722-6486 **Rivera, Reinaldo E.** (Assoc Justice App Div 2nd Dept) 45 Monroe Pl., Bklyn. 11201; **Fax:** (718) 722-6492; **E-mail:** rrivera@courts.state.ny.us
(347) 296-1113 **Riviezzo, Dineen A.** (J Ct of Claims & Acting Justice Sup Ct 2nd Jud Dist) 320 Jay St., Bklyn. 11201
(585) 428-2227 **Rivoli, John J.** (J Monroe Cty Family Ct) Hall of Justice, 3rd Fl., 99 Exchange Blvd., Rochester 14614-2187; **Fax:** (585) 428-2597
(516) 571-3259 **Robbins, Tammy S.** (J Nassau Cty Ct & Acting Justice Sup Ct 10th Jud Dist) West Wing, 252 Old Country Rd., Mineola 11501; **Fax:** (516) 571-1349; **E-mail:** trobbins@courts.state.ny.us
(718) 618-2200 **Roberts, Gayle P.** (J Family Ct of NYC) 900 Sheridan Ave., Bronx 10451
(518) 453-4680 **Robichaud, Kathleen Leahey** (J Rensselaer City Ct) 62 Washington St., Rensselaer 12144; **Fax:** (518) 462-3307
(718) 618-2510 **Rodriguez, Jose** (J Civil Ct of NYC Housing Part) Housing Ct., 1118 Grand Concourse, Bronx 10456

(718) 618-1416 **Rodriguez, Julia I.** (J Civil Ct of NYC & Acting Justice Sup Ct 12th Jud Dist Civil Term) 851 Grand Concourse, Bronx 10451

(716) 845-7487 **Rodwin, Lisa Bloch** (J Erie Cty Family Ct) One Niagara Plaza, Rm. 600, Buffalo 14202; **Fax:** (716) 858-7756

(315) 379-2217 **Rogers, Kathleen M.** (St Lawrence Cty Surro) Cthse., 48 Court St., Canton 13617-1199; **Fax:** (315) 379-2372

(518) 561-3700 **Rogers, Mark J.** (J Plattsburgh City Ct) 53 Court St., Plattsburgh 12901; **Fax:** (518) 563-3124

(315) 349-8741 **Roman, David J.** (J Oswego Cty Ct) Public Safety Center, 39 Churchill Rd., Oswego 13126

(212) 340-0400 **Roman, Nelson S.** (Assoc Justice App Div 1st Dept) 27 Madison Ave., N.Y.C. 10010

(718) 298-1441 **Roman, Sheri S.** (Assoc Justice App Div 2nd Dept) 125-01 Queens Blvd., Rm. 851, Kew Gardens 11415; **Fax:** (718) 520-8247; **E-mail:** sroman@courts.state.ny.us

(845) 208-7822 **Rooney, James T.** (J Putnam Cty Ct Family Ct & Surro) Putnam Cty. Cthse., 20 County Center, Carmel 10512

(718) 675-8640 **Rooney, Stephen J.** (J Ct of Claims & Acting Justice Sup Ct 13th Jud Dist) Cty. Cthse., 18 Richmond Terr., Staten Island 10301

(716) 845-9490 **Rosa, Janice M.** (Supv Justice Sup Ct 8th Jud Dist Matrimonial Matters) Erie Cty. Ct. Bldg., 2nd Fl., 25 Delaware Ave., Buffalo 14202; **Fax:** (716) 851-3225; **E-mail:** jrosa@courts.state.ny.us

(315) 823-1690 **Rose, Mark** (J Little Falls City Ct) City Hall, 659 E. Main St., Little Falls 13365; **Fax:** (315) 823-1623

(315) 363-0996 **Rose, Neal P.** (J Sherrill City Ct) 373 Sherrill Rd., Sherrill 13461; **Fax:** (315) 363-1176

(607) 778-2473 **Rose, Robert S.** (Assoc Justice App Div 3rd Dept) Broome Cty. Cthse., 92 Court St., P.O. Box 1766, Binghamton 13902-1766; **Fax:** (607) 778-2405

(585) 428-5288 **Rosenbaum, Matthew A.** (Justice Sup Ct 7th Jud Dist) 545 Hall of Justice, 99 Exchange Blvd., Rochester 14614-2184; **Fax:** (585) 428-2995

(347) 296-1513 **Rosenberg, Gerard H.** (Justice Sup Ct 2nd Jud Dist) 360 Adams St., Bklyn. 11201

(718) 298-1097 **Rosengarten, Roger N.** (Justice Sup Ct 11th Jud Dist) 88-11 Sutphin Blvd., Jamaica 11435

(315) 671-2775 **Rosenthal, Kate** (J Syracuse City Ct) 505 S. State St., Syracuse 13202-2104; **Fax:** (315) 671-2747; **E-mail:** krosenth@courts.state.ny.us

(646) 386-4666 **Ross, Neil E.** (J Crim Ct of NYC) 100 Centre St., N.Y.C. 10013; **Fax:** (212) 374-2579

(516) 571-0021 **Ross, Robert A.** (Supv J Sup Ct 10th Jud Dist Nassau Cty Matrimonial) Matrimonial Center, 400 County Seat Dr., Mineola 11501

(607) 273-2263 **Rossiter, Judith A.** (J Ithaca City Ct) 118 E. Clinton St., Ithaca 14850; **Fax:** (607) 277-3702

(347) 296-1533 **Rothenberg, Karen B.** (Justice Sup Ct 2nd Jud Dist) 360 Adams St., Bklyn. 11201

(607) 277-4957 **Rowley, John C.** (J Tompkins Cty Ct Family Ct & Surro) Cthse., 320 N. Tioga St., P.O. Box 70, Ithaca 14851-0070; **Fax:** (212) 457-2938

(347) 404-9061 **Rubin, Alice Fisher** (J Civil Ct of NYC) 141 Livingston St., Rm. 606, Bklyn. 11201

(347) 296-1521 **Ruchelsman, Leon** (Justice Sup Ct 2nd Jud Dist) 360 Adams St., Bklyn. 11201

(914) 289-2310 **Ruderman, Terry Jane** (J Ct of Claims) 140 Grand St., 5th Fl., White Plains 10601; **Fax:** (914) 289-2313

(585) 428-5488 **Ruhlmann, Dandrea Lynn** (J Monroe Cty Family Ct) Hall of Justice, 3rd Fl., 99 Exchange Blvd., Rochester 14614-2187; **Fax:** (585) 428-1807

(347) 401-9870 **Ruiz, Jeanette** (J Family Ct of NYC) 330 Jay St., Bklyn. 11201; **Fax:** (347) 401-9900

(718) 618-1435 **Ruiz, Norma** (Justice Sup Ct 12th Jud Dist Civil Term) 851 Grand Concourse, Bronx 10451

(607) 756-3480 **Rumsey, Phillip R.** (Justice Sup Ct 6th Jud Dist) 46 Greenbush St., Suite 301, Cortland 13045-2772; **Fax:** (607) 753-0854

(914) 831-6400 **Runes, Richard** (J Rye City Ct) 21 McCullough Pl., Rye 10580; **Fax:** (914) 967-4354

(716) 845-2623 **Russell, Robert T., Jr.** (J Buffalo City Ct) 50 Delaware Ave., Suite 250, Buffalo 14202; **Fax:** (716) 845-7574; **E-mail:** rrussell@courts.state.ny.us

(518) 565-4630 **Ryan, Kevin K.** (Clinton Cty Surro) Cty. Govt. Ctr., Suite 315, 137 Margaret St., Plattsburgh 12901-2933; **Fax:** (518) 565-4769

(718) 675-8800 **Sacco, Helene Donlan** (J Family Ct of NYC) 100 Richmond Terr., Staten Island 10301

(845) 794-9776 **Sackett, Robert A.** (Justice Sup Ct 3rd Jud Dist) 414 Broadway, Monticello 12701

(516) 571-3560 **St. George, Norman** (J Nassau Cty Ct & Acting Justice Sup Ct 10th Jud Dist) Cty. Cthse., 262 Old Country Rd., Mineola 11501; **Fax:** (516) 571-1600; **E-mail:** nstgeorg@courts.state.ny.us

(347) 296-1492 **Saitta, Wayne P.** (Justice Sup Ct 2nd Jud Dist) 360 Adams St., Bklyn. 11201

(718) 298-0204 **Salinitro, Barbara** (J Family Ct of NYC) 151-20 Jamaica Ave., Jamaica 11432; **Fax:** (718) 297-2530

(716) 845-2160 **Saltarelli, Mark E.** (Acting J Tonawanda City Ct) City Hall, 200 Niagara St., Tonawanda 14150; **Fax:** (716) 693-1612

(845) 486-2230 **Sammarco, Valentino T.** (J Dutchess Cty Family Ct & Acting Justice Sup Ct 9th Jud Dist) 50 Market St., Poughkeepsie 12601-3204; **Fax:** (845) 486-2510; **E-mail:** vsammarc@courts.state.ny.us

(718) 298-1671 **Sampson, Frederick D.R.** (Justice Sup Ct 11th Jud Dist) 25-10 Court Sq., Long Island City 11101; **E-mail:** fsampson@courts.state.ny.us

(646) 386-5709 **Samuels, Debra R.** (J Civil Ct of NYC) 111 Centre St., Rm. 673, N.Y.C. 10013; **Fax:** (212) 374-5709; **E-mail:** dsamuels@courts.state.ny.us

(631) 853-4918 **Santorelli, Joseph A.** (J Suffolk Cty Dist Ct) John P. Cohalan, Jr. Ct. Complex, 400 Carleton Ave., P.O. Box 9075, Central Islip 11722-9075

(718) 298-1087 **Santucci, Fred T.** (Assoc Justice App Div 2nd Dept) 88-11 Sutphin Blvd., Jamaica 11435; **Fax:** (718) 520-1464

(718) 875-1300 45 Monroe Pl., Bklyn. 11201

(718) 298-1095 **Satterfield, Patricia P.** (Justice Sup Ct 11th Jud Dist) 88-11 Sutphin Blvd., Jamaica 11435

(646) 386-5114 **Sattler, Lori** (J Civil Ct of NYC assigned to Family Ct) 60 Lafayette St., N.Y.C. 10013

(718) 466-3028 **Saunders, Verna** (J Civil Ct of NYC Housing Part) Housing Ct., 1118 Grand Concourse, Bronx 10456

(212) 340-0400 **Saxe, David B.** (Assoc Justice App Div 1st Dept) 27 Madison Ave., N.Y.C. 10010

(518) 451-8815 **Scarano, Jerry J.** (J Saratoga Cty Ct) 30 McMaster St., Ballston Spa 12020-0600

(914) 824-5654 **Scarpino, Anthony A., Jr.** (Westchester Cty Surro) 111 Dr. Martin Luther King, Jr. Blvd., 19th Fl., White Plains 10601; **Fax:** (914) 995-7593

(646) 386-5716 **Scarpulla, Saliann** (J Civil Ct of NYC & Acting Justice Sup Ct 1st Jud Dist) 111 Centre St., Rm. 335, N.Y.C. 10013; **E-mail:** sscarpulla@courts.state.ny.us

(914) 831-6980 **Scattaretico-Naber, Mary Anne** (J Yonkers City Ct) Robert W. Cacace Justice Center, 100 S. Broadway, Yonkers 10701

(914) 831-6513 (Acting J Westchester Cty Family Ct) 53 S. Broadway, Yonkers 10701; **Fax:** (914) 231-2809

(718) 618-1449 **Schachner, Larry** (J Civil Ct of NYC & Acting Justice Sup Ct 12th Jud Dist Civil Term) 851 Grand Concourse, Bronx 10451

(347) 296-1518 **Schack, Arthur M.** (Justice Sup Ct 2nd Jud Dist) 360 Adams St., Bklyn. 11201

(607) 721-8623 **Schaewe, Catherine C.** (J Ct of Claims) State Office Bldg., 18th Fl., 44 Hawley St., Binghamton 13901-4418; **Fax:** (607) 721-8590

(646) 386-5584 **Scheckowitz, Bruce** (J Civil Ct of NYC Housing Part) 111 Centre St., Rm. 1240, N.Y.C. 10013; **Fax:** (212) 374-5709

(646) 386-4648 **Schecter, Jennifer** (J Civil Ct of NYC assigned to Crim Ct) 100 Centre St., N.Y.C. 10013

(914) 824-5100 **Scheinkman, Alan D.** (Admin J Sup Ct 9th Jud Dist) 111 Dr. Martin Luther King Jr. Blvd., White Plains 10601; **Fax:** (212) 884-8939

(646) 386-3253 **Schlesinger, Alice** (Justice Sup Ct 1st Jud Dist) 60 Centre St., Rm. 525, N.Y.C. 10007

(347) 296-1501 **Schmidt, David I.** (Justice Sup Ct 2nd Jud Dist) 360 Adams St., Bklyn. 11201

(646) 386-5617 **Schneider, Jean** (Supv J Civil Ct of NYC Housing Part) 111 Centre St., Rm. 1240, N.Y.C. 10013; **Fax:** (212) 374-5709; **E-mail:** jschneider@courts.state.ny.us

(646) 386-3232 **Schoenfeld, Martin** (Justice Sup Ct 1st Jud Dist & Justice Sup Ct App Term 1st Jud Dept) 60 Centre St., Rm. 607, N.Y.C. 10007

(646) 386-5698 **Schreiber, Michelle D.** (J Civil Ct of NYC Housing Part) 111 Centre St., Rm. 1240, N.Y.C. 10013; **Fax:** (212) 374-5709; **E-mail:** mschreiber@courts.state.ny.us

(718) 298-1006 **Schulman, Martin J.** (Justice Sup Ct 11th Jud Dist) 88-11 Sutphin Blvd., Jamaica 11435; **E-mail:** mschulma@courts.state.ny.us

(585) 396-5011 **Schuppenhauer, John A.** (J Canandaigua City Ct) City Hall, 2 N. Main St., Canandaigua 14424-1448; **Fax:** (585) 396-5012

(585) 428-2450 **Schwartz, John R.** (Rochester City Ct & Supv J City Cts 7th Jud Dist & Acting J Monroe Cty Ct) 6 Hall of Justice, 99 Exchange Blvd., Rochester 14614; **Fax:** (585) 428-2737; **E-mail:** jschwart@courts.state.ny.us

(212) 361-8170 **Schweitzer, Melvin L.** (J Ct of Claims & Acting Justice Sup Ct 1st Jud Dist) 26 Broadway, 10th Floor, N.Y.C. 10004; **Fax:** (212) 361-8173; **E-mail:** mschweit@courts.state.ny.us

(315) 785-3019 **Schwerzmann, Peter A.** (Jefferson Cty Surro) Jefferson Cty. Ct. Complex, 3rd Fl., 163 Arsenal St., Watertown 13601-2562; **Fax:** (315) 785-5194

(646) 386-4686 **Sciarrino, Matthew A., Jr.** (J Crim Ct of NYC) 100 Centre St., N.Y.C. 10013; **E-mail:** msciarri@courts.state.ny.us

(716) 845-9495 **Sconiers, Rose H.** (Assoc Justice App Div 4th Dept) Buffalo City Ct. Bldg., 10th Fl., 50 Delaware Ave., Buffalo 14202; **Fax:** (716) 851-3328; **E-mail:** rsconier@courts.state.ny.us

(914) 289-2330 **Scuccimarra, Thomas H.** (J Ct of Claims) 140 Grand St., 9th Fl., White Plains 10601; **Fax:** (914) 289-2333

(607) 776-9623 **Scudder, Henry J.** (Pres Justice App Div 4th Dept) 19 E. Pulteney Sq., Bath 14810-1575; **Fax:** (607) 776-7168

(585) 530-3100 M. Dolores Denman Cthse., 50 East Ave., Rochester 14604

(315) 349-3350 **Seager, Kimberly M.** (J Oswego Cty Family Ct) Public Safety Center, 39 Churchill Rd., Oswego 13126; **Fax:** (315) 349-3457

(716) 278-1880 **Seaman, David E.** (J Niagara Cty Family Ct) Angelo A. DelSignore Civic Bldg., 775 3rd St., Niagara Falls 14302; **Fax:** (716) 278-1877; **E-mail:** dseaman@courts.state.ny.us

(716) 845-9351 **Sedita, Frank A., Jr.** (Justice Sup Ct 8th Jud Dist) Buffalo City Ct. Bldg., 9th Fl., 50 Delaware Ave., Buffalo 14202; **Fax:** (716) 851-3329; **E-mail:** fsedita@courts.state.ny.us

(718) 618-3675 **Seewald, Robert G.** (J Crim Ct of NYC & Acting Justice Sup Ct 12th Jud Dist Crim Term) Bronx Hall of Justice, 265 E. 161st St., Bronx 10451; **Fax:** (718) 618-3584

(518) 451-8830 **Seibert, Harry W., Jr.** (Saratoga Cty Surro) 30 McMaster St., Ballston Spa 12020-0600; **Fax:** (518) 884-4774

(914) 831-6463 **Seiden, Adam** (Assoc J Mount Vernon City Ct) Two Roosevelt Sq. N., 2nd Fl., Mount Vernon 10550-2019; **Fax:** (914) 699-1230

(607) 772-7006 **Seiden, Daniel L.** (J Binghamton City Ct) Governmental Plaza, 38 Hawley St., Binghamton 13901; **Fax:** (607) 772-7041

(315) 349-3270 **Seiter, Norman W., Jr.** (Justice Sup Ct 5th Jud Dist) Oswego Cty. Cthse., 25 E. Oneida St., Oswego 13126; **Fax:** (315) 349-3299

(718) 298-0925 **Serita, Toko** (J Crim Ct of NYC) 125-01 Queens Blvd., Kew Gardens 11415; **Fax:** (718) 520-4712

(631) 853-5138 **Sgroi, Sandra L.** (Assoc Justice App Div 2nd Dept) John P. Cohalan, Jr. Ct. Complex, 400 Carleton Ave., P.O. Box 9075, Central Islip 11722-9075; **Fax:** (631) 853-5798

(607) 687-0338 **Sgueglia, Vincent A.** (J Tioga Cty Ct Family Ct & Surro) Cthse., 20 Court St., P.O. Box 10, Owego 13827; **Fax:** (607) 687-1524

(315) 266-4297 **Shaheen, Anthony F.** (Justice Sup Ct 5th Jud Dist) Oneida Cty. Cthse., 200 Elizabeth St., Utica 13501; **Fax:** (315) 798-6431

(315) 253-1570 **Shamon, Thomas J.** (J Auburn City Ct) 157 Genesee St., Auburn 13021-3434; **Fax:** (315) 253-1085

(315) 343-0415 **Shanley, P. Michael** (J Oswego City Ct) Conway Munic. Center, 20 W. Oneida St., Oswego 13126; **Fax:** (315) 343-0531

(347) 404-9077 **Sheares, Robin K.** (J Civil Ct of NYC) 141 Livingston St., Bklyn. 11201

(518) 664-9876 **Sheehan, Joseph W.** (J Mechanicville City Ct) City Hall, 36 N. Main St., Mechanicville 12118; **Fax:** (518) 664-8606

(516) 571-2883 **Sher, Denise L.** (J Ct of Claims & Acting Justice Sup Ct 10th Jud Dist) 100 Supreme Court Dr., Mineola 11501; **E-mail:** dsher@courts.state.ny.us

(718) 618-1134 **Sherman, Carol R.** (J Family Ct of NYC) 900 Sheridan Ave., Bronx 10451
(718) 618-1451 **Sherman, Howard H.** (Justice Sup Ct 12th Jud Dist Civil Term) 851 Grand Concourse, Bronx 10451
(347) 296-1443 **Sherman, Kenneth P.** (J Civil Ct of NYC & Acting Justice Sup Ct 2nd Jud Dist) 360 Adams St., Bklyn. 11201
(607) 277-2355 **Sherman, M. John** (J Tompkins Cty Ct Family Ct & Surro) Cthse., 320 N. Tioga St., P.O. Box 70, Ithaca 14851-0070; **Fax:** (607) 272-0684
(646) 386-3807 **Sherwood, O. Peter** (J Ct of Claims & Acting Justice Sup Ct 1st Jud Dist) 60 Centre St., Rm. 615, N.Y.C. 10007; **Fax:** (212) 748-7793
(315) 266-4512 **Shkane, Joan E.** (J Oneida Cty Family Ct) Cthse., 301 W. Dominick St., Rome 13440-5196; **Fax:** (315) 337-0480
(646) 386-5687 **Shulman, Martin** (Justice Sup Ct 1st Jud Dist & Justice Sup Ct App Term 1st Jud Dept) 60 Centre St., Rm. 655, N.Y.C. 10007
(718) 298-1080 **Siegal, Bernice D.** (Justice Sup Ct 11th Jud Dist) 88-11 Sutphin Blvd., Jamaica 11435; **Fax:** (718) 298-1090
(315) 793-2184 **Siegel, Norman I.** (J Ct of Claims & Acting Justice Sup Ct 5th Jud Dist) State Office Bldg., 207 Genesee St., Utica 13501; **Fax:** (315) 793-2217
(347) 404-9085 **Sikowitz, Marcia** (J Civil Ct of NYC Housing Part) 141 Livingston St., Bklyn. 11201
(347) 401-9096 **Silber, Debra** (J Civil Ct of NYC & Acting Justice Sup Ct 2nd Jud Dist) 360 Adams St., Bklyn. 11201; **Fax:** (718) 643-3755
(315) 393-3941 **Silver, George E.** (J Ogdensburg City Ct) 330 Ford St., Ogdensburg 13669; **Fax:** (315) 393-6839
(646) 386-3271 **Silver, George J.** (J Civil Ct of NYC & Acting Justice Sup Ct 1st Jud Dist) 80 Centre St., N.Y.C. 10013
(718) 618-1480 **Silver, Howard R.** (Justice Sup Ct 12th Jud Dist Civil Term) 851 Grand Concourse, Bronx 10451
(646) 386-4676 **Simpson, ShawnDya L.** (J Civil Ct of NYC assigned to Crim Ct) 111 Centre St., N.Y.C. 10013
(516) 571-9010 **Singer, Conrad D.** (J Nassau Cty Family Ct) 1200 Old Country Rd., Westbury 11590; **Fax:** (516) 571-9395
(646) 386-5692 **Singh, Anil C.** (J Civil Ct of NYC & Acting Justice Sup Ct 1st Jud Dist) 111 Centre St., Rm. 1240, N.Y.C. 10013; **E-mail:** asingh@courts.state.ny.us
(518) 853-4432 **Sise, Joseph M.** (Justice Sup Ct 4th Jud Dist) Cthse., 58 Broadway, P.O. Box 1500, Fonda 12068-1500; **Fax:** (518) 853-8378
(518) 432-3435 **Sise, Richard E.** (Pres J Ct of Claims) P.O. Box 7344, Capitol Station, Albany 12224; **Fax:** (518) 432-3428
(716) 845-9354 **Siwek, Donna M.** (Supv Justice Sup Ct 8th Jud Dist Civil Matters) Buffalo City Ct. Bldg., 8th Fl., 50 Delaware Ave., Buffalo 14202; **Fax:** (716) 851-3318; **E-mail:** dsiwek@courts.state.ny.us
(516) 571-2727 **Skelos, Peter B.** (Assoc Justice App Div 2nd Dept) Supreme Ct. Bldg., 100 Supreme Court Dr., Mineola 11501; **Fax:** (516) 571-1281
(718) 875-1300 45 Monroe Pl., Bklyn. 11201
(518) 762-3840 **Skoda, Edward F.** (J Fulton Cty Family Ct) 11 N. William St., Johnstown 12095; **Fax:** (518) 762-9540
(845) 291-2107 **Slobod, Elaine** (Justice Sup Ct 9th Jud Dist) Cthse., 285 Main St., Goshen 10924
(315) 393-3941 **Small, William R.** (J Ogdensburg City Ct) 330 Ford St., Ogdensburg 13669; **Fax:** (315) 393-6839
(607) 778-2418 **Smith, Martin E.** (J Broome Cty Ct) Broome Cty. Family & Cty. Cts. Bldg., 65 Hawley St., P.O. Box 1766, Binghamton 13902-1766; **Fax:** (607) 778-6135
(914) 824-5431 **Smith, Mary H.** (Justice Sup Ct 9th Jud Dist) 111 Dr. Martin Luther King Jr. Blvd., White Plains 10601
(585) 530-3282 **Smith, Nancy E.** (Assoc Justice App Div 4th Dept) M. Dolores Denman Cthse., 50 East Ave., Rochester 14604; **Fax:** (585) 530-3193
(646) 386-3824 **Smith, Robert S.** (Assoc J Ct of App) 780 Third Ave., N.Y.C. 10017; **E-mail:** rssmith@courts.state.ny.us
(518) 455-7726 Court of Appeals Hall, 20 Eagle St., Albany 12207-1095
(718) 618-1016 **Smith, Ruth E.** (J Crim Ct of NYC & Acting Justice Sup Ct 12th Jud Dist Crim Term) Bronx Hall of Justice, 265 E. 161st St., Bronx 10451
(646) 386-3976 **Solomon, Charles H.** (J Crim Ct of NYC & Acting Justice Sup Ct 1st Jud Dist) 100 Centre St., N.Y.C. 10013
(646) 386-3181 **Solomon, Jane S.** (J Civil Ct of NYC & Acting Justice Sup Ct 1st Jud Dist) 60 Centre St., Rm. 647, N.Y.C. 10007
(347) 296-1495 **Solomon, Martin M.** (Justice Sup Ct 2nd Jud Dist) 360 Adams St., Bklyn. 11201
(646) 386-4503 **Sonberg, Michael R.** (J Crim Ct of NYC & Acting Justice Sup Ct 1st Jud Dist) 111 Centre St., N.Y.C. 10013; **E-mail:** msonberg@courts.state.ny.us
(646) 386-5104 **Sosa-Lintner, Gloria** (J Family Ct of NYC) 60 Lafayette St., N.Y.C. 10013
(212) 361-8160 **Soto, Faviola A.** (J Ct of Claims) 26 Broadway, 10th Fl., N.Y.C. 10004; **Fax:** (212) 361-8165
(518) 285-6159 **Spain, Edward O.** (Assoc Justice App Div 3rd Dept) Cthse., Congress and Second Sts., Troy 12180; **Fax:** (518) 270-0066
(646) 386-5589 **Spears, Brenda** (J Civil Ct of NYC Housing Part) 111 Centre St., Rm. 1240, N.Y.C. 10013; **Fax:** (212) 374-5709
(631) 853-7418 **Spelman, G. Ann** (J Suffolk Cty Dist Ct & Acting J Suffolk Cty Ct) John P. Cohalan, Jr. Ct. Complex, 400 Carleton Ave., P.O. Box 9075, Central Islip 11722-9075
(516) 572-2123 **Spergel, Robert H.** (J Nassau Cty Dist Ct) 99 Main St., Hempstead 11550
(716) 439-7140 **Sperrazza, Sara Sheldon** (J Niagara Cty Ct & Surro) Cthse., 175 Hawley St., Lockport 14094-2758; **Fax:** (716) 439-7149; **E-mail:** ssperraz@courts.state.ny.us
(631) 852-2309 **Spinner, Jeffrey Arlen** (J Suffolk Cty Ct & Acting Justice Sup Ct 10th Jud Dist) Supreme Ct. Bldg., 1 Court St., Riverhead 11901; **Fax:** (631) 852-3226; **E-mail:** jspinner@courts.state.ny.us
(347) 401-9312 **Spodek, Ellen** (Justice Sup Ct 2nd Jud Dist) 360 Adams St., Bklyn. 11201
(845) 486-2220 **Sproat, Christine A.** (Justice Sup Ct 9th Jud Dist) Cthse., 10 Market St., Poughkeepsie 12601; **Fax:** (845) 486-2014
(718) 618-3666 **Stadtmauer, David** (Justice Sup Ct 12th Jud Dist Crim Term) Bronx Hall of Justice, 265 E. 161st St., Bronx 10451; **Fax:** (718) 618-3584

(646) 386-3342 **Stallman, Michael D.** (J Civil Ct of NYC & Acting Justice Sup Ct 1st Jud Dist) 80 Centre St., N.Y.C. 10013

(585) 428-2082 **Stander, Thomas A.** (Justice Sup Ct 7th Jud Dist) 421 Hall of Justice, 99 Exchange Blvd., Rochester 14614-2184; **Fax:** (585) 428-2994

(347) 404-9084 **Stanley, John** (J Civil Ct of NYC Housing Part) 141 Livingston St., Bklyn. 11201

(518) 285-8939 **Stein, Leslie E.** (Assoc Justice App Div 3rd Dept) 50 Chapel St., 1st Fl., Albany 12207; **Fax:** (518) 434-5980

(347) 296-1545 **Steinhardt, Marsha L.** (Justice Sup Ct 2nd Jud Dist & Assoc Justice Sup Ct App Term 2nd 11th & 13th Jud Dists) 360 Adams St., Bklyn. 11201

(646) 386-4661 **Stephen, Larry R.C.** (J Crim Ct of NYC) 851 Grand Concourse, Bronx 10451; **Fax:** (212) 374-2579

(518) 453-4640 **Stiglmeier, Gary F.** (J Albany City Ct) 209 City Hall, Eagle & Corning Pl., Albany 12207; **Fax:** (518) 434-5034

(718) 618-1455 **Stinson, Betty Owen** (Justice Sup Ct 12th Jud Dist Civil Term) 851 Grand Concourse, Rm. 6M-21, Bronx 10451; **Fax:** (718) 590-3776

(718) 298-0204 **Stokinger, Carol A.** (Supv J Family Ct of NYC Queens Cty) 151-20 Jamaica Ave., Jamaica 11432; **Fax:** (718) 297-2530

(646) 386-3991 **Stolz, Robert M.** (J Crim Ct of NYC & Acting Justice Sup Ct 1st Jud Dist) 111 Centre St., N.Y.C. 10013

(646) 386-3984 **Stone, Lewis Bart** (Justice Sup Ct 1st Jud Dist) 100 Centre St., N.Y.C. 10013; **Fax:** (212) 608-7566

(518) 762-0007 **Stortecky, Frederick R.** (J Johnstown City Ct) City Hall, 33-41 E. Main St., Johnstown 12095; **Fax:** (518) 762-2720

(718) 675-8437 **Straniere, Philip S.** (Supv J Civil Ct of NYC) 927 Castleton Ave., West New Brighton, Staten Island 10310; **Fax:** (718) 390-8108; **E-mail:** pstranie@courts.state.ny.us

(718) 298-1081 **Strauss, Sidney F.** (Justice Sup Ct 11th Jud Dist) 88-11 Sutphin Blvd., Jamaica 11435; **E-mail:** strauss@courts.state.ny.us

(718) 618-1456 **Suarez, Lucindo** (Justice Sup Ct 12th Jud Dist Civil Term) 851 Grand Concourse, Bronx 10451; **Fax:** (718) 537-5076

(516) 571-2408 **Sullivan, David P.** (J Nassau Cty Ct & Acting Justice Sup Ct 10th Jud Dist & Supv J Village Cts Nassau Cty) West Wing, 252 Old Country Rd., Mineola 11501; **Fax:** (516) 571-1491; **E-mail:** dpsulliv@courts.state.ny.us

(347) 296-1049 **Sullivan, James P.** (Justice Sup Ct 2nd Jud Dist) 320 Jay St., Bklyn. 11201

(607) 337-1825 **Sullivan, W. Howard** (J Chenango Cty Ct Family Ct & Surro) Cty. Office Bldg., 5 Court St., Norwich 13815-1676; **Fax:** (607) 337-1834

(631) 952-4955 **Summa, Gina M. Lopez** (J Ct of Claims) State Office Bldg., 3rd Fl., Veterans Memorial Pkwy., Hauppauge 11788; **Fax:** (631) 952-2070

(347) 296-1527 **Sunshine, Jeffrey** (J Family Ct of NYC & Supv J Sup Ct 2nd Jud Dist Matrimonial Matters) 360 Adams St., Bklyn. 11201

(631) 853-2207 **Sweeney, Patrick A.** (J Suffolk Cty Family Ct & Acting Justice Sup Ct 10th Jud Dist) John P. Cohalan, Jr. Ct. Complex, 400 Carleton Ave., Central Islip 11722; **Fax:** (631) 853-8407

(347) 404-9060 **Sweeney, Peter P.** (Supv J Civil Ct of NYC) 141 Livingston St., Bklyn. 11201

(212) 340-0400 **Sweeny, John W., Jr.** (Assoc Justice App Div 1st Dept) 27 Madison Ave., N.Y.C. 10010
(845) 208-7825 Historic Courthouse, 44 Gleneida Ave., Carmel 10512

(716) 845-7481 **Szczur, Margaret Olszewski** (J Erie Cty Family Ct) One Niagara Plaza, Rm. 706, Buffalo 14202; **Fax:** (716) 858-7792

(585) 428-5541 **Taddeo, Ann Marie** (Justice Sup Ct 7th Jud Dist) 545 Hall of Justice, 99 Exchange Blvd., Rochester 14614-2184; **Fax:** (585) 428-4122

(607) 778-2201 **Tait, Jeffrey A.** (Justice Sup Ct 6th Jud Dist) Broome Cty. Cthse., 92 Court St., P.O. Box 1766, Binghamton 13902; **Fax:** (607) 778-2398; **E-mail:** taitjsc@courts.state.ny.us

(718) 618-3615 **Tallmer, Megan** (J Crim Ct of NYC & Acting Justice Sup Ct 12th Jud Dist Crim Term) Bronx Hall of Justice, 265 E. 161st St., Bronx 10451; **Fax:** (718) 618-3584

(718) 298-0204 **Tally, Linda** (J Family Ct of NYC) 151-20 Jamaica Ave., Jamaica 11432; **Fax:** (718) 297-2530

(631) 853-6323 **Tanenbaum, Melvyn** (Justice Sup Ct 10th Jud Dist & Assoc Justice Sup Ct App Term 9th and 10th Jud Dists) John P. Cohalan, Jr. Ct. Complex, Ctrm. S-32, 400 Carleton Ave., Central Islip 11722
Mailing Address: 400 Carleton Ave., Central Islip 11722

(718) 466-3175 **Tao, Elizabeth Y.** (J Civil Ct of NYC Housing Part) Housing Ct., 1118 Grand Concourse, Bronx 10456

(718) 618-2550 **Tapia, Fernando** (J Civil Ct of NYC & Acting Justice Sup Ct 12th Jud Dist Civil Term) 851 Grand Concourse, Bronx 10451

(631) 852-1960 **Tarantino, Andrew G., Jr.** (J Suffolk Cty Family Ct & Acting J Suffolk Cty Ct) Supreme Ct. Bldg., 1 Court St., Riverhead 11901; **Fax:** (631) 852-3351

(518) 798-4714 **Tarantino, Richard P.** (J Glens Falls City Ct) 42 Ridge St., 3rd Fl., Glens Falls 12801; **Fax:** (518) 798-0137

(718) 618-2549 **Taylor, Elizabeth A.** (J Civil Ct of NYC) 851 Grand Concourse, Bronx 10451

(718) 298-1194 **Taylor, Janice A.** (Justice Sup Ct 11th Jud Dist) 88-11 Sutphin Blvd., Jamaica 11435; **E-mail:** jataylor@courts.state.ny.us

(516) 431-1000 Ext. 7501 **Tepper, Roy** (J Long Beach City Ct) 1 West Chester St., Long Beach 11561; **Fax:** (516) 889-3511

(518) 285-8949 **Teresi, Joseph C.** (Justice Sup Ct 3rd Jud Dist) Cthse., Rm. 256, 16 Eagle St., Albany 12207

(347) 296-1539 **Thomas, Delores J.** (Justice Sup Ct 2nd Jud Dist) 360 Adams St., Bklyn. 11201

(718) 618-1459 **Thompson, Kenneth L., Jr.** (Justice Sup Ct 12th Jud Dist Civil Term) 851 Grand Concourse, Bronx 10451; **Fax:** (718) 618-3543

(646) 386-3178 **Tingling, Milton A., Jr.** (Justice Sup Ct 1st Jud Dist) 60 Centre St., Rm. 631, N.Y.C. 10007; **Fax:** (212) 374-3326

(914) 824-5435 **Tolbert, Bruce E.** (Justice Sup Ct 9th Jud Dist) 111 Dr. Martin Luther King, Jr. Blvd., White Plains 10601; **Fax:** (914) 995-4010

(212) 340-0400 **Tom, Peter** (Assoc Justice App Div 1st Dept) 27 Madison Ave., N.Y.C. 10010; **Fax:** (212) 340-0571

(347) 296-1010 **Tomei, Albert** (Justice Sup Ct 2nd Jud Dist) 320 Jay St., Bklyn. 11201
(518) 853-8108 **Tomlinson, Guy P.** (Montgomery Cty Surro) New Cthse., Rm. 50, 58 Broadway, P.O. Box 1500, Fonda 12068-1500; **Fax:** (518) 853-8230
(315) 789-6560 **Toole, Elisabeth A.** (J Geneva City Ct) Public Safety Bldg., 255 Exchange St., Geneva 14456; **Fax:** (315) 781-2802
(631) 853-4919 **Toomey, John J., Jr.** (J Suffolk Cty Dist Ct) John P. Cohalan, Jr. Ct. Complex, 400 Carleton Ave., P.O. Box 9075, Central Islip 11722-9075
(315) 671-1100 **Tormey, James C., III** (Admin J Sup Ct 5th Jud Dist) Onondaga Cty. Cthse., 401 Montgomery St., Syracuse 13202; **Fax:** (315) 671-1183
(646) 386-5219 **Torres, Analisa** (J Civil Ct of NYC & Acting Justice Sup Ct 1st Jud Dist) 111 Centre St., Rm. 1240, N.Y.C. 10013; **Fax:** (212) 374-5709
(347) 404-9744 **Torres, Margarita López** (Kings Cty Surro) 2 Johnson St., Bklyn. 11201; **Fax:** (718) 643-6237
(718) 618-1773 **Torres, Robert E.** (Justice Sup Ct 12th Jud Dist Civil Term) 851 Grand Concourse, Bronx 10451
(347) 404-9870 **Toussaint, Wavny** (J Civil Ct of NYC & Acting Justice Sup Ct 2nd Jud Dist) 330 Jay St., Bklyn. 11201; **Fax:** (347) 401-9900
(716) 845-2502 **Townsend, Sharon S.** (Justice Sup Ct 8th Jud Dist & Vice Dean for Family & Matrimonial Law NY State Judicial Institute) Erie Cty. Cthse., 3rd Fl., 92 Franklin St., Buffalo 14202-2721; **Fax:** (716) 845-7503; **E-mail:** stownsen@courts.state.ny.us
(914) 824-5800 84 N. Broadway, White Plains 10603
(716) 845-9378 **Troutman, Shirley** (Justice Sup Ct 8th Jud Dist) Erie Cty. Ct. Bldg., 25 Delaware Ave., Buffalo 14202; **Fax:** (716) 845-3224
(718) 618-1461 **Tuitt, Alison Y.** (Justice Sup Ct 12th Jud Dist Civil Term) 851 Grand Concourse, Bronx 10451; **Fax:** (718) 618-3590
(347) 401-9870 **Turbow, Daniel** (J Family Ct of NYC) 330 Jay St., Bklyn. 11201; **Fax:** (347) 401-9900
(518) 273-2434 **Turner, Matthew J.** (J Troy City Ct) 51 State St., Troy 12180; **Fax:** (518) 271-2360; **E-mail:** mjturner@courts.state.ny.us
(631) 854-1440 **Ukeiley, Stephen L.** (J Suffolk Cty Dist Ct) John P. Cohalan, Jr. Ct. Complex, 400 Carleton Ave., P.O. Box 9075, Central Islip 11722-9075
(631) 854-1440 Sixth District Court, 150 W. Main St., Patchogue 11772
(315) 671-2765 **Uplinger, Karen M.** (J Syracuse City Ct) 505 S. State St., Syracuse 13202-2104; **Fax:** (315) 671-2740; **E-mail:** kuplinge@courts.state.ny.us
(585) 428-2034 **Valentino, Joseph D.** (Justice Sup Ct 7th Jud Dist) 545 Hall of Justice, 99 Exchange Blvd., Rochester 14614-2184; **Fax:** (585) 428-1885; **E-mail:** jdvalenti@courts.state.ny.us
(585) 428-2885 **Van Strydonck, Thomas M.** (Admin J Sup Ct 7th Jud Dist) 545 Hall of Justice, 99 Exchange Blvd., Rochester 14614-2184; **Fax:** (585) 784-4225
(518) 233-2133 **Van Ullen, Stephen J.** (J Cohoes City Ct) City Hall, 1st Fl., Rm. 7, 97 Mohawk St., P.O. Box 678, Cohoes 12047-0678; **Fax:** (518) 233-8202
(347) 296-1455 **Vaughan, David B.** (Justice Sup Ct 2nd Jud Dist) 360 Adams St., Bklyn. 11201
(718) 262-7360 **Velasquez, Carmen R.** (J Civil Ct of NYC) 89-17 Sutphin Blvd., Jamaica 11435
(347) 296-1600 **Velasquez, Richard** (Justice Sup Ct 2nd Jud Dist) 360 Adams St., Bklyn. 11201
(718) 618-3653 **Villegas, George R.** (Justice Sup Ct 12th Jud Dist Crim Term) Bronx Hall of Justice, 265 E. 161st St., Bronx 10451; **Fax:** (718) 618-3571; **E-mail:** gvillega@courts.state.ny.us
(718) 466-3180 **Villella, Louis** (J Civil Ct of NYC Housing Part) Housing Ct., 1118 Grand Concourse, Bronx 10456
(716) 278-9820 **Violante, Mark Anthony** (Chief J Niagara Falls City Ct) Niagara Falls Munic. Complex, 1925 Main St., Niagara Falls 14305; **Fax:** (716) 278-9809; **E-mail:** maviolan@courts.state.ny.us
(716) 827-6486 **Violanti, Louis P.** (Assoc J Lackawanna City Ct) City Hall, 714 Ridge Rd., Lackawanna 14218-1588; **Fax:** (716) 825-1874
(718) 262-7385 **Viscovich, William A.** (J Civil Ct of NYC) 89-17 Sutphin Blvd., Jamaica 11435
(646) 386-3196 **Visitacion-Lewis, Laura** (Justice Sup Ct 1st Jud Dist) 60 Centre St., Rm. 669, N.Y.C. 10007; **E-mail:** lvlewis@courts.state.ny.us
(716) 278-9812 **Vitello, Diane L.** (J Niagara Falls City Ct) Niagara Falls Munic. Complex, 1925 Main St., Niagara Falls 14305; **Fax:** (716) 278-9809
(347) 404-9069 **Wade, Carolyn E.** (J Civil Ct of NYC) 141 Livingston St., Bklyn. 11201
(518) 451-8780 **Wait, Jeffrey D.** (J Saratoga Springs City Ct) City Hall, Suite 3, 474 Broadway, Saratoga Springs 12866-2295; **Fax:** (518) 584-3097
(718) 262-7121 **Waithe, Deighton S.** (J Civil Ct of NYC Housing Part) 89-17 Sutphin Blvd., Jamaica 11435
(718) 618-1465 **Walker, Edgar G.** (J Civil Ct of NYC & Acting Justice Sup Ct 12th Jud Dist Civil Term) 851 Grand Concourse, Bronx 10451; **Fax:** (212) 419-8494
(914) 824-5427 **Walker, Sam D.** (Justice Sup Ct 9th Jud Dist) Richard J. Daronco Cthse., Ctrm. 1001, 111 Dr. Martin Luther King, Jr. Blvd., White Plains 10601; **Fax:** (212) 401-9165; **E-mail:** chambersjusticesdwalker@nycourts.gov
(716) 845-7479 **Walker, Timothy J.** (J Ct of Claims & Acting Justice Sup Ct 8th Jud Dist) Erie Cty. Ct. Bldg., 3rd Fl., 25 Delaware Ave., Buffalo 14202; **Fax:** (716) 851-3440; **E-mail:** tjwalker@courts.state.ny.us **Fax:** (716) 851-3440
(518) 270-3761 Ext. 342 **Walsh, Elizabeth M.** (J Rensselaer Cty Family Ct) 1504 Fifth Ave., Troy 12180-4107; **Fax:** (518) 272-6573; **E-mail:** emwalsh@courts.state.ny.us
(347) 296-1055 **Walsh, John P.** (J Crim Ct of NYC & Acting Justice Sup Ct 2nd Jud Dist) 320 Jay St., Bklyn. 11201
(518) 285-8671 **Walsh, Margaret T.** (J Albany Cty Family Ct) 30 Clinton Ave., Albany 12207; **Fax:** (518) 462-4236; **E-mail:** mtwalsh@courts.state.ny.us
(518) 762-0007 **Walsh, Thomas C.** (J Johnstown City Ct) City Hall, 33-41 E. Main St., Johnstown 12095; **Fax:** (518) 762-2720
(845) 638-5365 **Walsh, Thomas E., II** (Rockland Cty Surro) 1 S. Main St., Suite 270, New City 10956; **Fax:** (845) 638-5632

(315) 671-1056 **Walsh, William D.** (J Onondaga Cty Ct) Crim. Cts. Bldg., Suite 370, 505 S. State St., Syracuse 13202; **Fax:** (315) 671-1188

(315) 428-3256 **Walsh Hood, Martha** (J Ct of Claims & Acting Justice Sup Ct 5th Jud Dist & Acting J Onondaga Cty Family Ct) State Office Bldg., 333 E. Washington St., Syracuse 13202; **Fax:** (315) 671-1163; **E-mail:** mhood@courts.state.ny.us

(716) 753-4188 **Ward, John T.** (J Chautauqua Cty Ct) Cthse., 1 N. Erie St., P.O. Box 292, Mayville 14757-0292; **Fax:** (716) 753-4993

(646) 386-4653 **Ward, Laura A.** (J Crim Ct of NYC & Acting Justice Sup Ct 1st Jud Dist) 100 Centre St., N.Y.C. 10013; **Fax:** (212) 295-4891

(914) 824-5400 **Warhit, Barry E.** (J Westchester Cty Ct) 111 Dr. Martin Luther King, Jr. Blvd., White Plains 10601; **Fax:** (914) 995-4946

(845) 638-5327 **Warren, William P.** (J Rockland Cty Family Ct) 1 S. Main St., Suite 300, New City 10956; **Fax:** (845) 638-5284

(516) 571-3351 **Warshawsky, Ira B.** (Justice Sup Ct 10th Jud Dist) Supreme Ct. Bldg., 100 Supreme Ct. Dr., Mineola 11501; **Fax:** (516) 571-0163; **E-mail:** iwarshaw@courts.state.ny.us

(716) 439-6684 **Watson, William J.** (J Lockport City Ct) Munic. Bldg., One Locks Plaza, Lockport 14094; **Fax:** (716) 439-6684

(718) 618-3620 **Webber, Troy K.** (Justice Sup Ct 12th Jud Dist Crim Term) Bronx Hall of Justice, 265 E. 161st St., Bronx 10451; **Fax:** (718) 618-3584

(631) 852-2176 **Weber, Gary J.** (J Suffolk Cty Ct & Acting Suffolk Cty Surro & Acting Justice Sup Ct 10th Jud Dist) Arthur M. Cromarty Ct. Complex, 210 Center Dr., Riverhead 11901-3310; **Fax:** (631) 852-3857

(646) 264-1318 **Weinberg, Richard** (J Crim Ct of NYC & Acting Justice Sup Ct 1st Jud Dist) Midtown Community Court, 314 W. 54th St., N.Y.C. 10019
(646) 386-4664 100 Centre St., N.Y.C. 10013

(845) 638-5355 **Weiner, Alfred J.** (Justice Sup Ct 9th Jud Dist) Cthse., 1 S. Main St., New City 10956; **Fax:** (845) 638-5834; **E-mail:** aweiner@courts.state.ny.us

(718) 298-1100 **Weinstein, Jeremy S.** (Admin J Sup Ct 11th Jud Dist Civil Term) 88-11 Sutphin Blvd., Jamaica 11435; **Fax:** (718) 298-1099; **E-mail:** jweinste@courts.state.ny.us

(347) 401-9870 **Weinstein, Stewart H.** (J Family Ct of NYC) 330 Jay St., Bklyn. 11201; **Fax:** (347) 401-9900

(718) 298-1184 **Weiss, Allan B.** (Justice Sup Ct 11th Jud Dist) 88-11 Sutphin Blvd., Jamaica 11435; **E-mail:** aweiss@courts.state.ny.us

(718) 466-3151 **Weissman, Steven** (J Civil Ct of NYC Housing Part) Housing Ct., 1118 Grand Concourse, Bronx 10456

(646) 386-5622 **Wendt, Peter M.** (J Civil Ct of NYC Housing Part) 111 Centre St., Rm. 1240, N.Y.C. 10013; **Fax:** (212) 374-5709; **E-mail:** pwendt@courts.state.ny.us

(347) 296-1480 **Weston, Michelle** (Justice Sup Ct 2nd Jud Dist & Assoc Justice Sup Ct App Term 2nd 11th & 13th Jud Dists) 360 Adams St., Bklyn. 11201; **Fax:** (718) 643-7325; **E-mail:** mweston@courts.state.ny.us

(716) 845-2750 **Whalen, Gerald J.** (Justice Sup Ct 8th Jud Dist) Erie Cty. Ct. Bldg., 4th Fl., 25 Delaware Ave., Buffalo 14202; **Fax:** (716) 851-3221

(631) 853-4935 **Whelan, Theresa** (J Suffolk Cty Family Ct) John P. Cohalan, Jr. Ct. Complex, 400 Carleton Ave., Central Islip 11722; **Fax:** (631) 853-7629

(631) 852-2365 **Whelan, Thomas F.** (Justice Sup Ct 10th Jud Dist) Supreme Ct. Bldg., Rm. A-258, 1 Court St., Riverhead 11901; **Fax:** (631) 852-1961

(646) 386-3970 **White, Renee Allyn** (J Crim Ct of NYC & Acting Justice Sup Ct 1st Jud Dist) 100 Centre St., N.Y.C. 10013

(646) 386-4655 **Whiten, Marc J.** (J Crim Ct of NYC) 100 Centre St., N.Y.C. 10013

(585) 243-7088 **Wiggins, Robert B.** (J Livingston Cty Ct Family Ct & Surro) Cthse., 2 Court St., Geneseo 14454-1030; **Fax:** (585) 243-7067

(646) 386-4433 **Wiley, Maxwell** (Ct of Claims & Acting Justice Sup Ct 1st Jud Dist) 100 Centre St., Rm. 1734, N.Y.C. 10013

(646) 386-3813 **Wilkins, Lottie E.** (Justice Sup Ct 1st Jud Dist) 71 Thomas St., Rm. 106, N.Y.C. 10013; **Fax:** (212) 374-8417

(347) 404-9472 **Williams, Betty J.** (J Civil Ct of NYC & Acting Justice Sup Ct 2nd Jud Dist) 120 Schermerhorn St., Bklyn. 11201; **Fax:** (718) 643-7733

(845) 340-3730 **Williams, Donald A., Jr.** (J Ulster Cty Ct) Cthse., 285 Wall St., Kingston 12401-0906; **Fax:** (845) 340-3739

(518) 581-9454 **Williams, Frank B.** (Justice Sup Ct 4th Jud Dist) Supreme Ct. Chambers, Suite 201, 433 Broadway, Saratoga Springs 12866; **Fax:** (518) 581-9458

(347) 404-9133 **Williams, Jacqueline D.** (J Civil Ct of NYC) 141 Livingston St., Bklyn. 11201

(718) 618-1467 **Williams, Patricia Anne** (J Crim Ct of NYC & Acting Justice Sup Ct 12th Jud Dist Crim Term) 851 Grand Concourse, Bronx 10451; **Fax:** (718) 618-3575

(315) 337-6440 **Wilson, Daniel C.** (J Rome City Ct) Justice Center, 100 W. Court St., Rome 13440; **Fax:** (315) 338-0343

(347) 404-9464 **Wilson, John H.** (J Civil Ct of NYC assigned to Crim Ct) 120 Schermerhorn St., Bklyn. 11201; **Fax:** (718) 643-7733

(516) 571-2480 **Winslow, F. Dana** (Justice Sup Ct 10th Jud Dist) Supreme Ct. Bldg., 100 Supreme Ct. Dr., Mineola 11501; **Fax:** (516) 571-0213

(585) 428-1891 **Winslow, Joanne M.** (Justice Sup Ct 7th Jud Dist) 545 Hall of Justice, 99 Exchange Blvd., Rochester 14614-2184; **Fax:** (585) 428-1889

(845) 858-4034 **Witherow, Matthew D.** (J Port Jervis City Ct) 20 Hammond St., Port Jervis 12771-2495; **Fax:** (845) 858-9883

(646) 386-4427 **Wittner, Bonnie G.** (J Crim Ct of NYC & Acting Justice Sup Ct 1st Jud Dist) 100 Centre St., N.Y.C. 10013; **E-mail:** bwittner@courts.state.ny.us

(718) 675-8800 **Wolff, Karen** (J Family Ct of NYC) 100 Richmond Terr., Staten Island 10301; **Fax:** (718) 390-5247

(716) 845-9363 **Wolfgang, Penny M.** (Justice Sup Ct 8th Jud Dist) Erie Cty. Ct. Bldg., 4th Fl., 25 Delaware Ave., Buffalo 14202; **Fax:** (716) 851-3331; **E-mail:** pwolfgan@courts.state.ny.us

(585) 428-4483 **Wolford, Kelly C.** (J Monroe Cty Ct & Acting J Monroe Cty Family Ct) Hall of Justice, 3rd Fl., 99 Exchange Blvd., Rochester 14614-2187; **Fax:** (585) 428-4482

(718) 298-1408 **Wong, Douglas S.** (J Crim Ct of NYC & Acting Justice Sup Ct 11th Jud Dist) 125-01 Queens Blvd., Kew Gardens 11415

(845) 486-6444 **Wood, Charles D.** (Justice Sup Ct 9th Jud Dist) Cthse., 10 Market St., Poughkeepsie 12601

(516) 571-2736 **Woodard, Michele M.** (Justice Sup Ct 10th Jud Dist) Supreme Ct. Bldg., 100 Supreme Ct. Dr., Mineola 11501; **Fax:** (516) 571-2170

(845) 291-7640 **Woods, Lori J. Currier** (J Orange Cty Family Ct) Orange Cty. Cthse., 285 Main St., Goshen 10924; **Fax:** (845) 291-7666

(646) 386-3604 **Wooten, Paul** (Justice Sup Ct 1st Jud Dist) 80 Centre St., Rm. 128, N.Y.C. 10013

(845) 340-3348 **Work, Mary M.** (Ulster Cty Surro) 244 Fair St., P.O. Box 1800, Kingston 12402-1800; **Fax:** (845) 340-3352

(718) 618-1432 **Wright, Geoffrey D.** (J Civil Ct of NYC & Acting Justice Sup Ct 12th Jud Dist Civil Term) 851 Grand Concourse, Bronx 10451; **Fax:** (718) 618-3511; **E-mail:** gdwright@courts.state.ny.us

(585) 428-1984 **Yacknin, Ellen M.** (J Rochester City Ct) 6 Hall of Justice, 99 Exchange Blvd., Rochester 14614; **Fax:** (585) 428-4386; **E-mail:** eyacknin@courts.state.ny.us

(646) 386-3985 **Yates, James A.** (Justice Sup Ct 1st Jud Dist) 100 Centre St., Rm. 1724, N.Y.C. 10013; **Fax:** (212) 374-0607; **E-mail:** jyates@courts.state.ny.us

(646) 386-4682 **Yavinsky, Michael** (J Crim Ct of NYC) 100 Centre St., N.Y.C. 10013

(718) 618-1034 **Yearwood, Alvin M.** (J Crim Ct of NYC & Acting Justice Sup Ct 12th Jud Dist Crim Term) Bronx Hall of Justice, 265 E. 161st St., Bronx 10451; **Fax:** (718) 618-3584; **E-mail:** ayearwood@courts.state.ny.us

(646) 386-3810 **York, Louis B.** (Justice Sup Ct 1st Jud Dist) 71 Thomas St., Rm. 207, N.Y.C. 10013

(315) 428-3215 **Young, Kevin G.** (Justice Sup Ct 5th Jud Dist) State Office Bldg., 8th Fl., 333 E. Washington St., Syracuse 13202; **E-mail:** kyoung@courts.state.ny.us

(914) 824-5439 **Zambelli, Barbara Gunther** (J Westchester Cty Ct & Acting Justice Sup Ct 9th Jud Dist) Richard J. Daronco Cthse., 111 Dr. Martin Luther King, Jr. Blvd., White Plains 10601; **Fax:** (914) 995-8653

(718) 298-0926 **Zaro, Stephanie** (J Crim Ct of NYC) 125-01 Queens Blvd., Kew Gardens 11415; **Fax:** (718) 520-4712

(718) 298-0924 **Zayas, Joseph** (J Crim Ct of NYC) 125-01 Queens Blvd., Kew Gardens 11415; **Fax:** (718) 520-4712

(516) 571-9005 **Zimmerman, Hope S.** (Supv J Nassau Cty Family Ct & Acting Justice Sup Ct 10th Jud Dist) Matrimonial Center, 400 County Seat Dr., Mineola 11501; **Fax:** (516) 571-9201

(518) 285-6170 **Zwack, Henry F.** (J Ct of Claims & Acting Justice Sup Ct 3rd Jud Dist) County Cthse., 3rd Fl., 80 Second St., Troy 12180

(646) 386-3987 **Zweibel, Ronald** (Ct of Claims & Acting Justice Sup Ct 1st Jud Dist) 100 Centre St., Rm. 1731, N.Y.C. 10013; **Fax:** (212) 748-5920

This NEW YORK Bar Directory
is kept up to date all year long.

If changes occur in your listing during the year,
please do not wait to notify us.

Contact us as soon as you know about a change in your listing.

NEW YORK LAWYERS DIARY AND MANUAL®

Attn: Mary Lurie
P.O. Box 50
Newark, New Jersey 07101-0050

(800) 444-4041, Ext. 131
Fax (973) 621-9027

E-mail: mlurie@lawdiary.com
Internet: www.lawdiary.com

2011
NEW YORK BAR DIRECTORY
ALPHABETICALLY ARRANGED

Explanatory Note: The date immediately following the name denotes the year of admission to the New York Bar. The "%" indicates the attorney is an associate/employee of the law firm. Parentheses around a firm name indicates a partner/shareholder/owner/officer/member/principal/responsible party of the firm.

Every effort has been made to insure accuracy. In cases where communications have elicited no response, existing addresses have been retained without comment.

This list includes information updated through August 1, 2010.

(917) 551-1300 .. **Aab,** Raymond J '78 OfCnsl Koehler & I LLP -61 Bway -NY 10006
(212) 225-2000 .. **Aaker,** Jos W '08 %Cleary GS&H -1 Lbrty Plz -NY 10006
(212) 446-4800 .. **Aandahl,** Soren W '10 %Kirkland & E LLP -153 E 53rd -NY 10022
(607) 778-2685 .. **Aaron,** Albert '87 Dept Soc Srvcs -36-42 Main -Bnghmtn 13905 **Fx:**778-2710
(718) 258-4774 .. **Aaron,** Allie '01 A Hertz,PC -934 E 19th -Brklyn 11230 **Fx:**258-4994
(516) 829-6959 .. **Aaron,** Andrew L '87 -27 Shorewood Dr -Pt Wash 11050
(212) 972-1000 .. **Aaron,** Clifford B '84 (London F LLP) -59 Maiden Ln -NY 10038
(845) 639-7800 .. **Aaron,** Colin J '97 SpclCnsl Mandel K&B,LLP -210 Route 303 -Vly Cottage 10989
(212) 684-4466 .. **Aaron,** Danl J '86 (D Aaron,PC) -437 Mad Av -NY 10022 **Fx:**684-5566
(716) 854-3015 .. **Aaron Dautch Sternberg & Lawson,LLP** -43 Court -Buffalo 14202 **Fx:**854-1716
(212) 537-2260 .. **Aaron,** Debra M '77 Morgan Stanley -1633 Bway -NY 10019
(516) 802-4140 .. **Aaron,** Fredric H '90 (F Aaron,PC) -14 Vanderventer Av -Pt Wash 11050 **Fx:**802-3807
(212) 848-4000 .. **Aaron,** Jaculin T '85 (Shearman & S LLP) -599 Lex Av -NY 10022
(212) 744-3300 .. **Aaron,** Jeffrey I '74 Larstrand Corp -22 E 65th -NY 10065
(212) 323-0474 .. **Aaron,** Lizbeth C '00 OppenheimerFunds,Inc -225 Lbrty -NY 10281
(516) 489-5000 .. **Aaron,** Merik R '94 %Town Atty -Town Hall -Hempstd 11550 **Fx:**489-5150
(212) 232-2500 .. **Aaron,** Mitchell K '83 (Torgan & C,PC) -17 State -NY 10004
(212) 735-3000 .. **Aaron,** Roger S '69 (Skadden ASM&F LLP) -4 Times Sq -NY 10036
(718) 298-7051 .. **Aaron,** Sherry E '71 Envrnmntl Cntrl Brd -144-06 94th Av -Jamaica 11435
(212) 715-1000 .. **Aaron,** Stewart D '84 (Arnold & P LLP) -399 Park Av -NY 10022
(212) 530-5000 .. **Aaron,** Wayne M '96 (Milbank TH&M LLP) -1 Chase Manh Plz -NY 10005
(718) 250-2000 .. **Aarons,** Judith C '04 %DA -350 Jay -Brklyn 11201 **Fx:**250-2314
(212) 751-1212 .. **Aarons,** Mark M '80 %Modells -498 7th Av -NY 10018
(212) 733-7950 .. **Aaronson,** Eric L '96 %Pfizer Inc -235 E 42nd -NY 10017
(212) 756-3152 .. **Aaronson,** Marc A '77 1st Manhattan Co -437 Mad Av -NY 10022 **Fx:**223-3185
(212) 593-6700 .. **Aaronson,** Mark J '70 (Aaronson RF&D,LLP) -757 3rd Av -NY 10017
(212) 704-6000 .. **Aaronson,** Matthew J '01 (Troutman S LLP) -405 Lex Av -NY 10174
(212) 331-5131 .. **Aaronson,** Nicola R '06 NYC Human Resources Admin Ofc -180 Water -NY 10038 **Fx:**331-4465
(212) 593-6700 .. **Aaronson Rappaport Feinstein & Deutsch,LLP** -757 3rd Av -NY 10017 **Fx:**593-6970
(516) 466-1700 .. **Aaronson,** Stacey Rebecca '00 %Day & Assoc,PC -11 Grace Av -Gt Neck 11021 **Fx:**466-7736
(212) 450-4000 .. **Aaronson,** Wm H '96 (Davis P&W LLP) -450 Lex Av -NY 10017
(607) 257-3540 .. **Aasen,** Nina C '94 -Bx3832 -Ithaca 14852
(716) 840-7901 .. **Aavik,** Karen M '00 %M&T Bank -465 Main -Buffalo 14203
(212) 714-2277 .. **Abad,** Leopoldo A '94 (Abad C&M,LLC) -350 5th Av -NY 10118 **Fx:**714-9331
(646) 394-3371 .. **Abad,** Luis A '98 %PricewaterhouseCoopers LLP -300 Mad Av -NY 10017
(347) 401-9047 .. **Abadi,** Gina Levy '02 %Supreme Ct -360 Adams -Brklyn 11201
(212) 310-8000 .. **Abadi,** Jos A '08 %Weil G&M LLP -767 5th Av -NY 10153
(212) 561-7700 .. **Abadir,** David A '08 %Pachulski SZ&J -780 3rd Av -NY 10017
(845) 359-7700 .. **Abadir,** Nader A '05 %Notaro M&Z PC -100 Dutch Hill Rd -Orangebrg 10962
(212) 763-5000 .. **Abady,** Jonathan S '91 (Emery CB&A LLP) -75 Rckfllr Plz -NY 10019
(718) 222-0043 .. **Abakporo,** I Eric '90 -60 4th Av -Brklyn 11217 **Fx:**222-0341
(516) 229-6000 .. **Abamont,** Brian A '02 %R Lau & Assoc -300 Jericho Quad Bx9040 -Jericho 11753 **Fx:**229-6167
(516) 742-8058 .. **Abamont,** Joyce Onorato '89 Abamont & Assoc -200 Grdn City Plz Bx9250 -Gdn Cty 11530 **Fx:**742-7308
(718) 779-6961 .. **Abarca,** Susana T '02 %Pena & K,PLLC -88-19 Roosevelt Av -Jcksn Hts 11372 **Fx:**779-6865
(212) 940-3705 .. **Abascal Sherwell,** Manuel '06 %Nixon P LLP -437 Mad Av -NY 10022
(212) 779-1414 .. **Abate,** Amy L '06 %Bernstein L LLP -10 E 40th -NY 10016
(718) 838-7878 .. **Abate,** Camille M '83 Bronx Defenders -860 Crtlandt Av -Bronx 10451 **Fx:**665-0100
(212) 366-4500 .. **Abate,** Catherine M '73 Cmty Hlthcare Ntwrk -79 Mad Av -NY 10016
(716) 662-4250 .. **Abate,** Jeffrey J '89 -4214 N Buffalo Rd -Orchard Pk 14127 **Fx:**662-9179
(845) 894-4633 .. **Abate,** Jos P '81 IBM -2070 Route 52 -Hopewell Junct 12533 **Fx:**892-6363
(212) 632-3367 .. **Abate,** M Katherine '98 Fiduciary Trust Co -600 5th Av -NY 10020
(212) 813-8800 .. **Abate,** Mark J '89 (Goodwin P LLP) -620 8th Av -NY 10018
(212) 779-0057 .. **Abate,** Philip S '01 %Hach & R,LLP -185 Mad Av -NY 10016
(212) 808-2700 .. **Abate,** Saml J Jr. '82 (Pepper H LLP) -620 8th Av -NY 10018
(212) 262-2390 .. **Abatemarco,** Christopher '05 %Connell F LLP -888 7th Av -NY 10106
(646) 837-0100 .. **Abatemarco,** David P '93 (Wenick & F,PC) -28 E 28th -NY 10016
(516) 741-9225 .. **Abatemarco,** Michl J '82 -46 Wellngtn Rd -Gdn Cty 11530 **Fx:**741-1624
(212) 490-3000 .. **Abatemarco,** Tracy J '92 (Wilson EME&D LLP) -150 E 42nd -NY 10017
(212) 558-5500 .. **Abato,** Anthony S '09 Weitz & L,PC -700 Bway -NY 10003
(718) 769-4021 .. **Abato,** Maureen A '85 -2732 E 21st -Brklyn 11235 **Fx:**769-8869
(646) 472-4000 .. **Abatzis,** Alice S '03 CNET Networks -28 E 28th -NY 10016
(914) 948-5550 .. **Abbagnaro,** Maria A '04 SrCnsl Cordia Corp -445 Hmltn Av -White Plns 10601
(212) 779-9800 .. **Abbamonte,** Lauren M '03 %Luboja & T,LLP -10 E 40th -NY 10016
(716) 852-1380 .. **Abbarno,** Anthony D '71 (Abbarno M&K) -314 Brisbane Bldg -Buffalo 14203
(716) 852-1380 .. **Abbarno McLaughlin & Kedzielawa** -314 Brisbane Bldg -Buffalo 14203
(718) 322-1525 .. **Abbasi,** Khalid Omair '05 -127-18 Lbrty Av -S Richmond Hll 11419 **Fx:**322-1101
(212) 259-8000 .. **Abbassi,** Rajab S '05 %Dewey & L LLP -1301 Av of Amer -NY 10019
(212) 227-8150 .. **Abbate,** Emanuel F '59 OfCnsl Treacy SM&M -111 Bway -NY 10006
(516) 542-1000 .. **Abbate,** John J '77 (Geisler & G,LLP) -100 Q Roosevelt Blvd -Gdn Cty 11530
(631) 586-0686 .. **Abbate,** Mary-Elizabeth '74 -1476 Deer Prk Av -N Babylon 11703 **Fx:**595-1072
(914) 423-1568 .. **Abbate,** Richd S '93 -297 Knollwood Rd -White Plns 10607 **Fx:**358-5728
(716) 881-4256 .. **Abbate,** Salvatore P '80 -215 Brcknrdg -Buffalo 14213 **Fx:**881-4256
(516) 496-0700 .. **Abbate,** Thos A '85 -100 Crsswys Park Dr W -Woodbury 11797
(585) 428-5210 .. **Abbatoy,** David M '04 Pub Def -10 N Fitzhugh -Rchstr 14614 **Fx:**428-2234
(212) 825-3348 .. **Abbenda,** Christine R '95 Dept of Bldgs Spcl Invstgtn Unit -83 Maiden Ln -NY 10038
(516) 674-4721 .. **Abbenda,** Jos P '76 -4 Nrthfld Rd -Glen Cove 11542
(212) 788-4694 .. **Abbene,** Norma C '90 Mayors Ofc -City Hall -NY 10007
(516) 227-7779 .. **Abberbock,** Ellen '88 %Dept Soc Srvcs -60 Chas Lindbergh Blvd -Uniondale 11553
(212) 889-3700 .. **Abbey,** Arthur N '59 (Abbey SR&A LLP) -212 E 39th -NY 10016
(212) 697-6262 .. **Abbey,** Maureen V '06 %Ward & O -380 Mad Av -NY 10017
(212) 889-3700 .. **Abbey Spanier Rodd & Abrams LLP** -212 E 39th -NY 10016 **Fx:**684-5191
(518) 486-7082 .. **Abbitt,** Viola I '92 %OCFS -52 Wshngtn -Rensselaer 12144 **Fx:**486-6361
(212) 610-6300 .. **Abbondante,** Thos D '89 (Allen & O) -1221 Av of Amer -NY 10020
(212) 696-5500 .. **Abbondola,** Victor A '84 -112 Mad Av -NY 10016
(516) 942-0244 .. **Abbondondelo,** Mary C '89 %Office oDA&R -375 N Bway -Jericho 11753 **Fx:**942-0353
(212) 981-4501 .. **Abbot,** Edw P '86 (Smith A,LLP) -90 Broad -NY 10004
(718) 286-6000 .. **Abbot,** Ellen C '87 %DA -125-01 Qns Blvd -Kew Gdns 11415
(212) 513-3200 .. **Abbott,** Allison N '01 %Holland & K LLP -31 W 52nd -NY 10019
(212) 832-3939 .. **Abbott,** Barry R '79 (R Felder & Prtnrs,PC) -437 Mad Av -NY 10022 **Fx:**838-1103
(718) 366-0464 .. **Abbott Bushlow & Schechner,LLP** -70-11 Fresh Pond Rd -Rdgwd 11385 **Fx:**366-4119
(631) 231-1199 .. **Abbott,** Christopher B '05 %Reynolds CGHL&Q,LLP -35 Arkay Dr -Hauppauge 11788
(516) 775-6800 .. **Abbott,** Courtney C '09 %CK Verkowitz -561 Lakevll Rd -New Hyde Pk 11040 **Fx:**775-0641
(212) 574-1200 .. **Abbott,** James E '85 (Seward & K LLP) -1 Bttry Pk Plz -NY 10004
(585) 546-5270 .. **Abbott,** Jason E '00 %Fitzsimmons NF&P,LLP -16 E Main -Rchstr 14614
(212) 574-1200 .. **Abbott,** Kathleen P '06 %Seward & K LLP -1 Bttry Pk Plz -NY 10004
(516) 222-1300 .. **Abbott,** Marc '78 (Abbott R&A,PC) -90 Merrick Av -E Meadow 11554
(518) 867-3001 .. **Abbott,** Marnie M '03 %Sciocchetti & Assoc,PLLC -12 Century Hill Dr -Latham 12110 **Fx:**867-3017
(212) 373-3000 .. **Abbott,** Matthew W '99 (Paul WRW&G LLP) -1285 Av of Amer -NY 10019
(607) 723-9511 .. **Abbott,** Rachel A '06 %Coughlin & G,LLP -19 Chenango Bx2039 -Bnghmtn 13902
(212) 449-6888 .. **Abbott,** Raymond T '85 Merrill Lynch -4 World Fncl Ctr -NY 10080
(516) 222-1300 .. **Abbott Reiss & Allen, PC** -90 Merrick Av -E Meadow 11554 **Fx:**222-1311
(716) 873-6765 .. **Abbott,** Richd G '81 (Pusatier S&A) -2464 Elmwood Av -Kenmore 14217
(716) 649-6700 .. **Abbott Tills & Knapp,LLP** -44 Union -Hambrg 14075 **Fx:**649-2264
(212) 351-4000 .. **Abbott,** Timothy C '09 %Gibson D&C LLP -200 Park Av -NY 10166
(585) 530-3100 .. **Abbott Hill,** Courtney A '10 %Appllt Div 4th Dept -50 East Av Ste 200 -Rchstr 14604 **Fx:**530-3247
(914) 422-6111 .. **Abbruzzese,** Michl '08 White Plains Police Dept -77 S Lex Av -White Plns 10601
(585) 428-5210 .. **Abdallah,** Wedade W '04 Pub Def -10 N Fitzhugh -Rchstr 14614 **Fx:**428-2234
(718) 250-2000 .. **Abdelhadi,** Nada '01 %DA -350 Jay -Brklyn 11201 **Fx:**250-2314

(212) 468-8000 .. **Abdelhamid,** Reema S '03 %Morrison & F LLP -1290 Av of Amer -NY 10104
(518) 725-9717 .. **Abdella,** George E '69 -8 W Fulton Bx673 -Gloversvll 12078 **Fx:**725-1910
(716) 483-6090 .. **Abdella,** H James '60 (Abdella & A) -901-903 Htl Jmstwn Ofc Bldg Bx3006 -Jamestwn 14702 **Fx:**483-3023
(585) 232-6500 .. **Abdella,** Peter H '88 (Harter S&E LLP) -1600 Bausch & Lomb Pl -Rchstr 14604
(518) 725-9717 .. **Abdella,** Robt E '01 -8 W Fulton Bx673 -Gloversvll 12078 **Fx:**725-1910
(716) 753-4247 .. **Abdella,** Stephen M '86 Cnty Atty -3 N Erie -Mayvll 14757 **Fx:**753-4129
(716) 483-6090 .. **Abdella,** Stephen M '86 (Abdella & A) -901-903 Htl Jmstwn Ofc Bldg Bx3006 -Jamestwn 14702 **Fx:**483-3023
(646) 252-2982 .. **Abdelrahman,** Aliaa Ezzat '02 %Transit Auth -2 Bway -NY 10004 **Fx:**252-5559
(212) 231-0009 .. **Abderrashmán,** Soraya Ruiz '04 SR Abderrashman,PC -648 Bway -NY 10012 **Fx:**231-1087
(516) 571-3800 .. **Abdi,** Zeena J '02 %DA -262 Old Cntry Rd -Mineola 11501 **Fx:**248-9479
(212) 974-7474 .. **Abdi,** Zehra J '06 %Cowan DA&S LLP -41 Mad Av -NY 10010
(212) 549-2517 .. **Abdo,** Alexander A '09 ACLU -125 Broad -NY 10004
(315) 461-4277 .. **Abdo,** Alexander J '04 %Falge & M,PC -3300 Vickery Rd -N Syracuse 13212
(212) 504-6000 .. **Abdo,** Michl N '04 %Cadwalader W&T LLP -1 World Fncl Ctr -NY 10281
(646) 435-0668 .. **Abdul Jaami,** Saboor H '03 -410 Park Av -NY 10022
(716) 566-1300 .. **Abdulla,** Karim A '00 %Hiscock & B,LLP -1100 M&T Ctr -Buffalo 14203
(212) 937-7247 .. **Abdullah,** Sadaf R '10 %WilmerHale -399 Park Av -NY 10022
(212) 983-1320 .. **Abdurrahim,** Salama '09 %Atadika & A -60 E 42nd -NY 10165 **Fx:**983-9167
(212) 275-7896 .. **Abedin,** Shahreen A '07 CNN Med News Unit -1 Time Warner Ctr -NY 10019
(716) 849-3500 .. **Abeel,** John E '06 %Hagelin & K LLC -135 Delaware Av -Buffalo 14202 **Fx:**849-3501
(212) 323-7070 .. **Abeel,** Timothy J '89 (Rawle & H LLP) -14 Wall -NY 10005
(845) 634-4700 .. **Abel & Brustein-Kampel,PC** -37 Congers Rd -New Cty 10956 **Fx:**634-1675
(212) 216-8000 .. **Abel,** Ira R '82 %Tarter K&D LLP -1350 Bway -NY 10018
(212) 998-6737 .. **Abel,** Laura Klein '95 Brennan Ctr for Justice -161 Av of Amer -NY 10013 **Fx:**995-4550
(212) 548-0131 .. **Abel,** Laura R '03 Open Society Inst -400 W 59th -NY 10019 **Fx:**548-4665
(212) 732-6460 .. **Abel,** Michl R '07 %Schwartz & S,PC -225 Bway -NY 10007
(212) 412-1442 .. **Abel,** Rebecca Gretchen '07 Barclays Cptl Inc -200 Park Av -NY 10166
(212) 403-6700 .. **Abel,** Robt W '07 %Gide LN LLP -120 W 45th -NY 10036
(315) 478-0560 .. **Abel,** Ryan L '04 %F Bersani Jr -224 Harrison -Syracuse 13202
(845) 634-4700 .. **Abel,** Steven L '73 (Abel & B-K,PC) -37 Congers Rd -New Cty 10956
(914) 703-6300 .. **Abele,** Leslie G '84 %Pillinger MT,LLP -570 Taxter Rd -Elmsfrd 10523
(212) 416-8870 .. **Abeles,** Michele L '92 %Dept of Law -120 Bway -NY 10271 **Fx:**416-8393
(212) 896-6500 .. **Abeles,** Sarah D '00 %Howrey LLP -601 Lex Av -NY 10022
(212) 415-9200 .. **Abelev,** Gary '96 (Dorsey & W LLP) -250 Park Av -NY 10177
(212) 732-5800 .. **Abelli,** Alicia '07 %Friedman & M LLP -233 Bway -NY 10279
(212) 949-9022 .. **Abelman Frayne & Schwab** -666 3rd Av -NY 10017 **Fx:**949-9190
(212) 949-9022 .. **Abelman,** Julianne '88 (Abelman F&S) -666 3rd Av -NY 10017
(212) 949-9022 .. **Abelman,** Lawr E '62 (Abelman F&S) -666 3rd Av -NY 10017
(212) 417-4357 .. **Abeloff,** Dianne '81 %Dept of Health -90 Church -NY 10007 **Fx:**417-4392
(315) 724-8102 .. **Abelove,** C Louis '65 -2110 Genesee Bx8010 -Utica 13505 **Fx:**724-8481
(516) 222-7000 .. **Abelove,** Jason L '97 -666 Old Cntry Rd -Gdn Cty 11530 **Fx:**228-8349
(518) 473-4282 .. **Abelove,** Joel E '95 Dept of Health -Corning Twr 24th Fl -Albany 12237 **Fx:**473-2430
(212) 497-4265 .. **Abelow,** Justin D '96 Houlihan Lokey Howard & Zukin -245 Park -NY 10167
(212) 655-3548 .. **Abelow,** Ross M '90 (Abelow & C LLP) -140 E 45th -NY 10017 **Fx:**655-3591
(516) 932-0068 .. **Abelow,** Ross M '90 (Abelow & C LLP) -410 Jericho Tpk -Jericho 11753 **Fx:**932-0072
(845) 279-5555 .. **Abels,** Stephen A '76 -154 Main -Brewstr 10509 **Fx:**278-6101
(212) 791-7805 .. **Abels,** Wendy S '00 %SPCC -161 William -NY 10038 **Fx:**791-2821
(585) 295-4400 .. **Abelson,** Gary H '76 (Hiscock & B,LLP) -2000 HSBC Plz -Rchstr 14604
(212) 259-8000 .. **Abelson,** Philip M '03 (Dewey & L LLP) -1301 Av of Amer -NY 10019
(315) 735-5050 .. **Abend,** Richd A '60 Staffworks -600 French Rd -New Hartfrd 13413 **Fx:**735-1113
(212) 532-7575 .. **Abend,** Richd H '03 (Abend & S,PLLC) -440 Park Av S -NY 10016 **Fx:**532-8180
(212) 849-7000 .. **Abensohn,** Adam M '95 (Quinn EU&S,LLP) -51 Mad Av -NY 10010
(212) 637-3224 .. **Aber,** Bruce H '90 %EPA -290 Bway -NY 10007 **Fx:**637-3096
(212) 272-2539 .. **Aber,** Cara E '94 %JP Morgan Chase -383 Mad Av -NY 10179
(212) 545-4720 .. **Aber,** M Joshua '55 OfCnsl Wolf HAF&H LLP -270 Mad Av -NY 10016
(212) 458-1498 .. **Aberasturi,** John A '96 AIG -175 Water -NY 10038
(845) 294-2852 .. **Aberasturi,** Mark G '89 -30 Matthews Bx176 -Goshen 10924 **Fx:**294-9102
(914) 908-5011 .. **Aberbach-Marolda,** Susanne '04 -30 Pocantico Rvr Rd -Plsntvll 10570
(212) 410-9777 .. **Aber-Cohen,** Lise '75 -49 E 86th -NY 10028
(212) 371-4500 .. **Abercrombie,** Chas D '78 (Seiff K&A) -444 Mad Av -NY 10022
(516) 759-7940 .. **Aberle,** Joi '99 %Genoa & Assoc,PC -12 Jaegger Dr -Old Brookvll 11545 **Fx:**674-9425
(516) 873-3040 .. **Aberle,** Richd M '88 (Kaston & A) -259 Mineola Blvd -Mineola 11501 **Fx:**873-5166
(212) 318-3000 .. **Abernethy,** Jonathan S '97 SrCnsl Fulbright & J LLP -666 5th Av -NY 10103
(212) 669-4531 .. **Abernethy,** Joyce A '97 %Comptroller -1 Centre -NY 10007 **Fx:**669-2884
(212) 545-1900 .. **Abernethy,** Saml F '75 (Menaker & H LLP) -10 E 40th -NY 10016
(718) 855-9000 .. **Abernethy,** Thos J '94 %Cullen and D LLP -177 Montague -Brklyn 11201
(516) 229-2360 .. **Abeshouse,** David J '83 -626 RXR Plz -Uniondale 11556 **Fx:**229-2361
(212) 545-4000 .. **Abeysekera,** Samantha K '03 %Jackson L LLP -666 3rd Av -NY 10017
(212) 269-7979 .. **Abilheira,** Elias '95 (Abilheira & Assoc,PC) -110 Wall -NY 10005 **Fx:** 269-7373
(646) 252-3239 .. **Abili,** John C '98 Cnsl MTA Captl Cnstrctn -2 Bway -NY 10004
(914) 253-4949 .. **Abinanti,** Jos P '74 -800 Wstchstr Av -Rye Brook 10573 **Fx:**696-0450
(914) 231-2700 .. **Abinanti,** Lauren R '08 %DA -104 S Bway -Ynkrs 10701 **Fx:**969-0574
(914) 328-9000 .. **Abinanti,** Thos J '75 -61 Kathwood Rd -White Plns 10607 **Fx:**328-9000
(845) 225-3641 .. **Abissi,** Heather M '07 %DA -40 Gleneida Av -Carmel 10512
(914) 328-0404 .. **Abitabilo,** Michl L '08 %Jackson L LLP -1 N Bway -White Plns 10601
(315) 706-0159 .. **Abitbol,** Gilles R '03 -121 Green Acres Dr -Liverpool 13090
(212) 806-5400 .. **Abitbol,** Sarah J '07 %Stroock &S&L LLP -180 Maiden Ln -NY 10038
(631) 321-8500 .. **Abiuso,** Robt A '96 -241-35 N Conduit Av -Rosedale 11422 **Fx:**321-8591
(212) 504-6000 .. **Ableman,** Mark D '07 %Cadwalader W&T LLP -1 World Fncl Ctr -NY 10281
(716) 884-2000 .. **Ables,** Jos A Jr. '80 %Doran & M -1234 Delaware Av -Buffalo 14209
(212) 836-8000 .. **Ablovatskiy,** Aleksander B O '05 %Kaye S LLP -425 Park Av -NY 10022
(516) 229-6000 .. **Abneri,** Michl D '91 %R Lau & Assoc -300 Jericho Quad Bx9040 -Jericho 11753 **Fx:**229-6167
(718) 590-2000 .. **Abodeely,** Cassandra M '05 %DA -198 E 161st -Bronx 10451 **Fx:**590-6477
(631) 239-6817 .. **Abola,** Michelle '04 %E Troy -44 Bway -Greenlawn 11740 **Fx:**239-6816
(212) 227-4716 .. **Abolafia,** Glenn R '88 (G Abolafia,PC) -299 Bway -NY 10007
(212) 227-4716 .. **Abolafia,** Leon '58 -299 Bway -NY 10007 **Fx:**227-4717
(212) 858-1000 .. **Abols,** Mara S '08 %Pillsbury WSP LLP -1540 Bway -NY 10036
(212) 558-1055 .. **Aboodi,** Nissim '68 %Questrion Research -150 E 52nd -NY 10022
(212) 504-6000 .. **Aborn,** Richd A '70 (Cadwalader W&T LLP) -1 World Fncl Ctr -NY 10281
(212) 350-2700 .. **Aborn,** Richd M '79 (Constantine C,PC) -450 Lex Av -NY 10017
(212) 688-2525 .. **Aborn,** Sargent L '82 Tams-Witmark Mus Lib -560 Lex Av -NY 10022 **Fx:**688-3232
(212) 684-1422 .. **Aboulafia,** David '98 -60 E 42nd -NY 10165 **Fx:**684-1428
(631) 853-4104 .. **Aboulafia,** Eric S '09 %DA -400 Carleton Av Bx9082 -Central Islip 11722 **Fx:**853-7838
(212) 684-1422 .. **Aboulafia,** Matthew S '86 (Aboulafia Law Firm LLC) -60 E 42nd -NY 10165 **Fx:**684-1428
(212) 705-7000 .. **Abou-Rahme,** Laila '00 (Bingham M LLP) -399 Park Av -NY 10022
(212) 216-8000 .. **Abraham,** Aaron N '96 (Tarter K&D LLP) -1350 Bway -NY 10018
(917) 518-2049 .. **Abraham,** Adrienne '95 -123 Main -White Plns 10601
(212) 693-0085 .. **Abraham,** Andrew E '69 Appellate Advocates -2 Rector -NY 10006 **Fx:**693-0878
(718) 286-6000 .. **Abraham,** Anisha '07 %DA -125-01 Qns Blvd -Kew Gdns 11415
(212) 829-9566 .. **Abraham,** Anthony M '82 -445 Park Av -NY 10022 **Fx:**829-8634
(646) 839-8575 .. **Abraham,** Antonia '09 Betaworks -416 W 13th -NY 10014
(212) 450-4000 .. **Abraham,** Aravindhan I '09 %Davis P&W LLP -450 Lex Av -NY 10017
(212) 504-6000 .. **Abraham,** Arun '09 %Cadwalader W&T LLP -1 World Fncl Ctr -NY 10281
(845) 292-4412 .. **Abraham,** Betsy Nalonnil '06 %Eisenberg & K -25 Darbee Ln Bx715 -Liberty 12754
(212) 297-5800 .. **Abraham,** Chas P '86 SrCnsl Day P LLP -7 Times Sq -NY 10036
(718) 782-3565 .. **Abraham,** Danl E '91 -236 Bway -Brklyn 11211 **Fx:**782-3566
(212) 613-2089 .. **Abraham,** Don '90 Cnsl Gibbons PC -1 Penn Plz -NY 10119 **Fx:**554-9692
(212) 328-6180 .. **Abraham,** Elyce Stuart '87 %CMW Lgl Search -845 3rd Av -NY 10022 **Fx:**328-6181
(212) 279-5050 .. **Abraham Fruchter & Twersky LLP** -1 Penn Plz -NY 10119 **Fx:**279-3655
(315) 471-1664 .. **Abraham,** Iman '07 %Meggesto C&V,LLP -313 E Willow -Syracuse 13203
(718) 848-3165 .. **Abraham,** Irwin D '03 (Abraham & A,LLC) -130-22 Rockaway Blvd -S Ozone Pk 11420 **Fx:**848-3166
(212) 506-1700 .. **Abraham,** Jaime L '10 %Kasowitz BT&F LLP -1633 Bway -NY 10019
(212) 279-5050 .. **Abraham,** Jeffrey S '88 (Abraham F&T LLP) -1 Penn Plz -NY 10119
(212) 686-4655 .. **Abraham,** Jonathan D '97 (Abraham L&A LLP) -292 Mad Av -NY 10017
(212) 336-2000 .. **Abraham,** Jos M '08 %Patterson BW&T LLP -1133 Av of Amer -NY 10036
(914) 993-5000 .. **Abraham,** Karen Miller '93 %Pearson Edu,Inc -10 Bank -White Plns 10606
(212) 236-8711 .. **Abraham,** Karen R '04 Merrill Lynch -2 World Fncl Ctr -NY 10281
(516) 873-6334 .. **Abraham,** Kimberlee C '96 Cnsl Ohrenstein & B,LLP -1010 Franklin Av Bx9243 -Gdn Cty 11530
(718) 848-3165 .. **Abraham,** Lauren F '04 (Abraham & A,LLC) -130-22 Rockaway Blvd -S Ozone Pk 11420 **Fx:**848-3166
(212) 686-4655 .. **Abraham Lerner & Arnold LLP** -292 Mad Av -NY 10017 **Fx:**532-3301
(212) 264-6113 .. **Abraham,** Mary Thottananiyil '03 US DHS/ICE Chief Cnsl Ofc -26 Fed Plz -NY 10278
(212) 333-8921 .. **Abraham,** Nancy '80 %PaineWebber Inc -590 Mad Av -NY 10022
(917) 454-1153 .. **Abraham,** Ricardo '07 Police Dept -2 Lafayette -NY 10007
(212) 298-5248 .. **Abraham,** Richd H '07 %Leg Aid -49 Thomas -NY 10013 **Fx:**298-5252

(212) 490-3000 .. **Abraham,** Scott R '08 %Wilson EME&D LLP -150 E 42nd -NY 10017
(914) 813-5800 .. **Abraham,** Shara J '03 %DA -475 North Av -New Rchll 10801 **Fx:**813-5806
(212) 791-0285 .. **Abraham,** Sharan R '06 %Malaby & B,LLC -150 Bway -NY 10038 **Fx:**791-0286
(631) 549-4677 .. **Abraham,** Shaun P '08 %Sobel K&S,PC -464 NY Av -Huntngtn 11743
(212) 431-2116 .. **Abraham,** Susan J '84 %NY Law Schl -185 W Bway -NY 10013 **Fx:**431-8193
(212) 909-6000 .. **Abraham,** V Mary '89 Cnsl Debevoise & P LLP -919 3rd Av -NY 10022
(212) 408-5100 .. **Abrahams,** Emily '06 %Chadbourne & P LLP -30 Rckfllr Plz -NY 10112
(212) 885-5000 .. **Abrahams,** George N '78 SrCnsl Blank R LLP -405 Lex Av -NY 10174
(718) 262-7376 .. **Abrahams,** Jay M '75 %Civil Ct -89-17 Sutphin Blvd -Jamaica 11435 **Fx:**262-7107
(516) 541-8900 .. **Abrahams,** Richd N '65 (Lederman & A,LLP) -567 Bway -Massapequa 11758
(212) 756-2000 .. **Abrahams,** Robt M '77 (Schulte R&Z LLP) -919 3rd Av -NY 10022
(516) 294-1333 .. **Abrahams,** Sheila M '06 %DeMartini & Y LLP -264 Hillside Av -Williston Pk 11596
(518) 897-1200 .. **Abrahamson,** Dale Scott '93 %DEC -1115 Route 86 Bx296 -Ray Brk 12977 **Fx:**897-1394
(516) 683-1102 .. **Abrahamson,** Jill M '04 Local 1102 -1587 Stewart Av -Westbury 11590
(212) 902-5077 .. **Abram,** Danl B '03 %Goldman Sachs -85 Broad -NY 10004
(212) 563-4100 .. **Abram,** Michl E '74 (Cohen W&S LLP) -330 W 42nd -NY 10036
(212) 709-1658 .. **Abram,** Sam L '71 %Banking Dept -1 State -NY 10004 **Fx:**709-1655
(516) 294-4180 .. **Abramchayeva,** Liliya '05 %Canfield M&R,LLP -1461 Franklin Av -Gdn Cty 11530
(516) 433-4900 .. **Abrami,** Stephen M '03 (SM Abrami PLLC) -500 N Bway -Jericho 11753 **Fx:**433-2314
(212) 319-3900 .. **Abramov,** B Roslyn '86 OfCnsl JE Bachelder LLP -437 Mad Av -NY 10022 **Fx:**319-3070
(212) 454-3794 .. **Abramov,** Igor '03 Deutsche Asset Mgmt -345 Park Av -NY 10154
(212) 617-3244 .. **Abramovich,** Caren E '99 Bloomberg,LP -731 Lex Av -NY 10022
(212) 803-5100 .. **Abramovitz,** Carole S '69 %NY Cnty Defender Srvcs -225 Bway -NY 10007 **Fx:**571-6035
(212) 682-6800 .. **Abramovitz,** David '93 Zetlin & D LLP -801 2nd Av -NY 10017
(212) 486-7005 .. **Abramovitz,** Rafael '79 Watanabe Law Firm,LLC -444 Mad Av -NY 10022 **Fx:**486-6010
(315) 443-1786 .. **Abramovsky,** Aviva '01 Syracuse Univ Cllg of Law -Wht Hall -Syracuse 13244 **Fx:**443-4213
(212) 685-7474 .. **Abramowitz,** Alton L '73 (Mayerson SA LLP) -292 Mad Av -NY 10017
(212) 416-8599 .. **Abramowitz,** Amy L '92 %Dept of Law -120 Bway -NY 10271 **Fx:**416-6075
(212) 489-8230 .. **Abramowitz,** Andrew H '98 (Davis WT LLP) -1633 Bway -NY 10019
(212) 208-3476 .. **Abramowitz,** David N '93 %Ambac Assurance -1 State Street Plz -NY 10004 **Fx:**785-1178
(212) 880-9500 .. **Abramowitz,** Elkan '64 (Morvillo AGIA&B,PC) -565 5th Av -NY 10017
(212) 836-8000 .. **Abramowitz,** Laurie P '88 (Kaye S LLP) -425 Park Av -NY 10022
(212) 692-1000 .. **Abramowitz,** Nathan '76 (Duane M LLP) -1540 Bway -NY 10036
(716) 568-0070 .. **Abramowitz,** Philip B '70 Cnsl Fncl Srvcs -6400 Main -Williamsvll 14221 **Fx:**568-0266
(631) 761-0800 .. **Abramowitz,** Robin S '90 (Lazer AR&Y,PC) -225 Old Cntry Rd -Melvll 11747
(212) 237-0000 .. **Abramowitz,** Steven M '91 (Vinson & E LLP) -666 5th Av -NY 10103
(518) 783-0200 .. **Abrams,** Aileen T '06 NYS Schl Bds Assn -24 Century Hill Dr -Latham 12110
(516) 621-8233 .. **Abrams,** Amy L '94 -Bx329 -Albertson 11507 **Fx:**621-8233
(212) 969-3000 .. **Abrams,** Bertram A '58 (Proskauer R LLP) -1585 Bway -NY 10036
(212) 854-4523 .. **Abrams,** Beryl A '76 %Columbia Univ -535 W 116th 412 Low Mem'l Library -NY 10027
(212) 530-5094 .. **Abrams,** Burt J '59 -1 Chase Manh Plz -NY 10005 **Fx:**530-5219
(212) 243-2681 .. **Abrams,** Carol L '04 C Abrams PC -360 W 21st -NY 10011 **Fx:**243-2639
(212) 335-9177 .. **Abrams,** Clark S '84 %DA -1 Hogan Pl -NY 10013 **Fx:**335-9807
(212) 782-7563 .. **Abrams,** Danal F '90 %Moore Capital Mgmt,Inc -1251 Av of Amer -NY 10020
(212) 664-6922 .. **Abrams,** Danl '93 %NBC -30 Rckfllr Plz -NY 10112
(212) 292-5663 .. **Abrams,** Danl L '96 -2 Penn Plz -NY 10121
(212) 930-9445 .. **Abrams,** Danl S '76 Istar Fincl -1114 Av of Amer -NY 10036
(212) 931-8300 .. **Abrams,** David A '86 (Strongin R&A,LLP) -5 Hanover Sq -NY 10004
(212) 506-1700 .. **Abrams,** David J '91 (Kasowitz BT&F LLP) -1633 Bway -NY 10019
(212) 897-5821 .. **Abrams,** David N '00 -305 Bway -NY 10007 **Fx:**897-5811
(212) 851-9366 .. **Abrams,** Donald L '86 Cardiovascular Rsrch Fndtn -55 E 59th -NY 10022 **Fx:**851-9367
(914) 683-2500 .. **Abrams,** Donna E '87 %Harold SS&S -81 Main -White Plns 10601
(212) 735-3000 .. **Abrams,** Elisia Brooke '06 %Skadden ASM&F LLP -4 Times Sq -NY 10036
(212) 859-8000 .. **Abrams,** Erin H '07 %Fried FHS&J LLP -1 NY Plz -NY 10004
(516) 328-2300 .. **Abrams Fensterman Fensterman Eisman Greenberg Formato & Einiger, LLP** -1111 Marcus Av -Lk Success 11042 **Fx:**328-6638
(212) 279-9200 .. **Abrams Fensterman Fensterman Eisman Greenberg Formato & Einiger, LLP** -630 3rd Av -NY 10017 **Fx:**279-0600
(585) 232-6002 .. **Abrams Fensterman Fensterman Eisman Greenberg Formato & Einiger, LLP** -45 Exchange Blvd -Rchstr 14614 **Fx:**232-6019
(518) 408-1495 .. **Abrams,** Florence E '77 %Dept of Health -Corning Twr 24th Fl -Albany 12237 **Fx:**486-4834
(212) 701-3000 .. **Abrams,** Floyd '61 (Cahill G&R LLP) -80 Pine -NY 10005 **Fx:**269-5420
(212) 695-0270 .. **Abrams,** Franklin S '67 (Abrams & A LLP) -7 Penn Plz -NY 10001 **Fx:**695-0919
(518) 334-6310 .. **Abrams,** Franklin S '97 %N Jain,PC -127 Lncstr -Albany 12210
(516) 739-8730 .. **Abrams,** Fred L '90 -224 7th -Gdn Cty 11530
(212) 201-1170 .. **Abrams Garfinkel Margolis Bergson,LLP** -237 W 35th -NY 10001 **Fx:**201-1171
(516) 794-5310 .. **Abrams Garfinkel Margolis Bergson,LLP** -125 Jericho Tpk -Jericho 11753 **Fx:**794-5311
(516) 336-2005 .. **Abrams Garfinkel Margolis Bergson,LLP** -2-12 W Park Av -Long Bch 11561 **Fx:**336-2009
(718) 377-5590 .. **Abrams,** Gary H '85 -2820 Av J -Brklyn 11210 **Fx:**377-1154
(718) 445-9108 .. **Abrams,** Gerald H '72 -139-19 31st Rd -Flushng 11354 **Fx:**445-9112
(212) 422-1200 .. **Abrams Gorelick Friedman & Jacobson, PC** -1 Bttry Pk Plz -NY 10004 **Fx:**968-7573
(212) 701-3000 .. **Abrams,** Hanna '09 %Cahill G&R LLP -80 Pine -NY 10005 **Fx:**269-5420
(631) 369-1112 .. **Abrams,** Hannah '06 %Nassau/Sflk Law Srvc -313 W Main -Rvrhead 11901 **Fx:**369-1612
(718) 541-3762 .. **Abrams,** Irwen C '90 -244 Amherst -Brklyn 11235
(212) 735-3000 .. **Abrams,** Jacob J '09 %Skadden ASM&F LLP -4 Times Sq -NY 10036
(914) 271-9529 .. **Abrams,** Jamie C '85 (Bass & A,PC) -109 Grand -Croton-On-Hud 10520 **Fx:**271-1184
(212) 963-5735 .. **Abrams,** Jason '88 %Ofc of Legal Affairs -UN -NY 10017
(212) 695-0270 .. **Abrams,** Jason T '02 (Abrams & A LLP) -7 Penn Plz -NY 10001 **Fx:**695-0919
(212) 753-9692 .. **Abrams,** Jed '68 (Lent & A) -286 Mad Av -NY 10017
(212) 458-7455 .. **Abrams,** Jennifer R '99 AIG -175 Water -NY 10038
(212) 889-3700 .. **Abrams,** Jill S '82 (Abbey SR&A LLP) -212 E 39th -NY 10016
(212) 972-1000 .. **Abrams,** Joshua B '09 %London F LLP -59 Maiden Ln -NY 10038
(212) 678-8642 .. **Abrams,** Larry H '88 %Gen Re-Ins Corp -560 Riverside Dr -NY 10027
(212) 655-2000 .. **Abrams,** Louis M '90 Tower Ins Co -120 Bway -NY 10271
(212) 728-8000 .. **Abrams,** Marc '85 (Willkie F&G LLP) -787 7th Av -NY 10019
(212) 382-3300 .. **Abrams,** Marc L '99 (Wollmuth M&D LLP) -500 5th Av -NY 10110
(212) 398-1940 .. **Abrams,** Mark '78 %S Hurwitz -19 W 44th -NY 10036 **Fx:**764-5982
(212) 557-9600 .. **Abrams,** Matthew B '08 %Russo & B -600 3rd Av -NY 10016
(212) 872-6927 .. **Abrams,** Miri Chaya '96 %KPMG LLP -757 3rd Av -NY 10017
(212) 208-8787 .. **Abrams,** Natalie '85 %Standard & Poor's -55 Water -NY 10041
(212) 314-3802 .. **Abrams,** Norman J '78 %AXA Financial Inc -1290 Av of Amer -NY 10104 **Fx:**707-1871
(631) 427-8778 .. **Abrams,** Norman S '53 -116 Nassau Rd -Huntngtn 11743 **Fx:**427-6734
(212) 867-9123 .. **Abrams,** Richd A '69 OfCnsl Berkman BN&R,LLP -521 5th Av -NY 10175
(212) 806-5400 .. **Abrams,** Robt '64 (Stroock &S&L LLP) -180 Maiden Ln -NY 10038
(516) 328-2300 .. **Abrams,** Robt '88 OfCnsl Abrams FFEGF&E,LLP -1111 Marcus Av -Lk Success 11042
(212) 545-4602 .. **Abrams,** Robt '93 OfCnsl Wolf HAF&H LLP -270 Mad Av -NY 10016
(212) 953-6000 .. **Abrams,** Robt A '92 (Katsky K LLP) -605 3rd Av -NY 10158
(212) 450-4000 .. **Abrams,** Ronnie '94 Cnsl Davis P&W LLP -450 Lex Av -NY 10017
(212) 848-4000 .. **Abrams,** Samara N '09 %Shearman & S LLP -599 Lex Av -NY 10022
(212) 698-3500 .. **Abrams,** Saml B '84 (Dechert LLP) -1095 Av of Amer -NY 10036
(518) 439-5700 .. **Abrams,** Saul M '76 -307 Maple Rd -Slingerlnds 12159
(212) 244-2999 .. **Abrams,** Seth A '08 %Kopff N&D LLP -440 9th Av -NY 10001
(518) 473-4631 .. **Abrams,** Seth M '79 %Dept of Health -Corning Twr 24th Fl -Albany 12237 **Fx:**473-2802
(212) 661-5000 .. **Abrams,** Stuart E '78 (Frankel & A) -230 Park Av -NY 10169
(212) 201-1170 .. **Abrams,** Wm L '90 (Abrams GMB,LLP) -237 W 35th -NY 10001
(212) 430-9276 .. **Abramson,** Adena R '98 COA -120 Wall -NY 10005
(212) 687-2655 .. **Abramson,** Alan B '73 %Abramson Bros -501 5th Av -NY 10017 **Fx:**490-0630
(212) 226-7098 .. **Abramson,** Alan M '86 (Abramson & M) -35 Worth -NY 10013
(212) 468-8000 .. **Abramson,** Cindy P '10 %Morrison & F LLP -1290 Av of Amer -NY 10104
(212) 250-3254 .. **Abramson,** David I '67 %Deutsche Bk -60 Wall -NY 10005
(212) 686-4401 .. **Abramson,** David S '81 (Abramson Law Grp PLLC) -570 Lex Av -NY 10022 **Fx:**686-6515
(212) 459-5282 .. **Abramson,** David S '95 Cnsl BBDO Worldwide -1285 Av of Amer -NY 10019
(718) 802-2723 .. **Abramson,** Deborah E '75 Family Ct Legal Srvcs -330 Jay -Brklyn 11201
(212) 233-0666 .. **Abramson,** Frederic R '97 -160 Bway -NY 10038 **Fx:**267-9177
(845) 291-2454 .. **Abramson,** Gary '74 %Leg Aid -2 Court Ln Bx328 -Goshen 10924 **Fx:**294-2638
(212) 788-4538 .. **Abramson,** Gerda '05 Family Crt Legal Srvcs -220 Church -NY 10013
(516) 294-5500 .. **Abramson,** Glenn J '87 -626 Reckson Plz -Uniondale 11556
(631) 761-7000 .. **Abramson,** Harold I '75 %Touro Cllg Law Ctr -225 Eastvw Dr -Central Islip 11722
(212) 683-7050 .. **Abramson,** James M '70 -375 5th Av -NY 10016 **Fx:**683-7076
(212) 468-4800 .. **Abramson,** Jason M '00 (Davis & G LLP) -1740 Bway -NY 10019
(212) 838-3830 .. **Abramson,** Jay B '87 Cramer Rosenthal McGlynn Inc -520 Mad Av -NY 10022
(212) 599-7700 .. **Abramson,** Joel E '70 (JE Abramson,PC) -271 Mad Av -NY 10016 **Fx:**213-3495
(212) 265-6888 .. **Abramson,** Joshua H '00 Cnsl Porzio B&N,PC -156 W 56th -NY 10019
(914) 777-1101 .. **Abramson,** Lauren B '87 -550 Mamaroneck Av -Harrison 10528
(212) 218-2100 .. **Abramson,** Marc A '08 %Fitzpatrick CH&S -1290 Av of Amer -NY 10104
(914) 603-3055 .. **Abramson,** Michelle R '88 -1010 E Main -Shrub Oak 10588
(212) 226-7098 .. **Abramson & Morak** -35 Worth -NY 10013 **Fx:**226-4559
(212) 964-3300 .. **Abramson,** Neil '87 (Rubin A LLP) -225 Bway -NY 10007
(212) 969-3000 .. **Abramson,** Neil H '89 (Proskauer R LLP) -1585 Bway -NY 10036
(212) 610-6300 .. **Abramson,** Paul B '85 SrCnsl Allen & O -1221 Av of Amer -NY 10020
(212) 382-0909 .. **Abramson,** Richd L '73 (Peckar & A,PC) -41 Mad Av -NY 10154
(212) 837-6000 .. **Abramson,** Ronald '78 (Hughes H&R LLP) -1 Bttry Pk Plz -NY 10004
(718) 478-5222 .. **Abramson,** Russell M '80 (Abramson & K) -6008 Woodside Av -Woodside 11377 **Fx:**478-5352
(212) 873-2430 .. **Abramson,** Stephanie W '69 -101 Cntrl Pk W -NY 10023

(212) 805-1009 ..**Abramson,** Stewart G '79 %Charter Financial Inc -530 5th Av -NY 10036

(516) 542-1000 ..**Abramson,** Tracy A '98 %Geisler & G,LLP -100 Q Roosevelt Blvd -Gdn Cty 11530

(845) 688-7250 ..**Abramson,** Wm I '53 -17 Grog Kill Rd -Willow 12495 **Fx:**688-7250

(212) 387-8400 ..**Abrandt,** Jeffrey G '78 (Goldfarb AS&K LLP) -350 5th Av -NY 10118

(212) 264-3299 ..**Abrash,** Ingrid H '01 %DHS -26 Fed Plz -NY 10278

(212) 998-6670 ..**Abresch,** Wm J '06 NYU Ctr Human Rts & Global Justice -110 W 3rd -NY 10012

(212) 592-1400 ..**Abreu,** Aismara J '04 %Herrick,F LLP -2 Park Av -NY 10016

(718) 823-5256 ..**Abreu,** Anny M '05 -3517 E Tremont Av -Bronx 10465 **Fx:**822-8036

(631) 665-3400 ..**Abreu,** Joan E '05 %Siben & S,LLP -90 E Main Bx149P -Bay Shr 11706

(212) 227-6821 ..**Abreu,** Johanna C '00 %Roura & M -233 Bway -NY 10279

(212) 335-4124 ..**Abreu,** Juan D '08 DA -80 Centre -NY 10013

(646) 458-6879 ..**Abreu,** Matthew A '08 Ace USA -140 Bway -NY 10005

(212) 225-2000 ..**Abreu,** Michelle '10 %Cleary GS&H -1 Lbrty Plz -NY 10006

(718) 250-2000 ..**Abriano,** Gerianne '94 %DA -350 Jay -Brklyn 11201 **Fx:**250-2314

(212) 431-2163 ..**Abrigo,** Anna '03 NY Law Schl -57 Worth -NY 10013

(315) 655-3810 ..**Abriola,** Frances Patterson '94 -6003 Nelson Rd -Canastota 13032 **Fx:**655-3810

(212) 271-0664 ..**Abrishamian,** Diana '09 %Lee AC LLP -350 5th Av -NY 10118

(212) 325-0401 ..**Abrusci,** Matthew D '96 Credit Suisse Securities LLC -11 Mad Av -NY 10010

(212) 512-1000 ..**Abrutyn,** Stephanie S '98 %HBO -1100 Av of Amer -NY 10036 **Fx:**512-1986

(516) 747-6461 ..**Abruzzese,** Kevin J '06 -200 Old Cntry Rd -Mineola 11501

(212) 715-9100 ..**Abruzzese,** Peter A '02 (Kramer LN&F,LLP) -1177 Av of Amer -NY 10036

(718) 243-2700 ..**Abruzzino,** Robt G '00 %Talisman & D,PC -409 Fulton -Brklyn 11201 **Fx:**243-2707

(212) 762-5139 ..**Abruzzo,** Craig T '95 Morgan Stanley -1221 Av of Amer -NY 10020

(516) 624-6150 ..**Abruzzo,** Martin P '83 %Town Atty -Town Hall -Oyster Bay 11771 **Fx:**624-6196

(914) 220-0110 ..**Abruzzo,** Ted J '86 (Weissmann A LLP) -445 Hmltn Av -White Plns 10601 **Fx:**(917) 368-6920

(212) 504-6000 ..**Absolonne,** Deirdre Long '99 SpclCnsl Cadwalader W&T LLP -1 World Fncl Ctr -NY 10281

(212) 237-1000 ..**Abt,** Josef F '99 %Windels ML&M,LLP -156 W 56th -NY 10019

(212) 403-1000 ..**Abt,** Steven R '10 %Wachtell LR&K -51 W 52nd -NY 10019

(212) 909-6000 ..**Abuhoff,** Danl M '79 (Debevoise & P LLP) -919 3rd Av -NY 10022

(212) 225-2000 ..**Abularach,** Nora K '07 %Cleary GS&H -1 Lbrty Plz -NY 10006

(212) 698-3500 ..**Abu-Shaar,** Muna '04 %Dechert LLP -1095 Av of Amer -NY 10036

(516) 479-6300 ..**Acampora,** Anthony C '84 (Silverman A LLP) -100 Jericho Quad -Jericho 11753

(212) 213-6110 ..**Acar,** Cigdem A '93 -404 Park Av S -NY 10016 **Fx:**689-3315

(845) 562-3366 ..**Acard,** Brian D '90 %Larkin AI&T,LLP -34 Route 17K -Newburgh 12550

(212) 687-2777 ..**Acasio,** Jenny '09 %Levine & S -60 E 42nd -NY 10165

(631) 665-0609 ..**Accardi,** James J '93 (Sherman FS&L LLP) -8 E Main -Bay Shr 11706

(607) 723-9404 ..**Accardi,** Vincent '78 -188 Court -Bnghmtn 13901 **Fx:**771-6134

(718) 590-3299 ..**Accardo,** Matthew G '09 %Law Dept -198 E 161st -Bronx 10451 **Fx:**590-2686

(732) 855-6411 ..**Accarrino,** Letitia J '92 %Wilentz G&S -110 William -NY 10038 **Fx:**726-6620

(914) 824-5655 ..**Accetta,** Jos M '93 %Surrogates Ct -111 Dr MLK Jr Blvd -White Plns 10601 **Fx:**995-3728

(914) 428-8800 ..**Accetta,** Susan Hegquist '94 %Stern KP&W,LLP -1025 Wstchstr Av -White Plns 10604

(914) 779-1100 ..**Accinelli,** Steven A '97 %Veneruso CS&C,LLP -35 E Grassy Sprain Rd -Ynkrs 10710

(718) 881-0418 ..**Accoo,** Ralph A '53 -859 E 216th -Bronx 10467

(914) 249-2000 ..**Accordino,** Gina Saline '00 Mastercard Intl -2000 Purchase -Purchase 10577

(914) 366-0201 ..**Accurso,** Nicholas J '89 %Reardon & S,PC -220 Wht Plns Rd -Tarrytwn 10591

(212) 845-5227 ..**Acer,** Eleanor A '89 %Human Rights First -333 7th Av -NY 10001 **Fx:**845-5289

(914) 949-6996 ..**Aceste,** Vincent J '75 OfCnsl Penino & M,LLP -180 E Post Rd -White Plns 10601

(212) 259-8000 ..**Acevedo,** Anthony '98 Cnsl Dewey & L LLP -1301 Av of Amer -NY 10019

(646) 746-9754 ..**Acevedo,** David '89 CFTC -140 Bway -NY 10005

(718) 590-2000 ..**Acevedo,** Elizabeth A '99 %DA -198 E 161st -Bronx 10451 **Fx:**590-6477

(631) 878-3280 ..**Acevedo,** Elsie '91 -111 Main -Ctr Moriches 11934 **Fx:**874-3346

(212) 460-3762 ..**Acevedo,** Enver R '96 Con Ed -4 Irving Pl -NY 10003

(212) 360-4124 ..**Acevedo,** Francis '92 %Harlem Cmmty Ct -170 E 121st -NY 10035

(212) 819-8200 ..**Acevedo,** Linda J '06 %White & C LLP -1155 Av of Amer -NY 10036

(212) 371-4500 ..**Acevedo,** Roland R '97 OfCnsl Seiff K&A -444 Mad Av -NY 10022

(212) 553-0300 ..**Acevedo,** Salhom N '96 Moodys Invstmnt Srvc -99 Church -NY 10007

(212) 455-2000 ..**Achi,** Ejim P '08 %Simpson T&B LLP -425 Lex Av -NY 10017

(212) 521-5400 ..**Achilles,** Jennifer L '04 %Reed S LLP -599 Lex Av -NY 10022

(212) 490-3000 ..**Achiron,** Andrew V '08 %Wilson EME&D LLP -150 E 42nd -NY 10017

(718) 463-7333 ..**Achiron,** Hope A '07 %M Mongelli II,PC -41-07 162nd -Flushng 11358 **Fx:**358-4872

(212) 715-9100 ..**Achkar,** Chas C '00 %Kramer LN&F,LLP -1177 Av of Amer -NY 10036

(212) 651-7500 ..**Acholonu,** Tomachukwu N '04 %Segal MS&M -850 3rd Av -NY 10022

(646) 328-0120 ..**Achtziger,** Erika M '08 %Bennett GM&P,LLP -494 8th Av -NY 10001

(718) 438-1100 ..**Acierno,** John L '84 Executive Change Inc -1440 39th -Brklyn 11218

(212) 801-6777 ..**Aciman,** Carole '91 (Greenberg T,LLP) -200 Park Av -NY 10166

(718) 487-1300 ..**Acinapura,** Paul J '75 %Leg Srvcs Corp A -80 Jamaica Av -Brklyn 11207 **Fx:**342-1780

(212) 460-5200 ..**Acito,** Richd A '73 -215 Park Av S -NY 10003

(845) 279-2986 ..**Acker,** Chas J '66 OfCnsl Hogan & R -1441 Route 22 -Brewstr 10509

(845) 225-3641 ..**Acker,** Christi J '93 %Hon J Rooney -40 Gleneida Av -Carmel 10512

(718) 286-7100 ..**Acker,** Derrick K '91 %FBI -80-02 Kew Grdn Blvd -Kew Gdns 11415

(212) 836-1135 ..**Acker,** Michele Landes '96 UJA-Federation -130 E 59th -NY 10022 **Fx:**888-7538

(212) 319-1000 ..**Acker,** Robt B '99 %Quirk & B,PC -845 3rd Av -NY 10022

(516) 798-9800 ..**Acker,** Robt T '81 (R Acker,PC) -727 N Bway -N Massapequa 11758 **Fx:**798-4736

(716) 362-1533 ..**Ackerhalt,** Arthur H '74 (Goldstein A&P,LLP) -70 Niagara -Buffalo 14202

(516) 676-4600 ..**Ackerly,** Shannon T '01 %Humes & W -147 Forest Av Bx546 -Locust Vly 11560

(518) 457-1260 ..**Ackerman,** Andra L '99 %DCJS -4 Twr Pl -Albany 12203 **Fx:**457-3089

(212) 259-0715 ..**Ackerman,** Corey B '99 Grtr NY Hsptl Assn -555 W 57th -NY 10019

(845) 485-3633 ..**Ackerman,** Denise A '95 %Law Dept -1 Overocker Rd -Poughkeepsie 12603

(212) 557-4000 ..**Ackerman,** Edw B '77 (Grunfeld DLS&K LLP) -399 Park Av -NY 10022

(212) 373-3000 ..**Ackerman,** Edw T '06 %Paul WRW&G LLP -1285 Av of Amer -NY 10019

(518) 756-3121 ..**Ackerman,** F Stanton '67 (Ackerman W&F) -Bx177 -Ravena 12143

(518) 463-2259 ..**Ackerman,** F Stanton '67 (Ackerman W&F) -90 State -Albany 12207

(212) 756-2000 ..**Ackerman,** Jos '06 %Schulte R&Z LLP -919 3rd Av -NY 10022

(516) 222-2333 ..**Ackerman,** Judith A '76 %Barbara Law Firm -401 Franklin Av -Gdn Cty 11530 **Fx:**222-2935

(914) 390-4124 ..**Ackerman,** Kathleen '95 %Hon M Fox -300 Quarropas -White Plns 10601

(212) 533-6300 ..**Ackerman,** Lena M '99 %NYSUT -52 Bway -NY 10004 **Fx:**995-2347

(631) 324-3942 ..**Ackerman,** Leonard I '65 (Ackerman OP&B,LLP) -34 Pantigo Rd -E Hampton 11937

(516) 829-6900 ..**Ackerman Levine Cullen Brickman & Limmer,LLP** -1010 Nrthrn Blvd -Gt Neck 11021 **Fx:**829-6966

(212) 326-2000 ..**Ackerman,** Marc E '93 (O'Melveny & M LLP) -7 Times Sq -NY 10036

(914) 686-4800 ..**Ackerman,** Marc J '97 %Harrington O&M,LLP -81 Main -White Plns 10601

(516) 877-1500 ..**Ackerman,** Michl S '03 (Ackerman & F) -6901 Jericho Tpk -Syosset 11791

(516) 747-0300 ..**Ackerman,** Neil H '82 (Meltzer LG&B,LLP) -190 Willis Av -Mineola 11501

(631) 324-3942 ..**Ackerman O'Brien Pachman & Brown,LLP** -34 Pantigo Rd -E Hampton 11937 **Fx:**324-3622

(212) 415-9200 ..**Ackerman,** Paul D '96 (Dorsey & W LLP) -250 Park Av -NY 10177

(914) 686-1200 ..**Ackerman,** Peter B '78 -202 Mamaroneck Av -White Plns 10601 **Fx:**686-1650

(518) 271-6807 ..**Ackerman,** Philip G '93 -65 2nd -Troy 12180

(212) 704-6000 ..**Ackerman,** Richd P '74 (Troutman S LLP) -405 Lex Av -NY 10174

(212) 788-1082 ..**Ackerman,** Stephen K '87 %Law Dept -100 Church -NY 10007 **Fx:**788-0367

(518) 463-2259 ..**Ackerman Wachs & Finton** -90 State -Albany 12207 **Fx:**463-6046

(518) 756-3121 ..**Ackerman Wachs & Finton** -Bx177 -Ravena 12143 **Fx:**756-3122

(516) 829-6900 ..**Ackerman,** Wm A '59 (Ackerman LCB&L,LLP) -1010 Nrthrn Blvd -Gt Neck 11021

(212) 757-8438 ..**Ackermann,** Candice L '04 %Levitt & N,PC -250 W 57th -NY 10107

(845) 451-4065 ..**Ackermann,** Paul F '06 Law Dept -Bx300 -Poughkeepsie 12602

(845) 357-5631 ..**Ackerson,** Richd H '67 -16 Claremont Ln -Suffern 10901 **Fx:**357-5631

(212) 683-6383 ..**Ackert,** Stanley M III '80 (Gersen B&A LLP) -270 Mad Av -NY 10016

(212) 859-8000 ..**Ackman,** Milton R '58 OfCnsl Fried FHS&J LLP -1 NY Plz -NY 10004

(518) 798-1013 ..**Ackner,** Lynne E '93 -110 Glen -Glens Fls 12801 **Fx:**798-1034

(914) 779-1500 ..**Acocella,** Frank A '01 -2088 Cntrl Pk Av -Ynkrs 10710 **Fx:**779-1573

(914) 723-1222 ..**Acocella,** Frank X '97 (F Acocella & Assoc) -68 Gaylor Rd -Scarsdale 10583 **Fx:**723-4600

(212) 468-8000 ..**Acocella,** Kerry S '06 %Morrison & F LLP -1290 Av of Amer -NY 10104

(631) 669-8600 ..**Acocella,** Peter R '87 (DeCarlo & A,PC) -175 W Main -Babylon 11702 **Fx:**669-2150

(212) 682-3025 ..**Acocelli,** Richd A Jr. '91 %Weiss & L -551 5th Av -NY 10176

(585) 494-1155 ..**Acomb-Wilcox,** Fern K '84 -741 Johnson Rd -Churchville 14428 **Fx:**494-1389

(212) 480-2733 ..**Acosta,** Carmen '94 Div of Human Rights -20 Exch Pl -NY 10005

(347) 404-9133 ..**Acosta,** Damaris B '08 %Civil Ct -141 Lvngstn -Brklyn 11201 **Fx:**(718) 643-3733

(212) 822-8300 ..**Acosta,** Douglas D '97 %NMIC -76 Wadsworth Av -NY 10033 **Fx:**740-9645

(212) 325-0679 ..**Acosta,** John J Jr. '07 Credit Suisse -11 Mad Av -NY 10010

(631) 232-0200 ..**Acosta,** Michelle C '02 %Fumuso KDSS&F,LLP -110 Marcus Blvd -Hauppauge 11788

(631) 271-6363 ..**Acosta,** Roger '90 (Cannon & A,LLP) -1923 NY Av -Huntngtn Sta 11746 **Fx:**271-7128

(212) 440-7027 ..**Acosta,** Tara E '01 CNA Ins -40 Wall -NY 10005

(212) 518-3005 ..**Acosta-Diaz,** Edwin '05 -5 Penn Plz -NY 10001

(516) 571-3800 ..**Acquafredda,** Anna '04 %DA -262 Old Cntry Rd -Mineola 11501 **Fx:**248-9479

(718) 351-5622 ..**Acquafredda,** Grace A '88 -15 Benedict Rd -Staten Isl 10304 **Fx:**351-5622

(518) 465-1473 ..**Acquario,** Stephen J '99 NYS Assn of Counties -540 Bway -Albany 12207

(646) 315-7300 ..**Acquavella,** Audra A '97 FINRA -14 Wall -NY 10005 **Fx:**315-7440

(516) 229-6000 ..**Acquaye,** Akwei Oko '04 R Lau & Assoc -300 Jericho Quad Bx9040 -Jericho 11753 **Fx:**229-6167

(718) 875-1300 .. **Acquista,** Angela '90 %Applt Div 2nd Dept -45 Monroe Pl -Brklyn 11201 **Fx:**858-2446
(718) 274-1010 .. **Acquista,** Salvatore J '05 -32-75 Steinway -Astoria 11103 **Fx:**274-1077
(718) 274-1600 .. **Acquista,** Vincent M '96 -31-10 37th Av -LIC 11101
(718) 422-4836 .. **Acri,** Corey '07 Ofc Emergency Mgmt -165 Cadman Plz E -Brklyn 11201
(212) 728-8000 .. **Acri,** Gabriel '02 %Willkie F&G LLP -787 7th Av -NY 10019
(212) 506-1700 .. **Acriche,** Marc '94 Kasowitz BT&F LLP -1633 Bway -NY 10019
(212) 384-0270 .. **Acton,** Edw J '77 -331 W 57th -NY 10019
(212) 530-4005 .. **Actor,** Mary E '87 %Home Ins -59 Maiden Ln -NY 10038
(212) 312-2260 .. **Acunis,** Benjie G '08 Leg Aid -60 Lafayette -NY 10013 **Fx:**349-0874
(212) 659-7300 .. **Acusar,** Dara C '07 %Haynes & B,LLP -1221 Av of Amer -NY 10020
(212) 225-5238 .. **Aczel,** Stephen M '07 Bank of Nove Scotia -1 Lbrty Plz -NY 10006
(212) 885-5000 .. **Adago,** Richd J '88 (Blank R LLP) -405 Lex Av -NY 10174
(585) 419-9000 .. **Adair,** Donald R '68 (Adair Law Firm LLP) -290 Linden Oaks -Rchstr 14625 **Fx:**419-8071
(518) 257-8319 .. **Adair,** John H '86 %Key Corp Capital -66 S Pearl -Albany 12207 **Fx:**257-8827
(518) 402-9507 .. **Adair,** Robyn M '05 %DEC -625 Bway -Albany 12233 **Fx:**402-9018
(212) 553-9206 .. **Adam,** Angelina L '04 %G Cannata -233 Bway -NY 10279 **Fx:**227-4141
(518) 346-7085 .. **Adam,** Gerhard K '60 -1130 Palmer Av -Schnctdy 12309 **Fx:**346-7085
(212) 661-8780 .. **Adam,** Richd '99 -275 Mad Av -NY 10016
(914) 271-5592 .. **Adami,** Guy M '64 -126 Grand Bx372 -Croton-On-Hud 10520
(212) 940-3000 .. **Adamidis,** Stavros D '02 (Nixon P LLP) -437 Mad Av -NY 10022
(914) 696-3800 .. **Adamis,** Demetrios '89 -2900 Wstchstr Av -Purchase 10577
(212) 285-1515 .. **Adamo,** John A Jr. '88 -277 Bway -NY 10007
(516) 328-2300 .. **Adamo,** Moriah R '07 %Abrams FFEGF&E,LLP -1111 Marcus Av -Lk Success 11042
(212) 964-7983 .. **Adamo,** Salvatore C '92 -350 5th Av -NY 10118
(212) 574-1200 .. **Adamolekun,** Olufolasade '03 %Seward & K LLP -1 Bttry Pk Plz -NY 10004
(212) 558-4000 .. **Adamovich,** Tracy L '10 %Sullivan & C LLP -125 Broad -NY 10004
(212) 351-4000 .. **Adams,** Aaron F '01 (Gibson D&C LLP) -200 Park Av -NY 10166
(212) 688-8671 .. **Adams,** Amy B '96 %Gould McCoy & Chadick -300 Park Av -NY 10022
(585) 232-6900 .. **Adams,** Anthony J Jr. '81 (Gates & A,PC) -28 E Main -Rchstr 14614
(212) 733-2782 .. **Adams,** Atiba D '97 %Pfizer Inc -235 E 42nd -NY 10017 **Fx:**573-7442
(212) 350-8524 .. **Adams,** Brian H '87 Douglas Elliman,LLC -485 Mad Av -NY 10022
(516) 763-4606 .. **Adams,** Bruce J '77 -169 Cleveland Av -Rockvll Ctr 11570
(212) 809-3700 .. **Adams,** Bruce L '70 (Adams & W) -17 Battery Pl -NY 10004
(718) 522-4563 .. **Adams,** C Murray '58 -185 Amity -Brklyn 11201 **Fx:**522-6786
(516) 466-4422 .. **Adams,** Carol M '80 OfCnsl R Fatoullah & Assoc -425 Nrthrn Blvd -Gt Neck 11021 **Fx:**466-2219
(212) 450-4000 .. **Adams,** Caroline R '04 %Davis P&W LLP -450 Lex Av -NY 10017
(631) 666-6200 .. **Adams,** Chas J '83 (PF Adams,PC) -49 5th Av Bx1089M -Bay Shr 11706 **Fx:**665-6739
(212) 847-8877 .. **Adams,** Colin McNeill '00 Citadel Securities LLC -601 Lex Av -NY 10022
(212) 783-4148 .. **Adams,** Cynthia Bookhart '97 Morgan Stanley -485 Lex Av -NY 10017
(718) 838-7878 .. **Adams,** Danl D '10 %Bronx Defenders -860 Crtlandt Av -Bronx 10451 **Fx:**665-0100
(845) 454-1200 .. **Adams,** Danl P '97 (Lewis & G,PC) -510 Haight Av Bx2990 -Poughkeepsie 12603
(716) 849-8900 .. **Adams,** David R '96 %Hurwitz & F,PC -1300 Lbrty Bldg -Buffalo 14202
(212) 510-0500 .. **Adams,** Diana Goldberg '89 %US Trustees Ofc -33 Whitehall -NY 10004 **Fx:**668-2255
(212) 331-5131 .. **Adams,** Diana M '05 HRA -180 Water -NY 10038
(212) 335-4129 .. **Adams,** Diane M '07 %DA -1 Hogan Pl -NY 10013
(908) 675-6181 .. **Adams,** E Regan '91 Information Law Practice -30 5th Av -NY 10011
(845) 567-0100 .. **Adams,** Edie A '92 %Ouimette G&A -843 Union Av -New Windsor 12553
(212) 385-0900 .. **Adams,** Edw R '79 -225 Bway -NY 10007
(212) 885-5000 .. **Adams,** Elise M '90 OfCnsl Blank R LLP -405 Lex Av -NY 10174
(212) 940-8800 .. **Adams,** Eric S '99 (Katten MR LLP) -575 Mad Av -NY 10022
(212) 947-7111 .. **Adams,** Ernest H '98 -19 W 34th -NY 10001
(585) 232-6900 .. **Adams,** Evelyn '81 %Gates & A,PC -28 E Main -Rchstr 14614
(212) 259-8000 .. **Adams,** Frank R III '94 (Dewey & L LLP) -1301 Av of Amer -NY 10019
(718) 272-8470 .. **Adams,** Gail A '99 G Adams,PC -1140 E 92nd -Brklyn 11236
(212) 909-6000 .. **Adams,** George B '57 Debevoise & P LLP -919 3rd Av -NY 10022
(516) 688-1700 .. **Adams,** Halvor N III '87 %IRS -1600 Stewart Av -Westbury 11590 **Fx:**688-1750
(585) 396-4411 .. **Adams,** Holly A '90 %Cnty Atty -27 N Main -Canandaigua 14424 **Fx:**396-4481
(212) 696-6000 .. **Adams,** J Dinsmore Jr. '70 (Curtis M-PC&M LLP) -101 Park Av -NY 10178
(212) 735-3000 .. **Adams,** J Phillip '73 (Skadden ASM&F LLP) -4 Times Sq -NY 10036
(212) 832-1977 .. **Adams,** James S '95 (Schreck RDA&H) -1790 Bway -NY 10019 **Fx:**832-2969
(212) 808-7800 .. **Adams,** Jason R '01 %Kelley D&W LLP -101 Park Av -NY 10178
(716) 635-1900 .. **Adams,** Jennifer Stashko '95 %Kaplan HMAF&F -20 Lawrence Bell Dr -Buffalo 14214 **Fx:**634-0431
(716) 568-8200 .. **Adams,** Joan Casilio '88 (J Adams & Assoc,PLLC) -500 Essjay Rd -Williamsvll 14221 **Fx:**568-8292
(516) 536-7119 .. **Adams,** Joann R '89 -166 Cleveland Av -Rockvll Ctr 11570
(845) 454-1110 .. **Adams,** Jon H '69 (Corbally G and R LLP) -35 Market -Poughkeepsie 12601
(212) 838-7797 .. **Adams,** Jon R '01 %Cohen MS&T,PLLC -88 Pine -NY 10005
(212) 688-8555 .. **Adams,** Jonathan C '96 %Fragomen DB&L LLP -7 Hanover Sq -NY 10004
(212) 223-4000 .. **Adams,** Jos A '88 (Crowell & M LLP) -590 Mad Av -NY 10022
(845) 353-2320 .. **Adams,** Jos H '78 JH Adams,PC -53 Burd -Nyack 10960 **Fx:**353-6934
(212) 735-3000 .. **Adams,** Julie B '05 %Skadden ASM&F LLP -4 Times Sq -NY 10036
(212) 713-9514 .. **Adams,** Karri June '03 UBS -1285 Av of Amer -NY 10019
(212) 996-2408 .. **Adams,** Kevin D '85 -2008 5th Av -NY 10035
(212) 701-3000 .. **Adams,** L Howard '86 (Cahill G&R LLP) -80 Pine -NY 10005 **Fx:**269-5420
(718) 618-2326 .. **Adams,** Laura A '84 %Surrogate's Ct -851 Grnd Cncrs -Bronx 10451 **Fx:**590-3575
(212) 297-5800 .. **Adams,** Lindsay Spencer '94 Cnsl Day P LLP -7 Times Sq -NY 10036
(917) 292-4154 .. **Adams,** Lori K '05 Exec Ofc for Immigration Review -26 Fed Plz -NY 10278
(718) 330-7713 .. **Adams,** Marcia E '91 %NLRB -2 Metrotech Ctr -Brklyn 11201 **Fx:**330-7579
(212) 720-7823 .. **Adams,** Marina I '96 %Fed Reserve Bk -33 Lbrty -NY 10045 **Fx:**785-5748
(212) 335-4500 .. **Adams,** Marjorie S '85 (DLA Piper LLP) -1251 Av of Amer -NY 10020
(845) 892-5578 .. **Adams,** Mark T '03 Cnsl IBM -2070 Route 52 -Hopewell Junct 12533
(212) 234-8155 .. **Adams,** Marlin L '90 -244 Mad Av -NY 10016
(212) 713-2214 .. **Adams,** Marnie A '02 UBS -1285 Av of Amer -NY 10019
(212) 785-1330 .. **Adams,** Martha C '82 %ABS -45 Bway -NY 10006
(212) 244-2999 .. **Adams,** Martin B '85 (Kopff N&D LLP) -440 9th Av -NY 10001
(212) 403-1000 .. **Adams,** Michl Jermaine O '10 %Wachtell LR&K -51 W 52nd -NY 10019
(516) 747-4082 .. **Adams,** Michl R '83 %Montfort HM&S LLP -1140 Franklin Av Bx7677 -Gdn Cty 11530
(212) 359-7355 .. **Adams,** Michl T '04 Polygon Invstmnt -399 Park Av -NY 10022
(212) 790-0200 .. **Adams,** Michelle V '90 Benj N Cardozo Schl of Law -55 5th Av -NY 10003 **Fx:**790-0345
(212) 872-1000 .. **Adams,** Nicholas C '10 -One Bryant Park -NY 10036 **Fx:**872-1002
(212) 389-5000 .. **Adams,** Otis Bert III '07 (Sutherland A&B LLP) -1114 Av of Amer -NY 10036
(631) 666-6200 .. **Adams,** Patrick F '55 (PF Adams,PC) -49 5th Av Bx1089M -Bay Shr 11706 **Fx:**665-6739
(212) 839-5300 .. **Adams,** Paul C '97 (Sidley A LLP) -787 7th Av -NY 10019
(914) 723-6400 .. **Adams,** Peter M '79 -2 Walworth Av -Scarsdale 10583 **Fx:**723-6363
(212) 455-2000 .. **Adams,** Rae C '10 %Simpson T&B LLP -425 Lex Av -NY 10017
(212) 336-3707 .. **Adams,** Raechel L '05 %EEOC -33 Whitehall -NY 10004
(212) 808-7800 .. **Adams,** Robt B '65 (Kelley D&W LLP) -101 Park Av -NY 10178
(718) 360-9953 .. **Adams,** Robt J Jr. '92 -300 Grdn City Plz -Gdn Cty 11530 **Fx:**360-9953
(518) 463-3385 .. **Adams,** Robt L '78 -600 Bway -Albany 12207 **Fx:**463-3440
(212) 977-9700 .. **Adams,** Robt M '04 (Phillips N LLP) -666 5th Av -NY 10103
(212) 350-2700 .. **Adams,** Roy M '95 (Constantine C,PC) -450 Lex Av -NY 10017
(716) 838-5515 .. **Adams,** Sandra H '92 %O Smukler -1438 Hertel Av -Buffalo 14216
(718) 262-7100 .. **Adams,** Sharon D '95 %Civil Ct -89-17 Sutphin Blvd -Jamaica 11435 **Fx:**262-7107
(718) 250-1400 .. **Adams,** Steven G '82 %BZ Green -12 MetroTech Ctr -Brklyn 11201 **Fx:**250-1401
(212) 766-1888 .. **Adams,** Suzanne J '99 %Morris DA&F -2 Rector -NY 10006
(607) 272-3442 .. **Adams Theisen May & Miller** -301 Clinton Hse -Ithaca 14850 **Fx:**272-4514
(718) 847-4572 .. **Adams,** Thos J Jr. '62 T Adams -114-06 Jamaica Av -Richmnd Hll 11418 **Fx:**847-5901
(212) 725-4423 .. **Adams,** Thos J III '91 (Paykin K&A LLP) -185 Mad Av -NY 10016
(315) 764-0513 .. **Adams,** Thos R '06 %Snider & S -252 Main -Massena 13662 **Fx:**764-9230
(212) 897-5804 .. **Adams,** Tisha N '01 (T Adams & Assoc,LLP) -305 Bway -NY 10007 **Fx:**897-5806
(212) 553-5400 .. **Adams,** Walter J '01 Zurich NA -1 Lbrty Plz -NY 10006
(212) 849-7000 .. **Adams,** Wm B '06 %Quinn EU&S,LLP -51 Mad Av -NY 10010
(212) 751-2600 .. **Adams,** Wm S '91 %Random House -1745 Bway -NY 10019
(315) 337-4171 .. **Adamski,** Bernard J '49 -400 N Wshngtn Bx208 -Rome 13442 **Fx:**339-3794
(212) 230-4500 .. **Adamski,** Michl D '05 One East Captl Advsrs -1 E 57th -NY 10022
(631) 423-4390 .. **Adams Nowak,** Karen J '95 %Mincone & M,PC -110 Walt Whitman Rd -South Huntington 11746 **Fx:**423-4408
(212) 210-9432 .. **Adamson,** Gary D '10 %Alston & B LLP -90 Park Av -NY 10016
(716) 884-2000 .. **Adamson,** George S '01 %Doran & M -1234 Delaware Av -Buffalo 14209
(716) 689-9646 .. **Adamy,** Richd A '64 -66 Kings Trl -Williamsvll 14221
(716) 882-4890 .. **Adamy,** Yasmin W '10 %Mosey P,LLP -625 Delaware Av -Buffalo 14202 **Fx:**882-5240
(518) 584-2200 .. **Adang,** Anthony P '73 (King A&A) -2911 Route 9 Bx4580 -Saratoga Spgs 12866
(212) 682-8811 .. **Adaszko,** Eva '89 %Dunnington B&M LLP -1359 Bway -NY 10018
(718) 268-0400 .. **Addabbo,** Dominic L '77 (Addabbo & G) -118-21 Qns Blvd -Frst Hlls 11375
(212) 261-8000 .. **Addabbo,** Grace M '09 %Mendes & M,LLP -750 7th Av -NY 10019
(718) 268-0400 .. **Addabbo & Greenberg** -118-21 Qns Blvd -Frst Hlls 11375 **Fx:**575-9869
(718) 268-0400 .. **Addabbo,** Jos P Jr. '93 OfCnsl Addabbo & G -118-21 Qns Blvd -Frst Hlls 11375
(718) 923-4206 .. **Addamo,** Sebastian J '83 %OTDA Fair Hearings -14 Boerum Pl -Brklyn 11201
(718) 923-4206 .. **Addamo,** Susan Bergman '76 %OTDA Fair Hearings -14 Boerum Pl -Brklyn 11201
(716) 856-4118 .. **Addelman,** David R '84 Cnsl D Addelman PC -69 Delaware Av -Buffalo 14202 **Fx:**856-6235
(716) 856-5500 .. **Addelman,** Kara M '09 %Damon M LLP -200 Delaware Av -Buffalo 14202
(914) 271-1020 .. **Addeo,** Annmarie F '91 -10 Teatown Rd -Croton-On-Hud 10520 **Fx:**271-1020
(914) 286-2913 .. **Addeo,** Kenneth P '91 OfCnsl Greenberg T,LLP -445 Hmltn Av -White Plns 10601
(914) 699-6052 .. **Addesso,** Jack A '73 -153 Stevens Av -Mt Vernon 10550 **Fx:**699-1769
(212) 238-2420 .. **Addison,** Andrea S '91 %UIA Bd -59 Maiden Ln -NY 10038 **Fx:**238-2451

(212) 318-3000 .. **Addison,** Linda L '07 (Fulbright & J LLP) -666 5th Av -NY 10103
(212) 728-8000 .. **Addison,** Lindsay M '09 %Willkie F&G LLP -787 7th Av -NY 10019
(212) 897-5840 .. **Addonizio,** Jennifer M '08 %Fishman & N -305 Bway -NY 10007 **Fx:**897-5841
(315) 479-8660 .. **Addonizio,** Peter J '03 %Alexander & C,LLC -115 E Jffrsn -Syracuse 13202
(212) 699-7085 .. **Addonizio,** Tarmi '04 Charmer Sunbelt Grp -60 E 42nd -NY 10165
(718) 795-0003 .. **Addo-Prempeh,** Kwadwo '04 -1263C Edward Grant Hwy -Bronx 10452
(716) 854-2100 .. **Adduci,** Kristin M '01 %Lewis & L,PC -37 Franklin -Buffalo 14202 **Fx:**854-0433
(212) 701-3000 .. **Addy,** Colin J '09 %Cahill G&R LLP -80 Pine -NY 10005 **Fx:**269-5420
(212) 965-2200 .. **Adegbile,** Debo P '95 %NAACP/LDF -99 Hudson -NY 10013 **Fx:**226-7592
(212) 309-1395 .. **Adejobi,** Adeola N '10 %Hunton & W -200 Park Av -NY 10166
(212) 878-8000 .. **Adekeye,** Akinbowale O '06 %Clifford C LLP -31 W 52nd -NY 10019
(212) 345-6000 .. **Adele,** Adeola I '01 Marsh,Inc -1166 Av of Amer -NY 10036
(718) 923-4206 .. **Adelekun,** Temitayo A M '94 %OTDA Fair Hearings -14 Boerum Pl -Brklyn 11201
(516) 432-6263 .. **Adell,** A Trudy '90 (Elovich & A) -164 W Park Av -Long Bch 11561
(631) 712-5633 .. **Adell,** April D '97 %Hon S Feuerstein -1014 Fed Plz Bx9014 -Central Islip 11722
(516) 357-3700 .. **Adelman,** Alvin '74 OfCnsl Cullen and D LLP -100 Q Roosevelt Blvd -Gdn Cty 11530
(718) 999-2916 .. **Adelman,** Amy K '86 %Fire Dept Bureau Leg Afrs -9 Metrotech Ctr -Brklyn 11201 **Fx:**999-2235
(347) 401-9556 .. **Adelman,** Barbara E '80 %Appellate Term -141 Lvngstn -Brklyn 11201
(212) 833-1107 .. **Adelman,** Barry A '70 (Friedman KS&A LLP) -1633 Bway -NY 10019 **Fx:**373-7907
(516) 745-0066 .. **Adelman,** Brian S '95 %Karol H&S,PC -600 Old Cntry Rd -Gdn Cty 11530
(212) 504-6000 .. **Adelman,** Chas M '74 (Cadwalader W&T LLP) -1 World Fncl Ctr -NY 10281
(212) 806-5400 .. **Adelman,** Jana L '07 %Stroock &S&L LLP -180 Maiden Ln -NY 10038
(212) 980-9400 .. **Adelman,** Jason T '95 Burnham Hill Ptrns -590 Mad Av -NY 10022
(212) 816-0418 .. **Adelman,** Marc B '94 Citibank NA -388 Greenwich -NY 10013
(212) 732-4343 .. **Adelman,** Martin B '67 (M Adelman,PC) -225 Bway -NY 10007 **Fx:**587-0570
(212) 248-3140 .. **Adelman,** Michl O '84 (Drinker B&R LLP) -140 Bway -NY 10005
(212) 675-3476 .. **Adelman,** Miriam R '67 -10 W 15th -NY 10011 **Fx:**229-9451
(718) 783-3500 .. **Adelman,** Peter A '95 -95 6th Av -Brklyn 11217
(212) 983-0072 .. **Adelman,** Richd B '80 (Cutler M&A LLP) -150 Wht Plns Rd -Tarrytwn 10591
(516) 239-7979 .. **Adelman,** Seymour '52 -30 Bayberry Rd W -Lawrence 11559 **Fx:**239-1841
(212) 341-2750 .. **Adelman Skarin,** Caryn B '96 %ACS -150 William -NY 10038
(516) 328-3500 .. **Adels,** Elizabeth '80 (McDonnell & A,PC) -401 Franklin Av -Gdn Cty 11530
(516) 569-6930 .. **Adelsberg,** Howard M '86 -445 Central Av -Cedarhrst 11516 **Fx:**569-6935
(212) 592-1400 .. **Adelsberg,** Jonathan A '93 (Herrick,F LLP) -2 Park Av -NY 10016
(212) 813-1314 .. **Adelsberg,** Kenneth E '80 Conway DelGenio Gries & Co,LLC -645 5th Av -NY 10022 **Fx:**813-0580
(212) 483-9490 .. **Adelsohn,** Marc J '73 OfCnsl McElroy DM&C,LLP -88 Pine -NY 10005
(212) 889-4009 .. **Adelson,** Amy '77 (Dershowitz E&A,PC) -220 5th Av -NY 10001
Adelson, Darlene '88 -3941 Salley Ln -Oceanside 11572 **Fx:**(516) 536-0500
(516) 294-5432 .. **Adelson,** David L '88 SrCnsl Kern AC&S,PC -1325 Franklin Av -Gdn Cty 11530
(212) 834-0600 .. **Adelson,** Dawn A '90 (Gordon & S,PC) -355 Lex Av -NY 10017
(212) 915-0110 .. **Adelson,** Jack L '76 Mitsubishi UFJ Trst & Bnkng -420 5th Av -NY 10018
(212) 759-4433 .. **Adelson,** Jonathan S '09 %Alvarez & Marsal -600 Lex Av -NY 10022 **Fx:**759-5532
(212) 708-9524 .. **Adelson,** Nancy R '85 %Museum of Modern Art -11 W 53rd -NY 10019
(212) 319-0990 .. **Adelson,** Robin J '94 %Toby Spitz Assoc -110 E 59th -NY 10022 **Fx:**319-1555
(631) 864-8084 .. **Adelson,** Sandra '82 -400 Townline Rd -Hauppauge 11788 **Fx:**864-8078
(212) 801-6822 .. **Adelstein,** Michl A '00 OfCnsl Greenberg T,LLP -200 Park Av -NY 10166
(914) 249-2000 .. **Adelstein,** Randi D '00 Mastercard -2000 Purchase -Purchase 10577
(212) 504-6000 .. **Aden,** Audrey J '08 %Cadwalader W&T LLP -1 World Fncl Ctr -NY 10281
(212) 859-8000 .. **Aden,** Leah C '08 %Fried FHS&J LLP -1 NY Plz -NY 10004
(212) 963-6108 .. **Adenuga,** Adeboye M '97 UN Invstgtns Div -1 UN Plz -NY 10017
(585) 344-2550 .. **Ader,** Jerry '85 Pub Def -1 W Main -Batavia 14020
(212) 578-2211 .. **Ader,** Lisa F '81 %MetLife -27-01 Qns Plz N -LIC 11101
(212) 921-8677 .. **Ades,** Albert '72 -19 W 44th -NY 10036 **Fx:**382-3362
(718) 237-2000 .. **Ades,** Danl '10 %Leg Aid -111 Lvngstn -Brklyn 11201 **Fx:**237-8737
(516) 560-6400 .. **Ades,** Janet '78 %Leg Aid -1 Helen Keller Way -Hempstd 11550 **Fx:**565-3694
(914) 472-5808 .. **Ades,** Maurice A '93 -19 Heathcote Rd -Scarsdale 10583
(631) 661-6800 .. **Ades,** Paul R '66 PR Ades,PLLC -181 W Main Bx790 -Babylon 11702 **Fx:**661-6266
(516) 234-0190 .. **Ades,** R David '93 -Bx220003 -Gt Neck 11022
(212) 921-8677 .. **Ades,** Rikki L '97 %A Ades -19 W 44th -NY 10036 **Fx:**382-3362
(718) 923-6300 .. **Ades,** Sharon Gursen '95 %Atty Grievance Comm -335 Adams -Brklyn 11201 **Fx:**624-2978
(212) 530-5000 .. **Adesanya,** Temitope M '06 %Milbank TH&M LLP -1 Chase Manh Plz -NY 10005
(718) 410-8564 .. **Adesina,** Olawunmi F '99 -1363 Jerome Av -Bronx 10452
(518) 745-0206 .. **Adeson,** Edwin M '95 -498 Glenn -Glens Fls 12801 **Fx:**745-0059
(718) 338-1971 .. **Adest,** Cheryl Fuchs '96 %H Freifeld -1318 Av J -Brklyn 11230
(516) 393-2200 .. **Adest,** Jeffry '97 (Garfunkel W,PC) -111 Grt Nck Rd -Gt Neck 11021
(718) 243-2862 .. **Adeyemi,** Michl O '92 -26 Court -Brklyn 11242 **Fx:**243-2863
(718) 657-4964 .. **Adeyemo,** Adeshola A '94 (A Adeyemo,PC) -90-79 Sutphin Blvd -Jamaica 11435 **Fx:**206-9502
(516) 742-1741 .. **Adges,** Michl C '87 -22 Jericho Tpk -Mineola 11501 **Fx:**742-1857
(212) 310-8000 .. **Adhinarayanan,** Priya B '08 %Weil G&M LLP -767 5th Av -NY 10153
(914) 862-5140 .. **Adimari,** Cynthia A '08 %DA -1940 Commerce -Yorktwn Hts 10598 **Fx:**862-5146
(212) 233-5000 .. **Adimey,** Marijo C '99 %Simonson HL&G,PC -15 Maiden Ln -NY 10038
(914) 995-2893 .. **Adin,** Justin R '07 %Cnty Atty -148 Martine Av -White Plns 10601 **Fx:**995-5858
(212) 977-9700 .. **Adinolfi,** Elizabeth A '01 Cnsl Phillips N LLP -666 5th Av -NY 10103
(718) 227-6050 .. **Adinolfi,** Thos R '90 TR Adinolfi,PC -340 Dewey Av -Staten Isl 10308 **Fx:**227-1644
(516) 483-1500 .. **Adipietro,** Frank '89 (Allen & A) -100 Main -Hempstd 11550 **Fx:**483-1560
(585) 258-2800 .. **Adiutori,** Anthony J '96 (Underberg & K LLP) -300 Bausch & Lomb Pl -Rchstr 14604
(212) 335-4500 .. **Adivari,** Heather S '01 %DLA Piper LLP -1251 Av of Amer -NY 10020
(212) 548-0600 .. **Adjami,** Mirna E '02 %Open Soc Jstc Initiative -400 W 59th -NY 10019 **Fx:**548-4679
(212) 626-6785 .. **Adjoua,** Hakim B '85 Reid R&R,LLP -1120 Av of Amer -NY 10036
(212) 906-1200 .. **Adkins,** Frances A '04 %Latham & W -885 3rd Av -NY 10022
(516) 496-5822 .. **Adkins,** Justin S '06 %T Spina -170 Froehlich Farm Blvd -Woodbury 11797 **Fx:**496-5420
(518) 478-0535 .. **Adkins,** Margaret I '91 -2 Overlook Dr -Voorheesvll 12186
(212) 880-6000 .. **Adkins,** Mark R T '01 %Torys LLP -237 Park Av -NY 10017
(212) 264-5916 .. **Adlam,** Chartrisse A '98 %DHS -26 Fed Plz -NY 10278
(212) 755-7500 .. **Adler,** Aaron S '05 %Marcus R&D LLP -488 Mad Av -NY 10022
(212) 819-8200 .. **Adler,** Abraham S '09 %White & C LLP -1155 Av of Amer -NY 10036
(212) 508-6100 .. **Adler,** Adam M '03 %Bracewell & G,LLP -1251 Av of Amer -NY 10020
(212) 859-8000 .. **Adler,** Adam R '07 %Fried FHS&J LLP -1 NY Plz -NY 10004
(212) 455-2000 .. **Adler,** Aimee M '01 %Simpson T&B LLP -425 Lex Av -NY 10017
(212) 309-6000 .. **Adler,** Allison J '06 %Morgan L&B LLP -101 Park Av -NY 10178
(212) 707-1402 .. **Adler,** Alyson K '76 %Music Theatre Intl -421 W 54th -NY 10019 **Fx:**397-4684
(212) 998-6645 .. **Adler,** Amy Mehler '93 NYU Law Schl -40 Wshngtn Sq S -NY 10012 **Fx:**995-4894
(646) 217-4404 .. **Adler,** Andrew N '96 OfCnsl Newman & S LLP -845 3rd Av -NY 10022
(212) 558-4000 .. **Adler,** Arthur S '83 (Sullivan & C LLP) -125 Broad -NY 10004
(212) 998-6660 .. **Adler,** Barry E '87 NYU Law Schl -40 Wshngtn Sq S -NY 10012
(212) 902-5761 .. **Adler,** Ben I '90 %Goldman Sachs -1 NY Plz -NY 10004
Adler, Beth S '87 -21 W 86th -NY 10024
(212) 344-2150 .. **Adler Cohn & Koeppel** -575 Lex Av -NY 10022 **Fx:**747-1068
(212) 875-9881 .. **Adler,** Cynthia M '01 -2 W 67th -NY 10023 **Fx:**875-9810
(845) 853-2994 .. **Adler,** Cyrus '59 -225 Tinker -Woodstock 12498
(212) 547-5400 .. **Adler,** David G '06 %McDermott W&E LLP -340 Mad Av -NY 10173
(212) 451-2300 .. **Adler,** David J '74 (Olshan GFR&W LLP) -65 E 55th -NY 10022
(212) 609-6800 .. **Adler,** David J '93 (McCarter & E,LLP) -245 Park Av -NY 10167
(718) 263-0677 .. **Adler,** David N '81 -125-10 Qns Blvd -Kew Gdns 11415 **Fx:**544-0033
(212) 489-8230 .. **Adler,** Deborah A '06 %Davis WT LLP -1633 Bway -NY 10019
(914) 323-7000 .. **Adler,** Debra A '00 (Wilson EME&D LLP) -3 Gannett Dr -White Plns 10604
(212) 837-6000 .. **Adler,** Derek J '89 (Hughes H&R LLP) -1 Bttry Pk Plz -NY 10004
(718) 780-7568 .. **Adler,** Dina L '89 Brooklyn Law Schl -1 Boerum Pl -Brklyn 11201
(212) 891-9100 .. **Adler,** Donald D '81 Cnsl Goldfarb & F LLP -345 Park Av -NY 10154
(212) 344-2150 .. **Adler,** Edw A K '73 (Adler C&K) -575 Lex Av -NY 10022
(516) 248-3722 .. **Adler,** Edw O '72 -666 Old Cntry Rd -Gdn Cty 11530 **Fx:**222-4585
(212) 878-8000 .. **Adler,** Elkan J '07 %Clifford C LLP -31 W 52nd -NY 10019
(516) 377-7100 .. **Adler,** Elliott '97 S Bilkis & Assoc -805 Smith -Baldwin 11510 **Fx:**377-7327
(212) 885-5000 .. **Adler,** Emanuel J '80 (Blank R LLP) -405 Lex Av -NY 10174
(845) 794-7600 .. **Adler,** Eric J '88 -41 Jffrsn Bx719 -Monticello 12701 **Fx:**794-7607
(212) 381-7000 .. **Adler,** Eric L '91 (Sabin B&G LLP) -4 Times Sq -NY 10036
(518) 339-2908 .. **Adler,** Eric L '09 -155 Water -Brklyn 11201
(212) 434-2120 .. **Adler,** Florence M '82 %Lenox Hill Hsptl -100 E 77th -NY 10075 **Fx:**434-2124
(212) 318-3000 .. **Adler,** Fredk R '52 OfCnsl Fulbright & J LLP -666 5th Av -NY 10103
(212) 502-2100 .. **Adler,** Fredric Lee '60 Océ Business Srvcs -460 W 34th -NY 10001 **Fx:**502-2113
(212) 705-7000 .. **Adler,** Gary A '81 (Bingham M LLP) -399 Park Av -NY 10022
(212) 371-8008 .. **Adler,** Gerald A '69 SrCnsl Guzov O,LLC -600 Mad Av -NY 10022
(212) 833-1118 .. **Adler,** Gerald I '82 (Friedman KS&A LLP) -1633 Bway -NY 10019 **Fx:**373-7978
(212) 267-7580 .. **Adler,** Gilbert '55 OfCnsl Adler & G -155 E 55th -NY 10022 **Fx:**546-9265
(212) 267-7580 .. **Adler & Gross** -155 E 55th -NY 10022
(914) 682-2055 .. **Adler,** Herbert '68 -50 Main -White Plns 10606 **Fx:**682-2093
(212) 799-4033 .. **Adler,** Hilary '97 -10 W 65th -NY 10023 **Fx:**724-1764
(212) 259-8000 .. **Adler,** Howard B '87 (Dewey & L LLP) -1301 Av of Amer -NY 10019
(516) 296-7000 .. **Adler,** Ira J '66 (Certilman BA&H,LLP) -90 Merrick Av -E Meadow 11554
(718) 260-9100 .. **Adler,** Jeff S '89 (Adler & K) -26 Court -Brklyn 11242 **Fx:**246-1423
(212) 450-4000 .. **Adler,** Jeremy T '10 %Davis P&W LLP -450 Lex Av -NY 10017
(212) 370-1300 .. **Adler,** Joan W '00 OfCnsl Ellenoff G&S LLP -150 E 42nd -NY 10017
(212) 855-9810 .. **Adler,** Joel M '06 %Goldman Sachs -1 NY Plz -NY 10004
(212) 450-4000 .. **Adler,** Jonathan L '06 %Davis P&W LLP -450 Lex Av -NY 10017
(212) 859-8000 .. **Adler,** Jonathan S '95 (Fried FHS&J LLP) -1 NY Plz -NY 10004
(212) 909-6000 .. **Adler,** Jonathan S '06 %Debevoise & P LLP -919 3rd Av -NY 10022
(212) 596-9000 .. **Adler,** Jordan S '08 %Ropes & G LLP -1211 Av of Amer -NY 10036
(718) 923-8200 .. **Adler,** Julian D '09 Red Hook Comm Jstc Ctr -888 Visitation Pl -Brklyn 11231
(212) 407-4000 .. **Adler,** Kenneth A '86 (Loeb & L,LLP) -345 Park Av -NY 10154

(212) 536-3900 .. **Adler**, Lani A '83 (K&L Gates LLP) -599 Lex Av -NY 10022
(212) 255-9108 .. **Adler**, Leonard '52 -146 W 29th -NY 10001 **Fx**:505-2345
(718) 520-3536 .. **Adler**, Linda P '80 %Supreme Ct Law Dept -88-11 Sutphin Blvd -Jamaica 11435
(516) 739-0000 .. **Adler**, Mady A '86 (Martyn T&M) -330 Old Cntry Rd -Mineola 11501
(516) 561-2877 .. **Adler**, Marjorie G '85 -753 Rockaway Av -Vly Stream 11581
(212) 233-4949 .. **Adler**, Mark S '77 (Adler & S) -110 Wall -NY 10005 **Fx**:(732) 748-2079
(212) 931-8300 .. **Adler**, Martin M '96 %Strongin R&A,LLP -5 Hanover Sq -NY 10004
(212) 317-5400 .. **Adler**, Matthew Q '02 %Swiss Re New Markets -55 E 52nd -NY 10055
(516) 496-5822 .. **Adler**, Meredith G '92 %T Spina -170 Froehlich Farm Blvd -Woodbury 11797 **Fx**:496-5420
(718) 377-7600 .. **Adler**, Michl '05 (Adler & F PC) -3006 Av M -Brklyn 11201 **Fx**:377-7603
(212) 557-7200 .. **Adler**, Michl A '92 %Davidoff M&H,LLP -605 3rd Av -NY 10158
(212) 770-7646 .. **Adler**, Michl E '90 %AIG -70 Pine -NY 10270
(718) 948-2100 .. **Adler**, Michl J '87 %Simonson & C,PC -4060 Amboy Rd -Staten Isl 10308
(212) 788-1019 .. **Adler**, Michl S '81 %Law Dept -100 Church -NY 10007 **Fx**:788-0367
(212) 563-4100 .. **Adler**, Michl S '03 %Cohen W&S LLP -330 W 42nd -NY 10036
(212) 726-7499 .. **Adler**, Mitchell A '05 Murray Hill Med Grp -317 E 34th -NY 10016
(212) 599-1717 .. **Adler**, Mitchell A '05 OfCnsl Barnett EGK&L,PC -122 E 42nd -NY 10168
(845) 358-8929 .. **Adler**, Naomi L '92 United Way of Rockland Cnty -135 Main -Nyack 10960 **Fx**:358-8250
(646) 478-7141 .. **Adler**, Nicholas C '03 -433 W 21st -NY 10011 **Fx**:292-5111
(212) 877-0748 .. **Adler**, Paul S '63 -165 West End Av -NY 10023
(212) 833-1119 .. **Adler**, Philippe '90 (Friedman KS&A LLP) -1633 Bway -NY 10019 **Fx**:373-7919
(631) 231-3775 .. **Adler**, Rita E '75 %Atty Grievance Comm -150 Motor Pkwy -Hauppauge 11788
(212) 406-0181 .. **Adler**, Roger B '71 (R Adler,PC) -233 Bway -NY 10279 **Fx**:406-2313
(212) 808-2700 .. **Adler**, Russell E '99 OfCnsl Pepper H LLP -620 8th Av -NY 10018
(212) 351-4500 .. **Adler**, Russell N '89 (Epstein B&G,PC) -250 Park Av -NY 10177
(212) 836-8000 .. **Adler**, Sara R '92 Cnsl Kaye S LLP -425 Park Av -NY 10022
(212) 735-3000 .. **Adler**, Sheldon S '80 (Skadden ASM&F LLP) -4 Times Sq -NY 10036
(212) 902-0495 .. **Adler**, Steven '05 %Goldman Sachs -85 Broad -NY 10004
(718) 250-1100 .. **Adler**, Steven A '88 %E Garfinkel -12 Metrotech Ctr -Brklyn 11201 **Fx**:250-1168
(516) 876-1105 .. **Adler**, Steven M '89 S Adler,PLLC -666 Old Cntry Rd -Gdn Cty 11530 **Fx**:997-7876
(516) 745-6666 .. **Adler**, Stuart J '87 -1 Old Cntry Rd -Carle Pl 11514 **Fx**:745-6667
(518) 438-9907 .. **Adler**, Sue H R '82 OfCnsl Young SWRB&M,LLC -5 Palisades Dr -Albany 12205
(212) 867-9595 .. **Adler**, Susan L '95 -630 3rd Av -NY 10017
(212) 883-1700 .. **Adler**, Terri L '97 (Duval & S LLP) -101 Park Av -NY 10178
(516) 364-7455 .. **Adler-Greene**, Laura A '94 -180 Froehlich Farm Blvd -Woodbury 11797 **Fx**:364-7459
(518) 402-0205 .. **Adlerman**, Catherine Anne '95 %UIA Bd -Troy Atrium Bx15126 -Albany 12212 **Fx**:402-6208
(212) 403-1000 .. **Adlerstein**, David M '03 %Wachtell LR&K -51 W 52nd -NY 10019
(212) 373-3000 .. **Adlerstein**, Jacob A '08 %Paul WRW&G LLP -1285 Av of Amer -NY 10019
(347) 821-5190 .. **Adlerstein**, Jo Anne C '77 Cnsl Cohen TS&W PC -420 Lex Av -NY 10170 **Fx**:(212) 504-3076
(212) 416-8610 .. **Adlerstein**, Lee Alan '73 %Dept of Law -120 Bway -NY 10271 **Fx**:416-6075
(914) 835-3111 .. **Admirand**, Wm R '71 %MSRI/The Richards Group -14 Calvert -Harrison 10528
(716) 662-1111 .. **Adner**, Jerome D '54 -425 Woodlnd Dr -Orchard Pk 14127
(212) 601-2680 .. **Adnopoz**, Stephen J '82 (Gonzalez S&H LLP) -350 5th Av -NY 10118
(212) 655-3580 .. **Adoff**, Leonard H '92 -140 E 45th -NY 10017 **Fx**:655-3581
(212) 238-8900 .. **Adolfsen**, Louis G '75 (Melito & A,PC) -233 Bway -NY 10279
(914) 997-1470 .. **Adolph**, Eleanor '88 -41 Lawrence Dr -N White Plns 10603 **Fx**:997-1470
(631) 853-4049 .. **Adolph**, Jeffrey A '80 %Cnty Atty -Dennison Bldg Bx6100 -Hauppauge 11788 **Fx**:853-5169
(212) 326-3939 .. **Adolphus**, Nicole Hunter '09 %Jones D -222 E 41st -NY 10017
(516) 932-0216 .. **Adomaites**, Vincent P '00 -410 Jericho Tpke -Jericho 11753 **Fx**:932-1394
(315) 487-0210 .. **Adorante**, Anthony P '67 (Adorante T & Assoc,PC) -5111 W Genesee Bx600 -Camillus 13031 **Fx**:487-2990
(212) 809-5700 .. **Adorno & Yoss LLP** -350 5th Av -NY 10118
(607) 429-5284 .. **Adour**, David L '81 IBM -1701 North -Endicott 13760 **Fx**:429-4119
(212) 269-4900 .. **Adrian**, James M '91 (Ford MEW&G,LLP) -Wall Street Plz -NY 10005
(631) 454-7677 .. **Adrian**, Marcy J '81 %Altana -60 Baylis Rd -Melvll 11747 **Fx**:454-6389
(716) 946-7594 .. **Adrian**, Mark A '82 -191 Canada -Holland 14080 **Fx**:537-2116
(212) 891-4082 .. **Adrion**, Harold L '89 Eisner LLP -750 3rd Av -NY 10017 **Fx**:891-4100
(315) 253-1391 .. **Adsit**, Diane M '87 %DA -95 Genesee -Auburn 13021 **Fx**:253-1521
(212) 728-8000 .. **Advani**, Sameer N '03 %Willkie F&G LLP -787 7th Av -NY 10019
(212) 471-6201 .. **Advocate**, Jason A '94 (Advocate & L,LLP) -780 3rd Av -NY 10017 **Fx**:935-1166
(212) 725-1818 .. **Adwar**, Stephanie Furgang '91 (Furgang & A,LLP) -1325 Av of Amer -NY 10019 **Fx**:941-9711
(914) 428-5300 .. **Adwar**, Stephanie Furgang '91 (Furgang & A,LLP) -11 Martine Av -White Plns 10606 **Fx**:428-0226
(845) 353-1818 .. **Adwar**, Stephanie Furgang '91 (Furgang & A,LLP) -2 Crosfld Av -W Nyack 10994 **Fx**:353-1996
(716) 852-0400 .. **Adymy**, Elizabeth G '94 (Roach BM&G,PC) -424 Main -Buffalo 14202
(212) 583-5224 .. **Aebersold**, Comer I '04 Park Hill Real Est Grp -345 Park Av -NY 10154 **Fx**:583-5713
(646) 471-4000 .. **Aeder**, Mitchel R '88 %PricewaterhouseCoopers LLP -300 Mad Av -NY 10017
(212) 218-2100 .. **Aeling**, Dennis C '10 %Fitzpatrick CH&S -1290 Av of Amer -NY 10104
(212) 259-8000 .. **Aerni**, John M '86 (Dewey & L LLP) -1301 Av of Amer -NY 10019
(212) 436-5013 .. **Afalonis**, Alicia '93 Deloitte & Touche,LLP -2 World Fncl Ctr -NY 10281
(718) 894-4401 .. **Affatato**, Domenick '62 -78-30 Metro Av -Middl Vllg 11379 **Fx**:894-4402
(516) 681-4030 .. **Affatato**, Peter T '49 -1055 Stewart Av -Bethpage 11714
(315) 479-3380 .. **Affleck**, Michl F '99 %UIA Bd -450 S Salina -Syracuse 13202 **Fx**:479-3418
(212) 298-5232 .. **Affler**, David B '91 %Leg Aid -49 Thomas -NY 10013 **Fx**:298-5252
(585) 248-0140 .. **Affronti**, Francis C '93 %Barney & A,LLP -130 D Linden Oaks -Rchstr 14625 **Fx**:248-0175
(718) 286-6000 .. **Affronti**, Kimberly A '85 %DA -125-01 Qns Blvd -Kew Gdns 11415
(585) 753-1380 .. **Affronti**, Leslie A '07 %Cnty Atty -307 Cnty Ofc Bldg -Rchstr 14614 **Fx**:753-1331
(716) 852-0400 .. **Affronti**, Mark R '09 %Roach BM&G,PC -424 Main -Buffalo 14202
(631) 582-5753 .. **Afran**, Neil H '88 (Afran & R,PC) -300 Rabro Dr -Hauppauge 11788 **Fx**:582-5754
(631) 761-7000 .. **Afran**, Neil H '88 %Touro Cllg Law Ctr -225 Eastvw Dr -Central Islip 11722
(716) 853-1616 .. **Africano**, Kenneth W '86 (Harter S&E LLP) -12 Fountain Plz -Buffalo 14202
(914) 997-9550 .. **Afriyie**, Adjoa S '05 %UIA Bd -120 Bloomingdale Rd -White Plns 10605 **Fx**:997-0014
(212) 846-5136 .. **Afriyie**, Xavier D '10 %MTV Networks -1515 Bway -NY 10036 **Fx**:258-8358
(212) 688-5151 .. **Afshar**, Houman '05 %Gibney A&F,LLP -665 5th Av -NY 10022
(212) 676-4039 .. **Afsharnik**, Miles '94 %Zurich US -1 Lbrty Plz -NY 10006 **Fx**:587-7092
(212) 906-1200 .. **Aftab**, Yousuf P '08 %Latham & W -885 3rd Av -NY 10022
(212) 735-4112 .. **Aftanas**, Richd B '95 (Skadden ASM&F LLP) -4 Times Sq -NY 10036
(718) 852-7298 .. **Afton**, John L '67 -101 Clark -Brklyn 11201 **Fx**:852-7298
(212) 730-8133 .. **Afzal**, Asna '07 %Gunderson DSVF&H,LLP -220 W 42nd -NY 10036
(212) 431-7166 .. **Agambila**, Apaamoore '95 (A Agambila & Assoc) -401 Bway -NY 10013
(607) 734-2271 .. **Agan**, Steven E '87 (Sayles & E) -1 W Church -Elmira 14901
(212) 973-9797 .. **Agar**, John S '94 %Saretsky KD&G,LLP -475 Park Av S -NY 10016
(212) 592-1800 .. **Agard**, Wayne A '05 Church Pension Fund -445 5th Av -NY 10016
(212) 244-4664 .. **Agarwal**, Nisha S '07 %NY Lawyers Pub Intrst -151 W 30th -NY 10001 **Fx**:244-4570
(212) 935-3000 .. **Agarwal**, Pooja '09 %Mintz LCFG&P,PC -666 3rd Av -NY 10017
(212) 833-1194 .. **Agarwal**, Rahul '07 %Friedman KS&A LLP -1633 Bway -NY 10019 **Fx**:373-7994
(212) 455-2000 .. **Agarwal**, Ravi K '10 %Simpson T&B LLP -425 Lex Av -NY 10017
(212) 278-1000 .. **Agarwala**, Kanishka '01 %Anderson K&O,PC -1251 Av of Amer -NY 10020
(212) 577-7700 .. **Agarwala**, Shelly '05 %Safe Horizon -2 Lafayette -NY 10007 **Fx**:385-0331
(716) 839-3200 .. **Agate**, John T '68 -4476 Main -Snyder 14226 **Fx**:839-3296
(212) 614-6464 .. **Agathocleous**, Alexis '04 Ctr for Constitutional Rts -666 Bway -NY 10012
(914) 933-0050 .. **Agatston**, Warren S '61 -15 Paddock Rd -Rye Brook 10573 **Fx**:937-7920
(516) 294-5555 .. **Agazarian**, Jaclene A '08 %Del Vecchio & R,LLP -1100 Franklin Av -Gdn Cty 11530 **Fx**:873-5336
(718) 739-6400 .. **Agbaje**, Ayisat Olatundun '00 DHCR -92-31 Union Hall -Jamaica 11433 **Fx**:262-7938
(718) 231-1353 .. **Agbaje**, Surajudeen Gbenga '00 -3550 Wht Plns Rd -Bronx 10467 **Fx**:324-0916
(212) 849-6938 .. **Agbayewa**, Adewole D '00 (A Agbayewa,LLC) -One Penn Plz -NY 10119 **Fx**:849-6901
(212) 805-0258 .. **Agcaoili**, Alastair J '06 %Hon K Wood -500 Pearl -NY 10007
(212) 233-6823 .. **Ageloff**, Kenneth M '68 -277 Bway -NY 10007
(212) 789-2000 .. **Ages**, Danl L '99 %NHL -1251 Av of Amer -NY 10020
(718) 250-2000 .. **Ageyeva**, Alla '06 %DA -350 Jay -Brklyn 11201 **Fx**:250-2314
(212) 455-2000 .. **Aggarwal**, Shalini M '05 %Simpson T&B LLP -425 Lex Av -NY 10017
(212) 581-3320 .. **Aggarwal**, Vashali M '03 Wasserman G&R,LLP -1700 Bway -NY 10019
(212) 947-4999 .. **Agi**, Murad '03 (Camacho MM,LLP) -350 5th Av -NY 10118
(212) 430-8020 .. **Agins**, Hillary Carlton '00 Cnsl LeClairRyan,PC -830 3rd Av -NY 10022
(212) 447-5599 .. **Agins**, Richd C '68 (Agins SR&B,LLP) -386 Park Av S -NY 10016
(212) 447-5599 .. **Agins Siegel Reiner & Bouklas,LLP** -386 Park Av S -NY 10016 **Fx**:447-5549
(914) 378-3900 .. **Aglietti**, Philip M '86 %Kaplan & M -1 Exec Blvd -Ynkrs 10701
(212) 508-6100 .. **Agnant**, Evelyn R '03 %Bracewell & G,LLP -1251 Av of Amer -NY 10020
(716) 851-2711 .. **Agnello**, Catherine M '83 %UIA Bd -290 Main -Buffalo 14202 **Fx**:851-2795
(212) 345-5069 .. **Agnello**, Patricia Anne '96 %Marsh USA -1166 Av of Amer -NY 10036 **Fx**:345-4808
(518) 434-7045 .. **Agnello**, Richd W '09 Research Fndtn SUNY -Bx9 -Albany 12201 **Fx**:434-8352
(212) 715-1000 .. **Agneshwar**, Anand '94 (Arnold & P LLP) -399 Park Av -NY 10022
(212) 728-8189 .. **Agnetti**, Peter M '07 %Willkie F&G LLP -787 7th Av -NY 10019
(516) 746-8000 .. **Agnew**, Linda S '95 (Jaspan S LLP) -300 Grdn City Plz -Gdn Cty 11530
(212) 554-7800 .. **Agnew**, Sheila A '04 %Moses & S LLP -405 Lex Av -NY 10174
(212) 750-7800 .. **Agnifilo**, Marc A '92 %Brafman & Assoc -767 3rd Av -NY 10017 **Fx**:750-3906
(212) 732-3200 .. **Agnihotri**, Bhavna M '04 %Carter L&M LLP -2 Wall -NY 10005
(212) 527-1000 .. **Agnitti**, Angelica '10 %Jones HC&B PC -1 Bttry Pk Plz -NY 10004
(212) 259-8000 .. **Agnos**, Dean '07 %Dewey & L LLP -1301 Av of Amer -NY 10019
(516) 396-0800 .. **Agoglia**, E Kevin '88 (Agoglia H&A,PC) -500 N Bway -Jericho 11753
(516) 396-0800 .. **Agoglia**, Emmet J '58 (Agoglia H&A,PC) -500 N Bway -Jericho 11753
(516) 396-0800 .. **Agoglia Holland & Agoglia,PC** -500 N Bway -Jericho 11753
(212) 265-5222 .. **Agoglia**, Thos A '91 -1650 Bway -NY 10019 **Fx**:265-5226

(347) 529-5226 .. **Agolia**, Anthony '07 -285 3rd Av -Brklyn 11215
(212) 848-4000 .. **Agor**, Andrew C '02 %Shearman & S LLP -599 Lex Av -NY 10022
(518) 387-7713 .. **Agosti**, Ann Marie M '93 GE -1 Rsrch Cir -Schnctdy 12309 **Fx**:387-7751
(585) 349-0222 .. **Agostinelli**, Gino '01 -12 Amity -Spencerprt 14559
(716) 855-3200 .. **Agostinelli**, Guy J '81 (Zdarsky S&A) -298 Main -Buffalo 14202
(315) 422-8191 .. **Agostinelli**, Jody L '10 %Leg Aid -351 S Warren -Syracuse 13202 **Fx**:472-2819
(718) 722-6472 .. **Agostino**, Aprilanne '85 %Appllt Div 2nd Dept -45 Monroe Pl -Brklyn 11201 **Fx**:858-2446
(718) 389-2427 .. **Agostino**, Frank '83 (Agostino & Assoc,PC) -500 Kngslnd Av -Brklyn 11222 **Fx**:349-6997
(516) 364-6501 .. **Agostino**, Joan '92 -7600 Jericho Tpk -Woodbury 11797 **Fx**:584-8348
(516) 431-1000 .. **Agostisi**, Robt M '02 %Corp Cnsl -1 W Chester -Long Bch 11561 **Fx**:431-1016
(516) 248-9880 .. **Agovino & Asselta,LLP** -330 Old Cntry Rd -Mineola 11501 **Fx**:248-9879
(212) 224-6925 .. **Agovino**, Eric M '03 Forest Labs,Inc -909 3rd Av -NY 10022
(516) 248-9880 .. **Agovino**, Peter L '73 (Agovino & A,LLP) -330 Old Cntry Rd -Mineola 11501
(212) 575-1557 .. **Agranoff**, Gerald N '76 OfCnsl Kupferman & K LLP -132 Titicus Rd Bx641 -N Salem 10560 **Fx**:937-3552
(212) 406-3911 .. **Agrapidis**, Evans C '85 (Leanza & A,PC) -521 5th Av -NY 10175
(212) 906-1200 .. **Agrati**, Paola '07 %Latham & W -885 3rd Av -NY 10022
(212) 446-4800 .. **Agrawal**, Jai '98 (Kirkland & E LLP) -153 E 53rd -NY 10022
(212) 909-6000 .. **Agrawal**, Kamal '08 %Debevoise & P LLP -919 3rd Av -NY 10022
(212) 935-3000 .. **Agrawal**, Priya '07 %Mintz LCFG&P,PC -666 3rd Av -NY 10017
(212) 336-8330 .. **Agrawal**, Suyash '09 (Susman G LLP) -560 Lex Av -NY 10022
(212) 852-7204 .. **Agress**, Ellen '73 %News America Inc -1211 Av of Amer -NY 10036
(212) 759-8882 .. **Agress**, Vivian H '53 -60 Sutton Pl S -NY 10022
(516) 294-9500 .. **Agresta**, Louis N Jr. '74 -114 Old Cntry Rd -Mineola 11501 **Fx**:294-9510
(718) 852-5894 .. **Agresta**, Maurizio M '83 -369 Jay -Brklyn 11201
(518) 486-2653 .. **Agresta**, Paul '84 %Dept Pub Srvc -3 ESP -Albany 12223
(212) 349-7511 .. **Agri**, Orin E '56 -291 Bway -NY 10007
(718) 969-1425 .. **Agrippina**, Anthony '95 -162-04 Union Tpk -Flushng 11366 **Fx**:969-1458
(718) 969-1425 .. **Agrippina**, Joanne S '01 -162-04 Union Tpk -Flushng 11366
(646) 252-5880 .. **Agritelley**, Ralph J '84 %Transit Auth -2 Bway -NY 10004 **Fx**:252-5559
(631) 642-2478 .. **Agro**, Nicholas J '94 NJ Agro,PC -1000 Main -Pt Jffrsn 11777
(631) 913-4444 .. **Agruso**, Joanne Smith '81 (Dell LT&V LLP) -5 Orvll Dr -Bohemia 11716
(718) 631-5750 .. **Agruso**, Joel A '84 (Northwoods Abstract) -445 Park Av -NY 10022
(212) 509-5050 .. **Agthe**, Thilo C '92 (Wuersch & G LLP) -100 Wall -NY 10005
(212) 261-8000 .. **Aguanno**, Giuseppe '10 %Mendes & M,LLP -750 7th Av -NY 10019
(212) 836-8000 .. **Agudelo**, Jonathan M '10 Kaye S LLP -425 Park Av -NY 10022
(212) 966-1320 .. **Agudo**, Dino R '02 -100 Lafayette -NY 10013
(718) 966-4141 .. **Agugliaro**, John P '99 -45 Page Av -Staten Isl 10309 **Fx**:966-4189
(212) 735-3000 .. **Aguiar**, Lauren E '96 (Skadden ASM&F LLP) -4 Times Sq -NY 10036
(646) 386-3040 .. **Aguiar**, Mark R '82 %Appellate Term-1st Dept -60 Centre -NY 10007
(516) 280-5387 .. **Aguiar**, Yvette '03 -114 Old Cntry Rd -Mineola 11501
(212) 702-1829 .. **Aguila**, Andres E '02 Bank of Montreal -3 Times Sq -NY 10036
(631) 467-0837 .. **Aguila**, Lorna C '85 -1311 Grundy Av -Holbrook 11741 **Fx**:471-8749
(646) 435-4866 .. **Aguilar**, Anna Conlon '01 -521 5th Av -NY 10175
(212) 640-1793 .. **Aguilar**, Michl J '01 Amer Exp -200 Vesey -NY 10285
(212) 388-3616 .. **Aguirre**, Gloria I '97 %32B-J Leg Srvcs -101 Av of Amer -NY 10013 **Fx**:388-3584
(212) 306-7184 .. **Aguirre**, Majalina G '04 Ofc of Collective Bargaining -40 Rector -NY 10006
(212) 756-2000 .. **Aguirre**, Nanette '04 %Schulte R&Z LLP -919 3rd Av -NY 10022
(718) 822-6999 .. **Aguirre**, Ricardo A '97 R Aguirre & Assoc,Inc -1967 Turnbull Av -Bronx 10473
(212) 612-4352 .. **Agulnek**, Barbara S '90 %Chubb Grp -55 Water -NY 10041
(212) 233-9500 .. **Agulnick**, Barry W '67 (Agulnick & G,LLC) -305 Bway -NY 10007 **Fx**:693-1666
(212) 571-2266 .. **Agulnick**, Peter M '99 (P Agulnick,PC) -305 Bway -NY 10007
(718) 352-4800 .. **Agulnick**, Scott E '00 (Greenblatt & A,PC) -55 Nrthrn Blvd -Gt Neck 11021 **Fx**:732-2110
(212) 603-6428 .. **Agun**, Igbeare Francis '96 -1633 Bway -NY 10019 **Fx**:489-8340
(516) 983-4885 .. **Agunwa**, Ebele T '05 Visiting Nurse Srvc of NY -11523 197th -St Albans 11412
(212) 902-3177 .. **Agus**, Raanan A '96 %Goldman Sachs & Co -1 NY Plz -NY 10004
(212) 376-5757 .. **Agus**, Stephen A '76 (Agus & Prtnrs,PC) -75 Maiden Ln -NY 10038 **Fx**:376-5752
(516) 355-2070 .. **Agusta**, Michl J '89 -1012 Maple Dr -Franklin Sq 11010 **Fx**:355-2074
(718) 739-4444 .. **Aguwa**, Placidus Nnanyere '96 (Placid & E PC) -161-10 Jamaica Av -Jamaica 11432 **Fx**:739-4440
(212) 474-1000 .. **Agyapong**, Eno G '10 %Cravath S&M LLP -825 8th Av -NY 10019
(212) 326-3939 .. **Agyeiwaah**, Maame Y '09 %Jones D -222 E 41st -NY 10017
(347) 296-1179 .. **Agyeman**, Kwaku B '07 Supreme Ct Law Dept -360 Adams -Brklyn 11201 **Fx**:643-6114
(212) 287-2839 .. **Ahamed**, Saleemah H '99 Sterling Stamos -450 Park Av -NY 10022
(212) 431-4455 .. **Ahari**, M Nader '90 -524 Bway -NY 10012 **Fx**:431-4457
(212) 605-0352 .. **Aharoni**, Danl J '77 -575 Mad Av -NY 10022 **Fx**:605-0319
(212) 854-5669 .. **Aharonson**, Donna Fenn '99 %Columbia Univ -535 W 116th 412 Low Mem'l Library -NY 10027
(718) 261-7700 .. **Ahdout**, Haleh '01 %Rappaport HC&R,PC -118-35 Qns Blvd -Frst Hlls 11375
(516) 431-4222 .. **A'Hearn**, Brian A '87 (A'Hearn & G) -161 Monroe Blvd -Long Bch 11561
(516) 538-2500 .. **A'Hearn**, Francis B '62 -600 Front -Hempstd 11550 **Fx**:538-4134
(212) 489-9809 .. **Ahearn**, Jos D '59 -445 W 54th -NY 10019
(518) 270-2802 .. **Ahearn**, Jos M '96 Cnty Conflict Defenders Ofc -61 State -Troy 12180 **Fx**:270-2686
(518) 690-7000 .. **Ahearn**, Kathy A '84 (Guercio & G,LLP) -24 Century Hill Dr -Latham 12110 **Fx**:690-0783
(646) 422-4319 .. **Ahearn**, Kristen M '03 Memorial Hospital -1275 York Av -NY 10065
(631) 283-4111 .. **Ahearn**, Michl '68 -41 Meeting House Ln -Southampton 11968 **Fx**:283-7711
(845) 744-3443 .. **Ahearn**, Timothy J '75 -11 Boniface Bx236 -Pine Bush 12566 **Fx**:744-3663
(718) 391-1720 .. **Ahearne**, Jane '80 %Dept Design & Cnstrctn -30-30 Thomson Av -LIC 11101 **Fx**:391-1894
(631) 435-8135 .. **Aheran**, Antonio '86 -651 Suffolk Av -Brentwd 11717 **Fx**:435-8306
(212) 909-6000 .. **Ahern**, Andrew M '06 %Debevoise & P LLP -919 3rd Av -NY 10022
(516) 571-3800 .. **Ahern**, Brendan M '08 %DA -262 Old Cntry Rd -Mineola 11501 **Fx**:248-9479
(631) 269-9500 .. **Ahern**, Dennis P '93 (Ahern & A) -One Main -Kings Pk 11754 **Fx**:269-9561
(631) 852-1650 .. **Ahern**, Michl J '75 %Leg Aid -300 Center Dr -Rvrhead 11901 **Fx**:852-1655
(631) 269-9500 .. **Ahern**, Wm F Jr. '58 (Ahern & A) -One Main -Kings Pk 11754 **Fx**:269-9561
(212) 626-4100 .. **Aherne**, Meredith A '07 %Baker & M LLP -1114 Av of Amer -NY 10036
(212) 449-6348 .. **Aherne**, Robt E '65 %Merrill Lynch -220 Bway -NY 10038
(212) 493-7566 .. **Ahlbaum**, Mitchel C '96 %NYC Partnership -1 Bttry Pk Plz -NY 10004 **Fx**:509-1280
(716) 856-5500 .. **Ahlers**, Christopher D '94 %Damon M LLP -200 Delaware Av -Buffalo 14202
(914) 428-3313 .. **Ahlers**, Keith J '84 (Curan AF&N,LLP) -14 Mamaroneck Av -White Plns 10601 **Fx**:949-5800
(212) 558-4000 .. **Ahlers**, Werner F '06 %Sullivan & C LLP -125 Broad -NY 10004
(716) 856-4000 .. **Ahlstrom**, Benjamin K '07 %Hodgson R LLP -140 Pearl -Buffalo 14202
(716) 858-2424 .. **Ahlstrom**, Kristi M '07 DA -25 Delaware Av -Buffalo 14202 **Fx**:858-7425
(631) 223-3046 .. **Ahlstrom**, Robt J '49 -4 Skylark Ct -Huntngtn Sta 11746 **Fx**:425-9774
(631) 223-3046 .. **Ahlstrom**, Robt J Jr. '89 -4 Skylark Ct -Huntngtn Sta 11746 **Fx**:425-9774
(212) 318-6000 .. **Ahluwalia**, Anupama '06 %Paul HJ&W LLP -75 E 55th -NY 10022
(212) 679-1104 .. **Ahluwalia**, Kuljit S '92 -Two Penn Plz -NY 10121 **Fx**:629-6568
(914) 683-1333 .. **Ahmad**, Hamra '04 My Sisters Place -1 Water -White Plns 10601 **Fx**:683-1412
(212) 419-0555 .. **Ahmad**, Hassan '04 -22 Crtlandt -NY 10007 **Fx**:419-0556
(212) 441-1694 .. **Ahmad**, Jamal '98 Aon Consulting,Inc -199 Water -NY 10038
(914) 946-4656 .. **Ahmad**, Khwaja Mohiuddin '96 (Ahmad & T) -199 Main -White Plns 10601 **Fx**:946 7828
(212) 259-8000 .. **Ahmad**, Usman '09 %Dewey & L LLP -1301 Av of Amer -NY 10019
(718) 482-7777 .. **Ahmad**, Usman B '00 -29-27 Qns Plz N -LIC 11101
(718) 254-6522 .. **Ahmad**, Zainab N '06 US Dist Ct-EDNY -271 Cadman Plz E -Brklyn 11201
(212) 566-4805 .. **Ahmed**, Eman '06 Dept of Bldgs -280 Bway -NY 10007
(212) 704-6000 .. **Ahmed**, Farah S '06 %Troutman S LLP -405 Lex Av -NY 10174
(212) 885-5000 .. **Ahmed**, Fatima H '10 %Blank R LLP -405 Lex Av -NY 10174
(212) 698-3500 .. **Ahmed**, Hassan '04 Dechert LLP -1095 Av of Amer -NY 10036
(718) 590-2000 .. **Ahmed**, Imran S '06 DA -198 E 161st -Bronx 10451 **Fx**:590-6477
(212) 839-5300 .. **Ahmed**, Saima S '01 %Sidley A LLP -787 7th Av -NY 10019
(212) 966-5932 .. **Ahmed**, Sameer '10 AALDEF -99 Hudson -NY 10013 **Fx**:966-4303
(516) 433-3394 .. **Ahmed**, Shamim '96 -15 North Rd -Oyster Bay 11771 **Fx**:433-3372
(646) 205-7880 .. **Ahmed**, Sheila '05 %Cruz & G & Assoc -110 William -NY 10038 **Fx**:(212) 233-9848
(914) 682-3900 .. **Ahmed**, Sumera M '05 Lawyers Title Ins -Ten Bank -White Plns 10606 **Fx**:682-3556
(516) 294-5433 .. **Ahmuty Demers & McManus** -200 IU Willets Rd -Albertson 11507 **Fx**:294-5387
(631) 727-2340 .. **Ahmuty Demers & McManus** -750 Roanoke Av -Rvrhead 11901 **Fx**:727-8198
(212) 513-7788 .. **Ahmuty Demers & McManus** -123 William -NY 10038 **Fx**:513-7843
(914) 584-9934 .. **Ahmuty Demers & McManus** -55 Church -White Plns 10601
(845) 223-3470 .. **Ahmuty Demers & McManus** -1531 Route 82 -Hopewell Junct 12533 **Fx**:223-3287
(516) 488-3300 .. **Ahmuty**, Steven J '79 (Shaub AC&S,LLP) -1983 Marcus Av -Lk Success 11042
(516) 294-5433 .. **Ahmuty**, Wm R III '71 (Ahmuty D&M) -200 IU Willets Rd -Albertson 11507
(212) 547-2062 .. **Ahn**, Bobi '95 %RCG Information Technology Inc -110 Wall -NY 10005
(212) 687-0100 .. **Ahn**, Bridgette Y '03 %Harris B PLLC -100 Wall -NY 10005
(518) 452-5600 .. **Ahn**, Caroline B '08 %Heslin RF&M PC -5 Columbia Cir -Albany 12203
(212) 907-9700 .. **Ahn**, Deana D '02 %Smith G&R,LLP -250 Park Av -NY 10177
(212) 439-4034 .. **Ahn**, Eunju '04 %Korean Mission to UN -335 E 45th -NY 10017
(212) 705-7000 .. **Ahn**, Flora '07 %Bingham M LLP -399 Park Av -NY 10022
(212) 521-5400 .. **Ahn**, Han J '04 %Reed S LLP -599 Lex Av -NY 10022
(212) 949-9022 .. **Ahn**, Harry K '00 (Abelman F&S) -666 3rd Av -NY 10017
(212) 335-9000 .. **Ahn**, Helen H '05 %DA -1 Hogan Pl -NY 10013
(212) 506-5000 .. **Ahn**, Jae-Hyon '07 %Orrick H&S LLP -51 W 52nd -NY 10019
(347) 648-2504 .. **Ahn**, James J '03 %Citigroup -2 Court Sq -LIC 11101
(212) 810-5300 .. **Ahn**, Janey J '01 BlackRock Inc -40 E 52nd -NY 10022
(212) 530-5000 .. **Ahn**, Jeeseon '09 %Milbank TH&M LLP -1 Chase Manh Plz -NY 10005
(212) 930-9700 .. **Ahn**, Jennifer '07 %Sichenzia RFF LLP -61 Bway -NY 10006
(718) 939-9400 .. **Ahn**, Jenny C '99 (Fields & A,LLP) -167-20 Nrthrn Blvd -Flushng 11358
(212) 596-9000 .. **Ahn**, Joshua J '10 %Ropes & G LLP -1211 Av of Amer -NY 10036
(212) 460-2764 .. **Ahn**, Kathleen Kyungsook '95 Con Ed -4 Irving Pl -NY 10003
(212) 269-4900 .. **Ahn**, Richd J '08 %Ford MEW&G,LLP -Wall Street Plz -NY 10005
(212) 464-2266 .. **Ahn**, Sandra R '95 JP Morgan -345 Park Av -NY 10154
(646) 840-3642 .. **Ahn**, Saul S '90 Linden Advisors LP -590 Mad Av -NY 10022
(212) 594-1035 .. **Ahne**, Saml Sang Hyun '86 -1220 Bway -NY 10001 **Fx**:967-1112
(585) 232-6500 .. **Aho**, Jon J '98 (Harter S&E LLP) -1600 Bausch & Lomb Pl -Rchstr 14604

(212) 670-0208 .. **Aholu,** Cadmus '00 Merrill Lynch -222 Bway -NY 10038
(845) 344-2524 .. **Ahrenholz,** Kevin P '09 %C Curcio -1 Edgewtr Dr -Middletwn 10940 **Fx:**344-2528
(212) 474-1000 .. **Ahrens,** Cherylyn H B '05 %Cravath S&M LLP -825 8th Av -NY 10019
(212) 450-4000 .. **Ahrens,** Emma L '09 %Davis P&W LLP -450 Lex Av -NY 10017
(607) 776-9631 .. **Ahrens,** Fredk H Jr. '72 (Cnty Atty) -3 E Pulteney Sq -Bath 14810 **Fx:**776-4930
(212) 906-1200 .. **Ahrens,** Matthew H '02 OfCnsl Latham & W -885 3rd Av -NY 10022
(516) 223-7100 .. **Ahronheim,** Keith B '80 -374 Franklin Blvd -Merrick 11566
(212) 963-9056 .. **Ahsan,** Ali '03 Exec Ofc Sec Gen -S3850B -NY 10017
(845) 897-2460 .. **Ahsan,** Aziz M '92 (Ahsan & Assoc,PLLC) -1330 Route 52 -Fishkill 12524 **Fx:**897-2461
(718) 850-1952 .. **Ahuja,** Anand M '98 -101-70 Lefferts Blvd -Richmnd Hll 11419
(212) 497-1500 .. **Ahuja,** Sima Saran '02 BNY ConvergEx Grp -1633 Bway -NY 10019
(914) 579-2100 .. **Aibara,** Jeffrey R '02 (Reed & A, PLLC) -586 Commerce -Thornwd 10594
(212) 765-7532 .. **Aibel,** Donald J '66 -250 W 57th -NY 10107 **Fx:**(201) 767-5583
(212) 635-1871 .. **Aibel,** James H '79 Bk of NY -1 Wall -NY 10286
(212) 929-6443 .. **Aibel,** Louise R '98 %Majestic Rayon Corp -116 W 23rd -NY 10011
(212) 929-6443 .. **Aibel,** Richd '72 -116 W 23rd -NY 10011
(516) 745-6622 .. **Aicher,** John G Jr. '90 -377 Oak -Gdn Cty 11530 **Fx:**465-0673
(212) 839-5300 .. **Aicher,** Robt D '06 (Sidley A LLP) -787 7th Av -NY 10019
(516) 745-6622 .. **Aicher,** Stacey Baumann '92 -377 Oak -Gdn Cty 11530
(718) 238-9898 .. **Aidala,** Arthur L '92 -8118 13th Av -Brklyn 11228 **Fx:**921-3292
(212) 750-9700 .. **Aidala,** Louis R '63 (Baratta B&A) -546 5th Av -NY 10036
(212) 622-5280 .. **Aidelson,** David B '93 Chase Manhattan Bk -277 Park Av -NY 10172
(212) 558-4000 .. **Aidinoff,** M Bernard '54 SrCnsl Sullivan & C LLP -125 Broad -NY 10004
(212) 310-8000 .. **Aidun,** Christopher K '81 (Weil G&M LLP) -767 5th Av -NY 10153
(718) 426-0444 .. **Aiello & Cannick** -69-06 Grand Av -Maspeth 11378 **Fx:**803-9764
(518) 482-0279 .. **Aiello,** James J '42 -744 Wstrn Av -Albany 12203
(212) 902-7370 .. **Aiello,** John F '00 Goldman Sachs -1 NY Plz -NY 10004
(212) 878-7900 .. **Aiello,** Kathleen M '09 %Fox R LLP -100 Park Av -NY 10017
(516) 747-1131 .. **Aiello,** Mary Ann '81 MA Aiello,PC -666 Old Cntry Rd -Gdn Cty 11530 **Fx:**794-3363
(631) 470-6889 .. **Aiello,** Maryann K '03 Garden City Grp Inc -105 Maxess Rd -Melvll 11747 **Fx:**940-6554
(212) 310-8000 .. **Aiello,** Michl J '95 (Weil G&M LLP) -767 5th Av -NY 10153
(212) 545-1740 .. **Aiello,** Philip '96 (Ateshoglou & A,PC) -381 Park Av S -NY 10016
(718) 426-0444 .. **Aiello,** Robt J '85 (Aiello & C) -69-06 Grand Av -Maspeth 11378
(914) 768-6988 .. **Aiello,** Rosalia Enea '97 Hudson Valley Bank -21 Scarsdale Rd -Ynkrs 10707
(516) 571-3800 .. **Aiello,** Teresa A '05 DA -262 Old Cntry Rd -Mineola 11501 **Fx:**248-9479
(212) 506-1700 .. **Aiello Rocha,** Karina C '06 Kasowitz BT&F LLP -1633 Bway -NY 10019
(212) 785-5050 .. **Aiena,** Michelle K '05 %Kardaras & K LLP -44 Wall -NY 10005
(212) 818-9200 .. **Aieta,** Mario '86 (Satterlee SB&B LLP) -230 Park Av -NY 10169
(212) 460-5757 .. **Aiken,** Candice D '99 %Gellis & M,LLP -137 5th Av -NY 10010
(212) 264-2819 .. **Aiken,** Chas F '02 Hon RK Musgrave -1 Fed Plz -NY 10278
(212) 563-5904 .. **Aiken,** Paul '86 %Authors Guild -116 W 23rd -NY 10011 **Fx:**564-5363
(914) 285-8500 .. **Aikman,** J David '73 %TK Moore -701 Wstchstr Av -White Plns 10604 **Fx:**285-8510
(212) 468-8000 .. **Aiko,** Tomohisa '03 %Morrison & F LLP -1290 Av of Amer -NY 10104
(212) 644-6006 .. **Aimone,** Jon C '68 OfCnsl Dickerson T&M -600 Mad Av -NY 10022
(212) 450-4000 .. **Ain,** Jennifer A '06 %Davis P&W LLP -450 Lex Av -NY 10017
(718) 278-2224 .. **Ain,** Jody M '87 -31-51 Crescent -LIC 11106
(212) 986-6000 .. **Ain,** Jonathan A '99 (Kleinberg KW&C,PC) -551 5th Av -NY 10176
(914) 750-5933 .. **Ainalakis-Barone,** Panagiota H '05 %Kissel H&W LLP -580 Wht Plns Rd -Tarrytwn 10591
(914) 417-3400 .. **Ainbinder,** Bruce D '94 (Littleton JUP&K LLP) -1 Manhattanvll Rd -Purchase 10577
(718) 265-1500 .. **Aini,** Jack A '97 (Aini & L,PLLC) -2615 Coney Isl Av -Brklyn 11223 **Fx:**265-1515
(212) 318-3000 .. **Ainscow,** Donald G '07 %Fulbright & J LLP -666 5th Av -NY 10103
(631) 265-3448 .. **Ainsley,** Fred M '92 -527 Townline Rd -Hauppauge 11788 **Fx:**265-0992
(631) 265-3448 .. **Ainsley,** Fred M Jr. '08 %F Ainsley,PC -527 Townline Rd -Hauppauge 11788 **Fx:**265-0992
(212) 935-3000 .. **Ainsworth,** Kevin N '95 (Mintz LCFG&P,PC) -666 3rd Av -NY 10017
(516) 357-3000 .. **Aiosa,** James V '92 (Rivkin R LLP) -926 RXR Plz -Uniondale 11556
(212) 340-0400 .. **Aisenson,** Tami J '81 Appllt Div 1st Dept -27 Mad Av -NY 10010 **Fx:**889-4412
(518) 285-8939 .. **Aitcheson,** Jessie A '96 Hon L Stein -50 Chapel -Albany 12207 **Fx:**434-5980
(631) 390-0010 .. **Aitken,** Richd C '94 (Bruno G&S,LLP) -445 Broad Hollow Rd -Melvll 11747
(516) 944-3000 .. **Aitken,** Robt L '76 (Ressa & A) -33 Main -Pt Wash 11050
(718) 590-3909 .. **Aivars,** Elizabeth '81 %Law Dept -198 E 161st -Bronx 10451 **Fx:**590-2686
(212) 222-3882 .. **Aiyar,** Chitra G '06 %African Srvcs Comm -429 W 127th -NY 10027 **Fx:**222-7067
(212) 450-4000 .. **Aizen,** Ron M '06 %Davis P&W LLP -450 Lex Av -NY 10017
(718) 797-9096 .. **Aizin,** Michl '86 -26 Court -Brklyn 11242 **Fx:**797-9670
(212) 422-0202 .. **Aizley,** Arthur H '96 %Sedgwick DM&A LLP -125 Broad -NY 10004
(718) 558-5656 .. **Ajah,** Jennifer C '98 (Ajah & Assoc,PC) -90-24 Sutphin Blvd -Jamaica 11435 **Fx:**558-8501
(585) 232-1420 .. **Ajaka,** Maroun G '02 -144 Exchange Blvd -Rchstr 14614
(212) 361-7993 .. **Ajami,** Tarik Fouad '97 %Dept Homeless Srvcs -33 Beaver -NY 10004 **Fx:**361-8002
(516) 571-3800 .. **Ajamu,** Ali '03 %DA -262 Old Cntry Rd -Mineola 11501 **Fx:**248-9479
(212) 361-8051 .. **Ajayi,** Katherine O '02 %Dept Homeless Srvcs -33 Beaver -NY 10004 **Fx:**361-8002
(212) 508-6335 .. **Ajayi-Obe,** Marcia '94 %Zesiger Capital Grp -320 Park Av -NY 10022 **Fx:**508-6329
(718) 494-3800 .. **Ajello,** Danl M '98 -1550 Richmond Av -Staten Isl 10314 **Fx:**494-3824
(914) 254-7500 .. **Ajello,** Gary '83 -1925 Commerce Box One -Yorktwn Hts 10598
(718) 876-6439 .. **Ajello,** Michl V '65 %Supreme Ct -355 Front -Staten Isl 10304
(718) 948-1140 .. **Ajello,** Nicole M '01 (Ajello & S) -3974 Amboy Rd -Staten Isl 10308 **Fx:**948-1160
(212) 753-7500 .. **Ajhar,** Marsha G '84 Cnsl Hartman & C LLP -488 Mad Av -NY 10022
(212) 906-1200 .. **Ajiashvili,** Nathan '06 %Latham & W -885 3rd Av -NY 10022
(516) 535-5555 .. **Ajlouny,** Paul '99 (P Ajlouny & Assoc PC) -320 Old Cntry Rd -Gdn Cty 11530 **Fx:**535-5556
(212) 326-3939 .. **Ajudua,** Helena O '10 %Jones D -222 E 41st -NY 10017
(212) 450-4000 .. **Ajzen,** Roman '08 %Davis P&W LLP -450 Lex Av -NY 10017
(212) 308-8505 .. **Akabas,** Seth A '82 (Akabas & S) -488 Mad Av -NY 10022
(212) 308-8505 .. **Akabas & Sproule** -488 Mad Av -NY 10022 **Fx:**308-8582
(631) 665-5884 .. **Akaike,** Kenji '95 %Marcos N&A,LLP -220 5th Av -Bay Shr 11706 **Fx:**968-0946
(718) 858-2488 .. **Akakwam,** Philip A '99 -303 Lvngstn -Brklyn 11217 **Fx:**858-2489
(845) 639-6627 .. **Akalonu,** Rosalyn B '94 -169 S Main -New Cty 10956 **Fx:**639-6628
(212) 408-2500 .. **Akalski,** Jos C '09 %Baker B,LLP -30 Rckfllr Plz -NY 10112
(718) 659-6900 .. **Akbar,** Al A '01 (Akbar & Assoc,LLC) -114-29 Lefferts Blvd -S Ozone Pk 11420 **Fx:**659-7900
(212) 998-6680 .. **Akbar,** Amna Amber '05 NYU Intl Human Rts Clinic -245 Sullivan -NY 10012
(917) 703-2326 .. **Akbik,** Mohamad Adel '05 -244 5th Av -NY 10001
(212) 387-0600 .. **Akbulut,** John C '98 -36 E 20th -NY 10003
(845) 563-9613 .. **Akerib,** David D E '95 Jacoby & M,LLP -1279 Route 300 Bx1111 -Newburgh 12550 **Fx:**562-3492
(212) 415-9200 .. **Akerman,** Nathaniel H '79 (Dorsey & W LLP) -250 Park Av -NY 10177
(212) 233-0880 .. **Akerman,** Robt '00 -11 Bway -NY 10004
(212) 880-3800 .. **Akerman Senterfitt** -335 Mad Av -NY 10017 **Fx:**880-8965
(516) 739-7200 .. **Akeson,** NancyAnn '94 %TPS Admin Srvcs -Bx8020 -Gdn Cty 11530 **Fx:**739-7202
(212) 336-0019 .. **Akhtar,** Mona Shams '03 SEC -3 World Fncl Ctr -NY 10281 **Fx:**336-1323
(518) 462-6831 .. **Akhtar,** Saima A '09 Empire Justice Ctr -119 Wshngtn Av -Albany 12210 **Fx:**462-6687
(516) 944-0301 .. **Akhtar-Gutman,** Halima '89 (Gutman & G) -33 Main -Pt Wash 11050 **Fx:**944-0310
(212) 436-2060 .. **Akian,** Steven '01 Deloitte & Touche LLP -2 World Fncl Ctr -NY 10281 **Fx:**653-2940
(212) 587-0760 .. **Akin,** Zafer A '95 (Akin & S,LLC) -30 Broad -NY 10004 **Fx:**587-4169
(718) 230-0050 .. **Akinola,** Oladipo C '00 (D Akinola,PC) -333 Nostrand Av -Brklyn 11216 **Fx:**230-0085
(718) 923-4225 .. **Akinrefon,** Akinwale Damilola '98 %OTDA Fair Hearings -14 Boerum Pl -Brklyn 11201
(212) 340-0649 .. **Akinrele,** Donna F '94 Counsel Press,LLC -520 8th Av -NY 10018
(212) 530-5000 .. **Akins,** Brittany T '10 %Milbank TH&M LLP -1 Chase Manh Plz -NY 10005
(212) 544-2000 .. **Akinsola,** Noel N '03 -4500 Bway -NY 10040 **Fx:**544-2054
(716) 568-1169 .. **Akiwumi,** Derek B '09 D Akiwumi,PLLC -848 Robin Rd -West Amherst 14228
(212) 735-3000 .. **Akiwumi-Assani,** Arlene A '10 %Skadden ASM&F LLP -4 Times Sq -NY 10036
(212) 858-1204 .. **Akiyama,** Shinya '95 (Pillsbury WSP LLP) -1540 Bway -NY 10036
(212) 858-1000 .. **Akiyama,** Takeo '85 (Pillsbury WSP LLP) -1540 Bway -NY 10036
(212) 512-4392 .. **Akkapeddi,** Prasanth Rao '01 %McGraw-Hill -1221 Av of Amer -NY 10020 **Fx:**512-4827
(315) 445-1831 .. **Akl,** Ronda T '91 %V Lang -333 Butternut Dr Bx503 -Syracuse 13214 **Fx:**445-1167
(212) 326-3939 .. **Aklufi,** Michl J '99 %Jones D -222 E 41st -NY 10017
(516) 227-6300 .. **Akmal,** Rizwan '05 %Ettelman & H,PC -100 Q Roosevelt Blvd -Gdn Cty 11530
(212) 309-1329 .. **Akman,** Michl L '10 %Hunton & W -200 Park Av -NY 10166
(212) 471-8459 .. **Akoglu,** Ningur '05 %Herzfeld & R,PC -125 Broad -NY 10004
(212) 630-3766 .. **Akohonae,** Rachael Arffa '01 Condé Nast -4 Times Sq -NY 10036
(718) 224-9824 .. **Akpinar,** Timur '94 -Horace Harding Station Bx620766 -Little Neck 11362
(212) 581-4540 .. **Akselrad,** Ira '89 US Realty Advsrs,LLC -1370 Av of Amer -NY 10019 **Fx:**581-4950
(212) 668-1700 .. **Akselrod,** Danl '05 %V Mandel,PC -80 Wall -NY 10005 **Fx:**668-1701
(212) 364-5340 .. **Akselrod,** Olga '03 %Innocence Project -100 5th Av -NY 10011 **Fx:**364-5341
(212) 735-3000 .. **Akselrod-Ifrah,** Michele '91 Cnsl Skadden ASM&F LLP -4 Times Sq -NY 10036
(212) 308-3999 .. **Akst,** George S '77 (Akst & A) -150 E 58th -NY 10155 **Fx:**317-2946
(212) 308-3999 .. **Akst,** Leslie K '79 (Akst & A) -150 E 58th -NY 10155 **Fx:**317-2946
(646) 471-5925 .. **Akunobera,** Festus '09 PricewaterhouseCoopers -300 Mad Av -NY 10017
(212) 635-7065 .. **Akyeampong,** Nathaniel E '09 Bank of NY -1 Wall -NY 10286
(212) 425-7200 .. **Akyuz,** Ishak David '02 %Kenyon & K,LLP -1 Bway -NY 10004
(718) 590-2000 .. **Alabre,** Rither '05 %DA -198 E 161st -Bronx 10451 **Fx:**590-6477
(516) 741-2100 .. **Alacqua,** S Marc '97 (Alacqua & B) -265 Post Av -Westbury 11590
(212) 770-6299 .. **Alade,** Bamidele H '00 %AIG -70 Pine -NY 10270
(516) 676-0322 .. **Alagheband,** Kamran Albert '09 -29 Glen Cove Av -Glen Cove 11542 **Fx:**676-6922
(914) 965-1515 .. **Alagna,** Roberta L '86 %J Romano -703 Ynkrs Av -Ynkrs 10704 **Fx:**965-0410
(716) 884-4602 .. **Alaimo,** Carol J '67 -556 Lafayette Av -Buffalo 14222
(718) 932-8130 .. **Alaimo,** Maria Pia '97 -2215 31st -Astoria 11105
(718) 381-3311 .. **Alaimo,** Richd '69 -65-09 Fresh Pond Rd -Rdgwd 11385
(631) 254-6300 .. **Alaimo,** Vincent S '84 -265 E Main -E Islip 11730 **Fx:**667-8176
(212) 816-4278 .. **Alalu,** Brian J '02 Citigroup -388 Greenwich -NY 10013
(212) 599-7299 .. **Alam,** M Najmul '01 (MN Alam,PC) -211 E 43rd -NY 10017 **Fx:**599-3450
(212) 302-9000 .. **Alam,** Navaid '95 Infrastucture Funding Grp -1500 Bway -NY 10036
(212) 272-5983 .. **Alamo,** Michl John '02 %JP Morgan Chase -383 Mad Av -NY 10179

(914) 323-7000 .. **Alampi,** Jennifer '04 %Wilson EME&D LLP -3 Gannett Dr -White Plns 10604
(646) 386-3359 .. **Alania,** Janel R '08 Hon B Fried Supreme Ct -60 Centre -NY 10007
(212) 446-4800 .. **Alankar,** Melinda Chow '07 %Kirkland & E LLP -153 E 53rd -NY 10022
(914) 636-5657 .. **Alarcon,** Ariel A '05 %Dryer D&W -271 North Av -New Rchll 10801 **Fx:**636-5890
(631) 867-2348 .. **Alarcon,** Rory M '07 -140 Fell Ct -Hauppauge 11788
(212) 232-1300 .. **Alarcon Demetri,** Patricia S '00 (Lewis BB&S LLP) -77 Water -NY 10005
(212) 770-7406 .. **Alarimo,** Lori A '95 %AIG Tech Srvcs -80 Pine -NY 10005
(315) 472-6676 .. **Alario,** Linda E '82 Alario & Assoc,PC -500 S Salina -Syracuse 13202
(718) 891-1200 .. **Alatsas & Taub,PC** -2115 Av U -Brklyn 11229 **Fx:**891-2274
(718) 891-1200 .. **Alatsas,** Theo '96 (Alatsas & T,PC) -2115 Av U -Brklyn 11229
(212) 790-4500 .. **Alazraki,** Marcia D '77 (Manatt P&P,LLP) -7 Times Sq -NY 10036
(212) 859-5080 .. **Alba,** Ana B '03 Alba Law,PC -110 Wall -NY 10005 **Fx:**943-2300
(212) 969-3000 .. **Alba,** Ilise S '98 %Proskauer R LLP -1585 Bway -NY 10036
(631) 367-7100 .. **Alba,** Mario Jr. '03 %Coughlin SGR&R LLP -58 S Srvc Rd -Melvll 11747
(631) 422-0500 .. **Alba,** Philip F '52 (P Alba,PC) -1250 Montauk Hwy -W Islip 11795 **Fx:**422-0967
(212) 940-8800 .. **Albakri,** Amina El-Sayad '05 %Katten MR LLP -575 Mad Av -NY 10022
(212) 541-2000 .. **Albakri,** Hassan '07 %Bryan C LLP -1290 Av of Amer -NY 10104
(516) 827-9713 .. **Albala,** Brent M '92 -19 Emmet Pl -Hicksvll 11801 **Fx:**827-9713
(212) 508-6100 .. **Albalah,** David C '92 (Bracewell & G,LLP) -1251 Av of Amer -NY 10020
(516) 248-7000 .. **Albanese & Albanese LLP** -1050 Franklin Av -Gdn Cty 11530 **Fx:**747-7777
(212) 310-8000 .. **Albanese,** Anthony J '97 (Weil G&M LLP) -767 5th Av -NY 10153
(914) 681-8700 .. **Albanese,** Christopher A '97 (Milber MP&S LLP) -3 Barker Av -White Plns 10601
(212) 613-2081 .. **Albanese,** Christopher A '08 %Gibbons PC -1 Penn Plz -NY 10119 **Fx:**554-9620
(516) 746-6000 .. **Albanese,** Christopher V '94 Albanese Devlpmnt Corp -1050 Franklin Av -Gdn Cty 11530 **Fx:**746-0580
(718) 250-2000 .. **Albanese,** Darren M '07 %DA -350 Jay -Brklyn 11201 **Fx:**250-2314
(212) 980-1900 .. **Albanese,** David J '07 %Donovan & G,LLP -261 Mad Av -NY 10016
(212) 244-6199 .. **Albanese,** Debra M '98 %Traflet & F -1001 Av of Amer -NY 10018
(845) 294-6765 .. **Albanese,** Jeffrey '87 J Albanese,PLLC -155 Main Bx119 -Goshen 10924
(585) 454-3377 .. **Albanese,** Jeffrey S '98 %Brown & T,LLC -19 Prince -Rchstr 14607
(607) 272-5212 .. **Albanese,** Jonathan O '83 OfCnsl Coughlin & G,LLP -401 E State -Ithaca 14850
(914) 725-7000 .. **Albanese,** Jos M '84 -700 Wht Plns Rd -Scarsdale 10583
(212) 281-5700 .. **Albanese,** Jos M '84 Women's Chamber of Commerce -1524 Amstrdm Av -NY 10031
(516) 248-7000 .. **Albanese,** Jos R '58 (Albanese & A LLP) -1050 Franklin Av -Gdn Cty 11530
(914) 725-5262 .. **Albanese,** Kathleen '89 -117 Walworth Av -Scarsdale 10583 **Fx:**725-5262
(518) 725-3575 .. **Albanese,** Mario M '55 (Albanese & A) -35 S Main -Gloversvll 12078 **Fx:**725-1829
(845) 291-2050 .. **Albanese,** Maryellen Black '87 %DA -255-275 Main -Goshen 10924 **Fx:**291-2085
(212) 335-9000 .. **Albanese,** Michl F '09 %DA -1 Hogan Pl -NY 10013
(518) 725-3575 .. **Albanese,** Michl M '87 (Albanese & A) -35 S Main -Gloversvll 12078 **Fx:**725-1829
(212) 208-9583 .. **Albanese,** Noelle P '02 Liberty Intl Underwriters -55 Water -NY 10041
(212) 801-9236 .. **Albanese,** Rachel Ehrlich '02 OfCnsl Greenberg T,LLP -200 Park Av -NY 10166
(212) 732-2929 .. **Albanese,** Sal F '90 OfCnsl Dansker & A Assoc -30 Vesey -NY 10007 **Fx:**732-8795
(631) 421-6011 .. **Albanese,** Toni J '86 -223 Wall #138 -Huntngtn 11743
(516) 248-7000 .. **Albanese,** Vincent A '93 %Albanese & A LLP -1050 Franklin Av -Gdn Cty 11530
(516) 248-7000 .. **Albanese,** Vincent M '49 (Albanese & A LLP) -1050 Franklin Av -Gdn Cty 11530
(646) 610-5400 .. **Albano,** Danl J '93 %NYPD -1 Police Plz -NY 10038
(646) 386-3176 .. **Albano,** Donna M '92 %Hon D Ling-Cohan -80 Centre -NY 10013
(212) 922-9700 .. **Albano,** Gabriella '84 %1st Amer Title -633 3rd Av -NY 10017 **Fx:**922-0881
(212) 406-3110 .. **Albano,** Geronimo C '90 -139 Fulton -NY 10038 **Fx:**406-3114
(516) 487-5900 .. **Albano,** Matthew N '98 GCP Capital Grp,LLC -60 Cuttermill Rd -Gt Neck 11021
(212) 225-2000 .. **Albano,** Michl J '02 (Cleary GS&H) -1 Lbrty Plz -NY 10006
(212) 408-5100 .. **Albarracin,** Carlos T '02 (Chadbourne & P LLP) -30 Rckfllr Plz -NY 10112
(212) 907-7300 .. **Albaugh,** Dallas L '00 %Golenbock EAB&P -437 Mad Av -NY 10022
(718) 720-2877 .. **Albee,** Christopher J '94 Votto & C,LLP -60 Bay -Staten Isl 10310
(718) 743-5739 .. **Albenda,** Louise S '84 -276 Exeter -Brklyn 11235 **Fx:**743-7950
(212) 969-3000 .. **Alber,** Christine '97 %Proskauer R LLP -1585 Bway -NY 10036
(212) 839-5300 .. **Alber,** Mark A '08 %Sidley A LLP -787 7th Av -NY 10019
(516) 572-2000 .. **Alber,** Michl J '08 %DA -99 Main -Hempstd 11550 **Fx:**572-2606
(631) 462-6900 .. **Alber,** Ronald T '03 (Alber & L) -5036 Jericho Tpk -Commack 11725 **Fx:**462-6999
(212) 258-8000 .. **Alberdingk-Thijm,** Yvette J '94 %MTV Networks -1515 Bway -NY 10036 **Fx:**258-8358
(914) 997-7600 .. **Alberga,** Jeanna M '98 %Penichet Firm,PC -140 Grand -White Plns 10601 **Fx:**997-8155
(914) 576-4710 .. **Alberi,** Danielle R '96 (Alberi A&A) -251 Broadvw Av -New Rchll 10804
(914) 576-4710 .. **Alberi,** Dante C '99 (Alberi A&A) -251 Broadvw Av -New Rchll 10804
(212) 533-3442 .. **Albers,** Rock '78 -4 Lex Av -NY 10010
(212) 715-9100 .. **Alberstadt,** Alexandra Kambouris C '95 SpclCnsl Kramer LN&F,LLP -1177 Av of Amer -NY 10036
(212) 880-3800 .. **Alberstadt,** Kenneth G '89 (Akerman S) -335 Mad Av -NY 10017
(212) 907-7300 .. **Albert,** Allyson R '06 %Golenbock EAB&P -437 Mad Av -NY 10022
(212) 302-6574 .. **Albert,** Amanda J '08 %Riker DSH&P LLP -500 5th Av -NY 10110
(212) 902-1000 .. **Albert,** Bruce A '96 %Goldman Sachs -85 Broad -NY 10004
(516) 872-5297 .. **Albert,** Bruce W '70 -877 N Corona Av -N Vly Strm 11580
(212) 209-3061 .. **Albert,** Craig J '83 (Reitler K&R LLC) -885 3rd Av -NY 10022
(212) 244-2999 .. **Albert,** Dana M '09 %Kopff N&D LLP -440 9th Av -NY 10001
(212) 250-2500 .. **Albert,** David M '04 Deutsche Bk -60 Wall -NY 10005
(212) 277-6500 .. **Albert,** Dawn Rudenko '98 (Dickstein S LLP) -1633 Bway -NY 10019
(718) 643-1805 .. **Albert,** Edw H '75 -250 Henry -Brklyn 11201
(212) 845-2604 .. **Albert,** Elizabeth '88 KBC Fncl Products -140 E 45th -NY 10017
(914) 332-6666 .. **Albert,** Eugene '88 (Albert & A) -100 Wht Plns Rd -Tarrytwn 10591 **Fx:**332-0806
(212) 837-6000 .. **Albert,** Garett J '70 SrCnsl Hughes H&R LLP -1 Bttry Pk Plz -NY 10004
(914) 667-1764 .. **Albert,** Ingrid S '87 -9 W Prospect Av -Mt Vernon 10550 **Fx:**664-1812
(212) 982-9604 .. **Albert,** Jack J '51 -301 E 21st -NY 10010 **Fx:**608-7415
(212) 974-7474 .. **Albert,** Jean C '00 (Cowan DA&S LLP) -41 Mad Av -NY 10010
(516) 227-0700 .. **Albert,** Jed C '86 (Farrell F,PC) -1320 RXR Plz -Uniondale 11556
(646) 943-8756 .. **Albert,** John Prakash '99 After-School Corp -1440 Bway -NY 10018
(914) 332-6666 .. **Albert,** Jos F '98 (Albert & A) -100 Wht Plns Rd -Tarrytwn 10591 **Fx:**332-0806
(212) 688-6262 .. **Albert,** Joshua J '97 -780 3rd Av -NY 10017
(212) 728-2200 .. **Albert,** Lauren S '89 (Axinn V&H LLP) -114 W 47th -NY 10036
(212) 556-2100 .. **Albert,** Lisa L '00 %King & S -1185 Av of Amer -NY 10036
(212) 227-0200 .. **Albert,** Louis I '82 -299 Bway -NY 10007 **Fx:**732-6972
(212) 584-0700 .. **Albert,** Marc S '96 (Seeger W LLP) -1 William -NY 10004
(718) 286-1500 .. **Albert,** Margot D '07 %Leg Srvcs -97-77 Qns Blvd -Rego Pk 11374 **Fx:**275-5352
(716) 858-2424 .. **Albert,** Matthew A '08 %DA -25 Delaware Av -Buffalo 14202 **Fx:**858-7425
(516) 463-4538 .. **Albert,** Miriam R '90 Hofstra Law Schl -121 Hofstra Univ -Hempstd 11549
(212) 312-2370 .. **Albert,** Natalie '78 %Leg Aid -60 Lafayette -NY 10013 **Fx:**349-0874
(212) 373-3000 .. **Albert,** Neale M '61 OfCnsl Paul WRW&G LLP -1285 Av of Amer -NY 10019
(631) 543-0003 .. **Albert,** Peter G '85 -356 Vets Mem'l Hwy -Commack 11725 **Fx:**864-3786
(212) 880-9560 .. **Albert,** Richd F '90 (Morvillo AGIA&B,PC) -565 5th Av -NY 10017
(212) 969-3000 .. **Albert,** Rory J '78 (Proskauer R LLP) -1585 Bway -NY 10036
(212) 566-4060 .. **Albert,** Shelley D '91 (Dario YS&A) -44 Wall -NY 10005
(212) 421-2233 .. **Albert,** Stephen A '77 (Wilk A LLP) -675 3rd Av -NY 10017
(212) 298-5122 .. **Albert,** Todd '03 %Leg Aid -49 Thomas -NY 10013 **Fx:**298-5252
(212) 578-8693 .. **Albertalli,** Roy C '79 %MetLife -27-01 Qns Plz N -LIC 11101
(516) 826-8938 .. **Albertelli,** Jennifer A '02 %R Young & Assoc -1321 Bellmore Av -Bellmore 11710 **Fx:**826-8932
(212) 557-4700 .. **Alberti,** Andrew A '75 -300 E 42nd -NY 10017
(631) 853-5761 .. **Alberti,** Frank J II '88 %Cnty Atty -400 Carleton Av -Central Islip 11722 **Fx:**853-7788
(585) 546-5530 .. **Alberti,** Michl F '02 West Group -50 Broad E -Rchstr 14694
(315) 422-1391 .. **Alberto,** Valerie L F '06 %Green & S,PLLC -One Lincoln Ctr #900 -Syracuse 13202
(212) 506-2500 .. **Alberts,** David W '97 (Mayer B LLP) -1675 Bway -NY 10019
(646) 386-5891 .. **Alberts,** Francesca '88 %MHLS -41 Mad Av -NY 10010
(718) 590-1900 .. **Alberts,** Francis T '95 -934 Sheridan Av -Bronx 10451 **Fx:**590-8189
(212) 637-1038 .. **Alberts,** Jeffrey E '02 %US Atty -1 St Andrews Plz -NY 10007
(212) 218-2100 .. **Alberts,** Melissa R '10 %Fitzpatrick CH&S -1290 Av of Amer -NY 10104
(212) 506-5000 .. **Alberts,** Patricia E '02 %Orrick H&S LLP -51 W 52nd -NY 10019
(516) 248-1700 .. **Alberts,** Stephanie M '07 %Forchelli CDSM&T,LLP -333 Earle Ovngton Blvd -Uniondale 11553
(631) 852-2500 .. **Albertson,** Janet M '88 %DA -200 Center Dr -Rvrhead 11901 **Fx:**852-1769
(212) 995-5965 .. **Albertson,** Joshua B '09 Curbed.com LLC -36 Cooper Sq -NY 10003
(212) 442-6806 .. **Albertus,** Angela M '92 %Law Dept -52 Duane -NY 10007 **Fx:**442-6868
(718) 261-7200 .. **Alberty,** Regina '94 -118-21 Qns Blvd -Frst Hlls 11375 **Fx:**261-7989
(212) 461-2323 .. **Albin,** Geri L '09 %Saiber LLC -44 Wall -NY 10005
(516) 794-4282 .. **Albin,** Lee M '54 -666 Old Cntry Rd -Gdn Cty 11530
(516) 572-2000 .. **Albin,** Stacy E '08 %DA -99 Main -Hempstd 11550 **Fx:**572-2606
(212) 619-5400 .. **Albin,** Suzanne R '83 OfCnsl Newman F LLP -1250 Bway -NY 10001
(212) 977-4800 .. **Albinder,** Wayne M '83 %Donald Zucker Co -101 W 55th -NY 10019 **Fx:**586-0258
(631) 727-3904 .. **Albinski,** Lindsey M '10 %H Arnoff -206 Roanoke Av -Rvrhead 11901 **Fx:**727-3940
(212) 592-1400 .. **Albinsky,** Julie '09 %Herrick,F LLP -2 Park Av -NY 10016
(718) 250-2000 .. **Albinson,** Grace E '08 %DA -350 Jay -Brklyn 11201 **Fx:**250-2314
(917) 637-3600 .. **Albisa,** Catherine '91 %Ctr for Reproductive Rts -120 Wall -NY 10005 **Fx:**637-3666
(718) 579-3000 .. **Albo,** Elisa Ann '90 %Leg Aid -1020 Grnd Cncrs -Bronx 10451 **Fx:**588-2611
(212) 966-5253 .. **Albom,** Barbara S '89 -166 Mercer -NY 10012 **Fx:**941-8566
(212) 259-8000 .. **Albrecht,** Matthew J '05 %Dewey & L LLP -1301 Av of Amer -NY 10019
(212) 407-4000 .. **Albrecht,** Michelle R '02 %Loeb & L,LLP -345 Park Av -NY 10154
(516) 942-0244 .. **Albrecht,** Randall J '82 %Office oDA&R -375 N Bway -Jericho 11753 **Fx:**942-0353
(845) 369-8989 .. **Albrecht,** Scott M '89 S Albrecht,PC -198 Orange Av -Suffern 10901 **Fx:**369-0944
(315) 234-8500 .. **Albright,** Audra A '04 US Dist Ct -100 S Clinton Bx7367 -Syracuse 13261
(518) 459-1819 .. **Albright,** Jennifer '07 %S Flaherty -21 Everett Rd Ext -Albany 12205 **Fx:**459-1827
(516) 921-2800 .. **Albright,** Joan Mongada '83 Ctr for Performing Arts -310 NY Av -Huntngtn 11743
(585) 342-4410 .. **Albright,** Johnson S II '77 (Burke AH&R,LLP) -1800 Hudson Av -Rchstr 14617

(718) 731-3114 .. **Albright,** Rhonda L '89 Citizens Advise Bur - Immigration Prgrm -2070 Grnd Cncrs -Bronx 10457
(631) 864-4967 .. **Albright,** Stephen '83 Cnsl Primary Land Srvcs LLC -368 Vets Mem'l Hwy -Commack 11725 **Fx:**864-4972
(212) 980-0010 .. **Albright,** Tina E '91 SrCnsl Kozusko HVW LLP -575 Mad Av -NY 10022 **Fx:**751-0084
(212) 596-9000 .. **Albro,** Amy E '09 %Ropes & G LLP -1211 Av of Amer -NY 10036
(212) 343-0708 .. **Albro,** George W '78 %Assn Leg Aid Attys -568 Bway -NY 10012 **Fx:**343-0966
(212) 221-5700 .. **Albstein,** Andrew W '82 (Goldberg WFG LLP) -1501 Bway -NY 10036
(212) 221-5700 .. **Albstein,** Iris A '79 (Goldberg WFG LLP) -1501 Bway -NY 10036
(585) 586-2510 .. **Album,** Betsy L '93 %B Album -100 Ofc Park Way -Pittsfrd 14534 **Fx:**387-9234
(585) 387-0500 .. **Album,** Marc D '93 (Olver K LLP) -100 Ofc Park Way -Pittsfrd 14534
(212) 969-3000 .. **Album,** Michl J '84 (Proskauer R LLP) -1585 Bway -NY 10036
(718) 720-4200 .. **Albunio,** Vincent A '91 -891 Forest Av -Staten Isl 10310
(212) 455-2000 .. **Alcabes,** Elisa Anne '89 SrCnsl Simpson T&B LLP -425 Lex Av -NY 10017
(212) 249-3800 .. **Alcamo,** Cris '93 Coral Realty -400 Broome -NY 10013
(212) 596-9000 .. **Alcantar Villagran,** Jose R '08 %Ropes & G LLP -1211 Av of Amer -NY 10036
(212) 408-5100 .. **Alcasabas,** Allison M '97 (Chadbourne & P LLP) -30 Rckfllr Plz -NY 10112
(315) 425-2700 .. **Alciati,** Wm C '10 %Hiscock & B,LLP -One Park Pl -Syracuse 13202
(212) 225-2000 .. **Alcock,** Mary E '95 Cnsl Cleary GS&H -1 Lbrty Plz -NY 10006
(914) 381-7600 .. **Alcott,** Danl R '93 (Dorf Law Firm,LLP) -740 W Bstn Post Rd -Mamaroneck 10543 **Fx:**381-7608
(315) 413-4050 .. **Alcott,** Lee '85 (French-Alcott) -One Park Pl -Syracuse 13202 **Fx:**413-4055
(212) 373-3000 .. **Alcott,** Mark H '65 OfCnsl Paul WRW&G LLP -1285 Av of Amer -NY 10019
(716) 934-3669 .. **Ald,** Steven M '95 -715 Central Av -Dunkirk 14048
(212) 268-6999 .. **Aldad,** Lior '96 (Aldad & Assoc) -350 5th Av -NY 10118 **Fx:**268-6998
(212) 655-5000 .. **Aldag,** James A '99 %Gannon R&M -120 Bway -NY 10271
(718) 286-6000 .. **Aldea,** Donna '99 %DA -125-01 Qns Blvd -Kew Gdns 11415
(631) 581-1923 .. **Alden,** Cameron '91 -33 Locust Av -Islip 11751
(212) 225-2000 .. **Alden,** Carissa L '09 %Cleary GS&H -1 Lbrty Plz -NY 10006
(212) 909-6000 .. **Alden,** Steven M '72 (Debevoise & P LLP) -919 3rd Av -NY 10022
(518) 792-6360 .. **Alden,** Timothy J '81 -513 Glen -Glens Fls 12801 **Fx:**792-6390
(212) 428-2140 .. **Alden,** Tricia Troy '84 OCA -25 Beaver -NY 10004 **Fx:**428-2197
(718) 250-2000 .. **Alderman,** Bruce '07 %DA -350 Jay -Brklyn 11201 **Fx:**250-2314
(212) 210-2100 .. **Alderman,** Cyna J '97 %Daily News,LP -450 W 33rd -NY 10001 **Fx:**643-7855
(315) 422-8131 .. **Alderman,** Edw B '57 (Alderman & A) -472 S Salina -Syracuse 13202 **Fx:**474-7507
(315) 415-1808 .. **Alderman,** Eric M '76 (E Alderman,PC) -123 Gadwell Ln -Manlius 13104 **Fx:**(800) 561-7929
(914) 499-4817 .. **Alderman,** Eric R '89 IBM -1 New Orchrd Rd -Armonk 10504 **Fx:**499-6085
(315) 329-0138 .. **Alderman,** Judith '84 -201 W Genesee -Fayettevll 13066 **Fx:**637-2122
(212) 847-3460 .. **Alderman,** Peter B '00 GoldenTree Asset Mgmt LP -300 Park Av -NY 10022
(315) 422-8131 .. **Alderman,** Richd B '69 (Alderman & A) -472 S Salina -Syracuse 13202 **Fx:**474-7507
(516) 294-8844 .. **Alderman,** Todd '07 %L'Abbate BC&C,LLP -1001 Franklin Av -Gdn Cty 11530
(212) 640-1008 .. **Alderoty,** Stuart '04 Amer Exp -200 Vesey -NY 10285
(212) 808-7800 .. **Alderson,** Jason R '08 %Kelley D&W LLP -101 Park Av -NY 10178
(212) 661-8000 .. **Alderson,** Robt E Jr. '99 (Lucas & M,LLP) -475 Park Av S -NY 10016
(212) 921-5959 .. **Aldoroty,** Lisa S '85 -57 W 38th -NY 10018 **Fx:**921-1083
(212) 922-2200 .. **Aldous,** Alexandros R '06 %Watson F&W LLP -1133 Av of Amer -NY 10036
(212) 969-3000 .. **Aldous,** Kenneth E '00 %Proskauer R LLP -1585 Bway -NY 10036
(518) 453-4640 .. **Aldrich,** Christopher R '87 Albany City Ct -209 City Hall -Albany 12207 **Fx:**434-5034
(518) 533-3000 .. **Aldrich,** John R '77 (Bond S&K,PLLC) -111 Wshngtn Av -Albany 12210
(212) 373-8085 .. **Aldrich,** Liberty '96 Ctr for Ct Innovation -520 8th Av -NY 10018
(212) 335-4500 .. **Aldrich,** Nicholas F '08 %DLA Piper LLP -1251 Av of Amer -NY 10020
(315) 358-6177 .. **Aldrich,** Vaughn N '80 -Bx430 -Hogansburg 13655 **Fx:**358-2430
(212) 753-5599 .. **Aldridge,** Christopher S '87 (Brill & M) -845 3rd Av -NY 10022
(718) 590-2000 .. **Aldridge,** Emily A '04 %DA -198 E 161st -Bronx 10451 **Fx:**590-6477
(212) 715-9100 .. **Aldridge,** Jeffrey C '07 %Kramer LN&F,LLP -1177 Av of Amer -NY 10036
(212) 834-5032 .. **Aldridge,** Joy L '92 %Chase Manhattan Bk -270 Park Av -NY 10017 **Fx:**834-6559
(516) 735-5266 .. **Aldridge,** Timothy D '90 -38 Constable Ln -Levittwn 11756
(212) 685-7101 .. **Aledort,** Eric S '89 Next Jump,Inc -261 5th Av -NY 10016 **Fx:**685-7081
(631) 755-0101 .. **Aledort,** Mark R '88 Cnsl Lewis JAA,LLP -425 Broad Hollow Rd -Melvll 11747
(212) 319-7759 .. **Alegria,** Anselmo A '88 -261 Mad Av -NY 10016
(212) 941-9090 .. **Aleguire,** Zabrina B '06 %The Door -121 Av of Amer -NY 10013 **Fx:**941-0714
(212) 909-6000 .. **Alekseyev,** Yaroslav '08 %Debevoise & P LLP -919 3rd Av -NY 10022
(212) 745-1380 .. **Aleman,** Jose L '01 -1230 Av of Amer -NY 10020
(212) 640-2676 .. **Aleman,** Michl S Jr. '09 AmEx -200 Vesey -NY 10285
(718) 401-8669 .. **Alemany,** Jack F '83 -840-11 Grnd Cncrs -Bronx 10451
(212) 907-9600 .. **Alenstein,** Ronald H '66 (Ingram YGC&B,LLP) -250 Park Av -NY 10177
(516) 873-0972 .. **Alesandro,** John A '95 Diocese of Rockeville Centre -120 5th -Gdn Cty 11530
(516) 248-1700 .. **Alesi,** Barbara Shaheen '83 (Forchelli CDSM&T,LLP) -333 Earle Ovngton Blvd -Uniondale 11553
(212) 468-8000 .. **Alesi,** Kara C '09 %Morrison & F LLP -1290 Av of Amer -NY 10104
(631) 755-5214 .. **Alesia,** Sal J '96 JP Morgan -395 N Srvc Rd -Melvll 11747
(914) 995-2683 .. **Alesio,** Lori A '92 %Cnty Atty -148 Martine Av -White Plns 10601 **Fx:**995-5858
(212) 661-3535 .. **Alessandro,** Alba '98 (Hodgson R LLP) -60 E 42nd -NY 10165
(716) 854-7900 .. **Alessi,** Donald A '70 -6215 Transit Rd -E Amherst 14051
(716) 856-4000 .. **Alessi,** John A '03 %Hodgson R LLP -140 Pearl -Buffalo 14202
(646) 279-8106 .. **Alessi,** Joy M '98 -244 5th Av -NY 10001
(212) 336-2000 .. **Alessi,** Kerri Lynn '00 %Patterson BW&T LLP -1133 Av of Amer -NY 10036
(516) 746-8000 .. **Alessi,** Marc S '05 OfCnsl Jaspan S LLP -300 Grdn City Plz -Gdn Cty 11530
(212) 701-3000 .. **Alessi,** Robt A '83 (Cahill G&R LLP) -80 Pine -NY 10005 **Fx:**269-5420
(518) 626-9000 .. **Alessi,** Robt J '86 (Dewey & L LLP) -99 Wshngtn Av -Albany 12210
(631) 243-1866 .. **Alessi,** Santo '87 -10 Smith -Deer Pk 11729
(315) 424-0300 .. **Alessio,** George P Jr. '88 -214 N State -Syracuse 13203 **Fx:**295-0956
(212) 416-8000 .. **Alestra,** Mary F '02 Dept of Law -120 Bway -NY 10271
(516) 316-4700 .. **Alevas,** Susan F '91 Alevas Consulting Grp Inc -Bx309 -Ctr Moriches 11934
(212) 907-0700 .. **Alex,** Martis '81 (Labaton S LLP) -140 Bway -NY 10005
(718) 250-2000 .. **Alexander,** Allana '04 %DA -350 Jay -Brklyn 11201 **Fx:**250-2314
(212) 768-6700 .. **Alexander,** Andris T '10 %Sonnenschein N&R LLP -2 World Fncl Ctr -NY 10281
(212) 298-5000 .. **Alexander,** Anju M '08 Leg Aid -49 Thomas -NY 10013 **Fx:**298-5252
(315) 474-2911 .. **Alexander,** Ann M '07 %Smith SK&S,PC -250 S Clinton -Syracuse 13202
(212) 715-9100 .. **Alexander,** Anne D '81 %Kramer LN&F,LLP -1177 Av of Amer -NY 10036
(212) 425-3000 .. **Alexander,** Arthur Lawr '69 AL Alexander PC -150 Bway -NY 10038 **Fx:**240-0365
(212) 710-3900 .. **Alexander,** Barry S '98 %Clyde & Co US LLP -405 Lex Av -NY 10174 **Fx:**710-3950
(718) 462-5162 .. **Alexander,** Bramwell H '81 -543 Ocean Av -Brklyn 11226
(212) 687-8181 .. **Alexander,** Brian J '97 (Kreindler & K) -750 3rd Av -NY 10017
(914) 749-8200 .. **Alexander,** Brooke A '09 %Boies S&F LLP -333 Main -Armonk 10504
(315) 479-8660 .. **Alexander & Catalano,LLC** -115 E Jffrsn -Syracuse 13202 **Fx:**479-8694
(212) 536-3900 .. **Alexander,** Darian '09 %K&L Gates LLP -599 Lex Av -NY 10022
(607) 756-4585 .. **Alexander,** David C '97 -Bx789 -Cortlnd 13045
(212) 764-6455 .. **Alexander,** David E '80 (Peyser & Alexander Mgt) -500 5th Av -NY 10110 **Fx:**921-4249
(716) 854-4300 .. **Alexander,** David H '73 (Gross SB&G,PC) -465 Main -Buffalo 14203
(212) 909-6000 .. **Alexander,** Derek P '09 %Debevoise & P LLP -919 3rd Av -NY 10022
(716) 847-8400 .. **Alexander,** Divitta M '05 %Phillips L LLP -3400 HSBC Ctr -Buffalo 14203
(212) 425-3240 .. **Alexander,** Elizabeth A '95 %Marrinan & MM,PC -26 Bway -NY 10004
(212) 318-6301 .. **Alexander,** Gerd S '09 Paul HJ&W LLP -75 E 55th -NY 10022
(212) 770-6575 .. **Alexander,** James I '01 AIG Risk Finance -70 Pine -NY 10270
(315) 479-8660 .. **Alexander,** James L '84 (Alexander & C,LLC) -115 E Jffrsn -Syracuse 13202
(516) 593-4948 .. **Alexander,** Jeannetta '98 -210 E Merrick Rd -Vly Stream 11580 **Fx:**593-4946
(212) 906-4645 .. **Alexander,** Jeffrey R '09 %Latham & W -885 3rd Av -NY 10022
(716) 688-6115 .. **Alexander,** Joan B '76 -196 Crestwood Ln -Williamsvll 14221 **Fx:**688-6254
(212) 857-2200 .. **Alexander,** John P '08 %Hon JM McLaughlin -40 Foley -NY 10007
(607) 734-2271 .. **Alexander,** John R '73 (Sayles & E) -1 W Church -Elmira 14901
(212) 612-9234 .. **Alexander,** Jos R '90 SrCnsl The Clearing House -450 W 33rd -NY 10001 **Fx:**612-9253
(516) 733-1810 .. **Alexander,** Joshua G '03 %J Beschel,PC -77 Newbrdg Rd -Hicksvll 11801
(718) 282-3553 .. **Alexander,** Kamari B I '02 -703 Flatbush Av -Brklyn 11225
(212) 265-6600 .. **Alexander,** Kim A '02 %RD Mgmt LLC -810 7th Av -NY 10019
(212) 306-7423 .. **Alexander,** Lanny R '86 %Comm on Human Rights -40 Rector -NY 10006 **Fx:**306-7414
(917) 353-7241 .. **Alexander,** Lawr '76 -305 Bway -NY 10007 **Fx:**(212) 619-0714
(518) 402-8537 .. **Alexander,** Louis A '86 DEC -625 Bway -Albany 12233 **Fx:**402-9016
Alexander, Michl '51 -150 E 69th -NY 10021
(212) 859-8000 .. **Alexander,** Michl '05 %Fried FHS&J LLP -1 NY Plz -NY 10004
(212) 403-1000 .. **Alexander,** Michele J '96 Cnsl Wachtell LR&K -51 W 52nd -NY 10019
(212) 822-1481 .. **Alexander,** Michelle L '02 -305 Bway -NY 10007
(212) 863-9170 .. **Alexander,** Nathan M '07 Phoenix Realty Grp -645 Mad Av -NY 10022
(914) 761-1300 .. **Alexander,** Neil J '96 (Cuddy & F LLP) -445 Hmltn Av -White Plns 10601
(212) 227-0347 .. **Alexander,** Raquel L '05 %Weiss W&W,PC -25 Park Pl -NY 10007
(212) 842-0700 .. **Alexander,** Richd B '98 %BBS Publishing Corp -252 W 38th -NY 10018
(585) 232-6500 .. **Alexander,** Richd E '84 (Harter S&E LLP) -1600 Bausch & Lomb Pl -Rchstr 14604
(718) 286-6000 .. **Alexander,** Robt D '73 %DA -125-01 Qns Blvd -Kew Gdns 11415
(518) 471-4815 .. **Alexander,** Sara K '09 Appellate 3rd Div -Bx7288 -Albany 12224
(212) 554-7800 .. **Alexander,** Shari A '06 %Moses & S LLP -405 Lex Av -NY 10174
(718) 286-8056 .. **Alexander,** Simon '74 Salomon Smith Barney -95-25 Qns Blvd -Rego Pk 11374
(631) 853-7604 .. **Alexander,** Susan D '81 %District Ct Law Dept -400 Carleton Av Bx9075 -Central Islip 11722
(212) 626-2067 .. **Alexander,** Thais Michelle '02 Prudential Ins Co -1114 Av of Amer -NY 10036
(212) 408-5100 .. **Alexander,** Todd E '95 (Chadbourne & P LLP) -30 Rckfllr Plz -NY 10112
(212) 819-8200 .. **Alexander,** Troy '88 (White & C LLP) -1155 Av of Amer -NY 10036
(718) 990-6630 .. **Alexander,** Vincent C '76 %St John's Law Schl -8000 Utopia Pkwy -Jamaica 11439 **Fx:**591-1855

(585) 232-5225 .. **Alexander,** Wm R '91 OfCnsl Remington GW&C,LLP -183 E Main -Rchstr 14604
(845) 279-7890 .. **Alexanderson,** Peter C '78 -1454 Route 22 -Brewstr 10509
(212) 668-2808 .. **Alexandrovskaya,** Gelena '04 Oppenheimer & Co Inc -125 Broad -NY 10004
(718) 357-2114 .. **Alexiades,** Hector '87 -42-40 Bell Blvd -Bayside 11361 **Fx:**357-2115
(212) 577-3500 .. **Alexion,** Gary '81 %Leg Aid -199 Water -NY 10038 **Fx:**809-1370
(718) 250-2000 .. **Alexis,** Jos P '92 %DA -350 Jay -Brklyn 11201 **Fx:**250-2314
(212) 474-1000 .. **Alexis,** Stephanie L '10 %Cravath S&M LLP -825 8th Av -NY 10019
(718) 694-3882 .. **Alexis-Hayes,** Melinda '00 %Transit Auth -130 Lvngstn -Brklyn 11201 **Fx:**694-5726
(585) 582-2330 .. **Alexson,** Timothy L '85 (Ohl & A) -Bx668 -Mendon 14506
(646) 878-0800 .. **Alfandary,** Francine L '91 SrCnsl Pearl CZL,LLP -1500 Bway -NY 10036
(718) 876-6429 .. **Alfano,** Jeffrey M '05 Supreme Ct -355 Front -Staten Isl 10304 **Fx:**876-6428
(914) 967-1404 .. **Alfano,** John L '65 (Alfano Law Ofc) -2 Griffon Pl -Rye 10580 **Fx:**967-7441
(212) 530-5000 .. **Alfano,** Justin A '07 %Milbank TH&M LLP -1 Chase Manh Plz -NY 10005
(212) 858-1000 .. **Alfano,** Peter J '98 (Pillsbury WSP LLP) -1540 Bway -NY 10036
(212) 298-5092 .. **Alfano,** Ronald D '86 Leg Aid -49 Thomas -NY 10013
(516) 746-8100 .. **Alfano,** Shawn M '99 %D Buttafuoco & Assoc -144 Woodbury Rd -Woodbury 11797 **Fx:**746-6473
(516) 741-1032 .. **Alfano,** Thos W '85 SrCnsl Manoussos & M,PLLC -595 Stewart Av -Gdn Cty 11530 **Fx:**741-7510
(212) 351-4000 .. **Alfaro,** Lisa A '98 (Gibson D&C LLP) -200 Park Av -NY 10166
(212) 788-1084 .. **Alfaro,** Martha Mann '82 %Law Dept -100 Church -NY 10007 **Fx:**788-0367
(718) 293-7660 .. **Alfasi,** Steven L '99 %Pub Admin -851 Grnd Cncrs -Bronx 10451 **Fx:**293-7851
(212) 449-9712 .. **Alfert,** Adam L '95 Merrill Lynch -220 Bway -NY 10038
(212) 751-8899 .. **Alfieri Frohman & Primoff,LLP** -460 Park Av -NY 10022 **Fx:**888-6094
(315) 471-8111 .. **Alfieri,** Jennifer L '07 %Scolaro SCF&B,PC -507 Plum -Syracuse 13204
(646) 497-3640 .. **Alfieri,** Lawr J '92 Amroc Investments LLC -535 Mad Av -NY 10022
(212) 490-3000 .. **Alfieri,** Lucinda H '95 (Wilson EME&D LLP) -150 E 42nd -NY 10017
(646) 723-5631 .. **Alfieri,** Michl J '89 Prestige Title Agency -15 W 39th -NY 10018
(212) 903-9000 .. **Alfieri,** Paul M '91 (Linklaters) -1345 Av of Amer -NY 10105
(212) 541-2000 .. **Alfieri,** Vincent '81 (Bryan C LLP) -1290 Av of Amer -NY 10104
(212) 261-5597 .. **Alfino Egler,** Geraldine '86 %Ace Guaranty Re -1325 Av of Amer -NY 10019
(212) 728-8000 .. **Alfonso,** Ana M '90 (Willkie F&G LLP) -787 7th Av -NY 10019
(212) 906-1200 .. **Alfonso,** Christina '10 %Latham & W -885 3rd Av -NY 10022
(212) 558-4000 .. **Alfonso,** Joel '07 %Sullivan & C LLP -125 Broad -NY 10004
(718) 479-0100 .. **Alfonso,** Julian L '87 -88-11 F Lewis Blvd -Qns Vllg 11427 **Fx:**468-0479
(212) 551-9473 .. **Alford,** Alvida R '07 %1st Amer Title -633 3rd Av -NY 10017 **Fx:**922-0881
(315) 394-0000 .. **Alford,** Gary R '99 -603 Caroline -Ogdensbrg 13669
(518) 828-5400 .. **Alford,** Nelson R Jr. '73 (Guterman S&A,PLLC) -21 N 7th -Hudson 12534
(212) 233-5511 .. **Alford,** Wm J III '88 -325 Bway -NY 10007
(212) 532-8100 .. **Alfson,** Brian C '06 %Stern & M,LLP -115 Bway -NY 10006
(917) 237-2926 .. **Algan,** Aylin '09 Axiom -75 Spring -NY 10012
(212) 643-1555 .. **Algase,** Roger C '64 -688 Av of Amer -NY 10010
(516) 747-0300 .. **Algava-Czik,** Esta '86 Cnsl Meltzer LG&B,LLP -190 Willis Av -Mineola 11501
(516) 486-4640 .. **Algazy,** Letal '05 %Cherry E&K,LLP -1 Old Cntry Rd -Carle Pl 11514
(914) 834-1052 .. **Alger Andrew & Rohlfs** -17 Dante -Larchmnt 10538
(212) 687-3000 .. **Alger,** Frances M A '09 Jaffe & A,LLP -600 3rd Av -NY 10016
(718) 875-1300 .. **Algeri,** Matthew D '04 Applt Div 2nd Dept -45 Monroe Pl -Brklyn 11201 **Fx:**858-2446
(212) 735-3000 .. **Algieri,** Philip D '10 %Skadden ASM&F LLP -4 Times Sq -NY 10036
(516) 739-0419 .. **Algios,** Louis '84 -200 Old Cntry Rd -Mineola 11501 **Fx:**741-7758
(212) 250-8607 .. **Alhadeff,** Marla F '83 %Deutsche Bank -60 Wall -NY 10005
(516) 745-0066 .. **Alhonte,** Marc '80 %Karol H&S,PC -600 Old Cntry Rd -Gdn Cty 11530
(212) 446-4800 .. **Ali,** Deola T '07 %Kirkland & E LLP -153 E 53rd -NY 10022
(315) 472-4481 .. **Ali,** Lucien P '56 (Ali P&C) -614 James -Syracuse 13203
(212) 406-9257 .. **Ali,** Mir Subhan '99 -41-43 Beekman -NY 10038
(212) 455-2000 .. **Ali,** Moiz '10 %Simpson T&B LLP -425 Lex Av -NY 10017
(718) 876-6300 .. **Ali,** Musa '08 DA -130 Styvsnt Pl -Staten Isl 10301
(315) 472-4481 .. **Ali Pappas & Cox** -614 James -Syracuse 13203 **Fx:**472-8299
(718) 382-2400 .. **Ali,** Shahid '08 (Ali & B PC) -118-35 Qns Blvd -Frst Hlls 11375
(212) 610-6300 .. **Ali,** Syed R '08 %Allen & O -1221 Av of Amer -NY 10020
(212) 768-6700 .. **Ali,** Syed Shujaat '03 %Sonnenschein N&R LLP -2 World Fncl Ctr -NY 10281
(914) 358-4934 .. **Aliaga,** Rocio T '96 %Ferro L&Z LLC -1025 Wstchstr Av -White Plns 10604
(212) 577-5000 .. **Aliano,** Robt J '77 (Aliano & Assoc,PC) -299 Bway -NY 10007 **Fx:**786-1503
(718) 845-4444 .. **Aliazzo McCloskey & Gonzalez** -94-03 101st Av -Ozone Pk 11416 **Fx:**738-2255
(212) 572-6282 .. **Alibatya,** Fred N '08 -300 Park Av -NY 10022
(212) 698-3500 .. **Alicandri,** Jay R '99 (Dechert LLP) -1095 Av of Amer -NY 10036
(212) 232-1300 .. **Alikakos,** Georgia S '01 (Lewis BB&S LLP) -77 Water -NY 10005
(212) 246-6700 .. **Alimanestianu,** Alexander A '85 %Town Sports Intl -5 Penn Plz -NY 10001
(718) 361-0075 .. **Alimaras,** Gus '83 (Kazazis & A,LLP) -36-12 34th Av -LIC 11106 **Fx:**361-5516
(718) 613-3500 .. **Alimaras,** Nicholas '96 %UIA Bd -Bx29002 -Brklyn 11201 **Fx:**613-3566
(914) 948-8044 .. **Alimonti,** Fredk P '90 -200 Mamaroneck Av #304 -White Plns 10601 **Fx:**948-8058
(212) 735-3000 .. **Alin,** Andrew P '05 %Skadden ASM&F LLP -4 Times Sq -NY 10036
(212) 935-3000 .. **Alin,** David M '01 (Mintz LCFG&P,PC) -666 3rd Av -NY 10017
(914) 821-9408 .. **Alin,** Robt D '78 Pentegra Retirement Srvcs -108 Corp Park Dr -White Plns 10604 **Fx:**694-9384
(212) 455-2000 .. **Alinauskas,** Karen A '00 %Simpson T&B LLP -425 Lex Av -NY 10017
(718) 816-8500 .. **Aliotta,** Randi P '83 -1358 Clove Rd -Staten Isl 10301
(716) 551-4931 .. **Aliouat,** Rhonda '81 %NLRB -130 S Elmwood Av -Buffalo 14202 **Fx:**551-4972
(212) 506-2500 .. **Aliouat,** Taos C '09 %Mayer B LLP -1675 Bway -NY 10019
(212) 696-6000 .. **Alisbah,** Kathryn L '96 Cnsl Curtis M-PC&M LLP -101 Park Av -NY 10178
(718) 984-5555 .. **Alishahi,** Amir H '91 A Alishahi,PC -3925 Hylan Blvd -Staten Isl 10308 **Fx:**984-1352
(646) 471-4000 .. **Alisiobi,** Ugochukwu C '09 PricewaterhouseCoopers LLP -300 Mad Av -NY 10017
(212) 237-0000 .. **Alix,** Noelle C '93 Cnsl Vinson & E LLP -666 5th Av -NY 10103
(516) 873-6062 .. **Alizio,** Peter J '99 -1551 Franklin Av -Mineola 11501
(212) 839-5300 .. **Aljure,** Algeria '08 %Sidley A LLP -787 7th Av -NY 10019
(212) 448-1100 .. **Alkalay,** Peter C '74 (McLaughlin & S,LLP) -260 Mad Av -NY 10016
(212) 237-1000 .. **Alkin,** Donna M '94 %Windels ML&M,LLP -156 W 56th -NY 10019
(212) 688-5151 .. **Allam,** Antonio '00 Cnsl Gibney A&F,LLP -665 5th Av -NY 10022
(212) 749-3693 .. **Allan,** Don W '85 -180 W 93rd -NY 10025 **Fx:**749-3693
(718) 780-7924 .. **Allan,** Richd '62 %Bklyn Law Schl -250 Joralemon -Brklyn 11201 **Fx:**780-0393
(315) 672-3360 .. **Allan,** Robt J '74 -43 Main -Camillus 13031 **Fx:**672-3361
(914) 285-0700 .. **Allan,** Scott C '01 %Renzulli Law Firm,LLP -81 Main -White Plns 10601 **Fx:**285-1213
(631) 264-0303 .. **Allar,** Joanne '89 (VanNostrand & M) -53 Bway Bx307 -Amityvll 11701
(212) 476-9000 .. **Allard,** Andrew B '97 %Neuberger Berman,LLC -605 3rd Av -NY 10158 **Fx:**476-9862
(914) 993-1962 .. **Allee,** Benjamin R '04 %US Atty -300 Quarropas -White Plns 10601 **Fx:**993-9036
(212) 963-5493 .. **Allee,** Susan S '87 United Nations -405 E 42nd -NY 10017
(212) 571-0550 .. **Allegaert Berger & Vogel LLP** -111 Bway -NY 10006 **Fx:**571-0555
(212) 571-0550 .. **Allegaert,** Christopher '90 (Allegaert B&V LLP) -111 Bway -NY 10006
(212) 732-3200 .. **Allegaert,** Theo '02 Cnsl Carter L&M LLP -2 Wall -NY 10005
(914) 921-5644 .. **Allegretti,** Frank P '92 -350 Theo Fremd Av -Rye 10580 **Fx:**921-0186
(212) 455-2000 .. **Allegretti,** Jill McClure '01 %Simpson T&B LLP -425 Lex Av -NY 10017
(914) 767-7749 .. **Allegretti-Davenport,** Regina M '87 %Pepsi Bottling Grp -1 Pepsi Way -Somers 10589
(212) 312-2354 .. **Allegro,** Marianne T '86 %Leg Aid -60 Lafayette -NY 10013 **Fx:**349-0874
(212) 735-3000 .. **Allehaut,** Anne-Laure '07 %Skadden ASM&F LLP -4 Times Sq -NY 10036
(212) 662-3098 .. **Allen,** Aimee M '04 -180 W 93rd -NY 10025
(212) 309-6000 .. **Allen,** Alexis L '09 %Morgan L&B LLP -101 Park Av -NY 10178
(212) 277-6500 .. **Allen,** Andrew J '08 %Dickstein S LLP -1633 Bway -NY 10019
(914) 620-0175 .. **Allen,** Anita B '87 (Allen & Assoc) -9 W Prospect Av -Mt Vernon 10550 **Fx:**620-0178
(212) 326-2000 .. **Allen,** Anya '08 %O'Melveny & M LLP -7 Times Sq -NY 10036
(212) 353-0040 .. **Allen,** Bernd '65 (Allen MT&S) -112 E 19th -NY 10003
(518) 487-7600 .. **Allen,** Bradley G '02 %Whiteman O&H LLP -1 Commerce Plz -Albany 12260
(845) 339-3115 .. **Allen,** Bree Manaton '02 Ethan Allen Entrprs Inc -113 Hunter -Kingston 12401
(212) 903-9000 .. **Allen,** Brian C '09 %Linklaters -1345 Av of Amer -NY 10105
(718) 286-6000 .. **Allen,** Brian F '05 %DA -125-01 Qns Blvd -Kew Gdns 11415
(718) 525-1336 .. **Allen,** Camille T '94 -203-20 Linden Blvd -St Albans 11412 **Fx:**525-1327
(914) 285-9800 .. **Allen,** Catherine S '89 %Kurzman EC&L,LLP -1 N Bway -White Plns 10601
(631) 694-2300 .. **Allen,** Cathleen D '98 (Lamb & B,LLP) -534 Broadhllw Rd Bx9034 -Melvll 11747
(212) 885-8013 .. **Allen,** Christopher D '03 Trenwith Securities -330 Mad Av -NY 10017
(607) 648-6113 .. **Allen,** Christopher J '82 -1946 Route 12 -Bnghmtn 13901
(716) 853-1616 .. **Allen,** Colleen M '08 %Harter S&E LLP -12 Fountain Plz -Buffalo 14202
(718) 549-2928 .. **Allen,** Cynthia Y '85 %New Direction LDC -21910 S Conduit Av -Sprngfld Gdns 11413
(518) 356-6000 .. **Allen,** David M '00 NY ISO -10 Krey Blvd -Rensselaer 12144
(516) 538-2500 .. **Allen,** David W '08 %Furey FLMW&D,PC -600 Front -Hempstd 11550
(212) 218-5500 .. **Allen,** Douglas F Jr. '77 OfCnsl Seyfarth S LLP -620 8th Av -NY 10018
(315) 838-1265 .. **Allen,** Douglas F '06 Goodrich -104 Otis -Rome 13441
(212) 324-2222 .. **Allen,** Felicia M '97 Ascend Venture Grp -1500 Bway -NY 10036
(212) 906-5115 .. **Allen,** Fiona M '06 UN Dvlpmnt Prgrmme -304 E 45th -NY 10017
(718) 835-5969 .. **Allen,** Frank E '93 -156-36 92nd -Jamaica 11414 **Fx:**835-5969
(212) 766-3366 .. **Allen,** Gerald G '84 (Goldberg & A) -49 W 37th -NY 10018 **Fx:**221-6867
(845) 306-1000 .. **Allen,** Gregory '04 Watchtower -100 Watchtower Dr -Patterson 12563 **Fx:**306-0709
(518) 437-4208 .. **Allen,** Gregory J '94 %State Ins Fund -15 Computer Dr W -Albany 12205 **Fx:**485-8761
(516) 483-1500 .. **Allen,** Guy J '85 (Allen & A) -100 Main -Hempstd 11550 **Fx:**483-1560
(516) 222-1300 .. **Allen,** Guy M '92 (Abbott R&A,PC) -90 Merrick Av -E Meadow 11554
(212) 317-5400 .. **Allen,** Harold D '99 Swiss Re Capital -55 E 52nd -NY 10055
(212) 696-6000 .. **Allen,** Heather E '10 %Curtis M-PC&M LLP -101 Park Av -NY 10178
(212) 848-4000 .. **Allen,** Hilary J '07 Shearman & S LLP -599 Lex Av -NY 10022
(716) 884-5600 .. **Allen,** James F '71 -1260 Delaware Av -Buffalo 14209
(212) 819-8200 .. **Allen,** Jason M '10 %White & C LLP -1155 Av of Amer -NY 10036
(315) 218-8000 .. **Allen,** John D '76 (Bond S&K,PLLC) -1 Lincoln Ctr -Syracuse 13202
(315) 343-9116 .. **Allen,** John D '76 (Bond S&K,PLLC) -130 E 2nd -Oswego 13126

(518) 487-7600 .. **Allen,** John L '77 (Whiteman O&H LLP) -1 Commerce Plz -Albany 12260
(212) 490-8600 .. **Allen,** John L '99 -60 E 42nd -NY 10165
(212) 909-6000 .. **Allen,** John M Jr. '78 (Debevoise & P LLP) -919 3rd Av -NY 10022
(718) 932-7375 .. **Allen,** John M '87 -3144 43rd -LIC 11103
(516) 694-9592 .. **Allen,** John R '83 -104 Hmpshr Dr -Farmngdl 11735
(315) 435-2518 .. **Allen,** John W '78 %Family Ct -Cnty Cthse -Syracuse 13202
(716) 551-5541 .. **Allen,** Jos W '90 US Trustee -42 Delaware Av -Buffalo 14202
(607) 273-6111 .. **Allen,** Jos Waldo '92 (Hines & A) -417 N Cayuga -Ithaca 14850 **Fx:**273-7920
(212) 969-3000 .. **Allen,** Julie M '84 (Proskauer R LLP) -1585 Bway -NY 10036
(518) 583-7300 .. **Allen,** Kimberly B '92 -376 Bway -Saratoga Spgs 12866
(212) 839-5300 .. **Allen,** Laura H '76 (Sidley A LLP) -787 7th Av -NY 10019
(212) 259-8000 .. **Allen,** Leon A Jr. '64 OfCnsl Dewey & L LLP -1301 Av of Amer -NY 10019
(716) 200-5050 .. **Allen,** Lisa J '91 (Harris B PLLC) -726 Exchange -Buffalo 14210
(212) 578-0686 .. **Allen,** Margaret M '09 MetLife -27-01 Qns Plz N -LIC 11101
(212) 696-6000 .. **Allen,** Marie-Therese F '82 (Curtis M-PC&M LLP) -101 Park Av -NY 10178
(718) 591-2100 .. **Allen,** Mark A '94 (Goldberg & A LLC) -77-07 Parsons Blvd -Fresh Mdws 11366 **Fx:**591-2102
(212) 222-7211 .. **Allen,** Marva A '78 -48 W 82nd -NY 10024
(518) 836-2310 .. **Allen,** Mary Ann Devane '82 Wildwood Programs Inc -2995 Curry Rd Ext -Schnctdy 12303 **Fx:**836-2301
(212) 969-3000 .. **Allen,** Mason L '07 %Proskauer R LLP -1585 Bway -NY 10036
(212) 972-4900 .. **Allen,** Michl I '89 (Shapiro FA&S LLP) -380 Mad Av -NY 10017
(315) 435-2470 .. **Allen,** Michl S '09 DA -505 S State -Syracuse 13202 **Fx:**435-3969
(585) 335-2333 .. **Allen,** Michl T '76 -180 Main -Dansvll 14437 **Fx:**335-9233
(516) 486-4640 .. **Allen,** Michelle I '94 %Cherry E&K,LLP -1 Old Cntry Rd -Carle Pl 11514
(212) 521-5400 .. **Allen,** Misty D '06 %Reed S LLP -599 Lex Av -NY 10022
(212) 353-0040 .. **Allen Morris Troisi & Simon** -112 E 19th -NY 10003 **Fx:**505-8652
(212) 803-5100 .. **Allen,** Neal C '77 %NY Cnty Defender Srvcs -225 Bway -NY 10007 **Fx:**571-6035
(585) 641-8001 .. **Allen & O'Brien** -625 Panorama Trl -Rchstr 14625 **Fx:**641-8017
(212) 566-7081 .. **Allen,** Otis G '98 (Cohen & H) -80 Maiden Ln -NY 10038
(212) 610-6300 .. **Allen & Overy** -1221 Av of Amer -NY 10020 **Fx:**610-6399
(212) 355-1500 .. **Allen,** Peter '92 OSL Shipping & Dvlpmnt -410 Park Av -NY 10022 **Fx:**355-6004
(516) 223-4700 .. **Allen,** Rita '51 (Allen & A) -1430 Grand Av Bx1007 -Baldwin 11510 **Fx:**223-4708
(212) 286-0200 .. **Allen,** Robt W '95 OfCnsl Hennessy & W,PC -574 Av of Amer -NY 10011 **Fx:**883-0475
(914) 448-0200 .. **Allen,** Ryan K '09 %Bartlett MB&M,LLP -81 Main -White Plns 10601
(315) 471-1318 .. **Allen,** Sandra A '03 %Lynch Law Ofc -2700 Bellevue Av -Syracuse 13219 **Fx:**471-1409
(518) 402-8537 .. **Allen,** Sandra L '89 %DEC -625 Bway -Albany 12233 **Fx:**402-8230
(518) 438-7139 .. **Allen,** Sandra M '00 -Bx8381 -Albany 12208 **Fx:**438-7139
(518) 486-7815 .. **Allen,** Sarah L '00 %Insurance Dept -99 Wshngtn Av -Albany 12257 **Fx:**474-3397
(585) 203-7574 .. **Allen,** Sharon L '09 -102 Main Bx214 -Naples 14512 **Fx:**374-8595
(607) 772-8440 .. **Allen,** Sian E '09 %R Perot -20-24 Wall -Bnghmtn 13901 **Fx:**772-8339
(212) 505-2880 .. **Allen,** Stephen W '04 %Raphael & M -276 Park Av S -NY 10010
(516) 662-4639 .. **Allen,** Thos J '98 -95 Pershing Av -Locust Vly 11560
(212) 773-2617 .. **Allen,** Wm D Jr. '09 Ernst & Young LLP -5 Times Sq -NY 10036
(212) 998-6327 .. **Allen,** Wm T '98 %NYU Law Schl -40 Wshngtn Sq S -NY 10012 **Fx:**995-4692
(212) 403-1261 .. **Allen,** Wm T '98 OfCnsl Wachtell LR&K -51 W 52nd -NY 10019
(718) 250-4209 .. **Allen,** Zoe G '99 %Leg Aid -111 Lvngstn -Brklyn 11201 **Fx:**250-4243
(631) 789-0707 .. **Allen-Bistakis,** Lisa L '95 -510 Bway -Amityvll 11701
(212) 250-2500 .. **Allenby,** Paul '97 Deutsche Bank -60 Wall -NY 10005
(212) 318-6000 .. **Allendorf,** Eric F '04 Paul HJ&W LLP -75 E 55th -NY 10022
(212) 909-6000 .. **Aller,** Jamie Bartholomew '07 %Debevoise & P LLP -919 3rd Av -NY 10022
(212) 310-8000 .. **Allerhand,** Jos S '79 (Weil G&M LLP) -767 5th Av -NY 10153
(212) 697-3122 .. **Allert,** James H '05 %Martin C&B LLP -220 E 42nd -NY 10017
(718) 390-5336 .. **Allerti,** Lauren E '08 %Law Dept -60 Bay -Staten Isl 10301 **Fx:**390-5338
(718) 449-3328 .. **Alleva,** Aldo E '58 -2280 McDonald Av -Brklyn 11223 **Fx:**265-4023
(212) 972-7373 .. **Alleva,** James '82 (Scatenato & A,PC) -276 5th Av -NY 10001 **Fx:**972-1311
(518) 563-4022 .. **Alley,** Danl J '80 %Leg Aid -100 Court Bx989 -Plattsbrgh 12901 **Fx:**563-4058
(914) 251-6055 .. **Alleyne,** Menelik R '98 Purchase College -735 Andrsn Hill Rd -Purchase 10577 **Fx:**251-6014
(646) 610-6351 .. **Alleyne,** Michelle Y '02 NYPD -1 Police Plz -NY 10038
(718) 250-2000 .. **Alleyne,** Wayne N '04 DA -350 Jay -Brklyn 11201 **Fx:**250-2314
(718) 466-3000 .. **Alleyne,** Yohance Omari '05 Civil Ct -1118 Grnd Cncrs -Bronx 10456 **Fx:**466-3006
(212) 284-2512 .. **Allgor,** Jos P '99 Jefferies @ Co -520 Mad Av -NY 10022
(516) 393-2200 .. **Alliance,** Danl '07 %Garfunkel W,PC -111 Grt Nck Rd -Gt Neck 11021
(518) 218-2088 .. **Allin,** Gurudev D '10 %Ruffo TM&M PC -300 Great Oaks Blvd -Albany 12203
(516) 296-7000 .. **Allinson,** Dale '81 (Certilman BA&H,LLP) -90 Merrick Av -E Meadow 11554
(212) 906-1200 .. **Allinson,** David S '97 (Latham & W) -885 3rd Av -NY 10022
(518) 869-6227 .. **Allinson,** Jennifer L '06 %Lavelle & F,LLP -29 British Amer Blvd -Latham 12110
(212) 596-9000 .. **Allison,** Lee E '98 (Ropes & G LLP) -1211 Av of Amer -NY 10036
(212) 259-8000 .. **Allison,** Mark D '96 (Dewey & L LLP) -1301 Av of Amer -NY 10019
(212) 972-1000 .. **Allison,** Sarah R '08 %London F LLP -59 Maiden Ln -NY 10038
(212) 819-1928 .. **Allister,** Jeffrey W '73 (Allister & N) -1430 Bway -NY 10018 **Fx:**819-1904
(212) 728-8000 .. **Allman,** Peter J '93 SpclCnsl Willkie F&G LLP -787 7th Av -NY 10019
(347) 296-1424 .. **Allman,** Richd N '86 Supreme Ct -360 Adams -Brklyn 11201
(914) 771-8318 .. **Allocco,** Christopher G '95 C Allocco,PC -8 Roy Pl -Eastchstr 10709 **Fx:**771-6878
(212) 262-2390 .. **Allogramento,** Philip W III '04 %Connell F LLP -888 7th Av -NY 10106
(718) 239-3339 .. **Allowe,** Jos '94 -914 Pelham Pkwy S -Bronx 10462 **Fx:**792-4110
(212) 969-3000 .. **Alloy,** Joshua F '02 %Proskauer R LLP -1585 Bway -NY 10036
(212) 538-7802 .. **Allsbrook,** R Colby '99 Credit Suisse -1 Mad Av -NY 10010
(212) 701-3000 .. **Allsman,** Julie A '03 %Cahill G&R LLP -80 Pine -NY 10005 **Fx:**269-5420
(212) 265-3687 .. **Allton,** Deborah J '02 Amer Guild for Musical Artists -1430 Bway -NY 10018 **Fx:**262-9088
(212) 661-7300 .. **Allweiss,** David H '00 %Malapero & P LLP -295 Mad Av -NY 10017
(212) 939-7511 .. **Ally,** Shahabuddeen Abid '02 -115 E 57th -NY 10022
(212) 213-8844 .. **Allyn & Fortuna LLP** -200 Mad Av -NY 10016 **Fx:**213-3318
(212) 213-8844 .. **Allyn,** James H '90 (Allyn & F LLP) -200 Mad Av -NY 10016
(212) 909-6000 .. **Almani,** Yossi '06 %Debevoise & P LLP -919 3rd Av -NY 10022
(631) 853-4104 .. **Almanzar-Paramio,** Omar '08 %DA -400 Carleton Av Bx9082 -Central Islip 11722 **Fx:**853-7838
(518) 433-8800 .. **Almas,** Scott R '98 %Lemery G LLC -50 Beaver -Albany 12207
(315) 769-9264 .. **Almasian,** Michl V '93 -31 Glenn -Massena 13662 **Fx:**769-9262
(212) 442-4553 .. **Almazan,** Annette Butiu '03 NYC Dept of Prob -100 Centre -NY 10013
(212) 691-8700 .. **Almazan,** Tracy A '92 (Almazan & Assoc,PC) -27 Union Sq W -NY 10003 **Fx:**691-8701
(212) 977-9700 .. **Almeda,** Dominador E '00 -666 5th Av -NY 10103 **Fx:**262-5152
(212) 455-2000 .. **Almeida,** Helena '02 %Simpson T&B LLP -425 Lex Av -NY 10017
(718) 721-5740 .. **Almeida,** Jessica A '09 %Latos L&D,PC -22-15 31st -Astoria 11105 **Fx:**721-9645
(845) 473-8100 .. **Almeida,** Michelle '04 %Iseman CR&H,LLP -2649 South Rd -Poughkeepsie 12601
(212) 805-1092 .. **Almeida,** Tico A '05 %Hon S Stein USDC -500 Pearl -NY 10007
(516) 374-6873 .. **Almeleh,** Morris '81 -11 Lotus -Cedarhrst 11516
(212) 688-4000 .. **Almodovar,** Priscilla '91 SONYMA -641 Lex Av -NY 10022 **Fx:**872-0789
(718) 250-2000 .. **Almog,** Danit '05 %DA -350 Jay -Brklyn 11201 **Fx:**250-2314
(212) 218-5500 .. **Almon,** Lorie E '95 (Seyfarth S LLP) -620 8th Av -NY 10018
(212) 468-8000 .. **Almonord,** Anne-Carmene '09 %Morrison & F LLP -1290 Av of Amer -NY 10104
(212) 683-2210 .. **Almonrode,** Patrick S '05 Childrens Rts Inc -330 7th Av -NY 10001 **Fx:**683-4015
(718) 232-2111 .. **Almonte,** Alexander '03 (Almonte & B,PLLC) -2652 Coney Isl Av -Brklyn 11223
(718) 222-2072 .. **Almonte,** Andrew T '09 %Law Dept -350 Jay -Brklyn 11201 **Fx:**222-2088
(718) 232-2111 .. **Almonte & Bratkovsky,PLLC** -2652 Coney Isl Av -Brklyn 11223 **Fx:**232-4333
(212) 698-3500 .. **Almonte,** Jose R '05 %Dechert LLP -1095 Av of Amer -NY 10036
(212) 688-8555 .. **Almonte,** Michl J '08 %Fragomen DB&L LLP -7 Hanover Sq -NY 10004
(212) 355-3505 .. **Al-Moosa,** Sarah '09 Permanent Mission of Oman to the UN -305 E 47th -NY 10017
(212) 735-3000 .. **Almroth,** David D '95 Cnsl Skadden ASM&F LLP -4 Times Sq -NY 10036
(212) 326-3939 .. **Alnajjar,** Joanne M '07 %Jones D -222 E 41st -NY 10017
(516) 694-3000 .. **Aloe,** Barbara Petraglia '85 (Guercio & G,LLP) -77 Conklin -Farmngdl 11735 **Fx:**694-4738
(212) 868-1010 .. **Aloe,** Paul H '84 (Kudman TA LLP) -350 5th Av -NY 10118
(914) 423-0800 .. **Aloeidat,** Mohd S '99 %N Sayegh,PC -10 Palisade Av -Ynkrs 10701 **Fx:**423-7870
(716) 636-7600 .. **Aloi,** Cheryl A '04 %HoganWillig -2410 N Forest Rd -Amherst 14068
(585) 262-3660 .. **Aloi,** Francis A '65 -Bx18186 -Rchstr 14618 **Fx:**262-3666
(718) 931-1888 .. **Aloi,** Leonard C '72 -1925 Wllmsbrdg Rd -Bronx 10461 **Fx:**829-0032
(585) 442-0760 .. **Aloi,** Paul M '78 -1596 Monroe Av -Rchstr 14618 **Fx:**442-3762
(212) 773-7683 .. **Aloi,** Peter R '96 Ernst & Young LLP -5 Times Sq -NY 10036
(516) 877-5600 .. **Aloia,** John L '87 %R Tusa -1225 Franklin Av -Gdn Cty 11530 **Fx:**877-5695
(212) 251-0101 .. **Aloia,** Mark N '89 %Aegon USA Realty -330 Mad Av -NY 10017
(718) 286-6000 .. **Aloise,** Nicole M '09 DA -125-01 Qns Blvd -Kew Gdns 11415
(212) 880-9480 .. **Aloisi,** Candice Leigh '05 %Morvillo AGIA&B,PC -565 5th Av -NY 10017
(718) 456-1845 .. **Alomar,** Karina E '00 (Alomar & Assoc,PC) -60-89 Myrtle Av -Rdgwd 11385 **Fx:**386-9299
(516) 571-1656 .. **Alonge,** Michl S '73 Nassau Cnty District Ct -99 Main -Hempstd 11550
(516) 333-8790 .. **Alongi,** Paul A '00 (Alongi & Assoc,LLC) -265 Post Av -Westbury 11590
(718) 590-2000 .. **Alongi,** Samantha '09 %DA -198 E 161st -Bronx 10451 **Fx:**590-6477
(212) 598-5900 .. **Alonso Andalkar & Kahn PC** -920 Bway -NY 10010 **Fx:**598-4650
(212) 766-1888 .. **Alonso,** Andrea M '82 (Morris DA&F) -2 Rector -NY 10006
(212) 267-6700 .. **Alonso,** Andres F '95 (Parker WA LLP) -111 John -NY 10038
(516) 466-6500 .. **Alonso,** Andres F '95 (Parker WA LLP) -6 Hrbr Park Dr S -Pt Wash 11050
(212) 688-8555 .. **Alonso,** Carmen '03 (Fragomen DB&L LLP) -7 Hanover Sq -NY 10004
(212) 335-9000 .. **Alonso,** Danl R '91 %DA -1 Hogan Pl -NY 10013
(212) 259-8000 .. **Alonso,** Ericka '09 %Dewey & L LLP -1301 Av of Amer -NY 10019
(718) 590-2000 .. **Alonso,** Marisol M '02 %DA -198 E 161st -Bronx 10451 **Fx:**590-6477
(212) 598-5900 .. **Alonso,** Mark J '81 (Alonso A&K PC) -920 Bway -NY 10010
(212) 226-7334 .. **Alonso,** Minerva L '07 %Meenan & Assoc,LLC -64 Fulton -NY 10038 **Fx:**226-7716
(718) 590-2000 .. **Alonso,** Odalys C '86 %DA -198 E 161st -Bronx 10451 **Fx:**590-6477
(212) 331-3371 .. **Alonso,** Philip E '03 HRA -180 Water -NY 10038
(718) 263-9591 .. **Alony,** Elliott P '03 %H Dalton & Assoc,PC -69-12 Austin -Frst Hlls 11375 **Fx:**263-9598
(212) 430-6040 .. **Alony,** Isaac '07 %Wasser & R LLP -80 Maiden Ln -NY 10038 **Fx:**430-6041
(212) 259-8000 .. **Alonzo,** Jos S '08 %Dewey & L LLP -1301 Av of Amer -NY 10019
(212) 751-7676 .. **Alosco,** Salvatore C '66 -1623 3rd Av -NY 10128
(212) 906-1200 .. **Alovisetti,** Chas S '10 %Latham & W -885 3rd Av -NY 10022

(518) 462-0300 .. **Aloy,** Paul M '06 %Girvin & F,PC -20 Corp Wds Blvd -Albany 12211
(212) 349-1121 .. **Alper,** David H '85 -225 E 70th -NY 10021
(212) 687-2770 .. **Alper,** Wm A '74 (Cohen PL&P) -551 5th Av -NY 10176
(914) 664-8400 .. **Alperin & Hufjay** -22 W 1st -Mt Vernon 10550 **Fx:**667-5960
(914) 623-0710 .. **Alperin,** Jos D '67 EVCI Career Colleges Holding Corp -1 Van Der Donck -Ynkrs 10701 **Fx:**964-8222
(914) 664-8400 .. **Alperin,** Lewis E '65 (Alperin & H) -22 W 1st -Mt Vernon 10550
(212) 735-3000 .. **Alperin,** Stuart N '77 (Skadden ASM&F LLP) -4 Times Sq -NY 10036
(516) 747-6300 .. **Alpern,** Jamie P '86 SrCnsl Koeppel M&L,LLP -155 First Bx863 -Mineola 11501
(212) 986-6330 .. **Alpern,** Richd L '73 Frederic W Cook & Co -90 Park Av -NY 10016
(212) 596-9000 .. **Alperovich,** Alexandra '04 %Ropes & G LLP -1211 Av of Amer -NY 10036
(212) 566-1096 .. **Alperstein,** Michl L '68 -30 Vesey -NY 10007 **Fx:**962-9696
(212) 888-3033 .. **Alperstein,** Robin Lee '97 (Becker GM&M LLP) -299 Park Av -NY 10171
(212) 436-3469 .. **Alpert,** Alan S '80 Deloitte & Touche LLP -2 World Fncl Ctr -NY 10281 **Fx:**436-7151
(212) 758-6958 .. **Alpert Butler & Weiss,PC** -90 Broad -NY 10004 **Fx:**758-2817
(718) 286-6000 .. **Alpert,** Carey B '06 %DA -125-01 Qns Blvd -Kew Gdns 11415
(212) 758-6958 .. **Alpert,** Clark E '94 (Alpert B&W,PC) -90 Broad -NY 10004
(212) 735-3000 .. **Alpert,** Cory E '09 %Skadden ASM&F LLP -4 Times Sq -NY 10036
(212) 662-2783 .. **Alpert,** Dee '86 -736 W End Av -NY 10025
(347) 592-2500 .. **Alpert,** Emma C '10 %Bklyn Fam Def Proj -177 Lvngstn -Brklyn 11201
(212) 474-9309 .. **Alpert,** Fredda '93 Chubb & Son -55 Water -NY 10041
(914) 725-5930 .. **Alpert,** Helaine Y '84 -10 Withington Rd -Scarsdale 10583 **Fx:**472-5577
(212) 582-8000 .. **Alpert,** Herbert H '57 (Feingold & A,LLP) -1330 Av of Amer -NY 10019
(212) 349-2000 .. **Alpert & Kaufman, LLP** -233 Bway -NY 10279 **Fx:**964-6161
(718) 822-0500 .. **Alpert & Kaufman, LLP** -2916 Bruckner Blvd -Bronx 10465
(212) 225-2000 .. **Alpert,** Laurent '73 (Cleary GS&H) -1 Lbrty Plz -NY 10006
(914) 643-8754 .. **Alpert,** Linda R '85 Harrison Childrens Ctr -480 Harrison Av -Harrison 10528
(212) 408-5100 .. **Alpert,** Marc A '87 (Chadbourne & P LLP) -30 Rckfllr Plz -NY 10112
(212) 578-2211 .. **Alpert,** Mark '87 %MetLife -27-01 Qns Plz N -LIC 11101
(631) 225-4603 .. **Alpert,** Michl W '98 -152 N Wellwood Av -Lindenhrst 11757 **Fx:**225-4602
(212) 349-2000 .. **Alpert,** Morton '58 (Alpert & K, LLP) -233 Bway -NY 10279
(212) 692-7851 .. **Alpert,** Nancy R '81 Ct TV Ntwrk -600 3rd Av -NY 10016 **Fx:**973-2870
(212) 833-1113 .. **Alpert,** Norman '74 Cnsl Friedman KS&A LLP -1633 Bway -NY 10019 **Fx:**373-7913
(516) 248-1700 .. **Alpert,** Peter M '81 (Forchelli CDSM&T,LLP) -333 Earle Ovngton Blvd -Uniondale 11553
(718) 544-3963 .. **Alpert,** Randy S '91 -118-21 Qns Blvd -Frst Hlls 11375
(212) 541-2000 .. **Alpert,** Robt '75 (Bryan C LLP) -1290 Av of Amer -NY 10104
(516) 679-8710 .. **Alpert,** Robt H '77 -2629 Silver Ct -E Meadow 11554
(212) 350-2700 .. **Alpert,** Stanley N '85 OfCnsl Constantine C,PC -450 Lex Av -NY 10017
(212) 661-9100 .. **Alpert,** Stephen H '90 OfCnsl Otterbourg SH&R,PC -230 Park Av -NY 10169
(212) 925-3429 .. **Alpert,** Tami J '07 DCTV -87 Lafayette -NY 10013
(516) 227-2121 .. **Alphonso,** Melaine C '04 %M Berkley,PC -585 Stewart Av -Gdn Cty 11530 **Fx:**227-1250
(212) 858-8158 .. **Alphonso-Napoli,** Geeta M '02 1st Investors Corp -110 Wall -NY 10005
(203) 270-5581 .. **Alpi,** Peter '67 -322 W 72nd -NY 10023 **Fx:**270-5583
(212) 762-7687 .. **Alprin,** Katherine J '00 %Morgan Stanley -1221 Av of Amer -NY 10020
(212) 455-2000 .. **Alpuche,** Maripat '92 (Simpson T&B LLP) -425 Lex Av -NY 10017
(315) 589-8864 .. **Alquist,** Mark H '89 -4046 Wayne -Williamson 14589
(315) 471-3151 .. **Alsante,** Cora A '90 (Hancock & E,LLP) -1500 AXA Twr I Bx4976 -Syracuse 13221
(212) 651-9502 .. **Al-Sati,** Ahmad A '02 Matlin Patterson Global Advisor,LLC -520 Mad Av -NY 10022
(212) 728-8000 .. **Al-Sayeh,** Dalia '05 %Willkie F&G LLP -787 7th Av -NY 10019
(212) 891-1600 .. **Alsdorf,** Matthew W '05 %Jenner & B LLP -919 3rd Av -NY 10022
(631) 435-0781 .. **Alsen,** Peter '82 (Borda KA&G,LLP) -1805 5th Av -Bay Shr 11706
(800) 479-9333 .. **Al-Shabazz,** Ikiesha Taquet '02 %Strazzullo Law Firm PC -100 Park Av -NY 10017
(212) 310-8000 .. **Al-Sharmani,** Mona M '02 %Weil G&M LLP -767 5th Av -NY 10153
(212) 521-5400 .. **Al-Shibib,** Luma S '03 %Reed S LLP -599 Lex Av -NY 10022
(518) 487-7600 .. **Alsina,** John C '81 OfCnsl Whiteman O&H LLP -1 Commerce Plz -Albany 12260
(212) 578-2211 .. **Alsina,** Neysa I '03 MetLife -27-01 Qns Plz N -LIC 11101
(718) 590-6176 .. **Alson,** Beth N '82 %Law Dept -198 E 161st -Bronx 10451 **Fx:**590-2686
(212) 848-4000 .. **Alsop,** Richd B '88 Shearman & S LLP -599 Lex Av -NY 10022
(212) 297-5800 .. **Alster,** Adam A '00 SrCnsl Day P LLP -7 Times Sq -NY 10036
(212) 270-7030 .. **Alster,** Dan '03 -270 Park Av -NY 10017
(212) 566-2566 .. **Alster,** Marc G '88 %Kahan & K -225 Bway -NY 10007 **Fx:**566-8165
(212) 225-2000 .. **Alster,** Sheldon H '82 (Cleary GS&H) -1 Lbrty Plz -NY 10006
(914) 381-7600 .. **Alster-Nelson,** Linda '92 Cnsl Dorf Law Firm,LLP -740 W Bstn Post Rd -Mamaroneck 10543 **Fx:**381-7608
(212) 210-9400 .. **Alston & Bird LLP** -90 Park Av -NY 10016 **Fx:**210-9444
(718) 231-7647 .. **Alston,** James H '66 -4035 Brnxwood Av -Bronx 10466
(718) 558-8478 .. **Alston,** Karla R '86 %LIRR -Jamaica Station -Jamaica 11435 **Fx:**558-8211
(585) 232-6500 .. **Alston,** Maureen T '83 (Harter S&E LLP) -1600 Bausch & Lomb Pl -Rchstr 14604
(518) 266-3000 .. **Alston,** Timothy J '85 %Div Tax Appls -500 Fed -Troy 12180 **Fx:**272-5178
(516) 229-4200 .. **Al-Sullami,** Yamile R '93 %Mendolia & S -875 Merrick Av -Westbury 11590
(845) 469-4900 .. **Alt,** Karen M '04 %Greenwald Law Ofc -99 Brookside Av -Chester 10918 **Fx:**469-2022
(212) 391-3993 .. **Alt,** Stanley A '55 -1501 Bway -NY 10036 **Fx:**764-6620
(212) 486-2004 .. **Altabef,** Douglas S '78 Matrix Asset Advsrs -747 3rd Av -NY 10017
(212) 325-5584 .. **Altabef,** Jeffrey A '93 Credit Suisse -11 Mad Av -NY 10010
(212) 975-3372 .. **Altabef,** Richd H '74 %CBS Inc -51 W 52nd -NY 10019 **Fx:**975-3930
(212) 478-7200 .. **Altamura,** Anthony '85 (Hahn & H LLP) -488 Mad Av -NY 10022
(516) 222-2880 .. **Altarac,** Jill A '96 Altarac Law Firm -600 Old Cntry Rd -Gdn Cty 11530 **Fx:**222-0828
(212) 506-5000 .. **Altarescu,** Howard S A '75 (Orrick H&S LLP) -51 W 52nd -NY 10019
(845) 292-6640 .. **Altbach,** Jeffrey S '74 -111 Sullivan Av Bx554 -Ferndale 12734 **Fx:**292-1780
(212) 969-3000 .. **Altchek,** Danl '01 %Proskauer R LLP -1585 Bway -NY 10036
(212) 541-2422 .. **Altchiler,** Robt Y '89 -590 Mad Av -NY 10022
(516) 333-3088 .. **Altebrando,** Nancy '80 -795 Oliver Av -Westbury 11590
(646) 684-3931 .. **Alter,** Amos '69 -11 Riverside Dr -NY 10023 **Fx:**684-4297
(845) 331-9373 .. **Alter,** Andrew C '86 %Leg Srvcs -101 Hurley Av -Kingston 12401 **Fx:**331-4813
(212) 859-8000 .. **Alter,** Ariel B '10 %Fried FHS&J LLP -1 NY Plz -NY 10004
(212) 558-4000 .. **Alter,** Avi S '07 %Sullivan & C LLP -125 Broad -NY 10004
(718) 237-0880 .. **Alter & Barbaro** -26 Court -Brklyn 11242 **Fx:**722-7887
(718) 237-0880 .. **Alter,** Bernard M '74 (Alter & B) -26 Court -Brklyn 11242
(212) 574-1200 .. **Alter,** Beth Hope '95 Cnsl Seward & K LLP -1 Bttry Pk Plz -NY 10004
(914) 670-0030 .. **Alter,** Bruce R '64 (Alter & G) -550 Mamaroneck Av -Harrison 10528
(212) 619-4350 .. **Alter,** Danl A '01 %Newman MKGH,PC -14 Wall -NY 10005
(212) 867-7777 .. **Alter,** Danl S '92 Alter & A -300 E 42nd -NY 10017
(212) 506-1700 .. **Alter,** Eleanor B '65 (Kasowitz BT&F LLP) -1633 Bway -NY 10019
(914) 670-0030 .. **Alter & Goldman** -550 Mamaroneck Av -Harrison 10528 **Fx:**670-0031
(845) 634-7909 .. **Alter,** Ilyssa Rothman '94 (Esbin & A,LLP) -497 S Main -New Cty 10956 **Fx:**634-4160
(212) 953-5500 .. **Alter,** Irving D '75 (Alter M LLP) -90 Park Av -NY 10016
(212) 867-7777 .. **Alter,** Ivan S '94 %Alter & A -300 E 42nd -NY 10017
(212) 906-1200 .. **Alter,** Jennifer M '10 %Latham & W -885 3rd Av -NY 10022
(212) 953-5500 .. **Alter Mantel LLP** -90 Park Av -NY 10016 **Fx:**953-5061
(516) 747-2200 .. **Alter,** Margaret S '93 -200 Old Cntry Rd -Mineola 11501 **Fx:**747-2200
(516) 747-2200 .. **Alter,** Mark E '92 -200 Old Cntry Rd -Mineola 11501 **Fx:**747-2200
(212) 801-9292 .. **Alter,** Paul R '65 OfCnsl Greenberg T,LLP -200 Park Av -NY 10166
(212) 818-1110 .. **Alter,** Regina M '97 %Butzel L,PC -380 Mad Av -NY 10017
(212) 867-7777 .. **Alter,** Stanley '61 (Alter & A) -300 E 42nd -NY 10017
(212) 867-7777 .. **Alter,** Stephanie S '83 (Alter & A) -300 E 42nd -NY 10017
(212) 554-7800 .. **Alterbaum,** James '78 (Moses & S LLP) -405 Lex Av -NY 10174
(315) 782-1800 .. **Alteri,** Steven J '01 -121 Sherman -Watertwn 13601
(212) 226-2800 .. **Alterman & Boop LLP** -35 Worth -NY 10013 **Fx:**431-3614
(212) 435-3431 .. **Alterman,** Cheryl N '08 Port Auth of NY/NJ -225 Park Av S -NY 10003 **Fx:**435-3555
(212) 226-2800 .. **Alterman,** Danl L '69 (Alterman & B LLP) -35 Worth -NY 10013
(212) 859-8000 .. **Alterman,** Edw M '83 SpclCnsl Fried FHS&J LLP -1 NY Plz -NY 10004
(212) 610-6300 .. **Alterman,** Owen S '06 %Allen & O -1221 Av of Amer -NY 10020
(212) 839-5300 .. **Alter-Nelson,** Marissa '08 %Sidley A LLP -787 7th Av -NY 10019
(212) 556-2100 .. **Altersohn,** Allison Hoch '98 (King & S) -1185 Av of Amer -NY 10036
(212) 288-3701 .. **Altfeder,** Nancy '92 -308 E 72nd -NY 10021
(212) 373-3000 .. **Altfest,** Rachel '05 %Paul WRW&G LLP -1285 Av of Amer -NY 10019
(212) 382-1588 .. **Altheim,** Marc A '89 Atlantic Dvlpmnt Grp -155 Av of Amer -NY 10013
(631) 754-2200 .. **Altholtz,** Lawr A '95 -68 S Srvc Rd -Melvll 11747 **Fx:**465-2158
(212) 422-1080 .. **Altholz,** Michl V '96 %D Magee -70 West -NY 10006 **Fx:**422-1090
(212) 269-4900 .. **Altier,** Catherine B '08 %Ford MEW&G,LLP -Wall Street Plz -NY 10005
(212) 564-9090 .. **Altier,** Jos P '56 (Altier & V,LLC) -450 7th Av -NY 10123
(212) 564-9090 .. **Altier & Vogt,LLC** -450 7th Av -NY 10123 **Fx:**268-8529
(716) 853-1616 .. **Altieri,** Danl J '10 %Harter S&E LLP -12 Fountain Plz -Buffalo 14202
(315) 646-2291 .. **Altieri,** David W '88 -352 Dodge Av -Sackets Hbr 13685
(212) 248-3140 .. **Altieri,** James M '76 (Drinker B&R LLP) -140 Bway -NY 10005
(212) 762-4000 .. **Altieri,** Nicholas P '00 Morgan Stanley -1221 Av of Amer -NY 10020
(212) 351-4500 .. **Altieri,** Peter L '81 (Epstein B&G,PC) -250 Park Av -NY 10177
(212) 391-6620 .. **Altieri,** Richd P '87 -420 5th Av -NY 10018 **Fx:**391-2035
(516) 248-8030 .. **Altimari,** Anthony F '78 -128 Front -Mineola 11501
(646) 386-5000 .. **Altizio,** Janice S '90 %Surrogates Ct -31 Chmbrs -NY 10007
(212) 344-8000 .. **Altman,** Aaron L '94 (Altman & S LLP) -225 Bway -NY 10007
(212) 417-4140 .. **Altman,** Alexandra '73 %Battery Pk City Auth -1 Wrld Fncl Ctr -NY 10281 **Fx:**417-2001
(917) 592-4779 .. **Altman,** Alvin '49 OfCnsl McMahon & K,LLP -545 W 45TH -NY 10036
(212) 471-8500 .. **Altman,** Amy F '08 %Herzfeld & R,PC -125 Broad -NY 10004
(914) 761-4040 .. **Altman,** Arthur L '68 -5 Woodlnd Pl -White Plns 10606 **Fx:**428-4531
(914) 421-2000 .. **Altman,** Chas '77 (Altman Law Grp LLC) -50 Main -White Plns 10606
(212) 867-4466 .. **Altman,** Danl T '89 (Belkin BW&G,LLP) -270 Mad Av -NY 10016
(212) 732-4800 .. **Altman,** David H '91 (Jeffer H&V) -150 Bway -NY 10038
(516) 222-0222 .. **Altman,** David N '91 (Brown & A,LLP) -510 Broadhllw Rd -Melvll 11747 **Fx:**222-0322
(212) 270-0775 .. **Altman,** Emily M '81 JP Morgan Chase -270 Park Av -NY 10017
(212) 351-4500 .. **Altman,** Eric L '87 (Epstein B&G,PC) -250 Park Av -NY 10177
(212) 779-9800 .. **Altman,** Erika L '02 %Luboja & T,LLP -10 E 40th -NY 10016
(518) 690-2828 .. **Altman,** Fredk M '75 (F Altman & Assoc) -6 Walker Way -Albany 12205 **Fx:**690-2809
(212) 435-3571 .. **Altman,** Gail C '06 Port Auth of NY/NJ -225 Park Av S -NY 10003 **Fx:**435-3555
(212) 788-7210 .. **Altman,** Gary L '79 %City Cncl Spkrs Ofc -City Hall -NY 10007 **Fx:**788-7207
(212) 619-4350 .. **Altman,** Howard B '02 %Newman MKGH,PC -14 Wall -NY 10005
(212) 541-2000 .. **Altman,** James M '82 (Bryan C LLP) -1290 Av of Amer -NY 10104
(914) 737-0200 .. **Altman,** Jared '82 -2125 Albany Post Rd -Montrose 10548 **Fx:**737-5504

(631) 777-2401 .. **Altman,** Jason C '95 J Altman,PC -425 Broadhllw Rd -Melvll 11747 **Fx:**777-2402
(585) 428-5210 .. **Altman,** Jonathan L '04 Pub Def -10 N Fitzhugh -Rchstr 14614 **Fx:**428-2234
(212) 848-4000 .. **Altman,** Jordan J '05 %Shearman & S LLP -599 Lex Av -NY 10022
(718) 328-0422 .. **Altman,** Jos A '84 (J Altman,PC) -951 Bruckner Blvd -Bronx 10459 **Fx:**378-4898
(631) 499-5046 .. **Altman,** Julie C '96 -15 Pickering Pl -Dix Hlls 11746 **Fx:**850-3125
(516) 333-2006 .. **Altman,** Leslie J '84 -1400 Old Cntry Rd -Westbury 11590 **Fx:**333-0200
(845) 853-5321 .. **Altman,** Louis N '94 -Bx154 -Hurley 12443
(212) 867-3820 .. **Altman,** Lyra J '01 %F Becker -122 E 42nd -NY 10168 **Fx:**983-5276
(845) 434-7380 .. **Altman,** Michl D '65 -Bx835 -S Fallsbrg 12779 **Fx:**434-5320
(212) 750-1200 .. **Altman,** Michl T '93 %Trolman G&L,PC -777 3rd Av -NY 10017
(212) 805-0427 .. **Altman,** Nicole Y C L '08 Hon G Lynch -500 Pearl -NY 10007
(212) 872-1000 .. **Altman,** Peter I '06 -One Bryant Park -NY 10036 **Fx:**872-1002
(212) 918-3000 .. **Altman,** Philip E '83 (Hogan L LLP) -875 3rd Av -NY 10022
(212) 633-0123 .. **Altman,** Richd A '78 -285 W 4th -NY 10014 **Fx:**(917) 463-1006
(718) 561-2356 .. **Altman,** Richd M '92 -3201 Grnd Cncrs -Bronx 10468 **Fx:**561-4855
(718) 906-2796 .. **Altman,** Richd S '90 Savino Del Bene -149-10 183rd -Jamaica 11413
(315) 471-3151 .. **Altman,** Robt H '70 (Hancock & E,LLP) -1500 AXA Twr I Bx4976 -Syracuse 13221
(212) 232-8713 .. **Altman,** Robt S '86 (RS Altman,PLLC) -27 Whitehall -NY 10004 **Fx:**232-8715
(845) 778-2121 .. **Altman,** Sanford R '80 %Jacobowitz & G,LLP -158 Orange Av Bx367 -Walden 12586
(212) 344-8000 .. **Altman & Schochet LLP** -225 Bway -NY 10007 **Fx:**344-8001
(845) 291-2050 .. **Altman,** Seth B '06 %DA -255-275 Main -Goshen 10924 **Fx:**291-2085
(212) 538-7997 .. **Altman,** Shirley L '07 Credit Suisse -1 Mad Av -NY 10010
(212) 683-7600 .. **Altman,** Steven '87 (Altman & Co PC) -260 Mad Av -NY 10016 **Fx:**683-7655
(516) 873-8872 .. **Altman,** Stewart N '68 -220 Mineola Blvd -Mineola 11501 **Fx:**873-8872
(212) 353-0674 .. **Altman,** Stuart M L '96 -264 E Bway -NY 10002 **Fx:**260-4534
(212) 335-4500 .. **Altman,** Theo '66 (DLA Piper LLP) -1251 Av of Amer -NY 10020
(212) 558-4000 .. **Altman,** Zvi Danl '06 %Sullivan & C LLP -125 Broad -NY 10004
(631) 878-7477 .. **Alto,** Laura '90 -3 Hrbrvw Pl -Ctr Moriches 11934
(212) 629-6151 .. **Alton,** Walter G Jr. '67 W Alton Jr & Assoc,PC -548 W 28th -NY 10001 **Fx:**629-5170
(518) 386-2266 .. **Altonberg,** Wendy '07 %Pub Def -519 State -Schnctdy 12305 **Fx:**386-2814
(212) 259-8000 .. **Altorelli,** John J '94 (Dewey & L LLP) -1301 Av of Amer -NY 10019
(716) 853-1150 .. **Altreuter Berlin** -617 Main -Buffalo 14203 **Fx:**853-1156
(716) 853-1150 .. **Altreuter,** Wm C '84 (Altreuter B) -617 Main -Buffalo 14203
(718) 855-9531 .. **Altruda,** Paul F '75 -44 Court -Brklyn 11201 **Fx:**(732) 972-8431
(914) 995-4038 .. **Altschiller,** Tami S '91 %Cnty Atty -148 Martine Av -White Plns 10601 **Fx:**995-2495
(212) 370-1880 .. **Altschul,** James S '89 %Aviation Advsry Srvc -230 Park Av -NY 10169 **Fx:**808-6553
(718) 248-2846 .. **Altschul,** Kimberly Ann '98 Citigroup -1 Court Sq -LIC 11120
(212) 924-1505 .. **Altschul,** Mark M '85 Altschul & A -18 E 12th -NY 10003 **Fx:**727-9615
(516) 496-7247 .. **Altschul,** Scott J '92 -93 Aspen Dr E -Woodbury 11797 **Fx:**496-7675
(212) 753-7500 .. **Altschul,** Sean A '00 (Hartman & C LLP) -488 Mad Av -NY 10022
(212) 422-2400 .. **Altschul,** Stanford M '59 (Altschul G&G) -17 Battery Place -NY 10004 **Fx:**732-1001
(212) 310-8000 .. **Altschuler,** Ashley R '00 (Weil G&M LLP) -767 5th Av -NY 10153
(212) 504-6000 .. **Altschuler,** Fredric L '73 (Cadwalader W&T LLP) -1 World Fncl Ctr -NY 10281
(877) 478-3529 .. **Altschuler,** Howard A '94 -545 8th Av -NY 10018
(212) 292-4222 .. **Altschuler,** Jonathan B '61 -521 5th Av -NY 10175 **Fx:**292-4219
(212) 682-4426 .. **Altschuler,** Jonathan R '05 %O'Shea Prtnrs LLP -521 5th Av -NY 10175 **Fx:**682-4437
(212) 613-2167 .. **Altschuler,** Kimberly B '04 %Gibbons PC -1 Penn Plz -NY 10119 **Fx:**554-9641
(212) 464-2337 .. **Altschuler,** Mark J '83 JP Morgan Chase Bk -345 Park Av -NY 10154
(212) 431-1300 .. **Altschuler,** Myron I '66 (Borah GAN&G PC) -377 Bway -NY 10013
(914) 332-1800 .. **Altschuller,** Debora R '89 %Cherry E&K,LLP -150 Wht Plns Rd -Tarrytwn 10591
(212) 834-0600 .. **Altshiler,** Florina '06 %Gordon & S,PC -355 Lex Av -NY 10017
(212) 859-8000 .. **Altun,** Nazar '05 %Fried FHS&J LLP -1 NY Plz -NY 10004
(212) 450-4000 .. **Altus,** Leslie J '84 Cnsl Davis P&W LLP -450 Lex Av -NY 10017
(315) 703-6600 .. **Altwarg,** Danl B '92 %Leg Aid -472 S Salina -Syracuse 13202 **Fx:**671-0062
(518) 785-1900 .. **Aluck,** Edw J '01 %PEF -1168-70 Troy-Schnctdy Rd Bx12414 -Albany 12212 **Fx:**785-1323
(212) 756-2000 .. **Aluko,** Michl A '03 %Schulte R&Z LLP -919 3rd Av -NY 10022
(212) 655-0880 .. **Alula,** Yared H '09 %NBPA -310 Lennox Av -NY 10027 **Fx:**655-0881
(518) 785-3300 .. **Alund,** Jos R '05 -426 Troy Schenectady Rd -Latham 12110 **Fx:**783-5691
(914) 766-1972 .. **Alutto,** Marjorie H '94 IBM -294 Route 100 -Somers 10589
(212) 450-4000 .. **Alva,** Marlene '75 SrCnsl Davis P&W LLP -450 Lex Av -NY 10017
(212) 964-6611 .. **Alvarado,** Alfredo J '92 (Lester SK&D) -120 Bway -NY 10271
(718) 923-4206 .. **Alvarado,** Douglas C '81 %OTDA Fair Hearings -14 Boerum Pl -Brklyn 11201
(973) 596-4529 .. **Alvarado,** Ivette P '05 %Gibbons PC -1 Penn Plz -NY 10119 **Fx:**639-6207
(516) 292-0101 .. **Alvarado,** Miguel A '99 (Mejias M&A,PC) -100 Main -Hempstd 11550 **Fx:**292-4694
(718) 537-7238 .. **Alvarado,** Phan T '06 %DA -198 E 161st -Bronx 10451 **Fx:**681-1129
(718) 590-2000 .. **Alvarez,** Alan S '01 %DA -198 E 161st -Bronx 10451 **Fx:**590-6477
(212) 906-1200 .. **Alvarez,** Carlos '87 (Latham & W) -885 3rd Av -NY 10022
(212) 752-5258 .. **Alvarez,** Chas J '07 %Schwartz SE&C LLC -845 3rd Av -NY 10022
(212) 310-8000 .. **Alvarez,** Denise '03 %Weil G&M LLP -767 5th Av -NY 10153
(212) 878-8000 .. **Alvarez,** Edgard '91 Cnsl Clifford C LLP -31 W 52nd -NY 10019
(212) 362-4173 .. **Alvarez,** Elizabeth M '00 Aquarius Hardware -601 Amstrdm Av -NY 10024
(212) 770-1569 .. **Alvarez,** Erin Gleason '02 AIG -80 Pine -NY 10005
(914) 328-0404 .. **Alvarez,** Francis P '91 (Jackson L LLP) -1 N Bway -White Plns 10601
(212) 416-8000 .. **Alvarez,** George A '93 %Dept of Law -120 Bway -NY 10271
(212) 947-9779 .. **Alvarez,** Gisela K '02 Advocates for Chldrn of NY -151 W 30th -NY 10001
(516) 227-6363 .. **Alvarez,** Gregory R '00 %Amato & Assoc,PC -666 Old Cntry Rd -Gdn Cty 11530 **Fx:**227-6367
(212) 269-3747 .. **Alvarez,** Janet '98 J Alvarez & Assoc,PC -14 Wall -NY 10005 **Fx:**269-2049
(212) 325-2421 .. **Alvarez,** Manuel J '84 %CSFP Cptl -11 Mad Av -NY 10010 **Fx:**325-8282
(212) 566-4530 .. **Alvarez,** Oscar '90 %Dept of Bldgs -280 Bway -NY 10007
(631) 465-2030 .. **Alvarez,** Richd I '83 -68 S Srvc Rd -Melvll 11747
(212) 965-9458 .. **Alvarez,** Virginia G '05 %Portela Law Firm,PC -177 Wadsworth Av -NY 10033 **Fx:**927-4690
(516) 822-8900 .. **Alventosa,** Leopoldo '85 Fiedelman & M -2 Jericho Plz -Jericho 11753
(212) 694-1000 .. **Alverio,** Daisy M '88 %Boricua College -3755 Bway -NY 10032
(212) 532-4434 .. **Alverson,** Margaret E '85 NYS Assn of Crim Def Lawyers -2 Wall -NY 10005 **Fx:**(888) 239-4665
(631) 928-8000 .. **Alves,** Ann M '05 %Winkler KW&K,LLP -310 Hallock Av -Pt Jffrsn Sta 11776
(212) 574-1200 .. **Alves,** Arlene R '85 Cnsl Seward & K LLP -1 Bttry Pk Plz -NY 10004
(212) 839-5300 .. **Alves,** Luis A T '07 %Sidley A LLP -787 7th Av -NY 10019
(212) 768-6700 .. **Alves,** Michelle K '09 %Sonnenschein N&R LLP -2 World Fncl Ctr -NY 10281
(914) 741-6100 .. **Alves,** Sergio '05 %Kaufman B&R -200 Summit Lk Dr -Valhalla 10595
(212) 370-1923 .. **Alvi,** Mumtaz H '87 Alvi & A -230 Park Av -NY 10169 **Fx:**370-1943
(917) 343-8382 .. **Alvi,** Rashid S '00 Goldman Sachs -1 NY Plz -NY 10004
(212) 547-5400 .. **Alvino,** Timothy J '82 (McDermott W&E LLP) -340 Mad Av -NY 10173
(718) 802-2725 .. **Alvord,** Kelly L '02 ACS -330 Jay -Brklyn 11201 **Fx:**802-2798
(516) 328-7181 .. **Alvy,** Norman D '71 (Alvy & T,LLP) -1979 Marcus Av -Lk Success 11042
(516) 328-7181 .. **Alvy & Tablante,LLP** -1979 Marcus Av -Lk Success 11042 **Fx:**328-7182
(718) 935-3967 .. **Alvy,** Vida M '78 NYC Dept Educ -335 Adams -Brklyn 11201
(212) 759-4888 .. **Alwais,** Jonathan D '06 %Phillips L LLP -437 Mad Av -NY 10022
(212) 906-1200 .. **Alwang,** Melissa Scharer '98 (Latham & W) -885 3rd Av -NY 10022
(315) 413-5400 .. **Alweis,** Kenneth M '86 (Goldberg S LLP) -5789 Widewaters Pkwy -Syracuse 13214
(516) 746-6766 .. **Alweiss,** Gary S '79 -229 7th -Gdn Cty 11530 **Fx:**741-9276
(212) 313-1200 .. **Aly,** Amal '93 %SIA -120 Bway -NY 10271 **Fx:**968-0705
(212) 775-8700 .. **Aly,** Amr '97 (Kilpatrick S,LLP) -31 W 52nd -NY 10019
(212) 836-8000 .. **Alyonycheva,** Tatiana N '01 %Kaye S LLP -425 Park Av -NY 10022
(212) 791-0285 .. **Alzadon,** Rula D '08 %Malaby & B,LLC -150 Bway -NY 10038 **Fx:**791-0286
(845) 562-0203 .. **Alzugaray,** Gustavo W '99 %Jacoby & M,LLP -1279 Route 300 Bx1111 -Newburgh 12550 **Fx:**562-3492
(718) 370-7030 .. **Amabile & Erman,PC** -1000 South Av -Staten Isl 10314 **Fx:**370-3656
(718) 852-9113 .. **Amabile & Erman,PC** -26 Court -Brklyn 11242 **Fx:**855-8811
(718) 220-4493 .. **Amachree,** Onimiteim Flagg '97 -3130 Grand Cncrs -Bronx 10458
(516) 292-6516 .. **Amadio,** Alfred J '97 (Clark & A,PC) -230 Hilton Av -Hempstd 11550
(718) 838-7878 .. **Amaez,** Leana E '06 %Bronx Defenders -860 Crtlandt Av -Bronx 10451 **Fx:**665-0100
(212) 425-3100 .. **Amagsila,** Jillian M '07 %McManus C&R,PC -48 Wall -NY 10005
(212) 807-4180 .. **Amah,** Udoka O '07 UF Amah,PC -305 Mad Av -NY 10165 **Fx:**957-1912
(973) 596-4829 .. **Amalfe,** Christine A '86 (Gibbons PC) -1 Penn Plz -NY 10119 **Fx:**639-6230
(845) 708-0123 .. **Amalfitano,** Gerard '82 -254 S Main -New Cty 10956 **Fx:**708-8727
(212) 735-3000 .. **Amamoo,** Agnesine R '07 %Skadden ASM&F LLP -4 Times Sq -NY 10036
(212) 506-1700 .. **Amamoo,** Paul Nii-Amar '08 %Kasowitz BT&F LLP -1633 Bway -NY 10019
(212) 225-2000 .. **Aman,** David E '00 (Cleary GS&H) -1 Lbrty Plz -NY 10006
(716) 845-7465 .. **Aman,** John J '78 %Family Ct -1 Niagara Plz -Buffalo 14202 **Fx:**858-6293
(718) 254-6024 .. **Amanat,** F Franklin '92 %US Atty -271 Cadman Plz E -Brklyn 11201 **Fx:**254-6479
(516) 470-1379 .. **Amanatides,** Alexander M '95 -400 Jericho Av -Jericho 11753
(718) 537-7447 .. **Amankwaa,** Kofi Owusu '96 Beak Brokerage Srvcs -1363 Jerome Av -Bronx 10452
(212) 675-4321 .. **Amann,** Anne T '95 Robbins Ent LLC -35 Worth -NY 10013 **Fx:**675-4441
(212) 403-1000 .. **Amar,** Stella E R '07 %Wachtell LR&K -51 W 52nd -NY 10019
(718) 643-8862 .. **Amar,** Suhail '99 Dept of Probation -283 Adams -Brklyn 11201
(212) 474-1000 .. **Amaral Surcan,** Camila '07 %Cravath S&M LLP -825 8th Av -NY 10019
(516) 249-3450 .. **Amarasinghe,** Jami C '00 %Carman C&I,LLP -266 Main -Farmngdl 11735
(212) 225-2000 .. **Amariglio,** Pierre F '10 %Cleary GS&H -1 Lbrty Plz -NY 10006
(212) 373-3000 .. **Amarnani,** Prem '09 %Paul WRW&G LLP -1285 Av of Amer -NY 10019
(212) 924-8961 .. **Amarosa,** Michl '82 -37 Carmine -NY 10014
(212) 297-0200 .. **Amarosa,** Ricci D '95 %American Bldg Maintenance -551 5th Av -NY 10176 **Fx:**338-8556
(212) 351-4000 .. **Amass,** Tyler H '08 %Gibson D&C LLP -200 Park Av -NY 10166
(516) 227-6363 .. **Amato,** Alfred L '91 (Amato & Assoc,PC) -666 Old Cntry Rd -Gdn Cty 11530 **Fx:**227-6367
(516) 931-1800 .. **Amato,** Alissa '06 %Catalano G&P LLP -100 Jericho Quadrangle -Jericho 11753
(516) 680-5874 .. **Amato,** Anthony W Jr. '92 (Amato & Assoc,LLC) -42 Old Pine Dr -Manhsst 11030

(516) 746-7780 .. **Amato,** Christopher '88 %Rossillo & L,PC -355 Post Av -Westbury 11590
(518) 402-8533 .. **Amato,** Christopher A '82 %DEC -625 Bway -Albany 12233 **Fx:**402-9016
(212) 320-0866 .. **Amato,** Jacob J III '01 Barclays Capital -1301 Av of Amer -NY 10019
(212) 259-8000 .. **Amato,** Jeffrey J '03 %Dewey & L LLP -1301 Av of Amer -NY 10019
(212) 277-6500 .. **Amato,** Jennifer Marciano '03 %Dickstein S LLP -1633 Bway -NY 10019
(212) 478-7200 .. **Amato,** John P '87 (Hahn & H LLP) -488 Mad Av -NY 10022
(516) 663-6600 .. **Amato,** Michl S '95 (Ruskin MF,PC) -1425 RXR Plz -Uniondale 11556
(845) 735-0900 .. **Amato,** Vincent N '79 -275 N Mddltwn Rd -Pearl Rvr 10965
(631) 265-4500 .. **Amato-Caypinar,** Laura '99 %Meyer M&K -28 Manor Rd -Smithtwn 11787
(718) 254-7000 .. **Amatruda,** Matthew Steven '99 %US Atty -271 Cadman Plz E -Brklyn 11201 **Fx:**254-6479
(212) 416-8000 .. **Ambachen,** Jensen '02 %Dept of Law -120 Bway -NY 10271
(212) 997-2445 .. **Ambalu,** Aaron C '96 -15 W 44th -NY 10036 **Fx:**869-2303
(212) 480-6796 .. **Ambaras,** Robt '82 %DHCR -25 Beaver -NY 10004 **Fx:**480-7416
(718) 243-6380 .. **Ambekar,** Deepa '06 %Leg Aid -111 Lvngstn -Brklyn 11201 **Fx:**237-8737
(212) 815-1818 .. **Ambia,** Ann Fawcett '95 %DC 37 MELS -125 Barclay -NY 10007 **Fx:**815-1343
(212) 943-9080 .. **Ambinder,** Lloyd R '90 (Virginia & A) -111 Bway -NY 10006
(212) 906-4603 .. **Ambler,** Susan M '09 %Latham & W -885 3rd Av -NY 10022
(212) 514-6111 .. **Ambos,** Paul H '77 (P Ambos,PC) -110 Wall -NY 10005 **Fx:**514-5222
(212) 588-1670 .. **Ambrecht,** Michl R '91 (Ambrecht & M LLP) -245 Park Av -NY 10167
(914) 997-9550 .. **Ambrecht,** Stephen J '89 %UIA Bd -120 Bloomingdale Rd -White Plns 10605 **Fx:**997-0014
(631) 852-2586 .. **Ambro,** Richd '85 Hon C Hinrichs -210 Center Dr -Rvrhead 11901
(631) 853-5212 .. **Ambro,** Susan D '86 %Leg Aid -400 Carleton Av Bx9082 -Central Islip 11722 **Fx:**853-7798
(212) 430-7992 .. **Ambron,** Mary Terri '98 West LB AG -1211 Av of Amer -NY 10036
(212) 735-3000 .. **Ambrose,** Amanda J '07 %Skadden ASM&F LLP -4 Times Sq -NY 10036
(212) 227-9163 .. **Ambrose,** Evan N '03 -111 Bway -NY 10006
(845) 338-1120 .. **Ambrose,** Nancy Fisher '82 %J Fisher,PC -261 Fair Bx3069 -Kingston 12402 **Fx:**338-2554
(212) 969-3000 .. **Ambrose,** Rebecca L '08 %Proskauer R LLP -1585 Bway -NY 10036
(212) 536-3900 .. **Ambrose,** Robt F '58 OfCnsl K&L Gates LLP -599 Lex Av -NY 10022
(631) 232-2400 .. **Ambrose,** Victor A '73 %Nassau/Sfflk Law Srv -1757 Vets Hwy -Islandia 11749 **Fx:**232-2489
(845) 638-5180 .. **Ambrose,** Wm '85 Cnty Atty -Cnty Ofc Bldg -New Cty 10956 **Fx:**638-5676
(516) 825-3670 .. **Ambrosino,** Cherie L '90 -692 Wyndgate Dr W -Vly Stream 11580
(516) 663-6600 .. **Ambrosino,** Edw A '90 OfCnsl Ruskin MF,PC -1425 RXR Plz -Uniondale 11556
(631) 724-4233 .. **Ambrosino,** Frank N '81 (Tonetti & A) -548 W Jericho Tpk -Smithtwn 11787 **Fx:**724-4776
(212) 513-7788 .. **Ambrosino,** Vincent S '92 (Ahmuty D&M) -123 William -NY 10038
(518) 457-6137 .. **Ambrosio,** Ralph F '85 %State Police -1220 Wshngtn Av -Albany 12226 **Fx:**485-1164
(212) 819-8200 .. **Ambruoso,** Andrew C '98 Cnsl White & C LLP -1155 Av of Amer -NY 10036
(212) 956-9500 .. **Amburgey,** David C '96 (Hand B&A LLP) -8 W 40th -NY 10018 **Fx:**376-6080
(212) 506-1700 .. **Amburgy,** Thos J '08 %Kasowitz BT&F LLP -1633 Bway -NY 10019
(516) 681-8200 .. **Ambus,** Gregory T '00 (Ambus R,PC) -380 N Bway -Jericho 11753 **Fx:**932-8353
(212) 403-1000 .. **Amdetsion,** Fasil '09 %Wachtell LR&K -51 W 52nd -NY 10019
(212) 310-8000 .. **Amdur,** Martin B '68 (Weil G&M LLP) -767 5th Av -NY 10153
(212) 906-1200 .. **Amdur,** Stephen B '05 %Latham & W -885 3rd Av -NY 10022
(315) 343-6363 .. **Amdursky Pelky Fennell & Wallen,PC** -26 E Oneida -Oswego 13126 **Fx:**343-0134
(212) 265-6888 .. **Amedeo,** Douglas A '92 Cnsl Porzio B&N,PC -156 W 56th -NY 10019
(518) 583-4123 .. **Amedio,** Gerard V '03 -18 Division -Saratoga Spgs 12866 **Fx:**583-4338
(718) 442-9000 .. **Ameduri,** Anthony L '80 (Ameduri G&F) -471 Bement Av -Staten Isl 10310
(718) 442-9000 .. **Ameduri Galante & Friscia** -471 Bement Av -Staten Isl 10310 **Fx:**273-5219
(212) 458-5134 .. **Ameel,** Susan M '09 ESP Technologies Corp -140 Bway -NY 10005
(646) 386-5000 .. **Amelar,** Jessica R '82 %Surrogates Ct -31 Chmbrs -NY 10007
(914) 468-0192 .. **Amelio,** Raffaele '92 %Corrigan & B,LLC -1311 Mamaroneck Av -White Plns 10605 **Fx:**468-0199
(516) 479-6313 .. **Amelkin,** Stanley P '62 OfCnsl Silverman A LLP -100 Jericho Quad -Jericho 11753 **Fx:**945-6313
(646) 487-9807 .. **Amen,** H M K '81 -Grnd Cntrl Sta Bx3023 -NY 10163
(212) 373-3000 .. **Amend,** Andrew W '10 %Paul WRW&G LLP -1285 Av of Amer -NY 10019
(716) 636-7600 .. **Amendola,** Amanda R '10 %HoganWillig -2410 N Forest Rd -Amherst 14068
(716) 883-3155 .. **Amendola,** Francis C '92 -403 Main -Buffalo 14203
(212) 593-9900 .. **Amendola,** Jos '97 AugustinPartners LLC -300 E 42nd -NY 10017 **Fx:**593-9997
(646) 386-3615 .. **Amendola,** Mary T '98 %Supreme Ct-Law Dept -60 Centre -NY 10007
(202) 225-8420 .. **Amendolara,** Lauren D '06 Rep ME McMahon(NY-13) -265 New Dorp Ln -Staten Isl 10306 **Fx:**226-1272
(212) 633-9300 .. **Amene,** Gabriel O '04 NY Foundling Hosptl -590 Av of the America -NY 10011
(212) 953-6000 .. **Amengual,** Randolph '75 (Katsky K LLP) -605 3rd Av -NY 10158
(917) 612-8854 .. **Ameno,** Lorenzo T '02 -306 Rudyard -Staten Isl 10306
(212) 455-2000 .. **Amer,** Andrew S '87 (Simpson T&B LLP) -425 Lex Av -NY 10017
(914) 421-0021 .. **Amer,** Harry '61 -140 Grand -White Plns 10601 **Fx:**421-0002
(212) 963-5361 .. **Amer,** Janette '90 UN-Div for the Advancement of Women -2 UN Plz -NY 10017
(516) 742-5290 .. **Amer,** Myron '55 -114 Old Cntry Rd -Mineola 11501 **Fx:**746-1298
(516) 683-5632 .. **Ameranti-Donnelly,** Cecilia '88 IRS -107 Charles Lindergh Blvd -Gdn Cty 11530
(646) 386-5000 .. **Ameres,** Timothy J '06 Surrogates Ct -31 Chmbrs -NY 10007
(518) 462-5300 .. **Amerling,** Andrew B '73 (DeGraff F&K LLP) -90 State -Albany 12207
(716) 856-4000 .. **Amershadian,** John P '77 (Hodgson R LLP) -140 Pearl -Buffalo 14202
(212) 425-9300 .. **Amery,** Brian F '75 (Bressler A&R,PC) -17 State -NY 10004
(212) 839-5300 .. **Amery,** Lindsey O '10 %Sidley A LLP -787 7th Av -NY 10019
(212) 730-8133 .. **Ames,** Allison A '05 %Gunderson DSVF&H,LLP -220 W 42nd -NY 10036
(607) 749-7255 .. **Ames,** David E '76 -23 S Main Bx96 -Homer 13077 **Fx:**749-7257
(607) 763-9200 .. **Ames,** Dorian D '82 (Levene G&T,LLP) -BxF-1706 -Bnghmtn 13902
(212) 605-0255 .. **Ames,** Elisabeth H W '98 -575 Mad Av -NY 10022 **Fx:**605-0259
(914) 696-9193 .. **Ames,** Gail A '82 -43 Crescent Ter -Bedfrd Hlls 10507
(212) 318-6000 .. **Ames,** Jill A '92 Paul HJ&W LLP -75 E 55th -NY 10022
(516) 681-3100 .. **Ames,** Jonathan R '92 %Donohue MC&B -555 N Bway Bx350 -Jericho 11753
(718) 312-4100 .. **Ames,** Kathleen L '89 %Empire Blue Cross -15 MetroTech Ctr -Brklyn 11201 **Fx:**312-6010
(212) 645-6360 .. **Ames,** Margery E '75 InterAgency Cncl -150 W 30th -NY 10001 **Fx:**627-8847
(315) 637-6398 .. **Ames,** Richd N '47 -201 Euclid Dr -Fayettevll 13066 **Fx:**637-2740
(315) 423-0282 .. **Ames,** Sharon L '83 Ames Immigration -472 S Salina -Syracuse 13202 **Fx:**476-9466
(718) 855-9000 .. **Ametrano,** Anthony '04 %Cullen and D LLP -177 Montague -Brklyn 11201
(212) 576-7000 .. **Amey-Hambric,** Keisha '01 NY Life Ins -51 Mad Av -NY 10010 **Fx:**447-0569
(631) 265-2550 .. **Amicizia,** Vincent M '96 (Greshin Z&A) -199 E Main Bx829 -Smithtwn 11787
(718) 622-2434 .. **Amico,** Jos C Jr. '83 -27 Prospect Park W -Brklyn 11215
(585) 454-2020 .. **Amico,** Richd P '89 (Cellino & B,PC) -16 W Main -Rchstr 14614
(917) 777-4200 .. **Amico,** Thos J '92 (Bingham M LLP) -1 Bttry Pk Plz -NY 10004
(518) 861-0133 .. **Amicone,** Bridget N '06 Protective Industrial Products -26 Computer Dr E -Albany 12205
(518) 427-9700 .. **Amicone,** Jos '98 SrCnsl Harris B PLLC -677 Bway -Albany 12207
(914) 251-1115 .. **Amicucci,** Paul G '91 (Walsh & A LLP) -2900 Wstchstr Av -Purchase 10577
(212) 858-7700 .. **Amieva,** Jorge L '02 %Budd L -140 Bway -NY 10005
(716) 852-1300 .. **Amigone,** Nicholas P III '75 (Amigone S&M,LLP) -350 Main -Buffalo 14202
(716) 852-1300 .. **Amigone Sanchez & Mattrey, LLP** -350 Main -Buffalo 14202 **Fx:**852-1344
(212) 506-1700 .. **Amin,** Eric S '05 Kasowitz BT&F LLP -1633 Bway -NY 10019
(212) 889-3700 .. **Amin-Giwner,** Stephanie D '03 %Abbey SR&A LLP -212 E 39th -NY 10016
(212) 490-4100 .. **Amini,** Bijan '85 (Storch A&M,PC) -140 E 45th -NY 10017
(212) 584-0700 .. **Aminolroaya,** Parvin K '09 %Seeger W LLP -1 William -NY 10004
(914) 681-0200 .. **Amir,** Jacob Eytan '96 %DelBello DWW&W,LLP -1 N Lex Av -White Plns 10601
(607) 734-1574 .. **Amir,** Leora '78 %JET,Inc -2205 Cllg Av -Elmira Hts 14903 **Fx:**734-5371
(212) 735-3000 .. **Amir,** Lior '06 %Skadden ASM&F LLP -4 Times Sq -NY 10036
(212) 715-1000 .. **Amir,** Michal '09 %Arnold & P LLP -399 Park Av -NY 10022
(518) 473-7051 .. **Amiraian,** David B '82 %OTDA-Fair Hearings -40 N Pearl -Albany 12243 **Fx:**473-6735
(212) 909-0000 .. **Amirfar,** Catherine M '01 (Debevoise & P LLP) -919 3rd Av -NY 10022
(917) 637-3600 .. **Amiri,** Brigitte A '00 %Ctr for Reproductive Rts -120 Wall -NY 10005 **Fx:**637-3666
(516) 482-9100 .. **Amirian,** Benjamin '95 (Amirian S& Assoc LLP) -40 Cuttermill Rd -Gt Neck 11021
(212) 259-8000 .. **Amirsaleh,** Alex G '10 %Dewey & L LLP -1301 Av of Amer -NY 10019
(607) 739-4511 .. **Amisano,** Guy L '06 Salient Corp -203 Colonial Rd -Horseheads 14845 **Fx:**739-4045
(585) 271-0060 .. **Amisano,** Jos R '78 -100 Meridian Ctr -Rchstr 14618 **Fx:**271-0061
(212) 554-0400 .. **Amit,** Lidore A '06 Grubman I&S,PC -152 W 57th -NY 10019
(718) 243-6302 .. **Amjad,** Ayisha Asmin '00 %Leg Aid -111 Lvngstn -Brklyn 11201 **Fx:**237-8737
(212) 969-3000 .. **Amladi,** Bela P '90 %Proskauer R LLP -1585 Bway -NY 10036
(212) 909-6000 .. **Amler,** James B '08 %Debevoise & P LLP -919 3rd Av -NY 10022
(212) 768-6700 .. **Amley,** Edw A Jr. '99 %Sonnenschein N&R LLP -2 World Fncl Ctr -NY 10281
(212) 421-2233 .. **Amlicke,** Thos R '62 (Wilk A LLP) -675 3rd Av -NY 10017
(631) 726-8069 .. **Ammar,** Brian Michl '94 -4 Farmstead Ln -Water Mill 11976
(516) 741-6355 .. **Ammendolea,** Francis J '02 %Nicolini PF&S -114 Old Cntry Rd Bx9006 -Mineola 11501
(516) 741-6355 .. **Ammendolea,** Mary-Katherine '06 %Nicolini PF&S -114 Old Cntry Rd Bx9006 -Mineola 11501
(631) 756-4255 .. **Ammerman,** Alisa A '96 %State Ins Fund -8 Corp Ctr Dr -Melvll 11747 **Fx:**756-4060
(212) 697-3122 .. **Ammerman,** Douglas G '01 (Martin C&B LLP) -220 E 42nd -NY 10017
(631) 473-5550 .. **Ammerman,** John E '82 -503 Main -Pt Jffrsn 11777
(718) 527-9862 .. **Amoachi,** Ala '10 %Stewart Law Firm,LLP -133-40 Hook Crk Blvd -Rosedale 11422 **Fx:**527-7624
(212) 940-8800 .. **Amoah,** Hannah C '07 %Katten MR LLP -575 Mad Av -NY 10022
(518) 438-2000 .. **Amodeo,** Anthony J '84 (Lombardi WWHA&D PC) -III Winners Cir -Albany 12205
(212) 474-1000 .. **Amodeo,** Cristina M '05 %Cravath S&M LLP -825 8th Av -NY 10019
(718) 618-2500 .. **Amodeo,** Mary Ann '93 %Civil Ct -851 Grnd Cncrs -Bronx 10451 **Fx:**590-7294
(518) 452-8787 .. **Amodeo,** Matthew P '92 (Drinker B&R LLP) -321 Great Oaks Blvd -Albany 12203
(716) 856-5500 .. **Amodeo,** Michl L '05 %Damon M LLP -200 Delaware Av -Buffalo 14202

(518) 257-3000 ..**Amodio**, Dena Tofte '95 %Dormitory Auth -515 Bway -Albany 12207 **Fx:**257-3101
(516) 747-4301 ..**Amodio**, Michl A '86 %Torino & B,PC -200 Old Cntry Rd -Mineola 11501
(914) 289-1961 ..**Amodio**, Michl P II '82 (McGovern & A) -2 William -White Plns 10601 **Fx:**289-1962
(212) 996-7708 ..**Amoils**, Nisa C '96 -21 E 96th -NY 10128
(212) 819-8200 ..**Amon**, Carl H III '69 (White & C LLP) -1155 Av of Amer -NY 10036
(845) 357-4000 ..**Amon**, Claudia J '89 (Rice & A) -4 Exec Blvd -Suffern 10901 **Fx:**357-0765
(212) 810-2430 ..**Amon**, Thos G '74 -250 W 57th -NY 10107 **Fx:**810-2427
(718) 923-6300 ..**Amon**, Thos G '09 %Atty Grievance Comm -335 Adams -Brklyn 11201 **Fx:**624-2978
(212) 259-8000 ..**Amoona**, Jonathan J '10 %Dewey & L LLP -1301 Av of Amer -NY 10019
(212) 863-6300 ..**Amore**, Marian E '99 HPD -100 Gold -NY 10038
(212) 244-6600 ..**Amorello**, Kenneth H '91 %Schechter & B,PC -350 5th Av -NY 10118
(973) 596-4835 ..**Amoresano**, Guy V '87 (Gibbons PC) -1 Penn Plz -NY 10119 **Fx:**639-6255
(212) 221-5200 ..**Amorese**, Sam A '82 OTB -1501 Bway -NY 10036
(516) 489-5000 ..**Amorini**, Federico A '01 %Town Atty -Town Hall -Hempstd 11550 **Fx:**489-5150
(212) 406-7000 ..**Amorosa**, Dominic F '77 -521 5th Av -NY 10175 **Fx:**233-7805
(212) 210-9467 ..**Amorosa**, Judith A '07 %Alston & B LLP -90 Park Av -NY 10016
(212) 450-4000 ..**Amorosi**, John D '96 (Davis P&W LLP) -450 Lex Av -NY 10017
(516) 572-2800 ..**Amoroso**, Dino G '86 Nassau Downs -220 Fulton Av -Hempstd 11550
(315) 733-0419 ..**Amoroso**, Gregory J '94 (Saunders K,LLP) -185 Genesee -Utica 13501
(212) 483-0105 ..**Amoroso**, Jos C '02 %Coughlin D LLP -88 Pine-Wall St Plz -NY 10005
(631) 853-4049 ..**Amoroso**, Michl A '85 %Cnty Atty -Dennison Bldg Bx6100 -Hauppauge 11788 **Fx:**853-5169
(914) 686-7272 ..**Amoroso**, Michl J '99 -500 Mamaroneck Av -Harrison 10528 **Fx:**517-7566
(212) 980-3500 ..**Amoroso**, Paolo G '09 %Pavia & H LLP -600 Mad Av -NY 10022
(212) 535-7026 ..**Amoroso**, Stephen D Jr. '76 -240 E 76th -NY 10021
(914) 253-9255 ..**Amoruso**, Michl J '95 (Amoruso & A,LLP) -800 Wstchstr Av -Rye Brook 10573 **Fx:**253-9162
(914) 253-9255 ..**Amoruso**, Sreelekha C '96 (Amoruso & A,LLP) -800 Wstchstr Av -Rye Brook 10573 **Fx:**253-9162
(315) 475-3127 ..**Amory**, Elaine Carnicelli '95 Leg Srvcs -472 S Salina -Syracuse 13202 **Fx:**475-2706
(212) 278-0400 ..**Amos**, Brian J '04 %Cooper & D LLP -30 Rckfllr Plz -NY 10112
(518) 447-2666 ..**Ampansiri**, Don Jr. '97 Tchrs Rtrmnt Sys -10 Corp Woods Dr -Albany 12211 **Fx:**447-2679
(212) 858-1000 ..**Amram**, Oren A '08 %Pillsbury WSP LLP -1540 Bway -NY 10036
(212) 922-0003 ..**Amrami**, Gil '02 -122 E 42nd -NY 10168
(518) 399-1000 ..**Amrhein**, Cynthia R '91 -1 Townley Dr -Burnt Hlls 12027 **Fx:**399-9020
(212) 788-1578 ..**Amron**, Susan E '86 %Law Dept -100 Church -NY 10007 **Fx:**788-0367
(212) 909-6000 ..**Ams**, Julianne '09 %Debevoise & P LLP -919 3rd Av -NY 10022
(212) 755-0808 ..**Amsel**, Jody B '95 %M Zimmett -126 E 56th -NY 10022 **Fx:**755-0888
(212) 310-8000 ..**Amsel**, Joshua S '01 %Weil G&M LLP -767 5th Av -NY 10153
(516) 670-8930 ..**Amsel**, Seena R '80 -963 Gerry Av -Lido Bch 11561
(212) 421-4100 ..**Amsellem**, Perry M '90 (Pryor C LLP) -7 Times Sq -NY 10036
(212) 889-2498 ..**Amsler**, Edw J '72 (Fager & A,LLP) -2 Park Av -NY 10016
(212) 715-9100 ..**Amster**, Jason S '06 %Kramer LN&F,LLP -1177 Av of Amer -NY 10036
(347) 401-9288 ..**Amster**, Jeffrey H '86 Supreme Ct Law Dept -360 Adams -Brklyn 11201 **Fx:**643-6114
(212) 336-8000 ..**Amster**, Morton '51 (Amster R&E) -90 Park Av -NY 10016
(212) 336-8000 ..**Amster Rothstein & Ebenstein** -90 Park Av -NY 10016 **Fx:**336-8001
(212) 986-8671 ..**Amster**, Sheldon '57 (Sydney A&G,PLLC) -122 E 42nd -NY 10168
(212) 725-6100 ..**Amsterdam & Lewinter** -9 E 40th -NY 10016 **Fx:**725-4799
(212) 725-6100 ..**Amsterdam**, Mark L '69 (Amsterdam & L) -9 E 40th -NY 10016
(718) 983-8800 ..**Amtzis**, Michl M '84 (Lee & A,LLP) -260 Christopher Ln -Staten Isl 10314
(845) 291-2454 ..**Amundson**, Karen A '01 %Leg Aid -2 Court Ln Bx328 -Goshen 10924 **Fx:**294-2638
(212) 588-0800 ..**Amundson**, Steven M '82 (Frommer L&H LLP) -745 5th Av -NY 10151
(315) 404-9902 ..**Amuso**, John P '99 (Reynolds-Amuso & A) -1 Kirkland Av Bx191 -Clinton 13323
(315) 788-3410 ..**Amyot**, John W '92 %Jefferson-Lewis BOCES -RD 1 Bx 130 -Watertwn 13601
(518) 746-2542 ..**Amyot**, Leah Soule '99 Hon T Mercure -383 Bway -Ft Edward 12828
(212) 801-3194 ..**An**, Christina H '06 %Greenberg T,LLP -200 Park Av -NY 10166
(212) 836-8000 ..**An**, Hwaja Kazuko '07 %Kaye S LLP -425 Park Av -NY 10022
(212) 863-8181 ..**An**, Jemma E '05 %HPD -100 Gold -NY 10038
(212) 563-3602 ..**An**, Richd W '85 -40 W 37th -NY 10018 **Fx:**563-3603
(516) 572-6818 ..**Anagnostopoulos**, Catherine '00 %MHLS -2201 Hempstd Tpk -E Meadow 11554 **Fx:**572-4926
(516) 536-3350 ..**Anand**, Jasleen Kaur '02 -500 Old Cntry Rd -Gdn Cty 11530 **Fx:**536-3352
(212) 796-5889 ..**Anand**, Kenneth J '03 -120 Bway -NY 10271
(212) 819-8200 ..**Anand**, Meeta '06 %White & C LLP -1155 Av of Amer -NY 10036
(631) 547-2321 ..**Anand**, Rachit '10 %OneBeacon Ins -201 Old Cntry Rd -Melvll 11747
(212) 451-2300 ..**Anand**, Safia A '03 %Olshan GFR&W LLP -65 E 55th -NY 10022
(212) 701-3000 ..**Anand**, Varuna '06 %Cahill G&R LLP -80 Pine -NY 10005 **Fx:**269-5420
(212) 750-8700 ..**Ananda**, Rajeev E '07 %Friedman & W,PC -600 Lex Av -NY 10022
(718) 625-0800 ..**Anandarangam**, Venkatesan P '94 %J Peltz,PC -26 Court -Brklyn 11242 **Fx:**624-5386
(212) 269-4900 ..**Anania**, Michl L '80 (Ford MEW&G,LLP) -Wall Street Plz -NY 10005
(315) 789-0775 ..**Anania**, Robt W Jr. '96 %Geneva Club Beverage Co -1 Pepsi Ln -Geneva 14456 **Fx:**789-0349
(516) 571-3800 ..**Anania**, Sheryl Hirsh '81 %DA -262 Old Cntry Rd -Mineola 11501 **Fx:**248-9479
(212) 223-4000 ..**Anastasia**, Jonathan J '10 %Crowell & M LLP -590 Mad Av -NY 10022
(212) 458-1340 ..**Anastasiades**, Michl J '04 AIGTS -175 Water -NY 10038
(212) 845-5000 ..**Anastasio**, Michl '94 %MBF Clearing Corp -1 North End Av -NY 10282
(212) 446-2300 ..**Anastasio**, Michl V '09 %Boies S&F LLP -575 Lex Av -NY 10022
(718) 263-8400 ..**Anastasiou**, Michl C '89 -125-10 Qns Blvd -Kew Gdns 11415 **Fx:**263-1705
(718) 474-3299 ..**Anaya**, Jeanmarie '01 -224 Beach 148th -Neponsit 11694 **Fx:**474-1936
(212) 239-4999 ..**Anbinder**, Jeffrey T '06 %Meyer SE&K,PC -1350 Bway Bx822 -NY 10018
(212) 679-2872 ..**Ancel**, Richd J '72 -330 E 33rd -NY 10016 **Fx:**532-7825
(516) 393-2200 ..**Ancona**, Lara Jean '00 %Garfunkel W,PC -111 Grt Nck Rd -Gt Neck 11021
(212) 245-0456 ..**Ancona**, Pamela C '02 Meso Scale Diagnostics LLC -371 W 49th -NY 10019
(516) 739-1803 ..**Ancona**, Vincent J '99 (Ancona Assoc) -220 Old Cntry Rd -Mineola 11501 **Fx:**739-1553
(917) 922-3020 ..**Ancowitz**, Richd B '83 OfCnsl Godosky & G,PC -61 Bway -NY 10006 **Fx:**(347) 214-3310
(212) 598-5900 ..**Andalkar**, Manoj R '98 (Alonso A&K PC) -920 Bway -NY 10010
(631) 765-1939 ..**Andaloro**, Jennifer A '03 Town of Southold -Bx1179 -Southold 11971 **Fx:**765-6639
(917) 379-2038 ..**Andaluz**, Rafael F '78 -145 E 149th -Bronx 10451 **Fx:**(718) 993-2156
(516) 625-9200 ..**Andelsman**, Lawr I '94 -79 Powerhse Rd -Roslyn Hts 11577 **Fx:**625-9205
(212) 505-7480 ..**Anderberg**, Robt K '81 %Open Space Institute -1350 Bway -NY 10018 **Fx:**353-2052
(516) 532-4999 ..**Anderman**, Arthur A '60 (Anderman & A) -39 Wensley Dr -Gt Neck 11021 **Fx:**(718) 228-2414
(718) 268-4000 ..**Anderman**, Lisa B '87 (Anderman & A) -108-18 Qns Blvd -Frst Hlls 11375 **Fx:**520-8175
(212) 267-1650 ..**Anderman**, Marvin '60 (Fine O&A,LLP) -39 Bway -NY 10006
(212) 474-1000 ..**Anderman**, Todd D C '08 %Cravath S&M LLP -825 8th Av -NY 10019
(718) 596-2150 ..**Anderocci**, Walter E '70 -32 Court -Brklyn 11201
(212) 403-1000 ..**Anders**, David B '95 Cnsl Wachtell LR&K -51 W 52nd -NY 10019
(212) 373-3000 ..**Anders**, Joshua D '08 %Paul WRW&G LLP -1285 Av of Amer -NY 10019
(212) 513-3200 ..**Andersen**, Anne-Mette E '99 (Holland & K LLP) -31 W 52nd -NY 10019
(212) 558-4000 ..**Andersen**, Christina '10 %Sullivan & C LLP -125 Broad -NY 10004
(212) 290-4700 ..**Andersen**, Elizabeth Ann '98 Human Rights Watch -350 5th Av -NY 10118 **Fx:**736-1300
(212) 789-3100 ..**Andersen**, Erik F '02 %Riemer & B LLP -7 Times Sq -NY 10036 **Fx:**719-0140
(212) 788-0870 ..**Andersen**, Jane E '09 %Law Dept -100 Church -NY 10007 **Fx:**788-0367
(646) 557-5100 ..**Andersen**, Richd E '82 (Patton B LLP) -1185 Av of Amer -NY 10036
(646) 315-7303 ..**Andersen**, Scott M '93 FINRA -14 Wall -NY 10005 **Fx:**315-7440
(212) 530-5000 ..**Andersen**, Sonja J '09 %Milbank TH&M LLP -1 Chase Manh Plz -NY 10005
(518) 786-1800 ..**Anderson**, Aaron R '91 OfCnsl Flink S LLC -23 British Amer Blvd -Latham 12110 **Fx:**786-1969
(212) 872-1000 ..**Anderson**, Alexander F '01 -One Bryant Park -NY 10036 **Fx:**872-1002
(631) 439-2450 ..**Anderson**, Alison M '90 %Leg Aid -320 Carleton Av -Central Islip 11722 **Fx:**439-2453
(516) 764-6061 ..**Anderson**, Anders A '83 -2941 Stevens -Oceanside 11572
(585) 263-1000 ..**Anderson**, Andrea E '03 %Nixon P LLP -1100 Clinton Sq -Rchstr 14604
(212) 969-3000 ..**Anderson**, Andrea N '05 %Proskauer R LLP -1585 Bway -NY 10036
(585) 722-9662 ..**Anderson**, Andrew J '90 %Eastman Kodak -343 State -Rchstr 14650
(802) 862-7070 ..**Anderson**, Arthur P '76 (Anderson & B PC) -186 US Oval -Plattsbrgh 12903 **Fx:**862-7227
(917) 637-3600 ..**Anderson**, Bebe J '82 %Ctr for Reproductive Rts -120 Wall -NY 10005 **Fx:**637-3666
(718) 625-9091 ..**Anderson**, Brown M '04 %NMASS -Bx130293 -NY 10013
(212) 403-1000 ..**Anderson**, Bryan C '10 %Wachtell LR&K -51 W 52nd -NY 10019
(212) 574-1200 ..**Anderson**, C Gerhard III '06 %Seward & K LLP -1 Bttry Pk Plz -NY 10004
(212) 847-8315 ..**Anderson**, Catherine E '96 (Giskan S&A) -11 Bway -NY 10004 **Fx:**(646) 520-3235
(212) 373-3000 ..**Anderson**, Christopher G '02 %Paul WRW&G LLP -1285 Av of Amer -NY 10019
(212) 715-1000 ..**Anderson**, Christopher P '03 %Arnold & P LLP -399 Park Av -NY 10022
(585) 325-7430 ..**Anderson**, Christopher S '97 %Anderson Law Firm -36 W Main -Rchstr 14614 **Fx:**546-6006
(518) 355-6268 ..**Anderson**, Danielle L '99 (Coughtry & A) -4382 Wstrn Tpk -Altamont 12009
(585) 663-4543 ..**Anderson**, David E '76 (Lacy K LLP) -4292 Lk Av -Rchstr 14612
(585) 454-5650 ..**Anderson**, David E '76 (Lacy K LLP) -130 E Main -Rchstr 14604
(518) 426-4600 ..**Anderson**, David G '97 (Couch W,LLP) -540 Bway Bx22222 -Albany 12201
(212) 277-0488 ..**Anderson**, David M '95 The Hartford -2 Park Av -NY 10016
(518) 746-2525 ..**Anderson**, Devin J '10 DA -383 Bway -Ft Edward 12828 **Fx:**746-2568
(631) 422-0500 ..**Anderson**, Donald A '70 -1250 Montauk Hwy -W Islip 11795 **Fx:**422-0967
(212) 538-2640 ..**Anderson**, Eric A '85 %Credit Suisse -11 Mad Av -NY 10010
(212) 619-4350 ..**Anderson**, Erica P '06 %Newman MKGH,PC -14 Wall -NY 10005
(718) 525-6878 ..**Anderson**, Ewan D '90 -200-31 Linden Blvd Bx120533 -St Albans 11412 **Fx:**525-7167

(212) 366-2384 ..**Anderson,** Gina Schachter '81 Penguin Putnam Inc -375 Hudson -NY 10014 **Fx:**366-2867
(914) 824-5070 ..**Anderson,** Gloria J '92 %Atty Grievance Comm -399 Knollwood Rd -White Plns 10603 **Fx:**949-0997
(718) 657-6480 ..**Anderson,** Greta Gainer '84 (GG Anderson & Assoc,PC) -114-14 Merrick Blvd -Jamaica 11434 **Fx:**657-6743
(914) 422-4667 ..**Anderson,** Horace E '97 %Pace Law Schl -78 N Bway -White Plns 10603 **Fx:**422-4039
(212) 791-6380 ..**Anderson,** Ian '83 I Anderson Intl -11 Park Pl -NY 10007 **Fx:**791-6381
(518) 499-1272 ..**Anderson,** James B '77 (Ryan S&C,PC) -134 Main Bx75 -Whitehall 12887
(914) 476-0600 ..**Anderson,** James R '94 OfCnsl Smith B&J,LLP -733 Ynkrs Av -Ynkrs 10704
(718) 667-9090 ..**Anderson,** Jared '02 Menicucci V & Assoc -2040 Victory Blvd -Staten Isl 10314 **Fx:**667-0700
(212) 490-1700 ..**Anderson,** Jay H '96 Cnsl Wiggin & D -450 Lex Av -NY 10017
(518) 785-4900 ..**Anderson,** Jeffrey K '83 (Anderson M&T,PLLC) -26 Century Hill Dr -Latham 12110
(212) 554-7800 ..**Anderson,** Jill E '08 OfCnsl Moses & S LLP -405 Lex Av -NY 10174
(716) 204-2400 ..**Anderson,** Jill S '02 %SJ Baum,PC -220 Nrthpnte Pkwy Bx1291 -Buffalo 14240 **Fx:**204-4600
(516) 627-3260 ..**Anderson,** Joanne Korakis '94 -85 Shore Rd -Manhsst 11030
(718) 783-7444 ..**Anderson,** John A Jr. '78 (Anderson & C) -255 Flatbush Av -Brklyn 11217 **Fx:**783-7423
(585) 232-6500 ..**Anderson,** John A '97 (Harter S&E LLP) -1600 Bausch & Lomb Pl -Rchstr 14604
(518) 388-7718 ..**Anderson,** Joyce Zehr '99 GE -1 River Rd -Schnctdy 12345
(212) 849-7000 ..**Anderson,** K McKenzie '08 %Quinn EU&S,LLP -51 Mad Av -NY 10010
(212) 682-5700 ..**Anderson,** Karen A '01 %Maya M,PC -261 Mad Av -NY 10016 **Fx:**697-4432
(607) 776-0540 ..**Anderson,** Karl V Jr. '72 -7161 State Route 54 Bx273 -Bath 14810 **Fx:**776-0541
(212) 897-5853 ..**Anderson,** Keith '01 -305 Bway -NY 10007 **Fx:**(201) 861-8057
(212) 963-3997 ..**Anderson,** Ken '00 UN Joint Appls Bd -304 E 45th -NY 10017
(212) 653-8700 ..**Anderson,** Kenneth B '83 SpclCnsl Sheppard MR&H LLP -30 Rckfllr Plz -NY 10112
(845) 331-2728 ..**Anderson,** Kent D '79 -Bx3243 -Kingston 12402
(212) 278-1000 ..**Anderson Kill & Olick,PC** -1251 Av of Amer -NY 10020 **Fx:**278-1733
(212) 464-0763 ..**Anderson,** Lauren E '06 JP Morgan Private Bk -345 Park Av -NY 10154
(607) 723-5341 ..**Anderson,** Lawr C '73 (Hinman H&K,LLP) -80 Exchange Bx5250 -Bnghmtn 13902
(716) 855-3424 ..**Anderson,** Leigh E '79 -69 Delaware Av -Buffalo 14202 **Fx:**855-2180
(631) 231-3775 ..**Anderson,** Leslie B '91 %Atty Grievance Comm -150 Motor Pkwy -Hauppauge 11788
(212) 264-4994 ..**Anderson,** Lisa Lee '99 %US HHS Ofc Civil Rts -26 Fed Plz -NY 10278
(212) 225-2000 ..**Anderson,** Marcel L '08 %Cleary GS&H -1 Lbrty Plz -NY 10006
(716) 759-6041 ..**Anderson,** Marie Volland '63 -4858 Smiley Terr -Clarence 14031
(518) 562-8383 ..**Anderson,** Mark E '95 -22 US Oval Bx2723 -Plattsbrgh 12901 **Fx:**562-8384
(212) 969-1428 ..**Anderson,** Mark R '96 Alliance Bernstein LP -1345 Av of Amer -NY 10105 **Fx:**554-4639
(716) 853-8100 ..**Anderson,** Martha M '88 (Nixon P LLP) -40 Fountain Plz -Buffalo 14202
(585) 753-4500 ..**Anderson,** Marty J '06 %DA -832 Watts Bldg -Rchstr 14614 **Fx:**753-4576
(212) 344-5400 ..**Anderson,** Mary W '77 OfCnsl Schlam S&D LLP -26 Bway -NY 10004
(212) 261-8000 ..**Anderson,** Matthew B '99 (Mendes & M,LLP) -750 7th Av -NY 10019
(212) 488-1200 ..**Anderson,** Matthew P '08 %Kobre & K,LLP -800 3rd Av -NY 10022
(212) 381-7000 ..**Anderson,** Michl J '00 (Sabin B&G LLP) -4 Times Sq -NY 10036
(518) 587-4905 ..**Anderson,** Michele L '97 (Anderson Law) -48 Union Av -Saratoga Spgs 12866 **Fx:**587-0128
(845) 562-3500 ..**Anderson,** Michelle '90 (Saffioti & A) -5031 Route 9W -Newburgh 12550 **Fx:**562-3117
(631) 725-4400 ..**Anderson,** Miles B '72 -16 Round Pond Ln -Sag Hbr 11963 **Fx:**725-2223
(212) 806-5400 ..**Anderson,** Morgan K '08 %Stroock &S&L LLP -180 Maiden Ln -NY 10038
(518) 785-4900 ..**Anderson Moschetti & Taffany,PLLC** -26 Century Hill Dr -Latham 12110 **Fx:**785-7990
(212) 558-4000 ..**Anderson,** Neil T '73 OfCnsl Sullivan & C LLP -125 Broad -NY 10004
(212) 489-1600 ..**Anderson,** Nicole Ann '94 %Deloitte LLP -1633 Bway -NY 10019 **Fx:**492-4201
Anderson, P Micheal '73 -47 Davis Av -White Plns 10605
(607) 257-8000 ..**Anderson,** Paige S '93 (Pinnisi & A,LLP) -111 Tioga -Ithaca 14850
(212) 450-4000 ..**Anderson,** Paul G '07 %Davis P&W LLP -450 Lex Av -NY 10017
(718) 993-2336 ..**Anderson,** Peter F Jr. '82 -370 E 149th -Bronx 10455
(718) 286-6000 ..**Anderson,** Philip D '98 %DA -125-01 Qns Blvd -Kew Gdns 11415
(212) 557-2800 ..**Anderson,** R Steven '70 (Barger & W LLP) -10 E 40th -NY 10016
(585) 325-7430 ..**Anderson,** Richd F '64 (Anderson Law Firm) -36 W Main -Rchstr 14614 **Fx:**546-6006
(518) 371-8888 ..**Anderson,** Richd F Jr. '77 (Ianniello A&R,PC) -805 Route 146 -Clifton Pk 12065
(631) 264-7137 ..**Anderson,** Richd W '87 Amity Law -23 Anthony Ct -Amityvll 11701
(212) 989-9100 ..**Anderson,** Robt J '72 (Finder NK LLP) -276 Park Av S -NY 10010
(212) 238-4800 ..**Anderson,** Robt J '06 %Landman CB&F,PC -120 Bway -NY 10271
(212) 742-3390 ..**Anderson,** Robt W '93 Lindabury ME&C,PC -26 Bway -NY 10004
(212) 236-6877 ..**Anderson,** Rozlyn L '81 %Merrill Lynch -2 World Fncl Ctr -NY 10281
(212) 268-5136 ..**Anderson,** Russell F Jr. '07 %Harwood L -350 5th Av -NY 10118
(212) 506-2500 ..**Anderson,** Sarah C '09 %Mayer B LLP -1675 Bway -NY 10019
(212) 345-6000 ..**Anderson,** Sean '91 %Marsh USA -1166 Av of Amer -NY 10036 **Fx:**345-4808
(914) 666-5600 ..**Anderson,** Stanley E Jr. '61 OfCnsl Shamberg MD&H,PC -55 Smith Av -Mt Kisco 10549
(646) 358-8501 ..**Anderson,** Steven H '86 Beecher Carlson -7 Times Sq -NY 10036
(212) 344-3600 ..**Anderson,** Steven S '83 (Anderson & O,LLP) -61 Bway -NY 10006 **Fx:**344-0970
(315) 448-0420 ..**Anderson,** Tania S '93 %Hon R Pooler -100 S Clinton Bx7395 -Syracuse 13261
(585) 232-6500 ..**Anderson,** Thos R '97 (Harter S&E LLP) -1600 Bausch & Lomb Pl -Rchstr 14604
(212) 768-6700 ..**Anderson,** Todd S '07 %Sonnenschein N&R LLP -2 World Fncl Ctr -NY 10281
(212) 808-7800 ..**Anderson,** Victoria E '06 %Kelley D&W LLP -101 Park Av -NY 10178
(212) 902-0043 ..**Anderson,** Wm D Jr. '95 %Goldman Sachs -1 NY Plz -NY 10004
(212) 408-2500 ..**Anderson,** Wm E '01 %Baker B,LLP -30 Rckfllr Plz -NY 10112
(718) 641-2430 ..**Anderson,** Wm M '85 -157-05 95th -Howard Bch 11414 **Fx:**641-4915
(212) 458-3409 ..**Anderson Adderly,** Roberta Ann '05 AIG -175 Water -NY 10038
(212) 537-6827 ..**Anderson-Bedford,** Charlotte G '96 -315 Mad Av -NY 10017
(914) 347-5522 ..**Andes,** James S '03 D Frum -565 Taxter Rd -Elmsfrd 10523 **Fx:**347-8760
(212) 788-0569 ..**Andes,** Marc S '93 %Law Dept -100 Church -NY 10007 **Fx:**788-0367
(631) 727-5780 ..**Andes,** Wm '59 (Andes & A) -224 Griffing Av Bx359 -Rvrhead 11901
(631) 727-5780 ..**Andes,** Wm F Jr. '88 (Andes & A) -224 Griffing Av Bx359 -Rvrhead 11901
(212) 481-1900 ..**Andino,** Lucas E '81 %Del Valle & Assoc -445 Park Av -NY 10022 **Fx:**481-4853
(212) 848-4000 ..**Andison,** Timothy A G '01 %Shearman & S LLP -599 Lex Av -NY 10022
(212) 455-2000 ..**Ando,** Alison J '02 Cnsl Simpson T&B LLP -425 Lex Av -NY 10017
(212) 878-8000 ..**Ando,** Mina J '06 %Clifford C LLP -31 W 52nd -NY 10019
(212) 490-4100 ..**Andoh,** Rena '04 %Storch A&M,PC -140 E 45th -NY 10017
(212) 813-8800 ..**Andolina,** Janet '95 (Goodwin P LLP) -620 8th Av -NY 10018
(585) 454-2181 ..**Andolina,** Lawr J '75 (Trevett CS&A,PC) -2 State -Rchstr 14614
(716) 633-9300 ..**Andolina Scott,** Karen M '10 %J Eiss PLLC -19 Limestone Dr -Buffalo 14221 **Fx:**633-0492
(212) 312-2274 ..**Andra,** Melinda L '04 %Leg Aid -60 Lafayette -NY 10013 **Fx:**349-0874
(212) 791-0890 ..**Andrade,** Bibiana C '94 -325 Bway -NY 10007
(212) 458-5682 ..**Andrade,** Robin P '03 AIG Domestic Claims,Inc -175 Water -NY 10038
(212) 619-5000 ..**Andre,** Astrid F '99 %EDC -110 William -NY 10038 **Fx:**312-3912
(212) 218-2100 ..**Andre,** Jude J '09 %Fitzpatrick CH&S -1290 Av of Amer -NY 10104
(516) 739-0081 ..**Andrea,** Frank A D III '82 (Andrea & T) -320 Old Cntry Rd -Gdn Cty 11530
(516) 739-0081 ..**Andrea & Towsky** -320 Old Cntry Rd -Gdn Cty 11530 **Fx:**739-0088
(212) 227-8150 ..**Andreadis,** Kleon C '88 -111 Bway -NY 10006 **Fx:**285-1968
(718) 726-6300 ..**Andreadis,** Nikos D '97 Andreadis Realty -46-02 Bway Bx3187 -Astoria 11103 **Fx:**956-4975
(212) 416-8000 ..**Andreadis,** Vicki F '03 %Dept of Law -120 Bway -NY 10271
(212) 547-5400 ..**Andreas,** Bronwyn D '92 (McDermott W&E LLP) -340 Mad Av -NY 10173
(646) 386-5891 ..**Andreasian,** Karen Gomes '88 %MHLS -41 Mad Av -NY 10010
(631) 421-4488 ..**Andree,** Mark S '86 (Serpe A&K) -149 Main Bx165 -Huntngtn 11743
(315) 425-9000 ..**Andreev,** Dmitrii '07 %Marjama MB&S LLP -250 S Clinton -Syracuse 13202
(212) 909-6000 ..**Andreeva,** Yulia '06 %Debevoise & P LLP -919 3rd Av -NY 10022
(212) 768-4343 ..**Andrei,** Elena Madalina '04 %Cantor E&M,LLP -40 W 37th -NY 10018
(212) 594-5300 ..**Andrejkovics,** Paul J '96 (Milberg LLP) -1 Penn Plz -NY 10119
(516) 571-2613 ..**Andren,** Joyce M '76 %Hon JM Galasso -100 Supreme Ct Dr -Mineola 11501 **Fx:**571-2164
(718) 979-0900 ..**Andreo,** Margaret Carasaniti '96 (Carasaniti & A) -1602 Richmond Rd -Staten Isl 10304 **Fx:**979-1991
(212) 335-4500 ..**Andreoli,** Brian E '83 (DLA Piper LLP) -1251 Av of Amer -NY 10020
(631) 686-6500 ..**Andreoli,** Christine '93 C Andreoli,PC -222 E Main -Smithtwn 11787 **Fx:**240-0059
(212) 504-6000 ..**Andreoli,** Ryan J '04 %Cadwalader W&T LLP -1 World Fncl Ctr -NY 10281
(631) 234-1500 ..**Andreolli,** Kathryn N '06 %Rubin & R LLC -1787 Vets Hwy -Islandia 11749
(718) 222-2381 ..**Andreopoulos,** Theodora '91 %Law Dept -350 Jay -Brklyn 11201 **Fx:**222-2373
(718) 625-8940 ..**Andreotta,** Joanne D '85 %B Lawrence -15 Metrotech Ctr N -Brklyn 11201 **Fx:**624-5756
(716) 565-1100 ..**Andreozzi Fickess LLP** -9145 Main -Clarence 14031 **Fx:**565-1920
(716) 565-1100 ..**Andreozzi,** Randall P '88 Andreozzi F LLP -9145 Main -Clarence 14031
(718) 254-7000 ..**Andres,** Greg D '97 %US Atty -271 Cadman Plz E -Brklyn 11201 **Fx:**254-6479
(212) 326-2000 ..**Andrescavage,** Michl J '06 %O'Melveny & M LLP -7 Times Sq -NY 10036
(212) 353-9005 ..**Andresen,** Erika L '06 De Novo Legal -150 E 42nd -NY 10017 **Fx:**353-3342
(212) 973-0572 ..**Andretta,** Gage '74 (Wolff & S PC) -140 Bway -NY 10005
(585) 419-8800 ..**Andreucci,** Christopher A '06 SrCnsl Harris B PLLC -99 Garnsey Rd -Pittsfrd 14534
(914) 631-6530 ..**Andrew,** Leonard D '68 -11 Pokahoe Dr -Sleepy Hollow 10591 **Fx:**332-4321
(718) 286-6000 ..**Andrews,** Alison L '06 %DA -125-01 Qns Blvd -Kew Gdns 11415
(845) 454-9700 ..**Andrews,** Arthur '80 (Ouimette G&A) -88 Market Bx192 -Poughkeepsie 12601
(716) 842-2200 ..**Andrews,** Benjamin J '67 (Andrews B&M,LLP) -69 Delaware Av -Buffalo 14202
(212) 972-7505 ..**Andrews,** Bradley H '07 -122 E 42nd -NY 10168 **Fx:**457-1147
(631) 727-1515 ..**Andrews,** Brian A '93 %TC Sledjeski II & Assoc,PLLC -18 1st Bx479 -Rvrhead 11901 **Fx:**727-7693
(212) 297-6157 ..**Andrews,** Christopher J '92 (Andrews & A) -420 Lex Av -NY 10170
(212) 708-9100 ..**Andrews,** Don J '04 Bessemer Trust Co -630 5th Av -NY 10111

(212) 822-8300 .. **Andrews,** E Michelle '06 OfCnsl NMIC -76 Wadsworth Av -NY 10033 **Fx:**740-9645
(516) 676-7193 .. **Andrews,** Edw A '99 E Andrews,PC -45 Dosoris Way -Glen Cove 11542 **Fx:**674-0040
(212) 297-6157 .. **Andrews,** Edw S '61 (Andrews & A) -420 Lex Av -NY 10170
(212) 351-4500 .. **Andrews,** Gordon C '70 (Epstein B&G,PC) -250 Park Av -NY 10177
(718) 250-2000 .. **Andrews,** Ishakia '08 %DA -350 Jay -Brklyn 11201 **Fx:**250-2314
(585) 987-2800 .. **Andrews,** Jaime M '04 %Woods OG LLP -2 State -Rchstr 14614
(212) 664-5951 .. **Andrews,** James F '88 NBC Universal Inc -30 Rockafeller Plz -NY 10112
(631) 473-5550 .. **Andrews,** John J '83 -503 Main -Pt Jffrsn 11777
(718) 237-3100 .. **Andrews,** Kaitlin '08 Leg Aid -111 Lvngstn -Brklyn 11201 **Fx:**250-4243
(212) 459-6990 .. **Andrews,** Karen E '86 BBDO Worldwide -1285 Av of Amer -NY 10019
(212) 504-6000 .. **Andrews,** Kathryn L '09 %Cadwalader W&T LLP -1 World Fncl Ctr -NY 10281
(212) 850-2800 .. **Andrews Kurth LLP** -450 Lex Av -NY 10017 **Fx:**850-2929
(718) 590-7000 .. **Andrews,** Leroi J '90 (Coleman & A LLC) -881 Gerard Av -Bronx 10452 **Fx:**590-6051
(518) 373-1228 .. **Andrews,** Lynne S '87 (Crescent Moon Law) -Bx4387 -Clifton Pk 12065 **Fx:**373-1228
(212) 557-7767 .. **Andrews,** Michl J '91 (M Andrews,PC) -60 E 42nd -NY 10165 **Fx:**557-7765
(716) 753-4347 .. **Andrews,** Paul H '82 %Hon J Ward -Cnty Cthse Bx292 -Mayvll 14757 **Fx:**753-4993
(716) 433-5941 .. **Andrews Pusateri Brandt Shoemaker & Roberson** -929 Lincoln Av -Lockprt 14094 **Fx:**434-3362
(315) 471-0405 .. **Andrews,** Ross P '93 (Satter & A,LLP) -217 S Salina -Syracuse 13202
(716) 635-9550 .. **Andrews,** Seth J '05 Bronson & M,LLP -415 Lawrence Bell Dr -Williamsvll 14221 **Fx:**635-9556
(212) 785-8561 .. **Andrews,** Suzanne E '84 Cnsl Healthcare Finance Grp -199 Water -NY 10038
(212) 525-8010 .. **Andrews,** Timothy W '00 HSBC Bk -452 5th Av -NY 10018
(914) 460-1640 .. **Andrews,** Vincent P '95 %MIM Corp -100 Clearbrook Rd -Elmsfrd 10523
(518) 473-0785 .. **Andrews,** Wm P '93 %Insurance Dept -99 Wshngtn Av -Albany 12257 **Fx:**473-4600
(315) 471-2413 .. **Andrews,** Wm S '53 -217 S Salina -Syracuse 13202
(914) 666-5600 .. **Andreycak,** Catherine B '85 (Shamberg MD&H,PC) -55 Smith Av -Mt Kisco 10549
(212) 455-2000 .. **Andrezo,** Andrea F '06 %Simpson T&B LLP -425 Lex Av -NY 10017
(518) 455-4264 .. **Andriano,** Jennifer R '10 %Ofc Cnsl to Minority -440 The Cptl -Albany 12248
(716) 847-0650 .. **Andriette,** Grace '88 %Leg Srvcs -237 Main -Buffalo 14203 **Fx:**847-0227
(516) 222-8500 .. **Andrieux,** Melissa G '04 %Martin C&B LLP -90 Merrick Av -E Meadow 11554
(845) 306-1000 .. **Andrik,** James E '03 %Watchtower -100 Watchtower Dr -Patterson 12563 **Fx:**306-0709
(212) 949-0100 .. **Andriko,** Kathy '82 %Cmmnwlth Land Title -140 E 45th -NY 10017 **Fx:**949-2438
(212) 521-5400 .. **Andriola,** James M '96 (Reed S LLP) -599 Lex Av -NY 10022
(516) 345-2600 .. **Andriola,** Philip P '97 Ameriprise Fncl Srvcs,Inc -401 Franklin Av -Gdn Cty 11530 **Fx:**345-2601
(212) 674-3230 .. **Andriolo,** Regina A '82 -115 E 9th -NY 10003
(845) 365-1455 .. **Andriotis,** Diana P '88 -7 Wheeler Ct -Blauvelt 10913 **Fx:**365-3911
(212) 373-3000 .. **Andrix,** Joshua '08 %Paul WRW&G LLP -1285 Av of Amer -NY 10019
(516) 741-6873 .. **Andron,** Anna Maria '87 A Andron,LLC -111 7th -Gdn Cty 11530 **Fx:**741-6874
(718) 834-7440 .. **Andron,** Rachel D '04 Safe Horizon Family Court -320 Jay -Brklyn 11201
(212) 451-2300 .. **Androphy,** Joshua S '06 %Olshan GFR&W LLP -65 E 55th -NY 10022
(212) 742-0310 .. **Androsiglio,** Robt G '91 %Powell & Assoc,LLC -110 Wall -NY 10005
(315) 425-2700 .. **Andrus,** Jeffrey B '82 (Hiscock & B,LLP) -One Park Pl -Syracuse 13202
(212) 806-5400 .. **Andruschak,** Keith M '97 (Stroock &S&L LLP) -180 Maiden Ln -NY 10038
(716) 652-1900 .. **Andruschat,** Thos E '66 -35 Park Ln S -E Aurora 14052
(716) 854-1111 .. **Andruschat,** Timothy J '96 %Spadafora & V -2 Symphony Cir -Buffalo 14201
(516) 942-0735 .. **Andruzzi,** Jos C '94 -2 Lincoln Gate -Plainvw 11803 **Fx:**942-5739
(212) 791-1511 .. **Andrzejewski,** Janusz W '93 -1 Whitehall -NY 10004 **Fx:**791-1396
(212) 872-9800 .. **Anduiza,** Juan A '73 SrCnsl Squire S&D LLP -30 Rckfllr Plz -NY 10112
(914) 969-3700 .. **Anduze,** Steve '86 -20 S Bway -Ynkrs 10701 **Fx:**969-6596
(212) 307-5500 .. **Anelli,** Stephanie T '08 %Venable LLP -1270 Av of Amer -NY 10020
(315) 473-0899 .. **Anelli,** Thos '97 (Anelli X,PC) -441 S Salina -Syracuse 13202 **Fx:**473-0530
(212) 416-6165 .. **Anello,** Rachael C '04 %Dept of Law -120 Bway -NY 10271
(212) 856-9600 .. **Anello,** Robt J '81 (Morvillo AGIA&B,PC) -565 5th Av -NY 10017
(212) 566-7500 .. **Anello,** Virginia E '07 Douglas & L -111 John -NY 10038
(212) 962-0360 .. **Anes Friedman Leventhal & Balistreri, PLLC** -299 Bway -NY 10007 **Fx:**233-2740
(631) 467-6337 .. **Anes Leventhal & Snyder PLLC** -266 Smithtown Blvd -Nesconset 11767 **Fx:**467-6376
(516) 747-7400 .. **Aneser,** Kenneth E '95 (Rosenberg C&B LLP) -100 Grdn City Plz -Gdn Cty 11530
(212) 232-1411 .. **Anesh,** Mark K '79 (Lewis BB&S LLP) -77 Water -NY 10005
(212) 684-6111 .. **Anesi,** Robt B '76 -2 Park Av -NY 10016 **Fx:**684-3008
(315) 866-6600 .. **Aney,** George Farber '60 -401 N Prospect -Herkimer 13350 **Fx:**866-7860
(212) 756-2000 .. **Ang,** Beverly J '03 %Schulte R&Z LLP -919 3rd Av -NY 10022
(716) 332-3680 .. **Ange,** Grace Marie '57 (Ange & A) -110 Pearl -Buffalo 14202
(716) 332-3680 .. **Ange,** John M '92 (Ange & A) -110 Pearl -Buffalo 14202
(212) 351-4000 .. **Angel,** Danl '04 %Gibson D&C LLP -200 Park Av -NY 10166
(914) 472-0820 .. **Angel,** Dennis '72 -1075 Central Av -Scarsdale 10583 **Fx:**472-0826
(212) 592-1400 .. **Angel,** Joshua J '59 Cnsl Herrick,F LLP -2 Park Av -NY 10016
(516) 741-3900 .. **Angel,** Marcia S '99 -170 Old Cntry Rd -Mineola 11501 **Fx:**741-3383
(516) 741-3900 .. **Angel,** Mitchell J '77 -170 Old Cntry Rd -Mineola 11501 **Fx:**741-3383
(718) 631-0800 .. **Angel,** Neil H '94 %Feinstein & N,PC -42-40 Bell Blvd -Bayside 11361
(631) 369-1700 .. **Angel,** Stephen R '75 (Esseks H&A,LLP) -108 E Main Bx279 -Rvrhead 11901
(516) 571-3800 .. **Angelakis,** Irene '03 %DA -262 Old Cntry Rd -Mineola 11501 **Fx:**248-9479
(718) 544-3499 .. **Angelakis,** Irene '08 Childrens Law Ctr -11821 Qns Blvd -Frst Hlls 11375
(212) 668-8888 .. **Angeles,** Anna V DeLeon '04 Prado & T,LLP -305 Bway -NY 10007 **Fx:**668-8494
(212) 764-1330 .. **Angeles,** Jos G B '01 %Philippine Consulate General -556 5th Av -NY 10036
(314) 259-2940 .. **Angelette,** Benjamin J '07 %Bryan C LLP -1290 Av of Amer -NY 10104 **Fx:**552-8940
(516) 745-0109 .. **Angeli,** Toni-Marie '03 -666 Old Cntry Rd -Gdn Cty 11530 **Fx:**745-0596
(212) 484-3900 .. **Angelich,** George P '05 (Arent F LLP) -1675 Bway -NY 10019
(914) 422-8755 .. **Angelico,** Elyse J '86 %Dept of Law -101 E Post Rd -White Plns 10601 **Fx:**422-8706
(718) 728-0900 .. **Angelides,** Harry '94 -23-58 Steinway -Astoria 11105 **Fx:**728-4320
(212) 474-1000 .. **Angelilli,** Lauren '01 (Cravath S&M LLP) -825 8th Av -NY 10019
(212) 233-5760 .. **Angelillo,** Gina M '95 -305 Bway -NY 10007 **Fx:**267-5183
(516) 741-6565 .. **Angelillo,** Robt C '99 (Meyer SE&K,PC) -990 Stewart Av Bx9194 -Gdn Cty 11530
(212) 723-6484 .. **Angelini,** Amanda M '98 Citigroup Global Mrkts -390 Greenwich -NY 10013
(315) 798-5925 .. **Angelini,** Peter L '93 %Family Ct -200 Elisabeth -Utica 13501 **Fx:**798-6404
(212) 758-3500 .. **Angelino,** Francis R '67 OfCnsl DeCampo D&A -747 3rd Av -NY 10017
(631) 777-2330 .. **Angelino,** Justin E '03 %O'Connor OH&D,LLP -1 Huntngtn Quad -Melvll 11747
(212) 752-9700 .. **Angelino,** Kristin J '96 %Gersten S LLP -600 Lex Av -NY 10022
(845) 486-6800 .. **Angelino,** Lorenzo L '06 %McCabe & M LLP -63 Wshngtn Bx509 -Poughkeepsie 12602
(716) 566-5400 .. **Angelino,** Sharon '95 (Goldberg S LLP) -665 Main -Buffalo 14203
(212) 336-2000 .. **Angell,** Christopher C '70 (Patterson BW&T LLP) -1133 Av of Amer -NY 10036
(212) 541-2000 .. **Angell,** Jean B '70 (Bryan C LLP) -1290 Av of Amer -NY 10104
(212) 880-6000 .. **Angell,** Julie A '08 %Torys LLP -237 Park Av -NY 10017
(212) 506-1700 .. **Angell,** Michele L '07 %Kasowitz BT&F LLP -1633 Bway -NY 10019
(845) 486-2280 .. **Angell,** Thos N N '82 %Pub Def -22 Market -Poughkeepsie 12601 **Fx:**486-2266
(212) 756-2000 .. **Angel-Lalanne,** Laura '01 %Schulte R&Z LLP -919 3rd Av -NY 10022
(718) 746-0500 .. **Angelo,** Jos C '85 -25-77 F Lewis Blvd -Flushng 11358 **Fx:**746-3215
(212) 335-4267 .. **Angelo,** Lauren R '09 DA -80 Centre -NY 10013
(516) 746-7799 .. **Angelo,** Michl J '83 (Reisman P&R LLP) -1305 Franklin Av -Gdn Cty 11530
(585) 865-4900 .. **Angelone,** Mary Jane '79 -3621 Lk Av -Rchstr 14612 **Fx:**865-4806
(212) 998-6430 .. **Angelos,** Claudia '78 %NYU Law Schl -245 Sullivan -NY 10012 **Fx:**995-4031
(516) 248-3750 .. **Angelou,** Jack D '97 -145 Willis Av -Mineola 11501
(212) 484-3900 .. **Angelov,** Mark A '07 %Arent F LLP -1675 Bway -NY 10019
(212) 801-2132 .. **Angelova,** Anastasia A '01 %Greenberg T,LLP -200 Park Av -NY 10166
(212) 297-6600 .. **Angelson,** Caryn E '01 %TMM -230 Park Av -NY 10169 **Fx:**297-6062
(212) 687-6900 .. **Angelson,** Stephen J '98 %Connell & W -555 5th Av -NY 10017 **Fx:**687-6999
(516) 663-0780 .. **Angerame,** Keith E '91 %D Green -175 Pinelawn Rd -Melvll 11747 **Fx:**740-9731
(212) 848-4000 .. **Angermueller,** Hans H '51 OfCnsl Shearman & S LLP -599 Lex Av -NY 10022
(718) 351-5244 .. **Angioletti,** Paul J '84 -38 Forest Rd -Staten Isl 10304
(212) 455-2000 .. **Angiolillo,** Bruce D '78 (Simpson T&B LLP) -425 Lex Av -NY 10017
(718) 855-9000 .. **Angiolillo,** Jos M '08 %Cullen and D LLP -177 Montague -Brklyn 11201
(914) 428-3000 .. **Angiolillo,** Jos V '53 -6 Chester Av -White Plns 10601 **Fx:**428-2647
(718) 468-7700 .. **Angione,** Howard F '90 -80-47 192nd -Jamaica 11423 **Fx:**468-6566
(718) 816-0005 .. **Angiuli,** Gary C '84 (Angiuli K&G,LLP) -60 Bay -Staten Isl 10301
(718) 816-0005 .. **Angiuli Katkin & Gentile, LLP** -60 Bay -Staten Isl 10301 **Fx:**727-5835
(516) 921-2077 .. **Angiulo,** Michl D '80 (M Angiulo & Assoc LLC) -6800 Jericho Tpk -Syosset 11791 **Fx:**921-1223
(212) 819-8200 .. **Angland,** Jos '77 (White & C LLP) -1155 Av of Amer -NY 10036
(914) 376-3757 .. **Angley,** Patricia L '88 %Leg Srvcs -30 S Bway -Ynkrs 10701 **Fx:**376-8739
(212) 504-6000 .. **Anglin,** Michl S '86 SpclCnsl Cadwalader W&T LLP -1 World Fncl Ctr -NY 10281
(212) 530-7490 .. **Anglum,** Angela C '82 Home Ins Co -59 Maiden Ln -NY 10038 **Fx:**299-4224
(212) 735-8600 .. **Anglum,** Peter K '82 (Morrison C LLP) -909 3rd Av -NY 10022
(212) 858-7515 .. **Angotti,** Donna L '91 -140 Bway -NY 10005 **Fx:**858-7750
(347) 517-4221 .. **Angri,** Louis '48 -8901 Shore Rd -Brklyn 11209 **Fx:**517-4221
(631) 577-7770 .. **Angstreich,** Wm T '06 K Dodson -100 Baylis Rd -Melvll 11747 **Fx:**577-7199
(212) 937-1030 .. **Angus,** Patricia M '93 Shelterwood Fncl Srvcs LLC -60 E 42nd -NY 10165
(212) 326-3939 .. **Angus,** S Wade '94 (Jones D) -222 E 41st -NY 10017

(212) 788-4753 ..**Anhouse,** Chari S '89 Dept Hlth & Mental Hygiene -125 Worth -NY 10013
(631) 321-0943 ..**Aniano,** Rita '97 R Aniano,PC -135 Anchorage Dr -W Islip 11795 **Fx:**321-4064
(718) 298-7058 ..**Anik,** Arthur L '89 Envrnmntl Cntrl Brd -144-06 94th Av -Jamaica 11435
(914) 683-1200 ..**Anile,** Jos S II '91 OfCnsl Harris B PLLC -445 Hmltn Av -White Plns 10601
(212) 479-6000 ..**Anisfeld,** Danl S '03 %Cooley LLP -1114 Av of Amer -NY 10036
(212) 526-9225 ..**Anisman,** Beth E '96 Barclays Capital Inc -745 7th Av -NY 10019
(212) 756-2000 ..**Anisman,** Debra R '83 SpclCnsl Schulte R&Z LLP -919 3rd Av -NY 10022
(212) 697-2800 ..**Anissi,** Andrew A '07 %Sofer & H,LLP -317 Mad Av -NY 10017
(518) 462-5300 ..**Anito,** Lawr F Jr. '68 (DeGraff F&K LLP) -90 State -Albany 12207
(718) 298-0279 ..**Anixiadis,** Kyriaki '90 Family Ct -89-14 Parsons Blvd -Jamaica 11432
(845) 225-2573 ..**Anker,** Benjamin R '79 -37 Fair -Carmel 10512 **Fx:**225-0468
(631) 755-0100 ..**Anker,** Kenneth B '84 (Smith & D,PA) -145 Pinelawn Rd -Melvll 11747
(212) 833-1244 ..**Anker,** Kent K '99 (Friedman KS&A LLP) -1633 Bway -NY 10019 **Fx:**373-7944
(212) 447-0800 ..**Anker,** Leslie K '83 -440 Park Av S -NY 10016 **Fx:**576-1414
(212) 230-8890 ..**Anker,** Philip D '05 (WilmerHale) -399 Park Av -NY 10022
(718) 643-1140 ..**Anker,** Robt T '62 -186 Montague -Brklyn 11201 **Fx:**643-1149
(631) 567-8871 ..**Anklowitz,** J Bret '99 -85 S Main -Sayvll 11782 **Fx:**567-8872
(718) 286-2000 ..**Ankra,** Nefertiti N '09 %Leg Aid -120-46 Qns Blvd -Kew Gdns 11415 **Fx:**286-2286
(212) 286-0423 ..**Ankrah,** Naakwama S '98 %Robinson T & Assoc -820 2nd Av -NY 10017
(914) 423-4967 ..**Annabi,** Majed Farid '98 -984 N Bway -Ynkrs 10701 **Fx:**963-6200
(212) 455-2000 ..**Annarumma,** Jeanne M '95 Cnsl Simpson T&B LLP -425 Lex Av -NY 10017
(585) 546-6448 ..**Annechino,** Dennis J '02 (Davidson F LLP) -28 E Main -Rchstr 14614
(585) 586-5668 ..**Annechino,** John A Jr. '97 -1844 Penfld Rd -Penfld 14526 **Fx:**586-3235
(212) 962-6289 ..**Annenberg,** Joshua '93 -111 John -NY 10038 **Fx:**406-3677
(212) 249-5506 ..**Annenberg,** Ted M '60 -30 E 65th -NY 10065
(516) 570-4000 ..**Annese,** Diann M '07 %M Mermel -98 Cuttermill Rd -Gt Neck 11021 **Fx:**570-4333
(212) 801-9323 ..**Annex,** Alan I '88 (Greenberg T,LLP) -200 Park Av -NY 10166
(646) 602-5600 ..**Annexstein,** Leslie T '06 %Urban Justice Ctr -123 William -NY 10038 **Fx:**(212) 533-4598
(516) 739-5600 ..**Annibale,** Fredk J Jr. '78 FJ Annibale,PC -226 7th -Gdn Cty 11530 **Fx:**739-5606
(516) 328-3500 ..**Annibale,** Lisa M '05 %McDonnell & A,PC 401 Franklin Av -Gdn Cty 11530
(516) 739-5600 ..**Annibale,** Michl J '06 MJ Annibale,PC -226 7th -Gdn Cty 11530 **Fx:**739-5606
(914) 693-4723 ..**Annicelli,** John P '65 -Troy Ln -Bedfrd 10506
(212) 455-2000 ..**Annis,** Robt M '09 %Simpson T&B LLP -425 Lex Av -NY 10017
(212) 440-4300 ..**Annobil,** Jojo '91 %Leg Aid -199 Water -NY 10038
(212) 806-5400 ..**Annoual,** Larissa '06 %Stroock &S&L LLP -180 Maiden Ln -NY 10038
(518) 457-4951 ..**Annucci,** Anthony J '81 %Dept Correctional Srvcs -1220 Wshngtn Av -Albany 12226 **Fx:**457-7555
(914) 725-5530 ..**Annunziata,** Albert M '75 -700 Wht Plns Rd -Scarsdale 10583
(917) 778-6600 ..**Annunziata,** Louis C '95 %J Toomey -485 Lex Av -NY 10017 **Fx:**778-7048
(631) 493-0909 ..**Annunziata,** Maria C '93 (Annunziata & R) -300 Commack Rd -Commack 11725 **Fx:**493-3081
(516) 248-6232 ..**Annunziata,** Mark A '99 M Annunziata,PC -229 7th -Gdn Cty 11530 **Fx:**248-4785
(585) 428-3491 ..**Annunziata,** Mark L '92 Surrogates Ct -541 Hall of Justice -Rchstr 14614
(914) 337-9724 ..**Annunziata,** Michl J '80 -35 E Grassy Sprain Rd -Ynkrs 10710 **Fx:**337-9756
(212) 506-2500 ..**Annunziata,** Michelle J '04 %Mayer B LLP -1675 Bway -NY 10019
(212) 227-5158 ..**Annunziato,** Thos C '88 -233 Bway -NY 10279
(845) 352-1340 ..**Anolik,** Irving '51 -130 Lbrty Rd -Tappan 10983
(212) 967-2011 ..**Anreder,** Scott '94 (Anreder & G) -143 W 29th -NY 10001 **Fx:**967-2013
(914) 682-2068 ..**Ansa Assuncao,LLP** -50 Main -White Plns 10606 **Fx:**682-7784
(914) 741-6100 ..**Ansaldi,** Vincent C '99 %Kaufman B&R -200 Summit Lk Dr -Valhalla 10595
(631) 598-0337 ..**Ansanelli,** Vincent W III '87 (Ansanelli K&S,LLP) -92 Bway -Amityvll 11701 **Fx:**598-0352
(718) 579-7900 ..**Ansari,** Bahar '07 %Leg Aid -900 Sheridan Av -Bronx 10451 **Fx:**293-8744
(212) 973-0572 ..**Ansari,** Farah N '02 %Wolff & S PC -140 Bway -NY 10005
(718) 250-2000 ..**Ansari,** Imran H '08 %DA -350 Jay -Brklyn 11201 **Fx:**250-2314
(212) 610-6300 ..**Ansari,** Nazish L '05 %Allen & O -1221 Av of Amer -NY 10020
(845) 592-7000 ..**Ansari,** Semira '08 %Donoghue TA&D LLP -2517 Route 52 -Hopewell Junct 12533
(212) 808-7800 ..**Ansari,** Talat M '89 (Kelley D&W LLP) -101 Park Av -NY 10178
(516) 349-6756 ..**Ansari,** Tanweer S '09 Bethpage Fed Credit Union -899 S Oyster Bay Rd -Bethpage 11714
(212) 506-5000 ..**Ansbro,** John '96 (Orrick H&S LLP) -51 W 52nd -NY 10019
(212) 845-7964 ..**Anscher,** Roger E '99 %Ramius Capital Grp,LLC -599 Lex Av -NY 10022 **Fx:**845-7905
(212) 940-3142 ..**Ansehl,** Robt '82 (Nixon P LLP) -437 Mad Av -NY 10022
(212) 407-4000 ..**Ansel,** David P '95 (Loeb & L,LLP) -345 Park Av -NY 10154
(212) 801-9393 ..**Ansell,** Danl J '87 (Greenberg T,LLP) -200 Park Av -NY 10166
(516) 479-6300 ..**Ansell,** Robt J '94 (Silverman A LLP) -100 Jericho Quad -Jericho 11753
(212) 558-4000 ..**Anselmi,** John J '03 %Sullivan & C LLP -125 Broad -NY 10004
(212) 576-7215 ..**Anselmi,** Robt A '82 %NYLIM -51 Mad Av -NY 10010 **Fx:**447-4262
(718) 222-9800 ..**Anselmo,** John A '09 Brecher FPWT&Z,PC -335 Adams -Brklyn 11201
(718) 761-4503 ..**Anselmo,** Thos P '94 -23 Shepard Av -Staten Isl 10314 **Fx:**761-1240
(518) 862-1200 ..**Ansert,** Jessica L '10 %Martin H&M LLP -Bx15141 -Albany 12212
(646) 756-2507 ..**Anslow,** Richd I '87 -1230 Av of Amer -NY 10020
(914) 286-3030 ..**Anson,** Brian M '97 %Insler & H LLP -80 Grasslands Rd -Elmsfrd 10523 **Fx:**372-1392
(718) 892-2770 ..**Ansoorian,** Haig Jr. '71 -1142 Castle Hill Av -Bronx 10462
(212) 484-8000 ..**Ansorge,** Mark D '89 %Warner Music Grp -75 Rckfllr Plz -NY 10019 **Fx:**489-3342
(212) 813-1000 ..**Ansour,** M Michl '83 March Prtnrs -555 5th Av -NY 10017
(716) 856-5012 ..**Anspach Meeks Ellenberger,LLP** -2400 Main Pl Twr -Buffalo 14202 **Fx:**852-2485
(716) 856-5012 ..**Anspach,** Robt M '99 (Anspach ME,LLP) -2400 Main Pl Twr -Buffalo 14202
(212) 416-8000 ..**Anspach,** Susan '75 %Dept of Law -120 Bway -NY 10271
(212) 354-4500 ..**Anspach,** Wm '94 (Friedman & W) -1500 Bway -NY 10036
(212) 440-2923 ..**Anstead,** Laura N '99 CNA -40 Wall -NY 10005 **Fx:**440-3700
(212) 688-8555 ..**Anstey,** Sarah R '09 %Fragomen DB&L LLP -7 Hanover Sq -NY 10004
(716) 648-3900 ..**Ansuini,** Thos M '74 -4819 S Park Av -Hambrg 14075 **Fx:**648-3979
(212) 720-3676 ..**Answini,** Dominick H '99 %Dept City Planning -22 Reade -NY 10007 **Fx:**720-3219
(212) 655-5000 ..**Antanesian,** Rojika '07 %Gannon R&M -120 Bway -NY 10271
(212) 488-6899 ..**Antao & Chuang** -521 5th Av -NY 10175 **Fx:**488-7076
(212) 488-6899 ..**Antao,** Roger S '91 (Antao & C) -521 5th Av -NY 10175
(516) 991-9671 ..**Antar,** Lana R '98 -Bx653 -Northprt 11768
(718) 769-3200 ..**Antar,** Solomon Edw '65 -42 Falmouth -Brklyn 11235 **Fx:**504-6138
(212) 944-2200 ..**Antell,** Stuart '94 (Ferber CE&C,LLP) -530 5th Av -NY 10036
(212) 849-7000 ..**Anten,** Todd S '07 %Quinn EU&S,LLP -51 Mad Av -NY 10010
(585) 787-7000 ..**Antetomaso,** Gerard G '88 -1674 Empire Blvd -Webster 14580 **Fx:**787-7007
(716) 898-8152 ..**Anthis,** Sara Lee '09 -14 Lafayette Sq -Buffalo 14203
(212) 737-9859 ..**Anthoine,** Alison '79 -1065 Lex Av -NY 10021
(212) 858-1000 ..**Anthoine,** Robt '49 SrCnsl Pillsbury WSP LLP -1540 Bway -NY 10036
(212) 737-7459 ..**Anthoine,** Robt N '89 -207 E 74th -NY 10021
(732) 855-6097 ..**Anthony,** Alfred M '94 (Wilentz G&S) -110 William -NY 10038 **Fx:**726-6533
(631) 277-7086 ..**Anthony,** Brooke L '05 %R Giusto,PC -136 E Main -E Islip 11730 **Fx:**277-7641
(212) 909-6000 ..**Anthony,** Christopher M '10 %Debevoise & P LLP -919 3rd Av -NY 10022
(212) 716-7094 ..**Anthony,** Eric '09 Russell Reynolds Assoc -200 Park Av -NY 10166
(212) 632-3000 ..**Anthony,** Eva-Maria G '97 Fiduciary Trust Co Intl -600 5th Av -NY 10020 **Fx:**632-3002
(212) 688-5151 ..**Anthony,** Fredk W '74 (Gibney A&F,LLP) -665 5th Av -NY 10022
(718) 260-8700 ..**Anthony,** Judith Shults '86 %Admin Children's Srvcs -345 Adams -Brklyn 11201
(212) 610-6300 ..**Anthony,** Lara S '07 %Allen & O -1221 Av of Amer -NY 10020
(845) 338-6322 ..**Anthony,** Richd A '70 Ulster Savings Bk -180 Schwenk Dr Bx3337 -Kingston 12402 **Fx:**339-8068
(646) 315-7300 ..**Anthony,** Willard S II '96 %FINRA -14 Wall -NY 10005 **Fx:**315-7440
(212) 697-3122 ..**Antico,** Jeanette '06 %Martin C&B LLP -220 E 42nd -NY 10017
(212) 762-4827 ..**Antico,** Joanne '01 Morgan Stanley -1221 Av of Amer -NY 10020
(212) 735-3000 ..**Anticoli,** Alain '05 %Skadden ASM&F LLP -4 Times Sq -NY 10036
(212) 596-9000 ..**Antier,** Cecile C '09 %Ropes & G LLP -1211 Av of Amer -NY 10036
(516) 571-3800 ..**Antignani,** Stephen M '92 %DA -262 Old Cntry Rd -Mineola 11501 **Fx:**248-9479
(212) 221-5999 ..**Antin Ehrlich & Epstein,LLP** -49 W 37th -NY 10018 **Fx:**221-6867
(212) 221-5999 ..**Antin,** Jeffrey S '84 (Antin E&E,LLP) -49 W 37th -NY 10018
(212) 406-1919 ..**Antin,** Mark L '88 (Gennet KA&R,PC) -140 Bway -NY 10005
(212) 259-8000 ..**Antiochos,** Brian T '08 %Dewey & L LLP -1301 Av of Amer -NY 10019
(718) 590-2000 ..**Antioco,** Gabriela Leal '07 %DA -198 E 161st -Bronx 10451 **Fx:**590-6477
(718) 855-1413 ..**Antioco,** Paul R '93 -26 Court -Brklyn 11242
(718) 855-1413 ..**Antioco,** Peter M '67 -26 Court -Brklyn 11242
(212) 425-7200 ..**Antis,** Michele Yael '06 %Kenyon & K,LLP -1 Bway -NY 10004
(212) 326-3939 ..**Antler,** Adriane M '91 (Jones D) -222 E 41st -NY 10017
(212) 918-3000 ..**Antler,** Ashley B '10 %Hogan L LLP -875 3rd Av -NY 10022
(845) 887-5026 ..**Antler,** David B I '01 %International Inc -Route 97 -Long Eddy 12760
(212) 397-3050 ..**Antoine,** Jethro M '98 Ctr for Ct Innovation -520 8th Av -NY 10018
(718) 566-6100 ..**Antoine,** Karen E '03 NYC Dept of Ed -1106 E 95th -Brklyn 11236
(212) 223-4000 ..**Antoine,** Olivier N '00 Cnsl Crowell & M LLP -590 Mad Av -NY 10022
(212) 310-8000 ..**Antoinette,** Vanessa L '09 %Weil G&M LLP -767 5th Av -NY 10153
(518) 370-2500 ..**Antokol Reisman & Coffin** -514 State -Schnctdy 12305 **Fx:**370-4929
(518) 370-2500 ..**Antokol,** Richd M '76 (Antokol R&C) -514 State -Schnctdy 12305
(518) 457-2070 ..**Antolick,** Lori P '01 %Dept of Tax & Fin -Bldg 9 State Campus -Albany 12227 **Fx:**457-6131
(212) 334-7397 ..**Antollino,** Gregory S '94 -116 W 22ns -NY 10011 **Fx:**334-7399
(718) 741-8409 ..**Antomattei,** Anton '80 %Div of Human Rights -1 Fordham Plz -Bronx 10458 **Fx:**741-8102
(516) 625-2499 ..**Anton,** Fredk J '89 NDP Grp,Inc -900 W Shore Rd -Pt Wash 11050
(347) 489-5765 ..**Anton,** Gene T '00 -Bx853 -Huntngtn 11743
(716) 285-3526 ..**Anton,** Ronald D '59 -800 Main -Niagara Fls 14301 **Fx:**282-7960
(516) 741-2190 ..**Antonacci,** Alessandro L '98 -499 Jericho Tpk -Mineola 11501
(212) 340-0400 ..**Antonacci,** Caroline M '83 %Appllt Div 1st Dept -27 Mad Av -NY 10010 **Fx:**889-4412
(212) 732-3200 ..**Antonacci,** Rita M '04 %Carter L&M LLP -2 Wall -NY 10005
(315) 437-2260 ..**Antonacci,** Robt E II '93 -6701 Manlius Ctr Rd -E Syracuse 13057 **Fx:**437-0977
(516) 782-6439 ..**Antonacci,** Salvatore M '99 -499 Jericho Tpk -Mineola 11501 **Fx:**741-2192
(914) 948-8044 ..**Antoncic,** Lydia S '95 %Alimonti Law Ofcs,PC -200 Mamaroneck Av #304 -White Plns 10601 **Fx:**948-8058
(212) 513-3200 ..**Antonecchia,** Marc L '01 %Holland & K LLP -31 W 52nd -NY 10019
(914) 232-3185 ..**Antonecchia,** Thos T '68 -159 Katonah Av -Katonah 10536 **Fx:**232-0974
(212) 318-6000 ..**Antonelli,** Anthony '07 %Paul HJ&W LLP -75 E 55th -NY 10022
(347) 245-6088 ..**Antonelli,** Ariana J '95 -32 Hillside Av -New Windsor 12553

(212) 227-2424 .. **Antonelli**, Danl R '07 (Antonelli & A) -225 Bway -NY 10007
(518) 359-7064 .. **Antonelli**, Laura '97 %MHLS -2445 State Route 30 -Tupper Lk 12986 **Fx**:359-4371
(212) 227-2424 .. **Antonelli**, Richd C '77 (Antonelli & A) -225 Bway -NY 10007
(914) 767-7210 .. **Antonetti**, Elena '99 %Pepsi Bottling Grp -1 Pepsi Way -Somers 10589
(516) 741-6565 .. **Antongiovanni**, Michl J '04 %Meyer SE&K,PC -990 Stewart Av Bx9194 -Gdn Cty 11530
(212) 262-2390 .. **Antonian**, Agnieszka '01 (Connell F LLP) -888 7th Av -NY 10106
(518) 762-5517 .. **Antonik**, Joan '91 Law Guardian Ofc -4 Wells -Johnstwn 12095
(212) 966-7775 .. **Antonio**, Lexter '99 %Ferro & C -100 Lafayette -NY 10013
(212) 878-8000 .. **Antonoff**, Rick B '90 (Clifford C LLP) -31 W 52nd -NY 10019
(212) 425-3100 .. **Antonovsky**, Alice '06 %McManus C&R,PC -48 Wall -NY 10005
(585) 325-3400 .. **Antonowicz**, Paul J '97 %Montemaggi & Assoc -130 W Main -Rchstr 14614 **Fx**:325-4161
(315) 337-4008 .. **Antonowicz**, Peter W '84 -1300 Floyd Av -Rome 13440 **Fx**:334-9592
(212) 278-1000 .. **Antonucci**, A Marcello '09 %Anderson K&O,PC -1251 Av of Amer -NY 10020
(212) 687-0100 .. **Antonucci**, Cynthia Weiss '84 (Harris B PLLC) -100 Wall -NY 10005
(315) 788-7300 .. **Antonucci**, David P '88 -12 Pub Sq -Watertwn 13601 **Fx**:788-1643
(518) 462-3000 .. **Antonucci**, Marc A '07 %Iseman CR&H,LLP -9 Thurlow Ter -Albany 12203
(212) 801-6867 .. **Antonucci**, Peter A '91 (Greenberg T,LLP) -200 Park Av -NY 10166
(718) 876-6300 .. **Antonucci**, Vincent F '68 %DA -130 Styvsnt Pl -Staten Isl 10301
(518) 462-6831 .. **Antos**, Susan C '80 %Empire Justice Ctr -119 Wshngtn Av -Albany 12210 **Fx**:462-6687
(212) 697-2800 .. **Antrim**, Gregory C '00 %Sofer & H,LLP -317 Mad Av -NY 10017
(212) 388-3600 .. **Antrobus**, Natalia L '93 %32B-J Leg Srvcs -101 Av of Amer -NY 10013 **Fx**:388-3061
(212) 398-9400 .. **Antwi**, Wm '03 (Siriboe & A) -110 W 40th -NY 10018 **Fx**:398-9411
(516) 746-1600 .. **Antwork**, David A '06 %Campanelli & Assoc,PC -623 Stewart Av -Gdn Cty 11530 **Fx**:746-2611
(212) 310-8000 .. **Anusionwu**, Ijeoma J '09 %Weil G&M LLP -767 5th Av -NY 10153
(718) 537-0490 .. **Anyikwa**, Eugene Chidiebere '99 -872 Gerard Av -Bronx 10452
(718) 896-2700 .. **Anzalone**, Lucille A '98 (Newman A & Assoc LLP) -97-45 Qns Blvd -Rego Pk 11374 **Fx**:896-2560
(212) 297-5800 .. **Anzalone**, Marco A '05 %Day P LLP -7 Times Sq -NY 10036
(718) 931-2100 .. **Anzalone**, Vincent '80 (Anzalone & L) -2027 Wllmsbrdg Rd -Bronx 10461
(212) 397-5531 .. **Anzalotta**, Jodye M '99 Soros Fund Mgmt LLC -888 7th Av -NY 10106 **Fx**:541-7751
(516) 883-5841 .. **Anzel**, Michl B '83 -29 Leeds Dr -Pt Wash 11050 **Fx**:767-3346
(516) 393-6127 .. **Anzelmo**, Barbara-Ann '91 SrCnsl N Linden -999 Stewart Av -Bethpage 11714
(212) 704-6000 .. **Anziska**, Danl N '01 (Troutman S LLP) -405 Lex Av -NY 10174
(201) 780-1959 .. **Anzuoni**, Nicole M '03 -80 Bay St Lndng -Staten Isl 10301
(212) 839-5300 .. **Aoun**, J Karim '09 %Sidley A LLP -787 7th Av -NY 10019
(212) 450-4000 .. **Aoyagi**, Melissa T '04 %Davis P&W LLP -450 Lex Av -NY 10017
(212) 909-6000 .. **Aoyama**, Naomi '00 Cnsl Debevoise & P LLP -919 3rd Av -NY 10022
(914) 422-4424 .. **Aoyama-Martin**, Jane '82 Pace Univ -78 N Bway -White Plns 10603
(716) 856-5500 .. **Apa**, Jill A '00 %Damon M LLP -200 Delaware Av -Buffalo 14202
(212) 664-5889 .. **Apadula**, John C '97 NBC -30 Rckfllr Plz -NY 10112
(212) 344-5680 .. **Apar**, Irving C '82 (Thompson H LLP) -335 Mad Av -NY 10017
(718) 661-2899 .. **Apat**, Burton J '52 -47-14 158th -Flushng 11358
(718) 261-9460 .. **Apat**, Richd H '89 (Pearlman AFS&S,LLP) -80-02 Kew Grdns Rd -Kew Gdns 11415
(914) 390-4324 .. **Apel**, Nicole R '09 Cypress Health Care Mgmt,LLC -4 W Red Oak Ln -West Harrison 10604
(516) 466-0090 .. **Apelboim**, Ory '04 %Yerushalmi & Assoc -17 Barstow Rd -Gt Neck 11021 **Fx**:466-8988
(914) 769-5900 .. **Aperans**, Gundars '72 Cnsl Robinson B&H -100 Summit Lk Dr -Valhalla 10595
(631) 586-1111 .. **Apfel**, Dennis M '72 (Miller A&C PLLC) -900 Grand Blvd -Deer Pk 11729
(212) 350-2772 .. **Apfel**, Robt J '81 -477 Mad Av -NY 10022
(212) 580-0733 .. **Apfel**, Wm A '77 -100 W 72nd -NY 10023
(212) 803-5108 .. **Apfelbaum**, Barry '76 NY Cnty Defender Srvcs -225 Bway -NY 10007 **Fx**:571-6035
(718) 243-9323 .. **Apfelbaum**, Melissa B '05 %Lewis & H -45 Main -Brklyn 11201 **Fx**:243-9326
(212) 984-8083 .. **Apfeldorf**, Morton '76 CB Richd Ellis -200 Park Av -NY 10166 **Fx**:370-7264
(212) 504-6000 .. **Apfelroth**, Joshua A '07 %Cadwalader W&T LLP -1 World Fncl Ctr -NY 10281
(914) 779-9099 .. **Apicella**, Francis J '71 -111 Lk Av Bx269 -Tuckahoe 10707 **Fx**:779-0726
(212) 803-5100 .. **Apicella**, John M '74 %NY Cnty Defender Srvcs -225 Bway -NY 10007 **Fx**:571-6035
(212) 849-7000 .. **Apicella**, Jolie A '06 %Quinn EU&S,LLP -51 Mad Av -NY 10010
(212) 723-3236 .. **Apicella**, Richd L '81 Smith Barney -250 West -NY 10013
(212) 568-4245 .. **Apicella & Schlesinger** -1454 St Nicholas Av -NY 10033 **Fx**:740-1470
(914) 699-1042 .. **Apicella**, Scott '83 -587 Manor Ln -Pelham Mnr 10803
(212) 568-4245 .. **Apicella**, Vincent A '61 (Apicella & S) -1454 St Nicholas Av -NY 10033
(516) 922-8030 .. **Apicella**, Vincent T '77 %Murphy & L,PC -1045 Oyster Bay Rd -E Norwich 11732
(212) 692-1000 .. **Apiscopa**, Richd T '01 %Duane M LLP -1540 Bway -NY 10036
(718) 694-8306 .. **Apisiga**, Michl B '93 -44 Court -Brklyn 11201 **Fx**:254-9201
(718) 987-5710 .. **Aplin**, Alison M '91 -281 Rhine Av -Staten Isl 10304 **Fx**:987-7551
(212) 980-2055 .. **Apollo**, Stephen M '83 -405 Lex Av -NY 10174 **Fx**:(206) 212-8516
(516) 229-6000 .. **Apollon**, Michaelle J '84 %R Lau & Assoc -300 Jericho Quad Bx9040 -Jericho 11753 **Fx**:229-6167
(212) 813-5900 .. **Apolzon**, Lawr E '88 (Fross ZL&Z,PC) -866 UN Plz -NY 10017
(718) 590-2000 .. **Aponte**, Rene '93 %DA -198 E 161st -Bronx 10451 **Fx**:590-6477
(914) 366-5700 .. **Aponte-Caferra**, Lillian '99 %MA Bjork -660 Wht Plns Rd -Tarrytwn 10591 **Fx**:366-5759
(718) 726-7070 .. **Apostle**, Basil N '68 -25-82 Steinway -LIC 11103 **Fx**:204-0941
(212) 530-3900 .. **Apostol**, Barbara J '08 %Hannum FP&M, LLC -55 Bway -NY 10006
(212) 766-1888 .. **Apostolakos**, Athanasia '93 (Morris DA&F) -2 Rector -NY 10006
(516) 229-4501 .. **Apoznanski**, Mark C '81 %Russo A&T -875 Merrick Av -Westbury 11590
(718) 286-2000 .. **Appadoo**, Ruth S '98 %Leg Aid -120-46 Qns Blvd -Kew Gdns 11415 **Fx**:286-2286
(212) 335-9000 .. **Apparicio**, Tanya C '01 %DA -1 Hogan Pl -NY 10013
(212) 541-2000 .. **Appel**, Alan I '77 Cnsl Bryan C LLP -1290 Av of Amer -NY 10104
(212) 806-5400 .. **Appel**, Albert M '69 OfCnsl Stroock &S&L LLP -180 Maiden Ln -NY 10038
(212) 450-0100 .. **Appel**, David M '97 Marubeni America -375 Lex Av -NY 10017 **Fx**:450-0706
(516) 681-1100 .. **Appel**, Douglas B '94 Kaufman DV&G,LLP -135 Crsswys Park Dr -Woodbury 11797
(914) 948-1400 .. **Appel**, Evelyn D '82 -399 Knollwood Rd -White Plns 10603 **Fx**:948-9656
(212) 552-7901 .. **Appel**, Grace Robinson '96 %JP Morgan Chase & Co -1 Chase Manh Plz -NY 10005
(212) 663-3143 .. **Appel**, Jacob M '04 -140 Claremont Av -NY 10027
(631) 979-3000 .. **Appel**, Jennifer B '97 (Certilman BA&H,LLP) -1393 Vets Mem'l Hwy -Hauppauge 11788
(212) 742-2232 .. **Appel**, Paul H '71 (P Appel,PC) -277 Bway -NY 10007 **Fx**:(973) 718-4368
(212) 471-2826 .. **Appel**, Richd M '92 Endurance Reinsurance Corp -750 3rd Av -NY 10017
(212) 753-5000 .. **Appel**, Robt S '66 OfCnsl Schiff H LLP -900 3rd Av -NY 10022
(212) 686-0770 .. **Appel**, Ronald M '60 -295 Mad Av -NY 10017 **Fx**:779-8208
(212) 661-5030 .. **Appel**, Ronit D '09 %Schoeman U&K,LLP -60 E 42nd -NY 10165
(212) 225-2000 .. **Appelbaum**, Alan '61 SrCnsl Cleary GS&H -1 Lbrty Plz -NY 10006
(718) 250-2000 .. **Appelbaum**, Amy Merrill '88 %DA -350 Jay -Brklyn 11201 **Fx**:250-2314
(212) 678-8804 .. **Appelbaum**, Ann H '74 Cnsl Jewish Theological Seminary -3080 Bway -NY 10027 **Fx**:678-8868
(212) 560-4934 .. **Appelbaum**, Arlen M '90 EBC -450 W 33rd -NY 10001 **Fx**:560-3191
(845) 897-7738 .. **Appelbaum**, Joel R '76 %Progressive Ins Co -1401 Route 52 -Fishkill 12524
(718) 286-6000 .. **Appelbaum**, Kenneth M '86 %DA -125-01 Qns Blvd -Kew Gdns 11415
(212) 986-3667 .. **Appelbaum**, Martin '84 -60 E 42nd -NY 10165 **Fx**:986-3669
(716) 856-5500 .. **Appelbaum**, Michl E '97 (Damon M LLP) -200 Delaware Av -Buffalo 14202
(212) 308-2200 .. **Appelbaum**, Michl W '60 (Grant & A,PC) -444 Mad Av -NY 10022
(516) 248-9200 .. **Appelbaum**, Morton R '87 %ICS Agency -310 Willis Av -Mineola 11501 **Fx**:248-9017
(718) 260-8700 .. **Appelbaum**, Sabrina L '01 ACS -345 Adams -Brklyn 11201
(516) 692-8888 .. **Appelbaum**, Scott L '97 %F Chau & Assoc,LLC -130 Woodbury Rd -Woodbury 11797 **Fx**:692-8889
(845) 291-2670 .. **Appel-Kaplan**, Jodi '02 %Childrens Rts Society -213 W Main Bx1002 -Goshen 10924 **Fx**:291-2679
(212) 538-1569 .. **Appell**, Gordon S '04 Credit Suisse -11 Mad Av -NY 10010
(212) 947-0101 .. **Appell**, John J '85 -3 W 35th -NY 10001
(212) 649-2000 .. **Appiah**, Egya '07 %Hearst Corp -300 W 57th -NY 10019 **Fx**:649-2035
(212) 247-1010 .. **Applbaum**, Allen D '90 FTI Consulting Inc -3 Times Sq -NY 10036
(516) 431-6900 .. **Apple**, Kenneth L '95 -30 W Park Av -Long Bch 11561
(518) 487-7600 .. **Apple**, Leslie M '76 (Whiteman O&H LLP) -1 Commerce Plz -Albany 12260
(845) 855-5459 .. **Apple**, Robt '84 -92 E Main -Pawling 12564 **Fx**:855-8166
(212) 818-8408 .. **Apple**, Thos N '90 Itochu Intl -335 Mad Av -NY 10017 **Fx**:818-8493
(212) 319-1900 .. **Applebaum**, Kenneth J '94 (Berger & W,LLP) -1633 Bway -NY 10019
(212) 880-3800 .. **Applebaum**, Lisa '10 %Akerman S -335 Mad Av -NY 10017
(212) 530-5000 .. **Applebaum**, Michl A '09 %Milbank TH&M LLP -1 Chase Manh Plz -NY 10005
(212) 335-9000 .. **Applebaum**, Seth J '06 %DA -1 Hogan Pl -NY 10013
(315) 782-9030 .. **Appleby**, Alison Bronwyn '07 Cnty Dept Socl Srvcs -250 Arsenal -Watertwn 13601
(212) 344-1800 .. **Appleby**, Richd '73 -42 Bway -NY 10004
(212) 446-4800 .. **Appleby**, Robt A '95 (Kirkland & E LLP) -153 E 53rd -NY 10022
(315) 894-9976 .. **Applegate**, Robt W '80 (Getman F&A,LLP) -38 Morgan Bx477 -Ilion 13357
(716) 566-5400 .. **Appler**, Carrie P '04 %Goldberg S LLP -665 Main -Buffalo 14203
(716) 774-3522 .. **Appler**, James M III '01 Cannon Design -2170 Whitehaven Rd -Grand Isl 14072
(315) 471-8111 .. **Appler**, John R '99 (Scolaro SCF&B,PC) -507 Plum -Syracuse 13204
(212) 253-2727 .. **Appleton**, Albert F '75 Regional Plan Assn -4 Irving Pl -NY 10003 **Fx**:253-5666
(516) 292-8100 .. **Appleton**, Candace Scott '80 %Nassau/Sfflk Law Srv -1 Helen Keller Way -Hempstd 11550 **Fx**:292-6529
(212) 403-1000 .. **Appleton**, Tracy O'Driscoll '10 %Wachtell LR&K -51 W 52nd -NY 10019
(516) 766-1384 .. **Applewhaite**, Leon B '51 -7 Lawrence Av -Rockvll Ctr 11570 **Fx**:255-0086
(718) 553-1608 .. **Applewhite**, Natasha H '04 %US Customs Srvc -Bldg 77 JFK Airport -Jamaica 11430
(212) 596-9000 .. **Appleyard**, Wm F '08 %Ropes & G LLP -1211 Av of Amer -NY 10036
(212) 298-5360 .. **Appling**, Rigodis T '07 %Leg Aid -49 Thomas -NY 10013 **Fx**:298-5252
(212) 839-6970 .. **Apploff**, Stuart A '83 %C Siegel -40 Wall -NY 10005 **Fx**:440-2385
(212) 637-2198 .. **Apps**, Antonia M '95 %US Atty -1 St Andrews Plz -NY 10007
(212) 306-7450 .. **Aprigliano**, Adam D '04 %Comm on Human Rights -40 Rector -NY 10006 **Fx**:306-7414
(516) 742-0009 .. **April**, Lori S '86 (Mason & A,LLC) -377 Oak -Gdn Cty 11530 **Fx**:742-0908
(212) 993-0076 .. **Aprile**, Dianna R '04 Riverstone Holdings -712 5th Av -NY 10019 **Fx**:993-0077
(212) 661-3344 .. **Apsan**, Moses '84 -225 Bway -NY 10007
(212) 589-4200 .. **Apte**, Anagha S '06 %Baker & H LLP -45 Rckfllr Plz -NY 10111
(716) 566-5400 .. **Apter**, Julie P '85 (Goldberg S LLP) -665 Main -Buffalo 14203

(631) 761-0800 .. **Aptheker,** Steven B '83 (Lazer AR&Y,PC) -225 Old Cntry Rd -Melvll 11747
(212) 655-5011 .. **Aptman,** Lowell D '93 Tower Grp Cos -120 Bway -NY 10271 **Fx:**655-5039
(212) 340-0400 .. **Apuzzo,** Dante W '04 %Appllt Div 1st Dept -27 Mad Av -NY 10010 **Fx:**889-4412
(212) 297-0885 .. **Apuzzo,** Wm J '67 (Apuzzo & C) -800 3rd Av -NY 10022 **Fx:**297-0887
(516) 877-2900 .. **Aquaro,** John R '86 (Bartlett MB&M,LLP) -300 Old Cntry Rd -Mineola 11501
(212) 705-7000 .. **Aquart,** Cassandra G '04 %Bingham M LLP -399 Park Av -NY 10022
(516) 742-0707 .. **Aquila,** Albert B '94 (Sullivan PBM&C PC) -55 Mineola Blvd -Mineola 11501
(212) 558-4000 .. **Aquila,** Francis J '84 (Sullivan & C LLP) -125 Broad -NY 10004
(718) 318-1714 .. **Aquilante,** Jeffrey M '79 -155 Beach 95th -Far Rckwy 11693
(585) 295-5753 .. **Aquilina,** Vivian M '91 %Leg Aid -1 W Main -Rchstr 14614 **Fx:**232-2352
(212) 804-5221 .. **Aquino,** Jennifer L '07 MSCI Barra -88 Pine -NY 10005
(212) 558-4000 .. **Aquino,** Maite '96 (Sullivan & C LLP) -125 Broad -NY 10004
(914) 761-2252 .. **Aquino,** Maria T '02 %Boeggeman G&C,PC -1 Water -White Plns 10601
(716) 683-2105 .. **Aquino,** Mark S '92 %Vllg of Lancaster -5423 Bway -Lancaster 14086 **Fx:**684-4830
(212) 438-3978 .. **Aquino,** Robt J '07 Standard & Poors -55 Water -NY 10041
(212) 966-7775 .. **Aquino,** Romben E '02 %Ferro & C -100 Lafayette -NY 10013
(212) 801-6834 .. **Aquino-Fike,** Alexandra '08 %Greenberg T,LLP -200 Park Av -NY 10166
(212) 277-6500 .. **Arabatzis,** C Elaine '91 Cnsl Dickstein S LLP -1633 Bway -NY 10019
(516) 670-3200 .. **Arad,** Graham N '92 (Beck & A,LLP) -670 Lng Bch Blvd -Long Bch 11561
(212) 825-0365 .. **Arad,** Guy '98 (AL Bailey,PC) -120 Bway -NY 10271 **Fx:**825-0999
(212) 980-0120 .. **Arad,** Iddo I '01 %Frankfurt KK&S,PC -488 Mad Av -NY 10022
(516) 747-4082 .. **Arad,** Matthew K '07 %Montfort HM&S LLP -1140 Franklin Av Bx7677 -Gdn Cty 11530
(631) 777-2330 .. **Arafat,** Jinan M '03 O'Connor OH&D,LLP -1 Huntngtn Quad -Melvll 11747
(212) 636-6678 .. **Aragaki,** Hiro N '05 %Fordham Univ -1790 Bway -NY 10019
(212) 859-8000 .. **Aragon,** Raquel L '09 %Fried FHS&J LLP -1 NY Plz -NY 10004
(212) 258-4000 .. **Aragona,** John T '78 %Siemens Corp -153 E 53rd -NY 10022 **Fx:**767-0580
(212) 455-2000 .. **Aragona,** Thos A '09 %Simpson T&B LLP -425 Lex Av -NY 10017
(718) 378-3913 .. **Arai,** Benjamin M '85 -1175 Forest Av -Bronx 10456 **Fx:**893-2949
(212) 849-7000 .. **Arain,** Ali M '06 %Quinn EU&S,LLP -51 Mad Av -NY 10010
(212) 326-3939 .. **Arakawa,** Scott T '04 %Jones D -222 E 41st -NY 10017
(212) 688-8555 .. **Araki,** Shintaro '96 OfCnsl Fragomen DB&L LLP -7 Hanover Sq -NY 10004
(518) 285-6152 .. **Aram,** Wm J '75 Cnty Cthse -Congress & 2nd -Troy 12180
(516) 889-0800 .. **Aramanda,** Maria J '00 (Aramanda & P,PC) -166 E Park Av -Long Bch 11561 **Fx:**889-2888
(585) 325-5820 .. **Aramini,** Mary E '86 Aramini Law Ofc -144 Exchange Blvd -Rchstr 14614 **Fx:**325-3839
(212) 770-7000 .. **Arana,** Christopher D '02 AIG -70 Pine -NY 10270
(646) 262-0275 .. **Arana,** Israel '92 (Arana & A) -299 Bway -NY 10007
(212) 297-5800 .. **Arana,** Jacqueline L '07 %Day P LLP -7 Times Sq -NY 10036
(212) 521-1771 .. **Arana,** Melissa N '05 ICC Industries -460 Park Av -NY 10022
(212) 956-9500 .. **Arana,** Michl A '98 %Hand B&A LLP -8 W 40th -NY 10018 **Fx:**376-6080
(212) 867-6000 .. **Aranda,** Ariel L '09 %Rosenberg & E,PC -733 3rd Av -NY 10017
(718) 263-2100 .. **Arandia,** Alex '84 (Arandia & A) -118-35 Qns Blvd -Frst Hlls 11375 **Fx:**263-7274
(718) 263-2100 .. **Arandia,** Olga M '89 (Arandia & A) -118-35 Qns Blvd -Frst Hlls 11375 **Fx:**263-7274
(631) 736-0400 .. **Araneo,** Albert E '72 -Bx453 -Farmngvll 11738 **Fx:**736-7480
(212) 685-2400 .. **Araneo,** Albert E Jr. '05 Writers Hse LLC -21 W 26th -NY 10010 **Fx:**685-1781
(212) 248-7200 .. **Arangio,** Jennifer '97 %McCabe & F,LLP -1 Whitehall -NY 10004
(212) 583-5193 .. **Arango,** Sebastian '07 Blackstone Grp -345 Park Av -NY 10154
(212) 953-6000 .. **Arani,** Shireen G '03 %Katsky K LLP -605 3rd Av -NY 10158
(212) 736-5300 .. **Aranki,** Fredk C '99 %Block O&M LLP -1 Penn Plz -NY 10119
(516) 773-3826 .. **Aranoff,** Howard N '90 -475 Nrthrn Blvd -Gt Neck 11021
(212) 406-1893 .. **Aranoff,** Michl S '84 -305 Bway -NY 10007
(212) 779-1414 .. **Aranoff,** Ronald J '96 (Bernstein L LLP) -10 E 40th -NY 10016
(212) 682-3454 .. **Aranov,** Valerie '09 %Rosenberg FS LLP -551 5th Av -NY 10176
(646) 414-6850 .. **Aranyos,** Stephanie L '04 %Lowenstein S PC -1251 Av of Amer -NY 10020 **Fx:**(973) 422-6841
(212) 407-4000 .. **Arar,** Roger M '83 (Loeb & L,LLP) -345 Park Av -NY 10154
(212) 455-2000 .. **Arastu,** Nermeen S '09 %Simpson T&B LLP -425 Lex Av -NY 10017
(516) 746-6718 .. **Arata,** Jos J '75 -124 Lipton Ln -Williston Pk 11596
(212) 709-0748 .. **Aratani,** Hitoshi '01 %Cushman & Wakefield -Wall Street Plz -NY 10005
(212) 282-3333 .. **Aratani,** Satoshi '99 Mizuho Corp Bank -1251 Av of Amer -NY 10020
(212) 490-3000 .. **Araten,** Jeffrey B '95 (Wilson EME&D LLP) -150 E 42nd -NY 10017
(631) 342-4387 .. **Arato,** Alexander G '02 CA,Inc -1 CA Plz -Islandia 11749 **Fx:**342-4866
(212) 479-6724 .. **Arato,** Cynthia '99 (Macht SA&I LLP) -1114 Av of Amer -NY 10036 **Fx:**202-6417
(212) 265-2877 .. **Araujo,** Derek C '05 Ctr for Inquiry -1 Rckfllr Plz -NY 10020 **Fx:**265-2844
(718) 757-9620 .. **Araujo,** John L '75 -421 DeGraw -Brklyn 11217
(718) 575-8552 .. **Araujo,** Jose M '01 JM Araujo PC -118-35 Qns Blvd -Frst Hlls 11375 **Fx:**263-9465
(315) 422-1234 .. **Araujo,** Theo L '86 Bankruptcy Law Ctr -313 E Willow -Syracuse 13203 **Fx:**422-9113
(212) 610-6300 .. **Aravind,** Vinod S '08 %Allen & O -1221 Av of Amer -NY 10020
(212) 557-3334 .. **Arbeeny,** Kenneth D '80 Beau Dietl & Assoc -1 Penn Plz -NY 10119 **Fx:**557-4737
(212) 237-1000 .. **Arbeeny,** Michele M '98 (Windels ML&M,LLP) -156 W 56th -NY 10019
(516) 766-1878 .. **Arbeit,** Michl A '98 (M Arbeit,PC) -23 S Main -Freeprt 11520 **Fx:**678-2266
(631) 234-4400 .. **Arbeit,** Robt S '76 (Pinks A&N) -140 Fell Ct -Hauppauge 11788
(212) 735-3000 .. **Arbeit,** Susan A '04 %Skadden ASM&F LLP -4 Times Sq -NY 10036
(914) 245-2738 .. **Arbelaez,** Claudia M '93 -18 Sun Hill Rd -Katonah 10536 **Fx:**245-3497
(516) 538-0009 .. **Arber,** Howard B '76 -64 Hilton Av -Hempstd 11550 **Fx:**486-0849
(212) 287-3125 .. **Arbess,** Danl J '86 %Perella Weinberg Ptnrs -767 5th Av -NY 10153 **Fx:**287-3201
(212) 770-1775 .. **Arbetman,** Lori E '95 %AIG -70 Pine -NY 10270
(212) 541-2000 .. **Arbisser,** Micah E '06 %Bryan C LLP -1290 Av of Amer -NY 10104
(631) 249-1976 .. **Arbiter,** Joan Sanalitro '83 JS Arbiter,PC -425 Broadhllw Rd -Melvll 11747 **Fx:**777-3204
(914) 323-7000 .. **Arbitrio,** Michelle M '03 %Wilson EME&D LLP -3 Gannett Dr -White Plns 10604
(315) 234-4229 .. **Arbon,** Mark T '88 (Sarofeen & A,PLLC) -1 Lincoln Ctr -Syracuse 13202 **Fx:**424-1011
(212) 806-5400 .. **Arbuse,** Jennifer '08 %Stroock &S&L LLP -180 Maiden Ln -NY 10038
(212) 227-3636 .. **Arbusman,** Shelli '09 %Spar & B,PC -225 Bway -NY 10007
(212) 918-3000 .. **Arca,** Emil '91 (Hogan L LLP) -875 3rd Av -NY 10022
(716) 845-2560 .. **Arcadi,** James V '67 Surrogates Ct -92 Franklin -Buffalo 14202 **Fx:**853-3741
(212) 735-3542 .. **Arcano,** Stephen F '89 (Skadden ASM&F LLP) -4 Times Sq -NY 10036
(716) 856-4200 .. **Arcara,** Mark D '98 (Gibson M&C,LLP) -69 Delaware Av -Buffalo 14202
(585) 428-4311 .. **Arcarese,** Vincent P '92 %Hon J Rivoli -Hall of Justice -Rchstr 14614
(631) 728-4005 .. **Arcate,** Ronald J '86 -9 Canoe Pl Rd -Hampton Bays 11946 **Fx:**728-0608
(212) 416-8508 .. **Arcati,** Michl A '02 %Dept of Law -120 Bway -NY 10271
(212) 735-3000 .. **Arce,** Alvaro '10 %Skadden ASM&F LLP -4 Times Sq -NY 10036
(212) 587-0760 .. **Arce,** Bryan S '10 %Akin & S,LLC -30 Broad -NY 10004 **Fx:**587-4169
(516) 565-0184 .. **Arce,** Martha L '99 -250 Fulton Av -Hempstd 11550
(347) 851-5048 .. **Arce,** Michl '92 -3144 E Tremont Av -Bronx 10461 **Fx:**851-5051
(212) 670-1119 .. **Arce,** Patricia '07 Merrill Lynch -222 Bway -NY 10038
(212) 525-6098 .. **Arce,** Rebecca E '84 %Republic Natl Bk -452 5th Av -NY 10018 **Fx:**525-8346
(212) 474-1000 .. **Arcella,** Craig F '99 (Cravath S&M LLP) -825 8th Av -NY 10019
(212) 708-9245 .. **Arcella,** David J '75 Bessemer Trst Co -630 5th Av -NY 10111 **Fx:**265-5826
(516) 742-8735 .. **Arceso,** Peter V '09 Athanata Arts,Ltd -152 Roxbury Rd -Gdn Cty 11530 **Fx:**742-7660
(607) 565-8155 .. **Arcesi,** Michl '01 %Friedlander & F,PC -425 Park Av Bx109 -Waverly 14892 **Fx:**565-8485
(212) 474-1000 .. **Archambault,** Misty L '07 %Cravath S&M LLP -825 8th Av -NY 10019
(718) 237-2556 .. **Archbald,** Anthony J '01 %New Start,LLC -32 Court -Brklyn 11201
(631) 249-6565 .. **Archer Byington Glennon & Levine, LLP** -425 Broadhllw Rd -Melvll 11747 **Fx:**777-6906
(212) 715-9100 .. **Archer,** Carol '06 %Kramer LN&F,LLP -1177 Av of Amer -NY 10036
(716) 648-3030 .. **Archer,** Christen D '04 %Chiacchia & F,LLP -5113 S Park Av -Hambrg 14075
(716) 853-1616 .. **Archer,** David T '07 %Harter S&E LLP -12 Fountain Plz -Buffalo 14202
(212) 431-2138 .. **Archer,** Deborah N '97 %NY Law Schl -185 W Bway -NY 10013 **Fx:**966-2053
(212) 318-3000 .. **Archer,** Judith Ann '89 (Fulbright & J LLP) -666 5th Av -NY 10103
(631) 393-6220 .. **Archer,** Keith H '83 (Harras B&A LLP) -445 Broad Hollow Rd -Melvll 11747
(212) 331-5053 .. **Archer,** Moira S '99 HRA -180 Water -NY 10038
(631) 249-6565 .. **Archer,** Robt M Jr. '72 (Archer BG&L,LLP) -425 Broadhllw Rd -Melvll 11747
(212) 902-2000 .. **Archibald,** Arthur B '06 Goldman Sachs -1 NY Plz -NY 10004
(212) 259-8000 .. **Archibald,** Catherine J '09 %Dewey & L LLP -1301 Av of Amer -NY 10019
(212) 277-6500 .. **Archibald,** Danl P '09 %Dickstein S LLP -1633 Bway -NY 10019
(718) 237-1111 .. **Archibald,** Roger V '91 (RV Archibald,PC) -26 Court -Brklyn 11242 **Fx:**237-1425
(516) 997-9711 .. **Archibong,** Archibong Mendie '99 -55 Jericho Tpk -Jericho 11753
(716) 856-0875 .. **Archilla,** Danl R '89 -170 Franklin -Buffalo 14202 **Fx:**853-1897
(718) 651-4363 .. **Arcia,** E Abel '93 -82-17 Roosevelt Av -Jcksn Hts 11372 **Fx:**651-4369
(631) 852-2500 .. **Arcidiacono,** Guy '84 %DA -200 Center Dr -Rvrhead 11901 **Fx:**852-2762
(718) 279-1659 .. **Arcidiacono,** Thos C '94 Cnsl Diacon Systems -240-24 42nd Av -Douglastn 11363
(516) 281-9800 .. **Arcieri,** Marianne '99 %Goldberg S LLP -200 Old Cntry Rd -Mineola 11501
(914) 946-0400 .. **Arciero,** Maureen Morris '91 (Schiavetti CDW&N,LLP) -709 Wstchstr Av -White Plns 10604
(212) 273-7305 .. **Arciero-Craig,** Patricia '93 %Gleacher & Co Securities,Inc -677 Bway -Albany 12207 **Fx:**(800) 887-4129
(631) 761-7000 .. **Arcila,** Fabio '02 %Touro Cllg Law Ctr -225 Eastvw Dr -Central Islip 11722
(212) 493-8496 .. **Arciola,** Danl J '00 %Brown Bros Harriman -140 Bway -NY 10005 **Fx:**493-8206
(212) 612-4200 .. **Arciold,** Christine '92 %Hoey KT&E -55 Water -NY 10041
(518) 272-2110 .. **Arcodia,** Anthony Jr. '91 (Ehrlich & A) -64 2nd -Troy 12180
(631) 667-1510 .. **Arcuri,** Andrew A '85 (Kelly L&A) -2023 Deer Prk Av -Deer Pk 11729
(914) 995-2696 .. **Arcuri,** Carol Fumanti '78 (Cnty Atty) -148 Martine Av -White Plns 10601 **Fx:**995-5858
(718) 931-3300 .. **Arcuri,** Frank D '78 (Reiss & A LLP) -2590 Frisby Av -Bronx 10461 **Fx:**829-3626
(716) 852-3540 .. **Arcuri,** Kristin Langdon '95 (Watson BCJ&S) -12 Fountain Plz -Buffalo 14202
(315) 793-8146 .. **Arcuri,** Michl A '85 -10 Broad -Utica 13501
(518) 489-1098 .. **Arcus,** Ian R '75 -21 Everett Road Ext -Albany 12205 **Fx:**489-3304

(212) 715-1000 .. **Arcyz,** Maja M '03 %Arnold & P LLP -399 Park Av -NY 10022
(212) 336-8330 .. **Ard,** Seth '09 %Susman G LLP -560 Lex Av -NY 10022
(631) 360-7800 .. **Ardam,** David M '79 (Spada A&S,PLLC) -64 Smithtwn Blvd -Smithtwn 11787
(718) 990-6614 .. **Ardan,** Jeanne Hogan '96 SJU Schl of Law -8000 Utopia Pkwy -Jamaica 11439 **Fx:**990-1918
(212) 326-3939 .. **Arden,** Glenn S '86 (Jones D) -222 E 41st -NY 10017
(212) 839-5300 .. **Arden,** James D '84 (Sidley A LLP) -787 7th Av -NY 10019
(631) 547-1500 .. **Arden,** Lisa '87 %Ewall & E -946 Park Av -Huntngtn 11743 **Fx:**424-6435
(212) 581-3320 .. **Arden,** Suzan S '97 %Wasserman G&R,LLP -1700 Bway -NY 10019
(212) 584-1139 .. **Arden Besunder,** Alison '99 -235 Park Av -NY 10003 **Fx:**(718) 228-7522
(718) 426-0444 .. **Arditi,** Jennifer '96 %Aiello & C -69-06 Grand Av -Maspeth 11378
(212) 735-3000 .. **Arditi,** Ralph R '74 (Skadden ASM&F LLP) -4 Times Sq -NY 10036
(516) 825-0500 .. **Ardito,** John A '91 -659 Franklin Av -Franklin Sq 11010 **Fx:**825-1195
(516) 825-0500 .. **Ardito,** Jos '93 -659 Franklin Av -Franklin Sq 11010 **Fx:**825-1195
(516) 535-1100 .. **Ardito,** Raymond V '95 (Valdebenito & A) -1399 Franklin Av -Gdn Cty 11530 **Fx:**535-3936
(516) 705-2766 .. **Ardizzone,** Leora F '93 Catholic Hlth Srvcs -992 N Vllg Av -Rockvll Ctr 11570
(518) 473-5115 .. **Ardolino,** Michelle I '04 Cnsl Ofc for Technology -State Cptl ESP Bx2062 -Albany 12220
(212) 903-9000 .. **Arellano,** Jorge Marcelo '02 %Linklaters -1345 Av of Amer -NY 10105
(212) 964-6611 .. **Arem,** Randee H '03 %Lester SK&D -120 Bway -NY 10271
(914) 686-5600 .. **Arena,** Augustine A '74 All NY Title Agency -180 E Post Rd -White Plns 10601 **Fx:**686-1440
(212) 484-8000 .. **Arena,** Christine L '00 Time Warner -1 Time Warner Ctr -NY 10019
(914) 337-6300 .. **Arena,** Debra A '01 OfCnsl Nobile M&D,LLP -111 Kraft Av -Bronxvll 10708
(212) 506-2500 .. **Arena,** Kimberly B '08 %Mayer B LLP -1675 Bway -NY 10019
(914) 946-6600 .. **Arena,** Nicole Janeen '95 %RL Geller,PC -280 N Central Av -Hartsdale 10530 **Fx:**614-7109
(718) 278-7191 .. **Arena,** Robt R '82 -21-83 Steinway -Astoria 11105 **Fx:**721-7981
(212) 660-6407 .. **Arena,** Salvatore '03 Chiomenti -1 Rckfllr Plz -NY 10020
(212) 972-2929 .. **Arena,** Stephen J '06 %Trachtenberg R&F LLP -545 5th Av -NY 10017 **Fx:**972-7581
(212) 530-5000 .. **Arena,** Thos A '91 (Milbank TH&M LLP) -1 Chase Manh Plz -NY 10005
(212) 878-0600 .. **Arenare,** Scott A '90 Warburg Pincus LLC -450 Lex Av -NY 10017 **Fx:**878-9351
(212) 487-1054 .. **Arenas,** Regla Guillermina '95 %Dept Cnsmr Affrs -42 Bway -NY 10004 **Fx:**487-4197
(212) 735-3000 .. **Areno,** Filipe B '07 %Skadden ASM&F LLP -4 Times Sq -NY 10036
(212) 768-7681 .. **Arens,** David '60 -36 W 44th -NY 10036
(212) 490-3600 .. **Arenson Dittmar & Karban** -295 Mad Av -NY 10017
(212) 687-1980 .. **Arenson,** Gregory K '78 (Kaplan F&K LLP) -850 3rd Av -NY 10022
(212) 697-5550 .. **Arenson,** Lois '86 %G & L Blumberg,LLP -521 5th Av -NY 10175 **Fx:**697-9570
(212) 490-3600 .. **Arenson,** Steven '87 (Arenson D&K) -295 Mad Av -NY 10017
(212) 679-3999 .. **Arenstein,** Robt D '73 -295 Mad Av -NY 10017 **Fx:**370-5822
(212) 484-3900 .. **Arent Fox LLP** -1675 Bway -NY 10019 **Fx:**484-3990
(516) 873-2000 .. **Arenth,** Terese L '90 (Moritt HH&H LLP) -400 Grdn City Plz -Gdn Cty 11530
(212) 801-6741 .. **Arentowicz,** Amy M '03 %Greenberg T,LLP -200 Park Av -NY 10166
(212) 471-8528 .. **Arentzen,** Roger E '77 (Herzfeld & R,PC) -125 Broad -NY 10004
(631) 476-5344 .. **Arevalo,** Edw J '86 -123 Mt Sinai Av -Mt Sinai 11766 **Fx:**331-6572
(914) 694-1000 .. **Arfa,** Jonathan P '78 (J Arfa,PC) -4 Gannett Dr -White Plns 10604 **Fx:**694-1800
(914) 390-4177 .. **Arfa,** Meredith A '09 Hon S Robinson USDC -300 Quarropas -White Plns 10601
(212) 455-2000 .. **Arfaania,** Maryam '10 %Simpson T&B LLP -425 Lex Av -NY 10017
(212) 709-8258 .. **Arfe,** Edw I '76 -150 E 37th -NY 10016
(212) 373-3000 .. **Arffa,** Allan J '82 (Paul WRW&G LLP) -1285 Av of Amer -NY 10019
(914) 773-1600 .. **Arfine,** Stephen '86 -245 Saw Mill Rvr Rd -Hawthorne 10532 **Fx:**372-1976
(716) 845-2560 .. **Argenio,** Modesto A '92 %Surrogates Ct -92 Franklin -Buffalo 14202 **Fx:**853-3741
(212) 355-1500 .. **Argentieri,** Marco G '03 OSL Shipping & Dvlpmt -410 Park Av -NY 10022
(718) 254-7000 .. **Argentieri,** Nicole M '03 %US Atty -271 Cadman Plz E -Brklyn 11201 **Fx:**254-6479
(607) 324-3232 .. **Argentieri,** Paul A '77 -188 Main -Hornell 14843 **Fx:**324-6188
(914) 772-2344 .. **Argentina,** Christine M '07 -600 Mamaroneck Av -Harrison 10528
(716) 884-3281 .. **Argentine,** Stephanie L '94 -18 Agassiz Cir -Buffalo 14214
(718) 816-9441 .. **Argento,** Elise L Genco '80 -418 St Marks Pl -Staten Isl 10301 **Fx:**816-9441
(585) 383-0020 .. **Argento,** Victoria M '88 -109 W Cmmrcial -E Rchstr 14445 **Fx:**383-1652
(212) 732-9000 .. **Argintar,** Clifford S '09 %Sullivan PBM&C PC -120 Bway -NY 10271
(718) 459-3300 .. **Argiriou & Finkel** -110-11 Qns Blvd -Frst Hlls 11375 **Fx:**459-8550
(516) 357-3700 .. **Argiriou,** George D '81 OfCnsl Cullen and D LLP -100 Q Roosevelt Blvd -Gdn Cty 11530
(212) 335-9000 .. **Arguello,** Che '01 %DA -1 Hogan Pl -NY 10013
(585) 425-5210 .. **Arguello,** Sue L '98 Maximus Federal Srvcs -50 Square Dr -Victor 14564 **Fx:**425-5301
(212) 258-4435 .. **Argueta,** Violetta V '95 Siemens Corp -153 E 53rd -NY 10022
(718) 777-1777 .. **Argyropoulos & Bender** -31-01 Bway -Astoria 11106 **Fx:**777-2737
(718) 777-1777 .. **Argyropoulos,** Philip '90 (Argyropoulos & B) -31-01 Bway -Astoria 11106
(212) 819-8200 .. **Argyrou,** Stella '08 %White & C LLP -1155 Av of Amer -NY 10036
(718) 254-7000 .. **Ariail,** J E Shreve '03 %US Atty -271 Cadman Plz E -Brklyn 11201 **Fx:**254-6479
(212) 840-3878 .. **Arias,** Betsy '99 %S Perlitsh,PC -110 W 34th -NY 10001 **Fx:**(917) 510-0872
(516) 571-3800 .. **Arias,** David '07 %DA -262 Old Cntry Rd -Mineola 11501 **Fx:**248-9479
(718) 899-6633 .. **Arias,** Fernando F Jr. '84 -37-32 75th -Jcksn Hts 11372 **Fx:**899-6919
(631) 844-9611 .. **Arias,** Jose A '00 %Shapiro D&B,LLP -105 Maxness Rd -Melvll 11747
(914) 417-3400 .. **Arias,** Kevin P '07 %Littleton JUP&K LLP -1 Manhattanvll Rd -Purchase 10577
(718) 824-2654 .. **Arias,** Larry Alfonso '95 LA Arias,PC -912 Soundvw Av -Bronx 10473
(212) 407-4529 .. **Arias,** Leslie Y '05 Banco Santander -45 E 53rd -NY 10022
(718) 476-7903 .. **Arias,** Teodora '03 Immigration Ctr -80-07 Roosevelt Av -Jcksn Hts 11372
(212) 223-4000 .. **Arias,** Vivian M '08 %Crowell & M LLP -590 Mad Av -NY 10022
(212) 232-1300 .. **Aribakan,** Suzanne E '06 %Lewis BB&S LLP -77 Water -NY 10005
(212) 363-3345 .. **Arida,** Paul N '75 -26 Bway -NY 10004 **Fx:**363-3544
(212) 441-2605 .. **Aries,** Christopher M '95 Aon Corp -199 Water -NY 10038 **Fx:**441-1929
(212) 571-7100 .. **Aripotch,** Steven A '91 %O'Dwyer & B,LLP -52 Duane -NY 10007
(718) 549-7735 .. **Aris,** Joram J '80 -3671 Hudson Manor Ter -Bronx 10463
(212) 259-8000 .. **Arisohn,** Joshua '07 %Dewey & L LLP -1301 Av of Amer -NY 10019
(212) 907-0840 .. **Arisohn,** Mark S '73 (Labaton S LLP) -140 Bway -NY 10005
(914) 684-2429 .. **Arisohn,** Sharon '89 S Arisohn,PC -399 Knollwood Dr -White Plns 10603 **Fx:**682-1512
(212) 224-4000 .. **Aristizabal,** Michl A '02 %Sumitomo Mitsui -277 Park Av -NY 10172 **Fx:**593-9522
(212) 305-9327 .. **Aristondo,** Linda E '83 -630 W 168th -NY 10032 **Fx:**305-7846
(212) 909-5000 .. **Aristova,** Arina E '96 KPMG LLP -757 3rd Av -NY 10017
(516) 374-3336 .. **Arker,** Sol '73 -15 Verbena Av -Floral Pk 11001
(212) 333-0200 .. **Arkin,** Alan R '97 Cnsl Arkin KR LLP -590 Mad Av -NY 10022
(212) 333-0200 .. **Arkin Kaplan Rice LLP** -590 Mad Av -NY 10022 **Fx:**333-2350
(212) 636-6850 .. **Arkin,** Marc M '84 %Fordham Univ Sch of Law -140 W 62nd -NY 10023 **Fx:**636-6899
(212) 333-0200 .. **Arkin,** Stanley S '63 (Arkin KR LLP) -590 Mad Av -NY 10022
(212) 836-8000 .. **Arkins,** Jonathan R C '02 Cnsl Kaye S LLP -425 Park Av -NY 10022
(212) 337-8550 .. **Arkles,** Z Gabriel '06 S Rivera Project -322 8th Av -NY 10001 **Fx:**337-1972
(914) 684-2100 .. **Arkontaky,** Adrienne J '05 %Littman K LLP -399 Knollwood Rd -White Plns 10603
(212) 696-6000 .. **Arkush,** Julie W '08 %Curtis M-PC&M LLP -101 Park Av -NY 10178
(718) 630-7000 .. **Arky,** Barbara Katz '78 Lutheran HealthCare -150 55th -Brklyn 11220
(212) 336-2588 .. **Arlein,** Michl S '01 (Patterson BW&T LLP) -1133 Av of Amer -NY 10036
(212) 992-8842 .. **Arlen,** Jennifer H '87 NYU Law Schl -40 Wshngtn Sq S -NY 10012
(518) 589-5264 .. **Arleo,** Robt L '91 -164 Sunset Park Rd -Haines Fls 12436
(212) 566-6262 .. **Arlia,** John '97 (Wenger & A,LLP) -20 Vesey -NY 10007
(212) 552-2670 .. **Armand,** Kelesha F '02 JP Morgan Chase & Co -1 Chase Manh Plz -NY 10081
(212) 637-2724 .. **Armand,** Pierre G '00 %US Atty -86 Chmbrs -NY 10007
(315) 468-1052 .. **Armani,** Dorina A '86 -4300 W Genesee -Syracuse 13219 **Fx:**468-0212
(315) 478-1583 .. **Armani,** Harry V Jr. '84 (H Armani & Assoc) -2700 Bellevue Av -Syracuse 13219
(315) 437-6100 .. **Armani,** Michl F '88 %O'Brien & G Ltd -5000 Brittonfld Pkwy Bx4873 -Syracuse 13221 **Fx:**463-7554
(516) 355-9600 .. **Armao,** Jos N '04 %Friedman HK&P -3000 Marcus Av -Lk Success 11042
(212) 903-9000 .. **Armao,** Jos P '85 (Linklaters) -1345 Av of Amer -NY 10105
(516) 256-3200 .. **Armao,** Michl A '10 Cnsl Armao Costa & Ricciardi -1055 Franklin Av -Gdn Cty 11530 **Fx:**256-4620
(212) 408-5100 .. **Armas,** Oliver J '91 (Chadbourne & P LLP) -30 Rckfllr Plz -NY 10112
(212) 445-7000 .. **Armatti-Epstein,** Linda T '85 %Jacoby & M,LLP -39 Bway -NY 10006
(212) 839-5300 .. **Armbrust,** Jos W Jr. '70 (Sidley A LLP) -787 7th Av -NY 10019
(212) 849-7000 .. **Armenio,** Peter J '95 (Quinn EU&S,LLP) -51 Mad Av -NY 10010
(212) 885-5000 .. **Armentano,** Catherine A '05 %Blank R LLP -405 Lex Av -NY 10174
(516) 227-0700 .. **Armentano,** John C '06 %Farrell F,PC -1320 RXR Plz -Uniondale 11556
(631) 777-2100 .. **Armentano,** Wm V '91 -175 Pinelawn Rd #300 -Melvll 11747
(212) 382-6625 .. **Armentrout,** Lynn '82 City Bar Justice Ctr -42 W 44th -NY 10036
(585) 586-4640 .. **Armer,** Karolyne '75 -2130 Five Mile Line Rd -Penfld 14526 **Fx:**586-6592
(631) 427-8789 .. **Armet,** Harold R '88 -121 Buttercup Ln -Huntngtn 11743 **Fx:**549-2566
(212) 809-7074 .. **Armienti DeBellis Guglielmo & Rhoden, LLP** -39 Bway -NY 10006 **Fx:**809-7713
(516) 877-1202 .. **Armienti DeBellis Guglielmo & Rhoden, LLP** -170 Old Cntry Rd -Mineola 11501 **Fx:**877-8099
(212) 809-7074 .. **Armienti,** Michl '80 (Armienti DG&R,LLP) -39 Bway -NY 10006
(212) 572-8511 .. **Armillei,** David C '04 MacAndrews & Forbes Holdings -35 E 62nd -NY 10065
(212) 918-3000 .. **Armillei,** Stacy M '06 %Hogan L LLP -875 3rd Av -NY 10022
(718) 608-1000 .. **Arminante,** Robt A '01 -4255 Amboy Rd -Staten Isl 10308 **Fx:**608-9128
(212) 863-5734 .. **Armour-Garb,** Allison Rees '96 %CUNY Task Force -100 Gold -NY 10038
(212) 403-1000 .. **Arms,** Martin J E '00 (Wachtell LR&K) -51 W 52nd -NY 10019
(646) 386-3348 .. **Armstrong,** Adrian N '91 NYS Supreme Ct -111 Centre -NY 10013
(718) 250-4254 .. **Armstrong,** Andrea N '08 %Leg Aid -111 Lvngstn -Brklyn 11201 **Fx:**250-4243
(646) 471-4000 .. **Armstrong,** Brian J '91 %PricewaterhouseCoopers LLP -300 Mad Av -NY 10017
(212) 752-7555 .. **Armstrong,** Danl V W '03 %Re P & Prtnrs -445 Park Av -NY 10022
(607) 756-7501 .. **Armstrong,** Donald C '80 (Pomeroy AC&M,LLP) -16 Tompkins Bx828 -Cortlnd 13045
(212) 964-3544 .. **Armstrong,** Edw W '89 E Armstrong,PC -233 Bway -NY 10279
(212) 854-3108 .. **Armstrong,** Joanne D S '84 -435 W 116th -NY 10027

(212) 450-4000 .. **Armstrong,** Jonathan E '08 %Davis P&W LLP -450 Lex Av -NY 10017
(315) 435-2470 .. **Armstrong,** Kari E '04 %DA -505 S State -Syracuse 13202 **Fx:**435-3969
(212) 735-3000 .. **Armstrong,** Katherine Anne '90 Cnsl Skadden ASM&F LLP -4 Times Sq -NY 10036
(516) 496-5822 .. **Armstrong,** Kelly E '09 T Spina -170 Froehlich Farm Blvd -Woodbury 11797 **Fx:**496-5420
(212) 736-4500 .. **Armstrong,** Laine A '01 %Nesenoff & M,LLP -363 7th Av -NY 10001
(718) 477-7700 .. **Armstrong,** Lance P '68 -900 South Av -Staten Isl 10314 **Fx:**477-5711
(212) 326-3939 .. **Armstrong,** Lee A '94 (Jones D) -222 E 41st -NY 10017
(315) 822-6890 .. **Armstrong,** Lee Palmer '69 -390 W Main Bx480 -W Winfld 13491 **Fx:**822-6890
(212) 504-6000 .. **Armstrong,** Matthew J '07 %Cadwalader W&T LLP -1 World Fncl Ctr -NY 10281
(212) 812-8926 .. **Armstrong,** Michl F '61 (Lankler & C,LLP) -845 3rd Av -NY 10022
(212) 468-8000 .. **Armstrong,** Naja R '09 %Morrison & F LLP -1290 Av of Amer -NY 10104
(518) 445-2311 .. **Armstrong,** Pamela J '87 Albany Law Schl -80 New Scotland Av -Albany 12208 **Fx:**445-2315
(212) 697-9280 .. **Armstrong,** Seymour '59 -122 E 42nd -NY 10168 **Fx:**697-9284
(516) 812-2000 .. **Armstrong,** Steven R '84 MSC -75 Maxess Rd -Melvll 11747
(718) 402-5143 .. **Armstrong,** Yvette '87 -1269 Mace Av -Bronx 10469 **Fx:**402-5144
(718) 522-3333 .. **Armstrong-Barrows,** Valerie F '99 %Children's Law Ctr -44 Court -Brklyn 11201 **Fx:**522-7376
(914) 846-7000 .. **Armstrong-Walker,** Diana L '08 NY Life Ins -1 Rockwood Rd -Sleepy Hollow 10591 **Fx:**846-4755
(212) 596-9000 .. **Arnaboldi,** Leo P III '86 (Ropes & G LLP) -1211 Av of Amer -NY 10036
(212) 538-3696 .. **Arnaboldi,** Nicole Sinek '86 CSFB Private Equity -11 Mad Av -NY 10010
(212) 331-2813 .. **Arnakis,** Pauline '99 Universal Music Grp -1755 Bway -NY 10019
(212) 972-3000 .. **Arnason,** Jon Y '75 OfCnsl Klestadt & W,LLP -292 Mad Av -NY 10017
(212) 559-0659 .. **Arnavat,** Gustavo '92 Citigroup Private Bk -399 Park Av -NY 10043
(212) 262-1000 .. **Arnay,** James D '89 (Levinsohn & A LLP) -1790 Bway -NY 10019
(631) 436-7100 .. **Arnberg,** Howard D '95 %Hirsch Intl Corp -200 Wireless Blvd Bx18004 -Hauppauge 11788 **Fx:**436-7054
(518) 449-3107 .. **Arndt,** Karen R '89 %Buckley M&C,PC -29 Wards Ln -Albany 12204
(516) 873-0011 .. **Arnedos,** Gina M '91 %S Goldstein,LLP -1 Old Cntry Rd -Carle Pl 11514 **Fx:**873-0120
(718) 875-5151 .. **Arnel,** Curt '82 -16 Court -Brklyn 11241 **Fx:**875-8951
(973) 376-5533 .. **Arnell,** Nathan E '85 -36 W 76th -NY 10023 **Fx:**376-5654
(631) 725-4778 .. **Arnel-Rudansky,** Meg '85 -36 Woodvale -Sag Hbr 11963 **Fx:**725-8685
(718) 205-3600 .. **Arnes,** Edwin '82 -9320A Roosevelt Av -Jcksn Hts 11372
(212) 806-5400 .. **Arnett,** Jennifer C '02 %Stroock &S&L LLP -180 Maiden Ln -NY 10038
(516) 496-5822 .. **Arnett,** Marshall D '08 T Spina -170 Froehlich Farm Blvd -Woodbury 11797 **Fx:**496-5420
(718) 833-9006 .. **Arniotes,** Steve C '55 -7206 5th Av -Brklyn 11209 **Fx:**680-4753
(315) 458-3331 .. **Arno,** Danl J '76 %Bertrand AW&P -107 S Main Bx277 -N Syracuse 13212
(631) 727-3904 .. **Arnoff,** Harvey A '68 -206 Roanoke Av -Rvrhead 11901 **Fx:**727-3940
(845) 471-1504 .. **Arnoff,** Lisa E '88 -1282 Dutchess Tpk -Poughkeepsie 12603
(212) 653-8700 .. **Arnold,** A Joy '92 (Sheppard MR&H LLP) -30 Rckfllr Plz -NY 10112
(315) 671-2094 .. **Arnold,** Aaron F '07 Ctr for Ct Innovation -600 S State -Syracuse 13202 **Fx:**671-2092
(212) 744-5022 .. **Arnold,** Alyssa L '04 Lenox Hill Neighborhood House -331 E 70th -NY 10021
(716) 439-7145 .. **Arnold,** Ann Freeland '93 %Supreme & Cnty Cts -175 Hawley -Lockprt 14094 **Fx:**439-7157
(607) 722-8272 .. **Arnold,** Becky L '90 -Bx126 -Bnghmtn 13904 **Fx:**722-8272
(516) 764-7811 .. **Arnold,** Bernadette M '85 -267 Hempstd Av -Rockvll Ctr 11570
(212) 715-1000 .. **Arnold,** Cameron W '07 %Arnold & P LLP -399 Park Av -NY 10022
(212) 686-4655 .. **Arnold,** Chas M '96 (Abraham L&A LLP) -292 Mad Av -NY 10017
(585) 338-6800 .. **Arnold,** Clay C '97 %Bausch & Lomb -One Bausch & Lomb Pl -Rchstr 14604 **Fx:**338-8706
(212) 336-8000 .. **Arnold,** Craig J '91 (Amster R&E) -90 Park Av -NY 10016
(914) 381-7400 .. **Arnold,** Dawn K '96 %Rattet P&G,LLP -550 Mamaroneck Av -Harrison 10528
(518) 457-5608 .. **Arnold,** Fredk B '84 %Agriculture & Mrkts -10B Airline Dr -Albany 12235 **Fx:**457-8842
(212) 269-0927 .. **Arnold,** Harry J Jr. '68 (D'Amato & L,LLP) -2 World Fncl Ctr -NY 10281
(585) 428-2757 .. **Arnold,** Jeanne T '99 %Hon D Ruhlmann -329 Hall of Justice -Rchstr 14614
(212) 762-4000 .. **Arnold,** Jill L '01 Morgan Stanley -522 5th Av -NY 10036
(518) 459-2495 .. **Arnold,** John Jay S '03 %Summers Law Firm,PC -125 Wolf Rd -Albany 12205 **Fx:**459-2571
(212) 335-9000 .. **Arnold,** Jordan S '01 %DA -1 Hogan Pl -NY 10013
(212) 504-6000 .. **Arnold,** Joshua P '09 %Cadwalader W&T LLP -1 World Fncl Ctr -NY 10281
(518) 474-2256 .. **Arnold,** Kathleen M '91 %Dept of Law -The Cptl -Albany 12224
(212) 715-1000 .. **Arnold,** Keri L '04 (Arnold & P LLP) -399 Park Av -NY 10022
(212) 336-0022 .. **Arnold,** Linda L '01 %SEC -3 World Fncl Ctr -NY 10281 **Fx:**336-1323
(303) 801-2705 .. **Arnold,** Lucy D '08 %Fulbright & J LLP -666 5th Av -NY 10103 **Fx:**801-2777
(585) 425-1060 .. **Arnold,** Michl H '85 (Place & A) -27 Plsnt -Fairprt 14450
(212) 935-3000 .. **Arnold,** Michl S '04 %Mintz LCFG&P,PC -666 3rd Av -NY 10017
(212) 969-3000 .. **Arnold,** Michelle E '10 %Proskauer R LLP -1585 Bway -NY 10036
(212) 302-1821 .. **Arnold,** Peter D '88 %CFDA -1412 Bway -NY 10018
(212) 566-3291 .. **Arnold,** Phyllis L '82 %Dept of Bldgs -280 Bway -NY 10007
(212) 715-1000 .. **Arnold & Porter LLP** -399 Park Av -NY 10022 **Fx:**715-1399
(212) 916-2649 .. **Arnold,** Rachel R '04 UBS AG -101 Park Av -NY 10178
(212) 484-3900 .. **Arnold,** Ronni N '07 %Arent F LLP -1675 Bway -NY 10019
(212) 883-8833 .. **Arnold,** Rosemarie '87 (Tacopina & A) -275 Mad Av -NY 10016
(315) 963-8909 .. **Arnold,** Stephen W '80 -527 Cnty Route 58 Bx296 -Mexico 13114 **Fx:**963-4040
(212) 335-9000 .. **Arnone,** Eric M '03 %DA -1 Hogan Pl -NY 10013
(716) 332-7860 .. **Arnone,** James R '86 %Hon H Scott -68 Court -Buffalo 14202 **Fx:**332-7865
(212) 787-1742 .. **Arnone,** Roberta Ann '94 -132 E 43rd -NY 10017
(212) 756-2000 .. **Arnot,** Mark J '09 %Schulte R&Z LLP -919 3rd Av -NY 10022
(212) 880-6000 .. **Arnot,** Michl J A '05 %Torys LLP -237 Park Av -NY 10017
(212) 839-7000 .. **Arnott,** Gordon S '86 (Hill B&N LLP) -200 Lbrty -NY 10281
(212) 478-7200 .. **Arnott,** Maria A '90 SpclCnsl Hahn & H LLP -488 Mad Av -NY 10022
(212) 697-3122 .. **Arnould,** Holly M '08 %Martin C&B LLP -220 E 42nd -NY 10017
(212) 335-9000 .. **Arnow,** Shira L '10 %DA -1 Hogan Pl -NY 10013
(914) 738-2220 .. **Arnowitz,** Seth J '96 %FN Peluso,PC -5 5th Av Bx327 -Pelham 10803
(631) 724-8833 .. **Arntsen,** David H '91 Cnsl Devitt SB,LLP -50 Route 111 -Smithtwn 11787
(212) 223-4000 .. **Arntsen,** Douglas R '03 Cnsl Crowell & M LLP -590 Mad Av -NY 10022
(212) 788-3159 .. **Arocho,** Jose A '01 %Law Dept -60 Lafayette -NY 10013 **Fx:**442-6865
(212) 776-5068 .. **Aron,** David J '90 %NYC Housing Auth -250 Bway -NY 10007 **Fx:**776-5039
(212) 346-9200 .. **Aron,** Kenneth L '83 -111 Bway -NY 10006 **Fx:**346-4665
(212) 755-6000 .. **Aronauer,** Jos '75 (Aronauer R&Y,LLP) -444 Mad Av -NY 10022
(212) 755-6000 .. **Aronauer Re & Yudell,LLP** -444 Mad Av -NY 10022 **Fx:**755-6006
(212) 845-7538 .. **Aronchick,** Martin C '79 Thacher Assoc,LLC -330 W 42nd -NY 10036 **Fx:**845-7549
(518) 457-8066 .. **Aron-DeFronzo,** Susan T '90 Crime Victims Bd -1 Columbia Cir -Albany 12203 **Fx:**457-8658
(212) 682-0700 .. **Aroniadis,** Anna V '02 G Vomvolakis -275 Mad Av -NY 10016 **Fx:**619-1028
(914) 803-0809 .. **Aronian,** John M '04 Venture Realty -1304 Mdlnd Av -Ynkrs 10704
(212) 213-9666 .. **Aronin,** Douglas D '83 OfCnsl L Atlas,PC -112 Mad Av -NY 10016 **Fx:**213-9896
(718) 875-4207 .. **Aronne,** Albert C '51 (Aronne & D) -186 Joralemon -Brklyn 11201 **Fx:**855-1112
(212) 635-6738 .. **Aronoff,** Andrea B '99 Bk of NY Mellon -1 Wall -NY 10286
(212) 655-5000 .. **Aronoff,** Jonathan D '02 %Gannon R&M -120 Bway -NY 10271
(212) 889-9250 .. **Aronoff,** Steven K '67 -499 Park Av -NY 10022 **Fx:**779-7605
(212) 682-7474 .. **Aronoff,** Yonaton '04 %Foley & L LLP -90 Park Av -NY 10016
(718) 432-0500 .. **Aronov,** Rachel R '09 %Krieger W&H -5602 Bway -Bronx 10463
(212) 689-1113 .. **Aronov,** Rita F '02 %Garbarini & S,PC -432 Park Av S -NY 10016
(718) 206-1555 .. **Aronov,** Robt '00 (R Aronov & Assoc,PC) -8802 136th -Richmnd Hll 11418 **Fx:**206-1227
(516) 741-4799 .. **Aronova,** Ester '07 %Baker SBGFM&N,LLC -100 Grdn City Plz -Gdn Cty 11530
(212) 373-3000 .. **Aronovitch,** Benjamin A '06 %Paul WRW&G LLP -1285 Av of Amer -NY 10019
(212) 607-2003 .. **Aronow,** David E '94 MetTel -55 Water -NY 10041
(212) 258-8000 .. **Aronow,** Gil '89 %MTV Networks -1515 Bway -NY 10036 **Fx:**258-8358
(212) 607-2000 .. **Aronow,** Jos M '65 %MetTel -55 Water -NY 10041
(516) 883-0167 .. **Aronow,** Michl '97 -53 Barkers Pnt Rd -Sands Pnt 11050 **Fx:**767-2374
(212) 373-3000 .. **Aronowicz,** Anat M '08 %Paul WRW&G LLP -1285 Av of Amer -NY 10019
(212) 267-9020 .. **Aronowitz,** David S '86 (Shapiro B&A LLP) -225 Bway -NY 10007
(212) 754-2233 .. **Aronowitz,** Debra M '97 Scientific Games Corp -750 Lex Av -NY 10022
(212) 878-8000 .. **Aronowitz,** Edmund S '06 %Clifford C LLP -31 W 52nd -NY 10019
(212) 681-2535 .. **Aronowitz,** Scott '07 %Greenberg & S,PC -275 Mad Av -NY 10016
(212) 416-6676 .. **Aronowitz,** Stacy P '00 Dept of Law -120 Bway -NY 10271
(212) 803-5100 .. **Aronowsky,** Courtney A '03 NY Cnty Defender Srvcs -225 Bway -NY 10007 **Fx:**571-6035
(718) 354-3200 .. **Aronowsky,** Michl '71 (Battiste A&S,Inc) -60 Bay -Staten Isl 10301
(212) 310-8000 .. **Arons,** Andrew R '09 %Weil G&M LLP -767 5th Av -NY 10153
(845) 362-6100 .. **Arons,** Edw M '04 (Weiss & A LLP) -1540 Route 202 -Pomona 10970 **Fx:**362-6111
(718) 225-0972 .. **Arons,** Eugene '52 -26910 Grnd Cntrl Pkwy -Floral Pk 11005 **Fx:**225-0972
(646) 386-4623 .. **Arons,** Jennifer G '99 %Hon AK Bartley Jr -111 Centre -NY 10013
(914) 666-2525 .. **Arons,** John L '69 (Arons & N LLP) -126 Barker -Mt Kisco 10549
(201) 388-9533 .. **Arons,** Lori E '95 -130 N Main -New Cty 10956 **Fx:**342-5772
(914) 666-2525 .. **Arons & Neary LLP** -126 Barker -Mt Kisco 10549 **Fx:**666-2325
(212) 586-2211 .. **Arons,** Nicholas G '05 %Orans EL&B LLP -875 3rd Av -NY 10022
(212) 770-2477 .. **Aronskind,** Michelle '93 %AIG -80 Pine -NY 10005 **Fx:**344-2357
(212) 577-6600 .. **Aronsky,** Jeffrey A '94 (J Aronsky,PC) -16 E 40th -NY 10016 **Fx:**577-6776
(212) 318-3000 .. **Aronson,** Alan L '72 (Fulbright & J LLP) -666 5th Av -NY 10103
(347) 408-4366 .. **Aronson,** Burton '54 -1 Bay Club Dr -Bayside 11360 **Fx:**408-4366
(212) 735-3000 .. **Aronson,** Clifford H '85 (Skadden ASM&F LLP) -4 Times Sq -NY 10036
(914) 664-6589 .. **Aronson,** Craig E '84 -401 Wstchstr Av -Mt Vernon 10552
(212) 521-3500 .. **Aronson,** David '75 (Aronson M&S, LLP) -485 Lex Av -NY 10017
(845) 226-9996 .. **Aronson,** Francine P '82 R Aronson -129 Clove Brnch Rd -Hopewell Junct 12533 **Fx:**226-9992
(914) 723-4300 .. **Aronson,** Howard N '76 (Lackenbach S LLP) -1 Chase Rd -Scarsdale 10583
(914) 428-2100 .. **Aronson,** Jeffrey A '76 OfCnsl Welby B&G,LLP -11 Martine Av -White Plns 10606
(212) 692-2000 .. **Aronson,** Jeffrey H '84 %Angelo Gordon & Co -245 Park Av -NY 10167 **Fx:**867-6395
(518) 431-5000 .. **Aronson,** Judith F '86 %Farm Family Ins -Bx656 -Albany 12201 **Fx:**431-5979
(212) 573-8920 .. **Aronson,** Kenneth J '75 -270 Mad Av -NY 10016 **Fx:**688-6457
(718) 237-1960 .. **Aronson,** Marc '78 -107 Smith -Brklyn 11201 **Fx:**624-1368
(212) 697-4956 .. **Aronson,** Marian '83 -244 Mad Av -NY 10016
(516) 572-2000 .. **Aronson,** Marisa A '10 %DA -99 Main -Hempstd 11550 **Fx:**572-2606
(212) 968-9199 .. **Aronson,** Mark I '77 -82 Wall -NY 10005

(212) 521-3500 .. **Aronson Mayefsky & Sloan, LLP** -485 Lex Av -NY 10017 **Fx:**838-5505
(212) 678-2767 .. **Aronson,** Paul '89 -2749 Bway -NY 10025
(212) 600-9531 .. **Aronson,** Peter E '83 P Aronson,PLLC -11 Bway -NY 10004 **Fx:**600-9532
(516) 482-3951 .. **Aronson,** Robin D '05 -30 Bayside Ter -Gt Neck 11023 **Fx:**482-3951
(518) 474-6800 .. **Aronson,** Saul '86 %Dept of Law -The Cptl -Albany 12224
(212) 354-6777 .. **Aronsson,** Jeffry M '78 %Oscar de la Renta -550 7th Av -NY 10018
(212) 949-6210 .. **Aronstam,** David J '85 -40 Exch Pl -NY 10005 **Fx:**689-1710
(212) 984-7748 .. **Aronstein,** Wm B '49 OfCnsl Warshaw BCS&K,LLP -555 5th Av -NY 10017
(212) 964-6611 .. **Aronwald,** Jeffrey B '92 (Lester SK&D) -120 Bway -NY 10271
(914) 946-6565 .. **Aronwald & Pykett** -81 Main -White Plns 10601 **Fx:**946-5906
(914) 946-6565 .. **Aronwald,** Wm I '66 (Aronwald & P) -81 Main -White Plns 10601
(212) 268-3580 .. **Arora,** Ajay K '95 A Arora PC -350 5th Av -NY 10118 **Fx:**268-3582
(212) 310-8000 .. **Arora,** Amanjit S '07 %Weil G&M LLP -767 5th Av -NY 10153
(212) 819-8200 .. **Arora,** Monica K '08 (White & C LLP) -1155 Av of Amer -NY 10036
(646) 471-1691 .. **Arora,** Puneet Singh '03 PricewaterhouseCoopers LLP -300 Mad Av -NY 10017
(212) 442-2715 .. **Aroubas,** Shlomit '08 %Law Dept -100 Church -NY 10007 **Fx:**788-0367
(718) 805-1271 .. **Arougheti,** Gerald '68 (Hashinsky & A) -101-05 Lefferts Blvd -S Richmond Hll 11419 **Fx:**805-1411
(212) 513-3200 .. **Arouh,** Jeffrey A '70 (Holland & K LLP) -31 W 52nd -NY 10019
(212) 764-3100 .. **Arounian,** Michl '09 %S Meissner LLC -450 7th Av -NY 10123 **Fx:**(646) 843-4964
(212) 446-4800 .. **Arovas,** Gregory S '93 (Kirkland & E LLP) -153 E 53rd -NY 10022
(212) 318-6000 .. **Arpajian,** Ralph E '84 OfCnsl Paul HJ&W LLP -75 E 55th -NY 10022
(518) 584-2200 .. **Arpey,** John W '79 (King A&A) -2911 Route 9 Bx4580 -Saratoga Spgs 12866
(631) 724-5251 .. **Arpino,** Arnold A '84 -155 E Main Bx830 -Smithtwn 11787 **Fx:**724-5527
(518) 373-9300 .. **Arquette,** Tammy J '91 -990 Route 146 -Clifton Pk 12065 **Fx:**373-9303
(212) 455-2000 .. **Arquit,** Kevin J '80 (Simpson T&B LLP) -425 Lex Av -NY 10017
(212) 655-5000 .. **Arrabito,** Marisa '02 %Gannon R&M -120 Bway -NY 10271
(212) 422-6111 .. **Arralde,** Noreen Dever '00 %Kenny S&Z -26 Bway -NY 10004
(212) 335-9000 .. **Arregui Labarca,** Daniela A '09 %DA -1 Hogan Pl -NY 10013
(212) 637-2218 .. **Arreola,** Anna E '03 %US Atty -1 St Andrews Plz -NY 10007
(718) 991-4758 .. **Arriaga,** Marisol '04 Leg Aid -953 Southrn Blvd -Bronx 10459
(718) 829-3509 .. **Arriaga-Torres,** Iris D '92 -2331 Gleason Av -Bronx 10462
(516) 295-5400 .. **Arrick,** Ronald M '74 (Jacobowitz & A) -650 Central Av Bx209 -Cedarhrst 11516
(914) 378-1010 .. **Arrieta,** Frank J '86 %Fitzgerald & F -538 Riverdale Av -Ynkrs 10705
(718) 984-5555 .. **Arrigali,** Christopher J '06 %A Alishahi,PC -3925 Hylan Blvd -Staten Isl 10308 **Fx:**984-1352
(718) 439-9200 .. **Arrigo,** Andrea M '04 -8118 13th Av -Brklyn 11228 **Fx:**921-3292
(585) 454-5650 .. **Arrington,** Lisa C '86 %Lacy K LLP -130 E Main -Rchstr 14604
(212) 732-3375 .. **Arroll,** Mark E '60 -125-10 Qns Blvd -Kew Gdns 11415
(914) 420-9307 .. **Arrospide,** Karin '01 -330 Mad Av -NY 10017
(212) 245-4580 .. **Arrow,** Allen H '54 (Shukat AHW&H,LLP) -111 W 57th -NY 10019
(212) 382-6600 .. **Arroyo,** Akira '02 %NYC Bar -42 W 44th -NY 10036 **Fx:**398-6634
(718) 624-7223 .. **Arroyo,** Armando '88 -50 Court -Brklyn 11201
(716) 879-6716 .. **Arroyo,** Corina M '99 Luvata NA,Inc -70 Sayre Bx981 -Buffalo 14240
(212) 236-6031 .. **Arroyo,** David E '98 Merril Lynch -2 World Fncl Ctr -NY 10281
(518) 464-6000 .. **Arroyo Copland,** Gloria '85 Arroyo Copland & Assoc,PLLC -300 Great Oaks Blvd -Albany 12203 **Fx:**464-6014
(212) 244-8190 .. **Arrufat Gracia,** Jose M '04 (Arrufat Gracia,PLLC) -350 5th Av -NY 10118 **Fx:**244-8193
(212) 564-7575 .. **Arschin,** Arthur N '83 -450 7th Av -NY 10123 **Fx:**564-1400
(718) 645-5947 .. **Arschin,** Leon '53 -2297 Coney Isl Av -Brklyn 11223
(212) 261-8000 .. **Arscott,** John R '80 (Mendes & M,LLP) -750 7th Av -NY 10019
(718) 643-1699 .. **Arsenakos,** Stella '85 -189 Montague -Brklyn 11201 **Fx:**404-9810
(518) 283-0373 .. **Arsenault,** Jos G '95 -20 S Lbrty Av -Wynantskill 12198
(212) 742-9280 .. **Arsenault,** Walter M '84 %Waterfront Comm -39 Bway -NY 10006 **Fx:**480-0587
(212) 582-6500 .. **Arshack,** Danl N '89 (Arshack H&L,PLLC) -1790 Bway -NY 10019
(212) 582-6500 .. **Arshack Hajek & Lehrman, PLLC** -1790 Bway -NY 10019 **Fx:**459-0568
(212) 735-8824 .. **Arsiotis,** Andrew M '86 (Morrison C LLP) -909 3rd Av -NY 10022
(212) 969-3000 .. **Arstark,** Reid Elliot '99 SrCnsl Proskauer R LLP -1585 Bway -NY 10036
(646) 386-3229 .. **Artal,** Orna Z '05 Hon C Ramos - Supreme Ct -60 Centre -NY 10007
(845) 352-0400 .. **Artale,** Louis J '63 -500 Chestnut Rdg Rd -Chestnut Rdg 10977 **Fx:**352-7568
(212) 455-2000 .. **Arteaga,** Juan A '03 %Simpson T&B LLP -425 Lex Av -NY 10017
(212) 697-6200 .. **Arteficio,** Enrico G '90 (Burke S&A,LLP) -370 Lex Av -NY 10017
(917) 626-6932 .. **Artel,** Craig A '00 -345 E 56th -NY 10022
(315) 443-2524 .. **Arterian,** Hannah R '74 Syracuse Univ Cllg of Law -Wht Hall -Syracuse 13244 **Fx:**443-4213
(212) 278-1246 .. **Artese,** Dennis J '03 %Anderson K&O,PC -1251 Av of Amer -NY 10020
(718) 250-2000 .. **Artese,** Lauren P '09 %DA -350 Jay -Brklyn 11201 **Fx:**250-2314
(718) 838-7878 .. **Arthur,** Brian G '05 Bronx Defenders -860 Crtlandt Av -Bronx 10451 **Fx:**665-0100
(212) 626-4100 .. **Arthur,** Brian P '09 %Baker & M LLP -1114 Av of Amer -NY 10036
(315) 798-5870 .. **Arthur,** David L '79 %Pub Def -321 Main -Utica 13501 **Fx:**798-6419
(518) 463-3200 .. **Arthur,** Gloria Herron '86 %NYS Bar Assn -1 Elk -Albany 12207 **Fx:**487-5544
(212) 902-1000 .. **Arthur,** Jacqueline Dupree '04 Goldman Sachs -32 Old Slip -NY 10005
(212) 735-3000 .. **Arthur,** Katherine F '08 %Skadden ASM&F LLP -4 Times Sq -NY 10036
(718) 376-4766 .. **Arthur,** Kent D '04 %Bukh & Assoc -1123 Av Z -Brklyn 11235 **Fx:**376-3033
(516) 248-1700 .. **Arthur,** Warren S '74 (Forchelli CDSM&T,LLP) -333 Earle Ovngton Blvd -Uniondale 11553
(212) 661-5030 .. **Artis,** Marvin A '96 (Schoeman U&K,LLP) -60 E 42nd -NY 10165
(607) 763-9200 .. **Artman,** John F '72 OfCnsl Levene G&T,LLP -BxF-1706 -Bnghmtn 13902
(718) 545-3614 .. **Artman,** Maureen '03 %Pappas & P -33-20 Bway -Astoria 11106 **Fx:**726-6545
(212) 250-2500 .. **Artmann,** Christian K '04 %Deutsche Bank -60 Wall -NY 10005
(845) 398-0361 .. **Artrip,** Jos J '04 %K Mulhearn,PC -60 Dutch Hill Rd -Orangebrg 10962 **Fx:**398-3836
(631) 880-7030 .. **Artukmac,** Emrah '01 -3239 Route 112 -Medfrd 11763
(631) 226-2100 .. **Artura,** Richd F '85 (Phillips WAC&M) -165 S Wellwood Av -Lindenhrst 11757
(914) 271-4849 .. **Arturo,** Lawr E '05 -80 Hastings Av -Croton-On-Hud 10520
(631) 761-7000 .. **Artusio,** Marianne '71 %Touro Cllg Law Ctr -225 Eastvw Dr -Central Islip 11722
(718) 928-3700 .. **Artz,** Alexander H '10 LSNYC-Bronx -579 Courtlandt Av -Bronx 10451 **Fx:**402-7586
(607) 772-6070 .. **Artz,** Philip J '82 (McDonough & A,PC) -89 Court Bx1740 -Bnghmtn 13902
(718) 879-8888 .. **Arulin,** Lubov '95 -2610 E 18th -Brklyn 11235
(718) 525-8823 .. **Aruti,** Ike '91 -257-37 149th Rd -Rosedale 11422
(718) 606-6570 .. **Arvanitakis,** Katerina '07 -4802 25th Av -Astoria 11103
(212) 816-6002 .. **Arvanitis,** Kyriakos G '03 Citigroup -388 Greenwich -NY 10013
(631) 942-6138 .. **Arvelo,** Adaline M '06 -166 E 11th -Huntngtn Sta 11746
(631) 673-3629 .. **Arweiler,** John E '72 -79 Green -Huntngtn 11743 **Fx:**385-1573
(212) 408-5100 .. **Aryani,** Lara G '09 %Chadbourne & P LLP -30 Rckfllr Plz -NY 10112
(212) 732-4992 .. **Arye,** Leonard A '50 OfCnsl Arye L&S,PC -20 Vesey -NY 10007
(212) 732-4992 .. **Arye Lustig & Sassower,PC** -20 Vesey -NY 10007 **Fx:**385-0875
(718) 261-0210 .. **Aryeh,** Elazar '92 (E Aryeh PC) -110-20 71st Rd -Frst Hlls 11375 **Fx:**261-2981
(212) 416-8633 .. **Arz,** Roderick L '06 %Dept of Law -120 Bway -NY 10271
(516) 364-7900 .. **Arzberger,** Christopher M '08 %Epstein F&G -45 Crsswys Park Dr W -Woodbury 11797
(718) 996-5600 .. **Arze,** Gerald G '01 (Arze & M,LLP) -2352 80th -Brklyn 11214 **Fx:**996-5800
(212) 318-6000 .. **Arzon,** Robin A '07 %Paul HJ&W LLP -75 E 55th -NY 10022
(212) 696-1469 .. **Arzoomanian,** Karekin '64 -50 E 42nd -NY 10017 **Fx:**779-4732
(516) 747-1136 .. **Arzt,** Jonathan J '98 Steinberg FB&F,PC -40 Crsswys Park Dr -Woodbury 11797
(212) 264-8819 .. **Arzt,** Robin J '79 SSA-ODAR -26 Fed Plz -NY 10278
(914) 668-4600 .. **Arzu,** Leticia '08 %Bozeman Law Firm,LLP -6 Gramatan Av -Mt Vernon 10550 **Fx:**668-4721
(212) 830-2000 .. **Arzuaga,** Danl J '90 EMI Music Pub -75 9th Av -NY 10011
(212) 848-4000 .. **Asaad,** Danielle '10 %Shearman & S LLP -599 Lex Av -NY 10022
(212) 388-3600 .. **Asad,** Eyad '00 %32B-J Leg Srvcs -101 Av of Amer -NY 10013 **Fx:**388-3061
(518) 565-4403 .. **Asadourian,** Amy '92 %Family Ct -137 Margaret -Plattsbrgh 12901 **Fx:**565-4688
(518) 561-4400 .. **Asadourian,** Ara '63 OfCnsl Stafford OC&T,PLLC -1 Cumberland Av Bx2947 -Plattsbrgh 12901
(585) 546-7620 .. **Asandrov,** Louis '84 -159 S Fitzhugh -Rchstr 14608
(212) 259-8000 .. **Asare,** Akua A '09 %Dewey & L LLP -1301 Av of Amer -NY 10019
(646) 358-8509 .. **Asaro,** Catherine Ann '98 Beecher Carlson -7 Times Sq -NY 10036
(212) 872-1000 .. **Asaro,** Michl A '99 -One Bryant Park -NY 10036 **Fx:**872-1002
(518) 689-1416 .. **Asaro,** Tricia A '98 (Greenberg T,LLP) -54 State -Albany 12207
(212) 751-8000 .. **Asaro Lawrence,** Bridget '86 OfCnsl Dankner & M,PC -41 E 57th -NY 10022
(631) 283-0046 .. **Asato,** Mary Jane '85 (Bourke F&A PC) -21 S Main -Southampton 11968
(212) 351-4000 .. **Asay,** Alma S '06 %Gibson D&C LLP -200 Park Av -NY 10166
(212) 708-3463 .. **Asbell,** Matthew D '08 %Ladas & P -26 W 61st -NY 10023
(518) 465-0400 .. **Ascenzo,** Maria Dracker '04 %O'Connor OB&F,PC -20 Corp Wds Blvd -Albany 12211
(212) 681-2535 .. **Asch,** Ian H '99 %Greenberg & S,PC -275 Mad Av -NY 10016
(212) 279-0757 .. **Asch,** Rosalind E '85 -481 8th Av -NY 10001
(212) 809-4500 .. **Asche,** Richd M '67 (Litman A&G,LLP) -140 Bway -NY 10005
(212) 949-9022 .. **Aschen,** Michl '85 (Abelman F&S) -666 3rd Av -NY 10017
(212) 294-6700 .. **Aschenbrand,** Jason S '99 %Winston & S -200 Park Av -NY 10166
(212) 693-0085 .. **Ascher,** Alexis A '01 %Appellate Advocates -2 Rector -NY 10006 **Fx:**693-0878
(212) 969-3000 .. **Ascher,** Andrea D '78 (Proskauer R LLP) -1585 Bway -NY 10036
(212) 426-3000 .. **Ascher,** Ann R '06 Leg Aid-HCLO -230 E 106th -NY 10029
(212) 351-4000 .. **Ascher,** Brian C '10 %Gibson D&C LLP -200 Park Av -NY 10166
(212) 335-9000 .. **Ascher,** Craig A '98 %DA -1 Hogan Pl -NY 10013
(212) 964-1515 .. **Ascher,** David M '93 -150 Bway -NY 10038 **Fx:**240-0365
(845) 352-4080 .. **Ascher,** David M '03 %Barr P & Assoc PLLC -664 Chestnut Rdg Rd Bx664 -Spg Vly 10977 **Fx:**352-6777
(917) 368-8200 .. **Ascher,** Paul B '70 -405 Lex Av -NY 10174
(212) 902-0901 .. **Ascher,** Rachel '90 %Goldman Sachs -1 NY Plz -NY 10004
(212) 891-1600 .. **Ascher,** Stephen L '93 (Jenner & B LLP) -919 3rd Av -NY 10022
(718) 275-7663 .. **Ascher,** Steven A '75 -67-66 108th -Frst Hlls 11375
(718) 490-3392 .. **Ascher,** Suzanne A '00 -88 New Dorp Plz -Staten Isl 10306
(212) 770-6502 .. **Aschheim,** Deborah S '82 %AIG -70 Pine -NY 10270
(212) 752-1000 .. **Aschkenasy,** Eric '03 %Eiseman LL&K,PC -805 3rd Av -NY 10022
(212) 422-1500 .. **Aschkenasy,** Jacob '57 OfCnsl Meyers TF&G LLP -14 Wall -NY 10005
(718) 595-3607 .. **Ascierto,** Greg L '92 %Water Board -59-17 Junction Blvd -Elmhrst 11373
(212) 907-0700 .. **Asciolla,** Gregory S '94 %Labaton S LLP -140 Bway -NY 10005
(516) 794-3500 .. **Ascione,** Lisa M '92 (Brunetti A&T,PLLC) -170 Old Cntry Rd -Mineola 11501 **Fx:**794-3696
(212) 761-7499 .. **Asciutto,** Steven A '96 %Morgan Stanley -1585 Bway -NY 10036
(212) 449-9930 .. **Asciutto,** Valerie '78 Merrill Lynch -4 World Fncl Ctr -NY 10080
(212) 566-0615 .. **Asekun,** Adebola O '95 -233 Bway -NY 10279
(212) 878-8000 .. **Asemota,** Osekpor '05 %Clifford C LLP -31 W 52nd -NY 10019
(212) 351-4500 .. **Asen,** Barry '74 (Epstein B&G,PC) -250 Park Av -NY 10177
(212) 768-3333 .. **Asen,** Michl Ira '74 -260 Mad Av -NY 10016 **Fx:**768-1323
(212) 613-2067 .. **Asfendis,** Paul E '00 %Gibbons PC -1 Penn Plz -NY 10119 **Fx:**554-9667
(347) 404-9133 .. **Asforis,** Evon M '96 %Civil Ct -141 Lvngstn -Brklyn 11201 **Fx:**(718) 643-3733

(212) 836-8000 .. **Asghar,** Muhammad Zafar '02 %Kaye S LLP -425 Park Av -NY 10022
(516) 932-6400 .. **Ash,** David C '77 %Sam Ash Music Corp -278 Duffy Av -Hicksvll 11801 **Fx:**931-3881
(212) 478-7200 .. **Ash,** Herbert L '65 OfCnsl Hahn & H LLP -488 Mad Av -NY 10022
(212) 940-8800 .. **Ash,** Karen Artz '81 (Katten MR LLP) -575 Mad Av -NY 10022
(212) 704-6000 .. **Ash,** Katherine Cooney '84 OfCnsl Troutman S LLP -405 Lex Av -NY 10174
(212) 670-0205 .. **Ash,** Mitchell S '92 %Merrill Lynch -220 Bway -NY 10038
(585) 454-5050 .. **Ash,** Spencer L '05 %Brown & H -2 State -Rchstr 14614
(212) 758-3500 .. **Ash,** Thos M III '86 (DeCampo D&A) -747 3rd Av -NY 10017
(212) 227-0414 .. **Ashanti,** Karl Jos '99 Law Dept -100 Church -NY 10007 **Fx:**788-0367
(718) 340-4200 .. **Ashar,** Sameer Mahendra '00 %CUNY Law Schl -65-21 Main -Flushng 11367 **Fx:**340-4482
(718) 279-2000 .. **Ashbahian,** Bruce H '89 (DeRose & S) -213-44 38th Av -Bayside 11361
(718) 279-2000 .. **Ashbahian,** Rosemarie L '99 %DeRose & S -213-44 38th Av -Bayside 11361
(646) 610-5400 .. **Ashbery,** Krista L '07 %NYPD -1 Police Plz -NY 10038
(866) 348-5819 .. **Ashby,** Douglas G '90 %SSA-ODAR -50 Fountain Plz -Buffalo 14202 **Fx:**(716) 551-4078
(212) 530-5000 .. **Ashby,** Kevin M '04 %Milbank TH&M LLP -1 Chase Manh Plz -NY 10005
(212) 454-7353 .. **Ashby,** Lynette D '04 %Deutsche Bank -60 Wall -NY 10005
(212) 903-9000 .. **Ashby,** Patrick C '08 %Linklaters -1345 Av of Amer -NY 10105
(212) 655-3500 .. **Ashby,** Stacey M '05 %Meister S&F LLP -140 E 45th -NY 10017
(585) 442-0540 .. **Ashcraft Franklin Young & Peters, LLP** -150 Allens Crk Rd -Rchstr 14618 **Fx:**442-6889
(585) 442-0540 .. **Ashcraft,** Sara Stout '96 (Ashcraft FY&P,LLP) -150 Allens Crk Rd -Rchstr 14618
(518) 885-2263 .. **Ashdown,** Jesse '00 %DA -25 W High -Ballston Spa 12020 **Fx:**884-8627
(518) 220-1850 .. **Ashdown,** Kristen L '00 %Schmeiser O&W -22 Century Hill Dr -Latham 12110
(718) 777-9595 .. **Ashe,** Adam S '93 %A Morgenstern -40-17 Bway Bx3223 -Astoria 11103
(518) 439-6713 .. **Ashe,** Bernard F '71 -7 Bedford Ct -Delmar 12054 **Fx:**439-3279
(212) 336-2000 .. **Ashe,** Danl P '08 %Patterson BW&T LLP -1133 Av of Amer -NY 10036
(914) 332-0700 .. **Ashe,** Patricia '93 %M Pollack -150 Wht Plns Rd -Tarrytwn 10591 **Fx:**684-6069
(518) 473-3233 .. **Asheld,** Barbara A '78 %Dept of Health -Corning Twr 24th Fl -Albany 12237 **Fx:**473-2019
(212) 453-5900 .. **Ashendorf,** Jeffrey S '75 (Ford & H LLP) -100 Park Av -NY 10017
(212) 258-8373 .. **Ashendorf,** Sondra Wexner '85 %MTV Networks -1515 Bway -NY 10036 **Fx:**258-8358
(212) 964-1200 .. **Asher,** Alan '66 -225 Bway -NY 10007 **Fx:**964-0444
(212) 277-4100 .. **Asher,** Amber A '03 Morgans Hotel Grp -475 10th Av -NY 10018
(212) 308-7171 .. **Asher,** Carlton R Jr. '69 OfCnsl Greenberg F LLP -110 E 59th -NY 10022 **Fx:**223-4912
(212) 553-8736 .. **Asher,** Gary P '78 %Cohen K & Assoc -2 Park Av -NY 10016 **Fx:**553-8721
(212) 649-2000 .. **Asher,** James M '75 %Hearst Corp -300 W 57th -NY 10019 **Fx:**649-2035
(212) 779-9910 .. **Asher,** Jeffrey A '97 (Eaton & V LLP) -3 Park Av -NY 10016
(212) 829-4816 .. **Asher,** Jos M '00 %Cantor Fitzgerald -110 E 59th -NY 10022
(212) 209-4800 .. **Asher,** Kenneth R '69 (Brown R LLP) -7 Times Sq -NY 10036
(212) 547-5400 .. **Asher,** Monica S '09 %McDermott W&E LLP -340 Mad Av -NY 10173
(914) 232-0934 .. **Asher,** Rachel S '90 (Asher G LLP) -223 Katonah Av -Katonah 10536 **Fx:**232-1144
(212) 697-2950 .. **Asher,** Robt S '64 -295 Mad Av -NY 10017 **Fx:**685-6862
(212) 227-5000 .. **Asher,** Roberta D '83 (Asher & Assoc,PC) -111 John -NY 10038 **Fx:**227-7117
(212) 227-5000 .. **Asher,** Ryan H '99 %Asher & Assoc,PC -111 John -NY 10038 **Fx:**227-7117
(212) 687-3000 .. **Asher,** Sanford S '70 (Jaffe & A,LLP) -600 3rd Av -NY 10016
(212) 450-4000 .. **Ashfaq,** Sarah '09 %Davis P&W LLP -450 Lex Av -NY 10017
(315) 423-1111 .. **Ashford,** Robt H A '80 %Syracuse Univ Cllg of Law -Wht Hall -Syracuse 13244 **Fx:**443-4213
(718) 222-2343 .. **Ashford,** Shannon R '09 %Law Dept -350 Jay -Brklyn 11201 **Fx:**222-2373
(212) 768-6700 .. **Ashinoff,** Reid L '74 (Sonnenschein N&R LLP) -1221 Av of Amer -NY 10020
(212) 909-6000 .. **Ashiru,** Oladipo M '08 %Debevoise & P LLP -919 3rd Av -NY 10022
(212) 458-5838 .. **Ashjian,** Tamara Madenlian '05 AIG Domestic Claims -175 Water -NY 10038
(212) 318-6000 .. **Ashkenazi,** Isaac S '07 %Paul HJ&W LLP -75 E 55th -NY 10022
(516) 568-1850 .. **Ashkenazy,** Hyman S '82 (Werner ZSS&A) -360 Merrick Rd -Lynbrk 11563
(212) 965-0010 .. **Ashkin,** Roberta E '79 -580 Bway -NY 10012 **Fx:**965-1301
(845) 348-3124 .. **Ashkinaze,** Alan S '04 -15 N Mill -Nyack 10960 **Fx:**358-4225
(212) 355-1724 .. **Ashley,** Bennett '81 (Janklow & A) -445 Park Av -NY 10022
(212) 449-3117 .. **Ashley,** Chase W '83 Merrill Lynch -4 World Fncl Ctr -NY 10080
(212) 258-4314 .. **Ashley,** Danl J '62 %Siemens Corp -153 E 53rd -NY 10022 **Fx:**767-0580
(212) 610-6300 .. **Ashley,** Jillian Shulman '08 %Allen & O -1221 Av of Amer -NY 10020
(212) 454-3465 .. **Ashley,** John B '96 %Deutsche Bank -60 Wall -NY 10005
(212) 798-6100 .. **Ashley,** Jonathan '92 %Fortress Invstmnt -1345 Av of Amer -NY 10105
(212) 408-5100 .. **Ashley,** Marc D '95 Cnsl Chadbourne & P LLP -30 Rckfllr Plz -NY 10112
(914) 276-2100 .. **Ashley,** Martin N '96 -268 Route 202 -Somers 10589
(212) 513-1300 .. **Ashley,** Mitchel H '94 Ashley Law Firm -100 William -NY 10038 **Fx:**385-1916
(914) 690-0070 .. **Ashley,** Perry '64 -211 S Ridge -Rye Brook 10573 **Fx:**690-0074
(212) 326-3939 .. **Ashley,** Robt da Silva '07 %Jones D -222 E 41st -NY 10017
(212) 848-4000 .. **Ashley,** Stephen C '05 %Shearman & S LLP -599 Lex Av -NY 10022
(516) 873-1902 .. **Ashman,** Emily R '09 %Morici & M -1399 Franklin Av -Gdn Cty 11530 **Fx:**873-3948
(212) 588-0880 .. **Ashman,** Richd A '90 %Michelstein & Assoc -485 Mad Av -NY 10022 **Fx:**588-0811
(212) 716-3940 .. **Ashman,** Vivienne M C '97 %Amer Arbtrtn Assn -1633 Bway -NY 10019 **Fx:**716-5902
(212) 574-1200 .. **Ashmead,** John R '91 (Seward & K LLP) -1 Bttry Pk Plz -NY 10004
(914) 948-1200 .. **Ashnault,** Richd W '96 %Cerussi & S,PC -1 N Lex Av -White Plns 10601
(585) 381-2021 .. **Ashnault,** Wallace F '58 (Wickins & A) -1828 Penfld Rd -Penfld 14526
(212) 969-3000 .. **Ashok,** Nima '07 %Proskauer R LLP -1585 Bway -NY 10036
(914) 864-7122 .. **Ashraf,** Michl J '06 %DA -25 Moore Av -Mt Kisco 10549
(716) 675-6300 .. **Ashton,** Christopher B '75 %Aldrich & Cox Inc -3075 Southwestern Blvd -Orchard Pk 14127 **Fx:**675-2098
(212) 309-1000 .. **Ashton,** John B '87 SrCnsl Hunton & W -200 Park Av -NY 10166
(212) 662-9904 .. **Ashton,** Robt W '65 -17 W 94th -NY 10025 **Fx:**932-0316
(212) 205-7000 .. **Ashurst LLP** -7 Times Sq -NY 10036 **Fx:**205-7020
(718) 250-2000 .. **Ashwal,** Lindsay Blake '07 %DA -350 Jay -Brklyn 11201 **Fx:**250-2314
(718) 237-2000 .. **Ashworth,** Danl S '83 %Leg Aid -111 Lvngstn -Brklyn 11201 **Fx:**237-8737
(585) 248-2382 .. **Ashworth,** Harold G '50 -57 Sky Ridge Dr -Rchstr 14625
(212) 906-1200 .. **Ashworth,** Julie A '08 %Latham & W -885 3rd Av -NY 10022
(718) 365-4100 .. **Asiedu,** Reginald Danquah '91 -2432 Grnd Cncrs -Bronx 10458 **Fx:**365-5943
(518) 455-7700 .. **Asiello,** John '78 %Ct of Appls -20 Eagle -Albany 12207
(212) 506-1700 .. **Askanase,** Eric S '04 %Kasowitz BT&F LLP -1633 Bway -NY 10019
(212) 878-8000 .. **Askenazi,** Lee A '04 %Clifford C LLP -31 W 52nd -NY 10019
(212) 403-1000 .. **Asker,** Nathaniel L '06 %Wachtell LR&K -51 W 52nd -NY 10019
(718) 990-0801 .. **Askew,** Darlene '86 %Queens Pub Library -89-11 Merrick Blvd -Jamaica 11432
(212) 735-3000 .. **Askew,** Justin G '98 Cnsl Skadden ASM&F LLP -4 Times Sq -NY 10036
(718) 780-0622 .. **Askin,** Jonathan '91 %Bklyn Law Schl -250 Joralemon -Brklyn 11201 **Fx:**780-0393
(631) 666-3300 .. **Askinas,** Steven C '75 (Askinas & M) -1991 Union Blvd -Bay Shr 11706 **Fx:**666-3392
(212) 849-7000 .. **Aslam,** Jehan '07 %Quinn EU&S,LLP -51 Mad Av -NY 10010
(212) 586-5100 .. **Aslan,** Donald B '71 %Wm Morris Agency -1325 Av of Amer -NY 10019 **Fx:**903-1473
(212) 906-1200 .. **Aslani-Far,** M Adel '97 (Latham & W) -885 3rd Av -NY 10022
(212) 702-0900 .. **Aslanova,** Kamilla '08 %Axelrod F&D -260 Mad Av -NY 10016 **Fx:**355-7365
(212) 667-4601 .. **Asman,** Matthew R '95 CIBC -300 Mad Av -NY 10017
(770) 391-0215 .. **Asman,** Sanford J '73 -52 Landfld Av -Monticello 12701 **Fx:**668-9144
(212) 736-4202 .. **Asmar,** Roger '06 (Ross & A LLC) -270 Mad Av -NY 10016 **Fx:**736-2873
(518) 387-4007 .. **Asmus,** Scott J '98 GE Global Research Cntr -1 Rsrch Cir -Schnctdy 12309
(516) 312-8249 .. **Asnen,** Neil E '10 -47 Shelter Hill Rd -Plainvw 11803
(212) 819-8200 .. **Asner,** Karen M '95 (White & C LLP) -1155 Av of Amer -NY 10036
(212) 715-1000 .. **Asner,** Marcus A '94 (Arnold & P LLP) -399 Park Av -NY 10022
(315) 866-8788 .. **Asnoe,** Jacquelyn M '81 -410 N Main Bx527 -Herkimer 13350 **Fx:**866-7132
(516) 377-9656 .. **Asonye,** Ngozi R '00 (Asonye & A,LLP) -121 Church -Freeprt 11520 **Fx:**377-0563
(516) 377-9656 .. **Asonye,** Nkwa '96 (Asonye & A,LLP) -121 Church -Freeprt 11520 **Fx:**377-0563
(914) 225-1000 .. **Aspen,** Andrew J '03 Morgan Stanley -2000 Wstchstr Av -Purchase 10577
(718) 588-1110 .. **Aspinall,** Michl H '86 (Aspinall & C) -177 E 161st -Bronx 10451 **Fx:**588-1294
(212) 858-2646 .. **Aspis,** Harold B '79 DVB Srvc (US) LLC -609 5th Av -NY 10017 **Fx:**858-2694
(518) 745-1400 .. **Aspland,** John D Jr. '00 (FitzGerald MBF) -16 Pearl Bx2017 -Glens Fls 12801
(212) 732-2929 .. **Aspromonte,** Salvatore '80 (Dansker & A Assoc) -30 Vesey -NY 10007 **Fx:**732-8795
(212) 552-0129 .. **Assa,** Ariel '03 JP Morgan Chase -1 Chase Manh Plz -NY 10005
(212) 458-1069 .. **Assa,** Jennifer D '95 %AIG -175 Water -NY 10038
(212) 861-6251 .. **Assael,** Michl '78 -200 E 74th -NY 10021
(518) 266-9060 .. **Assaf,** Michl D '87 (Assaf & M PLLC) -427 River -Troy 12180 **Fx:**266-9064
(212) 967-3000 .. **Assaf,** Wajeb W '09 %Levine & B,PLLC -350 5th Av -NY 10118
(212) 974-8875 .. **Assail,** Peter D '84 PD Assail,LLC -162 W 56th -NY 10019 **Fx:**974-8879
(631) 474-1752 .. **Assail,** Thos F '67 (T Assail,PC) -4 Gettysburg Dr -Pt Jffrsn Sta 11776 **Fx:**721-1904
(516) 248-9880 .. **Asselta,** Jos P '93 (Agovino & A,LLP) -330 Old Cntry Rd -Mineola 11501
(212) 227-1100 .. **Assenza,** Fredk J '89 -299 Bway -NY 10007
(212) 839-5300 .. **Assi,** Elisabetta M '05 %Sidley A LLP -787 7th Av -NY 10019
(518) 374-3399 .. **Assini,** Chas J Jr. '86 (Higgins RB&C,PC) -1430 Balltown Rd -Niskayuna 12309
(518) 388-4364 .. **Assini,** Jennifer Marindin '89 %DA -612 State -Schnctdy 12305 **Fx:**388-4569
(212) 944-7654 .. **Assis,** Moshe '94 -485 7th Av -NY 10018
(212) 907-7300 .. **Assor,** Nathan E '77 (Golenbock EAB&P) -437 Mad Av -NY 10022
(914) 682-2068 .. **Assuncao,** Robt A '93 (Ansa A,LLP) -50 Main -White Plns 10606
(212) 735-8600 .. **Ast,** Jordan A '06 %Morrison C LLP -909 3rd Av -NY 10022
(212) 644-3771 .. **Ast,** Paul A '81 (Ast Assoc) -1040 1st Av -NY 10022
(212) 644-3771 .. **Ast,** Therese M '85 -315 E 56th -NY 10022 **Fx:**644-3775
(516) 229-4501 .. **Asta,** John A '92 %Russo A&T -875 Merrick Av -Westbury 11590
(212) 244-6555 .. **Asta,** Michl J '89 -450 7th Av -NY 10123 **Fx:**244-4757
(585) 325-2520 .. **Astacio,** Leticia D '07 %Leg Assistance -1 W Main -Rchstr 14614 **Fx:**325-2559
(631) 283-4449 .. **Astarita,** Colin P '98 -33 Main -Southampton 11968
(212) 509-6544 .. **Astarita,** Mark J '81 (Beam & A) -110 Wall -NY 10005
(914) 253-2000 .. **Aste,** Louis J '70 %Pepsico -700 Andrsn Hill Rd -Purchase 10577

(718) 370-2900 .. **Asterita**, Jos J '00 (Bonfiglio & A,LLC) -900 South Av -Staten Isl 10314 **Fx**:370-2910
(212) 238-4800 .. **Astle**, Jason C '07 %Landman CB&F,PC -120 Bway -NY 10271
(212) 310-8000 .. **Astorga**, Patricia '09 %Weil G&M LLP -767 5th Av -NY 10153
(212) 785-1646 .. **Astorina**, John A '62 -40 Exch Pl -NY 10005 **Fx**:482-6050
(212) 504-6000 .. **Astorina**, Salvatore N '08 %Cadwalader W&T LLP -1 World Fncl Ctr -NY 10281
(212) 728-8000 .. **Astrachan**, Gregory B '93 (Willkie F&G LLP) -787 7th Av -NY 10019
(212) 922-6883 .. **Astwood**, Kiesha T '07 Dreyfus Corp -200 Park Av -NY 10166
(607) 722-3495 .. **Aswad & Ingraham** -46 Front -Bnghmtn 13905 **Fx**:722-2566
(212) 233-5500 .. **Aswad**, Kristin Dewitt '97 %SPCC -161 William -NY 10038 **Fx**:791-2821
(607) 722-3495 .. **Aswad**, Richd N '62 (Aswad & I) -46 Front -Bnghmtn 13905
(646) 386-3828 .. **Ata**, David W '09 Hon RS Smith -780 3rd Av -NY 10017
(212) 983-1320 .. **Atadika**, Agnes C '84 (Atadika & A) -60 E 42nd -NY 10165 **Fx**:983-9167
(212) 983-1320 .. **Atadika**, Michl R '83 (Atadika & A) -60 E 42nd -NY 10165 **Fx**:983-9167
(212) 506-2500 .. **Atamian**, Jean-Marie L '86 (Mayer B LLP) -1675 Bway -NY 10019
(631) 249-4480 .. **Atanasio**, Pamela D '96 -1121 Old Walt Whitman Rd -Melvll 11747 **Fx**:249-4766
(212) 713-1249 .. **Atanasio**, Paul '81 UBS -1285 Av of Amer -NY 10019
(212) 619-8119 .. **Atar**, Nursel '05 -299 Bway -NY 10007 **Fx**:619-0652
(212) 688-8555 .. **Atassi**, Isha '07 %Fragomen DB&L LLP -7 Hanover Sq -NY 10004
(718) 262-8032 .. **Atchison**, Dorothy M '99 (Atchison & Assoc,PC) -90-25 161st -Jamaica 11432 **Fx**:262-8284
(585) 232-6500 .. **Aten**, Fred G Jr. '77 (Harter S&E LLP) -1600 Bausch & Lomb Pl -Rchstr 14604
(212) 545-1740 .. **Ateshoglou & Aiello,PC** -381 Park Av S -NY 10016 **Fx**:545-7514
(212) 545-1740 .. **Ateshoglou**, Steven D '87 (Ateshoglou & A,PC) -381 Park Av S -NY 10016
(212) 436-7516 .. **Athanasidy Moran**, Janet E '90 Deloitte & Touche,LLP -2 World Fncl Ctr -NY 10281
(315) 733-9820 .. **Athari**, Mohammed J '99 Athari & Assoc,LLC -258 Genesee -Utica 13502 **Fx**:733-9821
(718) 403-3675 .. **Atik**, David C '88 %Dept of Finance -345 Adams -Brklyn 11201 **Fx**:403-3650
(212) 506-1700 .. **Atilade**, Adedapo A '04 %Kasowitz BT&F LLP -1633 Bway -NY 10019
(718) 585-1470 .. **Atilano**, Louis '90 -730 Grnd Cncrs -Bronx 10451 **Fx**:585-1458
(212) 303-1680 .. **Atinsky**, Lawr S '98 Cnsl Ascent Biomedical Ventures -142 W 57th -NY 10019 **Fx**:752-3633
(212) 506-1700 .. **Atkin**, Israel Jack '86 (Kasowitz BT&F LLP) -1633 Bway -NY 10019
(516) 248-1700 .. **Atkins**, Douglas W '06 %Forchelli CDSM&T,LLP -333 Earle Ovngton Blvd -Uniondale 11553
(212) 850-6220 .. **Atkins**, Elizabeth '87 (Lathrop & G LC) -230 Park Av -NY 10169
(212) 684-7676 .. **Atkins**, Erwin L '67 (Atkins & S) -220 5th Av -NY 10001
(212) 748-9599 .. **Atkins**, James E '99 J Atkins,PC -228 Park Av S -NY 10003 **Fx**:419-0966
(212) 504-6000 .. **Atkins**, Lisa A '10 %Cadwalader W&T LLP -1 World Fncl Ctr -NY 10281
(212) 735-3000 .. **Atkins**, Peter A '69 (Skadden ASM&F LLP) -4 Times Sq -NY 10036
(212) 373-3000 .. **Atkins**, Robt A '88 (Paul WRW&G LLP) -1285 Av of Amer -NY 10019
(914) 481-5781 .. **Atkins**, Robt E Jr. '73 %Riad & Assoc,PC -350 Theo Fremd Av -Rye 10580 **Fx**:315-0103
(212) 557-7700 .. **Atkins**, Ronald R '59 OfCnsl Davidson D&C LLP -60 E 42nd -NY 10165
(212) 858-7706 .. **Atkins**, Sally H '98 (Slowinski A,LLP) -140 Bway PMB 46039 -NY 10005
(518) 392-4806 .. **Atkins**, Steven T '69 -5 Stever Hill Rd Bx116 -Spencertown 12165 **Fx**:392-4809
(212) 684-7676 .. **Atkins & Sussman** -220 5th Av -NY 10001 **Fx**:684-7890
(212) 728-8000 .. **Atkinson**, Adrienne '95 (Willkie F&G LLP) -787 7th Av -NY 10019
(212) 421-4100 .. **Atkinson**, Anne S '72 OfCnsl Pryor C LLP -7 Times Sq -NY 10036
(212) 705-7000 .. **Atkinson**, Christopher W '96 OfCnsl Bingham M LLP -399 Park Av -NY 10022
(212) 859-7285 .. **Atkinson**, Jerome A '97 %Fortis,Inc -1 Chase Manh Plz -NY 10005 **Fx**:859-7034
(631) 653-4804 .. **Atkinson**, Matthew R '95 Peconic Baykeeper -Bx893 -Quogue 11959
(212) 918-3000 .. **Atkinson**, Meaghan L '08 %Hogan L LLP -875 3rd Av -NY 10022
(212) 804-4200 .. **Atkinson**, Philip H '90 %Mound CW&G -One Bttry Pk Plz -NY 10004
(716) 626-1564 .. **Atkinson**, Robt C '07 %Simpson & S PLLC -5555 Main -Williamsvll 14221 **Fx**:626-0366
(516) 593-1771 .. **Atkinson**, Thos D '00 (Ledwith & A) -14 St James Pl -Lynbrk 11563 **Fx**:593-1816
(315) 797-9261 .. **Atkinson**, Thos L '79 (Getnick LA&P,LLP) -258 Genesee -Utica 13502
(212) 450-4000 .. **Atkinson-Hope**, Laura-Lee '08 %Davis P&W LLP -450 Lex Av -NY 10017
(631) 477-3700 .. **Atkinson-Loveless**, Linnea J '87 -502 Carpenter -Greenprt 11944
(914) 448-0200 .. **Atlas**, Betty L '85 (Bartlett MB&M,LLP) -81 Main -White Plns 10601
(212) 455-2000 .. **Atlas**, Chad H '08 %Simpson T&B LLP -425 Lex Av -NY 10017
(212) 545-4000 .. **Atlas**, Clifford R '86 (Jackson L LLP) -666 3rd Av -NY 10017
(315) 437-7600 .. **Atlas**, Craig M '87 (Ferrara FLB&R,PC) -5010 Campuswood Dr -E Syracuse 13057
(212) 809-2500 .. **Atlas**, David Y '89 (Hernstadt A LLP) -11 Bway -NY 10004 **Fx**:214-0307
(631) 420-1212 .. **Atlas**, Howard J '88 (HJ Atlas,PC) -125 Baylis Rd -Melvll 11747
(212) 545-4703 .. **Atlas**, Jason B '97 (Wolf HAF&H LLP) -270 Mad Av -NY 10016
(607) 255-1348 .. **Atlas**, Joel B '85 %Cornell Law Schl -Myron Taylor Hall -Ithaca 14853 **Fx**:255-7193
(212) 450-4000 .. **Atlas**, Katharine M '07 %Davis P&W LLP -450 Lex Av -NY 10017
(718) 643-3985 .. **Atlas**, Linda '75 %Hon L Martin -360 Adams -Brklyn 11201
(212) 213-9666 .. **Atlas**, Louis M '81 (L Atlas,PC) -112 Mad Av -NY 10016 **Fx**:213-9896
(212) 415-8600 .. **Atlas**, Seth J '84 (Locke LB&L LLP) -3 World Fncl Ctr -NY 10281
(516) 229-4300 .. **Atlas**, Vicki S '78 %J Bilello & Assoc -875 Merrick Av -Westbury 11590
(914) 948-5152 .. **Atnally**, Edw V '60 -99 Court -White Plns 10601 **Fx**:948-5401
(631) 344-3440 .. **Atney**, Irene '88 US Dept of Energy -53 Bell Av -Upton 11973 **Fx**:344-3444
(607) 723-9511 .. **Aton**, Angel M '02 %Coughlin & G,LLP -19 Chenango Bx2039 -Bnghmtn 13902
(914) 273-9623 .. **Attaguile**, Paul F '76 -500 Main Bx255 -Armonk 10504 **Fx**:273-4512
(212) 722-2000 .. **Atta-Mensah**, Afua A '05 %Leg Aid -230 E 106th -NY 10029 **Fx**:876-5365
(212) 839-5300 .. **Attanasio**, Lee S '89 (Sidley A LLP) -787 7th Av -NY 10019
(914) 423-1616 .. **Attanasio**, Michl M '84 -656 Ynkrs Av -Ynkrs 10704 **Fx**:931-1008
(516) 625-8027 .. **Attanasio**, Peter J '09 -13 Engineers Rd -Roslyn 11576
(212) 867-3600 .. **Attardi**, Carolyn L '93 %S Tulman -369 Lex Av -NY 10017 **Fx**:867-1914
(585) 987-2800 .. **Attardo**, Robt S '93 %Woods OG LLP -2 State -Rchstr 14614
(212) 566-6780 .. **Attarian**, Tina F '07 %D Moss & Assoc -15 Maiden Ln -NY 10038 **Fx**:766-3362
(212) 878-8000 .. **Attawar**, Adithya R '10 %Clifford C LLP -31 W 52nd -NY 10019
(716) 649-4623 .. **Attea**, Brian F '93 (Attea & A) -7202 Bstn State Rd Bx120 -N Boston 14110 **Fx**:649-2951
(716) 847-8400 .. **Attea**, Fredk G '64 (Phillips L LLP) -3400 HSBC Ctr -Buffalo 14203
(716) 855-1222 .. **Attea**, Fredk G '96 %JJ Fromen -350 Main -Buffalo 14202
(716) 649-4623 .. **Attea**, Richd J '61 (Attea & A) -7202 Bstn State Rd Bx120 -N Boston 14110 **Fx**:649-2951
(212) 819-8200 .. **Atterbury**, S Ward '93 (White & C LLP) -1155 Av of Amer -NY 10036
(516) 803-4832 .. **Atteritano**, Dominique F '00 Rainbow Media Holdings -200 Jericho Quad -Jericho 11753
(718) 692-3007 .. **Attia**, Marc '85 -1091 E 3rd -Brklyn 11230 **Fx**:338-0391
(718) 725-7347 .. **Attia**, Sally Samir '03 -125-10 Qns Blvd -Kew Gdns 11415 **Fx**:(866) 929-0726
(914) 428-7124 .. **Attias**, Amy M '84 %Fed Def of NY Inc -300 Quarropas -White Plns 10601 **Fx**:997-6872
(212) 974-2400 .. **Attie**, Jeremy M '05 %J Burstein -1790 Bway -NY 10019 **Fx**:974-2944
(718) 237-5558 .. **Attie**, Jessica '02 Leg Srvcs -105 Court -Brklyn 11201 **Fx**:855-0733
(516) 746-6166 .. **Attie**, Murray S '68 -1 Old Cntry Rd -Carle Pl 11514 **Fx**:742-6474
(516) 747-7400 .. **Attner**, Diana G '88 %Rosenberg C&B LLP -100 Grdn City Plz -Gdn Cty 11530
(212) 310-8000 .. **Atton**, Corinne E '09 %Weil G&M LLP -767 5th Av -NY 10153
(212) 735-3000 .. **Attonito**, James M '07 %Skadden ASM&F LLP -4 Times Sq -NY 10036
(631) 265-6600 .. **Attonito**, Jos R '67 -59 Lndng Av -Smithtwn 11787 **Fx**:265-6672
(212) 935-3000 .. **Attonito**, Mekhala S '07 %Mintz LCFG&P,PC -666 3rd Av -NY 10017
(212) 670-1119 .. **Atukpawu**, Akudo A '06 Merrill Lynch-Ofc of Gen Counsel -222 Bway -NY 10038
(716) 854-4300 .. **Atwater**, Richd S '80 Gross SB&G,PC -465 Main -Buffalo 14203
(914) 422-4257 .. **Atwell**, Barbara L '84 %Pace Law Schl -78 N Bway -White Plns 10603 **Fx**:422-4039
(631) 267-2067 .. **Atwell**, Del '86 -39 5th -E Hampton 11937
(518) 402-6757 .. **Atwood**, Alyson E '99 %Workers Comp Bd -20 Park -Albany 12207
(631) 277-9760 .. **Atwood**, Frederic L '57 -272 Ocean Av -Islip 11751
(585) 262-6390 .. **Atwood**, Janice M '97 (Hamberger & W) -1 S Wshngtn -Rchstr 14614
(518) 462-0300 .. **Atwood**, Lauren A '10 %Girvin & F,PC -20 Corp Wds Blvd -Albany 12211
(718) 590-3255 .. **Atzmon**, Shira J '03 %Law Dept -900 Sheridan Av -Bronx 10451 **Fx**:590-2699
(646) 429-7500 .. **Au**, Alice '90 %Macys,Inc -11 Penn Plz -NY 10001 **Fx**:429-7521
(212) 506-1761 .. **Au**, Beverly '88 Kasowitz BT&F LLP -1633 Bway -NY 10019
(212) 571-7150 .. **Au**, Chris '96 (Au & Y,PC) -401 Bway -NY 10013 **Fx**:571-7153
(845) 677-3494 .. **Aubin**, Bruce M '77 (Miller & A) -110 Church BxC -Millbrook 12545
(212) 783-4150 .. **Aubry**, Rene '07 Citi Smith Barney -485 Lex Av -NY 10017
(212) 823-3663 .. **Auchincloss**, Andrew S '90 Bernstein Global Wealth Mgmt -1345 Av of Amer -NY 10105
(212) 245-4140 .. **Auchincloss**, Edw H '57 (Auchincloss & Lawrence) -610 5th Av -NY 10020 **Fx**:245-3589
(212) 805-0564 .. **Audain**, Raymond '05 US Courthouse -500 Pearl -NY 10007
(212) 696-6000 .. **Audal**, Jos P '10 %Curtis M-PC&M LLP -101 Park Av -NY 10178
(212) 921-2200 .. **Audena**, Mackens P '06 Update Legal -1140 Av of Americas -NY 10036 **Fx**:354-9480
(212) 819-8200 .. **Audette**, Danielle M '09 %White & C LLP -1155 Av of Amer -NY 10036
(518) 745-4343 .. **Audette**, Danielle N '10 %Stanclift L&M,PC -3 Warren Bx358 -Glens Fls 12801 **Fx**:745-4344
(212) 225-2000 .. **Audi**, Alan K '06 %Cleary GS&H -1 Lbrty Plz -NY 10006
(315) 425-2700 .. **Audunson**, Janet M '06 OfCnsl Hiscock & B,LLP -One Park Pl -Syracuse 13202
(212) 541-2000 .. **Auerbach**, Andrew E '02 (Bryan C LLP) -1290 Av of Amer -NY 10104
(718) 624-5634 .. **Auerbach**, Barry R '59 -125-10 Qns Blvd -Kew Gdns 11415
(716) 759-9759 .. **Auerbach**, Corey A '08 %Damon M LLP -9276 Main -Clarence 14031
(212) 421-4100 .. **Auerbach**, David L '56 SrCnsl Pryor C LLP -7 Times Sq -NY 10036
(212) 506-1700 .. **Auerbach**, Gregory J '05 Kasowitz BT&F LLP -1633 Bway -NY 10019
(212) 459-7894 .. **Auerbach**, Jacqueline A '85 %Dept of Tax & Fin -1740 Bway -NY 10019 **Fx**:459-7897
(212) 909-6000 .. **Auerbach**, Jason A '09 %Debevoise & P LLP -919 3rd Av -NY 10022
(212) 813-8800 .. **Auerbach**, Jonathan A '09 %Goodwin P LLP -620 8th Av -NY 10018
(516) 228-1300 .. **Auerbach**, Kenneth '77 (Sahn WC&B,PLLC) -333 Earle Ovngton Blvd -Uniondale 11553
(631) 654-4900 .. **Auerbach**, Kenneth A '87 (Cartier BA&D,PC) -100 Austin -Patchogue 11772
(914) 428-7171 .. **Auerbach**, Lee David '78 LD Auerbach,PC -81 Main -White Plns 10601 **Fx**:686-0168
(212) 759-3300 .. **Auerbach**, Martin '78 -747 3rd Av -NY 10017 **Fx**:753-7673
(212) 850-6100 .. **Auerbach**, Nicole A '00 %Levine SK&S,LLP -321 W 44th -NY 10036
(561) 775-2734 .. **Auerbach**, Paul I '55 -245 E 44th -NY 10017 **Fx**:694-0922

(917) 777-4200 .. **Auerbach,** Reed D '86 (Bingham M LLP) -1 Bttry Pk Plz -NY 10004

(516) 364-1095 .. **Auerbach,** Richd A '81 (McBreen & K) -500 N Bway -Jericho 11753

(212) 554-7800 .. **Auerbach,** Shira L '10 %Moses & S LLP -405 Lex Av -NY 10174

(914) 750-5933 .. **Auerbach,** Steven '97 %Kissel H&W LLP -580 Wht Plns Rd -Tarrytwn 10591

(212) 308-8505 .. **Auerbacher,** John '87 OfCnsl Akabas & S -488 Mad Av -NY 10022

(212) 506-1700 .. **Auerbach-Ziogas,** Mischa '04 %Kasowitz BT&F LLP -1633 Bway -NY 10019

(212) 720-8893 .. **Auer de Saram,** Jetsun '92 Fed Reserve Bk -33 Lbrty -NY 10045 **Fx:**720-8889

(516) 937-9800 .. **Aufenanger,** Jos A '95 ShopBistro Inc -500 N Bway -Jericho 11753

(518) 792-2117 .. **Auffredou,** Martin D '89 (Bartlett PS&R,PC) -1 Wshngtn Bx2168 -Glens Fls 12801

(212) 969-3000 .. **Aufiero-Peters,** Susan '02 %Proskauer R LLP -1585 Bway -NY 10036

(212) 557-5040 .. **Aufrichtig,** Paul S '53 OfCnsl McCarthy F LLP -747 3rd Av -NY 10017

(914) 946-3700 .. **Aufrichtig,** Peter D '84 (McCarthy F LLP) -11 Martine Av -White Plns 10606

(212) 715-9100 .. **Aufses,** Arthur H III '81 (Kramer LN&F,LLP) -1177 Av of Amer -NY 10036

(914) 397-2400 .. **Aufsesser,** Kenneth J '80 (Ferguson C,LLP) -1 N Lex Av -White Plns 10601 **Fx:**683-6956

(516) 357-3700 .. **Augello,** Cynthia A '09 %Cullen and D LLP -100 Q Roosevelt Blvd -Gdn Cty 11530

(716) 852-2500 .. **Augello & Matteliano LLP** -17 Court -Buffalo 14202 **Fx:**852-8263

(212) 268-5136 .. **Augello,** Michl A Jr. '08 %Harwood L -350 5th Av -NY 10118

(716) 852-2500 .. **Augello,** Thos R '79 (Augello & M LLP) -17 Court -Buffalo 14202

(212) 697-5550 .. **Augenbaum,** Todd H '83 %G & L Blumberg,LLP -521 5th Av -NY 10175 **Fx:**697-9570

(718) 509-9453 .. **Augenstein,** David '09 (Augenstein & S,PC) -1244 49th -Brklyn 11219 **Fx:**504-7755

(718) 298-8911 .. **Augente,** Lynda '87 %Leg Aid -153-01 Jamaica Av -Jamaica 11432 **Fx:**657-0537

(718) 625-1212 .. **Aughtry,** Dewette C '87 -68 Jay -Brklyn 11201 **Fx:**625-2236

(631) 447-5880 .. **Augi,** Craig H '99 -20 Medford Av -Patchogue 11772 **Fx:**447-6070

(212) 267-9040 .. **Augoustiniatos,** Evangelos '92 -299 Bway -NY 10007 **Fx:**732-6972

(631) 694-2400 .. **Augspach,** Enrique Francisco '05 %Hamburger MYK&M,LLP -225 Broadhllw Rd -Melvll 11747

(518) 393-5460 .. **Augspurger,** Robt B '84 -2272 Pinehaven Dr -Schnctdy 12309

(917) 817-8106 .. **August,** Brian M '87 -140 Hope -Brklyn 11211

(315) 443-1907 .. **August,** Elizabeth A '95 Syracuse Univ School of Law -267 Wht Hall -Syracuse 13210

(212) 695-8100 .. **August,** Ellen '79 (Goetz F,LLP) -1 Penn Plz -NY 10119

(716) 885-2360 .. **August,** James F '75 -744 Auburn Av -Buffalo 14222 **Fx:**885-2362

(212) 592-1400 .. **August,** John M '02 %Herrick,F LLP -2 Park Av -NY 10016

(212) 715-9100 .. **Auguste,** Christopher S '84 (Kramer LN&F,LLP) -1177 Av of Amer -NY 10036

(718) 286-2000 .. **Auguste,** Germaine '92 %Leg Aid -120-46 Qns Blvd -Kew Gdns 11415 **Fx:**286-2286

(516) 876-0800 .. **Augustin,** Hans H '05 %Druckman Law Grp PLLC -242 Drexel Av -Westbury 11590 **Fx:**876-0888

(212) 789-1500 .. **Augustin,** Nathalie A '96 Donna Karan Co -550 7th Av -NY 10018 **Fx:**789-1688

(917) 533-9251 .. **Augustine,** Edw E '01 -175 W 92nd -NY 10025 **Fx:**(212) 504-8169

(716) 853-6200 .. **Augustine,** Jos M '60 -438 Main -Buffalo 14202 **Fx:**856-3106

(212) 233-4185 .. **Augustine,** Jos P '93 (Augustine & E,LLP) -90 Broad -NY 10004 **Fx:**792-6580

(585) 454-6100 .. **Augustine,** Karanja A '01 Eltrex Industries -65 Sullivan -Rchstr 14605

(917) 842-9107 .. **Augustine,** Mark D '04 Schwartz & Feinsod Football -137 W 80th -NY 10024

(212) 609-6800 .. **Augustine,** Mary Jane '93 (McCarter & E,LLP) -245 Park Av -NY 10167

(631) 751-3285 .. **Augustine,** Peter '62 -36 Bonnie Ln -Stony Brk 11790

(631) 286-1755 .. **Augustine,** Scott B '87 -16 Station Rd Bx487 -Bellprt 11713 **Fx:**286-7041

(716) 691-3586 .. **Augustino,** Philip A '77 -656 N French Rd -Amherst 14228 **Fx:**691-3860

(718) 403-3600 .. **Augusto,** Maria '87 %Dept of Finance -345 Adams -Brklyn 11201 **Fx:**403-3650

(718) 558-4193 .. **Augustus,** Anthony '97 -89-31 161st -Jamaica 11432 **Fx:**504-4430

(718) 250-3917 .. **Aulbach,** Kevin C '07 %DA -350 Jay -Brklyn 11201 **Fx:**250-2314

(631) 473-6483 .. **Aulbach,** Philip E '77 -11 Yale -Pt Jffrsn Sta 11776 **Fx:**331-8646

(212) 319-2787 .. **Auld,** Alexei Ormani '99 VLA -1 E 53rd -NY 10022 **Fx:**752-6575

(212) 907-0700 .. **Auld,** Dominic J '99 OfCnsl Labaton S LLP -140 Bway -NY 10005

(212) 626-4100 .. **Auld,** Rekha '05 %Baker & M LLP -1114 Av of Amer -NY 10036

(718) 884-9013 .. **Auleta,** Vincent A '97 (V Auleta,PC) -3411 Irwin Av -Bronx 10463

(212) 269-7308 .. **Auletta,** Glenn E '01 %Leahey & J PC -120 Wall -NY 10005

(716) 856-5500 .. **Auletta,** Hedwig M '87 (Damon M LLP) -200 Delaware Av -Buffalo 14202

(212) 788-1357 .. **Auletta,** Steven J '08 %Law Dept -100 Church -NY 10007 **Fx:**788-0367

(212) 670-2812 .. **Auletta,** Suzanne E '91 %Merrill Lynch -220 Bway -NY 10038

(212) 935-3131 .. **Aulicino,** Jos V '00 %Gallet D&B,LLP -845 3rd Av -NY 10022

(631) 666-5766 .. **Aulivola,** Michelle '05 %Long TBSWJ&S -120 4th Av Bx5591 -Bay Shr 11706

(212) 373-3000 .. **Ault,** Saml S K '10 %Paul WRW&G LLP -1285 Av of Amer -NY 10019

(718) 446-0666 .. **Aumand,** Daria M '91 -37-06 82nd -Jcksn Hts 11372

(315) 473-0899 .. **Aumell,** Jeffrey A '02 Anelli X,PC -441 S Salina -Syracuse 13202 **Fx:**473-0530

(212) 483-9490 .. **Aumenta,** Wm Nicholas '01 OfCnsl McElroy DM&C,LLP -88 Pine -NY 10005

(212) 966-5932 .. **Aung,** Khin Mai '05 %AALDEF -99 Hudson -NY 10013 **Fx:**966-4303

(212) 688-3200 .. **Aung,** Khine Zin '08 %Scheichet & D,PC -767 3rd Av -NY 10017

(212) 788-3340 .. **Aung,** Sandra '02 Hlth & Hsptl Corp -125 Worth -NY 10013 **Fx:**267-6905

(585) 342-5681 .. **Aureli,** Danl L '78 -34 Orenda Dr -Rchstr 14622

(718) 209-4430 .. **Aurelien,** Pamela '99 -9915 Av L -Brklyn 11236

(212) 803-5705 .. **Auricchio,** Dina M '98 Bowery Residents Comm -324 Lafayette -NY 10012

(716) 675-3800 .. **Auricchio,** James F '01 Auricchio Law Firm -3800 Seneca -W Seneca 14224 **Fx:**608-4442

(315) 471-4319 .. **Auricchio,** Michl J '98 Auricchio Law Ofcs -144 Miles Av -Syracuse 13210 **Fx:**(610) 980-5873

(212) 676-0468 .. **Aurigemma,** Lisa Ann '91 %Law Dept -100 Church -NY 10007 **Fx:**788-0367

(631) 755-0101 .. **Aurilia,** Patrick '96 %Lewis JAA,LLP -425 Broad Hollow Rd -Melvll 11747

(914) 946-3700 .. **Aurnou,** Joel M '59 OfCnsl McCarthy F LLP -11 Martine Av -White Plns 10606

(914) 962-2071 .. **Auryansen,** Adrienne J '88 AEJA Inc -1795 Hunterbrook Rd -Yorktwn Hts 10598

(315) 592-4241 .. **Auser,** Wallace Van C III '76 (Sumner & A) -226 Oneida Bx549 -Fulton 13069

(631) 871-8373 .. **Ausili,** Fredrick M '03 -300 Grdn City Plz -Gdn Cty 11530

(914) 949-2700 .. **Ausili,** James T '96 OfCnsl Bleakley P&S,LLP -1 N Lex Av -White Plns 10601

(631) 712-5643 .. **Ausili,** Peter J '90 US Dist Ct -944 Fed Plz -Central Islip 11722

(212) 878-0000 .. **Auslander,** Andrew S '93 %MTA -2 Penn Plz -NY 10121

(212) 583-5609 .. **Auslander,** Dana E '99 Blackstone Grp -345 Park Av -NY 10154

(212) 421-2233 .. **Auslander,** Jay S '89 (Wilk A LLP) -675 3rd Av -NY 10017

(212) 728-8000 .. **Auslander,** Mitchell J '81 (Willkie F&G LLP) -787 7th Av -NY 10019

(212) 732-3200 .. **Auslander,** Rose '93 (Carter L&M LLP) -2 Wall -NY 10005

(212) 468-8046 .. **Auspitz,** Jack C '69 (Morrison & F LLP) -1290 Av of Amer -NY 10104

(516) 918-7823 .. **Auster,** Ellen Hostein '84 Deloitte & Touche,LLP -2 Jericho Plz -Jericho 11753

(212) 398-7900 .. **Auster,** Jay S '84 SpclCnsl Gerstein S&R LLP -57 W 38th -NY 10018

(914) 337-0700 .. **Auster,** Julie '88 %Sarah Lawrence College -1 Meadway -Bronxvll 10708

(518) 465-8085 .. **Auster,** Morris M '96 %Med Society -1 Commerce Plz -Albany 12210 **Fx:**465-0976

(845) 225-7700 .. **Auster,** Scott Y '76 -65 Highvw Dr -Carmel 10512

(212) 295-6484 .. **Austern,** Alyshea J '06 %WilmerHale -399 Park Av -NY 10022

(212) 577-2523 .. **Austern,** Bruce D '93 %Ctr for Appllt Litigation -74 Trinity Pl -NY 10006 **Fx:**577-2535

(631) 929-4541 .. **Austern,** Jonathan '89 (Austern & A PC) -2 Taconic Ct Bx558 -Wading Rvr 11792 **Fx:**929-4543

(718) 838-7878 .. **Austin,** Adrienne L '07 %Bronx Defenders -860 Crtlandt Av -Bronx 10451 **Fx:**665-0100

(212) 310-8000 .. **Austin,** Arthur Campbell '07 %Weil G&M LLP -767 5th Av -NY 10153

(212) 277-6031 .. **Austin,** Carolyn M '95 %Dickstein S LLP -1633 Bway -NY 10019 **Fx:**(917) 591-9661

(212) 590-2504 .. **Austin,** Chas E '98 -304 Park Av S -NY 10010 **Fx:**(646) 304-1901

(212) 225-2000 .. **Austin,** Christopher E '84 (Cleary GS&H) -1 Lbrty Plz -NY 10006

(718) 250-2000 .. **Austin,** Darryl E '09 %DA -350 Jay -Brklyn 11201 **Fx:**250-2314

(212) 880-9595 .. **Austin,** David C '04 %Morvillo AGIA&B,PC -565 5th Av -NY 10017

(315) 772-5261 .. **Austin,** Dwight E '88 %Ofc SJA -141 Lewis Av -Fort Drum 13602 **Fx:**772-5311

(212) 225-2000 .. **Austin,** Femi S '08 %Cleary GS&H -1 Lbrty Plz -NY 10006

(212) 460-2976 .. **Austin,** Garrett E '61 Con Ed -4 Irving Pl -NY 10003 **Fx:**260-8627

(718) 286-2000 .. **Austin,** Garrett L '99 %Leg Aid -120-46 Qns Blvd -Kew Gdns 11415 **Fx:**286-2286

(315) 471-3151 .. **Austin,** Holly Kozlowski '05 %Hancock & E,LLP -1500 AXA Twr I Bx4976 -Syracuse 13221

(518) 399-2625 .. **Austin,** Jason P '02 -928 Sacandaga Rd -Scotia 12302

(212) 251-4101 .. **Austin,** Jennifer Berkley '94 United Way -2 Park Av -NY 10016

(212) 351-4000 .. **Austin,** Jonathan B '08 %Gibson D&C LLP -200 Park Av -NY 10166

(212) 558-5330 .. **Austin,** Kenneth W '93 %Natl Urban League -120 Wall -NY 10005

(212) 610-6300 .. **Austin,** Kylene L '09 %Allen & O -1221 Av of Amer -NY 10020

(607) 277-4080 .. **Austin,** Lauren A '95 %Human Rights Comm -120 W State -Ithaca 14850

(607) 723-9511 .. **Austin,** Meiying Zhong '05 %Coughlin & G,LLP -19 Chenango Bx2039 -Bnghmtn 13902

(607) 639-2222 .. **Austin,** Meiying Zhong '05 %Coughlin & G,LLP -190 Main Bx462 -Afton 13730

(212) 969-3000 .. **Austin,** Nigel S '01 (Proskauer R LLP) -1585 Bway -NY 10036

(212) 512-2000 .. **Austin,** Terri D '84 McGraw-Hill -1221 Av of Amer -NY 10020 **Fx:**512-4827

(518) 436-1850 .. **Austin,** Timothy E '96 %Fed Pub Def -39 N Pearl -Albany 12207 **Fx:**436-1780

(212) 399-0899 .. **Austin,** Wanyong Lai '84 %LFCS -308 W 46th -NY 10036

(212) 622-4507 .. **Austin,** Wm A III '78 JP Morgan Chase -277 Park Av -NY 10172

(212) 360-4259 .. **Austrian,** Sarah G '85 Guggenheim Fndtn -345 Hudson -NY 10014

(718) 991-4600 .. **Austrie,** Elenor W '00 Leg Aid -953 Southrn Blvd -Bronx 10459 **Fx:**842-2867

(212) 859-8000 .. **Ausubel,** Marvin V '51 OfCnsl Fried FHS&J LLP -1 NY Plz -NY 10004

(212) 504-6000 .. **Auth,** Dorothy R '97 (Cadwalader W&T LLP) -1 World Fncl Ctr -NY 10281

(212) 277-1500 .. **Auth,** Thos P '96 One Equity Prtnrs LLC -320 Park Av -NY 10022

(718) 250-0400 .. **Autovino,** Benjamin '91 %R Tusa -1 MetroTech Ctr -Brklyn 11201 **Fx:**250-0591

(212) 765-5070 .. **Autuoro,** Michl F '05 %Fish & R,PC -153 E 53rd -NY 10022

(212) 218-2100 .. **Autz,** Will C '08 %Fitzpatrick CH&S -1290 Av of Amer -NY 10104

(718) 250-1400 .. **Auyeung,** Yvette Y W '95 %BZ Green -12 MetroTech Ctr -Brklyn 11201 **Fx:**250-1401

(212) 230-8845 .. **Avakian,** Stephanie '96 (WilmerHale) -399 Park Av -NY 10022

(212) 696-1760 .. **Avallone,** Albert J '79 -551 5th Av -NY 10176

(212) 373-3000 .. **Avallone,** Lauraine F '97 Paul WRW&G LLP -1285 Av of Amer -NY 10019

(914) 337-4400 .. **Avallone,** Michl '84 Bartech Abstract Srvcs -271 Main -Eastchstr 10709 **Fx:**337-6505

(631) 755-0101 .. **Avallone,** Robt J '80 (Lewis JAA,LLP) -425 Broad Hollow Rd -Melvll 11747

(516) 358-1700 .. **Avallone,** Rocco G '90 %Cronin & B,LLP -1983 Marcus Av -Lk Success 11042

(516) 829-0363 .. **Avalone,** Nancy Kramer '03 %Israel I&P,LLP -11 Grace Av -Gt Neck 11021 **Fx:**829-0366
(650) 614-7400 .. **Avalos,** Julio C '07 %Orrick H&S LLP -51 W 52nd -NY 10019 **Fx:**614-7401
(718) 802-1616 .. **Avanzino,** John K '84 (Avanzino & M,PC) -26 Court -Brklyn 11242 **Fx:**802-0189
(516) 681-1100 .. **Avdeychik,** Vadim '08 %Kaufman DV&G,LLP -135 Crsswys Park Dr -Woodbury 11797
(212) 687-8360 .. **Avedisian,** Craig '94 -60 E 42nd -NY 10165 **Fx:**(646) 213-3209
(212) 903-9000 .. **Avedissian,** Grace K '04 %Linklaters -1345 Av of Amer -NY 10105
(212) 732-9500 .. **Avelino,** A Jude '96 (Avelino N LLP) -225 Bway -NY 10007 **Fx:**732-4580
(516) 354-3346 .. **Avella,** Alexander A Jr. '68 -236 Fulton Av -Hempstd 11550 **Fx:**565-3029
(516) 496-5822 .. **Avella,** Erica '05 %T Spina -170 Froehlich Farm Blvd -Woodbury 11797 **Fx:**496-5420
(518) 455-2577 .. **Avella,** Michl A '90 %Senate Majority Cnsl -430 The Cptl -Albany 12247
(914) 798-9912 .. **Avella,** Terence M '02 Grant McCarthy Grp LLC -777 Wstchstr Av -White Plns 10604
(212) 223-0400 .. **Avellino,** John T '74 (Zeichner E&K LLP) -575 Lex Av -NY 10022
(212) 787-1275 .. **Avellone,** Anne C '81 -60 W 66th -NY 10023
(516) 393-2200 .. **Avena,** Suzanne M '95 Cnsl Garfunkel W,PC -111 Grt Nck Rd -Gt Neck 11021
(518) 473-5115 .. **Aveni,** John J '78 %Ofc for Technology -State Cptl ESP Bx2062 -Albany 12220
(518) 402-6969 .. **Avent,** Judith A '79 %Envrnmtl Facilities -625 Bway -Albany 12207 **Fx:**402-6972
(518) 427-2650 .. **Avent,** Michl T '09 %Nixon P LLP -677 Bway -Albany 12207
(914) 946-4777 .. **Aventuro,** Christopher J '95 OfCnsl Keane & B,PC -445 Hmltn Av -White Plns 10601
(212) 596-9000 .. **Averbug,** Flavio '09 %Ropes & G LLP -1211 Av of Amer -NY 10036
(212) 521-5400 .. **Averett,** Jill N '07 %Reed S LLP -599 Lex Av -NY 10022
(212) 504-6000 .. **Avergun,** Jodi Levine '88 (Cadwalader W&T LLP) -1 World Fncl Ctr -NY 10281
(212) 245-7300 .. **Averill,** Craig E '95 Serling R&F,LLP -119 5th Av -NY 10003
(516) 227-6300 .. **Averna,** Raymond J '86 (Ettelman & H,PC) -100 Q Roosevelt Blvd -Gdn Cty 11530
(716) 285-8825 .. **Aversa,** John M '81 -625 6th -Niagara Fls 14301 **Fx:**285-2313
(914) 946-3700 .. **Aversano,** Dina M '08 %McCarthy F LLP -11 Martine Av -White Plns 10606
(212) 715-1000 .. **Avery,** Alan W '99 (Arnold & P LLP) -399 Park Av -NY 10022
(518) 437-8300 .. **Avery,** Amanda A '03 Capital Dist Trans Auth -110 Watervliet Av -Albany 12206
(315) 357-6173 .. **Avery,** Chas W '47 -South Shore Rd Bx286 -Inlet 13360 **Fx:**357-3376
(716) 645-2074 .. **Avery,** Dianne '83 %SUNY Buffalo Lw Schl -O'Brian Hall -Buffalo 14260 **Fx:**645-5968
(914) 921-1352 .. **Avery,** Edw W Jr. '80 -495 Milton Rd -Rye 10580
(718) 444-4575 .. **Avery,** Elaine N '96 (Avery & A,PC) -5005 Av M -Brklyn 11234 **Fx:**444-7645
(607) 763-9200 .. **Avery,** Holly L '07 %Levene G&T,LLP -BxF-1706 -Bnghmtn 13902
(718) 590-7181 .. **Avery,** Patricia B '82 %Hon P Benitez -851 Grand Cncrs -Bronx 10451
(212) 759-4600 .. **Avery,** Patricia I '77 (Wolf P LLP) -845 3rd Av -NY 10022
(315) 218-8000 .. **Avery,** Paul J '06 %Bond S&K,PLLC -1 Lincoln Ctr -Syracuse 13202
(718) 262-7100 .. **Avery,** Susan '92 %Civil Ct -89-17 Sutphin Blvd -Jamaica 11435 **Fx:**262-7107
(718) 260-8186 .. **Averyhart,** Lisa Chrishon '96 -244 5th Av -NY 10001
(212) 756-3250 .. **Avicolli,** Anthony '98 1st Manhattan Co -437 Mad Av -NY 10022
(212) 218-6774 .. **Avicolli,** Jennifer A '01 Union Bancaire Privee -30 Rckfllr Plz -NY 10112
(212) 554-7800 .. **Avidon,** Michl E '81 (Moses & S LLP) -405 Lex Av -NY 10174
(518) 696-5268 .. **Avigdor,** David B '86 -8 Schl Bx159 -Lk Luzerne 12846 **Fx:**696-4515
(212) 541-2000 .. **Avigliano,** Chas M '02 %Bryan C LLP -1290 Av of Amer -NY 10104
(914) 323-7000 .. **Avila,** Allyson A '02 %Wilson EME&D LLP -3 Gannett Dr -White Plns 10604
(212) 506-2500 .. **Avila,** David A '09 %Mayer B LLP -1675 Bway -NY 10019
(212) 771-0505 .. **Avila,** Fredk A '91 CIT -505 5th Av -NY 10017
(212) 788-3300 .. **Aviles,** Alan D '78 %Hlth & Hsptl Corp -125 Worth -NY 10013 **Fx:**267-6905
(212) 460-3121 .. **Aviles,** Alexander C '92 ConEd Law Dept -4 Irving Pl -NY 10003
(631) 369-7600 .. **Aviles,** Deborah A '82 (Lewis JAA,LLP) -21 E 2nd -Rvrhead 11901
(800) 225-5224 .. **Aviles,** Elizabeth '08 CA Inc -One CA Plz -Islandia 11749
(212) 307-0023 .. **Aviles,** Michl J '99 (DeSimone AS&O LLP) -145 Hudson -NY 10013
(718) 403-4334 .. **Aviles,** Nelson '86 %Dept of Finance -345 Adams -Brklyn 11201
(718) 250-2000 .. **Avin,** Claudia '04 %DA -350 Jay -Brklyn 11201 **Fx:**250-2314
(212) 935-3000 .. **Avini,** Avisheh '96 %Mintz LCFG&P,PC -666 3rd Av -NY 10017
(716) 551-5755 .. **Avino,** Louis F Jr. '84 %HUD -465 Main -Buffalo 14203 **Fx:**551-5752
(212) 506-1700 .. **Avins,** Jon '01 %Kasowitz BT&F LLP -1633 Bway -NY 10019
(516) 572-2000 .. **Aviram,** Jesse M '08 %DA -99 Main -Hempstd 11550 **Fx:**572-2606
(212) 747-8787 .. **Avirom,** Jonathan E '63 (J Avirom & Assoc) -42 Bway -NY 10004
(212) 284-7131 .. **Avitabile,** Alex S '83 Enterprise Community Partners,Inc -1 Whitehall -NY 10004 **Fx:**262-9635
(212) 259-8000 .. **Avitabile,** Scott D '95 (Dewey & L LLP) -1301 Av of Amer -NY 10019
(518) 459-7911 .. **Avner,** Judith I '85 %Brain Injury Assn NYS -10 Colvin Av -Albany 12206
(212) 400-7151 .. **Avola,** Melyssa A Clevenger '07 (Avola & Assoc) -40 Wall -NY 10005 **Fx:**(626) 628-0436
(212) 696-6000 .. **Avram,** Dario D '08 %Curtis M-PC&M LLP -101 Park Av -NY 10178
(212) 613-5000 .. **Avrasina,** Olga '98 %Leg Assist Grp -450 W 33rd -NY 10001 **Fx:**750-0820
(212) 504-6000 .. **Avrutin,** Rebecca L '10 %Cadwalader W&T LLP -1 World Fncl Ctr -NY 10281
(516) 677-9400 .. **Avrutine,** Howard D '83 (Goldstein & A) -575 Underhill Blvd -Syosset 11791
(914) 874-2500 .. **Avrutova,** Zina '04 Sanford-Brown Institute -333 Wstchstr Av -White Plns 10604
(607) 687-1000 .. **Awad,** George C Jr. '82 -171 Main Bx507 -Owego 13827 **Fx:**687-6075
(516) 832-7777 .. **Awad,** Jos P '82 (Silberstein A&M,PC) -600 Old Cntry Rd -Gdn Cty 11530
(212) 698-3500 .. **Awad,** Mona S '10 %Dechert LLP -1095 Av of Amer -NY 10036
(516) 365-9191 .. **Awad,** Thos C '83 %S Friedman -1 Hllw Ln -New Hyde Pk 11042 **Fx:**365-6138
(212) 541-2000 .. **Awerdick,** Megan E '09 %Bryan C LLP -1290 Av of Amer -NY 10104
(212) 352-3430 .. **Awoyinfa,** Obayomi A '00 -27 Union Sq W -NY 10003
(800) 877-1373 .. **Awuku,** Ramseyer Hayford '04 %Workers Comp Bd -168-46 91st Av -Jamaica 11432
(212) 334-8725 .. **Axel,** Blair '80 Benjamin Prtnrs,Inc -589 Bway -NY 10012
(212) 732-8700 .. **Axel,** Ilyssa J '05 %McAloon & F,PC -123 William -NY 10038
(212) 686-3838 .. **Axelrad,** Alexis S '98 (Barst M&K LLP) -2 Park Av -NY 10016
(516) 496-5822 .. **Axelrad,** Danielle R '02 %T Spina -170 Froehlich Farm Blvd -Woodbury 11797 **Fx:**496-5420
(845) 566-5345 .. **Axelrod,** Alan J '74 (Larkin Al&T,LLP) -356 Meadow Av -Newburgh 12550
(212) 577-3688 .. **Axelrod,** Alan S '77 %Leg Aid -199 Water -NY 10038 **Fx:**509-8431
(516) 623-8800 .. **Axelrod,** Andrew R '87 %Love & Quiches -178 Hanse Av -Freeprt 11520 **Fx:**623-8817
(212) 869-6979 .. **Axelrod,** Chas F '72 -36 W 44th -NY 10036 **Fx:**997-3985
(518) 213-6000 .. **Axelrod,** Janet R '63 NYSUT -800 Troy-Schnctdy Rd -Latham 12110 **Fx:**213-6488
(516) 681-5359 .. **Axelrod,** Kenneth '78 -28 Pasadena Dr -Plainvw 11803
(212) 676-1361 .. **Axelrod,** Lauren Grant '05 City Cncl Gen Cnsl -250 Bway -NY 10007
(212) 651-7500 .. **Axelrod,** Madina Y '03 %Segal MS&M -850 3rd Av -NY 10022
(212) 315-5575 .. **Axelrod,** Margaret G '78 %Muchnick G&G,PC -200 Park Av S -NY 10003
(516) 296-7000 .. **Axelrod,** Michl C '74 (Certilman BA&H,LLP) -90 Merrick Av -E Meadow 11554
(718) 935-5849 .. **Axelrod,** Neil S '98 Dept Of Educ -65 Court -Brklyn 11201
(212) 702-0900 .. **Axelrod,** Peter A '81 (Axelrod F&D) -260 Mad Av -NY 10016 **Fx:**355-7365
(212) 661-1100 .. **Axelrod,** Robt J '96 (Pomerantz HG&G LLP) -100 Park Av -NY 10017
(212) 408-7174 .. **Axelrod,** Robt M '80 %Bank of NY -1290 Av of Amer -NY 10104
(585) 203-1020 .. **Axelrod,** Ronald J '70 (RJ Axelrod & Assoc,PC) -141 Sullys Trl -Pittsfrd 14534 **Fx:**203-1021
(212) 431-8073 .. **Axelrod,** Ruth E '86 (Axelrod & G) -100 Lafayette -NY 10013 **Fx:**431-8521
(212) 335-9000 .. **Axelrod,** Susan '85 %DA -1 Hogan Pl -NY 10013
(646) 315-7444 .. **Axelrod,** Susan F '90 %FINRA -14 Wall -NY 10005 **Fx:**315-7440
(212) 506-1700 .. **Axelrod,** Zachary T '06 %Kasowitz BT&F LLP -1633 Bway -NY 10019
(212) 341-6747 .. **Axinn,** David '97 %Liquidation Bur -123 William -NY 10038 **Fx:**608-3398
(212) 753-5599 .. **Axinn,** Mark N '82 (Brill & M) -845 3rd Av -NY 10022
(212) 728-2200 .. **Axinn,** Stephen M '62 (Axinn V&H LLP) -114 W 47th -NY 10036
(212) 728-2200 .. **Axinn Veltrop & Harkrider LLP** -114 W 47th -NY 10036 **Fx:**728-2201
(212) 693-1671 .. **Axisa,** Gary A '94 -111 John -NY 10038
(718) 298-1216 .. **Axler,** Andrew M '75 -88-11 Sutphin Blvd -Jamaica 11435
(212) 400-7223 .. **Axt,** Brian C '07 %Zaremba B&B PLLC -40 Wall -NY 10005 **Fx:**(646) 512-5607
(718) 418-7690 .. **Axt,** Deborah L '02 Make the Road by Walking -301 Grove -Brklyn 11237 **Fx:**418-9635
(212) 504-6000 .. **Axt,** Karen J '02 %Cadwalader W&T LLP -1 World Fncl Ctr -NY 10281
(212) 756-2000 .. **Ayala,** Christopher G '06 %Schulte R&Z LLP -919 3rd Av -NY 10022
(212) 683-7100 .. **Ayala,** Yolanda L '96 %Gallo V&K,LLP -90 Broad -NY 10004
(212) 819-8200 .. **Ayanruoh,** Felix E '00 White & C LLP -1155 Av of Amer -NY 10036
(212) 583-9600 .. **Ayazi,** Alex Ali '02 %Littler M,PC -900 3rd Av -NY 10022
(646) 386-5700 .. **Aybar,** Ingrid '00 %Civil Ct -111 Centre -NY 10013
(914) 946-7770 .. **Aydelott,** Gordon B '71 OfCnsl Westermann SKS&A,LLP -222 Bloomingdale Rd -White Plns 10605
(914) 946-7770 .. **Aydelott,** Judith A '80 OfCnsl Westermann SKS&A,LLP -222 Bloomingdale Rd -White Plns 10605
(718) 746-3440 .. **Aydiner,** Sinan '05 %Sacco & F,LLP -141-07 20th Av -Whitestone 11357
(212) 521-5400 .. **Ayer,** Nina V '09 %Reed S LLP -599 Lex Av -NY 10022
(212) 468-4800 .. **Ayerbe,** Maria J '09 %Davis & G LLP -1740 Bway -NY 10019
(518) 474-7330 .. **Ayers,** Andrew B '07 %Dept of Law -The Cptl -Albany 12224
(212) 686-4600 .. **Ayers,** Andrew M '03 %H Felcher -347 5th Av -NY 10016 **Fx:**686-4686
(518) 487-7600 .. **Ayers,** James B '67 (Whiteman O&H LLP) -1 Commerce Plz -Albany 12260
(212) 264-6426 .. **Ayers,** Kenneth I Jr. '01 %DHS -26 Fed Plz -NY 10278 **Fx:**264-1645
(518) 993-5211 .. **Ayers,** Kenneth L '83 -642 Paris Rd -Ft Plain 13339
(518) 673-8100 .. **Ayers,** Laura E '04 (Ayers Law Firm,PLLC) -Bx683 -Palatine Brdg 13428
(212) 227-2780 .. **Ayers,** Natascia '02 %Jaroslawicz & J -225 Bway -NY 10007
(212) 875-5000 .. **Ayers Shariff,** Kimberly '98 %Lincoln Ctr -70 Lincoln Ctr Plz -NY 10023
(212) 448-9570 .. **Ayes,** Mitchell R '07 %Callahan & F,LLC -40 Exch Pl -NY 10005
(716) 852-0400 .. **Aygun,** Serra '10 %Roach BM&G,PC -424 Main -Buffalo 14202
(212) 440-3224 .. **Aylesworth,** Arica D '07 CNA Ins -40 Wall -NY 10005
(212) 840-6400 .. **Aylesworth,** Jason '09 %Sendroff & B,LLP -1500 Bway -NY 10036 **Fx:**840-6401
(212) 667-8300 .. **Aylett,** Elizabeth Rose '94 CIBC World Mkts -425 Lex Av -NY 10017 **Fx:**667-8361
(646) 312-4555 .. **Aylman,** Carl E '88 Baruch College -1 Bernard Baruch Way -NY 10010
(716) 566-1300 .. **Aylward,** Gretchen P '96 OfCnsl Hiscock & B,LLP -1100 M&T Ctr -Buffalo 14203
(718) 834-8200 .. **Ayorinde,** Akintayo A '93 (A Ayorinde,PC) -16 Court -Brklyn 11241 **Fx:**834-9039
(212) 969-3000 .. **Ayorinde,** Ayokeji A '09 %Proskauer R LLP -1585 Bway -NY 10036
(914) 363-4370 .. **Ayoub,** Alexander M '06 -50 Main -White Plns 10606

(212) 967-1134 .. **Ayoub,** Chad P '05 %Marder E&N -450 7th Av -NY 10123
(212) 986-1544 .. **Ayoub,** Elsa '03 %Gleason & K,LLP -122 E 42nd -NY 10169 **Fx:**986-1379
(516) 536-2143 .. **Ayoung,** Kimberly A '92 -6 Glen Rd -W Hempstead 11552
(718) 250-2000 .. **Ayvazian,** Eileen K '87 %DA -350 Jay -Brklyn 11201 **Fx:**250-2314
(212) 624-5919 .. **Ayyappan,** Ajay '03 ExlSrvc Holdings,Inc -280 Park Av -NY 10017
(718) 672-8115 .. **Azam,** Khalid M '82 (Azam & H LLP) -74-09 37th Av -Jcksn Hts 11372 **Fx:**672-8117
(518) 640-6900 .. **Azam,** Syma S '06 %Phelan P&D,LLP -302 Wshngtn Av Ext -Albany 12203
(212) 819-8200 .. **Azar,** Ziad Raymond '02 %White & C LLP -1155 Av of Amer -NY 10036
(212) 538-2680 .. **Azarbad,** Shlomo '01 Credit Suisse -11 Mad Av -NY 10010
(212) 874-7945 .. **Azaria,** Murray '61 -585 West End Av -NY 10024
(212) 490-2900 .. **Azarian,** Philip H '94 %Marcus & P LLP -708 3rd Av -NY 10017 **Fx:**599-3167
(212) 474-1000 .. **Azarkh,** David W '07 %Cravath S&M LLP -825 8th Av -NY 10019
(212) 972-5252 .. **Azarm,** Sara '02 %Donohue & Prtnrs,PC -90 Broad -NY 10004 **Fx:**697-2737
(518) 399-6663 .. **Azarow,** Arnold P '61 -194 Westside Dr -Ballston Lk 12019 **Fx:**399-6664
(212) 768-6700 .. **Azarow,** Robt C '87 (Sonnenschein N&R LLP) -2 World Fncl Ctr -NY 10281
(718) 882-5700 .. **Azeez,** Ola '97 (O Azeez,PC) -3908 Wht Plns Rd -Bronx 10466 **Fx:**547-2116
(212) 578-2211 .. **Azer,** Irina K '00 %MetLife -27-01 Qns Plz N -LIC 11101
(212) 596-9000 .. **Azher,** Atif Imran '05 %Ropes & G LLP -1211 Av of Amer -NY 10036
(212) 709-3503 .. **Azia,** Jane M '78 %Banking Dept -1 State -NY 10004 **Fx:**709-1655
(718) 654-4299 .. **Azie,** Stella Uchenna '95 -3840 Wht Plns Rd -Bronx 10467
(212) 848-4000 .. **Aziz,** Azam H '97 (Shearman & S LLP) -599 Lex Av -NY 10022
(212) 259-8000 .. **Aziz,** Ziyad H '09 %Dewey & L LLP -1301 Av of Amer -NY 10019
(212) 839-5300 .. **Azizi,** Shabnam S '07 %Sidley A LLP -787 7th Av -NY 10019
(516) 688-1700 .. **Azmon,** Linda P '89 %IRS -1600 Stewart Av -Westbury 11590 **Fx:**688-1750
(516) 739-6200 .. **Azoulay,** Jacob '86 -864 Willis Av -Albertson 11507 **Fx:**739-6202
(516) 739-6200 .. **Azoulay,** Ouzy '07 J Azoulay -864 Willis Av -Albertson 11507 **Fx:**739-6202
(845) 300-5265 .. **Azran Greenwald,** Nicole '99 -10 Deerwood Rd -Spg Vly 10977 **Fx:**503-2236
(212) 869-8220 .. **Azriliant,** Evan B '93 (S&E Azriliant,PC) -36 W 44th -NY 10036 **Fx:**840-2540
(212) 570-5772 .. **Azriliant,** Janine R '95 -300 E 71st -NY 10021
(212) 869-8220 .. **Azriliant,** Sidney W '63 S&E Azriliant,PC -36 W 44th -NY 10036 **Fx:**840-2540
(212) 935-3131 .. **Azrin,** David I '99 (Gallet D&B,LLP) -845 3rd Av -NY 10022
(212) 701-3000 .. **Azulay,** Paula '08 %Cahill G&R LLP -80 Pine -NY 10005 **Fx:**269-5420
(716) 847-8400 .. **Azurin,** Sharon Prise '00 %Phillips L LLP -3400 HSBC Ctr -Buffalo 14203
(212) 938-0600 .. **Azurmendi,** Facundo '08 %Schwartz LLC -90 Broad -NY 10004 **Fx:**938-0601
(212) 282-5000 .. **Azzarelli,** Kim K '00 Avon Products -1345 Av of Amer -NY 10105
(516) 921-8600 .. **Azzaretto,** Mary C '02 %McAndrew C&P -95 Froehlich Farm Blvd -Woodbury 11797
(212) 668-2894 .. **Azzaro,** Christine V '02 %Hon A Gonzalez US Bnkrptcy Ct -One Bowling Grn -NY 10004
(631) 886-1357 .. **Azzato,** Lisa Ann '02 -150 Motor Pkwy -Hauppauge 11788
(212) 687-4900 .. **Azzinari,** Glenn M '92 (Wormser KG&J LLP) -825 3rd Av -NY 10022
(212) 756-2000 .. **Azzollini,** Phillip J '96 (Schulte R&Z LLP) -919 3rd Av -NY 10022
(212) 450-4000 .. **Azzopardi,** Franco '04 (Davis P&W LLP) -450 Lex Av -NY 10017
(631) 289-4600 .. **Baaden,** Kenneth J '98 %Jacoby & J -1737 N Ocean Av -Medfrd 11763 **Fx:**654-5095
(585) 247-9000 .. **Baader,** Alissa L '09 %Shapiro D&B,LLP -250 Mile Xing Blvd -Rchstr 14624
(914) 921-7508 .. **Baader,** Nadja M '03 Grewe & Prtnrs -11 Elm Pl -Rye 10580 **Fx:**967-1505
(716) 847-8400 .. **Baaki,** Wm H '05 %Phillips L LLP -3400 HSBC Ctr -Buffalo 14203
(212) 237-0000 .. **Baarez,** Nebiat Z '04 %Vinson & E LLP -666 5th Av -NY 10103
(716) 854-3400 .. **Baase,** Jeffrey F '95 (Rupp BPC&C LLC) -1600 Lbrty Bldg -Buffalo 14202
(212) 909-6000 .. **Bab,** Andrew L '93 (Debevoise & P LLP) -919 3rd Av -NY 10022
(212) 935-6000 .. **Bab,** Donald Stuart '63 Cnsl Lebow & S LLP -770 Lex Av -NY 10065
(914) 579-2200 .. **Babad,** Jessica Levine '05 %Dugan & D,PC -245 Saw Mill Rvr Rd -Hawthorne 10532 **Fx:**579-2201
(718) 222-2278 .. **Babaev,** Eli '07 %Law Dept -350 Jay -Brklyn 11201 **Fx:**222-2088
(914) 961-1359 .. **Babaja,** Sonia N '92 (Babaja & G) -35 E Grassy Sprain Rd -Ynkrs 10710 **Fx:**961-1339
(212) 782-7114 .. **Babakurban,** Dilek '92 Moore Capital Mgmt,Inc -1251 Av of Amer -NY 10020 **Fx:**782-7194
(518) 473-7793 .. **Babalola,** Anne I '07 NYSOCFS -52 Wshngtn -Rensselaer 12144
(718) 590-1000 .. **Babalola,** Olukayode L '95 -1035 Grnd Cncrs -Bronx 10452 **Fx:**590-1004
(212) 642-0950 .. **Babat,** Eric M '87 (Newman & O,PC) -8 W 38th -NY 10018
(716) 886-3517 .. **Babat,** Marla K '98 %MM Babat -460 Franklin -Buffalo 14202 **Fx:**886-0057
(716) 886-3517 .. **Babat,** Michl M '67 -460 Franklin -Buffalo 14202 **Fx:**886-0057
(212) 374-9300 .. **Babb,** Bernard J '59 OfCnsl Simons & W -45 Bway -NY 10006
(718) 250-2000 .. **Babb,** Colleen D '93 %DA -350 Jay -Brklyn 11201 **Fx:**250-2314
(212) 458-1863 .. **Babb,** Jenny E '00 AIGTS -175 Water -NY 10038
(212) 969-3000 .. **Babb,** Margaret J '91 %Proskauer R LLP -1585 Bway -NY 10036
(212) 839-5300 .. **Babb,** Robt L '08 %Sidley A LLP -787 7th Av -NY 10019
(212) 836-8000 .. **Babbitt,** Joshua D '06 %Kaye S LLP -425 Park Av -NY 10022
(718) 272-4500 .. **Babbush,** Glenn B '93 %Beyer Farms Inc -156-02 Lbrty Av -Jamaica 11433
(914) 470-0001 .. **Babchik,** Jack '78 (Babchik & Y,LLP) -200 E Post Rd -White Plns 10601
(212) 742-9280 .. **Babchik,** Paul E '06 Waterfront Comm -39 Bway -NY 10006 **Fx:**480-0587
(914) 470-0001 .. **Babchik & Young,LLP** -200 E Post Rd -White Plns 10601 **Fx:**470-0009
(518) 449-3300 .. **Babcock,** Christopher J '03 %Nolan & H,LLP -39 N Pearl -Albany 12207
(585) 343-5750 .. **Babcock,** Danl M '64 (Babcock & B) -534 E Main -Batavia 14020 **Fx:**343-8114
(585) 624-9611 .. **Babcock & Davies, PLLC** -Bx700 -Mendon 14506
(585) 624-9611 .. **Babcock,** Elizabeth A '01 (Babcock & D,PLLC) -Bx700 -Mendon 14506
(585) 624-9611 .. **Babcock,** Jeffrey J '01 (Babcock & D,PLLC) -Bx700 -Mendon 14506
(914) 730-3200 .. **Babcock,** Laura J '07 %Entwistle & C LLP -200 Business Park Dr -Armonk 10504
(315) 798-8272 .. **Babcock,** Matthew D '83 St Elizabeth Med Ctr -2209 Genesee -Utica 13501 **Fx:**235-7498
(845) 778-2121 .. **Babcock,** Michele L '04 %Jacobowitz & G,LLP -158 Orange Av Bx367 -Walden 12586
(585) 343-5750 .. **Babcock,** Stephen D '98 (Babcock & B) -534 E Main -Batavia 14020 **Fx:**343-8114
(212) 632-6205 .. **Babej,** Peter '91 %Lazard Freres -30 Rckfllr Plz -NY 10112 **Fx:**332-5975
(718) 881-7964 .. **Babel,** David J '89 DJ Babel,PC -2525 Eastchstr Rd -Bronx 10469
(718) 631-3272 .. **Babel,** Malcolm S '67 -213-38 40th Av -Bayside 11361
(631) 543-0219 .. **Babi,** Kenneth V '91 -8 Clover Dr -Smithtwn 11787 **Fx:**543-0219
(607) 277-7527 .. **Babiarz,** Lisa J '00 (Littman & B) -308 N Tioga -Ithaca 14850 **Fx:**275-9141
(212) 317-5151 .. **Babich,** Rory A '90 %Swiss Re New Markets -55 E 52nd -NY 10055
(315) 272-8755 .. **Babilon,** Thos R '03 -477 E Wshngtn -Syracuse 13202
(212) 460-2477 .. **Babinecz,** Richd W '73 Con Ed -4 Irving Pl -NY 10003
(718) 855-9000 .. **Babinecz,** Stephen M '10 %Cullen and D LLP -177 Montague -Brklyn 11201
(212) 779-8600 .. **Babinsky,** Ilona '05 %Silverman SS&B PLLC -381 Park Av S -NY 10016
(518) 465-3660 .. **Babiskin,** Lisa M '97 -35 Hmptn Av -Rensselaer 12144 **Fx:**465-3660
(518) 465-3002 .. **Babiskin,** Wm A '72 -79 Cptl Pl -Rensselaer 12144 **Fx:**465-3002
(212) 431-5876 .. **Babitch,** Debra L '88 -49 W 37th -NY 10018
(718) 424-3334 .. **Babitch,** Stuart N '68 -3744 75th -Jcksn Hts 11372
(516) 677-9400 .. **Babits,** Heather N '03 %Goldstein & A -575 Underhill Blvd -Syosset 11791
(212) 237-1000 .. **Babitt,** Roy '51 SpclCnsl Windels ML&M,LLP -156 W 56th -NY 10019
(212) 930-9700 .. **Babnick,** Richd J Jr. '97 (Sichenzia RFF LLP) -61 Bway -NY 10006
(212) 837-6000 .. **Babson,** Marshall B '89 (Hughes H&R LLP) -1 Bttry Pk Plz -NY 10004
(212) 446-4800 .. **Baca,** Robt C '09 %Kirkland & E LLP -153 E 53rd -NY 10022
(914) 767-0290 .. **Bacal,** Jessica '70 -200 Katonah Av -Katonah 10536 **Fx:**767-0294
(212) 450-4000 .. **Bacal,** Matthew J '06 %Davis P&W LLP -450 Lex Av -NY 10017
(212) 928-1100 .. **Bacallao,** Nise F '86 -615 W 179th -NY 10033 **Fx:**928-7086
(518) 793-2535 .. **Bacas,** Wm A '61 -257 Bay Rd Bx143 -Glens Fls 12801 **Fx:**793-6238
(212) 257-6690 .. **Baccari,** Louise B '89 Cnsl The Durst Orgn -One Bryant Park -NY 10036 **Fx:**257-6277
(212) 880-6000 .. **Baccus,** Darren D '01 (Torys LLP) -237 Park Av -NY 10017
(718) 852-8888 .. **Bacdayan,** Karen May '91 %LSNYC-Brooklyn -180 Lvngstn -Brklyn 11201 **Fx:**858-1786
(646) 337-8993 .. **Bach,** Amy '01 -2 Brnswck -Rchstr 14607
(212) 286-8585 .. **Bach,** Chas L Jr. '78 (Heidell PM&B,LLP) -99 Park Av -NY 10016
(518) 487-7600 .. **Bach,** Ellen M '93 OfCnsl Whiteman O&H LLP -1 Commerce Plz -Albany 12260
(585) 419-8800 .. **Bach,** Eric J '10 %Harris B PLLC -99 Garnsey Rd -Pittsfrd 14534
(845) 294-7941 .. **Bach,** John E Jr. '75 -20 Scotchtown Av Bx61 -Goshen 10924 **Fx:**294-7981
(212) 479-6000 .. **Bach,** Jonathan P '92 (Cooley LLP) -1114 Av of Amer -NY 10036
(917) 699-7193 .. **Bach,** Murray Danl '90 -38 W 32nd -NY 10001 **Fx:**(212) 563-9870
(212) 350-7448 .. **Bach,** Richd Jinyong '01 Korea Exchange Bk -460 Park Av -NY 10022
(315) 798-1055 .. **Bach,** Richd N '65 -258 Genesee -Utica 13502 **Fx:**738-7100
(212) 332-3330 .. **Bach,** Scott L '87 (Bach & Assoc) -767 3rd Av -NY 10017 **Fx:**332-3315
(718) 358-9400 .. **Bach,** Seyun '92 -134-01 20th Av -Cllg Pnt 11356
(718) 340-4200 .. **Bach,** Wendy Anne '97 %CUNY Law Schl -65-21 Main -Flushng 11367 **Fx:**340-4482
(914) 761-2030 .. **Bacharach,** Bernard R '63 -99 Court -White Plns 10601 **Fx:**428-4176
(212) 319-3900 .. **Bachelder,** Jos E III '59 -437 Mad Av -NY 10022 **Fx:**319-3070
(646) 865-0797 .. **Bacher,** James W '04 %Saftler Law Firm -275 Mad Av -NY 10016 **Fx:**865-0801
(212) 326-2000 .. **Bachman,** Chas Edw '79 (O'Melveny & M LLP) -7 Times Sq -NY 10036
(212) 326-2000 .. **Bachman,** Fredk M '84 (O'Melveny & M LLP) -7 Times Sq -NY 10036
(212) 210-9272 .. **Bachman,** Judith L '91 -100 Park Av -NY 10017 **Fx:**880-6499
(914) 285-8500 .. **Bachman,** Rik '82 %TK Moore -701 Wstchstr Av -White Plns 10604 **Fx:**285-8510
(212) 969-3000 .. **Bachman,** Timothy R '08 %Proskauer R LLP -1585 Bway -NY 10036
(516) 457-2009 .. **Bachmann,** Gregory W '95 G Bachmann PC -95 Ryder Rd -Manhsst 11030
(518) 587-4397 .. **Bachmann,** Vicki J '89 -4 Newington Av -Wilton 12831 **Fx:**587-4398
(917) 378-0176 .. **Bachner,** Larry S '80 (LS Bachner,PC) -153-01 Jamaica Av -Jamaica 11432 **Fx:**(201) 357-8547
(212) 344-7778 .. **Bachner,** Michl F '82 (Bachner & Assoc) -26 Bway -NY 10004
(212) 977-9700 .. **Bachner,** Robt L '59 Cnsl Phillips N LLP -666 5th Av -NY 10103
(518) 474-3018 .. **Bachrach,** Deborah '75 DOH-Ofc Hlth Ins Prgrms -Corning Twr ESP -Albany 12237
(212) 335-9000 .. **Bachrach,** Jaime '00 %DA -1 Hogan Pl -NY 10013
(212) 977-2400 .. **Bachrach,** Jonathan David '80 -55 Water -NY 10041
(212) 557-7747 .. **Bachrach,** Marion '78 (DePetris & B,LLP) -240 Mad Av -NY 10016 **Fx:**557-3383
(212) 929-0592 .. **Bachrach,** Michl K '01 -276 5th Av -NY 10001 **Fx:**(866) 328-1630
(718) 843-6464 .. **Bachu,** Darmin T '96 (Bachu & Assoc) -127-21 Lbrty Av -Richmnd Hll 11419 **Fx:**843-2192

(718) 291-3300 .. **Bachu**, Sharmela '97 -85-04 168th -Jamaica 11432
(212) 418-6100 .. **Bacich**, Cathleen A '84 %GM -767 5th Av -NY 10153 **Fx**:418-6123
(212) 645-8111 .. **Bacigalupi**, Robt F '88 Housing Works -320 W 13th -NY 10014
(212) 318-6000 .. **Bacigalupo**, Marc T '05 %Paul HJ&W LLP -75 E 55th -NY 10022
(516) 877-7000 .. **Bacigalupo**, Susan M '80 (McCoyd P&R,LLP) -1100 Franklin Av -Gdn Cty 11530
(212) 336-3702 .. **Back**, Christine J '09 EEOC -33 Whitehall -NY 10004
(212) 210-9570 .. **Backen**, Thos '85 Cnsl Alston & B LLP -90 Park Av -NY 10016
(212) 593-1100 .. **Backenroth**, Abraham J '77 (Backenroth F&K,LLP) -489 5th Av -NY 10017
(212) 909-6000 .. **Backenroth**, Danl '07 %Debevoise & P LLP -919 3rd Av -NY 10022
(212) 593-1100 .. **Backenroth Frankel & Krinsky, LLP** -489 5th Av -NY 10017 **Fx**:644-0544
(212) 478-7200 .. **Backenroth**, Gilbert '77 (Hahn & H LLP) -488 Mad Av -NY 10022
(212) 728-8000 .. **Backer**, Danl O '04 %Willkie F&G LLP -787 7th Av -NY 10019
(212) 686-7644 .. **Backer**, Glenn '76 -292 Mad Av -NY 10017 **Fx**:685-2425
(716) 372-4164 .. **Backhaus & Simon,PC** -Community Bk Bldg -Olean 14760 **Fx**:372-8560
(212) 309-6000 .. **Backhouse**, Denise E '00 %Morgan L&B LLP -101 Park Av -NY 10178
(212) 964-6611 .. **Backis**, Thos V '02 %Lester SK&D -120 Bway -NY 10271
(212) 833-5098 .. **Backman**, Jordan S '00 SONY Corp -550 Mad Av -NY 10022
(646) 822-1497 .. **Backofen**, Richd B '74 Signature Bk -565 5th Av -NY 10017
(212) 922-2200 .. **Backos**, Antonios Christos '98 (Watson F&W LLP) -1133 Av of Amer -NY 10036
(212) 839-5300 .. **Bacon**, David F '09 %Sidley A LLP -787 7th Av -NY 10019
(518) 782-9500 .. **Bacon**, David I '78 OfCnsl JD Kerr,PLLC -12 Cornell Rd -Latham 12110 **Fx**:782-9700
(845) 255-2026 .. **Bacon**, James B '92 -17 S Chestnut Bx575 -New Paltz 12561 **Fx**:255-8925
(585) 385-9689 .. **Bacon**, Jane L '83 -21 Brunson Way -Penfld 14526 **Fx**:385-9403
(212) 596-9000 .. **Bacon**, Kate E '10 %Ropes & G LLP -1211 Av of Amer -NY 10036
(718) 836-3800 .. **Bacotti**, Louis J '60 -8119 7th Av -Brklyn 11228 **Fx**:748-2061
(212) 309-6000 .. **Baczynski**, Ariane S '06 %Morgan L&B LLP -101 Park Av -NY 10178
(212) 957-7600 .. **Badaczewski**, Donald M '08 %Cohen & G LLP -800 3rd Av -NY 10022
(914) 669-8621 .. **Badagliacca**, Vincent J Jr. '83 -8 Chestnut Dr -N Salem 10560 **Fx**:277-3114
(212) 859-8000 .. **Badain**, David I '82 SpclCnsl Fried FHS&J LLP -1 NY Plz -NY 10004
(585) 385-2510 .. **Badain**, Lara R '94 Sercu & S LLP -31 N Main -Pittsfrd 14534
(212) 309-7879 .. **Badami**, Carolyn T '03 Lexis/Nexis -125 Park Av -NY 10017 **Fx**:309-8187
(631) 673-3222 .. **Badami**, David M '92 %J D'Elia -464 NY Av -Huntngtn 11743 **Fx**:673-4958
(646) 386-3500 .. **Badamo**, Angela J '96 %OCA -25 Beaver -NY 10004
(212) 857-1180 .. **Badamo**, Laura M '92 %Financial Info Srvcs -450 W 33rd -NY 10001
(631) 239-1702 .. **Badanes**, David P '04 -842 Route 25A -Northprt 11768 **Fx**:651-2859
(718) 746-3440 .. **Badash**, Larry I '99 %Sacco & F,LLP -141-07 20th Av -Whitestone 11357
(631) 242-9101 .. **Badash**, Mark '85 %Badash Crystal Inc -44G W Jeffryn Blvd -Deer Pk 11729
(212) 834-0115 .. **Badavas**, Christos P '95 Harry Fox Agncy -301 W 26th -NY 10001 **Fx**:(646) 487-6768
(212) 530-5000 .. **Badawi**, Husam '08 %Milbank TH&M LLP -1 Chase Manh Plz -NY 10005
(315) 443-3728 .. **Badawy**, Rami Shawky '01 SU-Judicial Affairs Ofc -310 Steele Hall -Syracuse 13244
(212) 529-2330 .. **Baddeley**, Gary C '91 Disinformation Co -163 3rd Av -NY 10003
(212) 578-6810 .. **Badeer**, Nancy Hamburg '85 %MetLife -27-01 Qns Plz N -LIC 11101 **Fx**:578-8144
(212) 297-5800 .. **Badejo**, Adetokunbo A '08 %Day P LLP -7 Times Sq -NY 10036
(212) 237-0000 .. **Baden**, Alan P '99 (Vinson & E LLP) -666 5th Av -NY 10103
(732) 219-7770 .. **Baden**, Linda Kenney '00 -15 W 53rd -NY 10019 **Fx**:(212) 397-2754
(212) 227-5000 .. **Baden**, Stacy N '98 %Asher & Assoc,PC -111 John -NY 10038 **Fx**:227-7117
(212) 344-5400 .. **Baden**, Wayne I '76 (Schlam S&D LLP) -26 Bway -NY 10004
(212) 425-7200 .. **Badenoch**, George E '70 (Kenyon & K,LLP) -1 Bway -NY 10004
(716) 633-2961 .. **Bader**, C Michl '81 %Zacher Healthcare -163 S Union -Williamsvll 14221 **Fx**:634-7721
(212) 850-0915 .. **Bader**, Gail I '84 -32 E 57th -NY 10022
(212) 575-7900 .. **Bader**, Howard D '75 (Ballon SB&N,PC) -729 7th Av -NY 10019
(914) 682-0072 .. **Bader**, I Walton '48 (Bader & B LLP) -50 Main PMB 1029 -White Plns 10606 **Fx**:682-0072
(212) 465-1110 .. **Bader**, Jeffrey W '80 (Bader Y&N LLP) -350 5th Av -NY 10118
(212) 880-9440 .. **Bader**, Lawr S '77 (Morvillo AGIA&B,PC) -565 5th Av -NY 10017
(212) 233-6255 .. **Bader**, Margo E '84 %Bloomberg S&B -425 Park Av -NY 10022
(716) 634-5525 .. **Bader**, Melissa Anne '96 %Ralabate & G -5792 Main -Buffalo 14221
(212) 576-6735 .. **Bader**, Randi J '79 %NY Life Ins -51 Mad Av -NY 10010 **Fx**:447-0569
(518) 478-0039 .. **Bader**, Richd W '92 -158 Swift Rd -Voorheesvll 12186
(212) 233-6255 .. **Bader**, Seth D '84 (Bloomberg S&B) -425 Park Av -NY 10022
(315) 422-1152 .. **Bader**, Warren W '71 OfCnsl Costello C&F,PLLC -500 Plum -Syracuse 13204
(212) 345-7000 .. **Bader**, Wm A '84 %Mercer HR Cnsltng -1166 Av of Amer -NY 10036
(212) 465-1110 .. **Bader Yakaitis & Nonnenmacher LLP** -350 5th Av -NY 10118
(315) 474-6896 .. **Badera**, Peter J '74 -217 Mntgmry -Syracuse 13202 **Fx**:422-7675
(914) 328-0404 .. **Baderian**, Steven D '75 (Jackson L LLP) -1 N Bway -White Plns 10601
(212) 986-1480 .. **Bader-York**, Judith '64 -331 Mad Av -NY 10017
(718) 482-5077 .. **Badger**, C Dion '87 %LaGuardia Comm Cllg -31-10 Thomson Av -LIC 11101
(212) 506-2500 .. **Badger**, Zoe Hart '09 %Mayer B LLP -1675 Bway -NY 10019
(631) 853-7718 .. **Badia**, Leonard J '07 NYS Ofc of Ct Admin -400 Carleton Av -Central Islip 11722
(212) 612-7000 .. **Badiak**, Mary L '95 Daiwa Securities Amer -32 Old Slip -NY 10005
(516) 877-2225 .. **Badiak & Will, LLP** -106 3rd -Mineola 11501 **Fx**:877-2230
(212) 407-4000 .. **Badian**, Sasha N '04 %Loeb & L,LLP -345 Park Av -NY 10154
(212) 244-5632 .. **Badie**, James W '65 -521 5th Av -NY 10175 **Fx**:244-1364
(212) 732-9000 .. **Badillo**, Herman '55 OfCnsl Sullivan PBM&C PC -120 Bway -NY 10271
(718) 613-3500 .. **Badillo**, Wm J '79 %UIA Bd -Bx29002 -Brklyn 11201 **Fx**:613-3566
(212) 259-8000 .. **Badini**, Aldo A '84 (Dewey & L LLP) -1301 Av of Amer -NY 10019
(212) 596-9000 .. **Badke**, Bradford J '82 (Ropes & G LLP) -1211 Av of Amer -NY 10036
(212) 576-7000 .. **Badler**, Sara L '85 NY Life Ins -51 Mad Av -NY 10010 **Fx**:447-0569
(212) 262-2390 .. **Badolato**, Richd J '81 (Connell F LLP) -888 7th Av -NY 10106
(212) 889-4100 .. **Badowski**, Michl J '94 %Realty Advisory Bd -292 Mad Av -NY 10017 **Fx**:889-4105
(516) 746-1144 .. **Badum**, Christopher J '77 %Kirschenbaum & P,PC -3000 Hempstd Tpk -Levittwn 11756
(845) 562-9100 .. **Badura**, Donna M '86 %Rider W&F,PC -655 Little Britain Rd -New Windsor 12553
(845) 357-2660 .. **Badura**, Wm S '86 (Kornfeld RN&S) -46 Wshngtn Av Bx177 -Suffern 10901
(973) 992-4800 .. **Badway**, Ernest E '93 (Fox R LLP) -100 Park Av -NY 10017 **Fx**:992-9125
(212) 319-6888 .. **Bae**, Christine M '95 (Kim & B PC) -110 E 59th -NY 10022
(212) 455-2000 .. **Bae**, Danl '09 %Simpson T&B LLP -425 Lex Av -NY 10017
(212) 695-7577 .. **Bae**, Danl C '10 %Sekas & Assoc,LLC -515 Mad Av -NY 10022 **Fx**:695-0152
(212) 468-4800 .. **Bae**, Elizabeth Costello '05 %Davis & G LLP -1740 Bway -NY 10019
(212) 878-8000 .. **Bae**, Hana '10 %Clifford C LLP -31 W 52nd -NY 10019
(212) 909-6000 .. **Bae**, Heeyoung '09 %Debevoise & P LLP -919 3rd Av -NY 10022
(800) 281-1515 .. **Bae**, Jinhee '09 %Power Law Firm LLP -590 Mad Av -NY 10022 **Fx**:903-1993
(212) 801-2216 .. **Bae**, John H '90 (Greenberg T,LLP) -200 Park Av -NY 10166
(212) 610-9140 .. **Bae**, Margaret C '05 ContourGlobal LP -650 Mad Av -NY 10022 **Fx**:610-9144
(212) 261-8000 .. **Bae**, Sojin '02 (Mendes & M,LLP) -750 7th Av -NY 10019
(212) 408-5100 .. **Baecher**, John T '83 (Chadbourne & P LLP) -30 Rckfllr Plz -NY 10112
(212) 788-7000 .. **Baecher**, Theo J '92 %City Cncl Leg Div -250 Bway -NY 10007 **Fx**:788-7034
(212) 696-6000 .. **Baecher-Scholz**, Catherine M '94 Cnsl Curtis M-PC&M LLP -101 Park Av -NY 10178
(212) 218-2100 .. **Baechtold**, Robt L '67 OfCnsl Fitzpatrick CH&S -1290 Av of Amer -NY 10104
(716) 439-7085 .. **Baehre**, Lisa M '97 %DA -175 Hawley -Lockprt 14094 **Fx**:439-7102
(716) 633-3363 .. **Baehre**, Mark A '87 (Katz & B) -8604 Main -Williamsvll 14221
(718) 875-5151 .. **Baello**, Ernest '09 %C Arnel -16 Court -Brklyn 11241 **Fx**:875-8951
(212) 343-6100 .. **Baender**, Margo B '95 Scholastic Inc -557 Bway -NY 10012
(212) 233-0318 .. **Baer**, Andrew J '88 -299 Bway -NY 10007 **Fx**:233-5737
(917) 206-8060 .. **Baer**, Andrew N '72 -666 5th Av -NY 10103
(516) 746-4373 .. **Baer**, Arthur A '87 %MHLS -170 Old Cntry Rd -Mineola 11501 **Fx**:746-0598
(212) 319-5656 .. **Baer**, Arthur D '78 -777 3rd Av -NY 10017 **Fx**:755-3174
(212) 669-8300 .. **Baer**, Barbara '83 Manhattan Boro Pres Ofc -1 Centre -NY 10007
(212) 810-5300 .. **Baer**, Edw B '95 BlackRock -40 E 52nd -NY 10022
(212) 867-4466 .. **Baer**, Edw G '83 (Belkin BW&G,LLP) -270 Mad Av -NY 10016
(212) 478-0000 .. **Baer**, F Brandon '98 DE Shaw & Co -120 W 45th -NY 10036
(212) 735-3000 .. **Baer**, Henry P '72 OfCnsl Skadden ASM&F LLP -4 Times Sq -NY 10036
(212) 230-8800 .. **Baer**, Lauren E '08 %WilmerHale -399 Park Av -NY 10022
(212) 310-8000 .. **Baer**, Lawr J '84 Cnsl Weil G&M LLP -767 5th Av -NY 10153
(212) 237-0000 .. **Baer**, Madeline F '93 Cnsl Vinson & E LLP -666 5th Av -NY 10103
(212) 446-2300 .. **Baer**, Matthew H '08 %Boies S&F LLP -575 Lex Av -NY 10022
(845) 794-3833 .. **Baer**, Michl D '93 (Billig L&B LLP) -146 Rck Hll Rd Bx780 -Rck Hll 12775 **Fx**:794-3827
(718) 780-7517 .. **Baer**, Miriam Hechler '97 %Bklyn Law Schl -250 Joralemon -Brklyn 11201 **Fx**:780-0393
(212) 374-8109 .. **Baer**, Myles S '78 Hon R Pickholz -111 Centre -NY 10013
(212) 227-1735 .. **Baer**, Robin B '92 (Bates & B) -60 E 42nd -NY 10165 **Fx**:(201) 518-2552
(914) 683-0068 .. **Baer**, Susan Taxin '86 ST Baer -399 Knollwood Rd -White Plns 10603 **Fx**:683-0086
(212) 980-3400 .. **Baer**, Thos H '61 -20 5th Av -NY 10011
(518) 828-9411 .. **Baer**, Willow F '08 %Cnty Dept Socl Srvcs -25 Railroad Av Bx458 -Hudson 12534
(212) 436-1091 .. **Baerga**, Carmen M '83 %IRS -290 Bwayr -NY 10007
(718) 262-7100 .. **Baer-Kuzniewski**, Jeannine M '87 %Civil Ct -89-17 Sutphin Blvd -Jamaica 11435 **Fx**:262-7107
(716) 857-7991 .. **Baetzhold**, James P '97 %Natl Fuel Gas -6363 Main -Williamsvll 14221 **Fx**:857-7614
(212) 416-6567 .. **Baez**, Ignacia Evelyn '02 %Dept of Law -120 Bway -NY 10271
(212) 213-9343 .. **Baez**, Jose Anibal '92 -347 5th Av -NY 10016 **Fx**:686-4686
(646) 458-5951 .. **Baez**, Lourdes M '03 ACE USA -140 Bway -NY 10005
(212) 673-6669 .. **Baez**, Peter '97 Ventura R&S -280 Park Av S -NY 10010
(516) 433-6677 .. **Baez**, Ricardo A '84 (Stewart GM&B) -6800 Jericho Tpk -Syosset 11791
(718) 592-3388 .. **Baez**, Ruth M '02 %Del Villar & Assoc -45-14 104th -Corona 11368 **Fx**:592-3775
(718) 920-6311 .. **Baez**, Yvonne '04 %Montefiore Med Ctr -3332 Rochambeau Av -Bronx 10467
(845) 228-4200 .. **Baffi**, Andrew L '03 %W Sayegh,PC -65 Gleneida Av -Carmel 10512 **Fx**:228-4832
(212) 250-7544 .. **Baganz**, Vivien '02 %Deutsche Bank -60 Wall -NY 10005
(212) 225-2000 .. **Bagarella**, Laura '10 %Cleary GS&H -1 Lbrty Plz -NY 10006
(212) 732-2000 .. **Bagatta**, Danl M '01 (Cullen and D LLP) -44 Wall -NY 10005 **Fx**:825-1531
(212) 504-6000 .. **Bagby**, Ingrid M '97 (Cadwalader W&T LLP) -1 World Fncl Ctr -NY 10281
(212) 964-9287 .. **Bagdasarian**, David '96 -321 Bway -NY 10007 **Fx**:964-9286
(845) 279-7000 .. **Bagen**, Gregory W '77 -317 Clock Twr Cmmns Dr Bx380 -Brewstr 10509 **Fx**:279-4900
(917) 833-8452 .. **Bagg**, Harvey M Jr. '79 -167 W 88th -NY 10024
(212) 918-3000 .. **Baggs**, Jordan K F '10 %Hogan L LLP -875 3rd Av -NY 10022

(212) 586-5800 .. **Baghban,** Giti '08 %Cohen TS&W PC -420 Lex Av -NY 10170
(212) 715-9100 .. **Baghdassarian,** Mark A '00 %Kramer LN&F,LLP -1177 Av of Amer -NY 10036
(315) 736-0816 .. **Bagley,** David A '88 OfCnsl Kernan Prof Grp,LLP -1310 Utica Bx750 -Oriskany 13424 **Fx:**736-8731
(212) 577-7700 .. **Bagley,** Lisa E '05 %Safe Horizon -2 Lafayette -NY 10007 **Fx:**385-0331
(212) 468-8000 .. **Bagley,** Luke T '10 %Morrison & F LLP -1290 Av of Amer -NY 10104
(212) 385-4410 .. **Bagley,** Nicolas '08 %Gersowitz L&K,PC -111 Bway -NY 10006
(212) 813-8800 .. **Bagley,** Parker H '84 (Goodwin P LLP) -620 8th Av -NY 10018
(212) 820-9497 .. **Bagley,** Roger J '81 (Hawkins D&W LLP) -One Chase Manh Plz -NY 10005
(212) 421-4100 .. **Bagley,** Ross M '09 %Pryor C LLP -7 Times Sq -NY 10036
(212) 310-8000 .. **Bagliebter,** Danl A '09 %Weil G&M LLP -767 5th Av -NY 10153
(212) 692-1000 .. **Bagliebter,** Wm M '77 (Duane M LLP) -1540 Bway -NY 10036
(718) 529-4242 .. **Baglino,** James '95 %Crasto & Assoc,PC -161-10A Crossbay Blvd -Howard Bch 11414 **Fx:**323-9407
(631) 427-7790 .. **Baglio,** Michl P '01 (Lewin GB,LLP) -900 Walt Whitman Rd -Melvll 11747
(212) 431-2884 .. **Baglio,** Rebecca S '03 %NY Law Schl -185 W Bway -NY 10013 **Fx:**274-1491
(212) 730-8133 .. **Baglio,** Steven L '04 (Gunderson DSVF&H,LLP) -220 W 42nd -NY 10036
(212) 859-8000 .. **Bagner,** Jeffrey '76 (Fried FHS&J LLP) -1 NY Plz -NY 10004
(516) 488-8090 .. **Bagni,** Cheryl A '90 -69 Maple Av -Floral Pk 11001
(518) 664-2951 .. **Bagnoli,** Jeffrey N '98 (Carola B&T,PLLC) -215 Park Av -Mechanicvll 12118 **Fx:**664-1150
(718) 423-4971 .. **Bagon,** Andrew R '86 -240-21B Oak Park Dr -Douglastn 11362
(212) 947-6600 .. **Bagshaw,** Duncan J '99 %Peak Cnsl Inc -25 W 31st -NY 10001
(212) 725-4650 .. **Bagwell,** Marvin N '85 Old Republic National Title Ins Co -192 Lex Av -NY 10016
(914) 747-7070 .. **Bagwin,** Steven C '87 -245 Saw Mill Rvr Rd -Hawthorne 10532 **Fx:**747-9201
(518) 533-3000 .. **Bagyi,** John M '97 (Bond S&K,PLLC) -111 Wshngtn Av -Albany 12210
(212) 336-0418 .. **Bah,** Ibrahim S '06 SEC -3 World Fncl Ctr -NY 10281 **Fx:**336-1323
(516) 783-9662 .. **Bahamonde,** James E '02 J Bahamonde,PC -2501 Jody Ct -N Bellmore 11710
(718) 442-5030 .. **Bahar,** Jody Lynn '89 -390 Manor Rd -Staten Isl 10314
(212) 558-4000 .. **Bahar,** Loni '06 %Sullivan & C LLP -125 Broad -NY 10004
(212) 233-1100 .. **Baharvar,** Sam '02 Cornell G -225 Bway -NY 10007 **Fx:**233-1110
(212) 326-3939 .. **Baher,** Julie M '07 %Jones D -222 E 41st -NY 10017
(212) 474-1000 .. **Bahgat,** Tamer O '07 %Cravath S&M LLP -825 8th Av -NY 10019
(212) 720-3700 .. **Bahler,** Gary M '77 %Foot Locker,Inc -112 W 34th -NY 10120 **Fx:**720-4116
(212) 310-8000 .. **Bahlke,** Conrad G '88 (Weil G&M LLP) -767 5th Av -NY 10153
(212) 818-9019 .. **Bahn,** Allan M '89 (Bahn H&M,LLP) -555 5th Av -NY 10017 **Fx:**986-5316
(607) 266-8842 .. **Bahn,** David S '05 -102 E State Bx5 -Ithaca 14851
(716) 845-6000 .. **Bahn,** Erin E '02 %Kavinoky C LLP -726 Exchange -Buffalo 14210
(212) 807-2829 .. **Bahn,** Michl S '93 Thomson Reuters -195 Bway -NY 10007
(718) 722-3100 .. **Bahn,** Susan C '85 %Leg Aid -111 Lvngstn -Brklyn 11201 **Fx:**722-3093
(585) 428-5210 .. **Bahr,** Robt P '07 Pub Def -10 N Fitzhugh -Rchstr 14614 **Fx:**428-2234
(212) 632-2241 .. **Bahrampour,** Firouzeh D '02 WPP Grp USA -125 Park Av -NY 10017
(212) 829-5437 .. **Bahrampour,** Robt F '00 Cantor Fitzgerald/Espeed -110 E 59th -NY 10022
(718) 725-3122 .. **Bahrenburg,** Diane M '07 ACS -15120 Jamaica Av -Jamaica 11432
(631) 727-2180 .. **Bahrenburg,** John Claude '84 OfCnsl Twomey LSKD&Q,LLP -33 W 2nd Bx9398 -Rvrhead 11901
(212) 878-8000 .. **Bahri,** Rana '09 %Clifford C LLP -31 W 52nd -NY 10019
(516) 466-1401 .. **Bai,** Jennifer '05 (Bai & S) -505 Nrthrn Blvd -Gt Neck 11021
(212) 404-5777 .. **Bai,** Michl H '98 (Littleton JUP&K LLP) -39 Bway -NY 10006
(212) 762-4719 .. **Bai,** Su Sun '92 Morgan Stanley -1221 Av of Amer -NY 10020
(212) 407-4000 .. **Bai,** Vivian Yun '03 %Loeb & L,LLP -345 Park Av -NY 10154
(516) 228-9181 .. **Baiamonte,** Rosalia '94 (Gassman BB&T,PC) -666 Old Cntry Rd -Gdn Cty 11530
(212) 626-0110 .. **Baiardi,** Jeanette '04 AKF Grp -1501 Bway -NY 10036
(212) 558-4000 .. **Baich,** Danl M '01 %Sullivan & C LLP -125 Broad -NY 10004
(212) 587-5859 .. **Baida,** David '82 %State Ins Fund -199 Church -NY 10007 **Fx:**385-9199
(212) 935-1400 .. **Baier,** Elena '02 %Seiden & S,PC -570 Lex Av -NY 10022
(315) 255-4316 .. **Baier,** James S '80 -152 Genesee -Auburn 13021 **Fx:**255-4324
(516) 873-1902 .. **Baier,** Wm B '93 Morici & M -1399 Franklin Av -Gdn Cty 11530 **Fx:**873-3948
(516) 741-2100 .. **Baierlein,** Raymond C '98 (Alacqua & B) -265 Post Av -Westbury 11590
(718) 418-5000 .. **Baig,** Mohamed Saif '01 -6609 Myrtle Av -Glendale 11385
(212) 449-1940 .. **Baik,** Je Young Han '96 Merrill Lynch -4 World Fncl Ctr -NY 10080
(212) 937-7275 .. **Baik,** Peter W '06 %WilmerHale -399 Park Av -NY 10022
(212) 225-2000 .. **Baik,** Robin J '08 %Cleary GS&H -1 Lbrty Plz -NY 10006
(585) 338-6800 .. **Bailey,** A Robt D '90 %Bausch & Lomb -One Bausch & Lomb Pl -Rchstr 14604 **Fx:**338-8706
(212) 825-0365 .. **Bailey,** Adam Leitman '96 (AL Bailey,PC) -120 Bway -NY 10271 **Fx:**825-0999
(212) 310-8000 .. **Bailey,** Andrew C '09 %Weil G&M LLP -767 5th Av -NY 10153
(212) 859-3530 .. **Bailey,** Anthony M '03 -110 Wall -NY 10005 **Fx:**943-2300
(716) 664-2967 .. **Bailey,** Arthur N '60 -111 W 2nd -Jamestwn 14701
(518) 436-9711 .. **Bailey,** Barbara A '07 Chicago Title Ins -80 State -Albany 12207 **Fx:**436-0891
(516) 741-2585 .. **Bailey,** Caren P '03 %Rosicki R & Assoc,PC -51 E Bethpage Rd -Plainvw 11803 **Fx:**741-4748
(845) 225-8404 .. **Bailey,** Celeste M '04 (Daniels & P,LLP) -102 Gleneida Av -Carmel 10512
(212) 244-3333 .. **Bailey,** Collin E '09 %Donovan H LLP -1350 Bway -NY 10018
(212) 210-1400 .. **Bailey,** Darci J '00 A&E TV Networks -235 E 45th -NY 10017
(718) 631-2500 .. **Bailey,** Edw G '85 (Bailey & S,PC) -42-21 Douglstn Pkwy -Douglastn 11363
(212) 526-8264 .. **Bailey,** Emma M '97 %Barclays Capital Inc -745 7th Av -NY 10019
(631) 249-6644 .. **Bailey,** Eric N '94 %Garcia & S -2076 Deer Prk Av -Deer Pk 11729
(212) 859-3530 .. **Bailey,** Gilda M '03 -110 Wall -NY 10005
(585) 781-5651 .. **Bailey,** Jack S '09 %Eastman Kodak -343 State -Rchstr 14650
(212) 626-4100 .. **Bailey,** James D '02 %Baker & M LLP -1114 Av of Amer -NY 10036
(212) 504-6000 .. **Bailey,** James T '98 (Cadwalader W&T LLP) -1 World Fncl Ctr -NY 10281
(315) 676-7314 .. **Bailey,** Jason B '06 %Sheats & Assoc,PC -9650 Brewertn Rd Bx820 -Brewertn 13029 **Fx:**676-7189
(631) 858-1762 .. **Bailey,** Jennifer A '95 Bisys Fund Srvcs -29 Spinning Wheel Ln -Dix Hlls 11746
(716) 662-0236 .. **Bailey,** John C '76 -3623 Eggert Rd -Orchard Pk 14127 **Fx:**662-0238
(518) 456-0082 .. **Bailey,** John W '80 (Bailey K&J,PC) -5 Pine West Plz -Albany 12205 **Fx:**456-4767
(516) 627-6919 .. **Bailey,** Julian J '76 SrCnsl J Bailey & Assoc -111 Vllg Rd -Manhsst 11030 **Fx:**365-3209
(718) 701-5915 .. **Bailey,** Lamont R '88 (Bailey & B,LLC) -123-20 82nd Av -Kew Gdns 11415 **Fx:**(877) 225-2932
(914) 949-2909 .. **Bailey,** Lawr R Jr. '75 (Eckert SC&M,LLC) -10 Bank -White Plns 10606
(917) 797-0577 .. **Bailey,** Louis Davenport '63 -1 Univ Pl -NY 10003
(212) 816-5831 .. **Bailey,** Martha Davenport '89 Citigroup Global Mrkts -388 Greenwich -NY 10013
(845) 294-9123 .. **Bailey,** Meg '99 %MHLS -5 Coates Dr -Goshen 10924 **Fx:**294-3506
(315) 671-2030 .. **Bailey,** Michele Pirro '86 Family Ct -401 Mntgmry -Syracuse 13202 **Fx:**671-1168
(212) 499-6644 .. **Bailey,** Morgan '03 %M Cohen & Assoc,PC -7 Penn Plz -NY 10001 **Fx:**818-0625
(212) 210-9466 .. **Bailey,** Nadjia Isaacs '10 %Alston & B LLP -90 Park Av -NY 10016
(212) 335-9000 .. **Bailey,** Patricia J '87 %DA -1 Hogan Pl -NY 10013
(631) 725-8680 .. **Bailey,** Paul '87 -Millstone Rd Bx86 -Sag Hbr 11963
(516) 320-6434 .. **Bailey,** Paula J '04 Bailey & Assoc PLLC -514 Merrick Rd -Baldwin 11510 **Fx:**320-6469
(212) 788-1191 .. **Bailey,** Percival '87 %Law Dept -100 Church -NY 10007 **Fx:**788-0367
(315) 536-9971 .. **Bailey,** Philip L '74 OfCnsl Heaton & V,LLP -118 Main Bx397 -Penn Yan 14527
(212) 635-1079 .. **Bailey,** Robt E '93 Bk of NY Mellon -1 Wall -NY 10286
(718) 631-2500 .. **Bailey & Sherman,PC** -42-21 Douglstn Pkwy -Douglastn 11363 **Fx:**631-2400
(716) 849-1333 .. **Bailey,** Teresa A '06 %Lipsitz GSC LLP -42 Delaware Av -Buffalo 14202
(716) 847-8400 .. **Bailey,** Thos C '75 (Phillips L LLP) -3400 HSBC Ctr -Buffalo 14203
(914) 949-2700 .. **Bailey,** Thos G Jr. '70 (Bleakley P&S,LLP) -1 N Lex Av -White Plns 10601
(516) 745-5605 .. **Bailey,** Thos J '95 (T Bailey & Assoc,PC) -175 W Old Cntry Rd -Hicksvll 11801
(212) 537-1518 .. **Bailey,** Valerie I '87 Morgan Stanley Dean Witter -1633 Bway -NY 10019
(212) 918-3000 .. **Bailey,** W Edw '75 OfCnsl Hogan L LLP -875 3rd Av -NY 10022
(212) 545-1900 .. **Bailey,** Yao Fu '99 (Menaker & H LLP) -10 E 40th -NY 10016
(631) 423-9150 .. **Bailey-Chen,** Zaralise P '95 -11 Westcliff Dr -Dix Hlls 11746 **Fx:**423-9150
(212) 267-1278 .. **Bailin,** Leonard '51 OfCnsl Bailin & S -299 Bway -NY 10007 **Fx:**285-0531
(212) 935-0900 .. **Bailin,** Marc L '78 (Rubin & B,LLP) -501 Mad Av -NY 10022
(212) 880-3800 .. **Bailkin,** Michl D '71 OfCnsl Akerman S -335 Mad Av -NY 10017
(212) 973-0572 .. **Bailliard,** Xavier M '08 %Wolff & S PC -140 Bway -NY 10005
(212) 949-0100 .. **Baillie,** Mark S '80 %Cmmnwlth Land Title -140 E 45th -NY 10017 **Fx:**949-2438
(518) 523-5555 .. **Baillie,** Martina '08 %Briggs N LLP -2296 Saranac Av -Lk Placid 12946 **Fx:**523-5559
(212) 716-6173 .. **Baillie,** Suzanne Irving '97 Episcopal Church -815 2nd Av -NY 10017
(914) 684-9100 .. **Bailly,** John J '85 (Bailly & M,LLP) -244 Wstchstr Av -White Plns 10604
(914) 684-9100 .. **Bailly & McMillan,LLP** -244 Wstchstr Av -White Plns 10604 **Fx:**684-9108
(518) 445-2311 .. **Bailly,** Rose Mary '77 Albany Law Schl -80 New Scotland Av -Albany 12208 **Fx:**445-2315
(518) 694-8875 .. **Bailly,** Stephen F '79 -750 Bway -Albany 12207 **Fx:**694-8877
(212) 340-0400 .. **Baily,** Jill B '81 %Appllt Div 1st Dept -27 Mad Av -NY 10010 **Fx:**889-4412
(212) 301-4455 .. **Bailyn,** Bradley R '04 Thomson West -530 5th Av -NY 10036
(718) 725-3200 .. **Baim,** Joan M '06 %Admin Children's Srvcs -151-20 Jamaica Av -Jamaica 11432
(607) 723-5341 .. **Bain,** Jacqueline A '09 %Hinman H&K,LLP -80 Exchange Bx5250 -Bnghmtn 13902
(212) 756-2000 .. **Bain,** Jos E '10 %Schulte R&Z LLP -919 3rd Av -NY 10022
(212) 436-6753 .. **Bain,** Karen A '83 Deloitte & Touche LLP -2 World Fncl Ctr -NY 10281
(646) 392-9250 .. **Bain,** Peter R '92 %M Klein & Assoc -200 Mad Av -NY 10016 **Fx:**(212) 779-1499
(212) 704-6471 .. **Bain,** Sonia Kaur '97 (Troutman S LLP) -405 Lex Av -NY 10174
(212) 264-5958 .. **Bain,** Terry A '81 Ofc of Immigration -26 Fed Plz -NY 10278
(212) 573-6703 .. **Baine,** Radley '96 %Giddins & C LLP -675 3rd Av -NY 10017 **Fx:**949-1923
(212) 732-5800 .. **Baines,** Jennifer A '08 %Friedman & M LLP -233 Bway -NY 10279
(914) 769-3886 .. **Bainlardi,** Alaina '96 -356 Manvll Rd -Plsntvll 10570 **Fx:**769-3886
(914) 769-3886 .. **Bainlardi,** John R '95 -356 Manvll Rd -Plsntvll 10570 **Fx:**769-3886
(718) 780-7963 .. **Bainnson,** Susan Dara '96 Bklyn Law Schl -250 Joralemon -Brklyn 11201 **Fx:**780-0374
(646) 723-2947 .. **Bains,** Deepika '08 %Sanford W&H,LLP -1350 Av of Amer -NY 10019
(718) 725-3026 .. **Bains,** Guljit Kaur '96 %Admin Children's Srvcs -151-20 Jamaica Av -Jamaica 11432
(347) 563-0162 .. **Bains,** Manavinder Singh '02 (Bains Law Grp,PC) -12 East 8th -NY 10003 **Fx:**(212) 674-1827
(718) 382-2400 .. **Bains,** Tejinder Singh '93 (Ali & B PC) -118-35 Qns Blvd -Frst Hlls 11375
(212) 907-9700 .. **Bainton,** J Jos '74 (Smith G&R,LLP) -250 Park Av -NY 10177

(716) 856-4650 .. **Baio,** Gayle R '94 %Price Waterhouse -3600 Marine Mdlnd Ctr -Buffalo 14203
(212) 728-8000 .. **Baio,** Jos T '79 (Willkie F&G LLP) -787 7th Av -NY 10019
(914) 793-9755 .. **Baio,** Regina '80 -140 Park Av -Bronxvll 10708
(212) 682-5700 .. **Baiocco,** Costanza N '87 Maya M,PC -261 Mad Av -NY 10016 **Fx:**697-4432
(914) 323-7000 .. **Baiocco,** Jos C '99 (Wilson EME&D LLP) -3 Gannett Dr -White Plns 10604
(212) 538-3712 .. **Bair,** Benjamin C '97 Credit Suisse -11 Mad Av -NY 10010
(212) 349-8173 .. **Bair,** Brian J '09 %Durkin & D -111 Bway -NY 10006 **Fx:**285-1968
(716) 200-5050 .. **Bair,** Teresa Brophy '97 (Harris B PLLC) -726 Exchange -Buffalo 14210
(716) 845-6000 .. **Baird,** Brian D '84 OfCnsl Kavinoky C LLP -726 Exchange -Buffalo 14210
(585) 263-5780 .. **Baird,** Bryce M '95 %Hon M Telesca -100 State -Rchstr 14614
(646) 471-4000 .. **Baird,** Erica Borden '76 %PricewaterhouseCoopers LLP -300 Mad Av -NY 10017
(518) 436-1850 .. **Baird,** George E Jr. '89 %Fed Pub Def -39 N Pearl -Albany 12207 **Fx:**436-1780
(646) 471-4000 .. **Baird,** Harry J Jr. '89 %PricewaterhouseCoopers LLP -300 Mad Av -NY 10017
(914) 696-3800 .. **Baird,** Lisa Gioffre '88 (Gioffre & G) -2900 Wstchstr Av -Purchase 10577 **Fx:**696-3833
(212) 474-1000 .. **Baird,** Michl D '10 %Cravath S&M LLP -825 8th Av -NY 10019
(585) 421-1000 .. **Baird,** Pamela Dintruff '00 ConServe -200 Crosskeys Ofc Park Bx7 -Fairprt 14450
(212) 637-2713 .. **Baird,** Susan D '84 %US Atty -86 Chmbrs -NY 10007
(718) 298-0013 .. **Bais,** Nicholas H '83 Supreme Ct -88-11 Sutphin Blvd -Jamaica 11435
(585) 428-5755 .. **Baisch,** Chas O '71 %Cnty Atty -50 W Main -Rchstr 14614 **Fx:**428-2031
(212) 966-0066 .. **Baisley,** Margaret D '80 -561 Bway -NY 10012 **Fx:**966-0234
(646) 227-2338 .. **Bajaj,** Shanti D '99 Memorial Sloan Kettering -633 3rd Av -NY 10017
(212) 449-7922 .. **Bajaj-Singh,** Monica Ashwani '95 %Merrill Lynch -220 Bway -NY 10038
(646) 386-3856 .. **Bajit,** John P '94 Supreme Ct -71 Thomas -NY 10013 **Fx:**(212) 374-8417
(212) 969-3000 .. **Bajkai,** Veronica K '08 Proskauer R LLP -1585 Bway -NY 10036 **Fx:**969-2900
(212) 962-2626 .. **Bajraktarevic,** Mirsade '00 %M Seitelman -111 Bway -NY 10006 **Fx:**962-5050
(212) 803-5100 .. **Bajuk,** Andrej S '03 NY Cnty Defender Srvcs -225 Bway -NY 10007 **Fx:**571-6035
(646) 673-5905 .. **Bajwa,** Deepan '07 -87-52 108th -Richmnd Hll 11418
(212) 318-6000 .. **Bajwa,** Hissan A '06 %Paul HJ&W LLP -75 E 55th -NY 10022
(631) 287-3065 .. **Bak,** Kara '94 %Town Atty -116 Hmptn Rd -Southampton 11968 **Fx:**287-3662
(212) 530-5000 .. **Bak,** Sander '99 (Milbank TH&M LLP) -1 Chase Manh Plz -NY 10005
(212) 804-4200 .. **Bakal,** Todd A '93 (Mound CW&G) -One Bttry Pk Plz -NY 10004
(212) 804-4200 .. **Bakal-Caplan,** Emilie L '87 (Mound CW&G) -One Bttry Pk Plz -NY 10004
(212) 319-1000 .. **Bakalor,** Richd '61 (Quirk & B,PC) -845 3rd Av -NY 10022
(914) 328-0404 .. **Baken,** Scott T '85 (Jackson L LLP) -1 N Bway -White Plns 10601
(212) 210-9400 .. **Baker,** Adam M '09 %Alston & B LLP -90 Park Av -NY 10016
(212) 577-3966 .. **Baker,** Allison M '01 Leg Aid -199 Water -NY 10038
(845) 294-5297 .. **Baker,** Alysia R '92 -305 Main -Goshen 10924 **Fx:**294-3075
(212) 906-1200 .. **Baker,** Andrew D '10 %Latham & W -885 3rd Av -NY 10022
(212) 964-7400 .. **Baker,** Angela Y '05 %Smith MDWY&Y,PC -111 John -NY 10038
(212) 805-1103 .. **Baker,** Anita Gidwani '98 Wells Fargo & Co -530 5th Av -NY 10036
(212) 974-7474 .. **Baker,** Anne C '83 OfCnsl Cowan DA&S LLP -41 Mad Av -NY 10010
(212) 696-3072 .. **Baker,** Anthony B '96 JP Morgan Chase & Co -349 5th Av -NY 10016
(585) 263-1000 .. **Baker,** Ashley E '09 %Nixon P LLP -1100 Clinton Sq -Rchstr 14604
(516) 775-7007 .. **Baker,** Beverly Ann '99 %Gutman MB&S,PC -813 Jericho Tpk -New Hyde Pk 11040
(212) 446-4800 .. **Baker,** Beverly M '00 %Kirkland & E LLP -153 E 53rd -NY 10022
(212) 373-8672 .. **Baker,** Bonnie M '96 Friedman KS&A LLP -1633 Bway -NY 10019 **Fx:**833-1250
(518) 449-2043 .. **Baker,** Bonnie S '97 %Chapter 13 Trustee -7 Southwoods Blvd -Albany 12211 **Fx:**449-2473
(212) 408-2500 .. **Baker Botts,LLP** -30 Rckfllr Plz -NY 10112 **Fx:**408-2501
(212) 704-6000 .. **Baker,** Brett R '98 (Troutman S LLP) -405 Lex Av -NY 10174
(516) 572-6063 .. **Baker,** Brian C '95 Nassau Hlth Care Corp -2201 Hempstd Tpk -E Meadow 11554 **Fx:**572-0160
(212) 679-3140 .. **Baker,** Brian R '89 -244 Mad Av -NY 10016
(585) 263-1000 .. **Baker,** Bruce J '80 (Nixon P LLP) -1100 Clinton Sq -Rchstr 14604
(518) 745-1400 .. **Baker,** Carl T '79 (FitzGerald MBF) -16 Pearl Bx2017 -Glens Fls 12801
(212) 610-6300 .. **Baker,** Carrie Moore '08 %Allen & O -1221 Av of Amer -NY 10020
(212) 335-4500 .. **Baker,** Chas H '86 (DLA Piper LLP) -1251 Av of Amer -NY 10020
(212) 218-2100 .. **Baker,** Chas P '68 OfCnsl Fitzpatrick CH&S -1290 Av of Amer -NY 10104
(607) 737-3560 .. **Baker,** Christopher P '96 %Hon J O'Shea -203 Lk Bx588 -Elmira 14902
(212) 730-0030 .. **Baker,** Cory M '02 Cnsl Iconix Brand Grp,Inc -1450 Bway -NY 10018
(212) 264-5916 .. **Baker,** Cynthia Gordon '94 DHS/ICE -26 Fed Plz -NY 10278
(718) 658-1912 .. **Baker,** Cynthia R '89 -90-04 161st -Jamaica 11432 **Fx:**739-8505
(516) 228-1300 .. **Baker,** Danl J '93 (Sahn WC&B,PLLC) -333 Earle Ovngton Blvd -Uniondale 11553
(212) 906-1200 .. **Baker,** David Jansing '01 (Latham & W) -885 3rd Av -NY 10022
(212) 752-5507 .. **Baker,** David R '63 OfCnsl Haskell SY&R,LLC -515 Mad Av -NY 10022
(212) 388-2060 .. **Baker,** Elizabeth A '96 %Local 32B-32J SEIU -101 Av of Amer -NY 10013 **Fx:**388-2180
(518) 584-6140 .. **Baker,** Ellen C '77 Pozefsky & B -48 State -Saratoga Spgs 12866
(845) 486-6800 .. **Baker,** Ellen L '83 (McCabe & M LLP) -63 Wshngtn Bx509 -Poughkeepsie 12602
(212) 613-1280 .. **Baker,** Eric S '97 Starbucks -330 5th Av -NY 10001
(212) 883-8833 .. **Baker,** Evan D '97 %Tacopina & A -275 Mad Av -NY 10016
(212) 223-3600 .. **Baker,** Gary B '70 -110 E 59th -NY 10022
(212) 227-5748 .. **Baker,** Gerald H '67 (Baker P&R) -44 Court -Brklyn 11201 **Fx:**(201) 659-1400
(516) 783-3300 .. **Baker Greenspan & Bernstein** -2099 Bellmore Av -Bellmore 11710 **Fx:**783-3311
(914) 468-0190 .. **Baker,** Gregg S '88 (Corrigan & B,LLC) -1311 Mamaroneck Av -White Plns 10605 **Fx:**468-0199
(212) 849-7000 .. **Baker,** H Gregory '05 %Quinn EU&S,LLP -51 Mad Av -NY 10010
(718) 858-7927 .. **Baker,** Harold C III '93 -32 Court -Brklyn 11201 **Fx:**260-9636
(212) 593-5400 .. **Baker,** Harold d' O '46 (Baker N&W) -515 Mad Av -NY 10022
(212) 450-4000 .. **Baker,** Hayden S '03 %Davis P&W LLP -450 Lex Av -NY 10017
(212) 747-1230 .. **Baker,** Heidi C '01 %McMahon M&G LLP -55 Washington -Brklyn 11201
(212) 589-4200 .. **Baker & Hostetler LLP** -45 Rckfllr Plz -NY 10111 **Fx:**589-4201
(631) 499-6606 .. **Baker,** Howard A '67 -12 Shelbourne Ln -Commack 11725
(212) 695-0060 .. **Baker,** Howard L '74 (Wilens & B,PC) -450 7th Av -NY 10123
(212) 345-1542 .. **Baker,** Irene M '03 Marsh & McLennan Cos -1166 Av of Amer -NY 10036
(416) 358-4665 .. **Baker,** Irwin C '09 -1623 Military Rd -Niagara Fls 14304
(212) 822-8300 .. **Baker,** James '74 NMIC -76 Wadsworth Av -NY 10033 **Fx:**740-9645
(607) 275-9916 .. **Baker,** James A '81 -148 The Cmmns -Ithaca 14850 **Fx:**275-9920
(631) 777-2330 .. **Baker,** James E '81 (O'Connor OH&D,LLP) -1 Huntngtn Quad -Melvll 11747
(212) 849-7000 .. **Baker,** James E '02 %Quinn EU&S,LLP -51 Mad Av -NY 10010
(212) 298-5441 .. **Baker,** Japheth T '06 %Leg Aid -49 Thomas -NY 10013 **Fx:**298-5252
(212) 267-1650 .. **Baker,** Jared E '08 %Fine O&A,LLP -39 Bway -NY 10006
(518) 438-9907 .. **Baker,** Jeffrey S '88 (Young SWRB&M,LLC) -5 Palisades Dr -Albany 12205
(585) 924-7550 .. **Baker,** Jeffrey W '71 Redcom Labs Inc -1 Redcom Ctr -Victor 14564
(516) 775-7007 .. **Baker,** Jesse R '82 (Gutman MB&S,PC) -813 Jericho Tpk -New Hyde Pk 11040
(716) 566-1300 .. **Baker,** Jessica M '04 %Hiscock & B,LLP -1100 M&T Ctr -Buffalo 14203
(516) 248-4503 .. **Baker,** John W '04 -65 E John -Hicksvll 11801
(518) 474-8390 .. **Baker,** Jos R III '88 %Governors Ofc -State Cptl -Albany 12224
(212) 715-9100 .. **Baker,** Katrina L '09 %Kramer LN&F,LLP -1177 Av of Amer -NY 10036
(212) 381-4221 .. **Baker,** Lauren M '03 Halstead Property -831 Bway -NY 10003
(716) 853-2888 .. **Baker,** Laurie A '10 %T Burton -716 Brisbane Bldg -Buffalo 14203 **Fx:**853-2892
(585) 621-1090 .. **Baker,** Lawr '79 -480 W Ridge Rd -Rchstr 14615 **Fx:**621-9501
(914) 681-9500 .. **Baker Leshko Saline & Blosser,LLP** -1 N Lex Av -White Plns 10601 **Fx:**681-9505
(516) 229-4300 .. **Baker,** Lisa A '98 %J Bilello & Assoc -875 Merrick Av -Westbury 11590
(212) 805-1007 .. **Baker,** Louisa L '89 Wells Fargo -530 5th Av -NY 10036 **Fx:**805-1119
(212) 962-0200 .. **Baker,** M David '61 -225 Bway -NY 10007 **Fx:**233-3859
(718) 237-2000 .. **Baker,** Margaret L '96 %Leg Aid -111 Lvngstn -Brklyn 11201 **Fx:**237-8737
(212) 849-7000 .. **Baker,** Mark D '03 %Quinn EU&S,LLP -51 Mad Av -NY 10010
(212) 750-7800 .. **Baker,** Mark M '73 Cnsl Brafman & Assoc -767 3rd Av -NY 10017 **Fx:**750-3906
(212) 742-1969 .. **Baker,** Mark R '80 NY Water Taxi -499 Van Brunt -Brklyn 11231
(212) 632-5500 .. **Baker,** Martin S '68 OfCnsl Salans LLP -620 5th Av -NY 10020
(212) 857-8230 .. **Baker McEvoy Morrissey & Moskovits,PC** -330 W 34th -NY 10001 **Fx:**857-8238
(212) 626-4100 .. **Baker & McKenzie LLP** -1114 Av of Amer -NY 10036 **Fx:**310-1600
(212) 848-4000 .. **Baker,** Michl S '99 (Shearman & S LLP) -599 Lex Av -NY 10022
(607) 778-2403 .. **Baker,** Michl T '98 %Pub Def -45 Hawley Bx1766 -Bnghmtn 13902 **Fx:**778-2432
(914) 681-9500 .. **Baker,** Mitchell J '81 (Baker LS&B,LLP) -1 N Lex Av -White Plns 10601
(212) 455-2000 .. **Baker,** Nicholas E '08 %Simpson T&B LLP -425 Lex Av -NY 10017
(315) 793-7000 .. **Baker,** Olli S '08 %Leg Aid -255 Genesee -Utica 13501 **Fx:**732-3202
(212) 483-2323 .. **Baker,** Paula M '84 %JP Morgan Chase -345 Park Av -NY 10154
(607) 243-5416 .. **Baker,** Peter H '79 (Hunt & B) -9 Main Bx7 -Dundee 14837 **Fx:**243-8409
(607) 569-2181 .. **Baker,** Peter H '79 Baker Law Ofcs -51 Main Bx398 -Hammondsprt 14840 **Fx:**569-2182
(518) 462-1015 .. **Baker,** R Linn '78 %ODAR-SSA -74 N Pearl -Albany 12207
(914) 517-5000 .. **Baker,** Richd C '83 (Meiselman DPC&E,PC) -1311 Mamaroneck Av -White Plns 10605
(716) 873-5610 .. **Baker,** Robt A Jr. '78 %Johnson Precision Inc -1516 Military Rd -Buffalo 14217
(914) 694-4444 .. **Baker,** Robt C '59 %Natl Rlty & Dvlpmnt -3 Manhattanvll Rd -Purchase 10577 **Fx:**694-5448
(516) 741-4799 .. **Baker,** Robt J '97 (Baker SBGFM&N,LLC) -100 Grdn City Plz -Gdn Cty 11530
(212) 230-8800 .. **Baker,** Robin L '90 Cnsl WilmerHale -399 Park Av -NY 10022
(212) 338-5110 .. **Baker,** Ryan S '05 -485 Lex Av -NY 10017 **Fx:**(646) 307-7106
(516) 741-4799 .. **Baker Sanders Barshay Grossman Fass Muhlstock & Neuwirth, LLC** -100 Grdn City Plz -Gdn Cty 11530 **Fx:**741-3777
(212) 758-2020 .. **Baker,** Scott L '89 -200 Park Av S -NY 10003
(914) 347-1292 .. **Baker,** Simon H '69 OfCnsl Rosenthal & M,LLP -45 Knollwood Rd -Elmsfrd 10523
Baker, Stephanie C '08 -996 Park Pl -Brklyn 11213
(518) 563-4022 .. **Baker,** Stephen '90 %Leg Aid -100 Court Bx989 -Plattsbrgh 12901 **Fx:**563-4058
(607) 434-9818 .. **Baker,** Stephen F '85 -252 Main -Oneonta 13820 **Fx:**432-4337
(212) 481-7007 .. **Baker,** Stephen L '69 (Baker & R) -1350 Bway -NY 10018
(212) 857-8230 .. **Baker,** Steven J '93 (Baker MM&M,PC) -330 W 34th -NY 10001
(212) 408-5100 .. **Baker,** Stuart D '60 (Chadbourne & P LLP) -30 Rckfllr Plz -NY 10112
(212) 450-4000 .. **Baker,** Susan Betteridge '85 Cnsl Davis P&W LLP -450 Lex Av -NY 10017
(212) 578-2211 .. **Baker,** Theresa Jeszeck '88 %MetLife -27-01 Qns Plz N -LIC 11101

(631) 715-7900 .. **Baker,** Wayne '97 %US Atty -610 Fed Plz -Central Islip 11722
(315) 422-7000 .. **Baker,** Wm F '89 Pyramid Cos -4 Clinton Sq -Syracuse 13202
(212) 210-9487 .. **Baker,** Wm H '05 Cnsl Alston & B LLP -90 Park Av -NY 10016
(212) 309-6000 .. **Baker,** Wm T Jr. '69 SrCnsl Morgan L&B LLP -101 Park Av -NY 10178
(212) 922-1500 .. **Baker-Cooper,** Lindsay '07 Ad Council,Inc -815 2nd Av -NY 10017
(914) 946-8900 .. **Baker Miller,** P Dawn '97 OfCnsl Clark G&M -99 Court -White Plns 10601
(212) 804-4200 .. **Bakert,** Vanessa M '03 %Mound CW&G -One Bttry Pk Plz -NY 10004
(516) 248-1180 .. **Bakhchi,** Laurie '07 %Continental Abstrct -1 Old Cntry Rd -Carle Pl 11514 **Fx:**248-7596
(845) 938-5544 .. **Bakken,** Timothy '86 US Military Academy -Dept of Law -West Pnt 10996 **Fx:**938-5541
(518) 487-7600 .. **Bakner,** Terresa M '88 (Whiteman O&H LLP) -1 Commerce Plz -Albany 12260
(718) 848-8515 .. **Baksh,** Affar '04 -147-26 Hillside Av -Jamaica 11435
(718) 590-2000 .. **Baksh,** Rasheeda '04 %DA -198 E 161st -Bronx 10451 **Fx:**590-6477
(212) 708-1942 .. **Bakshani,** Bharati H '90 (Ladas & P) -26 W 61st -NY 10023
(212) 570-1333 .. **Bakshi,** Manmohan K '87 -110 Wall -NY 10005
(845) 551-8237 .. **Bakshi,** Moneesh K '90 -1 Raymnd Av -Chestnut Rdg 10977
(716) 631-0004 .. **Bakshi,** Sunil '95 (Shelby B&W) -5662 Main -Williamsvll 14221 **Fx:**631-7546
(212) 506-2500 .. **Bakst,** David S '97 (Mayer B LLP) -1675 Bway -NY 10019
(212) 285-3038 .. **Bakst,** Dina Leshetz '98 %Better Balance -75 Maiden Ln -NY 10038 **Fx:**724-3535
(718) 284-8058 .. **Bakst,** Elliott '59 -180 E 18th -Brklyn 11226
(212) 268-7900 .. **Bakst,** Lyle A '85 (Fischer & B,PC) -888 7th Av -NY 10106
(516) 829-1900 .. **Bakst,** Lyle A '85 (Fischer & B,PC) -98 Cuttermill Rd -Gt Neck 11021
(917) 500-9039 .. **Balaban,** Barry '79 -8 Bond -Gt Neck 11021
(212) 757-0007 .. **Balaban,** Rachel Greer '00 (Scarola E LLP) -888 7th Av -NY 10106
(212) 906-1200 .. **Balaban,** Witold '94 (Latham & W) -885 3rd Av -NY 10022
(212) 552-6742 .. **Balacek,** Gerald T '93 JP Morgan Chase -1 Chase Manh Plz -NY 10081
(212) 436-1412 .. **Balachandran,** Murali '92 %IRS-Dist Cnsl -290 Bway -NY 10007
(212) 841-7712 .. **Balachandran,** Robt P '92 Cushman Wakefield -1290 Av of Amer -NY 10104
(212) 489-8230 .. **Balachandran,** Sona '08 %Davis WT LLP -1633 Bway -NY 10019
(718) 236-9300 .. **Balagur,** Perry '67 -8313 Bay Pkwy -Brklyn 11214 **Fx:**236-9318
(718) 981-6112 .. **Balahadia,** Modesto L '81 -552 Tompkins Av -Staten Isl 10305 **Fx:**981-6527
(212) 940-8800 .. **Balahan,** Cameron '08 %Katten MR LLP -575 Mad Av -NY 10022
(212) 962-1450 .. **Balahtsis,** Deana '97 -111 John -NY 10038 **Fx:**385-0235
(914) 384-1337 .. **Balaj,** Maria '02 -4 VA Pl -Plsntvll 10570
(212) 819-8200 .. **Balajee,** Aravind '07 %White & C LLP -1155 Av of Amer -NY 10036
(212) 344-1744 .. **Balakhovsky,** Yakov M '96 (Solton R&B LLP) -110 Wall -NY 10005 **Fx:**344-1734
(212) 964-7552 .. **Balakrishnan,** Rana '01 %RO Modupe -139 Fulton -NY 10038 **Fx:**693-1663
(516) 742-8058 .. **Balamoti,** Michl J '99 %Abamont & Assoc -200 Grdn City Plz Bx9250 -Gdn Cty 11530 **Fx:**742-7308
(212) 770-1889 .. **Balan,** Denise R '85 %AIG -80 Pine -NY 10005 **Fx:**344-2286
(516) 741-6996 .. **Balanoff,** Gilbert L '73 -1539 Franklin Av -Mineola 11501 **Fx:**877-7221
(914) 640-8100 .. **Balanoff,** Jamie E '02 Starwood Hotels & Resorts Worldwide,Inc -1111 Wstchstr Av -White Plns 10604
(315) 422-1391 .. **Balanoff,** Michl J '71 (Green & S,PLLC) -One Lincoln Ctr #900 -Syracuse 13202
(212) 888-2005 .. **Balardi,** Vincent A '88 %Morgenthau & G,LLP -575 Lex Av -NY 10022
(718) 560-2248 .. **Balas,** Matithyohu '04 The Knot,Inc -45 Main -Brklyn 11201
(212) 880-3800 .. **Balaschak,** Susan F '86 (Akerman S) -335 Mad Av -NY 10017
(212) 373-3000 .. **Balascio,** Michl A '08 %Paul WRW&G LLP -1285 Av of Amer -NY 10019
(212) 391-0170 .. **Balasiano,** Steven '88 Ventura Enterprises -512 Fashion Av -NY 10018
(212) 850-0603 .. **Balaskas,** Zoy '99 1st Amer Title -633 3rd Av -NY 10017 **Fx:**(646) 487-6931
(845) 454-1110 .. **Balassone,** Leah J '91 %Corbally G and R LLP -35 Market -Poughkeepsie 12601
(914) 946-5060 .. **Balazs,** Stephen R '87 -4 Bred Ln -White Plns 10605 **Fx:**288-9291
(212) 246-2400 .. **Balber,** Eric D '73 (Balber PM&VDT,PC) -1370 Av of Amer -NY 10019
(212) 246-2400 .. **Balber Pickard Maldonado & Van Der Tuin, PC** -1370 Av of Amer -NY 10019 **Fx:**765-4212
(212) 408-5100 .. **Balber,** Scott S '95 (Chadbourne & P LLP) -30 Rckfllr Plz -NY 10112
(212) 335-9000 .. **Balbert,** Coleen '99 %DA -1 Hogan Pl -NY 10013
(202) 315-5100 .. **Balboni,** Michl A L '85 Navigators Global -40 W 57th -NY 10019 **Fx:**315-5010
(212) 724-6396 .. **Balcacer,** Orlando I '95 -63 W 87th -NY 10024
(716) 856-5500 .. **Balcarczyk,** James E II '02 %Damon M LLP -200 Delaware Av -Buffalo 14202
(212) 735-3000 .. **Balch,** Michl J '94 Cnsl Skadden ASM&F LLP -4 Times Sq -NY 10036
(212) 225-2000 .. **Balcom,** Jonathan C '08 %Cleary GS&H -1 Lbrty Plz -NY 10006
(716) 938-9111 .. **Balcom,** Kelly M '03 DA -303 Court -Little Vly 14755
(212) 930-9700 .. **Balcombe-Francis,** Marcelle S '00 (Sichenzia RFF LLP) -61 Bway -NY 10006
(212) 790-0241 .. **Baldacci,** Paris R '88 %Benj N Cardozo Schl of Law -55 5th Av -NY 10003 **Fx:**790-0345
(212) 956-9500 .. **Baldachin,** Alan G '97 (Hand B&A LLP) -8 W 40th -NY 10018 **Fx:**376-6080
(212) 541-2000 .. **Baldasare,** Sharon L '06 %Bryan C LLP -1290 Av of Amer -NY 10104
(973) 596-4901 .. **Baldassare,** Michl A '00 (Gibbons PC) -1 Penn Plz -NY 10119 **Fx:**639-6274
(212) 657-0019 .. **Baldauf,** Andrew J '05 Citibank Glbl Mkts -111 Wall -NY 10005
(716) 886-0211 .. **Baldauf,** David H '77 %Benderson Dvlpmnt -570 Delaware Av -Buffalo 14202 **Fx:**886-2269
(716) 853-8507 .. **Baldauf,** Gary A '86 %Medicaid Fraud Cntrl -350 Main Pl Twr -Buffalo 14202 **Fx:**853-8525
(718) 529-2300 .. **Baldeo,** Albert J '92 A Baldeo,PC -106-11 Lbrty Av -Ozone Pk 11417 **Fx:**848-6203
(212) 966-4737 .. **Baldeo,** Krishna Jagdeo '92 -401 Bway -NY 10013
(212) 940-3041 .. **Balderston,** Kathleen M '83 (Nixon P LLP) -437 Mad Av -NY 10022
(212) 697-6266 .. **Baldi,** Paul L '56 -420 Lex Av -NY 10170 **Fx:**697-6149
(631) 224-5376 .. **Baldillo,** Aimee-Joan Caparas '02 Islip Law Enfrcmnt -655 Main -Islip 11751
(718) 627-1354 .. **Baldinger,** Harry M '86 -1546 E 7th -Brklyn 11230 **Fx:**339-3731
(718) 258-9066 .. **Baldinger,** Morris A '81 -2602 Av M -Brklyn 11210
(212) 872-1000 .. **Baldini,** Stephen M '91 -One Bryant Park -NY 10036 **Fx:**872-1002
(704) 749-8946 .. **Baldino,** Ralph J '01 %Bryan C LLP -1290 Av of Amer -NY 10104 **Fx:**749-9346
(516) 775-7007 .. **Baldinucci,** Edgardo L '99 (Gutman MB&S,PC) -813 Jericho Tpk -New Hyde Pk 11040
(212) 947-4855 .. **Baldonado,** Hector J '98 (Baldonado & Assoc,PC) -481 8th Av -NY 10001
(718) 298-8945 .. **Baldridge,** Buffy Maria '04 %Leg Aid -153-01 Jamaica Av -Jamaica 11432 **Fx:**657-0537
(212) 213-5500 .. **Balducci,** Delight D '04 %Periconi,LLC -708 3rd Av -NY 10017 **Fx:**213-5030
(315) 474-5533 .. **Balduf,** Wm L '80 W Balduf,PC -506 E Wshngtn -Syracuse 13202 **Fx:**701-4458
(212) 506-1700 .. **Balduzzi,** Julia A '09 %Kasowitz BT&F LLP -1633 Bway -NY 10019
(518) 474-2913 .. **Baldwin,** Aaron M '98 Dept of Law -The Cptl -Albany 12224 **Fx:**473-1572
(212) 417-4144 .. **Baldwin,** Danl '78 Battery Pk City Auth -1 Wrld Fncl Ctr -NY 10281 **Fx:**417-2001
(212) 374-3435 .. **Baldwin,** Elisa R '95 %NYC Dept Educ-OLS -52 Chmbrs -NY 10007 **Fx:**374-5939
(631) 324-8787 .. **Baldwin,** Elizabeth L '04 Town Atty -159 Pantigo Rd -E Hampton 11937 **Fx:**329-5371
(315) 934-4185 .. **Baldwin,** Gloria Flores '94 -8417 Oswego Rd PMB 231 -Baldwinsvll 13027 **Fx:**295-2550
(212) 747-1117 .. **Baldwin,** Irene M '91 %ANHD -50 Broad -NY 10004
(518) 477-8771 .. **Baldwin,** James N '80 %Questar III BOCES -10 Empire State Blvd -Castleton On Hudson 12033 **Fx:**477-9833
(315) 478-6551 .. **Baldwin,** Jeanella M '74 (Baldwin & W) -333 E Onondaga -Syracuse 13202
(212) 455-2000 .. **Baldwin,** Jeffrey E '09 %Simpson T&B LLP -425 Lex Av -NY 10017
(518) 457-2070 .. **Baldwin,** Jennifer L '04 Dept of Tax & Fin -Bldg 9 State Campus -Albany 12227 **Fx:**457-6131
(716) 856-5500 .. **Baldwin,** Jesse B '05 %Damon M LLP -200 Delaware Av -Buffalo 14202
(914) 824-5704 .. **Baldwin,** Linda M '94 OCA-Problem Solving Cts -140 Grand -White Plns 10601
(212) 577-3449 .. **Baldwin,** Michl T '06 %Leg Aid -199 Water -NY 10038
(516) 273-2222 .. **Baldwin,** Richd J '74 -173 Pine -Rockvll Ctr 11570
(212) 425-3730 .. **Baldwin,** Richd W '65 Brokerage & Mgmt Corp -90 Broad -NY 10004 **Fx:**363-4843
(315) 477-0100 .. **Baldwin,** Robt F Jr. '64 (Baldwin & S,LLP) -126 N Salina -Syracuse 13202
(212) 490-3000 .. **Baldwin,** Shelly L '99 (Wilson EME&D LLP) -150 E 42nd -NY 10017
(212) 402-6827 .. **Baldwin,** Summerfield M '93 -75 Maiden Ln -NY 10038
(315) 477-0100 .. **Baldwin & Sutphen,LLP** -126 N Salina -Syracuse 13202 **Fx:**477-5071
(315) 478-6551 .. **Baldwin & Wangerman** -333 E Onondaga -Syracuse 13202 **Fx:**478-0103
(212) 408-5100 .. **Baldwin Fuerst,** Marian E '92 (Chadbourne & P LLP) -30 Rckfllr Plz -NY 10112
(212) 310-8000 .. **Bale,** Morgan G '03 (Weil G&M LLP) -767 5th Av -NY 10153
(212) 998-6308 .. **Balendra,** Natasha Thiruni '00 %NYU Law Schl -245 Sullivan -NY 10012 **Fx:**995-4539
(212) 778-6801 .. **Bales,** Thos T '88 Pru Sec -1 NY Plz -NY 10292
(585) 530-3202 .. **Balestra,** Antonio Jr. '96 %Appllt Div 4th Dept -50 East Av Ste 200 -Rchstr 14604 **Fx:**530-3247
(315) 474-7541 .. **Balestra,** Michl J '09 %Menter R&T,PC -308 Maltbie -Syracuse 13204
(212) 374-5400 .. **Balestriere,** John G '99 (Balestriere L PLLC) -225 Bway -NY 10007 **Fx:**208-2613
(516) 214-0465 .. **Balestriere,** Louis '95 %S Salles -225 Bway -NY 10007 **Fx:**941-0791
(212) 907-7300 .. **Balestrino,** Rosa G L '01 %Golenbock EAB&P -437 Mad Av -NY 10022
(631) 501-1000 .. **Balfe & Holland,PC** -135 Pinelawn Rd -Melvll 11747 **Fx:**501-7699
(631) 501-1000 .. **Balfe,** Kevin E '84 (Balfe & H,PC) -135 Pinelawn Rd -Melvll 11747
(212) 446-4800 .. **Balfour,** Adam D J '08 %Kirkland & E LLP -153 E 53rd -NY 10022
(845) 486-5470 .. **Balga,** Andrea R '99 Cntrl Hudson Gas & Elec -284 South Av -Poughkeepsie 12601 **Fx:**486-5560
(212) 297-6600 .. **Balick,** Sanford E '83 %TMM -230 Park Av -NY 10169 **Fx:**297-6062
(212) 715-1000 .. **Baliga,** Vijay '05 %Arnold & P LLP -399 Park Av -NY 10022
(917) 981-0849 .. **Balile,** Sofia '03 -155 Water -Brklyn 11201
(516) 296-7000 .. **Balin,** Herbert M '52 (Certilman BA&H,LLP) -90 Merrick Av -E Meadow 11554
(212) 489-8230 .. **Balin,** Robt D '87 (Davis WT LLP) -1633 Bway -NY 10019
(914) 681-0200 .. **Balint,** Andrew J '60 Cnsl DelBello DWW&W,LLP -1 N Lex Av -White Plns 10601
(212) 944-9112 .. **Balint,** Marcie S '76 (Strategic Leg Solutions) -110 E 42nd -NY 10017 **Fx:**944-8448
(718) 389-5353 .. **Balis,** Keith W '83 -122 Nassau Av -Brklyn 11222 **Fx:**383-6720
(212) 962-0360 .. **Balistreri,** Chas M '78 (Anes FL&B,PLLC) -299 Bway -NY 10007
(718) 378-1100 .. **Balka,** Sigmund R '61 %Krasdale Foods Inc -400 Food Ctr Dr -Bronx 10474 **Fx:**893-0562
(516) 294-8844 .. **Balkan,** Kenneth J '73 Cnsl L'Abbate BC&C,LLP -1001 Franklin Av -Gdn Cty 11530
(716) 434-8891 .. **Balkin,** Patrick M '85 (Jackson & B) -365 Market Bx468 -Lockprt 14095
(212) 506-5000 .. **Ball,** Andrea '08 %Orrick H&S LLP -51 W 52nd -NY 10019
(631) 864-8700 .. **Ball,** Ann '82 A Ball PC -357 Vets Mem'l Hwy -Commack 11725
(212) 326-3939 .. **Ball,** Corinne '79 (Jones D) -222 E 41st -NY 10017

(212) 508-6100 .. **Ball,** David J '05 %Bracewell & G,LLP -1251 Av of Amer -NY 10020
(212) 752-3380 .. **Ball,** Deborah S '90 -880 3rd Av -NY 10022 **Fx:**(718) 544-3116
(607) 723-5341 .. **Ball,** Dwight R '60 SpclCnsl Hinman H&K,LLP -80 Exchange Bx5250 -Bnghmtn 13902
(212) 530-5000 .. **Ball,** James H Jr. '93 (Milbank TH&M LLP) -1 Chase Manh Plz -NY 10005
(607) 746-3944 .. **Ball,** James J '91 -Bx22 -Meridale 13806
(212) 909-6000 .. **Ball,** Jasmine '00 (Debevoise & P LLP) -919 3rd Av -NY 10022
(212) 556-2100 .. **Ball,** Jonathan D '03 %King & S -1185 Av of Amer -NY 10036
(518) 474-6740 .. **Ball,** Jos P '79 %Dept of State -41 State -Albany 12231 **Fx:**473-9211
(716) 853-3700 .. **Ball,** Kelly Lynn '96 %Harrington & M -70 Niagara -Buffalo 14202
(845) 338-6600 .. **Ball,** Lawr E '89 (Riseley & B) -111 Green Bx3296 -Kingston 12402
(716) 648-3030 .. **Ball,** Lisa A '09 %Chiacchia & F,LLP -5113 S Park Av -Hambrg 14075
(718) 817-3010 .. **Ball,** Margaret T '85 %Fordham Univ-Secretary -441 E Fordham Rd -Bronx 10458 **Fx:**817-3005
(914) 517-5000 .. **Ball,** Ronald A '79 OfCnsl Meiselman DPC&E,PC -1311 Mamaroneck Av -White Plns 10605
(212) 577-7700 .. **Ball,** Shonnie R '08 %Safe Horizon -2 Lafayette -NY 10007 **Fx:**385-0331
(914) 779-2600 .. **Ball,** Stuart '84 (Ball & F,PC) -2066 Cntrl Pk Av -Ynkrs 10710 **Fx:**779-2690
(516) 622-9200 .. **Ball,** Stuart S '84 (Westerman BEM&S,LLP) -1201 RXR Plz -Uniondale 11553
(716) 851-4343 .. **Ball,** Timothy A '05 %Law Dept -65 Niagara Sq -Buffalo 14202 **Fx:**851-4105
(212) 909-6000 .. **Balla,** Anne '09 %Debevoise & P LLP -919 3rd Av -NY 10022
(212) 238-4800 .. **Ballaine,** Wm G '72 (Landman CB&F,PC) -120 Bway -NY 10271
(212) 450-4000 .. **Ballan,** Harry R '93 (Davis P&W LLP) -450 Lex Av -NY 10017
(212) 935-3000 .. **Ballan,** Jonathan A '83 (Mintz LCFG&P,PC) -666 3rd Av -NY 10017
(315) 353-6614 .. **Ballan,** Robt H '82 -11 Baldwin Av -Norwd 13668 **Fx:**353-6615
(315) 379-2115 .. **Ballan,** Steven G '94 Pub Def -Cnty Cthse -Canton 13617 **Fx:**386-8241
(212) 506-1700 .. **Ballantyne,** Leslie MacDonald '02 %Kasowitz BT&F LLP -1633 Bway -NY 10019
(212) 896-6500 .. **Ballard,** Gregory G '93 (Howrey LLP) -601 Lex Av -NY 10022
(516) 466-6030 .. **Ballard,** Katrina W '97 %Mirkin & G,PC -98 Cuttermill Rd -Gt Neck 11021
(212) 626-4100 .. **Ballard,** Marcella '92 (Baker & M LLP) -1114 Av of Amer -NY 10036
(212) 825-5918 .. **Ballard,** Melissa A '07 Dept of Invstgtn -80 Maiden Ln -NY 10038 **Fx:**825-2860
(212) 720-5865 .. **Ballard,** Michl D II '98 %Fed Reserve Bk -33 Lbrty -NY 10045
(212) 552-2596 .. **Ballas,** Haroula Kordolemis '95 JP Morgan Chase -1 Chase Manh Plz -NY 10005
(212) 479-2000 .. **Ballas,** Stephen B '03 %TPG-Axon Captl Mgmt -888 7th Av -NY 10106
(516) 541-9080 .. **Ballato,** Anthony T '89 -5476 Merrick Rd -Massapequa 11758
(845) 634-3627 .. **Ballentine,** Gillian T '08 %Leg Aid -2 Congers Rd -New Cty 10956 **Fx:**634-8505
(212) 545-4640 .. **Baller,** Chas H '58 (Wolf HAF&H LLP) -270 Mad Av -NY 10016
(518) 395-5400 .. **Baller,** Russell H Jr. '60 %Racing & Wagering Bd -1 Bway Ctr -Schnctdy 12305 **Fx:**347-1250
(212) 465-1900 .. **Ballesteros,** Mary C '56 -350 5th Av -NY 10118 **Fx:**268-3076
(212) 775-3726 .. **Balletta,** Richd '88 NYS Dept Labor -75 Varick -NY 10013
(718) 625-8940 .. **Balletti,** Wm J '89 %B Lawrence -15 Metrotech Ctr N -Brklyn 11201 **Fx:**624-5756
(212) 715-9100 .. **Balliett,** Thos D '81 (Kramer LN&F,LLP) -1177 Av of Amer -NY 10036
(212) 732-8700 .. **Ballin,** Dawn C '05 %McAloon & F,PC -123 William -NY 10038
(585) 753-4500 .. **Balling,** Amanda Harris '09 %DA -832 Watts Bldg -Rchstr 14614 **Fx:**753-4576
(718) 237-3100 .. **Ballinger,** Kelly G '01 Leg Aid -111 Lvngstn -Brklyn 11201 **Fx:**250-4243
(585) 359-3840 .. **Ballister,** Jos C '91 -103 Parkmeadow Dr -Pittsfrd 14534 **Fx:**334-9775
(585) 394-8952 .. **Ballman,** Michl J '03 -70 S Main -Canandaigua 14424
(212) 594-2880 .. **Ballner,** Patricia R '91 -350 5th Av -NY 10118 **Fx:**736-5601
(212) 575-7900 .. **Ballon Stoll Bader & Nadler,PC** -729 7th Av -NY 10019 **Fx:**764-5060
(716) 634-0500 .. **Ballow,** John E '85 (Ballow Law Firm) -8226 Main -Williamsvll 14221 **Fx:**634-9075
(718) 981-0219 .. **Ballowe,** Melissa L '09 Leg Aid -60 Bay -Staten Isl 10301 **Fx:**981-6623
(212) 839-5300 .. **Balmer,** Reed W '06 %Sidley A LLP -787 7th Av -NY 10019
(212) 373-3000 .. **Balog,** Aliza J '06 %Paul WRW&G LLP -1285 Av of Amer -NY 10019
(718) 687-1737 .. **Balogun,** Safurat A '04 MTA -130 Lvngstn -Brklyn 11201
(716) 566-1300 .. **Balon,** Frank V '03 Cnsl Hiscock & B,LLP -1100 M&T Ctr -Buffalo 14203
(585) 232-2070 .. **Balonek,** Barry C '76 SrCnsl Stewart Title Ins -47 W Main -Rchstr 14614 **Fx:**232-4988
(212) 259-8000 .. **Baloul,** Gassan Adnan '05 %Dewey & L LLP -1301 Av of Amer -NY 10019
(518) 862-1386 .. **Balouskas,** Peter P '00 %Burke SM&H,LLP -302 Wshngtn Av Ext Bx15085 -Albany 12212
(914) 323-7000 .. **Baloy,** Donna Marie '94 (Wilson EME&D LLP) -3 Gannett Dr -White Plns 10604
(631) 324-0587 .. **Balsam,** Alexander I '07 Dayton & V -11 Muchmore Ln -E Hampton 11937 **Fx:**324-6593
(212) 473-9173 .. **Balsam,** Craig I '87 %Razor & Tie Music Corp -214 Sullivan -NY 10012
(631) 261-8834 .. **Balsam,** Ethan D '07 %Ingerman S LLP -150 Motor Pkwy -Hauppauge 11788
(212) 422-4600 .. **Balsam Felber & Goldfield** -99 Wall -NY 10005 **Fx:**422-4605
(718) 875-8341 .. **Balsam,** Helaine '83 %Envrnmntl Cntrl Brd -233 Schermerhorn -Brklyn 11201
(212) 543-9999 .. **Balsam,** Howard A '00 (Balsam J,LLP) -315 Mad Av -NY 10017 **Fx:**(888) 227-0711
(212) 838-7200 .. **Balsam,** Jerome M '82 %Gabriel Capital Grp -450 Park Av -NY 10022 **Fx:**838-9603
(212) 682-3025 .. **Balsam,** Moshe '82 %Weiss & L -551 5th Av -NY 10176
(212) 331-5865 .. **Balsam,** Richd F '92 HRA-Ofc Legal Affrs -180 Water -NY 10038 **Fx:**331-6136
(212) 422-4600 .. **Balsam,** Robt S '83 (Balsam F&G) -99 Wall -NY 10005
(718) 224-9038 .. **Balsam,** Steven '74 -50-35 207th -Oakland Gdns 11364
(212) 558-4000 .. **Balsam,** Yael S '98 SpclCnsl Sullivan & C LLP -125 Broad -NY 10004
(718) 858-7280 .. **Balsamo,** Andrea R '86 (Balsamo & R,PC) -80 Lvngstn -Brklyn 11201 **Fx:**855-4173
(212) 785-3434 .. **Balsamo,** Anthony '74 -40 Exch Pl -NY 10005 **Fx:**425-9237
(845) 357-2744 .. **Balsamo Byrne Cipriani & Ellsworth** -16 Chestnut Bx209 -Suffern 10901 **Fx:**357-3987
(718) 849-0021 .. **Balsamo,** Dolores D '81 -80-59 Lefferts Blvd -Kew Gdns 11415
(516) 742-0676 .. **Balsamo,** Michl N '79 -1325 Franklin Av -Gdn Cty 11530
(212) 400-7177 .. **Balsamo,** Stephen F '99 %Garrity GMG&F -40 Wall -NY 10005
(917) 421-4749 .. **Balsamo-Maniscalco,** Michelle L '04 IRS -33 Maiden Ln -NY 10038
(212) 576-5719 .. **Baltazar,** Lisa G '99 NY Life Ins -51 Mad Av -NY 10010
(516) 594-3471 .. **Baltch,** David L '65 -232 Thompson Av -Oceanside 11572 **Fx:**594-3014
(516) 766-5347 .. **Baltch,** Raymond J '65 -80 W Henrietta Av -Oceanside 11572 **Fx:**766-1153
(212) 732-8368 .. **Balter,** Ronald '84 (Caruso SLCU&S) -132 Nassau -NY 10038
(631) 267-8327 .. **Balterman,** Harry '47 -27 Pineway Bx1290 -Amagansett 11930 **Fx:**267-7642
(212) 474-1000 .. **Balthazaar,** M C Tania '02 %Cravath S&M LLP -825 8th Av -NY 10019
(718) 928-3700 .. **Baltimore,** Beth Dworkin '09 %LSNYC-Bronx -579 Courtlandt Av -Bronx 10451 **Fx:**402-7586
(718) 777-1233 .. **Baltrunas,** Evey '91 -23-56 Steinway -Astoria 11105 **Fx:**777-8998
(518) 459-6422 .. **Baltrush,** Jennifer A '06 SpclCnsl Capital District Ctr for Independence -875 Central Av -Albany 12206 **Fx:**459-7847
(212) 286-6100 .. **Baltzis,** Konstantinos G '01 %Rosenberg & P,LLP -420 Lex Av -NY 10170
(212) 857-8800 .. **Baluarte,** David C '08 US Ct of Appls -40 Foley Sq -NY 10007
(718) 286-6000 .. **Balvin,** Chas J '05 %DA -125-01 Qns Blvd -Kew Gdns 11415
(212) 758-9700 .. **Balzafiore,** Philip L '96 %KPMG LLP -345 Park Av -NY 10154
(212) 240-0099 .. **Balzano,** Vincent J '84 (Balzano & Assoc) -20 Vesey -NY 10007
(518) 432-9700 .. **Balzer,** Chad E '97 (Balzer & L,PLLC) -275½ Lark -Albany 12210 **Fx:**432-9722
(914) 316-3525 .. **Balzer,** Elyse G '77 -67 Grand Blvd -Scarsdale 10583
(212) 336-0027 .. **Bambach,** Alistaire '89 %SEC -3 World Fncl Ctr -NY 10281 **Fx:**336-1323
(212) 986-6840 .. **Bamberger,** David E '83 OfCnsl N Brickman -317 Mad Av -NY 10017 **Fx:**986-7691
(212) 857-2250 .. **Bamberger,** Kenneth A '01 %Hon A Kearse -40 Foley Sq -NY 10007
(212) 768-6700 .. **Bamberger,** Michl A '60 (Sonnenschein N&R LLP) -1221 Av of Amer -NY 10020
(518) 257-1443 .. **Bamberger,** Paul S '91 %CSEA,Inc -143 Wshngtn Av Bx7125 -Albany 12224 **Fx:**449-1525
(212) 848-4000 .. **Bambino,** Laurence M '83 (Shearman & S LLP) -599 Lex Av -NY 10022
(516) 747-2110 .. **Bambrick,** Gerard M '89 -1 Old Cntry Rd -Carle Pl 11514 **Fx:**(888) 419-0412
(516) 352-7266 .. **Bambrick,** Mary Ryan '95 -318 Carnation Av -Floral Pk 11001
(646) 610-5000 .. **Bambury,** John H '06 NYC Police Dept -1 Police Plz -NY 10038
(716) 856-7091 .. **Bambury,** Kevin J '89 %J Freedman -424 Main -Buffalo 14202 **Fx:**856-7097
(212) 230-8800 .. **Bamgboye,** Abimbola S '08 %WilmerHale -399 Park Av -NY 10022
(914) 941-0600 .. **Bamonte,** David J '89 -540 N State Rd -Briarclff Mnr 10510 **Fx:**941-0609
(212) 608-8840 .. **Bamundo,** Steven '80 (Bamundo Z&S,LLP) -111 John -NY 10038
(212) 608-8840 .. **Bamundo Zwal & Schermerhorn,LLP** -111 John -NY 10038 **Fx:**608-8039
(212) 541-5800 .. **Ban,** Jason M '99 Laurus Captl Mgmt -335 Mad Av -NY 10017 **Fx:**541-4434
(315) 682-7585 .. **Banac,** Mark A '87 M Banac,PC -224 Fayette -Manlius 13104 **Fx:**682-1490
(212) 237-1000 .. **Banahan,** Thos A '80 SpclCnsl Windels ML&M,LLP -156 W 56th -NY 10019
(716) 853-3087 .. **Banas,** Beata '99 %Leg Srvcs -237 Main -Buffalo 14203 **Fx:**856-5317
(716) 854-9283 .. **Banas,** Elissa M '94 -44 St James Pl -Buffalo 14222
(716) 856-0600 .. **Banas,** Mitchell J Jr. '86 (Jaeckle F&M,LLP) -12 Fountain Plz -Buffalo 14202
(212) 687-3000 .. **Banayan,** Sean D '05 %Jaffe & A,LLP -600 3rd Av -NY 10016
(914) 766-4384 .. **Bancone,** Jon J '90 IBM -294 Route 100 -Somers 10589
(212) 698-3500 .. **Bancroft,** Margaret A '72 OfCnsl Dechert LLP -1095 Av of Amer -NY 10036
(718) 722-6456 .. **Band,** Kenneth I '99 %Appllt Div 2nd Dept -45 Monroe Pl -Brklyn 11201 **Fx:**858-2446
(518) 785-5111 .. **Bandel,** Ralph W '74 -13 Green Mtn Dr -Cohoes 12047
(516) 222-0066 .. **Bandel,** Steven '94 (Bandel & B) -666 Old Cntry Rd -Gdn Cty 11530 **Fx:**222-0012
(212) 338-9898 .. **Bandelli,** Stanford J '90 -1611 Voorhies Av -Brklyn 11235 **Fx:**(718) 934-4579
(212) 735-3000 .. **Bander,** Deborah R '06 %Skadden ASM&F LLP -4 Times Sq -NY 10036
(718) 855-9000 .. **Bandlamudi,** Raghu N '95 %Cullen and D LLP -177 Montague -Brklyn 11201 **Fx:**935-1509
(212) 969-3000 .. **Bandler,** Aimee Taub '10 %Proskauer R LLP -1585 Bway -NY 10036
(212) 980-6800 .. **Bandler,** Alan E '56 -300 Park Av -NY 10022 **Fx:**326-1089
(212) 335-9000 .. **Bandler,** John T '03 %DA -1 Hogan Pl -NY 10013
(212) 682-0020 .. **Bandler,** Judy M '89 SpclCnsl Putney TH&H LLP -521 5th Av -NY 10175
(212) 693-1058 .. **Bandman,** Randi D '06 (Robbins GR&D LLP) -52 Duane -NY 10007 **Fx:**693-7423
(914) 479-5275 .. **Bando,** Diane Welch '84 -34 Mallard Rise -Irvngtn 10533 **Fx:**591-4275
(716) 856-4000 .. **Bandoblu,** James M Jr. '07 %Hodgson R LLP -140 Pearl -Buffalo 14202

(585) 258-2800 .. **Bandych,** Rachel Brody '88 SrCnsl Underberg & K LLP -300 Bausch & Lomb Pl -Rchstr 14604
(212) 596-9000 .. **Bane,** Mark I '86 (Ropes & G LLP) -1211 Av of Amer -NY 10036
(212) 373-3000 .. **Baneman,** Rebecca E '10 %Paul WRW&G LLP -1285 Av of Amer -NY 10019
(212) 848-4000 .. **Baneman,** Roger J '77 (Shearman & S LLP) -599 Lex Av -NY 10022
(212) 735-3000 .. **Banerjea,** Nirmal R '03 %Skadden ASM&F LLP -4 Times Sq -NY 10036
(212) 455-2000 .. **Banerjee,** Ishan '08 %Simpson T&B LLP -425 Lex Av -NY 10017
(212) 687-3000 .. **Banerjee,** Nabeena Chatterjee '05 %Jaffe & A,LLP -600 3rd Av -NY 10016
(607) 753-5392 .. **Banewicz,** Stacy L '00 Cnty DSS -60 Central Av -Cortlnd 13045
(212) 801-3173 .. **Banez,** Marissa '89 %Greenberg T,LLP -200 Park Av -NY 10166
(212) 883-6500 .. **Banfield,** Wm E '78 (Podell SS&B,LLP) -605 3rd Av -NY 10158
(914) 789-8100 .. **Bang,** Debra A '90 Fuji Photo -200 Summit Lk Dr -Valhalla 10595 **Fx:**789-8514
(718) 446-4400 .. **Bangel,** David J '94 (Bangel & C,LLP) -91-31 Qns Blvd -Elmhrst 11373 **Fx:**446-6537
(518) 432-1243 .. **Bangert-Drowns,** Diana K '88 -600 Bway -Albany 12207 **Fx:**432-0981
(917) 751-9115 .. **Bangiev,** Nisan L '08 -80-44 193rd -Hollis 11423
(716) 332-0990 .. **Bania,** Jos C '92 Childrens Legal Ctr -438 Main -Buffalo 14202
(516) 248-2474 .. **Banigan,** Lawr W '92 %S Hill & Assoc -41 Hilton Av -Hempstd 11550
(212) 593-6700 .. **Banik,** Rupa '05 %Aaronson RF&D,LLP -757 3rd Av -NY 10017
(516) 897-0719 .. **Banilower,** Samantha L '05 %NA Vinokur -100 W Park Av -Long Bch 11561 **Fx:**431-4219
(212) 490-9100 .. **Banino,** Bartholomew J '98 (Condon & F LLP) -7 Times Sq -NY 10036
(212) 687-4900 .. **Banino,** Chas G '72 (Wormser KG&J LLP) -825 3rd Av -NY 10022
(212) 735-8600 .. **Bank,** Andrew W '87 (Morrison C LLP) -909 3rd Av -NY 10022
(516) 538-2500 .. **Bank,** Arnold H '06 %Furey FLMW&D,PC -600 Front -Hempstd 11550
(516) 877-7100 .. **Bank,** Arnold R '53 (Bank T&B,PC) -400 Post Av -Westbury 11590
(212) 819-8200 .. **Bank,** Brian L '06 %White & C LLP -1155 Av of Amer -NY 10036
(516) 877-7100 .. **Bank,** Douglas M '91 (Bank T&B,PC) -400 Post Av -Westbury 11590
(516) 877-7100 .. **Bank,** Gladys S '91 %Bank T&B,PC -400 Post Av -Westbury 11590
(212) 964-1210 .. **Bank,** Glenn H '79 -325 Bway -NY 10007 **Fx:**732-0044
(212) 999-5800 .. **Bank,** Jeffrey '07 %Wilson SG&R -1301 Av of Americas -NY 10019
(914) 761-9111 .. **Bank,** Michl S '71 (Bank SS&H) -399 Knollwood Rd -White Plns 10603
(212) 408-5100 .. **Bank,** Scott A '08 %Chadbourne & P LLP -30 Rckfllr Plz -NY 10112
(914) 761-9111 .. **Bank Sheer Seymour & Hashmall** -399 Knollwood Rd -White Plns 10603 **Fx:**761-9262
(516) 877-7100 .. **Bank Tanen & Bank,PC** -400 Post Av -Westbury 11590 **Fx:**877-7105
(718) 520-7125 .. **Bank,** Todd C '97 -119-40 Union Tpk -Kew Gdns 11415
(212) 972-0534 .. **Banker,** Brooks Jr. '84 -551 5th Av -NY 10176
(212) 204-8692 .. **Banker,** David M '01 %Lowenstein S PC -1251 Av of Amer -NY 10020 **Fx:**(973) 422-6863
(716) 854-1744 .. **Banker,** Hilary C '97 %Burgio K&C -2150 Main Place Twr -Buffalo 14202
(718) 907-5960 .. **Banker,** Martin H '73 Brklyn Navy Yard Dvlpmnt Corp -63 Flushing Av -Brklyn 11205 **Fx:**643-9296
(212) 735-2760 .. **Banker,** Stephen M '78 (Skadden ASM&F LLP) -4 Times Sq -NY 10036
(646) 722-8500 .. **Banko,** James R '91 %Grant & E,PA -485 Lex Av -NY 10017
(212) 455-2000 .. **Bankole,** Taamiti M N '10 %Simpson T&B LLP -425 Lex Av -NY 10017
(212) 310-8000 .. **Banks,** Adam B '09 %Weil G&M LLP -767 5th Av -NY 10153
(212) 232-1300 .. **Banks,** Antoinette L '98 (Lewis BB&S LLP) -77 Water -NY 10005
(914) 666-8033 .. **Banks,** Chas G Jr. '66 (Banks SG&W,LLP) -118 N Bedford Rd Bx320 -Mt Kisco 10549
(631) 283-7215 .. **Banks,** Clarence R '78 -25 Bowden Sq -Southampton 11968 **Fx:**283-7685
(914) 666-2161 .. **Banks Curran Schwam & Squirrell, LLP** -61 Smith Av -Mt Kisco 10549 **Fx:**666-2450
(212) 318-3000 .. **Banks,** Glen P '82 (Fulbright & J LLP) -666 5th Av -NY 10103
(212) 701-3000 .. **Banks,** Helene R '89 (Cahill G&R LLP) -80 Pine -NY 10005 **Fx:**269-5420
(631) 261-7778 .. **Banks,** Jonathan F '94 %Brody O&O -7 Bayview Av -Northprt 11768
(212) 435-3571 .. **Banks,** Melissa L '09 Port Auth of NY/NJ -225 Park Av S -NY 10003 **Fx:**435-3555
(212) 858-1000 .. **Banks,** Michl C '90 (Pillsbury WSP LLP) -1540 Bway -NY 10036
(212) 609-6800 .. **Banks,** Open Weaver '03 %McCarter & E,LLP -245 Park Av -NY 10167
(914) 666-8033 .. **Banks Shapiro Gettinger & Waldinger,LLP** -118 N Bedford Rd Bx320 -Mt Kisco 10549 **Fx:**666-4459
(212) 416-8621 .. **Banks,** Steven L '96 %Dept of Law -120 Bway -NY 10271
(212) 440-4300 .. **Banks,** Steven R '82 %Leg Aid -199 Water -NY 10038
(315) 443-3678 .. **Banks,** Wm C '80 %Syracuse Univ Cllg of Law -Wht Hall -Syracuse 13244 **Fx:**443-4213
(914) 666-2161 .. **Banks,** Wm F '52 (Banks CS&S,LLP) -61 Smith Av -Mt Kisco 10549
(631) 852-2500 .. **Bannan,** Edw A '92 %DA -200 Center Dr -Rvrhead 11901 **Fx:**852-1769
(212) 318-6000 .. **Banner,** Matthew S '05 %Paul HJ&W LLP -75 E 55th -NY 10022
(845) 463-1200 .. **Banner,** Paul L '78 (Banner & B) -3 Sunrise Ln -Poughkeepsie 12603 **Fx:**463-3758
(212) 907-9600 .. **Banner,** Robt A '81 (Ingram YGC&B,LLP) -250 Park Av -NY 10177
(212) 395-6314 .. **Bannett,** Lon S '74 %Verizon -140 West -NY 10007
(718) 648-8300 .. **Banniettis,** Alden '97 -2972 Av X -Brklyn 11235 **Fx:**648-8730
(212) 259-8000 .. **Bannigan,** Elizabeth B '96 (Dewey & L LLP) -1301 Av of Amer -NY 10019
(212) 909-6000 .. **Bannigan,** Megan K '08 %Debevoise & P LLP -919 3rd Av -NY 10022
(718) 243-6896 .. **Bannister,** Erin M '03 Legal Aid Society -111 Lvngstn -Brklyn 11201
(212) 351-4000 .. **Bannister,** J Alan '89 (Gibson D&C LLP) -200 Park Av -NY 10166
(212) 446-2300 .. **Bannister,** John D '06 %Boies S&F LLP -575 Lex Av -NY 10022
(716) 842-2166 .. **Bannister,** Patrick J '85 %Workers Comp Bd -107 Delaware Av -Buffalo 14202
(212) 765-5070 .. **Bannon,** Edmond R '88 (Fish & R,PC) -153 E 53rd -NY 10022
(212) 259-8000 .. **Bannon,** Eileen '83 (Dewey & L LLP) -1301 Av of Amer -NY 10019
(212) 340-0400 .. **Bannon,** Elizabeth Anne '85 %Appllt Div 1st Dept -27 Mad Av -NY 10010 **Fx:**889-4412
(516) 571-9048 .. **Bannon,** Patricia E '77 Family Ct -1200 Old Cntry Rd -Westbury 11590 **Fx:**571-9335
(518) 828-3414 .. **Banovic,** Danl M '78 DA -325 Columbia -Hudson 12534 **Fx:**828-8491
(212) 637-2516 .. **Bansal,** Anirudh '94 %US Atty -1 St Andrews Plz -NY 10007
(212) 402-9400 .. **Bansal,** Sachin S '09 %McKool S,PC -1 Bryant Park -NY 10036
(585) 227-2610 .. **Bansbach,** John M '82 (Bansbach Z&W,PC) -31 Erie Canal Dr -Rchstr 14626
(631) 734-9700 .. **Bansbach,** Patricia '88 %Rizzo Grp,LLP -Bx986 -Cutchogue 11935 **Fx:**734-9702
(585) 227-2610 .. **Bansbach Zoghlin & Wahl,PC** -31 Erie Canal Dr -Rchstr 14626 **Fx:**227-2629
(973) 313-2571 .. **Bansile,** Moya S H '97 -261 E 57th -Brklyn 11203 **Fx:**313-2576
(212) 452-9188 .. **Banta,** Eugene M '59 (McAvoy & B) -322 E 86th -NY 10028
(718) 424-5560 .. **Banta,** Eugene M III '92 (Uvino & B) -33-07 102nd -Corona 11368 **Fx:**424-5569
(518) 891-4050 .. **Banta,** John S '95 %Adirondack Pk Agncy -Bx99 -Ray Brk 12977 **Fx:**891-3938
(212) 554-1234 .. **Banthin,** Christina '95 %AXA Financial Inc -1290 Av of Amer -NY 10104 **Fx:**707-3963
(212) 972-1000 .. **Bantis,** Spiro K '86 (London F LLP) -59 Maiden Ln -NY 10038
(585) 624-4395 .. **Bantle,** Douglas J '83 -30 Chillington Ln -Mendon 14506
(212) 228-9666 .. **Bantle,** Lee F '84 (Bantle & L LLP) -817 Bway -NY 10003 **Fx:**228-7654
(914) 664-1116 .. **Banton,** Veronica I '84 (V Banton,PC) -128 Stevens Av -Mt Vernon 10550 **Fx:**664-1333
(631) 424-4500 .. **Bantz,** Steven '77 -150 Broadhllw Rd -Melvll 11747 **Fx:**549-4175
(212) 449-2095 .. **Banziger,** Marc W '03 Merrill Lynch -4 World Fncl Ctr -NY 10080
(212) 326-3939 .. **Bapna,** Abhishek '10 %Jones D -222 E 41st -NY 10017
(716) 655-3900 .. **Bapst,** Rosemary L '85 -2901 Bowen Rd BxC -Elma 14059 **Fx:**655-0659
(212) 834-5402 .. **Baptista,** George A '97 JP Morgan Securities -270 Park Av -NY 10017
(212) 756-2000 .. **Baptiste,** Kim E '78 (Schulte R&Z LLP) -919 3rd Av -NY 10022
(212) 373-3000 .. **Baptiste,** Melanie N '10 %Paul WRW&G LLP -1285 Av of Amer -NY 10019
(631) 853-4049 .. **Baptiste,** Rudolph M '09 %Cnty Atty -Dennison Bldg Bx6100 -Hauppauge 11788 **Fx:**853-5169
(516) 746-8000 .. **Baquet,** Jessica M '09 %Jaspan S LLP -300 Grdn City Plz -Gdn Cty 11530
(212) 213-3111 .. **Baquet,** Robt P '00 %Weiser & Assoc -150 E 58th -NY 10155 **Fx:**213-5939
(212) 759-2300 .. **Bar,** Gillian R '00 %Carroll G&G,LLP -1790 Bway -NY 10019
(212) 766-1888 .. **Bara,** Cliff S '97 %Morris DA&F -2 Rector -NY 10006
(718) 250-3898 .. **Bara,** Louis J '07 %DA -350 Jay -Brklyn 11201 **Fx:**250-2314
(315) 798-5910 .. **Bara,** Raymond F '00 %Cnty Atty -800 Park Av -Utica 13501 **Fx:**798-5603
(914) 723-7255 .. **Bara,** Richd '79 -340 Ardsley Rd -Scarsdale 10583
(212) 781-0633 .. **Barab,** Jesse '82 -30 Park Cir -White Plns 10603 **Fx:**781-6203
(973) 992-4800 .. **Barabander,** Michl '80 (Fox R LLP) -100 Park Av -NY 10017 **Fx:**992-9125
(212) 318-2000 .. **Barabas,** Amy E '02 %Bloomberg LP -731 Lex Av -NY 10022
(212) 230-8800 .. **Barabas,** James P '01 Cnsl WilmerHale -399 Park Av -NY 10022
(718) 858-8258 .. **Barabash,** Claire '95 -101 Clark -Brklyn 11201
(212) 769-2534 .. **Barack,** Judith B '99 -34 W 65th -NY 10023 **Fx:**769-2534
(212) 874-7169 .. **Barad,** Elizabeth '53 -585 West End Av -NY 10024 **Fx:**769-0453
(212) 610-6300 .. **Baraff,** Andrew H '88 SrCnsl Allen & O -1221 Av of Amer -NY 10020
(631) 724-5031 .. **Barahal,** Paul '74 -31 New Mill Rd -Smithtwn 11787 **Fx:**724-8424
(845) 365-0136 .. **Barak,** Joanne H '76 %Crossways Consulting -136 Wshngtn Spring Rd -Palisades 10964
(631) 844-9611 .. **Barak,** Shari Seltzer '85 (Shapiro D&B,LLP) -105 Maxness Rd -Melvll 11747
(212) 973-0572 .. **Barakat,** Celine L '10 %Wolff & S PC -140 Bway -NY 10005
(212) 599-3322 .. **Barakat,** Charbel J '06 %Becker P,LLP -45 Bway -NY 10006
(212) 902-5349 .. **Barakat,** Mohammed I '02 Goldman Sachs -85 Broad -NY 10004
(718) 943-7536 .. **Baraket,** Tamara M '02 T Baraket PC -96-10 101st Av -Ozone Pk 11416 **Fx:**848-4865
(718) 250-2000 .. **Barall,** Victor P '87 %DA -350 Jay -Brklyn 11201 **Fx:**250-2314
(516) 222-2111 .. **Baram,** David E '82 (Baram & K) -600 Old Cntry Rd -Gdn Cty 11530 **Fx:**745-0456
(212) 431-4106 .. **Baran,** Roma '95 -350 Bway -NY 10013
(212) 218-5500 .. **Barancik,** Alysa M '06 (Seyfarth S LLP) -620 8th Av -NY 10018
(212) 558-4000 .. **Barancik,** Tia S '87 SpclCnsl Sullivan & C LLP -125 Broad -NY 10004
(718) 595-6537 .. **Baranczak,** Henry K Jr. '02 %DEP -59-17 Junction Blvd -Flushng 11373 **Fx:**595-6543
(212) 608-3500 .. **Barandes,** Gerald '59 OfCnsl Beckman L&B LLP -116 John -NY 10038
(212) 608-3500 .. **Barandes,** Robt '73 (Beckman L&B LLP) -116 John -NY 10038
(607) 758-8200 .. **Baranello,** James J '81 -39 Church -Cortlnd 13045 **Fx:**758-8201
(212) 374-5110 .. **Baranello,** Jos A '07 %NYC Dept Educ -52 Chmbrs -NY 10007
(718) 625-4200 .. **Barango-Tariah,** Da'Tekena A '00 -25 Bond -Brklyn 11201
(646) 386-3625 .. **Baranof,** Stephanie L '81 %Supreme Ct-Law Dept -60 Centre -NY 10007
(646) 202-9807 .. **Baranoff,** Adrienne R '97 (Baranoff Law Firm) -115 E 57th -NY 10022 **Fx:**202-9805
(212) 318-6000 .. **Baranowicz,** Adrienne C '09 %Paul HJ&W LLP -75 E 55th -NY 10022
(516) 747-4082 .. **Baranowicz,** Michl A '78 (Montfort HM&S LLP) -1140 Franklin Av Bx7677 -Gdn Cty 11530
(718) 261-7700 .. **Barany,** Kenneth T '85 (Rappaport HC&R,PC) -118-35 Qns Blvd -Frst Hlls 11375
(212) 888-3033 .. **Barari,** Mana '08 %Becker GM&M LLP -299 Park Av -NY 10171
(914) 422-4307 .. **Barasch,** Amy Pitcairn '97 %Pace Womens Justice Ctr -78 N Bway -White Plns 10603 **Fx:**422-4102

(212) 716-3500 .. **Barasch,** Candace Carmel '94 Williams Real Estate Co -380 Mad Av -NY 10017
(646) 471-4000 .. **Barasch,** Elizabeth A '89 %PricewaterhouseCoopers LLP -300 Mad Av -NY 10017
(212) 838-0286 .. **Barasch,** Lionel A '74 -425 Park Av -NY 10022 **Fx:**935-0947
(212) 940-8801 .. **Barasch,** Mal L '57 Cnsl Katten MR LLP -575 Mad Av -NY 10022
(518) 472-1320 .. **Barasch,** Maxine L '07 M Barasch & Assoc,PLLC -18 Corp Woolds Blvd -Albany 12211 **Fx:**472-1296
(212) 385-8000 .. **Barasch McGarry Salzman & Penson** -11 Park Pl -NY 10007 **Fx:**385-7845
(212) 385-8000 .. **Barasch,** Michl A '81 (Barasch MS&P) -11 Park Pl -NY 10007
(914) 934-8700 .. **Barasch,** Richd A '80 Amer Progressive Life & Hlth -6 Intl Dr -Rye Brook 10573
(212) 815-1860 .. **Barasch,** Sheldon '75 %DC 37 MELS -125 Barclay -NY 10007 **Fx:**815-1343
(516) 747-9700 .. **Barash,** Amy S '84 %Ryan & H,PC -1 Old Cntry Rd -Carle Pl 11514
(212) 701-3000 .. **Barash,** David L '08 %Cahill G&R LLP -80 Pine -NY 10005 **Fx:**269-5420
Barash, Gary A '80 -1075 Park Av -NY 10128
(212) 403-1000 .. **Barash,** Louis J '80 %Wachtell LR&K -51 W 52nd -NY 10019
(212) 815-1818 .. **Barash,** Salli J '92 %DC 37 MELS -125 Barclay -NY 10007 **Fx:**815-1343
(212) 596-9000 .. **Baratt,** Carly B '10 %Ropes & G LLP -1211 Av of Amer -NY 10036
(718) 802-9858 .. **Baratta,** Anthony '85 (Romeo & B) -411 Court -Brklyn 11231 **Fx:**802-9872
(212) 750-9700 .. **Baratta Baratta & Aidala** -546 5th Av -NY 10036 **Fx:**750-8297
(212) 750-9700 .. **Baratta,** Jos A '93 %Baratta B&A -546 5th Av -NY 10036
(212) 750-9700 .. **Baratta,** Jos P '63 (Baratta B&A) -546 5th Av -NY 10036
(718) 590-2000 .. **Barba,** Christina A '07 %DA -198 E 161st -Bronx 10451 **Fx:**590-6477
(518) 262-3830 .. **Barba,** James J '69 %Albany Med Ctr -New Scotland Av -Albany 12208 **Fx:**262-3825
(516) 623-6554 .. **Barbaccia,** Jos A '60 -300 Woodcleft Av -Freeprt 11520 **Fx:**623-4147
(516) 229-4400 .. **Barbakoff,** Dean A '92 %Kay & G -875 Merrick Av -Westbury 11590
(212) 685-5391 .. **Barbanel,** Gary A '74 -270 Mad Av -NY 10016
(718) 786-0048 .. **Barbanel,** Geraldine '86 -29-27 Qns Plz N -LIC 11101 **Fx:**392-9490
(212) 441-1333 .. **Barbanel,** Jerry F '92 Aon Consulting -199 Water -NY 10038
(718) 317-6984 .. **Barbanel,** Peggy Jo '94 -238 Rolling Hill Green -Staten Isl 10312 **Fx:**317-6984
(914) 995-6573 .. **Barbanes,** Elizabeth '90 %Cnty Atty -148 Martine Av -White Plns 10601 **Fx:**995-5858
(516) 222-2333 .. **Barbara,** Dominic A '71 (Barbara Law Firm) -401 Franklin Av -Gdn Cty 11530 **Fx:**222-2935
(516) 222-2333 .. **Barbara,** Jason M '00 %Barbara Law Firm -401 Franklin Av -Gdn Cty 11530 **Fx:**222-2935
(516) 248-6400 .. **Barbara,** Leslie F '92 (Davidoff M&H,LLP) -200 Grdn City Plz -Gdn Cty 11530
(212) 991-1300 .. **Barbaresi,** George P '92 Vero Captl Mmgt -220 5th Av -NY 10001 **Fx:**991-1301
(212) 351-4500 .. **Barbarino,** Jill '05 %Epstein B&G,PC -250 Park Av -NY 10177
(973) 848-4010 .. **Barbarisi,** Christopher A '00 (K&L Gates LLP) -599 Lex Av -NY 10022 **Fx:**848-4001
(718) 748-8078 .. **Barbaro,** Louis F '71 -9101 Shore Rd -Brklyn 11209
(212) 754-9400 .. **Barbaro,** Nicole V '02 %Todtman NS&J,PC -425 Park Av -NY 10022
(718) 237-0880 .. **Barbaro,** Stephen V '83 (Alter & B) -26 Court -Brklyn 11242
(973) 492-1190 .. **Barbarula,** John M '85 Barbarula Law Ofcs -4459 Amboy Rd -Staten Isl 10312 **Fx:**492-1307
(212) 541-2000 .. **Barbaruolo,** Christopher L '05 %Bryan C LLP -1290 Av of Amer -NY 10104
(518) 782-9100 .. **Barbaruolo,** Paula M '93 (Barbaruolo Law Firm PC) -12 Cornell Rd -Latham 12110 **Fx:**782-9101
(845) 638-5180 .. **Barbash,** Carol L '82 %Cnty Atty -Cnty Ofc Bldg -New Cty 10956 **Fx:**638-5676
(718) 828-8200 .. **Barbato,** Lucille M '85 (Spiegel & B,LLP) -2622 E Tremont Av -Bronx 10461
(212) 954-3142 .. **Barbella,** Jos '04 KPMG LLP -757 3rd Av -NY 10017
(516) 364-5100 .. **Barbella,** Nicole D '06 %Katz B&K -6900 Jericho Tpk -Syosset 11791 **Fx:**364-5166
(212) 405-4783 .. **Barbeosch,** Wm P '80 GenSpring Family Ofc -13-15 W 54th -NY 10019
(585) 475-7805 .. **Barber,** Andrea S '99 Cnsl RIT -124 Lomb Mem'l Dr -Rchstr 14623 **Fx:**475-7171
(212) 446-7000 .. **Barber,** Anna W '96 %McKinsey & Co -55 E 52nd -NY 10055 **Fx:**688-9521
(718) 763-4836 .. **Barber,** Beatrice '82 -226 Whitman Dr -Brklyn 11234
(518) 690-0096 .. **Barber,** Catherine Ann '92 OfCnsl Murphy BB&M,LLP -226 Great Oaks Blvd -Albany 12203
(845) 791-4808 .. **Barber,** Cindy L '94 -10 Hmltn Av Bx1068 -Monticello 12701 **Fx:**791-5355
(716) 849-6500 .. **Barber,** Janice A '78 (Brown & T,LLC) -14 Lafayette Sq -Buffalo 14203
(212) 813-8800 .. **Barber,** Jillian M '09 %Goodwin P LLP -620 8th Av -NY 10018
(518) 218-3840 .. **Barber,** Jonathan A '97 %AYCO -2 Wall -Albany 12205
(518) 596-6937 .. **Barber,** Kathryn M '91 -23 Fullerton -Albany 12209
(212) 870-5646 .. **Barber,** Lorie '89 %George Balachine Trust -20 Lincoln Ctr Plz -NY 10023 **Fx:**870-5651
(518) 220-1850 .. **Barber,** Melissa Knapp '04 %Schmeiser O&W -22 Century Hill Dr -Latham 12110
(518) 402-9521 .. **Barber,** Nathaniel H '94 %DEC -625 Bway -Albany 12233 **Fx:**402-9018
(518) 690-0096 .. **Barber,** Peter G '87 (Murphy BB&M,LLP) -226 Great Oaks Blvd -Albany 12203
(212) 373-3000 .. **Barber,** Philip G '85 Cnsl Paul WRW&G LLP -1285 Av of Amer -NY 10019
(607) 723-9511 .. **Barber,** Richd A '63 OfCnsl Coughlin & G,LLP -19 Chenango Bx2039 -Bnghmtn 13902
(212) 422-0202 .. **Barber,** Richd E '05 %Sedgwick DM&A LLP -125 Broad -NY 10004
(914) 967-3040 .. **Barber,** Richd J Jr. '64 -211 Purchase Bx570 -Rye 10580
(212) 309-8200 .. **Barber,** Scott J '90 ING Asset Mngt -230 Park Av -NY 10169
(212) 237-0000 .. **Barber,** Shelley A '91 (Vinson & E LLP) -666 5th Av -NY 10103
(845) 226-6107 .. **Barbera,** Ann Pooler '87 -138 Wilmont Ct -Hopewell Junct 12533
(718) 590-2000 .. **Barbera,** Bridget K '09 %DA -198 E 161st -Bronx 10451 **Fx:**590-6477
(212) 592-1414 .. **Barbera,** Gino C '04 Herrick,F LLP -2 Park Av -NY 10016 **Fx:**592-1500
(631) 473-5100 .. **Barbera,** Janine A '87 (Barbera & M,PC) -428 Route 25A Bx5595 -Miller Pl 11764 **Fx:**473-2648
(914) 686-1390 .. **Barbera,** John J '90 (Martin C&B LLP) -245 Main -White Plns 10601
(718) 461-6633 .. **Barbera,** Steven '06 %Mallilo & G -163-09 Nrthrn Blvd -Flushng 11358
(212) 834-0600 .. **Barbera,** Tricia L '10 %Gordon & S,PC -355 Lex Av -NY 10017
(914) 738-2266 .. **Barbera,** Wm T '77 -111 Wolfs Ln -Pelham 10803
(914) 328-8844 .. **Barberi,** Jeremy D '07 %Meagher & M -175 Main -White Plns 10601 **Fx:**328-8570
(212) 773-2613 .. **Barberot,** Jean-Baptiste P '04 Donahue & Prtnrs LLP -5 Times Sq -NY 10036 **Fx:**773-8814
(212) 541-2000 .. **Barber Schwartz,** Rachel E '03 %Bryan C LLP -1290 Av of Amer -NY 10104
(585) 454-2181 .. **Barbic,** Valerie L '92 (Trevett CS&A,PC) -2 State -Rchstr 14614
(212) 836-8000 .. **Barbiere,** Janet '84 (Kaye S LLP) -425 Park Av -NY 10022
(212) 450-4000 .. **Barbieri,** Dominick D '05 %Davis P&W LLP -450 Lex Av -NY 10017
(718) 932-2800 .. **Barbieri,** Guy '87 (Lopresto & B) -4502 Ditmars Blvd -Astoria 11105 **Fx:**721-6846
(212) 527-1000 .. **Barbieri,** John V '88 (Jones HC&B PC) -1 Bttry Pk Plz -NY 10004
(631) 277-0300 .. **Barbiero,** Anthony F '92 (Bartlett MB&M,LLP) -670 Main -Islip 11751
(631) 277-6800 .. **Barbiero,** Anthony V '65 (AV Barbiero,PC) -86 W Main -E Islip 11730 **Fx:**859-3916
(212) 695-5980 .. **Barbina,** Kenneth A '04 %Rizzo Grp LLP -11 Penn Plz -NY 10001
(607) 721-8771 .. **Barbosa,** Roberto '00 Dept of Law -44 Hawley -Bnghmtn 13901 **Fx:**721-8789
(212) 749-1820 .. **Barbot,** Herbert '92 WF Ryan Cmmnty Hlth Ctr -110 W 97th -NY 10025
(212) 783-4095 .. **Barbot,** Lawr G '04 Citigroup Global Mrkts,Inc -485 Lex Av -NY 10017
(914) 606-9790 .. **Barbour,** Edw J '84 %Cartafalsa ST&L -560 Wht Plns Rd -Tarrytwn 10591
(631) 271-4777 .. **Barbour,** Ross B '09 %D Kritzer & Assoc,PC -187 E Main -Huntngtn 11743 **Fx:**271-2530
(518) 447-3200 .. **Barbour,** Scott A '85 (McNamee LT&W,PC) -677 Bway -Albany 12207
(914) 765-6325 .. **Barbrack,** Joanne H '93 %IBM Credit LLC -North Castle Dr -Armonk 10504
(212) 474-1000 .. **Barbur,** Peter T '89 (Cravath S&M LLP) -825 8th Av -NY 10019
(212) 627-8100 .. **Barbur,** Ryan J '08 %Levy R,PC -80 8th Av -NY 10011
(516) 330-2893 .. **Barbuto,** Richd J '79 -26 Railroad Av PMB 118 -Babylon 11702
(914) 643-6301 .. **Barbuto,** Richd Lawr '66 -45 Radnor Av -Croton-On-Hud 10520
(914) 995-3497 .. **Barca,** Jos A III '09 %DA -111 Martin Luther King Blvd -White Plns 10601 **Fx:**995-3363
(212) 792-4311 .. **Barcarcel,** Sonia '89 -245 Park Av -NY 10167 **Fx:**792-4001
(212) 637-0179 .. **Barcelo,** Amy Ann '05 %US Atty -86 Chmbrs -NY 10007
(516) 294-8844 .. **Barcham,** Deborah S '87 (L'Abbate BC&C,LLP) -1001 Franklin Av -Gdn Cty 11530
(516) 742-3354 .. **Barcham,** Michl A '85 -108 Hazelwood Dr -Jericho 11753
(845) 485-3607 .. **Barcher,** Ann C '79 Town of Poughkeepsie -One Overocker Rd -Poughkeepsie 12603 **Fx:**462-4400
(212) 309-1000 .. **Barclay,** Amos W '09 %Hunton & W -200 Park Av -NY 10166
(212) 277-6500 .. **Barclay,** Bernays Thos '80 (Dickstein S LLP) -1633 Bway -NY 10019
(516) 759-1212 .. **Barclay,** Christopher R '98 Cnsl Mohen & T LLP -186 Birch Hill Rd -Locust Vly 11560
(315) 425-2700 .. **Barclay,** H Douglas '62 OfCnsl Hiscock & B,LLP -One Park Pl -Syracuse 13202
(718) 444-1068 .. **Barclay,** Ingrid '91 -295 Pulaski -Brklyn 11206
(518) 465-3553 .. **Barclay,** Kathleen A '08 %Maynard OS&C,LLP -6 Twr Pl -Albany 12203
(585) 262-8412 .. **Barclay,** Kirsten J '02 Rochester Schl Dist -131 W Broad -Rchstr 14614
(646) 562-3405 .. **Barclay,** Maria J '99 %PLC -747 3rd Av -NY 10017
(315) 425-2700 .. **Barclay,** Wm A '96 (Hiscock & B,LLP) -One Park Pl -Syracuse 13202
(212) 957-7600 .. **Barcroft,** Kathryn L '99 %Cohen & G LLP -800 3rd Av -NY 10022
(212) 735-3000 .. **Barcus,** Jessica A '08 %Skadden ASM&F LLP -4 Times Sq -NY 10036
(518) 320-1746 .. **Barczak,** Wm K '81 %State Univ Cnstrctn Fund -353 Bway -Albany 12246 **Fx:**689-2634
(631) 694-0033 .. **Bard,** Jeffrey '88 (Lawrence WR&B,PC) -425 Broadhllw Rd -Melvll 11747
(315) 474-7571 .. **Bard,** Jonathan H '09 %Mackenzie H LLP -101 S Salina Bx4967 -Syracuse 13221
(631) 777-2330 .. **Bard,** Robt J '82 %O'Connor OH&D,LLP -1 Huntngtn Quad -Melvll 11747
(212) 576-4000 .. **Bard,** Walter Eliot '90 Marvel Enterprises,Inc -417 5th Av -NY 10016
(716) 945-8471 .. **Bardak,** Tina M '94 Synergy Business Mgmt -255 Rochester -Salamanca 14779
(607) 754-3281 .. **Bardales,** Norman R '59 -2735 Alxndr -Endwell 13760
(212) 446-4800 .. **Barday,** Shireen A '09 %Kirkland & E LLP -153 E 53rd -NY 10022
(212) 292-6590 .. **Bardeen,** David P '03 %Ziff Bros Invstmts LLC -350 Park Av -NY 10022
(212) 848-4000 .. **Barden,** Jos N '09 %Shearman & S LLP -599 Lex Av -NY 10022
(585) 546-2500 .. **Barden,** Paul G '92 (McConville CC&M,PC) -25 E Main -Rchstr 14614
(212) 588-0800 .. **Bardenstein,** Rami '08 %Frommer L&H LLP -745 5th Av -NY 10151
(718) 487-4468 .. **Bardizbanian,** Simon '99 Cnsl Bardizbanian & Assoc,PC -135-24 Hillside Av -Richmnd Hll 11418 **Fx:**487-4230
(315) 448-4800 .. **Bardot,** Irene S '97 %OCTF -615 Erie Blvd W -Syracuse 13204 **Fx:**448-4858
(607) 758-9116 .. **Bardsley,** John L '88 -36 Main Bx166 -Cortlnd 13045 **Fx:**758-9062
(607) 753-1811 .. **Bardsley,** Margaret Shay '92 City Ct -Bx166 -Cortlnd 13045

(212) 858-1000 .. **Bardunias,** Kathleen D '09 %Pillsbury WSP LLP -1540 Bway -NY 10036
(607) 722-9348 .. **Bare,** Eric A '82 -1010 Pwdrhse Rd -Vestal 13850
(212) 225-2000 .. **Barefoot,** Luke A '05 %Cleary GS&H -1 Lbrty Plz -NY 10006
(646) 374-8515 .. **Barenbaum,** Bryan '08 -1205 47th -Brklyn 11219
(718) 871-8700 .. **Barenbaum,** Morris E '78 -1205 47th -Brklyn 11219 **Fx:**436-7936
(212) 854-2260 .. **Barenberg,** Mark '85 %Columbia Law Schl -435 W 116th -NY 10027 **Fx:**854-7946
(212) 252-0787 .. **Barenboim,** Natalie A '97 N Barenboim,PLLC -220 5th Av -NY 10001 **Fx:**(646) 356-7046
(212) 479-6000 .. **Barenholtz,** Celia Goldwag '80 (Cooley LLP) -1114 Av of Amer -NY 10036
(212) 236-6007 .. **Barenholtz,** Danl M '96 %Merrill Lynch -225 Lbrty -NY 10080
(212) 816-7291 .. **Barenholtz,** Paul K '79 Citigroup -388 Greenwich -NY 10013
(212) 225-2000 .. **Barenz,** Lindsay B '09 %Cleary GS&H -1 Lbrty Plz -NY 10006
(212) 661-2193 .. **Barer,** Harris A '60 -75 Rckfllr Plz -NY 10019 **Fx:**661-2195
(914) 788-0990 .. **Baresich,** Lara Rose '96 (Lima & B LLC) -30 Dickerson Rd -Cortlandt Manor 10567
(917) 848-0472 .. **Baretz,** Spencer Zane '98 -1325 Av of Amer -NY 10019
(212) 506-2500 .. **Barganz,** Marcella J '04 %Mayer B LLP -1675 Bway -NY 10019
(716) 488-0758 .. **Bargar,** Mark L '87 (Bly SBP&M) -3 Lakevw Av Bx3327 -Jamestwn 14702
(212) 701-3000 .. **Barger,** Katherine A '05 %Cahill G&R LLP -80 Pine -NY 10005 **Fx:**269-5420
(212) 557-2800 .. **Barger & Wolen LLP** -10 E 40th -NY 10016 **Fx:**557-2884
(212) 682-7474 .. **Bargmann,** Kelly M '05 %Foley & L LLP -90 Park Av -NY 10016
(716) 858-2424 .. **Bargnesi,** James P '97 %DA -25 Delaware Av -Buffalo 14202 **Fx:**858-7425
(716) 856-5500 .. **Bargnesi,** Julie M '88 (Damon M LLP) -200 Delaware Av -Buffalo 14202
(716) 842-2170 .. **Bargnesi,** Mona A '97 %Workers Comp Bd -107 Delaware Av -Buffalo 14202
(212) 259-8000 .. **Bargoz,** Roxana I '07 %Dewey & L LLP -1301 Av of Amer -NY 10019
(212) 474-1000 .. **Barg-Townsend,** Etienne '09 %Cravath S&M LLP -825 8th Av -NY 10019
(845) 784-1778 .. **Barham,** Nydia '93 -182 Grand -Newburgh 12550
(212) 267-6659 .. **Bari,** Frank '91 -305 Bway -NY 10007 **Fx:**732-2191
(516) 223-6890 .. **Baribault & Barry** -1113 South Dr -Baldwin 11510
(516) 223-6890 .. **Baribault,** Richd '77 (Baribault & B) -1113 South Dr -Baldwin 11510
(212) 446-4800 .. **Baribeau,** James L '06 %Kirkland & E LLP -153 E 53rd -NY 10022
(516) 742-2600 .. **Barics,** J Douglas '94 -1399 Franklin Av -Gdn Cty 11530
(212) 236-1020 .. **Barile,** Jos G '91 %Merrill Lynch -225 Lbrty -NY 10080
(718) 293-2263 .. **Barile,** Mary Ann '88 -901 Sheridan Av -Bronx 10451
(315) 793-0034 .. **Barile,** Monica R '94 -23 Oxford Rd -New Hartfrd 13413 **Fx:**793-0076
(212) 515-2832 .. **Barile,** Zabrina T '04 Hedge OP Compliance,LLC -3 Park Av -NY 10016
(212) 548-2100 .. **Barillari,** Alyssa C '05 %McGuire W LLP -1345 Av of Amer -NY 10105
(718) 273-4046 .. **Barillari,** Wm J '92 %Bosco B&M -857 Forest Av -Staten Isl 10310
(212) 788-1206 .. **Barillas,** Teressa M '91 %Law Dept -100 Church -NY 10007 **Fx:**788-0367
(212) 715-9100 .. **Baris,** Jay G '79 (Kramer LN&F,LLP) -1177 Av of Amer -NY 10036
(212) 684-0300 .. **Barisano,** Elvira '98 %Bauman K&G LLP -28 W 44th -NY 10036
(212) 236-8967 .. **Barisciano,** Robt T '09 Merrill Lynch -250 Vesey -NY 10281
(212) 750-1333 .. **Barish,** Jordana '91 (I Garr,PC) -777 3rd Av -NY 10017 **Fx:**486-2978
(212) 559-3333 .. **Barish,** Kenneth R '95 %Citigroup Private Bk -153 E 53rd -NY 10043 **Fx:**793-4860
(914) 285-9471 .. **Barish,** Wm L '77 -30 Glenn -White Plns 10603
(212) 986-8543 .. **Barish,** Wm L '77 -60 E 42nd -NY 10165
(516) 482-1831 .. **Baris-Rothstein,** Randy S '82 -72 Nassau Dr -Gt Neck 11021
(716) 849-1700 .. **Baritot,** Rebecca H '81 -70 Niagara -Buffalo 14202
(646) 435-9505 .. **Baritz & Colman LLP** -233 Bway -NY 10279 **Fx:**(212) 571-9149
(646) 435-9505 .. **Baritz,** Neil S '85 (Baritz & C LLP) -233 Bway -NY 10279
(631) 851-0400 .. **Bark & Karpf** -842 Route 25A -Northprt 11768
(718) 330-1909 .. **Bark & Karpf** -44 Court -Brklyn 11201 **Fx:**624-4748
(212) 450-4000 .. **Bark,** Lesley A '08 %Davis P&W LLP -450 Lex Av -NY 10017
(631) 851-0400 .. **Bark,** Peter '65 (Bark & K) -842 Route 25A -Northprt 11768
(212) 326-3939 .. **Bark,** Thos W '91 (Jones D) -222 E 41st -NY 10017
(212) 859-8000 .. **Barkan,** Andrew B '01 (Fried FHS&J LLP) -1 NY Plz -NY 10004
(212) 969-3000 .. **Barkan,** Lee A '80 SrCnsl Proskauer R LLP -1585 Bway -NY 10036
(212) 237-1000 .. **Barkan,** Mel P '68 Cnsl Windels ML&M,LLP -156 W 56th -NY 10019
(212) 227-5500 .. **Barkan,** Melissa '96 %HDC -110 William -NY 10038 **Fx:**227-6865
(347) 296-6178 .. **Barkan,** Neal S '96 %Supreme Ct Law Dept -360 Adams -Brklyn 11201 **Fx:**643-6114
(516) 358-3688 .. **Barkan,** Steven L '69 -445 Broad Hollow Rd -Melvll 11747
(718) 793-6999 .. **Barkas,** Loula '81 CLE Seminar & Publishing Srvcs -110-20 71st Rd -Frst Hlls 11375
(646) 502-7001 .. **Barkats,** Sunny Jos '05 (JSBarkats PLLC) -100 Church -NY 10007 **Fx:**607-5544
(212) 382-0700 .. **Barkaus,** Keith J '01 %Ostrolenk FG&S,LLP -1180 Av of Amer -NY 10036
(518) 435-1919 .. **Barker,** Christopher L '83 (Stockton B&M,LLP) -2 Twr Pl -Albany 12203
(212) 326-3939 .. **Barker,** Christopher R '09 %Jones D -222 E 41st -NY 10017
(631) 853-5212 .. **Barker,** Danl P '05 %Leg Aid -400 Carleton Av Bx9082 -Central Islip 11722 **Fx:**853-7798
(718) 590-2000 .. **Barker,** Georgia D '97 %DA -198 E 161st -Bronx 10451 **Fx:**590-6477
(212) 652-3890 .. **Barker,** Jane Lauer '77 (Pitta & G LLP) -120 Bway -NY 10271
(518) 587-3722 .. **Barker,** Joanne '87 -138 Elm -Saratoga Spgs 12866
(914) 448-0200 .. **Barker,** John W '92 (Bartlett MB&M,LLP) -81 Main -White Plns 10601
(212) 778-1202 .. **Barker,** Kami Z '07 %Law Dept -100 Church -NY 10007 **Fx:**788-0367
(212) 859-8000 .. **Barker,** Michl J '99 (Fried FHS&J LLP) -1 NY Plz -NY 10004
(718) 222-2330 .. **Barker,** Nikki L '07 %Law Dept -350 Jay -Brklyn 11201 **Fx:**222-2373
(585) 454-6820 .. **Barker,** Terrence G '77 -45 Exchange Blvd -Rchstr 14614 **Fx:**454-6824
(212) 259-3639 .. **Barker,** Timothy A '82 1st Republic Bank -1230 Av of Amer -NY 10020
(516) 745-1122 .. **Barket,** Bruce A '87 (Quadrino & S,PC) -666 Old Cntry Rd -Gdn Cty 11530
(212) 677-5776 .. **Barkey,** Albert H '82 -277 Bway #408 -NY 10007 **Fx:**(646) 219-3072
(212) 997-4644 .. **Barkham,** Graham E '66 -36 W 44th -NY 10036 **Fx:**221-0999
(646) 471-2118 .. **Barkhordar,** Arash G '04 PricewaterhouseCoopers LLP -300 Mad Av -NY 10017
(718) 417-1700 .. **Barkhordar,** Doris '00 %Deutsch & S LLP -79-37 Myrtle Av -Glendale 11385
(212) 541-2000 .. **Barkhorn,** Karin J '77 Cnsl Bryan C LLP -1290 Av of Amer -NY 10104
(516) 949-4217 .. **Barkin,** Saml L '89 Cnsl FINRA -2 Jericho Plz -Jericho 11753 **Fx:**949-4201
(718) 237-5547 .. **Barkley,** Danl W '00 %Leg Srvcs -105 Court -Brklyn 11201 **Fx:**855-0733
(212) 632-6484 .. **Barkoff,** Matthew B '05 Lazard Freres -30 Rckfllr Plz -NY 10112 **Fx:**632-6060
(212) 689-1113 .. **Bar-Kokhba,** Yuval D '95 (Garbarini & S,PC) -432 Park Av S -NY 10016
(212) 735-3000 .. **Bar-Kokhva,** Rotem '06 %Skadden ASM&F LLP -4 Times Sq -NY 10036
(212) 998-6611 .. **Barkow,** Anthony S '09 NYU Law Schl Ctr on Admin Crim Law -110 W 3rd -NY 10012 **Fx:**998-4600
(212) 735-3000 .. **Barksdale,** Wm R '09 %Skadden ASM&F LLP -4 Times Sq -NY 10036
(914) 941-3800 .. **Barlaam,** Raymond R '75 -500 Exec Blvd -Ossining 10562 **Fx:**941-3645
(212) 715-9100 .. **Barlekamp,** Jeffrey A '09 %Kramer LN&F,LLP -1177 Av of Amer -NY 10036
(845) 986-1988 .. **Barlet,** Peter D '77 -6 High Bx1010 -Warwick 10990 **Fx:**986-1940
(518) 473-6160 .. **Barletta,** C Thos '78 Banking Dept -80 Swan -Albany 12210 **Fx:**473-7204
(631) 847-6507 .. **Barletta,** Christopher J '00 CNA Ins Co -3 Huntngtn Quadrangle -Melvll 11747
(212) 687-0100 .. **Bar-Levav,** Doron M '80 (Harris B PLLC) -100 Wall -NY 10005
(212) 277-6500 .. **Barlia,** Neal S '82 (Dickstein S LLP) -1633 Bway -NY 10019
(212) 407-7700 .. **Barlin,** Danl J '06 %Vedder P,PC -1633 Bway -NY 10019
(212) 735-3000 .. **Barlow,** Christopher M '10 %Skadden ASM&F LLP -4 Times Sq -NY 10036
(212) 582-2300 .. **Barlow,** Edw L '65 %Whitcom Prtnrs -375 Park Av -NY 10152 **Fx:**582-2310
(212) 661-3535 .. **Barlow,** Emily J '03 %Hodgson R LLP -60 E 42nd -NY 10165
(212) 735-3000 .. **Barlow,** Erin K '10 %Skadden ASM&F LLP -4 Times Sq -NY 10036
(315) 785-3152 .. **Barlow,** Jeremy L '04 Pub Def -175 Arsenal -Watertwn 13601 **Fx:**785-5060
(516) 771-4290 .. **Barlow,** Paul K '87 -514 Merrick Rd -Baldwin 11510 **Fx:**546-2766
(212) 907-9700 .. **Barlow,** Peter B '10 (Smith G&R,LLP) -250 Park Av -NY 10177
(516) 364-7900 .. **Barman,** Ananya '06 Epstein F&G -45 Crsswys Park Dr W -Woodbury 11797
(212) 596-9000 .. **Barmash,** Inna '08 %Ropes & G LLP -1211 Av of Amer -NY 10036
(212) 732-0497 .. **Barna,** Elizabeth M '91 -305 Bway -NY 10007 **Fx:**732-0497
(212) 759-3300 .. **Barna,** Martin F '09 %Dornbush SS&V,LLP -747 3rd Av -NY 10017
(716) 854-3400 .. **Barna,** Timothy P '09 %Rupp BPC&C LLC -1600 Lbrty Bldg -Buffalo 14202
(646) 638-8209 .. **Barnabeo,** Susan P '86 In Demand LLC -345 Hudson -NY 10014 **Fx:**486-0861
(212) 354-8989 .. **Barnaby,** Michl J '94 -521 5th Av -NY 10175
(212) 848-4000 .. **Barnao,** Jaclyn A '07 %Shearman & S LLP -599 Lex Av -NY 10022
(212) 538-6273 .. **Barnard,** Alexander C B '03 Credit Suisse Securities LLC -1 Mad Av -NY 10010
(212) 538-9671 .. **Barnard,** Bernadette A '99 CSFB -1 Mad Av -NY 10010
(212) 373-3000 .. **Barnard,** Caroline D '09 %Paul WRW&G LLP -1285 Av of Amer -NY 10019
(212) 715-1000 .. **Barnard,** Kevin F '77 (Arnold & P LLP) -399 Park Av -NY 10022
(631) 661-0906 .. **Barnard,** R Kenneth '85 -384 W Main -Babylon 11702 **Fx:**661-0908
(212) 506-2500 .. **Barnard,** Robt N '03 (Mayer B LLP) -1675 Bway -NY 10019
(212) 344-5680 .. **Barnard,** Robt T '93 (Thompson H LLP) -335 Mad Av -NY 10017
(518) 385-7602 .. **Barnas,** Michl C '88 SrCnsl GE Intl,Inc -1 River Rd -Schnctdy 12345 **Fx:**385-8225
(716) 362-1139 .. **Barnashuk,** Robt F '08 %Long Firm,LLP -70 Niagara -Buffalo 14202
(212) 637-2679 .. **Barnea,** Jean-David '04 %US Atty -86 Chmbrs -NY 10007
(212) 451-2300 .. **Barnea,** Lori '06 %Olshan GFR&W LLP -65 E 55th -NY 10022
(212) 419-3934 .. **Barnes,** Aaron J '98 RNK Capital,LLC -527 Mad Av -NY 10022
(212) 728-8919 .. **Barnes,** Anthony M '01 -787 7th Av -NY 10019 **Fx:**728-9919
(212) 703-7996 .. **Barnes,** Brenda L '00 -1040 Av of Amer -NY 10018
(718) 286-6996 .. **Barnes,** Brooke '07 %DA -125-01 Qns Blvd -Kew Gdns 11415
(516) 794-5500 .. **Barnes,** Bruce Edw '79 -400 Grdn City Plz -Gdn Cty 11530 **Fx:**794-6179
(212) 973-0572 .. **Barnes,** Danl D '98 %Wolff & S PC -140 Bway -NY 10005
(716) 856-5222 .. **Barnes,** David K '93 -43 Court -Buffalo 14202
(914) 333-9693 .. **Barnes,** David L '03 Philips Electronics -345 Scarborough Rd Bx3001 -Briarclff Mnr 10510 **Fx:**332-0615
(212) 351-4000 .. **Barnes,** Douglas A '06 %Gibson D&C LLP -200 Park Av -NY 10166
(212) 693-2330 .. **Barnes,** Elisa A '85 -350 Bway -NY 10013 **Fx:**693-2334
(212) 326-3939 .. **Barnes,** Halia M '08 %Jones D -222 E 41st -NY 10017
(914) 592-5740 .. **Barnes Iaccarino & Shepherd, LLP** -258 Saw Mill Rvr Rd -Elmsfrd 10523 **Fx:**592-3213
(516) 483-2990 .. **Barnes Iaccarino & Shepherd, LLP** -3 Surrey Ln -Hempstd 11550 **Fx:**483-0566
(518) 452-1961 .. **Barnes,** James R '05 %Burke & C,PC -255 Washington Av Ext -Albany 12205
(718) 652-7800 .. **Barnes,** Jefferyson A '83 -3550 Wht Plns Rd -Bronx 10467
(212) 676-9218 .. **Barnes,** Jeffrey M '89 %Law Dept -100 Church -NY 10007 **Fx:**788-0367
(518) 388-4466 .. **Barnes,** Jennifer M '97 %Dept Soc Srvcs -106 Erie Blvd -Schnctdy 12307 **Fx:**382-1256

(631) 852-2500 .. **Barnes,** Kristin A '06 %DA -200 Center Dr -Rvrhead 11901 **Fx:**852-1769
(212) 506-2500 .. **Barnes,** Lawr M '05 %Mayer B LLP -1675 Bway -NY 10019
(516) 673-0674 .. **Barnes,** Leo K Jr. '97 (Barnes & B,PC) -1461 Franklin Av -Gdn Cty 11530
(845) 897-7770 .. **Barnes,** Linda L '82 (Kohler & B,PC) -300 Westage Business Ctr -Fishkill 12524 **Fx:**897-7711
(315) 841-3303 .. **Barnes,** Mark S '89 -122 E Main Bx86 -Waterville 13480 **Fx:**841-8105
(585) 425-5210 .. **Barnes,** Mary Jane '05 Maximus Federal Srvcs -50 Square Dr -Victor 14564 **Fx:**425-5292
(516) 673-0674 .. **Barnes,** Matthew J '02 (Barnes & B,PC) -1461 Franklin Av -Gdn Cty 11530
(212) 772-8740 .. **Barnes Morris & Yorn** -129 E 82nd -NY 10028
(212) 578-2324 .. **Barnes,** Paula L '00 %MetLife -1095 Av of Amer -NY 10036 **Fx:**578-3916
(518) 434-6195 .. **Barnes,** Richd E '87 %NYS Catholic Conf -465 State -Albany 12203 **Fx:**434-9796
(716) 854-2020 .. **Barnes,** Richd J '81 (Cellino & B,PC) -350 Main -Buffalo 14202
(212) 599-1744 .. **Barnes,** Richd L '61 (Opton H&F,LLP) -295 Mad Av -NY 10017
(914) 738-0575 .. **Barnes,** Richd M '75 -83 Harmon Av -Pelham 10803
(212) 725-0200 .. **Barnes Richardson & Colburn** -475 Park Av S -NY 10016 **Fx:**889-4135
(914) 592-5740 .. **Barnes,** Roy '70 (Barnes I&S,LLP) -258 Saw Mill Rvr Rd -Elmsfrd 10523
(716) 854-2020 .. **Barnes,** Stephen E '84 (Cellino & B,PC) -350 Main -Buffalo 14202
(718) 875-9264 .. **Barnes,** Tatia Djuana '05 %Warren & W,PC -185 Montague -Brklyn 11201 **Fx:**852-3069
(212) 696-6000 .. **Barnes,** Timothy A '07 (Curtis M-PC&M LLP) -101 Park Av -NY 10178
(212) 265-6888 .. **Barnes,** Timothy L '85 (Porzio B&N,PC) -156 W 56th -NY 10019
(212) 752-3575 .. **Barness,** Jordan G '85 (Steinberg BG&F,LLP) -767 3rd Av -NY 10017
(212) 732-3200 .. **Barnet,** Howard J Jr. '80 (Carter L&M LLP) -2 Wall -NY 10005
(212) 362-6174 .. **Barnett,** Alexander E '93 -144 W 72nd -NY 10023
(845) 358-2702 .. **Barnett,** Amy S '87 %Rockland Parent-Child Ctr -137 1st Av -Nyack 10960
(212) 806-5400 .. **Barnett,** Ayesha '96 SpclCnsl Stroock &S&L LLP -180 Maiden Ln -NY 10038
(212) 340-3149 .. **Barnett,** C Sue '80 %Metro-North -347 Mad Av -NY 10017 **Fx:**697-9079
(212) 788-8685 .. **Barnett,** Camille D '01 %Law Dept -100 Church -NY 10007 **Fx:**788-0367
(718) 286-6000 .. **Barnett,** Christopher E '06 %DA -125-01 Qns Blvd -Kew Gdns 11415
(212) 679-4666 .. **Barnett,** David A '87 %Frenkel H&S LLP -16 E 34th -NY 10016
(212) 593-5300 .. **Barnett,** David A '90 J L Advisors -400 Madision Av -NY 10017
(716) 856-5500 .. **Barnett,** E Meghan '09 %Damon M LLP -200 Delaware Av -Buffalo 14202
(212) 599-1717 .. **Barnett Edelstein Gross Kass & Lieber, PC** -122 E 42nd -NY 10168 **Fx:**599-2614
(212) 974-3612 .. **Barnett,** Elizabeth '83 -60 Lafayette -NY 10013
(718) 268-9090 .. **Barnett,** Frank '67 -71-58 Austin -Frst Hlls 11375 **Fx:**520-9081
(212) 464-2715 .. **Barnett,** Franya G '01 JP Morgan Private Bk -345 Park Av -NY 10154
(212) 903-9000 .. **Barnett,** Gary '87 (Linklaters) -1345 Av of Amer -NY 10105
(212) 286-0225 .. **Barnett,** Gregory G '95 (Casey & B LLC) -65 W 36th -NY 10018 **Fx:**286-0261
(212) 262-2390 .. **Barnett,** J Steve '95 OfCnsl Connell F LLP -888 7th Av -NY 10106
(212) 685-5545 .. **Barnett,** Jacalyn F '78 J Barnett -260 Mad Av -NY 10016 **Fx:**685-5695
(516) 506-6000 .. **Barnett,** Jason M '94 Rexcorp Realty -625 RXR Plz -Uniondale 11556
(212) 947-9779 .. **Barnett,** Jennifer L '02 Advocates for Chldrn of NY -151 W 30th -NY 10001
(212) 450-0131 .. **Barnett,** Jerome E '85 Marubeni America -375 Lex Av -NY 10017 **Fx:**450-0706
(914) 761-7041 .. **Barnett,** Jonathan S '96 -6 Harrows Ln -Purchase 10577 **Fx:**761-0002
(212) 227-0999 .. **Barnett,** Keith S '88 -321 Bway -NY 10007 **Fx:**693-1666
(212) 388-3600 .. **Barnett,** Kim L '86 %32B-J Leg Srvcs -101 Av of Amer -NY 10013 **Fx:**388-3061
(845) 452-5900 .. **Barnett,** Kyle W '97 (Van DeWater & V,LLP) -85 Civic Ctr Plz Bx112 -Poughkeepsie 12602
(212) 619-1555 .. **Barnett,** Lance E '82 -277 Bway -NY 10007 **Fx:**619-1522
(518) 280-3267 .. **Barnett,** Lara P '94 -2025 Bway -Schnctdy 12306 **Fx:**207-0924
(212) 527-4000 .. **Barnett,** Lucy '01 Revlon -237 Park Av -NY 10017 **Fx:**527-5299
(718) 205-2441 .. **Barnett,** Maria A '06 %Sacco & F,LLP -78-05 Roosevelt Av -Jcksn Hts 11372
(212) 512-1000 .. **Barnett,** Melissa Roper '93 %HBO -1100 Av of Amer -NY 10036 **Fx:**512-1986
(516) 294-6010 .. **Barnett,** Michl A '73 -1205 Franklin Av -Gdn Cty 11530 **Fx:**248-8036
(212) 697-1300 .. **Barnett,** Michl A '94 -1825 Park Av -NY 10035 **Fx:**297-0504
(212) 599-1717 .. **Barnett,** Michl H '73 (Barnett EGK&L,PC) -122 E 42nd -NY 10168
(516) 741-6600 .. **Barnett,** Mitchell M '90 -224 7th -Gdn Cty 11530
(914) 848-4676 .. **Barnett,** Penelope J '02 Pernod Ricard USA -100 Manhattanvll Rd -Purchase 10577
(516) 931-8100 .. **Barnett,** Robt S '88 (Capell BM&S,LLP) -100 Jericho Quadrangle -Jericho 11753
(212) 816-4477 .. **Barnett,** Rohan O '97 Citigroup -388 Greenwich -NY 10013
(212) 735-3000 .. **Barnett,** Rosemarie '02 %Skadden ASM&F LLP -4 Times Sq -NY 10036
(845) 695-2255 .. **Barnett,** Scott C '01 %Hannaford Bros Inc -30 Twr Dr -Middletwn 10941
(212) 605-0818 .. **Barnett,** Sloan N '94 Activated Holdings -767 5th Av -NY 10153
(212) 506-5000 .. **Barnett,** Steven R '95 %Orrick H&S LLP -51 W 52nd -NY 10019
(212) 728-8000 .. **Barnett,** Tyler E '10 %Willkie F&G LLP -787 7th Av -NY 10019
(315) 435-2170 .. **Barnette,** Devinn N '05 %Cnty Atty -421 Mntgmry -Syracuse 13202 **Fx:**435-5729
(212) 998-6732 .. **Barnette,** Margaret Ruhl '96 Brennan Ctr for Justice -161 Av of Amer -NY 10013 **Fx:**995-4550
(518) 457-9714 .. **Barnett-Mulligan,** Patrick M '83 -Bldg 8 State Campus -Albany 12227
(585) 248-0140 .. **Barney,** Brian J '79 (Barney & A,LLP) -130 D Linden Oaks -Rchstr 14625 **Fx:**248-0175
(607) 273-6841 .. **Barney Grossman Dubow Marcus & Orkin, LLP** -119 E Seneca -Ithaca 14850 **Fx:**272-8806
(212) 735-3000 .. **Barney,** Haylee D '09 %Skadden ASM&F LLP -4 Times Sq -NY 10036
(212) 244-4664 .. **Barney,** Jaclyn Okin '03 %NY Lawyers Pub Intrst -151 W 30th -NY 10001 **Fx:**244-4570
(315) 234-8624 .. **Barney,** Kerrie J '00 US Dist Ct -101 S Clinton Bx7345 -Syracuse 13261 **Fx:**234-8621
(212) 451-2300 .. **Barney,** Mason A '06 %Olshan GFR&W LLP -65 E 55th -NY 10022
(718) 892-2600 .. **Barnhard,** David W '84 -1978 Wllmsbrdg Rd -Bronx 10461
(845) 602-1842 .. **Barnhard,** Elizabeth M '82 Pfizer,Inc -401 N Mddltwn Rd -Pearl Rvr 10965 **Fx:**602-5666
(212) 532-8100 .. **Barnhardt,** Amanda Matthews '07 %Stern & M,LLP -115 Bway -NY 10006
(212) 210-9400 .. **Barnhart,** Jill C '08 %Alston & B LLP -90 Park Av -NY 10016
(718) 428-9180 .. **Barnhart,** Patrick R '07 %Rossi & C,LLP -42-24 235th -Douglastn 11363
(607) 721-8771 .. **Barnhill,** Laura M '88 %Dept of Law -44 Hawley -Bnghmtn 13901 **Fx:**721-8789
(631) 694-2300 .. **Barnosky,** Eugene R '80 (Lamb & B,LLP) -534 Broadhllw Rd Bx9034 -Melvll 11747
(516) 227-0700 .. **Barnosky,** John J '68 (Farrell F,PC) -1320 RXR Plz -Uniondale 11556
(212) 474-1000 .. **Barnstable-Brown,** Christopher D '09 %Cravath S&M LLP -825 8th Av -NY 10019
(607) 734-1216 .. **Barnstead,** Steven W '88 -420 Carroll -Elmira 14901
(212) 909-6000 .. **Barnum,** Lee Turnier '00 %Debevoise & P LLP -919 3rd Av -NY 10022
(212) 966-3761 .. **Barnum,** Nicole C '95 (Barnum & R,PC) -30 Vesey -NY 10007 **Fx:**651-9852
(516) 877-7554 .. **Barnwell,** Steven R '91 -50 Chas Lindbergh Blvd -Uniondale 11553
(212) 661-9100 .. **Barocas,** Michl P '90 (Otterbourg SH&R,PC) -230 Park Av -NY 10169
(212) 557-2800 .. **Barod,** Raenu '98 (Barger & W LLP) -10 E 40th -NY 10016
(212) 425-0055 .. **Baron,** Allison Merideth '97 %Sharretts PC&B -75 Broad -NY 10004
(212) 346-9200 .. **Baron,** Andrea J '87 OfCnsl K Aron -111 Bway -NY 10006 **Fx:**346-4665
(212) 382-3300 .. **Baron,** Andrew S '02 %Wollmuth M&D LLP -500 5th Av -NY 10110
(631) 852-8800 .. **Baron,** Anthony M '07 %DA -116 Hmptn Rd -Southampton 11968 **Fx:**852-8806
(212) 244-5670 .. **Baron Bergstein & Weinberg** -450 7th Av -NY 10123
(718) 934-6501 .. **Baron,** Bruce '88 Baron Assoc PC -2509 Av U -Brklyn 11229 **Fx:**648-7781
(516) 683-1717 .. **Baron,** Chas B '90 %V Russo & Assoc,PC -1600 Stewart Av -Westbury 11590 **Fx:**683-9393
(212) 261-8000 .. **Baron,** Craig D '03 (Mendes & M,LLP) -750 7th Av -NY 10019
(646) 328-0850 .. **Baron,** Danl E '00 %Outside Cnsl Solutns LLP -1430 Bway -NY 10018 **Fx:**360-5000
(718) 544-2700 .. **Baron,** David J '77 (Baron & B) -118-21 Qns Blvd -Frst Hlls 11375 **Fx:**544-2968
(646) 386-4520 .. **Baron,** Eileen J '78 %Criminal Ct -100 Centre -NY 10013
(914) 967-3332 .. **Baron,** Fredk U '83 %High Ridge Books -Bx286 -Rye 10580
(518) 434-6543 .. **Baron,** Gabriela P '96 Xerox Litigation Srvcs -80 State -Albany 12207 **Fx:**434-8457
(516) 328-3254 .. **Baron & Goodsell** -608 Jericho Tpk -New Hyde Pk 11040 **Fx:**328-0864
(212) 878-8465 .. **Baron,** Helayne L '85 (Clifford C LLP) -31 W 52nd -NY 10019
(212) 264-7500 .. **Baron,** Jeffrey E '82 (Baron & S,PC) -291 Bway -NY 10007
(631) 757-4493 .. **Baron,** Jeffrey T '96 (Baron Law Firm,PLLC) -166 Laurel Rd -E Northprt 11731 **Fx:**757-4486
(917) 684-8250 .. **Baron,** Kenneth I '91 -1400 5th Av -NY 10026
(212) 341-9005 .. **Baron,** Martin '74 %Admin Children's Srvcs -150 William -NY 10038
(212) 490-3000 .. **Baron,** Matthew I '06 %Wilson EME&D LLP -150 E 42nd -NY 10017
(212) 878-5131 .. **Baron,** Mitchell N '74 (Goulston & S,PC) -750 3rd Av -NY 10017
(631) 367-7000 .. **Baron & Pagliughi** -85 Main -Cold Spg Hbr 11724 **Fx:**367-7908
(212) 455-2000 .. **Baron,** Patrick M '02 %Simpson T&B LLP -425 Lex Av -NY 10017
(631) 367-7000 .. **Baron,** Peter D '87 (Baron & P) -85 Main -Cold Spg Hbr 11724
(716) 633-8300 .. **Baron,** Robt C '04 -5500 Main -Williamsvll 14221
(212) 474-1000 .. **Baron,** Robt H '82 (Cravath S&M LLP) -825 8th Av -NY 10019
(516) 822-3550 .. **Baron,** Ronald J '80 (Hoffmann & B LLP) -6900 Jericho Tpk -Syosset 11791 **Fx:**822-3582
(212) 337-0200 .. **Baron,** Sandra S '75 %MLRC -520 8th Av -NY 10018 **Fx:**337-9893
(718) 738-9800 .. **Baron,** Scott J '91 (S Baron & Assoc,PC) -159-49 Cross Bay Blvd -Howard Bch 11414 **Fx:**738-3912
(212) 603-1851 .. **Baron,** Seth F '04 Broadway Video -1619 Bway -NY 10019
(212) 264-7500 .. **Baron and Shelkin,PC** -291 Bway -NY 10007 **Fx:**264-7111
(718) 802-2714 .. **Baron,** Ted '83 ACS-DLS -330 Jay -Brklyn 11201
(212) 801-6960 .. **Baron,** Whitney S '08 %Greenberg T,LLP -200 Park Av -NY 10166
(212) 757-5800 .. **Baron,** Wm M '89 Titlevest Agncy,Inc -44 Wall -NY 10005 **Fx:**757-0466
(212) 832-3600 .. **Baronci,** Anthony '92 (Wertheimer F,LLC) -230 Park Av -NY 10169
(716) 854-7525 .. **Barone,** Anthony Jr. '74 %Serotte R&W -300 Delaware Av -Buffalo 14202
(718) 351-1600 .. **Barone,** Anthony P '64 (Barone & B LLP) -43 New Dorp Plz -Staten Isl 10306 **Fx:**980-2098
(845) 897-2210 .. **Barone,** Carl P '82 -1003 Main -Fishkill 12524 **Fx:**897-3796
(718) 836-1924 .. **Barone,** Claire '79 -426 81st -Brklyn 11209 **Fx:**836-1924
(518) 899-5700 .. **Barone,** Danielle M '06 %Lemire J,LLC -2534 Route 9 Bx2485 -Malta 12020 **Fx:**899-5487
(716) 667-0042 .. **Barone,** Deborah M '93 (Barone & B) -4467 S Buffalo -Orchard Pk 14127 **Fx:**667-0043
(845) 291-0011 .. **Barone,** Gardiner S '88 (Blustein SR&B,LLP) -10 Matthews -Goshen 10924
(315) 474-1511 .. **Barone,** Gregory '86 %National Grid -300 Erie Blvd W -Syracuse 13202 **Fx:**428-6149

(516) 364-7900 .. **Barone,** Jaime E '02 Epstein F&G -45 Crsswys Park Dr W -Woodbury 11797
(716) 856-4000 .. **Barone,** Kenneth F '79 (Hodgson R LLP) -140 Pearl -Buffalo 14202
(716) 667-0042 .. **Barone,** Michl F '77 (Barone & B) -4467 S Buffalo -Orchard Pk 14127 **Fx:**667-0043
(845) 294-7949 .. **Barone,** Michl F '09 %Norton & C -60 Erie Bx308 -Goshen 10924
(518) 447-7805 .. **Barone,** Michl Stephen '02 Police Dept -165 Henry Johnson Blvd -Albany 12210 **Fx:**447-7896
(914) 683-8200 .. **Barone,** Nicholas P '92 -44 Church -White Plns 10601 **Fx:**683-8824
(716) 849-6500 .. **Barone,** Robt D '94 (Brown & T,LLC) -14 Lafayette Sq -Buffalo 14203
(631) 287-4030 .. **Barone,** Rosemarie '98 R Barone PC -199 Mariners Dr -Southampton 11968 **Fx:**287-4034
(914) 750-5933 .. **Barone,** Salvatore '99 (Kissel H&W LLP) -580 Wht Plns Rd -Tarrytwn 10591
(888) 785-8566 .. **Barone,** Sestino S '09 -228 Park Av S -NY 10003 **Fx:**(718) 504-4280
(718) 351-1600 .. **Barone,** Toni Ann '92 (Barone & B LLP) -43 New Dorp Plz -Staten Isl 10306 **Fx:**980-2098
(585) 546-6440 .. **Barone,** Vincent M '78 -125 State -Rchstr 14614
(212) 637-2405 .. **Baroni,** Lisa A '95 US Atty -1 St Andrews Plz -NY 10007 **Fx:**637-0412
(914) 761-0300 .. **Baroni,** Roland A Jr. '78 (Stephens BR&L) -175 Main -White Plns 10601
(212) 508-1682 .. **Baronoff,** Kenneth D '88 Peter J Solomon Co -520 Mad Av -NY 10022
(212) 449-7020 .. **Baronoff,** Steven A '85 Merrill Lynch -2 World Fncl Ctr -NY 10281
(914) 253-0500 .. **Baronti,** Lynn Bianca '90 Baronti & B -2900 Wstchstr Av -Purchase 10577
(914) 253-0500 .. **Baronti,** Steven A '91 Baronti & B -2900 Wstchstr Av -Purchase 10577
(212) 596-9000 .. **Bar-Or,** Revital '07 %Ropes & G LLP -1211 Av of Amer -NY 10036
(917) 637-3600 .. **Barot,** Sneha Raghu '00 %Ctr for Reproductive Rts -120 Wall -NY 10005 **Fx:**637-3666
(212) 905-6536 .. **Barotz,** Nathan M '92 -52 Vndrblt Av -NY 10017 **Fx:**905-6537
(646) 264-3650 .. **Barouh,** Evan R '88 %US Dept of Labor -201 Varick -NY 10014 **Fx:**264-3660
(212) 541-9100 .. **Barous,** John E '97 %Schiavetti CDW&N,LLP -575 8th Av -NY 10018
(212) 861-2800 .. **Barovick,** Andrew J '89 AJ Barovick,PC -274 Mad Av -NY 10016 **Fx:**545-7211
(716) 551-4221 .. **Barovick,** Robin D '01 %Hon J Curtin -68 Court -Buffalo 14202
(631) 447-3400 .. **Barr,** Alan Raymond '99 AR Barr PC -98 S Ocean Av -Patchogue 11772 **Fx:**758-5894
(914) 220-8364 .. **Barr,** Beverly M '92 -445 Hmltn Av -White Plns 10601
(585) 964-8566 .. **Barr,** Culver K '61 -16 E Main -Rchstr 14614 **Fx:**964-2668
(212) 836-8000 .. **Barr,** David K '84 (Kaye S LLP) -425 Park Av -NY 10022
(212) 506-3900 .. **Barr,** Evan T '05 (Steptoe & J LLP) -750 7th Av -NY 10019
(212) 355-2323 .. **Barr,** Franklin J '76 (F Barr & Assoc) -866 UN Plz -NY 10017 **Fx:**355-0503
(631) 732-3775 .. **Barr,** Gene D '99 (G Barr,PC) -80 Medford Av -Patchogue 11772 **Fx:**654-0255
(212) 435-3571 .. **Barr,** Harry Kyle III '69 %Port Auth of NY/NJ -225 Park Av S -NY 10003 **Fx:**435-3555
(845) 352-4080 .. **Barr,** Harvey S '64 (Barr P & Assoc PLLC) -664 Chestnut Rdg Rd Bx664 -Spg Vly 10977 **Fx:**352-6777
(914) 997-7707 .. **Barr,** Harvey S '64 (Barr P & Assoc PLLC) -11 Martine Av -White Plns 10606 **Fx:**(845) 352-6777
(212) 869-4080 .. **Barr,** Harvey S '64 (Barr P & Assoc PLLC) -419 Park Av S -NY 10016 **Fx:**(845) 352-6777
(212) 821-9200 .. **Barr,** Jasmine '02 Lighthse Intl -111 E 59th -NY 10022 **Fx:**821-9713
(212) 521-5400 .. **Barr,** Jason M '08 %Reed S LLP -599 Lex Av -NY 10022
(212) 227-1834 .. **Barr,** Jeffrey A '84 -225 Bway -NY 10007 **Fx:**964-4360
(716) 845-1555 .. **Barr,** Jenifer Scalisi '97 Roswell Park Cancer Inst -Elm & Carlton -Buffalo 14263 **Fx:**845-8692
(212) 455-2000 .. **Barr,** Jeremy D '09 %Simpson T&B LLP -425 Lex Av -NY 10017
(212) 259-8000 .. **Barr,** Kenneth R '04 Cnsl Dewey & L LLP -1301 Av of Amer -NY 10019
(212) 237-1000 .. **Barr,** Leslie S '85 SpclCnsl Windels ML&M,LLP -156 W 56th -NY 10019
(518) 439-9013 .. **Barr,** Martin L '53 -46 Euclid Av -Delmar 12054
(718) 254-7000 .. **Barr,** Mary K '04 %US Atty -271 Cadman Plz E -Brklyn 11201 **Fx:**254-6479
(212) 530-5000 .. **Barr,** Matthew S '97 (Milbank TH&M LLP) -1 Chase Manh Plz -NY 10005
(212) 768-6700 .. **Barr,** Michl H '81 (Sonnenschein N&R LLP) -1221 Av of Amer -NY 10020
(212) 450-4000 .. **Barr,** Neil J '01 (Davis P&W LLP) -450 Lex Av -NY 10017
(716) 847-8400 .. **Barr,** Raymond H '73 (Phillips L LLP) -3400 HSBC Ctr -Buffalo 14203
(212) 326-3939 .. **Barr,** Ross S '04 %Jones D -222 E 41st -NY 10017
(212) 264-3650 .. **Barr,** Sheena V '01 SSA -26 Fed Plz -NY 10278 **Fx:**264-6372
(716) 856-5500 .. **Barr,** Trevor J '08 %Damon M LLP -200 Delaware Av -Buffalo 14202
(518) 402-1871 .. **Barra,** Daryl M '93 %Dept of Health -Corning Twr 24th Fl -Albany 12237 **Fx:**473-4896
(718) 300-9570 .. **Barra,** Thos D '97 -118-21 Qns Blvd -Frst Hlls 11375 **Fx:**261-9302
(212) 816-8744 .. **Barrack,** Craig S '95 Smith Barney -388 Greenwich -NY 10013
(212) 318-3000 .. **Barrack,** David L '90 (Fulbright & J LLP) -666 5th Av -NY 10103
(212) 867-6000 .. **Barrack,** Luise A '81 (Rosenberg & E,PC) -733 3rd Av -NY 10017
(212) 688-0782 .. **Barrack Rodos & Bacine** -1350 Bway -NY 10018 **Fx:**688-0783
(212) 651-5528 .. **Barrack,** Sarah G '01 NS Bienstock Inc -250 W 57th -NY 10107 **Fx:**757-6411
(845) 691-6789 .. **Barraco,** Anthony M '68 -3669 Route 9W Bx1545 -Highlnd 12528 **Fx:**691-2862
(585) 546-5980 .. **Barraco,** Ted A '83 -19 Main W -Rchstr 14614
(212) 878-7464 .. **Barraga,** Elaine M '94 %MTA -347 Mad Av -NY 10017
(212) 858-1000 .. **Barragan,** Sandra M '06 %Pillsbury WSP LLP -1540 Bway -NY 10036
(212) 326-3939 .. **Barragate,** Brett P '06 (Jones D) -222 E 41st -NY 10017
(212) 436-3555 .. **Barrameda,** Benedicto M '99 Deloitte & Touche,LLP -2 World Fncl Ctr -NY 10281
(212) 405-2255 .. **Barran,** Alana '00 A Barran,PC -109 Lafayette -NY 10013 **Fx:**405-2254
(212) 852-5916 .. **Barrantes,** Barbara '81 WestLB AG -1211 Av of Amer -NY 10036
(718) 556-0737 .. **Barravecchia,** Alexsis T '99 -60 Bay -Staten Isl 10301 **Fx:**448-8685
(718) 987-0481 .. **Barravecchio,** Judith-Marie '93 -20 Esther Depew -Staten Isl 10306 **Fx:**987-0616
(212) 351-4500 .. **Barravecchio,** Robt R '99 %Epstein B&G,PC -250 Park Av -NY 10177
(631) 696-0972 .. **Barravecchio,** Santo '02 -35 S Knndy Dr -Centereach 11720 **Fx:**696-4289
(718) 987-9178 .. **Barravecchio,** Santo A '93 -293 Park -Staten Isl 10306
(212) 310-8000 .. **Barraza,** Christopher D '07 %Weil G&M LLP -767 5th Av -NY 10153
(212) 584-0700 .. **Barreca,** Rick '99 %Seeger W LLP -1 William -NY 10004
(212) 408-5100 .. **Barredo,** Nilo J '05 %Chadbourne & P LLP -30 Rckfllr Plz -NY 10112
(718) 725-3200 .. **Barreira,** Elizabeth Pinheiro '98 %Admin Children's Srvcs -151-20 Jamaica Av -Jamaica 11432
(607) 763-9200 .. **Barreiro,** Alyssa M '93 (Levene G&T,LLP) -BxF-1706 -Bnghmtn 13902
(631) 753-4400 .. **Barrella,** Christopher J '00 OfCnsl Sferrazza & K,PLLC -532 Broad Hollow Rd -Melvll 11747
(212) 644-0100 .. **Barrella,** Vincent R '79 -909 3rd Av -NY 10022
(212) 504-6000 .. **Barrentine,** Glen P '06 SpclCnsl Cadwalader W&T LLP -1 World Fncl Ctr -NY 10281
(315) 671-2105 .. **Barrer,** Deborah M '84 %Hon P Wells -Cnty Cthse -Syracuse 13202
(315) 425-2700 .. **Barrer,** Robt A '83 (Hiscock & B,LLP) -One Park Pl -Syracuse 13202
(585) 338-6800 .. **Barrera,** Jos '08 %Bausch & Lomb -One Bausch & Lomb Pl -Rchstr 14604 **Fx:**338-8706
(212) 987-8700 .. **Barrera,** Naomi C '03 -103 E 125th -NY 10035
(212) 278-6754 .. **Barreras,** Bryan Lee '98 Societe Generale -1221 Av of Amer -NY 10020
(212) 935-3000 .. **Barres,** David L '93 (Mintz LCFG&P,PC) -666 3rd Av -NY 10017
(516) 228-8484 .. **Barrese,** Rocco S '73 (Dilworth & B,LLP) -1000 Woodbury Rd -Woodbury 11797
(212) 753-3468 .. **Barreto,** Rafael A '97 %Wildes & W,PC -515 Mad Av -NY 10022
(212) 416-6323 .. **Barrett,** Anita Fisher '72 %Dept of Law -120 Bway -NY 10271
(800) 879-1805 .. **Barrett,** B Jos '82 -26 Carroll -Amityvll 11701
(518) 637-4376 .. **Barrett,** Brian P '05 -72 Olympic Dr -Lk Placid 12946
(212) 701-3000 .. **Barrett,** Brian P '07 %Cahill G&R LLP -80 Pine -NY 10005 **Fx:**269-5420
(718) 462-9451 .. **Barrett,** Calvin A '00 -599 E 7th -Brklyn 11218
(914) 682-6830 .. **Barrett,** Christina Ann '91 -441 2nd Av -Pelham 10803
(718) 625-8568 .. **Barrett,** Clover M '85 CM Barrett,PC -338 Atl Av -Brklyn 11201 **Fx:**625-6646
(212) 442-3229 .. **Barrett,** Danielle J '08 %Law Dept -100 Church -NY 10007 **Fx:**788-0367
(212) 446-2300 .. **Barrett,** David A '75 (Boies S&F LLP) -575 Lex Av -NY 10022
(212) 735-3000 .. **Barrett,** David E '02 %Skadden ASM&F LLP -4 Times Sq -NY 10036
(212) 588-1000 .. **Barrett,** David I '65 -600 Mad Av -NY 10022 **Fx:**588-0118
(315) 437-7600 .. **Barrett,** Dennis T '70 (Ferrara FLB&R,PC) -5010 Campuswood Dr -E Syracuse 13057
(212) 323-7077 .. **Barrett,** Derek E '92 OfCnsl Rawle & H LLP -14 Wall -NY 10005
(585) 266-8884 .. **Barrett,** Donald C '56 -241 Norcrest Dr -Rchstr 14617
(212) 504-6000 .. **Barrett,** Elizabeth A '10 %Cadwalader W&T LLP -1 World Fncl Ctr -NY 10281
(585) 265-3730 .. **Barrett Greisberger LLP** -34 May -Webster 14580 **Fx:**265-1508
(212) 455-2000 .. **Barrett,** James P '62 OfCnsl Simpson T&B LLP -425 Lex Av -NY 10017
(718) 237-3400 .. **Barrett,** Jane N '77 -353 2nd -Brklyn 11215 **Fx:**222-5858
(212) 849-7000 .. **Barrett,** Jennifer Jackson '96 (Quinn EU&S,LLP) -51 Mad Av -NY 10010
(315) 331-4875 .. **Barrett,** John W Jr. '75 SrCnsl Underberg & K LLP -634 S Main -Newark 14513
(212) 815-1450 .. **Barrett,** Jos W '05 %DC 37 Gen Cnsl -125 Barclay -NY 10007 **Fx:**815-1440
(212) 415-8600 .. **Barrett,** Kathyrn A '09 %Locke LB&L LLP -3 World Fncl Ctr -NY 10281
(212) 715-1000 .. **Barrett,** Kelly M '06 %Arnold & P LLP -399 Park Av -NY 10022
(718) 268-4155 .. **Barrett Lazar,LLC** -109-01 72nd Rd -Frst Hlls 11375 **Fx:**268-5010
(212) 268-5136 .. **Barrett,** Levi W '09 %Harwood L -350 5th Av -NY 10118
(646) 471-4000 .. **Barrett,** Lori A '93 %PricewaterhouseCoopers LLP -300 Mad Av -NY 10017
(212) 487-4444 .. **Barrett,** Lori Ann '05 %Dept Cnsmr Affrs -42 Bway -NY 10004 **Fx:**487-4197
(845) 486-4300 .. **Barrett,** Maura Ann '95 (Ostertag OB&F) -17 Cllgvw Av -Poughkeepsie 12603
(212) 262-2390 .. **Barrett,** Meghan B '06 %Connell F LLP -888 7th Av -NY 10106
(585) 428-3889 .. **Barrett,** Melissa L '97 City Ct -6 Hall of Justice -Rchstr 14614 **Fx:**428-2746
(518) 457-1260 .. **Barrett,** Michl K '03 %DCJS -4 Twr Pl -Albany 12203 **Fx:**457-3089
(914) 332-5800 .. **Barrett,** Patrick J '82 Hitachi -50 Prospect Av -Tarrytwn 10591 **Fx:**332-5555
(516) 249-3450 .. **Barrett,** Paul A '99 (Carman C&I,LLP) -266 Main -Farmngdl 11735
(212) 460-4624 .. **Barrett,** Peter J '85 Con Ed -4 Irving Pl -NY 10003
(718) 980-9199 .. **Barrett,** Richd J '99 -88 New Dorp Plz S -Staten Isl 10306
(212) 558-4000 .. **Barrett,** Robb P '10 %Sullivan & C LLP -125 Broad -NY 10004
(212) 837-6000 .. **Barrett,** Sarah Copley '04 %Hughes H&R LLP -1 Bttry Pk Plz -NY 10004
(518) 463-3200 .. **Barrett,** Sebrina A '03 %NYS Bar Assn -1 Elk -Albany 12207 **Fx:**487-5544
(212) 248-8800 .. **Barrett,** Stephen J '09 %Callan KB&B LLP -1 Whitehall -NY 10004
(212) 773-9177 .. **Barrett,** Wm A '93 Ernst & Young LLP -5 Times Sq -NY 10036
(631) 724-8833 .. **Barrett,** Wm J '82 (Devitt SB,LLP) -50 Route 111 -Smithtwn 11787
(212) 818-1110 .. **Barrett,** Wm L D '64 OfCnsl Butzel L,PC -380 Mad Av -NY 10017
(914) 323-7000 .. **Barretta,** Rosemarie '02 %Wilson EME&D LLP -3 Gannett Dr -White Plns 10604

(212) 788-5021 .. **Barrett-Baisden,** Grace A '95 %Dept Hlth -125 Worth CN-30 -NY 10013 **Fx:**788-4300
(716) 852-7483 .. **Barrett O'Neill,** Julie M '00 Buffalo Niagara Riverkeeper -1250 Niagara -Buffalo 14213
(518) 487-7600 .. **Barrick,** Stacey M '06 %Whiteman O&H LLP -1 Commerce Plz -Albany 12260
(212) 541-2000 .. **Barrie,** John P '01 (Bryan C LLP) -1290 Av of Amer -NY 10104
(718) 487-2300 .. **Barrie,** Susan G '80 %Leg Srvcs Corp -256-260 Bway -Brklyn 11211 **Fx:**782-6790
(518) 426-4600 .. **Barriere,** James J '93 (Couch W,LLP) -540 Bway Bx22222 -Albany 12201 **Fx:**426-0533
(518) 432-1200 .. **Barringer,** Jeffrey P '08 %McGlinchey S PLLC -194 Wshngtn Av -Albany 12210
(212) 750-5560 .. **Barrison,** Earl '52 (Barrisons) -444 Mad Av -NY 10022 **Fx:**759-5551
(212) 269-0927 .. **Barrison,** Harvey '71 (D'Amato & L,LLP) -2 World Fncl Ctr -NY 10281
(212) 750-5560 .. **Barrison,** Steven M '87 (Barrisons) -444 Mad Av -NY 10022 **Fx:**759-5551
(516) 222-1350 .. **Barrocas & Rieger** -100 Q Roosevelt Blvd -Gdn Cty 11530 **Fx:**222-1654
(516) 222-1350 .. **Barrocas,** Sol '73 (Barrocas & R) -100 Q Roosevelt Blvd -Gdn Cty 11530
(516) 463-5246 .. **Barron,** Barbara S '85 %Hofstra Law Schl -121 Hofstra Univ -Hempstd 11549
(212) 907-9700 .. **Barron,** David W '06 %Smith G&R,LLP -250 Park Av -NY 10177
(212) 761-4000 .. **Barron,** Francis P '79 Morgan Stanley -1585 Bway -NY 10036
(212) 425-7854 .. **Barron,** Monica M '09 %Georgoulis & Assoc PLLC -45 Bway -NY 10006 **Fx:**422-5360
(212) 907-9700 .. **Barron,** Wm M '73 (Smith G&R,LLP) -250 Park Av -NY 10177
(212) 245-1000 .. **Barros,** Delyanne De Alves '09 %Outten & G LLP -3 Park Av -NY 10016
(212) 661-6109 .. **Barros,** Romeo J '77 -10 Lbrty -NY 10005
(646) 837-0100 .. **Barroso,** Carmen O '02 %Wenick & F,PC -28 E 28th -NY 10016
(718) 763-1010 .. **Barrow,** Audra J '96 -755 E 81st -Brklyn 11236
(212) 751-3001 .. **Barrow,** Hunter M '07 (Thompson & K LLP) -919 3rd Av -NY 10022
(518) 752-5567 .. **Barrow,** James '71 -31 Prospect Av -Gloversvll 12078 **Fx:**752-5567
(212) 310-8000 .. **Barrow,** Jodi L '08 %Weil G&M LLP -767 5th Av -NY 10153
(212) 661-9100 .. **Barrow-Bosshart,** Jenette A '85 (Otterbourg SH&R,PC) -230 Park Av -NY 10169
(212) 573-0979 .. **Barrows,** Michl C '04 M Barrows & Assoc PLLC -330 Mad Av -NY 10017
(212) 973-0572 .. **Barrows,** Warren E '91 Cnsl Wolff & S PC -140 Bway -NY 10005
(212) 701-3000 .. **Barrs,** Sarah E '08 %Cahill G&R LLP -80 Pine -NY 10005 **Fx:**269-5420
(212) 964-9282 .. **Barrun-Madla,** Mylene A '08 %N Weinrib & Assoc -305 Bway -NY 10007 **Fx:**964-9525
(212) 931-7900 .. **Barry,** Alexander D '02 MLB Properties -245 Park Av -NY 10167 **Fx:**949-5697
(315) 449-0876 .. **Barry,** Brian J '94 PMA Ins Grp -5789 Widewaters Pkwy -DeWitt 13214
(718) 590-2000 .. **Barry,** Colleen A '00 %DA -198 E 161st -Bronx 10451 **Fx:**590-6477
(718) 941-4400 .. **Barry,** Cuthbert J '75 -2809 Church Av -Brklyn 11226 **Fx:**941-4496
(315) 435-2470 .. **Barry,** Danl B '04 %DA -505 S State -Syracuse 13202 **Fx:**435-3969
(716) 853-9555 .. **Barry,** Danl E Jr. '62 %Leg Aid -237 Main -Buffalo 14203 **Fx:**853-3219
(212) 808-7800 .. **Barry,** David E '69 (Kelley D&W LLP) -101 Park Av -NY 10178
(516) 572-2000 .. **Barry,** David J '09 %DA -99 Main -Hempstd 11550 **Fx:**572-2606
(516) 223-6890 .. **Barry,** Dennis R '77 (Baribault & B) -1113 South Dr -Baldwin 11510
(212) 490-9100 .. **Barry,** Desmond T Jr. '74 (Condon & F LLP) -7 Times Sq -NY 10036
(718) 261-3047 .. **Barry,** Felice B '06 %Queens Law Assoc -118-21 Qns Blvd -Frst Hlls 11375 **Fx:**261-0798
(212) 536-8599 .. **Barry,** George C '82 %Amerada Hess -1185 Av of Amer -NY 10036 **Fx:**536-8390
(212) 819-8200 .. **Barry,** Hope B '09 %White & C LLP -1155 Av of Amer -NY 10036
(631) 269-7263 .. **Barry,** James C '40 -13 Lakebrdg Dr S -Kings Pk 11754
(845) 647-3250 .. **Barry,** James J '75 (J Barry,PC) -18 Warren Bx469 -Ellenvll 12428 **Fx:**647-3251
(914) 323-7000 .. **Barry,** Jeanne Ann '94 (Wilson EME&D LLP) -3 Gannett Dr -White Plns 10604
(212) 539-9056 .. **Barry,** John J '87 AT&T -32 Av of Amer -NY 10013
(631) 726-6230 .. **Barry,** John P '92 JDC Properties -99 Main -Westhmptn Bch 11978
(212) 969-3000 .. **Barry,** John P '98 (Proskauer R LLP) -1585 Bway -NY 10036
(315) 793-8101 .. **Barry,** Jos M '01 %Hon S Gerling -10 Broad -Utica 13501
(315) 448-8400 .. **Barry,** Jos W III '91 %Law Dept -233 E Wshngtn -Syracuse 13202 **Fx:**448-8381
(718) 643-7983 .. **Barry,** Justin A '90 Criminal Ct -120 Schermerhorn -Brklyn 11201
(718) 250-2000 .. **Barry,** Keith J '10 %DA -350 Jay -Brklyn 11201 **Fx:**250-2314
(516) 682-7231 .. **Barry,** Kevin '97 %T Spina -170 Froehlich Farm Blvd -Woodbury 11797 **Fx:**682-5337
(631) 261-1281 .. **Barry,** Kevin A '84 -23 Schooner Rd -Northprt 11768 **Fx:**261-1694
(631) 547-8400 .. **Barry,** Kevin J '75 Cnsl Farrell F,PC -290 Broad Hollow Rd -Melvll 11747
(914) 381-4774 .. **Barry,** Kevin J '88 -480 Mamaroneck Av -Harrison 10528
(845) 454-5705 .. **Barry,** Kevin P '91 -310 Mill -Poughkeepsie 12601 **Fx:**454-5710
(212) 541-2000 .. **Barry,** Leta M '06 %Bryan C LLP -1290 Av of Amer -NY 10104
(212) 269-0927 .. **Barry,** Mary Jo '82 (D'Amato & L,LLP) -2 World Fncl Ctr -NY 10281
(518) 447-3200 .. **Barry,** Mathew P '04 %McNamee LT&W,PC -677 Bway -Albany 12207
(212) 313-3600 .. **Barry McTiernan & Moore** -2 Rector -NY 10006 **Fx:**608-8901
(914) 946-1030 .. **Barry McTiernan & Moore** -55 Church -White Plns 10601 **Fx:**946-3814
(212) 935-3000 .. **Barry,** Michl B '94 (Mintz LCFG&P,PC) -666 3rd Av -NY 10017
(516) 285-1000 .. **Barry,** Michl C '83 (Barry & S) -700 Elmont Rd -Elmont 11003
(212) 735-8600 .. **Barry,** Michl Sherrin '98 SrCnsl Morrison C LLP -909 3rd Av -NY 10022
(914) 824-5108 .. **Barry,** Nancy J '89 %Hon F Nicolai -111 Dr MLK Blvd -White Plns 10601
(914) 253-4884 .. **Barry,** Patricia M '79 %State Ins Fund -105 Corp Park Dr -White Plns 10604
(212) 730-6709 .. **Barry,** Patrick H '94 %Barry Security Inc -317 Mad Av -NY 10017
(516) 576-8080 .. **Barry,** Rhonda H '86 -68 S Srvc Rd -Melvll 11747
(315) 253-0326 .. **Barry,** Robt E '77 (Boyle & A,PC) -110 Genesee -Auburn 13021
(631) 853-4161 .. **Barry,** Robt J '00 %DA -N Cnty Cmplx Bldg 77 -Hauppauge 11788 **Fx:**853-4192
(212) 685-8737 .. **Barry,** Robt P '69 -201 E 28th -NY 10016 **Fx:**685-5110
(917) 320-2500 .. **Barry,** Rosemary Q '86 %FDIC -350 5th Av -NY 10118 **Fx:**320-2917
(718) 250-2000 .. **Barry,** Rupert V '80 %DA -350 Jay -Brklyn 11201 **Fx:**250-2314
(914) 949-6996 .. **Barry,** Stephen L '89 %Penino & M,LLP -180 E Post Rd -White Plns 10601
(718) 739-6854 .. **Barry,** Stephen M '84 %Admin Children's Srvcs -151-20 Jamaica Av -Jamaica 11432
(607) 569-2181 .. **Barry,** Travis J '98 %Hunt & B -51 Main Bx398 -Hammondsprt 14840 **Fx:**569-2182
(646) 386-5700 .. **Barry,** Yacine '06 Civil Ct -111 Centre -NY 10013
(212) 460-4511 .. **Barsalona,** Roxana E '01 Con Ed -4 Irving Pl -NY 10003
(212) 698-3500 .. **Barsamian,** Bonnie A '90 (Dechert LLP) -1095 Av of Amer -NY 10036
(518) 281-1934 .. **Barsamian,** J Albert '61 -5 Sage Hill Ln -Albany 12204
(718) 382-3571 .. **Barsch,** Robt J '82 -3403 Av S -Brklyn 11234
(212) 888-2290 .. **Barse,** David M '87 MJ Whitman,Inc -622 3rd Av -NY 10017 **Fx:**888-6016
(516) 741-4799 .. **Barshay,** David M '00 (Baker SBGFM&N,LLC) -100 Grdn City Plz -Gdn Cty 11530
(631) 761-7000 .. **Barshay,** Ilene Hally '88 %Touro Cllg Law Ctr -225 Eastvw Dr -Central Islip 11722
(212) 859-8000 .. **Barshay,** Lawr N '92 (Fried FHS&J LLP) -1 NY Plz -NY 10004
(212) 474-1000 .. **Barshay,** Scott A '92 (Cravath S&M LLP) -825 8th Av -NY 10019
(212) 421-2150 .. **Barshov,** Steven M '83 OfCnsl Sive P&R,PC -460 Park Av -NY 10022
(212) 875-1359 .. **Barsky,** Danl J '82 Directrix Inc -215 W 90th -NY 10024
(212) 874-6157 .. **Barsky,** Leona L '85 -201 W 70th -NY 10023 **Fx:**874-4255
(718) 293-2222 .. **Barsky,** Michl J '87 -944 Gerard Av -Bronx 10452
(212) 479-6000 .. **Barsky,** Stanley A '07 %Cooley LLP -1114 Av of Amer -NY 10036
(585) 232-5300 .. **Barson,** Alan D '91 OfCnsl Boylan BCV&W,LLP -2400 Chase Sq -Rchstr 14604
(212) 686-3838 .. **Barst Mukamal & Kleiner LLP** -2 Park Av -NY 10016 **Fx:**481-9362
(212) 274-9099 .. **Barst Mukamal & Kleiner LLP** -168 Canal -NY 10013 **Fx:**274-9183
(212) 891-1600 .. **Bart,** Andrew H '79 (Jenner & B LLP) -919 3rd Av -NY 10022
(718) 380-2496 .. **Bart,** David A '83 -69-10 Utopia Pkwy -Fresh Mdws 11365 **Fx:**380-2692
(212) 848-9800 .. **Bart,** Hollis G '90 (Withers B LLP) -430 Park Av -NY 10022
(212) 806-5400 .. **Bart,** Jacob '80 (Stroock &S&L LLP) -180 Maiden Ln -NY 10038
(212) 815-1818 .. **Bart,** John A '92 %DC 37 MELS -125 Barclay -NY 10007 **Fx:**815-1343
(212) 233-2122 .. **Bartel,** Chas H '73 %Ferrara TH&G -711 3rd Av -NY 10017
(212) 450-4000 .. **Bartel,** Paul W '79 (Davis P&W LLP) -450 Lex Av -NY 10017
(631) 288-8600 .. **Bartel,** Richd R '98 -179 Montauk Hwy Bx5 -Remsenbrg 11960 **Fx:**288-2981
(212) 278-1883 .. **Bartelemucci,** Lawr J '01 (Anderson K&O,PC) -1251 Av of Amer -NY 10020
(516) 745-1100 .. **Bartell,** Lewis A '87 (Kaplan BRB,LLP) -666 Old Cntry Rd -Gdn Cty 11530
(212) 398-0055 .. **Bartelli,** Jan R '98 (Garwin G&F,LLP) -1501 Bway -NY 10036
(914) 681-7175 .. **Bartels & Feureisen LLP** -925 Wstchstr Av -White Plns 10604 **Fx:**681-0013
(914) 681-7175 .. **Bartels,** John R Jr. '60 OfCnsl Bartels & F LLP -925 Wstchstr Av -White Plns 10604
(212) 642-7800 .. **Bartels,** Natalia Maureira '02 ACE -1133 Av of Amer -NY 10036
(212) 477-3959 .. **Bartels,** Patricia McMonigle '79 -50 E 10th -NY 10003 **Fx:**(646) 452-4695
(516) 741-8585 .. **Bartels,** Paul A '10 %Bondi & I -1055 Franklin Av -Gdn Cty 11530
(914) 693-5851 .. **Bartels,** Robt '71 -19 Keller Ln -Dobbs Ferry 10522
(314) 259-2609 .. **Bartelsmeyer,** Fredk W Jr. '87 %Bryan C LLP -1290 Av of Amer -NY 10104 **Fx:**552-8609
(212) 504-6000 .. **Bartelstone,** Michl A '09 %Cadwalader W&T LLP -1 World Fncl Ctr -NY 10281
(212) 909-6000 .. **Bartenev,** Larry '10 %Debevoise & P LLP -919 3rd Av -NY 10022
(631) 853-4161 .. **Bartens,** James P '05 %DA -N Cnty Cmplx Bldg 77 -Hauppauge 11788 **Fx:**853-4192
(212) 521-5400 .. **Bartfeld,** Arnold L '75 (Reed S LLP) -599 Lex Av -NY 10022
(212) 530-5000 .. **Bartfeld,** Danl D '94 (Milbank TH&M LLP) -1 Chase Manh Plz -NY 10005
(212) 661-7100 .. **Bartfeld,** Peter M '76 OfCnsl Salon MDN&B,LLP -292 Mad Av -NY 10017
(212) 406-1700 .. **Bartfield,** Ira '52 OfCnsl Queller FWF&K LLP -233 Bway -NY 10279
(212) 268-3330 .. **Bartfield,** Jos '80 -6 Harrison -NY 10013 **Fx:**268-1989
(212) 788-0724 .. **Barth,** Amrita Prabhakar '02 %Law Dept -100 Church -NY 10007 **Fx:**788-0367
(315) 422-8191 .. **Barth,** Gerald T '71 %Leg Aid -351 S Warren -Syracuse 13202 **Fx:**472-2819
(212) 839-5300 .. **Barth,** Giselle M '04 (Sidley A LLP) -787 7th Av -NY 10019
(212) 872-1000 .. **Barth,** Mark H '78 -One Bryant Park -NY 10036 **Fx:**872-1002
(212) 385-0340 .. **Barth,** Patrick H '72 -299 Bway -NY 10007 **Fx:**202-5008
(716) 856-1300 .. **Barth,** Philip C III '89 (Barth SB) -43 Court -Buffalo 14202
(212) 319-4900 .. **Barth,** Richd S '83 (Frishauf HG&C) -220 5th Av -NY 10001
(716) 856-1300 .. **Barth,** Roger V '63 OfCnsl Barth SB -43 Court -Buffalo 14202
(716) 856-1300 .. **Barth Sullivan Behr** -43 Court -Buffalo 14202 **Fx:**856-1494
(315) 234-1864 .. **Barth Sullivan Behr** -224 Harrison -Syracuse 13202 **Fx:**422-4424
(212) 506-3900 .. **Barth,** Zachary M '03 %Steptoe & J LLP -750 7th Av -NY 10019
(212) 261-8000 .. **Barthel,** Michelle M '03 %Mendes & M,LLP -750 7th Av -NY 10019
(212) 388-3398 .. **Barthel,** Rory D '08 SEIU 32BJ -101 Av of Amer -NY 10013
(315) 472-6417 .. **Bartholomae,** Wm R '81 (Marris & B) -317 Mntgmry -Syracuse 13202
(518) 455-2424 .. **Bartholomew,** Edw M Jr. '75 NYS Senate -431 The Cptl -Albany 12247
(212) 885-5000 .. **Bartholomew,** Khianna N '08 %Blank R LLP -405 Lex Av -NY 10174
(212) 815-0896 .. **Bartholomew,** Mary Elizebeth '95 Supreme Ct -71 Thomas -NY 10013

(914) 696-7000 .. **Bartie,** Jared F '97 USTA -70 Red Oak Ln -White Plns 10604
(212) 297-5800 .. **Bartinik,** Douglas W '04 Cnsl Day P LLP -7 Times Sq -NY 10036
(516) 622-0606 .. **Bartkowski,** Alicia M '05 %P Rizzuto,PC -1 Old Cntry Rd -Carle Pl 11514 **Fx:**622-2112
(518) 587-7300 .. **Bartkowski,** Susan F '91 (Towne R & Prtnrs,PC) -137 Maple Av -Saratoga Spgs 12866
(212) 779-8111 .. **Bartle,** Christopher H '85 APC -60 Mad Av -NY 10010
(212) 610-3641 .. **Bartle,** Jennifer L '06 Cantor Fitzgerald -110 E 59th -NY 10022
(518) 274-3510 .. **Bartle McGrane Duffy & Jones,LLP** -251 River Bx448 -Troy 12181 **Fx:**274-3523
(518) 761-6463 .. **Bartlett,** Amy C '90 Warren Cnty Atty -1340 State Route 9 -Lk George 12845 **Fx:**761-6377
(516) 877-2900 .. **Bartlett,** Clifford A Jr. '63 (Bartlett MB&M,LLP) -300 Old Cntry Rd -Mineola 11501
(914) 333-9640 .. **Bartlett,** Ernestine Conner '82 %Philips Electronics -345 Scarborough Rd Bx3001 -Briarclff Mnr 10510 **Fx:**332-0615
(518) 457-2254 .. **Bartlett,** John W '83 Dept of Tax & Fin -Bldg 9 State Campus -Albany 12227 **Fx:**457-6131
(212) 660-3000 .. **Bartlett,** Jos W '81 OfCnsl Sullivan & W LLP -1290 Av of Amer -NY 10104
(914) 846-7000 .. **Bartlett,** Judy R '96 NY Life Ins -1 Rockwood Rd -Sleepy Hollow 10591 **Fx:**846-4755
(212) 878-5910 .. **Bartlett,** Kathy E '04 Amer Heart Assn -122 E 42nd -NY 10168
(646) 519-8446 .. **Bartlett,** Linda Gail '79 Amer Guild for Musical Artists -1430 Bway -NY 10018
(212) 558-4000 .. **Bartlett,** Margaret E '06 %Sullivan & C LLP -125 Broad -NY 10004
(212) 209-3033 .. **Bartlett,** Marshall P '70 Cnsl Reitler K&R LLC -885 3rd Av -NY 10022
(212) 504-6000 .. **Bartlett,** Maurine R '88 (Cadwalader W&T LLP) -1 World Fncl Ctr -NY 10281
(914) 285-1500 .. **Bartlett,** Mayo G '93 (Young & B,LLP) -81 Main -White Plns 10601 **Fx:**285-0055
(516) 877-2900 .. **Bartlett McDonough Bastone & Monaghan,LLP** -300 Old Cntry Rd -Mineola 11501 **Fx:**877-0732
(631) 277-0300 .. **Bartlett McDonough Bastone & Monaghan,LLP** -670 Main -Islip 11751 **Fx:**446-1671
(212) 983-2900 .. **Bartlett McDonough Bastone & Monaghan,LLP** -237 Park Av S -NY 10017 **Fx:**983-2901
(914) 448-0200 .. **Bartlett McDonough Bastone & Monaghan,LLP** -81 Main -White Plns 10601 **Fx:**448-0215
(518) 792-2117 .. **Bartlett Pontiff Stewart & Rhodes,PC** -1 Wshngtn Bx2168 -Glens Fls 12801 **Fx:**792-3309
(718) 931-1799 .. **Bartlett,** Randall D '88 Bartlett Law Grp LLC -1913 Tomlinson Av -Bronx 10461 **Fx:**931-0044
(212) 980-3883 .. **Bartlett,** Richd A '86 %Resource Hldngs Ltd -520 Mad Av -NY 10022 **Fx:**935-3851
(212) 768-7277 .. **Bartlett,** Theresa R '86 %DMA -1120 Av of Amer -NY 10036
(518) 859-3597 .. **Bartlette,** Lucien J '03 -3 Cheryl Ct -Ballston Spa 12020 **Fx:**584-2520
(518) 486-2921 .. **Bartley,** Elaine H '94 %OPRHP -Agncy Bldg 1 ESP -Albany 12238 **Fx:**474-5106
(212) 696-6000 .. **Bartley,** Myles K '99 Cnsl Curtis M-PC&M LLP -101 Park Av -NY 10178
(718) 216-6905 .. **Bartley,** Steven C '88 -299 Bway -NY 10007 **Fx:**(212) 385-4844
(212) 980-0369 .. **Bartley,** Timothy M '95 Aureole -34 E 61st -NY 10065
(516) 229-4300 .. **Bartling,** Dennis C '03 %J Bilello & Assoc -875 Merrick Av -Westbury 11590
(516) 248-3520 .. **Bartling,** Nancy L '05 %LaRusso & C -300 Old Cntry Rd -Mineola 11501 **Fx:**248-3522
(716) 875-8664 .. **Bartlo Hettler & Weiss** -22 Victoria Blvd -Kenmore 14217 **Fx:**875-6244
(716) 875-8664 .. **Bartlo,** Noel E '59 (Bartlo H&W) -22 Victoria Blvd -Kenmore 14217
(518) 464-2600 .. **Bartman,** Jerrold W '94 -Bx12099 -Albany 12212
(212) 848-8190 .. **Bartner,** Douglas P '83 (Shearman & S LLP) -599 Lex Av -NY 10022
(914) 995-5104 .. **Bartol,** Carl A '01 %Cnty Atty -148 Martine Av -White Plns 10601 **Fx:**995-5858
(516) 294-5100 .. **Bartol,** Ernest T '71 (Murphy B&O,LLP) -22 Jericho Tpk -Mineola 11501
(631) 755-0101 .. **Bartoldus,** Danl A '76 Cnsl Lewis JAA,LLP -425 Broad Hollow Rd -Melvll 11747
(518) 462-6765 .. **Bartolini,** Matthew C '09 %Leg Aid -55 Colvin Av -Albany 12206 **Fx:**427-8352
(212) 735-3000 .. **Bartolo,** Elizabeth M '93 %Skadden ASM&F LLP -4 Times Sq -NY 10036
(716) 282-2774 .. **Bartolomei & Grenga** -335 Buffalo Av -Niagara Fls 14303
(716) 282-2774 .. **Bartolomei,** John P '70 (Bartolomei & G) -335 Buffalo Av -Niagara Fls 14303
(212) 697-3122 .. **Bartolomeo,** Bradley J '08 %Martin C&B LLP -220 E 42nd -NY 10017
(212) 509-3456 .. **Bartolomeo,** Jamie A '07 %McGivney & K,PC -80 Broad -NY 10004
(631) 288-2876 .. **Bartolomeo,** Lisa A '03 %Kelly & H -323 Mill Rd -Westhmptn Bch 11978 **Fx:**288-1328
(718) 981-2399 .. **Bartolone,** Diane A '92 -55 Nicole Loop -Staten Isl 10301 **Fx:**981-3273
(212) 608-8840 .. **Bartolotta,** Ben '07 %Bamundo Z&S,LLP -111 John -NY 10038
(845) 225-3641 .. **Bartolotti,** Michl C '02 Cnty Clerk -40 Gleneida Av -Carmel 10512 **Fx:**228-0231
(212) 373-3000 .. **Barton,** Amy L '96 Cnsl Paul WRW&G LLP -1285 Av of Amer -NY 10019
(516) 248-1700 .. **Barton,** Anthony B '77 (Forchelli CDSM&T,LLP) -333 Earle Ovngton Blvd -Uniondale 11553
(212) 687-6262 .. **Barton Barton & Plotkin,LLP** -420 Lex Av -NY 10170 **Fx:**697-3043
(607) 734-1315 .. **Barton,** Christopher A '91 (Barton S&B,LLP) -304 E Church -Elmira 14901 **Fx:**734-1326
(212) 687-6262 .. **Barton,** Gerald C '59 (Barton B&P,LLP) -420 Lex Av -NY 10170
(212) 503-3563 .. **Barton,** Gregory E '87 Ziff Davis Media -28 E 28th -NY 10016
(646) 442-3100 .. **Barton,** James P III '76 %Legal Srvcs -90 John -NY 10038 **Fx:**(212) 227-9798
(212) 674-0016 .. **Barton,** Lindsay A '01 Corcoran Group -36 E 12th -NY 10003
(212) 906-1200 .. **Barton,** Maria A '92 Cnsl Latham & W -885 3rd Av -NY 10022
(518) 786-1800 .. **Barton,** Melissa R '02 %Flink S LLC -23 British Amer Blvd -Latham 12110 **Fx:**786-1969
(212) 458-2211 .. **Barton,** Patrice S '99 Natl Union Fire Ins Co -175 Water -NY 10038 **Fx:**458-1043
(607) 732-2222 .. **Barton,** Paul S '05 (Barton S&B,LLP) -304 E Church -Elmira 14901 **Fx:**734-1326
(607) 734-1647 .. **Barton,** Philip J '79 %Leg Srvcs -215 E Church -Elmira 14901 **Fx:**734-1018
(212) 715-9100 .. **Barton,** Reginald M '03 %Kramer LN&F,LLP -1177 Av of Amer -NY 10036
(212) 298-5382 .. **Barton,** Richd W '00 %Leg Aid -49 Thomas -NY 10013 **Fx:**298-5252
(212) 687-6262 .. **Barton,** Roger E '88 (Barton B&P,LLP) -420 Lex Av -NY 10170
(212) 301-1022 .. **Barton,** Stancil E Jr. '09 Natl Financial Prtnrs -340 Mad Av -NY 10173
(212) 616-3777 .. **Barton,** Wesley W '03 Trimaran Captial -1325 Av of Amer -NY 10019
(631) 859-0300 .. **Bartone,** Candace M '02 %Zaklukiewicz P&M,LLP -2701 Sunrise Hwy Bx389 -Islip Terr 11752
(516) 571-2768 .. **Bartow,** Cheryl L '00 Hon J McCormack -262 Old Cntry Rd -Mineola 11501 **Fx:**571-1093
(585) 428-5890 .. **Bartus,** Kelly K '00 Cnty Atty -300G Hall Of Justice -Rchstr 14614 **Fx:**428-2704
(212) 840-6400 .. **Baruch,** Jason P '94 (Sendroff & B,LLP) -1500 Bway -NY 10036 **Fx:**840-6401
(516) 393-2200 .. **Baruch,** Michl M '04 %Garfunkel W,PC -111 Grt Nck Rd -Gt Neck 11021
(212) 335-4500 .. **Barush,** Capricci G '05 %DLA Piper LLP -1251 Av of Amer -NY 10020
(212) 335-4500 .. **Barz,** Michl R '91 (DLA Piper LLP) -1251 Av of Amer -NY 10020
(212) 492-1100 .. **Barzelay,** Douglas E '74 WP Carey & Co,LLC -50 Rckfllr Plz -NY 10020
(212) 225-2000 .. **Barzell,** Dustin J '08 %Cleary GS&H -1 Lbrty Plz -NY 10006
(917) 822-7261 .. **Barzey,** Raymond C '90 -65 W 90th -NY 10024
(212) 373-3000 .. **Barzideh,** Sipoura '10 %Paul WRW&G LLP -1285 Av of Amer -NY 10019
(212) 962-3940 .. **Barzilai,** Arielle A '09 NY Living Solutions LLC -90 John -NY 10038
(212) 839-5300 .. **Barzilai,** Laura M '87 (Sidley A LLP) -787 7th Av -NY 10019
(212) 545-4664 .. **Basar,** Demet '92 (Wolf HAF&H LLP) -270 Mad Av -NY 10016
(212) 735-3000 .. **Basaran,** Alpaslan '09 %Skadden ASM&F LLP -4 Times Sq -NY 10036
(585) 899-3970 .. **Basch,** Duane C '95 (Basch & N) -1777 Penfld Rd -Penfld 14526
(845) 338-8884 .. **Basch,** Eli B '77 (Basch & K,LLP) -307 Clinton Av Bx4235 -Kingston 12402
(646) 435-6509 .. **Basch,** Laurie A '91 CMI Mrktng,Inc -401 Park Av S -NY 10016
(585) 899-3970 .. **Basch & Nickerson** -1777 Penfld Rd -Penfld 14526
(212) 878-8000 .. **Basch,** Pearl S '04 %Clifford C LLP -31 W 52nd -NY 10019
(212) 867-1200 .. **Basch,** Richd H '79 %D Buchwald & Assoc -10 E 44th -NY 10017 **Fx:**972-3209
(212) 227-0347 .. **Basch,** Solomon H '81 (Weiss W&W,PC) -25 Park Pl -NY 10007
(212) 933-0697 .. **Bascom,** Donna L '78 -15 W 81st -NY 10024 **Fx:**787-2780
(607) 432-9341 .. **Basdekis,** Theodoros '96 (Scarzafava & B) -48 Dietz -Oneonta 13820 **Fx:**432-1986
(718) 298-1200 .. **Basden-Clarke,** Latrice '04 %Supreme Ct -88-11 Sutphin Blvd -Jamaica 11435
(718) 224-7550 .. **Base,** Nick '91 (Base & B) -210-08 Nrthrn Blvd -Bayside 11361
(718) 224-7550 .. **Base,** Sofia '91 (Base & B) -210-08 Nrthrn Blvd -Bayside 11361
(631) 853-4336 .. **Baseer,** Arshia '05 Law Guardian -Bx9082 -Central Islip 11722
(718) 298-8904 .. **Bash,** Jessica E '04 Leg Aid -153-01 Jamaica Av -Jamaica 11432 **Fx:**657-0537
(718) 237-5500 .. **Bash,** Rachel E '07 %Leg Srvcs -105 Court -Brklyn 11201 **Fx:**855-0733
(212) 450-4000 .. **Bashago,** Sidney '08 %Davis P&W LLP -450 Lex Av -NY 10017
(212) 819-8200 .. **Bashan,** Dovrat '06 %White & C LLP -1155 Av of Amer -NY 10036
(646) 709-8120 .. **Bashani,** Tali A '06 (TAB Law Firm,PC) -65 Bway -NY 10006 **Fx:**403-4753
(914) 681-0200 .. **Bashar,** Stefanie A '01 %DelBello DWW&W,LLP -1 N Lex Av -White Plns 10601
(212) 268-3580 .. **Basheer,** Amjad Ahasan '05 A Arora PC -350 5th Av -NY 10118 **Fx:**268-3582
(212) 335-9000 .. **Bashford,** Martha S '80 %DA -1 Hogan Pl -NY 10013
(212) 859-8000 .. **Bashi,** Jonathan S '09 %Fried FHS&J LLP -1 NY Plz -NY 10004
(212) 455-2000 .. **Bashi,** Jonathan Solomon '10 %Simpson T&B LLP -425 Lex Av -NY 10017
(212) 682-8510 .. **Bashian,** Erik M '05 %S Landy & Assoc,PLLC -270 Mad Av -NY 10016 **Fx:**682-8514
(914) 946-5100 .. **Bashian & Farber, LLP** -235 Main -White Plns 10601 **Fx:**946-5111
(914) 946-5100 .. **Bashian,** Gary E '68 (Bashian & F,LLP) -235 Main -White Plns 10601
(212) 921-4110 .. **Bashian,** James V '83 -500 5th Av -NY 10110 **Fx:**921-4249
(212) 888-3033 .. **Bashner,** Richd S '86 (Becker GM&M LLP) -299 Park Av -NY 10171
(516) 222-4000 .. **Bashner,** Robt A '90 (Goldstein & B) -1778 Hempstd Tpk -E Meadow 11554
(315) 655-0631 .. **Basic,** Jennifer M '01 J Basic & Assoc,PLLC -130 Albany Bx423 -Cazenovia 13035 **Fx:**655-0639
(212) 476-0999 .. **Basichas,** Mark M '85 (M Basichas & Assoc,PC) -233 Bway -NY 10279 **Fx:**732-5431
(212) 351-4000 .. **Basil,** Jessica I '00 %Gibson D&C LLP -200 Park Av -NY 10166
(917) 512-3066 .. **Basil,** Robt J '92 (Collier & B,PC) -1270 Bway -NY 10001 **Fx:**(831) 536-1075
(631) 853-5761 .. **Basile,** Jennifer L '09 %Cnty Atty -400 Carleton Av -Central Islip 11722 **Fx:**853-7788
(212) 418-6130 .. **Basile,** Lisa J '08 GM Asset Mgmt -767 5th Av -NY 10153
(212) 808-7800 .. **Basile,** Matthew J '08 %Kelley D&W LLP -101 Park Av -NY 10178
(518) 374-3399 .. **Basile,** Michl '84 (Higgins RB&C,PC) -1430 Balltown Rd -Niskayuna 12309
(607) 778-2423 .. **Basile,** Rita M '94 %DA -45 Hawley Bx1766 -Bnghmtn 13902 **Fx:**778-8870
(718) 643-5262 .. **Basile,** Thos E '90 %Surrogates Ct -2 Johnson -Brklyn 11201
(917) 579-2216 .. **Basile,** Thos J R '03 Empire Solutions Consulting LLC -Bx1943 -New Cty 10956

(212) 818-9200 .. **Basilevsky,** Peter A '73 (Satterlee SB&B LLP) -230 Park Av -NY 10169
(973) 596-4755 .. **Basilo,** Christopher T '08 %Gibbons PC -1 Penn Plz -NY 10119 **Fx:**639-8326
(212) 626-4100 .. **Basinger,** John A '08 (Baker & M LLP) -1114 Av of Amer -NY 10036
(646) 602-5600 .. **Basinski,** Sean J '03 %Urban Justice Ctr -123 William -NY 10038 **Fx:**(212) 533-4598
(315) 473-0899 .. **Baska,** Robt S '07 %Anelli X,PC -441 S Salina -Syracuse 13202 **Fx:**473-0530
(646) 260-9936 .. **Baskerville,** Phillip L '99 PK Partners,LLC -Bx2865 -NY 10163
(646) 602-5600 .. **Baskin,** Gratienne G '08 Urban Justice Ctr -123 William -NY 10038 **Fx:**(212) 533-4598
(716) 845-2560 .. **Baskin,** Mona '84 %Surrogates Ct -92 Franklin -Buffalo 14202 **Fx:**853-3741
(212) 425-0055 .. **Baskin,** Peter Jay '68 %Sharretts PC&B -75 Broad -NY 10004
(914) 437-7670 .. **Baskin,** Ron '00 (Teitelbaum & B LLP) -3 Barker Av -White Plns 10601 **Fx:**437-7672
(212) 848-4000 .. **Baskin,** Stuart J '76 (Shearman & S LLP) -599 Lex Av -NY 10022
(646) 855-0705 .. **Baskin,** Todd M '97 Bank of Amer Securities LLC -1 Bryant Pk -NY 10036
(315) 475-9334 .. **Baskin,** Wm J '01 %Farchione & B LLP -217 Mntgmry -Syracuse 13202 **Fx:**475-9655
(518) 489-5596 .. **Basloe,** Evalyn G '65 (Basloe & B,PC) -Bx3145 -Albany 12203
(518) 489-5596 .. **Basloe,** Jos S '66 (Basloe & B,PC) -Bx3145 -Albany 12203
(718) 297-1717 .. **Basner,** Norman '75 (Viscardi B&B,PC) -148-45 Hillside Av -Jamaica 11435
(212) 450-4000 .. **Bason,** George R Jr. '79 (Davis P&W LLP) -450 Lex Av -NY 10017
(212) 644-1710 .. **Basralian,** Jos L '85 (Winne BH&B,PC) -286 Mad Av -NY 10017
(212) 982-8243 .. **Basri,** Carol L '79 -303 Mercer -NY 10003
(631) 271-7285 .. **Bass,** Brett S '78 -38 Hemingway Dr -Dix Hlls 11746
(631) 588-4000 .. **Bass,** Brian D '90 (Farr & B) -3100 Vets Mem'l Hwy -Bohemia 11716 **Fx:**588-0276
(212) 768-6700 .. **Bass,** Carole M '97 OfCnsl Sonnenschein N&R LLP -1221 Av of Amer -NY 10020
(914) 472-2300 .. **Bass,** Clifford I '78 (Jones G,LLP) -670 Wht Plns Rd -Scarsdale 10583
(212) 447-1111 .. **Bass,** Deborah A '82 (Ledy-Gurren B&S) -475 Park Av S -NY 10016
(585) 362-1154 .. **Bass,** Douglas A '01 -7630 Hillside Dr -Victor 14564
(718) 522-9705 .. **Bass,** Emily '80 -25 Wshngtn -Brklyn 11201 **Fx:**522-9707
(212) 801-3452 .. **Bass,** Franklin F '77 Catlin Inc -140 Bway -NY 10005
(212) 859-8000 .. **Bass,** Franklin L '52 OfCnsl Fried FHS&J LLP -1 NY Plz -NY 10004
(212) 259-8000 .. **Bass,** Fredric K '82 (Dewey & L LLP) -1301 Av of Amer -NY 10019
(212) 888-8200 .. **Bass,** Geoffrey A '75 (Feder K LLP) -845 3rd Av -NY 10022
(212) 839-5300 .. **Bass,** I Scott '76 (Sidley A LLP) -787 7th Av -NY 10019
(516) 741-5000 .. **Bass,** Jason B '92 (Bass & R) -1 Old Cntry Rd -Carle Pl 11514
(212) 873-6568 .. **Bass,** Judith B '77 -1325 Av of Amer -NY 10019
(212) 474-1000 .. **Bass,** Kimberly L '10 %Cravath S&M LLP -825 8th Av -NY 10019
(212) 685-7215 .. **Bass,** Lawr D '71 -11 E 86th -NY 10028 **Fx:**685-7277
(212) 755-5510 .. **Bass,** Leigh R '99 %Loeb B & Prtnrs -505 Park Av -NY 10022
(914) 271-9529 .. **Bass,** Mark K '85 (Bass & A,PC) -109 Grand -Croton-On-Hud 10520 **Fx:**271-1184
(716) 853-2330 .. **Bass,** Maureen T '01 %Buchanan I&R PC -50 Fountain Plz -Buffalo 14202
(212) 704-1239 .. **Bass,** Merlin III '95 %Interpublic Grp -1114 Av of Amer -NY 10036
(518) 473-4282 .. **Bass,** Michl G '99 %Dept of Health -Corning Twr 24th Fl -Albany 12237 **Fx:**473-2430
(516) 482-3344 .. **Bass,** Morton M '52 -185 Grt Nck Rd -Gt Neck 11021 **Fx:**466-6847
(212) 592-1400 .. **Bass,** Richd M '99 Herrick,F LLP -2 Park Av -NY 10016
(212) 848-4000 .. **Bass,** Richd S '10 %Shearman & S LLP -599 Lex Av -NY 10022
(212) 751-3001 .. **Bass,** Richd W '07 %Thompson & K LLP -919 3rd Av -NY 10022
(516) 741-5000 .. **Bass & Rubinowitz** -1 Old Cntry Rd -Carle Pl 11514 **Fx:**741-7018
(631) 588-4000 .. **Bass,** Sigmund '64 (Farr & B) -3100 Vets Mem'l Hwy -Bohemia 11716 **Fx:**588-0276
(212) 857-8760 .. **Bass,** Stanley A '74 %US Ct of Appls -US Cthse 40 Foley Sq -NY 10007 **Fx:**857-8755
(212) 876-0173 .. **Bass,** Timothy S T '98 Pardus Cptl Mgmt LP -590 Mad Av -NY 10022
(516) 876-0800 .. **Bass,** Vladimir '05 %Druckman Law Grp PLLC -242 Drexel Av -Westbury 11590 **Fx:**876-0888
(212) 664-4573 .. **Bass,** Wendy A '03 NBC Sports -30 Rckfllr Plz -NY 10112
(585) 546-5530 .. **Bassano,** Jos J '92 %Thomson West -50 E Broad -Rchstr 14694
(914) 949-2700 .. **Bassano,** Peter N '88 (Bleakley P&S,LLP) -1 N Lex Av -White Plns 10601
(212) 661-6800 .. **Bassel,** Stuart T '02 %Cyruli SH&Z LLP -420 Lex Av -NY 10170
(212) 837-6000 .. **Bassen,** Ned H '74 (Hughes H&R LLP) -1 Bttry Pk Plz -NY 10004
(212) 788-0428 .. **Bassett,** Amy H '06 %Law Dept -100 Church -NY 10007 **Fx:**788-0367
(212) 937-8858 .. **Bassett,** David B '07 (WilmerHale) -399 Park Av -NY 10022
(212) 808-7800 .. **Bassett,** David De La Garza '08 %Kelley D&W LLP -101 Park Av -NY 10178
(212) 962-2455 .. **Bassett,** Edw M '58 -110 Duane -NY 10007
(212) 297-5800 .. **Bassett,** Edwin F '95 SrCnsl Day P LLP -7 Times Sq -NY 10036
(315) 471-3151 .. **Bassett,** J Thos '73 (Hancock & E,LLP) -1500 AXA Twr I Bx4976 -Syracuse 13221
(631) 234-2511 .. **Bassett,** Jason '00 (Bassett & B,PC) -320 Carleton Av -Central Islip 11722
(631) 234-2511 .. **Bassett,** Kerry Sloane '02 (Bassett & B,PC) -320 Carleton Av -Central Islip 11722
(212) 903-9000 .. **Bassett,** Michl R '88 (Linklaters) -1345 Av of Amer -NY 10105
(212) 541-2000 .. **Bassett,** Morgan J '01 %Bryan C LLP -1290 Av of Amer -NY 10104
Bassetti, Karin J '88 -15 W 55th -NY 10019
(212) 588-0800 .. **Bassi,** Gina M '08 %Frommer L&H LLP -745 5th Av -NY 10151
(718) 721-1033 .. **Bassias,** George E '93 -6 Brixton Rd -Gdn Cty 11530 **Fx:**721-7981
(516) 487-4800 .. **Bassik,** Barry S '72 (Fine & B) -316 Grt Nck Rd -Gt Neck 11021
(212) 608-9700 .. **Bassin,** Steven Jay '78 -233 Bway -NY 10279 **Fx:**732-8486
(914) 698-9332 .. **Bassin,** Wm S '95 %Pres Air Trol Corp -1009 W Bstn Post Rd -Mamaroneck 10543
(518) 434-0600 .. **Bassinson,** D Scott '90 Cnsl Boies S&F LLP -10 N Pearl -Albany 12207
(212) 758-9700 .. **Bassiri,** Hassan A '09 KPMG LLP -345 Park Av -NY 10154
(212) 430-4504 .. **Bassis,** Barry T '74 OfCnsl Tressler LLP -One Penn Plz -NY 10119
(917) 670-2877 .. **Bassis,** Luke S '04 -3242 89th -E Elmhrst 11369
Basso, Diana J '06 -268 W 84th -NY 10024
(718) 931-1220 .. **Basso,** Gary S '74 -1937 Wllmsbrdg Rd -Bronx 10461 **Fx:**518-7680
(718) 286-6000 .. **Basso,** Hugo A '08 %DA -125-01 Qns Blvd -Kew Gdns 11415
(516) 393-5555 .. **Basso,** Jeffrey V '07 %Schneider M LLP -666 Old Cntry Rd -Gdn Cty 11530 **Fx:**393-5556
(845) 452-0200 .. **Basso,** John J '83 Basso & Assoc,PC -1171 Route 55 -LaGrangevll 12540 **Fx:**452-0261
(212) 966-8900 .. **Basso,** Peter A '08 %Eisenberg & S,LLP -233 Bway -NY 10279
(718) 984-2626 .. **Basso,** Wm '01 %Solomon & Assoc,PC -3309 Richmond Av -Staten Isl 10312 **Fx:**984-5820
(212) 326-3939 .. **Bassolino,** Thos J '10 %Jones D -222 E 41st -NY 10017
(718) 544-1076 .. **Bassrey,** Adiel '95 -108-18 Qns Blvd -Frst Hlls 11375 **Fx:**544-2055
(212) 530-5000 .. **Bast,** Ana M '06 %Milbank TH&M LLP -1 Chase Manh Plz -NY 10005
(212) 608-4040 .. **Bast,** Michl M '81 (Silverstein & B) -217 Bway -NY 10007
(212) 446-4800 .. **Basta,** Paul M '93 (Kirkland & E LLP) -153 E 53rd -NY 10022
(718) 250-0400 .. **Basterrechea,** Eric M '05 %R Tusa -1 MetroTech Ctr -Brklyn 11201 **Fx:**250-0591
(607) 751-4256 .. **Bastian,** Kenneth R '88 %Loral Fed Sys -1801 State Route 17C -Owego 13827
(212) 387-7787 .. **Bastian,** Mark '03 %P Kelley & Assoc -36 E 20th -NY 10003 **Fx:**387-0382
(716) 854-2020 .. **Bastible,** Denis J '95 (Cellino & B,PC) -350 Main -Buffalo 14202
(631) 271-8756 .. **Bastible,** Francis X '49 -21 Darby Dr -Huntngtn Sta 11746 **Fx:**271-8756
(516) 741-6565 .. **Bastible,** Kieran X '92 %Meyer SE&K,PC -990 Stewart Av Bx9194 -Gdn Cty 11530
(516) 358-6900 .. **Bastien,** Villard '97 %Cohen & J LLP -2001 Marcus Av -Lk Success 11042
(516) 746-0222 .. **Bastone,** Christine '90 %Harding & H -1055 Franklin Av -Gdn Cty 11530 **Fx:**746-0519
(914) 448-0200 .. **Bastone,** Frank D Jr. '66 OfCnsl Bartlett MB&M,LLP -81 Main -White Plns 10601
(718) 590-3758 .. **Bastone,** Josephine M '84 %Supreme Ct -851 Grnd Cncrs -Bronx 10451 **Fx:**590-8914
(631) 247-0404 .. **Bastone,** Stacey A '06 %Jackson L LLP -58 S Srvc Rd -Melvll 11747
(212) 905-9204 .. **Bastos,** Cecilia '03 Waterfront Comm -39 Bway -NY 10006 **Fx:**480-0587
(718) 237-5500 .. **Basu,** Shantonu J '05 %Leg Srvcs -105 Court -Brklyn 11201 **Fx:**855-0733
(914) 948-4500 .. **Basuk,** Philomena P '86 (O'Connor MCD&O) -1 Barker Av -White Plns 10601
(212) 918-3000 .. **Basuk,** Richd S '03 %Hogan L LLP -875 3rd Av -NY 10022
(212) 231-2349 .. **Basulto,** Vincent '96 %MacQuarie Holdings -125 W 55th -NY 10019
(212) 257-6960 .. **Baswell,** Karen C '08 %Chaffetz L LLP -1350 Av of Amer -NY 10019
(718) 585-2233 .. **Batalla,** Pedro J Jr. '87 -888 Grand Cncrs -Bronx 10451 **Fx:**585-8640
(212) 530-4480 .. **Batchelder,** Harry C Jr. '66 -40 Wall -NY 10005 **Fx:**530-4488
(212) 992-8156 .. **Batchelder,** Lily Lawr '06 NYU Law Schl -40 Wshngtn Sq S -NY 10012
(212) 308-0095 .. **Batcheler,** Wayne E '73 -161 W 16th -NY 10011
(518) 465-3524 .. **Batcheller,** Stephanie J '90 %NYS Defenders Assn -194 Wshngtn Av -Albany 12210 **Fx:**465-3249
(212) 732-3200 .. **Batchelor,** Ann M '05 %Carter L&M LLP -2 Wall -NY 10005
(212) 474-1000 .. **Batchelor,** Craig '06 %Cravath S&M LLP -825 8th Av -NY 10019
(518) 294-2039 .. **Batcher,** Jamie N '05 -296 Main Bx6 -Richmndvll 12149 **Fx:**294-2039
(212) 808-7800 .. **Batchoo,** Lystra '08 %Kelley D&W LLP -101 Park Av -NY 10178
(718) 273-2763 .. **Bate,** S John '76 -1444 Clove Rd -Staten Isl 10301
(516) 663-6600 .. **Bateman,** Alexander G Jr. '90 (Ruskin MF,PC) -1425 RXR Plz -Uniondale 11556
(212) 277-6500 .. **Bateman,** Chas L '04 %Dickstein S LLP -1633 Bway -NY 10019
(212) 574-1200 .. **Bateman,** Gregg S '06 %Seward & K LLP -1 Bttry Pk Plz -NY 10004
(212) 660-3000 .. **Bateman,** Margaret M '00 %Sullivan & W LLP -1290 Av of Amer -NY 10104
(914) 323-5468 .. **Bateman,** Maureen Scannell '69 Manhattanville College -2900 Purchase -Purchase 10577
(518) 474-2705 .. **Bateman,** Michele M '04 %NYS Div Human Rights -ESP Bx2049 -Albany 12220
(315) 253-2782 .. **Bates,** Douglas P '75 -203 Metcalf Plz -Auburn 13021 **Fx:**253-2784
(212) 556-2100 .. **Bates,** E Wm II '96 (King & S) -1185 Av of Amer -NY 10036
(212) 697-5204 .. **Bates,** Eric M '82 %E Bates & Assoc -630 3rd Av -NY 10017 **Fx:**697-5242
(212) 244-9000 .. **Bates,** Jeremy C '03 %Matalon SE -450 7th Av -NY 10123 **Fx:**244-4615
(518) 485-8412 .. **Bates,** Justyn P '03 NYS Educ Dept -80 Wolf Rd -Albany 12205
(914) 517-5000 .. **Bates,** Rebecca Rogers '07 %Meiselman DPC&E,PC -1311 Mamaroneck Av -White Plns 10605
(212) 227-1735 .. **Bates,** Robt K Jr. '91 (Bates & B) -60 E 42nd -NY 10165 **Fx:**(201) 518-2552
(212) 248-8800 .. **Bates,** Ryan M '10 %Callan KB&B LLP -1 Whitehall -NY 10004
(212) 837-6803 .. **Bates,** Tony C '10 %Hughes H&R LLP -1 Bttry Pk Plz -NY 10004 **Fx:**299-6803
(631) 727-0050 .. **Bates,** Wm F '75 -120 Court -Rvrhead 11901 **Fx:**369-4080
(518) 374-3344 .. **Bates,** Wm P '76 -650 Franklin -Schnctdy 12305 **Fx:**374-0828
(212) 701-3000 .. **Bateup,** Christine A '07 %Cahill G&R LLP -80 Pine -NY 10005 **Fx:**269-5420
(914) 946-6774 .. **Bath,** Jonathan A '90 (Pilkington & L,PC) -222 Bloomingdale Rd -White Plns 10605
(212) 558-4000 .. **Bathaee,** Yavar '09 %Sullivan & C LLP -125 Broad -NY 10004
(212) 421-4100 .. **Bathgate,** T P Lauren '99 %Pryor C LLP -7 Times Sq -NY 10036
(212) 513-3200 .. **Bathie,** Ryan M '08 %Holland & K LLP -31 W 52nd -NY 10019
(212) 350-3604 .. **Bathon,** James H '89 Banco Santander Cntrl Hispano, SA -45 E 53rd -NY 10022 **Fx:**350-3669
(212) 980-0070 .. **Batista,** Paul A '75 -26 Bway -NY 10004 **Fx:**344-7677
(212) 781-0355 .. **Batista,** Raquel E '05 Coalition for Immigrant Rights -665 W 182nd -NY 10033

(212) 269-7308 .. **Batista**, Rosa M '07 %Leahey & J PC -120 Wall -NY 10005
(212) 510-1400 .. **Batista**, Valerie Ann '94 %Spec Comm of Invstgtn -80 Maiden Ln -NY 10038 **Fx**:510-1550
(718) 898-6671 .. **Batista**, Victor R '88 -247 S 3rd -Brklyn 11211 **Fx**:898-7030
(212) 891-0700 .. **Batistich**, Zlatko '91 %FOJP Srvc Corp -28 E 28th -NY 10016 **Fx**:308-3911
(212) 530-5000 .. **Batkin**, Drew J '03 %Milbank TH&M LLP -1 Chase Manh Plz -NY 10005
(212) 264-8311 .. **Batley**, Lionel G Jr. '61 %US GSA -26 Fed Plz -NY 10278 **Fx**:264-1987
(212) 468-8000 .. **Batliboi**, Madhavi T '06 %Morrison & F LLP -1290 Av of Amer -NY 10104
(212) 941-9090 .. **Batra**, Monika '02 %The Door -121 Av of Amer -NY 10013 **Fx**:941-0714
(212) 545-1993 .. **Batra**, Ravi '81 (R Batra,PC) -142 Lex Av -NY 10016 **Fx**:545-0967
(212) 922-1330 .. **Batsedis**, Olga '05 %Zimmet B LLP -437 Mad Av -NY 10022
(718) 250-2000 .. **Batsidis**, Nicholas J '00 %DA -350 Jay -Brklyn 11201 **Fx**:250-2314
(212) 687-8500 .. **Batson**, James A '93 (Liddle & R,LLP) -800 3rd Av -NY 10022
(518) 445-2311 .. **Batson**, Robt C '76 Albany Law Schl -80 New Scotland Av -Albany 12208 **Fx**:445-2315
(716) 856-0600 .. **Batt**, Jamie J '06 %Jaeckle F&M,LLP -12 Fountain Plz -Buffalo 14202
(716) 854-3400 .. **Batt**, Jeffrey D '08 %Rupp BPC&C LLC -1600 Lbrty Bldg -Buffalo 14202
(716) 852-0400 .. **Batt**, Matthew J '06 %Roach BM&G,PC -424 Main -Buffalo 14202
(917) 551-1300 .. **Battaglia**, Chris J '90 %Koehler & I LLP -61 Bway -NY 10006
(212) 765-9100 .. **Battaglia**, Christopher J '97 (Halperin BR,LLP) -555 Mad Av -NY 10022
(212) 319-6898 .. **Battaglia**, Deborah A '96 %Lavin ORC&D -420 Lex Av -NY 10170
(585) 987-2800 .. **Battaglia**, Jack M '62 (Woods OG LLP) -2 State -Rchstr 14614
(212) 858-1738 .. **Battaglia**, John J '96 Cnsl Pillsbury WSP LLP -1540 Bway -NY 10036
(718) 236-5656 .. **Battaglia**, Jos G Jr. '91 -1168 68th -Brklyn 11219 **Fx**:236-7390
(212) 309-6000 .. **Battaglia**, Leni D '06 %Morgan L&B LLP -101 Park Av -NY 10178
(716) 250-1800 .. **Battaglia**, Paul A '73 (Jaeckle F&M,LLP) -400 Essjay Rd -Amherst 14221
(716) 854-2907 .. **Battaglia**, Peter J '73 Chicago Title Ins -424 Main -Buffalo 14202 **Fx**:852-7346
(716) 856-4000 .. **Battaglia**, Ronald J Jr. '04 %Hodgson R LLP -140 Pearl -Buffalo 14202
(315) 218-8000 .. **Battaglia**, S Paul '74 (Bond S&K,PLLC) -1 Lincoln Ctr -Syracuse 13202
(212) 964-6611 .. **Battaglia**, Sandro A '94 Cnsl Lester SK&D -120 Bway -NY 10271
(914) 834-2302 .. **Battalia**, Dolores A '79 (Stein & B) -2001 Palmer Av -Larchmnt 10538
(212) 705-7000 .. **Batten**, Peter R '83 OfCnsl Bingham M LLP -399 Park Av -NY 10022
(212) 478-7200 .. **Batterman**, Danl D '91 (Hahn & H LLP) -488 Mad Av -NY 10022
(516) 949-4216 .. **Batterman**, Jon S '91 SpclCnsl FINRA -2 Jericho Plz -Jericho 11753 **Fx**:949-4201
(212) 969-3000 .. **Batterman**, L Robt '67 (Proskauer R LLP) -1585 Bway -NY 10036
(212) 556-2100 .. **Batterson**, Angela L '09 (King & S) -1185 Av of Amer -NY 10036
(212) 490-9100 .. **Battista**, Anthony U '97 (Condon & F LLP) -7 Times Sq -NY 10036
(646) 862-2040 .. **Battista**, Gregory J '91 LRN Corp -1 E 52nd -NY 10022 **Fx**:862-2041
(631) 969-7777 .. **Battista**, Jos F III '00 %Frenkel LWW&G,LLP -20 W Main -Bay Shr 11706 **Fx**:206-0540
(716) 824-7200 .. **Battista**, Robt '85 %R Lorigo -101 Slade Av -W Seneca 14224 **Fx**:824-8728
(516) 747-4301 .. **Battista**, Vincent J '94 %Torino & B,PC -200 Old Cntry Rd -Mineola 11501
(718) 474-2918 .. **Battista**, Wm V '84 -11 Ocean Av -Rckwy Pnt 11697
(718) 354-3200 .. **Battiste Aronowsky & Suchow,Inc** -60 Bay -Staten Isl 10301 **Fx**:354-3210
(518) 587-6294 .. **Battiste**, Lynda '87 -8 Meghan Ct -Saratoga Spgs 12866
(516) 357-3000 .. **Battiste**, Michl J '10 %Rivkin R LLP -926 RXR Plz -Uniondale 11556
(718) 354-3200 .. **Battiste**, Paul A '72 (Battiste A&S,Inc) -60 Bay -Staten Isl 10301
(718) 846-5843 .. **Battisti**, Anthony M '89 -87-13 Myrtle Av -Glendale 11385
(212) 355-5575 .. **Battisti**, Brian L '06 %Smith & N,LLP -363 7th Av -NY 10001 **Fx**:486-3150
(607) 724-8529 .. **Battisti**, F Paul '05 (Battisti G&T) -19 Chenango -Bnghmtn 13901
(607) 724-8529 .. **Battisti Gartenman & Thayne** -19 Chenango -Bnghmtn 13901 **Fx**:724-1506
(516) 484-0284 .. **Battisti**, Rosa M '02 -1 Helen -Greenvale 11548
(845) 454-9611 .. **Battistoni**, Jeffrey S '85 (Battistoni & M) -97 Cannon -Poughkeepsie 12601 **Fx**:471-2035
(212) 753-5000 .. **Battistoni**, Thos P '85 (Schiff H LLP) -900 3rd Av -NY 10022
(516) 463-7014 .. **Battle**, Aiesha L '04 %Hofstra Law Schl -121 Hofstra Univ -Hempstd 11549
(212) 533-6300 .. **Battle**, Catherine V '94 %NYSUT -52 Bway -NY 10004 **Fx**:995-2347
(212) 965-2200 .. **Battle**, Marc Kevin '05 %NAACP/LDF -99 Hudson -NY 10013 **Fx**:226-7592
(212) 839-5300 .. **Batty**, Travis F '06 %Sidley A LLP -787 7th Av -NY 10019
(212) 909-6000 .. **Batzell**, Jessica E '10 %Debevoise & P LLP -919 3rd Av -NY 10022
(212) 244-4111 .. **Bau**, Alexander '07 %Shiboleth YR&Z,LLP -1 Penn Plz -NY 10119
(212) 969-3000 .. **Bau**, Lindy '07 %Proskauer R LLP -1585 Bway -NY 10036
(212) 506-1700 .. **Bauchner**, Joshua S '02 %Kasowitz BT&F LLP -1633 Bway -NY 10019
(212) 222-8900 .. **Bauchner**, Stuart E '88 -299 Riverside Dr -NY 10025 **Fx**:222-5900
(212) 836-8000 .. **Bauco**, John U '04 %Kaye S LLP -425 Park Av -NY 10022
(212) 474-1000 .. **Baudisch**, Matthias G '02 %Cravath S&M LLP -825 8th Av -NY 10019
(212) 310-8000 .. **Baudler**, Matthew B '09 %Weil G&M LLP -767 5th Av -NY 10153
(212) 610-6300 .. **Baudot**, Amelie D '09 %Allen & O -1221 Av of Amer -NY 10020
(212) 880-6000 .. **Bauer**, Alison D '96 (Torys LLP) -237 Park Av -NY 10017
(212) 836-8000 .. **Bauer**, Andrew '05 %Kaye S LLP -425 Park Av -NY 10022
(845) 565-1100 .. **Bauer**, Ari I '09 %Tarshis CLM&M,PLLC -One Corwin Ct -Newburgh 12550
(718) 260-8700 .. **Bauer**, Brenda L '00 %ACS -345 Adams -Brklyn 11201
(212) 692-1000 .. **Bauer**, Danl J '06 %Duane M LLP -1540 Bway -NY 10036
(716) 664-4705 .. **Bauer**, David A '00 %Goodell & G -617 Wshngtn -Jamestwn 14701 **Fx**:483-6481
(212) 450-4000 .. **Bauer**, David R '08 %Davis P&W LLP -450 Lex Av -NY 10017
(212) 945-1059 .. **Bauer**, Douglas F '70 -300 Rector Pl -NY 10280
(718) 297-2775 .. **Bauer**, Douglas J '93 -158-10 84th Rd -Jamaica 11432 **Fx**:297-3034
(516) 829-1040 .. **Bauer**, Fred L '77 -13 Terrace Cir -Gt Neck 11021 **Fx**:829-1041
(212) 735-3000 .. **Bauer**, Geoffrey '08 %Skadden ASM&F LLP -4 Times Sq -NY 10036
(212) 594-5300 .. **Bauer**, George A III '80 (Milberg LLP) -1 Penn Plz -NY 10119
(518) 436-0173 .. **Bauer**, Henry R '86 -20 Corp Wds Blvd -Albany 12211 **Fx**:436-0659
(516) 739-3838 .. **Bauer**, Jill W '89 -100 Grdn City Plz -Gdn Cty 11530 **Fx**:739-3838
(212) 318-3000 .. **Bauer**, John A '91 (Fulbright & J LLP) -666 5th Av -NY 10103
(631) 293-4525 .. **Bauer**, John T '87 (Littler M,PC) -290 Broadhllw Rd -Melvll 11747
(212) 277-6500 .. **Bauer**, Jonathan O '95 Cnsl Dickstein S LLP -1633 Bway -NY 10019
(315) 798-5766 .. **Bauer**, Joshua L '07 %DA -800 Park Av -Utica 13501 **Fx**:798-5582
(518) 270-2802 .. **Bauer**, Karen M '00 Cnty Conflict Defenders Ofc -61 State -Troy 12180 **Fx**:270-2686
(212) 839-5300 .. **Bauer**, Lawr A '82 (Sidley A LLP) -787 7th Av -NY 10019
(716) 856-4000 .. **Bauer**, Lisa A '00 %Hodgson R LLP -140 Pearl -Buffalo 14202
(212) 545-4000 .. **Bauer**, Lori D '89 (Jackson L LLP) -666 3rd Av -NY 10017
(212) 710-3900 .. **Bauer**, Matthew W '97 (Clyde & Co US LLP) -405 Lex Av -NY 10174 **Fx**:710-3950
(212) 308-6100 .. **Bauer**, Michl J '94 %Levi L&F LLP -1185 Av of Amer -NY 10036
(212) 336-2000 .. **Bauer**, Paul J '09 %Patterson BW&T LLP -1133 Av of Amer -NY 10036
(631) 249-1341 .. **Bauer**, Peter T '92 Minuteman Press -61 Exec Blvd -Farmngdl 11735
(631) 475-8340 .. **Bauer**, Robt G '57 -230 Hagerman Av -E Patchogue 11772 **Fx**:447-5815
(315) 798-5766 .. **Bauer**, Robt L '98 %DA -800 Park Av -Utica 13501 **Fx**:798-5582
(914) 286-3400 .. **Bauer**, Robin J '78 %Leg Aid -1 N Bway -White Plns 10601 **Fx**:682-4112
(914) 693-2484 .. **Bauer**, Sherylee F '84 -104 Nrthfld Av -Dobbs Ferry 10522
(631) 273-7187 .. **Bauer**, Valerie Loren '88 %A Quintana -1600 Islip Av -Brentwd 11717 **Fx**:273-7341
(585) 987-2800 .. **Bauer**, Wm G '82 (Woods OG LLP) -2 State -Rchstr 14614
(212) 826-0100 .. **Bauerfeld**, Richd J '85 %FSA -31 W 52nd -NY 10019 **Fx**:893-2710
(315) 253-1391 .. **Bauersfeld**, Brian N '05 DA -95 Genesee -Auburn 13021 **Fx**:253-1521
(516) 248-6400 .. **Baugh**, Cara A '00 %Davidoff M&H,LLP -200 Grdn City Plz -Gdn Cty 11530
(212) 768-2100 .. **Baugh**, Valerie A '96 %Kraditor & H,PC -75 9th Av -NY 10011
(585) 271-1430 .. **Baughan**, Sara B '79 -77 Mulberry -Rchstr 14620
(212) 373-3000 .. **Baughman**, John F '94 (Paul WRW&G LLP) -1285 Av of Amer -NY 10019
(516) 227-0700 .. **Bauknight**, Lucia DesChamps '02 %Farrell F,PC -1320 RXR Plz -Uniondale 11556
(212) 682-7474 .. **Baum**, Andrew '77 (Foley & L LLP) -90 Park Av -NY 10016
(914) 576-5860 .. **Baum**, Arnold '81 -60 Devonshr Rd -New Rchll 10804
(212) 312-2260 .. **Baum**, Brian S '09 Leg Aid -60 Lafayette -NY 10013 **Fx**:349-0874
(212) 335-4500 .. **Baum**, Christopher J '09 %DLA Piper LLP -1251 Av of Amer -NY 10020
(212) 389-2333 .. **Baum**, Claude A '85 Ore Hill Ptnrs LLC -650 5th Av -NY 10019
(212) 768-6700 .. **Baum**, David R '98 (Sonnenschein N&R LLP) -1221 Av of Amer -NY 10020
(212) 969-3000 .. **Baum**, Edwin M '85 (Proskauer R LLP) -1585 Bway -NY 10036
(845) 791-1000 .. **Baum**, Elizabeth R '96 %Baum Law Ofcs,LLP -438 Bway Bx1260 -Monticello 12701
(212) 353-8700 .. **Baum**, Eric M '94 (Simon E&B LLP) -24 Union Sq E -NY 10003 **Fx**:353-1708
(212) 382-6744 .. **Baum**, Frederic S '62 -42 W 44th -NY 10036 **Fx**:302-8219
(716) 854-0040 .. **Baum**, Holly '89 -14 Lafayette Sq -Buffalo 14203
(718) 991-4600 .. **Baum**, Howard J '91 Leg Aid -953 Southrn Blvd -Bronx 10459 **Fx**:842-2867
(718) 624-7791 .. **Baum**, Jack '55 (J Baum,PC) -26 Court -Brklyn 11242
(718) 980-5200 .. **Baum**, Jay S '82 -88 New Dorp Plz -Staten Isl 10306 **Fx**:351-2220
(516) 747-6900 .. **Baum**, Jeffrey I '88 JI Baum & Assoc,PC -666 Old Cntry Rd -Gdn Cty 11530 **Fx**:228-8349
(718) 990-1424 .. **Baum**, Jennifer '94 St John's Law Schl -8000 Utopia Pkwy -Jamaica 11439 **Fx**:591-1855
(631) 665-3400 .. **Baum**, Jonathan A '89 %Siben & S,LLP -90 E Main Bx149P -Bay Shr 11706
(718) 539-2100 .. **Baum**, Jos A '56 (Pliskin R&B) -137-11 Nrthrn Blvd -Flushng 11354
(518) 402-0570 .. **Baum**, Jos T '73 %UIA Bd -Troy Atrium Bx15126 -Albany 12212 **Fx**:402-6208
(315) 471-3151 .. **Baum**, Laurel E '98 (Hancock & E,LLP) -1500 AXA Twr I Bx4976 -Syracuse 13221
(212) 644-4414 .. **Baum**, Lauren A '94 L Baum,PC -307 E 53rd -NY 10022 **Fx**:644-8470
(516) 942-0244 .. **Baum**, Leonard '76 %Office oDA&R -375 N Bway -Jericho 11753 **Fx**:942-0353
(212) 969-3000 .. **Baum**, Leonard S '65 Cnsl Proskauer R LLP -1585 Bway -NY 10036
(845) 778-7305 .. **Baum**, Leslie A '91 -Bx706 -Walden 12586
(518) 474-0676 .. **Baum**, Lisa Henrikson '94 %Health Dept -2019 Corning Twr Empire St Plz -Albany 12237
(718) 254-0700 .. **Baum**, Michl Fred '79 %Bklyn Defender Srvcs -177 Lvngstn -Brklyn 11201 **Fx**:254-0897
(212) 488-1300 .. **Baum**, Michelle G '04 %Cohen & P LLP -444 Mad Av -NY 10022
(212) 468-4800 .. **Baum**, Miles A '68 (Davis & G LLP) -1740 Bway -NY 10019
(845) 887-4425 .. **Baum**, Morton I '61 -39 Lwr Main Bx248 -Callicoon 12723
(845) 791-1000 .. **Baum**, Morton I '61 -438 Bway Bx1260 -Monticello 12701
(845) 371-6888 .. **Baum**, Paul S '89 -50A S Main -Spg Vly 10977 **Fx**:371-8406
(718) 237-3100 .. **Baum**, Paula C '09 Leg Aid -111 Lvngstn -Brklyn 11201 **Fx**:250-4243
(315) 687-7215 .. **Baum**, Peter A '73 (Baum & W) -282 Genesee -Chittenango 13037
(516) 364-1600 .. **Baum**, Peter J '70 -6800 Jericho Tpk -Syosset 11791 **Fx**:364-1603
(845) 887-4425 .. **Baum**, Richd S '91 -39 Lwr Main Bx248 -Callicoon 12723
(845) 791-1000 .. **Baum**, Richd S '91 -438 Bway Bx1260 -Monticello 12701

(212) 417-8700 .. **Baum**, Robt M '72 %Fed Def of NY Inc -52 Duane -NY 10007 **Fx**:571-0392
(716) 833-2189 .. **Baum**, Ruth E '84 -738 Englewood Av -Buffalo 14223
(212) 355-6527 .. **Baum**, Simeon H '83 -575 Lex Av -NY 10022 **Fx**:753-0396
(212) 538-1777 .. **Baum**, Stephen '86 Credit Suisse -1 Mad Av -NY 10010
(212) 503-8811 .. **Baum**, Steven C '68 Paneth Haber & Zimmerman -622 3rd Av -NY 10017
(516) 422-8824 .. **Baum**, Steven D '93 Reliance 1st Cptl,LLC -270 S Srvc Rd -Melvll 11747 **Fx**:(866) 422-9775
(716) 204-2400 .. **Baum**, Steven J '87 SJ Baum,PC -220 Nrthpnte Pkwy Bx1291 -Buffalo 14240 **Fx**:204-4600
(585) 473-3100 .. **Baum**, Theo M B '91 (Ernstrom & D,LLP) -180 Canal Vw Blvd -Rchstr 14623
(315) 687-7215 .. **Baum & Wolfe** -282 Genesee -Chittenango 13037 **Fx**:687-7937
(212) 815-1818 .. **Bauman**, Andrew '79 %DC 37 MELS -125 Barclay -NY 10007 **Fx**:815-1343
(212) 564-3555 .. **Bauman**, Bert '58 OfCnsl Bauman & K,PC -14 Penn Plz -NY 10122
(845) 292-6571 .. **Bauman**, Harold J '72 -45 Delaware Av -Liberty 12754
(212) 835-2400 .. **Bauman**, John H '85 %Olnick Organization -110 E 59th -NY 10022 **Fx**:835-2458
(212) 684-0300 .. **Bauman Katz & Grill LLP** -28 W 44th -NY 10036 **Fx**:417-9380
(212) 564-3555 .. **Bauman & Kunkis,PC** -14 Penn Plz -NY 10122 **Fx**:564-2841
(914) 472-2300 .. **Bauman**, Louis W '56 OfCnsl Jones G,LLP -670 Wht Plns Rd -Scarsdale 10583
(212) 684-0300 .. **Bauman**, Mark S '77 (Bauman K&G LLP) -28 W 44th -NY 10036
(212) 354-4500 .. **Bauman**, Michl '91 (Friedman & W) -1500 Bway -NY 10036
(212) 969-3000 .. **Bauman**, Reuven '08 %Proskauer R LLP -1585 Bway -NY 10036
(212) 683-4565 .. **Bauman**, Stephen '68 -120 E 37th -NY 10016
(585) 232-5600 .. **Bauman**, Timothy R '94 (Blitman & K LLP) -16 W Main -Rchstr 14614
(212) 416-8000 .. **Bauman**, Wesley E '06 %Dept of Law -120 Bway -NY 10271
(212) 728-8000 .. **Baumann**, Corby J '04 %Willkie F&G LLP -787 7th Av -NY 10019
(212) 918-3000 .. **Baumann**, Kevin T '10 %Hogan L LLP -875 3rd Av -NY 10022
(212) 735-8600 .. **Baumann**, Richd M '88 (Morrison C LLP) -909 3rd Av -NY 10022
(516) 292-1111 .. **Baumann**, Robt E Jr. '69 -23 S Main -Freeprt 11520 **Fx**:678-2266
(212) 878-7900 .. **Baume**, Hal L '85 (Fox R LLP) -100 Park Av -NY 10017
(716) 852-1300 .. **Baumeister**, Arthur G Jr. '87 (Amigone S&M,LLP) -350 Main -Buffalo 14202
(212) 363-1200 .. **Baumeister**, Michel F '73 (Baumeister & S) -1 Exch Plz -NY 10006
(212) 363-1200 .. **Baumeister & Samuels** -1 Exch Plz -NY 10006 **Fx**:363-1346
(973) 912-7189 .. **Baumel**, Jeffrey A '84 (Sonnenschein N&R LLP) -1221 Av of Amer -NY 10020 **Fx**:912-7199
(212) 994-0260 .. **Baumel-Cornicello**, Susan '89 (Cornicello T&B-C,LLP) -2 Wall -NY 10005
(212) 259-8000 .. **Baumgaertner**, Peter A '98 (Dewey & L LLP) -1301 Av of Amer -NY 10019
(212) 355-6100 .. **Baumgardner**, Astrid R '77 %French Institute -22 E 60th -NY 10022
(212) 558-4000 .. **Baumgardner**, John E Jr. '76 (Sullivan & C LLP) -125 Broad -NY 10004
(212) 417-8700 .. **Baumgartel**, Sarah J '05 %Fed Def of NY Inc -52 Duane -NY 10007 **Fx**:571-0392
(212) 969-3000 .. **Baumgarten**, Jon A '68 (Proskauer R LLP) -1585 Bway -NY 10036
(212) 969-3000 .. **Baumgarten**, Jos '84 (Proskauer R LLP) -1585 Bway -NY 10036
(716) 843-5864 .. **Baumgarten**, Mary C '89 US Atty -138 Delaware Av -Buffalo 14202 **Fx**:551-3052
(917) 534-4942 .. **Baumgarten**, Michl D '92 Centre Grp Holdings Ltd -105 E 17th -NY 10003
(516) 868-6617 .. **Baumgarten**, Neil '56 -1885 Cynthia Ln -Merrick 11566 **Fx**:868-7666
(212) 940-8900 .. **Baumgarten**, Paul A '58 Cnsl Katten MR LLP -575 Mad Av -NY 10022
(914) 834-0610 .. **Baumgarten**, Philip A '84 -25 Woodlawn Av -New Rchll 10804
(212) 480-3030 .. **Baumgarten**, Robt H '85 M Pressman -125 Maiden Ln -NY 10038 **Fx**:480-2590
(212) 785-5959 .. **Baumgarten**, Sidney '61 (Devereaux B) -39 Bway -NY 10006 **Fx**:785-4487
(212) 858-4724 .. **Baumgartner**, Arthur G '95 FINRA -1 Lbrty Plz -NY 10006
(631) 777-2330 .. **Baumgartner**, Eileen M '99 %O'Connor OH&D,LLP -1 Huntngtn Quad -Melvll 11747
(718) 248-0338 .. **Baumgartner**, John E '92 %Citicorp Invstmnt Srvcs -1 Court Sq -LIC 11120
(845) 353-2200 .. **Baumgartner**, Jos P '82 (Bunyan & B) -500 Bradley Hill Rd -Blauvelt 10913
(718) 590-2000 .. **Baumgartner**, Susan E '04 %DA -198 E 161st -Bronx 10451 **Fx**:590-6477
(914) 765-4375 .. **Baumgartner-Bonanno**, Michele A '98 -1 New Castle Dr -Armonk 10504 **Fx**:765-7533
(718) 222-8880 .. **Baumholtz**, Melanie B '89 %Jones JO -45 Main -Brklyn 11201
(212) 787-5638 .. **Baumrin**, Bernard H '73 -590 West End Av -NY 10024
(212) 735-3000 .. **Baumstark**, Jonathan P '02 %Skadden ASM&F LLP -4 Times Sq -NY 10036
(212) 819-8200 .. **Baumstein**, Douglas P '98 Cnsl White & C LLP -1155 Av of Amer -NY 10036
(212) 436-2000 .. **Baumstein**, Jeffrey L '08 Deloitte Tax LLP -225 Lbrty -NY 10281
(212) 819-8200 .. **Baur**, Gerret J '04 %White & C LLP -1155 Av of Amer -NY 10036
(908) 221-1200 .. **Baurkot**, Danl J '88 (Pinczewski & B,PC) -2753 Coney Isl Av -Brklyn 11235 **Fx**:204-1350
(212) 930-0684 .. **Bausch**, Jacqueline F '88 %NY Public Lib -5th Av & 42nd -NY 10018 **Fx**:391-2503
(518) 426-4786 .. **Bauscher**, Rebecca M '03 -100 State -Albany 12207
(631) 266-3951 .. **Bausenwein**, Edw A '54 -235 Cedrus Av -E Northprt 11731
(718) 250-2000 .. **Bausk**, Heidi '06 %DA -350 Jay -Brklyn 11201 **Fx**:250-2314
(914) 323-7000 .. **Bautista**, Gregory J '08 %Wilson EME&D LLP -3 Gannett Dr -White Plns 10604
(212) 335-9000 .. **Bautista**, Sheila Lee '05 %DA -1 Hogan Pl -NY 10013
(646) 315-7300 .. **Bautz**, Michl W '94 %FINRA -14 Wall -NY 10005 **Fx**:315-7440
(212) 725-5755 .. **Bavagnoli**, Ronald C '99 (Bavagnoli & B) -232 Mad Av -NY 10016 **Fx**:(973) 785-9229
(212) 267-1950 .. **Bavaro**, Jos S '94 (Salenger SSK&B,LLP) -233 Bway -NY 10279
(516) 280-2091 .. **Bavaro**, Nicholas '09 -1010 Franklin Av -Gdn Cty 11530
(631) 854-9216 .. **Bavaro**, Ralph J '81 OCA -3105 Vets Hwy -Ronkonkoma 11779
(914) 686-9010 .. **Bave**, Wm H Jr. '74 (Wilson BCC&C,PC) -2 William -White Plns 10601
(212) 819-8200 .. **Bave**, Wm H III '09 %White & C LLP -1155 Av of Amer -NY 10036
(914) 633-7400 .. **Bave-Planell**, Patricia A '86 %Marcus O&K LLP -145 Huguenot -New Rchll 10801
(914) 995-3497 .. **Bavero**, James J '09 %DA -111 Martin Luther King Blvd -White Plns 10601 **Fx**:995-3363
(914) 997-7100 .. **Bavero**, Ronald J '75 (Berman BF&G pc) -123 Main -White Plns 10601
(212) 252-0004 .. **Bavli**, David H '07 %Carroll M&K LLC -570 Lex Av -NY 10022
(845) 856-4444 .. **Bavoso**, David W '10 Bavoso P&O -19 E Main Bx3139 -Pt Jervis 12771
(845) 856-4444 .. **Bavoso Plotsky & Onofry** -19 E Main Bx3139 -Pt Jervis 12771 **Fx**:858-8002
(845) 856-4444 .. **Bavoso**, Wm D '72 (Bavoso P&O) -19 E Main Bx3139 -Pt Jervis 12771
(212) 788-0454 .. **Bavuso**, Jos '97 %Law Dept -100 Church -NY 10007 **Fx**:788-0367
(716) 284-6407 .. **Bax**, Alfonso M '98 -460 Barton Dr -Lewiston 14092 **Fx**:298-1680
(212) 791-7200 .. **Baxley**, Chas E '58 (Hart BD&H) -90 John -NY 10038
(212) 325-1054 .. **Baxley**, Matthew W '91 -11 Mad Av -NY 10010
(212) 858-1222 .. **Baxter**, David S '00 (Pillsbury WSP LLP) -1540 Bway -NY 10036
(212) 371-8008 .. **Baxter**, James N '68 OfCnsl Guzov O,LLC -600 Mad Av -NY 10022
(914) 328-1272 .. **Baxter**, Janette A '99 J Baxter,PC -246 Central Av -White Plns 10606 **Fx**:328-1273
(212) 889-9811 .. **Baxter**, Jason M '05 -267 5th Av -NY 10016 **Fx**:889-9818
(518) 463-3200 .. **Baxter**, Kathleen R Mulligan '86 %NYS Bar Assn -1 Elk -Albany 12207 **Fx**:487-5544
(212) 768-6700 .. **Baxter**, Kathryn Howell '91 (Sonnenschein N&R LLP) -1221 Av of Amer -NY 10020
(212) 594-6747 .. **Baxter**, Michl J '10 -424 W 33rd -NY 10001
(212) 558-4000 .. **Baxter**, Michl N '09 %Sullivan & C LLP -125 Broad -NY 10004
(516) 997-7330 .. **Baxter**, Robt C '89 (Baxter S&S,PC) -99 N Bway -Hicksvll 11801
(212) 732-9800 .. **Baxter**, Robt C '89 (Baxter S&S,PC) -505 8th Av -NY 10018
(914) 749-8200 .. **Baxter**, Rosanne C '08 Cnsl Boies S&F LLP -333 Main -Armonk 10504
(516) 997-7330 .. **Baxter Smith & Shapiro,PC** -99 N Bway -Hicksvll 11801 **Fx**:997-7488
(212) 732-9800 .. **Baxter Smith & Shapiro,PC** -505 8th Av -NY 10018 **Fx**:732-0152
(914) 684-1055 .. **Baxter Smith & Shapiro,PC** -200 Mamaroneck Av -White Plns 10601 **Fx**:684-1058
(716) 854-6140 .. **Baxter Smith & Shapiro,PC** -182 Dwyer -W Seneca 14224 **Fx**:854-6540
(212) 720-5026 .. **Baxter**, Thos C Jr. '80 %Fed Reserve Bk -33 Lbrty -NY 10045 **Fx**:785-5748
(212) 373-3000 .. **Bayard**, Lynn Beth '96 (Paul WRW&G LLP) -1285 Av of Amer -NY 10019
(212) 219-1800 .. **Bayarin**, Gail S '04 %Lawyers Alliance NY -171 Mad Av -NY 10016 **Fx**:941-7458
(518) 462-6765 .. **Bayar Woods**, Elizabeth S '09 %Leg Aid -55 Colvin Av -Albany 12206 **Fx**:427-8352
(212) 909-6000 .. **Bayazitoglu**, Ahmet S '10 %Debevoise & P LLP -919 3rd Av -NY 10022
(212) 483-9490 .. **Bayda**, I Michl '65 OfCnsl McElroy DM&C,LLP -88 Pine -NY 10005
(212) 980-9600 .. **Baydala**, Betsy D '09 %Kaufman B&R -120 Bway -NY 10271
(516) 684-2900 .. **Baydar**, James B '87 (Pegalis & E,LLC) -1 Hllw Ln -Lk Success 11042
(718) 252-4700 .. **Baydar**, S John '86 -2186 Flatbush Av -Brklyn 11234 **Fx**:252-4555
(518) 359-7064 .. **Bayer**, Chas F '03 %MHLS -2445 State Route 30 -Tupper Lk 12986 **Fx**:359-4371
(315) 386-4583 .. **Bayer**, Genelle J '07 %Lekki HF&D,PC -21 Court Bx469 -Canton 13617
(212) 526-3129 .. **Bayer**, Jonathan L '99 %Barclays Capital Inc -745 7th Av -NY 10019
(212) 858-4382 .. **Bayer**, Katherine M '95 %FINRA -1 Lbrty Plz -NY 10006
(212) 335-9000 .. **Bayer**, Michele '04 %DA -1 Hogan Pl -NY 10013
(585) 428-5210 .. **Bayer**, Pamela '73 %Pub Def -10 N Fitzhugh -Rchstr 14614 **Fx**:428-2234
(212) 391-9500 .. **Bayer**, Richd '06 %Einbinder & D,PC -104 W 40th -NY 10018
(212) 848-4000 .. **Bayer**, Ronald M '02 (Shearman & S LLP) -599 Lex Av -NY 10022
(212) 446-4800 .. **Bayerd**, Jennifer J '09 %Kirkland & E LLP -153 E 53rd -NY 10022
(716) 662-8541 .. **Bayerl**, Lawr R '84 -104 Burbank Dr -Orchard Pk 14127
(212) 530-5000 .. **Bayeva**, Tatiana '09 %Milbank TH&M LLP -1 Chase Manh Plz -NY 10005
(212) 335-9000 .. **Bayles**, Danl J '96 %DA -1 Hogan Pl -NY 10013
(212) 319-1000 .. **Bayley**, Anoushka S '93 (Quirk & B,PC) -845 3rd Av -NY 10022
(212) 776-5000 .. **Bayley**, James E '94 NYC Housing Auth -250 Bway -NY 10007 **Fx**:776-5039
(516) 357-3700 .. **Baylis**, Thos S '89 (Cullen and D LLP) -100 Q Roosevelt Blvd -Gdn Cty 11530
(585) 428-5755 .. **Bayly-Henshaw**, Nicole E '07 Cnty Atty -50 W Main -Rchstr 14614 **Fx**:428-2031
(718) 262-7100 .. **Bayme**, Helene Asher '81 %Civil Ct -89-17 Sutphin Blvd -Jamaica 11435 **Fx**:262-7107
(212) 679-2205 .. **Bayne**, Andrew J '94 (Bayne Law Grp,LLC) -230 Park Av -NY 10169 **Fx**:679-2208
(212) 207-8400 .. **Bayne**, David F '89 (Kavanagh M&O LLP) -415 Mad Av -NY 10017
(518) 756-6000 .. **Baynes**, Brendan F '87 B Baynes,PLLC -130 Main -Ravena 12143 **Fx**:756-6007
(518) 487-5460 .. **Baynes**, Christopher P '95 %DA -6 Lodge -Albany 12207 **Fx**:487-5093
(212) 335-4500 .. **Baynes**, Katherine C '01 (DLA Piper LLP) -1251 Av of Amer -NY 10020
(518) 465-3484 .. **Baynes**, Kathleen McCaffrey '94 (Carter CCBM&L,PC) -20 Corp Wds Blvd -Albany 12211
(718) 990-6032 .. **Baynes**, Leonard M '84 St John's Law Schl -8000 Utopia Pkwy -Jamaica 11439 **Fx**:591-1855
(212) 770-7641 .. **Bayoneto**, M Victoria '96 %AIG -70 Pine -NY 10270
(718) 830-3200 .. **Bayrasli**, Ercument '01 (Rosado C&B,LLP) -31-00 47th Av -LIC 11101 **Fx**:830-3534
(212) 696-6000 .. **Bayrock**, David '95 (Curtis M-PC&M LLP) -101 Park Av -NY 10178
(516) 935-3600 .. **Bayroff**, Adam B '87 OfCnsl Seltzer SH&H LLP -100 Jericho Quad -Jericho 11753
(212) 836-8000 .. **Bays**, Lea M '08 %Kaye S LLP -425 Park Av -NY 10022

(718) 478-8583 .. **Bazan,** Ana Maria '03 -37-06 82nd -Jcksn Hts 11372 **Fx:**478-8560
(516) 739-1462 .. **Bazante,** Annabel '92 %Brosnan & H -1325 Franklin Av -Gdn Cty 11530
(212) 506-2500 .. **Bazar,** Jason S '97 (Mayer B LLP) -1675 Bway -NY 10019
(631) 265-6300 .. **Bazarsky,** Barrie E '87 (Birzon S&B) -222 E Main -Smithtwn 11787
(718) 999-2040 .. **Bazel,** Julian Robt '84 %Fire Dept Bureau Leg Afrs -9 Metrotech Ctr -Brklyn 11201
(516) 775-1555 .. **Bazhdari,** Mergim '77 -1111 Marcus Av -Lk Success 11042 **Fx:**592-5854
(212) 416-6152 .. **Bazile,** Bessie '89 %Dept of Law -120 Bway -NY 10271 **Fx:**416-6147
(845) 291-2650 .. **Bazile,** Stephanie '04 %Cnty Atty -285 Main -Goshen 10924 **Fx:**291-3014
(212) 735-3000 .. **Bazley,** Mathew C '04 %Skadden ASM&F LLP -4 Times Sq -NY 10036
(212) 450-4000 .. **Bazos,** Peter T '08 %Davis P&W LLP -450 Lex Av -NY 10017
(845) 361-3668 .. **Bazydlo,** Chas T '96 -5 Howard Seely Rd -Thompson Rdg 10985 **Fx:**361-3669
(212) 238-8900 .. **Bazzi,** Michl H '06 %Melito & A,PC -233 Bway -NY 10279
(718) 816-8266 .. **Bazzurro,** John T '95 -443 Cllg Av -Staten Isl 10314 **Fx:**816-0945
(415) 875-6600 .. **Bea,** Renée Beltranena '06 %Quinn EU&S,LLP -51 Mad Av -NY 10010 **Fx:**875-6700
(212) 364-8453 .. **Beach,** Janine Aneeka '05 Time Warner Cable -60 Columbus Cir -NY 10023
(212) 973-0572 .. **Beach,** Kevin J '06 %Wolff & S PC -140 Bway -NY 10005
(914) 323-7000 .. **Beach,** L Kellie '07 %Wilson EME&D LLP -3 Gannett Dr -White Plns 10604
(718) 286-6000 .. **Beach,** Melissa A '09 DA -125-01 Qns Blvd -Kew Gdns 11415
(518) 487-7600 .. **Beach,** Randall S '98 (Whiteman O&H LLP) -1 Commerce Plz -Albany 12260
(212) 509-3456 .. **Beacham,** Jeffrey B '86 (McGivney & K,PC) -80 Broad -NY 10004
(212) 519-7811 .. **Beacham,** Laurie Gindin '90 ACLU -125 Broad -NY 10004
(212) 297-5800 .. **Beacher,** Ronald S '94 (Day P LLP) -7 Times Sq -NY 10036
(585) 342-8142 .. **Beachman,** Robt G '55 -40 Hearthstone Ln -Rchstr 14617
(212) 697-6555 .. **Beadle,** Peter M '97 %Biedermann RH&R -570 Lex Av -NY 10022
(315) 624-3214 .. **Beakman,** Andrew W '04 Conmed Corp -525 French Rd -Utica 13502
(315) 361-8687 .. **Beakman,** Meghan M '02 %Oneida Indian Nation Enterprises -5218 Patrick Rd -Verona 13478 **Fx:**361-8009
(516) 938-0877 .. **Beal,** Carol Ann '87 (Beal & B) -34 Birchwood Park Cres -Jericho 11753 **Fx:**681-2161
(718) 250-2000 .. **Beal,** Elaine Liu '03 %DA -350 Jay -Brklyn 11201 **Fx:**250-2314
(212) 735-3000 .. **Beal,** Jamie A '06 %Skadden ASM&F LLP -4 Times Sq -NY 10036
(212) 905-2730 .. **Beal,** Jeremy A '04 %Morgan Stanley -330 Mad Av -NY 10017
(516) 938-0877 .. **Beal,** Kenneth I '88 (Beal & B) -34 Birchwood Park Cres -Jericho 11753 **Fx:**681-2161
(212) 888-0672 .. **Beale,** Christopher W '75 -301 E 52nd -NY 10022
(212) 949-0203 .. **Beale,** David A '75 -750 3rd Av -NY 10017
(212) 605-0272 .. **Beale,** Francesca Macartney '75 -301 E 52nd -NY 10022 **Fx:**605-0222
(585) 454-5190 .. **Beale,** Louise Rossi '82 (Des Marteau & B) -370 Rynlds Arcd -Rchstr 14614 **Fx:**454-4905
(607) 974-3921 .. **Beall,** Thos R '97 %Corning,Inc -Sp-FR-02-12 -Corning 14831
(212) 841-1000 .. **Beals,** Christopher L '08 %Covington & B LLP -620 8th Av -NY 10018
(212) 909-6000 .. **Beam,** Michl J '06 %Debevoise & P LLP -919 3rd Av -NY 10022
(212) 788-3757 .. **Beam,** Thos M '05 ACS -220 Church -NY 10013
(212) 504-6000 .. **Beaman,** Gregory D '10 %Cadwalader W&T LLP -1 World Fncl Ctr -NY 10281
(718) 445-8345 .. **Beaman,** Richd '70 -30-11 Murray -Flushng 11354
(212) 336-2000 .. **Beame,** Andrew P '97 Cnsl Patterson BW&T LLP -1133 Av of Amer -NY 10036
(212) 450-4000 .. **Beamon,** Martine M '93 (Davis P&W LLP) -450 Lex Av -NY 10017
(716) 856-4000 .. **Bean,** Edwin T Jr. '51 (Hodgson R LLP) -140 Pearl -Buffalo 14202
(585) 423-4520 .. **Bean,** Lloyd F II '94 %Xerox -100 Clinton Av S -Rchstr 14644
(518) 598-4810 .. **Bean,** Robt T '94 -457 W 57th -NY 10019
(212) 237-1000 .. **Bean,** Shaun A '10 %Windels ML&M,LLP -156 W 56th -NY 10019
(914) 946-4777 .. **Beane,** Edw F '67 (Keane & B,PC) -445 Hmltn Av -White Plns 10601
(212) 608-0919 .. **Beane,** Leona '69 -11 Park Pl -NY 10007
(718) 343-6779 .. **Bearak,** Corey B '82 -Bx135 -Glen Oaks 11004 **Fx:**225-3366
(212) 508-6700 .. **Beard,** Amy S '08 %Tannenbaum HS&H LLP -900 3rd Av -NY 10022
(212) 335-9000 .. **Beard,** Christopher J '91 %DA -1 Hogan Pl -NY 10013
(212) 885-5000 .. **Beard,** W Cameron III '87 (Blank R LLP) -405 Lex Av -NY 10174
(212) 244-4664 .. **Bearden,** Roger A '01 NY Lawyers Pub Intrst -151 W 30th -NY 10001 **Fx:**244-4570
(315) 469-3232 .. **Beardsley,** C Saml '72 -7106 S Salina -Nedrow 13120
(716) 847-8400 .. **Beardsley,** James M '63 OfCnsl Phillips L LLP -3400 HSBC Ctr -Buffalo 14203
(212) 758-9700 .. **Beardsley,** Joshua A '05 %KPMG LLP -345 Park Av -NY 10154
(212) 688-8555 .. **Beardsley,** Rachel J '07 %Fragomen DB&L LLP -7 Hanover Sq -NY 10004
(212) 837-6352 .. **Beardsley,** W Peter '07 %Hughes H&R LLP -1 Bttry Pk Plz -NY 10004 **Fx:**299-6352
(518) 487-3572 .. **Bearese,** George '75 Matthew Bender & Co,Inc -1275 Bway -Albany 12204 **Fx:**487-3573
(716) 842-2301 .. **Beaser,** Lisa Bertino '01 %M&T Bk -1 M & T Plz -Buffalo 14203 **Fx:**842-5376
(585) 272-0540 .. **Beasley,** Katherine M '09 Thomas & S LLP -693 East Av -Rchstr 14607
(718) 613-3500 .. **Beason,** Nicole A '05 %UIA Bd -Bx29002 -Brklyn 11201 **Fx:**613-3566
(914) 747-7410 .. **Beatley,** M Kathleen '92 (Stargiotti & B,PC) -48 Wheeler Av -Plsntvll 10570 **Fx:**747-7590
(212) 652-3890 .. **Beato,** Carlos E '08 %Pitta & G LLP -120 Bway -NY 10271
(212) 513-3200 .. **Beaton,** Neal N '79 (Holland & K LLP) -31 W 52nd -NY 10019
(212) 774-6818 .. **Beaton,** Regan M '00 %IMG Talent Agncy -1 N Lex Av -White Plns 10601
(212) 610-6300 .. **Beaton,** Shaun J '02 SrCnsl Allen & O -1221 Av of Amer -NY 10020
(212) 705-7000 .. **Beaton,** Todd M Jr. '06 %Bingham M LLP -399 Park Av -NY 10022
(914) 949-5896 .. **Beatrice,** Michl R '83 -200 N Cntrl Pk Av -Hartsdale 10530
(212) 964-6611 .. **Beattie,** John R '04 %Lester SK&D -120 Bway -NY 10271
(212) 655-5000 .. **Beattie,** Laura C '05 %Gannon R&M -120 Bway -NY 10271
(212) 668-1900 .. **Beattie,** Nina M '99 (Brune & R LLP) -80 Broad -NY 10004
(212) 824-5700 .. **Beattie,** Peter '07 Practising Law Inst -810 7th Av -NY 10019
(212) 455-2000 .. **Beattie,** Richd I '69 (Simpson T&B LLP) -425 Lex Av -NY 10017
(212) 421-4300 .. **Beatty,** Harry C '78 (Kent B&G,LLP) -425 Park Av -NY 10022
(212) 453-1140 .. **Beatty,** John F '72 %New Harbor Inc -546 5th Av -NY 10036
(212) 267-4177 .. **Beatty,** John P '07 %Kramer DL&M -217 Bway -NY 10007
(212) 766-5222 .. **Beatty,** Kathleen E '10 %Leav & S LLP -120 Bway -NY 10271 **Fx:**693-2377
(516) 746-8000 .. **Beatty,** Kerri K '08 %Jaspan S LLP -300 Grdn City Plz -Gdn Cty 11530
(212) 975-8926 .. **Beatty,** Mark Egan '08 CBS Corp -51 W 52nd -NY 10019
(212) 425-0230 .. **Beatty,** Michl C '83 (Feldman K&B) -42 Bway -NY 10004
(516) 482-2282 .. **Beatty,** Michl C '83 (Feldman K&B) -45 N Station Plz -Gt Neck 11021
(212) 269-0927 .. **Beatus,** Laurie P '87 %D'Amato & L,LLP -2 World Fncl Ctr -NY 10281
(518) 782-7700 .. **Beaty,** Danl H '98 %Plug Power Inc -968 Albany Shaker Rd -Latham 12110
(914) 995-3664 .. **Beaty,** Sara M '06 Cnty Atty -148 Martine Av -White Plns 10601 **Fx:**995-3132
(212) 449-2943 .. **Beauchesne,** Laura Rice '94 %Merrill Lynch -220 Bway -NY 10038
(212) 488-0231 .. **Beaudet,** Jacqueline B '06 Frenkel & Co Inc -350 Hudson -NY 10014
(518) 408-1495 .. **Beaudoin,** Cynthia H '05 %Dept of Health -Corning Twr 24th Fl -Albany 12237 **Fx:**486-4834
(518) 473-5115 .. **Beaudoin,** Susan E '84 Cnsl Ofc for Technology -State Cptl ESP Bx2062 -Albany 12220
(518) 833-6000 .. **Beaudoin,** Theresa A '00 %Dept Soc Srvcs -127 Bloomingrove Dr -Troy 12180 **Fx:**833-6121
(212) 649-4358 .. **Beaudoing,** Nicolas E '03 %Hearst Magazines Intl. -300 W 57th -NY 10019
(212) 839-5300 .. **Beaudry,** Francois '09 %Sidley A LLP -787 7th Av -NY 10019
(212) 530-5000 .. **Beaudry,** Jennifer Knesel '09 Milbank TH&M LLP -1 Chase Manh Plz -NY 10005
(718) 579-3139 .. **Beaulieu,** Sakeena '02 Leg Aid -1020 Grnd Cncrs -Bronx 10451
(212) 833-1245 .. **Beaumont,** Anne E '98 (Friedman KS&A LLP) -1633 Bway -NY 10019 **Fx:**373-7945
(518) 689-0966 .. **Beaumont,** John H '83 (Hite & B,PC) -20 Corp Wds Blvd -Albany 12211
(212) 837-6000 .. **Beausoleil,** Wm J '97 (Hughes H&R LLP) -1 Bttry Pk Plz -NY 10004
(914) 381-3534 .. **Beaver,** Thea S '91 (Rosenstrach & B) -740 W Bstn Post Rd -Mamaroneck 10543
(716) 675-6111 .. **Bebak,** Margaret C '92 %Greenan Law Ofc -3755 Seneca Bx188 -W Seneca 14224 **Fx:**674-2597
(646) 688-4375 .. **Bebchick,** Baruch M '03 Bebchick Law -120 W 31st -NY 10001 **Fx:**224-8289
(212) 859-8000 .. **Bebchick,** Lisa H '02 (Fried FHS&J LLP) -1 NY Plz -NY 10004
(646) 386-5700 .. **Bebelaar,** Kristin '98 Civil Ct -111 Centre -NY 10013
(718) 591-3512 .. **Beberfall,** Elmer H '73 -65-25 160th -Flushng 11365
(845) 340-3757 .. **Beccari,** Anthony 2nd '07 %Applt Div 3rd Dept -Capitol Station Bx7288 -Albany 12224 **Fx:**(518) 471-4750
(914) 448-0200 .. **Beccaro,** Lynne S '90 %Bartlett MB&M,LLP -81 Main -White Plns 10601
(716) 362-0991 .. **Bechakas,** Anastasios L '95 %Rupp BPC&C LLC -2495 Kensngtn Av -Amherst 14226
(716) 626-3040 .. **Bechakas,** Cheryl-Lane H '96 -300 Intl Dr -Buffalo 14221
(716) 204-2400 .. **Bechakas,** Elpiniki M '91 %SJ Baum,PC -220 Nrthpnte Pkwy Bx1291 -Buffalo 14240 **Fx:**204-4600
(718) 233-2755 .. **Bechara,** Margie '03 inMotion,Inc -2432 Grnd Cncrs -Bronx 10458 **Fx:**562-7514
(518) 473-5115 .. **Bechard,** Andrew W '91 %Ofc for Technology -State Cptl ESP Bx2062 -Albany 12220
(518) 457-4951 .. **Becher,** Leslie H '80 %Dept Correctional Srvcs -1220 Wshngtn Av -Albany 12226 **Fx:**457-7555
(518) 436-9525 .. **Becher,** Robt A '77 -5 Wilson -Albany 12207 **Fx:**436-4583
(212) 421-4100 .. **Bechhofer,** Samson R '79 (Pryor C LLP) -7 Times Sq -NY 10036
(212) 340-0400 .. **Becht,** Gretchen A '06 %Applt Div 1st Dept -27 Mad Av -NY 10010 **Fx:**889-4412
(718) 780-0342 .. **Bechtel,** Debra '84 %Bklyn Law Schl -250 Joralemon -Brklyn 11201 **Fx:**780-0393
(716) 856-4000 .. **Bechtel,** Lura Hess '04 %Hodgson R LLP -140 Pearl -Buffalo 14202
(516) 794-1900 .. **Bechtle,** Christopher T '00 %Bechtle & M -100 Grdn City Plz -Gdn Cty 11530
(516) 794-1900 .. **Bechtle,** Eugene W Jr. '70 (Bechtle & M) -100 Grdn City Plz -Gdn Cty 11530
(212) 768-6700 .. **Bechutsky,** Linda '09 %Sonnenschein N&R LLP -2 World Fncl Ctr -NY 10281
(212) 225-6522 .. **Becil,** Hector '93 Bank of Nova Scotia -1 Lbrty Plz -NY 10006
(212) 880-6000 .. **Beck,** Andrew J '73 (Torys LLP) -237 Park Av -NY 10017
(516) 670-3200 .. **Beck & Arad, LLP** -670 Lng Bch Blvd -Long Bch 11561
(212) 425-7200 .. **Beck,** Brian J '09 %Kenyon & K,LLP -1 Bway -NY 10004
(845) 228-2021 .. **Beck,** Connie K '80 %Guidepost A Church Corp -39 Seminary Hill Rd -Carmel 10512
(631) 390-0010 .. **Beck,** Gregory I '10 %Bruno G&S,LLP -445 Broad Hollow Rd -Melvll 11747
(212) 577-3530 .. **Beck,** John '84 %Leg Aid -199 Water -NY 10038 **Fx:**425-2465
(914) 949-5300 .. **Beck,** Kathleen M '86 (Brown & T,LLC) -1 N Bway -White Plns 10601
(914) 323-7000 .. **Beck,** Katrine Aliha '01 %Wilson EME&D LLP -3 Gannett Dr -White Plns 10604
(718) 847-1168 .. **Beck,** Laurence '88 -80-59 Lefferts Blvd -Kew Gdns 11415
(516) 228-8383 .. **Beck,** Leland Stuart '55 (Beck & S,PLLC) -50 Chas Lindbergh Blvd -Uniondale 11553
(914) 285-9500 .. **Beck Liebman Petrone, PC** -399 Knollwood Rd -White Plns 10603 **Fx:**285-9769
(718) 282-5575 .. **Beck,** Marc D '06 %CAMBA -885 Flatbush Av -Brklyn 11226
(716) 855-1111 .. **Beck,** Matthew J '03 (Duke HP&G LLP) -350 Main -Buffalo 14202
(212) 468-8000 .. **Beck,** Melissa D '04 %Morrison & F LLP -1290 Av of Amer -NY 10104

(646) 613-9633 .. **Beck,** Melissa M '95 LIFT -350 Bway -NY 10013
(212) 813-8800 .. **Beck,** Michl '00 %Goodwin P LLP -620 8th Av -NY 10018
(212) 407-4000 .. **Beck,** Michl D '81 (Loeb & L,LLP) -345 Park Av -NY 10154
(212) 735-3000 .. **Beck,** Monica H '02 %Skadden ASM&F LLP -4 Times Sq -NY 10036
(212) 455-2000 .. **Beck,** Noah D '04 %Simpson T&B LLP -425 Lex Av -NY 10017
(516) 670-3200 .. **Beck,** Philip D '85 (Beck & A,LLP) -670 Lng Bch Blvd -Long Bch 11561
(212) 431-2307 .. **Beck,** Richd C E '82 %NY Law Schl -185 W Bway -NY 10013 **Fx:**343-2039
(212) 269-4900 .. **Beck,** Robt G Jr. '07 %Ford MEW&G,LLP -Wall Street Plz -NY 10005
(914) 285-9500 .. **Beck,** Robt H '74 (Beck LP,PC) -399 Knollwood Rd -White Plns 10603
(212) 325-2000 .. **Beck,** Seanna B '03 Credit Suisse -11 Mad Av -NY 10010
(607) 724-2385 .. **Beck,** Stephanie G '90 (Paniccia & B,LLP) -53 Chenango -Bnghmtn 13901
(516) 228-8383 .. **Beck & Strauss,PLLC** -50 Chas Lindbergh Blvd -Uniondale 11553 **Fx:**228-8390
(212) 839-5300 .. **Beck,** Thos H '80 (Sidley A LLP) -787 7th Av -NY 10019
(631) 737-6500 .. **Beck,** Vincent James '65 -109 Forest Rd -Centereach 11720 **Fx:**737-6510
(631) 654-1061 .. **Beck,** Walter L '70 -73 N Ocean Av -Patchogue 11772 **Fx:**447-6662
(212) 517-6666 .. **Beckenstein,** Lawr A '82 (L Beckenstein,PC) -320 E 65th -NY 10065 **Fx:**517-2076
(212) 693-1500 .. **Becker,** Avrohom '89 (Becker & R) -111 John -NY 10038
(212) 351-4000 .. **Becker,** Barbara L '89 (Gibson D&C LLP) -200 Park Av -NY 10166
(212) 754-4800 .. **Becker,** Brad R '84 (Becker H LLP) -730 3rd Av -NY 10017 **Fx:**253-4198
(607) 723-5341 .. **Becker,** Bruce O '58 SpclCnsl Hinman H&K,LLP -80 Exchange Bx5250 -Bnghmtn 13902
(718) 252-0484 .. **Becker,** Carl H '85 -2425 Kings Hwy -Brklyn 11229
(718) 466-3000 .. **Becker,** Carri J '93 %Civil Ct -1118 Grnd Cncrs -Bronx 10456 **Fx:**466-3006
(212) 506-1700 .. **Becker,** Christian T '06 %Kasowitz BT&F LLP -1633 Bway -NY 10019
(212) 859-8000 .. **Becker,** Clinton K '09 %Fried FHS&J LLP -1 NY Plz -NY 10004
(212) 587-3023 .. **Becker,** Danl S '90 NYS Ins Fund -199 Church -NY 10007
(212) 735-3000 .. **Becker,** Danl W J '10 %Skadden ASM&F LLP -4 Times Sq -NY 10036
(718) 652-0847 .. **Becker,** David F '60 -2526 Wallace Av -Bronx 10467 **Fx:**652-2918
(212) 889-2021 .. **Becker,** David M '99 (Rele & B LLC) -1178 Bway -NY 10001 **Fx:**(646) 390-8000
(212) 732-8292 .. **Becker,** Donald W '79 -40 Fulton -NY 10038 **Fx:**732-8550
(212) 889-7460 .. **Becker,** Douglas A '89 %Jos P Day Realty -9 E 40th -NY 10016
(518) 462-5814 .. **Becker,** Ellen D B '82 (Becker & B) -148 Central Av Bx575 -Albany 12201 **Fx:**462-6836
(212) 431-3100 .. **Becker,** Eunice '80 -377 Bway -NY 10013 **Fx:**431-4460
(732) 855-6030 .. **Becker,** Frederic K '85 (Wilentz G&S) -110 William -NY 10038 **Fx:**726-6549
(212) 867-3820 .. **Becker,** Fredrick A '83 -122 E 42nd -NY 10168 **Fx:**983-5276
(212) 981-1980 .. **Becker,** Gary G '84 (G Becker,LLC) -200 W 57th -NY 10019 **Fx:**214-0901
(212) 888-3033 .. **Becker Glynn Melamed & Muffly LLP** -299 Park Av -NY 10171 **Fx:**888-0255
(845) 634-3696 .. **Becker,** Isabel L '70 (I Becker,LLC) -49 Maple Av Bx796 -New Cty 10956 **Fx:**634-3019
(212) 687-3860 .. **Becker,** Jack '60 (Snow BK,PC) -605 3rd Av -NY 10158
(212) 481-8199 .. **Becker,** James J '95 -222 E 31st -NY 10016
(212) 506-1700 .. **Becker,** Jason A '06 Kasowitz BT&F LLP -1633 Bway -NY 10019
(212) 351-4500 .. **Becker,** Jeffrey H '69 (Epstein B&G,PC) -250 Park Av -NY 10177
(718) 590-2000 .. **Becker,** Jennifer M '09 %DA -198 E 161st -Bronx 10451 **Fx:**590-6477
(800) 358-2550 .. **Becker,** Jerome M '62 NAM -990 Stewart Av -Gdn Cty 11530 **Fx:**(516) 794-8518
(646) 386-5891 .. **Becker,** Jillian C '01 %MHLS -41 Mad Av -NY 10010
(516) 393-2200 .. **Becker,** John E '03 %Garfunkel W,PC -111 Grt Nck Rd -Gt Neck 11021
(212) 788-1280 .. **Becker,** Jonathan S '80 %Law Dept -100 Church -NY 10007 **Fx:**788-0367
(212) 785-9100 .. **Becker,** Jordan D '87 (Paduano & W LLP) -1251 Av of Amer -NY 10020
(212) 888-3033 .. **Becker,** Jos D '55 Cnsl Becker GM&M LLP -299 Park Av -NY 10171
(212) 788-0514 .. **Becker,** Kenneth A '84 %Law Dept -100 Church -NY 10007 **Fx:**788-0367
(212) 355-6182 .. **Becker,** Laurie J '83 %EP Dine Inc -115 E 57th -NY 10022 **Fx:**755-8486
(718) 935-2720 .. **Becker,** Lawr E '80 %Bd of Educ -65 Court -Brklyn 11201
(518) 462-5814 .. **Becker,** Lawr E '80 (Becker & B) -148 Central Av Bx575 -Albany 12201 **Fx:**462-6836
(212) 374-6741 .. **Becker,** Lisa M '96 %NYC Dept Educ-OLS -52 Chmbrs -NY 10007 **Fx:**374-5596
(212) 891-9100 .. **Becker,** Marc J '84 (Goldfarb & F LLP) -345 Park Av -NY 10154
(800) 890-3090 .. **Becker,** Marc S '98 Jacoby & M,LLP -600 Old Cntry Rd -Gdn Cty 11530
(315) 437-4400 .. **Becker,** Marcella Zimmerman '91 -3333 James -Syracuse 13206
(718) 233-6480 .. **Becker,** Margaret A '06 %Leg Srvcs for NY -36 Richmond Ter -Staten Isl 10301
(212) 521-4430 .. **Becker Meisel LLC** -590 Mad Av -NY 10022 **Fx:**521-4431
(212) 336-2000 .. **Becker,** Michl A '05 %Patterson BW&T LLP -1133 Av of Amer -NY 10036
(212) 599-5799 .. **Becker,** Michl C '03 %Rutherford & C LLP -369 Lex Av -NY 10017
(212) 608-1808 .. **Becker,** Murray '79 -305 Bway -NY 10007 **Fx:**732-2191
(718) 875-1300 .. **Becker,** Patricia E '02 %Appllt Div 2nd Dept -45 Monroe Pl -Brklyn 11201 **Fx:**858-2446
(716) 854-0700 .. **Becker,** Paul B '99 %J Feroleto -438 Main -Buffalo 14202 **Fx:**854-0265
(845) 639-1130 .. **Becker,** Paul L '76 -6 Larkspur Ct -New Cty 10956 **Fx:**639-1062
(212) 723-3634 .. **Becker,** Philip H '79 Citigrp -250 West -NY 10013
(212) 599-3322 .. **Becker Poliakoff, LLP** -45 Bway -NY 10006 **Fx:**557-0295
(212) 226-2100 .. **Becker,** Richd C '95 OfCnsl Caesar & N -350 Bway -NY 10013
(212) 813-5900 .. **Becker,** Robt A '86 Cnsl Fross ZL&Z,PC -866 UN Plz -NY 10017
(212) 752-3380 .. **Becker,** Robt D '68 (Becker & D,PC) -880 3rd Av -NY 10022 **Fx:**593-3807
(212) 732-1200 .. **Becker,** Robt D '73 (Ginsberg B&W) -26 Bway -NY 10004
(212) 732-5400 .. **Becker,** Robt L '68 (Raff & B,LLP) -470 Park Av S -NY 10016
(212) 697-2310 .. **Becker Ross LLP** -317 Mad Av -NY 10017 **Fx:**490-0720
(212) 309-1000 .. **Becker,** Ryan A '03 %Hunton & W -200 Park Av -NY 10166
(212) 225-2000 .. **Becker,** Ryan T '08 %Cleary GS&H -1 Lbrty Plz -NY 10006
(716) 845-6000 .. **Becker,** Scott C '94 %Kavinoky C LLP -726 Exchange -Buffalo 14210
(518) 402-2134 .. **Becker,** Stephen A '03 NYS DMV Appeals Bd -6 ESP -Albany 12228
(516) 328-5123 .. **Becker,** Steven B '83 %Canon USA -1 Canon Plz -Lk Success 11042
(212) 626-4100 .. **Becker,** Steven H '81 (Baker & M LLP) -1114 Av of Amer -NY 10036
(212) 309-1000 .. **Becker,** Steven H '98 (Hunton & W) -200 Park Av -NY 10166
(212) 249-6038 .. **Becker,** Steven R '77 -215 E 68th -NY 10065
(212) 872-1000 .. **Becker,** Timothy J '06 -One Bryant Park -NY 10036 **Fx:**872-1002
(716) 753-4241 .. **Beckerink,** Laurie M '06 %DA -Cnty Cthse -Mayvll 14757 **Fx:**753-4628
(212) 589-4200 .. **Beckerlegge,** Robertson D '01 %Baker & H LLP -45 Rckfllr Plz -NY 10111
(585) 546-6010 .. **Beckerman,** Gerald '56 (Beckerman & B) -1 W Main -Rchstr 14614 **Fx:**546-7035
(212) 509-9400 .. **Beckerman,** Jason L '00 (Cozen O) -45 Bway Atrium -NY 10006
(646) 619-9810 .. **Beckerman,** Murray '52 -260 Mad Av -NY 10016 **Fx:**(212) 448-0066
(718) 544-3434 .. **Beckerman,** Ray '79 R Beckerman,PC -108-18 Qns Blvd -Frst Hlls 11375 **Fx:**559-6584
(516) 489-6100 .. **Beckerman,** Richd E '08 %Posner & G -215 Hilton Av Bx1200 -Hempstd 11551
(585) 546-6010 .. **Beckerman,** Steven M '84 (Beckerman & B) -1 W Main -Rchstr 14614 **Fx:**546-7035
(212) 391-8045 .. **Beckerman,** Stuart J '85 (Slater & B LLP) -61 Bway -NY 10006 **Fx:**391-8047
(845) 639-1636 .. **Beckerman,** Warren S '83 -30 Woodhvn Dr -New Cty 10956
(212) 872-1000 .. **Beckerman-Stenlake,** Lisa G '89 -One Bryant Park -NY 10036 **Fx:**872-1002
(315) 942-6116 .. **Beckert,** Karin Moore '93 -4 Main Bx216 -Boonvll 13309 **Fx:**942-6130
(212) 788-8681 .. **Becker-Zigodny,** Vicki S '09 %Law Dept -350 Jay -Brklyn 11201 **Fx:**(718) 222-2373
(212) 931-2708 .. **Beckett,** Deirdre C '88 LVMH Moet -19 E 57th -NY 10022 **Fx:**931-2729
(516) 463-6065 .. **Beckett,** Kathleen M '76 %Hofstra Law Schl -121 Hofstra Univ -Hempstd 11549
(212) 906-1200 .. **Beckett,** Mark D '88 (Latham & W) -885 3rd Av -NY 10022
(212) 577-3348 .. **Beckford,** Howard C '10 %Leg Aid -199 Water -NY 10038
(212) 788-7020 .. **Beckford,** Julene E '07 City Cncl Govt Affrs Div -250 Bway -NY 10007
(212) 858-1000 .. **Beckford-Young,** Tameka M '09 %Pillsbury WSP LLP -1540 Bway -NY 10036
(212) 506-5000 .. **Becking,** Laura Lee '03 OfCnsl Orrick H&S LLP -51 W 52nd -NY 10019
(212) 415-3300 .. **Beckler,** Andrew J '97 %WF Realty LLC -437 Mad Av -NY 10022
(917) 596-1917 .. **Beckler,** Laurence B '95 L Beckler,PLLC -575 Mad Av -NY 10022 **Fx:**(212) 504-2820
(212) 704-6327 .. **Beckler-Knoll,** Bryna R '91 -405 Lex Av -NY 10174
(212) 836-8000 .. **Beckles,** Tricia M '09 %Kaye S LLP -425 Park Av -NY 10022
(212) 596-9000 .. **Beckman,** Amy L '05 %Ropes & G LLP -1211 Av of Amer -NY 10036
(212) 218-2100 .. **Beckman,** Christopher V '05 %Fitzpatrick CH&S -1290 Av of Amer -NY 10104
(716) 326-3401 .. **Beckman,** John W '79 -98 S Portage -Westfld 14787
(212) 608-3500 .. **Beckman Lieberman & Barandes LLP** -116 John -NY 10038 **Fx:**608-9687
(315) 471-8111 .. **Beckman,** Marc S '95 (Scolaro SCF&B,PC) -507 Plum -Syracuse 13204
(212) 836-8000 .. **Beckman,** Mark A '95 %Kaye S LLP -425 Park Av -NY 10022
(212) 608-3500 .. **Beckman,** Michl '69 (Beckman L&B LLP) -116 John -NY 10038
(212) 808-4848 .. **Beckmann,** Bruce H '73 (Beckmann & Assoc LLC) -90 Park Av -NY 10016 **Fx:**986-4939
(212) 902-0542 .. **Beckmann,** Deborah R '92 Goldman Sachs -180 Maiden Ln -NY 10038
(516) 485-4888 .. **Beckmann,** Jeanne Marie '94 -64 Hilton Av -Hempstd 11550 **Fx:**485-1588
(716) 664-2346 .. **Beckstrom,** Chas G '71 OfCnsl Lundberg & G,LLP -202 W 4th -Jamestwn 14701
(607) 962-6885 .. **Becraft,** Chas D Jr. '67 -135 Cedar -Corning 14830 **Fx:**962-1810
(212) 465-5000 .. **Becton,** Donya-Gaye M '04 %Parsons Brinckerhoff -1 Penn Plz -NY 10119
(212) 735-3000 .. **Bedard,** Julie '02 Cnsl Skadden ASM&F LLP -4 Times Sq -NY 10036
(718) 237-5500 .. **Bedard,** Nancy '92 Leg Srvcs -105 Court -Brklyn 11201 **Fx:**855-0733
(315) 466-7161 .. **Bedard-Suddaby,** Judy '92 %Ct of Claims -205 S Salina -Syracuse 13202 **Fx:**466-7164
(212) 442-4900 .. **Beddoe,** Suzanne Alana '94 Ofc Admin Trials -40 Rector -NY 10006 **Fx:**442-4947
(516) 463-6079 .. **Bedell,** Amy E '03 %Hofstra Law Schl -121 Hofstra Univ -Hempstd 11549
(212) 880-1200 .. **Bedell,** Christopher J '77 %Chicago Title/Ticor -711 3rd Av -NY 10017 **Fx:**880-1400
(212) 450-4000 .. **Bedell,** Laureen F '78 (Davis P&W LLP) -450 Lex Av -NY 10017
(212) 461-2143 .. **Bedell,** Michl A '01 (Bedell & F LLP) -44 Wall -NY 10005 **Fx:**(646) 219-7441
(518) 873-9540 .. **Bedell,** Reginald H '99 -8 Williams Bx485 -Elizabethtwn 12932 **Fx:**873-9533
(716) 855-5710 .. **Bedenko,** Alan J '95 %J Quackenbush Jr -60 Lakefront Blvd -Buffalo 14202 **Fx:**855-5722
(212) 818-9600 .. **Bederka,** Anne C '94 (Greenfield S&S,LLP) -600 3rd Av -NY 10016
(212) 808-4000 .. **Bederman,** Steve M '81 Moinian Grp -530 5th Av -NY 10036

(212) 803-1293 .. **Bederow,** Mark A '99 -260 Mad Av -NY 10016 **Fx:**448-0066
(718) 738-1494 .. **Bedesi,** Nan K '86 -122-09 Lbrty Av -S Richmond Hll 11419
(718) 250-2000 .. **Bedford,** Amy E '04 %DA -350 Jay -Brklyn 11201 **Fx:**250-2314
(212) 705-7000 .. **Bedford,** Scott H '06 %Bingham M LLP -399 Park Av -NY 10022
(212) 994-0260 .. **Bedi,** Kuljyott Kaur '05 %Cornicello T&B-C,LLP -2 Wall -NY 10005
(718) 802-2790 .. **Bediako,** Kafui A '07 ACS-Legal -330 Jay -Brklyn 11201
(914) 948-2222 .. **Bedke,** Kathryn L '80 (Rabin P&H) -44 Church -White Plns 10601 **Fx:**948-2255
(212) 287-3200 .. **Bednar,** Andrew T '95 Perella Weinberg Prtnrs -767 5th Av -NY 10153 **Fx:**287-3201
(212) 326-2000 .. **Bednark,** B Andrew '03 Cnsl O'Melveny & M LLP -7 Times Sq -NY 10036
(917) 566-3493 .. **Bednark,** Katie Hughes '03 -121 Pacific -Brklyn 11201
(315) 435-2470 .. **Bednarski,** Christopher J '97 %DA -505 S State -Syracuse 13202 **Fx:**435-3969
(917) 847-3452 .. **Bedolis,** Audrey H '96 -215 W 78th -NY 10024
(212) 808-7800 .. **Bedoya,** Jennifer '07 %Kelley D&W LLP -101 Park Av -NY 10178
(914) 517-5000 .. **Bedwell-Coll,** Rebecca '09 %Meiselman DPC&E,PC -1311 Mamaroneck Av -White Plns 10605
(516) 746-5599 .. **Bee,** Peter A '77 (Bee RFH&D,LLP) -170 Old Cntry Rd -Mineola 11501
(516) 746-5599 .. **Bee Ready Fishbein Hatter & Donovan,LLP** -170 Old Cntry Rd -Mineola 11501 **Fx:**746-1045
(212) 373-3000 .. **Bee,** Satyam N '09 %Paul WRW&G LLP -1285 Av of Amer -NY 10019
(518) 487-5370 .. **Beebe,** Laura Oakley '89 %Hon T Breslin -16 Eagle -Albany 12207
(518) 373-1500 .. **Beebe,** Robt L '70 -514 Vischers Ferry Rd -Clifton Pk 12065 **Fx:**373-0030
(212) 980-0120 .. **Beeber,** Jessie F '96 (Frankfurt KK&S,PC) -488 Mad Av -NY 10022
(516) 433-8882 .. **Beeber,** Paul S '70 PS Beeber -130 Newbrdg Rd -Hicksvll 11801 **Fx:**433-8932
(845) 225-8851 .. **Beece,** Cheryl K '06 -138 Nimham Rd -Carmel 10512
(716) 847-8400 .. **Beecher,** Holly A '98 (Phillips L LLP) -3400 HSBC Ctr -Buffalo 14203
(212) 709-8367 .. **Beecher,** Robt '75 -110 Wall -NY 10005 **Fx:**(908) 771-0095
(914) 948-6050 .. **Beecher,** Roxanne Torres '83 -175 Main -White Plns 10601
(716) 847-8400 .. **Beecher,** Thos R Jr. '59 Cnsl Phillips L LLP -3400 HSBC Ctr -Buffalo 14203
(212) 703-2135 .. **Beechert,** Scott V '94 Venor Capital Mgmt -7 Times Sq -NY 10036
(212) 588-2176 .. **Beede,** Steven A '91 Centerline Holding Co -625 Mad Av -NY 10022
(718) 738-8888 .. **Beeharrilall,** Gerald '85 -104-15 123rd -S Richmond Hll 11419 **Fx:**843-4606
(607) 772-0360 .. **Beehm,** Robt S '90 -80 Court -Bnghmtn 13901 **Fx:**722-2842
(212) 909-6000 .. **Beeken,** Timothy K '92 Cnsl Debevoise & P LLP -919 3rd Av -NY 10022
(212) 557-7439 .. **Beekman,** Bernadette '83 -5 Tudor City Pl -NY 10017 **Fx:**973-9073
(516) 833-5630 .. **Beekman,** Jonathan D '03 (Beekman SK&L,LLP) -1050 Franklin Av -Gdn Cty 11530
(212) 351-4500 .. **Beekman,** Melissa J '03 %Epstein B&G,PC -250 Park Av -NY 10177
(516) 833-5630 .. **Beekman Schwartz Kaufman & Livoti, LLP** -1050 Franklin Av -Gdn Cty 11530 **Fx:**833-5631
(212) 909-6000 .. **Beekman,** Wm B '81 (Debevoise & P LLP) -919 3rd Av -NY 10022
(800) 358-2550 .. **Beeler,** Harold B '75 NAM -990 Stewart Av -Gdn Cty 11530
(212) 371-3300 .. **Beeler,** Joel I '70 -460 Park Av -NY 10022
(212) 841-1000 .. **Beeler,** Martin E '03 %Covington & B LLP -620 8th Av -NY 10018
(212) 894-7200 .. **Beemer,** Jonathan H '99 %Entwistle & C LLP -280 Park Av -NY 10017
(845) 291-2050 .. **Beemer,** Tanja M '09 %DA -255 275 Main -Goshen 10924 **Fx:**291-2085
(212) 998-6223 .. **Been,** Vicki L '84 %NYU Law Schl -40 Wshngtn Sq S -NY 10012 **Fx:**995-4341
(212) 558-4000 .. **Beeney,** Garrard R '80 (Sullivan & C LLP) -125 Broad -NY 10004
(212) 503-2157 .. **Beeney,** Marisa Janel '98 GSO Cptl Prtnr -280 Park Av -NY 10017
(212) 906-1200 .. **Beer,** Caitlin Pettit '10 %Latham & W -885 3rd Av -NY 10022
(212) 701-3000 .. **Beer,** Janet A '93 %Cahill G&R LLP -80 Pine -NY 10005 **Fx:**269-5420
(516) 569-4107 .. **Beer,** Michl E '92 -570 Longacre Av -Woodmere 11598 **Fx:**569-5136
(718) 938-0013 .. **Beer,** Omar L '05 -448 14th -Brklyn 11215
(212) 801-9294 .. **Beer,** Steven C '87 (Greenberg T,LLP) -200 Park Av -NY 10166
(212) 538-5385 .. **Beer,** Wendy '92 Credit Suisse -11 Mad Av -NY 10010
(212) 474-1000 .. **Beerbower,** John E '75 (Cravath S&M LLP) -825 8th Av -NY 10019
(212) 326-2000 .. **Beeri,** Doron '07 %O'Melveny & M LLP -7 Times Sq -NY 10036
(516) 327-4600 .. **Beerman,** Alen R '77 (Roseman BB LLP) -3000 Marcus Av -Lk Success 11042
(718) 250-2000 .. **Beerman,** Audra M '07 %DA -350 Jay -Brklyn 11201 **Fx:**250-2314
(212) 490-6600 .. **Beerman & Deutsch LLP** -122 E 42nd -NY 10168 **Fx:**983-5276
(212) 867-6000 .. **Beerman,** Hal N '03 %Rosenberg & E,PC -733 3rd Av -NY 10017
(212) 490-6600 .. **Beerman,** Robt L '62 (Beerman & D LLP) -122 E 42nd -NY 10168
(212) 335-9238 .. **Beermann,** Barbara A '90 %DA -1 Hogan Pl -NY 10013
(212) 360-3097 .. **Beermann,** Christopher M '82 Triborough Bridge & Tunnel Auth -Robert Moses Bldg -NY 10035
(212) 259-8000 .. **Beers,** Emily K '09 %Dewey & L LLP -1301 Av of Amer -NY 10019
(631) 368-8840 .. **Beers,** Henry S Jr. '91 -41 Bunkerhill Dr -Huntngtn 11743 **Fx:**261-2870
(585) 238-2000 .. **Beers,** Richd M Jr. '85 (Phillips L LLP) -1400 First Fed Plz -Rchstr 14614
(631) 698-7794 .. **Beers,** Robt Chas '75 -3 Linden -Selden 11784 **Fx:**736-7344
(516) 359-6859 .. **Beers,** Sharyn '04 S Beers,PC -119 Hrbr Rd -Cold Spg Hbr 11724
(212) 335-9000 .. **Beesch,** Wm O'Brien '98 %DA -1 Hogan Pl -NY 10013
(845) 534-4960 .. **Beesecker,** L A '77 -246 Main -Cornwall 12518 **Fx:**534-0378
(212) 882-5638 .. **Beeson,** Reba A '84 UBS -51 W 52nd -NY 10019
(212) 537-2448 .. **Beeson,** W Gary '94 Morgan Stanley -1633 Bway -NY 10019
(212) 772-8434 .. **Begelfer,** Constance A '82 -530 E 76th -NY 10021
(212) 382-0909 .. **Begg,** Gregory R '91 (Peckar & A,PC) -41 Mad Av -NY 10154
(212) 483-2323 .. **Beggs,** John F '96 %JP Morgan Chase & Co -345 Park Av -NY 10154
(212) 350-2700 .. **Begleiter,** Robt L '73 (Constantine C,PC) -450 Lex Av -NY 10017
(212) 435-3571 .. **Begley,** James M '75 %Port Auth of NY/NJ -225 Park Av S -NY 10003 **Fx:**435-3555
(718) 250-2000 .. **Begley,** Jamie R '07 %DA -350 Jay -Brklyn 11201 **Fx:**250-2314
(212) 297-5800 .. **Begley,** Kristine Russo '08 %Day P LLP -7 Times Sq -NY 10036
(212) 909-6000 .. **Begley,** Louis '60 SrCnsl Debevoise & P LLP -919 3rd Av -NY 10022
(516) 248-1895 .. **Begley,** Maria DeMarco '78 OfCnsl Franchina & G,PC -1100 Franklin Av -Gdn Cty 11530
(212) 705-7000 .. **Beglin,** Brian D '79 (Bingham M LLP) -399 Park Av -NY 10022
(914) 961-4441 .. **Begos Horgan & Brown LLP** -7 Pondfld Rd Bx369 -Bronxvll 10708 **Fx:**961-4442
(914) 961-4441 .. **Begos,** Patrick W '88 (Begos H&B LLP) -7 Pondfld Rd Bx369 -Bronxvll 10708
(516) 812-4500 .. **Beh,** Han Sheng '10 %Stagg TC&W LLP -401 Franklin Av -Gdn Cty 11530
(212) 868-3611 .. **Beh,** Lea L '04 -350 5th Av -NY 10118
(212) 571-0550 .. **Beha,** James A II '76 (Allegaert B&V LLP) -111 Bway -NY 10006
(212) 373-3000 .. **Beha,** James J '07 %Paul WRW&G LLP -1285 Av of Amer -NY 10019
(212) 732-3200 .. **Behan,** Edmund J '83 (Carter L&M LLP) -2 Wall -NY 10005
(914) 766-1684 .. **Behan,** Wm A Jr. '80 IBM -294 Route 100 -Somers 10589 **Fx:**766-1869
(212) 687-3000 .. **Behar,** Deric M '09 %Jaffe & A,LLP -600 3rd Av -NY 10016
(516) 746-5360 .. **Behar,** Ilene J '92 (Hoffman & B LLP) -94 Second -Mineola 11501
(631) 650-1200 .. **Behar,** Jarrett M '01 %Sinnreich K&M LLP -267 Carleton Av -Central Islip 11722
(212) 242-0500 .. **Behar,** Leon I '83 (L Behar,PC) -347 5th Av -NY 10016 **Fx:**242-0518
(212) 735-3000 .. **Behar,** Scott A '09 %Skadden ASM&F LLP -4 Times Sq -NY 10036
(646) 300-7200 .. **Behin,** Shahram D '01 Developer Grp LLC -115 E 23rd -NY 10010
(212) 696-6000 .. **Behmke,** Peter J '05 %Curtis M-PC&M LLP -101 Park Av -NY 10178
(631) 581-9494 .. **Behmoiram,** Claudia L '93 %Ferro KMS,PC -350 Motor Pkwy -Hauppauge 11788
(212) 752-9700 .. **Behnam,** Rostin '08 %Gersten S LLP -600 Lex Av -NY 10022
(518) 689-1450 .. **Behnke,** Heather P '99 %Greenberg T,LLP -54 State -Albany 12207
(607) 778-2117 .. **Behnke,** Robt G III '82 (Cnty Atty) -Cnty Ofc Bldg Bx1766 -Bnghmtn 13902 **Fx:**778-6122
(212) 210-9479 .. **Behr,** Alan '80 (Alston & B LLP) -90 Park Av -NY 10016
(212) 385-8088 .. **Behr,** James E '98 %Tsoi & Assoc -277 Bway -NY 10007 **Fx:**385-1887
(716) 856-1300 .. **Behr,** Laurence D '82 (Barth SB) -43 Court -Buffalo 14202
(212) 490-3000 .. **Behr,** Wm H '97 OfCnsl Wilson EME&D LLP -150 E 42nd -NY 10017
(212) 427-0677 .. **Behren,** Roderick J '89 (Behren & S) -185 E 85th -NY 10028 **Fx:**427-6414
(914) 741-5600 .. **Behren,** Roy D '87 %Wstchstr Cptl Mgt -100 Summit Lk Dr -Valhalla 10595
(212) 351-4000 .. **Behrendt,** John T '89 (Gibson D&C LLP) -200 Park Av -NY 10166
(212) 259-8000 .. **Behrens,** Jason L '06 %Dewey & L LLP -1301 Av of Amer -NY 10019
(212) 807-2813 .. **Behrens,** Kersten '95 %Thomson Reuters/RIA -195 Bway -NY 10007
(212) 310-8000 .. **Behrens,** Layne S '08 %Weil G&M LLP -767 5th Av -NY 10153
(212) 859-8000 .. **Behrens,** Matthew H '05 %Fried FHS&J LLP -1 NY Plz -NY 10004
(631) 283-7566 .. **Behringer,** Thos E Jr. '59 (Behringer & B) -71 Hill Bx5077 -Southampton 11969 **Fx:**283-4402
(631) 283-7566 .. **Behringer,** Thos E III '92 (Behringer & B) -71 Hill Bx5077 -Southampton 11969 **Fx:**283-4402
(718) 447-5540 .. **Behrins,** Bruce G '66 (Behrins & B,PC) -1 Edgewtr Plz -Staten Isl 10305 **Fx:**816-5483
(718) 447-5540 .. **Behrins,** Jonathan B '92 (Behrins & B,PC) -1 Edgewtr Plz -Staten Isl 10305 **Fx:**816-5483
(212) 957-9000 .. **Behrle,** Sandra G '74 (Cooper B&B,PC) -331 Mad Av -NY 10017
(212) 918-3000 .. **Behrman,** Andrew M '00 OfCnsl Hogan L LLP -875 3rd Av -NY 10022
(212) 490-3000 .. **Behrmann,** Thos '03 %Wilson EME&D LLP -150 E 42nd -NY 10017
(646) 473-6060 .. **Behroozi,** Mitra '87 1199 SEIU Natl Benefit Fund -330 W 42nd -NY 10036
(518) 474-9779 .. **Behuniak,** Jeanine D '95 %OTDA -40 N Pearl -Albany 12243 **Fx:**474-9389
(212) 975-7932 .. **Behuniak,** Julie B '91 CBS Corp -51 W 52nd -NY 10019
(518) 457-2070 .. **Behuniak,** Nicholas A '95 %Dept of Tax & Fin -Bldg 9 State Campus -Albany 12227 **Fx:**457-6131
(212) 986-1200 .. **Beier,** Carol Weiss '97 %Gordon HR&C LLP -355 Lex Av -NY 10017
(718) 779-5000 .. **Beier,** David L '78 -54-11 Qns Blvd -Woodside 11377 **Fx:**779-4645
(212) 336-2000 .. **Beier,** Jill Choate '06 %Patterson BW&T LLP -1133 Av of Amer -NY 10036
(516) 572-6908 .. **Beier,** Michele N '85 %Nassau Univ Med Ctr -2201 Hempstd Tpk -E Meadow 11554 **Fx:**572-0160
(212) 949-9022 .. **Beier,** Norman S '49 OfCnsl Abelman F&S -666 3rd Av -NY 10017
(212) 521-5400 .. **Beiersdorf,** Oliver K '98 (Reed S LLP) -599 Lex Av -NY 10022
(631) 231-7725 .. **Beige,** Jack S '94 -200 Motor Pkwy -Hauppauge 11788
(212) 779-1414 .. **Beige,** Jos R '96 Bernstein L LLP -10 E 40th -NY 10016
(212) 779-1414 .. **Beige,** Stephanie M '01 %Bernstein L LLP -10 E 40th -NY 10016
(212) 230-1300 .. **Beigelman,** Mark L '91 (Beigelman F&F,PC) -100 Wall -NY 10005 **Fx:**230-1090
(212) 548-2100 .. **Beil,** Marshall '72 (McGuire W LLP) -1345 Av of Amer -NY 10105
(212) 490-2700 .. **Beilis,** Shlomo A '76 (Beilis & P) -213 W 35th -NY 10001
(212) 659-7300 .. **Beim,** Aaron M '07 %Haynes & B,LLP -1221 Av of Amer -NY 10020
(212) 237-1000 .. **Beimfohr,** Douglas A '88 (Windels ML&M,LLP) -156 W 56th -NY 10019
(212) 237-1000 .. **Beimfohr,** Edw G '59 (Windels ML&M,LLP) -156 W 56th -NY 10019
(716) 631-3001 .. **Beimler,** Mary Beth '99 %Independent Hlth -511 Farber Lks Dr -Buffalo 14221 **Fx:**635-3838
(914) 779-0341 .. **Bein,** Joan C '81 -165 LaSalle Dr -Ynkrs 10710 **Fx:**337-3025
(212) 416-8460 .. **Bein,** Philip M '91 %Dept of Law -120 Bway -NY 10271
(212) 837-6000 .. **Beinecke,** Candace K '71 (Hughes H&R LLP) -1 Bttry Pk Plz -NY 10004

(718) 261-1100 .. **Beinert**, Jennifer L '98 (Fein & B,LLP) -80-02 Kew Grdns Rd -Kew Gdns 11415 **Fx:**575-9842
(718) 921-6601 .. **Beinert**, Thaniel J '96 -155 Bay Ridge Av -Brklyn 11220 **Fx:**921-6609
(973) 642-1307 .. **Beinfield**, Robt H '86 (Hawkins D&W LLP) -One Chase Manh Plz -NY 10005 **Fx:**642-6773
(716) 204-1055 .. **Beinhauer**, Chas W '77 (Pfalzgraf B&M LLP) -455 Cayuga Rd -Buffalo 14225 **Fx:**204-1080
(516) 747-9744 .. **Beinin**, Wm J '69 (Herman & B) -200 Willis Av -Mineola 11501
(212) 530-5000 .. **Beirne**, Andrew T '96 %Milbank TH&M LLP -1 Chase Manh Plz -NY 10005
(212) 558-4000 .. **Beirne**, B Logan '09 %Sullivan & C LLP -125 Broad -NY 10004
(518) 474-6915 .. **Beirne**, Eidin '81 %Dept of Law -The Cptl -Albany 12224
(845) 634-9225 .. **Beirne**, John P '86 -84 Havermill Rd -New Cty 10956
(212) 632-5500 .. **Beirne**, Kristina E '04 Cnsl Salans LLP -620 5th Av -NY 10020
(914) 681-0200 .. **Beirne**, Thos R '67 (DelBello DWW&W,LLP) -1 N Lex Av -White Plns 10601
(845) 340-0227 .. **Beisel**, John K '92 -1 N Front Bx3657 -Kingston 12402 **Fx:**338-0868
(845) 486-6800 .. **Beisner**, Ralph A '68 OfCnsl McCabe & M LLP -63 Wshngtn Bx509 -Poughkeepsie 12602
(212) 773-1718 .. **Beispel**, Steven '83 Gala Resources -1212 Av of Amer -NY 10036
(212) 661-9100 .. **Beitel**, Bernard '55 OfCnsl Otterbourg SH&R,PC -230 Park Av -NY 10169
(718) 222-2030 .. **Beitelman**, Pamela R '07 %Law Dept -350 Jay -Brklyn 11201 **Fx:**222-2088
(716) 566-5400 .. **Beiter**, Sean P '92 (Goldberg S LLP) -665 Main -Buffalo 14203
(212) 685-8300 .. **Beit-Halachmy**, Ron '98 -4 E 28th -NY 10016
(516) 488-3300 .. **Beitler**, Jeffrey R '03 %Shaub AC&S,LLP -1983 Marcus Av -Lk Success 11042
(212) 449-4974 .. **Beitler**, Richd I '89 %Merrill Lynch -220 Bway -NY 10038
(718) 624-1084 .. **Beitner**, Leo D '76 %S Rubenstein,PC -26 Court -Brklyn 11242 **Fx:**624-1980
(718) 408-1620 .. **Bejarano**, Mary Lency '00 -118-21 Qns Blvd -Frst Hlls 11375 **Fx:**261-9302
(212) 269-4900 .. **Beke**, David A '94 (Ford MEW&G,LLP) -Wall Street Plz -NY 10005
(212) 755-5510 .. **Bekele**, Danl '92 (Loeb B & Prtnrs) -505 Park Av -NY 10022
(516) 932-0151 .. **Bekerman**, Marc S '93 M Bekerman -Bx365 -Woodbury 11797 **Fx:**(800) 635-9834
(646) 674-2000 .. **Bekerman**, Matthew D '96 Liquidnet Holdings -498 7th Av -NY 10018
(516) 932-0151 .. **Bekerman**, Philip '64 OfCnsl M Bekerman -Bx365 -Woodbury 11797 **Fx:**(800) 635-9834
(212) 554-2645 .. **Bekian**, John '05 Daylight Forensic & Advisory LLC -1 Rckfllr Plz -NY 10020
(212) 608-1900 .. **Bekier**, James M '03 %Lovell SH LLP -61 Bway -NY 10006
(212) 808-0700 .. **Bekker**, Karen '02 %Norris M&M,PA -875 3rd Av -NY 10022
(212) 223-4000 .. **Bekker**, Pieter H F '92 (Crowell & M LLP) -590 Mad Av -NY 10022
(212) 455-2000 .. **Bekkerus**, Ryan R '02 %Simpson T&B LLP -425 Lex Av -NY 10017
(516) 408-3666 .. **Bekoff**, Ronald J '69 (Hession BC&L,LLP) -1103 Stewart Av -Gdn Cty 11530
(516) 742-8055 .. **Bekritsky**, Bruce R '74 -1551 Kellum Pl -Mineola 11501 **Fx:**294-5035
(212) 859-8000 .. **Beky**, Frederique '04 %Fried FHS&J LLP -1 NY Plz -NY 10004
(646) 471-1268 .. **Bel**, Maria J '03 %PricewaterhouseCoopers LLP -300 Mad Av -NY 10017 **Fx:**(813) 329-2242
(212) 344-3900 .. **Belair & Evans LLP** -61 Bway -NY 10006 **Fx:**514-6661
(212) 344-3900 .. **Belair**, Raymond W '74 (Belair & E LLP) -61 Bway -NY 10006
(914) 627-3000 .. **Belanger**, Elizabeth L '01 Diversified Invstmnt Advsrs -440 Mamaroneck Av -Harrison 10528
(212) 735-3000 .. **Belanger**, John H '09 %Skadden ASM&F LLP -4 Times Sq -NY 10036
(585) 325-5150 .. **Belanger**, Matthew F '91 (Faraci L,LLP) -28 E Main -Rchstr 14614
(212) 325-2000 .. **Belani**, Aarthi Kumar '05 Credit Suisse -1 Mad Av -NY 10010
(212) 269-1600 .. **Belani**, Akshay Nand '05 %Teigland-Hunt LLP -127 W 24th -NY 10011 **Fx:**269-1580
(631) 234-8234 .. **Belano**, Danl '98 -93 Wheeler Rd -Central Islip 11722 **Fx:**234-8754
(212) 310-2184 .. **Belasco**, Steven R '71 %Colgate-Palmolive -300 Park Av -NY 10022
(212) 681-1575 .. **Belasky**, Bryan D '96 (Belluck & F LLP) -546 5th Av -NY 10036
(718) 658-0500 .. **Belatsky**, Chester D '74 %Law Dept -151-20 Jamaica Av -Jamaica 11432 **Fx:**658-4025
(212) 852-1876 .. **Belaya**, Marina '03 Bank of America -114 W 47th -NY 10036
(212) 446-7000 .. **Belbusti**, John M '97 %McKinsey & Co -55 E 52nd -NY 10055 **Fx:**688-9521
(212) 788-2932 .. **Belcamino**, Gregory R '90 Ofc of Envrnmntl Coordination -100 Gold -NY 10038 **Fx:**788-2941
(631) 853-4104 .. **Belcastro**, Luigi A '08 %DA -400 Carleton Av Bx9082 -Central Islip 11722 **Fx:**853-7838
(212) 259-8000 .. **Belcher**, Aaron P '09 %Dewey & L LLP -1301 Av of Amer -NY 10019
(716) 743-9052 .. **Belczak**, Michl R '78 -1321 Harvard Av -N Tonawanda 14120 **Fx:**693-5617
(716) 284-0408 .. **Belden**, Willard N Jr. '59 -2706 Pine Av Bx2106 -Niagara Fls 14301
(212) 479-6000 .. **Beldner**, James A '74 (Cooley LLP) -1114 Av of Amer -NY 10036
(845) 267-4878 .. **Beldock**, Gerald J '55 OfCnsl Birbrower & B,PC -151 N Main -New Cty 10956
(800) 776-2060 .. **Beldock**, Howard N '53 -825 E Gate Blvd -Gdn Cty 11530 **Fx:**(516) 222-0726
(212) 490-0400 .. **Beldock Levine & Hoffman LLP** -99 Park Av -NY 10016 **Fx:**557-0565
(212) 277-5820 .. **Beldock**, Myron '58 (Beldock L&H LLP) -99 Park Av -NY 10016
(845) 267-4878 .. **Beldock**, Steven H '87 (Birbrower & B,PC) -151 N Main -New Cty 10956
(914) 287-0100 .. **Belefant**, Martin S '56 -2 William -White Plns 10601 **Fx:**287-0500
(914) 287-0100 .. **Belefant**, Peter T '86 -2 William -White Plns 10601 **Fx:**287-0500
(212) 474-1000 .. **Belelieu**, Christopher D '07 %Cravath S&M LLP -825 8th Av -NY 10019
(347) 404-9133 .. **Belen**, Joan E '83 %Civil Ct -141 Lvngstn -Brklyn 11201 **Fx:**(718) 643-3733
(718) 621-6611 .. **Belenitsky**, Olga '02 (O Belenitsky,PC) -3042 Ocean Av -Brklyn 11235 **Fx:**621-6613
(212) 326-3939 .. **Belenky**, Andrey '07 %Jones D -222 E 41st -NY 10017
(516) 328-2300 .. **Belesi**, John M '98 (Abrams FFEGF&E,LLP) -1111 Marcus Av -Lk Success 11042
(212) 732-8700 .. **Belessis**, Stephen J '00 %McAloon & F,PC -123 William -NY 10038
(516) 482-1970 .. **Belfer**, Andrew B '80 %Belfer Realty Dvlpmnt -80 Cuttermill Rd -Gt Neck 11021 **Fx:**482-6921
(212) 644-2200 .. **Belfer**, Laurence D '93 %Belco Oil & Gas Corp -767 5th Av -NY 10153 **Fx:**644-2230
(212) 432-9089 .. **Belfer**, Linda M '82 -375 South End Av -NY 10280
(212) 592-1400 .. **Belfi**, Catherine '10 %Herrick,F LLP -2 Park Av -NY 10016
(212) 907-0700 .. **Belfi**, Eric J '96 (Labaton S LLP) -140 Bway -NY 10005
(631) 862-8600 .. **Belford**, John L Jr. '69 (Bijesse & B) -217 Lk Av -St James 11780
(631) 231-2424 .. **Belford**, John L IV '95 %Dept of Law -300 Motor Pkwy -Hauppauge 11788 **Fx:**435-4757
(631) 665-4400 .. **Belford**, Michl K '73 -26 Saxon Av -Bay Shr 11706 **Fx:**665-6297
(212) 698-3500 .. **Belford**, Richd D '71 (Dechert LLP) -1095 Av of Amer -NY 10036
(212) 264-8819 .. **Belford**, Timothy C '98 Social Security Admin -26 Fed Plz -NY 10278
(212) 790-4500 .. **Belfort**, Robt '88 (Manatt P&P,LLP) -7 Times Sq -NY 10036
(212) 558-4000 .. **Belger**, James M '09 %Sullivan & C LLP -125 Broad -NY 10004
(585) 586-1430 .. **Belgiorno**, Michl T '73 -65A Monroe Av -Pittsfrd 14534 **Fx:**586-0245
(718) 522-3033 .. **Belgrave**, Carl C '92 -188 Montague -Brklyn 11201 **Fx:**522-7322
(718) 777-3800 .. **Belibasakis**, Emanuel J '97 (Kapetanos & B,LLP) -23-56 Steinway -Astoria 11105
(631) 445-7380 .. **Belil**, Jeena R '95 -150 Motor Pkwy -Hauppauge 11788 **Fx:**514-3615
(212) 735-3000 .. **Belin**, Rita Sinkfield '96 %Skadden ASM&F LLP -4 Times Sq -NY 10036
(212) 868-7347 .. **Belinfanti**, Ian M '99 -481 8th Av -NY 10001
(212) 471-6200 .. **Belinfanti**, Marka S '07 %Hinshaw & C LLP -780 3rd Av -NY 10017
(212) 894-8823 .. **Belinfanti**, Stefan M '02 CT Corp -111 8th Av -NY 10011
(212) 922-2200 .. **Belisle**, Christopher P '90 (Watson F&W LLP) -1133 Av of Amer -NY 10036
(516) 681-3100 .. **Belitsis**, Michl '95 (Donohue MC&B) -555 N Bway Bx350 -Jericho 11753
(212) 318-6000 .. **Belitsky**, Wm '07 %Paul HJ&W LLP -75 E 55th -NY 10022
(212) 770-2490 .. **Belitz**, Shari E '99 AIG -80 Pine -NY 10005
(212) 813-8800 .. **Beliveau**, Nicole M '07 %Goodwin P LLP -620 8th Av -NY 10018
(212) 335-9000 .. **Belizaire**, Raffaela S '10 %DA -1 Hogan Pl -NY 10013
(914) 333-9643 .. **Belk**, Michl E '01 %Philips Electronics -345 Scarborough Rd Bx3001 -Briarclff Mnr 10510 **Fx:**332-0615
(212) 867-4466 .. **Belkin Burden Wenig & Goldman,LLP** -270 Mad Av -NY 10016 **Fx:**867-0709
(212) 891-6745 .. **Belkin**, Harvey '72 %Amer Jewish Comm -165 E 56th -NY 10022 **Fx:**891-1495
(518) 785-5340 .. **Belkin**, M Randolph '92 Shantz & B -26 Century Hill Dr -Latham 12110 **Fx:**785-5470
(212) 207-8400 .. **Belkin**, Meredith D '01 %Kavanagh M&O LLP -415 Mad Av -NY 10017
(212) 867-4466 .. **Belkin**, Sherwin '77 (Belkin BW&G,LLP) -270 Mad Av -NY 10016
(212) 885-5000 .. **Belknap**, Thos H Jr. '97 (Blank R LLP) -405 Lex Av -NY 10174
(212) 759-8203 .. **Belkowski**, Anthony J '81 %Hedinger & L -110 Wall -NY 10005
(212) 506-1700 .. **Bell**, Aaron M '04 %Kasowitz BT&F LLP -1633 Bway -NY 10019
(212) 403-1000 .. **Bell**, Adrian L '08 %Wachtell LR&K -51 W 52nd -NY 10019
(212) 225-2000 .. **Bell**, Alexandra R '08 %Cleary GS&H -1 Lbrty Plz -NY 10006
(212) 838-3333 .. **Bell**, Andrew P '93 %Locks Law Firm,PLLC -747 3rd Av -NY 10017 **Fx:**838-3735
(718) 578-4983 .. **Bell**, Angus James '00 -26 Court -Brklyn 11242
(212) 468-8000 .. **Bell**, B Jeffery '01 %Morrison & F LLP -1290 Av of Amer -NY 10104
(914) 964-5519 .. **Bell**, Beverly L '92 Enhanced Sec 8 Outreach Prog -20 S Bway -Ynkrs 10701
(212) 455-2000 .. **Bell**, Blake A '84 SrCnsl Simpson T&B LLP -425 Lex Av -NY 10017
(518) 465-3553 .. **Bell**, Bruce A '82 (Maynard OS&C,LLP) -6 Twr Pl -Albany 12203
(716) 845-6000 .. **Bell**, Candace L '91 (Kavinoky C LLP) -726 Exchange -Buffalo 14210
(212) 619-2250 .. **Bell**, Cathy A '82 Loop Capital Mrkts,LLC -88 Pine -NY 10005
(212) 239-4001 .. **Bell**, Christine '01 (Rheem & B LLP) -302 5th Av -NY 10001 **Fx:**239-4125
(212) 455-2000 .. **Bell**, Christopher O '09 %Simpson T&B LLP -425 Lex Av -NY 10017
(212) 556-2100 .. **Bell**, Crayton L '92 (King & S) -1185 Av of Amer -NY 10036
(212) 998-6685 .. **Bell**, Derrick A '66 NYU Law Schl -40 Wshngtn Sq S -NY 10012
(212) 408-4389 .. **Bell**, Douglas C '88 Metro-North Railroad -347 Mad Av -NY 10017
(212) 967-5710 .. **Bell**, Erica '84 (Weiss B&B) -11 Park Pl -NY 10007
(914) 285-8500 .. **Bell**, Gary M '86 %TK Moore -701 Wstchstr Av -White Plns 10604 **Fx:**285-8510
(718) 888-7960 .. **Bell**, Glenn D '02 G Bell,PLLC -155-16 59th Av -Flushng 11355 **Fx:**888-7961
(212) 509-9400 .. **Bell**, Guy A '02 (Cozen O) -45 Bway Atrium -NY 10006
(845) 679-4860 .. **Bell**, H Clark '62 -23 Laura Ln Bx734 -Woodstock 12498 **Fx:**679-9790
(347) 404-9400 .. **Bell**, Hiram Lewis '83 %Criminal Ct -120 Schermerhorn -Brklyn 11201 **Fx:**(718) 643-3538
(212) 751-3001 .. **Bell**, J Michl '05 (Thompson & K LLP) -919 3rd Av -NY 10022
(914) 766-2627 .. **Bell**, Jaime N '02 IBM -294 Route 100 -Somers 10589
(585) 637-4275 .. **Bell**, James D '79 -62 Main Bx10 -Brockprt 14420 **Fx:**637-7858
(212) 818-9200 .. **Bell**, James H '66 (Satterlee SB&B LLP) -230 Park Av -NY 10169
(914) 723-9096 .. **Bell**, Janet Goldstein '76 -2 Penn Blvd -Scarsdale 10583
(212) 474-1000 .. **Bell**, Jefferson E '07 %Cravath S&M LLP -825 8th Av -NY 10019
(212) 885-5000 .. **Bell**, Jennifer L '08 %Blank R LLP -405 Lex Av -NY 10174
(718) 237-2000 .. **Bell**, Jerilyn L '99 %Leg Aid -111 Lvngstn -Brklyn 11201 **Fx:**237-8737
(516) 222-2434 .. **Bell**, Joanne Emily '83 %White Q&S -377 Oak Bx9304 -Gdn Cty 11530
(212) 792-8484 .. **Bell**, Jonathan R '78 (Stern T&B LLP) -380 Lex Av -NY 10168
(212) 758-4311 .. **Bell**, Jos B '84 (Longo & B) -430 Park Av -NY 10022 **Fx:**758-4312
(212) 872-1000 .. **Bell**, Justin H '07 -One Bryant Park -NY 10036 **Fx:**872-1002
(914) 288-0605 .. **Bell**, Karen Zelfman '74 -222 Bloomingdale Rd -White Plns 10605 **Fx:**683-0098

(212) 790-4500 .. **Bell,** Karyn E '02 %Manatt P&P,LLP -7 Times Sq -NY 10036
(212) 478-0000 .. **Bell,** Kevin '07 DE Shaw & Co,LP -120 W 45th -NY 10036
(212) 907-7300 .. **Bell,** Lawr M '77 (Golenbock EAB&P) -437 Mad Av -NY 10022
(212) 799-9638 .. **Bell,** Leonidas Beloyeannis '89 %West Side SRO Lw Prj -647 Columbus Av -NY 10025 **Fx:**721-1514
(212) 495-4595 .. **Bell,** Martin A '78 DH Blair -44 Wall -NY 10005
(212) 373-3000 .. **Bell,** Martin S '07 %Paul WRW&G LLP -1285 Av of Amer -NY 10019
(315) 349-3200 .. **Bell,** Matthew J '99 %DA -Pub Safety Ctr -Oswego 13126 **Fx:**349-3212
(212) 306-7239 .. **Bell,** Mayra E '89 %Mayors Ofc Labor Rel -40 Rector -NY 10006 **Fx:**306-7223
(212) 336-2000 .. **Bell,** Megan E '05 %Patterson BW&T LLP -1133 Av of Amer -NY 10036
(212) 310-8000 .. **Bell,** Michl D '09 %Weil G&M LLP -767 5th Av -NY 10153
(315) 422-1152 .. **Bell,** Nadine C '03 %Costello C&F,PLLC -500 Plum -Syracuse 13204
(718) 286-5880 .. **Bell,** Nathalie L '02 DA -125-01 Qns Blvd -Kew Gdns 11415
(212) 940-8800 .. **Bell,** Rebecca H '09 %Katten MR LLP -575 Mad Av -NY 10022
(212) 714-0988 .. **Bell,** Richd C '82 -545 8th Av -NY 10018 **Fx:**714-1768
(585) 232-6900 .. **Bell,** Richd T Jr. '98 %Gates & A,PC -28 E Main -Rchstr 14614
(212) 903-9000 .. **Bell,** Robt H '03 %Linklaters -1345 Av of Amer -NY 10105
(716) 851-4343 .. **Bell,** Sabrina R '08 Law Dept -65 Niagara Sq -Buffalo 14202 **Fx:**851-4105
(212) 997-4400 .. **Bell,** Sanford A '74 (Teitler & T,LLP) -1114 Av of Amer -NY 10036 **Fx:**997-4949
(212) 421-4100 .. **Bell,** Sarah E '05 %Pryor C LLP -7 Times Sq -NY 10036
(212) 545-4752 .. **Bell,** Seth J '05 %Wolf HAF&H LLP -270 Mad Av -NY 10016
(212) 237-1000 .. **Bell,** Stacey A '01 %Windels ML&M,LLP -156 W 56th -NY 10019
(212) 741-9311 .. **Bell,** Susan E '03 Inviva Inc -435 Hudson -NY 10014
(212) 455-2000 .. **Bell,** Thos H '85 (Simpson T&B LLP) -425 Lex Av -NY 10017
(212) 527-1000 .. **Bell,** Wm E '80 (Jones HC&B PC) -1 Bttry Pk Plz -NY 10004
(845) 306-1000 .. **Bell,** Wm R '84 %Watchtower -100 Watchtower Dr -Patterson 12563 **Fx:**306-0709
(212) 577-3349 .. **Bella,** Christine L '97 %Leg Aid -199 Water -NY 10038 **Fx:**577-3520
(212) 446-4800 .. **Bellacosa,** Peter A '89 (Kirkland & E LLP) -153 E 53rd -NY 10022
(914) 995-2597 .. **Bell-Adamo,** Sharon '91 %Cnty Atty -148 Martine Av -White Plns 10601 **Fx:**995-5858
(516) 679-2869 .. **Bellairs,** Chester K '90 Amer Exp -200 Vesey -NY 10285
(212) 326-7028 .. **Bellamy,** Carol '68 %UNICEF -3 UN Plz -NY 10017
(914) 253-2000 .. **Bellanca,** Christopher J '01 Pepsico -700 Andrsn Hill Rd -Purchase 10577
(631) 499-3030 .. **Bellantone,** Gregory D '91 (Dubi B,PC) -9 Cedar Ridge Ln -Dix Hlls 11746 **Fx:**462-4976
(914) 347-4500 .. **Bellantoni,** Amy L '99 %Lovett & B, LLP -37A Saw Mill Rvr Rd -Hawthorne 10532 **Fx:**347-4545
(914) 428-6602 .. **Bellantoni,** George S '88 -56 Greenrdg Av -White Plns 10605 **Fx:**948-4177
(914) 347-4500 .. **Bellantoni,** Rory J '96 (Lovett & B, LLP) -37A Saw Mill Rvr Rd -Hawthorne 10532 **Fx:**347-4545
(914) 428-1438 .. **Bellantoni,** Stephanie K '96 %T Bona,PC -123 Main -White Plns 10601 **Fx:**428-1413
(212) 406-9710 .. **Bellard,** Jos C '76 (Kral CRRP&G,LLP) -170 Bway -NY 10038
(212) 297-5800 .. **Bellard,** Lorraine M '02 %Day P LLP -7 Times Sq -NY 10036
(516) 741-8005 .. **Bellard,** Wm T '76 (Marshall & B) -1305 Franklin Av -Gdn Cty 11530
(212) 707-3028 .. **Bellarosa,** Erica B '04 Atlantic Records -1290 Av of Amer -NY 10104 **Fx:**707-5537
(718) 260-8700 .. **Bellarosa,** Jamine A '03 %Admin Children's Srvcs -345 Adams -Brklyn 11201
(516) 873-3000 .. **Bellavia,** Leonard A '83 (Bellavia G & Assoc,LLP) -200 Old Cntry Rd -Mineola 11501 **Fx:**873-9032
(914) 253-2000 .. **Bellavia,** Melissa L '01 Pepsico -700 Andrsn Hill Rd -Purchase 10577
(585) 232-8000 .. **Bellavia,** Timothy C '93 (Parisi & B) -16 W Main -Rchstr 14614 **Fx:**232-7245
(718) 590-2000 .. **Bell-Blair,** Miriam '91 %DA -198 E 161st -Bronx 10451 **Fx:**590-6477
(518) 436-9646 .. **Bellcourt,** Gwenn M '94 %Rutnik Law Firm -80 State -Albany 12207 **Fx:**436-9648
(212) 534-7800 .. **Belle,** Letta A '05 SCAN NY -307 E 116th -NY 10029
(212) 225-2000 .. **Beller,** Alan L '77 (Cleary GS&H) -1 Lbrty Plz -NY 10006
(212) 455-2000 .. **Beller,** Amy T '97 SrCnsl Simpson T&B LLP -425 Lex Av -NY 10017
(718) 590-1274 .. **Beller,** Beth '88 Hon J Lieb -215 E 161st -Bronx 10451
(212) 977-9700 .. **Beller,** Brian J '05 %Phillips N LLP -666 5th Av -NY 10103
(212) 373-3000 .. **Beller,** Danl J '73 (Paul WRW&G LLP) -1285 Av of Amer -NY 10019
(212) 839-5300 .. **Beller,** David S '08 %Sidley A LLP -787 7th Av -NY 10019
(212) 442-1400 .. **Beller,** Jessie M '06 Conflicts of Int Bd -2 Lafayette -NY 10007 **Fx:**442-1407
(212) 982-3000 .. **Bellet,** Ellen '89 -425 E 61st -NY 10065
(315) 422-7284 .. **Belletier,** Anthony Jr. '86 -120 E Wshngtn -Syracuse 13202
(212) 349-6009 .. **Bellew,** Kara M '05 %Sanctuary for Families -110 Wall -NY 10005 **Fx:**566-0344
(914) 461-4641 .. **Belli,** Josephine '87 Combe Inc -1101 Wstchstr Av -White Plns 10604 **Fx:**872-2376
(914) 358-5345 .. **Bellin,** Aytan Y '93 Bellin & Assoc,LLC -85 Miles Av -White Plns 10606
(212) 267-9100 .. **Bellin,** Eugene M '69 -233 Bway -NY 10279 **Fx:**349-0338
(718) 852-3710 .. **Bellina,** Nicole '99 (Stoll G&B) -71 Nevins -Brklyn 11217 **Fx:**852-3586
(212) 727-0725 .. **Bellinder,** Jessica '05 OfCnsl Prtnrshp for Homeless -305 7th Av -NY 10001 **Fx:**727-3820
(516) 746-6054 .. **Belline,** Dennis Dominick '99 %HMS Productions -72 Jericho Tpk -Mineola 11501
(516) 431-2031 .. **Belling,** Walter '75 W Belling & Assoc -20 W Park Av -Long Bch 11561
(212) 415-9200 .. **Bellinger,** G Michl '84 (Dorsey & W LLP) -250 Park Av -NY 10177
(631) 422-5029 .. **Bellinger,** Natasja V '91 -183 Anchorage Dr -W Islip 11795
(718) 273-1121 .. **Bellini,** Anthony M '02 -434 Port Richmond Av -Staten Isl 10302 **Fx:**273-1221
(212) 986-7353 .. **Bellinson,** Robt J '90 %Wingate R&S -420 Lex Av -NY 10170
(212) 909-6000 .. **Bellis,** Elizabeth O '07 %Debevoise & P LLP -919 3rd Av -NY 10022
(516) 358-1700 .. **Bellistri,** Christopher F '05 Cronin & B,LLP -1983 Marcus Av -Lk Success 11042
(516) 328-2300 .. **Bellizzi,** Angela C '03 %Abrams FFEGF&E,LLP -1111 Marcus Av -Lk Success 11042
(212) 739-7576 .. **Bellman,** Richd F '74 -99 Hudson -NY 10013
(914) 337-0052 .. **Bellman-McFadyen,** Carmella '85 -9 Avon Rd -Bronxvll 10708
(516) 228-6500 .. **Bello,** Cesar C '05 Ivy Asset Mgmt -1 Jericho Plz -Jericho 11753 **Fx:**228-6515
(631) 300-4960 .. **Bello,** John J Jr. '89 (Bello & L) -150 Motor Pkwy -Hauppauge 11788
(718) 981-9191 .. **Bello,** Judith C '81 -393 Lighthse Av -Staten Isl 10306 **Fx:**981-9588
(631) 300-4960 .. **Bello & Larkin** -150 Motor Pkwy -Hauppauge 11788 **Fx:**(603) 427-2119
(212) 898-4364 .. **Bello,** Marleen M '04 Liberty Intl Undrwriters -55 Water -NY 10041
(718) 981-9191 .. **Bello,** Thos F '86 Cnsl T Bello,PC -393 Lighthse Av -Staten Isl 10306 **Fx:**(347) 861-0845
(516) 248-1200 .. **Bellofatto,** Anthony R '63 -374 Hillside Av -Williston Pk 11596
(516) 877-9577 .. **Belloff,** Paul F '63 -100 Grdn City Plz -Gdn Cty 11530
(914) 769-9500 .. **Bellom,** Laurence J '87 -814 Commerce -Thornwd 10594 **Fx:**769-9549
(315) 463-5747 .. **Bellomo,** Deborah A '90 -4030 New Court Av -Syracuse 13206 **Fx:**463-5741
(212) 837-6520 .. **Bellomo,** Lisa N '07 %Hughes H&R LLP -1 Bttry Pk Plz -NY 10004
(212) 732-8579 .. **Bellone,** Robt M '85 %Sher HB&T,PC -277 Bway -NY 10007
(212) 732-8579 .. **Bellone,** Thos S '78 (Sher HB&T,PC) -277 Bway -NY 10007
(212) 408-5100 .. **Bellotti,** Wm L '77 Chadbourne & P LLP -30 Rckfllr Plz -NY 10112
(212) 481-5858 .. **Bellouny,** Kristin V '81 %Fidelity Natl Title Ins -1 Park Av -NY 10016 **Fx:**481-8747
(212) 750-1200 .. **Bellovin,** Dennis '75 (Trolman G&L,PC) -777 3rd Av -NY 10017
(212) 575-7900 .. **Bellovin,** Marshall B '85 (Ballon SB&N,PC) -729 7th Av -NY 10019
(212) 756-2000 .. **Bellow,** Marissa H '06 %Schulte R&Z LLP -919 3rd Av -NY 10022
(212) 310-8000 .. **Bellows,** Carl D '69 (Weil G&M LLP) -767 5th Av -NY 10153
(716) 856-0600 .. **Bellows,** George F '86 (Jaeckle F&M,LLP) -12 Fountain Plz -Buffalo 14202
(212) 932-3790 .. **Bellows,** Moshe Z '94 Bellows Productions -305 W 98th -NY 10025 **Fx:**749-0739
(914) 997-4535 .. **Bellsey,** Lisa E '83 March of Dimes -1275 Mamaroneck Av -White Plns 10605
(212) 530-5000 .. **Bellucci,** Michl J '94 (Milbank TH&M LLP) -1 Chase Manh Plz -NY 10005
(212) 681-1575 .. **Belluck & Fox LLP** -546 5th Av -NY 10036 **Fx:**681-1574
(212) 681-1575 .. **Belluck,** Jos W '95 (Belluck & F LLP) -546 5th Av -NY 10036
(914) 949-1305 .. **Bellus,** Melinda '98 %Leg Srvcs -90 Maple Av -White Plns 10601 **Fx:**949-6213
(516) 365-9802 .. **Bellus,** Stewart J '89 (Collard & R,PC) -1077 Nrthrn Blvd -Roslyn 11576
(516) 365-9802 .. **Bellus,** Stewart J '89 (Nolte N&H) -1077 Nrthrn Blvd -Roslyn 11576
(585) 454-4635 .. **Belluscio,** John A '72 -1 E Main -Rchstr 14614
(718) 445-1500 .. **Belluscio,** Robt F '79 -142-03 37th Av -Flushng 11354 **Fx:**358-9849
(212) 626-4100 .. **Bellwin,** Janna H J '73 (Baker & M LLP) -1114 Av of Amer -NY 10036
(212) 397-5530 .. **Belly,** Armando T '73 %Soros Fund Mgmt LLC -888 7th Av -NY 10106
(212) 964-6611 .. **Belmont,** Allyson B '97 %Lester SK&D -120 Bway -NY 10271
(212) 431-5757 .. **Belmont,** Dean G '86 -401 Bway -NY 10013
(212) 490-3000 .. **Belmont,** Kate B '10 %Wilson EME&D LLP -150 E 42nd -NY 10017
(718) 596-2648 .. **Belmont,** Peter A '96 -166 Columbia Hts -Brklyn 11201
(212) 695-0086 .. **Belmont,** Wm B '92 The Belmont Grp -118 E 60th -NY 10022 **Fx:**(917) 591-3361
(212) 279-9600 .. **Belmonte,** Alice Phillips '92 Cnsl Vintage Grp,LLC -15 W 39th -NY 10018
(212) 818-9200 .. **Belmonte,** Christopher R '77 (Satterlee SB&B LLP) -230 Park Av -NY 10169
(631) 439-2450 .. **Belmonte,** John B '96 %Leg Aid -320 Carleton Av -Central Islip 11722 **Fx:**439-2453
(212) 482-0001 .. **Belmonte,** Josefina A '93 %Russo K&T LLP -33 Whitehall -NY 10004
(212) 657-1568 .. **Belnap,** Brent J '90 %Citibank NA -111 Wall -NY 10043
(212) 553-5443 .. **Belniak,** Victoria '06 %Zurich NA -1 Lbrty Plz -NY 10006
(917) 679-3314 .. **Belnick,** Mark A '72 (MA Belnick,LLC) -300 Cntrl Pk W -NY 10024
(845) 357-1230 .. **Beloch,** John G '92 %Ramapo Manor Nursing Ctr -Bx248 -Suffern 10901 **Fx:**357-4210
(212) 696-6000 .. **Beloded,** Olga R '01 %Curtis M-PC&M LLP -101 Park Av -NY 10178
(914) 472-8528 .. **Belofsky,** Nathan '85 -500 Cntrl Pk Av -Scarsdale 10583 **Fx:**472-8560
(212) 416-8028 .. **Belohlavek,** Michl S '70 %Dept of Law -120 Bway -NY 10271
(516) 496-5822 .. **Belony,** Laurie '05 %T Spina -170 Froehlich Farm Blvd -Woodbury 11797 **Fx:**496-5420
(212) 940-8800 .. **Belosa,** Evan A '03 %Katten MR LLP -575 Mad Av -NY 10022
(516) 357-3000 .. **Belous,** Todd M '91 %Rivkin R LLP -926 RXR Plz -Uniondale 11556
(212) 346-2000 .. **Belova,** Rayka Trifonova '05 %T Sofer -115 Bway -NY 10006
(212) 627-8100 .. **Belovin,** Allyson L '97 (Levy R,PC) -80 8th Av -NY 10011
(718) 655-2900 .. **Belovin & Franzblau** -2311 Wht Plns Rd -Bronx 10467 **Fx:**655-2363
(718) 595-6003 .. **Belovin,** Heather J '95 NYC DEP -96-05 Horace Hrdng Expwy -Corona 11368
(718) 655-2900 .. **Belovin,** Jeffrey J '68 (Belovin & F) -2311 Wht Plns Rd -Bronx 10467
(718) 639-6700 .. **Belovin,** Robt S '69 -37-94 103rd -Corona 11368 **Fx:**426-3618
(914) 681-0200 .. **Belowich,** Brian T '00 (DelBello DWW&W,LLP) -1 N Lex Av -White Plns 10601
(845) 279-2986 .. **Belser,** Stephanie M '01 %Hogan & R -1441 Route 22 -Brewstr 10509 **Fx:**279-6425
(518) 474-1634 .. **Belsito,** Anthony M '07 Dept Pub Srvc -3 ESP -Albany 12223
(718) 855-9000 .. **Belsito,** Desiree '05 %Cullen and D LLP -177 Montague -Brklyn 11201

(516) 745-1100 .. **Belsky,** Bruce H '76 (Kaplan BRB,LLP) -666 Old Cntry Rd -Gdn Cty 11530
(518) 371-1536 .. **Belsky,** Michl J '96 -6 Chelsea Pl Bx424 -Clifton Pk 12065 **Fx:**373-1338
(718) 832-6500 .. **Belson,** I Victor '60 Belson & S -1310 8th Av -Brklyn 11215
(718) 286-6000 .. **Belson,** Jaclyn A '07 %DA -125-01 Qns Blvd -Kew Gdns 11415
(212) 941-9500 .. **Belson,** Jerome '49 -495 Bway -NY 10012
(718) 832-6500 .. **Belson & Szuflita** -1310 8th Av -Brklyn 11215
(716) 566-5400 .. **Belter,** Christopher J '94 (Goldberg S LLP) -665 Main -Buffalo 14203
(212) 371-8855 .. **Beltrametti Walker,** Viviana K R A '08 Stikeman E LLP -445 Park Av -NY 10022
(212) 883-4955 .. **Beltrami,** Jennifer Fletcher '99 (Cozen O) -277 Park Av -NY 10172 **Fx:**672-1155
(518) 463-1185 .. **Beltramo,** Jerry Wade '98 %NYCOM -119 Wshngtn Av -Albany 12210 **Fx:**463-1190
(914) 995-2660 .. **Beltran,** Karen T '07 %Cnty Atty -148 Martine Av -White Plns 10601 **Fx:**995-5858
(212) 545-4674 .. **Beltrani,** Maria I '89 (Wolf HAF&H LLP) -270 Mad Av -NY 10016
(917) 886-8540 .. **Beltrani,** Robt V '89 -35-31 85th -Jcksn Hts 11372
(631) 422-1321 .. **Beltrani,** Theresa P '99 Assblymn T Barraga -187 Sunrise Hwy -W Islip 11795 **Fx:**422-6085
(212) 318-3000 .. **Beltre,** Samantha E '06 %Fulbright & J LLP -666 5th Av -NY 10103
(718) 741-3400 .. **Beltre Rosado,** Llinet M '99 Childrens Law Ctr -2501 Grnd Cncrs -Bronx 10468
(212) 613-5023 .. **Beltz,** Amanda M '09 NY Legal Assistance Grp -450 W 33rd -NY 10001
(212) 883-4941 .. **Beltz,** Christian G '95 (Cozen O) -277 Park Av -NY 10172 **Fx:**672-1141
(716) 852-1000 .. **Beltz,** Paul W '54 (PW Beltz,PC) -36 Church -Buffalo 14202 **Fx:**852-5887
(212) 309-6000 .. **Beltzer,** Howard S '83 (Morgan L&B LLP) -101 Park Av -NY 10178
(212) 480-6785 .. **Belulovich,** Louise '93 %DHCR -25 Beaver -NY 10004 **Fx:**480-7416
(718) 787-4470 .. **Belushin,** Vel '02 -1712 Kings Hwy -Brklyn 11229
(212) 297-5800 .. **Belval,** Paul '90 (Day P LLP) -7 Times Sq -NY 10036
(212) 980-3500 .. **Belvisi,** Cindy M '08 %Pavia & H LLP -600 Mad Av -NY 10022
(212) 819-8200 .. **Belz,** Matthew R '10 %White & C LLP -1155 Av of Amer -NY 10036
(516) 483-7372 .. **Bembi,** Bruno J '89 -71 N Franklin -Hempstd 11550 **Fx:**483-4416
(914) 681-0200 .. **Bemporad,** Richd D '76 Cnsl DelBello DWW&W,LLP -1 N Lex Av -White Plns 10601
(716) 433-3836 .. **Ben,** Anthony C '54 (Ben & B) -193 East Av -Lockprt 14095 **Fx:**433-3838
(212) 212-4010 .. **Ben,** Cara M '09 Sup Ct-Deptmntl Disciplinary Cmmt-1st Dept -61 Bway -NY 10006
(716) 433-3836 .. **Ben,** Chas P II '82 (Ben & B) -193 East Av -Lockprt 14095 **Fx:**433-3838
(315) 682-5155 .. **Ben,** Sheila K '78 (Ben & B) -107 Fayette Bx421 -Manlius 13104 **Fx:**682-8521
(315) 682-5155 .. **Ben,** Stuart L '76 (Ben & B) -107 Fayette Bx421 -Manlius 13104 **Fx:**682-8521
(212) 903-9000 .. **Benabentos,** Lucia '10 %Linklaters -1345 Av of Amer -NY 10105
(212) 382-0909 .. **Benacchio,** Robt H '02 %Peckar & A,PC -41 Mad Av -NY 10154
(516) 739-3800 .. **Benack,** Richd A '61 -124 4th -Gdn Cty 11530 **Fx:**248-6001
(516) 487-1602 .. **Benak,** Galya R '93 %Zaccaria & S -175 E Shore Rd -Gt Neck 11023
(212) 216-8025 .. **Ben-Ami,** Andrew R '81 (Tarter K&D LLP) -1350 Bway -NY 10018
(212) 836-8000 .. **Ben-Ami,** Leora '85 (Kaye S LLP) -425 Park Av -NY 10022
(631) 499-0320 .. **Ben-Ami,** Oded '00 -26 Hamlet Dr -Commack 11725 **Fx:**(516) 977-3046
(518) 457-4317 .. **Ben-Amotz,** Pico Paul '87 Dept of Labor -State Campus Bldg 12 -Albany 12240
(212) 819-8200 .. **Benamram,** Oz '00 White & C LLP -1155 Av of Amer -NY 10036
(212) 679-7007 .. **Benard,** Jody C '87 (Brody B&B LLP) -205 Lex Av -NY 10016
(212) 207-1900 .. **Benardo,** Sanford M '95 -600 3rd Av -NY 10016
(212) 592-1400 .. **Ben-Ari,** Yariv C '03 %Herrick,F LLP -2 Park Av -NY 10016
(718) 442-9000 .. **Ben-Aron,** Marvin '88 %Ameduri G&F -471 Bement Av -Staten Isl 10310
(718) 258-4774 .. **Benasaraf,** Debbie Zacharia '92 A Hertz,PC -934 E 19th -Brklyn 11230 **Fx:**258-4994
(212) 321-7075 .. **Ben-Asher,** Jonathan J '81 (Ritz C&B-A LLP) -40 Exch Pl -NY 10005
(914) 422-4545 .. **Ben-Asher,** Noa '05 Pace Law Schl -78 N Bway -White Plns 10603 **Fx:**422-4039
(716) 632-4400 .. **Benatovich,** Sheldon B '67 -5350 Main -Williamsvll 14221
(516) 741-7676 .. **Ben-Bassat,** Ron '09 %Miranda SSSV LLP -240 Mineola Blvd -Mineola 11501
(646) 386-3986 .. **Benbow,** Christopher H '88 Hon M Kahn-Supreme Ct -100 Centre -NY 10013
(212) 728-8000 .. **Benchetrit,** Serge '91 (Willkie F&G LLP) -787 7th Av -NY 10019
(212) 455-2000 .. **Benchimol,** Gustavo '06 %Simpson T&B LLP -425 Lex Av -NY 10017
(716) 855-1111 .. **Bencini,** Robt L '94 (Duke HP&G LLP) -350 Main -Buffalo 14202
(212) 530-5000 .. **Bencivenga,** Tommaso '07 %Milbank TH&M LLP -1 Chase Manh Plz -NY 10005
(631) 581-3755 .. **Bencivinni,** Michele '90 -33 E Main -E Islip 11730 **Fx:**581-2949
(212) 756-2000 .. **Benda,** Jillian L '08 %Schulte R&Z LLP -919 3rd Av -NY 10022
(518) 370-2211 .. **Bendall,** James M '97 %Bendall & M -836 Plymouth Av -Schnctdy 12308 **Fx:**370-3840
(518) 370-2211 .. **Bendall,** James W '71 (Bendall & M) -836 Plymouth Av -Schnctdy 12308 **Fx:**370-3840
(212) 982-0269 .. **Ben Daniel,** Ran '04 -1010 W 79th -NY 10024 **Fx:**(646) 852-6697
(212) 969-3000 .. **Bender,** Audrey Ingber '80 Cnsl Proskauer R LLP -1585 Bway -NY 10036
(718) 780-1969 .. **Bender,** Austin S '95 College Hosp-HR -78 Amity -Brklyn 11201
(212) 687-0100 .. **Bender,** Brian A '98 (Harris B PLLC) -100 Wall -NY 10005
(845) 735-8385 .. **Bender,** Damon P '04 H Janow,LLC -1 Blue Hill Plz Bx1586 -Pearl Rvr 10965 **Fx:**735-1054
(914) 693-1890 .. **Bender,** David '71 -18 Eldredge Pl -Dobbs Ferry 10522
(716) 667-0061 .. **Bender,** Debra K '83 (Bender & P) -6459 W Quaker -Orchard Pk 14127
(212) 445-3424 .. **Bender,** Eric J '95 SrCnsl Bravado Intl Grp -245 5th Av -NY 10016 **Fx:**445-3499
(212) 326-2000 .. **Bender,** Gerald C '86 (O'Melveny & M LLP) -7 Times Sq -NY 10036
(914) 989-6650 .. **Bender,** Heath A '95 %Eustace & M -1133 Wstchstr Av -White Plns 10604
(212) 636-6000 .. **Bender,** Helen Hadjiyannakis '85 %Fordham Univ Sch of Law -140 W 62nd -NY 10023 **Fx:**636-6899
(914) 921-1998 .. **Bender,** Howard A '90 Coco Myles Inc -4 Kervan Rd -Rye 10580
(212) 605-0343 .. **Bender,** Jerome D '52 (Bender & B) -575 Mad Av -NY 10022
(914) 997-1100 .. **Bender,** Joel C '64 -1 N Lex Av -White Plns 10601 **Fx:**997-1324
(212) 362-4433 .. **Bender,** John C '68 -27 W 67th -NY 10023
(212) 421-2233 .. **Bender,** Jonathan K '95 %Wilk A LLP -675 3rd Av -NY 10017
(315) 443-4462 .. **Bender,** Leslie '92 %Syracuse Univ Cllg of Law -Wht Hall -Syracuse 13244 **Fx:**443-4213
(631) 547-5116 .. **Bender,** Mark E '92 (M Bender,LLC) -Bx385 -Greenlawn 11740 **Fx:**418-8501
(212) 605-0343 .. **Bender,** Martin S '83 (Bender & B) -575 Mad Av -NY 10022
(718) 777-1777 .. **Bender,** Michl S '81 (Argyropoulos & B) -31-01 Bway -Astoria 11106
(716) 856-3200 .. **Bender,** Paul A '89 (Bender & B LLP) -68 Niagara -Buffalo 14202 **Fx:**856-3270
(315) 926-5540 .. **Bender,** Paul F '78 -3775 S Main Bx220 -Marion 14505 **Fx:**926-1201
(516) 357-3634 .. **Bender,** Risa C '89 %Leventritt L&B -1010 Nrthrn Blvd -Gt Neck 11021
(212) 878-1044 .. **Bender,** Roberta '79 %MTA -347 Mad Av -NY 10017
(212) 725-7111 .. **Bender Rosenthal Isaacs & Richter LLP** -451 Park Av S -NY 10016 **Fx:**725-3737
(516) 357-3634 .. **Bender,** Sidney '54 (Leventritt L&B) -1010 Nrthrn Blvd -Gt Neck 11021
(914) 995-4457 .. **Bender,** Steven '81 %DA -111 Martin Luther King Blvd -White Plns 10601 **Fx:**995-3363
(212) 725-7111 .. **Bender,** Susan L '81 (Bender RI&R LLP) -451 Park Av S -NY 10016
(716) 856-3200 .. **Bender,** Thos W '80 (Bender & B LLP) -68 Niagara -Buffalo 14202 **Fx:**856-3270
(212) 816-2747 .. **Bendernagel,** Donald A '83 Citibank NA -250 West -NY 10013
(212) 735-3000 .. **Bender-Nash,** Sarah '07 %Skadden ASM&F LLP -4 Times Sq -NY 10036
(212) 308-4411 .. **Bendes,** Barry J '75 (Edwards AP&D LLP) -750 Lex Av -NY 10022
(212) 732-3320 .. **Bendik,** David L '91 %Short & B,PC -217 Bway -NY 10007
(516) 486-4600 .. **Bendik,** Edw '62 (Bendik & N) -250 Fulton Av -Hempstd 11550
(516) 486-4600 .. **Bendik & Nanos** -250 Fulton Av -Hempstd 11550
(212) 896-6500 .. **Bendinger,** Gary F '06 (Howrey LLP) -601 Lex Av -NY 10022
(914) 995-3420 .. **Bendish,** Brian J '05 %DA -111 Martin Luther King Blvd -White Plns 10601 **Fx:**995-3363
(914) 683-8484 .. **Bendish,** Bruce P '76 (Goodrich & B) -5 Old Rd -Elmsfrd 10523
(516) 357-3000 .. **Bendix,** Bruce A '84 (Rivkin R LLP) -926 RXR Plz -Uniondale 11556
(718) 388-2225 .. **Bendix,** Wm J '80 Bendix Law Ofc -692 Grand -Brklyn 11211 **Fx:**388-2521
(518) 641-5562 .. **Bendon Couch,** Mary Jane '86 Cnsl Cptl Dist Physicians Hlth Plan,Inc -500 Patroon Crk Blvd -Albany 12206 **Fx:**641-5505
(212) 701-3000 .. **Ben Dor,** Oren '10 %Cahill G&R LLP -80 Pine -NY 10005 **Fx:**269-5420
(212) 382-0909 .. **Ben-Dov,** Elana '96 (Peckar & A,PC) -41 Mad Av -NY 10154
(212) 506-1700 .. **Benecke,** Christopher B '09 %Kasowitz BT&F LLP -1633 Bway -NY 10019
(212) 583-9710 .. **Benedek,** M Lawr '80 -509 Mad Av -NY 10022 **Fx:**754-5907
(212) 586-8444 .. **Benedek,** Stephen D '02 Benedek Invstmnt Grp -145 W 57th -NY 10019
(212) 296-6969 .. **Benedetti,** Jos C '91 Morgan Stanley -522 5th Av -NY 10036
(718) 987-2768 .. **Benedetti,** Roland '76 -182 Rose Av -Staten Isl 10306
(212) 762-4697 .. **Benedetto,** Amie J '04 Morgan Stanley -1585 Bway -NY 10036
(631) 758-6500 .. **Benedetto,** Cathleen T '97 -629 Route 112 -Patchogue 11772 **Fx:**758-6383
(212) 838-5918 .. **Benedetto,** Marcello A '96 (Benedetto L,LLC) -122 E 42nd -NY 10168 **Fx:**591-6904
(718) 590-6177 .. **Benedetto,** Michelle M '09 %Law Dept -198 E 161st -Bronx 10451 **Fx:**590-2686
(212) 330-1000 .. **Benedetto,** Nicole M '04 %Buck Consultants -1 Penn Plz -NY 10119 **Fx:**695-4184
(516) 312-7465 .. **Benedetto,** Richd M '85 -2005 Merrick Rd -Merrick 11566
(212) 408-2500 .. **Benedetto,** Stephanie J '07 %Baker B,LLP -30 Rckfllr Plz -NY 10112
(315) 349-3350 .. **Benedetto,** Thos '92 Family Ct -39 Churchill Rd -Oswego 13126 **Fx:**349-3457
(607) 535-8932 .. **Benedict,** Alan S '10 %Fitzsimmons Law Firm -221 N Franklin -Watkins Glen 14891 **Fx:**535-5403
(716) 858-2424 .. **Benedict,** Amy B '03 %DA -25 Delaware Av -Buffalo 14202 **Fx:**858-7425
(845) 371-1800 .. **Benedict,** Anthony J '68 -664 Chestnut Rdg Rd -Chestnut Rdg 10977 **Fx:**371-2672
(212) 858-1000 .. **Benedict,** Bradley A '09 %Pillsbury WSP LLP -1540 Bway -NY 10036
(315) 448-0672 .. **Benedict,** Craig A '88 %US Atty -100 S Clinton Bx7198 -Syracuse 13261 **Fx:**448-0689
(212) 530-5000 .. **Benedict,** James N '75 (Milbank TH&M LLP) -1 Chase Manh Plz -NY 10005
(607) 776-9623 .. **Benedict,** Mary Hope M '87 %Supreme Ct-Appellate Div 4th Dept -19 E Pulteney Sq -Bath 14810 **Fx:**776-7168
(716) 433-5907 .. **Benedict,** Michl E '05 %Seaman JH&B,LLP -76 West Av -Lockprt 14094
(212) 756-2000 .. **Benedict,** Philippe '91 (Schulte R&Z LLP) -919 3rd Av -NY 10022
(646) 471-4000 .. **Benedict,** Rodman W '78 %PricewaterhouseCoopers LLP -300 Mad Av -NY 10017
(212) 827-4488 .. **Benedict,** Tabber B '03 Ace Grp Holdings Inc -1133 Av of Amer -NY 10036
(315) 338-6170 .. **Benedict,** Timothy A '00 -217 N Wshngtn Bx448 -Rome 13442 **Fx:**338-6172
(518) 828-9444 .. **Benedict,** Virginia Doney '89 (Rapport MWS&R,LLP) -436 Union -Hudson 12534
(516) 328-5113 .. **Benedis,** Maria '92 %Canon USA -1 Canon Plz -Lk Success 11042

(631) 271-3737 .. **Benelyahoo,** Dalia '05 %R Weiss,PC -734 Walt Whitman Rd -Melvll 11747 **Fx:**271-3784
(212) 506-1700 .. **Benenati,** Alycia Regan '99 SpclCnsl Kasowitz BT&F LLP -1633 Bway -NY 10019
(914) 949-2700 .. **Benenati,** Michl P '97 OfCnsl Bleakley P&S,LLP -1 N Lex Av -White Plns 10601
(212) 655-9583 .. **Benenson,** Anna E '00 -244 5th Av -NY 10001
(212) 819-8200 .. **Benenson,** Robt A '99 White & C LLP -1155 Av of Amer -NY 10036
(516) 512-6333 .. **Benes,** Christopher J '80 (Gold SKB LLP) -1025 Old Cntry Rd -Westbury 11590
(631) 467-9459 .. **Benesch,** Erin M '83 -1085 Main -Holbrook 11741
(216) 363-4500 .. **Benesch Friedlander Coplan & Aronoff, LLP** -50 Main -White Plns 10606 **Fx:**363-4588
(585) 454-6480 .. **Benesh,** Kathleen Brais '89 (Osborn R&B,LLP) -45 Exchange Blvd -Rchstr 14614
(212) 983-8500 .. **Benessere,** Lenore E '09 %Brown G&F LLP -355 Lex Av -NY 10017
(212) 836-8000 .. **Benett,** Katherine Petty '02 %Kaye S LLP -425 Park Av -NY 10022
(212) 687-8181 .. **Benett,** Megan Wolfe '00 %Kreindler & K -750 3rd Av -NY 10017
(914) 682-3300 .. **Beneventano,** Thos M '85 (La Sorsa & B) -3 Barker Av -White Plns 10601
(516) 577-9000 .. **Ben-Ezra,** Seth I '95 SI Ben-Ezra,PC -532 Broadhllw Rd -Melvll 11747 **Fx:**577-9008
(212) 227-4700 .. **Benfante,** Jos R '74 -225 Bway -NY 10007 **Fx:**406-6890
(212) 593-3255 .. **Benfeld,** Irina '00 IBE Trade Corp -950 3rd Av -NY 10022 **Fx:**308-3642
(212) 455-2000 .. **Benford,** R Justin '08 %Simpson T&B LLP -425 Lex Av -NY 10017
(212) 770-1601 .. **Bengali,** Shabbir '94 AIG -70 Pine -NY 10270
(716) 838-4600 .. **Bengart,** Steven B '86 -2655 Sheridan Dr -Tonawanda 14150 **Fx:**693-4685
(516) 747-1340 .. **Bengels,** Dennis A '65 -23 Tremont -Gdn Cty 11530
(212) 906-1684 .. **Bengels,** Jessica L '06 -885 3rd Av -NY 10022 **Fx:**751-4864
(212) 480-2317 .. **Benger,** Eugene '02 Cnsl Ins Dept Comm Mod Reg Fncl Srvcs -25 Beaver -NY 10004
(212) 837-6000 .. **Ben-Gera,** Avner '00 (Hughes H&R LLP) -1 Bttry Pk Plz -NY 10004
(212) 867-9646 .. **Benghiat,** Rebecca Hankin '06 Frnds of Birth Ctr -441 Lex Av -NY 10017
(631) 853-4104 .. **Bengis,** Joshua M '06 %DA -400 Carleton Av Bx9082 -Central Islip 11722 **Fx:**853-7838
(516) 714-7157 .. **Bengtsson,** Andrea L '05 %T Spina -170 Froehlich Farm Blvd -Woodbury 11797 **Fx:**496-5420
(212) 360-5516 .. **Bengualid,** Marc E '90 M Bengualid,PLLC -330 W 38th -NY 10018 **Fx:**427-7484
(212) 563-1710 .. **Benhaim,** David '03 %Schindel FLG&R LLP -14 Penn Plz -NY 10122
(212) 796-9373 .. **Benham,** Stephen M '92 Cohen & Steers Capital Mgmt Inc -280 Park Av -NY 10017
(212) 407-6322 .. **Ben-Harav,** Nurit '99 %Amer Technion Soc -55 E 59th -NY 10022
(315) 477-8100 .. **Benigno,** Anthony M '83 NYS Health Dept -217 S Salina -Syracuse 13202
(516) 593-9415 .. **Benigno,** Thos D '81 -333 Hempstd Av -Malverne 11565 **Fx:**593-9416
(212) 964-6462 .. **Benimowitz,** Michl K '69 -277 Bway -NY 10007 **Fx:**964-6931
(212) 538-9878 .. **Benincasa,** Gabriel A '89 Credit Suisse -1 Mad Av -NY 10010
(718) 993-3000 .. **Benintendi,** James P '91 %Getz & B,PC -172 E 161st -Bronx 10451
(516) 935-1903 .. **Benisatto,** Salvatore E '75 (S Benisatto,PC) -375 N Bway -Jericho 11753
(718) 590-2000 .. **Benischek,** Jennifer R '05 %DA -198 E 161st -Bronx 10451 **Fx:**590-6477
(585) 327-3216 .. **Benitez,** J Richd '99 %Dept of Law -144 Exchange Blvd -Rchstr 14614 **Fx:**546-7514
(585) 753-4500 .. **Benitez,** Raymond G '92 %DA -832 Watts Bldg -Rchstr 14614 **Fx:**753-4576
(212) 864-2246 .. **Benizeau,** Ernestine D '79 -160 W 97th -NY 10025
(212) 836-8000 .. **Ben-Jacob,** Michl '99 Kaye S LLP -425 Park Av -NY 10022
(212) 504-6000 .. **Benjamin,** Aaron J '99 SpclCnsl Cadwalader W&T LLP -1 World Fncl Ctr -NY 10281
(212) 891-2100 .. **Benjamin,** Alexander D '04 Cerberus Capital Mgmt,LP -299 Park Av -NY 10171
(212) 673-8350 .. **Benjamin,** Amy J '90 Benjamin Law.PC -111 E 14th -NY 10003
(212) 752-2171 .. **Benjamin,** Anthony M '75 -145 E 57th -NY 10022 **Fx:**355-3278
(516) 877-5600 .. **Benjamin,** Arthur E '90 %R Tusa -1225 Franklin Av -Gdn Cty 11530 **Fx:**877-5695
(212) 775-8783 .. **Benjamin,** Barry M '94 (Kilpatrick S,LLP) -31 W 52nd -NY 10019 **Fx:**775-8817
(212) 609-6800 .. **Benjamin,** Chas J '04 %McCarter & E,LLP -245 Park Av -NY 10167
(212) 843-8911 .. **Benjamin,** Dean S '90 Ascent Real Estate Advisors -1185 Av of Amer -NY 10036 **Fx:**843-6758
(516) 625-1772 .. **Benjamin,** Donald A '58 -1172 Willis Av Bx149 -Albertson 11507
(212) 614-5461 .. **Benjamin,** Elisabeth Ryden '93 Hlth Care Restructuring Initiatives -105 E 22nd -NY 10010 **Fx:**614-5305
(646) 252-7610 .. **Benjamin,** Goodwin E '90 MTA -2 Bway -NY 10004
(212) 407-8755 .. **Benjamin,** Harvey E '64 NBA -645 5th Av -NY 10022
(212) 832-3006 .. **Benjamin,** Howard '76 -437 Mad Av -NY 10022 **Fx:**829-1518
(212) 872-1000 .. **Benjamin,** James J Jr. '01 -One Bryant Park -NY 10036 **Fx:**872-1002
(212) 830-2466 .. **Benjamin,** Jeff '71 %Novartis Pharmaceuticals Corp -608 5th Av -NY 10020
(718) 263-1111 .. **Benjamin,** Jeffrey '00 (J Benjamin,PC) -118-21 Qns Blvd -Frst Hlls 11375 **Fx:**425-0692
(212) 450-4000 .. **Benjamin,** Joana Gesteira '06 %Davis P&W LLP -450 Lex Av -NY 10017
(212) 298-5200 .. **Benjamin,** Joshua A '99 Leg Aid -49 Thomas -NY 10013 **Fx:**298-5252
(914) 954-1312 .. **Benjamin,** Kenneth B '66 -6 Treelyn Ct -Bardonia 10954 **Fx:**(845) 623-0192
(718) 785-9665 .. **Benjamin,** Lesley V '98 (L Benjamin,PC) -1168 E 37th -Brklyn 11210 **Fx:**(866) 581-9665
(845) 735-0033 .. **Benjamin,** Marvin I '67 -300 N Mddltwn Rd -Pearl Rvr 10965
(212) 351-4000 .. **Benjamin,** Matthew '07 %Gibson D&C LLP -200 Park Av -NY 10166
(914) 824-5100 .. **Benjamin,** Melissa Sheryl '94 Hon B Warhit Cnty Ct -111 Martin Luther King Blvd -White Plns 10601
(212) 848-4000 .. **Benjamin,** Michl W '03 (Shearman & S LLP) -599 Lex Av -NY 10022
(516) 783-0330 .. **Benjamin,** Nicole Layne '04 %DP Weiss -406 Bedford Av -Bellmore 11710 **Fx:**783-8739
(845) 735-0510 .. **Benjamin,** Rhonda M '91 %M Manna & Assoc,PC -300 N Mddltwn Rd -Pearl Rvr 10965 **Fx:**(201) 447-6631
(914) 741-6100 .. **Benjamin,** Robt A '04 %Kaufman B&R -200 Summit Lk Dr -Valhalla 10595
(212) 512-3318 .. **Benjamin,** Robt K '83 %McGraw-Hill -1221 Av of Amer -NY 10020 **Fx:**512-4827
(212) 490-1700 .. **Benjamin,** Robt W '83 (Wiggin & D) -450 Lex Av -NY 10017
(607) 772-1442 .. **Benjamin,** Ronald R '78 R Benjamin -126 Riverside Dr Bx607 -Bnghmtn 13902 **Fx:**772-1678
(516) 625-1772 .. **Benjamin,** Scott Louis '87 -1172 Willis Av Bx149 -Albertson 11507
(718) 728-0555 .. **Benjamin,** Scott P '85 (Benjamin & V LLC) -2809 Ditmars Blvd -Astoria 11105
(518) 474-0846 .. **Benjamin,** Wayne L '77 %DMV -6 ESP -Albany 12228 **Fx:**474-0712
(315) 471-8111 .. **Benjamin,** Zachary R '06 %Scolaro SCF&B,PC -507 Plum -Syracuse 13204
(718) 523-3413 .. **Benjamin-George,** Beverly '02 -8931 161st -Jamaica 11432 **Fx:**523-3415
(212) 450-4000 .. **Benkard,** James W B '63 SrCnsl Davis P&W LLP -450 Lex Av -NY 10017
(212) 508-6724 .. **Benkov,** Judith L '84 %Tannenbaum HS&H LLP -900 3rd Av -NY 10022 **Fx:**(646) 607-9079
(212) 880-1304 .. **Benlevi,** Yosi Joe '02 Ticor Title Ins Co -711 3rd Av -NY 10017
(212) 474-1000 .. **Benloulou,** Jonathan S '06 %Cravath S&M LLP -825 8th Av -NY 10019
(212) 310-8000 .. **Ben-Menachem,** Ron S '05 %Weil G&M LLP -767 5th Av -NY 10153
(212) 210-9454 .. **Ben-Meyer,** Saul '79 (Alston & B LLP) -90 Park Av -NY 10016
(212) 267-5399 .. **Benmorits,** Sherri R '96 -325 Bway -NY 10007 **Fx:**267-5813
(212) 292-4290 .. **Ben-Moshe,** Jos S '92 -521 5th Av -NY 10175
(212) 326-3939 .. **Benn,** Jacqueline '02 (Jones D) -222 E 41st -NY 10017
(212) 403-1000 .. **Benn,** Michl S '08 %Wachtell LR&K -51 W 52nd -NY 10019
(212) 962-0800 .. **Benn,** Patrick G '94 (Estrin B&L) -225 Bway -NY 10007 **Fx:**732-1408
(516) 378-1110 .. **Bennardo,** Jack A '81 -2555 Linden Ln Bx360 -Merrick 11566 **Fx:**378-8588
(631) 361-2154 .. **Bennardo,** Raymond M '96 Sen J Flanagan -260 Middle Cntry Rd -Smithtwn 11787
(212) 849-7000 .. **Benner,** Jeffrey L '10 %Quinn EU&S,LLP -51 Mad Av -NY 10010
(212) 715-0300 .. **Benner,** Michl B '81 Cnsl Tishman Speyer Prop -45 Rckfllr Plz -NY 10111 **Fx:**332-6603
(716) 847-8400 .. **Bennes,** Cindy Kaplan '89 (Phillips L LLP) -3400 HSBC Ctr -Buffalo 14203
(315) 422-3029 .. **Bennet,** Tina C '00 -100 Kreischer Rd -N Syracuse 13212 **Fx:**422-3259
(212) 696-2116 .. **Bennett,** Alan J '89 (Bennett & M LLP) -575 Lex Av -NY 10022 **Fx:**696-2115
(516) 822-3550 .. **Bennett,** Anthony E '96 (Hoffmann & B LLP) -6900 Jericho Tpk -Syosset 11791 **Fx:**822-3582
(212) 407-1500 .. **Bennett,** Barbara M '91 %Kensington Publshng -119 W 40th -NY 10018 **Fx:**935-0699
(585) 232-6500 .. **Bennett,** Brian S '08 %Harter S&E LLP -1600 Bausch & Lomb Pl -Rchstr 14604
(212) 841-1000 .. **Bennett,** Bruce C '84 (Covington & B LLP) -620 8th Av -NY 10018
(212) 903-1488 .. **Bennett,** Catherine Gilbert '02 William Morris Agency,Inc -1325 Av of Amer -NY 10019
(518) 266-3000 .. **Bennett,** Catherine M '83 %Div Tax Appls -500 Fed -Troy 12180 **Fx:**272-5178
(212) 688-0353 .. **Bennett,** Chas H '71 -2 Sutton Pl S -NY 10022
(212) 209-4800 .. **Bennett,** Danielle M '09 Brown R LLP -7 Times Sq -NY 10036
(716) 652-9560 .. **Bennett DiFilippo & Kurtzhalts,LLP** -681 Main -E Aurora 14052 **Fx:**652-2164
(716) 537-2272 .. **Bennett DiFilippo & Kurtzhalts,LLP** -2 N Main -Holland 14080 **Fx:**537-9749
(212) 474-1000 .. **Bennett,** Donald Scott '07 %Cravath S&M LLP -825 8th Av -NY 10019
(716) 847-8400 .. **Bennett,** Ericka N '06 %Phillips L LLP -3400 HSBC Ctr -Buffalo 14203
(212) 298-5096 .. **Bennett,** Fredric B '74 %Leg Aid -49 Thomas -NY 10013 **Fx:**298-5252
(315) 946-4881 .. **Bennett,** Gary Lee '82 Dept Soc Srvcs -77 Water Bx10 -Lyons 14489 **Fx:**946-6810
(212) 229-0020 .. **Bennett,** Gary O '80 %Stonestreet Studios -48 W 21st -NY 10010
(646) 328-0120 .. **Bennett Giuliano McDonnell & Perrone,LLP** -494 8th Av -NY 10001 **Fx:**328-0121
(212) 935-3000 .. **Bennett,** Gregory R '05 %Mintz LCFG&P,PC -666 3rd Av -NY 10017
(315) 687-7369 .. **Bennett,** Harold C '68 -160 W Genesee -Chittenango 13037
(212) 806-5400 .. **Bennett,** Hillel M '79 (Stroock &S&L LLP) -180 Maiden Ln -NY 10038
(516) 227-0700 .. **Bennett,** James D '64 Cnsl Farrell F,PC -1320 RXR Plz -Uniondale 11556
(212) 681-6500 .. **Bennett,** James R '76 (Stempel BC&H,PC) -675 3rd Av -NY 10017
(631) 853-5212 .. **Bennett,** James S '76 %Leg Aid -400 Carleton Av Bx9082 -Central Islip 11722 **Fx:**853-7798
(716) 852-3540 .. **Bennett,** James W '72 (Watson BCJ&S) -12 Fountain Plz -Buffalo 14202
(212) 558-4000 .. **Bennett,** Jessica C '10 %Sullivan & C LLP -125 Broad -NY 10004
(212) 839-5300 .. **Bennett,** Jessica E '07 %Sidley A LLP -787 7th Av -NY 10019
(212) 435-3571 .. **Bennett,** Joan F '79 %Port Auth of NY/NJ -225 Park Av S -NY 10003 **Fx:**435-3555
(631) 423-7777 .. **Bennett,** John C '86 (Gathman & B,LLP) -191 NY Av -Huntngtn 11743 **Fx:**423-7784
(212) 483-2323 .. **Bennett,** John D '89 %JP Morgan Chase -345 Park Av -NY 10154
(516) 741-7985 .. **Bennett,** John Eldridge '63 -59 Grdn -Gdn Cty 11530 **Fx:**741-8759

(631) 283-9696 .. **Bennett**, John J '82 (Bennett & R) -212 Windmill Ln -Southampton 11968
(212) 455-2000 .. **Bennett**, John N '09 %Simpson T&B LLP -425 Lex Av -NY 10017
(212) 318-6000 .. **Bennett**, Joshua M '05 %Paul HJ&W LLP -75 E 55th -NY 10022
(516) 571-3800 .. **Bennett**, Karen B '93 %DA -262 Old Cntry Rd -Mineola 11501 **Fx**:248-9479
(212) 341-6400 .. **Bennett**, Karen L '78 %Liquidation Bur -123 William -NY 10038 **Fx**:608-3398
(315) 218-8000 .. **Bennett**, Kathleen M '99 (Bond S&K,PLLC) -1 Lincoln Ctr -Syracuse 13202
(212) 295-6349 .. **Bennett**, Kathryn A '09 %WilmerHale -399 Park Av -NY 10022
(518) 486-6470 .. **Bennett**, Kathy A '77 Cnsl Div of Budget -State Cptl -Albany 12224
(585) 346-6540 .. **Bennett**, Kenneth L '79 -Bx333 -Livonia 14487
(914) 323-7000 .. **Bennett**, Kirsten E '02 %Wilson EME&D LLP -3 Gannett Dr -White Plns 10604
(212) 735-3000 .. **Bennett**, Lauren R '09 %Skadden ASM&F LLP -4 Times Sq -NY 10036
(212) 444-6357 .. **Bennett**, Laurie M '01 Invstmnt Tchnlgy Grp Inc -380 Mad Av -NY 10017
(516) 222-6200 .. **Bennett**, Leslie R '74 (Berkman HPP&F,PC) -100 Grdn City Plz -Gdn Cty 11530
(718) 782-6200 .. **Bennett**, Lonny J '80 Dime Svngs Bk -209 Havemeyer -Brklyn 11211
(716) 845-3650 .. **Bennett**, Margot S '88 MHLS -438 Main -Buffalo 14202 **Fx**:874-7794
(585) 530-3149 .. **Bennett**, Mark W '98 %Appllt Div 4th Dept -50 East Av Ste 200 -Rchstr 14604 **Fx**:530-3247
(718) 250-2000 .. **Bennett**, Matthew J '09 %DA -350 Jay -Brklyn 11201 **Fx**:250-2314
(212) 756-2000 .. **Bennett**, Matthew P '02 %Schulte R&Z LLP -919 3rd Av -NY 10022
(845) 294-5401 .. **Bennett**, Matthew T '83 (Mirro & B) -176 Main BxB -Goshen 10924
(718) 282-5900 .. **Bennett**, Michl G '62 (Bennett & R) -1970 Flatbush Av -Brklyn 11234 **Fx**:(516) 826-9581
(646) 227-3516 .. **Bennett**, Pamela '86 Memorial Sloan Kettering -633 3rd Av -NY 10017
(212) 210-9559 .. **Bennett**, Philippe '84 (Alston & B LLP) -90 Park Av -NY 10016
(631) 283-9696 .. **Bennett & Read** -212 Windmill Ln -Southampton 11968 **Fx**:283-1259
(212) 727-1185 .. **Bennett**, Richd E '71 -520 LaGuardia Pl -NY 10012
(212) 888-9428 .. **Bennett**, Richd H '92 -110 E 59th -NY 10022 **Fx**:579-3420
(315) 474-7541 .. **Bennett**, Robt G '99 (Menter R&T,PC) -308 Maltbie -Syracuse 13204
(212) 650-0253 .. **Bennett**, Robt S '89 -1404 3rd Av -NY 10075 **Fx**:650-0253
(212) 918-3000 .. **Bennett**, Robt S '99 (Hogan L LLP) -875 3rd Av -NY 10022
(716) 537-2272 .. **Bennett**, Ronald P '63 (Bennett D&K,LLP) -2 N Main -Holland 14080
(518) 474-9502 .. **Bennett**, Russell C '75 %OTDA -40 N Pearl -Albany 12243 **Fx**:474-9389
(718) 624-1211 .. **Bennett**, Sandra Hope '05 (Zucker & B,PC) -186 Joralemon -Brklyn 11201 **Fx**:624-6037
(212) 512-3998 .. **Bennett**, Scott L '75 %McGraw-Hill -1221 Av of Amer -NY 10020 **Fx**:512-4827
(718) 250-0400 .. **Bennett**, Sharon L '97 %R Tusa -1 MetroTech Ctr -Brklyn 11201 **Fx**:250-0591
(212) 471-8500 .. **Bennett**, Stacie L '09 %Herzfeld & R,PC -125 Broad -NY 10004
(718) 579-3000 .. **Bennett**, Stephen M '72 %Leg Aid -1020 Grnd Cncrs -Bronx 10451 **Fx**:588-2611
(212) 326-3939 .. **Bennett**, Steven C '85 (Jones D) -222 E 41st -NY 10017
(212) 292-4488 .. **Bennett**, Steven C '91 -521 5th Av -NY 10175
(212) 558-4000 .. **Bennett**, Sultana '07 %Sullivan & C LLP -125 Broad -NY 10004
(718) 262-7100 .. **Bennett**, Susan A '84 %Civil Ct -89-17 Sutphin Blvd -Jamaica 11435 **Fx**:262-7107
(315) 474-7541 .. **Bennett**, Teresa M '08 %Menter R&T,PC -308 Maltbie -Syracuse 13204
(212) 308-6100 .. **Bennett**, Terrence M '86 (Levi L&F LLP) -1185 Av of Amer -NY 10036
(518) 408-0469 .. **Bennett**, Theo J '83 %Workers Comp Bd -20 Park -Albany 12207
(212) 209-4800 .. **Bennett**, Timothy C '05 Brown R LLP -7 Times Sq -NY 10036
(718) 579-3000 .. **Bennett**, Timothy J P '86 %Leg Aid -1020 Grnd Cncrs -Bronx 10451 **Fx**:588-2611
(315) 866-6648 .. **Bennett**, Todd D '92 -123 Court -Herkimer 13350 **Fx**:866-1079
(646) 328-0120 .. **Bennett**, Wm R III '93 (Bennett GM&P,LLP) -494 8th Av -NY 10001
(516) 768-8848 .. **Bennett-Brumm**, Karen S '88 -Bx2882 -Aquebogue 11931 **Fx**:(631) 779-3178
(914) 422-4333 .. **Bennett-Rodriguez**, Linda A '99 %Empire Justice Ctr -80 N Bway -White Plns 10603 **Fx**:422-4391
(212) 450-4000 .. **Bennetts**, Louise C '09 %Davis P&W LLP -450 Lex Av -NY 10017
(212) 308-2716 .. **Bennick**, Donna E '85 D Bennick,PC -20 Vesey -NY 10007 **Fx**:308-0058
(718) 236-3000 .. **Bennion**, David C '05 Catholic Migration Ofc -1258 65th -Brklyn 11219
(607) 776-0444 .. **Benno**, Deetza G '01 -7 E Steuben -Bath 14810
(212) 608-4140 .. **Beno**, Beti '03 %I Marku,PC -299 Bway -NY 10007 **Fx**:608-6256
(845) 429-3900 .. **Benoff**, Zeevyah A '03 %Stein & S -1 Railroad Sq -Haverstraw 10927 **Fx**:429-4392
(212) 384-1000 .. **Benoit**, Carl A Jr. '92 %FBI -26 Fed Plz -NY 10278
(212) 298-5196 .. **Benoit**, Michelle M '92 %Leg Aid -49 Thomas -NY 10013 **Fx**:298-5252
(917) 367-9246 .. **Benoit-Landale**, Brigitte P '02 UN Ofc of Leg Affrs -1 UN Plz -NY 10017 **Fx**:(212) 963-6430
(212) 506-1700 .. **Benor**, Miriam A '05 %Kasowitz BT&F LLP -1633 Bway -NY 10019
(914) 946-2400 .. **Benowich**, Leonard A '80 -1025 Wstchstr Av -White Plns 10604 **Fx**:946-9474
(631) 878-4329 .. **Benowitz**, Jerrold '63 -196 Bellevw Av -Ctr Moriches 11934 **Fx**:878-9238
(212) 797-3544 .. **Benowitz**, Lance E '96 %French & C,LLP -29 Bway -NY 10006
(212) 422-0488 .. **Benowitz**, Robt J '72 (Rick SF&B,LLP) -90 Broad -NY 10004
(516) 572-5834 .. **Benrubi**, Robt A '91 Nassau Health Care Corp -2201 Hempstd Tpke -E Meadow 11554
(914) 332-4144 .. **Bensal**, Nancy B '79 Housing Action Cncl -55 S Bway -Tarrytwn 10591
(212) 735-3000 .. **Bensch**, Jennifer A '08 (Skadden ASM&F LLP) -4 Times Sq -NY 10036
(212) 813-1600 .. **Benschar**, Tal S '97 %Kalow & S -488 Mad Av -NY 10022
(516) 486-2250 .. **Bensen**, Eric E '97 -384 Euston Rd S -Gdn Cty 11530
(212) 883-1700 .. **Ben Shimon**, Elsa '09 %Duval & S LLP -101 Park Av -NY 10178
(212) 725-6530 .. **Benshoof**, Janet '72 Global Justice Ctr -25 E 21st -NY 10010 **Fx**:725-6536
(516) 678-7875 .. **Bensi**, Andrew R '80 -2950 Hempstd Tpk -Levittwn 11756
(212) 326-3939 .. **Bensinger**, Chas N III '06 (Jones D) -222 E 41st -NY 10017
(212) 490-2525 .. **Bensinger**, Deborah R '05 ADL -605 3rd Av -NY 10158 **Fx**:867-0779
(212) 596-9000 .. **Bensinger**, Menachem M '07 %Ropes & G LLP -1211 Av of Amer -NY 10036
(212) 756-2000 .. **Bensky**, Eric A '97 SpclCnsl Schulte R&Z LLP -919 3rd Av -NY 10022
(212) 969-1333 .. **Bensley**, Adam M '03 %Alliance Bernstein LP -1345 Av of Amer -NY 10105 **Fx**:554-4639
(315) 732-5134 .. **Benson**, B Brooks '88 %Golden Law Firm -1412 Genesee -Utica 13502 **Fx**:732-5161
(212) 583-9600 .. **Benson**, Craig R '87 (Littler M,PC) -900 3rd Av -NY 10022
(212) 506-1700 .. **Benson**, Danl R '81 (Kasowitz BT&F LLP) -1633 Bway -NY 10019
(646) 471-1757 .. **Benson**, David J '09 PricewaterhouseCoopers -300 Mad Av -NY 10017
(212) 730-7750 .. **Benson**, Edw S '93 %Nicoletti GS&O,LLP -555 5th Av -NY 10017
(212) 836-8000 .. **Benson**, Gregg M '01 %Kaye S LLP -425 Park Av -NY 10022
(212) 922-2200 .. **Benson**, John J '04 %Watson F&W LLP -1133 Av of Amer -NY 10036
(212) 805-0684 .. **Benson**, Kelly E '05 DST CT SD NY -500 Pearl -NY 10007
(315) 474-2911 .. **Benson**, Kristen M '01 (Smith SK&S,PC) -250 S Clinton -Syracuse 13202
(716) 592-2900 .. **Benson**, Michl A '89 -77 N Buffalo -Sprngvll 14141 **Fx**:592-5170
(516) 571-3800 .. **Benson**, Mitchell H '87 %DA -262 Old Cntry Rd -Mineola 11501 **Fx**:248-9479
(516) 222-0200 .. **Benson**, Richd A '78 %Keith S&F -666 Old Cntry Rd -Gdn Cty 11530
(212) 474-1000 .. **Benson**, Robt E Jr. '10 %Cravath S&M LLP -825 8th Av -NY 10019
(315) 687-3993 .. **Benson**, Robt J '68 -234 Genesee Bx127 -Chittenango 13037 **Fx**:687-3994
(212) 449-1000 .. **Benson**, Shawn W '02 %Merrill Lynch -220 Bway -NY 10038
(315) 474-1267 .. **Benson**, Walter F '82 (Lynn Law Firm,LLP) -101 S Salina -Syracuse 13202 **Fx**:474-4514
(516) 571-3014 .. **Ben-Sorek**, Liora M '93 %Cnty Atty -1 West -Mineola 11501 **Fx**:571-6604
(914) 682-2634 .. **Bent**, Maureen A '91 (MannBent & Assoc,PC) -50 Main -White Plns 10606 **Fx**:682-7784
(212) 259-8000 .. **Bent**, Samantha N '10 %Dewey & L LLP -1301 Av of Amer -NY 10019
(212) 610-6300 .. **Bent**, Tamika P-G '09 %Allen & O -1221 Av of Amer -NY 10020
(212) 723-3122 .. **Bentch**, Adam C '02 Citigroup Global -250 West -NY 10013
(718) 780-7990 .. **Bentele**, Ursula '70 %Bklyn Law Schl -250 Joralemon -Brklyn 11201 **Fx**:780-0393
(718) 739-1529 .. **Bentham**, Yvette A '91 Edwards & Co,PC -175-20 Wexford Ter -Jamaica 11432 **Fx**:739-1583
(212) 459-4067 .. **Bentley**, Anthony M '71 SpclCnsl AM Bentley,PC -116 W 72nd -NY 10023 **Fx**:877-2868
(212) 243-1600 .. **Bentley**, Brandon C '00 Landmark Advisors -408 W 14th -NY 10014
(212) 815-1120 .. **Bentley**, Bruce K '83 DC 37 MELS -125 Barclay -NY 10007 **Fx**:815-1343
(212) 756-2000 .. **Bentley**, James T '03 %Schulte R&Z LLP -919 3rd Av -NY 10022
(516) 296-7000 .. **Bentley**, Jennifer A '05 %Certilman BA&H,LLP -90 Merrick Av -E Meadow 11554
(212) 728-8000 .. **Bentley**, Lisa Dennis '04 %Willkie F&G LLP -787 7th Av -NY 10019
(212) 715-9100 .. **Bentley**, Philip '85 (Kramer LN&F,LLP) -1177 Av of Amer -NY 10036
(518) 486-1336 .. **Bentley**, Susan R '00 %Dept of Health -Corning Twr 24th Fl -Albany 12237 **Fx**:486-4834
(212) 455-2000 .. **Bentley**, Taylor W '10 %Simpson T&B LLP -425 Lex Av -NY 10017
(516) 466-2130 .. **Benton**, Barry C '57 -9 Lincoln Rd -Gt Neck 11021
(631) 390-0010 .. **Benton**, Chas W '79 %Bruno G&S,LLP -445 Broad Hollow Rd -Melvll 11747
(212) 408-0003 .. **Benton**, Edw H '82 AXA Advisors,LLC -1633 Bway -NY 10019 **Fx**:408-9553
(212) 732-6666 .. **Benton**, Herbert M '59 -225 Bway -NY 10007
(212) 837-6000 .. **Benton**, Jason C '01 %Hughes H&R LLP -1 Bttry Pk Plz -NY 10004
(718) 520-3733 .. **Benton**, Josephine C '81 %Hon C Thomas -88-11 Sutphin Blvd -Jamaica 11435
(718) 243-6470 .. **Benton**, Marisa F '03 %Leg Aid -111 Lvngstn -Brklyn 11201 **Fx**:237-8737
(914) 948-1200 .. **Bentzen**, Richd D '79 SrCnsl Cerussi & S,PC -1 N Lex Av -White Plns 10601
(212) 708-6600 .. **Benudis**, Elissa Ganbarg '88 LeFrak Org -40 W 57th -NY 10019 **Fx**:708-6681
(212) 921-5525 .. **Benun**, Denise S '03 (Kaminer K&B LLP) -369 Lex Av -NY 10017 **Fx**:(646) 269-7669
(914) 347-2600 .. **Benvenuto**, Gerard '95 (Traub LS&S LLP) -7 Skyline Dr -Hawthorne 10532
(212) 450-4000 .. **Benvenuto**, Osmar J '08 %Davis P&W LLP -450 Lex Av -NY 10017
(516) 775-2236 .. **Benvenuto**, Thos J '85 (Santangelo B&S) -1800 Nrthrn Blvd -Roslyn 11576
(845) 565-1100 .. **Benvie**, Sally S '03 %Tarshis CLM&M,PLLC -One Corwin Ct -Newburgh 12550
(212) 845-7900 .. **Benwitt**, Michl G '05 Ramius Capital Grp,LLC -599 Lex Av -NY 10022
(212) 836-8000 .. **Benyacar**, David S '92 (Kaye S LLP) -425 Park Av -NY 10022
(212) 556-3402 .. **Benyacar**, Michelle J '94 Syska Hennessey -11 W 42nd -NY 10036
(212) 403-1000 .. **Ben-Yishai**, Shiri '03 %Wachtell LR&K -51 W 52nd -NY 10019
(585) 641-8000 .. **Benz**, David D '02 %Fix SB&G,PC -295 Woodcliff Dr -Fairprt 14450
(716) 856-5500 .. **Benz**, Susan A '92 (Damon M LLP) -200 Delaware Av -Buffalo 14202
(718) 312-4241 .. **Benza**, Louis L '87 Empire Blue Cross -15 MetroTech Ctr -Brklyn 11201 **Fx**:312-6010
(917) 351-1335 .. **Benzakarya**, Romina A '02 %Sperber D&K,PC -48 W 37th -NY 10018

(516) 922-9100 .. **Benzie,** Helen M '78 %V McNamara -1045 Oyster Bay Rd -E Norwich 11732 **Fx:**922-9208
(212) 667-0236 .. **Benziger,** Paul B '97 -1 Wall -NY 10005
(212) 765-9100 .. **Benzija,** Walter '96 (Halperin BR,LLP) -555 Mad Av -NY 10022
(212) 557-0167 .. **Ben-Zion,** Israel '81 (Ben-Zion & F) -60 E 42nd -NY 10165 **Fx:**557-1703
(212) 719-5300 .. **Ben-Zvi,** Leslie H '83 -100 Wall -NY 10005 **Fx:**666-6655
(212) 225-2000 .. **Bepko,** Arminda B '05 %Cleary GS&H -1 Lbrty Plz -NY 10006
(212) 458-1968 .. **Beqaj,** Vivian '01 AIG Domestic Claims -175 Water -NY 10038
(212) 382-0700 .. **Beran,** Martin J '58 OfCnsl Ostrolenk FG&S,LLP -1180 Av of Amer -NY 10036
(212) 815-1805 .. **Beranbaum,** Joan L '75 %DC 37 MELS -125 Barclay -NY 10007 **Fx:**815-1343
(212) 509-1616 .. **Beranbaum,** John A '82 (Beranbaum M LLP) -80 Pine -NY 10005
(212) 509-1616 .. **Beranbaum Menken LLP** -80 Pine -NY 10005 **Fx:**509-8088
(716) 285-3288 .. **Berard,** Wm D III '86 -770 Main -Niagara Fls 14301 **Fx:**282-0287
(718) 891-1937 .. **Berardelli,** Gene R '06 (G Berardelli,PLLC) -2817 Haring -Brklyn 11235
(716) 681-0069 .. **Berardi,** Rosanna '05 -33 Central Av -Lancaster 14086 **Fx:**683-3341
(914) 686-1041 .. **Berardino,** Michl S '84 (Mangialardi & B) -111 N Central Av -Hartsdale 10530 **Fx:**686-1043
(212) 446-4800 .. **Berardino,** Rita L '02 (Kirkland & E LLP) -153 E 53rd -NY 10022
(914) 686-1041 .. **Berardino,** S J '52 -111 N Central Av -Hartsdale 10530
(212) 558-4000 .. **Berarducci,** Patrick B '08 %Sullivan & C LLP -125 Broad -NY 10004
(716) 842-6350 .. **Berbary,** George A '74 -237 Main -Buffalo 14203
(718) 544-0198 .. **Berberian,** Raymond P '71 -80-02 Kew Grdns Rd -Kew Gdns 11415 **Fx:**520-8751
(212) 612-9550 .. **Berberich,** Karen Maria '98 %Dombroff & G,PC -40 Broad -NY 10004
(845) 357-0036 .. **Berbit,** Alexander F '08 SpclCnsl Lexow B&A,PC -56 Park Av Bx239 -Suffern 10901
(845) 357-0036 .. **Berbit,** Warren E '74 (Lexow B&A,PC) -56 Park Av Bx239 -Suffern 10901
(212) 872-1000 .. **Berchem,** Kerry E '92 -One Bryant Park -NY 10036 **Fx:**872-1002
(716) 847-8400 .. **Berchou,** Michl J '94 (Phillips L LLP) -3400 HSBC Ctr -Buffalo 14203
(212) 455-2000 .. **Berckholtz,** Rafael '07 %Simpson T&B LLP -425 Lex Av -NY 10017
(914) 472-8500 .. **Bercovici,** Paul B '94 -740 W Bstn Post Rd -Mamaroneck 10543 **Fx:**472-2106
(212) 682-1600 .. **Bercovitch,** Stephen J '77 %Diamant Katz Kahn & Co LLP -6 E 43rd -NY 10017 **Fx:**682-1661
(212) 461-7152 .. **Berd,** Alex '01 (Berd & K PLLC) -44 Wall -NY 10005 **Fx:**461-7153
(212) 260-9655 .. **Berde Mahl,** Olga '71 (O Berde Mahl,PC) -32 Union Sq E -NY 10003 **Fx:**260-9697
(516) 678-9797 .. **Berdnik,** Alison M '01 (Civardi O&B,LLP) -23 S Main -Freeprt 11520 **Fx:**678-2266
(212) 986-3750 .. **Berdon,** Allan J '63 -600 3rd Av -NY 10016 **Fx:**661-8002
(212) 849-7000 .. **Berdon,** Andrew M '88 (Quinn EU&S,LLP) -51 Mad Av -NY 10010
(212) 270-5920 .. **Berean,** Kevin J '03 JP Morgan Chase & Co -270 Park Av -NY 10017
(516) 545-5160 .. **Bereche,** Alfred C '91 %Natl Grid -175 E Old Cntry Rd -Hicksvll 11801 **Fx:**545-5029
(845) 634-6336 .. **Bereck,** Debra S '82 -120-126 N Main -New Cty 10956 **Fx:**638-9175
(718) 447-5499 .. **Berel,** Harold B '52 (Berel & M) -358 St Marks Pl -Staten Isl 10301
(718) 447-5499 .. **Berel & Mullen** -358 St Marks Pl -Staten Isl 10301
(212) 687-4900 .. **Berelson,** Stuart E '62 OfCnsl Wormser KG&J LLP -825 3rd Av -NY 10022
(212) 451-2300 .. **Berenblat,** Ron S '99 (Olshan GFR&W LLP) -65 E 55th -NY 10022
(212) 808-7800 .. **Berenbroick,** Jessica L '07 %Kelley D&W LLP -101 Park Av -NY 10178
(212) 909-9500 .. **Berend,** Robt W '55 (Wachtel & M,LLP) -885 2nd Av -NY 10017
(212) 259-8000 .. **Berengarten,** Joshua '03 %Dewey & L LLP -1301 Av of Amer -NY 10019
(212) 326-2000 .. **Berengarten,** Michl '06 %O'Melveny & M LLP -7 Times Sq -NY 10036
(212) 681-1548 .. **Berengarten,** Robt '67 R Berengarten -240 Mad Av -NY 10016 **Fx:**681-1593
(212) 858-1000 .. **Berens,** Michl C '08 %Pillsbury WSP LLP -1540 Bway -NY 10036
(516) 823-1800 .. **Berenshteyn,** Gary '09 Glassman Law Grp -34 Atl Av -Lynbrk 11563 **Fx:**823-4496
(212) 837-6000 .. **Berenson,** Harris T '98 Cnsl Hughes H&R LLP -1 Bttry Pk Plz -NY 10004
(212) 840-7383 .. **Berenson,** Harvey S '68 Schonbraun McCann Grp LLP -750 3rd Av -NY 10017
(212) 220-3000 .. **Berenson,** Marvin L '67 %Broadcast Music Inc -250 Greenwich -NY 10007
(212) 977-6800 .. **Berenson,** Richd A '60 -135 W 50th -NY 10020
(212) 286-8585 .. **Berent,** Anna '06 %Heidell PM&B,LLP -99 Park Av -NY 10016
(212) 302-9494 .. **Berenthal,** David W '98 %Berenthal & Assoc,PC -317 Mad Av -NY 10017 **Fx:**354-5625
(212) 302-9494 .. **Berenthal,** James L '70 (Berenthal & Assoc,PC) -317 Mad Av -NY 10017 **Fx:**354-5625
(631) 653-4875 .. **Beren-Wolff,** Ursula H '04 -43 Head of Lots Rd -E Quogue 11942
(212) 858-1000 .. **Berenyi,** Jessica R '08 %Pillsbury WSP LLP -1540 Bway -NY 10036
(212) 682-8811 .. **Beress,** Viktoria A '04 %Dunnington B&M LLP -1359 Bway -NY 10018
(212) 451-2300 .. **Berets,** Jessica A '03 %Olshan GFR&W LLP -65 E 55th -NY 10022
(585) 264-1380 .. **Beretta,** Frank J '85 -109 W Cmmrcial -E Rchstr 14445
(212) 850-0624 .. **Berey,** Michl J '77 %1st Amer Title -633 3rd Av -NY 10017 **Fx:**331-1511
(315) 734-2000 .. **Berez,** Lydia S '01 %Utica Natl Ins -180 Genesee Bx530 -Utica 13502 **Fx:**734-2662
(212) 619-5400 .. **Berezanskiy,** Glenn '06 %Newman F LLP -1250 Bway -NY 10001
(212) 310-8000 .. **Berezin,** Robt S '98 (Weil G&M LLP) -767 5th Av -NY 10153
(212) 385-4800 .. **Berfond,** Melvin B '84 -277 Bway -NY 10007 **Fx:**346-0858
(212) 909-6000 .. **Berg,** Andrew N '79 (Debevoise & P LLP) -919 3rd Av -NY 10022
(212) 637-2551 .. **Berg,** Arianna R '03 %US Atty -1 St Andrews Plz -NY 10007
(718) 545-1111 .. **Berg,** Brian H '03 Kokolakis & Assoc,PC -31-16 30th Av -Astoria 11102
(212) 238-3000 .. **Berg,** Bryant K '92 OfCnsl Emmet M&M,LLP -120 Bway -NY 10271
(631) 385-1746 .. **Berg,** Chas E '93 Berg & Assoc -Bx2728 -South Huntington 11746 **Fx:**385-1746
(516) 746-7799 .. **Berg,** David '06 %Reisman P&R LLP -1305 Franklin Av -Gdn Cty 11530
(212) 829-0400 .. **Berg,** David C '91 -425 Mad Av -NY 10017 **Fx:**829-9398
(212) 715-1000 .. **Berg,** David S '93 (Arnold & P LLP) -399 Park Av -NY 10022
(845) 623-1711 .. **Berg,** Egon E '64 -55 Old Tpk Rd -Nanuet 10954
(212) 819-8200 .. **Berg,** Eric L '82 (White & C LLP) -1155 Av of Amer -NY 10036
(917) 575-2830 .. **Berg,** Freddie J '90 -21 W 86th Bx87 -NY 10024
(212) 248-2220 .. **Berg,** Gabriel A '98 OfCnsl Kennedy JG LLC -99 Wall -NY 10005 **Fx:**248-0170
(212) 608-3103 .. **Berg,** Howard B '53 -150 Bway -NY 10038
(212) 981-3300 .. **Berg,** Ira S '02 Amida Cptl Mgmt LLC -415 Mad Av -NY 10017
(212) 480-4240 .. **Berg,** Irwin M '63 %Fuchsberg & F -29 Bway -NY 10006
(212) 279-3500 .. **Berg,** J Fredk Jr. '72 (Russin VB&B,LLP) -260 Mad Av -NY 10016
(212) 994-0260 .. **Berg,** Jay H '93 %Cornicello T&B-C,LLP -2 Wall -NY 10005
(212) 599-0990 .. **Berg,** Jonathan D '97 %J Lagemann -300 E 42nd -NY 10017 **Fx:**922-0518
(212) 538-5137 .. **Berg,** Kevin I '97 CSFB -11 Mad Av -NY 10010
(914) 397-1050 .. **Berg,** Kim Patricia '96 (Gould & B,LLP) -222 Bloomingdale Rd -White Plns 10605
(845) 356-0634 .. **Berg,** Leah '89 (Berg & B) -71 E Eckerson Rd -Spg Vly 10977
(212) 582-8000 .. **Berg,** Mark E '85 (Feingold & A,LLP) -1330 Av of Amer -NY 10019
(914) 517-5000 .. **Berg,** Michl A '97 OfCnsl Meiselman DPC&E,PC -1311 Mamaroneck Av -White Plns 10605
(646) 855-0706 .. **Berg,** Michl J '01 Bank of Amer -1 Bryant Pk -NY 10036
(607) 277-2355 .. **Berg,** Michl R '79 %Hon MJ Sherman -320 N Tioga Bx70 -Ithaca 14851 **Fx:**272-0684
(212) 373-3000 .. **Berg,** Mitchell L '82 (Paul WRW&G LLP) -1285 Av of Amer -NY 10019
(718) 340-4426 .. **Berg,** Paula E '83 %CUNY Law Schl -65-21 Main -Flushng 11367 **Fx:**340-4482
(212) 601-2680 .. **Berg,** Philip C '92 (Gonzalez S&H LLP) -350 5th Av -NY 10118
(212) 490-3000 .. **Berg,** Rebecca Wilen '98 (Wilson EME&D LLP) -150 E 42nd -NY 10017
(212) 940-3015 .. **Berg,** Roger E '70 (Nixon P LLP) -437 Mad Av -NY 10022
(315) 476-0806 .. **Berg,** Stefan D '92 -309 Arnold Av -Syracuse 13210 **Fx:**476-0806
(212) 224-5022 .. **Berg,** Steven M '93 SMBC Capital Mrkts Inc -277 Park Av -NY 10172
(516) 747-9494 .. **Berg,** Stuart R '78 -1205 Franklin Av -Gdn Cty 11530
(914) 285-9800 .. **Berg,** Stuart W '85 (Kurzman EC&L,LLP) -1 N Bway -White Plns 10601
(914) 995-4310 .. **Berg,** Tomme '79 %Hon F Nicolai -111 Martin Luther King Blvd -White Plns 10601
(212) 267-7575 .. **Bergam,** Mary A '87 (Dinerman B&D) -170 Bway -NY 10038 **Fx:**571-7475
(212) 527-8650 .. **Bergamo,** Anthony '78 -335 Mad Av -NY 10017 **Fx:**527-8653
(518) 465-1403 .. **Bergan,** Michl F '64 -219 Lncstr -Albany 12210 **Fx:**689-2113
(718) 694-9222 .. **Bergan,** Nancy A '82 (Bergan & W) -26 Court -Brklyn 11242
(315) 253-0326 .. **Bergan,** Robt K '82 (Boyle & A,PC) -110 Genesee -Auburn 13021
(212) 801-1444 .. **Bergdall,** Thos W '77 %Healthfirst, Inc -25 Bway -NY 10004 **Fx:**801-1799
(212) 226-4200 .. **Bergen,** Corinne M '08 Suckle S&L PLLC -224 W 35th -NY 10001
(716) 856-4200 .. **Bergen,** Elizabeth M '92 SpclCnsl Gibson M&C,LLP -69 Delaware Av -Buffalo 14202
(518) 285-8919 .. **Bergen,** Erika L '04 Appllt Div 3rd Dept -Capitol Station Bx7288 -Albany 12224 **Fx:**471-4750
(516) 767-3449 .. **Bergen,** G S Peter '63 -27 Pine -Pt Wash 11050 **Fx:**914-6640
(212) 925-2800 .. **Bergen,** James M '63 Dolgenos N&C LLP -271 Mad Av -NY 10016
(716) 633-3535 .. **Bergen,** Jos R '92 Cnsl W Mattar,PC -6720 Main -Williamsvll 14221 **Fx:**631-9804
(212) 536-3900 .. **Bergen,** Robt '74 (K&L Gates LLP) -599 Lex Av -NY 10022
(212) 269-0927 .. **Bergenfeld,** David '98 %D'Amato & L,LLP -2 World Fncl Ctr -NY 10281
(212) 969-2291 .. **Bergenfeld,** Jennifer L '00 Alliance Bernstein LP -1345 Av of Amer -NY 10105 **Fx:**554-4639
(212) 566-3039 .. **Berger,** Alex J '05 NYC Dept of Bldgs-Enforcement -280 Bway -NY 10007
(212) 209-3052 .. **Berger,** Alexander '01 %Reitler K&R LLC -885 3rd Av -NY 10022
(212) 492-1052 .. **Berger,** Alison S '88 Resources Global Professionals -512 7th Av -NY 10018
(212) 788-1093 .. **Berger,** Andrea J '84 %Law Dept -100 Church -NY 10007 **Fx:**788-0367
(212) 508-6700 .. **Berger,** Andrew '71 OfCnsl Tannenbaum HS&H LLP -900 3rd Av -NY 10022
(212) 323-2250 .. **Berger,** Barry I '73 %HHC-OLA-Medical Litigation -346 Bway -NY 10013 **Fx:**323-2251
(212) 876-3600 .. **Berger,** Barry N '62 -425 E 86th -NY 10028
(212) 646-2661 .. **Berger,** Barry S '79 JP Morgan -345 Park Av -NY 10154
(718) 254-7000 .. **Berger,** Berit A '03 %US Atty -271 Cadman Plz E -Brklyn 11201 **Fx:**254-6479
(718) 596-7800 .. **Berger,** Bonnie B '85 (Peters BK&G,PC) -26 Court -Brklyn 11242
(212) 571-1900 .. **Berger,** Bradley Ian '73 (Berger Atty PC) -321 Bway -NY 10007 **Fx:**(888) 529-4448
(914) 813-6850 .. **Berger,** Bruce B '82 Cnty Solid Waste Comm -100 E 1st -Mt Vernon 10550
(212) 753-2080 .. **Berger,** C Jaye '84 -110 E 59th -NY 10022
(845) 496-7833 .. **Berger,** Christopher G '98 -6 McNamara Dr -Campbell Hall 10916
(718) 588-4715 .. **Berger,** Danl '93 -189 E 163rd -Bronx 10451 **Fx:**588-4716
(212) 661-1100 .. **Berger,** Danl L '80 (Pomerantz HG&G LLP) -100 Park Av -NY 10017
(212) 541-6222 .. **Berger,** Darren S '87 (Kane K,PC) -1350 Av of Amer -NY 10019
(631) 271-2323 .. **Berger,** Darrin H '75 -83 Prospect -Huntngtn 11743
(212) 697-1890 .. **Berger,** David A '85 -230 Bergen -Brklyn 11217 **Fx:**697-1950
(212) 571-0550 .. **Berger,** David A '90 (Allegaert B&V LLP) -111 Bway -NY 10006
(718) 596-3800 .. **Berger,** David M '94 (Tenenbaum & B LLP) -26 Court -Brklyn 11242
(212) 602-0868 .. **Berger,** David P '97 Trinity Real Estate -74 Trinity Pl -NY 10006

(607) 239-6766 .. **Berger,** David S '89 -311 Exchange Av -Endicott 13760 **Fx:**(866) 460-3374
(631) 630-6982 .. **Berger,** Deborah '82 -1601 Vets Hwy -Islandia 11749 **Fx:**630-6983
(718) 254-7000 .. **Berger,** Emily E '77 %US Atty -271 Cadman Plz E -Brklyn 11201 **Fx:**254-6479
(212) 685-6100 .. **Berger,** Ephraim D '82 (Berger & S LLP) -295 Mad Av -NY 10017 **Fx:**685-6862
(212) 704-0444 .. **Berger,** Eric D '89 %Howard Sloan Leg Srch -261 Mad Av -NY 10016 **Fx:**869-7999
(212) 509-9400 .. **Berger,** Eric J '00 (Cozen O) -45 Bway Atrium -NY 10006
(212) 402-9400 .. **Berger,** Eric P '07 %McKool S,PC -1 Bryant Park -NY 10036
(212) 788-1346 .. **Berger,** Esther '87 Admin Childrens Srvcs -220 Church -NY 10013
(718) 338-5670 .. **Berger,** Ezra S '80 -946 E 27th -Brklyn 11210
(212) 925-6688 .. **Berger,** Frances C '77 -335 Bway -NY 10013 **Fx:**925-6987
(516) 229-9400 .. **Berger,** George '60 (Phillips N LLP) -600 Old Cntry Rd -Gdn Cty 11530
(212) 977-9700 .. **Berger,** George '60 (Phillips N LLP) -666 5th Av -NY 10103
(212) 687-3000 .. **Berger,** Glenn P '85 %Jaffe & A,LLP -600 3rd Av -NY 10016
(516) 746-8000 .. **Berger,** Harold D '65 OfCnsl Jaspan S LLP -300 Grdn City Plz -Gdn Cty 11530
(516) 747-1136 .. **Berger,** Heath S '93 (Steinberg FB&F,PC) -40 Crsswys Park Dr -Woodbury 11797
(212) 799-9378 .. **Berger,** Henry T '73 -127 W 77th -NY 10024 **Fx:**799-0886
(716) 855-1111 .. **Berger,** Howard E '82 (Duke HP&G LLP) -350 Main -Buffalo 14202
(718) 376-6699 .. **Berger,** Howard J '57 -1665 E 7th -Brklyn 11230
(212) 697-3122 .. **Berger,** Jacqueline D '99 (Martin C&B LLP) -220 E 42nd -NY 10017
(212) 318-6000 .. **Berger,** James E '95 %Paul HJ&W LLP -75 E 55th -NY 10022
(212) 756-2000 .. **Berger,** Jason H '04 %Schulte R&Z LLP -919 3rd Av -NY 10022
(212) 360-2380 .. **Berger,** Jason K '98 (Lincoln B LLP) -110 E 59th -NY 10022 **Fx:**360-2381
(212) 907-7300 .. **Berger,** Jeffrey S '85 (Golenbock EAB&P) -437 Mad Av -NY 10022
(212) 583-1291 .. **Berger,** Joan '78 Pzena Invstmnt Mgmt,LLC -120 W 45th -NY 10036
(212) 354-9300 .. **Berger,** Joel '66 %Meridian Leg Search/Leg Temp -25 W 43rd -NY 10036 **Fx:**921-1127
(212) 687-4911 .. **Berger,** Joel '68 OfCnsl Sonnenfeld & R -360 Lex Av -NY 10017 **Fx:**687-1406
(718) 229-8887 .. **Berger,** Joel Paul '63 -42-08 Bell Blvd -Bayside 11361
(212) 574-1200 .. **Berger,** Jonathan '66 Cnsl Seward & K LLP -1 Bttry Pk Plz -NY 10004
(212) 486-7272 .. **Berger,** Jonathan A '00 %Levisohn B,LLP -11 Bway -NY 10004
(631) 951-5204 .. **Berger,** Jonathan T '94 %Bestfood Baking Co -55 Paradise Ln -Bay Shr 11706
(518) 688-0755 .. **Berger,** Jos C '81 P Murray -10 Maxwell Dr -Clifton Pk 12065 **Fx:**688-0297
(212) 261-1227 .. **Berger,** Karen J '73 Elizabeth Arden -200 Park Av S -NY 10003 **Fx:**261-1316
(212) 357-5209 .. **Berger,** Keith A '01 %Goldman Sachs -1 NY Plz -NY 10004
(315) 435-2170 .. **Berger,** Kelly M '08 Cnty Atty -421 Mntgmry -Syracuse 13202 **Fx:**435-5729
(212) 227-1010 .. **Berger & Kramer** -225 Bway -NY 10007 **Fx:**267-9323
(516) 873-8600 .. **Berger,** Lawr A '78 (Mahon & B) -21 Glen -Glen Cove 11542 **Fx:**873-1937
(212) 532-0222 .. **Berger,** Lawr J '67 -200 Mad Av -NY 10016 **Fx:**532-0224
(212) 980-9600 .. **Berger,** Lee E '84 (Kaufman B&R) -120 Bway -NY 10271
(212) 532-0222 .. **Berger,** Leslie R '00 %L Berger -200 Mad Av -NY 10016 **Fx:**532-0224
(732) 855-6437 .. **Berger,** Lori Ann '99 %Wilentz G&S -110 William -NY 10038 **Fx:**726-6665
(212) 588-5500 .. **Berger,** Marc A '95 %Davies WP&V LLP -625 Mad Av -NY 10022
(212) 637-2207 .. **Berger,** Marc P '00 %US Atty -1 St Andrews Plz -NY 10007
(646) 610-6334 .. **Berger,** Mark D '04 NYPD Advocates Ofc -1 Police Plz -NY 10038 **Fx:**610-8938
(212) 247-4844 .. **Berger,** Marshall C '56 OfCnsl Margolin & P,LLP -111 W 57th -NY 10019
(212) 361-8132 .. **Berger,** MaryAnn '92 %Ct of Claims -26 Bway -NY 10004 **Fx:**361-8103
(212) 554-1400 .. **Berger,** Max W '72 (Bernstein LB&G LLP) -1285 Av of Amer -NY 10019
(718) 330-7563 .. **Berger,** Michl '07 NLRB -2 Metrotech Ctr -Brklyn 11201 **Fx:**330-7579
(716) 634-6500 .. **Berger,** Michl B '74 (Berger & B) -555 Intl Dr -Buffalo 14221 **Fx:**634-0415
(516) 560-6400 .. **Berger,** Michl F '66 %Leg Aid -1 Helen Keller Way -Hempstd 11550 **Fx:**565-3694
(212) 983-6000 .. **Berger,** Michl G '74 -250 Park Av -NY 10177 **Fx:**983-6008
(212) 336-8000 .. **Berger,** Michl J '70 (Amster R&E) -90 Park Av -NY 10016
(718) 630-2904 .. **Berger,** Michl J '07 %VA -800 Poly Pl -Brklyn 11209 **Fx:**630-2917
(212) 373-3000 .. **Berger,** Michl N '06 %Paul WRW&G LLP -1285 Av of Amer -NY 10019
(212) 594-5000 .. **Berger,** Neil '86 %Togut S&S LLP -1 Penn Plz -NY 10119
(516) 741-7400 .. **Berger,** Paul '51 %Breslin Rlty Dev -500 Old Cntry Rd -Gdn Cty 11530 **Fx:**741-7128
(718) 229-8887 .. **Berger,** Penny J G '86 -42-08 Bell Blvd -Bayside 11361
(212) 335-4500 .. **Berger,** Peri A '08 %DLA Piper LLP -1251 Av of Amer -NY 10020
(212) 486-7272 .. **Berger,** Peter L '69 (Levisohn B,LLP) -11 Bway -NY 10004
(845) 647-4000 .. **Berger,** Peter L '85 (Collier & B,PLLC) -130 S Main Bx509 -Ellenvll 12428
(212) 546-7300 .. **Berger,** Rachel L '00 Octagon Inc -919 3rd Av -NY 10022 **Fx:**546-7325
(718) 875-4186 .. **Berger,** Ralph S '79 ADR -60 Remsen -Brklyn 11201
(212) 371-6600 .. **Berger,** Randall K '93 (Kirby M LLP) -825 3rd Av -NY 10022
(718) 856-5100 .. **Berger,** Raphael '60 -111 Clarkson Av -Brklyn 11226 **Fx:**287-6801
(716) 852-8188 .. **Berger,** Richd G '74 -403 Main -Buffalo 14203 **Fx:**852-0923
(716) 282-5111 .. **Berger,** Richd G '74 -445 3rd -Niagara Fls 14301 **Fx:**284-5785
(212) 265-6600 .. **Berger,** Richd G '83 %RD Mgt Corp -810 7th Av -NY 10019 **Fx:**459-9133
(845) 639-7000 .. **Berger,** Ricki H '84 RH Berger,PC -254 S Main -New Cty 10956 **Fx:**639-3045
(315) 218-8000 .. **Berger,** Ronald C '78 (Bond S&K,PLLC) -1 Lincoln Ctr -Syracuse 13202
(212) 795-5637 .. **Berger,** Saml C '02 -1133 Bway -NY 10010 **Fx:**795-5698
(212) 693-0085 .. **Berger,** Sarah J '85 Appellate Advocates -2 Rector -NY 10006 **Fx:**693-0878
(212) 819-8200 .. **Berger,** Scott A '86 (White & C LLP) -1155 Av of Amer -NY 10036
(212) 776-5000 .. **Berger,** Sharon I '10 %NYC Housing Auth -250 Bway -NY 10007 **Fx:**776-5039
(212) 277-6500 .. **Berger,** Shaya M '03 %Dickstein S LLP -1633 Bway -NY 10019
(212) 412-3607 .. **Berger,** Shimon A '03 %Barclays Capital Inc -200 Park Av -NY 10166
(212) 830-8228 .. **Berger,** Shira E L '96 %Nautica Apparel -11 W 19th -NY 10011
(718) 731-1000 .. **Berger,** Solomon '61 -505 E 175th -Bronx 10457
(718) 370-7030 .. **Berger,** Stephanie M '00 %Amabile & E,PC -1000 South Av -Staten Isl 10314
(212) 319-1900 .. **Berger,** Steven A '69 (Berger & W,LLP) -1633 Bway -NY 10019
(212) 763-1300 .. **Berger,** Steven J '95 %JP Capital -1 North End Av -NY 10282
(212) 407-7700 .. **Berger,** Steven R '80 (Vedder P,PC) -1633 Bway -NY 10019
(212) 541-2000 .. **Berger,** Suzanne M '85 Cnsl Bryan C LLP -1290 Av of Amer -NY 10104
(212) 554-7800 .. **Berger,** Terrence B '90 OfCnsl Moses & S LLP -405 Lex Av -NY 10174
(631) 422-2130 .. **Berger,** Vincent G Jr. '63 -133 E Main -Babylon 11702
(212) 854-5521 .. **Berger,** Vivian O '74 %Columbia Law Schl -435 W 116th -NY 10027 **Fx:**595-0810
(212) 319-1900 .. **Berger & Webb,LLP** -1633 Bway -NY 10019 **Fx:**319-2017
(212) 867-9595 .. **Bergerbest,** Helene C '90 %L Fox -630 3rd Av -NY 10017 **Fx:**949-1857
(212) 266-7581 .. **Bergeron,** Christian '00 Commerzbank AG -2 World Fncl Ctr -NY 10281
(212) 277-4000 .. **Bergeron,** Ethan D '05 %Freshfields BD LLP -520 Mad Av -NY 10022
(518) 664-9816 .. **Bergeron,** Janice Serbalik '77 (Serbalik & S) -145 N Main -Mechanicvll 12118 **Fx:**664-1220
(315) 471-0405 .. **Bergeron,** Matthew E L '03 %Satter & A,LLP -217 S Salina -Syracuse 13202
(212) 848-4000 .. **Berges,** Paige L '08 %Shearman & S LLP -599 Lex Av -NY 10022
(716) 285-0640 .. **Bergevin,** Michele G '95 (Clayton & B) -650 4th -Niagara Fls 14301 **Fx:**285-0663
(315) 448-8400 .. **Bergh,** Jos Francis '02 %Law Dept -233 E Wshngtn -Syracuse 13202 **Fx:**448-8381
(212) 264-3449 .. **Bergida,** Robt D '92 DHS -26 Fed Plz -NY 10278 **Fx:**264-1645
(212) 259-8000 .. **Bergin,** Christine A '82 Cnsl Dewey & L LLP -1301 Av of Amer -NY 10019
(212) 468-8000 .. **Bergin,** James M '89 (Morrison & F LLP) -1290 Av of Amer -NY 10104
(212) 720-5017 .. **Bergin,** James P '01 Fed Reserve Bk -33 Lbrty -NY 10045
(212) 282-7254 .. **Bergin,** John M '72 %Avon Products -1251 Av of Amer -NY 10020
(212) 943-9000 .. **Bergin,** Keara A '95 (Dewey P&K LLP) -220 E 42nd -NY 10017
(585) 771-2294 .. **Bergin,** Robt J '74 %Rochester Gas & Elec -89 East Av -Rchstr 14649 **Fx:**724-8668
(845) 486-6800 .. **Bergin,** Scott D '86 (McCabe & M LLP) -63 Wshngtn Bx509 -Poughkeepsie 12602
(914) 681-0007 .. **Bergins,** Paul B '60 -6 Chester Av -White Plns 10601 **Fx:**428-2647
(718) 454-6700 .. **Berglas,** David '97 Cnsl Queens Fresh Meadows LLC -188-02 64th Av -Fresh Mdws 11365 **Fx:**(646) 723-9380
(914) 448-9448 .. **Berglas,** Lawr A '90 -17 Gilbert Pl -White Plns 10604 **Fx:**448-9447
(212) 227-4848 .. **Berglund,** Erik J '05 %Ceccarelli W PLLC -2 Wall -NY 10005
(518) 462-5601 .. **Berglund,** Wm F '04 %O'Connell & A -54 State -Albany 12207
(212) 944-1630 .. **Bergman,** Alan S '62 A Bergman,PC -529 W 42nd -NY 10036 **Fx:**944-1631
(212) 230-5500 .. **Bergman,** Andrew J '96 %Davis SLM&H LLP -689 5th Av -NY 10022
(212) 490-3000 .. **Bergman,** Arlene '91 (Wilson EME&D LLP) -150 E 42nd -NY 10017
(607) 778-2423 .. **Bergman,** Benjamin K '99 %DA -45 Hawley Bx1766 -Bnghmtn 13902 **Fx:**778-8870
(718) 275-3300 .. **Bergman Bergman Goldberg & Lamonsoff, LLP** -108-18 Qns Blvd -Frst Hlls 11375 **Fx:**275-0135
(212) 687-8080 .. **Bergman,** Brandy K '93 %Sard Verbinnen & Co -630 3rd Av -NY 10017
(516) 222-6200 .. **Bergman,** Bruce J '70 (Berkman HPP&F,PC) -100 Grdn City Plz -Gdn Cty 11530
(917) 363-4921 .. **Bergman,** David K '90 GlobalTransition Solutions -200 W 24th -NY 10011
(212) 554-7800 .. **Bergman,** Henry J '79 (Moses & S LLP) -405 Lex Av -NY 10174
(518) 485-9351 .. **Bergman,** Ilene R '81 Ofc of Professional Discipline -80 Wolf Rd -Albany 12205
(212) 417-5300 .. **Bergman,** Jacob M '05 %Medicaid Fraud Cntrl -120 Bway -NY 10271 **Fx:**417-5274
(212) 506-1700 .. **Bergman,** Jed I '98 (Kasowitz BT&F LLP) -1633 Bway -NY 10019
(212) 808-7800 .. **Bergman,** Jordan A '03 %Kelley D&W LLP -101 Park Av -NY 10178
(212) 728-8000 .. **Bergman,** Jos '98 %Willkie F&G LLP -787 7th Av -NY 10019
(516) 741-3441 .. **Bergman & King, PC** -500 Old Cntry Rd -Gdn Cty 11530 **Fx:**741-3436
(914) 993-0700 .. **Bergman,** Marc A '75 -1 Barker Av -White Plns 10601 **Fx:**993-9298
(718) 275-3300 .. **Bergman,** Marvin H '57 (Bergman BG&L,LLP) -108-18 Qns Blvd -Frst Hlls 11375
(212) 248-2220 .. **Bergman,** Meredith F '08 %Kennedy JG LLC -99 Wall -NY 10005 **Fx:**248-0170
(718) 275-3300 .. **Bergman,** Michl E '96 (Bergman BG&L,LLP) -108-18 Qns Blvd -Frst Hlls 11375
(914) 682-6813 .. **Bergman,** Michelle Duncan '95 OfCnsl Benesch FC&A,LLP -50 Main -White Plns 10606
(212) 889-4220 .. **Bergman,** Nicholas J '98 (Buchman Law Firm,LLP) -10 E 40th -NY 10016 **Fx:**889-4221
(212) 355-7711 .. **Bergman,** Paul B '68 -950 3rd Av -NY 10022 **Fx:**755-5509
(212) 962-1200 .. **Bergman,** Robt I '81 (Fogelgaren F&B,LLP) -277 Bway -NY 10007
(516) 837-6188 .. **Bergman,** Saml '73 Sutton Land Title -515 Rockaway Av -Vly Stream 11581
(914) 253-3646 .. **Bergman,** Sarah E '01 %Pepsico -700 Andrsn Hill Rd -Purchase 10577
(212) 593-6700 .. **Bergman,** Shanna E '05 %Aaronson RF&D,LLP -757 3rd Av -NY 10017

(212) 361-7996 .. **Bergman,** Steven '79 %Dept Homeless Srvcs -33 Beaver -NY 10004 **Fx:**361-8002
(212) 266-6022 .. **Bergmanis,** Imanta M '05 Raycliff Capital -5 E 59th -NY 10022
(631) 325-1600 .. **Bergmann,** Kathy G '89 -381 Montauk Hwy Bx904 -Remsenbrg 11960 **Fx:**325-1603
(212) 661-7300 .. **Bergmann,** Mary '86 %Malapero & P LLP -295 Mad Av -NY 10017
(518) 479-2055 .. **Bergmann,** Nancy A '84 -50 Morgan Rd -E Greenbush 12061
(212) 554-7800 .. **Bergner,** Eric P '92 (Moses & S LLP) -405 Lex Av -NY 10174
(212) 552-7317 .. **Bergold,** Francis J '79 %Chase Manhattan Bk -1 Chase Manh Plz -NY 10081
(212) 303-1126 .. **Bergovoy,** Richd R '90 Beanstalk Grp -28 E 28th -NY 10016
(212) 832-8500 .. **Bergreen,** Adele G '47 (Bergreen & B) -31 W 52nd -NY 10019 **Fx:**593-6241
(212) 201-1170 .. **Bergson,** Robt J '89 (Abrams GMB,LLP) -237 W 35th -NY 10001
(212) 318-6000 .. **Bergstein,** Danl G '68 (Paul HJ&W LLP) -75 E 55th -NY 10022
(718) 286-6000 .. **Bergstein,** Lee B '08 %DA -125-01 Qns Blvd -Kew Gdns 11415
(212) 244-5670 .. **Bergstein,** Martin '60 (Baron B&W) -450 7th Av -NY 10123
(516) 745-0066 .. **Bergstein,** Sheryl '93 %Karol H&S,PC -600 Old Cntry Rd -Gdn Cty 11530
(845) 469-1277 .. **Bergstein,** Stephen '94 (Bergstein & U,LLP) -15 Railroad Av -Chester 10918
(845) 469-1277 .. **Bergstein & Ullrich,LLP** -15 Railroad Av -Chester 10918 **Fx:**469-5904
(212) 878-7317 .. **Bergstrom,** Robin E '00 %MTA -347 Mad Av -NY 10017
(212) 442-7042 .. **Bergtraum,** Judith E '86 Dept Transportation -40 Worth -NY 10013 **Fx:**442-7733
(716) 484-7196 .. **Berhaupt,** Justin D '08 %Fessenden L&D -81 Forest Av Bx590 -Jamestwn 14702
(212) 903-9000 .. **Berick,** Joshua J G '98 (Linklaters) -1345 Av of Amer -NY 10105
(718) 575-3400 .. **Berinato,** Thos E '82 -123-40 83rd Av -Kew Gdns 11415
(212) 577-3530 .. **Beritan,** Juan C '91 %Leg Aid -199 Water -NY 10038 **Fx:**425-2465
(212) 850-2800 .. **Berk,** Danl I '97 %Andrews K LLP -450 Lex Av -NY 10017
(516) 571-5092 .. **Berk,** Donald J '85 %DA -262 Old Cntry Rd -Mineola 11501 **Fx:**248-9479
(917) 520-3969 .. **Berk,** Joan A '77 -25 Sutton Pl S -NY 10022 **Fx:**(201) 585-9464
(718) 250-2000 .. **Berk,** Lisa S '05 %DA -350 Jay -Brklyn 11201 **Fx:**250-2314
(718) 494-6500 .. **Berk,** Marc A '88 -706 Forest Av -Staten Isl 10310 **Fx:**983-6366
(212) 244-4664 .. **Berk,** Marnie Gilla '97 %NY Lawyers Pub Intrst -151 W 30th -NY 10001 **Fx:**244-4570
(212) 971-7600 .. **Berk,** Peretz B '03 Selfhelp Cmmnnty Srvcs,Inc -520 8th Av -NY 10018
(516) 222-4503 .. **Berk,** Ronald J '74 -200 Mad Av -NY 10016 **Fx:**(212) 244-1718
(631) 666-7400 .. **Berka,** Jerry G '67 (JG Berka,PC) -2115 Union Blvd -Bay Shr 11706 **Fx:**666-7995
(518) 489-1117 .. **Berke,** Alice K '87 -930 Mad Av -Albany 12208 **Fx:**446-1798
(212) 682-1230 .. **Berke,** Allan J '86 -60 E 42nd -NY 10165 **Fx:**601-9286
(212) 715-9100 .. **Berke,** Barry H '90 (Kramer LN&F,LLP) -1177 Av of Amer -NY 10036
(718) 505-6650 .. **Berke,** Danl S '97 %Kaplan & M -75-20 Astoria Blvd -E Elmhrst 11370
(914) 946-0400 .. **Berke,** Dena '92 %Schiavetti CDW&N,LLP -709 Wstchstr Av -White Plns 10604
(212) 755-5510 .. **Berke,** Howard B '78 (Loeb B & Prtnrs) -505 Park Av -NY 10022
(212) 373-3000 .. **Berke,** Janna I '07 %Paul WRW&G LLP -1285 Av of Amer -NY 10019
(212) 888-8787 .. **Berke,** Jeffrey R '75 (Berke & B) -590 Mad Av -NY 10022 **Fx:**888-5214
(212) 761-5051 .. **Berke,** Matthew E '90 Morgan Stanley -1585 Bway -NY 10036 **Fx:**761-0086
(718) 965-2915 .. **Berke,** Steven '72 -536 9th -Brklyn 11215
(212) 474-1000 .. **Berkebile,** Nathan J '08 %Cravath S&M LLP -825 8th Av -NY 10019
(212) 969-3000 .. **Berkebile,** Rebecca L '08 %Proskauer R LLP -1585 Bway -NY 10036
(914) 949-2700 .. **Berkelhamer,** Lester '58 (Bleakley P&S,LLP) -1 N Lex Av -White Plns 10601
(212) 526-2557 .. **Berkenfeld,** Steven L '85 Barclays Capital Inc -745 7th Av -NY 10019
(315) 468-6712 .. **Berkery,** Gerald P '70 -105 Forrest Way -Camillus 13031
(212) 506-2500 .. **Berkery,** John P '96 (Mayer B LLP) -1675 Bway -NY 10019
(518) 474-1331 .. **Berkery,** Peter P '90 %Ofc Mntl Health -44 Holland Av -Albany 12229 **Fx:**473-7863
(212) 449-2940 .. **Berkery,** Rosemary T '79 %Merrill Lynch -220 Bway -NY 10038
(212) 583-9500 .. **Berke-Weiss,** Laurie M '84 (Berke-Weiss & P LLP) -488 Mad Av -NY 10022 **Fx:**308-8582
(212) 935-3131 .. **Berkey,** David L '76 (Gallet D&B,LLP) -845 3rd Av -NY 10022
(212) 973-0572 .. **Berkey,** Mitchell S '84 (Wolff & S PC) -140 Bway -NY 10005
(914) 997-8100 .. **Berkley,** David M '84 %Burke LM&G -10 Bank -White Plns 10606
(212) 683-9880 .. **Berkley,** Herbert R '56 -870 5th Av -NY 10065
(516) 227-2121 .. **Berkley,** Michl P '90 -585 Stewart Av -Gdn Cty 11530 **Fx:**227-1250
(718) 403-8200 .. **Berkley,** Richd A '98 NYC Dept of Info Tech & Telecom -11 Metrotech Ctr -Brklyn 11201 **Fx:**403-8504
(212) 350-2750 .. **Berkman,** Andrew S '71 -450 Lex Av -NY 10017 **Fx:**350-2701
(212) 867-9123 .. **Berkman,** Barry '66 (Berkman BN&R,LLP) -521 5th Av -NY 10175
(212) 867-9123 .. **Berkman Bottger Newman & Rodd, LLP** -521 5th Av -NY 10175 **Fx:**983-8526
(212) 613-5000 .. **Berkman,** Deborah B '04 Leg Assist Grp -450 W 33rd -NY 10001 **Fx:**750-0820
(516) 222-6200 .. **Berkman Henoch Peterson Peddy & Fenchel,PC** -100 Grdn City Plz -Gdn Cty 11530 **Fx:**222-6209
(212) 820-9356 .. **Berkman,** Howard I '77 (Hawkins D&W LLP) -One Chase Manh Plz -NY 10005
(845) 225-5827 .. **Berkman & Hudak,PC** -38 Gleneida Av -Carmel 10512 **Fx:**225-5912
(212) 327-1654 .. **Berkman,** Jeffrey W '90 (Berkman Law Firm,PLLC) -2592 Overlook Pl -Baldwin 11510 **Fx:**208-0991
(845) 225-5827 .. **Berkman,** Jordan W '54 (Berkman & H,PC) -38 Gleneida Av -Carmel 10512
(718) 855-3627 .. **Berkman,** Marna F '95 -111 Lvngstn -Brklyn 11201 **Fx:**855-4696
(212) 661-4883 .. **Berkman,** Saul A '68 -185 Mad Av -NY 10016 **Fx:**661-4809
(518) 474-7330 .. **Berkman,** Thos S '98 %Dept of Law -The Cptl -Albany 12224
(631) 543-2900 .. **Berko,** Lloyd M '00 %Davis & H,LLP -1345 Motor Pkwy -Islandia 11749
(516) 746-4211 .. **Berko,** Paul R '66 -114 Old Cntry Rd -Mineola 11501 **Fx:**741-0912
(212) 577-3688 .. **Berko,** Steven R '86 %Leg Aid -199 Water -NY 10038 **Fx:**509-8431
(516) 873-2000 .. **Berkoff,** Leslie Ann '91 (Moritt HH&H LLP) -400 Grdn City Plz -Gdn Cty 11530
(212) 486-2400 .. **Berkon,** Fredk D '74 (Leader & B LLP) -630 3rd Av -NY 10017
(718) 484-7992 .. **Berkovich,** Alexander '88 -467 Troutman -Brklyn 11237
(212) 504-6000 .. **Berkovich,** Lawr V '97 SpclCnsl Cadwalader W&T LLP -1 World Fncl Ctr -NY 10281
(212) 310-8000 .. **Berkovich,** Ronit J '04 (Weil G&M LLP) -767 5th Av -NY 10153
(914) 723-7513 .. **Berkovits,** Leslie W '82 -5 Swarthmore Rd -Scarsdale 10583
(516) 918-7174 .. **Berkovitz,** Edw '02 Deloitte & Touche LLP -2 Jericho Plz -Jericho 11753
(212) 481-9600 .. **Berkow,** Bonnie Reid '81 (Wagner D,PC) -99 Mad Av -NY 10016
(212) 551-1158 .. **Berkowe,** Kathleen Hawkins '95 -122 E 42nd -NY 10168 **Fx:**551-1001
(212) 381-5006 .. **Berkower,** Elise '84 %Doulbeclick,Inc -111 8th Av -NY 10011
(212) 609-6800 .. **Berkower,** Howard M '86 (McCarter & E,LLP) -245 Park Av -NY 10167
(212) 969-3000 .. **Berkowitz,** Adam T '04 %Proskauer R LLP -1585 Bway -NY 10036
(212) 362-2999 .. **Berkowitz,** Adena K '86 -165 W 91st -NY 10024 **Fx:**799-3411
(631) 231-2184 .. **Berkowitz,** Alan B '89 %Dept of Law -300 Motor Pkwy -Hauppauge 11788 **Fx:**435-4757
(212) 228-1400 .. **Berkowitz,** Alan S '60 OfCnsl Loscalzo & L,PC -14 E 4th -NY 10012
(212) 538-3352 .. **Berkowitz,** Amy P '91 Credit Suisse -11 Mad Av -NY 10010
(212) 807-0454 .. **Berkowitz,** Benita F '81 -7 E 14th -NY 10003
(845) 638-9200 .. **Berkowitz,** Brian H '98 -216 Congers Rd -New Cty 10956
(516) 569-5001 .. **Berkowitz,** Brynde R '07 %Schonfeld & G,LLP -112 Spruce -Cedarhrst 11516
(212) 808-7800 .. **Berkowitz,** Chad R '05 %Kelley D&W LLP -101 Park Av -NY 10178
(718) 218-7000 .. **Berkowitz,** Chaim S '99 -268 Willoughby Av -Brklyn 11205
(718) 694-3865 .. **Berkowitz,** David E '89 %Transit Auth -130 Lvngstn -Brklyn 11201 **Fx:**694-5726
(631) 608-4114 .. **Berkowitz,** David H '93 (Riegler & B) -532 Broad Hollow Rd -Melvll 11747 **Fx:**396-1399
(631) 261-9545 .. **Berkowitz,** Gail M '02 -Bx185 -Centerprt 11721 **Fx:**261-3155
(914) 249-3784 .. **Berkowitz,** Hannah '79 %MasterCard Intl -2000 Purchase -Purchase 10577
(917) 454-1100 .. **Berkowitz,** Ilene '98 %Police Dept -2 Lafayette -NY 10007
(516) 294-5433 .. **Berkowitz,** Janice '89 (Ahmuty D&M) -200 IU Willets Rd -Albertson 11507
(212) 613-2093 .. **Berkowitz,** Jeffrey S '92 Cnsl Gibbons PC -1 Penn Plz -NY 10119 **Fx:**554-9691
(212) 431-4453 .. **Berkowitz,** Jess M '84 -401 Bway -NY 10013 **Fx:**431-4471
(212) 968-2300 .. **Berkowitz,** Jonathan L '08 %Chartwell Law Ofc,LLP -39 Bway -NY 10006 **Fx:**968-2400
(585) 421-9094 .. **Berkowitz,** Joyce B '95 -6605 Pttsfrd Palmyra Rd -Fairprt 14450
(516) 791-3294 .. **Berkowitz,** Leonard '61 -797 Caldwell Av -N Woodmere 11581
(716) 662-9808 .. **Berkowitz,** Leonard '73 (Berkowitz & P) -4513 S Buffalo Bx639 -Orchard Pk 14127
(646) 471-3000 .. **Berkowitz,** Leonard '07 PricewaterhouseCoopers -300 Mad Av -NY 10017
(718) 231-4300 .. **Berkowitz,** Leopold '84 Morris Park Nursing Home -1235 Pelham Pkwy N -Bronx 10469
(518) 587-1380 .. **Berkowitz,** Linda A '08 B Lee,PLLC -138 Church -Saratoga Spgs 12866 **Fx:**587-1393
(212) 336-8000 .. **Berkowitz,** Mark '08 %Amster R&E -90 Park Av -NY 10016
(718) 250-2000 .. **Berkowitz,** Mark '09 %DA -350 Jay -Brklyn 11201 **Fx:**250-2314
(212) 425-7200 .. **Berkowitz,** Matthew G '06 %Kenyon & K,LLP -1 Bway -NY 10004
(212) 935-3131 .. **Berkowitz,** Morrell I '75 (Gallet D&B,LLP) -845 3rd Av -NY 10022
(212) 414-4730 .. **Berkowitz,** Nancy Lee '97 Berko Prdctns -424 W 33rd -NY 10001
(212) 575-7900 .. **Berkowitz,** Norman R '62 (Ballon SB&N,PC) -729 7th Av -NY 10019
(716) 662-9808 .. **Berkowitz & Pace** -4513 S Buffalo Bx639 -Orchard Pk 14127 **Fx:**662-9546
(212) 583-9600 .. **Berkowitz,** Philip M '80 (Littler M,PC) -900 3rd Av -NY 10022
(212) 766-6300 .. **Berkowitz,** Robt J '93 (Eiges G&B,LLP) -225 Bway -NY 10007 **Fx:**233-5633
(718) 377-8174 .. **Berkowitz,** Steven C '79 -502 Av J -Brklyn 11230 **Fx:**338-5722
(212) 375-2031 .. **Berkowitz,** Steven J '86 ACA -140 Bway -NY 10005
(718) 643-2875 .. **Berkowitz,** Steven P '85 %Burke Supply -Bklyn Navy Yd Bldg 293 -Brklyn 11205 **Fx:**643-5648
(718) 590-8383 .. **Berkowitz,** Susan Ellen Ferkin '84 %Family Ct -900 Sheridan Av -Bronx 10451
(516) 227-0700 .. **Berkowitz,** Ted A '84 (Farrell F,PC) -1320 RXR Plz -Uniondale 11556
(516) 565-2486 .. **Berkowitz,** Warren S '80 -1445 Stephan Marc Ln -E Meadow 11554
(516) 791-1177 .. **Berkowitz-Ortiz,** Amy '01 -1225 Franklin Av -Gdn Cty 11530
(516) 432-4416 .. **Berkowsky,** Dennis Sr. '81 -68 W Park Av -Long Bch 11561
(212) 340-0400 .. **Berkowsky,** Peter '72 %Appllt Div 1st Dept -27 Mad Av -NY 10010 **Fx:**889-4412
(646) 344-1672 .. **Berks,** Andrew H '08 -45 Wall -NY 10005
(914) 968-2496 .. **Berkson,** Danl B '53 -1085 Warburton Av -Ynkrs 10701 **Fx:**478-3136
(212) 809-7600 .. **Berkson,** James H '96 %Cheven K&H -40 Wall -NY 10005
(518) 233-7218 .. **Berkun,** Jeffrey S '89 -Bx266 -Albany 12201
(716) 856-4080 .. **Berkun,** Robt D '90 -43 Court -Buffalo 14202
(212) 294-6700 .. **Berkwitt-Malefakis,** Susan '80 (Winston & S) -200 Park Av -NY 10166
(212) 335-9000 .. **Berland,** Jason H '03 %DA -1 Hogan Pl -NY 10013
(212) 508-6700 .. **Berland,** Judy L '96 %Tannenbaum HS&H LLP -900 3rd Av -NY 10022
(212) 576-7000 .. **Berland,** Merrill J '93 NY Life Ins -51 Mad Av -NY 10010 **Fx:**447-0569
(212) 277-6500 .. **Berland,** Sanford N '78 (Dickstein S LLP) -1633 Bway -NY 10019
(845) 225-8404 .. **Berlandi,** Brian L '00 OfCnsl Daniels & P,LLP -102 Gleneida Av -Carmel 10512
(914) 522-8879 .. **Berle,** Norman M '89 N Berle,PLLC -Bx34H -Scarsdale 10583 **Fx:**560-2181
(212) 759-5000 .. **Berley,** Alexander K '07 Abington Holding -950 3rd Av -NY 10022

(516) 796-1100 .. **Berley,** Debra S '85 Berley & B -4250 Hempstd Tpk -Bethpage 11714 **Fx:**796-1832
(212) 696-7100 .. **Berley,** Marc '08 Walter & Samuels,Inc -419 Park Av S -NY 10016
(631) 582-3700 .. **Berlin,** Aimee E '00 %Turley RR&R,LLP -3075 Vets Mem'l Hwy -Ronkonkoma 11779
(914) 694-5717 .. **Berlin,** Alan D '63 -2 Gannett Dr -White Plns 10604 **Fx:**694-1647
(212) 696-6000 .. **Berlin,** Alan S '73 (Curtis M-PC&M LLP) -101 Park Av -NY 10178
(646) 386-5130 .. **Berlin,** Amy '80 %Family Ct -60 Lafayette -NY 10013
(516) 626-0805 .. **Berlin,** Barbara G '87 -54 Cardinal Dr -East Hills 11576
(716) 853-1150 .. **Berlin,** Catherine Habermehl '88 (Altreuter B) -617 Main -Buffalo 14203
(212) 247-4650 .. **Berlin,** David C '90 -888 7th Av -NY 10106
(212) 832-1977 .. **Berlin,** David S '98 %Schreck RDA&H -1790 Bway -NY 10019 **Fx:**832-2969
(212) 643-5938 .. **Berlin,** Deborah H '95 Salomon Smith Barney -1 Penn Plz -NY 10119
(914) 948-8800 .. **Berlin,** Edw A '85 (E Berlin PLLC) -1 N Lex Av -White Plns 10601 **Fx:**948-6060
(516) 921-4466 .. **Berlin,** Jeremy S '97 %American Land Srvcs -6800 Jericho Tpk -Syosset 11791 **Fx:**921-3433
(212) 335-9000 .. **Berlin,** Joanna R '06 %DA -1 Hogan Pl -NY 10013
(516) 823-1020 .. **Berlin,** Laurie P '84 (Berlin & B) -444 Merrick Rd -Lynbrk 11563 **Fx:**823-1043
(212) 867-9595 .. **Berlin,** Martin '62 -630 3rd Av -NY 10017
(212) 610-6300 .. **Berlin,** Matthew B '08 %Allen & O -1221 Av of Amer -NY 10020
(212) 416-8453 .. **Berlin,** Michl A '97 %Dept of Law -120 Bway -NY 10271
(631) 859-3605 .. **Berlin,** Nils Hunter '95 (N H Berlin,PC) -130 W Main -E Islip 11730 **Fx:**277-5372
(718) 590-2000 .. **Berlin,** Rachel E '10 %DA -198 E 161st -Bronx 10451 **Fx:**590-6477
(212) 867-1100 .. **Berlin,** Raphael S '04 %Tratner & M -551 5th Av -NY 10176
(212) 648-9369 .. **Berlin,** Rita '96 %JP Morgan Chase & Co -60 Wall -NY 10260 **Fx:**648-5811
(914) 939-9261 .. **Berlin,** Robin L '87 -20 Magnolia Dr -Rye Brook 10573 **Fx:**939-4239
(516) 763-5543 .. **Berlin,** Roy A '84 -3507 Wstmnstr Rd -Oceanside 11572
(212) 850-6100 .. **Berlin,** Seth D '01 (Levine SK&S,LLP) -321 W 44th -NY 10036
(631) 694-2300 .. **Berlin,** Sharon N '92 (Lamb & B,LLP) -534 Broadhllw Rd Bx9034 -Melvll 11747
(212) 697-3122 .. **Berlin,** Steven M '81 (Martin C&B LLP) -220 E 42nd -NY 10017
(718) 876-6300 .. **Berliner,** Arnold D '70 %DA -130 Styvsnt Pl -Staten Isl 10301
(212) 774-8047 .. **Berliner,** Atara '85 Ramaz Middle Schl -114 E 85th -NY 10028
(718) 923-8405 .. **Berliner,** David L '88 %Forest City Ratner -1 Metrotech Ctr N -Brklyn 11201 **Fx:**923-8699
(516) 304-5555 .. **Berliner,** Eric L '86 (Berliner & P) -80 Cuttermill Rd -Gt Neck 11021
(914) 690-1050 .. **Berliner,** Ira E '73 -225 Wstchstr Av -Pt Chester 10573 **Fx:**690-1049
(718) 855-8599 .. **Berliner,** Jared M '98 -16 Court -Brklyn 11241
(516) 481-3121 .. **Berliner,** Jay '81 -141 Jackson -Hempstd 11550
(718) 998-6832 .. **Berliner,** Jos H '66 -1350 E 13th -Brklyn 11230
(516) 304-5555 .. **Berliner & Pilson** -80 Cuttermill Rd -Gt Neck 11021 **Fx:**304-5556
(718) 261-3000 .. **Berliner,** Rochelle S '92 -118-21 Qns Blvd -Frst Hlls 11375 **Fx:**793-0385
(914) 937-3100 .. **Berlingo & Carbone** -320 Wstchstr Av -Pt Chester 10573 **Fx:**937-3629
(914) 225-4954 .. **Berlow,** Rebecca Ann '94 Amaranth Grp -2000 Wstchstr Av -Purchase 10577
(212) 861-9569 .. **Berlow,** Rosalind Kent '85 -500 E 77th -NY 10162 **Fx:**861-6487
(212) 245-6440 .. **Berlowitz,** Allan J '68 -1700 Bway -NY 10019 **Fx:**245-6452
(914) 472-7564 .. **Berlstein,** Ann E '84 -249 Nelson Rd -Scarsdale 10583
(212) 335-4500 .. **Berlyne,** David A '00 (DLA Piper LLP) -1251 Av of Amer -NY 10020
(212) 430-8020 .. **Bermack,** Scott W '90 (LeClairRyan,PC) -830 3rd Av -NY 10022
(212) 268-1538 .. **Berman,** Adam A '92 (A Berman & Assoc) -11 Penn Plz -NY 10001 **Fx:**695-6058
(845) 357-5100 .. **Berman,** Alan B '79 %Ramapo Town Atty -237 Route 59 -Suffern 10901 **Fx:**357-2936
(212) 259-8000 .. **Berman,** Alan M '64 OfCnsl Dewey & L LLP -1301 Av of Amer -NY 10019
(914) 642-5847 .. **Berman,** Alec S '81 IBM -1133 Wstchstr Av -White Plns 10604
(212) 735-3000 .. **Berman,** Alison A '06 %Skadden ASM&F LLP -4 Times Sq -NY 10036
(212) 649-9700 .. **Berman,** Allison W '91 Greystone & Co -152 W 57th -NY 10019 **Fx:**649-9701
(212) 431-2114 .. **Berman,** Andrew R '89 NY Law Schl -185 W Bway -NY 10013 **Fx:**431-3295
(212) 867-5464 .. **Berman,** Ann Pinciss '88 A Pinciss Berman,PC -60 E 42nd -NY 10165 **Fx:**867-5017
(212) 237-0000 .. **Berman,** Ari M '00 (Vinson & E LLP) -666 5th Av -NY 10103
(914) 747-9500 .. **Berman,** Arnold L '69 -50 Bway -Hawthorne 10532 **Fx:**747-0935
(516) 829-2000 .. **Berman,** Barry J '77 -46 Deepdale Dr -Gt Neck 11021 **Fx:**487-3163
(914) 997-7100 .. **Berman Bavero Frucco & Gouz pc** -123 Main -White Plns 10601 **Fx:**949-4939
(212) 770-5926 .. **Berman,** Brad E '02 AIG Inc -70 Pine -NY 10270
(212) 697-3434 .. **Berman,** Brad L '84 Liberian Registry -99 Park Av -NY 10016 **Fx:**697-5655
(212) 558-4000 .. **Berman,** Brad W '96 SpclCnsl Sullivan & C LLP -125 Broad -NY 10004
(212) 382-6600 .. **Berman,** Dana M '97 %NYC Bar -42 W 44th -NY 10036 **Fx:**398-6634
(315) 471-3151 .. **Berman,** Danl B '83 (Hancock & E,LLP) -1500 AXA Twr I Bx4976 -Syracuse 13221
(212) 715-9100 .. **Berman,** Danl R '07 %Kramer LN&F,LLP -1177 Av of Amer -NY 10036
(212) 788-5027 .. **Berman,** David A '98 Dept Hlth -125 Worth CN-30 -NY 10013 **Fx:**788-4300
(212) 373-3000 .. **Berman,** David A '05 %Paul WRW&G LLP -1285 Av of Amer -NY 10019
(914) 834-3053 .. **Berman,** David H '56 -2005 Palmer Av -Larchmnt 10538 **Fx:**833-0138
(212) 773-0528 .. **Berman,** David I '86 Ernst & Young LLP -5 Times Sq -NY 10036
(914) 682-2010 .. **Berman,** Edw M '60 (Singer ND&B PLLC) -50 Main -White Plns 10606
(646) 414-6888 .. **Berman,** Elise S '83 Cnsl Lowenstein S PC -1251 Av of Amer -NY 10020 **Fx:**(973) 422-6889
(631) 486-4900 .. **Berman,** Eric M '82 (E Berman,PC) -100 Grdn City Plz -Gdn Cty 11530 **Fx:**486-4997
(631) 351-2100 .. **Berman,** Eugene D '74 (Fine F&B) -445 Broadhllw Rd -Melvll 11747 **Fx:**773-6766
(212) 768-6700 .. **Berman,** Evan R '08 %Sonnenschein N&R LLP -2 World Fncl Ctr -NY 10281
(212) 832-2797 .. **Berman,** Fredk J '77 (Shebitz B&C,PC) -1325 Av of Amer -NY 10019
(516) 364-8989 .. **Berman & Freedman** -6900 Jericho Tpk -Syosset 11791
(212) 451-2900 .. **Berman,** Garry C '90 (Robinson & C LLP) -885 3rd Av -NY 10022
(914) 419-8407 .. **Berman,** Geoffrey P '99 -2005 Palmer Av -Larchmnt 10538
(212) 782-8726 .. **Berman,** Gillian L '99 %Random House -1540 Bway -NY 10036
(212) 318-3000 .. **Berman,** Gregg J '88 (Fulbright & J LLP) -666 5th Av -NY 10103
(516) 333-2800 .. **Berman,** Harvey C '64 -1400 Old Cntry Rd -Westbury 11590
(646) 386-5700 .. **Berman,** Harvey M '78 %Civil Ct -111 Centre -NY 10013
(914) 997-7100 .. **Berman,** Henry S '67 (Berman BF&G pc) -123 Main -White Plns 10601
(914) 423-8880 .. **Berman,** Howard E '64 (Farrauto B&S) -1250 Cntrl Pk Av -Ynkrs 10704
(212) 801-9223 .. **Berman,** Howard J '78 (Greenberg T,LLP) -200 Park Av -NY 10166
(212) 436-2242 .. **Berman,** Howard J '87 Deloitte & Touche,LLP -2 World Fncl Ctr -NY 10281
(516) 683-1990 .. **Berman,** Jamie J '02 (Scupp & B LLP) -220 Old Cntry Rd -Mineola 11501 **Fx:**683-1992
(718) 643-7024 .. **Berman,** Jay R '76 %Hon G Held -360 Adams -Brklyn 11201
(212) 880-5836 .. **Berman,** Jean C '76 (ISLP) -31 W 52nd -NY 10019 **Fx:**878-8375
(718) 469-8787 .. **Berman,** Jeff R '94 %Mercury Paint Corp -4808 Farragut Rd -Brklyn 11203
(212) 298-5066 .. **Berman,** Jeffrey A '99 Leg Aid -49 Thomas -NY 10013 **Fx:**298-5252
(212) 849-7000 .. **Berman,** Jeffrey C '06 %Quinn EU&S,LLP -51 Mad Av -NY 10010
(212) 878-8000 .. **Berman,** Jeffrey D '96 (Clifford C LLP) -31 W 52nd -NY 10019
(212) 574-1200 .. **Berman,** Jeffrey M '01 %Seward & K LLP -1 Bttry Pk Plz -NY 10004
(212) 906-1200 .. **Berman,** Jennifer A '08 %Latham & W -885 3rd Av -NY 10022
(212) 237-0980 .. **Berman,** Jennifer E '01 Bank of NY -1633 Bway -NY 10019
(212) 735-2032 .. **Berman,** Jeremy A '82 SpclCnsl Skadden ASM&F LLP -4 Times Sq -NY 10036
(212) 298-5087 .. **Berman,** Jerrold '73 Leg Aid -49 Thomas -NY 10013 **Fx:**298-5252
(212) 431-4600 .. **Berman,** Jesse '69 -351 Bway -NY 10013 **Fx:**941-0980
(212) 789-2024 .. **Berman,** Jessica C '03 %NHL -1251 Av of Amer -NY 10020
(516) 741-6565 .. **Berman,** Jessica G '08 %Meyer SE&K,PC -990 Stewart Av Bx9194 -Gdn Cty 11530
(212) 755-4600 .. **Berman,** Jillian A '99 Park Av Bank -460 Park Av -NY 10022
(212) 637-2197 .. **Berman,** Jillian Blythe '01 %US Atty -1 St Andrews Plz -NY 10007
(212) 583-0005 .. **Berman,** Joel S '72 -780 3rd Av -NY 10017 **Fx:**583-0072
(718) 863-2300 .. **Berman,** Jonathan D '97 %Rosenberg Diamond Dvlpmnt Corp -1919 Wllmsbrdg Rd -Bronx 10461
(212) 494-0070 .. **Berman,** Jonathan S '82 -116 E 16th -NY 10003 **Fx:**494-0088
(212) 969-3000 .. **Berman,** Jordana Treger '00 %Proskauer R LLP -1585 Bway -NY 10036
(516) 747-0300 .. **Berman,** Joshua A '01 (Meltzer LG&B,LLP) -190 Willis Av -Mineola 11501
(212) 836-8000 .. **Berman,** Julius '61 SpclCnsl Kaye S LLP -425 Park Av -NY 10022
(212) 956-7767 .. **Berman,** Keith '80 (Bermans) -1775 Bway -NY 10019 **Fx:**956-1099
(212) 661-0009 .. **Berman,** Marjorie E '90 (Krantz & B LLP) -747 3rd Av -NY 10017 **Fx:**355-5009
(212) 922-9250 .. **Berman,** Mark A '91 (Ganfer & S LLP) -360 Lex Av -NY 10017
(212) 344-4619 .. **Berman,** Mark A '94 (Hartmann DR&B,LLC) -110 Wall -NY 10005
(617) 345-6037 .. **Berman,** Mark N '07 (Nixon P LLP) -437 Mad Av -NY 10022 **Fx:**(866) 382-5868
(212) 577-3658 .. **Berman,** Matthew J '05 Leg Aid -199 Water -NY 10038
(212) 679-3124 .. **Berman,** Matthew R '10 %T McCauley LLC -274 Mad Av -NY 10016 **Fx:**679-3105
(212) 528-1500 .. **Berman,** Michl J '81 (M Berman & Assoc,PC) -15 Maiden Ln -NY 10038 **Fx:**349-1887
(212) 964-7400 .. **Berman,** Michl K '81 Smith MDWY&Y,PC -111 John -NY 10038
(212) 301-6975 .. **Berman,** Michl P '03 (Berman & S LLC) -58 W 58th -NY 10019
(646) 638-8208 .. **Berman,** Michl S '91 IN DEMAND -345 Hudson -NY 10014
(212) 580-6500 .. **Berman,** Mitchell L '96 %Phillips K & Assoc,LLP -204 W 84th -NY 10024
(631) 761-7000 .. **Berman,** Myra Haskell '06 %Touro Cllg Law Ctr -225 Eastvw Dr -Central Islip 11722
(212) 889-5704 .. **Berman,** Myron P '58 (Berman & B) -234 E 40th -NY 10016 **Fx:**687-3878
(212) 483-9600 .. **Berman,** Peter E '77 %Costello S&G LLP -44 Wall -NY 10005
(212) 351-4500 .. **Berman,** Ralph A '87 (Epstein B&G,PC) -250 Park Av -NY 10177
(212) 415-9200 .. **Berman,** Randall M '08 %Dorsey & W LLP -250 Park Av -NY 10177
(212) 286-8585 .. **Berman,** Raphael J '90 (Heidell PM&B,LLP) -99 Park Av -NY 10016
(212) 869-5030 .. **Berman,** Robt H '74 Cnsl Kucker & B,LLP -747 3rd Av -NY 10017
(212) 986-6000 .. **Berman,** Robt L '78 (Kleinberg KW&C,PC) -551 5th Av -NY 10176
(212) 422-1414 .. **Berman,** Ronald P '75 -110 Wall -NY 10005 **Fx:**422-1464
(212) 269-7308 .. **Berman,** Ross A '07 %Leahey & J PC -120 Wall -NY 10005
(212) 479-6000 .. **Berman,** Russell S '68 (Cooley LLP) -1114 Av of Amer -NY 10036
(212) 225-2000 .. **Berman,** Sarah L '05 %Cleary GS&H -1 Lbrty Plz -NY 10006
(212) 208-1436 .. **Berman Sauter Record & Jardim,PC** -140 Bway -NY 10005 **Fx:**(973) 984-1632
(718) 853-8220 .. **Berman Schulman & Levine** -4607 Ft Hmltn Pkwy -Brklyn 11219 **Fx:**871-3225
(212) 833-1120 .. **Berman,** Scott M '83 (Friedman KS&A LLP) -1633 Bway -NY 10019 **Fx:**373-7920
(516) 832-7500 .. **Berman,** Seth L '08 %Nixon P LLP -50 Jericho Quadrangle -Jericho 11753
Berman, Seth W '95 -36-36 33rd -LIC 11106
(518) 371-8603 .. **Berman,** Sheila R '81 -12 Valencia Ln -Clifton Pk 12065
(212) 751-8088 .. **Berman,** Steven '76 -505 Park Av -NY 10022
(917) 534-4900 .. **Berman,** Stuart C '92 Zurich Capital Mrkts -105 E 17th -NY 10003
(718) 434-5757 .. **Berman,** Tehilah H '94 -653 E 17th -Brklyn 11230
(914) 244-6303 .. **Berman,** Valerie Juster '86 -53 Highbrdg Rd -Mt Kisco 10549

(646) 450-9529 .. **Berman,** Zachary L '05 ZL Berman,LLC -350 5th Av -NY 10118 **Fx:**915-1675
(718) 553-3285 .. **Berman,** Zachary M '88 %FAA -1 Aviation Plz -Jamaica 11434 **Fx:**995-5699
(718) 243-6828 .. **Berman-Rossi,** Simone '02 Leg Aid -111 Lvngstn -Brklyn 11201 **Fx:**237-8737
(212) 902-2609 .. **Bermanzohn,** Frances R '87 %Goldman Sachs -1 NY Plz -NY 10004
(516) 621-8221 .. **Bermas,** Roger E '64 -191 Salem Rd -Roslyn Hts 11577
(516) 482-1336 .. **Bermas,** Stephen '50 -9 Shelter Bay Dr -Gt Neck 11024
(914) 238-0320 .. **Bermel,** Michele L '80 -39 Grdn Ridge -Chappaqua 10514 **Fx:**238-1617
(212) 751-5959 .. **Bermingham,** Amy G '86 (Ehrenkranz & E,LLP) -375 Park Av -NY 10152 **Fx:**754-1905
(716) 841-4752 .. **Bermingham,** Ann B '80 HSBC -Bx803 -Buffalo 14240 **Fx:**841-4244
(718) 222-8040 .. **Bermingham,** John P '76 -16 Court -Brklyn 11241
(212) 232-0468 .. **Bermudez,** Ana Maria '93 %Dept Probation -33 Beaver -NY 10004 **Fx:**232-0599
(631) 851-0600 .. **Bermudez,** Emily '06 %I Rosenberg -320 Carleton Av -Central Islip 11722
(212) 289-9025 .. **Bermudez,** Flor '01 (Esperanza del Barrio,Inc) -2290 2nd Av -NY 10035 **Fx:**289-9026
(212) 837-6000 .. **Bermudez,** Jose V '10 %Hughes H&R LLP -1 Bttry Pk Plz -NY 10004
(518) 449-2037 .. **Bermudez,** Laurine A '03 OfCnsl Kriss K&B,LLP -350 Nrthrn Blvd -Albany 12204
(212) 801-9313 .. **Bermudez,** Marcela '01 %Greenberg T,LLP -200 Park Av -NY 10166
(212) 987-4000 .. **Bern,** Douglas M '92 (Kaufman BD&L,LLP) -888 7th Av -NY 10106
(212) 267-3700 .. **Bern,** Marc J '83 (Napoli BR LLP) -350 5th Av -NY 10118
(212) 350-2700 .. **Bernabe,** Axel A '03 (Constantine C,PC) -450 Lex Av -NY 10017
(212) 567-6296 .. **Bernace,** Victor A '94 (V Bernace,PC) -100 Cooper -NY 10034 **Fx:**(718) 504-5007
(718) 596-3800 .. **Bernache,** Damien E '07 %Tenenbaum & B LLP -26 Court -Brklyn 11242
(716) 842-6230 .. **Bernacki,** Jennifer Ann '97 %R Juda, Jr -37 Franklin -Buffalo 14202 **Fx:**842-6205
(585) 218-9550 .. **Bernacki,** John E Jr. '92 (J Bernacki Jr,PC) -11 State -Pittsfrd 14534 **Fx:**218-9551
(585) 454-3377 .. **Bernacki,** Thos M '95 (Brown & T,LLC) -19 Prince -Rchstr 14607
(718) 738-9800 .. **Bernadt,** W Bradford '99 %S Baron & Assoc,PC -159-49 Cross Bay Blvd -Howard Bch 11414 **Fx:**738-3912
(631) 425-4004 .. **Bernak,** Elliot D '96 Mercer -300 Broadhllw Rd -Melvll 11747
(718) 286-2000 .. **Bernal,** James A '06 %Leg Aid -120-46 Qns Blvd -Kew Gdns 11415 **Fx:**286-2286
(212) 269-4900 .. **Bernal,** Patrick J '05 %Ford MEW&G,LLP -Wall Street Plz -NY 10005
(212) 530-5000 .. **Bernanke,** Elise D '10 %Milbank TH&M LLP -1 Chase Manh Plz -NY 10005
(212) 759-3300 .. **Bernard,** Adler C '03 %Dornbush SS&V,LLP -747 3rd Av -NY 10017
(212) 859-8000 .. **Bernard,** Adrienne W '83 SpclCnsl Fried FHS&J LLP -1 NY Plz -NY 10004
(212) 310-2231 .. **Bernard,** Andrea Present '80 %Colgate-Palmolive -300 Park Av -NY 10022 **Fx:**310-3230
(212) 806-5400 .. **Bernard,** James L '96 (Stroock &S&L LLP) -180 Maiden Ln -NY 10038
(212) 310-8000 .. **Bernard,** Jon-Paul A '00 (Weil G&M LLP) -767 5th Av -NY 10153
(212) 940-8800 .. **Bernard,** Melissa A '02 SpclCnsl Katten MR LLP -575 Mad Av -NY 10022
(212) 727-2700 .. **Bernard,** Mitchell S '80 %NRDC -40 W 20th -NY 10011 **Fx:**727-1773
(914) 824-5481 .. **Bernard,** Raynette N '05 %Hon S Edlitz -111 Dr ML King Blvd -White Plns 10601
(212) 225-2000 .. **Bernard,** Ricardo O'Neil '08 %Cleary GS&H -1 Lbrty Plz -NY 10006
(212) 589-4200 .. **Bernard,** Richd J '02 OfCnsl Baker & H LLP -45 Rckfllr Plz -NY 10111
(718) 788-7553 .. **Bernard,** Robt A '78 -192 17th -Brklyn 11215
(212) 751-9800 .. **Bernard,** Thos G '07 %Morelli R PC -950 3rd Av -NY 10022
(585) 546-5530 .. **Bernardini,** Paul J '98 West Grp -50 E Broad -Rchstr 14614
(212) 318-6000 .. **Bernardo,** Nathalia Ann '05 %Paul HJ&W LLP -75 E 55th -NY 10022
(212) 688-4000 .. **Bernardo,** Remigio Z Jr. '96 %NYS HFA -641 Lex Av -NY 10022 **Fx:**872-0362
(212) 735-3000 .. **Bernardo,** Richd T '89 Cnsl Skadden ASM&F LLP -4 Times Sq -NY 10036
(212) 732-3200 .. **Bernards,** Bryce C '10 %Carter L&M LLP -2 Wall -NY 10005
(347) 592-2200 .. **Bernard Stines,** Sandra '99 Leg Srvcs -89-00 Sutphin Blvd -Jamaica 11435 **Fx:**(718) 937-5350
(716) 674-9100 .. **Bernas,** Kenneth P '85 -1299 Union Rd -W Seneca 14224
(212) 867-5800 .. **Bernasek,** Joyce M '09 %Osler H&H LLP -620 8th Av -NY 10018
(212) 326-3939 .. **Bernasky,** Jos J '06 %Jones D -222 E 41st -NY 10017
(212) 527-8400 .. **Bernbach,** Allison Scher '97 Cnsl Oak Hill Cptl Ptnrs -65 E 55th -NY 10022 **Fx:**527-8450
(914) 428-9100 .. **Bernbach,** Jason L '95 Bernbach Law Firm PLLC -245 Main -White Plns 10601 **Fx:**428-9106
(914) 428-9100 .. **Bernbach,** Jeffrey M '68 Bernbach Law Firm PLLC -245 Main -White Plns 10601 **Fx:**428-9106
(914) 939-1909 .. **Bernbaum,** Peter J '75 -5 Acker Dr -Rye Brook 10573 **Fx:**934-0036
(585) 232-6500 .. **Berndt,** Paul E '95 Cnsl Harter S&E LLP -1600 Bausch & Lomb Pl -Rchstr 14604
(212) 310-5906 .. **Berne,** Clement H '77 -875 3rd Av -NY 10022 **Fx:**644-4552
(718) 665-0220 .. **Berne,** Richd W '78 (Irom WFB&S,PC) -349 E 149th -Bronx 10451
(212) 721-7555 .. **Berner,** Adam J '95 -450 7th Av -NY 10123 **Fx:**(201) 836-6989
(212) 225-2000 .. **Berner,** Danl P '10 %Cleary GS&H -1 Lbrty Plz -NY 10006
(212) 752-7979 .. **Berner,** Richd O '78 (Berner & B) -485 Mad Av -NY 10022 **Fx:**735-0638
(212) 920-2800 .. **Berner,** Thos F '80 First Capital -565 5th Av -NY 10017 **Fx:**920-2820
(212) 752-7979 .. **Berner,** Thos R '74 (Berner & B) -485 Mad Av -NY 10022 **Fx:**735-0638
(631) 853-5761 .. **Bernet,** James G '02 %Cnty Atty -400 Carleton Av -Central Islip 11722 **Fx:**853-7788
(518) 474-0491 .. **Bernet,** Mary F '83 Exec Chamber Appointments Ofc -State Cptl -Albany 12224
(212) 838-7797 .. **Berney,** Elizabeth A '79 OfCnsl Cohen MS&T,PLLC -88 Pine -NY 10005
(212) 883-4900 .. **Berney,** Richd H '86 (Cozen O) -277 Park Av -NY 10172
(212) 661-1661 .. **Bernfeld,** David B '66 Bernfeld D&B -600 3rd Av -NY 10016 **Fx:**557-9610
(212) 661-1661 .. **Bernfeld,** Jeffrey L '94 (Bernfeld D&B) -600 3rd Av -NY 10016 **Fx:**557-9610
(212) 818-8800 .. **Bernfeld,** Lawr D '70 (Graubard M) -405 Lex Av -NY 10174
(212) 513-1988 .. **Bernfeld,** Randye F '87 -325 Bway -NY 10007 **Fx:**385-0564
(914) 422-4333 .. **Bernhard,** Adele '77 %John Jay Lgl Srvcs -80 N Bway -White Plns 10603 **Fx:**422-4391
(212) 223-0400 .. **Bernhard,** Greg M '89 %Zeichner E&K LLP -575 Lex Av -NY 10022
(518) 793-4382 .. **Bernhard,** John H '81 -28 Sanford Bx722 -Glens Fls 12801 **Fx:**793-4383
(212) 693-0085 .. **Bernhard,** Steven R '74 %Appellate Advocates -2 Rector -NY 10006 **Fx:**693-0878
(716) 674-2424 .. **Bernhardi,** Wm C '86 -950A Union Rd -W Seneca 14224 **Fx:**674-0388
(212) 951-6562 .. **Bernhardt,** Abigail S '89 %NYS Ed Dept-OLS -475 Park Av S -NY 10016 **Fx:**951-6573
(716) 542-5413 .. **Bernhardt,** Craig H '01 (Nicholas PSB&Z) -12364 Main Rd Bx176 -Akron 14001
(212) 788-0996 .. **Bernhardt,** Doris F '06 %Law Dept -100 Church -NY 10007 **Fx:**788-0367
(212) 957-7600 .. **Bernhardt,** Elizabeth F '89 %Cohen & G LLP -800 3rd Av -NY 10022
(716) 854-3400 .. **Bernhardt,** Eric S '07 %Rupp BPC&C LLC -1600 Lbrty Bldg -Buffalo 14202
(718) 390-5407 .. **Bernhardt,** Ralph P '84 %Surrogates Ct -18 Richmond Ter -Staten Isl 10301
(212) 538-6376 .. **Bernheim,** Carol S '80 Credit Suisse -11 Mad Av -NY 10010
(914) 271-6323 .. **Bernheim,** David '64 -6 E Mt Airy Rd Bx248 -Croton-On-Hud 10520 **Fx:**271-6323
(212) 262-1000 .. **Bernheim,** Douglas C '91 %Levinsohn & A LLP -1790 Bway -NY 10019
(718) 261-2300 .. **Bernheim,** Esther Chyzyk '83 %Sager & G -118-35 Qns Blvd -Frst Hlls 11375
(212) 682-5844 .. **Bernheim,** Gail '83 -521 5th Av -NY 10175
(212) 767-6917 .. **Bernheim,** Jennifer B '95 Hachette Fililpacchi -1633 Bway -NY 10019 **Fx:**767-5631
(516) 541-6200 .. **Bernheim,** Nancy '91 (Davis & B) -254 Pettit Av -Bellmore 11710 **Fx:**798-9097
(914) 345-0005 .. **Bernheimer,** Jason M '99 %Nesci K,PLLC -40 Saw Mill Rvr Rd -Hawthorne 10532
(516) 942-4020 .. **Bernheimer,** Melvin H '74 M Bernheimer,PC -76 N Bway -Hicksvll 11801 **Fx:**942-4088
(716) 845-7465 .. **Bernholz,** Neil J '92 %Family Ct -1 Niagara Plz -Buffalo 14202 **Fx:**858-6293
(516) 745-0066 .. **Bernier,** Alberthe '09 %Karol H&S,PC -600 Old Cntry Rd -Gdn Cty 11530
(607) 432-2950 .. **Bernier,** Lucy P '81 (Pantaleoni & B) -28 Watkins Av -Oneonta 13820
(212) 553-7132 .. **Berninger,** Michelle Lea '96 %Moody's Invstr Srvc -250 Greenwich -NY 10007
(518) 729-5230 .. **Bernini,** Anthony '76 Cnsl Eden Park Health Srvcs,Inc -45 Learned -Albany 12207 **Fx:**729-5238
(212) 230-8883 .. **Bernotas,** Tanya Stern '05 %WilmerHale -399 Park Av -NY 10022
(212) 384-1000 .. **Bernreuther,** Paul D '98 FBI -26 Fed Plz -NY 10278
(212) 407-7700 .. **Berns,** Amy S '88 %Vedder P,PC -1633 Bway -NY 10019
(914) 745-4000 .. **Berns,** Debra J '03 %Towers Watson -100 Summit Lk Dr -Valhalla 10595
(212) 332-3320 .. **Berns,** James A '79 (Berns & B) -767 3rd Av -NY 10017
(212) 332-3320 .. **Berns,** Michl H '76 (Berns & B) -767 3rd Av -NY 10017
(914) 251-0001 .. **Berns,** Mitchell '78 (Lane S&L LLP) -106 Corp Park Dr -White Plns 10604
(212) 332-3320 .. **Berns,** Rona B '79 OfCnsl Berns & B -767 3rd Av -NY 10017
(845) 294-4788 .. **Bernsley,** Richd A '93 -76 Boniface Dr -Pine Bush 12566 **Fx:**744-2599
(716) 845-9326 .. **Bernsohn,** David A '76 %Supreme Ct -92 Franklin -Buffalo 14202 **Fx:**856-4670
(212) 696-5500 .. **Bernstein,** Adam S '89 (Budin RK&B) -112 Mad Av -NY 10016
(212) 395-8099 .. **Bernstein,** Adam T '92 Verizon -1095 Av of Amer -NY 10036
(212) 964-7700 .. **Bernstein,** Alan D '77 (Warner B&B,LLP) -11 Park Pl -NY 10007 **Fx:**964-7730
(212) 732-3200 .. **Bernstein,** Alan J '84 (Carter L&M LLP) -2 Wall -NY 10005
(716) 842-2200 .. **Bernstein,** Alan L '60 (Andrews B&M,LLP) -69 Delaware Av -Buffalo 14202
(212) 604-2485 .. **Bernstein,** Alexander E '97 %St Vincent Catholic Med Ctr -170 W 12th -NY 10011
(212) 535-6449 .. **Bernstein,** Amy H '71 -155 E 76th -NY 10021
(212) 436-1141 .. **Bernstein,** Amy S '87 %IRS -290 Bway -NY 10007
(212) 310-8000 .. **Bernstein,** Andrea A '78 (Weil G&M LLP) -767 5th Av -NY 10153
(212) 935-3000 .. **Bernstein,** Andrew J '89 (Mintz LCFG&P,PC) -666 3rd Av -NY 10017
(718) 250-1100 .. **Bernstein,** Andrew M '79 %E Garfinkel -12 Metrotech Ctr -Brklyn 11201 **Fx:**250-1168
(718) 625-2200 .. **Bernstein,** Anita N '86 Bklyn Law Schl -250 Joralemon -Brklyn 11201 **Fx:**780-0393
(212) 578-2211 .. **Bernstein,** Annette '91 %MetLife -27-01 Qns Plz N -LIC 11101
(914) 997-6400 .. **Bernstein,** Arnold '75 -599 W Hartsdale Av -White Plns 10607 **Fx:**997-7518
(212) 969-3000 .. **Bernstein,** Avi '95 %Proskauer R LLP -1585 Bway -NY 10036
(212) 980-1212 .. **Bernstein,** Barry M '79 -245 E 63rd -NY 10065
(212) 490-3944 .. **Bernstein,** Barry S '72 (Livoti B&M,PC) -122 E 42nd -NY 10168
(212) 242-1054 .. **Bernstein,** Beatrice '46 -161 W 16th -NY 10011
(646) 672-6185 .. **Bernstein,** Benjamin K '02 MHLS-Manhattan Psychiatric Ctr -Meyer Bldg FL 10A Wards Isl -NY 10035
(212) 918-3000 .. **Bernstein,** Beth A '10 %Hogan L LLP -875 3rd Av -NY 10022

(718) 232-1250 .. **Bernstein,** Bonnie G '87 OfCnsl Polizzotto & P -6911 18th Av -Brklyn 11204 **Fx:**256-0966
(212) 449-9745 .. **Bernstein,** Brad N '89 %Merrill Lynch -220 Bway -NY 10038
(212) 227-3636 .. **Bernstein,** Bradford H '94 (Spar & B,PC) -225 Bway -NY 10007
(212) 980-4500 .. **Bernstein,** Bradley '78 (Cohen L LLP) -885 3rd Av -NY 10022
(718) 287-0010 .. **Bernstein,** Brenda '99 CAMBA -885 Flatbush Av -Brklyn 11226 **Fx:**282-5997
(212) 869-2300 .. **Bernstein,** Brian K '82 (Toback B&R,LLP) -15 W 44th -NY 10036
(212) 554-1400 .. **Bernstein,** Bruce D '98 OfCnsl Bernstein LB&G LLP -1285 Av of Amer -NY 10019
(718) 852-8800 .. **Bernstein,** Carey S '94 C Bernstein,PC -26 Court -Brklyn 11242 **Fx:**852-8733
(212) 447-5599 .. **Bernstein,** Carl D '66 OfCnsl Agins SR&B,LLP -386 Park Av S -NY 10016
(516) 482-2742 .. **Bernstein,** Carol Harrow '82 -14 Round Hill Rd -Gt Neck 11020
(212) 312-7551 .. **Bernstein,** Caryn S '86 %State Ins Fund -199 Church -NY 10007 **Fx:**385-9199
(212) 279-3500 .. **Bernstein,** Danl L '64 Russin VB&B,LLP -260 Mad Av -NY 10016
(212) 935-1400 .. **Bernstein,** Danl M '97 %Seiden & S,PC -570 Lex Av -NY 10022
(212) 909-6000 .. **Bernstein,** David H '90 (Debevoise & P LLP) -919 3rd Av -NY 10022
(212) 705-0765 .. **Bernstein,** David L '90 Cnsl Dexia Credit Local -445 Park Av -NY 10022 **Fx:**753-7522
(212) 536-3900 .. **Bernstein,** David W '62 (K&L Gates LLP) -599 Lex Av -NY 10022
(212) 216-8000 .. **Bernstein,** Debra Bodian '91 %Tarter K&D LLP -1350 Bway -NY 10018
(516) 223-0747 .. **Bernstein,** Diane L '86 (D Bernstein,PC) -2077 Byron Rd -Merrick 11566 **Fx:**223-0747
(212) 486-6000 .. **Bernstein,** Donald M '83 (Victor & B, PC) -18 E 41st -NY 10017 **Fx:**486-8668
(212) 450-4000 .. **Bernstein,** Donald S '79 (Davis P&W LLP) -450 Lex Av -NY 10017
(646) 414-6805 .. **Bernstein,** Douglas N '97 OfCnsl Lowenstein S PC -1251 Av of Amer -NY 10020 **Fx:**(973) 422-6843
(516) 868-6688 .. **Bernstein,** Edw A '73 -1745 Merrick Av -Merrick 11566 **Fx:**868-2040
(516) 364-5100 .. **Bernstein,** Edwin A '51 (Katz B&K) -6900 Jericho Tpk -Syosset 11791 **Fx:**364-5166
(516) 712-4000 .. **Bernstein,** Elana D '03 %Milber MP&S LLP -1000 Woodbury Rd -Woodbury 11797
(631) 941-9076 .. **Bernstein,** Elizabeth Cannarozzo '87 -Bx309 -E Setauket 11733 **Fx:**941-9361
(212) 683-1530 .. **Bernstein,** Eric R '99 (E Bernstein,PC) -260 Mad Av -NY 10016 **Fx:**448-0066
(212) 836-8000 .. **Bernstein,** Gary B '83 (Kaye S LLP) -425 Park Av -NY 10022
(212) 239-6000 .. **Bernstein,** Grace '80 %Div Of Parole -314 W 40th -NY 10018 **Fx:**239-6160
(718) 797-1012 .. **Bernstein,** Helene S '88 -44 Court -Brklyn 11201 **Fx:**624-0198
(845) 294-1632 .. **Bernstein,** Honey '83 -9 Winners Circle Ln -Goshen 10924
(718) 727-4555 .. **Bernstein,** Howard '73 -1444 Clove Rd -Staten Isl 10301 **Fx:**981-4666
(914) 961-5221 .. **Bernstein,** Jack '55 -Bx952 -Hartsdale 10530
(718) 798-6140 .. **Bernstein,** Jack '57 -2310 Vance -Bronx 10469
(516) 922-4040 .. **Bernstein,** Jacob '58 (Marino & B,PC) -Townsend Sq Bx180 -Oyster Bay 11771
(212) 406-4848 .. **Bernstein,** Jason M '01 %G Pillersdorf & Assoc,PC -225 Bway -NY 10007 **Fx:**406-5884
(212) 878-8527 .. **Bernstein,** Jay L '85 (Clifford C LLP) -31 W 52nd -NY 10019
(516) 466-4600 .. **Bernstein,** Jeffrey N '83 -525 Nrthrn Blvd -Gt Neck 11021
(516) 921-3838 .. **Bernstein,** Jennifer L '98 %Pitnick & M LLP -6800 Jericho Tpk -Syosset 11791 **Fx:**921-3824
(212) 885-5000 .. **Bernstein,** Jerry D '83 (Blank R LLP) -405 Lex Av -NY 10174
(212) 815-1818 .. **Bernstein,** Jill V '84 %DC 37 MELS -125 Barclay -NY 10007 **Fx:**815-1343
(212) 907-0869 .. **Bernstein,** Joel H '76 (Labaton S LLP) -140 Bway -NY 10005
(212) 545-8611 .. **Bernstein,** Joel S '77 (Solomon & B) -351 Bway -NY 10013
(212) 371-0033 .. **Bernstein,** Jonathan A '98 (Levy D&M,LLP) -29 Bway -NY 10006
(212) 506-2500 .. **Bernstein,** Jonathan H '09 %Mayer B LLP -1675 Bway -NY 10019
(518) 463-5400 .. **Bernstein,** Jonathan M '03 %Goldberg S LLP -8 Southwoods Blvd -Albany 12211
(212) 226-1900 .. **Bernstein,** Jonathan M '07 %Tesser & C -591 Bway -NY 10012
(516) 812-4500 .. **Bernstein,** Jonathan M '08 %Stagg TC&W LLP -401 Franklin Av -Gdn Cty 11530
(212) 730-7700 .. **Bernstein,** Jordan R '06 %Michelman & R,LLP -114 W 47th -NY 10036
(212) 774-5825 .. **Bernstein,** Jordan S '94 Cl Capitol Prtnrs LLC -500 Park Av -NY 10022
(917) 365-3651 .. **Bernstein,** Jos E '76 -1045 5th Av -NY 10028
(212) 682-4100 .. **Bernstein,** Joshua A '10 %M Risk, PC -60 E 42nd -NY 10165 **Fx:**682-4775
(212) 421-4100 .. **Bernstein,** Joshua D '02 %Pryor C LLP -7 Times Sq -NY 10036
(212) 763-6800 .. **Bernstein,** Joshua M '04 (Vandenberg & F,LLP) -60 E 42nd -NY 10165
(212) 757-5531 .. **Bernstein,** Julian H '02 JB Natl Entrprs,Inc -110 E 59th -NY 10022
(212) 373-3000 .. **Bernstein,** Justin P '10 %Paul WRW&G LLP -1285 Av of Amer -NY 10019
(212) 339-9955 .. **Bernstein,** Karen J '02 -100 Park Av -NY 10017
(516) 747-4301 .. **Bernstein,** Kenneth A '82 (Torino & B,PC) -200 Old Cntry Rd -Mineola 11501
(914) 288-8100 .. **Bernstein,** Kenneth F '87 Acadia Rlty Trust -1311 Mamoroneck Av -White Plns 10605
(845) 486-2242 .. **Bernstein,** Kenneth M '83 %Hon JD Pagones -10 Market -Poughkeepsie 12601 **Fx:**486-2245
(315) 218-8000 .. **Bernstein,** Kevin M '87 (Bond S&K,PLLC) -1 Lincoln Ctr -Syracuse 13202
(212) 836-8000 .. **Bernstein,** Lauren M '98 Cnsl Kaye S LLP -425 Park Av -NY 10022
(718) 871-4840 .. **Bernstein,** Lawr M '98 Jonas Equities -725 Church Av -Brklyn 11218
(212) 683-3800 .. **Bernstein,** Leigh W '87 %Dinkes & S,PC -112 Mad Av -NY 10016
(631) 874-7334 .. **Bernstein,** Leonard '52 -348 Seabreeze Ct -Moriches 11955 **Fx:**283-3556
(212) 779-1414 .. **Bernstein Liebhard LLP** -10 E 40th -NY 10016 **Fx:**779-3218
(212) 798-7500 .. **Bernstein,** Lisa Barse '89 %Interbrand -130 5th Av -NY 10011
(914) 235-0989 .. **Bernstein,** Lisa M '93 -50 Verdun Av -New Rchll 10804 **Fx:**235-4776
(212) 554-1400 .. **Bernstein Litowitz Berger & Grossmann LLP** -1285 Av of Amer -NY 10019 **Fx:**554-1444
(212) 318-6000 .. **Bernstein,** Marc E '90 OfCnsl Paul HJ&W LLP -75 E 55th -NY 10022
(718) 823-2600 .. **Bernstein,** Mark F '86 (Siriano & B,PC) -2027 Wllmsbrdg Rd -Bronx 10461
(914) 941-2800 .. **Bernstein,** Mark F '86 (Siriano & B,PC) -515 N State Rd -Briarcliff 10510
(212) 310-8000 .. **Bernstein,** Mark I '05 %Weil G&M LLP -767 5th Av -NY 10153
(516) 741-5252 .. **Bernstein,** Mark R '92 %Sanders SBWV&G,PC -100 Hrrcks Rd -Mineola 11501
(516) 357-3700 .. **Bernstein,** Marna E '93 (Cullen and D LLP) -100 Q Roosevelt Blvd -Gdn Cty 11530
(212) 688-2700 .. **Bernstein,** Marshall A '72 -950 3rd Av -NY 10022
(212) 603-6300 .. **Bernstein,** Marshall E '62 (Robinson BLGG&G PC) -875 3rd Av -NY 10022
(212) 422-0202 .. **Bernstein,** Michl H '87 (Sedgwick DM&A LLP) -125 Broad -NY 10004
(646) 253-2300 .. **Bernstein,** Michl I '63 (Bond S&K,PLLC) -330 Mad Av -NY 10017
(212) 385-0723 .. **Bernstein,** Michl I '96 (M Bernstein,PA) -1580 Ocean Av -Brklyn 11230 **Fx:**(646) 390-2219
(914) 995-3497 .. **Bernstein,** Michelle K '09 %DA -111 Martin Luther King Blvd -White Plns 10601 **Fx:**995-3363
(212) 765-5070 .. **Bernstein,** Mitchell '05 %Fish & R,PC -153 E 53rd -NY 10022
(212) 592-1400 .. **Bernstein,** Mitchell G '77 Cnsl Herrick,F LLP -2 Park Av -NY 10016
(516) 742-4343 .. **Bernstein,** Peter I '95 (Scully SM&P PC) -400 Grdn City Plz -Gdn Cty 11530
(516) 222-0440 .. **Bernstein,** Philip M '73 -595 Stewart Av -Gdn Cty 11530 **Fx:**222-2971
(212) 381-7000 .. **Bernstein,** Richd A '82 (Sabin B&G LLP) -4 Times Sq -NY 10036
(212) 292-4573 .. **Bernstein,** Richd F '83 OfCnsl T McInnis -521 5th Av -NY 10175 **Fx:**292-4574
(718) 693-7500 .. **Bernstein,** Richd L '59 -1431 Nostrand Av -Brklyn 11226
(212) 763-6800 .. **Bernstein,** Robt B '82 (Vandenberg & F,LLP) -60 E 42nd -NY 10165
(212) 705-4811 .. **Bernstein,** Robt J '77 -488 Mad Av -NY 10022
(516) 783-3300 .. **Bernstein,** Robt L Jr. '88 (Baker G&B) -2099 Bellmore Av -Bellmore 11710
(914) 472-8455 .. **Bernstein,** Robt M '87 (Bernstein & S) -670 Wht Plns Rd -Scarsdale 10583 **Fx:**472-8755
(914) 698-3986 .. **Bernstein,** Robt S '66 -500 Rushmore Av -Mamaroneck 10543
(212) 609-6800 .. **Bernstein,** Robt S '96 (McCarter & E,LLP) -245 Park Av -NY 10167
(212) 214-9246 .. **Bernstein,** Robin A '86 Rent Stblztn Assn -123 William -NY 10038 **Fx:**732-0617
(212) 209-0784 .. **Bernstein,** Roderick S '06 Zenta Global Ltd -485 Lex Av -NY 10017
(212) 338-9188 .. **Bernstein,** Roger J '85 -331 Mad Av -NY 10017 **Fx:**338-9102
(212) 757-5531 .. **Bernstein,** Roy J '71 -110 E 59th -NY 10022 **Fx:**582-0176
(212) 888-6688 .. **Bernstein,** Ruth E '91 -271 Mad Av -NY 10016 **Fx:**888-9399
(718) 855-5110 .. **Bernstein,** Saml A '85 -26 Court -Brklyn 11242
(212) 593-7700 .. **Bernstein,** Scott B '83 %Caxton Corp -500 Park Av -NY 10022
(516) 829-2400 .. **Bernstein,** Scott H '90 Schottenstein/Bernstein Capital Grp LLC -1010 Nrthrn Blvd -Gt Neck 11021 **Fx:**829-2404
(212) 309-1000 .. **Bernstein,** Scott H '03 %Hunton & W -200 Park Av -NY 10166
(212) 474-1000 .. **Bernstein,** Scott S '10 %Cravath S&M LLP -825 8th Av -NY 10019
(212) 895-4447 .. **Bernstein,** Sol W '85 Amalgamated Bnk -275 7th -NY 10001
(212) 779-1414 .. **Bernstein,** Stanley D '81 (Bernstein L LLP) -10 E 40th -NY 10016
(212) 686-4300 .. **Bernstein,** Stephen M '65 -10 E 40th -NY 10016 **Fx:**689-2079
(718) 875-7900 .. **Bernstein,** Steven C '83 -189 Montague -Brklyn 11201
(212) 248-8800 .. **Bernstein,** Stuart '91 (Callan KB&B LLP) -1 Whitehall -NY 10004
(212) 756-2000 .. **Bernstein,** Susan E '95 SpclCnsl Schulte R&Z LLP -919 3rd Av -NY 10022
(914) 376-2782 .. **Bernstein,** Susan F '81 -19 Fanshaw Av -Ynkrs 10705 **Fx:**376-7114
(516) 775-9400 .. **Bernstein,** Susan P '93 %Jeffrey Goldberg,PC -2001 Marcus Av -Lk Success 11042 **Fx:**775-4477
(516) 228-9660 .. **Bernstein,** Terry S '64 TS Bernstein -600 Old Cntry Rd -Gdn Cty 11530
(212) 631-0200 .. **Bernstein,** Tracey S '94 (Himmel & B LLP) -928 Bway -NY 10010
(212) 836-8000 .. **Bernstein,** Warren J '81 (Kaye S LLP) -425 Park Av -NY 10022
(212) 267-6456 .. **Bernstein,** Wendy J '94 %Fischer Bros -217 Bway -NY 10007 **Fx:**267-6468
(631) 654-4900 .. **Bernstein,** Wm J '76 (Cartier BA&D,PC) -100 Austin -Patchogue 11772
(212) 790-4500 .. **Bernstein,** Wm S '83 (Manatt P&P,LLP) -7 Times Sq -NY 10036
(212) 859-8000 .. **Bernstein,** Zachary B '06 %Fried FHS&J LLP -1 NY Plz -NY 10004
(718) 722-5495 .. **Bernstein-Gold,** Gail '88 Independence Community Bank -195 Montague -Brklyn 11201
(212) 490-3000 .. **Bernstock,** Christine A '00 (Wilson EME&D LLP) -150 E 42nd -NY 10017
(212) 532-1200 .. **Bernstone,** Alvin M '59 -292 Mad Av -NY 10017 **Fx:**532-6330
(212) 652-9379 .. **Bernthal,** Danielle J '03 Six Flags,Inc -1540 Bway -NY 10036
(212) 361-7770 .. **Beroff,** Carole L '86 %Dept Consumer Affrs -66 John -NY 10038
(212) 490-3000 .. **Beron,** Helmut '87 (Wilson EME&D LLP) -150 E 42nd -NY 10017
(914) 323-7000 .. **Beron,** Helmut '87 (Wilson EME&D LLP) -3 Gannett Dr -White Plns 10604
(718) 260-8210 .. **Berotti,** Wm G '89 -31 Smith -Brklyn 11201 **Fx:**522-1388
(212) 513-1713 .. **Berowitz,** Irwin J '94 (Thaker B LLP) -225 Bway -NY 10007 **Fx:**513-7737
(212) 771-9528 .. **Beroza,** Anne '77 CIT Grp,Inc -505 5th Av -NY 10017
(212) 267-3091 .. **Berquist,** Darron E '08 %Wilentz G&S -110 William -NY 10038 **Fx:**(732) 726-6513
(516) 747-0300 .. **Berra,** José L '86 Cnsl Meltzer LG&B,LLP -190 Willis Av -Mineola 11501
(212) 576-7000 .. **Berrafati,** Jos F '95 NY Life Ins -51 Mad Av -NY 10010 **Fx:**447-0569
(212) 351-3400 .. **Berrebi,** Jason '08 %Desmarais LLP -230 Park Av -NY 10169 **Fx:**351-3401
(212) 446-4800 .. **Berrebi,** Rebecca K '08 %Kirkland & E LLP -153 E 53rd -NY 10022
(212) 937-7513 .. **Berrent,** Jennifer C '01 Cnsl WilmerHale -399 Park Av -NY 10022
(212) 230-8892 .. **Berrent,** Steven K '05 WilmerHale -399 Park Av -NY 10022

(212) 965-2200 .. **Berrien,** Jacqueline A '87 %NAACP/LDF -99 Hudson -NY 10013 **Fx:**226-7592
(716) 285-1535 .. **Berrigan,** Patrick J '58 SrCnsl Harris B PLLC -800 Main Bx712 -Niagara Fls 14302
(212) 521-5400 .. **Berringer,** John B '81 (Reed S LLP) -599 Lex Av -NY 10022
(212) 386-3980 .. **Berrios,** Annabelle '01 Hon E Padro -100 Centre -NY 10013
(585) 454-2181 .. **Berrittella,** Lisa Giovanna '05 %Trevett CS&A,PC -2 State -Rchstr 14614
(212) 848-4000 .. **Berry,** Abigail J '04 %Shearman & S LLP -599 Lex Av -NY 10022
(212) 715-1000 .. **Berry,** Chas '78 (Arnold & P LLP) -399 Park Av -NY 10022
(212) 267-9340 .. **Berry,** Christiane Simone '99 -132 Nassau -NY 10038
(212) 417-4357 .. **Berry,** Courtney Ann '93 %Dept of Health -90 Church -NY 10007 **Fx:**417-4392
(212) 626-4100 .. **Berry,** Dean C '83 (Baker & M LLP) -1114 Av of Amer -NY 10036
(212) 355-0777 .. **Berry,** Eric '85 -132 Nassau -NY 10038 **Fx:**758-2817
(212) 455-2000 .. **Berry,** Eric Z '09 %Simpson T&B LLP -425 Lex Av -NY 10017
(212) 871-5770 .. **Berry,** Francine J '07 (Berry & Assoc PC) -551 Mad Av -NY 10022 **Fx:**871-5774
(914) 332-1500 .. **Berry,** Gregory J '88 (Berry & N,LLP) -660 Wht Plns Rd -Tarrytwn 10591 **Fx:**332-1777
(212) 980-0120 .. **Berry,** Hamish R '03 %Frankfurt KK&S,PC -488 Mad Av -NY 10022
(212) 449-1000 .. **Berry,** Henry T '82 %Merrill Lynch -220 Bway -NY 10038
(914) 232-5094 .. **Berry,** I Wm '61 -115 Lily Pond Ln -Katonah 10536 **Fx:**232-4499
(212) 753-5000 .. **Berry,** Jill L '07 %Schiff H LLP -900 3rd Av -NY 10022
(516) 573-7000 .. **Berry,** John F Jr. '98 %Cnty Police -1490 Franklin Av -Mineola 11501
(212) 872-1000 .. **Berry,** John W '99 -One Bryant Park -NY 10036 **Fx:**872-1002
(212) 879-5246 .. **Berry,** Joshua D '83 -404 E 88th -NY 10128 **Fx:**722-7228
(212) 336-2000 .. **Berry,** Karen R '96 Cnsl Patterson BW&T LLP -1133 Av of Amer -NY 10036
(212) 336-3620 .. **Berry,** Kevin J '89 %EEOC -33 Whitehall -NY 10004
(212) 267-3091 .. **Berry,** Kevin M '86 (Wilentz G&S) -110 William -NY 10038 **Fx:**(732) 726-6593
(212) 756-2000 .. **Berry,** Laura J '07 %Schulte R&Z LLP -919 3rd Av -NY 10022
(212) 259-8000 .. **Berry,** Linda Potter '89 Cnsl Dewey & L LLP -1301 Av of Amer -NY 10019
(315) 422-9295 .. **Berry,** Martha L '87 (Longstreet & B,LLP) -313 Mntgmry -Syracuse 13202
(518) 474-4614 .. **Berry,** Mary Ann '95 Dept of Law -The Cptl -Albany 12224
(315) 423-1104 .. **Berry,** Paul R '81 %Medicaid Fraud Cntrl -615 Erie Blvd W -Syracuse 13204
(212) 307-7890 .. **Berry,** Richd S '71 -311 W 43rd -NY 10036
(212) 756-2000 .. **Berry,** Sean P D '07 %Schulte R&Z LLP -919 3rd Av -NY 10022
(518) 447-7150 .. **Berry,** Timothy J '95 Pub Def -60 S Pearl -Albany 12207 **Fx:**449-2903
(716) 853-3087 .. **Berry,** Wm W '79 %Leg Srvcs -237 Main -Buffalo 14203 **Fx:**856-5317
(914) 948-8511 .. **Berry Harding,** Alison '85 -300 Hmltn Av -White Plns 10601 **Fx:**948-8696
(212) 259-8000 .. **Bers,** Rebecca A '09 %Dewey & L LLP -1301 Av of Amer -NY 10019
(315) 478-0560 .. **Bersani,** Frank A Jr. '81 -224 Harrison -Syracuse 13202
(585) 454-2181 .. **Bersani,** Kenneth '76 (Trevett CS&A,PC) -2 State -Rchstr 14614
(315) 253-3293 .. **Bersani,** Michl G '94 (Michaels & S,PC) -71 South -Auburn 13021
(212) 218-2100 .. **Berschadsky,** Jonathan '01 (Fitzpatrick CH&S) -1290 Av of Amer -NY 10104
(212) 373-3000 .. **Berse,** Farrah R '03 %Paul WRW&G LLP -1285 Av of Amer -NY 10019
(315) 422-7000 .. **Bersin,** Adam S '87 %Pyramid -4 Clinton Sq -Syracuse 13202 **Fx:**422-2717
(212) 964-1000 .. **Bersin,** Andrew '75 (Durst Law Firm,PC) -319 Bway -NY 10007 **Fx:**964-1400
(212) 824-5700 .. **Bersofsky,** Danielle T '07 Practising Law Inst -810 7th Av -NY 10019
(212) 945-5000 .. **Berson & Budashewitz, PC** -15 Maiden Ln -NY 10038
(347) 296-1677 .. **Berson,** Dale '91 %Supreme Ct Law Dept -360 Adams -Brklyn 11201 **Fx:**643-6114
(212) 945-5000 .. **Berson,** Jeffrey A '93 (Berson & B, PC) -15 Maiden Ln -NY 10038
(212) 661-3535 .. **Berson,** Joel I '52 OfCnsl Hodgson R LLP -60 E 42nd -NY 10165
(212) 788-0408 .. **Berson,** Lesley A '09 %Law Dept -100 Church -NY 10007 **Fx:**788-0367
(845) 566-5526 .. **Berson,** Marilyn D '78 -263 Route 17K -Newburgh 12550 **Fx:**566-9416
(646) 315-7300 .. **Berson,** Neil M '70 %FINRA -14 Wall -NY 10005 **Fx:**315-7440
(845) 365-9100 .. **Berson,** Robt M '64 -30 Ramland Rd -Orangebrg 10962 **Fx:**365-9190
(212) 408-5100 .. **Berson,** Scott D '96 (Chadbourne & P LLP) -30 Rckfllr Plz -NY 10112
(212) 676-7832 .. **Berstell,** Mitchell F '85 Child Support Lit -220 Church -NY 10013
(718) 742-1688 .. **Bertan,** David K '86 -888 Grnd Cncrs -Bronx 10451
(914) 276-3040 .. **Berte,** Georgianne M '86 %Premier Abstract Ltd -Routes 100 & 202 -Somers 10589 **Fx:**276-2429
(212) 909-6000 .. **Berthou,** Erica E '04 (Debevoise & P LLP) -919 3rd Av -NY 10022
(212) 250-5404 .. **Berti,** Christina M '90 %Deutsche Bank -60 Wall -NY 10005
(607) 772-1225 .. **Berti,** David J '80 Connerton & Berti -57 Front -Bnghmtn 13905 **Fx:**723-4765
(914) 472-7700 .. **Bertine Hufnagel Headley Zeltner Drummond & Dohn,LLP** -700 Wht Plns Rd -Scarsdale 10583 **Fx:**472-1946
(212) 837-1883 .. **Bertini,** Jos J '96 %JP Morgan Chase & Co -522 5th Av -NY 10036
(718) 266-6528 .. **Bertino,** Frank A '98 -8756 25th Av -Brklyn 11214 **Fx:**266-6528
(212) 279-5299 .. **Bertisch,** Sharyn F '99 (Feinbloom B LLP) -40 Worth -NY 10013
(212) 425-3220 .. **Bertocci,** Richd A '69 (Gilmartin P&S LLP) -845 Third Av -NY 10022
(845) 358-9700 .. **Bertolino,** Danl E '79 -407 N Highland Av -Upper Nyack 10960 **Fx:**358-9707
(631) 277-5292 .. **Bertolino,** Steven P '95 S Bertolino,PC -130 W Main -E Islip 11730 **Fx:**277-5372
(212) 457-9680 .. **Bertoni,** Fabio B '98 Incisive Media,LLC -120 Bway -NY 10271
(212) 213-9752 .. **Bertram,** Jonathan W '95 Civil Solutns Inc -31 E 32nd -NY 10016 **Fx:**213-9756
(212) 909-6000 .. **Bertram-Nothnagel,** Hans '76 OfCnsl Debevoise & P LLP -919 3rd Av -NY 10022
(212) 860-4733 .. **Bertram-Nothnagel,** Jutta F '83 -55 E 86th -NY 10028
(315) 458-3331 .. **Bertrand Arno Welch & Putzer** -107 S Main Bx277 -N Syracuse 13212 **Fx:**458-3571
(212) 504-6000 .. **Bertrand,** Jean M '00 SpclCnsl Cadwalader W&T LLP -1 World Fncl Ctr -NY 10281
(212) 883-1700 .. **Bertrand,** Marie C '08 %Duval & S LLP -101 Park Av -NY 10178
(315) 656-3990 .. **Bertrand,** Perley A Jr. '54 %Untd Methodist Fndtn -250 East Av -Minoa 13116
(315) 458-3331 .. **Bertrand,** Robt J '78 %Bertrand AW&P -107 S Main Bx277 -N Syracuse 13212
(212) 256-8441 .. **Bertron,** Dennis C '97 Atticus Capital LP -767 5th Av -NY 10153 **Fx:**256-8704
(516) 626-4700 .. **Bertsch,** Robt A '91 (Bertsch & Assoc) -2 Seaview Blvd -Pt Wash 11050 **Fx:**626-6265
(845) 482-4288 .. **Bertsch-Brustman,** Lori '96 -688 Cnty Rd 95 -N Branch 12766 **Fx:**482-4106
(917) 551-1300 .. **Bertschi,** Michl Robt '98 %Koehler & I LLP -61 Bway -NY 10006
(212) 244-5670 .. **Bertstein,** Sheryl '93 (Baron B&W) -450 7th Av -NY 10123
(212) 788-0466 .. **Bertulfo,** Annette J '08 %Law Dept -100 Church -NY 10007 **Fx:**788-0367
(516) 746-3500 .. **Bertuna,** Jason P '09 %Brand G&B,PC -600 Old Cntry Rd -Gdn Cty 11530
(718) 238-9898 .. **Bertuna,** Marianne E '03 %A Aidala & Assoc,PC -8118 13th Av -Brklyn 11228 **Fx:**921-3292
(212) 612-3270 .. **Berube,** Mark A '98 (Mishcon de R NY LLP) -200 Park Av -NY 10166
(518) 792-2117 .. **Berube,** Paula Nadeau '92 (Bartlett PS&R,PC) -1 Wshngtn Bx2168 -Glens Fls 12801
(845) 462-0001 .. **Berube,** Richd A '02 (Serino M&B,PLLC) -12 Walker Rd -Poughkeepsie 12603
(212) 819-8200 .. **Berwanger,** Lara A '06 %White & C LLP -1155 Av of Amer -NY 10036
(516) 742-4343 .. **Berweger,** Drew R '09 %Scully SM&P PC -400 Grdn City Plz -Gdn Cty 11530
(212) 705-0137 .. **Berwitt,** Katherine L '09 CARU -70 W 36th -NY 10018
(718) 544-7200 .. **Berwitz,** Barbara J '79 -118-21 Qns Blvd -Frst Hlls 11375 **Fx:**544-7921
(516) 747-3200 .. **Berwitz,** Lawr N '80 (Berwitz & D LLP) -310 Old Cntry Rd -Gdn Cty 11530
(516) 794-2323 .. **Berzak,** Robt A '80 (Lester M&B) -325 Merrick Av -E Meadow 11554
(716) 833-8455 .. **Berzer,** Cheryl A '99 -2140 Eggert Rd -Amherst 14226
(631) 661-3540 .. **Berzins,** Ivars '65 (I Berzins,PC) -484 W Main -Babylon 11702 **Fx:**661-2722
(516) 663-6600 .. **Berzow,** Harold S '72 (Ruskin MF,PC) -1425 RXR Plz -Uniondale 11556
(716) 667-2207 .. **Besanceney,** Robt L '78 -73 Briar Hill Rd -Orchard Pk 14127
(516) 733-1810 .. **Beschel,** Jared W '02 -77 Newbrdg Rd -Hicksvll 11801
(212) 371-1000 .. **Beschta,** Susan M '91 %Catholic Charities -1011 1st Av -NY 10022 **Fx:**319-8265
(212) 854-1384 .. **Besek,** June M '82 %Columbia Law Schl -435 W 116th -NY 10027 **Fx:**854-7946
(212) 848-4000 .. **Besen,** Stephen M '84 (Shearman & S LLP) -599 Lex Av -NY 10022
(516) 745-1800 .. **Besen,** Stuart P '91 (Besen & T,LLP) -825 E Gate Blvd -Gdn Cty 11530
(516) 745-1800 .. **Besen and Trop,LLP** -825 E Gate Blvd -Gdn Cty 11530 **Fx:**745-1801
(212) 705-7000 .. **Beser,** Joshua A '07 %Bingham M LLP -399 Park Av -NY 10022
(518) 402-2032 .. **Besha,** Katie Beaudette '05 Appellate Div 3rd Dept -Bx7350 -Albany 12224
(212) 474-1000 .. **Beshar,** Christine '60 OfCnsl Cravath S&M LLP -825 8th Av -NY 10019
(212) 351-4084 .. **Beshar,** Peter J '90 Marsh USA -1166 Av of Amer -NY 10036 **Fx:**345-4808
(212) 450-4000 .. **Beshar,** Sarah E '86 (Davis P&W LLP) -450 Lex Av -NY 10017
(212) 450-4000 .. **Beshara,** Michel '06 %Davis P&W LLP -450 Lex Av -NY 10017
(646) 942-7993 .. **Beshara,** Renee T '02 Zurich NA -1 Lbrty Plz -NY 10006
(212) 925-0258 .. **Beshay,** Samy A '01 -401 Bway -NY 10013
(315) 732-5121 .. **Besig,** Jennifer M '05 %Helmer JM&K -405 Court -Utica 13502
(212) 407-4000 .. **Besikof,** Danl B '05 %Loeb & L,LLP -345 Park Av -NY 10154
(518) 465-1500 .. **Beskid,** Melissa M '98 (Cannon H&W,LLP) -54 State -Albany 12207
(631) 665-0609 .. **Beskin,** Kenneth S '74 (Sherman FS&L LLP) -8 E Main -Bay Shr 11706
(212) 698-1171 .. **Beslow,** Wm S '73 -620 5th Av -NY 10020 **Fx:**698-1182
(718) 434-8300 .. **Bespechny,** Alena E '96 %A Bespechny -1122 Coney Isl Av -Brklyn 11230 **Fx:**434-6112
(718) 434-8300 .. **Bespechny,** Alexander '96 -1122 Coney Isl Av -Brklyn 11230 **Fx:**434-6112
(718) 792-4800 .. **Bespechny,** Alexander '96 -2931 Wstchstr Av -Bronx 10461
(212) 331-5065 .. **Bess,** Linda S '73 %HRA -180 Water -NY 10038
(917) 454-1100 .. **Besse,** Matthew J '02 %Police Dept -2 Lafayette -NY 10007
(212) 538-8325 .. **Bessel,** Michl J '97 Credit Suisse -11 Mad Av -NY 10010
(518) 481-5000 .. **Bessette,** James P '77 (Fischer B&M) -Cntry Clb Rd Bx420 -Malone 12953
(315) 769-3898 .. **Bessette,** Shannon A '98 %Pease & G -40 Main -Massena 13662 **Fx:**769-5018
(631) 549-1938 .. **Bessich,** John A '81 (Follick & B,PC) -33 Walt Whitman Rd -Huntngtn Sta 11746
(718) 590-8584 .. **Bessim,** Indji '90 %Admin Children's Srvcs -900 Sheridan Av -Bronx 10451
(212) 813-5900 .. **Bessinger,** Tamar Niv '98 Cnsl Fross ZL&Z,PC -866 UN Plz -NY 10017
(631) 666-5766 .. **Besso,** David H '73 (Long TBSWJ&S) -120 4th Av Bx5591 -Bay Shr 11706
(631) 447-6121 .. **Besso,** Eric B '85 E Besso,LLC -25 Candee Av -Sayvll 11782
(212) 715-9100 .. **Bessonette,** John C '99 (Kramer LN&F,LLP) -1177 Av of Amer -NY 10036
(718) 213-8020 .. **Best,** C Wm '94 -1053 Lincoln Pl -Brklyn 11213 **Fx:**953-5875
(315) 393-3130 .. **Best,** Jeremy J '99 %MHLS -804 Commerce Park Dr -Ogdensbrg 13669 **Fx:**393-9633
(585) 637-2550 .. **Best,** Joanne L '93 -86 Main -Brockprt 14420 **Fx:**637-8840

(212) 701-3000 .. **Best,** Landis Cox '97 (Cahill G&R LLP) -80 Pine -NY 10005 **Fx:**269-5420
(212) 374-0220 .. **Best,** Michl '92 NYC Dept Educ-OLS -52 Chmbrs -NY 10007 **Fx:**374-5596
(212) 549-2500 .. **Best,** Norman F E '03 ACLU -125 Broad -NY 10004 **Fx:**549-2651
(212) 353-2407 .. **Best,** Paula Whitney '89 -435 E 9th -NY 10009
(212) 656-3000 .. **Best,** Richd R '94 NYSE,Inc -14 Wall -NY 10005
(315) 789-2345 .. **Best,** Willard C '64 -379 S Main -Geneva 14456 **Fx:**789-2392
(914) 872-8400 .. **Besteiro,** Donna Renzetti '92 %The Dannon Co -100 Hillside Av -White Plns 10603
(716) 881-3010 .. **Bestine,** Katherine J '90 (Cohen & L,PC) -343 Elmwood Av Bx5204 -Buffalo 14213
(716) 688-1600 .. **Bestry,** Sherwood L '49 -10 JJ Audobon Pkwy -Amherst 14228 **Fx:**688-1678
(631) 234-9240 .. **Besunder,** Harvey B '67 -1 Suffolk Sq -Islandia 11749 **Fx:**234-9278
(718) 250-2000 .. **Besunder,** Jon L '75 %DA -350 Jay -Brklyn 11201 **Fx:**250-2314
(212) 210-9402 .. **Betancourt,** Brian A '96 (Alston & B LLP) -90 Park Av -NY 10016
(718) 336-8076 .. **Betancourt,** Melissa '96 -155 Kings Hwy -Brklyn 11223
(212) 297-0050 .. **Betancourt,** Ronald '91 (Betancourt VHG&K LLC) -46 Trinity Pl -NY 10006
(212) 297-0050 .. **Betancourt Van Hemmen Greco & Kenyon LLC** -46 Trinity Pl -NY 10006 **Fx:**(732) 530-9536
(212) 909-6000 .. **Betancourt,** Viviana M '09 %Debevoise & P LLP -919 3rd Av -NY 10022
(914) 333-0700 .. **Betensky,** Keith R '03 %Snyder & S -94 Wht Plns Rd -Tarrytwn 10591 **Fx:**333-0743
(212) 906-1200 .. **Betensky,** Steven M '90 (Latham & W) -885 3rd Av -NY 10022
(516) 683-6200 .. **Betesh,** Shimon I '99 (Betesh & Assoc PLLC) -585 Stewart Av -Gdn Cty 11530
(212) 408-5100 .. **Betheil,** Blake G '09 %Chadbourne & P LLP -30 Rckfllr Plz -NY 10112
(212) 421-4100 .. **Betheil,** Richd M '81 (Pryor C LLP) -7 Times Sq -NY 10036
(212) 417-5387 .. **Bethel,** Cassandra M '92 %Medicaid Fraud Cntrl -120 Bway -NY 10271 **Fx:**417-5274
(212) 451-2300 .. **Bethel,** Jayme M '10 %Olshan GFR&W LLP -65 E 55th -NY 10022
(212) 317-1717 .. **Bethel,** Jeremy J '03 %Chemtob MF&T LLP -3 E 54th -NY 10022
(212) 768-6700 .. **Bethill,** Chas D '75 (Sonnenschein N&R LLP) -2 World Fncl Ctr -NY 10281
(212) 661-7300 .. **Bethmann,** Mark A '90 %Malapero & P LLP -295 Mad Av -NY 10017
(518) 449-8893 .. **Betke,** Alexander L II '03 %Wilson EME&D LLP -677 Bway -Albany 12207
(212) 593-1400 .. **Betlesky,** Richd '63 (Fisher F PC) -30 Vesey -NY 10007
(212) 326-3939 .. **Betman,** Amanda M '05 %Jones D -222 E 41st -NY 10017
(631) 821-1500 .. **Betro,** Dean '00 -131 Route 25A -Rocky Pnt 11778 **Fx:**744-7179
(315) 363-3602 .. **Betro,** James W '89 (Vindigni & B,PLLC) -146 Madison -Oneida 13421
(516) 739-0400 .. **Betron,** Eric B '03 %Kelly R&K,LLP -330 Old Cntry Rd -Mineola 11501
(212) 446-2300 .. **Bettan,** Richd J '06 %Boies S&F LLP -575 Lex Av -NY 10022
(516) 560-6400 .. **Bettenhauser,** Meredith A '06 %Leg Aid -1 Helen Keller Way -Hempstd 11550 **Fx:**565-3694
(518) 486-9564 .. **Better,** Craig S '04 %Workers Comp Bd -20 Park -Albany 12207
(518) 465-3351 .. **Better,** J Michl '78 -393 Wshngtn Av -Albany 12206 **Fx:**449-5631
(518) 758-1511 .. **Better,** Wm J '82 -1 Albany Av Bx406 -Kinderhook 12106 **Fx:**758-1227
(212) 446-4800 .. **Betterly,** Patricia E '06 (Kirkland & E LLP) -153 E 53rd -NY 10022
(212) 850-2665 .. **Bettex,** Donald A '55 -700 Park Av -NY 10021
(212) 884-7555 .. **Bettex,** John N '01 %GMAC Commercial Credit -1290 Av of Amer -NY 10104
(631) 543-4184 .. **Betti,** Walter V '65 -2 Deepdale Dr -Commack 11725
(315) 218-8000 .. **Bettinger,** Blaine T '10 %Bond S&K,PLLC -1 Lincoln Ctr -Syracuse 13202
(212) 878-7900 .. **Bettinger,** Matthew I '09 %Fox R LLP -100 Park Av -NY 10017
(212) 854-8364 .. **Bettinger-Lopez,** Caroline S '04 %Columbia Law Schl -435 W 116th -NY 10027 **Fx:**854-3554
(212) 222-3882 .. **Bettinger-Lopez,** Sean C '04 African Srvcs Comm,Inc -429 W 127th -NY 10027
(212) 966-9091 .. **Bettison,** Leslie N '06 Sol de Ibiza -52 Greene -NY 10013
(212) 789-2000 .. **Bettman,** Gary B '78 %NHL -1185 Av of Amer -NY 10036 **Fx:**789-2020
(914) 328-7020 .. **Bettman,** Steven J '85 -280 Dobbs Ferry Rd -White Plns 10607
(516) 228-9181 .. **Betts,** Charlotte Marian '94 (Gassman BB&T,PC) -666 Old Cntry Rd -Gdn Cty 11530
(212) 574-1200 .. **Betts,** Derick W Jr. '71 (Seward & K LLP) -1 Bttry Pk Plz -NY 10004
(631) 727-4100 .. **Betts,** Gair G '76 (Smith FLI&Y) -456 Griffing Av Bx389 -Rvrhead 11901
(212) 735-3000 .. **Bettwy,** Andrew J '98 Cnsl Skadden ASM&F LLP -4 Times Sq -NY 10036
(212) 577-3001 .. **Betz,** Heather L '02 HIV Law Project -15 Maiden Ln -NY 10038
(212) 267-3700 .. **Betz,** Justin S '08 Napoli BR LLP -350 5th Av -NY 10118
(516) 877-2900 .. **Betz,** Robt J '84 (Bartlett MB&M,LLP) -300 Old Cntry Rd -Mineola 11501
(212) 822-7247 .. **Betz,** T Paige '98 NY Academy of Medicine -1216 5th Av -NY 10029
(516) 641-9906 .. **Betz,** Wm E '84 -50-A Sagamore Hill Dr -Pt Wash 11050
(212) 574-1200 .. **Betzing,** Christine I '09 %Seward & K LLP -1 Bttry Pk Plz -NY 10004
(607) 776-4200 .. **BetzJitomir,** Susan M '01 -8 Buell -Bath 14810 **Fx:**776-4212
(212) 819-8200 .. **Beuchaw,** Meredith J '07 %White & C LLP -1155 Av of Amer -NY 10036
(212) 801-6986 .. **Beury,** Katherine J '10 %Greenberg T,LLP -200 Park Av -NY 10166
(845) 565-3074 .. **Beutel,** Julie Restivo '98 Newburgh City Ct -57 Bway -Newburgh 12550
(607) 721-8440 .. **Bevacqua,** A Laura '94 %MHLS -44 Hawley -Bnghmtn 13901 **Fx:**721-8447
(212) 538-0677 .. **Bevacqua,** Allison M '97 Credit Suisse -1 Mad Av -NY 10010 **Fx:**538-4596
(212) 579-1172 .. **Bevan Mosca Giudutta & Zarillo, PC** -200 Mad Av -NY 10016
(212) 699-4597 .. **Bevans,** Jane '82 -1 Penn Plz -NY 10119 **Fx:**942-9967
(212) 848-4000 .. **Beveridge,** David J '87 (Shearman & S LLP) -599 Lex Av -NY 10022
(212) 702-5400 .. **Beveridge & Diamond,PC** -477 Mad Av -NY 10022 **Fx:**702-5450
(212) 407-4000 .. **Beveridge,** Norwood P III '92 (Loeb & L,LLP) -345 Park Av -NY 10154
(212) 530-5000 .. **Beverley,** Constance E '08 %Milbank TH&M LLP -1 Chase Manh Plz -NY 10005
(914) 997-4530 .. **Beverly,** Wanda E '91 March of Dimes Fndtn -1275 Mamaroneck Av -White Plns 10605
(212) 903-9000 .. **Beverly-Graham,** Kiah D '09 %Linklaters -1345 Av of Amer -NY 10105
(845) 341-0008 .. **Beverson,** Cheryl Ann '05 -12 Evergreen Dr -Middletwn 10940 **Fx:**341-0068
(212) 670-0110 .. **Bevilacqua,** John P '88 Merrill Lynch -222 Bway -NY 10038
(716) 691-7444 .. **Bevilacqua,** Jonathan '07 Bevilacqua Development LP -9332 Transit Rd -E Amherst 14051 **Fx:**691-7557
(212) 506-1700 .. **Bevilacqua,** Kathryn S '05 %Kasowitz BT&F LLP -1633 Bway -NY 10019
(212) 504-6000 .. **Bevilacqua,** Louis J '78 (Cadwalader W&T LLP) -1 World Fncl Ctr -NY 10281
(718) 457-8044 .. **Bevilacqua,** Silvia A '95 -37-21 75th -Jcksn Hts 11372 **Fx:**457-2408
(631) 608-4100 .. **Bevolas,** Leo G '95 %K Mollins,PC -425 Broadhllw Rd -Melvll 11747 **Fx:**608-4107
(518) 474-7330 .. **Bewlay,** Shoshanah V '97 %Dept of Law -The Cptl -Albany 12224
(212) 449-1000 .. **Bey,** Wm F Jr. '06 %Merrill Lynch -250 Vesey -NY 10080
(212) 225-7700 .. **Beyda,** David R '89 %Cartafalsa ST&L -165 Bway -NY 10006
(347) 643-9960 .. **Beyda,** Jeremy '05 Copper Grp -752 Pacific -Brklyn 11238
(212) 317-1717 .. **Beyda,** Michl F '01 (Chemtob MF&T LLP) -3 E 54th -NY 10022
(718) 725-3060 .. **Beyda,** Tamara '01 %Admin Children's Srvcs -151-20 Jamaica Av -Jamaica 11432
(212) 483-9490 .. **Beyel,** John P '88 (McElroy DM&C,LLP) -88 Pine -NY 10005
(716) 852-1300 .. **Beyer,** David W '72 OfCnsl Amigone S&M,LLP -350 Main -Buffalo 14202
(914) 715-8111 .. **Beyer,** Elyse R '84 -22 Crestvw Dr -Plsntvll 10570 **Fx:**747-8130
(518) 439-1989 .. **Beyer,** Harold G Jr. '70 -4 North -Delmar 12054
(518) 474-6400 .. **Beyer,** Howard S '02 %Dept of Ed -89 Wshngtn Av -Albany 12234 **Fx:**473-2925
(212) 248-3140 .. **Beyer,** Jeffrey M '02 %Drinker B&R LLP -140 Bway -NY 10005
(212) 803-3100 .. **Beyer,** Jonathan '80 %Empire State Dvlmnt Corp -633 3rd Av -NY 10017
(212) 489-1600 .. **Beyer,** Linda M '90 %Deloitte LLP -1633 Bway -NY 10019 **Fx:**492-4201
(516) 294-4014 .. **Beyer,** Martin A '86 (Waldron W&B) -49 Robin Rd -Westbury 11590
(914) 993-5500 .. **Beyer,** Phillip M '07 HRH Construction,LLC -50 Main -White Plns 10606 **Fx:**993-5700
(631) 427-0100 .. **Beyer,** Stephen W '93 OfCnsl Pezold SH&S,LLC -120 Main -Huntngtn 11743
(212) 279-9090 .. **Beyer,** Vicki Woody '93 (Stark & S) -One Penn Plz -NY 10119 **Fx:**279-9113
(585) 786-3148 .. **Beyer,** Wm C '82 %Surrogates Ct -147 N Main -Warsaw 14569
(212) 816-4290 .. **Beyers,** A Julie '92 Citibank -388 Greenwich -NY 10013
(585) 258-2800 .. **Beyma,** Michl J '70 (Underberg & K LLP) -300 Bausch & Lomb Pl -Rchstr 14604
(212) 935-5500 .. **Beyman,** Richd '86 (Franklin WR&V) -488 Mad Av -NY 10022
(516) 365-9191 .. **Beyrer,** Inez-Mary '91 %S Friedman -1 Hllw Ln -New Hyde Pk 11042 **Fx:**365-6138
(516) 248-1200 .. **Beyrer,** John A '95 %Mulholland M&R -374 Hillside Av -Williston Pk 11596
(631) 420-7795 .. **Bezack,** Ira '73 -510 Broadhllw Rd -Melvll 11747 **Fx:**622-2322
(212) 508-6100 .. **Bezanson,** Philip J '05 %Bracewell & G,LLP -1251 Av of Amer -NY 10020
(212) 957-7600 .. **Bezanson,** Thos E '75 Cnsl Cohen & G LLP -800 3rd Av -NY 10022
(212) 848-4000 .. **Bezbatchenko,** Timothy M '09 %Shearman & S LLP -599 Lex Av -NY 10022
(585) 753-4500 .. **Bezer,** Michl J '07 %DA -832 Watts Bldg -Rchstr 14614 **Fx:**753-4576
(315) 422-1311 .. **Bezigian,** Thos Jr. '08 %Melvin & M,PLLC -217 S Salina -Syracuse 13202
(518) 427-9700 .. **Bezio,** Kevin T '04 %Harris B PLLC -677 Bway -Albany 12207
(212) 529-1919 .. **Bezozi,** Alan M '85 -31 E 12th -NY 10003
(212) 659-7300 .. **Bezozo,** Kenneth K '81 (Haynes & B,LLP) -1221 Av of Amer -NY 10020
(212) 558-4000 .. **Bezrukova,** Marina A '02 %Sullivan & C LLP -125 Broad -NY 10004
(718) 526-6700 .. **Bhairam,** Roy Persaud '87 -146-04 Hillside Av -Jamaica 11435 **Fx:**526-6189
(212) 412-9500 .. **Bhalla,** Archena '06 %Flemming ZWZ LLP -1 Lbrty Plz -NY 10006
(212) 969-2310 .. **Bhalla,** Mona '96 Alliance Bernstein LP -1345 Av of Amer -NY 10105 **Fx:**554-4639
(212) 878-8000 .. **Bhandari,** Amita Kumari '07 Clifford C LLP -31 W 52nd -NY 10019
(212) 250-2825 .. **Bhandari,** Prabha S '97 Deutsche Bk AG -60 Wall -NY 10005
(212) 269-5600 .. **Bhandari,** Rishi '05 (Mandel B LLP) -11 Bway -NY 10004 **Fx:**(646) 964-6667
(845) 562-9100 .. **Bhandarkar,** Sarita '03 %Rider W&F,PC -655 Little Britain Rd -New Windsor 12553
(212) 637-2200 .. **Bharara,** Preetinder '94 US Atty -1 St Andrews Plz -NY 10007
(212) 376-0542 .. **Bharara,** Vinit '97 Topps Co Inc -1 Whitehall -NY 10004
(212) 805-5352 .. **Bharatiya,** Jay '03 L-3 Communications Corp -600 3rd Av -NY 10016
(716) 842-6558 .. **Bhargava,** Ambar '99 -22 Evans -Williamsvll 14221
(212) 264-5916 .. **Bhargava,** Anne Yun '01 %DHS -26 Fed Plz -NY 10278
(212) 374-2990 .. **Bhargava,** Anurima '03 NYC Dept of Ed -52 Chmbrs -NY 10007
(646) 315-7309 .. **Bhargava,** Radhika '00 %FINRA -14 Wall -NY 10005 **Fx:**315-7440
(212) 848-4000 .. **Bhashyam,** Shriram '10 Shearman & S LLP -599 Lex Av -NY 10022
(212) 698-3500 .. **Bhasin,** Amarpreet S '09 %Dechert LLP -1095 Av of Amer -NY 10036
(212) 770-0785 .. **Bhasin,** Rajika '03 AIG -80 Pine -NY 10005
(718) 250-2000 .. **Bhasin,** Richa '10 %DA -350 Jay -Brklyn 11201 **Fx:**250-2314
(212) 909-6000 .. **Bhaskaran,** Rushmi '10 %Debevoise & P LLP -919 3rd Av -NY 10022
(212) 617-6319 .. **Bhaskaran,** Yamuna '03 Bloomberg LP -731 Lex Av -NY 10022
(212) 530-5000 .. **Bhatia,** Karen Hakime '07 %Milbank TH&M LLP -1 Chase Manh Plz -NY 10005

(212) 295-6419 ..**Bhatia,** Minni '04 WilmerHale -399 Park Av -NY 10022
(212) 479-1581 ..**Bhatia,** Neil S '04 Fortress Invstmnt Grp,LLC -1345 Av of Amer -NY 10105
(212) 594-7980 ..**Bhatia,** Satish Kumar '98 -38 W 32nd -NY 10001
(212) 335-9000 ..**Bhatia,** Vimi '01 %DA -1 Hogan Pl -NY 10013
(212) 519-7840 ..**Bhatnagar,** Chandra S '03 ACLU -125 Broad -NY 10004
(718) 590-2000 ..**Bhatnagar,** Pooja '08 %DA -198 E 161st -Bronx 10451 **Fx:**590-6477
(631) 654-7118 ..**Bhatnagar,** Rashmi C '04 Brookhaven Memorial -101 Hsptl Rd -Patchogue 11772
(212) 728-8000 ..**Bhatt,** Aparnaa '10 %Willkie F&G LLP -787 7th Av -NY 10019
(718) 694-3908 ..**Bhatt,** Kavita K '05 %Transit Auth -130 Lvngstn -Brklyn 11201 **Fx:**694-5726
(845) 331-6615 ..**Bhatt,** Milan A '07 %Workers Rts Law Ctr -101 Hurley Av -Kingston 12401
(716) 507-9995 ..**Bhatt,** Monika '10 -2470 Sheridan Dr -Tonawanda 14150
(315) 386-4583 ..**Bhatt,** Neil Tarak '05 (Lekki HF&D,PC) -21 Court Bx469 -Canton 13617
(212) 964-9282 ..**Bhatt,** Samir '07 %N Weinrib & Assoc -305 Bway -NY 10007 **Fx:**964-9525
(212) 382-3300 ..**Bhattacharji,** Sandip '91 (Wollmuth M&D LLP) -500 5th Av -NY 10110
(212) 506-1700 ..**Bhattacharyya,** Monica V '99 (Kasowitz BT&F LLP) -1633 Bway -NY 10019
(212) 806-5400 ..**Bhattacharyya,** Sayan '07 %Stroock &S&L LLP -180 Maiden Ln -NY 10038
(212) 450-4000 ..**Bhattacharyya,** Somnath '09 %Davis P&W LLP -450 Lex Av -NY 10017
(917) 592-2983 ..**Bhatti,** Thakur Alyas Raj '70 Cnsl Shaws Regstrtn Law -Bx509 -NY 10008 **Fx:**(212) 348-8040
(516) 747-1990 ..**Bhavnani,** Ajay C '06 %Cascone & K,LLP -1399 Franklin Av -Gdn Cty 11530
(914) 251-0001 ..**Bhimani,** Riyaz Gulam '01 OfCnsl Lane S&L LLP -106 Corp Park Dr -White Plns 10604
(212) 210-7124 ..**Bhonslay,** Stephanie T '90 J Walter Thompson -466 Lex Av -NY 10017
(212) 790-4500 ..**Bhoumik,** Arunabha '05 %Manatt P&P,LLP -7 Times Sq -NY 10036
(212) 695-1515 ..**Bhouraskar,** Megha D '87 (Poppe & B,LLP) -350 5th Av -NY 10118
(516) 797-9797 ..**Bhukta,** Arnab '09 A Donofrio,PLLC -5518 Merrick Rd -Massapequa 11758 **Fx:**977-6700
(212) 687-1736 ..**Bhurtel,** Durga P '04 %R Schwartzberg & Assoc,PLLC -60 E 42nd -NY 10165
(718) 891-9802 ..**Bhushan,** Raj '93 -2793 Brighton 8th -Brklyn 11235 **Fx:**891-4746
(212) 233-8000 ..**Biaggi,** Mario Jr. '84 -220 5th Av -NY 10001 **Fx:**679-1099
(212) 233-8000 ..**Biaggi,** Richd M '82 -220 5th Av -NY 10001 **Fx:**679-1099
(845) 294-9447 ..**Biagi,** James B '91 (Dickover DD&B LLP) -28 Bruen Pl Bx610 -Goshen 10924
(212) 553-8300 ..**Biagi,** Robt E '98 %Cohen K & Assoc -2 Park Av -NY 10016 **Fx:**553-8721
(212) 867-9500 ..**Bial,** Ernest L '65 OfCnsl Kurzman K&F,LLP -230 Park Av -NY 10169
(212) 504-6000 ..**Bial,** Jos J '03 SpclCnsl Cadwalader W&T LLP -1 World Fncl Ctr -NY 10281
(212) 382-3300 ..**Bialek,** Adam M '03 %Wollmuth M&D LLP -500 5th Av -NY 10110
(212) 490-3000 ..**Bialek,** Adam R '92 (Wilson EME&D LLP) -150 E 42nd -NY 10017
(914) 323-7000 ..**Bialek,** Adam R '92 (Wilson EME&D LLP) -3 Gannett Dr -White Plns 10604
(845) 639-6031 ..**Bialek,** Jay '67 (Bialek & B,LLP) -337 N Main -New Cty 10956 **Fx:**639-6034
(845) 639-6031 ..**Bialek,** Keith A '02 (Bialek & B,LLP) -337 N Main -New Cty 10956 **Fx:**639-6034
(212) 213-5500 ..**Bialik,** Ezra I '70 Cnsl Periconi,LLC -708 3rd Av -NY 10017 **Fx:**213-5030
(212) 735-3000 ..**Bialkin,** Kenneth J '53 (Skadden ASM&F LLP) -4 Times Sq -NY 10036
(212) 421-4722 ..**Bialkin,** Lisa B '92 -37 W 57th -NY 10019
(212) 859-3460 ..**Bialkowski,** Stephen W '88 (McLellan & B) -110 Wall -NY 10005
(212) 238-3000 ..**Bialo,** Kenneth M '72 (Emmet M&M,LLP) -120 Bway -NY 10271
(212) 889-0707 ..**Bialostok,** Lee '87 %Platte KL&L,LLP -10 E 40th -NY 10016
(718) 250-2000 ..**Bialo Y Padin,** Deirdre A '86 %DA -350 Jay -Brklyn 11201 **Fx:**250-2314
(716) 856-0600 ..**Bialy,** Marjorie A '91 %Jaeckle F&M,LLP -12 Fountain Plz -Buffalo 14202
(212) 596-9000 ..**Biamonte,** Marc N '07 %Ropes & G LLP -1211 Av of Amer -NY 10036
(212) 225-2000 ..**Bianca,** Salvatore F '05 %Cleary GS&H -1 Lbrty Plz -NY 10006
(516) 741-7015 ..**Biancanello,** Dennis P '01 DP Biancanello,PC -500 Jericho Tpk -Mineola 11501 **Fx:**741-4438
(516) 741-7015 ..**Biancanello,** Michl P '02 -500 Jericho Tpk Bx607 -Mineola 11501 **Fx:**741-4438
(718) 261-2323 ..**Biancaniello,** Christine M '07 %J Gemelli,PC -105-15 Metro Av -Frst Hlls 11375 **Fx:**520-1669
(631) 852-2500 ..**Biancavilla,** Robt P '86 %DA -200 Center Dr -Rvrhead 11901 **Fx:**852-1769
(518) 474-6400 ..**Bianchi,** Alison B '08 Dept of Ed -89 Wshngtn Av -Albany 12234 **Fx:**473-2925
(212) 553-8300 ..**Bianchi,** Angelantonio '88 %Cohen K & Assoc -2 Park Av -NY 10016 **Fx:**553-8721
(914) 286-3400 ..**Bianchi,** Anne B '85 %Leg Aid -1 N Bway -White Plns 10601 **Fx:**682-4112
(516) 408-7908 ..**Bianchi,** Anthony G '92 Bianchi, PC -25 Carle Rd -Westbury 11590 **Fx:**203-4235
(212) 889-2121 ..**Bianchi,** Bruno P '88 %Kellner HG&F -470 Park Av S -NY 10016
(212) 355-3233 ..**Bianchi,** Carlos J '85 -150 E 58th -NY 10155
(518) 457-4181 ..**Bianchi,** Gina L '92 %DCJS -4 Twr Pl -Albany 12203 **Fx:**457-3089
(914) 631-0440 ..**Bianchi,** John F '62 -65 S Bway -Tarrytwn 10591 **Fx:**332-5725
(631) 680-0685 ..**Bianchi,** Kerri E '92 -998 Old Cntry Rd -Plainvw 11803
(914) 684-9330 ..**Bianchi,** Ronald B '64 -5 Tam O'Shanter Dr -Purchase 10577 **Fx:**684-9667
(516) 932-5700 ..**Bianco,** Alan Richd '86 -998 Old Cntry Rd -Plainvw 11803
(516) 746-5599 ..**Bianco,** Angelo M '05 %Bee RFH&D,LLP -170 Old Cntry Rd -Mineola 11501
(212) 907-0700 ..**Bianco,** Benjamin D '03 %Labaton S LLP -140 Bway -NY 10005
(631) 462-4911 ..**Bianco Byrnes & Finkel, LLP** -5036 Jericho Tpk Bx49 -Commack 11725 **Fx:**462-4922
(516) 248-2002 ..**Bianco,** Dominic R '78 (Gallagher WB&P) -98 Willis Av -Mineola 11501
(914) 737-7735 ..**Bianco,** Fred J Jr. '63 -1200 Brown -Peekskill 10566 **Fx:**737-5130
(516) 255-1800 ..**Bianco,** John Jr. '91 (Rosenblum & B LLP) -100 Merrick Rd -Rockvll Ctr 11570
(212) 773-3807 ..**Bianco,** Jos G '96 Ernst & Young LLP -5 Times Sq -NY 10036
(646) 855-2776 ..**Bianco,** Michele J '06 %Banc of Amer Securities -1 Bryant Pk -NY 10036
(914) 941-2450 ..**Bianco,** Phyllis A '98 %Victoria Home -25 N Malcolm -Ossining 10562 **Fx:**941-2962
(315) 424-0744 ..**Bianco,** Randi Juda '89 -247 W Fayette -Syracuse 13202
(212) 566-8120 ..**Bianco,** Rossana '07 Day One -Bx1507 -NY 10013
(212) 697-1900 ..**Bianco,** S Anthony '75 %Booz Allen Hamilton -101 Park Av -NY 10178
(516) 747-0300 ..**Bianco,** Thos J '86 (Meltzer LG&B,LLP) -190 Willis Av -Mineola 11501
(516) 742-7747 ..**Bianco,** Vincent '00 (Ginsberg & B) -114 Old Cntry Rd -Mineola 11501 **Fx:**742-7748
(212) 754-8135 ..**Bianco,** Wm A '02 Sandler Capital Mgmt -711 5th Av -NY 10022
(718) 366-2600 ..**Bianco,** Wm F '62 (Bianco & B) -66-24 Fresh Pond Rd -Rdgwd 11385
(718) 366-2600 ..**Bianco,** Wm T '88 (Bianco & B) -66-24 Fresh Pond Rd -Rdgwd 11385
(212) 661-1888 ..**Biancone,** Louis '78 (Biancone & W,LLP) -230 Park Av -NY 10169
(212) 661-1888 ..**Biancone & Wilinsky,LLP** -230 Park Av -NY 10169 **Fx:**661-4774
(212) 277-6500 ..**BianRosa,** Jennifer L '04 %Dickstein S LLP -1633 Bway -NY 10019
(212) 374-6888 ..**Bibbs,** Malika R '01 %NYC Dept Educ-OLS -52 Chmbrs -NY 10007 **Fx:**374-5596
(212) 788-5033 ..**Bibelnieks,** Dzintra B '78 %Dept Hlth -125 Worth CN-30 -NY 10013 **Fx:**788-4300
(212) 416-8000 ..**Biben,** Ellen Nachtigal '93 %Dept of Law -120 Bway -NY 10271
(212) 685-7081 ..**Biben,** Matthew L '93 Next Jump Inc -261 5th Av -NY 10016
(212) 541-6050 ..**Biberaj,** Ken C '09 RTR Funding Grp Inc -234 W 56th -NY 10019
(212) 416-6699 ..**Biberman,** Dana H '90 %Dept of Law -120 Bway -NY 10271
(718) 232-3625 ..**Bibicheff,** Alexander V '00 (Bibicheff & Assoc) -2568 86th -Brklyn 11214 **Fx:**232-4943
(212) 635-1487 ..**Bibko,** Kenneth C '01 BNY Capital Mrkts -1 Wall -NY 10260
(212) 442-1503 ..**Bibla,** Philip J '78 %DCAS Ofc Discip Advocate -1 Centre -NY 10007
(631) 752-4040 ..**Biblo,** Larry A '91 (Weiner & B,LLP) -555 Broadhllw Rd -Melvll 11747 **Fx:**752-4049
(516) 227-0700 ..**Biblow,** Charlotte A '82 (Farrell F,PC) -1320 RXR Plz -Uniondale 11556
(212) 859-8000 ..**Bibona,** John M '92 (Fried FHS&J LLP) -1 NY Plz -NY 10004
(212) 986-2233 ..**Bibro,** Mark R '99 %Early & S LLC -360 Lex Av Bx3601 -NY 10163
(718) 243-2700 ..**Bibuld,** Paul '89 %Talisman & D,PC -409 Fulton -Brklyn 11201
(607) 778-2685 ..**Bice,** Mark A '80 Dept Soc Srvcs -36-42 Main -Bnghmtn 13905 **Fx:**778-2710
(212) 804-2187 ..**Bice,** Michl R Jr. '95 Bank of NY -32 Old Slip -NY 10286
(212) 530-5000 ..**Bice,** Wm B '96 (Milbank TH&M LLP) -1 Chase Manh Plz -NY 10005
(212) 643-9932 ..**BichouPan,** Abraham '89 -140 W 57th -NY 10019
(516) 482-1186 ..**Bichoupan,** Carolyn Corn '92 %R Bichoupan,PC -175 E Shore Rd -Gt Neck 11023
(516) 482-1186 ..**Bichoupan,** Robt '92 (R Bichoupan,PC) -175 E Shore Rd -Gt Neck 11023
(212) 450-4000 ..**Bick,** John A '84 (Davis P&W LLP) -450 Lex Av -NY 10017
(973) 228-5700 ..**Bick,** Jonathan D '85 Cnsl Brach E LLC -100 Park Av -NY 10017 **Fx:**228-7852
(212) 415-9200 ..**Bickal,** Ellen Jane '81 (Dorsey & W LLP) -250 Park Av -NY 10177
(212) 489-1400 ..**Bickel & Brewer** -767 5th Av -NY 10153 **Fx:**489-2384
(212) 489-1400 ..**Bickel,** John W II '89 (Bickel & B) -767 5th Av -NY 10153
(518) 561-7035 ..**Bickel,** Oliver L '92 -92 Montcalm -Plattsbrgh 12901
(212) 298-5238 ..**Bickel,** Robt J '07 %Leg Aid -49 Thomas -NY 10013 **Fx:**298-5252
(212) 889-7384 ..**Bickford,** Peter H '64 -50 Park Av -NY 10016
(212) 808-7800 ..**Bickford,** Robt D Jr. '75 (Kelley D&W LLP) -101 Park Av -NY 10178
(516) 829-0600 ..**Bickler,** Sharon G '87 -3 Baker Hill Rd -Gt Neck 11023
(212) 336-0086 ..**Bickley,** Lee S '99 %SEC -3 World Fncl Ctr -NY 10281 **Fx:**336-1323
(212) 687-3000 ..**Bicknese,** Fredk H '04 %Jaffe & A,LLP -600 3rd Av -NY 10016
(212) 227-4000 ..**Bickoff,** Eliot S '08 Mirman M&L,PC -291 Bway -NY 10007
(212) 259-8000 ..**Bicks,** David P '59 OfCnsl Dewey & L LLP -1301 Av of Amer -NY 10019
(212) 768-6700 ..**Bicks,** John A '86 (Sonnenschein N&R LLP) -1221 Av of Amer -NY 10020
(212) 506-5000 ..**Bicks,** Peter A '87 (Orrick H&S LLP) -51 W 52nd -NY 10019
(212) 363-1380 ..**Bicocchi,** LisaAnne Rega '92 %Herten BSCBL&H,LLC -747 3rd Av -NY 10017
(212) 337-4263 ..**Bicovny,** Wendy C '97 RIA -195 Bway -NY 10007
(212) 596-9000 ..**Biddinger,** Brian P '07 %Ropes & G LLP -1211 Av of Amer -NY 10036
(646) 442-3302 ..**Biddle,** Ann Pegg '93 Legal Srvcs NYC -350 Bway -NY 10013 **Fx:**(212) 966-9571
(212) 484-3900 ..**Biderman,** Eric A '06 %Arent F LLP -1675 Bway -NY 10019
(212) 318-6000 ..**Biderman,** Stephanie Alperin '09 %Paul HJ&W LLP -75 E 55th -NY 10022
(212) 922-0050 ..**Bidner,** Michl P '86 %Stewart Title Ins -300 E 42nd -NY 10017 **Fx:**983-1133
(212) 325-2000 ..**Bidwell,** Anna L '02 Credit Suisse -1 Mad Av -NY 10010
(212) 660-3000 ..**Bidwell,** J Truman Jr. '59 (Sullivan & W LLP) -1290 Av of Amer -NY 10104
(315) 423-3232 ..**Bidwell,** Mark E '90 -300 Demong Dr -Syracuse 13214
(212) 361-1731 ..**Biebel,** Ann M '84 Envrnmntl Cntrl Brd -66 John -NY 10038 **Fx:**361-1900
(212) 922-1330 ..**Bieber,** Bruce W '92 (Zimmet B LLP) -437 Mad Av -NY 10022
(518) 473-6882 ..**Bieber,** Eric D '81 %Dept of Law -The Cptl -Albany 12224
(914) 949-1305 ..**Bieber,** Gary W '80 %Leg Srvcs -90 Maple Av -White Plns 10601 **Fx:**949-6213

(914) 640-1609 .. **Bieber**, Jacquelyn R '02 Jones Apparel Grp -1129 Wstchstr Av -White Plns 10604
(718) 746-5900 .. **Bieber**, Susan J '91 GNYADA -1810 Whitestone Expy -Whitestone 11357
(212) 848-4000 .. **Bieber**, Tammy P '96 (Shearman & S LLP) -599 Lex Av -NY 10022
(718) 590-2000 .. **Bieder**, John W '07 %DA -198 E 161st -Bronx 10451 **Fx:**590-6477
(917) 912-6073 .. **Bieder**, Stacy L '06 -391 Arbuckle Av -Cedarhrst 11516
(212) 605-0477 .. **Biederman**, Susan Duke '79 -575 Mad Av -NY 10022 **Fx:**308-9834
(212) 697-6555 .. **Biedermann**, Kurt E '74 (Biedermann RH&R) -570 Lex Av -NY 10022
(212) 697-6555 .. **Biedermann Reif Hoenig & Ruff** -570 Lex Av -NY 10022 **Fx:**986-3509
(212) 422-0202 .. **Biedermann**, Theresa M '08 %Sedgwick DM&A LLP -125 Broad -NY 10004
(646) 471-3588 .. **Biegeleisen**, Alan J '84 PricewaterhouseCoopers LLP -300 Mad Av -NY 10017
(516) 393-2200 .. **Biehl**, David J '88 (Garfunkel W,PC) -111 Grt Nck Rd -Gt Neck 11021
(914) 235-5299 .. **Biehl**, Fredk R '58 -252 Oxford Rd -New Rchll 10804
(516) 861-7880 .. **Biel**, Amy E '05 Sleepys LLC -1000 S Oyster Bay Rd -Hicksvll 11801
(845) 433-1157 .. **Biela**, Jos A '88 IBM -2455 South Rd -Poughkeepsie 12601
(212) 956-3905 .. **Bielaska**, Mary G '86 -355 W 52nd -NY 10019
(518) 455-7700 .. **Bielawski**, Julia Smead '96 %Ct of Appls -20 Eagle -Albany 12207
(585) 419-8800 .. **Bielecki**, Julie R '07 %Harris B PLLC -99 Garnsey Rd -Pittsfrd 14534
(212) 269-1098 .. **Bielefeld**, Wm J '73 -3 Hanover Sq -NY 10004 **Fx:**269-1099
(212) 735-3000 .. **Bielen**, Sofie '03 %Skadden ASM&F LLP -4 Times Sq -NY 10036
(212) 325-2976 .. **Bielenberg**, Aaron C '03 Credit Suisse -11 Mad Av -NY 10010
(212) 670-0436 .. **Bieler**, I Scott '83 %Merrill Lynch -222 Bway -NY 10038
(212) 944-5104 .. **Bielesz**, Maria Christine '94 -500 5th Av -NY 10110 **Fx:**944-8720
(585) 567-2676 .. **Bielewicz**, Roy D '05 -10 W Main Bx179 -Fillmore 14735 **Fx:**567-2670
(914) 833-0506 .. **Bieley**, Patricia D '83 -121 Devonshr Rd -Larchmnt 10538 **Fx:**833-0518
(212) 351-4500 .. **Bielik**, Linda C '00 (Epstein B&G,PC) -250 Park Av -NY 10177
(516) 328-9201 .. **Bielli**, Damien M '03 %Ruffo TM&M PC -3000 Marcus Av -Lk Success 11042
(212) 245-1000 .. **Bien**, Rachel M '06 %Outten & G LLP -3 Park Av -NY 10016
(212) 506-1700 .. **Bienenfeld**, Eric S '08 %Kasowitz BT&F LLP -1633 Bway -NY 10019
(212) 973-0572 .. **Bienenfeld**, Morris '82 (Wolff & S PC) -140 Bway -NY 10005
(212) 363-7701 .. **Bienenfeld**, Saul W '90 Bienenfeld & Assoc,PC -26 Bway -NY 10004 **Fx:**363-7703
(718) 250-2000 .. **Bienenfeld**, Sue-Ellen '91 %DA -350 Jay -Brklyn 11201 **Fx:**250-2314
(914) 834-3500 .. **Bienenstock**, Jennifer L '10 %McMillan CM&P LLP -2180 Bstn Post Rd -Larchmnt 10538
(212) 259-8000 .. **Bienenstock**, Martin J '78 (Dewey & L LLP) -1301 Av of Amer -NY 10019
(212) 779-9777 .. **Bienstock**, Caroline '84 %Carlin America Inc -126 E 38th -NY 10016 **Fx:**779-7920
(212) 599-8200 .. **Bienstock**, Craig G '02 %Shaub AC&S,LLP -655 3rd Av -NY 10017
(212) 208-3443 .. **Bienstock**, Gregg L '92 Ambac Assurance Corp -1 State Street Plz -NY 10004
(718) 459-5050 .. **Bienstock**, Joshua E '81 (Bienstock & B LLP) -105-25 65th Av -Frst Hlls 11375 **Fx:**459-5055
(212) 720-5026 .. **Bienstock**, Lori Ann '93 %Fed Reserve Bk -33 Lbrty -NY 10045 **Fx:**785-5748
(518) 449-8893 .. **Bienstock**, Martin '91 (Wilson EME&D LLP) -677 Bway -Albany 12207
(212) 247-0848 .. **Bienstock & Michael, PC** -250 W 57th -NY 10107 **Fx:**247-0910
(212) 512-0807 .. **Bienstock**, Peter '74 (Cohen HB&R,PC) -11 W 42nd -NY 10036
(212) 779-7977 .. **Bienstock**, Robt H '86 %Carlin America Inc -126 E 38th -NY 10016 **Fx:**779-7920
(212) 247-0848 .. **Bienstock**, Ronald S '84 (Bienstock & M,PC) -250 W 57th -NY 10107
(516) 295-1256 .. **Bienstock**, Walter '59 -799 Arbuckle Av -Woodmere 11598 **Fx:**569-5913
(631) 863-1788 .. **Bienz**, Frederic C '86 -305 E Main -Smithtwn 11787 **Fx:**863-1790
(212) 481-4900 .. **Bier**, Bruno C '98 -38 W 32nd -NY 10001
(212) 237-1000 .. **Bier**, Richd I '74 (Windels ML&M,LLP) -156 W 56th -NY 10019
(212) 676-7502 .. **Bier**, Richd M '94 %Admin Children's Srvcs -150 William -NY 10038
(212) 698-3889 .. **Bier**, Stephen H '90 (Dechert LLP) -1095 Av of Amer -NY 10036
(212) 909-6000 .. **Bierbauer**, Erik C '00 Cnsl Debevoise & P LLP -919 3rd Av -NY 10022
(212) 840-0080 .. **Bierce & Kenerson,PC** -420 Lex Av -NY 10170 **Fx:**840-6210
(212) 840-0080 .. **Bierce**, Wm B '76 (Bierce & K,PC) -420 Lex Av -NY 10170
(212) 651-7700 .. **Bierfriend**, Gary A '93 %Mortgage It.com -33 Maiden Ln -NY 10038
(585) 546-2434 .. **Bierley**, Sarah M '03 %Hirsch & T PC -1000 Rynlds Arcd Bldg -Rchstr 14614
(212) 474-1000 .. **Bierman**, Carrie R '10 %Cravath S&M LLP -825 8th Av -NY 10019
(516) 677-0444 .. **Bierman**, Ira '77 -485 Underhill Blvd -Syosset 11791 **Fx:**677-1911
(212) 248-8800 .. **Bierman**, Kenneth T '02 %Callan KB&B LLP -1 Whitehall -NY 10004
(518) 474-3444 .. **Bierman**, Luke J '83 %State Comptroller -110 State -Albany 12236 **Fx:**473-9104
(212) 232-2055 .. **Bierman**, Mark H '82 (Bierman & P LLP) -74 Trinity Pl -NY 10006 **Fx:**232-2056
(718) 390-5422 .. **Bierman**, Paul C '83 %Civil Ct -927 Castleton Av -Staten Isl 10310 **Fx:**390-8108
(212) 905-1180 .. **Bierman**, Rick S '78 -600 3rd Av -NY 10016 **Fx:**905-1184
(212) 839-5300 .. **Bierman**, Steven M '77 (Sidley A LLP) -787 7th Av -NY 10019
(212) 448-1100 .. **Biermann**, Rodney C '08 %McLaughlin & S,LLP -260 Mad Av -NY 10016
(212) 310-8000 .. **Biernacki**, Jakub '08 %Weil G&M LLP -767 5th Av -NY 10153
(585) 546-2350 .. **Biernbaum**, Alan S '67 (Biernbaum & M LLP) -19 W Main -Rchstr 14614
(585) 546-2350 .. **Biernbaum & Meyer LLP** -19 W Main -Rchstr 14614 **Fx:**546-7365
(212) 788-0967 .. **Biernoff**, Ari '03 %Law Dept -100 Church -NY 10007 **Fx:**788-0367
(212) 790-0352 .. **Bierschbach**, Rick A '03 Benj N Cardozo Schl of Law -55 5th Av -NY 10003 **Fx:**790-0345
(212) 522-3217 .. **Bierstedt**, Robin '79 %Time Inc -1271 Av of Amer -NY 10020 **Fx:**522-0437
(212) 784-6400 .. **Bierstein**, Andrea B '85 (Hanly CBSF&H LLP) -112 Mad Av -NY 10016
(212) 545-4738 .. **Biesanz**, Zachary W '09 %Wolf HAF&H LLP -270 Mad Av -NY 10016
(212) 269-1304 .. **Biester**, David R '94 WTC Captive Ins Co,Inc -100 William -NY 10038
(212) 416-8000 .. **Biesty**, Thos M '03 %Dept of Law -120 Bway -NY 10271
(518) 429-4200 .. **Bifera**, Frank V '76 (Hiscock & B,LLP) -50 Beaver -Albany 12207
(877) 786-7552 .. **Bifulci Kocal**, Danielle M '09 %E Swire Falker,PC -42 Lovell Ln -New Rchll 10804 **Fx:**(914) 738-5654
(718) 848-6940 .. **Bifulco**, Maryanne '00 (Bifulco & R,LLP) -160-36 91st -Howard Bch 11414 **Fx:**848-6664
(212) 446-7000 .. **Bigalow**, Tamara S '91 %McKinsey & Co -55 E 52nd -NY 10055 **Fx:**688-9521
(212) 349-5730 .. **Bigel**, Madeline K '77 -2 5th Av -NY 10011 **Fx:**385-1410
(212) 326-3939 .. **Bigelow**, Bronson J '04 %Jones D -222 E 41st -NY 10017
(212) 947-3793 .. **Bigelow**, Francis D '02 OfCnsl Sadis & G LLP -551 5th Av -NY 10176
(516) 378-1700 .. **Bigelow**, Joyce G '92 %Chesney & M -2305 Grand Av -Baldwin 11510
(212) 924-4890 .. **Bigelow**, Kirk L '88 %AFL-CIO Local 3369 -Bx601 -NY 10014
(718) 297-1717 .. **Bigelow**, Luke J '93 (Viscardi B&B,PC) -148-45 Hillside Av -Jamaica 11435
(646) 602-5600 .. **Bigelow**, Madeline Garcia '94 %Urban Justice Ctr -123 William -NY 10038 **Fx:**(212) 533-4598
(908) 812-6671 .. **Bigelow**, Robt W '94 -22 Crtland -NY 10007
(212) 556-2100 .. **Biggar**, Barry P '82 (King & S) -1185 Av of Amer -NY 10036
(914) 253-2000 .. **Biggart**, Robt K '80 %Pepsico -700 Andrsn Hill Rd -Purchase 10577
(212) 698-3500 .. **Bigge**, David M '02 %Dechert LLP -1095 Av of Amer -NY 10036
(212) 813-5900 .. **Bigger**, Stephen '67 (Fross ZL&Z,PC) -866 UN Plz -NY 10017
(212) 541-2000 .. **Biggers**, Michl G '86 (Bryan C LLP) -1290 Av of Amer -NY 10104
(518) 475-9500 .. **Biggerstaff**, Laura K '04 Biggerstaff Law Firm,LLP -1280 New Scotland Rd -Slingerlnds 12159 **Fx:**475-7677
(518) 475-9500 .. **Biggerstaff**, Robt E '74 Biggerstaff Law Firm,LLP -1280 New Scotland Rd -Slingerlnds 12159 **Fx:**475-7677
(516) 682-8555 .. **Biggiani**, Michl A '86 -2 Roosevelt Av -Syosset 11791
(716) 566-5400 .. **Biggie**, Brian R '04 %Goldberg S LLP -665 Main -Buffalo 14203
(212) 999-5800 .. **Biggio**, Chas E '86 (Wilson SG&R) -1301 Av of Americas -NY 10019
(212) 735-3000 .. **Biggio**, Jessica L '94 (Skadden ASM&F LLP) -4 Times Sq -NY 10036
(518) 562-0600 .. **Biggs**, Donald W '96 (O'Connell & A) -206 W Bay Plz -Plattsbrgh 12901
(212) 619-4350 .. **Bigham**, Stephen M '99 (Newman MKGH,PC) -14 Wall -NY 10005
(212) 779-1414 .. **Bigin**, Michl S '00 %Bernstein L LLP -10 E 40th -NY 10016
(516) 545-5160 .. **Biging**, Elizabeth K '87 %Natl Grid -175 E Old Cntry Rd -Hicksvll 11801 **Fx:**545-5029
(212) 232-1300 .. **Biging**, Peter J '87 (Lewis BB&S LLP) -77 Water -NY 10005
(212) 340-2865 .. **Bigler**, Esta R '75 %Cornell Univ-ILR -16 E 34th -NY 10016 **Fx:**340-2822
(516) 409-6565 .. **Bigler**, John M '77 -1421 Wantagh Av -Wantagh 11793 **Fx:**409-6522
(516) 327-1112 .. **Bigman**, Laurie G '91 %GreenPoint Bk -1981 Marcus Av -Lk Success 11042
(315) 475-4410 .. **Bigsby**, Arthur J Jr. '82 (Fallon F&B) -501 E Wshngtn -Syracuse 13202 **Fx:**475-0759
(631) 582-1919 .. **Bigus**, Caryn M '07 %V Russo & Assoc,PC -3740 Expwy Dr S -Islandia 11749 **Fx:**582-8484
(631) 862-8600 .. **Bijesse & Belford** -217 Lk Av -St James 11780 **Fx:**862-8618
(212) 902-2041 .. **Bijou**, Leon J '82 Goldman Sachs -1 NY Plz -NY 10004
(212) 931-8300 .. **Bikel**, Dror Moshe '93 %Strongin R&A,LLP -5 Hanover Sq -NY 10004
(718) 376-0216 .. **Bikhman**, Karl '03 (Bikhman & V,PC) -1909 E 17th -Brklyn 11229 **Fx:**228-6633
(914) 683-5300 .. **Bikkal**, Cecilia G '86 %Silverman B&S,LLP -81 Main -White Plns 10601
(914) 683-5300 .. **Bikkal**, Robin A '83 (Silverman B&S,LLP) -81 Main -White Plns 10601
(646) 602-5600 .. **Biklen**, Molly K '05 %Urban Justice Ctr -123 William -NY 10038 **Fx:**(212) 533-4598
(212) 788-1411 .. **Bila**, Anthony '03 %Law Dept -100 Church -NY 10007 **Fx:**788-0367
(212) 909-6000 .. **Bilar**, Sharon R '08 %Debevoise & P LLP -919 3rd Av -NY 10022
(917) 778-6600 .. **Bilbao**, Cesar O '97 %J Toomey -485 Lex Av -NY 10017 **Fx:**778-7048
(212) 916-7800 .. **Bilbao**, Guillermo G '85 Rabobank Nederland -245 Park Av -NY 10167
(718) 332-1114 .. **Bildner**, Ira J '93 -3235 Emmons Av -Brklyn 11235
(718) 464-4289 .. **Bildstein**, Bernd '61 -79-34 212th -Oakland Gdns 11364
(718) 340-4200 .. **Bilek**, Marylu '81 %CUNY Law Schl -65-21 Main -Flushng 11367 **Fx:**340-4482
(516) 997-8383 .. **Bilello**, Anthony J '99 %S Zlotolow -1025 Old Cntry Rd -Westbury 11590 **Fx:**997-7876
(315) 445-8670 .. **Bilello**, Barney F '90 %MA Bjork -5784 Widewaters Pkwy -DeWitt 13214 **Fx:**445-8688
(516) 746-6066 .. **Bilello**, Chas J '94 (Cammarasana & B) -500 Old Cntry Rd -Gdn Cty 11530 **Fx:**746-6411
(516) 229-4300 .. **Bilello**, James G '86 (J Bilello & Assoc) -875 Merrick Av -Westbury 11590
(914) 328-1844 .. **Bilello**, Lauren K '09 %Miano & C,LLP -550 Mamaroneck Av -Harrison 10528
(212) 506-1700 .. **Bileris**, Monika O '04 Kasowitz BT&F LLP -1633 Bway -NY 10019
(212) 669-2376 .. **Biletsky**, Samantha M '96 %Comptroller -1 Centre -NY 10007 **Fx:**669-2884
(516) 746-8000 .. **Bilewich**, Igor '76 (Jaspan S LLP) -300 Grdn City Plz -Gdn Cty 11530
(718) 250-2000 .. **Bilfield**, Pamela J '97 %DA -350 Jay -Brklyn 11201 **Fx:**250-2314

(585) 262-4700 .. **Bilgore,** Donald L '52 (Bilgore RLK&K) -950 Rynlds Arcd Bldg -Rchstr 14614
(585) 262-4700 .. **Bilgore Reich Levine Kroll & Kantor** -950 Rynlds Arcd Bldg -Rchstr 14614 **Fx:**262-4118
(516) 992-1850 .. **Bilich,** Chas A '73 Cnsl Westerman BEM&S,LLP -1201 RXR Plz -Uniondale 11553
(716) 626-0276 .. **Bilicki,** Byron '86 -17 Beresford Ct -Williamsvll 14221
(716) 664-5600 .. **Bilicki,** Byron '86 (Bilicki Law Firm,PC) -1285 N Main -Jamestwn 14701 **Fx:**664-5606
(518) 213-6000 .. **Bilik,** James D '84 %NYSUT -800 Troy-Schnctdy Rd -Latham 12110 **Fx:**213-6488
(315) 425-2700 .. **Bilinski,** Peter J '93 (Hiscock & B,LLP) -One Park Pl -Syracuse 13202
(212) 819-8200 .. **Bilkis,** David '89 (White & C LLP) -1155 Av of Amer -NY 10036
(516) 377-7100 .. **Bilkis,** Stephen H '97 (S Bilkis & Assoc) -805 Smith -Baldwin 11510 **Fx:**377-7327
(212) 966-5350 .. **Billah,** Mohammad W '01 (Billah Law Firm,PLLC) -100 Church -NY 10007 **Fx:**(646) 845-4771
(212) 425-7200 .. **Billah,** Zaed M '07 %Kenyon & K,LLP -1 Bway -NY 10004
(212) 924-1633 .. **Billard,** Mary A '97 -247 W 12th -NY 10014
(631) 249-5600 .. **Billeci,** Craig J '08 Sheps Law Grp,PC -35 Pinelawn Rd -Melvll 11747 **Fx:**249-5613
(212) 962-0001 .. **Biller,** Bradlee G '80 NY Career Institute -11 Park Pl -NY 10007
(646) 885-5002 .. **Biller,** Holly M '85 %Dept of Sanitation -125 Worth -NY 10013 **Fx:**(212) 442-9090
(516) 921-8461 .. **Biller,** Susan G '86 -42 Bristol Dr -Woodbury 11797 **Fx:**921-0942
(613) 599-0376 .. **Billet,** Kevin R '79 -Bx661 -Buffalo 14217
(212) 867-4466 .. **Billet,** Phillip L '81 %Belkin BW&G,LLP -270 Mad Av -NY 10016
(212) 608-6972 .. **Billett,** Donald R '84 -142 W End Av -NY 10023
(212) 689-8390 .. **Billig,** Darin S '95 Billig Law,PC -80 Broad -NY 10004
(845) 794-3833 .. **Billig,** Jacob R '84 (Billig L&B LLP) -146 Rck Hll Rd Bx780 -Rck Hll 12775 **Fx:**794-3827
(212) 907-9600 .. **Billig,** Melissa Tabako '98 (Ingram YGC&B,LLP) -250 Park Av -NY 10177
(212) 689-8390 .. **Billig,** Suzanne M '96 (Billig Law,PC) -80 Broad -NY 10004 **Fx:**(646) 862-8726
(212) 474-1000 .. **Billings,** Ryan M '05 %Cravath S&M LLP -825 8th Av -NY 10019
(212) 487-9700 .. **Billings,** Wm M '82 OfCnsl White F&F,LLP -61 Bway -NY 10006
(716) 434-5783 .. **Billingsley,** Gary M '80 -4421 Lwr Mtn Rd -Lockprt 14094 **Fx:**434-5784
(212) 849-7000 .. **Billington,** Sharon H '07 %Quinn EU&S,LLP -51 Mad Av -NY 10010
(315) 471-6265 .. **Billinson,** Craig J '82 (CJ Billinson & Assoc) -342 S Salina -Syracuse 13202 **Fx:**474-3153
(212) 805-3900 .. **Billis,** Peter N '07 %Clausen M PC -1 Chase Manh Plz -NY 10005
(212) 319-3737 .. **Billman,** Martha G '78 J Silberman Assoc,PC -145 E 57th -NY 10022 **Fx:**319-8188
(716) 851-5775 .. **Billman,** Scott C '93 Urban Renewal Agency -920 City Hall -Buffalo 14202
(212) 574-1200 .. **Billotti,** Keith J '07 %Seward & K LLP -1 Bttry Pk Plz -NY 10004
(212) 698-3500 .. **Billy,** Jason O '06 %Dechert LLP -1095 Av of Amer -NY 10036
(212) 732-3320 .. **Billy,** Michl '76 (Short & B,PC) -217 Bway -NY 10007
(718) 923-4206 .. **Bilmes,** Steven J '77 %OTDA Fair Hearings -14 Boerum Pl -Brklyn 11201
(845) 639-3445 .. **Bilotta,** Cassandra '75 -14 S Main -New Cty 10956 **Fx:**639-3442
(212) 302-5151 .. **Bilotta,** Frank B '91 Global Sec Srvcs,LLC -114 W 47th -NY 10036
(631) 588-8778 .. **Bilotti,** Doris Waldmann '02 %Germano & C,PC -4250 Vets Mem'l Hwy -Holbrook 11741
(516) 962-7943 .. **Bilotti,** Douglas J '01 Merchant Srvcs,Inc -515 Broadhllw Rd -Melvll 11747
(212) 999-5800 .. **Bilotto,** Darren J '08 %Wilson SG&R -1301 Av of Americas -NY 10019
(914) 683-9487 .. **Bilotto,** Gerard '97 (G Bilotto,PC) -80 Winding Ridge Rd -White Plns 10603 **Fx:**683-8027
(718) 515-0300 .. **Bilski,** Christopher P '97 (D'Angelica & B,PLLC) -2705 Eastchstr Rd -Bronx 10469 **Fx:**515-4366
(716) 565-1327 .. **Biltekoff,** Dara B '05 Energy Curtailment Specialists,Inc -4455 Genesee -Buffalo 14225 **Fx:**565-1703
(716) 633-3200 .. **Biltekoff,** Robt A '89 (Lipman B&J,LLP) -333 Intl Dr -Williamsvll 14221
(914) 253-3443 .. **Bilus,** Elizabeth N '78 %Pepsico -700 Andrsn Hill Rd -Purchase 10577
(631) 423-4390 .. **Bily,** Karen A '04 %Mincone & M,PC -110 Walt Whitman Rd -South Huntington 11746 **Fx:**423-4408
(212) 974-7474 .. **Bimbler,** Fredk P '95 (Cowan DA&S LLP) -41 Mad Av -NY 10010
(718) 318-4724 .. **Binckes,** Wm G '86 -142 Beach 128th -Far Rckwy 11694 **Fx:**318-8558
(212) 859-8000 .. **Bindek,** Ewa P '07 %Fried FHS&J LLP -1 NY Plz -NY 10004
(212) 977-9700 .. **Bindelglass,** Howard '55 Cnsl Phillips N LLP -666 5th Av -NY 10103
(800) 742-9696 .. **Binder,** Chas E '76 (Binder & B,PC) -33-00 Nrthrn Blvd -LIC 11101 **Fx:**(718) 512-2424
(212) 225-2000 .. **Binder,** Grant M '05 %Cleary GS&H -1 Lbrty Plz -NY 10006
(631) 361-6699 .. **Binder,** Harry J '72 (Binder & B,PC) -300 Rabro Dr -Hauppauge 11788 **Fx:**361-6475
(631) 582-1200 .. **Binder,** Harry J '72 (DeHaan B LLP) -300 Rabro Dr -Hauppauge 11788
(212) 903-8700 .. **Binder,** Jason K '06 %Roberts & H,LLP -825 8th Av -NY 10019
(516) 333-2737 .. **Binder,** Jay S '78 (Binder & C) -265 Post Av -Westbury 11590 **Fx:**333-1262
(914) 946-3191 .. **Binder,** Jeffrey A '03 J Binder PC -68 E Post Rd -White Plns 10601
(914) 946-3191 .. **Binder,** Jeffrey M '97 J Binder PC & Assoc -68 E Post Rd -White Plns 10601 **Fx:**946-4344
(518) 402-9184 .. **Binder,** Jonathan A '09 DEC -625 Bway -Albany 12233 **Fx:**402-9018
(212) 909-9500 .. **Binder,** Karen '87 OfCnsl Wachtel & M,LLP -885 2nd Av -NY 10017
(212) 264-9271 .. **Binder,** Karen P '78 %US Customs -26 Fed Plz -NY 10278
(212) 574-1200 .. **Binder,** Laurie R '84 %Seward & K LLP -1 Bttry Pk Plz -NY 10004
(212) 530-1800 .. **Binder,** Neil S '96 %Richards K&O LLP -1 World Fncl Ctr -NY 10281
(212) 788-0818 .. **Binder,** Robin '79 %Law Dept -100 Church -NY 10007 **Fx:**788-0367
(212) 837-6376 .. **Binder,** Sarah A '05 %Hughes H&R LLP -1 Bttry Pk Plz -NY 10004
(212) 474-1000 .. **Binder,** Stephanie J '09 %Cravath S&M LLP -825 8th Av -NY 10019
(212) 732-8700 .. **Binder,** Wm H '03 %McAloon & F,PC -123 William -NY 10038
(212) 986-0100 .. **Binderman,** Wm N '65 -110 Wall -NY 10005
(212) 922-6844 .. **Bindert,** Thos W '86 Bk of NY Mellon Corp -200 Park Av -NY 10166 **Fx:**922-7565
(212) 237-1000 .. **Bindler,** Deborah Hilsenrath '81 SpclCnsl Windels ML&M,LLP -156 W 56th -NY 10019
(212) 450-4000 .. **Bindra,** Priya '10 %Davis P&W LLP -450 Lex Av -NY 10017
(212) 687-0090 .. **Bindra,** Saranjit S '99 %Fairchild Properties -20 E 46th -NY 10017
(518) 474-5487 .. **Bing,** Andrew D '83 %Dept of Law -The Cptl -Albany 12224
(212) 605-0937 .. **Bing,** Jonathan L '96 NYS Assembly -132 E 43rd -NY 10017 **Fx:**605-9948
(845) 246-2888 .. **Bing,** Marie F '83 OfCnsl Rosenblum & L -41 Market Bx270 -Saugerties 12477
(845) 354-9226 .. **Bing,** Robt W '77 -278 Route 306 -Monsey 10952 **Fx:**354-9226
(212) 286-1666 .. **Bing,** Steven E '79 -276 5th Av -NY 10001 **Fx:**286-1616
(212) 348-7449 .. **Bing,** Tracey A '98 %Legal Srvcs -1 W 125th -NY 10027 **Fx:**348-4093
(845) 362-6477 .. **Binger,** Alan J '77 -PMB#378-169 S Main -New Cty 10956 **Fx:**354-8255
(631) 261-0960 .. **Binger,** Julia R '80 -168 Laurel Av -Northprt 11768 **Fx:**261-0932
(212) 336-0462 .. **Binger,** Sharon B '02 SEC -3 World Fncl Ctr -NY 10281 **Fx:**336-1323
(845) 220-8313 .. **Bingham-Hall,** Pamela '05 -Bx377 -Dover Plns 12522 **Fx:**877-3223
(212) 515-2813 .. **Bingham,** Kara B '05 Hedgeop Compliance -3 Park Av -NY 10016
(212) 517-7174 .. **Bingham,** Karen Koch '74 -20 E 74th -NY 10021
(212) 909-6000 .. **Bingham,** Laura M '08 %Debevoise & P LLP -919 3rd Av -NY 10022
(212) 705-7000 .. **Bingham McCutchen LLP** -399 Park Av -NY 10022 **Fx:**752-5378
(917) 777-4200 .. **Bingham McCutchen LLP** -1 Bttry Pk Plz -NY 10004 **Fx:**777-4299
(212) 758-0050 .. **Bingham,** Michelle Cruz '86 Title Assoc -825 3rd Av -NY 10022 **Fx:**758-8223
(718) 237-3100 .. **Bingham,** Nicole P '99 Leg Aid -111 Lvngstn -Brklyn 11201 **Fx:**250-4243
(212) 335-4081 .. **Bini,** Mark E '01 %DA -1 Hogan Pl -NY 10013
(212) 227-3636 .. **Biniakewitz,** Michl J '03 %Spar & B,PC -225 Bway -NY 10007
(585) 546-5530 .. **Binimow,** Jason '92 %Thomson West -50 E Broad -Rchstr 14694
(716) 668-5000 .. **Biniszkiewicz,** Wm M '59 -2448 Union Rd -Cheektowaga 14227
(212) 230-8800 .. **Binkley,** Alex F '09 %WilmerHale -399 Park Av -NY 10022
(716) 895-5500 .. **Binko,** Richd S '83 -2427 William -Buffalo 14206 **Fx:**895-1029
(518) 457-6207 .. **Binseel,** Anne J '85 %Dept Civil Srvc -Harriman Campus Bldg 1 -Albany 12239 **Fx:**457-6654
(518) 474-7091 .. **Binseel,** John '82 %OTDA -40 N Pearl -Albany 12243 **Fx:**474-9389
(212) 943-1550 .. **Binsky,** Mark Ian '81 (Speyer & P,LLP) -26 Bway -NY 10004
(212) 625-8910 .. **Binson,** David E '08 %B Kogan & Assoc,PC -277 Bway -NY 10007 **Fx:**219-2728
(212) 253-6911 .. **Binstock,** Gregory E '07 %Kurland B& Assoc,PC -304 Park Av S -NY 10010
(212) 757-4305 .. **Binstok,** Joel I '82 York Consulting -7 W 51st -NY 10019 **Fx:**757-3212
(347) 561-4704 .. **Biolsi,** Steven A '05 -107-23 71st Rd -Frst Hlls 11375
(212) 836-8607 .. **Bionda,** Jeanette C '98 (Kaye S LLP) -425 Park Av -NY 10022 **Fx:**836-7156
(914) 946-5093 .. **Biondi,** Lawr P '84 -81 Main -White Plns 10601 **Fx:**946-7372
(212) 421-2233 .. **Biondi,** Sabino '99 %Wilk A LLP -675 3rd Av -NY 10017
(347) 404-9400 .. **Biondo,** Christina G '95 %Criminal Ct -120 Schermerhorn -Brklyn 11201 **Fx:**(718) 643-3538
(631) 668-1000 .. **Biondo,** George F '74 (Biondo & H LLP) -The Plz Bx5030 -Montauk 11954 **Fx:**668-3971
(914) 686-6100 .. **Biondo,** James F '96 (Rosenblum & T LLC) -50 Main -White Plns 10606
(212) 888-8001 .. **Biondo,** James F '96 (Rosenblum & T LLC) -405 Lex Av -NY 10174
(516) 742-8620 .. **Biondo,** John '06 Cnsl V Stempel -1205 Franklin Av -Gdn Cty 11530 **Fx:**742-6859
(212) 506-2500 .. **Biondo,** Vanessa M '05 %Mayer B LLP -1675 Bway -NY 10019
(212) 972-2721 .. **Biow,** Thos J '83 -551 5th Av -NY 10176
(212) 764-2468 .. **Birbach,** Stuart '78 -15 W 44th -NY 10036 **Fx:**869-2303
(914) 737-1020 .. **Birbrower,** Adam L '98 Birbrower Law Firm,PC -1 Park Pl -Peekskill 10566 **Fx:**737-5311
(914) 737-1020 .. **Birbrower,** Barry '69 Birbrower Law Firm,PC -1 Park Pl -Peekskill 10566 **Fx:**737-5311
(845) 267-4878 .. **Birbrower & Beldock,PC** -151 N Main -New Cty 10956 **Fx:**634-5979
(845) 267-4878 .. **Birbrower,** Leonard J '63 (Birbrower & B,PC) -151 N Main -New Cty 10956
(518) 851-7733 .. **Birch,** David A '68 -Bx83 -Livingston 12541
(212) 944-0500 .. **Birch,** David L '74 (Hofheimer G&G,LLP) -530 5th Av -NY 10036 **Fx:**897-4996
(718) 442-1295 .. **Birch,** James H '87 %J Stern -1189 Forest Av -Staten Isl 10310 **Fx:**442-1114
(718) 442-1295 .. **Birch,** Jerome S '53 -1189 Forest Av -Staten Isl 10310 **Fx:**442-1114
(607) 547-5253 .. **Birch,** Robt W '83 (Schlather & B) -192 Main Bx391 -Cooperstwn 13326 **Fx:**547-2420
(585) 586-8060 .. **Bircher,** Ronald T '73 (Sutton DC&D,PLLC) -359 N Wshngtn -Rchstr 14625
(212) 344-3100 .. **Bird,** Christie M '02 %Frenkel LWW&G,LLP -1 Whitehall -NY 10004
(212) 205-7000 .. **Bird,** Douglas A '01 (Ashurst LLP) -7 Times Sq -NY 10036
(212) 909-6000 .. **Bird,** Paul S '89 (Debevoise & P LLP) -919 3rd Av -NY 10022
(585) 248-2340 .. **Bird,** Robt J '74 -361 N Wshngtn -Rchstr 14625 **Fx:**248-2340
(516) 997-4800 .. **Bird,** Wm III '01 %TK Murtha & Assoc,PC -45 Post Av -Westbury 11590 **Fx:**997-9027
(212) 425-7200 .. **Birde,** Patrick J '83 (Kenyon & K,LLP) -1 Bway -NY 10004
(516) 750-3919 .. **Birdie,** Alyson J '06 Wright Risk Mgmt -333 Earl Ovington Blvd -Uniondale 11553
(212) 931-8709 .. **Birdoff,** David C '70 OfCnsl Feldman W&S LLP -420 Lex Av -NY 10170

(516) 572-7501 .. **Birdoff,** Joyce W '71 Nassau Comm College -One Educ Dr -Gdn Cty 11530
(212) 265-6600 .. **Birdoff,** Richd J '84 -810 7th Av -NY 10019
(212) 969-3000 .. **Birdsall,** Nathaniel W '09 %Proskauer R LLP -1585 Bway -NY 10036
(718) 793-5000 .. **Birdsall,** Nikki '07 %Tarshis & H,LLP -118-35 Qns Blvd -Frst Hlls 11375
(212) 361-1727 .. **Biren,** Richd M '77 %Envrnmntl Cntrl Brd -66 John -NY 10038 **Fx:**361-1900
(914) 332-0222 .. **Biren,** Steven R '74 %Philips Electronics -345 Scarborough Rd Bx3001 -Briarclff Mnr 10510 **Fx:**332-0615
(212) 294-6700 .. **Birenbaum,** Jonathan '79 (Winston & S) -200 Park Av -NY 10166
(212) 373-3000 .. **Birenboim,** Bruce A '83 (Paul WRW&G LLP) -1285 Av of Amer -NY 10019
(212) 381-7000 .. **Birenz,** Jerry S '81 (Sabin B&G LLP) -4 Times Sq -NY 10036
(212) 479-6000 .. **Birger,** Laura Grossfield '94 (Cooley LLP) -1114 Av of Amer -NY 10036
(212) 315-4000 .. **Birkhahn,** Jonathan '81 King World Productions -1700 Bway -NY 10019
(212) 909-6000 .. **Birkland,** Berglind H '10 %Debevoise & P LLP -919 3rd Av -NY 10022
(212) 455-2000 .. **Birkmann,** Stefanie '03 Cnsl Simpson T&B LLP -425 Lex Av -NY 10017
(212) 592-1400 .. **Birle,** Joann Berardo '91 Cnsl Herrick,F LLP -2 Park Av -NY 10016
(914) 630-4680 .. **Birman,** Carl D '04 (C Birman,PLLC) -235 Mamaroneck Av -White Plns 10605 **Fx:**630-4681
(212) 208-9585 .. **Birman,** Mindy J '96 Liberty Intl Underwriters -55 Water -NY 10041
(716) 856-4000 .. **Birmingham,** Brad A '98 (Hodgson R LLP) -140 Pearl -Buffalo 14202
(212) 820-9563 .. **Birmingham,** Danl G '96 %Hawkins D&W LLP -One Chase Manh Plz -NY 10005
(716) 856-0600 .. **Birmingham,** Kristen M '98 (Jaeckle F&M,LLP) -12 Fountain Plz -Buffalo 14202
(716) 847-8400 .. **Birmingham,** Richd G '57 OfCnsl Phillips L LLP -3400 HSBC Ctr -Buffalo 14203
(718) 596-3300 .. **Birn,** Harold M '95 P Schneider & Assoc PLLC -335 Adams -Brklyn 11201
(212) 685-4322 .. **Birn,** Martin J '75 -16 E 34th -NY 10016 **Fx:**685-4534
(212) 697-0024 .. **Birnant,** Danl A '51 (Fastenberg & B) -60 E 42nd -NY 10165
(516) 829-6305 .. **Birnbach,** Howard R '80 -111 Grt Nck Rd -Gt Neck 11021 **Fx:**829-0651
(212) 259-8000 .. **Birnbaum,** Abbie G '09 %Dewey & L LLP -1301 Av of Amer -NY 10019
(212) 291-4818 .. **Birnbaum,** Alan R '84 %Citigroup -125 Broad -NY 10004
(718) 797-5700 .. **Birnbaum,** Arthur '74 OfCnsl Wenig S LLP -26 Court -Brklyn 11242
(212) 310-8000 .. **Birnbaum,** Ashley '10 %Weil G&M LLP -767 5th Av -NY 10153
(516) 248-2750 .. **Birnboim,** Barry N '74 -2 Birchwood Ct -Mineola 11501
(516) 222-5073 .. **Birnbaum,** Bruce '83 -1600 Stewart Av -Westbury 11590 **Fx:**222-5040
(212) 586-5800 .. **Birnbaum,** Courtney L '99 %Cohen TS&W PC -420 Lex Av -NY 10170
(718) 767-6800 .. **Birnbaum,** Dave A '76 (Birnbaum & S) -149-40 14th Av Bx156 -Whitestone 11357 **Fx:**746-8715
(516) 621-7205 .. **Birnbaum,** Dave A '76 -62 Highland Av -Roslyn 11576
(718) 590-2000 .. **Birnbaum,** David '91 %DA -198 E 161st -Bronx 10451 **Fx:**590-6477
(212) 449-9746 .. **Birnbaum,** David M '84 %Merrill Lynch -220 Bway -NY 10038
(516) 248-8000 .. **Birnbaum,** Donald H '72 (Sandback B&M) -200 Old Cntry Rd -Mineola 11501
(212) 471-8540 .. **Birnbaum,** Edw L '64 (Herzfeld & R,PC) -125 Broad -NY 10004
(212) 779-9910 .. **Birnbaum,** George P '75 (Eaton & V LLP) -3 Park Av -NY 10016
(212) 450-4000 .. **Birnbaum,** Harold M '09 %Davis P&W LLP -450 Lex Av -NY 10017
(212) 684-5050 .. **Birnbaum,** Jaeson L '03 Birnbaum & Assoc,PC -280 Mad Av -NY 10016 **Fx:**684-5086
(845) 825-8023 .. **Birnbaum,** James M '05 %Prudential Rand Realty -10 Schriever Ln -New Cty 10956
(212) 513-7970 .. **Birnbaum,** Janice L '87 %Law Dept -100 Church -NY 10007 **Fx:**788-0940
(718) 722-3500 .. **Birnbaum,** John K '96 %Forest City Ratner -1 Metrotech Ctr N -Brklyn 11201
(718) 741-8328 .. **Birnbaum,** Julian R '84 Div of Human Rights -1 Fordham Plz -Bronx 10458 **Fx:**741-8279
(718) 634-3794 .. **Birnbaum,** Julius '51 -318 Beach 144th -Neponsit 11694
(516) 742-0009 .. **Birnbaum,** Keren G '09 %Mason & A,LLC -377 Oak -Gdn Cty 11530 **Fx:**742-0908
(646) 386-5700 .. **Birnbaum,** Kimberly S '07 Civil Ct -111 Centre -NY 10013
(646) 386-3660 .. **Birnbaum,** Lawr '75 %Supreme Ct-Law Dept -60 Centre -NY 10007
(516) 379-7818 .. **Birnbaum,** Lenore S '75 -1997 Lowell Ln -Merrick 11566
(914) 997-2022 .. **Birnbaum,** Linda D '81 -123 Main -White Plns 10601 **Fx:**328-0916
(516) 498-2900 .. **Birnbaum,** Mark D '77 (Naidich WB&M,LLP) -80 Cuttermill Rd -Gt Neck 11021 **Fx:**466-3555
(845) 256-1341 .. **Birnbaum,** Marvin R '01 -Bx784 -New Paltz 12561 **Fx:**255-6877
(212) 336-0523 .. **Birnbaum,** Michl D '00 %SEC -3 World Fncl Ctr -NY 10281 **Fx:**336-1323
(212) 874-0383 .. **Birnbaum,** Mindy A '84 Citarella -2135 Bway -NY 10023
(212) 301-3000 .. **Birnbaum,** Nancy L '01 %Fox News -1211 Av of Amer -NY 10036
(914) 428-4565 .. **Birnbaum,** Richd S '73 -200 Mamaroneck Av -White Plns 10601 **Fx:**997-1965
(718) 828-1400 .. **Birnbaum,** Robt A '88 %Stillman & S,PC -2622 E Tremont Av -Bronx 10461
(212) 682-8383 .. **Birnbaum,** Robt M '61 OfCnsl Kantor DWMT&G,PC -51 E 42nd -NY 10017
(212) 819-8200 .. **Birnbaum,** Scott D '10 %White & C LLP -1155 Av of Amer -NY 10036
(212) 735-3000 .. **Birnbaum,** Sheila L '65 (Skadden ASM&F LLP) -4 Times Sq -NY 10036
(631) 329-3491 .. **Birnbaum,** Stanley I '73 -10 Pantigo Rd Bx4234 -E Hampton 11937
(212) 468-8000 .. **Birnbaum,** Stephanie M '09 %Morrison & F LLP -1290 Av of Amer -NY 10104
(212) 335-4500 .. **Birnbaum,** Timothy H '09 %DLA Piper LLP -1251 Av of Amer -NY 10020
(516) 747-7400 .. **Birney,** Wm J '84 (Rosenberg C&B LLP) -100 Grdn City Plz -Gdn Cty 11530
(212) 474-1000 .. **Birnhak,** Danl A '05 %Cravath S&M LLP -825 8th Av -NY 10019
(716) 837-1070 .. **Birnholz,** Alan C '91 -39 Gatehse Ln -E Amherst 14051
(212) 446-2300 .. **Birns,** Richd J '98 (Boies S&F LLP) -575 Lex Av -NY 10022
(212) 705-7000 .. **Biron,** Kevin J '04 Cnsl Bingham M LLP -399 Park Av -NY 10022
(716) 853-4340 .. **Biryla,** Richd J '79 (Getman & B) -800 Rand Bldg -Buffalo 14203
(631) 265-6300 .. **Birzon,** Mitchell J '85 (Birzon S&B) -222 E Main -Smithtwn 11787
(516) 942-9100 .. **Birzon,** Peter M '85 P Birzon & Assoc -400 Jericho Tpk -Jericho 11753 **Fx:**942-0596
(631) 265-6300 .. **Birzon Strang & Bazarsky** -222 E Main -Smithtwn 11787 **Fx:**265-6799
(631) 574-4462 .. **Bisca,** Robt A '86 -105 Maxess Rd -Melvll 11747
(212) 766-4700 .. **Biscardi,** Toni J '03 %Katz & R -116 John -NY 10038 **Fx:**766-4705
(212) 451-2300 .. **Bisceglie,** Kyle C '95 (Olshan GFR&W LLP) -65 E 55th -NY 10022
(631) 277-0300 .. **Bisch,** Jos M '97 %Bartlett MB&M,LLP -670 Main -Islip 11751
(716) 630-6500 .. **Bischof,** Dennis J Jr. '90 (DJ Bischof,LLC) -6720 Main -Williamsvll 14221
(212) 867-9120 .. **Bischof,** George L '94 GL Bischof,PLLC -230 Park Av -NY 10169 **Fx:**661-2153
(212) 636-6000 .. **Bischoff,** Christina P '00 %Fordham Univ Sch of Law -140 W 62nd -NY 10023 **Fx:**636-6899
(212) 906-1200 .. **Bischoff,** Senet S '00 %Latham & W -885 3rd Av -NY 10022
(516) 248-4444 .. **Biscone,** Craig G '87 -1399 Franklin Av -Gdn Cty 11530
(518) 756-7333 .. **Biscone,** John T '71 (Biscone & N) -186 Main -Ravena 12143 **Fx:**756-3293
(518) 465-2239 .. **Biscone,** John T '71 (Biscone & N) -311 State -Albany 12210 **Fx:**426-7139
(516) 357-3000 .. **Biscone,** Merril S '88 %Rivkin R LLP -926 RXR Plz -Uniondale 11556
(518) 756-2002 .. **Biscone,** Michl J '75 -151 Main -Ravena 12143 **Fx:**756-3334
(518) 756-7333 .. **Biscone,** Sarah M '01 %Biscone & N -186 Main -Ravena 12143 **Fx:**756-3293
(518) 465-2239 .. **Biscone,** Sarah M '01 %Biscone & N -311 State -Albany 12210 **Fx:**426-7139
(212) 735-3000 .. **Bisek,** Veronica A '99 Cnsl Skadden ASM&F LLP -4 Times Sq -NY 10036
(212) 797-9000 .. **Biser,** Mordechai '97 %Agudath Israel -42 Bway -NY 10004 **Fx:**(646) 254-1650
(212) 609-6800 .. **Biser,** Sarah B '84 (McCarter & E,LLP) -245 Park Av -NY 10167
(631) 577-7770 .. **Bishai,** Sylvia '02 %K Dodson -100 Baylis Rd -Melvll 11747 **Fx:**577-7199
(716) 285-4200 .. **Bishara,** Danl W '56 -2027 Main Bx253 -Niagara Fls 14305
(914) 347-1292 .. **Bishko,** Sherry A '04 %Rosenthal & M,LLP -45 Knollwood Rd -Elmsfrd 10523
(212) 701-3000 .. **Bishoff,** Noah H '07 %Cahill G&R LLP -80 Pine -NY 10005 **Fx:**269-5420
(212) 656-2370 .. **Bishop,** Allison A '88 NYSE -11 Wall -NY 10005
(212) 272-2545 .. **Bishop,** Barbara W '77 %JP Morgan Chase -383 Mad Av -NY 10179
(212) 869-3000 .. **Bishop,** Christopher '83 %Centro US -420 Lex Av -NY 10170 **Fx:**302-4776
(212) 371-6600 .. **Bishop,** David A S '94 (Kirby M LLP) -825 3rd Av -NY 10022
(212) 309-6000 .. **Bishop,** Dennis W '96 %Morgan L&B LLP -101 Park Av -NY 10178
(631) 853-4049 .. **Bishop,** Diana T '86 %Cnty Atty -Dennison Bldg Bx6100 -Hauppauge 11788 **Fx:**853-5169
(631) 288-0440 .. **Bishop,** Hermon J '84 -110 Mill Rd Bx1469 -Westhmptn Bch 11978 **Fx:**288-0468
(607) 746-2271 .. **Bishop & Hill** -120 Main Bx191 -Delhi 13753 **Fx:**746-7407
(212) 490-9100 .. **Bishop,** Kevin J '06 %Condon & F LLP -7 Times Sq -NY 10036
(212) 354-4500 .. **Bishop,** Nathan V '99 (Friedman & W) -1500 Bway -NY 10036
(718) 286-6000 .. **Bishop,** Pamela L '97 %DA -125-01 Qns Blvd -Kew Gdns 11415
(973) 228-5700 .. **Bishop,** Paul M '06 %Brach E LLC -100 Park Av -NY 10017 **Fx:**228-7852
(518) 449-3320 .. **Bishop,** Robt J '76 (Pitta BD&G LLP) -111 Wshngtn Av -Albany 12210
(212) 652-3890 .. **Bishop,** Robt J '76 (Pitta & G LLP) -120 Bway -NY 10271
(914) 682-6866 .. **Bishop,** Scott Marshall '98 -50 Main -White Plns 10606
(718) 520-0413 .. **Bishop,** Wendy '98 %S Siegel -123-12 82nd Av -Kew Gdns 11415 **Fx:**544-7044
(718) 273-4046 .. **Bisignano,** Anthony F III '83 (Bosco B&M) -857 Forest Av -Staten Isl 10310
(646) 267-0518 .. **Bisio,** Gabriel A '02 SrCnsl Diageo NA,Inc -530 5th Av -NY 10036
(212) 969-3000 .. **Biskupska,** Alicja I '08 %Proskauer R LLP -1585 Bway -NY 10036
(718) 828-4517 .. **Bisogno,** Gloria L '94 -1754 Seminole Av -Bronx 10461 **Fx:**828-9091
(718) 745-0880 .. **Bisogno,** Patrick F '90 (Bisogno & M) -7018 Ft Hmltn Pkwy -Brklyn 11228 **Fx:**680-3891
(607) 277-2043 .. **Bissel,** Heather L '06 -119 S Cayuga -Ithaca 14850
(212) 506-1700 .. **Bissell,** Catherine E '07 %Kasowitz BT&F LLP -1633 Bway -NY 10019
(518) 426-4600 .. **Bissell,** Garrett E '05 %Couch W,LLP -540 Bway Bx22222 -Albany 12201
(585) 591-0824 .. **Bissell,** Merlyn E '92 -1600 Clinton St Rd -Attica 14011 **Fx:**591-2346
(914) 328-0068 .. **Bistany,** Chas T '67 -399 Knollwood Rd -White Plns 10603 **Fx:**285-9769
(914) 730-3200 .. **Bitanga,** James '07 %Entwistle & C LLP -200 Business Park Dr -Armonk 10504
(212) 237-1000 .. **Bitar,** John B '02 %Windels ML&M,LLP -156 W 56th -NY 10019
(212) 801-2160 .. **Bitar,** Karen Y '87 (Greenberg T,LLP) -200 Park Av -NY 10166
(585) 546-6435 .. **Bitetti,** Gary '80 -16 E Main -Rchstr 14614 **Fx:**546-4749
(516) 296-7000 .. **Bitetto,** Eileen O'Boyle '95 (Certilman BA&H,LLP) -90 Merrick Av -E Meadow 11554
(212) 922-6000 .. **Bitetto,** James '97 Dreyfus -200 Park Av -NY 10166
(516) 496-3868 .. **Bitetto,** James J '95 (Keusey T&B,PC) -20 Crsswys Park Dr N -Woodbury 11797
(718) 590-2000 .. **Bitetto,** Kristen Shields '06 DA -198 E 161st -Bronx 10451 **Fx:**590-6477
(516) 394-4200 .. **Bithorn,** Edw G '86 Cnsl Duffy & D -1370 RXR Plz -Uniondale 11556
(718) 254-7000 .. **Bitkower,** David M '03 US Atty -271 Cadman Plz E -Brklyn 11201 **Fx:**254-6479

(212) 309-6000 .. **Bitman,** Craig A '97 (Morgan L&B LLP) -101 Park Av -NY 10178
(631) 342-0687 .. **Bitman,** David B '91 D Bitman,PC -1300 Vets Mem'l Hwy -Hauppauge 11788
(212) 527-1000 .. **Biton,** Merav '05 %Jones HC&B PC -1 Bttry Pk Plz -NY 10004
(212) 773-1621 .. **Biton,** Rivi '02 Ernst & Young LLP -5 Times Sq -NY 10036
(631) 234-3030 .. **Bitsimis,** Gina Raio '89 %Davidow DS&S,LLP -1601 Vets Mem'l Hwy -Islandia 11749
(212) 869-5030 .. **Bittens,** Andrew B '98 (Kucker & B,LLP) -747 3rd Av -NY 10017
(518) 792-2117 .. **Bitter,** Stefanie DiLallo '01 (Bartlett PS&R,PC) -1 Wshngtn Bx2168 -Glens Fls 12801
(914) 323-7000 .. **Bitterman,** Aaron '10 %Wilson EME&D LLP -3 Gannett Dr -White Plns 10604
(212) 626-1184 .. **Bittker,** Donald L '70 %Bank Leumi USA -562 5th Av -NY 10036 **Fx:**626-1195
(585) 987-2800 .. **Bittker,** Morton L '60 OfCnsl Woods OG LLP -2 State -Rchstr 14614
(914) 472-3600 .. **Bittlingmaier,** Fred T '83 (Tibaldi & B) -1075 Cntrl Pk Av -Scarsdale 10583 **Fx:**472-8943
(212) 715-1000 .. **Bittman,** Lauren R '06 %Arnold & P LLP -399 Park Av -NY 10022
(212) 223-4000 .. **Bittman,** Scott L '06 %Crowell & M LLP -590 Mad Av -NY 10022
(315) 423-2932 .. **Bittner,** Amy M '94 %Workers Comp Bd -935 James -Syracuse 13203 **Fx:**423-2938
(845) 485-6226 .. **Bittner,** Fredk Jr. '68 -2 Cannon -Poughkeepsie 12601 **Fx:**485-4609
(212) 728-2200 .. **Bitton,** Danl S '05 %Axinn V&H LLP -114 W 47th -NY 10036
(212) 530-3900 .. **Biundo,** Vito A '03 %Hannum FP&M, LLC -55 Bway -NY 10006
(212) 450-4000 .. **Bivens,** Frances E '93 (Davis P&W LLP) -450 Lex Av -NY 10017
(716) 856-5500 .. **Bivona,** Beth Ann '98 (Damon M LLP) -200 Delaware Av -Buffalo 14202
(212) 363-3100 .. **Bivona & Cohen,PC** -88 Pine -NY 10005 **Fx:**363-9824
(212) 363-3100 .. **Bivona,** John V '68 (Bivona & C,PC) -88 Pine -NY 10005
(518) 436-3404 .. **Bixby Crable & Stiglmeier, PLLC** -19 Dove -Albany 12210 **Fx:**426-3204
(518) 436-3404 .. **Bixby,** Robt Hardwick '79 (Bixby C&S,PLLC) -19 Dove -Albany 12210
(212) 761-4000 .. **Bixler,** Amanda M '04 Morgan Stanley -1585 Bway -NY 10036 **Fx:**761-0086
(607) 277-7286 .. **Bixler,** Elizabeth J '72 (Blumkin F&B) -401 E State -Ithaca 14850
(212) 575-7900 .. **Bizar,** Irving '57 (Ballon SB&N,PC) -729 7th Av -NY 10019
(716) 881-5800 .. **Bizub,** Scott J '07 %Siegel K&K -426 Franklin -Buffalo 14202
(516) 294-8844 .. **Bizzaro,** Matthew J '04 %L'Abbate BC&C,LLP -1001 Franklin Av -Gdn Cty 11530
(516) 296-7000 .. **Bizzaro,** Thos A '00 %Certilman BA&H,LLP -90 Merrick Av -E Meadow 11554
(718) 833-8246 .. **Bizzarro,** C Laurie '02 -100 Marine Av -Brklyn 11209 **Fx:**680-6807
(631) 853-4049 .. **Bizzarro,** Lynne Anne '88 %Cnty Atty -Dennison Bldg Bx6100 -Hauppauge 11788 **Fx:**853-5169
(212) 889-1196 .. **Bizzell,** Kinchen C '77 -71 Park Av -NY 10016
(212) 643-1153 .. **Bizzoco,** Domenica '81 -350 5th Av -NY 10118 **Fx:**465-9104
(212) 259-8000 .. **Bjarnson,** Jos R '10 %Dewey & L LLP -1301 Av of Amer -NY 10019
(212) 733-1768 .. **Bjegovic,** Sandra '08 Pfizer,Inc -150 E 42nd -NY 10017
(212) 225-2000 .. **Bjerke,** Alina G '04 %Cleary GS&H -1 Lbrty Plz -NY 10006
(212) 450-4000 .. **Bjerke,** Bjorn '01 (Davis P&W LLP) -450 Lex Av -NY 10017
(917) 637-3600 .. **Bjerregaard,** Alisha S '09 %Ctr for Reproductive Rts -120 Wall -NY 10005 **Fx:**637-3666
(212) 751-3001 .. **Bjorck,** Dorothy Heisner '98 (Thompson & K LLP) -919 3rd Av -NY 10022
(716) 852-5211 .. **Bjork,** Mary Audi '79 -350 Main -Buffalo 14202 **Fx:**852-8149
(518) 456-5249 .. **Bjork,** Mary Audi '79 -500 New Karner Rd -Albany 12205 **Fx:**456-1288
(914) 366-5700 .. **Bjork,** Mary Audi '79 -660 Wht Plns Rd -Tarrytwn 10591 **Fx:**366-5759
(315) 445-8670 .. **Bjork,** Mary Audi '79 -5784 Widewaters Pkwy -DeWitt 13214 **Fx:**445-8688
(845) 695-6811 .. **Bjork,** Mary Audi '79 -100 Crystal Run Rd -Middletwn 10941 **Fx:**695-6818
(585) 454-3616 .. **Bjork,** Mary Audi '79 -2 State -Rchstr 14614 **Fx:**454-3664
(716) 569-2481 .. **Bjork,** Sherry Ann '96 -Bx492 -Frewsburg 14738
(516) 627-6512 .. **Bjorklund,** J Hank '81 -27 Colonial Dr -Manhsst 11030
(212) 455-2000 .. **Bjorklund,** Victoria Baum '84 (Simpson T&B LLP) -425 Lex Av -NY 10017
(212) 807-7338 .. **Bjorkman,** James J '87 -10 W 15th -NY 10011 **Fx:**(708) 585-3867
(516) 571-9362 .. **Bjorneby,** Eric '74 Hon K Diamond -1200 Old Cntry Rd -Westbury 11590
(716) 439-7085 .. **Bjornholm,** Susan B '00 %DA -175 Hawley -Lockprt 14094 **Fx:**439-7102
(518) 429-4200 .. **Blabey,** David E '68 OfCnsl Hiscock & B,LLP -50 Beaver -Albany 12207
(212) 715-9100 .. **Blabey,** David E Jr. '05 %Kramer LN&F,LLP -1177 Av of Amer -NY 10036
(212) 259-8000 .. **Blabey,** Virginia A '06 %Dewey & L LLP -1301 Av of Amer -NY 10019
(516) 227-5380 .. **Blachor,** Isaac '64 -1565 Franklin Av -Mineola 11501
(718) 858-8675 .. **Black,** Andrew S '79 (Gelb & B) -26 Court -Brklyn 11201 **Fx:**858-7342
(212) 935-3131 .. **Black,** Barry '98 (Gallet D&B,LLP) -845 3rd Av -NY 10022
(718) 466-3000 .. **Black,** Bernadette G '94 %Civil Ct -1118 Grnd Cncrs -Bronx 10456 **Fx:**466-3006
(631) 462-5200 .. **Black,** Bronwyn M '86 (Black & B) -145 Pinelawn Rd -Melvll 11747 **Fx:**462-5221
(631) 715-7800 .. **Black,** Christine H '81 %US Trustees Ofc -560 Fed Plz -Central Islip 11722 **Fx:**715-7777
(212) 768-6700 .. **Black,** Claire Wong '07 %Sonnenschein N&R LLP -1221 Av of Amer -NY 10020
(212) 825-1080 .. **Black,** Courtney E '07 %Bonjean Law Grp,PLLC -119 W 23rd -NY 10011 **Fx:**529-0644
(585) 340-2962 .. **Black,** D Eric '97 Paetec Comm -600 Wllwbrk Ofc Pk -Fairprt 14450
(212) 661-5030 .. **Black,** David '97 %Schoeman U&K,LLP -60 E 42nd -NY 10165
(716) 645-2982 .. **Black,** Dennis R '82 %SUNY -542 Capen Hall -Buffalo 14260 **Fx:**645-5966
(631) 462-5200 .. **Black,** Edwin F '81 (Black & B) -145 Pinelawn Rd -Melvll 11747 **Fx:**462-5221
(212) 732-3200 .. **Black,** Elizabeth C '09 %Carter L&M LLP -2 Wall -NY 10005
(631) 462-5200 .. **Black,** Gregory A '88 %Black & B -145 Pinelawn Rd -Melvll 11747 **Fx:**462-5221
(914) 285-9800 .. **Black,** Gregory Kevin '99 %Kurzman EC&L,LLP -1 N Bway -White Plns 10601
(646) 654-5069 .. **Black,** Harris '88 %VNU USA -770 Bway -NY 10003
(212) 558-4000 .. **Black,** James I III '77 (Sullivan & C LLP) -125 Broad -NY 10004
(516) 496-1825 .. **Black,** James M II '87 OMSC -175 Crsswys Park Dr W -Woodbury 11797
(716) 373-1920 .. **Black,** Jeffrey A '94 (Dwyer B&L,LLP) -1616 W State Bx648 -Olean 14760
(212) 880-3800 .. **Black,** Jerry B '66 (Akerman S) -335 Mad Av -NY 10017
(607) 754-6086 .. **Black,** John A '71 -2309 North -Endicott 13760 **Fx:**754-0767
(315) 448-8400 .. **Black,** John C Jr. '78 Law Dept -233 E Wshngtn -Syracuse 13202 **Fx:**448-8381
(518) 436-0751 .. **Black,** John F '75 (Hinman S PC) -121 State -Albany 12207
(516) 522-2873 .. **Black,** Keith D '07 -626 RXR Plz -Uniondale 11556
(914) 347-2600 .. **Black,** Lisa J '99 (Traub LS&S LLP) -7 Skyline Dr -Hawthorne 10532
(917) 656-6263 .. **Black,** Louis E '72 -350 5th Av -NY 10118
(212) 596-9000 .. **Black,** Matthew E '10 %Ropes & G LLP -1211 Av of Amer -NY 10036
(914) 682-7800 .. **Black,** Meredith '05 %Zarin & S -81 Main -White Plns 10601
(212) 297-9090 .. **Black,** Michl Ian '68 -270 Mad Av -NY 10016 **Fx:**297-0527
(212) 355-3550 .. **Black,** Noble B '02 Corcoran Grp -660 Mad Av -NY 10065
(212) 918-3000 .. **Black,** R Brian '04 (Hogan L LLP) -875 3rd Av -NY 10022
(212) 705-7000 .. **Black,** R Jeffrey '08 %Bingham M LLP -399 Park Av -NY 10022
(716) 835-2492 .. **Black,** Robt C '03 -3500 Main -Amherst 14226
(646) 442-3100 .. **Black,** Rosalind '98 %Legal Srvcs -90 John -NY 10038 **Fx:**(212) 227-9798
(631) 784-7820 .. **Black,** Scott B '98 (Jones & B,PC) -23 Green -Huntngtn 11743 **Fx:**784-7821
(212) 336-0029 .. **Black,** Scott L '96 %SEC -3 World Fncl Ctr -NY 10281 **Fx:**336-1323
(845) 566-4400 .. **Black,** Scott T '04 %D Kenny,PC -288 N Plnk Rd -Newburgh 12550
(716) 631-4844 .. **Black,** Sharon L '03 -5813 Main -Williamsvll 14221
(516) 466-3033 .. **Black,** Walter '60 -98 Cuttermill Rd -Gt Neck 11021 **Fx:**487-1803
(212) 527-5531 .. **Blackburn,** Julie M '90 %Revlon -237 Park Av -NY 10017 **Fx:**527-5299
(212) 408-5100 .. **Blackburn,** Marcelo M '05 %Chadbourne & P LLP -30 Rckfllr Plz -NY 10112
(212) 336-1050 .. **Blackburn,** Robt B '72 %SEC -3 World Fncl Ctr -NY 10281 **Fx:**336-1323
(845) 398-5725 .. **Blackburn,** Robt E '71 Union State Bank -100 Dutch Hill Rd -Orangebrg 10962
(212) 218-5500 .. **Blackiston,** Henry C III '68 (Seyfarth S LLP) -620 8th Av -NY 10018
(716) 433-8539 .. **Blackley,** David E '95 -Bx443 -Lockprt 14095
(212) 309-1000 .. **Blacklocks,** Stephen R '93 (Hunton & W) -200 Park Av -NY 10166
(212) 225-2000 .. **Blacklow,** Kimberly R '95 (Cleary GS&H) -1 Lbrty Plz -NY 10006
(212) 859-8000 .. **Blackman,** Amy Loren '04 %Fried FHS&J LLP -1 NY Plz -NY 10004
(212) 336-2000 .. **Blackman,** Burke A H '09 %Patterson BW&T LLP -1133 Av of Amer -NY 10036
(212) 964-6611 .. **Blackman,** Christopher A '04 %Lester SK&D -120 Bway -NY 10271
(718) 590-3494 .. **Blackman,** Duane G '07 %Law Dept -198 E 161st -Bronx 10451 **Fx:**590-2686
(212) 430-6537 .. **Blackman,** Gregory A '00 -65 Bway -NY 10006
(718) 499-6030 .. **Blackman,** Joshua D '93 Legal Options, Inc -123 7th Av -Brklyn 11215
(212) 309-6000 .. **Blackman,** Joshua R '03 %Morgan L&B LLP -101 Park Av -NY 10178
(212) 909-6000 .. **Blackman,** Keith E '02 %Debevoise & P LLP -919 3rd Av -NY 10022
(212) 859-8000 .. **Blackman,** Kenneth R '66 OfCnsl Fried FHS&J LLP -1 NY Plz -NY 10004
(212) 791-2530 .. **Blackman,** Laura A '90 %Hudson River Park Trust -Pier 40 - W Houston & West -NY 10014
(646) 386-5700 .. **Blackman,** Lauren Ann '95 %Civil Ct -111 Centre -NY 10013
(212) 832-8500 .. **Blackman,** Martin '50 (Bergreen & B) -31 W 52nd -NY 10019 **Fx:**593-6241
(646) 610-6352 .. **Blackman,** Michelle L '00 NYPD-Advocates Dept -1 Police Plz -NY 10038
(718) 576-1646 .. **Blackman,** Nigel E '05 (N Blackman PC) -172-29 Brocher Rd -Jamaica 11434
(718) 237-2753 .. **Blackman,** Robt I '51 -1 Tiffany Pl -Brklyn 11231 **Fx:**858-3155
(212) 878-8000 .. **Blackman,** Sarah '07 %Clifford C LLP -31 W 52nd -NY 10019
(718) 222-8880 .. **Blackmer,** Ryan F '05 %Jones JO -45 Main -Brklyn 11201
(845) 331-2725 .. **Blackmon,** Dana D '05 -1 N Front -Kingston 12401 **Fx:**338-0868
(716) 636-7600 .. **Blackmon,** David H '98 %HoganWillig -2410 N Forest Rd -Amherst 14068
(518) 465-3484 .. **Blackmore,** James C '69 (Carter CCBM&L,PC) -20 Corp Wds Blvd -Albany 12211
(718) 243-4186 .. **Black-Pennington,** Dale A '90 %Transit Auth -370 Jay -Brklyn 11201
(212) 776-5019 .. **Blackstock,** Mindy M '93 NYC Housing Auth -250 Bway -NY 10007 **Fx:**776-5159
(212) 268-1000 .. **Blackstone,** Laureve D '07 %Broach & S,LLP -1 Penn Plz -NY 10119
(212) 632-5500 .. **Blackwell,** Christopher A '06 %Salans LLP -620 5th Av -NY 10020
(518) 402-6969 .. **Blackwell,** Judith A '84 Envrnmtl Facilities -625 Bway -Albany 12207 **Fx:**402-6972
(516) 560-6400 .. **Blackwood,** Monique S '06 %Leg Aid -1 Helen Keller Way -Hempstd 11550 **Fx:**565-3694
(212) 902-1000 .. **Blades,** Alexander B '98 %Goldman Sachs -1 NY Plz -NY 10004
(845) 382-1200 .. **Blades,** J Lawr '73 %Healthcare Assoc -24 Lohmaier Ln -Lk Katrine 12449
(718) 538-3151 .. **Blades,** Lisa Y '02 -176-25 Union Tpk #245 -Fresh Mdws 11366 **Fx:**341-5656
(212) 715-9100 .. **Blades,** Melissa S '05 %Kramer LN&F,LLP -1177 Av of Amer -NY 10036

(212) 355-5575 .. **Blaeser**, Alycia K '06 %Smith & N,LLP -363 7th Av -NY 10001 **Fx:**486-3150
(212) 530-4838 .. **Blaha**, Eric P '94 (LaRocca HRG&B LLP) -40 Wall -NY 10005
(845) 486-6800 .. **Blahut**, Rebecca Mayfield '02 %McCabe & M LLP -63 Wshngtn Bx509 -Poughkeepsie 12602
(212) 213-6996 .. **Blain**, J Ellen E '05 %Spears & I LLP -51 Mad Av -NY 10010
(212) 768-3333 .. **Blaine**, Alison I '98 OfCnsl MI Asen,PC -260 Mad Av -NY 10016 **Fx:**768-1323
(518) 487-5460 .. **Blain-Lewis**, Jessica E '06 %DA -6 Lodge -Albany 12207 **Fx:**487-5093
(212) 295-6369 .. **Blair**, Arnold G III '03 WilmerHale -399 Park Av -NY 10022
(212) 819-8200 .. **Blair**, Clifford F '08 %White & C LLP -1155 Av of Amer -NY 10036
(212) 319-4000 .. **Blair**, Elliot S '61 -600 Mad Av -NY 10022
(212) 697-7207 .. **Blair**, Harry F '63 %Creative Hlth Cncpts -305 Mad Av -NY 10165
(212) 478-0553 .. **Blair**, Hilda R '98 DE Shaw & Co LP -120 W 45th -NY 10036
(914) 762-2379 .. **Blair**, James F '72 -139 Cedar Ln -Ossining 10562
(212) 455-0326 .. **Blair**, James N '71 OfCnsl Snow BK,PC -605 3rd Av -NY 10158
(212) 655-3500 .. **Blair**, Jeanette R '03 %Meister S&F LLP -140 E 45th -NY 10017
(212) 879-5500 .. **Blair**, Jeffrey N '99 %Metropolitan Museum -1000 5th Av -NY 10028 **Fx:**570-3850
(716) 834-9181 .. **Blair**, Jeffrey T '07 Blair & R,LLP -2645 Sheridan Dr -Tonawanda 14150
(716) 834-9181 .. **Blair**, John N '73 (Blair & R,LLP) -2645 Sheridan Dr -Tonawanda 14150
(212) 536-3900 .. **Blair**, Koren B '83 (K&L Gates LLP) -599 Lex Av -NY 10022
(212) 355-8555 .. **Blair**, Lauren H '89 Cnsl Potters & D LLP -546 5th Av -NY 10036
(917) 734-8662 .. **Blair**, Margo '09 -201 W 92nd -NY 10025
(212) 909-6000 .. **Blair**, Michl W '82 (Debevoise & P LLP) -919 3rd Av -NY 10022
(212) 354-0020 .. **Blair**, Noel '93 (Blair & Assoc) -1501 Bway -NY 10036 **Fx:**354-1343
(917) 282-8816 .. **Blair**, Norman '05 %Baker & Henderson Inc -Bx556 -NY 10163
(585) 546-1980 .. **Blair**, Patricia Ann '97 Fulton F&G LLP -28 E Main -Rchstr 14614
(631) 363-8600 .. **Blair**, Patricia Byrne '90 (Mazzei & B) -9B Montauk Hwy -Blue Pnt 11715
(716) 834-9181 .. **Blair & Roach, LLP** -2645 Sheridan Dr -Tonawanda 14150 **Fx:**834-9197
(315) 685-9900 .. **Blair**, Thos M '01 (Cheney & B LLP) -3895 Fennell -Skaneateles 13152 **Fx:**685-9910
(212) 637-2627 .. **Blais**, Brian R '09 %US Atty -1 St Andrews Plz -NY 10007
(607) 272-5212 .. **Blaise**, Oliver N III '98 (Coughlin & G,LLP) -401 E State -Ithaca 14850
(607) 723-9511 .. **Blaise**, Oliver N III '98 (Coughlin & G,LLP) -19 Chenango Bx2039 -Bnghmtn 13902
(212) 949-7500 .. **Blaivas**, David G '88 (Sasson B LLP) -1350 Bway -NY 10018 **Fx:**949-7502
(212) 772-3900 .. **Blaivas**, Kimberly '98 Euro Center of NY -445 E 77th -NY 10075
(718) 250-2000 .. **Blake**, Ayanna T '06 DA -350 Jay -Brklyn 11201 **Fx:**250-2314
(347) 404-9133 .. **Blake**, Diane '86 %Civil Ct -141 Lvngstn -Brklyn 11201 **Fx:**(718) 643-3733
(845) 471-4455 .. **Blake**, Janet W '86 %Steinberg S&P,LLP -27 Grdn -Poughkeepsie 12601
(516) 803-4811 .. **Blake**, Jerome D '93 Rainbow Media Holdings -200 Jericho Quad -Jericho 11753
(516) 627-2015 .. **Blake**, Jos P Jr. '67 -55 Revere Rd -Manhsst 11030
(212) 556-3906 .. **Blake**, Juliette L '86 %The NY Times Co -620 8th Av -NY 10018 **Fx:**556-4634
(518) 402-2373 .. **Blake**, Kathryn J '93 %Dept of Law -The Cptl -Albany 12224 **Fx:**408-2057
(518) 377-2225 .. **Blake**, Lynn M '87 (Friedman H&M,LLP) -100 Great Oaks Blvd Bx38279 -Albany 12203
(914) 472-2300 .. **Blake**, Marcy '94 %Jones G,LLP -670 Wht Plns Rd -Scarsdale 10583
(718) 546-0950 .. **Blake**, Martha-Ibis '92 Dept of Correction -75-20 Astoria Blvd -E Elmhrst 11370
(212) 458-6162 .. **Blake**, Maxine '81 AIG -175 Water -NY 10038
(631) 874-4100 .. **Blake**, Patricia M '84 (P Blake,PC) -451 Montauk Hwy -E Moriches 11940
(347) 462-9900 .. **Blake**, Sonia V '97 %Shapiro & S,LLP -3145 Coney Isl Av -Brklyn 11235
(718) 237-2000 .. **Blakeley**, Chas H '78 %Leg Aid -111 Lvngstn -Brklyn 11201 **Fx:**237-8737
(516) 328-2300 .. **Blakeman**, Bruce A '84 (Abrams FFEGF&E,LLP) -1111 Marcus Av -Lk Success 11042
(212) 336-2000 .. **Blakeman**, Janet L '58 Cnsl Patterson BW&T LLP -1133 Av of Amer -NY 10036
(212) 683-6383 .. **Blakeman**, Richd R '74 (Gersen B&A LLP) -270 Mad Av -NY 10016
(516) 825-7575 .. **Blakeman**, Robt M '49 -108 S Franklin Av -Vly Stream 11580 **Fx:**825-7249
(516) 825-7590 .. **Blakeman**, Royal E '47 -108 S Franklin Av -Vly Stream 11580 **Fx:**825-7249
(212) 984-1677 .. **Blaker**, Richd H '74 Case Pomeroy & Co -521 5th Av -NY 10175
(631) 852-2500 .. **Blakey**, Michl H '85 %DA -200 Center Dr -Rvrhead 11901 **Fx:**852-1769
(212) 564-5005 .. **Blanaru**, Mirela G '04 L Kucherovsky -212 W 35th -NY 10001 **Fx:**564-5121
(212) 788-9087 .. **Blanc**, Diane E '88 NYC Cncl-Human Srvcs -250 Bway -NY 10007
(212) 728-8000 .. **Blanc**, Roger D '71 (Willkie F&G LLP) -787 7th Av -NY 10019
(914) 332-5723 .. **Blancato**, Richd T '69 -65 S Bway -Tarrytwn 10591 **Fx:**332-5725
(212) 422-0202 .. **Blancett**, John W '80 (Sedgwick DM&A LLP) -125 Broad -NY 10004
(212) 668-0340 .. **Blanch**, Marianna '02 %Ambac Assurance -1 State Street Plz -NY 10004 **Fx:**785-1178
(212) 736-9721 .. **Blanch**, Ryan G '00 (R Blanch,PC) -350 5th Av -NY 10118
(212) 909-6000 .. **Blanchard**, A Elliott '05 %Debevoise & P LLP -919 3rd Av -NY 10022
(212) 891-1430 .. **Blanchard**, Avital K '08 Amer Jewish Comm -165 E 56th -NY 10022 **Fx:**891-1495
(212) 349-9090 .. **Blanchard**, Deborah Grant '02 Ctr for Seafarers Rights -241 Water -NY 10038
(212) 259-8000 .. **Blanchard**, Eric W '00 (Dewey & L LLP) -1301 Av of Amer -NY 10019
(212) 336-2000 .. **Blanchard**, Hal E '06 Patterson BW&T LLP -1133 Av of Amer -NY 10036
(212) 310-8000 .. **Blanchard**, Kimberly S '82 (Weil G&M LLP) -767 5th Av -NY 10153
(914) 377-6240 .. **Blanchard**, Mark W '04 Law Dept -300 City Hall -Ynkrs 10701 **Fx:**964-0563
(718) 590-2000 .. **Blanchard**, Mary Jo L '99 %DA -198 E 161st -Bronx 10451 **Fx:**590-6477
(716) 634-0500 .. **Blanchard**, Robyn L '01 %Ballow Law Firm -8226 Main -Williamsvll 14221 **Fx:**634-9075
(315) 422-8284 .. **Blanchard**, Thos J '89 %Metro Dvlpmnt Assn -1900 State Twr Bldg -Syracuse 13202
(212) 345-5610 .. **Blanchard**, Wm A '72 %Marsh USA -1166 Av of Amer -NY 10036 **Fx:**345-4808
(212) 637-2494 .. **Blanche**, Todd W '04 %US Atty -1 St Andrews Plz -NY 10007
(212) 446-4800 .. **Blanchet**, Joel A '08 (Kirkland & E LLP) -153 E 53rd -NY 10022
(212) 416-8595 .. **Blanchette**, Antoinette W '98 %Dept of Law -120 Bway -NY 10271
(518) 268-1916 .. **Blanchfield**, Mark W '95 OfCnsl D Coffey -119 Wshngtn Av -Albany 12210 **Fx:**207-1916
(518) 447-7150 .. **Blanchfield**, Peter J '93 %Pub Def -60 S Pearl -Albany 12207 **Fx:**447-5533
(212) 489-1600 .. **Blanchini**, Patricia '99 %Deloitte LLP -1633 Bway -NY 10019 **Fx:**492-4201
(212) 236-3112 .. **Blanco**, Bruce E '85 %Merrill Lynch -225 Lbrty -NY 10080
(212) 906-1200 .. **Blanco**, Heather E '09 %Latham & W -885 3rd Av -NY 10022
(212) 909-6000 .. **Blanco**, Lindsay K '02 %Debevoise & P LLP -919 3rd Av -NY 10022
(212) 696-6000 .. **Blanco**, Marco '84 (Curtis M-PC&M LLP) -101 Park Av -NY 10178
(212) 450-4000 .. **Blanco**, Maurice '02 (Davis P&W LLP) -450 Lex Av -NY 10017
(212) 909-6000 .. **Blanco**, Vivian M '04 %Debevoise & P LLP -919 3rd Av -NY 10022
(212) 431-5576 .. **Bland**, Eric M '92 (Siskind SB) -430 W 14th -NY 10014
(212) 705-7000 .. **Bland**, J Goodwin '88 (Bingham M LLP) -399 Park Av -NY 10022
(716) 854-6424 .. **Bland**, Kevin John '02 %K Ricotta -350 Main -Buffalo 14202 **Fx:**854-6425
(646) 366-5014 .. **Bland**, Marushka A '08 Practical Law Co,Inc -747 3rd Av -NY 10017
(718) 585-7668 .. **Bland**, Sharol A '97 -362 E 137th -Bronx 10454
(212) 685-7600 .. **Blander**, Stuart A '80 (Heller H&F,PC) -292 Mad Av -NY 10017
(315) 735-3556 .. **Blando**, Frank E '70 -811 Court -Utica 13502
(212) 682-5702 .. **Blane**, Roger S '88 %Hutton & S -475 5th Av -NY 10017
(212) 808-0700 .. **Blaney**, Bryan '88 (Norris M&M,PA) -875 3rd Av -NY 10022
(212) 616-5400 .. **Blaney**, Catherine A '92 -150 Bway -NY 10038
(347) 418-4253 .. **Blaney**, James B '87 British Airways -75-20 Astoria Blvd -Jcksn Hts 11370 **Fx:**418-4204
(212) 223-3900 .. **Blaney**, Natalie T '84 -1185 Park Av -NY 10128
(516) 844-8810 .. **Blank**, Adam S '97 Cnsl Sleepys Inc -1000 S Oyster Bay Rd -Hicksvll 11801
(212) 925-4475 .. **Blank**, Allan A '77 (Blank G&D) -111 John -NY 10038
(718) 965-0860 .. **Blank**, Bette Folkenflik '78 -257 6th Av -Brklyn 11215
(585) 295-4400 .. **Blank**, Christopher E '87 (Hiscock & B,LLP) -2000 HSBC Plz -Rchstr 14604
(718) 250-2000 .. **Blank**, Christopher P '85 %DA -350 Jay -Brklyn 11201 **Fx:**250-2314
(212) 752-5258 .. **Blank**, David L '98 (Schwartz SE&C LLC) -845 3rd Av -NY 10022
(212) 792-8484 .. **Blank**, Ellen I '87 %Stern T&B LLP -380 Lex Av -NY 10168
(212) 925-4475 .. **Blank Goolnick & Dittenhoefer** -111 John -NY 10038 **Fx:**925-2935
(718) 498-3333 .. **Blank**, Helene E '78 (Blank & S) -387 New Lots Av -Brklyn 11207 **Fx:**498-4715
(212) 836-8000 .. **Blank**, James S '93 (Kaye S LLP) -425 Park Av -NY 10022
(718) 260-8700 .. **Blank**, Jane S '88 %Admin Children's Srvcs -345 Adams -Brklyn 11201
(718) 802-2647 .. **Blank**, Jeffrey S '06 %Admin Children's Srvcs -330 Jay -Brklyn 11201
(212) 530-1800 .. **Blank**, Jonas L '05 %Richards K&O LLP -1 World Fncl Ctr -NY 10281
(212) 998-6271 .. **Blank**, Joshua D '03 NYU Schl of Law -40 Wshngtn Sq S -NY 10012
(212) 463-2099 .. **Blank**, Joshua T '07 Saatchi & Saatchi -375 Hudson -NY 10014
(212) 275-4736 .. **Blank**, Kristy '05 Warner Music Grp -75 Rckfllr Plz -NY 10019
(212) 794-5347 .. **Blank**, Laura B '74 %CUNY -535 E 80th -NY 10075 **Fx:**794-5667
(315) 538-8026 .. **Blank**, Lynne M '02 Blank Patent -Bx613 -Macedon 14502
(212) 837-6815 .. **Blank**, Rebecca L '10 %Hughes H&R LLP -1 Bttry Pk Plz -NY 10004 **Fx:**299-6815
(212) 353-0446 .. **Blank**, Richd M '95 -123 5th Av -NY 10003
(212) 885-5000 .. **Blank Rome LLP** -405 Lex Av -NY 10174 **Fx:**885-5001
(212) 831-3440 .. **Blank**, Stephen Paul '72 (SP Blank,PC) -360 E 72nd -NY 10021
(585) 419-4070 .. **Blank**, Thos W '74 HHC,LLC -400 Linden Oaks Office Pk -Rchstr 14625 **Fx:**419-4010
(212) 471-6726 .. **Blanke**, Todd A '05 BNP Paribas -787 7th Av -NY 10019
(914) 273-0777 .. **Blank-Ecker**, Tammi L '87 (Ecker E & Assoc LLP) -80 Business Park Dr -Armonk 10504 **Fx:**273-1787
(716) 843-8300 .. **Blankenberg**, Kelly S '07 US Customs & Border Protection -726 Exchange -Buffalo 14210
(646) 223-4200 .. **Blankenship**, Carolyn H '90 %Reuters -3 Times Sq -NY 10036 **Fx:**223-4250
(914) 741-0382 .. **Blankenship**, John G '90 -98 Sunnyside Av -Plsntvll 10570
(212) 848-4000 .. **Blankenship**, Michl J '09 %Shearman & S LLP -599 Lex Av -NY 10022
(516) 676-4437 .. **Blankfein**, Richd S '64 -11 Lincoln Av -Glen Head 11545 **Fx:**676-4030
(212) 940-8800 .. **Blankley**, Adrienne Woods '05 %Katten MR LLP -575 Mad Av -NY 10022
(631) 757-1262 .. **Blankman**, Steven C '85 -30 Jericho Tpk -Commack 11725
(585) 263-1000 .. **Blankopf**, Marion '86 Cnsl Nixon P LLP -1100 Clinton Sq -Rchstr 14604
(516) 745-1800 .. **Blankowitz**, Vilma '99 %Besen & T,LLP -825 E Gate Blvd -Gdn Cty 11530
(212) 259-8000 .. **Blankrot**, Orit B '08 %Dewey & L LLP -1301 Av of Amer -NY 10019
(516) 334-1100 .. **Blankstein**, Jeffrey L '86 -400 Post Av -Westbury 11590 **Fx:**334-4954
(516) 571-3800 .. **Blanshaft**, Stacey S '95 %DA -262 Old Cntry Rd -Mineola 11501 **Fx:**248-9479
(516) 826-6500 .. **Blansky**, David A '98 (LaMonica H&M LLP) -3305 Jerusalem Av -Wantagh 11793

(516) 496-5822 .. **Blansky,** Stacey R '99 %T Spina -170 Froehlich Farm Blvd -Woodbury 11797 **Fx:**496-5420
(212) 684-7920 .. **Blant,** Ian L '83 -475 Park Av S -NY 10016
(585) 704-9241 .. **Blanton,** Andrew '03 SEIU 200 United -1150 Univ Av -Rchstr 14607
(212) 448-1100 .. **Blasband,** David '62 (McLaughlin & S,LLP) -260 Mad Av -NY 10016
(516) 747-0300 .. **Blasberg,** Jason K '99 Cnsl Meltzer LG&B,LLP -190 Willis Av -Mineola 11501
(516) 747-0300 .. **Blasberg,** Laura R '97 OfCnsl Meltzer LG&B,LLP -190 Willis Av -Mineola 11501
(516) 229-4400 .. **Blascetta,** Margaret G '01 %Kay & G -875 Merrick Av -Westbury 11590
(607) 842-6189 .. **Blasdell,** Regina L '98 -6320 Academy -Truxton 13158 **Fx:**842-6189
(212) 756-2000 .. **Blase,** Kristie M '07 %Schulte R&Z LLP -919 3rd Av -NY 10022
(212) 446-4800 .. **Blasenheim,** Itay '06 %Kirkland & E LLP -153 E 53rd -NY 10022
(212) 318-6000 .. **Blaser,** Danl B '07 %Paul HJ&W LLP -75 E 55th -NY 10022
(212) 777-4755 .. **Blash,** Justin S '96 Blash Firm,PLLC -280 Mad Av -NY 10016 **Fx:**(917) 595-5313
(212) 407-4000 .. **Blasi,** Gregory J '77 (Loeb & L,LLP) -345 Park Av -NY 10154
(315) 425-9000 .. **Blasiak,** George S '94 (Marjama MB&S LLP) -250 S Clinton -Syracuse 13202
(716) 664-2346 .. **Blasius,** Myra Vignovic '94 %Lundberg & G,LLP -202 W 4th -Jamestwn 14701
(212) 267-1650 .. **Blask,** Jordan S '05 %Fine O&A,LLP -39 Bway -NY 10006
(631) 854-9933 .. **Blass,** Gregory J '75 Cnty Dept Social Srvcs -Bx18100 -Hauppauge 11788 **Fx:**854-9996
(845) 639-7800 .. **Blass,** Ilana B '04 %Mandel K&B,LLP -210 Route 303 -Vly Cottage 10989
(212) 465-1718 .. **Blass,** Jonathan A '87 (Adler B&B) -89 5th Av -NY 10003 **Fx:**629-4005
(212) 484-3900 .. **Blass,** Michl S '80 (Arent F LLP) -1675 Bway -NY 10019
(212) 465-1718 .. **Blass,** Norman '53 (Adler B&B) -89 5th Av -NY 10003 **Fx:**629-4005
(845) 452-5900 .. **Blass,** Ronald C Jr. '79 (Van DeWater & V,LLP) -85 Civic Ctr Plz Bx112 -Poughkeepsie 12602
(212) 909-6000 .. **Blassberg,** Franci J '78 (Debevoise & P LLP) -919 3rd Av -NY 10022
(212) 790-0200 .. **Blasser,** Jennifer R '99 Benj N Cardozo Schl of Law -55 5th Av -NY 10003 **Fx:**790-0345
(718) 722-4545 .. **Blassman,** Angela M '87 %PERB -55 Hanson Pl -Brklyn 11217 **Fx:**722-4550
(518) 402-6757 .. **Blassman,** George A '81 %Workers Comp Bd -20 Park -Albany 12207
(631) 447-6500 .. **Blaszcyk,** Theo W '90 (Gilbert B&M,LLP) -440 Waverly Av -Patchogue 11772
(212) 554-1400 .. **Blatchley,** Michl D '10 %Bernstein LB&G LLP -1285 Av of Amer -NY 10019
(518) 565-4770 .. **Blatchley,** Timothy G '02 %DA -137 Margaret -Plattsbrgh 12901 **Fx:**565-4777
(845) 255-4600 .. **Blatchly,** Bruce D '77 (Blatchly & S,PC) -3 Academy Bx280 -New Paltz 12561
(845) 255-4600 .. **Blatchly & Simonson,PC** -3 Academy Bx280 -New Paltz 12561 **Fx:**255-2627
(212) 468-8000 .. **Blatnik,** EJW '00 %Morrison & F LLP -1290 Av of Amer -NY 10104
(845) 638-0660 .. **Blatt,** Arnold W '59 -120-126 N Main -New Cty 10956 **Fx:**634-0223
(212) 675-3699 .. **Blatt,** David '02 D Blatt,PLLC -119 W 23rd -NY 10011 **Fx:**675-8078
(212) 599-8000 .. **Blatt,** Jason M '02 Fincl Fed Credit Inc -730 3rd Av -NY 10017 **Fx:**286-5885
(845) 708-8700 .. **Blatt & Koppelman,PC** -151 N Main -New Cty 10956 **Fx:**708-8811
(718) 624-8633 .. **Blatt,** Mindy L '82 -189 Montague -Brklyn 11201 **Fx:**404-9810
(718) 225-5046 .. **Blatt,** Richd L '88 Parkoff Mgt -98 Cuttermill Rd -Gt Neck 11021
(516) 873-3000 .. **Blatt,** Steven H '89 %Bellavia G & Assoc,LLP -200 Old Cntry Rd -Mineola 11501 **Fx:**873-9032
(347) 418-3830 .. **Blattberg,** Chas P '02 %L Miles -36-01 43rd Av -LIC 11101 **Fx:**418-3838
(516) 505-5948 .. **Blatteis,** Michl H '67 -424 Grdn -E Meadow 11554 **Fx:**505-5951
(718) 461-6633 .. **Blatti,** Nicholas G '10 Mallilo & G -163-09 Nrthrn Blvd -Flushng 11358
(212) 756-2000 .. **Blattmachr,** Jonathan D '09 %Schulte R&Z LLP -919 3rd Av -NY 10022
(212) 903-9000 .. **Blatz,** Jessica T '04 %Linklaters -1345 Av of Amer -NY 10105
(212) 605-0423 .. **Blau,** Andrea F '07 A Blau & Assoc -575 Mad Av -NY 10022
(212) 450-4000 .. **Blau,** Andrew G '04 %Davis P&W LLP -450 Lex Av -NY 10017
(212) 521-5400 .. **Blau,** Craig '97 (Reed S LLP) -599 Lex Av -NY 10022
(212) 407-7700 .. **Blau,** Denise L '78 (Vedder P,PC) -1633 Bway -NY 10019
(518) 439-5956 .. **Blau,** Joel '75 -32 Windsor Ct -Delmar 12054 **Fx:**439-2083
(718) 792-5639 .. **Blau,** Ronna B '74 %MHLS -1500 Waters Pl -Bronx 10461 **Fx:**597-7385
(646) 252-2740 .. **Blau,** Seth J '98 MTA NYC Transit -2 Bway -NY 10004
(800) 910-0529 .. **Blau,** Steven Bennett '75 (Blau B&L,LLC) -224 W 30th -NY 10001 **Fx:**(212) 488-4848
(212) 848-4000 .. **Blau,** Steven R '09 %Shearman & S LLP -599 Lex Av -NY 10022
(516) 823-1020 .. **Blau,** Stuart M '84 (Berlin & B) -444 Merrick Rd -Lynbrk 11563 **Fx:**823-1043
(212) 906-1200 .. **Blauch,** Kevin Craig '85 (Latham & W) -885 3rd Av -NY 10022
(718) 325-4200 .. **Blauman & McCabe** -4234 Vireo Av -Bronx 10470 **Fx:**325-4201
(718) 325-4200 .. **Blauman,** Simon L '60 (Blauman & M) -4234 Vireo Av -Bronx 10470
(212) 284-4300 .. **Blauner,** Stephen J '79 Solus Alternative Asset Mgmt -430 Park Av -NY 10022 **Fx:**284-4320
(212) 808-7800 .. **Blaustein,** Benjamin '06 %Kelley D&W LLP -101 Park Av -NY 10178
(845) 639-6666 .. **Blaustein,** Caryn F '84 (Kleinman S&B,PC) -151 N Main Bx947 -New Cty 10956
(877) 833-4150 .. **Blaustein,** Howard A '89 Kurtzman Carson Cnsltnts LLC -599 Lex Av -NY 10022
(212) 595-9529 .. **Blaustein,** Karen E '89 -180 W End Av -NY 10023 **Fx:**921-2422
(516) 229-2756 .. **Blaustein,** Lisa S '86 -50 Chas Lindbergh Blvd -Uniondale 11553 **Fx:**484-3321
(516) 248-5800 .. **Blaustein,** Mark R '87 (M Blaustein,PC) -1325 Franklin Av -Gdn Cty 11530 **Fx:**248-5839
(212) 446-4800 .. **Blaustein,** Robt C '06 %Kirkland & E LLP -153 E 53rd -NY 10022
(212) 558-4000 .. **Blaut,** Ari B '08 %Sullivan & C LLP -125 Broad -NY 10004
(212) 571-0111 .. **Blaxill,** David C '88 %Hardin KM&P,PA -110 William -NY 10038
(718) 837-4000 .. **Blay & Liss** -8778 Bay Pkwy -Brklyn 11214 **Fx:**837-4016
(212) 902-0215 .. **Blayer,** Stacey D '00 %Goldman Sachs -1 NY Plz -NY 10004
(212) 373-3000 .. **Blaylock,** Madhuri P '99 Paul WRW&G LLP -1285 Av of Amer -NY 10019
(516) 625-1700 .. **Blaymore,** Michl D '78 (Salamon GB&S,PC) -97 Powerhse Rd -Roslyn Hts 11577
(516) 625-1700 .. **Blaymore,** Russell B '07 %Salamon GB&S,PC -97 Powerhse Rd -Roslyn Hts 11577
(212) 225-2000 .. **Blazejewski,** Kenneth S '08 %Cleary GS&H -1 Lbrty Plz -NY 10006
(212) 468-8000 .. **Blazejewski,** Rosa L '01 Morrison & F LLP -1290 Av of Amer -NY 10104
(212) 610-6300 .. **Blazek,** Zuzana '10 %Allen & O -1221 Av of Amer -NY 10020
(315) 829-2525 .. **Blazer,** Frances E '94 -Bx807 -Vernon 13476 **Fx:**829-2772
(212) 310-8000 .. **Blazer,** Natalie R '09 %Weil G&M LLP -767 5th Av -NY 10153
(716) 856-4000 .. **Blazkow,** Geanne M '08 %Hodgson R LLP -140 Pearl -Buffalo 14202
(516) 747-9700 .. **Blazowski,** Maureen P '06 %Ryan & H,PC -1 Old Cntry Rd -Carle Pl 11514
(914) 723-7801 .. **Blea,** Lori S '89 -78 Brook -Scarsdale 10583 **Fx:**337-2368
(914) 337-2112 .. **Blea,** Lori S '89 -25 Park Pl -Bronxvll 10708 **Fx:**337-2368
(315) 759-5905 .. **Bleakley,** Carrie A '04 -33 Seneca -Geneva 14456
(315) 789-2362 .. **Bleakley,** Paul W '96 (Gage G&B) -33 Seneca Bx1187 -Geneva 14456 **Fx:**781-1663
(914) 949-2700 .. **Bleakley Platt & Schmidt, LLP** -1 N Lex Av -White Plns 10601 **Fx:**683-6956
(516) 470-1950 .. **Blech,** Richd B '95 (Blech & Assoc) -530 Old Cntry Rd -Westbury 11590 **Fx:**794-1581
(212) 558-4000 .. **Blecher,** Jennifer H '10 %Sullivan & C LLP -125 Broad -NY 10004
(212) 736-4430 .. **Blecher Mendel & Fedele** -1501 Bway -NY 10036 **Fx:**827-0494
(212) 552-3814 .. **Blecher,** Stacey L '90 JP Morgan Chase -1 Chase Manh Plz -NY 10081
(212) 732-1900 .. **Blecher,** Tedd '77 -225 Bway -NY 10007 **Fx:**732-1901
(212) 692-1000 .. **Blechman,** Jason G '04 %Duane M LLP -1540 Bway -NY 10036
(607) 723-5341 .. **Blechman,** Jon S '71 SpclCnsl Hinman H&K,LLP -80 Exchange Bx5250 -Bnghmtn 13902
(212) 836-8000 .. **Blechman,** Michl D '66 (Kaye S LLP) -425 Park Av -NY 10022
(212) 309-3400 .. **Blechner,** Howard K '84 %Towers Watson -335 Mad Av -NY 10017
(212) 504-6000 .. **Blechynden,** Ellisha A '08 %Cadwalader W&T LLP -1 World Fncl Ctr -NY 10281
(212) 442-6856 .. **Blecker,** Elizabeth A '00 %Law Dept -52 Duane -NY 10007 **Fx:**442-6868
(212) 431-2873 .. **Blecker,** Robt I '75 %NY Law Schl -185 W Bway -NY 10013 **Fx:**431-1830
(212) 279-4490 .. **Bleckner,** David J '87 (D Bleckner,PC) -350 5th Av -NY 10118 **Fx:**279-4495
(212) 363-6900 .. **Blee,** David I '91 (Faust GS&B LLP) -2 Rector -NY 10006
(212) 564-6633 .. **Bleecker,** Renaud T '84 %White & M,PC -875 Av of Amer -NY 10001
(212) 909-6000 .. **Bleeker,** Danl A '10 %Debevoise & P LLP -919 3rd Av -NY 10022
(212) 949-6490 .. **Bleemer,** Russell E '90 %CPR Inst -575 Lex Av -NY 10022 **Fx:**949-8859
(212) 408-5100 .. **Bleiberg,** Benjamin D '07 %Chadbourne & P LLP -30 Rckfllr Plz -NY 10112
(212) 682-7474 .. **Bleiberg,** Chas M '67 (Foley & L LLP) -90 Park Av -NY 10016
(718) 875-1430 .. **Bleiberg,** Isadore C '53 -3010 Dwight Av -Far Rckwy 11691
(212) 758-0050 .. **Bleiberg,** Richd B '87 %Title Assoc -825 3rd Av -NY 10022 **Fx:**758-8223
(212) 848-8033 .. **Bleich,** David L '68 OfCnsl Shearman & S LLP -599 Lex Av -NY 10022
(718) 306-1100 .. **Bleich,** Sanford J '83 -16 Court -Brklyn 11241
(845) 371-7700 .. **Bleichman,** Joshua N '83 (Bleichman & K) -267 Route 59 W -Spg Vly 10977 **Fx:**(267) 295-8430
(212) 907-0700 .. **Bleichmar,** Javier '99 (Labaton S LLP) -140 Bway -NY 10005
(718) 927-5228 .. **Bleier,** David S '95 Lenox Academy -100-01 Flatlands Av -Brklyn 11236
(585) 454-2190 .. **Bleier,** Donald R '82 -31 E Main -Rchstr 14614
(718) 591-7500 .. **Bleier,** Jack B '80 (Bleier B&B) -80-30 164th -Jamaica 11432 **Fx:**969-0994
(718) 292-2850 .. **Bleifer,** Paul '66 -60 E 42nd -NY 10165 **Fx:**(201) 944-8630
(518) 583-0171 .. **Bleikamp,** Joan B '84 (Walsh & W,LLP) -42 Long Alley -Saratoga Spgs 12866 **Fx:**583-1025
(607) 277-0416 .. **Bleiwas,** Pamela B '91 -408 N Tioga -Ithaca 14850 **Fx:**273-8449
(212) 643-0700 .. **Blejec,** Ivan F '86 -236 W 30th -NY 10001 **Fx:**643-0701
(631) 853-5212 .. **Blekht,** Angela '98 %Leg Aid -400 Carleton Av Bx9082 -Central Islip 11722 **Fx:**853-7798
(518) 782-1929 .. **Blendell,** James '84 -40 British Amer Blvd -Latham 12110 **Fx:**782-3429
(212) 250-2500 .. **Blennau,** Thos F '03 %Deutsche Bank -60 Wall -NY 10005
Bleser, Marilyn J '05 -1436 Altamont Av PMB 298 -Schnctdy 12303
(315) 435-2170 .. **Bleskoski,** Karen Ann '89 %Cnty Atty -421 Mntgmry -Syracuse 13202 **Fx:**435-5729
(212) 269-1400 .. **Blessey,** Robt L '73 OfCnsl Gusrae KB&N PLLC -120 Wall -NY 10005
(212) 425-7200 .. **Blessing,** Carolyn A '09 %Kenyon & K,LLP -1 Bway -NY 10004
(212) 848-4000 .. **Blessing,** Peter H '78 (Shearman & S LLP) -599 Lex Av -NY 10022
(212) 788-1144 .. **Bletsch,** Christopher M '06 %Law Dept -100 Church -NY 10007 **Fx:**788-0367
(212) 645-7660 .. **Bletter,** Gloria '77 -350 W 24th -NY 10011
(212) 310-8000 .. **Blevin,** John W '05 %Weil G&M LLP -767 5th Av -NY 10153
(716) 881-3010 .. **Blewett,** Richd N '51 (Cohen & L,PC) -343 Elmwood Av Bx5204 -Buffalo 14213
(212) 504-6000 .. **Bley,** Danl J '10 %Cadwalader W&T LLP -1 World Fncl Ctr -NY 10281
(631) 724-2300 .. **Bleyer,** Penny '91 F Schwartz -317 Middle Cntry Rd -Smithtwn 11787
(212) 333-8997 .. **Blick,** Jeffrey S '96 UBS -590 Mad Av -NY 10022
(212) 450-4000 .. **Bligh,** Gur '08 %Davis P&W LLP -450 Lex Av -NY 10017

(631) 265-2550 .. **Bligh,** Matthew H '04 %Greshin Z&A -199 E Main Bx829 -Smithtwn 11787
(212) 504-6000 .. **Bliley,** Jonathan H '09 %Cadwalader W&T LLP -1 World Fncl Ctr -NY 10281
(212) 577-2800 .. **Blinder,** Albert A '49 Cnsl Sexter & W -115 Bway -NY 10006
(212) 225-2000 .. **Blinder,** Seth B '08 %Cleary GS&H -1 Lbrty Plz -NY 10006
(212) 969-3000 .. **Blinderman,** Eric H '00 %Proskauer R LLP -1585 Bway -NY 10036
(212) 545-3258 .. **Blinderman,** Larisa '02 -Bx1177 -NY 10274
(212) 867-9595 .. **Blindman,** Stanley '67 (Blindman & U) -630 3rd Av -NY 10017
(212) 867-9595 .. **Blindman & Uram** -630 3rd Av -NY 10017 **Fx:**949-1857
(212) 878-9335 .. **Blinken,** Anthony J '89 -466 Lex Av -NY 10017
(212) 307-5500 .. **Blinken,** Sally '92 (Venable LLP) -1270 Av of Amer -NY 10020
(716) 875-8916 .. **Blinkoff,** Andrew D '01 (Blinkoff & B) -1207 Delaware Av -Buffalo 14209 **Fx:**332-6183
(516) 248-1188 .. **Blinkoff,** Jeffrey L '90 (Carrieri & C,PC) -200 Old Cntry Rd -Mineola 11501 **Fx:**248-1794
(716) 875-8916 .. **Blinkoff,** Michl M '76 (Blinkoff & B) -1207 Delaware Av -Buffalo 14209 **Fx:**332-6183
(212) 307-5500 .. **Blinkoff,** Sharon A '89 OfCnsl Venable LLP -1270 Av of Amer -NY 10020
(718) 590-2000 .. **Blira-Koessler,** Christopher J '01 %DA -198 E 161st -Bronx 10451 **Fx:**590-6477
(585) 588-2720 .. **Blish,** Nelson A '98 Eastman Kodak -343 State -Rchstr 14650
(516) 229-6000 .. **Blishteyn,** Alexander '03 %R Lau & Assoc -300 Jericho Quad Bx9040 -Jericho 11753 **Fx:**229-6167
(516) 327-4641 .. **Blisko,** Larry '89 -311 Meacham Av -Elmont 11003 **Fx:**327-4645
(516) 249-3450 .. **Bliss,** David J '09 %Carman C&I,LLP -266 Main -Farmngdl 11735
(516) 437-7419 .. **Bliss,** James Jr. '79 -84 Prnctn -Gdn Cty 11530
(212) 318-6000 .. **Bliss,** James R '99 (Paul HJ&W LLP) -75 E 55th -NY 10022
(518) 523-9900 .. **Bliss,** Janet H '83 -12 Morningside Dr -Lk Placid 12946 **Fx:**523-1406
(914) 723-2728 .. **Bliss,** John G '93 %Central Taxi -East Pkwy -Scarsdale 10583
(914) 499-4867 .. **Bliss,** Larry A '03 IBM -1 New Orchrd Rd -Armonk 10504 **Fx:**499-6085
(631) 853-4104 .. **Bliss,** Melisa D '08 %DA -400 Carleton Av Bx9082 -Central Islip 11722 **Fx:**853-7838
(914) 428-9050 .. **Bliss,** Patrick J '85 -399 Knollwood Rd -White Plns 10603 **Fx:**946-6301
(212) 741-8808 .. **Bliss,** Richd H '77 -275 Mad Av -NY 10016 **Fx:**202-9631
(212) 541-2000 .. **Bliss,** Ronald J '07 %Bryan C LLP -1290 Av of Amer -NY 10104
(718) 849-6900 .. **Blissett,** Anokye Soyini '07 %G Russo & Assoc PC -101-05 Lefferts Blvd -S Richmond Hll 11419 **Fx:**849-6930
(212) 858-7119 .. **Blissett,** Roger A '88 RBC Capital Mrkts -1 Lbrty Plz -NY 10006 **Fx:**858-7480
(212) 487-7350 .. **Blit,** Marnie Lee '95 %CCPC -17 Battery Pl -NY 10004
(212) 967-3000 .. **Blit,** Matthew J '01 (Levine & B,PLLC) -350 5th Av -NY 10118
(315) 422-7111 .. **Blitman,** Chas E '70 (Blitman & K LLP) -443 N Franklin -Syracuse 13204
(315) 422-7111 .. **Blitman & King LLP** -443 N Franklin -Syracuse 13204 **Fx:**471-2623
(585) 232-5600 .. **Blitman & King LLP** -16 W Main -Rchstr 14614 **Fx:**232-7738
(518) 785-4387 .. **Blitman & King LLP** -800 Troy-Schnctdy Rd -Latham 12110 **Fx:**785-9264
(212) 310-8329 .. **Blittner,** David M '92 (Weil G&M LLP) -767 5th Av -NY 10153
(212) 735-3000 .. **Blitz,** Brian A '02 %Skadden ASM&F LLP -4 Times Sq -NY 10036
(212) 314-4085 .. **Blitz,** Harvey '72 %AXA Fncl Inc -1290 Av of Amer -NY 10104
(212) 871-1300 .. **Blitz,** Justin M '04 (Schulman B&W,LLP) -980 Av of Amer -NY 10018 **Fx:**(646) 599-9320
(212) 237-0000 .. **Blitzer,** Caroline B '08 (Vinson & E LLP) -666 5th Av -NY 10103
(212) 735-3000 .. **Blitzer,** Rachel R '06 %Skadden ASM&F LLP -4 Times Sq -NY 10036
(718) 250-2000 .. **Blitzer,** Ronn M '08 %DA -350 Jay -Brklyn 11201 **Fx:**250-2314
(212) 264-5916 .. **Blivaiss,** Jeffrey E '04 %DHS -26 Fed Plz -NY 10278
(914) 468-0968 .. **Bliven,** David I '98 -445 Hmltn Av -White Plns 10601
(212) 246-2400 .. **Blivess,** Steven N '04 %Balber PM&VDT,PC -1370 Av of Amer -NY 10019
(212) 389-5000 .. **Bliwise,** Lester M '71 (Sutherland A&B LLP) -1114 Av of Amer -NY 10036
(212) 880-1210 .. **Bliwise,** Matthew S '99 %Chicago Title/Ticor -711 3rd Av -NY 10017 **Fx:**880-1400
(716) 632-5809 .. **Bliznik,** Mary Ann '93 -Bx315 -Clarence 14031
(516) 248-2474 .. **Bliznikas,** Tomas '03 %S Hill & Assoc -41 Hilton Av -Hempstd 11550
(212) 417-4450 .. **Bloch,** Claudia Morales '81 %Dept of Health -145 Huguenot -New Rchll 10801 **Fx:**(914) 654-7050
(212) 438-3654 .. **Bloch,** Colleen S '02 Standard & Poors -55 Water -NY 10041
(212) 803-3100 .. **Bloch,** Darren S '05 %Empire State Dvlmnt Corp -633 3rd Av -NY 10017
(585) 419-8076 .. **Bloch,** Howard A '82 -349 W Cmmrcial -E Rchstr 14445
(212) 310-8000 .. **Bloch,** Matthew D '86 (Weil G&M LLP) -767 5th Av -NY 10153
(914) 725-0222 .. **Bloch,** Mitchell R '80 -700 Wht Plns Rd -Scarsdale 10583 **Fx:**725-6160
(212) 344-5680 .. **Bloch,** Norman A '78 (Thompson H LLP) -335 Mad Av -NY 10017
(212) 459-7894 .. **Bloch,** Peter M '74 %Dept of Tax & Fin -1740 Bway -NY 10019 **Fx:**459-7897
(718) 522-6773 .. **Bloch,** Przemyslaw J '98 -26 Court -Brklyn 11242
(718) 461-6633 .. **Bloch,** Russell A '09 %Mallilo & G -163-09 Nrthrn Blvd -Flushng 11358
(212) 218-5500 .. **Bloch,** Stanley E '68 (Seyfarth S LLP) -620 8th Av -NY 10018
(212) 442-6360 .. **Bloch,** Tracy L '06 %NYC Mayors Ofc of Contracts -253 Boradway -NY 10007
(716) 847-0650 .. **Block,** Alan B '80 %Leg Srvcs -237 Main -Buffalo 14203 **Fx:**847-0227
(516) 622-9200 .. **Block,** Andrea G '04 %Westerman BEM&S,LLP -1201 RXR Plz -Uniondale 11553
(212) 364-8442 .. **Block,** Andrew T '94 Time Warner Cable -60 Columbus Av -NY 10023 **Fx:**364-8460
(516) 741-5252 .. **Block,** Ann C '93 -100 Hrrcks Rd -Mineola 11501 **Fx:**741-0799
(212) 405-3838 .. **Block,** Arthur R '77 -230 Park Av -NY 10169 **Fx:**599-1759
(718) 897-9700 .. **Block,** Barry H '92 -Bx750129 -Frst Hlls 11375
(212) 661-6800 .. **Block,** Caryn J '88 Cyruli SH&Z LLP -420 Lex Av -NY 10170
(212) 755-5510 .. **Block,** Chas J '59 Cnsl Loeb B & Prtnrs -505 Park Av -NY 10022
(212) 661-2370 .. **Block,** Chas P '78 -305 Mad Av -NY 10165
(212) 269-5500 .. **Block,** Christopher B '07 (Gordon & R LLP) -90 Broad -NY 10004
(716) 854-4080 .. **Block Colucci & Longo, PC** -1 Niagara Sq -Buffalo 14202 **Fx:**854-0059
(518) 348-1000 .. **Block Colucci Spellman & Peller,LLP** -9 Exec Park Dr -Clifton Pk 12065 **Fx:**348-2000
(518) 523-4671 .. **Block Colucci Spellman & Peller,LLP** -2276 Saranac Av -Lk Placid 12946 **Fx:**523-4672
(845) 638-5180 .. **Block,** Danl J '82 Cnty Atty -Cnty Ofc Bldg -New Cty 10956 **Fx:**638-5676
(716) 852-5211 .. **Block,** David M '94 %MA Bjork -350 Main -Buffalo 14202 **Fx:**852-8149
(212) 504-6000 .. **Block,** Dennis J '68 (Cadwalader W&T LLP) -1 World Fncl Ctr -NY 10281
(212) 628-2904 .. **Block,** Devra Anne '96 -165 E 66th -NY 10065
(518) 402-2028 .. **Block,** Elaine L '97 Law Dept -The Cptl -Albany 12224
(212) 416-8197 .. **Block,** Elizabeth '76 %Dept of Law -120 Bway -NY 10271
(212) 286-8585 .. **Block,** Fern H '83 OfCnsl Heidell PM&B,LLP -99 Park Av -NY 10016
(212) 244-6825 .. **Block,** Gilad O '99 GNS Funding Corp -265 W 37th -NY 10018
(845) 583-6183 .. **Block,** Howard '85 -Bx480 -Kauneonga Lk 12749 **Fx:**583-8693
(716) 886-0211 .. **Block,** Howard '96 %Benderson Dvlpmnt -570 Delaware Av -Buffalo 14202 **Fx:**886-2269
(212) 728-8000 .. **Block,** Howard T '09 %Willkie F&G LLP -787 7th Av -NY 10019
(212) 221-5200 .. **Block,** Ira H '72 OTB -1501 Bway -NY 10036 **Fx:**221-8025
(212) 736-5300 .. **Block,** Jeffrey A '88 (Block O&M LLP) -1 Penn Plz -NY 10119
(914) 921-1515 .. **Block,** Jennifer Leigh '96 Travel Loft -120 Bloomingdale Rd -White Plns 10605
(212) 605-6270 .. **Block,** Jerome H '01 (Levy P&K,LLP) -800 3rd Av -NY 10022
(212) 506-5000 .. **Block,** Jill D '89 (Orrick H&S LLP) -51 W 52nd -NY 10019
(212) 506-1700 .. **Block,** Jonah M '08 Cnsl Kasowitz BT&F LLP -1633 Bway -NY 10019
(212) 891-1600 .. **Block,** Joshua A '06 %Jenner & B LLP -919 3rd Av -NY 10022
(585) 530-3158 .. **Block,** Joshua B '09 NY Unified Courts System -50 East Av -Rchstr 14604
(914) 834-3227 .. **Block,** Julian '68 -3 Wshngtn Sq -Larchmnt 10538 **Fx:**834-3227
(718) 897-9700 .. **Block,** Julie '05 -Bx750129 -Frst Hlls 11375
(631) 582-1717 .. **Block,** Justin M '88 (J Block,PC) -1 Suffolk Sq -Islandia 11749 **Fx:**582-1737
(212) 715-9100 .. **Block,** Justine J '99 %Kramer LN&F,LLP -1177 Av of Amer -NY 10036
(212) 508-6700 .. **Block,** Kenneth M '72 (Tannenbaum HS&H LLP) -900 3rd Av -NY 10022
(212) 376-6400 .. **Block,** Laura V '10 %Marshall DWC&G -88 Pine -NY 10005
(212) 594-5300 .. **Block,** Lauren '86 %Milberg LLP -1 Penn Plz -NY 10119
(914) 307-7020 .. **Block,** Lawr S '93 Kenmar Grp Inc -900 King -Pt Chester 10573
(212) 869-5030 .. **Block,** Marc J '00 %Kucker & B,LLP -747 3rd Av -NY 10017
(516) 741-5252 .. **Block,** Martin '65 (Sanders SBWV&G,PC) -100 Hrrcks Rd -Mineola 11501
(212) 227-9008 .. **Block,** Michl '86 -277 Bway -NY 10007 **Fx:**693-0368
(212) 732-9000 .. **Block,** Michl N '67 (Sullivan PBM&C PC) -120 Bway -NY 10271
(212) 697-3122 .. **Block,** Nancy J '96 (Martin C&B LLP) -220 E 42nd -NY 10017
(631) 261-8834 .. **Block,** Neil M '88 (Ingerman S LLP) -150 Motor Pkwy -Hauppauge 11788
(845) 358-7633 .. **Block,** Noah '74 -11 Richard Dr -W Nyack 10994
(914) 769-3100 .. **Block,** Norman M '88 (N Block,PC) -245 Saw Mill Rvr Rd -Hawthorne 10532 **Fx:**769-3156
(212) 736-5300 .. **Block O'Toole & Murphy LLP** -1 Penn Plz -NY 10119 **Fx:**971-9840
(212) 935-3000 .. **Block,** Richd H '78 (Mintz LCFG&P,PC) -666 3rd Av -NY 10017
(914) 332-4700 .. **Block,** Richd J '93 (Mirsky & B,PLLC) -303 S Bway -Tarrytwn 10591 **Fx:**332-1671
(212) 725-2404 .. **Block,** Richd M '83 (R Block) -245 Park Av -NY 10167
(212) 661-2370 .. **Block,** Robt D '77 -305 Mad Av -NY 10165
(212) 922-3260 .. **Block,** Stephen H '93 SrCnsl Harry Fox Agency -601 W 26th -NY 10001
(516) 663-6600 .. **Block,** Steven P '88 (Ruskin MF,PC) -1425 RXR Plz -Uniondale 11556
(212) 750-9320 .. **Block,** Wendy Brenner '94 %Beginning With Children Fndtn -575 Lex Av -NY 10022
(212) 687-1313 .. **Block,** Wm K '77 (WK Block,PC) -150 Bway -NY 10038 **Fx:**687-7823
(914) 332-0222 .. **Blocker,** Edw M '81 %Philips Electronics -345 Scarborough Rd Bx3001 -Briarclff Mnr 10510 **Fx:**332-0615
(212) 836-8000 .. **Blocker,** Tanya N '10 Kaye S LLP -425 Park Av -NY 10022
(845) 482-9345 .. **Blocker,** Wendy J '93 -Schlhse Rd Bx216 -Jffrsnvll 12748 **Fx:**482-3701
(212) 572-9700 .. **Blockinger,** Jeffrey C '97 Och-Ziff Capital Mgmnt Grp -9 W 57th -NY 10019
(212) 636-6782 .. **Block-Lieb,** Susan '83 Fordham Univ Sch of Law -140 W 62nd -NY 10023 **Fx:**636-6899
(315) 788-6352 .. **Blodgett,** Peter S '74 -200 Wshngtn -Watertwn 13601
(516) 280-7105 .. **Blodnick,** Edw K '58 (Blodnick F & Assoc,PC) -1325 Franklin Av -Gdn Cty 11530 **Fx:**280-7102
(516) 921-4305 .. **Blodnick,** Peter L '89 -316 Jackson Av -Syosset 11791
(212) 545-1900 .. **Bloemsma,** Michiel A '93 (Menaker & H LLP) -10 E 40th -NY 10016
(607) 937-5205 .. **Bloise,** John R '75 -283½ S Hmltn -Painted Post 14870 **Fx:**937-5170
(518) 330-0214 .. **Bloise,** John R Jr. '94 -34 Devonshr Way -Clifton Pk 12065
(212) 715-9100 .. **Blom,** Leah A '10 %Kramer LN&F,LLP -1177 Av of Amer -NY 10036
(914) 946-7850 .. **Blomberg,** Troy G '86 -365 North Av -New Rchll 10801 **Fx:**946-7860
(800) 225-6560 .. **Blond,** Jason C '04 Ski-Safe -1 Hllw Ln -New Hyde Pk 11042
(212) 563-2200 .. **Blond,** Peter E '98 %Brandt S&L LLP -386 Park Av S -NY 10016
(718) 206-3008 .. **Blond,** Suzanne '86 -153-01 Jamaica Av -Jamaica 11432 **Fx:**(516) 295-7434
(631) 812-6497 .. **Blonder,** Meir Yehuda '95 Leviton -201 N Srvc Rd -Melvll 11747
(212) 709-8180 .. **Bloodsaw,** Tracey A '98 -110 Wall -NY 10005 **Fx:**943-2300
(518) 473-7051 .. **Bloodstein,** Danl '81 %OTDA-Fair Hearings -40 N Pearl -Albany 12243 **Fx:**473-6735

(212) 967-1800 .. **Bloodworth,** Joshua D '04 %Bryant BJ&R LLP -140 Bway -NY 10005
(212) 788-0969 .. **Bloom,** Aaron M '04 %Law Dept -100 Church -NY 10007 **Fx:**788-0367
(212) 318-6000 .. **Bloom,** Allan S '96 (Paul HJ&W LLP) -75 E 55th -NY 10022
(212) 903-9000 .. **Bloom,** Andrew D '08 %Linklaters -1345 Av of Amer -NY 10105
(212) 532-3553 .. **Bloom,** Andrew J '01 Hudson Realty Capital LLC -250 Park Av S -NY 10003
(631) 864-3033 .. **Bloom,** Audrey '98 -823 W Jericho Tpk -Smithtwn 11787 **Fx:**864-3133
(212) 521-2930 .. **Bloom,** Barry L '85 Tisch Fncl Mgt -655 Mad Av -NY 10065 **Fx:**521-2983
(212) 710-0011 .. **Bloom,** Barry M '62 Cnsl Drohan L,LLP -489 5th Av -NY 10017
(212) 696-2666 .. **Bloom,** Barry S '68 OfCnsl Weisberg F&K -261 5th Av -NY 10016
(516) 741-1116 .. **Bloom,** Brett I '90 (Bloom & N,LLP) -170 Old Cntry Rd -Mineola 11501 **Fx:**741-0546
(212) 279-9200 .. **Bloom,** Brian A '03 (Abrams FFEGF&E,LLP) -630 3rd Av -NY 10017
(212) 728-2200 .. **Bloom,** Bryan L '08 %Axinn V&H LLP -114 W 47th -NY 10036
(212) 664-4444 .. **Bloom,** Craig A '94 %NBC -30 Rckfllr Plz -NY 10112
(516) 627-7000 .. **Bloom,** Craig D '05 %Weiss & Z,PC -3333 New Hyde Pk Rd -New Hyde Pk 11042
(212) 836-8000 .. **Bloom,** Danl A '09 %Kaye S LLP -425 Park Av -NY 10022
(845) 561-6920 .. **Bloom,** Danl J '66 (Bloom & B,PC) -530 Blooming Grove Tpk Bx4323 -New Windsor 12553 **Fx:**561-0978
(212) 674-0404 .. **Bloom,** Danl J '73 -35 W 9th -NY 10011
(716) 373-0004 .. **Bloom,** Darryl R '08 %Pub Def -175 N Union -Olean 14760 **Fx:**373-3462
(914) 993-1900 .. **Bloom,** Douglas B '06 %US Atty -300 Quarropas -White Plns 10601 **Fx:**993-9036
(585) 419-8800 .. **Bloom,** Edw D '70 (Harris B PLLC) -99 Garnsey Rd -Pittsfrd 14534
(516) 739-5300 .. **Bloom,** Eliot F '86 -114 Old Cntry Rd -Mineola 11501 **Fx:**739-3202
(212) 969-3000 .. **Bloom,** Elise M '84 (Proskauer R LLP) -1585 Bway -NY 10036
(516) 571-2870 .. **Bloom,** Elizabeth A '02 %Supreme Ct -100 Supreme Ct Dr -Mineola 11501 **Fx:**571-2555
(212) 227-4016 .. **Bloom,** Emanuel '50 (Bloom & M) -225 Bway -NY 10007
(716) 856-5500 .. **Bloom,** Eric A '81 SpclCnsl Damon M LLP -200 Delaware Av -Buffalo 14202
(718) 250-4273 .. **Bloom,** Evan K '09 Leg Aid -111 Lvngstn -Brklyn 11201 **Fx:**250-4243
(516) 393-2200 .. **Bloom,** Greg E '91 (Garfunkel W,PC) -111 Grt Nck Rd -Gt Neck 11021
(518) 445-2355 .. **Bloom,** Ira M '70 %Albany Law Schl -80 New Scotland Av -Albany 12208 **Fx:**445-2315
(845) 791-8167 .. **Bloom,** Jane M '98 -Bx818 -Rck Hll 12775 **Fx:**791-8168
(212) 943-1090 .. **Bloom,** Jeffrey B '80 (Gair GCSMB&R) -80 Pine -NY 10005
(718) 237-2000 .. **Bloom,** Jeffrey C '95 Leg Aid -111 Lvngstn -Brklyn 11201 **Fx:**237-8737
(718) 402-1100 .. **Bloom,** Jeffrey M '99 -888 Grnd Cncrs -Bronx 10451 **Fx:**585-8640
(212) 412-9500 .. **Bloom,** Jennifer L '10 %Flemming ZWZ LLP -1 Lbrty Plz -NY 10006
(646) 315-7310 .. **Bloom,** Jeremy S '02 %FINRA -14 Wall -NY 10005 **Fx:**315-7440
(212) 310-8000 .. **Bloom,** Jonathan '92 Cnsl Weil G&M LLP -767 5th Av -NY 10153
(914) 421-3085 .. **Bloom,** Jonathan '93 -44 S Bway -White Plns 10601 **Fx:**686-5141
(631) 853-5212 .. **Bloom,** Jonathan R '96 %Leg Aid -400 Carleton Av Bx9082 -Central Islip 11722 **Fx:**853-7798
(212) 326-3939 .. **Bloom,** K Adam '09 %Jones D -222 E 41st -NY 10017
(845) 561-6920 .. **Bloom,** Kathleen Lyons '10 (Bloom & B,PC) -530 Blooming Grove Tpk Bx4323 -New Windsor 12553 **Fx:**561-0978
(212) 759-5800 .. **Bloom,** Kenneth A '82 (Gartner + B,PC) -801 2nd Av -NY 10017
(845) 561-6920 .. **Bloom,** Kevin D '99 (Bloom & B,PC) -530 Blooming Grove Tpk Bx4323 -New Windsor 12553 **Fx:**561-0978
(716) 853-8100 .. **Bloom,** Laurie S '84 Cnsl Nixon P LLP -40 Fountain Plz -Buffalo 14202
(212) 964-3502 .. **Bloom,** Lawr H '80 -11 Park Pl -NY 10007 **Fx:**267-3165
(877) 222-1814 .. **Bloom,** Leonora '92 %B Rothenberg -100 Duffy Av -Hicksvll 11801 **Fx:**(866) 894-2182
(212) 973-6752 .. **Bloom,** Lisa Read '87 Court TV -600 3rd Av -NY 10016 **Fx:**973-3355
(212) 484-3900 .. **Bloom,** Mark A '95 (Arent F LLP) -1675 Bway -NY 10019
(914) 834-5050 .. **Bloom,** Mark N '69 -104 Edgewood Av -Larchmnt 10538 **Fx:**834-4121
(516) 367-6104 .. **Bloom,** Marvin J '73 -2 Maple Way -Woodbury 11797
(212) 474-1000 .. **Bloom,** Matthew H '09 %Cravath S&M LLP -825 8th Av -NY 10019
(212) 227-4016 .. **Bloom & Mintz** -225 Bway -NY 10007 **Fx:**385-9785
(518) 842-8213 .. **Bloom,** Nadine A '84 %Wollman Law Firm -41 Market -Amsterdam 12010 **Fx:**842-3420
(516) 741-4000 .. **Bloom,** Neil A '97 %Shanker Law Grp -101 Front -Mineola 11501 **Fx:**741-4665
(631) 393-6220 .. **Bloom,** Paul '72 (Harras B&A LLP) -445 Broad Hollow Rd -Melvll 11747
(845) 561-6920 .. **Bloom,** Peter E '68 (Bloom & B,PC) -530 Blooming Grove Tpk Bx4323 -New Windsor 12553 **Fx:**561-0978
(212) 286-8585 .. **Bloom,** Rachel S '09 %Heidell PM&B,LLP -99 Park Av -NY 10016
(212) 624-3300 .. **Bloom,** Richd I '01 UGO Networks, Inc -670 Bway -NY 10012
(516) 222-6200 .. **Bloom,** Robt T '72 OfCnsl Berkman HPP&F,PC -100 Grdn City Plz -Gdn Cty 11530
(212) 984-7775 .. **Bloom,** Roger F '59 OfCnsl Warshaw BCS&K,LLP -555 5th Av -NY 10017 **Fx:**972-9150
(212) 541-2000 .. **Bloom,** Steven D '70 (Bryan C LLP) -1290 Av of Amer -NY 10104
(212) 336-2000 .. **Bloom,** Susan F '80 (Patterson BW&T LLP) -1133 Av of Amer -NY 10036
(212) 218-5500 .. **Bloom,** Susan K '91 %Seyfarth S LLP -620 8th Av -NY 10018
(845) 732-7536 .. **Bloom,** Susan M '94 %Medicaid Fraud Cntrl -1 Blue Hill Plz Bx1557 -Pearl Rvr 10965 **Fx:**732-7555
(212) 259-8000 .. **Bloom,** Suzanne Jaffe '89 (Dewey & L LLP) -1301 Av of Amer -NY 10019
(716) 847-8400 .. **Bloomberg,** Edw S '73 (Phillips L LLP) -3400 HSBC Ctr -Buffalo 14203
(518) 434-1121 .. **Bloomberg & Magguilli** -Bx714 -Newtonville 12128
(917) 841-2124 .. **Bloomberg,** Mark A '90 -85 W Cedarvw Av -Staten Isl 10306
(212) 596-9000 .. **Bloomberg,** Mark H '85 (Ropes & G LLP) -1211 Av of Amer -NY 10036
(212) 259-8000 .. **Bloomberg,** Sheri E '94 (Dewey & L LLP) -1301 Av of Amer -NY 10019
(212) 233-6255 .. **Bloomberg Steinberg & Bader** -425 Park Av -NY 10022 **Fx:**587-3375
(914) 337-0142 .. **Bloomer,** Suzanne M '86 -85 Pondfld Rd -Bronxvll 10708 **Fx:**337-0436
(518) 434-0600 .. **Bloomer,** Tricia J '02 (Boies S&F LLP) -10 N Pearl -Albany 12207
(718) 544-0500 .. **Bloomfield,** Allan R '76 -118-21 Qns Blvd -Frst Hlls 11375 **Fx:**360-9704
(718) 665-5900 .. **Bloomfield,** Clifford D '02 %ME Bloomfield -349 E 149th -Bronx 10451
(718) 951-5608 .. **Bloomfield,** David C '84 Brooklyn Cllg CUNY -2900 Bedford Av -Brklyn 11210 **Fx:**951-4816
(212) 878-7205 .. **Bloomfield,** Donald R '78 %MTA -347 Mad Av -NY 10017 **Fx:**878-0162
(212) 265-2266 .. **Bloomfield,** Jay L '74 (Schneider GB LLP) -90 Broad -NY 10004
(212) 859-8000 .. **Bloomfield,** Kathryn-Ann '08 %Fried FHS&J LLP -1 NY Plz -NY 10004
(212) 888-5222 .. **Bloomfield,** Keith M '97 Cnsl 3rd Av Mgmt,LLC -622 3rd Av -NY 10017
(718) 665-5900 .. **Bloomfield,** Marshall E '68 ME Bloomfield -349 E 149th -Bronx 10451
(212) 806-5400 .. **Bloomfield,** Micah W '79 (Stroock &S&L LLP) -180 Maiden Ln -NY 10038
(718) 665-5900 .. **Bloomfield,** Michl P '03 OfCnsl ME Bloomfield -349 E 149th -Bronx 10451
(631) 853-4104 .. **Bloomfield,** Pamela J '06 %DA -400 Carleton Av Bx9082 -Central Islip 11722 **Fx:**853-7838
(631) 757-4694 .. **Bloomgarden,** Gerald A '57 -21 Griggs Dr -Greenlawn 11740 **Fx:**754-5999
(212) 816-8142 .. **Bloomgarden,** Nancy L '81 Citigroup -388 Greenwich -NY 10013
(518) 325-3141 .. **Bloomstein,** Alexander W '92 Baldwin & B,LLC -Bx248 -Hillsdale 12529 **Fx:**325-3490
(212) 750-7300 .. **Bloomstein,** Joshua M '99 Ares Mgmt LLC -280 Park Av -NY 10017 **Fx:**750-1777
(212) 593-6700 .. **Bloomstein,** Larry D '93 (Aaronson RF&D,LLP) -757 3rd Av -NY 10017
(212) 267-9020 .. **Bloomstein,** Morris J '52 %Shapiro B&A LLP -225 Bway -NY 10007
(212) 903-9000 .. **Bloor,** Martin S '01 %Linklaters -1345 Av of Amer -NY 10105
(914) 961-1300 .. **Blose,** James P '94 (Griffin CB&S,PC) -51 Pondfld Rd -Bronxvll 10708
(914) 681-9500 .. **Blosser,** Michele L '05 (Baker LS&B,LLP) -1 N Lex Av -White Plns 10601
(212) 571-0805 .. **Blossner,** Robt '69 -30 Vesey -NY 10007 **Fx:**571-0938
(212) 245-1000 .. **Blostein,** Katherine '08 %Outten & G LLP -3 Park Av -NY 10016
(212) 689-8808 .. **Blosveren,** Joshua L '03 %Hoguet NR&K,LLP -10 E 40th -NY 10016
(212) 559-0909 .. **Blotner,** Sara B '92 %Citibank -425 Park Av -NY 10043
(716) 847-6500 .. **Blotnik,** Michl M '75 (Steiner & B) -300 Delaware Av -Buffalo 14202
(212) 558-5500 .. **Blouin,** Danl P '05 Weitz & L,PC -700 Bway -NY 10003
(914) 665-2397 .. **Blount,** Andrea K '01 Mount Vernon City Ct -2 Roosevelt Sq -Mt Vernon 10550
(212) 593-5223 .. **Bloustein,** Elise A '82 OfCnsl A Hillman -41 E 57th -NY 10022 **Fx:**593-4633
(212) 259-8000 .. **Bloustein,** Esther E '99 %Dewey & L LLP -1301 Av of Amer -NY 10019
(518) 474-7469 .. **Bloustein,** Marc C '76 %OCA -Agncy Bldg 4 ESP -Albany 12223 **Fx:**473-5514
(518) 474-6955 .. **Blow,** Steven '80 %Dept Pub Srvc -3 ESP -Albany 12223
(212) 837-6000 .. **Bluck,** James H '83 (Hughes H&R LLP) -1 Bttry Pk Plz -NY 10004
(212) 841-4590 .. **Blue,** David J '99 Millennium Prtnrs -666 5th Av -NY 10103
(212) 750-6776 .. **Blue,** Gregory A '96 (Morgenstern & B,LLC) -885 3rd Av -NY 10022
(585) 388-9018 .. **Blue,** J Tyson '91 -4064 Cnty Line Rd -Macedon 14502
(716) 633-3200 .. **Bluestein,** Gary '85 (Bluestein & M,PC) -333 Intl Dr -Williamsvll 14221
(212) 239-4999 .. **Bluestein,** Irwin '70 (Meyer SE&K,PC) -1350 Bway Bx822 -NY 10018
(914) 276-3935 .. **Bluestein,** Lisa M '88 (LM Bluestein,LLC) -5 Sun Valley Hghts Rd -N Salem 10560
(914) 763-3250 .. **Bluestein,** Martin J '68 (Bluestein & S,LLP) -333 Salem Rd -Pound Rdg 10576 **Fx:**763-3296
(716) 633-3200 .. **Bluestein & Muhlbauer,PC** -333 Intl Dr -Williamsvll 14221 **Fx:**633-0301
(212) 791-5600 .. **Bluestone,** Andrew Lavoott '79 -233 Bway -NY 10279 **Fx:**513-7206
(212) 849-7000 .. **Blum,** Alan '82 (Quinn EU&S,LLP) -51 Mad Av -NY 10010
(516) 294-9292 .. **Blum,** Andrew D '83 (Tabat CB&Y,LLP) -1205 Franklin Av -Gdn Cty 11530
(212) 609-1500 .. **Blum,** Chas F '78 %VNSNY -107 E 70th -NY 10021 **Fx:**794-6357
(212) 458-2261 .. **Blum,** Christopher V '97 %AIG -175 Water -NY 10038
(212) 947-9416 .. **Blum,** David M '93 (Burstein & B,LLP) -286 Mad Av -NY 10017 **Fx:**947-0907
(516) 560-6400 .. **Blum,** Deborah J '06 %Leg Aid -1 Helen Keller Way -Hempstd 11550 **Fx:**565-3694
(212) 906-1200 .. **Blum,** Erin K '09 %Latham & W -885 3rd Av -NY 10022
(212) 245-5872 .. **Blum,** Herbert H '54 -1740 Bway -NY 10019 **Fx:**246-1912
(646) 878-0800 .. **Blum,** Hili '03 %Pearl CZL,LLP -1500 Bway -NY 10036
(212) 557-3000 .. **Blum,** Howard '72 (Rivelis P&B,LLP) -286 Mad Av -NY 10017
(212) 687-2770 .. **Blum,** Ian R '99 %Cohen PL&P -551 5th Av -NY 10176
(718) 461-6633 .. **Blum,** Jeffrey M '93 %Mallilo & G -163-09 Nrthrn Blvd -Flushng 11358
(518) 789-3613 .. **Blum,** John R H '56 -1 John BxZ -Millerton 12546
(212) 969-3000 .. **Blum,** Kevin S '10 %Proskauer R LLP -1585 Bway -NY 10036
(212) 259-8000 .. **Blum,** Leonard '68 OfCnsl Dewey & L LLP -1301 Av of Amer -NY 10019
(585) 423-1611 .. **Blum,** Mark R '76 -203 Irving Pl -Rchstr 14614
(718) 876-5723 .. **Blum,** Matthew P '02 DA -67 Targee -Staten Isl 10304
(212) 449-8486 .. **Blum,** Michl A '90 Merrill Lynch -250 Vesey -NY 10080
(212) 865-1793 .. **Blum,** Mitchell E '85 -251 W 101st -NY 10025
(212) 705-7000 .. **Blum,** Philip L '00 (Bingham M LLP) -399 Park Av -NY 10022

(212) 323-1905 .. **Blum,** Rebecca I '09 Chief Med Exmnr Ofc -421 E 26th -NY 10016
(212) 679-3918 .. **Blum,** Reuben '61 -286 Mad Av -NY 10017 **Fx:**679-3919
(212) 440-4300 .. **Blum,** Richd E '90 %Leg Aid -199 Water -NY 10038
(518) 402-2900 .. **Blum,** Robt M '53 (Dept of Law) -The Cptl -Albany 12224
(212) 790-4500 .. **Blum,** Ronald G '83 (Manatt P&P,LLP) -7 Times Sq -NY 10036
(518) 736-5511 .. **Blum,** Ronald G '09 %DA -223 W Main -Johnstwn 12095 **Fx:**762-2042
(631) 444-8250 .. **Blum,** Susan B '85 %SUNY Univ Cnsl -221 Admin Bldg -Stony Brk 11794 **Fx:**444-6101
(212) 687-3272 .. **Blum,** Tibby '71 (Blum & M) -271 Mad Av -NY 10016 **Fx:**949-0469
(212) 267-7600 .. **Blum,** Wm L '87 (Solomon PBH&S LLP) -40 Wall -NY 10005
(631) 789-4000 .. **Blumberg Cherkoss FitzGibbons & Blumberg** -330 Bway -Amityvll 11701 **Fx:**789-4005
(212) 346-0808 .. **Blumberg,** Craig A '92 -15 Maiden Ln -NY 10038 **Fx:**346-0777
(607) 334-5656 .. **Blumberg,** Edith '64 -Bx847 -New Berlin 13411
(631) 789-4000 .. **Blumberg,** H Lee '64 (Blumberg CF&B) -330 Bway -Amityvll 11701
(212) 417-3700 .. **Blumberg,** Jason S '08 MFY Legal Srvcs -299 Bway -NY 10007 **Fx:**417-3890
(631) 789-4000 .. **Blumberg,** Joshua P '00 (Blumberg CF&B) -330 Bway -Amityvll 11701
(718) 786-7777 .. **Blumberg,** Kenneth M '93 %Feldman Lumber -300 N Henry -Brklyn 11222
(212) 697-5550 .. **Blumberg,** Lawr S '74 (G & L Blumberg,LLP) -521 5th Av -NY 10175 **Fx:**697-9570
(212) 335-9000 .. **Blumberg,** Nicole J '99 %DA -1 Hogan Pl -NY 10013
(212) 761-2820 .. **Blumberg,** Philip M '02 Morgan Stanley -1585 Bway -NY 10036
(516) 248-1700 .. **Blumberg,** Richd A '94 (Forchelli CDSM&T,LLP) -333 Earle Ovngton Blvd -Uniondale 11553
(212) 431-5000 .. **Blumberg,** Robt H '64 %BlumbergExcelsior,Inc -62 White -NY 10013 **Fx:**431-5111
(914) 948-8466 .. **Blumberg,** Shawn B '06 Westchester Hispanic Coalition Inc -46 Waller Av -White Plns 10605
(631) 232-0800 .. **Blumberg,** Stuart G '60 (Blumberg & B) -129 Carleton Av -Central Islip 11722 **Fx:**232-1118
(516) 239-9653 .. **Blumberg,** Thelma C '51 -61 Margaret Av -Lawrence 11559
(212) 808-7235 .. **Blumberg,** Theo L '86 -230 Park Av -NY 10169
(212) 282-2127 .. **Blume,** Gerald W '83 %Rockefeller Grp -1221 Av of Amer -NY 10020 **Fx:**282-2005
(718) 618-0462 .. **Blumen,** Alan '02 -2753 Coney Isl Av -Brklyn 11235
(212) 969-3000 .. **Blumenauer,** Kerri R '08 %Proskauer R LLP -1585 Bway -NY 10036
(518) 884-4795 .. **Blumenberg,** Andrew C '95 %Pub Def -40 McMaster -Ballston Spa 12020 **Fx:**884-4789
(516) 327-2700 .. **Blumencranz,** Eric S '91 BWD Grp LLC -BWD Plz Bx9050 -Jericho 11753 **Fx:**327-2800
(718) 769-7000 .. **Blumenfeld,** Alan '88 %V Gartenstein,PC -3711 Shore Pkwy Bx350179 -Brklyn 11235 **Fx:**769-4302
(718) 292-2222 .. **Blumenfeld,** Franklin H '67 -327 E 149th -Bronx 10451 **Fx:**292-1190
(212) 298-5132 .. **Blumenfeld,** Joshua M '06 Leg Aid -49 Thomas -NY 10013 **Fx:**298-5252
(212) 785-2929 .. **Blumenfeld,** Michl T '89 (Conway FC&K,PC) -48 Wall -NY 10005
(914) 761-9008 .. **Blumenfeld,** Philip '59 -12 Murchison Pl -White Plns 10605 **Fx:**761-9008
(212) 756-2000 .. **Blumenfeld,** Robt D '07 %Schulte R&Z LLP -919 3rd Av -NY 10022
(914) 934-6002 .. **Blumenfeld,** Seth D '66 %MCI Intl -2 Intl Dr -Rye Brook 10573
(212) 762-4000 .. **Blumenfeld,** Stephen J '02 Morgan Stanley -1221 Av of Amer -NY 10020
(212) 447-0500 .. **Blumenfield,** Deborah B '06 %Graubard & Assoc,PC -65 W 36th -NY 10018 **Fx:**447-7505
(518) 463-4481 .. **Blumenkopf,** Alan '73 %Cade & S -4 Pine -Albany 12207
(212) 323-1905 .. **Blumenkopf,** Rebecca A '09 %OCME -421 E 26th -NY 10016
(212) 336-2000 .. **Blumenkrantz,** Adam P '07 %Patterson BW&T LLP -1133 Av of Amer -NY 10036
(212) 647-0450 .. **Blumenstein,** Danl G '82 -1123 Bway -NY 10010 **Fx:**859-7302
(212) 479-6000 .. **Blumenstein,** Ian B '90 (Cooley LLP) -1114 Av of Amer -NY 10036
(212) 964-7700 .. **Blumenstock,** John U H '83 (Warner B&B,LLP) -11 Park Pl -NY 10007 **Fx:**964-7730
(718) 643-7410 .. **Blumenthal,** Abbe Schwartz '81 Supreme Ct -120 Schermerhorn -Brklyn 11201
(212) 245-3860 .. **Blumenthal,** Andrew F '74 -250 W 57th -NY 10107 **Fx:**956-5463
(516) 584-6127 .. **Blumenthal,** Arthur H '68 -6900 Jericho Tpke -Syosset 11791
(516) 747-5566 .. **Blumenthal,** Dan M '93 (Ezratty E&L) -80 E Old Cntry Rd -Mineola 11501
(212) 603-6300 .. **Blumenthal,** David M '82 (Robinson BLGG&G PC) -875 3rd Av -NY 10022
(212) 480-3030 .. **Blumenthal,** Dustin C '06 %M Pressman -125 Maiden Ln -NY 10038 **Fx:**480-2590
(212) 440-4400 .. **Blumenthal,** Elliot J '93 Cnsl Buchanan I&R PC -620 8th Av -NY 10018
(516) 361-0412 .. **Blumenthal,** Gail '92 -7 Lord Av -Lawrence 11559 **Fx:**371-4370
(212) 245-3860 .. **Blumenthal,** Henry L '62 -250 W 57th -NY 10107 **Fx:**956-5463
(212) 719-9688 .. **Blumenthal,** Hillary B '97 -251 W 39th -NY 10018 **Fx:**719-9462
(212) 935-3000 .. **Blumenthal,** Ivan K '91 (Mintz LCFG&P,PC) -666 3rd Av -NY 10017
(914) 332-1270 .. **Blumenthal,** Michl A '79 -150 Wht Plns Rd -Tarrytwn 10591 **Fx:**332-1744
(212) 223-4000 .. **Blumenthal,** Michl V '75 (Crowell & M LLP) -590 Mad Av -NY 10022
(212) 943-1550 .. **Blumenthal,** Thos A '68 -26 Bway -NY 10004
(516) 228-5939 .. **Blumenthal-Stechman,** Jane '86 Defense Contract Mgt Agency -605 Stewart Av -Gdn Cty 11530 **Fx:**228-3647
(516) 229-4300 .. **Blumer,** Jarred W '09 J Bilello & Assoc -875 Merrick Av -Westbury 11590
(212) 685-9660 .. **Blumert,** Stephen J '80 (Schwartz & B) -295 Mad Av -NY 10017 **Fx:**599-6272
(212) 655-3500 .. **Bluming,** Sidney D '68 (Meister S&F LLP) -140 E 45th -NY 10017
(607) 277-7286 .. **Blumkin,** Joy A '81 (Blumkin F&B) -401 E State -Ithaca 14850
(212) 768-6700 .. **Blumm,** Carol A '03 %Sonnenschein N&R LLP -1221 Av of Amer -NY 10020
(212) 446-4800 .. **Blumsack,** Emily '07 %Kirkland & E LLP -153 E 53rd -NY 10022
(212) 751-7480 .. **Blumstein,** Stephanie J '04 %B Oberman -160 E 56th -NY 10022 **Fx:**935-8425
(212) 319-1000 .. **Blunda,** Stephen K '75 (Quirk & B,PC) -845 3rd Av -NY 10022
(845) 920-7100 .. **Blundetto,** Sandra G '94 US Re Company -Bx1574 -Pearl Rvr 10965
(212) 442-4016 .. **Blundi,** Suzanne S '93 NYC Health & Hospitals Corp -346 Bway -NY 10013
(516) 393-2200 .. **Blustein,** Andrew '91 (Garfunkel W,PC) -111 Grt Nck Rd -Gt Neck 11021
(845) 291-0011 .. **Blustein,** Burt J '64 (Blustein SR&B,LLP) -10 Matthews -Goshen 10924
(845) 291-0011 .. **Blustein,** Michl S '93 (Blustein SR&B,LLP) -10 Matthews -Goshen 10924
(845) 291-0011 .. **Blustein Shapiro Rich & Barone,LLP** -10 Matthews -Goshen 10924 **Fx:**291-0021
(212) 448-1130 .. **Bluth,** Marshall S '85 -733 3rd Av -NY 10017 **Fx:**354-2221
(516) 364-1095 .. **Bluth,** Norman N '93 (McBreen & K) -500 N Bway -Jericho 11753
(518) 455-7506 .. **Bluth,** Randall G '87 Leg Bill Drafting Comm -308 State Cptl -Albany 12224
(212) 407-7700 .. **Bluth,** Valerie J '09 %Vedder P,PC -1633 Bway -NY 10019
(212) 683-9700 .. **Bluthman,** Alvin P '74 GNY Mutual Ins -200 Mad Av -NY 10016 **Fx:**843-1962
(212) 483-9600 .. **Blutman,** Alan T '82 (Costello S&G LLP) -44 Wall -NY 10005
(212) 483-9600 .. **Blutman,** Paul E '78 (Costello S&G LLP) -44 Wall -NY 10005
(516) 433-7777 .. **Blutter,** Arthur I '80 (Blutter & B) -497 S Oyster Bay Rd -Plainvw 11803 **Fx:**938-2915
(516) 433-7777 .. **Blutter,** Joanne D '87 (Blutter & B) -497 S Oyster Bay Rd -Plainvw 11803 **Fx:**938-2915
(516) 433-7777 .. **Blutter,** Paul C '97 %Blutter & B -497 S Oyster Bay Rd -Plainvw 11803 **Fx:**938-2915
(716) 488-0758 .. **Bly,** Loren L '65 (Bly SBP&M) -3 Lakevw Av Bx3327 -Jamestwn 14702
(716) 488-0758 .. **Bly Sheffield Bargar Pillittieri & MacCallum** -3 Lakevw Av Bx3327 -Jamestwn 14702 **Fx:**483-3351
(917) 406-1533 .. **Blyangov,** Dimiter N '05 -419 Lafayette -NY 10003
(212) 605-6200 .. **Blydenburgh,** Donald P '06 %Levy P&K,LLP -800 3rd Av -NY 10022
(718) 330-7700 .. **Blyer,** Alvin P '70 %NLRB -2 Metrotech Ctr -Brklyn 11201 **Fx:**330-7579
(212) 788-1170 .. **Blyn,** Kathy E '83 %Law Dept -100 Church -NY 10007 **Fx:**788-0367
(845) 913-6093 .. **Blythe,** Michl D '03 -320 Jackson Av -New Windsor 12553 **Fx:**497-3255
(212) 514-7800 .. **Blythe,** Wendy E '93 %C DiGiulio,PC -111 John -NY 10038 **Fx:**514-7838
(212) 696-6000 .. **Bninski,** Roman A '76 (Curtis M-PC&M LLP) -101 Park Av -NY 10178
(212) 259-8000 .. **Boado,** Paolo C S '08 %Dewey & L LLP -1301 Av of Amer -NY 10019
(212) 336-8000 .. **Boag,** David A '02 %Amster R&E -90 Park Av -NY 10016
(212) 506-1700 .. **Boakye,** Abena A '06 Kasowitz BT&F LLP -1633 Bway -NY 10019
(212) 455-2000 .. **Boan,** Adrienne Escousse '99 Simpson T&B LLP -425 Lex Av -NY 10017
(212) 804-4200 .. **Boardingham,** Brian F '91 (Mound CW&G) -One Bttry Pk Plz -NY 10004
(585) 475-1100 .. **Boardman,** Erin F '05 %Segar & S -400 Meridian Centre -Rchstr 14618
(631) 367-7100 .. **Boardman,** Erin W '08 %Coughlin SGR&R LLP -58 S Srvc Rd -Melvll 11747
(212) 909-8404 .. **Boas,** Andrew M '81 Carl Marks & Co -900 3rd Av -NY 10022 **Fx:**980-2631
(516) 481-3339 .. **Boas,** Arlene L '85 -330 Eagle Av -W Hempstead 11552
(917) 583-5974 .. **Boatti,** Robt P '86 -323 W 96th -NY 10025
(212) 688-8555 .. **Boaz,** Reina '09 Fragomen DB&L LLP -7 Hanover Sq -NY 10004
(212) 440-3241 .. **Bob,** Rachel H '05 Lawyers Prof Liablty Claims-CNA -40 Wall -NY 10005
(518) 487-6219 .. **Bobarakis,** Stephen H Jr. '91 %IBM -80 State -Albany 12207
(212) 421-1000 .. **Bobb,** Julian A '01 %Jennison Assoc -466 Lex Av -NY 10017
(212) 819-8200 .. **Bobb,** Marcia Nesbitt '97 White & C LLP -1155 Av of Amer -NY 10036
(212) 363-8048 .. **Bobchin,** Peter C '90 -140 Bway PMB 46013 -NY 10005 **Fx:**(201) 848-6808
(518) 474-4552 .. **Bobear,** Theresa M '98 %Insurance Dept -99 Wshngtn Av -Albany 12257 **Fx:**486-2218
(716) 847-8400 .. **Bobeck,** Glenn J '93 (Phillips L LLP) -3400 HSBC Ctr -Buffalo 14203
(212) 637-2718 .. **Bober,** David V '03 US Atty -86 Chmbrs -NY 10007
(212) 331-5139 .. **Bober,** Michaele J '87 %HRA -180 Water -NY 10038
(212) 682-7474 .. **Bober,** Sandra A '03 %Foley & L LLP -90 Park Av -NY 10016
(212) 574-1200 .. **Bobinger,** Jonathan D '09 %Seward & K LLP -1 Bttry Pk Plz -NY 10004
(718) 990-6016 .. **Bobis,** Chas S '68 %St John's Law Schl -8000 Utopia Pkwy -Jamaica 11439 **Fx:**591-1855
(212) 213-2210 .. **Bobker,** Avi '03 -11 E 36th -NY 10016 **Fx:**213-2886
(212) 213-2210 .. **Bobker,** Benny B '02 -11 E 36th -NY 10016 **Fx:**213-2886
(212) 836-8000 .. **Bobker,** Dov '10 Kaye S LLP -425 Park Av -NY 10022
(212) 213-2210 .. **Bobker,** Eli M '00 -11 E 36th -NY 10016 **Fx:**213-2886
(914) 485-1185 .. **Bobolia,** Stephen J '77 -62 June Rd Bx512 -N Salem 10560 **Fx:**669-0018
(212) 776-5000 .. **Boboris,** Panagiotis D '04 NYC Housing Auth -250 Bway -NY 10007 **Fx:**776-5039
(315) 218-8000 .. **Bobrek,** Andrew D '08 %Bond S&K,PLLC -1 Lincoln Ctr -Syracuse 13202
(212) 969-3000 .. **Bobroff,** Bradley R '04 %Proskauer R LLP -1585 Bway -NY 10036
(212) 751-4300 .. **Bobrow,** Alvan L '74 (Hodgson R LLP) -1540 Bway -NY 10036
(212) 249-1550 .. **Bobrow,** Irving S '38 (Bobrow & R) -40 E 69th -NY 10021 **Fx:**249-5451
(718) 403-3600 .. **Bobrow,** Joy A '94 Dept of Finance -345 Adams -Brklyn 11201 **Fx:**403-3650
(315) 853-4436 .. **Bobrow,** Kenneth L '84 (Felt E,LLP) -4-6 N Park Row -Clinton 13323
(315) 853-4436 .. **Bobrow,** Patricia Shaffer '84 (Felt E,LLP) -4-6 N Park Row -Clinton 13323
(914) 632-5151 .. **Bobrow & Sosis** -271 North Av -New Rchll 10801 **Fx:**632-5252

(315) 422-1311 .. **Bobrycki,** Kenneth J '77 (Melvin & M,PLLC) -217 S Salina -Syracuse 13202
(716) 679-0404 .. **Bobseine,** Michl K '99 %Brautigam & B -32 White Bx210 -Fredonia 14063 **Fx:**679-0406
(212) 715-1000 .. **Boccanfuso,** Anthony D '89 %Arnold & P LLP -399 Park Av -NY 10022
(212) 909-6000 .. **Boccardi,** Lauren M '07 %Debevoise & P LLP -919 3rd Av -NY 10022
(914) 225-5591 .. **Boccardi,** Susan M '93 Morgan Stanley -2000 Wstchstr Av -Purchase 10577
(845) 831-0670 .. **Boccia,** Julius S '54 (Phillips H&S) -33 Henry Bx430 -Beacon 12508
(845) 452-3350 .. **Boccia,** Michl R '55 %Quaker Abstract -304 Main -Poughkeepsie 12601 **Fx:**452-8759
(212) 922-9221 .. **Boccia-Kovarcik,** Annamaria '93 -590 Mad Av -NY 10022
(718) 658-0500 .. **Boccio,** Danielle M '04 Law Dept -151-20 Jamaica Av -Jamaica 11432 **Fx:**658-4025
(716) 845-2504 .. **Boccio,** Diana M '88 %Supreme Ct -92 Franklin -Buffalo 14202 **Fx:**851-3293
(716) 845-7444 .. **Boccio,** Frank J '56 %Family Ct -1 Niagara Plz -Buffalo 14202 **Fx:**858-8432
(718) 557-6543 .. **Boccio,** Joy Freitas '95 OHA-SSA -Bx319300 -Jamaica 11431
(973) 496-2174 .. **Boccio,** Lynn A '79 AVIS -Bx4319 -Huntngtn 11743
(718) 389-7668 .. **Boccio,** Richd J '94 (Malewski M&B LLP) -657 Manh Av -Brklyn 11222
(516) 488-3300 .. **Boccio,** Robt '01 %Shaub AC&S,LLP -1983 Marcus Av -Lk Success 11042
(516) 541-7897 .. **Boccio,** Virginia A '84 -977 N Bway -Massapequa 11758 **Fx:**541-7760
(516) 294-5106 .. **Boccio,** Wm R '82 (W Boccio,PC) -22 Jericho Tpk -Mineola 11501 **Fx:**294-1657
(914) 693-0293 .. **Boccumini,** Carole M '87 -35 Nrthfld Av -Dobbs Ferry 10522
(212) 225-2000 .. **Boccuzzi,** Carmine D '95 (Cleary GS&H) -1 Lbrty Plz -NY 10006
(607) 734-5204 .. **Bocek,** Timothy J '04 (Personius MP&B) -150 Lk Bx146 -Elmira 14902
(516) 222-8060 .. **Bochat,** Christine A '04 %LJ Bochat,PC -377 Oak -Gdn Cty 11530
(516) 222-8060 .. **Bochat,** Lawr J '83 (LJ Bochat,PC) -377 Oak -Gdn Cty 11530
(212) 216-1245 .. **Bochenek,** Michl G '96 Human Rights Watch -350 5th Av -NY 10118 **Fx:**736-1300
(516) 747-0300 .. **Bochicchio,** Salvatore '04 %Meltzer LG&B,LLP -190 Willis Av -Mineola 11501
(516) 294-4876 .. **Bochner,** Alan S '82 -1225 Franklin Av -Gdn Cty 11530 **Fx:**877-2586
(516) 944-7474 .. **Bochner,** Lisa J '85 -62A Barkers Pnt Rd -Sands Pnt 11050 **Fx:**944-8224
(914) 251-0001 .. **Bochner,** Paul M '78 Cnsl Lane S&L LLP -106 Corp Park Dr -White Plns 10604
(718) 298-0235 .. **Bochner,** Suzanne M '89 Family Ct -151-20 Jamaica Av -Jamaica 11432
(212) 688-4000 .. **Bocina,** Joan S '84 NYS HFA -641 Lex Av -NY 10022 **Fx:**872-0362
(914) 245-6060 .. **Bock,** Aaron C '78 (Durante B&T,PLLC) -2000 Maple Hill -Yorktwn Hts 10598
(212) 440-4300 .. **Bock,** Jane S '86 %Leg Aid -199 Water -NY 10038
(631) 913-4444 .. **Bock,** Jennifer J '99 %Dell LT&V LLP -5 Orvll Dr -Bohemia 11716
(212) 587-3001 .. **Bock,** Norman P '86 (Leibowitz & B) -225 Bway -NY 10007 **Fx:**587-8699
(212) 840-8300 .. **Bock,** Simon '93 Natter & N -501 5th Av -NY 10017 **Fx:**302-0295
(212) 481-1300 .. **Bock,** Wallace '58 (Collier HNN&B,LLP) -355 Lex Av -NY 10017
(716) 853-5100 .. **Bocketti,** Brian J '99 %Lippes MWF LLP -665 Main -Buffalo 14203
(212) 233-5340 .. **Bocketti,** Phillip A '71 (Mazur & B) -225 Bway -NY 10007
(212) 530-5000 .. **Bockos,** Peter C '08 %Milbank TH&M LLP -1 Chase Manh Plz -NY 10005
(212) 885-5000 .. **Bockstein,** Herbert '72 (Blank R LLP) -405 Lex Av -NY 10174
(212) 988-9252 .. **Bockstein,** Martin H '60 -875 5th Av -NY 10065
(212) 907-0700 .. **Bockwoldt,** John B '08 %Labaton S LLP -140 Bway -NY 10005
(212) 418-6028 .. **Boczar,** Thos J '87 %Twenty-First Securities Corp -780 3rd Av -NY 10017
(212) 403-1000 .. **Boczko,** Ian '01 (Wachtell LR&K) -51 W 52nd -NY 10019
(718) 579-7902 .. **Bodack,** Sarah F '02 Leg Aid -900 Sheridan Av -Bronx 10451 **Fx:**293-8744
(212) 596-9000 .. **Bodade,** Nikhil L '08 %Ropes & G LLP -1211 Av of Amer -NY 10036
(315) 478-1583 .. **Bodah,** Scott F '90 %H Armani & Assoc -2700 Bellevue Av -Syracuse 13219
(212) 440-4300 .. **Bodden,** Marlen S '88 Leg Aid -199 Water -NY 10292
(718) 403-9655 .. **Bodden,** Wayne C '88 -45 Main -Brklyn 11201 **Fx:**403-0495
(212) 480-7652 .. **Boddie,** Corey D '02 (Boddie & Assoc,PC) -40 Exch Pl -NY 10005 **Fx:**480-6581
(212) 431-2371 .. **Boddie,** Elise C '98 %NY Law Schl -185 W Bway -NY 10013 **Fx:**406-0103
(718) 254-7000 .. **Bode,** Allen L '98 %US Atty -271 Cadman Plz E -Brklyn 11201 **Fx:**254-6479
(631) 853-4343 .. **Bode,** Kim E '03 %Leg Aid -400 Carleton Av Bx9082 -Central Islip 11722 **Fx:**853-7798
(212) 557-4000 .. **Bodek,** Arthur W '88 (Grunfeld DLS&K LLP) -399 Park Av -NY 10022
(212) 488-1200 .. **Bodel,** Alexandra Parra '07 %Kobre & K,LLP -800 3rd Av -NY 10022
(212) 973-8000 .. **Boden,** Eric A '07 %Schnader HS&L LLP -140 Bway -NY 10005
(516) 249-3450 .. **Boden,** Stephanie L '97 (Carman C&I,LLP) -266 Main -Farmngdl 11735 **Fx:**843-6390
(212) 589-4200 .. **Bodenheimer,** Henry C '06 %Baker & H LLP -45 Rckfllr Plz -NY 10111
(718) 459-0255 .. **Bodenstein,** Gail M '82 -108-31 65th Rd -Frst Hlls 11375
(212) 237-3649 .. **Boder,** Robt M '95 -26 Deer Tree Ln -Briarclff Mnr 10510
(585) 324-0500 .. **Bodewes,** Andrew V '01 Conifer Realty,LLC -183 E Main -Rchstr 14604
(631) 249-3900 .. **Bodian,** David H '95 (Bodian & B) -425 Broad Hollow Rd -Melvll 11747 **Fx:**249-4298
(631) 249-3900 .. **Bodian,** Martin H '59 (Bodian & B) -425 Broad Hollow Rd -Melvll 11747 **Fx:**249-4298
(212) 935-3000 .. **Bodian,** Robt I '81 (Mintz LCFG&P,PC) -666 3rd Av -NY 10017
(212) 974-7474 .. **Bodine,** Susan H '82 SpclCnsl Cowan DA&S LLP -41 Mad Av -NY 10010
(212) 310-8000 .. **Bodkin,** Lynn M '84 %Weil G&M LLP -767 5th Av -NY 10153
(212) 340-0400 .. **Bodkin,** Wm P '02 Appllt Div 1st Dept -27 Mad Av -NY 10010 **Fx:**889-4412
(518) 640-5000 .. **Bodmer,** Bradley '86 AYCO -25 British Amer Blvd -Latham 12110
(212) 848-4000 .. **Bodmer,** Zachary W '10 Shearman & S LLP -599 Lex Av -NY 10022
(914) 997-2500 .. **Bodnar,** Peter O '71 (Bodnar & M LLP) -140 Grand -White Plns 10601 **Fx:**997-8155
(212) 344-5633 .. **Bodner,** Allen Jay '64 -45 Bway -NY 10006 **Fx:**742-2626
(212) 777-7388 .. **Bodner,** Bruce '70 -Bx469 -Bearsville 12409
(518) 436-0751 .. **Bodner,** Fredric L '76 (Hinman S PC) -121 State -Albany 12207
(631) 249-7500 .. **Bodner,** Gerald T '82 (Bodner & O LLP) -425 Broadhllw Rd -Melvll 11747 **Fx:**249-4508
(212) 841-1000 .. **Bodner,** Jack S '95 (Covington & B LLP) -620 8th Av -NY 10018
(516) 222-7800 .. **Bodner,** Karen L '81 %S Hirsch PC -666 Old Cntry Rd -Gdn Cty 11530 **Fx:**222-0518
(212) 669-4952 .. **Bodner,** Marilyn S '95 %Comptroller -1 Centre -NY 10007 **Fx:**669-2884
(212) 486-3000 .. **Bodner,** Mark L '83 (M Bodner,PC) -470 Park Av S -NY 10016 **Fx:**(646) 514-0888
(212) 902-1000 .. **Bodoff,** Amy P '97 Goldman Sachs & Co -85 Broad -NY 10004
(718) 923-6361 .. **Bodoff,** Fred A '68 Committee Character & Fitness -335 Adams -Brklyn 11201
(212) 686-4401 .. **Bodoff,** Jeffrey A '89 %Abramson Law Grp PLLC -570 Lex Av -NY 10022 **Fx:**686-6515
(516) 357-3000 .. **Bodoff,** Stuart M '97 (Rivkin R LLP) -926 RXR Plz -Uniondale 11556
(718) 403-3600 .. **Bodon,** Zulma A '91 Dept of Finance -345 Adams -Brklyn 11201 **Fx:**403-3650
(212) 819-8200 .. **Bodony,** Rebecca M '08 %White & C LLP -1155 Av of Amer -NY 10036
(212) 919-3076 .. **Bodovitz,** James P '85 Guardian Life -7 Hanover Sq -NY 10004
(315) 422-1234 .. **Bodow,** Wayne R '75 -8184 Bluffvw Dr -Manlius 13104 **Fx:**422-9113
(212) 872-3054 .. **Bodrato,** Michl F '97 %KPMG LLP -345 Park Av -NY 10154 **Fx:**954-2786
(315) 703-6600 .. **Bodwitch,** Wm '76 %Leg Aid -472 S Salina -Syracuse 13202 **Fx:**671-0062
(631) 324-4428 .. **Bodziner,** Steven '78 -38 Gould -E Hampton 11937 **Fx:**324-4428
(716) 897-4896 .. **Boeck,** Danl P '90 -1332 Walden Av -Cheektowaga 14211
(212) 474-1000 .. **Boeckman,** Philip J '92 (Cravath S&M LLP) -825 8th Av -NY 10019
(631) 715-7900 .. **Boeckmann,** Nicole '98 US Atty -610 Fed Plz -Central Islip 11722
(718) 979-7874 .. **Boegel,** Ellen K '85 -200 Jacques Av -Staten Isl 10306
(212) 350-2700 .. **Boegem,** Sacha A '06 %Constantine C,PC -450 Lex Av -NY 10017
(914) 761-2252 .. **Boeggeman George & Corde,PC** -1 Water -White Plns 10601 **Fx:**761-5211
(518) 465-1100 .. **Boeggeman George & Corde,PC** -46 Columbia -Albany 12207 **Fx:**465-1800
(585) 545-0380 .. **Boehler,** James R '68 -16 E Main -Rchstr 14614 **Fx:**325-4559
(518) 388-1270 .. **Boehlert,** Robt J '78 %CQC -401 State -Schnctdy 12305 **Fx:**388-1275
(516) 627-8660 .. **Boehm,** Brian B '77 -47 Plandome Rd -Manhsst 11030 **Fx:**869-0697
(212) 349-6460 .. **Boehm,** Geoffrey A '97 NY PIRG -9 Murray -NY 10007
(716) 854-3015 .. **Boehm,** Robt C '73 (Aaron DS&L,LLP) -43 Court -Buffalo 14202
(212) 504-6000 .. **Boehm,** Shlomo M '04 %Cadwalader W&T LLP -1 World Fncl Ctr -NY 10281
(212) 418-0540 .. **Boehner,** Leonard B '56 (Morris & M LLP) -767 3rd Av -NY 10017
(212) 373-3000 .. **Boehning,** H Christopher '95 (Paul WRW&G LLP) -1285 Av of Amer -NY 10019
(518) 828-1792 .. **Boeringer,** Margaret J '04 Hudson Area Assoc Library -400 State -Hudson 12534
(212) 408-2500 .. **Boerman,** Brian S '09 %Baker B,LLP -30 Rckfllr Plz -NY 10112
(718) 664-1956 .. **Boerner,** Brittney '07 ACS -900 Sheridan Av -Bronx 10451
(718) 330-7713 .. **Boerschinger,** Tabitha E '02 %NLRB -2 Metrotech Ctr -Brklyn 11201 **Fx:**330-7579
(646) 624-5924 .. **Boersma,** Diana L '81 Genpact -105 Mad Av -NY 10016
(516) 255-3780 .. **Boes,** Lawr E '94 SrCnsl Lincoln Land Srvcs LLC -265 Sunrise Hwy -Rockvll Ctr 11570 **Fx:**255-3701
(516) 997-2996 .. **Boes,** Lawr W '65 -256 Asbury Av -Westbury 11590
(212) 449-3495 .. **Boesch,** Leslina Wen-Ling '03 Merrill Lynch -4 World Fncl Ctr -NY 10080
(585) 423-5778 .. **Boesel,** Scott R '01 %Xerox -100 Clinton Av S -Rchstr 14644
(212) 421-5333 .. **Boesky,** Stuart J '82 %Related Capital -625 Mad Av -NY 10022 **Fx:**593-6131
(212) 326-2000 .. **Boettjer,** Shannon '03 Cnsl O'Melveny & M LLP -7 Times Sq -NY 10036
(212) 637-2748 .. **Boeving,** James N '06 US Atty -86 Chmbrs -NY 10007
(585) 798-1615 .. **Bogan,** Katherine Kersch '94 -517 Main Bx14 -Medina 14103 **Fx:**798-1615
(585) 590-4127 .. **Bogan,** Katherine Kersch '94 %DA -13925 Route 31 -Albion 14411 **Fx:**590-4129
(212) 687-8300 .. **Bogard,** Mark D '09 PLC Law Grp -245 Park Av -NY 10167 **Fx:**867-8301
(585) 530-3111 .. **Bogardus,** Amy I '99 %Appllt Div 4th Dept -50 East Av Ste 200 -Rchstr 14604 **Fx:**530-3247
(917) 421-4741 .. **Bogardus,** Wm C '99 IRS -33 Maiden Ln -NY 10038
(716) 858-2424 .. **Bogart,** Mary Ann '97 %DA -25 Delaware Av -Buffalo 14202 **Fx:**858-7425
(212) 684-8282 .. **Bogart,** Michl R '04 Cnsl Maxwell-Kates,Inc -9 E 38th -NY 10016 **Fx:**545-6718
(212) 876-1840 .. **Bogart,** Nelson '88 -1636 3rd Av -NY 10128 **Fx:**876-2467
(212) 490-4100 .. **Bogart,** Russell L '97 %Storch A&M,PC -140 E 45th -NY 10017
(212) 971-7693 .. **Bogart,** Valerie J '83 Selfhelp Commnty Srvcs Inc -520 8th Av -NY 10018
(212) 406-9065 .. **Bogatin,** Marc '82 -277 Bway -NY 10007 **Fx:**406-1560
(212) 481-7797 .. **Bogaty,** A Paul '77 -470 Park Av S -NY 10016 **Fx:**686-3822
(631) 247-0404 .. **Bogaty,** Ian B '04 %Jackson L LLP -58 S Srvc Rd -Melvll 11747
(914) 674-4047 .. **Bogaty,** Lewis '80 -923 Saw Mill Rvr Rd -Ardsley 10502 **Fx:**674-6494
(914) 220-0038 .. **Bogatz,** Susan A '98 %Pattison & F -1 N Lex Av -White Plns 10601

(212) 837-6000 .. **Bogdan,** Alexander W '07 %Hughes H&R LLP -1 Bttry Pk Plz -NY 10004
(518) 434-9000 .. **Bogdan,** Edw A III '93 %Bogdan L&K LLC -111 Wshngtn Av -Albany 12210 **Fx:**434-2510
(631) 225-5300 .. **Bogdan,** Ewa B '97 -100 Montauk Hwy -Copiague 11726 **Fx:**225-3400
(212) 761-4000 .. **Bogdan,** Fredk W '86 Morgan Stanley -88 Pine -NY 10005
(315) 646-2877 .. **Bogdan,** Robt P '92 -Bx286 -Sackets Hbr 13685 **Fx:**646-2878
(518) 862-1200 .. **Bogdan,** Rosemarie Riddell '93 (Martin H&M LLP) -Bx15141 -Albany 12212
(914) 245-1100 .. **Bogdanoff,** Suzanne '90 Montrose Mgmt Assoc Inc -3666 Hill Blvd Bx590 -Jffrsn Vly 10535 **Fx:**245-0797
(212) 849-7000 .. **Bogdanos,** Claudia T '96 OfCnsl Quinn EU&S,LLP -51 Mad Av -NY 10010
(212) 335-9000 .. **Bogdanos,** Matthew F '84 %DA -1 Hogan Pl -NY 10013
(212) 583-0100 .. **Bogdanos,** Natalie '00 Enzo Biochem -527 Mad Av -NY 10022
(212) 302-3300 .. **Bogdashevsky,** Dmitry '01 Graf Repetti & Co,LLP -1114 Av of Amer -NY 10036 **Fx:**302-9660
(212) 530-5000 .. **Bogdashevsky,** Irene '04 %Milbank TH&M LLP -1 Chase Manh Plz -NY 10005
(212) 715-1000 .. **Bogen,** Andrew S '85 Cnsl Arnold & P LLP -399 Park Av -NY 10022
(518) 452-5600 .. **Boger,** John W '96 %Heslin RF&M PC -5 Columbia Cir -Albany 12203
(212) 426-3000 .. **Boggia,** Silvana '01 Leg Aid -230 E 106th -NY 10029 **Fx:**876-5365
(212) 756-2000 .. **Boggiano,** Kristin '02 SpclCnsl Schulte R&Z LLP -919 3rd Av -NY 10022
(914) 946-3700 .. **Boggio,** Gail M '98 (McCarthy F LLP) -11 Martine Av -White Plns 10606
(718) 643-6277 .. **Boggio,** Linda M '88 %Family Ct -283 Adams -Brklyn 11201
(914) 699-7772 .. **Boggio,** Miriam A '77 Supreme Ct -80 Centre -NY 10013
(718) 237-2000 .. **Boggs,** Wm D '02 Leg Aid -111 Lvngstn -Brklyn 11201 **Fx:**237-8737
(212) 679-5100 .. **Boghosian,** Heidi E '07 Natl Lawyers Guild -132 Nassau -NY 10038 **Fx:**679-2811
(212) 586-5800 .. **Boghosian,** Robt A '88 (Cohen TS&W PC) -420 Lex Av -NY 10170
(718) 264-3340 .. **Bogin,** Adam T '06 %MHLS -80-45 Wnchstr Blvd -Qns Vllg 11427 **Fx:**264-3559
(518) 445-6050 .. **Bogin,** James M '85 %Prisoners' Leg Srvcs -41 State -Albany 12207 **Fx:**445-6053
(212) 421-2150 .. **Bogin,** Michl S '90 (Sive P&R,PC) -460 Park Av -NY 10022
(212) 530-7000 .. **Bogin,** Russell G '92 %Home Ins -59 Maiden Ln -NY 10038
(845) 486-2110 .. **Bogle,** Carol A '84 %Cnty Atty -22 Market -Poughkeepsie 12601 **Fx:**486-2002
(212) 705-7000 .. **Bogle,** Chas R '95 (Bingham M LLP) -399 Park Av -NY 10022
(212) 785-2929 .. **Bogle,** Richd '89 %Conway FC&K,PC -48 Wall -NY 10005
(516) 571-2070 .. **Bogle,** Robt G '83 %Cnty Ct -262 Old Cntry Rd -Mineola 11501 **Fx:**571-2160
(845) 454-1110 .. **Bogle,** Wm F Jr. '84 (Corbally G and R LLP) -35 Market -Poughkeepsie 12601
(212) 836-8000 .. **Boglioli,** Danl M '01 Cnsl Kaye S LLP -425 Park Av -NY 10022
(716) 878-9626 .. **Boglioli,** James A '99 Benderson Development Co,LLC -570 Delaware Av -Buffalo 14202
(212) 969-3000 .. **Boglivi,** Lauren K '93 (Proskauer R LLP) -1585 Bway -NY 10036
(212) 715-1000 .. **Bogner,** Barri Lynn '00 Cnsl Arnold & P LLP -399 Park Av -NY 10022
(716) 852-5875 .. **Bogner,** Brian J '10 %Feldman K LLP -110 Pearl -Buffalo 14202
(212) 969-3000 .. **Bogner,** Ira G '91 (Proskauer R LLP) -1585 Bway -NY 10036
(212) 272-9893 .. **Bogner,** Jennifer Tillem '91 %JP Morgan Chase -383 Mad Av -NY 10179
(212) 373-3000 .. **Bogner,** Michl S '06 %Paul WRW&G LLP -1285 Av of Amer -NY 10019
(631) 844-7422 .. **Bogni,** Jason R '03 %Adecco USA -175 Broadhllw Rd -Melvll 11747 **Fx:**844-7266
(212) 404-6988 .. **Bogorad,** Lyle A '04 %R Yellen & Assoc LLP -111 Bway -NY 10006 **Fx:**404-7857
(845) 225-1382 .. **Bogosian,** Gary P '75 (Della Cioppa & B) -64 Gleneida Av -Carmel 10512 **Fx:**225-1385
(631) 282-7338 .. **Bogosian,** Margaret C '68 %Brookhaven Natl Lab -Bldg 902C Bx5000 -Upton 11973 **Fx:**282-3729
(212) 877-8082 .. **Bograd,** Harriet M '67 -165 West End Av -NY 10023
(212) 229-8923 .. **Bogre,** Michelle L '04 %Parsons Design Schl -66 5th Av -NY 10011
(212) 417-5638 .. **Bogren,** Elizabeth T '77 %Medicaid Fraud Cntrl -120 Bway -NY 10271 **Fx:**417-5335
(516) 739-1950 .. **Bogucki,** Robt H '69 -666 Old Cntry Rd -Gdn Cty 11530 **Fx:**227-1126
(212) 458-3987 .. **Bogue,** Martin J '99 AIG -175 Water -NY 10038
(212) 819-8200 .. **Bogush,** Olga '05 %White & C LLP -1155 Av of Amer -NY 10036
(212) 449-1261 .. **Boguslavsky,** Ilya '04 Merrill Lynch -4 World Fncl Ctr -NY 10281
(516) 822-9000 .. **Bogut,** John F '65 OfCnsl J O'Brien -500 N Bway -Jericho 11753 **Fx:**822-1050
(212) 327-3684 .. **Bohan,** Alice Anne '95 -1225 Park Av -NY 10128 **Fx:**327-3694
(914) 834-0102 .. **Bohan,** Jos P Jr. '60 (Bohan TB&W) -2001 Palmer Av -Larchmnt 10538
(914) 834-0102 .. **Bohan Trask Bohan & Winter** -2001 Palmer Av -Larchmnt 10538 **Fx:**833-1350
(212) 848-4000 .. **Bohannon,** Amy E '05 %Shearman & S LLP -599 Lex Av -NY 10022
(917) 777-4200 .. **Bohensky,** Harlyn D '02 Cnsl Bingham M LLP -1 Bttry Pk Plz -NY 10004
(718) 252-6942 .. **Bohensky,** Jay '95 -2115 Av O -Brklyn 11210
(914) 273-1000 .. **Bohm,** Alex A '51 -10 Hunter Dr -Armonk 10504 **Fx:**273-5533
(718) 928-3245 .. **Bohm,** Elyse K '77 -902 Kings Hwy -Brklyn 11223 **Fx:**627-2361
(212) 909-6000 .. **Bohm,** Richd D '79 (Debevoise & P LLP) -919 3rd Av -NY 10022
(212) 972-3557 .. **Bohmart,** Joel K '60 Bohmart & S,PC -60 E 42nd -NY 10165 **Fx:**972-3607
(516) 357-3700 .. **Bohn,** Douglas J '99 %Cullen and D LLP -100 Q Roosevelt Blvd -Gdn Cty 11530
(212) 787-0319 .. **Bohn,** Theo R '91 -501 5th Av -NY 10017 **Fx:**787-0716
(917) 279-2495 .. **Bohnenfield,** Murray Z '78 -1325 Penn Av -Brklyn 11239 **Fx:**(718) 642-3676
(212) 748-2367 .. **Bohner,** Christine Ramsey '99 %Zurich Amer Ins Co -One Lbrty Plz -NY 10006
(212) 732-9000 .. **Bohner,** Robt J '59 OfCnsl Sullivan PBM&C PC -120 Bway -NY 10271
(718) 636-1155 .. **Bohnett,** Elizabeth H '09 %Leg Srvcs -1368 Fulton -Brklyn 11216 **Fx:**398-6414
(212) 318-3000 .. **Bohnett,** Wm H '75 OfCnsl Fulbright & J LLP -666 5th Av -NY 10103
(212) 589-4200 .. **Bohorquez,** Fernando A Jr. '00 (Baker & H LLP) -45 Rckfllr Plz -NY 10111
(212) 610-6300 .. **Bohr,** Bernd '01 SrCnsl Allen & O -1221 Av of Amer -NY 10020
(212) 751-8000 .. **Bohrer,** Abram I '92 OfCnsl Dankner & M,PC -41 E 57th -NY 10022
(315) 423-2932 .. **Bohrer,** Andrew '95 %Workers Comp Bd -935 James -Syracuse 13203 **Fx:**423-2938
(212) 880-9550 .. **Bohrer,** Barry A '76 (Morvillo AGIA&B,PC) -565 5th Av -NY 10017
(212) 732-8700 .. **Bohrer,** David K '00 (McAloon & F,PC) -123 William -NY 10038
(212) 560-2941 .. **Bohrer,** Jessica A '06 Wnet.org -450 W 33rd -NY 10001
(631) 853-5761 .. **Bohrer,** Karin A '01 %Cnty Atty -400 Carleton Av -Central Islip 11722 **Fx:**853-7788
(914) 835-1414 .. **Bohrman,** Darren M '08 Vail Chevrolet Inc -Bx370 -Bedfrd Hlls 10507
(212) 526-9523 .. **Boidman,** Mark A '01 Barclays Capital Inc -745 7th Av -NY 10019
(212) 446-2300 .. **Boies,** Christopher A '95 (Boies S&F LLP) -575 Lex Av -NY 10022
(212) 806-5400 .. **Boies,** Christopher G '08 %Stroock &S&L LLP -180 Maiden Ln -NY 10038
(914) 749-8200 .. **Boies,** David '67 (Boies S&F LLP) -333 Main -Armonk 10504
(212) 446-2300 .. **Boies,** Judith '65 Cnsl Boies S&F LLP -575 Lex Av -NY 10022
(914) 234-3700 .. **Boies,** Mary M '88 Boies & M -Empire Bldg -Bedfrd 10506 **Fx:**234-0929
(518) 434-0600 .. **Boies Schiller & Flexner LLP** -10 N Pearl -Albany 12207 **Fx:**434-0665
(914) 749-8200 .. **Boies Schiller & Flexner LLP** -333 Main -Armonk 10504 **Fx:**749-8300
(212) 446-2300 .. **Boies Schiller & Flexner LLP** -575 Lex Av -NY 10022 **Fx:**446-2350
(518) 257-3000 .. **Boiko,** Stephan A '76 %Dormitory Auth -515 Bway -Albany 12207 **Fx:**257-3101
(585) 454-1130 .. **Boillat,** Louise A '83 Cnsl FR Michel -28 E Main -Rchstr 14614 **Fx:**454-6118
(212) 209-3058 .. **Boillot,** David A '75 SrCnsl Reitler K&R LLC -885 3rd Av -NY 10022
(716) 664-5600 .. **Boinski,** Jos J '05 %Bilicki Law Firm,PC -1285 N Main -Jamestwn 14701 **Fx:**664-5606
(212) 259-8000 .. **Boisseau,** Jane '86 (Dewey & L LLP) -1301 Av of Amer -NY 10019
(212) 626-0240 .. **Boisseau,** Justin L '00 Gates Capital Mgmt -1177 Av of Amer -NY 10036
(212) 475-1100 .. **Boissevain,** Benjamin M '88 Agile Equity -381 Park S -NY 10016
(516) 594-1234 .. **Boitel,** Henry J '66 -324 Brower Av -Rockvll Ctr 11570 **Fx:**536-8766
(518) 473-5093 .. **Boivin,** Bruce J '92 %Dept of Law -The Cptl -Albany 12224
(212) 262-2390 .. **Bojbasa,** Michl '07 %Connell F LLP -888 7th Av -NY 10106
(212) 506-1700 .. **Bojesen,** Andreas K '04 Kasowitz BT&F LLP -1633 Bway -NY 10019
(631) 451-7900 .. **Bokar,** Andrew W '97 %Rosenberg & G,LLP -1176 Portion Rd -Holtsvll 11742
(315) 946-5905 .. **Bokelman,** Christopher '05 DA -54 Broad -Lyons 14489 **Fx:**946-5911
(212) 468-4800 .. **Bokert,** Mark E '95 (Davis & G LLP) -1740 Bway -NY 10019
(212) 277-4000 .. **Bokhari,** Kiran '01 %Freshfields BD LLP -520 Mad Av -NY 10022
(631) 396-1980 .. **Boklak,** John '98 -4250 Vets Mem'l Hwy -Holbrook 11741 **Fx:**396-1983
(516) 889-1107 .. **Bokor,** Jason D '96 (Goldberg & B,LLP) -138 E Park Av -Long Bch 11561
(212) 664-7152 .. **Bokor,** Jonathan D '90 %NBC -30 Rckfllr Plz -NY 10112
(718) 579-7900 .. **Boksenbaum,** Anna V '06 Leg Aid -900 Sheridan Av -Bronx 10451 **Fx:**293-8744
(718) 834-1904 .. **Bokser,** Andrew A '83 -26 Court -Brklyn 11242 **Fx:**834-1830
(212) 533-6300 .. **Bokser,** Sherry B '88 %NYSUT -52 Bway -NY 10004 **Fx:**995-2347
(718) 298-5251 .. **Bolaji,** Oladeji O '99 -91-16 Sutphin Blvd -Jamaica 11435 **Fx:**298-5279
(212) 406-1919 .. **Bolan,** Brian J '00 %Gennet KA&R,PC -140 Bway -NY 10005
(212) 201-6825 .. **Bolan Jahnsen Salter & Sachs** -One Lbrty Plz -NY 10006 **Fx:**201-6824
(716) 845-2761 .. **Boland,** Ann Marie '87 Supreme Ct -25 Delaware Av -Buffalo 14202 **Fx:**851-3293
(212) 995-7496 .. **Boland,** Claire E '87 Cabrini Medical Ctr -227 E 19th -NY 10003
(212) 940-3122 .. **Boland,** Constance M '87 (Nixon P LLP) -437 Mad Av -NY 10022
(716) 285-6953 .. **Boland,** Danl P '88 %Rice RB&W -800 Main Bx219 -Niagara Fls 14302
(516) 741-8850 .. **Boland,** Donald J '63 -320 Old Cntry Rd -Gdn Cty 11530 **Fx:**294-1767
(516) 379-9035 .. **Boland,** Donald J '63 -33 N Babylon Tpk -Merrick 11566
(516) 922-9100 .. **Boland,** John F '87 %V McNamara -1045 Oyster Bay Rd -E Norwich 11732 **Fx:**922-9208
(518) 474-3032 .. **Boland,** Kathleen A '96 %Medicaid Fraud Cntrl -The Cptl -Albany 12223 **Fx:**474-4519
(631) 244-2904 .. **Boland,** Lyn Batzar '83 (Boland & C) -222 E Mian -Smithtwn 11787 **Fx:**472-5153
(212) 442-4191 .. **Boland,** Mary B '92 Hlth & Hsptl Corp -346 Bway -NY 10013
(631) 329-1411 .. **Boland,** Nicholas J '90 -38 Bucks Path -E Hampton 11937
(212) 998-7274 .. **Boland,** Robt A '96 NYU -10 Astor Pl -NY 10003
(516) 248-1200 .. **Boland,** Susan B '06 %Mulholland M&R -374 Hillside Av -Williston Pk 11596
(718) 990-7428 .. **Boland-DeVito,** Joyce E '85 St John's Univ Law Schl -8000 Utopia Pkwy -Jamaica 11439
(212) 351-4000 .. **Bolander,** Bruce D '85 (Gibson D&C LLP) -200 Park Av -NY 10166
(212) 647-1138 .. **Bolano,** Maritza F '94 -241 Av of Amer -NY 10014 **Fx:**633-8766
(585) 419-8800 .. **Bolaños,** Karlee S '02 (Harris B PLLC) -99 Garnsey Rd -Pittsfrd 14534
(212) 363-3782 .. **Bolatti,** Silvia L '88 (Bolatti & G) -45 Bway -NY 10006 **Fx:**363-3790
(516) 733-1810 .. **Boldi,** Danl L '03 %J Beschel,PC -77 Newbrdg Rd -Hicksvll 11801
(516) 733-1822 .. **Boldi,** Elizabeth '03 %Rivers Edge Land Srvcs -77 Newbrdg Rd -Hicksvll 11801 **Fx:**320-8096
(631) 360-7333 .. **Boldi,** Greta S '04 De Sena & S -1383 Vets Mem'l Hwy -Hauppauge 11788

(585) 428-2680 .. **Boldt**, Margaret M '84 %Family Ct -309B Hall of Justice -Rchstr 14614
(585) 473-3100 .. **Boldt**, Timothy D '06 %Ernstrom & D,LLP -180 Canal Vw Blvd -Rchstr 14623
(212) 984-8013 .. **Bolen**, Anne E '02 CB Richd Ellis -200 Park Av -NY 10166
(212) 801-9315 .. **Bolen**, David E '99 (Greenberg T,LLP) -200 Park Av -NY 10166
(716) 753-3333 .. **Bolender**, Michl J '78 -Bx154 -Mayvll 14757
(518) 274-2501 .. **Bolgatz**, Abraham E '58 -127 Elmgrove Av -Troy 12180
(845) 528-4410 .. **Bolger Hinz & Zutt** -Bx8 -Putnam Vly 10579 **Fx:**528-2566
(212) 918-3000 .. **Bolger**, Katherine M '99 (Hogan L LLP) -875 3rd Av -NY 10022
(212) 208-1187 .. **Bolger**, Rita M '83 %Standard & Poor's -55 Water -NY 10041
(212) 586-8329 .. **Bolin**, Ngozi E '91 -30 Lincoln Plz -NY 10023 **Fx:**(646) 314-8851
(212) 314-8000 .. **Bolkin**, Eve B '89 %Capgemini NA -623 5th Av -NY 10022
(212) 279-9090 .. **Boll**, Alisa C '04 %Stark & S -One Penn Plz -NY 10119 **Fx:**279-9113
(212) 446-4800 .. **Boll**, Deanna D '00 (Kirkland & E LLP) -153 E 53rd -NY 10022
(518) 463-3990 .. **Boll**, Jennifer M '00 (Tuczinski CG&C,PC) -54 State -Albany 12207
(212) 867-4100 .. **Bolla**, Evan W '08 %Furman K&B LLP -61 Bway -NY 10006
(518) 833-1322 .. **Bollam**, Jeremy O '05 Emma Willard School -285 Pawling Av -Troy 12180
(518) 474-4552 .. **Bollam**, Rebecca L '05 %Insurance Dept -99 Wshngtn Av -Albany 12257 **Fx:**486-2218
(212) 915-8190 .. **Bollati**, Albana '05 %Willis of NY -200 Lbrty -NY 10281 **Fx:**915-8511
(845) 651-4644 .. **Bollenbach**, John D '90 -757 Seward Hwy -Florida 10921
(212) 509-0918 .. **Bollepalli**, Sumanth '09 %Weissman & M LLC -80 Pine -NY 10005
(212) 351-4000 .. **Boller**, Jennifer L '08 %Gibson D&C LLP -200 Park Av -NY 10166
(212) 872-1000 .. **Boller**, Robt J '07 -One Bryant Park -NY 10036 **Fx:**872-1002
(212) 867-3636 .. **Boller**, Rosemary B '84 (Levin & G,PC) -420 Lex Av -NY 10170
(212) 783-3619 .. **Bollerman**, Jeffrey C '03 Citigroup -485 Lex Av -NY 10017
(518) 457-7012 .. **Bolles**, David M '81 %Dept Of Labor Ofc of Inspector Genl -State Campus Bldg 12 -Albany 12240 **Fx:**457-4954
(631) 584-0100 .. **Bollhofer**, Jos A '85 -291 Lk Av -St James 11780 **Fx:**584-2304
(212) 704-6000 .. **Bollinger**, James M '87 (Troutman S LLP) -405 Lex Av -NY 10174
(631) 379-6452 .. **Bollon**, Kathleen M '00 -Bx1331 -Commack 11725
(716) 649-7940 .. **Bolm**, Robt J '68 -5629 Coachman's Ln -Hambrg 14075
(201) 671-0124 .. **Bolnick**, David R '81 %Merrill Lynch -201 E 80th -NY 10075 **Fx:**671-3705
(845) 639-6666 .. **Bolnick**, Garry M '78 (Kleinman S&B,PC) -151 N Main Bx947 -New Cty 10956
(914) 328-0404 .. **Bologna**, Jenifer M '94 %Jackson L LLP -1 N Bway -White Plns 10601
(212) 909-6000 .. **Bolotin**, Michl I '05 %Debevoise & P LLP -919 3rd Av -NY 10022
(212) 446-4771 .. **Bolsinger**, Cristin A '03 -153 E 53rd -NY 10022
(212) 446-4800 .. **Bolsinger**, Markus P '98 (Kirkland & E LLP) -153 E 53rd -NY 10022
(212) 578-2211 .. **Bolstad**, Max '01 %MetLife -27-01 Qns Plz N -LIC 11101
(212) 902-2649 .. **Bolster**, Brian W '01 Goldman Sachs -85 Broad -NY 10004
(315) 471-3151 .. **Bolster**, Jennifer R '04 %Hancock & E,LLP -1500 AXA Twr I Bx4976 -Syracuse 13221
(212) 701-3000 .. **Bolster**, Karen L '09 %Cahill G&R LLP -80 Pine -NY 10005 **Fx:**269-5420
(212) 999-5800 .. **Bolton**, Craig E '09 %Wilson SG&R -1301 Av of Americas -NY 10019
(212) 345-5932 .. **Bolton**, Dana J '87 %Marsh USA -1166 Av of Amer -NY 10036 **Fx:**345-4808
(516) 222-0600 .. **Bolton**, David '90 (D Bolton,PC) -666 Old Cntry Rd -Gdn Cty 11530 **Fx:**222-1110
(516) 832-7568 .. **Bolton**, Jennifer G '95 %Nixon P LLP -50 Jericho Quadrangle -Jericho 11753
(212) 358-8244 .. **Bolton**, John F '96 Phoenix Partners Grp LP -315 Park Av S -NY 10010
(212) 872-1000 .. **Bolton**, Victoria Fisher '04 -One Bryant Park -NY 10036 **Fx:**872-1002
(716) 854-6140 .. **Boltrek**, Wm III '01 %Baxter S&S,PC -182 Dwyer -W Seneca 14224
(212) 954-6337 .. **Boltz**, Mark A '00 %KPMG LLP -345 Park Av -NY 10154
(718) 459-9000 .. **Bolz**, Francis A III '84 (Sweeney GR&B,LLP) -95-25 Qns Blvd -Rego Pk 11374
(518) 589-6290 .. **Bolz**, Michl R '85 -Colgate Rd Bx63 -E Jewett 12424
(212) 859-8000 .. **Bomba**, Abigail P '04 %Fried FHS&J LLP -1 NY Plz -NY 10004
(212) 513-1112 .. **Bomba**, Margaret Ann '83 -2 Wall -NY 10005 **Fx:**495-2379
(718) 579-3000 .. **Bomba**, Thos F '88 %Leg Aid -1020 Grnd Cncrs -Bronx 10451 **Fx:**588-2611
(718) 845-4283 .. **Bombara**, Robt George '74 -98-16 163rd Av -Howard Bch 11414 **Fx:**845-2516
(212) 341-0793 .. **Bombard**, Steven R '94 %Law Dept -100 Church -NY 10007 **Fx:**788-0367
(914) 765-1900 .. **Bomberger**, Gregory '78 IBM -1 New Orchrd Rd -Armonk 10504 **Fx:**765-7533
(516) 482-3934 .. **Bommarito**, Robt '01 R Bommarito,PC -80 Cuttermill Rd -Gt Neck 11021 **Fx:**829-8801
(716) 842-1222 .. **Bommer**, Loran Martin '00 -485 Mich Av -Buffalo 14203
(718) 997-7778 .. **Bompart**, Nina S '04 (Bompart & B,LLC) -96-62 Qns Blvd -Rego Pk 11374 **Fx:**459-7228
(718) 997-7778 .. **Bompart**, Timothy L '92 (Bompart & B,LLC) -96-62 Qns Blvd -Rego Pk 11374 **Fx:**459-7228
(212) 762-8386 .. **Bompey**, Mitchell S '95 Morgan Stanley -1221 Av of Amer -NY 10020
(212) 574-1200 .. **Bomrind**, Benjamin A '01 %Seward & K LLP -1 Bttry Pk Plz -NY 10004
(212) 479-6000 .. **Bomrind**, Zev M '97 %Cooley LLP -1114 Av of Amer -NY 10036
(917) 602-5142 .. **Bomser**, Alan H '55 (Winslett SM&B LLP) -6 E 39th -NY 10016 **Fx:**(212) 207-4298
(516) 742-6546 .. **Bomze**, Alyssa F '00 %L Stober Jr,LLC -350 Old Cntry Rd -Gdn Cty 11530 **Fx:**742-8603
(212) 297-5800 .. **Bomzer**, T David '01 Cnsl Day P LLP -7 Times Sq -NY 10036
(646) 610-5400 .. **Bona**, Steven L '01 %NYPD -1 Police Plz -NY 10038
(914) 428-1438 .. **Bona**, Thos M '83 (T Bona,PC) -123 Main -White Plns 10601 **Fx:**428-1413
(212) 803-5100 .. **Bonacarti**, Alexandra '89 %NY Cnty Defender Srvcs -225 Bway -NY 10007 **Fx:**571-6035
(718) 250-0400 .. **Bonacci**, Edw H Jr. '81 R Tusa -1 MetroTech Ctr -Brklyn 11201 **Fx:**250-0591
(518) 474-6750 .. **Bonacci**, Lisa M '04 Liquor Auth -80 S Swan -Albany 12210 **Fx:**402-2304
(585) 420-7013 .. **Bonaccio**, Cecilia '98 Cnsl Genesee Mgmt -1265 Scottsvll Rd -Rchstr 14624 **Fx:**420-7012
(518) 743-2259 .. **Bonacic**, Andrew M '83 %Adirondack Comm Cllg -Bay Rd -Glens Fls 12801
(845) 703-3101 .. **Bonacic**, J Scott '95 (Bonacic KCM&B,LLP) -90 Crystal Run Rd -Middletwn 10941
(845) 703-3101 .. **Bonacic**, John J '69 OfCnsl Bonacic KCM&B,LLP -90 Crystal Run Rd -Middletwn 10941
(845) 703-3101 .. **Bonacic Krahulik Cuddeback McMahon & Brady, LLP** -90 Crystal Run Rd -Middletwn 10941 **Fx:**703-3110
(845) 986-1156 .. **Bonacic Krahulik Cuddeback McMahon & Brady, LLP** -2 Bank Bx391 -Warwick 10990 **Fx:**986-9421
(845) 856-5178 .. **Bonacic Krahulik Cuddeback McMahon & Brady, LLP** -17 E Main Bx1114 -Pt Jervis 12771 **Fx:**856-5515
(518) 457-8413 .. **Bonacquist**, Mark '86 %DCJS -4 Twr Pl -Albany 12203 **Fx:**457-3089
(212) 839-5300 .. **Bonacum**, John J III '83 (Sidley A LLP) -787 7th Av -NY 10019
(212) 554-1234 .. **Bonadonna**, Mary Jean Elizabeth '98 %AXA Financial Inc -1290 Av of Amer -NY 10104 **Fx:**707-3963
(315) 926-4206 .. **Bonafede**, Saml J '73 -3819 S Main Bx53 -Marion 14505
(716) 856-4000 .. **Bonaguide**, Christine A '99 (Hodgson R LLP) -140 Pearl -Buffalo 14202
(212) 728-8000 .. **Bonagura**, Rebecca A '10 %Willkie F&G LLP -787 7th Av -NY 10019
(516) 437-6100 .. **Bonagura**, Salvatore R '78 -122 Plainfld Av Bx444 -Floral Pk 11002 **Fx:**437-6197
(718) 797-5151 .. **Bonaldes**, Melissa E '96 -26 Court -Brklyn 11242 **Fx:**504-5009
(212) 434-0103 .. **Bonalsky**, James M '02 %Litchfield C LLP -420 Lex Av -NY 10170
(718) 921-1300 .. **Bonamassa**, James D '88 -9001 5th Av -Brklyn 11209 **Fx:**921-0926
(718) 222-4500 .. **Bonan**, Anthony P '06 Cremat Asset Mgt -78 Delavan -Brklyn 11231
(518) 464-6770 .. **Bonanni**, Maureen S '81 (Thorn GT&B,LLP) -5 Wembley Ct Bx15054 -Albany 12212
(941) 730-8590 .. **Bonanno**, John D '86 -14656 Bayside Av -Flushng 11354
(212) 213-1220 .. **Bonanno**, John P '97 (Weiner MM&B,LLC) -220 5th Av -NY 10001
(914) 377-6240 .. **Bonanno**, Jos T '81 %Law Dept -300 City Hall -Ynkrs 10701 **Fx:**964-0563
(212) 922-9250 .. **Bonanno**, Justin R '01 (Ganfer & S LLP) -360 Lex Av -NY 10017
(914) 948-5545 .. **Bonanno**, Patsy '96 -175 Main -White Plns 10601
(716) 858-2424 .. **Bonanno**, Paul E '06 %DA -25 Delaware Av -Buffalo 14202 **Fx:**858-7425
(212) 357-3184 .. **Bonanno**, Peter V '07 Goldman Sachs -1 NY Plz -NY 10004
(212) 801-3777 .. **Bonanno**, Raquel A '03 Related Companies LP -60 Columbus Cir -NY 10023
(914) 968-0045 .. **Bonante**, Christopher T '01 (US Asset Recovery Srvcs) -11 Brnx Rvr Rd -Ynkrs 10704 **Fx:**968-0028
(585) 344-1994 .. **Bonarigo**, Benjamin J '83 (Bonarigo & M) -18 Ellicott -Batavia 14020 **Fx:**344-1996
(315) 734-2000 .. **Bonaros**, Thos P '66 %Utica Natl Ins -180 Genesee Bx530 -Utica 13502 **Fx:**734-2662
(212) 323-2250 .. **Bonas Benjamin**, Laura Z '03 %HHC-OLA-Medical Litigation -346 Bway -NY 10013 **Fx:**323-2251
(607) 274-5461 .. **Bonavia**, Andrew J '98 %DA -320 N Tioga -Ithaca 14850 **Fx:**274-5429
(585) 546-7830 .. **Bonavilla**, Jon E '97 %Culley MT&P,LLP -36 W Main -Rchstr 14614
(718) 590-2057 .. **Bonavoglia**, Marie Z '82 %DA -198 E 161st -Bronx 10451 **Fx:**590-6477
(516) 829-7270 .. **Bonchonsky**, Larry J '83 -96 Bayview Av -Northprt 11768
(516) 747-1400 .. **Bonchonsky**, Peter R '82 (Bonchonsky & Z,LLP) -226 7th -Gdn Cty 11530
(516) 747-1400 .. **Bonchonsky & Zaino,LLP** -226 7th -Gdn Cty 11530 **Fx:**747-1455
(718) 286-6000 .. **Boncy**, Talia S '08 %DA -125-01 Qns Blvd -Kew Gdns 11415
(212) 406-2300 .. **Bond**, Adam M '90 (Stumpp & B,LLP) -One Lbrty Plz -NY 10006
(212) 209-4800 .. **Bond**, Clifford J '91 Brown R LLP -7 Times Sq -NY 10036
(212) 837-6000 .. **Bond**, Erik B '05 %Hughes H&R LLP -1 Bttry Pk Plz -NY 10004
(212) 609-6800 .. **Bond**, Jeannette M '80 SpclCnsl McCarter & E,LLP -245 Park Av -NY 10167
(718) 260-8700 .. **Bond**, Jeffrey V '89 %Admin Children's Srvcs -345 Adams -Brklyn 11201
(716) 878-8000 .. **Bond**, Jill K '86 %Rich Products -1 Robert Rich Way -Buffalo 14213 **Fx:**878-8767
(914) 375-7111 .. **Bond**, John L '95 -125 Corp Blvd -Ynkrs 10701 **Fx:**969-2425
(716) 856-1636 .. **Bond**, Keith N '84 (Walsh R&G) -14 Lafayette Sq -Buffalo 14203
(212) 872-9817 .. **Bond**, Kenneth W '74 (Squire S&D LLP) -30 Rckfllr Plz -NY 10112
(845) 291-2050 .. **Bond**, Kerry M '04 %DA -255-275 Main -Goshen 10924 **Fx:**291-2085
(315) 789-8480 .. **Bond McDonald & Lehman, PC** -91 Genesee -Geneva 14456 **Fx:**789-0449
(518) 371-8888 .. **Bond**, Megan M '93 %Ianniello A&R,PC -805 Route 146 -Clifton Pk 12065
(212) 732-8700 .. **Bond**, Melissa A '09 %McAloon & F,PC -123 William -NY 10038
(212) 969-3000 .. **Bond**, Philippa M '00 %Proskauer R LLP -1585 Bway -NY 10036
(315) 218-8000 .. **Bond Schoeneck & King,PLLC** -1 Lincoln Ctr -Syracuse 13202 **Fx:**218-8100
(518) 533-3000 .. **Bond Schoeneck & King,PLLC** -111 Wshngtn Av -Albany 12210 **Fx:**533-3299
(716) 566-2800 .. **Bond Schoeneck & King,PLLC** -40 Fountian Plz -Buffalo 14202 **Fx:**566-2808
(646) 253-2300 .. **Bond Schoeneck & King,PLLC** -330 Mad Av -NY 10017 **Fx:**253-2301
(516) 267-6300 .. **Bond Schoeneck & King,PLLC** -1399 Franklin Av -Gdn Cty 11530 **Fx:**267-6301
(585) 362-4700 .. **Bond Schoeneck & King,PLLC** -350 Linden Oaks -Rchstr 14625 **Fx:**362-4701
(315) 343-9116 .. **Bond Schoeneck & King,PLLC** -130 E 2nd -Oswego 13126 **Fx:**343-1231

(607) 330-4000 .. **Bond Schoeneck & King,PLLC** -10 Brown Rd -Ithaca 14850 **Fx:**330-4001
(315) 738-1223 .. **Bond Schoeneck & King,PLLC** -501 Main -Utica 13501 **Fx:**724-2074
(212) 310-8000 .. **Bond,** W Michl '00 (Weil G&M LLP) -767 5th Av -NY 10153
(212) 733-2085 .. **Bondada,** Vijay V '00 %Pfizer Inc -235 E 42nd -NY 10017
(212) 506-2500 .. **Bondard,** Celine L '07 Mayer B LLP -1675 Bway -NY 10019
(718) 339-7777 .. **Bondarenko-Hoffman,** Irina M '06 -2370 Coney Isl Av -Brklyn 11223
(212) 708-1800 .. **Bondell,** Jay A '78 OfCnsl Ladas & P -26 W 61st -NY 10023
(518) 452-7718 .. **Bonder,** Moshe H '04 Crompton Greaves Ltd -403 New Karner Rd -Albany 12205
(212) 267-9020 .. **Bonder,** Sandra L '91 (Shapiro B&A LLP) -225 Bway -NY 10007
(212) 735-3000 .. **Bonderoff,** Amy K '07 %Skadden ASM&F LLP -4 Times Sq -NY 10036
(212) 373-3000 .. **Bonderoff,** Saml E '03 %Paul WRW&G LLP -1285 Av of Amer -NY 10019
(631) 289-4600 .. **Bond-Hirschey,** Kerri E '98 %Jacoby & J -1737 N Ocean Av -Medfrd 11763 **Fx:**654-5095
(516) 741-8585 .. **Bondi & Iovino** -1055 Franklin Av -Gdn Cty 11530 **Fx:**741-8598
(516) 741-8585 .. **Bondi,** Jos C '73 (Bondi & I) -1055 Franklin Av -Gdn Cty 11530
(516) 684-2900 .. **Bondi-Stoddard,** Annamarie '84 (Pegalis & E,LLC) -1 Hllw Ln -Lk Success 11042
(718) 548-4000 .. **Bondor,** Page '94 %Horace Mann School -231 W 246th -Bronx 10471
(212) 446-4800 .. **Bondor,** Paul A '94 (Kirkland & E LLP) -153 E 53rd -NY 10022
(718) 643-1600 .. **Bondorowsky,** Barry R '74 -26 Court -Brklyn 11242 **Fx:**643-1133
(212) 274-9260 .. **Bondy,** Craig M '86 -350 Bway -NY 10013 **Fx:**274-9264
(212) 554-7800 .. **Bondy,** David A '00 %Moses & S LLP -405 Lex Av -NY 10174
(212) 973-0572 .. **Bondy,** Jonathan '92 (Wolff & S PC) -140 Bway -NY 10005
(212) 219-3572 .. **Bondy,** Jos A '95 -20 Vesey -NY 10007 **Fx:**219-8456
(212) 944-0900 .. **Bondy,** Matthew A '99 %Mishaan D&L -1370 Bway -NY 10018
(212) 512-1000 .. **Bondy,** Meeka Jun '95 %HBO -1100 Av of Amer -NY 10036 **Fx:**512-1986
(212) 279-8833 .. **Bondy,** Thos L '77 (Zuller & B) -42 W 38th -NY 10018
(212) 286-8585 .. **Bone,** John H '05 %Heidell PM&B,LLP -99 Park Av -NY 10016
(212) 818-1110 .. **Boneau,** Maria C '09 %Butzel L,PC -380 Mad Av -NY 10017
(212) 204-8694 .. **Boneberg,** Robt C '84 (Lowenstein S PC) -1251 Av of Amer -NY 10020 **Fx:**(973) 422-6845
(212) 815-1818 .. **Bonelli,** Anette '86 %DC 37 MELS -125 Barclay -NY 10007 **Fx:**815-1343
(212) 750-2009 .. **Bonem,** Franklin S '64 -770 Lex Av -NY 10065 **Fx:**935-4865
(212) 259-8000 .. **Bonenfant,** Genevieve B '10 %Dewey & L LLP -1301 Av of Amer -NY 10019
(212) 704-6000 .. **Boneparth,** Harvey M '70 OfCnsl Troutman S LLP -405 Lex Av -NY 10174
(516) 248-1700 .. **Bonesso,** Wm F '86 (Forchelli CDSM&T,LLP) -333 Earle Ovngton Blvd -Uniondale 11553
(212) 906-1200 .. **Bonewitz,** Paul L '09 %Latham & W -885 3rd Av -NY 10022
(212) 592-1400 .. **Bonéy,** Lenora B '01 %Herrick,F LLP -2 Park Av -NY 10016
(718) 738-1763 .. **Bonfa,** Stephen A '99 -244 5th Av -NY 10001
(631) 423-5855 .. **Bonfante,** Chas '00 -1 Earl Rd -Melvll 11747
(914) 684-6800 .. **Bonfield,** Howard S '93 %Collier HNN&B,LLP -1 N Lex Av -White Plns 10601
(718) 370-2900 .. **Bonfiglio,** Thos J '88 (Bonfiglio & A,LLC) -900 South Av -Staten Isl 10314 **Fx:**370-2910
(212) 225-2000 .. **Bongartz,** Georg A '07 %Cleary GS&H -1 Lbrty Plz -NY 10006
(631) 232-0800 .. **Bongermino,** Ernest M '80 (Blumberg & B) -129 Carleton Av -Central Islip 11722 **Fx:**232-1118
(212) 373-3000 .. **Bongiorni,** Phillip J '08 %Paul WRW&G LLP -1285 Av of Amer -NY 10019
(908) 385-4289 .. **Bongiorno,** Andrew W '70 %Bevan MG&Z,PC -200 Mad Av -NY 10016
(516) 294-5433 .. **Bongiorno,** Angelo J '00 (Ahmuty D&M) -200 IU Willets Rd -Albertson 11507
(212) 975-2721 .. **Bongiorno,** Anthony '85 %CBS Inc -51 W 52nd -NY 10019 **Fx:**975-3930
(516) 741-2405 .. **Bongiorno,** Jos R '85 (Geoghan C&B LLC) -250 Mineola Blvd -Mineola 11501
(914) 422-8700 .. **Bongiorno,** Michl E '82 %OCTF -101 E Post Rd -White Plns 10601 **Fx:**422-8795
(212) 937-7220 .. **Bongiorno,** Michl G '05 (WilmerHale) -399 Park Av -NY 10022
(516) 741-4170 .. **Bongiorno,** Peter C '86 (Bongiorno Law Firm,PLLC) -250 Mineola Blvd -Mineola 11501 **Fx:**741-4240
(516) 741-4170 .. **Bongiorno,** Richd M '93 (Bongiorno Law Firm,PLLC) -250 Mineola Blvd -Mineola 11501 **Fx:**741-4240
(718) 625-8940 .. **Bongiorno,** Robt J '98 %B Lawrence -15 Metrotech Ctr N -Brklyn 11201 **Fx:**624-5756
(631) 208-9007 .. **Bonheim,** Karl E '73 -431 Griffing Av -Rvrhead 11901
(212) 253-6911 .. **Bonica,** Gina M '04 (Kurland B& Assoc,PC) -304 Park Av S -NY 10010
(716) 285-4300 .. **Boniello,** David G '80 -2902 Pine Av at 29th -Niagara Fls 14301 **Fx:**285-1708
(518) 465-3553 .. **Boniewski,** Dana M '01 %Maynard OS&C,LLP -6 Twr Pl -Albany 12203
(845) 727-4000 .. **Boniface,** Courtney E '01 %B Cane -50 Piermont Av -Nyack 10960 **Fx:**727-4023
(914) 245-1541 .. **Bonifacio,** Adrianne F '83 -2280 Mark Rd -Yorktwn Hts 10598 **Fx:**245-1541
(516) 365-9191 .. **Bonifati,** Wm L '87 %S Friedman -1 Hllw Ln -New Hyde Pk 11042 **Fx:**365-6138
(212) 849-7000 .. **Bonifield,** Gregory D '07 OfCnsl Quinn EU&S,LLP -51 Mad Av -NY 10010
(518) 442-3300 .. **Bonilla,** Adrienne D '03 University at Albany, SUNY -1400 Wshngtn Av -Albany 12222
(212) 331-5136 .. **Bonilla,** Grace C '06 HRA -180 Water -NY 10038
(212) 815-1818 .. **Bonilla,** Noemi '89 %DC 37 MELS -125 Barclay -NY 10007 **Fx:**815-1343
(212) 858-4374 .. **Bonilla,** Wm N '79 %FINRA -1 Lbrty Plz -NY 10006
(212) 554-2690 .. **Bonime-Blanc,** Andrea '88 Daylight Forensic & Advsry LLC -1 Rckfllr Plz -NY 10020
(718) 522-1786 .. **Bonina,** Andrea E '92 (Bonina & B,PC) -16 Court -Brklyn 11241 **Fx:**243-0414
(718) 522-1786 .. **Bonina,** John '90 (Bonina & B,PC) -16 Court -Brklyn 11241 **Fx:**243-0414
(212) 335-4500 .. **Bonitatibus,** Kara M '03 %DLA Piper LLP -1251 Av of Amer -NY 10020
(212) 788-0521 .. **Bonitatibus,** Marie A '08 %Law Dept -100 Church -NY 10007 **Fx:**788-0367
(212) 288-6123 .. **Boniuk,** Vivien '80 -530 E 84th -NY 10028
(212) 825-1080 .. **Bonjean,** Jennifer A '05 (Bonjean Law Grp,PLLC) -119 W 23rd -NY 10011 **Fx:**529-0644
(212) 310-8000 .. **Bonk,** Jason B '07 %Weil G&M LLP -767 5th Av -NY 10153
(212) 437-1924 .. **Bonn,** David E '98 Royal Bk of Canada -1 Lbrty Plz -NY 10006
(212) 374-1511 .. **Bonnaig,** Denise K '89 (Bonnaig & Assoc) -25 Murray -NY 10007 **Fx:**374-1703
(212) 351-4500 .. **Bonnefil,** Pierre Georges '89 (Epstein B&G,PC) -250 Park Av -NY 10177
(212) 450-4000 .. **Bonner,** Anjali S '10 %Davis P&W LLP -450 Lex Av -NY 10017
(516) 240-8025 .. **Bonner,** Arthur H '74 -1225 Franklin Av -Gdn Cty 11530 **Fx:**(866) 845-1824
(315) 425-2700 .. **Bonner,** Christopher J '88 OfCnsl Hiscock & B,LLP -One Park Pl -Syracuse 13202
(212) 239-4340 .. **Bonner,** James P '93 (Shalov SB&R LLP) -485 7th Av -NY 10018
(516) 730-1912 .. **Bonner,** Karin L '98 Yellow Book USA -398 RXR Plz -Uniondale 11556
(212) 268-7535 .. **Bonner Kiernan Trebach & Crociata,LLP** -350 5th Av -NY 10118 **Fx:**268-4965
(212) 274-1226 .. **Bonner,** Lisa H '09 Bonner Law PC -100 Wall -NY 10005 **Fx:**658-9395
(212) 223-2100 .. **Bonner,** Patrick D Jr. '91 (Menz B&K LLP) -444 Mad Av -NY 10022
(212) 425-1900 .. **Bonner,** Patrick J '79 (Freehill H&M LLP) -80 Pine -NY 10005
(212) 894-7200 .. **Bonner,** Thos J '70 OfCnsl Entwistle & C LLP -280 Park Av -NY 10017
(212) 474-1000 .. **Bonnes,** Andrew R '08 %Cravath S&M LLP -825 8th Av -NY 10019
(718) 694-3877 .. **Bonnet,** Miriam P '87 %Transit Auth -130 Lvngstn -Brklyn 11201 **Fx:**694-5726
(518) 433-8800 .. **Bonneville,** Michl J '09 %Lemery G LLC -50 Beaver -Albany 12207
(845) 928-5318 .. **Bonney,** Jeanne '93 -11 Abrams Rd Bx67 -Centrl Vly 10917 **Fx:**928-5321
(315) 539-9211 .. **Bonney,** Sam C '75 -20 W Main Bx316 -Waterloo 13165 **Fx:**539-7110
(212) 266-0400 .. **Bonnick,** Sandra M '96 %Krez & F,LLP -225 Bway -NY 10007
(212) 455-2000 .. **Bonnie,** Joshua F '97 (Simpson T&B LLP) -425 Lex Av -NY 10017
(914) 921-4820 .. **Bonnist,** Craig M '92 (Bonnist & C,LLP) -800 Wstchstr Av -Rye Brook 10573 **Fx:**921-4823
(212) 267-1900 .. **Bono,** Michl A '96 (Wade CM) -111 Bway -NY 10006
(212) 455-2000 .. **Bono,** Simone E '02 %Simpson T&B LLP -425 Lex Av -NY 10017
(212) 489-1600 .. **Bonomi,** John Jr. '87 %Deloitte LLP -1633 Bway -NY 10019 **Fx:**492-4201
(516) 365-6690 .. **Bonomo,** Anthony J '85 Adm for the Prof -1800 Nrthrn Blvd -Roslyn 11576
(212) 553-8300 .. **Bonomo,** Tara A '00 %Cohen K & Assoc -2 Park Av -NY 10016 **Fx:**553-8721
(718) 698-0194 .. **Bonomo,** Wm P '96 -160 Dinsmore -Staten Isl 10314
(914) 333-0700 .. **Bonomolo,** Cara Marie '98 %Snyder & S -94 Wht Plns Rd -Tarrytwn 10591 **Fx:**333-0743
(631) 581-3046 .. **Bonsignore,** Edw J '06 -3330 Vets Mem'l Hwy -Bohemia 11716 **Fx:**857-7892
(585) 641-8000 .. **Bonsignore,** James J '06 (Fix SB&G,PC) -295 Woodcliff Dr -Fairprt 14450
(914) 261-1854 .. **Bonsignore,** Michele Marianna '98 MM Bonsignore PC -11-44 Jackson Av -Scarsdale 10583 **Fx:**793-6303
(212) 747-1230 .. **Bonsignore,** Paul '72 (McMahon M&G LLP) -55 Washington -Brklyn 11201
(212) 599-8000 .. **Bonsignore,** Robt T '95 Fincl Fed Credit Inc -730 3rd Av -NY 10017 **Fx:**286-5885
(212) 586-5504 .. **Bonstrom,** Kim Patrick '87 (Bonstrom & M) -200 W 57th -NY 10019
(518) 392-6471 .. **Bonstrom & Murphy** -76 Phelps Rd -Old Chatham 12136 **Fx:**392-7916
(212) 586-5504 .. **Bonstrom & Murphy** -200 W 57th -NY 10019 **Fx:**980-2968
(516) 747-1364 .. **Bontempo,** Ralph A '62 -162 Schley Av -Albertson 11507 **Fx:**741-0870
(212) 841-1000 .. **Bonthuis,** Mari K '06 %Covington & B LLP -620 8th Av -NY 10018
(845) 352-8378 .. **Bonura,** Frank J '65 -4 Angela Ct -Monsey 10952
(212) 344-5680 .. **Bonuso,** Cristina M '09 %Thompson H LLP -335 Mad Av -NY 10017
(516) 508-0389 .. **Bonventre,** Ann-Margaret '96 -135 E Melrose -Vly Stream 11580
(212) 238-4800 .. **Bonventre,** John A '83 (Landman CB&F,PC) -120 Bway -NY 10271
(212) 692-7200 .. **Bonventre,** Jos S '02 Lexington Corp Prop Trust -1 Penn Plz -NY 10119
(518) 445-2311 .. **Bonventre,** Vincent M '77 %Albany Law Schl -80 New Scotland Av -Albany 12208 **Fx:**445-2315
(516) 794-7500 .. **Bonventre Deverteuil,** Anna-Lisa '94 OfCnsl Westermann SKS&A,LLP -333 Earle Ovngton Blvd -Uniondale 11553
(212) 373-3000 .. **Bonvino,** Angelo '97 (Paul WRW&G LLP) -1285 Av of Amer -NY 10019
(212) 656-5621 .. **Bon Viso,** Peter '97 NYSE -20 Broad -NY 10005
(718) 834-0501 .. **Bonwich,** Peter S '61 -6 Montague Ter -Brklyn 11201
(212) 702-4346 .. **Bonyne,** Gregory L '01 Icahn Assoc Corp -767 5th Av -NY 10153
(914) 499-6618 .. **Bonzani,** Andrew '90 IBM -1 New Orchrd Rd -Armonk 10504 **Fx:**765-7533
(518) 436-0751 .. **Boochever,** Jos '50 OfCnsl Hinman S PC -121 State -Albany 12207
(518) 474-6400 .. **Boochever,** Patricia Levine '93 %Dept of Ed -89 Wshngtn Av -Albany 12234 **Fx:**473-2925
(518) 452-8787 .. **Boochever,** Stephen S '90 (Drinker B&R LLP) -321 Great Oaks Blvd -Albany 12203
(516) 742-5995 .. **Boockvar,** Alan I '70 -120 Front Bx30 -Mineola 11501 **Fx:**742-3987
(212) 589-2706 .. **Boockvar,** Danl M '97 Weight Watchers -11 Mad Av -NY 10010
(212) 952-0602 .. **Boodhoo,** Gaitri '04 %Brualdi Law -29 Bway -NY 10006 **Fx:**952-0608
(212) 687-8181 .. **Boody,** Michl T '08 %Kreindler & K -750 3rd Av -NY 10017
(914) 631-4800 .. **Boogaard,** Paul M P '97 %J Shumejda -47 Beekman Av -Sleepy Hollow 10591 **Fx:**631-5388

(212) 259-8000 .. **Booher,** Martin T '99 (Dewey & L LLP) -1301 Av of Amer -NY 10019
(914) 377-6240 .. **Booher,** Sean C '79 %Law Dept -300 City Hall -Ynkrs 10701 **Fx:**964-0563
(212) 221-7999 .. **Book,** Chaim B '91 (Moskowitz B&W,LLP) -345 7th Av -NY 10001
(518) 270-4040 .. **Book,** Christa M '06 %DA -80 2nd -Troy 12180 **Fx:**270-4025
(631) 852-2500 .. **Bookamer,** Dari R '84 %DA -200 Center Dr -Rvrhead 11901 **Fx:**852-1769
(212) 801-6948 .. **Bookbinder,** Julie P '06 %Greenberg T,LLP -200 Park Av -NY 10166
(212) 944-9112 .. **Bookbinder,** Sara D '01 %Strategic Leg Solutions -110 E 42nd -NY 10017 **Fx:**944-8448
(212) 408-5100 .. **Booke,** Nicholas S '94 %Chadbourne & P LLP -30 Rckfllr Plz -NY 10112
(212) 455-2000 .. **Booken,** Adam S '08 %Simpson T&B LLP -425 Lex Av -NY 10017
(212) 261-7055 .. **Booker,** David B '91 %Calyon -1301 Av of Amer -NY 10019
(212) 735-3000 .. **Booker,** Kelly A '08 %Skadden ASM&F LLP -4 Times Sq -NY 10036
(718) 722-3949 .. **Booker-Williams,** Lois M '92 Dept of Law -55 Hanson Pl -Brklyn 11217 **Fx:**722-3951
(718) 953-4419 .. **Bookhard-Dimoh,** Irene '96 -1141 Eastern Pkwy -Brklyn 11213 **Fx:**953-7491
(315) 655-3770 .. **Bookhout,** Wm R '77 -Bx123 -Cazenovia 13035 **Fx:**655-2871
(607) 432-5200 .. **Bookhout,** Wm R '77 -353 Main -Oneonta 13820 **Fx:**432-5202
(212) 506-1700 .. **Bookman,** Karla R '07 %Kasowitz BT&F LLP -1633 Bway -NY 10019
(212) 513-1988 .. **Bookman,** Robt S '80 (Pesetsky & B) -325 Bway -NY 10007
(212) 310-8000 .. **Bookspan,** Tracy K '09 %Weil G&M LLP -767 5th Av -NY 10153
(718) 275-7500 .. **Bookstein,** Scott L '91 -125-10 Qns Blvd -Kew Gdns 11415 **Fx:**275-2364
(845) 897-3504 .. **Boolukos,** Robt '78 -1065 Main -Fishkill 12524 **Fx:**897-3509
(212) 837-6000 .. **Boomstein,** Anita L '77 (Hughes H&R LLP) -1 Bttry Pk Plz -NY 10004
(212) 227-0347 .. **Boomstra,** Stacie L '04 %Weiss W&W,PC -25 Park Pl -NY 10007
(212) 848-4000 .. **Boon,** Kevin H '09 %Shearman & S LLP -599 Lex Av -NY 10022
(212) 578-2211 .. **Boon,** Melissa K '03 %MetLife -27-01 Qns Plz N -LIC 11101
(212) 848-4000 .. **Boon,** Rebecca E '08 %Shearman & S LLP -599 Lex Av -NY 10022
(212) 363-6900 .. **Boone,** Dominic '02 %Faust GS&B LLP -2 Rector -NY 10006
(212) 918-3000 .. **Boone,** Laural S '03 %Hogan L LLP -875 3rd Av -NY 10022
(212) 474-1000 .. **Boone,** Robt L '09 %Cravath S&M LLP -825 8th Av -NY 10019
(212) 586-8329 .. **Boone,** W Dan '73 -30 Lincoln Plz -NY 10023 **Fx:**(646) 314-8851
(212) 603-6300 .. **Boonshoft,** Stephen '76 (Robinson BLGG&G PC) -875 3rd Av -NY 10022
(212) 226-2800 .. **Boop,** Arlene F '76 (Alterman & B LLP) -35 Worth -NY 10013
(212) 909-6000 .. **Boorman,** Pamela Gay '93 %Debevoise & P LLP -919 3rd Av -NY 10022
(212) 345-7136 .. **Boorstein,** Carol '82 %Mercer HR Cnsltng -1166 Av of Amer -NY 10036
(212) 809-4800 .. **Boorstein,** Wm S '77 %N Kanzer -30 Broad -NY 10004 **Fx:**363-3097
(212) 489-8230 .. **Boose,** R Andrew '64 (Davis WT LLP) -1633 Bway -NY 10019
(212) 295-6507 .. **Boot,** Jeannette K '96 (WilmerHale) -399 Park Av -NY 10022
(718) 250-2000 .. **Booth,** Amatullah K '08 %DA -350 Jay -Brklyn 11201 **Fx:**250-2314
(718) 246-7398 .. **Booth,** Chan D '91 -Bx20852 -Brklyn 11202 **Fx:**246-4999
(212) 269-4900 .. **Booth,** Chas A '79 (Ford MEW&G,LLP) -Wall Street Plz -NY 10005
(212) 768-6700 .. **Booth,** Chas D '85 SrCnsl Sonnenschein N&R LLP -1221 Av of Amer -NY 10020
(212) 363-6969 .. **Booth,** Christopher '89 (Lipman & B,LLC) -11 Bway #967 -NY 10004
(212) 854-0286 .. **Booth,** Jane E '77 %Columbia Univ -535 W 116th 412 Low Mem'l Library -NY 10027
(212) 450-4000 .. **Booth,** Karla J '06 %Davis P&W LLP -450 Lex Av -NY 10017
(718) 838-7878 .. **Booth,** Katherine A '09 %Bronx Defenders -860 Crtlandt Av -Bronx 10451 **Fx:**665-0100
(716) 852-1888 .. **Booth,** Michl V '04 %Cantor LD&P,PC -350 Main -Buffalo 14202
(212) 977-2525 .. **Booth,** Mitchell B '52 -75 E End Av -NY 10028
(212) 769-5867 .. **Booth,** Rachel Dillon '06 Amer Museum of Natl History -200 Cntrl Pk W -NY 10024
(607) 255-4025 .. **Booth,** Richd S '73 %Cornell Univ -117 W Sibley Hall -Ithaca 14853 **Fx:**255-1971
(845) 471-2667 .. **Bopp,** Bryan C '94 -303 Mill -Poughkeepsie 12601 **Fx:**471-7597
(845) 471-4455 .. **Bopp,** Ellen Fischer '94 (Steinberg S&P,LLP) -27 Grdn -Poughkeepsie 12601
(631) 225-9870 .. **Bopp,** Herman John '81 -218 N Wellwood Av -Lindenhrst 11757
(631) 271-2548 .. **Borack,** Alan N '76 -738 Verona Dr -Melvll 11747
(212) 310-8000 .. **Boragine,** Ellie D '09 %Weil G&M LLP -767 5th Av -NY 10153
(212) 431-1300 .. **Borah Goldstein Altschuler Nahins & Goidel PC** -377 Bway -NY 10013 **Fx:**334-0960
(212) 431-1300 .. **Borah,** Gregory D '09 %Borah GAN&G PC -377 Bway -NY 10013
(212) 581-2157 .. **Borah,** Jeffrey '76 -1825 Park Av -NY 10035 **Fx:**581-1637
(212) 836-8000 .. **Borah,** Matthew J '06 %Kaye S LLP -425 Park Av -NY 10022
(212) 529-5055 .. **Borak,** Gregory S '07 Thor Equities LLC -25 W 39th -NY 10018
(914) 472-6278 .. **Boral,** Jacques '54 -281 Garth Rd -Scarsdale 10583
(718) 264-3340 .. **Boranian,** Lisa Caligiuri '89 %MHLS -80-45 Wnchstr Blvd -Qns Vllg 11427 **Fx:**264-3559
(516) 747-4082 .. **Boranian,** Michl J '89 %Montfort HM&S LLP -1140 Franklin Av Bx7677 -Gdn Cty 11530
(212) 790-9200 .. **Borchard,** Wm M '64 (Cowan L&L,PC) -1133 Av of Amer -NY 10036
(718) 767-3333 .. **Borchert Genovesi LaSpina & Landicino,PC** -19-02 Whitestone Expy -Whitestone 11357 **Fx:**767-3309
(718) 767-3333 .. **Borchert,** Helmut '82 (Borchert GL&L,PC) -19-02 Whitestone Expy -Whitestone 11357
(212) 407-4000 .. **Borchetta,** Frank J '06 %Loeb & L,LLP -345 Park Av -NY 10154
(212) 446-2300 .. **Borchini,** Andrew E '09 %Boies S&F LLP -575 Lex Av -NY 10022
(631) 435-0781 .. **Borda Kennedy Alsen & Gold,LLP** -1805 5th Av -Bay Shr 11706 **Fx:**435-1550
(631) 435-0781 .. **Borda,** Richd '61 (Borda KA&G,LLP) -1805 5th Av -Bay Shr 11706
(212) 233-7195 .. **Bordan,** Erika A '93 %Lewis JAA,LLP -61 Bway -NY 10006
(212) 221-5700 .. **Bordanaro,** Stephen A '94 %Goldberg WFG LLP -1501 Bway -NY 10036
(212) 816-3134 .. **Borde,** David C '02 Citigroup -388 Greenwich -NY 10013
(716) 856-5500 .. **Borden,** Andrew A '08 %Damon M LLP -200 Delaware Av -Buffalo 14202
(212) 631-7447 .. **Borden,** Anthony P '86 -20 Vesey -NY 10007 **Fx:**631-7448
(516) 747-4301 .. **Borden,** Barbara A '91 %Torino & B,PC -200 Old Cntry Rd -Mineola 11501
(516) 795-5800 .. **Borden,** George L '66 -20 Amherst Pl -Massapequa 11758 **Fx:**795-5801
(914) 995-3000 .. **Borden,** Kenneth P Jr. '08 DA -111 Martin Luther King Blvd -White Plns 10601 **Fx:**995-3363
(212) 704-6000 .. **Borden,** Miles M '87 (Troutman S LLP) -405 Lex Av -NY 10174
(518) 786-9069 .. **Borden,** Rebecca '02 Schiller & K LLP -950 New Loudon Rd -Latham 12110
(212) 975-3610 .. **Borden,** Rebecca '03 %CBS Inc -51 W 52nd -NY 10019 **Fx:**975-3930
(212) 922-1800 .. **Borden,** Seth H '98 (McKenna L&A) -230 Park Av -NY 10169
(516) 741-3300 .. **Borden Skidell Fleck & Stackel** -666 Old Cntry Rd -Gdn Cty 11530 **Fx:**873-9108
(212) 838-8400 .. **Borden,** Valerie Wynn '02 Artstor -140 E 62nd -NY 10065
(212) 688-0008 .. **Bordetsky,** Barry M '98 -570 Lex Av -NY 10022
(718) 250-2000 .. **Bordley,** Ann '85 %DA -350 Jay -Brklyn 11201 **Fx:**250-2314
(212) 478-7200 .. **Bordoff,** Ninette S '79 (Hahn & H LLP) -488 Mad Av -NY 10022
(914) 684-6800 .. **Bordon,** Gregory A '07 %Collier HNN&B,LLP -1 N Lex Av -White Plns 10601
(315) 448-4800 .. **Bordonaro,** Patricia M '86 %Dept of Law -615 Erie Blvd W -Syracuse 13204 **Fx:**448-4853
(212) 813-8800 .. **Bordoni,** Christopher A '01 (Goodwin P LLP) -620 8th Av -NY 10018
(914) 323-7000 .. **Bordoni,** David M '96 OfCnsl Wilson EME&D LLP -3 Gannett Dr -White Plns 10604
(315) 218-8000 .. **Bordoni,** R Danl '80 (Bond S&K,PLLC) -1 Lincoln Ctr -Syracuse 13202
(718) 881-5600 .. **Bordowitz,** Harold R '86 (Lazarus L&W) -3699 Bainbrdg Av -Bronx 10467 **Fx:**881-5666
(516) 571-9041 .. **Bordowitz,** Shari Landecker '86 %Cnty Atty -1200 Old Cntry Rd -Westbury 11590
(631) 421-8282 .. **Bordwin,** Matthew '95 KPMG Corp Finance -1305 Walt Whitman Rd -Melvll 11747 **Fx:**794-2448
(631) 351-7800 .. **Bordwin,** Moe '63 Keen Consultants LLC -1305 Walt Whitman Rd -Melvll 11747
(716) 849-1333 .. **Boreanaz,** Robt L '90 (Lipsitz GSC LLP) -42 Delaware Av -Buffalo 14202
(716) 839-4321 .. **Borek,** Gary D '81 -Bx2167 -Buffalo 14231
(212) 566-7188 .. **Borek,** Jennifer '00 Cnsl Genova B&G -115 Bway -NY 10006
(212) 859-8000 .. **Borek,** John A '82 SpclCnsl Fried FHS&J LLP -1 NY Plz -NY 10004
(212) 456-1204 .. **Borell,** Stephen '06 Walt Disney -77 W 66th -NY 10023 **Fx:**456-6565
(212) 949-5800 .. **Borelli,** Alison Doviak '96 %Brady K&W,LLP -501 5th Av -NY 10017
(631) 852-2500 .. **Borelli,** Carl A '01 %DA -200 Center Dr -Rvrhead 11901 **Fx:**852-1769
(516) 746-7780 .. **Borelli,** Danielle M '03 %Rossillo & L,PC -355 Post Av -Westbury 11590
(212) 218-2100 .. **Borello,** Christopher P '03 %Fitzpatrick CH&S -1290 Av of Amer -NY 10104
(212) 575-1292 .. **Borenkind,** Alan '72 (Uncyk B&N,LLP) -555 5th Av -NY 10017
(845) 369-3457 .. **Borenkoff,** Darryl C '91 -Bx278 -Suffern 10901
(212) 391-2444 .. **Borenstein,** Abraham '75 (A Borenstein & Assoc,PC) -292 Mad Av -NY 10017 **Fx:**(973) 379-4620
(718) 463-3369 .. **Borenstein,** Debra B '84 -42-02 Main -Flushng 11355
(212) 891-0888 .. **Borenstein,** Eugene R '69 FOJP Srvc Corp -28 E 28th -NY 10016
(212) 696-6000 .. **Borenstein,** Evan S '99 (Curtis M-PC&M LLP) -101 Park Av -NY 10178
(718) 575-0100 .. **Borenstein,** Jacob '86 -70-41 136th -Flushng 11367 **Fx:**261-3939
(718) 802-2790 .. **Borenstein,** Joel '07 ACS-Legal -330 Jay -Brklyn 11201
(718) 286-6000 .. **Borenstein,** Mariana Zelig '88 %DA -125-01 Qns Blvd -Kew Gdns 11415
(212) 267-1873 .. **Borenstein,** Rosa '83 -368B Greenwich -NY 10013
(212) 831-4444 .. **Borer,** Brondi '97 -47 E 88th -NY 10128 **Fx:**831-4515
(718) 596-2605 .. **Borer,** Jaime J '70 JJ Borer & Assoc -26 Court -Brklyn 11242 **Fx:**596-2610
(212) 294-6700 .. **Boresta,** Robt A '85 (Winston & S) -200 Park Av -NY 10166
(212) 742-3390 .. **Boretz,** Stacey Edelbaum '87 (Lindabury ME&C,PC) -26 Bway -NY 10004
(212) 272-5805 .. **Borg,** Claudia L '98 %JP Morgan Chase -383 Mad Av -NY 10179
(212) 751-4165 .. **Borg,** Jerome J '55 -750 Lex Av -NY 10022 **Fx:**838-2427
(212) 297-5800 .. **Borg,** Jonathan M '99 SrCnsl Day P LLP -7 Times Sq -NY 10036
(212) 248-8800 .. **Borg,** Meredith B '98 %Callan KB&B LLP -1 Whitehall -NY 10004
(212) 268-7222 .. **Borg,** Michl A '89 (Soffer R&B LLP) -48 Wall -NY 10005
(212) 571-5454 .. **Borg,** Neil G '90 -305 Bway -NY 10007 **Fx:**571-4111
(212) 983-9611 .. **Borg,** Solomon J '77 (S Borg,PC) -630 3rd Av -NY 10017 **Fx:**983-9613
(212) 980-9600 .. **Borgeest,** Wayne E '83 (Kaufman B&R) -120 Bway -NY 10271
(718) 990-6600 .. **Borgen,** Christopher J '98 %St John's Law Schl -8000 Utopia Pkwy -Jamaica 11439 **Fx:**591-1855
(917) 699-6889 .. **Borgen,** Craig A '00 -387 New Lots Av -Brklyn 11207 **Fx:**(718) 498-4715
(646) 429-7500 .. **Borger,** Mitchell F '83 %Macys,Inc -11 Penn Plz -NY 10001 **Fx:**429-7521
(718) 855-9000 .. **Borges,** Jos J '90 %Cullen and D LLP -177 Montague -Brklyn 11201
(516) 677-8200 .. **Borges,** Wanda '79 (Borges & Assoc,LLC) -575 Underhill Blvd -Syosset 11791 **Fx:**677-0806
(914) 967-1999 .. **Borgeson,** Bruce W '73 -45 Fulton Av -Rye 10580
(718) 613-2150 .. **Borghard,** Aleah Stern '08 US Dist Ct-EDNY -225 Cadman Plz E -Brklyn 11201
(631) 724-8833 .. **Borghardt,** Chas W '09 %Devitt SB,LLP -50 Route 111 -Smithtwn 11787
(718) 340-4200 .. **Borgmann,** Caitlin E '92 %CUNY Law Schl -65-21 Main -Flushng 11367 **Fx:**340-4482
(212) 417-3700 .. **Borgmann,** Jota L '07 %MFY Legal Srvcs -299 Bway -NY 10007 **Fx:**417-3890
(646) 654-4901 .. **Borgna,** Cari Lyn '09 Nielsen Co -770 Bway -NY 10003

(212) 259-8000 .. **Borgogni,** Lorenzo '96 (Dewey & L LLP) -1301 Av of Amer -NY 10019
(518) 793-4900 .. **Borgos & Del Signore,PC** -82 Glenwood Av Bx4392 -Queensbury 12804 **Fx:**793-4902
(518) 793-4900 .. **Borgos,** Michl S '96 (Borgos & D,PC) -82 Glenwood Av Bx4392 -Queensbury 12804
(718) 590-2402 .. **Borgstedt,** Astrid A '89 %DA -198 E 161st -Bronx 10451 **Fx:**590-6477
(607) 547-8500 .. **Borgstrom,** Donna F '09 %Trosset Grp -31 Pioneer Bx28 -Cooperstwn 13326
(212) 468-8000 .. **Borho,** Ryan W '04 %Morrison & F LLP -1290 Av of Amer -NY 10104
(917) 937-3000 .. **Borik,** Michl J Jr. '91 %Guy Carpenter & Co,Inc -1166 Av of Amer -NY 10036
(212) 806-5400 .. **Borin,** Glenn '80 SpclCnsl Stroock &S&L LLP -180 Maiden Ln -NY 10038
(716) 854-5200 .. **Borins Setel Snitzer & Brownstein** -403 Main -Buffalo 14203 **Fx:**854-5204
(718) 263-3800 .. **Boris,** Fran R '91 %Muss Devel Corp -118-35 Qns Blvd -Frst Hlls 11375
(212) 708-6689 .. **Boris,** Howard L '60 %LeFrak Org -40 W 57th -NY 10019 **Fx:**708-6681
(212) 209-3898 .. **Boris,** Richd S '65 (Moss & B) -708 3rd Av -NY 10017
(718) 596-9000 .. **Boris,** Shirley '86 %Cohen HEP&T -25 Chapel -Brklyn 11201
(212) 819-8200 .. **Boris,** Stanley J '09 %White & C LLP -1155 Av of Amer -NY 10036
(315) 734-4472 .. **Boris,** Traci Anne '98 St Elizabeth Med Ctr -2209 Genesee -Utica 13501 **Fx:**798-8220
(516) 222-6200 .. **Boriskin,** Sara Z '04 %Berkman HPP&F,PC -100 Grdn City Plz -Gdn Cty 11530
(212) 225-2000 .. **Borisky,** Scott Douglas '87 Cnsl Cleary GS&H -1 Lbrty Plz -NY 10006
(212) 373-3000 .. **Borisoff,** Richd S '71 OfCnsl Paul WRW&G LLP -1285 Av of Amer -NY 10019
(212) 770-1917 .. **Borjas,** Helen '03 AIG Tech Srvcs -80 Pine -NY 10005
(914) 629-6361 .. **Bork,** Rhona M '02 -333 Mamaroneck Av -White Plns 10605
(212) 301-6969 .. **Borkan,** Howard '88 (H Borkan,PC) -1501 Bway -NY 10036 **Fx:**221-6350
(718) 553-7565 .. **Borkan,** Stephen '69 %Traffic Violations Bur -168-35 Rockaway Blvd -Jamaica 11434
(212) 918-3000 .. **Borkin,** Elizabeth Mullins '07 %Hogan L LLP -875 3rd Av -NY 10022
(718) 590-2000 .. **Borko,** Nancy L '78 %DA -198 E 161st -Bronx 10451 **Fx:**590-6477
(718) 261-4146 .. **Borko,** Susan Lynn '87 -125-10 Qns Blvd -Kew Gdns 11415
(212) 412-1707 .. **Borkow,** Allan J '89 %Barclays Capital -200 Park Av -NY 10166
(914) 946-4777 .. **Borkowski,** James W '88 OfCnsl Keane & B,PC -445 Hmltn Av -White Plns 10601
(914) 286-3415 .. **Borkowski,** Yvonne K '86 %Leg Aid -1 N Bway -White Plns 10601 **Fx:**682-4112
(631) 231-3775 .. **Borkowsky,** Mitchell T '94 %Atty Grievance Comm -150 Motor Pkwy -Hauppauge 11788
(631) 501-5700 .. **Borland,** Harold A '07 %Carter DF&S LLP -445 Broadhallow Rd -Melvll 11747
(212) 837-6000 .. **Borman,** Reuben L '04 %Hughes H&R LLP -1 Bttry Pk Plz -NY 10004
(585) 272-0540 .. **Born,** Sarah M '09 %Thomas & S LLP -693 East Av -Rchstr 14607
(212) 225-2000 .. **Borneo,** Catherine '92 %Cleary GS&H -1 Lbrty Plz -NY 10006
(914) 738-1600 .. **Borner,** Wm J '85 Spraylat Corp -143 Sparks Av -Pelham 10803 **Fx:**712-2838
(212) 857-8252 .. **Bornes,** Marjorie E '79 -330 W 34th -NY 10001 **Fx:**857-8210
(516) 692-2911 .. **Bornes,** Marjorie E '79 -75 Harvard Dr -Plainvw 11803
(212) 450-4000 .. **Bornhorst,** Christopher R '10 %Davis P&W LLP -450 Lex Av -NY 10017
(212) 592-1400 .. **Bornstein,** Benjamin A '89 Cnsl Herrick,F LLP -2 Park Av -NY 10016
(212) 458-1104 .. **Bornstein,** Brian D '88 %AIG -175 Water -NY 10038 **Fx:**458-1048
(212) 619-3730 .. **Bornstein,** Carl M '68 -217 Bway -NY 10007 **Fx:**962-5037
(516) 227-3777 .. **Bornstein & Emanuel,PC** -200 Grdn City Plz -Gdn Cty 11530 **Fx:**228-3299
(212) 474-1000 .. **Bornstein,** Gary A '98 (Cravath S&M LLP) -825 8th Av -NY 10019
(516) 227-3777 .. **Bornstein,** Kenneth '89 (Bornstein & E,PC) -200 Grdn City Plz -Gdn Cty 11530
(718) 545-0400 .. **Bornstein,** Philip J '94 -46-02 Bway -Astoria 11103
(631) 962-2000 .. **Bornstein,** Richd A '98 OSI Pharm -41 Pinelawn Rd -Melvll 11747
(718) 579-3000 .. **Bornstein,** Robt J '70 %Leg Aid -1020 Grnd Cncrs -Bronx 10451 **Fx:**588-2611
(212) 801-2172 .. **Bornstein,** Scott J '96 (Greenberg T,LLP) -200 Park Av -NY 10166
(212) 478-0750 .. **Bornstein,** Stephen A '81 DE Shaw & Co -120 W 45th -NY 10036 **Fx:**845-1750
(646) 471-4000 .. **Boro,** Michl J '91 %PricewaterhouseCoopers LLP -300 Mad Av -NY 10017
(212) 609-6800 .. **Borod,** Donald L '73 (McCarter & E,LLP) -245 Park Av -NY 10167
(212) 765-5070 .. **Borodach,** Saml '94 (Fish & R,PC) -153 E 53rd -NY 10022
(212) 447-5599 .. **Boroff,** Jason D '98 (Agins SR&B,LLP) -386 Park Av S -NY 10016
(212) 719-5620 .. **Borofsky,** Jeffrey M '83 -570 7th Av -NY 10018
(212) 572-8600 .. **Borofsky,** Michl C '00 MacAndrews & Forbes -35 E 62nd -NY 10065
(516) 228-1050 .. **Borofsky,** Steven J '00 %A Rosner -600 Old Cntry Rd -Gdn Cty 11530 **Fx:**228-1055
(716) 855-2800 .. **Boron,** Eric T '97 %Mura & S,PLLC -14 Lafayette Sq #930 -Buffalo 14203
(516) 227-5353 .. **Boronow,** Paul A '95 SrCnsl P Boronow,PC -200 Grdn City Plz -Gdn Cty 11530 **Fx:**227-0181
(516) 746-8000 .. **Boros,** Jerome S '50 OfCnsl Jaspan S LLP -300 Grdn City Plz -Gdn Cty 11530
(631) 630-1101 .. **Borovina,** Anton J '76 -445 Broad Hollow Rd -Melvll 11747 **Fx:**465-8935
(516) 572-2000 .. **Borovina,** Stefan A '09 %DA -99 Main -Hempstd 11550 **Fx:**572-2606
(914) 238-6306 .. **Borowick,** Howard R '80 -50 Carolyn Pl -Chappaqua 10514
(516) 625-8578 .. **Borowick,** Jeffrey M '88 -2 The Birches -Roslyn 11576
(718) 222-2313 .. **Borowiecki,** Kathrine M '08 %Law Dept -350 Jay -Brklyn 11201 **Fx:**222-2088
(212) 909-6000 .. **Borowitz,** Peter L '79 SrCnsl Debevoise & P LLP -919 3rd Av -NY 10022
(516) 739-7777 .. **Borowka,** Melvin N '69 (M Borowka,PC) -707 Walt Whitman Dr -Melvll 11747 **Fx:**742-4106
(201) 452-2158 .. **Borowski,** John P '82 -50 Raymnd Av -Staten Isl 10314
(518) 456-7200 .. **Borowski,** John P '82 %Solomon & S,PC -5 Columbia Cir Bx15019 -Albany 12212
(212) 750-4430 .. **Borrack,** E J '95 Farley Cptl LP -780 3rd Av -NY 10017
(212) 713-1477 .. **Borreggine,** Angela A '92 UBS Financial Srvcs Inc -1285 Av of Amer -NY 10019
(718) 667-8600 .. **Borrell,** Jeffrey F P '84 (Borrell & R,LLP) -1500 Hylan Blvd -Staten Isl 10305 **Fx:**980-1745
(212) 789-1500 .. **Borrelli,** Antonio '00 %Donna Karan Co -550 7th Av -NY 10018 **Fx:**789-1688
(631) 324-5209 .. **Borrelli,** Carmela L '92 (Ongioni & B) -15 Railroad Av -E Hampton 11937 **Fx:**324-7521
(212) 425-9300 .. **Borrelli,** Cynthia J '98 (Bressler A&R,PC) -17 State -NY 10004
(516) 485-0400 .. **Borrelli,** Gary F '06 %Muscarella & D -42 Nassau Blvd -Gdn Cty 11530
(914) 864-7122 .. **Borrelli,** Michl J Jr. '96 %DA -25 Moore Av -Mt Kisco 10549
(516) 248-5550 .. **Borrelli,** Michl J '02 (Borelli & Assoc,PC) -1 Old Cntry Rd -Carle Pl 11514
(516) 342-2200 .. **Borrelli,** Richd M '90 %Schwartzapfel Prtnrs -300 Jericho Quad -Jericho 11753
(212) 373-3000 .. **Borrero,** Jos D '06 %Paul WRW&G LLP -1285 Av of Amer -NY 10019
(845) 562-0203 .. **Borrero,** Robt E '99 Jacoby & M,LLP -1279 Route 300 Bx1111 -Newburgh 12550 **Fx:**562-3492
(845) 339-8800 .. **Borrero,** Stuart L '91 -71 Albany Av -Kingston 12401 **Fx:**331-7766
(212) 980-8866 .. **Borri,** Gregg J '85 -61 Bway -NY 10006 **Fx:**208-0969
(315) 792-0171 .. **Borrill,** Wm M '90 %Law Dept -1 Knndy Plz -Utica 13502 **Fx:**792-0175
(718) 680-5778 .. **Borrino,** Grace M '06 %Caruso C&B, PC -7302 13th Av -Brklyn 11228
(845) 226-6050 .. **Borrok,** Peter A '73 -75 Spy Glass Hill Rd -Hopewell Junct 12533 **Fx:**226-6036
(212) 578-8909 .. **Borrow,** J Stewart '86 %MetLife -27-01 Qns Plz N -LIC 11101 **Fx:**743-0605
(212) 797-3000 .. **Borrup,** Kevin T '00 %Cncl on Accreditation -120 Wall -NY 10005
(347) 401-9312 .. **Borruso,** Kristen A '00 %Hon E Spodek -360 Adams -Brklyn 11201
(516) 832-7506 .. **Borruso,** Santo '98 %Nixon P LLP -50 Jericho Quadrangle -Jericho 11753
(212) 571-0111 .. **Borsa,** Lilas K '98 %Hardin KM&P,PA -110 William -NY 10038
(631) 451-7900 .. **Borsella,** Lisa J '07 Rosenberg & G,LLP -1176 Portion Rd -Holtsvll 11742
(631) 327-2687 .. **Borsetti,** Chas V '81 -1021 Skyline Dr -Coram 11727
(212) 977-9700 .. **Borsody,** Robt P '65 Cnsl Phillips N LLP -666 5th Av -NY 10103
(212) 458-1064 .. **Borst,** Alan W Jr. '85 %AIG Adjustment -70 Pine -NY 10270
(212) 460-2837 .. **Borstein,** Carole A '70 Con Ed -4 Irving Pl -NY 10003
(212) 506-1700 .. **Borstein,** Jos I '06 %Kasowitz BT&F LLP -1633 Bway -NY 10019
(212) 687-1600 .. **Borstein,** Leon B '68 (Borstein & S) -420 Lex Av -NY 10170
(212) 687-1600 .. **Borstein & Sheinbaum** -420 Lex Av -NY 10170 **Fx:**687-8710
(212) 418-8600 .. **Bort,** Ina R '96 %Kornstein VW&P,LLP -757 3rd Av -NY 10017
(212) 664-5767 .. **Borteck,** Andrew E '05 NBC Universal,Inc -30 Rckfllr Plz -NY 10112
(212) 883-0350 .. **Borteck,** Mark B '93 Gordon Haskett Cptl -441 Lex Av -NY 10017 **Fx:**697-4587
(212) 683-2210 .. **Borten,** Laurence D '03 %Childrens Rts Inc -330 7th Av -NY 10001 **Fx:**683-4015
(212) 687-3860 .. **Borten,** Mark S '75 (Snow BK,PC) -605 3rd Av -NY 10158
(212) 949-7120 .. **Borter,** Lisa Levaggi '90 %Meeks & S -330 Mad Av -NY 10017
(212) 878-8000 .. **Bortner,** Carolyn Older '91 -31 W 52nd -NY 10019 **Fx:**878-8375
(212) 687-8500 .. **Bortnick,** Blaine H '91 (Liddle & R,LLP) -800 3rd Av -NY 10022
(212) 986-6000 .. **Bortnick,** Jeffrey '83 (Kleinberg KW&C,PC) -551 5th Av -NY 10176
(212) 808-2700 .. **Bortnick,** Steven D '89 (Pepper H LLP) -620 8th Av -NY 10018
(646) 240-4872 .. **Bortstein,** Lawr A '95 (Bortstein & I LLC) -275 Mad Av -NY 10016 **Fx:**(866) 955-9403
(718) 459-2299 .. **Borukhov,** Aron B '99 -97-29 64th Rd -Rego Pk 11374 **Fx:**459-2229
(212) 909-6000 .. **Borut,** Ezra B '97 (Debevoise & P LLP) -919 3rd Av -NY 10022
(212) 336-0113 .. **Boryshansky,** Jos O '03 %SEC -3 World Fncl Ctr -NY 10281 **Fx:**336-1323
(212) 557-9405 .. **Borzykowski,** Marc D '06 Vector Media -708 3rd Av -NY 10017
(212) 233-1988 .. **Bos,** John E '85 -305 Bway -NY 10007
(212) 837-6794 .. **Bosch,** Richd W III '05 Hughes H&R LLP -1 Bttry Pk Plz -NY 10004 **Fx:**299-6794
(212) 682-9655 .. **Boschini,** Francesco '01 F Boschini PLLC -590 Mad Av -NY 10022
(212) 250-2359 .. **Bosco,** Anthony J P '87 Deutsche Bk Sec -60 Wall -NY 10005
(718) 273-4046 .. **Bosco Bisignano & Mascolo** -857 Forest Av -Staten Isl 10310 **Fx:**273-3388
(516) 935-5555 .. **Bosco,** Carol A '81 Beechwood Org -500 N Bway -Jericho 11753 **Fx:**935-3005
(212) 566-7188 .. **Bosco,** Celia S '93 (Genova B&G) -115 Bway -NY 10006
(607) 263-2267 .. **Bosco,** Chas J '78 -552 Pegg Rd -Morris 13808
(212) 709-8203 .. **Bosco,** Damien M '01 -110 Wall -NY 10005
(845) 938-6532 .. **Bosco,** David D '90 US JAG -USMA -West Pnt 10996
(631) 475-5800 .. **Bosco,** Francis L '80 -38 Church -Patchogue 11772 **Fx:**475-5805
(914) 277-2704 .. **Bosco,** John I '59 -658A Heritage Hills -Somers 10589
(718) 273-4046 .. **Bosco,** John M '83 (Bosco B&M) -857 Forest Av -Staten Isl 10310
(718) 966-4141 .. **Bosco,** Michl S '99 -45 Page Av -Staten Isl 10309
(212) 558-5500 .. **Bosek,** Edw S '74 %Weitz & L,PC -700 Bway -NY 10003
(973) 992-4800 .. **Boshak,** Heather R '95 (Fox R LLP) -100 Park Av -NY 10017 **Fx:**992-9125
(914) 946-1405 .. **Boshart,** Tracy W '94 -33 Prescott Av -White Plns 10605
(212) 940-3068 .. **Boshkov,** Stefan R '76 (Nixon P LLP) -437 Mad Av -NY 10022
(516) 466-9355 .. **Boshnack,** Leonard '73 -8 Cathy Ln -Gt Neck 11024
(212) 209-4800 .. **Bosi,** Tanya D '05 %Brown R LLP -7 Times Sq -NY 10036
(212) 461-2370 .. **Bosland,** Christopher L '99 Saber Prtnrs,LLC -44 Wall -NY 10005
(212) 932-1058 .. **Bosley,** Lawr M '01 Dept of Ed -209 W 125th -NY 10027
(315) 336-9130 .. **Bosman,** A J '87 -6599 Martin -Rome 13440

(518) 464-9958 .. **Bosman,** Robt A '74 SrCnsl Bosman & Assoc,PLLC -1 Exec Centre Dr -Albany 12203 **Fx:**464-0968
(212) 259-8000 .. **Boss,** Gary D '97 (Dewey & L LLP) -1301 Av of Amer -NY 10019
(516) 294-0077 .. **Boss,** George '88 -245 Hillside Av -Williston Pk 11596 **Fx:**294-0252
(516) 739-1462 .. **Boss,** Lorraine Stacknowitz '90 %Brosnan & H -1325 Franklin Av -Gdn Cty 11530
(212) 373-3000 .. **Boss,** Michelle A '98 Cnsl Paul WRW&G LLP -1285 Av of Amer -NY 10019
(585) 621-4760 .. **Boss,** Ralph H Jr. '72 -2691 Dewey Av -Rchstr 14616 **Fx:**264-0815
(716) 856-3200 .. **Bosse,** Diane F '77 OfCnsl Bender & B LLP -68 Niagara -Buffalo 14202 **Fx:**856-3270
(212) 442-2000 .. **Bosse,** Jon C '89 SrCnsl NYC Dept Bldgs -11 Park Pl -NY 10007 **Fx:**442-2072
(212) 445-8000 .. **Bosses,** David K '98 %Weber Shandwick -919 3rd Av -NY 10022
(914) 723-9060 .. **Bosses,** Stevan J '63 (ADR Pro LLC) -19 Sprngdl Rd -Scarsdale 10583 **Fx:**472-5024
(516) 248-5757 .. **Bosso,** Michl D '07 %Colleran O&M,LLP -1225 Franklin Av -Gdn Cty 11530
(845) 562-0203 .. **Bossom,** Joel '65 OfCnsl Finkelstein & Prtnrs,LLP -1279 Route 300 Bx1111 -Newburgh 12550
(212) 832-0400 .. **Bosswick,** Mark G '87 Berdon LLP -360 Mad Av -NY 10017
(212) 818-9200 .. **Bosswick,** Pamela A '90 %Satterlee SB&B LLP -230 Park Av -NY 10169
(212) 530-4400 .. **Bostany,** John P '89 Bostany Law Firm -40 Wall -NY 10005 **Fx:**530-4488
(212) 558-4000 .. **Bostelman,** John T '80 (Sullivan & C LLP) -125 Broad -NY 10004
(212) 536-3900 .. **Bostick,** Calvina L '07 %K&L Gates LLP -599 Lex Av -NY 10022
(212) 728-8000 .. **Boston,** David K '92 (Willkie F&G LLP) -787 7th Av -NY 10019
(212) 577-3530 .. **Boston,** John F '76 %Leg Aid -199 Water -NY 10038 **Fx:**425-2465
(212) 765-3040 .. **Boston,** Kari D '07 NS Bienstock Inc -250 W 57th -NY 10107
(212) 836-7197 .. **Boston,** Sheila S '94 (Kaye S LLP) -425 Park Av -NY 10022 **Fx:**836-7158
(646) 471-4000 .. **Bostrom,** Lisa Klaiman '91 %PricewaterhouseCoopers LLP -300 Mad Av -NY 10017
(212) 649-2000 .. **Bostron,** Catherine A '81 %Hearst Corp -300 W 57th -NY 10019 **Fx:**649-2035
(212) 704-6000 .. **Bost Seaton,** Christina H '05 %Troutman S LLP -405 Lex Av -NY 10174
(212) 940-8800 .. **Boswell,** Jonathan M '09 %Katten MR LLP -575 Mad Av -NY 10022
(631) 331-2494 .. **Boswell,** Linda M '89 -Bx478 -Pt Jffrsn 11777
(914) 337-3626 .. **Bosworth Gray & Fuller** -116 Kraft Av -Bronxvll 10708 **Fx:**337-3630
(518) 455-4881 .. **Bosworth,** Lynelle K '07 NYS Assembly -80 S Swan -Albany 12248
(212) 637-1079 .. **Bosworth,** Michl S '04 US Atty -1 St Andrews Plz -NY 10007
(212) 577-3688 .. **Bota,** Heidi '94 %Leg Aid -199 Water -NY 10038 **Fx:**509-8431
(212) 431-2161 .. **Botein,** Michl '69 %NY Law Schl -185 W Bway -NY 10013 **Fx:**966-2053
(212) 385-8780 .. **Both,** Kieran A '89 -299 Bway -NY 10007 **Fx:**385-0249
(718) 729-2485 .. **Bothos,** Demetrios A '03 -3343 Vernon Blvd -Astoria 11106
(631) 874-4826 .. **Botjer,** Wm L '76 -Bx478 -Ctr Moriches 11934
(845) 638-5180 .. **Botta,** Brigitte M '03 Cnty Atty -Cnty Ofc Bldg -New Cty 10956 **Fx:**638-5676
(315) 422-3466 .. **Bottar,** Anthony S '77 (Bottar L,PLLC) -120 Madison -Syracuse 13202
(315) 422-3466 .. **Bottar Leone, PLLC** -120 Madison -Syracuse 13202 **Fx:**422-4621
(315) 422-3466 .. **Bottar,** Michl A '04 %Bottar L,PLLC -120 Madison -Syracuse 13202
(212) 490-3000 .. **Bottari,** Paul J '77 (Wilson EME&D LLP) -150 E 42nd -NY 10017
(516) 222-6500 .. **Botter,** Allan S '59 OfCnsl Galasso LC&L,LLP -377 Oak -Gdn Cty 11530
(212) 872-1000 .. **Botter,** David H '90 -One Bryant Park -NY 10036 **Fx:**872-1002
(212) 835-1572 .. **Botter,** Theo I '50 OfCnsl Lampf LP&P -5 Penn Plz 19th Fl -NY 10119
(212) 867-9123 .. **Bottger,** Walter F '65 (Berkman BN&R,LLP) -521 5th Av -NY 10175
(585) 396-4575 .. **Botti,** Nicole J '95 %Hon J Harvey -27 N Main -Canandaigua 14424
(845) 294-2325 .. **Botti,** Peter G '81 P Botti -14 Scotchtown Av Bx388 -Goshen 10924 **Fx:**294-2088
(914) 762-6136 .. **Botticelli,** Elizabeth J '84 -18 Susquehanna Rd -Ossining 10562
(516) 484-5752 .. **Botticelli,** Giuliano '98 -1 Wakefld Dr -Glen Head 11545
(646) 386-5891 .. **Botticelli,** Jessica M '99 %MHLS -41 Mad Av -NY 10010
(631) 435-3535 .. **Botticelli,** Robt D '01 %UFC Aerospace -25 Drexel Dr -Bay Shr 11706
(914) 668-4040 .. **Bottiglieri,** Wm A '85 -9 W Prospect Av -Mt Vernon 10550 **Fx:**668-6260
(212) 906-1200 .. **Bottner,** Morgan L '09 %Latham & W -885 3rd Av -NY 10022
(212) 269-6720 .. **Bottoms,** David N Jr. '67 %Fudiciary Admin Srvcs -30 Wall -NY 10005
(212) 670-0408 .. **Bottoms,** Tonia P '93 Merrill Lynch -222 Bway -NY 10038
(212) 590-7161 .. **Botway,** Jill R '81 OMD USA -11 Mad Av -NY 10010
(516) 571-2250 .. **Botwin,** Elizabeth Dvorkin '79 %Cnty Comptroller -240 Old Cntry Rd -Mineola 11501
(718) 522-6118 .. **Botwinick,** Dina N '09 %A Scarlato & Assoc -26 Court -Brklyn 11242 **Fx:**596-2610
(212) 818-9600 .. **Botwinick,** Jeffrey '85 %Greenfield S&S,LLP -600 3rd Av -NY 10016
(212) 399-4280 .. **Botwinick,** Jonathan S '98 %Gerschel & Co -600 Mad Av -NY 10022
(718) 875-1300 .. **Botwinik,** Nancy A '94 %Appllt Div 2nd Dept -45 Monroe Pl -Brklyn 11201 **Fx:**858-2446
(212) 508-6700 .. **Botwinoff,** Neil E '82 (Tannenbaum HS&H LLP) -900 3rd Av -NY 10022
(212) 506-1700 .. **Boucai,** Michl D '06 %Kasowitz BT&F LLP -1633 Bway -NY 10019
(212) 768-6700 .. **Boucard,** Robin J '07 %Sonnenschein N&R LLP -2 World Fncl Ctr -NY 10281
(585) 232-4424 .. **Bouchard,** John D '82 %Riedman Corp -45 East Av -Rchstr 14604
(518) 459-1684 .. **Bouchard,** Michl G '88 -4 Atrium Dr -Albany 12205 **Fx:**459-1688
(212) 209-4800 .. **Bouchard,** Nicole M '09 %Brown R LLP -7 Times Sq -NY 10036
(631) 852-1429 .. **Boucher,** Anne Molloy '79 %Hon J Jones Jr -210 Center Dr -Rvrhead 11901
(914) 225-5719 .. **Boucher,** Evan J '08 Morgan Stanley & Co -2000 Wstchstr Av -Purchase 10577
(718) 797-5145 .. **Boucher,** Rebecca Q '87 -225 Kane -Brklyn 11231
(212) 474-1000 .. **Bouchoux,** Christopher J '08 Cravath S&M LLP -825 8th Av -NY 10019
(212) 351-4000 .. **Boudreau,** Chas Jos '02 %Gibson D&C LLP -200 Park Av -NY 10166
(212) 558-4000 .. **Boudreau,** Jean-Michel '09 %Sullivan & C LLP -125 Broad -NY 10004
(212) 294-6700 .. **Boudreau,** Robt J '09 %Winston & S -200 Park Av -NY 10166
(518) 262-3828 .. **Bougen,** Harriet '82 %Albany Med Ctr -43 New Scotland Av -Albany 12208 **Fx:**262-4184
(212) 484-3900 .. **Bougher,** Jennifer L '04 %Arent F LLP -1675 Bway -NY 10019
(212) 661-9100 .. **Bougiamas,** John A '93 %Otterbourg SH&R,PC -230 Park Av -NY 10169
(212) 336-0032 .. **Bougiamas,** Panayiota Kilaras '00 %SEC -3 World Fncl Ctr -NY 10281 **Fx:**336-1323
(914) 375-0100 .. **Bougopoulos,** Gregory S '07 %Novick ELRW&L,PC -733 Ynkrs Av -Ynkrs 10704
(212) 447-5599 .. **Bouklas,** Philip V '96 (Agins SR&B,LLP) -386 Park Av S -NY 10016
(212) 858-1000 .. **Boulanger,** Carol Seabrook '70 (Pillsbury WSP LLP) -1540 Bway -NY 10036
(716) 270-2431 .. **Boulanger,** Raymond M '87 %IRS -300 Pearl -Buffalo 14202
(212) 825-9457 .. **Boulbol,** Chas E '84 C Boulbol,PC -26 Bway -NY 10004 **Fx:**825-9414
(212) 490-3000 .. **Boule,** Eugene T '94 (Wilson EME&D LLP) -150 E 42nd -NY 10017
(212) 490-3000 .. **Boulhosa,** Michl L '87 (Wilson EME&D LLP) -150 E 42nd -NY 10017
(914) 323-7000 .. **Boulhosa,** Michl L '87 (Wilson EME&D LLP) -3 Gannett Dr -White Plns 10604
(518) 463-4491 .. **Boulia,** Trudy L '99 %JP Harvey,PLLC -677 Bway -Albany 12207 **Fx:**463-5665
(631) 727-3059 .. **Boulier,** Wm B '96 -Bx791 -Manorvll 11949 **Fx:**727-1425
(212) 808-0700 .. **Boulougouris,** Christina '95 %Norris M&M,PA -875 3rd Av -NY 10022
(212) 450-4000 .. **Boulyjenkova,** Irina '09 %Davis P&W LLP -450 Lex Av -NY 10017
(607) 723-9511 .. **Bouman,** Peter H '76 OfCnsl Coughlin & G,LLP -19 Chenango Bx2039 -Bnghmtn 13902
(212) 820-7700 .. **Boundas Skarzynski Walsh & Black,LLC** -1 Bttry Pk Plz -NY 10004 **Fx:**820-7740
(212) 820-7700 .. **Boundas,** Theo A '93 (Boundas SW&B,LLC) -1 Bttry Pk Plz -NY 10004
(212) 417-5300 .. **Bounds,** Twan V '01 %Medicaid Fraud Cntrl -120 Bway -NY 10271 **Fx:**417-5274
(212) 294-7848 .. **Boundy,** David E '98 %Cantor Fitzgerald -110 E 59th -NY 10022
(716) 852-3540 .. **Bouquard,** Leah A '08 %Watson BCJ&S -12 Fountain Plz -Buffalo 14202
(518) 487-7600 .. **Bourassa,** Beth A '91 (Whiteman O&H LLP) -1 Commerce Plz -Albany 12260
(718) 590-2000 .. **Bourbon,** Jessica I '05 %DA -198 E 161st -Bronx 10451 **Fx:**590-6477
(315) 531-3233 .. **Bourcy,** Bernetta A '88 Yates Cnty Atty -415 Lbrty Bx635 -Penn Yan 14527 **Fx:**531-3234
(585) 263-1000 .. **Bourdeau,** James O '96 (Nixon P LLP) -1100 Clinton Sq -Rchstr 14604
(212) 450-4000 .. **Bourdeaut,** Thos '07 %Davis P&W LLP -450 Lex Av -NY 10017
(212) 732-3200 .. **Bourgasser-Ketterling,** Sandra '02 %Carter L&M LLP -2 Wall -NY 10005
(212) 891-0782 .. **Bourgeois,** David A '92 FOJP Srvc Corp -28 E 28th -NY 10016
(212) 460-6753 .. **Bourgeois,** Karen A '96 Con Ed -4 Irving Pl -NY 10003
(212) 318-3000 .. **Bourgeois,** Richd P '78 (Fulbright & J LLP) -666 5th Av -NY 10103
(212) 238-3000 .. **Bourgerie,** Richd P '69 OfCnsl Emmet M&M,LLP -120 Bway -NY 10271
(212) 704-6000 .. **Bourguignon,** Robt L '96 (Troutman S LLP) -405 Lex Av -NY 10174
(212) 326-3939 .. **Bourjolly,** Lissa S '06 %Jones D -222 E 41st -NY 10017
(212) 521-5400 .. **Bourke,** Aaron Z '10 %Reed S LLP -599 Lex Av -NY 10022
(631) 283-0046 .. **Bourke Flanagan & Asato PC** -21 S Main -Southampton 11968 **Fx:**287-1255
(631) 283-0046 .. **Bourke,** Thos J '57 OfCnsl Bourke F&A PC -21 S Main -Southampton 11968
(212) 360-8743 .. **Bournas-Ney,** Michl '79 Harlem Cmmnty Justice Ctr -170 E 121st -NY 10035
(212) 967-3322 .. **Bournazos,** Steven '95 (Bournazos & M,PC) -111 Bway -NY 10006 **Fx:**268-5012
(845) 791-4074 .. **Bourne,** Alexandra '00 -30 Glen Wild Rd Bx1093 -Rck Hll 12775 **Fx:**791-7480
(212) 506-1700 .. **Bourne,** Andrew N '03 %Kasowitz BT&F LLP -1633 Bway -NY 10019
(718) 741-8400 .. **Bourne-Clarke,** Sharon Ann '94 %Div of Human Rights -1 Fordham Plz -Bronx 10458 **Fx:**741-8102
(212) 310-8000 .. **Bourque,** Lisa R '09 %Weil G&M LLP -767 5th Av -NY 10153
(212) 455-2000 .. **Bourque,** Robt A '83 (Simpson T&B LLP) -425 Lex Av -NY 10017
(212) 755-5551 .. **Boursereau,** Dominique G '87 -575 Mad Av -NY 10022 **Fx:**755-6385
(212) 558-4000 .. **Bourtin,** Nicolas '97 (Sullivan & C LLP) -125 Broad -NY 10004
(212) 446-2300 .. **Bourtin,** Stephen M '04 %Boies S&F LLP -575 Lex Av -NY 10022
(585) 325-4300 .. **Bourtis,** Eftihia '92 (Pelton DDD&B) -45 Exchange Blvd -Rchstr 14614 **Fx:**325-6075
(212) 434-0100 .. **Boury,** Jos E '83 %Litchfield C LLP -420 Lex Av -NY 10170
(718) 442-4600 .. **Bousanti,** Anthony J '75 (Jacobi SBP&F,PC) -235 Forest Av -Staten Isl 10301
(212) 952-0100 .. **Bouscaren,** Anthony G '78 US Aviation -199 Water -NY 10038
(315) 422-1391 .. **Bousquet,** Laurence Gere '81 (Green & S,PLLC) -One Lincoln Ctr #900 -Syracuse 13202
(718) 876-6300 .. **Bousquet,** Michl J '79 %DA -130 Styvsnt Pl -Staten Isl 10301
(315) 422-1391 .. **Bousquet,** Phillip S '90 (Green & S,PLLC) -One Lincoln Ctr #900 -Syracuse 13202
(914) 682-3911 .. **Boustead,** Cheryl L '82 -18 Idlewood Rd -White Plns 10605
(631) 689-8600 .. **Boutcher,** Robt F '75 (Trump & B,LLP) -46 Route 25A Bx830 -E Setauket 11733
(518) 474-6436 .. **Bouteiller,** Wm L '88 %Dept Pub Srvc -3 ESP -Albany 12223
(518) 873-3880 .. **Boutelle,** Brandon E '00 %Pub Def -Bx217 -Elizabethtwn 12932 **Fx:**873-3888
(212) 269-0927 .. **Boutin,** Arturo M '97 %D'Amato & L,LLP -2 World Fncl Ctr -NY 10281

(212) 770-7000 .. **Boutin,** Japhet '98 AIG Domestic Claims -175 Water -NY 10038
(518) 257-3000 .. **Bouton,** Susan J '99 %Dormitory Auth -515 Bway -Albany 12207 **Fx:**257-3101
(845) 562-0203 .. **Bova,** Frances M '94 Finkelstein & Prtnrs,LLP -1279 Route 300 Bx1111 -Newburgh 12550
(212) 788-0705 .. **Bova Hiatt,** Lisa Ann '95 %Law Dept -100 Church -NY 10007 **Fx:**788-0367
(212) 480-7748 .. **Bove,** Brian R '87 %DHCR -25 Beaver -NY 10004 **Fx:**480-7416
(585) 546-7430 .. **Bove,** Emil J Jr. '74 %Dept of Law -144 Exchange Blvd -Rchstr 14614 **Fx:**546-7514
(585) 243-7948 .. **Bove,** Emil J III '09 Hon RJ Sullivan -500 Pearl -NY 10007
(212) 940-3180 .. **Bove,** John G '72 (Nixon P LLP) -437 Mad Av -NY 10022
(518) 477-7951 .. **Bove,** John J '90 OfCnsl Maney M&L -77 Troy Rd -E Greenbush 12061
(718) 590-5400 .. **Bove,** Jos '92 %M Ridge -910 Grnd Cncrs -Bronx 10451 **Fx:**681-0285
(212) 561-7700 .. **Bove,** Maria A '01 OfCnsl Pachulski SZ&J -780 3rd Av -NY 10017
(516) 489-5000 .. **Bove,** Mario S '93 %Town Atty -Town Hall -Hempstd 11550 **Fx:**489-5150
(212) 902-1000 .. **Bove,** Peter A '03 Goldman Sachs -1 NY Plz -NY 10004
(212) 335-9000 .. **Bovell,** Kavita M '01 %DA -1 Hogan Pl -NY 10013
(212) 450-4000 .. **Bovenzi,** Giorgio '96 %Davis P&W LLP -450 Lex Av -NY 10017
(718) 237-0193 .. **Bovers,** Wm H '83 -106 Cromwell Cir -Staten Isl 10304
(845) 291-2050 .. **Bovill,** Luke E '06 %DA -255-275 Main -Goshen 10924 **Fx:**291-2085
(718) 380-3842 .. **Bowden,** David W '74 -81-18 167th -Jamaica 11432
(516) 801-9524 .. **Bowden,** Jason T '07 Pall Corp -25 Hrbr Park Dr -Pt Wash 11050
(212) 446-4800 .. **Bowden,** S Christopher '08 %Kirkland & E LLP -153 E 53rd -NY 10022
(212) 837-6122 .. **Bowden,** Yohance L '01 %Hughes H&R LLP -1 Bttry Pk Plz -NY 10004 **Fx:**299-6122
(808) 384-9140 .. **Bowe,** Jos G '89 %US Marine Corps -Bx528 -Jamesprt 11947 **Fx:**254-3462
(212) 788-0878 .. **Bowe,** Martin J '01 %Law Dept -100 Church -NY 10007 **Fx:**788-0367
(315) 471-3151 .. **Bowe,** Melinda B '07 %Hancock & E,LLP -1500 AXA Twr I Bx4976 -Syracuse 13221
(212) 506-1700 .. **Bowe,** Michl J '93 (Kasowitz BT&F LLP) -1633 Bway -NY 10019
(212) 635-6609 .. **Bowe,** Michelle K '97 SrCnsl Bank of NY Mellon -1 Wall -NY 10286 **Fx:**635-1098
(212) 422-0202 .. **Bowen,** Abigail '07 %Sedgwick DM&A LLP -125 Broad -NY 10004
(212) 644-4420 .. **Bowen,** Anita D '95 (Fabiani C&H,LLP) -570 Lex Av -NY 10022
(607) 777-2441 .. **Bowen,** C Scott '78 %Binghamton Univ -222 Water -Bnghmtn 13901 **Fx:**777-6530
(212) 299-2000 .. **Bowen,** Christopher K '97 %NYMEX -1 North End Av -NY 10282 **Fx:**301-4700
(585) 454-1130 .. **Bowen,** David F '85 Cnsl FR Michel -28 E Main -Rchstr 14614 **Fx:**454-6118
(646) 428-3806 .. **Bowen,** Felice A '02 %Dept of Educ -32 Old Slip -NY 10005 **Fx:**428-3843
(212) 758-0050 .. **Bowen,** James Milton '72 %Title Assoc -825 3rd Av -NY 10022 **Fx:**758-8223
(585) 232-6500 .. **Bowen,** Jeffrey H '81 (Harter S&E LLP) -1600 Bausch & Lomb Pl -Rchstr 14604
(212) 474-1000 .. **Bowen,** Lindsay W Jr. '10 %Cravath S&M LLP -825 8th Av -NY 10019
(212) 903-9000 .. **Bowen,** Lorna M '01 (Linklaters) -1345 Av of Amer -NY 10105
(212) 314-3813 .. **Bowen,** Margretta Jeffers '77 %AXA Financial Inc -1290 Av of Amer -NY 10104 **Fx:**707-1880
(212) 506-1700 .. **Bowen,** Michl P '93 (Kasowitz BT&F LLP) -1633 Bway -NY 10019
(212) 906-1200 .. **Bowen,** Sharon Y '84 (Latham & W) -885 3rd Av -NY 10022
(212) 506-2500 .. **Bowen,** Todd E '04 %Mayer B LLP -1675 Bway -NY 10019
(585) 546-5530 .. **Bower,** Carolyn '83 %Thomson West -50 E Broad -Rchstr 14694
(212) 274-5664 .. **Bower,** Jaime S '03 Admin Children's Srvcs -220 Church -NY 10013
(516) 431-1177 .. **Bower,** Jessica G '08 %Galgano & Assoc,PLLC -20 W Park Av -Long Bch 11561
(212) 599-0900 .. **Bower & Lawrence, PC** -261 Mad Av -NY 10016 **Fx:**599-4560
(212) 240-0700 .. **Bower,** Mark R '72 M Bower,PC -11 Park Pl -NY 10007
(212) 599-0900 .. **Bower,** Peter R '81 (Bower & L,PC) -261 Mad Av -NY 10016
(212) 820-9300 .. **Bowerman,** Faustino N '10 (Hawkins D&W LLP) -One Chase Manh Plz -NY 10005
(716) 852-5200 .. **Bowers,** Francis D '94 (Hamberger & W) -700 Main Pl Twr -Buffalo 14202
(212) 837-6717 .. **Bowers,** James C '07 %Hughes H&R LLP -1 Bttry Pk Plz -NY 10004
(631) 669-0894 .. **Bowers,** James H '65 -107 Cooper Bx490 -Babylon 11702 **Fx:**669-0260
(845) 644-4356 .. **Bowers,** John C '01 -Bx123 -Wurtsboro 12790
(315) 338-0181 .. **Bowers,** Keith D '89 -201 W Court -Rome 13440
(315) 866-0006 .. **Bowers,** Keith D '89 -209 N Wshngtn -Herkimer 13350 **Fx:**866-0689
(516) 680-0215 .. **Bowers,** Kerrin A '09 -272 Foster Av -Sayvll 11782
(212) 269-0927 .. **Bowers,** Meleena M '02 %D'Amato & L,LLP -2 World Fncl Ctr -NY 10281
(518) 392-4267 .. **Bowers,** Morgen M '00 %S Del Peral -22 Park Row -Chatham 12037 **Fx:**392-4389
(212) 353-2200 .. **Bowers,** Nicholas E '07 %Turkel F&D LLP -304 Park Av S -NY 10010
(212) 880-3800 .. **Bowers,** Richd N '76 (Akerman S) -335 Mad Av -NY 10017
(212) 909-6000 .. **Bowers,** Scott Ethan '05 %Debevoise & P LLP -919 3rd Av -NY 10022
(212) 858-1000 .. **Bowers,** Wm C '88 (Pillsbury WSP LLP) -1540 Bway -NY 10036
(212) 979-0505 .. **Bowes,** Christopher J '95 %Ctr For Disability Advcy Rights -100 Lafayette -NY 10013 **Fx:**979-8778
(518) 283-5412 .. **Bowes,** Donald C '55 -1060 Spring Av -Troy 12180
(212) 794-5382 .. **Bowes,** Kristen M '02 CUNY -535 E 80th -NY 10075 **Fx:**794-5426
(585) 419-8800 .. **Bowes,** Robt J III '08 %Harris B PLLC -99 Garnsey Rd -Pittsfrd 14534
(212) 852-3575 .. **Bowes-McCann,** Jennifer '05 %US Trust Co,NA -114 W 47th -NY 10036 **Fx:**852-1310
(212) 529-6445 .. **Bowie,** Alexandra S '85 %Graham-Windham -33 Irving Pl -NY 10003 **Fx:**614-9811
(914) 618-2394 .. **Bowie,** April D '02 -29 Chase Rd -Scarsdale 10583
(914) 216-9555 .. **Bowie,** Darren A '08 Nokia Inc -102 Corp Park Dr -White Plns 10604
(212) 297-5800 .. **Bowie,** Morris Alexander II '90 (Day P LLP) -7 Times Sq -NY 10036
(212) 903-9000 .. **Bowie,** Scott O '03 (Linklaters) -1345 Av of Amer -NY 10105
(518) 434-0327 .. **Bowitch,** Gary S '87 -119 Wshngtn Av -Albany 12210 **Fx:**434-0328
(202) 663-6558 .. **Bowker,** David W '04 (WilmerHale) -399 Park Av -NY 10022 **Fx:**663-6363
(212) 867-3171 .. **Bowker,** Julie Lee '93 -60 E 42nd -NY 10165
(212) 941-5025 .. **Bowler,** Anne Marie '01 (Gabay-Rafiy & B LLP) -299 Bway -NY 10007 **Fx:**202-3883
(585) 724-2577 .. **Bowler,** John R '02 Eastman Kodak Co -343 State -Rchstr 14650
(718) 298-8923 .. **Bowler,** Norah E '96 %Leg Aid -153-01 Jamaica Av -Jamaica 11432 **Fx:**657-0537
(914) 993-0936 .. **Bowler,** Richd J '83 R Bowler -10 Bank -White Plns 10606 **Fx:**683-1369
(646) 264-3650 .. **Bowles,** Allison L '07 %US Dept of Labor -201 Varick -NY 10014 **Fx:**264-3660
(646) 419-4264 .. **Bowles,** David K '99 (Bowles C&C LLP) -54 W 21st -NY 10010 **Fx:**(866) 844-8305
(212) 952-6200 .. **Bowles,** Lawr J '67 (Nourse & B,LLP) -55 Bway -NY 10006
(212) 937-4000 .. **Bowles,** Paul N '09 %Fitzpatrick & HTCPA,LLP -12 E 49th -NY 10017
(518) 238-4359 .. **Bowles,** Sharon R '87 NYS Judicial Inst -98 Niver -Cohoes 12047
(212) 765-5070 .. **Bowley,** Christopher C '10 %Fish & R,PC -153 E 53rd -NY 10022
(203) 330-2102 .. **Bowman,** Aaron G '06 %Pullman & C,LLC -50 Main -White Plns 10606
(212) 458-1180 .. **Bowman,** Amy J '04 AIG -175 Water -NY 10038
(718) 237-5500 .. **Bowman,** Catherine Ford '95 %Leg Srvcs -105 Court -Brklyn 11201 **Fx:**855-0733
(212) 909-6000 .. **Bowman,** Craig A '93 (Debevoise & P LLP) -919 3rd Av -NY 10022
(212) 514-9700 .. **Bowman,** David B '82 (Bowman & V) -575 Mad Av -NY 10022 **Fx:**202-4897
(718) 263-6800 .. **Bowman,** Dustin B '03 OfCnsl S Zalewski & Assoc,PC -125-10 Qns Blvd -Kew Gdns 11415 **Fx:**520-9401
(585) 705-8877 .. **Bowman,** Jason J '03 -2106 Bailey Rd -Ontario 14519 **Fx:**(315) 524-2510
(718) 243-2700 .. **Bowman,** Kelby N '87 %Talisman & D,PC -409 Fulton -Brklyn 11201 **Fx:**243-2707
(585) 263-1000 .. **Bowman,** Lori A '01 %Nixon P LLP -1100 Clinton Sq -Rchstr 14604
(716) 692-3988 .. **Bowman,** Mary-Jean '98 -319 Wheatfld -N Tonawanda 14120
(212) 446-2300 .. **Bowman,** Philip M '02 (Boies S&F LLP) -575 Lex Av -NY 10022
(212) 576-8323 .. **Bowman,** Richd P '98 %NY Life Ins -51 Mad Av -NY 10010 **Fx:**447-0569
(212) 636-6000 .. **Bowman,** Scott J '07 %Fordham Univ Sch of Law -140 W 62nd -NY 10023 **Fx:**636-6899
(315) 475-9334 .. **Bowman,** Stephen S '89 (Farchione & B LLP) -217 Mntgmry -Syracuse 13202 **Fx:**475-9655
(914) 347-2600 .. **Bowman,** Victoria Tiburzi '97 %Traub LS&S LLP -7 Skyline Dr -Hawthorne 10532
(347) 404-9133 .. **Bowman,** Wm D '93 %Civil Ct -141 Lvngstn -Brklyn 11201 **Fx:**(718) 643-3733
(585) 232-3730 .. **Bowman,** Wynn L '01 %Chamberlain D LLP -1600 Crssrds Bldg -Rchstr 14614
(212) 709-8170 .. **Bowmaster,** Harry J '94 -110 Wall -NY 10005
(212) 664-5211 .. **Bowyer,** Elizabeth Caldwell '03 NBC News -30 Rckfllr Plz -NY 10112
(212) 969-3000 .. **Boxer,** Abby C '08 %Proskauer R LLP -1585 Bway -NY 10036
(212) 981-9060 .. **Boxer,** Barry J '66 (Rose & B) -1065 Av of Amer -NY 10018
(212) 770-6181 .. **Boxer,** Gene '00 AIG,Inc -70 Pine -NY 10270
(212) 922-0050 .. **Boxer,** Harold S '77 SrCnsl Stewart Title Ins -300 E 42nd -NY 10017 **Fx:**983-1133
(212) 419-1522 .. **Boxer,** Harriette N '89 -31 E 32nd -NY 10016
(212) 521-2776 .. **Boxer,** Jason T '96 %Loews Corp -667 Mad Av -NY 10065 **Fx:**521-2997
(212) 732-3200 .. **Boxer,** Jeffrey S '93 (Carter L&M LLP) -2 Wall -NY 10005
(516) 627-7000 .. **Boxer,** Joshua A '06 %Weiss & Z,PC -3333 New Hyde Pk Rd -New Hyde Pk 11042
(212) 806-5400 .. **Boxer,** Leonard '63 (Stroock &S&L LLP) -180 Maiden Ln -NY 10038
(516) 484-3800 .. **Boxer,** Michl A '87 %Avant Garde Optics -44 Hrbr Park Dr -Pt Wash 11050
(212) 845-7980 .. **Boxer,** Michl D '93 %Ramius Capital Grp -599 Lex Av -NY 10022
(212) 210-9470 .. **Boxer,** Nelson A '88 (Alston & B LLP) -90 Park Av -NY 10016
(585) 383-6803 .. **Boxer,** Robt L '78 %MOSCOM Corp -3750 Monroe Av -Pittsfrd 14534
(212) 813-8800 .. **Boyadjian,** Livia D '81 %Goodwin P LLP -620 8th Av -NY 10018
(212) 695-8100 .. **Boyajian,** Aaron D '99 %Goetz F,LLP -1 Penn Plz -NY 10119
(518) 463-7784 .. **Boyajian,** Donald W '81 (Dreyer B LLP) -75 Columbia -Albany 12210
(845) 897-2487 .. **Boyajian,** Michl G '94 -291 Main -Beacon 12508
(212) 768-6700 .. **Boyajian,** Victor H '04 (Sonnenschein N&R LLP) -1221 Av of Amer -NY 10020
(212) 297-5800 .. **Boyan,** James W III '07 %Day P LLP -7 Times Sq -NY 10036
(212) 759-8203 .. **Boyan,** Jos M '98 %Hedinger & L -110 Wall -NY 10005
(845) 557-8319 .. **Boyar,** Andrew '69 -592 Route 55 -Eldred 12732 **Fx:**557-8310
(212) 269-0927 .. **Boyar,** David A '82 (D'Amato & L,LLP) -2 World Fncl Ctr -NY 10281
(212) 667-2430 .. **Boyar,** Gabriel L '93 %UBS Warburg -1285 Av of Amer -NY 10019
(631) 427-3533 .. **Boyar,** Jeffrey N '75 %Widlitz & S,PC -700 NY Av -Huntngtn 11743
(212) 995-8300 .. **Boyar,** Jonathan '07 M Boyar & Co -35 E 21st -NY 10010
(212) 841-8115 .. **Boyarski,** Jason R '01 Universal Music Publishing -1755 Bway -NY 10019
(212) 972-0000 .. **Boyarsky,** Jay F '90 -60 E 42nd -NY 10165
(212) 506-1700 .. **Boyarsky,** Stuart M '03 Kasowitz BT&F LLP -1633 Bway -NY 10019
(718) 638-6298 .. **Boyce,** Cynthia L '85 (CL Boyce & Assoc) -269 St James Pl -Brklyn 11238 **Fx:**398-1393
(631) 650-1200 .. **Boyce,** James M '02 %Sinnreich K&M LLP -267 Carleton Av -Central Islip 11722
(718) 875-1300 .. **Boyce,** Michl T '77 %Appllt Div 2nd Dept -45 Monroe Pl -Brklyn 11201 **Fx:**858-2446

(585) 454-2000 .. **Boyce,** Sheldon W Jr. '80 (Brenna B&B,PLLC) -31 E Main -Rchstr 14614
(212) 319-7600 .. **Boychuk,** George E '86 Cnsl Ziegler Z & Assoc LLP -570 Lex Av -NY 10022 **Fx:**319-7605
(631) 434-1500 .. **Boyd,** Allison J '90 (A Crain,PC) -130 3rd Av -Brentwd 11717 **Fx:**434-3200
(212) 872-1000 .. **Boyd,** Christopher L '10 -One Bryant Park -NY 10036 **Fx:**872-1002
(631) 755-0101 .. **Boyd,** Claudia L '99 (Lewis JAA,LLP) -425 Broad Hollow Rd -Melvll 11747
(212) 259-8000 .. **Boyd,** David A '09 %Dewey & L LLP -1301 Av of Amer -NY 10019
(212) 244-4664 .. **Boyd,** Dennis R '88 %NY Lawyers Pub Intrst -151 W 30th -NY 10001 **Fx:**244-4570
(631) 765-1555 .. **Boyd,** Edw J V '69 -54655 Main Rd Bx1468 -Southold 11971
(212) 777-5714 .. **Boyd,** Gail W '80 G Boyd,PC -305 Mad Av -NY 10165 **Fx:**777-2396
(212) 297-5800 .. **Boyd,** Julia '08 %Day P LLP -7 Times Sq -NY 10036
(518) 542-2128 .. **Boyd,** Kathleen M '02 -26 Brookside Av -Menands 12204 **Fx:**935-9343
(518) 408-0469 .. **Boyd,** Kathleen M '02 Workers Comp Bd -20 Park -Albany 12207
(516) 522-2610 .. **Boyd,** Kenneth T '88 -626 RXR Plz -Uniondale 11556 **Fx:**522-2620
(212) 577-3688 .. **Boyd,** Laura D '89 %Leg Aid -199 Water -NY 10038 **Fx:**509-8431
(585) 244-4541 .. **Boyd,** Marcia J '76 -290 Linden Oaks Dr -Rchstr 14625 **Fx:**641-2203
(212) 576-7000 .. **Boyd,** Michl W '98 %NYLIM -51 Mad Av -NY 10010
(212) 839-5300 .. **Boyd,** Robt L '89 (Sidley A LLP) -787 7th Av -NY 10019
(212) 964-6611 .. **Boyd,** Rosemarie P '01 %Lester SK&D -120 Bway -NY 10271
(212) 468-4942 .. **Boyd,** S Gregory '05 %Davis & G LLP -1740 Bway -NY 10019 **Fx:**621-0916
(718) 636-1155 .. **Boyd,** Sandhya S '00 %Leg Srvcs -1368 Fulton -Brklyn 11216 **Fx:**398-6414
(716) 839-7777 .. **Boyd,** Stephen '99 (O'Brien B PC) -40 N Forest Rd -Williamsvll 14221
(212) 730-8133 .. **Boyd,** Steven D '03 Gunderson DSVF&H,LLP -220 W 42nd -NY 10036
(212) 484-8000 .. **Boyd,** Virginia Bennett '06 %Warner Music Grp -75 Rckfllr Plz -NY 10019 **Fx:**489-3342
(212) 735-3000 .. **Boydell,** Tiffany Tran '96 Cnsl Skadden ASM&F LLP -4 Times Sq -NY 10036
(914) 946-8084 .. **Boydstun,** Robt L '80 -15 Chester Av -White Plns 10601 **Fx:**946-8085
(718) 250-2000 .. **Boye,** Richd M '00 %DA -350 Jay -Brklyn 11201 **Fx:**250-2314
(646) 315-7300 .. **Boyer,** Allen D '91 %FINRA -14 Wall -NY 10005 **Fx:**315-7440
(718) 979-5200 .. **Boyer,** Kathleen D '90 %W Leininger,PC -34 Dumont Av -Staten Isl 10305 **Fx:**667-7128
(212) 918-3000 .. **Boyer,** Nathaniel S '10 %Hogan L LLP -875 3rd Av -NY 10022
(845) 790-1454 .. **Boyer,** Ruth L '96 -1 Civic Cntr Plz -Poughkeepsie 12601
(212) 943-1090 .. **Boyers,** Seymour '54 (Gair GCSMB&R) -80 Pine -NY 10005
(315) 793-2502 .. **Boykin,** Carl J '90 %Dept of Law -207 Genesee -Utica 13501 **Fx:**793-2228
(212) 773-3189 .. **Boykin,** Roberta M '06 Ernst & Young LLP -5 Times Sq -NY 10036
(718) 434-1700 .. **Boyko,** Yekaterina '01 -2021 Nostrand Av -Brklyn 11210 **Fx:**434-8953
(585) 232-5300 .. **Boylan Brown Code Vigdor & Wilson,LLP** -2400 Chase Sq -Rchstr 14604 **Fx:**232-3528
(516) 571-3800 .. **Boylan,** Dana R '05 %DA -262 Old Cntry Rd -Mineola 11501 **Fx:**248-9479
(212) 335-9000 .. **Boylan,** Danl C '04 %DA -1 Hogan Pl -NY 10013
(212) 578-7758 .. **Boylan,** James J '90 %MetLife -1095 Av of Amer -NY 10036
(585) 768-8148 .. **Boylan,** Laurence W '67 -45 W Main Bx307 -Le Roy 14482 **Fx:**768-7738
(585) 768-8148 .. **Boylan,** Mark S '94 -45 W Main Bx307 -Le Roy 14482 **Fx:**768-7738
(585) 768-8148 .. **Boylan,** Paul S '66 -45 W Main Bx307 -Le Roy 14482 **Fx:**768-7738
(315) 253-0326 .. **Boyle & Anderson,PC** -110 Genesee -Auburn 13021 **Fx:**253-4968
(212) 813-5900 .. **Boyle,** Cara A '02 (Fross ZL&Z,PC) -866 UN Plz -NY 10017
(212) 803-5100 .. **Boyle,** Christopher '92 %NY Cnty Defender Srvcs -225 Bway -NY 10007 **Fx:**571-6035
(718) 694-3899 .. **Boyle,** David C '90 %Transit Auth -130 Lvngstn -Brklyn 11201 **Fx:**694-5726
(631) 331-6198 .. **Boyle,** Douglas J '91 -285 Sheep Pasture Rd -E Setauket 11733
(212) 490-3000 .. **Boyle,** Edw J '67 OfCnsl Wilson EME&D LLP -150 E 42nd -NY 10017
(212) 307-5500 .. **Boyle,** Edw P '96 (Venable LLP) -1270 Av of Amer -NY 10020
(914) 963-4433 .. **Boyle,** Ellen M '81 -52 Radford -Ynkrs 10705 **Fx:**376-0537
(212) 660-3100 .. **Boyle,** James B '82 Eltman E&C,PC -140 Bway -NY 10005
(212) 319-1000 .. **Boyle,** Jeanne M '05 %Quirk & B,PC -845 3rd Av -NY 10022
(516) 571-3800 .. **Boyle,** Jennifer A '07 %DA -262 Old Cntry Rd -Mineola 11501 **Fx:**248-9479
(516) 545-5160 .. **Boyle,** John P '92 %Natl Grid -175 E Old Cntry Rd -Hicksvll 11801 **Fx:**545-5029
(212) 735-3000 .. **Boyle,** John P '96 Cnsl Skadden ASM&F LLP -4 Times Sq -NY 10036
(973) 503-5920 .. **Boyle,** Jos A '90 (Kelley D&W LLP) -101 Park Av -NY 10178 **Fx:**503-5950
(845) 294-7901 .. **Boyle,** Patrick J '60 -1 Harriman Sq Bx716 -Goshen 10924 **Fx:**294-7889
(631) 923-0940 .. **Boyle,** Patrick J '93 -151 W Carver -Huntngtn 11743 **Fx:**923-0941
(212) 980-0120 .. **Boyle,** Patrick J '98 (Frankfurt KK&S,PC) -488 Mad Av -NY 10022
(212) 819-8200 .. **Boyle,** Patrick J '08 %White & C LLP -1155 Av of Amer -NY 10036
(631) 277-7300 .. **Boyle,** Philip M '88 (Steinberg & B,LLP) -136 E Main -E Islip 11730
(212) 431-0229 .. **Boyle,** Robt J '81 -299 Bway -NY 10007
(914) 225-4548 .. **Boyle,** Robt K '93 %Morgan Stanley -2000 Wstchstr Av -Purchase 10577
(718) 990-6609 .. **Boyle,** Robin A '90 %St John's Law Schl -8000 Utopia Pkwy -Jamaica 11439 **Fx:**591-1855
(212) 980-0404 .. **Boyle,** Thos A Jr. '03 %J Dearie & Assoc -515 Mad Av -NY 10022 **Fx:**980-0555
(212) 458-6007 .. **Boyle,** Wm M '89 AIGTS -175 Water -NY 10038
(718) 518-4395 .. **Boyle,** Wm P '06 %CUNY Citizenshp & Immig Prjct -120 E 49th -Bronx 10451
(212) 291-3288 .. **Boyle-Devine,** Jennifer R '00 Citigroup,Inc -125 Broad -NY 10004
(212) 547-5400 .. **Boyles,** Jonathan J '01 %McDermott W&E LLP -340 Mad Av -NY 10173
(212) 506-5000 .. **Boyne,** Victoria K '10 %Orrick H&S LLP -51 W 52nd -NY 10019
(914) 948-9200 .. **Boynton,** Sally J '84 (S Boynton,LLC) -81 Main -White Plns 10601
(585) 419-8800 .. **Boysen,** David C '67 (Harris B PLLC) -99 Garnsey Rd -Pittsfrd 14534
(212) 916-6047 .. **Bozek,** Matthew J Jr. '77 -730 3rd Av -NY 10017
(914) 668-4600 .. **Bozeman,** Bruce L '69 (Bozeman Law Firm,LLP) -6 Gramatan Av -Mt Vernon 10550 **Fx:**668-4721
(716) 847-8400 .. **Bozer,** Alan J '85 (Phillips L LLP) -3400 HSBC Ctr -Buffalo 14203
(212) 458-2415 .. **Bozovic,** Victoria H '06 %AIG -175 Water -NY 10038
(212) 553-5602 .. **Bozza,** Amanda R '08 %Zurich NA -1 Lbrty Plz -NY 10006
(646) 315-7300 .. **Bozza,** Kenneth R '86 %FINRA -14 Wall -NY 10005 **Fx:**315-7440
(212) 708-6685 .. **Bozzo,** Paul P '79 %LeFrak Org -40 W 57th -NY 10019 **Fx:**708-6681
(212) 226-5054 .. **Bozzuti,** Jos J '05 %Powley & G,PC -304 Hudson -NY 10013 **Fx:**266-5085
(212) 969-3000 .. **Braatz,** John R '96 %Proskauer R LLP -1585 Bway -NY 10036
(212) 530-5000 .. **Brabant,** Lisa A '99 %Milbank TH&M LLP -1 Chase Manh Plz -NY 10005
(212) 988-4874 .. **Brabec,** Jeffrey J '70 -322 E 73rd -NY 10021 **Fx:**988-4874
(585) 226-5369 .. **Bracci,** Leo J '79 %DEC -6274 E Avon-Lima Rd -Avon 14414 **Fx:**226-9485
(518) 374-3545 .. **Braccini,** Michl '93 -Bx3339 -Schnctdy 12303 **Fx:**374-2784
(716) 856-4000 .. **Braccio,** Jos L '85 (Hodgson R LLP) -140 Pearl -Buffalo 14202
(718) 250-1400 .. **Bracco,** Ann V '02 %BZ Green -12 MetroTech Ctr -Brklyn 11201 **Fx:**250-1401
(718) 377-2300 .. **Bracco,** Steven '93 -5122 Av N -Brklyn 11234
(718) 921-6601 .. **Bracconier,** Jos J '09 %T Beinert -155 Bay Ridge Av -Brklyn 11220 **Fx:**921-6609
(212) 310-8000 .. **Brace,** Jennifer M '08 %Weil G&M LLP -767 5th Av -NY 10153
(212) 508-6100 .. **Bracewell & Giuliani,LLP** -1251 Av of Amer -NY 10020 **Fx:**508-6101
(212) 373-3000 .. **Brach,** Jessica L '06 %Paul WRW&G LLP -1285 Av of Amer -NY 10019
(585) 428-5210 .. **Brach,** Kevin P '01 Pub Def -10 N Fitzhugh -Rchstr 14614 **Fx:**428-2234
(212) 530-5000 .. **Brach,** Richd S '73 (Milbank TH&M LLP) -1 Chase Manh Plz -NY 10005
(212) 868-2751 .. **Brachfeld,** Zev '08 -30 Broad -NY 10004
(631) 369-7600 .. **Bracken,** Anne M '95 %Lewis JAA,LLP -21 E 2nd -Rvrhead 11901
(914) 287-7047 .. **Bracken,** Gary V '78 %Chase Manhattan Bk -11 Martine Av -White Plns 10606
(716) 856-3500 .. **Bracken,** James P '81 SpclCnsl Magavern MG LLP -1100 Rand Bldg -Buffalo 14203
(631) 234-8585 .. **Bracken,** John P '63 (Bracken & M,LLP) -1 Suffolk Sq -Islandia 11749
(631) 751-8916 .. **Bracken,** Lawr J '58 -Bx69 -E Setauket 11733
(631) 234-8585 .. **Bracken & Margolin,LLP** -1 Suffolk Sq -Islandia 11749 **Fx:**234-8702
(212) 974-7474 .. **Bracken,** Michl '81 OfCnsl Cowan DA&S LLP -41 Mad Av -NY 10010
(212) 513-1075 .. **Bracken,** Thos J '95 (Stalker VB&F, LLP) -80 Broad -NY 10004
(718) 969-9392 .. **Bracker,** Lorraine K '83 -69-40 174th -Flushng 11365
(212) 889-2200 .. **Bracker,** Suzanne K '87 -280 Mad Av -NY 10016
(212) 264-3650 .. **Brackett,** Christopher J '09 %SSA Ofc Genl Cnsl -26 Fed Plz -NY 10278 **Fx:**264-6372
(718) 625-5884 .. **Brackley,** Albert J '61 -233 Bway -NY 10279 **Fx:**625-5737
(212) 334-3736 .. **Brackley,** Patrick J '92 -233 Bway -NY 10279 **Fx:**513-7068
(914) 939-0305 .. **Brackman,** Jody H '85 -76 Tamarack Rd -Rye Brook 10573 **Fx:**939-0305
(212) 669-7778 .. **Brackman,** Robt T '79 %Comptroller -1 Centre -NY 10007 **Fx:**669-2884
(212) 808-8100 .. **Brackney,** Megan L '01 %Kostelanetz & F,LLP -7 Wrld Trd Ctr -NY 10007
(518) 561-1980 .. **Bracy,** Evan I '94 (Niles P&B) -46-48 Cornelia Bx2729 -Plattsbrgh 12901
(212) 701-3000 .. **Bradburd,** Nathaniel L '09 %Cahill G&R LLP -80 Pine -NY 10005 **Fx:**269-5420
(212) 835-1536 .. **Bradbury,** John P '03 -1 Penn Plz -NY 10119
(518) 457-3160 .. **Braden,** Elaine Wallace '81 %Dept Tax & Fin -WA Harriman Campus Bldg 8 -Albany 12227 **Fx:**457-5174
(716) 566-5400 .. **Braden,** Richd A '96 (Goldberg S LLP) -665 Main -Buffalo 14203
(212) 216-2000 .. **Bradford,** Elizabeth '80 %Jacob K Javits Cnvntn Ctr -655 W 34th -NY 10001 **Fx:**216-2588
(212) 416-6060 .. **Bradford,** Emily B '07 Atty Gen -120 Bway -NY 10271 **Fx:**417-5274
(716) 687-3758 .. **Bradford,** Ian A '91 Fisher-Price Inc -636 Girard Av -E Aurora 14052 **Fx:**687-3660
(212) 292-9652 .. **Bradford,** Pamela G '88 Calvin Klein,Inc -205 W 39th -NY 10018
(212) 261-8000 .. **Bradford,** R James '83 (Mendes & M,LLP) -750 7th Av -NY 10019
(212) 599-0700 .. **Bradham,** John M '00 (Mazzeo S&B LLP) -708 3rd Av -NY 10017 **Fx:**599-8400
(914) 422-1200 .. **Bradley,** Adam T '90 Mayor -255 Main -White Plns 10601
(212) 558-4000 .. **Bradley,** Catherine Megan '09 %Sullivan & C LLP -125 Broad -NY 10004
(914) 949-9510 .. **Bradley,** Cheryl J '71 -16 Little John Pl -White Plns 10605 **Fx:**682-9232
(212) 619-4444 .. **Bradley,** Christopher T '85 (Marshall CW&B,PC) -116 John -NY 10038
(716) 882-5905 .. **Bradley,** David V L '87 %Osmose Inc -980 Ellicott -Buffalo 14209
(212) 641-6632 .. **Bradley,** Diane '87 Pearson Assessments & Info -1330 Av of Amer -NY 10019
(516) 572-2000 .. **Bradley,** Edw '07 %DA -99 Main -Hempstd 11550 **Fx:**572-2606
(516) 829-6900 .. **Bradley,** James A '74 OfCnsl Ackerman LCB&L,LLP -1010 Nrthrn Blvd -Gt Neck 11021
(516) 766-8800 .. **Bradley,** James J '98 -55 Maple Av -Rockvll Ctr 11570
(585) 226-5366 .. **Bradley,** James L '87 DEC -6274 E Avon-Lima Rd -Avon 14414 **Fx:**226-9485
(718) 237-6282 .. **Bradley,** Jocelyn D '89 %Family Ct Leg Affrs Ofc -283 Adams -Brklyn 11201
(212) 407-7700 .. **Bradley,** John E '80 (Vedder P,PC) -1633 Bway -NY 10019
(845) 794-4094 .. **Bradley,** John J '85 %Leg Aid -11 Bank -Monticello 12701 **Fx:**794-0119
(212) 488-1840 .. **Bradley,** John K '89 Frenkel & Co -350 Hudson -NY 10014
(212) 312-7415 .. **Bradley,** John P '82 %State Ins Fund -199 Church -NY 10007 **Fx:**385-9199

(585) 428-5210 .. **Bradley,** John T '97 %Pub Def -10 N Fitzhugh -Rchstr 14614 **Fx:**428-2234
(315) 423-7525 .. **Bradley,** Kelly Ann '98 Invstmnt Proprty Exchng Srvcs -201 E Jffrsn -Syracuse 13202 **Fx:**423-7549
(315) 425-2700 .. **Bradley,** Lisa G '81 OfCnsl Hiscock & B,LLP -One Park Pl -Syracuse 13202
(718) 520-3850 .. **Bradley,** Maria Fury '91 %Supreme Ct -88-11 Sutphin Blvd -Jamaica 11435
(212) 446-4800 .. **Bradley,** Melanie '01 OfCnsl Kirkland & E LLP -153 E 53rd -NY 10022
(212) 756-2000 .. **Bradley,** Michl P '06 %Schulte R&Z LLP -919 3rd Av -NY 10022
(718) 590-2000 .. **Bradley,** Michaela E '08 %DA -198 E 161st -Bronx 10451 **Fx:**590-6477
(609) 524-2044 .. **Bradley,** Patrick E '87 (Reed S LLP) -599 Lex Av -NY 10022 **Fx:**951-0824
(516) 742-1095 .. **Bradley,** Patrick J '90 -18 Elm -Gdn Cty 11530
(716) 856-4000 .. **Bradley,** Peter K '86 (Hodgson R LLP) -140 Pearl -Buffalo 14202
(315) 422-1311 .. **Bradley,** Roger W '70 (Melvin & M,PLLC) -217 S Salina -Syracuse 13202
(212) 788-0958 .. **Bradley,** Ruby E '84 %Law Dept -100 Church -NY 10007 **Fx:**788-0367
(212) 937-4281 .. **Bradley,** Stephanie F '06 Watkins B&C,LLP -228 Park Av S -NY 10003
(212) 872-1182 .. **Bradley,** Timothy P '90 Signal Equity Prtnrs -10 E 53rd -NY 10022
(585) 427-4022 .. **Bradley,** Valerie Curry '98 Cnsl Xerox -100 Clinton Av S -Rchstr 14644
(845) 485-3900 .. **Bradley,** Vincent G Jr. '96 %Dept of Law -235 Main -Poughkeepsie 12601 **Fx:**452-3303
(212) 389-5000 .. **Bradley,** Wm H '04 (Sutherland A&B LLP) -1114 Av of Amer -NY 10036
(212) 791-0285 .. **Bradley,** Wm J III '97 (Malaby & B,LLC) -150 Bway -NY 10038 **Fx:**791-0286
(585) 663-5432 .. **Bradshaw,** Alexander H '76 -5000 Mt Read Blvd -Rchstr 14612
(315) 422-2255 .. **Bradshaw,** Arlene '98 %Macht B&G -510 State Twr Bldg -Syracuse 13202
(917) 783-8125 .. **Bradshaw,** Diane '09 -307 E 89th -NY 10128 **Fx:**(212) 831-3486
(315) 568-0911 .. **Bradshaw,** Eugene B '70 -69 Fall -Seneca Fls 13148 **Fx:**568-0910
(718) 931-4400 .. **Bradshaw,** Kathleen R '92 -3114 E Tremont Av -Bronx 10461 **Fx:**931-5509
(212) 255-8833 .. **Bradshaw,** Melanie K '96 %M Liu & Assoc PLLC -107 Grand -NY 10013 **Fx:**255-4981
(212) 255-8833 .. **Bradshaw,** Melanie L '08 M Liu & Assoc PLLC -107 Grand -NY 10013 **Fx:**255-4981
(914) 813-6880 .. **Bradshaw-Soto,** Jill C '93 %Leg Srvcs -100 E 1st -Mt Vernon 10550 **Fx:**813-6890
(315) 422-6900 .. **Bradt,** Wm H '83 %1st Amer Title -351 S Warren -Syracuse 13202 **Fx:**422-7400
(212) 493-8356 .. **Brady,** Alison M '05 Brown Brothers Harriman & Co -140 Bway -NY 10005
(845) 291-2303 .. **Brady,** Amanda B '01 %Hon R Onofry -30 Park Pl -Goshen 10924
(518) 886-4000 .. **Brady,** Amy Berke '93 AYCO -321 Bway Bx860 -Saratoga Spgs 12866
(914) 332-4880 .. **Brady,** Arthur R '82 -150 Wht Plns Rd -Tarrytwn 10591 **Fx:**631-5827
(845) 294-6181 .. **Brady,** Bernard '70 -75 Main Bx639 -Goshen 10924 **Fx:**294-9185
(516) 227-2260 .. **Brady,** Bruce M '76 (Callan KB&B LLP) -333 Earle Ovngton Blvd -Uniondale 11553
(212) 248-8800 .. **Brady,** Bruce M '76 (Callan KB&B LLP) -1 Whitehall -NY 10004
(212) 706-0248 .. **Brady,** Christopher '76 (Hollyer B LLP) -60 E 42nd -NY 10165 **Fx:**(646) 652-5336
(315) 422-7111 .. **Brady,** Colleen M '02 %Blitman & K LLP -443 N Franklin -Syracuse 13204
(212) 431-1354 .. **Brady,** Colleen Quinn '98 -99 Hudson -NY 10013
(845) 703-3101 .. **Brady,** Damian J '01 %Bonacic KCM&B,LLP -90 Crystal Run Rd -Middletwn 10941
(917) 777-4200 .. **Brady,** Deirdre R '09 %Bingham M LLP -1 Bttry Pk Plz -NY 10004
(718) 423-6800 .. **Brady,** Dennis J '93 (MacKay W&B LLP) -40-26 235th -Douglastn 11363
(516) 745-1199 .. **Brady,** Donna M '82 -900 Merchants Cncrs -Westbury 11590 **Fx:**227-6594
(212) 326-2000 .. **Brady,** Emma K A '09 Cnsl O'Melveny & M LLP -7 Times Sq -NY 10036
(914) 690-0800 .. **Brady,** Enoch C '89 E Brady & Assoc -130 N Main -Pt Chester 10573 **Fx:**937-1386
(716) 945-2000 .. **Brady,** Erin M '02 %Brady & S -41 Main -Salamanca 14779
(518) 486-4505 .. **Brady,** Francis A III '87 %Dept of Law -The Cptl -Albany 12224
(914) 428-2100 .. **Brady,** Gerard P '86 (Welby B&G,LLP) -11 Martine Av -White Plns 10606
(315) 431-6600 .. **Brady,** James C '80 %Brady & C -443 Electronics Pkwy -Liverpool 13088 **Fx:**431-6605
(212) 533-6300 .. **Brady,** James J '68 %NYSUT -52 Bway -NY 10004 **Fx:**995-2347
(516) 674-8686 .. **Brady,** James J '87 -333 Glen Head Rd -Old Brookvll 11545 **Fx:**674-8118
(212) 801-6961 .. **Brady,** Jennifer E '98 %Greenberg T,LLP -200 Park Av -NY 10166
(212) 909-6000 .. **Brady,** John B Jr. '78 OfCnsl Debevoise & P LLP -919 3rd Av -NY 10022
(718) 835-7800 .. **Brady,** Jos Edw '66 (JE Brady,PC) -101-02 159th Av -Howard Bch 11414 **Fx:**843-0923
(631) 852-2332 .. **Brady,** Jos H '74 %Family Ct -877 E Main -Rvrhead 11901
(845) 454-2540 .. **Brady,** Kelly Romano '04 (Brooke & B,LLP) -31 Cllgvw Av -Poughkeepsie 12603 **Fx:**454-2542
(212) 351-4500 .. **Brady,** Kevin R '01 %Epstein B&G,PC -250 Park Av -NY 10177
(212) 949-5800 .. **Brady Klein & Weissman,LLP** -501 5th Av -NY 10017 **Fx:**949-5085
(212) 949-5800 .. **Brady,** Margaret '88 (Brady K&W,LLP) -501 5th Av -NY 10017
(212) 604-8332 .. **Brady,** Marie E '95 -511 Av of the Americas -NY 10011
(716) 851-7190 .. **Brady,** Maureen A '85 %DEC -270 Mich Av -Buffalo 14203 **Fx:**851-7211
(914) 478-4293 .. **Brady McGuire & Steinberg,PC** -603 Warburton Av -Hastings-On-Hud 10706 **Fx:**478-4142
(716) 856-9443 .. **Brady,** Michl A '76 (Hagerty & B) -69 Delaware Av -Buffalo 14202
(212) 268-5136 .. **Brady,** Michl J '82 (Harwood L) -350 5th Av -NY 10118
(631) 369-3617 .. **Brady,** Michl S '94 Asset Preservation Inc -125 Baylis Rd -Melvll 11747 **Fx:**614-7954
(845) 486-2280 .. **Brady,** Michl W '04 %Pub Def -22 Market -Poughkeepsie 12601 **Fx:**486-2266
(516) 829-8265 .. **Brady,** Nancy J '01 (Brady & M,LLP) -4523 Arcadia Ln -Gt Neck 11020 **Fx:**482-2688
(212) 973-3431 .. **Brady,** Orla M '08 %Kreindler & K -750 3rd Av -NY 10017
(212) 335-9000 .. **Brady,** Penelope J '02 %DA -1 Hogan Pl -NY 10013
(716) 626-9999 .. **Brady,** Peter F '80 (Brady & S LLP) -4367 Harlem Rd -Buffalo 14226
(212) 808-7800 .. **Brady,** Richd W '56 (Kelley D&W LLP) -101 Park Av -NY 10178
(516) 883-0800 .. **Brady,** Robt A '65 -31 S Bayles Av -Pt Wash 11050
(973) 596-4617 .. **Brady,** Robt C '02 (Gibbons PC) -1 Penn Plz -NY 10119 **Fx:**639-8380
(212) 582-0380 .. **Brady,** Ross '96 Interstate Environmental Comm -311 W 43rd -NY 10036
(914) 995-3740 .. **Brady,** Shannon S '96 %Cnty Atty -148 Martine Av -White Plns 10601 **Fx:**995-5858
(716) 858-5155 .. **Brady,** Stephen R '83 -40 Fountain Plz -Buffalo 14202
(716) 945-2000 .. **Brady & Swenson** -41 Main -Salamanca 14779 **Fx:**945-3566
(212) 310-8000 .. **Brady,** Teresa M '07 %Weil G&M LLP -767 5th Av -NY 10153
(212) 815-1818 .. **Brady,** Theresa '86 %DC 37 MELS -125 Barclay -NY 10007 **Fx:**815-1343
(716) 945-2000 .. **Brady,** Thos C '73 (Brady & S) -41 Main -Salamanca 14779
(212) 474-1000 .. **Brady,** Wm B '08 %Cravath S&M LLP -825 8th Av -NY 10019
(212) 661-5000 .. **Brady,** Wm J III '77 %Frankel & A -230 Park Av -NY 10169
(212) 697-3122 .. **Brady,** Wm P '81 (Martin C&B LLP) -220 E 42nd -NY 10017
(718) 752-5052 .. **Brady-Phillips,** Vivian L '97 NYC Leadership Academy -3030 Thompson Av -LIC 11101
(212) 448-1100 .. **Braegelmann,** Tom H '08 %McLaughlin & S,LLP -260 Mad Av -NY 10016
(212) 558-4000 .. **Braff,** David H '85 (Sullivan & C LLP) -125 Broad -NY 10004
(212) 599-2085 .. **Braff Harris & Sukoneck** -305 Bway -NY 10007 **Fx:**822-1479
(212) 836-8000 .. **Braff,** Michl '83 (Kaye S LLP) -425 Park Av -NY 10022
(212) 750-7800 .. **Brafman,** Benjamin '75 (Brafman & Assoc) -767 3rd Av -NY 10017 **Fx:**750-3906
(212) 308-5858 .. **Bragar,** Raymond A '73 (Bragar WE&S,PC) -885 3rd Av -NY 10022
(212) 308-5858 .. **Bragar Wexler Eagel & Squire, PC** -885 3rd Av -NY 10022 **Fx:**486-0462
(212) 788-9131 .. **Bragg,** Alvin L '00 City Cncl -250 Bway -NY 10007
(212) 233-2141 .. **Bragg,** Brian E '92 -11 Hanover Sq -NY 10005
(585) 473-3100 .. **Braggins,** Todd R '91 (Ernstrom & D,LLP) -180 Canal Vw Blvd -Rchstr 14623
(212) 982-0131 .. **Bragin,** Abraham M '84 -504 Grand -NY 10002
(212) 751-7326 .. **Bragin Stein & Pacht,PC** -320 E 58th -NY 10022 **Fx:**751-7326
(212) 643-7000 .. **Braginsky,** Philip '92 (Sills C&G PC) -One Rckfllr Plz -NY 10020
(631) 324-3737 .. **Bragman,** Jeffrey L '78 JL Bragman,PC -15 Railroad Av -E Hampton 11937 **Fx:**324-7888
(631) 423-7755 .. **Bragoli,** Christopher C '98 (Bragoli & Assoc,PC) -999 Walt Whitman Rd -Melvll 11747 **Fx:**423-5299
(646) 723-1286 .. **Braha,** Sokol '03 -1357 Bway -NY 10018
(212) 446-5802 .. **Brahms,** Marisa Ilana '05 Dvlpmnt Corp Israel -575 Lex Av -NY 10022 **Fx:**644-7102
(212) 819-8200 .. **Brahmst,** Oliver C '97 (White & C LLP) -1155 Av of Amer -NY 10036
(212) 513-3200 .. **Braid,** Fredk D '72 (Holland & K LLP) -31 W 52nd -NY 10019
(914) 995-3460 .. **Brailey,** Susan Heine '80 %DA -111 Martin Luther King Blvd -White Plns 10601 **Fx:**995-3363
(212) 813-8800 .. **Braiman,** Jason O '10 %Goodwin P LLP -620 8th Av -NY 10018
(315) 568-9456 .. **Brainard,** Calvin A '71 -51 State -Seneca Fls 13148 **Fx:**568-8221
(607) 273-4200 .. **Brainard,** Hayden R '99 (Miller M,LLP) -202 E State -Ithaca 14850
(212) 391-5200 .. **Brainin,** David N '58 OfCnsl Locker G&B,PC -420 5th Av -NY 10018
(718) 448-6040 .. **Braisted,** David W '89 (Braisted & B) -686 Forest Av -Staten Isl 10310 **Fx:**720-6033
(716) 634-8882 .. **Braisted,** Michl D '92 -40 N Forest Rd -Williamsvll 14221
(212) 837-6000 .. **Braiterman,** Andrew H '81 (Hughes H&R LLP) -1 Bttry Pk Plz -NY 10004
(585) 232-6500 .. **Braithwaite,** Cody R '05 %Harter S&E LLP -1600 Bausch & Lomb Pl -Rchstr 14604
(212) 786-8272 .. **Braithwaite,** Martha '00 Cnsl EMI Music NA -150 5th Av -NY 10011
(631) 543-2828 .. **Braitman,** Elinor '95 -7 Holly Dr -Smithtwn 11787 **Fx:**543-7018
(212) 508-6100 .. **Brake,** Patrick E Jr. '05 %Bracewell & G,LLP -1251 Av of Amer -NY 10020
(212) 837-6885 .. **Braker,** Kevin '07 %Hughes H&R LLP -1 Bttry Pk Plz -NY 10004
(212) 210-2893 .. **Bralow,** David S '07 (Thomas L&B PL) -220 E 42nd -NY 10017 **Fx:**210-2883
(212) 379-4976 .. **Bralow,** Paula Block '91 %SWN Comm,Inc -224 W 30th -NY 10001
(212) 813-8800 .. **Bralower,** Jennifer K '02 (Goodwin P LLP) -620 8th Av -NY 10018
(212) 246-7417 .. **Bralower,** John I '81 Ironstone Grp -200 Cntrl Pk S -NY 10019
(518) 433-8800 .. **Braman,** James E '87 %Lemery G LLC -50 Beaver -Albany 12207
(212) 336-2000 .. **Braman,** Leonard M '06 %Patterson BW&T LLP -1133 Av of Amer -NY 10036
(718) 625-5525 .. **Bramante,** Anthony M '83 -32 Court -Brklyn 11201 **Fx:**625-5522
(212) 547-1561 .. **Bramante,** Mark S '89 Mizuho Capital -1440 Bway -NY 10018
(212) 759-3300 .. **Bramhall,** Park S '06 %Dornbush SS&V,LLP -747 3rd Av -NY 10017
(212) 269-0927 .. **Bramham,** Chas '70 (D'Amato & L,LLP) -2 World Fncl Ctr -NY 10281
(585) 423-1775 .. **Bramlet,** Robt E '89 %Xerox -100 Clinton Av S -Rchstr 14644
(518) 434-2622 .. **Bramley,** Bruce C '76 (Pozefsky B&M) -90 State -Albany 12207
(212) 692-1044 .. **Bramnik,** Robt P '74 (Duane M LLP) -1540 Bway -NY 10036 **Fx:**(312) 277-2326
(914) 946-3700 .. **Bramson,** Howell '78 (McCarthy F LLP) -11 Martine Av -White Plns 10606
(212) 576-7000 .. **Bramson,** Laura M '85 %NY Life Ins -51 Mad Av -NY 10010 **Fx:**447-0569
(212) 563-1710 .. **Bramson,** Philip A '92 %Schindel FLG&R LLP -14 Penn Plz -NY 10122
(212) 530-5000 .. **Bramwell,** Austin W '04 %Milbank TH&M LLP -1 Chase Manh Plz -NY 10005

(718) 442-3105 .. **Bramwell,** George Y '62 -45 Park Ln -Staten Isl 10301 **Fx:**720-4595
(212) 637-2804 .. **Branagan,** Susan C '97 %US Atty -86 Chmbrs -NY 10007
(718) 492-7600 .. **Branca,** Ross M '75 -517 54th -Brklyn 11220 **Fx:**492-0945
(914) 995-4172 .. **Branca-Santos,** Paula '00 DA -111 Martin Luther King Blvd -White Plns 10601 **Fx:**995-3363
(518) 689-1448 .. **Brancatella,** Caroline B '08 %Greenberg T,LLP -54 State -Albany 12207
(212) 813-8800 .. **Brancati,** Christopher W '08 %Goodwin P LLP -620 8th Av -NY 10018
(914) 948-1200 .. **Brancato,** Deborah R '08 %Cerussi & S,PC -1 N Lex Av -White Plns 10601
(212) 335-9000 .. **Brancato,** John J '79 %DA -1 Hogan Pl -NY 10013
(516) 222-2800 .. **Brancato,** Jos A Jr. '79 (Brancato B&B) -585 Stewart Av -Gdn Cty 11530
(718) 238-6500 .. **Brancato,** Laura M '04 %Connors & S,PC -7408 5th Av -Brklyn 11209
(516) 222-2800 .. **Brancato,** Louis J '80 (Brancato B&B) -585 Stewart Av -Gdn Cty 11530
(516) 869-1111 .. **Brancato,** Mark F '95 MF Brancato,PC -47 Plandome Rd -Manhsst 11030 **Fx:**869-0697
(212) 455-2000 .. **Branch,** Beatrice C '07 %Simpson T&B LLP -425 Lex Av -NY 10017
(718) 246-6525 .. **Branch,** Clifton R Jr. '01 %NYC Housing Ct -350 Lvngstn -Brklyn 11217
(585) 546-8426 .. **Branch Dewart & Wise** -45 Exchange Blvd -Rchstr 14614 **Fx:**546-5798
(718) 522-3333 .. **Branch,** Pamela '96 %Children's Law Ctr -44 Court -Brklyn 11201 **Fx:**522-7376
(212) 679-7007 .. **Branch,** Tanya M '95 (Brody B&B LLP) -205 Lex Av -NY 10016
(516) 228-1300 .. **Branciforte,** Ralph '02 %Sahn WC&B,PLLC -333 Earle Ovngton Blvd -Uniondale 11553
(212) 808-0448 .. **Brand Brand Nomberg & Rosenbaum,LLP** -286 Mad Av -NY 10017 **Fx:**808-8009
(914) 946-5650 .. **Brand Brand Nomberg & Rosenbaum,LLP** -50 Main -White Plns 10606
(212) 867-4466 .. **Brand,** David R '06 %Belkin BW&G,LLP -270 Mad Av -NY 10016
(516) 746-3500 .. **Brand,** David W '76 (Brand G&B,PC) -600 Old Cntry Rd -Gdn Cty 11530
(914) 251-0190 .. **Brand,** Deborah Proner '92 -One Stoneleigh Manor Ln -Purchase 10577
(516) 746-3500 .. **Brand Glick & Brand, PC** -600 Old Cntry Rd -Gdn Cty 11530 **Fx:**294-9744
(716) 479-1885 .. **Brand,** Harold J Jr. '67 -88 Oakview Dr -Williamsvll 14221
(212) 664-4178 .. **Brand,** Irving '68 %NBC -30 Rckfllr Plz -NY 10112
(212) 643-7000 .. **Brand,** Jessica R '06 %Sills C&G PC -One Rckfllr Plz -NY 10020
(516) 627-8494 .. **Brand,** Karen G '76 K Brand,PC -36 Maple Pl -Manhsst 11030 **Fx:**627-6533
(716) 847-8400 .. **Brand,** Mark E '91 (Phillips L LLP) -3400 HSBC Ctr -Buffalo 14203
(212) 661-9100 .. **Brand,** Mitchell M '82 (Otterbourg SH&R,PC) -230 Park Av -NY 10169
(212) 446-4800 .. **Brand,** Richd M '08 %Kirkland & E LLP -153 E 53rd -NY 10022
(212) 989-6272 .. **Brand,** Richd S '77 -158 W 13th -NY 10011 **Fx:**633-1276
(212) 475-6096 .. **Brand,** Susan E '84 -515 E 14th -NY 10009
(718) 680-5778 .. **Branda,** Rose Ann '85 (Caruso C&B, PC) -7302 13th Av -Brklyn 11228
(212) 223-6700 .. **Brandeis,** Clifford A '80 (Zukerman GB&C,LLP) -875 3rd Av -NY 10022
(212) 279-2000 .. **Brandel,** Justin D '09 %D Resnick & Assoc,PC -450 7th Av -NY 10123
(212) 460-4333 .. **Brandenburg,** Brent L '71 Con Ed -4 Irving Pl -NY 10003 **Fx:**260-8627
(212) 237-1000 .. **Brandenburg,** Neal A '07 %Windels ML&M,LLP -156 W 56th -NY 10019
(845) 639-0607 .. **Brandenburg,** Wendy K '87 -Bx68 -New Cty 10956 **Fx:**639-6638
(800) 416-5454 .. **Brandenstein,** Richd J '76 (Fusco B&R) -9207 Flatlands Av -Brklyn 11236
(800) 416-5454 .. **Brandenstein,** Richd J '76 (Fusco B&R) -11 Penn Plz -NY 10001
(800) 416-5454 .. **Brandenstein,** Richd J '76 (Fusco B&R) -180 Froehlich Farm Blvd -Woodbury 11797
(800) 416-5454 .. **Brandenstein,** Richd J '76 (Fusco B&R) -2116 Wllmsbrdg Rd -Bronx 10461
(800) 416-5454 .. **Brandenstein,** Richd J '76 (Fusco B&R) -3253 Route 112 -Medfrd 11763
(516) 568-3014 .. **Brander,** Norman P '83 -221 Mineola Blvd -Mineola 11501
(212) 558-4000 .. **Brander,** Saul '03 %Sullivan & C LLP -125 Broad -NY 10004
(212) 504-6000 .. **Brandes,** Ari J '10 %Cadwalader W&T LLP -1 World Fncl Ctr -NY 10281
(212) 406-0150 .. **Brandes,** Barbara J '80 -225 Bway -NY 10007 **Fx:**566-2488
(212) 373-1919 .. **Brandes,** David M '79 %Krusch & M -10 Rckfllr Plz -NY 10020
(212) 310-8000 .. **Brandes,** Katherine M '09 %Weil G&M LLP -767 5th Av -NY 10153
(212) 816-6710 .. **Brandes,** Kenneth T '96 Citigroup -388 Greenwich -NY 10013
(212) 335-4500 .. **Brandes,** Lawr I '75 (DLA Piper LLP) -1251 Av of Amer -NY 10020
(646) 386-5206 .. **Brandes,** Marcelle Z '89 Family Ct -60 Lafayette -NY 10013
(212) 506-2500 .. **Brandes,** Philip O '95 (Mayer B LLP) -1675 Bway -NY 10019
(212) 613-5000 .. **Brandfield,** Julie '92 %Leg Assist Grp -450 W 33rd -NY 10001 **Fx:**750-0820
(212) 504-6000 .. **Brandfon,** Nicholas E '10 %Cadwalader W&T LLP -1 World Fncl Ctr -NY 10281
(212) 301-3441 .. **Brandi,** Dianne D '95 %Fox News -1211 Av of Amer -NY 10036 **Fx:**391-4818
(718) 746-3440 .. **Brandimarte,** Luigi '02 %Sacco & F,LLP -141-07 20th Av -Whitestone 11357
(212) 558-5500 .. **Brandis,** Ambre J '06 Weitz & L,PC -700 Bway -NY 10003
(716) 634-1179 .. **Brandl,** James D '91 -34 Patton Pl -Williamsvll 14221
(718) 590-2000 .. **Brandler,** Elizabeth A '03 %DA -198 E 161st -Bronx 10451 **Fx:**590-6477
(212) 725-2285 .. **Brandler,** Simon G '08 %NYS Democratic Cmte -461 Park Av S -NY 10016
(212) 309-1000 .. **Brandley,** David F Jr. '81 (Hunton & W) -200 Park Av -NY 10166
(631) 845-2600 .. **Brandman,** Brian S '88 (Morenus CG&B) -58 S Srvc Rd -Melvll 11747
(212) 806-5400 .. **Brandman,** Etta '80 SpclCnsl Stroock &S&L LLP -180 Maiden Ln -NY 10038
(212) 855-0747 .. **Brandman,** Lawr S '86 %Goldman Sachs -1 NY Plz -NY 10004
(212) 626-4100 .. **Brandman,** Scott L '93 (Baker & M LLP) -1114 Av of Amer -NY 10036
(516) 933-4160 .. **Brandoff,** Mark A '76 M Brandoff,PC -212 Halsey Av Bx97 -Jericho 11753 **Fx:**933-4169
(212) 267-5600 .. **Brandofino,** Elaine M '83 -Bx286744 -NY 10128
(212) 759-4888 .. **Brandofino,** Keith M '02 (Phillips L LLP) -437 Mad Av -NY 10022
(212) 506-5000 .. **Brandon,** Alexandra L '09 %Orrick H&S LLP -51 W 52nd -NY 10019
(845) 225-7040 .. **Brandon,** Alice '83 -110 Old Route 6 -Carmel 10512
(212) 455-2000 .. **Brandon,** D Rhett '80 (Simpson T&B LLP) -425 Lex Av -NY 10017
(718) 981-0219 .. **Brandon,** Joni '95 Leg Aid -60 Bay -Staten Isl 10301 **Fx:**981-6623
(718) 590-2000 .. **Brandon,** M Elizabeth '04 %DA -198 E 161st -Bronx 10451 **Fx:**590-6477
(212) 465-6320 .. **Brandon,** Robt A '85 %Madison Sq Grdn,LP -2 Penn Plz -NY 10121 **Fx:**465-6011
(212) 319-2787 .. **Brandow,** Benjamin J '08 VLA -1 E 53rd -NY 10022 **Fx:**752-6575
(212) 450-4000 .. **Brandow,** John M '84 (Davis P&W LLP) -450 Lex Av -NY 10017
(212) 918-3000 .. **Brandriss,** Chava '09 %Hogan L LLP -875 3rd Av -NY 10022
(212) 472-8340 .. **Brandrup,** Douglas W '69 (Griggs B&B) -305 Mad Av -NY 10165
(212) 221-5700 .. **Brandstatter,** Dov B '04 %Goldberg WFG LLP -1501 Bway -NY 10036
(212) 878-8000 .. **Brandstetter,** Kelley R '10 %Clifford C LLP -31 W 52nd -NY 10019
(716) 433-5941 .. **Brandt,** Albert R Jr. '61 (Andrews PBS&R) -929 Lincoln Av -Lockprt 14094
(212) 563-2200 .. **Brandt,** Hubert J '53 (Brandt S&L LLP) -386 Park Av S -NY 10016
(212) 682-2900 .. **Brandt,** Ian J '04 %Braverman & Assoc,PC -331 Mad Av -NY 10017 **Fx:**682-7718
(212) 906-1200 .. **Brandt,** James E '83 (Latham & W) -885 3rd Av -NY 10022
(212) 751-3001 .. **Brandt,** Jane Politz '05 (Thompson & K LLP) -919 3rd Av -NY 10022
(212) 554-2600 .. **Brandt,** Jeffrey L '00 Daylight Forensic -1 Rckfllr Plz -NY 10020
(315) 671-1107 .. **Brandt,** John W '73 %Supreme Ct -401 Mntgmry -Syracuse 13202 **Fx:**671-1181
(315) 349-3350 .. **Brandt,** Karen M '02 Family Ct -39 Churchill Rd -Oswego 13126 **Fx:**349-3457
(212) 344-5680 .. **Brandt,** Katherine D '04 (Thompson H LLP) -335 Mad Av -NY 10017
(212) 563-2200 .. **Brandt,** Kathryn Weg '83 %Brandt S&L LLP -386 Park Av S -NY 10016
(631) 853-5212 .. **Brandt,** Kirk R '84 %Leg Aid -400 Carleton Av Bx9082 -Central Islip 11722 **Fx:**853-7798
(212) 790-2789 .. **Brandt,** Laura McCabe '97 %Apple Core Hotels,Inc -15 W 39th -NY 10018 **Fx:**790-2791
(212) 728-8000 .. **Brandt,** Michl E '06 %Willkie F&G LLP -787 7th Av -NY 10019
(212) 530-1800 .. **Brandt,** Shari A '97 %Richards K&O LLP -1 World Fncl Ctr -NY 10281
(212) 563-2200 .. **Brandt Steinberg & Lewis LLP** -386 Park Av S -NY 10016 **Fx:**629-4272
(716) 433-5941 .. **Brandt,** Thos H '82 %Andrews PBS&R -929 Lincoln Av -Lockprt 14094
(917) 663-3572 .. **Brandt,** Wm A Jr. '82 %Philip Morris Mgt Corp -120 Park Av -NY 10017 **Fx:**663-5707
(585) 263-1000 .. **Brandt,** Wm S '72 SrCnsl Nixon P LLP -1100 Clinton Sq -Rchstr 14604
(212) 613-5000 .. **Brandt-Young,** Christina L '03 %Leg Assist Grp -450 W 33rd -NY 10001 **Fx:**750-0820
(212) 655-0880 .. **Brandveen,** Sean A '09 %NBPA -310 Lennox Av -NY 10027 **Fx:**655-0881
(718) 849-1235 .. **Brandwein,** Edw C '94 -85-37 124th -Kew Gdns 11415
(516) 747-1990 .. **Brandwein,** Howard R '94 %Cascone & K,LLP -1399 Franklin Av -Gdn Cty 11530
(212) 362-1060 .. **Brandys,** Mark W '93 -225 Bway -NY 10007
(212) 558-5500 .. **Braniff,** Edw III '96 %Weitz & L,PC -700 Bway -NY 10003
(518) 270-3724 .. **Branigan,** Loretta E '86 Surrogates Ct -80 2nd -Troy 12180
(718) 286-6000 .. **Branigan,** Wm H '02 %DA -125-01 Qns Blvd -Kew Gdns 11415
(518) 785-6904 .. **Brankman,** Anthony C '68 -8 Conway Cir -Loudonvll 12211
(212) 614-6471 .. **Brannelly,** Kevi Patricia '00 Ctr Cnstnl Rights -666 Bway -NY 10012 **Fx:**614-6499
(212) 909-6000 .. **Brannen,** Stephanie S '08 %Debevoise & P LLP -919 3rd Av -NY 10022
(516) 248-1200 .. **Brannigan,** Eugene J '53 OfCnsl Mulholland M&R -374 Hillside Av -Williston Pk 11596
(212) 262-2390 .. **Brannigan,** Patrick S '03 %Connell F LLP -888 7th Av -NY 10106
(212) 863-5019 .. **Brannon,** Ralph '97 HPD -100 Gold -NY 10038
(212) 269-1400 .. **Branower,** Danl M '02 %Gusrae KB&N PLLC -120 Wall -NY 10005
(212) 448-0702 .. **Brant,** Gerald '08 Prospect Admin LLC -11 E 40th -NY 10016
(212) 446-4800 .. **Brant,** W Josh '06 %Kirkland & E LLP -153 E 53rd -NY 10022
(212) 949-9022 .. **Branthover,** Ned W '80 (Abelman F&S) -666 3rd Av -NY 10017
(914) 693-3026 .. **Brantl,** Robt F '80 -52 Mulligan Ln -Irvngtn 10533 **Fx:**693-1807
(718) 298-0057 .. **Brantley,** Ayesha Keri '05 %Family Ct -151-20 Jamaica Av -Jamaica 11432
(585) 317-1127 .. **Brantley,** Hugh F '75 -10 Arvine Park -Rchstr 14611
(917) 921-9601 .. **Brantley,** Mark S '00 -2289 5th Av -NY 10037 **Fx:**(212) 748-0035
(212) 961-4408 .. **Brantley,** Reginald '83 %OCFS -163 W 125th -NY 10027
(516) 681-3456 .. **Brantman,** Lisa M '93 -333 Jericho Tpk -Jericho 11753
(212) 509-9400 .. **Brantz,** Jonathan S '09 %Cozen O -45 Bway Atrium -NY 10006
(212) 267-2500 .. **Brasch,** Justin C '93 -30 Vesey -NY 10007 **Fx:**233-3130
(212) 446-4800 .. **Brashares,** Wm C '01 (Kirkland & E LLP) -153 E 53rd -NY 10022
(212) 768-6700 .. **Brasher,** Douglas B '06 %Sonnenschein N&R LLP -1221 Av of Amer -NY 10020
(212) 421-4100 .. **Brasile,** Jos L '97 (Pryor C LLP) -7 Times Sq -NY 10036
(585) 719-9848 .. **Brasley,** John A '87 -132 Clay Av -Rchstr 14613
(631) 422-2900 .. **Braslow,** John '55 -816 Deer Prk Av -N Babylon 11703 **Fx:**422-0987
(315) 448-3334 .. **Brass,** Tyler G '04 Smith Barney -1500 AXA Twr I -Syracuse 13202
(212) 530-5000 .. **Brassel,** Thallen J '10 %Milbank TH&M LLP -1 Chase Manh Plz -NY 10005
(914) 995-7710 .. **Brathwaite,** Delores Scott '03 Cnty Human Rights Comm -112 E Post Rd -White Plns 10601 **Fx:**995-7720
(718) 655-6750 .. **Brathwaite,** Harold D '60 -939 E 229th -Bronx 10466

(212) 286-9510 .. **Brathwaite,** Marcia W '93 -240 Mad Av -NY 10016 **Fx:**286-9076
(718) 232-2111 .. **Bratkovsky,** Mark '99 (Almonte & B,PLLC) -2652 Coney Isl Av -Brklyn 11223
(212) 874-1864 .. **Bratsafolis,** Michelle S '83 -440 W End Av -NY 10024
(212) 841-1000 .. **Bratt,** Andrew M '06 %Covington & B LLP -620 8th Av -NY 10018
(347) 296-1518 .. **Bratt,** Ronald D '93 %Supreme Ct -360 Adams -Brklyn 11201
(518) 462-5601 .. **Bratten,** Kurt E '08 %O'Connell & A -54 State -Albany 12207
(516) 671-3210 .. **Bratter,** Benjamin P '03 -450 7th Av -NY 10123 **Fx:**671-6786
(212) 340-0400 .. **Bratton,** Andral N '78 %Appllt Div 1st Dept -27 Mad Av -NY 10010 **Fx:**889-4412
(914) 323-7000 .. **Braude,** Danl M '07 %Wilson EME&D LLP -3 Gannett Dr -White Plns 10604
(718) 871-4311 .. **Braude,** Jacob '86 -3904 15th Av -Brklyn 11218
(518) 457-3177 .. **Braude,** Jeffrey M '93 %Dept Civil Srvc -Harriman Campus Bldg 1 -Albany 12239 **Fx:**457-6654
(914) 457-2300 .. **Brauer,** Marlena J '87 %Kanterman & S,LLP -50 Main -White Plns 10606
(212) 556-7127 .. **Brauer,** Rhonda L '85 %The NY Times Co -620 8th Av -NY 10018 **Fx:**556-4634
(212) 813-8800 .. **Braum,** Edw J '00 (Goodwin P LLP) -620 8th Av -NY 10018
(914) 949-2700 .. **Braumuller,** Robt '99 (Bleakley P&S,LLP) -1 N Lex Av -White Plns 10601
(914) 681-7175 .. **Braun,** Barbara K '09 Bartels & F LLP -925 Wstchstr Av -White Plns 10604
(631) 864-9400 .. **Braun,** Bernard '54 -357 Vets Mem'l Hwy -Commack 11725 **Fx:**864-3599
(716) 856-0600 .. **Braun,** Beverley S '08 %Jaeckle F&M,LLP -12 Fountain Plz -Buffalo 14202
(212) 836-8000 .. **Braun,** Christine A '03 %Kaye S LLP -425 Park Av -NY 10022
(914) 962-5655 .. **Braun,** Donald '76 -2025 Crompond Rd -Yorktwn Hts 10598 **Fx:**962-6250
(212) 715-9100 .. **Braun,** Jeffrey L '73 (Kramer LN&F,LLP) -1177 Av of Amer -NY 10036
(212) 374-0346 .. **Braun,** Jill H '04 %NY Dept of Ed-Legal Srvcs -52 Chmbrs -NY 10007
(212) 502-1870 .. **Braun,** Judith F '03 Polaris Mgmt Prtnrs -38 E 32nd -NY 10016
(718) 590-2000 .. **Braun,** Justin J '08 %DA -198 E 161st -Bronx 10451 **Fx:**590-6477
(212) 373-3000 .. **Braun,** Karen M '88 %Paul WRW&G LLP -1285 Av of Amer -NY 10019
(516) 873-2000 .. **Braun,** Keith S '82 OfCnsl Moritt HH&H LLP -400 Grdn City Plz -Gdn Cty 11530
(212) 953-2436 .. **Braun,** Laurie E '84 -60 E 42nd -NY 10165
(212) 310-8368 .. **Braun,** Lynda M '92 Cnsl Weil G&M LLP -767 5th Av -NY 10153
(212) 468-8000 .. **Braun,** Michl O '74 (Morrison & F LLP) -1290 Av of Amer -NY 10104
(917) 777-4200 .. **Braun,** Michl P '86 (Bingham M LLP) -1 Bttry Pk Plz -NY 10004
(716) 849-1333 .. **Braun,** Michele A '92 (Lipsitz GSC LLP) -42 Delaware Av -Buffalo 14202
(718) 834-6020 .. **Braun,** Pauline E '89 -26 Court -Brklyn 11242
(716) 847-8400 .. **Braun,** Peter D '75 (Phillips L LLP) -3400 HSBC Ctr -Buffalo 14203
(845) 592-2412 .. **Braun,** Randy L '86 -33 Innsbruck Blvd -Hopewell Junct 12533 **Fx:**592-2413
(631) 853-4049 .. **Braun,** Robt A '77 %Cnty Atty -Dennison Bldg Bx6100 -Hauppauge 11788 **Fx:**853-5169
(212) 294-6700 .. **Braun,** Ruth Anne '02 %Winston & S -200 Park Av -NY 10166
(212) 750-0040 .. **Braun,** Seymour '82 Braun & G -110 E 59th -NY 10022 **Fx:**826-9315
(212) 770-1789 .. **Braun,** Suzanne '95 %AIG -80 Pine -NY 10005 **Fx:**344-2357
(212) 296-6180 .. **Braun,** Victoria '07 Morgan Stanley -522 5th Av -NY 10036
(212) 588-0800 .. **Braunel,** Bryan J '07 %Frommer L&H LLP -745 5th Av -NY 10151
(212) 237-1000 .. **Brauner,** David A '67 Cnsl Windels ML&M,LLP -156 W 56th -NY 10019
(212) 583-9600 .. **Brauner,** Lisa Michelle '95 OfCnsl Littler M,PC -900 3rd Av -NY 10022
(845) 634-7701 .. **Braunfotel,** Keith I '95 (Braunfotel & F LLC) -49 Maple Av -New Cty 10956 **Fx:**634-7710
(716) 847-8400 .. **Braun-Kolbe,** Karla '07 %Phillips L LLP -3400 HSBC Ctr -Buffalo 14203
(212) 370-6703 .. **Braunsberg,** Linda C '90 -60 E 42nd -NY 10165
(212) 239-3300 .. **Braunschweig,** Robt S '57 -350 5th Av -NY 10118
(212) 801-3760 .. **Braunschweiger,** Adam W '96 Michael L&R LLP -60 Columbus Cir -NY 10023
(585) 419-8800 .. **Braunsdorf,** Paul R '68 (Harris B PLLC) -99 Garnsey Rd -Pittsfrd 14534
(516) 735-9251 .. **Braunstein,** Carol S '91 -167 Springtime Ln -Levittwn 11756
(516) 937-1010 .. **Braunstein,** Franklin '90 %F Laine,PC -449 S Oyster Bay Rd -Plainvw 11803
(516) 802-0700 .. **Braunstein,** Harry P '75 (Braunstein T LLP) -7600 Jericho Tpk -Woodbury 11797
(718) 934-0504 .. **Braunstein,** Jacob '76 -1422 E 70th -Brklyn 11234
(516) 937-5900 .. **Braunstein,** Jill T '94 %Moomjian WW&C LLP -100 Jericho Quad -Jericho 11753
(212) 689-5700 .. **Braunstein,** Laurence M '80 LMB Grp,Inc -286 Mad Av -NY 10017
(914) 997-6220 .. **Braunstein,** Lawr J '83 (Braunstein & Z) -123 Main -White Plns 10601 **Fx:**328-0916
(516) 739-3441 .. **Braunstein,** Lee S '82 -1025 Old Cntry Rd -Westbury 11590 **Fx:**739-3442
(212) 980-1900 .. **Braunstein,** Matthew R '04 %Donovan & G,LLP -261 Mad Av -NY 10016
(516) 802-0700 .. **Braunstein,** Michl E '10 %Braunstein T LLP -7600 Jericho Tpk -Woodbury 11797
(845) 356-2570 .. **Braunstein,** Michl L '97 %Kantrowitz G&G,PC -747 Chestnut Rdg Rd -Chestnut Rdg 10977
(212) 758-7690 .. **Braunstein,** Mordecai B '63 -485 Mad Av -NY 10022 **Fx:**588-0471
(212) 859-8000 .. **Braunstein,** Rachel L '04 %Fried FHS&J LLP -1 NY Plz -NY 10004
(212) 455-2000 .. **Braunstein,** Samantha S '09 %Simpson T&B LLP -425 Lex Av -NY 10017
(516) 802-0700 .. **Braunstein Turkish LLP** -7600 Jericho Tpk -Woodbury 11797 **Fx:**802-0701
(212) 756-2000 .. **Braunstein,** Yehuda M '00 SpclCnsl Schulte R&Z LLP -919 3rd Av -NY 10022
(212) 788-0650 .. **Braut,** Bradley S '93 %Law Dept -100 Church -NY 10007 **Fx:**788-0367
(732) 855-6084 .. **Brauth,** Marvin J '88 (Wilentz G&S) -110 William -NY 10038 **Fx:**726-6651
(716) 679-0404 .. **Brautigam,** Daryl P '82 (Brautigam & B) -32 White Bx210 -Fredonia 14063 **Fx:**679-0406
(585) 567-8911 .. **Brautigam,** David C '80 -9888 Cnty Rd 23 -Houghton 14744 **Fx:**567-2722
(845) 357-0000 .. **Brautigam,** Donna M '00 %AB Brill,PC -49 N Airmont Rd -Suffern 10901 **Fx:**357-7192
(716) 679-0404 .. **Brautigam,** Sharon E '83 (Brautigam & B) -32 White Bx210 -Fredonia 14063 **Fx:**679-0406
(718) 623-9452 .. **Brautigam,** Steven N '95 -183 St James Pl -Brklyn 11238
(718) 286-6000 .. **Brave,** Gerard '84 %DA -125-01 Qns Blvd -Kew Gdns 11415
(585) 389-2004 .. **Braveman,** Daan '82 Nazereth College -4245 East Av -Rchstr 14618 **Fx:**586-2452
(518) 465-5551 .. **Braveman,** Deanne M '08 %Meyer SE&K,PC -One Commerce Plz -Albany 12260
(516) 248-1434 .. **Braverman,** Alfred P '74 (Braverman & R) -200 Old Cntry Rd -Mineola 11501
(212) 233-2910 .. **Braverman,** Danl S '95 -225 Bway -NY 10007 **Fx:**766-2298
(212) 854-2943 .. **Braverman,** Deborah S '89 %Barnard Cllg-Instit Advancement -3009 Bway -NY 10027
(212) 599-0900 .. **Braverman,** Dylan C '01 %Bower & L,PC -261 Mad Av -NY 10016
(212) 682-2900 .. **Braverman,** Edw T '63 (Braverman & Assoc,PC) -331 Mad Av -NY 10017 **Fx:**682-7718
(212) 446-7000 .. **Braverman,** Eric S '03 McKinsey & Co -55 E 52nd -NY 10055 **Fx:**688-9521
(516) 627-3900 .. **Braverman,** Gordon L '88 (Braverman & L) -1205 Nrthrn Blvd -Manhsst 11030
(212) 693-1000 .. **Braverman,** Ivan M '03 %Golub & G,LLP -225 Bway -NY 10007 **Fx:**693-0090
(718) 237-3100 .. **Braverman,** Jessica '10 Leg Aid -111 Lvngstn -Brklyn 11201 **Fx:**250-4243
(212) 619-5000 .. **Braverman,** Jill I '88 %EDC -110 William -NY 10038 **Fx:**312-3912
(718) 403-3600 .. **Braverman,** Joan K '02 %Dept of Finance -345 Adams -Brklyn 11201 **Fx:**403-3650
(212) 721-7625 .. **Braverman,** Lori J '85 -280 Riverside Dr -NY 10025
(212) 385-0066 .. **Braverman,** Marc D '08 %Dealy & S,LLP -225 Bway -NY 10007
(631) 234-1500 .. **Braverman,** Mark R '96 %Rubin & R LLC -1787 Vets Hwy -Islandia 11749
(718) 993-3000 .. **Braverman,** Michl I '91 (Getz & B,PC) -172 E 161st -Bronx 10451
(516) 822-0022 .. **Braverman,** Peter A '78 Winthrop Financial Assoc -2 Jericho Plz -Jericho 11753
(212) 553-1497 .. **Braverman,** Philip '81 Moody's Invstr Srvc -250 Greenwich -NY 10007
(516) 365-3838 .. **Braverman,** Richd '66 -50 Chas Lindbergh Blvd -Uniondale 11553 **Fx:**365-3261
(212) 682-2900 .. **Braverman,** Robt J '92 (Braverman & Assoc,PC) -331 Mad Av -NY 10017 **Fx:**682-7718
(718) 293-1977 .. **Braverman,** Saml M '93 -901 Sheridan Av -Bronx 10451 **Fx:**293-5395
(516) 365-3838 .. **Braverman,** Shari H '95 -50 Chas Lindbergh Blvd -Uniondale 11553 **Fx:**365-3261
(631) 234-1500 .. **Braverman,** Shari L '07 %Rubin & R LLC -1787 Vets Hwy -Islandia 11749
(646) 878-0800 .. **Braverman,** Todd J '91 (Pearl CZL,LLP) -1500 Bway -NY 10036
(212) 532-0800 .. **Bravo,** Dominique T '92 %AFTRA -260 Mad Av -NY 10016 **Fx:**545-1238
(516) 829-2940 .. **Brawer,** Marc H '70 OfCnsl B Resnicoff -287 Nrthrn Blvd -Gt Neck 11021 **Fx:**829-0130
(516) 292-8100 .. **Braxter,** Milton J '91 %Nassau/Sfflk Law Srv -1 Helen Keller Way -Hempstd 11550 **Fx:**292-6529
(845) 294-5466 .. **Braxton,** Gladys E '81 -Bx328 -Goshen 10924
(518) 266-3000 .. **Bray,** Arthur '77 %Div Tax Appls -500 Fed -Troy 12180 **Fx:**272-5178
(315) 894-8330 .. **Bray,** Christopher R '06 Radley & R -85 Otsego Bx360 -Ilion 13357
(212) 277-4000 .. **Bray,** Daina '05 %Freshfields BD LLP -520 Mad Av -NY 10022
(518) 457-2070 .. **Bray,** Donald H '71 %Dept of Tax & Fin -Bldg 9 State Campus -Albany 12227 **Fx:**457-6131
(716) 674-9100 .. **Bray,** John R '61 (Morris & B,PC) -1299 Union Rd -Buffalo 14224
(212) 801-2228 .. **Bray,** Karen I '96 (Greenberg T,LLP) -200 Park Av -NY 10166
(212) 857-8819 .. **Bray,** Matthew A '07 US Ct of Appls -500 Pearl -NY 10007
(518) 455-7527 .. **Bray,** Paul M '70 %Legis Bill Drftng Comm -The Cptl -Albany 12224 **Fx:**455-7516
(716) 674-9100 .. **Bray,** Stephen N '98 (Morris & B,PC) -1299 Union Rd -Buffalo 14224
(585) 288-3200 .. **Brayley,** Nancy E '82 -460 Winton Rd N -Rchstr 14610 **Fx:**288-3204
(212) 474-1000 .. **Braylovskaya,** Inna '10 %Cravath S&M LLP -825 8th Av -NY 10019
(585) 530-3157 .. **Brayman,** Glenda K '80 Appllt Div 4th Dept -50 East Av Ste 200 -Rchstr 14604 **Fx:**530-3247
(212) 891-5721 .. **Brayshaw,** Jon W '97 %CDC Mortgage Capital -9 W 57th -NY 10019
(212) 556-1234 .. **Brayton,** Diane M '97 %The NY Times Co -620 8th Av -NY 10018 **Fx:**556-4634
(212) 464-0892 .. **Braz,** Darline K '87 %JP Morgan Chase & Co -345 Park Av -NY 10154
(718) 994-8323 .. **Brazil,** John C '60 -332 E 240th -Bronx 10470 **Fx:**944-1155
(212) 819-8200 .. **Brazil,** Jos H '97 (White & C LLP) -1155 Av of Amer -NY 10036
(585) 428-5210 .. **Brazill,** Roger '78 %Pub Def -10 N Fitzhugh -Rchstr 14614 **Fx:**428-2234
(845) 434-2000 .. **Braziller,** Kenneth A '89 %SYDA Fndtn -371 Brickman Rd -Hurleyville 12747 **Fx:**436-2100
(516) 270-4292 .. **Braziller,** Scott L '88 OfCnsl S Braziller,PC -1 Old Cntry Rd -Carle Pl 11514 **Fx:**776-9444
(516) 825-8910 .. **Brazin,** Stewart A '98 -210 Sunrise Hwy -Vly Stream 11581
(212) 344-5680 .. **Brazzano,** Rebecca A '96 OfCnsl Thompson H LLP -335 Mad Av -NY 10017
(516) 616-4440 .. **Brea,** Patrick J '86 (Brea Y,PC) -35 N Tyson Av -Floral Pk 11001
(516) 616-4440 .. **Brea Yankowitz,PC** -35 N Tyson Av -Floral Pk 11001 **Fx:**616-1450
(212) 227-8865 .. **Breadbar Garfield & Schmelkin** -11 Park Pl -NY 10007 **Fx:**791-4129

(518) 869-5552 .. **Breakell,** Walter G '78 Breakell PC -10 Airline Dr -Albany 12205 **Fx:**869-4222
(516) 723-4620 .. **Breakstone,** Jay L T '77 SrCnsl Parker WA LLP -6 Hrbr Park Dr S -Pt Wash 11050 **Fx:**723-4720
(516) 781-7734 .. **Breakstone,** Rhonda Wiener '80 -2698 Boundary Rd -Bellmore 11710 **Fx:**409-6838
(518) 785-4537 .. **Brearton,** James J '76 (Wager TH&B) -950 New London Rd Bx889 -Latham 12110
(212) 558-4000 .. **Breau,** David L '09 %Sullivan & C LLP -125 Broad -NY 10004
(518) 464-9075 .. **Breault,** Adam M '04 %Meyers & M,LLP -1734 Wstrn Av -Albany 12203 **Fx:**464-9078
(212) 336-2000 .. **Breaux,** Diana S '06 %Patterson BW&T LLP -1133 Av of Amer -NY 10036
(212) 688-8555 .. **Breaux,** Marie-Anne N '09 Fragomen DB&L LLP -7 Hanover Sq -NY 10004
(212) 558-4000 .. **Brebner,** Adam R '00 %Sullivan & C LLP -125 Broad -NY 10004
(212) 286-0747 .. **Brecher,** Dan S '69 -99 Park Av -NY 10016 **Fx:**808-4155
(212) 468-4800 .. **Brecher,** David '83 (Davis & G LLP) -1740 Bway -NY 10019
(917) 286-2230 .. **Brecher,** Elliot E '89 Metromedia -810 7th Av -NY 10019
(516) 741-4100 .. **Brecher,** Eric '97 -1 Old Cntry Rd Bx125 -Carle Pl 11514 **Fx:**741-7485
(212) 687-8500 .. **Brecher,** Ethan A '92 (Liddle & R,LLP) -800 3rd Av -NY 10022
(212) 341-7900 .. **Brecher Fishman Pasternack Walsh Tilker & Ziegler, PC** -233 Bway -NY 10279 **Fx:**267-8235
(516) 742-3636 .. **Brecher Fishman Pasternack Walsh Tilker & Ziegler, PC** -1325 Franklin Av -Gdn Cty 11530 **Fx:**742-3994
(718) 222-9800 .. **Brecher Fishman Pasternack Walsh Tilker & Ziegler, PC** -335 Adams -Brklyn 11201 **Fx:**222-0179
(914) 328-8500 .. **Brecher Fishman Pasternack Walsh Tilker & Ziegler, PC** -1 N Bway -White Plns 10601 **Fx:**328-8751
(718) 677-0582 .. **Brecher Fishman Pasternack Walsh Tilker & Ziegler, PC** -1957 Flatbush Av -Brklyn 11234 **Fx:**677-0572
(718) 222-9800 .. **Brecher Fishman Pasternack Walsh Tilker & Ziegler, PC** -118-21 Qns Blvd -Frst Hlls 11375 **Fx:**268-9431
(718) 222-9800 .. **Brecher Fishman Pasternack Walsh Tilker & Ziegler, PC** -369 E 149th -Bronx 10455 **Fx:**742-5739
(631) 348-1668 .. **Brecher Fishman Pasternack Walsh Tilker & Ziegler, PC** -868 Church -Bohemia 11716 **Fx:**218-0401
(631) 348-1668 .. **Brecher Fishman Pasternack Walsh Tilker & Ziegler, PC** -168 Old Cntry Rd -Speonk 11972
(718) 222-9800 .. **Brecher,** George '63 (Brecher FPWT&Z,PC) -335 Adams -Brklyn 11201
(212) 949-9009 .. **Brecher,** Harvey '67 -350 5th Av -NY 10118 **Fx:**695-4248
(212) 907-1500 .. **Brecher,** Howard A '80 Value Line,Inc -220 E 42nd -NY 10017 **Fx:**682-5779
(631) 247-0404 .. **Brecher,** Jeffrey W '00 (Jackson L LLP) -58 S Srvc Rd -Melvll 11747
(212) 969-3000 .. **Brecher,** Stephen I '00 %Proskauer R LLP -1585 Bway -NY 10036
(212) 340-2872 .. **Brecher,** Susan '79 %Cornell Univ-ILR -16 E 34th -NY 10016 **Fx:**340-2822
(716) 332-0990 .. **Brechtel,** Christopher J '06 Childrens Legal Ctr -438 Main -Buffalo 14202
(212) 207-8400 .. **Breckenridge,** James R '80 OfCnsl Kavanagh M&O LLP -415 Mad Av -NY 10017
(212) 902-1000 .. **Breckenridge,** Jonathan E '93 Goldman Sachs -1 NY Plz -NY 10004
(212) 742-9700 .. **Brecker,** Jeffrey R '79 %Godosky & G,PC -61 Bway -NY 10006
(212) 831-7780 .. **Brecker,** Mark L '75 -1562 3rd Av -NY 10128
(315) 379-1466 .. **Breda,** Jos P '95 (Oot & Assoc,PLLC) -63 Main -Canton 13617 **Fx:**379-1433
(315) 471-6687 .. **Breda,** Jos P '95 (Oot & Assoc,PLLC) -503 E Wshngtn -Syracuse 13202 **Fx:**476-7603
(212) 791-1468 .. **Bredin,** David A '01 -9 Pell -NY 10013
(212) 578-2590 .. **Bredin,** Emma J '03 %MetLife -27-01 Qns Plz N -LIC 11101
(518) 690-4200 .. **Breding,** Alice M '04 %Piedmont Law Firm -4 British Amer Blvd -Latham 12110 **Fx:**690-4207
(212) 687-6767 .. **Breed,** Barnabas B B '70 (B Breed & Assoc) -420 Lex Av -NY 10170 **Fx:**687-1197
(212) 532-0500 .. **Breed,** Maxwell K '07 %Heiberger & Assoc,PC -205 Lex Av -NY 10016 **Fx:**532-2040
(518) 383-9400 .. **Breedlove,** Brian H '87 (Pennock B&N) -1407 Route 9 -Clifton Pk 12065
(518) 452-5600 .. **Breedlove,** Jill M '88 OfCnsl Heslin RF&M PC -5 Columbia Cir -Albany 12203
(516) 496-9745 .. **Breen,** Anne T '82 -3 Walnut Dr Bx171 -Syosset 11791 **Fx:**496-9754
(631) 981-5584 .. **Breen,** Barbara A '87 -5 Doyle Ct -Lk Grove 11755 **Fx:**467-5877
(212) 506-5000 .. **Breen,** Bradford S '82 SrCnsl Orrick H&S LLP -51 W 52nd -NY 10019
(212) 685-7411 .. **Breen,** Dennis A '82 %Lurie IM&R,LLP -475 Park Av S -NY 10016 **Fx:**685-9827
(212) 598-5900 .. **Breen,** Erin Elizabeth O'Brien '10 %Alonso A&K PC -920 Bway -NY 10010
(716) 332-7193 .. **Breen,** Gail R '89 -43 Court -Buffalo 14202 **Fx:**332-7194
(516) 847-0267 .. **Breen,** James L '88 -395 Fulton -Farmngdl 11735 **Fx:**847-0271
(212) 455-2000 .. **Breen,** Jason C '08 %Simpson T&B LLP -425 Lex Av -NY 10017
(631) 273-2222 .. **Breen,** John J '87 (Breen & C,PC) -1355 Motor Pkwy -Hauppauge 11749 **Fx:**273-1111
(212) 701-3000 .. **Breen,** Justin C '03 %Cahill G&R LLP -80 Pine -NY 10005 **Fx:**269-5420
(212) 318-6000 .. **Breen,** Kenneth M '93 (Paul HJ&W LLP) -75 E 55th -NY 10022
(716) 645-2167 .. **Breen,** Lauren E '90 %SUNY Buffalo Lw Schl -O'Brian Hall -Buffalo 14260 **Fx:**645-5968
(718) 250-2000 .. **Breen,** Linda Susan '81 %DA -350 Jay -Brklyn 11201 **Fx:**250-2314
(212) 683-6699 .. **Breen,** Maura E '89 %Raab SG&G,LLP -317 Mad Av -NY 10017
(212) 756-2000 .. **Breen,** Meghan '06 %Schulte R&Z LLP -919 3rd Av -NY 10022
(914) 251-1618 .. **Breen,** Michl K '95 (Price MS&D,PC) -106 Corp Park Dr -White Plns 10604
(518) 827-4320 .. **Breen,** Michl L '74 -109 Railroad Av Bx982 -Middleburgh 12122 **Fx:**827-7381
(315) 393-6662 .. **Breen,** Ramona A '89 -623 Ford -Ogdensbrg 13669 **Fx:**394-0836
(212) 883-8833 .. **Breen,** Sheri Ann '95 %Tacopina & A -275 Mad Av -NY 10016
(516) 775-6800 .. **Breen,** Tara L '04 %CK Verkowitz -561 Lakevll Rd -New Hyde Pk 11040 **Fx:**775-0641
(212) 269-0927 .. **Breen,** Thos F '77 (D'Amato & L,LLP) -2 World Fncl Ctr -NY 10281
(212) 521-5400 .. **Breene,** Paul E '84 (Reed S LLP) -599 Lex Av -NY 10022
(212) 277-0485 .. **Breen Guy,** Laura '86 %Hartford -2 Park Av -NY 10016
(518) 439-9936 .. **Breeze,** John H '72 -1397 New Scotland Rd Bx279 -Slingerlnds 12159 **Fx:**439-7915
(212) 730-8133 .. **Breeze,** Ward '98 %Gunderson DSVF&H,LLP -220 W 42nd -NY 10036
(212) 759-6930 .. **Breger,** David S '88 (Breger & B LLP) -1501 Bway -NY 10022 **Fx:**980-5105
(212) 759-6930 .. **Breger,** Edw E '50 (Breger & B LLP) -1501 Bway -NY 10022 **Fx:**980-5105
(518) 445-2328 .. **Breger,** Melissa L '95 Law Clinic & Justice Ctr -80 New Scotland Av -Albany 12208 **Fx:**434-8612
(212) 878-7311 .. **Breger,** Peter '79 -347 Mad Av -NY 10017
(212) 373-3000 .. **Breglio,** John F '72 OfCnsl Paul WRW&G LLP -1285 Av of Amer -NY 10019
(212) 804-4200 .. **Breglio,** Kristen M '04 %Mound CW&G -One Bttry Pk Plz -NY 10004
(631) 283-0200 .. **Bregman,** Eric '69 (Gilmartin & B) -320 Hmptn Rd Bx5071 -Southampton 11969
(212) 696-6000 .. **Bregman,** Jerrold L '03 Cnsl Curtis M-PC&M LLP -101 Park Av -NY 10178
(212) 837-6298 .. **Bregman,** Neil A '03 Hughes H&R LLP -1 Bttry Pk Plz -NY 10004 **Fx:**299-6298
(212) 940-8800 .. **Bregstein,** Henry '94 (Katten MR LLP) -575 Mad Av -NY 10022
(845) 561-1951 .. **Breheney,** Mary Fern '97 (Glenn & B PLLC) -372 S Plnk Rd -Newburgh 12550 **Fx:**561-5651
(516) 249-3450 .. **Breheny,** Peter F '89 (Carman C&I,LLP) -266 Main -Farmngdl 11735
(212) 422-0202 .. **Brehony,** Dawn M '01 %Sedgwick DM&A LLP -125 Broad -NY 10004
(516) 487-4143 .. **Breidbart,** Jill Carey '90 -52 Arleigh Rd -Gt Neck 11021
(212) 685-3260 .. **Breidbart,** Randy M '80 %Park Av Financial Advsrs -92 Michelle Dr -Jericho 11753 **Fx:**684-5433
(212) 310-8000 .. **Breidenbach,** Michl N '05 %Weil G&M LLP -767 5th Av -NY 10153
(212) 791-3900 .. **Breier Deutschmeister Urban & Fromme PC** -111 Bway -NY 10006 **Fx:**791-4072
(212) 791-3900 .. **Breier,** Miriam M '82 (Breier DU&F PC) -111 Bway -NY 10006
(212) 993-2818 .. **Breinholt,** Jacob T '06 -1 Wrld Fncl Ctr -NY 10281
(646) 471-1149 .. **Breinin,** Bartley J '84 PricewaterhouseCoopers LLP -300 Mad Av -NY 10017
(212) 267-6364 .. **Breisblatt,** Lester '98 %Kossoff & U -217 Bway -NY 10007
(631) 383-2862 .. **Breit,** Jason R '07 Nwstrn Mutual Fncl Ntwrk -246 Railroad Av -Sayvll 11782
(212) 784-6400 .. **Breit,** Mitchell M '90 (Hanly CBSF&H LLP) -112 Mad Av -NY 10016 **Fx:**213-5949
(917) 566-5650 .. **Breitbart,** David '69 -152 W 57th -NY 10019
(212) 580-6500 .. **Breite,** Harley D '01 -204 W 84th -NY 10024 **Fx:**(973) 305-9112
(518) 585-2881 .. **Breitenbach,** John C Jr. '00 (Carney & B) -12 Father Joques Pl -Ticonderoga 12883 **Fx:**585-2608
(516) 393-2200 .. **Breitenbach,** Roy W '92 (Garfunkel W,PC) -111 Grt Nck Rd -Gt Neck 11021
(212) 332-7592 .. **Breitenecker,** Rudiger L Jr. '93 (Breitenecker & Assoc) -45 Rckfllr Plz -NY 10111 **Fx:**332-7597
(516) 539-7900 .. **Breiter,** Jeanne C '84 (Breiter & G,LLP) -377 Oak -Gdn Cty 11530
(718) 977-3653 .. **Breiterman,** Seymour '52 -127-08 Merrick Blvd -Sprngfld Gdns 11434 **Fx:**977-3658
(212) 479-4545 .. **Breitman,** Eric D '99 Coty Inc -2 Park Av -NY 10016
(212) 885-5000 .. **Breitman,** Matthew K '94 (Blank R LLP) -405 Lex Av -NY 10174
(516) 826-9004 .. **Breitman,** Steven E '80 -2471 Hrbr Ln -Bellmore 11710 **Fx:**826-9003
(516) 832-7777 .. **Breitner,** Dennis A '75 (Silberstein A&M,PC) -600 Old Cntry Rd -Gdn Cty 11530
(516) 763-2996 .. **Breitner,** Renee Ann '89 %L Rogak,LLC -3355 Lawson Blvd -Oceanside 11572 **Fx:**763-2998
(212) 272-3626 .. **Breitstein,** Melissa B '99 %JP Morgan Chase -383 Mad Av -NY 10179
(718) 748-8080 .. **Breitstein,** Norman R '74 (Heitner & B) -26 Court -Brklyn 11242
(516) 747-0300 .. **Breitstone,** Stephen M '83 (Meltzer LG&B,LLP) -190 Willis Av -Mineola 11501
(631) 905-7024 .. **Brems,** Andrew F '97 -155 Private Rd -E Patchogue 11772
(212) 799-5984 .. **Brenan,** C Kane '97 Goldman Sachs & Co -32 Old Slip -NY 10005
(646) 386-3165 .. **Brendler,** Andrea M '83 %Hon S Sklar -60 Centre -NY 10007
(212) 750-6256 .. **Brenenson,** Chanah S '00 -174 E 74th -NY 10021
(646) 837-0688 .. **Brenenson,** Shoshana R '00 -267 NY Av -Brklyn 11216 **Fx:**(718) 560-3079
(212) 265-2171 .. **Brener,** Judith M '83 Solil Mgmt -640 5th Av -NY 10019 **Fx:**265-1669
(212) 450-4000 .. **Brener,** Katia '00 %Davis P&W LLP -450 Lex Av -NY 10017
(212) 909-6000 .. **Brener,** Liora '05 %Debevoise & P LLP -919 3rd Av -NY 10022
(973) 520-2319 .. **Brener,** Robt J '95 Cnsl Edwards AP&D LLP -750 Lex Av -NY 10022 **Fx:**520-2600
(718) 590-7816 .. **Brenes,** Jessica '01 %Admin Children's Srvcs -900 Sheridan Av -Bronx 10451
(212) 593-6700 .. **Brenes,** Neil F '89 (Aaronson RF&D,LLP) -757 3rd Av -NY 10017
(315) 422-2255 .. **Brenizer,** Jon W '72 (Macht B&G) -510 State Twr Bldg -Syracuse 13202
(212) 687-7410 .. **Brenlla,** George F '96 %Clifton B&D,LLP -420 Lex Av -NY 10170
(212) 237-1000 .. **Brenna,** Michl A '00 %Windels ML&M,LLP -156 W 56th -NY 10019
(585) 454-2000 .. **Brenna,** Robt L Jr. '79 (Brenna B&B,PLLC) -31 E Main -Rchstr 14614
(516) 364-1095 .. **Brennan,** Aileen M '09 %McBreen & K -500 N Bway -Jericho 11753
(718) 884-1689 .. **Brennan,** Arthur D '77 -2475 Palisade Av -Bronx 10463
(212) 788-0782 .. **Brennan,** Ave Maria '83 %Law Dept -100 Church -NY 10007 **Fx:**788-0367
(212) 788-0841 .. **Brennan,** Bernadette M '90 %Law Dept -100 Church -NY 10007 **Fx:**788-0367
(212) 577-3688 .. **Brennan,** Bonnie C '90 %Leg Aid -199 Water -NY 10038 **Fx:**509-8431
(212) 335-9000 .. **Brennan,** Bridget G '84 %DA -1 Hogan Pl -NY 10013
(212) 223-2100 .. **Brennan,** Bridget R '09 %Menz B&K LLP -444 Mad Av -NY 10022

(518) 471-4777 .. **Brennan**, Cailin Connors '05 Appllt Div 3rd Dept -Capitol Station Bx7288 -Albany 12224 **Fx:**471-4750
(631) 232-0200 .. **Brennan**, Catherine Ann '97 %Fumuso KDSS&F,LLP -110 Marcus Blvd -Hauppauge 11788
(516) 766-1619 .. **Brennan**, Chas F '61 %Dergarabedian D & Assoc -11 Clinton Av -Rockvll Ctr 11570 **Fx:**766-6121
(718) 423-6800 .. **Brennan**, Christine '05 %MacKay W&B LLP -40-26 235th -Douglastn 11363
(212) 319-7600 .. **Brennan**, Christopher '92 Cnsl Ziegler Z & Assoc LLP -570 Lex Av -NY 10022 **Fx:**319-7605
(516) 571-4170 .. **Brennan**, Cristina M '06 Nassau Cnty Legislature -1550 Franklin Av -Mineola 11501
(315) 255-3854 .. **Brennan**, Cynthia Beauter '91 (Leone & B) -7 Court Bx188 -Auburn 13021 **Fx:**253-0091
(518) 471-4734 .. **Brennan**, Danl C '81 %Appllt Div 3rd Dept -Capitol Station Bx7288 -Albany 12224 **Fx:**471-4750
(518) 438-9907 .. **Brennan**, David C '99 (Young SWRB&M,LLC) -5 Palisades Dr -Albany 12205
(631) 293-6060 .. **Brennan**, Dylan J '02 (Cellino & B,PC) -445 Broad Hollow Rd -Melvll 11747
(914) 961-4441 .. **Brennan**, Eileen D '91 OfCnsl Begos H&B LLP -7 Pondfld Rd Bx369 -Bronxvll 10708
(516) 248-5757 .. **Brennan**, Erin O '07 %Colleran O&M,LLP -1225 Franklin Av -Gdn Cty 11530
(518) 449-3300 .. **Brennan**, Francis J '98 (Nolan & H,LLP) -39 N Pearl -Albany 12207
(516) 248-9880 .. **Brennan**, Frank W '03 %Agovino & A,LLP -330 Old Cntry Rd -Mineola 11501
(718) 788-7221 .. **Brennan**, James F '83 %State Assmbly -641 LOB -Albany 12248
(518) 449-3900 .. **Brennan**, James G '52 SrCnsl Cooper E&S,LLP -39 N Pearl -Albany 12207
(212) 373-3000 .. **Brennan**, James J '06 %Paul WRW&G LLP -1285 Av of Amer -NY 10019
(718) 590-2000 .. **Brennan**, James T '94 %DA -198 E 161st -Bronx 10451 **Fx:**590-6477
(631) 969-3100 .. **Brennan**, Jennifer R '01 %Frenkel LWW&G,LLP -20 W Main -Bay Shr 11706
(585) 428-6754 .. **Brennan**, Johanna F '82 %Law Dept -30 Church -Rchstr 14614 **Fx:**428-6950
(315) 867-1185 .. **Brennan**, John J '86 NYS Supreme Ct -301 N Wshngtn -Herkimer 13350 **Fx:**867-1531
(516) 328-1100 .. **Brennan**, John O '91 (Ryan B&D LLP) -131 Tulip Av -Floral Pk 11001
(607) 737-5577 .. **Brennan**, John P '07 %Pub Advocate Ofc -219 Mad Av Bx588 -Elmira 14902 **Fx:**737-2955
(315) 474-6448 .. **Brennan**, John R '87 (Byrne C&P PC) -100 Madison -Syracuse 13202
(914) 761-2700 .. **Brennan**, John T '75 (Henderson & B) -222 Mamaroneck Av -White Plns 10605
(518) 451-9252 .. **Brennan**, Jos M '71 -397 Kenwood Av -Delmar 12054 **Fx:**451-9254
(518) 793-3424 .. **Brennan**, Jos R '67 (Brennan & W LLP) -163 Haviland Rd -Queensbury 12804 **Fx:**793-3422
(212) 345-6508 .. **Brennan**, Katherine J '04 Marsh & McClennan Co,Inc -1166 Av of Amer -NY 10036
(716) 845-5972 .. **Brennan**, Kathleen Ann '96 %Roswell Pk Cancer Hsptl -Elm & Carlton -Buffalo 14263
(718) 422-2853 .. **Brennan**, Kathleen M '02 %Leg Aid -111 Lvngstn -Brklyn 11201 **Fx:**722-3093
(518) 474-1331 .. **Brennan**, Keith J '94 %Ofc Mntl Health -44 Holland Av -Albany 12229 **Fx:**473-7863
(212) 858-1000 .. **Brennan**, Kerry A '90 (Pillsbury WSP LLP) -1540 Bway -NY 10036
(212) 571-4067 .. **Brennan**, Kevin J '78 (Dwyer & B) -7 Dey -NY 10007
(845) 534-7545 .. **Brennan**, Kevin V '76 -284 Main -Cornwall 12518 **Fx:**534-4150
(212) 490-3000 .. **Brennan**, Lawr B '78 (Wilson EME&D LLP) -150 E 42nd -NY 10017
(516) 227-2300 .. **Brennan**, Lawr J '78 Wright Risk Mgmt -333 Earle Ovngton Blvd -Uniondale 11553 **Fx:**227-2352
(212) 949-6490 .. **Brennan**, Lorraine M '86 Intl Inst for Conflict Prevention & Resolution -575 Lex Av -NY 10022 **Fx:**949-8859
(212) 558-4000 .. **Brennan**, Matthew J '87 SpclCnsl Sullivan & C LLP -125 Broad -NY 10004
(212) 835-2400 .. **Brennan**, Matthew P '96 %Olnick Organization -110 E 59th -NY 10022
(718) 575-4529 .. **Brennan**, Melissa A '10 NYC Family Justice Ctr -12602 82nd Av -Kew Gdns 11415
(718) 270-3019 .. **Brennan**, Michl C '82 %SUNY Hlth Sci Ctr -450 Clarkson Av -Brklyn 11203
(631) 852-2500 .. **Brennan**, Michl J '92 %DA -200 Center Dr -Rvrhead 11901 **Fx:**852-1769
(212) 384-8340 .. **Brennan**, Niall P '96 %FBI -26 Fed Plz -NY 10278
(212) 319-7480 .. **Brennan**, Patricia B '87 -488 Mad Av -NY 10022
(212) 309-6000 .. **Brennan**, Patricia F '91 (Morgan L&B LLP) -101 Park Av -NY 10178
(212) 867-4100 .. **Brennan**, Patrick J '88 (Furman K&B LLP) -61 Bway -NY 10006
(212) 627-9898 .. **Brennan**, Paul R '96 -555 W 25th -NY 10001 **Fx:**627-9498
(718) 548-2100 .. **Brennan**, Pierce V '51 -165 W 231st -Bronx 10463
(585) 454-2181 .. **Brennan**, Robt E '76 (Trevett CS&A,PC) -2 State -Rchstr 14614
(914) 846-7000 .. **Brennan**, Stephen W '90 %NY Life Ins -1 Rockwood Rd -Sleepy Hollow 10591 **Fx:**846-4755
(716) 773-3626 .. **Brennan**, Terrance C '82 -1693 Grand Isl Blvd -Grand Isl 14072 **Fx:**773-2479
(718) 286-6000 .. **Brennan**, Thos '07 %DA -125-01 Qns Blvd -Kew Gdns 11415
(518) 485-7515 .. **Brennan**, Thos F '88 %Dept Civil Srvc -Harriman Campus Bldg 1 -Albany 12239 **Fx:**457-6654
(914) 993-9600 .. **Brennan**, Timothy J '81 -1 N Bway -White Plns 10601 **Fx:**993-9603
(212) 224-6400 .. **Brennan**, Timothy P '85 %Apple Bk -122 E 42nd -NY 10168
(518) 640-6900 .. **Brennan**, Timothy S '02 %Phelan P&D,LLP -302 Wshngtn Av Ext -Albany 12203
(631) 581-8105 .. **Brennan**, Victoria E '98 Highlander Consultants -103 W Main -E Islip 11730 **Fx:**581-8205
(315) 472-0161 .. **Brennan**, Wm H '82 -201 E Jffrsn -Syracuse 13202 **Fx:**472-7225
(716) 847-8400 .. **Brennan**, Wm J '77 (Phillips L LLP) -3400 HSBC Ctr -Buffalo 14203
(518) 474-3752 .. **Brennan**, Wm J '94 Vet Affrs -5 ESP -Albany 12223
(212) 422-0202 .. **Brennan**, Wm J '07 %Sedgwick DM&A LLP -125 Broad -NY 10004
(212) 248-8800 .. **Brennan**, Wm L '84 (Callan KB&B LLP) -1 Whitehall -NY 10004
(315) 426-1648 .. **Brenneck**, Scott A '02 Cambareri & C,LLP -305 Mntgmry -Syracuse 13202
(212) 225-2000 .. **Brenneman**, Adam J '08 %Cleary GS&H -1 Lbrty Plz -NY 10006
(212) 762-9255 .. **Brenneman**, David C '05 Morgan Stanley -1221 Av of Amer -NY 10020
(315) 785-3088 .. **Brennen**, Terence M '05 %Cnty Atty -175 Arsenal -Watertwn 13601 **Fx:**785-5178
(212) 455-2000 .. **Brenner**, Alan G '86 (Simpson T&B LLP) -425 Lex Av -NY 10017
(585) 753-4620 .. **Brenner**, Allen S '06 DA -832 Watts Bldg -Rchstr 14614 **Fx:**753-4576
(518) 785-0175 .. **Brenner**, Barbara C '90 (Copland & B) -410 Troy Schenectady Rd -Latham 12110 **Fx:**786-1541
(847) 295-7892 .. **Brenner**, Christopher K '98 AYCO -1 Wall Bx15073 -Albany 12212
(212) 964-0725 .. **Brenner**, David J '85 (Brenner & B,PC) -170 Bway -NY 10038
(212) 788-1039 .. **Brenner**, Deborah A '95 %Law Dept -100 Church -NY 10007 **Fx:**788-0367
(845) 359-2210 .. **Brenner**, Donald '61 -4 Indpndnc Av -Tappan 10983 **Fx:**359-8070
(914) 749-8200 .. **Brenner**, Eric J '97 (Boies S&F LLP) -333 Main -Armonk 10504
(845) 452-2022 .. **Brenner Gordon & Lane** -219 Church -Poughkeepsie 12601 **Fx:**452-6954
(212) 417-5377 .. **Brenner**, Jill D '04 %Medicaid Fraud Cntrl -120 Bway -NY 10271 **Fx:**417-5274
(212) 808-2700 .. **Brenner**, John F '88 (Pepper H LLP) -620 8th Av -NY 10018
(212) 582-8000 .. **Brenner**, Jonathan S '81 (Feingold & A,LLP) -1330 Av of Amer -NY 10019
(516) 742-2400 .. **Brenner**, Jos '65 (Matturro & Assoc) -1025 Old Cntry Rd -Westbury 11590 **Fx:**742-2233
(212) 554-0400 .. **Brenner**, Jos M '90 (Grubman I&S,PC) -152 W 57th -NY 10019
(212) 504-6000 .. **Brenner**, Justin S '09 %Cadwalader W&T LLP -1 World Fncl Ctr -NY 10281
(212) 610-6300 .. **Brenner**, Kieran B '06 %Allen & O -1221 Av of Amer -NY 10020
(718) 630-2909 .. **Brenner**, Lawr A '78 %VA -800 Poly Pl -Brklyn 11209 **Fx:**630-2917
(212) 964-0725 .. **Brenner**, Leonard '58 -170 Bway -NY 10038
(212) 734-1551 .. **Brenner**, Lois M '81 -12 E 86th -NY 10028 **Fx:**734-3856
(212) 935-3131 .. **Brenner**, Mark B '77 (Gallet D&B,LLP) -845 3rd Av -NY 10022
(845) 452-2022 .. **Brenner**, Marshall L '60 (Brenner G&L) -219 Church -Poughkeepsie 12601
(718) 250-2000 .. **Brenner**, Michl L '05 %DA -350 Jay -Brklyn 11201 **Fx:**250-2314
(718) 250-2000 .. **Brenner**, Michl S '09 %DA -350 Jay -Brklyn 11201 **Fx:**250-2314
(212) 659-7300 .. **Brenner**, Nancy '88 OfCnsl Haynes & B,LLP -1221 Av of Amer -NY 10020
(914) 238-5635 .. **Brenner**, Nancy G '74 -27 Neustadt Ln -Chappaqua 10514
(212) 431-4880 .. **Brenner**, Paul S '73 -401 Bway -NY 10013
(516) 482-6224 .. **Brenner**, Richd L '61 -34 Hawthorne Ln -Gt Neck 11023 **Fx:**482-6225
(212) 964-0725 .. **Brenner**, Robt J '83 (Brenner & B,PC) -170 Bway -NY 10038
(212) 593-1000 .. **Brenner**, Robt M '84 %Kroll Assoc -1166 Av of Amer -NY 10036 **Fx:**593-2631
(212) 344-8756 .. **Brenner**, Sara P '85 -76 Pearl -NY 10004
(212) 832-0400 .. **Brenner**, Saul B '80 Berdon LLP -360 Mad Av -NY 10017
(212) 355-0292 .. **Brenner**, Scott M '85 -220 E 63rd -NY 10065 **Fx:**750-3804
(718) 727-7700 .. **Brenner**, Stephen G '90 (Minchew S&B,LLP) -1741 Victory Blvd -Staten Isl 10314
(212) 231-1347 .. **Brenner**, Terence D '03 MacQuarie Securities -125 W 55th -NY 10019
(716) 439-7085 .. **Brenner**, Theo A '85 %DA -175 Hawley -Lockprt 14094 **Fx:**439-7102
(845) 985-7411 .. **Brenner**, Wm A '66 -157 Main Bx369 -Grahamsvll 12740 **Fx:**985-0274
(845) 477-9284 .. **Brenner-DeAngelo**, Nancy B '86 -35 Oak Bx1650 -Greenwd Lk 10925 **Fx:**477-9285
(716) 633-7860 .. **Brenon**, John G '73 (Ward B&D) -5500 Main -Williamsvll 14221
(212) 839-5300 .. **Brensilver**, Peter C '03 %Sidley A LLP -787 7th Av -NY 10019
(212) 538-6584 .. **Brensilver**, Stephanie D '06 Credit Suisse -11 Mad Av -NY 10010 **Fx:**322-9866
(845) 434-3973 .. **Brent**, Florence '92 -1500 Route 52 -Liberty 12754
(516) 775-7007 .. **Brent**, Jann S '03 %Gutman MB&S,PC -813 Jericho Tpk -New Hyde Pk 11040
(718) 261-8114 .. **Brent**, Robt H '96 %Wittenstein & W -108-18 Qns Blvd -Frst Hlls 11375 **Fx:**263-4999
(585) 424-5330 .. **Brent**, Stephen M '75 -95 Allens Crk Rd -Rchstr 14618
(716) 863-9143 .. **Brentjens**, Joanneke K '01 -2821 Wehrle Dr -Buffalo 14221 **Fx:**565-3801
(631) 853-7530 .. **Brentson**, Laurie A '04 %Supreme Ct Law Lib -400 Carleton Av -Central Islip 11722
(212) 698-3500 .. **Brereton**, Kira N '08 %Dechert LLP -1095 Av of Amer -NY 10036
(212) 701-3000 .. **Bresa**, Lindita '10 %Cahill G&R LLP -80 Pine -NY 10005 **Fx:**269-5420
(212) 876-7700 .. **Bresch**, Debora M '99 %ASPCA -424 E 92nd -NY 10128 **Fx:**860-3560
(212) 594-3445 .. **Breschel**, David C '83 -525 7th Av -NY 10018 **Fx:**869-0775
(212) 490-3000 .. **Brescia**, Christina M '04 %Wilson EME&D LLP -150 E 42nd -NY 10017
(914) 670-0030 .. **Brescia**, Dana P '01 %Alter & G -550 Mamaroneck Av -Harrison 10528
(914) 777-0804 .. **Brescia**, Jean Marie '86 -534 Prospect Av -Mamaroneck 10543
(516) 739-1462 .. **Brescia**, Michl J '05 %Brosnan & H -1325 Franklin Av -Gdn Cty 11530
(646) 602-5600 .. **Brescia**, Raymond H '93 %Urban Justice Ctr -123 William -NY 10038 **Fx:**(212) 533-4598
(516) 228-3214 .. **Brescia**, Ronald J '68 -600 Old Cntry Rd -Gdn Cty 11530 **Fx:**228-4232
(212) 487-9701 .. **Brescia**, Vincent A '83 %Robin HK&F -1 Bttry Pk Plz -NY 10014
(518) 465-0400 .. **Bresee**, Dianne C '80 (O'Connor OB&F,PC) -20 Corp Wds Blvd -Albany 12211
(518) 533-3000 .. **Breselor**, Franklin K '75 OfCnsl Bond S&K,PLLC -111 Wshngtn Av -Albany 12210
(516) 227-2700 .. **Bresky**, Hunt F '86 (Lipsky B&L,LLP) -585 Stewart Av -Gdn Cty 11530
(718) 335-5400 .. **Bresky**, Marc S '82 -91-31 Qns Blvd -Flushng 11373 **Fx:**899-8906
(518) 485-8063 .. **Bresler**, Barry M '78 Dept of Tax & Fin -Bldg 9 State Campus -Albany 12227 **Fx:**485-8070

(212) 574-1200 .. **Bresler,** Danl H '10 %Seward & K LLP -1 Bttry Pk Plz -NY 10004
(212) 697-3122 .. **Bresler,** Jason H '09 %Martin C&B LLP -220 E 42nd -NY 10017
(212) 417-4450 .. **Bresler,** Jean C '79 %Dept of Health -145 Huguenot -New Rchll 10801 **Fx:**(914) 654-7050
(212) 848-9800 .. **Bresler,** Judith A '75 OfCnsl Withers B LLP -430 Park Av -NY 10022
(718) 336-2219 .. **Breslin,** Danl '80 -2226 E 15th -Brklyn 11229
(631) 200-6346 .. **Breslin,** Eileen Mary '85 Cnsl NBTY,Inc -2100 Smithtown Av -Ronkonkoma 11779
(914) 723-0282 .. **Breslin,** John J '63 -48 Whistler Rd -Scarsdale 10583
(516) 741-7400 .. **Breslin,** Kenneth A '87 %Breslin Rlty Dev -500 Old Cntry Rd -Gdn Cty 11530 **Fx:**741-7128
(212) 867-0707 .. **Breslin,** Michl E '00 FullServe Grp -570 7th Av -NY 10018
(518) 447-7040 .. **Breslin,** Michl G '72 (Cnty Exec Ofc) -112 State -Albany 12207 **Fx:**447-5589
(212) 384-1000 .. **Breslin,** Michl T '95 %FBI -26 Fed Plz -NY 10278
(518) 455-2411 .. **Breslin,** Molly Adams '10 NYS Senate -617 Lgsltv Ofc Bldg -Albany 12247
(518) 429-4200 .. **Breslin,** Neil D '72 OfCnsl Hiscock & B,LLP -50 Beaver -Albany 12207
(607) 337-1405 .. **Breslin,** Richd W '75 SrCnsl Cnty Atty -5 Court -Norwich 13815 **Fx:**337-1435
(518) 463-7784 .. **Breslin,** Saml C '10 %Dreyer B LLP -75 Columbia -Albany 12210
(631) 543-1191 .. **Breslow,** Allen B '65 -6165 Jericho Tpke -Commack 11725 **Fx:**543-8305
(212) 832-1930 .. **Breslow,** Howard S '65 (Breslow & W,LLP) -767 3rd Av -NY 10017
(212) 492-6182 .. **Breslow,** Lauren Hammer '03 JFN Philanthropic Srvcs -150 W 30th -NY 10001
(845) 486-0300 .. **Breslow,** Lawr A '96 %Rutberg Pl Law -3344 Route 9 N -Poughkeepsie 12601 **Fx:**486-0270
(212) 832-1930 .. **Breslow,** Leonard J '93 (Breslow & W,LLP) -767 3rd Av -NY 10017
(212) 909-5400 .. **Breslow,** Richd M '83 KPMG LLP -757 3rd Av -NY 10017
(212) 756-2000 .. **Breslow,** Stephanie R '86 (Schulte R&Z LLP) -919 3rd Av -NY 10022
(212) 538-9000 .. **Breslow,** Stuart J M '85 Credit Suisse -1 Mad Av -NY 10010
(212) 832-1930 .. **Breslow & Walker,LLP** -767 3rd Av -NY 10017 **Fx:**888-4955
(718) 286-6000 .. **Bresnahan,** Danl S '03 DA -125-01 Qns Blvd -Kew Gdns 11415
(718) 286-6000 .. **Bresnahan,** Debra J '01 %DA -125-01 Qns Blvd -Kew Gdns 11415
(212) 697-3122 .. **Bresnan,** Jessica A '09 %Martin C&B LLP -220 E 42nd -NY 10017
(212) 969-3000 .. **Bresnan,** Mary I '07 %Proskauer R LLP -1585 Bway -NY 10036
(212) 849-7000 .. **Bresnick,** Sandra A '93 (Quinn EU&S,LLP) -51 Mad Av -NY 10010
(212) 572-4890 .. **Bresnick,** Sidney R '66 Meredith & K PLLC -300 Park Av -NY 10022
(914) 428-0770 .. **Bress,** Dean S '66 -399 Knollwood Rd -White Plns 10603 **Fx:**428-5663
(212) 431-2389 .. **Bress,** Frank A '73 %NY Law Schl -185 W Bway -NY 10013 **Fx:**944-2053
(212) 876-7700 .. **Bressant-Kibwe,** Kim W '79 %ASPCA -424 E 92nd -NY 10128 **Fx:**860-3560
(212) 425-9300 .. **Bressler Amery & Ross,PC** -17 State -NY 10004 **Fx:**425-9337
(212) 554-7800 .. **Bressler,** Arnold N '75 (Moses & S LLP) -405 Lex Av -NY 10174 **Fx:**377-6036
(631) 298-8353 .. **Bressler,** Eric J '76 (Wickham BG&G,PC) -13015 Main Rd Bx1424 -Mattituck 11952
(631) 249-9480 .. **Bressler,** Eric J '76 (Wickham BG&G,PC) -275 Broad Hollow Rd -Melvll 11747
(212) 357-7426 .. **Bressler,** Gregory N '92 Goldman Sachs & Co -32 Old Slip -NY 10005
(212) 506-1700 .. **Bressler,** Howard L '92 SpclCnsl Kasowitz BT&F LLP -1633 Bway -NY 10019
(212) 873-2863 .. **Bressler,** Jane C '77 -115 Cntrl Pk W -NY 10023 **Fx:**362-1520
(212) 885-5000 .. **Bressler,** Kenneth L '85 (Blank R LLP) -405 Lex Av -NY 10174
(516) 742-4343 .. **Bressler,** Marvin '69 (Scully SM&P PC) -400 Grdn City Plz -Gdn Cty 11530
(585) 262-2120 .. **Bressler,** Melvin '68 (Bressler & K) -16 W Main -Rchstr 14614 **Fx:**262-2625
(718) 967-1720 .. **Bressler,** Robt N '63 -109 Carlyle Green -Staten Isl 10312
(212) 906-1200 .. **Bressler,** Shira E '09 %Latham & W -885 3rd Av -NY 10022
(212) 455-2000 .. **Bressler,** Vanessa '03 %Simpson T&B LLP -425 Lex Av -NY 10017
(212) 840-8555 .. **Bressman,** David L '76 Urban Zen,LLC -570 7th Av -NY 10018 **Fx:**840-8266
(212) 728-8000 .. **Bressman,** Robt Ian '81 (Willkie F&G LLP) -787 7th Av -NY 10019
(212) 969-3000 .. **Bressman,** Stuart '86 (Proskauer R LLP) -1585 Bway -NY 10036
(212) 450-4000 .. **Bretholz,** Michl '07 %Davis P&W LLP -450 Lex Av -NY 10017
(212) 267-1922 .. **Bretillot Levaillant,** Audrey S '96 %NYTAB, Inc -Bx566 -NY 10272
(518) 527-6628 .. **Breton,** Robt O '89 -6219 Empire Av -Schnctdy 12306 **Fx:**630-0041
(212) 266-2163 .. **Bretous,** Stella '04 Admn Child Srvcs -150 William -NY 10038
(212) 297-1272 .. **Bretstein,** Joshua A '99 CTI Legal Staffing -331 Mad Av -NY 10017 **Fx:**697-1244
(212) 704-6000 .. **Brett,** Barry J '65 (Troutman S LLP) -405 Lex Av -NY 10174
(585) 383-1850 .. **Brett,** Elizabeth J '98 %Birdeye Foods Inc -90 Linden Oaks -Rchstr 14625
(718) 631-7733 .. **Brett,** Errol A '66 -26910 Grnd Cntrl Pkwy -Floral Pk 11005 **Fx:**631-7765
(914) 323-7000 .. **Brett,** Harry P '79 (Wilson EME&D LLP) -3 Gannett Dr -White Plns 10604
(716) 834-9181 .. **Brett,** Jay E '58 (Blair & R,LLP) -2645 Sheridan Dr -Tonawanda 14150
(516) 432-0703 .. **Brett,** Jennifer L '04 -23 Biarritz -Lido Bch 11561 **Fx:**432-0776
(212) 883-1700 .. **Brett,** Kirk L '92 (Duval & S LLP) -101 Park Av -NY 10178
(212) 867-4466 .. **Brett,** Matthew S '99 (Belkin BW&G,LLP) -270 Mad Av -NY 10016
(718) 263-0123 .. **Brett,** Thos E '58 -125-10 Qns Blvd -Kew Gdns 11415 **Fx:**263-0134
(212) 727-8260 .. **Brettler,** June Hollie '79 -10 W 15th -NY 10011
(212) 449-6313 .. **Bretton-Granatoor,** Marianne J '83 %Merrill Lynch -225 Lbrty WFC -NY 10080
(212) 747-8787 .. **Brettschneider,** Elizabeth R '05 %J Avirom & Assoc -42 Bway -NY 10004
(212) 487-8284 .. **Brettschneider,** Eric '83 ACT -2 Wshngtn -NY 10004 **Fx:**487-8581
(516) 869-9000 .. **Brettschneider,** Glenn D '84 Kimco Realty Corp -3333 New Hyde Pk Rd -New Hyde Pk 11042
(631) 367-3111 .. **Brettschneider,** Jos M '87 (Brettschneider & B,LLP) -83 Prospect -Huntngtn 11743 **Fx:**427-6912
(631) 337-1977 .. **Brettschneider,** Mark '84 %C Petroske,PC -4875 Sunrise Hwy -Bohemia 11716 **Fx:**337-1966
(631) 367-3111 .. **Brettschneider,** Rita R F '61 (Brettschneider & B,LLP) -83 Prospect -Huntngtn 11743 **Fx:**427-6912
(212) 267-2555 .. **Bretz & Coven,LLP** -305 Bway -NY 10007 **Fx:**267-2129
(212) 267-2555 .. **Bretz,** Eileen Collins '96 (Bretz & C,LLP) -305 Bway -NY 10007
(212) 267-2555 .. **Bretz,** Kerry Wm '92 (Bretz & C,LLP) -305 Bway -NY 10007
(631) 234-1154 .. **Breud,** Albert A '05 %S Mishkin,PC -1 Suffolk Sq -Islandia 11749 **Fx:**234-5048
(718) 782-1500 .. **Breuer,** M David '04 -211 Ross -Brklyn 11211 **Fx:**782-3350
(212) 250-5032 .. **Breuvart,** Alexia '03 %Deutsche Bank -60 Wall -NY 10005
(212) 536-3900 .. **Brevetti,** Laura A '77 (K&L Gates LLP) -599 Lex Av -NY 10022
(914) 682-8440 .. **Brevetti,** Louis A '54 -7 Fairway Dr -White Plns 10605 **Fx:**682-7550
(716) 332-3740 .. **Brevorka,** Jillian E '09 P Brevorka,PC -4476 Main -Amherst 14226
(212) 609-6800 .. **Brew,** Gerard G '89 (McCarter & E,LLP) -245 Park Av -NY 10167
(516) 378-1700 .. **Brew,** Harold T III '89 %Chesney & M -2305 Grand Av -Baldwin 11510
(631) 501-5700 .. **Brew,** Michl R '93 (Carter DF&S LLP) -445 Broadhallow Rd -Melvll 11747
(212) 859-8000 .. **Brewer,** John W '94 SpclCnsl Fried FHS&J LLP -1 NY Plz -NY 10004
(716) 852-5200 .. **Brewer,** Kim M '93 %Hamberger & W -700 Main Pl Twr -Buffalo 14202
(212) 876-5500 .. **Brewer,** M Weldon '73 %Neighborhood Def Srv -317 Lenox Av -NY 10027 **Fx:**876-5586
(212) 697-9400 .. **Brewer,** Shaleen D '04 (Cheifetz IM,PC) -275 Mad Av -NY 10016
(518) 897-1227 .. **Brewer,** Steven L '81 %DEC -1115 Route 86 Bx296 -Ray Brk 12977 **Fx:**897-1394
(212) 489-1400 .. **Brewer,** Wm A III '79 (Bickel & B) -767 5th Av -NY 10153
(212) 294-6793 .. **Brewer,** Wm D '95 (Winston & S) -200 Park Av -NY 10166
(212) 223-0400 .. **Brewer,** Wm L '95 (Zeichner E&K LLP) -575 Lex Av -NY 10022
(212) 460-6614 .. **Brewi,** Stephen T '94 Con Ed -4 Irving Pl -NY 10003
(516) 489-6959 .. **Brewington,** Fredk K '86 -556 Peninsula Blvd -Hempstd 11550 **Fx:**489-6958
(716) 631-5767 .. **Brewster,** Melissa A '07 Stamm R&S -5555 Main -Williamsvll 14221
(212) 222-4084 .. **Brewster,** Reginald T '51 -356 W 122nd -NY 10027
(212) 416-8650 .. **Brewster,** Richd W '68 %Dept of Law -120 Bway -NY 10271
(212) 222-4084 .. **Brewster,** Roland T '96 -356 W 122nd -NY 10027
(914) 714-7352 .. **Breyer,** Robt C '93 %Verizon -4 Centerock Rd -W Nyack 10994 **Fx:**714-7125
(212) 450-4000 .. **Breyfogle,** Molly C '07 %Davis P&W LLP -450 Lex Av -NY 10017
(518) 886-4501 .. **Breyo,** John '72 AYCO -321 Bway Bx860 -Saratoga Spgs 12866
(212) 446-4800 .. **Brez,** Zachary S '00 (Kirkland & E LLP) -153 E 53rd -NY 10022
(212) 473-0255 .. **Brezenoff,** Kenneth S '00 Seedco -915 Bway -NY 10010
(212) 506-1700 .. **Brezinsky,** Helene '76 OfCnsl Kasowitz BT&F LLP -1633 Bway -NY 10019
(212) 581-4700 .. **Breznick,** Martin F '77 (Breznick & C) -630 9th Av -NY 10036 **Fx:**247-1407
(516) 869-7157 .. **Briamonte,** Barbara E '84 %Kimco Realty Corp -3333 New Hyde Pk Rd -New Hyde Pk 11042 **Fx:**869-7199
(718) 628-6191 .. **Brian,** Anthony J '93 -6223 74th Av -Rdgwd 11385
(212) 924-1704 .. **Brian,** Conley E Jr. '75 -7 E 14th -NY 10003 **Fx:**924-1704
(716) 849-8900 .. **Briandi,** Jody E '97 (Hurwitz & F,PC) -1300 Lbrty Bldg -Buffalo 14202
(914) 946-5900 .. **Briccetti Calhoun & Lawrence,LLP** -81 Main -White Plns 10601 **Fx:**946-5906
(212) 859-8000 .. **Briccetti,** Christina E '10 %Fried FHS&J LLP -1 NY Plz -NY 10004
(518) 455-3413 .. **Briccetti,** Heather C '90 %NYS Senate -The Cptl -Albany 12247
(914) 946-5900 .. **Briccetti,** Vincent L '81 (Briccetti C&L,LLP) -81 Main -White Plns 10601
(315) 422-7111 .. **Brice,** Danl R '04 (Blitman & K LLP) -443 N Franklin -Syracuse 13204
(212) 696-6000 .. **Brice,** Karen R '05 %Curtis M-PC&M LLP -101 Park Av -NY 10178
(212) 331-5861 .. **Brice,** Lisa C '04 %HRA -180 Water -NY 10038
(718) 553-3285 .. **Brice,** Stephen W '99 %FAA -1 Aviation Plz -Jamaica 11434 **Fx:**995-5699
(212) 277-6500 .. **Brice,** Susan M '04 %Dickstein S LLP -1633 Bway -NY 10019
(518) 489-9423 .. **Brick,** Andrew '95 %D Zee,PC -1 Winners Cir -Albany 12205 **Fx:**489-9429
(212) 698-3500 .. **Brick,** Brian H '02 %Dechert LLP -1095 Av of Amer -NY 10036
(716) 693-2335 .. **Brick Brick & Elmer,PC** -91 Tremont Bx604 -N Tonawanda 14120 **Fx:**693-4972
(716) 693-2335 .. **Brick,** Danl E '70 (Brick B&E,PC) -91 Tremont Bx604 -N Tonawanda 14120
(516) 596-6000 .. **Brick,** Marc L '86 -366 Pearsall -Cedarhrst 11516
(212) 302-6574 .. **Brick,** Wm D '97 (Riker DSH&P LLP) -500 5th Av -NY 10110
(914) 238-7501 .. **Brick-Cabot,** Helaine S '77 -26 Gedney Way -Chappaqua 10514 **Fx:**238-0473
(212) 421-4100 .. **Brickell,** Jamie M '84 (Pryor C LLP) -7 Times Sq -NY 10036
(212) 979-3092 .. **Bricker,** Denise L '94 %Natl Audubon Society -225 Varick -NY 10014
(718) 286-6000 .. **Bricker,** Emil S '81 %DA -125-01 Qns Blvd -Kew Gdns 11415
(212) 223-4000 .. **Bricker,** John F '81 Cnsl Crowell & M LLP -590 Mad Av -NY 10022
(212) 355-0346 .. **Bricker,** Mark H '95 %KLS Profsnl Advsrs -111 5th Av -NY 10003
(212) 696-6000 .. **Bricker,** Wm L Jr. '72 (Curtis M-PC&M LLP) -101 Park Av -NY 10178
(914) 935-9705 .. **Brickfield,** Paul B '82 (P Brickfield,PC) -219 Wstchstr Av -Pt Chester 10573 **Fx:**(201) 488-9559
(518) 464-6464 .. **Brickman,** David '88 -1664 Wstrn Av -Albany 12203 **Fx:**464-6688
(516) 829-6900 .. **Brickman,** John M '69 (Ackerman LCB&L,LLP) -1010 Nrthrn Blvd -Gt Neck 11021
(718) 318-8805 .. **Brickman,** Leon '49 L Brickman -224 Beach 147th -Rckwy Pk 11694 **Fx:**318-8806
(212) 790-0327 .. **Brickman,** Lester '77 %Benj N Cardozo Schl of Law -55 5th Av -NY 10003 **Fx:**790-0345
(212) 986-6840 .. **Brickman,** Neal '82 -317 Mad Av -NY 10017 **Fx:**986-7691
(518) 474-7700 .. **Brickman,** Stephen K '88 %NYS OPWDD -44 Holland Av -Albany 12229 **Fx:**474-7382

(718) 624-1550 .. **Brickner,** Howard M '79 (Brickner M,LLP) -292 Warren -Brklyn 11201 **Fx:**855-1094
(212) 906-1200 .. **Brickner,** Jed W '93 (Latham & W) -885 3rd Av -NY 10022
(315) 423-3302 .. **Brickwedde,** Richd J '70 Brickwedde Law Firm -300 S State -Syracuse 13202 **Fx:**426-0489
(914) 995-3224 .. **Brickwood,** Dale R '05 %DA -111 Martin Luther King Blvd -White Plns 10601 **Fx:**995-3363
(212) 450-4000 .. **Bridge,** Anna T '05 %Davis P&W LLP -450 Lex Av -NY 10017
(716) 856-4200 .. **Bridge,** C Christopher '87 (Gibson M&C,LLP) -69 Delaware Av -Buffalo 14202
(716) 551-4741 .. **Bridge,** Carol A '88 %US DHS -130 Delaware Av -Buffalo 14202
(716) 874-8010 .. **Bridge,** Chas P '65 (Bridge & B) -Bx336 -Tonawanda 14223 **Fx:**874-8113
(212) 957-7600 .. **Bridge,** Colin C '05 %Cohen & G LLP -800 3rd Av -NY 10022
(212) 506-5000 .. **Bridge,** Scott P '05 %Orrick H&S LLP -51 W 52nd -NY 10019
(716) 874-8010 .. **Bridge,** Timothy P '99 %Bridge & B -Bx336 -Tonawanda 14223 **Fx:**874-8113
(212) 728-8000 .. **Bridgeford,** Soh Hyong '02 %Willkie F&G LLP -787 7th Av -NY 10019
(212) 816-9942 .. **Bridgers,** Darrell N '99 Citigrp Glbl Mkts -388 Greenwich -NY 10013
(718) 556-3096 .. **Bridgers,** Linda A '96 -368 Victory Blvd -Staten Isl 10301 **Fx:**556-3097
(212) 756-2000 .. **Bridges,** Misti M '98 %Schulte R&Z LLP -919 3rd Av -NY 10022
(516) 536-0900 .. **Bridges,** Robt M '74 (Jacobson & S) -510 Merrick Rd Bx46 -Rockvll Ctr 11571
(212) 682-8969 .. **Bridgewater,** Christiana J '82 -333 E 45th -NY 10017 **Fx:**(718) 659-5171
(518) 434-4926 .. **Bridgham,** Ruth T '74 -524 Mad Av -Albany 12208
(646) 386-3043 .. **Brieant,** Chas III '83 Supreme Ct-Law Dept -60 Centre -NY 10007
(212) 832-5570 .. **Brief Carmen & Kleiman,LLP** -805 3rd Av -NY 10022 **Fx:**832-7221
(212) 832-5570 .. **Brief,** Matthew J '81 (Brief C&K,LLP) -805 3rd Av -NY 10022
(212) 805-6387 .. **Brief,** Tania C '05 %Hon W Pauley III -500 Pearl -NY 10007
(212) 382-0700 .. **Brieger,** George '94 OfCnsl Ostrolenk FG&S,LLP -1180 Av of Amer -NY 10036
(914) 347-2600 .. **Briem,** Jeffrey '06 %Traub LS&S LLP -7 Skyline Dr -Hawthorne 10532
(845) 221-4099 .. **Brien,** Scott M '08 %Campanaro & T -867 Route 376 Bx123 -Hopewell Junct 12533 **Fx:**221-1570
(914) 422-4628 .. **Briendel,** Natanya '86 Pace Womens Justice Ctr -78 N Bway -White Plns 10603
(212) 801-2107 .. **Briendel,** Wm D '85 (Greenberg T,LLP) -200 Park Av -NY 10166
(212) 656-2870 .. **Brienza,** Mary L '80 NYSE -20 Broad -NY 10005 **Fx:**656-2460
(212) 885-5000 .. **Brier,** David '98 %Blank R LLP -405 Lex Av -NY 10174
(212) 326-3939 .. **Brier,** Gabriel P '05 %Jones D -222 E 41st -NY 10017
(212) 735-3000 .. **Brier,** Shane '99 Cnsl Skadden ASM&F LLP -4 Times Sq -NY 10036
(212) 786-2999 .. **Briere,** Robt W '02 -110 Wall -NY 10005
(845) 838-2045 .. **Brierton,** Maureen J '03 -Bx253 -Beacon 12508 **Fx:**838-2040
(718) 262-7100 .. **Briese,** June M '91 %Civil Ct -89-17 Sutphin Blvd -Jamaica 11435 **Fx:**262-7107
(212) 944-6611 .. **Briess,** Craig C '09 %Tompkins & D,LLP -5 Hanover Sq -NY 10004
(212) 854-2638 .. **Briffault,** Richd '79 %Columbia Law Schl -435 W 116th -NY 10027 **Fx:**854-7946
(718) 224-3100 .. **Brigandi,** Douglas C J '78 -214-11 Nrthrn Blvd -Bayside 11361 **Fx:**224-0902
(212) 310-9800 .. **Briganti,** Lorraine '90 %Bayerische Landesbank -560 Lex -NY 10022 **Fx:**310-9822
(914) 997-0500 .. **Briganti,** Vincent '97 (Lowey DC&H,PC) -1 N Bway -White Plns 10601
(212) 723-3808 .. **Brigantic,** Patricia E '83 Citigroup Global Mrkts -250 West -NY 10013
(212) 736-0900 .. **Brigantic,** Robt M '87 -875 Av of Amer -NY 10001
(212) 758-4000 .. **Briger,** Peter L '60 (P Briger & Assoc) -230 Park Av -NY 10169
(631) 427-5635 .. **Briggs,** Benjamin R '88 -11 Vllg Dr -Huntngtn 11743
(585) 262-8412 .. **Briggs,** Cara M '88 Rochester Schl Dist -131 W Broad -Rchstr 14614
(518) 523-5555 .. **Briggs,** Jenifer R '03 %Briggs N LLP -2296 Saranac Av -Lk Placid 12946 **Fx:**523-5559
(212) 692-9666 .. **Briggs,** Lincoln W '87 (Gilbride TL&S LLC) -708 3rd Av -NY 10017
(212) 885-5000 .. **Briggs,** Lindsey V '07 %Blank R LLP -405 Lex Av -NY 10174
(716) 842-2366 .. **Briggs,** Marissa K '94 %M&T Bk -One M&T Plz -Buffalo 14203 **Fx:**842-5376
(718) 286-2450 .. **Briggs,** Melissa J '04 %Leg Aid -120-46 Qns Blvd -Kew Gdns 11415 **Fx:**263-4234
(518) 372-5689 .. **Briggs,** Paul '82 (Pemberton & B) -202 Union -Schnctdy 12305 **Fx:**372-5768
(518) 523-5555 .. **Briggs,** Ronald J '76 (Briggs N LLP) -2296 Saranac Av -Lk Placid 12946 **Fx:**523-5559
(646) 386-3223 .. **Briggs,** Wm C '98 %Hon W McCooe -60 Centre -NY 10007
(212) 318-6000 .. **Brigham,** Matthew G '07 %Paul HJ&W LLP -75 E 55th -NY 10022
(516) 437-1719 .. **Brighindi,** Vittorio B '97 -122 Plainfld Av -Floral Pk 11001
(212) 228-6320 .. **Bright,** Danl R '89 (Schwartz L&B,PC) -275 7th Av -NY 10001
(212) 421-2233 .. **Bright,** Jonathan K '90 (Wilk A LLP) -675 3rd Av -NY 10017
(212) 259-8000 .. **Bright,** Nicole M '05 %Dewey & L LLP -1301 Av of Amer -NY 10019
(212) 474-1000 .. **Bright,** Patrick J '06 %Cravath S&M LLP -825 8th Av -NY 10019
(212) 768-6700 .. **Bright,** W Edw '82 (Sonnenschein N&R LLP) -2 World Fncl Ctr -NY 10281
(631) 232-2400 .. **Briglio,** Robt '88 %Nassau/Sfflk Law Srv -1757 Vets Hwy -Islandia 11749 **Fx:**232-2489
(212) 759-6556 .. **Brignati,** Thos G '98 %Starr & Co,LLC -850 3rd Av -NY 10022
(518) 449-2037 .. **Brignola,** Dominick J '84 (Kriss K&B,LLP) -350 Nrthrn Blvd -Albany 12204
(212) 407-4600 .. **Brignoni,** David P '07 %GAM USA Inc -1 Rckfllr Plz -NY 10020 **Fx:**407-4684
(718) 434-1700 .. **Brignoni,** Yanitza N '01 OfCnsl Boyko & Assoc,PC -2021 Nostrand Av -Brklyn 11210 **Fx:**434-8953
(585) 428-4373 .. **Brilbeck,** Thos J '85 %Hon A Renzi-Supreme Ct -545 Hall of Justice -Rchstr 14614 **Fx:**428-4371
(212) 407-1200 .. **Briley,** Siobhan '10 %Joseph Law Ofcs LLC -485 Lex Av -NY 10017 **Fx:**407-1299
(845) 357-0000 .. **Brill,** Alan B '80 (AB Brill,PC) -49 N Airmont Rd -Suffern 10901 **Fx:**357-7192
(212) 753-5599 .. **Brill,** Allen H '68 (Brill & M) -845 3rd Av -NY 10022
(212) 903-8700 .. **Brill,** Arthur '66 OfCnsl Roberts & H,LLP -825 8th Av -NY 10019
(716) 835-8719 .. **Brill,** B Kastle '78 -207 Summit Av -Buffalo 14214
(212) 975-1164 .. **Brill,** Craig J '01 %CBS Inc -51 W 52nd -NY 10019 **Fx:**975-3930
(212) 332-6303 .. **Brill,** Cynthia M '78 Journalism Online -25 W 52nd -NY 10019
(212) 969-3000 .. **Brill,** Edw A '73 (Proskauer R LLP) -1585 Bway -NY 10036
(212) 909-6000 .. **Brill,** Elizabeth K '02 %Debevoise & P LLP -919 3rd Av -NY 10022
(212) 374-9101 .. **Brill,** Haydn J '85 (Brill & Assoc,PC) -111 John -NY 10038 **Fx:**374-9108
(516) 489-8786 .. **Brill,** Howard R '87 (HR Brill,PC) -250 Fulton Av -Hempstd 11550 **Fx:**486-4933
(212) 735-3000 .. **Brill,** Jeffrey A '99 (Skadden ASM&F LLP) -4 Times Sq -NY 10036
(716) 853-1616 .. **Brill,** John W '10 %Harter S&E LLP -12 Fountain Plz -Buffalo 14202
(212) 885-5000 .. **Brill,** Laura A '00 %Blank R LLP -405 Lex Av -NY 10174
(212) 848-4000 .. **Brill,** Lisa M '01 (Shearman & S LLP) -599 Lex Av -NY 10022
(718) 833-2100 .. **Brill,** Lori A '97 %Elhilow & Assoc -259 86th -Brklyn 11209 **Fx:**833-0476
(516) 489-8786 .. **Brill,** Marilyn I '84 HR Brill,PC -250 Fulton Av -Hempstd 11550 **Fx:**486-4933
(212) 753-5599 .. **Brill & Meisel** -845 3rd Av -NY 10022 **Fx:**486-6587
(212) 509-9400 .. **Brill,** Melissa F '99 (Cozen O) -45 Bway Atrium -NY 10006
(212) 416-8000 .. **Brill,** Nathan A '05 %Dept of Law -120 Bway -NY 10271
(212) 233-3800 .. **Brill,** Peter E '98 %Karasyk & M,LLP -225 Bway -NY 10007
(212) 935-7900 .. **Brill,** Robt M '82 -880 3rd Av -NY 10022 **Fx:**935-6524
(212) 326-2000 .. **Brill,** Stephanie Lloyd '07 Cnsl O'Melveny & M LLP -7 Times Sq -NY 10036
(212) 566-1000 .. **Brill,** Steven G '95 (Sullivan & B LLP) -115 Bway -NY 10006 **Fx:**566-1068
(631) 726-5435 .. **Brill,** Wendy '73 -Bx205 -Water Mill 11976 **Fx:**726-0026
(212) 608-4100 .. **Brill,** Wendy '73 -9 Murray -NY 10007 **Fx:**732-4443 ***[Social Security Law]***
(212) 702-5400 .. **Brillault,** Megan R '04 %Beveridge & D,PC -477 Mad Av -NY 10022
(212) 709-8210 .. **Brilleman,** Louis A '91 -110 Wall -NY 10005 **Fx:**943-2300
(212) 306-3293 .. **Briller,** Julius '84 %Housing Auth -250 Bway -NY 10007 **Fx:**306-3455
(212) 698-3500 .. **Brilliant,** Allan S '01 (Dechert LLP) -1095 Av of Amer -NY 10036
(718) 634-1057 .. **Brilliant,** Corinne L '51 -150 Beach 140th -Belle Hbr 11694 **Fx:**634-1056
(212) 571-7800 .. **Brilliant,** Robyn M '91 -16 Penn Plz -NY 10001 **Fx:**571-4846
(518) 473-5246 .. **Brilling,** Jaclyn A '80 %Dept Pub Srvc -3 ESP -Albany 12223 **Fx:**486-6081
(914) 995-2697 .. **Brimais,** Patricia '96 %Cnty Atty -148 Martine Av -White Plns 10601 **Fx:**995-5858
(585) 530-3163 .. **Brimlow,** Joan P '80 %Appllt Div 4th Dept -50 East Av Ste 200 -Rchstr 14604 **Fx:**530-3247
(716) 674-1407 .. **Brimmer,** George A II '87 -81 Crystal Ln -Buffalo 14224 **Fx:**674-1407
(631) 712-5600 .. **Brin,** Katherine R '03 %Hon T Platt -100 Fed Plz -Central Islip 11722
(631) 439-4200 .. **Brin,** Marcia Mae '75 %R Tusa -898 Vets Mem'l Hwy -Hauppauge 11788 **Fx:**439-4292
(212) 468-8000 .. **Brin,** Sara D '08 %Morrison & F LLP -1290 Av of Amer -NY 10104
(516) 466-3100 .. **Brinberg,** Simeon '59 %Gould Investors -60 Cuttermill Rd -Gt Neck 11021 **Fx:**466-3132
(212) 984-0706 .. **Brinberg,** Todd Michl '79 (Nadborny & B LLP) -100 Park Av -NY 10017 **Fx:**656-1660
(212) 486-7465 .. **Brinck,** Jeffrey K '70 %Transoceanic Marine -39 E 51st -NY 10022
(212) 763-5000 .. **Brinckerhoff,** Matthew D '91 (Emery CB&A LLP) -75 Rckfllr Plz -NY 10019
(315) 733-2396 .. **Brindisi,** Anthony J '04 (Brindisi MBPJ&P,LLP) -2713 Genesee -Utica 13501
(315) 733-2396 .. **Brindisi,** Louis T '60 (Brindisi MBPJ&P,LLP) -2713 Genesee -Utica 13501
(315) 733-2396 .. **Brindisi Murad Brindisi Pearlman Julian & Pertz, LLP** -2713 Genesee -Utica 13501 **Fx:**733-7933
(212) 330-8151 .. **Brinen,** Joshua D '98 (Brinen & Assoc,LLC) -7 Dey -NY 10007 **Fx:**202-5330
(212) 370-1300 .. **Bring,** Martin R '68 (Ellenoff G&S LLP) -150 E 42nd -NY 10017
(845) 639-0272 .. **Bring,** Robt D '61 -Bx628 -New Cty 10956 **Fx:**639-0416
(212) 617-8504 .. **Bringardner,** Lindsay R '03 %Bloomberg,LP -731 Lex Av -NY 10022
(718) 273-3588 .. **Bringslid,** Kerri L '01 -1882 Victory Blvd -Staten Isl 10314
(212) 435-3571 .. **Brink,** Christopher R '10 Port Auth of NY/NJ -225 Park Av S -NY 10003 **Fx:**435-3555
(212) 558-4000 .. **Brinkman,** Andrew S C '08 %Sullivan & C LLP -125 Broad -NY 10004
(716) 858-2200 .. **Brinkworth,** Kelly Anne '90 %Cnty Atty -95 Franklin -Buffalo 14202 **Fx:**858-2281
(716) 851-4403 .. **Brinkworth,** Kevin J '99 Buffalo Police Dept -74 Franklin -Buffalo 14202
(716) 823-3936 .. **Brinkworth,** Thos F '65 -1038 Abbott Rd -Buffalo 14220
(718) 260-5124 .. **Brin Moran,** Marissa '91 %City Tech-Law & Paralegal Studies -300 Jay -Brklyn 11201
(516) 764-3335 .. **Brinn,** Alan '64 %Rubin C&S -330 Sunrise Hwy -Rockvll Ctr 11570
(212) 661-3535 .. **Brinn,** Elissa R '99 %Hodgson R LLP -60 E 42nd -NY 10165
(631) 425-4100 .. **Brino,** Janine '06 %Ré NH&C,LLP -36 N NY Av -Huntngtn 11743
(631) 724-8833 .. **Brino,** Nicholas M '05 %Devitt SB,LLP -50 Route 111 -Smithtwn 11787
(516) 746-7660 .. **Brint,** Roland P '63 %Klemanowicz H&VS,LLP -300 Old Cntry Rd -Mineola 11501 **Fx:**747-7292
(718) 746-2235 .. **Brintle,** Jos A '93 (J Brintle,PC) -14-46 Utopia Pkwy -Whitestone 11357
(212) 878-8276 .. **Brinton,** G David '86 (Clifford C LLP) -31 W 52nd -NY 10019
(914) 428-4034 .. **Brinton & January** -50 Main -White Plns 10606 **Fx:**948-2152
(212) 938-5000 .. **Brinton,** Michl D '09 %Cantor Fitzgerald -110 E 59th -NY 10022
(914) 428-4034 .. **Brinton,** Robt L '67 (Brinton & J) -50 Main -White Plns 10606
(212) 402-9400 .. **Briody,** John C '04 %McKool S,PC -1 Bryant Park -NY 10036
(646) 473-3943 .. **Briody,** Maureen O '00 USPS-Law Dept -380 W 33rd -NY 10199

(212) 426-3000 .. **Brisbane,** Kamber L '00 Leg Aid -230 E 106th -NY 10029
(212) 503-7954 .. **Briscoe,** Colleen M '05 Bank of America -335 Mad Av -NY 10017
(212) 577-3688 .. **Briskey,** Mitchell J '88 %Leg Aid -199 Water -NY 10038 **Fx:**509-8431
(518) 842-2508 .. **Briskie,** Robt L '57 -214 Mannys Crnr Rd -Amsterdam 12010 **Fx:**842-2508
(212) 608-7778 .. **Briskin,** Peter E '06 (Fishbeyn & B,PC) -225 Bway -NY 10007 **Fx:**608-7779
(212) 975-4915 .. **Briskman,** Louis J '09 CBS Inc -51 W 52nd -NY 10019 **Fx:**975-3930
(212) 546-9255 .. **Brisman,** Yaacov M '05 %Scarinci H -107 Grand -NY 10013
(516) 683-8500 .. **Brissenden,** Matthew W '00 (Scaring & B,PLLC) -666 Old Cntry Rd -Gdn Cty 11530 **Fx:**683-8410
(212) 790-4500 .. **Brissette,** Renée '88 (Manatt P&P,LLP) -7 Times Sq -NY 10036
(212) 903-9000 .. **Brisson,** Jean-Philippe W '99 Cnsl Linklaters -1345 Av of Amer -NY 10105
(914) 769-1136 .. **Brisson,** John Phillips '86 (Brisson & B) -10 North Pl -Plsntvll 10570 **Fx:**769-5540
(914) 769-1136 .. **Brisson,** Robt Pierre '53 (Brisson & B) -10 North Pl -Plsntvll 10570 **Fx:**769-5540
(716) 853-3801 .. **Brister,** Richd C '07 Cnsl Kenney SL&N,LLP -14 Lafayette Sq -Buffalo 14203
(212) 788-1374 .. **Bristol,** Gary L '95 %Law Dept -100 Church -NY 10007 **Fx:**788-0367
(516) 409-6200 .. **Bristol,** Lauren B '87 %Furey KWM&C,PC -2174 Jackson Av -Seafrd 11783
(212) 735-3000 .. **Bristor,** Katherine M '81 (Skadden ASM&F LLP) -4 Times Sq -NY 10036
(212) 416-8648 .. **Bristow,** Wm H III '90 %Dept of Law -120 Bway -NY 10271
(845) 566-0015 .. **Brite,** Paul C '89 -1661 Route 300 -Newburgh 12550 **Fx:**566-0196
(212) 259-8000 .. **Britell,** Peter S '66 (Dewey & L LLP) -1301 Av of Amer -NY 10019
(631) 247-0404 .. **Briton,** Roger H '73 (Jackson L LLP) -58 S Srvc Rd -Melvll 11747
(718) 721-4837 .. **Britt,** Burl R III '84 -21-70 24th -Astoria 11105
(212) 363-3100 .. **Britt,** Kenneth O '05 %Bivona & C,PC -88 Pine -NY 10005
(212) 340-6175 .. **Britt,** Lynne M '07 Fortis Cptl Corp -520 Mad Av -NY 10022
(315) 471-8113 .. **Britt,** Patrick S '95 (McDermott & B,PC) -103 E Water -Syracuse 13202
(845) 496-1112 .. **Britt,** Phaedra '01 (Britt & T,PLLC) -290 Larkin Dr -Monroe 10950 **Fx:**496-1112
(516) 741-1717 .. **Britt,** Susan Fagen '85 (Hirsch B&M) -1225 Franklin Av -Gdn Cty 11530
(212) 225-2000 .. **Britt,** Tamara J '10 %Cleary GS&H -1 Lbrty Plz -NY 10006
(212) 909-6347 .. **Brittenham,** David A '86 (Debevoise & P LLP) -919 3rd Av -NY 10022
(315) 548-2011 .. **Britting,** John C '53 -30 Orchrd Pk -Phelps 14532
(718) 286-6000 .. **Brittle,** Kathryn M '10 %DA -125-01 Qns Blvd -Kew Gdns 11415
(585) 232-6500 .. **Britton,** A Paul '79 Cnsl Harter S&E LLP -1600 Bausch & Lomb Pl -Rchstr 14604
(718) 390-5464 .. **Britton,** Angela M '98 %Family Ct -100 Richmond Ter -Staten Isl 10301
(212) 836-8000 .. **Britton,** Christopher B '04 %Kaye S LLP -425 Park Av -NY 10022
(212) 349-2727 .. **Britton,** Gerard A '92 (Targum B&T,LLP) -233 Bway -NY 10279 **Fx:**672-0094
(212) 350-2700 .. **Britton,** Gerard J '91 OfCnsl Constantine C,PC -450 Lex Av -NY 10017
(212) 530-5000 .. **Britton,** John R '05 %Milbank TH&M LLP -1 Chase Manh Plz -NY 10005
(212) 848-4000 .. **Britton,** Robt A '08 %Shearman & S LLP -599 Lex Av -NY 10022
(646) 471-1000 .. **Britton,** Wayne M '07 PricewaterhouseCoopers LLP -300 Mad Av -NY 10017
(516) 496-2222 .. **Britvan,** Aaron '61 -7600 Jericho Tpk -Woodbury 11797 **Fx:**496-3450
(212) 556-2100 .. **Brivanlou,** Margaret Bolce '96 (King & S) -1185 Av of Amer -NY 10036
(212) 451-3838 .. **Brizel,** Michl A '81 Saks Inc -12 E 49th -NY 10017
(212) 687-1736 .. **Brizel,** Steven I '80 R Schwartzberg & Assoc,PLLC -60 E 42nd -NY 10165
(212) 268-1000 .. **Broach,** Judith P '76 (Broach & S,LLP) -1 Penn Plz -NY 10119
(212) 268-1000 .. **Broach & Stulberg,LLP** -1 Penn Plz -NY 10119 **Fx:**947-6010
(716) 856-4200 .. **Broad,** Sally J '96 (Gibson M&C,LLP) -69 Delaware Av -Buffalo 14202
(212) 474-1000 .. **Broad,** Trevor M '09 %Cravath S&M LLP -825 8th Av -NY 10019
(315) 724-3164 .. **Broadbent,** Michelle Elwood '07 %Kowalczyk TD&H,LLP -185 Genesee -Utica 13501
(718) 579-3000 .. **Broadie,** Kissa '04 Leg Aid -1020 Grnd Cncrs -Bronx 10451 **Fx:**588-2611
(212) 323-5012 .. **Broadrup,** Garrett C '02 OppenheimerFunds,Inc -225 Lbrty -NY 10281
(212) 446-4800 .. **Broadwater,** Brett J '09 %Kirkland & E LLP -153 E 53rd -NY 10022
(212) 577-7700 .. **Broadwin,** Jos L '55 %Safe Horizon -2 Lafayette -NY 10007 **Fx:**385-0331
(212) 576-7398 .. **Brobston,** Irena S '01 %NY Life Ins -51 Mad Av -NY 10010 **Fx:**447-0569
(631) 828-5831 .. **Brocato,** Christopher C '03 -713 Main -Pt Jffrsn 11777
(914) 517-5000 .. **Brocchini,** Lawr V '90 (Meiselman DPC&E,PC) -1311 Mamaroneck Av -White Plns 10605
(718) 392-0200 .. **Broccole,** Carmine J '92 Standard Motor Products -37-18 Nrthrn Blvd -LIC 11101
(212) 964-3855 .. **Broccolo,** Anthony '06 %R Cardali & Assoc,LLP -39 Bway -NY 10006 **Fx:**634-4856
(212) 468-4800 .. **Brochin,** Gregg L '02 %Davis & G LLP -1740 Bway -NY 10019
(212) 297-5800 .. **Brochin,** Heather Weine '02 Cnsl Day P LLP -7 Times Sq -NY 10036
(212) 373-3000 .. **Brochin,** James L '92 (Paul WRW&G LLP) -1285 Av of Amer -NY 10019
(516) 876-2319 .. **Brochin,** Lawr S '74 -355 Post Av -Westbury 11590 **Fx:**876-2652
(212) 613-5000 .. **Brochstein,** Phyllis R '72 Leg Assist Grp -450 W 33rd -NY 10001 **Fx:**750-0820
(518) 213-6000 .. **Brock,** Anthony J '91 %NYSUT -800 Troy-Schnctdy Rd -Latham 12110 **Fx:**213-6488
(212) 878-0000 .. **Brock,** Chas C '87 MTA -2 Penn Plz -NY 10121
(212) 517-5170 .. **Brock,** Chas L '70 (Brock Prtnrs) -765 Park Av -NY 10021
(716) 856-0600 .. **Brock,** David G '73 (Jaeckle F&M,LLP) -12 Fountain Plz -Buffalo 14202
(212) 903-8700 .. **Brock,** Gia G '06 %Roberts & H,LLP -825 8th Av -NY 10019
(716) 847-0650 .. **Brock,** Jorien L '04 Leg Srvcs -237 Main -Buffalo 14203 **Fx:**847-0227
(212) 558-4000 .. **Brock,** Mitchell '54 SrCnsl Sullivan & C LLP -125 Broad -NY 10004
(212) 836-8000 .. **Brock,** Piper A '85 Cnsl Kaye S LLP -425 Park Av -NY 10022
(516) 222-6200 .. **Brock,** Steven '79 (Berkman HPP&F,PC) -100 Grdn City Plz -Gdn Cty 11530
(607) 277-3995 .. **Brock,** Susan H '89 -12 Pheasant Way -Ithaca 14850 **Fx:**277-8042
(973) 596-4597 .. **Brock,** Suzanne Herrmann '06 %Gibbons PC -1 Penn Plz -NY 10119 **Fx:**639-6347
(212) 818-9200 .. **Brock,** Timothy T '85 (Satterlee SB&B LLP) -230 Park Av -NY 10169
(518) 374-6815 .. **Brockbank,** Michl T '75 -1494 Wendell Av -Schnctdy 12308 **Fx:**374-6805
(212) 849-7000 .. **Brockett,** Danl L '85 (Quinn EU&S,LLP) -51 Mad Av -NY 10010
(212) 357-0634 .. **Brockett,** Scott D '97 Goldman Sachs & Co -1 NY Plz -NY 10004
(585) 394-3758 .. **Brocklebank,** Derek G '98 (Brocklebank Law Firm) -51 N Main -Canandaigua 14424 **Fx:**394-3585
(585) 394-3758 .. **Brocklebank,** Richd G '60 OfCnsl Brocklebank Law Firm -51 N Main -Canandaigua 14424 **Fx:**394-3585
(212) 885-5000 .. **Brockman,** Alan J '57 SrCnsl Blank R LLP -405 Lex Av -NY 10174
(585) 374-6343 .. **Brockman,** Edw J '72 -159 S Main Bx457 -Naples 14512
(212) 840-6444 .. **Brockman,** Marvin '63 (Lipsky S&L,PC) -120 W 45th -NY 10036
(212) 223-4996 .. **Brocks,** Jason M '01 -14 E 60th -NY 10022
(518) 465-9313 .. **Brocks,** Kevin R '81 (Read and L,LLP) -25 Eagle -Albany 12207
(212) 776-2072 .. **Brocks,** Sarah R '01 %Coalition for the Homeless -129 Fulton -NY 10038
(516) 739-5100 .. **Brocks,** Wm R Jr. '94 (Farber B&Z LLP) -51 Charles -Mineola 11501
(212) 334-4800 .. **Brockway,** Barry J '84 -191 Canal -NY 10013 **Fx:**343-2597
(716) 854-7888 .. **Brockway,** Bryan G '79 (Venzon B,LLP) -300 Delaware Av -Buffalo 14202 **Fx:**854-0294
(212) 355-0346 .. **Brod,** Alan J '79 KLS Prof Advisors -111 5th Av -NY 10003 **Fx:**355-0413
(212) 848-4000 .. **Brod,** Benjamin G '10 Shearman & S LLP -599 Lex Av -NY 10022
(212) 225-2000 .. **Brod,** Craig B '81 (Cleary GS&H) -1 Lbrty Plz -NY 10006
(212) 593-1000 .. **Brod,** Ernest '62 %Kroll Assoc -1166 Av of Amer -NY 10036 **Fx:**593-2631
(212) 455-2000 .. **Brod,** Mark A '02 %Simpson T&B LLP -425 Lex Av -NY 10017
(518) 272-0580 .. **Broda,** Douglas J '86 -Bx239 -Troy 12182
(917) 923-9090 .. **Brodack,** Michl A '99 AXA Advisors,LLC -1633 Bway -NY 10019
(212) 813-0620 .. **Brodegaard,** Robt F '76 (Brodegaard & S,LLC) -110 E 59th -NY 10022 **Fx:**(646) 355-1920
(518) 457-4380 .. **Broden,** Kristen L '03 %Dept of Labor -State Campus Bldg 12 -Albany 12240 **Fx:**485-1819
(212) 244-2000 .. **Broder,** Aaron J '49 -350 5th Av -NY 10118 **Fx:**244-2006
(212) 455-2000 .. **Broder,** Amie N '08 %Simpson T&B LLP -425 Lex Av -NY 10017
(212) 244-2000 .. **Broder,** Deborah M '87 -350 5th Av -NY 10118 **Fx:**244-2006
(212) 536-3900 .. **Broder,** Douglas F '78 (K&L Gates LLP) -599 Lex Av -NY 10022
(585) 385-0893 .. **Broder,** Howard K '73 -Bx92561 -Rchstr 14692
(212) 940-8800 .. **Broder,** Kimberly L '06 %Katten MR LLP -575 Mad Av -NY 10022
(718) 923-6300 .. **Broder,** Melissa D '92 %Atty Grievance Comm -335 Adams -Brklyn 11201 **Fx:**624-2978
(212) 592-1400 .. **Broder,** Robt S '92 %Herrick,F LLP -2 Park Av -NY 10016
(516) 674-8285 .. **Broder,** Wm I '65 -109 Cmbrdg Ct -Glen Cove 11542 **Fx:**674-8376
(718) 447-1324 .. **Broderick,** Ann '95 %Law Dept -60 Bay -Staten Isl 10301 **Fx:**981-4459
(212) 403-1000 .. **Broderick,** Christina O '08 %Wachtell LR&K -51 W 52nd -NY 10019
(718) 830-0700 .. **Broderick,** David J '91 -70-20 Austin -Frst Hlls 11375
(212) 566-7188 .. **Broderick,** David K '08 %Genova B&G -115 Bway -NY 10006
(212) 610-6300 .. **Broderick,** David S '93 (Allen & O) -1221 Av of Amer -NY 10020
(212) 687-5353 .. **Broderick,** Edwin T '73 Williamson Pickett Gross Inc -51 E 42nd -NY 10017
(516) 921-8310 .. **Broderick,** James P '92 -32 Pine Rd -Syosset 11791 **Fx:**921-8310
(212) 297-5800 .. **Broderick,** Jane H '06 %Day P LLP -7 Times Sq -NY 10036
(516) 921-8310 .. **Broderick,** John J '61 -32 Pine Rd -Syosset 11791 **Fx:**921-8310
(518) 474-0571 .. **Broderick,** Kieran P '89 Ofc Gnl Srvcs -Corning Twr ESP -Albany 12242 **Fx:**473-4973
(516) 560-6400 .. **Broderick,** Lauren T '04 %Leg Aid -1 Helen Keller Way -Hempstd 11550 **Fx:**565-3694
(718) 229-6070 .. **Broderick,** Mark T '98 -42-40 Bell Blvd -Bayside 11361 **Fx:**224-2938
(718) 590-3668 .. **Broderick,** Patricia '78 Supreme Ct -851 Grnd Cncrs -Bronx 10451
(718) 229-6070 .. **Broderick,** Patrick F '67 -42-40 Bell Blvd -Bayside 11361 **Fx:**224-2938
(212) 698-3500 .. **Broderick,** Patrick G '98 %Dechert LLP -1095 Av of Amer -NY 10036
(212) 513-7788 .. **Broderick,** Peter F '69 (Ahmuty D&M) -123 William -NY 10038
(914) 686-4800 .. **Broderick,** Sean M '98 %Harrington O&M,LLP -81 Main -White Plns 10601
(212) 310-8000 .. **Broderick,** Vernon S '89 (Weil G&M LLP) -767 5th Av -NY 10153
(716) 285-6953 .. **Broderick,** Wm D '63 (Rice RB&W) -800 Main Bx219 -Niagara Fls 14302
(716) 285-6953 .. **Broderick,** Wm D Jr. '92 %Rice RB&W -800 Main Bx219 -Niagara Fls 14302
(212) 528-1340 .. **Broderick,** Wm M '76 -7 Dey -NY 10007
(212) 697-3122 .. **Broderson,** Jeanne R '05 %Martin C&B LLP -220 E 42nd -NY 10017
(212) 373-3000 .. **Brodhead,** David C '60 OfCnsl Paul WRW&G LLP -1285 Av of Amer -NY 10019
(212) 764-4044 .. **Brodherson,** Alan S '90 -36 W 44th -NY 10036
(914) 323-7000 .. **Brodie,** Alice L '08 %Wilson EME&D LLP -3 Gannett Dr -White Plns 10604
(212) 735-3000 .. **Brodie,** Bradley H '10 %Skadden ASM&F LLP -4 Times Sq -NY 10036
(212) 858-1000 .. **Brodie,** Fredk A '89 (Pillsbury WSP LLP) -1540 Bway -NY 10036
(518) 862-1090 .. **Brodie,** Hal '82 NYSERDA -17 Columbia Cir -Albany 12203 **Fx:**862-1091
(718) 522-0666 .. **Brodie,** Jordan B '89 (Sanders G&B,PC) -26 Court -Brklyn 11242

(718) 254-6277 .. **Brodie,** Margo K '92 %US Atty -271 Cadman Plz E -Brklyn 11201 **Fx:**254-6479
(212) 788-8861 .. **Brodie,** Nancy F '79 %Law Dept -100 Church -NY 10007 **Fx:**788-0367
(212) 592-1400 .. **Brodie,** Stephen D '76 (Herrick,F LLP) -2 Park Av -NY 10016
(212) 362-6336 .. **Brodlieb,** Barbara S '81 -1 Sherman Sq -NY 10023 **Fx:**874-5825
(718) 239-7110 .. **Brodman,** David M '97 -627 Lydig Av -Bronx 10462
(845) 228-1400 .. **Brodnick,** Andrew D '86 Cnsl Camarda Rlty Invstmnts -1699 Route 6 -Carmel 10512
(212) 374-6044 .. **Brodnicki,** Catherine A '04 %NYC Dept Educ -52 Chmbrs -NY 10007
(212) 259-8000 .. **Brodnicki,** Paul J II '04 %Dewey & L LLP -1301 Av of Amer -NY 10019
(212) 449-1731 .. **Brodoff,** Jennifer N '01 Merrill Lynch -4 World Fncl Ctr -NY 10080
(212) 977-9700 .. **Brodrick,** R Brian '82 (Phillips N LLP) -666 5th Av -NY 10103
(516) 741-3060 .. **Brodrick,** Robt H '60 (Moran B&E) -300 Grdn City Plz -Gdn Cty 11530
(212) 319-1900 .. **Brodsky,** Adam H '01 %Berger & W,LLP -1633 Bway -NY 10019
(212) 750-8200 .. **Brodsky,** Adam M '99 (Hakim Org) -3 W 57th -NY 10019 **Fx:**421-3241
(516) 572-7809 .. **Brodsky,** Alla '06 Nassau Community Cllg -1 Educ Dr -Gdn Cty 11530
(718) 250-2000 .. **Brodsky,** Beth A '09 %DA -350 Jay -Brklyn 11201 **Fx:**250-2314
(845) 928-2190 .. **Brodsky,** David A '84 -45 Florance Dr -Centrl Vly 10917 **Fx:**928-5805
(212) 225-2000 .. **Brodsky,** David E '85 (Cleary GS&H) -1 Lbrty Plz -NY 10006
(212) 906-1200 .. **Brodsky,** David M '68 (Latham & W) -885 3rd Av -NY 10022
(212) 374-7954 .. **Brodsky,** David M '94 %NYC Dept of Ed -52 Chmbrs -NY 10007
(716) 434-0024 .. **Brodsky,** Felice A '94 -125B Prof Pkwy Bx557 -Lockprt 14095 **Fx:**434-0046
(718) 491-6400 .. **Brodsky & Gordina,PC** -539 86th -Brklyn 11209 **Fx:**491-6318
(212) 687-2220 .. **Brodsky,** Grace L '62 -60 E 42nd -NY 10165
(718) 591-6900 .. **Brodsky,** Jeffrey P '90 %Ginsberg & K -77-53 Main -Flushng 11367
(212) 355-8555 .. **Brodsky,** Jodi S '89 Cnsl Potters & D LLP -546 5th Av -NY 10036
(212) 373-3000 .. **Brodsky,** Joshua I '06 %Paul WRW&G LLP -1285 Av of Amer -NY 10019
(718) 332-5125 .. **Brodsky,** Judith T '89 -2790 Bragg -Brklyn 11235
(212) 577-3300 .. **Brodsky,** Katherine A '07 %Leg Aid -199 Water -NY 10038
(212) 613-5000 .. **Brodsky,** Kirsten K '05 Leg Assist Grp -450 W 33rd -NY 10001 **Fx:**750-0820
(718) 254-7000 .. **Brodsky,** Leslie '82 %US Atty -271 Cadman Plz E -Brklyn 11201 **Fx:**254-6479
(212) 753-7500 .. **Brodsky,** Marc S '97 (Hartman & C LLP) -488 Mad Av -NY 10022
(212) 506-2999 .. **Brodsky,** Mark D '78 %Stonington Mgt Corp -712 5th Av -NY 10019
(516) 571-3800 .. **Brodsky,** Marta '04 %DA -262 Old Cntry Rd -Mineola 11501 **Fx:**248-9479
(718) 491-6400 .. **Brodsky,** Merrick J '89 (Brodsky & G,PC) -539 86th -Brklyn 11209
(212) 523-2162 .. **Brodsky,** Nina '85 %Beth Israel Med Ctr -555 W 57th -NY 10019
(914) 381-2525 .. **Brodsky & Peck** -550 Mamaroneck Av -Harrison 10528 **Fx:**381-6331
(212) 833-5391 .. **Brodsky,** Peter S '91 SONY -550 Mad Av -NY 10022
(212) 637-2492 .. **Brodsky,** Reed M '98 %US Atty -1 St Andrews Plz -NY 10007
(914) 381-2525 .. **Brodsky,** Robt A '82 (Brodsky & P) -550 Mamaroneck Av -Harrison 10528
(212) 346-1274 .. **Brodsky,** Stephen '82 Pace Univ Cnsl -156 William -NY 10038 **Fx:**346-1682
(212) 223-3900 .. **Brodsky,** Stephen L '94 SrCnsl Zwerling S&Z,LLP -41 Mad Av -NY 10010
(646) 827-8702 .. **Brodsky,** Steven C '97 -11 Penn Plz -NY 10001
(212) 532-8100 .. **Brodsky,** Tamarah E '02 %Stern & M,LLP -115 Bway -NY 10006
(212) 480-4800 .. **Brodsky,** Wm M '76 (Fox H&C LLP) -825 3rd Av -NY 10022
(718) 286-6000 .. **Brodt,** Sharon Y '94 %DA -125-01 Qns Blvd -Kew Gdns 11415 **Fx:**286-6930
(212) 720-3700 .. **Brodwin,** Randolph M '92 %Foot Locker,Inc -112 W 34th -NY 10120 **Fx:**720-4116
(212) 687-7230 .. **Brody,** Aaron L '96 Stull S&B -6 E 45th -NY 10017
(212) 679-7007 .. **Brody Benard & Branch LLP** -205 Lex Av -NY 10016 **Fx:**679-7123
(718) 643-5262 .. **Brody,** Chas '73 %Surrogates Ct -2 Johnson -Brklyn 11201
(516) 681-1100 .. **Brody,** Danl H '07 %Kaufman DV&G,LLP -135 Crsswys Park Dr -Woodbury 11797
(212) 335-4143 .. **Brody,** Danl S '09 %DA -1 Hogan Pl -NY 10013
(716) 633-5432 .. **Brody,** David A '80 -5547 Main -Williamsvll 14221
(212) 431-1300 .. **Brody,** David R '80 (Borah GAN&G PC) -377 Bway -NY 10013
(516) 932-5700 .. **Brody,** Denis '67 (D Brody,PC) -998 Old Cntry Rd -Plainvw 11803 **Fx:**932-5725
(212) 773-6297 .. **Brody,** Douglas M '98 %Ernst & Young LLP -5 Times Sq -NY 10036
(212) 461-2337 .. **Brody,** Elizabeth Diane '02 -44 Wall -NY 10005
(212) 903-8712 .. **Brody,** Ellen Seiler '95 (Roberts & H,LLP) -825 8th Av -NY 10019
(845) 338-7494 .. **Brody,** Jeffrey M '73 (J Brody & Assoc) -236 Clinton Av Bx4116 -Kingston 12402 **Fx:**338-7497
(212) 983-1545 .. **Brody,** Joan P '78 -75 Rckfllr Plz -NY 10019
(212) 715-9100 .. **Brody,** Joshua K '03 %Kramer LN&F,LLP -1177 Av of Amer -NY 10036
(212) 687-7230 .. **Brody,** Jules '64 Stull S&B -6 E 45th -NY 10017
(212) 414-9161 .. **Brody,** Lauren Reiter '80 (Brody & B LLP) -1 Penn Plz -NY 10119
(914) 683-5414 .. **Brody,** Leslie Ann '84 Career Strategies Intl -19 Court -White Plns 10601 **Fx:**683-5456
(212) 574-1200 .. **Brody,** Mark A '88 (Seward & K LLP) -1 Bttry Pk Plz -NY 10004
(518) 474-9717 .. **Brody,** Mark D '82 %Dept of Law -The Cptl -Albany 12224
(212) 679-7007 .. **Brody,** Neil '75 (Brody B&B LLP) -205 Lex Av -NY 10016
(631) 261-7778 .. **Brody O'Connor & O'Connor** -7 Bayview Av -Northprt 11768 **Fx:**261-6411
(212) 233-2505 .. **Brody O'Connor & O'Connor** -111 John -NY 10038 **Fx:**233-2506
(212) 206-6011 .. **Brody,** Philip S '82 %Time Equities Inc -55 5th Av -NY 10003 **Fx:**727-0563
(212) 216-1206 .. **Brody,** Reed K '79 %Human Rights Watch -350 5th Av -NY 10118 **Fx:**736-1300
(212) 564-7399 .. **Brody,** Robt G '89 Brody & Assoc,LLC -110 Wall -NY 10005 **Fx:**(203) 965-0569
(212) 819-8200 .. **Brody,** Ronald S '88 (White & C LLP) -1155 Av of Amer -NY 10036
(212) 233-2505 .. **Brody,** Scott A '85 (Brody O&O) -111 John -NY 10038
(212) 705-7000 .. **Brody,** Steven G '87 (Bingham M LLP) -399 Park Av -NY 10022
(518) 429-4200 .. **Brody,** Stuart H '87 OfCnsl Hiscock & B,LLP -50 Beaver -Albany 12207
(914) 428-7124 .. **Brody,** Susanne B '88 %Fed Def of NY Inc -300 Quarropas -White Plns 10601 **Fx:**997-6872
(212) 336-0080 .. **Brody,** Todd D '95 %SEC -3 World Fncl Ctr -NY 10281 **Fx:**336-1323
(212) 687-7230 .. **Brody,** Tzivia '96 Stull S&B -6 E 45th -NY 10017
(631) 847-5445 .. **Brody,** Wayne M '81 Arrow Electronics -50 Marcus Dr -Melvll 11747 **Fx:**847-5458
(516) 248-2727 .. **Brodzansky,** Karl '83 -300 Grdn City Plz -Gdn Cty 11530 **Fx:**248-6929
(212) 902-9690 .. **Broeckel,** Janet A '91 Goldman Sachs -1 NY Plz -NY 10004
(212) 735-3000 .. **Broer,** Paul H '09 %Skadden ASM&F LLP -4 Times Sq -NY 10036
(212) 598-8000 .. **Broer,** Stephen H '04 %Guardian Life Ins -7 Hanover Sq -NY 10004 **Fx:**919-2693
(516) 627-7000 .. **Brofman,** Michl D '79 (Weiss & Z,PC) -3333 New Hyde Pk Rd -New Hyde Pk 11042
(212) 603-6300 .. **Brog,** Avron I '57 (Robinson BLGG&G PC) -875 3rd Av -NY 10022
(718) 694-1820 .. **Brogan,** Danielle T '06 %Transit Auth -130 Lvngstn -Brklyn 11201 **Fx:**694-5726
(718) 250-2000 .. **Brogan,** Denis T '03 %DA -350 Jay -Brklyn 11201 **Fx:**250-2314
(212) 906-1200 .. **Brogan,** Kevin J '07 %Latham & W -885 3rd Av -NY 10022
(212) 588-0800 .. **Brogan,** Marilyn Matthes '83 (Frommer L&H LLP) -745 5th Av -NY 10151
(914) 391-6700 .. **Brogan,** Peter '77 %Judicial Title -800 Wstchstr Av -Rye Brook 10573
(718) 468-6100 .. **Brogdon,** Gerard E '02 (Brogdon & B LLP) -205-20 Jamaica Av -Hollis 11423 **Fx:**468-6110
(845) 294-7200 .. **Broge,** Brett A '07 Lerch S LLP -140 Main -Goshen 10924
(212) 223-6444 .. **Broggi,** Donald A '10 Scott +S,LLP -500 5th Av -NY 10110 **Fx:**223-6334
(518) 435-1770 .. **Brogoch,** Carla A '05 Womans Bar Assn Legal Proj -6 Exec Park Dr -Albany 12203
(917) 778-6500 .. **Broido,** Gregory W '99 %K Dodson -485 Lex Av -NY 10017
(212) 850-4317 .. **Broido,** Michl W '68 Emigrant Bk/Emigrant Realty Fnc -6 E 43rd -NY 10017
(585) 987-2800 .. **Broikos,** Gregory G '93 (Woods OG LLP) -2 State -Rchstr 14614
(585) 546-5530 .. **Broikos,** Philip V '99 %Thomson West -50 E Broad -Rchstr 14694
(212) 980-1000 .. **Broitman,** Elana '92 %UJA Federation -130 E 59th -NY 10022
(212) 681-0600 .. **Broitman,** Joshua S '94 (Ostrager CF&B,PC) -570 Lex Av -NY 10022
(212) 688-5151 .. **Brokate,** Brian W '80 (Gibney A&F,LLP) -665 5th Av -NY 10022
(631) 283-2233 .. **Brokaw,** Clifford V III '57 -Bx5002 -Southampton 11969 **Fx:**283-7773
(212) 632-6000 .. **Brokaw,** George R '95 %Lazard Freres -30 Rckfllr Plz -NY 10112 **Fx:**632-6060
(212) 752-5258 .. **Brollesy,** Hany S '95 Cnsl Schwartz SE&C LLC -845 3rd Av -NY 10022
(212) 248-7906 .. **Bromberg,** Brian L '92 (Bromberg Law Ofc,PC) -40 Exch Pl -NY 10005 **Fx:**248-7908
(212) 957-7600 .. **Bromberg,** Karen H '88 (Cohen & G LLP) -800 3rd Av -NY 10022
(212) 209-4800 .. **Bromberg,** Katherine S '03 %Brown R LLP -7 Times Sq -NY 10036
(212) 537-3355 .. **Bromberg,** Laurence J '92 Morgan Stanley -1633 Bway -NY 10019
(212) 265-6888 .. **Bromberg,** Lisa M '85 (Porzio B&N,PC) -156 W 56th -NY 10019
(212) 635-1985 .. **Bromberg,** Matthew J '00 Bk of NY Mellon -1 Wall -NY 10286
(212) 265-6888 .. **Bromberg,** Myron J '81 OfCnsl Porzio B&N,PC -156 W 56th -NY 10019
(516) 560-6400 .. **Bromberg,** Nicole V '05 Leg Aid -1 Helen Keller Way -Hempstd 11550 **Fx:**565-3694
(646) 386-3629 .. **Bromberg,** Roy G '86 %Supreme Ct-Law Dept -60 Centre -NY 10007
(646) 722-8500 .. **Bromberg,** Talja T '06 %Grant & E,PA -485 Lex Av -NY 10017
(212) 479-6000 .. **Bromfeld,** Andrea C '96 %Cooley LLP -1114 Av of Amer -NY 10036
(516) 742-0707 .. **Bromfeld,** Jeffrey B '94 %Sullivan PBM&C PC -55 Mineola Blvd -Mineola 11501
(212) 458-7016 .. **Bromfield,** Lise A '98 AIG -175 Water -NY 10038
(516) 295-4301 .. **Bromley,** Ira J '77 -610 Oaklnd Av -Cedarhrst 11516 **Fx:**295-4399
(212) 225-2000 .. **Bromley,** James L '90 (Cleary GS&H) -1 Lbrty Plz -NY 10006
(212) 909-6000 .. **Bromley,** Kyra K '94 Cnsl Debevoise & P LLP -919 3rd Av -NY 10022
(212) 964-3502 .. **Bromsen,** Ellen K '82 -11 Park Pl -NY 10007 **Fx:**(201) 894-1120
(212) 859-8000 .. **Bromwich,** Michl R '05 (Fried FHS&J LLP) -1 NY Plz -NY 10004
(212) 310-8000 .. **Bronder,** Vigdis '08 %Weil G&M LLP -767 5th Av -NY 10153
(914) 285-0700 .. **Brondo,** Edwin T Jr. '06 %Renzulli Law Firm,LLP -81 Main -White Plns 10601 **Fx:**285-1213
(212) 608-1686 .. **Bronfeld,** Alan M '04 Bronfeld & Assoc -225 Bway -NY 10007 **Fx:**(646) 356-7047
(212) 631-7436 .. **Bronfeld,** Allen S '89 (Bronfeld & S) -352 7th Av -NY 10001 **Fx:**379-8311
(718) 250-2000 .. **Bronfeld,** Ian '06 DA -350 Jay -Brklyn 11201 **Fx:**250-2314
(212) 759-3300 .. **Bronfman,** Leonid '05 %Dornbush SS&V,LLP -747 3rd Av -NY 10017
(212) 583-9600 .. **Bronfman,** Meredith L '09 %Littler M,PC -900 3rd Av -NY 10022
(718) 238-6800 .. **Bronfman,** Zina '03 %DiConza LD&K -478 Bay Ridge Pkwy -Brklyn 11209
(585) 454-2000 .. **Brongo,** Wm J '77 %Brenna B&B,PLLC -31 E Main -Rchstr 14614
(585) 475-1100 .. **Bronk,** Danl A '92 Segar & S -400 Meridian Centre -Rchstr 14618
(914) 347-2600 .. **Bronk,** Megan E '02 %Traub LS&S LLP -7 Skyline Dr -Hawthorne 10532
(631) 582-3700 .. **Bronnberg,** Diana P '01 %Turley RR&R,LLP -3075 Vets Mem'l Hwy -Ronkonkoma 11779
(212) 907-9600 .. **Bronner,** Caitlin L '07 %Ingram YGC&B,LLP -250 Park Av -NY 10177
(212) 335-9000 .. **Bronner,** George D '04 %DA -1 Hogan Pl -NY 10013
(212) 529-7002 .. **Bronner,** Leonard E '89 -95 Delancey -NY 10002 **Fx:**677-2900
(716) 842-5837 .. **Bronson,** Arthur J '87 %M&T Bk -1 M & T Plz -Buffalo 14203 **Fx:**842-5376
(716) 635-9550 .. **Bronson,** H Bruce Jr. '80 (Bronson & M,LLP) -415 Lawrence Bell Dr -Williamsvll 14221 **Fx:**635-9556

(212) 594-5300 .. **Bronson,** Kent A '99 (Milberg LLP) -1 Penn Plz -NY 10119
(212) 682-7474 .. **Bronson,** Matthew B '08 %Foley & L LLP -90 Park Av -NY 10016
(646) 855-1492 .. **Bronson,** Regina '00 Bank of Amer Securities LLC -1 Bryant Pk -NY 10036
(212) 863-8202 .. **Bronson,** Susan C '03 HPD -100 Gold -NY 10038
(718) 261-5235 .. **Bronstein,** Caryn '85 -108-18 Qns Blvd -Frst Hlls 11375
(212) 770-1047 .. **Bronstein,** Glen M '87 AIG -80 Pine -NY 10005
(516) 338-7520 .. **Bronstein,** Joshua R '04 %Daniels & N,PC -900 Merchants Cncrs -Westbury 11590
(212) 697-6484 .. **Bronstein,** Peretz '86 (Bronstein G&G,LLC) -60 E 42nd -NY 10165 **Fx:**697-0877
(212) 956-8300 .. **Bronstein,** Peter E '68 (Bronstein Van V LLC) -650 Mad Av -NY 10022
(212) 373-3000 .. **Bronstein,** Richd J '77 (Paul WRW&G LLP) -1285 Av of Amer -NY 10019
(631) 234-0080 .. **Bronstein,** Richd M '69 -14 Cornwallis Rd -E Setauket 11733 **Fx:**232-1758
(212) 956-8300 .. **Bronstein Van Veen LLC** -650 Mad Av -NY 10022 **Fx:**644-0574
(212) 237-1000 .. **Bronster,** Bruce F '93 (Windels ML&M,LLP) -156 W 56th -NY 10019
(518) 373-9000 .. **Bronsther,** Brian H '86 -930 Route 146 -Clifton Pk 12065 **Fx:**373-9042
(212) 883-4942 .. **Bronston,** David E '86 (Cozen O) -277 Park Av -NY 10172 **Fx:**672-1142
(212) 573-7297 .. **Bronzo,** John F '75 %Pfizer Inc -235 E 42nd -NY 10017
(212) 530-5000 .. **Brook,** Anna '08 %Milbank TH&M LLP -1 Chase Manh Plz -NY 10005
(212) 801-2197 .. **Brook,** Brian C '06 %Greenberg T,LLP -200 Park Av -NY 10166
(212) 943-1090 .. **Brook,** Danl L '01 %Gair GCSMB&R -80 Pine -NY 10005
(212) 460-2117 .. **Brook,** Helman R '70 Con Ed -4 Irving Pl -NY 10003
(212) 449-1485 .. **Brook,** Jonathan E '98 Merrill Lynch -4 World Fncl Ctr -NY 10080
(212) 277-4000 .. **Brook,** Lara V '04 %Freshfields BD LLP -520 Mad Av -NY 10022
(212) 239-4999 .. **Brook,** Richd A '92 (Meyer SE&K,PC) -1350 Bway Bx822 -NY 10018
(516) 944-5700 .. **Brook,** Richd E '76 R Brook,PC -8 Maple -Pt Wash 11050 **Fx:**944-5799
(516) 741-8400 .. **Brook,** Richd S '67 -114 Old Cntry Rd -Mineola 11501
(631) 289-4600 .. **Brooke,** John P '07 %Jacoby & J -1737 N Ocean Av -Medfrd 11763 **Fx:**654-5095
(845) 454-2540 .. **Brooke,** Saml P '74 (Brooke & B,LLP) -31 Cllgvw Av -Poughkeepsie 12603 **Fx:**454-2542
(585) 458-0310 .. **Brooker,** James G '91 -1347 Lyell Av -Rchstr 14606
(212) 373-3000 .. **Brooker,** Katharine E G '08 %Paul WRW&G LLP -1285 Av of Amer -NY 10019
(212) 264-0657 .. **Brookes,** Debra C '99 %US DOJ Antitrust Div -26 Fed Plz Ste 3630 -NY 10278
(315) 461-4277 .. **Brookins,** Claire T '99 OfCnsl Falge & M,PC -3300 Vickery Rd -N Syracuse 13212
(212) 801-9200 .. **Brookins,** Irene Lippa '07 %Greenberg T,LLP -200 Park Av -NY 10166
(212) 758-4200 .. **Brookman,** Michl D '62 (Brookman & B,PC) -480 Park Av -NY 10022 **Fx:**753-1319
(212) 574-1200 .. **Brookman,** Seth A '06 %Seward & K LLP -1 Bttry Pk Plz -NY 10004
(516) 227-6300 .. **Brookmeyer,** Philip R '80 %Ettelman & H,PC -100 Q Roosevelt Blvd -Gdn Cty 11530
(516) 222-6200 .. **Brookmeyer,** Stephen J '83 (Berkman HPP&F,PC) -100 Grdn City Plz -Gdn Cty 11530
(212) 808-0800 .. **Brookoff,** Bruce M '86 %D Skrilow -551 5th Av -NY 10176 **Fx:**808-0807
(212) 819-8683 .. **Brooks,** Aaron T '04 -1155 Av of Amer -NY 10036 **Fx:**354-8113
(518) 474-5490 .. **Brooks,** Albert W '85 %State Comptroller -110 State -Albany 12236 **Fx:**473-9104
(212) 318-6000 .. **Brooks,** Barry A '90 (Paul HJ&W LLP) -75 E 55th -NY 10022
(212) 272-6601 .. **Brooks,** Brant '94 JP Morgan Chase -383 Mad Av -NY 10179
(212) 735-3000 .. **Brooks,** Bryan A '07 %Skadden ASM&F LLP -4 Times Sq -NY 10036
(718) 590-2000 .. **Brooks,** Candace C '04 %DA -198 E 161st -Bronx 10451 **Fx:**590-6477
(718) 250-0400 .. **Brooks,** Charmaine '97 %R Tusa -1 MetroTech Ctr -Brklyn 11201 **Fx:**250-0591
(914) 347-2600 .. **Brooks,** Chevon Andre '06 %Traub LS&S LLP -7 Skyline Dr -Hawthorne 10532
(718) 232-6525 .. **Brooks,** Dana '97 -33 Bay 22nd -Brklyn 11214
(212) 973-8000 .. **Brooks,** Danl J '74 (Schnader HS&L LLP) -140 Bway -NY 10005
(973) 596-4719 .. **Brooks,** David A '99 %Gibbons PC -1 Penn Plz -NY 10119 **Fx:**639-8342
(212) 318-6000 .. **Brooks,** David M '95 (Paul HJ&W LLP) -75 E 55th -NY 10022
(212) 798-6100 .. **Brooks,** David N '97 Fortress Invstmnt Grp LLC -1345 Av of Amer -NY 10105
(212) 486-1400 .. **Brooks & Distler** -110 E 59th -NY 10022 **Fx:**486-2266
(212) 574-1200 .. **Brooks,** Douglas J '05 %Seward & K LLP -1 Bttry Pk Plz -NY 10004
(212) 264-0300 .. **Brooks,** Eric H '93 %NLRB -26 Fed Plz -NY 10278 **Fx:**264-8427
(212) 458-1204 .. **Brooks,** Faye D '83 %AIG -175 Water -NY 10038 **Fx:**458-1259
(212) 277-6500 .. **Brooks,** Fredric M '93 Cnsl Dickstein S LLP -1633 Bway -NY 10019
(212) 878-8000 .. **Brooks,** Gary A '94 (Clifford C LLP) -31 W 52nd -NY 10019
(212) 709-1641 .. **Brooks,** Gene C '80 %Banking Dept -1 State -NY 10004 **Fx:**709-1655
(212) 839-5300 .. **Brooks,** George H '08 %Sidley A LLP -787 7th Av -NY 10019
(212) 245-7300 .. **Brooks,** Gregory W '06 %Serling R&F,LLP -119 5th Av -NY 10003
(212) 578-2211 .. **Brooks,** Helen A '83 %MetLife -27-01 Qns Plz N -LIC 11101
(212) 722-2000 .. **Brooks,** J Lorch '78 %Leg Aid -230 E 106th -NY 10029 **Fx:**876-5365
(518) 523-1555 .. **Brooks,** James M '67 J Brooks -72 Olympic Dr -Lk Placid 12946 **Fx:**523-4486
(914) 636-8900 .. **Brooks,** Jason '07 %McCabe W&C,PC -145 Huguenot -New Rchll 10801
(212) 735-8600 .. **Brooks,** Jeffrey D '98 %Morrison C LLP -909 3rd Av -NY 10022
(914) 367-0111 .. **Brooks,** Jill L '81 -500 Mamaroneck Av -Harrison 10528
(516) 338-0533 .. **Brooks,** Joel L '83 (J Brooks & Assoc,PC) -25 S Srvc Rd -Jericho 11753
(516) 229-9400 .. **Brooks,** Jon S '85 (Phillips N LLP) -600 Old Cntry Rd -Gdn Cty 11530
(212) 977-9700 .. **Brooks,** Jon S '85 (Phillips N LLP) -666 5th Av -NY 10103
(631) 962-2000 .. **Brooks,** Jonathan B '02 OSI Pharm,Inc -41 Pinelawn Rd -Melvll 11747 **Fx:**752-3880
(212) 759-9585 .. **Brooks,** Jordan M '07 %Citak & C -270 Mad Av -NY 10016
(212) 446-4800 .. **Brooks,** Justin S '09 %Kirkland & E LLP -153 E 53rd -NY 10022
(716) 938-9133 .. **Brooks,** Kameron K G '78 -207 Court -Little Vly 14755
(212) 416-8514 .. **Brooks,** Katherine S '79 %Dept of Law -120 Bway -NY 10271
(516) 538-7100 .. **Brooks,** Katrina R '94 Town of Hempstead -200 N Franklin -Hempstd 11550
(212) 554-1234 .. **Brooks,** Kermitt J '90 AXA Financial Inc -1290 Av of Amer -NY 10104 **Fx:**707-3963
(212) 530-5000 .. **Brooks,** LaTonya D '09 %Milbank TH&M LLP -1 Chase Manh Plz -NY 10005
(631) 632-8521 .. **Brooks,** Lauren B '09 %Ctr for Biotech -SUNY at Stony Brook -Stony Brk 11794 **Fx:**632-8577
(212) 336-2000 .. **Brooks,** Lia M '09 %Patterson BW&T LLP -1133 Av of Amer -NY 10036
(212) 980-0120 .. **Brooks,** Lia N '04 %Frankfurt KK&S,PC -488 Mad Av -NY 10022
(646) 386-3626 .. **Brooks,** Lyle D '88 %Supreme Ct-Law Dept -60 Centre -NY 10007
(585) 672-2600 .. **Brooks,** M Sue '05 OfCnsl Burns & S LLP -28 E Main -Rchstr 14614 **Fx:**(866) 825-7217
(212) 486-1400 .. **Brooks,** Marsha S '75 (Brooks & D) -110 E 59th -NY 10022
(716) 433-5907 .. **Brooks,** Matthew E '95 (Seaman JH&B,LLP) -76 West Av -Lockprt 14094
(212) 710-3900 .. **Brooks,** Matthew P '10 Clyde & Co US LLP -405 Lex Av -NY 10174 **Fx:**710-3950
(845) 883-5539 .. **Brooks,** Maureen '95 -25 Faro Ln Bx367 -Clintondale 12515
(914) 241-7817 .. **Brooks,** Michl P '91 %Brooks Org -61 Crow Hill Rd -Mt Kisco 10549
(212) 715-9100 .. **Brooks,** Michl T '06 %Kramer LN&F,LLP -1177 Av of Amer -NY 10036
(212) 455-2000 .. **Brooks,** Michera N '10 %Simpson T&B LLP -425 Lex Av -NY 10017
(212) 245-1000 .. **Brooks,** Molly A '05 %Outten & G LLP -3 Park Av -NY 10016
(646) 641-1829 .. **Brooks,** Peter L '89 Brooksie -37 Wall -NY 10005
(212) 474-1000 .. **Brooks,** Roger G '89 (Cravath S&M LLP) -825 8th Av -NY 10019
(212) 594-5300 .. **Brooks,** Ross B '99 (Milberg LLP) -1 Penn Plz -NY 10119
(212) 310-8000 .. **Brooks,** Russell B '10 %Weil G&M LLP -767 5th Av -NY 10153
(800) 854-6011 .. **Brooks,** Sherri J '04 METLIFE -31 British Amer Blvd -Latham 12110
(716) 938-9133 .. **Brooks,** Stephen E '02 -207 Court -Little Vly 14755
(646) 865-1541 .. **Brooks,** Stephen G '81 %NYS IOLA -11 E 44th -NY 10017
(716) 852-1544 .. **Brooks,** Stephen P '87 (Smith M&S,LLC) -786 Ellicott Sq Bldg -Buffalo 14203
(716) 938-9133 .. **Brooks,** Teddar S '74 -207 Court -Little Vly 14755 **Fx:**938-6155
(631) 761-7000 .. **Brooks,** Wm M '80 %Touro Cllg Law Ctr -225 Eastvw Dr -Central Islip 11722
(212) 294-6700 .. **Brooksher,** Anne A '07 %Winston & S -200 Park Av -NY 10166
(646) 292-3511 .. **Brooks-Rigolosi,** Robin M '03 RBR Realty -376 Bway -NY 10013
(212) 541-2000 .. **Brooks Rincón,** Carolyn K '06 %Bryan C LLP -1290 Av of Amer -NY 10104
(212) 227-4226 .. **Broome,** Alvin H '73 (A Broome & Assoc,PC) -225 Bway -NY 10007 **Fx:**608-0101
(212) 689-4670 .. **Broome,** Bernard H '84 -386 Park Av S -NY 10016 **Fx:**545-9016
(718) 263-3790 .. **Broome,** Bernard L '54 B Broome,PC -123-12 82nd Av -Kew Gdns 11415 **Fx:**263-3933
(212) 849-7000 .. **Broome,** Stephen A '07 %Quinn EU&S,LLP -51 Mad Av -NY 10010
(718) 493-6339 .. **Broomfield,** Archibald H '60 -868 Nostrand Av -Brklyn 11225
(212) 877-6502 .. **Broomfield,** Michl A '68 -15 W 81st -NY 10024
(212) 324-8758 .. **Brophy,** Aileen B '07 %Rainbow Media -11 Penn Plz -NY 10001
(914) 946-3700 .. **Brophy,** Jos J '74 (McCarthy F LLP) -11 Martine Av -White Plns 10606
(845) 225-8466 .. **Brophy,** Patrick J '73 Legal Aid Soc -20 Fair -Carmel 10512 **Fx:**225-0517
(212) 747-1230 .. **Brophy,** Patrick Walsh '92 (McMahon M&G LLP) -55 Washington -Brklyn 11201
(631) 852-2500 .. **Brosco,** Patricia L '88 %DA -200 Center Dr -Rvrhead 11901 **Fx:**852-1769
(631) 454-8282 .. **Broscritto,** Anthony Jr. '87 -534 Broadhllw Rd -Melvll 11747 **Fx:**420-1030
(631) 439-4200 .. **Brosdal,** Mary L '99 %R Tusa -898 Vets Mem'l Hwy -Hauppauge 11788 **Fx:**439-4292
(212) 839-5300 .. **Brose,** Jonathan P '96 (Sidley A LLP) -787 7th Av -NY 10019
(212) 327-7340 .. **Brosgol,** David S '96 Rockerfeller University -1230 York Av -NY 10065
(585) 263-1000 .. **Broshears,** Timothy S '03 %Nixon P LLP -1100 Clinton Sq -Rchstr 14604
(212) 661-0065 .. **Brosius,** Martha J '03 (Brosius & Assoc,PC) -420 Lex Av -NY 10170 **Fx:**661-0601
(212) 415-6500 .. **Brosnahan,** Martina A '02 American Realty Capital -405 Park Av -NY 10022
(631) 661-8631 .. **Brosnahan,** Patrick K Jr. '75 -73 W Main -Babylon 11702 **Fx:**661-3902
(631) 261-7778 .. **Brosnan,** Aisha K '97 %Brody O&O -7 Bayview Av -Northprt 11768
(845) 497-2350 .. **Brosnan,** David J '91 -25 South -Washingtnvll 10992 **Fx:**497-2351
(516) 739-1462 .. **Brosnan & Hegler** -1325 Franklin Av -Gdn Cty 11530 **Fx:**739-1463
(516) 739-1462 .. **Brosnan,** Mark J '88 (Brosnan & H) -1325 Franklin Av -Gdn Cty 11530
(518) 374-3545 .. **Brosnan,** Michl W '05 %M Braccini -Bx3339 -Schnctdy 12303 **Fx:**374-2784
(845) 639-7800 .. **Brosnan,** Tracy J '90 (Mandel K&B,LLP) -210 Route 303 -Vly Cottage 10989
(212) 818-1110 .. **Brosnick,** Richd B '97 (Butzel L,PC) -380 Mad Av -NY 10017
(212) 446-4800 .. **Brosse,** Michl A '95 (Kirkland & E LLP) -153 E 53rd -NY 10022
(212) 756-2000 .. **Brossman,** Mark E '79 (Schulte R&Z LLP) -919 3rd Av -NY 10022
(212) 681-0117 .. **Brost,** John T '05 %Starr GD&R -530 5th Av -NY 10036
(212) 909-6000 .. **Brosterman,** Megan MacDonald '07 %Debevoise & P LLP -919 3rd Av -NY 10022
(212) 806-5400 .. **Brosterman,** Melvin A '75 (Stroock &S&L LLP) -180 Maiden Ln -NY 10038
(212) 656-2365 .. **Brostoff,** Steve J '84 NYSE,Inc -14 Wall -NY 10005 **Fx:**656-2366

(212) 931-9694 .. **Brostowin,** Terry A '99 Brostowin & Assoc,PC -111 John -NY 10038 **Fx:**812-9286
(718) 780-7963 .. **Brot,** Marni S '06 Bklyn Law Schl -250 Joralemon -Brklyn 11201 **Fx:**780-0374
(631) 232-2400 .. **Brothers,** Irene '89 %Nassau/Sfflk Law Srv -1757 Vets Hwy -Islandia 11749 **Fx:**232-2489
(914) 276-1392 .. **Brothers,** Martin L '65 -7 Livery Ln -N Salem 10560 **Fx:**276-1394
(716) 200-5050 .. **Brothman,** Phillip '63 (Harris B PLLC) -726 Exchange -Buffalo 14210
(212) 264-9271 .. **Brotman,** Beth E '84 %US Customs -26 Fed Plz -NY 10278
(212) 713-7935 .. **Brotman,** Eric B '02 UBS Financial Srvcs Inc -1285 Av of Amer -NY 10019
(212) 733-5029 .. **Brotman,** Marc '93 %Pfizer Inc -235 E 42nd -NY 10017
(212) 422-0010 .. **Brotman,** Susan '81 -150 E 58th -NY 10155
(914) 694-6200 .. **Brotmann,** Andrew K '89 (Brotmann Law Grp) -2 Gannett Dr -White Plns 10604 **Fx:**509-5444
(914) 694-6200 .. **Brotmann,** Stephen J M '91 (Brotmann Law Grp) -2 Gannett Dr -White Plns 10604 **Fx:**509-1917
(315) 448-0672 .. **Broton,** Edw R '80 %US Atty -100 S Clinton Bx7198 -Syracuse 13261 **Fx:**448-0689
(212) 483-9490 .. **Brotspies,** Kevin S '09 %McElroy DM&C,LLP -88 Pine -NY 10005
(716) 847-8400 .. **Brott,** Irving D Jr. '55 OfCnsl Phillips L LLP -3400 HSBC Ctr -Buffalo 14203
(518) 627-0202 .. **Brott,** Jason A '97 -4193 State Hwy 30 -Amsterdam 12010 **Fx:**627-0303
(212) 906-1200 .. **Broude,** Mark A '90 (Latham & W) -885 3rd Av -NY 10022
(212) 973-0311 .. **Broudo,** Aaron '07 Sontag Advisory -261 Mad Av -NY 10016
(212) 310-8000 .. **Broudy,** Barbra J '04 %Weil G&M LLP -767 5th Av -NY 10153
(212) 661-7100 .. **Broudy,** Louis L '64 (Salon MDN&B,LLP) -292 Mad Av -NY 10017
(212) 233-0130 .. **Broudy,** Wm K '74 Nelson Ld&H -120 Bway -NY 10271
(212) 318-6000 .. **Broughel,** Kevin P '04 %Paul HJ&W LLP -75 E 55th -NY 10022
(315) 798-5925 .. **Brouillette,** Julia M '02 %Family Ct -200 Elizabeth -Utica 13501
(212) 964-6611 .. **Brouk,** Aaron '01 %Lester SK&D -120 Bway -NY 10271
(718) 796-2210 .. **Broumand,** Heddyeh P '91 (Doyle & B,LLP) -3152 Albany Crescent -Bronx 10463
(718) 281-4000 .. **Brounstein,** Steven L '83 (Papa D&B) -42-40 Bell Blvd -Bayside 11361 **Fx:**281-4030
(212) 997-8500 .. **Brountas,** Nicholas P Jr. '93 %Amerada Hess -1185 Av of Amer -NY 10036 **Fx:**536-8390
(516) 479-6300 .. **Brountzas,** Katina '02 %Silverman A LLP -100 Jericho Quad -Jericho 11753
(212) 989-5469 .. **Brous,** Edith Ann '00 -118 E 28th -NY 10016
(516) 803-3000 .. **Broussard,** Robt '86 Rainbow Prog -1111 Stewart Av -Bethpage 11714
(518) 455-7723 .. **Brousseau,** Cara E '99 Ct of Appls -20 Eagle -Albany 12207
(518) 862-9292 .. **Brousseau,** Shawn F '95 (Napierski V&N,LLP) -296 Wshngtn Av Ext -Albany 12203
(516) 328-2300 .. **Broutman,** Eric '03 %Abrams FFEGF&E,LLP -1111 Marcus Av -Lk Success 11042
(212) 384-1000 .. **Brouwer,** Wendy B '89 %FBI -26 Fed Plz -NY 10278
(585) 641-8000 .. **Brovitz,** Richd S '77 (Fix SB&G,PC) -295 Woodcliff Dr -Fairprt 14450
(212) 416-8734 .. **Brovner,** Lesley Allison '96 %Dept of Law -120 Bway -NY 10271
(718) 286-6000 .. **Brovner,** Michl E '96 %DA -125-01 Qns Blvd -Kew Gdns 11415
(212) 530-5000 .. **Browand,** Nathaniel T '05 %Milbank TH&M LLP -1 Chase Manh Plz -NY 10005
(212) 967-8202 .. **Browand,** Nicole McGee '06 %Pagan Law Firm,PC -245 5th Av -NY 10016 **Fx:**967-8794
(914) 861-9119 .. **Browde,** David A '01 (D Browde,PC) -604 Quaker Rd -Chappaqua 10514 **Fx:**861-6799
(212) 756-2000 .. **Browder,** Vanessa K '09 %Schulte R&Z LLP -919 3rd Av -NY 10022
(212) 373-3000 .. **Browdy,** Jos E '62 OfCnsl Paul WRW&G LLP -1285 Av of Amer -NY 10019
(212) 816-0329 .. **Brower,** Alan G '78 Citigroup -388 Greenwich -NY 10013
(212) 501-9000 .. **Brower,** David A P '83 (Brower P,PC) -488 Mad Av -NY 10022 **Fx:**501-0300
(516) 378-1700 .. **Brower,** Gregory E '97 (Chesney & M) -2305 Grand Av -Baldwin 11510
(518) 862-7300 .. **Brower,** Murry Spencer '89 Cnsl T Puleo -900 Watervliet Shaker Rd Bx12699 -Albany 12212 **Fx:**862-7322
(212) 216-1257 .. **Brown,** A Widney '95 %Human Rights Watch -350 5th Av -NY 10118 **Fx:**736-1300
(212) 226-0350 .. **Brown,** Adam J '05 (Mercader & B PLLC) -100 Church -NY 10007 **Fx:**226-0391
(914) 946-6774 .. **Brown,** Adam T '98 %Pilkington & L,PC -222 Bloomingdale Rd -White Plns 10605
(516) 482-6166 .. **Brown,** Aimee Kleiger '84 (Kleiger & K) -80 Cuttermill Rd -Gt Neck 11021 **Fx:**482-6240
(212) 302-2900 .. **Brown,** Alan I '69 (Tannenbaum D&R) -1140 Av of Amer -NY 10036
(212) 815-1450 .. **Brown,** Alan M '83 %DC 37 Gen Cnsl -125 Barclay -NY 10007 **Fx:**815-1440
(212) 277-6500 .. **Brown,** Alana L '00 Cnsl Dickstein S LLP -1633 Bway -NY 10019
(212) 751-3001 .. **Brown,** Alex J '08 (Thompson & K LLP) -919 3rd Av -NY 10022
(914) 225-5536 .. **Brown,** Althea A '06 Morgan Stanley -2000 Wstchstr Av -Purchase 10577
(212) 455-2000 .. **Brown,** Alvin H '75 (Simpson T&B LLP) -425 Lex Av -NY 10017
(212) 574-1200 .. **Brown,** Amanda K '07 %Seward & K LLP -1 Bttry Pk Plz -NY 10004
(212) 833-1239 .. **Brown,** Amy C '00 (Friedman KS&A LLP) -1633 Bway -NY 10019 **Fx:**373-7939
(212) 213-0610 .. **Brown,** Andrea '82 -108 E 30th -NY 10016
(212) 669-0600 .. **Brown,** Andrew R '07 %Hill R LLP -45 Bway -NY 10006
(212) 310-8000 .. **Brown,** Andrew S '09 %Weil G&M LLP -767 5th Av -NY 10153
(212) 455-2000 .. **Brown,** Anita Yuen '08 %Simpson T&B LLP -425 Lex Av -NY 10017
(718) 262-7100 .. **Brown,** Annamarie Policriti '52 Civil Ct -89-17 Sutphin Blvd -Jamaica 11435 **Fx:**262-7107
(212) 788-9045 .. **Brown,** Anne B '05 NYC Council-Finance Div -250 Bway -NY 10007
(212) 417-3700 .. **Brown,** Anne Elise '04 %MFY Legal Srvcs -299 Bway -NY 10007 **Fx:**417-3890
(718) 459-5050 .. **Brown,** Anne Lantz '92 %Bienstock & B LLP -105-25 65th Av -Frst Hlls 11375 **Fx:**459-5055
(516) 599-2020 .. **Brown,** Anthony M '04 %A Chianese & Assoc -100 Merrick Rd -Rockvll Ctr 11570 **Fx:**599-6476
(518) 226-0210 .. **Brown,** Arlene P '82 (Cipriano & B,PC) -24 Horseshoe Dr -Saratoga Spgs 12866
(212) 836-8000 .. **Brown,** Arthur E '95 (Kaye S LLP) -425 Park Av -NY 10022
(212) 448-1100 .. **Brown,** Arthur H Jr. '72 (McLaughlin & S,LLP) -260 Mad Av -NY 10016
(212) 547-5400 .. **Brown,** Banks '78 (McDermott W&E LLP) -340 Mad Av -NY 10173
(212) 732-3200 .. **Brown,** Barbara Block '80 Cnsl Carter L&M LLP -2 Wall -NY 10005
(917) 237-2900 .. **Brown,** Bernadette E '04 %Axiom Legal -75 Spring -NY 10012
(212) 446-4800 .. **Brown,** Binta N '99 (Kirkland & E LLP) -153 E 53rd -NY 10022
(212) 277-6500 .. **Brown,** Bradley M '08 %Dickstein S LLP -1633 Bway -NY 10019
(631) 755-0101 .. **Brown,** Brian '79 Cnsl Lewis JAA,LLP -425 Broad Hollow Rd -Melvll 11747
(212) 514-8040 .. **Brown,** Brian A '92 %Freedom Hse -120 Wall -NY 10005 **Fx:**514-8050
(914) 633-2570 .. **Brown,** Brian E '88 %Iona Cllg -715 North Av -New Rchll 10801
(212) 458-1211 .. **Brown,** Brian L '07 AIG Inc -175 Water -NY 10038
(212) 400-7226 .. **Brown,** Brian M '03 (Zaremba B&B PLLC) -40 Wall -NY 10005 **Fx:**(646) 512-5607
(212) 446-2300 .. **Brown,** Bridget E '08 %Boies S&F LLP -575 Lex Av -NY 10022
(845) 624-1966 .. **Brown Burgoon & Hartnagel,PC** -365 Route 304 -Bardonia 10954 **Fx:**624-1977
(607) 734-2271 .. **Brown,** Carla '07 %Sayles & E -1 W Church -Elmira 14901
(518) 447-7110 .. **Brown,** Catherine E '04 Cnty Atty -112 State -Albany 12207
(718) 297-7711 .. **Brown,** Cedric A '57 -150-49 Hillside Av -Jamaica 11432 **Fx:**297-5588
(518) 736-5511 .. **Brown,** Chad W '01 %DA -223 W Main -Johnstwn 12095 **Fx:**762-2042
(212) 768-6700 .. **Brown,** Chas D '52 OfCnsl Sonnenschein N&R LLP -2 World Fncl Ctr -NY 10281
(212) 908-0626 .. **Brown,** Chas D '86 %Fitch IBCA -1 State Street Plz -NY 10004 **Fx:**968-8839
(315) 792-0171 .. **Brown,** Chas N '76 %Law Dept -1 Knndy Plz -Utica 13502 **Fx:**792-0175
(716) 886-0211 .. **Brown,** Cheryl A '85 %Benderson Dvlpmnt -570 Delaware Av -Buffalo 14202 **Fx:**886-2269
(716) 681-7190 .. **Brown Chiari LLP** -5775 Bway -Lancaster 14086 **Fx:**681-8136
(716) 681-7190 .. **Brown Chiari LLP** -69 Delaware Av -Buffalo 14202 **Fx:**681-8136
(914) 961-4441 .. **Brown,** Christopher G '93 (Begos H&B LLP) -7 Pondfld Rd Bx369 -Bronxvll 10708
(212) 971-8680 .. **Brown,** Clarence O'Neill '80 %Anavista Entertainment -347 W 39th -NY 10018
(516) 204-4678 .. **Brown,** Clifford J '85 (C Brown,PC) -1938 Lowell Ln -Merrick 11566
(518) 257-1443 .. **Brown,** Constance R '90 %CSEA,Inc -143 Wshngtn Av Bx7125 -Albany 12224 **Fx:**449-1525
(518) 885-9292 .. **Brown Craig & Hunt** -1 E High -Ballston Spa 12020 **Fx:**884-2738
(212) 883-1700 .. **Brown,** Craig L '94 (Duval & S LLP) -101 Park Av -NY 10178
(212) 944-9112 .. **Brown,** Craig S '85 Strategic Legal Solutions -500 5th Av -NY 10110
(845) 566-5345 .. **Brown,** Craig Stephen '97 %Larkin AI&T,LLP -356 Meadow Av -Newburgh 12550
(607) 722-1263 .. **Brown,** Craig W '76 -64 Front Bx1766 -Bnghmtn 13902
(718) 596-0025 .. **Brown,** Damien M '98 -26 Court -Brklyn 11242 **Fx:**228-7292
(631) 852-2500 .. **Brown,** Dana E '96 %DA -200 Center Dr -Rvrhead 11901 **Fx:**852-1769
(716) 856-5500 .. **Brown,** Danl F '82 (Damon M LLP) -200 Delaware Av -Buffalo 14202
(212) 999-5800 .. **Brown,** Danl G '94 (Wilson SG&R) -1301 Av of Americas -NY 10019
(212) 653-8700 .. **Brown,** Danl L '99 (Sheppard MR&H LLP) -30 Rckfllr Plz -NY 10112
(212) 259-8000 .. **Brown,** Danl S '89 SrCnsl Dewey & L LLP -1301 Av of Amer -NY 10019
(212) 337-2639 .. **Brown,** Danl S '97 %US DOJ INS -201 Varick -NY 10014
(212) 836-8000 .. **Brown,** DaShondra L '08 %Kaye S LLP -425 Park Av -NY 10022
(516) 222-9449 .. **Brown,** David A '94 BLS Funding -125 Jericho Tpk -Jericho 11753
(212) 809-7600 .. **Brown,** David A '00 %Cheven K&H -40 Wall -NY 10005
(585) 454-3377 .. **Brown,** David E '71 (Brown & T,LLC) -19 Prince -Rchstr 14607
(914) 949-5300 .. **Brown,** David E '71 (Brown & T,LLC) -1 N Bway -White Plns 10601
(607) 231-6529 .. **Brown,** David M '85 -89 Court -Bnghmtn 13901 **Fx:**231-6530
(212) 225-2000 .. **Brown,** David P '10 %Cleary GS&H -1 Lbrty Plz -NY 10006
(212) 957-9000 .. **Brown,** David S '59 (Cooper B&B,PC) -331 Mad Av -NY 10017
(212) 468-8000 .. **Brown,** David S '02 %Morrison & F LLP -1290 Av of Amer -NY 10104
(518) 783-2200 .. **Brown,** David Simon '83 (Brown & B) -11 Century Hill Dr -Latham 12110 **Fx:**783-2225
(212) 373-3000 .. **Brown,** David W '02 (Paul WRW&G LLP) -1285 Av of Amer -NY 10019
(718) 596-3300 .. **Brown,** Dean R '83 P Schneider & Assoc PLLC -335 Adams -Brklyn 11201
(212) 788-9113 .. **Brown,** Deborah A '99 NYC Cncl -250 Bway -NY 10007
(212) 849-7000 .. **Brown,** Deborah K '03 %Quinn EU&S,LLP -51 Mad Av -NY 10010
(631) 853-4049 .. **Brown,** Dennis M '84 %Cnty Atty -Dennison Bldg Bx6100 -Hauppauge 11788 **Fx:**853-5169
(315) 788-3360 .. **Brown Dierdorf & Renzi** -165 Mullin -Watertwn 13601 **Fx:**788-1752
(845) 452-7400 .. **Brown,** Donald D Jr. '73 (Spiegel BF&C,LLP) -272 Mill -Poughkeepsie 12601
(516) 794-9100 .. **Brown,** Donna J '87 East Coast Abstract -100 Q Roosevelt Blvd -Gdn Cty 11530 **Fx:**794-2725
(212) 325-2000 .. **Brown,** Douglas B Jr. '06 Credit Suisse -1 Mad Av -NY 10010
(315) 474-8218 .. **Brown,** E Parker II '79 -108 Lockwood Rd -Syracuse 13214
(212) 878-0000 .. **Brown,** Earamichia N '98 %MTA -2 Penn Plz -NY 10121
(914) 633-7900 .. **Brown,** Edw H '54 Boyle F&H -271 North Av -New Rchll 10801 **Fx:**576-0947
(845) 268-0844 .. **Brown,** Edw J '65 -32 Burnside Av -Congers 10920 **Fx:**268-8308
(315) 423-4400 .. **Brown,** Edw M '95 (Wolff G&G,LLP) -217 Mntgmry -Syracuse 13202
(516) 571-2788 .. **Brown,** Edw T '49 %Supreme Ct -100 Supreme Ct Dr -Mineola 11501

(212) 244-2999 .. **Brown,** Eileen M '06 %Kopff N&D LLP -440 9th Av -NY 10001
(212) 935-5500 .. **Brown,** Elliot H '76 (Franklin WR&V) -488 Mad Av -NY 10022
(718) 979-5291 .. **Brown,** Elliott J '87 -2409 Richmond Rd -Staten Isl 10306 **Fx:**(866) 301-8300
(315) 218-8000 .. **Brown,** Emily M D '10 %Bond S&K,PLLC -1 Lincoln Ctr -Syracuse 13202
(631) 324-3942 .. **Brown,** Eric N '95 (Ackerman OP&B,LLP) -34 Pantigo Rd -E Hampton 11937
(516) 883-8868 .. **Brown,** Eric S '79 -1 Sloanes Ct -Sands Pnt 11050
(212) 935-5500 .. **Brown,** Eric S '90 (Franklin WR&V) -488 Mad Av -NY 10022
(212) 306-1000 .. **Brown,** Eric S '97 %Amer Stock Exch -86 Trinity Pl -NY 10006
(914) 993-0303 .. **Brown,** Felicia D '94 %Vanguard Inc -244 Wstchstr Av -White Plns 10604 **Fx:**993-0364
(845) 735-0088 .. **Brown,** Frank I '76 (Brown B&K,LLP) -275 N Mddltwn Rd -Pearl Rvr 10965 **Fx:**735-7660
(212) 761-2754 .. **Brown,** G Wm Jr. '81 Morgan Stanley -1585 Bway -NY 10036 **Fx:**761-0052
(631) 342-5224 .. **Brown,** Gary R '89 %CA,Inc -1 CA Plz -Islandia 11749 **Fx:**342-4866
(914) 995-2155 .. **Brown,** Gary S '80 Dept of Consumer Protection -112 E Post Rd -White Plns 10601 **Fx:**995-3115
(212) 983-8500 .. **Brown Gavalas & Fromm LLP** -355 Lex Av -NY 10017 **Fx:**983-5946
(516) 938-6385 .. **Brown,** George F '83 -2 Campus Pl -Hicksvll 11801
(212) 471-2990 .. **Brown,** George R '94 %Merle B&N,PC -90 Broad -NY 10004
(914) 949-7791 .. **Brown,** Gerald '58 -175 Main -White Plns 10601
(212) 859-8000 .. **Brown,** Gerald H '07 %Fried FHS&J LLP -1 NY Plz -NY 10004
(716) 855-6711 .. **Brown,** Gillian D '90 %BMHA -300 Perry -Buffalo 14204 **Fx:**855-6761
(516) 741-2585 .. **Brown,** Gillian P '94 %Rosicki R & Assoc,PC -51 E Bethpage Rd -Plainvw 11803 **Fx:**741-4748
(716) 675-8620 .. **Brown,** Gordon M '96 -3590 Seneca -W Seneca 14224 **Fx:**675-1619
(212) 750-9898 .. **Brown,** Gregory A '06 %B Levinson -747 3rd Av -NY 10017 **Fx:**750-2536
(718) 386-4345 .. **Brown,** Gregory J '77 (Ramo N&B) -75-19 Myrtle Av -Glendale 11385
(716) 843-5700 .. **Brown,** Gregory L '88 %US Atty -138 Delaware Av -Buffalo 14202 **Fx:**551-3052
(315) 442-0100 .. **Brown,** Gregory M '92 (Gilberti SH&S,PC) -555 E Genesee -Syracuse 13202
(212) 366-4600 .. **Brown & Gropper,LLP** -275 7th Av -NY 10001 **Fx:**366-6950
(315) 453-6530 .. **Brown,** Harold C III '94 %State Ins Fund -1045 7th N -Liverpool 13088 **Fx:**453-6540
(212) 407-4000 .. **Brown,** Harris B '09 %Loeb & L,LLP -345 Park Av -NY 10154
(516) 829-0363 .. **Brown,** Harvey R '75 %Israel I&P,LLP -11 Grace Av -Gt Neck 11021 **Fx:**829-0366
(212) 536-6135 .. **Brown,** Harvey S '75 -530 5th Av -NY 10036 **Fx:**719-0951
(585) 454-5050 .. **Brown & Hutchinson** -2 State -Rchstr 14614 **Fx:**454-5066
(516) 482-4567 .. **Brown,** Ira L '84 OfCnsl Camardella & B,LLC -98 Cuttermill Rd -Gt Neck 11021
(718) 229-4300 .. **Brown,** Ira L '84 Cnsl Briarwood Org -3635 Bell Blvd -Bayside 11361 **Fx:**225-3746
(845) 353-1874 .. **Brown,** Ira P '69 -Bx826 -Nyack 10960 **Fx:**353-1874
(212) 374-5110 .. **Brown,** J M '93 %NYC Dept Educ -52 Chmbrs -NY 10007
(212) 366-4600 .. **Brown,** James A '87 (Brown & G,LLP) -275 7th Av -NY 10001
(518) 474-7151 .. **Brown,** James C '04 %Dept of Law -The Cptl -Albany 12224
(718) 923-4206 .. **Brown,** James E '73 %OTDA Fair Hearings -14 Boerum Pl -Brklyn 11201
(716) 681-7190 .. **Brown,** James E '73 (Brown C LLP) -5775 Bway -Lancaster 14086
(716) 858-6537 .. **Brown,** James E '84 %Dept Soc Srvcs -95 Franklin -Buffalo 14202 **Fx:**858-8072
(212) 615-2200 .. **Brown,** James H L '05 %Butler FF&M,PC -36 W 44th -NY 10036
(212) 412-4000 .. **Brown,** James P '98 Barclays Capital -200 Park Av -NY 10166
(212) 728-8000 .. **Brown,** James R Jr. '04 (Willkie F&G LLP) -787 7th Av -NY 10019
(212) 490-3000 .. **Brown,** James S '73 (Wilson EME&D LLP) -150 E 42nd -NY 10017
(212) 735-3000 .. **Brown,** James W '93 Cnsl Skadden ASM&F LLP -4 Times Sq -NY 10036
(212) 397-2800 .. **Brown,** Jan H '78 (JH Brown,PC) -1150 Av of Amer -NY 10036 **Fx:**397-7376
(718) 570-7761 .. **Brown,** Janet L '98 -89-31 161st -Jamaica 11432 **Fx:**228-9421
(917) 674-2300 .. **Brown,** Janice E '91 -520 E 81st -NY 10028
(212) 696-1700 .. **Brown,** Jared '75 (Brown & G LLP) -274 Mad Av -NY 10016 **Fx:**545-7211
(212) 640-4807 .. **Brown,** Jason K '98 Amer Exp -200 Vesey -NY 10285
(212) 435-3571 .. **Brown,** Jason P '09 %Port Auth of NY/NJ -225 Park Av S -NY 10003 **Fx:**435-3555
(800) 910-0529 .. **Brown,** Jason T '06 (Blau B&L,LLC) -224 W 30th -NY 10001 **Fx:**(212) 488-4848
(315) 342-3366 .. **Brown,** Jean A '97 -110 W 2nd -Oswego 13126
(607) 723-9511 .. **Brown,** Jeffrey A '87 (Coughlin & G,LLP) -19 Chenango Bx2039 -Bnghmtn 13902
(212) 637-1110 .. **Brown,** Jeffrey A '00 %US Atty -1 St Andrews Plz -NY 10007
(315) 474-7571 .. **Brown,** Jeffrey D '92 (Mackenzie H LLP) -101 S Salina Bx4967 -Syracuse 13221
(516) 873-9550 .. **Brown,** Jeffrey K '97 (Leeds M&B) -1 Old Cntry Rd -Carle Pl 11514
(212) 225-2000 .. **Brown,** Jennifer '00 %Cleary GS&H -1 Lbrty Plz -NY 10006
(212) 336-4094 .. **Brown,** Jennifer K '95 Morrison & F LLP -1290 Av of Amer -NY 10104
(212) 417-8700 .. **Brown,** Jennifer L '97 %Fed Def of NY Inc -52 Duane -NY 10007 **Fx:**571-0392
(212) 916-2864 .. **Brown,** Jennifer M '06 %UBS AG -101 Park Av -NY 10178
(212) 422-2660 .. **Brown,** Jennifer P '02 %Family Law Ctr -11 Bway -NY 10004 **Fx:**422-2666
(212) 336-2000 .. **Brown,** Jennifer Weitz '03 %Patterson BW&T LLP -1133 Av of Amer -NY 10036
(212) 969-3000 .. **Brown,** Jeremy M '97 SrCnsl Proskauer R LLP -1585 Bway -NY 10036
(212) 702-1767 .. **Brown,** Jerome J '96 Harris Nesbitt Corp -3 Times Sq -NY 10036
(646) 871-8773 .. **Brown,** Jesse B '09 %W Forsythe -36 E 20th -NY 10003 **Fx:**(212) 624-0236
(212) 859-3490 .. **Brown,** Joan B '99 -110 Wall -NY 10005
(646) 428-0914 .. **Brown,** John F '95 Hoplite Capital Mgmt,LLC -810 7th Av -NY 10019
(212) 618-1250 .. **Brown,** John Lewis '77 (Maher & B) -14 Wall -NY 10005 **Fx:**618-1251
(631) 727-3947 .. **Brown,** Jonathan D '83 -737 Roanoke Av -Rvrhead 11901
(212) 530-5000 .. **Brown,** Jonathan H '07 %Milbank TH&M LLP -1 Chase Manh Plz -NY 10005
(716) 849-1333 .. **Brown,** Jonathan W '01 (Lipsitz GSC LLP) -42 Delaware Av -Buffalo 14202
(516) 537-1130 .. **Brown,** Jos A '80 Glinkenhouse F&Q -116 Spruce -Cedarhrst 11516
(845) 294-1622 .. **Brown,** Jos P '68 -154 Main Bx376 -Goshen 10924 **Fx:**294-1633
(716) 856-4000 .. **Brown,** Jos S '05 %Hodgson R LLP -140 Pearl -Buffalo 14202
(212) 964-0725 .. **Brown,** Joyce '89 %Brenner & B,PC -170 Bway -NY 10038
(212) 708-1449 .. **Brown,** Joyce A '00 %Showtime Networks Inc -1633 Bway -NY 10019
(212) 815-1818 .. **Brown,** Judith A '85 %DC 37 MELS -125 Barclay -NY 10007 **Fx:**815-1343
(315) 379-2410 .. **Brown,** Judith H '94 Family Ct -48 Court -Canton 13617 **Fx:**386-3197
(914) 606-9790 .. **Brown,** Judy L '88 %Cartafalsa ST&L -560 Wht Plns Rd -Tarrytwn 10591
(212) 912-0520 .. **Brown,** Julie M '97 (Gaschler & B) -375 South End Av -NY 10280 **Fx:**(917) 591-6322
(585) 352-2420 .. **Brown,** Karen M '03 %Monroe 2-Orleans BOCES -3599 Big Ridge Rd -Spencerprt 14559
(212) 834-1070 .. **Brown,** Katharine B '78 %GreenPoint Bk -90 Park Av -NY 10016 **Fx:**834-1402
(212) 906-1200 .. **Brown,** Katherine M '09 %Latham & W -885 3rd Av -NY 10022
(845) 894-6919 .. **Brown,** Katherine S '04 IBM -294 Route 100 -Somers 10589
(718) 390-5321 .. **Brown,** Keith E '04 %Law Dept -60 Bay -Staten Isl 10301 **Fx:**981-4459
(914) 241-2400 .. **Brown,** Keith M '04 %Novenstern F&G -69 S Bedford Rd -Mt Kisco 10549
(516) 222-0222 .. **Brown,** Keith P '95 (Brown & A,LLP) -510 Broadhllw Rd -Melvll 11747 **Fx:**222-0322
(518) 943-1111 .. **Brown Kelleher & Zwickel,LLP** -370 Main -Catskill 12414 **Fx:**943-4549
(585) 987-2800 .. **Brown,** Kelley Ross '92 (Woods OG LLP) -2 State -Rchstr 14614
(212) 872-1000 .. **Brown,** Kelly L '08 -One Bryant Park -NY 10036 **Fx:**872-1002
(716) 854-2620 .. **Brown & Kelly,LLP** -1500 Lbrty Bldg -Buffalo 14202 **Fx:**854-0082
(646) 471-4000 .. **Brown,** Kelly P '99 %PricewaterhouseCoopers LLP -300 Mad Av -NY 10017
(631) 393-6220 .. **Brown,** Kenneth A '88 Cnsl Harras B&A LLP -445 Broad Hollow Rd -Melvll 11747
(917) 778-6600 .. **Brown,** Kenneth B '87 %J Toomey -485 Lex Av -NY 10017 **Fx:**778-7048
(914) 949-2700 .. **Brown,** Kenneth C '84 (Bleakley P&S,LLP) -1 N Lex Av -White Plns 10601
(718) 597-7070 .. **Brown,** Kenneth D '81 -1106 Allerton Av -Bronx 10469
(718) 297-7711 .. **Brown,** Kenneth Lloyd '55 (Brown & B) -150-49 Hillside Av -Jamaica 11432 **Fx:**297-5588
(212) 530-5000 .. **Brown,** Kevin A '08 %Milbank TH&M LLP -1 Chase Manh Plz -NY 10005
(315) 233-8300 .. **Brown,** Kevin C '02 (Burr & B) -101 S Salina -Syracuse 13202
(212) 728-8000 .. **Brown,** Kevin C '09 %Willkie F&G LLP -787 7th Av -NY 10019
(716) 855-1118 .. **Brown,** Kevin D '02 %JE Morris -424 Main -Buffalo 14202 **Fx:**855-1119
(315) 442-0100 .. **Brown,** Kevin J '85 (Gilberti SH&S,PC) -555 E Genesee -Syracuse 13202
(518) 427-1636 .. **Brown,** Kevin J '92 -471 Hudson Av -Albany 12203 **Fx:**437-1636
(212) 696-4848 .. **Brown,** Kevin M '06 %Mintz & G LLP -470 Park Av S -NY 10016
(212) 790-4500 .. **Brown,** Kim S '07 %Manatt P&P,LLP -7 Times Sq -NY 10036
(212) 490-3000 .. **Brown,** Kimberly '10 %Wilson EME&D LLP -150 E 42nd -NY 10017
(212) 609-6800 .. **Brown,** Kristina Rak '98 %McCarter & E,LLP -245 Park Av -NY 10167
(212) 698-3500 .. **Brown,** Kristopher D '93 (Dechert LLP) -1095 Av of Amer -NY 10036
(716) 831-1994 .. **Brown,** Lawr C '78 -385 Cleveland Dr -Buffalo 14215 **Fx:**831-1200
(315) 633-5583 .. **Brown,** Lawr P '85 -363 Route 31 Bx669 -Brdgprt 13030 **Fx:**633-8225
(212) 637-2638 .. **Brown,** Leslie C '96 %US Atty -1 St Andrews Plz -NY 10007
(212) 471-8514 .. **Brown,** Linda M '89 (Herzfeld & R,PC) -125 Broad -NY 10004
(212) 318-3000 .. **Brown,** Lindsay Hamilton '05 %Fulbright & J LLP -666 5th Av -NY 10103
(518) 456-6767 .. **Brown,** Lisa E '98 (Young FK&B,PC) -1881 Wstrn Av -Albany 12203
(212) 635-7595 .. **Brown,** Lloyd W II '96 %Bk of NY -1 Wall -NY 10286 **Fx:**635-7403
(212) 335-4500 .. **Brown,** Loren H '93 (DLA Piper LLP) -1251 Av of Amer -NY 10020
(518) 584-1500 .. **Brown,** Loren N '60 OfCnsl Snyder KTC&C,LLP -160 West Av Bx4367 -Saratoga Spgs 12866
(716) 885-9700 .. **Brown,** Luke A '08 (Collins & B,LLP) -267 North -Buffalo 14201
(516) 741-6565 .. **Brown,** Lynn M '84 OfCnsl Meyer SE&K,PC -990 Stewart Av Bx9194 -Gdn Cty 11530
(212) 545-4714 .. **Brown,** Malcolm T '98 %Wolf HAF&H LLP -270 Mad Av -NY 10016
(718) 590-2000 .. **Brown,** Marc A '04 %DA -198 E 161st -Bronx 10451 **Fx:**590-6477
(585) 295-4400 .. **Brown,** Marc S '95 (Hiscock & B,LLP) -2000 HSBC Plz -Rchstr 14604
(716) 847-8400 .. **Brown,** Marc W '00 %Phillips L LLP -3400 HSBC Ctr -Buffalo 14203
(718) 774-0026 .. **Brown,** Margaret O '96 -1370 Union -Brklyn 11213
(716) 836-3946 .. **Brown,** Marla Depan '87 -109 Depew Av -Buffalo 14214
(516) 560-6400 .. **Brown,** Marva C '07 %Leg Aid -1 Helen Keller Way -Hempstd 11550 **Fx:**565-3694
(212) 682-8811 .. **Brown,** Marvin M '66 (Dunnington B&M LLP) -1359 Bway -NY 10018
(212) 553-3200 .. **Brown,** Mary K '00 %Marulli LE&T,LLP -5 Hanover Sq -NY 10004
(518) 842-5580 .. **Brown,** Mary S '02 -2096 Cnty Hwy 107 -Amsterdam 12010 **Fx:**212-6518
(585) 473-3100 .. **Brown,** Matthew D '00 %Ernstrom & D,LLP -180 Canal Vw Blvd -Rchstr 14623

(516) 558-7115 .. **Brown,** Matthew D '02 MD Brown PC -35 Roosevelt Av -Syosset 11791
(518) 474-5288 .. **Brown,** Megan Maureen '94 %Dept of Law -The Cptl -Albany 12224
(347) 592-2560 .. **Brown,** Megan S '09 Family Defense Project -177 Lvngstn -Brklyn 11201
(212) 259-8000 .. **Brown,** Meghan A '08 %Dewey & L LLP -1301 Av of Amer -NY 10019
(716) 852-5533 .. **Brown,** Meghan M '07 %Connors & V,LLP -1000 Lbrty Bldg -Buffalo 14202
(212) 815-1450 .. **Brown,** Melissa '85 %DC 37 Gen Cnsl -125 Barclay -NY 10007 **Fx:**815-1440
(212) 713-1366 .. **Brown,** Melissa Vogel '93 UBS Securities -1285 Av of Amer -NY 10019
(212) 909-6000 .. **Brown,** Meredith M '65 SrCnsl Debevoise & P LLP -919 3rd Av -NY 10022
(212) 219-3516 .. **Brown,** Michl A '86 -39 E Bway -NY 10002
(516) 873-6334 .. **Brown,** Michl D '71 (Ohrenstein & B,LLP) -1010 Franklin Av Bx9243 -Gdn Cty 11530
(607) 256-2000 .. **Brown,** Michl F '81 (Brown & M,PC) -118 N Tioga -Ithaca 14850
(212) 756-2000 .. **Brown,** Michl G '01 SpclCnsl Schulte R&Z LLP -919 3rd Av -NY 10022
(631) 232-9700 .. **Brown,** Michl J '93 -320 Carleton Av -Central Islip 11722 **Fx:**232-9701
(212) 643-8007 .. **Brown,** Michl K '90 -1270 Bway -NY 10001 **Fx:**643-9868
(212) 730-7750 .. **Brown,** Michl S '94 %Nicoletti GS&O,LLP -555 5th Av -NY 10017
(212) 902-1000 .. **Brown,** Michl T '04 %Goldman Sachs -1 NY Plz -NY 10004
(607) 256-2000 .. **Brown & Michaels,PC** -118 N Tioga -Ithaca 14850 **Fx:**256-3628
(585) 641-0790 .. **Brown & Michaels,PC** -1250 Pttsfrd Victor Rd -Pittsfrd 14534 **Fx:**641-0795
(716) 332-0990 .. **Brown,** Michele A '80 Childrens Leg Ctr -438 Main -Buffalo 14202
(212) 336-1023 .. **Brown,** Nancy A '86 %SEC -3 World Fncl Ctr -NY 10281 **Fx:**336-1323
(212) 246-2400 .. **Brown,** Neal A '61 (Balber PM&VDT,PC) -1370 Av of Amer -NY 10019
(718) 886-1100 .. **Brown,** Neil G '04 %F Regan Jr -159-18 Nrthrn Blvd -Flushng 11358 **Fx:**461-5651
(212) 335-4500 .. **Brown,** Nia M '03 %DLA Piper LLP -1251 Av of Amer -NY 10020
(212) 839-5300 .. **Brown,** Nicholas R '93 (Sidley A LLP) -787 7th Av -NY 10019
(212) 267-1900 .. **Brown,** Nicole Y '99 (Wade CM) -111 Bway -NY 10006
(845) 471-1375 .. **Brown,** Norbert H Jr. '60 -Bx3329 -Poughkeepsie 12603
(518) 427-7350 .. **Brown,** Patrick E '84 (Brown & W PLLC) -79 Columbia -Albany 12210
(716) 855-3761 .. **Brown,** Patrick J '77 (LoTempio & B,PC) -181 Franklin -Buffalo 14202 **Fx:**855-3437
(315) 449-2616 .. **Brown,** Paul A '74 Martin GBM&C,PC -5790 Widewaters Pkwy -DeWitt 13214
(212) 818-9200 .. **Brown,** Paul M '63 (Satterlee SB&B LLP) -230 Park Av -NY 10169
(212) 325-4859 .. **Brown,** Paul W Jr. '95 %Credit Suisse First Boston -11 Mad Av -NY 10010
(212) 589-4200 .. **Brown,** Peter '74 (Baker & H LLP) -45 Rckfllr Plz -NY 10111
(518) 432-1600 .. **Brown,** Peter M '96 Meridian Capital Ptnrs -20 Corp Wds Blvd -Albany 12211
(212) 425-1999 .. **Brown,** Philip S '80 Edelsteins F&B,LLP -61 Bway -NY 10006
(212) 696-6000 .. **Brown,** Preston '62 (Curtis M-PC&M LLP) -101 Park Av -NY 10178
(718) 270-5129 .. **Brown,** Racquel Delsita '01 %Medgar Evers Cllg CUNY -1650 Bedford Av -Brklyn 11225
(212) 735-3000 .. **Brown,** Rebecca S '09 %Skadden ASM&F LLP -4 Times Sq -NY 10036
(212) 815-1818 .. **Brown,** Regina J '86 %DC 37 MELS -125 Barclay -NY 10007 **Fx:**815-1343
(212) 674-5151 .. **Brown,** Rhonda S '89 %Macmillan -175 5th Av -NY 10010 **Fx:**529-0594
(585) 461-2167 .. **Brown,** Rhonda T '81 -96 Fonthill Pk -Rchstr 14618
(718) 286-6000 .. **Brown,** Richd A '56 (DA) -125-01 Qns Blvd -Kew Gdns 11415
(516) 294-5200 .. **Brown,** Richd B '97 %Picciano & S -900 Merchants Cncrs -Westbury 11590
(607) 547-4359 .. **Brown,** Richd E '93 Support Magistrate -32 Chestnut -Cooperstwn 13326 **Fx:**547-6412
(212) 297-5800 .. **Brown,** Richd H '94 (Day P LLP) -7 Times Sq -NY 10036
(212) 592-1400 .. **Brown,** Richd J '77 (Herrick,F LLP) -2 Park Av -NY 10016
(212) 836-8000 .. **Brown,** Richd S '98 Cnsl Kaye S LLP -425 Park Av -NY 10022
(631) 360-7333 .. **Brown,** Robt B '99 %De Sena & S -1383 Vets Mem'l Hwy -Hauppauge 11788
(973) 596-4831 .. **Brown,** Robt D '99 %Gibbons PC -1 Penn Plz -NY 10119 **Fx:**639-8377
(585) 232-5300 .. **Brown,** Robt E '70 (Boylan BCV&W,LLP) -2400 Chase Sq -Rchstr 14604
(718) 979-9779 .. **Brown,** Robt E '01 -2409 Richmond Rd -Staten Isl 10306 **Fx:**979-9784
(718) 261-6991 .. **Brown,** Robt H '95 -108-18 Qns Blvd -Frst Hlls 11375 **Fx:**261-6990
(212) 983-8500 .. **Brown,** Robt J '82 (Brown G&F LLP) -355 Lex Av -NY 10017
(212) 261-8000 .. **Brown,** Robt J '84 (Mendes & M,LLP) -750 7th Av -NY 10019
(518) 274-8578 .. **Brown,** Robt M '77 -10 East Rd -Troy 12180
(212) 421-1845 .. **Brown,** Rodney A '76 (Brown & W,PC) -711 3rd Av -NY 10017 **Fx:**421-8418
(212) 297-5800 .. **Brown,** Ronald Erik '88 SrCnsl Day P LLP -7 Times Sq -NY 10036
(212) 533-7500 .. **Brown,** Ronna D '82 %Better Bus Bur -257 Park Av S -NY 10010 **Fx:**477-4912
(212) 209-4800 .. **Brown Rudnick LLP** -7 Times Sq -NY 10036 **Fx:**209-4801
(212) 596-9000 .. **Brown,** S Jason '88 (Ropes & G LLP) -1211 Av of Amer -NY 10036
(212) 587-5966 .. **Brown,** Saul C '92 -305 Bway -NY 10007 **Fx:**897-1437
(212) 819-0089 .. **Brown,** Scott F '95 %Edmonds & Co,PC -112 Mad Av -NY 10016 **Fx:**819-0189
(716) 549-1565 .. **Brown,** Scott M '84 -Bx7 -Angola 14006
(212) 589-4200 .. **Brown,** Seanna Rose '07 %Baker & H LLP -45 Rckfllr Plz -NY 10111
(845) 462-2700 .. **Brown,** Sharon A '88 %DG Ellis -2076 South Rd -Poughkeepsie 12601 **Fx:**462-4895
(212) 820-9657 .. **Brown,** Sharon L '98 %Hawkins D&W LLP -One Chase Manh Plz -NY 10005
(845) 624-1966 .. **Brown,** Shawn M '91 (Brown B&H,PC) -365 Route 304 -Bardonia 10954
(212) 532-8585 .. **Brown,** Shayne L '01 %S Feldman -12 E 41st -NY 10017 **Fx:**532-8598
(212) 417-5300 .. **Brown,** Sherrie E '81 %Medicaid Fraud Cntrl -120 Bway -NY 10271 **Fx:**417-5274
(212) 419-2899 .. **Brown,** Spencer L '92 Excelsior Radio Ntwk -220 W 42nd -NY 10036 **Fx:**285-0174
(212) 918-3000 .. **Brown,** Stanley J '06 (Hogan L LLP) -875 3rd Av -NY 10022
(631) 424-8484 .. **Brown,** Stephen A '87 -191 NY Av -Huntngtn 11743 **Fx:**425-7030
(914) 779-1100 .. **Brown,** Stephen J '05 %Veneruso CS&C,LLP -35 E Grassy Sprain Rd -Ynkrs 10710
(212) 332-8900 .. **Brown,** Stephenie L '97 Simon & Prtnrs LLP -551 5th Av -NY 10176 **Fx:**332-8909
(212) 788-1004 .. **Brown,** Steven C '82 %Law Dept -100 Church -NY 10007 **Fx:**788-0367
(212) 762-4723 .. **Brown,** Steven L '91 Morgan Stanley -1221 Av of Amer -NY 10020
(518) 783-2200 .. **Brown,** Steven S '82 (Brown & B) -11 Century Hill Dr -Latham 12110 **Fx:**783-2225
(212) 735-3000 .. **Brown,** Susan A '95 %Skadden ASM&F LLP -4 Times Sq -NY 10036
(914) 686-0108 .. **Brown,** Susan S '88 (Glassman & B) -99 Court -White Plns 10601
(716) 852-0400 .. **Brown,** T Alan '63 (Roach BM&G,PC) -424 Main -Buffalo 14202
(585) 454-5050 .. **Brown,** T Andrew '85 (Brown & H) -2 State -Rchstr 14614
(212) 815-1818 .. **Brown,** Tammy L '92 %DC 37 MELS -125 Barclay -NY 10007 **Fx:**815-1343
(585) 454-3377 .. **Brown & Tarantino,LLC** -19 Prince -Rchstr 14607 **Fx:**232-5883
(716) 849-6500 .. **Brown & Tarantino,LLC** -14 Lafayette Sq -Buffalo 14203 **Fx:**849-6503
(914) 949-5300 .. **Brown & Tarantino,LLC** -1 N Bway -White Plns 10601 **Fx:**949-6284
(212) 872-1000 .. **Brown,** Taryn C '10 -One Bryant Park -NY 10036 **Fx:**872-1002
(914) 681-6200 .. **Brown,** Terryl L '93 %NYPA -123 Main -White Plns 10601 **Fx:**390-8038
(212) 586-2211 .. **Brown,** Thos A II '95 (Orans EL&B LLP) -875 3rd Av -NY 10022
(212) 637-2194 .. **Brown,** Thos G A '97 %US Atty -1 St Andrews Plz -NY 10007
(212) 751-5959 .. **Brown,** Tinika M '04 %Ehrenkranz & E,LLP -375 Park Av -NY 10152 **Fx:**754-1905
(518) 877-7857 .. **Brown,** Tracey A '02 -Bx4760 -Clifton Pk 12065 **Fx:**877-8387
(212) 553-9215 .. **Brown,** Tracey L '04 (Cochran Firm) -233 Bway -NY 10279
(845) 897-1600 .. **Brown,** Tyrone S '07 %Rosicki R & Assoc,PC -2 Summit Ct -Fishkill 12524 **Fx:**897-2648
(212) 742-0002 .. **Brown,** Van '02 (V Brown,PC) -26 Bway -NY 10004 **Fx:**809-4753
(845) 735-0088 .. **Brown,** Vera G '89 (Brown B&K,LLP) -275 N Mddltwn Rd -Pearl Rvr 10965 **Fx:**735-7660
(516) 357-3700 .. **Brown,** Verley A '09 %Cullen and D LLP -100 Q Roosevelt Blvd -Gdn Cty 11530
(212) 847-2300 .. **Brown,** Vernon J '97 -888 7th Av -NY 10106 **Fx:**847-2350
(212) 227-7373 .. **Brown,** Victor M '92 -11 Park Pl -NY 10007
(212) 909-6000 .. **Brown,** Victoria G J '10 %Debevoise & P LLP -919 3rd Av -NY 10022
(212) 874-6181 .. **Brown,** Victoria M '83 -324 W 83rd -NY 10024
(718) 645-3111 .. **Brown,** Violet Lee '02 %Leg Aid Society Ofc for the Aging -111 Lvngstn -Brklyn 11201 **Fx:**260-4722
(914) 725-7243 .. **Brown,** Virginia R '89 -137 Edgemont Rd -Scarsdale 10583 **Fx:**725-0158
(518) 427-7350 .. **Brown & Weinraub PLLC** -79 Columbia -Albany 12210 **Fx:**427-7792
(212) 566-4600 .. **Brown & Weinraub PLLC** -233 Bway -NY 10279 **Fx:**566-4063
(212) 527-1000 .. **Brown,** Wm C III '80 OfCnsl Jones HC&B PC -1 Bttry Pk Plz -NY 10004
(716) 847-8400 .. **Brown,** Wm J '80 (Phillips L LLP) -3400 HSBC Ctr -Buffalo 14203
(212) 759-4888 .. **Brown,** Wm J '80 (Phillips L LLP) -437 Mad Av -NY 10022
(607) 778-2403 .. **Brown,** Wm L '84 %Pub Def -45 Hawley Bx1766 -Bnghmtn 13902 **Fx:**778-2432
(914) 345-9001 .. **Brown,** Wm M '99 %Taro Pharmaceuticals USA Inc -5 Skyline Dr -Hawthorne 10532 **Fx:**345-8728
(212) 349-6009 .. **Brownback,** Elizabeth Ann '98 %Sanctuary for Families -110 Wall -NY 10005 **Fx:**566-0344
(914) 995-6317 .. **Brownbill-Vega,** Susan '95 %DA -111 Martin Luther King Blvd -White Plns 10601 **Fx:**995-3362
(212) 572-6214 .. **Browndorf,** Matthew C '04 -300 Park Av -NY 10022 **Fx:**572-6499
(718) 990-2703 .. **Brown-Douglas,** Victoria L '93 %St John's Law Schl -8000 Utopia Pkwy -Jamaica 11439 **Fx:**591-1855
(516) 678-6795 .. **Browne,** Arthur J '79 -17 Hewitt Rd -Rockvll Ctr 11570
(212) 815-1304 .. **Browne,** Audrey A '82 DC 37 Hlth & Security Plan -125 Barclay -NY 10007
(631) 761-0800 .. **Browne,** Christian P '05 %Lazer AR&Y,PC -225 Old Cntry Rd -Melvll 11747
(212) 548-2100 .. **Browne,** Christopher P '87 %McGuire W LLP -1345 Av of Amer -NY 10105
(212) 986-4030 .. **Browne,** Cori '02 Driscoll & R -521 5th Av -NY 10175 **Fx:**986-4050
(212) 768-6700 .. **Browne,** Diana G '86 Cnsl Sonnenschein N&R LLP -2 World Fncl Ctr -NY 10281
(212) 238-4800 .. **Browne,** Erika C '06 %Landman CB&F,PC -120 Bway -NY 10271
(718) 664-1808 .. **Browne,** Erin E '07 ACS -900 Sheridan Av -Bronx 10451
(212) 414-9161 .. **Browne,** Frances K '89 (Brody & B LLP) -1 Penn Plz -NY 10119
(631) 692-8600 .. **Browne,** Helen T '97 %Cold Spring Harbor High Sch -82 Turkey Ln -Cold Spg Hbr 11724
(516) 671-2197 .. **Browne,** Jo-Ann '88 -Bx418 -Locust Vly 11560
(212) 554-1400 .. **Browne,** John C '00 (Bernstein LB&G LLP) -1285 Av of Amer -NY 10019
(631) 547-4200 .. **Browne,** John P '76 Nikon Inc -1300 Walt Whitman Rd -Melvll 11747 **Fx:**547-6261
(212) 770-7000 .. **Browne,** Kathleen B '90 AIG Ins -70 Pine -NY 10270
(347) 882-0033 .. **Browne,** Laura C '06 -751 Cmmnwlth Av -Bronx 10473 **Fx:**(718) 542-6630
(212) 839-6511 .. **Browne,** N Patricia '01 Dept of Transportation -55 Water -NY 10041
(212) 902-1000 .. **Browne,** Nancy D '88 %Goldman Sachs -1 NY Plz -NY 10004
(212) 407-8218 .. **Browne,** Timothy J '02 NBA -645 5th Av -NY 10022
(718) 250-2000 .. **Browne-Lee,** Sharlene W '83 %DA -350 Jay -Brklyn 11201 **Fx:**250-2314

(315) 789-3922 .. **Brownell**, Carlton K '66 Town Atty -3750 Cnty Road 6 -Geneva 14456
(716) 854-4055 .. **Brownell**, Carlton K III '90 (O'Neill & B) -298 Main -Buffalo 14202 **Fx:**854-4062
(518) 869-9500 .. **Brownell**, Conor E '06 %Ganz W&S,LLP -1 Columbia Cir -Albany 12203
(518) 374-9832 .. **Brownell**, Glen W '85 -600 Franklin -Schnctdy 12305 **Fx:**374-2914
(212) 400-7225 .. **Brownell**, Richd J '90 (Zaremba B&B PLLC) -40 Wall -NY 10005 **Fx:**(646) 512-5607
(212) 605-9228 .. **Brownell**, Serena R '94 -660 Mad Av -NY 10065
(607) 725-7516 .. **Browning**, Chas L '90 -76 Genesee Bx237 -Greene 13778
(212) 872-9832 .. **Browning**, Jackson B Jr. '76 (Squire S&D LLP) -30 Rckfllr Plz -NY 10112
(518) 449-3900 .. **Browning**, Lindsay N '09 %Cooper E&S,LLP -39 N Pearl -Albany 12207
(914) 253-9400 .. **Browning**, Renita D '89 Browning Metals Corp -2975 Wstchstr Av -Purchase 10577 **Fx:**253-9411
(718) 858-7152 .. **Brown-Inz**, Steven D '77 -25 Joralemon -Brklyn 11201
(631) 749-0405 .. **Brownlie**, Heather Gordon '95 -25 Shore Rd Bx623 -Shelter Isl 11964
(212) 373-3000 .. **Brownlow**, Winston R '09 %Paul WRW&G LLP -1285 Av of Amer -NY 10019
(212) 218-5500 .. **Brownridge**, Lawr B '81 (Seyfarth S LLP) -620 8th Av -NY 10018
(631) 853-5212 .. **Browns**, Bryan L '04 -Bx9082 -Central Islip 11722
(718) 243-6460 .. **Brownscheidle**, Gretchen '01 Leg Aid -111 Lvngstn -Brklyn 11201 **Fx:**237-8737
(212) 704-8234 .. **Brownstein**, Alexander C '94 %Edelman Public Relations -1500 Bway -NY 10036 **Fx:**704-0128
(212) 403-1000 .. **Brownstein**, Andrew R '80 (Wachtell LR&K) -51 W 52nd -NY 10019
(718) 969-8010 .. **Brownstein**, Chas S '57 -69-36 174th -Flushng 11365 **Fx:**969-8140
(516) 466-1100 .. **Brownstein**, Danl J '60 -98 Cutter Mill Rd -Gt Neck 11021 **Fx:**466-1286
(718) 993-2556 .. **Brownstein**, Elfreda '82 Envrnmntl Cntrl Brd -3030 3rd Av -Bronx 10455
(212) 506-1700 .. **Brownstein**, Henry B '07 %Kasowitz BT&F LLP -1633 Bway -NY 10019
(718) 585-6495 .. **Brownstein**, Howard K '75 -909 Sheridan Av -Bronx 10451 **Fx:**293-4040
(516) 286-5442 .. **Brownstein**, Ilissa R '04 -22 Crtlandt -NY 10007 **Fx:**(212) 608-5442
(716) 854-5200 .. **Brownstein**, Joel '58 (Borins SS&B) -403 Main -Buffalo 14203
(212) 885-4727 .. **Brownstein**, Jonathan L '96 %CIBC World Markets -425 Lex Av -NY 10017
(914) 949-2700 .. **Brownstein**, Judy B '75 OfCnsl Bleakley P&S,LLP -1 N Lex Av -White Plns 10601
(212) 839-5300 .. **Brownstein**, Katharine F '06 %Sidley A LLP -787 7th Av -NY 10019
(212) 536-9062 .. **Brownstein**, Megan L '06 Jones Apparel Grp -1411 Bway -NY 10018
(212) 207-8889 .. **Brownstein**, Michl A '95 (M Brownstein,PLLC) -11 Penn Plz -NY 10001 **Fx:**207-8994
(212) 885-5000 .. **Brownstein**, Michl Z '74 (Blank R LLP) -405 Lex Av -NY 10174
(212) 504-6000 .. **Brownstein**, Miller B '05 %Cadwalader W&T LLP -1 World Fncl Ctr -NY 10281
(585) 381-4320 .. **Brown-Steiner**, Terrence C '86 OfCnsl Odorisi Law Firm -311 S Wshngtn Bx69 -E Rchstr 14445 **Fx:**586-5624
(914) 937-6672 .. **Brown-Weissman**, Holly S '84 %Weissman Mgmt -225 Wstchstr Av -Pt Chester 10573 **Fx:**937-5129
(212) 474-1000 .. **Brownwood**, David O '69 SrCnsl Cravath S&M LLP -825 8th Av -NY 10019
(516) 756-5100 .. **Brownyard**, Ryan L '02 %Lavallee Law Ofc -4 West Gate Rd -Farmngdl 11735 **Fx:**756-4629
(516) 663-6600 .. **Browser**, Adam L '92 OfCnsl Ruskin MF,PC -1425 RXR Plz -Uniondale 11556
(585) 325-6202 .. **Broyles**, Mark K '89 (Relin G&C LLP) -28 E Main -Rchstr 14614
(212) 574-1200 .. **Broz**, Michl W '10 %Seward & K LLP -1 Bttry Pk Plz -NY 10004
(212) 391-9500 .. **Brozik**, Matthew D '99 %Einbinder & D,PC -104 W 40th -NY 10018
(631) 544-6331 .. **Brozinsky**, Edw '69 -152 Lakebrdg Dr N -Kings Pk 11754 **Fx:**544-6221
(212) 878-8000 .. **Brozman**, Andrew P '76 (Clifford C LLP) -31 W 52nd -NY 10019
(212) 259-8000 .. **Brozost**, Marshall '95 (Dewey & L LLP) -1301 Av of Amer -NY 10019
(212) 952-0602 .. **Brualdi**, Richd B '89 -29 Bway -NY 10006 **Fx:**952-0608
(212) 697-3122 .. **Brubaker**, Dana L '05 %Martin C&B LLP -220 E 42nd -NY 10017
(917) 450-4018 .. **Brubaker**, Lisa N '05 -94 E 4th -NY 10003 **Fx:**591-4175
(716) 852-9800 .. **Brucato**, Robt C Jr. '91 %Counsel Press,LLC -295 Main -Buffalo 14203
(716) 843-5700 .. **Bruce**, Anthony M '75 %US Atty -138 Delaware Av -Buffalo 14202 **Fx:**551-3052
(585) 546-7430 .. **Bruce**, Benjamin A '90 %Dept of Law -144 Exchange Blvd -Rchstr 14614 **Fx:**546-7514
(212) 801-9200 .. **Bruce**, Cameron N '10 %Greenberg T,LLP -200 Park Av -NY 10166
(212) 815-1818 .. **Bruce**, Diane L '93 %DC 37 MELS -125 Barclay -NY 10007 **Fx:**815-1343
(212) 521-5400 .. **Bruce**, Keri S '08 %Reed S LLP -599 Lex Av -NY 10022
(212) 701-3000 .. **Bruce**, R Banks '08 %Cahill G&R LLP -80 Pine -NY 10005 **Fx:**269-5420
(315) 422-6154 .. **Bruce**, Sherry R '92 (Greene H&S) -1 Lincoln Ctr -Syracuse 13202
(212) 654-8376 .. **Bruce**, Valerie C '99 Sundance Channel LLC -1633 Bway -NY 10019
(212) 450-4000 .. **Bruck**, Andrew J '09 %Davis P&W LLP -450 Lex Av -NY 10017
(212) 610-6300 .. **Bruck**, Jaime E '03 Allen & O -1221 Av of Amer -NY 10020
(631) 385-1944 .. **Bruckart**, David L '89 -14 Old Northport Rd -Huntngtn 11743
(212) 244-6600 .. **Brucker**, Andrew P '76 (Schechter & B,PC) -350 5th Av -NY 10118
(212) 695-8100 .. **Bruckman**, George T '60 (Goetz F,LLP) -1 Penn Plz -NY 10119
(516) 256-3370 .. **Bruckman**, Jennifer E '08 Foundation Src -777 Sunrise Hwy -Lynbrk 11563
(212) 521-3700 .. **Bruckmann**, Bruce C '82 BRS & Co,LLC -126 E 56th -NY 10022 **Fx:**521-3799
(212) 850-8500 .. **Bruckmann**, Mark F '76 (Bruckmann & V,LLP) -420 Lex Av -NY 10170
(212) 850-8500 .. **Bruckmann & Victory,LLP** -420 Lex Av -NY 10170 **Fx:**850-8505
(516) 747-2000 .. **Bruckner**, Frederic N '82 %Margolin Winer Evens,LLP -400 Grdn City Plz -Gdn City 11530 **Fx:**747-6707
(212) 545-4605 .. **Bruckner**, Gustavo F '93 OfCnsl Wolf HAF&H LLP -270 Mad Av -NY 10016
(631) 360-7333 .. **Bruckner**, James D '88 %De Sena & S -1383 Vets Mem'l Hwy -Hauppauge 11788
(212) 610-6300 .. **Bruckner**, Matthew A '08 %Allen & O -1221 Av of Amer -NY 10020
(212) 210-9596 .. **Bruckner**, Willa Cohen '82 (Alston & B LLP) -90 Park Av -NY 10016
(718) 224-1390 .. **Bruder**, Howard '85 -212-09 67th Av -Oakland Gdns 11364
(212) 963-6583 .. **Bruderlein**, Claude '97 %United Nations -1 UN Plz -NY 10017
(516) 571-0338 .. **Brudie**, Barbara A '88 Nassau Cty Clerk -240 Old Cntry Rd -Mineola 11501
(212) 318-6000 .. **Brudner**, Alan J '86 (Paul HJ&W LLP) -75 E 55th -NY 10022
(516) 741-4799 .. **Brudoley**, Michl '08 %Baker SBGFM&N,LLC -100 Grdn City Plz -Gdn Cty 11530
(718) 445-1613 .. **Brue**, Fred A '56 -171-52 46th Av -Flushng 11358
(631) 691-2600 .. **Bruechert**, Robt G '94 -140A Bway -Amityvll 11701 **Fx:**691-2662
(212) 848-4000 .. **Brueck**, Michl P '06 %Shearman & S LLP -599 Lex Av -NY 10022
(585) 258-2800 .. **Brueckner**, Wm E III '90 SrCnsl Underberg & K LLP -300 Bausch & Lomb Pl -Rchstr 14604
(518) 457-6137 .. **Bruen**, Kevin P '90 %State Police -1220 Wshngtn Av -Albany 12226 **Fx:**485-1164
(518) 474-1310 .. **Bruening**, Glen T '90 %Gov's Cnsls Ofc -242 State Cptl -Albany 12224
(212) 237-1000 .. **Bruenner**, Eric W '76 Cnsl Windels ML&M,LLP -156 W 56th -NY 10019
(212) 446-4800 .. **Bruens**, Craig A '99 (Kirkland & E LLP) -153 E 53rd -NY 10022
(631) 765-4343 .. **Bruer**, Rudolph H '65 -5500 Main Rd Bx1466 -Southold 11971 **Fx:**765-2752
(718) 250-2000 .. **Bruffee**, Anthea H '80 %DA -350 Jay -Brklyn 11201 **Fx:**250-2314
(315) 474-2943 .. **Bruffett**, David C Jr. '03 %Sugarman Law Firm,LLP -211 W Jffrsn -Syracuse 13202
(212) 410-0100 .. **Bruh**, Mark E '01 %R Geltzer -1556 3rd Av -NY 10128 **Fx:**410-0400
(212) 869-5030 .. **Bruh**, Saul D '80 (Kucker & B,LLP) -747 3rd Av -NY 10017
(212) 833-8000 .. **Bruh**, Tara A '01 Sony BMG Music Entrtnmnt -550 Mad Av -NY 10022 **Fx:**833-8406
(845) 331-5058 .. **Bruhn**, J Michl Jr. '95 -85 John Bx4487 -Kingston 12402 **Fx:**331-2753
(212) 760-2681 .. **Bruhn**, Jarrett D '96 %JP Morgan Chase -60 Wall -NY 10260
(516) 663-6600 .. **Brum**, Irvin '80 (Ruskin MF,PC) -1425 RXR Plz -Uniondale 11556
(212) 262-6699 .. **Brum**, Richd J '08 %Tenzer & L LLP -1775 Bway -NY 10019
(646) 416-6262 .. **Brumer**, Michl B '95 -1 Lincoln Plz -NY 10023
(845) 306-1000 .. **Brumley**, Philip '88 %Watchtower -100 Watchtower Dr -Patterson 12563 **Fx:**306-0709
(212) 605-2000 .. **Brumm**, James E '69 %Mitsubishi Intl -655 3rd Av -NY 10017 **Fx:**605-2129
(212) 705-8868 .. **Brumm**, Nicholas D S '93 QVT Financial -1177 Av of Amer -NY 10036
(212) 806-5400 .. **Brummer**, Diana M '99 (Stroock &S&L LLP) -180 Maiden Ln -NY 10038
(914) 332-0700 .. **Brundage**, Laura M '95 %M Pollack -150 Wht Plns Rd -Tarrytwn 10591 **Fx:**684-6069
(585) 442-2551 .. **Brundage**, Saml G '51 (Johnson M&B,PC) -1399 Monroe Av -Rchstr 14618
(914) 785-5300 .. **Brundage**, Steven J '92 %A Lamer -555 Taxter Rd -Elmsfrd 10523 **Fx:**347-4269
(914) 328-0335 .. **Brundage**, Theo J '81 -500 Mamaroneck Av -Harrison 10528
(201) 536-9220 .. **Brundige**, Robt W Jr. '70 SrCnsl Hughes H&R LLP -1 Bttry Pk Plz -NY 10004 **Fx:**536-0799
(212) 668-1900 .. **Brune & Richard LLP** -80 Broad -NY 10004 **Fx:**668-0315
(212) 668-1900 .. **Brune**, Susan E '89 (Brune & R LLP) -80 Broad -NY 10004
(315) 423-4400 .. **Brune**, Tracy Alexander '94 (Wolff G&G,LLP) -217 Mntgmry -Syracuse 13202
(716) 852-1088 .. **Brunea**, Chris T '80 -170 Franklin -Buffalo 14202 **Fx:**845-6457
(716) 753-4241 .. **Brunecz**, Tracey '89 %DA -Cnty Cthse -Mayvll 14757 **Fx:**753-4628
(212) 809-9100 .. **Brunelle**, George '75 (Brunelle & H,PC) -1 Whitehall -NY 10004 **Fx:**809-3219
(516) 222-2626 .. **Brunengraber**, Marc B '97 %Feldherr & F -900 Merchnts Cncrs -Westbury 11590 **Fx:**222-2651
(212) 508-6100 .. **Brunette**, Jeris D '09 %Bracewell & G,LLP -1251 Av of Amer -NY 10020
(716) 855-7254 .. **Brunette**, Vicky-Marie J '95 %NFTA -181 Ellicott -Buffalo 14203 **Fx:**855-7657
(718) 332-7766 .. **Brunetti**, Christopher J '06 Eaton & T,LLP -1662 Sheepshead Bay Rd -Brklyn 11235 **Fx:**332-5898
(212) 546-9255 .. **Brunetti**, Frank L '82 (Scarinci H) -107 Grand -NY 10013
(516) 794-3500 .. **Brunetti**, Robt J '90 (Brunetti A&T,PLLC) -170 Old Cntry Rd -Mineola 11501 **Fx:**794-3696
(212) 558-4000 .. **Bruney**, Craig W '07 %Sullivan & C LLP -125 Broad -NY 10004
(646) 845-1123 .. **Bruni**, Gennaro '90 Standard Chartered Bk -1 Mad Av -NY 10010
(212) 702-1829 .. **Bruning**, Dianne N '01 Bank of Montreal -3 Times Sq -NY 10036 **Fx:**(646) 366-1724
(212) 458-3219 .. **Brunje**, Richd J '94 %AIG -175 Water -NY 10038
(860) 256-8539 .. **Brunjes**, John A '90 (Bracewell & G,LLP) -1251 Av of Amer -NY 10020 **Fx:**760-6928
(212) 319-1000 .. **Brunk**, Danl B '08 Quirk & B,PC -845 3rd Av -NY 10022
(585) 232-5300 .. **Brunner**, Adam H '07 %Boylan BCV&W,LLP -2400 Chase Sq -Rchstr 14604
(212) 903-8700 .. **Brunner**, Emily S '07 %Roberts & H,LLP -825 8th Av -NY 10019
(646) 264-3650 .. **Brunner**, Jane S '77 %US Dept of Labor -201 Varick -NY 10014 **Fx:**264-3660
(212) 450-4000 .. **Brunner**, Janice G '01 %Davis P&W LLP -450 Lex Av -NY 10017
(212) 809-1166 .. **Brunnock**, Timothy J '91 (Brunnock & F,PC) -204 W 84th -NY 10024 **Fx:**809-1155
(718) 286-6000 .. **Bruno**, Anthony '09 %DA -125-01 Qns Blvd -Kew Gdns 11415
(212) 949-0100 .. **Bruno**, Christopher J '87 %Cmmnwlth Land Title -140 E 45th -NY 10017 **Fx:**983-8430
(631) 390-0010 .. **Bruno**, Craig J '82 (Bruno G&S,LLP) -445 Broad Hollow Rd -Melvll 11747

(516) 877-2900 .. **Bruno,** Danielle T '01 %Bartlett MB&M,LLP -300 Old Cntry Rd -Mineola 11501
(212) 384-1000 .. **Bruno,** Dawn C '92 %FBI -26 Fed Plz -NY 10278
(845) 361-3671 .. **Bruno,** Edw C '98 -15 Bruyn Av Bx987 -Pine Bush 12566 **Fx:**913-9200
(914) 345-2600 .. **Bruno,** Erasmo S '85 (ES Bruno Law Firm,PC) -30 Lark Av -White Plns 10607 **Fx:**345-2604
(212) 345-2136 .. **Bruno,** Francesca '83 %Mercer HR Cnsltng -1166 Av of Amer -NY 10036
(212) 613-2043 .. **Bruno,** Frank A '00 (Gibbons PC) -1 Penn Plz -NY 10119 **Fx:**554-9662
(212) 839-5300 .. **Bruno,** Frank P '80 (Sidley A LLP) -787 7th Av -NY 10019
(631) 543-8811 .. **Bruno,** Frank P '03 %C altese -1050 W Jericho Tpk -Smithtwn 11787 **Fx:**543-1718
(718) 418-5000 .. **Bruno,** Frank X Jr. '97 Bruno Law Ofc -66-09 Myrtle Av -Glendale 11385 **Fx:**418-3266
(315) 363-4690 .. **Bruno,** Gary F '77 (Dunn B&S LLP) -1507 Uppr Lenox Av -Oneida 13421
(631) 390-0010 .. **Bruno Gerbino & Soriano,LLP** -445 Broad Hollow Rd -Melvll 11747 **Fx:**393-5497
(845) 454-2385 .. **Bruno,** Glenn R '93 -11 Market -Poughkeepsie 12601 **Fx:**454-2387
(201) 200-2033 .. **Bruno,** Joanne Z '92 -32 Gramercy Park S -NY 10003 **Fx:**200-3434
(212) 952-1111 .. **Bruno,** John J '95 (H Gladstein & Prtnrs LLC) -110 Wall -NY 10005 **Fx:**943-7427
(212) 980-9600 .. **Bruno,** Jonathan B '96 (Kaufman B&R) -120 Bway -NY 10271
(212) 872-3062 .. **Bruno,** Jos J '00 KPMG LLP -345 Park Av -NY 10154
(518) 561-2130 .. **Bruno,** Keith M '86 -62 Brinkerhoff -Plattsbrgh 12901 **Fx:**561-2194
(518) 279-1217 .. **Bruno,** Kenneth R '91 -3991 NY Rte 2 Bx159 -Cropseyville 12052 **Fx:**279-9434
(212) 458-1520 .. **Bruno,** Lori Ann '96 %AIG -175 Water -NY 10038 **Fx:**458-0859
(516) 281-9800 .. **Bruno,** Matthew V '07 %Goldberg S LLP -200 Old Cntry Rd -Mineola 11501
(518) 479-2011 .. **Bruno,** Nicholas J Jr. '80 -469 Miller Rd -E Greenbush 12061 **Fx:**479-2011
(516) 328-9500 .. **Bruno,** Patrick L '80 (Bruno G&V) -99 Tulip Av -Floral Pk 11001 **Fx:**775-8326
(212) 474-1000 .. **Bruno,** Roberto '98 %Cravath S&M LLP -825 8th Av -NY 10019
(631) 979-3480 .. **Bruno,** Rosemarie '03 R Bruno,PLLC -4250 Vets Mem'l Hwy -Holbrook 11741 **Fx:**716-7171
(212) 656-5464 .. **Bruno,** Thos C '89 NYSE -11 Wall -NY 10005
(212) 986-4500 .. **Bruns,** Alyson C '04 %Horwitz H&P -405 Lex Av -NY 10174
(607) 273-2202 .. **Bruns,** Diane Vargo '93 (Schlather SP&S) -200 E Buffalo Bx353 -Ithaca 14851
(212) 826-1054 .. **Bruns,** Emerson E '96 (EE Bruns,PLLC) -1790 Bway -NY 10019 **Fx:**832-2969
(212) 856-9600 .. **Brunsden,** Andrew C '10 %Morvillo AGIA&B,PC -565 5th Av -NY 10017
(718) 634-4444 .. **Brunstein,** Irene Y '87 -124-04 Cronston Av -Rckwy Pk 11694 **Fx:**634-4448
(585) 244-4239 .. **Brunsting,** Suzanne L '88 -202 Clovercrest Dr -Rchstr 14618
(914) 220-0020 .. **Brusca,** Raymond J '92 -2 Gannett Dr -White Plns 10604 **Fx:**220-0016
Brusca, Robt L '90 -105 Devonshr Dr -E Norwich 11732
(518) 862-1200 .. **Bruschini,** Robt S '94 %Martin H&M LLP -Bx15141 -Albany 12212
(718) 680-5000 .. **Brusco,** Ann Marie '94 %JJ Visci -8302 13th Av -Brklyn 11228 **Fx:**833-2912
(212) 526-3218 .. **Brusco,** F Robt '92 Lehman Brothers Inc -399 Park Av -NY 10022 **Fx:**(646) 758-4635
(212) 799-3205 .. **Brusco,** Nicholas E '89 -165 W 74th -NY 10023
(212) 799-3205 .. **Brusco,** Paul A '90 -163 W 74th -NY 10023
(646) 395-8582 .. **Brusewitz,** Mary Rose '83 (Strasburger & P LLP) -750 Lex Av -NY 10022
(518) 765-2503 .. **Brusgul,** Justin C '90 -Bx474 -Voorheesvll 12186
(516) 496-5822 .. **Brush,** Jesse R '10 %T Spina -170 Froehlich Farm Blvd -Woodbury 11797 **Fx:**496-5420
(516) 512-8981 .. **Brush,** Louis F '80 -1225 Franklin Av -Gdn Cty 11530 **Fx:**742-9038
(212) 326-2000 .. **Brush,** Matthew R '10 %O'Melveny & M LLP -7 Times Sq -NY 10036
(212) 909-6000 .. **Brusiloff,** Paul D '92 (Debevoise & P LLP) -919 3rd Av -NY 10022
(212) 318-6000 .. **Bruso,** Michl M '06 %Paul HJ&W LLP -75 E 55th -NY 10022
(518) 473-4982 .. **Bruso,** Wm F Jr. '86 %Ofc Gnl Srvcs -Corning Twr ESP -Albany 12242 **Fx:**473-4973
(631) 501-5700 .. **Brussel,** Dana A '01 (Carter DF&S LLP) -445 Broadhallow Rd -Melvll 11747
(212) 836-8000 .. **Brustein,** Andrea H '06 %Kaye S LLP -425 Park Av -NY 10022
(212) 676-0987 .. **Brustein,** Evan C '08 %Law Dept -60 Lafayette -NY 10013 **Fx:**442-6865
(845) 634-4700 .. **Brustein-Kampel,** Lynn J '80 (Abel & B-K,PC) -37 Congers Rd -New Cty 10956
(212) 965-9081 .. **Brustin,** Nick J '97 (Neufeld S&B) -99 Hudson -NY 10013
(914) 681-9100 .. **Brustman,** Jayson A '82 -399 Knollwood Rd -White Plns 10603 **Fx:**681-5109
(212) 474-1000 .. **Brutlag,** Benjamin D '08 %Cravath S&M LLP -825 8th Av -NY 10019
(212) 277-6500 .. **Brutman,** Laura C '01 (Dickstein S LLP) -1633 Bway -NY 10019
(718) 627-1659 .. **Brutten,** Alan I '67 -1341 Ocean Pkwy -Brklyn 11230 **Fx:**375-2469
(212) 248-1126 .. **Brutten,** Caren S '72 -17 Battery Pl -NY 10004 **Fx:**248-1128
(212) 969-6751 .. **Bruttomesso,** Frank J '94 %Alliance Bernstein LP -1345 Av of Amer -NY 10105 **Fx:**554-4639
(585) 987-2800 .. **Bruu,** Christen C '93 %Woods OG LLP -2 State -Rchstr 14614
(631) 283-7007 .. **Bruyn,** Wayne D '92 (O'Shea M&B,LLP) -250 N Sea Rd -Southampton 11968
(212) 872-1000 .. **Bruynes,** John P '91 -One Bryant Park -NY 10036 **Fx:**872-1002
(212) 269-1114 .. **Bruzga,** Chas E '86 -11 Bway -NY 10004 **Fx:**943-1238
(212) 732-2000 .. **Bruzina,** John S '08 %Cullen and D LLP -44 Wall -NY 10005
(914) 347-2600 .. **Bruzzese,** Sheryl A '02 %Traub LS&S LLP -7 Skyline Dr -Hawthorne 10532
(212) 808-7800 .. **Bruzzese-Szczygiel,** Pamela '00 (Kelley D&W LLP) -101 Park Av -NY 10178
(914) 642-3530 .. **Bruzzone,** Lauren C '92 %IBM -1133 Wstchstr Av -White Plns 10604 **Fx:**642-5788
(718) 773-2400 .. **Bryan,** A Lorenzo '88 (AL Bryan,LLC) -366 Styvsnt Av -Brklyn 11233 **Fx:**773-2444
(212) 909-6000 .. **Bryan,** Barry R '59 SrCnsl Debevoise & P LLP -919 3rd Av -NY 10022
(518) 455-4311 .. **Bryan,** Bernard H '74 %NYS Assembly -80 State -Albany 12248
(315) 476-1800 .. **Bryan,** Bruce R '81 -333 E Onondaga -Syracuse 13202
(212) 541-2000 .. **Bryan Cave LLP** -1290 Av of Amer -NY 10104 **Fx:**541-4630
(212) 504-6000 .. **Bryan,** Chas E '75 (Cadwalader W&T LLP) -1 World Fncl Ctr -NY 10281
(212) 232-1300 .. **Bryan,** Christopher D '09 %Lewis BB&S LLP -77 Water -NY 10005
(212) 403-1000 .. **Bryan,** David C '93 (Wachtell LR&K) -51 W 52nd -NY 10019
(212) 664-4444 .. **Bryan,** Donna M '95 %NBC Olympics -30 Rckfllr Plz -NY 10112
(212) 788-1341 .. **Bryan,** Kim '96 %Law Dept -100 Church -NY 10007 **Fx:**788-0367
(646) 434-8172 .. **Bryan,** Richd '96 R Bryan PLLC -350 1st Av -NY 10010 **Fx:**(212) 658-9581
(212) 592-1400 .. **Bryan,** T James '71 -2 Park Av -NY 10016 **Fx:**592-1500
(212) 878-8000 .. **Bryant,** Adrain L '08 %Clifford C LLP -31 W 52nd -NY 10019
(212) 967-1800 .. **Bryant,** B Seth '97 (Bryant BJ&R LLP) -140 Bway -NY 10005
(718) 852-3682 .. **Bryant,** Bruce K '77 -16 Court -Brklyn 11241 **Fx:**855-2727
(212) 967-1800 .. **Bryant Burgher Jaffe & Roberts LLP** -140 Bway -NY 10005 **Fx:**967-1811
(212) 918-3000 .. **Bryant,** Christopher R '01 %Hogan L LLP -875 3rd Av -NY 10022
(518) 474-3882 .. **Bryant,** David D '88 %Dept of Ed -89 Wshngtn Av -Albany 12234 **Fx:**486-7336
(212) 732-2000 .. **Bryant,** Deborah Ann '90 %Cullen and D LLP -44 Wall -NY 10005
(518) 474-5209 .. **Bryant,** Eileen E '80 %Dept of Law -The Cptl -Albany 12224
(914) 997-1346 .. **Bryant,** Gina M '03 %Seham SM&P,LLP -445 Hmltn Av -White Plns 10601
(518) 295-7500 .. **Bryant,** James M '79 -279 Main Bx653 -Schoharie 12157 **Fx:**295-7574
(212) 859-8000 .. **Bryant,** Jared M '10 %Fried FHS&J LLP -1 NY Plz -NY 10004
(631) 577-2400 .. **Bryant,** Kevin J '85 %Tromello M&K -25 Melvll Park Rd Bx9038 -Melvll 11747
(845) 339-9344 .. **Bryant,** Kevin R '99 -85 John Bx4487 -Kingston 12402 **Fx:**331-2753
(212) 458-2332 .. **Bryant,** Kyle D '07 AIG -175 Water -NY 10038
(212) 969-6791 .. **Bryant,** Marc R '07 Alliance Bernstein LP -1345 Av of Amer -NY 10105 **Fx:**554-4639
(516) 873-6334 .. **Bryant,** Matthew '03 %Ohrenstein & B,LLP -1010 Franklin Av Bx9243 -Gdn Cty 11530
(315) 422-4727 .. **Bryant,** Michl M '91 -239 E Water -Syracuse 13202
(212) 903-5187 .. **Bryant,** Saleda S '05 Oprah Magazine -1700 Bway -NY 10019
(518) 465-3524 .. **Bryant,** Susan C '02 %NYS Defenders Assn -194 Wshngtn Av -Albany 12210 **Fx:**465-3249
(718) 340-4200 .. **Bryant,** Susan J '77 %CUNY Law Schl -65-21 Main -Flushng 11367 **Fx:**340-4482
(646) 557-5100 .. **Bryant,** Veronica '08 %Patton B LLP -1185 Av of Amer -NY 10036
(212) 756-2000 .. **Bryce,** Nathan A '10 %Schulte R&Z LLP -919 3rd Av -NY 10022
(212) 909-8351 .. **Bryce,** Philip R '92 -919 3rd Av -NY 10022
(212) 981-3085 .. **Bryde,** Steven P '80 Marcum & Kliegman LLP -655 3rd Av -NY 10017
(585) 232-6500 .. **Brydges,** Jerauld E '97 (Harter S&E LLP) -1600 Bausch & Lomb Pl -Rchstr 14604
(716) 856-0600 .. **Brydges,** Thos E '74 (Jaeckle F&M,LLP) -12 Fountain Plz -Buffalo 14202
(212) 906-1200 .. **Bryer,** Barry A '73 (Latham & W) -885 3rd Av -NY 10022
(212) 708-1800 .. **Bryer,** Lanning G '85 (Ladas & P) -26 W 61st -NY 10023
(212) 370-0630 .. **Bryer,** Madeline L '86 (M Bryer,PC) -60 E 42nd -NY 10165
(212) 727-2700 .. **Bryk,** Dale S '94 %NRDC -40 W 20th -NY 10011 **Fx:**727-1773
(718) 625-5430 .. **Bryk,** Laurie S '82 (Stern B&H,PC) -26 Court -Brklyn 11242
(347) 497-5972 .. **Bryk,** Wm '90 -578 74th -Brklyn 11209 **Fx:**497-5972
(212) 807-2875 .. **Brylski,** Steve '00 Thomson Reuters/RIA -195 Bway -NY 10007
(585) 494-1382 .. **Bryson,** Danl S '92 (Lacy K LLP) -16 N Lake -Bergen 14416
(585) 454-5650 .. **Bryson,** Danl S '92 (Lacy K LLP) -130 E Main -Rchstr 14604
(212) 576-5738 .. **Bryson,** Elizabeth A '83 NY Life Ins -51 Mad Av -NY 10010 **Fx:**589-4470
(585) 424-3270 .. **Brzezinski,** Kevin E '06 %Dollinger & Assoc,PC -777 Canal Vw Blvd -Rchstr 14623
(516) 487-5900 .. **Brzostovski,** Adam '88 GCP Capital Grp LLC -60 Cutter Mill Rd -Gt Neck 11021 **Fx:**487-5944
(212) 407-1200 .. **Bschorr,** Paul J '65 OfCnsl Joseph Law Ofcs LLC -485 Lex Av -NY 10017 **Fx:**407-1299
(516) 745-6830 .. **Buatti,** Maryanne '83 (Golden W&B PC) -900 Merchants Cncrs -Westbury 11590
(212) 858-7575 .. **Buba,** Barbara J '99 (Wilbraham L&B PC) -140 Bway -NY 10005
(973) 539-6500 .. **Bubb,** Michl S '86 (Bubb G&C,LLP) -65 W 36th -NY 10018 **Fx:**539-6409
(212) 438-8674 .. **Bubeck,** Thos F '96 %Capital IQ Inc -55 Water -NY 10041
(212) 336-2000 .. **Bubel,** Henry P '78 (Patterson BW&T LLP) -1133 Av of Amer -NY 10036
(516) 572-2380 .. **Bucaria,** Thos A '86 Dist Ct Law Dept -99 Main -Hempstd 11550
(718) 982-2000 .. **Bucaro,** Thos A '05 CUNY Cllg Staten Isl -2800 Victory Blvd -Staten Isl 10314
(518) 589-9797 .. **Bucca,** Anthony C '69 -6055 Main Bx907 -Tannersvll 12485 **Fx:**589-9959
(518) 719-3590 .. **Bucca,** Chas O '00 %DA -411 Main -Catskill 12414 **Fx:**719-3792
(212) 572-8600 .. **Buccella,** Wm '68 %MacAndrews & Forbes -35 E 62nd -NY 10065
(718) 286-6000 .. **Buccheri,** Rosemary '91 %DA -125-01 Qns Blvd -Kew Gdns 11415
(518) 393-8900 .. **Bucci,** Earl M '54 Cnsl Bucci & B -1539 Dean -Schnctdy 12309 **Fx:**393-8900
(914) 323-7000 .. **Bucci,** Gregg '88 (Wilson EME&D LLP) -3 Gannett Dr -White Plns 10604
(914) 400-4333 .. **Bucci,** Michl A II '83 -78 Willow Av -Larchmnt 10538
(212) 408-5100 .. **Bucci,** Peter H '79 (Chadbourne & P LLP) -30 Rckfllr Plz -NY 10112
(315) 635-9944 .. **Bucci,** Rosemary E '64 (Bucci Law Firm,PLLC) -104 Syracuse Bx207 -Baldwinsvll 13027 **Fx:**638-1827
(518) 285-8581 .. **Buccini,** Lisa M '03 OfCnsl Surrogates Ct -30 Clinton Av -Albany 12207
(646) 756-2586 .. **Bucci-Orozco,** Maria W '05 -1230 Av of Amer -NY 10020 **Fx:**756-2999
(716) 852-1300 .. **Buch,** David '51 OfCnsl Amigone S&M,LLP -350 Main -Buffalo 14202
(646) 696-3116 .. **Buch,** Hannah M '08 %US DOJ -26 Fed Plz -NY 10278

(212) 788-0964 .. **Buch,** June R '80 %Law Dept -100 Church -NY 10007 **Fx:**788-0367
(212) 628-1443 .. **Buch,** Leslie N '70 -404 E 66th -NY 10065
(516) 222-1300 .. **Buchalter,** Donald J '63 (Abbott R&A,PC) -90 Merrick Av -E Meadow 11554
(845) 454-6011 .. **Buchalter,** Stephen '80 -30 MacGhee Rd -Poughkeepsie 12603
(315) 623-7133 .. **Buchan,** Wm M '91 (Buchan & S) -21 Lakeshr Dr -Constantia 13044 **Fx:**623-7130
(212) 788-0023 .. **Buchanan,** Adam E '09 Mayors Ofc Contract Srvcs -253 Bway -NY 10007
(518) 434-3518 .. **Buchanan,** Charlotte S '81 -115 Van Wies Pnt Rd -Glenmont 12077
(212) 584-0700 .. **Buchanan,** David R '94 (Seeger W LLP) -1 William -NY 10004
(212) 325-7907 .. **Buchanan,** Deborah J '08 %Credit Suisse -11 Mad Av -NY 10010
(718) 768-4313 .. **Buchanan,** Dennis '01 %NY Methodist Hospital -506 6th Av -Brklyn 11215
(212) 335-9000 .. **Buchanan,** Heather D '07 %DA -1 Hogan Pl -NY 10013
(212) 440-4400 .. **Buchanan Ingersoll & Rooney PC** -620 8th Av -NY 10018 **Fx:**440-4401
(716) 853-2330 .. **Buchanan Ingersoll & Rooney PC** -50 Fountain Plz -Buffalo 14202 **Fx:**854-4227
(212) 336-2000 .. **Buchanan,** Michl F '93 (Patterson BW&T LLP) -1133 Av of Amer -NY 10036
(212) 637-3274 .. **Buchanan,** Patricia L '91 US Atty -86 Chmbrs -NY 10007
(212) 407-8013 .. **Buchanan,** Richd '95 NBA -645 5th Av -NY 10022
(518) 783-3843 .. **Buchanan,** Thos D '99 %Hacker & M,LLP -7 Airport Park Blvd -Latham 12110
(212) 809-7800 .. **Buchanan-Alleyne,** Athena T '09 %Jaffe & K,LLP -40 Wall -NY 10005
(718) 980-7334 .. **Buchansky-Francesco,** Amy B '93 -159 New Dorp Plz -Staten Isl 10306
(718) 599-7070 .. **Buchbinder,** Brian T '76 %Grand Renovation -249 Huron -Brklyn 11222 **Fx:**599-6969
(212) 435-3571 .. **Buchbinder,** Darrell '72 %Port Auth of NY/NJ -225 Park Av S -NY 10003 **Fx:**435-3555
(212) 613-8344 .. **Buchbinder,** Gad '02 Orthodox Union -11 Bway -NY 10004
(212) 237-1000 .. **Buchbinder,** Julian B '07 %Windels ML&M,LLP -156 W 56th -NY 10019
(212) 416-8019 .. **Buchbinder,** Marion R '76 %Dept of Law -120 Bway -NY 10271
(212) 336-8330 .. **Buchdahl,** Jacob '98 (Susman G LLP) -560 Lex Av -NY 10022
(646) 878-0800 .. **Buchek,** Nathaniel B '00 %Pearl CZL,LLP -1500 Bway -NY 10036
(516) 393-5555 .. **Buchel,** Justin S '09 %Schneider M LLP -666 Old Cntry Rd -Gdn Cty 11530 **Fx:**393-5556
(516) 785-7855 .. **Buchenberger,** Thos E '75 -2067 Jackson Av -Seafrd 11783 **Fx:**785-1243
(718) 741-8315 .. **Buchenholz,** Peter G '98 %Div of Human Rights -1 Fordham Plz -Bronx 10458 **Fx:**741-8102
(718) 575-1822 .. **Bucher,** Linda '91 -125-10 Qns Blvd -Kew Gdns 11415 **Fx:**575-1826
(212) 225-2000 .. **Buchheit,** Lee C '85 (Cleary GS&H) -1 Lbrty Plz -NY 10006
(212) 982-1125 .. **Buchholz,** Bernard '57 -1 Univ Pl -NY 10003
(516) 746-8100 .. **Buchholz,** Ellen '83 (D Buttafuoco & Assoc) -144 Woodbury Rd -Woodbury 11797 **Fx:**746-6473
(914) 725-3200 .. **Buchicchio,** Michl F '75 -700 Wht Plns Rd -Scarsdale 10583 **Fx:**725-5780
(212) 715-9100 .. **Buchinsky,** M Frances '76 SpclCnsl Kramer LN&F,LLP -1177 Av of Amer -NY 10036
(212) 859-8000 .. **Buchman,** Emil '97 (Fried FHS&J LLP) -1 NY Plz -NY 10004
(845) 340-7553 .. **Buchman,** Gail A '85 %DEP -71 Smith Av -Kingston 12401 **Fx:**340-7564
(212) 682-8383 .. **Buchman,** Joel '63 OfCnsl Kantor DWMT&G,PC -51 E 42nd -NY 10017
(718) 732-3820 .. **Buchman,** Julie '99 Buchman & Assoc,PC -2626 E 14th -Brklyn 11235 **Fx:**732-3823
(914) 703-6300 .. **Buchman,** Lawr J '93 %Pillinger MT,LLP -570 Taxter Rd -Elmsfrd 10523
(212) 661-1100 .. **Buchman,** Michl M '93 (Pomerantz HG&G LLP) -100 Park Av -NY 10017
(315) 493-3000 .. **Buchman,** Seth B '84 -20298 S Shore Rd -Three Mile Bay 13693 **Fx:**649-4195
(212) 408-5100 .. **Buchman,** Stephen L '63 OfCnsl Chadbourne & P LLP -30 Rckfllr Plz -NY 10112
(212) 701-3000 .. **Buchner,** Jennifer L '09 %Cahill G&R LLP -80 Pine -NY 10005 **Fx:**269-5420
(212) 971-0416 .. **Bucholtz,** Jesse R '03 %J Schwartz & Assoc,PLLC -245 5th Av -NY 10016 **Fx:**971-0417
(212) 431-8700 .. **Bucholz,** Seymour H '65 OfCnsl Garvey SB -100 Wall -NY 10005
(212) 480-4118 .. **Buchsbaum,** Alan H '56 -132 Nassau -NY 10038
(212) 233-9385 .. **Buchsbaum,** Andrew V '86 (Friedman J&B LLP) -132 Nassau -NY 10038
(212) 509-9400 .. **Buchstein,** Shari R '93 Cozen O -45 Bway Atrium -NY 10006
(718) 286-6000 .. **Buchter,** Rachel E '98 %DA -125-01 Qns Blvd -Kew Gdns 11415
(212) 373-3000 .. **Buchwald,** David E '08 %Paul WRW&G LLP -1285 Av of Amer -NY 10019
(212) 808-7800 .. **Buchwald,** Don '70 (Kelley D&W LLP) -101 Park Av -NY 10178
(212) 715-9100 .. **Buchwald,** Jules '63 Cnsl Kramer LN&F,LLP -1177 Av of Amer -NY 10036
(212) 735-3000 .. **Buchwald,** Michl E '09 %Skadden ASM&F LLP -4 Times Sq -NY 10036
(212) 297-5800 .. **Buchwalter,** Ruth L '02 Cnsl Day P LLP -7 Times Sq -NY 10036
(516) 747-4544 .. **Buchwalter,** Theo '59 -174 Mineola Blvd -Mineola 11501 **Fx:**747-2069
(212) 310-8000 .. **Buchweitz,** Yehudah L '03 %Weil G&M LLP -767 5th Av -NY 10153
(212) 698-3500 .. **Buck,** Andrew L '97 %Dechert LLP -1095 Av of Amer -NY 10036
(607) 734-8161 .. **Buck Danaher Ryan & McGlenn** -100 Baldwin -Elmira 14901 **Fx:**734-4209
(212) 615-7342 .. **Buck,** Jane R '84 %NBLI -333 W 34th -NY 10001 **Fx:**615-7308
(607) 734-8161 .. **Buck,** Jos C '51 (Buck DR&M) -100 Baldwin -Elmira 14901
(212) 667-9368 .. **Buck,** Juliet F '93 Nomura Securities Intl -2 World Fncl Ctr -NY 10281
(212) 825-0489 .. **Buck,** Michl P '96 (Cinotti & B LLP) -445 Park Av -NY 10022 **Fx:**825-0117
(212) 809-8585 .. **Buckel,** David '88 Lambda Leg Def -120 Wall -NY 10005 **Fx:**809-0055
(315) 471-3151 .. **Buckel,** Thos C Jr. '82 (Hancock & E,LLP) -1500 AXA Twr I Bx4976 -Syracuse 13221
(518) 487-7600 .. **Buckey,** Christopher E '99 (Whiteman O&H LLP) -1 Commerce Plz -Albany 12260
(212) 984-7700 .. **Buckhardt,** Danielle L '03 %Warshaw BCS&K,LLP -555 5th Av -NY 10017
(845) 357-0265 .. **Buckheit,** John L '92 (Buckheit & W,PC) -49 N Airmont Rd -Suffern 10901 **Fx:**357-7192
(212) 335-9000 .. **Buckheit,** Richd A '93 %DA -1 Hogan Pl -NY 10013
(212) 558-4000 .. **Buckholz,** Robt E Jr. '80 (Sullivan & C LLP) -125 Broad -NY 10004
(212) 889-2121 .. **Buckhout,** Scott E '07 %Kellner HG&F -470 Park Av S -NY 10016
(716) 847-8400 .. **Bucki,** Craig R '07 %Phillips L LLP -3400 HSBC Ctr -Buffalo 14203
(212) 431-2182 .. **Buckler,** Carol A '83 %NY Law Schl -185 W Bway -NY 10013 **Fx:**965-8841
(212) 909-6000 .. **Buckley,** Alison E '09 %Debevoise & P LLP -919 3rd Av -NY 10022
(212) 728-8000 .. **Buckley,** Branwen '09 %Willkie F&G LLP -787 7th Av -NY 10019
(718) 520-3985 .. **Buckley,** Brian F '98 %Family Ct -89-14 Parsons Blvd -Jamaica 11432
(516) 542-1000 .. **Buckley,** Colleen M '05 %Geisler & G,LLP -100 Q Roosevelt Blvd -Gdn Cty 11530
(212) 514-7400 .. **Buckley & Curtis, PA** -225 Bway -NY 10007 **Fx:**514-7404
(716) 854-2100 .. **Buckley,** D Jeffrey '94 (Lewis & L,PC) -37 Franklin -Buffalo 14202 **Fx:**854-0433
(516) 248-2222 .. **Buckley,** Eileen C '85 %LI Advocacy Ctr -999 Hrrcks Rd -New Hyde Pk 11040 **Fx:**248-2290
(585) 753-4500 .. **Buckley,** Elizabeth Dillon '06 DA -832 Watts Bldg -Rchstr 14614 **Fx:**753-4576
(212) 956-8300 .. **Buckley,** Eric A '08 %Bronstein Van V LLC -650 Mad Av -NY 10022
(212) 416-6096 .. **Buckley,** Erica L '05 %Dept of Law -120 Bway -NY 10271
(212) 269-0927 .. **Buckley,** Frances M '92 (D'Amato & L,LLP) -2 World Fncl Ctr -NY 10281
(518) 449-3107 .. **Buckley,** James E '69 (Buckley M&C,PC) -29 Wards Ln -Albany 12204
(212) 656-2534 .. **Buckley,** James G '85 NYSE EuroNext -20 Broad -NY 10005
(518) 885-2263 .. **Buckley,** Jennifer L '03 %DA -25 W High -Ballston Spa 12020 **Fx:**884-8627
(718) 590-3867 .. **Buckley,** John P '77 %NYS Supreme Ct -851 Grnd Cncrs -Bronx 10451
(646) 252-4931 .. **Buckley,** Judith F '91 NYC Transit Auth -2 Bway -NY 10004
(212) 768-6700 .. **Buckley,** Kate F '05 %Sonnenschein N&R LLP -2 World Fncl Ctr -NY 10281
(212) 451-2300 .. **Buckley,** Kathleen J '97 %Olshan GFR&W LLP -65 E 55th -NY 10022
(212) 804-4200 .. **Buckley,** Kevin F '98 (Mound CW&G) -One Bttry Pk Plz -NY 10004
(212) 309-1000 .. **Buckley,** Kevin J '99 (Hunton & W) -200 Park Av -NY 10166
(845) 359-0606 .. **Buckley,** Laura '86 %MHLS -140 Old Orangebrg Rd -Orangebrg 10962 **Fx:**365-1773
(212) 421-4100 .. **Buckley,** Lisa M '91 (Pryor C LLP) -7 Times Sq -NY 10036
(718) 722-6498 .. **Buckley,** Loretta C '06 Appellate Div - 2nd Dept -195 Montague -Brklyn 11201
(716) 634-2497 .. **Buckley,** Mary White '94 (Kelly & S) -5678 Main -Williamsvll 14221
(518) 449-3107 .. **Buckley Mendleson & Criscione,PC** -29 Wards Ln -Albany 12204 **Fx:**449-3108
(212) 514-7400 .. **Buckley,** Michl B '83 (Buckley & C,PA) -225 Bway -NY 10007
(516) 357-3000 .. **Buckley,** Michl E '90 (Rivkin R LLP) -926 RXR Plz -Uniondale 11556
(585) 232-6500 .. **Buckley,** Michl F '68 (Harter S&E LLP) -1600 Bausch & Lomb Pl -Rchstr 14604
(212) 331-5195 .. **Buckley,** Michele N '09 HR Admin -180 Water -NY 10038
(212) 608-3500 .. **Buckley,** Robt A '04 OfCnsl Beckman L&B LLP -116 John -NY 10038
(212) 961-8317 .. **Buckley,** Robt F '82 %Liquor Auth -105 W 125th -NY 10027
(212) 637-2261 .. **Buckley,** Sean S '04 %US Atty -1 St Andrews Plz -NY 10007
(212) 701-3000 .. **Buckley,** Susan '78 (Cahill G&R LLP) -80 Pine -NY 10005 **Fx:**269-5420
(631) 543-3030 .. **Buckley,** Terrence '72 -356 Vets Mem'l Hwy -Commack 11725 **Fx:**543-2888
(315) 781-1455 .. **Buckley,** Timothy J '75 -117 Wshngtn Bx308 -Geneva 14456 **Fx:**781-1397
(212) 689-1113 .. **Buckley,** Wm D '90 %Garbarini & S,PC -432 Park Av S -NY 10016
(518) 463-3200 .. **Bucklin,** Patricia K '79 %NYS Bar Assn -1 Elk -Albany 12207 **Fx:**487-5544
(212) 455-2000 .. **Buckman,** Anne T '06 %Simpson T&B LLP -425 Lex Av -NY 10017
(212) 300-1300 .. **Buckman,** James E '69 York Cptl Mgmt LLC -767 5th Av -NY 10153 **Fx:**300-1301
(212) 867-5800 .. **Buckmann,** Carol I '77 Cnsl Osler H&H LLP -620 8th Av -NY 10018
(212) 833-3305 .. **Bucknam,** James R '87 %Kroll Assoc -1166 Av of Amer -NY 10036 **Fx:**593-2631
(585) 232-8314 .. **Buckner & Kourofsky** -1 S Wshngtn -Rchstr 14614 **Fx:**327-7101
(315) 233-8300 .. **Buckner,** Nicole J '02 %Burr & B -101 S Salina -Syracuse 13202
(585) 232-8314 .. **Buckner,** Raymond T Jr. '74 (Buckner & K) -1 S Wshngtn -Rchstr 14614
(212) 554-1463 .. **Buckser-Schulz,** Lisa '93 AB Data Ltd -244 Mad Av -NY 10016
(212) 220-3000 .. **Buckstein,** Evelyn '52 %Broadcast Music Inc -250 Greenwich -NY 10007
(212) 962-2173 .. **Buckvar,** Eric J '88 -305 Bway -NY 10007 **Fx:**406-7265
(212) 962-2173 .. **Buckvar,** Morton '59 -305 Bway -NY 10007 **Fx:**406-7265
(212) 788-8681 .. **Buckwalter,** Ellen L '08 %Law Dept -100 Church -NY 10007 **Fx:**788-0367
(914) 681-6200 .. **Bucobo,** Javier E '98 NYPA -123 Main -White Plns 10601 **Fx:**390-8038
(716) 204-9480 .. **Buczkowski,** Marin Lee '05 %SJ Baum,PC -900 Merchants Cncrs -Westbury 11590 **Fx:**204-9680
(212) 279-9200 .. **Buda,** Denise '90 %Abrams FFEGF&E,LLP -630 3rd Av -NY 10017
(212) 945-5000 .. **Budashewitz,** Elliot G '89 (Berson & B, PC) -15 Maiden Ln -NY 10038
(212) 838-2609 .. **Budd,** Aviva D '66 -812 5th Av -NY 10065
(631) 929-4560 .. **Budd,** Bernadette Smith '99 -Bx619 -Wading Rvr 11792
(212) 571-0111 .. **Budd,** Eileen T '99 %Hardin KM&P,PA -110 William -NY 10038
(212) 858-7700 .. **Budd Larner** -140 Bway -NY 10005 **Fx:**858-7699

(212) 418-0500 .. **Budd,** Macdonald '59 (Morris & M LLP) -767 3rd Av -NY 10017
(212) 687-7410 .. **Budd,** Thos W '65 (Clifton B&D,LLP) -420 Lex Av -NY 10170
(212) 422-0202 .. **Budelman,** Robt B Jr. '63 SpclCnsl Sedgwick DM&A LLP -125 Broad -NY 10004
(315) 253-1391 .. **Budelmann,** Jon E '93 %DA -95 Genesee -Auburn 13021 **Fx:**253-1521
(914) 761-3700 .. **Buderwitz,** Jos M '83 OfCnsl Gaines GP&N,LLP -1 N Bway -White Plns 10601 **Fx:**(866) 442-1933
(212) 609-6800 .. **Budesheim,** Adam J '05 %McCarter & E,LLP -245 Park Av -NY 10167
(212) 446-4800 .. **Budetti,** John L '06 %Kirkland & E LLP -153 E 53rd -NY 10022
(212) 813-8800 .. **Budewitz,** Michl '10 %Goodwin P LLP -620 8th Av -NY 10018
(718) 694-5719 .. **Budhwa,** Christine A '03 %Transit Auth -130 Lvngstn -Brklyn 11201 **Fx:**694-5726
(212) 696-5500 .. **Budin,** Harlan S '82 (Budin RK&B) -112 Mad Av -NY 10016
(212) 696-5500 .. **Budin,** Jay '60 (Budin RK&B) -112 Mad Av -NY 10016
(914) 234-6737 .. **Budin,** Laura J '90 -7 Peters Ln -Bedfrd 10506
(212) 696-5500 .. **Budin Reisman Kupferberg & Bernstein** -112 Mad Av -NY 10016 **Fx:**889-3978
(212) 969-3000 .. **Budish,** Lawr H '75 (Proskauer R LLP) -1585 Bway -NY 10036
(212) 530-1800 .. **Budlong,** Scott C '93 (Richards K&O LLP) -1 World Fncl Ctr -NY 10281
(516) 222-1010 .. **Budman,** Theo M '77 (Kafka & B) -585 Stewart Av -Gdn Cty 11530
(315) 437-7600 .. **Budmen,** Donald E '91 (Ferrara FLB&R,PC) -5010 Campuswood Dr -E Syracuse 13057
(212) 651-7500 .. **Budner,** Jennifer L '01 %Segal MS&M -850 3rd Av -NY 10022
(212) 577-3688 .. **Budner,** Robt J '88 %Leg Aid -199 Water -NY 10038 **Fx:**509-8431
(718) 793-0101 .. **Budnetz,** Joel E '71 OfCnsl J Plotner -108-18 Qns Blvd -Frst Hlls 11375
(212) 872-1000 .. **Budoff,** Jessica S '06 -One Bryant Park -NY 10036 **Fx:**872-1002
(212) 450-4000 .. **Budofsky,** Danl N '91 (Davis P&W LLP) -450 Lex Av -NY 10017
(212) 382-0909 .. **Budorick,** Danl E '03 %Peckar & A,PC -41 Mad Av -NY 10154
(212) 977-9700 .. **Budow,** Leonard N '81 (Phillips N LLP) -666 5th Av -NY 10103
(212) 735-8668 .. **Budow,** Stephen I '73 (Morrison C LLP) -909 3rd Av -NY 10022
(212) 885-5000 .. **Budzenski,** Scott F '08 %Blank R LLP -405 Lex Av -NY 10174
(212) 669-7778 .. **Budzik,** Valerie '90 %Comptroller -1 Centre -NY 10007 **Fx:**669-2884
(716) 856-5500 .. **Budzinski,** Stacey L '10 %Damon M LLP -200 Delaware Av -Buffalo 14202
(212) 735-3000 .. **Budzynski,** Catherine A '10 %Skadden ASM&F LLP -4 Times Sq -NY 10036
(914) 614-7000 .. **Buebel,** Felicia P '83 Cnsl Icon Enterprises -445 Hmltn Av -White Plns 10601
(212) 859-8000 .. **Bueche,** Jos T '10 %Fried FHS&J LLP -1 NY Plz -NY 10004
(212) 861-8845 .. **Buechley,** Susan E '89 -66 E 80th -NY 10075 **Fx:**861-8845
(212) 446-7000 .. **Buehler,** Kevin S '91 %McKinsey & Co -55 E 52nd -NY 10055 **Fx:**688-9521
(212) 918-3000 .. **Buehler,** Robt B '90 (Hogan L LLP) -875 3rd Av -NY 10022
(212) 937-4000 .. **Buehner,** Maura L '09 %Fitzpatrick & HTCPA,LLP -12 E 49th -NY 10017
(212) 967-5710 .. **Buell,** Carol L '81 (Weiss B&B) -11 Park Pl -NY 10007
(914) 937-1000 .. **Buell,** Curtiss N '82 (C Buell,PC) -219 Wstchstr Av -Pt Chester 10573
(212) 225-2000 .. **Buell,** Deborah M '82 (Cleary GS&H) -1 Lbrty Plz -NY 10006
(212) 701-3000 .. **Buell,** Guillaume O '10 %Cahill G&R LLP -80 Pine -NY 10005 **Fx:**269-5420
(212) 803-5100 .. **Buell,** Scott A '87 %NY Cnty Defender Srvcs -225 Bway -NY 10007 **Fx:**571-6035
(212) 696-6000 .. **Buenger,** Peter J '10 %Curtis M-PC&M LLP -101 Park Av -NY 10178
(646) 273-7335 .. **Bueno,** Lauro M '01 Rainbow Media -11 Penn Plz -NY 10001
(718) 590-2000 .. **Buentello,** Jennifer L '08 %DA -198 E 161st -Bronx 10451 **Fx:**590-6477
(718) 237-2000 .. **Buenzle,** Desiree '91 %Leg Aid -111 Lvngstn -Brklyn 11201 **Fx:**237-8737
(212) 373-3000 .. **Buergel,** Susanna M '02 (Paul WRW&G LLP) -1285 Av of Amer -NY 10019
(716) 854-6140 .. **Buerger,** Paul T Jr. '81 %Baxter S&S,PC -182 Dwyer -W Seneca 14224
(716) 847-8400 .. **Buerk,** Caroline Hassett '81 OfCnsl Phillips L LLP -3400 HSBC Ctr -Buffalo 14203
(315) 464-8309 .. **Buerkle,** Ann Marie M '96 %Dept of Law -750 E Adams -Syracuse 13210 **Fx:**464-8327
(585) 419-8800 .. **Buerman,** Gunther K '68 (Harris B PLLC) -99 Garnsey Rd -Pittsfrd 14534
(212) 804-4200 .. **Buermann,** George H Jr. '02 %Mound CW&G -One Bttry Pk Plz -NY 10004
(212) 885-5000 .. **Buerstetta,** Grant E '97 (Blank R LLP) -405 Lex Av -NY 10174
(212) 998-6730 .. **Buery,** Richd R '98 %The Brennan Ctr for Justice -161 Av of Amer -NY 10013 **Fx:**995-4550
(516) 248-9880 .. **Bues,** John P '98 %Agovino & A,LLP -330 Old Cntry Rd -Mineola 11501
(212) 701-3000 .. **Buescher,** Michl L '09 %Cahill G&R LLP -80 Pine -NY 10005 **Fx:**269-5420
(212) 907-9600 .. **Buesser,** Jennifer G '97 %Ingram YGC&B,LLP -250 Park Av -NY 10177
(631) 852-2920 .. **Buetow,** Jennifer Ann '87 Family Ct -877 E Main -Rvrhead 11901
(631) 853-4934 .. **Buetow,** Mary C '95 Family Ct -400 Carleton Av -Central Islip 11722
(585) 454-1760 .. **Buettner,** Brian C '90 -430 Rynlds Arcd Bldg -Rchstr 14614 **Fx:**454-1611
(518) 792-2117 .. **Buettner,** Karla Williams '03 %Bartlett PS&R,PC -1 Wshngtn Bx2168 -Glens Fls 12801
(212) 225-2000 .. **Buettner,** Peter F '99 %Cleary GS&H -1 Lbrty Plz -NY 10006
(315) 437-7600 .. **Bufano,** Jos J '09 %Ferrara FLB&R,PC -5010 Campuswood Dr -E Syracuse 13057
(516) 248-9880 .. **Buff,** Robt C '68 OfCnsl Agovino & A,LLP -330 Old Cntry Rd -Mineola 11501
(212) 248-9100 .. **Buffa,** Michl A '84 %Epstein M&M -1 Whitehall -NY 10004
(631) 451-7900 .. **Buffa,** Michl V '96 (Rosenberg & G,LLP) -1176 Portion Rd -Holtsvll 11742
(212) 455-2000 .. **Buffa,** Philip A '08 %Simpson T&B LLP -425 Lex Av -NY 10017
(718) 855-9000 .. **Buffaloe,** Kenneth S '92 (Cullen and D LLP) -177 Montague -Brklyn 11201
(212) 848-4000 .. **Buffier,** Beau W '01 (Shearman & S LLP) -599 Lex Av -NY 10022
(716) 652-3151 .. **Buffomante,** Angelo A '73 -Bx226 -Elma 14059
(716) 631-9981 .. **Buffomante,** Frank J '75 (Labin & B) -531 Farber Lks Dr -Williamsvll 14221
(212) 538-9352 .. **Buffone,** Douglas C '96 CSFB -11 Mad Av -NY 10010
(212) 351-4000 .. **Buffone,** Steven P '93 (Gibson D&C LLP) -200 Park Av -NY 10166
Bugbee, Robt T '89 -Bx151 -E Greenbush 12061
(718) 875-1300 .. **Bugge,** Bari L '09 %Appllt Div 2nd Dept -45 Monroe Pl -Brklyn 11201 **Fx:**858-2446
(718) 591-7500 .. **Buggy,** Kevin J '94 (Bleier B&B) -80-30 164th -Jamaica 11432 **Fx:**969-0994
(212) 264-0655 .. **Bughman,** Bryan C '05 US DOJ -26 Fed Plz -NY 10278
(212) 969-3000 .. **Buglione,** Ariane R A '08 %Proskauer R LLP -1585 Bway -NY 10036
(914) 946-6774 .. **Bugliosi,** John M '90 %Pilkington & L,PC -222 Bloomingdale Rd -White Plns 10605
(212) 922-0050 .. **Bugoni,** Paul F '87 %Stewart Title Ins -300 E 42nd -NY 10017 **Fx:**983-1133
(212) 310-8000 .. **Buhl,** Miriam A '93 Cnsl Weil G&M LLP -767 5th Av -NY 10153
(212) 310-8000 .. **Buhle,** Warren T '77 (Weil G&M LLP) -767 5th Av -NY 10153
(845) 265-2636 .. **Buhler,** Gregory W '75 -Bx246 -Cold Spg 10516
(212) 888-3033 .. **Buhofer,** Stephen '06 %Becker GM&M LLP -299 Park Av -NY 10171
(585) 232-5885 .. **Buholtz,** Eileen E '80 (Connors & C,LLP) -45 Exchange -Rchstr 14614
(518) 689-1432 .. **Buhr,** Stephen M '95 OfCnsl Greenberg T,LLP -54 State -Albany 12207
(585) 419-8800 .. **Buhrman,** John R '09 %Harris B PLLC -99 Garnsey Rd -Pittsfrd 14534
(518) 402-9003 .. **Buhrmaster,** Edw I '82 %DEC -625 Bway -Albany 12233 **Fx:**402-9018
(212) 788-0874 .. **Buhta,** John M '10 %Law Dept -100 Church -NY 10007 **Fx:**788-0367
(716) 565-1100 .. **Bui,** Teia M '09 %Andreozzi F LLP -9145 Main -Clarence 14031
(212) 248-3144 .. **Bui,** Thuy T '06 %Drinker B&R LLP -140 Bway -NY 10005
(212) 557-7700 .. **Buice,** Wm T III '67 (Davidson D&C LLP) -60 E 42nd -NY 10165
(201) 736-2948 .. **Builder,** Jane P '92 -12 Debbie Ln -Cross Rvr 10518 **Fx:**833-1661
(212) 698-3500 .. **Buino,** James S '06 %Dechert LLP -1095 Av of Amer -NY 10036
(212) 980-8470 .. **Buitrago,** Marcelo A '05 %J Melcer,PLLC -39 Bway -NY 10006 **Fx:**980-8256
(585) 546-7430 .. **Buitrago,** Maritza C '00 %Dept of Law -144 Exchange Blvd -Rchstr 14614 **Fx:**546-7514
(212) 773-3644 .. **Buitron,** Cristina A '06 Ernst & Young -5 Times Sq -NY 10036
(315) 422-1080 .. **Buitron,** Steven C '07 -333 E Onondaga -Syracuse 13202
(212) 221-5700 .. **Bukary,** Gerald '00 Goldberg WFG LLP -1501 Bway -NY 10036
(315) 636-0900 .. **Bukata,** Alison A '95 -1107 Wolf -Syracuse 13208 **Fx:**636-0999
(212) 801-3142 .. **Bukchin,** Evelyn '02 %Greenberg T,LLP -200 Park Av -NY 10166
(718) 376-4766 .. **Bukh,** Arkady '03 (Bukh & Assoc) -1123 Av Z -Brklyn 11235 **Fx:**376-3033
(212) 635-1132 .. **Buki,** Gary A '84 Bk of NY Mellon -1 Wall -NY 10286 **Fx:**635-1698
(518) 561-8800 .. **Bukolt-Ryder,** MaryAnne F '82 -61 Clinton Bx3043 -Plattsbrgh 12901 **Fx:**561-8861
(212) 316-5490 .. **Bukowski,** Jacqueline M Hansen '92 -527 Cathedral Pkwy -NY 10025 **Fx:**280-1613
(917) 454-1040 .. **Bukszpan,** Joanna Miller '77 DOJ Immigration Ct -26 Fed Plz -NY 10278 **Fx:**(212) 644-1070
(212) 277-6300 .. **Bulcao,** Scott W '05 %Schindler C&H LLP -100 Wall -NY 10005
(646) 471-0179 .. **Bulekbayeva,** Natalia V '98 PricewaterhouseCoopers -300 Mad Av -NY 10017
(518) 427-7350 .. **Buley,** Jeffrey T '88 (Brown & W PLLC) -79 Columbia -Albany 12210
(212) 530-1800 .. **Bulger,** James A '04 %Richards K&O LLP -1 World Fncl Ctr -NY 10281
(585) 325-7440 .. **Bulger,** John L '74 Kaman BMJ&G LLP -135 Corp Woods -Rchstr 14623
(212) 224-4000 .. **Bulger,** Robt W '84 %Sumitomo Mitsui -277 Park Av -NY 10172 **Fx:**593-9522
(518) 692-8504 .. **Bulger,** Timothy M '84 -138 Main -Greenwich 12834 **Fx:**692-8505
(646) 223-4200 .. **Bulka,** Shmuel R '94 %Reuters -3 Times Sq -NY 10036 **Fx:**223-4250
(212) 751-3001 .. **Bulkeley,** J Russell '91 OfCnsl Thompson & K LLP -919 3rd Av -NY 10022
(212) 527-1000 .. **Bull,** Bartle '66 (Jones HC&B PC) -1 Bttry Pk Plz -NY 10004
(212) 804-5752 .. **Bull,** Collin D '78 -110 Wall -NY 10005
(845) 695-2002 .. **Bull Morreale Judelson & Diamond,PC** -90 Crystal Run Rd -Middletwn 10941 **Fx:**695-2902
(212) 504-6000 .. **Bull,** Nathan M '06 %Cadwalader W&T LLP -1 World Fncl Ctr -NY 10281
(212) 213-6222 .. **Bull,** Peter D '93 (Bull & L,LLP) -18 E 41st -NY 10017
(212) 761-4000 .. **Bullard,** Dennine '95 Morgan Stanley -1221 Av of Amer -NY 10020
(516) 622-9200 .. **Bullard,** Edw J Jr. '98 (Westerman BEM&S,LLP) -1201 RXR Plz -Uniondale 11553
(585) 419-8800 .. **Bullard,** H Todd '88 (Harris B PLLC) -99 Garnsey Rd -Pittsfrd 14534
(718) 204-2300 .. **Bullaro,** Gabriel J '76 -25-19 Steinway -Astoria 11103 **Fx:**728-5840
(518) 474-7735 .. **Bullen,** Audrey V A '99 %Dept of Law -The Cptl -Albany 12224
(212) 836-8000 .. **Bullerman,** Michl S '07 %Kaye S LLP -425 Park Av -NY 10022
(518) 465-9500 .. **Bullett,** Tracy L '02 %Tabner R&K,LLP -18 Corp Wds Blvd -Albany 12211
(607) 763-9200 .. **Bullis,** Robt G '77 (Levene G&T,LLP) -BxF-1706 -Bnghmtn 13902
(212) 309-6000 .. **Bullitt,** P Georgia '88 (Morgan L&B LLP) -101 Park Av -NY 10178
(800) 877-1373 .. **Bullitt,** Tiffany R '02 %Workers Comp Bd -215 W 125th -NY 10027
(212) 506-2500 .. **Bullock,** Henninger S '02 %Mayer B LLP -1675 Bway -NY 10019
(718) 595-2857 .. **Bullock,** Jacquelyn R '77 -26 Court -Brklyn 11242 **Fx:**246-2713
(914) 997-1346 .. **Bullock,** Jaimee E '06 %Seham SM&P,LLP -445 Hmltn Av -White Plns 10601
(716) 652-0828 .. **Bullock,** Michelle S '97 %Hall RM&G -471 Main -E Aurora 14052
(516) 572-6064 .. **Bullock,** Reginald Jr. '90 Cnsl Nassau Hlth Care Corp -2201 Hempstd Tpke -E Meadow 11554
(212) 227-4000 .. **Bullock,** Scott D '06 (Mirman M&L,PC) -291 Bway -NY 10007

(518) 443-5101 .. **Bulluck,** Dona S '82 %SUNY Univ Cnsl -S333 SUNY Plz -Albany 12246 **Fx:**443-5409
(212) 230-8814 .. **Bulsara,** Sanket J '03 Cnsl WilmerHale -399 Park Av -NY 10022
(315) 453-2866 .. **Bulsiewicz,** Wm J Sr. '75 OCRRA -100 Elwood Davis Rd -N Syracuse 13212 **Fx:**453-7692
(716) 933-8792 .. **Bulson,** Raymond W '70 -6 S Main Bx248 -Portvll 14770 **Fx:**933-8793
(716) 838-4300 .. **Bulson,** Sara M '06 %Bulan CH&I -1320 Millersport Hwy -Williamsvll 14221 **Fx:**204-9728
(914) 948-1556 .. **Bulua,** Stanley E '80 (Danziger & M LLP) -123 Main -White Plns 10601
(212) 573-1556 .. **Bulzacchelli,** Paul F '80 Pfizer Inc -150 E 42nd -NY 10017 **Fx:**973-7321
(716) 685-2640 .. **Bumbalo,** Paul T '81 -5476 Bway -Lancaster 14086 **Fx:**681-7247
(212) 906-1200 .. **Bumby,** Colin B '08 %Latham & W -885 3rd Av -NY 10022
(845) 225-7100 .. **Bumgarner,** Craig T '94 -1717 Route 6 -Carmel 10512 **Fx:**225-7109
(845) 808-1150 .. **Bumgarner,** Jennifer S '98 %Cnty Atty -48 Gleneida Av -Carmel 10512 **Fx:**808-1903
(212) 768-6700 .. **Bunbury,** Donna M '07 %Sonnenschein N&R LLP -2 World Fncl Ctr -NY 10281
(718) 468-6100 .. **Bunch,** Joy S '02 (Brogdon & B LLP) -205-20 Jamaica Av -Hollis 11423 **Fx:**468-6110
(212) 225-2000 .. **Bunda,** Matthew M '07 %Cleary GS&H -1 Lbrty Plz -NY 10006
(212) 852-7046 .. **Bunder,** Michl L '94 %News America Inc -1211 Av of Amer -NY 10036
(212) 425-1900 .. **Bundy,** Carolyn E '04 %Freehill H&M LLP -80 Pine -NY 10005
(212) 685-8500 .. **Bundy,** Lakeeda M '06 %Greenstein & M,LLP -1825 Park Av -NY 10035
(212) 587-0563 .. **Bunescu,** Ana P '88 -7117 12th Av -Brklyn 11228 **Fx:**(718) 745-0066
(212) 878-8000 .. **Bunevich,** Cheryl A '99 %Clifford C LLP -31 W 52nd -NY 10019
(212) 257-6109 .. **Buni,** Ronny '00 R Buni,PC -817 Bway -NY 10003
(212) 683-0083 .. **Bunim,** Mark J '76 Case Closure -9 E 40th -NY 10016
(212) 637-7074 .. **Bunin,** Jacob '80 %US Customs Srvc -1 Penn Plz -NY 10119
(212) 210-9492 .. **Bunin,** Martin G '77 (Alston & B LLP) -90 Park Av -NY 10016
(585) 325-7086 .. **Bunis,** Harvey S '77 -1 E Main -Rchstr 14614 **Fx:**325-7087
(212) 902-0952 .. **Bunkin,** Steven M '92 %Goldman Sachs -1 NY Plz -NY 10004
(212) 226-4200 .. **Bunks,** Abe '58 -224 W 35th -NY 10001 **Fx:**226-4226
(212) 609-6800 .. **Bunn,** Andrew O '91 (McCarter & E,LLP) -245 Park Av -NY 10167
(212) 688-3020 .. **Bunn,** George R Jr. '69 -126 E 56th -NY 10022 **Fx:**888-0669
(212) 801-9318 .. **Bunning,** David W '92 (Greenberg T,LLP) -200 Park Av -NY 10166
(914) 288-0103 .. **Buno,** Jessica '09 %R Steinvurzel,PC -34 S Bway -White Plns 10601
(212) 604-2483 .. **Bunshaft,** Jess A '92 St Vincents Hospital -153 W 11th -NY 10011
(516) 745-0006 .. **Bunsis,** Barry A '83 (Bunsis,PC) -1101 Stewart Av -Gdn Cty 11530 **Fx:**745-0237
(516) 745-0006 .. **Bunsis,** Michl O '88 (Bunsis,PC) -1101 Stewart Av -Gdn Cty 11530 **Fx:**745-0237
(516) 358-8825 .. **Bunting,** Gerald A II '94 (Bunting G & Assoc PC) -60 E 42nd -NY 10165 **Fx:**450-3510
(914) 682-8837 .. **Bunting,** Kenneth L '89 (Bunting-Smith & B) -125 Dobbs Ferry Rd -White Plns 10607 **Fx:**682-5250
(518) 885-1600 .. **Bunting,** Nancy E '77 -20 Prospect -Ballston Spa 12020 **Fx:**885-1610
(914) 286-3400 .. **Bunting,** Valissa L '06 %Leg Aid -1 N Bway -White Plns 10601 **Fx:**682-4112
(914) 682-8837 .. **Bunting-Smith,** Eve '77 (Bunting-Smith & B) -125 Dobbs Ferry Rd -White Plns 10607 **Fx:**682-5250
(718) 618-2500 .. **Bunyan,** Jamie L '10 Civil Ct -851 Grnd Cncrs -Bronx 10451 **Fx:**590-7294
(845) 353-2200 .. **Bunyan,** Richd P '92 (Bunyan & B) -500 Bradley Hill Rd -Blauvelt 10913
(646) 386-3646 .. **Bunyar,** Kathleen A '89 %Supreme Ct-Law Dept -60 Centre -NY 10007
(607) 231-5900 .. **Bunzey,** Charlotte H '90 %Leg Aid -30 Fayette -Bnghmtn 13901 **Fx:**724-7211
(212) 770-1964 .. **Buonamassa,** Eric '91 AIG -80 Pine -NY 10005
(914) 288-9200 .. **Buonamici,** A Albert '82 (Buonamici & L,LLP) -222 Bloomingdale Rd -White Plns 10605 **Fx:**997-2666
(212) 309-1000 .. **Buonanno,** Jos B '90 (Hunton & W) -200 Park Av -NY 10166
(718) 761-4602 .. **Buonincontri,** Cara '01 -2156 Victory Blvd -Staten Isl 10314 **Fx:**761-4603
(518) 758-1979 .. **Buono,** Anthony G '96 -2880 Route 9 Bx300 -Valatie 12184 **Fx:**758-1978
(518) 429-4200 .. **Buono,** Nicholas J '04 %Hiscock & B,LLP -50 Beaver -Albany 12207
(212) 292-9678 .. **Buonocore,** Dawn N '97 %Calvin Klein,Inc -205 W 39th -NY 10018 **Fx:**292-9988
(845) 352-9240 .. **Buonocore,** Ernest S '95 Jacoby & M,LLP -296 Main -Spg Vly 10977 **Fx:**344-2090
(914) 423-0505 .. **Buonocore,** Kristine J '98 %N Leo Jr,PC -111 Lockwood Av -Ynkrs 10701 **Fx:**423-0606
(212) 326-3939 .. **Buonome,** Lauren M '10 %Jones D -222 E 41st -NY 10017
(718) 324-9100 .. **Buonomo,** Donald G '59 (Buonomo & B) -4200 Wht Plns Rd -Bronx 10466 **Fx:**324-9128
(631) 853-4161 .. **Buonora,** John L '66 %DA -N Cnty Cmplx Bldg 77 -Hauppauge 11788 **Fx:**853-5820
(631) 952-6400 .. **Buonpastore,** Alan N '81 %Medicaid Fraud Cntrl -300 Motor Pkwy -Hauppauge 11788 **Fx:**952-6382
(631) 582-1919 .. **Buquicchio,** Frank L '94 (V Russo & Assoc,PC) -3740 Expwy Dr S -Islandia 11749 **Fx:**582-8484
(516) 935-8747 .. **Burack,** Elyssa J '94 (Jurissolutions.com) -550 W Old Cntry Rd -Hicksvll 11801 **Fx:**935-8748
(212) 987-0600 .. **Burack,** Jeffrey P '89 -412 E 88th -NY 10128
(212) 776-5143 .. **Bura-Drago,** Jane B '88 %NYC Housing Auth -250 Bway -NY 10007 **Fx:**776-5039
(212) 940-8870 .. **Burak,** H Paul '58 OfCnsl Katten MR LLP -575 Mad Av -NY 10022
(212) 525-6533 .. **Burak,** Janet L '82 HSBC USA Inc -452 5th Av -NY 10018 **Fx:**525-8447
(212) 336-8000 .. **Burak,** Robt D '08 %Amster R&E -90 Park Av -NY 10016
(212) 259-8000 .. **Burakoff,** Julie R '10 %Dewey & L LLP -1301 Av of Amer -NY 10019
(802) 862-7070 .. **Buran,** David C '88 (Anderson & B PC) -186 US Oval -Plattsbrgh 12903 **Fx:**862-7227
(212) 471-8451 .. **Buratti,** Jodi A '02 %Herzfeld & R,PC -125 Broad -NY 10004
(212) 538-1728 .. **Burba,** Andre J '01 Credit Suisse -11 Mad Av -NY 10010
(212) 313-3600 .. **Burbage,** James S '90 %Barry M&M -2 Rector -NY 10006
(212) 902-1000 .. **Burban,** Elizabeth M '91 %Goldman Sachs -1 NY Plz -NY 10004
(585) 327-5040 .. **Burbank,** Paul Whittaker '83 (Burbank Law Firm) -125 State -Rchstr 14614 **Fx:**454-1254
(631) 390-0010 .. **Burbol,** Lauren E '09 %Bruno G&S,LLP -445 Broad Hollow Rd -Melvll 11747
(718) 855-9000 .. **Burbridge,** John J III '93 %Cullen and D LLP -177 Montague -Brklyn 11201
(212) 210-9512 .. **Burce,** Simon B '09 %Alston & B LLP -90 Park Av -NY 10016
(315) 425-2700 .. **Burch,** David G Jr. '07 %Hiscock & B,LLP -One Park Pl -Syracuse 13202
(212) 998-6550 .. **Burch,** Micah J '00 %NYU Law Schl -245 Sullivan -NY 10012
(212) 848-4000 .. **Burch,** Seth E '08 %Shearman & S LLP -599 Lex Av -NY 10022
(518) 285-8327 .. **Burch,** Thos J III '83 Unified Ct Sys -90 State -Albany 12208 **Fx:**426-6098
(516) 747-4324 .. **Burcheri,** Russell C '86 -50 Chas Lindbergh Blvd -Uniondale 11553 **Fx:**747-4326
(212) 458-2874 .. **Burchetta,** James D Jr. '02 AIG -175 Water -NY 10038
(212) 351-7064 .. **Burchill,** Andrew S '99 Monster Worldwide -622 3rd Av -NY 10017
(516) 359-3558 .. **Burck,** Shirley Strachman '90 -5 Sunken Orchrd Ln -Oyster Bay 11771
(518) 455-7924 .. **Burckard,** Nicole A '03 -500-D The Cptl -Albany 12247
(607) 225-4234 .. **Burd,** James P '82 J Burd,PC -2609 Main Bx967 -Greenwood 14839 **Fx:**225-4236
(212) 553-5400 .. **Burd,** Samantha M '04 %Zurich NA -1 Lbrty Plz -NY 10006
(718) 625-6052 .. **Burden,** Crystal J '92 (C Burden,PC) -26 Court -Brklyn 11242 **Fx:**222-1335
(716) 849-6800 .. **Burden,** Donna L '88 (Burden G&H,LLC) -403 Main -Buffalo 14203 **Fx:**849-6806
(212) 867-4466 .. **Burden,** Jos '75 (Belkin BW&G,LLP) -270 Mad Av -NY 10016
(516) 365-6400 .. **Burden,** Michl J '96 Excess Space -1 Hllw Ln -New Hyde Pk 11042
(631) 608-2858 .. **Burden,** Patricia '00 -Bx1117 -Copiague 11726 **Fx:**532-4843
(212) 788-6084 .. **Burdess,** Andrew G '02 Ofc of Mgmt & Budget -75 Park Pl -NY 10007
(516) 742-1295 .. **Burdi,** James F '80 Burdi & B -229 7th -Gdn Cty 11530 **Fx:**742-6347
(212) 532-0800 .. **Burdick,** Ann M '00 %AFTRA -260 Mad Av -NY 10016 **Fx:**545-1238
(212) 922-0509 .. **Burdick,** Christopher W '83 %Stewart Title Ins -300 E 42nd -NY 10017 **Fx:**922-1593
(718) 579-3000 .. **Burdick,** Vanessa M '89 %Leg Aid -1020 Grnd Cncrs -Bronx 10451 **Fx:**588-2611
(516) 248-7575 .. **Burdo,** Wm T '95 OfCnsl Levine & G -114 Old Cntry Rd -Mineola 11501
(212) 436-6416 .. **Burekhovich,** Inga '00 Deloitte & Touche LLP -2 World Fncl Ctr -NY 10281
(212) 455-2000 .. **Buresh,** James C '89 (Simpson T&B LLP) -425 Lex Av -NY 10017
(718) 254-7000 .. **Buretta,** John D '97 %US Atty -271 Cadman Plz E -Brklyn 11201 **Fx:**254-6479
(914) 946-7770 .. **Burford,** Kenneth J '84 OfCnsl Westermann SKS&A,LLP -222 Bloomingdale Rd -White Plns 10605
(212) 532-8100 .. **Burg,** Daniela B '07 %Stern & M,LLP -115 Bway -NY 10006
(845) 454-1200 .. **Burg,** Debra M '00 %Lewis & G,PC -510 Haight Av Bx2990 -Poughkeepsie 12603
(212) 872-1000 .. **Burg,** Michelle A '01 -One Bryant Park -NY 10036 **Fx:**872-1002
(212) 909-6000 .. **Burg,** Sarah S '10 %Debevoise & P LLP -919 3rd Av -NY 10022
(212) 309-1000 .. **Burgard,** Nadia St George '92 (Hunton & W) -200 Park Av -NY 10166
(716) 843-5700 .. **Burgasser,** George C '79 %US Atty -138 Delaware Av -Buffalo 14202 **Fx:**551-3052
(716) 854-2620 .. **Burgasser,** Jessica J '03 %Brown & K,LLP -1500 Lbrty Bldg -Buffalo 14202
(716) 692-1783 .. **Burgasser,** R Thos '70 (RT Burgasser,PLLC) -825 Payne Av -N Tonawanda 14120 **Fx:**692-6614
(212) 906-1200 .. **Burgaud,** Celine A '07 %Latham & W -885 3rd Av -NY 10022
(585) 263-1000 .. **Burgdorf,** Robt W '88 (Nixon P LLP) -1100 Clinton Sq -Rchstr 14604
(585) 263-6201 .. **Burger,** Anne Mary '95 Fed Pub Def -28 E Main -Rchstr 14614 **Fx:**263-5871
(212) 949-6126 .. **Burger,** Barbara '72 (Burger Y&G LLP) -60 E 42nd -NY 10165 **Fx:**681-6999
(212) 857-8813 .. **Burger,** Benjamin S '06 %Ct of Appls-2nd Cir -40 Foley Sq -NY 10007
(212) 704-6000 .. **Burger,** Carol F '81 (Troutman S LLP) -405 Lex Av -NY 10174
(718) 522-1910 .. **Burger,** Chas H '57 -32 Court -Brklyn 11201
(212) 603-6300 .. **Burger,** David C '84 Cnsl Robinson BLGG&G PC -875 3rd Av -NY 10022
(914) 332-0700 .. **Burger,** Eilleen M '99 %M Pollack -150 Wht Plns Rd -Tarrytwn 10591 **Fx:**684-6069
(212) 984-7845 .. **Burger,** Howard M '72 (Warshaw BCS&K,LLP) -555 5th Av -NY 10017
(212) 614-5311 .. **Burger,** Jacqueline '88 %Community Srvc Soc -105 E 22nd -NY 10010 **Fx:**614-9441
(516) 932-4300 .. **Burger,** Mark A '83 Technology Practice Grp LLC -1010 Nrthrn Blvd -Gt Neck 11021
(718) 217-2200 .. **Burger,** Martin '78 -219-51 Jamaica Av -Qns Vllg 11428 **Fx:**217-5518
(585) 546-6448 .. **Burger,** Michl A '95 (Davidson F LLP) -28 E Main -Rchstr 14614
(212) 998-6550 .. **Burger,** Michl H '04 %NYU Law Schl -245 Sullivan -NY 10012
(718) 522-1910 .. **Burger,** Randi L '87 -32 Court -Brklyn 11201
(212) 732-3200 .. **Burger,** Stephen V '81 (Carter L&M LLP) -2 Wall -NY 10005
(212) 450-4000 .. **Burgess,** Angela T '96 (Davis P&W LLP) -450 Lex Av -NY 10017
(212) 259-8000 .. **Burgess,** Christina B '06 %Dewey & L LLP -1301 Av of Amer -NY 10019
(845) 897-5199 .. **Burgess,** Craig A '07 %Feldman K&C,LLP -995 Main BxA -Fishkill 12524
(315) 797-9850 .. **Burgess,** Danl A '97 %Hage & H LLC -283 Genesee -Utica 13501 **Fx:**797-1721

(585) 865-5750 .. **Burgess DiRaddo & Case** -2725 Dewey Av -Rchstr 14616 **Fx:**865-5829
(585) 581-1060 .. **Burgess,** Douglas R '73 -480 W Ridge Rd -Rchstr 14615
(518) 486-1765 .. **Burgess,** Fredk W '76 %Dept of Ed -Cultural Educ Ctr Rm 3021 -Albany 12231 **Fx:**474-3863
(518) 482-0038 .. **Burgess,** Kathleen Hughes '84 Maternity & Early Childhd Fndtn -50 Colvin Av -Albany 12206
(315) 475-3083 .. **Burgess,** Kevin D '88 %Affordable Legal Srvcs -313 E Willow -Syracuse 13203 **Fx:**478-5336
(518) 648-5603 .. **Burgess,** Lisa A '02 -Bx440 -Indian Lk 12842 **Fx:**648-5603
(518) 371-0052 .. **Burgess,** Peter L '92 (Burgess & Assoc PC) -646 Plnk Rd -Clifton Pk 12065 **Fx:**371-0053
(585) 391-3441 .. **Burgess,** Susan N '88 -13 Market -Brockprt 14420 **Fx:**391-3442
(212) 310-8000 .. **Burgess,** Tracy A '10 %Weil G&M LLP -767 5th Av -NY 10153
(718) 590-2000 .. **Burgess Capers,** Kimberly K '00 %DA -198 E 161st -Bronx 10451 **Fx:**590-6477
(716) 488-3090 .. **Burgett,** Dalton J '66 (Burgett & R) -15 E 5th Bx3090 -Jamestwn 14702
(716) 488-3090 .. **Burgett & Robbins** -15 E 5th Bx3090 -Jamestwn 14702 **Fx:**483-3765
(212) 967-1800 .. **Burgher,** Gopal M '98 (Bryant BJ&R LLP) -140 Bway -NY 10005
(716) 854-1744 .. **Burgio,** James P '75 (Burgio K&C) -2150 Main Place Twr -Buffalo 14202
(716) 854-1744 .. **Burgio Kita & Curvin** -2150 Main Place Twr -Buffalo 14202 **Fx:**854-1749
(212) 371-4386 .. **Burgman,** Dierdre A '82 -345 E 56th -NY 10022
(212) 506-1700 .. **Burgo,** Paul J '07 %Kasowitz BT&F LLP -1633 Bway -NY 10019
(212) 949-8989 .. **Burgoon,** Gary M '93 %Lifshutz & L,PC -501 5th Av -NY 10017 **Fx:**922-9620
(845) 624-1966 .. **Burgoon,** Kelly Anne '91 (Brown B&H,PC) -365 Route 304 -Bardonia 10954
(212) 755-5510 .. **Burgos,** Arlene '98 %Loeb B & Prtnrs -505 Park Av -NY 10022
(646) 374-0028 .. **Burgos,** Christina N '06 (Ginsberg & B,PLLC) -12 E 49th -NY 10017 **Fx:**355-0202
(914) 631-5050 .. **Burgos,** Ioanna N '04 -95 Beekman Av -Sleepy Hollow 10591
(212) 940-3000 .. **Burgos,** Joel D '07 %Nixon P LLP -437 Mad Av -NY 10022
(718) 741-8400 .. **Burgos,** Luis R '82 %Div of Human Rights -1 Fordham Plz -Bronx 10458 **Fx:**741-8102
(212) 532-8100 .. **Burgos,** Sandra P '98 (Stern & M,LLP) -115 Bway -NY 10006
(914) 738-9000 .. **Burgoyne,** Allen G '63 -311 5th Av -Pelham 10803 **Fx:**738-3414
(585) 344-1087 .. **Burhans,** Debra L '83 -104 Bank Bx566 -Batavia 14021 **Fx:**344-1317
(716) 434-2825 .. **Burhans,** Mark E '86 %Ticor Title Ins -Bx551 -Lockprt 14095
(716) 854-4300 .. **Burhyte,** Janet G '82 %Gross SB&G,PC -465 Main -Buffalo 14203
(585) 678-7149 .. **Buri,** Mark D '96 Constellation Brands Inc -207 Hgh Pnt Dr -Victor 14564
(516) 803-2300 .. **Burian,** Lawr J '96 %Cablevision Sys -1111 Stewart Av -Bethpage 11714
(518) 486-7398 .. **Burianek,** Lisa M '92 %Dept of Law -The Cptl -Albany 12224
(518) 761-6405 .. **Burin,** Matthew D '05 %DA -Cnty Mncpl Ctr -Lk George 12845
(212) 761-3233 .. **Burk,** Adam D '04 Morgan Stanley-Invstmnt Banking Div -1585 Bway -NY 10036
(212) 455-2000 .. **Burk,** Erika H '03 %Simpson T&B LLP -425 Lex Av -NY 10017
(212) 878-8000 .. **Burka,** Jennifer L '07 %Clifford C LLP -31 W 52nd -NY 10019
(718) 250-2000 .. **Burka,** Thos S '89 %DA -350 Jay -Brklyn 11201 **Fx:**250-2314
(212) 872-6464 .. **Burkard,** Arthur C E '96 %KPMG LLP -345 Park Av -NY 10154
(845) 279-2986 .. **Burkart,** David P '04 %Hogan & R -1441 Route 22 -Brewstr 10509
(716) 566-5400 .. **Burkart,** Elisha J '06 %Goldberg S LLP -665 Main -Buffalo 14203
(516) 249-3450 .. **Burkart,** Michl M '95 %Carman C&I,LLP -266 Main -Farmngdl 11735
(516) 560-6400 .. **Burkavage,** Erin '06 %Leg Aid -1 Helen Keller Way -Hempstd 11550 **Fx:**565-3694
(718) 243-6467 .. **Burkavage,** Jennifer A '07 %Leg Aid -111 Lvngstn -Brklyn 11201 **Fx:**237-8737
(585) 232-5958 .. **Burke,** Adrian J '87 (Burke & B) -16 W Main -Rchstr 14614
(516) 463-4243 .. **Burke,** Alafair S '00 %Hofstra Law Schl -121 Hofstra Univ -Hempstd 11549
(585) 342-4410 .. **Burke Albright Harter & Reddy,LLP** -1800 Hudson Av -Rchstr 14617 **Fx:**342-4514
(516) 571-3800 .. **Burke,** Amanda '06 %DA -262 Old Cntry Rd -Mineola 11501 **Fx:**248-9479
(212) 728-8000 .. **Burke,** Amanda M '09 %Willkie F&G LLP -787 7th Av -NY 10019
(212) 450-4000 .. **Burke,** Arthur J '94 (Davis P&W LLP) -450 Lex Av -NY 10017
(716) 856-0600 .. **Burke,** B Kevin Jr. '00 (Jaeckle F&M,LLP) -12 Fountain Plz -Buffalo 14202
(212) 953-2381 .. **Burke,** Brendan M Jr. '00 %Rubin F&F,LLP -292 Mad Av -NY 10017
(212) 848-4000 .. **Burke,** Brian G '06 %Shearman & S LLP -599 Lex Av -NY 10022
(518) 445-2311 .. **Burke,** Bridgit M '90 %Law Clinic & Justice Ctr -80 New Scotland Av -Albany 12208
(518) 452-1961 .. **Burke & Casserly,PC** -255 Washington Av Ext -Albany 12205 **Fx:**452-4230
(585) 758-7613 .. **Burke,** Christine E '78 %Univ of Rochester Med Ctr -Bx278979 -Rchstr 14627 **Fx:**272-9311
(516) 571-3800 .. **Burke,** Christine E '94 %DA -262 Old Cntry Rd -Mineola 11501 **Fx:**248-9479
(315) 443-4532 .. **Burke,** Christopher E '93 %Student Lgl Srvcs -760 Ostrum Av -Syracuse 13244
(212) 695-8090 .. **Burke,** Coleman P '73 %Waterfront Realty -224 12th Av -NY 10001 **Fx:**269-8768
(212) 969-6169 .. **Burke,** Colin T '88 %Alliance Bernstein LP -1345 Av of Amer -NY 10105 **Fx:**554-4639
(212) 506-5000 .. **Burke,** Colman J '95 (Orrick H&S LLP) -51 W 52nd -NY 10019
(212) 571-9596 .. **Burke,** Constance M '82 -14 Wall -NY 10005 **Fx:**577-6702
(516) 833-5135 .. **Burke,** Cynthia M '98 -265 Post Av -Westbury 11590 **Fx:**908-4043
(516) 466-6500 .. **Burke,** Danl C '94 %Parker WA LLP -6 Hrbr Park Dr S -Pt Wash 11050
(516) 802-0560 .. **Burke,** Danl P '86 (DP Burke & Assoc,PLLC) -240 Townsend Sq -Oyster Bay 11771
(212) 344-0464 .. **Burke,** Donald '63 OfCnsl Cardillo & C -29 Bway -NY 10006
(212) 435-3571 .. **Burke,** Donald F '83 %Port Auth of NY/NJ -225 Park Av S -NY 10003 **Fx:**435-3555
(212) 858-1000 .. **Burke,** Donovan W '97 (Pillsbury WSP LLP) -1540 Bway -NY 10036
(716) 852-1380 .. **Burke,** Edmund W '68 OfCnsl Abbarno M&K -314 Brisbane Bldg -Buffalo 14203
(631) 283-4111 .. **Burke,** Edw D '69 (Burke & S,PLLC) -41 Meeting House Ln -Southampton 11968
(631) 725-3131 .. **Burke,** Edw D Jr. '91 E Burke Jr & Assoc,LLC -62 Main Bx3319 -Sag Hbr 11963 **Fx:**725-7327
(212) 756-9251 .. **Burke,** Edw J Jr. '91 %Santander Investments -45 E 53rd -NY 10022
(607) 755-9700 .. **Burke,** Edw M '72 %IBM -1701 North -Endicott 13760
(212) 530-4823 .. **Burke,** Erin K '98 %LaRocca HRG&B LLP -40 Wall -NY 10005
(716) 631-8444 .. **Burke,** Eugene V '77 -5754 Main -Williamsvll 14221
(716) 883-7272 .. **Burke,** F Brendan Jr. '76 (McGee & G) -200 Summer -Buffalo 14222
(631) 249-3978 .. **Burke,** Gary E '89 (Burke & B,PC) -500 Bi-Cnty Blvd -Farmngdl 11735 **Fx:**249-3994
(518) 463-1269 .. **Burke,** George B III '92 (Walsh & H) -18 Corp Wds Blvd -Albany 12211
(212) 818-9200 .. **Burke,** Gilman S '62 Cnsl Satterlee SB&B LLP -230 Park Av -NY 10169
(212) 819-8200 .. **Burke,** Heather M '07 %White & C LLP -1155 Av of Amer -NY 10036
(518) 884-4770 .. **Burke,** Hugh G '86 %Cnty Atty -Cnty Mncpl Ctr -Ballston Spa 12020 **Fx:**884-4720
(518) 346-2450 .. **Burke,** J David '68 -835 Union -Schnctdy 12308 **Fx:**346-2417
(212) 859-8000 .. **Burke,** Jacquelyn M '07 %Fried FHS&J LLP -1 NY Plz -NY 10004
(845) 562-3366 .. **Burke,** James Alexander '85 %Larkin AI&T,LLP -34 Route 17K -Newburgh 12550
(914) 323-7000 .. **Burke,** James F '97 (Wilson EME&D LLP) -3 Gannett Dr -White Plns 10604
(631) 755-0101 .. **Burke,** James M '88 Cnsl Lewis JAA,LLP -425 Broad Hollow Rd -Melvll 11747
(718) 254-0700 .. **Burke,** Jamie '90 %Bklyn Defender Srvcs -177 Lvngstn -Brklyn 11201 **Fx:**254-0897
(518) 462-5601 .. **Burke,** Jane Bello '82 OfCnsl O'Connell & A -54 State -Albany 12207
(212) 294-6700 .. **Burke,** Jeffrey R '02 (Winston & S) -200 Park Av -NY 10166
(716) 648-3020 .. **Burke,** Jennifer L '00 %Shaw & S -4819 S Park Av -Hambrg 14075 **Fx:**648-3730
(212) 554-1234 .. **Burke,** Jennifer Woods '02 AXA Financial Inc -1290 Av of Amer -NY 10104 **Fx:**707-3963
(516) 739-3090 .. **Burke,** Jessie James '97 %Mason & M,PC -394 Old Cntry Rd -Gdn Cty 11530 **Fx:**739-5060
(585) 232-5958 .. **Burke,** John F '54 OfCnsl Burke & B -16 W Main -Rchstr 14614
(845) 641-5760 .. **Burke,** John F '04 -24 Graney Ct -Pearl Rvr 10965 **Fx:**735-1563
(845) 294-1611 .. **Burke,** John F X '78 -210 Main Bx943 -Goshen 10924 **Fx:**294-9667
(212) 460-3121 .. **Burke,** John J '77 Con Ed -4 Irving Pl -NY 10003
(631) 439-3230 .. **Burke,** John J Jr. '92 D'Addario & Co -595 Smith -Farmngdl 11735
(212) 557-9600 .. **Burke,** Jos M '71 (Russo & B) -600 3rd Av -NY 10016
(718) 250-2000 .. **Burke,** Jos M '04 %DA -350 Jay -Brklyn 11201 **Fx:**250-2314
(631) 287-3065 .. **Burke,** Jos M '06 %Town Atty -116 Hmptn Rd -Southampton 11968 **Fx:**287-3662
(646) 386-5700 .. **Burke,** Jos P Jr. '94 %Civil Ct -111 Centre -NY 10013
(315) 598-8552 .. **Burke,** Judith P '98 -163 S 1st -Fulton 13069 **Fx:**598-1830
(212) 626-4100 .. **Burke,** June Anne '09 (Baker & M LLP) -1114 Av of Amer -NY 10036
(631) 853-4049 .. **Burke,** Kathleen A '89 %Cnty Atty -Dennison Bldg Bx6100 -Hauppauge 11788 **Fx:**853-5169
(212) 746-4075 .. **Burke,** Kathleen M '76 %NY Presbyterian Hsptl -525 E 68th Bx88 -NY 10065 **Fx:**746-8603
(212) 310-8000 .. **Burke,** Kathlene M '09 %Weil G&M LLP -767 5th Av -NY 10153
(518) 388-4368 .. **Burke,** Kevin A '94 Cnty Atty -106 Erie Blvd -Schnctdy 12305 **Fx:**382-1256
(212) 896-6500 .. **Burke,** Kevin A '96 (Howrey LLP) -601 Lex Av -NY 10022
(212) 857-8230 .. **Burke,** Kevin B '91 %Baker MM&M,PC -330 W 34th -NY 10001
(212) 701-3000 .. **Burke,** Kevin John '80 (Cahill G&R LLP) -80 Pine -NY 10005 **Fx:**269-5420
(212) 460-1110 .. **Burke,** Kevin M '78 Con Ed -4 Irving Pl -NY 10003
(212) 854-5573 .. **Burke,** Kevin M '04 Columbia Univ -535 W 116th -NY 10027
(518) 862-1386 .. **Burke,** Kevin P '89 (Burke SM&H,LLP) -302 Wshngtn Av Ext Bx15085 -Albany 12212
(212) 687-7410 .. **Burke,** Kristin M '90 (Clifton B&D,LLP) -420 Lex Av -NY 10170
(212) 941-9090 .. **Burke,** Lauren A '10 The Door -121 Av of Amer -NY 10013 **Fx:**941-0714
(347) 404-9133 .. **Burke,** Lauren E '09 %Civil Ct -141 Lvngstn -Brklyn 11201 **Fx:**(718) 643-3733
(718) 270-5101 .. **Burke,** Levar N '09 Medgar Evers Cllg-CUNY -1637 Bedford Av -Brklyn 11225
(914) 997-8100 .. **Burke Lipton McCarthy & Gordon** -10 Bank -White Plns 10606 **Fx:**997-8473
(516) 571-3337 .. **Burke,** Lisa M '81 %Hon E McCabe -100 Supreme Ct Dr -Mineola 11501
(646) 654-5084 .. **Burke,** Lois A '77 VNU USA -770 Bway -NY 10003
(212) 682-1700 .. **Burke,** Louis F '73 (L Burke,PC) -460 Park Av -NY 10022 **Fx:**808-4280
(518) 378-7758 .. **Burke,** Martin G '97 -Bx1025 -Albany 12201
(212) 577-3688 .. **Burke,** Mary Katherine '09 %Leg Aid -199 Water -NY 10038 **Fx:**509-8431
(914) 946-7770 .. **Burke,** Mary Pat '90 (Westermann SKS&A,LLP) -222 Bloomingdale Rd -White Plns 10605
(716) 853-3801 .. **Burke,** Melissa B '08 %Kenney SL&N,LLP -14 Lafayette Sq -Buffalo 14203
(212) 839-5300 .. **Burke,** Michl A '82 (Sidley A LLP) -787 7th Av -NY 10019
(212) 258-7500 .. **Burke,** Michl A '02 %Nickelodeon -1515 Bway -NY 10036
(716) 375-5130 .. **Burke,** Michl D '94 (Driscoll & B) -2646 W State -Olean 14760 **Fx:**375-5131
(212) 629-8899 .. **Burke,** Michl F '63 (Burke B&B) -350 5th Av -NY 10118 **Fx:**629-3889
(212) 839-5300 .. **Burke,** Michl G '03 %Sidley A LLP -787 7th Av -NY 10019
(914) 703-6300 .. **Burke,** Michl J '89 %Pillinger MT,LLP -570 Taxter Rd -Elmsfrd 10523

(845) 294-4080 .. **Burke,** Michl Kennedy '97 (Burke M&G) -40 Matthews Bx216 -Goshen 10924
(212) 593-6700 .. **Burke,** Michl L '01 %Aaronson RF&D,LLP -757 3rd Av -NY 10017
(212) 382-3300 .. **Burke,** Michl P '04 %Wollmuth M&D LLP -500 5th Av -NY 10110
(631) 380-2360 .. **Burke,** Michelle J '02 Cnsl BASF Corp -50 Health Sciences Dr -Stony Brk 11790
(212) 265-6888 .. **Burke,** Michelle Molinaro '06 %Porzio B&N,PC -156 W 56th -NY 10019
(845) 294-4080 .. **Burke Miele & Golden** -40 Matthews Bx216 -Goshen 10924 **Fx:**294-7673
(845) 357-7500 .. **Burke Miele & Golden** -Bx397 -Suffern 10901 **Fx:**357-7321
(212) 858-1000 .. **Burke,** Nora E '09 %Pillsbury WSP LLP -1540 Bway -NY 10036
(212) 354-3800 .. **Burke & Parsons** -100 Park Av -NY 10017 **Fx:**221-1432
(516) 741-6611 .. **Burke,** Patricia Farrell '92 (Farrell F&B) -212 Station Plaza N -Mineola 11501
(212) 629-8899 .. **Burke,** Patrick G Jr. '60 (Burke B&B) -350 5th Av -NY 10118 **Fx:**629-3889
(212) 582-6500 .. **Burke,** Patrick G III '91 %Arshack H&L,PLLC -1790 Bway -NY 10019
(585) 232-5958 .. **Burke,** Patrick J '80 (Burke & B) -16 W Main -Rchstr 14614
(646) 920-3744 .. **Burke,** Patrick J '88 Guidance Software,Inc -551 5th Av -NY 10176
(845) 357-7500 .. **Burke,** Patrick T '66 (Burke M&G) -Bx397 -Suffern 10901
(845) 294-4080 .. **Burke,** Patrick T '66 (Burke M&G) -40 Matthews Bx216 -Goshen 10924
(212) 742-3390 .. **Burke,** Peter M '89 Lindabury ME&C,PC -26 Bway -NY 10004
(585) 987-2800 .. **Burke,** Philip L '82 (Woods OG LLP) -2 State -Rchstr 14614
(212) 944-7333 .. **Burke,** R Brian '83 (Rode & Q) -55 W 39th -NY 10018
(212) 354-3800 .. **Burke,** Raymond J Jr. '68 (Burke & P) -100 Park Av -NY 10017
(716) 826-8749 .. **Burke,** Raymond M '87 -71 Olcott Av -Buffalo 14220
(212) 629-8899 .. **Burke,** Richd A '68 (Burke B&B) -350 5th Av -NY 10118 **Fx:**629-3889
(212) 418-4206 .. **Burke,** Richd F Jr. '94 %Gleacher Partners LLC -660 Mad Av -NY 10065
(631) 249-3978 .. **Burke,** Richd J '82 (Burke & B,PC) -500 Bi-Cnty Blvd -Farmngdl 11735 **Fx:**249-3994
(845) 452-6400 .. **Burke,** Richd J Jr. '85 OfCnsl O'Neil & B -301 Mnchstr Rd -Poughkeepsie 12603
(212) 687-1736 .. **Burke,** Robt E '00 %R Schwartzberg & Assoc,PLLC -60 E 42nd -NY 10165
(585) 342-4410 .. **Burke,** Robt J '67 (Burke AH&R,LLP) -1800 Hudson Av -Rchstr 14617
(212) 425-0700 .. **Burke,** Ronald C '84 Cnsl Kelner & K -140 Bway -NY 10005
(212) 464-0444 .. **Burke,** Rose Marie '88 JP Morgan Chase & Co -345 Park Av -NY 10154
(518) 862-1386 .. **Burke Scolamiero Mortati & Hurd,LLP** -302 Wshngtn Av Ext Bx15085 -Albany 12212 **Fx:**862-1393
(518) 671-6004 .. **Burke Scolamiero Mortati & Hurd,LLP** -437 E Allen -Hudson 12534 **Fx:**671-6008
(212) 435-3571 .. **Burke,** Sean P '09 Port Auth of NY/NJ -225 Park Av S -NY 10003 **Fx:**435-3555
(212) 737-5146 .. **Burke,** Sheila Ann '89 -330 E 85th -NY 10028
(212) 335-4500 .. **Burke,** Sidney '03 (DLA Piper LLP) -1251 Av of Amer -NY 10020
(516) 571-3800 .. **Burke,** Stephanie N '05 %DA -262 Old Cntry Rd -Mineola 11501 **Fx:**248-9479
(631) 421-1211 .. **Burke,** Stephen P '76 Martin F&M -100 E Carver -Huntngtn 11743
(212) 697-6200 .. **Burke Stone & Arteficio, LLP** -370 Lex Av -NY 10017 **Fx:**687-3333
(631) 283-4111 .. **Burke & Sullivan,PLLC** -41 Meeting House Ln -Southampton 11968 **Fx:**283-7711
(914) 828-8832 .. **Burke,** Susan E '98 %Swiss Re America -175 King -Armonk 10504 **Fx:**828-7000
(516) 227-0700 .. **Burke,** Suzanne Q '02 %Farrell F,PC -1320 RXR Plz -Uniondale 11556
(518) 449-3300 .. **Burke,** Terence J '72 SrCnsl Nolan & H,LLP -39 N Pearl -Albany 12207
(516) 465-8090 .. **Burke,** Theresa F '95 %North Shore-LIJ Hlth Systm -145 Community Dr -Gt Neck 11021 **Fx:**465-8013
(518) 886-4190 .. **Burke,** Thos A '99 AYCO -321 Bway Bx860 -Saratoga Spgs 12866 **Fx:**(917) 977-3414
(585) 454-6480 .. **Burke,** Thos C '64 (Osborn R&B,LLP) -45 Exchange Blvd -Rchstr 14614
(914) 997-8100 .. **Burke,** Thos J '80 (Burke LM&G) -10 Bank -White Plns 10606
(212) 629-8899 .. **Burke,** Thos P '59 (Burke B&B) -350 5th Av -NY 10118 **Fx:**629-3889
(212) 596-9000 .. **Burke,** Thos P '95 Cnsl Ropes & G LLP -1211 Av of Amer -NY 10036
(716) 632-1644 .. **Burke,** Timothy L '81 %UAW Lgl Srvcs Plan -307 Cayuga Rd -Cheektowaga 14225 **Fx:**632-1897
(845) 794-4094 .. **Burke,** Timothy P '92 %Leg Aid -11 Bank -Monticello 12701 **Fx:**794-0119
(518) 452-1961 .. **Burke,** Walter T '79 (Burke & C,PC) -255 Washington Av Ext -Albany 12205
(212) 858-1000 .. **Burke,** Wm L '68 (Pillsbury WSP LLP) -1540 Bway -NY 10036
(845) 452-6400 .. **Burke,** Wm T '82 (O'Neil & B) -301 Mnchstr Rd -Poughkeepsie 12603
(914) 332-1800 .. **Burke,** Wm T '91 (Cherry E&K,LLP) -150 Wht Plns Rd -Tarrytwn 10591
(585) 396-0670 .. **Burkett,** Alexandra '96 -66 N Main -Canandaigua 14424 **Fx:**396-0871
(518) 792-2117 .. **Burkett,** James R '92 (Bartlett PS&R,PC) -1 Wshngtn Bx2168 -Glens Fls 12801
(212) 582-1951 .. **Burkett,** Perry C '68 -617 11th Av -NY 10036 **Fx:**246-0856
(212) 250-2572 .. **Burkhard,** Raymond T '89 %Deutsche Bk -60 Wall -NY 10005
(914) 289-0200 .. **Burkhardt,** John F '75 -445 Hmltn Av -White Plns 10601
(914) 946-4777 .. **Burkhardt,** John F '75 OfCnsl Keane & B,PC -445 Hmltn Av -White Plns 10601
(212) 345-0045 .. **Burkhardt,** Suzanne Pence '95 %Marsh USA -1166 Av of Amer -NY 10036 **Fx:**345-4808
(212) 705-7000 .. **Burkhart,** Benjamin C '99 OfCnsl Bingham M LLP -399 Park Av -NY 10022
(516) 222-2230 .. **Burkhart,** Errol A '64 (Burkhart W&H,LLP) -585 Stewart Av -Gdn Cty 11530
(516) 222-2230 .. **Burkhart Wexler & Hirschberg, LLP** -585 Stewart Av -Gdn Cty 11530 **Fx:**222-8803
(585) 325-1750 .. **Burkhart,** Wm E Jr. '96 -16 E Main -Rchstr 14614
(516) 746-7371 .. **Burkhoff,** Jeffrey M '94 (Burns RT&R,LLP) -390 Old Cntry Rd -Gdn Cty 11530
(212) 833-6800 .. **Burkin,** Brian L '90 Sony Corp of America -555 Mad Av -NY 10022
(212) 460-3332 .. **Burkland,** Elizabeth A '88 Con Ed -4 Irving Pl -NY 10003
(914) 249-2000 .. **Burkley,** John H '99 %MasterCard Intl -2000 Purchase -Purchase 10577
(518) 695-3050 .. **Burkly,** Catherine A '90 -74 Broad -Schuylrvll 12871 **Fx:**695-4511
(212) 838-1937 .. **Burko,** Elliott J '78 -245 5th Av -NY 10016
(718) 625-2300 .. **Burko,** Louis R '00 (Severance B&S,PC) -16 Court -Brklyn 11241
(716) 853-9555 .. **Burko,** Paula '84 %Leg Aid -237 Main -Buffalo 14203 **Fx:**853-3219
(212) 937-6304 .. **Burkoff,** David M '04 Cnsl WilmerHale -399 Park Av -NY 10022
(585) 295-7316 .. **Burkwit,** Chas F '97 (Cellino & B,PC) -16 W Main -Rchstr 14614
(585) 546-1588 .. **Burkwit,** Robt L '62 -450 Rynlds Arcd Bldg -Rchstr 14614 **Fx:**232-2802
(212) 421-9630 .. **Burlant,** Brian Lee '85 Smythe Masterson & Judd -230 Park Av -NY 10169 **Fx:**421-9665
(212) 525-7638 .. **Burlant,** Gail A '85 HSBC Securities -452 5th Av -NY 10018
(212) 841-5975 .. **Burlant,** Michl N '87 %Cushman & Wakefield -1290 Av of Amer -NY 10104
(212) 762-4772 .. **Burlazzi,** Susan Young '03 Morgan Stanley -1221 Av of Amer -NY 10020
(212) 909-6000 .. **Burleigh,** Jennifer J '95 (Debevoise & P LLP) -919 3rd Av -NY 10022
(212) 207-8787 .. **Burleigh,** John F '84 (Jacobs & B LLP) -445 Park Av -NY 10022
(212) 813-8800 .. **Burleson,** Sarah M '09 %Goodwin P LLP -620 8th Av -NY 10018
(212) 596-9000 .. **Burling,** Michl S '04 %Ropes & G LLP -1211 Av of Amer -NY 10036
(212) 223-0400 .. **Burlingame,** Glenn D '92 (Zeichner E&K LLP) -575 Lex Av -NY 10022
(631) 969-3100 .. **Burlingame,** Nancy G '91 %Frenkel LWW&G,LLP -20 W Main -Bay Shr 11706
(718) 254-7000 .. **Burlingame,** Roger A '01 %US Atty -271 Cadman Plz E -Brklyn 11201 **Fx:**254-6479
(212) 609-6800 .. **Burman,** Cheryl Fisher '95 %McCarter & E,LLP -245 Park Av -NY 10167
(518) 455-3313 .. **Burman,** Diane Long '92 Senate Minority Cnsl Ofc -4 ESP -Albany 12223
(212) 770-5373 .. **Burman,** Jeffrey S '97 AIG -70 Pine -NY 10270
(518) 474-1201 .. **Burman,** Jonathan D '92 Dept of Ed -89 Wshngtn Av -Albany 12234
(212) 968-1001 .. **Burman,** Roberta '79 (Gwertzman LBS&M) -80 Broad -NY 10004
(516) 883-6055 .. **Burman,** Russell S '81 -18 Haven Av -Pt Wash 11050 **Fx:**883-6052
(212) 935-1600 .. **Burman,** Sheldon V '60 (SV Burman,PC) -110 E 59th -NY 10022 **Fx:**223-4911
(718) 250-2000 .. **Burnazaki,** Yekaterina '09 %DA -350 Jay -Brklyn 11201 **Fx:**250-2314
(212) 938-5000 .. **Burnazian,** Lara M '99 %Cantor Fitzgerald -110 E 59th -NY 10022
(212) 682-4002 .. **Burnbaum,** Edw H '79 (Novack BC LLP) -300 E 42nd -NY 10017
(212) 686-7996 .. **Burnbaum,** Marian C '80 -333 E 34th -NY 10016
(212) 309-1000 .. **Burner,** Eric R '99 (Hunton & W) -200 Park Av -NY 10166
(631) 941-3434 .. **Burner,** Nancy '88 (Burner S & Assoc LLP) -46 Route 25A -Setauket 11733 **Fx:**941-3443
(212) 336-0037 .. **Burnett,** Burk E '99 %SEC -3 World Fncl Ctr -NY 10281 **Fx:**336-1323
(212) 849-7000 .. **Burnett,** David D '08 %Quinn EU&S,LLP -51 Mad Av -NY 10010
(212) 872-9800 .. **Burnett,** Douglas R '82 (Squire S&D LLP) -30 Rckfllr Plz -NY 10112
(718) 526-6596 .. **Burnett,** Glen A '86 -107-28 171st -Jamaica 11433
(212) 223-4000 .. **Burnett,** Henry G '90 (Crowell & M LLP) -590 Mad Av -NY 10022
(718) 738-9800 .. **Burnett,** John J '86 S Baron & Assoc,PC -159-49 Cross Bay Blvd -Howard Bch 11414 **Fx:**738-3912
(516) 867-3280 .. **Burnett,** Lawr W '80 -2128 Seneca Dr S -Merrick 11566 **Fx:**867-4554
(646) 386-5269 .. **Burnett,** Marva A '88 Family Ct -60 Lafayette -NY 10013
(212) 264-3650 .. **Burnett,** Sybil L '96 %SSA Ofc Genl Cnsl -26 Fed Plz -NY 10278 **Fx:**264-6372
(212) 909-6000 .. **Burnett,** Tracy A '06 %Debevoise & P LLP -919 3rd Av -NY 10022
(212) 457-9545 .. **Burnett-Cole,** Antoinette D '97 %IncisiveMedia /NYLJ -120 Bway -NY 10271
(212) 660-5550 .. **Burney,** Nathaniel E '99 OfCnsl MC Rakower,PC -747 3rd Av -NY 10017 **Fx:**660-5551
(212) 340-2077 .. **Burney,** Raymond '84 %Metro-North -345 Mad Av -NY 10017 **Fx:**340-2391
(716) 849-1333 .. **Burnham,** Thos C '04 (Lipsitz GSC LLP) -42 Delaware Av -Buffalo 14202
(518) 782-2733 .. **Burnham,** Todd C '01 (Burnham Law Firm,PLLC) -11 Century Hill Dr -Latham 12110
(212) 465-5688 .. **Burnley,** Anissa S '05 Parsons Brinckerhoff -1 Penn Plz -NY 10119
(212) 450-4000 .. **Burnovski,** Brian M '07 %Davis P&W LLP -450 Lex Av -NY 10017
(516) 328-3500 .. **Burns,** Alisa A '04 %McDonnell & A,PC -401 Franklin Av -Gdn Cty 11530
(212) 373-3000 .. **Burns,** Aliza F '06 %Paul WRW&G LLP -1285 Av of Amer -NY 10019
(718) 630-2900 .. **Burns,** Amanda M '07 %VA -800 Poly Pl -Brklyn 11209 **Fx:**630-2917
(585) 672-2600 .. **Burns,** Andrew M '93 (Burns & S LLP) -28 E Main -Rchstr 14614 **Fx:**(866) 825-7217
(212) 728-8000 .. **Burns,** Anna C '10 %Willkie F&G LLP -787 7th Av -NY 10019
(212) 956-3037 .. **Burns,** Arnold I '53 Quanstar Grp,LLC -75 Rckfllr Plz -NY 10019
(518) 434-5050 .. **Burns,** Bradford D '02 %Law Dept -106 City Hall -Albany 12207 **Fx:**434-5070
(518) 583-0595 .. **Burns,** Brandi '95 -229 Wshngtn Bx 11 -Saratoga Spgs 12866 **Fx:**583-0783
(212) 696-1999 .. **Burns,** Brent A '94 (Lax & N LLP) -1412 Bway -NY 10018
(212) 883-1700 .. **Burns,** Brian A '94 (Duval & S LLP) -101 Park Av -NY 10178
(212) 983-9700 .. **Burns,** Brian J '91 %Gallagher H&L LLP -380 Lex Av -NY 10168
(516) 270-3260 .. **Burns,** Carolyn '85 -25 Larch Av -Floral Pk 11001 **Fx:**354-7225
(845) 338-8085 .. **Burns,** Christopher A '99 (C Burns,PC) -369 Wshngtn Av -Kingston 12401 **Fx:**338-8085
(518) 785-9522 .. **Burns,** Danl R '81 -1187 Troy Schenectady Rd -Latham 12110 **Fx:**785-9286

(212) 909-5848 .. **Burns,** David A '84 %KPMG LLP -280 Park Av -NY 10017
(212) 449-2773 .. **Burns,** David E '99 Merrill Lynch & Co -250 Vesey -NY 10080
(212) 373-3000 .. **Burns,** Douglas M '05 %Paul WRW&G LLP -1285 Av of Amer -NY 10019
(516) 997-3200 .. **Burns,** Douglas T '85 -675 Old Cntry Rd -Westbury 11590 **Fx:**997-3278
(212) 221-6900 .. **Burns,** Dove Ann E '07 (Winget S&S,LLP) -45 Bway -NY 10006
(212) 339-7838 .. **Burns,** Edmund C '91 %Baseball Cmmssnr -245 Park Av -NY 10167
(212) 964-2469 .. **Burns,** Edmund J '67 (Burns KS&O,PC) -120 Bway -NY 10271
(212) 335-9000 .. **Burns,** Edw M '06 %DA -1 Hogan Pl -NY 10013
(718) 630-2900 .. **Burns,** George J '81 %VA -800 Poly Pl -Brklyn 11209 **Fx:**630-2917
(212) 310-8000 .. **Burns,** Gregory C '08 %Weil G&M LLP -767 5th Av -NY 10153
(212) 393-1000 .. **Burns & Harris** -233 Bway -NY 10279 **Fx:**267-2110
(212) 227-4450 .. **Burns,** Howard W Jr. '76 -170 Bway -NY 10038 **Fx:**227-4566
(212) 687-8080 .. **Burns,** Hugh L '93 %Citigate Sard Verbinnen -630 3rd Av -NY 10017 **Fx:**687-8344
(718) 618-2227 .. **Burns,** Jacqueline M '99 Family Ct -900 Sheridan Av -Bronx 10451
(212) 715-9100 .. **Burns,** Jade A '08 %Kramer LN&F,LLP -1177 Av of Amer -NY 10036
(607) 776-3306 .. **Burns,** James H '91 OfCnsl Cole & V,PC -7 E Steuben Bx232 -Bath 14810 **Fx:**776-4189
(518) 690-0096 .. **Burns,** James J '88 (Murphy BB&M,LLP) -226 Great Oaks Blvd -Albany 12203
(212) 806-5400 .. **Burns,** James L '83 Stroock &S&L LLP -180 Maiden Ln -NY 10038
(631) 928-8359 .. **Burns,** James R '93 -27 Westmoylan Ln -Coram 11727 **Fx:**928-8359
(718) 634-2342 .. **Burns,** James W '74 -46 W Market -Rckwy Pnt 11697
(212) 306-1822 .. **Burns,** Jeffrey P '94 Amer Stock Exch -86 Trinity Pl -NY 10006
(212) 637-2315 .. **Burns,** Jennifer E '04 US Atty -1 St Andrews Plz -NY 10007
(212) 964-8038 .. **Burns,** John W '88 %Worth L&L,LLP -111 John -NY 10038
(315) 428-7632 .. **Burns,** Jos T '06 -333 E Wshngtn -Syracuse 13202 **Fx:**472-4157
(212) 903-9000 .. **Burns,** Joshua D '07 %Linklaters -1345 Av of Amer -NY 10105
(212) 393-1000 .. **Burns,** Katherine M '80 OfCnsl Burns & H -233 Bway -NY 10279
(718) 725-3070 .. **Burns,** Kelley A '02 ACS -92-31 Union Hall -Jamaica 11433
(212) 964-2469 .. **Burns Kennedy Schilling & O'Shea,PC** -120 Bway -NY 10271 **Fx:**962-4140
(914) 798-5400 .. **Burns,** Kevin '98 %Goldberg S LLP -11 Martine Av -White Plns 10606
(212) 265-2323 .. **Burns,** Kevin L '03 Palisades Media Corp -40 Cntrl Pk S -NY 10019
(585) 238-2033 .. **Burns,** Kevin T '00 Origin LLC -2604 Elmwood Av -Rchstr 14618 **Fx:**238-7866
(518) 474-7700 .. **Burns,** Kristina A '76 NYS OPWDD -44 Holland Av -Albany 12229 **Fx:**474-7382
(212) 323-7070 .. **Burns,** Laura J '07 %Rawle & H LLP -14 Wall -NY 10005
(315) 797-8300 .. **Burns,** Leighton R '58 (Kernan and K,PC) -258 Genesee -Utica 13502 **Fx:**797-6467
(212) 207-9009 .. **Burns,** Linda A '07 %J Siegel -233 Bway -NY 10007
(212) 302-9494 .. **Burns,** Loretta M '81 (Berenthal & Assoc,PC) -317 Mad Av -NY 10017 **Fx:**354-5625
(212) 962-8020 .. **Burns,** Mary Elizabeth '85 %Julien & S,PC -1 Whitehall -NY 10004
(212) 416-6341 .. **Burns,** Mary Ellen '75 %Dept of Law -120 Bway -NY 10271
(718) 634-7143 .. **Burns,** Mary K '47 -137 Beach 133rd -Belle Hbr 11694
(518) 486-2970 .. **Burns,** Mary L '85 %Insurance Dept -99 Wshngtn Av -Albany 12257 **Fx:**474-3397
(718) 875-1060 .. **Burns,** Nancy E '83 -96 Henry -Brklyn 11201 **Fx:**875-1060
(212) 949-9022 .. **Burns,** Natasha J '01 (Abelman F&S) -666 3rd Av -NY 10017
(212) 224-1558 .. **Burns,** Patrick A '72 %Mutual of America -320 Park Av -NY 10022
(718) 250-2000 .. **Burns,** Paul F '84 %DA -350 Jay -Brklyn 11201 **Fx:**250-2314
(212) 867-3636 .. **Burns,** Paul G '79 (Levin & G,PC) -420 Lex Av -NY 10170
(718) 590-5438 .. **Burns,** Rebecca F '95 %Admin Children's Srvcs -900 Sheridan Av -Bronx 10451
(914) 238-0931 .. **Burns,** Richd E '61 -44 Pinecliff Rd -Chappaqua 10514 **Fx:**238-0306
(845) 356-0300 .. **Burns,** Richd Owen '67 -500 Chestnut Rdg Rd -Chestnut Rdg 10977 **Fx:**356-0033
(212) 416-1745 .. **Burns,** Robt G '03 Monarch Alt Captl -375 Park Av -NY 10152
(212) 513-3200 .. **Burns,** Robt J '01 %Holland & K LLP -31 W 52nd -NY 10019
(516) 746-7371 .. **Burns Russo Tamigi & Reardon,LLP** -390 Old Cntry Rd -Gdn Cty 11530 **Fx:**747-7682
(212) 323-7070 .. **Burns,** Ryan M '09 %Rawle & H LLP -14 Wall -NY 10005
(212) 998-6430 .. **Burns,** Sarah E '89 %NYU Law Schl -245 Sullivan -NY 10012 **Fx:**995-4031
(212) 252-0004 .. **Burns,** Sean T '99 %Carroll M&K LLC -570 Lex Av -NY 10022
(914) 946-4777 .. **Burns,** Stephanie L '98 (Keane & B,PC) -445 Hmltn Av -White Plns 10601
(212) 474-1000 .. **Burns,** Stephen L '91 (Cravath S&M LLP) -825 8th Av -NY 10019
(716) 845-0401 .. **Burns,** Theo J '67 -19 Rabin Ter -Buffalo 14201 **Fx:**845-5526
(585) 343-0311 .. **Burns,** Thos A '89 -200 E Main -Batavia 14020 **Fx:**343-5377
(516) 487-1602 .. **Burns,** Thos J '88 %Zaccaria & S -175 E Shore Rd -Gt Neck 11023
(585) 238-2000 .. **Burns,** Thos R '72 (Phillips L LLP) -1400 First Fed Plz -Rchstr 14614
(212) 218-2100 .. **Burns,** Thos R '06 %Fitzpatrick CH&S -1290 Av of Amer -NY 10104
(914) 846-3879 .. **Burns,** Wm J '88 NY Life Ins Co -1 Rockwood Rd -Sleepy Hollow 10591
(631) 537-1166 .. **Burnside,** Susan '78 (Burnside & G) -264 Butter Ln Bx1285 -Brdghmptn 11932 **Fx:**537-7348
(212) 770-1827 .. **Burns-Sagalow,** Teresa K '83 %AIG -80 Pine -NY 10005 **Fx:**344-0972
(914) 323-7000 .. **Burnstin,** Stephen J '07 %Wilson EME&D LLP -3 Gannett Dr -White Plns 10604
(518) 388-4364 .. **Burock,** Amy E '00 %DA -612 State -Schnctdy 12305 **Fx:**388-4569
(516) 688-1700 .. **Burow,** Margaret '04 %IRS -1600 Stewart Av -Westbury 11590 **Fx:**688-1750
(914) 248-6055 .. **Burpee,** Linda R '84 -Bx206 -Lincolndale 10540 **Fx:**248-7057
(315) 233-8300 .. **Burr & Brown** -101 S Salina -Syracuse 13202 **Fx:**233-8320
(607) 798-1521 .. **Burr,** Frederic W '80 OfCnsl Burr & R,LLP -Bx2308 -Bnghmtn 13902
(212) 458-5811 .. **Burr,** Karen R '01 AIG -175 Water -NY 10038
(716) 849-0701 .. **Burr,** Kathleen A '91 %Lipsitz & P LLC -135 Delaware Av -Buffalo 14202
(607) 798-1521 .. **Burr & Reid,LLP** -Bx2308 -Bnghmtn 13902 **Fx:**798-1913
(315) 233-8300 .. **Burr,** Stephen P '98 (Burr & B) -101 S Salina -Syracuse 13202
(845) 735-7301 .. **Burrascano,** Dominick '52 -161 N Mddltwn Rd -Pearl Rvr 10965 **Fx:**623-2219
(718) 722-5722 .. **Burrell,** Andre K '98 Independence Community Bank -195 Montague -Brklyn 11201
(212) 895-4070 .. **Burrell,** Colin A '95 %Genworth Fncl -666 3rd Av -NY 10017
(212) 889-3700 .. **Burrell,** James S II '06 %Abbey SR&A LLP -212 E 39th -NY 10016
(212) 761-7509 .. **Burrell,** Jamila Deas '03 Morgan Stanley -1585 Bway -NY 10036
(212) 696-6000 .. **Burrell,** Lizabeth L '81 Cnsl Curtis M-PC&M LLP -101 Park Av -NY 10178
(347) 592-2516 .. **Burrell,** Michelle L '09 Family Def Proj-Leg Srvcs -177 Lvngstn -Brklyn 11201
(212) 567-8590 .. **Burrell,** Walter P '92 (Burrell R LLC) -110 Wall -NY 10005 **Fx:**567-2630
(212) 374-6741 .. **Burrell-Newman,** Julianne '95 %NYC Dept Educ-OLS -52 Chmbrs -NY 10007 **Fx:**374-5596
(516) 255-1800 .. **Burrell-Rubel,** Joan '92 %Rosenblum & B LLP -100 Merrick Rd -Rockvll Ctr 11570
(518) 474-6331 .. **Burriesci,** Donald J '78 %Dept of Law -The Cptl -Albany 12224
(212) 742-3390 .. **Burris,** Anne S '00 Lindabury ME&C,PC -26 Bway -NY 10004
(212) 504-6000 .. **Burris,** C Kawezya '07 %Cadwalader W&T LLP -1 World Fncl Ctr -NY 10281
(212) 508-7200 .. **Burris,** Joel G '84 Brown Harris Stevens -770 Lex Av -NY 10065
(914) 846-7000 .. **Burris,** Susanne '86 %NY Life Ins -1 Rockwood Rd -Sleepy Hollow 10591 **Fx:**846-4755
(212) 218-5500 .. **Burritt,** Jason E '07 %Seyfarth S LLP -620 8th Av -NY 10018
(518) 457-2854 .. **Burritt,** Nancy L '84 %PERB -80 Wolf Rd -Albany 12205 **Fx:**457-2664
(718) 637-2019 .. **Burroughs,** Blair V '03 NYS PEF -205 Montague -Brklyn 11201
(718) 838-7878 .. **Burroughs,** Gaylynn '06 %Bronx Defenders -860 Crtlandt Av -Bronx 10451 **Fx:**665-0100
(212) 532-0800 .. **Burrow,** Stephen '79 %AFTRA -260 Mad Av -NY 10016 **Fx:**545-1238
(212) 819-8200 .. **Burrowes,** Michelle A '07 %White & C LLP -1155 Av of Amer -NY 10036
(212) 880-1200 .. **Burrows,** Anthony D '05 Fidelity Natl Title Grp -711 3rd Av -NY 10017
(914) 683-3520 .. **Burrows,** Gordon A '86 -445 Hmltn Av -White Plns 10601 **Fx:**428-1660
(315) 786-0266 .. **Burrows,** James A '90 (Slye & B) -104 Wshngtn -Watertwn 13601
(212) 980-6922 .. **Burrows,** Kenneth D '71 -950 3rd Av -NY 10022 **Fx:**980-6161
(212) 801-6757 .. **Burrows,** Michl '74 (Greenberg T,LLP) -200 Park Av -NY 10166
(212) 318-6000 .. **Burrows,** Sarah N '10 %Paul HJ&W LLP -75 E 55th -NY 10022
(212) 854-0681 .. **Burrows,** Thos H Jr. '06 %Columbia Univ -535 W 116th 412 Low Mem'l Library -NY 10027
(718) 298-8900 .. **Burrows,** Thos J '88 Leg Aid -153-01 Jamaica Av -Jamaica 11432 **Fx:**657-0537
(631) 852-2500 .. **Burrows,** Tisha A '06 %DA -200 Center Dr -Rvrhead 11901 **Fx:**852-1769
(716) 883-0500 .. **Burruano,** Albert A '98 -420 Franklin -Buffalo 14202
(516) 719-9884 .. **Burruano,** Jos D '75 %LI Power Auth -333 Earle Ovngton Blvd -Uniondale 11553 **Fx:**222-9137
(212) 458-2783 .. **Burruano,** Jos J '02 AIG Domestic Claims -175 Water -NY 10038
(716) 566-1300 .. **Burruano,** Saml J Jr. '94 (Hiscock & B,LLP) -1100 M&T Ctr -Buffalo 14203
(212) 341-6522 .. **Burruss,** Melvin A '95 %Liquidation Bur -123 William -NY 10038 **Fx:**608-3398
(212) 310-8000 .. **Burshtine,** Ram '02 Cnsl Weil G&M LLP -767 5th Av -NY 10153
(212) 558-5500 .. **Burshtyn,** Patti L '00 %Weitz & L,PC -700 Bway -NY 10003
(212) 848-4000 .. **Burski,** Todd M '09 %Shearman & S LLP -599 Lex Av -NY 10022
(212) 859-8000 .. **Bursky,** Danl J '95 (Fried FHS&J LLP) -1 NY Plz -NY 10004
(516) 371-3077 .. **Bursky,** Herman A '63 -25 Muriel Av -Lawrence 11559 **Fx:**371-3079
(631) 300-2426 .. **Bursky,** Robt M '86 -775 Park Av -Huntngtn 11743
(212) 416-8000 .. **Burson,** Kate C '08 %Dept of Law -120 Bway -NY 10271
(212) 989-9113 .. **Bursor,** Scott A '97 -369 Lex Av -NY 10017 **Fx:**989-9163
(315) 471-8111 .. **Burstein,** Alan S '66 (Scolaro SCF&B,PC) -507 Plum -Syracuse 13204
(212) 728-8000 .. **Burstein,** Danl M '05 %Willkie F&G LLP -787 7th Av -NY 10019
(212) 350-2580 .. **Burstein,** David '72 %East NY Svngs Bk -350 Park Av -NY 10022 **Fx:**350-2594
(212) 761-4961 .. **Burstein,** Deborah S '96 Morgan Stanley -1585 Bway -NY 10036
(212) 661-6191 .. **Burstein,** Devin J '04 %Hon J Kaye US Ct of Appls -230 Park Av -NY 10169
(718) 286-6000 .. **Burstein,** Ernest '86 %DA -125-01 Qns Blvd -Kew Gdns 11415
(516) 829-1900 .. **Burstein,** Harry H '75 (Fischer & B,PC) -98 Cuttermill Rd -Gt Neck 11021
(212) 268-7900 .. **Burstein,** Harry H '75 (Fischer & B,PC) -888 7th Av -NY 10106
(212) 974-2400 .. **Burstein,** Judd '82 -1790 Bway -NY 10019 **Fx:**974-2944
(212) 696-4282 .. **Burstein,** Lawr S '68 -245 5th Av -NY 10016
(212) 984-7777 .. **Burstein,** Lucien '49 OfCnsl Warshaw BCS&K,LLP -555 5th Av -NY 10017
(718) 897-4433 .. **Burstein,** Matthew '98 (Burstein & R PC) -11325 Qns Blvd -Frst Hlls 11375
(914) 347-3440 .. **Burstein,** Matthew S '00 Calvary Invstmnts -7 Skyline Dr -Hawthorne 10532
(212) 545-9514 .. **Burstein,** Neil A '77 -370 Lex Av -NY 10017
(518) 449-3300 .. **Burstein,** Richd L '75 Nolan & H,LLP -39 N Pearl -Albany 12207
(212) 947-9416 .. **Burstein,** Robt A '77 (Burstein & B,LLP) -286 Mad Av -NY 10017 **Fx:**947-0907
(212) 922-2200 .. **Burstein,** Susanne M '06 %Watson F&W LLP -1133 Av of Amer -NY 10036
(518) 435-9000 .. **Burstein,** Wm M '72 Wade & B,PLLC -250 Osborne Rd -Albany 12205
(518) 453-9000 .. **Burstein,** Wm M '72 Gateway Title Agency,LLC -250 Osborne Rd -Albany 12205 **Fx:**438-8700
(212) 964-3030 .. **Burstin,** Brian J '82 -160 Bway -NY 10038 **Fx:**732-1425
(845) 634-3627 .. **Bursztein,** Alexander '79 %Leg Aid -2 Congers Rd -New Cty 10956 **Fx:**634-8505
(646) 386-5138 .. **Burt,** Jennifer S '94 %Family Ct -60 Lafayette -NY 10013
(585) 385-4252 .. **Burt,** Margaret A '80 -63 Callingham Rd -Pittsfrd 14534 **Fx:**385-7717

(212) 545-4669 .. **Burt,** Thos H '98 (Wolf HAF&H LLP) -270 Mad Av -NY 10016
(212) 573-2323 .. **Burt,** Wm P '99 Pfizer Inc -219 E 42nd -NY 10017
(607) 723-5341 .. **Burtis,** Wm C Jr. '62 SpclCnsl Hinman H&K,LLP -80 Exchange Bx5250 -Bnghmtn 13902
(212) 819-8200 .. **Burton,** Adam M '05 %White & C LLP -1155 Av of Amer -NY 10036
(212) 326-2000 .. **Burton,** Allen W '03 Cnsl O'Melveny & M LLP -7 Times Sq -NY 10036
(212) 715-9100 .. **Burton,** Angela M '10 %Kramer LN&F,LLP -1177 Av of Amer -NY 10036
(718) 340-4200 .. **Burton,** Angela O '92 %CUNY Law Schl -65-21 Main -Flushng 11367 **Fx:**340-4482
(516) 889-9841 .. **Burton,** Bernard L '56 -26 W Bway -Long Bch 11561
(212) 969-3000 .. **Burton,** Brian '07 %Proskauer R LLP -1585 Bway -NY 10036
(212) 318-6000 .. **Burton,** Chas '57 Paul HJ&W LLP -75 E 55th -NY 10022
(516) 536-2345 .. **Burton,** David J '90 (Burton & B,PC) -360 Merrick Rd -Lynbrk 11563 **Fx:**536-2342
(212) 649-2000 .. **Burton,** Eve B '90 Hearst Corp -300 W 57th -NY 10019 **Fx:**649-2035
(631) 580-5389 .. **Burton,** Jeanne R '88 -Bx697 -Central Islip 11722
(845) 486-2280 .. **Burton,** Jennifer '90 %Pub Def -22 Market -Poughkeepsie 12601 **Fx:**486-2266
(718) 579-3000 .. **Burton,** Katherine A '83 %Leg Aid -1020 Grnd Cncrs -Bronx 10451 **Fx:**588-2611
(516) 536-2345 .. **Burton,** Linda S '91 (Burton & B,PC) -360 Merrick Rd -Lynbrk 11563 **Fx:**536-2342
(212) 891-9100 .. **Burton,** Ronald E '92 (Goldfarb & F LLP) -345 Park Av -NY 10154
(631) 580-5389 .. **Burton,** Steven M '81 -Bx697 -Central Islip 11722
(716) 858-5043 .. **Burton,** Terry C '82 Delaware North Cos,Inc -40 Fountain Plz -Buffalo 14202
(716) 853-2888 .. **Burton,** Thos H '80 -716 Brisbane Bldg -Buffalo 14203 **Fx:**853-2892
(518) 449-3107 .. **Burton,** Wayne L '74 OfCnsl Buckley M&C,PC -29 Wards Ln -Albany 12204
(212) 672-1840 .. **Burton,** Wm C '75 (Sagat B LLP) -245 Park Av -NY 10167 **Fx:**672-1842
(718) 254-7000 .. **Burwell,** Carter H '05 %US Atty -271 Cadman Plz E -Brklyn 11201 **Fx:**254-6479
(212) 250-8991 .. **Burwell,** Steven R '99 %Deutsche Bank -60 Wall -NY 10005 **Fx:**797-4561
(212) 728-8000 .. **Burwick,** Jonathan C '09 %Willkie F&G LLP -787 7th Av -NY 10019
(716) 856-2239 .. **Burwick,** Michl C '72 -43 Court -Buffalo 14202 **Fx:**845-6475
(212) 385-1997 .. **Bury,** Stephen J '84 -120 Bway -NY 10271 **Fx:**227-6166
(631) 277-9175 .. **Bury,** Wayne R '95 (O'Connor & B) -34 Overlook Dr -E Islip 11730
(516) 570-4343 .. **Burzichelli,** Robt J '90 (Greenberg BG PC) -3000 Marcus Av -New Hyde Pk 11042 **Fx:**570-4348
(718) 366-3800 .. **Burzio,** Stephen S '04 Ridgewood Senior Citizens Cncl -217 Wyckoff Av -Brklyn 11237
(718) 254-7000 .. **Busa,** Amy L '00 US Atty -271 Cadman Plz E -Brklyn 11201 **Fx:**254-6479
(212) 450-4000 .. **Busath,** Lynn Earl '80 Cnsl Davis P&W LLP -450 Lex Av -NY 10017
(212) 577-3688 .. **Busby,** Helene J '09 %Leg Aid -199 Water -NY 10038 **Fx:**509-8431
(212) 418-6247 .. **Buscaglia,** Anne M '94 GM -767 5th Av -NY 10153 **Fx:**418-6123
(716) 856-4000 .. **Buscaglia,** Elizabeth K '06 %Hodgson R LLP -140 Pearl -Buffalo 14202
(716) 631-0004 .. **Buscaglia,** Kara A '03 OfCnsl Shelby B&W -5662 Main -Williamsvll 14221 **Fx:**631-7546
(716) 892-5294 .. **Buscaglia,** Wm K Jr. '74 DeSpirt Mosaic & Marble -1085 E Delavan Av -Buffalo 14215 **Fx:**892-5321
(212) 962-4688 .. **Buscemi,** Francis R '80 (Mehler & B) -305 Bway -NY 10007
(212) 399-3600 .. **Buscemi,** Gary '80 %Tishman Rlty & Constrctn -666 5th Av -NY 10103
(212) 715-9100 .. **Busch,** Adam M '07 %Kramer LN&F,LLP -1177 Av of Amer -NY 10036
(212) 661-3600 .. **Busch,** Glenn '86 -1775 Bway -NY 10019 **Fx:**661-5297
(914) 761-0082 .. **Busch,** John R '72 -989 N Bway -N White Plns 10603 **Fx:**948-3606
(212) 558-5500 .. **Busch,** Lisa Nathanson '94 %Weitz & L,PC -180 Maiden Ln -NY 10038 **Fx:**344-5461
(212) 735-3000 .. **Busch,** Michl F '05 %Skadden ASM&F LLP -4 Times Sq -NY 10036
(718) 875-0070 .. **Busch,** Richd L '72 -26 Court -Brklyn 11242
(212) 450-4000 .. **Busch,** Tamara L '08 %Davis P&W LLP -450 Lex Av -NY 10017
(212) 341-0900 .. **Busching,** Laurence E '91 Admin for Childrens Srvcs -150 William -NY 10038
(212) 471-8500 .. **Buschkin,** Samuil '06 %Herzfeld & R,PC -125 Broad -NY 10004
(315) 253-4050 .. **Buschman,** Steven H '98 (Williams HM&B) -11 Court -Auburn 13021 **Fx:**253-4223
(718) 390-5383 .. **Buschmann,** Odette N '89 %Supreme Ct Law Dept -18 Richmond Ter -Staten Isl 10301
(516) 829-9595 .. **Busell,** Sandra N '77 (Busell & S PLLC) -98 Cuttermill Rd -Gt Neck 11021
(914) 220-0110 .. **Busell,** Sheryl P '09 %Weissmann A LLP -445 Hmltn Av -White Plns 10601 **Fx:**(917) 368-6920
(516) 829-9595 .. **Busell & Stier PLLC** -98 Cuttermill Rd -Gt Neck 11021 **Fx:**829-9617 ***[Estate Planning & Administration]***
(212) 661-5306 .. **Bush,** Anne Donnelly '05 OfCnsl I Wallace,PLLC -501 5th Av -NY 10017
(518) 452-8787 .. **Bush,** Brett Avery '09 %Drinker B&R LLP -321 Great Oaks Blvd -Albany 12203
(212) 689-8808 .. **Bush,** Caitlin N '09 %Hoguet NR&K,LLP -10 E 40th -NY 10016
(212) 906-1200 .. **Bush,** Christopher F '09 %Latham & W -885 3rd Av -NY 10022
(212) 482-0001 .. **Bush,** Denise M '03 %Russo K&T LLP -33 Whitehall -NY 10004
(914) 376-3757 .. **Bush,** Ellen Parker '90 %Leg Srvcs -30 S Bway -Ynkrs 10701 **Fx:**376-8739
(315) 689-9486 .. **Bush,** Fredk A '73 -34 N Main Bx583 -Jordan 13080 **Fx:**689-6650
(212) 642-1712 .. **Bush,** James F II '02 Intl Trademark Assn -655 3rd Av -NY 10017
(212) 848-4000 .. **Bush,** Jocelyn Hill '10 Shearman & S LLP -599 Lex Av -NY 10022
(518) 473-7051 .. **Bush,** John D '83 %OTDA-Fair Hearings -40 N Pearl -Albany 12243 **Fx:**473-6735
(212) 268-8200 .. **Bush,** Lauren R '06 %B Raphan,PC -7 Penn Plz -NY 10001 **Fx:**244-3075
(212) 277-6500 .. **Bush,** Lindsay A '03 %Dickstein S LLP -1633 Bway -NY 10019
(631) 393-9439 .. **Bush,** Martin J '51 (Hayt H&L LLP) -500 Bi-Cnty Blvd -Farmngdl 11735
(718) 987-8444 .. **Bush,** Michl H '95 %Chelli & B -149 New Dorp Ln -Staten Isl 10306
(212) 983-8866 .. **Bush,** Michl R '84 (Einig & B) -420 Lex Av -NY 10170
(914) 779-3165 .. **Bush,** Myron '57 -3 Hayes Dr -Eastchstr 10709
(585) 442-8385 .. **Bush,** Peter J '72 -55 Dunbarton Dr -Rchstr 14618
(718) 987-8444 .. **Bush,** Robt D '66 (Chelli & B) -149 New Dorp Ln -Staten Isl 10306
(518) 477-4575 .. **Bush,** Scott W '83 (Corrigan M&B) -220 Columbia Tpk -Rensselaer 12144
(212) 972-3000 .. **Bush,** Stacy E '97 %Klestadt & W,LLP -292 Mad Av -NY 10017
(212) 289-3896 .. **Bush,** Wm C '65 -64 E 94th -NY 10128
(718) 549-9000 .. **Bushell,** Kenneth M '69 -6132 Riverdale Av -Bronx 10471 **Fx:**601-8225
(631) 261-7777 .. **Bushell Kleczka & Minasi** -7 Bayview Av -Northprt 11768 **Fx:**261-7757
(631) 261-7777 .. **Bushell,** Theo G '51 (Bushell K&M) -7 Bayview Av -Northprt 11768
(212) 949-4700 .. **Bushell,** Victor C '90 (Bushell SO&G LLP) -60 E 42nd -NY 10165 **Fx:**286-0513
(212) 749-5900 .. **Bushin,** Howard I '62 -251 W 93rd -NY 10025 **Fx:**749-0237
(212) 471-8500 .. **Bushkanets,** Regina '02 %Herzfeld & R,PC -125 Broad -NY 10004
(718) 366-7171 .. **Bushlow,** Alan L '92 (Abbott B&S,LLP) -70-11 Fresh Pond Rd -Rdgwd 11385 **Fx:**366-7676
(718) 366-0464 .. **Bushlow,** Bruce E '66 (Abbott B&S,LLP) -70-11 Fresh Pond Rd -Rdgwd 11385
(845) 627-1627 .. **Bushman,** David M '87 -101 N Mddltwn Rd -Nanuet 10954 **Fx:**(201) 731-5350
(212) 572-7855 .. **Bushnell,** George E III '86 %Vivendi,SA -800 3rd Av -NY 10022 **Fx:**572-7496
(212) 964-7400 .. **Bushneva,** O Alina '05 Smith MDWY&Y,PC -111 John -NY 10038
(212) 556-6754 .. **Bushong,** Heather Hansen '00 %ICM -825 8th Av -NY 10019 **Fx:**556-5665
(516) 357-3000 .. **Bushwack,** Jacqueline D '08 %Rivkin R LLP -926 RXR Plz -Uniondale 11556
(516) 572-2000 .. **Bushwack,** Michl J '08 %DA -99 Main -Hempstd 11550 **Fx:**572-2606
(716) 853-4080 .. **Bushway,** Todd C '93 %Colucci & G,PC -424 Main -Buffalo 14202
(212) 715-1000 .. **Busillo,** John J '85 (Arnold & P LLP) -399 Park Av -NY 10022
(315) 435-2470 .. **Buske,** Kerry L '05 %DA -505 S State -Syracuse 13202 **Fx:**435-3969
(212) 238-4800 .. **Buskin,** Jason A '05 %Landman CB&F,PC -120 Bway -NY 10271
(518) 474-6697 .. **Buskus,** Michl S '80 %Dept of Law -The Cptl -Albany 12224
(212) 571-0550 .. **Busloff,** Ronald I '00 %Allegaert B&V LLP -111 Bway -NY 10006
(914) 946-6555 .. **Busman,** Kenneth '79 -175 Main -White Plns 10601 **Fx:**946-6556
(212) 335-4500 .. **Buss,** David B '87 (DLA Piper LLP) -1251 Av of Amer -NY 10020
(914) 476-0600 .. **Buss,** Jeffrey D '80 (Smith B&J,LLP) -733 Ynkrs Av -Ynkrs 10704
(518) 474-8012 .. **Buss,** Wm E '74 %Dept of Law -The Cptl -Albany 12224
(631) 582-1200 .. **Busse,** Patrick Henry '97 (DeHaan B LLP) -300 Rabro Dr -Hauppauge 11788
(212) 839-5300 .. **Busse,** Stephanie L '06 %Sidley A LLP -787 7th Av -NY 10019
(212) 775-8700 .. **Bussey,** Megan E '09 %Kilpatrick S,LLP -31 W 52nd -NY 10019
(716) 856-1700 .. **Bussiere,** Evan Y '10 %Cannon H&W,LLP -726 Exchange -Buffalo 14210
(212) 225-2000 .. **Bussigel,** Emily A '10 %Cleary GS&H -1 Lbrty Plz -NY 10006
(212) 261-7000 .. **Busson,** Ingrid '00 Calyon -1301 Av of Amer -NY 10019
(212) 326-2000 .. **Bustany,** Christine B '08 %O'Melveny & M LLP -7 Times Sq -NY 10036
(212) 225-2000 .. **Bustin,** George L '74 SrCnsl Cleary GS&H -1 Lbrty Plz -NY 10006
(516) 747-6700 .. **Bustos,** Pablo E '03 %Kirschenbaum & K -200 Grdn City Plz -Gdn Cty 11530 **Fx:**747-6781
(212) 578-2590 .. **Buszko,** Scott E '06 Metropolitan Life Ins Co -1095 Av of Amer -NY 10036
(212) 642-8716 .. **Butala,** Smita G '96 Polo Ralph Lauren -625 Mad Av -NY 10022 **Fx:**705-8386
(718) 260-4750 .. **Butani,** Susan D '89 %Leg Aid -111 Lvngstn -Brklyn 11201 **Fx:**260-4744
(212) 335-4500 .. **Butch,** Mary Susan '83 DLA Piper LLP -1251 Av of Amer -NY 10020
(716) 566-1300 .. **Butchello,** Marie A '07 %Hiscock & B,LLP -1100 M&T Ctr -Buffalo 14203
(212) 803-5100 .. **Butchen,** Michl R '78 %NY Cnty Defender Srvcs -225 Bway -NY 10007 **Fx:**571-6035
(845) 634-7010 .. **Butcher,** Martin S '06 %Montalbano C&F,PC -67 N Main Bx1070 -New Cty 10956
(212) 728-8000 .. **Butcher,** Melanie L '06 %Willkie F&G LLP -787 7th Av -NY 10019
(585) 263-2444 .. **Butcher,** Steve Sr. '81 (S Butcher Sr) -36 W Main -Rchstr 14614 **Fx:**263-2428
(718) 264-3340 .. **Butchin,** Jamie M '99 %MHLS -80-45 Wnchstr Blvd -Qns Vllg 11427 **Fx:**264-3559
(516) 357-3000 .. **Butera,** Celeste M '90 (Rivkin R LLP) -926 RXR Plz -Uniondale 11556
(716) 691-6212 .. **Butera,** Leo C '88 Charlestowne Floors -2965 Niagara Flls Blvd -Amherst 14228
(212) 436-3231 .. **Butera,** Thos A '92 Deloitte & Touche LLP -2 World Fncl Ct -NY 10281
(212) 642-1710 .. **Butkiewicz,** Lisa A '99 Intl Trademark Assn -655 3rd Av -NY 10017 **Fx:**768-7796
(212) 770-6626 .. **Butkovic,** Denis M '99 AIG -70 Pine -NY 10270
(212) 701-3000 .. **Butler,** Andrea Rose '99 %Cahill G&R LLP -80 Pine -NY 10005 **Fx:**269-5420
(212) 318-6000 .. **Butler,** Aoife E '07 %Paul HJ&W LLP -75 E 55th -NY 10022
(212) 788-6898 .. **Butler,** Barbara B '70 City Cncl Gen Cnsl -250 Bway -NY 10007
(716) 847-0650 .. **Butler,** Bernardine M '95 %Leg Srvcs -237 Main -Buffalo 14203 **Fx:**847-0227
(315) 218-8000 .. **Butler,** Brian J '97 (Bond S&K,PLLC) -1 Lincoln Ctr -Syracuse 13202
(631) 921-0330 .. **Butler,** Brian P '02 BP Butler,PC -80 Orvll Rd -Bohemia 11716 **Fx:**207-8310
(718) 403-4305 .. **Butler,** Carlton T '80 NYC Dept Educ-OLS -345 Adams -Brklyn 11201
(518) 447-7150 .. **Butler,** Christina M '00 %Pub Def -60 S Pearl -Albany 12207 **Fx:**447-5533
(607) 748-9907 .. **Butler,** David E '96 (Butler & B,LLP) -231 Main -Vestal 13850 **Fx:**754-0780

(212) 425-9300 .. **Butler**, David J '01 %Bressler A&R,PC -17 State -NY 10004
(607) 748-9907 .. **Butler**, Earl D '64 (E Butler,PC) -231 Main -Vestal 13850 **Fx**:754-0780
(212) 969-3000 .. **Butler**, Elana '81 (Proskauer R LLP) -1585 Bway -NY 10036
(212) 504-6000 .. **Butler**, Elizabeth Ann '98 SpclCnsl Cadwalader W&T LLP -1 World Fncl Ctr -NY 10281
(212) 615-2200 .. **Butler Fitzgerald Fiveson & McCarthy, PC** -36 W 44th -NY 10036 **Fx**:615-2215
(212) 259-8000 .. **Butler**, Geoffrey L '08 %Dewey & L LLP -1301 Av of Amer -NY 10019
(212) 644-1010 .. **Butler**, J Patrick '04 %Kauff M&M LLP -950 3rd Av -NY 10022
(516) 229-6000 .. **Butler**, James F '90 %R Lau & Assoc -300 Jericho Quad Bx9040 -Jericho 11753 **Fx**:229-6167
(718) 739-6400 .. **Butler**, Janet E '83 %DHCR -92-31 Union Hall -Jamaica 11433 **Fx**:262-7938
(631) 754-2477 .. **Butler**, Janine M '97 -23 Suffolk Pl -E Northprt 11731
(212) 878-8000 .. **Butler**, Jeff E '97 (Clifford C LLP) -31 W 52nd -NY 10019
(212) 326-3939 .. **Butler**, Jeffrey M '90 (Jones D) -222 E 41st -NY 10017
(212) 858-1000 .. **Butler**, Joanne '99 %Pillsbury WSP LLP -1540 Bway -NY 10036
(315) 452-2468 .. **Butler**, Jodi Lynn '00 AJM Mgmt Srvcs,Inc -5112 W Taft Rd -Liverpool 13088 **Fx**:452-2030
(315) 472-4489 .. **Butler**, John E Jr. '75 -825 Univ Bldg -Syracuse 13210 **Fx**:472-1456
(607) 273-3210 .. **Butler**, John E '88 %Tompkins Cnty Trst -Bx460 -Ithaca 14851
(212) 450-4000 .. **Butler**, John H '95 (Davis P&W LLP) -450 Lex Av -NY 10017
(718) 453-9194 .. **Butler**, John L '65 -713 MacDonough Bx330702 -Brklyn 11233 **Fx**:453-9195
(585) 258-2800 .. **Butler**, José A '03 %Underberg & K LLP -300 Bausch & Lomb Pl -Rchstr 14604
(518) 455-9952 .. **Butler**, Karen A '96 (Thuillez FGB&Y,LLP) -20 Corp Wds Blvd -Albany 12211
(631) 969-3100 .. **Butler**, Kevin M '04 %Frenkel LWW&G,LLP -20 W Main -Bay Shr 11706
(212) 484-8000 .. **Butler**, Kwanza R '99 %Time Warner -1 Time Warner Ctr -NY 10019
(212) 218-2100 .. **Butler**, Lisa '07 %Fitzpatrick CH&S -1290 Av of Amer -NY 10104
(212) 761-4000 .. **Butler**, Lisa Anne '99 Morgan Stanley -1585 Bway -NY 10036
(212) 756-2000 .. **Butler**, Margaret Isa '04 %Schulte R&Z LLP -919 3rd Av -NY 10022
(716) 839-5411 .. **Butler**, Mark C '85 -5166 Main -Williamsvll 14221 **Fx**:839-5422
(518) 463-3148 .. **Butler**, Mary E '91 AT&T -111 Wshngtn Av -Albany 12210 **Fx**:463-5943
(607) 748-9907 .. **Butler**, Matthew C '99 (Butler & B,LLP) -231 Main -Vestal 13850 **Fx**:754-0780
(347) 627-9006 .. **Butler**, Mauverine D '95 M Butler,PLLC -4811 Murdock Av -Bronx 10470 **Fx**:627-9007
(212) 479-2078 .. **Butler**, Michl L '04 TPG Axon Capital Mgt Lp -888 7th Av -NY 10106
(516) 408-6314 .. **Butler**, Michl W '87 (Butler & B) -377 Oak -Gdn Cty 11530 **Fx**:222-2508
(646) 964-5749 .. **Butler**, Niisha Karima '02 (Walker GW&B,LLC) -1825 Park Av -NY 10035 **Fx**:(866) 422-4858
(212) 883-8833 .. **Butler**, Paige R '09 %Tacopina & A -275 Mad Av -NY 10016
(718) 590-2000 .. **Butler**, Patrick G '08 %DA -198 E 161st -Bronx 10451 **Fx**:590-6477
(845) 359-2500 .. **Butler**, Paula S '04 Subaru Distributors Corp -6 Ramland Rd -Orangebrg 10962
(212) 474-1000 .. **Butler**, Saml C '57 SpclCnsl Cravath S&M LLP -825 8th Av -NY 10019
(845) 291-3150 .. **Butler**, Stacy Ann '07 %Cnty Atty -255 Main -Goshen 10924 **Fx**:291-3167
(347) 401-9580 .. **Butler**, Steven S '73 %Appllt Term -141 Lvngstn -Brklyn 11201 **Fx**:(718) 643-7889
(716) 773-9400 .. **Butler**, Thos E '69 -592 E River Rd -Grand Isl 14072 **Fx**:773-2455
(212) 408-5100 .. **Butler**, Thos E '92 (Chadbourne & P LLP) -30 Rckfllr Plz -NY 10112
(631) 577-1870 .. **Butler**, Thos G '80 Grant Thornton LLP -445 Broadhllw Rd -Melvll 11747 **Fx**:249-6144
(212) 559-8741 .. **Butler**, Thos J '83 Citigroup -787 7th Av -NY 10019
(212) 326-3939 .. **Butler**, Wendy C '03 (Jones D) -222 E 41st -NY 10017
(212) 725-5505 .. **Butler**, Wm J '50 -280 Mad Av -NY 10016 **Fx**:685-3615
(212) 688-1904 .. **Butner**, Lawr '60 -16 Sutton Pl -NY 10022 **Fx**:688-1904
(212) 734-6750 .. **Butner**, Robin L '84 -505 E 79th -NY 10075
(212) 506-2500 .. **Butowsky**, Michl R '87 (Mayer B LLP) -1675 Bway -NY 10019
(516) 746-8100 .. **Buttafuoco**, Danl P '81 (D Buttafuoco & Assoc) -144 Woodbury Rd -Woodbury 11797 **Fx**:746-6473
(516) 746-8100 .. **Buttafuoco**, Kristen N '08 %D Buttafuoco & Assoc -144 Woodbury Rd -Woodbury 11797 **Fx**:746-6473
(212) 940-8560 .. **Buttenwieser**, Lawr B '56 Cnsl Katten MR LLP -575 Mad Av -NY 10022
(212) 408-2500 .. **Butter**, Gary M '91 (Baker B,LLP) -30 Rckfllr Plz -NY 10112
(845) 896-4520 .. **Butterfass**, Stephen E '77 -1065 Main -Fishkill 12524 **Fx**:896-0286
(631) 351-3042 .. **Butterfield**, Deirdre M '75 Town Atty -100 Main -Huntngtn 11743 **Fx**:351-3032
(631) 668-0006 .. **Butterfield**, Edwin L '81 -576 Montauk Hwy Bx17 -Montauk 11954 **Fx**:668-1660
(212) 573-1229 .. **Butterfield**, Garth C '99 %Pfizer Inc -235 E 42nd -NY 10017
(631) 261-9463 .. **Butterfield**, Kenneth C '62 -168 Laurel Av -Northprt 11768 **Fx**:757-2664
(212) 974-7474 .. **Butterfield**, Toby M J '92 (Cowan DA&S LLP) -41 Mad Av -NY 10010
(716) 877-4490 .. **Butterini**, David F '84 -919 Kenmore Av -Buffalo 14223 **Fx**:875-8359
(212) 460-1089 .. **Butterklee**, Neil H '93 Con Ed -4 Irving Pl -NY 10003
(718) 997-1000 .. **Butterly**, Casey J '09 %Mitchell & I -98-20 Metro Av -Frst Hlls 11375
(212) 308-7697 .. **Butterman**, Jay R '89 (Butterman & K,LLP) -425 Park Av -NY 10022
(212) 308-7697 .. **Butterman & Kahn,LLP** -425 Park Av -NY 10022 **Fx**:223-4209
(212) 692-1000 .. **Butterman**, Michl D '61 OfCnsl Duane M LLP -1540 Bway -NY 10036
(212) 229-1516 .. **Buttermore Newman Delanney & Foltz, LLP** -111 Bway -NY 10006 **Fx**:676-7497
(646) 624-5916 .. **Butterworth**, Gabriella A '04 Genpact -105 Mad Av -NY 10016
(631) 281-6320 .. **Buttitta**, Claudio '99 Leviton Manfctrng Co -201 N Srvc Rd -Melvll 11747
(212) 318-6000 .. **Button**, Christine A '97 %Paul HJ&W LLP -75 E 55th -NY 10022
(518) 447-9698 .. **Buttridge**, Jos W '94 -20 Corp Wds Blvd Bx1690 -Albany 12201 **Fx**:426-7209
(845) 471-1600 .. **Butts**, Robt R '72 -75 Wshngtn BxG -Poughkeepsie 12601 **Fx**:452-0150
(845) 471-4221 .. **Butts**, Roland E '74 -224 Church -Poughkeepsie 12601 **Fx**:471-4239
(212) 554-7800 .. **Butvick**, Declan M '01 %Moses & S LLP -405 Lex Av -NY 10174
(212) 326-2000 .. **Butwin**, Bradley J '86 (O'Melveny & M LLP) -7 Times Sq -NY 10036
(212) 336-2000 .. **Butzel**, Laura E '92 (Patterson BW&T LLP) -1133 Av of Amer -NY 10036
(212) 818-1110 .. **Butzel Long, PC** -380 Mad Av -NY 10017 **Fx**:818-0494
(212) 480-6254 .. **Buxbaum**, Ellen R '83 %Insurance Dept -25 Beaver -NY 10004 **Fx**:480-5272
(646) 414-6820 .. **Buxbaum**, Michl A '86 (Lowenstein S PC) -1251 Av of Amer -NY 10020 **Fx**:(973) 422-6847
(914) 785-5300 .. **Buxbaum**, Scott A '89 %A Lamer -555 Taxter Rd -Elmsfrd 10523 **Fx**:347-4269
(212) 808-7800 .. **Buxton**, James J '05 %Kelley D&W LLP -101 Park Av -NY 10178
(212) 210-9448 .. **Buxton**, Tiffany A '04 (Alston & B LLP) -90 Park Av -NY 10016
(212) 513-6720 .. **Buyer**, Deborah A '95 Dept Business Srvcs -110 William -NY 10038 **Fx**:618-8989
(716) 652-4413 .. **Buyer**, Martha R '96 -Bx305 -E Aurora 14052 **Fx**:655-9176
(212) 355-9946 .. **Buza**, John P '09 %DA -1 Hogan Pl -NY 10013
(585) 419-8800 .. **Buzard**, A Vincent '68 (Harris B PLLC) -99 Garnsey Rd -Pittsfrd 14534 **Fx**:419-8812
(212) 318-6000 .. **Buzard**, Robt R '99 OfCnsl Paul HJ&W LLP -75 E 55th -NY 10022
(212) 530-5000 .. **Buzdugan**, Maria '01 %Milbank TH&M LLP -1 Chase Manh Plz -NY 10005
(212) 869-3500 .. **Buzin**, Andrew S '07 %J Fuchsberg Law Firm,LLP -500 5th Av -NY 10110 **Fx**:398-1532
(212) 580-6500 .. **Buzin**, Heath T '97 %Phillips K & Assoc,LLP -204 W 84th -NY 10024
(518) 891-1000 .. **Buzzell**, Stephen L '76 -648 Lk Flower Av -Saranac Lk 12983 **Fx**:891-1000
(212) 801-9217 .. **Buzzetta**, Danl J '95 (Greenberg T,LLP) -200 Park Av -NY 10166
(212) 225-2000 .. **Buzzetta**, Jerilin '10 %Cleary GS&H -1 Lbrty Plz -NY 10006
(212) 564-9009 .. **Buzzetti**, Albert L '95 (A Buzzetti & Assoc,LLC) -2 Penn Plz -NY 10121
(212) 474-1000 .. **Byars**, Michl Brent '10 %Cravath S&M LLP -825 8th Av -NY 10019
(212) 637-2793 .. **Byars**, Michl J '01 %US Atty -86 Chmbrs -NY 10007
(716) 823-2558 .. **Bybel**, Frank L '89 -674 Ridge Rd -Lackawanna 14218 **Fx**:822-0009
(212) 752-9700 .. **Bycer**, Jaclyn '05 %Gersten S LLP -600 Lex Av -NY 10022
(718) 303-8999 .. **Bychok**, Olga '98 -2610 E 18th -Brklyn 11235
(516) 358-1700 .. **Byczek**, Christopher S '74 %Cronin & B,LLP -1983 Marcus Av -Lk Success 11042
(212) 310-8000 .. **Byeff**, David P '09 %Weil G&M LLP -767 5th Av -NY 10153
(718) 286-6000 .. **Byer**, Pamela J '92 %DA -125-01 Qns Blvd -Kew Gdns 11415
(212) 668-8000 .. **Byer**, Peter '81 Oppenheimer & Co -125 Broad -NY 10004
(212) 695-4435 .. **Byers**, Eugene S '91 (Byers & B) -48 Wall -NY 10005
(212) 867-6000 .. **Byers**, Wm R '01 (Rosenberg & E,PC) -733 3rd Av -NY 10017
(212) 858-1000 .. **Byington**, John H Jr. '62 SrCnsl Pillsbury WSP LLP -1540 Bway -NY 10036
(631) 249-6565 .. **Byington**, John H III '89 (Archer BG&L,LLP) -425 Broadhllw Rd -Melvll 11747
(718) 615-0044 .. **Byk**, Michl '10 %Lozner & M -1901 Emmons Av -Brklyn 11235
(914) 272-3323 .. **Bykov**, Kim F '03 %Energy Nuclear Operatns Inc -440 Hmltn Av -White Plns 10601
(212) 736-4500 .. **Byler**, Philip A '79 OfCnsl Nesenoff & M,LLP -363 7th Av -NY 10001
(716) 688-3800 .. **Bylewski**, Scott A '99 %Nesper F&D,LLP -501 JJ Audobon Pkwy -Amherst 14228
(718) 923-4206 .. **Byne**, Eric '74 %OTDA Fair Hearings -14 Boerum Pl -Brklyn 11201
(718) 923-7143 .. **Bynoe-Kasden**, Valerie A '01 Visting Nurse -111 Lvngstn -Brklyn 11201
(212) 373-3000 .. **Byon**, Youjung '09 Paul WRW&G LLP -1285 Av of Amer -NY 10019
(212) 480-3030 .. **Byoun**, Steven D '00 %M Pressman -125 Maiden Ln -NY 10038 **Fx**:480-2590
(212) 403-1000 .. **Byowitz**, Michl H '83 (Wachtell LR&K) -51 W 52nd -NY 10019
(212) 922-9550 .. **Byram**, Ellen J '09 Clutch Grp -370 Lex Av -NY 10017
(212) 846-6463 .. **Byrd**, Aja C '07 MTV Networks -1515 Bway -NY 10036
(212) 541-2000 .. **Byrd**, Leslie R '84 %Bryan C LLP -1290 Av of Amer -NY 10104
(585) 263-1000 .. **Byrd**, Roger W '91 (Nixon P LLP) -1100 Clinton Sq -Rchstr 14604
(607) 274-3909 .. **Byrd**, Traevena L '06 Ithaca College -953 Danby Rd -Ithaca 14850
(212) 709-8261 .. **Byrialsen**, Jane H '06 (Fisher & B,PLLC) -110 Wall -NY 10005 **Fx**:943-2300
(516) 868-6984 .. **Byrn**, Francis X '51 -709 W Carl Av -Baldwin 11510
(718) 286-2000 .. **Byrne**, Barbara '90 %Leg Aid -120-46 Qns Blvd -Kew Gdns 11415 **Fx**:286-2286
(212) 247-2500 .. **Byrne**, Carolyn Ann '00 OfCnsl A Daniele -75 Rckfllr Plz -NY 10019 **Fx**:202-7930
(718) 999-2039 .. **Byrne**, Catherine B '88 %Fire Dept Bureau Leg Afrs -9 Metrotech Ctr -Brklyn 11201
(315) 474-6448 .. **Byrne Costello & Pickard PC** -100 Madison -Syracuse 13202 **Fx**:424-8556
(212) 615-0495 .. **Byrne**, Danl E '99 Cnsl Group Health Inc -441 9th Av -NY 10001 **Fx**:563-8577
(845) 291-2050 .. **Byrne**, David J '97 %DA -255-275 Main -Goshen 10924 **Fx**:291-2085
(631) 589-7242 .. **Byrne**, Douglas P '03 %Zabell & Assoc,LLP -4875 Sunrise Hwy -Bohemia 11716
(516) 766-3200 .. **Byrne**, Edw T '76 (Murtagh C&B) -100 N Park Av -Rockvll Ctr 11570
(631) 439-4200 .. **Byrne**, Eileen E '86 %R Tusa -898 Vets Mem'l Hwy -Hauppauge 11788 **Fx**:439-4292
(646) 471-4000 .. **Byrne**, Gregory D '06 %PricewaterhouseCoopers LLP -300 Mad Av -NY 10017
(212) 259-8000 .. **Byrne**, H Michl '05 (Dewey & L LLP) -1301 Av of Amer -NY 10019

(212) 344-1231 .. **Byrne,** J Bruce '63 -31 S Bayles Av -Pt Wash 11050 **Fx:**363-8762
(914) 995-3419 .. **Byrne,** James P '93 %DA -111 Martin Luther King Blvd -White Plns 10601 **Fx:**995-3363
(212) 250-1869 .. **Byrne,** James T Jr. '65 %Deutsche Bk -60 Wall -NY 10005
(212) 849-7000 .. **Byrne,** Jane M '89 (Quinn EU&S,LLP) -51 Mad Av -NY 10010
(315) 425-2700 .. **Byrne,** Jennifer M S '84 Cnsl Hiscock & B,LLP -One Park Pl -Syracuse 13202
(718) 482-6471 .. **Byrne,** John F III '85 %DEC -1 Hunters Pnt Plz -LIC 11101 **Fx:**482-4962
(516) 766-2775 .. **Byrne,** John J '67 -3 Pembroke Ct -Rockvll Ctr 11570
(212) 336-0041 .. **Byrne,** Kenneth V '98 %SEC -3 World Fncl Ctr -NY 10281 **Fx:**336-1323
(718) 935-9339 .. **Byrne,** Kevin J '01 -327 Clinton -Brklyn 11231
(914) 366-3155 .. **Byrne,** Kevin T '80 %Phelps Mem Hsptl -701 N Bway -N Tarrytwn 10591
(212) 328-8732 .. **Byrne,** Lauren Taylor '00 %Alvarez & Marsal -125 Park Av -NY 10017
(212) 903-9000 .. **Byrne,** Lawr '85 (Linklaters) -1345 Av of Amer -NY 10105
(212) 340-0400 .. **Byrne,** Linda M '94 %Appllt Div 1st Dept -27 Mad Av -NY 10010 **Fx:**889-4412
(212) 916-4657 .. **Byrne,** Margaret Mary '81 %TIAA-CREF -730 3rd Av -NY 10017
(585) 325-4064 .. **Byrne,** Marie C '95 (LaFay B&L,PC) -36 W Main -Rchstr 14614 **Fx:**325-4064
(845) 357-2744 .. **Byrne,** Matthew J '93 (Balsamo BC&E) -16 Chestnut Bx209 -Suffern 10901
(516) 795-1621 .. **Byrne,** Matthew L '69 -977 N Bway -Massapequa 11758 **Fx:**541-7760
(212) 931-8569 .. **Byrne,** Matthew T '99 (Byrne P LLP) -11 Bway -NY 10004 **Fx:**931-8521
(315) 474-6448 .. **Byrne,** Matthew V III '84 (Byrne C&P PC) -100 Madison -Syracuse 13202
(607) 334-8150 .. **Byrne,** Maureen A '84 -Bx427 -Norwich 13815 **Fx:**334-2610
(518) 456-6705 .. **Byrne,** Melissa L '06 %Shevy Law Firm,LLC -7 Exec Centre Dr -Albany 12203 **Fx:**456-6709
(212) 848-4000 .. **Byrne,** Michl A '09 %Shearman & S LLP -599 Lex Av -NY 10022
(212) 779-8600 .. **Byrne,** Michl C '95 (Silverman SS&B PLLC) -381 Park Av S -NY 10016
(315) 474-6448 .. **Byrne,** Michl J '75 (Byrne C&P PC) -100 Madison -Syracuse 13202
(212) 422-9424 .. **Byrne,** Michl J '83 (Gogick B&O,LLP) -11 Bway -NY 10004
(212) 465-5000 .. **Byrne,** Michl R '03 Cnsl Parsons Brinckerhoff -1 Penn Plz -NY 10119
(212) 674-9120 .. **Byrne,** Olga K '05 %University Settlement -184 Eldrdg -NY 10002
(516) 877-0800 .. **Byrne,** Richd C '65 -100 E Old Cntry Rd -Mineola 11501 **Fx:**873-0513
(516) 294-8844 .. **Byrne,** Richd P '83 (L'Abbate BC&C,LLP) -1001 Franklin Av -Gdn Cty 11530
(914) 921-0026 .. **Byrne,** Robt L '88 -350 Theo Fremd Av -Rye 10580 **Fx:**921-0028
(518) 457-1260 .. **Byrne,** Sean M '83 %DCJS -4 Twr Pl -Albany 12203 **Fx:**457-3089
(516) 656-5300 .. **Byrne,** Steven '00 Mullooly JR&F LLP -6851 Jericho Tpk Bx9036 -Syosset 11791
(212) 218-2100 .. **Byrne,** Tara Ann '95 (Fitzpatrick CH&S) -1290 Av of Amer -NY 10104
(914) 376-0289 .. **Byrne,** Thos J '83 -197 St Johns Av -Ynkrs 10704 **Fx:**376-7921
(212) 225-2000 .. **Byrne,** Timothy J '91 Cleary GS&H -1 Lbrty Plz -NY 10006
(212) 438-1916 .. **Byrnes,** Bernard C '87 Standard & Poor's -55 Water -NY 10041
(631) 462-4911 .. **Byrnes,** Beth Ann '06 (Bianco B&F,LLP) -5036 Jericho Tpk Bx49 -Commack 11725
(212) 809-5663 .. **Byrnes,** Christine A '02 HDG Mansur Cptl Grp,LLC -780 3rd Av -NY 10017
(718) 816-4980 .. **Byrnes,** Danl J '03 -4459 Amboy Rd -Staten Isl 10312 **Fx:**816-4981
(631) 585-1942 .. **Byrnes,** Debra A '83 D Byrnes,PC -Bx458 -Holbrook 11741 **Fx:**981-2356
(718) 579-3000 .. **Byrnes,** Edmund J '73 %Leg Aid -1020 Grnd Cncrs -Bronx 10451 **Fx:**588-2611
(212) 669-0600 .. **Byrnes,** George D '61 OfCnsl Hill R LLP -45 Bway -NY 10006
(585) 292-1040 .. **Byrnes,** James M '75 -45 Exchange -Rchstr 14614 **Fx:**292-1075
(212) 417-8700 .. **Byrnes,** John J '72 %Fed Def of NY Inc -52 Duane -NY 10007 **Fx:**571-0392
(631) 589-3754 .. **Byrnes,** John R '81 (Byrnes & D) -284 W Main -Sayvll 11782 **Fx:**589-3907
(212) 233-8070 .. **Byrnes,** John W '89 (Callan & B) -225 Bway -NY 10007
(718) 727-2444 .. **Byrnes,** Paul F '84 -333 Lathrop Av -Staten Isl 10302
(212) 972-7040 .. **Byrnes,** Richd Henry '84 %R Ferrari -630 3rd Av -NY 10017 **Fx:**922-1939
(631) 462-4911 .. **Byrnes,** Timothy J '07 %Bianco B&F,LLP -5036 Jericho Tpk Bx49 -Commack 11725
(212) 808-7800 .. **Byroade,** Melissa E '07 %Kelley D&W LLP -101 Park Av -NY 10178
(845) 486-2110 .. **Byron,** Keith P '85 %Cnty Atty -22 Market -Poughkeepsie 12601 **Fx:**486-2002
(914) 528-1726 .. **Byron,** Patricia J '78 -Bx739 -Baldwin Place 10505
(212) 542-2105 .. **Byron,** Stuart D '59 -200 Mad Av -NY 10016 **Fx:**542-2185
(718) 923-0690 .. **Byron,** Tanisha J '05 %R Santoriella PC -335 Adams -Brklyn 11201 **Fx:**923-0683
(718) 442-1700 .. **Bystritskaya,** Alexandra '07 Connors & C,PC -766 Castleton Av -Staten Isl 10310 **Fx:**442-1717
(516) 741-0066 .. **Bythewood,** David A '84 -85 Willis Av -Mineola 11501 **Fx:**741-0072
(650) 843-5000 .. **Byun,** Brian '07 %Cooley LLP -1114 Av of Amer -NY 10036 **Fx:**857-0663
(518) 785-4400 .. **Bywater,** Angelique M '00 CSEA -1 Lear Jet Ln -Latham 12110
(516) 877-2525 .. **Bzura,** Steven '67 OfCnsl Weinstein K&C,PC -1325 Franklin Av -Gdn Cty 11530
(212) 788-1023 .. **Caal,** Philip M '99 Law Dept -100 Church -NY 10007 **Fx:**788-0367
(212) 809-1111 .. **Caamaño,** Penelope '99 %Morgan MA -39 Bway -NY 10006
(212) 422-1200 .. **Caballero,** Vanessa '05 %Abrams GF&J,PC -1 Bttry Pk Plz -NY 10004
(914) 385-0292 .. **Cabanillas,** Christopher R '02 (Cabanillas & Assoc,PC) -245 Main -White Plns 10601 **Fx:**470-2988
(518) 429-4200 .. **Cabaniss,** David B '92 (Hiscock & B,LLP) -50 Beaver -Albany 12207
(212) 223-3900 .. **Cabassa-Torres,** Ana M '01 %Zwerling S&Z,LLP -41 Mad Av -NY 10010
(212) 816-1508 .. **Cabasso,** Sheri L '91 Citigroup Alternative Invstmnts -388 Greenwich -NY 10013
(631) 231-3775 .. **Cabble,** Robt H '79 Atty Grievance Comm -150 Motor Pkwy -Hauppauge 11788
(718) 883-1560 .. **Cabelly,** Alan S '80 (Cabelly & C) -153-01 Jamaica Av -Jamaica 11432 **Fx:**883-1562
(585) 262-1771 .. **Cable,** Susan K '80 %Monroe Comm Cllg -228 E Main -Rchstr 14604
(518) 387-6480 .. **Cabou,** Christain G '01 GE Corp R&D -1 Rsrch Dr -Niskayuna 12309
(212) 558-4000 .. **Cabral,** Jason J '08 %Sullivan & C LLP -125 Broad -NY 10004
(212) 626-1149 .. **Cabrales,** Carlos A '92 %Bank Leumi USA -562 5th Av -NY 10036 **Fx:**626-1195
(212) 218-5500 .. **Cabrera,** Anjanette '01 %Seyfarth S LLP -620 8th Av -NY 10018
(212) 947-6555 .. **Cabrera,** Anna M '92 OfCnsl S Tashman -3 W 35th -NY 10001 **Fx:**594-0019
(212) 431-1300 .. **Cabrera,** David B '92 (Borah GAN&G PC) -377 Bway -NY 10013
(212) 417-4357 .. **Cabrera,** Gerard A '00 %Dept of Health -90 Church -NY 10007 **Fx:**417-4392
(718) 439-3600 .. **Cabrera,** Heriberto A '86 -5615 5th Av -Brklyn 11220 **Fx:**439-1452
(212) 849-4556 .. **Cabrera,** Ivonne M '91 Dover Corp -280 Park Av -NY 10017
(212) 236-1000 .. **Cabrera,** Maribel '00 Merrill Lynch -225 Lbrty -NY 10080
(212) 335-9000 .. **Cabrera,** Reynaldo '00 %DA -1 Hogan Pl -NY 10013
(212) 852-5020 .. **Cabrera,** Stephanie M '06 Girl Scouts USA -420 5th Av -NY 10018
(212) 969-3000 .. **Cacace,** Anthony S '09 %Proskauer R LLP -1585 Bway -NY 10036
(914) 377-6363 .. **Cacace,** Claudia M '93 %Hon R Liebowitz -100 S Bway -Ynkrs 10701
(212) 403-7300 .. **Cacace,** Karen '00 %Vladeck WE&E,PC -1501 Bway -NY 10036
(212) 969-3000 .. **Cacace,** Perry A '80 (Proskauer R LLP) -1585 Bway -NY 10036
(718) 722-4545 .. **Cacavas,** Elena '85 %PERB -55 Hanson Pl -Brklyn 11217 **Fx:**722-4550
(646) 855-1109 .. **Caccamise,** Wm C '89 Bk of Amer -1 Bryant Pk -NY 10036
(212) 640-5326 .. **Caccamo,** Anthony R '04 AmEx -200 Vesey -NY 10285
(212) 267-1950 .. **Caccese,** Carolyn M '05 %Salenger SSK&B,LLP -233 Bway -NY 10279
(718) 238-8018 .. **Caccese,** Vincent E '38 -1724 86th -Brklyn 11214 **Fx:**331-4750
(212) 735-3000 .. **Caccia,** John M '96 (Skadden ASM&F LLP) -4 Times Sq -NY 10036
(631) 439-2450 .. **Cacciabaudo,** Heidi '89 %Leg Aid -320 Carleton Av -Central Islip 11722 **Fx:**439-2453
(631) 439-4200 .. **Cacciabaudo,** Scott M '85 %R Tusa -898 Vets Mem'l Hwy -Hauppauge 11788 **Fx:**439-4292
(716) 692-5100 .. **Cacciato,** Louis M '64 -535 Delaware Av -Tonawanda 14150 **Fx:**692-8728
(516) 868-1070 .. **Cacciatore,** V Roy '74 -30 S Ocean Av -Freeprt 11520 **Fx:**868-4315
(914) 722-0070 .. **Cacciola,** Rocco N '91 -240 Main -Eastchstr 10709
(718) 428-6868 .. **Caccioppoli,** Diana L '07 %N Horowitz,LLC -38-50 Bell Blvd -Bayside 11361 **Fx:**423-5373
(718) 847-9838 .. **Caceres,** Hernan '98 (H Caceres,PLLC) -89-32 83rd Av -Glendale 11385 **Fx:**849-3888
(212) 264-4994 .. **Cachero,** Cathleen G '98 Dept of H&HS -26 Fed Plz -NY 10278
(631) 751-8946 .. **Cacioppo,** Eileen Coen '79 -1353 Stony Brk Rd -Stony Brk 11790 **Fx:**751-8949
(212) 341-6400 .. **Cacioppo,** Lauren M '06 %Liquidation Bur -123 William -NY 10038 **Fx:**608-3398
(212) 521-4430 .. **Cacoulidis,** George '89 -590 Mad Av -NY 10022 **Fx:**521-4431
(518) 884-4703 .. **Cacozza,** Mark F '78 Hon T Nolan Jr -30 McMaster -Ballston Spa 12020 **Fx:**884-4761
(212) 788-0688 .. **Cacuci,** Gabriela P '84 %Law Dept -100 Church -NY 10007 **Fx:**788-0450
(718) 442-1212 .. **Caddell,** Joan Nerlino '82 SrCnsl JN Caddell & Assoc,PLLC -358 St Marks Pl -Staten Isl 10301 **Fx:**442-4988
(631) 424-4900 .. **Cadden,** Kevin P '89 -1641 Deer Prk Av -Deer Pk 11729
(516) 922-8400 .. **Caddick,** Helen Grosso '79 -19 W Main -Oyster Bay 11771
(212) 925-0101 .. **Cade,** Jason A '06 %C Slovinsky -401 Bway -NY 10013 **Fx:**219-9412
(518) 463-4481 .. **Cade & Saunders** -4 Pine -Albany 12207 **Fx:**426-3183
(212) 756-2000 .. **Cade,** Shannon L '07 %Schulte R&Z LLP -919 3rd Av -NY 10022
(518) 463-4481 .. **Cade,** Wm J '71 (Cade & S) -4 Pine -Albany 12207
(212) 552-5699 .. **Cadel,** Andrew N '93 %JP Morgan Chase & Co -1 Chase Manh Plz -NY 10081
(516) 338-5130 .. **Cadel,** Wm A '75 -1400 Old Cntry Rd -Westbury 11590
(212) 421-4100 .. **Caden,** Colleen L '00 (Pryor C LLP) -7 Times Sq -NY 10036
(516) 408-3666 .. **Cader,** Jonathan M '07 %Hession BC&L,LLP -1103 Stewart Av -Gdn Cty 11530
(718) 297-0004 .. **Cadet,** Vladimir '99 -8931 161st -Jamaica 11432
(516) 747-6300 .. **Cadet-Osse,** Myrna A '95 %Koeppel M&L,LLP -155 First Bx863 -Mineola 11501
(315) 475-3127 .. **Cadin,** Christopher '81 %Leg Srvcs -472 S Salina -Syracuse 13202 **Fx:**475-2706
(716) 853-8436 .. **Cadle,** Delia D '05 %Dept of Law -350 Main Pl Twr -Buffalo 14202 **Fx:**853-8571
(716) 838-4300 .. **Cadmus,** Howard D '04 %Bulan CH&I -1320 Millersport Hwy -Williamsvll 14221 **Fx:**204-9728
(607) 777-9407 .. **Cadore,** John D '94 -34 Chenango -Bnghmtn 13901 **Fx:**777-9408
(914) 478-7317 .. **Cadoux,** Robt L '82 -18 Fairmont Av -Hastings-On-Hud 10706
(212) 504-6000 .. **Cadwalader, Wickersham & Taft LLP** -1 World Fncl Ctr -NY 10281 **Fx:**504-6666
(716) 664-3906 .. **Cadwell,** Sherwood S '53 OfCnsl Phillips L LLP -8 E 3rd Bx1279 -Jamestwn 14702
(914) 779-1691 .. **Cady,** John L '51 -46 Summit Av -Bronxvll 10708 **Fx:**779-1691
(718) 596-7200 .. **Caesar,** Edw E '84 -26 Court -Brklyn 11242
(212) 414-6449 .. **Caesar,** Francis M '89 barnesandnoble.com LLC -76 9th Av -NY 10011
(212) 226-2100 .. **Caesar & Napoli** -350 Bway -NY 10013 **Fx:**226-3224
(212) 804-5744 .. **Caesar,** Sharon A '94 -110 Wall -NY 10005
(585) 530-3100 .. **Cafarell,** Frances E '86 %Appllt Div 4th Dept -50 East Av Ste 200 -Rchstr 14604 **Fx:**530-3247
(716) 285-1479 .. **Cafarella,** Jason J '05 -727 Main -Niagara Fls 14301
(518) 474-4552 .. **Cafarelli,** Todd R '06 %Insurance Dept -99 Wshngtn Av -Albany 12257 **Fx:**473-4600

(516) 203-7555 .. **Cafaro,** Bridget M '91 %J Cara,PLLC -37 Boylston -Gdn Cty 11530 **Fx:**741-1813
(516) 747-4082 .. **Cafaro,** Christopher T '89 (Montfort HM&S LLP) -1140 Franklin Av Bx7677 -Gdn Cty 11530
(516) 747-4082 .. **Cafaro,** Frank J '63 (Montfort HM&S LLP) -1140 Franklin Av Bx7677 -Gdn Cty 11530
(212) 583-7400 .. **Cafaro,** Wm '81 -19 W 44th -NY 10036
(718) 286-6000 .. **Caferri,** Nicoletta J '86 %DA -125-01 Qns Blvd -Kew Gdns 11415
(212) 884-6242 .. **Caffarelli,** Danl J '00 Guggenheim Advisors -135 E 57th -NY 10022
(212) 558-4000 .. **Caffarone,** Allison '05 %Sullivan & C LLP -125 Broad -NY 10004
(585) 263-1000 .. **Caffera,** Stephanie M '93 (Nixon P LLP) -1100 Clinton Sq -Rchstr 14604
(716) 856-1344 .. **Caffery,** Michl P '80 SpclCnsl Bouvier Prtnrshp,LLP -350 Main -Buffalo 14202 **Fx:**856-1369
(716) 855-5718 .. **Caffrey,** Danl J '03 -60 Lakefront Blvd -Buffalo 14202
(212) 608-8840 .. **Caffrey,** James M '95 (Bamundo Z&S,LLP) -111 John -NY 10038
(718) 637-4739 .. **Caffrey,** Maureen A '92 -314 Beach Rd -Staten Isl 10312
(646) 414-6791 .. **Caffrey,** Michl J '05 Cnsl Lowenstein S PC -1251 Av of Amer -NY 10020 **Fx:**(973) 597-2547
(212) 450-4000 .. **Caffrey,** Seth I '07 %Davis P&W LLP -450 Lex Av -NY 10017
(631) 694-2400 .. **Caffrey,** Wm P '00 %Hamburger MYK&M,LLP -225 Broadhllw Rd -Melvll 11747
(518) 792-1582 .. **Caffry & Flower** -100 Bay -Glens Fls 12801 **Fx:**793-0541
(518) 792-1582 .. **Caffry,** John W '85 (Caffry & F) -100 Bay -Glens Fls 12801
(646) 442-3447 .. **Caffuzzi,** Carlo R '63 -228 E 45th -NY 10017
(212) 464-0894 .. **Caffuzzi,** Claudia F '93 JP Morgan -345 Park Av -NY 10154
(212) 735-3000 .. **Caffuzzi,** Marco P '97 (Skadden ASM&F LLP) -4 Times Sq -NY 10036
(212) 770-6879 .. **Cafiero,** John M '96 AIG -70 Pine -NY 10270
(315) 724-5177 .. **Cafruny,** Danl N '10 %S Lockwood,PC -285 Genesee -Utica 13501 **Fx:**368-0084
(212) 867-9123 .. **Cagan,** Meredith B '04 %Berkman BN&R,LLP -521 5th Av -NY 10175
(212) 440-7360 .. **Cagan,** Nancy M '91 %CNA Ins Co -40 Wall -NY 10005 **Fx:**440-7644
(631) 821-7700 .. **Caggiano,** Gregory '02 (Miller & C,LLP) -3400 Vets Mem'l Hwy -Bohemia 11716 **Fx:**821-8700
(631) 395-1727 .. **Caggiano,** Karen Marie '91 -198 Crestwood Dr -Shirley 11967 **Fx:**399-3729
(212) 622-2466 .. **Caggiano,** Marco J '97 %JP Morgan Chase & Co -270 Park Av -NY 10017
(212) 790-4500 .. **Caginalp,** Aydin S '76 (Manatt P&P,LLP) -7 Times Sq -NY 10036
(212) 703-4034 .. **Caginalp,** Oggie '83 Commerzbank Cptl Mkts Corp -2 World Fncl Ctr -NY 10281
(518) 431-0247 .. **Cagino,** Diane J '88 %US Atty -445 Bway -Albany 12207 **Fx:**431-0249
(518) 473-0518 .. **Cagino,** Paul F '86 %Dept of Law -The Cptl -Albany 12224
(212) 751-3001 .. **Cagle,** Jason L '06 %Thompson & K LLP -919 3rd Av -NY 10022
(212) 506-1700 .. **Cagle,** Kimberly Kabnick '05 %Kasowitz BT&F LLP -1633 Bway -NY 10019
(212) 267-4177 .. **Cagney,** John D '10 %Kramer DL&M -217 Bway -NY 10007
(212) 909-6000 .. **Cagney,** Lawr K '82 (Debevoise & P LLP) -919 3rd Av -NY 10022
(212) 237-1000 .. **Cagney,** Wm C '77 (Windels ML&M,LLP) -156 W 56th -NY 10019
(315) 423-7025 .. **Cagnina,** Christina G '94 -120 E Wshngtn -Syracuse 13202 **Fx:**234-5774
(631) 425-9600 .. **Cahalan,** Eric M '82 (Cahalan & C,PC) -191 NY Av -Huntngtn 11743
(212) 836-8000 .. **Cahalan,** John S '07 %Kaye S LLP -425 Park Av -NY 10022
(631) 425-9600 .. **Cahalan,** Lynn T '86 (Cahalan & C,PC) -191 NY Av -Huntngtn 11743
(315) 474-2911 .. **Cahalan,** Robt P '96 (Smith SK&S,PC) -250 S Clinton -Syracuse 13202
(212) 925-9100 .. **Cahalane,** Brian A '97 %Reddy L&Z,PC -85 Worth -NY 10013
(212) 418-7282 .. **Cahan,** Michl S '99 ICON Sprts & Entertnmt Mktng -1 Dag Hmmrskjld Plz -NY 10017
(914) 681-6200 .. **Cahill,** Anne B '81 NYPA -123 Main -White Plns 10601 **Fx:**390-8038
(212) 474-5843 .. **Cahill,** Brian T '05 Televest Daytime Programs -825 8th Av -NY 10019
(631) 324-4134 .. **Cahill,** Catherine Anne '82 %Town Ct -159 Pantigo Rd -E Hampton 11937
(845) 398-4121 .. **Cahill,** Christine M '03 St Thomas Aquinas College -125 Route 340 -Sparkill 10976
(518) 464-2444 .. **Cahill,** Danl J '80 AYCO -1 Wall Bx15073 -Albany 12212
(518) 584-1991 .. **Cahill,** Danl S '97 (Cahill/Wink LLP) -60 Railroad Pl -Saratoga Spgs 12866
(212) 481-6100 .. **Cahill,** David R '80 Structure-Tone Inc -770 Bway -NY 10003 **Fx:**685-9267
(718) 250-4282 .. **Cahill,** Genevieve M '10 Leg Aid -111 Lvngstn -Brklyn 11201 **Fx:**250-4243
(718) 855-4076 .. **Cahill,** James H Sr. '59 (Cahill & C) -161 Atl Av -Brklyn 11201 **Fx:**855-0030
(718) 855-4076 .. **Cahill,** James H Jr. '94 (Cahill & C) -161 Atl Av -Brklyn 11201 **Fx:**855-0030
(518) 465-3669 .. **Cahill,** James J '52 -600 Bway -Albany 12207 **Fx:**465-3671
(607) 748-7481 .. **Cahill,** James N '63 (Cahill Law Ofc) -145 Wshngtn Av Bx119 -Endicott 13761 **Fx:**748-4831
(212) 318-6000 .. **Cahill,** John A '89 (Paul HJ&W LLP) -75 E 55th -NY 10022
(518) 439-4005 .. **Cahill,** John J III '78 -848 Kenwood Av Bx326 -Slingerlnds 12159 **Fx:**439-4535
(212) 408-5100 .. **Cahill,** John P '86 Cnsl Chadbourne & P LLP -30 Rckfllr Plz -NY 10112
(212) 719-4400 .. **Cahill,** John R '88 (Lynn & C,LLP) -58 W 40th -NY 10018 **Fx:**719-4440
(631) 854-8426 .. **Cahill,** John R '08 Suffolk Cnty Police Dept -345 Old Willets Path -Hauppauge 11787
(845) 562-0203 .. **Cahill,** Kristine M '00 %Finkelstein & Prtnrs,LLP -1279 Route 300 Bx1111 -Newburgh 12550
(212) 837-6000 .. **Cahill,** Lisa A '91 Cnsl Hughes H&R LLP -1 Bttry Pk Plz -NY 10004
(518) 429-4200 .. **Cahill,** M Cornelia '84 (Hiscock & B,LLP) -50 Beaver -Albany 12207
(212) 922-9700 .. **Cahill,** Matthew C '95 %1st Amer Title -633 3rd Av -NY 10017 **Fx:**922-0881
(631) 588-8778 .. **Cahill,** Michl J '80 (Germano & C,PC) -4250 Vets Mem'l Hwy -Holbrook 11741
(212) 773-3000 .. **Cahill,** Peter J '88 %Ernst & Young,LLP -5 Times Sq -NY 10036
(845) 331-2525 .. **Cahill,** Richd T Jr. '97 %Ryan R&R,LLP -115 Green Bx3153 -Kingston 12402
(631) 501-7128 .. **Cahill,** Susanne M '02 Gentria Hlth Srvcs -3 Huntngtn Quad -Melvll 11747
(212) 818-9200 .. **Cahill,** Thos J '91 (Satterlee SB&B LLP) -230 Park Av -NY 10169
(718) 783-7444 .. **Cahill,** Wm A Jr. '79 (Anderson & C) -255 Flatbush Av -Brklyn 11217 **Fx:**783-7423
(516) 355-7901 .. **Cahill,** Wm E '81 %Paganini GCC&F -1979 Marcus Av -Lk Success 11042
(518) 584-1991 .. **Cahill/Wink LLP** -60 Railroad Pl -Saratoga Spgs 12866 **Fx:**584-1962
(646) 434-1661 .. **Cahill/Wink LLP** -5 Penn Plz -NY 10001 **Fx:**(518) 584-1962
(212) 930-9700 .. **Cahlon,** Jeff A '01 %Sichenzia RFF LLP -61 Bway -NY 10006
(212) 732-3200 .. **Cahn,** Aaron R '75 Cnsl Carter L&M LLP -2 Wall -NY 10005
(212) 693-1313 .. **Cahn,** Adam D '95 -150 Bway -NY 10038
(212) 715-9100 .. **Cahn,** Avram J '88 SpclCnsl Kramer LN&F,LLP -1177 Av of Amer -NY 10036
(212) 310-8000 .. **Cahn,** Blaire A '09 %Weil G&M LLP -767 5th Av -NY 10153
(631) 752-1600 .. **Cahn,** Danl K '02 (Cahn & C LLP) -22 High -Huntngtn 11743 **Fx:**752-1555
(212) 594-5300 .. **Cahn,** Herman '56 OfCnsl Milberg LLP -1 Penn Plz -NY 10119
(212) 715-9100 .. **Cahn,** Joshua Baron '09 %Kramer LN&F,LLP -1177 Av of Amer -NY 10036
(212) 686-1180 .. **Cahn,** Karen L '80 -232 Mad Av -NY 10016
(718) 250-4202 .. **Cahn,** Laura Potter '83 %Leg Aid -111 Lvngstn -Brklyn 11201 **Fx:**250-4243
(516) 741-0001 .. **Cahn,** Neil R '75 N Cahn PLLC -1 Old Cntry Rd -Carle Pl 11514 **Fx:**741-9673
(516) 571-9054 .. **Cahn,** Penelope B '76 Family Ct -1200 Old Cntry Rd -Westbury 11590
(631) 752-1600 .. **Cahn,** Richd C '56 (Cahn & C LLP) -22 High -Huntngtn 11743 **Fx:**752-1555
(516) 371-4400 .. **Cahn,** Steven P '80 %Wascomat Of America -461 Doughty Blvd -Inwood 11096
(212) 412-4077 .. **Cai,** Xiang '07 Barclays Capital Inc -745 7th Av -NY 10019
(914) 524-5600 .. **Caiazzo,** Christopher C '92 %L Fishman -303 S Bway -Tarrytwn 10591 **Fx:**524-5742
(516) 746-3066 .. **Caiazzo,** Jos E '81 -29 Spruce -Gdn Cty 11530
(212) 490-3000 .. **Caiazzo,** Nicholas R '89 (Wilson EME&D LLP) -150 E 42nd -NY 10017
(518) 455-4258 .. **Cail,** Laura J '07 Assembly Minority Cnsl Ofc -440 The Cptl -Albany 12248
(212) 906-1200 .. **Caillavet,** Cynthia A '06 %Latham & W -885 3rd Av -NY 10022
(212) 310-8904 .. **Cailteux,** Konrad L '86 (Weil G&M LLP) -767 5th Av -NY 10153
(607) 734-8161 .. **Cain,** Danl J '06 (Buck DR&M) -100 Baldwin -Elmira 14901
(315) 634-7663 .. **Cain,** Douglas M '06 Pyramid Mgmt Grp Inc -4 Clinton Sq -Syracuse 13202
(718) 991-4600 .. **Cain,** Heidi Lee '06 %Leg Aid -953 Southrn Blvd -Bronx 10459 **Fx:**842-2867
(212) 506-1700 .. **Cain,** James T '00 SpclCnsl Kasowitz BT&F LLP -1633 Bway -NY 10019
(212) 450-4000 .. **Cain,** Juliet '83 (Davis P&W LLP) -450 Lex Av -NY 10017
(212) 403-1000 .. **Cain,** Karessa Lin '06 %Wachtell LR&K -51 W 52nd -NY 10019
(212) 815-1818 .. **Cain,** Rashana E '05 %DC 37 MELS -125 Barclay -NY 10007 **Fx:**815-1343
(718) 802-4804 .. **Cain,** Sheila T '80 %Dept of Finance -210 Joralemon -Brklyn 11201
(516) 688-1700 .. **Caine,** Marc L '02 %IRS -1600 Stewart Av -Westbury 11590 **Fx:**688-1750
(212) 233-1050 .. **Caine,** Martin L '62 -217 Bway -NY 10007 **Fx:**233-1060
(516) 571-2777 .. **Caine,** Robt S '66 %Supreme Ct -100 Supreme Ct Dr -Mineola 11501
(516) 825-7700 .. **Caiola,** Bennett A '97 %Property Services LLC -104 S Central Av -Vly Stream 11580
(212) 759-4888 .. **Caiola,** Eugene P '01 %Phillips L LLP -437 Mad Av -NY 10022
(212) 935-0273 .. **Cairns,** John B '80 -418 E 59th -NY 10022
(631) 853-7915 .. **Cairns,** John P Jr. '04 Suffolk Cnty Fam Ct -400 Carleton Av -Central Islip 11722
(212) 373-3000 .. **Cairns,** Kellie A '10 %Paul WRW&G LLP -1285 Av of Amer -NY 10019
(212) 878-4669 .. **Cairns,** Richd J '89 MTA -347 Mad Av -NY 10017
(516) 825-1222 .. **Cairo,** Jos G Jr. '71 -877 N Corona Av -N Vly Strm 11580
(518) 237-9434 .. **Cairo,** Jos M '69 -25 Wshngtn Av Bx437 -Waterfrd 12188 **Fx:**237-8394
(516) 746-8000 .. **Cairo,** Lisa A '03 %Jaspan S LLP -300 Grdn City Plz -Gdn Cty 11530
(212) 407-4000 .. **Caixeiro,** Manny J '04 %Loeb & L,LLP -345 Park Av -NY 10154
(718) 237-0411 .. **Cajoux,** Marjory '93 -406 Atl Av -Brklyn 11217
(212) 962-8020 .. **Cakani,** Ylli '08 %Julien & S,PC -1 Whitehall -NY 10004
(716) 483-2252 .. **Cala,** Philip A '79 -111 W 2nd -Jamestwn 14701 **Fx:**661-3468
(518) 487-5460 .. **Calabrese,** Christina M '05 %DA -6 Lodge -Albany 12207 **Fx:**487-5093
(585) 546-5600 .. **Calabrese,** Christopher '93 (Pheterson SCN&S,LLP) -1 E Main -Rchstr 14614
(212) 549-2500 .. **Calabrese,** Christopher R '01 %ACLU -125 Broad -NY 10004 **Fx:**549-2651
(718) 250-2000 .. **Calabrese,** Danl J '09 %DA -350 Jay -Brklyn 11201 **Fx:**250-2314
(212) 541-2000 .. **Calabrese,** David '86 (Bryan C LLP) -1290 Av of Amer -NY 10104
(718) 274-1072 .. **Calabrese,** Dominic J '59 -22-45 31st -Astoria 11105 **Fx:**274-8858
(631) 486-4900 .. **Calabrese,** Ellen M '98 %E Berman,PC -100 Grdn City Plz -Gdn Cty 11530 **Fx:**486-4997
(518) 434-1493 .. **Calabrese,** Gennaro D '10 %Kindlon & S,PC -74 Chapel -Albany 12207
(718) 990-1848 .. **Calabrese,** Gina M '97 %St John's Law Schl -8000 Utopia Pkwy -Jamaica 11439 **Fx:**591-1855
(585) 232-6500 .. **Calabrese,** Jeffrey J '96 (Harter S&E LLP) -1600 Bausch & Lomb Pl -Rchstr 14604
(212) 530-5000 .. **Calabrese,** John A '10 %Milbank TH&M LLP -1 Chase Manh Plz -NY 10005
(212) 816-6000 .. **Calabrese,** Jos L '92 Citigroup Global Mrkts -77 Water -NY 10005

(516) 357-3000 .. **Calabrese,** Justin A '04 %Rivkin R LLP -926 RXR Plz -Uniondale 11556
(212) 728-8000 .. **Calabrese,** Katie M '07 %Willkie F&G LLP -787 7th Av -NY 10019
(718) 579-7915 .. **Calabrese,** Kristen '05 %Leg Aid -900 Sheridan Av -Bronx 10451 **Fx:**293-8744
(716) 649-3311 .. **Calabrese,** Kyle W '94 -265 Union -Hambrg 14075
(212) 940-8800 .. **Calabrese,** Madelyn '03 %Katten MR LLP -575 Mad Av -NY 10022
(212) 237-1000 .. **Calabrese,** Marianne '99 %Windels ML&M,LLP -156 W 56th -NY 10019
(585) 243-5150 .. **Calabrese,** Mary C '70 -4177 Lima Rd -Geneseo 14454
(631) 598-1400 .. **Calabrese,** Mary Sullivan '92 %R Handler -50 Bway Bx427 -Amityvll 11701 **Fx:**598-0952
(212) 986-7070 .. **Calabrese,** Michl '77 (Calabrese & T) -280 Mad Av -NY 10016 **Fx:**661-2876
(585) 232-4724 .. **Calabrese,** Richd A '59 (Elliott S&C,LLP) -1 E Main -Rchstr 14614
(516) 255-1800 .. **Calabrese,** Richd J '08 %Rosenblum & B LLP -100 Merrick Rd -Rockvll Ctr 11570
(914) 478-5104 .. **Calabrese,** Rosa M '87 (Calabrese & C,LLP) -82 Donald Dr -Hastings-On-Hud 10706
(914) 478-5104 .. **Calabrese,** Salvatore J '83 (Calabrese & C,LLP) -82 Donald Dr -Hastings-On-Hud 10706
(212) 889-1101 .. **Calabrese,** Teresa D '90 -233 5th Av -NY 10016
(212) 805-7176 .. **Calabrese,** Theo S '06 %Computershare -17 State -NY 10004
(516) 931-2600 .. **Calabria,** Nicholas P Jr. '89 (Churbuck CJ&M PC) -43A E Barclay -Hicksvll 11801
(914) 421-0080 .. **Calabro,** Fortunato John '91 Cohen & S LLP -14 Mamaroneck Av -White Plns 10601 **Fx:**421-0035
(646) 688-6095 .. **Calabro,** Gregory G '88 (Calabro & Assoc,PC) -450 7th Av -NY 10123 **Fx:**688-6096
(212) 849-7000 .. **Calabro,** Jason T '09 %Quinn EU&S,LLP -51 Mad Av -NY 10010
(212) 556-2100 .. **Calabro,** John A '05 %King & S -1185 Av of Amer -NY 10036
(347) 404-9133 .. **Calabro,** Miriam '80 %Civil Ct -141 Lvngstn -Brklyn 11201 **Fx:**(718) 643-3733
(212) 626-4100 .. **Calabro,** Nicole C '99 %Baker & M LLP -1114 Av of Amer -NY 10036
(631) 232-2400 .. **Calabro,** Patricia I '00 Nassau/Sfflk Law Srv -1757 Vets Hwy -Islandia 11749 **Fx:**232-2489
(212) 310-8000 .. **Calabro,** Sheryl L '05 %Weil G&M LLP -767 5th Av -NY 10153
(212) 813-8800 .. **Calaf,** Maria A '05 %Goodwin P LLP -620 8th Av -NY 10018
(212) 878-8000 .. **Calafiore,** Valeria '04 %Clifford C LLP -31 W 52nd -NY 10019
(212) 209-4800 .. **Calagione,** Jessica C '08 %Brown R LLP -7 Times Sq -NY 10036
(315) 422-1152 .. **Calagiovanni,** Alicia S '78 (Costello C&F,PLLC) -500 Plum -Syracuse 13204
(212) 752-9700 .. **Calaguio,** Cheryll June '07 %Gersten S LLP -600 Lex Av -NY 10022
(718) 833-9006 .. **Calakos,** Demetra Arniotes '05 -7206 5th Av -Brklyn 11209
(212) 336-0042 .. **Calamari,** Andrew M '86 %SEC -3 World Fncl Ctr -NY 10281 **Fx:**336-1323
(718) 990-6009 .. **Calamari,** Jos A '42 %St John's Law Schl -8000 Utopia Pkwy -Jamaica 11439 **Fx:**(516) 352-4522
(212) 474-1000 .. **Calamari,** Jos L '90 Cravath S&M LLP -825 8th Av -NY 10019
(212) 849-7000 .. **Calamari,** Nicholas J '07 %Quinn EU&S,LLP -51 Mad Av -NY 10010
(212) 849-7000 .. **Calamari,** Peter E '74 (Quinn EU&S,LLP) -51 Mad Av -NY 10010
(212) 435-3571 .. **Calamia,** Angela '83 %Port Auth of NY/NJ -225 Park Av S -NY 10003 **Fx:**435-3555
(631) 462-9339 .. **Calamis,** James P '79 -5036 Jericho Tpk -Commack 11725 **Fx:**462-6960
(212) 547-5400 .. **Calandra,** John J '92 (McDermott W&E LLP) -340 Mad Av -NY 10173
(212) 558-4000 .. **Calandra,** Meredith A '10 %Sullivan & C LLP -125 Broad -NY 10004
(646) 772-7211 .. **Calandra,** Michl A Sr. '71 OfCnsl Peltz & W -222 Bway -NY 10038
(212) 768-6700 .. **Calandra,** Michl A Jr. '06 %Sonnenschein N&R LLP -2 World Fncl Ctr -NY 10281
(585) 349-3922 .. **Calandra,** Thos D '66 -31 N Union -Spencerprt 14559 **Fx:**352-2929
(631) 360-7570 .. **Calandrino,** Fred '95 %Town Atty -99 W Main -Smithtwn 11787 **Fx:**360-7719
(212) 685-3500 .. **Calano,** Janet Madonia '86 OfCnsl Calano & C,LLP -370 Lex Av -NY 10017 **Fx:**(914) 946-6000
(914) 686-3000 .. **Calano,** Janet Madonia '86 OfCnsl Calano & C,LLP -14 Mamaroneck Av -White Plns 10601 **Fx:**946-6000
(914) 686-3000 .. **Calano,** Michl A '84 (Calano & C,LLP) -14 Mamaroneck Av -White Plns 10601 **Fx:**946-6000
(212) 685-3500 .. **Calano,** Michl A '84 (Calano & C,LLP) -370 Lex Av -NY 10017 **Fx:**(914) 946-6000
(315) 331-8080 .. **Calarco,** Michl D '90 -605 Mason -Newark 14513 **Fx:**331-8140
(518) 487-7600 .. **Calareso,** John P Jr. '99 %Whiteman O&H LLP -1 Commerce Plz -Albany 12260
(518) 452-1961 .. **Calareso,** Julie Ann '04 %Burke & C,PC -255 Washington Av Ext -Albany 12205
(212) 318-6000 .. **Calatozzo,** Peter A '06 %Paul HJ&W LLP -75 E 55th -NY 10022
(212) 574-1200 .. **Calay,** Sharan K '01 (Seward & K LLP) -1 Bttry Pk Plz -NY 10004
(212) 728-8000 .. **Calbert,** Tonisha M '08 %Willkie F&G LLP -787 7th Av -NY 10019
(631) 582-5151 .. **Calcagni,** John R '81 (Haley W&C,LLP) -1601 Vets Mem'l Hwy -Islandia 11749
(914) 277-2255 .. **Calcagnini,** George J '79 -376 Route 202 -Somers 10589 **Fx:**277-2299
(212) 244-4100 .. **Calcagno,** Andrew John '91 (Calcagno & Assoc,LLC) -30 Vesey -NY 10007
(718) 980-2464 .. **Calcagno,** Steven R '88 (S Calcagno PC) -1272 Richmond Rd -Staten Isl 10304 **Fx:**980-4545
(718) 243-6895 .. **Calcaterra,** Elisabeth R '04 %Leg Aid -111 Lvngstn -Brklyn 11201 **Fx:**237-8737
(212) 688-0782 .. **Calcaterra,** Regina Marie '97 (Barrack R&B) -1350 Bway -NY 10018
(212) 592-1400 .. **Caldarola,** Chas E '98 %Herrick,F LLP -2 Park Av -NY 10016
(212) 455-2000 .. **Calder,** Andrew T '03 %Simpson T&B LLP -425 Lex Av -NY 10017
(212) 940-8800 .. **Calder,** James J '78 (Katten MR LLP) -575 Mad Av -NY 10022
(631) 475-4400 .. **Calder,** Linda D '82 Cnsl Roe TT&P,LLP -One Corp Dr -Bohemia 11716
(212) 804-4200 .. **Calder,** Michl L '07 %Mound CW&G -One Bttry Pk Plz -NY 10004
(631) 577-7611 .. **Calder Greene,** Desa Onika '05 K Dodson -100 Baylis Rd -Melvll 11747 **Fx:**577-7199
(516) 712-4000 .. **Calderon,** Bruce R '98 (Milber MP&S LLP) -1000 Woodbury Rd -Woodbury 11797
(914) 668-8900 .. **Calderon,** Carlos M '91 (Weisman & C LLP) -6 Gramatan Av -Mt Vernon 10550
(518) 487-5460 .. **Calderon,** Francisco '98 %DA -6 Lodge -Albany 12207 **Fx:**487-5093
(718) 515-4807 .. **Calderon,** Jos '80 -2705 Wllmsbrdg Rd -Bronx 10469 **Fx:**790-0039
(718) 883-1560 .. **Calderon,** Lewis S '94 (Cabelly & C) -153-01 Jamaica Av -Jamaica 11432 **Fx:**883-1562
(212) 610-6300 .. **Calderon-Barrera,** Dennise A '04 %Allen & O -1221 Av of Amer -NY 10020
(516) 228-8484 .. **Calderone,** Adrian T '86 %Dilworth & B,LLP -1000 Woodbury Rd -Woodbury 11797
(516) 626-9200 .. **Calderone,** Philip D '82 %Banfi Vintners -1111 Cedar Swamp Rd -Old Brookvll 11545
(718) 319-1400 .. **Calderoni,** Dominick M '94 (Klein C&S LLP) -1614 Wllmsbrdg Rd -Bronx 10461
(212) 909-6000 .. **Calderon Rizzo,** Julie M '05 %Debevoise & P LLP -919 3rd Av -NY 10022
(212) 863-6300 .. **Calderwood,** Wm '77 %HPD -100 Gold -NY 10038 **Fx:**863-8201
(518) 766-2616 .. **Caldes,** Theo G '59 Zweig & Caldes -32 Lyons Lk Rd Bx616 -Nassau 12123
(212) 446-4800 .. **Caldis,** Grant H '06 %Kirkland & E LLP -153 E 53rd -NY 10022
(212) 610-6300 .. **Caldon,** Brendan W '07 %Allen & O -1221 Av of Amer -NY 10020
(716) 439-7085 .. **Caldwell,** Claudette S '98 %DA -175 Hawley -Lockprt 14094 **Fx:**439-7102
(718) 783-2000 .. **Caldwell,** Gillian B '93 Witness -80 Hanson Pl -Brklyn 11217
(212) 553-0300 .. **Caldwell,** J McGinnis Jr. '91 %Moody's Invstr Srvc -250 Greenwich -NY 10007
(212) 216-2000 .. **Caldwell,** Jeffrey D '82 %Jacob K Javits Cnvntn Ctr -655 W 34th -NY 10001 **Fx:**216-2588
(212) 596-9000 .. **Caldwell,** Joel R '10 %Ropes & G LLP -1211 Av of Amer -NY 10036
(315) 736-1969 .. **Caldwell,** Jos D '78 -1 Ellinwood Ct Bx799 -New Hartfrd 13413
(212) 253-1710 .. **Caldwell,** Katherine L '07 NESRI -90 John -NY 10038
(212) 309-6000 .. **Caldwell,** Leslie R '83 (Morgan L&B LLP) -101 Park Av -NY 10178
(212) 492-3607 .. **Caldwell,** Victor F '98 Deloitte Touche Tohmatsu -1633 Bway -NY 10019
(212) 416-6346 .. **Caldwell-Brown,** Dorothea '96 %Dept of Law -120 Bway -NY 10271
(212) 785-2577 .. **Cale,** Tiffany E '01 %Rosner & N -26 Bway -NY 10004 **Fx:**785-5203
(631) 329-0400 .. **Caleca,** Johanna E '83 (Caleca & T,PC) -257 Pantigo Rd -E Hampton 11937
(631) 329-0400 .. **Caleca & Towner, PC** -257 Pantigo Rd -E Hampton 11937 **Fx:**329-0004
(212) 237-1000 .. **Calella,** Patrick M '96 %Windels ML&M,LLP -156 W 56th -NY 10019
(718) 631-4489 .. **Calender,** David B '88 -38-50 Bell Blvd -Bayside 11361 **Fx:**423-2987
(212) 808-7800 .. **Caley,** Steven P '82 (Kelley D&W LLP) -101 Park Av -NY 10178
(212) 455-2000 .. **Calheiros,** Grenfel Schwartz '05 %Simpson T&B LLP -425 Lex Av -NY 10017
(845) 534-0400 .. **Calhelha & Doyle,LLC** -2640 Route 9W -Cornwall 12518 **Fx:**534-0420
(845) 534-0400 .. **Calhelha,** Moacyr R '80 (Calhelha & D,LLC) -2640 Route 9W -Cornwall 12518
(212) 741-7229 .. **Calhoun,** Carol A '75 -46 Carmine -NY 10014 **Fx:**627-1001
(914) 946-5900 .. **Calhoun,** Clinton W III '83 (Briccetti C&L,LLP) -81 Main -White Plns 10601
(212) 788-0923 .. **Calhoun,** Martha A '93 %Law Dept -100 Church -NY 10007 **Fx:**788-0367
(716) 858-2200 .. **Calhoun,** Stephanie J '09 Cnty Atty -95 Franklin -Buffalo 14202 **Fx:**858-2281
(718) 948-2922 .. **Calhoun,** Wm F '81 -145 Corbin Av -Staten Isl 10308
(212) 791-9730 .. **Cali,** Frank '93 %PF Adams,PC -30 Vesey -NY 10007
(315) 435-2470 .. **Cali,** Jeremy P '07 %DA -505 S State -Syracuse 13202 **Fx:**435-3969
(212) 951-6550 .. **Caliano,** Melba T '99 -475 Park Av S -NY 10016
(212) 506-2500 .. **Calica,** Andrew J '05 %Mayer B LLP -1675 Bway -NY 10019
(516) 747-7400 .. **Calica,** Robt M '70 (Rosenberg C&B LLP) -100 Grdn City Plz -Gdn Cty 11530
(518) 689-1434 .. **Calicchia,** Erin Kate '03 %Greenberg T,LLP -54 State -Albany 12207
(646) 722-8500 .. **Caliendo,** Chas T '96 SrCnsl Grant & E,PA -485 Lex Av -NY 10017
(212) 732-3355 .. **Caliendo,** Gary W '02 %Pops & Assoc -225 Bway -NY 10007 **Fx:**732-8844
(718) 590-2000 .. **Caliendo,** Robt '05 %DA -198 E 161st -Bronx 10451 **Fx:**590-6477
(212) 670-0179 .. **Califano,** Andrea C '94 Merrill Lynch -222 Bway -NY 10038
(718) 250-0400 .. **Califano,** Claudia M '91 %R Tusa -1 MetroTech Ctr -Brklyn 11201 **Fx:**250-0591
(212) 841-5200 .. **Califano,** Jos A Jr. '55 %CASA/Columbia Univ -633 3rd Av -NY 10017
(212) 335-4500 .. **Califano,** Thos R '89 (DLA Piper LLP) -1251 Av of Amer -NY 10020
(716) 854-3455 .. **Caligiuri,** Jos A '98 (Gielowski F&C,LLP) -135 Delaware Av -Buffalo 14202 **Fx:**854-2797
(516) 238-0367 .. **Caliguiri,** Michl '80 -2 Whitman Ridge Dr -Melvll 11747
(631) 981-7293 .. **Calimano,** John '00 -6 Dusk Dr -Centereach 11720
(212) 826-8800 .. **Calinoff & Katz,LLP** -245 5th Av -NY 10016 **Fx:**644-5123
(212) 826-8800 .. **Calinoff,** Robt A '71 (Calinoff & K,LLP) -245 5th Av -NY 10016
(212) 925-3456 .. **Calip,** Christine L '04 %Sedlmayr & Assoc -200 Park Av S -NY 10003 **Fx:**925-0554
(732) 962-1510 .. **Calise,** Albert A '04 -86 Court -Brklyn 11201 **Fx:**962-1502
(631) 232-0030 .. **Calisto,** Edw A '94 (Ferruggia & C,LLP) -150 Motor Pkwy -Hauppauge 11788 **Fx:**232-2330
(212) 788-8682 .. **Calistro,** Phyllis G '89 %Law Dept -100 Church -NY 10007 **Fx:**788-0367
(212) 673-6669 .. **Calistro,** Valerie B '90 Ventura R&S -280 Park Av S -NY 10010
(212) 422-0202 .. **Calkins,** Allison M '05 %Sedgwick DM&A LLP -125 Broad -NY 10004

(516) 931-0064 .. **Calkins,** Steven P '77 (Kingsley K&C) -91 W Cherry -Hicksvll 11801 **Fx:**931-4313
(212) 468-8000 .. **Call,** Richd C '08 %Morrison & F LLP -1290 Av of Amer -NY 10104
(585) 345-0894 .. **Call,** W Douglas '66 -6230 E Morganvll Rd -Stafford 14143
(212) 613-2015 .. **Callaghan,** Anthony P '97 (Gibbons PC) -1 Penn Plz -NY 10119 **Fx:**554-9610
(516) 365-9802 .. **Callaghan,** Edw J '02 %Collard & R,PC -1077 Nrthrn Blvd -Roslyn 11576
(914) 472-1500 .. **Callaghan,** Georgann M '00 %Colucci & U -670 Wht Plns Rd -Scarsdale 10583
(212) 578-6842 .. **Callaghan,** Katherine M '98 %MetLife -1 Mad Av -NY 10010
(212) 556-1107 .. **Callaghan,** Kevin R '94 The NY Times -620 8th Av -NY 10018
(516) 522-2695 .. **Callaghan,** Leo G '95 (Callaghan P LLP) -626 RXR Plz -Uniondale 11556 **Fx:**(866) 269-3969
(518) 474-4453 .. **Callaghan,** Thos A '66 %MHLS -40 Steuben -Albany 12207 **Fx:**473-5849
(718) 991-4600 .. **Callagy,** Ann Kimmerling '94 %Leg Aid -953 Southrn Blvd -Bronx 10459 **Fx:**842-2867
(212) 533-6300 .. **Callagy,** Christopher M '92 %NYSUT -52 Bway -NY 10004 **Fx:**995-2347
(212) 808-7800 .. **Callagy,** John M '69 (Kelley D&W LLP) -101 Park Av -NY 10178
(845) 471-0058 .. **Callagy,** Paul G '93 %Leg Srvcs -29 N Hmltn -Poughkeepsie 12601 **Fx:**471-0244
(631) 283-1625 .. **Callahan,** Alfred J Jr. '79 -40 Barnhart -Southampton 11968 **Fx:**283-3512
(212) 839-5300 .. **Callahan,** Andrew J '09 %Sidley A LLP -787 7th Av -NY 10019
(518) 485-2346 .. **Callahan,** Brian M '98 %Comm of Correction -80 Wolf Rd -Albany 12205 **Fx:**485-2467
(631) 853-4049 .. **Callahan,** Brian P '75 %Cnty Atty -Dennison Bldg Bx6100 -Hauppauge 11788 **Fx:**853-5169
(914) 600-4224 .. **Callahan,** Brian R '04 (B Callahan & Assoc,PLLC) -120 Bedford Rd -Plsntvll 10570 **Fx:**206-4743
(212) 373-3000 .. **Callahan,** Corey R '10 %Paul WRW&G LLP -1285 Av of Amer -NY 10019
(212) 490-6050 .. **Callahan,** Darin L '09 %Lennon M&L LLC -420 Lex Av -NY 10170 **Fx:**490-6070
(212) 489-8230 .. **Callahan,** David P '73 (Davis WT LLP) -1633 Bway -NY 10019
(212) 595-5315 .. **Callahan,** Edw T '57 -225 Cntrl Pk W -NY 10024
(716) 566-5400 .. **Callahan,** Elizabeth Y '00 %Goldberg S LLP -665 Main -Buffalo 14203
(315) 443-3673 .. **Callahan,** Elletta Sangrey '85 %Syracuse Univ School of Mgmt -Crouse Hinds Hall -Syracuse 13244
(212) 687-4900 .. **Callahan,** Eugene J '68 (Wormser KG&J LLP) -825 3rd Av -NY 10022
(212) 448-9570 .. **Callahan & Fusco,LLC** -40 Exch Pl -NY 10005 **Fx:**448-9772
(516) 573-0636 .. **Callahan,** James J III '94 Cnty Ofc Emergency Mgmt -100 Carman Av -E Meadow 11554 **Fx:**378-7633
(315) 471-3151 .. **Callahan,** Janet D '81 (Hancock & E,LLP) -1500 AXA Twr I Bx4976 -Syracuse 13221
(212) 376-3035 .. **Callahan,** Jean C '95 Vera Inst of Justice -233 Bway -NY 10279
(914) 422-1241 .. **Callahan,** John G '76 Law Dept -255 Main -White Plns 10601 **Fx:**422-1231
(315) 218-8000 .. **Callahan,** John H '82 (Bond S&K,PLLC) -1 Lincoln Ctr -Syracuse 13202
(315) 472-5201 .. **Callahan,** Jos M '87 (Mackay C&C,PC) -103 E Water -Syracuse 13202
(212) 344-1013 .. **Callahan,** Jos P '69 (Callahan & W) -88 Pine -NY 10005
(516) 742-9743 .. **Callahan & Malone** -263 Mineola Blvd -Mineola 11501 **Fx:**742-9749
(518) 473-1403 .. **Callahan,** Mary T '90 %Dept of Health -Corning Twr 24th Fl -Albany 12237 **Fx:**473-2019
(212) 969-3000 .. **Callahan,** Michl E '02 %Proskauer R LLP -1585 Bway -NY 10036
(914) 600-4224 .. **Callahan,** Nicole A '04 %B Callahan & Assoc,PLLC -120 Bedford Rd -Plsntvll 10570 **Fx:**206-4743
(716) 853-2050 .. **Callahan,** Paul J '03 %Sliwa & L -237 Main -Buffalo 14203
(518) 370-1233 .. **Callahan,** Paul M '76 -179½ Jay -Schnctdy 12305 **Fx:**370-1818
(518) 895-2334 .. **Callahan,** Paul M '76 -4886 Wstrn Tpk Bx100 -Duanesbrg 12056 **Fx:**895-8327
(212) 578-7311 .. **Callahan,** Robt F '82 %MetLife -27-01 Qns Plz N -LIC 11101
(518) 473-1707 .. **Callahan,** Robt J '78 %Dept of Health -Corning Twr 24th Fl -Albany 12237 **Fx:**486-1858
(212) 425-9300 .. **Callahan,** Sean C '01 %Bressler A&R,PC -17 State -NY 10004
(631) 273-8822 .. **Callahan,** Sean P '95 NYSUT -150 Motor Pkwy -Hauppauge 11788
(212) 935-3000 .. **Callahan,** Steven B '80 OfCnsl Mintz LCFG&P,PC -666 3rd Av -NY 10017
(516) 545-5160 .. **Callahan,** Thos F '81 SrCnsl Natl Grid -175 E Old Cntry Rd -Hicksvll 11801 **Fx:**545-5029
(212) 889-3000 .. **Callahan,** Wm P '64 -17 Battery Pl -NY 10004 **Fx:**889-3242
(212) 344-1013 .. **Callahan & Wolkoff** -88 Pine -NY 10005
(631) 234-1154 .. **Callan,** Andrea L '08 S Mishkin,PC -1 Suffolk Sq -Islandia 11749 **Fx:**234-5048
(631) 851-9300 .. **Callan,** Bernard T '65 BT Callan,PC -320 Carleton Av -Central Islip 11722 **Fx:**232-9701
(212) 233-8070 .. **Callan & Byrnes** -225 Bway -NY 10007 **Fx:**732-8167
(212) 233-8070 .. **Callan,** Cesar A '84 (Callan & B) -225 Bway -NY 10007
(212) 323-7070 .. **Callan,** James R '97 %Rawle & H LLP -14 Wall -NY 10005
(212) 248-8800 .. **Callan Koster Brady & Brennan LLP** -1 Whitehall -NY 10004 **Fx:**248-6815
(516) 227-2260 .. **Callan Koster Brady & Brennan LLP** -333 Earle Ovngton Blvd -Uniondale 11553 **Fx:**227-2264
(315) 733-0419 .. **Callan,** Michl D '10 %Saunders K,LLP -185 Genesee -Utica 13501
(585) 266-6574 .. **Callan,** Michelle L '84 -13 Anchor Ter -Rchstr 14617 **Fx:**266-6574
(212) 248-8800 .. **Callan,** Paul F '76 (Callan KB&B LLP) -1 Whitehall -NY 10004
(516) 227-2260 .. **Callan,** Paul F '76 (Callan KB&B LLP) -333 Earle Ovngton Blvd -Uniondale 11553
(516) 248-1840 .. **Callan,** Thos J '67 -320 Old Cntry Rd -Gdn Cty 11530 **Fx:**294-1767
(716) 204-2400 .. **Callanan,** Casey '84 %SJ Baum,PC -220 Nrthpnte Pkwy Bx1291 -Buffalo 14240 **Fx:**204-4600
(845) 744-5934 .. **Callanan,** John W '84 -269 Hardenburgh Rd Bx147 -Pine Bush 12566 **Fx:**744-6448
(585) 546-7830 .. **Callanan,** Karen Smith '83 -36 W Main -Rchstr 14614
(512) 921-9640 .. **Callanan,** Kevin M '96 Gemini Pharmaceuticals -87 Modular Av -Commack 11725
(716) 845-3630 .. **Callanan,** Margaret C '87 %Atty Grievance Comm -438 Main -Buffalo 14202 **Fx:**856-2701
(315) 724-1600 .. **Callanen Foley & Hobika,LLP** -1417 Genesee -Utica 13501 **Fx:**735-0521
(212) 307-5500 .. **Callari,** Carollynn H G '95 (Venable LLP) -1270 Av of Amer -NY 10020
(516) 364-7900 .. **Callari,** Michl III '97 Epstein F&G -45 Crsswys Park Dr W -Woodbury 11797
(212) 809-4220 .. **Callaway,** Danl C '94 (Goldstein Law Grp,PC) -61 Bway -NY 10006 **Fx:**809-4228
(212) 480-1600 .. **Calle,** G Victoria '98 Calle & Assoc -11 E Bway -NY 10038 **Fx:**480-1611
(631) 273-6222 .. **Calle,** Maureen D '02 -1836 5th Av -Bay Shr 11706
(607) 656-2311 .. **Callea,** Louis J '86 Raymond Corp -20 S Canal Bx130 -Greene 13778 **Fx:**656-9005
(585) 425-5210 .. **Callear,** Chas L '81 Maximus Federal Srvcs -50 Square Dr -Victor 14564 **Fx:**425-5292
(718) 286-2000 .. **Callender,** Glenda '87 %Leg Aid -120-46 Qns Blvd -Kew Gdns 11415 **Fx:**286-2286
(212) 644-4420 .. **Callender,** Melissa R '95 %Fabiani C&H,LLP -570 Lex Av -NY 10022
(718) 466-3000 .. **Callender,** Tracia C '99 %Civil Ct -1118 Grnd Cncrs -Bronx 10456 **Fx:**466-3006
(212) 328-4641 .. **Calleo,** Peter J '02 Arch Ins Grp -1 Lbrty Plz -NY 10006
(718) 438-2525 .. **Caller,** Carl N '85 (NC Caller,PC) -4309 13th Av -Brklyn 11219 **Fx:**972-4154
(585) 232-4840 .. **Calleri,** Angelo T '62 -95 Bittner -Rchstr 14604 **Fx:**546-3622
(585) 454-4060 .. **Callery,** Catherine M '83 %Empire Justice Ctr -1 W Main -Rchstr 14614 **Fx:**454-4019
(212) 878-7049 .. **Calley,** Danl P '98 %MTA -347 Mad Av -NY 10017 **Fx:**878-0162
(315) 733-0455 .. **Calli Calli & Cully** -510 Bleecker -Utica 13501 **Fx:**733-4301
(315) 733-0455 .. **Calli Calli & Cully** -Fletcher Rd -Old Forge 13420 **Fx:**733-4301
(212) 265-6888 .. **Calli,** Lawr A '05 %Porzio B&N,PC -156 W 56th -NY 10019
(315) 733-0455 .. **Calli,** Robt R '10 %Calli C&C -510 Bleecker -Utica 13501
(315) 733-0455 .. **Calli,** Wm S '49 (Calli C&C) -Fletcher Rd -Old Forge 13420
(315) 733-0455 .. **Calli,** Wm S '49 (Calli C&C) -510 Bleecker -Utica 13501
(315) 733-0455 .. **Calli,** Wm S Jr. '93 (Calli C&C) -510 Bleecker -Utica 13501
(315) 733-0455 .. **Calli,** Wm S Jr. '93 (Calli C&C) -Fletcher Rd -Old Forge 13420
(516) 229-6000 .. **Callies,** Lisa E '93 %R Lau & Assoc -300 Jericho Quad Bx9040 -Jericho 11753 **Fx:**229-6167
(631) 390-0010 .. **Callinan,** Michl A '03 (Bruno G&S,LLP) -445 Broad Hollow Rd -Melvll 11747
(516) 489-6959 .. **Calliste,** Gregory Jr. '04 %F Brewington -556 Peninsula Blvd -Hempstd 11550 **Fx:**489-6958
(212) 986-3663 .. **Callo,** Dominick F '60 -295 Mad Av -NY 10017 **Fx:**972-8572
(716) 856-5500 .. **Callocchia,** Frank C '04 %Damon M LLP -200 Delaware Av -Buffalo 14202
(212) 225-2000 .. **Callow,** Amy Mikolajczyk '08 %Cleary GS&H -1 Lbrty Plz -NY 10006
(212) 285-2290 .. **Calluori,** Jos '79 -225 Bway -NY 10007 **Fx:**964-4506
(212) 267-6659 .. **Callwood,** June B '77 -305 Bway -NY 10007 **Fx:**732-2191
(718) 222-8880 .. **Cally,** Diana J '97 (Jones JO) -45 Main -Brklyn 11201
(914) 683-3933 .. **Cally,** Wm V '94 (W Cally,PC) -50 Main -White Plns 10606 **Fx:**683-7955
(212) 909-6000 .. **Calman,** Camille '07 %Debevoise & P LLP -919 3rd Av -NY 10022
(212) 461-2323 .. **Calmann,** Arnold B '81 (Saiber LLC) -44 Wall -NY 10005
(845) 473-4440 .. **Calnero,** Shari '97 Scenic Hudson -1 Civic Ctr Plz -Poughkeepsie 12601
(646) 823-7196 .. **Calone,** David L '00 Jove Equity Prtnrs -69 Clinton -Babylon 11702
(718) 520-2859 .. **Caloras,** Robt '86 %Hon J Robinson -125-01 Qns Blvd -Kew Gdns 11415
(917) 545-3500 .. **Calotta,** John G '82 (J Calotta,PC) -Bx3223 -NY 10008
(212) 841-1000 .. **Caloza,** Alexis I '09 %Covington & B LLP -620 8th Av -NY 10018
(845) 454-2569 .. **Caltagirone,** Paul '81 (Sall C&C) -3 Cannon -Poughkeepsie 12601
(212) 878-8000 .. **Calto,** Jos T '99 Cnsl Clifford C LLP -31 W 52nd -NY 10019
(631) 501-3012 .. **Calvacca,** Anthony S '85 %J Humphreys -3 Huntngtn Quad Bx9028 -Melvll 11747 **Fx:**501-3085
(516) 683-1000 .. **Calvanese,** Peter J '85 %Abstracts, Inc -585 Stewart Av -Gdn Cty 11530 **Fx:**683-0089
(212) 261-8000 .. **Calvano,** Heather K '99 (Mendes & M,LLP) -750 7th Av -NY 10019
(212) 808-7800 .. **Calvaruso,** Andrea L '97 (Kelley D&W LLP) -101 Park Av -NY 10178
(212) 506-5000 .. **Calvaruso,** Jos A '75 (Orrick H&S LLP) -51 W 52nd -NY 10019
(646) 312-3593 .. **Calvelli,** Maria DiMeo '89 %Baruch College -17 Lex Av Bx 316 -NY 10010
(212) 393-9441 .. **Calvello,** Susan '84 -110 Wall -NY 10005
(212) 619-4350 .. **Calvert,** Adam C '10 %Newman MKGH,PC -14 Wall -NY 10005
(845) 676-3986 .. **Calvert,** Elizabeth S '85 -165 Delaware Av -Andes 13731 **Fx:**676-3987
(212) 906-1200 .. **Calvert,** Sarah M '09 %Latham & W -885 3rd Av -NY 10022
(315) 451-7955 .. **Calvert,** Virginia Freeman '83 Melvin & C,PC -6834 Buckley Rd -N Syracuse 13212 **Fx:**451-7958
(585) 594-9450 .. **Calvete,** Michl L '73 -3161 Union -N Chili 14514 **Fx:**594-8883
(914) 963-8852 .. **Calvi,** Carlo J '80 -42 Valentine -Ynkrs 10704 **Fx:**963-8156
(914) 376-8450 .. **Calvi,** Janet Ann '90 %School 25 -579 Warburton Av -Ynkrs 10701
(914) 813-5800 .. **Calvi,** Michelle A '07 %DA -475 North Av -New Rchll 10801 **Fx:**813-5806
(347) 645-7649 .. **Calvin,** Jane E '00 Corcoran Grp -49 E 10th -NY 10003
(718) 340-4200 .. **Calvo,** Janet M '74 %CUNY Law Schl -65-21 Main -Flushng 11367 **Fx:**340-4482
(845) 294-9392 .. **Calzaretta,** Craig M '97 -37 Murray Av -Goshen 10924
(631) 439-4690 .. **Cama,** Franklin A '74 %F Cama,PC -4250 Vets Mem'l Hwy -Holbrook 11741 **Fx:**439-4696
(845) 639-7800 .. **Cama,** Spenta R '00 %Mandel K&B,LLP -210 Route 303 -Vly Cottage 10989
(212) 878-8434 .. **Camacho,** Alejandro E '85 (Clifford C LLP) -31 W 52nd -NY 10019
(212) 947-4999 .. **Camacho,** Andrea Sacco '92 (Camacho MM,LLP) -350 5th Av -NY 10118
(212) 661-7300 .. **Camacho,** Cynthia P '99 %Malapero & P LLP -295 Mad Av -NY 10017
(212) 947-4999 .. **Camacho Mauro Mulholland,LLP** -350 5th Av -NY 10118 **Fx:**947-8099

(212) 937-4000 .. **Camacho,** Nelson '08 %Fitzpatrick & HTCPA,LLP -12 E 49th -NY 10017
(718) 876-9065 .. **Camacho,** Valerie J '95 -100 Kirshon Av -Staten Isl 10314 **Fx:**907-7917
(212) 331-5134 .. **Camaiore,** Marguerite Ann '93 HRA -180 Water -NY 10038
(212) 530-5000 .. **Camara,** Felipe R L '09 %Milbank TH&M LLP -1 Chase Manh Plz -NY 10005
(212) 801-2141 .. **Camarata,** Candace M '06 %Greenberg T,LLP -200 Park Av -NY 10166
(516) 564-1740 .. **Camarda,** Catherine M '93 -392 Woodfld Rd -W Hempstead 11552 **Fx:**564-8163
(516) 482-4567 .. **Camardella & Brown,LLC** -98 Cuttermill Rd -Gt Neck 11021 **Fx:**482-4599
(516) 482-4567 .. **Camardella,** James V '69 (Camardella & B,LLC) -98 Cuttermill Rd -Gt Neck 11021
(631) 247-0404 .. **Camardella,** Matthew J '99 (Jackson L LLP) -58 S Srvc Rd -Melvll 11747
(315) 252-3846 .. **Camardo,** Jos A Jr. '87 (Camardo Law Firm,PC) -127 Genesee -Auburn 13021 **Fx:**252-3508
(315) 426-1648 .. **Cambareri & Cambareri, LLP** -305 Mntgmry -Syracuse 13202 **Fx:**426-1676
(315) 426-1648 .. **Cambareri,** Dom '87 (Cambareri & C,LLP) -305 Mntgmry -Syracuse 13202
(914) 631-6900 .. **Cambareri,** Jo-Ann '01 %Guttridge & C,PC -303 S Bway -Tarrytwn 10591 **Fx:**631-6644
(516) 712-4000 .. **Cambareri,** Jos V '93 (Milber MP&S LLP) -1000 Woodbury Rd -Woodbury 11797
(845) 638-3012 .. **Cambareri,** Mark P '97 %R Neimark & Assoc,LLP -37 Congers Rd -New Cty 10956 **Fx:**638-3093
(315) 426-1648 .. **Cambareri,** Stefano '90 (Cambareri & C,LLP) -305 Mntgmry -Syracuse 13202
(315) 471-3151 .. **Cambier,** Thos C '06 %Hancock & E,LLP -1500 AXA Twr I Bx4976 -Syracuse 13221
(212) 225-2000 .. **Cambouris,** Alexandra E '10 %Cleary GS&H -1 Lbrty Plz -NY 10006
(914) 390-8007 .. **Cambouris,** Arthur T '71 %NYPA -123 Main -White Plns 10601 **Fx:**390-8038
(718) 250-2000 .. **Cambre,** Caren M '01 DA -350 Jay -Brklyn 11201 **Fx:**250-2314
(212) 558-4000 .. **Cambria,** Allison J '08 %Sullivan & C LLP -125 Broad -NY 10004
(718) 227-0630 .. **Cambria,** Anthony R '93 -422 Retford Av -Staten Isl 10312 **Fx:**356-0404
(212) 210-9583 .. **Cambria,** John F '77 (Alston & B LLP) -90 Park Av -NY 10016
(716) 849-1333 .. **Cambria,** Paul J Jr. '73 (Lipsitz GSC LLP) -42 Delaware Av -Buffalo 14202
(516) 572-2000 .. **Cambridge,** Beatrice W '84 %DA -99 Main -Hempstd 11550 **Fx:**572-2606
(315) 484-1200 .. **Cambs,** Denise P '86 Cambs Law Firm,LLP -3208 W Genesee -Syracuse 13219 **Fx:**484-7200
(516) 466-6500 .. **Cambs,** Peter J '84 Parker WA LLP -6 Hrbr Park Dr S -Pt Wash 11050 **Fx:**466-6665
(212) 873-8774 .. **Camche,** Joel T '60 -150 West End Av -NY 10023 **Fx:**873-3295
(516) 802-7007 .. **Camelo,** Dianne M '86 (Levy S&C,LLP) -1425 RXR Plz -Uniondale 11556
(212) 704-1343 .. **Camera,** Nicholas J '73 Cnsl Interpublic Grp -1114 Av of Amer -NY 10036 **Fx:**704-1201
(845) 562-0203 .. **Camera,** Robt J '84 (Finkelstein & Prtnrs,LLP) -1279 Route 300 Bx1111 -Newburgh 12550
(212) 773-1521 .. **Camera,** Susan C '81 %Ernst & Young,LLP -5 Times Sq -NY 10036
(212) 480-4800 .. **Camerini,** David C '98 (Fox H&C LLP) -825 3rd Av -NY 10022
(212) 480-4800 .. **Camerini,** Ezequiel A '75 (Fox H&C LLP) -825 3rd Av -NY 10022
(914) 640-3666 .. **Cameron,** Brian E '00 Starwood Hotels -111 Wstchstr Av -White Plns 10601
(631) 589-0083 .. **Cameron,** Bryan E '94 -52 Main -Sayvll 11782 **Fx:**589-0728
(212) 468-8000 .. **Cameron,** Danusia K '08 %Morrison & F LLP -1290 Av of Amer -NY 10104
(212) 233-3348 .. **Cameron,** Donald E '84 -139 Fulton -NY 10038
(914) 945-3244 .. **Cameron,** Douglas W '84 IBM -Bx218 -Yorktwn Hts 10598
(212) 244-3333 .. **Cameron,** Duncan G '92 (Donovan H LLP) -1350 Bway -NY 10018
(212) 371-8855 .. **Cameron,** Gordon N '04 %Stikeman E LLP -445 Park Av -NY 10022
(646) 840-6666 .. **Cameron & Hornbostel** -230 Park Av -NY 10169 **Fx:**304-1080
(718) 667-0897 .. **Cameron,** James N '66 -74 Lincoln Av -Staten Isl 10306 **Fx:**987-0742
(716) 853-8579 .. **Cameron,** Jane Coleman '88 %Dept of Law -350 Main Pl Twr -Buffalo 14202 **Fx:**853-8571
(845) 291-2107 .. **Cameron,** John B '68 Hon E Slobod -255-285 Main -Goshen 10924 **Fx:**291-2595
(607) 847-8888 .. **Cameron,** John D '89 -12 Green BxE -New Berlin 13411 **Fx:**847-8492
(212) 852-7000 .. **Cameron,** Michl G '05 %News Corp -1211 Av of Amer -NY 10036 **Fx:**852-7147
(212) 468-4800 .. **Cameron,** Sean P '07 %Davis & G LLP -1740 Bway -NY 10019
(212) 627-8100 .. **Cameron,** Susan J '07 %Levy R,PC -80 8th Av -NY 10011
(516) 409-6200 .. **Cameron,** Timothy D '05 %Furey KWM&C,PC -2174 Jackson Av -Seafrd 11783
(212) 474-1000 .. **Cameron,** Timothy G '99 (Cravath S&M LLP) -825 8th Av -NY 10019
(212) 297-6113 .. **Camhi,** Brooke A '06 (Camhi & M LLC) -420 Lex Av -NY 10170 **Fx:**479-2521
(212) 588-9460 .. **Camhi,** Evan J '05 %Kent & M,PC -420 Lex Av -NY 10170 **Fx:**588-9818
(646) 613-4000 .. **Camhi,** Jason A '99 Getty Images -75 Varick -NY 10013
(516) 746-8000 .. **Camhi,** Stanley A '80 (Jaspan S LLP) -300 Grdn City Plz -Gdn Cty 11530
(631) 422-2594 .. **Camillery,** Rachel A '00 (RA Camillery,PC) -103 Cooper -Babylon 11702 **Fx:**422-2784
(212) 788-6992 .. **Camilo,** Lisette '03 NYC Council -250 Bway -NY 10007
(212) 286-8585 .. **Caminiti,** Danielle E '01 %Heidell PM&B,LLP -99 Park Av -NY 10016
(631) 765-5900 .. **Caminiti,** Paul A '56 -53345 Main Rd Bx992 -Southold 11971 **Fx:**765-5902
(212) 687-8080 .. **Caminiti,** Paul J '93 (Sard Verbinnen & Co) -630 3rd Av -NY 10017
(718) 410-0940 .. **Camins & Hirsch PLLC** -930 Grnd Cncrs -Bronx 10451 **Fx:**410-0941
(718) 410-0940 .. **Camins,** Leslie L '92 (Camins & H PLLC) -930 Grnd Cncrs -Bronx 10451
(516) 741-0005 .. **Camisa,** Anthony M '99 (AM Camisa PC) -323 Willis Av -Mineola 11501 **Fx:**(866) 831-2098
(212) 403-1000 .. **Cammaker,** Joshua R '95 (Wachtell LR&K) -51 W 52nd -NY 10019
(212) 248-3140 .. **Cammarano,** Marita Erbeck '03 %Drinker B&R LLP -140 Bway -NY 10005
(631) 757-7471 .. **Cammarasana,** Enza M '93 -18 Martin Pl -Northprt 11768 **Fx:**757-3434
(516) 746-6066 .. **Cammarasana,** James M '95 (Cammarasana & B) -500 Old Cntry Rd -Gdn Cty 11530 **Fx:**746-6411
(516) 922-4660 .. **Cammarata,** James '98 -Bx180 -Oyster Bay 11771
(585) 325-7440 .. **Cammarata,** Ross J '78 (Kaman BMJ&G LLP) -135 Corp Woods -Rchstr 14623
(212) 244-2999 .. **Cammarosano,** Jos R '82 (Kopff N&D LLP) -440 9th Av -NY 10001
(917) 421-4637 .. **Cammarota,** Nicole F '05 %IRS Ofc Chf Cnsl -33 Maiden Ln -NY 10038
(212) 490-0900 .. **Cammisa,** Zjantelle '04 OfCnsl Margolis Law Firm -11 E 44th -NY 10017
(718) 222-8880 .. **Camo,** Lauren A '06 %Jones JO -45 Main -Brklyn 11201
(212) 312-2260 .. **Camp,** Courtney C '09 Leg Aid -60 Lafayette -NY 10013 **Fx:**349-0874
(518) 862-5555 .. **Camp,** John W II '00 OfCnsl A Dell -450 New Karner Rd -Albany 12205 **Fx:**862-5545
(212) 727-6184 .. **Camp,** Katherine E '02 Douglas Elliman,LLC -26 W 17th -NY 10011
(212) 610-6300 .. **Camp,** Lawton Mortimer '96 (Allen & O) -1221 Av of Amer -NY 10020
(212) 549-2632 .. **Camp,** Susan Talcott '95 ACLU -125 Broad -NY 10004 **Fx:**549-2652
(716) 852-4191 .. **Campagna,** Dennis J '88 Cornell Univ -9120 Michl Douglas Dr -Clarence Ctr 14032 **Fx:**741-7056
(631) 501-5700 .. **Campagna,** Giuseppina M '05 %Carter DF&S LLP -445 Broadhallow Rd -Melvll 11747
(631) 737-8200 .. **Campagna,** Thos K '87 -4949 Express Dr N -Ronkonkoma 11779 **Fx:**737-8687
(212) 788-2903 .. **Campagna,** Vanessa R '08 %Law Dept -100 Church -NY 10007 **Fx:**788-0367
(212) 354-5650 .. **Campaign,** H John '55 (Graham C PC) -36 W 44th -NY 10036
(716) 843-5700 .. **Campana,** Paul J '83 %US Atty -138 Delaware Av -Buffalo 14202 **Fx:**551-3052
(845) 221-4099 .. **Campanaro,** Patricia L '85 (Campanaro & T) -867 Route 376 Bx123 -Hopewell Junct 12533 **Fx:**221-1570
(914) 686-0634 .. **Campanaro,** Steven A '03 -244 Wstchstr Av -West Harrison 10604
(212) 908-1729 .. **Campanella,** Janis '97 %Waterhouse Invstr Srvcs -100 Wall -NY 10005
(516) 364-9578 .. **Campanella,** Lewis J '68 -140 The Knoll -Syosset 11791
(585) 454-2181 .. **Campanella,** Mark M '02 %Trevett CS&A,PC -2 State -Rchstr 14614
(607) 733-1580 .. **Campanella,** Ottavio '94 -311 Lk -Elmira 14901 **Fx:**732-0479
(716) 542-5413 .. **Campanella,** Santo '86 %Nicholas PSB&Z -12364 Main Rd Bx176 -Akron 14001
(516) 739-0000 .. **Campanella,** Timothy J '96 %Martyn T&M -330 Old Cntry Rd -Mineola 11501
(516) 746-1600 .. **Campanelli,** Andrew J '93 (Campanelli & Assoc,PC) -623 Stewart Av -Gdn Cty 11530 **Fx:**746-2611
(718) 896-2500 .. **Campanelli,** Edw L '04 ACQC -16121 Jamaica Av -Jamaica 11432 **Fx:**459-7405
(212) 816-7559 .. **Campanelli,** Jeanne M '91 Citigroup -388 Greenwich -NY 10013
(347) 296-1455 .. **Campanelli,** Joy '93 Hon D Vaughan Supreme Ct -360 Adams -Brklyn 11201
(212) 480-5284 .. **Campanelli,** Michl J '92 %Insurance Dept -25 Beaver -NY 10004 **Fx:**480-5272
(315) 363-0585 .. **Campanie,** Abigail N '10 %Campanie & W PLLC -60 E State Bx70 -Sherrill 13461 **Fx:**363-1952
(315) 363-0585 .. **Campanie,** S John '79 (Campanie & W PLLC) -60 E State Bx70 -Sherrill 13461 **Fx:**363-1952
(212) 766-1888 .. **Campanile,** Michl V '92 (Morris DA&F) -2 Rector -NY 10006
(518) 786-8000 .. **Campano,** Deborah Fox '81 -17 British Amer Blvd -Latham 12110
(212) 773-6511 .. **Campano,** Fredk W '95 Ernst & Young LLP -5 Times Sq -NY 10036
(212) 746-1360 .. **Campano,** John V '85 %NY Presbyterian Hsptl -525 E 68th Bx88 -NY 10065 **Fx:**746-8603
(516) 741-6266 .. **Campano,** Teresa '04 %McCabe CM&F,LLP -346 Westbury Av Bx9000 -Carle Pl 11514
(315) 376-9445 .. **Campany,** Thos A '76 Campany Law Firm,PLLC -7571 State Bx311 -Lowvll 13367 **Fx:**376-9479
(631) 242-1888 .. **Campasano,** Nicholas V '72 -2000 Deer Prk Av -Deer Pk 11729
(631) 242-1888 .. **Campasano,** Vincent '88 -2000 Deer Prk Av -Deer Pk 11729
(585) 275-5211 .. **Campbell,** Amy T '04 U of R Med Ctr-Psychiatry -300 Crittenden Blvd -Rchstr 14642
(212) 661-2490 .. **Campbell,** Andrew P '08 %Delany & O -80 Broad -NY 10004
(716) 849-6500 .. **Campbell,** Ann M '92 (Brown & T,LLC) -14 Lafayette Sq -Buffalo 14203
(212) 416-8000 .. **Campbell,** Brant B '00 Dept of Law -120 Bway -NY 10271
(212) 504-6000 .. **Campbell,** Bret A '96 (Cadwalader W&T LLP) -1 World Fncl Ctr -NY 10281
(212) 310-8000 .. **Campbell,** Caitlyn M '06 %Weil G&M LLP -767 5th Av -NY 10153
(212) 480-2689 .. **Campbell,** Camielle A M '99 %Insurance Dept -25 Beaver -NY 10004 **Fx:**480-5272
(914) 406-7000 .. **Campbell,** Catherine S '90 %Rand RR&G LLP -50 Main -White Plns 10606
(716) 842-2166 .. **Campbell,** Christine V '01 %Workers Comp Bd -107 Delaware Av -Buffalo 14202
(212) 265-6888 .. **Campbell,** D Jeffrey '87 (Porzio B&N,PC) -156 W 56th -NY 10019
(585) 263-1000 .. **Campbell,** Dana K '98 %Nixon P LLP -1100 Clinton Sq -Rchstr 14604
(516) 352-0300 .. **Campbell,** Danl T '77 (Campbell & Assoc) -99 Tulip Av -Floral Pk 11001 **Fx:**775-0352
(212) 566-7520 .. **Campbell,** Denise '93 Campbell Lgl Assoc,PLLC -111 John -NY 10038 **Fx:**566-7522
(212) 252-0300 .. **Campbell,** Denise M '01 %Kagan LLLG&C,LLP -200 Mad Av -NY 10016

(607) 273-3666 .. **Campbell,** Diane L '99 %Leg Srvcs -215 N Cayuga -Ithaca 14850 **Fx:**273-5521
(607) 723-5341 .. **Campbell,** Donald R '73 SpclCnsl Hinman H&K,LLP -80 Exchange Bx5250 -Bnghmtn 13902
(914) 285-1400 .. **Campbell,** Donald S '95 Cnsl Danzig F&D -1 N Bway -White Plns 10601
(914) 948-7700 .. **Campbell,** Edgar P '59 -2 Mad Av -Valhalla 10595 **Fx:**948-7795
(212) 267-3600 .. **Campbell,** Emily '93 (The Campbell Firm PLLC) -80 Broad -NY 10004 **Fx:**267-3601
(212) 752-5200 .. **Campbell,** Emily Thornton '96 Greene Levin Snyder LLC -150 E 58th -NY 10155
(516) 997-7330 .. **Campbell,** Harold '00 %Baxter S&S,PC -99 N Bway -Hicksvll 11801
(718) 882-2681 .. **Campbell,** Hugh W '83 (Rodman & C,PC) -1428 E Gun Hill Rd -Bronx 10469
(914) 238-3555 .. **Campbell,** Jacqueline R '92 %Campbell Engineering -25 Mem'l Dr Bx255 -Chappaqua 10514
(212) 381-9700 .. **Campbell,** James R '97 %Lambos Firm,LLP -303 S Bway -Tarrytwn 10591 **Fx:**797-9213
(585) 624-5030 .. **Campbell,** James W Jr. '93 (Kruk & C) -7312 E Main Bx30-A -Lima 14485 **Fx:**624-3972
(914) 304-4353 .. **Campbell,** Jay S '04 %Lynch S, PLLC -75 S Bway -White Plns 10601 **Fx:**304-4378
(212) 816-6186 .. **Campbell,** Jeanne A '02 Citigroup Global Mrkts -388 Greenwich -NY 10013
(914) 833-9785 .. **Campbell,** John E '04 (Tilem & C,LLP) -188 E Post Rd -White Plns 10601 **Fx:**833-9788
(516) 571-3800 .. **Campbell,** John F III '06 %DA -262 Old Cntry Rd -Mineola 11501 **Fx:**248-9479
(646) 264-3650 .. **Campbell,** John G '95 %US Dept of Labor -201 Varick -NY 10014 **Fx:**264-3660
(212) 788-1203 .. **Campbell,** John M '06 %Law Dept -100 Church -NY 10007 **Fx:**788-0367
(212) 227-1980 .. **Campbell,** Jos P '88 (Meltzer FM&C) -225 Bway -NY 10007
(718) 276-6996 .. **Campbell,** Judy T '02 -11401 F Lewis Blvd -Cambria Hts 11411 **Fx:**276-7408
(845) 562-0203 .. **Campbell,** Kara Lyn '99 %Finkelstein & Prtnrs,LLP -1279 Route 300 Bx1111 -Newburgh 12550
(212) 232-1300 .. **Campbell,** Karen L '88 (Lewis BB&S LLP) -77 Water -NY 10005
(914) 948-7700 .. **Campbell,** Kathleen E '93 OfCnsl E Campbell -2 Mad Av -Valhalla 10595 **Fx:**948-7795
(315) 453-8300 .. **Campbell,** Kathleen S '97 %State Ins Fund -1045 7th N -Liverpool 13088 **Fx:**453-6540
(631) 754-1686 .. **Campbell,** Kevin B '86 -315 Woodbine Av -Northprt 11768
(516) 741-5050 .. **Campbell,** Kevin M '88 %Fidelity Natl Title Ins -1415 Kellum Pl -Gdn Cty 11530 **Fx:**741-5363
(585) 454-5050 .. **Campbell,** Kimberly J '00 %Brown & H -2 State -Rchstr 14614
(212) 663-6609 .. **Campbell,** Laura B '88 %Envrnmtl Law Intl -740 West End Av -NY 10025 **Fx:**663-0944
(212) 728-8000 .. **Campbell,** Leah C '83 (Willkie F&G LLP) -787 7th Av -NY 10019
(212) 259-8000 .. **Campbell,** Leah M '02 %Dewey & L LLP -1301 Av of Amer -NY 10019
(315) 428-9393 .. **Campbell,** Linda M '82 -333 E Onondaga -Syracuse 13202 **Fx:**422-7741
(516) 222-0121 .. **Campbell,** Lois S '80 -600 Old Cntry Rd -Gdn Cty 11530 **Fx:**222-0828
(212) 596-9000 .. **Campbell,** Margaret Harrison '06 %Ropes & G LLP -1211 Av of Amer -NY 10036
(914) 948-7700 .. **Campbell,** Mark A '86 OfCnsl E Campbell -2 Mad Av -Valhalla 10595 **Fx:**948-7795
(212) 483-2323 .. **Campbell,** Mary G '85 %JP Morgan Chase -345 Park Av -NY 10154
(212) 720-5038 .. **Campbell,** Michl V '97 %Fed Reserve Bk -33 Lbrty -NY 10045 **Fx:**785-5748
(212) 471-8500 .. **Campbell,** Natalie E '10 %Herzfeld & R,PC -125 Broad -NY 10004
(718) 523-6868 .. **Campbell,** Nathalee Venice '05 %Comm Mediation Svcs -89-64 163rd -Jamaica 11432
(315) 422-9951 .. **Campbell,** Patricia C '97 -307 S Townsend -Syracuse 13202 **Fx:**234-4244
(212) 589-4200 .. **Campbell,** Patrick T '09 %Baker & H LLP -45 Rckfllr Plz -NY 10111
(585) 344-2580 .. **Campbell,** Paula Ann '93 %Cnty Atty -5130 E Main Rd -Batavia 14020 **Fx:**343-5548
(212) 735-3000 .. **Campbell,** Peter I '05 %Skadden ASM&F LLP -4 Times Sq -NY 10036
(716) 992-9300 .. **Campbell,** R Colin '92 (Campbell & S,LLP) -8274 N Main -Eden 14057
(716) 856-4000 .. **Campbell,** Richd F '76 (Hodgson R LLP) -140 Pearl -Buffalo 14202
(716) 759-2952 .. **Campbell,** Richd L '73 (Campbell & Assoc,LLP) -10535 Main -Clarence 14031 **Fx:**759-8609
(646) 346-7203 .. **Campbell,** Roger C '79 BGC Partners Inc -199 Water -NY 10038
(212) 238-4800 .. **Campbell,** Roxanna S '01 (Landman CB&F,PC) -120 Bway -NY 10271
(607) 723-5341 .. **Campbell,** Sarah Grace '92 SpclCnsl Hinman H&K,LLP -80 Exchange Bx5250 -Bnghmtn 13902
(212) 878-8000 .. **Campbell,** Sarah N '01 %Clifford C LLP -31 W 52nd -NY 10019
(212) 552-2363 .. **Campbell,** Scott G '76 JP Morgan Chase & Co -1 Chase Manh Plz -NY 10005
(212) 449-1969 .. **Campbell,** Sean E '86 %Merrill Lynch -220 Bway -NY 10038
(718) 262-7100 .. **Campbell,** Shannon R N '95 %Civil Ct -89-17 Sutphin Blvd -Jamaica 11435 **Fx:**262-7107
(716) 992-9300 .. **Campbell & Shelton,LLP** -8274 N Main -Eden 14057 **Fx:**992-9350
(212) 532-8100 .. **Campbell,** Soraya '96 %Stern & M,LLP -115 Bway -NY 10006
(315) 218-8000 .. **Campbell,** Stephanie M '10 %Bond S&K,PLLC -1 Lincoln Ctr -Syracuse 13202
(212) 837-6000 .. **Campbell,** Susan M '76 (Hughes H&R LLP) -1 Bttry Pk Plz -NY 10004
(212) 344-1500 .. **Campbell,** Thos M '84 (Smith C,LLP) -110 Wall -NY 10005
(212) 715-9100 .. **Campbell,** Valerie G '88 SpclCnsl Kramer LN&F,LLP -1177 Av of Amer -NY 10036
(845) 858-0990 .. **Campbell,** Victoria Brace '88 (V Campbell,PC) -18 E Broome Bx814 -Pt Jervis 12771 **Fx:**856-2118
(585) 621-1820 .. **Campbell,** Vincent B '69 -1100 Long Pond Rd -Rchstr 14626
(914) 686-1700 .. **Campbell,** Wanda Smith '94 %O'Connor R,LLP -200 Mamaroneck Av -White Plns 10601
(212) 806-5400 .. **Campbell,** Wm '86 (Stroock &S&L LLP) -180 Maiden Ln -NY 10038
(212) 351-4000 .. **Campbell,** Wm R '77 (Gibson D&C LLP) -200 Park Av -NY 10166
(212) 909-6000 .. **Campbell,** Woodrow W Jr. '74 (Debevoise & P LLP) -919 3rd Av -NY 10022
(212) 661-7300 .. **Campbell,** Youngmin Oh '04 %Malapero & P LLP -295 Mad Av -NY 10017
(212) 804-5776 .. **Campbell Priveterre,** Joyce D '98 -110 Wall -NY 10005 **Fx:**943-2300
(631) 501-7214 .. **Camperlengo,** John N '89 Gentiva Health Srvcs -3 Huntngtn Quadrangle -Melvll 11747
(212) 306-7234 .. **Campese,** Matthew '96 %NYC Ofc Labor Relations -40 Rector -NY 10006
(212) 336-2000 .. **Campi,** J Ella '08 %Patterson BW&T LLP -1133 Av of Amer -NY 10036
(516) 741-7676 .. **Campiglia,** Gabriella M '06 %Miranda SSSV LLP -240 Mineola Blvd -Mineola 11501
(518) 885-2263 .. **Campion,** Patrick J '05 %DA -25 W High -Ballston Spa 12020 **Fx:**884-8627
(631) 342-9100 .. **Campion,** Phyllis '87 -300 Rabro Dr -Hauppauge 11788
(212) 248-3140 .. **Campion,** Thos F Jr. '88 (Drinker B&R LLP) -140 Bway -NY 10005
(212) 425-9300 .. **Campione,** Ronald J '05 %Bressler A&R,PC -17 State -NY 10004
(212) 446-7000 .. **Campisano,** Mark S '83 %McKinsey & Co -55 E 52nd -NY 10055 **Fx:**688-9521
(212) 509-9400 .. **Campise,** James F '75 (Cozen O) -45 Bway Atrium -NY 10006
(212) 687-1980 .. **Campisi,** Jeffrey P '01 %Kaplan F&K LLP -850 3rd Av -NY 10022
(212) 962-2800 .. **Campisi,** Jos '96 (Schwartz G&C,LLP) -90 Broad -NY 10004
(516) 465-8090 .. **Campisi,** Lauren E '98 %North Shore-LIJ Hlth Systm -145 Community Dr -Gt Neck 11021 **Fx:**465-8013
(212) 309-6000 .. **Campisi,** Lisa M '93 OfCnsl Morgan L&B LLP -101 Park Av -NY 10178
(516) 622-9200 .. **Campisi,** Philip J Jr. '98 (Westerman BEM&S,LLP) -1201 RXR Plz -Uniondale 11553
(212) 216-8000 .. **Campitiello,** Peter '96 (Tarter K&D LLP) -1350 Bway -NY 10018
(518) 436-6001 .. **Campito,** Laurie A '92 -120 Bway -Albany 12204 **Fx:**436-4992
(518) 786-1800 .. **Campito,** Paul J '79 OfCnsl Flink S LLC -23 British Amer Blvd -Latham 12110 **Fx:**786-1969
(212) 809-7600 .. **Campo,** Chas J '01 %Cheven K&H -40 Wall -NY 10005
(631) 543-5031 .. **Campo,** Jerome A '54 -48 Sun Flower Dr -Hauppauge 11788
(212) 613-2091 .. **Campo,** John P '81 (Gibbons PC) -1 Penn Plz -NY 10119 **Fx:**554-9685
(212) 421-4100 .. **Campoli,** Michl T '01 %Pryor C LLP -7 Times Sq -NY 10036
(585) 428-7410 .. **Campolieto,** John M '98 %Law Dept -30 Church -Rchstr 14614 **Fx:**428-6950
(631) 738-9100 .. **Campolo,** Jos N '98 (Campolo M&M,LLP) -3340 Vets Mem'l Hwy -Bohemia 11716 **Fx:**738-0659
(212) 878-8000 .. **Campolonghi,** Stefano '08 %Clifford C LLP -31 W 52nd -NY 10019
(914) 241-6407 .. **Campolongo,** Robt P '91 %Merrill Lynch -105 S Bedford Rd -Mt Kisco 10549
(718) 724-1000 .. **Campomanes,** Arturo A '81 (Arthur & Assoc,Ltd) -1090 Coney Isl Av -Brklyn 11230 **Fx:**724-0232
(718) 250-2000 .. **Campomanes,** Caroline '01 %DA -350 Jay -Brklyn 11201 **Fx:**250-2314
(845) 450-5100 .. **Camporeale,** Carlo J '95 Kohl Construction Grp -225 N Route 303 -Congers 10920 **Fx:**450-5195
(212) 458-3477 .. **Camporeale,** Michl '03 AIGTS -175 Water -NY 10038
(212) 464-2423 .. **Camporine,** Garrett A '98 JP Morgan Private Bank -270 Park Av -NY 10017
(718) 454-4040 .. **Campos,** George C '57 (Campos & P,PC) -186-09 Union Tpk -Flushng 11366
(631) 207-4300 .. **Campos,** Mario A '00 -224 E Main -Patchogue 11772
(718) 454-4040 .. **Campos & Pavlides,PC** -186-09 Union Tpk -Flushng 11366 **Fx:**454-9413
(631) 277-2600 .. **Campos,** Victor M '89 -1215 Suffolk Av -Brentwd 11717 **Fx:**822-7700
(631) 421-4820 .. **Campos,** Victoria Luz '00 (V Campos,PC) -1677 NY Av -Huntngtn Sta 11746 **Fx:**421-2427
(718) 254-7000 .. **Campos,** Wm P '94 %US Atty -271 Cadman Plz E -Brklyn 11201 **Fx:**254-6479
(212) 709-8285 .. **Campos-Marquetti,** Roberto '88 (Campos-Marquetti & P,PLLC) -110 Wall -NY 10005 **Fx:**943-2300
(212) 541-2000 .. **Campriello,** Austin V '71 (Bryan C LLP) -1290 Av of Amer -NY 10104
(914) 769-9332 .. **Campriello,** Cristina M '79 -40 Nannahagan Rd -Plsntvll 10570
(212) 941-0792 .. **Campson,** Paul J '91 (Miller & C) -377 Bway -NY 10013 **Fx:**431-4460
(212) 902-0843 .. **Campuzano,** Consuelo I '99 Goldman Sachs -85 Broad -NY 10004
(212) 536-4222 .. **Camuffo,** Jessica Y '98 Ann Taylor -7 Times Sq -NY 10036
(718) 522-1969 .. **Camuso,** Henry F Jr. '85 -8225 3rd Av -Brklyn 11209
(212) 759-4888 .. **Canaan,** Eva '04 %Phillips L LLP -437 Mad Av -NY 10022
(212) 223-4000 .. **Canada,** Jerry '06 (Crowell & M LLP) -590 Mad Av -NY 10022
(718) 836-7800 .. **Canade,** Austen D '60 -7703 5th Av -Brklyn 11209
(631) 414-7040 .. **Canale,** Anadel '95 A Canale PC -1111 Route 110 -Farmngdl 11735 **Fx:**414-7038
(212) 716-5790 .. **Canale,** Anthony P '98 %Cohen Lgl Grp,LLC -230 Park Av -NY 10169
(518) 338-3404 .. **Canale,** Gregory V '90 -456 Bay Rd -Queensbury 12804 **Fx:**338-3409
(716) 856-1344 .. **Canale,** John F '48 SpclCnsl Bouvier Prtnrshp,LLP -350 Main -Buffalo 14202 **Fx:**856-1369
(518) 793-5108 .. **Canale,** Wm V '60 -6 Sherman Av Bx639 -Glens Fls 12801 **Fx:**793-3434
(212) 752-9700 .. **Canales,** Jason '05 %Gersten S LLP -600 Lex Av -NY 10022
(212) 878-8000 .. **Canales,** Paola A '08 %Clifford C LLP -31 W 52nd -NY 10019
(212) 686-7700 .. **Canarick,** Lisa B '08 %Mazur CR&S PC -1250 Bway -NY 10001
(518) 736-5533 .. **Canary,** Mark V '86 Hon R Aulisi -223 W Main -Johnstwn 12095 **Fx:**762-1158
(914) 993-9393 .. **Canavan,** Gerard F '88 %Stewart Title Ins -707 Wstchstr Av -White Plns 10604 **Fx:**997-1698
(212) 225-2000 .. **Canavan,** Jason G '08 %Cleary GS&H -1 Lbrty Plz -NY 10006

(631) 537-3100 .. **Canavan,** Kelly M '92 Cnsl Farrell F,PC -2488 Montauk Hwy Bx1980 -Brdghmptn 11932
(585) 546-5530 .. **Canavan,** Matthew J '79 %Thomson West -50 E Broad -Rchstr 14694
(212) 265-6888 .. **Canberg,** Sarah M '07 %Porzio B&N,PC -156 W 56th -NY 10019
(212) 885-5000 .. **Canby,** Margaret L '90 %Blank R LLP -405 Lex Av -NY 10174
(631) 234-2121 .. **Cancellare,** Chas G '91 -1770 Motor Pkwy -Islandia 11749
(516) 626-6500 .. **Cancellare,** Michl W '85 -76 Brookvll Rd -Muttontwn 11545
(516) 571-3800 .. **Cancellieri,** Robt L '09 %DA -262 Old Cntry Rd -Mineola 11501 **Fx:**248-9479
(315) 266-0030 .. **Cancilla,** Michl J '96 -1 Hopper -Utica 13501
(914) 969-7791 .. **Cancro,** Steven M '80 -67 Courter Av -Ynkrs 10705
(516) 739-7979 .. **Cancro,** Susannah M '99 %Hooghuis Inc -176 Mineola Blvd -Mineola 11501
(718) 852-5700 .. **Candal,** Luis F '76 -40 Wall -NY 10005 **Fx:**852-5760
(631) 577-7224 .. **Candee,** Don L '83 %Travelers -100 Baylis Rd Bx9093 -Melvll 11747
(914) 242-1717 .. **Candee,** Richd S '74 -116 Radio Cir -Mt Kisco 10549
(212) 272-7437 .. **Candela,** Gregory P '89 %JP Morgan Chase -383 Mad Av -NY 10179
(516) 229-4584 .. **Candela,** Jos '89 %G Lauzon -875 Merrick Av -Westbury 11590
(914) 946-5100 .. **Candela,** Michl '07 %Bashian & F,LLP -235 Main -White Plns 10601
(212) 859-8000 .. **Candela,** Sarah J '07 %Fried FHS&J LLP -1 NY Plz -NY 10004
(212) 689-1131 .. **Candela,** Steven '92 (Mannarino & C,PC) -315 Mad Av -NY 10017
(718) 317-9004 .. **Candelaria,** Maria T '78 -114 Seguine Av -Staten Isl 10309 **Fx:**317-7495
(212) 351-4000 .. **Candelaria,** Wm A '98 (Gibson D&C LLP) -200 Park Av -NY 10166
(212) 450-4000 .. **Candelario,** Jennifer S '05 Davis P&W LLP -450 Lex Av -NY 10017
(516) 294-5200 .. **Candelario,** Mary Ann '94 %Picciano & S -900 Merchants Cncrs -Westbury 11590
(212) 506-2500 .. **Candia,** Eileen M '08 %Mayer B LLP -1675 Bway -NY 10019
(212) 878-8000 .. **Candido,** Anthony M '98 (Clifford C LLP) -31 W 52nd -NY 10019
(212) 931-7967 .. **Candido,** Domna L '91 %MLB Properties -245 Park Av -NY 10167 **Fx:**949-5697
(212) 308-8505 .. **Candido,** Larry S '83 Cnsl Akabas & S -488 Mad Av -NY 10022
(718) 447-5499 .. **Candiloros,** Wm N '84 %Berel & M -358 St Marks Pl -Staten Isl 10301
(716) 674-8900 .. **Candino,** Dominic Paul '95 -1395 Union Rd -Buffalo 14224 **Fx:**674-3932
(516) 579-6500 .. **Candiotti,** Howard P '84 %A Clark & Assoc,LLC -650 Wantagh Av -Levittwn 11756 **Fx:**579-6604
(631) 589-3838 .. **Candito,** Marianne Norato '88 -4875 Sunrise Hwy -Bohemia 11716 **Fx:**589-6096
(631) 224-9141 .. **Candito,** Steven A '86 %Natl Response Corp -3500 Sunrise Hwy -Great Rvr 11739 **Fx:**224-9082
(646) 386-3514 .. **Candreva,** Elizabeth '84 %OCA -25 Beaver -NY 10004 **Fx:**(212) 457-2669
(212) 704-6292 .. **Candreva,** Jeremiah H '97 (Troutman S LLP) -405 Lex Av -NY 10174 **Fx:**704-5991
(212) 484-3900 .. **Candreva,** Karen F '95 (Arent F LLP) -1675 Bway -NY 10019
(212) 709-8351 .. **Cane,** Alexander R '87 -110 Wall -NY 10005
(845) 727-4000 .. **Cane,** Barbara H '85 -50 Piermont Av -Nyack 10960 **Fx:**727-4023
(516) 677-0066 .. **Cane,** Paul G '01 (Nichols & C,LLP) -6800 Jericho Tpk -Syosset 11791
(212) 922-9800 .. **Cane,** Peter S '90 P Cane & Assoc LLC -230 Park Av -NY 10169 **Fx:**922-9822
(212) 223-9654 .. **Canelias,** Peter S '91 -420 Lex Av -NY 10170 **Fx:**223-9651
(212) 612-4000 .. **Canell,** Sari B '94 %Chubb Grp -55 Water -NY 10041
(212) 336-1020 .. **Canellos,** George S '90 SEC -3 World Fncl Ctr -NY 10281 **Fx:**336-1323
(212) 403-1000 .. **Canellos,** Peter C '67 (Wachtell LR&K) -51 W 52nd -NY 10019
(718) 651-5454 .. **Canepa,** Jos G '92 (JG Canepa,PLLC) -37-38 75th -Jcksn Hts 11372
(212) 735-3000 .. **Canepari,** Megan E '10 %Skadden ASM&F LLP -4 Times Sq -NY 10036
(212) 336-2000 .. **Caner,** Krista D '08 %Patterson BW&T LLP -1133 Av of Amer -NY 10036
(631) 838-0087 .. **Caner,** Timothy K '04 -Bx201 -Lindenhrst 11757
(845) 356-9340 .. **Canetti & Troodler,LLP** -3 Arcadian Dr -Spg Vly 10977
(212) 425-1900 .. **Canevari,** Thos M '90 (Freehill H&M LLP) -80 Pine -NY 10005
(212) 698-3500 .. **Caney,** Lee D '94 (Dechert LLP) -1095 Av of Amer -NY 10036
(516) 294-4180 .. **Canfield,** David J '93 (Canfield M&R,LLP) -1461 Franklin Av -Gdn Cty 11530
(212) 788-8703 .. **Canfield,** Donna A '03 %Law Dept -100 Church -NY 10007 **Fx:**788-0367
(315) 425-2700 .. **Canfield,** James J '80 (Hiscock & B,LLP) -One Park Pl -Syracuse 13202
(516) 294-4180 .. **Canfield,** James W Jr. '50 OfCnsl Canfield M&R,LLP -1461 Franklin Av -Gdn Cty 11530
(212) 504-6000 .. **Canfield,** Jonathan D '07 %Cadwalader W&T LLP -1 World Fncl Ctr -NY 10281
(212) 326-3939 .. **Canfield,** Kenneth '07 %Jones D -222 E 41st -NY 10017
(212) 966-5780 .. **Canfield,** Kevin M '88 -111 John -NY 10038
(516) 294-4180 .. **Canfield Madden & Ruggiero,LLP** -1461 Franklin Av -Gdn Cty 11530 **Fx:**294-4188
(212) 949-4646 .. **Canfield Madden & Ruggiero,LLP** -230 Park Av -NY 10169 **Fx:**661-2153
(212) 397-5551 .. **Canfield,** Maryann '93 Soros Fund Mgmt LLC -888 7th Av -NY 10106 **Fx:**(917) 206-0790
(212) 465-2526 .. **Cangemi,** Agostino '95 NSI -505 Park Av -NY 10022 **Fx:**465-2531
(516) 741-1130 .. **Cangemi,** Andrew G '79 (Herman KC&C,LLP) -400 Grdn City Plz -Gdn Cty 11530
(631) 852-2500 .. **Cangero,** Dina M '02 %DA -200 Center Dr -Rvrhead 11901 **Fx:**852-1769
(212) 644-1710 .. **Cangialosi,** Thos J '83 (Winne BH&B,PC) -286 Mad Av -NY 10017
(212) 684-1111 .. **Cangiano,** Christian Vincent '96 %Deutsch M&D,LLP -18 East 41st -NY 10017
(212) 532-9736 .. **Cangiano,** Gregory '07 %R Skyer & Assoc,LLP -276 5th Av -NY 10001 **Fx:**532-9846
(718) 494-4593 .. **Cangro,** Chas R '83 -45 Sleepy Hllw Rd -Staten Isl 10314
(516) 496-1903 .. **Cangro,** Janene M '05 %Fazio R & Assoc LLP -175 Eileen Way -Syosset 11791 **Fx:**496-0912
(914) 366-5700 .. **Caniglia-Nanni,** Camille '89 %MA Bjork -660 Wht Plns Rd -Tarrytwn 10591 **Fx:**366-5759
(518) 486-5005 .. **Canino,** John R '75 Chldrn & Fam Srvcs -52 Wshngtn -Rensselaer 12144
(845) 338-4500 .. **Canino,** Jos L '71 -90 St James Bx4380 -Kingston 12402 **Fx:**338-0638
(212) 902-4313 .. **Canisius,** Karen A '03 %Goldman Sachs -85 Broad -NY 10004
(212) 259-8000 .. **Canizales Muller,** Adan '08 %Dewey & L LLP -1301 Av of Amer -NY 10019
(212) 460-3188 .. **Canizio,** Candida L '83 Con Ed -4 Irving Pl -NY 10003
(212) 692-1000 .. **Canizio,** Mark A '83 (Duane M LLP) -1540 Bway -NY 10036
(212) 408-5100 .. **Cankorel,** Turgut I '07 %Chadbourne & P LLP -30 Rckfllr Plz -NY 10112
(212) 286-8585 .. **Cann,** Deborah J '99 %Heidell PM&B,LLP -99 Park Av -NY 10016
(212) 247-3003 .. **Canna,** Brett G '99 -75 Rckfllr Plz -NY 10019
(800) 890-3090 .. **Cannata,** Benedene C '87 (Jacoby & M,LLP) -39 Bway -NY 10002 **Fx:**(212) 344-9400
(212) 553-9206 .. **Cannata,** Gregory J '78 -233 Bway -NY 10279 **Fx:**227-4141
(631) 549-4677 .. **Cannata,** Lisa M '03 %Sobel K&S,PC -464 NY Av -Huntngtn 11743
(516) 357-3000 .. **Cannata,** Michl C '08 %Rivkin R LLP -926 RXR Plz -Uniondale 11556
(646) 386-3813 .. **Cannataro,** Anthony '97 Hon L Wilkins -71 Thomas Part 18 -NY 10013 **Fx:**(212) 227-2322
(516) 678-5995 .. **Cannataro,** Frank K '50 -64 N Park Av -Rockvll Ctr 11570 **Fx:**678-5995
(516) 472-7300 .. **Cannatella,** Anthony S '89 -53 Orchrd -Manhsst 11030
(607) 748-1533 .. **Cannavino,** Thos F '80 -10 Mad Av -Endicott 13760
(212) 776-5000 .. **Cannavo,** John J '85 %NYC Housing Auth -250 Bway -NY 10007 **Fx:**776-5039
(716) 362-1207 .. **Cannavo,** Thos J '94 (McCabe CM&F,LLP) -651 Delaware Av -Buffalo 14202
(212) 732-9000 .. **Cannavo,** Vito A '79 (Sullivan PBM&C PC) -120 Bway -NY 10271
(212) 779-9910 .. **Cannella,** Jos L '78 (Eaton & V LLP) -3 Park Av -NY 10016
(212) 455-2000 .. **Cannella,** Meghan E '08 %Simpson T&B LLP -425 Lex Av -NY 10017
(212) 564-6633 .. **Cannella,** Michl A '92 %White & M,PC -875 Av of Amer -NY 10001
(212) 218-2100 .. **Cannella,** Nicholas M '77 (Fitzpatrick CH&S) -1290 Av of Amer -NY 10104
(212) 980-0120 .. **Canner,** Mara P '91 OfCnsl Frankfurt KK&S,PC -488 Mad Av -NY 10022
(607) 432-1521 .. **Canner,** Patricia L '07 %W Terry III -22 Dietz Bx945 -Oneonta 13820 **Fx:**432-1527
(212) 836-8000 .. **Canner,** Steven G '91 (Kaye S LLP) -425 Park Av -NY 10022
(212) 973-0572 .. **Cannici,** Wm J '09 %Wolff & S PC -140 Bway -NY 10005
(718) 426-0444 .. **Cannick,** Deveraux L '85 (Aiello & C) -69-06 Grand Av -Maspeth 11378
(212) 264-3650 .. **Canning,** Dennis J '91 %SSA Ofc Genl Cnsl -26 Fed Plz -NY 10278 **Fx:**264-6372
(212) 474-1000 .. **Canning,** James E '00 Cravath S&M LLP -825 8th Av -NY 10019
(516) 671-9758 .. **Canning,** John W C '90 -60 Roslyn Av Bx140 -Sea Cliff 11579 **Fx:**759-6762
(212) 715-1000 .. **Canning,** Michl J '72 (Arnold & P LLP) -399 Park Av -NY 10022
(646) 733-3200 .. **Canning,** Suzanne N '05 US Customs & Border Protectn -1 Penn Plz -NY 10119 **Fx:**733-3243
(212) 658-6210 .. **Cannistra,** Allyson A '09 T-Systems NA Inc -32 Avnune of the Americas -NY 10013
(212) 974-7474 .. **Cannistraci,** Andrea F '90 OfCnsl Cowan DA&S LLP -41 Mad Av -NY 10010
(212) 687-6444 .. **Cannistraci,** John A '65 -230 Park Av -NY 10169 **Fx:**687-2270
(516) 877-7000 .. **Cannizzaro,** Louis A '09 %McCoyd P&R,LLP -1100 Franklin Av -Gdn Cty 11530
(315) 789-7176 .. **Cannon,** A Clark '73 -4067 W Lake Rd -Geneva 14456 **Fx:**789-1938
(914) 723-4854 .. **Cannon,** Allan T '57 -47 Brwstr Rd -Scarsdale 10583
(212) 943-9000 .. **Cannon,** Ariel P '01 %Dewey P&K LLP -220 E 42nd -NY 10017
(212) 723-4931 .. **Cannon,** Cade R '06 US Fixed Income Corp -390 Greenwich -NY 10013
(315) 422-1391 .. **Cannon,** Cecelia R '09 %Green & S,PLLC -One Lincoln Ctr #900 -Syracuse 13202
(212) 755-3100 .. **Cannon,** David A '87 OfCnsl Kaufmann GR&O LLP -777 3rd Av -NY 10017
(518) 465-1500 .. **Cannon,** Geoffrey J '89 (Cannon H&W,LLP) -54 State -Albany 12207
(518) 465-1500 .. **Cannon Heyman & Weiss, LLP** -54 State -Albany 12207 **Fx:**465-6678
(716) 856-1700 .. **Cannon Heyman & Weiss, LLP** -726 Exchange -Buffalo 14210 **Fx:**856-2311
(212) 558-4000 .. **Cannon,** John F '62 SrCnsl Sullivan & C LLP -125 Broad -NY 10004
(212) 848-8159 .. **Cannon,** John J III '87 (Shearman & S LLP) -599 Lex Av -NY 10022
(212) 307-5500 .. **Cannon,** Lameke E '08 %Venable LLP -1270 Av of Amer -NY 10020
(518) 474-3148 .. **Cannon,** Lisa S '99 %Dept of Law -The Cptl -Albany 12224
(718) 273-0265 .. **Cannon,** Maria E '88 -34 Moody Pl -Staten Isl 10310 **Fx:**273-0753
(212) 417-5346 .. **Cannon,** Mark P '93 %Medicaid Fraud Cntrl -120 Bway -NY 10271 **Fx:**417-5274
(516) 712-4000 .. **Cannon,** Michl J '91 %Milber MP&S LLP -1000 Woodbury Rd -Woodbury 11797
(631) 271-6363 .. **Cannon,** Patrick W '85 (Cannon & A,LLP) -1923 NY Av -Huntngtn Sta 11746 **Fx:**271-7128
(585) 243-9330 .. **Cannon,** Scott D '92 -28 Main Bx446 -Geneseo 14454 **Fx:**243-9335
(631) 298-4387 .. **Cannon,** Susan Couture '82 -Aldrich Extn -Mattituck 11952 **Fx:**298-3512
(212) 586-9000 .. **Cannon,** Thos J '02 Flag Wharf Inc -888 7th Av -NY 10106 **Fx:**586-9765
(212) 587-2383 .. **Cannon,** Vivian Storch '92 -305 Bway -NY 10007 **Fx:**732-7080
(212) 613-2180 .. **Cannone,** Frank T '92 (Gibbons PC) -1 Penn Plz -NY 10119 **Fx:**(973) 639-8340
(212) 489-1600 .. **Cannon-Geary,** Irene S '86 %Deloitte LLP -1633 Bway -NY 10019 **Fx:**492-4201

(516) 745-1122 .. **Cannova,** Barbara A '04 Cnsl Quadrino & S,PC -666 Old Cntry Rd -Gdn Cty 11530
(516) 877-5600 .. **Canny,** Michl J '87 %R Tusa -1225 Franklin Av -Gdn Cty 11530 **Fx:**877-5695
(516) 741-7575 .. **Cano,** Gina-Marie '04 %Vecchione V&C LLP -147 Hrrcks Rd -Gdn Cty Pk 11040 **Fx:**294-4636
(718) 389-2427 .. **Cano,** Jairo G '10 Agostino & Assoc,PC -500 Kngslnd Av -Brklyn 11222
(718) 505-8506 .. **Cano,** Mercedes S '00 -40-26 82nd -Elmhrst 11373 **Fx:**505-8507
(518) 436-0344 .. **Cano,** Pilar A '05 %Deily M&G,LLP -8 Thurlow Ter -Albany 12203
(212) 762-4763 .. **Canon,** Carlos A '02 Morgan Stanley -1221 Av of Amer -NY 10020
(212) 506-1700 .. **Canoni,** John C '94 (Kasowitz BT&F LLP) -1633 Bway -NY 10019
(212) 323-2250 .. **Canosa,** Claudia L '93 %HHC-OLA-Medical Litigation -346 Bway -NY 10013 **Fx:**323-2251
(845) 371-4700 .. **Canova,** Nicholas J '05 %Fein SK&S,PC -747 Chestnut Rdg Rd -Spg Vly 10977
(212) 388-3600 .. **Canovas,** Jos W '09 %32B-J Leg Srvcs -101 Av of Amer -NY 10013 **Fx:**388-3061
(212) 918-3000 .. **Canovas,** Maria Luisa '00 (Hogan L LLP) -875 3rd Av -NY 10022
(518) 395-5400 .. **Cansdale,** John G '89 Racing & Wagering Bd -1 Bway Ctr -Schnctdy 12305 **Fx:**347-1250
(212) 683-4141 .. **Cantanno,** James E '95 OfCnsl Lynch & Assoc -462 7th Av -NY 10018 **Fx:**208-0948
(516) 308-3760 .. **Cantanno,** Rose Marie '97 (Liotta & C LLP) -519 Central Av -Massapequa 11758
(212) 632-5500 .. **Cantarella,** Claudia '92 (Salans LLP) -620 5th Av -NY 10020
(718) 330-7861 .. **Cantarella,** Tina F '00 %ODAR-SSA -111 Lvngstn -Brklyn 11201 **Fx:**330-2009
(212) 768-3878 .. **Cantarutti,** Steven D '03 %Smith SWH&B,LLP -100 Park Av -NY 10017
(212) 832-4000 .. **Cantelli,** Luca '04 %Eisen & S,LLP -18 E 48th -NY 10017
(212) 715-9100 .. **Canter,** Jonathan H '91 (Kramer LN&F,LLP) -1177 Av of Amer -NY 10036
(212) 837-6674 .. **Canter,** Megan E '06 %Hughes H&R LLP -1 Bttry Pk Plz -NY 10004
(845) 371-7500 .. **Canter,** Mitchell J '83 -103 Airport Exec Pk -Nanuet 10954 **Fx:**352-4464
(914) 948-3011 .. **Canter,** Nelson E '88 Canter Law Firm PC -123 Main -White Plns 10601 **Fx:**948-3066
(212) 816-2007 .. **Canter,** Wade M '99 Salomon Smith Barney -388 Greenwich -NY 10013
(914) 378-3900 .. **Cantin,** Bruce S '95 %Kaplan & M -1 Exec Blvd -Ynkrs 10701
(212) 806-5400 .. **Cantine,** Chas E '00 SpclCnsl Stroock &S&L LLP -180 Maiden Ln -NY 10038
(516) 625-1234 .. **Cantius,** Carole J '88 -332 Willis Av -Roslyn Hts 11577 **Fx:**625-4321
(212) 593-6700 .. **Canton,** J David '99 %Aaronson RF&D,LLP -757 3rd Av -NY 10017
(516) 409-6200 .. **Canton,** John A '00 %Furey KWM&C,PC -2174 Jackson Av -Seafrd 11783
(845) 291-2100 .. **Canton,** Leah C '05 %DA -255-275 Main -Goshen 10924 **Fx:**291-2125
(212) 488-4210 .. **Canton,** Melissa '08 Derivatives Cnsltng Grp -420 W 14th -NY 10014
(315) 484-9255 .. **Cantone,** Danl G '82 (Cantone Law Firm,PC) -5426 W Genesee Bx475 -Camillus 13031 **Fx:**484-9270
(212) 969-3000 .. **Cantone,** Robt A '78 (Proskauer R LLP) -1585 Bway -NY 10036
(718) 923-8432 .. **Cantone,** Scott C '97 Forest City Ratner Co -1 Metrotech Ctr N -Brklyn 11201
(718) 286-5837 .. **Cantoni,** Linda '84 %DA -125-01 Qns Blvd -Kew Gdns 11415 **Fx:**286-6540
(212) 878-7900 .. **Cantor,** Adam B '98 (Fox R LLP) -100 Park Av -NY 10017
(212) 326-2000 .. **Cantor,** Danl L '90 (O'Melveny & M LLP) -7 Times Sq -NY 10036
(212) 768-4343 .. **Cantor Epstein & Mazzola, LLP** -49 W 37th -NY 10018 **Fx:**719-0717
(845) 297-7777 .. **Cantor,** Jay S '81 (Tendy & C) -62 E Main -Wappingers Fls 12590
(212) 972-1000 .. **Cantor,** Jeremy B '04 %London F LLP -59 Maiden Ln -NY 10038
(212) 455-2000 .. **Cantor,** Jonathan E '98 Cnsl Simpson T&B LLP -425 Lex Av -NY 10017
(212) 907-0700 .. **Cantor,** Lindsay R '08 %Labaton S LLP -140 Bway -NY 10005
(716) 852-1888 .. **Cantor Lukasik Dolce & Panepinto,PC** -350 Main -Buffalo 14202 **Fx:**852-3588
(716) 852-1888 .. **Cantor,** Mark H '77 (Cantor LD&P,PC) -350 Main -Buffalo 14202
(212) 474-1000 .. **Cantor,** Matthew '09 %Cravath S&M LLP -825 8th Av -NY 10019
(212) 616-2113 .. **Cantor,** Matthew A '90 Normandy Hill Capital,LP -150 E 52nd -NY 10022
(212) 350-2700 .. **Cantor,** Matthew L '96 (Constantine C,PC) -450 Lex Av -NY 10017
(212) 455-2000 .. **Cantor,** Melvyn L '69 OfCnsl Simpson T&B LLP -425 Lex Av -NY 10017
(212) 679-7820 .. **Cantor,** Mitchell '87 -470 Park Av S -NY 10016 **Fx:**686-3822
(212) 350-7200 .. **Cantor,** Paul S '64 %Cantor Weiss & Friedner -880 3rd Av -NY 10022 **Fx:**350-7295
(212) 237-0000 .. **Cantor,** Rebecca J '09 %Vinson & E LLP -666 5th Av -NY 10103
(845) 452-1834 .. **Cantor,** Richd I '67 OfCnsl Teahan & C -2780 South Rd Bx1969 -Poughkeepsie 12601
(212) 873-6700 .. **Cantor,** Robt '67 -250 W 57th -NY 10107 **Fx:**315-2948
(212) 768-4343 .. **Cantor,** Robt I '71 (Cantor E&M,LLP) -49 W 37th -NY 10018
(212) 788-0736 .. **Cantor,** Sharon R '80 %Law Dept -100 Church -NY 10007 **Fx:**788-0367
(518) 869-2542 .. **Cantore,** Anthony S '73 Ret Pub Employee Assn -435 New Karner Rd -Albany 12205 **Fx:**869-0631
(718) 265-1500 .. **Cantrell,** James H '01 Aini & L,PLLC -2615 Coney Isl Av -Brklyn 11223 **Fx:**265-1515
(212) 249-6046 .. **Cantrell,** Lana E '94 -300 E 71st -NY 10021 **Fx:**249-6046
(212) 225-2000 .. **Cantu Estevez,** G Angelica '05 %Cleary GS&H -1 Lbrty Plz -NY 10006
(716) 853-1300 .. **Cantwell,** E Carey '70 Cnsl EC Cantwell,PC -295 Main -Buffalo 14203 **Fx:**853-1303
(716) 849-8900 .. **Cantwell,** Earl K II '80 (Hurwitz & F,PC) -1300 Lbrty Bldg -Buffalo 14202
(518) 474-5841 .. **Cantwell,** Ginger J '03 Gov Ofc Emply Rel -2 ESP -Albany 12223
(212) 909-6000 .. **Cantwell,** Helen V '96 (Debevoise & P LLP) -919 3rd Av -NY 10022
(518) 561-9251 .. **Cantwell,** Lori Ann '91 (Cantwell Law Firm,PLLC) -178 Broad -Plattsbrgh 12901 **Fx:**561-9254
(518) 483-1511 .. **Cantwell,** Paul M Jr. '66 (Cantwell & C) -14 Elm -Malone 12953 **Fx:**483-1530
(518) 561-9251 .. **Cantwell,** Richd E '91 (Cantwell Law Firm,PLLC) -178 Broad -Plattsbrgh 12901 **Fx:**561-9254
(212) 833-8000 .. **Cantwell-Sweeney,** Ann Christie '86 Sony BMG Music Entrtnmnt -550 Mad Av -NY 10022 **Fx:**833-8406
(212) 578-2983 .. **Canty,** Meghan E '04 %MetLife -1095 Av of Amer -NY 10036 **Fx:**578-3916
(516) 571-3800 .. **Canty,** Michl P '05 %DA -262 Old Cntry Rd -Mineola 11501 **Fx:**248-9479
(315) 253-1391 .. **Canzano,** Romolo '01 DA -95 Genesee -Auburn 13021 **Fx:**253-1521
(516) 873-1902 .. **Canzoneri,** Carolyn M '02 %Morici & M -1399 Franklin Av -Gdn Cty 11530 **Fx:**873-3948
(516) 354-9026 .. **Canzoneri,** Jos '67 (Canzoneri & C,LLP) -248 Scherer Blvd -Franklin Sq 11010 **Fx:**354-9295
(718) 361-1514 .. **Canzoneri,** Matthew A D '07 %N Isserlis -36-01 43rd Av -LIC 11101 **Fx:**(347) 418-3839
(516) 354-9026 .. **Canzoneri,** Patricia M '95 (Canzoneri & C,LLP) -248 Scherer Blvd -Franklin Sq 11010 **Fx:**354-9295
(212) 684-4143 .. **Cao,** Jin '90 -12 E 33rd -NY 10016
(646) 502-7001 .. **Cao,** Liangrong '07 SpclCnsl JSBarkats PLLC -100 Church -NY 10007 **Fx:**607-5544
(212) 940-8800 .. **Cao,** Yue Stephanie '06 SpclCnsl Katten MR LLP -575 Mad Av -NY 10022
(516) 714-7287 .. **Capalbo,** Angelo '06 Geico -170 Froehlich Farm Blvd -Woodbury 11797
(585) 377-7260 .. **Capanna,** Paloma A '92 -2060 Fairport 9 Mile Pnt Rd -Penfld 14526 **Fx:**377-7268
(212) 629-5950 .. **Caparas,** Aurelio L '85 -225 W 34th -NY 10122 **Fx:**629-5833
(212) 629-5950 .. **Caparas,** Raymund D '06 -225 W 34th -NY 10122
(212) 880-6000 .. **Caparelli,** Christopher M '00 %Torys LLP -237 Park Av -NY 10017
(646) 471-2363 .. **Capassakis,** Evelyn M '83 %PricewaterhouseCoopers LLP -300 Mad Av -NY 10017
(718) 531-4282 .. **Capasso,** Andrew M '91 -2744 Arkansas Dr -Brklyn 11234 **Fx:**531-6737
(212) 972-1000 .. **Capasso,** Anthony D '03 %London F LLP -59 Maiden Ln -NY 10038
(212) 554-1234 .. **Capasso,** Armando '03 AXA Financial Inc -1290 Av of Amer -NY 10104 **Fx:**707-3963
(631) 878-8194 .. **Capasso,** Louis J '95 -43 Montauk Hwy -Ctr Moriches 11934 **Fx:**874-3346
(518) 374-1800 .. **Capasso & Massaroni LLP** -215 State Bx1088 -Schnctdy 12301 **Fx:**374-4726
(631) 732-7407 .. **Capasso,** Michl M '73 (Capasso & C) -3650 Route 112 -Coram 11727 **Fx:**732-7116
(631) 732-7407 .. **Capasso,** Thos A '81 (Capasso & C) -3650 Route 112 -Coram 11727 **Fx:**732-7116
(518) 374-1800 .. **Capasso,** Vincent Jr. '78 (Capasso & M LLP) -215 State Bx1088 -Schnctdy 12301
(212) 667-8300 .. **Capatides,** Michl G '81 %CIBC World Mkts -425 Lex Av -NY 10017 **Fx:**667-8361
(516) 496-1919 .. **Capece,** Nicholas R Jr. '93 (Keller O&W,PC) -242 Crsswys Park Dr W -Woodbury 11797
(315) 735-4999 .. **Capecelatro,** Salvador J III '82 -421 Broad -Utica 13501 **Fx:**735-4562
(212) 698-3500 .. **Capeless,** Catherine L '08 %Dechert LLP -1095 Av of Amer -NY 10036
(212) 326-2000 .. **Capelin,** Laura J '08 %O'Melveny & M LLP -7 Times Sq -NY 10036
(516) 931-8100 .. **Capell Barnett Matalon & Schoenfeld, LLP** -100 Jericho Quadrangle -Jericho 11753 **Fx:**931-8101
(212) 867-4466 .. **Capell,** Heela D '06 %Belkin BW&G,LLP -270 Mad Av -NY 10016
(516) 931-8100 .. **Capell,** Howard '66 (Capell BM&S,LLP) -100 Jericho Quadrangle -Jericho 11753
(212) 286-8585 .. **Capell,** Jesse D '06 %Heidell PM&B,LLP -99 Park Av -NY 10016
(516) 496-7576 .. **Capell,** Philip J '91 -135 Crsswys Park Dr -Woodbury 11797 **Fx:**496-7803
(585) 546-6448 .. **Capell,** Walter R '74 (Davidson F LLP) -28 E Main -Rchstr 14614
(718) 261-0181 .. **Capellas,** Andrea Marie '10 %M Kule-Korgood -118-35 Qns Blvd -Frst Hlls 11375 **Fx:**268-2633
(914) 288-0022 .. **Capelli,** Christopher J '94 OfCnsl Leason E LLP -81 Main -White Plns 10601
(914) 945-0198 .. **Capelli,** Ivy M '94 -75 Pheasant Run -Millwd 10546
(914) 962-3311 .. **Capellini,** Albert A '67 -1767 Front -Yorktwn Hts 10598 **Fx:**962-8145
(212) 270-5892 .. **Capello,** Gene '82 JP Morgan Chase & Co -270 Park Av -NY 10017
(845) 339-8077 .. **Capen,** Elizabeth B '89 -23 Rogers -Kingston 12401
(516) 378-2540 .. **Caperna,** Aldo J '55 -19 Merrick Av -Merrick 11566
(212) 815-1818 .. **Capers,** Cecilia Tikura '04 DC 37 MELS -125 Barclay -NY 10007 **Fx:**815-1343
(516) 463-5232 .. **Capers,** I Bennett '92 %Hofstra Law Schl -121 Hofstra Univ -Hempstd 11549
(718) 254-7000 .. **Capers,** Robt L '97 %US Atty -271 Cadman Plz E -Brklyn 11201 **Fx:**254-6479
(212) 557-7200 .. **Capetanakis,** Chas '90 (Davidoff M&H,LLP) -605 3rd Av -NY 10158
(845) 359-8147 .. **Capetanakis,** John G '61 -72 Stephens Rd -Tappan 10983
(516) 746-2300 .. **Capetola,** Anthony A '71 -2C Hillside Av -Williston Pk 11596 **Fx:**746-2318
(631) 293-6060 .. **Capetola,** Jos J '85 (Cellino & B,PC) -445 Broad Hollow Rd -Melvll 11747
(516) 746-2300 .. **Capetola,** Michelle M '01 %A Capetola -2C Hillside Av -Williston Pk 11596 **Fx:**746-2318
(212) 351-4500 .. **Capezza,** Michelle '97 (Epstein B&G,PC) -250 Park Av -NY 10177
(518) 431-0247 .. **Capezza,** Thos A '94 US Atty -445 Bway -Albany 12207 **Fx:**431-0249
(212) 336-0590 .. **Capezzuto,** James A '91 %SEC -3 World Fncl Ctr -NY 10281 **Fx:**336-1323
(516) 739-2225 .. **Capicotto,** Rina M '88 -94 Willis Av -Mineola 11501
(516) 378-4210 .. **Capitano,** Francesca M '87 %Hmpstd Sanitation Dept -1600 Merrick Rd -Merrick 11566

(212) 616-0407 .. **Capitano,** Michelle Fava '05 Bizzi & Prtnrs Dvlpmnt LLC -712 5th Av -NY 10019
(516) 747-4301 .. **Capitolo,** Christine M '85 %Torino & B,PC -200 Old Cntry Rd -Mineola 11501
(212) 693-6924 .. **Capitti,** Linda M '93 %HRA -60 Lafayette -NY 10013
(212) 504-6000 .. **Capitummino,** Brian J '09 %Cadwalader W&T LLP -1 World Fncl Ctr -NY 10281
(716) 681-7190 .. **Capizzi,** Saml J '89 (Brown C LLP) -5775 Bway -Lancaster 14086
(212) 973-2376 .. **Caplan,** Brian D '85 (Caplan & R,LLP) -270 Mad Av -NY 10016 **Fx:**661-4290
(212) 381-7000 .. **Caplan,** Cindy L '00 %Sabin B&G LLP -4 Times Sq -NY 10036
(212) 450-4000 .. **Caplan,** David L '88 (Davis P&W LLP) -450 Lex Av -NY 10017
(212) 406-2181 .. **Caplan,** Glenn S '93 (G Caplan PC) -160 Bway -NY 10038 **Fx:**732-1425
(212) 728-8000 .. **Caplan,** Gordon R '92 (Willkie F&G LLP) -787 7th Av -NY 10019
(646) 471-4000 .. **Caplan,** John D '77 %PricewaterhouseCoopers LLP -300 Mad Av -NY 10017
(212) 715-9100 .. **Caplan,** Jonathan S '94 (Kramer LN&F,LLP) -1177 Av of Amer -NY 10036
(518) 457-2070 .. **Caplan,** Justine Clarke '94 %Dept of Tax & Fin -Bldg 9 State Campus -Albany 12227 **Fx:**457-6131
(518) 464-6644 .. **Caplan,** Murray N '80 (Caplan & C) -1707 Central Av -Albany 12205 **Fx:**464-0202
(212) 259-8000 .. **Caplan,** Richd B '08 %Dewey & L LLP -1301 Av of Amer -NY 10019
(212) 723-6453 .. **Caplan,** Richd J '93 %Salomon Smith Barney -390 Greenwich -NY 10013
(212) 593-6700 .. **Caplan,** Richd V '68 (Aaronson RF&D,LLP) -757 3rd Av -NY 10017
(212) 336-2000 .. **Caplan,** Scott C '10 %Patterson BW&T LLP -1133 Av of Amer -NY 10036
(212) 909-6000 .. **Caplan,** Sherri G '87 (Debevoise & P LLP) -919 3rd Av -NY 10022
(212) 768-6700 .. **Caplan,** Stuart A '86 (Sonnenschein N&R LLP) -1221 Av of Amer -NY 10020
(315) 471-9393 .. **Caple,** Nancy '82 %US SBA -224 Harrison -Syracuse 13202 **Fx:**471-9288
(212) 474-1000 .. **Caples,** Alyssa K '01 (Cravath S&M LLP) -825 8th Av -NY 10019
(212) 688-9812 .. **Caples,** Richd J '78 -470 Park Av -NY 10022 **Fx:**221-7938
(845) 651-4484 .. **Caplicki,** Dennis P '75 -Bx940 -Goshen 10924 **Fx:**651-4911
(845) 483-0983 .. **Caplicki,** Edmund V Jr. '70 (E Caplicki Jr,PC) -1133 Route 55 Bx15 -LaGrangevll 12540 **Fx:**483-0938
(845) 651-4484 .. **Caplicki,** Matthew J '06 -Bx940 -Goshen 10924
(845) 223-5204 .. **Caplicki,** Patricia Miller '94 -122 Todd Hill Rd -LaGrangevll 12540 **Fx:**223-3067
(212) 319-7125 .. **Caplin & Drysdale** -375 Park Av -NY 10152 **Fx:**644-6755
(914) 244-3300 .. **Caplin,** Susan M '93 S Caplin,PC -344 Main -Mt Kisco 10549 **Fx:**244-1756
(212) 269-0927 .. **Caplinger,** Roy T '95 %D'Amato & L,LLP -2 World Fncl Ctr -NY 10281
(718) 780-7944 .. **Caplow,** Stacy '73 %Bklyn Law Schl -250 Joralemon -Brklyn 11201 **Fx:**780-0393
(914) 481-5000 .. **Capobianco,** Jerri-Lynn '00 Blackacre Title Agncy -2900 Wstchstr Av -Purchase 10577 **Fx:**481-5005
(516) 746-7799 .. **Capobianco,** Jos '86 (Reisman P&R LLP) -1305 Franklin Av -Gdn Cty 11530
(212) 588-5500 .. **Capobianco,** Melanie Anne '05 %Davies WP&V LLP -625 Mad Av -NY 10022
(212) 218-5500 .. **Capobianco,** Neil A '89 (Seyfarth S LLP) -620 8th Av -NY 10018
(516) 488-4444 .. **Capobianco,** Sandra D '97 (S Capobianco,PC) -1981 Marcus Av -Lk Success 11042 **Fx:**488-3042
(212) 252-0004 .. **Capobianco,** Steven C '00 %Carroll M&K LLC -570 Lex Av -NY 10022
(212) 446-4800 .. **Capocasale,** Louis J '07 %Kirkland & E LLP -153 E 53rd -NY 10022
(718) 876-5723 .. **Capofari,** Paul A '81 %DA -67 Targee -Staten Isl 10304
(212) 509-7700 .. **Capogrosso,** Eleanor '88 E Capogrosso,PLLC -211 E 43rd -NY 10017 **Fx:**509-7600
(212) 637-3163 .. **Capon,** Virginia '89 %EPA -290 Bway -NY 10007 **Fx:**637-3096
(315) 788-3030 .. **Capone,** Andrew N '92 -120 Wshngtn -Watertwn 13601 **Fx:**788-3780
(212) 363-1200 .. **Capone,** Dorothea McGann '99 (Baumeister & S) -1 Exch Plz -NY 10006
(845) 528-3149 .. **Capone,** Gina C '97 -17 Oscawana Lk Rd Bx396 -Putnam Vly 10579 **Fx:**528-1374
(718) 558-7740 .. **Capone,** Michl '96 %LIRR -Jamaica Station -Jamaica 11435 **Fx:**558-8211
(315) 788-3030 .. **Capone,** Richd M '60 -120 Wshngtn -Watertwn 13601
(212) 450-4000 .. **Capone,** Russell '06 %Davis P&W LLP -450 Lex Av -NY 10017
(914) 497-7854 .. **Capone,** Victoria Ann '85 -2088 Cntrl Pk Av -Ynkrs 10710
(518) 869-1200 .. **Caponera,** Philip S '67 -10 Enterprise Av -Clifton Pk 12065 **Fx:**869-4200
(518) 453-8381 .. **Caponera,** Victor A '77 -3 Atrium Dr -Albany 12205 **Fx:**453-8385
(212) 450-4000 .. **Caponi,** Carlo M '09 %Davis P&W LLP -450 Lex Av -NY 10017
(631) 853-5212 .. **Caponi,** Sabato '86 %Leg Aid -400 Carleton Av Bx9082 -Central Islip 11722 **Fx:**853-7798
(718) 979-3300 .. **Caporal,** Georgeann '00 %MHLS -777 Seaview Av -Staten Isl 10305 **Fx:**667-2666
(585) 244-1852 .. **Capossere,** Julie Karowe '91 -215 Fair Oaks Av -Rchstr 14618
(877) 222-1814 .. **Capote,** Alexia J '07 %B Rothenberg -100 Duffy Av -Hicksvll 11801 **Fx:**(866) 894-2182
(516) 488-3300 .. **Capowski,** Timothy R '95 (Shaub AC&S,LLP) -1983 Marcus Av -Lk Success 11042
(516) 572-3259 .. **Capoziello,** James L '80 Nassau Hlth Care Corp -2201 Hempstd Tpk -E Meadow 11554
(315) 425-2700 .. **Capozza,** Richd R '92 (Hiscock & B,LLP) -One Park Pl -Syracuse 13202
(718) 745-3300 .. **Capozzi,** Anthony G '84 -9201 4th Av -Brklyn 11209 **Fx:**921-4526
(212) 335-2700 .. **Capozzi,** James G '87 %FBI -26 Fed Plz -NY 10278
(212) 907-9600 .. **Capozzi,** Michl D '03 %Ingram YGC&B,LLP -250 Park Av -NY 10177
(518) 584-5133 .. **Capozzola,** Theresa A '89 -57 Gilbert Rd -Saratoga Spgs 12866 **Fx:**584-3315
(718) 254-6454 .. **Capozzolo,** Anthony M '95 %US Atty -271 Cadman Plz E -Brklyn 11201 **Fx:**254-6479
(718) 225-9223 .. **Cappa,** James A '84 -42-40 Bell Blvd -Bayside 11361 **Fx:**225-9093
(212) 512-4563 .. **Cappabianca,** Rosemarie '83 McGraw-Hill Co,Inc -2 Penn Plz -NY 10121 **Fx:**512-4827
(212) 309-6000 .. **Cappell,** Shana R '03 %Morgan L&B LLP -101 Park Av -NY 10178
(718) 847-6100 .. **Cappellani,** Jerome E '75 -80-59 Lefferts Blvd -Kew Gdns 11415 **Fx:**441-9405
(518) 833-6000 .. **Cappellano,** Edw L '93 %Dept Soc Srvcs -127 Bloomingrove Dr -Troy 12180 **Fx:**833-6121
(518) 210-8962 .. **Cappellano,** Tamara M '02 -1128 Hoosick Rd -Troy 12180
(718) 447-7428 .. **Cappelli,** Allen P '89 -148 Kissel Av -Staten Isl 10310
(716) 883-3222 .. **Cappelli,** Emil J '77 -420 Franklin -Buffalo 14202 **Fx:**885-3369
(212) 798-6100 .. **Cappelli,** Stephen F '96 %Fortress Invsmt Grp -1345 Av of Amer -NY 10105
(212) 697-5030 .. **Cappellini,** Bruno John '61 -5 Tudor City Pl -NY 10017
(585) 968-1390 .. **Cappellini,** John Albert Jr. '98 -1 E Main Bx105 -Cuba 14727 **Fx:**968-1198
(718) 478-7390 .. **Cappello,** Dennis S '82 -83-04 54th Av -Elmhrst 11373 **Fx:**672-6438
(315) 386-4595 .. **Cappello,** Francis P '73 (Oliver Law Firm) -117 Main -Canton 13617 **Fx:**379-1240
(315) 265-2747 .. **Cappello,** Francis P '73 (Cappello L&L) -76 Market Bx5153 -Potsdam 13676
(845) 778-2121 .. **Cappello,** John C '87 (Jacobowitz & G,LLP) -158 Orange Av Bx367 -Walden 12586
(315) 265-2747 .. **Cappello Linden & Ladouceur** -76 Market Bx5153 -Potsdam 13676 **Fx:**265-2749
(646) 610-5400 .. **Cappello,** Michl J '05 %NYPD -1 Police Plz -NY 10038
(212) 551-8908 .. **Cappello,** Paula I '89 %Israel Discount Bk -511 5th Av -NY 10017 **Fx:**551-8916
(718) 448-6400 .. **Cappello,** Thos J '99 (Slater S&C,PC) -1298 Victory Blvd -Staten Isl 10301
(646) 386-5700 .. **Cappelluti-Tessler,** Martha '91 %Civil Ct -111 Centre -NY 10013
(516) 949-4225 .. **Cappeto,** Patricia A '00 FINRA -2 Jericho Plz -Jericho 11753 **Fx:**949-4201
(631) 853-5212 .. **Cappiello,** Renee Bysheim '91 %Leg Aid -400 Carleton Av Bx9082 -Central Islip 11722 **Fx:**853-7798
(845) 855-5444 .. **Cappillino,** Donald '77 (Cappillino & R LLP) -7 Broad Bx390 -Pawling 12564
(845) 471-5535 .. **Cappillino,** Donald '77 (Cappillino & R LLP) -2 Cannon -Poughkeepsie 12601
(845) 855-5444 .. **Cappillino & Rothschild LLP** -7 Broad Bx390 -Pawling 12564 **Fx:**855-5895
(845) 471-5535 .. **Cappillino & Rothschild LLP** -2 Cannon -Poughkeepsie 12601 **Fx:**855-5895
(212) 801-2247 .. **Cappo,** Anthony '09 %Greenberg T,LLP -200 Park Av -NY 10166
(718) 250-2000 .. **Cappock,** Patrick F '98 %DA -350 Jay -Brklyn 11201 **Fx:**250-2314
(585) 225-0386 .. **Cappon,** Robt E '53 -56 Briar Hill -Rchstr 14626
(518) 392-3288 .. **Cappozzo,** Fred J '78 -14 Park Row -Chatham 12037 **Fx:**392-3285
(212) 715-9100 .. **Capps,** Pamela M '93 (Kramer LN&F,LLP) -1177 Av of Amer -NY 10036
(212) 894-7200 .. **Cappucci,** Robt N '94 (Entwistle & C LLP) -280 Park Av -NY 10017
(212) 894-7200 .. **Cappucci,** Vincent R '85 (Entwistle & C LLP) -280 Park Av -NY 10017
(315) 471-8111 .. **Cappuccilli,** Timothy J '95 %Scolaro SCF&B,PC -507 Plum -Syracuse 13204
(212) 484-7980 .. **Cappuccio,** Paul T '02 %Time Warner -1 Time Warner Ctr -NY 10019
(212) 872-1000 .. **Cappuyns,** Elisabeth J '99 -One Bryant Park -NY 10036 **Fx:**872-1002
(212) 636-6855 .. **Capra,** Danl J '78 %Fordham Univ Sch of Law -140 W 62nd -NY 10023 **Fx:**636-6899
(212) 556-2100 .. **Capra,** James J Jr. '79 (King & S) -1185 Av of Amer -NY 10036
(718) 590-2000 .. **Capra-Cunningham,** Marisa M '04 %DA -198 E 161st -Bronx 10451 **Fx:**590-6477
(516) 747-4082 .. **Caprari-Dempsey,** Susan H '79 %Montfort HM&S LLP -1140 Franklin Av Bx7677 -Gdn Cty 11530
(212) 269-3444 .. **Capriano Lichtman & Flach,LLP** -80 Wall -NY 10005 **Fx:**363-7437
(212) 269-3444 .. **Capriano,** Michl P '58 (Capriano L&F,LLP) -80 Wall -NY 10005
(315) 423-7100 .. **Capriotti,** David M '93 (Harris B PLLC) -300 S State -Syracuse 13202
(212) 208-3287 .. **Capruso,** James M '97 %Ambac Assurance Corp -1 State St Plz -NY 10004
(914) 347-6360 .. **Capshaw,** Wm K '81 %Epstein & R -565 Taxter Rd -Elmsfrd 10523
(212) 564-2233 .. **Capsuto,** Ira R '66 -212 W 29th -NY 10001
(212) 374-3441 .. **Captan,** Solange B '02 %NYC Dept Educ -52 Chmbrs -NY 10007
(315) 476-2921 .. **Captor,** Renee S '83 Assigned Cnsl Prgm,Inc -State Twr Bldg -Syracuse 13202 **Fx:**476-0576
(516) 357-3700 .. **Capuano,** Justin F '03 %Cullen and D LLP -100 Q Roosevelt Blvd -Gdn Cty 11530
(212) 551-1192 .. **Capuano,** Nicholas '04 (Capuano & L LLP) -380 Lex Av -NY 10168 **Fx:**(646) 558-0238
(212) 468-8000 .. **Capucilli,** David C '04 %Morrison & F LLP -1290 Av of Amer -NY 10104
(212) 509-9595 .. **Capuder,** Douglas '80 (Capuder FG LLP) -90 Broad -NY 10004
(212) 509-9595 .. **Capuder Fazio Giacoia LLP** -90 Broad -NY 10004 **Fx:**509-9597
(631) 853-4049 .. **Caputi,** Jacqueline '87 %Cnty Atty -Dennison Bldg Bx6100 -Hauppauge 11788 **Fx:**853-5169
(716) 841-2326 .. **Caputi,** Renee M '07 HSBC Bank -1 HSBC Ctr -Buffalo 14203
(631) 421-2500 .. **Caputi,** Robt R '48 OfCnsl Caputi W&N -50 Elm -Huntngtn 11743
(631) 421-2500 .. **Caputi Weintraub & Neary** -50 Elm -Huntngtn 11743 **Fx:**421-2565
(914) 337-8900 .. **Caputo,** A Fredric '78 -7 Pondfld Rd -Bronxvll 10708
(914) 664-2002 .. **Caputo,** Anthony J '59 -Bx310 -Somers 10589 **Fx:**664-3130
(718) 980-9820 .. **Caputo,** Anthony R '63 -221 Jffrsn Av -Staten Isl 10306
(212) 332-7880 .. **Caputo,** Bruce F '84 (Caputo Legal,PC) -1270 Av of Amer -NY 10020 **Fx:**337-7885
(718) 420-0750 .. **Caputo,** Christopher '92 (C Caputo PC) -1860 Clove Rd -Staten Isl 10304 **Fx:**420-0780
(212) 455-2000 .. **Caputo,** Christopher J '10 %Simpson T&B LLP -425 Lex Av -NY 10017
(516) 742-0707 .. **Caputo,** Deanne M '05 %Sullivan PBM&C PC -55 Mineola Blvd -Mineola 11501

(212) 788-1055 .. **Caputo,** Francis F '74 %Law Dept -100 Church -NY 10007 **Fx:**788-0367
(212) 578-2211 .. **Caputo,** Frank '89 %MetLife -27-01 Qns Plz N -LIC 11101
(212) 363-6900 .. **Caputo,** Ida A '01 %Faust GS&B LLP -2 Rector -NY 10006
(516) 997-2700 .. **Caputo,** Jacqueline M '04 %A Core,PC -173 Schl -Westbury 11590 **Fx:**997-7334
(212) 728-8000 .. **Caputo,** James F '08 %Willkie F&G LLP -787 7th Av -NY 10019
(585) 428-5210 .. **Caputo,** Jean A '98 %Pub Def -10 N Fitzhugh -Rchstr 14614 **Fx:**428-2234
(212) 603-6300 .. **Caputo,** Nicholas R '94 %Robinson BLGG&G PC -875 3rd Av -NY 10022
(212) 873-4768 .. **Caputo,** Patricia C '88 -149 W 85th -NY 10024 **Fx:**873-4768
(631) 884-1010 .. **Caputo,** Robt '00 -309 N Ontario Av -Lindenhrst 11757 **Fx:**884-0015
(518) 434-0117 .. **Caputo Granich,** Christine A '94 Hon J Egan Jr -50 Chapel -Albany 12207 **Fx:**434-5979
(914) 632-4700 .. **Cara,** Frank T '92 (McDonough Law Firm, LLP) -145 Huguenot -New Rchll 10801
(516) 203-7555 .. **Cara,** Jacqueline A '92 -37 Boylston -Gdn Cty 11530 **Fx:**741-1813
(212) 732-3200 .. **Caraballo,** Chloé D '10 %Carter L&M LLP -2 Wall -NY 10005
(212) 213-8860 .. **Caraballo,** Dolly '95 (Caraballo & M,LLC) -10 E 40th -NY 10016
(646) 833-0900 .. **Caraballo,** Elizabeth F '08 %Tressler LLP -One Penn Plz -NY 10119
(718) 388-5400 .. **Caraballo,** F Louis '73 Caraballo Law Ofcs -701 Bway -Brklyn 11206 **Fx:**388-8687
(212) 969-3000 .. **Caraballo-Garrison,** Phil J '08 %Proskauer R LLP -1585 Bway -NY 10036
(212) 430-6400 .. **Carabba,** Anthony '94 (Carabba L LLP) -100 William -NY 10038
(212) 430-6400 .. **Carabba Locke LLP** -100 William -NY 10038 **Fx:**430-6405
(516) 997-6000 .. **Carabell,** Barbara N '79 %Marshall & M -30 Jericho Exec Plz -Jericho 11753 **Fx:**997-0860
(914) 381-5715 .. **Caraccio,** Noël F '77 (NF Caraccio PLLC) -875 Mamaroneck Av -Mamaroneck 10543 **Fx:**698-4646
(315) 343-1939 .. **Caraccioli,** Kevin C '91 SrCnsl Caraccioli & N,PLLC -120 E 1st -Oswego 13126 **Fx:**343-1822
(718) 624-2898 .. **Caracciolo,** Anthony A '55 -26 Court -Brklyn 11242
(212) 335-9000 .. **Caracciolo,** Claudine '04 %DA -1 Hogan Pl -NY 10013
(212) 773-2543 .. **Caracciolo,** David '03 Ernst & Young LLP -5 Times Sq -NY 10036
(212) 295-8260 .. **Caracciolo,** Vincent G '92 Integro Ins -1 State -NY 10004
(212) 277-4000 .. **Caracristi,** Dennis '07 %Freshfields BD LLP -520 Mad Av -NY 10022
(212) 232-2394 .. **Caracta,** Michl F '95 -80 Wall -NY 10005 **Fx:**344-5437
(631) 589-7788 .. **Caradonna,** Anne Marie '94 Cnsl Enright Court Reporting,Inc -100 S Main -Sayvll 11782 **Fx:**589-1103
(315) 431-6600 .. **Carafa,** Thos P '88 %Brady & C -443 Electronics Pkwy -Liverpool 13088 **Fx:**431-6605
(646) 386-4743 .. **Caragine,** Judith A '01 Criminal Ct -100 Centre -NY 10013
(212) 326-9415 .. **Caramagna,** Carmel Ann '93 HCCIG -600 Lex Av -NY 10022 **Fx:**751-8444
(631) 242-2020 .. **Caramagno,** Eileen G '86 -1641 Deer Prk Av -Deer Pk 11729 **Fx:**242-2034
(631) 242-2020 .. **Caramagno,** Jos S '90 -1641 Deer Prk Av -Deer Pk 11729 **Fx:**242-2034
(718) 855-9000 .. **Caran,** Djordje '05 %Cullen and D LLP -177 Montague -Brklyn 11201
(212) 732-8700 .. **Caran,** Juliana '04 %McAloon & F,PC -123 William -NY 10038
(518) 388-2680 .. **Carangelo,** Justin B '98 MVP Hlth Plan,Inc -625 State -Schnctdy 12305
(212) 310-8499 .. **Carangelo,** Robt F Jr. '92 (Weil G&M LLP) -767 5th Av -NY 10153
(212) 407-7700 .. **Caranicas,** Chas S '02 %Vedder P,PC -1633 Bway -NY 10019
(646) 562-3400 .. **Carannante,** Jerry J '04 Practical Law Co,Inc -747 3rd Av -NY 10017
(212) 474-1000 .. **Carapiet,** Jos J '09 %Cravath S&M LLP -825 8th Av -NY 10019
(212) 788-7000 .. **Caras,** James '89 %City Cncl Leg Div -250 Bway -NY 10007 **Fx:**788-7034
(718) 979-0900 .. **Carasaniti,** Victor T '63 (Carasaniti & A) -1602 Richmond Rd -Staten Isl 10304 **Fx:**979-1991
(212) 732-0500 .. **Carasso,** Jos M '82 -305 Bway -NY 10007 **Fx:**385-1977
(212) 686-7999 .. **Caravela,** Dana M '07 %N Dennis -1040 Av of Amer -NY 10018 **Fx:**686-0630
(631) 608-1346 .. **Caravella,** John J '04 -49 Culver Hill -Southampton 11968
(718) 725-4205 .. **Caravello,** Barbara J '94 -153-01 Jamaica Av -Jamaica 11432 **Fx:**725-4206
(212) 930-8908 .. **Caravello,** G John '84 %Lloyds Bk -1095 Av of Amer -NY 10036
(212) 840-6711 .. **Caraway,** David A '95 (Caraway & S,LLP) -44 Wall -NY 10005
(212) 839-9461 .. **Caraway,** Erica '95 Dept of Transportation -55 Water -NY 10041
(212) 661-5030 .. **Carb,** Stephen A '58 OfCnsl Schoeman U&K,LLP -60 E 42nd -NY 10165
(212) 878-7900 .. **Carberry,** Andrez '06 %Fox R LLP -100 Park Av -NY 10017
(212) 326-3939 .. **Carberry,** Chas M '77 (Jones D) -222 E 41st -NY 10017
(212) 819-8200 .. **Carberry,** Paul B '98 (White & C LLP) -1155 Av of Amer -NY 10036
(212) 278-0400 .. **Carbo,** Gregory J '06 %Cooper & D LLP -30 Rckfllr Plz -NY 10112
(914) 767-3313 .. **Carbonari,** Wm L Jr. '89 -Bx569 -Goldens Bridge 10526
(315) 472-4481 .. **Carbonaro,** Brianne M '05 %Ali P&C -614 James -Syracuse 13203
(516) 742-7777 .. **Carbonaro,** Jos W '86 %Frazer & F,LLP -1415 Kellum Pl -Gdn Cty 11530
(315) 252-2352 .. **Carbonaro,** Patrick A '06 (Carbonaro Law,PC) -110 Genesee -Auburn 13021 **Fx:**252-0575
(315) 252-2352 .. **Carbonaro,** Paul '79 -110 Genesee Bx549 -Auburn 13021
(917) 587-8940 .. **Carbonaro Arrabito,** Jane G '95 -3619 Av S -Brklyn 11234 **Fx:**(718) 998-4922
(518) 462-5300 .. **Carbone,** Aaron '09 %DeGraff F&K LLP -90 State -Albany 12207
(516) 747-7007 .. **Carbone,** Andrea L '03 (Scherer & Assoc,PLLC) -600 Old Cntry Rd -Gdn Cty 11530 **Fx:**747-7008
(914) 937-3100 .. **Carbone,** Anthony A '77 (Berlingo & C) -320 Wstchstr Av -Pt Chester 10573
(212) 705-7000 .. **Carbone,** Anthony J '82 (Bingham M LLP) -399 Park Av -NY 10022
(212) 407-4000 .. **Carbone,** Christian D '97 (Loeb & L,LLP) -345 Park Av -NY 10154
(212) 848-8244 .. **Carbone,** Danielle '90 (Shearman & S LLP) -599 Lex Av -NY 10022
(212) 695-8100 .. **Carbone,** Donald J '78 (Goetz F,LLP) -1 Penn Plz -NY 10119
(315) 724-4216 .. **Carbone,** Enessa M '87 %Don-Al Mngmnt -5700 Horatio -Utica 13502 **Fx:**724-4248
(631) 979-9800 .. **Carbone,** Jos Jr. '94 (McCarthy & C,PC) -400 Townline Rd -Hauppauge 11788
(212) 839-5300 .. **Carbone,** Karen Murphy '04 %Sidley A LLP -787 7th Av -NY 10019
(212) 460-3995 .. **Carbone,** Larry '89 Con Ed -4 Irving Pl -NY 10003
(914) 684-0201 .. **Carbone,** Louis J '89 (Carbone & Assoc) -111 N Central Av -Hartsdale 10530
(315) 369-3544 .. **Carbone,** Malorie A '99 (Frye F&C) -2973 State Route 28 Bx291 -Old Forge 13420
(315) 733-7549 .. **Carbone,** Malorie A '99 (Frye F&C) -2219 Genesee -Utica 13501
(518) 283-1245 .. **Carbone,** Martin A '07 (Carbone & C LLP) -53 Kuhl Blvd -Wynantskill 12198 **Fx:**326-0366
(518) 668-3711 .. **Carbone,** Martin A Sr. '73 (Carbone & C LLP) -Bx502 -Lk George 12845 **Fx:**326-0366
(718) 709-2276 .. **Carbone,** Michl P '98 Jet Blue Airways -118-29 Qns Blvd -Frst Hlls 11375
(212) 940-8800 .. **Carbone,** Neil V '96 (Katten MR LLP) -575 Mad Av -NY 10022
(914) 995-3400 .. **Carbone,** Peter A '90 %DA -111 Martin Luther King Blvd -White Plns 10601 **Fx:**995-3363
(646) 855-0720 .. **Carbone,** Peter J '95 Bk of Amer -1 Bryant Pk -NY 10036
(718) 739-6400 .. **Carbone,** Ralph F '81 %DHCR -92-31 Union Hall -Jamaica 11433 **Fx:**262-7938
(212) 716-5800 .. **Carbone,** Sasha A '97 %Amer Arbtrtn Assn -1633 Bway -NY 10019
(212) 645-6918 .. **Carbonell,** Vincent A '03 United Reprographic Svcs -40 W 25th -NY 10010
(716) 836-4285 .. **Carbonell-Medina,** Doris A '89 -254 Rounds Av -Buffalo 14215 **Fx:**884-3279
(212) 225-2000 .. **Carbonetto,** Antonino G '04 %Cleary GS&H -1 Lbrty Plz -NY 10006
(212) 732-9000 .. **Carboy,** Andrew J '93 (Sullivan PBM&C PC) -120 Bway -NY 10271
(212) 587-3788 .. **Carbuccia,** Gladys '86 %State Ins Fund -199 Church -NY 10007 **Fx:**385-9199
(212) 373-3000 .. **Carbullido,** Mitchel R '09 %Paul WRW&G LLP -1285 Av of Amer -NY 10019
(212) 785-4823 .. **Carcagno,** Jos J '89 SrCnsl Carcagno & Assoc -80 Broad -NY 10004 **Fx:**785-0437
(914) 833-2695 .. **Carcano,** James R III '94 -15 Hudson Pl -Larchmnt 10538 **Fx:**833-2695
(212) 386-1945 .. **Carcano,** Robt '82 NAIC -48 Wall -NY 10005
(212) 436-2096 .. **Carchman,** Fred M '99 Deloitte & Touche,LLP -2 World Fncl Ctr -NY 10281
(917) 663-3722 .. **Carcich,** Claire C '96 PMI Global Srvcs Inc -120 Park Av -NY 10017
(212) 220-3830 .. **Carcich,** Michl J '74 (Nicoletti H&S) -88 Pine -NY 10005
(845) 291-2454 .. **Card,** Donald M Jr. '92 %Leg Aid -2 Court Ln Bx328 -Goshen 10924 **Fx:**294-2638
(516) 488-7100 .. **Cardalena,** Kim M '91 Washington Title Ins Co -31 Stewart -Floral Pk 11001
(516) 328-3599 .. **Cardalena,** Peter P Jr. '85 -31 Stewart -Floral Pk 11001 **Fx:**488-6311
(212) 964-3855 .. **Cardali,** Robt A '93 (R Cardali & Assoc,LLP) -39 Bway -NY 10006 **Fx:**634-4856
(212) 487-9700 .. **Cardali,** Wendy K '91 (White F&F,LLP) -61 Bway -NY 10006
(716) 856-5500 .. **Cardamone,** Danielle M '03 %Damon M LLP -200 Delaware Av -Buffalo 14202
(518) 346-0833 .. **Cardamone,** Jos R '76 -249 Green -Schnctdy 12305 **Fx:**370-4129
(518) 561-1389 .. **Cardany,** Jos T '86 -44 Oak Bx3082 -Plattsbrgh 12901 **Fx:**561-1797
(716) 668-3416 .. **Cardarelli,** Antonio '81 (Cardarelli & L,LLP) -144 Woodgate Dr -Cheektowaga 14227 **Fx:**668-3416
(212) 513-7788 .. **Cardascia,** Nicholas M '88 (Ahmuty D&M) -123 William -NY 10038
(212) 406-1600 .. **Cardeli,** Seth L '09 %Gurfein D LLP -11 Park Pl -NY 10007
(212) 998-1268 .. **Cardeli-Arroyo,** Barbara '01 NYU Human Resrcs -7 E 12th -NY 10003
(516) 873-2000 .. **Cardello,** Michl III '97 (Moritt HH&H LLP) -400 Grdn City Plz -Gdn Cty 11530
(315) 435-2470 .. **Carden,** Clifton C '07 %DA -505 S State -Syracuse 13202 **Fx:**435-3969
(212) 613-5000 .. **Carden,** Constance P '73 %Leg Assist Grp -450 W 33rd -NY 10001 **Fx:**750-0820
(212) 326-3939 .. **Carden,** David L '01 (Jones D) -222 E 41st -NY 10017
(212) 878-8000 .. **Carden,** Donald G '87 (Clifford C LLP) -31 W 52nd -NY 10019
(914) 345-6510 .. **Cardenas,** Barak P '02 Miranda SSSV LLP -570 Taxter Rd -Elmsfrd 10523
(212) 977-7095 .. **Cardenas,** J Roberto '95 (Cardenas & Assoc) -119 W 57th -NY 10019 **Fx:**977-7085
(212) 232-1300 .. **Cardenas,** James A '98 (Lewis BB&S LLP) -77 Water -NY 10005
(516) 571-9038 .. **Cardenas-Curry,** Celeste '87 Family Ct -1200 Old Cntry Rd -Westbury 11590 **Fx:**571-9335
(212) 627-8100 .. **Carder,** Ezekiel Daystar '05 %Levy R,PC -80 8th Av -NY 10011
(212) 709-1650 .. **Cardi,** Christine R '91 %Banking Dept -1 State -NY 10004 **Fx:**709-1655
(212) 481-7770 .. **Cardi,** Dawn M '80 (D Cardi & Assoc) -2 Park Av -NY 10016 **Fx:**684-3008
(212) 572-8350 .. **Cardi,** Patricia M '80 -575 Lex Av -NY 10022 **Fx:**573-8304
(631) 207-2500 .. **Cardiello,** Nicole M '02 (N Cardiello,PC) -66A Medford Av -Patchogue 11772
(718) 833-6355 .. **Cardieri,** Jos V '91 -623 80th -Brklyn 11209
(716) 759-9759 .. **Cardillo,** Christopher A '94 (Damon M LLP) -9276 Main -Clarence 14031
(212) 344-0464 .. **Cardillo & Corbett** -29 Bway -NY 10006 **Fx:**797-1212
(212) 297-0050 .. **Cardillo,** Jos P '06 %Betancourt VHG&K LLC -46 Trinity Pl -NY 10006
(516) 222-0101 .. **Cardillo,** Maren Paige '05 Divorce Mdtn Prof -585 Stewart Av -Gdn Cty 11530
(518) 792-1151 .. **Cardinal,** Paul A '85 %Evergreen Bancorp -237 Glen -Glens Fls 12801
(585) 546-5530 .. **Cardinale,** Cara M '05 %Thomson West -50 E Broad -Rchstr 14694
(518) 473-6217 .. **Cardinale,** Carin M '04 Ofc Emp Rltns -Agncy Bldg 2 ESP -Albany 12223
(718) 274-1750 .. **Cardinale,** Dominick S '94 -2176 36th -Astoria 11105 **Fx:**274-1327

(718) 250-2000 .. **Cardinale,** Melissa K '92 %DA -350 Jay -Brklyn 11201 **Fx:**250-2314
(315) 698-9630 .. **Cardinale,** Michl R '97 Cardinale Law Firm PC -8432 Brewerton Rd -Cicero 13039 **Fx:**698-8829
(631) 722-4744 .. **Cardinale,** Philip J '74 (Cardinale & C) -Main Rd Bx2021 -Jamesprt 11947 **Fx:**722-4877
(718) 624-9391 .. **Cardinale,** Richd J '92 (Cardinale H&M) -26 Court -Brklyn 11242
(631) 722-4744 .. **Cardinale,** Susan M '74 (Cardinale & C) -Main Rd Bx2021 -Jamesprt 11947 **Fx:**722-4877
(212) 421-2111 .. **Cardinali,** Raymond J '99 %Granoff W&F,PC -747 3rd Av -NY 10017
(212) 465-2140 .. **Cardinez,** Benjamin F '93 -421 7th Av -NY 10001 **Fx:**465-2012
(212) 465-2140 .. **Cardinez,** Jason B '01 -421 7th Av -NY 10001
(631) 264-1200 .. **Cardino,** Frank J '91 (Cardino & C) -825 Montauk Hwy -Copiague 11726 **Fx:**264-1210
(631) 218-0100 .. **Cardino,** Jos Jr. '86 Primerica -4580 Sunrise Hwy -Oakdale 11769
(212) 953-2381 .. **Cardo,** Leila '81 (Rubin F&F,LLP) -292 Mad Av -NY 10017
(212) 532-3651 .. **Cardon,** Paul E '02 Marwood Grp -733 3rd Av -NY 10017
(518) 434-9807 .. **Cardona,** Anthony V Jr. '93 (D'Agostino KM&C,PC) -16 Sage Estate -Menands 12204
(518) 487-5344 .. **Cardona,** Jamie S '93 %Cnty Supreme Ct -16 Eagle -Albany 12207
(212) 538-0026 .. **Cardona,** John R '03 Credit Suisse -1 Mad Av -NY 10010
(315) 437-3321 .. **Cardona,** Laura Estela '89 Kall & R -3522 James -Syracuse 13206 **Fx:**437-0091
(518) 452-5600 .. **Cardona,** Victor A '99 (Heslin RF&M PC) -5 Columbia Cir -Albany 12203
(585) 590-4127 .. **Cardone,** Jos V '84 (DA) -13925 Route 31 -Albion 14411 **Fx:**590-4129
(516) 593-2440 .. **Cardone,** Nunzio J '52 -21 Hempstd Av -Lynbrk 11563 **Fx:**593-2486
(212) 267-4876 .. **Cardone,** Susan Ann '98 %Hoagland LMD&D,LLP -1501 Bway -NY 10036
(585) 798-3010 .. **Cardone,** Vincent D '49 -116 Park Av Bx109 -Medina 14103 **Fx:**798-2317
(212) 515-4641 .. **Cardoni,** Douglas J '98 Fortress Invstmt Grp -1345 Av of Amer -NY 10105
(516) 334-4500 .. **Cardoso,** Anthony F '09 %Sokoloff S LLP -355 Post Av -Westbury 11590 **Fx:**334-4501
(212) 406-2886 .. **Cardoso,** Patricia '81 (Glicksman & C) -150 Bway -NY 10038
(212) 838-6120 .. **Cardozo,** Benjamin M '42 Cardozo & C,PC -488 Mad Av -NY 10022 **Fx:**486-0701
(212) 335-4500 .. **Cardozo,** Camilo '01 %DLA Piper LLP -1251 Av of Amer -NY 10020
(212) 788-0800 .. **Cardozo,** Michl A '66 %Law Dept -100 Church -NY 10007 **Fx:**227-5641
(212) 567-4858 .. **Cardran,** Cheryl M '93 -125 Seaman Av -NY 10034
(585) 263-6760 .. **Carducci,** Grace M '04 %US Atty -620 Fed Bldg -Rchstr 14614 **Fx:**263-6226
(212) 705-7000 .. **Care,** M Derek '07 %Bingham M LLP -399 Park Av -NY 10022
(212) 651-7500 .. **Careathers,** Benjamin L '04 %Segal MS&M -850 3rd Av -NY 10022
(585) 263-1000 .. **Carello,** Jos A '08 %Nixon P LLP -1100 Clinton Sq -Rchstr 14604
(718) 875-5418 .. **Carena,** Lori H '79 Envrnmntl Cntrl Brd -233 Schermerhorn -Brklyn 11201
(917) 589-9234 .. **Caretto,** Howard R '80 (H Caretto,PC) -394A 9th -Brklyn 11215 **Fx:**(718) 832-6222
(718) 243-6428 .. **Caretto,** Matthew M '07 %Leg Aid -111 Lvngstn -Brklyn 11201 **Fx:**237-8737
(914) 824-5571 .. **Carew,** Colleen F '85 Surrogates Ct -111 Dr MLK Jr Blvd -White Plns 10601 **Fx:**995-3728
(914) 997-8100 .. **Carew,** Sean T '04 %Burke LM&G -10 Bank -White Plns 10606
(718) 330-2847 .. **Carew-Belfiore,** Tracy '92 %NLRB -2 Metrotech Ctr -Brklyn 11201 **Fx:**330-7579
(212) 225-2000 .. **Carew-Watts,** Antonia '10 %Cleary GS&H -1 Lbrty Plz -NY 10006
(212) 460-1122 .. **Carey,** Barbara Jane '77 Con Ed -4 Irving Pl -NY 10003
(518) 869-9500 .. **Carey,** Beth E '07 %Ganz W&S,LLP -1 Columbia Cir -Albany 12203
(212) 483-9490 .. **Carey,** Brian J '88 %McElroy DM&C,LLP -88 Pine -NY 10005
(212) 558-4000 .. **Carey,** Brie Ann '10 %Sullivan & C LLP -125 Broad -NY 10004
(716) 712-0888 .. **Carey,** Catherine A '88 %W Piotrowski -3881 Seneca -W Seneca 14224 **Fx:**712-0622
(212) 935-3000 .. **Carey,** Chas E '80 (Mintz LCFG&P,PC) -666 3rd Av -NY 10017
(212) 476-9000 .. **Carey,** Danl E '05 %Neuberger Berman,LLC -605 3rd Av -NY 10158 **Fx:**476-9862
(212) 858-4333 .. **Carey,** David L '86 FINRA -1 Lbrty Plz -NY 10006
(518) 474-4709 .. **Carey,** Edw J '85 %Appllt Div 3rd Dept -Capitol Station Bx7288 -Albany 12224 **Fx:**471-4750
(212) 373-3000 .. **Carey,** Emily J '08 %Paul WRW&G LLP -1285 Av of Amer -NY 10019
(212) 687-0100 .. **Carey,** Hugh L '51 (Harris B PLLC) -100 Wall -NY 10005
(212) 373-3000 .. **Carey,** Jessica S '04 %Paul WRW&G LLP -1285 Av of Amer -NY 10019
(212) 735-3855 .. **Carey,** John '97 NYSE -11 Wall -NY 10005
(212) 598-8000 .. **Carey,** Kevin F '86 %Guardian Life Ins -7 Hanover Sq -NY 10004 **Fx:**919-2693
(914) 238-0735 .. **Carey,** Kimberly '90 -20 Prospect Dr -Chappaqua 10514 **Fx:**238-0964
(631) 654-5997 .. **Carey,** Lisa A '82 -83 John -Patchogue 11772
(716) 838-5550 .. **Carey,** Louise E '69 (Carey & R) -360 Crescent Av -Buffalo 14214
(631) 366-2397 .. **Carey,** Maria Forte '92 -23 Jasmine Ln -Kings Pk 11754
(212) 245-0900 .. **Carey,** Meaghan E '09 %R Michaels,PC -150 E 52nd -NY 10022 **Fx:**245-5459
(212) 687-0100 .. **Carey,** Michl G '80 OfCnsl Harris B PLLC -100 Wall -NY 10005
(914) 682-2626 .. **Carey,** Michl L '91 SrCnsl Pannone LD&W LLC -81 Main -White Plns 10606
(212) 758-0076 .. **Carey,** Michl Q '72 (Carey & Assoc LLC) -521 5th Av -NY 10175 **Fx:**758-0069
(315) 474-0077 .. **Carey,** Paul G '88 (Carey Law Ofc,PC) -333 E Onondaga -Syracuse 13202 **Fx:**474-0425
(212) 889-4220 .. **Carey,** Paulette R '84 %Buchman Law Firm,LLP -10 E 40th -NY 10016 **Fx:**889-4221
(212) 277-4000 .. **Carey,** R Reed '08 %Freshfields BD LLP -520 Mad Av -NY 10022
(516) 682-0100 .. **Carey,** Raymond '80 R Carey,PC -9 Paige Ln -Moriches 11955 **Fx:**682-5883
(516) 832-7642 .. **Carey,** Robt H '62 Cnsl Nixon P LLP -50 Jericho Quadrangle -Jericho 11753
(212) 508-6100 .. **Carey,** Robt T '95 (Bracewell & G,LLP) -1251 Av of Amer -NY 10020
(607) 722-3686 .. **Carey,** Robt W '86 -122 State -Bnghmtn 13901 **Fx:**722-2842
(716) 773-3304 .. **Carey,** Shawn W '97 -1730 Grand Isl Blvd -Grand Isl 14072
(315) 426-0177 .. **Carey,** Susan C '93 -472 S Salina -Syracuse 13202
(212) 483-9490 .. **Carey,** Wm C '84 Cnsl McElroy DM&C,LLP -88 Pine -NY 10005
(212) 637-2711 .. **Cargo,** Shane P '03 %US Atty -86 Chmbrs -NY 10007
(212) 909-6000 .. **Cariappa,** Priya M '10 %Debevoise & P LLP -919 3rd Av -NY 10022
(212) 325-2000 .. **Caridi,** Joan '76 CSFB -1 Mad Av -NY 10010
(718) 531-6765 .. **Caridi,** Marco R '03 -546 3rd Av -Brklyn 11215
(212) 547-5400 .. **Cariello,** Bari M '93 (McDermott W&E LLP) -340 Mad Av -NY 10173
(516) 745-8310 .. **Cariello,** Denise A '97 (Perez & V) -333 Earle Ovngton Blvd Bx9372 -Uniondale 11553
(212) 768-6700 .. **Cariello,** Dennis M '00 Sonnenschein N&R LLP -1221 Av of Amer -NY 10020
(718) 463-7333 .. **Cariello,** Wm J III '94 %M Mongelli II,PC -41-07 162nd -Flushng 11358 **Fx:**358-4872
(718) 236-3140 .. **Carilli,** Albert F '87 -1646 85th -Brklyn 11214
(917) 454-1100 .. **Carinci,** Elaine M '00 NYPD-Civil Enfrcmnt -2 Lafayette -NY 10007
(718) 520-1212 .. **Carini,** Dominic L '67 -125-10 Qns Blvd -Kew Gdns 11415
(646) 722-8500 .. **Carino,** Michele S '00 %Grant & E,PA -485 Lex Av -NY 10017
(212) 714-2277 .. **Carino,** Tomas D J '02 %Abad C&M,LLC -350 5th Av -NY 10118 **Fx:**714-9331
(585) 454-7145 .. **Cariola,** Elena F '05 %Gallo & I,LLP -39 State -Rchstr 14614
(212) 588-9460 .. **Caristo-Perez,** Lisa A '05 %Kent & M,PC -420 Lex Av -NY 10170 **Fx:**588-9818
(315) 798-5890 .. **Carl,** Aniela J '76 -200 Elisabeth -Utica 13501
(585) 385-6090 .. **Carl,** Stephen J '93 Clover Capital Mgmt Inc -400 Meridian Ctr -Rchstr 14618
(716) 565-2000 .. **Carland,** Edw J '51 -17 Beresford Ct -Williamsvll 14221 **Fx:**565-2002
(212) 374-9840 .. **Carle,** Kevin P '08 %Wenig & W -150 Bway -NY 10038 **Fx:**374-9844
(212) 558-4000 .. **Carle,** Nathaniel M '09 %Sullivan & C LLP -125 Broad -NY 10004
(845) 638-5180 .. **Carle,** Patrick '83 %Cnty Atty -Cnty Ofc Bldg -New Cty 10956 **Fx:**638-5676
(347) 592-2200 .. **Carlea,** Azaleea S '03 Leg Srvcs -89-00 Sutphin Blvd -Jamaica 11435 **Fx:**(718) 937-5350
(212) 785-3041 .. **Carlebach,** P David '91 -40 Exch Pl -NY 10005 **Fx:**785-3618
(212) 859-8000 .. **Carleen,** Donald P '84 (Fried FHS&J LLP) -1 NY Plz -NY 10004
(212) 869-2147 .. **Carlet Garrison Klein & Zaretsky** -645 5th Av -NY 10022
(212) 820-7700 .. **Carleton,** Edw C '06 %Boundas SW&B,LLC -1 Bttry Pk Plz -NY 10004
(518) 276-3777 .. **Carletta,** Chas F '69 Cnsl RPI -110 8th -Troy 12180 **Fx:**276-3665
(718) 726-6993 .. **Carley,** Brian '85 %G Poulos -29-16 23rd Av -Astoria 11105 **Fx:**721-7793
(914) 251-0001 .. **Carley,** J Patrick III '05 %Lane S&L LLP -106 Corp Park Dr -White Plns 10604
(212) 460-2097 .. **Carley,** John L '83 Con Ed -4 Irving Pl -NY 10003
(646) 442-3100 .. **Carlier,** Milton J '89 %Legal Srvcs -90 John -NY 10038 **Fx:**(212) 227-9798
(212) 406-5502 .. **Carlin,** Alexander M '90 -299 Bway -NY 10007
(212) 935-8300 .. **Carlin,** Allan H '76 -708 3rd Av -NY 10017
(212) 530-4835 .. **Carlin,** Amy D '90 %LaRocca HRG&B LLP -40 Wall -NY 10005
(845) 225-6467 .. **Carlin,** Brian E '96 (Ryder C&C) -45 Gleneida Av Bx150 -Carmel 10512 **Fx:**225-1664
(917) 841-4101 .. **Carlin,** David H '67 -993 Park Av -NY 10028
(607) 762-3366 .. **Carlin,** Donald P '71 United Hlth Srvcs, Inc -10-42 Mitchell Av -Bnghmtn 13903
(212) 406-5502 .. **Carlin,** Francine Galante '92 A Carlin -299 Bway -NY 10007
(716) 854-4300 .. **Carlin,** Hugh C '88 (Gross SB&G,PC) -465 Main -Buffalo 14203
(212) 538-4602 .. **Carlin,** Jane D '83 Credit Suisse -11 Mad Av -NY 10010
(212) 218-2100 .. **Carlin,** John D '93 (Fitzpatrick CH&S) -1290 Av of Amer -NY 10104
(607) 763-9200 .. **Carlin,** John J '68 (Levene G&T,LLP) -BxF-1706 -Bnghmtn 13902
(212) 697-4589 .. **Carlin,** Judith L '63 -330 E 38th -NY 10016 **Fx:**697-4589
(212) 622-7180 .. **Carlin,** Larry M '73 -437 Mad Av -NY 10022 **Fx:**754-2508
(212) 788-9110 .. **Carlin,** Matthew W '00 %City Cncl Leg Div -250 Bway -NY 10007 **Fx:**788-7034
(212) 269-3100 .. **Carlin,** Michl D '78 -26 Bway -NY 10004 **Fx:**269-7032
(516) 681-9757 .. **Carlin,** Robt F II '84 -2 Robbins Ln -Jericho 11753 **Fx:**681-9766
(212) 508-6700 .. **Carlin,** Roy H '64 OfCnsl Tannenbaum HS&H LLP -900 3rd Av -NY 10022
(212) 238-3000 .. **Carlin,** Sean M '87 (Emmet M&M,LLP) -120 Bway -NY 10271
(212) 909-5400 .. **Carlin,** Steven B '88 KPMG -757 3rd Av -NY 10017
(212) 403-1000 .. **Carlin,** Wayne M '85 (Wachtell LR&K) -51 W 52nd -NY 10019
(914) 390-8009 .. **Carline,** Jos '75 %NYPA -123 Main -White Plns 10601 **Fx:**390-8040
(212) 758-7600 .. **Carling,** Francis '72 (Collazo C&M) -747 3rd Av -NY 10017
(585) 672-2600 .. **Carling,** Steven G '04 %Burns & S LLP -28 E Main -Rchstr 14614 **Fx:**(866) 825-7217
(845) 452-3434 .. **Carlini,** Anthony C Jr. '95 (Handel & C,LLP) -112 Delafld -Poughkeepsie 12601 **Fx:**471-0105
(212) 483-9490 .. **Carlino,** Anthony M '89 (McElroy DM&C,LLP) -88 Pine -NY 10005
(716) 566-5400 .. **Carlino,** Jeffrey A '99 SpclCnsl Goldberg S LLP -665 Main -Buffalo 14203
(516) 622-0099 .. **Carlinsky Dunn & Pasquariello,PLLC** -8 Duffy Av -Hicksvll 11801 **Fx:**622-9280
(212) 849-7000 .. **Carlinsky,** Michl B '89 (Quinn EU&S,LLP) -51 Mad Av -NY 10010
(516) 622-0099 .. **Carlinsky,** Mitchell J '81 (Carlinsky D&P,PLLC) -8 Duffy Av -Hicksvll 11801
(716) 856-8200 .. **Carlisle,** Benjamin S '09 %Williams & W -43 Court -Buffalo 14202 **Fx:**856-0559
(212) 213-0172 .. **Carlisle,** Frances '84 -20 Waterside Plz -NY 10010 **Fx:**213-2342
(914) 422-4234 .. **Carlisle,** Jay C II '70 %Pace Law Schl -78 N Bway -White Plns 10603 **Fx:**422-4039
(212) 636-2000 .. **Carlisle,** Keith M '96 Christie's -20 Rckfllr Plz -NY 10020
(315) 393-1111 .. **Carlisle,** Preston C '61 Carlisle C&C,PC -602 State Bx757 -Ogdensbrg 13669 **Fx:**393-1181

(716) 856-3500 .. **Carlo,** James N '58 (Magavern MG LLP) -1100 Rand Bldg -Buffalo 14203
(631) 348-7500 .. **Carlo,** Margaret '09 %Chase S Law Grp,LLP -64 Smithtwn Blvd -Smithtwn 11787 **Fx:**348-7501
(212) 943-1550 .. **Carlock,** J Gregory '74 Cnsl Speyer & P,LLP -26 Bway -NY 10004
(631) 543-0713 .. **Carlomagno,** Alexander D '89 -26 Radburn Dr -Commack 11725
(718) 359-2786 .. **Carlomusto,** Michl '94 -1065 Old Cntry Rd -Westbury 11590 **Fx:**(516) 945-3269
(212) 474-1000 .. **Carlon,** Andrew M '08 %Cravath S&M LLP -825 8th Av -NY 10019
(212) 250-5548 .. **Carlon,** Carlo-Edoardo '00 %Deutsche Bank -60 Wall -NY 10005
(212) 808-7800 .. **Carlon,** James P '00 %Kelley D&W LLP -101 Park Av -NY 10178
(212) 631-7442 .. **Carlos,** Don A Jr. '93 -352 7th Av -NY 10001 **Fx:**631-7452
(212) 492-1742 .. **Carlos,** Suzana '09 EMI Music Publishing -75 9th Av -NY 10011
(718) 590-2000 .. **Carlow,** Nina C '87 %DA -198 E 161st -Bronx 10451 **Fx:**590-6477
(212) 545-4000 .. **Carlozzi,** Linda R '99 (Jackson L LLP) -666 3rd Av -NY 10017
(212) 710-3900 .. **Carlsen,** Christopher '84 (Clyde & Co US LLP) -405 Lex Av -NY 10174 **Fx:**710-3950
(718) 366-0058 .. **Carlsen,** Robt C '64 R Carlsen,PC -73-35 Myrtle Av -Glendale 11385 **Fx:**497-8329
(212) 521-5400 .. **Carlson,** A Sonali '02 %Reed S LLP -599 Lex Av -NY 10022
(516) 222-6500 .. **Carlson,** Amanda L '06 %Galasso LC&L,LLP -377 Oak -Gdn Cty 11530
(914) 681-0200 .. **Carlson,** Ann Farrissey '88 (DelBello DWW&W,LLP) -1 N Lex Av -White Plns 10601
(631) 870-3961 .. **Carlson,** Brian '95 Fuoco Grp,LLP -200 Pkwy Dr S -Hauppauge 11788 **Fx:**870-3911
(917) 743-2594 .. **Carlson,** Carl M '04 -158 Guernsey -Brklyn 11222
(718) 590-2000 .. **Carlson,** Cynthia A '08 %DA -198 E 161st -Bronx 10451 **Fx:**590-6477
(212) 790-0210 .. **Carlson,** David G '78 %Benj N Cardozo Schl of Law -55 5th Av -NY 10003 **Fx:**790-0345
(212) 425-1900 .. **Carlson,** Edw J '08 %Freehill H&M LLP -80 Pine -NY 10005
(716) 856-4000 .. **Carlson,** Elizabeth D '02 %Hodgson R LLP -140 Pearl -Buffalo 14202
(212) 762-4000 .. **Carlson,** Eric J '99 Morgan Stanley -1221 Av of Amer -NY 10020
(212) 308-1000 .. **Carlson,** Eric R '98 %RFR Holding LLC -390 Park Av -NY 10022
(212) 600-3116 .. **Carlson,** Irene A '01 United Business Media -11 W 19th -NY 10011
(212) 506-2500 .. **Carlson,** James B '93 (Mayer B LLP) -1675 Bway -NY 10019
(212) 474-1000 .. **Carlson,** James W '10 %Cravath S&M LLP -825 8th Av -NY 10019
(518) 713-2144 .. **Carlson,** Jennifer L '04 %Rehfuss L & Assoc,PC -40 British Amer Blvd -Latham 12110 **Fx:**713-2148
(516) 378-1338 .. **Carlson,** John '83 -5 Winifred Dr -Merrick 11566
(607) 637-4542 .. **Carlson,** John L '49 -Bx444 -Hancock 13783 **Fx:**637-4542
(518) 457-6410 .. **Carlson,** Kenneth S '95 %PERB -80 Wolf Rd -Albany 12205 **Fx:**457-2664
(631) 424-6100 .. **Carlson,** Kerry Ann '95 Advantage Title Agncy -410 new York Av -Huntngtn 11743
(212) 408-5100 .. **Carlson,** Kirsten M '06 %Chadbourne & P LLP -30 Rckfllr Plz -NY 10112
(212) 297-5800 .. **Carlson,** Mat D '03 %Day P LLP -7 Times Sq -NY 10036
(212) 261-7000 .. **Carlson,** Richd V '82 %Calyon -1301 Av of Amer -NY 10019
(212) 839-5300 .. **Carlson,** Robt E Jr. '99 (Sidley A LLP) -787 7th Av -NY 10019
(212) 558-4000 .. **Carlson,** Sarah D '10 %Sullivan & C LLP -125 Broad -NY 10004
(631) 589-1221 .. **Carlsson,** Kathleen A '66 (Carlsson & C) -85 S Main -Sayvll 11782
(212) 858-1000 .. **Carlston,** Mats G '87 (Pillsbury WSP LLP) -1540 Bway -NY 10036
(212) 208-9592 .. **Carlton,** Eileen S '97 Liberty Intl Underwriters -55 Water -NY 10041
(212) 683-9559 .. **Carlton,** Gary M '79 (Goldberg & C,PLLC) -31 E 32nd -NY 10016 **Fx:**683-7901
(607) 723-0600 .. **Carlton,** Jason M '01 (Gitto & N,LLP) -71 State -Bnghmtn 13901 **Fx:**723-0634
(212) 489-1600 .. **Carlucci,** Amy '01 %Deloitte LLP -1633 Bway -NY 10019 **Fx:**492-4201
(914) 428-2100 .. **Carlucci,** Anthony P Jr. '00 %Welby B&G,LLP -11 Martine Av -White Plns 10606
(646) 865-1590 .. **Carlucci,** Don D '78 (Carlucci & G,LLP) -11 E 44th -NY 10017
(646) 865-1590 .. **Carlucci & Giardina,LLP** -11 E 44th -NY 10017 **Fx:**865-1319
(518) 822-1435 .. **Carlucci,** James '90 -21 N 7th -Hudson 12534 **Fx:**822-1437
(914) 761-1300 .. **Carlucci,** Jos P '69 (Cuddy & F LLP) -445 Hmltn Av -White Plns 10601
(212) 651-7500 .. **Carlucci,** Maria C '05 %Segal MS&M -850 3rd Av -NY 10022
(212) 279-3334 .. **Carlucci,** Michl A '86 (Collopy & C) -5 Penn Plz -NY 10001
(516) 249-3450 .. **Carman Callahan & Ingham, LLP** -266 Main -Farmngdl 11735 **Fx:**843-6390
(212) 596-9000 .. **Carman,** Eva Ciko '96 (Ropes & G LLP) -1211 Av of Amer -NY 10036
(516) 249-3450 .. **Carman,** Gregory W Jr. '92 (Carman C&I,LLP) -266 Main -Farmngdl 11735 **Fx:**249-3782
(516) 249-3450 .. **Carman,** James M '93 (Carman C&I,LLP) -266 Main -Farmngdl 11735
(516) 683-3600 .. **Carman,** John F '90 -666 Old Cntry Rd -Gdn Cty 11530 **Fx:**683-8410
(516) 249-3450 .. **Carman,** Willis B Jr. '57 (Carman C&I,LLP) -266 Main -Farmngdl 11735
(516) 249-3450 .. **Carman,** Willis B '90 (Carman C&I,LLP) -266 Main -Farmngdl 11735
(212) 585-1600 .. **Carmel,** Dorothy D '96 Cadogan Cptl Mgmt -149 5th Av -NY 10010
(212) 453-5900 .. **Carmell,** Wm Abel '66 (Ford & H LLP) -100 Park Av -NY 10017
(212) 319-4000 .. **Carmen,** Allison N '92 OfCnsl Weiss & H,PC -600 Mad Av -NY 10022
(516) 992-1848 .. **Carmen,** Michl E '00 (M Carmen & Assoc,PLLC) -1201 RXR Plz -Uniondale 11556 **Fx:**739-0981
(315) 361-8687 .. **Carmen,** Peter D '92 %Oneida Indian Nation Enterprises -5218 Patrick Rd -Verona 13478 **Fx:**361-8009
(212) 758-6160 .. **Carmen,** Richd E '80 (Brief C&K,LLP) -805 3rd Av -NY 10022
(212) 704-6000 .. **Carmen,** Robt M '79 OfCnsl Troutman S LLP -405 Lex Av -NY 10174
(347) 404-9133 .. **Carmenaty,** Rudolph J '91 %Civil Ct -141 Lvngstn -Brklyn 11201 **Fx:**(718) 643-3733
(212) 407-4000 .. **Carmichael,** Tamara F '03 (Loeb & L,LLP) -345 Park Av -NY 10154
(212) 554-1234 .. **Carmicino,** Benedict G '93 AXA Financial Inc -1290 Av of Amer -NY 10104 **Fx:**707-3963
(718) 259-5558 .. **Carmine,** Jos N '56 -1904 86th -Brklyn 11214
(212) 715-9100 .. **Carmine,** R Sean '01 Kramer LN&F LLP -1177 Av of Amer -NY 10036 **Fx:**715-8000
(518) 581-8800 .. **Carminucci,** James A '86 (Lemery G LLC) -60 Railroad Pl -Saratoga Spgs 12866
(516) 739-8300 .. **Carmody,** Brian J '82 -355 Post Av -Westbury 11590
(845) 679-4500 .. **Carmody,** Don T '76 -1407 Bway -NY 10018
(914) 995-3496 .. **Carmody,** John J '90 %DA -111 Martin Luther King Blvd -White Plns 10601 **Fx:**995-3363
(716) 278-9814 .. **Carmody,** Kathleen M '89 %City Ct -1925 Main -Niagara Fls 14305
(212) 268-8200 .. **Carmody,** Matthew D '99 %B Raphan,PC -7 Penn Plz -NY 10001 **Fx:**244-3075
(212) 239-9777 .. **Carmody,** Michl '85 (Parker & C,LLP) -331 Mad Av -NY 10017 **Fx:**239-9175
(516) 365-8819 .. **Carmody,** Robt C Jr. '85 -26 Sargent Pl -Manhsst 11030
(212) 336-8330 .. **Carmody,** Wm C '07 (Susman G LLP) -560 Lex Av -NY 10022
(212) 751-0406 .. **Carmon,** Rakeffet '86 Carmon & C -767 3rd Av -NY 10017 **Fx:**751-0409
(845) 278-0072 .. **Carmona,** Paul A Jr. '96 (P Carmona & Assoc,PLLC) -96 Main -Brewstr 10509 **Fx:**278-5441
(212) 373-3000 .. **Carmona Parent,** David '07 %Paul WRW&G LLP -1285 Av of Amer -NY 10019
(585) 342-4410 .. **Carnahan,** Christine Albright '03 %Burke AH&R,LLP -1800 Hudson Av -Rchstr 14617
(212) 556-2100 .. **Carnaval,** Christopher C '05 %King & S -1185 Av of Amer -NY 10036
(914) 668-6458 .. **Carnegie,** Christa L '76 -380 Hayward Av -Mt Vernon 10552 **Fx:**668-6458
(212) 943-1090 .. **Carnemolla,** Diana M '98 (Gair GCSMB&R) -80 Pine -NY 10005
(631) 543-7667 .. **Carner,** Michl '92 (Carner & D) -350 Vets Mem'l Hwy -Commack 11725 **Fx:**543-7901
(631) 543-7667 .. **Carner,** Ronald S '67 (Sarisohn Law Prtnrs LLP) -350 Vets Mem'l Hwy -Commack 11725 **Fx:**543-7901
(585) 268-9410 .. **Carnes,** Nora K '08 %Cnty Atty -7 Court -Belmont 14813 **Fx:**268-9651
(516) 512-8914 .. **Carnesi,** Chas F '75 -1225 Franklin Av -Gdn Cty 11530 **Fx:**227-1902
(212) 430-8020 .. **Carnesi,** Kim A '97 Cnsl LeClairRyan,PC -830 3rd Av -NY 10022
(212) 425-1900 .. **Carnevale,** Barbara Grose '86 %Freehill H&M LLP -80 Pine -NY 10005
(212) 425-7200 .. **Carnevale,** Eric P '10 %Kenyon & K,LLP -1 Bway -NY 10004
(212) 732-3200 .. **Carnevale,** Lawr F '82 (Carter L&M LLP) -2 Wall -NY 10005
(914) 288-0022 .. **Carney,** Bonnie K '91 Leason E LLP -81 Main -White Plns 10601
(212) 872-1000 .. **Carney,** Brian T '06 -One Bryant Park -NY 10036 **Fx:**872-1002
(516) 483-2990 .. **Carney,** Danielle M '95 %Barnes I&S,LLP -3 Surrey Ln -Hempstd 11550
(718) 505-6660 .. **Carney,** Dawn S '02 %S Swenton & Assoc -75-20 Astoria Blvd -E Elmhrst 11370
(212) 449-5884 .. **Carney,** Faith E '72 %Merrill Lynch -220 Bway -NY 10038
(212) 373-3000 .. **Carney,** Gary R Jr. '88 Cnsl Paul WRW&G LLP -1285 Av of Amer -NY 10019
(518) 388-4331 .. **Carney,** Jean T '96 Pub Def -620 State -Schnctdy 12305 **Fx:**388-4308
(914) 738-4001 .. **Carney,** John F '66 (Carney & M) -4810 Bstn Post Rd -Pelham 10803
(716) 854-5311 .. **Carney,** John J '56 -43 Court -Buffalo 14202
(716) 854-5311 .. **Carney,** John J III '84 -43 Court -Buffalo 14202 **Fx:**854-4857
(212) 589-4200 .. **Carney,** John J '05 (Baker & H LLP) -45 Rckfllr Plz -NY 10111
(212) 484-8000 .. **Carney,** Jos E '91 Warner Music Grp -75 Rckfllr Plz -NY 10019 **Fx:**489-3342
(716) 854-5311 .. **Carney,** Mark S '87 -43 Court -Buffalo 14202
(716) 854-5311 .. **Carney,** Mary G '01 -43 Court -Buffalo 14202 **Fx:**854-4857
(516) 742-6600 .. **Carney & McKay** -1050 Franklin Av -Gdn Cty 11530 **Fx:**742-6671
(914) 738-4001 .. **Carney & McKay** -4810 Bstn Post Rd -Pelham 10803 **Fx:**738-3944
(212) 701-3000 .. **Carney,** Michl R '05 %Cahill G&R LLP -80 Pine -NY 10005 **Fx:**269-5420
(518) 585-2881 .. **Carney,** Patrick J '74 (Carney & B) -12 Father Joques Pl -Ticonderoga 12883 **Fx:**585-2608
(212) 964-6611 .. **Carney,** Paul E '99 %Lester SK&D -120 Bway -NY 10271
(518) 388-4364 .. **Carney,** Robt M '79 (DA) -612 State -Schnctdy 12305 **Fx:**388-4569
(212) 577-3688 .. **Carney,** Wm B '90 %Leg Aid -199 Water -NY 10038 **Fx:**509-8431
(212) 351-4500 .. **Carney D'Angelo,** Erin '98 SrCnsl Epstein B&G,PC -250 Park Av -NY 10177
(212) 425-7200 .. **Carniaux,** Michelle M '94 (Kenyon & K,LLP) -1 Bway -NY 10004
(718) 591-2400 .. **Carniol,** Norman M '76 -179-14 Union Tpk -Fresh Mdws 11366
(212) 973-0572 .. **Carniol,** Rhonda E '83 OfCnsl Wolff & S PC -140 Bway -NY 10005
(212) 264-0659 .. **Carnival,** Mary Anne '87 %Dept Justice -26 Fed Plz -NY 10278
(845) 340-3315 .. **Carnright,** D Holley '78 DA -285 Wall -Kingston 12401 **Fx:**340-3185
(315) 448-8400 .. **Carnrike,** Catherine E '04 %Law Dept -233 E Wshngtn -Syracuse 13202 **Fx:**448-8381
(315) 425-2700 .. **Carnrike,** Thos A '06 %Hiscock & B,LLP -One Park Pl -Syracuse 13202
(315) 448-8400 .. **Carnrike,** Thos M '76 %Law Dept -233 E Wshngtn -Syracuse 13202 **Fx:**448-8381
(716) 856-4000 .. **Carnrite,** Troy M '09 %Hodgson R LLP -140 Pearl -Buffalo 14202
(718) 250-2000 .. **Carny,** Ronny '03 %DA -350 Jay -Brklyn 11201 **Fx:**250-2314
(716) 881-3010 .. **Caro,** Danl C '96 OfCnsl Cohen & L,PC -343 Elmwood Av Bx5204 -Buffalo 14213
(212) 966-6420 .. **Caro,** Shirley '01 %Lwyrs For Children -110 Lafayette -NY 10013 **Fx:**966-0531
(718) 678-8900 .. **Carofano,** Jos A '92 (JA Carofano,PC) -3651 E Tremont Av -Bronx 10465 **Fx:**678-8901
(516) 229-6000 .. **Carola,** Jos III '91 %R Lau & Assoc -300 Jericho Quad Bx9040 -Jericho 11753 **Fx:**229-6167
(212) 209-4800 .. **Carolan,** Christopher J '01 (Brown R LLP) -7 Times Sq -NY 10036
(845) 223-3470 .. **Carolei,** Carmine J '89 (Ahmuty D&M) -1531 Route 82 -Hopewell Junct 12533
(718) 238-9555 .. **Carollo,** Cristina '05 %Gullo & Assoc,LLP -520 86th -Brklyn 11209 **Fx:**238-9552
(914) 681-0444 .. **Carollo,** Frank J '74 (Rende R&D,LLP) -202 Mamaroneck Av -White Plns 10601
(718) 444-3301 .. **Carone,** Anthony J '02 (Carone & Assoc,PLLC) -2132 Flatbush Av -Brklyn 11234

(212) 223-8868 .. **Carone,** Frank V '95 -9306 Flatlands Av -Brklyn 11236 **Fx:**(718) 872-7984
(631) 231-1199 .. **Caronia,** Peter R '72 (Reynolds CGHL&Q,LLP) -35 Arkay Dr -Hauppauge 11788
(718) 522-5717 .. **Caronna,** Anthony A '93 -26 Court -Brklyn 11242
(716) 282-3322 .. **Carosella,** Jos W '73 -151 Buffalo Av -Niagara Fls 14303 **Fx:**282-5693
(212) 819-8200 .. **Carosi,** Brendan J '08 %White & C LLP -1155 Av of Amer -NY 10036
(212) 225-7700 .. **Carotenuto,** Louis '84 %Cartafalsa ST&L -165 Bway -NY 10006
(212) 471-8515 .. **Caroti,** Gisella Levi '86 (Herzfeld & R,PC) -125 Broad -NY 10004
(914) 235-1498 .. **Carozza,** Carol '94 (Carozza Law Ofc) -2525 Palmer Av -New Rchll 10801 **Fx:**235-1499
(914) 302-6285 .. **Carozza,** Rekha M '01 -39 Braddock Ct -Yorktwn Hts 10598 **Fx:**962-4589
(212) 508-0164 .. **Carp,** David J '02 -717 5th Av -NY 10022
(212) 686-7700 .. **Carp,** Gerald I '63 (Mazur CR&S PC) -1250 Bway -NY 10001
(914) 993-1546 .. **Carparelli,** Peter '75 %Town Atty -177 Hillside Av -Greenburgh 10607 **Fx:**993-1656
(212) 289-6593 .. **Carpeni,** Marcia E '68 -1150 Park Av -NY 10128
(212) 210-9582 .. **Carpenito,** Craig '02 (Alston & B LLP) -90 Park Av -NY 10016
(212) 312-2368 .. **Carpenter,** Bruce A '91 %Leg Aid -60 Lafayette -NY 10013 **Fx:**349-0874
(716) 672-5354 .. **Carpenter,** Bruce K '67 -33 Church Bx111 -Fredonia 14063
(212) 906-1200 .. **Carpenter,** Chas E '00 (Latham & W) -885 3rd Av -NY 10022
(212) 797-4362 .. **Carpenter,** George J '85 Rafter & Assoc,PLLC -29 Bway -NY 10006 **Fx:**797-4363
(518) 374-3344 .. **Carpenter,** Howard G Jr. '67 -650 Franklin -Schnctdy 12305 **Fx:**374-0828
(212) 218-2100 .. **Carpenter,** James R '09 %Fitzpatrick CH&S -1290 Av of Amer -NY 10104
(516) 571-9038 .. **Carpenter,** Jeffrey M '92 %Family Ct -1200 Old Cntry Rd -Westbury 11590
(315) 867-1155 .. **Carpenter,** Jeffrey S '93 %DA -301 N Wshngtn -Herkimer 13350 **Fx:**867-1348
(718) 250-2000 .. **Carpenter,** Jordan Ryan '05 %DA -350 Jay -Brklyn 11201 **Fx:**250-2314
(315) 453-4282 .. **Carpenter,** Karen B '94 Carpenter Law Ofc,PC -716 7th N St -Liverpool 13088 **Fx:**453-4285
(914) 684-1055 .. **Carpenter,** Kimberley A '90 %Baxter S&S,PC -200 Mamaroneck Av -White Plns 10601
(646) 386-3666 .. **Carpenter,** Lelan K '04 %Supreme Ct-Law Dept -60 Centre -NY 10007
(212) 788-0903 .. **Carpenter,** Megan '07 %Law Dept -100 Church -NY 10007 **Fx:**788-0367
(914) 712-1100 .. **Carpenter,** Paul D '78 %Murphy & H,LLP -1 Radisson Plz -New Rchll 10801
(914) 834-6669 .. **Carpenter,** Randle B Jr. '65 -29 Hazel Ln -Larchmnt 10538 **Fx:**834-3109
(212) 506-5000 .. **Carpenter,** Stephanie L '08 %Orrick H&S LLP -51 W 52nd -NY 10019
(914) 241-6346 .. **Carpenter,** Susan E '76 %Westchester Land Trust -403 Harris Rd -Bedfrd Hlls 10507 **Fx:**241-4508
(845) 485-2529 .. **Carpenter,** Todd W '07 J Spilbor,LLC -35 Main -Poughkeepsie 12601
(212) 547-5400 .. **Carpentier,** Joan-Elisse '84 (McDermott W&E LLP) -340 Mad Av -NY 10173
(516) 248-7000 .. **Carpentier,** Robt A '82 OfCnsl Albanese & A LLP -1050 Franklin Av -Gdn Cty 11530
(212) 422-1200 .. **Carpentiere,** Marisa '97 %Abrams GF&J,PC -1 Bttry Pk Plz -NY 10004
(212) 751-2700 .. **Carpinello,** Anthony J '74 JAMS -620 8th Av -NY 10018 **Fx:**751-4099
(518) 434-0600 .. **Carpinello,** George F '76 (Boies S&F LLP) -10 N Pearl -Albany 12207
(518) 478-0245 .. **Carpinello,** Melissa A '95 -20 Bender Ln -Delmar 12054 **Fx:**439-6855
(914) 995-2897 .. **Carpiniello,** James R '97 %Cnty Atty -148 Martine Av -White Plns 10601 **Fx:**995-5858
(212) 367-9600 .. **Carponter,** Candace C '82 -60 Broad -NY 10004
(315) 785-3053 .. **Carr,** Aaron D '03 %DA -175 Arsenal -Watertwn 13601 **Fx:**785-3371
(212) 681-6000 .. **Carr,** Aaron J '69 Fed Home Loan Bk -101 Park Av -NY 10178
(518) 465-3484 .. **Carr,** Brian D '07 %Carter CCBM&L,PC -20 Corp Wds Blvd -Albany 12211
(212) 637-3170 .. **Carr,** Brian E '92 %EPA -290 Bway -NY 10007 **Fx:**637-3096
(212) 471-8500 .. **Carr,** Brian T '02 %Herzfeld & R,PC -125 Broad -NY 10004
(518) 668-5412 .. **Carr,** Bruce G '86 (Stafford C&M,PC) -175 Ottawa -Lk George 12845
(716) 645-3030 .. **Carr,** Chas E Jr. '78 %SUNY Buffalo Lw Schl -O'Brian Hall -Buffalo 14260 **Fx:**645-5968
(212) 456-7777 .. **Carr,** Cherylyn D '89 %ABC -77 W 66th -NY 10023 **Fx:**456-6202
(212) 704-1443 .. **Carr,** Christine D '04 Interpublic Grp of Companies,Inc -1114 Av of Amer -NY 10036
(866) 931-6092 .. **Carr,** Christopher T '91 ODAR-SSA -155-10 Jamaica Av Bx319300 -Jamaica 11431 **Fx:**(718) 557-6575
(716) 856-5012 .. **Carr,** Daria A '04 %Anspach ME,LLP -2400 Main Pl Twr -Buffalo 14202
(585) 455-7192 .. **Carr,** Denine K '93 -344 Warren Av -Rchstr 14618 **Fx:**899-4454
(212) 735-3000 .. **Carr,** Elizabeth L '03 %Skadden ASM&F LLP -4 Times Sq -NY 10036
(212) 808-7955 .. **Carr,** James S '88 (Kelley D&W LLP) -101 Park Av -NY 10178
(716) 372-4450 .. **Carr,** Jay D '96 (Carr S LLP) -235 N Union -Olean 14760 **Fx:**372-4011
(212) 207-8044 .. **Carr,** John J '65 OfCnsl Mulholland & K,LLP -230 Park Av -NY 10169 **Fx:**599-1759
(212) 455-2000 .. **Carr,** John W '88 (Simpson T&B LLP) -425 Lex Av -NY 10017
(518) 449-5131 .. **Carr,** Jos B '76 McGinn Smith & Co -99 Pine -Albany 12207
(212) 334-4494 .. **Carr,** Kelly C '99 Bur Emrgncy Mgmt -125 Worth -NY 10013
(518) 408-1495 .. **Carr,** Mary Frances '03 %Dept of Health -Corning Twr 24th Fl -Albany 12237 **Fx:**486-4834
(212) 525-3378 .. **Carr,** Maxwell A '09 HSBC Securities(USA) -452 5th Av -NY 10018
(518) 862-0662 .. **Carr,** Murray S '80 -1683 Wstrn Av -Albany 12203 **Fx:**862-0921
(212) 935-7100 .. **Carr,** Pamela J '91 -488 Mad Av -NY 10022 **Fx:**935-7125
(914) 472-5636 .. **Carr,** Patrick J '64 -21 Rodney Rd -Scarsdale 10583
(315) 422-1311 .. **Carr,** Ronald S '74 OfCnsl Melvin & M,PLLC -217 S Salina -Syracuse 13202
(914) 347-7039 .. **Carr,** Sara Jane '03 Student Advocacy Inc -3 W Main -Elmsfrd 10523
(212) 336-2000 .. **Carr,** Shaun L '04 Patterson BW&T LLP -1133 Av of Amer -NY 10036
(716) 856-5012 .. **Carr,** Steven E '06 %Anspach ME,LLP -2400 Main Pl Twr -Buffalo 14202
(631) 749-0322 .. **Carr,** Thos A '88 -Bx575 -Shelter Isl 11964
(518) 218-7100 .. **Carr,** Thos J '98 Cnsl Tully R,PLLC -441 New Karner Rd -Albany 12205
(516) 652-7624 .. **Carr,** Victor A '81 -88 2nd -Mineola 11501 **Fx:**747-2574
(585) 546-6350 .. **Carra,** Josephine R '84 %Ticor Title -19 W Main -Rchstr 14614 **Fx:**546-5465
(716) 631-3001 .. **Carra,** Laurie Boreanaz '88 %Independent Hlth -511 Farber Lks Dr -Buffalo 14221 **Fx:**635-3838
(516) 742-1135 .. **Carra,** Lawr V '79 -114 Old Cntry Rd -Mineola 11501
(212) 812-8911 .. **Carragher,** Owen B Jr. '89 (Lankler & C,LLP) -845 3rd Av -NY 10022
(212) 361-1725 .. **Carraher,** Laura '81 Envrnmntl Cntrl Brd -66 John -NY 10038 **Fx:**361-1900
(212) 688-5000 .. **Carrara,** John J '80 %Westvaco -299 Park Av -NY 10171
(212) 232-1300 .. **Carrasco,** Michl A '00 %Lewis BB&S LLP -77 Water -NY 10005
(718) 742-6550 .. **Carrasquillo,** Lisa M '01 Dept of Ed -501 Courtland Av -Bronx 10451 **Fx:**742-6569
(212) 613-2051 .. **Carrasquillo,** Rogelio J '00 Cnsl Gibbons PC -1 Penn Plz -NY 10119 **Fx:**554-9652
(518) 462-0110 .. **Carraway,** Natalie A '00 (Sheehan GCG&J LLP) -54 State -Albany 12207
(212) 232-1300 .. **Carre,** Nicholas A '05 %Lewis BB&S LLP -77 Water -NY 10005
(716) 634-2511 .. **Carrel,** Jerome D '63 -17 Beresford Ct -Williamsvll 14221 **Fx:**565-2002
(212) 483-0105 .. **Carrer,** Michl E '06 %Coughlin D LLP -88 Pine-Wall St Plz -NY 10005
(518) 734-6037 .. **Carreras,** Marilyn T '83 -5465 Main Bx759 -Windham 12496
(212) 732-3640 .. **Carreras & McCallen PLLC** -11 Park Pl -NY 10007 **Fx:**732-3670
(212) 326-3939 .. **Carrero,** Kelly A '04 %Jones D -222 E 41st -NY 10017
(212) 319-8500 .. **Carrey,** Bernard S '65 OfCnsl Stevens & L PC -485 Mad Av -NY 10022
(716) 652-5821 .. **Carr-Hoagland,** Deborah '85 -842 E Fillmore -E Aurora 14052
(212) 768-4343 .. **Carrick,** Brett L '05 %Cantor E&M,LLP -49 W 37th -NY 10018
(212) 522-1112 .. **Carrico,** Lynn M '03 %Time Inc -1271 Av of Amer -NY 10020 **Fx:**522-0437
(212) 880-9489 .. **Carrico,** Matthew S '04 %Morvillo AGIA&B,PC -565 5th Av -NY 10017
(914) 767-7552 .. **Carriello,** Amy E '00 Pepsi Bottling Grp,Inc -1 Pepsi Way -Somers 10589
(516) 248-1188 .. **Carrieri,** Jos R '61 (Carrieri & C,PC) -200 Old Cntry Rd -Mineola 11501 **Fx:**248-1794
(516) 248-1188 .. **Carrieri,** Ralph R '80 (Carrieri & C,PC) -200 Old Cntry Rd -Mineola 11501 **Fx:**248-1794
(716) 854-4080 .. **Carrier-LaMarca,** Joy '03 %Block C&L,PC -1 Niagara Sq -Buffalo 14202
(518) 483-1511 .. **Carriero,** Craig P '02 (Cantwell & C) -14 Elm -Malone 12953 **Fx:**483-1530
(718) 446-8600 .. **Carriero,** J James '79 Carriero & Assoc,PLLC -108-54 Ditmars Blvd -E Elmhrst 11369 **Fx:**446-6672
(315) 823-2331 .. **Carrig,** Bart M '77 (Blumberg & C) -37 N Ann Bx1049 -Little Fls 13365 **Fx:**823-2729
(212) 858-1000 .. **Carrig,** Erica E '02 %Pillsbury WSP LLP -1540 Bway -NY 10036
(516) 877-0450 .. **Carrigan,** F Scott '90 -100 Grdn City Plz -Gdn Cty 11530 **Fx:**280-5740
(212) 530-5000 .. **Carrillo,** Arturo '98 %Milbank TH&M LLP -1 Chase Manh Plz -NY 10005
(212) 818-9200 .. **Carrillo,** Roberto C '04 %Satterlee SB&B LLP -230 Park Av -NY 10169
(315) 349-8296 .. **Carrington,** Christa L '03 Cnty Atty -46 E Brdg -Oswego 13126 **Fx:**349-8298
(203) 330-2285 .. **Carrington,** Michl P '10 %Pullman & C,LLC -50 Main -White Plns 10606
(716) 853-8530 .. **Carrington,** Patricia I '86 %OCTF -350 Main Pl Twr -Buffalo 14202 **Fx:**853-8550
(212) 230-8891 .. **Carrion,** Christopher W '04 WilmerHale -399 Park Av -NY 10022
(212) 428-2540 .. **Carrion,** Fabiola '09 Unified Ct Systm -25 Beaver -NY 10004
(212) 861-4400 .. **Carrion,** Gladys '77 %Inwood House -320 E 82nd -NY 10028
(212) 213-5005 .. **Carro Carro & Mitchell,LLP** -475 Park Av S -NY 10016 **Fx:**213-5004
(212) 213-5005 .. **Carro,** John '56 (Carro C&M,LLP) -475 Park Av S -NY 10016
(212) 213-5005 .. **Carro,** John S '84 (Carro C&M,LLP) -475 Park Av S -NY 10016
(212) 972-1000 .. **Carro,** Michl J '88 %London F LLP -59 Maiden Ln -NY 10038
(718) 401-6100 .. **Carro,** Robt A '97 NY Natl Bk -369 E149th -Bronx 10455
(800) 208-8565 .. **Carroccio,** Benjamin '93 Sunrise Credit Srvcs,Inc -260 Airport Plz Bx9100 -Farmngdl 11735 **Fx:**(631) 501-8529
(716) 691-0596 .. **Carrol,** Jed L '90 Americas Choice -20 Nrthpnte Pkwy -Amherst 14228 **Fx:**691-0650
(718) 694-6711 .. **Carroll,** Ann Catherine '98 %Bishop Mugavero Geriatric Ctr -155 Dean -Brklyn 11217
(212) 210-2341 .. **Carroll,** Anne B '92 Daily News,LP -450 W 33rd -NY 10001 **Fx:**643-7843
(212) 224-1572 .. **Carroll,** Anne Marie '92 %Mutual of America -320 Park Av -NY 10022
(212) 632-5554 .. **Carroll,** Anthony J '80 (Salans LLP) -620 5th Av -NY 10020
(646) 829-3908 .. **Carroll,** Chas F '84 Terra-Gen Power,LLC -565 5th Av -NY 10017
(212) 252-0004 .. **Carroll,** Christopher R '92 (Carroll M&K LLC) -570 Lex Av -NY 10022
(585) 232-4090 .. **Carroll,** Cynthia J '96 %Leg Aid -1 W Main -Rchstr 14614 **Fx:**232-2352
(212) 248-3140 .. **Carroll,** Danl B '95 (Drinker B&R LLP) -140 Bway -NY 10005
(212) 907-9600 .. **Carroll,** Danl L '70 (Ingram YGC&B,LLP) -250 Park Av -NY 10177
(212) 640-5783 .. **Carroll,** David S '80 Amer Exp -200 Vesey -NY 10285 **Fx:**619-7099

(518) 450-0325 .. **Carroll,** David S '96 OfCnsl Anderson Law -48 Union Av -Saratoga Spgs 12866 **Fx:**587-0128
(631) 501-1101 .. **Carroll,** Diane C '86 D Carroll,PC -445 Broadhllw Rd -Melvll 11747
(212) 480-5284 .. **Carroll,** Donald T '74 %Insurance Dept -25 Beaver -NY 10004 **Fx:**480-5272
(845) 338-5977 .. **Carroll,** Edw J '77 E Carroll -2733 Route 209 -Kingston 12401 **Fx:**338-5975
(718) 250-2000 .. **Carroll,** Edw J '97 %DA -350 Jay -Brklyn 11201 **Fx:**250-2314
(212) 728-8000 .. **Carroll,** Erin L '10 %Willkie F&G LLP -787 7th Av -NY 10019
(866) 419-7490 .. **Carroll,** Francis X '81 Ticor Title Ins -70 Niagara -Buffalo 14202 **Fx:**(716) 362-0779
(212) 554-1234 .. **Carroll,** Gerald J Jr. '85 %AXA Financial Inc -1290 Av of Amer -NY 10104 **Fx:**707-3963
(212) 759-2300 .. **Carroll Guido & Groffman,LLP** -1790 Bway -NY 10019 **Fx:**759-9556
(315) 448-0672 .. **Carroll,** Gwendolyn E '08 US Atty -100 S Clinton Bx7198 -Syracuse 13261 **Fx:**448-0689
(212) 225-2000 .. **Carroll,** J Speed '64 OfCnsl Cleary GS&H -1 Lbrty Plz -NY 10006
(212) 635-2230 .. **Carroll,** James E '99 (Cetrulo & C LLP) -14 Wall -NY 10005
(631) 676-5692 .. **Carroll,** James G '98 (JG Carroll,PC) -751 Coates Av -Holbrook 11741 **Fx:**676-5708
(607) 273-7373 .. **Carroll,** James W '70 -103 W Seneca Bx417 -Ithaca 14851
(973) 228-5700 .. **Carroll,** Jenny '00 %Brach E LLC -100 Park Av -NY 10017 **Fx:**228-7852
(518) 474-1331 .. **Carroll,** John B '78 %Ofc Mntl Health -44 Holland Av -Albany 12229 **Fx:**473-7863
(315) 474-5356 .. **Carroll,** John Benjamin '51 Carroll & C,PC -440 S Warren -Syracuse 13202 **Fx:**474-5451
(212) 416-8173 .. **Carroll,** John F '94 %Dept of Law -120 Bway -NY 10271
(212) 735-3000 .. **Carroll,** John K '93 (Skadden ASM&F LLP) -4 Times Sq -NY 10036
(212) 403-3610 .. **Carroll,** John M '82 %Rothschild Inc -1251 Av of Amer -NY 10020
(212) 233-0314 .. **Carroll,** John W '78 (Wolfson & C) -233 Bway -NY 10279 **Fx:**349-4911
(631) 852-2500 .. **Carroll,** Jos F Jr. '87 %DA -200 Center Dr -Rvrhead 11901 **Fx:**852-1769
(516) 546-8233 .. **Carroll,** Jos J '64 -647 Stratford Rd -Baldwin 11510 **Fx:**546-8233
(212) 360-1346 .. **Carroll,** Justin A '06 Dept of Parks & Rec -830 5th Av -NY 10065
(212) 326-3939 .. **Carroll,** Justin F '09 %Jones D -222 E 41st -NY 10017
(518) 561-2000 .. **Carroll,** Kevin J '71 %CVPH Med Ctr -75 Beekman -Plattsbrgh 12901
(518) 886-4000 .. **Carroll,** Laura B '09 Ayco Co -321 Bway Bx860 -Saratoga Spgs 12866
(516) 572-2000 .. **Carroll,** Laura E '97 %DA -99 Main -Hempstd 11550 **Fx:**572-2606
(212) 863-8228 .. **Carroll,** Marie L '99 HPD -100 Gold -NY 10038
(718) 539-4949 .. **Carroll,** Maureen A '81 -150-24 60th Av -Flushng 11355 **Fx:**539-4949
(212) 252-0004 .. **Carroll McNulty & Kull LLC** -570 Lex Av -NY 10022 **Fx:**252-0444
(516) 747-7400 .. **Carroll,** Megan F '99 %Rosenberg C&B LLP -100 Grdn City Plz -Gdn Cty 11530
(212) 328-2100 .. **Carroll,** Michl C '98 Medallion Financial Corp -437 Mad Av -NY 10022
(212) 450-4000 .. **Carroll,** Michl P '94 (Davis P&W LLP) -450 Lex Av -NY 10017
(212) 571-7100 .. **Carroll,** Michl P '98 %O'Dwyer & B,LLP -52 Duane -NY 10007
(516) 571-3891 .. **Carroll,** Patricia M '85 %Hon G Kohn -100 Supreme Ct Dr -Mineola 11501
(914) 243-5990 .. **Carroll,** Patricia M '98 -1825 Maple Hill -Yorktwn Hts 10598 **Fx:**243-5991
(914) 949-6996 .. **Carroll,** Patrick C '00 %Penino & M,LLP -180 E Post Rd -White Plns 10601
(212) 476-9000 .. **Carroll,** Philip R '62 %Neuberger Berman,LLC -605 3rd Av -NY 10158 **Fx:**476-9862
(212) 608-1917 .. **Carroll,** Raymond S '82 %Davis S&S,PC -44 Wall -NY 10005
(914) 332-1800 .. **Carroll,** Robt E '82 (Cherry E&K,LLP) -150 Wht Plns Rd -Tarrytwn 10591
(212) 525-4727 .. **Carroll,** Robt F Jr. '06 WTAS -452 5th Av -NY 10018
(718) 390-5168 .. **Carroll,** Robt S '87 %Hon L Marrero -18 Richmond Ter -Staten Isl 10301
(212) 759-2300 .. **Carroll,** Rosemary '82 (Carroll G&G,LLP) -1790 Bway -NY 10019
(212) 484-3900 .. **Carroll,** Schuyler G '93 (Arent F LLP) -1675 Bway -NY 10019
(716) 712-2767 .. **Carroll,** Scott V '01 Palladian Health -2732 Transit Rd -W Seneca 14224 **Fx:**712-2308
(212) 952-6200 .. **Carroll,** Shaun F '81 (Nourse & B,LLP) -55 Bway -NY 10006
(212) 837-6779 .. **Carroll,** Sinead '09 %Hughes H&R LLP -1 Bttry Pk Plz -NY 10004
(518) 471-4811 .. **Carroll,** Stephen M '08 %Appllt Div 3rd Dept -Capitol Station Bx7288 -Albany 12224 **Fx:**471-4750
(516) 328-1126 .. **Carroll,** Thos L '73 -83 Laurel Dr -New Hyde Pk 11040
(212) 416-8000 .. **Carroll,** Thos T '99 %Dept of Law -120 Bway -NY 10271
(718) 286-6000 .. **Carroll,** Vincent J Jr. '77 %DA -125-01 Qns Blvd -Kew Gdns 11415
(516) 931-2300 .. **Carroll,** Walter J '57 -117 Newbrdg Rd -Hicksvll 11801 **Fx:**938-0452
(845) 638-2042 .. **Carroll,** Wm P '59 -69 W Church -Spg Vly 10977
(315) 474-5356 .. **Carroll,** Woodruff Lee '84 Carroll & C,PC -440 S Warren -Syracuse 13202 **Fx:**474-5451
(315) 393-1111 .. **Carrothers,** Alice J '92 (Carlisle C&C,PC) -602 State Bx757 -Ogdensbrg 13669 **Fx:**393-1181
(716) 664-7933 .. **Carrow,** Allison B '05 Carrow Law Ofc,PC -3406 N Main St Ext Bx489 -Jamestwn 14702 **Fx:**664-7933
(718) 224-4746 .. **Carrozza,** Ann Margaret '96 -213-38 40th Av -Bayside 11361 **Fx:**224-4794
(718) 829-4500 .. **Carrozza,** Jos P '57 -2027 Wllmsbrdg Rd -Bronx 10461
(718) 359-9700 .. **Carrozzo,** Peter M '97 -133-47 Sanford Av -Flushng 11355 **Fx:**762-9385
(516) 355-0500 .. **Carrozzo,** Robt A '86 -114 Jericho Tpk -Floral Pk 11001
(516) 222-6200 .. **Carruba,** Robt A '97 %Berkman HPP&F,PC -100 Grdn City Plz -Gdn Cty 11530
(716) 862-8853 .. **Carrubba,** Jeffrey V '89 -120 LeBrun Rd -Buffalo 14215
(716) 661-3010 .. **Carrubba,** Marie T '83 %SILC -843 N Main -Jamestwn 14701 **Fx:**661-3011
(631) 577-7770 .. **Carrubba,** Theresa M '05 %K Dodson -100 Baylis Rd -Melvll 11747 **Fx:**577-7199
(212) 326-2000 .. **Carruthers,** Thos G '81 (O'Melveny & M LLP) -7 Times Sq -NY 10036
(212) 715-9100 .. **Carruzzo,** Fabien L '05 %Kramer LN&F,LLP -1177 Av of Amer -NY 10036
(516) 485-4872 .. **Carsey,** Kevin R '77 (Carsey & H PC) -230 Hilton Av -Hempstd 11550 **Fx:**538-7303
(518) 581-3200 .. **Carsky,** Christine M '81 (DeGraff F&K LLP) -47 W Harrison -Saratoga Spgs 12866
(212) 506-5000 .. **Carso,** Brad C '02 %Orrick H&S LLP -51 W 52nd -NY 10019
(212) 408-5100 .. **Carson,** Benjamin G '08 %Chadbourne & P LLP -30 Rckfllr Plz -NY 10112
(518) 473-8418 .. **Carson,** Chas A '83 %OCFS -52 Wshngtn -Rensselaer 12144 **Fx:**486-6361
(212) 801-6855 .. **Carson,** Deirdre A '77 (Greenberg T,LLP) -200 Park Av -NY 10166
(914) 253-3956 .. **Carson,** Kathryn L '84 %Pepsico -700 Andrsn Hill Rd -Purchase 10577
(212) 836-8000 .. **Carson,** Patricia A '93 (Kaye S LLP) -425 Park Av -NY 10022
(212) 222-1137 .. **Carson,** Sandra P '82 -885 West End Av -NY 10025
(212) 552-0950 .. **Carson,** Sheila E '99 JP Morgan Chase Bnk,NA -1 Chase Manh Plz -NY 10005
(212) 450-4000 .. **Carson,** Tyler B '08 %Davis P&W LLP -450 Lex Av -NY 10017
(212) 575-9080 .. **Carson-Selman,** Mark L '80 Klotz & G,PC -36 W 44th -NY 10036
(212) 271-9153 .. **Carss,** Jason B '04 Kohlberg Kravis Roberts & Co -9 W 57th -NY 10019
(212) 848-7010 .. **Carswell,** Robt '52 OfCnsl Shearman & S LLP -599 Lex Av -NY 10022
(914) 606-9790 .. **Cartafalsa,** John B Jr. '87 (Cartafalsa ST&L) -560 Wht Plns Rd -Tarrytwn 10591
(212) 682-0020 .. **Cartafalsa,** Jos B '93 (Putney TH&H LLP) -521 5th Av -NY 10175
(914) 606-9790 .. **Cartafalsa Slattery Turpin & Lenoff** -560 Wht Plns Rd -Tarrytwn 10591 **Fx:**606-9791
(212) 225-7700 .. **Cartafalsa Slattery Turpin & Lenoff** -165 Bway -NY 10006 **Fx:**225-7745
(212) 614-5462 .. **Cartagena,** Juan '82 Community Srvc Soc -105 E 22nd -NY 10010 **Fx:**260-6218
(518) 455-4371 .. **Cartagena,** Nicholas R '04 NYS Assembly Program & Cnsl -Cptl -Albany 12248
(212) 820-7700 .. **Cartaina,** Helene L '99 OfCnsl Boundas SW&B,LLC -1 Bttry Pk Plz -NY 10004
(914) 993-0100 .. **Cartelli,** James A '74 -81 Main -White Plns 10601 **Fx:**993-0199
(914) 993-0100 .. **Cartelli,** Trisha L '01 %J Cartelli -81 Main -White Plns 10601 **Fx:**993-0199
(212) 854-4291 .. **Carter,** Alexandra B '05 %Columbia Law Schl -435 W 116th -NY 10027 **Fx:**854-7946
(212) 335-9000 .. **Carter,** Antoinette D '92 %DA -1 Hogan Pl -NY 10013
(631) 727-1666 .. **Carter,** Benjamin E '58 -220 Roanoke Av Bx118 -Rvrhead 11901 **Fx:**727-1710
(718) 579-3000 .. **Carter,** Carol A '88 %Leg Aid -1020 Grnd Cncrs -Bronx 10451 **Fx:**588-2611
(315) 946-7463 .. **Carter,** Chelsea B '09 Leg Aid -9 Pearl -Lyons 14489 **Fx:**946-5964
(518) 465-3484 .. **Carter Conboy Case Blackmore Maloney & Laird,PC** -20 Corp Wds Blvd -Albany 12211 **Fx:**465-1843
(212) 371-8008 .. **Carter,** D Reeves '97 %Guzov O,LLC -600 Mad Av -NY 10022
(631) 501-5700 .. **Carter,** David M '85 (Carter DF&S LLP) -445 Broadhallow Rd -Melvll 11747
(631) 501-5700 .. **Carter DeLuca Farrell & Schmidt LLP** -445 Broadhallow Rd -Melvll 11747 **Fx:**501-3526
(212) 869-3500 .. **Carter,** Elena D H '03 %J Fuchsberg Law Firm,LLP -500 5th Av -NY 10110 **Fx:**398-1532
(212) 806-5400 .. **Carter,** Elizabeth C '10 %Stroock &S&L LLP -180 Maiden Ln -NY 10038
(212) 513-3200 .. **Carter,** Faith L '07 %Holland & K LLP -31 W 52nd -NY 10019
(585) 654-0621 .. **Carter,** Harold M Jr. '78 Rochester-Genesee Reg Trans Auth -1372 E Main -Rchstr 14609
(212) 484-3900 .. **Carter,** Hunter T '02 (Arent F LLP) -1675 Bway -NY 10019
(315) 788-7300 .. **Carter,** J R Santana '08 D Antonucci -12 Pub Sq -Watertwn 13601 **Fx:**788-1643
(212) 558-4000 .. **Carter,** James H '71 (Sullivan & C LLP) -125 Broad -NY 10004
(718) 590-2000 .. **Carter,** Janene D '08 %DA -198 E 161st -Bronx 10451 **Fx:**590-6477
(212) 937-7271 .. **Carter,** Janet Rhiannon '06 Cnsl WilmerHale -399 Park Av -NY 10022
(323) 656-7044 .. **Carter,** Jeffrey C '73 -110 Wall -NY 10005 **Fx:**656-7796
(212) 816-5388 .. **Carter,** Jessica F '03 Citigroup Global Mrkts -388 Greenwich -NY 10013
(212) 336-2000 .. **Carter,** Jessica S '97 %Patterson BW&T LLP -1133 Av of Amer -NY 10036
(518) 471-4825 .. **Carter,** John E Jr. '71 Appllt Div 3rd Dept -Capitol Station Bx7288 -Albany 12224 **Fx:**471-4750
(212) 688-8555 .. **Carter,** John H '88 (Fragomen DB&L LLP) -7 Hanover Sq -NY 10004
(212) 667-0197 .. **Carter,** John M '98 Standard Chtd Bnk -1 Mad Av -NY 10010
(212) 446-4800 .. **Carter,** Jonathan R '09 %Kirkland & E LLP -153 E 53rd -NY 10022
(212) 944-7000 .. **Carter,** Julia Vance '79 Carter Mgmt -22 Cntrl Pk S -NY 10019
(585) 263-1000 .. **Carter,** Kathleen T '03 %Nixon P LLP -1100 Clinton Sq -Rchstr 14604
(212) 854-3688 .. **Carter,** Kenneth R '98 %Columbia Inst for Teleinformation -3022 Bway -NY 10027
(315) 266-4174 .. **Carter,** Kristie M '03 Utica Natl Ins Grp -180 Genesee -New Hartfrd 13413
(718) 590-2000 .. **Carter,** Latasha N '09 %DA -198 E 161st -Bronx 10451 **Fx:**590-6477
(212) 799-5000 .. **Carter,** Laurie A '94 %Juilliard -60 Lincoln Ctr Plz -NY 10023
(212) 732-3200 .. **Carter Ledyard & Milburn LLP** -2 Wall -NY 10005 **Fx:**732-3232
(212) 858-1000 .. **Carter,** Lee C '06 (Pillsbury WSP LLP) -1540 Bway -NY 10036
(212) 421-2233 .. **Carter,** Leonard H '59 Cnsl Wilk A LLP -675 3rd Av -NY 10017
(212) 735-3000 .. **Carter,** Melissa A '06 %Skadden ASM&F LLP -4 Times Sq -NY 10036
(212) 841-1000 .. **Carter,** Pamela A '06 %Covington & B LLP -620 8th Av -NY 10018
(212) 418-4700 .. **Carter,** Philip Gifford '03 ICON Captl -100 5th Av -NY 10011
(212) 826-9033 .. **Carter,** Philip R '78 Urban Prtnrs,LLC -457 Mad Av -NY 10022 **Fx:**220-3776
(212) 996-4549 .. **Carter,** Priscilla D '87 -49 E 86th -NY 10028 **Fx:**996-4483
(315) 686-5572 .. **Carter Ramseier & Holcombe PLLC** -229 John -Clayton 13624 **Fx:**686-2271

(212) 779-9910 .. **Carter,** Richd J Jr. '72 OfCnsl Eaton & V LLP -3 Park Av -NY 10016
(315) 472-7868 .. **Carter,** Robt E L '03 %Weisberg & Z,PLLC -109 S Warren -Syracuse 13202 **Fx:**472-7070
(516) 296-7000 .. **Carter,** Tobi J '03 %Certilman BA&H,LLP -90 Merrick Av -E Meadow 11554
(212) 331-5058 .. **Carter,** Uwonda Shabrette '98 %NYC HRA Ofc Lgl Affrs -180 Water -NY 10038
(718) 634-2374 .. **Carter,** Vivian Rattay '86 -155 Beach 137th -Far Rckwy 11694
(212) 899-7395 .. **Carter,** Warwick M Jr. '95 %Chase Manhattan Bk -1211 Av of Amer -NY 10036
(212) 415-9200 .. **Carter,** Zachary W '76 (Dorsey & W LLP) -250 Park Av -NY 10177
(718) 262-2140 .. **Carter-Dais,** Olga '82 CUNY York College -94-20 Guy R Brewer Blvd -Jamaica 11451
(631) 654-4900 .. **Cartier Bernstein Auerbach & Dazzo,PC** -100 Austin -Patchogue 11772 **Fx:**654-0724
(516) 488-3300 .. **Cartier,** Christopher P '97 %Shaub AC&S,LLP -1983 Marcus Av -Lk Success 11042
(631) 654-4900 .. **Cartier,** Rudolph H Jr. '76 (Cartier BA&D,PC) -100 Austin -Patchogue 11772
(518) 473-4631 .. **Cartier,** Susan Gallup '05 Dept of Health -Corning Twr 24th Fl -Albany 12237 **Fx:**473-2802
(516) 877-0800 .. **Cartiglia Connolly & Russo** -1050 Franklin Av -Gdn Cty 11530 **Fx:**873-0513
(212) 290-4700 .. **Cartner,** Holly Ann '88 %Human Rights Watch -350 5th Av -NY 10118 **Fx:**736-1300
(212) 620-2437 .. **Cartolano,** MariaRosa '86 %Forbes Inc -60 5th Av -NY 10011 **Fx:**620-1890
(914) 517-5000 .. **Carton,** Jeffrey I '91 (Meiselman DPC&E,PC) -1311 Mamaroneck Av -White Plns 10605
(914) 949-6700 .. **Carton,** Robin D '83 (Carton & R,PC) -5 Waller Av -White Plns 10601 **Fx:**381-7158
(914) 949-6700 .. **Carton,** Robin D '83 (Carton & R,PC) -450 7th Av -NY 10123 **Fx:**381-7158
(516) 221-3700 .. **Carton,** Ruya '90 (Eisenberg & C) -2631 Merrick Rd -Bellmore 11710 **Fx:**977-3337
(212) 859-8000 .. **Carton,** Sean M '05 %Fried FHS&J LLP -1 NY Plz -NY 10004
(718) 624-0154 .. **Carton,** Thos G '86 Cnsl Katz & Assoc -26 Court -Brklyn 11242 **Fx:**624-4212
(914) 631-0575 .. **Cartoon,** Stuart F '60 -33 McKeel Av -Tarrytwn 10591 **Fx:**631-8810
(516) 489-6959 .. **Cartright,** Valerie M '04 %F Brewington -556 Peninsula Blvd -Hempstd 11550 **Fx:**489-6958
(212) 383-1730 .. **Cartusciello,** Anthony T '89 State Comptroller -59 Maiden Ln -NY 10038 **Fx:**383-3901
(212) 532-8203 .. **Cartusciello,** Neil S '79 -470 Park Av S -NY 10016
(516) 921-6645 .. **Cartwright,** Rachel A '09 %A Pearl & Assoc,PC -6800 Jericho Tpk -Syosset 11791 **Fx:**921-6774
(914) 995-2660 .. **Cartwright,** Rashida D '02 %Cnty Atty -148 Martine Av -White Plns 10601 **Fx:**995-5858
(212) 741-9238 .. **Carty,** James E III '88 (JE Carty III,PC) -11 Penn Plz -NY 10001
(212) 973-8000 .. **Carty,** Mary Christine '78 (Schnader HS&L LLP) -140 Bway -NY 10005
(914) 828-8000 .. **Carty,** Patrick J '91 Swiss Re Life & Hlth -175 King -Armonk 10504
(845) 362-8610 .. **Carty-Ward,** Heather D '93 %Cejjus Institute -5 Cooper Morris Dr -Pomona 10970
(212) 619-4350 .. **Caruana,** Patrick M '07 %Newman MKGH,PC -14 Wall -NY 10005
(212) 848-4000 .. **Carucci,** Michl S '09 %Shearman & S LLP -599 Lex Av -NY 10022
(212) 458-3382 .. **Carucci,** Saml D '95 AIGTS -175 Water -NY 10038
(212) 922-0450 .. **Carulli,** Thos G '81 OfCnsl Kaplan M&A,LLC -70 E 55th -NY 10022
(516) 365-1400 .. **Carus,** Barry R '89 Cnsl Cooperman LM LLP -1129 Nrthrn Blvd -Manhsst 11030
(914) 785-5300 .. **Caruso,** Alexander '78 %A Lamer -555 Taxter Rd -Elmsfrd 10523 **Fx:**347-4269
(518) 387-7354 .. **Caruso,** Andrew J '04 %GE -1 Rsrch Ctr -Niskayuna 12309
(315) 474-7541 .. **Caruso,** Antonio E '80 (Menter R&T,PC) -308 Maltbie -Syracuse 13204
(718) 680-5778 .. **Caruso Caruso & Branda, PC** -7302 13th Av -Brklyn 11228 **Fx:**680-9671
(212) 554-7800 .. **Caruso,** Christopher J '01 (Moses & S LLP) -405 Lex Av -NY 10174
(518) 379-1391 .. **Caruso,** David A '77 Cnsl Golub Corp -501 Duanesburg Rd Bx1074 -Schnctdy 12306 **Fx:**379-3536
(212) 381-9700 .. **Caruso,** Donato '67 (Lambos Firm,LLP) -303 S Bway -Tarrytwn 10591 **Fx:**797-9213
(212) 267-4876 .. **Caruso,** Frank J '04 %Hoagland LMD&D,LLP -1501 Bway -NY 10036
(212) 450-4000 .. **Caruso,** Gina '97 Cnsl Davis P&W LLP -450 Lex Av -NY 10017
(212) 407-4000 .. **Caruso,** Giovanni '00 (Loeb & L,LLP) -345 Park Av -NY 10154
(518) 270-3761 .. **Caruso,** James A '83 Hon L Griffin -1504 5th Av -Troy 12180 **Fx:**272-6573
(845) 808-1150 .. **Caruso,** Jennifer L '09 %Cnty Atty -48 Gleneida Av -Carmel 10512 **Fx:**808-1903
(212) 758-0050 .. **Caruso,** John A '91 %Title Assoc -825 3rd Av -NY 10022 **Fx:**758-8223
(212) 819-1726 .. **Caruso,** Jos J '83 -1261 Bway -NY 10001
(212) 508-6100 .. **Caruso,** Kenneth A '78 (Bracewell & G,LLP) -1251 Av of Amer -NY 10020
(718) 680-5778 .. **Caruso,** Mark J '78 (Caruso C&B, PC) -7302 13th Av -Brklyn 11228
(518) 386-2266 .. **Caruso,** Mark J '93 %Pub Def -519 State -Schnctdy 12305 **Fx:**386-2814
(212) 541-2000 .. **Caruso,** Michl J '09 %Bryan C LLP -1290 Av of Amer -NY 10104
(212) 237-1000 .. **Caruso,** Michl R '08 %Windels ML&M,LLP -156 W 56th -NY 10019
(518) 402-9188 .. **Caruso,** Michl S '98 %DEC -625 Bway -Albany 12233 **Fx:**402-9018
(914) 949-6400 .. **Caruso,** Michl V '08 %McCullough G&S,LLP -1311 Mamaroneck Av -White Plns 10605
(212) 894-7418 .. **Caruso,** Pamela J '91 Vornado Realty Trust -888 7th Av -NY 10106
(516) 524-3402 .. **Caruso,** Patricia D '00 -45 Richmond Blvd -Ronkonkoma 11779 **Fx:**(631) 676-5822
(716) 885-0444 .. **Caruso,** Ronald H '70 -110 Oaklnd Pl -Buffalo 14222
(585) 325-7440 .. **Caruso,** Saml H Jr. '85 (Kaman BMJ&G LLP) -135 Corp Woods -Rchstr 14623
(914) 656-1837 .. **Caruso,** Sandra R '97 -170 Maple Av -White Plns 10601
(518) 402-9509 .. **Caruso,** Scott W '04 %DEC -625 Bway -Albany 12233 **Fx:**402-9018
(212) 732-8368 .. **Caruso Spillane Leighton Contrastano Ulaner & Savino** -132 Nassau -NY 10038 **Fx:**962-5523
(212) 458-1537 .. **Caruso,** Stephen V '92 AIGTS -175 Water -NY 10038
(212) 837-7908 .. **Caruso,** Steven B '81 (Maddox H&C,PC) -80 Broad -NY 10004 **Fx:**837-7998
(914) 698-6392 .. **Caruso,** Thos G '92 (Caruso & D) -100 Mamaroneck Av -Mamaroneck 10543 **Fx:**698-2038
(914) 288-9268 .. **Caruso,** Thos J '90 -333 Mamaroneck Av -White Plns 10605
(516) 622-0250 .. **Carusona,** Thos M '73 -111 South Bx180 -Oyster Bay 11771 **Fx:**922-4046
(518) 761-6405 .. **Carusone,** Jason M '96 %DA -Cnty Mncpl Ctr -Lk George 12845
(518) 584-3240 .. **Carusone,** John J Jr. '66 Carusone & C -491 Bway Bx478 -Saratoga Spgs 12866 **Fx:**584-7451
(212) 684-3933 .. **Carvajal,** Carlos M '96 %Hantman & Assoc -1515 Bway -NY 10036 **Fx:**520-4301
(718) 250-2000 .. **Carvajal,** Melissa L '04 %DA -350 Jay -Brklyn 11201 **Fx:**250-2314
(212) 589-4200 .. **Carvalho,** Melissa M '05 %Baker & H LLP -45 Rckfllr Plz -NY 10111
(212) 530-1800 .. **Carvalho,** Rebecca C '06 %Richards K&O LLP -1 World Fncl Ctr -NY 10281
(212) 323-7070 .. **Carvell,** Diane B '03 %Rawle & H LLP -14 Wall -NY 10005
(914) 824-5642 .. **Carvelli,** Amy Elise Thompson '98 %Surrogates Ct -111 Dr MLK Jr Blvd -White Plns 10601 **Fx:**995-3728
(212) 505-5066 .. **Carver,** Danielle Fawn '94 %B Levy Assoc Intl Ltd -2 Penn Plz -NY 10121 **Fx:**505-5771
(212) 238-3000 .. **Carver,** Robt P '93 %Emmet M&M,LLP -120 Bway -NY 10271
(315) 798-5766 .. **Carville,** Todd C '03 %DA -800 Park Av -Utica 13501 **Fx:**798-5582
(212) 490-3000 .. **Carvino,** Leanne M '08 %Wilson EME&D LLP -150 E 42nd -NY 10017
(212) 748-1636 .. **Carvlin,** Stephanie M '88 -111 Bway -NY 10006
(516) 741-2000 .. **Carway & Flipse** -194 Old Cntry Rd -Mineola 11501 **Fx:**739-0428
(516) 741-2000 .. **Carway,** Jacqueline S '78 (Carway & F) -194 Old Cntry Rd -Mineola 11501
(212) 868-6300 .. **Cary Kane LLP** -1350 Bway -NY 10018 **Fx:**868-6302
(212) 868-6300 .. **Cary,** Larry '84 (Cary K LLP) -1350 Bway -NY 10018
(585) 546-6300 .. **Casaceli,** Frank O '62 -300 Rynlds Arcd Bldg -Rchstr 14614
(914) 376-0113 .. **Casadevall,** Alberto '85 -538 Riverdale Av -Ynkrs 10705 **Fx:**378-1092
(212) 334-4577 .. **Casado,** Carmen '07 (Jones C LLP) -225 Bway -NY 10007 **Fx:**406-6890
(518) 213-6000 .. **Casagrande,** Richd E '76 NYSUT -800 Troy-Schnctdy Rd -Latham 12110 **Fx:**213-6488
(212) 308-4411 .. **Casais,** John D '96 (Edwards AP&D LLP) -750 Lex Av -NY 10022
(518) 661-5001 .. **Casale,** Anthony S '03 -2431 State Hwy 30 BxXX -Mayfield 12117 **Fx:**661-4664
(212) 233-4700 .. **Casale,** Donald D '80 %Rosato & L,PC -233 Bway -NY 10279 **Fx:**233-6500
(516) 229-4501 .. **Casale,** Doreen E '96 %Russo A&T -875 Merrick Av -Westbury 11590
(631) 293-3332 .. **Casale,** Francis X Jr. '81 -115 Broad Hollow Rd -Melvll 11747 **Fx:**293-2060
(516) 357-3000 .. **Casale,** George N '79 (Rivkin R LLP) -926 RXR Plz -Uniondale 11556
(516) 747-9700 .. **Casale,** Nicole A '08 %Ryan & H,PC -1 Old Cntry Rd -Carle Pl 11514
(516) 688-1700 .. **Casali,** Joan M '95 %IRS -1600 Stewart Av -Westbury 11590 **Fx:**688-1750
(212) 828-9101 .. **Casaly,** John P '76 -1170 5th Av -NY 10029
(212) 415-8600 .. **Casamento,** Gregory T '98 (Locke LB&L LLP) -3 World Fncl Ctr -NY 10281
(212) 610-6300 .. **Casani,** Marina Martino '98 SrCnsl Allen & O -1221 Av of Amer -NY 10020
(212) 335-9000 .. **Casanova,** David J '02 %DA -1 Hogan Pl -NY 10013
(718) 507-4800 .. **Casanova,** Lorenzo '68 -78-27 37th Av -Jcksn Hts 11372 **Fx:**397-5477
(212) 708-1600 .. **Casanova,** Tiffany '08 %Showtime Networks Inc -1633 Bway -NY 10019 **Fx:**708-1391
(212) 801-9200 .. **Casareale,** Anthony B '84 OfCnsl Greenberg T,LLP -200 Park Av -NY 10166
(212) 237-1000 .. **Casas,** Antonio Jose '93 %Windels ML&M,LLP -156 W 56th -NY 10019
(212) 269-0927 .. **Casavant,** Catherine L '91 %D'Amato & L,LLP -2 World Fncl Ctr -NY 10281
(646) 855-1582 .. **Casavechia,** Richd M '92 Banc of Amer Securities LLC -One Bryant Pk -NY 10036 **Fx:**(212) 378-5963
(646) 536-3004 .. **Casazza,** Christopher L '06 Take Two Interactive Software -622 Bway -NY 10012
(845) 496-9166 .. **Casazza,** James '77 -19 South -Washingtnvll 10992 **Fx:**496-9005
(212) 446-4800 .. **Casazza,** Lauren Oland '02 (Kirkland & E LLP) -153 E 53rd -NY 10022
(212) 688-8555 .. **Casazza,** Robt J Jr. '97 %Fragomen DB&L LLP -7 Hanover Sq -NY 10004
(631) 563-7799 .. **Cascardo,** Rosa Prestia '88 -5 Gibbons Ct -Sayvll 11782 **Fx:**563-7778
(212) 832-7400 .. **Cascella,** Christopher N '03 %Weidenbaum & H,LLP -708 3rd Av -NY 10017
(212) 566-4807 .. **Casciano,** Jos M '06 NYC Dept of Bldgs -280 Bway -NY 10007
(516) 542-5900 .. **Cascino,** Gregory A '02 %Congdon FORDT&F -333 Earle Ovngton Blvd -Uniondale 11553
(516) 463-5858 .. **Cascino,** Laurie B '02 %Hofstra Law Schl -121 Hofstra Univ -Hempstd 11549
(212) 714-1720 .. **Cascino,** Margaret J '04 %Tompkins MW&B LLP -140 Bway -NY 10005
(718) 250-0400 .. **Cascio,** Carmine '56 %R Tusa -1 MetroTech Ctr -Brklyn 11201 **Fx:**250-0591
(914) 422-8755 .. **Cascio,** Vincent M '84 %Dept of Law -101 E Post Rd -White Plns 10601 **Fx:**422-8706
(516) 357-3700 .. **Cascione,** Angela N '85 OfCnsl Cullen and D LLP -100 Q Roosevelt Blvd -Gdn Cty 11530
(212) 964-9640 .. **Cascione Purcigliotti & Galluzzi,PC** -20 Vesey -NY 10007 **Fx:**406-2857
(212) 964-9640 .. **Cascione,** Thos G '83 (Cascione P&G,PC) -20 Vesey -NY 10007
(914) 961-1263 .. **Cascione,** Thos G '83 -35 E Grassy Sprain Rd -Ynkrs 10710

(212) 599-4747 .. **Cascone Cole & Collyer** -711 3rd Av -NY 10017 **Fx:**599-7909
(212) 599-4747 .. **Cascone,** Kenneth T '66 (Cascone C&C) -711 3rd Av -NY 10017
(516) 747-1990 .. **Cascone & Kluepfel,LLP** -1399 Franklin Av -Gdn Cty 11530 **Fx:**747-1992
(716) 855-1660 .. **Cascone & Kluepfel LLP** -110 Pearl -Buffalo 14202 **Fx:**855-1665
(516) 747-1990 .. **Cascone,** Leonard M '95 (Cascone & K,LLP) -1399 Franklin Av -Gdn Cty 11530
(516) 627-3203 .. **Case,** Berna '89 -34 Acorn Ponds Dr -Roslyn 11576
(716) 204-2400 .. **Case,** Chas D J '04 %SJ Baum,PC -220 Nrthpnte Pkwy Bx1291 -Buffalo 14240 **Fx:**204-4600
(212) 732-3200 .. **Case,** Clifford P III '70 (Carter L&M LLP) -2 Wall -NY 10005
(585) 325-6202 .. **Case,** David P '03 (Relin G&C LLP) -28 E Main -Rchstr 14614
(585) 865-5750 .. **Case,** Deborah Ann '82 (Burgess D&C) -2725 Dewey Av -Rchstr 14616
(315) 793-9571 .. **Case,** Donna J '95 %Hon D Hurd -10 Broad -Utica 13501 **Fx:**793-8034
(585) 758-7610 .. **Case,** Edw G '89 Univ of Rochester Med Ctr -Bx278979 -Rchstr 14627 **Fx:**272-9311
(716) 853-9555 .. **Case,** Kenneth F '88 Leg Aid -237 Main -Buffalo 14203 **Fx:**853-3219
(315) 287-2000 .. **Case & Leader LLP** -107 E Main Bx13 -Gouverneur 13642 **Fx:**287-2002
(212) 754-2233 .. **Case,** Leslie K '86 %Scientific Games Corp -750 Lex Av -NY 10022 **Fx:**754-2372
(212) 697-6555 .. **Case,** Michl J '88 (Biedermann RH&R) -570 Lex Av -NY 10022
(212) 317-2252 .. **Case,** Stephen H '69 Cohen & Co -800 3rd Av -NY 10022
(585) 454-4060 .. **Case Grammatico,** Rebecca '04 %Empire Justice Ctr -1 W Main -Rchstr 14614 **Fx:**454-4019
(631) 661-8000 .. **Casel,** Jerry D '78 -384 W Main -Babylon 11702 **Fx:**661-2870
(212) 998-6849 .. **Casell,** Jason H '02 NYU -25 W 4th -NY 10012
(212) 725-2450 .. **Casella,** Anthony J '66 (Casella & H) -110 W 40th -NY 10018 **Fx:**725-2452
(646) 223-4200 .. **Casella,** Cecilia '97 %Reuters -3 Times Sq -NY 10036 **Fx:**223-4250
(607) 773-0363 .. **Casella,** F Danl '78 -64 Front -Bnghmtn 13905
(914) 824-5070 .. **Casella,** Gary L '73 %Atty Grievance Comm -399 Knollwood Rd -White Plns 10603 **Fx:**949-0997
(212) 813-8800 .. **Casella,** Jason M '00 %Goodwin P LLP -620 8th Av -NY 10018
(718) 979-1137 .. **Casella,** Keith M '03 (Casella & C,LLP) -1200 South Av -Staten Isl 10314 **Fx:**273-4847
(718) 979-1137 .. **Casella,** Ralph P '68 (Casella & C,LLP) -1200 South Av -Staten Isl 10314 **Fx:**273-4847
(315) 507-6404 .. **Casella,** Thos '10 -505 Henry -Utica 13502 **Fx:**413-6326
(212) 455-2000 .. **Casella,** Valentina M '08 %Simpson T&B LLP -425 Lex Av -NY 10017
(212) 255-5556 .. **Casellas,** Andrea Landis '06 %Feifer & G LLP -27 Union Sq W -NY 10003
(585) 758-7614 .. **Caselli,** Diane G '94 %Univ of Rochester Med Ctr -Bx278979 -Rchstr 14627 **Fx:**272-9311
(212) 547-5400 .. **Casero,** Jason P '06 %McDermott W&E LLP -340 Mad Av -NY 10173
(212) 547-5400 .. **Casero,** Susan S '04 %McDermott W&E LLP -340 Mad Av -NY 10173
(718) 837-7900 .. **Caserta,** Richd A '66 -8108 18th Av -Brklyn 11214
(716) 284-7886 .. **Caserta,** Thos J Jr. '81 -800 Main -Niagara Fls 14301
(518) 877-4900 .. **Casey,** Ann J '86 (Casey & C) -308 Ushers Rd Bx463 -Clifton Pk 12065 **Fx:**877-4727
(518) 877-4900 .. **Casey,** Arthur F '69 (Casey & C) -308 Ushers Rd Bx463 -Clifton Pk 12065 **Fx:**877-4727
(518) 429-4200 .. **Casey,** Brian D '94 (Hiscock & B,LLP) -50 Beaver -Albany 12207
(516) 488-3300 .. **Casey,** Brian J '02 %Shaub AC&S,LLP -1983 Marcus Av -Lk Success 11042
(845) 634-3345 .. **Casey,** Bridget M '84 %Jade Abstract -151 S Main -New Cty 10956 **Fx:**634-3108
(212) 909-6000 .. **Casey,** Chan E '08 %Debevoise & P LLP -919 3rd Av -NY 10022
(212) 675-7150 .. **Casey,** Dennis P '69 -465 W 23rd -NY 10011
(212) 872-6052 .. **Casey,** Donal P '93 KPMG LLP -345 Park Av -NY 10154
(212) 403-1000 .. **Casey,** Donald P '08 %Wachtell LR&K -51 W 52nd -NY 10019
(315) 425-2700 .. **Casey,** Eileen Ann '05 %Hiscock & B,LLP -One Park Pl -Syracuse 13202
(212) 670-0112 .. **Casey,** Ellen J '90 Merrill Lynch -222 Bway -NY 10038
(585) 325-3050 .. **Casey,** Erin F '05 Farmworker Lgl Srvcs -1187 Culver Rd -Rchstr 14609 **Fx:**325-7614
(212) 848-4000 .. **Casey,** George A '95 (Shearman & S LLP) -599 Lex Av -NY 10022
(212) 906-1200 .. **Casey,** Jason M '05 %Latham & W -885 3rd Av -NY 10022
(585) 454-0700 .. **Casey,** Jeffrey D '10 %Ward GH&R LLP -300 State -Rchstr 14614
(718) 206-4685 .. **Casey,** Jeffrey R '03 Law Dept -89-17 Sutphin Blvd -Jamaica 11435 **Fx:**206-4702
(516) 294-5433 .. **Casey,** Jennifer A '98 (Ahmuty D&M) -200 IU Willets Rd -Albertson 11507
(518) 463-7784 .. **Casey,** John B '95 %Dreyer B LLP -75 Columbia -Albany 12210
(212) 239-6000 .. **Casey,** John F '96 %Div Of Parole -314 W 40th -NY 10018 **Fx:**239-6160
(518) 429-4200 .. **Casey,** John R '71 (Hiscock & B,LLP) -50 Beaver -Albany 12207
(518) 274-4830 .. **Casey,** John T Jr. '88 -47 2nd -Troy 12180 **Fx:**274-4383
(718) 278-7373 .. **Casey,** John W '73 -38-12 30th Av -LIC 11103 **Fx:**728-4151
(631) 470-7407 .. **Casey,** Karen A '00 KA Casey,LLC -780 NY Av -Huntngtn 11743 **Fx:**470-7414
(631) 421-1145 .. **Casey,** Kathleen A '99 %T Casey -6 Red Deer Ln -Huntngtn 11743 **Fx:**421-3855
(716) 795-9700 .. **Casey,** Kathleen E '91 -9240 Haight Rd -Barker 14012
(631) 853-4161 .. **Casey,** Kathleen J '98 %DA -N Cnty Cmplx Bldg 77 -Hauppauge 11788 **Fx:**853-4192
(718) 250-2000 .. **Casey,** Kelly T '99 %DA -350 Jay -Brklyn 11201 **Fx:**250-2314
(212) 442-4900 .. **Casey,** Kevin F '86 %Ofc Admin Trials -40 Rector -NY 10006 **Fx:**442-4947
(212) 456-7281 .. **Casey,** Kevin G '95 ABC -77 W 66th -NY 10023 **Fx:**456-6202
(212) 762-6994 .. **Casey,** Kevin M '09 Morgan Stanley -1221 Av of Amer -NY 10020
(518) 457-1446 .. **Casey,** Kristen G '01 NYS Educ Dept -80 Wolf Rd -Albany 12205
(518) 465-3484 .. **Casey,** Leah Walker '04 %Carter CCBM&L,PC -20 Corp Wds Blvd -Albany 12211
(212) 286-0225 .. **Casey,** Martin F '86 (Casey & B LLC) -65 W 36th -NY 10018 **Fx:**286-0261
(516) 294-5433 .. **Casey,** Maureen '93 (Ahmuty D&M) -200 IU Willets Rd -Albertson 11507
(718) 428-5292 .. **Casey,** Moira E '84 (French & C,LLP) -42-24 235th -Douglastn 11363
(212) 797-3544 .. **Casey,** Moira E '84 (French & C,LLP) -29 Bway -NY 10006
(212) 906-1200 .. **Casey,** Morgan R '09 %Latham & W -885 3rd Av -NY 10022
(585) 344-1050 .. **Casey,** Peter M '09 %M Del Plato -73 Main -Batavia 14020 **Fx:**344-4165
(631) 421-1145 .. **Casey,** Richd P '00 %T Casey -6 Red Deer Ln -Huntngtn 11743 **Fx:**421-3855
(518) 525-2617 .. **Casey,** Sandra Mulay '89 -5 Groot Dr -Altamont 12009
(212) 454-4045 .. **Casey,** Sean P '96 Deutsche Bnk -345 Park Av -NY 10154
(212) 488-1200 .. **Casey,** Sean Patrick '00 (Kobre & K,LLP) -800 3rd Av -NY 10022
(212) 701-3000 .. **Casey,** Shannon C '09 %Cahill G&R LLP -80 Pine -NY 10005 **Fx:**269-5420
(585) 428-5210 .. **Casey,** Tamara F '80 %Pub Def -10 N Fitzhugh -Rchstr 14614 **Fx:**428-2234
(718) 250-2000 .. **Casey,** Thos E '08 %DA -350 Jay -Brklyn 11201 **Fx:**250-2314
(631) 421-1145 .. **Casey,** Thos J '59 -6 Red Deer Ln -Huntngtn 11743 **Fx:**421-3855
(212) 336-1014 .. **Casey,** Timothy J '05 %SEC -3 World Fncl Ctr -NY 10281 **Fx:**336-1323
(212) 506-5000 .. **Casey,** Vincent '91 OfCnsl Orrick H&S LLP -51 W 52nd -NY 10019
(212) 297-5800 .. **Casey,** Warren J '76 (Day P LLP) -7 Times Sq -NY 10036
(212) 490-3000 .. **Cash,** Joshua '07 %Wilson EME&D LLP -150 E 42nd -NY 10017
(212) 685-9660 .. **Cash,** Mark '57 -295 Mad Av -NY 10017
(212) 431-2147 .. **Cash,** Melanie L '03 Ctr for NYC Law NY Law Schl -47 Worth -NY 10013
(202) 370-7429 .. **Cash,** Steven A '88 (Harris CC&H LLP) -111 Bway -NY 10006 **Fx:**(212) 202-6206
(518) 851-7021 .. **Cashen,** James A '58 -73 Roxbury Rd -Hudson 12534 **Fx:**851-7021
(914) 487-7330 .. **Casher,** Scott H '98 (White and W LLP) -427 Bedford Rd -Plsntvll 10570
(914) 487-7330 .. **Casher,** Scott H '98 (White and W LLP) -427 Bedford Rd -Plsntvll 10570
(718) 982-0423 .. **Cashin,** Margarette Berg '95 -112 Roswell Av -Staten Isl 10314 **Fx:**982-0423
(212) 421-4100 .. **Cashman,** Gideon '54 (Pryor C LLP) -7 Times Sq -NY 10036
(516) 742-0729 .. **Cashman,** Judith L '87 -2 Keenan Pl -Gdn Cty 11530
(212) 612-4000 .. **Cashman,** Raymond '92 Chubb Grp -55 Water -NY 10041
(212) 351-4000 .. **Cashman,** Richd '69 OfCnsl Gibson D&C LLP -200 Park Av -NY 10166
(914) 995-3646 .. **Cashman,** Richd P '85 %Cnty Atty -148 Martine Av -White Plns 10601 **Fx:**995-5858
(716) 856-5500 .. **Cashmore,** Timothy C '81 (Damon M LLP) -200 Delaware Av -Buffalo 14202
(718) 261-6604 .. **Casil,** James S '74 (Casil P&Z) -118-21 Qns Blvd -Frst Hlls 11375 **Fx:**261-6609
(716) 633-9933 .. **Casilio,** Paul J '97 %P&R Casilio Enterprises -2457 Wehrle Dr -Williamsvll 14221
(212) 521-5400 .. **Casimir,** Gary '94 Cnsl Reed S LLP -599 Lex Av -NY 10022
(212) 448-9570 .. **Casinelli,** Selena M '07 %Callahan & F,LLC -40 Exch Pl -NY 10005
(585) 454-6480 .. **Casini,** Christian C '96 (Osborn R&B,LLP) -45 Exchange Blvd -Rchstr 14614
(718) 305-3600 .. **Casino,** Andrew P R '96 -69-07 Roosevelt Av -Woodside 11377 **Fx:**305-3800
(212) 336-8000 .. **Casino,** Jos M '97 (Amster R&E) -90 Park Av -NY 10016
(585) 232-6500 .. **Casion,** Jos G '00 (Harter S&E LLP) -1600 Bausch & Lomb Pl -Rchstr 14604
(585) 232-4090 .. **Casion,** Kathia M '01 %Leg Aid -1 W Main -Rchstr 14614 **Fx:**232-2352
(315) 379-2355 .. **Casiuk,** Amy V '04 %Dept Soc Srvcs -6 Judson -Canton 13617 **Fx:**386-2782
(212) 681-0800 .. **Caslin,** John J Jr. '65 Cnsl Wyatt G&O,LLP -99 Park Av -NY 10016
(518) 371-6125 .. **Caslin,** Kevin G '88 %EG Watkins -1745 Rt 9 -Clifton Pk 12065 **Fx:**371-6183
(212) 455-2000 .. **Casner,** Alina E '06 %Simpson T&B LLP -425 Lex Av -NY 10017
(516) 379-9000 .. **Caso,** George R III '81 -2174 N Hewlett Av -Merrick 11566 **Fx:**379-4402
(516) 294-5200 .. **Caso,** Peter J '87 %Picciano & S -900 Merchants Cncrs -Westbury 11590
(716) 856-3500 .. **Caso,** Raymond H Jr. '98 %Magavern MG LLP -1100 Rand Bldg -Buffalo 14203
(516) 248-2500 .. **Caso,** Ronald G '62 Cnsl Redmond P&C, LLP -1461 Franklin Av -Gdn Cty 11530
(516) 248-1399 .. **Casolaro,** Chas J '99 (Casolaro & Assoc,PC) -1050 Franklin Av -Gdn Cty 11530
(212) 732-3200 .. **Casolaro,** John R '78 (Carter L&M LLP) -2 Wall -NY 10005
(212) 335-9000 .. **Casolaro,** Peter T '79 %DA -1 Hogan Pl -NY 10013
(212) 421-2150 .. **Casowitz,** Paul D '89 (Sive P&R,PC) -460 Park Av -NY 10022
(718) 613-2163 .. **Caspari,** Alexander P '85 US Dist Ct -225 Cadman Plz E -Brklyn 11201
(212) 856-3637 .. **Casparian,** Kathryn G '82 CIBC World Mkts -300 Mad Av -NY 10017 **Fx:**885-4829
(631) 273-4400 .. **Casper,** Barry J '89 -330 Motor Pkwy -Hauppauge 11788 **Fx:**273-4451
(518) 436-2840 .. **Casper,** Peter M '02 %Thruway Auth -200 Southrn Blvd Bx189 -Albany 12201 **Fx:**471-4340
(212) 761-4000 .. **Casper,** Robt Y '92 Morgan Stanley -1585 Bway -NY 10036
(914) 242-4900 .. **Casper,** Thos P '81 (Casper & F,LLP) -38 Smith Av -Mt Kisco 10549 **Fx:**242-4902
(718) 797-4100 .. **Caspi,** Avi D '93 A Caspi,PLLC -26 Court -Brklyn 11242 **Fx:**797-4716
(212) 349-3420 .. **Cass,** Alan M '74 -225 Bway -NY 10007 **Fx:**349-3462
(212) 815-1818 .. **Cass,** Barbara A '81 %DC 37 MELS -125 Barclay -NY 10007 **Fx:**815-1343
(212) 785-5778 .. **Cass,** Barry M '76 Orion & Glbl Chrtring Co, Inc -29 Bway -NY 10006 **Fx:**785-5779
(857) 222-1714 .. **Cass,** Jean-Paul '01 -1230 Av of Amer -NY 10020
(631) 712-5763 .. **Cass,** Luke V '04 US Dist Crt- Eastern NY -100 Fed Pk -Central Islip 11722
(212) 326-5728 .. **Cass,** Michelle T '95 Columbia Univ Med Ctr -14 E 60th -NY 10022

(585) 275-7777 .. **Cassada,** Thos L '92 %Univ of Rochester -601 Elmwood Av -Rchstr 14642
(315) 671-6702 .. **Cassady,** Margaret M '85 Excellus Blue Cross Blue Shield -333 Butternut Dr -Syracuse 13214 **Fx:**671-6700
(212) 878-3590 .. **Cassagnol,** Joel H '05 Ave Cptl Grp -535 Mad Av -NY 10022
(315) 798-5926 .. **Cassalia Barry,** Christine M '85 %Family Ct -Cnty Cthse -Utica 13501
(212) 988-0366 .. **Cassan,** Vito J '55 -301 E 66th -NY 10065 **Fx:**288-8479
(917) 838-7550 .. **Cassandra,** Jennifer M '97 -12 Shepard Av -Staten Isl 10314
(516) 932-0068 .. **Cassandro,** Robt J '90 (Abelow & C LLP) -410 Jericho Tpk -Jericho 11753 **Fx:**932-0072
(716) 636-7600 .. **Cassano,** Thos R '71 Cnsl HoganWillig -2410 N Forest Rd -Amherst 14068
(212) 859-8000 .. **Cassanos,** Robt '82 (Fried FHS&J LLP) -1 NY Plz -NY 10004
(646) 386-4683 .. **Cassanova,** Zoila Soledad '05 Criminal Ct -100 Centre -NY 10013
(631) 271-6596 .. **Cassar,** Christopher J '89 (C Cassar,PC) -13 E Carver -Huntngtn 11743
(585) 247-9000 .. **Cassara,** Frank M '91 %Shapiro D&B,LLP -250 Mile Xing Blvd -Rchstr 14624
(718) 720-2877 .. **Cassata,** Serafina M '96 (Votto & C,LLP) -60 Bay -Staten Isl 10310
(212) 403-1000 .. **Cassata,** Valentina '09 %Wachtell LR&K -51 W 52nd -NY 10019
(518) 943-7033 .. **Casscles,** J Stephen '85 -308 Route 385 -Catskill 12414
(212) 848-4000 .. **Cassedy,** Colin H '09 %Shearman & S LLP -599 Lex Av -NY 10022
(212) 907-7300 .. **Cassell,** Barry A '91 OfCnsl Golenbock EAB&P -437 Mad Av -NY 10022
(516) 942-4700 .. **Cassell,** Michl D '95 (Lefkowitz H&C) -500 N Bway -Jericho 11753
(718) 896-2500 .. **Cassell,** Ruth N '74 ACQC -16121 Jamaica Av -Jamaica 11432
(212) 373-3000 .. **Casselman,** Carolyn J '04 %Paul WRW&G LLP -1285 Av of Amer -NY 10019
(518) 785-3032 .. **Casserly,** Michelle I '85 -4 Edge Of Woods -Latham 12110
(518) 452-1961 .. **Casserly,** Timothy E '85 (Burke & C,PC) -255 Washington Av Ext -Albany 12205
(212) 952-0100 .. **Cassese,** Anthony P '85 US Aviation -199 Water -NY 10038
(718) 590-2070 .. **Cassetta,** Irene '88 %DA -198 E 161st -Bronx 10451 **Fx:**590-6477
(212) 726-6296 .. **Cassetta,** Samantha L '02 Oxford Univ Press -198 Mad Av -NY 10016
(631) 277-8080 .. **Cassidy,** Brian P '01 (Cassidy R&L,PC) -70 W Main -E Islip 11730 **Fx:**277-4908
(212) 301-5835 .. **Cassidy,** Carlotta '04 %Fox News Corp -1211 Av of Amer -NY 10036
(607) 754-0061 .. **Cassidy,** Carole M '00 -137 Wshngtn Av -Endicott 13760
(212) 766-4300 .. **Cassidy,** Cathleen Pringle '07 %A Ferrini,PC -200 Park Av S -NY 10003 **Fx:**(646) 390-8314
(212) 417-8700 .. **Cassidy,** Colleen P '82 %Fed Def of NY Inc -52 Duane -NY 10007 **Fx:**571-0392
(914) 899-3100 .. **Cassidy,** Danl D '93 (Mead HC&G) -109 Spencer Pl -Mamaroneck 10543
(516) 357-3000 .. **Cassidy,** David M '86 (Rivkin R LLP) -926 RXR Plz -Uniondale 11556
(914) 286-3400 .. **Cassidy,** Debra Ann '89 %Leg Aid -1 N Bway -White Plns 10601 **Fx:**682-4112
(845) 778-2121 .. **Cassidy,** Elizabeth K '09 %Jacobowitz & G,LLP -158 Orange Av Bx367 -Walden 12586
(718) 625-8940 .. **Cassidy,** James P '79 %B Lawrence -15 Metrotech Ctr N -Brklyn 11201 **Fx:**624-5756
(315) 461-4277 .. **Cassidy,** Jason L '04 %Falge & M,PC -3300 Vickery Rd -N Syracuse 13212
(212) 537-6616 .. **Cassidy,** Joanne '06 (Cassidy & V) -4315 Webster Av -Bronx 10470
(212) 720-5957 .. **Cassidy,** John S '82 %Fed Reserve Bk -33 Lbrty -NY 10045
(607) 274-5525 .. **Cassidy,** Jos R '01 Dept Soc Srvcs -320 W State -Ithaca 14850
(212) 849-7000 .. **Cassidy,** Kate E '06 %Quinn EU&S,LLP -51 Mad Av -NY 10010
(212) 479-6000 .. **Cassidy,** Kathleen E '07 %Cooley LLP -1114 Av of Amer -NY 10036
(212) 207-7000 .. **Cassidy,** Kyran E '91 %HarperCollins Pub -10 E 53rd -NY 10022 **Fx:**207-7552
(212) 826-8438 .. **Cassidy,** M Sharon '92 %US Steel & Carnegie -350 Park Av -NY 10022
(212) 803-3100 .. **Cassidy,** Maria E '84 %Empire State Dvlmnt Corp -633 3rd Av -NY 10017
(518) 561-3088 .. **Cassidy,** Michl E '92 %Prisoners' Leg Srvcs -121 Brdg -Plattsbrgh 12901 **Fx:**561-3262
(212) 906-1200 .. **Cassidy,** Robt Chas III '06 %Latham & W -885 3rd Av -NY 10022
(716) 874-0078 .. **Cassidy,** Sandra '86 -381 Ontario -Buffalo 14207
(212) 776-5000 .. **Cassidy,** Susan F '84 %NYC Housing Auth -250 Bway -NY 10007 **Fx:**776-5039
(212) 587-5396 .. **Cassidy,** Vickie R '94 %State Ins Fund -199 Church -NY 10007 **Fx:**385-9199
(212) 972-6161 .. **Cassin & Cassin LLP** -711 3rd Av -NY 10017 **Fx:**557-2952
(212) 832-1930 .. **Cassin,** Jeffrey K '06 %Breslow & W,LLP -767 3rd Av -NY 10017
(212) 972-6161 .. **Cassin,** Jos M '67 (Cassin & C LLP) -711 3rd Av -NY 10017
(212) 440-4300 .. **Cassin,** Olivia L '89 %Leg Aid -199 Water -NY 10038
(212) 358-6587 .. **Cassino,** Nicholas P '96 Berkadia Commercial Mortgage LLC -315 Park Av S -NY 10010
(212) 504-6000 .. **Cassino,** Thos N '04 %Cadwalader W&T LLP -1 World Fncl Ctr -NY 10281
(212) 704-6000 .. **Cassirer,** Aurora '76 (Troutman S LLP) -405 Lex Av -NY 10174
(516) 294-5050 .. **Cassisi,** Frank J '85 (Cassisi & C,PC) -114 Old Cntry Rd -Mineola 11501
(718) 441-5050 .. **Cassisi,** O John '85 Cassisi Law Firm,PC -102-08 101st Av -Ozone Pk 11416 **Fx:**441-5055
(212) 836-8000 .. **Casson,** Benjamin S '08 %Kaye S LLP -425 Park Av -NY 10022
(212) 425-7200 .. **Casson,** Lawr P '02 Cnsl Kenyon & K,LLP -1 Bway -NY 10004
(212) 594-4077 .. **Cassuto,** Jeffrey M '95 -111 3rd Av -NY 10003
(845) 638-2889 .. **Castagna,** David '88 -10 Esquire Rd -New Cty 10956 **Fx:**638-3500
(516) 495-7906 .. **Castagna,** Jeanine F '97 -1225 Franklin Av -Gdn Cty 11530 **Fx:**908-7773
(914) 378-1010 .. **Castagnozzi,** Maria I '00 %Fitzgerald & F -538 Riverdale Av -Ynkrs 10705
(718) 643-7437 .. **Castaldi,** Jennifer L '91 Family Ct - Ofc Ct Admin -283 Adams -Brklyn 11201
(718) 556-1800 .. **Castaldi,** Philip S '93 (Lucarelli & C) -1491 Richmond Rd -Staten Isl 10304 **Fx:**556-1775
(212) 816-8643 .. **Castaldo,** Andrew P '96 Citigroup -388 Greenwich -NY 10013
(212) 819-8200 .. **Castaldo,** Catherine R '03 %White & C LLP -1155 Av of Amer -NY 10036
(716) 566-1300 .. **Castaldo,** Jennifer N '09 %Hiscock & B,LLP -1100 M&T Ctr -Buffalo 14203
(212) 785-9100 .. **Castaldo,** Steven '05 %Paduano & W LLP -1251 Av of Amer -NY 10020
(212) 554-7800 .. **Castanaro,** Valeria M '10 %Moses & S LLP -405 Lex Av -NY 10174
(914) 939-8594 .. **Castaneda,** Jose O '92 -219 Wstchstr Av -Pt Chester 10573 **Fx:**937-9407
(212) 751-2700 .. **Castano,** Gregory J '56 JAMS -620 8th Av -NY 10018 **Fx:**751-4099
(212) 458-3561 .. **Castano,** Thos J '01 American Home Assurance -175 Water -NY 10038 **Fx:**458-5861
(212) 351-4000 .. **Castelino,** Rachel F '01 %Gibson D&C LLP -200 Park Av -NY 10166
(212) 408-5100 .. **Castell,** Ted P '04 %Chadbourne & P LLP -30 Rckfllr Plz -NY 10112
(315) 495-6224 .. **Castellane,** Richd '83 -4899 Bear Path Rd -Munnsville 13409 **Fx:**495-6224
(212) 310-8000 .. **Castellani,** Anne K '09 %Weil G&M LLP -767 5th Av -NY 10153
(718) 982-9090 .. **Castellano,** Anthony J '68 AJCastellano,PC -300 W Srvc Rd -Staten Isl 10314 **Fx:**982-9102
(212) 232-1300 .. **Castellano,** Carmine J '06 %Lewis BB&S LLP -77 Water -NY 10005
(212) 450-4000 .. **Castellano,** Gina M '09 %Davis P&W LLP -450 Lex Av -NY 10017
(631) 581-7100 .. **Castellano,** John F '77 %Mercy Advocacy Program -859 Connetquot Av -Islip Terr 11752 **Fx:**581-9310
(718) 286-6000 .. **Castellano,** John M '84 %DA -125-01 Qns Blvd -Kew Gdns 11415
(585) 256-1927 .. **Castellano,** June M '84 -125 Dunbarton Dr -Rchstr 14618 **Fx:**242-7873
(516) 746-3340 .. **Castellano,** Louis J Jr. '50 -85 Boathouse Ln -Bay Shr 11706 **Fx:**(631) 665-1344
(212) 261-3744 .. **Castellano,** Peter J '05 Calyon -1301 Av of Amer -NY 10019
(631) 366-5300 .. **Castellano,** Philip Jr. '76 (P Castellano Jr,PC) -181 Smithtown Blvd -Nesconset 11767 **Fx:**366-5313
(914) 779-1100 .. **Castellano,** Vincent '99 -35 E Grassy Sprain Rd -Ynkrs 10710 **Fx:**779-0369
(718) 250-2000 .. **Castelli,** John A '97 %DA -350 Jay -Brklyn 11201 **Fx:**250-2314
(516) 409-6200 .. **Castelli,** Meredith B '07 %Furey KWM&C,PC -2174 Jackson Av -Seafrd 11783
(212) 298-5063 .. **Castelli,** Victor '64 %Leg Aid -49 Thomas -NY 10013 **Fx:**298-5252
(607) 737-2901 .. **Castellino,** Saml D '98 Family Ct -203 William -Elmira 14901
(914) 347-2600 .. **Castellitto,** Mario '94 (Traub LS&S LLP) -7 Skyline Dr -Hawthorne 10532
(212) 403-1000 .. **Castelli Villa,** Franco '06 %Wachtell LR&K -51 W 52nd -NY 10019
(973) 503-5900 .. **Castello,** Geoffrey W III '96 (Kelley D&W LLP) -101 Park Av -NY 10178 **Fx:**503-5920
(212) 599-8200 .. **Castello,** Raymond R '78 (Shaub AC&S,LLP) -655 3rd Av -NY 10017
(718) 990-6633 .. **Castello,** Rosa C '07 St John's Law Schl -8000 Utopia Pkwy -Jamaica 11439 **Fx:**591-1855
(212) 318-3000 .. **Castelluccio,** Jos A III '07 %Fulbright & J LLP -666 5th Av -NY 10103
(914) 225-5576 .. **Castelly,** John L '02 %Morgan Stanley Dean Witter -200 Wstchstr Av -Purchase 10577
(212) 693-1139 .. **Castiblanco,** Jaime H '94 -315 Bway -NY 10007
(914) 835-3339 .. **Castiglia,** Ferdinando J '65 -241 Harrison Av -Harrison 10528
(516) 626-8400 .. **Castiglia Canino,** Catherine T '96 Cnsl E Realty Title Agency -333 Jericho Tpk -Jericho 11753 **Fx:**626-7556
(631) 232-3400 .. **Castiglia-Rubinstein,** Christine '03 OfCnsl G Obedin -320 Carleton Av -Central Islip 11722 **Fx:**232-5343
(716) 845-2758 .. **Castiglione,** Donna M '86 Family Ct -1 Niagara Plz -Buffalo 14202 **Fx:**858-4739
(516) 248-9595 .. **Castiglione,** Frank P '94 (Palmieri C & Assoc,PC) -250 Mineola Blvd -Mineola 11501
(212) 906-1200 .. **Castiglione,** John D '07 %Latham & W -885 3rd Av -NY 10022
(518) 438-9907 .. **Castiglione,** Jos F '04 %Young SWRB&M,LLC -5 Palisades Dr -Albany 12205
(212) 455-2000 .. **Castiglione,** Michl J '08 %Simpson T&B LLP -425 Lex Av -NY 10017
(914) 684-0090 .. **Castiglioni,** Richd E '01 (Diserio MO&C LLP) -50 Main -White Plns 10606
(212) 622-4959 .. **Castilla,** Rafael E '93 JP Morgan Chase -277 Park Av -NY 10172
(212) 341-2572 .. **Castillo,** Camille J '08 Admin Child Srvcs -150 William -NY 10038
(212) 450-4000 .. **Castillo,** Elvira '08 %Davis P&W LLP -450 Lex Av -NY 10017
(718) 654-5046 .. **Castillo,** Epifanio Jr. '82 (Castillo Assoc LLP) -2718 Seymour Av -Bronx 10469 **Fx:**654-5046
(212) 839-5300 .. **Castillo,** Eric W '04 %Sidley A LLP -787 7th Av -NY 10019
(518) 456-2722 .. **Castillo,** Gaspar M Jr. '81 (Parker & C) -3 Wembley Ct -Albany 12205
(212) 412-1872 .. **Castillo,** Jerome P A '01 Barclays Capital -200 Park Av -NY 10166
(516) 621-8646 .. **Castillo,** Nelson A Rivas '02 Castillo Law Firm,PLLC -99 Powerhse Rd -Roslyn Hts 11577
(516) 933-4080 .. **Castillo,** Pauline Tran '00 %Davis & V -176 Woodbury Rd -Hicksvll 11801
(212) 942-0200 .. **Castillo,** Raysa A '94 -800 Riverside Dr -NY 10032
(212) 735-3000 .. **Castillo,** Veronica '06 %Skadden ASM&F LLP -4 Times Sq -NY 10036
(212) 227-2865 .. **Castillo,** Walfredo P '83 -30 Vesey -NY 10007 **Fx:**227-2867
(212) 692-1000 .. **Castillo Jiménez,** Marlene F '05 %Duane M LLP -1540 Bway -NY 10036
(212) 644-8600 .. **Castle,** David A '91 Branford Castle Inc -150 E 58th -NY 10155
(315) 866-7401 .. **Castle,** Michl A '80 M Castle -110 W Albany -Herkimer 13350 **Fx:**866-6960
(585) 422-6634 .. **Castle,** Wm H Jr. '98 %Xerox Corp -800 Phillips Rd -Webster 14580
(212) 479-6000 .. **Castleberry,** W Lesse '70 (Cooley LLP) -1114 Av of Amer -NY 10036
(212) 247-1010 .. **Castleman,** Danl J '80 FTI Consulting Inc -3 Times Sq -NY 10036 **Fx:**841-9350
(212) 558-4000 .. **Castleman,** David A '07 %Sullivan & C LLP -125 Broad -NY 10004
(212) 819-8200 .. **Castleman,** Lauriston Jr. '60 OfCnsl White & C LLP -1155 Av of Amer -NY 10036

(718) 701-3100 .. **Castorina,** Ronald Jr. '06 -1336 Clove Rd -Staten Isl 10301 **Fx:**701-3133
(914) 666-2574 .. **Castrataro,** Barbara A '90 -Bx132 -Chappaqua 10514 **Fx:**666-6399
(212) 455-2000 .. **Castro,** Aby D '09 %Simpson T&B LLP -425 Lex Av -NY 10017
(914) 944-4087 .. **Castro,** Andréa I '96 (Castro & R,PC) -30 State -Ossining 10562 **Fx:**944-4103
(914) 939-0002 .. **Castro,** Antonio D '88 OfCnsl Gallo F&N,LLP -211 S Ridge -Rye Brook 10573
(914) 323-7000 .. **Castro,** Christian R '08 %Wilson EME&D LLP -3 Gannett Dr -White Plns 10604
(212) 826-3800 .. **Castro,** Claude '76 (C Castro & Assoc,PLLC) -355 Lex Av -NY 10017 **Fx:**486-6583
(718) 793-9060 .. **Castro,** Deron R '93 -11835 Qns Blvd -Frst Hlls 11375 **Fx:**268-4812
(212) 340-0400 .. **Castro,** Elba Iris '01 %Appllt Div 1st Dept -27 Mad Av -NY 10010 **Fx:**889-4412
(212) 836-8000 .. **Castro,** H Stephen '00 (Kaye S LLP) -425 Park Av -NY 10022
(212) 788-0976 .. **Castro,** Johana V '06 %Law Dept -100 Church -NY 10007 **Fx:**788-0367
(718) 533-8090 .. **Castro,** John C '07 Castro Law,PLLC -82-11 37th Av -Jcksn Hts 11372 **Fx:**533-8091
(631) 686-5426 .. **Castro,** Kevin M '06 -4 Aspen Cir -St James 11780
(917) 551-1300 .. **Castro,** Liam L '04 %Koehler & I LLP -61 Bway -NY 10006
(631) 382-7979 .. **Castro,** Michl C '98 (Castro & T,LLC) -29 Bellemeade Av -Smithtwn 11787 **Fx:**382-7974
(212) 532-9736 .. **Castro,** Sonia M '94 %R Skyer & Assoc,LLP -276 5th Av -NY 10001 **Fx:**532-9846
(347) 851-5048 .. **Castro-Arce,** Yolanda '99 -3144 E Tremont Av -Bronx 10461 **Fx:**851-5051
(914) 323-7000 .. **Castro-Blanco,** James F '92 OfCnsl Wilson EME&D LLP -3 Gannett Dr -White Plns 10604
(212) 530-5000 .. **Castro Escobar,** Adlin M '09 %Milbank TH&M LLP -1 Chase Manh Plz -NY 10005
(212) 837-7788 .. **Castronovo,** Paul R '00 -80 Broad -NY 10004
(212) 482-0001 .. **Castronuovo,** Marie A '87 %Russo K&T LLP -33 Whitehall -NY 10004
(631) 265-2077 .. **Castrovinci,** Philip J '86 (Castrovinci & M) -1 Edgewood Av -Smithtwn 11787 **Fx:**265-0627
(607) 756-7501 .. **Casullo,** Francis J '91 (Pomeroy AC&M,LLP) -16 Tompkins Bx828 -Cortlnd 13045
(212) 474-1000 .. **Casusol,** Audry X '08 %Cravath S&M LLP -825 8th Av -NY 10019
(518) 486-2801 .. **Casutto,** Kevin J '84 Dept Pub Srvc -3 ESP -Albany 12223 **Fx:**473-3263
(212) 357-0383 .. **Caswell,** Bradford L '97 %Goldman Sachs & Co -32 Old Slip -NY 10005
(315) 472-5201 .. **Caswell,** John J '61 OfCnsl Mackay C&C,PC -103 E Water -Syracuse 13202
(516) 239-8818 .. **Catafago,** Jacques '84 (Catafago Law Firm) -595 Stewart Av -Gdn Cty 11530
(212) 239-9669 .. **Catafago,** Jacques '84 (Catafago Law Firm) -350 5th Av -NY 10118 **Fx:**239-9688
(585) 454-6480 .. **Catalana,** Bernadette '96 (Osborn R&B,LLP) -45 Exchange Blvd -Rchstr 14614
(631) 289-6440 .. **Catalanello,** Danl J '00 %TJ Worsoe Jr -997 Waverly Av -Holtsvll 11742 **Fx:**289-6040
(212) 692-1000 .. **Catalanello,** Gerard S '93 (Duane M LLP) -1540 Bway -NY 10036
(716) 205-0017 .. **Catalano,** A Jos '99 -730 Main -Niagara Fls 14301
(718) 250-2000 .. **Catalano,** Anthony '88 %DA -350 Jay -Brklyn 11201 **Fx:**250-2314
(212) 969-3000 .. **Catalano,** Benjamin J '96 (Proskauer R LLP) -1585 Bway -NY 10036
(585) 615-4005 .. **Catalano,** Christian A '04 -1 E Main -Rchstr 14614 **Fx:**232-6674
(212) 318-3000 .. **Catalano,** Douglas P '73 (Fulbright & J LLP) -666 5th Av -NY 10103
(518) 432-5810 .. **Catalano,** Frank A Jr. '86 -10 Colvin Av -Albany 12206
(516) 931-1800 .. **Catalano Gallardo & Petropoulos LLP** -100 Jericho Quadrangle -Jericho 11753 **Fx:**931-1033
(518) 433-5257 .. **Catalano,** Jane D '83 Natl Grid USA -1125 Bway -Albany 12204 **Fx:**433-5220
(212) 733-5431 .. **Catalano,** Jodi A '92 Pfizer Inc -235 E 42nd -NY 10017
(518) 797-9456 .. **Catalano,** Jos M '89 -Bx219 -Rensselaervll 12147 **Fx:**797-9457
(718) 990-6626 .. **Catalano,** Lisa A '94 %St John's Law Schl -8000 Utopia Pkwy -Jamaica 11439 **Fx:**591-1855
(631) 324-5605 .. **Catalano,** Mark J '92 -10 Pantigo Rd -E Hampton 11937 **Fx:**324-2943
(315) 479-8660 .. **Catalano,** Peter '92 (Alexander & C,LLC) -115 E Jffrsn -Syracuse 13202
(516) 931-1800 .. **Catalano,** Ralph A '89 (Catalano G&P LLP) -100 Jericho Quadrangle -Jericho 11753
(212) 878-8421 .. **Catalano,** Richd '92 (Clifford C LLP) -31 W 52nd -NY 10019
(212) 964-6611 .. **Catalano,** Thos A '83 (Lester SK&D) -120 Bway -NY 10271
(516) 681-3100 .. **Catalano,** Thos C Jr. '78 (Donohue MC&B) -555 N Bway Bx350 -Jericho 11753
(845) 454-1919 .. **Catalano,** Vincent J Jr. '84 -4 Lbrty -Poughkeepsie 12601
(631) 367-3111 .. **Catalanotto,** Michl C '06 %Brettschneider & B,LLP -83 Prospect -Huntngtn 11743 **Fx:**427-6912
(716) 845-9367 .. **Cataldi,** Lawr F '77 %Supreme Ct -25 Delaware Av -Buffalo 14202 **Fx:**851-3293
(631) 563-0555 .. **Cataldo,** Sal J '09 %D O'Doherty Jr -25 Candee Av -Sayvll 11782 **Fx:**563-0737
(631) 650-1200 .. **Cataldo-Barile,** Annalee J '91 (Sinnreich K&M LLP) -267 Carleton Av -Central Islip 11722
(518) 692-9645 .. **Catalfimo,** James A '61 (Catalfimo Law Firm) -18 Hill Bx184 -Greenwich 12834 **Fx:**692-2833
(518) 465-3484 .. **Catalfimo,** Michl J '86 (Carter CCBM&L,PC) -20 Corp Wds Blvd -Albany 12211
(518) 692-9645 .. **Catalfimo,** Michl J '86 Cnsl Catalfimo Law Firm -18 Hill Bx184 -Greenwich 12834 **Fx:**692-2833
(914) 736-0087 .. **Catalina,** Frank A '82 -1013 Brown -Peekskill 10566
(845) 246-3666 .. **Catalinotto,** Michl E '61 (Maynard OS&C,LLP) -Bx180 -Saugerties 12477
(845) 246-3666 .. **Catalinotto,** Michl E Jr. '93 (Maynard OS&C,LLP) -Bx180 -Saugerties 12477
(212) 648-0344 .. **Catana,** Mark C '91 JP Morgan Chase -245 Park Av -NY 10167
(914) 761-7190 .. **Catanese,** Louis M Jr. '96 %ODAR-SSA -75 S Bway -White Plns 10601 **Fx:**682-7006
(212) 559-0622 .. **Catania,** Bruce C '85 %Citibank -399 Park Av -NY 10043
(212) 317-5546 .. **Catania,** John A '85 Swiss Re -55 E 52nd -NY 10055
(845) 565-1100 .. **Catania,** Jos A Jr. '78 (Tarshis CLM&M,PLLC) -One Corwin Ct -Newburgh 12550
(212) 461-2323 .. **Catania,** Matthew A '07 %Saiber LLC -44 Wall -NY 10005
(845) 565-1100 .. **Catania,** Michl E '07 %Tarshis CLM&M,PLLC -One Corwin Ct -Newburgh 12550
(516) 742-4343 .. **Catania,** Richd L '89 (Scully SM&P PC) -400 Grdn City Plz -Gdn Cty 11530
(516) 478-5700 .. **Catanzano,** Raymond A '74 -162 Post Av -Westbury 11590
(212) 608-1234 .. **Catanzaro,** Dana M '10 %Peluso & T -70 Lafayette -NY 10013
(315) 476-1273 .. **Catanzaro,** Jos B '05 Pemco Grp,Inc -217 Mntgmry -Syracuse 13202
(212) 949-9022 .. **Catanzaro,** Jos J '69 (Abelman F&S) -666 3rd Av -NY 10017
(212) 226-1234 .. **Catanzaro,** Leonard J '93 -555 Malcolm X Blvd -NY 10037
(212) 344-3900 .. **Catapano,** Amy E '08 %Belair & E LLP -61 Bway -NY 10006
(212) 779-8600 .. **Catapano,** Anne F '04 %Silverman SS&B PLLC -381 Park Av S -NY 10016
(315) 788-5100 .. **Catapano,** Krystal M '09 %Conboy MB&K,LLP -407 Sherman -Watertwn 13601
(212) 342-9009 .. **Catapano,** Patricia Sachs '79 %Columbia Univ -535 W 116th 412 Low Mem'l Library -NY 10027
(516) 747-4082 .. **Catapano,** Philip J '73 (Montfort HM&S LLP) -1140 Franklin Av Bx7677 -Gdn Cty 11530
(718) 298-1186 .. **Catapano-Fox,** Tracy Ann '98 Supreme Ct -88-11 Sutphin Blvd -Jamaica 11435
(518) 463-7501 .. **Catapano-Friedman,** Robt S '88 (R Catapano-Friedman,PC) -744 Bway -Albany 12207 **Fx:**463-7502
(607) 763-9200 .. **Catarella,** Greg S '00 (Levene G&T,LLP) -BxF-1706 -Bnghmtn 13902
(718) 286-6000 .. **Catarisano,** Francesco '80 %DA -125-01 Qns Blvd -Kew Gdns 11415
(212) 259-8000 .. **Cate,** Elizabeth A '09 %Dewey & L LLP -1301 Av of Amer -NY 10019
(516) 538-2500 .. **Catelli,** Frank '82 OfCnsl Furey FLMW&D,PC -600 Front -Hempstd 11550
(845) 634-0888 .. **Caterina,** Laura '02 OfCnsl Freeman & L RLLP -4 Laurel Rd -New Cty 10956
(212) 259-8000 .. **Caterini,** Mark A '92 (Dewey & L LLP) -1301 Av of Amer -NY 10019
(212) 258-8368 .. **Cates,** Melissa B '86 %MTV Networks -1515 Bway -NY 10036 **Fx:**258-8358
(212) 549-2500 .. **Cates,** Paul J III '88 ACLU -125 Broad -NY 10004 **Fx:**549-2651
(315) 685-4551 .. **Cates,** Sarah D '91 %Welch Allyn,Inc -4341 State Street Rd -Skaneateles Fls 13153
(212) 708-1800 .. **Cathcart,** Ralph H '91 (Ladas & P) -26 W 61st -NY 10023
(914) 377-6240 .. **Cathcart,** Thos '06 %Law Dept -300 City Hall -Ynkrs 10701 **Fx:**964-0563
(716) 634-3320 .. **Catherine,** David M '05 %Pope Law Firm,PLLC -6580 Main -Williamsvll 14221 **Fx:**204-2770
(518) 478-9314 .. **Cathers,** Michl D '77 -113 Jordan Blvd -Delmar 12054 **Fx:**478-9314
(315) 781-1556 .. **Cathy,** Donna M '89 -Bx551 -Waterloo 13165 **Fx:**781-1556
(585) 232-6500 .. **Catillaz,** Margaret Artale '77 (Harter S&E LLP) -1600 Bausch & Lomb Pl -Rchstr 14604
(845) 627-8500 .. **Catina,** Laura M '03 %Condon & Assoc,PLLC -55 Old Tpk Rd -Nanuet 10954
(212) 458-1561 .. **Catina,** Michl P '00 AIG -175 Water -NY 10038
(212) 232-1300 .. **Catlett,** George '81 (Lewis BB&S LLP) -77 Water -NY 10005
(212) 935-3000 .. **Catlow,** Jessica W '04 %Mintz LCFG&P,PC -666 3rd Av -NY 10017
(718) 579-7900 .. **Cato,** Alexa U '04 %Leg Aid -900 Sheridan Av -Bronx 10451 **Fx:**293-8744
(212) 819-8200 .. **Cato,** Finn R '98 White & C LLP -1155 Av of Amer -NY 10036
(212) 735-3000 .. **Catoir,** Damien '09 %Skadden ASM&F LLP -4 Times Sq -NY 10036
(212) 715-9100 .. **Caton,** Amy D '00 (Kramer LN&F,LLP) -1177 Av of Amer -NY 10036
(518) 452-0802 .. **Catone,** Paul J '88 %Taylor & Assoc -1 Columbia Cir -Albany 12203 **Fx:**452-1863
(718) 590-2000 .. **Catros,** Stephanie E '06 DA -198 E 161st -Bronx 10451 **Fx:**590-6477
(718) 250-0400 .. **Catsandonis,** Paul D '98 %R Tusa -1 MetroTech Ctr -Brklyn 11201 **Fx:**250-0591
(212) 455-2000 .. **Cattell,** Andrew D W '06 %Simpson T&B LLP -425 Lex Av -NY 10017
(516) 222-6500 .. **Catterson,** Jeffrey L '99 (Galasso LC&L,LLP) -377 Oak -Gdn Cty 11530
(212) 751-4300 .. **Catterson,** John '75 (Hodgson R LLP) -1540 Bway -NY 10036
(516) 334-2414 .. **Catterson,** John T '86 OfCnsl Reynolds CGHL&Q,LLP -35 Arkay Dr -Hauppauge 11788 **Fx:**334-5921
(516) 826-3674 .. **Catterson,** Thos '95 -1801 Mad Av -N Bellmore 11710
(212) 761-3058 .. **Cattier,** Jennifer A '98 Morgan Stanley -1585 Bway -NY 10036
(212) 446-4800 .. **Catto,** Iskender H '01 (Kirkland & E LLP) -153 E 53rd -NY 10022
(212) 613-2001 .. **Catullo,** Kim M '92 (Gibbons PC) -1 Penn Plz -NY 10119 **Fx:**(973) 639-6280
(212) 538-6274 .. **Caudill,** Matthew D '03 CSFB -1 Mad Av -NY 10010
(518) 473-4596 .. **Caudle,** Rebecca L '85 %Gov Ofc Emply Rel -ESP Bldg 2 -Albany 12223
(212) 808-7800 .. **Caufield,** Carolyn R '83 (Kelley D&W LLP) -101 Park Av -NY 10178
(315) 428-5418 .. **Cauger,** A Scott '86 %National Grid -300 Erie Blvd W -Syracuse 13202 **Fx:**428-6149
(315) 788-6700 .. **Caughlin,** Keith B '90 (Schwerzmann & W,PC) -215 Wshngtn Bx704 -Watertwn 13601
(315) 782-9295 .. **Caughlin,** Mary D '87 %Hon H Gilbert -317 Wshngtn -Watertwn 13601
(212) 999-5800 .. **Cauley,** Kashana '07 %Wilson SG&R -1301 Av of Americas -NY 10019
(716) 856-4000 .. **Cauley,** Katherine E '00 (Hodgson R LLP) -140 Pearl -Buffalo 14202
(718) 767-3333 .. **Caulfield,** Caroline G '91 %Borchert GL&L,PC -19-02 Whitestone Expy -Whitestone 11357
(845) 657-2573 .. **Caulfield,** George J '86 -Route 28A Bx36 -W Shokan 12494
(212) 732-3200 .. **Caulfield,** Jerome J '76 (Carter L&M LLP) -2 Wall -NY 10005

(845) 561-2727 .. **Caulfield,** John G '89 %A Lewis -425 Robnsn Av -Newburgh 12550 **Fx:**561-6961
(212) 495-9506 .. **Caulfield,** Justin P '02 (Caulfield LLC) -240 Main Bx176 -Northprt 11768 **Fx:**(631) 486-8825
(631) 422-8400 .. **Caulfield,** Marilyn Milligan '88 %J Milligan -200 W Main Bx328 -Babylon 11702 **Fx:**422-8483
(718) 442-1700 .. **Caulfield,** Michl J '79 %Connors & C,PC -766 Castleton Av -Staten Isl 10310 **Fx:**442-1717
(212) 314-3823 .. **Caulfield,** Patrick J Jr. '76 AXA Client Solutions -1290 Av of Amer -NY 10104
(212) 773-0761 .. **Caulfield,** Saml A '97 Ernst & Young -5 Times Sq -NY 10036
(631) 723-3721 .. **Caulfield,** Thos W '83 -5 Squires Av -E Quogue 11942 **Fx:**723-3721
(516) 823-0100 .. **Causin,** Harriet '89 -104 S Central Av -Vly Stream 11580 **Fx:**823-0105
(631) 669-8849 .. **Cava,** Robt J '81 (R Cava,PC) -1038 Little East Neck Rd -W Babylon 11704 **Fx:**669-8577
(914) 668-4600 .. **Cavaco,** Luanda E '09 %Bozeman Law Firm,LLP -6 Gramatan Av -Mt Vernon 10550 **Fx:**668-4721
(716) 849-1333 .. **Cavagnaro,** Melissa A '06 %Lipsitz GSC LLP -42 Delaware Av -Buffalo 14202
(212) 770-2985 .. **Cavagnaro,** Patricia A '92 %AIG -80 Pine -NY 10005
(347) 643-3095 .. **Cavagnaro,** Rhonda M '99 -335 Adams -Brklyn 11201
(631) 439-2960 .. **Cavalier,** Dorothy '97 (Cavalier & Assoc) -144-1 Remngtn Blvd -Ronkonkoma 11779 **Fx:**439-2961
(631) 439-2960 .. **Cavalier,** Matthew J '97 (Cavalier & Assoc) -144-1 Remngtn Blvd -Ronkonkoma 11779 **Fx:**439-2961
(212) 306-1404 .. **Cavalier,** Michl '87 %Amer Stock Exch -86 Trinity Pl -NY 10006
(518) 463-3990 .. **Cavalier,** Roland M '71 (Tuczinski CG&C,PC) -54 State -Albany 12207
(914) 761-4200 .. **Cavaliere,** Kevin F '84 (Steinberg & C,LLP) -50 Main -White Plns 10606
(631) 851-1090 .. **Cavaliere,** Melissa A '07 Weinstein Grp,PC -10 Newton Pl -Hauppauge 11788
(212) 592-1400 .. **Cavaliere,** Natalia '01 %Herrick,F LLP -2 Park Av -NY 10016
(212) 219-3551 .. **Cavaliere,** Paul C '02 -335 Bway -NY 10013
(212) 885-5000 .. **Cavaliere,** Rocco A '01 %Blank R LLP -405 Lex Av -NY 10174
(212) 788-6405 .. **Cavalieri,** Meghan Ann '05 %Law Dept -100 Church -NY 10007 **Fx:**788-0367
(716) 856-4022 .. **Cavall,** Diana B '96 %Mattar D&G,LLP -17 Court -Buffalo 14202
(212) 977-3535 .. **Cavallaro,** Alfred '87 -1 Rckfllr Plz -NY 10020 **Fx:**247-5202
(646) 315-7319 .. **Cavallaro,** Anthony J '92 %FINRA -14 Wall -NY 10005 **Fx:**315-7440
(212) 533-6300 .. **Cavallaro,** Antonio M '00 %NYSUT -52 Bway -NY 10004 **Fx:**995-2347
(212) 261-8000 .. **Cavallaro,** Dana L '05 %Mendes & M,LLP -750 7th Av -NY 10019
(914) 631-3636 .. **Cavallaro,** John D '97 John D Cavallaro,PLLC -200 Wht Plns Rd -Tarrytwn 10591 **Fx:**631-1501
(212) 785-9100 .. **Cavallaro,** Meredith Rosen '00 %Paduano & W LLP -1251 Av of Amer -NY 10020
(212) 490-9505 .. **Cavallaro,** Patricia A '01 %Sterling Natl Bk -145 E 40th -NY 10016
(516) 408-5704 .. **Cavallaro,** Robt '99 Arc Excess & Surplus LLC -1122 Franklin Av -Gdn Cty 11530
(845) 357-5555 .. **Cavalli,** Sergio P '03 %R Reda,PC -1 Exec Blvd -Suffern 10901 **Fx:**357-3333
(212) 792-6070 .. **Cavallo,** Carrie A '99 (Schpoont & C,LLP) -50 Bway -NY 10004 **Fx:**792-6071
(212) 361-1400 .. **Cavallo,** Ernest J '87 Envrnmntl Cntrl Brd -66 John -NY 10038 **Fx:**361-1900
(914) 750-5933 .. **Cavallo,** Jessica '10 %Kissel H&W LLP -580 Wht Plns Rd -Tarrytwn 10591
(212) 581-4700 .. **Cavallo,** John '82 (Breznick & C) -630 9th Av -NY 10036 **Fx:**247-1407
(914) 251-1900 .. **Cavallo,** Maria C '90 %G Febbraio,PC -110 Corp Park Dr -White Plns 10604 **Fx:**251-1490
(718) 822-2203 .. **Cavallo,** Orlando A '88 (Cavallo & C) -3396 E Tremont Av -Bronx 10461 **Fx:**597-4617
(516) 571-3800 .. **Cavallo,** Robt L '98 DA -262 Old Cntry Rd -Mineola 11501 **Fx:**248-9479
(212) 753-2224 .. **Cavallo,** Robt M '58 R Cavallo,PC -163 Amstrdm Av -NY 10023 **Fx:**753-7113
(718) 822-2203 .. **Cavallo,** Vincent A '84 (Cavallo & C) -3396 E Tremont Av -Bronx 10461 **Fx:**597-4617
(914) 694-2100 .. **Cavaluzzi,** Gerard P '87 %Malcolm Pirnie Inc -104 Corp Park Dr Bx751 -White Plns 10602 **Fx:**694-2145
(716) 852-8222 .. **Cavan,** Joe R '84 (Paladino C&Q) -295 Main -Buffalo 14203
(718) 526-9150 .. **Cavanagh,** Chas M '96 %Little Flower Chldrns Srvcs -89-12 162nd -Jamaica 11432 **Fx:**526-9421
(718) 990-6621 .. **Cavanagh,** Edw D '75 %St John's Law Schl -8000 Utopia Pkwy -Jamaica 11439 **Fx:**591-1855
(631) 379-7736 .. **Cavanagh,** Francis A '08 Hon J Seybert USDC -100 Fed Plz Bx9014 -Central Islip 11722
(212) 720-5026 .. **Cavanagh,** Gregory P '04 %Fed Reserve Bk -33 Lbrty -NY 10045 **Fx:**785-5748
(914) 332-1800 .. **Cavanagh,** James U '95 (Cherry E&K,LLP) -150 Wht Plns Rd -Tarrytwn 10591
(518) 465-0400 .. **Cavanagh,** Michl P '95 (O'Connor OB&F,PC) -20 Corp Wds Blvd -Albany 12211
(516) 877-2424 .. **Cavanagh,** Terese A '87 Weinberg G&P LLP -400 Grdn City Plz -Gdn Cty 11530
(212) 408-5100 .. **Cavanagh,** Wm G '80 (Chadbourne & P LLP) -30 Rckfllr Plz -NY 10112
(212) 572-4724 .. **Cavanaugh,** Andrew J '76 %Estee Lauder -767 5th Av -NY 10153 **Fx:**572-3989
(212) 293-9431 .. **Cavanaugh,** Christopher S '03 Ruben Cap Mgt -600 Mad Av -NY 10022
(212) 856-7210 .. **Cavanaugh,** Dennis H '89 -555 5th Av -NY 10017
(718) 286-7900 .. **Cavanaugh,** Jennifer H '00 JetBlue -118-29 Qns Blvd -Frst Hlls 11375
(518) 862-1386 .. **Cavanaugh,** Judith B '07 %Burke SM&H,LLP -302 Wshngtn Av Ext Bx15085 -Albany 12212
(212) 297-6600 .. **Cavanaugh,** Lisa P '95 %TMM -230 Park Av -NY 10169 **Fx:**297-6062
(212) 758-9300 .. **Cavanaugh,** Michl E '87 (Lazare P&G LLP) -950 3rd Av -NY 10022
(716) 852-1300 .. **Cavanaugh,** Stephen E '61 (Amigone S&M,LLP) -350 Main -Buffalo 14202
(212) 336-2000 .. **Cavanaugh,** Wm F Jr. '81 (Patterson BW&T LLP) -1133 Av of Amer -NY 10036
(212) 453-5900 .. **Cavanna-Wilk,** Linda A '92 OfCnsl Ford & H LLP -100 Park Av -NY 10017
(716) 847-2523 .. **Cavarello,** Danl T '96 (Sugarman Law Firm,LLP) -14 Lafayette Sq -Buffalo 14203
(516) 478-5818 .. **Cavayero,** Harvey J '80 H Cavayero & Assoc -57 Old Cntry Rd -Westbury 11590 **Fx:**478-5817
(212) 506-3900 .. **Cavazos,** Sandra E '99 SpclCnsl Steptoe & J LLP -750 7th Av -NY 10019
(212) 373-3000 .. **Cave,** David Mark '03 %Paul WRW&G LLP -1285 Av of Amer -NY 10019
(212) 222-7005 .. **Cave,** LaVerne M '80 OfCnsl Rawlins & G,LLP -103 E 125th -NY 10035 **Fx:**222-7187
(212) 849-7000 .. **Cave,** Neil G '04 %Quinn EU&S,LLP -51 Mad Av -NY 10010
(212) 837-6000 .. **Cave,** Sarah Loomis '98 (Hughes H&R LLP) -1 Bttry Pk Plz -NY 10004
(718) 261-8762 .. **Caveglia,** Ronald C '78 -110-20 71st Rd -Frst Hlls 11375
(845) 679-7207 .. **Cavell,** Rachel Lee '93 %Wapner K&F,PLLC -45 Mill Hill Rd Bx572 -Woodstock 12498
(845) 331-0100 .. **Cavell,** Rachel Lee '93 %Wapner K&F,PLLC -239 Wall Bx3268 -Kingston 12402
(212) 859-5005 .. **Cavera,** RoseMarie '86 -110 Wall -NY 10005 **Fx:**472-9596
(212) 298-5207 .. **Cavet,** Keith J '90 %Leg Aid -49 Thomas -NY 10013 **Fx:**298-5252
(845) 471-0044 .. **Caviglia,** Marco '81 -329 Main -Poughkeepsie 12601 **Fx:**471-0041
(212) 556-2100 .. **Cavino,** Michl W '05 %King & S -1185 Av of Amer -NY 10036
(212) 504-6000 .. **Cavior,** Saml S '04 %Cadwalader W&T LLP -1 World Fncl Ctr -NY 10281
(212) 558-4000 .. **Cavo,** Andrew J '10 %Sullivan & C LLP -125 Broad -NY 10004
(212) 530-5000 .. **Cavoli,** James G '93 (Milbank TH&M LLP) -1 Chase Manh Plz -NY 10005
(518) 886-4000 .. **Cavoli,** Mae A '90 %AYCO -321 Bway Bx860 -Saratoga Spgs 12866
(212) 533-7000 .. **Cavolina,** Ellen '93 %Time Cafe -380 Lafayette -NY 10003
(212) 269-7658 .. **Cavuoto,** Barbara '04 %Ingalls & Snyder -61 Bway -NY 10006
(212) 449-2277 .. **Cavuotti,** Christopher D '83 %Merrill Lynch -220 Bway -NY 10038
(516) 409-6200 .. **Cawley,** Cornelius M '95 %Furey KWM&C,PC -2174 Jackson Av -Seafrd 11783
(631) 395-3336 .. **Cawley,** Danl R '84 -30 Jericho Tpke -Commack 11725
(716) 635-9550 .. **Cawley,** Jonathan P '05 %Bronson & M,LLP -415 Lawrence Bell Dr -Williamsvll 14221 **Fx:**635-9556
(607) 778-2431 .. **Cawley,** Jos F Jr. '85 Broome Cnty Ct -65 Hawley -Bnghmtn 13901
(212) 371-8008 .. **Cawley,** Mark P '85 %Guzov O,LLC -600 Mad Av -NY 10022
(845) 794-3000 .. **Cawley,** Thos J '93 %Cnty Atty -100 North Bx5012 -Monticello 12701 **Fx:**794-4924
(212) 314-7300 .. **Cawthorn,** Stuart C '03 IAC -555 W 18th -NY 10011
(212) 701-3907 .. **Cawthra,** Robt '71 -80 Pine -NY 10005 **Fx:**269-5420
(212) 601-2680 .. **Cayea,** Donald J '76 (Gonzalez S&H LLP) -350 5th Av -NY 10118
(212) 657-3922 .. **Cayne,** Louise E '85 %Citibank -111 Wall -NY 10005 **Fx:**657-3744
(917) 805-4120 .. **Caytas,** Ivo G '92 (Caytas & Assoc) -146 W 57th -NY 10019 **Fx:**591-9340
(716) 845-9382 .. **Caywood,** David C '95 %Supreme Ct -25 Delaware Av -Buffalo 14202 **Fx:**851-3293
(212) 841-1000 .. **Caywood,** Warren G Jr. '77 (Covington & B LLP) -620 8th Av -NY 10018
(845) 687-0061 .. **Cazakoff,** Martin D '71 -400 Scarawan Rd Bx279 -Stone Rdg 12484 **Fx:**687-7421
(718) 852-5900 .. **Cea,** Richd J '78 (Wingate K&C) -45 Main -Brklyn 11201
(516) 285-2060 .. **Cean Owens,** Cassandra N '02 Cean Owens LLC -867 W Merrick Rd -Vly Stream 11580
(718) 222-2048 .. **Ceballo,** Brian P '05 %Law Dept -350 Jay -Brklyn 11201 **Fx:**222-2088
(718) 590-2000 .. **Ceballos,** Marta '87 %DA -198 E 161st -Bronx 10451 **Fx:**590-6477
(631) 225-9410 .. **Cebula,** Janet D '94 -443 N Wellwood Av -Lindenhrst 11757 **Fx:**225-6590
(585) 343-5450 .. **Cebula,** John W '72 %Leg Srvcs -5073 Clinton St Rd -Batavia 14020 **Fx:**343-5503
(212) 398-0055 .. **Cebulash,** Brett H '94 (Garwin G&F,LLP) -1501 Bway -NY 10036
(212) 593-6700 .. **Cecala,** Robt J '92 (Aaronson RF&D,LLP) -757 3rd Av -NY 10017
(718) 875-1300 .. **Ceccacci,** Diana '97 %Appllt Div 2nd Dept -45 Monroe Pl -Brklyn 11201 **Fx:**858-2446
(212) 227-4848 .. **Ceccarelli,** Jos J '81 (Ceccarelli W PLLC) -2 Wall -NY 10005
(212) 227-4848 .. **Ceccarelli Weprin PLLC** -2 Wall -NY 10005 **Fx:**227-4636
(914) 995-3460 .. **Cecchini,** Craig A '00 %DA -111 Martin Luther King Blvd -White Plns 10601 **Fx:**995-3363
(518) 766-5469 .. **Cecchini,** Peter G '96 %Peter Gerard Assoc Inc -Bx267 -N Chatham 12132
(516) 227-6363 .. **Ceccorulli,** Michl A '07 %Amato & Assoc,PC -666 Old Cntry Rd -Gdn Cty 11530 **Fx:**227-6367
(212) 563-4100 .. **Ceccotti,** Babette '84 (Cohen W&S LLP) -330 W 42nd -NY 10036
(516) 294-5433 .. **Cecere,** Frank A Jr. '85 (Ahmuty D&M) -200 IU Willets Rd -Albertson 11507
(718) 459-6000 .. **Cecere,** Robt J '93 (Pennisi D&N LLP) -97-77 Qns Blvd -Rego Pk 11374
(585) 292-2108 .. **Cecero,** Diane M '79 Monroe Community Cllg -1000 E Henrietta Rd -Rchstr 14623 **Fx:**424-5249
(212) 303-1825 .. **Cech,** Scott M '99 %Rosen Seymour Shapss Martin & Co -757 3rd Av -NY 10017
(718) 448-1000 .. **Ceci,** David J '89 Northfield Savings Bk -1731 Victory Blvd -Staten Isl 10314 **Fx:**981-1572
(212) 526-8912 .. **Cecil,** John L '81 %Lehman Bros -399 Park Av -NY 10022
(315) 435-2585 .. **Cecile,** Julie A '93 %Dept Social Srvcs -421 Mntgmry -Syracuse 13202
(212) 274-0777 .. **Cecutti,** Anthony '06 %Romano & K,PLLC -100 Lafayette -NY 10013
(212) 536-3900 .. **Cedar,** Philip M '78 (K&L Gates LLP) -599 Lex Av -NY 10022
(212) 695-0060 .. **Cedeno,** Peter L '94 %Wilens & B,PC -450 7th Av -NY 10123
(718) 250-2000 .. **Cedeno,** Vivian R '01 %DA -350 Jay -Brklyn 11201 **Fx:**250-2314
(212) 387-5400 .. **Cederqvist,** L Fredrik '95 AT&T -32 Av of Amer -NY 10013
(212) 319-6898 .. **Cedrone,** Gerard '99 (Lavin ORC&D) -420 Lex Av -NY 10170

(212) 957-7600 .. **Cefo,** Damir '01 %Cohen & G LLP -800 3rd Av -NY 10022
(646) 252-2936 .. **Ceglian,** Marissa C '06 MTA -2 Bway -NY 10004
(212) 592-6700 .. **Ceitlin,** Andrew D '01 %Bovis Lend Lease Hldngs -200 Park Av -NY 10166 **Fx:**592-6997
(212) 596-9000 .. **Celada,** M Cristina '86 %Ropes & G LLP -1211 Av of Amer -NY 10036
(914) 366-5700 .. **Celano,** Josephine M '88 %MA Bjork -660 Wht Plns Rd -Tarrytwn 10591 **Fx:**366-5759
(212) 244-6222 .. **Celauro,** Steven '90 (Melucci C&S,LLP) -26 Bway -NY 10004 **Fx:**244-7165
(212) 503-6203 .. **Celedonia,** Baila H '76 (Cowan L&L,PC) -1133 Av of Amer -NY 10036
(212) 219-7533 .. **Celedonio,** Francisco '87 -401 Bway -NY 10013
(212) 422-0202 .. **Celentano,** Christopher J '04 %Sedgwick DM&A LLP -125 Broad -NY 10004
(518) 402-6193 .. **Celentano,** Paul '99 %Workers Comp Bd -20 Park -Albany 12207
(914) 761-7190 .. **Celentano,** Ralph A '58 %ODAR-SSA -75 S Bway -White Plns 10601 **Fx:**682-7006
(718) 875-1300 .. **Celenza,** Christine E '98 %Applt Div 2nd Dept -45 Monroe Pl -Brklyn 11201 **Fx:**858-2446
(914) 665-2440 .. **Celestin,** Alexis S '05 %DA -Roosevelt Sq -Mt Vernon 10550 **Fx:**668-2314
(212) 262-1103 .. **Celestin,** Robt A '86 -250 W 57th -NY 10107 **Fx:**262-1173
(718) 286-6000 .. **Celestin,** Scottie '08 %DA -125-01 Qns Blvd -Kew Gdns 11415
(212) 635-2730 .. **Celis,** Maria E '00 %Neville P LLP -17 State -NY 10004
(212) 509-6300 .. **Cella,** Glenn P '08 Melli GW&M -17 Battery Pl -NY 10004
(631) 853-5761 .. **Cella,** Mara E '07 %Cnty Atty -400 Carleton Av -Central Islip 11722 **Fx:**853-7788
(516) 348-0604 .. **Cella,** Mario V '78 (Cella Law Firm) -900 Merchants Cncrs -Westbury 11590 **Fx:**832-8435
(516) 348-0609 .. **Cella,** Vincent M '03 %Cella Law Firm -900 Merchants Cncrs -Westbury 11590 **Fx:**832-8435
(518) 449-2043 .. **Celli,** Andrea E '89 (Chapter 13 Trustee) -7 Southwoods Blvd -Albany 12211 **Fx:**449-2473
(212) 763-5000 .. **Celli,** Andrew G Jr. '91 (Emery CB&A LLP) -75 Rckfllr Plz -NY 10019
(212) 532-8100 .. **Cellilli,** Thos H III '03 (Stern & M,LLP) -115 Bway -NY 10006
(716) 857-7991 .. **Cellino,** Anna Marie '82 (Natl Fuel Gas) -6363 Main -Williamsvll 14221 **Fx:**857-7614
(716) 854-2020 .. **Cellino & Barnes, PC** -350 Main -Buffalo 14202 **Fx:**854-6291
(585) 454-2020 .. **Cellino & Barnes, PC** -16 W Main -Rchstr 14614 **Fx:**454-3279
(631) 293-6060 .. **Cellino & Barnes, PC** -445 Broad Hollow Rd -Melvll 11747 **Fx:**(877) 227-8020
(716) 854-2020 .. **Cellino,** Ross M Jr. '83 (Cellino & B,PC) -350 Main -Buffalo 14202
(212) 578-3067 .. **Cellupica,** Paul G '06 %MetLife -27-01 Qns Plz N -LIC 11101
(631) 622-5219 .. **Cellura,** Davin P '99 Amer Home Mortgage -538 Broadhllw Rd -Melvll 11747
(716) 854-1002 .. **Celniker,** Philip '64 (Miserendino CS&E,PC) -295 Main -Buffalo 14203
(845) 638-5001 .. **Cember,** Alicia B '88 DA -1 S Main -New Cty 10956 **Fx:**638-5070
(212) 310-2184 .. **Cember,** Jonathan '82 %Colgate-Palmolive -300 Park Av -NY 10022
(845) 358-7078 .. **Cember,** Wm '87 (Cember & C,PC) -10 S Bway Bx555 -Nyack 10960 **Fx:**358-8625
(212) 815-7530 .. **Cempa,** Richd S '83 PELS -125 Barclay -NY 10007 **Fx:**815-7534
(212) 306-7200 .. **Cenac,** Maxine N '04 Mayors Ofc Labor Rel -40 Rector -NY 10006 **Fx:**306-7223
(212) 637-2705 .. **Cenawood,** Sean C '92 %US Atty -86 Chmbrs -NY 10007
(518) 453-4600 .. **Cenci,** Cathleen S '85 %Comm Judicial Cndct -ESP -Albany 12223 **Fx:**486-1850
(212) 446-4800 .. **Cendali,** Dale M '85 (Kirkland & E LLP) -153 E 53rd -NY 10022
(212) 277-4000 .. **Cendan,** Danl L '04 %Freshfields BD LLP -520 Mad Av -NY 10022
(212) 634-1228 .. **Cender,** Joshua Fielding '97 ME Zuckerman & Co Inc -450 Park Av -NY 10022
(212) 552-0328 .. **Cenedella,** Linda W '98 JP Morgan Chase & Co -1 Chase Manh Plz -NY 10005
(607) 729-1539 .. **Cenesky Alenik Stefanski & Gallagher** -251 Main -Johnson Cty 13790 **Fx:**729-2472
(607) 729-1539 .. **Cenesky,** John F '49 (Cenesky AS&G) -251 Main -Johnson Cty 13790
(212) 480-3030 .. **Cennamo,** Alison B '08 %M Pressman -125 Maiden Ln -NY 10038 **Fx:**480-2590
(718) 520-0065 .. **Censor,** Martin A '90 -141-05 68th Dr -Flushng 11367 **Fx:**793-0822
(914) 641-2018 .. **Centeio,** Elena '97 %ITT Corp -1133 Wstchstr Av -White Plns 10604
(518) 452-3710 .. **Centi,** Danl J '78 (Feeney C&M) -116 Great Oaks Blvd -Albany 12203
(212) 237-0000 .. **Centner,** Danl B '09 %Vinson & E LLP -666 5th Av -NY 10103
(212) 964-7400 .. **Centner,** Erik W '03 %Smith MDWY&Y,PC -111 John -NY 10038
(516) 357-3000 .. **Centola,** Gary D '77 (Rivkin R LLP) -926 RXR Plz -Uniondale 11556
(315) 422-1391 .. **Centolella,** Jason J '05 %Green & S,PLLC -One Lincoln Ctr #900 -Syracuse 13202 **Fx:**423-2874
(315) 422-1391 .. **Centolella,** Kathleen M '05 %Green & S,PLLC -One Lincoln Ctr #900 -Syracuse 13202
(914) 993-5095 .. **Centone,** Anthony J '87 (A Centone,PC) -244 Wstchstr Av -White Plns 10604 **Fx:**993-0654
(212) 267-2600 .. **Centor,** Irving '52 -61 Bway -NY 10006 **Fx:**267-3024
(315) 425-2700 .. **Centore,** Christopher J '99 (Hiscock & B,LLP) -One Park Pl -Syracuse 13202
(585) 262-8100 .. **Centrone,** Bethany A '02 City School Dist -131 W Broad -Rchstr 14614 **Fx:**282-8381
(718) 835-1100 .. **Centrone,** D Marjorie '55 -108-14 Crossbay Blvd -Ozone Pk 11417 **Fx:**323-0270
(607) 723-5341 .. **Ceparano,** Laurie M '99 SpclCnsl Hinman H&K,LLP -80 Exchange Bx5250 -Bnghmtn 13902
(914) 517-5000 .. **Cepelewicz,** Barry B '92 (Meiselman DPC&E,PC) -1311 Mamaroneck Av -White Plns 10605
(212) 255-6200 .. **Cephas,** Derrick D '80 Amalgamated Bk -275 7th Av -NY 10001
(845) 894-8051 .. **Cepiel,** Donald M Jr. '96 %IBM Corp -2070 State Hwy 52 -Hopewell Junct 12533
(516) 571-3800 .. **Cepriano,** Jessica '07 %DA -262 Old Cntry Rd -Mineola 11501 **Fx:**248-9479
(212) 537-6269 .. **Cera,** Kenneth B '03 (Schwartz & C LLP) -350 5th Av -NY 10118 **Fx:**(917) 591-5184
(607) 231-6735 .. **Cerabino,** Renzo A '00 M & T Bank -2 Court Bx5250 -Bnghmtn 13902
(212) 728-8000 .. **Cerabino,** Thos M '82 (Willkie F&G LLP) -787 7th Av -NY 10019
(212) 259-8000 .. **Cerasani,** Denise A '85 (Dewey & L LLP) -1301 Av of Amer -NY 10019
(518) 792-2117 .. **Cerasano,** Mark E '83 (Bartlett PS&R,PC) -1 Wshngtn Bx2168 -Glens Fls 12801
(516) 873-8600 .. **Cerasi,** Luciano '84 %Mahon & B -21 Glen -Glen Cove 11542 **Fx:**873-1937
(212) 218-5500 .. **Cerasia,** Edw II '91 (Seyfarth S LLP) -620 8th Av -NY 10018
(203) 330-2246 .. **Ceraso,** Cara Ann '05 %Pullman & C,LLC -50 Main -White Plns 10606 **Fx:**576-8888
(212) 205-7000 .. **Cerasuolo,** Jacquelyn Dinielli '98 Cnsl Ashurst LLP -7 Times Sq -NY 10036
(212) 608-0012 .. **Ceraulo,** Andrew J '80 -150 Bway -NY 10038 **Fx:**608-0658
(212) 608-0656 .. **Ceraulo,** Anna M '79 -150 Bway -NY 10038 **Fx:**608-0658
(718) 596-1829 .. **Cerbin,** Scott G '03 -26 Court -Brklyn 11242 **Fx:**228-4612
(212) 852-3538 .. **Cerbone,** Gregory B '90 %US Trust Co,NA -114 W 47th -NY 10036 **Fx:**852-1310
(212) 478-7200 .. **Cerbone,** Janine M '03 %Hahn & H LLP -488 Mad Av -NY 10022
(914) 328-0500 .. **Cerbone,** Wm A '83 -81 Main -White Plns 10601
(914) 664-6151 .. **Cerchiara,** Anthony V '51 -560 N Columbus Av -Mt Vernon 10552 **Fx:**664-6151
(212) 285-3800 .. **Cerchione,** Gregory T '86 (Subin Assoc LLP) -150 Bway -NY 10007
(212) 735-3000 .. **Cerciello,** Amy Findlay '07 %Skadden ASM&F LLP -4 Times Sq -NY 10036
(716) 854-3400 .. **Cercone,** Marco '03 (Rupp BPC&C LLC) -1600 Lbrty Bldg -Buffalo 14202
(716) 830-2061 .. **Cercone,** Paul Albert '91 -52 Chateau Ter -Buffalo 14226 **Fx:**839-3021
(716) 883-3300 .. **Cercone,** Roland M '86 -484 Delaware Av -Buffalo 14202 **Fx:**883-2163
(212) 969-1000 .. **Ceres,** Rudyard W II '98 Alliance Bernstein LP -1345 Av of Amer -NY 10105 **Fx:**554-4639
(518) 274-1500 .. **Ceresia,** Richd D '79 (Ceresia S&M) -1 State -Troy 12180
(518) 674-2836 .. **Ceresia,** Richd D '79 (Ceresia S&M) -2977 NY 43 -Averill Pk 12018
(212) 351-4000 .. **Ceresia,** Scott P '09 %Gibson D&C LLP -200 Park Av -NY 10166
(518) 274-1500 .. **Ceresia Singiser & Malone** -1 State -Troy 12180 **Fx:**274-7730
(518) 674-2836 .. **Ceresia Singiser & Malone** -2977 NY 43 -Averill Pk 12018 **Fx:**674-2837
(212) 909-6000 .. **Ceresney,** Andrew J '97 (Debevoise & P LLP) -919 3rd Av -NY 10022
(212) 471-8520 .. **Ceresney,** Ian '70 (Herzfeld & R,PC) -125 Broad -NY 10004
(516) 466-8005 .. **Cereste,** Saverio V Jr. '09 %Tashlik KG&C PC -40 Cuttermill Rd -Gt Neck 11021
(212) 598-8000 .. **Cerezola,** Theresa A '79 %Guardian Life Ins -7 Hanover Sq -NY 10004 **Fx:**919-2693
(212) 672-6000 .. **Cerick,** M Richd '82 %Hypo und Vereins Bk -150 E 42nd -NY 10017
(212) 940-3019 .. **Ceriello,** Lawr A '82 (Nixon P LLP) -437 Mad Av -NY 10022
(212) 259-8000 .. **Cerini,** Olga B '91 (Dewey & L LLP) -1301 Av of Amer -NY 10019
(607) 732-0719 .. **Cerio,** Fredk M '94 -460 E Market -Elmira 14901 **Fx:**732-0733
(212) 596-9000 .. **Cerio,** Jeffrey M '10 %Ropes & G LLP -1211 Av of Amer -NY 10036
(315) 697-3987 .. **Cerio,** Marian J '80 -104 Center Bx362 -Canastota 13032
(315) 422-8769 .. **Cerio,** Thos J '96 -407 S Warren -Syracuse 13202 **Fx:**476-8002
(914) 428-2100 .. **Cermele,** Mark '05 %Welby B&G,LLP -11 Martine Av -White Plns 10606
(516) 746-0033 .. **Cerniglia,** Nat '75 -72 Jericho Tpk -Mineola 11501 **Fx:**746-0124
(212) 768-6700 .. **Cerniglia,** Stephen '97 (Sonnenschein N&R LLP) -2 World Fncl Ctr -NY 10281
(516) 742-6000 .. **Cernigliaro,** Frank '93 (Landers & C,PC) -1 Old Cntry Rd -Carle Pl 11514 **Fx:**742-6066
(518) 689-1410 .. **Cernik,** Christopher A '77 (Greenberg T,LLP) -54 State -Albany 12207
(516) 536-0900 .. **Cernitz,** Henry J '76 (Jacobson & S) -510 Merrick Rd Bx46 -Rockvll Ctr 11571
(212) 903-9000 .. **Cerny,** Corinne N '10 %Linklaters -1345 Av of Amer -NY 10105
(845) 855-8900 .. **Cerny,** Marilyn-Joy '91 (Cerny Assoc,PC) -24 Smith -Pawling 12564 **Fx:**855-8904
(845) 855-8900 .. **Cerny,** Michl V '87 (Cerny Assoc,PC) -24 Smith -Pawling 12564 **Fx:**855-8904
(212) 238-3000 .. **Cerow,** Stephen P '78 (Emmet M&M,LLP) -120 Bway -NY 10271
(914) 423-1616 .. **Cerrato,** Anthony J Jr. '67 -656 Ynkrs Av -Ynkrs 10704 **Fx:**423-8150
(516) 742-7900 .. **Cerrato,** Louis J '95 (Frommer & C,LLP) -42 Nassau Blvd Bx8134 -Gdn Cty 11530 **Fx:**742-7999
(718) 250-2000 .. **Cerrato,** Perry A '05 %DA -350 Jay -Brklyn 11201 **Fx:**250-2314
(914) 686-1700 .. **Cerrato,** Stephen A '03 %O'Connor R,LLP -200 Mamaroneck Av -White Plns 10601
(212) 909-6000 .. **Cerreta,** John W '07 %Debevoise & P LLP -919 3rd Av -NY 10022
(914) 939-5208 .. **Cerreto,** Anthony M '86 %Village Atty -222 Grace Church -Pt Chester 10573
(212) 340-0400 .. **Cerreto,** Jos D '75 %Applt Div 1st Dept -27 Mad Av -NY 10010 **Fx:**889-4412
(716) 679-0100 .. **Cerrie,** Michl R '07 -221 Central Av -Fredonia 14063 **Fx:**679-0600
(212) 326-3939 .. **Cerrito,** F Dominic '92 (Jones D) -222 E 41st -NY 10017
(315) 422-7111 .. **Cerrito,** Jonathan M '04 (Blitman & K LLP) -443 N Franklin -Syracuse 13204
(315) 474-7571 .. **Cerrito,** Nicole Allen '04 %Mackenzie H LLP -101 S Salina Bx4967 -Syracuse 13221
(718) 855-9000 .. **Cerritos,** Danl E '97 %Cullen and D LLP -177 Montague -Brklyn 11201
(716) 688-1305 .. **Cerrone,** Anthony F '70 -1701 N Forest Rd Bx477 -Getzvll 14068
(716) 843-5700 .. **Cerrone,** Michl S '00 %US Atty -138 Delaware Av -Buffalo 14202 **Fx:**551-3052
(212) 431-2815 .. **Cerruti,** Eugene '71 %NY Law Schl -185 W Bway -NY 10013 **Fx:**343-2039
(212) 687-7800 .. **Certain,** Gary T '94 (Certain & Z,PLLC) -909 3rd Av -NY 10017 **Fx:**687-7801

(516) 296-7000 .. **Certilman Balin Adler & Hyman,LLP** -90 Merrick Av -E Meadow 11554 **Fx:**296-7111
(631) 979-3000 .. **Certilman Balin Adler & Hyman,LLP** -1393 Vets Mem'l Hwy -Hauppauge 11788 **Fx:**979-7070
(516) 296-7000 .. **Certilman,** Morton L '56 (Certilman BA&H,LLP) -90 Merrick Av -E Meadow 11554
(212) 956-3425 .. **Certilman,** Steven A '82 (S Certilman,PC) -488 Mad Av -NY 10022 **Fx:**(203) 425-8600
(516) 349-6100 .. **Certner,** David J '83 %Episcopal Health Srvcs -700 Hicksvll Rd -Bethpage 11714
(212) 323-7070 .. **Certo,** Cynthia M '00 (Rawle & H LLP) -14 Wall -NY 10005
(585) 275-5269 .. **Cerulli,** Catherine '93 Univ of Rochester Med Ctr-Psych Dept -300 Crittenden Blvd -Rchstr 14642
(585) 454-3323 .. **Cerulli Massare & Lembke** -339 East Av -Rchstr 14604 **Fx:**262-6015
(212) 883-2420 .. **Cerullo,** Alfred C III '87 Grand Cntrl Prtnrshp -122 E 42nd -NY 10168
(212) 309-8100 .. **Cerullo,** Michele C '01 Lexis Nexis -125 Park Av -NY 10017
(212) 506-2500 .. **Cerullo,** Norman R '05 %Mayer B LLP -1675 Bway -NY 10019
(718) 590-2678 .. **Cerussi,** Albert Jr. '67 %Supreme Ct -851 Grnd Cncrs -Bronx 10451
(516) 745-1300 .. **Cerussi,** Chas A '97 (Cerussi & G,PC) -1325 Franklin Av -Gdn Cty 11530 **Fx:**745-1310
(914) 948-1200 .. **Cerussi,** Michl A Jr. '77 (Cerussi & S,PC) -1 N Lex Av -White Plns 10601
(914) 948-1200 .. **Cerussi & Spring,PC** -1 N Lex Av -White Plns 10601 **Fx:**948-1579
(914) 948-1200 .. **Cerussi,** Thos F '90 (Cerussi & S,PC) -1 N Lex Av -White Plns 10601
(212) 879-6465 .. **Cerutti,** Dino '53 -320 E 72nd -NY 10021
(718) 250-2000 .. **Cervantes,** Julia V '08 %DA -350 Jay -Brklyn 11201 **Fx:**250-2314
(516) 292-8100 .. **Cervantes-Ospina,** Keiko '09 %Nassau/Sfflk Law Srv -1 Helen Keller Way -Hempstd 11550 **Fx:**292-6529
(914) 995-4172 .. **Cervasio,** Christine E '01 %DA -111 Martin Luther King Blvd -White Plns 10601 **Fx:**995-3363
(716) 856-5222 .. **Cervi,** Anthony J '02 -43 Court -Buffalo 14202
(212) 754-9400 .. **Cervini,** Jos P Jr. '99 (Todtman NS&J,PC) -425 Park Av -NY 10022
(718) 779-8910 .. **Cervini,** Michl A '87 (MA Cervini) -Bx800018 -Elmhrst 11380 **Fx:**205-5830
(845) 240-1700 .. **Cervone,** Jos V '94 J Cervone,PC -2610 South Av -Wappingers Fls 12590 **Fx:**240-1701
(212) 506-2500 .. **Cervoni,** Domenic C '08 %Mayer B LLP -1675 Bway -NY 10019
(516) 825-0500 .. **Cervoni,** Roberto '06 %Ardito & A,LLP -659 Franklin Av -Franklin Sq 11010 **Fx:**825-1195
(212) 425-7200 .. **Cerwinski,** Robt V '98 (Kenyon & K,LLP) -1 Bway -NY 10004
(212) 808-2700 .. **Cerza,** Frank J '81 (Pepper H LLP) -620 8th Av -NY 10018
(212) 232-1300 .. **Cesani,** Serena A '09 %Lewis BB&S LLP -77 Water -NY 10005
(212) 335-9000 .. **Cesarano,** James C '02 %DA -1 Hogan Pl -NY 10013
(212) 351-4500 .. **Cesaratto,** Brian G '88 (Epstein B&G,PC) -250 Park Av -NY 10177
(845) 831-6672 .. **Cesaratto,** Mercedes '93 %US DOJ INS -Red Schlhse Rd -Fishkill 12524
(212) 541-2000 .. **Cesare,** Christine B '85 (Bryan C LLP) -1290 Av of Amer -NY 10104
(718) 330-1200 .. **Cesare,** Heidi C '92 %Fed Def of NY Inc -1 Pierrepont Plz -Brklyn 11201 **Fx:**855-0760
(212) 774-5918 .. **Cesare,** James J '01 Point Lookout Cptl Prtnrs -275 Mad Av -NY 10016 **Fx:**774-5919
(212) 681-4486 .. **Cesare,** Lisa A '94 NYS Comptrollers Ofc -633 3rd Av -NY 10017
(518) 408-0469 .. **Cesare,** Lucy DeWitt '94 Workers Comp Bd -20 Park -Albany 12207
(212) 705-7000 .. **Cesar-Fabian,** Eugenie M '05 %Bingham M LLP -399 Park Av -NY 10022
(212) 326-2000 .. **Cesaro,** Angela L '10 %O'Melveny & M LLP -7 Times Sq -NY 10036
(212) 605-6200 .. **Cesaro,** Erica V '06 %Levy P&K,LLP -800 3rd Av -NY 10022
(718) 409-2212 .. **Cesarski,** Walter J '96 %Wstchstr Sq Chiroprctc -2744 E Tremont Av -Bronx 10461
(212) 419-3978 .. **Cesnik,** Eric A '01 RNK Capital LLC -527 Mad Av -NY 10022
(212) 576-7000 .. **Cespedes,** Carol '04 %NY Life Ins -51 Mad Av -NY 10010 **Fx:**447-0569
(516) 741-4799 .. **Cespedes,** Edw A '04 %Baker SBGFM&N,LLC -100 Grdn City Plz -Gdn Cty 11530
(914) 347-2600 .. **Cestaro,** Shawn M '02 %Traub LS&S LLP -7 Skyline Dr -Hawthorne 10532
(631) 361-7979 .. **Cetero,** Frank A '00 -141 John -Babylon 11702
(212) 819-8200 .. **Cetina,** Luisa H '07 %White & C LLP -1155 Av of Amer -NY 10036
(212) 476-9000 .. **Cetron,** Brad E '01 %Neuberger Berman,LLC -605 3rd Av -NY 10158 **Fx:**476-9862
(212) 635-2230 .. **Cetrulo & Capone LLP** -14 Wall -NY 10005 **Fx:**635-2239
(212) 635-2230 .. **Cetrulo,** Lawr G '99 (Cetrulo & C LLP) -14 Wall -NY 10005
(646) 356-8600 .. **Ceurvels,** Jacqueline M '04 Ambrose Employer Grp -199 Water -NY 10038
(516) 560-6400 .. **Cevasco,** Christopher M '98 %Leg Aid -1 Helen Keller Way -Hempstd 11550 **Fx:**565-3694
(212) 819-8200 .. **Cevher Conti,** Mehtap '03 %White & C LLP -1155 Av of Amer -NY 10036
(212) 969-3000 .. **Cha,** Jos S '95 (Proskauer R LLP) -1585 Bway -NY 10036
(212) 271-0664 .. **Cha,** Kyuchul '07 %Lee AC LLP -350 5th Av -NY 10118
(212) 801-6902 .. **Cha,** Moonhee '08 %Greenberg T,LLP -200 Park Av -NY 10166
(718) 888-9500 .. **Cha,** Stephen H '96 (Kim & C,LLP) -158-14 Nrthrn Blvd -Flushng 11358
(716) 881-5800 .. **Chaas,** Michelle G '92 %Siegel K&K -426 Franklin -Buffalo 14202
(212) 541-6741 .. **Chabin,** Lee G '91 Fund for Modern Courts -351 W 54th -NY 10019 **Fx:**541-7301
(718) 618-2500 .. **Chabot,** Ann C '79 %Civil Ct -851 Grnd Cncrs -Bronx 10451 **Fx:**590-7294
(516) 222-0888 .. **Chabus,** Lance P '89 %Lehman & E LLP -50 Chas Lindbergh Blvd -Uniondale 11553
(585) 232-6500 .. **Chacchia,** Bartholomew '07 %Harter S&E LLP -1600 Bausch & Lomb Pl -Rchstr 14604
(914) 595-8224 .. **Chach,** Kristin L '99 Visant Corp -357 Main -Armonk 10504
(646) 356-0550 .. **Chachanashvili,** Gershon '00 Hire Cnsl -575 Mad Av -NY 10022 **Fx:**356-0585
(718) 997-8255 .. **Chachanashvili,** Revaz '04 -108-18 72nd Av -Frst Hlls 11375
(212) 822-8300 .. **Chachere,** Matthew J '87 %NMIC -76 Wadsworth Av -NY 10033 **Fx:**740-9645
(212) 506-5000 .. **Chachkes,** Alex V '00 (Orrick H&S LLP) -51 W 52nd -NY 10019
(212) 965-2200 .. **Chachkin,** Norman J '74 %NAACP/LDF -99 Hudson -NY 10013 **Fx:**226-7592
(516) 545-5160 .. **Chacko,** Anna S '88 %Natl Grid -175 E Old Cntry Rd -Hicksvll 11801 **Fx:**545-5029
(914) 333-7420 .. **Chacko,** Jacob S '02 %Akzo Nobel -120 Wht Plns Rd -Tarrytwn 10591
(914) 785-5300 .. **Chaconas,** John G '91 %A Lamer -555 Taxter Rd -Elmsfrd 10523 **Fx:**347-4269
(212) 906-1200 .. **Chadakoff,** Richd L '73 (Latham & W) -885 3rd Av -NY 10022
(914) 923-8499 .. **Chadbourne O'Neill Thomson Whalen & Fitzgerald** -Bx701 -Sleepy Hollow 10591 **Fx:**923-8499
(212) 408-5100 .. **Chadbourne & Parke LLP** -30 Rckfllr Plz -NY 10112 **Fx:**541-5369
(315) 472-6742 .. **Chadick,** Christopher J '81 -620 Erie Blvd W -Syracuse 13204
(212) 788-0647 .. **Chadirjian,** Michl Jr. '99 %Law Dept -100 Church -NY 10007 **Fx:**788-0367
(212) 888-0063 .. **Chadrjian,** Nancy '88 -1173A 2nd Av -NY 10065
(716) 845-6000 .. **Chadsey,** Deborah J '88 SpclCnsl Kavinoky C LLP -726 Exchange -Buffalo 14210
(914) 245-4468 .. **Chadurjian,** Frank '57 -3496 Kamhi Dr -Yorktwn Hts 10598
(585) 454-5650 .. **Chadwick,** Jennifer L '95 (Lacy K LLP) -130 E Main -Rchstr 14604
(585) 454-5650 .. **Chadwick,** Jennifer L '95 (Lacy K LLP) -319 W Main -Batavia 14020
(718) 460-5600 .. **Chae,** Ji Hyun '06 YKASEC -136-19 41st Av -Flushng 11355 **Fx:**445-0032
(212) 583-5541 .. **Chae,** Michl Soo-Hyun '99 %Blackstone Grp -345 Park Av -NY 10154
(212) 969-3000 .. **Chae,** Peter '06 %Proskauer R LLP -1585 Bway -NY 10036
(607) 737-2944 .. **Chafee,** Amanda M '09 DA -226 Lk Bx588 -Elmira 14902 **Fx:**737-2965
(212) 594-5000 .. **Chafetz,** Eric S '05 %Togut S&S LLP -1 Penn Plz -NY 10119
(212) 788-6811 .. **Chaffee,** Chelsea H '04 Crmnl Justice Coordntr -1 Centre -NY 10007
(607) 776-9631 .. **Chaffee,** Ruth A '09 %Cnty Atty -3 E Pulteney Sq -Bath 14810 **Fx:**776-4930
(212) 257-6960 .. **Chaffetz Lindsey LLP** -1350 Av of Amer -NY 10019 **Fx:**257-6950
(212) 257-6960 .. **Chaffetz,** Peter R '79 (Chaffetz L LLP) -1350 Av of Amer -NY 10019
(347) 269-4460 .. **Chaffin,** Eric T '03 (Chaffin L LLP) -330 Mad Av -NY 10017 **Fx:**(888) 499-1123
(212) 269-0927 .. **Chafiian,** Liza A '90 %D'Amato & L,LLP -2 World Fncl Ctr -NY 10281
(914) 683-1200 .. **Chafizadeh,** Darius P '98 (Harris B PLLC) -445 Hmltn Av -White Plns 10601
(212) 416-8322 .. **Chahal,** Harkiranjit K '09 %Dept of Law -120 Bway -NY 10271
(212) 716-5790 .. **Chaice,** Christopher '00 %Cohen Lgl Grp,LLC -230 Park Av -NY 10169
(212) 408-1078 .. **Chaice,** Stephanie D '00 %Chadbourne & P LLP -30 Rckfllr Plz -NY 10112
(516) 827-4300 .. **Chaiet,** Clifford P '78 (Naness C&N LLC) -375 N Bway -Jericho 11753
(212) 594-9410 .. **Chaifetz,** Lawr B '87 (Chaifetz & C) -488 Mad Av -NY 10022 **Fx:**594-0814
(212) 594-9410 .. **Chaifetz,** Malcolm '57 (Chaifetz & C) -488 Mad Av -NY 10022 **Fx:**594-0814
(646) 855-0723 .. **Chaiken,** Steve M '88 Bank of America -1 Bryant Pk -NY 10036
(212) 688-0888 .. **Chaikin,** Eric B '72 (Chaikin & C) -444 Mad Av -NY 10022 **Fx:**594-5064
(212) 742-0476 .. **Chaikin,** Ian M '05 I Chaikin,PLLC -17 State -NY 10004 **Fx:**742-8701
(212) 845-7943 .. **Chaikin,** Lee D '99 Ramius Capital Grp -599 Lex Av -NY 10022
(212) 688-0888 .. **Chaikin,** Stacey '83 (Chaikin & C) -444 Mad Av -NY 10022 **Fx:**594-5064
(914) 788-6582 .. **Chaikin,** Steven J '86 -21 Elena Dr -Cortlandt Manor 10567 **Fx:**788-6579
(718) 286-6000 .. **Chain,** Bradley H '06 %DA -125-01 Qns Blvd -Kew Gdns 11415
(718) 403-3600 .. **Chain,** Heidi H '78 %Dept of Finance -345 Adams -Brklyn 11201 **Fx:**403-3650
(718) 225-3200 .. **Chain,** Risa Greenberg '93 (Greenberg & H,PC) -254-10 Nrthrn Blvd -Little Neck 11362
(212) 538-4178 .. **Chaisanguanthum,** Michl B '04 %Credit Suisse -11 Mad Av -NY 10010
(718) 487-2300 .. **Chait,** Linda R '84 %Leg Srvcs Corp -256-260 Bway -Brklyn 11211 **Fx:**782-6790
(716) 883-0355 .. **Chait,** Mark L '91 %R Perk -995 Elmwood Av -Buffalo 14222
(585) 325-3545 .. **Chait,** Mitchell A '84 -440 Wilder Bldg -Rchstr 14614 **Fx:**325-1544
(212) 599-3322 .. **Chaitman,** Helen D '78 (Becker P,LLP) -45 Bway -NY 10006
(212) 447-0291 .. **Chaitovitz,** Ann E '88 %AFTRA -260 Mad Av -NY 10016 **Fx:**545-1238
(718) 250-2000 .. **Cha-Jua-Lee,** Jamila A '02 %DA -350 Jay -Brklyn 11201 **Fx:**250-2314
(845) 356-2570 .. **Chakan,** John M '73 %Kantrowitz G&G,PC -747 Chestnut Rdg Rd -Chestnut Rdg 10977
(212) 244-5121 .. **Chakansky,** Michl I '82 -245 5th Av -NY 10016
(631) 232-6600 .. **Chakmakian,** Edmond C '94 (E Chakmakian,PC) -200 Motor Pkwy -Hauppauge 11788
(212) 735-3000 .. **Chakrabarti,** Monami '09 %Skadden ASM&F LLP -4 Times Sq -NY 10036
(914) 686-5000 .. **Chakrabarty,** Sreelekha '96 %Westminster USA -4 W Red Oak Ln -White Plns 10604 **Fx:**697-5050
(212) 259-8000 .. **Chakraborty,** Suman '02 %Dewey & L LLP -1301 Av of Amer -NY 10019
(646) 473-1301 .. **Chakwin,** Stephen D Jr. '79 -3 W 35th -NY 10001
(518) 828-9444 .. **Chale,** Christine M '93 (Rapport MWS&R,LLP) -436 Union -Hudson 12534
(315) 478-1111 .. **Chalenski,** Arthur A '69 -109 S Warren -Syracuse 13202 **Fx:**703-6076
(212) 546-7515 .. **Chalfin,** David A '89 Asset Mgmt Finance Corp -65 E 55th -NY 10022 **Fx:**644-2243
(212) 349-6290 .. **Chalfin,** Mark '76 -11 Park Pl -NY 10007
(212) 751-4300 .. **Chalian,** Shant H '95 (Hodgson R LLP) -1540 Bway -NY 10036

(631) 852-2500 .. **Chalifoux,** James G '93 %DA -200 Center Dr -Rvrhead 11901 **Fx:**852-1769
(585) 232-5300 .. **Chalifoux,** Sheila M '93 %Boylan BCV&W,LLP -2400 Chase Sq -Rchstr 14604
(631) 843-5500 .. **Challed,** Carol A '00 Henry Schein Inc -135 Duryea Rd -Melvll 11747
(718) 250-2000 .. **Challenger-Nibbs,** Kendra '05 %DA -350 Jay -Brklyn 11201 **Fx:**250-2314
(212) 552-1065 .. **Chalnick,** Andrew T '93 %JP Morgan Chase & Co -1 Chase Manh Plz -NY 10005
(212) 292-4208 .. **Chaloff,** Rhoda '72 -521 5th Av -NY 10175
(212) 648-0252 .. **Chalom,** Elliot E '05 JP Morgan Chase -245 Park Av -NY 10167
(917) 790-8455 .. **Chalom,** Esther '86 US Army Corp of Engineers -26 Fed Plz -NY 10278
(212) 810-5433 .. **Chalom,** Jos A '98 BlackRock Solutns -55 E 52nd -NY 10055
(516) 767-3600 .. **Chalos,** George M '98 (Chalos O&D) -366 Main -Pt Wash 11050
(516) 767-3600 .. **Chalos,** Michl G '76 (Chalos O&D) -366 Main -Pt Wash 11050
(516) 767-3600 .. **Chalos O'Connor & Duffy** -366 Main -Pt Wash 11050 **Fx:**767-3605
(718) 392-3232 .. **Chalpin,** Marc S '97 %CON-DEA Supply Corp -21-21 44th Rd -LIC 11101
(212) 530-5000 .. **Chalsen,** Christopher E '84 (Milbank TH&M LLP) -1 Chase Manh Plz -NY 10005
(212) 326-3939 .. **Chalson,** Andrew S '06 %Jones D -222 E 41st -NY 10017
(718) 222-2072 .. **Cham,** Marissa D '98 %Law Dept -350 Jay -Brklyn 11201 **Fx:**222-2088
(212) 705-7000 .. **Chamberlain,** Ann F '81 (Bingham M LLP) -399 Park Av -NY 10022
(585) 232-3730 .. **Chamberlain D'Amanda LLP** -1600 Crssrds Bldg -Rchstr 14614 **Fx:**232-3882
(212) 504-6000 .. **Chamberlain,** Holly Marcille '98 SpclCnsl Cadwalader W&T LLP -1 World Fncl Ctr -NY 10281
(718) 263-1505 .. **Chamberlain,** James O '81 -70 Greenway Ter -Frst Hlls 11375
(607) 336-3489 .. **Chamberlain,** James P '98 -92 S Broad -Norwich 13815 **Fx:**336-3837
(518) 435-9426 .. **Chamberlain,** Jeffrey F '77 (Chamberlain K&J) -35 Fuller Rd -Albany 12205 **Fx:**435-9102
(212) 710-0000 .. **Chamberlain,** Stephen J '07 %Drohan L,LLP -489 5th Av -NY 10017
(212) 267-5353 .. **Chamberlain Willi Ouchterloney & Watson** -575 8th Av -NY 10018 **Fx:**791-2564
(212) 998-2240 .. **Chamberlin,** Leona S '76 %NYU Ofc Leg Cnsl -70 Wshngtn Sq S -NY 10012 **Fx:**995-3048
(646) 289-5410 .. **Chamberlin,** Michl M '76 %EMTA -360 Mad Av -NY 10017 **Fx:**289-5429
(718) 859-9155 .. **Chambers,** Allan G '01 (A Chambers & Assoc) -1721 Bklyn Av -Brklyn 11210 **Fx:**421-7687
(212) 577-3342 .. **Chambers,** Cara A '03 %Leg Aid -199 Water -NY 10038 **Fx:**577-3520
(631) 979-7044 .. **Chambers,** Caryn A '80 -53 Oak -Smithtwn 11787 **Fx:**979-4522
(716) 851-4343 .. **Chambers,** Cavette A '05 Law Dept -65 Niagara Sq -Buffalo 14202 **Fx:**851-4105
(716) 823-6262 .. **Chambers,** David J G '82 %Sorrento Lactalis,Inc -2376 S Park Av -Buffalo 14220
(212) 661-8400 .. **Chambers,** John '81 (J Chambers,PC) -60 E 42nd -NY 10165 **Fx:**661-1242
(212) 645-5279 .. **Chambers,** John S '84 (JS Chambers & Assoc) -89 5th Av -NY 10003 **Fx:**242-0551
(914) 237-3348 .. **Chambers,** Michele A '94 %A Heilbraun,PC -1046 McLean Av -Ynkrs 10704
(914) 997-1380 .. **Chambers,** Milton A '72 (Marino & C,PC) -1 Barker Av -White Plns 10601
(718) 776-1200 .. **Chambers,** Roberta '99 -110-21 F Lewis Blvd -Qns Vllg 11429 **Fx:**776-1283
(718) 522-3333 .. **Chambers,** Taisha L '09 %Children's Law Ctr -44 Court -Brklyn 11201 **Fx:**522-7376
(212) 417-5300 .. **Chambers,** Vernitta N '03 %Medicaid Fraud Cntrl -120 Bway -NY 10271 **Fx:**417-5274
(315) 331-3181 .. **Chambers,** Victor B '71 -105 Maple Ct -Newark 14513 **Fx:**331-7610
(212) 837-6025 .. **Chamie,** Ramsey '07 %Hughes H&R LLP -1 Bttry Pk Plz -NY 10004 **Fx:**299-6025
(212) 407-4000 .. **Chamlin,** Marc A '81 (Loeb & L,LLP) -345 Park Av -NY 10154
(716) 433-5907 .. **Chamot,** Philip S '88 %Seaman JH&B,LLP -76 West Av -Lockprt 14094
(212) 758-7377 .. **Chamousis,** Nicholas '77 -260 Mad Av -NY 10016 **Fx:**813-9600
(718) 590-2000 .. **Chamoy,** Noah J '08 %DA -198 E 161st -Bronx 10451 **Fx:**590-6477
(212) 336-1100 .. **Champ,** Norman B III '90 %SEC -3 World Fncl Ctr -NY 10281 **Fx:**336-1323
(518) 481-1544 .. **Champagne,** Derek P '96 (DA) -Ct Hse -Malone 12953 **Fx:**481-1545
(212) 233-7195 .. **Champey,** Christine A '07 %Lewis JAA,LLP -61 Bway -NY 10006
(212) 351-4000 .. **Champion,** Anne M '06 %Gibson D&C LLP -200 Park Av -NY 10166
(315) 255-3414 .. **Champion,** Erin P '01 (Bentkofsky & C,LLC) -144 Genesee -Auburn 13021 **Fx:**255-2262
(518) 533-3000 .. **Champion,** Gregory J '92 (Bond S&K,PLLC) -111 Wshngtn Av -Albany 12210
(315) 255-3414 .. **Champion,** Maxsen D '01 (Bentkofsky & C,LLC) -144 Genesee -Auburn 13021 **Fx:**255-2262
(212) 407-7700 .. **Champion,** Sara S '92 (Vedder P,PC) -1633 Bway -NY 10019
(212) 336-2000 .. **Champlin,** Kimberly A '06 %Patterson BW&T LLP -1133 Av of Amer -NY 10036
(315) 482-3306 .. **Champney,** Richd K '76 R Champney,PC -4 Market -Alexandria Bay 13607 **Fx:**482-3887
(315) 298-6611 .. **Champney,** Richd K '76 R Champney,PC -3790 State Route 13 Bx241 -Pulaski 13142 **Fx:**298-2147
(212) 223-4000 .. **Champoux,** Barbara E '87 (Crowell & M LLP) -590 Mad Av -NY 10022
(212) 687-4900 .. **Chamulak,** Elizabeth L '94 %Wormser KG&J LLP -825 3rd Av -NY 10022
(631) 847-2000 .. **Chan,** Alan L '01 Arrow Electronics -50 Marcus Dr -Melvll 11747
(212) 425-7200 .. **Chan,** Albert '09 %Kenyon & K,LLP -1 Bway -NY 10004
(718) 799-1000 .. **Chan,** Albert Wai-Kit '93 -141-07 20th Av -Whitestone 11357 **Fx:**357-8615
(212) 937-4000 .. **Chan,** Alice '98 Fitzpatrick & HTCPA,LLP -12 E 49th -NY 10017
(718) 222-2015 .. **Chan,** Andrea M '07 %Law Dept -350 Jay -Brklyn 11201 **Fx:**222-2088
(212) 465-1890 .. **Chan,** Andrew C '10 %J Rice -377 Ashford Av -Dobbs Ferry 10522 **Fx:**629-3055
(212) 878-8000 .. **Chan,** Cecilia '02 %Clifford C LLP -31 W 52nd -NY 10019
(718) 296-4200 .. **Chan,** Danl '83 -8201 Rockaway Blvd -Ozone Pk 11416
(212) 576-7000 .. **Chan,** David '01 %NYLIM -51 Mad Av -NY 10010
(212) 875-6299 .. **Chan,** David K '88 Sesame Workshop -1 Lincoln Plz -NY 10023
(212) 343-0881 .. **Chan,** Deborah '91 (D Chan,PC) -401 Bway -NY 10013 **Fx:**343-0908
(212) 921-8399 .. **Chan,** Derek '06 %Lankler S&W LLP -500 5th Av -NY 10110
(718) 886-0663 .. **Chan,** Diane '97 (Chan & Associates PLLC) -39-07 Prince -Flushng 11354 **Fx:**886-5615
(212) 274-9930 .. **Chan,** Dylan Wen '99 -401 Bway -NY 10013 **Fx:**274-8613
(212) 398-0055 .. **Chan,** Elena K '05 %Garwin G&F,LLP -1501 Bway -NY 10036
(212) 843-2344 .. **Chan,** Frances '92 ABCI -62 William -NY 10005 **Fx:**843-2711
(212) 371-8855 .. **Chan,** Gawain K W '04 %Stikeman E LLP -445 Park Av -NY 10022
(718) 260-5500 .. **Chan,** Gilen '93 SpclCnsl NYC Cllg of Tech/CUNY -300 Jay -Brklyn 11201
(212) 226-5354 .. **Chan,** H Rebecca '99 HR Chan,PLLC -191 Canal -NY 10013 **Fx:**431-7418
(917) 415-3559 .. **Chan,** Henry '06 -345 E 93rd -NY 10128
(212) 504-6000 .. **Chan,** Jane K '01 %Cadwalader W&T LLP -1 World Fncl Ctr -NY 10281
(212) 735-3000 .. **Chan,** Janice W '10 %Skadden ASM&F LLP -4 Times Sq -NY 10036
(212) 805-0246 .. **Chan,** Jessica Wai-Chung '08 Hon S Scheindlin -500 Pearl -NY 10007
(212) 326-2000 .. **Chan,** Joanna K W '09 %O'Melveny & M LLP -7 Times Sq -NY 10036
(212) 478-0408 .. **Chan,** Justin H Y '03 DE Shaw & Co LP -120 W 45th -NY 10036
(718) 396-0035 .. **Chan,** Kai-Ko '03 -86-16 Qns Blvd -Elmhrst 11373
(212) 504-6000 .. **Chan,** Keala F '10 %Cadwalader W&T LLP -1 World Fncl Ctr -NY 10281
(212) 635-0202 .. **Chan,** Linda H '99 Investigators Ofc -17 Battery Pl -NY 10004
(212) 940-8800 .. **Chan,** Linda S '98 %Katten MR LLP -575 Mad Av -NY 10022
(718) 760-6600 .. **Chan,** Lo Y '03 %Dept of Parks & Rec -Olmsted Ctr -Flushng 11368 **Fx:**760-6730
(212) 349-2206 .. **Chan,** Loi N '92 -2 Mott -NY 10013
(212) 559-2821 .. **Chan,** Marion S L '90 Citigroup Private Bk -153 E 53rd -NY 10022
(716) 886-1257 .. **Chan,** Mary C '06 %Perla & P,LLP -367 Linwood Av -Buffalo 14209 **Fx:**886-2720
(212) 868-6300 .. **Chan,** Melissa S '10 %Cary K LLP -1350 Bway -NY 10018
(212) 548-7956 .. **Chan,** Min '99 West Group -530 5th Av -NY 10036
(718) 250-2000 .. **Chan,** Norma L '10 %DA -350 Jay -Brklyn 11201 **Fx:**250-2314
(212) 944-2200 .. **Chan,** Robt N '74 (Ferber CE&C,LLP) -530 5th Av -NY 10036
(212) 506-1700 .. **Chan,** Roy L '01 Kasowitz BT&F LLP -1633 Bway -NY 10019
(212) 373-3000 .. **Chan,** Sebastian W C '08 %Paul WRW&G LLP -1285 Av of Amer -NY 10019
(718) 330-7713 .. **Chan,** Sharon Siu-Yee '91 %NLRB -2 Metrotech Ctr -Brklyn 11201 **Fx:**330-7579
(845) 639-7800 .. **Chan,** Siu Lan '90 (Mandel K&B,LLP) -210 Route 303 -Vly Cottage 10989
(212) 878-8000 .. **Chan,** Siu-Yan '03 %Clifford C LLP -31 W 52nd -NY 10019
(212) 490-9550 .. **Chan,** Wai K '06 %C Trinko -16 W 46th -NY 10036 **Fx:**986-0158
(212) 819-8200 .. **Chan,** Wai Sing Jonathan '99 White & C LLP -1155 Av of Amer -NY 10036
(212) 554-7800 .. **Chan,** Wai Y '95 (Moses & S LLP) -405 Lex Av -NY 10174
(212) 837-1212 .. **Chan,** Wayne H '98 JP Morgan Chase & Co -522 5th Av -NY 10036
(212) 361-8016 .. **Chan,** Wendy W H '07 Dept Homeless Srvcs -33 Beaver -NY 10004 **Fx:**361-8002
(212) 530-1800 .. **Chan,** Yvonne Y '06 %Richards K&O LLP -1 World Fncl Ctr -NY 10281
(212) 373-3000 .. **Chan,** Yvonne Y F '90 (Paul WRW&G LLP) -1285 Av of Amer -NY 10019
(212) 592-1400 .. **Chanales,** Sheldon '81 (Herrick,F LLP) -2 Park Av -NY 10016
(212) 335-9000 .. **Chananie,** Jonathan D '07 %DA -1 Hogan Pl -NY 10013
(718) 920-6566 .. **Chananie,** Judith W '88 %Montefiore Med Ctr -111 E 210th -Bronx 10467 **Fx:**920-2637
(516) 393-2200 .. **Chananie,** Steven J '84 (Garfunkel W,PC) -111 Grt Nck Rd -Gt Neck 11021
(212) 848-4000 .. **Chanayil,** Ajay '05 %Shearman & S LLP -599 Lex Av -NY 10022
(212) 431-1300 .. **Chancas,** Jeffrey C '80 (Borah GAN&G PC) -377 Bway -NY 10013
(518) 487-5460 .. **Chance,** Tracey J '04 %DA -6 Lodge -Albany 12207 **Fx:**487-5093
(631) 577-2400 .. **Chancellor,** A G III '97 %Tromello M&K -25 Melvll Park Rd Bx9038 -Melvll 11747
(718) 846-6380 .. **Chand,** Shawn D '03 (Chand & G LLP) -110-13 Jamaica Av -Richmnd Hll 11418 **Fx:**846-4019
(212) 530-5000 .. **Chanda,** Ateesh S '09 %Milbank TH&M LLP -1 Chase Manh Plz -NY 10005
(212) 848-4000 .. **Chanda,** Parthapratim '05 %Shearman & S LLP -599 Lex Av -NY 10022
(646) 264-3633 .. **Chanda,** Sudwiti '02 US Dept of Labor -201 Varick -NY 10014
(646) 471-5855 .. **Chander,** Ameet '01 PricewaterhouseCoopers LLP -300 Mad Av -NY 10017
(212) 310-8000 .. **Chandis,** Vanessa '07 %Weil G&M LLP -767 5th Av -NY 10153
(716) 847-0650 .. **Chandler,** Cindy '96 Leg Srvcs -237 Main -Buffalo 14203 **Fx:**847-0227
(212) 558-5500 .. **Chandler,** David A '01 %Weitz & L,PC -700 Bway -NY 10003
(212) 237-8753 .. **Chandler,** Elsie '87 %John Jay College -445 W 59th -NY 10019
(315) 788-5100 .. **Chandler,** Floyd J '74 (Conboy MB&K,LLP) -407 Sherman -Watertwn 13601
(518) 828-4331 .. **Chandler,** John B '98 %Hudson River Park Trust -Bx76 -Hudson 12534
(914) 948-8044 .. **Chandler,** Kathryn M '08 %Alimonti Law Ofcs,PC -200 Mamaroneck Av #304 -White Plns 10601 **Fx:**948-8058
(347) 417-7683 .. **Chandler,** Monte M '00 -45 Main -Brklyn 11201
(212) 909-6000 .. **Chandler,** Robt H '03 %Debevoise & P LLP -919 3rd Av -NY 10022
(212) 796-1706 .. **Chandler,** Sara M '08 King St Capital Mgmt LP -65 E 55th -NY 10022

(212) 310-8000 .. **Chandler,** Todd R '09 (Weil G&M LLP) -767 5th Av -NY 10153
(718) 857-7498 .. **Chandler,** Violet A '85 -17 Jffrsn Av -Brklyn 11238 **Fx:**857-7828
(212) 868-4400 .. **Chandler,** Wm F '77 Spectrum Cnsltng Prtnrs -Bx20036 -NY 10001 **Fx:**(646) 758-8176
(212) 918-3000 .. **Chandra,** Arun '99 %Hogan L LLP -875 3rd Av -NY 10022
(212) 230-8800 .. **Chandrasekhar,** Charu A '05 %WilmerHale -399 Park Av -NY 10022
(212) 554-1400 .. **Chandrasekhar,** Jai K '01 SrCnsl Bernstein LB&G LLP -1285 Av of Amer -NY 10019
(212) 336-2000 .. **Chandrasoma,** Nishka G '07 %Patterson BW&T LLP -1133 Av of Amer -NY 10036
(212) 336-3706 .. **Chandy,** Sunu P '99 US EEOC -33 Whitehall -NY 10004
(212) 971-1315 .. **Chanel,** Lisa D '99 LD Chanel,LLC -350 5th Av PMB#18G -NY 10118
(212) 552-7443 .. **Chanen,** Lawr '75 JP Morgan Chase -1 Chase Manh Plz -NY 10081
(212) 541-2000 .. **Chaney,** Frank E '06 %Bryan C LLP -1290 Av of Amer -NY 10104
(212) 318-6000 .. **Chaney,** Lisa A '06 %Paul HJ&W LLP -75 E 55th -NY 10022
(718) 888-9500 .. **Chang,** Agnes Jooyeon '06 %Kim & C,LLP -158-14 Nrthrn Blvd -Flushng 11358
(212) 984-9166 .. **Chang,** Aileen '98 Radian Asset Assurance -335 Mad Av -NY 10017
(212) 506-2500 .. **Chang,** Alanna '09 %Mayer B LLP -1675 Bway -NY 10019
(212) 474-1000 .. **Chang,** Albert '10 %Cravath S&M LLP -825 8th Av -NY 10019
(212) 450-4000 .. **Chang,** Alicia L '07 %Davis P&W LLP -450 Lex Av -NY 10017
(212) 336-0048 .. **Chang,** Brenda Wai Ming '01 %SEC -3 World Fncl Ctr -NY 10281 **Fx:**336-1323
(212) 450-4000 .. **Chang,** Catherine Paskoff '07 %Davis P&W LLP -450 Lex Av -NY 10017
(646) 562-3405 .. **Chang,** Catherine So Young '96 %PLC -747 3rd Av -NY 10017
(212) 416-8000 .. **Chang,** Cecelia '05 %Dept of Law -120 Bway -NY 10271
(212) 483-0105 .. **Chang,** Chas K '07 %Coughlin D LLP -88 Pine-Wall St Plz -NY 10005
(516) 739-0000 .. **Chang,** Chi Wai '99 %Martyn T&M -330 Old Cntry Rd -Mineola 11501
(212) 769-1756 .. **Chang,** Chia-Yu '05 -2109 Bway -NY 10023
(917) 237-2900 .. **Chang,** Ch'iu Lien '94 Axion Legal Solutions -75 Spring -NY 10012
(718) 250-2000 .. **Chang,** Chris '08 %DA -350 Jay -Brklyn 11201 **Fx:**250-2314
(212) 208-1470 .. **Chang,** Christopher E '79 -140 Bway -NY 10005 **Fx:**208-1468
(718) 445-0405 .. **Chang,** David Shao-Chieh '82 -39-01 Main -Flushng 11354 **Fx:**358-6833
(212) 450-4000 .. **Chang,** Daysun Sun '09 %Davis P&W LLP -450 Lex Av -NY 10017
(212) 940-8800 .. **Chang,** Dexter T '98 %Katten MR LLP -575 Mad Av -NY 10022
(212) 225-2000 .. **Chang,** Elizabeth A '00 %Cleary GS&H -1 Lbrty Plz -NY 10006
(212) 918-3000 .. **Chang,** Eric '03 %Hogan L LLP -875 3rd Av -NY 10022
(212) 728-8000 .. **Chang,** Eugene L W '96 (Willkie F&G LLP) -787 7th Av -NY 10019
(212) 872-1000 .. **Chang,** Eunice J '09 -One Bryant Park -NY 10036 **Fx:**872-1002
(212) 474-1000 .. **Chang,** Frederic '10 %Cravath S&M LLP -825 8th Av -NY 10019
(212) 670-0185 .. **Chang,** Gale K '01 Merrill Lynch -220 Bway -NY 10038
(212) 839-5300 .. **Chang,** Gladys '07 %Sidley A LLP -787 7th Av -NY 10019
(212) 980-4200 .. **Chang,** Helen J '07 %Levy HP&D,LLP -950 3rd Av -NY 10022
(212) 596-9000 .. **Chang,** Hyeyun Catharine '02 %Ropes & G LLP -1211 Av of Amer -NY 10036
(212) 962-2300 .. **Chang,** Irene '92 Lower Manhattan Devlpmt Corp -1 Lbrty Plz -NY 10006 **Fx:**962-2431
(718) 286-6000 .. **Chang,** Jasmine H J '03 %DA -125-01 Qns Blvd -Kew Gdns 11415
(718) 834-0200 .. **Chang,** Jason '82 -185 Montague -Brklyn 11201
(212) 357-3559 .. **Chang,** Jeffay F '95 Goldman Sachs Trust Co -1 NY Plz -NY 10004
(212) 872-5587 .. **Chang,** Ji Young '06 KPMG LLP -345 Park Av -NY 10154
(718) 358-8430 .. **Chang,** Jih-Kuei '81 -35-16 Farrington -Flushng 11354 **Fx:**358-8002
(212) 925-1937 .. **Chang,** John '84 -401 Bway -NY 10013 **Fx:**941-7504
(212) 450-4000 .. **Chang,** Jonathan '07 %Davis P&W LLP -450 Lex Av -NY 10017
(212) 403-8036 .. **Chang,** Julie '07 DE Shaw & Co -120 W 45th -NY 10036
(212) 594-8793 .. **Chang,** Kyung Hee '85 -1220 Bway -NY 10001
(212) 819-8200 .. **Chang,** Laura L '08 %White & C LLP -1155 Av of Amer -NY 10036
(718) 961-1507 .. **Chang,** Lee-Lee '90 -136-21 Roosevelt Av -Flushng 11354 **Fx:**961-4583
(212) 922-2200 .. **Chang,** Leo '79 (Watson F&W LLP) -1133 Av of Amer -NY 10036
(646) 313-8798 .. **Chang,** Lily '91 Cnsl Banc of Amer Securities -1 Bryant Pk -NY 10036 **Fx:**313-4803
(212) 259-8000 .. **Chang,** Lily S-W '08 %Dewey & L LLP -1301 Av of Amer -NY 10019
(212) 872-9800 .. **Chang,** Mary M '95 (Squire S&D LLP) -30 Rckfllr Plz -NY 10112
(212) 962-0114 .. **Chang,** Melody A '93 (Chang Law Assoc) -11 E 36th -NY 10016 **Fx:**962-2541
(212) 425-7200 .. **Chang,** Michl S '10 %Kenyon & K,LLP -1 Bway -NY 10004
(212) 548-0694 .. **Chang,** Nancy '79 Open Society Institute -400 W 59th -NY 10019
(212) 766-4336 .. **Chang,** Randy '05 -7 Chatham Sq -NY 10038 **Fx:**267-3028
(212) 937-6268 .. **Chang,** Rebecca G '04 %WilmerHale -399 Park Av -NY 10022
(917) 673-5029 .. **Chang,** Serk H '05 -16 W 32nd -NY 10001 **Fx:**(201) 292-1899
(212) 872-1000 .. **Chang,** Shinah '09 -One Bryant Park -NY 10036 **Fx:**872-1002
(716) 566-5400 .. **Chang,** Soo-Young '97 %Goldberg S LLP -665 Main -Buffalo 14203
(212) 762-7236 .. **Chang,** Stefanie V '92 Morgan Stanley -1221 Av of Amer -NY 10020
(212) 219-3920 .. **Chang,** Stephen '83 -7 Chatham Sq -NY 10038 **Fx:**219-3932
(212) 461-2388 .. **Chang,** Ta Kuang '84 (Chang & Co,LLC) -44 Wall -NY 10005 **Fx:**461-2399
(212) 284-4755 .. **Chang,** Terry E '07 Fletcher Asset Mgmt -48 Wall -NY 10005
(212) 868-9190 .. **Chang,** Tony C '91 -299 Bway -NY 10007 **Fx:**868-9335
(212) 382-3300 .. **Chang,** Vincent T '90 (Wollmuth M&D LLP) -500 5th Av -NY 10110
(212) 524-5000 .. **Chang,** Wayne '04 %Jacob M&F -1270 Av of Amer -NY 10020
(212) 530-5000 .. **Chang,** Wayne R '09 %Milbank TH&M LLP -1 Chase Manh Plz -NY 10005
(212) 551-8907 .. **Chang,** Wen-Chi '97 %Israel Discount Bk -511 5th Av -NY 10017 **Fx:**551-8916
(212) 765-5070 .. **Chang,** Willy '08 %Fish & R,PC -153 E 53rd -NY 10022
(212) 508-6100 .. **Chang,** Won Kyung '06 %Bracewell & G,LLP -1251 Av of Amer -NY 10020
(718) 250-2000 .. **Chang,** Yea-Jiun '10 %DA -350 Jay -Brklyn 11201 **Fx:**250-2314
(212) 349-6009 .. **Chang,** Yi-jen '06 Sanctuary for Families -110 Wall -NY 10005 **Fx:**566-0344
(212) 318-6000 .. **Chang,** Yoon Kyung '07 %Paul HJ&W LLP -75 E 55th -NY 10022
(212) 232-1300 .. **Changrani,** Bhavna '05 %Lewis BB&S LLP -77 Water -NY 10005
(516) 496-5822 .. **Chanice,** Lawr J '02 %T Spina -170 Froehlich Farm Blvd -Woodbury 11797 **Fx:**496-5420
(845) 551-9255 .. **Chanin,** Geoffrey E '80 -4 Hmptn Rd -Goshen 10924
(212) 969-2831 .. **Chanin,** Kathryn S '94 Alliance Bernstein LP -1345 Av of Amer -NY 10105 **Fx:**554-4639
(212) 385-1191 .. **Chanin,** Lester L '92 (Goodman & J LLP) -75 Broad -NY 10004
(631) 694-2300 .. **Chanin,** Lloyd K '61 OfCnsl Lamb & B,LLP -534 Broadhllw Rd Bx9034 -Melvll 11747
(516) 880-8484 .. **Chanis,** Robt J '88 (Harris B PLLC) -333 Earle Ovngton Blvd -Uniondale 11553
(212) 338-7202 .. **Chan King,** Harriet L '82 Verizon -240 E 38th -NY 10016
(646) 654-8300 .. **Chan Lau,** Flora W L '98 Nielsen Media Resrch -770 Bway -NY 10003
(585) 546-5530 .. **Chanmugam,** Sheani Dilrukshi '02 %Thomson West -50 E Broad -Rchstr 14694
(716) 626-3616 .. **Channa,** Pardeep Singh '05 -300 Intl Dr -Williamsvll 14221
(718) 250-2000 .. **Channapati,** Anita T '02 %DA -350 Jay -Brklyn 11201 **Fx:**250-2314
(212) 878-1035 .. **Channer,** Colleen J '88 %MTA -347 Mad Av -NY 10017
(516) 571-2331 .. **Channer-Lundy,** Sheryl A '97 Hon F Gulotta,Jr -262 Old Cntry Rd -Mineola 11501
(212) 644-3013 .. **Channing,** Nicole David '96 Anomaly Cptl Ptnrs LLC -68 Quaker Brdg Rd -Croton-On-Hud 10520
(212) 506-2500 .. **Chanoine,** Hannah Y S '06 %Mayer B LLP -1675 Bway -NY 10019
(212) 615-4351 .. **Chansler,** Jeffrey D '81 Group Hlth Inc -441 9th Av -NY 10001
(718) 590-2000 .. **Chanza,** Nadia J '00 %DA -198 E 161st -Bronx 10451 **Fx:**590-6477
(718) 590-2000 .. **Chao,** Alice '08 %DA -198 E 161st -Bronx 10451 **Fx:**590-6477
(516) 466-2033 .. **Chao,** Brendan '97 -67 Cutter Mill Rd -Gt Neck 11021 **Fx:**466-2007
(914) 243-0073 .. **Chao,** Chia-Hui '95 %Chia's Intl -1260 Park Ln -Yorktwn Hts 10598 **Fx:**243-0073
(212) 326-3939 .. **Chao,** Eva '10 %Jones D -222 E 41st -NY 10017
(212) 841-1000 .. **Chao,** Karen K Y '07 %Covington & B LLP -620 8th Av -NY 10018
(718) 286-6000 .. **Chao,** Rosemary '01 %DA -125-01 Qns Blvd -Kew Gdns 11415
(212) 806-5400 .. **Chao,** Sean '07 %Stroock &S&L LLP -180 Maiden Ln -NY 10038
(212) 999-5649 .. **Chapell,** Alan P '02 Cheetahmail,Inc -29 Bway -NY 10006
(718) 465-6355 .. **Chapian,** Edw M '52 -85-24 215th -Qns Vllg 11427
(516) 922-6448 .. **Chapian,** Lynne M '82 -1 Surrey Pl -E Norwich 11732 **Fx:**922-0048
(212) 756-2000 .. **Chapin,** Alexis Victoria '09 %Schulte R&Z LLP -919 3rd Av -NY 10022
(212) 702-8509 .. **Chapin,** Allan M '70 Compass Advisors -825 3rd Av -NY 10022
(212) 238-3000 .. **Chapin,** Bayard S '91 (Emmet M&M,LLP) -120 Bway -NY 10271
(212) 374-7930 .. **Chapin,** Florence R '03 NYC Dept Educ-OLS -52 Chmbrs -NY 10007 **Fx:**374-5596
(914) 372-2225 .. **Chapin,** Georganne '05 Hudson Hlth Plan -303 S Bway -Tarrytwn 10591
(646) 278-0370 .. **Chapin-Horowitz,** Deborah '85 EdsLink LLC -1140 Av of Amer -NY 10036
(212) 566-7188 .. **Chapland,** Lisa A '07 %Genova B&G -115 Bway -NY 10006
(201) 631-7449 .. **Chaplin,** Mark A '98 AIG -70 Pine -NY 10270
(212) 417-3700 .. **Chapman,** Allegra A '04 %MFY Legal Srvcs -299 Bway -NY 10007 **Fx:**417-3890
(516) 803-3000 .. **Chapman,** Brent A '90 Rainbow Prog -1111 Stewart Av -Bethpage 11714
(914) 323-7000 .. **Chapman,** Carmen S '00 %Wilson EME&D LLP -3 Gannett Dr -White Plns 10604
(212) 749-3553 .. **Chapman,** Clare J '95 %Commn on Christian Unity -475 Riverside Dr -NY 10115 **Fx:**749-3556
(212) 839-5300 .. **Chapman,** Craig E '81 (Sidley A LLP) -787 7th Av -NY 10019
(212) 655-6000 .. **Chapman and Cutler LLP** -330 Mad Av -NY 10017 **Fx:**697-7210
(212) 872-1000 .. **Chapman,** Dean L Jr. '09 -One Bryant Park -NY 10036 **Fx:**872-1002
(212) 504-6000 .. **Chapman,** Drew G L '99 (Cadwalader W&T LLP) -1 World Fncl Ctr -NY 10281
(212) 867-4466 .. **Chapman,** Jamie B '09 %Belkin BW&G,LLP -270 Mad Av -NY 10016
(607) 762-7939 .. **Chapman,** Janine N '83 %Electric & Gas Corp -4500 Vestal Pkwy E -Bnghmtn 13902
(212) 558-4000 .. **Chapman,** Jeffrey J '99 (Sullivan & C LLP) -125 Broad -NY 10004
(212) 945-9159 .. **Chapman,** John D '83 -10 Lbrty -NY 10005
(212) 854-1666 .. **Chapman,** Karen Boyes '94 %Columbia Univ Law Schl -435 W 116th -NY 10027
(212) 594-5300 .. **Chapman,** Kirk '91 (Milberg LLP) -1 Penn Plz -NY 10119
(845) 703-3101 .. **Chapman,** Langdon C '00 %Bonacic KCM&B,LLP -90 Crystal Run Rd -Middletwn 10941
(516) 741-6601 .. **Chapman,** Mark A '96 (Chapman Z LLP) -114 Old Cntry Rd -Mineola 11501 **Fx:**741-6602
(212) 425-7200 .. **Chapman,** Mark A '99 (Kenyon & K,LLP) -1 Bway -NY 10004
(914) 723-4300 .. **Chapman,** Nancy Dwyer '83 %Lackenbach S LLP -1 Chase Rd -Scarsdale 10583
(315) 472-5827 .. **Chapman,** Paul '80 -250 Harrison -Syracuse 13202
(212) 306-7450 .. **Chapman,** R Keith '09 %Comm on Human Rights -40 Rector -NY 10006 **Fx:**306-7414
(585) 419-8800 .. **Chapman,** Richd N '70 (Harris B PLLC) -99 Garnsey Rd -Pittsfrd 14534
(212) 455-2000 .. **Chapnick,** David B '63 OfCnsl Simpson T&B LLP -425 Lex Av -NY 10017
(212) 854-2675 .. **Chapnick,** Ellen P '81 %Columbia Law Schl -435 W 116th -NY 10027 **Fx:**854-7946
(212) 309-6000 .. **Chapnick,** Michl A '69 (Morgan L&B LLP) -101 Park Av -NY 10178
(212) 788-9737 .. **Chapnik,** Elaine '80 %Hlth & Hsptl Corp -125 Worth -NY 10013 **Fx:**267-6905
(212) 506-1700 .. **Chapoulie,** Adrienne M '05 %Kasowitz BT&F LLP -1633 Bway -NY 10019
(212) 403-1321 .. **Chappell,** Claire D '91 -51 W 52nd -NY 10019 **Fx:**403-2321
(212) 264-8080 .. **Chappell,** Nicole K '94 %HUD -26 Fed Plz -NY 10278
(212) 815-1818 .. **Chappell,** Ralph B '84 %DC 37 MELS -125 Barclay -NY 10007 **Fx:**815-1343
(212) 593-6700 .. **Chappell,** Robt J '96 %Aaronson RF&D,LLP -757 3rd Av -NY 10017

(315) 472-0124 .. **Chappell-Daly**, Diane R '94 -430 E Genesee -Syracuse 13202 **Fx:**472-0400
(585) 263-5894 .. **Chapus**, David P '87 %Hon D Larimer -100 State -Rchstr 14614
(914) 824-5410 .. **Chapyak Pernicone**, Mary C '86 Appllt Div 2nd Dept -45 Monroe Pl -Brklyn 11201 **Fx:**(212) 401-9170
(212) 696-4912 .. **Char**, Edw M '03 (Char & H,LLP) -183 Mad Av -NY 10016
(212) 484-3900 .. **Charap**, Ross J '74 (Arent F LLP) -1675 Bway -NY 10019
(212) 922-6000 .. **Charatan**, Joni Lacks '84 Dreyfus -200 Park Av -NY 10166
(845) 279-5445 .. **Charbonneau**, Jos A '93 -1441 Route 22 -Brewstr 10509 **Fx:**278-6135
(718) 923-0690 .. **Charbonneau**, Michelle C '08 %R Santoriella PC -335 Adams -Brklyn 11201 **Fx:**923-0683
(212) 701-3000 .. **Charbonneau**, Thos E '83 Cnsl Cahill G&R LLP -80 Pine -NY 10005 **Fx:**269-5420
(845) 986-3700 .. **Charde**, Luke M Jr. '75 -19 West Bx712 -Warwick 10990 **Fx:**986-3750
(212) 243-1027 .. **Charen**, Steven C '77 -562 Hudson -NY 10014
(212) 839-5300 .. **Charest**, Stephen T '02 %Sidley A LLP -787 7th Av -NY 10019
(917) 320-2500 .. **Charet**, Linda S '88 %FDIC -350 5th Av -NY 10118 **Fx:**320-2917
(212) 478-7200 .. **Chari**, Roger S '92 (Hahn & H LLP) -488 Mad Av -NY 10022
(212) 255-3070 .. **Charie**, Craig S '93 Charie Properties LLC -100 W 23rd -NY 10011
(607) 724-3300 .. **Chariff**, Wayne M '77 -19 Chenango -Bnghmtn 13901 **Fx:**724-5381
(718) 590-2000 .. **Chariott**, Julia Lien '98 %DA -198 E 161st -Bronx 10451 **Fx:**590-6477
(845) 371-4700 .. **Charipper**, Douglas S '90 OfCnsl Fein SK&S,PC -747 Chestnut Rdg Rd -Spg Vly 10977
(212) 230-8800 .. **Charish**, Debra L '08 %WilmerHale -399 Park Av -NY 10022
(212) 806-5400 .. **Charity**, Courtney M '09 %Stroock &S&L LLP -180 Maiden Ln -NY 10038
(212) 238-4800 .. **Charkow**, Andrew B '96 (Landman CB&F,PC) -120 Bway -NY 10271
(212) 336-8000 .. **Charkow**, Benjamin '04 %Amster R&E -90 Park Av -NY 10016
(212) 294-6700 .. **Charkow**, Jason S '03 %Winston & S -200 Park Av -NY 10166
(718) 838-7878 .. **Charland**, Stacy E '05 %Bronx Defenders -860 Crtlandt Av -Bronx 10451 **Fx:**665-0100
(607) 271-9089 .. **Charlap**, Allan G '82 Charlap Law Firm -315 Lk -Elmira 14901 **Fx:**271-9155
(718) 694-4817 .. **Charles**, Alice '00 %Transit Auth -130 Lvngstn -Brklyn 11201 **Fx:**694-5726
(212) 785-4100 .. **Charles**, Allison Mattera '06 %Fensterstock & Prtnrs LLP -30 Wall -NY 10005
(212) 556-2100 .. **Charles**, Andrew H '87 (King & S) -1185 Av of Amer -NY 10036
(212) 408-5100 .. **Charles**, Cassandre L '06 %Chadbourne & P LLP -30 Rckfllr Plz -NY 10112
(212) 726-1016 .. **Charles**, Claude A '03 -244 5th Av -NY 10001
(718) 875-1300 .. **Charles**, Claudia J '03 %Appllt Div 2nd Dept -45 Monroe Pl -Brklyn 11201 **Fx:**858-2446
(212) 935-3000 .. **Charles**, Faith L '87 (Mintz LCFG&P,PC) -666 3rd Av -NY 10017
(347) 414-6721 .. **Charles**, Fred V '06 -1428 Granada Pl -Far Rckwy 11691
(212) 269-1600 .. **Charles**, GuyLaine '97 (Teigland-Hunt LLP) -127 W 24th -NY 10011 **Fx:**269-1580
(716) 851-7050 .. **Charles**, James '82 %DEC -270 Mich Av -Buffalo 14203 **Fx:**851-7211
(518) 457-4380 .. **Charles**, John D '75 Dept of Labor -State Campus Bldg 12 -Albany 12240 **Fx:**485-1819
(212) 408-2500 .. **Charles**, Lee D '89 (Baker B,LLP) -30 Rckfllr Plz -NY 10112
(516) 466-6571 .. **Charles**, Pamela F '88 -26 Old Field Ln -Gt Neck 11020 **Fx:**977-1510
(212) 490-3000 .. **Charles**, Rose M J '99 (Wilson EME&D LLP) -150 E 42nd -NY 10017
(212) 403-1000 .. **Charles**, Scott K '85 (Wachtell LR&K) -51 W 52nd -NY 10019
(518) 457-2411 .. **Charles**, Suzanne H '76 DOT -50 Wolf Rd -Albany 12232 **Fx:**457-4021
(212) 440-4400 .. **Charles**, Valerie C '08 Buchanan I&R PC -620 8th Av -NY 10018
(718) 802-9749 .. **Charles**, Vernita C '00 -44 Court -Brklyn 11201 **Fx:**(347) 823-2720
(718) 590-3784 .. **Charles**, Winnifred '06 Supreme Ct-Bronx Cnty Civil -851 Grnd Cncrs -Bronx 10451
(212) 428-2799 .. **Charles-Cator**, Martine Myriame '02 %OCA -25 Beaver -NY 10004 **Fx:**428-2819
(516) 791-9111 .. **Charleston**, Joel S '69 -11 Pearl -N Woodmere 11581 **Fx:**791-3324
(212) 682-2900 .. **Charleston**, Kelly A '10 %Braverman & Assoc,PC -331 Mad Av -NY 10017 **Fx:**682-7718
(212) 701-3000 .. **Charleston**, Lucas T '10 %Cahill G&R LLP -80 Pine -NY 10005 **Fx:**269-5420
(585) 546-7430 .. **Charlesworth**, Denis J '98 %Dept of Law -144 Exchange Blvd -Rchstr 14614 **Fx:**546-7514
(212) 468-8000 .. **Charlesworth**, Jacqueline C '94 OfCnsl Morrison & F LLP -1290 Av of Amer -NY 10104
(516) 463-5166 .. **Charlow**, Robin '82 %Hofstra Law Schl -121 Hofstra Univ -Hempstd 11549
(315) 425-2700 .. **Charlton**, J Eric '77 (Hiscock & B,LLP) -One Park Pl -Syracuse 13202
(718) 250-2000 .. **Charlton**, Joshua R '02 DA -350 Jay -Brklyn 11201 **Fx:**250-2314
(212) 720-5026 .. **Charlton**, Richd E III '97 %Fed Reserve Bk -33 Lbrty -NY 10045 **Fx:**785-5748
(212) 980-6800 .. **Charnas**, Scott E '01 Charnas Law Firm, PC -455 E 51st -NY 10022 **Fx:**980-1871
(718) 358-3322 .. **Charnas**, Wm V '94 -37-44 75th -Jcksn Hts 11372 **Fx:**358-8947
(212) 878-8000 .. **Charney**, Aaron Brett '04 %Clifford C LLP -31 W 52nd -NY 10019
(212) 548-2100 .. **Charney**, Allison '07 %McGuire W LLP -1345 Av of Amer -NY 10105
(212) 614-6464 .. **Charney**, Darius '02 Ctr for Constitutionsl Rts -666 Bway -NY 10012 **Fx:**614-6499
(212) 637-3181 .. **Charney**, Lauren P '09 US EPA -290 Bway -NY 10007
(212) 819-0994 .. **Charney**, Leon H '65 -1441 Bway -NY 10018 **Fx:**921-2785
(212) 880-0863 .. **Charney**, Leonard J '66 -60 E 42nd -NY 10165 **Fx:**983-0415
(212) 298-5166 .. **Charney**, Richd M '74 %Leg Aid -49 Thomas -NY 10013 **Fx:**298-5252
(212) 382-0909 .. **Charney**, Steven M '88 (Peckar & A,PC) -41 Mad Av -NY 10154
(718) 793-3707 .. **Charnis**, Jonathan '86 -105-05 69th Av -Frst Hlls 11375
(212) 400-9292 .. **Charno**, Steven R '90 Douglaston Devlpmnt -42-09 235th -Douglastn 11363 **Fx:**400-9294
(718) 250-2000 .. **Charnoff**, Adam S '88 %DA -350 Jay -Brklyn 11201 **Fx:**250-2314
(212) 586-5100 .. **Charnoff**, Richd W '81 %Wm Morris Agency -1325 Av of Amer -NY 10019 **Fx:**903-1473
(516) 463-5326 .. **Charnov**, Bruce H '91 -134 Hofstra Univ -Hempstd 11549
(718) 624-7220 .. **Charnov**, Richd H '80 -61 Pierrepont -Brklyn 11201 **Fx:**624-6205
(646) 654-8319 .. **Charny**, Carla '99 SrCnsl The Nielsen Co -770 Bway -NY 10003 **Fx:**654-8325
(212) 326-2000 .. **Charon**, Garrett T '06 %O'Melveny & M LLP -7 Times Sq -NY 10036
(845) 339-8080 .. **Charpentier**, Rosalee '86 %Family Advocates Inc -209 Clinton Av -Kingston 12401 **Fx:**339-8089
(914) 461-3222 .. **Charpilloz**, Sylvia S '94 OfCnsl Kipness & Assoc -460 Old Post Rd -Bedfrd 10506 **Fx:**(800) 414-2044
(718) 578-4422 .. **Charrington-Medard**, Karen H '00 Charrington Medard,PC -One Cross Isl Plz -Rosedale 11422
(631) 608-1100 .. **Charron**, Christian D '99 (Charron & Assoc) -534 Broadhllw Rd -Melvll 11747 **Fx:**608-1114
(212) 869-7000 .. **Charron**, Robt F '99 (Feldman W&S LLP) -420 Lex Av -NY 10170
(212) 421-4100 .. **Charron**, Wm L '99 (Pryor C LLP) -7 Times Sq -NY 10036
(718) 590-2000 .. **Chartan**, Eric J '06 DA -198 E 161st -Bronx 10451 **Fx:**590-6477
(516) 773-8300 .. **Chartan**, Lauren Seides '85 %Wisselman H & Assoc,PC -1010 Nrthrn Blvd -Gt Neck 11021 **Fx:**773-8304
(212) 692-1000 .. **Chartan**, Michl L '82 (Duane M LLP) -1540 Bway -NY 10036
(212) 593-6700 .. **Chartan**, Rebecca J '06 %Aaronson RF&D,LLP -757 3rd Av -NY 10017
(212) 785-5050 .. **Charters**, Susan M '02 %Kardaras & K LLP -44 Wall -NY 10005
(585) 271-1500 .. **Chartier**, Craig D '00 %Dibble & M,PC -55 Canterbury Rd -Rchstr 14607
(718) 892-8588 .. **Chartier**, Jeffrey P '98 -2027 Wllmsbrdg Rd -Bronx 10461
(845) 334-9775 .. **Charuk**, Catherine '80 -26 Pearl Bx4011 -Kingston 12402 **Fx:**334-9776
(516) 294-8844 .. **Charwat**, Mark S '59 OfCnsl L'Abbate BC&C,LLP -1001 Franklin Av -Gdn Cty 11530
(845) 485-5918 .. **Charwat**, Martin A '76 -7 Crk Bend Rd -Poughkeepsie 12603 **Fx:**485-5164
(212) 577-3530 .. **Chasan**, Jonathan S '81 %Leg Aid -199 Water -NY 10038 **Fx:**425-2465
(212) 596-9000 .. **Chasan**, Michl J '08 %Ropes & G LLP -1211 Av of Amer -NY 10036
(646) 610-5400 .. **Chasan**, Rebecca K '07 NYPD -1 Police Plz -NY 10038
(212) 819-8200 .. **Chase**, Aaron '06 %White & C LLP -1155 Av of Amer -NY 10036
(914) 378-1010 .. **Chase**, Ann B '84 (Fitzgerald & F) -538 Riverdale Av -Ynkrs 10705
(585) 753-4500 .. **Chase**, Ann E '84 %DA -832 Watts Bldg -Rchstr 14614 **Fx:**753-4576
(212) 688-4000 .. **Chase**, Arlo Monell '00 %NYS HFA -641 Lex Av -NY 10022 **Fx:**872-0362
(212) 450-4000 .. **Chase**, Beverly Fanger '75 (Davis P&W LLP) -450 Lex Av -NY 10017
(212) 336-0049 .. **Chase**, Celeste Ann '98 %SEC -3 World Fncl Ctr -NY 10281 **Fx:**336-1323
(212) 980-0120 .. **Chase**, Christopher R '03 %Frankfurt KK&S,PC -488 Mad Av -NY 10022
(212) 922-2200 .. **Chase**, Clark Greg '02 %Watson F&W LLP -1133 Av of Amer -NY 10036
(212) 297-0885 .. **Chase**, David D '99 (Apuzzo & C) -800 3rd Av -NY 10022 **Fx:**297-0887
(631) 348-7500 .. **Chase**, Dennis R '91 (Chase S Law Grp,LLP) -64 Smithtwn Blvd -Smithtwn 11787 **Fx:**348-7501
(212) 735-8684 .. **Chase**, Donald H '83 (Morrison C LLP) -909 3rd Av -NY 10022
(212) 217-6300 .. **Chase**, Douglas W '97 %Capital Lease Funding -1065 Av of Amer -NY 10018
(914) 665-3015 .. **Chase**, Edw T '69 -70 Elmsmere Rd -Mt Vernon 10552 **Fx:**665-3017
(212) 425-9300 .. **Chase**, Eric L '83 (Bressler A&R,PC) -17 State -NY 10004
(315) 423-4400 .. **Chase**, Eric R '03 %Wolff G&G,LLP -217 Mntgmry -Syracuse 13202
(845) 486-2300 .. **Chase**, Frank F '84 %DA -236 Main -Poughkeepsie 12601 **Fx:**486-2324
(518) 463-1269 .. **Chase**, Glenn D '88 (Walsh & H) -18 Corp Wds Blvd -Albany 12211
(212) 715-9100 .. **Chase**, Heather J '03 %Kramer LN&F,LLP -1177 Av of Amer -NY 10036
(212) 471-8460 .. **Chase**, Jeffrey L '75 (Herzfeld & R,PC) -125 Broad -NY 10004
(212) 351-4000 .. **Chase**, Jeremy A '10 Gibson D&C LLP -200 Park Av -NY 10166
(516) 671-5880 .. **Chase**, John M '78 (Chase R&C,LLP) -48 Forest Av -Glen Cove 11542
(845) 534-4400 .. **Chase**, Jonathan A '88 -1 Taft Pl Bx367 -Cornwall-On-Hud 12520 **Fx:**534-0440
(518) 457-2070 .. **Chase**, Kathleen D '98 %Dept of Tax & Fin -Bldg 9 State Campus -Albany 12227 **Fx:**457-6131
(718) 858-3100 .. **Chase**, Marc J '80 (Weinstein CM&P) -26 Court -Brklyn 11242
(212) 906-1200 .. **Chase**, Matthew J '06 %Latham & W -885 3rd Av -NY 10022
(716) 551-4228 .. **Chase**, Michl E '98 %Hon J Elfvin -68 Court -Buffalo 14202
(212) 819-1130 .. **Chase**, Oliver G '04 %Hirschen S&E -902 Bway -NY 10010
(212) 998-6217 .. **Chase**, Oscar G '66 %NYU Law Schl -40 Wshngtn Sq S -NY 10012 **Fx:**995-4881
(516) 671-5880 .. **Chase Rathkopf & Chase,LLP** -48 Forest Av -Glen Cove 11542 **Fx:**671-0740
(718) 298-1077 .. **Chase**, Richd A '94 Hon AN Price -8811 Sutphin Blvd -Jamaica 11435
(315) 589-4411 .. **Chase**, Richd E '65 -4071 W Main Bx70 -Williamson 14589
(518) 746-2216 .. **Chase**, Sara E '10 Cnty Atty -383 Bway -Ft Edward 12828 **Fx:**746-2137
(516) 333-1690 .. **Chase**, Seth Nolan '94 -1565 Franklin Ave -Mineola 11501 **Fx:**333-4182
(315) 435-2470 .. **Chase**, Shaun M '08 %DA -505 S State -Syracuse 13202 **Fx:**435-3969
(718) 520-1600 .. **Chase**, Steven D '84 %Kramer & S -80-02 Kew Grdns Rd -Kew Gdns 11415
(212) 426-3000 .. **Chase**, Susan Hardison '95 Leg Aid -230 E 106th -NY 10029 **Fx:**876-5365
(212) 326-3939 .. **Chase**, Terri L '98 (Jones D) -222 E 41st -NY 10017
(212) 661-3080 .. **Chase**, Thos E '96 %Rottenberg LR,PC -369 Lex Av -NY 10017

(718) 250-1400 .. **Chaseman,** Thos A '95 %BZ Green -12 MetroTech Ctr -Brklyn 11201 **Fx:**250-1401
(212) 306-2330 .. **Chasen,** Michl E '94 FINRA -165 Bway -NY 10006
(212) 782-1140 .. **Chasey,** Jacqueline '84 %Bertelsmann Inc -1540 Bway -NY 10036 **Fx:**782-1010
(212) 761-3105 .. **Chasin,** Chas '84 Morgan Stanley -1585 Bway -NY 10036
(718) 250-2000 .. **Chasin,** Farin R '98 %DA -350 Jay -Brklyn 11201 **Fx:**250-2314
(212) 727-2700 .. **Chasis,** Sarah '73 %NRDC -40 W 20th -NY 10011 **Fx:**727-1773
(607) 274-5022 .. **Chason,** Katherine Ann '90 DSS -320 W State -Ithaca 14850
(212) 715-9100 .. **Chass,** Mark I '91 %Kramer LN&F,LLP -1177 Av of Amer -NY 10036
(585) 786-8450 .. **Chassin,** Edw L '70 %Leg Aid -18 Linwood Av -Warsaw 14569 **Fx:**786-8478
(212) 888-3033 .. **Chassin,** Richd N '85 (Becker GM&M LLP) -299 Park Av -NY 10171
(212) 986-9700 .. **Chastain,** Edw B '97 Cnsl Eilenberg & K LLP -11 E 44th -NY 10017
(212) 294-6700 .. **Chastaine,** Kathleen M '07 %Winston & S -200 Park Av -NY 10166
(516) 688-1700 .. **Chastanet,** Catherine R '85 %IRS -1600 Stewart Av -Westbury 11590 **Fx:**688-1750
(212) 735-3000 .. **Chatain,** Miles R '02 %Skadden ASM&F LLP -4 Times Sq -NY 10036
(212) 632-5500 .. **Chateau,** Francois M '89 (Salans LLP) -620 5th Av -NY 10020
(212) 206-1761 .. **Chater,** Galal '99 -27 Union Sq W -NY 10003 **Fx:**206-1767
(212) 902-4148 .. **Chaterjee,** Nabanita '01 Goldman Sachs -1 NY Plz -NY 10004
(212) 455-2000 .. **Chatfield,** Kellin M '09 %Simpson T&B LLP -425 Lex Av -NY 10017
(315) 636-7911 .. **Chatfield,** Scott F '76 -3100 Brewer Rd Bx70 -Marietta 13110 **Fx:**636-7913
(212) 768-6700 .. **Chatillon,** M Devereux '80 (Sonnenschein N&R LLP) -1221 Av of Amer -NY 10020
(212) 268-2920 .. **Chatrath,** Sanddeep '95 (Chatrath Law Firm,PC) -494 8th Av -NY 10001 **Fx:**268-2921
(212) 837-6000 .. **Chattaway,** Kristy A '07 %Hughes H&R LLP -1 Bttry Pk Plz -NY 10004
(718) 418-7690 .. **Chatterjee,** Anusuya '01 Make the Road by Walking -301 Grove -Brklyn 11237
(212) 956-9500 .. **Chatterjee,** Sharmila '04 Hand B&A LLP -8 W 40th -NY 10018 **Fx:**376-6080
(212) 558-4000 .. **Chatterjee,** Whitney A '02 (Sullivan & C LLP) -125 Broad -NY 10004
(845) 294-8950 .. **Chatterton,** Mary Lou '89 OfCnsl J Haspel -40 Mathews -Goshen 10924 **Fx:**294-3843
(212) 481-1220 .. **Chattoraj,** Partha Pratim '99 (Markowitz & C LLP) -271 Mad Av -NY 10016 **Fx:**481-1221
(585) 247-9000 .. **Chatwin,** Michl J '02 %Shapiro D&B,LLP -250 Mile Xing Blvd -Rchstr 14624
(212) 310-8000 .. **Chatzinoff,** Howard '78 (Weil G&M LLP) -767 5th Av -NY 10153
(516) 357-3000 .. **Chatzinoff,** Peter R '87 (Rivkin R LLP) -926 RXR Plz -Uniondale 11556
(914) 729-9816 .. **Chatzky,** John A '84 %Prop Resources Corp -10 Bank -White Plns 10606 **Fx:**644-1903
(516) 822-3550 .. **Chau,** Anna C '07 %Hoffmann & B LLP -6900 Jericho Tpk -Syosset 11791 **Fx:**822-3582
(212) 938-1080 .. **Chau,** Brian K '07 %Conway & C -1700 Bway -NY 10019 **Fx:**938-1207
(516) 692-8888 .. **Chau,** Frank '89 (F Chau & Assoc,LLC) -130 Woodbury Rd -Woodbury 11797 **Fx:**692-8889
(212) 878-8000 .. **Chau,** Lai Lee '05 %Clifford C LLP -31 W 52nd -NY 10019
(212) 317-8100 .. **Chau,** Winnie Y '07 %E Grosz -757 3rd Av -NY 10017 **Fx:**679-7426
(212) 563-3223 .. **Chaubey,** Sanjay '00 -350 5th Av -NY 10118 **Fx:**563-4534
(212) 848-4000 .. **Chaudhari,** Gaurav '09 %Shearman & S LLP -599 Lex Av -NY 10022
(212) 790-9200 .. **Chaudhri,** Sujata '01 %Cowan L&L,PC -1133 Av of Amer -NY 10036
(212) 267-4876 .. **Chaudhri-deWit,** Shazia '01 %Hoagland LMD&D,LLP -1501 Bway -NY 10036
(917) 526-1362 .. **Chaudhry,** Muhammad-Omar Q '05 -80 Mt Misery Rd -Huntngtn 11743
(518) 474-7330 .. **Chaudhry,** Zainab A '99 %Dept of Law -The Cptl -Albany 12224
(845) 638-5001 .. **Chaudhury,** Nabeela '07 %DA -1 S Main -New Cty 10956 **Fx:**638-5070
(718) 275-3660 .. **Chaudhury,** Siddiquah '10 Harris Law Grp,LLP -96-14 63rd Dr -Rego Pk 11374 **Fx:**275-3405
(212) 735-3000 .. **Chaudry,** Yasmeena F '01 %Skadden ASM&F LLP -4 Times Sq -NY 10036
(212) 730-2351 .. **Chauhan,** Asha '85 -36 W 44th -NY 10036 **Fx:**730-5162
(212) 505-9080 .. **Chaut,** Alan M '84 %Loscalzo & L,PC -14 E 4th -NY 10012
(518) 885-2263 .. **Chauvin,** Matthew J '05 %DA -25 W High -Ballston Spa 12020 **Fx:**884-8627
(518) 371-5010 .. **Chauvin,** Robt J '76 -661B Plnk Rd Bx1258 -Clifton Pk 12065 **Fx:**383-4743
(585) 325-5110 .. **Chauvin-Bezinque,** Mark C '94 -45 Exchange Blvd -Rchstr 14614
(212) 259-8000 .. **Chavarria,** Ciarra A '09 %Dewey & L LLP -1301 Av of Amer -NY 10019
(212) 924-3732 .. **Chave,** Carolyn M '80 -693 Wshngtn -NY 10014 **Fx:**675-4530
(212) 349-5618 .. **Chaves,** Herbert H '62 -116 John -NY 10038 **Fx:**349-5624
(212) 785-5959 .. **Chaves,** Thos J '84 %Devereaux B -39 Bway -NY 10006 **Fx:**785-4487
(212) 239-6000 .. **Chavez,** Barbara P '90 Div Of Parole -314 W 40th -NY 10018 **Fx:**239-6160
(718) 294-4030 .. **Chavez,** Danl '81 -835 Walton Av -Bronx 10451 **Fx:**731-5054
(646) 303-6915 .. **Chavez,** Hector Francisco '99 -2565 Bway -NY 10025
(212) 815-0140 .. **Chavez,** Jacqueline C '09 DA -80 Centre -NY 10013
(212) 692-1000 .. **Chavez,** Javier Jr. '07 %Duane M LLP -1540 Bway -NY 10036
(212) 682-4001 .. **Chavez,** Jennifer T '01 %Lynch R LLP -630 3rd Av -NY 10017
(212) 768-3878 .. **Chavez,** Omar-John C '05 %Smith SWH&B,LLP -100 Park Av -NY 10017
(718) 579-3000 .. **Chavez,** Steven M '05 Leg Aid -1020 Grnd Cncrs -Bronx 10451 **Fx:**588-2611
(212) 361-9647 .. **Chavez-Garcia,** Gisela '05 -11 E 44th -NY 10017 **Fx:**(888) 500-1506
(518) 273-0000 .. **Chavin,** Bonnie P '88 %S Fox,PC -219 River Bx869 -Troy 12181 **Fx:**273-2030
(315) 733-7079 .. **Chavis,** Clifford W '87 -20 Finevw Dr Bx46 -Utica 13503 **Fx:**733-7079
(718) 250-2000 .. **Chavis,** Nicole L '03 %DA -350 Jay -Brklyn 11201 **Fx:**250-2314
(631) 712-6500 .. **Chavis,** Randi L '83 %Fed Def of NY Inc -770 Fed Plz -Central Islip 11722 **Fx:**712-6505
(845) 340-3315 .. **Chavkin,** Cindy B '05 %DA -285 Wall -Kingston 12401 **Fx:**340-3185
(212) 541-2000 .. **Chavkin,** Jeffrey S '76 (Bryan C LLP) -1290 Av of Amer -NY 10104
(212) 935-3000 .. **Chavkin,** Peter A '78 (Mintz LCFG&P,PC) -666 3rd Av -NY 10017
(212) 969-3000 .. **Chawla,** Aditi '09 %Proskauer R LLP -1585 Bway -NY 10036
(212) 317-1717 .. **Chawla,** Mudita '01 %Chemtob MF&T LLP -3 E 54th -NY 10022
(212) 563-4999 .. **Chawla,** Shagun '06 Cnsl Kemistre 8 LLC -31 W 34th -NY 10001
(212) 788-1465 .. **Chawla,** Vineet '04 ACS -220 Church -NY 10013
(212) 259-8000 .. **Chawla Dharwarkar,** Mayankita '07 %Dewey & L LLP -1301 Av of Amer -NY 10019
(212) 848-4000 .. **Chayko,** Erin E '08 %Shearman & S LLP -599 Lex Av -NY 10022
(718) 746-2163 .. **Chayt,** Maurice '53 (M Chayt,PC) -166-25 Powells Cove Blvd -Whitestone 11357
(212) 757-4044 .. **Chayut,** Jason T '01 %Sportstars Inc -142 W 57th -NY 10019
(212) 957-0039 .. **Chazan,** Paul M '76 -250 W 57th -NY 10107 **Fx:**957-0096
(718) 237-3100 .. **Chazen,** Jonathan B '07 Leg Aid -111 Lvngstn -Brklyn 11201 **Fx:**250-4243
(212) 841-1000 .. **Chazen,** Leonard '69 (Covington & B LLP) -620 8th Av -NY 10018
(212) 771-0749 .. **Chazin,** Susan '81 Aspen Law & Business -76 9th Av -NY 10011
(212) 314-7457 .. **Cheah,** Michl A '01 IAC -555 W 18th -NY 10011
(212) 610-6300 .. **Cheatham,** J Allie '06 %Allen & O -1221 Av of Amer -NY 10020
(718) 243-0900 .. **Cheatham,** Michl B '02 -161 Lvngstn -Brklyn 11201 **Fx:**858-3115
(212) 504-6000 .. **Chebli,** Brian E '05 %Cadwalader W&T LLP -1 World Fncl Ctr -NY 10281
(212) 506-2500 .. **Chebli,** Leslie E '99 %Mayer B LLP -1675 Bway -NY 10019
(212) 878-8000 .. **Chebli,** Michele Mathers '05 %Clifford C LLP -31 W 52nd -NY 10019
(212) 351-4000 .. **Checa Chong,** Jana N '10 Gibson D&C LLP -200 Park Av -NY 10166
(212) 819-8200 .. **Checchio,** Leigh M '08 %White & C LLP -1155 Av of Amer -NY 10036
(718) 830-3200 .. **Chechanover,** Michl D '83 (Rosado C&B,LLP) -31-00 47th Av -LIC 11101 **Fx:**830-3534
(212) 735-3000 .. **Check,** Carolyn M '10 %Skadden ASM&F LLP -4 Times Sq -NY 10036
(212) 225-2000 .. **Check,** Raymond B '87 (Cleary GS&H) -1 Lbrty Plz -NY 10006
(212) 989-7939 .. **Checki,** Donald J '67 -30 Greenwich Av -NY 10011
(212) 714-0500 .. **Checkla,** Ira J '84 %J Hughes -421 7th Av -NY 10001 **Fx:**714-0518
(212) 264-9940 .. **Checkman,** Neil B '71 -111 Bway -NY 10006 **Fx:**346-4665
(212) 335-9000 .. **Cheeks,** Benjamin J '05 %DA -1 Hogan Pl -NY 10013
(914) 683-1333 .. **Cheeks-Lomax,** Karen N '92 My Sisters Place -1 Water -White Plns 10601 **Fx:**683-1412
(212) 589-4200 .. **Cheema,** Bikramjit S '03 %Baker & H LLP -45 Rckfllr Plz -NY 10111
(212) 563-4464 .. **Cheerath,** Ram M '91 -147 W 35th -NY 10001 **Fx:**563-4708
(516) 378-8472 .. **Cheeseboro,** Jacqueline P '92 -63 Underhill Av -Roosevelt 11575 **Fx:**378-8472
(516) 288-1583 .. **Cheeseman-Bak,** Kara L '94 -99B Main -Westhmptn Bch 11978
(212) 715-0335 .. **Cheever,** Bethany H '02 Tishman Speyer Prop -45 Rckfllr Plz -NY 10111 **Fx:**332-6603
(516) 333-3232 .. **Chefec,** David W '81 (D Chefec,PC) -100 Q Roosevelt Blvd -Gdn Cty 11530 **Fx:**333-8359
(212) 735-2183 .. **Cheffo,** Mark '91 (Skadden ASM&F LLP) -4 Times Sq -NY 10036
(212) 596-9000 .. **Chegwidden,** Bryan C '04 (Ropes & G LLP) -1211 Av of Amer -NY 10036
(212) 230-8800 .. **Chehardy,** Kimberly N '10 %WilmerHale -399 Park Av -NY 10022
(914) 945-0783 .. **Chehebar,** Anne McMahon '83 -390 Old Briarcliff Rd -Briarclff Mnr 10510
(212) 889-2121 .. **Chehebar,** Chas '78 (Chehebar D&P LLP) -470 Park Av S -NY 10016 **Fx:**684-6224
(212) 806-5400 .. **Cheifetz,** David M '07 %Stroock &S&L LLP -180 Maiden Ln -NY 10038
(212) 697-9400 .. **Cheifetz Iannitelli Marcolini, PC** -275 Mad Av -NY 10016 **Fx:**697-9401
(212) 559-7801 .. **Cheifetz,** Ralph A '69 %Citibank -153 E 53rd -NY 10043
(631) 265-1600 .. **Chekenian,** Haig '61 -332 Edgewood Av -Smithtwn 11787 **Fx:**360-7715
(212) 574-1200 .. **Chelf,** Ryan E C '08 %Seward & K LLP -1 Bttry Pk Plz -NY 10004
(212) 530-5000 .. **Cheliotis,** Kostas '03 %Milbank TH&M LLP -1 Chase Manh Plz -NY 10005
(718) 987-8444 .. **Chelli,** Angelo F '66 (Chelli & B) -149 New Dorp Ln -Staten Isl 10306
(718) 987-8444 .. **Chelli & Bush** -149 New Dorp Ln -Staten Isl 10306 **Fx:**667-8187
(212) 335-9000 .. **Chelmow,** Marcy B '98 %DA -1 Hogan Pl -NY 10013
(212) 506-5000 .. **Chelney,** Konstantin '00 (Orrick H&S LLP) -51 W 52nd -NY 10019
(212) 319-3900 .. **Chelnitsky,** Dmitriy '08 %JE Bachelder LLP -437 Mad Av -NY 10022 **Fx:**319-3070
(716) 852-3600 .. **Chelus Herdzik Speyer & Monte,PC** -438 Main -Buffalo 14202 **Fx:**852-0038
(716) 608-7664 .. **Chelus Herdzik Speyer & Monte,PC** -2448 Union Rd -Cheektowaga 14225 **Fx:**608-7063
(716) 852-3600 .. **Chelus,** Michl F '68 (Chelus HS&M,PC) -438 Main -Buffalo 14202
(716) 852-3600 .. **Chelus,** Michl M '04 %Chelus HS&M,PC -438 Main -Buffalo 14202
(212) 318-3000 .. **Chemcham Cannarozzi,** Chehrazade '07 %Fulbright & J LLP -666 5th Av -NY 10103
(212) 244-4111 .. **Chemtob,** Lilach '04 Wender Law Grp -1 Penn Plz -NY 10119
(212) 317-1717 .. **Chemtob Moss Forman & Talbert LLP** -3 E 54th -NY 10022 **Fx:**317-1555
(212) 317-1717 .. **Chemtob,** Nancy Nadel '92 (Chemtob MF&T LLP) -3 E 54th -NY 10022
(212) 715-9100 .. **Chen,** Albert B '97 SpclCnsl Kramer LN&F,LLP -1177 Av of Amer -NY 10036
(212) 530-5000 .. **Chen,** Alecia '09 %Milbank TH&M LLP -1 Chase Manh Plz -NY 10005
(212) 270-2447 .. **Chen,** Alice F '82 JP Morgan Chase -270 Park Av -NY 10167
(212) 487-4444 .. **Chen,** Alison J '01 %Dept Cnsmr Affrs -42 Bway -NY 10004 **Fx:**487-4197

(718) 321-8056 .. **Chen,** Amy Y '06 AY Chen,PLLC -41-25 Kissena Blvd -Flushng 11355 **Fx:**321-8057
(212) 310-8000 .. **Chen,** Andrew J '05 %Weil G&M LLP -767 5th Av -NY 10153
(212) 588-0800 .. **Chen,** Angus '06 %Frommer L&H LLP -745 5th Av -NY 10151
(212) 788-1270 .. **Chen,** Caroline L '07 %Law Dept -100 Church -NY 10007 **Fx:**788-0367
(212) 490-3000 .. **Chen,** Catherine Ping '04 %Wilson EME&D LLP -150 E 42nd -NY 10017
(718) 321-3636 .. **Chen,** Christopher '03 -136-56 39th Av -Flushng 11354 **Fx:**321-3591
(212) 735-3000 .. **Chen,** Cindy '05 %Skadden ASM&F LLP -4 Times Sq -NY 10036
(212) 937-4281 .. **Chen,** Clifford Y '09 Watkins B&C,LLP -228 Park Av S -NY 10003
(718) 286-6000 .. **Chen,** David '88 %DA -125-01 Qns Blvd -Kew Gdns 11415
(718) 613-2154 .. **Chen,** David H '10 %Hon DL Irizarry -225 Cadman Plz E -Brklyn 11201
(212) 373-3000 .. **Chen,** Elaine '07 %Paul WRW&G LLP -1285 Av of Amer -NY 10019
(212) 645-0010 .. **Chen,** Elaine C Y '95 RGE Monitor -131 Varick -NY 10013 **Fx:**645-0023
(212) 788-0303 .. **Chen,** Elaine J S '07 %Law Dept -100 Church -NY 10007 **Fx:**788-0367
(212) 421-4100 .. **Chen,** Elizabeth Fei '05 OfCnsl Pryor C LLP -7 Times Sq -NY 10036
(212) 891-6151 .. **Chen,** Elizabeth K '01 Ixis Cap Mkts -9 W 57th -NY 10019
(212) 533-6300 .. **Chen,** Eric W '01 %NYSUT -52 Bway -NY 10004 **Fx:**995-2347
(212) 455-2000 .. **Chen,** Estella F '08 %Simpson T&B LLP -425 Lex Av -NY 10017
(212) 530-5000 .. **Chen,** Ginni E '10 %Milbank TH&M LLP -1 Chase Manh Plz -NY 10005
(347) 404-9133 .. **Chen,** Grace I '08 Civil Ct -141 Lvngstn -Brklyn 11201 **Fx:**(718) 643-3733
(212) 385-4003 .. **Chen,** Graeme H '95 (G Chen & Assoc PC) -305 Bway -NY 10007
(212) 326-3939 .. **Chen,** Gwendolynne M '08 %Jones D -222 E 41st -NY 10017
(212) 733-1025 .. **Chen,** Heidi C '93 %Pfizer Inc -235 E 42nd -NY 10017
(212) 230-8800 .. **Chen,** Henry '08 %WilmerHale -399 Park Av -NY 10022
(212) 571-0550 .. **Chen,** Howard '00 (Allegaert B&V LLP) -111 Bway -NY 10006
(516) 488-3300 .. **Chen,** Hsiuen F '07 %Shaub AC&S,LLP -1983 Marcus Av -Lk Success 11042
(212) 335-4500 .. **Chen,** I-Ann Annie '10 %DLA Piper LLP -1251 Av of Amer -NY 10020
(212) 565-8628 .. **Chen,** Iris S '02 Google,Inc -76 9th Av -NY 10011
(212) 279-2080 .. **Chen,** Iris Y '05 Teach for America -315 W 36th -NY 10018
(212) 735-3000 .. **Chen,** Ivan '09 %Skadden ASM&F LLP -4 Times Sq -NY 10036
(212) 596-9000 .. **Chen,** Jack J '10 %Ropes & G LLP -1211 Av of Amer -NY 10036
(212) 317-5700 .. **Chen,** Jack Jia-Horng '97 Centerline Capital -625 Mad Av -NY 10022 **Fx:**751-3550
(212) 408-2500 .. **Chen,** Jack L '06 %Baker B,LLP -30 Rckfllr Plz -NY 10112
(347) 401-9075 .. **Chen,** Janice E '03 %Supreme Ct -360 Adams -Brklyn 11201
(212) 984-5340 .. **Chen,** Jaye '97 Inst of Intl Educ -809 UN Plz -NY 10017
(212) 455-2000 .. **Chen,** Jean '07 %Simpson T&B LLP -425 Lex Av -NY 10017
(212) 450-4000 .. **Chen,** Jiabei '10 %Davis P&W LLP -450 Lex Av -NY 10017
(212) 478-8185 .. **Chen,** Jo E '04 DE Shaw & Co -120 W 45th -NY 10036 **Fx:**478-0100
(212) 816-1689 .. **Chen,** John Y '03 Citigroup -388 Greenwich -NY 10013
(212) 506-5000 .. **Chen,** Joyce '05 %Orrick H&S LLP -51 W 52nd -NY 10019
(212) 230-8800 .. **Chen,** Joyce H '09 %WilmerHale -399 Park Av -NY 10022
(212) 474-1000 .. **Chen,** Julie S '10 %Cravath S&M LLP -825 8th Av -NY 10019
(718) 316-6538 .. **Chen,** Kai Wm '96 -86-16 Qns Blvd -Elmhrst 11373 **Fx:**396-6548
(212) 255-5001 .. **Chen,** Katharine M '91 -Bx20053 -NY 10014
(212) 468-8000 .. **Chen,** Kelvin D '05 %Morrison & F LLP -1290 Av of Amer -NY 10104
(212) 494-0061 .. **Chen,** Kenneth S '06 Asian Amer Writers Workshop -16 W 32nd -NY 10001 **Fx:**494-0062
(718) 309-7347 .. **Chen,** Ledan C '07 -2061 31st -Astoria 11105
(914) 378-1010 .. **Chen,** Liu-Ming '02 Fitzgerald & F -538 Riverdale Av -Ynkrs 10705
(212) 859-8000 .. **Chen,** Liwen '06 %Fried FHS&J LLP -1 NY Plz -NY 10004
(212) 218-2100 .. **Chen,** Lucian C '03 %Fitzpatrick CH&S -1290 Av of Amer -NY 10104
(212) 431-2155 .. **Chen,** Lung-Chu '85 %NY Law Schl -185 W Bway -NY 10013 **Fx:**431-3295
(212) 326-3939 .. **Chen,** M David '09 %Jones D -222 E 41st -NY 10017
(718) 353-7779 .. **Chen,** Mei Sun '98 -39-15 Main -Flushng 11354
(646) 223-4200 .. **Chen,** Meivile '97 %Reuters -3 Times Sq -NY 10036 **Fx:**223-4250
(212) 859-8000 .. **Chen,** Michl '10 %Fried FHS&J LLP -1 NY Plz -NY 10004
(718) 939-4633 .. **Chen,** Mingli '05 %KK Tung PC -38-21 Main -Flushng 11354 **Fx:**939-4468
(212) 859-5004 .. **Chen,** Nancy '89 -110 Wall -NY 10005
(718) 254-7575 .. **Chen,** Pamela Ki Mai '03 %US Atty -271 Cadman Plz E -Brklyn 11201 **Fx:**254-6479
(212) 756-2000 .. **Chen,** Pamela Poland '05 %Schulte R&Z LLP -919 3rd Av -NY 10022
(212) 218-2100 .. **Chen,** Patrick L '10 %Fitzpatrick CH&S -1290 Av of Amer -NY 10104
(718) 552-2509 .. **Chen,** Patrick P Y '09 CTG Atheletics,LLC -2417 3rd Av -Bronx 10451
(212) 259-8000 .. **Chen,** Paul P '97 (Dewey & L LLP) -1301 Av of Amer -NY 10019
(212) 468-4800 .. **Chen,** Peggy S '04 %Davis & G LLP -1740 Bway -NY 10019
(212) 608-6500 .. **Chen,** Peter G '80 (DeHeng C,LLC) -225 Bway -NY 10007
(718) 886-8181 .. **Chen,** Richd Alan '80 -41-60 Main -Flushng 11355
(212) 715-1000 .. **Chen,** Richd Leeway '99 Cnsl Arnold & P LLP -399 Park Av -NY 10022
(212) 403-1000 .. **Chen,** Ronald C '05 %Wachtell LR&K -51 W 52nd -NY 10019
(212) 415-8600 .. **Chen,** Sarah M '07 %Locke LB&L LLP -3 World Fncl Ctr -NY 10281
(607) 248-1253 .. **Chen,** Siwen '01 %Corning Inc -SP-TI-3-1 -Corning 14831
(212) 839-5300 .. **Chen,** Steven '08 %Sidley A LLP -787 7th Av -NY 10019
(718) 353-1234 .. **Chen,** Steven C '95 -133-47 41st Rd -Flushng 11355 **Fx:**358-2320
(212) 637-2790 .. **Chen,** Sue '02 %US Atty -86 Chmbrs -NY 10007
(212) 403-1000 .. **Chen,** Tian-Wei Dianna '00 Cnsl Wachtell LR&K -51 W 52nd -NY 10019
(212) 474-1000 .. **Chen,** Ting S '07 %Cravath S&M LLP -825 8th Av -NY 10019
(212) 965-9988 .. **Chen,** Tisha '98 -401 Bway -NY 10013 **Fx:**965-9987
(212) 878-8000 .. **Chen,** Vivian H '07 %Clifford C LLP -31 W 52nd -NY 10019
(212) 891-1600 .. **Chen,** Walter H '10 %Jenner & B LLP -919 3rd Av -NY 10022
(212) 754-9400 .. **Chen,** Wesley '81 SpclCnsl Todtman NS&J,PC -425 Park Av -NY 10022
(212) 326-3939 .. **Chen,** Xi '08 %Jones D -222 E 41st -NY 10017
(212) 294-3550 .. **Chen,** Xi '10 %Winston & S -200 Park Av -NY 10166
(212) 608-6500 .. **Chen,** Xiaomin '94 (DeHeng C,LLC) -225 Bway -NY 10007
(718) 228-7206 .. **Chen,** Yang '91 Asian Amer Bar Assn of NY -Grnd Cntrl Station Bx3656 -NY 10163
(212) 370-1300 .. **Chen,** Yingying '09 %Ellenoff G&S LLP -150 E 42nd -NY 10017
(212) 408-2500 .. **Chen,** Yong '08 %Baker B,LLP -30 Rckfllr Plz -NY 10112
(212) 351-4000 .. **Chen,** Zern-Shun '08 Gibson D&C LLP -200 Park Av -NY 10166
(212) 450-4000 .. **Chenard,** James A '08 %Davis P&W LLP -450 Lex Av -NY 10017
(212) 460-4600 .. **Chenard,** Rebecca Hanson '01 Con Ed -4 Irving Pl -NY 10003
(212) 537-1791 .. **Chenchinski,** Amir '06 %Morgan Stanley -1633 Bway -NY 10019
(212) 574-1200 .. **Chender,** Robt L '81 Cnsl Seward & K LLP -1 Bttry Pk Plz -NY 10004
(518) 489-0026 .. **Chenel,** Michl P '05 -11 Computer Dr W -Albany 12205 **Fx:**489-0034
(516) 229-4501 .. **Chenery,** Tina M '90 %Russo A&T -875 Merrick Av -Westbury 11590
(212) 728-8000 .. **Cheney,** Alexander L '08 %Willkie F&G LLP -787 7th Av -NY 10019
(315) 685-9900 .. **Cheney,** Donald J '02 (Cheney & B LLP) -3895 Fennell -Skaneateles 13152 **Fx:**685-9910
(212) 335-4500 .. **Cheney,** Helen H Nichols '06 %DLA Piper LLP -1251 Av of Amer -NY 10020
(212) 788-3489 .. **Cheney,** Jacqueline B '06 ACS Fam Ct Leg Svcs -220 Church -NY 10013
(212) 692-1000 .. **Cheney,** Kathleen Carver '95 (Duane M LLP) -1540 Bway -NY 10036
(516) 354-7255 .. **Cheng,** Archie T '78 -87 Covert Av -Floral Pk 11001 **Fx:**775-1056
(212) 848-4000 .. **Cheng,** Benjamin M '00 Cnsl Shearman & S LLP -599 Lex Av -NY 10022
(631) 852-3850 .. **Cheng,** Bernard Che Ho '95 %Hon J Hudson -210 Center Dr -Rvrhead 11901 **Fx:**852-3225
(212) 373-3000 .. **Cheng,** Brian '07 %Paul WRW&G LLP -1285 Av of Amer -NY 10019
(212) 918-3000 .. **Cheng,** Carol F '00 Hogan L LLP -875 3rd Av -NY 10022
(212) 489-1600 .. **Cheng,** Caroline K '04 %Deloitte LLP -1633 Bway -NY 10019 **Fx:**492-4201
(718) 250-2000 .. **Cheng,** Chin Ho '07 %DA -350 Jay -Brklyn 11201 **Fx:**250-2314
(212) 403-1000 .. **Cheng,** Christina '09 %Wachtell LR&K -51 W 52nd -NY 10019
(718) 780-7550 .. **Cheng,** Edw K '04 Bklyn Law Schl -250 Joralemon -Brklyn 11201 **Fx:**780-0393
(212) 688-4000 .. **Cheng,** Elaine May '97 %NYS Affordable Hsng -641 Lex Av -NY 10022
(914) 323-7000 .. **Cheng,** Eric G '98 (Wilson EME&D LLP) -3 Gannett Dr -White Plns 10604
(917) 368-3567 .. **Cheng,** Eugenia R '02 ABP Invstmnts US Inc -666 3rd Av -NY 10017
(212) 841-2000 .. **Cheng,** Everett S '99 BNP Paribas -787 7th Av -NY 10019
(212) 233-9377 .. **Cheng,** Horkeen '92 -7-8 Chatham Sq -NY 10038
(212) 416-6695 .. **Cheng,** Isaac C '09 %Dept of Law -120 Bway -NY 10271
(212) 403-1000 .. **Cheng,** Jessie '09 %Wachtell LR&K -51 W 52nd -NY 10019
(212) 766-2466 .. **Cheng,** Julia '00 (DiSanto LLP) -15 Maiden Ln -NY 10038 **Fx:**(866) 746-0504
(212) 687-2770 .. **Cheng,** Kent H '91 (Cohen PL&P) -551 5th Av -NY 10176
(212) 450-4000 .. **Cheng,** Loyti '87 Cnsl Davis P&W LLP -450 Lex Av -NY 10017
(212) 553-7832 .. **Cheng,** Lulu Y '99 Moody's Invstr Srvc -250 Greenwich -NY 10007
(212) 264-3510 .. **Cheng,** Mary M '98 DHS -26 Fed Plz -NY 10278
(516) 741-2200 .. **Cheng,** Meng '06 %Zisholtz & Z,LLP -170 Old Cntry Rd -Mineola 11501 **Fx:**746-1024
(212) 385-2122 .. **Cheng,** Nolan '97 -11 E Bway -NY 10038 **Fx:**385-2022
(914) 681-8700 .. **Cheng,** Otto '05 %Milber MP&S LLP -3 Barker Av -White Plns 10601
(212) 762-7136 .. **Cheng,** Patricia Mun '94 Morgan Stanley -1221 Av of Amer -NY 10020
(212) 592-1839 .. **Cheng,** Patrick S '95 Church Pension Fund -445 5th Av -NY 10016 **Fx:**592-9428
(212) 608-1234 .. **Cheng,** Pei Pei '01 (Peluso & T) -70 Lafayette -NY 10013
(718) 937-8480 .. **Cheng,** Pui Chi '91 Cheng & Assoc PLLC -27-28 Thomson Av -LIC 11101 **Fx:**937-8444
(718) 694-4157 .. **Cheng,** Saml '98 %Transit Auth -130 Lvngstn -Brklyn 11201 **Fx:**694-5726
(718) 643-4673 .. **Cheng,** Sharon G '88 Surrogates Ct -2 Johnson -Brklyn 11201 **Fx:**643-4743
(212) 326-3939 .. **Cheng,** Susie S '99 %Jones D -222 E 41st -NY 10017
(212) 431-2834 .. **Cheng,** Tai-Heng '04 %NY Law Schl -185 W Bway -NY 10013 **Fx:**406-0103
(212) 969-3000 .. **Cheng,** Theo K '98 %Proskauer R LLP -1585 Bway -NY 10036
(212) 227-5577 .. **Cheng,** Victor W '85 (Lee & C,PC) -7 Chatham Sq -NY 10038 **Fx:**732-2671
(732) 855-6192 .. **Cheng,** Vincent '04 %Wilentz G&S -110 William -NY 10038 **Fx:**726-4708
(212) 310-8000 .. **Cheng,** Wing Ting Jennifer '09 %Weil G&M LLP -767 5th Av -NY 10153
(212) 909-6000 .. **Cheng,** Xi Lucy '08 %Debevoise & P LLP -919 3rd Av -NY 10022
(718) 658-5999 .. **Cheng,** Yafang '95 (Cheng & F,LLP) -246-11 F Lewis Blvd -Rosedale 11422 **Fx:**528-5708
(718) 658-0500 .. **Cheng,** Yvette '08 %Law Dept -151-20 Jamaica Av -Jamaica 11432 **Fx:**658-4025
(212) 336-2000 .. **Chen-Josephson,** YiLing Livia '09 %Patterson BW&T LLP -1133 Av of Amer -NY 10036
(212) 223-0400 .. **Chenkin,** David B '83 (Zeichner E&K LLP) -575 Lex Av -NY 10022
(212) 563-2049 .. **Chenn,** Fletcher H '93 Savant Consulting Grp,Inc -30 Elizabeth -NY 10013
(718) 694-3864 .. **Chenn,** June-Annette Fletcher '90 %Transit Auth -130 Lvngstn -Brklyn 11201 **Fx:**694-5726
(212) 733-5095 .. **Chenoweth,** Laura A '90 Pfizer Inc -235 E 42nd -NY 10017
(212) 455-2000 .. **Cheong,** Yoo Sun '10 %Simpson T&B LLP -425 Lex Av -NY 10017
(212) 373-3000 .. **Chepiga,** Geoffrey '08 %Paul WRW&G LLP -1285 Av of Amer -NY 10019
(212) 455-2000 .. **Chepiga,** Michl J '80 (Simpson T&B LLP) -425 Lex Av -NY 10017
(212) 610-6300 .. **Chepiga,** Pamela A R '74 (Allen & O) -1221 Av of Amer -NY 10020
(347) 404-9720 .. **Chepiga,** Stephen F '78 Surrogates Ct -2 Johnson -Brklyn 11201

(212) 450-4000 .. **Chepiga,** Tenley Laserson '09 %Davis P&W LLP -450 Lex Av -NY 10017
(212) 337-2341 .. **Cherasard,** Paul '01 %US Dept Labor OSHA -201 Varick -NY 10014
(631) 928-5500 .. **Cherches,** Eric D '90 -220 E Main -Pt Jffrsn 11777
(212) 859-3490 .. **Cherchian,** Ralph '79 -110 Wall -NY 10005 **Fx:**943-2300
(718) 579-7926 .. **Cherena,** Vanessa D '96 %Leg Aid -900 Sheridan Av -Bronx 10451 **Fx:**293-8744
(718) 928-3700 .. **Cherenfant,** Guilene '91 %LSNYC-Bronx -579 Courtlandt Av -Bronx 10451 **Fx:**402-7586
(716) 853-9555 .. **Cherian,** Nina S '06 Leg Aid -237 Main -Buffalo 14203 **Fx:**853-3219
(914) 948-2299 .. **Cherico,** John B '94 (JB Cherico & Assoc) -308 Battle Av -White Plns 10606 **Fx:**948-4248
(914) 948-2299 .. **Cherico,** Julie Ann '95 OfCnsl JB Cherico & Assoc -308 Battle Av -White Plns 10606 **Fx:**948-4248
(212) 285-4100 .. **Cheriff,** Bernard '54 OfCnsl Cheriff & F,PC -2 Rector -NY 10006
(212) 285-4100 .. **Cheriff,** Bruce J '87 (Cheriff & F,PC) -2 Rector -NY 10006
(212) 285-4100 .. **Cheriff & Fink,PC** -2 Rector -NY 10006 **Fx:**285-4101
(212) 407-1200 .. **Cherington,** Rachel M '06 %Joseph Law Ofcs LLC -485 Lex Av -NY 10017 **Fx:**407-1299
(718) 739-6718 .. **Cheris,** Ann Zetoony '89 %Admin Children's Srvcs -151-20 Jamaica Av -Jamaica 11432
(212) 455-2000 .. **Cheriyan,** Ashwin N '09 %Simpson T&B LLP -425 Lex Av -NY 10017
(718) 222-2350 .. **Cherizard,** Sarrah '03 %Law Dept -151-20 Jamaica Av -Jamaica 11432 **Fx:**658-4025
(212) 335-9000 .. **Cherkasky,** Eli K '07 %DA -1 Hogan Pl -NY 10013
(212) 345-3550 .. **Cherkasky,** Michl G '79 MMC -1166 Av of Amer -NY 10036
(212) 237-0000 .. **Cherkis,** Laurence D '67 OfCnsl Vinson & E LLP -666 5th Av -NY 10103
(212) 964-7400 .. **Cherkis,** Louise M '84 Smith MDWY&Y,PC -111 John -NY 10038
(631) 789-4000 .. **Cherkoss,** Val S '83 (Blumberg CF&B) -330 Bway -Amityvll 11701
(212) 458-1205 .. **Chermak,** Sarah Anne '90 %AIG -175 Water -NY 10038
(212) 801-2146 .. **Chern,** Richd '00 OfCnsl Greenberg T,LLP -200 Park Av -NY 10166
(914) 701-4000 .. **Cherneff,** Peter R '72 (Watkins & C) -106 Corp Park Dr -White Plns 10604 **Fx:**701-4001
(212) 309-6000 .. **Cherner-Ranft,** Meghan E '06 %Morgan L&B LLP -101 Park Av -NY 10178
(518) 747-0609 .. **Cherney,** Elan '76 -354 Main -Hudson Fls 12839 **Fx:**747-0285
(212) 836-8000 .. **Cherney,** Emanuel S '78 (Kaye S LLP) -425 Park Av -NY 10022
(718) 442-7004 .. **Cherniak,** George A '82 %Johnson & L,PC -1688 Victory Blvd -Staten Isl 10314 **Fx:**442-9086
(646) 386-3647 .. **Cherniak,** Saml A '81 %Supreme Ct-Law Dept -60 Centre -NY 10007
(212) 819-8200 .. **Chernichaw,** Adam '96 (White & C LLP) -1155 Av of Amer -NY 10036
(718) 739-2879 .. **Chernick,** Albert D '57 -140-35 Burden Cres -Jamaica 11435
(914) 238-0999 .. **Chernick,** Chas M '78 -5 Stornowaye -Chappaqua 10514
(212) 532-8686 .. **Chernick,** Glen M '88 SrCnsl Kensington Vanguard -39 W 37th -NY 10018
(212) 318-6000 .. **Chernick,** Michl K '91 (Paul HJ&W LLP) -75 E 55th -NY 10022
(212) 272-2557 .. **Chernick,** Sharon Lee '79 %JP Morgan Chase -383 Mad Av -NY 10179
(718) 590-2000 .. **Chernin,** Hilary K '09 %DA -198 E 161st -Bronx 10451 **Fx:**590-6477
(212) 448-1100 .. **Chernin,** Oliver R '86 %McLaughlin & S,LLP -260 Mad Av -NY 10016
(212) 779-8600 .. **Chernis,** Paul '62 OfCnsl Silverman SS&B PLLC -381 Park Av S -NY 10016
(212) 877-9935 .. **Chernis,** Steven A '66 -27 W 86th -NY 10024 **Fx:**877-5865
(212) 859-8000 .. **Cherno,** Marc P '61 OfCnsl Fried FHS&J LLP -1 NY Plz -NY 10004
(516) 647-1307 .. **Cherno,** Wm A '80 -Bx1668 -Lindenhrst 11757 **Fx:**203-4362
(212) 225-2000 .. **Chernobilsky,** Yana '09 %Cleary GS&H -1 Lbrty Plz -NY 10006
(212) 506-1700 .. **Chernock,** Larissa R '08 %Kasowitz BT&F LLP -1633 Bway -NY 10019
(212) 637-2481 .. **Chernoff,** Harry A '98 %US Atty -1 St Andrews Plz -NY 10007
(212) 696-4411 .. **Chernofsky,** Chas B '67 (Chernofsky & deN) -360 W 22nd -NY 10011 **Fx:**239-4463
(212) 717-2900 .. **Chernofsky,** Melissa R '02 Dontzin Law Firm -6 E 81st -NY 10028 **Fx:**717-8088
(212) 350-2700 .. **Chernov,** Joel A '84 OfCnsl Constantine C,PC -450 Lex Av -NY 10017
(212) 487-9700 .. **Chernow,** Jonathan S '97 (White F&F,LLP) -61 Bway -NY 10006
(917) 991-4360 .. **Chern-Thompson,** Gail S '82 -140 Pinehurst Av -NY 10033
(212) 728-8000 .. **Chernuchin,** Cindy '85 SpclCnsl Willkie F&G LLP -787 7th Av -NY 10019
(718) 449-5100 .. **Cherny,** Aleksandr S '04 (Cherny & P,PLLC) -8778 Bay Pkwy -Brklyn 11214 **Fx:**449-6661
(516) 739-1500 .. **Cherny,** Rachel L '01 %Weiss & W -300 Old Cntry Rd -Mineola 11501 **Fx:**739-2189
(212) 446-4800 .. **Cherny,** Steven C '92 (Kirkland & E LLP) -153 E 53rd -NY 10022
(212) 715-9100 .. **Chernyak,** Yekaterina '07 %Kramer LN&F,LLP -1177 Av of Amer -NY 10036
(917) 454-1100 .. **Chernyavsky,** Oleg '02 NYPD-Civil Enfcmnt -2 Lafayette -NY 10007
(845) 353-0789 .. **Cherofsky,** Robt D '81 -53 Burd -Nyack 10960 **Fx:**353-5997
(718) 250-2000 .. **Cherofsky,** Robt J '09 %DA -350 Jay -Brklyn 11201 **Fx:**250-2314
(212) 962-6442 .. **Cherot,** Nicholas M '73 Cherot & M -305 Bway -NY 10007 **Fx:**571-0570
(212) 263-3277 .. **Cherrick,** Ellen R '82 NYU School of Medicine Div Cardiothoracic Surgery -530 First Av -NY 10016 **Fx:**263-2246
(718) 428-4806 .. **Cherrick,** Tara A '03 %K Litwack,PC -38-08 Bell Blvd -Bayside 11361 **Fx:**947-2794
(212) 310-8000 .. **Cherry,** Brandon '08 %Weil G&M LLP -767 5th Av -NY 10153
(212) 405-9602 .. **Cherry,** Carnell L '08 Alvin Ailey Dance Fndtn,Inc -405 W 55th -NY 10019
(718) 298-0239 .. **Cherry,** Cheryl Ann '98 Family Ct -151-20 Jamaica Av -Jamaica 11432
(516) 486-4640 .. **Cherry Edson & Kelly, LLP** -1 Old Cntry Rd -Carle Pl 11514 **Fx:**486-7732
(914) 332-1800 .. **Cherry Edson & Kelly, LLP** -150 Wht Plns Rd -Tarrytwn 10591 **Fx:**332-4062
(212) 599-2085 .. **Cherry,** Gloria B '59 (Braff H&S) -305 Bway -NY 10007
(212) 980-0010 .. **Cherry,** Jennie L '89 OfCnsl Kozusko HVW LLP -575 Mad Av -NY 10022 **Fx:**751-0084
(212) 872-1000 .. **Cherry,** Jessica '02 -One Bryant Park -NY 10036 **Fx:**872-1002
(212) 351-4000 .. **Cherry,** Kevin W '05 %Gibson D&C LLP -200 Park Av -NY 10166
(212) 878-8000 .. **Cherry,** Marye C '04 %Clifford C LLP -31 W 52nd -NY 10019
(212) 709-1663 .. **Cherry,** Sharon A '89 %Banking Dept -1 State -NY 10004 **Fx:**709-1655
(718) 798-6287 .. **Cherry,** Steven E '70 -Lenox Hill Station Bx2249 -NY 10021 **Fx:**(212) 734-9727
(212) 490-3000 .. **Cherry,** Thos R '85 (Wilson EME&D LLP) -150 E 42nd -NY 10017
(914) 323-7000 .. **Cherry,** Thos R '85 (Wilson EME&D LLP) -3 Gannett Dr -White Plns 10604
(646) 442-3100 .. **Cherry-Slack,** Montel '00 %Legal Srvcs -90 John -NY 10038 **Fx:**(212) 227-9798
(718) 261-7700 .. **Cherson,** Eliot Jay '77 (Rappaport HC&R,PC) -118-35 Qns Blvd -Frst Hlls 11375
(212) 285-3800 .. **Chertock,** Gene '83 Subin Assoc LLP -150 Bway -NY 10007
(516) 771-6900 .. **Chertock,** Richd J '87 -2174 Hewlett Av -Merrick 11566 **Fx:**771-9870
(212) 349-5554 .. **Chertoff,** Andrew M '76 -61 Bway -NY 10006 **Fx:**962-3123
(212) 382-0909 .. **Chertoff,** Gregory H '95 (Peckar & A,PC) -41 Mad Av -NY 10154
(718) 694-3903 .. **Chertoff,** Kenneth J '76 %Transit Auth -130 Lvngstn -Brklyn 11201 **Fx:**694-5726
(518) 583-4600 .. **Chertok,** Danl G '92 (LeCours C&Y,LLP) -59 Church -Saratoga Spgs 12866 **Fx:**583-4642
(212) 421-2150 .. **Chertok,** Mark A '71 (Sive P&R,PC) -460 Park Av -NY 10022
(212) 277-4000 .. **Chertudi,** Danl S '08 %Freshfields BD LLP -520 Mad Av -NY 10022
(518) 427-7350 .. **Cherubin,** David M '87 OfCnsl Brown & W PLLC -79 Columbia -Albany 12210
(718) 624-3894 .. **Cherubin,** Sidney '02 Brooklyn Bar Assn Volunteer Lwyrs Proj Inc -123 Remsen -Brklyn 11201
(845) 364-9745 .. **Cherveny-Brown,** Jacqueline '92 -8 Cooper Morris Dr -Pomona 10970 **Fx:**364-9745
(212) 541-7800 .. **Chervin,** Carole I '91 %Planned Parenthood -434 W 33rd -NY 10001 **Fx:**868-4677
(212) 504-6000 .. **Chervokas,** Leslie W '86 SpclCnsl Cadwalader W&T LLP -1 World Fncl Ctr -NY 10281
(212) 678-2323 .. **Cherwin,** Ric '88 -124 W 93rd -NY 10025 **Fx:**666-1351
(631) 422-1471 .. **Chery,** Francis P '90 -510 Sunrise Hwy -W Babylon 11704 **Fx:**422-1481
(518) 474-1968 .. **Chery-Sekhobo,** Marie '02 %Dept of Law -The Cptl -Albany 12224
(212) 770-2729 .. **Cheshire,** Sandra K '01 AIG -80 Pine -NY 10005 **Fx:**770-2730
(212) 506-2500 .. **Chesin,** Scott A '03 %Mayer B LLP -1675 Bway -NY 10019
(212) 697-7220 .. **Chesir,** Seymour N '57 (Stein SC&R,LLP) -140 E 45th -NY 10017
(212) 338-2630 .. **Chesir-Teran,** Ian '96 -1065 Av of Amer -NY 10018
(212) 340-0400 .. **Chesler,** Ariel D '04 %Appllt Div 1st Dept -27 Mad Av -NY 10010 **Fx:**889-4412
(212) 474-1000 .. **Chesler,** Evan R '76 (Cravath S&M LLP) -825 8th Av -NY 10019
(718) 520-3363 .. **Chesler,** Ivan '77 %Criminal Ct -125-01 Qns Blvd -Kew Gdns 11415
(212) 761-4000 .. **Chesler,** Jill D '04 %Morgan Stanley -1633 Bway -NY 10019
(914) 946-8200 .. **Chesler Messafi,** Stephanie '00 R Peirce & Assoc -8 Cottage Pl -White Plns 10601
(718) 522-3055 .. **Chesley,** Stephen R '82 (SR Chesley,LLC) -16 Court -Brklyn 11241 **Fx:**855-2900
(518) 434-1022 .. **Chesley,** Stephen R '07 Sullivan KO&V, LLP -152 Central Av -Albany 12206
(718) 330-7861 .. **Cheslow,** Frieda R '97 %ODAR-SSA -111 Lvngstn -Brklyn 11201 **Fx:**330-2009
(516) 378-1700 .. **Chesney & Murphy** -2305 Grand Av -Baldwin 11510 **Fx:**378-7633
(516) 378-1700 .. **Chesney,** Richd E '78 (Chesney & M) -2305 Grand Av -Baldwin 11510
(516) 378-1700 .. **Chesney,** Richd E Jr. '09 %Chesney & M -2305 Grand Av -Baldwin 11510
(516) 626-6132 .. **Chesnik,** Edw J '77 -68 Wheatley Rd -Brookvll 11545 **Fx:**626-6129
(212) 861-9332 .. **Chess,** Stanley D '74 %LawTV -330 E 75th -NY 10021 **Fx:**202-5025
(212) 265-6888 .. **Chesson,** Thos R '82 OfCnsl Porzio B&N,PC -156 W 56th -NY 10019
(212) 793-6027 .. **Chester,** Alison B '99 Citigroup Inc -909 3rd Av -NY 10043
(212) 637-3213 .. **Chester,** Amy R '92 %EPA -290 Bway -NY 10007 **Fx:**637-3096
(212) 682-8228 .. **Chester,** Cathy S '85 -711 3rd Av -NY 10017 **Fx:**957-9229
(212) 391-9500 .. **Chester,** Jeffrey A '86 (Einbinder & D,PC) -104 W 40th -NY 10018
(212) 820-7700 .. **Chester,** Michl B '02 %Boundas SW&B,LLC -1 Bttry Pk Plz -NY 10004
(212) 681-4499 .. **Chester,** Paula L '86 %State Comptroller -633 3rd Av -NY 10017
(212) 318-7000 .. **Chesterman,** Tracie R '00 Polo Ralph Lauren -650 Mad Av -NY 10022
(212) 788-0991 .. **Chestnov,** Michl S '04 %Law Dept -100 Church -NY 10007 **Fx:**788-0367
(585) 899-1414 .. **Chesworth,** Donald O '72 (Harris COJW&L) -300 Linden Oaks -Rchstr 14625
(516) 338-2888 .. **Chetkof,** Howard A '96 (Levin & C,LLP) -265 Post Av -Westbury 11590 **Fx:**338-4343
(631) 360-7333 .. **Chetkof,** Linda M '93 De Sena & S -1383 Vets Mem'l Hwy -Hauppauge 11788
(516) 873-7200 .. **Chetkof,** Michl '64 (Saltzman C&R,LLP) -300 Grdn City Plz -Gdn Cty 11530
(212) 557-5830 .. **Chetrick,** Harold '61 (H Chetrick PC) -60 E 42nd -NY 10165 **Fx:**679-9195
(212) 557-5830 .. **Chetrick,** Kenneth A '91 %H Chetrick PC -60 E 42nd -NY 10165 **Fx:**679-9195
(212) 791-0285 .. **Chetta,** Rosario '99 %Malaby & B,LLC -150 Bway -NY 10038 **Fx:**791-0286
(212) 998-6093 .. **Chettiar,** Inimai M '04 NYU Law Schl -245 Sullivan -NY 10012
(212) 687-2770 .. **Chettih,** Mindy H '80 %Cohen PL&P -551 5th Av -NY 10176
(212) 788-0437 .. **Cheuk,** Fei Y '05 Law Dept -100 Church -NY 10007 **Fx:**788-8896
(212) 226-6366 .. **Cheuk,** Lydia L '98 Blue Man Productions,Inc -411 Lafayette -NY 10003
(212) 403-1000 .. **Cheung,** Andrew J '97 Cnsl Wachtell LR&K -51 W 52nd -NY 10019

(212) 436-7508 .. **Cheung,** Brian W H '06 Deloitte Fncl Advssry Srvcs LLP -1 Wrld Fncl Ctr -NY 10281
(718) 286-6000 .. **Cheung,** Carla L '08 %DA -125-01 Qns Blvd -Kew Gdns 11415
(212) 506-5000 .. **Cheung,** Chi '09 %Orrick H&S LLP -51 W 52nd -NY 10019
(212) 732-7811 .. **Cheung,** Chiu K '95 -17-23 E Bway -NY 10002 **Fx:**732-7828
(212) 323-2299 .. **Cheung,** David C Y '90 Hlth & Hosp Corp -346 Bway -NY 10013
(212) 374-5110 .. **Cheung,** Elizabeth K '02 %NYC Dept Educ -52 Chmbrs -NY 10007
(212) 259-8000 .. **Cheung,** Eric D '10 %Dewey & L LLP -1301 Av of Amer -NY 10019
(516) 605-6634 .. **Cheung,** Linda '98 NMHCRX -26 Hrbr Park Dr -Pt Wash 11050 **Fx:**802-8095
(212) 226-6248 .. **Cheung,** Ronald T '97 (Lee & C,PLLC) -150 Bway -NY 10038
(212) 558-4000 .. **Cheung,** Rosita '79 %Sullivan & C LLP -125 Broad -NY 10004
(212) 239-4001 .. **Cheung,** Thos L '08 %Rheem & B LLP -302 5th Av -NY 10001 **Fx:**239-4125
(646) 837-0100 .. **Chevalier,** Carol Lee '89 (Wenick & F,PC) -28 E 28th -NY 10016
(212) 218-2100 .. **Chevalier,** Chas H '05 %Fitzpatrick CH&S -1290 Av of Amer -NY 10104
(518) 474-8241 .. **Chevalier,** Michele Viger '93 %OCFS -52 Wshngtn -Rensselaer 12144 **Fx:**486-6361
(212) 577-3658 .. **Chevalier,** Rebecca '07 %Leg Aid -199 Water -NY 10038
(718) 875-1300 .. **Chevat,** Alan '78 %Appllt Div 2nd Dept -45 Monroe Pl -Brklyn 11201 **Fx:**858-2446
(212) 809-7600 .. **Cheven,** Barbara A '73 (Cheven K&H) -40 Wall -NY 10005
(212) 809-7600 .. **Cheven,** Candice Starr '94 %Cheven K&H -40 Wall -NY 10005
(212) 809-7600 .. **Cheven Keely & Hatzis** -40 Wall -NY 10005 **Fx:**809-4793
(914) 949-2909 .. **Cheverko,** Geraldine A '02 %Eckert SC&M,LLC -10 Bank -White Plns 10606
(212) 969-3000 .. **Chevlowe,** Roberta K '91 SrCnsl Proskauer R LLP -1585 Bway -NY 10036
(718) 232-0052 .. **Chevtsov,** Vladimir '01 -32 Av O -Brklyn 11204 **Fx:**234-5925
(212) 720-5026 .. **Chew,** Denley Y '94 %Fed Reserve Bk -33 Lbrty -NY 10045 **Fx:**785-5748
(212) 878-7900 .. **Chew,** Elizabeth A '08 %Fox R LLP -100 Park Av -NY 10017
(212) 972-1000 .. **Chew,** Emily '05 %London F LLP -59 Maiden Ln -NY 10038
(518) 640-5144 .. **Chew,** Eric M '83 AYCO -25 British Amer Blvd -Latham 12110
(212) 361-7996 .. **Chew,** Rebecca D '02 %Dept Homeless Srvcs -33 Beaver -NY 10004 **Fx:**361-8002
(212) 556-5600 .. **Cheyette,** Herbert '58 %ICM -825 8th Av -NY 10019 **Fx:**556-5665
(718) 286-6000 .. **Chheda,** Ajay D '08 %DA -125-01 Qns Blvd -Kew Gdns 11415
(212) 326-3939 .. **Chheda,** Jennifer J '03 OfCnsl Jones D -222 E 41st -NY 10017
(212) 503-2100 .. **Chhim,** Viravyne '07 GSO Captl Ptnrs -280 Park Av -NY 10017 **Fx:**503-6930
(518) 449-0044 .. **Chi,** Elaine '10 %Hoffman W&D LLC -75 State -Albany 12207 **Fx:**449-0047
(212) 761-7634 .. **Chia,** Donny '09 Morgan Stanley -1585 Bway -NY 10036
(716) 648-3030 .. **Chiacchia,** Danl J '89 (Chiacchia & F,LLP) -5113 S Park Av -Hambrg 14075
(716) 648-3030 .. **Chiacchia & Fleming,LLP** -5113 S Park Av -Hambrg 14075
(631) 368-5698 .. **Chiacchiaro,** Suanne Linder '82 -45 Wintercress Ln -E Northprt 11731 **Fx:**368-2629
(212) 525-4852 .. **Chiafari,** Anthony J Jr. '06 %WTAS -452 5th Av -NY 10018
(718) 238-6900 .. **Chiaino,** Stephen D '96 %L DiGiovanna -357 Bay Ridge Pkwy -Brklyn 11209 **Fx:**921-0753
(716) 630-2400 .. **Chiampou,** Chas W '81 (Chiampou Travis Besaw & Kershner) -45 Bryant Woods N -Buffalo 14228
(212) 547-5400 .. **Chiampou,** Madeline M '06 %McDermott W&E LLP -340 Mad Av -NY 10173
(212) 640-1567 .. **Chiamprasert,** Chatchada '01 AmEx Co -200 Vesey -NY 10285
(516) 599-2020 .. **Chianese,** Albert W '76 (A Chianese & Assoc) -100 Merrick Rd -Rockvll Ctr 11570 **Fx:**599-6476
(718) 762-7452 .. **Chiang,** Chao-Houng '93 -35-18 Farrington -Flushng 11354
(718) 286-6000 .. **Chiang,** David H '01 %DA -125-01 Qns Blvd -Kew Gdns 11415
(212) 998-6730 .. **Chiang,** Emily '02 %Brennan Ctr for Justice -161 Av of Amer -NY 10013
(212) 636-6835 .. **Chiang,** Frank '74 %Fordham Univ Sch of Law -140 W 62nd -NY 10023 **Fx:**636-6899
(212) 250-5317 .. **Chiang,** Grace Y '04 Deutsche Bk Mtg Cptl -60 Wall -NY 10005
(212) 696-6000 .. **Chiang,** Kuang-Chu '01 Cnsl Curtis M-PC&M LLP -101 Park Av -NY 10178
(212) 839-5300 .. **Chiang,** Tun-Yu Esther '10 %Sidley A LLP -787 7th Av -NY 10019
(516) 775-7007 .. **Chiantella,** Jos J '06 %Gutman MB&S,PC -813 Jericho Tpk -New Hyde Pk 11040
(212) 918-3000 .. **Chiappa,** Carl J '79 (Hogan L LLP) -875 3rd Av -NY 10022
(212) 818-9200 .. **Chiappari,** Ted J '93 (Satterlee SB&B LLP) -230 Park Av -NY 10169
(212) 813-5900 .. **Chiappetta,** Michl R '00 Cnsl Fross ZL&Z,PC -866 UN Plz -NY 10017
(212) 850-2800 .. **Chiappetta,** Russell A '03 %Andrews K LLP -450 Lex Av -NY 10017
(585) 464-3650 .. **Chiappinelli,** John A '93 -89 Genesee -Rchstr 14611
(212) 335-9000 .. **Chiara,** John B '07 %DA -1 Hogan Pl -NY 10013
(212) 302-8989 .. **Chiara,** Nicholas P '02 %Hedman & C,PC -1185 Av of Amer -NY 10036
(845) 304-0215 .. **Chiaramonte,** Paul S '93 (P Chiaramonte,LLC) -75A Lk Rd -Congers 10920 **Fx:**268-4634
(212) 827-7130 .. **Chiaramonte,** Philip G '88 %TD Securities -31 W 52nd -NY 10019
(212) 267-0380 .. **Chiaravalloti,** Mariangela '89 (Friedman FC&G) -2 Rector -NY 10006
(212) 464-1282 .. **Chiaravalloti,** Michl J '00 JP Morgan Chase -345 Park Av -NY 10154
(716) 626-3604 .. **Chiaravalloti,** Paul A '86 -300 Intl Dr -Williamsvll 14221
(212) 937-4000 .. **Chiarchiaro,** Frank J '77 Fitzpatrick & HTCPA,LLP -12 E 49th -NY 10017
(212) 692-1000 .. **Chiarelli,** Lawr '94 SpclCnsl Duane M LLP -1540 Bway -NY 10036
(718) 923-8400 .. **Chiarelli,** Linda A '88 %Forest City Ratner -1 Metrotech Ctr N -Brklyn 11201 **Fx:**923-8722
(212) 910-6000 .. **Chiarenza,** Rosario '07 Cnsl ISDA -360 Mad Av -NY 10017 **Fx:**910-6001
(716) 681-7190 .. **Chiari,** Donald P '84 (Brown C LLP) -5775 Bway -Lancaster 14086
(716) 838-4300 .. **Chiari,** Gerald '72 (Bulan CH&I) -1320 Millersport Hwy -Williamsvll 14221 **Fx:**204-9728
(516) 801-8100 .. **Chiariello,** Dominic L '91 (Chiariello & C) -147 Glen -Glen Cove 11542
(516) 801-8100 .. **Chiariello,** Gerald '54 (Chiariello & C) -147 Glen -Glen Cove 11542
(516) 801-8100 .. **Chiariello,** Gerald II '95 (Chiariello & C) -147 Glen -Glen Cove 11542
(212) 837-6000 .. **Chiarini,** Lisa A '01 (Hughes H&R LLP) -1 Bttry Pk Plz -NY 10004
(716) 635-0550 .. **Chiarolanza,** David M '72 %Essex Homes -8940 Main -Clarence 14031
(212) 564-9090 .. **Chiatto,** Elizabeth '98 %Altier & V,LLC -450 7th Av -NY 10123
(212) 318-3000 .. **Chiaviello,** Robt M Jr. '80 (Fulbright & J LLP) -666 5th Av -NY 10103
(212) 627-7087 .. **Chibututu,** Ignatius '84 -307 7th Av -NY 10001 **Fx:**627-1416
(518) 372-3300 .. **Chicatelli,** Louis W Jr. '00 (Fazzone F&C,PLLC) -1536 Union -Schnctdy 12309 **Fx:**372-7400
(516) 248-1700 .. **Chicco,** Robt '81 (Forchelli CDSM&T,LLP) -333 Earle Ovngton Blvd -Uniondale 11553
(212) 728-8000 .. **Chich,** Geri A '09 %Willkie F&G LLP -787 7th Av -NY 10019
(212) 259-8000 .. **Chichi,** Francesca Alessandra '05 %Dewey & L LLP -1301 Av of Amer -NY 10019
(212) 319-4900 .. **Chick,** Marshall J '75 (Frishauf HG&C) -220 5th Av -NY 10001
(212) 440-2454 .. **Chick,** Wileen '02 CNA Ins Co -40 Wall -NY 10005
(516) 671-6577 .. **Chiclacos,** Chas J '74 -15 Karen Rd -Glen Cove 11542 **Fx:**801-4634
(516) 832-7538 .. **Chiclacos,** Jessica A '04 %Nixon P LLP -50 Jericho Quadrangle -Jericho 11753
(212) 335-9000 .. **Chicon,** Kerry L '00 %DA -1 Hogan Pl -NY 10013
(212) 259-8000 .. **Chida,** Junaid H '84 (Dewey & L LLP) -1301 Av of Amer -NY 10019
(212) 448-1800 .. **Chidekel,** David H '87 (Roberts RLSC&F LLP) -235 Park Av S -NY 10003
(212) 605-0161 .. **Chidekel,** David M '91 -575 Mad Av -NY 10022 **Fx:**605-0166
(315) 735-7566 .. **Chieco,** Mark O '03 %Petrone & P,PC -1624 Genesee -Utica 13502
(518) 218-7100 .. **Chieco,** Tracy D '04 %Tully R,PLLC -441 New Karner Rd -Albany 12205
(212) 504-6000 .. **Chien,** Andrew C '04 %Cadwalader W&T LLP -1 World Fncl Ctr -NY 10281
(212) 556-2100 .. **Chien,** Jason C '09 %King & S -1185 Av of Amer -NY 10036
(212) 455-2000 .. **Ch'ien,** Kay '07 %Simpson T&B LLP -425 Lex Av -NY 10017
(845) 282-7022 .. **Chiera,** Randall John '88 RJ Chiera & Assoc -20 Church -Carmel 10512 **Fx:**231-0541
(516) 358-7200 .. **Chigirinsky,** Tatyana '10 %Mavrides M & Assoc,LLP -3000 Marcus Av -Lk Success 11042 **Fx:**358-7250
(212) 289-1062 .. **Chikofsky,** Edw M '72 -301 E 87th -NY 10128 **Fx:**369-8823
(212) 335-9000 .. **Chilaka,** Andrea Ngozi '05 %DA -1 Hogan Pl -NY 10013
(212) 723-3807 .. **Childers,** Carol E '98 Citigroup -250 West -NY 10013
(212) 871-1578 .. **Childs,** George L '99 Zurich Alternative Asset Mgmt -105 E 17th -NY 10003
(212) 556-2100 .. **Childs,** Louisa B '06 %King & S -1185 Av of Amer -NY 10036
(914) 946-3444 .. **Childs,** Ronald C '82 Horne & C -399 Knollwood Rd -White Plns 10603
(518) 487-5460 .. **Childs,** Sean T '05 %DA -6 Lodge -Albany 12207 **Fx:**487-5093
(212) 692-8257 .. **Chill,** Adam J '93 %Angelo Gordon & Co -245 Park Av -NY 10167
(212) 818-8800 .. **Chill,** C Danl '61 (Graubard M) -405 Lex Av -NY 10174
(212) 907-7300 .. **Chill,** Steven G '82 (Golenbock EAB&P) -437 Mad Av -NY 10022
(212) 617-5924 .. **Chiller,** Andrea J '03 Bloomberg LP -731 Lex Av -NY 10022
(212) 722-4900 .. **Chilliest,** Anthony S '95 (Donaldson C&M,LLP) -1825 Park Av -NY 10035
(212) 564-7560 .. **Chillino,** Gregory T '98 S Klein -99 Mad Av -NY 10016 **Fx:**564-7845
(212) 878-8000 .. **Chilstrom,** Per Benjamin '01 %Clifford C LLP -31 W 52nd -NY 10019
(212) 735-3000 .. **Chilstrom,** Robt M '75 (Skadden ASM&F LLP) -4 Times Sq -NY 10036
(516) 867-7747 .. **Chimeri,** Wm F '81 -113 W Sunrise Hwy -Freeprt 11520 **Fx:**867-1187
(716) 854-4705 .. **Chimes,** Deborah Ann '90 Lippman O -300 Pearl -Buffalo 14202
(212) 682-6800 .. **Chimos,** Bill P '99 (Zetlin & D LLP) -801 2nd Av -NY 10017
(646) 265-1468 .. **Chin,** Albert '92 (Pollack,PC) -132 E 43rd -NY 10017 **Fx:**253-1276
(212) 969-3000 .. **Chin,** Bettina M '10 Proskauer R LLP -1585 Bway -NY 10036 **Fx:**969-2900
(212) 878-1037 .. **Chin,** Ching Wah '91 MTA -347 Mad Av -NY 10017
(212) 267-7895 .. **Chin,** Chris Chou '98 %Boquen Realty -31 Catherine -NY 10038
(646) 392-9250 .. **Chin,** Christopher '95 %M Klein & Assoc -200 Mad Av -NY 10016 **Fx:**(212) 779-1499
(212) 237-1000 .. **Chin,** Christopher L '87 SpclCnsl Windels ML&M,LLP -156 W 56th -NY 10019
(646) 428-3900 .. **Chin,** Coleen '00 %Dept of Educ -32 Old Slip -NY 10005 **Fx:**428-3890
(212) 508-6700 .. **Chin,** Danica '04 %Tannenbaum HS&H LLP -900 3rd Av -NY 10022
(212) 331-5908 .. **Chin,** David T '84 HRA Child Support Litgtn -180 Water -NY 10038
(212) 515-4659 .. **Chin,** De Wayne '92 Fortress Invstmt Grp LLC -1345 Av of Amer -NY 10105
(212) 326-3939 .. **Chin,** Dickson C '99 (Jones D) -222 E 41st -NY 10017
(212) 852-3884 .. **Chin,** Donald J '97 %US Trust Co,NA -114 W 47th -NY 10036 **Fx:**852-3852
(718) 250-2000 .. **Chin,** Ernest G '06 DA -350 Jay -Brklyn 11201 **Fx:**250-2314
(718) 780-7597 .. **Chin,** Francis H '01 Bklyn Law Schl -250 Joralemon -Brklyn 11201 **Fx:**780-0368
(914) 762-1595 .. **Chin,** Hazel F '88 -1 Mancuso Dr -Ossining 10562 **Fx:**923-3129
(212) 676-6208 .. **Chin,** Ilene '84 %Business Integrity Comm -100 Church -NY 10007 **Fx:**676-6204
(212) 219-3360 .. **Chin,** Jackson '87 %Latino Justice PRLDEF -99 Hudson -NY 10013 **Fx:**431-4276
(212) 493-7593 .. **Chin,** James Y '92 %NYC Chamber of Commerce -1 Bttry Pk Plz -NY 10004
(718) 321-7785 .. **Chin,** Jenifer M '89 -13620 Roosevelt Av -Flushng 11354 **Fx:**321-7736
(212) 538-8077 .. **Chin,** Jennifer R '02 Credit Suisse -11 Mad Av -NY 10010
(631) 247-0404 .. **Chin,** K Joy '91 (Jackson L LLP) -58 S Srvc Rd -Melvll 11747
(212) 504-6000 .. **Chin,** Kathy H '81 (Cadwalader W&T LLP) -1 World Fncl Ctr -NY 10281
(212) 715-9100 .. **Chin,** Kenneth '88 (Kramer LN&F,LLP) -1177 Av of Amer -NY 10036

(212) 965-0569 .. **Chin,** Kenneth '94 -401 Bway -NY 10013 **Fx:**625-1731
(212) 756-2000 .. **Chin,** Kirby '96 (Schulte R&Z LLP) -919 3rd Av -NY 10022
(516) 822-3550 .. **Chin,** Linda Dione '06 %Hoffmann & B LLP -6900 Jericho Tpk -Syosset 11791 **Fx:**822-3582
(718) 990-7457 .. **Chin,** Linda T '87 St John's Univ -8000 Utopia Pkwy -Jamaica 11439 **Fx:**591-1855
(212) 701-3000 .. **Chin,** Matthew J '08 %Cahill G&R LLP -80 Pine -NY 10005 **Fx:**269-5420
(845) 340-7617 .. **Chin,** May Kin-Yu '93 %DEP -71 Smith Av -Kingston 12401 **Fx:**340-7564
(516) 747-4082 .. **Chin,** Michl K '94 %Montfort HM&S LLP -1140 Franklin Av Bx7677 -Gdn Cty 11530
(917) 421-4626 .. **Chin,** Michl Y '09 IRS -33 Maiden Ln -NY 10038
(718) 321-7000 .. **Chin,** Michelle A '07 %Shih & F -136-20 38th Av -Flushng 11354 **Fx:**762-7679
(212) 417-3700 .. **Chin,** Natalie M '05 %MFY Legal Srvcs -299 Bway -NY 10007 **Fx:**417-3890
(212) 270-4409 .. **Chin,** Peter '99 JP Morgan Chase & Co -270 Park Av -NY 10017
(212) 406-2240 .. **Chin,** Raymond W M '89 -305 Bway -NY 10007 **Fx:**406-2271
(212) 621-7761 .. **Chin,** Rockwell J '84 -Bx674 -NY 10008 **Fx:**233-5231
(212) 536-3900 .. **Chin,** Sophia J '98 %K&L Gates LLP -599 Lex Av -NY 10022
(212) 514-8645 .. **Chin,** Stephen M '95 (Von Simson & C) -62 William -NY 10005 **Fx:**514-8648
(212) 836-8000 .. **Chin,** Steven C '06 %Kaye S LLP -425 Park Av -NY 10022
(212) 506-1700 .. **Chin,** Steven D '98 SpclCnsl Kasowitz BT&F LLP -1633 Bway -NY 10019
(212) 819-8200 .. **Chin,** Sylvia Fung '78 (White & C LLP) -1155 Av of Amer -NY 10036
(212) 864-4445 .. **Chinaud,** Juliette Y C '02 OfCnsl Stevens H&W,PC -116 W 111th -NY 10026
(718) 526-2900 .. **Chinboukas,** Bessie '92 -147-32 Jamaica Av -Jamaica 11435 **Fx:**526-4600
(212) 326-3939 .. **Chin Eng,** Catharina J '95 %Jones D -222 E 41st -NY 10017
(917) 685-9399 .. **Ching,** Adriana A C '05 -220 Riverside Blvd -NY 10069
(212) 655-3500 .. **Ching,** Cassandra A T '07 %Meister S&F LLP -140 E 45th -NY 10017
(212) 474-1000 .. **Ching,** Chas Y '04 %Cravath S&M LLP -825 8th Av -NY 10019
(212) 696-6000 .. **Ching,** Dienna '09 %Curtis M-PC&M LLP -101 Park Av -NY 10178
(212) 373-3000 .. **Ching,** Ellen N '08 %Paul WRW&G LLP -1285 Av of Amer -NY 10019
(212) 335-9000 .. **Ching,** Emily C '05 %DA -1 Hogan Pl -NY 10013
(212) 735-3000 .. **Ching,** George '08 %Skadden ASM&F LLP -4 Times Sq -NY 10036
(212) 834-3265 .. **Ching,** Jonathan J '04 JP Morgan Chase Bk -270 Park Av -NY 10017
(718) 238-8787 .. **Ching,** Leslie D '87 -8778 Bay Pkwy -Brklyn 11214
(212) 465-8840 .. **Chinigo,** Dario A '96 %Hofmann & S -360 W 31st -NY 10001 **Fx:**465-8849
(212) 885-5000 .. **Chinitz,** Marilyn B '82 (Blank R LLP) -405 Lex Av -NY 10174
(212) 599-1515 .. **Chinitz,** Mark I '84 OfCnsl Stein RM,LLP -405 Lex Av -NY 10174
(718) 824-6500 .. **Chinitz,** Michl A '80 (Coiro WC&S) -1206 Castle Hill Av -Bronx 10462
(212) 246-2400 .. **Chinitz,** Stanley A '88 (Balber PM&VDT,PC) -1370 Av of Amer -NY 10019
(718) 625-2200 .. **Chin-Kee-Fatt,** Camille '90 Bklyn Law Schl -250 Joralemon -Brklyn 11201 **Fx:**780-0393
(212) 380-2650 .. **Chinn,** Adam D '88 Centerview Ptnrs LLC -640 5th Av -NY 10019 **Fx:**380-2651
(212) 626-4100 .. **Chinn,** Christopher K '05 %Baker & M LLP -1114 Av of Amer -NY 10036
(212) 969-3000 .. **Chinn,** Lloyd B '97 (Proskauer R LLP) -1585 Bway -NY 10036
(212) 261-9408 .. **Chinn,** Samantha Niele '98 NY Life Ins Co -120 Bway -NY 10271
(212) 430-6491 .. **Chin-Nobile,** Lorna L '94 -65 Bway -NY 10006 **Fx:**430-6492
(631) 643-8438 .. **Chin Quee,** Michelle T '01 -1940 Deer Prk Av -Deer Pk 11729 **Fx:**643-1011
(212) 416-8000 .. **Chinta,** Padmaja '01 %Dept of Law -120 Bway -NY 10271
(212) 848-4000 .. **Chinwuba,** Emeka C '07 %Shearman & S LLP -599 Lex Av -NY 10022
(914) 761-1300 .. **Chiocchio,** Lucia '02 %Cuddy & F LLP -445 Hmltn Av -White Plns 10601
(212) 325-6724 .. **Chiodi,** Maria '95 %Credit Suisse First Boston -1 Mad Av -NY 10010
(212) 922-6754 .. **Chioffi,** Jos '00 Dreyfus -200 Park Av -NY 10166
(718) 505-6650 .. **Chiofolo,** Thos L '90 %Kaplan & M -75-20 Astoria Blvd -E Elmhrst 11370
(516) 571-3800 .. **Chionchio,** Anthony M '07 %DA -262 Old Cntry Rd -Mineola 11501 **Fx:**248-9479
(516) 921-8600 .. **Chionchio,** Nadia M '07 %McAndrew C&P -95 Froehlich Farm Blvd -Woodbury 11797
(212) 384-1000 .. **Chios,** James N '02 %FBI -26 Fed Plz -NY 10278
(212) 310-8000 .. **Chiperfield,** Robt N Jr. '91 (Weil G&M LLP) -767 5th Av -NY 10153
(516) 229-4300 .. **Chipkin,** Laia C '01 %J Bilello & Assoc -875 Merrick Av -Westbury 11590
(516) 248-2234 .. **Chipkin,** Leonard B '87 %Sackstein S&L,LLP -1140 Franklin Av -Gdn Cty 11530
(212) 355-9500 .. **Chiplock,** Danl P '01 (Lieff CH&B,LLP) -250 Hudson -NY 10013
(212) 826-7179 .. **Chira,** Robt '68 (R Chira & Assoc) -488 Mad Av -NY 10022 **Fx:**486-0701
(212) 747-9370 .. **Chirayilparambu,** Govind M '04 %Rasul & Assoc,LLC -110 Wall -NY 10005
(212) 859-8000 .. **Chirco,** Michele J '10 %Fried FHS&J LLP -1 NY Plz -NY 10004
(315) 252-1563 .. **Chirco,** Norman J '87 -95 Genesee -Auburn 13021 **Fx:**255-2434
(716) 856-5012 .. **Chiriboga,** J Christine '94 %Anspach ME,LLP -2400 Main Pl Twr -Buffalo 14202
(516) 931-8100 .. **Chirichigno,** Brian G '08 %Capell BM&S,LLP -100 Jericho Quadrangle -Jericho 11753
(518) 589-9765 .. **Chirico,** Guy W '87 -237 Main Bx67 -Tannersvll 12485
(212) 779-8600 .. **Chirico,** Vincent '94 (Silverman SS&B PLLC) -381 Park Av S -NY 10016
(212) 848-4000 .. **Chirita,** Laura R '08 %Shearman & S LLP -599 Lex Av -NY 10022
(212) 351-4000 .. **Chirlin,** Danl '07 %Gibson D&C LLP -200 Park Av -NY 10166
(212) 506-5000 .. **Chirls,** Richd '77 (Orrick H&S LLP) -51 W 52nd -NY 10019
(516) 280-2281 .. **Chisari,** Louis F '00 (Marcote & Assoc,PC) -403 Merrick Av -E Meadow 11554 **Fx:**280-2283
(631) 472-1562 .. **Chisari,** Thos V '73 -223 Gainsboro Rd -Holbrook 11741
(212) 992-8844 .. **Chishti,** Muzaffar A '83 %NYU Law Schl Migration Policy Inst -245 Sullivan -NY 10012 **Fx:**995-4031
(212) 455-2000 .. **Chisling,** Brian E '02 SrCnsl Simpson T&B LLP -425 Lex Av -NY 10017
(518) 462-3000 .. **Chisolm,** Laurie K '82 %Iseman CR&H,LLP -9 Thurlow Ter -Albany 12203
(516) 249-3450 .. **Chitalia,** Santosh N '09 %Carman C&I,LLP -266 Main -Farmngdl 11735
(212) 903-9000 .. **Chithran,** Sheila J '09 %Linklaters -1345 Av of Amer -NY 10105
(212) 370-0447 .. **Chittur,** Krishnan S '86 Chittur & Assoc,PC -285 Mad Av -NY 10017 **Fx:**370-0465
(212) 735-3000 .. **Chitwood,** Christopher M '04 %Skadden ASM&F LLP -4 Times Sq -NY 10036
(516) 773-6090 .. **Chitwood Harley Harnes LLP** -185 Grt Nck Rd -Gt Neck 11021 **Fx:**(888) 873-3999
(718) 445-7580 .. **Chiu,** Allen P '78 -142-03 37th Av -Flushng 11354
(212) 402-1131 .. **Chiu,** Christopher T '00 NY Cares -214 W 29th -NY 10001
(212) 297-5800 .. **Chiu,** Conrad K '99 Cnsl Day P LLP -7 Times Sq -NY 10036
(212) 788-1158 .. **Chiu,** Danl '98 %Law Dept -100 Church -NY 10007 **Fx:**788-0367
(212) 417-3700 .. **Chiu,** Donna '06 %MFY Legal Srvcs -299 Bway -NY 10007 **Fx:**417-3890
(718) 990-6657 .. **Chiu,** Elaine M '95 %St John's Law Schl -8000 Utopia Pkwy -Jamaica 11439 **Fx:**591-1855
(212) 230-8800 .. **Chiu,** Eugene '09 %WilmerHale -399 Park Av -NY 10022
(212) 385-1500 .. **Chiu,** Franklin K '00 %H Mo,PC -225 Bway -NY 10007 **Fx:**385-1870
(917) 418-2553 .. **Chiu,** Harry '96 -54 Florence -Staten Isl 10308 **Fx:**(718) 227-2095
(212) 761-4000 .. **Chiu,** Iris Yee-Ching '99 %Morgan Stanley -1585 Bway -NY 10036
(718) 883-8125 .. **Chiu,** Maria J '84 %Leg Aid -153-01 Jamaica Av -Jamaica 11432 **Fx:**657-0537
(212) 450-4000 .. **Chiu,** Ning Shyh '96 Cnsl Davis P&W LLP -450 Lex Av -NY 10017
(212) 619-3329 .. **Chiu,** Peter F '83 -17 E Bway -NY 10002 **Fx:**962-6064
(718) 701-5511 .. **Chiu,** Phoebe Hui-Ying '97 (PH Chiu & Assoc,PLLC) -87-08 Justice Av -Elmhrst 11373 **Fx:**(347) 374-8450
(212) 839-5300 .. **Chiu,** Victor T '98 %Sidley A LLP -787 7th Av -NY 10019
(212) 225-2000 .. **Chiu,** Victor Y '02 %Cleary GS&H -1 Lbrty Plz -NY 10006
(212) 388-3600 .. **Chiu,** Viven Yih-Wen '97 32B-J Leg Srvcs -101 Av of Amer -NY 10013 **Fx:**388-3061
(617) 733-4591 .. **Chiungos,** Byron D '03 -131 W 86th -NY 10024
(212) 769-6589 .. **Chiusano,** Brian S '04 Prudential-Douglas Elliman -1995 Bway -NY 10023
(212) 541-2000 .. **Chivate,** Madhura J '08 %Bryan C LLP -1290 Av of Amer -NY 10104
(212) 310-8000 .. **Chivers,** Corey R '92 (Weil G&M LLP) -767 5th Av -NY 10153
(607) 723-5341 .. **Chivers,** James L '67 (Hinman H&K,LLP) -80 Exchange Bx5250 -Bnghmtn 13902
(518) 238-4339 .. **Chivers,** Matthew L '02 %OCA -187 Wolf Rd -Albany 12205 **Fx:**438-3518
(212) 962-2626 .. **Chivily,** Nicholas A '90 -111 Bway -NY 10006
(914) 287-7680 .. **Chivily,** Nicholas J '86 (Mayo C LLC) -600 N Bway -White Plns 10603 **Fx:**287-7685
(718) 522-3814 .. **Chiwaya-Sibande,** Henry F '88 -66 Bond -Brklyn 11217
(212) 310-8000 .. **Chizzik,** Andrew I '05 %Weil G&M LLP -767 5th Av -NY 10153
(212) 483-9490 .. **Chkolnikova,** Elena '05 %McElroy DM&C,LLP -88 Pine -NY 10005
(212) 855-0481 .. **Chlapowski,** Francis Stefan '91 Goldman Sachs -1 NY Plz -NY 10004
(518) 286-5000 .. **Chlastawa,** Allan F '98 -62 Indn Pipe Dr -Wynantskill 12198 **Fx:**286-2500
(212) 450-4000 .. **Chlipala,** Jason A '10 %Davis P&W LLP -450 Lex Av -NY 10017
(212) 335-4500 .. **Chludzinski,** Gregory T '09 %DLA Piper LLP -1251 Av of Amer -NY 10020
(212) 532-9736 .. **Chlupsa,** Jaime L '05 %R Skyer & Assoc,LLP -276 5th Av -NY 10001 **Fx:**532-9846
(716) 852-3600 .. **Chmiel,** Michl J '00 %Chelus HS&M,PC -438 Main -Buffalo 14202
(212) 940-8800 .. **Chmil,** Bonnie L '05 %Katten MR LLP -575 Mad Av -NY 10022
(718) 726-9700 .. **Chmura,** Eugene E '91 -14-47 Bway -Astoria 11106 **Fx:**726-4189
(212) 454-2568 .. **Chmura,** Lisa L '98 Deutsche Bank -280 Park Av -NY 10017
(212) 906-1200 .. **Chmura,** Meaghan Blaine '05 %Latham & W -885 3rd Av -NY 10022
(212) 819-8200 .. **Cho,** Adela K H '08 %White & C LLP -1155 Av of Amer -NY 10036
(212) 967-1001 .. **Cho,** Alice Y '05 %J Cho -1220 Bway -NY 10001 **Fx:**967-1112
(212) 837-8918 .. **Cho,** Ann S '00 -522 5th Av -NY 10036
(212) 715-9100 .. **Cho,** Dannie '09 %Kramer LN&F,LLP -1177 Av of Amer -NY 10036
(212) 683-5136 .. **Cho,** David '90 %Top Fashion Trading Co -53 W 28th -NY 10001
(212) 719-8356 .. **Cho,** David P '03 NYS Society of CPAs -530 5th Av -NY 10036
(212) 947-3330 .. **Cho,** Dean T '89 (Tuan & C,LLP) -225 Bway -NY 10007
(212) 735-3000 .. **Cho,** Edgar '09 %Skadden ASM&F LLP -4 Times Sq -NY 10036
(212) 704-6000 .. **Cho,** Elizabeth Yoona '05 %Troutman S LLP -405 Lex Av -NY 10174
(631) 853-4161 .. **Cho,** Eun K '06 %DA -N Cnty Cmplx Bldg 77 -Hauppauge 11788 **Fx:**853-4192
(212) 878-0069 .. **Cho,** Gregory D '00 %MTA -2 Penn Plz -NY 10121
(212) 661-8000 .. **Cho,** Hyun Soon '05 %Lucas & M,LLP -475 Park Av S -NY 10016
(212) 454-2568 .. **Cho,** Jaiho '00 Standard & Poor's -55 Water -NY 10041
(718) 254-6519 .. **Cho,** James R '05 %US Atty -271 Cadman Plz E -Brklyn 11201 **Fx:**254-6479
(212) 218-5500 .. **Cho,** Jay W '07 %Seyfarth S LLP -620 8th Av -NY 10018
(212) 702-3705 .. **Cho,** Jean M '96 %Sirius America -120 W 45th -NY 10036
(212) 753-5000 .. **Cho,** Jeanne '05 %Schiff H LLP -900 3rd Av -NY 10022
(718) 353-2699 .. **Cho,** Jin D '04 -13656 39th Av -Flushng 11354
(212) 825-1565 .. **Cho,** Julie '00 %Ptashnik & Assoc -45 Bway -NY 10006 **Fx:**825-1559
(212) 839-5300 .. **Cho,** Linda '05 %Sidley A LLP -787 7th Av -NY 10019
(212) 909-6000 .. **Cho,** Margaret G '09 %Debevoise & P LLP -919 3rd Av -NY 10022
(212) 909-6000 .. **Cho,** Mark S '07 %Debevoise & P LLP -919 3rd Av -NY 10022
(516) 684-9897 .. **Cho,** Mukang '00 Crown Street Capital,LLC -300 Nrthrn Blvd -Gt Neck 11021
(212) 259-8000 .. **Cho,** Roy D '10 %Dewey & L LLP -1301 Av of Amer -NY 10019

(212) 610-9000 .. **Cho,** Stephen P '98 Reservoir Cptl Grp -650 Mad Av -NY 10022
(212) 310-8000 .. **Cho,** Su-Yeon '06 %Weil G&M LLP -767 5th Av -NY 10153
(212) 268-3607 .. **Cho,** Sukjin Henry '88 (Pak & C,PC) -230 Park Av -NY 10169 **Fx:**(201) 886-0111
(212) 779-7770 .. **Cho,** Tai Y '82 -445 5th Av -NY 10016 **Fx:**779-7862
(212) 487-4166 .. **Cho,** Y David '06 Dept Cnsmr Affrs -42 Bway -NY 10004 **Fx:**487-4197
(212) 643-2828 .. **Chobor,** John J L '90 %GNYHCFA -360 W 31st -NY 10001 **Fx:**643-2956
(516) 486-4600 .. **Chocron,** Miriam '03 %Bendik & N -250 Fulton Av -Hempstd 11550
(212) 407-7348 .. **Chodkowski,** Adam P '99 Swiss Re Products -55 E 52nd -NY 10055
(212) 792-7600 .. **Chodos,** Justin P '04 Peak Counsel,Inc -25 W 31st -NY 10001
(716) 597-7440 .. **Chodos,** Linda W '94 -4511 Harlem Rd -Buffalo 14226
(212) 227-5018 .. **Chodosh,** Bernard '58 -120 Duane -NY 10007 **Fx:**385-0266
(212) 858-4771 .. **Chodosh,** Gary A '88 FINRA -1 Lbrty Plz -NY 10006 **Fx:**858-4389
(212) 334-9556 .. **Chodosh,** Loren '83 L Chodosh,PC -18 Harrison -NY 10013 **Fx:**334-9771
(212) 975-6961 .. **Chodosh,** Reuben '93 %CBS -524 W 57th -NY 10019
(212) 816-0716 .. **Choe,** Anna Hajin '99 Citigroup Global Mrkts,Inc -388 Greenwich -NY 10013
(212) 969-3000 .. **Choe,** Carol S '10 %Proskauer R LLP -1585 Bway -NY 10036
(212) 213-4400 .. **Choe,** Jane K '01 -1261 Bway -NY 10001
(212) 504-6000 .. **Choe,** Jennifer '08 %Cadwalader W&T LLP -1 World Fncl Ctr -NY 10281
(212) 696-5710 .. **Choe,** Jerry '93 -34 W 27th -NY 10001 **Fx:**696-5833
(212) 230-8800 .. **Choe,** Julie H '08 WilmerHale -399 Park Av -NY 10022
(212) 447-7220 .. **Choe,** KiYoung Peter '89 (Choe & O,PC) -15 E 32nd -NY 10016 **Fx:**447-0968
(212) 225-2000 .. **Choe,** Shiwon '08 %Cleary GS&H -1 Lbrty Plz -NY 10006
(914) 576-5000 .. **Choe Friedman,** Chong Alexandra '99 Simone Devlpmnt -1000 Main -New Rchll 10801
(212) 859-8000 .. **Choi,** Alice Won Jung '05 %Fried FHS&J LLP -1 NY Plz -NY 10004
(212) 334-5346 .. **Choi,** Andy H '95 -55 Chrystie -NY 10002 **Fx:**334-0278
(212) 450-4000 .. **Choi,** Boyoon '09 %Davis P&W LLP -450 Lex Av -NY 10017
(212) 455-2000 .. **Choi,** Chang Won '09 %Simpson T&B LLP -425 Lex Av -NY 10017
(212) 506-1700 .. **Choi,** Charlene '09 %Kasowitz BT&F LLP -1633 Bway -NY 10019
(212) 836-8000 .. **Choi,** Christopher S '06 %Kaye S LLP -425 Park Av -NY 10022
(212) 478-0000 .. **Choi,** David '05 DE Shaw & Co -120 W 45th -NY 10036 **Fx:**478-0100
(516) 222-2230 .. **Choi,** David '09 %Burkhart W&H,LLP -585 Stewart Av -Gdn Cty 11530
(914) 285-9800 .. **Choi,** David Y '00 %Kurzman EC&L,LLP -1 N Bway -White Plns 10601
(212) 728-8000 .. **Choi,** Dong Hyuk '09 %Willkie F&G LLP -787 7th Av -NY 10019
(201) 592-7710 .. **Choi,** E Sandy '05 ES Choi,LLC -292 Mad Av -NY 10017 **Fx:**592-7107
(718) 613-2490 .. **Choi,** Eun Young '07 Ct of Appls 2nd Circ -225 Cadman Plz E -Brklyn 11201
(212) 925-4759 .. **Choi,** Gavin M '84 -109 Lafayette -NY 10013 **Fx:**941-1330
(516) 488-3300 .. **Choi,** Gilbert H '99 %Shaub AC&S,LLP -1983 Marcus Av -Lk Success 11042
(212) 858-7700 .. **Choi,** Hailey '07 %Budd L -140 Bway -NY 10005
(212) 916-5647 .. **Choi,** Hye-Won '90 %TIAA-CREF -730 3rd Av -NY 10017
(718) 321-8586 .. **Choi,** Hyuck Bai '93 -4522 162nd -Flushng 11358
(631) 547-0300 .. **Choi,** Jakyung '10 %Novick & Assoc,PC -202 E Main -Huntngtn 11743 **Fx:**547-0212
(212) 848-4000 .. **Choi,** Janet C '10 %Shearman & S LLP -599 Lex Av -NY 10022
(516) 741-6565 .. **Choi,** Jayson J R '92 %Meyer SE&K,PC -990 Stewart Av Bx9194 -Gdn Cty 11530
(212) 468-8000 .. **Choi,** Jinyoung '10 %Morrison & F LLP -1290 Av of Amer -NY 10104
(212) 949-9022 .. **Choi,** John H '04 %Abelman F&S -666 3rd Av -NY 10017
(212) 325-5352 .. **Choi,** Jos '04 Credit Suisse -11 Mad Av -NY 10010
(212) 969-3000 .. **Choi,** Jos Y '03 %Proskauer R LLP -1585 Bway -NY 10036
(518) 664-1840 .. **Choi,** Joyce Serbalik '94 -44 N Main -Mechanicvll 12118 **Fx:**664-1806
(718) 658-0500 .. **Choi,** Justin '08 %Law Dept -151-20 Jamaica Av -Jamaica 11432 **Fx:**658-4025
(212) 326-3939 .. **Choi,** Kathleen J '09 %Jones D -222 E 41st -NY 10017
(212) 762-3337 .. **Choi,** Kenneth '98 Morgan Stanley -750 7th Av -NY 10019 **Fx:**507-3709
(212) 848-4000 .. **Choi,** Kwang-Duk '09 %Shearman & S LLP -599 Lex Av -NY 10022
(212) 808-7800 .. **Choi,** Marie E '08 %Kelley D&W LLP -101 Park Av -NY 10178
(718) 463-3500 .. **Choi,** Michl Hyungmoo '91 -36-09 Main -Flushng 11354 **Fx:**463-8297
(646) 315-7300 .. **Choi,** Michl S '98 %FINRA -14 Wall -NY 10005 **Fx:**315-7440
(973) 315-4423 .. **Choi,** Michl W '02 %Budd L -140 Bway -NY 10005
(516) 688-1700 .. **Choi,** Nina E '06 IRS -1600 Stewart Av -Westbury 11590 **Fx:**688-1750
(212) 823-3121 .. **Choi,** Pil Sun '03 Alliance Bernstein LP -1345 Av of Amer -NY 10105 **Fx:**554-4639
(212) 836-8000 .. **Choi,** Richd '08 %Kaye S LLP -425 Park Av -NY 10022
(212) 728-8000 .. **Choi,** S J Robin '01 %Willkie F&G LLP -787 7th Av -NY 10019
(212) 219-6000 .. **Choi,** Sandy Suh-Moon '01 Tower Rsrch Cptl LLC -377 Bway -NY 10013
(212) 837-6000 .. **Choi,** Selyn '09 %Hughes H&R LLP -1 Bttry Pk Plz -NY 10004
(212) 458-1038 .. **Choi,** Seon Young '95 %AIG -175 Water -NY 10038
(212) 806-5400 .. **Choi,** Sharon H '10 %Stroock &S&L LLP -180 Maiden Ln -NY 10038
(718) 460-5600 .. **Choi,** Steven K '05 YKASEC -136-19 41st Av -Flushng 11355
(212) 318-6000 .. **Choi,** Sung Ho '08 %Paul HJ&W LLP -75 E 55th -NY 10022
(212) 696-1201 .. **Choi,** Tae Ethan '07 OfCnsl ML Pfeifer,PC -350 Old Cntry Rd -Gdn Cty 11530
(718) 224-0888 .. **Choi,** Thos '97 (Choi & S,PLLC) -38-39 Bell Blvd -Bayside 11361 **Fx:**224-0868
(212) 661-7300 .. **Choi,** Won Jong '98 %Malapero & P LLP -295 Mad Av -NY 10017
(718) 888-7774 .. **Choi,** Yohan '02 -15408 Nrthrn Blvd -Flushng 11354
(212) 216-1657 .. **Choi,** Yon K '04 SL Green Realty Corp -420 Lex Av -NY 10170
(718) 939-0200 .. **Choi,** Youngsoo '01 (Sung & C,PC) -38-12 150th -Flushng 11354 **Fx:**939-2179
(212) 697-3122 .. **Choi,** Younie '05 %Martin C&B LLP -220 E 42nd -NY 10017
(212) 450-4000 .. **Choi,** Yun Jung '08 %Davis P&W LLP -450 Lex Av -NY 10017
(718) 460-2512 .. **Choi,** Yunsung '03 (Y Choi,PC) -3625 Union -Flushng 11354 **Fx:**460-1240
(212) 788-1159 .. **Choi-Hausman,** Susan '96 %Law Dept -100 Church -NY 10007 **Fx:**788-0367
(516) 571-3800 .. **Choinski,** Michelle '07 %DA -262 Old Cntry Rd -Mineola 11501 **Fx:**248-9479
(212) 513-7788 .. **Chojnacki,** Thos G '93 %Ahmuty D&M -123 William -NY 10038
(212) 609-6800 .. **Chokshi,** Sanjiv M '00 %McCarter & E,LLP -245 Park Av -NY 10167
(212) 237-0000 .. **Cholak,** Lyndsey R '08 %Vinson & E LLP -666 5th Av -NY 10103
(518) 402-6969 .. **Cholakis,** George N '90 %Envrnmtl Facilities -625 Bway -Albany 12207 **Fx:**402-6972
(518) 274-0766 .. **Cholakis,** Gregory D '93 -514 Grand -Troy 12180 **Fx:**274-0945
(518) 286-3063 .. **Cholakis,** Nia C '89 -7 Coyote Ln -Troy 12180 **Fx:**286-3065
(212) 490-3000 .. **Cholewa,** Ilysa W '03 %Wilson EME&D LLP -150 E 42nd -NY 10017
(212) 480-3030 .. **Cholewa,** Stuart B '04 %M Pressman -125 Maiden Ln -NY 10038 **Fx:**480-2590
(212) 687-7770 .. **Cholst,** Bruce A '78 (Rosen L&C LLP) -275 Mad Av -NY 10016
(212) 626-1181 .. **Chomsky,** Maryellen '81 %Bank Leumi USA -562 5th Av -NY 10036 **Fx:**626-1195
(516) 446-5515 .. **Chon,** El Woong '00 -11 Northen Blvd -Gt Neck 11021
(212) 816-2182 .. **Chon,** Song Won '96 Citigroup Alternative Invstmnts -388 Greenwich -NY 10013
(212) 274-8001 .. **Chong,** Chak C '93 -80 Bowery -NY 10013 **Fx:**274-8196
(212) 259-8000 .. **Chong,** Jonathan J-M '08 %Dewey & L LLP -1301 Av of Amer -NY 10019
(212) 681-0600 .. **Chong,** Leighton K '75 OfCnsl Ostrager CF&B,PC -570 Lex Av -NY 10022
(212) 468-4800 .. **Chong,** Wendy K '09 %Davis & G LLP -1740 Bway -NY 10019
(212) 986-6000 .. **Chonoles,** Andrew M '88 (Kleinberg KW&C,PC) -551 5th Av -NY 10176
(212) 574-1200 .. **Choo,** Aileen Y '08 %Seward & K LLP -1 Bttry Pk Plz -NY 10004
(212) 801-6952 .. **Choo,** Sohyoung '08 %Greenberg T,LLP -200 Park Av -NY 10166
(212) 735-3000 .. **Chopp,** Sarah M '07 %Skadden ASM&F LLP -4 Times Sq -NY 10036
(212) 656-9000 .. **Chopra,** Rupali '00 %Cashedge -215 Park Av S -NY 10003
(212) 683-3800 .. **Chopra,** Sameer '07 Dinkes & S,PC -112 Mad Av -NY 10016
(212) 294-6700 .. **Chopra,** Sanjana '03 %Winston & S -200 Park Av -NY 10166
(212) 455-2000 .. **Chorazak,** Mark J '07 %Simpson T&B LLP -425 Lex Av -NY 10017
(212) 880-1470 .. **Chorba,** Kyle H '03 %Fidelity Natl Title Grp -711 3rd Av -NY 10017
(212) 770-7000 .. **Chorengel,** Christopher B '03 AIG Inc -70 Pine -NY 10270
(516) 357-3000 .. **Choriatis,** George '02 %Rivkin R LLP -926 RXR Plz -Uniondale 11556
(212) 526-0469 .. **Chormanski,** Joanne '92 %Barclays Capital Inc -1271 Av of Amer -NY 10020
(212) 349-9100 .. **Chorne,** Alan R '82 -41 Mad Av -NY 10010 **Fx:**(866) 655-8465
(718) 923-3321 .. **Chorney,** Alan D '77 %OTDA Fair Hearings -14 Boerum Pl -Brklyn 11201
(212) 325-2000 .. **Chorney,** David A '05 Credit Suisse -11 Mad Av -NY 10010
(718) 266-5512 .. **Chorney,** Kevin M '93 NYS DMV -2875 W 8th -Brklyn 11224
(212) 880-1200 .. **Chorny,** Dennis T '91 Chicago Title/Ticor -711 3rd Av -NY 10017 **Fx:**880-1400
(212) 421-2150 .. **Chorost,** Danl D '97 (Sive P&R,PC) -460 Park Av -NY 10022
(914) 948-4500 .. **Chorzewski,** Linda M '06 %O'Connor MCD&O -1 Barker Av -White Plns 10601
(212) 489-8230 .. **Choset,** Kevan D '05 %Davis WT LLP -1633 Bway -NY 10019
(516) 877-2424 .. **Choset,** Seth M '93 (Weinberg G&P LLP) -400 Grdn City Plz -Gdn Cty 11530
(212) 225-2000 .. **Chotiros,** Kathleya '06 %Cleary GS&H -1 Lbrty Plz -NY 10006
(212) 349-6775 .. **Chou,** Corinna H '07 %Peltz & W -222 Bway -NY 10038
(212) 697-6555 .. **Chou,** Elaine N '96 %Biedermann RH&R -570 Lex Av -NY 10022
(212) 836-8000 .. **Chou,** Henry '08 %Kaye S LLP -425 Park Av -NY 10022
(212) 872-1000 .. **Chou,** James P '97 -One Bryant Park -NY 10036 **Fx:**872-1002
(212) 984-0694 .. **Chou,** Jean L '10 -100 Park Av -NY 10017 **Fx:**600-0601
(212) 226-2610 .. **Chou,** Luna '99 -401 Bway -NY 10013 **Fx:**226-3978
(212) 848-9800 .. **Chouchana,** Yael '07 %Withers B LLP -430 Park Av -NY 10022
(202) 783-6881 .. **Choudhary,** Dharmendra N '09 %Grunfeld DLS&K LLP -399 Park Av -NY 10022
(212) 455-2000 .. **Choudhri,** Nihara K '00 %Simpson T&B LLP -425 Lex Av -NY 10017
(212) 809-7600 .. **Choudhry,** Shafiq Ahmad '98 %Cheven K&H -40 Wall -NY 10005
(212) 279-2800 .. **Choudhury,** H Taufiq '91 (HT Choudhury,PC) -61 Bway Bx1402 -NY 10268 **Fx:**514-6165
(845) 592-7000 .. **Choudhury,** Neelanjan '06 %Donoghue TA&D LLP -2517 Route 52 -Hopewell Junct 12533
(212) 756-2000 .. **Chough,** Mimi '08 %Schulte R&Z LLP -919 3rd Av -NY 10022
(212) 891-9100 .. **Chouinard,** Jos W '93 %Goldfarb & F LLP -345 Park Av -NY 10154
(212) 756-2000 .. **Choung,** Peter Y '10 %Schulte R&Z LLP -919 3rd Av -NY 10022
(212) 669-3500 .. **Choupres,** Maria Caliope '02 Comptrollers Ofc -1 Centre -NY 10007
(212) 318-6000 .. **Chouraqui,** Sara A '07 %Paul HJ&W LLP -75 E 55th -NY 10022
(212) 856-0131 .. **Chovnick,** Stanley L '81 -60 E 42nd -NY 10165 **Fx:**856-0135
(212) 964-9282 .. **Chow,** Andrew K '88 %N Weinrib & Assoc -305 Bway -NY 10007 **Fx:**964-9525
(212) 918-3000 .. **Chow,** Arlene L '04 (Hogan L LLP) -875 3rd Av -NY 10022
(212) 310-8000 .. **Chow,** Bernice J '09 %Weil G&M LLP -767 5th Av -NY 10153
(212) 668-5927 .. **Chow,** Blaise U '01 %Ropers MK&B -17 State -NY 10004
(212) 735-3000 .. **Chow,** Deborah M '03 %Skadden ASM&F LLP -4 Times Sq -NY 10036
(212) 858-7119 .. **Chow,** Edw C '84 RBC Capital Mrkts Corp -165 Bway -NY 10006
(212) 331-5059 .. **Chow,** Eric '08 HRA -180 Water -NY 10038
(212) 705-7000 .. **Chow,** Gary K '07 %Bingham M LLP -399 Park Av -NY 10022
(212) 957-0500 .. **Chow,** Katherine King Yee '06 %R Goldstein,PC -145 W 57th -NY 10019 **Fx:**957-2020
(212) 450-4000 .. **Chow,** Margaret '09 %Davis P&W LLP -450 Lex Av -NY 10017
(212) 373-3000 .. **Chow,** Marianne W '08 %Paul WRW&G LLP -1285 Av of Amer -NY 10019

(718) 463-7333 .. **Chow,** Martin C '95 %M Mongelli II,PC -41-07 162nd -Flushng 11358 **Fx:**358-4872
(212) 326-3939 .. **Chow,** Matthew S '10 %Jones D -222 E 41st -NY 10017
(212) 848-4000 .. **Chowdhary,** Ranbir S '09 %Shearman & S LLP -599 Lex Av -NY 10022
(212) 922-1920 .. **Chowdhury,** Aleya J '96 %West Group -530 5th Av -NY 10036 **Fx:**867-2404
(212) 431-9550 .. **Chowes,** Helene '87 -401 Bway -NY 10013
(212) 837-6000 .. **Chowhan,** Amera Zaka '98 Cnsl Hughes H&R LLP -1 Bttry Pk Plz -NY 10004
(212) 264-9271 .. **Choy,** Chi S '87 %US Customs -26 Fed Plz -NY 10278
(212) 999-5800 .. **Choy,** Eliot S '98 OfCnsl Wilson SG&R -1301 Av of Americas -NY 10019
(212) 326-3939 .. **Choy,** Jennifer Y '08 %Jones D -222 E 41st -NY 10017
(212) 608-5866 .. **Choy,** Lana '86 %Summit Assoc -100 Lafayette -NY 10013
(516) 593-2440 .. **Choy,** Michl E '95 %Claim Srvc Bureau of NY Inc -21 Hempstd Av -Lynbrk 11563
(646) 833-0900 .. **Choy,** Peter '03 %Tressler LLP -One Penn Plz -NY 10119
(212) 340-0400 .. **Choy,** Victoria L '06 %Appllt Div 1st Dept -27 Mad Av -NY 10010 **Fx:**889-4412
(914) 345-3701 .. **Choyne,** David J '09 %Marks OO&C,PC -530 Saw Mill Rvr Rd -Elmsfrd 10523
(212) 428-2695 .. **Chresomales,** Emmy '97 OCA -25 Beaver -NY 10004
(518) 786-3900 .. **Chrimes,** Shari G '82 Kelleher & Assoc -17 British Amer Blvd -Latham 12110 **Fx:**786-6446
(718) 459-5400 .. **Chriqui,** Jonathan '02 %Farber R&K PC -97-77 Qns Blvd -Rego Pk 11374
(212) 458-3674 .. **Chris,** Sloane Fleckman '02 AIG -175 Water -NY 10038
(718) 726-4600 .. **Chrisafis,** Jerry '81 -21-83 Steinway -Astoria 11105 **Fx:**721-7981
(518) 673-8100 .. **Chrisman,** Jennifer L '05 %Ayers Law Firm,PLLC -Bx683 -Palatine Brdg 13428
(914) 524-9400 .. **Chrisomalis,** Dana S '08 %Cushner & G LLP -155 Wht Plns Rd -Tarrytwn 10591 **Fx:**524-0422
(718) 855-9531 .. **Chrisomalis,** Jack S '73 -44 Court -Brklyn 11201
(516) 488-3300 .. **Chrisomallides,** Kyriaki '07 %Shaub AC&S,LLP -1983 Marcus Av -Lk Success 11042
(212) 558-4000 .. **Chrisope,** Bret T '08 %Sullivan & C LLP -125 Broad -NY 10004
(716) 664-1558 .. **Chrispell,** David J '93 -815 Busti Sugar Grove Rd -Jamestwn 14701
(212) 558-4000 .. **Christ,** Donald C '64 SrCnsl Sullivan & C LLP -125 Broad -NY 10004
(646) 252-7000 .. **Christ,** Julia R '90 %TBTA -2 Bway -NY 10004
(212) 770-1727 .. **Christ,** Kathryn L '91 %AIG -80 Pine -NY 10005 **Fx:**344-2357
(718) 792-1200 .. **Christ,** Paul J '03 %Cohen & S,LLP -1325 Castle Hill Av -Bronx 10462
(516) 944-4247 .. **Christ,** Susan E '99 Publishers Clearing House -382 Channel Dr -Pt Wash 11050
(716) 847-8400 .. **Christ,** Wm D '91 (Phillips L LLP) -3400 HSBC Ctr -Buffalo 14203
(212) 878-8011 .. **Christenfeld,** Alan M '77 (Clifford C LLP) -31 W 52nd -NY 10019
(607) 776-4126 .. **Christensen,** Amy L '86 %Leg Srvcs -104 E Steuben -Bath 14810 **Fx:**776-4029
(212) 836-8000 .. **Christensen,** Andrea S '66 (Kaye S LLP) -425 Park Av -NY 10022
(631) 712-6200 .. **Christensen,** Catherine '89 Hon D Eisenberg -200 Fed Plz -Central Islip 11722
(212) 490-9100 .. **Christensen,** Christopher R '88 (Condon & F LLP) -7 Times Sq -NY 10036
(212) 574-1200 .. **Christensen,** Dale C Jr. '77 (Seward & K LLP) -1 Bttry Pk Plz -NY 10004
(212) 558-4000 .. **Christensen,** Erik H '09 %Sullivan & C LLP -125 Broad -NY 10004
(212) 310-8000 .. **Christensen,** Evert J Jr. '10 %Weil G&M LLP -767 5th Av -NY 10153
(212) 547-5400 .. **Christensen,** Henry III '70 (McDermott W&E LLP) -340 Mad Av -NY 10173
(845) 294-7949 .. **Christensen,** Henry N Jr. '70 (Norton & C) -60 Erie Bx308 -Goshen 10924
(212) 210-9589 .. **Christensen,** Janice A '03 %Alston & B LLP -90 Park Av -NY 10016
(516) 877-2424 .. **Christensen,** Jeanne-Marie '81 OfCnsl Weinberg G&P LLP -400 Grdn City Plz -Gdn Cty 11530
(914) 946-1981 .. **Christensen,** Jeanne-Marie Bates '94 -1025 Wstchstr Av -West Harrison 10604
(212) 399-3600 .. **Christensen,** Linda '79 %TishmanRlty&Cnstrctn -666 5th Av -NY 10103 **Fx:**843-3992
(212) 701-3000 .. **Christenson,** Michelle L '09 %Cahill G&R LLP -80 Pine -NY 10005 **Fx:**269-5420
(718) 645-3111 .. **Christenson,** Nora E '08 Leg Aid Society Ofc for the Aging -111 Lvngstn -Brklyn 11201 **Fx:**260-4722
(518) 449-3900 .. **Christenson,** Terrence P '73 (Cooper E&S,LLP) -39 N Pearl -Albany 12207
(212) 454-1039 .. **Christerson,** Blanche Lark '87 %Deutsche Bk -280 Park Av -NY 10017
(631) 232-0200 .. **Christesen,** Scott G '92 (Fumuso KDSS&F,LLP) -110 Marcus Blvd -Hauppauge 11788
(516) 471-1900 .. **Christian,** Amol N '05 Havkins RR&V,LLP -114 Old Cntry Rd -Mineola 11501
(212) 335-9000 .. **Christian,** Catherine Ann '90 %DA -1 Hogan Pl -NY 10013
(518) 402-9512 .. **Christian,** Deborah Whipple '83 %DEC -625 Bway -Albany 12233 **Fx:**402-9018
(212) 872-1000 .. **Christian,** Edw P '09 -One Bryant Park -NY 10036 **Fx:**872-1002
(518) 482-0209 .. **Christian,** George '77 -49 Brookline Av -Albany 12203
(212) 294-6700 .. **Christian,** Glynna K '05 (Winston & S) -200 Park Av -NY 10166
(212) 878-8290 .. **Christian,** John M '77 (Clifford C LLP) -31 W 52nd -NY 10019
(518) 387-4595 .. **Christian,** Jos J '00 GE -1 Rsrch Cir -Schnctdy 12309
(516) 683-1717 .. **Christian,** Kim N '05 %V Russo & Assoc,PC -1600 Stewart Av -Westbury 11590 **Fx:**683-9393
(212) 829-4776 .. **Christian,** Nathaniel H '88 %Castle Oak Securities -110 E 59th -NY 10022
(845) 227-8977 .. **Christian,** Stephen J '77 -690 Route 376 -Hopewell Junct 12533
(212) 335-4500 .. **Christian,** Tiffany Lee '03 %DLA Piper LLP -1251 Av of Amer -NY 10020
(518) 842-2100 .. **Christian,** Wm P '41 -18 Knollwood Av -Amsterdam 12010
(845) 339-2989 .. **Christiana,** Mary Lou P '89 -243 Wall Bx3505 -Kingston 12402 **Fx:**339-2986
(585) 232-5768 .. **Christiano,** Albert R '59 (Christiano G&C) -16 E Main -Rchstr 14614
(585) 232-5768 .. **Christiano Gallant & Coletti** -16 E Main -Rchstr 14614 **Fx:**232-4004
(585) 232-5768 .. **Christiano,** Gary A '87 (Christiano G&C) -16 E Main -Rchstr 14614
(315) 471-8111 .. **Christiansen,** Carol Ann '95 %Scolaro SCF&B,PC -507 Plum -Syracuse 13204
(212) 318-6000 .. **Christiansen,** Jason T '06 %Paul HJ&W LLP -75 E 55th -NY 10022
(585) 924-3252 .. **Christiansen,** Judith E '92 %Victor Central Schools -933 High -Victor 14564
(516) 488-2806 .. **Christiansen,** Peter V '01 -48 E Poplar -Floral Pk 11001
(718) 643-0480 .. **Christiansen,** Peter V '01 -26 Court -Brklyn 11242 **Fx:**797-5554
(516) 481-3121 .. **Christiansen,** Steven F '98 (McAndrews & C) -141 Jackson -Hempstd 11550
(212) 657-0645 .. **Christie,** Christopher R '93 Citigroup Global Mrkts -77 Water -NY 10005
(585) 753-4500 .. **Christie,** F James III '97 %DA -832 Watts Bldg -Rchstr 14614 **Fx:**753-4576
(212) 876-5500 .. **Christie,** John O '07 %Neighborhood Def Srv -317 Lenox Av -NY 10027 **Fx:**876-5586
(646) 378-2192 .. **Christie Pabarue Mortensen & Young, PC** -5 Penn Plz -NY 10001 **Fx:**378-2001
(212) 609-6800 .. **Christie,** Scott S '90 (McCarter & E,LLP) -245 Park Av -NY 10167
(585) 546-7430 .. **Christie,** Tamara Bill '97 Dept of Law -144 Exchange Blvd -Rchstr 14614 **Fx:**546-7514
(212) 779-4046 .. **Christman,** Audrey '75 Virgil Mountain Inc -1 E 28th -NY 10016
(212) 364-8446 .. **Christman,** David A '94 Time Warner Cable -60 Columbus Av -NY 10023 **Fx:**364-8460
(212) 878-1700 .. **Christman,** Steven M '99 %Marshall DWC&G -140 Bway -NY 10005
(212) 401-0800 .. **Christmas,** Angela '88 Disciplinary Comm -61 Bway -NY 10006 **Fx:**287-1045
(607) 974-7715 .. **Christmas,** Danl P '08 Cnsl Corning Inc -1 Rvrfrnt Plz -Corning 14831
(212) 940-3103 .. **Christmas,** Robt N H '88 (Nixon P LLP) -437 Mad Av -NY 10022
(212) 446-4800 .. **Christo,** Pauline M '04 %Kirkland & E LLP -153 E 53rd -NY 10022
(212) 264-0677 .. **Christodoulou,** Helen '07 US DOJ Antitrust Div -26 Fed Plz Ste 3630 -NY 10278
(212) 922-2200 .. **Christoffersen,** Svein-Erik M '97 %Watson F&W LLP -1133 Av of Amer -NY 10036
(212) 422-1200 .. **Christofides,** Chris '80 (Abrams GF&J,PC) -1 Bttry Pk Plz -NY 10004
(212) 425-9300 .. **Christofides,** Glenn J '09 %Bressler A&R,PC -17 State -NY 10004
(914) 937-3900 .. **Christoforatos,** Areti '08 Euro Grp of Cos -10 Mdlnd Av -Pt Chester 10573
(718) 721-1250 .. **Christoforatos,** Jerry '07 (TCP Law Group) -3501 30th Av -Astoria 11103 **Fx:**721-1270
(718) 726-5400 .. **Christoforatos,** Kate D '85 (Kulakis & C) -21-74 Steinway -Astoria 11105 **Fx:**726-8777
(212) 277-0400 .. **Christon,** Chris R '06 %Hartford Fncl Products -2 Park -NY 10016
(718) 932-0072 .. **Christoph,** Joel D '98 -3423 Steinway -Astoria 11101
(212) 344-3800 .. **Christophe,** Chas '97 (Christophe & Assoc,PC) -2 Wall -NY 10005 **Fx:**344-3212
(516) 571-3800 .. **Christophe,** Cliff A '06 %DA -262 Old Cntry Rd -Mineola 11501 **Fx:**248-9479
(212) 335-4500 .. **Christopher,** Jason M '05 %DLA Piper LLP -1251 Av of Amer -NY 10020
(716) 856-4000 .. **Christopher,** John J '88 (Hodgson R LLP) -140 Pearl -Buffalo 14202
(516) 228-1300 .. **Christopher,** John P '08 %Sahn WC&B,PLLC -333 Earle Ovngton Blvd -Uniondale 11553
(212) 610-6300 .. **Christopher,** Maria A '07 %Allen & O -1221 Av of Amer -NY 10020
(212) 613-2165 .. **Christopher,** Nick P '06 %Gibbons PC -1 Penn Plz -NY 10119 **Fx:**554-9630
(718) 835-3300 .. **Christopher,** Patrick '74 -158-01 Cross Bay Blvd -Howard Bch 11414 **Fx:**835-9441
(212) 446-4800 .. **Christopher,** Thos W '98 (Kirkland & E LLP) -153 E 53rd -NY 10022
(516) 625-2426 .. **Christophorou,** Chris '86 NPD Grp -900 W Shore Rd -Pt Wash 11050
(212) 225-2000 .. **Christophorou,** Penelope L '90 Cnsl Cleary GS&H -1 Lbrty Plz -NY 10006
(201) 488-1825 .. **Christopoulos,** George '01 -949 Cnty Route 53 -Oswego 13126 **Fx:**488-1826
(845) 634-4027 .. **Christos,** Joan A '79 -692 S Mtn Rd -New Cty 10956
(212) 728-8000 .. **Christy,** Ian M '10 %Willkie F&G LLP -787 7th Av -NY 10019
(315) 428-9446 .. **Christy,** Nancy J '92 -120 E Wshngtn -Syracuse 13202 **Fx:**656-2341
(212) 571-7000 .. **Christy,** Peter B N '84 (Petrocelli & C) -217 Bway -NY 10007 **Fx:**571-6454
(315) 386-8335 .. **Christy,** Walter R '57 -64½ State -Canton 13617
(212) 509-5050 .. **Chromow,** Chas E '74 SrCnsl Wuersch & G LLP -100 Wall -NY 10005
(212) 940-8800 .. **Chromow,** Sheri P '72 (Katten MR LLP) -575 Mad Av -NY 10022
(516) 393-2200 .. **Chronakis,** Philip C '00 (Garfunkel W,PC) -111 Grt Nck Rd -Gt Neck 11021
(212) 425-3100 .. **Chrysanthem,** Nicholas P '89 (McManus C&R,PC) -48 Wall -NY 10005
(516) 694-3976 .. **Chryssos,** Dean '89 -27 E Park Dr -Old Bethpage 11804
(315) 422-9390 .. **Chryst,** Robt D '77 -170 Seymour -Syracuse 13202
(914) 834-6205 .. **Chrystal,** Margot C '82 -686 Forest Av -Larchmnt 10538
(212) 972-4903 .. **Chrzanowski,** Lech '92 -501 5th Av -NY 10017 **Fx:**953-2215
(212) 425-7200 .. **Chu,** Alex K '08 %Kenyon & K,LLP -1 Bway -NY 10004
(212) 219-9000 .. **Chu,** Alexander F '78 %Eastbank,NA -183 Centre -NY 10013 **Fx:**219-9010
(212) 947-3330 .. **Chu,** Alvin Y '99 %Tuan & C,LLP -225 Bway -NY 10007
(212) 719-0200 .. **Chu,** Amanda '02 %BAR/BRI -1500 Bway -NY 10036 **Fx:**719-1421
(212) 430-6400 .. **Chu,** Amy '04 %Carabba L LLP -100 William -NY 10038
(845) 897-2004 .. **Chu,** Carl S '85 -725 Route 9 Bx438 -Fishkill 12524
(212) 225-2000 .. **Chu,** Carolyn '09 %Cleary GS&H -1 Lbrty Plz -NY 10006
(631) 393-9439 .. **Chu,** Clifford J '60 (Hayt H&L LLP) -500 Bi-Cnty Blvd -Farmngdl 11735

(212) 416-8187 .. **Chu,** Danl '99 %Dept of Law -120 Bway -NY 10271
(212) 869-8188 .. **Chu,** Danl D '98 -60 E 42nd -NY 10165
(212) 520-1027 .. **Chu,** David L '04 ImaginAsian Entertnmt -1515 Bway -NY 10036 **Fx:**660-3941
(212) 643-1112 .. **Chu,** Douglas J '91 (Hynes & C,LLP) -1350 Bway -NY 10018 **Fx:**643-0777
(212) 219-9000 .. **Chu,** Eric S H '79 %Eastbank,NA -183 Centre -NY 10013 **Fx:**219-9010
(212) 762-4825 .. **Chu,** Erica A '06 Morgan Stanley -1585 Bway -NY 10036
(212) 735-3000 .. **Chu,** Grace '09 %Skadden ASM&F LLP -4 Times Sq -NY 10036
(516) 746-0804 .. **Chu,** Howard '79 -6 Greenrdg Pk -Gdn Cty 11530 **Fx:**746-6523
(212) 909-6000 .. **Chu,** Jennifer L '07 %Debevoise & P LLP -919 3rd Av -NY 10022
(212) 758-9700 .. **Chu,** Jimmy '99 %KPMG LLP -345 Park Av -NY 10154
(212) 609-6800 .. **Chu,** Justin Y K '91 (McCarter & E,LLP) -245 Park Av -NY 10167
(212) 532-6078 .. **Chu,** Karl K '93 -1123 Bway -NY 10010
(212) 336-3740 .. **Chu,** Kenneth W '78 EEOC -33 Whitehall -NY 10004
(212) 558-4000 .. **Chu,** King Kai '09 %Sullivan & C LLP -125 Broad -NY 10004
(212) 521-5400 .. **Chu,** Luanne K '08 %Reed S LLP -599 Lex Av -NY 10022
(212) 620-9009 .. **Chu,** Lynn T '83 -116 W 14th -NY 10011 **Fx:**620-0023
(212) 909-6000 .. **Chu,** Nancy S '07 %Debevoise & P LLP -919 3rd Av -NY 10022
(212) 925-9000 .. **Chu & Partners** -183 Centre -NY 10013 **Fx:**925-9003
(718) 250-2000 .. **Chu,** Phyllis '91 %DA -350 Jay -Brklyn 11201 **Fx:**250-2314
(212) 219-0612 .. **Chu,** Ricky W '06 Cnsl RW Chu,PC -55-59 Chrystie -NY 10002 **Fx:**219-0613
(212) 872-3211 .. **Chu,** Sherry L '99 KPMG LLP -345 Park Av -NY 10154
(212) 705-9469 .. **Chu,** Vernon G '87 %BBC Worldwide Americas -747 3rd Av -NY 10017 **Fx:**705-9338
(212) 819-8200 .. **Chu,** Yahn-Rurng '08 %White & C LLP -1155 Av of Amer -NY 10036
(212) 416-6588 .. **Chu,** Yueh-Ru '92 NY Atty Gen -120 Bway -NY 10271
(212) 613-5088 .. **Chua,** Melissa L '06 %Leg Assist Grp -450 W 33rd -NY 10001 **Fx:**750-0820
(212) 488-6899 .. **Chuang,** Enna '91 (Antao & C) -521 5th Av -NY 10175
(212) 561-5522 .. **Chuang,** Jane '06 (Gil Y&C) -636 Bway -NY 10012
(718) 353-4700 .. **Chuang,** Saml J '98 -135-11 40th Rd -Flushng 11354 **Fx:**(212) 202-4527
(347) 542-8529 .. **Chuang,** Wm '07 (Jakubowitz & C LLP) -401 Bway -NY 10013 **Fx:**532-1344
(212) 446-7000 .. **Chubak,** David B '06 %McKinsey & Co -55 E 52nd -NY 10055 **Fx:**688-9521
(212) 259-8000 .. **Chubak,** Jeffrey S '08 %Dewey & L LLP -1301 Av of Amer -NY 10019
(212) 490-1700 .. **Chubb,** Laura A '07 %Wiggin & D -450 Lex Av -NY 10017
(212) 566-7188 .. **Chubenko,** Kristina E '06 %Genova B&G -115 Bway -NY 10006
(212) 848-4000 .. **Chubin,** Yasmine '07 %Shearman & S LLP -599 Lex Av -NY 10022
(718) 579-3000 .. **Chubinsky,** James H '77 %Leg Aid -1020 Grnd Cncrs -Bronx 10451 **Fx:**588-2611
(914) 273-4545 .. **Chubinsky,** Leonard I '73 %MBIA Ins Corp -113 King -Armonk 10504
(212) 813-8800 .. **Chuchev,** Krum S '10 Goodwin P LLP -620 8th Av -NY 10018
(212) 450-4000 .. **Chudd,** Wm J '03 %Davis P&W LLP -450 Lex Av -NY 10017
(212) 682-7474 .. **Chudnovsky,** Christine Pardo '84 %Foley & L LLP -90 Park Av -NY 10016
(212) 858-1000 .. **Chudy,** James T '85 (Pillsbury WSP LLP) -1540 Bway -NY 10036
(212) 506-5000 .. **Chudy,** Patryk J '01 %Orrick H&S LLP -51 W 52nd -NY 10019
(212) 455-2000 .. **Chuebon,** Gregory T '08 %Simpson T&B LLP -425 Lex Av -NY 10017
(212) 455-2000 .. **Chueh,** Kuang-Wei '08 %Simpson T&B LLP -425 Lex Av -NY 10017
(212) 408-2500 .. **Chumney,** Jason C '04 %Baker B,LLP -30 Rckfllr Plz -NY 10112
(212) 596-9000 .. **Chun,** David S '03 %Ropes & G LLP -1211 Av of Amer -NY 10036
(518) 455-4371 .. **Chun,** Elsie J '03 NYS Assembly -522 State Cptl -Albany 12248 **Fx:**455-4693
(212) 357-8719 .. **Chun,** Eric S '02 Goldman Sachs & Co -1 NY Plz -NY 10004
(212) 446-4890 .. **Chun,** Eunu '92 (Kirkland & E LLP) -153 E 53rd -NY 10022
(212) 489-5060 .. **Chun,** Howard C '07 -769 9th Av -NY 10019
(212) 354-4500 .. **Chun,** Jae W '02 %Friedman & W -1500 Bway -NY 10036
(212) 849-7000 .. **Chun,** John H '98 OfCnsl Quinn EU&S,LLP -51 Mad Av -NY 10010
(212) 857-8200 .. **Chun,** Lena '05 Amer Transit Ins Co -330 W 34th -NY 10001
(212) 733-4018 .. **Chun,** Lisa Soyoung '04 %Pfizer Inc -235 E 42nd -NY 10017
(516) 659-7493 .. **Chun,** Richd '00 Winter Grp -14 Park Pl -Floral Pk 11001
(212) 977-9700 .. **Chung,** Alexander J '06 Phillips N LLP -666 5th Av -NY 10103
(212) 225-2000 .. **Chung,** Amy '03 %Cleary GS&H -1 Lbrty Plz -NY 10006
(212) 408-5100 .. **Chung,** Amy H '07 %Chadbourne & P LLP -30 Rckfllr Plz -NY 10112
(212) 849-7000 .. **Chung,** Christine H '04 (Quinn EU&S,LLP) -51 Mad Av -NY 10010
(518) 445-2311 .. **Chung,** Christine Sgarlata '94 Albany Law Schl -80 New Scotland Av -Albany 12208 **Fx:**445-2315
(212) 335-9000 .. **Chung,** Cindy K '03 DA -1 Hogan Pl -NY 10013
(212) 310-2000 .. **Chung,** Connie Hae Won '04 Colgate-Palmolive -300 Park Av -NY 10022 **Fx:**310-3406
(212) 846-4649 .. **Chung,** Danl '92 %MTV Networks -1515 Bway -NY 10036 **Fx:**258-8358
(718) 590-2000 .. **Chung,** Danl P '07 DA -198 E 161st -Bronx 10451 **Fx:**590-6477
(212) 637-2417 .. **Chung,** Danl Park '04 %US Atty -1 St Andrews Plz -NY 10007
(718) 389-2427 .. **Chung,** Eduardo S '06 %Agostino & Assoc,PC -500 Kngslnd Av -Brklyn 11222
(212) 455-2000 .. **Chung,** Edw J H '93 (Simpson T&B LLP) -425 Lex Av -NY 10017
(212) 885-5000 .. **Chung,** Ernest W '97 (Blank R LLP) -405 Lex Av -NY 10174
(212) 735-3000 .. **Chung,** Eun Joo '10 %Skadden ASM&F LLP -4 Times Sq -NY 10036
(212) 308-4411 .. **Chung,** Huhnsik '90 (Edwards AP&D LLP) -750 Lex Av -NY 10022
(212) 538-9042 .. **Chung,** Hyun '94 Credit Suisse -1 Mad Av -NY 10010
(212) 434-0100 .. **Chung,** Hyun-Baek '04 %Litchfield C LLP -420 Lex Av -NY 10170
(315) 422-8191 .. **Chung,** J Gloria '05 %Leg Aid -351 S Warren -Syracuse 13202 **Fx:**472-2819
(212) 334-7118 .. **Chung,** Jack Wing Chee '02 -401 Bway -NY 10013
(212) 909-6000 .. **Chung,** Jae-Sun '02 %Debevoise & P LLP -919 3rd Av -NY 10022
(718) 520-3508 .. **Chung,** Jaewon '93 %Supreme Ct -125-01 Qns Blvd -Kew Gdns 11415
(718) 461-8808 .. **Chung,** James '04 -35-48 Union -Flushng 11354
(212) 610-6300 .. **Chung,** Jane '09 %Allen & O -1221 Av of Amer -NY 10020
(212) 563-3111 .. **Chung,** Janice Y '03 JY Chung,PC -363 7th Av -NY 10001 **Fx:**(732) 662-7984
(212) 584-0058 .. **Chung,** Jennifer '08 %Yoon & K LLP -11 E 44th -NY 10017
(212) 474-1000 .. **Chung,** Jinhee Jennifer '10 %Cravath S&M LLP -825 8th Av -NY 10019
(212) 819-8200 .. **Chung,** John H '99 (White & C LLP) -1155 Av of Amer -NY 10036
(212) 269-0927 .. **Chung,** Judy Yan '95 %D'Amato & L,LLP -2 World Fncl Ctr -NY 10281
(212) 504-6000 .. **Chung,** Julian S H '96 (Cadwalader W&T LLP) -1 World Fncl Ctr -NY 10281
(347) 404-9133 .. **Chung,** Michl J '96 %Civil Ct -141 Lvngstn -Brklyn 11201 **Fx:**(718) 643-3733
(212) 278-1000 .. **Chung,** Michl S '09 %Anderson K&O,PC -1251 Av of Amer -NY 10020
(212) 872-1000 .. **Chung,** Nancy '99 -One Bryant Park -NY 10036 **Fx:**872-1002
(212) 872-1000 .. **Chung,** Olivia Mi '09 -One Bryant Park -NY 10036 **Fx:**872-1002
(212) 415-9200 .. **Chung,** Rebecca I '08 %Dorsey & W LLP -250 Park Av -NY 10177
(212) 259-8000 .. **Chung,** Robt Nakhyun '09 %Dewey & L LLP -1301 Av of Amer -NY 10019
(212) 278-1039 .. **Chung,** Robt Y '98 (Anderson K&O,PC) -1251 Av of Amer -NY 10020
(585) 232-4090 .. **Chung,** Sandra H '01 %Leg Aid -1 W Main -Rchstr 14614 **Fx:**232-2352
(212) 969-3000 .. **Chung,** Seung Min '09 %Proskauer R LLP -1585 Bway -NY 10036
(516) 742-4343 .. **Chung,** Wm '08 %Scully SM&P PC -400 Grdn City Plz -Gdn Cty 11530
(607) 723-2043 .. **Chupp,** Frank M '53 -62 Davis -Bnghmtn 13905
(212) 592-1400 .. **Churaman,** Mahendra N '01 Cnsl Herrick,F LLP -2 Park Av -NY 10016
(516) 931-2600 .. **Churbuck Calabria Jones & Materazo PC** -43A E Barclay -Hicksvll 11801 **Fx:**931-2641
(516) 931-2600 .. **Churbuck,** Robt B '88 (Churbuck CJ&M PC) -43A E Barclay -Hicksvll 11801
(716) 849-8900 .. **Church,** Diane K '85 (Hurwitz & F,PC) -1300 Lbrty Bldg -Buffalo 14202
(607) 277-0696 .. **Church,** James H '86 -1395 Danby Rd -Ithaca 14850 **Fx:**277-9158
(212) 909-6186 .. **Church,** Judith L '93 Cnsl Debevoise & P LLP -919 3rd Av -NY 10022
(631) 878-4044 .. **Church,** Kristin B '01 -18 Railroad Av Bx682 -Ctr Moriches 11934 **Fx:**878-1453
(212) 626-4100 .. **Church,** Pamela T '83 (Baker & M LLP) -1114 Av of Amer -NY 10036
(212) 278-5810 .. **Church,** S Chris '99 SG Amer Securities,LLC -1221 Av of Amer -NY 10020 **Fx:**(646) 365-4764
(585) 589-5525 .. **Church,** Sanford A '85 -3 E Bank -Albion 14411 **Fx:**589-7544
(212) 907-0700 .. **Church,** Tara '06 %Labaton S LLP -140 Bway -NY 10005
(212) 850-8500 .. **Church,** Timothy G '99 %Bruckmann & V,LLP -420 Lex Av -NY 10170
(212) 779-9910 .. **Churchill,** Robt S '71 (Eaton & V LLP) -3 Park Av -NY 10016
(845) 624-3820 .. **Churgin,** Jos A '94 %P Savad & Assoc -55 Old Tpk Rd -Nanuet 10954 **Fx:**624-3821
(212) 732-0480 .. **Churin,** Kenneth S '92 -277 Bway -NY 10007 **Fx:**732-0414
(212) 869-5030 .. **Churneftsky,** John M '97 (Kucker & B,LLP) -747 3rd Av -NY 10017
(212) 417-4411 .. **Churnetski,** Megan A '07 Battery Pk City Auth -1 Wrld Fncl Ctr -NY 10281 **Fx:**417-2001
(212) 332-2345 .. **Chusid,** Ann L '87 %E Gelman -350 5th Av -NY 10118 **Fx:**332-8301
(212) 838-6188 .. **Chusid,** Candee B '83 -14 E 60th -NY 10022 **Fx:**759-2525
(917) 254-4670 .. **Chusid,** Richd D '82 (McDaniel & C,LLP) -350 5th Av -NY 10018 **Fx:**(201) 845-3777
(516) 496-5822 .. **Chustek,** David S '00 T Spina -170 Froehlich Farm Blvd -Woodbury 11797 **Fx:**496-5420
(212) 483-0105 .. **Chuven,** Michl S '07 %Coughlin D LLP -88 Pine-Wall St Plz -NY 10005
(315) 479-3900 .. **Chwalek,** John P '51 %SSA-ODAR -300 S State -Syracuse 13202 **Fx:**479-3933
(516) 364-5100 .. **Chwat,** Lara R '00 %Katz B&K -6900 Jericho Tpk -Syosset 11791 **Fx:**364-5166
(212) 816-0578 .. **Chwe,** Jane S '04 Citigroup Global Mrkts -388 Greenwich -NY 10013
(518) 656-3002 .. **Chwiecko,** Joanne Case '06 -5 Boathouse Rd -Queensbury 12804
(212) 218-5500 .. **Chylinski,** Jeremi L '01 %Seyfarth S LLP -620 8th Av -NY 10018
(860) 524-3926 .. **Ciabarra,** Laura G '01 (Dechert LLP) -1095 Av of Amer -NY 10036 **Fx:**524-3930
(212) 682-3454 .. **Ciacci,** Richd S '95 (Rosenberg FS LLP) -551 5th Av -NY 10176
(718) 405-1500 .. **Ciacci,** Walter F '83 (Della Mura & C LLP) -981 Allerton Av -Bronx 10469 **Fx:**405-2500
(585) 262-2740 .. **Ciaccio,** Christopher S '86 -30 W Broad -Rchstr 14614 **Fx:**325-4696
(212) 556-2100 .. **Ciaccio,** Franklin '67 Cnsl King & S -1185 Av of Amer -NY 10036
(585) 423-5955 .. **Ciaccio,** Richd T '79 -203 Irving Pl -Rchstr 14614
(718) 278-3900 .. **Ciafone,** John J '95 -25-59 Steinway -Astoria 11103 **Fx:**278-6900
(212) 980-9600 .. **Ciallella,** Janine C '01 %Kaufman B&R -120 Bway -NY 10271
(212) 788-7021 .. **Ciampa,** Felix A '93 %City Cncl Leg Div -250 Bway -NY 10007 **Fx:**788-7034
(516) 327-3000 .. **Ciampi,** Anthony R '83 %Astoria Fed Svngs & Loan -1 Astoria Fed Plz -Lk Success 11042 **Fx:**327-7421
(212) 269-2453 .. **Ciampi,** Arthur J '87 (Ciampi LLC) -39 Bway -NY 10006 **Fx:**(866) 254-8302
(212) 269-2453 .. **Ciampi,** Maria '87 OfCnsl Ciampi LLC -39 Bway -NY 10006 **Fx:**(866) 254-8302
(212) 381-9700 .. **Ciampi,** Richd J Jr. '88 %Lambos Firm,LLP -303 S Bway -Tarrytwn 10591 **Fx:**797-9213
(646) 471-4000 .. **Ciampi,** Sabrina '05 %PricewaterhouseCoopers LLP -300 Mad Av -NY 10017
(518) 455-2166 .. **Ciampoli,** John J N '85 NYS Senate -The Cptl -Albany 12247
(518) 436-3865 .. **Ciampoli,** John J N '85 -677 Bway -Albany 12207
(585) 428-5210 .. **Cianca,** Julie Ann '93 %Pub Def -10 N Fitzhugh -Rchstr 14614 **Fx:**428-2234
(718) 318-5830 .. **Ciancimino,** Albert F '59 -156 Beach 149th -Neponsit 11694
(716) 858-2424 .. **Cianciosa,** Michelle L '04 %DA -25 Delaware Av -Buffalo 14202 **Fx:**858-7425

(607) 231-6786 .. **Cianciosi,** Leo A '54 OfCnsl Hinman H&K,LLP -80 Exchange Bx5250 -Bnghmtn 13902 **Fx:**722-1919
(516) 683-0901 .. **Cianciulli,** Emil V '57 (Cianciulli M&P) -Bx246 -Uniondale 11553
(516) 683-0901 .. **Cianciulli Meng & Panos** -Bx246 -Uniondale 11553 **Fx:**683-0907
(315) 343-0362 .. **Cianfarano,** Michl G '95 -Bx1024 -Oswego 13126 **Fx:**343-6336
(585) 948-5201 .. **Cianfrini,** Raymond F '73 -87 N Main Bx167 -Oakfld 14125 **Fx:**948-5202
(212) 373-3000 .. **Ciani,** Mark T '07 %Paul WRW&G LLP -1285 Av of Amer -NY 10019
(914) 798-5400 .. **Ciano,** Frank J '91 (Goldberg S LLP) -11 Martine Av -White Plns 10606
(646) 253-5400 .. **Ciano,** Frank J '91 (Goldberg S LLP) -1200 Av of Amer -NY 10036
(212) 563-4100 .. **Ciantra,** Thos N '90 (Cohen W&S LLP) -330 W 42nd -NY 10036
(212) 788-0708 .. **Ciappetta,** Nicholas R '05 %Law Dept -100 Church -NY 10007 **Fx:**788-0367
(914) 420-7483 .. **Ciaramella,** Christina '06 (Ciaramella & S,LLP) -1 Renaissance Sq -White Plns 10601
(516) 794-4700 .. **Ciaravino,** Lucia M '03 %T Liotti -600 Old Cntry Rd -Gdn Cty 11530 **Fx:**794-2816
(516) 561-6645 .. **Ciaravino,** Michl J '00 %E Schlissel -479 Merrick Rd -Lynbrk 11563 **Fx:**561-6716
(607) 754-1310 .. **Ciaravino,** Wm J '77 -101 Jffrsn Av -Endicott 13760 **Fx:**748-4220
(315) 428-1380 .. **Ciardullo,** Frances A '80 %Fager & A,LLP -2 Clinton Sq -Syracuse 13202
(212) 715-9100 .. **Ciardullo,** Jean-Paul '07 %Kramer LN&F,LLP -1177 Av of Amer -NY 10036
(631) 369-5100 .. **Ciarelli,** John L '77 (Ciarelli & D) -737 Roanoke Av -Rvrhead 11901 **Fx:**369-5132
(212) 317-9500 .. **Ciarlo,** Michl '99 %Nadel & Assoc,PC -3 E 54th -NY 10022 **Fx:**317-9849
(212) 239-4340 .. **Ciarlone,** Thos G Jr. '02 (Shalov SB&R LLP) -485 7th Av -NY 10018
(518) 447-2734 .. **Ciarmiello-Hewig,** Rosemarie '01 %Tchrs Rtrmnt Sys -10 Corp Woods Dr -Albany 12211 **Fx:**447-2679
(212) 307-5500 .. **Ciatto,** Frank A '95 (Venable LLP) -1270 Av of Amer -NY 10020
(518) 782-0056 .. **Ciavardoni,** John J '83 -1 Jessica Ct -Latham 12110
(212) 521-5400 .. **Ciavarella,** Angelo '94 (Reed S LLP) -599 Lex Av -NY 10022
(212) 455-2000 .. **Ciavarella,** Margaret K '08 %Simpson T&B LLP -425 Lex Av -NY 10017
(212) 818-1880 .. **Cibella,** Michl V '97 (M Cibella,LLC) -60 E 42nd -NY 10165 **Fx:**697-4689
(212) 858-7552 .. **Cicala,** Criston E '01 ARX Holdings LLC -501 5th Av -NY 10017
(212) 371-6600 .. **Cicala,** Joanne M '95 (Kirby M LLP) -825 3rd Av -NY 10022
(631) 853-7770 .. **Cicale,** Alfred J '59 %Leg Aid -400 Carlton Av -Central Islip 11722 **Fx:**853-4336
(516) 496-5822 .. **Cicalo,** Melissa A '04 %T Spina -170 Froehlich Farm Blvd -Woodbury 11797 **Fx:**496-5420
(716) 839-0401 .. **Ciccarelli,** F J '51 -206 Bentham Pkwy E -Snyder 14226
(716) 854-2620 .. **Ciccarelli,** Patricia S '94 (Brown & K,LLP) -1500 Lbrty Bldg -Buffalo 14202
(718) 353-0464 .. **Ciccarone,** Lilin M '99 -36-09 Main -Flushng 11354 **Fx:**353-3660
(212) 209-4800 .. **Cicchetti,** Paul W '84 (Brown R LLP) -7 Times Sq -NY 10036
(315) 425-1801 .. **Cicci,** Stephen A '93 %Case Supply Inc -Bx1032 -Syracuse 13201 **Fx:**476-4729
(212) 509-9400 .. **Ciccia,** Maria J '02 %Cozen O -45 Bway Atrium -NY 10006
(718) 833-1116 .. **Ciccone,** Andrea '89 -8304 13th Av -Brklyn 11228 **Fx:**232-8014
(212) 227-1489 .. **Ciccone,** Diane '79 -770 Bway -NY 10003
(631) 424-1080 .. **Ciccone,** Glenn T '93 -116 Barrett Cir -Melvll 11747 **Fx:**547-8247
(585) 263-6201 .. **Ciccone,** Jeffrey L '02 Cnsl Fed Pub Def -28 E Main -Rchstr 14614 **Fx:**263-5871
(585) 232-9080 .. **Ciccone,** Kelly M '00 -30 W Broad -Rchstr 14614
(212) 421-4100 .. **Ciccone,** Louis M '98 %Pryor C LLP -7 Times Sq -NY 10036
(518) 433-6012 .. **Ciccone,** Nicholas J '09 GE Co RESO -12 Corp Wds Blvd -Albany 12211
(914) 633-7400 .. **Ciccone,** Rachel F '07 Marcus O&K LLP -145 Huguenot -New Rchll 10801
(212) 640-6660 .. **Ciccone,** Robt V '02 Amer Exp -200 Vesey -NY 10285
(646) 386-5700 .. **Cicoletto,** Theresa M '91 %Civil Ct -111 Centre -NY 10013
(518) 474-4535 .. **Cicerani,** Jane '91 %Dept Pub Srvc -3 ESP -Albany 12223
(212) 455-2000 .. **Cicerani Kahney,** Dana '05 %Simpson T&B LLP -425 Lex Av -NY 10017
(212) 788-5536 .. **Cicero,** Alethea U '05 ACS -220 Church -NY 10013
(718) 340-4200 .. **Cicero,** C John '78 %CUNY Law Schl -65-21 Main -Flushng 11367 **Fx:**340-4482
(585) 385-3100 .. **Cicero,** Jill M '85 J Cicero & Assoc -290 Linden Oaks -Rchstr 14625 **Fx:**385-3340
(212) 326-2000 .. **Cicero,** Paul N '04 Cnsl O'Melveny & M LLP -7 Times Sq -NY 10036
(212) 704-6000 .. **Cices,** Simon D '80 (Troutman S LLP) -405 Lex Av -NY 10174
(212) 344-7042 .. **Cichanowicz Callan Keane Vengrow & Textor,LLP** -61 Bway -NY 10006 **Fx:**344-7285
(914) 969-1900 .. **Cichowlas,** Andrij B '00 (Kozicky & C,PLLC) -125 Corp Blvd -Ynkrs 10701
(516) 742-8058 .. **Cicio,** Susan L '89 %Abamont & Assoc -200 Grdn City Plz Bx9250 -Gdn Cty 11530 **Fx:**742-7308
(212) 809-7600 .. **Cicolello,** Thos '92 %Cheven K&H -40 Wall -NY 10005
(212) 388-3600 .. **Ciechanov,** Jocelyn '80 %32B-J Leg Srvcs -101 Av of Amer -NY 10013 **Fx:**388-3061
(212) 799-7560 .. **Ciechanover,** Jos '82 -115 Cntrl Pk W -NY 10023 **Fx:**769-1485
(212) 799-7560 .. **Ciechanover,** Tamar '91 -115 Cntrl Pk W -NY 10023
(212) 759-8777 .. **Cielusniak,** David M '00 %Conquest Capital Grp LLC -540 Mad Av -NY 10022
(718) 250-3197 .. **Cienava,** Maria E '93 %DA -350 Jay -Brklyn 11201 **Fx:**250-2314
(212) 756-2000 .. **Cieplinski,** Michal P '05 %Schulte R&Z LLP -919 3rd Av -NY 10022
(315) 435-2470 .. **Ciereck,** Geoffrey Jon Karol '05 %DA -505 S State -Syracuse 13202 **Fx:**435-3969
(212) 446-4800 .. **Cieri,** Richd M '04 (Kirkland & E LLP) -153 E 53rd -NY 10022
(518) 374-6344 .. **Ciervo,** John J '63 -422 Penn -Schnctdy 12303
(212) 408-9434 .. **Ciervo,** Lourdes M '01 %Manhattan Skyline Legal Dept -103 W 55th -NY 10019 **Fx:**489-3749
(716) 895-3367 .. **Ciesielski,** Robt M '74 -2511 Harlem Rd -Cheektowaga 14225
(516) 747-4343 .. **Ciesinski,** Kim M '90 %JP DiMascio & Assoc,LLP -300 Grdn City Plz -Gdn Cty 11530 **Fx:**747-0204
(718) 286-6000 .. **Ciesla,** Robt S '89 %DA -125-01 Qns Blvd -Kew Gdns 11415
(716) 692-0341 .. **Cieslik,** Karlene L '84 -2424 Rvr Rd -Niagara Fls 14304
(716) 849-1333 .. **Cieslik,** Paul J '80 (Lipsitz GSC LLP) -42 Delaware Av -Buffalo 14202
(315) 593-2793 .. **Cieszeski,** Chas H '80 -189 S 1st -Fulton 13069 **Fx:**598-5022
(518) 694-1923 .. **Cifarelli,** Jos P II '99 -255 Washington Av Ext -Albany 12205
(845) 223-3470 .. **Ciffone,** Louis A '75 %Ahmuty D&M -1531 Route 82 -Hopewell Junct 12533
(914) 472-5500 .. **Cifone,** Nancy '88 -670 Wht Plns Rd -Scarsdale 10583 **Fx:**725-7724
(212) 418-0100 .. **Cifu,** Douglas A '90 (Virtu Mgmt) -645 Mad Av -NY 10022
(212) 373-3000 .. **Cifuentes,** Brian K '06 %Paul WRW&G LLP -1285 Av of Amer -NY 10019
(212) 766-5800 .. **Cifuni,** Nicholas G '03 (Ungaro & C) -291 Bway -NY 10007
(845) 638-5001 .. **Ciganek,** Carrie A '89 %DA -1 S Main -New Cty 10956 **Fx:**638-5070
(845) 641-0756 .. **Ciganek,** Kristine A '99 -3 Eberling Dr -New Cty 10956 **Fx:**709-6231
(845) 942-4300 .. **Cigna,** Edw M '97 E Cigna,PC -148 S Lbrty Dr -Stony Pnt 10980 **Fx:**942-4925
(716) 651-0102 .. **Cignarale,** Vincent P '07 V Cignarale,LLC -5100 Transit Rd -Depew 14043
(212) 209-3933 .. **Cilenti,** Giustino(Justin) '98 (Cilenti & C,PLLC) -708 3rd Av -NY 10017 **Fx:**209-7102
(212) 219-1800 .. **Cilenti,** Maria '92 %Lawyers Alliance NY -171 Mad Av -NY 10016 **Fx:**941-7458
(718) 876-6300 .. **Cilia,** Jennifer S '06 %DA -130 Styvsnt Pl -Staten Isl 10301
(212) 421-2233 .. **Cilia,** Julie A '02 Wilk A LLP -675 3rd Av -NY 10017
(212) 223-1581 .. **Cilio,** Bruno '00 (Cilio & Ptrnrs,PC) -405 Park Av -NY 10022 **Fx:**223-1578
(646) 394-6758 .. **Cilluffo,** Jos A '97 %PricewaterhouseCoopers LLP -300 Mad Av -NY 10017
(212) 269-7444 .. **Cilmi,** John M '87 (Cilmi & Assoc PLLC) -39 Bway -NY 10006 **Fx:**269-3958
(212) 574-1200 .. **Cima,** Ronald P '80 (Seward & K LLP) -1 Bttry Pk Plz -NY 10004
(212) 223-0330 .. **Cimbal,** Marc A '81 -120 E 56th -NY 10022
(212) 904-1015 .. **Ciment,** Ivan S '97 Morningside Evaluation & Consulting -450 7th Av -NY 10123
(917) 778-6600 .. **Ciment,** Wm M '80 %J Toomey -485 Lex Av -NY 10017 **Fx:**778-7048
(716) 655-8514 .. **Ciminelli,** Danl '94 -478 Linden Av -E Aurora 14052
(716) 833-1134 .. **Ciminelli,** James A '90 -1700 Hertel Av -Buffalo 14216
(585) 235-0980 .. **Ciminelli,** Paul V '88 -4 Van Auker -Rchstr 14608 **Fx:**328-2503
(585) 232-6500 .. **Ciminello,** Dominic P '07 %Harter S&E LLP -1600 Bausch & Lomb Pl -Rchstr 14604
(212) 448-9933 .. **Ciminera,** Joanne '01 %Finder & C LLP -9 E 38th -NY 10016
(914) 834-8504 .. **Ciminesi,** David J '73 -58 Chatsworth Av -Larchmnt 10538
(212) 799-8900 .. **Cimino,** Gregory P II '00 Visconti & Boren -11 W 67th -NY 10023 **Fx:**799-8332
(212) 272-8505 .. **Cimino,** Margaret M '92 %JP Morgan Chase -383 Mad Av -NY 10179
(212) 661-7300 .. **Cimino,** Peter '83 %Malapero & P LLP -295 Mad Av -NY 10017
(631) 755-0101 .. **Cimino,** Robt J '73 Cnsl Lewis JAA,LLP -425 Broad Hollow Rd -Melvll 11747
(315) 428-1000 .. **Cimino,** Stephen Lance '74 -307 S Clinton -Syracuse 13202 **Fx:**428-1002
(212) 428-2310 .. **Cimino,** Toni M '93 %OCA -25 Beaver -NY 10004
(212) 326-3939 .. **Cimmiyotti,** Jason B '08 %Jones D -222 E 41st -NY 10017
(212) 969-3000 .. **Cinamon,** Aliza R '99 %Proskauer R LLP -1585 Bway -NY 10036
(212) 949-9022 .. **Cinamon,** Jay S '63 %Abelman F&S -666 3rd Av -NY 10017
(718) 463-3700 .. **Cinamon,** Warren A '03 %H Katz,PC -61-25 Utopia Pkwy -Fresh Mdws 11365
(646) 344-8517 .. **Cinardo,** Claudia '88 %Arch Ins Grp -1 Lbrty Plz -NY 10006
(212) 530-5000 .. **Cinco,** Victor R '08 %Milbank TH&M LLP -1 Chase Manh Plz -NY 10005
(516) 364-2266 .. **Cincotta,** Anthony J '63 -100 Crossway Park Dr -Woodbury 11797 **Fx:**364-2109
(215) 446-6264 .. **Cincotta,** Jos M '80 (Gibbons PC) -1 Penn Plz -NY 10119 **Fx:**446-6315
(716) 565-3800 .. **Cinelli,** Brian L '03 (Marcus & C LLP) -2821 Wehrle Dr -Buffalo 14221 **Fx:**565-3801
(914) 244-7277 .. **Cinelli,** Jean Martin '92 -50 Lk Marie Ln -Bedfrd Hlls 10507
(718) 742-6541 .. **Cinelli,** Johncarlo R '02 NYCDOE-Student Susp -501 Courtlandt Av -Bronx 10451
(716) 332-0990 .. **Cinelli,** Ronald M '77 SrCnsl Children's Legal Cntr -438 Main -Buffalo 14202 **Fx:**332-0997
(212) 335-4500 .. **Ciner,** Jonathan A '99 OfCnsl DLA Piper LLP -1251 Av of Amer -NY 10020
(212) 385-1545 .. **Cini,** Robt A '92 -363 7th Av -NY 10001
(212) 307-5500 .. **Cinotti,** David N '04 %Venable LLP -1270 Av of Amer -NY 10020
(212) 825-0489 .. **Cinotti,** Filippo M '97 (Cinotti & B LLP) -445 Park Av -NY 10022 **Fx:**825-0117
(212) 759-5515 .. **Cinque & Cinque,PC** -845 3rd Av -NY 10022 **Fx:**759-7737
(212) 759-5515 .. **Cinque,** James P '77 (Cinque & C,PC) -845 3rd Av -NY 10022
(914) 761-0300 .. **Cinque,** Kristen L '05 %Stephens BR&L -175 Main -White Plns 10601
(845) 278-2000 .. **Cinque,** Robt A '96 (Goldsand & C) -864 Route 22 -Brewstr 10509 **Fx:**278-9650
(212) 759-5515 .. **Cinque,** Robt W '68 (Cinque & C,PC) -845 3rd Av -NY 10022
(718) 267-1300 .. **Cinquemani,** Elia S '88 AAH Construction Corp -18-55 42nd -Astoria 11105 **Fx:**726-1474
(914) 632-2300 .. **Cinquemani,** Jos J '95 -145 Hugenot -New Rchll 10801 **Fx:**632-9603
(516) 409-6200 .. **Cinquemani,** Rosemary A '85 (Furey KWM&C,PC) -2174 Jackson Av -Seafrd 11783
(212) 752-5200 .. **Cintron,** Lisa Ann '97 Greene Levin Snyder LLC -150 E 58th -NY 10155
(718) 917-8633 .. **Cintron,** Michl A '89 -16801 Rockaway Blvd -Jamaica 11434
(716) 854-2020 .. **Ciocca,** Stephen C '97 (Cellino & B,PC) -350 Main -Buffalo 14202
(516) 355-7901 .. **Cioci,** Susan Ann '93 (Paganini GCC&F) -1979 Marcus Av -Lk Success 11042

(718) 243-6232 .. **Cioffero,** Erica Gerarde '95 %Leg Aid -111 Lvngstn -Brklyn 11201 **Fx:**237-8737
(518) 377-6700 .. **Cioffi,** Cristine '79 (Cioffi SW PC) -2310 Nott E -Niskayuna 12309
(212) 574-1200 .. **Cioffi,** Greg B '88 (Seward & K LLP) -1 Bttry Pk Plz -NY 10004
(914) 765-4280 .. **Cioffi,** James J '02 IBM -1 N Castle Dr -Armonk 10504
(212) 468-4800 .. **Cioffi,** Jos '98 (Davis & G LLP) -1740 Bway -NY 10019
(518) 377-6700 .. **Cioffi Slezak Wildgrube PC** -2310 Nott E -Niskayuna 12309 **Fx:**377-6110
(518) 474-1331 .. **Cioffi,** Thos R '78 %Ofc Mntl Health -44 Holland Av -Albany 12229 **Fx:**473-7863
(631) 853-4104 .. **Cione,** Denise L '89 %DA -400 Carleton Av Bx9082 -Central Islip 11722 **Fx:**853-7838
(845) 294-4273 .. **Cione,** Thos J '85 -One Railroad Av Bx615 -Goshen 10924 **Fx:**294-5974
(914) 285-9797 .. **Cioppa,** Diana A '10 %Kitson LLP -50 Main -White Plns 10606
(315) 451-3810 .. **Ciotoli,** Stephen '03 (O'Hara O&C,PC) -7207 E Genesee -Fayettevll 13066
(516) 747-1900 .. **Ciotti,** John Jos '80 (Ciotti & D,LLP) -1551 Kellum Pl -Mineola 11501 **Fx:**746-4709
(516) 671-2178 .. **Ciovacco,** Robt J '67 -12 Highland Av -Sea Cliff 11579
(212) 308-4440 .. **Cipani,** Sara Keyhan '05 OfCnsl Ferrante,PLLC -5 W 19th -NY 10011 **Fx:**888-3839
(718) 528-1551 .. **Cipolla,** Chas '54 -241-28 S Conduit Av -Rosedale 11422 **Fx:**528-3818
(716) 890-7100 .. **Cipolla,** John S '99 Verizon Business,Inc -325 Delaware Av -Buffalo 14202
(716) 848-3241 .. **Cipolla,** Kevin S '98 %M & T Bk -1 Fountain Plz -Buffalo 14203 **Fx:**848-3177
(212) 232-1300 .. **Cipolla,** Mark '93 (Lewis BB&S LLP) -77 Water -NY 10005
(212) 373-3000 .. **Cipolla,** Matthew D '08 %Paul WRW&G LLP -1285 Av of Amer -NY 10019
(212) 696-6000 .. **Cipolla,** Oreste '07 %Curtis M-PC&M LLP -101 Park Av -NY 10178
(914) 824-5070 .. **Cipollone,** Antonia Pia '95 %Atty Grievance Comm -399 Knollwood Rd -White Plns 10603 **Fx:**949-0997
(212) 854-8158 .. **Cipollone,** Christine M '96 %Columbia Univ Law Schl Library -435 W 116th -NY 10027
(914) 428-8800 .. **Cipollone,** Deanna M '08 %Stern KP&W,LLP -1025 Wstchstr Av -White Plns 10604
(212) 267-1650 .. **Cipollone,** Teresa E '05 %Fine O&A,LLP -39 Bway -NY 10006
(516) 247-7010 .. **Cippitelli,** Robt J '01 -333 Earle Ovngton Blvd -Uniondale 11553
(212) 605-0422 .. **Ciprian,** Muriel '98 -575 Mad Av -NY 10022
(631) 849-5396 .. **Cipriani,** Terry '98 T Cipriani PLLC -595 Route 25A -Miller Pl 11764
(518) 226-0210 .. **Cipriano,** Frank J '81 (Cipriano & B,PC) -24 Horseshoe Dr -Saratoga Spgs 12866
(212) 213-1220 .. **Cipriano,** Peter J '07 %Weiner MM&B,LLC -220 5th Av -NY 10001
(631) 224-1587 .. **Cipriano,** Robt M '89 -136 E Main -E Islip 11730 **Fx:**224-1643
(716) 857-7991 .. **Ciprich,** Paula M '86 %Natl Fuel Gas -6363 Main -Williamsvll 14221 **Fx:**857-7614
(718) 522-3333 .. **Cira,** Alexandra '07 %Children's Law Ctr -44 Court -Brklyn 11201 **Fx:**522-7376
(212) 613-2047 .. **Ciraco,** Vito N '03 %Gibbons PC -1 Penn Plz -NY 10119 **Fx:**554-9687
(212) 530-5000 .. **Ciraldo Stabile,** Gina Y '08 %Milbank TH&M LLP -1 Chase Manh Plz -NY 10005
(315) 474-1285 .. **Cirando,** John A '66 (DJ & JA Cirando) -101 S Salina -Syracuse 13202
(212) 326-3939 .. **Cirando,** Lisa M '97 OfCnsl Jones D -222 E 41st -NY 10017
(631) 858-7365 .. **Ciraolo,** Michl F '04 Forest Labs -49 Mall Dr -Commack 11725
(212) 940-8800 .. **Cirel,** Alexis L '04 %Katten MR LLP -575 Mad Av -NY 10022
(212) 448-1800 .. **Cirelli,** Michl A '94 Cnsl Roberts RLSC&F LLP -235 Park Av S -NY 10003
(212) 564-2244 .. **Cires,** Adriana S '95 -277 Bway -NY 10007 **Fx:**564-2244
(845) 291-2050 .. **Cirigliano,** Marcello A '06 %DA -255-275 Main -Goshen 10924 **Fx:**291-2085
(518) 598-9907 .. **Cirilla,** Killeen M '03 -1346 Sterling Rd -Pattersonville 12137 **Fx:**887-2218
(212) 637-3203 .. **Cirillo,** Argie Korkidis '86 %EPA -290 Bway -NY 10007 **Fx:**637-3096
(315) 433-2629 .. **Cirillo,** David V '00 OCM BOCES -6820 Thompson Rd -Syracuse 13211
(914) 835-6790 .. **Cirillo,** Frank G '86 -10 Sharon Ln -Rye 10580 **Fx:**921-0274
(646) 315-7332 .. **Cirillo,** Jeanne R '84 FINRA -14 Wall -NY 10005
(212) 449-1974 .. **Cirillo,** Patricia N '84 %Merrill Lynch -220 Bway -NY 10038
(212) 556-2100 .. **Cirillo,** Richd A '76 (King & S) -1185 Av of Amer -NY 10036
(518) 432-1100 .. **Cirincione,** Martin J '77 NYPTI -107 Columbia -Albany 12210 **Fx:**432-1180
(315) 449-2616 .. **Cirincione,** Michl J '96 Martin GBM&C,PC -5790 Widewaters Pkwy -DeWitt 13214
(518) 447-3200 .. **Cirincione,** Richd D '94 (McNamee LT&W,PC) -677 Bway -Albany 12207
(631) 287-5750 .. **Cirincione,** Sandra '03 %Town Manager -116 Hmptn Rd -Southampton 11968
(718) 699-8863 .. **Cirino,** Gloria A '53 -52-10 108th -Corona 11368
(631) 271-8722 .. **Cirino,** Jerri Ann '90 -35 Pinelawn Rd -Melvll 11747 **Fx:**271-8699
(212) 385-1191 .. **Cirone,** Thos J '91 (Goodman & J LLP) -75 Broad -NY 10004
(718) 931-1220 .. **Cirrincione,** James '79 -1937 Wllmsbrdg Rd -Bronx 10461 **Fx:**518-7680
(516) 292-1818 .. **Cirrito,** Mary Ellen '79 (White C&N,LLP) -58 Hilton Av -Hempstd 11550
(516) 292-1818 .. **Cirrito,** Michl L '79 (White C&N,LLP) -58 Hilton Av -Hempstd 11550
(631) 390-0010 .. **Ciscone,** James '09 %Bruno G&S,LLP -445 Broad Hollow Rd -Melvll 11747
(914) 422-4333 .. **Cisneros,** Robt '95 %Empire Justice Ctr -80 N Bway -White Plns 10603 **Fx:**422-4391
(212) 558-4000 .. **Cisse-Green,** Anta '04 %Sullivan & C LLP -125 Broad -NY 10004
(212) 759-9585 .. **Citak,** Burton '52 (Citak & C) -270 Mad Av -NY 10016
(212) 759-9585 .. **Citak & Citak** -270 Mad Av -NY 10016 **Fx:**759-2979
(212) 759-9585 .. **Citak,** Donald L '81 (Citak & C) -270 Mad Av -NY 10016
(212) 770-5280 .. **Citardi,** Paul T '98 AIG -70 Pine -NY 10270
(914) 995-8114 .. **Citarella,** Lisa M '95 Hon R DiBella -111 Martin Luther King Blvd -White Plns 10601 **Fx:**995-4010
(212) 450-4000 .. **Citera,** Gerard S '81 Cnsl Davis P&W LLP -450 Lex Av -NY 10017
(212) 818-9200 .. **Citera,** Kathleen M '90 Cnsl Satterlee SB&B LLP -230 Park Av -NY 10169
(212) 326-3939 .. **Citera,** Toni-Ann '02 (Jones D) -222 E 41st -NY 10017
(212) 753-7500 .. **Citrin,** Caryn B '85 (Hartman & C LLP) -488 Mad Av -NY 10022
(516) 255-4160 .. **Citrin,** Jonathan M '92 %Kardisch L & Assoc PC -80 E Old Cntry Rd -Mineola 11501 **Fx:**255-4163
(516) 488-3300 .. **Citrin,** Marc J '83 (Shaub AC&S,LLP) -1983 Marcus Av -Lk Success 11042
(212) 506-2500 .. **Citron,** Allison D '02 %Mayer B LLP -1675 Bway -NY 10019
(212) 804-5759 .. **Citron,** Andrew '85 -110 Wall -NY 10005
(212) 969-3000 .. **Citron,** Evan B '08 %Proskauer R LLP -1585 Bway -NY 10036
(212) 557-7200 .. **Citron,** Jeffrey I '76 (Davidoff M&H,LLP) -605 3rd Av -NY 10158
(516) 227-0700 .. **Citron,** Jill S '95 Cnsl Farrell F,PC -1320 RXR Plz -Uniondale 11556
(212) 687-3860 .. **Citron,** Kenneth E '00 (Snow BK,PC) -605 3rd Av -NY 10158
(646) 414-6819 .. **Citron,** Lowell A '95 (Lowenstein S PC) -1251 Av of Amer -NY 10020 **Fx:**(973) 422-6809
(516) 747-1010 .. **Citron,** Nadine G '82 %Dollinger G&G -1 Old Cntry Rd -Carle Pl 11514
(631) 761-7115 .. **Citron,** Rodger D '07 %Touro Cllg Law Ctr -225 Eastvw Dr -Central Islip 11722
(973) 327-4516 .. **Cittone,** Henry J '03 (Cittone & L LLP) -122 W 27th -NY 10001 **Fx:**(212) 624-0244
(212) 506-1700 .. **Ciuffani,** Cara M '03 %Kasowitz BT&F LLP -1633 Bway -NY 10019
(518) 884-4795 .. **Ciulla,** John H Jr. '75 (Pub Def) -40 McMaster -Ballston Spa 12020 **Fx:**884-4789
(212) 635-8609 .. **Ciulla,** John R '95 %Bk of NY -1 Wall -NY 10286
(516) 747-7400 .. **Ciulla,** John S '88 %Rosenberg C&B LLP -100 Grdn City Plz -Gdn Cty 11530
(516) 280-8782 .. **Ciurcina,** John '94 -1461 Franklin Av -Gdn Cty 11530 **Fx:**280-8783
(716) 849-0140 .. **Ciurczak,** Diane M '91 -295 Main -Buffalo 14203
(212) 735-3000 .. **Civale,** Michl A '03 %Skadden ASM&F LLP -4 Times Sq -NY 10036
(516) 678-9797 .. **Civardi,** Stephen '77 (Civardi O&B,LLP) -23 S Main -Freeprt 11520 **Fx:**678-2266
(212) 259-8000 .. **Civetta,** Margaret '94 (Dewey & L LLP) -1301 Av of Amer -NY 10019
(518) 587-4400 .. **Civic,** Susan J '93 -376 Bway -Saratoga Spgs 12866 **Fx:**885-7744
(516) 338-3081 .. **Civile,** Robt J '93 -144 Glenn Curtiss Blvd -Uniondale 11556 **Fx:**338-3370
(716) 366-2010 .. **Civilette,** David M '73 (Spann & C,PC) -643 Central Av Bx262 -Dunkirk 14048
(631) 298-3200 .. **Civiletti,** Denise '83 News Review Newspaper Corp -Bx1500 -Mattituck 11952
(716) 282-8863 .. **Civiletto,** Samual J '66 (Grossman & C) -331 Buffalo Av -Niagara Fls 14303
(718) 264-3340 .. **Civitano,** Jacqueline F '98 %MHLS -80-45 Wnchstr Blvd -Qns Vllg 11427 **Fx:**264-3559
(212) 458-2208 .. **Civitano-Lombardi,** Christine A '04 AIG -175 Water -NY 10038
(631) 804-9186 .. **Civitello,** Donna Ann '84 -17 E Gate Rd -Huntngtn 11743
(516) 741-1342 .. **Civitello,** Therese M '92 -211 Collins Av -Williston Pk 11596 **Fx:**742-0795
(845) 486-2110 .. **Civitillo,** Victor A '93 %Cnty Atty -22 Market -Poughkeepsie 12601 **Fx:**486-2002
(212) 308-4411 .. **Cizmarik,** Andre K '94 Cnsl Edwards AP&D LLP -750 Lex Av -NY 10022
(212) 318-6000 .. **Claassen,** Robt A '93 (Paul HJ&W LLP) -75 E 55th -NY 10022
(716) 852-1300 .. **Clack,** Richd A '76 (Amigone S&M,LLP) -350 Main -Buffalo 14202
(212) 880-3800 .. **Claeson,** Robt W '69 (Akerman S) -335 Mad Av -NY 10017
(518) 238-2575 .. **Claeys,** Jos V '76 -17 Hyland Dr -Troy 12182
(718) 590-8377 .. **Claffee,** Wendy J '90 %Admin Children's Srvcs -900 Sheridan Av -Bronx 10451
(212) 233-4200 .. **Claffey,** Kevin P '88 (K Claffey,PC) -19 Fulton -NY 10038 **Fx:**233-1323
(212) 237-1000 .. **Clain,** Michl J '82 (Windels ML&M,LLP) -156 W 56th -NY 10019
(212) 300-1100 .. **Clair,** Bernard E '77 (Clair G LLP) -555 Mad Av -NY 10022 **Fx:**300-1111
(914) 472-6202 .. **Clair,** Ira S '79 (Clair & G) -720 Wht Plns Rd -Scarsdale 10583 **Fx:**472-1936
(212) 940-8800 .. **Clair,** J Bradley '09 %Katten MR LLP -575 Mad Av -NY 10022
(212) 363-3100 .. **Clair,** James '78 %Bivona & C,PC -88 Pine -NY 10005
(646) 240-4872 .. **Clair,** Meredith L '99 %Bortstein & I LLC -275 Mad Av -NY 10016 **Fx:**(866) 955-9403
(212) 681-6500 .. **Claman,** Richd L '81 (Stempel BC&H,PC) -675 3rd Av -NY 10017
(212) 573-6703 .. **Claman,** Scott '83 (Giddins & C LLP) -675 3rd Av -NY 10017 **Fx:**949-1923
(212) 407-4000 .. **Clampitt,** Erika L '09 %Loeb & L,LLP -345 Park Av -NY 10154
(212) 747-1744 .. **Clancy,** Donna H '91 -40 Wall -NY 10005 **Fx:**747-1763
(212) 858-4381 .. **Clancy,** Elizabeth R '71 %FINRA -1 Lbrty Plz -NY 10006
(212) 728-8000 .. **Clancy,** Jeffrey B '01 %Willkie F&G LLP -787 7th Av -NY 10019
(845) 294-3004 .. **Clancy,** John M '84 -2004 State Route 17M -Goshen 10924 **Fx:**294-3017
(631) 273-2222 .. **Clancy,** Michl T '85 (Breen & C,PC) -1355 Motor Pkwy -Hauppauge 11749 **Fx:**273-1111
(212) 318-6000 .. **Clancy,** Quinn E '06 %Paul HJ&W LLP -75 E 55th -NY 10022
(518) 285-8959 .. **Clancy,** Rebecca A '07 Cnty Supreme Ct -16 Eagle -Albany 12207
(212) 549-2500 .. **Clapman,** Alice J '04 %ACLU -125 Broad -NY 10004 **Fx:**549-2651
(212) 852-1000 .. **Clapp,** Ada '92 %US Trust Co,NA -114 W 47th -NY 10036 **Fx:**852-1310
(212) 222-4200 .. **Clapp,** Alison E '76 -7 Dey -NY 10007
(212) 517-4631 .. **Clapp,** Constance L '85 -160 E 72nd -NY 10021
(212) 953-2626 .. **Clapp,** James E '78 OfCnsl Kelly & H -380 Lex Av -NY 10168 **Fx:**983-5271
(212) 344-5680 .. **Clapp,** John M '88 (Thompson H LLP) -335 Mad Av -NY 10017
(212) 735-3000 .. **Claps,** Thos E '99 Cnsl Skadden ASM&F LLP -4 Times Sq -NY 10036
(212) 294-6700 .. **Clar,** Brandon S '08 %Winston & S -200 Park Av -NY 10166
(585) 419-8800 .. **Clar,** David M '98 (Harris B PLLC) -99 Garnsey Rd -Pittsfrd 14534
(518) 458-7806 .. **Clar,** Lonnie D '66 -15 Cliff Top Dr -Loudonvll 12211
(585) 271-4800 .. **Clar,** Rachel I '04 Norry Mgmt Corp -1465 Monroe Av -Rchstr 14618
(315) 331-1334 .. **Clar,** Wendy '99 %Nesbitt & W -180 E Union Bx226 -Newark 14513 **Fx:**331-1033

(631) 499-4644 .. **Clare,** Edwin S '53 -357 Vets Mem'l Hwy -Commack 11725 **Fx:**499-4921
(212) 918-3000 .. **Clare,** James '08 %Hogan L LLP -875 3rd Av -NY 10022
(212) 538-6045 .. **Clare,** Laura M '03 Credit Suisse -1 Mad Av -NY 10010
(631) 757-1589 .. **Clare,** Mark T '91 -104 Laurel Ct -Northprt 11768
(212) 220-8211 .. **Clare,** Ronald J Jr. '05 Manhattan Cmmnty Cllg -199 Chmbrs -NY 10007
(631) 567-0050 .. **Clare,** Timothy W '80 -Bx702 -E Northprt 11731
(212) 751-1585 .. **Clareman,** Jack '40 -121 E 61st -NY 10065
(212) 751-1585 .. **Clareman,** Lloyd S '77 -121 E 61st -NY 10065
(212) 373-3000 .. **Clareman,** Wm A '07 %Paul WRW&G LLP -1285 Av of Amer -NY 10019
(212) 450-4000 .. **Clarens,** Margarita S '09 %Davis P&W LLP -450 Lex Av -NY 10017
(212) 633-4310 .. **Clarick,** Gregory A '91 (Clarick GR LLP) -40 W 25th -NY 10010 **Fx:**(646) 478-9484
(212) 790-9200 .. **Clarida,** Robt W '94 %Cowan L&L,PC -1133 Av of Amer -NY 10036
(845) 291-3121 .. **Clarino,** Richd '80 Hon J Berry -255 Main -Goshen 10924 **Fx:**291-2101
(631) 249-6565 .. **Clarity,** Paula A '08 %Archer BG&L,LLP -425 Broadhllw Rd -Melvll 11747
(212) 373-3000 .. **Clark,** Abigail Wells '10 %Paul WRW&G LLP -1285 Av of Amer -NY 10019
(585) 899-1414 .. **Clark,** Adam M '06 %Harris COJW&L -300 Linden Oaks -Rchstr 14625
(516) 579-6500 .. **Clark,** Alan W '78 (A Clark & Assoc,LLC) -650 Wantagh Av -Levittwn 11756 **Fx:**579-6604
(914) 833-2890 .. **Clark,** Alice M '79 -5 Beach Av -Larchmnt 10538
(516) 292-6516 .. **Clark & Amadio,PC** -230 Hilton Av -Hempstd 11550 **Fx:**292-6517
(212) 403-7300 .. **Clark,** Anne L '91 (Vladeck WE&E,PC) -1501 Bway -NY 10036
(212) 806-5400 .. **Clark,** Beth K '00 %Stroock &S&L LLP -180 Maiden Ln -NY 10038
(516) 579-6500 .. **Clark,** Brandon S '04 %A Clark & Assoc,LLC -650 Wantagh Av -Levittwn 11756 **Fx:**579-6604
(212) 687-7410 .. **Clark,** Brian J '86 (Clifton B&D,LLP) -420 Lex Av -NY 10170
(212) 732-3200 .. **Clark,** Brooks S '92 (Carter L&M LLP) -2 Wall -NY 10005
(212) 558-4000 .. **Clark,** Bruce E '71 (Sullivan & C LLP) -125 Broad -NY 10004
(516) 767-1200 .. **Clark,** Bruce G '66 (B Clark & Assoc,PC) -22 S Bayles Av -Pt Wash 11050 **Fx:**767-1702
(315) 598-8552 .. **Clark,** Bruce N '75 -163 S 1st -Fulton 13069
(845) 268-0316 .. **Clark,** Bryant G '88 -114 Snedecker Av -Congers 10920
(212) 530-5334 .. **Clark,** Carolyn C '69 -1 Chase Manh Plz -NY 10005 **Fx:**530-5219
(212) 370-4220 .. **Clark,** Celia R '80 -570 Lex Av -NY 10022 **Fx:**370-4270
(212) 506-5000 .. **Clark,** Charity R '06 %Orrick H&S LLP -51 W 52nd -NY 10019
(518) 853-4432 .. **Clark,** Chas M '90 Supreme Ct -58 Bway Bx1500 -Fonda 12068
(212) 259-8000 .. **Clark,** Christopher J '97 (Dewey & L LLP) -1301 Av of Amer -NY 10019
(212) 259-8000 .. **Clark,** Christopher R '09 %Dewey & L LLP -1301 Av of Amer -NY 10019
(516) 545-5160 .. **Clark,** Cynthia R '85 %Natl Grid -175 E Old Cntry Rd -Hicksvll 11801 **Fx:**545-5029
(212) 872-9800 .. **Clark,** D Lewis Jr. '02 (Squire S&D LLP) -30 Rckfllr Plz -NY 10112
(607) 902-9260 .. **Clark,** Dale J '82 Corning Community College -1 Academic Dr -Corning 14830
(718) 613-2422 .. **Clark,** Danl E '07 Hon F Block -225 Cadman Plz E -Brklyn 11201
(212) 351-4500 .. **Clark,** David J '97 %Epstein B&G,PC -250 Park Av -NY 10177
(845) 635-9860 .. **Clark,** David M '02 -Bx454 -Plsnt Vlly 12569
(212) 566-4949 .. **Clark,** Deanna D '03 %Shayne Law Grp,PC -64 Fulton -NY 10038 **Fx:**202-5423
(518) 761-6500 .. **Clark,** Donald H Jr. '85 %Family Ct -1340 State Route 9 -Lk George 12845 **Fx:**761-6230
(518) 449-8893 .. **Clark,** Douglas S '98 (Wilson EME&D LLP) -677 Bway -Albany 12207
(845) 562-0203 .. **Clark,** Duncan W '79 (Finkelstein & Prtnrs,LLP) -1279 Route 300 Bx1111 -Newburgh 12550
(212) 454-1603 .. **Clark,** Elise C '03 Deutsche Asset Mgmt -345 Park Av -NY 10154
(212) 238-3000 .. **Clark,** Elizabeth M '96 (Emmet M&M,LLP) -120 Bway -NY 10271
(212) 657-1098 .. **Clark,** Eugene V '82 Citigroup Global Mrkts -77 Water -NY 10005
(212) 268-7535 .. **Clark,** Ewan M '00 OfCnsl Bonner KT&C,LLP -350 5th Av -NY 10118
(347) 404-9133 .. **Clark,** Francis J '79 %Civil Ct -141 Lvngstn -Brklyn 11201 **Fx:**(718) 643-3733
(315) 701-5990 .. **Clark,** Frank A '75 -300 S State -Syracuse 13202
(631) 266-1881 .. **Clark,** Frank E '78 -382 Larkfld Rd -E Northprt 11731 **Fx:**266-1646
(518) 438-2000 .. **Clark,** Fredk W III '98 %Lombardi WWHA&D PC -III Winners Cir -Albany 12205
(212) 644-1010 .. **Clark,** G Peter '74 SrCnsl Kauff M&M LLP -950 3rd Av -NY 10022
(914) 946-8900 .. **Clark Gagliardi & Miller** -99 Court -White Plns 10601 **Fx:**946-8960
(212) 906-1200 .. **Clark,** Gareth P '07 %Latham & W -885 3rd Av -NY 10022
(585) 753-4598 .. **Clark,** Gregory C '02 DA -832 Watts Bldg -Rchstr 14614 **Fx:**753-4576
(212) 225-2000 .. **Clark,** James C '05 %Cleary GS&H -1 Lbrty Plz -NY 10006
(631) 539-8889 .. **Clark,** James E '02 -57 W Main -Babylon 11702 **Fx:**956-9114
(212) 701-3000 .. **Clark,** James J '80 (Cahill G&R LLP) -80 Pine -NY 10005 **Fx:**269-5420
(516) 357-3700 .. **Clark,** James P '95 (Cullen and D LLP) -100 Q Roosevelt Blvd -Gdn Cty 11530
(518) 402-2227 .. **Clark,** James R '90 NYS Ofc Homeland Security -1220 Wshngtn Av -Albany 12242
(212) 705-7000 .. **Clark,** Jared R '96 (Bingham M LLP) -399 Park Av -NY 10022
(212) 259-8000 .. **Clark,** Jason D '04 %Dewey & L LLP -1301 Av of Amer -NY 10019
(585) 771-2291 .. **Clark,** Jeffrey R '87 %Rochester Gas & Elec -89 East Av -Rchstr 14649 **Fx:**724-8668
(315) 422-7111 .. **Clark,** Jennifer A '82 (Blitman & K LLP) -443 N Franklin -Syracuse 13204
(212) 509-9400 .. **Clark,** Jennifer L '09 %Cozen O -45 Bway Atrium -NY 10006
(212) 972-1000 .. **Clark,** Jessica A '08 %London F LLP -59 Maiden Ln -NY 10038
(212) 225-2000 .. **Clark,** John A '08 %Cleary GS&H -1 Lbrty Plz -NY 10006
(212) 351-4500 .. **Clark,** John E '96 (Epstein B&G,PC) -250 Park Av -NY 10177
(518) 758-6214 .. **Clark,** John H III '91 -Bx654 -Valatie 12184
(917) 778-6600 .. **Clark,** John P '96 %J Toomey -485 Lex Av -NY 10017 **Fx:**778-7048
(518) 373-1482 .. **Clark,** John W '77 (DuCharme H&C,LLP) -10 Maxwell Dr -Clifton Pk 12065
(212) 940-8800 .. **Clark,** Jonathan K '08 %Katten MR LLP -575 Mad Av -NY 10022
(212) 450-4000 .. **Clark,** Jonathan M '65 SrCnsl Davis P&W LLP -450 Lex Av -NY 10017
(845) 365-9100 .. **Clark,** Jos A III '70 OfCnsl Davidson & G -30 Ramland Rd -Orangebrg 10962
(516) 328-3500 .. **Clark,** Jos A '82 %McDonnell & A,PC -401 Franklin Av -Gdn Cty 11530
(716) 564-3288 .. **Clark,** Jos D '04 %K Hiller -2001 Niagara Flls Blvd -Amherst 14228 **Fx:**564-3291
(212) 836-8000 .. **Clark,** Jos F '09 %Kaye S LLP -425 Park Av -NY 10022
(718) 625-6888 .. **Clark,** Julie A '84 -32 Court -Brklyn 11201 **Fx:**625-6977
(212) 732-3200 .. **Clark,** Justine M '82 (Carter L&M LLP) -2 Wall -NY 10005
(212) 310-8000 .. **Clark,** Kathleen E '08 %Weil G&M LLP -767 5th Av -NY 10153
(212) 756-2000 .. **Clark,** Kerri L '09 %Schulte R&Z LLP -919 3rd Av -NY 10022
(585) 753-4500 .. **Clark,** Kevin R '08 DA -832 Watts Bldg -Rchstr 14614 **Fx:**753-4576
(212) 326-3939 .. **Clark,** Landon R '10 %Jones D -222 E 41st -NY 10017
(607) 746-2125 .. **Clark,** Lauren A '85 Cnty Ct -3 Court -Delhi 13753 **Fx:**746-3253
(518) 429-4200 .. **Clark,** Linda J '92 (Hiscock & B,LLP) -50 Beaver -Albany 12207
(914) 669-5896 .. **Clark,** Margaret A '81 -Bx505 -N Salem 10560 **Fx:**669-8715
(914) 232-0707 .. **Clark,** Margaret A '81 -215 Katonah Av -Katonah 10536 **Fx:**232-6984
(914) 576-6500 .. **Clark,** Mary N '83 (Clark & C) -225 Broadvw Av -New Rchll 10804 **Fx:**576-6502
(716) 845-2560 .. **Clark,** Marylou E '75 %Surrogates Ct -92 Franklin -Buffalo 14202 **Fx:**853-3741
(585) 428-5210 .. **Clark,** Matthew J '91 %Pub Def -10 N Fitzhugh -Rchstr 14614 **Fx:**428-2234
(212) 992-8639 .. **Clark,** Melanca D '03 Brennan Ctr for Justice/NYU Law Schl -161 Av of the Americas -NY 10013 **Fx:**995-4550
(212) 858-1000 .. **Clark,** Merrell E Jr. '48 SrCnsl Pillsbury WSP LLP -1540 Bway -NY 10036
(646) 706-7031 .. **Clark,** Merrill J '89 -110 Wall -NY 10005 **Fx:**706-7041
(516) 292-6516 .. **Clark,** Michl C '93 (Clark & A,PC) -230 Hilton Av -Hempstd 11550
(917) 554-1215 .. **Clark,** Michelle A '03 -229 W 16th -NY 10011
(212) 321-7075 .. **Clark,** Miriam F '85 (Ritz C&B-A LLP) -40 Exch Pl -NY 10005
(212) 381-7000 .. **Clark,** Patricia Ann '92 (Sabin B&G LLP) -4 Times Sq -NY 10036
(212) 267-1900 .. **Clark,** Paul F '85 (Wade CM) -111 Bway -NY 10006
(516) 431-1521 .. **Clark,** Paul J '88 -750 Lido Blvd -Lido Bch 11561 **Fx:**431-1256
(212) 504-6000 .. **Clark,** Peter B '66 (Cadwalader W&T LLP) -1 World Fncl Ctr -NY 10281
(716) 673-1361 .. **Clark,** Peter D '74 (Schaack WCN PC) -2 W Main Bx109 -Fredonia 14063
(315) 471-3151 .. **Clark,** R John '88 (Hancock & E,LLP) -1500 AXA Twr I Bx4976 -Syracuse 13221
(212) 252-9550 .. **Clark,** Rachael N '06 Freiberg & P -49 W 37th -NY 10018
(585) 586-8060 .. **Clark,** Rae A Jr. '79 (Sutton DC&D,PLLC) -359 N Wshngtn -Rchstr 14625
(212) 989-6613 .. **Clark,** Ramsey '70 -37 W 12th -NY 10011
(212) 530-5000 .. **Clark,** Randy J '10 %Milbank TH&M LLP -1 Chase Manh Plz -NY 10005
(315) 474-3742 .. **Clark,** Richd E '77 Stanley Law Ofcs -500 S Salina -Syracuse 13202 **Fx:**471-1536
(718) 625-0202 .. **Clark,** Robt D '59 (Clark C&M,LLP) -Bx26515 -Brklyn 11202 **Fx:**625-2644
(212) 704-6000 .. **Clark,** Rory S '09 %Troutman S LLP -405 Lex Av -NY 10174
(718) 286-6000 .. **Clark,** Ryan J '07 %DA -125-01 Qns Blvd -Kew Gdns 11415
(716) 842-6400 .. **Clark,** Sanford L '74 -69 Delaware Av -Buffalo 14202
(585) 781-7889 .. **Clark,** Scott A '03 Eastman Kodak -343 State -Rchstr 14650
(212) 768-6700 .. **Clark,** Scott B '85 (Sonnenschein N&R LLP) -1221 Av of Amer -NY 10020
(718) 286-6000 .. **Clark,** Shawn '97 %DA -125-01 Qns Blvd -Kew Gdns 11415
(315) 793-2370 .. **Clark,** Stephen C '98 %MHLS -207 Genesee -Utica 13501 **Fx:**793-2371
(212) 708-9791 .. **Clark,** Stephen W '91 %MOMA -11 W 53rd -NY 10019 **Fx:**708-9856
(917) 320-2500 .. **Clark,** Thos M '98 %FDIC -350 5th Av -NY 10118 **Fx:**320-2917
(212) 841-1000 .. **Clark,** Timothy J '89 (Covington & B LLP) -620 8th Av -NY 10018
(212) 969-3000 .. **Clark,** Timothy M '92 (Proskauer R LLP) -1585 Bway -NY 10036
(212) 857-8866 .. **Clark,** Toby D '05 2nd Circuit -233 Bway -NY 10279
(212) 837-6814 .. **Clark,** Valerie N '10 %Hughes H&R LLP -1 Bttry Pk Plz -NY 10004 **Fx:**299-6814
(212) 455-2000 .. **Clark,** Vanessa L '10 %Simpson T&B LLP -425 Lex Av -NY 10017
(914) 576-6500 .. **Clark,** Walter T III '71 (Clark & C) -225 Broadvw Av -New Rchll 10804 **Fx:**576-6502
(631) 853-5368 .. **Clark,** Warren G '85 Dist Admin Judges Ofc -400 Carleton Av -Central Islip 11722
(518) 474-6740 .. **Clark,** Whitney A '97 %Dept of State -41 State -Albany 12231 **Fx:**473-9211
(212) 428-2965 .. **Clark,** Wm J III '84 %OCA -25 Beaver -NY 10004 **Fx:**428-2973
(212) 353-8223 .. **Clark,** Wm K III '04 Lisa Mgmt Inc -225 E 6th -NY 10003 **Fx:**353-0586
(716) 885-9700 .. **Clark,** Wm P '07 Collins C&D -267 North -Buffalo 14201 **Fx:**885-9770
(914) 995-3000 .. **Clark-DiRusso,** Mary A '87 %DA -111 Martin Luther King Blvd -White Plns 10601 **Fx:**995-3363
(718) 250-2000 .. **Clarke,** Andrea E '07 %DA -350 Jay -Brklyn 11201 **Fx:**250-2314
(212) 381-7000 .. **Clarke,** Ashley H '08 %Sabin B&G LLP -4 Times Sq -NY 10036
(646) 233-1403 .. **Clarke,** B Neil S '91 -110 Wall -NY 10005
(631) 439-2450 .. **Clarke,** Barbara Walsh '86 %Leg Aid -320 Carleton Av -Central Islip 11722 **Fx:**439-2453
(646) 386-3900 .. **Clarke,** Barry R '03 Supreme Ct Criminal Term -100 Centre -NY 10013
(212) 269-7308 .. **Clarke,** Christopher D '92 (Leahey & J PC) -120 Wall -NY 10005
(212) 221-5700 .. **Clarke,** Christopher R '04 %Goldberg WFG LLP -1501 Bway -NY 10036
(518) 402-9188 .. **Clarke,** Cristin M '01 DEC -625 Bway -Albany 12233 **Fx:**402-9018
(718) 579-3000 .. **Clarke,** David C '77 %Leg Aid -1020 Grnd Cncrs -Bronx 10451 **Fx:**588-2611
(212) 793-4912 .. **Clarke,** Denis J '95 Citigroup,Inc -425 Park Av -NY 10022
(212) 446-2300 .. **Clarke,** Diana M '00 OfCnsl Boies S&F LLP -575 Lex Av -NY 10022
(212) 261-8000 .. **Clarke,** Ellen R '84 (Mendes & M,LLP) -750 7th Av -NY 10019
(718) 284-5771 .. **Clarke,** George A '92 -15 Ocean Av -Brklyn 11225

(718) 888-8880 .. **Clarke,** George W '77 SrCnsl Dai & Assoc,PC -136-20 38th Av -Flushng 11354 **Fx:**888-9270
(718) 354-3200 .. **Clarke,** Gregory C '71 %Battiste A&S,Inc -60 Bay -Staten Isl 10301
(212) 336-2000 .. **Clarke,** Harry S III '06 %Patterson BW&T LLP -1133 Av of Amer -NY 10036
(716) 882-1549 .. **Clarke,** Hillary G '92 %NYPIRG-206 Cassety Hall -1300 Elmwood Av -Buffalo 14222
(212) 771-4629 .. **Clarke,** J Elizabeth '02 Trust Co of the West -1251 Av of Amer -NY 10020
(631) 952-6400 .. **Clarke,** James P '89 %Medicaid Fraud Cntrl -300 Motor Pkwy -Hauppauge 11788 **Fx:**952-6382
(212) 752-8000 .. **Clarke,** Jennifer E D '94 SpclCnsl Cole SMF&L,PA -900 3rd Av -NY 10022
(518) 783-1100 .. **Clarke,** Jennifer L '03 %Luibrand Law Firm,PLLC -950 New Loudon Rd -Latham 12110
(212) 264-1630 .. **Clarke,** Jessica '04 %DHS -26 Fed Plz -NY 10278
(845) 486-2280 .. **Clarke,** John B '91 %Pub Def -22 Market -Poughkeepsie 12601 **Fx:**486-2266
(212) 335-4500 .. **Clarke,** John J Jr. '91 (DLA Piper LLP) -1251 Av of Amer -NY 10020
(516) 248-1490 .. **Clarke,** John P '57 -35 Broad -Williston Pk 11596 **Fx:**873-9567
(212) 687-0100 .. **Clarke,** John W '67 (Harris B PLLC) -100 Wall -NY 10005
(212) 474-1000 .. **Clarke,** Jonathan J '01 Cravath S&M LLP -825 8th Av -NY 10019
(212) 969-3911 .. **Clarke,** Karen E '90 %Proskauer R LLP -1585 Bway -NY 10036
(516) 486-2693 .. **Clarke,** Lance D '79 Cooke & C -510 S Franklin Bx4852 -Hempstd 11551 **Fx:**564-9493
(716) 845-9475 .. **Clarke,** Lynn A '84 %Supreme Ct -25 Delaware Av -Buffalo 14202 **Fx:**851-3293
(212) 233-2311 .. **Clarke,** Mary A '83 -305 Bway -NY 10007 **Fx:**233-2005
(518) 471-4813 .. **Clarke,** Michl C '06 %Supreme Ct -Bx7350 -Albany 12224
(212) 335-9000 .. **Clarke,** Randolph W '01 %DA -1 Hogan Pl -NY 10013
(212) 705-7000 .. **Clarke,** Raquel S '05 %Bingham M LLP -399 Park Av -NY 10022
(212) 578-3652 .. **Clarke,** Richd G '75 %MetLife -27-01 Qns Plz N -LIC 11101
(212) 720-4477 .. **Clarke,** Sheilagh M '96 Foot Locker,Inc -112 W 34th -NY 10120 **Fx:**720-4116
(212) 450-4000 .. **Clarke,** Thos J '10 %Davis P&W LLP -450 Lex Av -NY 10017
(845) 343-3000 .. **Clarke,** Thos P Jr. '88 (MacVean LS&M,PC) -34 Grove Bx310 -Middletwn 10940
(914) 422-4128 .. **Clarke,** Virginia J '89 %Pace Law Schl -78 N Bway -White Plns 10603 **Fx:**422-4039
(212) 735-3000 .. **Clarke,** Wm F Jr. '98 %Skadden ASM&F LLP -4 Times Sq -NY 10036
(212) 558-4000 .. **Clarkin,** Catherine M '96 (Sullivan & C LLP) -125 Broad -NY 10004
(212) 553-0300 .. **Clarkson,** Brian M '88 %Moody's Invstr Srvc -250 Greenwich -NY 10007
(212) 306-2469 .. **Clarkson,** Theresa C '03 FINRA -65 Bway -NY 10006
(212) 447-7070 .. **Clark-Weintraub,** Deborah '87 (Whatley D&K LLC) -1540 Bway -NY 10036
(718) 596-3800 .. **Claro,** Jos M '08 Tenenbaum & B LLP -26 Court -Brklyn 11242
(516) 803-3000 .. **Claro,** Karen Au '89 Rainbow Prog -1111 Stewart Av -Bethpage 11714
(212) 269-2500 .. **Claro,** Thos P '04 %Gorlick K&L,PC -17 State -NY 10004
(718) 725-3076 .. **Clarry,** Tracy N '05 Admin Childrens Srvcs -151-20 Jamaica Av -Jamaica 11432
(716) 754-4869 .. **Clary,** Dennis A '86 -755 Center Bx1044 -Lewiston 14092 **Fx:**754-2819
(212) 267-4405 .. **Clary,** Rhoda Lipp '81 -111 Bway -NY 10006 **Fx:**206-6711
(212) 474-1000 .. **Clary,** Richd W '81 (Cravath S&M LLP) -825 8th Av -NY 10019
(212) 451-2900 .. **Clasen,** Jos L '81 (Robinson & C LLP) -885 3rd Av -NY 10022
(516) 229-6000 .. **Clasen,** Robt J '84 %R Lau & Assoc -300 Jericho Quad Bx9040 -Jericho 11753 **Fx:**229-6167
(914) 478-1681 .. **Classon,** Gregory B '82 -62 Strafford Ln -Hastings-On-Hud 10706
(212) 909-8440 .. **Claster,** Mark L '78 Carl Marks & Co -900 3rd Av -NY 10022 **Fx:**980-2631
(212) 770-5570 .. **Clateman,** Michl G '94 %AIG -70 Pine -NY 10270 **Fx:**785-1584
(212) 382-6600 .. **Claudio-Blum,** Lillian I '08 NYC Bar -42 W 44th -NY 10036 **Fx:**398-6634
(212) 425-2200 .. **Claugus,** Bruce A '77 (Claugus & M) -110 Wall -NY 10005
(212) 425-2200 .. **Claugus & Mitchell** -110 Wall -NY 10005
(585) 546-7686 .. **Claus Curry Schuster & Schwartzman** -19 W Main -Rchstr 14614 **Fx:**546-7365
(718) 318-3301 .. **Claus,** Jessica L '03 %J Trainor & Assoc -225 Beach 116th -Rckwy Pk 11694 **Fx:**318-3308
(212) 250-8190 .. **Clausen,** Christopher N '87 %Deutsche Bank -60 Wall -NY 10005
(212) 735-3000 .. **Clausen,** Curt R '08 %Skadden ASM&F LLP -4 Times Sq -NY 10036
(212) 698-3500 .. **Clausen,** Danl L '09 %Dechert LLP -1095 Av of Amer -NY 10036
(212) 805-3900 .. **Clausen Miller PC** -1 Chase Manh Plz -NY 10005 **Fx:**805-3939
(212) 220-3830 .. **Clausen,** Scott D '04 %Nicoletti H&S -88 Pine -NY 10005
(631) 841-3333 .. **Clauss,** Amy C '97 Able Equipmnt Rntl -21 Dixon Av -Copiague 11726
(212) 279-3500 .. **Clauss,** Eliot R '78 (Russin VB&B,LLP) -260 Mad Av -NY 10016
(585) 428-5210 .. **Clauss,** Wm G '83 Pub Def -10 N Fitzhugh -Rchstr 14614 **Fx:**428-2234
(516) 571-2325 .. **Clavin,** Virginia Ann '90 %Hon G O'Connell -100 Supreme Ct Dr -Mineola 11501
(212) 593-5400 .. **Clay,** Henry J Jr. '78 (Baker N&W) -515 Mad Av -NY 10022
(212) 973-0572 .. **Claybrook,** Graham H '08 %Wolff & S PC -140 Bway -NY 10005
(212) 922-1080 .. **Clayman,** Chas E '70 (Clayman & R,LLP) -305 Mad Av -NY 10165
(212) 922-1080 .. **Clayman & Rosenberg, LLP** -305 Mad Av -NY 10165 **Fx:**949-8255
(212) 940-8800 .. **Clayton,** Allison S '08 %Katten MR LLP -575 Mad Av -NY 10022
(212) 613-2071 .. **Clayton,** Catherine M '99 (Gibbons PC) -1 Penn Plz -NY 10119 **Fx:**554-9651
(631) 261-8834 .. **Clayton,** Christopher J '93 (Ingerman S LLP) -150 Motor Pkwy -Hauppauge 11788
(716) 285-0640 .. **Clayton,** H James '92 (Clayton & B) -650 4th -Niagara Fls 14301 **Fx:**285-0663
(212) 523-2162 .. **Clayton,** Jill E '86 %Beth Israel Med Ctr -555 W 57th -NY 10019
(212) 373-3000 .. **Clayton,** Lewis R '79 (Paul WRW&G LLP) -1285 Av of Amer -NY 10019
(212) 210-9573 .. **Clayton,** Natalie C '06 %Alston & B LLP -90 Park Av -NY 10016
(518) 213-6000 .. **Clayton,** Paul D '85 NYSUT -800 Troy-Schnctdy Rd -Latham 12110 **Fx:**213-6488
(212) 218-2100 .. **Clayton,** Ronald A '81 (Fitzpatrick CH&S) -1290 Av of Amer -NY 10104
(212) 791-7536 .. **Clayton,** Thos A '95 %Morgan Stanley -1585 Bway -NY 10036
(212) 558-4000 .. **Clayton,** W Jay III '95 (Sullivan & C LLP) -125 Broad -NY 10004
(212) 608-1900 .. **Clayton,** Writer C '02 %Lovell SH LLP -61 Bway -NY 10006
(212) 553-0300 .. **Cleary,** Andrew T '08 Moody's Invstr Srvc -250 Greenwich -NY 10007
(716) 634-3320 .. **Cleary,** Brian P '97 %Pope Law Firm,PLLC -6580 Main -Williamsvll 14221 **Fx:**204-2770
(212) 551-0600 .. **Cleary,** Danl M '06 Mutual Marine Ofc Inc -919 3rd Av -NY 10022
(716) 855-1111 .. **Cleary,** Dennis P '84 (Duke HP&G LLP) -350 Main -Buffalo 14202
(718) 358-3432 .. **Cleary,** Edw F '94 %Elite Academy -136-56 39th Av -Flushng 11354
(212) 415-3355 .. **Cleary,** Eric J '01 Omnicom Group -437 Mad Av -NY 10022 **Fx:**415-3470
(212) 909-6000 .. **Cleary,** Erin L '09 %Debevoise & P LLP -919 3rd Av -NY 10022
(212) 225-2000 .. **Cleary Gottlieb Steen & Hamilton** -1 Lbrty Plz -NY 10006 **Fx:**225-3999
(585) 336-1000 .. **Cleary,** James C '93 ESL Fed Credit Union -225 Chestnut -Rchstr 14604 **Fx:**336-1014
(518) 474-5367 .. **Cleary,** Jean K '71 %Dept Pub Srvc -3 ESP -Albany 12223
(212) 259-8000 .. **Cleary,** John C '85 (Dewey & L LLP) -1301 Av of Amer -NY 10019
(212) 574-1200 .. **Cleary,** John J '88 (Seward & K LLP) -1 Bttry Pk Plz -NY 10004
(718) 254-7000 .. **Cleary,** Kevan '81 %US Atty -271 Cadman Plz E -Brklyn 11201 **Fx:**254-6479
(518) 474-6740 .. **Cleary,** Linda Dwyer '84 %Dept of State -41 State -Albany 12231 **Fx:**473-9211
(212) 336-2000 .. **Cleary,** Lisa E '85 (Patterson BW&T LLP) -1133 Av of Amer -NY 10036
(212) 771-9519 .. **Cleary,** Michl J '73 CIT Grp Inc -505 5th Av -NY 10017
(212) 261-8000 .. **Cleary,** Michl S '07 %Mendes & M,LLP -750 7th Av -NY 10019
(212) 973-0572 .. **Cleary,** Patricia D '07 %Wolff & S PC -140 Bway -NY 10005
(716) 759-6841 .. **Cleary,** Paul G '77 -4210 Harris Hill Rd -Williamsvll 14221 **Fx:**759-6978
(917) 421-4616 .. **Cleary,** Philip R '09 IRS -33 Maiden Ln -NY 10038
(212) 969-3000 .. **Cleary,** Robt J '82 (Proskauer R LLP) -1585 Bway -NY 10036
(212) 697-3122 .. **Cleary,** Ryan M '08 %Martin C&B LLP -220 E 42nd -NY 10017
(518) 436-0751 .. **Cleary,** Stephen M '71 (Hinman S PC) -121 State -Albany 12207
(631) 367-4328 .. **Cleary,** Timothy J '88 -250 Round Swamp Rd -Melvll 11747
(212) 468-8000 .. **Cleary,** Timothy J '10 %Morrison & F LLP -1290 Av of Amer -NY 10104
(718) 250-1400 .. **Cleary,** Wm J '87 %BZ Green -12 MetroTech Ctr -Brklyn 11201 **Fx:**250-1401
(212) 455-2000 .. **Cleary,** Yahonnes S '10 %Simpson T&B LLP -425 Lex Av -NY 10017
(917) 680-3503 .. **Cleaver,** Carole M '86 -380 Rector Pl -NY 10280
(631) 598-0337 .. **Cleere,** Thos P '99 OfCnsl Ansanelli K&S,LLP -92 Bway -Amityvll 11701 **Fx:**598-0352
(845) 331-7966 .. **Clegg,** David J '78 (D Clegg & Assoc) -48 Main Bx3448 -Kingston 12402 **Fx:**331-6994
(914) 637-1922 .. **Clegg,** Deborah D '94 -455 Main -New Rchll 10801 **Fx:**636-2971
(212) 728-8000 .. **Clegg,** Dorota Niechwiej '05 %Willkie F&G LLP -787 7th Av -NY 10019
(212) 269-0061 .. **Cleland,** E Gordon '87 -29 Bway -NY 10006 **Fx:**269-0172
(845) 398-3540 .. **Clemen,** John D '84 -One Kings Hwy -Tappan 10983 **Fx:**(201) 802-0613
(716) 992-2900 .. **Clemens,** David A '75 -8226 N Main -Eden 14057 **Fx:**992-2950
(914) 834-8258 .. **Clemens,** Frank J Jr. '66 -89 Colonial Av -Larchmnt 10538
(585) 203-3400 .. **Clemens,** Margaret A '85 (Littler M,PC) -400 Linden Oaks -Rchstr 14625
(914) 995-2687 .. **Clemens,** Shari E '00 %Cnty Atty -148 Martine Av -White Plns 10601 **Fx:**995-5858
(212) 446-4800 .. **Clemens,** Steven E '98 (Kirkland & E LLP) -153 E 53rd -NY 10022
(845) 358-8688 .. **Clemensen,** C Robt '74 -609 N Bway -Nyack 10960 **Fx:**358-8116
(315) 424-1750 .. **Clemens-Sponenburg,** Heather A '99 SEIU/AFL-CIO -1153 W Fayette -Syracuse 13204
(212) 415-8600 .. **Clement,** Alan B '91 (Locke LB&L LLP) -3 World Fncl Ctr -NY 10281
(212) 752-7555 .. **Clement,** Christelle G '01 %Re P & Prtnrs -445 Park Av -NY 10022
(212) 701-3000 .. **Clement,** Christopher W '10 %Cahill G&R LLP -80 Pine -NY 10005 **Fx:**269-5420
(212) 683-9551 .. **Clement,** Danl E '87 -220 5th Av -NY 10001 **Fx:**583-9661
(516) 512-8908 .. **Clement,** Debra A '99 -1225 Franklin Av -Gdn Cty 11530 **Fx:**973-8881
(315) 783-2927 .. **Clement,** Julia Rizer '03 -Bx98 -Henderson Harbor 13651
(212) 577-3634 .. **Clement,** Susan J '89 %Leg Aid -199 Water -NY 10038 **Fx:**577-3520
(212) 227-0347 .. **Clemente,** Alejandro A '02 %Weiss W&W,PC -25 Park Pl -NY 10007
(718) 643-3780 .. **Clemente,** Ann Marie L '88 %Hon TT Jones Jr -360 Adams -Brklyn 11201
(845) 887-6344 .. **Clemente,** Frances S '82 -32 Lwr Main Bx866 -Callicoon 12723 **Fx:**887-6341
(212) 269-5900 .. **Clemente,** Irma '88 %Regal Abstract Corp -90 Broad -NY 10004
(212) 969-3000 .. **Clemente,** Jean A '10 %Proskauer R LLP -1585 Bway -NY 10036
(845) 252-3033 .. **Clemente,** Jeffrey P '78 -Bx12 -Narrowsburg 12764 **Fx:**252-3035
(845) 294-9900 .. **Clemente,** Laurence A '83 (L Clemente,PC) -1 W Main at 1 Harriman Sq -Goshen 10924 **Fx:**294-2760
(518) 283-9099 .. **Clemente,** Linda Mandel '90 (Mandel Clemente,PC) -120 DeFreest Dr -North Greenbush 12180
(212) 425-5005 .. **Clemente Mueller & Tobia,PA** -14 Wall -NY 10005
(718) 921-2588 .. **Clemente,** Paul S '84 -7206 5th Av -Brklyn 11209
(212) 972-3099 .. **Clemente,** Peter C '64 Clemente Cnsltng Srvcs -324 E 41st -NY 10017
(631) 696-6200 .. **Clemente,** Robt P '65 -1150 Portion Rd -Holtsvll 11742 **Fx:**696-0052
(718) 615-1057 .. **Clemente,** Robt S '82 -153 Amherst -Brklyn 11235
(212) 727-4473 .. **Clements,** Allison S '05 NRDC -40 W 20th -NY 10011 **Fx:**727-1773
(518) 745-0978 .. **Clements,** Bernadine Morielli '89 (Clements Firm) -21 Bay Bx598 -Glens Fls 12801 **Fx:**745-0979

(212) 358-8930 .. **Clements,** Cathleen Ann '93 Chldrn's Aid Society -105 E 22nd -NY 10010
(212) 318-7000 .. **Clements,** Jacqueline M '95 %Polo Ralph Lauren Corp -650 Mad Av -NY 10022 **Fx:**318-7183
(212) 278-1244 .. **Clements,** James G '72 (Anderson K&O,PC) -1251 Av of Amer -NY 10020
(315) 375-6789 .. **Clements,** Mahlon T '60 -912 Main -Morristwn 13664 **Fx:**375-6662
(518) 474-8211 .. **Clements,** Maureen L '89 %Law Reporting Bur -1 Commerce Plz -Albany 12210 **Fx:**463-6869
(212) 836-8000 .. **Clements,** Pamela J '08 %Kaye S LLP -425 Park Av -NY 10022
(212) 819-8200 .. **Clements,** S Carter '05 %White & C LLP -1155 Av of Amer -NY 10036
(518) 745-0978 .. **Clements,** Thos G '87 (Clements Firm) -21 Bay Bx598 -Glens Fls 12801 **Fx:**745-0979
(718) 205-0287 .. **Clemenza,** Anthony '02 Queens Blvd Extended Care -6111 Qns Blvd -Woodside 11377
(212) 967-1134 .. **Clemmens,** C Michelle '06 %Marder E&N -450 7th Av -NY 10123
(212) 321-8136 .. **Clemons,** Keefe B '06 %Verizon -140 West -NY 10007
(518) 455-2711 .. **Clenahan,** Bryan Michl '97 %Senate Minority Cnsl -500 The Cptl -Albany 12247
(631) 588-6244 .. **Clennan,** John F '76 -2206 Ocean Av Bx1143 -Ronkonkoma 11779 **Fx:**588-9428
(212) 406-9710 .. **Clerkin,** James C '82 (Kral CRRP&G,LLP) -170 Bway -NY 10038
(914) 725-3332 .. **Clerkin,** John J '58 -27 Woods Ln -Scarsdale 10583
(518) 474-6400 .. **Clerkin,** Mary Ellen '83 %Dept of Ed -89 Wshngtn Av -Albany 12234 **Fx:**473-2925
(607) 255-5189 .. **Clermont,** Kevin M '74 Cornell Law Schl -Myron Taylor Hall -Ithaca 14853 **Fx:**255-7193
(607) 272-5656 .. **Clermont,** Pamela A '80 -935 Taughannock Blvd -Ithaca 14850
(516) 741-2585 .. **Cleveland-Duke,** Sherril-Anne F '99 %Rosicki R & Assoc,PC -51 E Bethpage Rd -Plainvw 11803 **Fx:**741-4748
(914) 337-3626 .. **Clewell,** Paul A '04 OfCnsl Bosworth G&F -116 Kraft Av -Bronxvll 10708
(516) 466-6030 .. **Cliff,** Donna M '86 %Mirkin & G,PC -98 Cuttermill Rd -Gt Neck 11021
(212) 836-1063 .. **Cliff,** Patricia Warburg '80 The Corcoran Grp -660 Mad Av -NY 10065
(212) 504-6000 .. **Clifford,** Alicia M '02 %Cadwalader W&T LLP -1 World Fncl Ctr -NY 10281
(518) 462-6714 .. **Clifford,** Allison M '04 %City Ct - Crim Part -Pub Safety Bldg -Albany 12202 **Fx:**447-8778
(212) 878-8000 .. **Clifford Chance US LLP** -31 W 52nd -NY 10019 **Fx:**878-8375
(973) 596-4843 .. **Clifford,** Debra A '96 (Gibbons PC) -1 Penn Plz -NY 10119 **Fx:**639-6498
(585) 546-6448 .. **Clifford,** Eugene T '67 OfCnsl Davidson F LLP -28 E Main -Rchstr 14614
(516) 897-7420 .. **Clifford,** John A '84 -370 W Bway -Long Bch 11561 **Fx:**897-7420
(716) 845-0333 .. **Clifford,** Martin J III '82 -403 Main -Buffalo 14203
(914) 428-1292 .. **Clifford,** Matthew S '99 %Watkins & W,LLP -150 Grand -White Plns 10601 **Fx:**428-4104
(631) 852-2500 .. **Clifford,** Nancy B '99 %DA -200 Center Dr -Rvrhead 11901 **Fx:**852-1769
(914) 834-0100 .. **Clifford & Purves** -1890 Palmer Av -Larchmnt 10538 **Fx:**834-0888
(914) 834-0757 .. **Clifford,** Richd C '79 -1890 Palmer Av -Larchmnt 10538 **Fx:**834-0888
(212) 687-7410 .. **Clifton Budd & DeMaria,LLP** -420 Lex Av -NY 10170 **Fx:**687-3285
(212) 419-1500 .. **Clifton,** Danl E '78 (Lewis C&N,PC) -350 7th Av -NY 10001
(631) 293-5700 .. **Clinard,** Robt A '97 RA Clinard PLLC -445 Broadhllw Rd -Melvll 11747
(646) 678-2645 .. **Cline,** Benjamin M '08 -130 Chruch -NY 10007
(718) 721-2000 .. **Cline,** Christina '94 %Drobenko & Assoc,PC -25-84 Steinway -Astoria 11103 **Fx:**721-8812
(516) 678-8627 .. **Cline,** Jerome Z '66 -14 St James Pl -Lynbrk 11563 **Fx:**593-1240
(716) 849-6500 .. **Cline,** Kimberly A '00 %Brown & T,LLC -14 Lafayette Sq -Buffalo 14203
(516) 463-5125 .. **Cline,** Kimberly R '88 %Hofstra Univ -1000 Fulton Av -Hempstd 11550 **Fx:**463-6870
(631) 244-2904 .. **Cline,** Regina T '03 (Boland & C) -222 E Mian -Smithtwn 11787 **Fx:**472-5153
(607) 563-8910 .. **Cline,** Thos R '92 -9 Division -Sidney 13838
(212) 837-6000 .. **Clines,** Kevin F '01 (Hughes H&R LLP) -1 Bttry Pk Plz -NY 10004
(212) 864-0188 .. **Cling,** B J '88 -325 Riverside Dr -NY 10025 **Fx:**316-3256
(518) 359-7064 .. **Clingman,** Nan B '91 %MHLS -2445 State Route 30 -Tupper Lk 12986 **Fx:**359-4371
(607) 547-2522 .. **Clinton,** David J '87 (Gozigian W&C) -103 Main Bx431 -Cooperstwn 13326
(315) 671-2792 .. **Clinton,** John P '73 Cnsl City Ct -505 S State -Syracuse 13202
(607) 336-4657 .. **Clippinger,** Scott J '82 Clippinger -48 Hale -Norwich 13815 **Fx:**336-1628
(607) 627-6811 .. **Clippinger,** Scott J '82 Clippinger -1 W Main Bx272 -Smyrna 13464 **Fx:**627-6816
(212) 335-9000 .. **Cliver,** C Andrew '09 %DA -1 Hogan Pl -NY 10013
(518) 725-1200 .. **Clo,** John N '93 -32 Spring -Gloversvll 12078 **Fx:**725-0779
(607) 729-5032 .. **Clobridge,** Robt R '58 -68 Grand Blvd -Bnghmtn 13905
(516) 426-2350 .. **Clodfelter,** Kristen A '02 -734 Franklin Av -Gdn Cty 11530
(716) 845-1837 .. **Clohessy,** Michl P '84 %Supreme Ct -92 Franklin -Buffalo 14202 **Fx:**856-4670
(518) 943-3100 .. **Cloke,** Edw G '68 -420 Hambrg Rd Bx325 -Catskill 12414
(845) 353-3202 .. **Cloney Dedyo,** Shannon '96 -1059 Route 9W S -Nyack 10960
(845) 331-0702 .. **Cloonan,** Wm N '75 (Cook NCK&M,PC) -85 Main Bx3939 -Kingston 12402
(212) 637-2716 .. **Clopper,** John D '00 US Atty -86 Chmbrs -NY 10007
(716) 855-1111 .. **Clor,** Bernadette J '03 SpclCnsl Duke HP&G LLP -350 Main -Buffalo 14202
(212) 691-4228 .. **Clor,** Kevin C '00 Local 72-IBT -265 W 14th -NY 10011
(212) 872-1000 .. **Clore,** Christopher J '09 -One Bryant Park -NY 10036 **Fx:**872-1002
(212) 676-0936 .. **Close,** Beatrice A '78 %Hlth & Hsptl Corp -346 Bway -NY 10013 **Fx:**676-0892
(212) 682-0020 .. **Close,** Sean H '96 (Putney TH&H LLP) -521 5th Av -NY 10175
(212) 821-0801 .. **Cloud,** Christopher H '94 %Weill Cornell Med Cllg -525 E 68th -NY 10065
(212) 782-4632 .. **Cloud,** Mio E '92 %Bk of Tokyo-Mitsubishi -1251 Av of Amer -NY 10020 **Fx:**782-6420
(212) 839-5300 .. **Cloud,** Ryan T '09 %Sidley A LLP -787 7th Av -NY 10019
(315) 393-1111 .. **Clough,** Molly E '97 (Carlisle C&C,PC) -602 State Bx757 -Ogdensbrg 13669 **Fx:**393-1181
(518) 756-6636 .. **Clouse,** Peter T '89 -Bx945 -Coeymans 12045 **Fx:**756-6636
(518) 473-1577 .. **Clune,** Albert E '78 OCFS -52 Wshngtn -Rensselaer 12144 **Fx:**402-6526
(607) 563-1152 .. **Clune,** Albert E '78 -3 Main -Sidney 13838
(212) 720-2799 .. **Clune,** David K '03 %Fed Reserve Bk -33 Lbrty -NY 10045 **Fx:**785-5748
(212) 481-1312 .. **Clune,** James W '93 Gulotta Law Grp PLLC -271 Mad Av -NY 10016 **Fx:**481-1316
(607) 273-3339 .. **Clune,** Robt J '61 (Williamson C&S) -317 N Tioga Bx126 -Ithaca 14850
(518) 432-7861 .. **Clune,** Timothy A '87 %Disability Advocates,Inc -5 Clinton Sq -Albany 12207 **Fx:**427-6561
(212) 373-3000 .. **Clunie,** David G '06 %Paul WRW&G LLP -1285 Av of Amer -NY 10019
(914) 798-5400 .. **Clunis,** Jennaydra D '05 %Goldberg S LLP -11 Martine Av -White Plns 10606
(516) 222-1650 .. **Clurfeld,** Hyman '53 (H Clurfeld,PC) -1205 Franklin Av -Gdn Cty 11530 **Fx:**227-0551
(917) 848-0974 .. **Clurman,** David '52 -201 E 37th -NY 10016 **Fx:**(212) 876-5554
(518) 563-4884 .. **Clute,** James Wm '75 (Clute C&T) -121 Brdg Bx2885 -Plattsbrgh 12901 **Fx:**563-5845
(518) 563-4884 .. **Clute,** John E Jr. '78 (Clute C&T) -121 Brdg Bx2885 -Plattsbrgh 12901 **Fx:**563-5845
(914) 935-3336 .. **Clyatt,** Wonda Liu '86 -189 Milton Rd -Rye 10580 **Fx:**935-1494
(212) 421-2233 .. **Clyman,** Mark S '06 %Wilk A LLP -675 3rd Av -NY 10017
(315) 448-0672 .. **Clymer,** Steven D '96 %US Atty -100 S Clinton Bx7198 -Syracuse 13261 **Fx:**448-0689
(518) 449-8893 .. **Clyne,** Donna M '84 OfCnsl Wilson EME&D LLP -677 Bway -Albany 12207
(518) 436-0786 .. **Clyne,** Elizabeth K '86 (Featherstonhaugh W&C,LLP) -99 Pine -Albany 12207
(212) 696-6000 .. **Clyne,** Jos F '84 Curtis M-PC&M LLP -101 Park Av -NY 10178
(516) 741-1130 .. **Clyne,** Kevin M '00 (Herman KC&C,LLP) -400 Grdn City Plz -Gdn Cty 11530
(518) 626-0015 .. **Clyne,** Matthew J '78 -90 State -Albany 12207 **Fx:**626-0118
(212) 669-0600 .. **Clyne,** Robt G '89 (Hill R LLP) -45 Bway -NY 10006
(212) 859-5084 .. **Clyne,** Wm C '91 -110 Wall -NY 10005
(212) 248-9100 .. **Clynes,** James G '86 %Epstein H&M -1 Whitehall -NY 10004
(212) 661-3535 .. **Cmielewski,** Margaret M '00 %Hodgson R LLP -60 E 42nd -NY 10165
(718) 304-4122 .. **Co,** Catherine May '06 -10 5th -Vly Stream 11581 **Fx:**412-3212
(212) 635-1152 .. **Coad,** Brian D '84 Bank of NY Mellon -1 Wall -NY 10286
(212) 839-5300 .. **Coad,** C Sarah '08 %Sidley A LLP -787 7th Av -NY 10019
(718) 286-2000 .. **Coakley,** Bryan J '87 %Leg Aid -120-46 Qns Blvd -Kew Gdns 11415 **Fx:**286-2286
(212) 909-6000 .. **Coakley,** Josephine D '05 %Debevoise & P LLP -919 3rd Av -NY 10022
(212) 872-5504 .. **Coakley,** Monica M '95 (KPMG LLP) -345 Park Av -NY 10154 **Fx:**409-8320
(518) 463-3990 .. **Coan,** Alison M '96 %Tuczinski CG&C,PC -54 State -Albany 12207
(212) 940-8800 .. **Coan,** Rachel B '85 (Katten MR LLP) -575 Mad Av -NY 10022
(518) 377-9096 .. **Coan,** Robt P '93 (Parisi C&S,PLLC) -376 Bway Bx1087 -Schnctdy 12305 **Fx:**377-9108
(914) 472-5857 .. **Coape-Arnold,** Karen '89 -1000 Post Rd -Scarsdale 10583 **Fx:**472-5817
(585) 352-0700 .. **Coapman,** Carl A '88 %Kennedy & S -43 Nichols Bx102 -Spencerprt 14559 **Fx:**352-0701
(212) 357-1247 .. **Coar,** Lisa M '04 Goldman Sachs -85 Broad -NY 10004
(212) 809-7800 .. **Coates,** Peter F '02 %Jaffe & K,LLP -40 Wall -NY 10005
(212) 775-8700 .. **Coates,** Stephen J '07 %Kilpatrick S,LLP -31 W 52nd -NY 10019
(516) 674-1556 .. **Coates,** W Shelby Jr. '61 -Bx186 -Oyster Bay 11771 **Fx:**624-6802
(212) 489-1600 .. **Coats,** Shari Fallek '01 %Deloitte LLP -1633 Bway -NY 10019 **Fx:**492-4201
(212) 993-0076 .. **Coats,** Stephen S '02 Riverstone Holdings -712 5th Av -NY 10019 **Fx:**993-0077
(718) 597-2100 .. **Cobaj,** Merima '00 (M Cobaj,PC) -3651 E Tremont Av -Bronx 10465 **Fx:**597-2150
(212) 849-7000 .. **Cobb,** Alicia K '09 %Quinn EU&S,LLP -51 Mad Av -NY 10010
(716) 885-9700 .. **Cobb,** Chas H '04 %Collins & B,LLP -267 North -Buffalo 14201
(212) 759-4888 .. **Cobb,** Chester L '78 (Phillips L LLP) -437 Mad Av -NY 10022
(212) 545-4704 .. **Cobb,** Christopher '01 %Wolf HAF&H LLP -270 Mad Av -NY 10016
(212) 635-1507 .. **Cobb,** Cristina '94 Bk of NY Mellon -1 Wall -NY 10286
(212) 596-9000 .. **Cobb,** Emily A '01 %Ropes & G LLP -1211 Av of Amer -NY 10036
(212) 259-8000 .. **Cobb,** John H Jr. '96 (Dewey & L LLP) -1301 Av of Amer -NY 10019
(845) 565-0500 .. **Cobb,** John W '93 (Cobb & C) -724 Bway -Newburgh 12550 **Fx:**565-1035
(718) 997-5775 .. **Cobb,** Katharine T '77 Queens College -65-30 Kissena Blvd -Flushng 11367 **Fx:**997-5738
(845) 298-2000 .. **Cobb,** Lisa M '96 Vergilis SRD&D,LLP -1136 Route 9 -Wappingers Fls 12590
(212) 440-4300 .. **Cobb,** Peter V Z '80 Leg Aid -199 Water -NY 10038
(845) 565-0500 .. **Cobb,** Verna W '81 (Cobb & C) -724 Bway -Newburgh 12550 **Fx:**565-1035
(914) 824-5388 .. **Cobbinah,** Dafina O '06 %Hon L Martin -111 Dr ML King Jr Blvd -White Plns 10601
(585) 454-5050 .. **Cobbs,** Michl '98 (Brown & H) -2 State -Rchstr 14614
(516) 248-7844 .. **Cobert Haber & Haber** -1050 Franklin Av -Gdn Cty 11530 **Fx:**248-8124
(212) 279-5979 .. **Cobin,** David A '70 OfCnsl Kates NRE&F,LLP -845 3rd Av -NY 10022
(212) 593-9191 .. **Coblence,** Alain '75 (Coblence & Assoc) -200 Park Av S -NY 10003 **Fx:**593-0011
(212) 918-4868 .. **Cobos,** Franz '04 (Cobos EM&M,LLC) -48 Wall -NY 10005 **Fx:**918-4801
(212) 541-7800 .. **Cobrin,** Jill A '78 %Planned Parenthood -434 W 33rd -NY 10001 **Fx:**868-4677
(212) 274-6750 .. **Coburn,** Christine '84 ACS-Legal Dept -220 Church -NY 10013

(212) 422-7533 .. **Coburn**, Gregory B '77 -160 Water -NY 10038 **Fx:**422-7532
(845) 744-6131 .. **Coburn**, Jos W '80 -30 Main Bx67 -Pine Bush 12566 **Fx:**744-3152
(212) 288-5100 .. **Coburn**, Richd J '85 -880 5th Av -NY 10021 **Fx:**472-2216
(212) 643-7000 .. **Cocariu**, Dacia C '05 %Sills C&G PC -One Rckfllr Plz -NY 10020
(212) 816-6000 .. **Cocchiarella**, John C '99 Citigroup Global Mrkts -388 Greenwich -NY 10013
(607) 721-8771 .. **Cocchiola**, Carol A '86 %Dept of Law -44 Hawley -Bnghmtn 13901 **Fx:**721-8789
(607) 432-5331 .. **Coccoma**, Ellen Leary '82 SpclCnsl Hinman H&K,LLP -Five Ford Av -Oneonta 13820
(212) 715-9100 .. **Coch**, Nicholas L '62 (Kramer LN&F,LLP) -1177 Av of Amer -NY 10036
(212) 918-3000 .. **Cochet**, Sabrina H '06 %Hogan L LLP -875 3rd Av -NY 10022
(315) 735-1813 .. **Cochi**, Carl J '55 -104 Mayro Bldg -Utica 13501 **Fx:**735-4641
(212) 909-6000 .. **Cochran**, Alexander R '06 %Debevoise & P LLP -919 3rd Av -NY 10022
(518) 474-4402 .. **Cochran**, David L '88 %Dept of Law -The Cptl -Albany 12224
(212) 735-3000 .. **Cochran**, Eric L '87 (Skadden ASM&F LLP) -4 Times Sq -NY 10036
(212) 553-9215 .. **The Cochran Firm** -233 Bway -NY 10279 **Fx:**227-8763
(212) 558-4000 .. **Cochran**, Zachary L '09 %Sullivan & C LLP -125 Broad -NY 10004
(212) 450-4000 .. **Cochran-Becchina**, Ann M '96 %Davis P&W LLP -450 Lex Av -NY 10017
(212) 558-4000 .. **Cochrane**, Kathleen M '10 %Sullivan & C LLP -125 Broad -NY 10004
(212) 334-1300 .. **Cockburn**, Chloe F '08 Vera Inst of Justice -233 Bway -NY 10279 **Fx:**941-9407
(212) 736-1940 .. **Cockburn**, Shelia A '07 %Davidson D&K LLC -485 7th Av -NY 10018
(212) 909-5400 .. **Cockfield**, Susan Cary '87 KPMG LLP -757 3rd Av -NY 10017
(973) 912-7101 .. **Cockren**, Robt W '80 (Sonnenschein N&R LLP) -1221 Av of Amer -NY 10020
(212) 735-3000 .. **Coco**, Jos A '82 (Skadden ASM&F LLP) -4 Times Sq -NY 10036
(212) 450-4000 .. **Coco**, Kevin J '10 %Davis P&W LLP -450 Lex Av -NY 10017
(718) 444-4530 .. **Coco**, Maria L '91 (ML Coco & Assoc) -6601 Av U -Brklyn 11234 **Fx:**251-4058
(516) 759-2100 .. **Coco**, Michl '73 -15 Glen -Glen Cove 11542
(212) 382-6600 .. **Coco**, Tina G '93 %NYC Bar -42 W 44th -NY 10036 **Fx:**398-6634
(212) 688-8555 .. **Cococcia**, Amy C '00 %Fragomen DB&L LLP -7 Hanover Sq -NY 10004
(845) 855-3671 .. **Cocola**, John F '83 -5 Mtn Vw Dr -Holmes 12531
(212) 312-4800 .. **Cocoros**, James E '99 %Stuyvesant High Schl -345 Chmbrs -NY 10282
(914) 476-0162 .. **Cocozza**, Frank P '56 -707 Ynkrs Av -Ynkrs 10704 **Fx:**476-2950
(914) 476-2881 .. **Cocozza**, Paul F '75 PFC Title Ins Agency Ltd -707 Ynkrs Av -Ynkrs 10704 **Fx:**476-2950
(585) 464-9400 .. **Cocquyt**, Ronald A '76 %Wilmorite -1265 Scottsvll Rd -Rchstr 14624 **Fx:**328-1784
(585) 546-1734 .. **Cocuzzi**, Thos F '74 -45 Exchange Blvd -Rchstr 14614
(607) 324-7118 .. **Coddington**, David E '95 -238 Main -Hornell 14843 **Fx:**324-5719
(718) 590-2000 .. **Coddington**, Peter D '74 %DA -198 E 161st -Bronx 10451 **Fx:**590-6477
(914) 285-8500 .. **Code**, Howard T '81 %TK Moore -701 Wstchstr Av -White Plns 10604 **Fx:**285-8510
(585) 232-5300 .. **Code**, Ralph J III '71 (Boylan BCV&W,LLP) -2400 Chase Sq -Rchstr 14604
(718) 931-2575 .. **Codelia & Socorro PC** -1967 Turnbull Av -Bronx 10473 **Fx:**931-1121
(516) 222-0007 .. **Coden**, Jennifer L '02 -600 Old Cntry Rd -Gdn Cty 11530 **Fx:**222-0088
(212) 962-6525 .. **Codispoti**, Bruno F '89 (Codispoti & Assoc,PC) -111 John -NY 10038 **Fx:**962-6791
(845) 639-7800 .. **Codispoti**, Lawr A '87 (Mandel K&B,LLP) -210 Route 303 -Vly Cottage 10989
(914) 323-7000 .. **Codispoti**, Marianna '07 %Wilson EME&D LLP -3 Gannett Dr -White Plns 10604
(716) 856-9704 .. **Codjovi**, Jamie L '08 %Feuerstein & S,LLP -17 St Louis Pl -Buffalo 14202 **Fx:**856-9707
(212) 722-2000 .. **Codling**, L Antonia '93 %Leg Aid -230 E 106th -NY 10029 **Fx:**876-5365
(718) 206-4735 .. **Cody**, Brian D '96 %Law Dept -89-17 Sutphin Blvd -Jamaica 11435 **Fx:**206-4702
(518) 262-3828 .. **Cody**, John C '95 %Albany Med Ctr -43 New Scotland Av -Albany 12208 **Fx:**262-4184
(585) 546-8303 .. **Cody**, Lynne P '95 %Rochester Business Journal -45 East Av -Rchstr 14604 **Fx:**546-3398
(315) 474-7571 .. **Cody**, Mary Anne '91 (Mackenzie H LLP) -101 S Salina Bx4967 -Syracuse 13221
(212) 687-4900 .. **Cody**, Patricia Ann '97 Cnsl Wormser KG&J LLP -825 3rd Av -NY 10022
(585) 724-3167 .. **Cody**, Peter C '93 Eastman Kodak -343 State -Rchstr 14650
(212) 309-8695 .. **Cody**, Thalia M '86 %ING-Legal Dept -230 Park Av -NY 10169
(845) 639-1500 .. **Cody**, Thos J '65 -5 Moreland Rd -New Cty 10956 **Fx:**639-9714
(585) 637-7560 .. **Cody**, Wm J '82 -109 Main -Brockprt 14420 **Fx:**637-7457
(607) 432-2980 .. **Coe**, Christy A '89 %MHLS -28 Hill -Oneonta 13820
(914) 631-7768 .. **Coe**, Laurie MacDonald '85 (Hulnick & C) -54 Main -Tarrytwn 10591
(914) 761-1857 .. **Coe**, Robt '59 -134 Soundvw Av -White Plns 10606 **Fx:**761-1857
(212) 310-8000 .. **Coelho**, Sara '08 %Weil G&M LLP -767 5th Av -NY 10153
(212) 574-1200 .. **Coelho-Adam**, Yvette D '02 %Seward & K LLP -1 Bttry Pk Plz -NY 10004
(212) 643-5402 .. **Coello**, Marjorie Y '04 %SA Rubin & Assoc,PLLC -350 5th Av -NY 10118 **Fx:**594-4082
(212) 325-2000 .. **Coen**, Maureen R '88 Credit Suisse -11 Mad Av -NY 10010
(631) 501-3100 .. **Coen**, Merilee K '94 %J Humphreys -3 Huntngtn Quad Bx9028 -Melvll 11747 **Fx:**501-3085
(212) 455-2000 .. **Coen**, R Davis '09 %Simpson T&B LLP -425 Lex Av -NY 10017
(718) 875-8808 .. **Coen**, Seth E '77 (S Coen,PC) -44 Court -Brklyn 11201 **Fx:**852-8365
(212) 225-2000 .. **Coenen**, Thos J '09 %Cleary GS&H -1 Lbrty Plz -NY 10006
(212) 574-1200 .. **Cofer**, James C '01 (Seward & K LLP) -1 Bttry Pk Plz -NY 10004
(212) 425-5750 .. **Coffee**, Evanthia '93 Gard NA,Inc -30 Broad -NY 10004
(212) 854-2833 .. **Coffee**, John C Jr. '70 %Columbia Law Schl -435 W 116th -NY 10027 **Fx:**854-7946
(845) 638-5599 .. **Coffey**, Brian P '94 %Hon W Kelly -1 S Main -New Cty 10956
(212) 417-3700 .. **Coffey**, Carolyn E '05 MFY Legal Srvcs -299 Bway -NY 10007 **Fx:**417-3890
(718) 298-0204 .. **Coffey**, Christopher W '91 Family Ct -151-20 Jamaica Av -Jamaica 11432
(518) 268-1916 .. **Coffey**, Danl W '91 D Coffey -119 Wshngtn Av -Albany 12210 **Fx:**207-1916
(212) 532-0500 .. **Coffey**, Francis A '02 %Heiberger & Assoc,PC -205 Lex Av -NY 10016 **Fx:**532-2040
(845) 639-8100 .. **Coffey**, Gregg A '94 (Masch C & Assoc,LLP) -254 S Main -New Cty 10956 **Fx:**639-8104
(518) 561-5510 .. **Coffey**, James J '75 -62 Brinkerhoff Bx158 -Plattsbrgh 12901 **Fx:**561-5332
(212) 356-4792 .. **Coffey**, Jennifer M '99 St Vincents Leg Affrs -450 W 33rd -NY 10001
(212) 533-6300 .. **Coffey**, Jennifer N '05 %NYSUT -52 Bway -NY 10004 **Fx:**995-2347
(516) 599-7917 .. **Coffey**, John F K '96 (Coffey & C,LLP) -304A Hempstd Av -Malverne 11565 **Fx:**599-4324
(914) 997-9550 .. **Coffey**, John P '91 %UIA Bd -120 Bloomingdale Rd -White Plns 10605 **Fx:**997-0014
(212) 838-0950 .. **Coffey**, Jos J '93 Executive Media Ntwrk -750 3rd Av -NY 10017
(646) 473-3958 .. **Coffey**, M Kevin '90 USPS-Law Dept -380 W 33rd -NY 10199
(718) 254-7000 .. **Coffey**, Martin E '76 %US Atty -271 Cadman Plz E -Brklyn 11201 **Fx:**254-6479
(914) 323-7000 .. **Coffey**, Michl W '95 (Wilson EME&D LLP) -3 Gannett Dr -White Plns 10604
(212) 490-3000 .. **Coffey**, Michl W '95 (Wilson EME&D LLP) -150 E 42nd -NY 10017
(212) 309-6000 .. **Coffey**, Michele A '89 (Morgan L&B LLP) -101 Park Av -NY 10178
(516) 599-7917 .. **Coffey**, Monica A '97 (Coffey & C,LLP) -304A Hempstd Av -Malverne 11565 **Fx:**599-4324
(518) 370-4645 .. **Coffey**, Peter V '65 (Englert CM&F,LLP) -224 State Bx1092 -Schnctdy 12301
(845) 897-5199 .. **Coffey**, Richd J '84 (Feldman K&C,LLP) -995 Main BxA -Fishkill 12524
(845) 695-6811 .. **Coffey**, Seth J '08 %MA Bjork -100 Crystal Run Rd -Middletwn 10941 **Fx:**695-6818
(518) 462-5601 .. **Coffey**, Stephen R '70 (O'Connell & A) -54 State -Albany 12207
(646) 344-8454 .. **Coffey**, Steven M '03 Pzena Invstmnt Mgmt LLC -120 W 45th -NY 10036 **Fx:**(212) 308-0010
(212) 265-6888 .. **Coffey**, Thos J '04 %Porzio B&N,PC -156 W 56th -NY 10019
(845) 856-3557 .. **Coffill**, Randall V '85 -15 Jersey Av Bx3158 -Pt Jervis 12771 **Fx:**856-3419
(212) 208-4175 .. **Coffin**, Kenneth J '96 Liberty Natl Underwriters -55 Water -NY 10041
(315) 366-2360 .. **Coffin**, W Benjamin '88 %Hon H Humphreys -Bx607 -Wampsville 13163
(212) 732-9000 .. **Coffinas**, Eleni '86 (Sullivan PBM&C PC) -120 Bway -NY 10271
(845) 638-3012 .. **Coffinas**, George G '83 (Coffinas Law Firm,PLLC) -37 Congers Rd -New Cty 10956 **Fx:**(888) 288-6174
(718) 643-7078 .. **Coffinas**, GiGi '88 %Hon L Scholnick -360 Adams -Brklyn 11201
(718) 238-4004 .. **Coffinas**, Gustav '52 Cnsl Coffinas Law Firm,PLLC -251 86th -Brklyn 11209
(718) 488-7900 .. **Coffinas & Lusthaus,PC** -186 Joralemon -Brklyn 11201 **Fx:**625-3210
(718) 488-7900 .. **Coffinas**, Maria '85 (Coffinas & L,PC) -186 Joralemon -Brklyn 11201
(518) 761-6547 .. **Coffinger**, Tatiana N '01 Supreme Ct -1340 State Route 9 -Lk George 12845 **Fx:**761-6465
(212) 841-1000 .. **Coffino**, Dianne F '89 (Covington & B LLP) -620 8th Av -NY 10018
(631) 265-1355 .. **Coffman**, James '80 (Coffman & M) -4 Tiffany Ln -Smithtwn 11787
(212) 421-1611 .. **Coffman**, Richd W '87 Institute of Intl Bankers -299 Park Av -NY 10171
(212) 335-9000 .. **Cofield**, Jason G '07 DA -1 Hogan Pl -NY 10013
(718) 708-4560 .. **Cofino**, Jos A '84 -1711 Wht Plns Rd -Bronx 10462
(212) 878-1700 .. **Cofresi**, John T '05 %Marshall DWC&G -140 Bway -NY 10005
(718) 557-6539 .. **Cofresi**, Manuel '87 OHA-SSA -Bx319300 -Jamaica 11431
(212) 640-4221 .. **Cogan**, Bruce A '78 %Amer Exp -200 Vesey -NY 10285
(212) 885-5000 .. **Cogan**, Harris N '79 (Blank R LLP) -405 Lex Av -NY 10174
(212) 683-7100 .. **Cogan**, Howard L '94 (Gallo V&K,LLP) -90 Broad -NY 10004
(212) 488-1200 .. **Cogan**, Jonathan D '03 (Kobre & K,LLP) -800 3rd Av -NY 10022
(518) 489-8302 .. **Cogan**, Kathleen A '82 -184 Whitehall Rd -Albany 12209 **Fx:**489-8370
(212) 455-2000 .. **Cogan**, Sarah E '82 (Simpson T&B LLP) -425 Lex Av -NY 10017
(518) 427-2650 .. **Cogen**, Richd M '80 (Nixon P LLP) -677 Bway -Albany 12207
(212) 728-8000 .. **Coggin**, Kara E '07 %Willkie F&G LLP -787 7th Av -NY 10019
(212) 765-5070 .. **Coggio**, Brian D '75 SrCnsl Fish & R,PC -153 E 53rd -NY 10022
(212) 421-2150 .. **Coghlan**, Jennifer L '04 %Sive P&R,PC -460 Park Av -NY 10022
(917) 777-4200 .. **Cogill**, Jean '92 (Bingham M LLP) -1 Bttry Pk Plz -NY 10004
(585) 232-3730 .. **Cognata**, Suzanne L '94 (Chamberlain D LLP) -1600 Crssrds Bldg -Rchstr 14614
(212) 728-8000 .. **Cognetti**, Mark A '99 (Willkie F&G LLP) -787 7th Av -NY 10019
(315) 476-6487 .. **Cognetti**, Ralph A '79 (Mevec & C) -206 N Townsend -Syracuse 13203
(212) 822-2216 .. **Cogsville**, Donald P '96 Cogsville Grp LLC -213 W 138th -NY 10030
(315) 689-3529 .. **Cogswell**, Michl C '71 -106 E Main Bx1006 -Elbrdg 13060 **Fx:**689-7182
(212) 455-2000 .. **Cogut**, Chas Ingram '74 (Simpson T&B LLP) -425 Lex Av -NY 10017
(212) 909-6000 .. **Cogut**, Pamela G '08 %Debevoise & P LLP -919 3rd Av -NY 10022
(212) 839-5300 .. **Cogut**, Stephen J '99 Cnsl Sidley A LLP -787 7th Av -NY 10019
(516) 296-7000 .. **Cohan**, Danl S '57 OfCnsl Certilman BA&H,LLP -90 Merrick Av -E Meadow 11554
(212) 925-1220 .. **Cohan**, Evan S '92 %DLS,Inc -401 Bway -NY 10013 **Fx:**941-0235
(212) 373-3000 .. **Cohan**, Keith Y '10 %Paul WRW&G LLP -1285 Av of Amer -NY 10019
(212) 633-6967 .. **Cohan**, Marc '80 %Natl Ctr Law & Economic Justice -275 7th Av -NY 10001 **Fx:**633-6371
(914) 592-8844 .. **Cohan**, Robt J '78 -160 S Central Av -Elmsfrd 10523 **Fx:**592-8627
(212) 715-9100 .. **Cohan**, S Elliott '81 Cnsl Kramer LN&F,LLP -1177 Av of Amer -NY 10036

(212) 206-6118 .. **Cohan,** Stacey P '03 Time Equities Inc -55 5th Av -NY 10003 **Fx:**727-0563
(716) 856-0600 .. **Coheley,** Marissa A '09 %Jaeckle F&M,LLP -12 Fountain Plz -Buffalo 14202
(212) 808-7800 .. **Cohen,** Aaron M '94 %Kelley D&W LLP -101 Park Av -NY 10178
(212) 716-5790 .. **Cohen,** Adam B '98 (Cohen Lgl Grp,LLC) -230 Park Av -NY 10169
(212) 841-9393 .. **Cohen,** Adam I '94 FTI Consulting -3 Times Sq -NY 10036
(212) 474-1000 .. **Cohen,** Adam J '10 %Cravath S&M LLP -825 8th Av -NY 10019
(212) 541-6222 .. **Cohen,** Adam M '89 (Kane K,PC) -1350 Av of Amer -NY 10019
(212) 351-4000 .. **Cohen,** Adam P '09 Gibson D&C LLP -200 Park Av -NY 10166
(718) 937-4545 .. **Cohen,** Adam R '08 Major World -4340 Nrthrn Blvd -LIC 11101
(914) 421-0080 .. **Cohen,** Adam S '92 (Cohen & S LLP) -14 Mamaroneck Av -White Plns 10601 **Fx:**421-0035
(914) 798-4234 .. **Cohen,** Adam S '99 Mariner Invstmt Grp -500 Mamaroneck Av -Harrison 10528
(212) 499-6644 .. **Cohen,** Adam S '01 %M Cohen & Assoc,PC -7 Penn Plz -NY 10001 **Fx:**818-0625
(212) 682-7474 .. **Cohen,** Akiva Meir '05 %Foley & L LLP -90 Park Av -NY 10016
(718) 948-0453 .. **Cohen,** Alan '95 -495 Eltingvll Blvd -Staten Isl 10312
(516) 679-5936 .. **Cohen,** Alan Ian '95 -339 St Marks Av -Bellmore 11710
(212) 902-1000 .. **Cohen,** Alan M '80 Goldman Sachs & Co -85 Broad -NY 10004
(212) 318-6000 .. **Cohen,** Alan S '79 (Paul HJ&W LLP) -75 E 55th -NY 10022
(212) 479-6000 .. **Cohen,** Alan S '87 (Cooley LLP) -1114 Av of Amer -NY 10036
(516) 746-5360 .. **Cohen,** Alexandra N '03 %Hoffman & B LLP -94 Second -Mineola 11501
(212) 269-1400 .. **Cohen,** Alison Bender '06 %Gusrae KB&N PLLC -120 Wall -NY 10005
(212) 351-7463 .. **Cohen,** Allan B '94 Hudson Global Rsrcs -560 Lex Av -NY 10022
(516) 832-7522 .. **Cohen,** Allan H '89 (Nixon P LLP) -50 Jericho Quadrangle -Jericho 11753
(516) 466-8331 .. **Cohen,** Allen A '72 (Kirschner & C) -305 Nrthrn Blvd -Gt Neck 11021
(212) 536-3900 .. **Cohen,** Alyssa B '08 K&L Gates LLP -599 Lex Av -NY 10022
(718) 590-7342 .. **Cohen,** Amy E '88 %Hon B Newman -851 Grand Cncrs -Bronx 10451
(518) 867-4010 .. **Cohen,** Amy W '97 -6 Twr Pl -Albany 12203 **Fx:**867-4010
(212) 790-4500 .. **Cohen,** Andrea G '96 Cnsl Manatt P&P,LLP -7 Times Sq -NY 10036
(212) 554-1234 .. **Cohen,** Andrea Harris '80 %AXA Financial Inc -1290 Av of Amer -NY 10104 **Fx:**707-3963
(212) 788-0741 .. **Cohen,** Andrea Lee '83 %Law Dept -100 Church -NY 10007 **Fx:**788-0367
(212) 715-0338 .. **Cohen,** Andrew I '92 %Tishman Speyer Prop -45 Rckfllr Plz -NY 10111 **Fx:**332-6603
(212) 230-8800 .. **Cohen,** Andrew I '02 WilmerHale -399 Park Av -NY 10022
(585) 621-4000 .. **Cohen,** Andrew J '78 (Cohen & Assoc,PC) -2300 Ridge Rd W -Rchstr 14626
(718) 618-1465 .. **Cohen,** Andrew J '99 Hon E Walker - Supreme Ct -851 Grnd Cncrs -Bronx 10451
(845) 426-0600 .. **Cohen,** Andrew L '86 (A Cohen,PC) -150 Airport Exec Pk -Nanuet 10954 **Fx:**426-0624
(212) 244-0595 .. **Cohen,** Andrew M '93 -250 W 57th -NY 10107
(212) 909-6000 .. **Cohen,** Andrew M '08 %Debevoise & P LLP -919 3rd Av -NY 10022
(516) 333-2737 .. **Cohen,** Andrew S '77 (Binder & C) -265 Post Av -Westbury 11590 **Fx:**333-1262
(212) 268-3222 .. **Cohen,** Andrew S '99 %Raphaelson & L,PC -14 Penn Plz -NY 10122 **Fx:**268-3313
(212) 351-4500 .. **Cohen,** Anna A '04 %Epstein B&G,PC -250 Park Av -NY 10177
(212) 909-6000 .. **Cohen,** Anne E '86 (Debevoise & P LLP) -919 3rd Av -NY 10022
(718) 590-2000 .. **Cohen,** April R '04 %DA -198 E 161st -Bronx 10451 **Fx:**590-6477
(212) 940-8800 .. **Cohen,** Ariele L '04 %Katten MR LLP -575 Mad Av -NY 10022
(212) 790-9200 .. **Cohen,** Arlana S '82 (Cowan L&L,PC) -1133 Av of Amer -NY 10036
(516) 484-9412 .. **Cohen,** Arnold '69 -46 Grdn Dr -Albertson 11507
(212) 645-3444 .. **Cohen,** Arnold S '79 Prtnrshp for the Homeless -305 7th Av -NY 10001
(212) 834-0600 .. **Cohen,** Arthur G '76 (Gordon & S,PC) -355 Lex Av -NY 10017
(212) 820-9359 .. **Cohen,** Arthur M '76 (Hawkins D&W LLP) -One Chase Manh Plz -NY 10005
(212) 558-4000 .. **Cohen,** Audra D '93 (Sullivan & C LLP) -125 Broad -NY 10004
(212) 640-2000 .. **Cohen,** Avi '02 Amer Exp -200 Vesey -NY 10285
(212) 506-1700 .. **Cohen,** Avinoam '06 Kasowitz BT&F LLP -1633 Bway -NY 10019
(212) 349-5890 .. **Cohen,** Barbara '83 NYS Trial Lawyers Assn -132 Nassau -NY 10038 **Fx:**608-2310
(516) 679-5936 .. **Cohen,** Barbara E '00 -339 St Marks Av -Bellmore 11710
(718) 261-6780 .. **Cohen,** Barbara G '86 %A Talero -71-50 Austin -Frst Hlls 11375 **Fx:**261-6478
(212) 475-3333 .. **Cohen,** Barbara Gratch '91 -36 Cooper Sq -NY 10003 **Fx:**505-1698
(914) 949-9700 .. **Cohen,** Barry C '92 (BC Cohen,PLLC) -Bx274 -Mt Kisco 10549 **Fx:**949-9799
(631) 979-3000 .. **Cohen,** Barry S '88 (Certilman BA&H,LLP) -1393 Vets Mem'l Hwy -Hauppauge 11788
(646) 290-5289 .. **Cohen,** Barry S '02 -845 3rd Av -NY 10022
(212) 701-3000 .. **Cohen,** Benjamin J '81 (Cahill G&R LLP) -80 Pine -NY 10005 **Fx:**269-5420
(212) 906-1200 .. **Cohen,** Benjamin J '10 %Latham & W -885 3rd Av -NY 10022
(212) 839-5300 .. **Cohen,** Benson R '05 %Sidley A LLP -787 7th Av -NY 10019
(516) 488-7000 .. **Cohen,** Bernard H '69 -98 Cuttermill Rd -Gt Neck 11021 **Fx:**488-8351
(212) 506-2500 .. **Cohen,** Berwin '00 %Mayer B LLP -1675 Bway -NY 10019
(212) 335-9000 .. **Cohen,** Beth F '97 %DA -1 Hogan Pl -NY 10013
(212) 480-5249 .. **Cohen,** Beth R '96 %Insurance Dept -25 Beaver -NY 10004 **Fx:**480-5272
(518) 445-3339 .. **Cohen,** Beverly '88 (Albany Law Schl) -80 New Scotland Av -Albany 12208 **Fx:**445-2315
(518) 465-4000 .. **Cohen,** Bob '89 Citizen Action of NY -94 Central Av -Albany 12206 **Fx:**465-2980
(718) 520-4416 .. **Cohen,** Bonnie R '79 %Hon S Roman -125-01 Qns Blvd -Kew Gdns 11415
(212) 849-7000 .. **Cohen,** Brad E '06 %Quinn EU&S,LLP -51 Mad Av -NY 10010
(212) 506-2999 .. **Cohen,** Brett F '00 %Elliott Assoc,LP -712 5th Av -NY 10019
(914) 701-5260 .. **Cohen,** Brian L '03 Schultze Asset Mgmt -3000 Wstchstr Av -Purchase 10577
(212) 779-1414 .. **Cohen,** Brian S '98 %Bernstein L LLP -10 E 40th -NY 10016
(212) 372-2178 .. **Cohen,** Brian S '07 Newmark Knight Frank -125 Park Av -NY 10017
(212) 406-0588 .. **Cohen,** Bruce D '83 -129 W 27th -NY 10001 **Fx:**385-0339
(516) 763-6700 .. **Cohen,** Bruce E '81 (Davidson & C,PC) -265 Sunrise Hwy -Rockvll Ctr 11570
(516) 938-1270 .. **Cohen,** Bruce J '80 -410 Jericho Tpke -Jericho 11753 **Fx:**942-3758
(212) 684-1919 .. **Cohen,** Bruce M '84 (Cohen & F) -286 Mad Av -NY 10017 **Fx:**686-8367
(914) 723-2038 .. **Cohen,** Bryna '88 -10 Ft Hill Ln -Scarsdale 10583
(516) 741-0123 .. **Cohen,** Carl G '60 (Cohen & P) -130 Newbrdg Rd -Hicksvll 11801
(914) 238-5893 .. **Cohen,** Carolyn F '83 -48 Brevoort Rd -Chappaqua 10514 **Fx:**238-5893
(212) 637-2264 .. **Cohen,** Carrie H '94 %US Atty -1 St Andrews Plz -NY 10007 **Fx:**637-2937
(212) 838-1800 .. **Cohen,** Chas S '79 -750 Lex Av -NY 10022 **Fx:**755-8070
(212) 837-6000 .. **Cohen,** Chas W '96 (Hughes H&R LLP) -1 Bttry Pk Plz -NY 10004
(631) 243-0097 .. **Cohen,** Craig F '93 -123 Millet N -Dix Hlls 11746
(212) 238-3000 .. **Cohen,** Craig H '94 %Emmet M&M,LLP -120 Bway -NY 10271
(212) 610-6300 .. **Cohen,** Craig M '04 %Allen & O -1221 Av of Amer -NY 10020
(516) 933-1700 .. **Cohen,** D David '66 -500 N Bway -Jericho 11753 **Fx:**933-8454
(516) 577-2641 .. **Cohen,** Dalia S '99 Honeywell -2 Corp Ctr Dr -Melvll 11747
(718) 243-6491 .. **Cohen,** Dana J '95 %Leg Aid -111 Lvngstn -Brklyn 11201 **Fx:**237-8737
(212) 418-8600 .. **Cohen,** Danl A '95 %Kornstein VW&P,LLP -757 3rd Av -NY 10017
(212) 697-5277 .. **Cohen,** Danl Antell '58 -295 Mad Av -NY 10017 **Fx:**685-6862
(212) 888-2797 .. **Cohen,** Danl I A '88 -420 E 54th -NY 10022 **Fx:**319-7824
(212) 819-8200 .. **Cohen,** Danl R '09 %White & C LLP -1155 Av of Amer -NY 10036
(315) 798-8830 .. **Cohen,** Danl S '62 (Cohen & C) -258 Genesee -Utica 13502 **Fx:**798-8034
(631) 361-8194 .. **Cohen,** Daphne Bicher '86 -116 Oakside Dr -Smithtwn 11787
(212) 521-5400 .. **Cohen,** Darren B '92 (Reed S LLP) -599 Lex Av -NY 10022
(646) 264-3684 .. **Cohen,** Darren J '05 US Dept of Labor -201 Varick -NY 10014
(212) 398-2913 .. **Cohen,** David '83 OfCnsl Sichenzia RFF LLP -61 Bway -NY 10006 **Fx:**208-2408
(212) 489-1600 .. **Cohen,** David '99 %Deloitte LLP -1633 Bway -NY 10019 **Fx:**492-4201
(516) 364-6006 .. **Cohen,** David A '80 (Cohen & S,LLP) -199 Crsswys Park Dr Bx9004 -Woodbury 11797
(212) 735-8600 .. **Cohen,** David A '07 %Morrison C LLP -909 3rd Av -NY 10022
(212) 310-8000 .. **Cohen,** David A '09 %Weil G&M LLP -767 5th Av -NY 10153
(212) 237-0000 .. **Cohen,** David B '08 (Vinson & E LLP) -666 5th Av -NY 10103
(516) 248-6400 .. **Cohen,** David E '88 %Davidoff M&H,LLP -200 Grdn City Plz -Gdn Cty 11530
(607) 797-1231 .. **Cohen,** David H '67 -142 Front -Bnghmtn 13905 **Fx:**729-5981
(718) 522-4604 .. **Cohen,** David H '77 (Tantleff C&T,PC) -188 Montague -Brklyn 11201
(516) 873-2000 .. **Cohen,** David H '84 (Moritt HH&H LLP) -400 Grdn City Plz -Gdn Cty 11530
(212) 766-9111 .. **Cohen,** David J '95 (Cohen & F,LLP) -40 Fulton -NY 10038 **Fx:**766-9166
(212) 715-9100 .. **Cohen,** David K '06 %Kramer LN&F,LLP -1177 Av of Amer -NY 10036
(718) 793-1553 .. **Cohen,** David L '71 -125-10 Qns Blvd -Kew Gdns 11415 **Fx:**793-4719
(516) 803-3318 .. **Cohen,** David L '92 Cablevision Systems Corp -1111 Stewart Av -Bethpage 11714
(914) 368-0417 .. **Cohen,** David L '99 Nokia Inc -102 Corp Park Dr -White Plns 10604
(212) 903-9000 .. **Cohen,** David L '06 %Linklaters -1345 Av of Amer -NY 10105
(212) 580-0277 .. **Cohen,** David M '58 -440 West End Av -NY 10024 **Fx:**580-0280
(631) 293-6061 .. **Cohen,** David M '79 (Cooper S&C,PC) -560 Broadhllw Rd -Melvll 11747
(631) 424-7000 .. **Cohen,** David M '87 %Five Towns Cllg -305 N Srvc Rd -Dix Hlls 11746 **Fx:**424-7006
(212) 408-2500 .. **Cohen,** David M '87 (Baker B,LLP) -30 Rckfllr Plz -NY 10112
(212) 756-2000 .. **Cohen,** David M '90 (Schulte R&Z LLP) -919 3rd Av -NY 10022
(718) 553-3270 .. **Cohen,** David M '03 FAA -1 Aviation Plz -Jamaica 11434
(914) 286-2900 .. **Cohen,** David N '88 (Greenberg T,LLP) -445 Hmltn Av -White Plns 10601
(718) 565-4397 .. **Cohen,** David P '96 %Sterling Doubleday -Shea Stadium -Flushng 11368
(212) 340-0400 .. **Cohen,** David S '87 %Appllt Div 1st Dept -27 Mad Av -NY 10010 **Fx:**889-4412
(718) 250-2000 .. **Cohen,** Deborah '95 %DA -350 Jay -Brklyn 11201 **Fx:**250-2314
(914) 824-5432 .. **Cohen,** Deborah L '83 %Hon M Smith -111 Martin Luther King Blvd -White Plns 10601 **Fx:**955-4184
(212) 765-9100 .. **Cohen,** Debra J '92 %Halperin BR,LLP -555 Mad Av -NY 10022
(718) 515-7500 .. **Cohen,** Debra S '99 (McLaughlin G&C) -959 E 233rd -Bronx 10466 **Fx:**515-5557
(718) 488-5755 .. **Cohen,** Della R '79 %DMV -625 Atl Av -Brklyn 11217
(212) 592-1400 .. **Cohen,** Dena '88 Cnsl Herrick,F LLP -2 Park Av -NY 10016
(212) 589-4200 .. **Cohen,** Dennis O '04 %Baker & H LLP -45 Rckfllr Plz -NY 10111
(516) 364-6040 .. **Cohen,** Diane D '98 -7600 Jericho Tpk -Woodbury 11797 **Fx:**364-6041
(212) 316-4048 .. **Cohen,** Diane R '81 -162 W 94th -NY 10025
(914) 684-2100 .. **Cohen,** Dina B '08 %Littman K LLP -399 Knollwood Rd -White Plns 10603
(212) 801-2171 .. **Cohen,** Donald N '84 (Greenberg T,LLP) -200 Park Av -NY 10166
(631) 694-6012 .. **Cohen,** Donald R '86 -72 Allen Blvd -Farmngdl 11735 **Fx:**694-6002
(212) 294-8092 .. **Cohen,** Douglas N '97 %Cantor Fitzgerald -110 E 59th -NY 10022
(212) 541-4684 .. **Cohen,** Drew H '94 Music Theatre Intl -421 W 54th -NY 10019
(212) 294-6700 .. **Cohen,** Edmund S '72 (Winston & S) -200 Park Av -NY 10166
(212) 772-9020 .. **Cohen,** Edw B '71 -525 E 86th -NY 10028
(212) 940-8580 .. **Cohen,** Edw H '64 Cnsl Katten MR LLP -575 Mad Av -NY 10022
(212) 925-4044 .. **Cohen,** Edw I '61 -299 Bway -NY 10007 **Fx:**925-4044
(631) 665-3400 .. **Cohen,** Edw J '76 %Siben & S,LLP -90 E Main Bx149P -Bay Shr 11706
(212) 755-0500 .. **Cohen,** Eliezer A '82 -63 White Dr -Cedarhrst 11516 **Fx:**791-9795
(212) 416-6500 .. **Cohen,** Elizabeth '07 %Dept of Law -120 Bway -NY 10271
(212) 833-8000 .. **Cohen,** Elizabeth S '07 Sony BMG Music Entrtnmnt -550 Mad Av -NY 10022 **Fx:**833-8406
(212) 762-6859 .. **Cohen,** Ella Dlin '99 Morgan Stanley Invstmnt Mgmt -1221 Av of Amer -NY 10020

(212) 704-6000 .. **Cohen,** Elliot '74 (Troutman S LLP) -405 Lex Av -NY 10174
(516) 294-8844 .. **Cohen,** Elyssa W '07 %L'Abbate BC&C,LLP -1001 Franklin Av -Gdn Cty 11530
(212) 788-0718 .. **Cohen,** Emily '04 %Law Dept -100 Church -NY 10007 **Fx:**788-0367
(718) 250-4222 .. **Cohen,** Emily J '95 %Leg Aid -111 Lvngstn -Brklyn 11201 **Fx:**250-4243
(212) 335-9000 .. **Cohen,** Emily R '09 %DA -1 Hogan Pl -NY 10013
(212) 331-0571 .. **Cohen,** Eric N '99 E Cohen & Assoc,PLLC -276 5th Av -NY 10001 **Fx:**(646) 219-5539
(212) 244-3333 .. **Cohen,** Eric S '03 %Donovan H LLP -1350 Bway -NY 10018
(212) 269-2500 .. **Cohen,** Erica H '04 %Gorlick K&L,PC -17 State -NY 10004
(315) 785-3001 .. **Cohen,** Erica L '06 Jefferson Cnty Family Ct -163 Arsenal -Watertwn 13601
(516) 742-8058 .. **Cohen,** Evan B '90 %Abamont & Assoc -200 Grdn City Plz Bx9250 -Gdn Cty 11530 **Fx:**742-7308
(212) 455-2000 .. **Cohen,** Evan I '08 %Simpson T&B LLP -425 Lex Av -NY 10017
(212) 878-8000 .. **Cohen,** Evan J '88 (Clifford C LLP) -31 W 52nd -NY 10019
(718) 980-4680 .. **Cohen,** Francine Pickett '92 -1110 South Av -Staten Isl 10314 **Fx:**(347) 273-1383
(212) 732-0002 .. **Cohen Frankel & Ruggiero,LLP** -20 Vesey -NY 10007 **Fx:**293-7224
(516) 684-9891 .. **Cohen,** Fred J '05 -1180 Nrthrn Blvd -Manhsst 11030
(917) 376-0598 .. **Cohen,** Fred R '81 -1215 5th Av -NY 10029
(212) 692-1000 .. **Cohen,** Fredk S '68 (Duane M LLP) -1540 Bway -NY 10036
(212) 632-3253 .. **Cohen,** Gail E '86 Fiduciary Trust Co Intl -600 5th Av -NY 10020 **Fx:**632-4104
(917) 455-0077 .. **Cohen,** Gary '78 -141 Joralemon -Brklyn 11201
(914) 968-4432 .. **Cohen,** George I '41 -501 Riverdale Av -Ynkrs 10705
(212) 374-9115 .. **Cohen,** Gerald M '05 (Cohen & F LLP) -225 Bway -NY 10007 **Fx:**406-6890
(212) 994-8730 .. **Cohen,** Gerald S '71 Ackman-Ziff Real Estate Grp -110 E 42nd -NY 10017
(212) 537-9000 .. **Cohen Goldstein & Silpe,LLP** -850 3rd Av -NY 10022 **Fx:**537-9010
(212) 957-7600 .. **Cohen & Gresser LLP** -800 3rd Av -NY 10022 **Fx:**957-4514
(212) 468-4800 .. **Cohen,** Guy R '94 (Davis & G LLP) -1740 Bway -NY 10019
(212) 558-4000 .. **Cohen,** H Rodgin '71 (Sullivan & C LLP) -125 Broad -NY 10004
(212) 836-8000 .. **Cohen,** Hanna Glomska '07 %Kaye S LLP -425 Park Av -NY 10022
(646) 386-5700 .. **Cohen,** Hannah '98 %Civil Ct -111 Centre -NY 10013
(212) 992-8124 .. **Cohen,** Harlan G '04 %NYU Law Schl -137 MacDougal -NY 10012
(212) 512-0801 .. **Cohen,** Harriet Newman '75 (Cohen HB&R,PC) -11 W 42nd -NY 10036
(212) 223-4000 .. **Cohen,** Harry P '82 (Crowell & M LLP) -590 Mad Av -NY 10022
(516) 766-3200 .. **Cohen,** Harvey '48 (Murtagh C&B) -100 N Park Av -Rockvll Ctr 11570
(315) 625-3215 .. **Cohen,** Heather L '98 CONMED Corp -525 French Rd -Utica 13502 **Fx:**793-8929
(646) 761-6907 .. **Cohen,** Helen L '02 (Wolpin & C) -220 Salina Meadow -Syracuse 13212
(212) 575-0007 .. **Cohen Hennessey Bienstock & Rabin, PC** -11 W 42nd -NY 10036 **Fx:**764-3925
(914) 683-3519 .. **Cohen Hennessey Bienstock & Rabin, PC** -445 Hmltn Av -White Plns 10601 **Fx:**428-1060
(212) 755-2800 .. **Cohen,** Herbert L '74 (Stiefel & C) -770 Lex Av -NY 10065
(607) 754-5990 .. **Cohen,** Herbert N '60 -Bx426 -Bnghmtn 13902 **Fx:**754-7826
(212) 846-6758 .. **Cohen,** Hillary S '95 %MTV Networks -1515 Bway -NY 10036 **Fx:**258-8358
(212) 704-6000 .. **Cohen,** Hollace T '73 (Troutman S LLP) -405 Lex Av -NY 10174
(716) 854-4300 .. **Cohen,** Howard B '84 (Gross SB&G,PC) -465 Main -Buffalo 14203
(516) 374-4317 .. **Cohen,** Howard I '50 -376 Central Av -Lawrence 11559
(212) 984-7750 .. **Cohen,** Howard M '49 OfCnsl Warshaw BCS&K,LLP -555 5th Av -NY 10017
(212) 964-6611 .. **Cohen,** Howard R '71 Cnsl Lester SK&D -120 Bway -NY 10271
(914) 766-4385 .. **Cohen,** Howard S '80 IBM -N Castle Dr -Armonk 10504
(212) 973-2972 .. **Cohen,** Howard S '98 AECOM Tech Corp -605 3rd Av -NY 10158 **Fx:**986-4713
(718) 596-9000 .. **Cohen Hurkin Ehrenfeld Pomerantz & Tenenbaum** -25 Chapel -Brklyn 11201 **Fx:**596-9536
(212) 756-2000 .. **Cohen,** Ian R '10 %Schulte R&Z LLP -919 3rd Av -NY 10022
(516) 621-6689 .. **Cohen,** Ilene H '87 -Bx221 -Roslyn 11576 **Fx:**621-0259 ***[Per Diem Services]***
(516) 374-1594 .. **Cohen,** Ilene Rosen '83 -1365 Hrbr Rd -Hewlett 11557
(516) 223-8822 .. **Cohen,** Ira A '67 -2322 Grand Av Bx0066 -Baldwin 11510
(212) 672-6000 .. **Cohen,** Ira D '97 %Hypo und Vereins Bk -150 E 42nd -NY 10017
(212) 964-2544 .. **Cohen,** Irving '67 -233 Bway -NY 10279 **Fx:**732-1339
(212) 791-5500 .. **Cohen,** Irving '88 Cohen P PLLC -156 William -NY 10038
(212) 686-4401 .. **Cohen,** Irwin J '77 %Abramson Law Grp PLLC -570 Lex Av -NY 10022 **Fx:**686-6515
(212) 728-8000 .. **Cohen,** Jack D '07 %Willkie F&G LLP -787 7th Av -NY 10019
(212) 440-2350 .. **Cohen,** Jack L '80 %C Siegel -40 Wall -NY 10005 **Fx:**440-2385
(212) 258-6000 .. **Cohen,** Jack S '87 %Viacom -1515 Bway -NY 10036
(212) 310-8000 .. **Cohen,** Jaclyn L '98 %Weil G&M LLP -767 5th Av -NY 10153
(212) 558-4000 .. **Cohen,** Jacob E '10 %Sullivan & C LLP -125 Broad -NY 10004
(212) 984-2935 .. **Cohen,** Jacob M '08 TRG Mgmt LP -280 Park Av -NY 10075
(516) 358-6900 .. **Cohen & Jaffe LLP** -2001 Marcus Av -Lk Success 11042 **Fx:**358-6903
(212) 688-4500 .. **Cohen,** James A '71 %P & E Properties -444 Mad Av -NY 10022 **Fx:**888-5025
(212) 636-6822 .. **Cohen,** James A '77 %Fordham Univ Sch of Law -140 W 62nd -NY 10023 **Fx:**636-6899
(212) 986-6000 .. **Cohen,** James R '66 (Kleinberg KW&C,PC) -551 5th Av -NY 10176
(718) 948-2100 .. **Cohen,** James R '76 (Simonson & C,PC) -4060 Amboy Rd -Staten Isl 10308
(212) 988-3338 .. **Cohen,** Janet A '88 -19 W 34th -NY 10001 **Fx:**794-3680
(518) 471-4766 .. **Cohen,** Janis '83 %Appllt Div 3rd Dept -Capitol Station Bx7288 -Albany 12224 **Fx:**471-4750
(212) 758-8575 .. **Cohen,** Jason A '98 Lazard Middle Mrkt -11 W 42nd -NY 10036
(212) 521-5400 .. **Cohen,** Jason A '04 %Reed S LLP -599 Lex Av -NY 10022
(914) 640-8100 .. **Cohen,** Jason F '00 Starwood Hotels & Resorts -1111 Wstchstr Av -White Plns 10604 **Fx:**640-8250
(212) 412-9500 .. **Cohen,** Jason T '87 OfCnsl Flemming ZWZ LLP -1 Lbrty Plz -NY 10006
(212) 373-3000 .. **Cohen,** Jay '81 (Paul WRW&G LLP) -1285 Av of Amer -NY 10019
(718) 237-1200 .. **Cohen,** Jay D '77 (Jacobs & C) -26 Court -Brklyn 11242
(718) 537-4958 .. **Cohen,** Jay L '82 %ODAR-SSA -226 E 161st -Bronx 10451 **Fx:**590-1673
(212) 373-3000 .. **Cohen,** Jayson L '06 %Paul WRW&G LLP -1285 Av of Amer -NY 10019
(212) 712-2891 .. **Cohen,** Jeffrey B '99 Salomon Smith Barney -250 West -NY 10013
(518) 474-2523 .. **Cohen,** Jeffrey C '70 Dept Pub Srvc -3 ESP -Albany 12223
(212) 903-9000 .. **Cohen,** Jeffrey C '98 (Linklaters) -1345 Av of Amer -NY 10105
(516) 577-5708 .. **Cohen,** Jeffrey D '89 Oyster Bay -150 Miller Pl -Syosset 11791
(212) 626-4100 .. **Cohen,** Jeffrey E '83 (Baker & M LLP) -1114 Av of Amer -NY 10036
(718) 365-4310 .. **Cohen,** Jeffrey F '80 -617 E 188th -Bronx 10458 **Fx:**367-7386
(718) 370-7030 .. **Cohen,** Jeffrey J '77 (Amabile & E,PC) -1000 South Av -Staten Isl 10314
(212) 479-6000 .. **Cohen,** Jeffrey L '00 (Cooley LLP) -1114 Av of Amer -NY 10036
(518) 436-5409 .. **Cohen,** Jeffrey M '84 -7 Thurlow Ter -Albany 12203 **Fx:**445-8907
(212) 705-5030 .. **Cohen,** Jeffrey P '94 Island Capital Grp -717 5th Av -NY 10022
(212) 537-9000 .. **Cohen,** Jeffrey R '72 (Cohen G&S,LLP) -850 3rd Av -NY 10022
(212) 259-8000 .. **Cohen,** Jeffrey W '91 Cnsl Dewey & L LLP -1301 Av of Amer -NY 10019
(212) 715-9100 .. **Cohen,** Jeremy A '01 %Kramer LN&F,LLP -1177 Av of Amer -NY 10036
(212) 998-6169 .. **Cohen,** Jerome Alan '82 NYU Law Schl -40 Wshngtn Sq S -NY 10012 **Fx:**995-3662
(212) 319-3900 .. **Cohen,** Jerome J '62 OfCnsl JE Bachelder LLP -437 Mad Av -NY 10022 **Fx:**319-3070
(516) 248-1100 .. **Cohen,** Jerrold N '64 J Cohen -155 Mineola Blvd Bx229 -Mineola 11501 **Fx:**248-1194
(212) 735-3000 .. **Cohen,** Jessica Newill '00 Cnsl Skadden ASM&F LLP -4 Times Sq -NY 10036
(212) 788-1895 .. **Cohen,** Jessica T '07 %Law Dept -100 Church -NY 10007 **Fx:**788-0367
(718) 643-3985 .. **Cohen,** Joanne Minsky '84 Hon B Bunyan -360 Adams -Brklyn 11201
(212) 288-5040 .. **Cohen,** Joel '63 Cohen & C -Cherokee Station Bx20562 -NY 10021 **Fx:**(646) 349-4060
(212) 806-5400 .. **Cohen,** Joel '68 (Stroock &S&L LLP) -180 Maiden Ln -NY 10038
(845) 356-5176 .. **Cohen,** Joel A '64 -17 Eastvw Rd -Monsey 10952
(212) 735-3000 .. **Cohen,** Joel A '09 %Skadden ASM&F LLP -4 Times Sq -NY 10036
(212) 351-4000 .. **Cohen,** Joel M '89 (Gibson D&C LLP) -200 Park Av -NY 10166
(212) 450-4000 .. **Cohen,** Joel M '94 (Davis P&W LLP) -450 Lex Av -NY 10017
(212) 571-8899 .. **Cohen,** Joel S '79 (J Cohen,PC) -128 Mott -NY 10013 **Fx:**571-9065
(646) 454-0744 .. **Cohen,** Jonathan A '03 Forrest Partners LLC -133 Ludlow -NY 10002
(646) 602-5600 .. **Cohen,** Jonathan D '93 %Urban Justice Ctr -123 William -NY 10038 **Fx:**(212) 533-4598
(518) 828-2918 .. **Cohen,** Jonathan E '96 -4 E Court -Hudson 12534
(516) 222-6200 .. **Cohen,** Jonathan M '95 %Berkman HPP&F,PC -100 Grdn City Plz -Gdn Cty 11530
(212) 643-2800 .. **Cohen,** Jonathan T K '89 -1350 Bway -NY 10018 **Fx:**643-4386
(212) 487-6279 .. **Cohen,** Jordan P '07 NYC Dept of Consumer Affairs -42 Bway -NY 10004
(212) 578-2211 .. **Cohen,** Jos B '94 %MetLife -27-01 Qns Plz N -LIC 11101
(212) 969-3000 .. **Cohen,** Jos C '08 %Proskauer R LLP -1585 Bway -NY 10036
(212) 509-0999 .. **Cohen,** Jos J '01 %H Weber -61 Bway -NY 10006 **Fx:**509-1222
(212) 687-3000 .. **Cohen,** Jos M '06 %Jaffe & A,LLP -600 3rd Av -NY 10016
(212) 478-7200 .. **Cohen,** Joshua J '05 %Hahn & H LLP -488 Mad Av -NY 10022
(212) 742-8700 .. **Cohen,** Joshua R '92 (Garson D&C LLP) -110 Wall -NY 10005
(212) 287-6864 .. **Cohen,** Joshua S '05 %Highbridge Captl Mgt -1350 Av of Amer -NY 10019
(212) 297-5800 .. **Cohen,** Joshua W '97 (Day P LLP) -7 Times Sq -NY 10036
(212) 756-2000 .. **Cohen,** Joya '08 %Schulte R&Z LLP -919 3rd Av -NY 10022
(212) 587-9690 .. **Cohen,** Judah Zvi '98 %J Samel & Partners -150 Bway -NY 10038 **Fx:**587-9673
(516) 488-3300 .. **Cohen,** Judd '86 (Shaub AC&S,LLP) -1983 Marcus Av -Lk Success 11042
(212) 655-3500 .. **Cohen,** Judd H '96 (Meister S&F LLP) -140 E 45th -NY 10017
(516) 678-7433 .. **Cohen,** Judith H '89 -3356 Fredrck -Oceanside 11572
(212) 277-6500 .. **Cohen,** Judith R '77 Cnsl Dickstein S LLP -1633 Bway -NY 10019
(212) 832-2797 .. **Cohen,** Julia R '95 (Shebitz B&C,PC) -1325 Av of Amer -NY 10019
(212) 708-1800 .. **Cohen,** Julian H '60 OfCnsl Ladas & P -26 W 61st -NY 10023
(212) 735-3000 .. **Cohen,** Julie E '09 %Skadden ASM&F LLP -4 Times Sq -NY 10036
(212) 915-7787 .. **Cohen,** Justin H '04 Willis M&A Grp -200 Lbrty -NY 10281 **Fx:**915-8511
(212) 553-0437 .. **Cohen,** Kathyanne S '03 %Moody's Invstr Srvc -250 Greenwich -NY 10007
(716) 845-6000 .. **Cohen,** Kenneth A '70 (Kavinoky C LLP) -726 Exchange -Buffalo 14210
(212) 719-3959 .. **Cohen,** Kenneth M '92 -570 7th Av -NY 10018 **Fx:**944-1237
(212) 559-5103 .. **Cohen,** Kenneth S '83 %Citicorp/Citibank NA -425 Park Av -NY 10043
(914) 949-3411 .. **Cohen,** Kevin H '96 -30 Glenn -White Plns 10603 **Fx:**949-3444
(212) 371-0330 .. **Cohen & Khani** -444 Mad Av -NY 10022 **Fx:**486-2016
(212) 751-9800 .. **Cohen,** Koren L '06 %Morelli R PC -950 3rd Av -NY 10022
(212) 564-1900 .. **Cohen & Krassner** -450 7th Av -NY 10123 **Fx:**244-6219
(212) 758-9300 .. **Cohen,** Lainie E '07 %Lazare P&G LLP -950 3rd Av -NY 10022
(212) 980-4500 .. **Cohen Lans LLP** -885 3rd Av -NY 10022 **Fx:**980-3448
(212) 487-9701 .. **Cohen,** Laura R '08 %Robin HK&F -1 Bttry Pk Plz -NY 10014
(212) 728-8000 .. **Cohen,** Lauren C '06 %Willkie F&G LLP -787 7th Av -NY 10019
(516) 783-0062 .. **Cohen,** Laurence I '93 %Pike & P,PC -1921 Bellmore Av -Bellmore 11710 **Fx:**783-0082
(212) 751-5959 .. **Cohen,** Laurence W '88 (Ehrenkranz & E,LLP) -375 Park Av -NY 10152 **Fx:**754-1905
(212) 325-2000 .. **Cohen,** Lauri '01 Credit Suisse -1 Mad Av -NY 10010
(718) 391-5500 .. **Cohen,** Laurie '88 Taxi & Limo Comm -32-02 Qns Blvd -LIC 11101
(518) 449-8893 .. **Cohen,** Laurie T '90 (Wilson EME&D LLP) -677 Bway -Albany 12207
(212) 613-2037 .. **Cohen,** Lawr '86 (Gibbons PC) -1 Penn Plz -NY 10119 **Fx:**554-9640
(212) 889-0320 .. **Cohen,** Lawr A '55 (Rankow C&I) -220 E 42nd -NY 10017

(212) 551-1770 .. **Cohen,** Lawr A '80 %Capital Senior Living Corp -300 Park Av -NY 10022
(212) 527-9905 .. **Cohen,** Lawr J '81 Pembroke Co -70 E 55th -NY 10022
(212) 267-2321 .. **Cohen & Leavitt PC** -277 Bway -NY 10007 **Fx:**227-7140
(212) 839-5300 .. **Cohen,** Leigh M '10 %Sidley A LLP -787 7th Av -NY 10019
(212) 416-8597 .. **Cohen,** Leonard A '90 %Dept of Law -120 Bway -NY 10271 **Fx:**416-6075
(315) 437-5549 .. **Cohen,** Leslie H '60 -115 Stillwtr Dr Bx158 -E Syracuse 13057 **Fx:**437-5549
(212) 878-8000 .. **Cohen,** Lewis R '87 (Clifford C LLP) -31 W 52nd -NY 10019
(518) 470-4995 .. **Cohen,** Linda J '83 -24 Century Hill Dr -Latham 12110
(212) 373-3000 .. **Cohen,** Lindsay F '06 %Paul WRW&G LLP -1285 Av of Amer -NY 10019
(212) 277-6300 .. **Cohen,** Lisa C '88 (Schindler C&H LLP) -100 Wall -NY 10005
(914) 723-5759 .. **Cohen,** Lisa R '89 -180 Old Colony Rd -Hartsdale 10530
(516) 775-2236 .. **Cohen,** Lloyd B '01 %Santangelo B&S -1800 Nrthrn Blvd -Roslyn 11576
(716) 881-3010 .. **Cohen & Lombardo,PC** -343 Elmwood Av Bx5204 -Buffalo 14213 **Fx:**881-2755
(212) 431-1228 .. **Cohen,** Lori '87 (Cohen & F,PC) -145 Hudson -NY 10013 **Fx:**307-0187
(212) 949-9022 .. **Cohen,** Lori B '85 %Abelman F&S -666 3rd Av -NY 10017
(212) 349-6009 .. **Cohen,** Lori L '00 %Sanctuary for Families -110 Wall -NY 10005 **Fx:**566-0344
(718) 250-2743 .. **Cohen,** Louise '85 DA -350 Jay -Brklyn 11201 **Fx:**250-2314
(518) 455-9952 .. **Cohen,** Marc E '88 OfCnsl Thuillez FGB&Y,LLP -20 Corp Wds Blvd -Albany 12211
(914) 993-1902 .. **Cohen,** Marcia S '94 %US Atty -300 Quarropas -White Plns 10601 **Fx:**993-9036
(646) 424-6159 .. **Cohen,** Marcy S '79 SrCnsl ING Financial Srvcs LLC -1325 Av of Amer -NY 10019
(212) 326-3939 .. **Cohen,** Marissa J '08 %Jones D -222 E 41st -NY 10017
(212) 489-1600 .. **Cohen,** Mark A '93 %Deloitte LLP -1633 Bway -NY 10019 **Fx:**492-4201
(212) 832-9170 .. **Cohen,** Mark C '77 %Natl Enterprises -830 3rd Av -NY 10022 **Fx:**755-1410
(718) 258-1500 .. **Cohen,** Mark E '91 -108-18 Qns Blvd -Frst Hlls 11375 **Fx:**793-1627
(718) 792-1200 .. **Cohen,** Mark H '91 (Cohen & S,LLP) -1325 Castle Hill Av -Bronx 10462
(212) 732-0002 .. **Cohen,** Mark I '86 (Cohen F&R,LLP) -20 Vesey -NY 10007
(516) 742-4343 .. **Cohen,** Mark J '85 (Scully SM&P PC) -400 Grdn City Plz -Gdn Cty 11530
(212) 478-7200 .. **Cohen,** Mark S '82 SpclCnsl Hahn & H LLP -488 Mad Av -NY 10022
(212) 957-7600 .. **Cohen,** Mark S '88 (Cohen & G LLP) -800 3rd Av -NY 10022
(646) 878-0800 .. **Cohen,** Mark S '94 (Pearl CZL,LLP) -1500 Bway -NY 10036
(212) 488-1300 .. **Cohen,** Marshall J '77 (Cohen & P LLP) -444 Mad Av -NY 10022
(212) 674-1985 .. **Cohen,** Martin '89 Cohen & Co -357 Grand -NY 10002 **Fx:**673-6294
(845) 561-6000 .. **Cohen,** Martin A '76 -450 Bway Bx1402 -Newburgh 12551 **Fx:**561-6095
(518) 745-1400 .. **Cohen,** Martin A '98 %FitzGerald MBF -16 Pearl Bx2017 -Glens Fls 12801
(212) 986-8282 .. **Cohen,** Martin J '64 (Cohen & S) -360 Lex Av -NY 10017
(631) 424-7000 .. **Cohen,** Martin L '88 %Five Towns Cllg -305 N Srvc Rd -Dix Hlls 11746 **Fx:**424-7006
(212) 762-7292 .. **Cohen,** Martin M '88 Morgan Stanley -1633 Bway -NY 10019
(516) 763-1212 .. **Cohen,** Martin P '76 -100 Merrick Rd -Rockvl Ctr 11570
(212) 417-8700 .. **Cohen,** Martin S '04 %Fed Def of NY Inc -52 Duane -NY 10007 **Fx:**571-0392
(516) 546-9115 .. **Cohen,** Marvin H '53 (Sperry W&C) -62 Lena Av -Freeprt 11520
(212) 362-6291 .. **Cohen,** Matthew '82 -215 W 91st -NY 10024
(718) 237-2000 .. **Cohen,** Matthew B '86 %Leg Aid -111 Lvngstn -Brklyn 11201 **Fx:**237-8737
(212) 868-1010 .. **Cohen,** Matthew H '04 %Kudman TA LLP -350 5th Av -NY 10118
Cohen, Matthew I '96 -746 The Pkwy -Mamaroneck 10543
(516) 295-7699 .. **Cohen,** Matthew S '66 %Interboro Systems Corp -123 Maple Av -Cedarhrst 11516 **Fx:**295-7696
(212) 751-3001 .. **Cohen,** Matthew S '92 (Thompson & K LLP) -919 3rd Av -NY 10022
(212) 227-3787 .. **Cohen,** Max '54 -160 Bway -NY 10038 **Fx:**227-3789
(212) 683-2210 .. **Cohen,** Melissa A '10 %Childrens Rts Inc -330 7th Av -NY 10001 **Fx:**683-4015
(212) 340-0400 .. **Cohen,** Melissa Ann '86 Appllt Div 1st Dept -27 Mad Av -NY 10010 **Fx:**889-4412
(212) 854-4522 .. **Cohen,** Melissa Paige '06 Columbia Univ -535 W 116th 412 Low Mem'l Library -NY 10027
(212) 735-3000 .. **Cohen,** Meredith S '10 %Skadden ASM&F LLP -4 Times Sq -NY 10036
(212) 499-6644 .. **Cohen,** Merrill R '92 (M Cohen & Assoc,PC) -7 Penn Plz -NY 10001 **Fx:**818-0625
(718) 596-3800 .. **Cohen,** Michl '93 %Tenenbaum & B LLP -26 Court -Brklyn 11242
(516) 280-6806 .. **Cohen,** Michl A '94 -400 Grdn City Plz -Gdn Cty 11530 **Fx:**873-8009
(212) 446-4800 .. **Cohen,** Michl A '00 (Kirkland & E LLP) -153 E 53rd -NY 10022
(212) 836-3212 .. **Cohen,** Michl D '92 Trump Org -725 5th Av -NY 10022
(631) 265-0010 .. **Cohen,** Michl F '85 %Cohen & W,PC -80 Maple Av Bx768 -Smithtwn 11787
(212) 267-6364 .. **Cohen,** Michl I '85 %Kossoff & U -217 Bway -NY 10007
(212) 504-6000 .. **Cohen,** Michl J '03 %Cadwalader W&T LLP -1 World Fncl Ctr -NY 10281
(718) 279-4700 .. **Cohen,** Michl M '74 (Cohen S LLP) -214-11 Nrthrn Blvd -Bayside 11361 **Fx:**279-1651
(212) 220-0390 .. **Cohen,** Michl Marks '66 OfCnsl Nicoletti H&S -88 Pine -NY 10005 **Fx:**220-3784
(212) 831-4400 .. **Cohen,** Michl R '94 (Green & C,PC) -319 E 91st -NY 10128 **Fx:**831-8390
(516) 426-6003 .. **Cohen,** Michl Ross '07 -16 W 16th -NY 10011
(516) 832-7544 .. **Cohen,** Michl S '80 (Nixon P LLP) -50 Jericho Quadrangle -Jericho 11753
(212) 318-6000 .. **Cohen,** Michele J '90 (Paul HJ&W LLP) -75 E 55th -NY 10022
(516) 296-7000 .. **Cohen,** Michelle E '08 Certilman BA&H,LLP -90 Merrick Av -E Meadow 11554
(212) 336-2000 .. **Cohen,** Michelle K '05 %Patterson BW&T LLP -1133 Av of Amer -NY 10036
(212) 838-7797 .. **Cohen Milstein Sellers & Toll,PLLC** -88 Pine -NY 10005 **Fx:**838-7745
(212) 972-1000 .. **Cohen,** Miriam Beth '07 %London F LLP -59 Maiden Ln -NY 10038
(212) 407-4000 .. **Cohen,** Miriam L '87 (Loeb & L,LLP) -345 Park Av -NY 10154
(212) 407-7700 .. **Cohen,** Mitchell D '99 (Vedder P,PC) -1633 Bway -NY 10019
(212) 847-7900 .. **Cohen,** Mitchell S '85 (Wechsler & C,LLP) -17 State -NY 10004
(212) 838-3333 .. **Cohen,** Mitchell S '93 (Locks Law Firm,PLLC) -747 3rd Av -NY 10017 **Fx:**838-3735
(845) 735-7000 .. **Cohen,** Mitchell Y '86 (Johnson & C,LLP) -1 Blue Hill Plz -Pearl Rvr 10965
(718) 859-8009 .. **Cohen,** Morris E '95 -1122 Coney Isl Av -Brklyn 11230
(516) 496-3091 .. **Cohen,** Morton A '72 -133 Woodlake Dr -Woodbury 11797
(212) 759-3300 .. **Cohen,** Myron '83 (Dornbush SS&V,LLP) -747 3rd Av -NY 10017
(212) 309-1000 .. **Cohen,** Myron D '63 SrCnsl Hunton & W -200 Park Av -NY 10166
(212) 286-8585 .. **Cohen,** Natalie J R '05 %Heidell PM&B,LLP -99 Park Av -NY 10016
(212) 836-8000 .. **Cohen,** Nathan '05 %Kaye S LLP -425 Park Av -NY 10022
(718) 876-6300 .. **Cohen,** Neal S '04 %DA -130 Styvsnt Pl -Staten Isl 10301
(212) 765-9100 .. **Cohen,** Neal W '96 %Halperin BR,LLP -555 Mad Av -NY 10022
(718) 624-3246 .. **Cohen,** Neil '72 -32 Court -Brklyn 11201 **Fx:**875-5883
(516) 742-6575 .. **Cohen,** Neil L '85 (Decolator C&D,LLP) -1399 Franklin Av -Gdn Cty 11530
(516) 877-1800 .. **Cohen,** Neil S '85 %Schlissel OK,PLLC -200 Grdn City Plz -Gdn Cty 11530
(212) 705-7000 .. **Cohen,** Neil S '02 Cnsl Bingham M LLP -399 Park Av -NY 10022
(212) 878-8217 .. **Cohen,** Ness '98 (Clifford C LLP) -31 W 52nd -NY 10019
(212) 455-2000 .. **Cohen,** Nicholas F '06 %Simpson T&B LLP -425 Lex Av -NY 10017
(718) 891-9096 .. **Cohen,** Noah D '82 (Hecht & Assoc) -728 Av U -Brklyn 11223 **Fx:**891-2555
(212) 533-6300 .. **Cohen,** Noel D '67 %NYSUT -52 Bway -NY 10004 **Fx:**995-2347
(516) 877-2720 .. **Cohen,** Norman H '52 (Cohen & R) -1100 Franklin Av -Gdn Cty 11530 **Fx:**877-2736
(718) 448-2889 .. **Cohen,** Orin J '83 -1162 Victory Blvd -Staten Isl 10301 **Fx:**650-9965
(716) 843-4100 .. **Cohen,** Pamela D '85 %US SBA -130 S Elmwood Av -Buffalo 14202
(516) 922-6626 .. **Cohen,** Pamela Wolff '87 %J Shein & Assoc,PC -575 Underhill Blvd -Syosset 11791 **Fx:**922-2797
(516) 576-1044 .. **Cohen,** Paul '72 (P Cohen,PC) -54 Sunnyside Blvd -Plainvw 11803
(212) 248-9100 .. **Cohen,** Paul '79 (Epstein M&M) -1 Whitehall -NY 10004
(212) 259-8000 .. **Cohen,** Paul H '99 %Dewey & L LLP -1301 Av of Amer -NY 10019
(212) 488-1300 .. **Cohen & Perfetto LLP** -444 Mad Av -NY 10022 **Fx:**813-0767
(212) 754-9400 .. **Cohen,** Perry L '78 (Todtman NS&J,PC) -425 Park Av -NY 10022
(212) 869-7000 .. **Cohen,** Peter B '83 (Feldman W&S LLP) -420 Lex Av -NY 10170
(914) 682-9262 .. **Cohen,** Peter H '87 -10 Bank -White Plns 10606
(212) 493-7587 .. **Cohen,** Peter M '97 NYC Invstmnt Fund -1 Bttry Pk Plz -NY 10004
(516) 962-7942 .. **Cohen,** Peter S '85 EVO Merchant Srvcs -515 Broadhllw Rd -Melvll 11747 **Fx:**962-7520
(212) 801-2145 .. **Cohen,** Philip H '90 (Greenberg T,LLP) -200 Park Av -NY 10166
(212) 687-2770 .. **Cohen Pontani Lieberman & Pavane** -551 5th Av -NY 10176 **Fx:**972-5487
(516) 741-0123 .. **Cohen & Prizer** -130 Newbrdg Rd -Hicksvll 11801 **Fx:**741-9470
(212) 553-8300 .. **Cohen,** Rachelle D '77 Cohen K & Assoc -2 Park Av -NY 10016 **Fx:**553-8721
(212) 619-5000 .. **Cohen,** Randi S '93 %EDC -110 William -NY 10038 **Fx:**312-3912
(718) 485-3682 .. **Cohen,** Raymond A '99 Maverick Mgmt Corp -1000 Penn Av -Brklyn 11207 **Fx:**927-1625
(212) 977-5000 .. **Cohen,** Richd A '79 Stonehenge Mgmt LLC -888 7th Av -NY 10106
(212) 687-1736 .. **Cohen,** Richd A '84 %R Schwartzberg & Assoc,PLLC -60 E 42nd -NY 10165
(315) 798-8830 .. **Cohen,** Richd A '97 (Cohen & C) -258 Genesee -Utica 13502 **Fx:**798-8034
(212) 878-7900 .. **Cohen,** Richd B '78 (Fox R LLP) -100 Park Av -NY 10017
(212) 535-9794 .. **Cohen,** Richd B '86 -325 Bway -NY 10007
(212) 858-1000 .. **Cohen,** Richd G '56 (Pillsbury WSP LLP) -1540 Bway -NY 10036
(718) 588-1110 .. **Cohen,** Richd G '85 (Aspinall & C) -177 E 161st -Bronx 10451 **Fx:**588-1294
(646) 253-5400 .. **Cohen,** Richd J '91 (Goldberg S LLP) -1200 Av of Amer -NY 10036
(716) 566-5400 .. **Cohen,** Richd J '91 (Goldberg S LLP) -665 Main -Buffalo 14203
(631) 475-7572 .. **Cohen,** Richd J '92 -122 Medford Av -Patchogue 11772 **Fx:**447-2265
(212) 829-9090 .. **Cohen,** Richd N '87 (Friedberg CC&P,LLP) -767 3rd Av -NY 10017
(914) 332-9700 .. **Cohen,** Richd S '78 %Walden Grp -560 Wht Plns Rd -Tarrytwn 10591
(914) 997-0500 .. **Cohen,** Richd W '81 (Lowey DC&H,PC) -1 N Bway -White Plns 10601
(212) 698-3500 .. **Cohen,** Robt A '71 (Dechert LLP) -1095 Av of Amer -NY 10036
(631) 587-5100 .. **Cohen,** Robt A '80 (Tabat CB&Y,LLP) -500 Montauk Hwy -W Islip 11795
(212) 835-9500 .. **Cohen,** Robt A '81 RA Cohen & Assoc,Inc -60 E 42nd -NY 10165 **Fx:**835-9501
(212) 773-3000 .. **Cohen,** Robt G '77 %Ernst & Young,LLP -5 Times Sq -NY 10036
(518) 296-8866 .. **Cohen,** Robt H '62 OfCnsl Towne R & Prtnrs,PC -2668 State Route 7 -Cobleskill 12043
(212) 801-6907 .. **Cohen,** Robt H '79 (Greenberg T,LLP) -200 Park Av -NY 10166
(631) 694-2300 .. **Cohen,** Robt H '84 (Lamb & B,LLP) -534 Broadhllw Rd Bx9034 -Melvll 11747
(212) 415-3721 .. **Cohen,** Robt H '97 Omnicom Group -437 Mad Av -NY 10022 **Fx:**415-3530
(212) 736-6800 .. **Cohen,** Robt L '69 -1350 Bway -NY 10018 **Fx:**643-1882
(518) 877-5552 .. **Cohen,** Robt M '72 -181 Wood Dale Dr -Ballston Lk 12019 **Fx:**877-5099
(718) 948-2100 .. **Cohen,** Robt M '79 (Simonson & C,PC) -4060 Amboy Rd -Staten Isl 10308
(212) 759-2300 .. **Cohen,** Robt M '87 Carroll G&G,LLP -1790 Bway -NY 10019
(516) 877-2525 .. **Cohen,** Robt N '79 (Weinstein K&C,PC) -1325 Franklin Av -Gdn Cty 11530
(212) 980-4500 .. **Cohen,** Robt S '63 (Cohen L LLP) -885 3rd Av -NY 10022
(516) 873-2000 .. **Cohen,** Robt S '87 (Moritt HH&H LLP) -400 Grdn City Plz -Gdn Cty 11530

(212) 446-4800 .. **Cohen,** Robt S '02 (Kirkland & E LLP) -153 E 53rd -NY 10022
(212) 719-0200 .. **Cohen,** Robt W '85 %BAR/BRI -1500 Bway -NY 10036 **Fx:**719-1421
(212) 319-0990 .. **Cohen,** Robin E '82 %Toby Spitz Assoc -110 E 59th -NY 10022 **Fx:**319-1555
(212) 506-1700 .. **Cohen,** Robin L '89 (Kasowitz BT&F LLP) -1633 Bway -NY 10019
(212) 788-0714 .. **Cohen,** Rochelle H '87 %Law Dept -100 Church -NY 10007 **Fx:**788-0367
(212) 710-2500 .. **Cohen,** Rodney S '91 Pegasus Capital Advisors -505 Park Av -NY 10022
(212) 969-3000 .. **Cohen,** Roger A '07 %Proskauer R LLP -1585 Bway -NY 10036
(718) 590-0268 .. **Cohen,** Ronald H '94 Family Ct -900 Sheridan Av -Bronx 10451
(845) 291-1900 .. **Cohen,** Ronald Jay '81 (Cohen E & Assoc,LLP) -40 Matthews -Goshen 10924 **Fx:**291-8601
(212) 574-1200 .. **Cohen,** Ronald L '76 (Seward & K LLP) -1 Bttry Pk Plz -NY 10004
(212) 307-5500 .. **Cohen,** Rory M '95 (Venable LLP) -1270 Av of Amer -NY 10020
(212) 265-6888 .. **Cohen,** Roy Alan '86 (Porzio B&N,PC) -156 W 56th -NY 10019
(212) 806-5400 .. **Cohen,** Royce F '02 SpclCnsl Stroock &S&L LLP -180 Maiden Ln -NY 10038
(212) 282-4377 .. **Cohen,** Saara Berenson '81 Mizuho Corp Bank -1251 Av of Amer -NY 10020
(212) 867-5800 .. **Cohen,** Sandra Wieder '99 (Osler H&H LLP) -620 8th Av -NY 10018
(917) 637-3600 .. **Cohen,** Sanford M '80 Ctr for Reproductive Rts -120 Wall -NY 10005 **Fx:**637-3666
(212) 848-4000 .. **Cohen,** Saralyn M '89 Cnsl Shearman & S LLP -599 Lex Av -NY 10022
(212) 922-0166 .. **Cohen,** Saul E '06 (Cohen Law Firm,LLP) -275 Mad Av -NY 10016
(212) 980-7915 .. **Cohen,** Saul S '61 -870 UN Plz -NY 10017
(516) 785-0101 .. **Cohen,** Scott R '90 -1921 Bellmore Av -Bellmore 11710
(212) 705-5092 .. **Cohen,** Seth A '00 Island Capital Grp -717 5th Av -NY 10022
(516) 746-3500 .. **Cohen,** Seth D '99 %Brand G&B,PC -600 Old Cntry Rd -Gdn Cty 11530
(646) 435-1614 .. **Cohen,** Seth G '05 Weiser LLP -135 W 50th -NY 10020
(212) 872-6460 .. **Cohen,** Seth M '96 KPMG LLP -345 Park Av -NY 10154
(212) 506-5000 .. **Cohen,** Seth M '06 %Orrick H&S LLP -51 W 52nd -NY 10019
(212) 586-0491 .. **Cohen,** Seymour I '52 -1674 Bway -NY 10019 **Fx:**977-7620
(315) 471-8111 .. **Cohen,** Shari R '92 (Scolaro SCF&B,PC) -507 Plum -Syracuse 13204
(212) 797-5400 .. **Cohen,** Sheldon '60 (Cohen & G,LLP) -32 Bway -NY 10004 **Fx:**943-3295
(212) 618-7076 .. **Cohen,** Sheldon L '81 CB Richard Ellis -140 Bway -NY 10005
(212) 563-5500 .. **Cohen,** Sherri North '00 ARIS Corp -340 Mad Av -NY 10173 **Fx:**563-6500
(212) 401-0800 .. **Cohen,** Sherry K '87 %Disciplinary Comm -61 Bway -NY 10006 **Fx:**287-1045
(718) 539-8448 .. **Cohen,** Sheryl Lynn '84 DMV -30-56 Whitestone Expwy -Flushng 11354
(212) 986-8282 .. **Cohen & Silverman** -360 Lex Av -NY 10017 **Fx:**986-8332
(516) 364-6006 .. **Cohen & Slamowitz,LLP** -199 Crsswys Park Dr Bx9004 -Woodbury 11797 **Fx:**364-3431
(212) 442-3093 .. **Cohen,** Stacey L '92 %Law Dept -100 Church -NY 10007 **Fx:**788-0367
(212) 735-3000 .. **Cohen,** Stacey L '04 %Skadden ASM&F LLP -4 Times Sq -NY 10036
(212) 840-0050 .. **Cohen,** Stanley A '63 (Cohen & T) -1501 Bway -NY 10036
(212) 686-8200 .. **Cohen,** Stanley Dale '77 -41 Park Av -NY 10016 **Fx:**686-4900
(212) 979-7572 .. **Cohen,** Stanley L '84 -119 Av D -NY 10009 **Fx:**995-5574
(718) 792-1200 .. **Cohen & Stark,LLP** -1325 Castle Hill Av -Bronx 10462 **Fx:**792-4594
(212) 609-6800 .. **Cohen,** Stephanie J '01 (McCarter & E,LLP) -245 Park Av -NY 10167
(212) 819-8200 .. **Cohen,** Stephanie L '03 %White & C LLP -1155 Av of Amer -NY 10036
(212) 735-8705 .. **Cohen,** Stephen A '62 (Morrison C LLP) -909 3rd Av -NY 10022
(212) 930-9700 .. **Cohen,** Stephen A '06 %Sichenzia RFF LLP -61 Bway -NY 10006
(315) 471-8111 .. **Cohen,** Stephen H '71 (Scolaro SCF&B,PC) -507 Plum -Syracuse 13204
(718) 446-4400 .. **Cohen,** Stephen H '93 (Bangel & C,LLP) -91-31 Qns Blvd -Elmhrst 11373 **Fx:**446-6537
(212) 407-4000 .. **Cohen,** Stephen H '94 (Loeb & L,LLP) -345 Park Av -NY 10154
(516) 358-6900 .. **Cohen,** Stephen M '74 (Cohen & J LLP) -2001 Marcus Av -Lk Success 11042
(212) 644-4420 .. **Cohen,** Stephen M '86 (Fabiani C&H,LLP) -570 Lex Av -NY 10022
(212) 226-1900 .. **Cohen,** Steven '88 (Tesser & C) -591 Bway -NY 10012
(212) 403-1000 .. **Cohen,** Steven A '93 (Wachtell LR&K) -51 W 52nd -NY 10019
(212) 553-8462 .. **Cohen,** Steven Balson '85 %Cohen K & Assoc -2 Park Av -NY 10016 **Fx:**553-8721
(516) 741-2405 .. **Cohen,** Steven E '79 (Geoghan C&B LLC) -250 Mineola Blvd -Mineola 11501
(516) 228-3131 .. **Cohen,** Steven E '86 (Franklin G&C,PC) -666 Old Cntry Rd -Gdn Cty 11530
(212) 541-6222 .. **Cohen,** Steven E '90 (Kane K,PC) -1350 Av of Amer -NY 10019
(212) 840-3737 .. **Cohen,** Steven E '95 %Goidel & SL LLP -122 E 42nd -NY 10168 **Fx:**840-3793
(212) 431-1300 .. **Cohen,** Steven H '75 Cnsl Borah GAN&G PC -377 Bway -NY 10013
(212) 480-3030 .. **Cohen,** Steven H '85 -125 Maiden Ln -NY 10038 **Fx:**480-2590
(845) 298-2870 .. **Cohen,** Steven H '86 (Finkelstein & Prtnrs,LLP) -1778 South Rd -Wappingers Fls 12590
(212) 597-8342 .. **Cohen,** Steven H '87 WestLB AG NY Brnch -1211 Av of Amer -NY 10036
(212) 564-1900 .. **Cohen,** Steven J '81 (Cohen & K) -450 7th Av -NY 10123
(212) 909-9500 .. **Cohen,** Steven J '83 (Wachtel & M,LLP) -885 2nd Av -NY 10017
(212) 261-5542 .. **Cohen,** Steven J '95 Assured Guaranty Co -1325 Av of the Americas -NY 10019
(212) 416-8000 .. **Cohen,** Steven M '89 %Dept of Law -120 Bway -NY 10271
(716) 636-7600 .. **Cohen,** Steven M '89 %HoganWillig -2410 N Forest Rd -Amherst 14068
(212) 504-6000 .. **Cohen,** Steven N '82 (Cadwalader W&T LLP) -1 World Fncl Ctr -NY 10281
(516) 487-4994 .. **Cohen,** Stuart A '87 -66 Beverly Rd -Gt Neck 11021
(914) 397-2400 .. **Cohen,** Stuart M '70 (Ferguson C,LLP) -1 N Lex Av -White Plns 10601 **Fx:**683-6956
(518) 455-7700 .. **Cohen,** Stuart M '80 %Ct of Appls -20 Eagle -Albany 12207
(718) 761-4054 .. **Cohen,** Susan L '82 -1015 Westwood Av -Staten Isl 10314 **Fx:**761-0952
(646) 442-3100 .. **Cohen,** Susan M '83 %Legal Srvcs -90 John -NY 10038 **Fx:**(212) 227-9798
(212) 806-5400 .. **Cohen,** Susan R '95 SpclCnsl Stroock &S&L LLP -180 Maiden Ln -NY 10038
(212) 586-5800 .. **Cohen Tauber Spievack & Wagner PC** -420 Lex Av -NY 10170 **Fx:**586-5095
(212) 937-7209 .. **Cohen,** Terese R '82 WilmerHale -399 Park Av -NY 10022
(212) 819-2000 .. **Cohen,** Theo J '72 Cnsl Eastern Funding LLC -213 W 35th -NY 10001 **Fx:**819-9764
(212) 686-4401 .. **Cohen,** Thos F '80 SpclCnsl Abramson Law Grp PLLC -570 Lex Av -NY 10022 **Fx:**686-6515
(212) 770-8111 .. **Cohen,** Todd S '96 %AIG -70 Pine -NY 10270
(212) 725-0200 .. **Cohen,** Tsiona '00 %Barnes R&C -475 Park Av S -NY 10016
(212) 840-0050 .. **Cohen & Tucker** -1501 Bway -NY 10036
(212) 867-3636 .. **Cohen,** Victor '79 (Levin & G,PC) -420 Lex Av -NY 10170
(212) 566-7081 .. **Cohen,** Walter '61 (Cohen & H) -80 Maiden Ln -NY 10038
(914) 793-2933 .. **Cohen,** Warren L '77 -107 Lk Av -Tuckahoe 10707 **Fx:**793-2114
(631) 265-0010 .. **Cohen & Warren,PC** -80 Maple Av Bx768 -Smithtwn 11787 **Fx:**265-0853
(212) 719-7368 .. **Cohen,** Wayne N '02 Och Ziff Capital Mgmt -9 W 57th -NY 10019
(212) 563-4100 .. **Cohen Weiss & Simon LLP** -330 W 42nd -NY 10036 **Fx:**695-5436
(718) 875-1300 .. **Cohen,** Wendy '85 %Appllt Div 2nd Dept -45 Monroe Pl -Brklyn 11201 **Fx:**858-2446
(212) 940-8800 .. **Cohen,** Wendy E '87 SpclCnsl Katten MR LLP -575 Mad Av -NY 10022
(212) 578-2581 .. **Cohen,** Winifred A '85 %MetLife -1 Mad Av -NY 10010
(212) 586-5800 .. **Cohen,** Y Jerry '87 (Cohen TS&W PC) -420 Lex Av -NY 10170
(212) 756-2000 .. **Cohen,** Yocheved '78 SpclCnsl Schulte R&Z LLP -919 3rd Av -NY 10022
(212) 836-8000 .. **Cohen,** Yossi '07 %Kaye S LLP -425 Park Av -NY 10022
(212) 790-0248 .. **Cohen,** Ziva '03 %Benj N Cardozo Schl of Law -55 5th Av -NY 10003 **Fx:**790-0345
(716) 753-4241 .. **Cohen Brown,** Randi E '87 %DA -Cnty Cthse -Mayvll 14757 **Fx:**753-4628
(516) 377-1350 .. **Cohen-Lieberman,** Terri H '03 -2994 Judith Dr -Merrick 11566
(212) 903-9000 .. **Cohen-Millstein,** Peter L '03 %Linklaters -1345 Av of Amer -NY 10105
(718) 875-7584 .. **Cohen-Vigder,** Jennifer L '03 -105 Court -Brklyn 11201
(646) 878-0800 .. **Cohen-Zedek,** Dor '06 (Pearl CZL,LLP) -1500 Bway -NY 10036
(212) 789-2780 .. **Cohig,** Susan E '03 NHL Enterprises,LP -1185 Av of Amer -NY 10036 **Fx:**789-2020
(914) 949-2826 .. **Cohlan,** Richd M '75 (Robinowitz CD&D,LLP) -199 Main -White Plns 10601
(646) 419-4264 .. **Cohn,** Adam '07 (Bowles C&C LLP) -54 W 21st -NY 10010 **Fx:**(866) 844-8305
(212) 903-9000 .. **Cohn,** Andrew S '09 %Linklaters -1345 Av of Amer -NY 10105
(718) 897-2700 .. **Cohn,** Arthur B '67 -63-52 Saunders -Rego Pk 11374 **Fx:**897-2703
(516) 663-2206 .. **Cohn,** Bruce M '84 Winthrop Univ Hospital -288 Old Cntry Rd -Mineola 11501
(212) 284-2300 .. **Cohn,** Clifford D '02 Jefferies & Co Inc -520 Mad Av -NY 10022
(212) 259-8000 .. **Cohn,** David J '05 %Dewey & L LLP -1301 Av of Amer -NY 10019
(212) 335-9000 .. **Cohn,** David M '97 %DA -1 Hogan Pl -NY 10013
(212) 704-6000 .. **Cohn,** David S '05 (Troutman S LLP) -405 Lex Av -NY 10174
(212) 355-1444 .. **Cohn,** Donald J '56 -425 Park Av -NY 10022 **Fx:**223-1942
(718) 403-3606 .. **Cohn,** Douglas R '89 %Dept of Finance -345 Adams -Brklyn 11201 **Fx:**403-3650
(212) 759-2600 .. **Cohn,** Edw '79 (Irwin LC&L,PC) -845 3rd Av -NY 10022
(516) 877-5600 .. **Cohn,** Edw H '79 %R Tusa -1225 Franklin Av -Gdn Cty 11530 **Fx:**877-5695
(914) 632-4700 .. **Cohn,** Eli S '58 (McDonough Law Firm, LLP) -145 Huguenot -New Rchll 10801
(914) 366-5700 .. **Cohn,** Erica A '99 %MA Bjork -660 Wht Plns Rd -Tarrytwn 10591 **Fx:**366-5759
(212) 267-2600 .. **Cohn,** Fredk H '66 -61 Bway -NY 10006 **Fx:**267-3024
(212) 571-6200 .. **Cohn,** Gerald '57 (Cohn & C,PC) -116 John -NY 10038 **Fx:**571-6201
(516) 921-8881 .. **Cohn & Goldstein,PC** -100 Crsswys Park W -Woodbury 11797 **Fx:**802-5895
(212) 728-8000 .. **Cohn,** Henry M '81 (Willkie F&G LLP) -787 7th Av -NY 10019
(518) 473-3818 .. **Cohn,** Janet S '87 %Dept of Health -Corning Twr 24th Fl -Albany 12237 **Fx:**473-2802
(212) 227-0347 .. **Cohn,** Jerry A '88 %Weiss W&W,PC -25 Park Pl -NY 10007
(212) 751-3001 .. **Cohn,** John R '05 (Thompson & K LLP) -919 3rd Av -NY 10022
(212) 571-6200 .. **Cohn,** Jonathan D '91 (Cohn & C,PC) -116 John -NY 10038 **Fx:**571-6201
(212) 506-2500 .. **Cohn,** Joshua D '81 (Mayer B LLP) -1675 Bway -NY 10019
(914) 428-0505 .. **Cohn,** Julius W '64 (Cohn & S) -200 E Post Rd -White Plns 10601
(212) 264-3650 .. **Cohn,** Kristina D '04 %SSA Ofc Genl Cnsl -26 Fed Plz -NY 10278 **Fx:**264-6372
(212) 578-0594 .. **Cohn,** Marc A '94 %MetLife -1 Mad Av -NY 10010 **Fx:**578-8978
(212) 705-7000 .. **Cohn,** Matthew D '09 %Bingham M LLP -399 Park Av -NY 10022
(516) 571-0645 .. **Cohn,** Melissa B '04 %Cnty Atty -1 West -Mineola 11501 **Fx:**571-6604
(516) 747-3030 .. **Cohn,** Michl H '77 (Cohn & R) -100 E Old Cntry Rd -Mineola 11501
(212) 798-6100 .. **Cohn,** Michl J '99 Fortress Investment Grp -1345 Av of Amer -NY 10105
(718) 491-7184 .. **Cohn,** Nancy E '88 %Metropolitan Jewish Health System -6323 7th Av -Brklyn 11220
(212) 880-1303 .. **Cohn,** Naomi '99 Fidelity Ntl Fncl Inc -711 3rd Av -NY 10017
(212) 310-8000 .. **Cohn,** Paul T '88 (Weil G&M LLP) -767 5th Av -NY 10153
(212) 871-4000 .. **Cohn,** Richd L '86 -55 Lbrty -NY 10005 **Fx:**716-1143
(212) 360-1757 .. **Cohn,** Robt L '91 Incidental Funding Corp -1075 Park Av -NY 10128 **Fx:**(646) 349-1422
(516) 747-3030 .. **Cohn & Roth** -100 E Old Cntry Rd -Mineola 11501 **Fx:**747-3046
(212) 344-2150 .. **Cohn,** Sarah '88 (Adler C&K) -575 Lex Av -NY 10022
(212) 484-3900 .. **Cohn,** Scott A '84 Cnsl Arent F LLP -1675 Bway -NY 10019

(212) 644-4420 .. **Cohn,** Seth H '04 %Fabiani C&H,LLP -570 Lex Av -NY 10022
(914) 428-0505 .. **Cohn & Spector** -200 E Post Rd -White Plns 10601 **Fx:**428-0519
(516) 294-6410 .. **Cohn,** Steven '75 -1 Old Cntry Rd -Carle Pl 11514 **Fx:**294-0094
(718) 875-2400 .. **Cohn,** Steven D '74 (Goldberg & C LLP) -16 Court -Brklyn 11241
(212) 371-6600 .. **Cohn,** Steven D '05 %Kirby M LLP -825 3rd Av -NY 10022
(212) 492-4974 .. **Cohn,** Teri '91 Deloitte Consulting LLP -1633 Bway -NY 10019
(212) 307-5500 .. **Cohn,** Thos A '99 OfCnsl Venable LLP -1270 Av of Amer -NY 10020
(516) 248-1700 .. **Cohn,** Wm S '53 Cnsl Forchelli CDSM&T,LLP -333 Earle Ovngton Blvd -Uniondale 11553
(212) 701-3000 .. **Cohn,** Yafit '05 %Cahill G&R LLP -80 Pine -NY 10005 **Fx:**269-5420
(585) 235-6611 .. **Coia,** Richd '84 (Panzarella & C) -1411 Chili Av -Rchstr 14624 **Fx:**436-9706
(212) 770-1219 .. **Coilparampil,** Meera S '01 AIG -80 Pine -NY 10005
(212) 351-4000 .. **Coindreau,** Bernardo '00 %Gibson D&C LLP -200 Park Av -NY 10166
(516) 822-7700 .. **Coiro,** Christopher J '00 %M Mikelinich,PC -6800 Jericho Tpk -Syosset 11791 **Fx:**822-7714
(718) 824-6500 .. **Coiro,** Jos T '66 (Coiro WC&S) -1206 Castle Hill Av -Bronx 10462
(718) 824-6500 .. **Coiro Wardi Chinitz & Silverstein** -1206 Castle Hill Av -Bronx 10462 **Fx:**(347) 691-3321
(212) 981-5600 .. **Coke Cohen,** Vanessa E '03 Silver Lk Ptnrs -9 W 57th -NY 10019 **Fx:**981-3535
(516) 739-3090 .. **Cokinos,** Paula '90 %Mason & M,PC -394 Old Cntry Rd -Gdn Cty 11530 **Fx:**739-5060
(212) 644-3880 .. **Col,** Sonia V '80 -400 Park Av -NY 10022 **Fx:**758-9678
(914) 686-9010 .. **Cola,** Erin M '04 Wilson BCC&C,PC -2 William -White Plns 10601
(914) 741-7430 .. **Colacurcio,** Jos '97 Verizon Corp -500 Summit Lk Dr -Valhalla 10595
(800) 755-3100 .. **Colagiacomo,** Carlo Jr. '04 Amer Home Mortgage -538 Broadhllw Rd -Melvll 11747
(516) 877-7000 .. **Colagiacomo,** Marcus A '00 %McCoyd P&R,LLP -1100 Franklin Av -Gdn Cty 11530
(716) 856-1344 .. **Colaiacovo,** Emilio L '02 (Bouvier Prtnrshp,LLP) -350 Main -Buffalo 14202 **Fx:**856-1369
(716) 200-5050 .. **Colaiacovo,** Kimberly A '07 %Harris B PLLC -726 Exchange -Buffalo 14210
(212) 250-1207 .. **Colaluca,** Kenneth A Jr. '00 Deutsche Bk Sec -60 Wall -NY 10005
(212) 425-3100 .. **Colamarino,** Lee Anne '07 %McManus C&R,PC -48 Wall -NY 10005
(212) 513-7788 .. **Colameo,** Thos J '98 (Ahmuty D&M) -123 William -NY 10038
(917) 532-8585 .. **Colan,** Gregory C '93 -788 Columbus Av -NY 10025
(212) 867-5800 .. **Colan,** Kevin P Jr. '02 %Osler H&H LLP -620 8th Av -NY 10018
(212) 314-3826 .. **Colan,** Robt '82 %AXA Financial Inc -1290 Av of Amer -NY 10104 **Fx:**707-7864
(212) 287-4900 .. **Colandrea,** Eric F '00 Highbridge Cptl Mgt -40 W 57th -NY 10019
(914) 328-1844 .. **Colangelo,** Arlene '88 (Miano & C,LLP) -550 Mamaroneck Av -Harrison 10528
(914) 693-8864 .. **Colangelo,** Faith '75 -64 Bellair Dr -Dobbs Ferry 10522
(914) 939-0002 .. **Colangelo,** John B '80 -211 S Ridge -Rye Brook 10573 **Fx:**939-2665
(212) 689-3819 .. **Colangelo,** Kevin E '95 %Pangea3 LLC -18 E 41st -NY 10017 **Fx:**820-9784
(212) 490-9550 .. **Colangelo,** Lori E '92 %C Trinko -16 W 46th -NY 10036 **Fx:**986-0158
(212) 965-2200 .. **Colangelo,** Matthew B '04 NAACP/LDF -99 Hudson -NY 10013 **Fx:**226-7592
(212) 415-9200 .. **Colangelo-Bryan,** Joshua N '03 %Dorsey & W LLP -250 Park Av -NY 10177
(212) 635-6989 .. **Colaninno,** Marie B '90 Bank of NY -1 Wall -NY 10286
(516) 741-1032 .. **Colantonio,** Anthony L '04 %Manoussos & M,PLLC -595 Stewart Av -Gdn Cty 11530 **Fx:**741-7510
(212) 310-8000 .. **Colao,** Andrew J '90 (Weil G&M LLP) -767 5th Av -NY 10153
(212) 461-2323 .. **Colao,** Danalynn Tolento '00 (Saiber LLC) -44 Wall -NY 10005
(212) 759-8203 .. **Colao,** Gregory J '00 %Hedinger & L -110 Wall -NY 10005
(212) 486-2400 .. **Colao,** Jos G '86 (Leader & B LLP) -630 3rd Av -NY 10017
(607) 763-9200 .. **Colapietro,** Bruno '60 OfCnsl Levene G&T,LLP -71 State -Bnghmtn 13902
(914) 946-2777 .. **Colarusso,** Jos J '83 -245 Main -White Plns 10601 **Fx:**(203) 325-3066
(516) 378-4466 .. **Colarusso,** Robt J '86 %State Farm -3346 Lng Bch Rd -Oceanside 11572
(914) 251-1111 .. **Colasurdo,** Jos T '86 (J Colasurdo & Assoc,PC) -2900 Wstchstr Av -Purchase 10577 **Fx:**251-0011
(212) 756-2000 .. **Colasurdo,** Lindsay K '10 %Schulte R&Z LLP -919 3rd Av -NY 10022
(212) 809-7074 .. **Colatrella,** Laura M '95 %Armienti DG&R,LLP -39 Bway -NY 10006
(631) 755-0101 .. **Colavecchio,** Michl T '91 (Lewis JAA,LLP) -425 Broad Hollow Rd -Melvll 11747
(914) 793-1222 .. **Colavita,** Anthony J '61 -575 Wht Plns Rd -Eastchstr 10709
(516) 294-8844 .. **Colavita,** Anthony P '78 (L'Abbate BC&C,LLP) -1001 Franklin Av -Gdn Cty 11530
(914) 793-1222 .. **Colavita,** Anthony S '88 -575 Wht Plns Rd -Eastchstr 10709
(718) 923-4206 .. **Colavita,** Katherine T '92 OTDA Fair Hearings -14 Boerum Pl -Brklyn 11201
(516) 408-1600 .. **Colavito,** Elaine M '08 %Heidell PM&B,LLP -1050 Franklin Av -Gdn Cty 11530
(516) 942-9100 .. **Colavito,** Jeanine D '06 %P Birzon & Assoc -400 Jericho Tpk -Jericho 11753 **Fx:**942-0596
(518) 457-7069 .. **Colavito,** Maria L '80 Dept of Labor -State Campus Bldg 12 -Albany 12240 **Fx:**457-1164
(212) 579-6260 .. **Colavito,** Wm D '95 -140 W 69th -NY 10023
(212) 351-4000 .. **Colb,** Sara A '08 %Gibson D&C LLP -200 Park Av -NY 10166
(212) 310-8000 .. **Colbath,** Bruce A '85 (Weil G&M LLP) -767 5th Av -NY 10153
(212) 407-4000 .. **Colbath,** Paula K '91 (Loeb & L,LLP) -345 Park Av -NY 10154
(212) 777-7270 .. **Colberg,** Michl D '80 -301 E 21st -NY 10010
(212) 736-1770 .. **Colbert,** Douglas M '72 -350 5th Av -NY 10118 **Fx:**947-0375
(212) 252-0300 .. **Colbert,** Jos G '93 (Kagan LLLG&C,LLP) -200 Mad Av -NY 10016
(518) 235-4520 .. **Colbert,** Scott D '90 -Bx382 -Troy 12182 **Fx:**235-4530
(212) 558-4000 .. **Colbran,** Philip L '87 SpclCnsl Sullivan & C LLP -125 Broad -NY 10004
(585) 753-4500 .. **Colburn,** Martha Brownell '00 %DA -832 Watts Bldg -Rchstr 14614 **Fx:**753-4576
(212) 408-5100 .. **Colby,** A Robt '83 (Chadbourne & P LLP) -30 Rckfllr Plz -NY 10112
(716) 842-2800 .. **Colby,** Jeremy A '05 %Webster S LLP -1400 Lbrty Bldg -Buffalo 14202
(716) 883-7272 .. **Colca,** Laura Wutz '94 %McGee & G -200 Summer -Buffalo 14222
(212) 357-8724 .. **Colchamiro,** Eric D '98 Goldman Sachs -1 NY Plz -NY 10004
(212) 490-2020 .. **Coldwell,** Mark F '95 %Littman K LLP -655 3rd Av -NY 10017
(212) 801-3183 .. **Cole,** Adam D '91 (Greenberg T,LLP) -200 Park Av -NY 10166
(212) 697-4200 .. **Cole,** Beverly P '99 Milberg Factors -99 Park Av -NY 10016
(212) 384-7047 .. **Cole,** Chas D Jr. '80 (Newman MKGH,PC) -14 Wall -NY 10005
(212) 504-6000 .. **Cole,** Chauncey D '07 %Cadwalader W&T LLP -1 World Fncl Ctr -NY 10281
(315) 349-3200 .. **Cole,** Chelsey A '06 %DA -Pub Safety Ctr -Oswego 13126 **Fx:**349-3212
(212) 209-3050 .. **Cole,** David P '08 %Reitler K&R LLC -885 3rd Av -NY 10022
(212) 998-2176 .. **Cole,** Debra R '05 New York Univ -194 Mercer -NY 10012
(516) 739-0639 .. **Cole,** Denis E '68 -1301 Franklin Av -Gdn Cty 11530
(585) 530-8465 .. **Cole,** Elaine Zipp '78 %Dept of Tax & Fin -340 E Main -Rchstr 14604 **Fx:**530-2017
(212) 259-8000 .. **Cole,** Eva Wolaniuk '04 %Dewey & L LLP -1301 Av of Amer -NY 10019
(315) 445-1700 .. **Cole,** Heather M '05 %Wladis Law Firm,PC -5795 Widewaters Pkwy -Syracuse 13214 **Fx:**251-1073
(212) 403-1000 .. **Cole,** James Jr. '97 (Wachtell LR&K) -51 W 52nd -NY 10019
(518) 465-7933 .. **Cole,** James David '74 %Assn of Towns of NYS -146 State -Albany 12207 **Fx:**465-0724
(516) 572-2000 .. **Cole,** James W '08 %DA -99 Main -Hempstd 11550 **Fx:**572-2606
(415) 882-8023 .. **Cole,** Jeffrey M '73 (K&L Gates LLP) -599 Lex Av -NY 10022 **Fx:**882-8220
(212) 237-0000 .. **Cole,** Jonathan C '09 %Vinson & E LLP -666 5th Av -NY 10103
(212) 506-5000 .. **Cole,** Jonathan H '01 %Orrick H&S LLP -51 W 52nd -NY 10019
(914) 287-7680 .. **Cole,** Joshua S '03 %Mayo C LLC -600 N Bway -White Plns 10603 **Fx:**287-7685
(845) 235-5846 .. **Cole,** Justin L '04 J Cole,PLLC -Bx351 -Rhinecliff 12574 **Fx:**(917) 254-4678
(516) 227-0700 .. **Cole,** Kathryn Carney '03 %Farrell F,PC -1320 RXR Plz -Uniondale 11556
(212) 403-1000 .. **Cole,** Keia D '10 %Wachtell LR&K -51 W 52nd -NY 10019
(212) 361-1400 .. **Cole,** Leo W '50 Envrnmntl Cntrl Brd -66 John -NY 10038 **Fx:**361-1900
(212) 806-5400 .. **Cole,** Lewis G '54 OfCnsl Stroock &S&L LLP -180 Maiden Ln -NY 10038
(212) 929-0606 .. **Cole,** Martin S '56 -110 Wall -NY 10005 **Fx:**608-7266
(646) 459-3326 .. **Cole,** Melissa Anne '98 Music Choice -328 W 34th -NY 10001
(585) 546-5530 .. **Cole,** Melvin C '84 %Thomson West -50 E Broad -Rchstr 14694
(212) 599-4747 .. **Cole,** Michl S '80 (Cascone C&C) -711 3rd Av -NY 10017
(716) 856-3646 .. **Cole,** Richd H '96 (Cole SHH&G,PC) -37 Franklin -Buffalo 14202
(716) 240-2262 .. **Cole,** Richd W '80 -17 Beresford Ct -Williamsvll 14221
(212) 763-4100 .. **Cole,** Robt B G '94 Cnsl Reavis PL LLP -41 Mad Av -NY 10010
(212) 752-8000 .. **Cole Schotz Meisel Forman & Leonard,PA** -900 3rd Av -NY 10022 **Fx:**752-8393
(518) 439-0805 .. **Cole,** Sheila S '77 -80 Huntersfld Rd -Delmar 12054
(716) 856-3646 .. **Cole Sorrentino Hurley Hewner & Gambino,PC** -37 Franklin -Buffalo 14202 **Fx:**854-2531
(716) 286-8319 .. **Cole,** Stephanie A '01 Cnsl Niagara Univ -Bx2025 -Niagara University 14109
(585) 327-4100 .. **Cole,** Steven E '95 (Leclair KGC,LLP) -150 State -Rchstr 14614 **Fx:**327-4200
(212) 576-4752 .. **Cole,** Susan Tamarkin '95 NY Life Ins -51 Mad Av -NY 10010
(212) 589-4200 .. **Cole,** Tracy L '96 (Baker & H LLP) -45 Rckfllr Plz -NY 10111
(212) 455-2000 .. **Cole,** Victor '03 %Simpson T&B LLP -425 Lex Av -NY 10017
(845) 639-5845 .. **Cole-Hatchard,** Stephen J '89 -315 Route 210 -Stony Pnt 10980
(315) 442-0100 .. **Colella,** Brenda D '06 %Gilberti SH&S,PC -555 E Genesee -Syracuse 13202
(315) 510-3328 .. **Colella,** Donald P '65 -216 Genesee Bx210 -Chittenango 13037 **Fx:**510-3329
(212) 566-5880 .. **Colella,** Frank G '89 -217 Bway -NY 10007 **Fx:**385-9229
(585) 335-3168 .. **Colella,** Louis J '76 -88 Ossian -Dansvll 14437
(212) 577-3563 .. **Colella,** Patricia S '90 %Leg Aid -199 Water -NY 10038 **Fx:**577-3520
(518) 478-1133 .. **Colello,** Anna Diane '82 %Ofc of Continuing Care -161 Delaware Av -Delmar 12054
(212) 825-5900 .. **Coleman,** Anastasia '97 %Dept of Invstgtn -80 Maiden Ln -NY 10038 **Fx:**825-2860
(212) 655-3500 .. **Coleman,** Bruce S '72 Cnsl Meister S&F LLP -140 E 45th -NY 10017
(212) 858-1000 .. **Coleman,** C Payson Jr. '77 (Pillsbury WSP LLP) -1540 Bway -NY 10036
(718) 260-5124 .. **Coleman,** Chas E '86 NYC Technical College -300 Jay -Brklyn 11201 **Fx:**573-1303
(518) 436-5790 .. **Coleman,** Cheryl F '86 -100 State -Albany 12207
(212) 869-3200 .. **Coleman,** Christopher M '07 %Molod S&D,PC -104 W 40th -NY 10018
(845) 454-2569 .. **Coleman,** Christopher S '91 (Sall C&C) -3 Cannon -Poughkeepsie 12601
(212) 877-9298 .. **Coleman,** Columbus Jr. '05 -308 W 92nd -NY 10025 **Fx:**769-2418
(718) 590-2000 .. **Coleman,** Debbie A '94 -215 E 161st -Bronx 10451
(518) 369-0478 .. **Coleman,** Douglas E '05 DE Coleman,PC -445 Warren -Hudson 12534 **Fx:**828-2362
(212) 349-5890 .. **Coleman,** Elizabeth J '98 NYS Trial Assn -132 Nassau -NY 10038 **Fx:**608-2310
(212) 310-8000 .. **Coleman,** Erica A '09 %Weil G&M LLP -767 5th Av -NY 10153
(212) 541-2000 .. **Coleman,** Glenn B '91 Cnsl Bryan C LLP -1290 Av of Amer -NY 10104
(212) 836-8000 .. **Coleman,** Gregory '10 %Kaye S LLP -425 Park Av -NY 10022
(212) 735-3000 .. **Coleman,** Hayden A '97 Cnsl Skadden ASM&F LLP -4 Times Sq -NY 10036
(212) 558-4000 .. **Coleman,** Heather L '08 %Sullivan & C LLP -125 Broad -NY 10004
(212) 259-8000 .. **Coleman,** Ilona B '09 %Dewey & L LLP -1301 Av of Amer -NY 10019

(607) 535-7694 .. **Coleman**, James P '69 -311 S Franklin Bx271 -Watkins Glen 14891 **Fx**:535-0008
(607) 277-1916 .. **Coleman**, Jeff '83 -107 S Albany -Ithaca 14850 **Fx**:277-7519
(212) 837-6000 .. **Coleman**, Jeffrey R '86 (Hughes H&R LLP) -1 Bttry Pk Plz -NY 10004
(212) 682-0020 .. **Coleman**, Jerome P '76 (Putney TH&H LLP) -521 5th Av -NY 10175
(212) 829-9090 .. **Coleman**, John A Jr. '91 (Friedberg CC&P,LLP) -767 3rd Av -NY 10017
(716) 284-2706 .. **Coleman**, Jos D '86 -2902 Pine Av -Niagara Fls 14301
(212) 526-7637 .. **Coleman**, Jos P Jr. '88 %Barclays Capital Inc -745 7th Av -NY 10019
(212) 816-2779 .. **Coleman**, Jos R '04 Citigroup Cptl Mrkts -388 Greenwich -NY 10013
(212) 859-8000 .. **Coleman**, Joshua T '04 %Fried FHS&J LLP -1 NY Plz -NY 10004
(212) 837-6000 .. **Coleman**, Kathryn A '06 (Hughes H&R LLP) -1 Bttry Pk Plz -NY 10004
(518) 455-2381 .. **Coleman**, Kathryn J '10 Sen R McDonald -306 Lgsltv Ofc Bldg -Albany 12247
(212) 610-6300 .. **Coleman**, Kenneth P '82 (Allen & O) -1221 Av of Amer -NY 10020
(914) 828-8144 .. **Coleman**, Kevin M '92 Swiss Re America -175 King -Armonk 10504 **Fx**:828-7144
(212) 825-1212 .. **Coleman**, Kimberly N '08 %Morrison M LLP -17 State -NY 10004
(212) 715-9100 .. **Coleman**, Kristen A '09 %Kramer LN&F,LLP -1177 Av of Amer -NY 10036
(718) 250-2000 .. **Coleman**, Lindsay B '08 %DA -350 Jay -Brklyn 11201 **Fx**:250-2314
(914) 946-0150 .. **Coleman**, Lisandre S '83 (Coleman & S) -41 Winslow Rd -White Plns 10606 **Fx**:997-0375
(516) 937-5900 .. **Coleman**, Lonnie '89 (Moomjian WW&C LLP) -100 Jericho Quad -Jericho 11753
(212) 489-8230 .. **Coleman**, M Graham 2nd '84 (Davis WT LLP) -1633 Bway -NY 10019
(718) 855-7562 .. **Coleman**, Marjorie T '77 -155 Willow -Brklyn 11201
(646) 487-3650 .. **Coleman**, Mark J '04 YES Ntwrk -405 Lex Av -NY 10174
(212) 693-0501 .. **Coleman**, Marshal '83 -32 Bway -NY 10004 **Fx**:693-2167
(516) 802-5960 .. **Coleman**, Martin J '91 -100 Crsswys Park Dr W -Woodbury 11797 **Fx**:802-5961
(646) 728-5300 .. **Coleman**, Matthew J '01 DE Shaw & Co -120 W 45th -NY 10036
(518) 402-2797 .. **Coleman**, Maureen A '97 %DEC -625 Bway -Albany 12233 **Fx**:402-9018
(212) 438-2000 .. **Coleman**, Maureen N '93 %Standard & Poor's -55 Water -NY 10041
(914) 750-5933 .. **Coleman**, Meredith A '07 %Kissel H&W LLP -580 Wht Plns Rd -Tarrytwn 10591
(212) 803-5100 .. **Coleman**, Michl '74 %NY Cnty Defender Srvcs -225 Bway -NY 10007 **Fx**:571-6035
(212) 804-4200 .. **Coleman**, Michl P '09 %Mound CW&G -One Bttry Pk Plz -NY 10004
(607) 778-2403 .. **Coleman**, Michele A '04 %Pub Def -45 Hawley Bx1766 -Bnghmtn 13902 **Fx**:778-2432
(518) 455-7924 .. **Coleman**, Nicola T '07 NYS Senate Majority Cnsl -The Cptl -Albany 12247
(212) 422-0202 .. **Coleman**, Nora '04 %Sedgwick DM&A LLP -125 Broad -NY 10004
(718) 590-7000 .. **Coleman**, Philip W Sr. '88 (Coleman & A LLC) -881 Gerard Av -Bronx 10452 **Fx**:590-6051
(315) 475-8461 .. **Coleman**, Ralph E '80 OfCnsl Coulter V&M,LLP -636 Old Liverpool Rd -Liverpool 13088
(516) 798-7800 .. **Coleman**, Richd H '78 (Shapiro & C,PC) -727 N Bway -N Massapequa 11758
(212) 682-7050 .. **Coleman**, Robt Emmet '95 %Geringer & D -5 Hanover Sq -NY 10004
(212) 695-8100 .. **Coleman**, Ronald D '89 (Goetz F,LLP) -1 Penn Plz -NY 10119
(212) 883-4039 .. **Coleman**, Scott R '87 %Cluett American Corp -48 W 38th -NY 10018 **Fx**:883-4040
(212) 806-5400 .. **Coleman**, Stuart H '80 (Stroock &S&L LLP) -180 Maiden Ln -NY 10038
(718) 590-2000 .. **Coleman**, Victoria T '08 %DA -198 E 161st -Bronx 10451 **Fx**:590-6477
(718) 875-8555 .. **Coleman**, Wm R '73 -155 Willow -Brklyn 11201
(914) 289-0800 .. **Coleman**, Wm V '94 %Solomon & T,PC -707 Wstchstr Av -White Plns 10604
(212) 474-1000 .. **Coleman Tio**, Jose R '09 %Cravath S&M LLP -825 8th Av -NY 10019
(518) 274-7252 .. **Cole-Paul**, Donna '01 DC Paul,PC -54 2nd -Troy 12180 **Fx**:274-0348
(212) 969-3000 .. **Coles**, Anthony C '90 SrCnsl Proskauer R LLP -1585 Bway -NY 10036
(212) 335-4500 .. **Coles**, Anthony Paul '81 (DLA Piper LLP) -1251 Av of Amer -NY 10020
(518) 426-8111 .. **Coles**, Lynn M '00 %Morris & M LLP -19 Dove -Albany 12210
(212) 819-1130 .. **Coletta**, Christine A '09 %Hirschen S&E -902 Bway -NY 10010
(212) 220-3000 .. **Coletta**, John J '98 %Broadcast Music Inc -250 Greenwich -NY 10007
(718) 613-3500 .. **Coletti**, Alterio A '79 %UIA Bd -Bx29002 -Brklyn 11201 **Fx**:613-3566
(585) 232-5768 .. **Coletti**, David R '91 (Christiano G&C) -16 E Main -Rchstr 14614
(718) 482-1815 .. **Coletti**, Robt J Jr. '83 -37-18 Railroad Av -LIC 11101
(212) 446-4800 .. **Coletti**, Ryan H '07 %Kirkland & E LLP -153 E 53rd -NY 10022
(212) 691-5631 .. **Colfin**, Bruce E '82 (B Colfin Law,PC) -1178 Mad Av -NY 10001
(212) 335-9000 .. **Colgan**, Danl M '93 %DA -1 Hogan Pl -NY 10013
(212) 431-9380 .. **Colgan**, David M '99 %Goldberger & D,PC -401 Bway -NY 10013
(718) 981-5505 .. **Colgan**, Erin K '02 E Colgan PC -390 Manor Rd -Staten Isl 10314 **Fx**:971-1034
(516) 338-5780 .. **Colgan**, Patricia M '86 %Macri G&M -393 Old Cntry Rd -Carle Pl 11514
(212) 566-5000 .. **Colgate**, James P '03 Dept of Bldgs -280 Bway -NY 10007
(516) 227-0700 .. **Colgrove**, Peter B '85 Cnsl Farrell F,PC -1320 RXR Plz -Uniondale 11556
(516) 393-5500 .. **Colica**, Brian '99 -3601 Hempstd Tpk -Levittwn 11756
(585) 232-5225 .. **Colicchio**, Roy E '56 (Remington GW&C,LLP) -183 E Main -Rchstr 14604
(212) 626-4100 .. **Colihan**, James C '80 (Baker & M LLP) -1114 Av of Amer -NY 10036
(718) 488-7788 .. **Colihan**, Michl J '84 -44 Court -Brklyn 11201
(718) 380-3708 .. **Colin**, Andrew '81 (Colin & S) -164-16 73rd Av -Fresh Mdws 11366 **Fx**:591-8535
(212) 218-2100 .. **Colin**, Jeffrey R '09 %Fitzpatrick CH&S -1290 Av of Amer -NY 10104
(914) 328-8028 .. **Colin**, Lisa F '90 (Martin & C,PC) -44 Church -White Plns 10601 **Fx**:206-3619
(646) 392-9250 .. **Colin**, Robt P '99 %M Klein & Assoc -200 Mad Av -NY 10016 **Fx**:(212) 779-1499
(718) 834-0190 .. **Colinayo**, Margie P '07 Figeroux & Assoc -26 Court -Brklyn 11242 **Fx**:222-3153
(212) 734-1561 .. **Colin-Greene**, Robin '76 -2 W 45th -NY 10036
(212) 929-3453 .. **Colinvaux**, Sally '79 -331 W 11th -NY 10014
(212) 732-3200 .. **Colish**, Faith '60 Cnsl Carter L&M LLP -2 Wall -NY 10005
(914) 946-0600 .. **Colistra**, Brian W '98 %Pino & Assoc -50 Main -White Plns 10606 **Fx**:946-0650
(212) 506-5000 .. **Coll**, J Peter Jr. '69 (Orrick H&S LLP) -51 W 52nd -NY 10019
(631) 273-8444 .. **Collado Collado & Fiore,PLLC** -14 Wshngtn Av -Brentwd 11717 **Fx**:273-8499
(631) 273-8444 .. **Collado**, John J '91 (Collado C&F,PLLC) -14 Wshngtn Av -Brentwd 11717
(347) 404-9133 .. **Collado**, Julissa '10 %Civil Ct -141 Lvngstn -Brklyn 11201 **Fx**:(718) 643-3733
(212) 909-2989 .. **Collado**, Michl A '93 Talkpoint Communications -100 William -NY 10038 **Fx**:404-1525
(631) 273-8444 .. **Collado**, Wm J '84 (Collado C&F,PLLC) -14 Wshngtn Av -Brentwd 11717
(516) 365-9802 .. **Collard**, Allison C '69 (Collard & R,PC) -1077 Nrthrn Blvd -Roslyn 11576
(516) 365-9802 .. **Collard & Roe, PC** -1077 Nrthrn Blvd -Roslyn 11576 **Fx**:365-9805
(516) 365-9802 .. **Collard**, Wm C '98 %Collard & R,PC -1077 Nrthrn Blvd -Roslyn 11576
(914) 376-9160 .. **Collarile**, Paul J '80 -711 Ynkrs Av -Ynkrs 10704 **Fx**:476-1205
(212) 758-7600 .. **Collazo Carling & Mish** -747 3rd Av -NY 10017 **Fx**:758-7609
(212) 758-7600 .. **Collazo**, Ernest J '75 (Collazo C&M) -747 3rd Av -NY 10017
(212) 309-6000 .. **Collazo**, Gretchen P '08 %Morgan L&B LLP -101 Park Av -NY 10178
(718) 293-0555 .. **Collazo**, Salvador '80 -1015 Grnd Cncrs -Bronx 10452 **Fx**:293-0848
(516) 512-6590 .. **Colleary**, Michl J '96 %Pieret & Assoc -400 Grdn City Plz -Gdn Cty 11530 **Fx**:742-4116
(516) 741-3400 .. **Colleluori**, Anthony J '85 (A Colleluori & Assoc) -180 Froehlich Farm Blvd -Woodbury 11797 **Fx**:921-8845
(718) 250-4275 .. **Collentine**, Alexis C '07 %Leg Aid -111 Lvngstn -Brklyn 11201 **Fx**:250-4243
(212) 944-2200 .. **Coller**, Edmond M '67 (Ferber CE&C,LLP) -530 5th Av -NY 10036
(516) 248-5757 .. **Colleran O'Hara & Mills,LLP** -1225 Franklin Av -Gdn Cty 11530 **Fx**:742-1765
(212) 552-2552 .. **Colleran**, Robt '69 JP Morgan Chase -1 Chase Manh Plz -NY 10081
(212) 355-6182 .. **Collery**, Melissa Anne '93 %EP Dine Inc -115 E 57th -NY 10022 **Fx**:755-8486
(212) 313-3600 .. **Collesano**, Mark A '93 %Barry M&M -2 Rector -NY 10006
(212) 227-6879 .. **Collesano**, Michl J '96 -155 E 34th -NY 10016
(716) 856-1010 .. **Collesano**, Stanley J '69 (S Collesano,LLC) -69 Delaware Av -Buffalo 14202
(212) 763-4700 .. **Collet**, Brian C '09 Partners Grp Inc -450 Lex Av -NY 10017
(212) 250-5122 .. **Collett**, Gregory S '98 %Deutsche Bank -60 Wall -NY 10005
(212) 438-2000 .. **Collett**, Lucy Anne '89 %Standard & Poor's -55 Water -NY 10041
(212) 558-4000 .. **Colletta**, Anthony J '89 (Sullivan & C LLP) -125 Broad -NY 10004
(212) 227-0347 .. **Colletta**, Mary '93 %Weiss W&W,PC -25 Park Pl -NY 10007
(914) 533-2867 .. **Colletti**, Paul J '65 -19 Kingswood Way -S Salem 10590 **Fx**:533-2867
(212) 588-0800 .. **Colletti**, Robt E '99 (Frommer L&H LLP) -745 5th Av -NY 10151
(212) 573-7596 .. **Colletti**, Salvatore '86 %Pfizer Inc -235 E 42nd -NY 10017
(914) 277-4800 .. **Colley**, Bryan O '81 -Bx779 -Croton Fls 10519
(212) 788-1613 .. **Colley**, Drake A '90 %Law Dept -100 Church -NY 10007 **Fx**:788-0367
(212) 440-2745 .. **Colliau Elenius Murphy Carluccio Keener & Morrow** -40 Wall -NY 10005 **Fx**:440-2749
(845) 647-4000 .. **Collier & Berger,PLLC** -130 S Main Bx509 -Ellenvll 12428 **Fx**:647-6029
(845) 626-0655 .. **Collier & Berger,PLLC** -37 Main Bx310 -Accord 12404 **Fx**:626-3817
(718) 579-7909 .. **Collier**, Chas D '03 %Leg Aid -900 Sheridan Av -Bronx 10451 **Fx**:293-8744
(718) 989-4714 .. **Collier**, David T Jr. '09 -26 Court -Brklyn 11242
(914) 684-6800 .. **Collier Halpern Newberg Nolletti & Bock,LLP** -1 N Lex Av -White Plns 10601 **Fx**:684-6986
(212) 481-1300 .. **Collier Halpern Newberg Nolletti & Bock,LLP** -355 Lex Av -NY 10017 **Fx**:696-4064
(212) 306-7450 .. **Collier**, Mikki P '05 %Comm on Human Rights -40 Rector -NY 10006 **Fx**:306-7414
(845) 647-4000 .. **Collier**, Wm H III '79 (Collier & B,PLLC) -130 S Main Bx509 -Ellenvll 12428
(845) 626-0655 .. **Collier**, Wm H III '79 (Collier & B,PLLC) -37 Main Bx310 -Accord 12404
(914) 684-6800 .. **Collier**, Wm J Jr. '60 (Collier HNN&B,LLP) -1 N Lex Av -White Plns 10601
(716) 852-3540 .. **Colligan**, David J '78 (Watson BCJ&S) -12 Fountain Plz -Buffalo 14202
(914) 285-8500 .. **Colligan**, Patrick '76 %TK Moore -701 Wstchstr Av -White Plns 10604 **Fx**:285-8510
(585) 263-1000 .. **Collin**, Dwight R '68 OfCnsl Nixon P LLP -1100 Clinton Sq -Rchstr 14604
(585) 492-1691 .. **Colling**, John Kirby '85 (JK Colling,PC) -270 Main Bx26 -Arcade 14009 **Fx**:492-1948
(212) 837-6031 .. **Collings**, Brett M '09 %Hughes H&R LLP -1 Bttry Pk Plz -NY 10004
(212) 247-1400 .. **Collins**, Adrian A '68 (A Collins,PC) -630 9th Av -NY 10036 **Fx**:247-1407
(212) 477-6141 .. **Collins**, Alice A '75 -11 5th Av -NY 10003
(212) 687-2770 .. **Collins**, Alphonso A '96 %Cohen PL&P -551 5th Av -NY 10176
(212) 277-5883 .. **Collins**, Aoife '02 %Beldock L&H LLP -99 Park Av -NY 10016

(631) 265-9494 .. **Collins,** Brian M '01 %D Collins -523 Townline Rd -Hauppauge 11788 **Fx:**265-9496
(716) 885-9700 .. **Collins & Brown, LLP** -267 North -Buffalo 14201 **Fx:**885-9770
(914) 946-1400 .. **Collins,** Chas A Jr. '76 (Vouté LM&C,LLP) -170 Hmltn Av -White Plns 10601
(718) 222-8880 .. **Collins,** Christa M '98 (Jones JO) -45 Main -Brklyn 11201
(212) 788-8661 .. **Collins,** Christopher '80 Bd of Standards -40 Rector -NY 10006
(212) 808-7800 .. **Collins,** Christopher J '91 %Kelley D&W LLP -101 Park Av -NY 10178
(631) 421-6955 .. **Collins,** Colleen P '89 -9 Mallard Dr -Huntngtn 11743 **Fx:**351-0983
(716) 854-4920 .. **Collins,** Cornelius '63 -295 Main -Buffalo 14203 **Fx:**849-1112
(631) 265-9494 .. **Collins,** Danl '87 -523 Townline Rd -Hauppauge 11788 **Fx:**265-9496
(585) 232-6500 .. **Collins,** Danl W '09 %Harter S&E LLP -1600 Bausch & Lomb Pl -Rchstr 14604
(212) 906-1200 .. **Collins,** Davon '08 %Latham & W -885 3rd Av -NY 10022
(212) 269-0927 .. **Collins,** Deborah M '91 (D'Amato & L,LLP) -2 World Fncl Ctr -NY 10281
(631) 331-0642 .. **Collins,** Dennis C '80 (D Collins,PC) -407 E Main Bx391 -Pt Jffrsn 11777 **Fx:**473-9054
(631) 420-0958 .. **Collins,** Diane M '88 -329 Carnation Dr -Farmngdl 11735
(212) 587-2400 .. **Collins Dobkin & Miller,LLP** -277 Bway -NY 10007 **Fx:**587-2410
(212) 536-4005 .. **Collins,** Elwood F Jr. '72 (K&L Gates LLP) -599 Lex Av -NY 10022
(718) 286-6000 .. **Collins,** Emily F '07 %DA -125-01 Qns Blvd -Kew Gdns 11415
(212) 318-6000 .. **Collins,** Erika C '05 (Paul HJ&W LLP) -75 E 55th -NY 10022
(212) 693-0085 .. **Collins,** Erin R '07 Appellate Advocates -2 Rector -NY 10006 **Fx:**693-0878
(518) 463-9877 .. **Collins,** George V III '91 -311 State -Albany 12210 **Fx:**463-9869
(716) 856-1344 .. **Collins,** George W Jr. '85 (Bouvier Prtnrshp,LLP) -350 Main -Buffalo 14202 **Fx:**856-1369
(518) 473-2275 .. **Collins,** Henry C '84 %Dept of Law -The Cptl -Albany 12224
(212) 997-8500 .. **Collins,** J Barclay '69 %Amerada Hess -1185 Av of Amer -NY 10036 **Fx:**536-8390
(845) 897-5199 .. **Collins,** J Peter '69 OfCnsl Feldman K&C,LLP -995 Main BxA -Fishkill 12524
(607) 692-3344 .. **Collins,** James C '59 -6107 NY Rte 26 Bx713 -Whitney Pnt 13862 **Fx:**692-2299
(212) 705-7000 .. **Collins,** James F Jr. '07 %Bingham M LLP -399 Park Av -NY 10022
(516) 741-6266 .. **Collins,** James J '80 (McCabe CM&F,LLP) -346 Westbury Av Bx9000 -Carle Pl 11514
(716) 849-1333 .. **Collins,** John A '83 (Lipsitz GSC LLP) -42 Delaware Av -Buffalo 14202
(631) 852-2500 .. **Collins,** John B '82 %DA -200 Center Dr -Rvrhead 11901 **Fx:**852-1769
(716) 885-9700 .. **Collins,** John F '72 (Collins C&D) -267 North -Buffalo 14201 **Fx:**885-9770
(212) 259-8000 .. **Collins,** John F '74 (Dewey & L LLP) -1301 Av of Amer -NY 10019
(518) 640-5000 .. **Collins,** John J III '81 AYCO -25 British Amer Blvd -Latham 12110
(315) 386-8506 .. **Collins,** John K '98 (Silver & C) -44 Court -Canton 13617 **Fx:**386-8507
(212) 947-4999 .. **Collins,** John M '96 OfCnsl Camacho MM,LLP -350 5th Av -NY 10118
(646) 428-3900 .. **Collins,** John P '95 %Dept of Educ -32 Old Slip -NY 10005 **Fx:**428-3890
(914) 993-1919 .. **Collins,** John Patrick Jr. '99 %US Atty -300 Quarropas -White Plns 10601 **Fx:**993-9036
(716) 649-1118 .. **Collins,** Jos A '78 -4255 Clark -Hambrg 14075 **Fx:**646-5855
(212) 819-8200 .. **Collins,** Jos E III '08 %White & C LLP -1155 Av of Amer -NY 10036
(518) 402-6190 .. **Collins,** K Brian '85 %Workers Comp Bd -20 Park -Albany 12207
(718) 250-2000 .. **Collins,** Kathleen A '08 Cnsl DA -350 Jay -Brklyn 11201 **Fx:**250-2314
(212) 435-3571 .. **Collins,** Kathleen M '83 %Port Auth of NY/NJ -225 Park Av S -NY 10003 **Fx:**435-3555
(212) 867-4100 .. **Collins,** Kathryn C '02 %Furman K&B LLP -61 Bway -NY 10006
(212) 813-8800 .. **Collins,** Kevin T '81 (Goodwin P LLP) -620 8th Av -NY 10018
(518) 447-7150 .. **Collins,** Lavonda S '05 %Pub Def -60 S Pearl -Albany 12207 **Fx:**447-5533
(212) 592-1400 .. **Collins,** Lisamarie F '08 %Herrick,F LLP -2 Park Av -NY 10016
(212) 854-2088 .. **Collins,** Mark E '91 Barnard Cllg -3009 Bway -NY 10027
(315) 471-0065 .. **Collins,** Martin C '87 (Mangano L&C) -201 E Jffrsn -Syracuse 13202
(516) 294-0300 .. **Collins McDonald & Gann** -138 Mineola Blvd -Mineola 11501 **Fx:**294-0477
(914) 666-5600 .. **Collins,** Megan K '07 %Shamberg MD&H,PC -55 Smith Av -Mt Kisco 10549
(646) 943-5913 .. **Collins,** Melissa J '01 Beazley Grp PLC -1270 Av of Amer -NY 10020
(516) 437-5649 .. **Collins,** Michl J '78 -26 Cmbrdg Av -Gdn Cty 11530
(212) 355-7100 .. **Collins,** Michl P '81 -725 5th Av -NY 10022
(646) 253-2300 .. **Collins,** Michl P '92 SrCnsl Bond S&K,PLLC -330 Mad Av -NY 10017
(718) 590-8394 .. **Collins,** Noreen '04 ACS -900 Sheridan Av -Bronx 10451
(718) 923-6368 .. **Collins,** Patricia '78 Comm on Character & Fitness -335 Adams -Brklyn 11201 **Fx:**624-5258
(212) 609-6800 .. **Collins,** Patrick M '91 (McCarter & E,LLP) -245 Park Av -NY 10167
(516) 227-0700 .. **Collins,** Patrick T '96 (Farrell F,PC) -1320 RXR Plz -Uniondale 11556
(212) 753-5000 .. **Collins,** Paul J '85 Cnsl Schiff H LLP -900 3rd Av -NY 10022
(518) 474-6367 .. **Collins,** Paul M '75 Bd of Elections -40 Steuben -Albany 12207
(212) 706-0248 .. **Collins,** Peter M '69 (Hollyer B LLP) -60 E 42nd -NY 10165 **Fx:**(646) 652-5336
(212) 310-8000 .. **Collins,** Reed L '08 %Weil G&M LLP -767 5th Av -NY 10153
(516) 294-0300 .. **Collins,** Richd D '85 (Collins M&G) -138 Mineola Blvd -Mineola 11501
(716) 631-5700 .. **Collins,** Richd G '75 (Sargent & C,LLP) -6245 Sheridan Dr -Williamsvll 14221 **Fx:**631-9120
(212) 578-2211 .. **Collins,** Richd S '71 %MetLife -27-01 Qns Plz N -LIC 11101
(607) 687-1899 .. **Collins,** Robt A '55 -1470 State Route 38 -Owego 13827 **Fx:**687-1899
(212) 692-9222 .. **Collins,** Robt Kirkman '76 -551 5th Av -NY 10176 **Fx:**692-9229
(212) 872-1000 .. **Collins,** Russell J '04 -One Bryant Park -NY 10036 **Fx:**872-1002
(212) 962-8020 .. **Collins,** Sara A '04 %Julien & S,PC -1 Whitehall -NY 10004
(718) 457-8707 .. **Collins,** Sharon M '90 -33-28 81st -Jcksn Hts 11372
(518) 447-7150 .. **Collins,** Shauna M '03 %Pub Def -60 S Pearl -Albany 12207 **Fx:**447-5533
(516) 443-6403 .. **Collins,** Stephen A '95 -998 Old Cntry Rd -Plainvw 11803 **Fx:**443-6404
(716) 675-6813 .. **Collins,** Susan B '89 -735 Union Rd -W Seneca 14224 **Fx:**675-6833
(212) 238-2420 .. **Collins,** Tammy B '01 UIA Bd -59 Maiden Ln -NY 10038 **Fx:**238-2451
(212) 298-5009 .. **Collins,** Tara A '99 %Leg Aid -49 Thomas -NY 10013 **Fx:**298-5252
(315) 451-3810 .. **Collins,** Timothy A '04 %O'Hara O&C,PC -7207 E Genesee -Fayettevll 13066
(212) 587-2400 .. **Collins,** Timothy L '86 (Collins D&M,LLP) -277 Bway -NY 10007
(315) 788-5100 .. **Collins,** Victoria Hasseler '07 %Conboy MB&K,LLP -407 Sherman -Watertwn 13601
(212) 245-7300 .. **Collins,** Wallace '88 OfCnsl Serling R&F,LLP -119 5th Av -NY 10003
(212) 848-4000 .. **Collins,** Wayne Dale '79 (Shearman & S LLP) -599 Lex Av -NY 10022
(716) 885-9700 .. **Collins,** Wm B '82 (Collins & B,LLP) -267 North -Buffalo 14201
(518) 455-4191 .. **Collins,** Wm F '77 %Ofc Cnsl to Majority -448M State Cptl -Albany 12248 **Fx:**455-4103
(212) 841-1000 .. **Collins,** Wm R '86 (Covington & B LLP) -620 8th Av -NY 10018
(516) 802-0630 .. **Collins,** Wm T '00 %Simmons J,LLP -115 Eileen Way -Syosset 11791
(718) 643-5004 .. **Collins-Hooks,** Gail '89 %Hon G Dabiri -283 Adams -Brklyn 11201
(718) 250-2000 .. **Collis,** Zulan D '97 %DA -350 Jay -Brklyn 11201 **Fx:**250-2314
(212) 850-6220 .. **Collison,** Bert A '52 OfCnsl Lathrop & G LC -230 Park Av -NY 10169
(607) 754-0410 .. **Collison,** Chas H '65 (Thomas C&M) -1201 Monroe Bx329 -Endicott 13761
(315) 701-5768 .. **Collison,** Gary H '94 -1000 7th N -Liverpool 13088 **Fx:**701-5770
(315) 422-8191 .. **Collmer,** Veda M '09 %Leg Aid -351 S Warren -Syracuse 13202 **Fx:**472-2819
(212) 238-3000 .. **Colloff,** Margery A '82 (Emmet M&M,LLP) -120 Bway -NY 10271
(212) 279-3334 .. **Collopy,** Alice F '83 (Collopy & C) -5 Penn Plz -NY 10001
(212) 279-3334 .. **Collopy & Carlucci** -5 Penn Plz -NY 10001 **Fx:**(973) 539-4774
(212) 425-3100 .. **Collura,** Anthony M '86 OfCnsl McManus C&R,PC -48 Wall -NY 10005
(518) 463-3990 .. **Collura,** Thos J '89 (Tuczinski CG&C,PC) -54 State -Albany 12207
(518) 565-4770 .. **Collyer,** Douglas G N '09 DA -137 Margaret -Plattsbrgh 12901 **Fx:**565-4777
(212) 832-7400 .. **Collyer,** Gerald F '63 -110 E 59th -NY 10022 **Fx:**832-7761
(212) 449-6759 .. **Colm,** Mark E '94 Merrill Lynch -250 Vesey-World Fncl Ctr -NY 10281
(212) 336-2000 .. **Colman,** Chas E '10 %Patterson BW&T LLP -1133 Av of Amer -NY 10036
(718) 225-8313 .. **Colman,** Mark S '72 -1 Bay Club Dr -Bayside 11360
(315) 446-7084 .. **Colman,** Peter A '71 (Colman & U) -7030 E Genesee -Fayettevll 13066
(315) 446-7084 .. **Colman & Underwood** -7030 E Genesee -Fayettevll 13066 **Fx:**446-7086
(716) 650-7532 .. **Colmerauer,** Michl J '84 %Seneca Rsrcs Corp -300 Essjay Rd -Williamsvll 14221
(212) 428-2160 .. **Colodner,** Michl '67 %OCA -25 Beaver -NY 10004 **Fx:**428-2155
(212) 536-3900 .. **Colodner,** Warren H '66 (K&L Gates LLP) -599 Lex Av -NY 10022
(646) 602-5600 .. **Colodny,** David A '06 Urban Justice Ctr -123 William -NY 10038 **Fx:**(212) 533-4598
(212) 878-9213 .. **Colodny,** Mark M '96 Warburg Pincus LLC -450 Lex Av -NY 10017
(718) 855-3179 .. **Colodny,** Richd '82 -185 Montague -Brklyn 11201
(212) 925-9000 .. **Colombini,** Anthony P '78 (Chu & Prtnrs) -183 Centre -NY 10013
(518) 449-8893 .. **Colombo,** Elizabeth F '05 %Wilson EME&D LLP -677 Bway -Albany 12207
(212) 756-2000 .. **Colombo,** Jason M '09 %Schulte R&Z LLP -919 3rd Av -NY 10022
(585) 242-9990 .. **Colombo,** Jeanne M '80 -774 Monroe Av -Rchstr 14607 **Fx:**242-9105
(516) 463-5931 .. **Colombo,** Ronald J '99 Hofstra Law Schl -121 Hofstra Univ -Hempstd 11549
(212) 551-0154 .. **Colombo Ball,** Mary Ann A '03 Brookwood Co Inc -25 W 45th -NY 10036
(718) 390-0555 .. **Colon,** Christopher '01 %Gabor & M LLC -1878 Victory Blvd -Staten Isl 10314
(516) 572-2000 .. **Colon,** Cristina '08 %DA -99 Main -Hempstd 11550 **Fx:**572-2606
(646) 386-3500 .. **Colon,** Diana '00 %OCA -25 Beaver -NY 10004 **Fx:**(212) 748-5085
(212) 428-2150 .. **Colon,** Eugene '85 OCA -25 Beaver -NY 10004
(585) 423-5200 .. **Colon,** Flor M '89 %Xerox -100 Clinton Av S -Rchstr 14644
(646) 252-7000 .. **Colon,** Gloria E '83 %TBTA -2 Bway -NY 10004
(212) 636-6000 .. **Colon,** Jeffrey M '90 %Fordham Univ Sch of Law -140 W 62nd -NY 10023 **Fx:**636-6899
(212) 264-4136 .. **Colon,** Linda C '86 US DHHS -26 Fed Plz -NY 10278
(347) 404-9133 .. **Colon,** Lizette '99 %Civil Ct -141 Lvngstn -Brklyn 11201 **Fx:**(718) 643-3733
(718) 858-4080 .. **Colon,** Lovemarie '02 -9 Adelphi -Brklyn 11205 **Fx:**858-0520
(212) 481-1900 .. **Colon,** Luis N '02 %Del Valle & Assoc -445 Park Av -NY 10022 **Fx:**481-4853
(212) 480-6727 .. **Colón,** Mark C '02 %DHCR -25 Beaver -NY 10004 **Fx:**480-7416
(212) 269-2091 .. **Colon,** Michl N '85 (Espinosa & E,LLP) -61 Bway -NY 10006
(212) 668-5632 .. **Colon,** Miriam G '91 %Hon C Blackshear -1 Bowling Grn -NY 10004
(516) 747-8830 .. **Colon,** Norman R '98 %Jaghab & J -176 Mineola Blvd -Mineola 11501 **Fx:**747-8770
(212) 964-8030 .. **Colon,** Raymond L '89 -233 Bway -NY 10279 **Fx:**964-2575
(585) 475-6932 .. **Colon,** Robt A '93 SrCnsl RIT -154 Lomb Mem'l Dr -Rchstr 14623 **Fx:**475-5360
(212) 455-2000 .. **Colon,** Sara C '10 %Simpson T&B LLP -425 Lex Av -NY 10017
(646) 610-5400 .. **Colon,** Steven J '06 NYPD -1 Police Plz -NY 10038
(212) 310-8000 .. **Colon-Bosolet,** Melissa '08 %Weil G&M LLP -767 5th Av -NY 10153
(646) 386-5700 .. **Colon-Greenaway,** Denise '05 %Civil Ct -111 Centre -NY 10013
(212) 833-3371 .. **Colonna,** Danielle F '03 Kroll Assoc -1166 Av of Amer -NY 10036 **Fx:**593-2631

(718) 882-7995 .. **Colonna,** James J '51 -3617A Wht Plns Rd -Bronx 10467 **Fx:**798-9480
(516) 747-5757 .. **Colonna,** John A '92 (Colonna & U,LLP) -1551 Kellum Pl -Mineola 11501 **Fx:**747-2107
(212) 709-1836 .. **Colonna,** Karen Leshowitz '93 %SOREMA NA -199 Water -NY 10038
(212) 833-1198 .. **Colorado,** Christopher M '07 %Friedman KS&A LLP -1633 Bway -NY 10019 **Fx:**373-7998
(607) 273-2900 .. **Colosi,** Christopher B '06 %Shaw Law Firm -109 E Seneca -Ithaca 14850 **Fx:**273-2933
(716) 845-7480 .. **Colosi,** Darryl J '90 %Supreme Ct -25 Delaware Av -Buffalo 14202 **Fx:**851-3293
(212) 315-8239 .. **Colosi,** Michl F '94 Kenneth Cole Prdctns -603 W 50th -NY 10019 **Fx:**315-8288
(212) 859-8000 .. **Colosimo,** Andrew J '01 (Fried FHS&J LLP) -1 NY Plz -NY 10004
(516) 248-7000 .. **Colozzi,** Arthur L '85 (Albanese & A LLP) -1050 Franklin Av -Gdn Cty 11530
(315) 424-8023 .. **Colozzi,** Gaetano L '79 -217 Mntgmry -Syracuse 13202 **Fx:**424-6826
(212) 257-6455 .. **Colson,** Deborah A '96 (Colson & H LLP) -10 E 40th -NY 10016 **Fx:**257-6453
(718) 229-1215 .. **Colson,** Grace M '98 G Colson,PC -1979 Marcus Av -Lk Success 11042 **Fx:**425-8999
(716) 427-8180 .. **Colson,** Thos J '89 IP.COM -150 Lucius Gorden Dr -W Henrietta 14586
(212) 788-0462 .. **Colt,** Suzanne K '81 %Law Dept -100 Church -NY 10007 **Fx:**788-0367
(845) 282-8595 .. **Colthirst,** June C M '03 -43 Wyndham Ln -Carmel 10512 **Fx:**282-8596
(631) 499-7616 .. **Coltoff,** Paul M '82 -150 Candlewood Path -Dix Hlls 11746
(212) 768-6700 .. **Colton,** Glenn C '90 (Sonnenschein N&R LLP) -1221 Av of Amer -NY 10020
(516) 377-2249 .. **Colton,** Howard E '95 Village Atty -46 N Ocean Av -Freeprt 11520
(518) 392-2789 .. **Colton,** Michl A '66 (M Colton,PC) -63 Norton Rd Bx65 -Austerlitz 12017 **Fx:**392-2754
(212) 701-3000 .. **Colton,** Scott E '06 %Cahill G&R LLP -80 Pine -NY 10005 **Fx:**269-5420
(718) 376-2645 .. **Colton,** Wm A '79 -208 Van Sicklen -Brklyn 11223
(716) 854-4080 .. **Colucci,** Anthony J '58 (Block C&L,PC) -1 Niagara Sq -Buffalo 14202
(716) 853-4080 .. **Colucci,** Anthony J III '84 (Colucci & G,PC) -424 Main -Buffalo 14202
(212) 416-8634 .. **Colucci,** Clement J III '83 %Dept of Law -120 Bway -NY 10271 **Fx:**416-6075
(212) 335-4500 .. **Colucci,** Dean M '94 (DLA Piper LLP) -1251 Av of Amer -NY 10020
(212) 935-5700 .. **Colucci,** Frank J '65 (Colucci & U) -218 E 50th -NY 10022
(716) 853-4080 .. **Colucci & Gallaher,PC** -424 Main -Buffalo 14202 **Fx:**854-4070
(914) 472-1500 .. **Colucci,** Gregory J '94 (Colucci & U) -670 Wht Plns Rd -Scarsdale 10583
(212) 715-9100 .. **Colucci,** Marcus A '03 %Kramer LN&F,LLP -1177 Av of Amer -NY 10036
(914) 741-6100 .. **Colucci,** Paul J '96 (Kaufman B&R) -200 Summit Lk Dr -Valhalla 10595
(212) 935-5700 .. **Colucci & Umans** -218 E 50th -NY 10022 **Fx:**935-5728
(914) 472-1500 .. **Colucci & Umans** -670 Wht Plns Rd -Scarsdale 10583 **Fx:**472-1551
(516) 766-1619 .. **Coluccio,** Jos G '03 %Dergarabedian D & Assoc -11 Clinton Av -Rockvll Ctr 11570 **Fx:**766-6121
(212) 940-3183 .. **Columbo,** Elizabeth M '95 (Nixon P LLP) -437 Mad Av -NY 10022
(718) 442-7171 .. **Columbo,** James R Jr. '95 (Columbo & E,PC) -207 Forest Av -Staten Isl 10301 **Fx:**273-9526
(212) 704-6000 .. **Columbres,** Candice '04 %Troutman S LLP -405 Lex Av -NY 10174
(212) 819-8200 .. **Columbres,** Claudine '04 %White & C LLP -1155 Av of Amer -NY 10036
(315) 798-5766 .. **Coluzza,** Michl A '91 %DA -800 Park Av -Utica 13501 **Fx:**798-5582
(212) 220-3830 .. **Coluzzi,** Saml C '97 (Nicoletti H&S) -88 Pine -NY 10005
(631) 424-8495 .. **Colvin,** Amy Gibbons '86 Farmingdale State Cllg -2350 Broadhllw Rd -Farmngdl 11735
(212) 878-8000 .. **Colvin,** Caitlin L '09 %Clifford C LLP -31 W 52nd -NY 10019
(516) 803-4859 .. **Colvin,** Cathleen M '93 Rainbow Media Holdings LLC -200 Jericho Quadrangle -Jericho 11753
(212) 715-9100 .. **Colvin,** Christopher A '01 (Kramer LN&F,LLP) -1177 Av of Amer -NY 10036
(212) 757-1544 .. **Colvin,** Geoffrey J '78 %CEW Prtnrs -780 3rd Av -NY 10017
(212) 225-7200 .. **Colvin,** Mary A '89 %Fed Emrgncy MgtAgncy -26 Fed Plz -NY 10278
(516) 593-0202 .. **Colway,** Mary H '83 -340 Atl Av -E Rockaway 11518 **Fx:**593-0297
(518) 462-4242 .. **Colwell Colwell & Petroccione,LLP** -20 Corp Wds Blvd -Albany 12211 **Fx:**462-4031
(518) 462-4242 .. **Colwell,** Kevin M '98 (Colwell C&P,LLP) -20 Corp Wds Blvd -Albany 12211
(518) 462-4242 .. **Colwell,** Mary T '02 (Colwell C&P,LLP) -20 Corp Wds Blvd -Albany 12211
(212) 269-5500 .. **Colwin,** Mercedes '92 (Gordon & R LLP) -90 Broad -NY 10004
(212) 859-8000 .. **Colyer,** Jennifer L '93 SpclCnsl Fried FHS&J LLP -1 NY Plz -NY 10004
(212) 336-8000 .. **Comack,** Brian '99 %Amster R&E -90 Park Av -NY 10016
(718) 816-0005 .. **Comas,** Stephanie S '05 %Angiuli K&G,LLP -60 Bay -Staten Isl 10301
(914) 993-4567 .. **Comas,** Waldemar A '76 %NY Medical Cllg -Sunshine Cottage -Valhalla 10595 **Fx:**993-4328
(845) 452-5900 .. **Comatos,** Gerard J '79 (Van DeWater & V,LLP) -85 Civic Ctr Plz Bx112 -Poughkeepsie 12602
(914) 725-6165 .. **Combe,** Cynthia M '79 -22 River Rd -Scarsdale 10583
(845) 433-1402 .. **Combe,** Daniela Kresic '90 %IBM -522 South Rd M/S-P905 -Poughkeepsie 12601 **Fx:**432-9797
(212) 762-7580 .. **Combs,** Tom '98 Morgan Stanley -750 7th Av -NY 10019
(516) 616-0245 .. **Comeau,** Lisa M '87 -1225 Franklin Av -Gdn Cty 11530 **Fx:**706-3458
(518) 873-2068 .. **Comeau,** Louis P '83 -High Bx6 -Elizabethtwn 12932
(716) 856-4000 .. **Comeau,** Paul R '74 (Hodgson R LLP) -140 Pearl -Buffalo 14202
(518) 457-0972 .. **Comenzo,** Susan A '79 %PERB -80 Wolf Rd -Albany 12205 **Fx:**457-2664
(914) 683-5400 .. **Comer,** Neal S '74 -445 Hmltn Av -White Plns 10601 **Fx:**428-1660
(212) 697-3122 .. **Comer,** Thos W '98 %Martin C&B LLP -220 E 42nd -NY 10017
(716) 551-3341 .. **Comerford,** Brian P '06 Fed Pub Def -300 Pearl -Buffalo 14202 **Fx:**551-3346
(716) 849-6500 .. **Comerford,** Danl K '10 %Brown & T,LLC -14 Lafayette Sq -Buffalo 14203
(516) 248-4817 .. **Comerford & Dougherty, LLP** -1122 Franklin Av -Gdn Cty 11530 **Fx:**248-1302
(212) 867-5800 .. **Comerford,** Jason J '01 %Osler H&H LLP -620 8th Av -NY 10018
(716) 849-0701 .. **Comerford,** John P '96 (Lipsitz & P LLC) -135 Delaware Av -Buffalo 14202
(212) 770-1930 .. **Comerford,** Mary Guerin '94 %AIG -70 Pine -NY 10270
(212) 530-5000 .. **Comerford,** Michl E '03 %Milbank TH&M LLP -1 Chase Manh Plz -NY 10005
(516) 248-4817 .. **Comerford,** Michl J '80 (Comerford & D,LLP) -1122 Franklin Av -Gdn Cty 11530
(212) 682-4001 .. **Comerford,** Patrick J '97 (Lynch R LLP) -630 3rd Av -NY 10017
(315) 332-7100 .. **Comerford,** Peter Flynn '83 %Ultralife Batteries,Inc -2000 Tech Pkwy -Newark 14513 **Fx:**331-7048
(212) 558-5812 .. **Comerford,** Thos M '01 %Weitz & L,PC -700 Bway -NY 10003
(212) 310-8000 .. **Comet,** Howard B '76 (Weil G&M LLP) -767 5th Av -NY 10153
(212) 788-7970 .. **Comfrey,** Kathleen M '77 %Law Dept -100 Church -NY 10007 **Fx:**788-0367
(716) 566-1300 .. **Cominsky,** Roger F '88 (Hiscock & B,LLP) -1100 M&T Ctr -Buffalo 14203
(315) 475-3425 .. **Cominsky,** Sidney P '76 -1500 State Twr Bldg -Syracuse 13202 **Fx:**475-2932
(718) 694-3861 .. **Comiskey,** Beatrix Seisdedos '85 %Transit Auth -130 Lvngstn -Brklyn 11201 **Fx:**694-5726
(516) 248-9880 .. **Comiskey,** John M '99 %Agovino & A,LLP -330 Old Cntry Rd -Mineola 11501
(212) 510-1461 .. **Comiskey,** Thos F '80 %Spec Comm of Invstgtn -80 Maiden Ln -NY 10038 **Fx:**510-1550
(518) 457-2070 .. **Comiskey,** Wm J '79 %Dept of Tax & Fin -Bldg 9 State Campus -Albany 12227 **Fx:**457-6131
(212) 336-2000 .. **Commandeur,** Nicolas '01 Cnsl Patterson BW&T LLP -1133 Av of Amer -NY 10036
(212) 661-4333 .. **Commender,** David G '80 -52 Vndrblt Av -NY 10017 **Fx:**697-2773
(631) 243-5886 .. **Commins,** Mark A '94 -1793 Deer Prk Av -Deer Pk 11729 **Fx:**242-4911
(518) 482-4922 .. **Commins,** Stephen D '88 -125 Wolf Rd -Albany 12205 **Fx:**677-1011
(212) 277-4000 .. **Commission,** Jeffery P '02 %Freshfields BD LLP -520 Mad Av -NY 10022
(518) 462-5601 .. **Commisso,** Cristina D '10 %O'Connell & A -54 State -Albany 12207
(718) 286-6000 .. **Communiello,** Anthony M Jr. '77 %DA -125-01 Qns Blvd -Kew Gdns 11415
(631) 537-6000 .. **Comnas,** Aspasia G '81 Sotheby's Intl Realty -Bx1799 -Brdghmptn 11932
(212) 735-3000 .. **Comnenos,** Pallas A '99 %Skadden ASM&F LLP -4 Times Sq -NY 10036
(718) 459-8700 .. **Como,** Anthony '01 -125-10 Qns Blvd -Kew Gdns 11415
(607) 565-2461 .. **Como,** Frank M '78 -440 Waverly Bx111 -Waverly 14892 **Fx:**565-7826
(718) 298-8900 .. **Como,** Irena '09 Leg Aid -153-01 Jamaica Av -Jamaica 11432 **Fx:**657-0537
(646) 746-9742 .. **Compa,** Gregory '02 CFTC -140 Bway -NY 10005 **Fx:**746-9939
(315) 471-8111 .. **Compagni,** Michl J '87 (Scolaro SCF&B,PC) -507 Plum -Syracuse 13204
(212) 232-1300 .. **Comparato,** Carolyn '06 %Lewis BB&S LLP -77 Water -NY 10005
(212) 478-3474 .. **Comparato,** Susan B '95 Syncora -825 8th Av -NY 10019
(212) 966-6700 .. **Compas,** Nicole '08 %Gray K LLP -207 W 25th -NY 10001 **Fx:**966-6051
(718) 273-0909 .. **Competiello,** Mark A '88 -444 Kissel Av -Staten Isl 10301 **Fx:**815-9885
(631) 451-6500 .. **Compitello,** Jeanne Alda '91 %Brookhaven Law Dept -1 Indpndnc Hill -Farmngvll 11738 **Fx:**698-4489
(212) 728-8000 .. **Composti,** Jeanna L '09 %Willkie F&G LLP -787 7th Av -NY 10019
(718) 875-5199 .. **Composto,** Andrea F '03 (Composto & C) -142 Joralemon -Brklyn 11201 **Fx:**639-7586
(718) 875-5199 .. **Composto,** Frank A '72 (Composto & C) -142 Joralemon -Brklyn 11201 **Fx:**639-7586
(315) 724-5147 .. **Compson Eannace & Pierro PLLC** -2621 Genesee -Utica 13501 **Fx:**724-2534
(315) 724-5147 .. **Compson,** Richd G '68 (Compson E&P PLLC) -2621 Genesee -Utica 13501
(212) 906-1200 .. **Compton,** Andrew C '08 %Latham & W -885 3rd Av -NY 10022
(212) 863-8225 .. **Compton,** Jeffrey M '06 HPD -100 Gold -NY 10038
(212) 850-0647 .. **Compton,** S H Spencer '90 %1st Amer Title -633 3rd Av -NY 10017 **Fx:**331-1680
(917) 750-3374 .. **Comstock,** Kristin B '97 ACE USA -140 Bway -NY 10005
(631) 390-5000 .. **Cona,** Jennifer B '97 (Genser DG&C,LLP) -445 Broad Hollow Rd -Melvll 11747
(315) 218-8000 .. **Conan,** Edw Ryan '81 (Bond S&K,PLLC) -1 Lincoln Ctr -Syracuse 13202
(212) 888-3033 .. **Conan,** Jesse T '06 %Becker GM&M LLP -299 Park Av -NY 10171
(315) 448-0909 .. **Conan,** Marguerite A '89 %US Dist Ct -100 S Clinton -Syracuse 13261
(315) 448-0672 .. **Conan,** Paula R '76 %US Atty -100 S Clinton Bx7198 -Syracuse 13261 **Fx:**448-0689
(315) 422-1152 .. **Conan,** Timothy J '87 (Costello C&F,PLLC) -500 Plum -Syracuse 13204
(212) 943-1090 .. **Conason,** Leslie A '78 -80 Pine -NY 10005
(212) 701-3000 .. **Conaty,** Matthew L '07 %Cahill G&R LLP -80 Pine -NY 10005 **Fx:**269-5420
(845) 482-5522 .. **Conaty,** Philip E '80 Callicoon Coop Ins -15 Chapel Bx675 -Jffrsnvll 12748
(212) 907-6442 .. **Conaway,** Danl M '04 (Conaway & S,PC) -4045 Lex Av -NY 10174
(631) 390-0010 .. **Conboy,** Christine M '08 %Bruno G&S,LLP -445 Broad Hollow Rd -Melvll 11747

(518) 899-5700 .. **Conboy,** Jacinda H '00 %Lemire J,LLC -2534 Route 9 Bx2485 -Malta 12020 **Fx:**899-5487
(518) 853-8250 .. **Conboy,** James E '81 (DA) -Bway Bx1500 -Fonda 12068 **Fx:**853-8212
(518) 465-3484 .. **Conboy,** James M '58 SrCnsl Carter CCBM&L,PC -20 Corp Wds Blvd -Albany 12211
(518) 474-5774 .. **Conboy,** Jenika '00 State Comptroller -110 State -Albany 12236 **Fx:**486-3106
(212) 906-1200 .. **Conboy,** Kenneth '65 (Latham & W) -885 3rd Av -NY 10022
(212) 458-6038 .. **Conboy,** Maureen A '86 AIGTS -175 Water -NY 10038
(315) 788-5100 .. **Conboy McKay Bachman & Kendall,LLP** -407 Sherman -Watertwn 13601 **Fx:**788-3463
(315) 493-0030 .. **Conboy McKay Bachman & Kendall,LLP** -307 State -Carthage 13619 **Fx:**493-7549
(315) 386-8544 .. **Conboy McKay Bachman & Kendall,LLP** -2 Judson -Canton 13617 **Fx:**379-0126
(516) 921-8600 .. **Conboy,** Michl P '87 (McAndrew C&P) -95 Froehlich Farm Blvd -Woodbury 11797
(518) 463-8858 .. **Conboy,** Wm J II '76 -112 State -Albany 12207
(212) 318-6000 .. **Conca,** David M '00 %Paul HJ&W LLP -75 E 55th -NY 10022
(212) 962-2727 .. **Concagh,** Kevin '69 (K Concagh,PC) -225 Bway -NY 10007 **Fx:**608-7492
(212) 850-2800 .. **Concannon,** David L '92 (Andrews K LLP) -450 Lex Av -NY 10017
(212) 813-1801 .. **Concannon,** Paul J '06 %Finnerty C&D,PC -488 Mad Av -NY 10022
(212) 808-7800 .. **Concannon,** Richd J '61 (Kelley D&W LLP) -101 Park Av -NY 10178
(212) 732-6460 .. **Concannon,** Timothy M '01 %Schwartz & S,PC -225 Bway -NY 10007
(212) 792-6490 .. **Concepcion,** Natasha P '03 Meridian Fund Srvcs(USA)LLC -370 Lex Av -NY 10017
(516) 794-6630 .. **Concepcion,** Nilo V '77 -2115 Hempstd Tpk -E Meadow 11554 **Fx:**794-7971
(212) 849-7000 .. **Conciatori,** Jeffrey A '81 (Quinn EU&S,LLP) -51 Mad Av -NY 10010
(914) 251-1618 .. **Conciatori,** Paul A '90 OfCnsl Price MS&D,PC -106 Corp Park Dr -White Plns 10604
(631) 577-7153 .. **Concu,** Sal G '91 The Travelers Co,Inc -100 Baylis Rd -Melvll 11747 **Fx:**(866) 781-1211
(212) 218-2100 .. **Conde,** Dominick A '91 (Fitzpatrick CH&S) -1290 Av of Amer -NY 10104
(212) 506-5000 .. **Conde,** Michelle R '85 OfCnsl Orrick H&S LLP -51 W 52nd -NY 10019
(212) 813-8800 .. **Conde,** Sarah Nicholson '08 %Goodwin P LLP -620 8th Av -NY 10018
(212) 732-3665 .. **Conde Da Silveira,** Marion A '01 %Harmon L&R -42 Bway -NY 10004
(212) 977-9700 .. **Condell,** Henry '86 (Phillips N LLP) -666 5th Av -NY 10103
(718) 259-4500 .. **Condello,** Mary Grace E '90 OfCnsl Vanchieri & F -1724 86th -Brklyn 11214
(718) 780-0382 .. **Condliffe,** David C '81 Bklyn Law Schl -250 Joralemon -Brklyn 11201 **Fx:**643-4726
(212) 225-2000 .. **Condlin,** Christopher S '10 %Cleary GS&H -1 Lbrty Plz -NY 10006
(845) 294-3596 .. **Condoluci,** Marie '95 %S Haysom LLC -1 Railroad Av Bx487 -Goshen 10924 **Fx:**294-8495
(845) 627-8500 .. **Condon,** Brian K '96 (Condon & Assoc,PLLC) -55 Old Tpk Rd -Nanuet 10954
(212) 506-1700 .. **Condon,** Brian L '03 %Kasowitz BT&F LLP -1633 Bway -NY 10019
(631) 724-8833 .. **Condon,** Brian S '09 %Devitt SB,LLP -50 Route 111 -Smithtwn 11787
(716) 845-5500 .. **Condon,** Carol A '82 -420 Main -Buffalo 14202 **Fx:**845-5516
(212) 848-7628 .. **Condon,** Creighton O '83 (Shearman & S LLP) -599 Lex Av -NY 10022
(212) 269-4900 .. **Condon,** Cushing O'Malley II '82 (Ford MEW&G,LLP) -Wall Street Plz -NY 10005
(518) 447-7110 .. **Condon,** Eugenia K '90 %Cnty Atty -112 State -Albany 12207
(212) 490-9100 .. **Condon & Forsyth LLP** -7 Times Sq -NY 10036 **Fx:**370-4453
(716) 434-5332 .. **Condon,** James E '65 -419 S Transit -Lockprt 14094
(716) 649-6700 .. **Condon,** Kevin C '02 %Abbott T&K,LLP -44 Union -Hambrg 14075
(631) 694-2626 .. **Condon,** Kevin G '92 %Grenier H&N LLP -445 Broadhllw Rd -Melvll 11747
(631) 421-8600 .. **Condon,** Patricia A '90 (McGuire C,PC) -775 Park Av -Huntngtn 11743 **Fx:**427-5106
(212) 660-3000 .. **Condon,** Robt V III '05 %Sullivan & W LLP -1290 Av of Amer -NY 10104
(914) 333-0700 .. **Condon,** Sean F '99 %Snyder & S -94 Wht Plns Rd -Tarrytwn 10591 **Fx:**333-0743
(845) 634-7010 .. **Condon,** Thos A '73 (Montalbano C&F,PC) -67 N Main Bx1070 -New Cty 10956
(585) 987-2800 .. **Condon,** Timothy D '09 %Woods OG LLP -2 State -Rchstr 14614
(212) 552-0939 .. **Condren,** James L '84 JP Morgan Chase -1 Chase Manh Plz -NY 10081
(716) 854-3400 .. **Condren,** John R '93 (Rupp BPC&C LLC) -1600 Lbrty Bldg -Buffalo 14202
(518) 474-7735 .. **Conduzio,** Arthur L '74 %Dept of Law -The Cptl -Albany 12224
(212) 688-3637 .. **Condzal,** Paul F '91 -29 Bway -NY 10006 **Fx:**(646) 924-3406
(212) 878-8000 .. **Cone,** Clifford R '06 %Clifford C LLP -31 W 52nd -NY 10019
(914) 481-6249 .. **Cone,** John E '69 (Cone & K) -83 S Bedford Rd -Mt Kisco 10549
(212) 635-2730 .. **Cone,** Michl T '98 OfCnsl Neville P LLP -17 State -NY 10004
(718) 250-2000 .. **Cone,** Stephanie Bond '08 %DA -350 Jay -Brklyn 11201 **Fx:**250-2314
(212) 225-2000 .. **Cone,** Sydney M III '70 SrCnsl Cleary GS&H -1 Lbrty Plz -NY 10006
(212) 431-2379 .. **Cone,** Sydney M III '70 %NY Law Schl -185 W Bway -NY 10013 **Fx:**966-6393
(212) 643-2828 .. **Cone,** Thos J '94 %GNYHCFA -360 W 31st -NY 10001 **Fx:**643-2956
(973) 848-4048 .. **Conenello,** Gail Howie '94 (K&L Gates LLP) -599 Lex Av -NY 10022 **Fx:**848-4001
(212) 374-3442 .. **Coneys,** Michl P '86 %NYC Dept Educ-OLS -52 Chmbrs -NY 10007 **Fx:**374-5596
(914) 968-3483 .. **Confalone,** Wm F '55 -169 Wstmnstr Dr -Ynkrs 10710 **Fx:**476-6531
(845) 485-3900 .. **Conflitti,** Robt J '85 %Dept of Law -235 Main -Poughkeepsie 12601 **Fx:**452-3303
(631) 232-1111 .. **Conforti,** Anthony T '74 (Conforti & W) -140 Fell Ct -Hauppauge 11788 **Fx:**232-2380
(914) 738-4575 .. **Conforti,** Martha L '78 (Conforti & T) -14 Clifford Av -Pelham 10803 **Fx:**738-4684
(516) 812-4503 .. **Confusione,** Lisa M '88 (Stagg TC&W LLP) -401 Franklin Av -Gdn Cty 11530
(516) 542-5900 .. **Congdon Flaherty O'Callaghan Reid Donlon Travis & Fishlinger** -333 Earle Ovngton Blvd -Uniondale 11553 **Fx:**542-5912
(518) 437-9300 .. **Congdon Flaherty O'Callaghan Reid Donlon Travis & Fishlinger** -12 Metro Park Rd -Colonie 12205 **Fx:**437-1182
(516) 542-5900 .. **Congdon,** Michl S '83 (Congdon FORDT&F) -333 Earle Ovngton Blvd -Uniondale 11553
(716) 945-3060 .. **Congdon Perreault Dohl & Rickert** -107 Main -Salamanca 14779 **Fx:**945-3062
(516) 785-5359 .. **Congero,** Kurt W '93 -2297 S Seamans Neck -Seafrd 11783
(212) 594-5300 .. **Congress,** Jerome M '66 (Milberg LLP) -1 Penn Plz -NY 10119
(212) 331-5047 .. **Conheim,** Susan '82 %HRA OLA -180 Water -NY 10038
(914) 253-2583 .. **Coniaris,** Jeffrey J '83 Pepsico -700 Andrsn Hill Rd -Purchase 10577
(315) 479-3900 .. **Coniber,** Constance J '97 SSA-ODAR -300 S State -Syracuse 13202 **Fx:**479-3933
(716) 854-3400 .. **Conidi,** Kimberly S '05 Rupp BPC&C LLC -1600 Lbrty Bldg -Buffalo 14202
(718) 351-1111 .. **Conigatti,** Thos R '96 (Conigatti & R,LLP) -67 New Dorp Plz -Staten Isl 10306 **Fx:**351-8616
(212) 367-0454 .. **Conigliaro,** James G '95 DJ Knight -101 5th Av -NY 10003
(585) 658-3120 .. **Coniglio,** Gerald A '02 -115 Main -Mt Morris 14510
(585) 258-2800 .. **Coniglio,** James A '78 (Underberg & K LLP) -300 Bausch & Lomb Pl -Rchstr 14604
(212) 530-5000 .. **Conis,** Andrea M '09 %Milbank TH&M LLP -1 Chase Manh Plz -NY 10005
(212) 463-0299 .. **Conkey,** Kathleen M '92 -353 W 11th -NY 10014
(516) 294-5433 .. **Conklin,** David S '94 (Ahmuty D&M) -200 IU Willets Rd -Albertson 11507
(845) 647-1106 .. **Conklin,** Dawn M '97 -24 Beaver Dam Rd -Ellenvll 12428 **Fx:**647-3875
(212) 455-2000 .. **Conklin,** Donald D '07 %Simpson T&B LLP -425 Lex Av -NY 10017
(518) 486-1841 .. **Conklin,** Jeffrey J '79 %Dept of Health -Corning Twr 24th Fl -Albany 12237 **Fx:**473-2430
(914) 899-3100 .. **Conklin,** Kevin T '80 (Mead HC&G) -109 Spencer Pl -Mamaroneck 10543
(845) 638-5001 .. **Conklin,** Kristen A '04 %DA -1 S Main -New Cty 10956 **Fx:**638-5070
(516) 294-8844 .. **Conklin,** Marianne S '91 OfCnsl L'Abbate BC&C,LLP -1001 Franklin Av -Gdn Cty 11530
(585) 394-5470 .. **Conklin,** Patrick J '05 -70 S Main -Canandaigua 14424
(716) 856-4000 .. **Conklin,** Robt B '68 Cnsl Hodgson R LLP -140 Pearl -Buffalo 14202
(845) 357-4242 .. **Conklin,** Robt V '87 (Licata & C) -222 Route 59 -Suffern 10901
(212) 435-3571 .. **Conkling,** Howard D '91 %Port Auth of NY/NJ -225 Park Av S -NY 10003 **Fx:**435-3555
(914) 834-4013 .. **Conkling,** Robt L '50 -3 Wshngtn Sq -Larchmnt 10538
(212) 318-6000 .. **Conlan,** Lawr J '06 %Paul HJ&W LLP -75 E 55th -NY 10022
(518) 487-5460 .. **Conley,** Brian W '03 %DA -6 Lodge -Albany 12207 **Fx:**487-5093
(212) 589-4200 .. **Conley,** S Jeanine '03 %Baker & H LLP -45 Rckfllr Plz -NY 10111
(585) 232-4090 .. **Conley,** Tanya '01 %Leg Aid -1 W Main -Rchstr 14614 **Fx:**232-2352
(518) 782-9400 .. **Conley,** Wm M '97 %NYS Nurses Assn -11 Cornell Rd -Latham 12110 **Fx:**782-9530
(516) 764-4467 .. **Conlin,** Elizabeth '87 -100 N Centre Av -Rockvll Ctr 11570 **Fx:**255-3725
(212) 440-3774 .. **Conlin,** Sylvia Meneses '97 %CNA Ins Co -40 Wall -NY 10005
(518) 402-9522 .. **Conlon,** Benjamin A '90 %DEC -625 Bway -Albany 12233 **Fx:**402-9018
(516) 741-7400 .. **Conlon,** Christopher M '90 %Breslin Rlty DevCorp -500 Old Cntry Rd -Gdn Cty 11530 **Fx:**741-7128
(516) 759-1212 .. **Conlon,** Edw M '04 %Mohen & T LLP -186 Birch Hill Rd -Locust Vly 11560
(718) 990-1595 .. **Conlon,** James A '97 St John's Law Schl -8000 Utopia Pkwy -Jamaica 11439 **Fx:**591-1855
(212) 506-2500 .. **Conlon,** John M '91 (Mayer B LLP) -1675 Bway -NY 10019
(212) 509-6009 .. **Conlon,** Kieran J '92 (Ryan & C LLP) -2 Wall -NY 10005
(315) 789-2795 .. **Conlon,** Matthew D '90 -82 Seneca -Geneva 14456
(516) 822-7700 .. **Conlon,** Scott A '95 -380 N Bway -Jericho 11753 **Fx:**932-8353
(607) 723-5341 .. **Conlon,** Thos A Jr. '92 (Hinman H&K,LLP) -80 Exchange Bx5250 -Bnghmtn 13902
(631) 589-4003 .. **Conlon,** Walter M '52 -280 Versa Pl -Sayvll 11782
(212) 670-0364 .. **Conlon-Lamberto,** Kathleen A '07 Bk of America -222 Bway -NY 10038
(718) 886-0995 .. **Conlon-Muller,** Jane M '98 -120-16 9th Av -Cllg Pnt 11356 **Fx:**939-2972
(212) 351-4000 .. **Conn,** Jennifer L '96 (Gibson D&C LLP) -200 Park Av -NY 10166
(212) 335-9000 .. **Conn,** Tracy L '05 %DA -1 Hogan Pl -NY 10013
(212) 237-0000 .. **Connally,** John B IV '08 (Vinson & E LLP) -666 5th Av -NY 10103
(212) 801-6496 .. **Connaughton,** Alice L '03 %Greenberg T,LLP -200 Park Av -NY 10166
(631) 360-2626 .. **Connaughton,** Clare B '84 -1038 W Jericho Tpk -Smithtwn 11787 **Fx:**360-2636
(516) 357-3000 .. **Conneely,** Brian S '78 (Rivkin R LLP) -926 RXR Plz -Uniondale 11556
(845) 794-9776 .. **Conneely,** Mary G '93 Hon R Sackett -414 Bway -Monticello 12701
(516) 571-3800 .. **Connell,** Cristin N '03 %DA -262 Old Cntry Rd -Mineola 11501 **Fx:**248-9479
(518) 465-3484 .. **Connell,** Edw M '01 %Carter CCBM&L,PC -20 Corp Wds Blvd -Albany 12211
(212) 262-2390 .. **Connell Foley LLP** -888 7th Av -NY 10106 **Fx:**262-0050
(518) 457-7069 .. **Connell,** Joan A '86 %Dept of Labor -State Campus Bldg 12 -Albany 12240 **Fx:**457-1164
(716) 838-5977 .. **Connell,** Mary Anne '80 -51 Univ Cir -Buffalo 14214
(212) 416-8610 .. **Connell,** Monica Anne '99 %Dept of Law -120 Bway -NY 10271

(212) 773-3914 .. **Connell**, Patricia A '82 %Ernst & Young,LLP -5 Times Sq -NY 10036
(212) 233-0440 .. **Connell**, Raymond A '66 (McMahon & C,PC) -132 Nassau -NY 10038
(518) 833-6000 .. **Connell**, Timothy J '88 %Dept Soc Srvcs -127 Bloomingrove Dr -Troy 12180 **Fx**:833-6121
(212) 687-6900 .. **Connell**, Wm F '71 (Connell & W) -555 5th Av -NY 10017 **Fx**:687-6999
(315) 474-2943 .. **Connell-Brady**, Sara M '03 %Sugarman Law Firm,LLP -211 W Jffrsn -Syracuse 13202
(716) 842-2200 .. **Connelly**, Andrew J '05 %Andrews B&M,LLP -69 Delaware Av -Buffalo 14202
(212) 906-1200 .. **Connelly**, Blair G '99 (Latham & W) -885 3rd Av -NY 10022
(212) 755-0100 .. **Connelly**, Ciaran P A '05 %Grais & E LLP -40 E 52nd -NY 10022
(914) 632-9300 .. **Connelly**, Frank H Jr. '61 (McGovern C&D) -145 Huguenot -New Rchll 10801
(631) 712-6354 .. **Connelly**, Jennifer E '02 US Probation -202 Fed Plz -Central Islip 11722
(516) 741-6266 .. **Connelly**, John J '96 (McCabe CM&F,LLP) -346 Westbury Av Bx9000 -Carle Pl 11514
(716) 856-3500 .. **Connelly**, Jos R '75 (Magavern MG LLP) -1100 Rand Bldg -Buffalo 14203
(518) 473-0939 .. **Connelly**, Lisa M '85 Applt Div 3rd Dept -Cptl Sta -Albany 12224
(518) 285-8301 .. **Connelly**, Lisa M '95 %Appllt Div 3rd Dept -Capitol Station Bx7288 -Albany 12224 **Fx**:471-4750
(212) 294-6700 .. **Connelly**, Luke A '97 (Winston & S) -200 Park Av -NY 10166
(212) 648-4950 .. **Connelly**, Mindy R '79 %JP Morgan Chase -60 Wall -NY 10260
(914) 328-4100 .. **Connelly**, Neil B '80 (N Connelly,PLLC) -99 Church -White Plns 10601 **Fx**:684-0401
(845) 225-3641 .. **Connelly**, Patricia A '03 Putnam Cnty Supreme Ct Library -40 Gleneida Av -Carmel 10512
(631) 586-4500 .. **Connelly**, Peter R '89 (Connelly & C,PC) -1390 Deer Prk Av -N Babylon 11703 **Fx**:586-7748
(212) 490-9100 .. **Connelly**, Sarah R '06 %Condon & F LLP -7 Times Sq -NY 10036
(212) 259-8000 .. **Connelly**, Sharon M '07 %Dewey & L LLP -1301 Av of Amer -NY 10019
(716) 551-4741 .. **Connelly**, Steven J '91 %US DHS -130 Delaware Av -Buffalo 14202
(212) 343-6968 .. **Connelly**, Teresa M '98 Scholastic Corp -557 Bway -NY 10012
(631) 586-4500 .. **Connelly**, Thos J '60 (Connelly & C,PC) -1390 Deer Prk Av -N Babylon 11703 **Fx**:586-7748
(212) 742-3390 .. **Connelly-Agnostak**, Kathleen '91 (Lindabury ME&C,PC) -26 Bway -NY 10004
(585) 428-5210 .. **Conner**, Amanda C '06 %Pub Def -10 N Fitzhugh -Rchstr 14614 **Fx**:428-2234
(212) 294-6700 .. **Conner**, Darwin L '00 %Winston & S -200 Park Av -NY 10166
(212) 325-6688 .. **Conner**, Robbin W '90 Credit Suisse -1 Mad Av -NY 10010
(518) 738-0136 .. **Conner**, Sharalyn S '07 Plug Power Inc -968 Albany Shaker Rd -Latham 12110
(716) 565-2000 .. **Conners**, Adam B '93 %Freid & K -17 Beresford Ct -Williamsvll 14221 **Fx**:565-2002
(315) 343-6363 .. **Conners**, John D '92 (Amdursky PF&W,PC) -26 E Oneida -Oswego 13126
(212) 803-5145 .. **Conners**, Stephanie G '88 NY Cnty Defender Srvcs -225 Bway -NY 10007 **Fx**:571-6035
(518) 885-5359 .. **Conners**, Stephen J '92 (Rosch & C,PLLC) -20 Church Av Bx463 -Ballston Spa 12020
(212) 661-5030 .. **Connery**, Nancy '79 (Schoeman U&K,LLP) -60 E 42nd -NY 10165
(212) 421-4100 .. **Connery**, Sean M '07 %Pryor C LLP -7 Times Sq -NY 10036
(516) 873-3900 .. **Connick**, Chas X '76 -114 Old Cntry Rd -Mineola 11501 **Fx**:873-3904
(518) 257-1443 .. **Connick**, Timothy '81 %CSEA,Inc -143 Wshngtn Av Bx7125 -Albany 12224 **Fx**:449-1525
(212) 596-9000 .. **Conniff**, Christopher P '92 (Ropes & G LLP) -1211 Av of Amer -NY 10036
(212) 859-8248 .. **Conniff**, Danl '98 -1 NY Plz 25th Fl -NY 10004 **Fx**:859-6719
(212) 309-6000 .. **Conniff**, Martin F '74 (Morgan L&B LLP) -101 Park Av -NY 10178
(718) 855-9000 .. **Conniff**, Thos A '62 (Cullen and D LLP) -177 Montague -Brklyn 11201
(646) 487-3948 .. **Connolly**, Bridget '95 BT Americas Inc -350 Mad Av -NY 10017 **Fx**:487-3500
(516) 742-7600 .. **Connolly**, Bruce R '08 OfCnsl Raiser & K,PC -1517 Franklin Av -Mineola 11501
(212) 508-6100 .. **Connolly**, Danl S '89 (Bracewell & G,LLP) -1251 Av of Amer -NY 10020
(212) 848-4000 .. **Connolly**, David P '03 %Shearman & S LLP -599 Lex Av -NY 10022
(212) 598-8000 .. **Connolly**, Deborah J '80 %Guardian Life Ins -7 Hanover Sq -NY 10004 **Fx**:919-2693
(716) 334-0170 .. **Connolly**, Dennis Michl '98 %Integrated Nano-Technologies -999 LeHigh Station Rd -Henrietta 14467
(212) 801-6429 .. **Connolly**, Elizabeth M '09 %Greenberg T,LLP -200 Park Av -NY 10166
(212) 788-8864 .. **Connolly**, Elizabeth M '09 %Law Dept -100 Church -NY 10007 **Fx**:788-0367
(516) 326-9608 .. **Connolly Frey Eschmann & LaPasta** -250-A Jericho Tpk -Floral Pk 11001 **Fx**:326-9636
(516) 877-0800 .. **Connolly**, Gerard A Jr. '81 (Cartiglia C&R) -1050 Franklin Av -Gdn Cty 11530
(718) 260-8732 .. **Connolly**, Heidi S '02 ACS -345 Adams -Brklyn 11201 **Fx**:260-8773
(518) 457-2070 .. **Connolly**, James P '89 %Dept of Tax & Fin -Bldg 9 State Campus -Albany 12227 **Fx**:457-6131
(516) 764-2800 .. **Connolly**, Janet M '81 (Goldberg & C) -66 N Vllg Av -Rockvll Ctr 11570
(212) 530-1800 .. **Connolly**, Jon J '03 %Richards K&O LLP -1 World Fncl Ctr -NY 10281
(631) 236-4105 .. **Connolly**, June '92 (Goldson NC,PC) -145 Marcus Blvd -Hauppauge 11788 **Fx**:236-4110
(518) 455-2342 .. **Connolly**, Kenneth J '68 %NYS Senate Majority Cnsls Ofc -431 The Cptl -Albany 12247
(646) 442-4342 .. **Connolly**, Kerry E '90 (K Connolly) -1 Bttry Pk Plz -NY 10004 **Fx**:(917) 591-4858
(212) 278-1000 .. **Connolly**, Kevin J '90 (Anderson K&O,PC) -1251 Av of Amer -NY 10020
(518) 877-7647 .. **Connolly**, Kevin S '89 -Bx7306 -Albany 12224
(914) 345-3701 .. **Connolly**, Kevin W '91 %Marks OO&C,PC -530 Saw Mill Rvr Rd -Elmsfrd 10523
(585) 473-3100 .. **Connolly**, Martha A '90 (Ernstrom & D,LLP) -180 Canal Vw Blvd -Rchstr 14623
(516) 571-3800 .. **Connolly**, Matthew J '08 %DA -262 Old Cntry Rd -Mineola 11501 **Fx**:248-9479
(212) 735-8788 .. **Connolly**, Michl '86 (Morrison C LLP) -909 3rd Av -NY 10022
(518) 487-5140 .. **Connolly**, Michl J '86 %Hon J Teresi -433A Cthse -Albany 12207
(212) 474-1000 .. **Connolly**, Michele '07 %Cravath S&M LLP -825 8th Av -NY 10019
(212) 576-7000 .. **Connolly**, Patrick J '83 %NY Life Ins -51 Mad Av -NY 10010 **Fx**:447-0569
(212) 225-2000 .. **Connolly**, Paul K III '02 Cleary GS&H -1 Lbrty Plz -NY 10006
(516) 746-5599 .. **Connolly**, Robt '94 (Bee RFH&D,LLP) -170 Old Cntry Rd -Mineola 11501
(315) 422-1152 .. **Connolly**, Robt W '93 (Costello C&F,PLLC) -500 Plum -Syracuse 13204
(716) 532-0904 .. **Connolly**, Sean W '01 -Bx607 -Fredonia 14063 **Fx**:532-1204
(212) 383-1671 .. **Connolly**, Steven M '91 OCFS- Bur of Special Hearings -80 Maiden Ln -NY 10038 **Fx**:383-2537
(518) 285-8776 .. **Connolly**, Steven M '98 %Hon R McDonough -309 Albany Cnty Judcl Ctr -Albany 12207
(631) 231-2178 .. **Connolly**, Susan Medeiros '87 %Dept of Law -300 Motor Pkwy -Hauppauge 11788 **Fx**:435-4757
(212) 259-8000 .. **Connolly**, Tatiana '04 %Dewey & L LLP -1301 Av of Amer -NY 10019
(212) 906-1200 .. **Connolly**, Terrence J '80 (Latham & W) -885 3rd Av -NY 10022
(718) 366-9504 .. **Connolly**, Thos Anthony '01 -1647 Norman -Rdgwd 11385 **Fx**:793-3934
(718) 855-9000 .. **Connolly**, Thos G '93 %Cullen and D LLP -177 Montague -Brklyn 11201
(518) 447-3200 .. **Connolly**, Thos P '62 OfCnsl McNamee LT&W,PC -677 Bway -Albany 12207
(516) 832-4295 .. **Connolly**, Wm P '03 Arbor Cmmrcl Mortgage LLC -333 Earle Ovngton Blvd -Uniondale 11553
(518) 456-0082 .. **Connor**, Aaron E '07 %Bailey K&J,PC -5 Pine West Plz -Albany 12205 **Fx**:456-4767
(315) 536-5550 .. **Connor**, Allison M '07 DA -415 Lbrty -Penn Yan 14527 **Fx**:536-5556
(631) 462-2500 .. **Connor**, Andrew F '79 -5036 Jericho Tpk -Commack 11725 **Fx**:462-2837
(716) 826-9778 .. **Connor**, Angela R '04 Advantage Energy -3556 Lk Shr Rd -Buffalo 14219
(212) 227-0347 .. **Connor**, Brian J '95 %Weiss W&W,PC -25 Park Pl -NY 10007
(516) 746-0707 .. **Connor**, Brian V '06 %Hammill OCDP&K,PC -6851 Jericho Tpk -Syosset 11791
(516) 881-3540 .. **Connor**, Dennis S '87 -444 Merrick Rd -Lynbrk 11563 **Fx**:887-2069
(212) 480-6707 .. **Connor**, Gary R '74 %DHCR -25 Beaver -NY 10004 **Fx**:480-7416
(212) 632-2650 .. **Connor**, Ian C '00 %Lazard Freres -30 Rckfllr Plz -NY 10112 **Fx**:632-6060
(607) 773-2892 .. **Connor**, James W '92 %Hon T McAvoy -15 Henry -Bnghmtn 13901
(518) 828-2712 .. **Connor**, John G Jr. '85 -76 Green Bx427 -Hudson 12534 **Fx**:822-8442
(315) 471-6265 .. **Connor**, John J Jr. '90 %CJ Billinson & Assoc -342 S Salina -Syracuse 13202 **Fx**:474-3153
(212) 878-7017 .. **Connor**, Margaret M '86 %MTA -347 Mad Av -NY 10017 **Fx**:878-7398
(718) 875-1010 .. **Connor**, Martin E '71 -61 Pierrepont -Brklyn 11201 **Fx**:875-6044
(212) 791-0285 .. **Connor**, Maryellen '04 (Malaby & B,LLC) -150 Bway -NY 10038 **Fx**:791-0286
(516) 255-3717 .. **Connor**, Peter T '79 -77 N Centre Av -Rockvll Ctr 11570 **Fx**:255-9183
(212) 376-6400 .. **Connor**, Wm R III '75 OfCnsl Marshall DWC&G -88 Pine -NY 10005
(585) 232-5885 .. **Connors & Corcoran,LLP** -45 Exchange -Rchstr 14614 **Fx**:546-3631
(212) 553-8300 .. **Connors**, Danl L '87 %Cohen K & Assoc -2 Park Av -NY 10016 **Fx**:553-8721
(716) 881-3010 .. **Connors**, Danl R '00 (Cohen & L,PC) -343 Elmwood Av Bx5204 -Buffalo 14213
(585) 262-2667 .. **Connors & Ferris,LLP** -3445 Winton Pl -Rchstr 14623 **Fx**:262-2670
(585) 262-2667 .. **Connors**, Gregory R '96 (Connors & F,LLP) -3445 Winton Pl -Rchstr 14623
(518) 464-2330 .. **Connors**, James B '96 AYCO -1 Wall Bx15073 -Albany 12212
(212) 449-1000 .. **Connors**, James E '76 %Merrill Lynch -220 Bway -NY 10038
(212) 751-3939 .. **Connors**, James J II '88 %Kelso & Co -320 Park Av -NY 10022 **Fx**:223-2379
(914) 946-8800 .. **Connors**, James P Jr. '53 (Smith RC&M,PC) -235 Main -White Plns 10601
(212) 527-1000 .. **Connors**, James P '78 (Jones HC&B PC) -1 Bttry Pk Plz -NY 10004
(516) 931-1800 .. **Connors**, James P '00 (Catalano G&P LLP) -100 Jericho Quadrangle -Jericho 11753
(518) 475-9601 .. **Connors**, Jaya L '86 -Bx424 -Delmar 12054 **Fx**:475-9601
(212) 468-7745 .. **Connors**, Jennifer Ann '91 %BNY ESI&Co Inc -1633 Bway -NY 10019
(718) 442-1700 .. **Connors**, John P Jr. '82 (Connors & C,PC) -766 Castleton Av -Staten Isl 10310 **Fx**:442-1717
(518) 445-2328 .. **Connors**, Jos M '89 %Law Clinic & Justice Ctr -80 New Scotland Av -Albany 12208
(716) 854-3400 .. **Connors**, Kelly A '08 %Rupp BPC&C LLC -1600 Lbrty Bldg -Buffalo 14202
(516) 433-6677 .. **Connors**, Lauretta L '89 %Stewart GM&B -6800 Jericho Tpk -Syosset 11791
(716) 853-9555 .. **Connors**, Marc J '08 Leg Aid -237 Main -Buffalo 14203 **Fx**:853-3219
(718) 238-6500 .. **Connors**, Michl N '80 (Connors & S,PC) -7408 5th Av -Brklyn 11209
(631) 755-0100 .. **Connors**, Michl P '93 (Smith & D,PA) -145 Pinelawn Rd -Melvll 11747

(518) 445-2311 .. **Connors,** Patrick M '89 Albany Law Schl -80 New Scotland Av -Albany 12208 **Fx:**445-2315
(212) 506-5000 .. **Connors,** Peter J '77 (Orrick H&S LLP) -51 W 52nd -NY 10019
(212) 335-9000 .. **Connors,** Ryan C '06 %DA -1 Hogan Pl -NY 10013
(516) 741-7575 .. **Connors,** Steven F '92 (Vecchione V&C LLP) -147 Hrrcks Rd -Gdn Cty Pk 11040 **Fx:**294-4636
(718) 238-6500 .. **Connors & Sullivan,PC** -7408 5th Av -Brklyn 11209 **Fx:**238-2616
(212) 737-2700 .. **Connors & Sullivan,PC** -110 E 59th -NY 10022 **Fx:**(718) 238-2616
(718) 225-7200 .. **Connors & Sullivan,PC** -200-20 Nrthrn Blvd -Bayside 11361 **Fx:**238-2616
(718) 238-6500 .. **Connors & Sullivan,PC** -78-30 Metro Av -Middl Vllg 11379 **Fx:**238-2616
(716) 852-5533 .. **Connors,** Terrence M '73 (Connors & V,LLP) -1000 Lbrty Bldg -Buffalo 14202
(716) 852-5533 .. **Connors & Vilardo, LLP** -1000 Lbrty Bldg -Buffalo 14202 **Fx:**852-5649
(914) 925-9709 .. **Connors,** Wm R '88 -108 Claremont Av -Rye 10580
(212) 820-9305 .. **Connorton,** John V Jr. '71 (Hawkins D&W LLP) -One Chase Manh Plz -NY 10005
(212) 335-4500 .. **Connuck,** Eric S '92 OfCnsl DLA Piper LLP -1251 Av of Amer -NY 10020
(518) 482-2828 .. **Conole,** Thos D '77 -40 Hawthorne Av -Albany 12203 **Fx:**482-2828
(212) 588-9080 .. **Conover,** Bradford D '85 -75 Rckfllr Pl -NY 10019 **Fx:**763-5001
(516) 294-5433 .. **Conover,** Christopher J '89 (Ahmuty D&M) -200 IU Willets Rd -Albertson 11507
(212) 687-3000 .. **Conover,** David C '02 %Jaffe & A,LLP -600 3rd Av -NY 10016
(212) 779-8600 .. **Conquest,** Deborah A '97 %Silverman SS&B PLLC -381 Park Av S -NY 10016
(212) 683-3520 .. **Conrad,** Francis G '78 OfCnsl Jager S,PC -485 Mad Av -NY 10022
(212) 636-7975 .. **Conrad,** Mark A '83 %Fordham Univ Schl of Bus Adm -113 W 60th -NY 10023 **Fx:**717-4716
(212) 969-3000 .. **Conrad,** Peter D '78 (Proskauer R LLP) -1585 Bway -NY 10036
(212) 450-4000 .. **Conrad,** Winthrop B Jr. '72 SrCnsl Davis P&W LLP -450 Lex Av -NY 10017
(518) 785-0134 .. **Conrad Regan,** Terri Jo '91 Marvin & Co,PC -11 British Amer Blvd -Latham 12110
(607) 723-9511 .. **Conrow,** Mary Louise '92 (Coughlin & G,LLP) -19 Chenango Bx2039 -Bnghmtn 13902
(585) 419-8800 .. **Conroy,** Andrew Q '06 %Harris B PLLC -99 Garnsey Rd -Pittsfrd 14534
(917) 367-4337 .. **Conroy,** Brian T '06 UN -1 UN Plz -NY 10017
(212) 530-5000 .. **Conroy,** Chas J '79 (Milbank TH&M LLP) -1 Chase Manh Plz -NY 10005
(212) 335-9000 .. **Conroy,** Christopher R '97 %DA -1 Hogan Pl -NY 10013
(212) 326-3939 .. **Conroy,** David E '00 %Jones D -222 E 41st -NY 10017
(718) 262-7100 .. **Conroy,** Eric S '05 %Civil Ct -89-17 Sutphin Blvd -Jamaica 11435 **Fx:**262-7107
(718) 852-6763 .. **Conroy,** Gary R '91 (Epstein & C) -410 Myrtle Av -Brklyn 11205 **Fx:**834-7631
(212) 510-1400 .. **Conroy,** Gerald P '83 %Spec Comm of Invstgtn -80 Maiden Ln -NY 10038 **Fx:**510-1550
(212) 506-2500 .. **Conroy,** Gregory M '09 %Mayer B LLP -1675 Bway -NY 10019
(917) 454-1100 .. **Conroy,** James J '01 NYPD -2 Lafayette -NY 10007
(212) 784-6400 .. **Conroy,** Jayne '97 (Hanly CBSF&H LLP) -112 Mad Av -NY 10016
(516) 535-3360 .. **Conroy,** John M '57 %Hon JW Burke -100 Supreme Ct Dr -Mineola 11501
(914) 948-4700 .. **Conroy,** Katharine W '81 (Kent HWCV&F,LLP) -111 Church -White Plns 10601
(212) 506-1700 .. **Conroy,** Kim '05 %Kasowitz BT&F LLP -1633 Bway -NY 10019
(212) 224-9562 .. **Conroy,** Matthew G '07 Octavian Advisors LP -650 Mad Av -NY 10022
(516) 248-2425 .. **Conroy,** Matthew J '02 (MJ Conroy & Assoc) -350 Old Cntry Rd -Gdn Cty 11530 **Fx:**248-2427
(212) 310-8000 .. **Conroy,** Melanie A '09 %Weil G&M LLP -767 5th Av -NY 10153
(718) 876-6300 .. **Conroy,** Michl T '93 %DA -130 Styvsnt Pl -Staten Isl 10301
(516) 433-6677 .. **Conroy,** Patrick M '03 %Stewart GM&B -6800 Jericho Tpk -Syosset 11791
(212) 342-8700 .. **Conroy,** Sasha C '04 CSTV Networks,Inc -85 10th Av -NY 10011 **Fx:**342-8899
(212) 839-5300 .. **Conroy,** Tara M '09 %Sidley A LLP -787 7th Av -NY 10019
(585) 232-6500 .. **Conroy,** Theresa Anne '90 (Harter S&E LLP) -1600 Bausch & Lomb Pl -Rchstr 14604
(845) 294-5151 .. **Conroy,** Wm '81 %Hon PC Patsalos -255-275 Main -Goshen 10924
(516) 229-4400 .. **Conroy Domingo,** Noreen E '03 %Kay & G -875 Merrick Av -Westbury 11590
(212) 659-8105 .. **Considine,** Christopher A '91 %Mt Sinai Med Ctr -1 Gustave L Levy Pl Bx 1099 -NY 10029 **Fx:**348-2230
(518) 452-8787 .. **Considine,** Eileen M '81 (Drinker B&R LLP) -321 Great Oaks Blvd -Albany 12203
(212) 759-5400 .. **Considine,** John E '81 Marjac Grp,Ltd -575 Mad Av -NY 10022 **Fx:**688-7449
(585) 546-2500 .. **Considine,** John J Jr. '55 (McConville CC&M,PC) -25 E Main -Rchstr 14614
(212) 248-8800 .. **Considine,** Kimberly A '10 %Callan KB&B LLP -1 Whitehall -NY 10004
(212) 297-5800 .. **Considine,** Michl G '85 (Day P LLP) -7 Times Sq -NY 10036
(212) 326-3939 .. **Considine,** Michl P '06 %Jones D -222 E 41st -NY 10017
(917) 438-1562 .. **Considine,** Wm M '74 American Arbitration Assn -65 Bway -NY 10006
(718) 520-2357 .. **Consigli,** Francis M '87 %Hon M Hirsch -125-01 Qns Blvd -Kew Gdns 11415
(914) 834-3500 .. **Constabile,** Thos R Jr. '68 (McMillan CM&P LLP) -2180 Bstn Post Rd -Larchmnt 10538
(212) 227-3550 .. **Constable,** Cody D '06 %Waesche S&O,PC -111 Bway -NY 10006
(212) 541-6222 .. **Constable,** Gary E '97 %Kane K,PC -1350 Av of Amer -NY 10019
(212) 736-5300 .. **Constable,** Sean P '98 %Block O&M LLP -1 Penn Plz -NY 10119
(631) 789-2359 .. **Constain,** Monica P '05 -143 Schleigel Blvd -Amityvll 11701
(212) 715-9100 .. **Constance,** Thos E '65 (Kramer LN&F,LLP) -1177 Av of Amer -NY 10036
(631) 853-4161 .. **Constant,** Emily A '80 %DA -N Cnty Cmplx Bldg 77 -Hauppauge 11788 **Fx:**853-4192
(212) 478-3456 .. **Constant,** Mary Jane '94 Syncora -825 8th Av -NY 10019
(631) 852-2500 .. **Constant,** Thos R '88 %DA -200 Center Dr -Rvrhead 11901 **Fx:**852-1769
(212) 898-4363 .. **Constant,** Wm C '89 Liberty Intl Underwriters -55 Water -NY 10041
(518) 402-9184 .. **Constantakes,** Blaise W '91 %DEC -625 Bway -Albany 12233 **Fx:**402-9018
(212) 350-2700 .. **Constantine Cannon,PC** -450 Lex Av -NY 10017 **Fx:**350-2701
(585) 530-3178 .. **Constantine,** Christine A '91 %Appllt Div 4th Dept -50 East Av Ste 200 -Rchstr 14604 **Fx:**530-3247
(516) 333-1666 .. **Constantine,** George A '89 -Bx732 -Westbury 11590
(212) 578-2211 .. **Constantine,** Heidi C '00 %MetLife -27-01 Qns Plz N -LIC 11101
(212) 350-2700 .. **Constantine,** Jan Friedman '74 (Constantine C,PC) -450 Lex Av -NY 10017
(212) 350-2700 .. **Constantine,** Lloyd '73 Cnsl Constantine C,PC -450 Lex Av -NY 10017
(914) 237-1474 .. **Constantine,** Peter J '07 -618 Mdlnd Av -Ynkrs 10704 **Fx:**965-0630
(212) 381-7000 .. **Constantine,** Richd M '87 (Sabin B&G LLP) -4 Times Sq -NY 10036
(716) 841-0355 .. **Constantine,** Robt W '75 HSBC Bank USA -Bx803 -Buffalo 14240 **Fx:**841-4244
(212) 250-9837 .. **Constantine,** Russell '09 Deutsche Bk -60 Wall -NY 10005
(212) 571-2000 .. **Constantine,** Scott A '00 %Ottinger Firm,PC -19 Fulton -NY 10038 **Fx:**571-0505
(212) 530-5000 .. **Constantinides,** Julie A '09 %Milbank TH&M LLP -1 Chase Manh Plz -NY 10005
(718) 204-1500 .. **Constantinidis,** Gus J '96 SrCnsl Constantinidis & Assoc,PC -35-01 30th Av -LIC 11103 **Fx:**956-8668
(585) 225-3080 .. **Constantino,** Jacqueline A '92 %Parrs & P LLP -105 Canal Lndng Blvd -Rchstr 14626 **Fx:**225-0459
(845) 452-1834 .. **Constantino,** James P '80 (Teahan & C) -2780 South Rd Bx1969 -Poughkeepsie 12601
(585) 454-5650 .. **Constantino,** Joanne '92 %Lacy K LLP -130 E Main -Rchstr 14604
(212) 417-3700 .. **Constantinou,** Maro A '02 OfCnsl MFY Legal Srvcs -299 Bway -NY 10007 **Fx:**417-3890
(718) 204-9681 .. **Constantopes,** Alex '95 (Wasserman C&S,LLC) -48-02 25th Av -Astoria 11103 **Fx:**204-8550
(845) 634-0023 .. **Constant-Rouzard,** Judeline T '04 (Rouzard & R,LLP) -490 Route 304 -New Cty 10956 **Fx:**503-2224
(516) 759-4642 .. **Constants,** Alfred C III '01 -52 Ayers Rd -Locust Vly 11560
(646) 386-5891 .. **Constas,** Dorothea '77 %MHLS -41 Mad Av -NY 10010
(212) 210-9420 .. **Conston,** Henry S '59 SrCnsl Alston & B LLP -90 Park Av -NY 10016
(212) 804-5767 .. **Consumano,** Dennis '87 D Consumano,PLLC -110 Wall -NY 10005
(914) 238-9472 .. **Conta,** Annmarie '96 (A Conta,PC) -36 Pebblebrook Way -Chappaqua 10514 **Fx:**238-9473
(914) 593-1700 .. **Conta,** Raymond A '96 -22 Saw Mill Rvr Rd -Hawthorne 10532 **Fx:**741-0862
(212) 363-1380 .. **Contant,** Richd J '88 (Herten BSCBL&H,LLC) -747 3rd Av -NY 10017
(718) 739-6916 .. **Contaratos,** Katerina '90 %Admin Children's Srvcs -151-20 Jamaica Av -Jamaica 11432
(516) 741-9300 .. **Contardo,** Anthony '08 %Toscano & Assoc,PC -200 Old Cntry Rd -Mineola 11501 **Fx:**741-0345
(631) 262-8618 .. **Conte,** Barbara J '94 %BAE Systems -One Hazeltime Way -Greenlawn 11740
(212) 876-5500 .. **Conte,** Felice '05 Neighborhood Def Srv -317 Lenox Av -NY 10027
(914) 948-1200 .. **Conte,** Lisa '97 %Cerussi & S,PC -1 N Lex Av -White Plns 10601
(914) 948-4500 .. **Conte,** Rocco '67 (O'Connor MCD&O) -1 Barker Av -White Plns 10601
(212) 264-3650 .. **Conte,** Stephen P '93 %SSA Ofc Genl Cnsl -26 Fed Plz -NY 10278 **Fx:**264-6372
(518) 437-6964 .. **Conte,** Tommasino S '98 %State Ins Fund -15 Computer Dr W -Albany 12205 **Fx:**485-8761
(212) 547-5400 .. **Contegiacomo,** Jennifer J H '96 %McDermott W&E LLP -340 Mad Av -NY 10173
(718) 442-0900 .. **Conti,** Alfredo P '99 %Russo S&D,PC -1010 Forest Av -Staten Isl 10310
(516) 486-5256 .. **Conti,** Danl A Jr. '86 -165 EAB Plz -Uniondale 11556 **Fx:**486-5295
(516) 877-2525 .. **Conti,** Erika L '06 %Weinstein K&C,PC -1325 Franklin Av -Gdn Cty 11530
(518) 434-4440 .. **Conti,** Jacqueline R '01 -614 Route 9W -Glenmont 12077 **Fx:**(866) 218-5370
(212) 416-2164 .. **Conti,** Jason P '03 Dow Jones -1211 Av of Amer -NY 10036
(212) 756-2000 .. **Conti,** Pat S '86 (Schulte R&Z LLP) -919 3rd Av -NY 10022
(718) 852-3710 .. **Conti-Cook,** Cynthia H '07 %Stoll G&B -71 Nevins -Brklyn 11217 **Fx:**852-3586
(315) 252-7515 .. **Contiguglia,** David A '96 -100 Genesee -Auburn 13021 **Fx:**252-7535
(315) 252-7515 .. **Contiguglia,** Louis P '56 -100 Genesee -Auburn 13021 **Fx:**252-7535
(516) 538-5300 .. **Conti-Levine,** Audrey '85 -599 Jerusalem Av -Uniondale 11553 **Fx:**538-5353
(718) 390-5422 .. **Conti-Maiorana,** Daniela '98 %Civil Ct -927 Castleton Av -Staten Isl 10310 **Fx:**390-8108
(516) 294-8844 .. **Contini,** Peter L '77 (L'Abbate BC&C,LLP) -1001 Franklin Av -Gdn Cty 11530
(716) 847-8400 .. **Contino,** James J '82 (Phillips L LLP) -3400 HSBC Ctr -Buffalo 14203
(516) 357-3000 .. **Contino,** Peter C '78 (Rivkin R LLP) -926 RXR Plz -Uniondale 11556
(212) 490-3000 .. **Contino,** Victoria M '86 (Wilson EME&D LLP) -150 E 42nd -NY 10017
(518) 449-8893 .. **Contino,** Victoria M '86 (Wilson EME&D LLP) -677 Bway -Albany 12207
(516) 472-0460 .. **Contos,** Gus M '98 -33 Plandome Rd -Manhsst 11030
(212) 318-6000 .. **Contoudis Buzard,** Karen K '03 %Paul HJ&W LLP -75 E 55th -NY 10022
(212) 732-8368 .. **Contrastano,** Mauro A '76 (Caruso SLCU&S) -132 Nassau -NY 10038

(718) 237-3100 .. **Contratto,** Justin M '09 Leg Aid -111 Lvngstn -Brklyn 11201 **Fx:**250-4243
(718) 928-3700 .. **Contreras,** Gatsby M '04 %LSNYC-Bronx -579 Courtlandt Av -Bronx 10451 **Fx:**402-7586
(516) 572-2000 .. **Contreras,** Jennifer A '08 %DA -99 Main -Hempstd 11550 **Fx:**572-2606
(212) 836-8000 .. **Contreras,** Monica '04 %Kaye S LLP -425 Park Av -NY 10022
(315) 597-5337 .. **Converse & Morell,LLP** -224 E Main Bx215 -Palmyra 14522 **Fx:**597-5584
(718) 233-3785 .. **Convery,** Thos V '96 (Tansey T&C) -221 Jffrsn Av -Staten Isl 10306
(716) 856-1969 .. **Convissar,** Robt N '77 -112 Franklin -Buffalo 14202 **Fx:**332-0907
(212) 848-4000 .. **Conway,** Adam B '10 %Shearman & S LLP -599 Lex Av -NY 10022
(518) 426-4600 .. **Conway,** Adam T '10 %Couch W,LLP -540 Bway Bx22222 -Albany 12201
(585) 454-1370 .. **Conway,** Andrew W '82 -18 Wd Crk Dr -Pittsfrd 14534
(914) 995-3420 .. **Conway,** Brian J '87 %DA -111 Martin Luther King Blvd -White Plns 10601 **Fx:**995-3363
(212) 530-5000 .. **Conway,** Caroline '07 %Milbank TH&M LLP -1 Chase Manh Plz -NY 10005
(212) 577-3500 .. **Conway,** Claudia C '77 %Leg Aid -199 Water -NY 10038 **Fx:**809-1370
(631) 669-0001 .. **Conway,** Darrell J '82 -179 Little East Neck Rd -W Babylon 11704 **Fx:**669-4011
(212) 808-7855 .. **Conway,** E Virgil '56 -101 Park Av -NY 10178 **Fx:**808-7897
(212) 931-9694 .. **Conway,** Eugene D '88 -111 John -NY 10038 **Fx:**812-9286
(212) 785-2929 .. **Conway Farrell Curtin & Kelly,PC** -48 Wall -NY 10005 **Fx:**785-7229
(914) 422-4424 .. **Conway,** Gail C '98 Pace Womens Justice Ctr -78 N Bway -White Plns 10603
(315) 655-3456 .. **Conway,** George F '65 -87 Albany Bx437 -Cazenovia 13035 **Fx:**655-2115
(845) 462-2700 .. **Conway,** George P '92 DG Ellis -2076 South Rd -Poughkeepsie 12601 **Fx:**462-4895
(212) 403-1000 .. **Conway,** George T III '89 (Wachtell LR&K) -51 W 52nd -NY 10019
(518) 465-8085 .. **Conway,** Gerard L '65 Med Society -1 Commerce Plz -Albany 12210 **Fx:**465-0976
(518) 782-7700 .. **Conway,** Gerard Lawr Jr. '98 Plug Power Inc -968 Albany Shaker Rd -Latham 12110
(518) 862-7306 .. **Conway,** James E '88 Cnsl Travelers -900 Watervliet-Shaker Rd -Albany 12205 **Fx:**(800) 470-9416
(631) 265-5485 .. **Conway,** Jane E '72 -120 Lndng Av -Smithtwn 11787
(212) 474-1000 .. **Conway,** Jennifer S '02 (Cravath S&M LLP) -825 8th Av -NY 10019
(212) 952-6200 .. **Conway,** John B '75 OfCnsl Nourse & B,LLP -55 Bway -NY 10006
(518) 449-4098 .. **Conway,** John J III '76 -152 Central Av -Albany 12206
(516) 248-3520 .. **Conway,** Jos R '88 (LaRusso & C) -300 Old Cntry Rd -Mineola 11501 **Fx:**248-3522
(518) 581-9454 .. **Conway,** Karla Barz '92 Hon F Williams -433 Bway -Saratoga Spgs 12866
(631) 845-2600 .. **Conway,** Keith J '88 (Morenus CG&B) -58 S Srvc Rd -Melvll 11747
(212) 407-5272 .. **Conway,** Kevin J '86 %Clayton Dubilier&Rice -375 Park Av -NY 10152
(212) 938-1080 .. **Conway,** Kevin P '79 (Conway & C) -1700 Bway -NY 10019 **Fx:**938-1207
(845) 353-3500 .. **Conway,** Kevin T '87 (Dorfman K&C LLP) -51 N Bway -Nyack 10960
(212) 788-0865 .. **Conway,** Kimberly D '03 %Law Dept -100 Church -NY 10007 **Fx:**788-0367
(518) 533-1050 .. **Conway & Kirby LLP** -9 Cornell Rd -Latham 12110 **Fx:**533-1073
(212) 265-6888 .. **Conway,** Laura C '99 Cnsl Porzio B&N,PC -156 W 56th -NY 10019
(718) 618-2324 .. **Conway,** Louise G '88 Surrogate's Ct -851 Grnd Cncrs -Bronx 10451 **Fx:**590-3575
(212) 450-4000 .. **Conway,** Mary B '94 (Davis P&W LLP) -450 Lex Av -NY 10017
(585) 232-3051 .. **Conway,** Mary Beth '88 %Legal Srvcs -1 W Main -Rchstr 14614 **Fx:**232-5103
(518) 436-1661 .. **Conway,** Michl C '96 (Harris C&D,PLLC) -5 Clinton Sq -Albany 12207
(516) 739-0000 .. **Conway,** Michl G '90 %Martyn T&M -330 Old Cntry Rd -Mineola 11501
(518) 464-2363 .. **Conway,** Michl K '84 AYCO -1 Wall Bx15073 -Albany 12212
(212) 430-8020 .. **Conway,** Michl T '97 (LeClairRyan,PC) -830 3rd Av -NY 10022
(631) 424-0999 .. **Conway,** Mona R '04 (Conway Business Law Grp,PC) -33 Walt Whitman Rd -Huntngtn Sta 11746 **Fx:**824-9116
(518) 786-4541 .. **Conway,** Robt G Jr. '98 Cnsl Div Miltry & Naval Affrs -330 Old Niskayuna Rd -Latham 12110 **Fx:**786-4944
(212) 619-4444 .. **Conway,** Robt J '77 (Marshall CW&B,PC) -116 John -NY 10038
(516) 627-4014 .. **Conway,** Rosanne M '85 -Bx931 -Plandome 11030
(631) 952-1788 .. **Conway,** Sean J '95 -1 Suffolk Sq -Islandia 11749 **Fx:**951-3682
(212) 972-4900 .. **Conway,** Tamara L '07 %Shapiro FA&S LLP -380 Mad Av -NY 10017
(518) 533-1050 .. **Conway,** Thos A '76 (Conway & K LLP) -9 Cornell Rd -Latham 12110
(518) 474-7553 .. **Conway,** Thos G '78 %Dept of Health -Corning Twr 24th Fl -Albany 12237 **Fx:**473-2802
(201) 447-5600 .. **Conway,** Wm J III '95 (Johnson & C,LLP) -307 7th Av -NY 10001 **Fx:**447-2080
(518) 402-9512 .. **Conyers,** Carol R '93 %DEC -625 Bway -Albany 12233 **Fx:**402-9018
(212) 788-3300 .. **Conyers,** Diane M '88 %Hlth & Hsptl Corp -125 Worth -NY 10013 **Fx:**267-6905
(212) 705-7000 .. **Conyers,** Sabrina N '05 %Bingham M LLP -399 Park Av -NY 10022
(212) 803-5100 .. **Conza,** Jos M '99 %NY Cnty Defender Srvcs -225 Bway -NY 10007 **Fx:**571-6035
(718) 845-5555 .. **Conza,** Peter J '61 -94-01 101st Av -Ozone Pk 11416 **Fx:**848-8939
(212) 225-3455 .. **Conza,** Richd V '78 Cleary GS&H -1 Lbrty Plz -NY 10006
(212) 415-3600 .. **Conzelmann,** Kevin R '77 %Omnicom Group -437 Mad Av -NY 10022 **Fx:**415-3530
(914) 961-1300 .. **Coogan,** James M '67 (Griffin CB&S,PC) -51 Pondfld Rd -Bronxvll 10708
(516) 742-2500 .. **Coogan,** John P '71 -1010 Franklin Av -Gdn Cty 11530 **Fx:**742-2516
(212) 921-8399 .. **Coogan,** Matthew G '02 %Lankler S&W LLP -500 5th Av -NY 10110
(212) 487-9700 .. **Coogler,** Gilbert M '99 (White F&F,LLP) -61 Bway -NY 10006
(212) 585-3435 .. **Cook,** Andrew J '86 -530 E 76th -NY 10021 **Fx:**570-6357
(212) 556-2100 .. **Cook,** Ann Marie '99 (King & S) -1185 Av of Amer -NY 10036
(212) 533-3181 .. **Cook,** Barbara Ann '71 -2 Stuvesant Oval -NY 10009 **Fx:**529-5022
(516) 747-4082 .. **Cook,** Bruce A '76 %Montfort HM&S LLP -1140 Franklin Av Bx7677 -Gdn Cty 11530
(212) 489-1400 .. **Cook,** Candice S '10 %Bickel & B -767 5th Av -NY 10153
(315) 218-8000 .. **Cook,** Christa R '01 (Bond S&K,PLLC) -1 Lincoln Ctr -Syracuse 13202
(315) 410-1415 .. **Cook,** Christine M '89 -333 E Onondaga -Syracuse 13202
(718) 590-2000 .. **Cook,** Clorisa L '05 %DA -198 E 161st -Bronx 10451 **Fx:**590-6477
(585) 872-2050 .. **Cook,** David B '79 -153 W Main -Webster 14580 **Fx:**872-2098
(212) 687-8181 .. **Cook,** David C '73 (Kreindler & K) -750 3rd Av -NY 10017
(212) 533-3181 .. **Cook,** David S '77 -2 Styvsnt Oval -NY 10009 **Fx:**529-5022
(212) 261-7000 .. **Cook,** Douglas G '84 %Calyon -1301 Av of Amer -NY 10019
(585) 368-9898 .. **Cook,** E Michl '87 (EM Cook,PC) -1151 Titus Av -Rchstr 14617 **Fx:**368-9852
(212) 782-4620 .. **Cook,** Elaine A '95 Bk of Tokyo-Mitsubishi -1251 Av of Amer -NY 10020 **Fx:**782-6420
(646) 386-4981 .. **Cook,** Elliot J '71 %Hon JP Walsh -100 Centre -NY 10013
(973) 992-4800 .. **Cook,** Francis V '92 (Fox R LLP) -100 Park Av -NY 10017 **Fx:**992-9125
(518) 445-6050 .. **Cook,** Gavin A '89 %Prisoners' Leg Srvcs -41 State -Albany 12207 **Fx:**445-6053
(516) 248-6437 .. **Cook,** George V '53 -Bx8049 -Gdn Cty 11530
(212) 574-1200 .. **Cook,** H Clayton Jr. '60 Cnsl Seward & K LLP -1 Bttry Pk Plz -NY 10004
(718) 590-2000 .. **Cook,** Heather E '07 %DA -198 E 161st -Bronx 10451 **Fx:**590-6477
(646) 386-5150 .. **Cook,** Ivy I '92 %Family Ct -60 Lafayette -NY 10013
(212) 272-3295 .. **Cook,** J Todd '94 %JP Morgan Chase -383 Mad Av -NY 10179
(212) 382-0909 .. **Cook,** Jacques '03 (Peckar & A,PC) -41 Mad Av -NY 10154
(212) 784-1060 .. **Cook,** Jan Myers '82 -301 Cathedral Pkwy -NY 10026
(315) 536-5550 .. **Cook,** Jason L '98 DA -415 Lbrty -Penn Yan 14527 **Fx:**536-5556
(212) 880-3800 .. **Cook,** Jeffrey T '99 (Akerman S) -335 Mad Av -NY 10017
(315) 425-2700 .. **Cook,** John D '02 %Hiscock & B,LLP -One Park Pl -Syracuse 13202
(212) 351-4500 .. **Cook,** John Wm '94 %Epstein B&G,PC -250 Park Av -NY 10177
(585) 328-2550 .. **Cook,** Julie M '09 Wegmans Food Mrkts -1500 Brooks Av Bx30844 -Rchstr 14603 **Fx:**464-4636
(212) 509-3456 .. **Cook,** Kerryann M '04 %McGivney & K,PC -80 Broad -NY 10004
(212) 937-4000 .. **Cook,** Kevin F '76 Fitzpatrick & HTCPA,LLP -12 E 49th -NY 10017
(212) 587-0523 .. **Cook,** Kevin L '85 -233 Bway -NY 10279 **Fx:**227-6534
(315) 635-9944 .. **Cook,** Linda M '74 %Bucci Law Firm,PLLC -104 Syracuse Bx207 -Baldwinsvll 13027 **Fx:**638-1827
(212) 408-4260 .. **Cook,** Martha J '91 Bank of NY -1290 Av of Amer -NY 10104
(646) 386-5700 .. **Cook,** Melissa '92 %Civil Ct -111 Centre -NY 10013
(212) 834-0600 .. **Cook,** Meredith L '02 %Gordon & S,PC -355 Lex Av -NY 10017
(212) 756-2000 .. **Cook,** Michl L '69 (Schulte R&Z LLP) -919 3rd Av -NY 10022
(845) 331-0702 .. **Cook,** Michl T '99 %Cook NCK&M,PC -85 Main Bx3939 -Kingston 12402
(845) 331-0702 .. **Cook Netter Cloonan Kurtz & Murphy, PC** -85 Main Bx3939 -Kingston 12402 **Fx:**331-1003
(212) 430-6324 .. **Cook,** Peter A '98 -65 Bway -NY 10006 **Fx:**(646) 219-4287
(212) 310-8000 .. **Cook,** Richd R '08 %Weil G&M LLP -767 5th Av -NY 10153
(315) 471-3151 .. **Cook,** Richd W '76 (Hancock & E,LLP) -1500 AXA Twr I Bx4976 -Syracuse 13221
(845) 331-0702 .. **Cook,** Robt D '78 (Cook NCK&M,PC) -85 Main Bx3939 -Kingston 12402
(212) 441-1078 .. **Cook,** Robt E '91 AON Risk Srvcs -199 Water -NY 10038
(212) 278-1203 .. **Cook,** Robt S Jr. '66 (Anderson K&O,PC) -1251 Av of Amer -NY 10020
(631) 265-0102 .. **Cook,** Ronald S '04 -45 Derby Pl -Smithtwn 11787 **Fx:**265-5306
(718) 793-1311 .. **Cook,** Sharon E '83 (Cooper PC&C) -80-02 Kew Grdns Rd -Kew Gdns 11415 **Fx:**575-4070
(585) 546-6448 .. **Cook,** Stuart M '66 OfCnsl Davidson F LLP -28 E Main -Rchstr 14614
(585) 381-1988 .. **Cook,** Thos D '74 -7 State -Pittsfrd 14534
(212) 980-0120 .. **Cook,** Victoria S '99 (Frankfurt KK&S,PC) -488 Mad Av -NY 10022
(212) 237-1000 .. **Cook,** Wayne S Jr. '99 %Windels ML&M,LLP -156 W 56th -NY 10019
(212) 434-0100 .. **Cooke,** Bradford '79 (Litchfield C LLP) -420 Lex Av -NY 10170
(212) 859-8000 .. **Cooke,** Brenda E '03 %Fried FHS&J LLP -1 NY Plz -NY 10004
(315) 798-5870 .. **Cooke,** David A '05 %Pub Def -321 Main -Utica 13501 **Fx:**798-6419
(212) 455-2000 .. **Cooke,** David M L '09 %Simpson T&B LLP -425 Lex Av -NY 10017
(212) 566-7188 .. **Cooke,** David P '87 OfCnsl Genova B&G -115 Bway -NY 10006
(518) 402-0205 .. **Cooke,** Deane M '80 %UIA Bd -Troy Atrium Bx15126 -Albany 12212 **Fx:**402-6208
(845) 794-5110 .. **Cooke,** Edw M '66 -Ten Hmltn Av Bx1444 -Monticello 12701 **Fx:**794-8455
(212) 790-4500 .. **Cooke,** George A Jr. '85 (Manatt P&P,LLP) -7 Times Sq -NY 10036
(516) 338-5780 .. **Cooke,** James W '85 %Macri G&M -393 Old Cntry Rd -Carle Pl 11514
(212) 788-0751 .. **Cooke,** Jay C '75 %Law Dept -100 Church -NY 10007 **Fx:**788-0367
(716) 853-3801 .. **Cooke,** Jesse J '06 %Kenney SL&N,LLP -14 Lafayette Sq -Buffalo 14203
(516) 712-4000 .. **Cooke,** Jos J '84 OfCnsl Milber MP&S LLP -1000 Woodbury Rd -Woodbury 11797
(212) 455-2000 .. **Cooke,** Justin S '06 %Simpson T&B LLP -425 Lex Av -NY 10017
(212) 307-5500 .. **Cooke,** Lawr H II '92 (Venable LLP) -1270 Av of Amer -NY 10020
(212) 269-7308 .. **Cooke,** Michl B '08 %Leahey & J PC -120 Wall -NY 10005
(607) 776-9631 .. **Cooke,** Michelle A '10 Cnty Atty -3 E Pulteney Sq -Bath 14810 **Fx:**776-4930
(585) 232-7210 .. **Cooke & Miller** -183 Main E -Rchstr 14604 **Fx:**232-7455
(212) 697-3122 .. **Cooke,** Peggy Anne '04 %Martin C&B LLP -220 E 42nd -NY 10017
(845) 735-1415 .. **Cooke & Santomauro** -30 N William -Pearl Rvr 10965
(212) 375-2048 .. **Cooke,** Stephen D '81 American Capital Access -140 Bway -NY 10005
(212) 815-1450 .. **Cooke,** Thos M '99 %DC 37 Gen Cnsl -125 Barclay -NY 10007 **Fx:**815-1440
(718) 237-5500 .. **Cook-Mack,** Rebekah B '09 %Leg Srvcs -105 Court -Brklyn 11201 **Fx:**855-0733

(716) 639-5236 .. **Cookson,** Chas P '94 %Dunlop Tire -Bx1109 -Buffalo 14240 **Fx:**639-5451
(212) 483-9490 .. **Cookson,** John P '85 OfCnsl McElroy DM&C,LLP -88 Pine -NY 10005
(631) 324-5909 .. **Cooley,** Alice G '09 %MacLachlan & E LLP -241 Pantigo Rd -E Hampton 11937
(212) 450-4000 .. **Cooley,** Alicyn L '09 %Davis P&W LLP -450 Lex Av -NY 10017
(315) 548-8036 .. **Cooley,** Brent D '90 -57 Main -Phelps 14532 **Fx:**548-8036
(716) 856-4000 .. **Cooley,** Catherine Grantier '02 (Hodgson R LLP) -140 Pearl -Buffalo 14202
(212) 479-6000 .. **Cooley LLP** -1114 Av of Amer -NY 10036 **Fx:**479-6275
(315) 435-2470 .. **Coolican,** Jos T '92 %DA -505 S State -Syracuse 13202 **Fx:**435-3969
(585) 546-2500 .. **Cooman,** Kevin S '79 (McConville CC&M,PC) -25 E Main -Rchstr 14614
(518) 431-0247 .. **Coombe,** Elizabeth C '93 %US Atty -445 Bway -Albany 12207 **Fx:**431-0249
(212) 596-9000 .. **Cooms,** Lisa C '09 %Ropes & G LLP -1211 Av of Amer -NY 10036
(518) 584-6300 .. **Coon,** Dean M '79 -188 Church -Saratoga Spgs 12866 **Fx:**584-5673
(212) 974-5766 .. **Coon,** Douglas W '07 Brevet Capital -666 3rd Av -NY 10017
(212) 698-3500 .. **Coon,** Jennifer E '01 %Dechert LLP -1095 Av of Amer -NY 10036
(914) 323-7000 .. **Coon,** Timothy P '81 (Wilson EME&D LLP) -3 Gannett Dr -White Plns 10604
(212) 490-3000 .. **Coon,** Timothy P '81 (Wilson EME&D LLP) -150 E 42nd -NY 10017
(212) 532-0532 .. **Coonerty,** Sean E '98 %Geller & S,LLP -419 Park Av S -NY 10016 **Fx:**532-1871
(516) 248-9586 .. **Cooney,** Dennis F '92 -245 Hillside Av -Williston Pk 11596 **Fx:**248-9588
(718) 694-3905 .. **Cooney,** Elizabeth A '77 %Transit Auth -130 Lvngstn -Brklyn 11201 **Fx:**694-5726
(914) 323-7000 .. **Cooney,** James B '09 %Wilson EME&D LLP -3 Gannett Dr -White Plns 10604
(516) 663-6600 .. **Cooney,** John J '09 %Ruskin MF,PC -1425 RXR Plz -Uniondale 11556
(212) 402-9400 .. **Cooney,** John P Jr. '70 (McKool S,PC) -1 Bryant Park -NY 10036
(516) 463-5934 .. **Cooney,** John R '94 Hofstra Univ -108 Hofstra Univ -Hempstd 11549
(585) 263-1000 .. **Cooney,** Michl J '89 (Nixon P LLP) -1100 Clinton Sq -Rchstr 14604
(212) 265-5131 .. **Cooney,** Nicholas J '60 -116 Cntrl Pk S -NY 10019 **Fx:**265-5131
(585) 396-1640 .. **Cooney,** Patrick J '75 -23 Coach -Canandaigua 14424 **Fx:**396-0729
(516) 294-5433 .. **Cooney,** Patrick J '91 (Ahmuty D&M) -200 IU Willets Rd -Albertson 11507
(646) 678-4957 .. **Cooney,** Robt J '07 -511 E 81st -NY 10028
(716) 852-1888 .. **Cooney,** Sean E '08 %Cantor LD&P,PC -350 Main -Buffalo 14202
(585) 394-5670 .. **Cooney,** Susan S '73 -70 N Main -Canandaigua 14424 **Fx:**394-6665
(718) 742-6572 .. **Cooney,** Tracy '99 NYC Dept of Ed -501 Courtlandt Av -Bronx 10451
(212) 313-3600 .. **Cooney,** Wm A '90 %Barry M&M -2 Rector -NY 10006
(518) 385-2298 .. **Cooney,** Wm F '88 GE Co -1 River Rd -Schnctdy 12345
(212) 710-3900 .. **Cooney,** Wm M '02 %Clyde & Co US LLP -405 Lex Av -NY 10174 **Fx:**710-3950
(914) 682-2068 .. **Coons,** James S '04 %Ansa A,LLP -50 Main -White Plns 10606
(516) 837-8000 .. **Coope,** Dara Anne Levy '97 Treeline Co -200 Grdn City Plz -Gdn Cty 11530 **Fx:**837-8500
(212) 929-5500 .. **Coope,** Simon P '95 %MacKenzie Partners -105 Mad Av -NY 10016 **Fx:**929-0308
(212) 297-5800 .. **Cooper,** A Blake '07 %Day P LLP -7 Times Sq -NY 10036
(718) 793-1311 .. **Cooper,** Adam '92 (Cooper PC&C) -80-02 Kew Grdns Rd -Kew Gdns 11415 **Fx:**575-4070
(212) 243-2129 .. **Cooper,** Adam D '09 Vastardis Capital Srvcs -41 Mad Av -NY 10010
(518) 465-3484 .. **Cooper,** Adam H '05 %Carter CCBM&L,PC -20 Corp Wds Blvd -Albany 12211
(212) 558-5500 .. **Cooper,** Adam R '94 %Weitz & L,PC -700 Bway -NY 10003
(516) 294-0250 .. **Cooper,** Adrienne S '93 OfCnsl M Haskel -167 Willis Av -Mineola 11501 **Fx:**294-0854
(212) 249-4435 .. **Cooper,** Albert B '80 -20 E 74th -NY 10021
(212) 357-0383 .. **Cooper,** Alexander M '98 Goldman Sachs -1 NY Plz -NY 10004
(516) 741-1973 .. **Cooper,** Alfred D Sr. '87 SrCnsl AD Cooper,PC -114 Old Cntry Rd -Mineola 11501 **Fx:**741-3059
(212) 526-5811 .. **Cooper,** Andrew D '07 %Barclays Capital Inc -745 7th Av -NY 10019
(516) 408-3666 .. **Cooper,** Andrew P '90 (Hession BC&L,LLP) -1103 Stewart Av -Gdn Cty 11530
(212) 246-9500 .. **Cooper,** Andrew R '71 -1700 Bway -NY 10019 **Fx:**956-5255
(212) 455-2000 .. **Cooper,** Ariana S '09 %Simpson T&B LLP -425 Lex Av -NY 10017
(585) 546-7430 .. **Cooper,** Audrey C '86 %Dept of Law -144 Exchange Blvd -Rchstr 14614 **Fx:**546-7514
(212) 684-3900 .. **Cooper,** Barry A '71 (Gottlieb R&R,PC) -270 Mad Av -NY 10016
(646) 285-9881 .. **Cooper,** Bethany J '99 %Lehman Bros -1271 Av of Amer -NY 10020
(212) 402-9400 .. **Cooper,** Brett E '02 %McKool S,PC -1 Bryant Park -NY 10036
(212) 659-7300 .. **Cooper,** Brian Michl '97 OfCnsl Haynes & B,LLP -1221 Av of Amer -NY 10020
(212) 957-9000 .. **Cooper Brown & Behrle,PC** -331 Mad Av -NY 10017 **Fx:**843-9191
(212) 652-3890 .. **Cooper,** Bruce J '73 (Pitta & G LLP) -120 Bway -NY 10271
(607) 776-9631 .. **Cooper,** Byrum W Jr. '99 %Pub Def -3 E Pulteney Sq -Bath 14810 **Fx:**664-2496
(212) 490-2277 .. **Cooper,** Chas A '55 %NY Land Srvcs -630 3rd Av -NY 10017 **Fx:**490-8012
(212) 239-9777 .. **Cooper,** Christina S '07 %Parker & C,LLP -331 Mad Av -NY 10017 **Fx:**239-9175
(212) 336-2000 .. **Cooper,** Christopher E '09 %Patterson BW&T LLP -1133 Av of Amer -NY 10036
(716) 851-4343 .. **Cooper,** Cindy Tyrene '06 Law Dept -65 Niagara Sq -Buffalo 14202 **Fx:**851-4105
(212) 265-0369 .. **Cooper,** Danl J '80 -350 W 50th -NY 10019
(212) 474-1000 .. **Cooper,** Dashene A '08 %Cravath S&M LLP -825 8th Av -NY 10019
(914) 682-7800 .. **Cooper,** David J '04 %Zarin & S -81 Main -White Plns 10601
(518) 527-0455 .. **Cooper,** David M '96 -113 Marsdale Ct -Selkirk 12158
(212) 326-3939 .. **Cooper,** David M '05 %Jones D -222 E 41st -NY 10017
(212) 280-4473 .. **Cooper,** Deborah E '79 Cooke Ctr for Learning & Devlpmnt -475 Riverside Dr -NY 10115 **Fx:**280-4477
(718) 479-9500 .. **Cooper,** Denrick W '98 -207-23 Hillside Av -Qns Vllg 11427
(516) 767-1200 .. **Cooper,** Diane C '98 %B Clark & Assoc,PC -22 S Bayles Av -Pt Wash 11050 **Fx:**767-1702
(516) 663-6600 .. **Cooper,** Douglas '73 (Ruskin MF,PC) -1425 RXR Plz -Uniondale 11556
(212) 278-0400 .. **Cooper & Dunham LLP** -30 Rckfllr Plz -NY 10112 **Fx:**391-0525
(716) 645-3030 .. **Cooper,** Edw '92 %SUNY Buffalo Lw Schl -O'Brian Hall -Buffalo 14260 **Fx:**645-5968
(212) 232-2500 .. **Cooper,** Edw T '93 (Torgan & C,PC) -17 State -NY 10004
(212) 906-1200 .. **Cooper,** Elana C '10 %Latham & W -885 3rd Av -NY 10022
(212) 666-4865 .. **Cooper,** Elizabeth '76 -425 Riverside Dr -NY 10025
(212) 455-2000 .. **Cooper,** Elizabeth A '02 %Simpson T&B LLP -425 Lex Av -NY 10017
(212) 636-7067 .. **Cooper,** Elizabeth B '89 %Fordham Univ Sch of Law -140 W 62nd -NY 10023 **Fx:**636-6899
(212) 506-1700 .. **Cooper,** Emilie B '05 %Kasowitz BT&F LLP -1633 Bway -NY 10019
(212) 947-4999 .. **Cooper,** Eric L '95 %Camacho MM,LLP -350 5th Av -NY 10118
(518) 449-3900 .. **Cooper Erving & Savage,LLP** -39 N Pearl -Albany 12207 **Fx:**432-3111
(718) 286-6000 .. **Cooper,** Eva L '83 %DA -125-01 Qns Blvd -Kew Gdns 11415
(212) 610-6300 .. **Cooper,** Felise G '04 %Allen & O -1221 Av of Amer -NY 10020
(212) 909-5400 .. **Cooper,** Frederic J '89 %KPMG LLP -757 3rd Av -NY 10017
(212) 687-6884 .. **Cooper,** Glenn Roy '67 -232 Mad Av -NY 10016
(212) 608-4828 .. **Cooper,** Gregory '71 -20 Vesey -NY 10007 **Fx:**964-2926
(212) 513-3200 .. **Cooper,** Helen Adrian '09 %Holland & K LLP -31 W 52nd -NY 10019
(718) 222-2331 .. **Cooper,** Holly E '08 %Law Dept -350 Jay -Brklyn 11201 **Fx:**222-2373
(516) 227-0700 .. **Cooper,** Ilene S '80 (Farrell F,PC) -1320 RXR Plz -Uniondale 11556
(516) 390-4365 .. **Cooper,** Ira '85 -1 Old Cntry Rd -Carle Pl 11514
(718) 793-1311 .. **Cooper,** Ira G '75 (Cooper PC&C) -80-02 Kew Grdns Rd -Kew Gdns 11415 **Fx:**575-4070
(516) 605-1063 .. **Cooper,** Ira S '63 -410 Jericho Tpk -Jericho 11753 **Fx:**605-1064
(212) 474-1000 .. **Cooper,** James D '81 (Cravath S&M LLP) -825 8th Av -NY 10019
(212) 323-7081 .. **Cooper,** Jared R '08 %Rawle & H LLP -14 Wall -NY 10005
(212) 277-9000 .. **Cooper,** Jason M '03 Creative Artists Agency -162 5th Av -NY 10010 **Fx:**277-9099
(518) 486-3183 .. **Cooper,** Jason N '00 %State Comptroller -110 State -Albany 12236 **Fx:**473-9104
(212) 312-2260 .. **Cooper,** Jayne E '09 %Leg Aid -60 Lafayette -NY 10013 **Fx:**349-0874
(212) 841-7981 .. **Cooper,** Jeffrey H '71 %Cushman & Wakefield -51 W 52nd -NY 10019 **Fx:**841-7715
(212) 201-8602 .. **Cooper,** Jeffrey M '84 (Reis C LLP) -250 W 57th -NY 10107 **Fx:**201-8699
(585) 325-7792 .. **Cooper,** Jennie M '86 -134 S Fitzhugh -Rchstr 14608 **Fx:**325-6716
(212) 450-4000 .. **Cooper,** Jennifer Grant '05 %Davis P&W LLP -450 Lex Av -NY 10017
(516) 881-3535 .. **Cooper,** Jerome '55 -444 Merrick Rd -Lynbrk 11563
(516) 791-5700 .. **Cooper,** Jonathan M '97 -483 Chestnut -Cedarhrst 11516 **Fx:**791-8188
(631) 586-1621 .. **Cooper,** Justin L '53 -17 Quail Run Dr -Deer Pk 11729
(212) 723-3456 .. **Cooper,** Karl D '89 Citigroup Global Mrkts -250 West -NY 10013
(212) 225-2000 .. **Cooper,** Katherine B '07 %Cleary GS&H -1 Lbrty Plz -NY 10006
(212) 640-5702 .. **Cooper,** Kevin J '93 %Amer Exp -200 Vesey -NY 10285
(212) 735-3000 .. **Cooper,** Kristina L '10 %Skadden ASM&F LLP -4 Times Sq -NY 10036
(646) 414-6873 .. **Cooper,** Kylie '08 %Lowenstein S PC -1251 Av of Amer -NY 10020 **Fx:**(973) 422-6811
(646) 315-7326 .. **Cooper,** Laura Anne '90 %FINRA -14 Wall -NY 10005 **Fx:**315-7440
(212) 403-1000 .. **Cooper,** Lauren E '07 %Wachtell LR&K -51 W 52nd -NY 10019
(718) 548-2100 .. **Cooper,** Lawr R '76 -165 W 231st -Bronx 10463 **Fx:**548-2140
(914) 738-6276 .. **Cooper,** Leonard '81 -999 Grant Av -Pelham 10803
(914) 741-6100 .. **Cooper,** Leonard B '92 %Kaufman B&R -200 Summit Lk Dr -Valhalla 10595
(212) 549-2500 .. **Cooper,** Leslie J '96 %ACLU -125 Broad -NY 10004 **Fx:**549-2651
(607) 644-3283 .. **Cooper,** Linda L '94 -34 Chenango -Bnghmtn 13901
(212) 733-7447 .. **Cooper,** Mark J '95 %Pfizer Inc -235 E 42nd -NY 10017
(212) 451-2300 .. **Cooper,** Martin S '70 Cnsl Olshan GFR&W LLP -65 E 55th -NY 10022
(212) 788-2381 .. **Cooper,** Maya L '06 %ACS-Education Unit -150 William -NY 10038
(212) 759-3300 .. **Cooper,** Melissa E '99 (Dornbush SS&V,LLP) -747 3rd Av -NY 10017
(212) 558-4000 .. **Cooper,** Michl A '61 OfCnsl Sullivan & C LLP -125 Broad -NY 10004
(716) 648-5695 .. **Cooper,** Michl G '89 -71 Main Bx238 -Hambrg 14075 **Fx:**648-4450
(718) 590-2000 .. **Cooper,** Michl H '84 %DA -198 E 161st -Bronx 10451 **Fx:**590-6477
(716) 854-2020 .. **Cooper,** Michl J '87 (Cellino & B,PC) -350 Main -Buffalo 14202
(516) 759-2722 .. **Cooper,** Michl J '08 %Ryan M&L,LLP -90 Forest Av -Locust Vly 11560
(212) 545-4000 .. **Cooper,** Michl R '74 (Jackson L LLP) -666 3rd Av -NY 10017
(212) 969-3000 .. **Cooper,** Michl R D '93 Proskauer R LLP -1585 Bway -NY 10036
(516) 747-8877 .. **Cooper,** Mitchell J '80 (Spizz & C,LLP) -114 Old Cntry Rd -Mineola 11501
(516) 484-0554 .. **Cooper,** Neil J '75 -17 Marwill Pl -Roslyn Hts 11577
(212) 946-2616 .. **Cooper,** Nicholas C '69 -11 Penn Plz -NY 10001 **Fx:**946-2808
(516) 222-8500 .. **Cooper,** Patricia J '08 %Martin C&B LLP -90 Merrick Av -E Meadow 11554
(212) 209-3933 .. **Cooper,** Peter H '96 (Cilenti & C,PLLC) -708 3rd Av -NY 10017 **Fx:**209-7102
(212) 267-6456 .. **Cooper,** Richd A '80 OfCnsl Fischer Bros -217 Bway -NY 10007 **Fx:**267-6468
(212) 450-4000 .. **Cooper,** Richd A '07 %Davis P&W LLP -450 Lex Av -NY 10017
(212) 957-9000 .. **Cooper,** Richd B '58 (Cooper B&B,PC) -331 Mad Av -NY 10017
(212) 225-2000 .. **Cooper,** Richd J '87 (Cleary GS&H) -1 Lbrty Plz -NY 10006

(585) 292-1920 .. **Cooper,** Robt S '84 -1425 Jffrsn Rd -Rchstr 14623 **Fx:**292-1925
(212) 225-2000 .. **Cooper,** Roger A '04 %Cleary GS&H -1 Lbrty Plz -NY 10006
(607) 739-8763 .. **Cooper,** Roger R '60 (Cooper P&W,LLP) -2854 Wstnghse Rd -Horseheads 14845 **Fx:**739-9373
(631) 293-6061 .. **Cooper Sapir & Cohen,PC** -560 Broadhllw Rd -Melvll 11747 **Fx:**293-6127
(718) 260-8762 .. **Cooper,** Sarah Pnina '96 %Admin Children's Srvcs -345 Adams -Brklyn 11201 **Fx:**260-8773
(718) 729-7114 .. **Cooper,** Scott W '95 -47-16 44th -Woodside 11377 **Fx:**729-8004
(212) 907-0600 .. **Cooper,** Sharon F '93 (Gardner W&R LLP) -270 Mad Av -NY 10016
(212) 687-6884 .. **Cooper,** Sonja J M '87 -232 Mad Av -NY 10016
(631) 298-5000 .. **Cooper,** Stacey M '85 %North Folk Bk -275 Broad Hollow Rd -Melvll 11747
(212) 756-2000 .. **Cooper,** Stacy J '94 SpclCnsl Schulte R&Z LLP -919 3rd Av -NY 10022
(212) 605-0221 .. **Cooper,** Stephanie R '88 (SR Cooper,PC) -575 Mad Av -NY 10022 **Fx:**605-0517
(212) 513-1722 .. **Cooper,** Stephen C '74 -111 Bway -NY 10006 **Fx:**513-1798
(518) 766-4090 .. **Cooper,** Stephen E '75 -8 John -Nassau 12123
(518) 445-2311 .. **Cooper,** Stephen H '65 %Albany Law Schl -80 New Scotland Av -Albany 12208 **Fx:**445-2315
(212) 521-5400 .. **Cooper,** Steven '84 (Reed S LLP) -599 Lex Av -NY 10022
(914) 725-4800 .. **Cooper,** Steven J '93 (S Cooper & Assoc,PC) -455 S Central Av -Scarsdale 10583 **Fx:**725-3217
(585) 232-3680 .. **Cooper,** Stuart B '81 %1st Amer Title -16 W Main -Rchstr 14614 **Fx:**423-8273
(516) 485-3200 .. **Cooper,** Stuart K '80 -390 Willis Av -Mineola 11501 **Fx:**292-7349
(845) 624-3820 .. **Cooper,** Susan '81 %P Savad & Assoc -55 Old Tpk Rd -Nanuet 10954 **Fx:**624-3821
(716) 278-1833 .. **Cooper,** Timothy J '81 Family Ct -775 3rd -Niagara Fls 14301
(212) 232-0155 .. **Cooper,** Varonica R '98 (Maduegbuna C,LLP) -110 Wall -NY 10005
(212) 529-6530 .. **Cooper,** W Clifford '87 -541 E 20th -NY 10010
(212) 314-3828 .. **Cooper,** Wendy E '79 %AXA Financial Inc -1290 Av of Amer -NY 10104 **Fx:**770-1890
(516) 766-6736 .. **Cooper,** Wm D '75 (Rubin C&S) -330 Sunrise Hwy -Rockvll Ctr 11570
(914) 428-9200 .. **Cooper,** Wm H '91 (M Cooper,PC) -245 Main -White Plns 10601 **Fx:**428-4126
(516) 371-0657 .. **Cooperberg,** Shevy '84 -65 Margaret Av -Lawrence 11559
(718) 264-7715 .. **Cooper-Gregory,** Helen A '84 -111-36 Farmers Blvd -St Albans 11412 **Fx:**264-7714
(516) 228-0033 .. **Cooperman,** Cindy B '86 (Pollack C&F,PC) -5372 Merrick Rd -Massapequa 11758 **Fx:**797-1227
(212) 835-1592 .. **Cooperman,** Don A '96 -5 Penn Plz -NY 10001 **Fx:**849-6901
(212) 490-3000 .. **Cooperman,** Janice L '08 %Wilson EME&D LLP -150 E 42nd -NY 10017
(212) 808-7800 .. **Cooperman,** Jonathan K '86 (Kelley D&W LLP) -101 Park Av -NY 10178
(212) 818-1110 .. **Cooperman,** Katie L '06 %Butzel L,PC -380 Mad Av -NY 10017
(516) 365-1400 .. **Cooperman Lester Miller LLP** -1129 Nrthrn Blvd -Manhsst 11030 **Fx:**365-1404
(212) 688-7000 .. **Cooperman Lester Miller LLP** -767 3rd Av -NY 10017 **Fx:**371-7634
(212) 337-5331 .. **Cooperman,** M James '88 %Relativity Records -79 5th Av -NY 10003
(718) 923-4206 .. **Cooperman,** Mark N '83 OTDA Fair Hearings -14 Boerum Pl -Brklyn 11201
(212) 732-7184 .. **Cooperman,** Paige E '04 %Leser HT&T -17 State -NY 10004
(718) 264-0190 .. **Cooperman,** Peter R '71 -118-21 Qns Blvd -Frst Hlls 11375
(516) 365-1400 .. **Cooperman,** Robt N '60 (Cooperman LM LLP) -1129 Nrthrn Blvd -Manhsst 11030
(212) 735-8600 .. **Cooperman,** Steven M '93 (Morrison C LLP) -909 3rd Av -NY 10022
(845) 368-2783 .. **Coopersmith,** Marsha F '90 -Cherry Ln Bx397 -Tallman 10982
(212) 625-8505 .. **Coopersmith,** Richd D '65 Coopersmith & C -233 Bway -NY 10279 **Fx:**625-8508
(212) 788-0871 .. **Cooperstein,** David C '07 %Law Dept -100 Church -NY 10007 **Fx:**788-0367
(631) 754-7777 .. **Cooperstein,** Kenneth S '79 -54 Hrbr Park Dr -Centerprt 11721
(212) 964-3300 .. **Cooperstein,** Paul '81 %Rubin A LLP -225 Bway -NY 10007
(315) 478-3500 .. **Copani,** Anthony F '84 (Mannion & C) -224 Harrison -Syracuse 13202
(212) 576-7241 .. **Cope,** Marian M '88 NY Life Ins -51 Mad Av -NY 10010
(212) 836-8000 .. **Copeland,** David S '86 (Kaye S LLP) -425 Park Av -NY 10022
(212) 246-2400 .. **Copeland,** Edw '79 (Balber PM&VDT,PC) -1370 Av of Amer -NY 10019
(212) 909-6000 .. **Copeland,** Gregory P '10 %Debevoise & P LLP -919 3rd Av -NY 10022
(716) 856-4000 .. **Copeland,** Jessica L '05 %Hodgson R LLP -140 Pearl -Buffalo 14202
(718) 579-3000 .. **Copeland,** Jordan C '01 %Leg Aid -1020 Grnd Cncrs -Bronx 10451 **Fx:**588-2611
(212) 551-8500 .. **Copeland,** Julie '76 %Israel Discount Bk -511 5th Av -NY 10017 **Fx:**551-8916
(212) 560-7154 .. **Copeland,** Karen '85 -521 5th Av -NY 10175 **Fx:**(516) 594-9061
(212) 940-8800 .. **Copell,** Alexandra B '10 %Katten MR LLP -575 Mad Av -NY 10022
(212) 735-3000 .. **Copen,** Robt A '90 (Skadden ASM&F LLP) -4 Times Sq -NY 10036
(212) 878-0000 .. **Copertino,** Carl J '81 %MTA -2 Penn Plz -NY 10121
(212) 281-5838 .. **Copes,** Laverne B '85 -30 W 141st -NY 10037
(212) 479-6000 .. **Coplan,** Jennifer B '94 (Cooley LLP) -1114 Av of Amer -NY 10036
(914) 422-4343 .. **Coplan,** Karl S '85 %Envrnmtl Lit Clinic -78 N Bway -White Plns 10603 **Fx:**422-4437
(518) 785-0175 .. **Copland,** Eric K '69 (Copland & B) -410 Troy Schenectady Rd -Latham 12110 **Fx:**786-1541
(518) 464-6000 .. **Copland,** Gloria Arroyo '85 (Arroyo Copland & Assoc,PLLC) -300 Great Oaks Blvd -Albany 12203 **Fx:**464-6014
(212) 229-5100 .. **Copland,** Laura '92 Eugene Lang Univ -65 W 11th -NY 10011
(718) 519-6000 .. **Copland,** Richd M '58 -3475 Bstn Rd Bx690010 -Bronx 10469
(212) 782-5902 .. **Coplar,** Nancy Lockhart '84 %Bk of Tokyo Mitsubishi -1251 Av of Amer -NY 10020
(212) 788-4294 .. **Copleman,** Martha '79 Dept Hlth & Mental Hygiene -125 Worth Bx 30B -NY 10013 **Fx:**788-4296
(646) 557-5100 .. **Copley,** James O '82 OfCnsl Patton B LLP -1185 Av of Amer -NY 10036
(914) 761-4200 .. **Coploff,** Steven A '75 Cnsl Steinberg & C,LLP -50 Main -White Plns 10606
(212) 530-5000 .. **Copp,** Brianne A '08 %Milbank TH&M LLP -1 Chase Manh Plz -NY 10005
(212) 468-8000 .. **Coppedge,** Alexis M '02 %Morrison & F LLP -1290 Av of Amer -NY 10104
(212) 732-0076 .. **Copperman,** Joel N '86 %CASES -346 Bway -NY 10013 **Fx:**571-0292
(212) 406-9710 .. **Coppersmith,** Robt '79 %Kral CRRP&G,LLP -170 Bway -NY 10038
(718) 423-2733 .. **Coppin,** Dennis B '90 -47-03 Bell Blvd -Bayside 11361 **Fx:**423-2512
(516) 877-2900 .. **Coppinger,** Christian B '01 %Bartlett MB&M,LLP -300 Old Cntry Rd -Mineola 11501
(212) 949-9022 .. **Coppola,** Anthony A '88 (Abelman F&S) -666 3rd Av -NY 10017
(716) 852-4100 .. **Coppola,** Douglas S '76 -37 Franklin -Buffalo 14202 **Fx:**852-0002
(914) 963-6368 .. **Coppola,** Frank '54 -49 Valley Vw Dr -Ynkrs 10710
(212) 425-7200 .. **Coppola,** Jos A '95 Cnsl Kenyon & K,LLP -1 Bway -NY 10004
(212) 277-0728 .. **Coppola,** Jos M '85 The Hartford Ins -2 Park Av -NY 10016
(716) 375-2520 .. **Coppola,** Leibert F '84 St Bonaventure Univ -Jrnlism Dept BxJ -St Bonaventure 14778 **Fx:**375-2588
(716) 854-3400 .. **Coppola,** Lisa A '90 (Rupp BPC&C LLC) -1600 Lbrty Bldg -Buffalo 14202
(212) 732-2000 .. **Coppola,** Richd A '08 %Cullen and D LLP -44 Wall -NY 10005
(212) 964-6611 .. **Coppola,** Thos B '95 Cnsl Lester SK&D -120 Bway -NY 10271
(914) 271-5592 .. **Coppola Adami,** Nancy C '64 -126 Grand Bx372 -Croton-On-Hud 10520
(212) 361-7996 .. **Coppola-Baldwin,** Rosemarie M '01 %Dept Homeless Srvcs -33 Beaver -NY 10004 **Fx:**361-8002
(518) 457-1260 .. **Coppolo,** Lisa Marie '94 %DCJS -4 Twr Pl -Albany 12203 **Fx:**457-3089
(212) 833-3487 .. **Coppotelli,** Blake A '88 Knoll Inc -1166 Av of Amer -NY 10036
(518) 436-4170 .. **Copps,** Anne Reynolds '82 -126 State -Albany 12207 **Fx:**436-1456
(518) 408-0469 .. **Copps,** Carl D '81 %Workers Comp Bd -20 Park -Albany 12207
(212) 389-5000 .. **Copps,** Robt E '04 (Sutherland A&B LLP) -1114 Av of Amer -NY 10036
(631) 691-2050 .. **Corallo,** Gerald A Jr. '98 (Corallo & C) -134 Ireland Pl -Amityvll 11701 **Fx:**691-2045
(631) 691-2050 .. **Corallo,** Laurie A '98 (Corallo & C) -134 Ireland Pl -Amityvll 11701 **Fx:**691-2045
(718) 767-1177 .. **Coran Ober, PC** -25-02 F Lewis Blvd -Flushng 11358 **Fx:**767-2455
(212) 859-8000 .. **Corapi,** Kristin D '03 %Fried FHS&J LLP -1 NY Plz -NY 10004
(315) 797-8375 .. **Corasanti,** Jos J '90 %Conmed -310 Broad -Utica 13501 **Fx:**797-0321
(718) 442-4424 .. **Corash & Hollender,PC** -1200 South Av -Staten Isl 10314 **Fx:**273-4847
(315) 437-8453 .. **Corbacio,** Vincent G '75 %Hillsberg SC&V -346 N Midler Av Bx275 -Syracuse 13206
(845) 876-4091 .. **Corbally Gartland and Rappleyea LLP** -6369 Mill Bx366 -Rhinebeck 12572 **Fx:**876-7192
(845) 677-5539 .. **Corbally Gartland and Rappleyea LLP** -30 Front -Millbrook 12545 **Fx:**677-6297
(845) 454-1110 .. **Corbally Gartland and Rappleyea LLP** -35 Market -Poughkeepsie 12601 **Fx:**454-4857
(845) 454-1110 .. **Corbally,** Richd V '58 OfCnsl Corbally G and R LLP -35 Market -Poughkeepsie 12601
(718) 286-6000 .. **Corbett,** Christine M '04 %DA -125-01 Qns Blvd -Kew Gdns 11415
(212) 984-4178 .. **Corbett,** Christopher J '79 %L'Oreal USA -575 5th Av -NY 10017 **Fx:**984-4946
(212) 277-6500 .. **Corbett,** Donald A '95 (Dickstein S LLP) -1633 Bway -NY 10019
(516) 679-9494 .. **Corbett,** James J '92 -254 Pettit Av -Bellmore 11710 **Fx:**679-7406
(212) 582-9526 .. **Corbett,** John J '66 (Corbett & R) -250 W 57th -NY 10019
(212) 227-4210 .. **Corbett,** Jonathan C '09 %Weg & M,PC -52 Duane -NY 10007
(516) 931-1800 .. **Corbett,** Karen '97 OfCnsl Catalano G&P LLP -100 Jericho Quadrangle -Jericho 11753
(518) 584-1500 .. **Corbett,** Kathleen A '81 (Snyder KTC&C,LLP) -160 West Av Bx4367 -Saratoga Spgs 12866
(516) 880-8484 .. **Corbett,** Keith M '08 %Harris B PLLC -333 Earle Ovngton Blvd -Uniondale 11553
(212) 436-6509 .. **Corbett,** Kevin R '04 Deloitte & Touche LLP -2 World Fncl Ctr -NY 10281 **Fx:**653-3361
(518) 792-1174 .. **Corbett,** Lawr E '52 OfCnsl McPhillips F&C,LLP -288 Glen Bx299 -Glens Fls 12801
(212) 880-1200 .. **Corbett,** Michl L '73 Fidelity National Fncl -711 3rd Av -NY 10017
(518) 436-1850 .. **Corbett,** Molly K '97 %Fed Pub Def -39 N Pearl -Albany 12207 **Fx:**436-1780
(212) 839-5300 .. **Corbett,** Nancy H '94 (Sidley A LLP) -787 7th Av -NY 10019
(212) 953-2381 .. **Corbett,** Patrick J '89 (Rubin F&F,LLP) -292 Mad Av -NY 10017
(212) 582-9526 .. **Corbett & Rebak** -250 W 57th -NY 10019 **Fx:**977-6802
(212) 344-0464 .. **Corbett,** Robt V '66 (Cardillo & C) -29 Bway -NY 10006
(516) 775-6849 .. **Corbett,** Wm J '66 -113 S Tyson Av -Floral Pk 11001 **Fx:**328-2545
(212) 969-3000 .. **Corbi,** Richd J '06 %Proskauer R LLP -1585 Bway -NY 10036
(516) 922-5211 .. **Corbin,** Bari Brandes '99 -1518 Laurel Hllw Rd -Laurel Hollow 11791
(212) 854-0069 .. **Corbin,** Caroline M '03 Columbia Law Schl -435 W 116th Bx D-28 -NY 10027 **Fx:**854-7946
(646) 386-3045 .. **Corbin,** Catherine M '83 %Appellate Term -60 Centre -NY 10007
(212) 230-8800 .. **Corbin,** Danl R '07 %WilmerHale -399 Park Av -NY 10022
(212) 682-6300 .. **Corbin,** I Jeffrey '91 %KCSA Public Relations -880 3rd Av -NY 10022
(914) 285-9800 .. **Corbin,** Lee H '69 (Kurzman EC&L,LLP) -1 N Bway -White Plns 10601
(212) 232-1300 .. **Corbin,** Steven T '07 %Lewis BB&S LLP -77 Water -NY 10005
(518) 487-5460 .. **Corbitt,** Shannon K '98 %DA -6 Lodge -Albany 12207 **Fx:**487-5093
(718) 258-4774 .. **Corbo,** Louis W '07 %A Hertz,PC -934 E 19th -Brklyn 11230 **Fx:**258-4994
(718) 987-3600 .. **Corbo,** Paschal A '74 -2141 Richmond Rd -Staten Isl 10306
(646) 386-3665 .. **Corbo,** Victoria Goodspeed '05 %Supreme Ct-Law Dept -60 Centre -NY 10007
(212) 809-7074 .. **Corchia,** Vanessa M '85 %Armienti DG&R,LLP -39 Bway -NY 10006

(212) 351-4500 .. **Corcoran,** Carrie B '00 %Epstein B&G,PC -250 Park Av -NY 10177
(585) 454-5850 .. **Corcoran,** Christopher H '77 (Wiedman VC&V,PC) -5 S Fitzhugh -Rchstr 14614
(646) 610-5400 .. **Corcoran,** Ethel H '84 %NYPD -1 Police Plz -NY 10038
(718) 520-3378 .. **Corcoran,** Geralyn '95 NYS Supreme Ct -88-11 Sutphin Blvd -Jamaica 11435
(212) 564-9090 .. **Corcoran,** James M '98 %Altier & V,LLC -450 7th Av -NY 10123
(212) 249-1580 .. **Corcoran,** James P '69 -239 E 79th -NY 10075
(914) 750-5933 .. **Corcoran,** Jennifer B '04 (Kissel H&W LLP) -580 Wht Plns Rd -Tarrytwn 10591
(518) 218-7100 .. **Corcoran,** Jennifer J '97 Tully R,PLLC -441 New Karner Rd -Albany 12205
(315) 471-3151 .. **Corcoran,** John F '94 (Hancock & E,LLP) -1500 AXA Twr I Bx4976 -Syracuse 13221
(212) 506-1700 .. **Corcoran,** John T '92 Kasowitz BT&F LLP -1633 Bway -NY 10019
(518) 465-0400 .. **Corcoran,** Justin O C '95 (O'Connor OB&F,PC) -20 Corp Wds Blvd -Albany 12211
(631) 765-1889 .. **Corcoran,** Kieran M '95 Town of Southold -53095 Main Rd Bx1179 -Southold 11971
(212) 857-8253 .. **Corcoran,** Matthew G '09 %R Reinstein PC -330 W 34th -NY 10001 **Fx:**857-8233
(212) 896-6500 .. **Corcoran,** Neil D '09 %Howrey LLP -601 Lex Av -NY 10022
(212) 468-4800 .. **Corcoran,** Paul F '72 (Davis & G LLP) -1740 Bway -NY 10019
(315) 655-3463 .. **Corcoran,** Rhonda M '08 %Mitchell G&S,LLC -5 Mill Bx312 -Cazenovia 13035
(914) 328-0404 .. **Corcoran,** Susan M '90 (Jackson L LLP) -1 N Bway -White Plns 10601
(212) 867-5800 .. **Corcoran,** Wm J '06 (Osler H&H LLP) -620 8th Av -NY 10018
(212) 708-1800 .. **Cord,** Janet I '88 (Ladas & P) -26 W 61st -NY 10023
(631) 265-7200 .. **Cordano,** Richd T '99 (Russo KW&C) -400 Townline Rd -Hauppauge 11788
(212) 637-2745 .. **Cordaro,** Jos N '04 US Atty -86 Chmbrs -NY 10007
(212) 973-0572 .. **Cordaro,** Stephen G '94 Cnsl Wolff & S PC -140 Bway -NY 10005
(212) 455-2000 .. **Cordaro,** Susan M '05 %Simpson T&B LLP -425 Lex Av -NY 10017
(212) 527-1000 .. **Corde,** Danl S '87 (Jones HC&B PC) -1 Bttry Pk Plz -NY 10004
(914) 761-2252 .. **Corde,** Richd G '85 (Boeggeman G&C,PC) -1 Water -White Plns 10601
(212) 821-3158 .. **Cordell,** Robt L II '96 %UBS Warburg -299 Park Av -NY 10171
(212) 421-2800 .. **Cordella,** Paul R '01 %Lanier Law Firm,PLLC -126 E 56th -NY 10022 **Fx:**421-2878
(212) 689-6272 .. **Cordelli,** Luca '03 Wilton & Prtnrs,LLP -420 5th Av -NY 10018
(585) 258-2800 .. **Cordello,** Elizabeth A '03 %Underberg & K LLP -300 Bausch & Lomb Pl -Rchstr 14604
(585) 272-0540 .. **Cordello,** Justin M '03 %Thomas & S LLP -693 East Av -Rchstr 14607
(212) 848-4000 .. **Cordera,** Michl W '02 %Shearman & S LLP -599 Lex Av -NY 10022
(212) 425-7200 .. **Cordero,** Rose '05 %Kenyon & K,LLP -1 Bway -NY 10004
(212) 207-8400 .. **Cordero,** Steven M '00 %Kavanagh M&O LLP -415 Mad Av -NY 10017
(212) 836-8000 .. **Cordes,** Dana E '09 %Kaye S LLP -425 Park Av -NY 10022
(631) 694-2400 .. **Cordiale,** Inna N '07 %Hamburger MYK&M,LLP -225 Broadhllw Rd -Melvll 11747
(518) 457-2449 .. **Cordier,** Danielle C '92 %Agriculture & Mrkts -10B Airline Dr -Albany 12235 **Fx:**457-8842
(212) 403-1000 .. **Cording,** Chas D '09 %Wachtell LR&K -51 W 52nd -NY 10019
(845) 561-0550 .. **Cordisco,** Dominic R '95 %Drake LHKGG&R PLLC -555 Hudson Valley Av -New Windsor 12553
(212) 756-2000 .. **Cordo,** Gabriela '01 %Schulte R&Z LLP -919 3rd Av -NY 10022
(518) 445-2535 .. **Cordo,** John L '96 (Cordo & Co LLC) -90 State -Albany 12207 **Fx:**445-2539
(212) 519-4281 .. **Cordobes,** Sean P '04 Verizon -560 Lex Av -NY 10022
(716) 852-5200 .. **Cordon,** John M Jr. '06 %Hamberger & W -700 Main Pl Twr -Buffalo 14202
(631) 694-0033 .. **Cordova,** Chas R '00 %Lawrence WR&B,PC -425 Broadhllw Rd -Melvll 11747
(516) 741-0070 .. **Cordova,** Debra Lynne '96 (Cordova & S,LLP) -666 Old Cntry Rd -Gdn Cty 11530 **Fx:**741-4225
(212) 279-2666 .. **Cordova,** Jessica '04 Teach for America -315 W 36th -NY 10018
(212) 839-5300 .. **Cordova,** Marcus A '05 %Sidley A LLP -787 7th Av -NY 10019
(845) 691-4200 .. **Cordovano,** Peter M '87 P Cordovano,PC -1 N Roberts Rd -Highlnd 12528 **Fx:**691-5725
(212) 471-8461 .. **Cordrey,** Matthew M '82 %Herzfeld & R,PC -125 Broad -NY 10004
(516) 997-2700 .. **Core,** Anthony E '90 (A Core,PC) -173 Schl -Westbury 11590 **Fx:**997-7334
(516) 741-3720 .. **Corea,** Jeanne M '97 (J Corea,PLLC) -250 Mineola Blvd -Mineola 11501 **Fx:**741-4240
(212) 765-2100 .. **Corello,** Sara Anne '93 (Spivak L LLP) -1700 Bway -NY 10019
(212) 351-4000 .. **Coren,** Jeffrey D '10 Gibson D&C LLP -200 Park Av -NY 10166
(518) 587-0080 .. **Coreno,** M Elizabeth '04 %Jones F -68 West Av Bx4400 -Saratoga Spgs 12866
(212) 841-1000 .. **Corenswet,** Ellen B '90 (Covington & B LLP) -620 8th Av -NY 10018
(212) 788-1022 .. **Corenthal,** Norman T '75 %Law Dept -100 Church -NY 10007 **Fx:**788-0367
(212) 239-4999 .. **Corenthal,** Richd S '80 (Meyer SE&K,PC) -1350 Bway Bx822 -NY 10018
(212) 686-2224 .. **Corenthal,** Seymour F '57 -330 5th Av -NY 10001 **Fx:**481-3274
(631) 549-7900 .. **Corey,** Peter '02 %Macco & S,LLP -135 Pinelawn Rd -Melvll 11747
(716) 753-4247 .. **Corey,** Shawn M '03 %Cnty Atty -3 N Erie -Mayvll 14757 **Fx:**753-4129
(518) 225-9707 .. **Corey-Mongue,** Heather Ann '97 -10 E High -Ballston Spa 12020 **Fx:**885-5376
(914) 946-0400 .. **Corgan,** John J '76 (Schiavetti CDW&N,LLP) -709 Wstchstr Av -White Plns 10604
(718) 250-2000 .. **Corhan,** Suzanne M '88 %DA -350 Jay -Brklyn 11201 **Fx:**250-2314
(631) 969-3100 .. **Corigliano,** Cheryll L '93 Frenkel LWW&G,LLP -20 W Main -Bay Shr 11706
(212) 764-4222 .. **Corigliano,** Dina M '99 %S Jeffries & Assoc -1560 Bway -NY 10036 **Fx:**764-4229
(845) 628-0271 .. **Corigliano,** Frank J '96 -577 N Main -Brewstr 10509 **Fx:**(914) 206-4000
(914) 235-0784 .. **Corini,** Robt O '74 -542 Main -New Rchll 10801
(631) 324-0596 .. **Corio,** Jamie T '00 (JT Corio,PLLC) -34 Alewive Brook Rd -E Hampton 11937 **Fx:**614-4407
(718) 204-0437 .. **Coritsidis,** Demetrios '77 (Coritsidis S&S) -25-61 Steinway -LIC 11103 **Fx:**267-0330
(212) 264-2920 .. **Coritsidis,** Gus '05 %Hon N Tsoucalas -1 Fed Plz -NY 10278
(212) 797-4600 .. **Coritsidis & Lambros,PLLC** -46 Trinity Pl -NY 10006 **Fx:**797-4601
(212) 797-4600 .. **Coritsidis,** Michl N '82 (Coritsidis & L,PLLC) -46 Trinity Pl -NY 10006
(914) 762-1787 .. **Corke,** Robt G '86 -11 Lakevw Rd -Ossining 10562
(516) 747-1100 .. **Corker,** W Russell '75 (Shayne DCS&D) -114 Old Cntry Rd -Mineola 11501
(212) 821-5260 .. **Corkery,** F Danl '85 UBS Financial Srvcs Inc -299 Park Av -NY 10171
(718) 254-7000 .. **Corkery,** Susan '80 %US Atty -271 Cadman Plz E -Brklyn 11201 **Fx:**254-6479
(212) 849-7000 .. **Corkhill,** Andrew S '10 %Quinn EU&S,LLP -51 Mad Av -NY 10010
(315) 699-9585 .. **Corl,** James E '01 -6035 State Route 31 -Cicero 13039
(212) 931-9950 .. **Corleone,** Douglas S '01 (Corleone Law Firm,PLLC) -111 John -NY 10038 **Fx:**406-3677
(914) 323-7000 .. **Corleto,** Anthony B '89 (Wilson EME&D LLP) -3 Gannett Dr -White Plns 10604
(631) 249-6644 .. **Corleto,** Raymond A '60 %Garcia & S -2076 Deer Prk Av -Deer Pk 11729
(585) 546-5072 .. **Corletta,** Thos A '81 -16 Main W -Rchstr 14614 **Fx:**546-2256
(212) 750-1200 .. **Corley,** David B '87 (Trolman G&L,PC) -777 3rd Av -NY 10017
(607) 737-2902 .. **Corley,** Elizabeth A '86 %Family Ct -203-209 William Bx588 -Elmira 14902
(212) 751-3001 .. **Corley,** O Paul Jr. '04 (Thompson & K LLP) -919 3rd Av -NY 10022
(212) 278-6194 .. **Corley,** Patricia G '99 %Societe Generale -1221 Av of Amer -NY 10020
(914) 304-1751 .. **Corliss,** George F '79 ITT Corp -1133 Wstchstr Av -West Harrison 10604
(914) 232-5161 .. **Corliss,** Marie A '86 (Covey RC&C) -200 Katonah Av -Katonah 10536
(212) 318-6000 .. **Cormack,** Michl C '03 %Paul HJ&W LLP -75 E 55th -NY 10022
(212) 816-0499 .. **Cormier,** Rosalynn H '03 CitiGroup Global Mrkts,Inc -388 Greenwich -NY 10013
(212) 818-9600 .. **Corn,** Harvey E '74 (Greenfield S&S,LLP) -600 3rd Av -NY 10016
(212) 558-4000 .. **Corn,** Richd M '05 %Sullivan & C LLP -125 Broad -NY 10004
(718) 730-6333 .. **Cornacchia,** Louis T III '07 (Skenderis & C PC) -45-07 Davis -LIC 11101 **Fx:**730-6334
(646) 278-4297 .. **Cornacchia,** Michl T III '77 -260 Mad Av -NY 10016
(212) 286-8585 .. **Cornacchio,** Elizabeth '82 (Heidell PM&B,LLP) -99 Park Av -NY 10016
(914) 253-6533 .. **Cornachio,** Albert W '65 -800 Wstchstr Av -Rye Brook 10573 **Fx:**696-0450
(914) 253-6533 .. **Cornachio,** Albert W III '93 -800 Wstchstr Av -Rye Brook 10573 **Fx:**696-0450
(516) 662-4600 .. **Cornachio,** Anthony W '72 (A Cornachio,PC) -100 15th -Gdn Cty 11530 **Fx:**742-5278
(914) 995-4172 .. **Cornachio,** Julia D '91 %DA -111 Martin Luther King Blvd -White Plns 10601 **Fx:**995-3363
(516) 357-3000 .. **Cornachio,** Wm '78 (Rivkin R LLP) -926 RXR Plz -Uniondale 11556
(646) 557-5100 .. **Corneal,** Devon A '08 %Patton B LLP -1185 Av of Amer -NY 10036
(212) 972-3000 .. **Corneau,** Jos C '03 %Klestadt & W,LLP -292 Mad Av -NY 10017
(212) 765-3144 .. **Corneck,** Lawr J '72 -211 W 56th -NY 10019
(212) 592-1400 .. **Cornehls,** Grant R '00 %Herrick,F LLP -2 Park Av -NY 10016
(212) 269-1600 .. **Cornejo,** Florencia '09 %Teigland-Hunt LLP -127 W 24th -NY 10011 **Fx:**269-1580
(212) 523-2010 .. **Cornelius,** Diane Y '96 %St Luke's-Rsvlt Hosp -1111 Amstrdm Av -NY 10025 **Fx:**523-3935
(518) 719-3220 .. **Cornelius,** Dominic Jos '96 Pub Def -411 Main -Catskill 12414 **Fx:**719-3785
(212) 225-2000 .. **Cornelius,** John B '10 %Cleary GS&H -1 Lbrty Plz -NY 10006
(585) 546-2500 .. **Cornelius,** Raymond E '63 Cnsl McConville CC&M,PC -25 E Main -Rchstr 14614
(718) 322-8867 .. **Cornelius Nightingale,** Catherine H '93 Law Ctr -95-03 101st Av -Ozone Pk 11416
(585) 593-5829 .. **Cornell,** Andrew J '04 -3460 Riverside Dr Bx1307 -Wellsvll 14895 **Fx:**593-3284
(212) 742-3390 .. **Cornell,** Athina Lekas '00 Lindabury ME&C,PC -26 Bway -NY 10004
(212) 729-8180 .. **Cornell,** George V III '83 -350 5th Av -NY 10118 **Fx:**(866) 400-6194
(607) 763-9200 .. **Cornell,** Heather M '99 (Levene G&T,LLP) -BxF-1706 -Bnghmtn 13902
(212) 233-1100 .. **Cornell,** Janet O'Connor '84 (Cornell G) -225 Bway -NY 10007 **Fx:**233-1110
(212) 326-3939 .. **Cornell,** John R '69 (Jones D) -222 E 41st -NY 10017
(845) 634-7901 .. **Cornell,** Keith J '93 Cornell & C -82 Maple Av -New Cty 10956 **Fx:**634-7963
(516) 741-4682 .. **Corner Finn Nicholson & Charles** -35 Hilton Av -Gdn Cty 11530
(212) 833-1114 .. **Corngold,** Eric O '85 (Friedman KS&A LLP) -1633 Bway -NY 10019 **Fx:**373-7914
(212) 994-0260 .. **Cornicello,** Anthony J '87 (Cornicello T&B-C,LLP) -2 Wall -NY 10005
(212) 994-0260 .. **Cornicello Tendler & Baumel-Cornicello, LLP** -2 Wall -NY 10005
(212) 275-4199 .. **Cornick,** Susan A '96 Elektra Ent Grp -75 Rckfllr Plz -NY 10019 **Fx:**275-1800
(212) 587-9690 .. **Cornish,** Christopher L '97 %J Samel & Partners -150 Bway -NY 10038 **Fx:**587-9673
(315) 425-2700 .. **Cornish,** Kathryn M '07 %Hiscock & B,LLP -One Park Pl -Syracuse 13202
(212) 373-3000 .. **Cornish,** Kelley Ann '84 (Paul WRW&G LLP) -1285 Av of Amer -NY 10019
(212) 664-3969 .. **Cornis-Pop,** Anca L '04 %NBC Universal -30 Rckfllr Plz -NY 10112
(212) 708-1800 .. **Cornman,** Michl A '62 OfCnsl Ladas & P -26 W 61st -NY 10023
(212) 965-9081 .. **Cornwall,** Deborah L '01 %Neufeld S&B -99 Hudson -NY 10013
(518) 640-5000 .. **Cornwell,** Craig G '06 AYCO -25 British Amer Blvd -Latham 12110

(607) 797-5123 .. **Cornwell**, Stephen K Jr. '05 -53 Chenango -Bnghmtn 13901 **Fx**:723-3671
(800) 281-1515 .. **Coron**, Jennifer D '08 %Power Law Firm LLP -590 Mad Av -NY 10022 **Fx**:903-1993
(518) 438-2000 .. **Corona**, Jennifer K '97 OfCnsl Lombardi WWHA&D PC -III Winners Cir -Albany 12205
(212) 515-2800 .. **Coronel**, Rinarisa G '02 HedgeOp -3 Park Av -NY 10016
(212) 408-5100 .. **Coronios**, Andrew C '78 (Chadbourne & P LLP) -30 Rckfllr Plz -NY 10112
(718) 925-9200 .. **Corozzo & Greenberg,PC** -158-01 Cross Bay Blvd -Howard Bch 11414
(212) 545-8777 .. **Corozzo**, Jos R Jr. '91 (Rubinstein & C,PC) -260 Mad Av -NY 10016
(718) 925-9200 .. **Corozzo**, Rocco J '98 (Corozzo & G,PC) -158-01 Cross Bay Blvd -Howard Bch 11414
(315) 471-3151 .. **Corp**, Michl L '82 (Hancock & E,LLP) -1500 AXA Twr I Bx4976 -Syracuse 13221
(718) 515-6000 .. **Corpina**, Jos B '63 (Corpina PK&P,LLP) -2344 Eastchstr Rd -Bronx 10469
(718) 515-6000 .. **Corpina Piergrossi Klar & Peterman,LLP** -2344 Eastchstr Rd -Bronx 10469 **Fx**:515-0511
(315) 425-2700 .. **Corpus**, Karla M '86 (Hiscock & B,LLP) -One Park Pl -Syracuse 13202
(212) 695-5282 .. **Corpuz**, Benjy M '03 Corpuz & Assoc,PC -370 7th Av -NY 10001 **Fx**:563-2664
(212) 330-7201 .. **Corr**, Dennis G '89 -800 Grnd Cncrs -Bronx 10451
(518) 435-1536 .. **Corr**, Janice K '70 -1 Winners Cir Bx15056 -Albany 12212 **Fx**:438-4349
(212) 848-4000 .. **Corr**, Stacey L '10 Shearman & S LLP -599 Lex Av -NY 10022
(607) 731-2039 .. **Corradini**, Paul R '70 -63 Larchmont Rd -Elmira 14905
(212) 554-7892 .. **Corradino**, Elizabeth A '92 (Moses & S LLP) -405 Lex Av -NY 10174
(718) 979-4300 .. **Corrado**, Christine '95 %Decker DD&I,LLP -1610 Richmond Rd -Staten Isl 10304
(845) 454-3250 .. **Corrado**, Elizabeth M '06 %Gellert & K,PC -75 Wshngtn -Poughkeepsie 12601
(212) 838-0600 .. **Corrado**, Giacomo J '92 -1 Astor Pl -NY 10003
(516) 622-0606 .. **Corrado**, Jason R '99 %P Rizzuto,PC -1 Old Cntry Rd -Carle Pl 11514 **Fx**:622-2112
(518) 457-2411 .. **Corrado**, Marie A '83 %DOT -50 Wolf Rd -Albany 12232 **Fx**:457-4021
(516) 564-6473 .. **Corrado**, Melissa P '88 -58 Hilton Av -Hempstd 11550 **Fx**:489-1940
(212) 401-0800 .. **Corrado**, Nicole '91 %Disciplinary Comm -61 Bway -NY 10006 **Fx**:287-1045
(212) 225-2982 .. **Corrales**, Carmen A '91 (Cleary GS&H) -1 Lbrty Plz -NY 10006
(212) 328-6180 .. **Corrao**, Laura S '81 %CMW Lgl Search -845 3rd Av -NY 10022 **Fx**:328-6181
(914) 381-2525 .. **Corrao**, Maria Concetta '05 OfCnsl Brodsky & P -550 Mamaroneck Av -Harrison 10528
(212) 226-4200 .. **Corrao**, Melissa K '05 Suckle S&L PLLC -224 W 35th -NY 10001
(646) 386-4800 .. **Correa**, Brenda '01 %Comm Judicial Cndct -61 Bway -NY 10006 **Fx**:458-0037
(917) 777-4200 .. **Correa**, Laura R '08 %Bingham M LLP -1 Bttry Pk Plz -NY 10004
(718) 585-7000 .. **Corredine**, Roger A '94 (Rogers WKC&Z) -800 Grnd Cncrs -Bronx 10451 **Fx**:585-8969
(718) 923-8400 .. **Corredor**, Livia M '85 %Forest City Ratner -1 Metrotech Ctr N -Brklyn 11201 **Fx**:923-8722
(315) 946-7472 .. **Correia**, Andrew D '00 %Pub Def -26 Church -Lyons 14489 **Fx**:946-7478
(212) 487-9701 .. **Correia**, Doreen J '88 %Robin HK&F -1 Bttry Pk Plz -NY 10014
(516) 229-4300 .. **Correia**, Umberto O '02 %J Bilello & Assoc -875 Merrick Av -Westbury 11590
(212) 710-3900 .. **Correll**, Danl E '03 %Clyde & Co US LLP -405 Lex Av -NY 10174 **Fx**:710-3950
(877) 718-8250 .. **Correll**, Donna E '00 Sun Microsystems Inc -101 Park Av -NY 10178
(212) 475-3070 .. **Correll**, P Kent '82 -300 Park Av -NY 10022 **Fx**:475-2378
(585) 265-1343 .. **Corretore**, David T '83 -66 E Main -Webster 14580 **Fx**:265-0482
(212) 686-2042 .. **Corriero**, Michl A '68 Big Brothers Big Sisters NYC -223 E 30th -NY 10016
(212) 513-3200 .. **Corrigan**, Brian P '02 (Holland & K LLP) -31 W 52nd -NY 10019
(718) 590-3795 .. **Corrigan**, Edw V '85 Bronx Cnty Ct -851 Grnd Cncrs -Bronx 10451
(516) 810-8231 .. **Corrigan**, James W III '92 -Bx1268 -Selden 11784
(212) 572-4382 .. **Corrigan**, Jason M '99 Estee Lauder -767 5th Av -NY 10153 **Fx**:572-3989
(212) 248-9100 .. **Corrigan**, John K '86 %Epstein M&M -1 Whitehall -NY 10004
(914) 468-0190 .. **Corrigan**, John P '90 (Corrigan & B,LLC) -1311 Mamaroneck Av -White Plns 10605 **Fx**:468-0199
(212) 526-0582 .. **Corrigan**, Karen Barlow '97 %Lehman Bros -1271 Av of Amer -NY 10020
(212) 809-7074 .. **Corrigan**, Mary Breen '86 %Armienti DG&R,LLP -39 Bway -NY 10006
(518) 477-4575 .. **Corrigan McCoy & Bush** -220 Columbia Tpk -Rensselaer 12144 **Fx**:477-4578
(212) 455-2000 .. **Corrigan**, Michl V '69 OfCnsl Simpson T&B LLP -425 Lex Av -NY 10017
(518) 477-4575 .. **Corrigan**, Peter J '75 (Corrigan M&B) -220 Columbia Tpk -Rensselaer 12144
(212) 849-6980 .. **Corrigan**, Peter M '91 Submedia LLC -250 W 34tth -NY 10119
(212) 490-1700 .. **Corrigan**, Scott D '93 (Wiggin & D) -450 Lex Av -NY 10017
(212) 318-3000 .. **Corrigan**, Sean F '87 (Fulbright & J LLP) -666 5th Av -NY 10103
(212) 745-7626 .. **Corrigan**, Terence J '99 IBM -590 Mad Av -NY 10022
(212) 889-0575 .. **Corriggio**, Jennifer Hu '03 %Perlman & P -41 Mad Av -NY 10010 **Fx**:743-8120
(212) 482-0001 .. **Corring**, John A '97 %Russo K&T LLP -33 Whitehall -NY 10004
(212) 756-2000 .. **Corriss**, Stephen C '80 SpclCnsl Schulte R&Z LLP -919 3rd Av -NY 10022
(212) 262-2390 .. **Corriston**, Timothy E '87 (Connell F LLP) -888 7th Av -NY 10106
(212) 450-4000 .. **Corry**, John A '57 SrCnsl Davis P&W LLP -450 Lex Av -NY 10017
(516) 767-3600 .. **Corsa**, LeRoy S '62 OfCnsl Chalos O&D -366 Main -Pt Wash 11050
(718) 409-3431 .. **Corsa**, Lorraine C '88 -80 Wstchstr Sq -Bronx 10461 **Fx**:409-4685
(718) 250-1100 .. **Corsair**, Bradley J '93 E Garfinkel -12 Metrotech Ctr -Brklyn 11201 **Fx**:250-1168
(212) 326-2000 .. **Corsaro**, Maria A '03 Cnsl O'Melveny & M LLP -7 Times Sq -NY 10036
(212) 969-3000 .. **Corsaro**, Paula M '00 %Proskauer R LLP -1585 Bway -NY 10036
(845) 433-5715 .. **Corsello**, Kenneth R '93 %IBM -2455 South Rd -Poughkeepsie 12601
(212) 259-8000 .. **Corsello**, Philip F '93 Cnsl Dewey & L LLP -1301 Av of Amer -NY 10019
(212) 788-1090 .. **Corsi**, Alexandra '10 %Law Dept -100 Church -NY 10007 **Fx**:788-0367
(212) 693-0085 .. **Corsi**, Denise A '94 %Appellate Advocates -2 Rector -NY 10006 **Fx**:693-0878
(518) 489-8424 .. **Corsi**, Ennio J '94 Cnsl AFSCME Council 82 -63 Colvin Av -Albany 12206 **Fx**:435-1523
(212) 238-4800 .. **Corsi**, Louis G '73 (Landman CB&F,PC) -120 Bway -NY 10271
(212) 474-1000 .. **Corsico**, Jonathan L '04 %Cravath S&M LLP -825 8th Av -NY 10019
(212) 225-2000 .. **Corsiglia**, James G '94 Cleary GS&H -1 Lbrty Plz -NY 10006
(516) 333-9500 .. **Corso**, Frank M '54 F Corso,PC -350 Jericho Tpk -Jericho 11753 **Fx**:333-9114
(212) 949-4700 .. **Corso**, Keith W '02 (Bushell SO&G LLP) -60 E 42nd -NY 10165 **Fx**:286-0513
(914) 843-3600 .. **Corso**, Louis M '94 -23 Fraser -Pelham 10803
(212) 799-0849 .. **Corso**, Philip F Jr. '82 -142 West End Av -NY 10023
(631) 390-4900 .. **Corso**, Victor P '91 Bouchard Transportation -58 S Srvc Rd -Melvll 11747 **Fx**:390-4905
(516) 794-3500 .. **Corson**, David A '90 Brunetti A&T,PLLC -170 Old Cntry Rd -Mineola 11501 **Fx**:794-3696
(212) 578-5613 .. **Corson**, Nicholas W C '97 MetLife -1095 Av of Amer -NY 10036 **Fx**:578-3916
(212) 758-1219 .. **Corson**, Rochelle M '78 -340 E 52nd -NY 10022 **Fx**:812-0722
(212) 888-7300 .. **Corsun**, Lori A '87 -444 Mad Av -NY 10022 **Fx**:888-7306
(212) 335-9735 .. **Cort**, Danl G '89 %DA -1 Hogan Pl -NY 10013 **Fx**:335-8992
(646) 386-3190 .. **Cort**, Julia A '91 %Hon J Madden -60 Centre -NY 10007
(718) 286-6000 .. **Cort**, Michelle Y '03 %DA -125-01 Qns Blvd -Kew Gdns 11415
(631) 465-5000 .. **Cort**, Yvonne '84 %K Tenenbaum,PC -225 Old Cntry Rd -Melvll 11747 **Fx**:465-5003
(516) 248-1188 .. **Cortazzo**, James '90 (Carrieri & C,PC) -200 Old Cntry Rd -Mineola 11501 **Fx**:248-1794
(718) 894-9500 .. **Cortegiano**, Mark L '97 -65-12 69th Pl -Middl Vllg 11379 **Fx**:326-3781
(212) 661-7100 .. **Cortellessa**, Wm J '02 %Salon MDN&B,LLP -292 Mad Av -NY 10017
(914) 288-9191 .. **Cortelli**, Terrence J '02 %Lever & S,LLP -303 Old Tarrytown Rd -White Plns 10603
(718) 286-6000 .. **Cortes**, Denise I '09 DA -125-01 Qns Blvd -Kew Gdns 11415
(212) 468-4800 .. **Cortes**, Jessica Golden '02 %Davis & G LLP -1740 Bway -NY 10019
(631) 852-2500 .. **Cortes**, John W '03 %DA -200 Center Dr -Rvrhead 11901 **Fx**:852-1769
(347) 401-9911 .. **Cortes**, Karen M C '04 Hon T McElrath - Family Ct -330 Jay -Brklyn 11201
(212) 836-8000 .. **Cortes**, Lee M Jr. '04 %Kaye S LLP -425 Park Av -NY 10022
(212) 259-8000 .. **Cortes**, Robt E '05 %Dewey & L LLP -1301 Av of Amer -NY 10019
(631) 863-1262 .. **Cortes de Torres**, Juana '92 J Cortes de Torres,PLLC -341 MacArthur Blvd -Hauppauge 11788 **Fx**:863-1262
(718) 590-2000 .. **Cortese**, Maria T '84 %DA -198 E 161st -Bronx 10451 **Fx**:590-6477
(212) 691-0950 .. **Cortese**, Michele '88 Ctr for Family Representation -116 John -NY 10038 **Fx**:691-0951
(212) 407-4000 .. **Cortese**, Nichole D '05 %Loeb & L,LLP -345 Park Av -NY 10154
(516) 741-1818 .. **Corteselli**, Karen P '83 (O'Reilly M&C,PC) -222 Old Cntry Rd -Mineola 11501
(212) 446-4800 .. **Cortesi**, Shane V '06 %Kirkland & E LLP -153 E 53rd -NY 10022
(212) 894-7200 .. **Cortez**, Jordan A '06 %Entwistle & C LLP -280 Park Av -NY 10017
(212) 909-6000 .. **Cortez**, Natalia L '07 %Debevoise & P LLP -919 3rd Av -NY 10022
(914) 766-1900 .. **Corthell**, Jon '84 IBM -294 Route 100 -Somers 10589
(212) 326-3939 .. **Coruzzi**, Laura A '86 (Jones D) -222 E 41st -NY 10017
(212) 964-3290 .. **Corvino**, Thos R '87 %Levidow L&O -299 Bway -NY 10007
(973) 491-3359 .. **Corvo**, Laura H '98 %LeClairRyan,PC -830 3rd Av -NY 10022 **Fx**:491-3555
(212) 683-3086 .. **Corwin**, Chas A '02 Original Media,LLC -38 E 29th -NY 10016
(516) 482-7098 .. **Corwin**, Christopher C '03 -98 Cuttermill Rd -Gt Neck 11021 **Fx**:706-6891
(914) 698-0100 .. **Corwin**, Garrison R Jr. '60 (Meighan & N) -100 Mamaroneck Av -Mamaroneck 10543
(212) 979-9242 .. **Corwin**, John W '74 -303 Mercer -NY 10003
(212) 889-1059 .. **Corwin**, Jules A '74 -333 E 30th -NY 10016 **Fx**:963-7456
(212) 801-3113 .. **Corwin**, Leslie D '74 (Greenberg T,LLP) -200 Park Av -NY 10166
(631) 462-2323 .. **Corwin**, Melissa '03 %Somer & H LLP -2171 Jericho Tpk -Commack 11725 **Fx**:462-2338
(516) 741-6565 .. **Corwin**, Nathaniel L '87 (Meyer SE&K,PC) -990 Stewart Av Bx9194 -Gdn Cty 11530
(212) 637-2707 .. **Corwin**, Neil M '86 %US Atty -86 Chmbrs -NY 10007
(212) 986-1000 .. **Corwin**, Paul M '80 (Goldberg C&G,LLP) -331 Mad Av -NY 10017 **Fx**:986-8039
(516) 223-3722 .. **Coryat**, R Jos '00 (RJ Coryat,PC) -431 N Main -Freeprt 11520 **Fx**:223-3776
(516) 228-1300 .. **Coschignano**, Chris J '90 (Sahn WC&B,PLLC) -333 Earle Ovngton Blvd -Uniondale 11553
(212) 237-1000 .. **Coscia**, Anthony R '85 (Windels ML&M,LLP) -156 W 56th -NY 10019
(718) 727-7100 .. **Coscia**, John B '74 %Custom Title Srvcs -690 Forest Av -Staten Isl 10310 **Fx**:727-7542
(917) 816-2206 .. **Coscia**, Mark F '09 -206 Benedict Av -Staten Isl 10314
(718) 238-1400 .. **Coscia**, Michl A '87 (Cantor C&S,LLP) -8778 Bay Pkwy -Brklyn 11214 **Fx**:238-7642
(212) 525-4772 .. **Coscia**, Peter J '92 Advisory Srvcs -452 5th Av -NY 10018
(914) 592-4275 .. **Coscia**, Risa Kriegel '85 %MHLS -100 Clearbrook Rd -Elmsfrd 10523 **Fx**:592-2634
(516) 822-8900 .. **Coscio**, Neil L '89 Fiedelman & M -2 Jericho Plz -Jericho 11753

(212) 259-8000 .. **Cosentino,** Jos A '01 %Dewey & L LLP -1301 Av of Amer -NY 10019
(585) 815-0288 .. **Cosentino,** Kelly '10 %Rosicki R & Assoc,PC -26 Harvester Av -Batavia 14020 **Fx:**815-0299
(631) 513-2900 .. **Cosentino,** Meryl R '87 -3 Haskel Ct -Stony Brk 11790 **Fx:**689-1126
(212) 513-7788 .. **Cosentino,** Ralph A '09 %Ahmuty D&M -123 William -NY 10038
(315) 834-6621 .. **Cosentino,** Richd N '64 -8941 N Seneca -Weedsport 13166 **Fx:**834-6029
(914) 948-4500 .. **Cosentino,** Robt E '98 %O'Connor MCD&O -1 Barker Av -White Plns 10601
(315) 822-4141 .. **Cosentino Snyder & Quinn** -379 W Main Bx596 -W Winfld 13491 **Fx:**822-6328
(315) 733-9900 .. **Cosentino Snyder & Quinn** -605 French Rd -New Hartfrd 13413
(718) 558-7993 .. **Cosenza,** Albert C '71 %LIRR -Jamaica Station -Jamaica 11435 **Fx:**558-8211
(212) 752-8000 .. **Cosenza,** Michele E '01 %Cole SMF&L,PA -900 3rd Av -NY 10022
(212) 270-6000 .. **Cosenza,** Thos M '99 JP Morgan Chase & Co -270 Park Av -NY 10017
(212) 728-8000 .. **Cosenza,** Todd G '99 %Willkie F&G LLP -787 7th Av -NY 10019
(518) 584-5030 .. **Coseo,** John P '75 (McMahon & C,PC) -16 Lake Av Bx587 -Saratoga Spgs 12866
(518) 385-7858 .. **Coseo,** Mary K '09 GE -1 River Rd -Schnctdy 12345
(518) 584-5030 .. **Coseo,** Matthew R '06 %McMahon & C,PC -16 Lake Av Bx587 -Saratoga Spgs 12866
(518) 584-5030 .. **Coseo,** Peter L '78 (McMahon & C,PC) -16 Lake Av Bx587 -Saratoga Spgs 12866
(914) 995-3577 .. **Cosgriff,** Irma W '88 %Cnty Atty -148 Martine Av -White Plns 10601 **Fx:**995-5858
(800) 521-1260 .. **Cosgriff,** James H III '85 %Petrone & P,PC -5500 Main -Williamsvll 14221
(914) 741-5315 .. **Cosgriff,** John P '88 %Verizon -500 Summit Lk Dr -Valhalla 10595
(212) 466-7700 .. **Cosgrove,** Britten L '10 %Sandler O'Neill & Prtnrs,LP -919 3rd Av -NY 10022 **Fx:**466-7998
(212) 735-3000 .. **Cosgrove,** Catherine M '04 %Skadden ASM&F LLP -4 Times Sq -NY 10036
(212) 705-7000 .. **Cosgrove,** David B '99 (Bingham M LLP) -399 Park Av -NY 10022
(716) 854-2211 .. **Cosgrove,** Edw C '63 -525 Delaware Av -Buffalo 14202 **Fx:**854-8122
(716) 854-2211 .. **Cosgrove,** Edw J '01 E Cosgrove -525 Delaware Av -Buffalo 14202 **Fx:**854-8122
(518) 459-5179 .. **Cosgrove,** Francis A '77 -33 Fairlawn Av -Albany 12203
(716) 854-2211 .. **Cosgrove,** James C '01 %E Cosgrove -525 Delaware Av -Buffalo 14202 **Fx:**854-8122
(845) 638-3240 .. **Cosgrove,** Jeanne Schofield '89 (Schofield S&C,LLP) -9 Elyse Dr -New Cty 10956
(518) 485-7728 .. **Cosgrove,** Jeremiah P '89 %Agriculture & Mrkts -10B Airline Dr -Albany 12235 **Fx:**457-8842
(716) 200-5050 .. **Cosgrove,** Nelson H '75 OfCnsl Harris B PLLC -726 Exchange -Buffalo 14210
(212) 696-4848 .. **Cosgrove,** Noreen English '95 Mintz & G LLP -470 Park Av S -NY 10016
(716) 858-2424 .. **Cosgrove,** Peter M '89 %DA -25 Delaware Av -Buffalo 14202 **Fx:**858-7425
(212) 756-2000 .. **Cosgrove,** Richd T '02 %Schulte R&Z LLP -919 3rd Av -NY 10022
(212) 267-1900 .. **Cosgrove,** Robt J '00 (Wade CM) -111 Bway -NY 10006
(212) 349-8173 .. **Cosgrove,** Robt S '97 (Durkin & D) -111 Bway -NY 10006 **Fx:**285-1968
(914) 345-9001 .. **Cossin,** Alexander '74 Taro Pharmaceuticals USA Inc -5 Skyline Dr -Hawthorne 10532 **Fx:**345-8728
(212) 715-9100 .. **Cossin,** Rebecca L '10 %Kramer LN&F,LLP -1177 Av of Amer -NY 10036
(914) 288-9595 .. **Cossu,** Denise M '83 (Gaines GP&N,LLP) -1 N Bway -White Plns 10601
(718) 852-8047 .. **Cossuto,** Mark S '89 -32 Court -Brklyn 11201
(212) 319-3900 .. **Cost,** Bradley P '80 -437 Mad Av -NY 10022 **Fx:**319-3070
(518) 429-4200 .. **Cost,** David M Jr. '07 %Hiscock & B,LLP -50 Beaver -Albany 12207
(914) 286-3615 .. **Costa,** Donna '88 %Mitsubishi Chem Amer -1 N Lex Av -White Plns 10601 **Fx:**761-0108
(212) 408-2500 .. **Costa,** Doreen Leavens '81 (Baker B,LLP) -30 Rckfllr Plz -NY 10112
(212) 310-8000 .. **Costa,** Jessica L '10 %Weil G&M LLP -767 5th Av -NY 10153
(845) 353-5155 .. **Costa,** John A '71 OfCnsl Costa & Assoc -135 Main -Nyack 10960 **Fx:**353-8643
(845) 691-5851 .. **Costa,** John G '91 -Bx948 -Highlnd 12528 **Fx:**691-5852
(212) 848-4000 .. **Costa,** Jordan A '06 %Shearman & S LLP -599 Lex Av -NY 10022
(718) 894-2301 .. **Costa,** Jos S '74 -6328 Plsntvw -Middl Vllg 11379 **Fx:**377-2072
(212) 880-3800 .. **Costa,** Keith N '85 (Akerman S) -335 Mad Av -NY 10017
(914) 235-1053 .. **Costa,** Matthew J '04 -1333A North Av -New Rchll 10804 **Fx:**235-1054
(212) 250-3116 .. **Costa,** Michl A '82 Deutsche Bank -60 Wall -NY 10005
(646) 562-1000 .. **Costa,** Michl R '87 Cowen Grp -1221 Av of Amer -NY 10020
(716) 853-4340 .. **Costa,** Peter L '51 OfCnsl Getman & B -800 Rand Bldg -Buffalo 14203
(212) 264-5916 .. **Costa,** Philip J '93 %DHS -26 Fed Plz -NY 10278
(212) 816-6000 .. **Costa,** Randall D '93 Citibank -390 Greenwich -NY 10013
(212) 788-1600 .. **Costa,** Richd J '99 %Law Dept -100 Church -NY 10007 **Fx:**788-0367
(315) 471-1212 .. **Costa,** Saml J '77 (S Costa,PC) -2 Clinton Sq -Syracuse 13202 **Fx:**471-4843
(212) 424-9712 .. **Costa,** Saverio R '97 %Benedetto Gartland & Co -1330 Av of Amer -NY 10019
(631) 752-0303 .. **Costa,** Thos L '77 -510 Broadhllw Rd -Melvll 11747 **Fx:**845-8779
(212) 859-8000 .. **Costabile,** Sommer '10 %Fried FHS&J LLP -1 NY Plz -NY 10004
(718) 556-9545 .. **Costagliola,** John A '92 -2110 Clove Rd -Staten Isl 10305 **Fx:**556-9547
(212) 692-1000 .. **Costantini,** Anthony J '73 (Duane M LLP) -1540 Bway -NY 10036
(718) 322-9824 .. **Costantino,** Andrew A '49 -160-40 80th -Howard Bch 11414
(212) 755-8686 .. **Costantino,** John R '71 %Walden Prtnrs Ltd -708 3rd Av -NY 10017 **Fx:**755-8894
(631) 842-0255 .. **Costantino,** Jos A '91 (Costantino & C) -632 Merrick Rd -Copiague 11726 **Fx:**842-0412
(212) 389-1528 .. **Costantino,** Kevin M '01 Greenhill & Co,LLC -300 Park Av -NY 10022
(716) 832-2626 .. **Costantino,** Nicholas C '72 -2626 Main -Buffalo 14214 **Fx:**836-3449
(631) 842-0255 .. **Costantino,** Steven A '84 (Costantino & C) -632 Merrick Rd -Copiague 11726 **Fx:**842-0412
(585) 218-9438 .. **Costantino,** Tracy L '85 -9 Pearl Stone Dr -Penfld 14526
(585) 232-3600 .. **Costanza,** Andrew A '87 (Costanza Entrprs) -14 Franklin -Rchstr 14604 **Fx:**423-0779
(718) 855-3374 .. **Costanza,** Denise J '83 -26 Court -Brklyn 11242
(585) 454-6480 .. **Costanza,** L Damien '87 %Osborn R&B,LLP -45 Exchange Blvd -Rchstr 14614
(212) 298-5123 .. **Costanzo,** Antoinette '93 %Leg Aid -49 Thomas -NY 10013 **Fx:**298-5252
(212) 779-7070 .. **Costanzo,** Arlene E '96 %Ronemus & V -112 Mad Av -NY 10016
(518) 828-3414 .. **Costanzo,** David M '00 %DA -325 Columbia -Hudson 12534 **Fx:**828-8491
(718) 876-7311 .. **Costanzo,** Diane '88 %Hon P DiMango -355 Front -Staten Isl 10304
(914) 949-1800 .. **Costanzo,** Jason P '04 (Hirshfield & C,PC) -62 Waller Av -White Plns 10605 **Fx:**949-5880
(212) 344-0464 .. **Costas,** Christophil B '68 (Cardillo & C) -29 Bway -NY 10006
(845) 353-5155 .. **Costa-Trahan,** Cynthia '97 %Costa & Assoc -135 Main -Nyack 10960 **Fx:**353-8643
(212) 422-0202 .. **Coste,** Stephanie C '08 %Sedgwick DM&A LLP -125 Broad -NY 10004
(631) 852-3076 .. **Costell,** Alan T '83 Supreme Ct -210 Center Dr -Rvrhead 11901
(516) 747-0377 .. **Costella,** Andrew J Jr. '92 (Costella & G,LLP) -7 12th -Gdn Cty 11530 **Fx:**248-0023
(212) 309-6000 .. **Costello,** Andrew C '07 %Morgan L&B LLP -101 Park Av -NY 10178
(212) 980-9600 .. **Costello,** Barbara M '00 %Kaufman B&R -120 Bway -NY 10271
(518) 436-0751 .. **Costello,** Bartley J III '73 (Hinman S PC) -121 State -Albany 12207
(212) 294-6700 .. **Costello,** Christopher C '05 %Winston & S -200 Park Av -NY 10166
(315) 422-1152 .. **Costello Cooney & Fearon,PLLC** -500 Plum -Syracuse 13204 **Fx:**422-1139
(315) 422-1152 .. **Costello Cooney & Fearon,PLLC** -220 Columbia Tpk -Rensselaer 12144 **Fx:**422-1139
(315) 422-1152 .. **Costello Cooney & Fearon,PLLC** -5701 W Genesee -Camillus 13031 **Fx:**484-7350
(212) 652-3890 .. **Costello,** Danl J '02 %Pitta & G LLP -120 Bway -NY 10271
(718) 222-2361 .. **Costello,** Edw J '04 %Law Dept -350 Jay -Brklyn 11201 **Fx:**222-2373
(845) 225-1900 .. **Costello & Folchetti,LLP** -1875 Route 6 -Carmel 10512 **Fx:**228-4228
(212) 765-2100 .. **Costello,** Gillian '97 (Spivak L LLP) -1700 Bway -NY 10019
(914) 606-9790 .. **Costello,** J McGarry '91 %Cartafalsa ST&L -560 Wht Plns Rd -Tarrytwn 10591
(518) 455-7700 .. **Costello,** James A '92 %Ct of Appls -20 Eagle -Albany 12207
(646) 369-6857 .. **Costello,** Janet '07 J Costello,LLC -80 Broad -NY 10004
(631) 727-1090 .. **Costello,** Jeanmarie P '81 -455 Griffing Av Bx295 -Rvrhead 11901 **Fx:**727-4528
(718) 624-5446 .. **Costello,** Jeannie '92 Bklyn Volunteer Lawyers Project -123 Remsen -Brklyn 11201
(212) 808-7800 .. **Costello,** John J '47 (Kelley D&W LLP) -101 Park Av -NY 10178
(315) 474-6448 .. **Costello,** John J Jr. '54 (Byrne C&P PC) -100 Madison -Syracuse 13202
(585) 546-5960 .. **Costello,** John J '80 -36 W Main -Rchstr 14614 **Fx:**546-6389
(585) 394-5831 .. **Costello,** John M '82 Cnty Family Ct -27 N Main -Canandaigua 14424
(212) 839-5300 .. **Costello,** John M Jr. '78 (Sidley A LLP) -787 7th Av -NY 10019
(866) 331-3271 .. **Costello,** John P '79 SSA-ODAR -100 State -Rchstr 14614 **Fx:**(585) 263-5792
(718) 331-4600 .. **Costello,** Jos G '58 (Costello & C,PC) -5919 20th Av -Brklyn 11204 **Fx:**331-2400
(718) 331-4600 .. **Costello,** Jos R '98 (Costello & C,PC) -5919 20th Av -Brklyn 11204 **Fx:**331-2400
(718) 357-5705 .. **Costello,** Kevin '82 -4333 194th -Flushng 11358
(716) 634-2753 .. **Costello,** Kyle M '06 %HJ Marcus,PC -5888 Main -Williamsvll 14221
(585) 232-5300 .. **Costello,** Mark A '81 (Boylan BCV&W,LLP) -2400 Chase Sq -Rchstr 14604
(212) 813-8800 .. **Costello,** Meagan E '03 %Goodwin P LLP -620 8th Av -NY 10018
(607) 277-1517 .. **Costello,** Michl J '83 %Family Ct -Cnty Cthse Bx70 -Ithaca 14851
(518) 463-1177 .. **Costello,** Michl L '74 (Tobin & D,LLP) -33 Elk -Albany 12207
(518) 473-5843 .. **Costello,** Morgan A '04 NYS Ofc of Att Gen -The Cptl -Albany 12222
(585) 987-2800 .. **Costello,** P Keely '72 OfCnsl Woods OG LLP -2 State -Rchstr 14614
(212) 259-8000 .. **Costello,** Patrick B '03 Cnsl Dewey & L LLP -1301 Av of Amer -NY 10019
(212) 779-8600 .. **Costello,** Patrick S '94 (Silverman SS&B PLLC) -381 Park Av S -NY 10016
(631) 361-4844 .. **Costello,** Paul G '73 -1 Spruce -Smithtwn 11787
(518) 862-1090 .. **Costello,** Peter J '04 NYSERDA -17 Columbia Cir -Albany 12203 **Fx:**862-1091
(212) 765-8600 .. **Costello,** Phillip R '98 (Costello & G LLP) -1790 Bway -NY 10019
(516) 572-7713 .. **Costello,** Robt G '99 %Nassau Comm College -1 Educ Dr -Gdn Cty 11530
(212) 949-8770 .. **Costello,** Robt J '73 (Levy T&C,LLP) -630 3rd Av -NY 10017
(716) 854-3400 .. **Costello,** Sean W '10 %Rupp BPC&C LLC -1600 Lbrty Bldg -Buffalo 14202
(212) 846-5338 .. **Costello,** Selene H '00 %MTV Networks -1515 Bway -NY 10036 **Fx:**258-8358
(212) 483-9600 .. **Costello Shea & Gaffney LLP** -44 Wall -NY 10005 **Fx:**344-7680
(516) 764-9090 .. **Costello Shea & Gaffney LLP** -100 Merrick Rd -Rockvll Ctr 11570 **Fx:**764-9104
(631) 852-2500 .. **Costello,** Thos C '93 %DA -200 Center Dr -Rvrhead 11901 **Fx:**852-1769
(845) 225-1900 .. **Costello,** Thos J '77 (Costello & F,LLP) -1875 Route 6 -Carmel 10512
(585) 427-5400 .. **Costello,** Timothy J '82 %Xerox -100 Clinton Av S -Rchstr 14644

(212) 755-4321 .. **Costello,** Timothy M '90 Costello & Assoc,PC -551 5th Av -NY 10176 **Fx:**755-2806
(914) 428-3313 .. **Costello,** Wm F '75 Curan AF&N,LLP -14 Mamaroneck Av -White Plns 10601 **Fx:**949-5800
(716) 773-3600 .. **Costello,** Wm J II '76 -2263 Grand Isl Blvd -Grand Isl 14072 **Fx:**773-3693
(212) 818-9200 .. **Coster,** James J '92 (Satterlee SB&B LLP) -230 Park Av -NY 10169
(516) 479-5171 .. **Costiera,** Cindy E '93 Utica Natl Ins Co -1 Jericho Plz -Jericho 11753
(516) 229-6000 .. **Costiera,** Richd J '94 %R Lau & Assoc -300 Jericho Quad Bx9040 -Jericho 11753 **Fx:**229-6167
(212) 218-8760 .. **Costigan,** Andrew J '90 (Hargraves M&C,PC) -420 Lex Av -NY 10170
(718) 822-7419 .. **Costigan,** Dennis P '70 -2120 E Tremont Av -Bronx 10462
(212) 302-8989 .. **Costigan,** James V '67 (Hedman & C,PC) -1185 Av of Amer -NY 10036
(212) 302-8989 .. **Costigan,** Kathleen A '99 %Hedman & C,PC -1185 Av of Amer -NY 10036
(631) 928-8000 .. **Costigan,** Peter J '57 Cnsl Winkler KW&K,LLP -310 Hallock Av -Pt Jffrsn Sta 11776
(631) 854-1954 .. **Costigan,** Philip P '72 %District Ct Law Dept -400 Carleton Av Bx9075 -Central Islip 11722
(212) 803-5100 .. **Costigan,** Susan E '89 %NY Cnty Defender Srvcs -225 Bway -NY 10007 **Fx:**571-6035
(212) 759-3300 .. **Costigan,** Wm F '81 OfCnsl Dornbush SS&V,LLP -747 3rd Av -NY 10017
(718) 222-2331 .. **Costigliacci,** Steven J '09 %Law Dept -350 Jay -Brklyn 11201 **Fx:**222-2373
(212) 373-3000 .. **Costikyan,** Edw N '49 OfCnsl Paul WRW&G LLP -1285 Av of Amer -NY 10019
(718) 618-0589 .. **Costin,** Delmas A Jr. '00 -177 E 161st -Bronx 10451 **Fx:**(347) 510-0099
(212) 821-3000 .. **Costin,** Sandra Ward '87 %USB PaineWebber -299 Park Av -NY 10171
(917) 783-1505 .. **Costo,** James R '01 -465 W 23rd -NY 10011
(646) 562-7834 .. **Costom,** Mitchell '00 Bain & Co -3 Times Sq Plz -NY 10036
(212) 682-3198 .. **Cotchett,** Jos W '06 (Cotchett P&M) -100 Park Av -NY 10017
(212) 682-3198 .. **Cotchett Pitre & McCarthy** -100 Park Av -NY 10017
(585) 654-0200 .. **Cote,** Amy R '03 Rochester Genesee Rgnl Trnsprtn Auth -1372 E Main -Rchstr 14609
(315) 478-3074 .. **Cote,** Jos S III '88 (Cote & V,LLP) -214 N State -Syracuse 13203 **Fx:**478-3094
(845) 452-7400 .. **Coté,** Michl A '98 (Spiegel BF&C,LLP) -272 Mill -Poughkeepsie 12601
(914) 597-7800 .. **Cote,** Raymond A '02 %Lewis S&C,LLC -11 Martine Av -White Plns 10606 **Fx:**597-7801
(212) 402-9400 .. **Cote,** Robt A '90 (McKool S,PC) -1 Bryant Park -NY 10036
(315) 451-2383 .. **Cote,** Robt M '97 %D'Arrigo -7515 Morgan Rd -Liverpool 13090 **Fx:**451-4106
(516) 484-3111 .. **Cotelidis,** Peter C '79 -200 Old Cntry Rd -Mineola 11501 **Fx:**484-0201
(914) 592-4411 .. **Cotellessa,** Susan Domenica '94 %NYSUT -520 Wht Plns Rd -Tarrytwn 10591
(212) 442-8388 .. **Cotenoff,** Scott A '88 Dept Pub Health-Cmty Health Works -40 Worth -NY 10013
(631) 447-2606 .. **Cotes,** Teresa A '99 -124 Medford Av -Patchogue 11772
(212) 785-7520 .. **Coti,** Ralph '78 (Coti & S) -17 State -NY 10004
(212) 785-7520 .. **Coti & Sugrue** -17 State -NY 10004 **Fx:**785-7511
(212) 964-6611 .. **Cotignola,** Felice J '85 (Lester SK&D) -120 Bway -NY 10271
(212) 267-2300 .. **Cotignola,** Michl N '80 -108 Greenwich -NY 10006 **Fx:**267-8279
(212) 768-6700 .. **Cotins,** Arthur James '90 (Sonnenschein N&R LLP) -2 World Fncl Ctr -NY 10281
(800) 610-5126 .. **Cotler,** Robin '90 -11 S Wshngtn Av -Hartsdale 10530
(212) 408-5100 .. **Cotrim,** Amanda L '09 %Chadbourne & P LLP -30 Rckfllr Plz -NY 10112
(914) 682-2929 .. **Cotronei,** P Christopher '78 -81 Main -White Plns 10601
(585) 987-2800 .. **Cotroneo,** Anthony '90 (Woods OG LLP) -2 State -Rchstr 14614
(212) 635-2244 .. **Cotroneo,** Anthony L '01 %Rosner N&R LLP -110 Wall -NY 10005
(212) 277-0849 .. **Cotroneo,** Jennifer L '01 Hartford Fncl Products -2 Park Av -NY 10016
(212) 570-3940 .. **Cott,** Sharon Hooper '86 %Metropolitan Museum -1000 5th Av -NY 10028 **Fx:**570-3850
(212) 848-4000 .. **Cottafavi,** Vittorio '07 %Shearman & S LLP -599 Lex Av -NY 10022
(212) 971-5607 .. **Cotten,** Marya N '03 Hudson Yards Devel Corp -225 W 34th -NY 10122
(315) 475-3700 .. **Cotter,** Brendan V '06 %Synapse Risk Mgmt LLC -325 E Water -Syracuse 13202
(845) 454-9460 .. **Cotter,** Catherine E '04 %MHLS -One Civic Ctr Plz -Poughkeepsie 12601 **Fx:**471-9308
(718) 590-6559 .. **Cotter,** Catherine L '82 %Law Dept -198 E 161st -Bronx 10451 **Fx:**590-2686
(212) 574-1200 .. **Cotter,** Chas A III '04 %Seward & K LLP -1 Bttry Pk Plz -NY 10004
(716) 847-8400 .. **Cotter,** Christina M '10 %Phillips L LLP -3400 HSBC Ctr -Buffalo 14203
(716) 634-7920 .. **Cotter,** David B '94 (Cotter & C PC) -5109 Main -Williamsvll 14221 **Fx:**634-5362
(212) 817-4330 .. **Cotter,** Debra J '01 Weight Watchers Intl -11 Mad Av -NY 10010
(917) 343-5314 .. **Cotter,** Eleanor '04 Goldman Sachs -1 NY Plz -NY 10004
(212) 871-6835 .. **Cotter,** Ellen M '93 Reading Intl Inc -189 2nd Av -NY 10003
(212) 455-2000 .. **Cotter,** James M '67 OfCnsl Simpson T&B LLP -425 Lex Av -NY 10017
(914) 989-6650 .. **Cotter,** Rose M '94 (Eustace & M) -1133 Wstchstr Av -White Plns 10604
(718) 250-2000 .. **Cotter,** Theo A '09 %DA -350 Jay -Brklyn 11201 **Fx:**250-2314
(716) 270-2431 .. **Cotter,** Timothy M '76 %IRS -300 Pearl -Buffalo 14202
(716) 634-7920 .. **Cotter,** Wm J '55 (Cotter & C PC) -5109 Main -Williamsvll 14221 **Fx:**634-5362
(212) 264-9245 .. **Cottet,** Mikki '91 %US DOJ -26 Fed Plz -NY 10278 **Fx:**264-1916
(212) 813-8800 .. **Cottler,** Michl B '07 %Goodwin P LLP -620 8th Av -NY 10018
(914) 644-8162 .. **Cottler,** Steven B '87 -14 Mad Av -Valhalla 10595 **Fx:**644-8167
(718) 250-2000 .. **Cotto,** Wilfredo '91 %DA -350 Jay -Brklyn 11201 **Fx:**250-2314
(718) 939-6454 .. **Cotton,** Andrew M '96 %DG Cotton -18-17 Cllg Pnt Blvd -Cllg Pnt 11356 **Fx:**461-3919
(212) 449-1652 .. **Cotton,** Christina A '91 %Merrill Lynch -4 World Fncl Ctr -NY 10080
(718) 939-6454 .. **Cotton,** David G '68 -18-17 Cllg Pnt Blvd -Cllg Pnt 11356 **Fx:**461-3919
(212) 940-8800 .. **Cotton,** Howard E '84 (Katten MR LLP) -575 Mad Av -NY 10022
(212) 903-8700 .. **Cotton,** Quincy '87 (Roberts & H,LLP) -825 8th Av -NY 10019
(212) 297-0275 .. **Cotton,** Richd B '83 -230 Park Av -NY 10169 **Fx:**972-7896
(212) 804-4200 .. **Cotton,** Stuart '68 (Mound CW&G) -One Bttry Pk Plz -NY 10004
(718) 998-0714 .. **Cottone,** Annalise F '91 -2920 Av R -Brklyn 11229 **Fx:**998-0740
(212) 336-1056 .. **Cottrell,** Amelia A '01 %SEC -3 World Fncl Ctr -NY 10281 **Fx:**336-1323
(518) 431-0247 .. **Cottrell,** Barbara D '85 %US Atty -445 Bway -Albany 12207 **Fx:**431-0249
(914) 592-1919 .. **Cottrell,** Floyd G '84 -5 W Main -Elmsfrd 10523 **Fx:**592-2987
(516) 678-3114 .. **Cotty,** Kenneth J '78 -124 Dartmth -Rockvll Ctr 11570
(908) 277-4100 .. **Couch,** Bryan P '01 (Clyde & Co US LLP) -405 Lex Av -NY 10174 **Fx:**277-4110
(518) 220-9577 .. **Couch Dale PC** -29 British Amer Blvd -Latham 12110 **Fx:**220-9587
(518) 220-9577 .. **Couch,** Mark W '86 (Couch D PC) -29 British Amer Blvd -Latham 12110
(518) 426-4600 .. **Couch White, LLP** -540 Bway Bx22222 -Albany 12201 **Fx:**426-0376
(212) 483-0105 .. **Coughlin Duffy LLP** -88 Pine-Wall St Plz -NY 10005 **Fx:**480-3899
(212) 534-2447 .. **Coughlin,** Francis J '54 -352 E 87th -NY 10128 **Fx:**860-8192
(212) 826-0100 .. **Coughlin,** Francis J Jr. '81 %FSA -31 W 52nd -NY 10019 **Fx:**893-2710
(607) 723-9511 .. **Coughlin & Gerhart, LLP** -19 Chenango Bx2039 -Bnghmtn 13902 **Fx:**723-1530
(607) 369-3811 .. **Coughlin & Gerhart, LLP** -176 Main Bx429 -Unadilla 13849 **Fx:**369-3315
(607) 272-5212 .. **Coughlin & Gerhart, LLP** -401 E State -Ithaca 14850 **Fx:**272-0155
(607) 687-0567 .. **Coughlin & Gerhart, LLP** -27-29 Lk Bx250 -Owego 13827 **Fx:**687-9860
(607) 637-3707 .. **Coughlin & Gerhart, LLP** -125 Wheeler -Hancock 13783 **Fx:**723-1530
(607) 467-4010 .. **Coughlin & Gerhart, LLP** -105 Front Bx147 -Deposit 13754 **Fx:**467-4700
(607) 639-2222 .. **Coughlin & Gerhart, LLP** -190 Main Bx462 -Afton 13730 **Fx:**639-3726
(585) 232-6500 .. **Coughlin,** Gregory J '04 %Harter S&E LLP -1600 Bausch & Lomb Pl -Rchstr 14604
(718) 250-2000 .. **Coughlin,** James E '09 %DA -350 Jay -Brklyn 11201 **Fx:**250-2314
(631) 425-4100 .. **Coughlin,** John J '03 (Ré NH&C,LLP) -36 N NY Av -Huntngtn 11743
(212) 350-2700 .. **Coughlin,** Kerin E '03 %Constantine C,PC -450 Lex Av -NY 10017
(212) 483-0105 .. **Coughlin,** Kevin T '80 (Coughlin D LLP) -88 Pine-Wall St Plz -NY 10005
(518) 474-3592 .. **Coughlin,** Robt E '82 %State Comptroller -110 State -Albany 12236 **Fx:**473-9104
(518) 786-1800 .. **Coughlin,** Robt H Jr. '82 (Flink S LLC) -23 British Amer Blvd -Latham 12110 **Fx:**786-1969
(212) 657-1127 .. **Coughlin,** Sean J '89 Citigroup -77 Water -NY 10005
(631) 367-7100 .. **Coughlin Stoia Geller Rudman & Robbins LLP** -58 S Srvc Rd -Melvll 11747 **Fx:**367-1173
(212) 693-1058 .. **Coughlin Stoia Geller Rudman & Robbins LLP** -52 Duane -NY 10007 **Fx:**693-7423
(718) 286-6000 .. **Coughlin,** Tara A '02 %DA -125-01 Qns Blvd -Kew Gdns 11415
(716) 753-4376 .. **Coughlin,** Wm F '91 Pub Def -7 N Erie -Mayvll 14757 **Fx:**753-4751
(518) 355-6268 .. **Coughtry & Anderson** -4382 Wstrn Tpk -Altamont 12009 **Fx:**357-9723
(518) 355-6268 .. **Coughtry,** JoAnn E '91 (Coughtry & A) -4382 Wstrn Tpk -Altamont 12009
(718) 298-0500 .. **Coulman,** Lee J '84 %Surrogate's Ct -88-11 Sutphin Blvd -Jamaica 11435 **Fx:**520-5048
(607) 778-2685 .. **Coulson,** Thos P '83 %Dept Soc Srvcs -36-42 Main -Bnghmtn 13905 **Fx:**778-2710
(212) 446-4800 .. **Coulston,** Christopher V '08 %Kirkland & E LLP -153 E 53rd -NY 10022
(718) 664-6600 .. **Coulston,** Gerald F '70 -825 E 233rd -Bronx 10466 **Fx:**664-6691
(212) 755-4016 .. **Coulston,** Judith '80 -228 E 45th -NY 10017 **Fx:**751-2707
(212) 746-1702 .. **Coulston,** Michl S '96 %NY Presbyterian Hsptl -525 E 68th Bx88 -NY 10065 **Fx:**746-8603
(212) 838-7000 .. **Coulter,** Chad W '99 Delphi Capital Mgmt -590 Mad Av -NY 10022 **Fx:**319-6171
(845) 454-9400 .. **Coulter,** John M '65 -42 Catharine BxR -Poughkeepsie 12602 **Fx:**454-5934
(212) 588-0677 .. **Coulter,** John V Jr. '80 -675 3rd Av -NY 10017 **Fx:**588-0861
(518) 695-6866 .. **Coulter,** Livingston T '62 -106 Broad Bx5 -Schuylrvll 12871
(315) 475-8461 .. **Coulter,** Robt F '53 OfCnsl Coulter V&M,LLP -636 Old Liverpool Rd -Liverpool 13088
(315) 475-8461 .. **Coulter Ventre & McCarthy,LLP** -636 Old Liverpool Rd -Liverpool 13088 **Fx:**475-4314
(212) 660-3000 .. **Coultrap,** Martha F '75 (Sullivan & W LLP) -1290 Av of Amer -NY 10104
(315) 435-2470 .. **Counihan,** Brian J '02 %DA -505 S State -Syracuse 13202 **Fx:**435-3969
(212) 819-8200 .. **Counihan,** Robt E '08 %White & C LLP -1155 Av of Amer -NY 10036
(518) 486-3287 .. **Countryman,** Elizabeth H '02 %State Comptroller -110 State -Albany 12236 **Fx:**473-9104
(518) 370-7972 .. **Countryman,** Patricia L '87 -2334 Harrison -Schnctdy 12306
(631) 852-2500 .. **Courbois,** Sandra '01 %DA -200 Center Dr -Rvrhead 11901 **Fx:**852-1769
(212) 751-4300 .. **Cournot,** Pierre '78 (Hodgson R LLP) -1540 Bway -NY 10036
(212) 806-5400 .. **Cournoyer,** Stephanie A '10 %Stroock &S&L LLP -180 Maiden Ln -NY 10038
(212) 538-7907 .. **Courpas,** Katherine Ann '95 %Credit Suisse First Boston -11 Mad Av -NY 10010
(212) 310-8000 .. **Coursant,** Caroline S '08 %Weil G&M LLP -767 5th Av -NY 10153
(315) 655-5530 .. **Coursen,** Alexandra '82 -3169 Windy Hill Ln -Manlius 13104

(212) 216-1826 .. **Coursen-Neff**, Zama '99 %Human Rights Watch -350 5th Av -NY 10118 **Fx:**736-1300
(585) 546-5530 .. **Courtade**, Colleen '85 %Thomson West -50 E Broad -Rchstr 14694
(631) 851-8700 .. **Courten**, Dorothy A '86 -33 Kings Hwy -Hauppauge 11788 **Fx:**851-8703
(212) 918-3000 .. **Courtheoux**, Karen L '10 %Hogan L LLP -875 3rd Av -NY 10022
(212) 545-4000 .. **Courtian**, Jennifer B '92 (Jackson L LLP) -666 3rd Av -NY 10017
(914) 750-5933 .. **Courtman**, Sarah C '05 %Kissel H&W LLP -580 Wht Plns Rd -Tarrytwn 10591
(646) 525-3276 .. **Courtney**, Cornelius M '86 NYFIX,Inc -100 Wall -NY 10005
(631) 722-5333 .. **Courtney**, John J '61 -18 Southflds Rd -Rvrhead 11901 **Fx:**722-5444
(631) 267-6161 .. **Courtney**, John P '74 -530 Montauk Hwy Bx720 -Amagansett 11930 **Fx:**267-6177
(585) 454-4060 .. **Courtney**, Katherine E '07 %Empire Justice Ctr -1 W Main -Rchstr 14614 **Fx:**454-4019
(518) 262-3828 .. **Courtney**, Kathleen H '01 Albany Med Ctr -43 New Scotland Av -Albany 12208 **Fx:**262-4184
(646) 502-8611 .. **Courtney**, Kimberly '02 Courtney Law Grp -75 W End Av -NY 10023 **Fx:**417-7421
(212) 370-7421 .. **Courtney**, Lisa A '93 LexisNexis -125 Park Av -NY 10017
(212) 428-5519 .. **Courtney**, Lisa M '00 %OCA -25 Beaver -NY 10004
(585) 428-5827 .. **Courtney**, Loretta S '84 %DA -832 Watts Bldg -Rchstr 14614 **Fx:**753-4576
(212) 891-0728 .. **Courtney**, Marian E '98 FOJP Service Corp -28 E 28th -NY 10016
(845) 331-0062 .. **Courtney**, Marshall A '89 -41 Pearl Bx3611 -Kingston 12402 **Fx:**331-2754
(914) 725-5409 .. **Courtney**, Michl W '78 -180 Griffen Av -Scarsdale 10583
(518) 473-0586 .. **Courtney**, Nathan M '94 %Dept of Law -The Cptl -Albany 12224 **Fx:**473-8153
(212) 417-5822 .. **Courtney**, Sean P '87 %Welfare Inspector Genl -22 Crtlandt -NY 10007 **Fx:**417-5849
(212) 474-1000 .. **Coury**, Larry A '04 %Cravath S&M LLP -825 8th Av -NY 10019
(212) 735-3000 .. **Coury**, Steven E '00 Cnsl Skadden ASM&F LLP -4 Times Sq -NY 10036
(718) 788-5052 .. **Coury**, Wm J '86 (Hagan C & Assoc) -908 4th Av -Brklyn 11232
(212) 218-5500 .. **Cousin**, Brian S '89 (Seyfarth S LLP) -620 8th Av -NY 10018
(212) 834-0600 .. **Cousin**, Wayne E '95 (Gordon & S,PC) -355 Lex Av -NY 10017
(518) 433-8800 .. **Cousineau**, Lauren M '05 %Lemery G LLC -50 Beaver -Albany 12207
(212) 969-3000 .. **Cousins**, Abigail F '81 %Proskauer R LLP -1585 Bway -NY 10036
(212) 688-5151 .. **Cousins**, Peter N '82 (Gibney A&F,LLP) -665 5th Av -NY 10022
(212) 385-0097 .. **Cousins Neil**, Racquel A '03 -299 Bway -NY 10007 **Fx:**385-0098
(914) 249-2000 .. **Cousquer**, Sandrine A '01 %MasterCard Intl -2000 Purchase -Purchase 10577
(518) 473-3303 .. **Coutant**, Richd N '82 %Dept of Health -Corning Twr 24th Fl -Albany 12237 **Fx:**473-2019
(315) 793-3622 .. **Coutlée**, Ryan F '03 %Estate Planning Law Ctr -555 French Rd -New Hartfrd 13413
(716) 853-2050 .. **Coutu**, Michl T '99 %Sliwa & L -237 Main -Buffalo 14203
(212) 586-4700 .. **Couture**, Jerold L '62 (Fitelson LA&C) -551 5th Av -NY 10176
(914) 686-9010 .. **Couzens**, John C Jr. '77 (Wilson BCC&C,PC) -2 William -White Plns 10601
(212) 261-5543 .. **Cove**, Ruth Lynn '91 Assured Guaranty Corp -1325 Av of Amer -NY 10019
(646) 878-2914 .. **Covell**, Jennifer A '95 Legacy Benefits,LLC -350 5th Av -NY 10118 **Fx:**878-2915
(315) 786-2261 .. **Covell**, Larry G '83 %Jefferson Cmmnty Cllg -Outer Coffeen -Watertwn 13601
(212) 697-3250 .. **Coven**, Brad '03 %Goldberg & R PLLC -115 Bway -NY 10006 **Fx:**227-4533
(212) 267-2555 .. **Coven**, Jules E '58 (Bretz & C,LLP) -305 Bway -NY 10007
(212) 267-2555 .. **Coven**, Michele R '85 %Bretz & C,LLP -305 Bway -NY 10007
(718) 447-1300 .. **Coven**, Mitchell S '83 -1578 Forest Av -Staten Isl 10302 **Fx:**447-2300
(212) 326-3939 .. **Cover**, Jason M '08 %Jones D -222 E 41st -NY 10017
(718) 233-6480 .. **Cover**, Leah M '05 %Leg Srvcs for NY -36 Richmond Ter -Staten Isl 10301
(716) 849-1333 .. **Covert**, Barry Nelson '90 (Lipsitz GSC LLP) -42 Delaware Av -Buffalo 14202
(631) 232-2544 .. **Covert**, Cory J '93 C Covert PC -519 Route 111 -Hauppauge 11788 **Fx:**582-2555
(716) 551-3341 .. **Covert**, Marybeth '92 %Fed Pub Def -300 Pearl -Buffalo 14202 **Fx:**551-3346
(212) 687-3440 .. **Covey**, Bonnie S '78 (Goldstick WF&G,PC) -7 Penn Plz -NY 10001
(212) 422-0202 .. **Covey**, David M '75 (Sedgwick DM&A LLP) -125 Broad -NY 10004
(212) 906-1200 .. **Covey**, Mark A '09 %Latham & W -885 3rd Av -NY 10022
(212) 732-3200 .. **Covey**, Richd B '58 SrCnsl Carter L&M LLP -2 Wall -NY 10005
(914) 232-5161 .. **Covey Roberts Corliss & Carmody-Roberts** -200 Katonah Av -Katonah 10536 **Fx:**232-0574
(718) 260-2434 .. **Covey Fayngold**, Julia '97 %Hon R Dearie -225 Cadman Plz E -Brklyn 11201 **Fx:**260-2437
(315) 425-9000 .. **Coviello**, Garth E '09 %Marjama MB&S LLP -250 S Clinton -Syracuse 13202
(212) 382-3300 .. **Coviello**, Gerald '01 (Wollmuth M&D LLP) -500 5th Av -NY 10110
(212) 455-2000 .. **Coviello**, Jeffrey '04 %Simpson T&B LLP -425 Lex Av -NY 10017
(212) 487-9700 .. **Coviello**, Jennifer L '99 %White F&F,LLP -61 Bway -NY 10006
(212) 696-4848 .. **Coviello**, Nicole A '07 %Mintz & G LLP -470 Park Av S -NY 10016
(212) 461-2323 .. **Coviello**, Nino A '87 (Saiber LLC) -44 Wall -NY 10005
(914) 995-2665 .. **Covill**, Kitley S '83 %Cnty Atty -148 Martine Av -White Plns 10601 **Fx:**995-5858
(516) 623-6499 .. **Coville**, John D '94 (Coville & G,PC) -2174 Hewlett Av -Merrick 11566 **Fx:**623-5365
(315) 685-5211 .. **Coville**, Robt A '93 (R Coville,PC) -3750 Fisher Rd -Skaneateles 13152 **Fx:**685-4827
(212) 841-1000 .. **Covington & Burling LLP** -620 8th Av -NY 10018 **Fx:**841-1010
(718) 857-0557 .. **Covington**, Wm J '73 -325 Flatbush Av -Brklyn 11217 **Fx:**789-8636
(973) 315-4446 .. **Covino**, A Michl '92 (Budd L) -140 Bway -NY 10005
(315) 463-1313 .. **Covino**, John D '68 -7000 E Genesee -Fayettevll 13066
(212) 464-2349 .. **Covino**, Serena '00 JP Morgan Chase Bank -345 Park Av -NY 10154 **Fx:**464-2312
(212) 294-6700 .. **Covino**, Teisha G '06 %Winston & S -200 Park Av -NY 10166
(212) 455-2000 .. **Covit**, Barrie B '99 (Simpson T&B LLP) -425 Lex Av -NY 10017
(516) 488-3300 .. **Covitt**, Adam S '00 %Shaub AC&S,LLP -1983 Marcus Av -Lk Success 11042
(212) 259-8000 .. **Covitt**, Renee I '05 %Dewey & L LLP -1301 Av of Amer -NY 10019
(212) 974-7474 .. **Cowan DeBaets Abrahams & Sheppard LLP** -41 Mad Av -NY 10010 **Fx:**974-8474
(212) 909-6000 .. **Cowan**, Jennifer R '98 Cnsl Debevoise & P LLP -919 3rd Av -NY 10022
(212) 790-9200 .. **Cowan**, Lewis R '54 SrCnsl Cowan L&L,PC -1133 Av of Amer -NY 10036
(212) 790-9200 .. **Cowan Liebowitz & Latman,PC** -1133 Av of Amer -NY 10036 **Fx:**575-0671
(212) 790-9200 .. **Cowan**, Marvin S '48 SrCnsl Cowan L&L,PC -1133 Av of Amer -NY 10036
(646) 328-0120 .. **Cowan**, Matthew J '07 %Bennett GM&P,LLP -494 8th Av -NY 10001
(212) 768-6700 .. **Cowan**, Miles B '08 %Sonnenschein N&R LLP -2 World Fncl Ctr -NY 10281
(718) 590-2000 .. **Cowan**, Robin I '91 %DA -198 E 161st -Bronx 10451 **Fx:**590-6477
(212) 514-5300 .. **Cowan**, Roger Brian '58 -355 Lex Av -NY 10017 **Fx:**514-5983
(914) 725-5379 .. **Cowan**, Ruth E '83 -22 Dorset Rd -Scarsdale 10583
(718) 497-1800 .. **Coward**, Kathryn L '02 Sen S Maltese -71-04 Myrtle Av -Glendale 11385 **Fx:**386-7803
(212) 607-8160 .. **Coward**, Nicole J '04 %MoloLamken -540 Mad Av -NY 10022 **Fx:**607-8161
(212) 637-2693 .. **Cowart**, Brandon H '03 US Atty -86 Chmbrs -NY 10007
(212) 661-1100 .. **Cowart**, Jason S '00 (Pomerantz HG&G LLP) -100 Park Av -NY 10017
(212) 425-7200 .. **Cowell**, Richd M '08 %Kenyon & K,LLP -1 Bway -NY 10004
(917) 778-6600 .. **Cowen**, Gerald G '78 %J Toomey -485 Lex Av -NY 10017 **Fx:**778-7048
(518) 561-6800 .. **Cowen**, Mark V '04 -10 Oak -Plattsbrgh 12901 **Fx:**563-1196
(212) 450-4000 .. **Cowgill**, Elyse J '09 %Davis P&W LLP -450 Lex Av -NY 10017
(212) 506-1700 .. **Cowherd**, Matthew K '07 Kasowitz BT&F LLP -1633 Bway -NY 10019
(718) 474-0111 .. **Cowhey-Macron**, Marilyn '89 (Macron & C, PC) -257 Beach 116th -Rckwy Pk 11694
(516) 984-5483 .. **Cowie**, Ellin Regis '95 -46 Prnctn -Gdn Cty 11530 **Fx:**706-0839
(212) 841-1000 .. **Cowie**, Kevin K '07 %Covington & B LLP -620 8th Av -NY 10018
(212) 381-7000 .. **Cowit**, Elizabeth '92 OfCnsl Sabin B&G LLP -4 Times Sq -NY 10036
(212) 868-1010 .. **Cowit**, Evan Scott '95 %Kudman TA LLP -350 5th Av -NY 10118
(845) 225-3026 .. **Cowle**, Rick S '04 -95 Gleneida Av -Carmel 10512 **Fx:**225-3026
(646) 502-7001 .. **Cowles**, Jane CoCo '06 OfCnsl JSBarkats PLLC -100 Church -NY 10007 **Fx:**607-5544
(516) 877-5600 .. **Cowley**, James J '77 %R Tusa -1225 Franklin Av -Gdn Cty 11530 **Fx:**877-5695
(212) 344-3100 .. **Cowling**, Dennis O '88 %Frenkel LWW&G,LLP -1 Whitehall -NY 10004
(716) 841-4265 .. **Cownie**, George L '74 %HSBC Bank -1 HSBC Ctr -Buffalo 14203 **Fx:**841-5087
(516) 280-2281 .. **Cox**, Andrew G '93 (Marcote & Assoc,PC) -403 Merrick Av -E Meadow 11554 **Fx:**280-2283
(212) 596-9000 .. **Cox**, Brianna J '08 %Ropes & G LLP -1211 Av of Amer -NY 10036
(212) 735-3000 .. **Cox**, Christopher D '98 %Skadden ASM&F LLP -4 Times Sq -NY 10036
(212) 701-3000 .. **Cox**, Christopher T '94 (Cahill G&R LLP) -80 Pine -NY 10005 **Fx:**269-5420
(718) 786-0543 .. **Cox**, Deborah A '03 M Parisi & Son Constructn Co,Inc -54-65 48th -Maspeth 11378
(718) 340-4241 .. **Cox**, Douglas C '03 CUNY Law Schl -65-21 Main -Flushng 11367 **Fx:**340-4482
(914) 945-3593 .. **Cox**, Ellen Gillerman '97 %IBM -1101 Kitchawan Rd Bx218 -Yorktwn Hts 10598 **Fx:**945-2973
(518) 584-1500 .. **Cox**, James S '90 (Snyder KTC&C,LLP) -160 West Av Bx4367 -Saratoga Spgs 12866
(518) 457-8901 .. **Cox**, Jean M '92 %Emergency Mgmt Ofc -1220 Wshngtn Av -Albany 12226
(315) 435-2170 .. **Cox**, Jeanne N '08 %Cnty Atty -421 Mntgmry -Syracuse 13202 **Fx:**435-5729
(212) 501-3592 .. **Cox**, John J '85 -34-23 Steinway -LIC 11101
(716) 881-3010 .. **Cox**, Jonathan D '02 (Cohen & L,PC) -343 Elmwood Av Bx5204 -Buffalo 14213
(516) 921-3298 .. **Cox**, Jos E '76 -172 Berry Hill Rd -Syosset 11791
(212) 724-1496 .. **Cox**, Judith B '89 -316 W 84th -NY 10024
(212) 423-3500 .. **Cox**, Judith S '85 Guggenheim Fndtn -1071 5th Av -NY 10128 **Fx:**423-3650
(212) 963-6802 .. **Cox**, Katherine E '99 UN Station -405 E 42nd -NY 10017
(716) 856-5012 .. **Cox**, Kevin D '56 OfCnsl Anspach ME,LLP -2400 Main Pl Twr -Buffalo 14202
(315) 252-3846 .. **Cox**, Kevin M '97 %Camardo Law Firm,PC -127 Genesee -Auburn 13021 **Fx:**252-3508
(718) 452-1457 .. **Cox**, Marcelino Edmundo '83 -220 Patchen Av -Brklyn 11233
(607) 757-2361 .. **Cox**, Marcy L '91 -3550 George F Hwy -Endicott 13760
(631) 226-2100 .. **Cox**, Michl S '92 (Phillips WAC&M) -165 S Wellwood Av -Lindenhrst 11757
(212) 449-6577 .. **Cox**, Mitchell M '91 %Merrill Lynch -225 Lbrty -NY 10080
(212) 953-6633 .. **Cox Padmore Skolnik & Shakarchy LLP** -630 3rd Av -NY 10017 **Fx:**949-6943
(212) 209-4800 .. **Cox**, Patrick M '97 (Brown R LLP) -7 Times Sq -NY 10036
(585) 238-4590 .. **Cox**, Ralph W II '73 Excellus Hlth Plan,Inc -165 Court -Rchstr 14647 **Fx:**238-3619
(315) 472-4481 .. **Cox**, Robt B '70 (Ali P&C) -614 James -Syracuse 13203
(914) 323-7000 .. **Cox**, Ryan T '09 %Wilson EME&D LLP -3 Gannett Dr -White Plns 10604
(212) 506-1700 .. **Cox**, Sarah M '09 %Kasowitz BT&F LLP -1633 Bway -NY 10019
(212) 479-5861 .. **Cox**, Stephen D '02 Eurohypo AG -1114 Av of Amer -NY 10036
(315) 798-5766 .. **Cox**, Steven G '97 %DA -800 Park Av -Utica 13501 **Fx:**798-5582
(212) 925-1208 .. **Cox**, Theo N '83 -401 Bway -NY 10013 **Fx:**925-5188
(718) 874-8227 .. **Cox**, Timothy C '05 Quadra Srvcs -Bx676 -NY 10101
(845) 586-1400 .. **Cox**, Timothy E '97 Catskill Watershed Corp -Bx569 -Margaretvll 12455 **Fx:**586-1401
(212) 986-1200 .. **Cox**, Wm H '83 (Gordon HR&C LLP) -355 Lex Av -NY 10017

(914) 762-3688 .. **Coxen,** Erin '07 Triad Grp -400 Exec Blvd -Ossining 10562
(518) 463-2927 .. **Coxeter,** Danl T '78 (Coxeter & C) -Bx219 -Duanesbrg 12056
(518) 463-2927 .. **Coxeter,** Susan J '80 (Coxeter & C) -Bx219 -Duanesbrg 12056
(518) 474-4552 .. **Cox-Gietman,** Judith L '02 Insurance Dept -99 Wshngtn Av -Albany 12257 **Fx:**486-2218
(631) 331-4013 .. **Coy,** Gayle L '95 -9A Oliver -Pt Jffrsn Sta 11776 **Fx:**(877) 406-1299
(518) 884-5000 .. **Coy,** Julie P '91 %State Farm -100 State Farm Pl Bx8000 -Ballston Spa 12020
(631) 732-3080 .. **Coy,** Kenneth G '97 -17 Edna Ln -Selden 11784
(718) 250-2000 .. **Coy,** Michelle P '01 %DA -350 Jay -Brklyn 11201 **Fx:**250-2314
(716) 285-3525 .. **Coykendall,** Wm Maxwell '95 (Tisdale C&W) -800 Main -Niagara Fls 14302 **Fx:**285-8574
(212) 351-4000 .. **Coyle,** Anne M '07 %Gibson D&C LLP -200 Park Av -NY 10166
(516) 745-0160 .. **Coyle,** Denise R '83 Benjamin Cos -377 Oak Bx739 -Gdn Cty 11530
(212) 458-1630 .. **Coyle,** Jeffrey M '89 %AIG -175 Water -NY 10038
(716) 854-4705 .. **Coyle,** John M '04 Lippman O -300 Pearl -Buffalo 14202
(212) 943-9080 .. **Coyle,** Leonor Hidalgo '07 %Virginia & A -111 Bway -NY 10006
(212) 225-2000 .. **Coyle,** Lisa M '06 %Cleary GS&H -1 Lbrty Plz -NY 10006
(718) 543-2200 .. **Coyle,** Lorraine '81 (Coyle & Assoc,LLP) -5911 Riverdale Av -Bronx 10471 **Fx:**543-2156
(212) 312-7254 .. **Coyle,** Michl F '80 %State Ins Fund -199 Church -NY 10007 **Fx:**385-9199
(631) 853-5212 .. **Coyle,** Robt J Jr. '06 %Leg Aid -400 Carleton Av Bx9082 -Central Islip 11722 **Fx:**853-7798
(718) 474-4955 .. **Coyle,** Susan M '96 -609 Cross Bay Blvd -Broad Channel 11693 **Fx:**474-8402
(212) 558-4000 .. **Coyle,** Victoria A '09 %Sullivan & C LLP -125 Broad -NY 10004
(212) 816-3772 .. **Coyle,** Vincent J Jr. '86 Citi Global Transaction Srvcs -388 Greenwich -NY 10013
(212) 841-5277 .. **Coyle,** Wm P '92 Natl Ctr Addctn & Substnc Abuse -633 3rd Av -NY 10017
(607) 739-3841 .. **Coyles,** Donald B '76 Shull & C -2300 Grnd Cntrl Av -Horseheads 14845 **Fx:**739-4608
(212) 931-7859 .. **Coyles,** Jonathan D '06 MLB -245 Park Av -NY 10167
(212) 964-6611 .. **Coyne,** Bridget E '90 %Lester SK&D -120 Bway -NY 10271
(518) 455-4637 .. **Coyne,** Carol E '88 %NYS Assembly -440 Cptl -Albany 12224 **Fx:**455-5930
(585) 899-1414 .. **Coyne,** Ellen J '89 (Harris COJW&L) -300 Linden Oaks -Rchstr 14625
(631) 549-8382 .. **Coyne,** Francis J '61 -240 Wshngtn Dr -Centerprt 11721
(917) 778-6600 .. **Coyne,** Jeffrey M '96 %J Toomey -485 Lex Av -NY 10017 **Fx:**778-7048
(212) 878-7049 .. **Coyne,** Laureen McDermott '92 MTA -347 Mad Av -NY 10017 **Fx:**878-0162
(212) 307-9300 .. **Coyne,** Marissa L '01 Prada USA Corp -610 W 52nd -NY 10019
(212) 552-0941 .. **Coyne,** Michl F '84 JP Morgan Chase -1 Chase Manh Plz -NY 10081
(212) 644-1010 .. **Coyne,** Michele Ann '96 %Kauff M&M LLP -950 3rd Av -NY 10022
(212) 747-1230 .. **Coyne,** Roderick '90 (McMahon M&G LLP) -55 Washington -Brklyn 11201
(516) 294-4141 .. **Coyne,** Russell J '75 -72 Jericho Tpk -Mineola 11501 **Fx:**294-4600
(718) 254-7000 .. **Coyne,** Sarah M '01 %US Atty -271 Cadman Plz E -Brklyn 11201 **Fx:**254-6479
(718) 286-2000 .. **Coyne,** Stephen M '01 %Leg Aid -120-46 Qns Blvd -Kew Gdns 11415 **Fx:**286-2286
(718) 729-9395 .. **Coyne,** Thos P '87 -36-11 36th -LIC 11106
(315) 471-3151 .. **Coyne,** W Carroll '57 OfCnsl Hancock & E,LLP -1500 AXA Twr I Bx4976 -Syracuse 13221
(718) 520-3614 .. **Coz,** Sol Edgar '87 %Civil Ct -89-17 Sutphin Blvd -Jamaica 11435 **Fx:**262-7107
(212) 883-4900 .. **Cozen O'Connor** -277 Park Av -NY 10172 **Fx:**986-0604
(212) 509-9400 .. **Cozen O'Connor** -45 Bway Atrium -NY 10006 **Fx:**509-9492
(212) 351-4500 .. **Cozier,** Barry A '76 (Epstein B&G,PC) -250 Park Av -NY 10177
(212) 698-3500 .. **Cozier,** Keith C '09 Dechert LLP -1095 Av of Amer -NY 10036
(914) 686-9010 .. **Cozza,** Michl J '79 (Wilson BCC&C,PC) -2 William -White Plns 10601
(518) 828-3414 .. **Cozzolino,** Beth G '86 (DA) -325 Columbia -Hudson 12534 **Fx:**828-8491
(518) 828-3414 .. **Cozzolino,** Michl A '97 %DA -325 Columbia -Hudson 12534 **Fx:**828-8491
(718) 263-8025 .. **Crabill,** John C '77 (Gasser & H) -106-19 Metro Av -Frst Hlls 11375
(518) 436-3404 .. **Crable,** Paige E '95 (Bixby C&S,PLLC) -19 Dove -Albany 12210
(631) 753-0200 .. **Crabtree,** Andrew L '93 -225 Broadhllw Rd -Melvll 11747 **Fx:**753-0950
(212) 416-8000 .. **Crabtree,** Sarah D '02 %Dept of Law -120 Bway -NY 10271
(631) 271-5000 .. **Craco & Ellsworth, LLP** -7 High -Huntngtn 11743 **Fx:**271-7290
(631) 271-5000 .. **Craco,** Louis A '58 OfCnsl Craco & E,LLP -7 High -Huntngtn 11743
(212) 571-0550 .. **Craco,** Louis A Jr. '89 (Allegaert B&V LLP) -111 Bway -NY 10006
(631) 271-5000 .. **Craco,** Paul V '95 (Craco & E,LLP) -7 High -Huntngtn 11743
(212) 326-3939 .. **Craddock,** Clark '05 %Jones D -222 E 41st -NY 10017
(212) 310-8000 .. **Craddock,** Erin M '09 %Weil G&M LLP -767 5th Av -NY 10153
(212) 822-9541 .. **Craemer,** Rebecca A '07 Advocates for Children -151 W 30th -NY 10001
(516) 766-6200 .. **Crafa,** Jos R '85 (Crafa & S PC) -100 N Centre Av -Rockvll Ctr 11570 **Fx:**766-1109
(212) 576-5617 .. **Craft,** Cindy M '93 NY Life Ins -51 Mad Av -NY 10010
(212) 513-3200 .. **Craft,** Randal R Jr. '69 (Holland & K LLP) -31 W 52nd -NY 10019
(212) 676-7804 .. **Crafton,** James S '06 %HRA -220 Church -NY 10013
(718) 579-7900 .. **Crafton,** Jessica M '06 Leg Aid -900 Sheridan Av -Bronx 10451 **Fx:**293-8744
(845) 791-7676 .. **Cragan,** Thos H '01 %Shawn Law Ofcs -30 North Bx1320 -Monticello 12701 **Fx:**791-4660
(212) 715-1000 .. **Cragg,** Simon R '04 %Arnold & P LLP -399 Park Av -NY 10022
(914) 723-0769 .. **Craig,** A Douglas P '61 -16 Wyndham Rd -Scarsdale 10583
(212) 308-0070 .. **Craig,** Alicyn B '01 (McCusker AR&C,PC) -805 3rd Av -NY 10022
(212) 232-1300 .. **Craig,** AnneMarie F '04 %Lewis BB&S LLP -77 Water -NY 10005
(914) 428-1707 .. **Craig,** Benjamin M '08 US House of Rep -222 Mamaroneck Av -White Plns 10605
(516) 764-2800 .. **Craig,** Brian P '87 %Goldberg & C -66 N Vllg Av -Rockvll Ctr 11570
(212) 918-3000 .. **Craig,** Derek J '05 %Hogan L LLP -875 3rd Av -NY 10022
(518) 885-9292 .. **Craig,** James P '92 (Brown C&H) -1 E High -Ballston Spa 12020
(718) 858-0306 .. **Craig,** Joan L '76 -28 Old Fulton -Brklyn 11201 **Fx:**254-9156
(212) 909-6000 .. **Craig,** John S '05 %Debevoise & P LLP -919 3rd Av -NY 10022
(518) 885-9292 .. **Craig,** Kimberly A '06 (Brown C&H) -1 E High -Ballston Spa 12020
(585) 586-1060 .. **Craig,** Peter J '85 (P Craig & Assoc.PC) -Bx439 -Pittsfrd 14534 **Fx:**264-1442
(212) 455-2000 .. **Craig,** Summer '04 %Simpson T&B LLP -425 Lex Av -NY 10017
(718) 546-0950 .. **Craig-Trauner,** Jessica J '01 %Dept of Correction -75-20 Astoria Blvd -E Elmhrst 11370
(212) 848-4000 .. **Craigwell-Graham,** Jeannetta K '10 Shearman & S LLP -599 Lex Av -NY 10022
(212) 318-6000 .. **Crain,** Angelique M '05 %Paul HJ&W LLP -75 E 55th -NY 10022
(585) 428-6753 .. **Crain,** Michele Romance '88 -30 Church -Rchstr 14614
(518) 257-1443 .. **Crain,** Steven A '82 %CSEA,Inc -143 Wshngtn Av Bx7125 -Albany 12224 **Fx:**449-1525
(212) 218-5500 .. **Crainer,** Steven M '98 (Seyfarth S LLP) -620 8th Av -NY 10018
(914) 253-3774 .. **Cram,** Douglas M '69 %Pepsico -700 Andrsn Hill Rd -Purchase 10577
(646) 428-3900 .. **Cramer,** Anna Maria '90 %Dept of Educ -32 Old Slip -NY 10005 **Fx:**428-3890
(212) 421-3350 .. **Cramer,** Edw M '50 -110 E 59th -NY 10022 **Fx:**826-9315
(212) 589-4200 .. **Cramer,** Jonathan P '82 (Baker & H LLP) -45 Rckfllr Plz -NY 10111
(518) 270-2950 .. **Cramer,** Kelly A '00 %Cnty Atty -1600 7th Av -Troy 12180 **Fx:**270-2954
(212) 867-5800 .. **Cramer,** Kevin D '93 (Osler H&H LLP) -620 8th Av -NY 10018
(212) 448-1100 .. **Cramer,** Lauren B '96 %McLaughlin & S,LLP -260 Mad Av -NY 10016
(212) 931-0704 .. **Cramer,** Martin R '61 -80 Maiden Ln -NY 10038 **Fx:**(201) 692-1139
(212) 259-3900 .. **Cramer,** Roger L '88 -250 W 57th -NY 10107
(212) 504-6000 .. **Cramer,** Shanell M '02 %Cadwalader W&T LLP -1 World Fncl Ctr -NY 10281
(315) 492-3000 .. **Cramer Smith & Miller,PC** -3175 E Genesee -Syracuse 13224 **Fx:**492-4007
(212) 684-0300 .. **Cramer,** Steven C '94 (Bauman K&G LLP) -28 W 44th -NY 10036
(607) 272-2314 .. **Cramer,** Thos D '87 (Thaler & T) -309 N Tioga Bx266 -Ithaca 14851 **Fx:**272-8466
(212) 450-4000 .. **Crames,** Michl J '61 SrCnsl Davis P&W LLP -450 Lex Av -NY 10017
(212) 468-8000 .. **Crampe,** Michiko Ito '76 (Morrison & F LLP) -1290 Av of Amer -NY 10104
(607) 255-5251 .. **Cramton,** Chas D '84 %Cornell Law Schl -Myron Taylor Hall -Ithaca 14853 **Fx:**255-7193
(315) 474-2943 .. **Crance,** Rebecca Ann '05 %Sugarman Law Firm,LLP -211 W Jffrsn -Syracuse 13202
(212) 996-4513 .. **Cranch,** Constance W '82 -1125 Park Av -NY 10128 **Fx:**996-4513
(212) 969-1646 .. **Cranch,** Laurence E '74 Alliance Bernstein LP -1345 Av of Amer -NY 10105 **Fx:**554-4639
(607) 936-3785 .. **Crandall,** Catherine B '88 %J Ullman & Assoc -51 E Market -Corning 14830 **Fx:**936-8361
(315) 866-1445 .. **Crandall,** Chas E III '80 -410 N Main -Herkimer 13350 **Fx:**866-7132
(212) 848-7540 .. **Crandall,** Jeffrey P '83 (Shearman & S LLP) -599 Lex Av -NY 10022
(315) 867-1155 .. **Crandall,** John H '83 (DA) -301 N Wshngtn -Herkimer 13350 **Fx:**867-1348
(518) 374-4500 .. **Crandall,** Karen R '87 -115 Clinton -Schnctdy 12305
(516) 466-8005 .. **Crandell,** Brenda M '88 (Tashlik KG&C PC) -40 Cuttermill Rd -Gt Neck 11021
(716) 847-8400 .. **Crandell,** Patrick D '09 %Phillips L LLP -3400 HSBC Ctr -Buffalo 14203
(718) 590-2000 .. **Crane,** Catherine A '09 %DA -198 E 161st -Bronx 10451 **Fx:**590-6477
(212) 465-6000 .. **Crane,** Christopher J '06 %Madison Sq Grdn,LP -2 Penn Plz -NY 10121 **Fx:**465-6011
(212) 373-3000 .. **Crane,** Danl A '00 Cnsl Paul WRW&G LLP -1285 Av of Amer -NY 10019
(585) 325-6202 .. **Crane,** Howard R '81 (Relin G&C LLP) -28 E Main -Rchstr 14614
(518) 432-8000 .. **Crane,** James B II '84 (Crane & P) -48 Howard -Albany 12207
(914) 937-7272 .. **Crane,** John M II '97 (J Crane,PC) -342 N Main -Pt Chester 10573 **Fx:**937-7277
(212) 486-4430 .. **Crane,** Jonah M A '06 Cnsl Sen C Schumer -757 3rd Av -NY 10017 **Fx:**486-7693
(212) 725-7111 .. **Crane,** Lauren G '05 %Bender RI&R LLP -451 Park Av S -NY 10016
(585) 768-8946 .. **Crane,** Manley C '91 -43 Myrtle -Le Roy 14482 **Fx:**768-8946
(212) 340-0400 .. **Crane,** Melissa A '92 Applt Div 1st Dept -27 Mad Av -NY 10010 **Fx:**889-4412
(212) 773-3815 .. **Crane,** Michl J '87 %Ernst & Young,LLP -5 Times Sq -NY 10036
(518) 432-8000 .. **Crane & Parente** -48 Howard -Albany 12207 **Fx:**432-0086
(212) 536-3900 .. **Crane,** Roger R Jr. '74 (K&L Gates LLP) -599 Lex Av -NY 10022
(212) 415-3600 .. **Crane,** Ronald L '76 %Omnicom Group -437 Mad Av -NY 10022 **Fx:**415-3530
(585) 530-3050 .. **Crane,** Samantha J '95 %MHLS -50 East Av -Rchstr 14604 **Fx:**530-3079
(212) 450-4000 .. **Crane,** Sharon L '03 Davis P&W LLP -450 Lex Av -NY 10017
(212) 751-2700 .. **Crane,** Stephen G '63 %JAMS -620 8th Av -NY 10018 **Fx:**751-4099
(212) 788-0928 .. **Crane,** Thos C '71 %Law Dept -100 Church -NY 10007 **Fx:**788-0367
(607) 257-3282 .. **Crane,** Wm D '04 CFCU Comm Credit Union -1030 Craft Rd -Ithaca 14850
(845) 454-5150 .. **Crane,** Wm G '58 -11 Market -Poughkeepsie 12601 **Fx:**454-6612
(212) 938-2337 .. **Craner,** John A '90 (Craner SS&S,PC) -60 E 42nd -NY 10165
(212) 478-7200 .. **Craner,** Katharine G '03 %Hahn & H LLP -488 Mad Av -NY 10022
(212) 506-5000 .. **Craner,** Matthew L '98 (Orrick H&S LLP) -51 W 52nd -NY 10019
(212) 218-5660 .. **Craner,** Mitchel B '62 -60 E 42nd -NY 10165 **Fx:**218-5653
(212) 938-2337 .. **Craner Satkin Scheer & Schwartz, PC** -60 E 42nd -NY 10165 **Fx:**321-2101
(716) 853-4080 .. **Crangle,** Jos F '60 OfCnsl Colucci & G,PC -424 Main -Buffalo 14202
(518) 828-9252 .. **Cranna,** Kenneth G '92 -5 Bayley Blvd -Hudson 12534 **Fx:**828-9252
(518) 822-0453 .. **Cranna,** Wm '87 %Hon P Czajka-Surrogate -401 Union -Hudson 12534
(845) 357-4422 .. **Crannage,** Sonia B '88 %Sichol & H -139 Lafayette Av Bx359 -Suffern 10901

(212) 957-7600 .. **Cranston,** Duane A '02 %Cohen & G LLP -800 3rd Av -NY 10022
(914) 422-4069 .. **Cranstoun,** Jennifer B '00 Pace Womens Justice Ctr -78 N Bway -White Plns 10603
(212) 506-2500 .. **Craparo,** Therese '04 %Mayer B LLP -1675 Bway -NY 10019
(716) 847-7680 .. **Crapsi,** Paul V '94 %Div of Human Rights -65 Court -Buffalo 14202 **Fx:**847-7625
(914) 763-8647 .. **Crary,** Calvert D '68 -Bx192 -Waccabuc 10597
(212) 935-3000 .. **Crasson,** Sara J '06 %Mintz LCFG&P,PC -666 3rd Av -NY 10017
(718) 529-4242 .. **Crasto,** Anthony C '90 (Crasto & Assoc,PC) -161-10A Crossbay Blvd -Howard Bch 11414 **Fx:**323-9407
(212) 474-1000 .. **Cravath Swaine & Moore LLP** -825 8th Av -NY 10019 **Fx:**474-3700
(518) 587-7812 .. **Craven,** Judith A '88 -163 Phila -Saratoga Spgs 12866 **Fx:**587-7809
(516) 294-5200 .. **Craven,** Thos R Jr. '99 %Picciano & S -900 Merchants Cncrs -Westbury 11590
(518) 455-4257 .. **Craw,** Marc D '90 %Minority Cnsl's Ofc -The Cptl -Albany 12248 **Fx:**455-5930
(518) 465-7933 .. **Crawford,** A Kevin '79 %Assn of Towns of NYS -146 State -Albany 12207 **Fx:**465-0724
(631) 854-8515 .. **Crawford,** Alexander J '98 OfCnsl Police Dept -30 Yaphank Av -Yaphank 11980 **Fx:**854-8519
(718) 273-9414 .. **Crawford,** Allyn J '95 -1882 Victory Blvd -Staten Isl 10314 **Fx:**273-9418
(718) 838-7878 .. **Crawford,** Amy L '02 %Bronx Defenders -860 Crtlandt Av -Bronx 10451 **Fx:**665-0100
(212) 323-2250 .. **Crawford,** Andrea L '98 %HHC-OLA-Medical Litigation -346 Bway -NY 10013 **Fx:**323-2251
(212) 451-2300 .. **Crawford,** Aneliya S '09 %Olshan GFR&W LLP -65 E 55th -NY 10022
(212) 326-3939 .. **Crawford,** Bridget A '09 %Jones D -222 E 41st -NY 10017
(914) 422-4416 .. **Crawford,** Bridget J '97 %Pace Law Schl -78 N Bway -White Plns 10603 **Fx:**422-4039
(212) 819-2106 .. **Crawford,** Carla R '06 Iconix Brand Grp Inc -1450 Bway -NY 10018
(518) 481-1544 .. **Crawford,** Elizabeth M '04 %DA -Ct Hse -Malone 12953 **Fx:**481-1545
(212) 318-3000 .. **Crawford,** James R '95 Cnsl Fulbright & J LLP -666 5th Av -NY 10103
(212) 804-4200 .. **Crawford,** Jeffrey C '88 (Mound CW&G) -One Bttry Pk Plz -NY 10004
(212) 777-8395 .. **Crawford,** John A III '71 %Allworth Press -10 E 23rd -NY 10010 **Fx:**777-8261
(212) 751-9800 .. **Crawford,** Kalisha M '07 %Morelli R PC -950 3rd Av -NY 10022
(212) 425-5191 .. **Crawford,** Lynne E '90 Mischel & H,PC -1 Whitehall -NY 10004
(518) 465-3524 .. **Crawford,** Mardi E '98 %NYS Defenders Assn -194 Wshngtn Av -Albany 12210 **Fx:**465-3249
(718) 776-0001 .. **Crawford,** Mark A '98 (Drummond & C PC) -221-10 Jamaica Av -Qns Vllg 11428
(718) 680-6204 .. **Crawford,** Patricia A '04 -Bx90022 -Brklyn 11209 **Fx:**680-6204
(973) 596-4803 .. **Crawford,** Philip W '07 (Gibbons PC) -1 Penn Plz -NY 10119 **Fx:**639-6327
(716) 853-3801 .. **Crawford,** Robt A Jr. '88 (Kenney SL&N,LLP) -14 Lafayette Sq -Buffalo 14203
(212) 735-3000 .. **Crawford,** Robt A III '09 %Skadden ASM&F LLP -4 Times Sq -NY 10036
(914) 683-5313 .. **Crawford,** Roger C '84 SrCnsl CEO Title Agency -399 Knollwood Rd -White Plns 10603 **Fx:**683-3265
(518) 438-3585 .. **Crawford,** Stefanie D '09 Special Funds Conservation Committee -2 Twr Pl -Albany 12203
(212) 816-9276 .. **Crawford-Neher,** T Addison '96 %Salomon Smith Barney -388 Greenwich -NY 10013
(914) 738-6076 .. **Crawley,** Anne M '99 (Pinto & C,LLP) -210 6th Av -Pelham 10803 **Fx:**712-0647
(866) 931-4494 .. **Crawley,** Brian J '86 Social Security Admin -375 N Bway -Jericho 11753
(212) 713-8268 .. **Crawley,** Georgina D '04 College Bd -45 Columbus Av -NY 10023
(212) 558-4000 .. **Crawshaw,** Donald R '84 (Sullivan & C LLP) -125 Broad -NY 10004
(212) 969-3000 .. **Crawshaw-Sparks,** Sandra A '89 (Proskauer R LLP) -1585 Bway -NY 10036
(212) 460-3245 .. **Cray,** Brian E '85 Con Ed -4 Irving Pl -NY 10003
(212) 906-1200 .. **Craythorn,** Dennis G '06 %Latham & W -885 3rd Av -NY 10022
(718) 625-2200 .. **Crea,** Jos '47 %Bklyn Law Schl -250 Joralemon -Brklyn 11201 **Fx:**780-0393
(917) 226-1881 .. **Creadore,** Donald E Jr. '87 Creadore Law Firm PC -305 Bway -NY 10007
(585) 530-3050 .. **Creahan,** Emmett J '82 %MHLS -50 East Av -Rchstr 14604 **Fx:**530-3079
(716) 881-3010 .. **Cream,** Douglas S '70 (Cohen & L,PC) -343 Elmwood Av Bx5204 -Buffalo 14213
(212) 558-4000 .. **Creamer,** Ronald E Jr. '92 (Sullivan & C LLP) -125 Broad -NY 10004
(845) 268-1828 .. **Crean,** James R '92 -20 Old Lk Rd -Congers 10920
(212) 697-3122 .. **Crean,** Peter T '82 (Martin C&B LLP) -220 E 42nd -NY 10017
(585) 586-8480 .. **Creary,** Wm J Jr. '85 (Creary & C) -18 N Main -Pittsfrd 14534
(518) 474-8816 .. **Creaser,** Michl K '93 %Comm Prof Standrds -40 Steuben -Albany 12207 **Fx:**474-0389
(212) 250-2500 .. **Creasman,** Melinda Anne '05 Deutsche Bank -60 Wall -NY 10005
(212) 408-5100 .. **Creazzo,** Felipe E '06 %Chadbourne & P LLP -30 Rckfllr Plz -NY 10112
(212) 588-0330 .. **Creditor,** Paul '60 -747 3rd Av -NY 10017 **Fx:**588-0440
(212) 421-2111 .. **Creditor,** Paul '60 OfCnsl Granoff W&F,PC -747 3rd Av -NY 10017
(718) 793-1331 .. **Creditor,** Richd M '64 -118-21 Qns Blvd -Frst Hlls 11375
(516) 802-0630 .. **Creech,** Jason W '07 %Simmons J,LLP -115 Eileen Way -Syosset 11791
(212) 906-1200 .. **Creed,** Ayano K '98 %Latham & W -885 3rd Av -NY 10022
(212) 455-2000 .. **Creed,** John J '86 (Simpson T&B LLP) -425 Lex Av -NY 10017
(212) 225-2000 .. **Creede,** Ellen M '79 SpclCnsl Cleary GS&H -1 Lbrty Plz -NY 10006
(631) 656-9220 .. **Creedon,** Peter J Jr. '83 (Creedon & G,PC) -24 Woodbine Av -Northprt 11768 **Fx:**686-6718
(212) 578-6476 .. **Creegan,** Patrick J '93 %MetLife -27-01 Qns Plz N -LIC 11101
(845) 569-9110 .. **Creekmore,** Lewis G '90 %Leg Srvcs -123 Grand -Newburgh 12550 **Fx:**569-9120
(212) 421-4213 .. **Creel,** Thos L '67 T Creel LLC -25 Beekman Pl -NY 10022
(212) 891-1600 .. **Creelan,** Jeremy M '97 (Jenner & B LLP) -919 3rd Av -NY 10022
(718) 293-3100 .. **Cregan,** Mark T '90 -1465 Nelson Av -Bronx 10452
(518) 465-2333 .. **Cregg,** George W Jr. '72 (Hodgson R LLP) -677 Bway -Albany 12207
(585) 324-0669 .. **Crego,** Frank T '69 SrCnsl Forsyth HOK&M,PC -1 Chase Sq -Rchstr 14604
(716) 854-0007 .. **Creighton,** Catherine '91 (Creighton PJ&G) -295 Main -Buffalo 14203 **Fx:**854-0004
(631) 852-2500 .. **Creighton,** Elizabeth A '02 %DA -200 Center Dr -Rvrhead 11901 **Fx:**852-1769
(914) 761-4200 .. **Creighton,** James F '95 %Steinberg & C,LLP -50 Main -White Plns 10606
(516) 355-0800 .. **Creighton,** Michl J '81 Cnsl Millenium Abstract Corp -35 N Tyson Av -Floral Pk 11001 **Fx:**282-0222
(516) 227-0700 .. **Creighton,** Robt C '86 (Farrell F,PC) -1320 RXR Plz -Uniondale 11556
(718) 834-6000 .. **Creinis,** Paul D '89 -16 Court -Brklyn 11241
(212) 351-4000 .. **Creizman,** Eric M '00 %Gibson D&C LLP -200 Park Av -NY 10166
(845) 592-7000 .. **Crelin-Mayle,** Judith M '04 %Donoghue TA&D LLP -2517 Route 52 -Hopewell Junct 12533
(212) 969-3000 .. **Crelinsten,** Jason C '05 %Proskauer R LLP -1585 Bway -NY 10036
(212) 696-6000 .. **Cremades Roman,** Bernardo M '10 %Curtis M-PC&M LLP -101 Park Av -NY 10178
(212) 661-9100 .. **Cremer,** Allen '97 %Otterbourg SH&R,PC -230 Park Av -NY 10169
(212) 701-3000 .. **Cremins,** Megan E '08 %Cahill G&R LLP -80 Pine -NY 10005 **Fx:**269-5420
(518) 474-0665 .. **Cremo,** John V '95 %Dept of Law -The Cptl -Albany 12224
(518) 408-0469 .. **Cremo,** Patrick J '99 %Workers Comp Bd -20 Park -Albany 12207
(212) 836-8000 .. **Cremona,** Nicholas J '00 Cnsl Kaye S LLP -425 Park Av -NY 10022
(914) 967-7019 .. **Cresap,** Joan M '89 -1 Greenacres Dr -Rye 10580
(212) 592-1400 .. **Crescenti,** Brooke E '07 %Herrick,F LLP -2 Park Av -NY 10016
(212) 233-8300 .. **Cresci,** Carl '60 (Epstein & C) -7 Dey -NY 10007
(518) 402-0549 .. **Cresho,** Anthony J '00 %UIA Bd -Troy Atrium Bx15126 -Albany 12212 **Fx:**402-6208
(212) 973-0572 .. **Crespi,** Robt H '95 (Wolff & S PC) -140 Bway -NY 10005
(212) 458-2902 .. **Crespo,** Kimberly L '00 %AIGTS -175 Water -NY 10038
(646) 386-3794 .. **Crespo,** Louis '87 Supreme Ct Spcl Referee -71 Thomas -NY 10013 **Fx:**(212) 374-8417
(718) 345-4519 .. **Crespo,** Margaret '03 -556 Van Siclen Av -Brklyn 11207
(585) 272-0540 .. **Cressman,** Sarah E '02 %Thomas & S LLP -693 East Av -Rchstr 14607
(212) 661-9100 .. **Cretella,** James M '05 %Otterbourg SH&R,PC -230 Park Av -NY 10169
(212) 373-3000 .. **Crew,** Jesse S '09 %Paul WRW&G LLP -1285 Av of Amer -NY 10019
(347) 404-9133 .. **Crew,** Kelsey C '09 Civil Ct -141 Lvngstn -Brklyn 11201 **Fx:**(718) 643-3733
(518) 402-9512 .. **Crew,** Michelle Ann '95 %DEC -625 Bway -Albany 12233 **Fx:**402-9018
(516) 229-6000 .. **Crewe Gerbasi,** Marcella J '93 %R Lau & Assoc -300 Jericho Quad Bx9040 -Jericho 11753 **Fx:**229-6167
(914) 949-1095 .. **Cribari,** Arnold D '77 -175 Main -White Plns 10601 **Fx:**949-5348
(212) 871-5770 .. **Crichlow,** Anne C '07 %Berry & Assoc PC -551 Mad Av -NY 10022 **Fx:**871-5774
(212) 858-1000 .. **Crichlow,** David A '90 (Pillsbury WSP LLP) -1540 Bway -NY 10036
(315) 443-2524 .. **Criddle,** Evan J '04 %Syracuse Univ Cllg of Law -Wht Hall -Syracuse 13244 **Fx:**443-4213
(212) 455-2000 .. **Crider,** S Todd '92 (Simpson T&B LLP) -425 Lex Av -NY 10017
(212) 593-6700 .. **Cridland,** Peter C '07 %Aaronson RF&D,LLP -757 3rd Av -NY 10017
(518) 325-4100 .. **Crill,** Juliette M '94 -119 Rodman Rd -Hillsdale 12529 **Fx:**325-5100
(212) 619-1919 .. **Crilley,** Patrick C '95 -233 Bway -NY 10279 **Fx:**214-0311
(212) 850-1864 .. **Crilly,** Dennis J '96 %J&W Seligman & Co -100 Park Av -NY 10017 **Fx:**922-5731
(516) 561-6622 .. **Crimeni,** Carmela '99 %Simon & M -99 W Hawthorne Av -Vly Stream 11580
(585) 753-3480 .. **Crimi,** Jos P '89 Conflict Def -30 W Broad -Rchstr 14614 **Fx:**753-3489
(718) 990-6018 .. **Crimm,** Nina J '88 %St John's Law Schl -8000 Utopia Pkwy -Jamaica 11439 **Fx:**591-1855
(718) 330-7861 .. **Crimmins,** Elaine C '84 %ODAR-SSA -111 Lvngstn -Brklyn 11201 **Fx:**330-2009
(212) 833-6760 .. **Crimmins,** Frank L '76 Sony BMG Music Entrtnmnt -550 Mad Av -NY 10022 **Fx:**833-8406
(518) 794-8708 .. **Crimmins,** Ian Lyle '05 %J Kleinbaum -18 Park Row -Chatham 12037 **Fx:**794-8709
(212) 536-3900 .. **Crimmins,** Stephen J '74 (K&L Gates LLP) -599 Lex Av -NY 10022
(315) 524-6040 .. **Crippen,** Patricia M '78 -6301 Furnace Rd -Ontario 14519 **Fx:**524-6221
(212) 326-3939 .. **Crippin,** Marlena S '10 %Jones D -222 E 41st -NY 10017
(212) 277-4000 .. **Cripps,** Stephanie Brown '09 %Freshfields BD LLP -520 Mad Av -NY 10022
(315) 471-9151 .. **Crisafulli,** John S '82 -214 N State -Syracuse 13203
(518) 464-1104 .. **Crisafulli,** Mario S '92 -3 Wshngtn Sq -Albany 12205
(212) 541-6222 .. **Crisafulli,** Sara J '05 %Kane K,PC -1350 Av of Amer -NY 10019
(518) 402-9521 .. **Crisafulli,** Scott W '94 %DEC -625 Bway -Albany 12233 **Fx:**402-9018
(315) 471-3151 .. **Crisafulli,** Timothy P '07 %Hancock & E,LLP -1500 AXA Twr I Bx4976 -Syracuse 13221
(914) 421-1800 .. **Crisalli,** Noelle V '07 %Hocherman T&W LLP -1 N Bway -White Plns 10601
(212) 943-8940 .. **Crisci,** Vincent P '75 (Crisci W&H) -17 State -NY 10004 **Fx:**425-3428
(518) 449-1680 .. **Criscione,** Guy J '81 -817 Mad Av -Albany 12208 **Fx:**427-6720
(518) 408-1495 .. **Criscione,** Joanne E '90 %Dept of Health -Corning Twr 24th Fl -Albany 12237 **Fx:**486-4834
(518) 449-3107 .. **Criscione,** John J '82 (Buckley M&C,PC) -29 Wards Ln -Albany 12204
(518) 462-6677 .. **Criscione,** Nicholas J '69 Criscione Law Firm LLC -120 Bway -Albany 12204 **Fx:**462-6603
(518) 455-7500 .. **Criscione,** Nicole A '97 %Legis Bill Drftng Comm -310 The Cptl -Albany 12224 **Fx:**455-7598

(516) 775-0837 .. **Criscitelli,** Perry T '82 -57 Maple Av -Floral Pk 11001 **Fx:**775-0837
(631) 361-9494 .. **Criscito,** Tricia M '01 %A Vardaro,PC -732 Smithtwn Bypass -Smithtwn 11787 **Fx:**361-8752
(585) 232-3240 .. **Criscuolo,** Vincent Jr. '84 -16 E Main -Rchstr 14614
(212) 949-9022 .. **Crisona,** Richd L '85 (Abelman F&S) -666 3rd Av -NY 10017
(315) 443-4645 .. **Crisp,** Jennifer M '96 %Syracuse Univ-Tech Transfer -2-220 Ctr Sci & Tech -Syracuse 13244 **Fx:**443-8469
(212) 596-9000 .. **Crisp,** Martin J '05 %Ropes & G LLP -1211 Av of Amer -NY 10036
(212) 818-0600 .. **Crispi,** Pat James '84 (Keogh C,PC) -521 5th Av -NY 10175 **Fx:**818-0180
(914) 948-1200 .. **Crispi,** Ronald G '88 (Cerussi & S,PC) -1 N Lex Av -White Plns 10601
(212) 753-5000 .. **Crispi,** Thos M '94 (Schiff H LLP) -900 3rd Av -NY 10022
(845) 638-5001 .. **Crispino,** Dominic A '03 DA -1 S Main -New Cty 10956 **Fx:**638-5070
(212) 371-7000 .. **Crispo,** Pasquale J '75 OfCnsl Todtman NS&J,PC -425 Park Av -NY 10022
(212) 841-1000 .. **Criss,** Jason P '00 SpclCnsl Covington & B LLP -620 8th Av -NY 10018
(212) 277-6500 .. **Crisses,** Andrew M '74 SpclCnsl Dickstein S LLP -1633 Bway -NY 10019
(518) 463-7784 .. **Crist,** Craig M '96 %Dreyer B LLP -75 Columbia -Albany 12210
(516) 739-0102 .. **Cristal,** Jane '87 -200 Old Cntry Rd -Mineola 11501
(914) 946-1400 .. **Cristantello,** Elliot A '67 OfCnsl Vouté LM&C,LLP -170 Hmltn Av -White Plns 10601
(631) 844-9611 .. **Cristiano,** Jennifer Rando '04 %Shapiro D&B,LLP -105 Maxness Rd -Melvll 11747
(718) 298-0500 .. **Cristiano,** Jos A '77 %Surrogate's Ct -88-11 Sutphin Blvd -Jamaica 11435 **Fx:**520-5048
(212) 576-7000 .. **Cristina,** Donnamarie '91 %NYLIM -51 Mad Av -NY 10010
(585) 263-1000 .. **Cristman,** Scott F '74 (Nixon P LLP) -1100 Clinton Sq -Rchstr 14604
(585) 454-2181 .. **Cristo,** Louis B '85 (Trevett CS&A,PC) -2 State -Rchstr 14614
(518) 436-7687 .. **Cristo,** Peter A '78 -Bx11580 -Albany 12211
(212) 373-3000 .. **Cristofalo,** Helen R '04 Paul WRW&G LLP -1285 Av of Amer -NY 10019
(516) 932-0400 .. **Cristofano,** Lauren B '87 %Friedman & S -333 Jericho Tpk -Jericho 11753 **Fx:**932-0455
(718) 639-1100 .. **Cristofari,** Fabio '92 (Masone WP&C) -69-34 Grand Av -Maspeth 11378
(212) 813-8800 .. **Cristovici,** Yvonne M '03 (Goodwin P LLP) -620 8th Av -NY 10018
(212) 245-6565 .. **Criswell,** Thos O IV '96 %Levine P&M,LLP -1740 Bway -NY 10019
(212) 262-2390 .. **Critchley,** Jennifer C '03 %Connell F LLP -888 7th Av -NY 10106
(212) 626-4100 .. **Critchlow,** Chas H '76 (Baker & M LLP) -1114 Av of Amer -NY 10036
(516) 742-7608 .. **Critelli,** Christopher W '86 (C Critelli,PC) -999 Franklin Av -Gdn Cty 11530 **Fx:**742-6356
(315) 853-6183 .. **Critelli,** Steven M '80 Power Line Constructors,Inc -24 Robnsn Rd Bx385 -Clinton 13323 **Fx:**853-3176
(212) 524-5000 .. **Crittenden,** David R '97 %Jacob M&F -1270 Av of Amer -NY 10020
(607) 273-6444 .. **Crittenden,** Don R '83 SrCnsl Harris B PLLC -119 E Seneca -Ithaca 14850
(212) 808-2256 .. **Crittenden,** Laurie S '97 NTT America,Inc -101 Park Av -NY 10178 **Fx:**661-1078
(212) 770-2578 .. **Crivelli,** Robt A '80 %AIG -80 Pine -NY 10005
(212) 723-9250 .. **Crivelli,** Rosanna J '81 Citigroup Global Mrkts -388 Greenwich -NY 10013
(212) 455-2000 .. **Crnkovich,** Sean P '09 %Simpson T&B LLP -425 Lex Av -NY 10017
(518) 690-4410 .. **Croak,** Richd '76 (R Croak & Assoc) -314 Great Oaks Blvd -Albany 12203 **Fx:**690-4435
(631) 853-4104 .. **Croce,** Alfred J '07 %DA -400 Carleton Av Bx9082 -Central Islip 11722 **Fx:**853-7838
(212) 980-0404 .. **Croce,** Michl J '97 %J Dearie & Assoc -515 Mad Av -NY 10022 **Fx:**980-0555
(518) 682-2400 .. **Crocetta,** Kimberly A '04 -48 Union Av -Saratoga Spgs 12866 **Fx:**587-0128
(914) 766-4660 .. **Crockatt,** Jo Ann Kealy '92 IBM -294 Route 100 -Somers 10589
(518) 402-9185 .. **Crocker,** Alison H '87 %DEC -625 Bway -Albany 12233 **Fx:**402-9018
(607) 652-7327 .. **Crocker,** J D '47 (Rushmore MM&C) -11 Harper -Stamfrd 12167
(631) 694-2300 .. **Crocker,** Lindsay T '04 %Lamb & B,LLP -534 Broadhllw Rd Bx9034 -Melvll 11747
(212) 768-6700 .. **Crocker,** Mason L '90 (Sonnenschein N&R LLP) -2 World Fncl Ctr -NY 10281
(585) 724-6533 .. **Crocker,** Pamela R '97 SpclCnsl Eastman Kodak -343 State -Rchstr 14650 **Fx:**477-4646
(646) 471-4000 .. **Crockett,** Julie '91 %PricewaterhouseCoopers LLP -300 Mad Av -NY 10017
(518) 565-3316 .. **Crockett,** Van '78 %Dept Social Srvcs -13 Durkee -Plattsbrgh 12901 **Fx:**565-3626
(212) 238-3000 .. **Croes,** Jane E '83 (Emmet M&M,LLP) -120 Bway -NY 10271
(585) 987-2800 .. **Croessmann,** Robt W '79 (Woods OG LLP) -2 State -Rchstr 14614
(212) 903-9000 .. **Croffoot-Suede,** Lance R '91 (Linklaters) -1345 Av of Amer -NY 10105
(212) 225-2000 .. **Croft,** James A '08 %Cleary GS&H -1 Lbrty Plz -NY 10006
(212) 558-4000 .. **Crofton,** Scott B '10 %Sullivan & C LLP -125 Broad -NY 10004
(718) 590-2000 .. **Crofts,** James J '00 %DA -198 E 161st -Bronx 10451 **Fx:**590-6477
(716) 285-2606 .. **Crogan-Mazur,** Bonnie L '92 -800 Main -Niagara Fls 14301
(212) 450-4000 .. **Crohn,** Alexander A '10 %Davis P&W LLP -450 Lex Av -NY 10017
(212) 506-5000 .. **Croke,** James J Jr. '85 (Orrick H&S LLP) -51 W 52nd -NY 10019
(631) 673-5548 .. **Croker,** Jeffrey T '04 -4 Gramercy Pl -Huntngtn 11743 **Fx:**673-5548
(212) 448-1100 .. **Croly,** Mary Sembrot '89 %McLaughlin & S,LLP -260 Mad Av -NY 10016
(212) 532-1200 .. **Croly,** Peter B '87 %A Bernstone -292 Mad Av -NY 10017 **Fx:**532-6330
(212) 468-4800 .. **Cromartie,** Dominick R '04 %Davis & G LLP -1740 Bway -NY 10019
(631) 666-5766 .. **Cromarty,** Arthur M '49 OfCnsl Long TBSWJ&S -120 4th Av Bx5591 -Bay Shr 11706
(212) 345-1605 .. **Crombie,** Timothy J '77 %Marsh USA -1166 Av of Amer -NY 10036 **Fx:**345-4808
(718) 525-3600 .. **Cromer,** Gail K '90 -232-12 Linden Blvd -Cambria Hts 11411 **Fx:**525-7090
(518) 885-8451 .. **Cromie,** John J '74 -132 Bath -Ballston Spa 12020 **Fx:**884-8599
(914) 745-0700 .. **Cromwell,** John M '90 -135 Mntgmry Av -Scarsdale 10583
(212) 442-6814 .. **Cromwell,** Laura Lee '92 %Law Dept -60 Lafayette -NY 10013 **Fx:**442-6865
(212) 418-6125 .. **Cromwell,** Robt D '88 %GM -767 5th Av -NY 10153 **Fx:**418-6123
(631) 734-5100 .. **Cron,** James J '81 -Bx973 -Cutchogue 11935
(212) 637-2779 .. **Cronan,** John Peter '02 %US Atty -1 St Andrews Plz -NY 10007
(516) 747-7800 .. **Cronin,** Brad W '82 (Cronin C&H,PC) -200 Old Cntry Rd -Mineola 11501
(516) 358-1700 .. **Cronin & Byczek,LLP** -1983 Marcus Av -Lk Success 11042 **Fx:**358-1730
(518) 756-6700 .. **Cronin,** Christina A '04 %McHugh,PC -149 Main -Ravena 12143 **Fx:**756-9753
(631) 232-6130 .. **Cronin,** Colleen M '94 (Weiner L LLP) -888 Vets Mem'l Hwy -Hauppauge 11788
(516) 747-7800 .. **Cronin Cronin & Harris,PC** -200 Old Cntry Rd -Mineola 11501 **Fx:**741-8354
(631) 374-8419 .. **Cronin,** Danl J '00 DJ Cronin,PC -1353 Stony Brk Rd -Stony Brk 11790 **Fx:**751-8949
(212) 237-0000 .. **Cronin,** Denis F '73 (Vinson & E LLP) -666 5th Av -NY 10103
(212) 857-8800 .. **Cronin,** Elizabeth '84 %US Ct of Appls -40 Foley Sq -NY 10007
(212) 925-2800 .. **Cronin,** Eugene M '78 (Dolgenos N&C LLP) -271 Mad Av -NY 10016
(516) 795-2500 .. **Cronin,** James P '92 J Cronin,PC -5510 Merrick Rd -Massapequa 11758 **Fx:**797-1111
(516) 358-1700 .. **Cronin,** Linda M '84 (Cronin & B,LLP) -1983 Marcus Av -Lk Success 11042
(516) 747-7800 .. **Cronin,** Matthew J '50 (Cronin C&H,PC) -200 Old Cntry Rd -Mineola 11501
(212) 576-7000 .. **Cronin,** Maureen A '03 NY Life Invstmnt Mgmt LLC -51 Mad Av -NY 10010
(914) 765-1900 .. **Cronin,** Michl I '82 IBM -1 New Orchrd Rd -Armonk 10504 **Fx:**765-7533
(718) 250-2000 .. **Cronin,** Nora M '07 %DA -350 Jay -Brklyn 11201 **Fx:**250-2314
(212) 885-5000 .. **Cronin,** Ryan E '09 %Blank R LLP -405 Lex Av -NY 10174
(516) 747-7800 .. **Cronin,** Sean M '05 %Cronin C&H,PC -200 Old Cntry Rd -Mineola 11501
(212) 335-9000 .. **Cronin,** Stephen M '74 %DA -1 Hogan Pl -NY 10013
(212) 247-5100 .. **Cronin,** Wm H Jr. '81 -180 Cntrl Pk S -NY 10019 **Fx:**247-2233
(212) 949-6490 .. **Cronin Harris,** Catherine E '72 %The CPR Inst Dispute Res -575 Lex Av -NY 10022
(212) 806-5400 .. **Cronise,** Elizabeth H '05 %Stroock &S&L LLP -180 Maiden Ln -NY 10038
(212) 325-2000 .. **Cronk,** Henry H '92 Credit Suisse -1 Mad Av -NY 10010
(585) 295-4400 .. **Cronmiller,** Thos B '88 (Hiscock & B,LLP) -2000 HSBC Plz -Rchstr 14604
(212) 966-4439 .. **Cronquist,** Mary M '84 -110 William -NY 10038 **Fx:**226-7554
(716) 832-0996 .. **Cronyn,** Robt L '92 -3795 Harlem -Cheektowaga 14215
(585) 530-3162 .. **Croog,** Laura E '83 %Appllt Div 4th Dept -50 East Av Ste 200 -Rchstr 14604 **Fx:**530-3247
(585) 724-3294 .. **Croog,** Robt D '69 %Eastman Kodak -343 State -Rchstr 14650 **Fx:**724-9657
(914) 789-8394 .. **Croog,** Tamar Y '08 Fujifilm Hldngs Amer Corp -200 Summit Lk Dr -Valhalla 10595
(212) 878-8000 .. **Crook,** Keridy S '09 %Clifford C LLP -31 W 52nd -NY 10019
(212) 310-8000 .. **Crooker,** Kerianne '07 %Weil G&M LLP -767 5th Av -NY 10153
(718) 927-4100 .. **Crooks,** Ene E '05 -5009 Av N -Brklyn 11234 **Fx:**927-1507
(212) 335-9000 .. **Crooks,** Mark W '03 %DA -1 Hogan Pl -NY 10013
(212) 752-5258 .. **Croot,** John E Jr. '96 (Schwartz SE&C LLC) -845 3rd Av -NY 10022
(585) 589-9400 .. **Cropsey,** Conrad F '76 (Cropsey & C) -109 N Main Bx386 -Albion 14411 **Fx:**589-4735
(212) 849-7000 .. **Crosa Di Vergagni,** Celine C '09 %Quinn EU&S,LLP -51 Mad Av -NY 10010
(212) 676-1874 .. **Crosa,** Eduardo L '04 Law Dept -100 Church -NY 10007 **Fx:**788-0367
(212) 559-6096 .. **Crosa,** Pablo E '02 Citigroup Private Bank -485 Lex Av -NY 10017
(716) 856-4200 .. **Crosby,** Brian P '70 (Gibson M&C,LLP) -69 Delaware Av -Buffalo 14202
(607) 664-2138 .. **Crosby,** David M '88 Family Ct -3 E Pulteney Sq -Bath 14810 **Fx:**776-7857
(646) 452-2300 .. **Crosby,** Mark R '89 (Crosby & H LLP) -350 Bway -NY 10013 **Fx:**452-2301
(585) 230-7575 .. **Crosby,** Michl J '83 -22 Parkvw Manor Cir -Honeoye Fls 14472
(212) 704-1347 .. **Crosby,** Wm H Jr. '94 Interpublic Grp -1114 Av of Amer -NY 10036 **Fx:**704-2236
(585) 263-1000 .. **Crosnicker,** Michl J '09 %Nixon P LLP -1100 Clinton Sq -Rchstr 14604
(212) 906-1200 .. **Cross,** Christopher G '97 (Latham & W) -885 3rd Av -NY 10022
(212) 805-0234 .. **Cross,** David D '03 US Judiciary -500 Pearl -NY 10007
(845) 838-3400 .. **Cross,** Francois R '64 (Pagones & C,PC) -355 Main Bx550 -Beacon 12508
(718) 643-7074 .. **Cross,** Iris J '90 %Hon MW Patterson -360 Adams -Brklyn 11201
(212) 455-2000 .. **Cross,** James D '91 (Simpson T&B LLP) -425 Lex Av -NY 10017
(914) 682-7800 .. **Cross,** Jody T '02 %Zarin & S -81 Main -White Plns 10601
(212) 408-5100 .. **Cross,** Jonathan C '02 Cnsl Chadbourne & P LLP -30 Rckfllr Plz -NY 10112
(716) 853-5100 .. **Cross,** Kevin J '00 %Lippes MWF LLP -665 Main -Buffalo 14203
(212) 872-1000 .. **Cross,** Michl K '10 -One Bryant Park -NY 10036 **Fx:**872-1002
(212) 596-9000 .. **Cross,** Nicole L '10 %Ropes & G LLP -1211 Av of Amer -NY 10036
(212) 417-8700 .. **Cross,** Peggy M '02 %Fed Def of NY Inc -52 Duane -NY 10007 **Fx:**571-0392
(212) 643-7000 .. **Cross,** Peter A '73 (Sills C&G PC) -One Rckfllr Plz -NY 10020
(518) 474-7278 .. **Cross,** Richd W '77 %Dept of Law -The Cptl -Albany 12224
(212) 831-3941 .. **Cross,** Robt W '65 -1435 Lex Av -NY 10128 **Fx:**(215) 297-8050
(716) 856-4200 .. **Cross,** Tara Karch '03 %Gibson M&C,LLP -69 Delaware Av -Buffalo 14202
(212) 374-6029 .. **Crossan,** Kerri Ann '04 %Dept of Ed -49-51 Chmbrs -NY 10007
(212) 981-4500 .. **Crossdale,** Carol Fredericka '96 PeterSan Grp -1450 Bway -NY 10018 **Fx:**981-4560
(212) 878-8000 .. **Crosse,** Katrina L '08 (Clifford C LLP) -31 W 52nd -NY 10019

(212) 750-4483 .. **Crossett,** Carol A '02 %F Sembler,PLLC -501 Mad Av -NY 10022 **Fx:**750-4491
(518) 402-6969 .. **Crossett,** Lance C '96 %Envrnmtl Facilities -625 Bway -Albany 12207 **Fx:**402-6972
(315) 425-2700 .. **Crossett,** Peter J '90 (Hiscock & B,LLP) -One Park Pl -Syracuse 13202
(315) 471-1664 .. **Crossett,** Wm W IV '82 (Meggesto C&V,LLP) -313 E Willow -Syracuse 13203
(914) 834-5441 .. **Crossin,** Wm J '63 Crossin & C -65 Prospect Av -Larchmnt 10538 **Fx:**833-2926
(516) 746-7730 .. **Crossley,** Dennis J '76 %AAA NY -1415 Kellum Pl -Gdn Cty 11530
(607) 273-5787 .. **Crossmore,** Edw Y '74 -115 W Green -Ithaca 14850 **Fx:**273-0291
(516) 299-4246 .. **Crosson,** Elaine M '86 Long Island Univ -Univ Ctr Bush Brown Hall -Brookvll 11548 **Fx:**299-2072
(518) 474-0871 .. **Crossway,** Dinah M '83 %DMV -6 ESP -Albany 12228 **Fx:**486-4485
(212) 998-4505 .. **Crosswhite,** Anastasia B '03 NYU Faculty Housing -244 Greene -NY 10003 **Fx:**995-4158
(212) 506-5000 .. **Crost,** Katharine Ingersoll '79 (Orrick H&S LLP) -51 W 52nd -NY 10019
(631) 435-0700 .. **Croston,** Alyssa Silver '95 %M Silver,PC -330 Motor Pkwy -Hauppauge 11788 **Fx:**435-8253
(631) 474-0900 .. **Croston,** Michl J '93 -18 Crescent Rd -Pt Jffrsn 11777 **Fx:**474-2930
(212) 906-1200 .. **Croswell,** Alexandra H '09 %Latham & W -885 3rd Av -NY 10022
(646) 387-6248 .. **Croswell,** Annmarie '99 Kinetic Prtnrs LLP -675 3rd Av -NY 10017
(516) 741-4799 .. **Croteau,** James J '06 %Baker SBGFM&N,LLC -100 Grdn City Plz -Gdn Cty 11530
(212) 593-6700 .. **Crothers,** Erin N '08 %Aaronson RF&D,LLP -757 3rd Av -NY 10017
(212) 480-3474 .. **Crotty,** Christopher C '05 Farina & Assoc,Inc -20 Broad -NY 10005
(212) 312-7129 .. **Crotty,** Elizabeth R '01 (Crotty & S LLP) -52 Duane -NY 10007 **Fx:**918-9375
(518) 561-1980 .. **Crotty,** John M '77 Niles P&B -46-48 Cornelia Bx2729 -Plattsbrgh 12901
(212) 858-4341 .. **Crotty,** Julie M '01 FINRA -1 Lbrty Plz -NY 10006
(212) 336-2000 .. **Crotty,** Kathleen M '00 Cnsl Patterson BW&T LLP -1133 Av of Amer -NY 10036
(518) 474-4785 .. **Crotty,** Peter '67 %Industrial Bd of Appls -Agncy Bldg 2 -Albany 12223
(716) 845-9373 .. **Crotty,** Peter J '97 %Supreme Ct -25 Delaware Av -Buffalo 14202 **Fx:**851-3293
(845) 563-4630 .. **Crotty,** Philip A Jr. '74 Town Atty -555 Union Av -New Windsor 12553
(212) 808-7800 .. **Crotty,** Robt E '73 (Kelley D&W LLP) -101 Park Av -NY 10178
(212) 374-2990 .. **Crotty,** Theresa '02 NYC Law Dept-Edu -52 Chmbrs -NY 10007
(212) 267-1650 .. **Crouch,** Donald A Jr. '92 (Fine O&A,LLP) -39 Bway -NY 10006
(585) 394-2665 .. **Croucher Jones & Johns** -70 S Main -Canandaigua 14424 **Fx:**396-0247
(212) 839-5300 .. **Crough,** Maureen M '95 Cnsl Sidley A LLP -787 7th Av -NY 10019
(845) 294-5953 .. **Croughan,** Richd J '97 -Bx426 -Chester 10918 **Fx:**294-3974
(518) 869-9200 .. **Crouse,** Jessica K '10 %Rose Law Firm,PLLC -501 New Karner Rd -Albany 12205 **Fx:**869-3334
(212) 878-8000 .. **Crouse,** Rebecca M '09 %Clifford C LLP -31 W 52nd -NY 10019
(212) 836-8000 .. **Croushore,** Amanda C '10 Kaye S LLP -425 Park Av -NY 10022
(516) 746-0707 .. **Croutier,** Wm J Sr. '59 Cnsl Hammill OCDP&K,PC -6851 Jericho Tpk -Syosset 11791
(516) 746-0707 .. **Croutier,** Wm J Jr. '79 (Hammill OCDP&K,PC) -6851 Jericho Tpk -Syosset 11791
(212) 416-2000 .. **Crovitz,** Gordon '88 Wall St Jrnl -1211 Av of Amer -NY 10036
(212) 576-2670 .. **Crow,** Danl H '06 %J Osborn,PC -841 Bway -NY 10003 **Fx:**686-4023
(212) 577-3688 .. **Crow,** David A '85 %Leg Aid -199 Water -NY 10038 **Fx:**509-8431
(646) 419-4264 .. **Crow,** John C '91 (Bowles C&C LLP) -54 W 21st -NY 10010 **Fx:**(866) 844-8305
(718) 780-0338 .. **Crow,** Melissa E '95 Brklyn Law Schl -1 Boerum Pl -Brklyn 11201
(212) 725-7373 .. **Crow,** Michele J '89 Asheville Grp LLC -14 Wshngtn Pl -NY 10003 **Fx:**725-7117
(585) 256-2109 .. **Crowder,** Debra A '93 -620 Park Av -Rchstr 14607
(845) 348-1160 .. **Crowe,** Alice T '96 -99 Main -Nyack 10960
(845) 348-1160 .. **Crowe,** Alicia Marie '94 -99 Main -Nyack 10960
(212) 906-1200 .. **Crowe,** Andrea L '94 OfCnsl Latham & W -885 3rd Av -NY 10022
(212) 306-7237 .. **Crowe,** Elizabeth N '07 NY Ofc of Labor Relations -40 Rector -NY 10006
(718) 366-0940 .. **Crowe,** Eugene F '89 %Kerzner & H,LLC -74-09 Myrtle Av -Glendale 11385 **Fx:**366-0922
(212) 779-8600 .. **Crowe,** Gerard J '97 (Silverman SS&B PLLC) -381 Park Av S -NY 10016
(212) 728-8000 .. **Crowe,** James M '08 %Willkie F&G LLP -787 7th Av -NY 10019
(212) 526-1544 .. **Crowe,** John C '94 Barclays Capital Inc -745 7th Av -NY 10019
(212) 421-4100 .. **Crowe,** John J '88 (Pryor C LLP) -7 Times Sq -NY 10036
(585) 258-2800 .. **Crowe,** John W '73 OfCnsl Underberg & K LLP -300 Bausch & Lomb Pl -Rchstr 14604
(315) 379-0007 .. **Crowe,** Michl C '73 -49 Main Bx696 -Canton 13617 **Fx:**379-1871
(718) 981-6200 .. **Crowe,** Steven P '89 (Duskin & C) -1688 Victory Blvd -Staten Isl 10314 **Fx:**981-0433
(914) 949-2700 .. **Crowe,** Vincent W '86 (Bleakley P&S,LLP) -1 N Lex Av -White Plns 10601
(347) 365-9544 .. **Crowe,** Walter M Jr. '77 -5718 Ft Hmltn Pkwy -Brklyn 11219
(212) 655-5000 .. **Crowe,** Wm J '00 %Gannon R&M -120 Bway -NY 10271
(716) 631-5767 .. **Crowe,** Wm R '75 -5555 Main -Williamsvll 14221
(212) 373-3000 .. **Crowell,** Aaron H '07 %Paul WRW&G LLP -1285 Av of Amer -NY 10019
(518) 581-1006 .. **Crowell,** Ann Cummings '93 Hon Ferradino -Bx2380 -Malta 12020 **Fx:**581-0825
(212) 788-3013 .. **Crowell,** Anthony W '98 Cnsl NYC Ofc of the Mayor -City Hall -NY 10007 **Fx:**788-9869
(212) 878-8000 .. **Crowell,** David J '99 %Clifford C LLP -31 W 52nd -NY 10019
(212) 907-0700 .. **Crowell,** Joshua L '07 %Labaton S LLP -140 Bway -NY 10005
(212) 223-4000 .. **Crowell & Moring LLP** -590 Mad Av -NY 10022 **Fx:**223-4134
(212) 839-5300 .. **Crowell,** Nicholas P '99 (Sidley A LLP) -787 7th Av -NY 10019
(212) 490-7770 .. **Crowell,** Thos A '03 (Saperstein & C,LLP) -275 Mad Av -NY 10016 **Fx:**321-7082
(518) 487-7600 .. **Crowell,** Wm Y III '77 (Whiteman O&H LLP) -1 Commerce Plz -Albany 12260
(718) 423-5500 .. **Crowley,** Bernadette M '95 -42-24 235th -Douglastn 11363
(212) 473-1972 .. **Crowley,** Catherine J '86 -30 E 9th -NY 10003 **Fx:**473-1972
(212) 883-1300 .. **Crowley,** Chas L Jr. '83 (Sandler T&R,PA) -551 5th Av -NY 10176
(212) 450-4000 .. **Crowley,** Christopher '67 SrCnsl Davis P&W LLP -450 Lex Av -NY 10017
(718) 651-1948 .. **Crowley Crowley & Kaufman** -84-56 Grand Av -Elmhrst 11373 **Fx:**565-9228
(212) 506-2500 .. **Crowley,** David E '09 %Mayer B LLP -1675 Bway -NY 10019
(607) 723-5408 .. **Crowley,** David F '63 (Shaw OC&R) -55 Main -Bnghmtn 13905
(212) 947-1999 .. **Crowley,** Donald L '82 (Methfessel & W,PC) -450 7th Av -NY 10123
(516) 505-0600 .. **Crowley,** Erin M '07 %J McCormack,PC -1035 Stewart Av -Gdn Cty 11530 **Fx:**505-0632
(718) 474-5782 .. **Crowley,** James J '72 -537 Beach 132nd -Belle Hbr 11694
(917) 454-1100 .. **Crowley,** Jessie A '04 %Police Dept -2 Lafayette -NY 10007
(212) 450-4000 .. **Crowley,** John G '91 (Davis P&W LLP) -450 Lex Av -NY 10017
(646) 855-0742 .. **Crowley,** Jos A '03 Banc of Amer Securities -1 Bryant Pk -NY 10036
(716) 845-7448 .. **Crowley,** Kathleen A '88 %Family Ct -1 Niagara Plz -Buffalo 14202 **Fx:**858-4739
(607) 723-5408 .. **Crowley,** Kiernan Meeker '93 %Shaw OC&R -55 Main -Bnghmtn 13905
(212) 858-1000 .. **Crowley,** Leo T '81 (Pillsbury WSP LLP) -1540 Bway -NY 10036
(212) 297-5800 .. **Crowley,** Marc D '97 SrCnsl Day P LLP -7 Times Sq -NY 10036
(315) 435-3839 .. **Crowley,** Mary Lou '51 Hon W Roy -403 Cnty Cthse -Syracuse 13202 **Fx:**435-3394
(212) 909-6000 .. **Crowley,** Meagan E '08 %Debevoise & P LLP -919 3rd Av -NY 10022
(212) 952-6200 .. **Crowley,** Michl E '84 (Nourse & B,LLP) -55 Bway -NY 10006
(212) 262-2390 .. **Crowley,** Michl J '85 (Connell F LLP) -888 7th Av -NY 10106
(212) 513-3200 .. **Crowley,** Richd A '78 (Holland & K LLP) -31 W 52nd -NY 10019
(718) 423-5500 .. **Crowley,** Rosaleen M '99 -42-24 235th -Douglastn 11363
(212) 965-9081 .. **Crowley,** Sarah A '07 Neufeld S&B -99 Hudson -NY 10013
(212) 557-7200 .. **Crowley,** Sean E '94 (Davidoff M&H,LLP) -605 3rd Av -NY 10158
(315) 785-3152 .. **Crowley,** Sheila M '98 %Pub Def -175 Arsenal -Watertwn 13601 **Fx:**785-5060
(718) 428-9180 .. **Crowley,** Theresa E '93 (Rossi & C,LLP) -42-24 235th -Douglastn 11363
(914) 253-2000 .. **Crowley,** Wm J III '04 %Pepsico -700 Andrsn Hill Rd -Purchase 10577
(212) 593-9191 .. **Crown,** Patricia '83 OfCnsl Coblence & Assoc -200 Park Av S -NY 10003 **Fx:**593-0011
(845) 429-5371 .. **Crown,** Valerie J '84 -90 New Main Bx360 -Haverstraw 10927 **Fx:**429-5375
(716) 856-2626 .. **Crowther,** David C '06 %Tronolone & S,PC -298 Main -Buffalo 14202
(585) 344-2550 .. **Croyle,** Robt J '83 Family Ct -1 W Main -Batavia 14020 **Fx:**344-8520
(914) 377-6240 .. **Crozier,** Kevin D '79 %Law Dept -300 City Hall -Ynkrs 10701 **Fx:**964-0563
(914) 366-5700 .. **Cru,** Andrea '82 %MA Bjork -660 Wht Plns Rd -Tarrytwn 10591 **Fx:**366-5759
(800) 416-5454 .. **Crudden,** Vincent P '86 %Fusco B&R -3253 Route 112 -Medfrd 11763
(800) 416-5454 .. **Crudden,** Vincent P '86 %Fusco B&R -353 Vets Mem'l Hwy -Commack 11725
(212) 474-1000 .. **Cruess,** Danl G '08 %Cravath S&M LLP -825 8th Av -NY 10019
(518) 563-5964 .. **Cruikshank,** Allan B '99 -49 Clinton -Plattsbrgh 12901 **Fx:**563-5965
(212) 415-3742 .. **Cruikshank,** Ronald G '97 %Omnicom Group -437 Mad Av -NY 10022 **Fx:**415-3530
(631) 423-4764 .. **Cruise,** James J Jr. '62 -11 Lake Rd -Huntngtn Sta 11746
(845) 291-3136 .. **Cruise,** Kathleen Ann McSweeney '86 %Hon J Alessandro -255 Main -Goshen 10924
(212) 471-8531 .. **Crum,** Chas A '68 OfCnsl Herzfeld & R,PC -125 Broad -NY 10004
(585) 428-6990 .. **Crumb,** Donald L Jr. '91 %Law Dept -30 Church -Rchstr 14614 **Fx:**428-6950
(212) 541-5996 .. **Crumiller,** Susan K '07 Housing Conservation Coordinators,Inc -777 10th Av -NY 10019
(518) 426-9648 .. **Crummey,** Peter G '83 -90 State -Albany 12207
(585) 275-6649 .. **Crummins,** Richd S '90 %Univ of Rochester Med Ctr -Bx278979 -Rchstr 14627 **Fx:**272-9311
(516) 931-1800 .. **Crumpton,** Judith E '88 OfCnsl Catalano G&P LLP -100 Jericho Quadrangle -Jericho 11753
(212) 529-4000 .. **Crupain,** Danl '67 -225 Bway -NY 10007 **Fx:**406-6890
(212) 335-5657 .. **Crupi,** Karen M '90 Fidelity Invstmnts -200 Lbrty -NY 10281
(212) 554-1234 .. **Crupi,** Lisa L '84 AXA Financial Inc -1290 Av of Amer -NY 10104 **Fx:**707-3963
(718) 286-6000 .. **Crusco,** Peter A '81 %DA -125-01 Qns Blvd -Kew Gdns 11415
(516) 870-3020 .. **Cruse,** Suzanne A '96 Kozy Shack Enterprises,Inc -83 Ludy -Hicksvll 11801 **Fx:**870-3021
(631) 539-0375 .. **Cruser Mitchell & Novitz,LLP** -175 Pinelawn Rd -Melvll 11747 **Fx:**539-0379
(212) 735-3000 .. **Crusey,** H Matthew '05 %Skadden ASM&F LLP -4 Times Sq -NY 10036
(845) 562-9100 .. **Crush,** Maureen '86 (Rider W&F,PC) -655 Little Britain Rd -New Windsor 12553
(212) 688-8555 .. **Crusha,** Jeffrey M '05 %Fragomen DB&L LLP -7 Hanover Sq -NY 10004
(212) 226-2376 .. **Crusius,** Eric S '01 %Oved & O LLP -101 Av of Amer -NY 10013 **Fx:**226-7555
(212) 848-4000 .. **Crutchfield,** Michelle A '06 %Shearman & S LLP -599 Lex Av -NY 10022
(212) 474-1000 .. **Cruz,** Alejandro H '10 %Cravath S&M LLP -825 8th Av -NY 10019
(646) 386-3241 .. **Cruz,** Angel '05 Hon L Suarez -60 Centre -NY 10007
(718) 222-2048 .. **Cruz,** Angela R '07 %Law Dept -350 Jay -Brklyn 11201 **Fx:**222-2088
(516) 741-4170 .. **Cruz,** Brandon M '98 %Bongiorno Law Firm,PLLC -250 Mineola Blvd -Mineola 11501 **Fx:**741-4240
(914) 666-6700 .. **Cruz,** Carlos E Jr. '83 (Zuckerman & C) -121 Smith Av -Mt Kisco 10549 **Fx:**666-0605

(718) 681-1111 .. **Cruz,** Carlos E Jr. '83 (Zuckerman & C) -910 Sheridan Av -Bronx 10451
(646) 205-7880 .. **Cruz,** Francisco '98 Cruz & G & Assoc -110 William -NY 10038 **Fx**:(212) 233-9848
(212) 735-3000 .. **Cruz,** Heather S '96 (Skadden ASM&F LLP) -4 Times Sq -NY 10036
(718) 590-2000 .. **Cruz,** Jennifer Estrella '04 %DA -198 E 161st -Bronx 10451 **Fx**:590-6477
(212) 213-0128 .. **Cruz,** Jose M '96 -20 Waterside Plz -NY 10010
(212) 578-2211 .. **Cruz,** Joselyn A '03 %MetLife -27-01 Qns Plz N -LIC 11101
(212) 947-8800 .. **Cruz,** Julio '95 NY Elevator -519 8th Av -NY 10018 **Fx**:947-9555
(718) 428-1555 .. **Cruz,** Louis A '81 -4727 Little Neck Pkwy -Douglastn 11362
(212) 867-4466 .. **Cruz,** Magda L '86 (Belkin BW&G,LLP) -270 Mad Av -NY 10016
(212) 339-0653 .. **Cruz,** Margarita E '98 Population Cncl -1 Dag Hmmrskjld Plz -NY 10017
(212) 521-5400 .. **Cruz,** Mariel E '10 %Reed S LLP -599 Lex Av -NY 10022
(212) 788-7619 .. **Cruz,** Martha '01 NYC Loft Bd -100 Gold -NY 10038
(212) 668-5632 .. **Cruz,** Tracy F '96 %Hon C Blackshear -1 Bowling Grn -NY 10004
(212) 803-5125 .. **Cruz,** Wendell '96 NY Cnty Defender Srvcs -225 Bway -NY 10007 **Fx**:571-6035
(212) 351-4000 .. **Cruz-Abrams,** Carlos F '01 %Gibson D&C LLP -200 Park Av -NY 10166
(212) 210-9571 .. **Cruz-Backman,** Ana E '03 Cnsl Alston & B LLP -90 Park Av -NY 10016
(212) 735-3000 .. **Cruz Melendez,** Maria E '07 %Skadden ASM&F LLP -4 Times Sq -NY 10036
(631) 283-4111 .. **Cryan,** Ann E '89 %Burke & S,PLLC -41 Meeting House Ln -Southampton 11968
(212) 484-3900 .. **Cryan,** Michl S '96 (Arent F LLP) -1675 Bway -NY 10019
(212) 692-9030 .. **Crystal,** David II '65 (Crystal & D) -708 3rd Av -NY 10017
(212) 682-4002 .. **Crystal,** Howard C '79 (Novack BC LLP) -300 E 42nd -NY 10017
(212) 728-8000 .. **Crystal,** Jeremy '07 %Willkie F&G LLP -787 7th Av -NY 10019
(212) 869-3000 .. **Crystal,** Joel F '69 %Centro US -420 Lex Av -NY 10170 **Fx**:302-4776
(212) 813-8800 .. **Crystal,** Jos B '06 %Goodwin P LLP -620 8th Av -NY 10018
(212) 759-4888 .. **Crystal,** Kenneth R '81 (Phillips L LLP) -437 Mad Av -NY 10022
(315) 476-2121 .. **Crystal,** Milton J '53 -447 E Wshngtn -Syracuse 13202 **Fx**:478-4352
(212) 218-5500 .. **Crystal,** Richd '67 OfCnsl Seyfarth S LLP -620 8th Av -NY 10018
(212) 603-2000 .. **Csaszar,** Greg '98 Cnsl URS Corp -One Penn Plz -NY 10119
(516) 482-6633 .. **Cserhalmi,** Michl L '75 (M Cserhalmi,PC) -437 Middle Nck Rd -Gt Neck 11023 **Fx**:482-8406
(212) 421-5500 .. **Ctorides,** Christina '94 (Goldsmith C&R,LLP) -747 3rd Av -NY 10017
(212) 450-4000 .. **Cua,** Albert A '99 Cnsl Davis P&W LLP -450 Lex Av -NY 10017
(718) 590-5944 .. **Cuadrado,** Jessica Ines '05 ACS-DLS -900 Sheridan Av -Bronx 10451
(914) 576-2203 .. **Cuba,** Gary M '75 -271 North Av -New Rchll 10801
(718) 237-2000 .. **Cubbage,** Alexandria R '01 %Leg Aid -111 Lvngstn -Brklyn 11201 **Fx**:237-8737
(212) 961-4408 .. **Cubbedge,** Debra A '94 %OCFS -163 W 125th -NY 10027
(914) 848-4680 .. **Cubbon,** Michelle McKee '01 %Pernod Ricard -100 Manhattanvll Rd -Purchase 10577
(212) 310-8000 .. **Cubell,** Michl B '07 %Weil G&M LLP -767 5th Av -NY 10153
(212) 909-6000 .. **Cubitto,** Robt J '79 SrCnsl Debevoise & P LLP -919 3rd Av -NY 10022
(212) 506-2500 .. **Cuccaro,** Mark '07 %Mayer B LLP -1675 Bway -NY 10019
(646) 252-7000 .. **Cucchi,** Diane M '82 %TBTA -2 Bway -NY 10004
(718) 254-7000 .. **Cucchissi,** Grace M '90 %US Atty -271 Cadman Plz E -Brklyn 11201 **Fx**:254-6479
(212) 527-8400 .. **Cucci,** Gardenia P '95 Cnsl Oak Hill Cptl Ptnrs -65 E 55th -NY 10022 **Fx**:527-8450
(631) 265-7200 .. **Cucci,** John Jr. '93 %Russo KW&C -400 Townline Rd -Hauppauge 11788
(212) 274-0190 .. **Cucci,** Richd C '77 American Construction -44 W 18th -NY 10011 **Fx**:274-0199
(212) 931-4642 .. **Cucci,** Sergio O '00 -520 8th Av -NY 10018
(212) 966-7775 .. **Cuccia,** Edw J '90 (Ferro & C) -100 Lafayette -NY 10013
(914) 834-8900 .. **Cuccia,** Fredk J '70 -1865 Palmer Av -Larchmnt 10538 **Fx**:834-8911
(212) 819-8200 .. **Cuccinello,** Glen R '90 Cnsl White & C LLP -1155 Av of Amer -NY 10036
(212) 425-9300 .. **Cuccio,** Frank J '94 (Bressler A&R,PC) -17 State -NY 10004
(212) 586-9500 .. **Cucin,** Robt L '86 -40 Cntrl Pk S -NY 10019 **Fx**:586-9529
(914) 949-2696 .. **Cucinell,** Robt G '67 -25 Highvw Rd -Pound Rdg 10576 **Fx**:949-2477
(212) 326-2000 .. **Cucinella,** Brooke E '07 %O'Melveny & M LLP -7 Times Sq -NY 10036
(845) 786-2826 .. **Cucolo,** K Jody '90 KJ Cucolo,PC -15 Thiells Rd -Stony Pnt 10980 **Fx**:786-3121
(518) 457-4380 .. **Cucolo,** Richd J '77 Cnsl Dept of Labor -State Campus Bldg 12 -Albany 12240 **Fx**:485-1819
(212) 813-5900 .. **Cucurella,** Carlos '01 (Fross ZL&Z,PC) -866 UN Plz -NY 10017
(518) 568-2423 .. **Cuda,** Francis T '72 -4 E Main Bx57 -St Johnsvll 13452 **Fx**:568-3348
(415) 268-6904 .. **Cudd,** Robt A N '75 (Morrison & F LLP) -1290 Av of Amer -NY 10104 **Fx**:268-7522
(516) 775-3998 .. **Cuddahy,** John P '56 -1736 West End Av -New Hyde Pk 11040
(518) 457-6468 .. **Cuddeback,** Ryan C '99 %Agriculture & Mrkts -10B Airline Dr -Albany 12235 **Fx**:457-8842
(718) 590-2000 .. **Cudden,** James P '96 DA -198 E 161st -Bronx 10451 **Fx**:590-6477
(716) 868-9103 .. **Cuddy,** Andrew K '96 -Bx636 -Auburn 13021 **Fx**:204-2041
(631) 369-8200 .. **Cuddy,** Chas R '67 -445 Griffing Av Bx1547 -Rvrhead 11901 **Fx**:369-9080
(212) 687-3860 .. **Cuddy,** Edw Michl III '79 (Snow BK,PC) -605 3rd Av -NY 10158
(914) 761-1300 .. **Cuddy & Feder LLP** -445 Hmltn Av -White Plns 10601 **Fx**:761-5372
(845) 896-2229 .. **Cuddy & Feder LLP** -300 Westage Business Ctr -Fishkill 12524 **Fx**:896-3672
(212) 541-2000 .. **Cudrin,** Matthew E '03 %Bryan C LLP -1290 Av of Amer -NY 10104
(212) 285-2290 .. **Cueto,** Anthony R '88 -225 Bway -NY 10007 **Fx**:964-4506
(718) 368-5563 .. **Cueva,** Maria Elizabeth J '98 Kingsborough Comm Cllg -2001 Oriental Blvd -Brklyn 11235 **Fx**:368-4609
(914) 964-7060 .. **Cuevas,** Carlos J '83 -1250 Cntrl Pk Av -Ynkrs 10704 **Fx**:964-7064
(212) 335-3674 .. **Cuevas,** Julio A Jr. '97 %DA -1 Hogan Pl -NY 10013
(212) 310-6766 .. **Cuevas,** Lisa I '94 Weil G&M LLP -767 5th Av -NY 10153
(518) 464-1300 .. **Cuevas,** Michl R '79 OfCnsl Roemer WG&M LLP -13 Columbia Cir -Albany 12203
(212) 290-3207 .. **Cuevas,** Myrna I '97 %VNSNY -1250 Bway -NY 10001
(315) 443-2524 .. **Cuevas-Rodriguez,** Melanie '01 %Syracuse Univ Cllg of Law -Wht Hall -Syracuse 13244 **Fx**:443-4213
(718) 434-4878 .. **Cuff,** Walter G '83 -725 Rugby Rd -Brklyn 11230
(607) 337-1833 .. **Cuffney,** Robt E '89 Family Ct -5 Court -Norwich 13815 **Fx**:337-1835
(315) 435-2170 .. **Cuffy,** Gordon J '90 Cnty Atty -421 Mntgmry -Syracuse 13202 **Fx**:435-5729
(914) 722-6571 .. **Cugini,** Anthony J Jr. '88 -717 Wht Plns Rd -Scarsdale 10583
(212) 819-8200 .. **Cuillerier Dit Spooner,** Ian '96 (White & C LLP) -1155 Av of Amer -NY 10036
(212) 925-4545 .. **Cuisinier,** Lori G '96 %Friedman & G,LLP -568 Bway -NY 10012
(516) 463-5858 .. **Cuison-Villazor,** Rose C '01 %Hofstra Law Schl -121 Hofstra Univ -Hempstd 11549
(212) 696-6000 .. **Cukier,** Eduardo A '90 (Curtis M-PC&M LLP) -101 Park Av -NY 10178
(212) 935-3000 .. **Cukier,** Jennifer A '08 %Mintz LCFG&P,PC -666 3rd Av -NY 10017
(212) 613-2013 .. **Cukor,** Michl '01 (Gibbons PC) -1 Penn Plz -NY 10119 **Fx**:554-9658
(212) 907-9600 .. **Cukras,** Roger '67 (Ingram YGC&B,LLP) -250 Park Av -NY 10177
(212) 903-9000 .. **Culas,** Bindu M '99 (Linklaters) -1345 Av of Amer -NY 10105
(212) 848-4000 .. **Culbert,** Craig R '07 %Shearman & S LLP -599 Lex Av -NY 10022
(212) 348-7449 .. **Culbert,** Jennifer R '00 %Legal Srvcs -1 W 125th -NY 10027 **Fx**:348-4093
(212) 848-4000 .. **Culhane,** Catherine K '08 %Shearman & S LLP -599 Lex Av -NY 10022
(212) 326-3939 .. **Culhane,** Danl R '10 %Jones D -222 E 41st -NY 10017
(631) 218-3419 .. **Culhane,** Eileen Ann '93 -230 Waterford Rd -Oakdale 11769
(516) 249-1342 .. **Culhane,** Frank J '90 %Grey & G,LLP -360 Main -Farmngdl 11735
(212) 903-9000 .. **Culhane,** Stephen '94 (Linklaters) -1345 Av of Amer -NY 10105
(212) 685-3500 .. **Culhane,** Thos A '83 (Calano & C,LLP) -370 Lex Av -NY 10017 **Fx**:(914) 946-6000
(914) 686-3000 .. **Culhane,** Thos A '83 (Calano & C,LLP) -14 Mamaroneck Av -White Plns 10601 **Fx**:946-6000
(518) 447-7110 .. **Culihan,** Karry L '09 %Cnty Atty -112 State -Albany 12207
(518) 783-4406 .. **Culkin,** Jeffrey T '90 %Epstein & R -950 New Loudon Rd -Latham 12110
(212) 874-0100 .. **Cullen,** Ann C R '93 Bellmarc Realty LLC -424 Columbus Av -NY 10024
(845) 486-2110 .. **Cullen,** Christian R '88 %Cnty Atty -22 Market -Poughkeepsie 12601 **Fx**:486-2002
(212) 770-6692 .. **Cullen,** Clare D '87 %AIG -70 Pine -NY 10270
(914) 286-3400 .. **Cullen,** Dina L '83 %Leg Aid -1 N Bway -White Plns 10601 **Fx**:682-4112
(718) 855-9000 .. **Cullen and Dykman LLP** -177 Montague -Brklyn 11201 **Fx**:855-4282
(516) 357-3700 .. **Cullen and Dykman LLP** -100 Q Roosevelt Blvd -Gdn Cty 11530 **Fx**:357-3792
(212) 732-2000 .. **Cullen and Dykman LLP** -44 Wall -NY 10005 **Fx**:571-2838
(718) 359-2200 .. **Cullen and Dykman LLP** -158-14 Nrthrn Blvd -Flushng 11358 **Fx**:359-1722
(212) 581-4180 .. **Cullen,** Elizabeth '80 %Rosedale Mgmt -1775 Bway -NY 10019
(914) 962-4300 .. **Cullen,** Frank '75 -1875 Glenrock -Yorktwn Hts 10598 **Fx**:962-4386
(212) 278-1565 .. **Cullen,** James P '70 (Anderson K&O,PC) -1251 Av of Amer -NY 10020
(718) 897-1600 .. **Cullen,** James R '89 -80-02 Kew Grdns Rd -Kew Gdns 11415
(914) 632-7275 .. **Cullen,** John E '71 (Reville & C) -540 North Av -New Rchll 10801
(212) 490-3000 .. **Cullen,** Jos P '06 %Wilson EME&D LLP -150 E 42nd -NY 10017
(212) 233-9772 .. **Cullen,** Kevin D Jr. '98 (Cullen & T,PC) -2 Rector -NY 10006
(212) 558-4000 .. **Cullen,** Matthew K '09 %Sullivan & C LLP -125 Broad -NY 10004
(212) 732-2000 .. **Cullen,** Matthew P '99 %Cullen and D LLP -44 Wall -NY 10005
(914) 765-3924 .. **Cullen,** Pauline M '82 %MBIA Ins Corp -113 King -Armonk 10504
(631) 329-3981 .. **Cullen,** Scott M '98 -Bx5125 -E Hampton 11937
(914) 946-7770 .. **Cullen,** Thos A '97 %Westermann SKS&A,LLP -222 Bloomingdale Rd -White Plns 10605
(212) 233-9772 .. **Cullen & Troia,PC** -2 Rector -NY 10006 **Fx**:233-9771
(212) 836-8000 .. **Cullen,** Wm J J '86 (Kaye S LLP) -425 Park Av -NY 10022
(914) 761-0707 .. **Culleton,** James J '74 (Culleton & M) -245 Main -White Plns 10601 **Fx**:761-0795
(212) 401-0800 .. **Culley,** Kevin P '91 (Disciplinary Comm) -61 Bway -NY 10006 **Fx**:287-1045
(914) 698-5188 .. **Culley,** Lawr T '81 -421 Waverly Av -Mamaroneck 10543
(585) 546-7830 .. **Culley Marks Tanenbaum & Pezzulo,LLP** -36 W Main -Rchstr 14614 **Fx**:546-6456
(212) 416-6039 .. **Culley,** Rebecca D K '07 Atty Gen -120 Bway -NY 10271
(212) 813-8800 .. **Culligan,** Kevin J '81 (Goodwin P LLP) -620 8th Av -NY 10018
(516) 365-6690 .. **Cullinan,** Kristen M '04 PRI -1800 Nrthrn Blvd -Roslyn 11576
(516) 712-4000 .. **Cullinan,** Marybeth '92 (Milber MP&S LLP) -1000 Woodbury Rd -Woodbury 11797
(631) 897-4111 .. **Cullinane,** Shawn S '01 -183 Texas -Lindenhrst 11757
(718) 923-6312 .. **Cullinane Mollica,** Shaun K '05 Law Guardian Prog -335 Adams -Brklyn 11201 **Fx**:624-5603
(716) 858-2424 .. **Culliton,** Alyson C '07 %DA -25 Delaware Av -Buffalo 14202 **Fx**:858-7425
(631) 853-8500 .. **Cullity,** Carolyn J '02 Health Dept -Bx6100 -Hauppauge 11788
(518) 792-1174 .. **Cullum,** James E '68 (McPhillips F&C,LLP) -288 Glen Bx299 -Glens Fls 12801
(212) 479-6000 .. **Cullum,** Janet L '07 (Cooley LLP) -1114 Av of Amer -NY 10036
(315) 733-0455 .. **Cully,** Herbert J '78 (Calli C&C) -510 Bleecker -Utica 13501
(212) 967-1800 .. **Cully,** Kathleen G '83 OfCnsl Bryant BJ&R LLP -140 Bway -NY 10005
(845) 340-3315 .. **Culmone,** Elizabeth A '07 %DA -285 Wall -Kingston 12401 **Fx**:340-3185
(518) 462-3000 .. **Culnan,** Brian M '93 (Iseman CR&H,LLP) -9 Thurlow Ter -Albany 12203
(212) 326-2000 .. **Culvahouse,** Arthur B Jr. '06 (O'Melveny & M LLP) -7 Times Sq -NY 10036

(646) 253-2300 .. **Culver,** Amy M '06 %Bond S&K,PLLC -330 Mad Av -NY 10017
(212) 218-5500 .. **Culver,** Marjorie R '09 (Seyfarth S LLP) -620 8th Av -NY 10018
(212) 776-5000 .. **Culverhouse,** Cecilia '09 %NYC Housing Auth -250 Bway -NY 10007 **Fx:**776-5039
(646) 871-6739 .. **Cumber,** Anishah A '09 Advocates for Children of NY -151 W 30th -NY 10001
(212) 804-5710 .. **Cumberbatch,** Lawr S '73 -110 Wall -NY 10005 **Fx:**943-2300
(212) 442-9025 .. **Cumberbatch,** Yvette Stacey '87 %Law Dept -100 Church -NY 10007 **Fx:**788-0367
(585) 256-2702 .. **Cumbo,** James A '94 -69 Wilshire Rd -Rchstr 14618
(212) 946-4781 .. **Cumby,** Dorothy E '87 (Cumby + W LLP) -11 Penn Plz -NY 10001
(212) 525-5000 .. **Cumings,** Victoria E '05 Cnsl HSBC Bank -452 5th Av -NY 10018
(212) 425-0055 .. **Cumins,** Gail T '63 (Sharretts PC&B) -75 Broad -NY 10004
(516) 686-2236 .. **Cumming,** Chas S '95 Sheffield Investments -55 Brookvll Rd -Brookvll 11545
(914) 686-0108 .. **Cumming,** Elizabeth A '06 %Glassman & B -99 Court -White Plns 10601
(631) 574-4520 .. **Cummings,** Anthony W '88 (Cummings Law Ofc,PC) -105 Maxess Rd -Melvll 11747
(914) 921-1000 .. **Cummings,** Barbara W '74 -14 Elm Pl -Rye 10580 **Fx:**921-1056
(716) 856-5012 .. **Cummings,** C DeForest Jr. '62 OfCnsl Anspach ME,LLP -2400 Main Pl Twr -Buffalo 14202
(212) 626-4100 .. **Cummings,** Chas B '74 (Baker & M LLP) -1114 Av of Amer -NY 10036
(212) 756-2000 .. **Cummings,** David L '10 %Schulte R&Z LLP -919 3rd Av -NY 10022
(212) 373-3000 .. **Cummings,** Desiree R '05 %Paul WRW&G LLP -1285 Av of Amer -NY 10019
(914) 948-1200 .. **Cummings,** Douglas J Jr. '07 %Cerussi & S,PC -1 N Lex Av -White Plns 10601
(518) 377-1076 .. **Cummings,** Edw J Jr. '68 -1121 Glen Meadown Ct -Schnctdy 12309
(518) 471-4777 .. **Cummings,** Edw L '05 Appllt Div 3rd Dept -Capitol Station Bx7288 -Albany 12224 **Fx:**471-4750
(212) 984-7807 .. **Cummings,** Fredk R Jr. '74 (Warshaw BCS&K,LLP) -555 5th Av -NY 10017
(914) 631-6900 .. **Cummings,** Glenn P '00 %Guttridge & C,PC -303 S Bway -Tarrytwn 10591 **Fx:**631-6644
(585) 663-2150 .. **Cummings,** James J III '86 -1577 W Ridge Rd -Rchstr 14615 **Fx:**663-3962
(518) 388-4364 .. **Cummings,** Laurie M '07 DA -612 State -Schnctdy 12305 **Fx:**388-4569
(516) 628-3168 .. **Cummings,** LoRetta '84 -Bx103 -Bayvll 11709
(646) 414-1741 .. **Cummings,** Louise E '06 -45 Wall -NY 10005
(212) 325-2000 .. **Cummings,** Michl E '99 CSFB -1 Mad Av -NY 10010
(212) 841-1000 .. **Cummings,** Michl O '95 OfCnsl Covington & B LLP -620 8th Av -NY 10018
(212) 969-3000 .. **Cummings,** Neil '94 (Proskauer R LLP) -1585 Bway -NY 10036
(607) 772-9262 .. **Cummings,** Patricia A '88 (O'Connor GL&C,LLP) -84 Court -Bnghmtn 13901
(315) 376-6565 .. **Cummings,** Richd C '55 %Dunckel & K LLP -5423 Shady Av Bx473 -Lowvll 13367 **Fx:**376-8418
(716) 856-4000 .. **Cummings,** Ryan K '03 (Hodgson R LLP) -140 Pearl -Buffalo 14202
(718) 537-6707 .. **Cummings,** Sherine F '08 %Law Dept -198 E 161st -Bronx 10451 **Fx:**590-2686
(212) 688-3025 .. **Cummings,** Terence P '82 (Hitchcock & C,LLP) -757 3rd Av -NY 10017 **Fx:**688-3040
(716) 285-9555 .. **Cummings,** Wm H Jr. '74 (Viola C&L) -770 Main Bx948 -Niagara Fls 14302
(845) 628-7415 .. **Cummins,** Don M III '98 -34 Mayfair Ln -Mahopac 10541
(212) 285-0510 .. **Cummins,** Harry A '86 (Wilkofsky FK&C) -299 Bway -NY 10007
(212) 839-5300 .. **Cummins,** J Gerard '93 (Sidley A LLP) -787 7th Av -NY 10019
(212) 309-1040 .. **Cummins,** Jennifer L '10 %Hunton & W -200 Park Av -NY 10166
(716) 847-3513 .. **Cummins,** Judith M '89 %Div of Parole -460 Main -Buffalo 14202 **Fx:**847-3464
(585) 232-6500 .. **Cummins,** Kathleen L '08 %Harter S&E LLP -1600 Bausch & Lomb Pl -Rchstr 14604
(212) 351-4000 .. **Cummins,** Megan L '07 %Gibson D&C LLP -200 Park Av -NY 10166
(914) 238-9787 .. **Cummins,** Richd M '64 -236 N Bedford Rd -Chappaqua 10514
(718) 422-4618 .. **Cummins,** Seth J '79 NYC OEM -165 Cadman Plz E -Brklyn 11201
(212) 695-8100 .. **Cummiskey,** Timothy B '95 %Goetz F,LLP -1 Penn Plz -NY 10119
(212) 768-6700 .. **Cummo,** Aimee M '99 (Sonnenschein N&R LLP) -2 World Fncl Ctr -NY 10281
(518) 487-7600 .. **Cumo,** Tammy L '03 %Whiteman O&H LLP -1 Commerce Plz -Albany 12260
(212) 902-5734 .. **Cundiff,** Richd M Jr. '97 Goldman Sachs -1 NY Plz -NY 10004
(212) 318-6000 .. **Cundiff,** Victoria A '81 (Paul HJ&W LLP) -75 E 55th -NY 10022
(518) 886-4189 .. **Cuneo,** Brian C '97 %AYCO -Bx860 -Saratoga Spgs 12866
(516) 248-3506 .. **Cuneo,** Chas R '85 -114 Old Cntry Rd -Mineola 11501
(845) 473-5371 .. **Cuneo,** Eileen '85 -Bx205 -LaGrangevll 12540 **Fx:**473-3645
(212) 403-1000 .. **Cuneo,** James D '08 %Wachtell LR&K -51 W 52nd -NY 10019
(212) 294-6700 .. **Cuneo,** Lauren E '09 %Winston & S -200 Park Av -NY 10166
(212) 848-4000 .. **Cunha,** Kirsten Nelson '05 (Shearman & S LLP) -599 Lex Av -NY 10022
(212) 455-2000 .. **Cunha,** Mark G '81 (Simpson T&B LLP) -425 Lex Av -NY 10017
(914) 761-1300 .. **Cunnane,** Thos A '06 %Cuddy & F LLP -445 Hmltn Av -White Plns 10601
(212) 277-4000 .. **Cunning,** Andrea M '03 %Freshfields BD LLP -520 Mad Av -NY 10022
(518) 402-1871 .. **Cunningham,** Andrea P '94 %Dept of Health -Corning Twr 24th Fl -Albany 12237 **Fx:**473-4896
(518) 474-1620 .. **Cunningham,** Audrey M '01 OCTF -The Cptl -Albany 12224 **Fx:**474-7258
(516) 746-2133 .. **Cunningham,** Brian G '92 (Cunningham & C,LLP) -22 Jericho Tpk -Mineola 11501 **Fx:**294-5385
(212) 963-3887 .. **Cunningham,** C Lynette '88 %UN Legal Ofc -DC-408 UN -NY 10017 **Fx:**963-5847
(914) 835-1988 .. **Cunningham,** Carolyn C '89 -18 Soundvw Av -Rye 10580 **Fx:**835-3526
(212) 964-6611 .. **Cunningham,** Clare M '02 %Lester SK&D -120 Bway -NY 10271
(845) 794-3000 .. **Cunningham,** Colleen M '91 %Div of Hlth & Fam Srvcs -Govt Center-100 North -Monticello 12701 **Fx:**807-0507
(518) 431-1000 .. **Cunningham,** Danl D '99 %Siegal,LLC -16 Corp Wds Blvd -Albany 12211 **Fx:**465-7200
(212) 849-7000 .. **Cunningham,** Danl P '80 (Quinn EU&S,LLP) -51 Mad Av -NY 10010
(516) 248-4908 .. **Cunningham,** Deborah M '89 -150 Lafayette -Williston Pk 11596
(315) 472-8655 .. **Cunningham,** Diana G '92 -109 S Warren -Syracuse 13202 **Fx:**472-5800
(516) 328-3705 .. **Cunningham,** Edw F '78 -62 Cmbrdg Av -Gdn Cty 11530 **Fx:**775-6835
(845) 452-5900 .. **Cunningham,** Edw V K Jr. '62 Cnsl Van DeWater & V,LLP -85 Civic Ctr Plz Bx112 -Poughkeepsie 12602
(914) 723-2404 .. **Cunningham Galloway & Marett** -220 Harwood Bldg -Scarsdale 10583 **Fx:**723-1951
(212) 207-8400 .. **Cunningham,** Geraldine M '97 (Kavanagh M&O LLP) -415 Mad Av -NY 10017
(212) 679-0404 .. **Cunningham,** Gerard W '63 (Cunningham & C,LLP) -451 Park Av S -NY 10016 **Fx:**683-0404
(212) 302-2435 .. **Cunningham,** Glen T '83 (Cunningham & C) -19 W 44th -NY 10036
(631) 577-7770 .. **Cunningham,** Glenda R '03 %K Dodson -100 Baylis Rd -Melvll 11747 **Fx:**577-7199
(212) 483-9600 .. **Cunningham,** Gregory E '05 %Costello S&G LLP -44 Wall -NY 10005
(646) 534-8775 .. **Cunningham,** Jacqueline G '96 JP Morgan Chase & Co -270 Park Av -NY 10017
(212) 415-2000 .. **Cunningham,** James T '97 DDB Worldwode Communications -437 Mad Av -NY 10022
(315) 474-2911 .. **Cunningham,** James W '95 (Smith SK&S,PC) -250 S Clinton -Syracuse 13202
(212) 351-4000 .. **Cunningham,** Jason C '09 Gibson D&C LLP -200 Park Av -NY 10166
(212) 310-8000 .. **Cunningham,** Jessica V '08 %Weil G&M LLP -767 5th Av -NY 10153
(518) 434-1022 .. **Cunningham,** John J '58 OfCnsl Sullivan KO&V, LLP -152 Central Av -Albany 12206
(212) 728-8000 .. **Cunningham,** Jos P '00 OfCnsl Willkie F&G LLP -787 7th Av -NY 10019
(212) 885-5000 .. **Cunningham,** Kathleen A '00 (Blank R LLP) -405 Lex Av -NY 10174
(516) 571-2722 .. **Cunningham,** Kathryn A '83 %County Ct -262 Old Cntry Rd -Mineola 11501 **Fx:**571-2160
(212) 335-4500 .. **Cunningham,** Kerry F '98 %DLA Piper LLP -1251 Av of Amer -NY 10020
(212) 225-2000 .. **Cunningham,** Kevin C '08 %Cleary GS&H -1 Lbrty Plz -NY 10006
(718) 990-7616 .. **Cunningham,** Larry H '01 St John's Law Schl -8000 Utopia Pkwy -Jamaica 11439 **Fx:**591-1855
(212) 790-0214 .. **Cunningham,** Laura E '88 %Benj N Cardozo Schl of Law -55 5th Av -NY 10003 **Fx:**790-0345
(516) 573-7000 .. **Cunningham,** Lewis W '97 %Cnty Police -1490 Franklin Av -Mineola 11501
(646) 386-4707 .. **Cunningham,** Lisa K '01 %Hon J Newton -100 Centre -NY 10013
(212) 458-1049 .. **Cunningham,** Mary Lee K '91 %AIG -175 Water -NY 10038
(914) 232-9696 .. **Cunningham,** Maryanne '86 NextGen Networks -200 Katonah Av -Katonah 10536
(212) 302-2435 .. **Cunningham,** Maureen P '84 (Cunningham & C) -19 W 44th -NY 10036
(518) 462-3000 .. **Cunningham,** Michl J '74 (Iseman CR&H,LLP) -9 Thurlow Ter -Albany 12203
(212) 768-6700 .. **Cunningham,** Michl M '08 %Sonnenschein N&R LLP -2 World Fncl Ctr -NY 10281
(914) 253-3474 .. **Cunningham,** Patrick C '97 %Pepsico Aviation -150 Airport Rd Hangar V -White Plns 10604
(212) 697-3122 .. **Cunningham,** Rebecca R '08 %Martin C&B LLP -220 E 42nd -NY 10017
(212) 318-3000 .. **Cunningham,** Richd J Jr. '62 OfCnsl Fulbright & J LLP -666 5th Av -NY 10103
(212) 351-4000 .. **Cunningham,** Robt L Jr. '73 (Gibson D&C LLP) -200 Park Av -NY 10166
(716) 853-5100 .. **Cunningham,** Roy H '99 %Lippes MWF LLP -665 Main -Buffalo 14203
(914) 948-7000 .. **Cunningham,** Stephen C '87 (Keidel W&C LLP) -925 Wstchstr Av -White Plns 10604
(845) 223-3888 .. **Cunningham,** Thos F '69 -6 Trinity Way -LaGrangevll 12540
(516) 229-4300 .. **Cunningham,** Thos J '60 %J Bilello & Assoc -875 Merrick Av -Westbury 11590
(716) 854-3400 .. **Cunningham,** Thos P '93 (Rupp BPC&C LLC) -1600 Lbrty Bldg -Buffalo 14202
(212) 608-8840 .. **Cunningham,** Wm B '83 %Bamundo Z&S,LLP -111 John -NY 10038
(518) 474-4246 .. **Cunningham,** Wm J III '77 Governors Ofc -State Cptl -Albany 12224 **Fx:**473-7619
(516) 873-6330 .. **Cuocci,** Vincent '97 (Feinsilver & C,LLC) -1 Old Cntry Rd -Carle Pl 11514
(518) 474-7330 .. **Cuomo,** Andrew M '84 Dept of Law -The Cptl -Albany 12224
(212) 456-2042 .. **Cuomo,** Christopher C '96 %ABC News -147 Columbus Av -NY 10023
(716) 839-4001 .. **Cuomo,** Frank N '55 (Hellerer C&O) -4536 Main -Amherst 14226 **Fx:**839-0964
(212) 688-8555 .. **Cuomo,** G Martine '96 (Fragomen DB&L LLP) -7 Hanover Sq -NY 10004
(212) 238-4800 .. **Cuomo,** Jerry A '97 (Landman CB&F,PC) -120 Bway -NY 10271
(516) 248-1700 .. **Cuomo,** Jos V '92 (Forchelli CDSM&T,LLP) -333 Earle Ovngton Blvd -Uniondale 11553
(631) 853-5212 .. **Cuomo,** Leo '04 Leg Aid -400 Carleton Av Bx9082 -Central Islip 11722 **Fx:**853-7798
(315) 366-2241 .. **Cuomo,** Lisa Sapino '90 Family Ct -Bx507 -Wampsville 13163 **Fx:**366-2828
(212) 728-8000 .. **Cuomo,** Mario M '56 OfCnsl Willkie F&G LLP -787 7th Av -NY 10019
(212) 448-9933 .. **Cuomo,** Matthew A '92 (Finder & C LLP) -9 E 38th -NY 10016
(718) 579-7919 .. **Cuomo,** Meghan '04 %Leg Aid -900 Sheridan Av -Bronx 10451 **Fx:**293-8744
(716) 839-4001 .. **Cuomo,** Neil N '86 %Hellerer C&O -4536 Main -Amherst 14226 **Fx:**839-0964

(914) 584-4949 .. **Cuono,** Vincent '00 -33 Hubbells Dr -Mt Kisco 10549 **Fx:**666-6743
(212) 858-7706 .. **Cuonzo,** Angelo A '90 (Slowinski A,LLP) -140 Bway PMB 46039 -NY 10005
(718) 590-2000 .. **Cuozzo,** Diana M '09 %DA -198 E 161st -Bronx 10451 **Fx:**590-6477
(845) 294-1060 .. **Cupero,** James J '80 (J Cupero,PLLC) -50 N Church -Goshen 10924 **Fx:**294-1525
(518) 566-6666 .. **Cuppett,** Danl C '06 %MA Schneider -57 Court -Plattsbrgh 12901 **Fx:**566-6667
(212) 440-2547 .. **Curan,** Michl B '97 %CNA-ENS -40 Wall -NY 10005 **Fx:**440-2536
(914) 428-3313 .. **Curan,** Michl E '64 (Curan AF&N,LLP) -14 Mamaroneck Av -White Plns 10601 **Fx:**949-5800
(516) 364-9446 .. **Curasi,** Gary M '97 -Bx1142 -Syosset 11791 **Fx:**364-9447
(212) 577-8785 .. **Curbelo,** Maria C '89 %Criminal Justice Agncy -52 Duane -NY 10007 **Fx:**577-0586
(718) 590-2000 .. **Curbelo,** Rafael A '98 %DA -198 E 161st -Bronx 10451 **Fx:**590-6477
(212) 455-2000 .. **Curbow,** Wm E '91 (Simpson T&B LLP) -425 Lex Av -NY 10017
(718) 851-4766 .. **Curchack,** Susan L '77 -415 Albemarle Rd -Brklyn 11218
(212) 407-4000 .. **Curchack,** Walter H '76 (Loeb & L,LLP) -345 Park Av -NY 10154
(212) 244-2999 .. **Curcillo,** Tara K '93 (Kopff N&D LLP) -440 9th Av -NY 10001
(845) 344-2524 .. **Curcio,** Craig P '86 -1 Edgewtr Dr -Middletwn 10940 **Fx:**344-2528
(212) 319-1000 .. **Curcio,** Dominic S '92 (Quirk & B,PC) -845 3rd Av -NY 10022
(718) 412-4790 .. **Curcio,** Donna C '01 (Curcio L & Assoc,PLLC) -259 Lbrty Av -Staten Isl 10305 **Fx:**980-3858
(718) 558-8352 .. **Curcio,** John B '69 %LIRR -Jamaica Station -Jamaica 11435 **Fx:**558-8211
(917) 612-5178 .. **Curcio,** Lindsay A '97 -9508 4th Av -Brklyn 11209
(212) 768-6700 .. **Curcio,** Louis A '02 %Sonnenschein N&R LLP -1221 Av of Amer -NY 10020
(631) 249-9230 .. **Curcio,** Philip L '04 -445 Broadhllw Rd -Melvll 11747
(212) 448-1800 .. **Curcio,** Tanya M '08 %Roberts RLSC&F LLP -235 Park Av S -NY 10003
(516) 767-6106 .. **Curd,** Ann Marie '91 A Curd PLLC -14 Vanderventer Av -Pt Wash 11050 **Fx:**706-2650
(718) 237-3144 .. **Cure,** Ira S '84 -161 Remsen -Brklyn 11201
(212) 768-6700 .. **Curi,** Eli Jr. '97 (Sonnenschein N&R LLP) -2 World Fncl Ctr -NY 10281
(212) 224-1540 .. **Curiale,** Salvatore R '70 Mutual of America -320 Park Av -NY 10022 **Fx:**224-2520
(607) 723-5341 .. **Curinga,** Megan E '07 %Hinman H&K,LLP -80 Exchange Bx5250 -Bnghmtn 13902
(718) 579-3000 .. **Curkin,** Seth T '04 %Leg Aid -1020 Grnd Cncrs -Bronx 10451 **Fx:**588-2611
(646) 282-5839 .. **Curl,** Suzanne B '05 Davidson Kempner Cptl Mgmt,LLC -65 E 55th -NY 10022
(212) 385-1215 .. **Curley,** Amy J '04 %P Lange -445 Park Av -NY 10022 **Fx:**608-1215
(315) 379-2115 .. **Curley,** Christopher R '96 %Pub Def -Cnty Cthse -Canton 13617 **Fx:**386-8241
(212) 269-0927 .. **Curley,** Gavin J '03 %D'Amato & L,LLP -2 World Fncl Ctr -NY 10281
(212) 551-5723 .. **Curley,** Gregory M '95 %Royal Alliance Assoc -1 World Fncl Ctr -NY 10281 **Fx:**551-5620
(212) 909-6000 .. **Curley,** John P '09 %Debevoise & P LLP -919 3rd Av -NY 10022
(631) 342-4943 .. **Curley,** Kelley Dowd '01 %Computer Assocs Intl,Inc -1 Computer Associates Plz -Islandia 11749
(315) 798-5870 .. **Curley,** Mark C '03 %Pub Def -321 Main -Utica 13501 **Fx:**798-6419
(914) 749-8560 .. **Curley,** Mary S '04 USI Hldngs Corp -555 Plsntvll Rd -Briarclff Mnr 10510 **Fx:**(610) 537-9324
(646) 378-2231 .. **Curley,** Michl A '89 (Curley & M LLP) -5 Penn Plz -NY 10001 **Fx:**378-2232
(212) 704-1348 .. **Curley,** Paul J '95 %Interpublic Grp -1114 Av of Amer -NY 10036 **Fx:**704-1201
(212) 980-9600 .. **Curley,** Paul T '98 (Kaufman B&R) -120 Bway -NY 10271
(212) 935-3000 .. **Curley,** Stephen C '72 (Mintz LCFG&P,PC) -666 3rd Av -NY 10017
(718) 945-4709 .. **Curley,** Thos E '84 -106-20 Shore Front Pkwy -Rckwy Pk 11694
(212) 806-5400 .. **Curnin,** Kevin '96 (Stroock &S&L LLP) -180 Maiden Ln -NY 10038
(212) 455-2000 .. **Curnin,** Paul C '88 (Simpson T&B LLP) -425 Lex Av -NY 10017
(212) 867-5800 .. **Curpen,** Radha Devinaigi '07 (Osler H&H LLP) -620 8th Av -NY 10018
(315) 446-0033 .. **Curran,** Ann M '94 %Medical Mgt Resources -Bx2000 -E Syracuse 13057
(585) 235-4250 .. **Curran,** Brian F '84 -56 Elmwood Av -Rchstr 14611 **Fx:**235-3115
(516) 741-6355 .. **Curran,** Brian F '95 %Nicolini PF&S -114 Old Cntry Rd Bx9006 -Mineola 11501
(516) 333-8099 .. **Curran,** Brian P '85 -2 Douglas -Carle Pl 11514
(585) 232-6500 .. **Curran,** Candace M '08 %Harter S&E LLP -1600 Bausch & Lomb Pl -Rchstr 14604
(212) 776-5000 .. **Curran,** Elizabeth '89 %NYC Housing Auth -250 Bway -NY 10007 **Fx:**776-5039
(631) 586-1111 .. **Curran,** James P '92 (Miller A&C PLLC) -900 Grand Blvd -Deer Pk 11729
(516) 571-3056 .. **Curran,** Joanne T '04 %Cnty Atty -1 West -Mineola 11501 **Fx:**571-6604
(212) 981-6540 .. **Curran,** John F Jr. '88 %Stroz Friedberg LLC -32 Av of Amer -NY 10013 **Fx:**981-6545
(585) 454-6180 .. **Curran,** John G '58 -36 W Main -Rchstr 14614 **Fx:**454-2867
(704) 988-4459 .. **Curran,** John P '82 %TIAA-CREF -730 3rd Av -NY 10017
(212) 732-2000 .. **Curran,** John T '83 (Cullen and D LLP) -44 Wall -NY 10005
(212) 508-6700 .. **Curran,** John-Patrick S '92 (Tannenbaum HS&H LLP) -900 3rd Av -NY 10022
(585) 454-0700 .. **Curran,** Jos G '89 (Ward GH&R LLP) -300 State -Rchstr 14614
(212) 902-0805 .. **Curran,** Kenneth G '90 %Goldman Sachs & Co -85 Broad -NY 10004
(212) 465-5000 .. **Curran,** Kevin J '76 %Parsons Brinckerhoff -1 Penn Plz -NY 10119
(585) 394-8340 .. **Curran,** M Kathleen '85 -47 Ontario -Canandaigua 14424
(212) 701-3000 .. **Curran,** Mary C '02 %Cahill G&R LLP -80 Pine -NY 10005 **Fx:**269-5420
(914) 666-2161 .. **Curran,** Maurice F '58 OfCnsl Banks CS&S,LLP -61 Smith Av -Mt Kisco 10549
(718) 830-7741 .. **Curran,** Michl R '97 -98-120 Qns Blvd -Rego Pk 11374 **Fx:**830-9088
(212) 578-2211 .. **Curran,** Patricia Ann '96 %MetLife -27-01 Qns Plz N -LIC 11101
(212) 335-9000 .. **Curran,** Patricia J '80 %DA -1 Hogan Pl -NY 10013
(716) 856-5500 .. **Curran,** Patrick B '82 (Damon M LLP) -200 Delaware Av -Buffalo 14202
(212) 849-7000 .. **Curran,** Patrick D '08 %Quinn EU&S,LLP -51 Mad Av -NY 10010
(518) 449-3440 .. **Curran,** Patrick J III '80 %Energy Assn NYS -111 Wshngtn Av -Albany 12210 **Fx:**449-3446
(212) 382-0909 .. **Curran,** Thos J '90 (Peckar & A,PC) -41 Mad Av -NY 10154
(516) 571-3800 .. **Curran,** Victoria A '90 %DA -262 Old Cntry Rd -Mineola 11501 **Fx:**248-9479
(212) 306-1000 .. **Curran,** Wm A '03 %Amer Stock Exch -86 Trinity Pl -NY 10006
(212) 450-4000 .. **Curran,** Wm A '10 %Davis P&W LLP -450 Lex Av -NY 10017
(518) 457-2854 .. **Curreri,** Richd A '77 %PERB -80 Wolf Rd -Albany 12205 **Fx:**457-2664
(212) 474-1000 .. **Currey,** Ralph B III '83 Cravath S&M LLP -825 8th Av -NY 10019
(212) 225-2000 .. **Currie,** Katherine S '10 %Cleary GS&H -1 Lbrty Plz -NY 10006
(212) 223-4000 .. **Currie,** Kelly T '95 (Crowell & M LLP) -590 Mad Av -NY 10022
(718) 797-3117 .. **Currie,** Neil B '04 %MS Flamm -26 Court -Brklyn 11242 **Fx:**522-2026
(315) 449-2616 .. **Currie,** Thos F '75 Martin GBM&C,PC -5790 Widewaters Pkwy -DeWitt 13214
(212) 335-4500 .. **Currie,** Wm D '09 %DLA Piper LLP -1251 Av of Amer -NY 10020
(518) 692-2494 .. **Currin,** Cailie Ann '89 -14 Main Bx90 -Greenwich 12834
(212) 709-8174 .. **Curro,** Isabelle L '90 -110 Wall -NY 10005 **Fx:**943-2300
(518) 464-6644 .. **Curro,** Kelly M '93 %Caplan & C -1707 Central Av -Albany 12205 **Fx:**464-0202
(212) 753-5000 .. **Curro,** Matthew L '08 %Schiff H LLP -900 3rd Av -NY 10022
(212) 318-6000 .. **Curry,** Amy F '08 %Paul HJ&W LLP -75 E 55th -NY 10022
(718) 618-3000 .. **Curry,** Christina E '91 Hon E Foley -265 E 161st -Bronx 10451
(212) 709-8274 .. **Curry,** Danl J '99 -110 Wall -NY 10005
(516) 227-0700 .. **Curry,** David M '04 %Farrell F,PC -1320 RXR Plz -Uniondale 11556
(212) 218-2100 .. **Curry,** Donald J '81 (Fitzpatrick CH&S) -1290 Av of Amer -NY 10104
(518) 648-5113 .. **Curry,** James T '80 DA -Bx277 -Indian Lk 12842 **Fx:**648-5724
(516) 485-5577 .. **Curry,** John E '60 (Rosenthal C&K,LLP) -1600 Front -E Meadow 11554
(212) 909-6000 .. **Curry,** John T III '82 (Debevoise & P LLP) -919 3rd Av -NY 10022
(212) 687-0100 .. **Curry,** Judi Abbott '87 (Harris B PLLC) -100 Wall -NY 10005
(212) 698-3500 .. **Curry,** Niamh A '98 %Dechert LLP -1095 Av of Amer -NY 10036
(516) 485-5577 .. **Curry,** Patrick W '89 (Rosenthal C&K,LLP) -1600 Front -E Meadow 11554
(516) 227-0700 .. **Curry,** Peter L '79 (Farrell F,PC) -1320 RXR Plz -Uniondale 11556
(212) 637-3134 .. **Curry,** Virginia A '89 %EPA -290 Bway -NY 10007 **Fx:**637-3096
(718) 254-0700 .. **Curry,** Virginia B '85 %Bklyn Defender Srvcs -177 Lvngstn -Brklyn 11201 **Fx:**254-0897
(212) 407-4000 .. **Cursio,** Ralph M '79 OfCnsl Loeb & L,LLP -345 Park Av -NY 10154
(914) 995-3420 .. **Curti,** Michl V '05 %DA -111 Martin Luther King Blvd -White Plns 10601 **Fx:**995-3363
(516) 223-5500 .. **Curti,** Shana '05 %R Nelson -2249 Derby Rd -Baldwin 11510 **Fx:**223-5505
(212) 872-7742 .. **Curtin,** Andrew J '83 KPMG LLP -345 Park Av -NY 10154 **Fx:**409-8729
(518) 758-9480 .. **Curtin,** Anne F '83 Church of the Holy Cross -138 8th -Troy 12180
(518) 387-6446 .. **Curtin,** Christopher E '02 GE -1 Rsrch Cir -Schnctdy 12309
(212) 318-6000 .. **Curtin,** Cynthia A '07 %Paul HJ&W LLP -75 E 55th -NY 10022
(845) 452-4353 .. **Curtin,** Danl F '69 -90 Market -Poughkeepsie 12601
(518) 561-4400 .. **Curtin,** Dennis D '86 Stafford OC&T,PLLC -1 Cumberland Av Bx2947 -Plattsbrgh 12901
(212) 752-9700 .. **Curtin,** Edw R '69 -101 E 52nd -NY 10022 **Fx:**980-5192
(212) 265-6888 .. **Curtin,** Kelly D '10 %Porzio B&N,PC -156 W 56th -NY 10019
(212) 770-8111 .. **Curtin,** Melissa C '02 %AIG -70 Pine -NY 10270
(212) 336-3620 .. **Curtin,** Nora E '89 %EEOC -33 Whitehall -NY 10004
(607) 763-9200 .. **Curtin,** Patricia M '84 (Levene G&T,LLP) -BxF-1706 -Bnghmtn 13902
(212) 785-2929 .. **Curtin,** Patrick E Jr. '72 (Conway FC&K,PC) -48 Wall -NY 10005
(716) 853-9555 .. **Curtin,** Paul B '99 %Leg Aid -237 Main -Buffalo 14203 **Fx:**853-3219
(315) 424-8944 .. **Curtin,** Paul J Jr. '77 (Shulman CG&R,PC) -250 S Clinton -Syracuse 13202
(914) 347-4300 .. **Curtin,** Paul S '95 %Acorda Therapeutics -15 Skyline Dr -Hawthorne 10532
(212) 249-8070 .. **Curtin,** Philip J '61 -444 E 82nd -NY 10028 **Fx:**504-3243
(212) 558-5500 .. **Curtin,** Teresa A '89 %Weitz & L,PC -700 Bway -NY 10003
(212) 850-6220 .. **Curtin,** Thos H '87 (Lathrop & G LC) -230 Park Av -NY 10169
(212) 918-3000 .. **Curtin,** Wm J III '08 (Hogan L LLP) -875 3rd Av -NY 10022
(212) 363-3100 .. **Curtis,** Adam B '89 (Bivona & C,PC) -88 Pine -NY 10005
(914) 961-4400 .. **Curtis,** Barbara '94 OfCnsl Elefante & P,LLP -141 Hillside Pl -Eastchstr 10709
(212) 230-8802 .. **Curtis,** Douglas F '89 (WilmerHale) -399 Park Av -NY 10022
(212) 416-8641 .. **Curtis,** Edw J '88 Dept of Law -120 Bway -NY 10271
(914) 276-2920 .. **Curtis,** Frank R '72 (Rembar & C) -Bx908 -Croton Fls 10519
(315) 624-7777 .. **Curtis,** George E '68 OfCnsl P Hobaica,LLC -2045 Genesee -Utica 13501 **Fx:**624-7781
(212) 850-1864 .. **Curtis,** James M '96 %J&W Seligman & Co -100 Park Av -NY 10017 **Fx:**922-5731
(212) 596-9000 .. **Curtis,** Jeanne C '92 (Ropes & G LLP) -1211 Av of Amer -NY 10036
(516) 328-4481 .. **Curtis,** Jill R '94 %Canon USA -1 Canon Plz -Lk Success 11042
(212) 902-6268 .. **Curtis,** John W '77 %Goldman Sachs -1 NY Plz -NY 10004
(212) 696-6000 .. **Curtis Mallet-Prevost Colt & Mosle LLP** -101 Park Av -NY 10178 **Fx:**697-1559
(212) 214-6064 .. **Curtis,** Mary H '02 Wachovia -375 Park Av -NY 10152
(212) 791-0285 .. **Curtis,** Michl J '91 %Malaby & B,LLC -150 Bway -NY 10038 **Fx:**791-0286
(212) 451-2300 .. **Curtis,** Patrick J '09 %Olshan GFR&W LLP -65 E 55th -NY 10022
(212) 715-1000 .. **Curtis,** Philip H '73 (Arnold & P LLP) -399 Park Av -NY 10022
(585) 325-7440 .. **Curtis,** Richd G '80 (Kaman BMJ&G LLP) -135 Corp Woods -Rchstr 14623
(212) 969-3000 .. **Curtis,** Susan G '75 %Proskauer R LLP -1585 Bway -NY 10036
(212) 735-3000 .. **Curtis,** Susan M '82 (Skadden ASM&F LLP) -4 Times Sq -NY 10036
(212) 734-4915 .. **Curtis,** Thos M '66 -1385 York Av -NY 10021 **Fx:**535-4688
(212) 312-2350 .. **Curtis,** Thos V '72 %Leg Aid -60 Lafayette -NY 10013 **Fx:**349-0874

(212) 587-0200 .. **Curtis,** W Robt '87 Curtis & Assoc,PC -155 Duane -NY 10013 **Fx:**587-0218
(518) 731-6118 .. **Curtis Warren & Fori** -46 Reed -Coxsackie 12051 **Fx:**731-2233
(716) 857-7991 .. **Curtiss,** Alice A '89 %Natl Fuel Gas -6363 Main -Williamsvll 14221 **Fx:**857-7614
(585) 396-4411 .. **Curtiss,** Gary L '78 %Cnty Atty -27 N Main -Canandaigua 14424 **Fx:**396-4481
(845) 225-5500 .. **Curtiss & Leibell, PC** -20 Church -Carmel 10512 **Fx:**225-5946
(845) 225-5500 .. **Curtiss,** Timothy J '77 (Curtiss & L,PC) -20 Church -Carmel 10512
(212) 704-4400 .. **Curtner,** Gregory L '01 (Miller CP&S,PLLC) -500 5th Av -NY 10110
(516) 248-1700 .. **Curto,** Andrew E '92 (Forchelli CDSM&T,LLP) -333 Earle Ovngton Blvd -Uniondale 11553
(516) 248-1700 .. **Curto,** Anthony V '60 (Forchelli CDSM&T,LLP) -333 Earle Ovngton Blvd -Uniondale 11553
(914) 779-1100 .. **Curto,** Jos R '83 (Veneruso CS&C,LLP) -35 E Grassy Sprain Rd -Ynkrs 10710
(914) 779-1100 .. **Curto,** Michl J '96 (Veneruso CS&C,LLP) -35 E Grassy Sprain Rd -Ynkrs 10710
(646) 264-3650 .. **Curtwright,** Esther D '74 %US Dept of Labor -201 Varick -NY 10014 **Fx:**264-3660
(716) 854-2100 .. **Curvin,** Carrie Q '06 %Lewis & L,PC -37 Franklin -Buffalo 14202 **Fx:**854-0433
(716) 854-1744 .. **Curvin,** Steven P '80 (Burgio K&C) -2150 Main Place Twr -Buffalo 14202
(212) 440-3488 .. **Curwood,** James M '84 %CNA Ins Co -40 Wall -NY 10005
(212) 261-5526 .. **Curzan,** Elisabeth R '93 %Assured Guaranty -31 W 52nd -NY 10019
(212) 309-6000 .. **Cusack,** Clare M '06 %Morgan L&B LLP -101 Park Av -NY 10178
(212) 701-3000 .. **Cusack,** Elizabeth Kells '09 %Cahill G&R LLP -80 Pine -NY 10005 **Fx:**269-5420
(718) 876-7228 .. **Cusack,** Eva M '01 %Pub Admin Ofc -130 Styvsnt Pl -Staten Isl 10301
(518) 272-6565 .. **Cusack,** Jennifer A '91 %Martin SWD&J -279 River Bx1530 -Troy 12181
(212) 335-4500 .. **Cusack,** John T J '84 (DLA Piper LLP) -1251 Av of Amer -NY 10020
(518) 438-9907 .. **Cusack,** Michl E '91 OfCnsl Young SWRB&M,LLC -5 Palisades Dr -Albany 12205
(212) 459-1300 .. **Cusack,** Thos F III '91 %Prudential Prfrd Fncl -630 5th Av -NY 10111 **Fx:**262-0291
(716) 853-9555 .. **Cusack,** Treneeka '06 %Leg Aid -237 Main -Buffalo 14203 **Fx:**853-3219
(212) 490-3000 .. **Cusack,** Wm F III '06 %Wilson EME&D LLP -150 E 42nd -NY 10017
(516) 229-4501 .. **Cusanelli,** Thos W '90 %Russo A&T -875 Merrick Av -Westbury 11590
(914) 245-7200 .. **Cusano,** Gary A '86 OfCnsl G Kuczinski,PC -2649 Strang Blvd -Yorktwn Hts 10598 **Fx:**245-7208
(212) 998-2240 .. **Cusano,** Louis J '86 NYU Ofc Leg Cnsl -70 Wshngtn Sq S -NY 10012 **Fx:**995-3048
(585) 258-2800 .. **Cusato,** Patrick L '88 (Underberg & K LLP) -300 Bausch & Lomb Pl -Rchstr 14604
(718) 466-3000 .. **Cuscione,** Jeannie A '87 %Civil Ct -1118 Grnd Cncrs -Bronx 10456 **Fx:**466-3006
(212) 715-9100 .. **Cushenberry,** Tamika S '05 %Kramer LN&F,LLP -1177 Av of Amer -NY 10036
(518) 862-1200 .. **Cushing,** Craig A '05 %Martin H&M LLP -Bx15141 -Albany 12212
(518) 895-8306 .. **Cushing,** George A '73 -2014 Mudge Rd -Delanson 12053
(516) 488-3300 .. **Cushing,** Gerard J '88 (Shaub AC&S,LLP) -1983 Marcus Av -Lk Success 11042
(212) 799-9986 .. **Cushman,** Constance '74 -38 W 89th -NY 10024 **Fx:**799-6632
(516) 571-3164 .. **Cushman,** Elissa Stein '89 %Cnty Atty -1 West -Mineola 11501 **Fx:**571-6604
(607) 334-2562 .. **Cushman,** James G '75 -15 Eaton Av -Norwich 13815 **Fx:**334-2820
(212) 788-0730 .. **Cushman,** Steven Stein '88 %Law Dept -100 Church -NY 10007 **Fx:**788-0367
(914) 524-9400 .. **Cushner,** Todd Steven '02 (Cushner & G LLP) -155 Wht Plns Rd -Tarrytwn 10591 **Fx:**524-0422
(212) 784-8800 .. **Cusí,** José M '01 %Cuatrecasas LLP -110 E 55th -NY 10022 **Fx:**758-1028
(212) 556-2100 .. **Cusick,** James P '02 (King & S) -1185 Av of Amer -NY 10036
(212) 277-6500 .. **Cusick,** Michl F '73 (Dickstein S LLP) -1633 Bway -NY 10019
(212) 312-7995 .. **Cusick,** Peter '93 State Ins Fund -199 Church -NY 10007 **Fx:**385-9199
(212) 754-9400 .. **Cusimano,** Donna M '99 %Todtman NS&J,PC -425 Park Av -NY 10022
(212) 941-2413 .. **Cusimano,** John M '95 (Watch Ent, Inc) -900 Bway -NY 10003
(607) 723-5341 .. **Cusimano,** Thos W Jr. '83 (Hinman H&K,LLP) -80 Exchange Bx5250 -Bnghmtn 13902
(585) 724-4578 .. **Cusker,** Dorothy H '87 %Eastman Kodak -343 State -Rchstr 14650 **Fx:**724-6611
(585) 321-9976 .. **Cusker,** Richd E '76 LexisNexis -542 Pttsfrd Henrietta Tl Rd -Pittsfrd 14534 **Fx:**(866) 960-3447
(585) 338-3880 .. **Cusker,** Thos J '65 Cusker & C -2121 N Clinton Av -Rchstr 14617 **Fx:**338-3886
(212) 735-3000 .. **Cusker Gonzalez,** Mara C '06 %Skadden ASM&F LLP -4 Times Sq -NY 10036
(212) 408-5100 .. **Cusmano,** Christopher J '10 %Chadbourne & P LLP -30 Rckfllr Plz -NY 10112
(315) 422-0420 .. **Custer,** C Gay '85 (Field & C) -4933 Jamesvll Rd -Jamesvll 13078
(718) 520-8550 .. **Cusumano,** Jos A '55 -92-01 68th Av -Frst Hlls 11375 **Fx:**793-2889
(516) 355-7901 .. **Cusumano,** Peter A '81 %Paganini GCC&F -1979 Marcus Av -Lk Success 11042
(212) 827-4411 .. **Cusumano,** Robt F '81 Ace Grp Holdings -1133 Av of Amer -NY 10036
(845) 527-7882 .. **Cusumano,** Robt P '85 -2537 Route 52 -Hopewell Junct 12533 **Fx:**896-1472
(716) 856-4000 .. **Cutaia,** Alfonzo I '08 %Hodgson R LLP -140 Pearl -Buffalo 14202
(212) 909-6000 .. **Cuthbertson,** Douglas I '08 %Debevoise & P LLP -919 3rd Av -NY 10022
(631) 351-3501 .. **Cuthbertson,** Mark A '93 -434 NY Av -Huntngtn 11743 **Fx:**614-4314
(212) 504-6000 .. **Cuthbertson,** Sophie K '99 %Cadwalader W&T LLP -1 World Fncl Ctr -NY 10281
(212) 489-8230 .. **Cuti,** John R '91 (Davis WT LLP) -1633 Bway -NY 10019
(212) 526-8339 .. **Cuticello,** Vincent J '97 Neuberger Berman Grp LLC -1271 Av of Amer -NY 10020
(212) 756-2000 .. **Cutini,** Michl G '03 %Schulte R&Z LLP -919 3rd Av -NY 10022
(212) 983-1199 .. **Cutler,** Andrew N '85 (Cutler M&A,LLP) -708 3rd Av -NY 10017
(212) 464-1896 .. **Cutler,** Anne Fox '89 JP Morgan -345 Park Av -NY 10154
(212) 575-7900 .. **Cutler,** Avraham Z '09 OfCnsl Ballon SB&N,PC -729 7th Av -NY 10019
(212) 679-6669 .. **Cutler,** Bruce '75 -260 Mad Av -NY 10016 **Fx:**679-3628
(518) 899-9200 .. **Cutler,** Daryl S '93 (Cutler T&C LLP) -2 Hemphill Pl -Malta 12020
(518) 899-9200 .. **Cutler,** Debbie '88 (Cutler T&C LLP) -2 Hemphill Pl -Malta 12020
(212) 397-3370 .. **Cutler,** Gary L '84 (Harris CC&H LLP) -111 Bway -NY 10006 **Fx:**202-6206
(212) 788-0733 .. **Cutler,** Jason '72 %Law Dept -100 Church -NY 10007 **Fx:**788-0367
(212) 532-9736 .. **Cutler,** Jesse C '04 (R Skyer & Assoc,LLP) -276 5th Av -NY 10001 **Fx:**532-9846
(516) 766-3200 .. **Cutler,** Joel B '83 (Murtagh C&B) -100 N Park Av -Rockvll Ctr 11570
(718) 613-3500 .. **Cutler,** Joyce Marie Antoni '02 %UIA Bd -Bx29002 -Brklyn 11201 **Fx:**613-3566
(212) 983-1199 .. **Cutler Minikes & Adelman, LLP** -708 3rd Av -NY 10017 **Fx:**983-2443
(212) 983-1199 .. **Cutler Minikes & Adelman LLP** -150 Wht Plns Rd -Tarrytwn 10591 **Fx:**983-2443
(212) 521-4333 .. **Cutler,** Randall M '95 -590 Mad Av -NY 10022 **Fx:**521-4099
(212) 683-0220 .. **Cutler,** Richd W '70 -60 Mad Av -NY 10010 **Fx:**683-2523
(212) 880-3800 .. **Cutler,** Robt A '04 %Akerman S -335 Mad Av -NY 10017
(718) 398-4776 .. **Cutler,** Timothy R '95 -358 Putnam Av -Brklyn 11216 **Fx:**398-4776
(518) 899-9200 .. **Cutler Trainor & Cutler LLP** -2 Hemphill Pl -Malta 12020 **Fx:**899-9300
(212) 447-8690 .. **Cutner,** David A '71 (Lamson & C,PC) -9 E 40th -NY 10016 **Fx:**447-8691
(212) 847-2389 .. **Cutner,** Rolande '78 -60 Broad -NY 10004 **Fx:**(646) 349-2240
(516) 496-1919 .. **Cutone,** Angela A '95 %Keller O&W,PC -242 Crsswys Park Dr W -Woodbury 11797
(212) 750-5233 .. **Cutro,** James J '94 (Bonnist & C,LLP) -444 Mad Av -NY 10022
(607) 722-3495 .. **Cutrona,** Angelina '91 (Aswad & I) -46 Front -Bnghmtn 13905
(718) 981-9200 .. **Cutrona,** Jennifer Gotlin '95 -1082 Forest Av -Staten Isl 10310
(718) 698-0569 .. **Cutrona,** Robt S '93 (Cutrona & F,PC) -41 Kell Av -Staten Isl 10314
(718) 381-8238 .. **Cutrone,** Francesca L '97 -472 Suydam -Brklyn 11237
(516) 826-8938 .. **Cutrone,** Jack '03 %R Young & Assoc -1321 Bellmore Av -Bellmore 11710 **Fx:**826-8932
(718) 631-5500 .. **Cutrone,** Paul W '82 -42-24 235th -Douglastn 11363
(718) 456-6700 .. **Cutrone,** Ralph F '60 -65-15 Myrtle Av -Glendale 11385 **Fx:**497-2534
(212) 998-6671 .. **Cutter,** Gail E '88 %NYU Law Schl-Career Ofc -110 W 3rd -NY 10012 **Fx:**995-4076
(212) 385-8000 .. **Cutting,** Dana A '05 OfCnsl Barasch MS&P -11 Park Pl -NY 10007
(212) 310-8000 .. **Cutting,** Dionne Y '09 %Weil G&M LLP -767 5th Av -NY 10153
(212) 679-0355 .. **Cuttita,** Francis V '94 (Cuttita LLP) -128 E 35th -NY 10016 **Fx:**679-0073
(914) 750-5933 .. **Cuttita,** Victoria '94 OfCnsl Kissel H&W LLP -580 Wht Plns Rd -Tarrytwn 10591
(212) 679-0355 .. **Cuttita,** Vincent J '62 (Cuttita LLP) -128 E 35th -NY 10016 **Fx:**679-0073
(718) 625-0202 .. **Cuyler,** Renaye Brown '80 (Clark C&M,LLP) -Bx26515 -Brklyn 11202 **Fx:**625-2644
(914) 381-7400 .. **Cvek,** Julie A '05 %Rattet P&G,LLP -550 Mamaroneck Av -Harrison 10528
(212) 753-3468 .. **Cvjeticanin,** Marijan '10 %Wildes & W,PC -515 Mad Av -NY 10022
(716) 648-9611 .. **Cwick,** Craig M '91 -180 Main -Hambrg 14075 **Fx:**648-9614
(212) 756-2000 .. **Cybul,** Bruce S '84 (Schulte R&Z LLP) -919 3rd Av -NY 10022
(212) 553-8300 .. **Cygan,** Jeanne A '78 Cohen K & Assoc -2 Park Av -NY 10016 **Fx:**553-8721
(212) 661-9100 .. **Cyganowski,** Melanie L '82 (Otterbourg SH&R,PC) -230 Park Av -NY 10169
(212) 929-9689 .. **Cylkowski,** Jeffrey '85 -55 Bethune -NY 10014
(212) 661-9100 .. **Cymbler,** Jeffrey K '84 Otterbourg SH&R,PC -230 Park Av -NY 10169
(845) 473-8100 .. **Cymerman,** Jacquelyn R '10 %Iseman CR&H,LLP -2649 South Rd -Poughkeepsie 12601
(212) 558-4000 .. **Cymrot,** Peter H '09 %Sullivan & C LLP -125 Broad -NY 10004
(718) 847-5277 .. **Cyperstein,** Aaron I '94 JCC -8246 Lefferts Blvd -Kew Gdns 11415
(212) 684-0661 .. **Cypher,** Margaret A '79 -163 3rd Av -NY 10003
(914) 837-4671 .. **Cypher,** Robt S Jr. '80 -75 Orchrd Ln -Rye 10580 **Fx:**967-1304
(212) 944-8910 .. **Cyphers,** Kenneth R '98 %Continental Guest Srvcs -1501 Bway -NY 10036
(212) 808-7800 .. **Cyr,** Brendan J '06 %Kelley D&W LLP -101 Park Av -NY 10178
(212) 918-3000 .. **Cyr,** Jos P '81 (Hogan L LLP) -875 3rd Av -NY 10022
(212) 661-6800 .. **Cyruli,** Robt J '88 (Cyruli SH&Z LLP) -420 Lex Av -NY 10170
(212) 661-6800 .. **Cyruli Shanks Hart & Zizmor LLP** -420 Lex Av -NY 10170 **Fx:**661-5350
(914) 749-8200 .. **Cyrulnik,** Jason C '05 %Boies S&F LLP -333 Main -Armonk 10504
(212) 755-0100 .. **Cyrulnik,** Owen L '01 Grais & E LLP -40 E 52nd -NY 10022
(212) 343-4562 .. **Cyrus,** Kaye A '02 Scholastic,Inc -557 Bway -NY 10012
(718) 584-9000 .. **Cytron,** Sara R '03 Bronx VA Med Ctr -130 W Kngsbrdg Rd -Bronx 10468
(212) 848-4396 .. **Cywiak,** Frayda U '06 %Shearman & S LLP -599 Lex Av -NY 10022
(212) 848-4000 .. **Czachor,** Bruce '88 (Shearman & S LLP) -599 Lex Av -NY 10022
(212) 826-7060 .. **Czaja,** Richd F '76 Stahl Real Estate -277 Park Av -NY 10172 **Fx:**223-4609
(518) 487-5460 .. **Czajka,** John M '05 %DA -6 Lodge -Albany 12207 **Fx:**487-5093
(631) 853-4647 .. **Czajkowski,** Christine C '85 %Family Ct -400 Carleton Av -Central Islip 11722
(585) 271-1500 .. **Czajkowski,** Mark E '97 %Dibble & M,PC -55 Canterbury Rd -Rchstr 14607
(212) 325-7542 .. **Czapiewska,** Malgorzata '95 CSFB -11 Mad Av -NY 10010

(585) 753-3491 .. **Czapranski,** Kimberly J '88 -30 W Broad -Rchstr 14614
(212) 218-2100 .. **Czarnecki,** Robt J '10 %Fitzpatrick CH&S -1290 Av of Amer -NY 10104
(212) 735-3000 .. **Czarniak,** Julia A '98 (Skadden ASM&F LLP) -4 Times Sq -NY 10036
(607) 936-8057 .. **Czarples,** Anna C '09 %J Welch -8 Denison Pkwy E -Corning 14830 **Fx:**936-6815
(607) 936-8057 .. **Czarples,** Thos C M '09 %J Welch -8 Denison Pkwy E -Corning 14830 **Fx:**936-6815
(212) 594-5300 .. **Czeisler,** Jennifer L '00 %Milberg LLP -1 Penn Plz -NY 10119
(212) 836-4857 .. **Czepiel,** Lori A '99 -445 Park Av -NY 10105 **Fx:**(917) 322-2105
(212) 526-7000 .. **Czepyha,** Eric N '05 %Barclays Capital Inc -745 7th Av -NY 10019
(212) 460-3285 .. **Czerepak,** Andrew J '82 %Con Ed -4 Irving Pl -NY 10003
(212) 418-9600 .. **Czerewacka,** Elzbieta '02 Cnsl Columbus Nova -153 E 53rd -NY 10022
(212) 308-4411 .. **Czerniawski,** Jos E '02 %Edwards AP&D LLP -750 Lex Av -NY 10022
(212) 820-9546 .. **Czerwinski,** Alicia '05 %Hawkins D&W LLP -One Chase Manh Plz -NY 10005
(212) 363-6900 .. **Czeslowski,** Stephen '00 %Faust GS&B LLP -2 Rector -NY 10006
(646) 252-2356 .. **Czik,** Jayne '88 MTA Cptl Construction Co -2 Bway -NY 10004
(212) 413-4462 .. **Czik,** Steven J '96 -101 Av of Amer -NY 10013 **Fx:**226-7555
(516) 801-0157 .. **Czik,** Thos D '86 -30 Eagle Ln -Roslyn 11576 **Fx:**801-0158
(845) 623-5800 .. **Czubak,** Teresa M '09 Rockland Bakery,Inc -94 Demarest Mill Rd -Nanuet 10954
(516) 747-0377 .. **Czuchman,** Stephen S '06 %Costella & G,LLP -7 12th -Gdn Cty 11530 **Fx:**248-0023
(212) 310-8000 .. **Da,** Xiaofeng '08 %Weil G&M LLP -767 5th Av -NY 10153
(516) 739-3737 .. **Daab,** Michl C '98 %Alexander P,LLC -666 Old Cntry Rd -Gdn Cty 11530
(631) 758-1976 .. **Daal,** Jeannie V '95 -Bx305 -Medfrd 11763
(212) 981-4500 .. **Dabagian-Paul,** Patricia G '93 PeterSan Grp -1450 Bway -NY 10018 **Fx:**981-4560
(718) 658-0500 .. **D'Abate,** Danielle N '09 %Law Dept -151-20 Jamaica Av -Jamaica 11432 **Fx:**658-4025
(212) 878-8000 .. **Dabbasi,** Ronnie I '09 %Clifford C LLP -31 W 52nd -NY 10019
(212) 637-2212 .. **Dabbs,** Jenna Minicucci '02 %US Atty -1 St Andrews Plz -NY 10007
(212) 373-3000 .. **Dabela,** Albab A '03 %Paul WRW&G LLP -1285 Av of Amer -NY 10019
(212) 808-7800 .. **D'Ablemont,** Eugene T '60 (Kelley D&W LLP) -101 Park Av -NY 10178
(212) 556-2100 .. **Dabney,** Hovey S Jr. '05 (King & S) -1185 Av of Amer -NY 10036
(212) 859-8000 .. **Dabney,** James W '80 (Fried FHS&J LLP) -1 NY Plz -NY 10004
(716) 848-4898 .. **Dabney,** Phillip Jr. '03 -69 Delaware Av -Buffalo 14202
(516) 496-5822 .. **Dabrowski,** Jill F '01 %T Spina -170 Froehlich Farm Blvd -Woodbury 11797 **Fx:**496-5420
(718) 680-1900 .. **Dacchille,** Lawr D '88 -8601 4th Av -Brklyn 11209 **Fx:**680-3700
(917) 606-5500 .. **Daccord,** Julie Ann '98 %Miramax Films -161 Av of Amer -NY 10013
(212) 972-4900 .. **Dacey-Seib,** Joan '69 OfCnsl Shapiro FA&S LLP -380 Mad Av -NY 10017
(631) 423-7755 .. **D'Achilli,** Adrienne E '00 %Bragoli & Assoc,PC -999 Walt Whitman Rd -Melvll 11747 **Fx:**423-5299
(212) 595-6776 .. **Dachs,** Ann T '86 -175 W 72nd -NY 10023
(516) 747-1100 .. **Dachs,** Jonathan A '84 (Shayne DCS&D) -114 Old Cntry Rd -Mineola 11501
(516) 747-1100 .. **Dachs,** Norman H '54 (Shayne DCS&D) -114 Old Cntry Rd -Mineola 11501
(718) 849-6900 .. **Dachtera,** Irene L '79 -101-05 Lefferts Blvd -S Richmond Hll 11419
(212) 687-0100 .. **DaCunzo,** Daniella D '04 %Harris B PLLC -100 Wall -NY 10005
(212) 259-8000 .. **Dada,** James '09 %Dewey & L LLP -1301 Av of Amer -NY 10019
(212) 513-3200 .. **Dadakis,** John D '77 (Holland & K LLP) -31 W 52nd -NY 10019
(914) 631-8000 .. **D'Adamio,** Anthony '89 Bayer Hlthcare -511 Benedict Av -Tarrytwn 10591 **Fx:**524-3594
(585) 591-1100 .. **Dadd,** Eric T '75 (Dadd N&W) -11 Exchange Bx238 -Attica 14011
(585) 753-4500 .. **Dadd,** Hayden M '08 %DA -832 Watts Bldg -Rchstr 14614 **Fx:**753-4576
(585) 591-1111 .. **Dadd,** Margaret B '73 (Dadd & R,PLLC) -17 Exchange Bx206 -Attica 14011 **Fx:**591-1116
(585) 591-1100 .. **Dadd Nelson & Wilkinson** -11 Exchange Bx238 -Attica 14011 **Fx:**591-1722
(315) 476-4041 .. **D'Addario,** Francis R '72 -407 S Warren -Syracuse 13202 **Fx:**476-8002
(212) 259-8000 .. **Daddario,** Gregory R '08 %Dewey & L LLP -1301 Av of Amer -NY 10019
(631) 224-2796 .. **D'Addario,** Jos R '97 %J Guadagno -136 E Main -E Islip 11730 **Fx:**224-1643
(914) 995-3338 .. **D'Addario,** Michl A '88 %DA -111 Martin Luther King Blvd -White Plns 10601 **Fx:**995-3363
(631) 756-9433 .. **D'Addario,** Richd '01 %Bio Systems Inc -210 Sherwood Av -Farmngdl 11735
(212) 637-2306 .. **Daddario,** Richd C '78 %US Atty -1 St Andrews Plz -NY 10007
(718) 389-0240 .. **D'Addario,** Ron '76 (Piazza D&F) -824 Manh Av -Brklyn 11222
(212) 818-0964 .. **Dade,** Cynthia A '84 -60 E 42nd -NY 10165
(315) 435-2470 .. **Dadey,** Brenton P '08 DA -505 S State -Syracuse 13202 **Fx:**435-3969
(646) 522-8423 .. **Dadian,** Talene '98 (Dadian & W) -Bx203 -Mt Kisco 10549
(212) 666-9924 .. **Dadoun,** Pascal A '89 -46 W 96th -NY 10025
(212) 992-8984 .. **Dadush,** Sarah Valeria '05 Inst for Intl Law & Justice NYU Schl of Law -110 W 3rd -NY 10012
(212) 756-2000 .. **Dady,** Andrew J '90 (Schulte R&Z LLP) -919 3rd Av -NY 10022
(716) 674-5550 .. **Daetsch,** Wm H '78 -1299 Union Rd -W Seneca 14224 **Fx:**674-5768
(212) 744-5022 .. **Daffan,** Kathleen B '06 Lenox Hill Neighborhood Hse -331 E 70th -NY 10021 **Fx:**744-5150
(845) 452-2057 .. **D'Afflitto,** Jennifer L '03 -1133 Route 55 -LaGrangevll 12540 **Fx:**452-2058
(516) 485-3395 .. **Daffner,** Gerald N '59 OfCnsl Lawrence and W,PC -215 Hilton Av Bx1200 -Hempstd 11551 **Fx:**538-2079
(718) 298-8900 .. **Daftary,** Marjan '09 %Leg Aid -153-01 Jamaica Av -Jamaica 11432 **Fx:**657-0537
(631) 454-9800 .. **Dagan,** Eitan '01 %Support Claim Srvcs -125 Baylis Rd -Melvll 11747
(212) 878-8000 .. **Dagan,** Jacqueline '02 %Clifford C LLP -31 W 52nd -NY 10019
(212) 436-1613 .. **Dagati,** Patricia Chin '91 %IRS -290 Bway -NY 10007
(212) 286-5800 .. **Dagenais,** Sophie G '89 Rockwood Rlty Assoc,LLC -555 5th Av -NY 10017
(718) 237-5500 .. **Dagg,** Christopher W '00 %Leg Srvcs -105 Court -Brklyn 11201 **Fx:**855-0733
(212) 715-9100 .. **Daggan,** Clinton N '10 %Kramer LN&F,LLP -1177 Av of Amer -NY 10036
(212) 244-6600 .. **Daglieri,** Christian P '02 %Schechter & B,PC -350 5th Av -NY 10118
(607) 324-6690 .. **Dagon,** John N '90 -29 Church -Hornell 14843 **Fx:**324-0537
(718) 250-2000 .. **Dagonese,** Catherine Ann '95 %DA -350 Jay -Brklyn 11201 **Fx:**250-2314
(716) 837-1596 .. **Dagonese,** Jos C '69 -305 Woodward Av -Buffalo 14214
(914) 682-1993 .. **D'Agostino,** A Chas '50 (D'Agostino & S) -445 Hmltn Av -White Plns 10601
(516) 872-7400 .. **D'Agostino,** Albert A '70 (Minerva & D) -107 S Central Av -Vly Stream 11580
(212) 269-0927 .. **D'Agostino,** Alfred A Jr. '77 (D'Amato & L,LLP) -2 World Fncl Ctr -NY 10281
(212) 408-5100 .. **D'Agostino,** Amy E '04 %Chadbourne & P LLP -30 Rckfllr Plz -NY 10112
(914) 422-4146 .. **D'Agostino,** Angela M '01 %Pace Law Schl -78 N Bway -White Plns 10603 **Fx:**422-4039
(518) 489-1098 .. **D'Agostino,** Carolyn A '95 -21 Everett Rd Ext -Albany 12205 **Fx:**489-3304
(914) 747-4455 .. **D'Agostino,** Chas A Jr. '78 -427 Bedford Rd -Plsntvll 10570 **Fx:**747-3626
(212) 455-2000 .. **D'Agostino,** Chase J '09 %Simpson T&B LLP -425 Lex Av -NY 10017
(315) 474-2911 .. **D'Agostino,** David A '01 %Smith SK&S,PC -250 S Clinton -Syracuse 13202
(914) 328-4000 .. **D'Agostino,** Ernest N '98 %King Abstract LLC -180 Brook -Scarsdale 10583
(518) 463-2251 .. **D'Agostino,** Harry J '55 (D'Agostino HF&J,PC) -187 Wolf Rd -Albany 12205
(518) 463-2251 .. **D'Agostino Hoblock Flannery & Jeram,PC** -187 Wolf Rd -Albany 12205 **Fx:**463-0311
(516) 227-0700 .. **D'Agostino,** Jaclene '07 %Farrell F,PC -1320 RXR Plz -Uniondale 11556
(212) 564-9800 .. **D'Agostino,** John '80 (D'Agostino L&L,LLP) -345 7th Av -NY 10001
(718) 967-1600 .. **D'Agostino,** Jonathan '90 -3309 Richmond Av -Staten Isl 10312 **Fx:**967-8677
(718) 442-9000 .. **D'Agostino,** Jos A '89 %Ameduri G&F -471 Bement Av -Staten Isl 10310
(516) 741-4799 .. **D'Agostino,** Jos A '04 %Baker SBGFM&N,LLC -100 Grdn City Plz -Gdn Cty 11530
(212) 825-1212 .. **D'Agostino,** Julia '07 %Morrison M LLP -17 State -NY 10004
(518) 434-9807 .. **D'Agostino Krackeler Maguire & Cardona, PC** -16 Sage Estate -Menands 12204 **Fx:**434-9826
(212) 564-9800 .. **D'Agostino Levine & Landesman,LLP** -345 7th Av -NY 10001 **Fx:**564-9802
(914) 559-3100 .. **D'Agostino,** Linda M '09 %Heidell PM&B,LLP -81 Main -White Plns 10601
(718) 523-1111 .. **D'Agostino,** Lisa A '08 Gildin Z&S,PC -138-44 Qns Blvd -Briarwd 11435
(914) 261-5124 .. **D'Agostino,** Luigi '00 (D'Agostino & Co,PC) -9101 Shore Rd -Brklyn 11209
(518) 434-9807 .. **D'Agostino,** Mae A '81 (D'Agostino KM&C,PC) -16 Sage Estate -Menands 12204
(212) 752-3380 .. **D'Agostino,** Michl '79 (Becker & D,PC) -880 3rd Av -NY 10022 **Fx:**593-3807
(315) 471-3151 .. **D'Agostino,** Raymond R '68 (Hancock & E,LLP) -1500 AXA Twr I Bx4976 -Syracuse 13221
(914) 682-1993 .. **D'Agostino,** Rocco F '91 -445 Hmltn Av -White Plns 10601 **Fx:**682-1994
(914) 682-1993 .. **D'Agostino & Salvi** -445 Hmltn Av -White Plns 10601 **Fx:**682-1994
(716) 992-4461 .. **D'Agostino,** Sam J '72 -9687 New Oregon Rd Bx220 -Eden 14057 **Fx:**992-4140
(914) 997-6945 .. **D'Agostino,** Thos A '92 -87 Cloverdale Av -White Plns 10603
(716) 856-4022 .. **D'Agostino,** Thos C '65 (Mattar D&G,LLP) -17 Court -Buffalo 14202
(212) 279-3355 .. **Daguanno,** James E '90 (Tiger & D,LLP) -31 E 32nd -NY 10016 **Fx:**683-2338
(518) 474-7330 .. **Dague,** C Harris '05 %Dept of Law -The Cptl -Albany 12224
(315) 422-2052 .. **Dague,** Raymond J '79 R Dague,PLLC -472 S Salina -Syracuse 13202 **Fx:**474-4334
(718) 891-1200 .. **Dahan,** Chaim '96 (Alatsas & T,PC) -2115 Av U -Brklyn 11229
(212) 935-5700 .. **Dahan,** David M '95 (Colucci & U) -218 E 50th -NY 10022
(212) 504-6000 .. **Dahan,** Israel '98 (Cadwalader W&T LLP) -1 World Fncl Ctr -NY 10281
(212) 753-0300 .. **Dahan,** M Marc '68 (Dahan & N LLP) -1700 Bway -NY 10019
(212) 753-0300 .. **Dahan & Nowick LLP** -1700 Bway -NY 10019 **Fx:**753-0375
(212) 382-3300 .. **Dahill,** Wm F '92 (Wollmuth M&D LLP) -500 5th Av -NY 10110
(212) 766-8000 .. **Dahiya,** Karamvir '99 K Dahiya LLC -350 Bway -NY 10007 **Fx:**766-8001
(212) 839-5300 .. **Dahiya,** Neal K '04 %Sidley A LLP -787 7th Av -NY 10019
(212) 335-9000 .. **Dahl,** Mark E '02 %DA -1 Hogan Pl -NY 10013
(212) 335-4500 .. **Dahl,** Meredith J '09 %DLA Piper LLP -1251 Av of Amer -NY 10020
(212) 207-8400 .. **Dahl,** Sarah Ann '97 %Kavanagh M&O LLP -415 Mad Av -NY 10017
(518) 431-5186 .. **Dahl,** Tiffany L '07 Farm Family Life Ins Co -Bx656 -Albany 12201
(585) 724-4899 .. **Dahl,** Torger N '73 Eastman Kodak -343 State -Rchstr 14650 **Fx:**724-5515
(212) 607-2800 .. **Dahlberg,** Karen A '03 FTC -1 Bowling Grn -NY 10004 **Fx:**607-2822
(212) 549-2500 .. **Dahlberg,** Robin L '85 %ACLU -125 Broad -NY 10004 **Fx:**549-2651
(914) 949-5300 .. **Dahle,** Bridget K '97 (Brown & T,LLC) -1 N Bway -White Plns 10601

(212) 450-4000 .. **Dahlen,** Jenny M '05 %Davis P&W LLP -450 Lex Av -NY 10017
(607) 723-5341 .. **Dahlgren,** Wilbur D '84 (Hinman H&K,LLP) -80 Exchange Bx5250 -Bnghmtn 13902
(315) 218-8000 .. **Dahline,** Susan Lee '09 %Bond S&K,PLLC -1 Lincoln Ctr -Syracuse 13202
(518) 372-3848 .. **Dahlke,** Lawr T '83 -115 Clinton -Schnctdy 12305 **Fx:**372-3882
(212) 836-8000 .. **Dahlman,** Marilee P '06 %Kaye S LLP -425 Park Av -NY 10022
(212) 375-2494 .. **Dahlman,** Nora J '91 ACA Capital Holdings -140 Bway -NY 10005
(212) 661-1100 .. **Dahlstrom,** Patrick V '88 (Pomerantz HG&G LLP) -100 Park Av -NY 10017
(212) 586-7522 .. **Dahn,** Mark D '97 Wilf Law Firm -13-15 W 54th -NY 10019
(718) 447-0400 .. **Dai,** Christopher J '97 -136 Bay -Staten Isl 10301 **Fx:**815-1872
(718) 486-6800 .. **Dai,** Miwako '97 Central Amrcn Legal Assistance -240 Hooper -Brklyn 11211
(718) 888-8880 .. **Dai,** Shang '05 (Dai & Assoc,PC) -136-20 38th Av -Flushng 11354 **Fx:**888-9270
(212) 848-4000 .. **Dai,** Xin '10 Shearman & S LLP -599 Lex Av -NY 10022
(212) 643-0099 .. **Daibee,** P Ashoka '92 %Spitz Friedman Libien -225 W 34th -NY 10122
(212) 541-6222 .. **Daichman,** Jeffrey H '75 (Kane K,PC) -1350 Av of Amer -NY 10019
(718) 338-7555 .. **Daiell,** Michl S '78 M Daiell,PC -1401 Ocean Av -Brklyn 11230 **Fx:**338-7545
(212) 286-6100 .. **Daigle,** Alexander J '09 %Rosenberg & P,LLP -420 Lex Av -NY 10170
(212) 872-1000 .. **Daigle,** Brian T '05 -One Bryant Park -NY 10036 **Fx:**872-1002
(212) 806-5400 .. **Daignault,** Ronald M '92 (Stroock &S&L LLP) -180 Maiden Ln -NY 10038
(212) 880-3738 .. **Daigneault,** Christina E '03 Orchard Strategies,Inc -915 Bway -NY 10010
(585) 589-0360 .. **Dailey,** John M '55 -20 Hazard Pkwy -Albion 14411 **Fx:**589-0360
(212) 867-1475 .. **Dailey,** Jos P '70 (Dailey & S) -405 Lex Av -NY 10174
(518) 371-4865 .. **Dailey,** Kevin M '77 -1 Sam Brook Edge -Rexfrd 12148 **Fx:**371-2759
(315) 673-4864 .. **Dailey,** Mary Reagan '91 (Reagan & D) -18 E Main Bx196 -Marcellus 13108 **Fx:**673-3438
(212) 897-5877 .. **Dailey,** Michl F '95 -305 Bway -NY 10007
(212) 326-3939 .. **Dailey,** Michl J '10 %Jones D -222 E 41st -NY 10017
(212) 678-6238 .. **Dailey,** Peter H '86 -468 Riverside Dr -NY 10027 **Fx:**222-4152
(212) 735-3000 .. **Dailey,** Sean M '05 %Skadden ASM&F LLP -4 Times Sq -NY 10036
(212) 618-0666 .. **Dailey,** Wm M '94 Bear Wagner Specialists LLC -40 Wall -NY 10005
(718) 834-4850 .. **Daillie,** Simon '04 %Gerber & G LLP -26 Court -Brklyn 11242 **Fx:**858-8119
(716) 842-2166 .. **Dailor,** Jos F '97 %Workers Comp Bd -107 Delaware Av -Buffalo 14202
(212) 401-3580 .. **Daingerfield,** Richd P '87 %Royal Bank of Scotland -101 Park Av -NY 10178 **Fx:**401-3632
(212) 885-9230 .. **Dainow,** J David '65 OfCnsl Abelman F&S -666 3rd Av -NY 10017
(718) 585-1300 .. **Dairo,** Helen Abimbola '92 -573 Grnd Cncrs -Bronx 10451
(212) 537-9341 .. **Daiter,** Ian C '95 IC Daiter,PLLC -270 Mad Av -NY 10016 **Fx:**937-2460
(212) 788-0775 .. **Daitz,** Elizabeth M '06 %Law Dept -100 Church -NY 10007 **Fx:**788-0367
(212) 382-0909 .. **Daitz,** Jeffrey M '01 (Peckar & A,PC) -41 Mad Av -NY 10154
(212) 310-8000 .. **Daitz,** Ronald F '66 SrCnsl Weil G&M LLP -767 5th Av -NY 10153
(718) 979-4657 .. **Daiuto,** Ralph A '69 -298 Barbara -Staten Isl 10306 **Fx:**980-5175
(718) 383-0909 .. **Dajka,** Damian D '03 (Dajka & P,PLLC) -596 Manh Av -Brklyn 11222 **Fx:**383-0350
(212) 854-3600 .. **Dakin,** Brett '05 %Columbia Law Schl -435 W 116th -NY 10027 **Fx:**854-7946
(212) 849-7000 .. **Dakis,** Robt K '05 %Quinn EU&S,LLP -51 Mad Av -NY 10010
(518) 782-0600 .. **Dalbec,** A Andre '07 %School Admin Assn NYS -8 Airport Park Blvd -Latham 12110 **Fx:**782-9552
(212) 361-2980 .. **D'Albis,** Ceasar '77 %Traffic Violations Bur -19 Rector -NY 10006
(212) 906-1200 .. **Dalbokova,** Svetla I '07 %Latham & W -885 3rd Av -NY 10022
(516) 496-5822 .. **Dale,** Dominick R '07 %T Spina -170 Froehlich Farm Blvd -Woodbury 11797 **Fx:**496-5420
(212) 451-2900 .. **Dale,** Eric J '90 (Robinson & C LLP) -885 3rd Av -NY 10022
(212) 998-6161 .. **Dale,** Harvey P '62 %NYU Law Schl -110 W 3rd -NY 10012 **Fx:**995-3149
(518) 220-9577 .. **Dale,** Kimberlee J '97 (Couch D PC) -29 British Amer Blvd -Latham 12110
(212) 969-3000 .. **Dale,** Margaret Antinori '90 (Proskauer R LLP) -1585 Bway -NY 10036
(212) 310-8000 .. **Dale,** Sarah Stickney '08 %Weil G&M LLP -767 5th Av -NY 10153
(585) 798-4200 .. **Dale,** T Gregory '95 -309 W Center Bx27 -Medina 14103 **Fx:**798-4155
(516) 487-2252 .. **Dale,** Todd '07 %Rothkrug R&S,LLP -55 Watermill Ln -Gt Neck 11021
(212) 465-5349 .. **Dale,** Wm E '80 %Parsons Brinckerhoff -1 Penn Plz -NY 10119
(212) 669-0600 .. **Dalen,** Keith B '74 (Hill R LLP) -45 Bway -NY 10006
(516) 294-2508 .. **D'Aleo,** Robt I '83 %Bk of NY -82 7th -Gdn Cty 11530
(518) 370-4785 .. **Dales,** Douglas S Jr. '63 -2012 Lex Pkwy -Schnctdy 12309
(212) 859-8000 .. **Dalesandro,** David P '10 %Fried FHS&J LLP -1 NY Plz -NY 10004
(212) 770-5856 .. **D'Alessandri,** Richd J '83 %AIG -70 Pine -NY 10270
(631) 653-6665 .. **D'Alessandro,** Girolama M '53 -76 W Montauk hwy -Hampton Bays 11946 **Fx:**653-6665
(914) 997-0555 .. **D'Alessandro,** John '09 %Quinn & M,LLP -399 Knollwood Rd -White Plns 10603
(718) 590-6360 .. **D'Alessandro,** John P '80 %Hon B Katz -851 Grnd Cncrs -Bronx 10451
(212) 850-1703 .. **D'Alessandro,** Jos '00 %J&W Seligman & Co -100 Park Av -NY 10017 **Fx:**922-5731
(914) 681-8700 .. **D'Alessandro,** Leonardo A '95 (Milber MP&S LLP) -3 Barker Av -White Plns 10601
(518) 449-1421 .. **D'Alessandro,** Richd V '66 -69 Columbia -Albany 12210 **Fx:**449-3193
(518) 456-7084 .. **D'Alessandro,** Ronald A Jr. '99 Keohane & D,PLLC -1881 Wstrn Av -Albany 12203 **Fx:**456-7004
(212) 513-3200 .. **D'Alessandro,** Steven L '97 (Holland & K LLP) -31 W 52nd -NY 10019
(914) 995-5103 .. **D'Alessio,** Christie L '03 %Cnty Atty -148 Martine Av -White Plns 10601 **Fx:**995-5858
(212) 269-7444 .. **D'Alessio,** Louis A '03 Cilmi & Assoc PLLC -39 Bway -NY 10006 **Fx:**269-3958
(914) 682-5300 .. **D'Alessio,** Michl '02 Greenburgh Police Dept -188 Tarrytown Rd -White Plns 10607
(212) 577-3507 .. **D'Alessio,** Selene '97 %Leg Aid -199 Water -NY 10038 **Fx:**577-3520
(212) 792-7600 .. **Dalewitz,** Michl B '05 (Peak Cnsl) -25 W 31st -NY 10001
(315) 435-2470 .. **Daley,** James R '04 %DA -505 S State -Syracuse 13202 **Fx:**435-3969
(718) 238-6500 .. **Daley,** Justin P '08 %Connors & S,PC -7408 5th Av -Brklyn 11209
(212) 815-1818 .. **Daley,** Lisa A M '98 DC 37 MELS -125 Barclay -NY 10007 **Fx:**815-1343
(212) 560-3941 .. **Daley,** M Teresa '82 -520 8th Av -NY 10018 **Fx:**(917) 351-0983
(212) 323-7070 .. **Daley,** Maureen E '09 (Rawle & H LLP) -14 Wall -NY 10005
(315) 218-8000 .. **Daley,** Stephen C '88 (Bond S&K,PLLC) -1 Lincoln Ctr -Syracuse 13202
(518) 465-3553 .. **Daley,** Thos G '80 (Maynard OS&C,LLP) -6 Twr Pl -Albany 12203
(212) 632-5500 .. **Dalfen,** Sahra '99 %Salans LLP -620 5th Av -NY 10020
(914) 612-4000 .. **Dalfonso,** Lisa Marie '96 Cadbury Schweppes -900 King -Rye Brook 10573 **Fx:**612-6302
(212) 758-9700 .. **Dalgleish,** Jack Jr. '93 %KPMG LLP -345 Park Av -NY 10154
(845) 534-2200 .. **Dalgoutte,** Christopher N '97 -Bx296 -Cornwall 12518
(212) 820-9631 .. **Daliana,** Michela '87 (Hawkins D&W LLP) -One Chase Manh Plz -NY 10005
(212) 848-4000 .. **D'Alimonte,** Christa Ann '94 (Shearman & S LLP) -599 Lex Av -NY 10022
(212) 768-6700 .. **Dalin,** Andrew '87 %Sonnenschein N&R LLP -1221 Av of Amer -NY 10020
(718) 543-5566 .. **Dall,** Carol L '79 -2600 Netherland Av -Bronx 10463 **Fx:**543-5582
(845) 331-5111 .. **Dall Vechia & Kraft LLP** -115 Green -Kingston 12401 **Fx:**853-7600
(212) 735-8600 .. **Dal Lago,** Michl R '01 (Morrison C LLP) -909 3rd Av -NY 10022
(212) 345-5512 .. **Dallara,** Mark J '80 %Marsh USA -1166 Av of Amer -NY 10036 **Fx:**345-4808
(212) 352-3220 .. **Dallas,** Andra H '03 Amer Conference Inst -41 W 25th -NY 10010
(212) 343-0240 .. **Dallas,** Michl J '02 Leary Firefighters Fndt -594 Bway -NY 10012
(212) 558-4000 .. **Dallas,** Wm M Jr. '75 OfCnsl Sullivan & C LLP -125 Broad -NY 10004
(212) 801-2140 .. **Dalla Val,** Anna '04 %Greenberg T,LLP -200 Park Av -NY 10166
(212) 632-5500 .. **Dallendorfer,** Viktoria Lof '00 %Salans LLP -620 5th Av -NY 10020
(212) 931-5500 .. **Dalley,** John A R '92 OfCnsl McCue S&Z,PC -521 5th Av -NY 10175
(516) 292-4700 .. **Dalli,** John '95 (Dalli & M,LLP) -231 Mineola Blvd -Mineola 11501 **Fx:**292-5198
(631) 727-2180 .. **Dalli,** Kathryn '83 (Twomey LSKD&Q,LLP) -33 W 2nd Bx9398 -Rvrhead 11901
(212) 906-1200 .. **Dalling,** Brandon O '03 %Latham & W -885 3rd Av -NY 10022
(212) 530-5000 .. **Dalling,** Kristi L '08 %Milbank TH&M LLP -1 Chase Manh Plz -NY 10005
(917) 572-9449 .. **Dallos,** Laurie E '91 -76 Taymil Rd -New Rchll 10804
(718) 238-0091 .. **Dalloul,** Rimonda K '03 Lenihan &T,LLP -265 86th -Brklyn 11209
(845) 343-4070 .. **Dallow,** Howard S '70 (H Dallow,PC) -225 Dolson Av -Middletwn 10940 **Fx:**343-7199
(845) 331-5111 .. **Dall Vechia,** John T '69 (Dall Vechia &K LLP) -115 Green -Kingston 12401
(518) 374-8494 .. **Dalmata,** Cory R '08 %DeLorenzo Law Firm -201 Nott Ter -Schnctdy 12307 **Fx:**374-5906
(718) 236-6659 .. **Dalmazio,** Christine R '96 -2269 65th -Brklyn 11204 **Fx:**256-1932
(212) 617-6396 .. **Dalnekoff,** Danl J '02 Bloomberg LP -731 Lex Av -NY 10022
(516) 248-2500 .. **Daloia,** James F '07 Redmond P&C, LLP -1461 Franklin Av -Gdn Cty 11530
(914) 946-8900 .. **D'Aloise,** Lawr T Jr. '70 (Clark G&M) -99 Court -White Plns 10601
(516) 883-8484 .. **D'Alonzo,** Augustino D Jr. '93 %Cow Bay Contracting -105 Hrbr Rd -Pt Wash 11050 **Fx:**883-9692
(516) 883-8484 .. **D'Alonzo,** Jos R '95 %Cow Bay Contracting -105 Hrbr Rd -Pt Wash 11050 **Fx:**883-9692
(212) 944-1970 .. **Dalpiaz,** Christopher C '85 -300 West End Av -NY 10023
(914) 428-9330 .. **Dalrymple,** James E '02 (Oestreicher ED&D,LLP) -235 Mamaroneck Av -White Plns 10605
(914) 428-9330 .. **Dalrymple,** John E '66 (Oestreicher ED&D,LLP) -235 Mamaroneck Av -White Plns 10605
(518) 587-9600 .. **Dalton,** Alisa M '87 (Dalton Law Firm) -96 Lake Av -Saratoga Spgs 12866 **Fx:**587-9602
(516) 739-0400 .. **Dalton,** Barbara A '89 %Kelly R&K,LLP -330 Old Cntry Rd -Mineola 11501
(917) 778-6600 .. **Dalton,** Brian J '84 %J Toomey -485 Lex Av -NY 10017 **Fx:**778-7048
(716) 835-5249 .. **Dalton,** Gregory L '83 -83 Coniston Rd -Amherst 14226
(718) 263-9591 .. **Dalton,** Helen F '95 (H Dalton & Assoc,PC) -69-12 Austin -Frst Hlls 11375 **Fx:**263-9598
(212) 803-3585 .. **Dalton,** Jacqueline T '79 Empire State Devpt Corp -633 3rd Av -NY 10017 **Fx:**803-3595
(718) 923-2987 .. **Dalton,** James J '78 OTDA -14 Boerum Pl -Brklyn 11201
(631) 423-4390 .. **Dalton,** Jeanette C '01 %Mincone & M,PC -110 Walt Whitman Rd -South Huntington 11746 **Fx:**423-4408
(516) 883-6400 .. **Dalton,** John G Jr. '64 -12 Monfort Rd -Pt Wash 11050 **Fx:**767-9176
(518) 474-6011 .. **Dalton,** John K '73 %State Comptroller -110 State -Albany 12236 **Fx:**473-9104
(718) 448-1303 .. **Dalton,** John M '79 -406 Forest Av -Staten Isl 10301 **Fx:**876-6910
(718) 761-9300 .. **Dalton,** Kenneth M '81 Vaslas LH&D LLP -201 Edward Curry Av -Staten Isl 10314
(585) 530-3116 .. **Dalton,** Lawr X Jr. '87 %Appllt Div 4th Dept -50 East Av Ste 200 -Rchstr 14604 **Fx:**530-3247
(585) 419-8800 .. **Dalton,** Patrick J '87 (Harris B PLLC) -99 Garnsey Rd -Pittsfrd 14534
(212) 557-8060 .. **Dalton,** Rachel J '98 %Superstar Exp -230 Park Av -NY 10169
(718) 250-2000 .. **Dalton,** Shannah S '87 %DA -350 Jay -Brklyn 11201 **Fx:**250-2314
(516) 334-1111 .. **Dalto-Schettino,** Patricia A '01 -220 Westbury Av -Carle Pl 11514
(212) 549-2633 .. **Dalven,** Jennifer E '96 %ACLU -125 Broad -NY 10004 **Fx:**549-2651

(914) 448-0200 .. **D'Alvia,** Patricia '64 %Bartlett MB&M,LLP -81 Main -White Plns 10601
(212) 247-9193 .. **Daly,** Brian T '97 Millennium Prtnrs LLP -666 5th Av -NY 10103
(914) 961-2909 .. **Daly,** Carol McEwen '78 -68 Algonquin Rd -Ynkrs 10710 **Fx:**961-2077
(718) 590-2000 .. **Daly,** Christine E '04 %DA -198 E 161st -Bronx 10451 **Fx:**590-6477
(516) 227-0700 .. **Daly,** Christopher P '93 (Farrell F,PC) -1320 RXR Plz -Uniondale 11556
(212) 756-2000 .. **Daly,** Conor W '07 %Schulte R&Z LLP -919 3rd Av -NY 10022
(212) 238-3000 .. **Daly,** David M '65 OfCnsl Emmet M&M,LLP -120 Bway -NY 10271
(516) 571-5811 .. **Daly,** Eileen C '97 Nassau Cnty Ct -262 Old Cntry Rd -Mineola 11501
(212) 446-4800 .. **Daly,** Elizabeth F '08 %Kirkland & E LLP -153 E 53rd -NY 10022
(212) 599-6232 .. **Daly,** Eugene J '74 -437 Mad Av -NY 10022
(518) 449-2245 .. **Daly,** J Kevin '89 (Erwin M&D) -23 Elk -Albany 12207 **Fx:**449-7890
(516) 868-8000 .. **Daly,** James C '64 -111 W Sunrise Hwy -Freeprt 11520
(516) 877-1756 .. **Daly,** James J '63 %McKeen Fund -1055 Franklin Av -Gdn Cty 11530 **Fx:**877-1758
(518) 374-9125 .. **Daly,** James S '85 (Wemple & D) -508 Union -Schnctdy 12305
(845) 778-3793 .. **Daly,** Jayne E '96 Meadow Creek Dvlpmnt -110 Orange Av -Walden 12586
(914) 739-2080 .. **Daly,** Jennifer E '91 -125 Burke Ct -Buchanan 10511 **Fx:**788-5292
(212) 556-2100 .. **Daly,** Jennifer E '04 (King & S) -1185 Av of Amer -NY 10036
(914) 242-7837 .. **Daly,** Jill E '05 Prof Indemnity Agency -37 Radio Circle Dr -Mt Kisco 10549
(646) 394-6759 .. **Daly,** John E '95 %PricewaterhouseCoopers LLP -300 Mad Av -NY 10017 **Fx:**394-6717
(914) 378-1010 .. **Daly,** John M '89 -538 Riverdale Av -Ynkrs 10705 **Fx:**378-1092
(914) 323-7000 .. **Daly,** Kathleen A '91 %Wilson EME&D LLP -3 Gannett Dr -White Plns 10604
(716) 854-3400 .. **Daly,** Kathryn A '08 %Rupp BPC&C LLC -1600 Lbrty Bldg -Buffalo 14202
(212) 513-3200 .. **Daly,** Kathryn Blythe '09 %Holland & K LLP -31 W 52nd -NY 10019
(845) 278-7815 .. **Daly,** Kenneth C '85 -701 Essex Ct -Brewstr 10509
(212) 966-6420 .. **Daly,** Laura B '09 %Lwyrs For Children -110 Lafayette -NY 10013 **Fx:**966-0531
(914) 941-7000 .. **Daly Lavery & Hall** -500 Exec Blvd -Ossining 10562 **Fx:**941-0391
(212) 552-1814 .. **Daly,** Linda R '93 JP Morgan Chase -1 Chase Manh Plz -NY 10081
(631) 423-5350 .. **Daly,** Margaret Easa '88 -20 Carnegie Av -Cold Spg Hbr 11724
(315) 797-0890 .. **Daly,** Martin J '78 -185 Genesee -Utica 13501 **Fx:**797-0892
(212) 878-0000 .. **Daly,** Maura E '93 %MTA -2 Penn Plz -NY 10121
(845) 735-7000 .. **Daly,** Maureen A '10 %Johnson & C,LLP -1 Blue Hill Plz -Pearl Rvr 10965
(212) 487-9700 .. **Daly,** Michl F '05 %White F&F,LLP -61 Bway -NY 10006
(315) 471-3036 .. **Daly,** Michl P '77 -8195 Cazenovia Rd -Manlius 13104 **Fx:**682-4924
(202) 263-3711 .. **Daly,** Michl P '03 %Mayer B LLP -1675 Bway -NY 10019
(212) 382-2044 .. **Daly,** Nicholas G '09 %Marshall Firm -271 Mad Av -NY 10016 **Fx:**382-3610
(212) 384-1000 .. **Daly,** Patrick C '02 FBI -26 Fed Plz -NY 10278
(212) 656-3000 .. **Daly,** Patrick F '99 NYSE -20 Broad -NY 10005
(716) 835-2200 .. **Daly,** Richd F '82 -4249 Maple Rd -Amherst 14226 **Fx:**834-5814
(516) 739-5200 .. **Daly,** Russell D '97 -310 Old Cntry Rd -Gdn Cty 11530 **Fx:**739-5267
(516) 766-1619 .. **Daly,** Timothy F '94 %Dergarabedian D & Assoc -11 Clinton Av -Rockvll Ctr 11570 **Fx:**766-6121
(212) 789-2000 .. **Daly,** Wm L III '91 %NHL -1251 Av of Amer -NY 10020
(718) 665-5124 .. **Daly-Rivera,** Victor G '79 -840 Grnd Cncrs -Bronx 10451
(212) 710-2643 .. **Dalzine,** Marcus E '02 OfCnsl Wahab & M,LLC -1115 Bway -NY 10011 **Fx:**(646) 619-4195
(516) 880-4811 .. **Damadeo,** Maria '90 -37 Netto Ln -Plainvw 11803
(631) 271-7400 .. **Damadeo,** Nicholas J '79 (NJ Damadeo,PC) -27 W Neck Rd -Huntngtn 11743
(585) 232-3730 .. **D'Amanda,** John F '85 (Chamberlain D LLP) -1600 Crssrds Bldg -Rchstr 14614
(914) 591-5400 .. **D'Amanda,** Kathleen M '88 %D'Ambrosio & D,PC -42 Main -Irvngtn 10533 **Fx:**591-5122
(585) 232-3730 .. **D'Amanda,** Louis '62 OfCnsl Chamberlain D LLP -1600 Crssrds Bldg -Rchstr 14614
(585) 473-8799 .. **D'Amanda,** Richd '86 -171 Pearl -Rchstr 14607
(212) 756-2000 .. **Damania,** Farzad F '02 %Schulte R&Z LLP -919 3rd Av -NY 10022
(516) 357-3000 .. **D'Amaro,** Louis '87 OfCnsl Rivkin R LLP -926 RXR Plz -Uniondale 11556
(212) 352-9248 .. **Damasco,** Gino Paul '90 -156 W 22nd -NY 10011 **Fx:**924-3899
(212) 552-8267 .. **Damascus,** Dennis A '87 JP Morgan Chase Bk -1 Chase Manh Plz -NY 10005
(212) 788-6616 .. **Damashek,** Jay B '83 Dept of Info Tchnlgy & Telecom -75 Park Pl -NY 10007
(212) 490-5700 .. **Damashek,** Jonathan S '98 (Hecht KP&D) -19 W 44th -NY 10036
(212) 532-9736 .. **Damashek,** Lara '07 %R Skyer & Assoc,LLP -276 5th Av -NY 10001 **Fx:**532-9846
(212) 839-6503 .. **Damashek,** Philip '72 %Dept of Transportation -55 Water -NY 10041
(212) 836-8000 .. **Damast,** Michl J '99 (Kaye S LLP) -425 Park Av -NY 10022
(914) 779-2211 .. **Damast,** Robt '78 (Lauterbach GD&H LLP) -35 E Grassy Sprain Rd -Ynkrs 10710
(212) 883-5608 .. **D'Amato,** Alfonse M '62 (Park Strategies) -101 Park Av -NY 10178
(212) 883-5608 .. **D'Amato,** Armand P '70 Park Strategies -101 Park Av -NY 10178
(212) 237-1000 .. **Damato,** Chas A '79 (Windels ML&M,LLP) -156 W 56th -NY 10019
(716) 854-2020 .. **D'Amato,** Christopher D '98 (Cellino & B,PC) -350 Main -Buffalo 14202
(212) 883-5608 .. **D'Amato,** Christopher P '97 Park Strategies -101 Park Av -NY 10178
(212) 883-5608 .. **D'Amato,** Katuria E '01 %Park Strategies -101 Park Av -NY 10178
(212) 422-0202 .. **D'Amato,** Kristine L '04 %Sedgwick DM&A LLP -125 Broad -NY 10004
(718) 423-3000 .. **D'Amato,** Lawr L '72 (Dayton & D,PC) -42-40 Bell Blvd -Bayside 11361
(585) 987-2800 .. **D'Amato,** Louis M '80 (Woods OG LLP) -2 State -Rchstr 14614
(212) 269-0927 .. **D'Amato & Lynch, LLP** -2 World Fncl Ctr -NY 10281 **Fx:**269-3559
(212) 261-8000 .. **D'Amato,** Mary Ann '76 (Mendes & M,LLP) -750 7th Av -NY 10019
(212) 209-4800 .. **D'Amato,** Neal A '08 %Brown R LLP -7 Times Sq -NY 10036
(585) 226-5366 .. **D'Amato,** Paul J '83 %DEC -6274 E Avon-Lima Rd -Avon 14414 **Fx:**226-9485
(516) 922-8030 .. **Damato,** Paul L '87 (Murphy & L,PC) -1045 Oyster Bay Rd -E Norwich 11732
(212) 756-2000 .. **Dambacher,** Joshua '02 (Schulte R&Z LLP) -919 3rd Av -NY 10022
(212) 279-9090 .. **Dambeck,** Amy Beth '05 %Stark & S -One Penn Plz -NY 10119 **Fx:**279-9113
(516) 560-6400 .. **D'Ambra,** Cindy E '84 Leg Aid -1 Helen Keller Way -Hempstd 11550 **Fx:**565-3694
(914) 262-8444 .. **Dambroff,** David '77 -115 Beacon Hill Dr -Dobbs Ferry 10522 **Fx:**231-7550
(315) 425-2700 .. **D'Ambrogio,** Emanuela '03 %Hiscock & B,LLP -One Park Pl -Syracuse 13202
(212) 506-5333 .. **D'Ambrosio,** Alan A '73 (Orrick H&S LLP) -51 W 52nd -NY 10019
(914) 390-8003 .. **D'Ambrosio,** Denise J '80 NYPA -123 Main -White Plns 10601 **Fx:**390-8038
(914) 591-5400 .. **D'Ambrosio,** James J '88 (D'Ambrosio & D,PC) -42 Main -Irvngtn 10533 **Fx:**591-5122
(914) 681-8700 .. **D'Ambrosio,** Jason C '05 %Milber MP&S LLP -3 Barker Av -White Plns 10601
(914) 375-0100 .. **D'Ambrosio,** Jennifer L '04 -733 Ynkrs Av -Ynkrs 10704 **Fx:**375-0699
(212) 859-8000 .. **D'Ambrosio,** Jocelyn M '09 %Fried FHS&J LLP -1 NY Plz -NY 10004
(914) 591-5400 .. **D'Ambrosio,** John P '58 (D'Ambrosio & D,PC) -42 Main -Irvngtn 10533 **Fx:**591-5122
(212) 701-3000 .. **D'Ambrosio,** John P '10 %Cahill G&R LLP -80 Pine -NY 10005 **Fx:**269-5420
(212) 269-4900 .. **D'Ambrosio,** Jos '98 (Ford MEW&G,LLP) -Wall Street Plz -NY 10005
(518) 785-1138 .. **D'Ambrosio,** Mary Vinciguerra '82 (Vinciguerra Law Firm) -10 Utica Av -Latham 12110 **Fx:**785-1265
(914) 725-1717 .. **D'Ambrosio,** Michl T '75 -700 Wht Plns Rd -Scarsdale 10583 **Fx:**725-5780
(518) 533-3000 .. **D'Ambrosio,** Nicholas J Jr. '81 (Bond S&K,PLLC) -111 Wshngtn Av -Albany 12210
(718) 875-7100 .. **D'Ambrosio,** Rosellen '97 Home Abstract Corp -8225 3rd Av -Brklyn 11209
(718) 931-1220 .. **D'Ambrosio,** Susan M '04 -1937 Wllmsbrdg Rd -Bronx 10461 **Fx:**518-7680
(212) 309-6000 .. **D'Ambrosio,** Thos V '92 (Morgan L&B LLP) -101 Park Av -NY 10178
(914) 773-0047 .. **D'Ambrozio,** Dominick N '86 -245 Saw Mill Rvr Rd -Hawthorne 10532 **Fx:**773-0518
(631) 736-2698 .. **D'Ambruoso,** Jos A '52 -192 Theodore Dr -Coram 11727
(212) 373-3000 .. **D'Ambruoso Martinelli,** Julie M '06 %Paul WRW&G LLP -1285 Av of Amer -NY 10019
(518) 862-1386 .. **D'Amelia,** Gerald D Jr. '90 %Burke SM&H,LLP -302 Wshngtn Av Ext Bx15085 -Albany 12212
(315) 453-4860 .. **Damelio,** Anthony J Jr. '09 (Damelio G&M) -103 Commerce Blvd -Liverpool 13088 **Fx:**453-4828
(315) 266-6100 .. **D'Amelio,** Dean P '93 %Pub Def -235 Elizabeth -Utica 13501 **Fx:**266-6105
(585) 442-7360 .. **Damelio,** Jos S '87 -125 State -Rchstr 14614 **Fx:**461-3666
(914) 287-2000 .. **Damen,** Amy K '87 -470 Mamaroneck Av -White Plns 10605
(212) 596-9000 .. **Damerville,** Laura M '08 %Ropes & G LLP -1211 Av of Amer -NY 10036
(646) 386-4082 .. **Dames,** Helen S '93 %Hon C Solomon -100 Centre -NY 10013
(585) 232-6500 .. **Damia,** Michl A '86 Cnsl Harter S&E LLP -1600 Bausch & Lomb Pl -Rchstr 14604
(845) 639-7711 .. **Damiani,** Gerard M '66 -499 Route 304 Bx1135 -New Cty 10956 **Fx:**639-7719
(212) 792-8484 .. **Damiano,** Brian J '04 %Stern T&B LLP -380 Lex Av -NY 10168
(315) 422-5618 .. **Damiano,** Linda A '85 -215 Kenwick Dr -Syracuse 13208
(212) 819-6520 .. **Damiano,** Peter A '00 AMC -500 7th Av -NY 10018
(617) 686-3377 .. **Damianos,** Elexis Z '09 -14 Blueberry Ridge Rd -E Setauket 11733
(631) 360-9000 .. **Damianos,** John E '82 (DRG Realty) -222 Middle Cntry Rd -Smithtwn 11787 **Fx:**360-0103
(212) 262-2390 .. **D'Amico,** Daniela R '04 %Connell F LLP -888 7th Av -NY 10106
(315) 474-1154 .. **Damico,** Donald A '82 -315 W Fayette -Syracuse 13202 **Fx:**471-4238
(716) 857-7991 .. **Damico,** Edw J '08 Natl Fuel Gas -6363 Main -Williamsvll 14221 **Fx:**857-7614
(585) 338-1330 .. **D'Amico,** Edw L '58 -1171 Titus Av -Rchstr 14617 **Fx:**338-9664
(212) 474-1000 .. **D'Amico,** Evan M '09 %Cravath S&M LLP -825 8th Av -NY 10019
(516) 798-3276 .. **D'Amico,** Gregory M '01 State Farm Ins -1026 Park Blvd -Massapequa Pk 11762
(315) 474-1267 .. **Damico,** J David '71 -M&T Bldg -Syracuse 13202 **Fx:**474-4514
(212) 504-6000 .. **D'Amico,** Jeannine F '03 %Cadwalader W&T LLP -1 World Fncl Ctr -NY 10281
(516) 222-2021 .. **D'Amico,** Jeffrey R '93 (D'Amico & Assoc,PLLC) -585 Stewart Av -Gdn Cty 11530 **Fx:**222-0265
(585) 225-5440 .. **Damico,** John A '53 -857 N Greece Rd -Rchstr 14626
(718) 984-3100 .. **D'Amico,** Jos A '82 -114 Seguine Av -Staten Isl 10309 **Fx:**227-0431
(585) 240-7500 .. **D'Amico,** Lance E '95 %Ziff-Davis -500 Canal Vw Blvd -Rchstr 14623
(585) 428-5755 .. **D'Amico,** Marie C '94 %Cnty Atty -50 W Main -Rchstr 14614 **Fx:**428-2031
(212) 541-2000 .. **D'Amico,** Matthew P '86 (Bryan C LLP) -1290 Av of Amer -NY 10104
(716) 885-2889 .. **D'Amico,** Michl L '99 (Eoannou L&D) -484 Delaware Av -Buffalo 14202
(212) 309-7892 .. **D'Amico,** Richd J '96 %Lexis/Nexis -125 Park Av -NY 10017 **Fx:**309-8187
(212) 436-1121 .. **D'Amico,** Sean A '94 IRS -290 Bway -NY 10007 **Fx:**436-1063
(585) 436-7720 .. **D'Amico,** Wm P '82 %UAW Leg Srvcs Plan -1200C Scottsvll Rd -Rchstr 14624 **Fx:**436-7741
(212) 625-2614 .. **Damien,** Javier '88 -325 Bway -NY 10007 **Fx:**625-2615
(518) 869-9200 .. **Damin,** Peter M '04 %Rose Law Firm,PLLC -501 New Karner Rd -Albany 12205 **Fx:**869-3334

(516) 747-1900 .. **Damm,** Harold F '79 (Ciotti & D,LLP) -1551 Kellum Pl -Mineola 11501 **Fx:**746-4709
(607) 277-8601 .. **Damm,** Kelly A '00 -308 N Tioga Bx256 -Ithaca 14851 **Fx:**277-2185
(718) 519-6281 .. **Dammar,** Merrick J '93 -782 Burke Av -Bronx 10467 **Fx:**325-3233
(914) 948-8600 .. **D'Ammora,** Victor J '80 (Lucchese & D,LLP) -10 Bank -White Plns 10606
(212) 259-8000 .. **Damon,** Jonathan A '94 (Dewey & L LLP) -1301 Av of Amer -NY 10019
(716) 856-5500 .. **Damon Morey LLP** -200 Delaware Av -Buffalo 14202 **Fx:**856-5510
(585) 232-3640 .. **Damon Morey LLP** -16 W Main -Rchstr 14614
(716) 759-9759 .. **Damon Morey LLP** -9276 Main -Clarence 14031
(212) 468-8000 .. **D'Amore,** Matthew M '95 (Morrison & F LLP) -1290 Av of Amer -NY 10104
(516) 802-0560 .. **Damoulakis,** Georgia '05 %DP Burke & Assoc,PLLC -240 Townsend Sq -Oyster Bay 11771
(212) 653-8700 .. **D'Amour,** David J '08 %Sheppard MR&H LLP -30 Rckfllr Plz -NY 10112
(718) 250-2000 .. **Dampf,** Gayle '91 %DA -350 Jay -Brklyn 11201 **Fx:**250-2314
(914) 693-2476 .. **Damplo,** Susan M '00 -923 Saw Mill Rvr Rd Bx219 -Ardsley 10502
(607) 324-6006 .. **Damrath,** Jos E '81 -24 Church -Hornell 14843
(212) 854-2675 .. **Damrosch,** Lori Fisler '82 %Columbia Law Schl -435 W 116th -NY 10027 **Fx:**854-7946
(631) 393-9400 .. **Damsky,** Edw J '86 %Forster & G -500 Bi-Cnty Blvd Bx9030 -Farmngdl 11735
(516) 294-5200 .. **Dana,** Isaac M '94 %Picciano & S -900 Merchants Cncrs -Westbury 11590
(718) 520-0300 .. **Dana,** John R '86 -113-25 Qns Blvd -Frst Hlls 11375 **Fx:**520-8211
(516) 571-1476 .. **Dana,** Thos V '70 Supreme Ct -100 Supreme Ct Dr -Mineola 11501
(212) 996-4611 .. **Dana-Bashian,** Pauline '76 -401 E 89th -NY 10128 **Fx:**996-4611
(315) 424-8944 .. **Danaher,** Christian J '97 (Shulman CG&R,PC) -250 S Clinton -Syracuse 13202
(607) 721-8796 .. **Danaher,** Michl J Jr. '85 %Dept of Law -44 Hawley -Bnghmtn 13901 **Fx:**721-8789
(518) 270-2950 .. **Danaher,** Philip J '86 %Cnty Atty -1600 7th Av -Troy 12180 **Fx:**270-2954
(518) 463-4383 .. **Danaher,** Philip J '86 -252 Bway -Rensselaer 12144 **Fx:**463-4386
(212) 532-8585 .. **Danchuk,** Emily A '02 %S Feldman -12 E 41st -NY 10017 **Fx:**532-8598
(315) 637-3663 .. **Dancks,** Therese Wiley '92 (Gale & D,LLC) -Bx6527 -Syracuse 13217
(631) 912-8839 .. **D'ancona,** Philip A '01 BAE Systems -40 E Pulaski Rd -Greenlawn 11740
(212) 310-8541 .. **Dandeneau,** Debra A '87 (Weil G&M LLP) -767 5th Av -NY 10153
(631) 454-0606 .. **Dandeneau,** Gerald V '74 (Dandeneau & L) -425 Broadhllw Rd -Melvll 11747 **Fx:**454-9250
(718) 961-6927 .. **Dandola,** John A '78 -27-31 164th -Flushng 11358 **Fx:**939-7760
(631) 738-6761 .. **Dandola,** Susan '95 -500 Portion Rd -Ronkonkoma 11779
D'Andrea, Dennis '88 NYS Law Judge -Bx127 -Wainscott 11975
(518) 452-8787 .. **D'Andrea,** John J '91 (Drinker B&R LLP) -321 Great Oaks Blvd -Albany 12203
(518) 884-4770 .. **D'Andrea,** Karen E S '02 Cnty Atty -Cnty Mncpl Ctr -Ballston Spa 12020 **Fx:**884-4720
(631) 852-2325 .. **D'Andrea,** Mary C '87 %MHLS -One Court -Rvrhead 11901 **Fx:**852-2392
(914) 472-0800 .. **D'Andrea,** Vincent P '60 D'Andrea & G -700 Wht Plns Rd -Scarsdale 10583
(914) 697-4708 .. **D'Andrea-McCullagh,** Roxann '99 Private Ofc Inc -800 Wstchstr Av -Rye Brook 10573
(718) 658-6770 .. **Dandridge,** Lance K '86 -90-50 Parsons Blvd -Jamaica 11432
(716) 849-8900 .. **Dandridge-Richburg,** Tasha T '99 %Hurwitz & F,PC -1300 Lbrty Bldg -Buffalo 14202
(212) 612-4398 .. **Dandrige,** Danielle M '02 Hoey KT&E -55 Water -NY 10041
(914) 949-5300 .. **Dandy,** Katherine W '93 (Brown & T,LLC) -1 N Bway -White Plns 10601
(212) 966-6420 .. **Dane,** Ronnie '84 %Lwyrs For Children -110 Lafayette -NY 10013 **Fx:**966-0531
(212) 373-3000 .. **Danek,** Jane D '04 %Paul WRW&G LLP -1285 Av of Amer -NY 10019
(518) 640-6900 .. **Danek,** Marie Flynn '92 (Phelan P&D,LLP) -302 Wshngtn Av Ext -Albany 12203
(585) 987-2800 .. **Danella,** Dennis B '04 (Woods OG LLP) -2 State -Rchstr 14614
(212) 735-3000 .. **Danella,** Nicholas A '07 %Skadden ASM&F LLP -4 Times Sq -NY 10036
(212) 520-8320 .. **Danenberg,** Gregory E '97 -825 3rd Av -NY 10022 **Fx:**520-8321
(646) 414-6879 .. **Danenhauer,** George P '01 Cnsl Lowenstein S PC -1251 Av of Amer -NY 10020 **Fx:**(973) 422-6855
(631) 727-2340 .. **Daneri,** Eugene L Jr. '88 %Ahmuty D&M -750 Roanoke Av -Rvrhead 11901
(212) 584-0700 .. **Danes,** Asa R '04 %Seeger W LLP -1 William -NY 10004
(718) 250-3214 .. **Danet,** Gloria J '92 %DA -350 Jay -Brklyn 11201 **Fx:**250-4860
(212) 319-3405 .. **Danetti,** Gina T '04 -60 E 42nd -NY 10165
(718) 575-0045 .. **Danetz,** Stephen S '65 -118-21 Qns Blvd -Frst Hlls 11375 **Fx:**793-7928
(646) 562-3405 .. **Danford,** Caroline S '95 %PLC -747 3rd Av -NY 10017
(212) 762-6794 .. **Dang,** Bao-Ngoc V '04 Morgan Stanley -1221 Av of Amer -NY 10020
(212) 446-2300 .. **Danganan,** Jobe G '05 %Boies S&F LLP -575 Lex Av -NY 10022
(718) 515-0300 .. **D'Angelica,** Leonard '00 (D'Angelica & B,PLLC) -2705 Eastchstr Rd -Bronx 10469 **Fx:**515-4366
(631) 360-5600 .. **D'Angelillo,** Robt M '92 %Grabie & G,LLP -162 Terry Rd -Smithtwn 11787 **Fx:**360-3370
(212) 374-3379 .. **D'Angelo,** Anthony J '93 %NYC Dept Educ-OLS -52 Chmbrs -NY 10007 **Fx:**374-5596
(212) 763-6800 .. **D'Angelo,** Christopher A '85 (Vandenberg & F,LLP) -60 E 42nd -NY 10165
(212) 626-4100 .. **D'Angelo,** Erica S '10 %Baker & M LLP -1114 Av of Amer -NY 10036
(212) 373-3000 .. **D'Angelo,** Frank D '10 %Paul WRW&G LLP -1285 Av of Amer -NY 10019
(516) 742-7601 .. **D'Angelo,** Frank G Jr. '86 F D'Angelo & Assoc -901 Stewart Av -Gdn Cty 11530 **Fx:**742-6070
(631) 462-6908 .. **D'Angelo,** James '92 -1772 E Jericho Tpk -Huntngtn 11743 **Fx:**462-7548
(631) 981-4400 .. **D'Angelo,** Janet M '91 Nationwide Ct Srvcs -4250 Vets Mem'l Hwy -Holbrook 11741 **Fx:**981-4731
(212) 592-1400 .. **D'Angelo,** Jason A '98 Cnsl Herrick,F LLP -2 Park Av -NY 10016
(585) 987-2800 .. **D'Angelo,** Jeffrey C '90 %Woods OG LLP -2 State -Rchstr 14614
(212) 848-0274 .. **D'Angelo,** John R '83 Plymouth Partners Ltd -645 5th Av -NY 10022
(631) 224-1133 .. **D'Angelo,** Mario '88 (Hariton & D,LLP) -3500 Sunrise Hwy -Great Rvr 11739
(212) 756-2000 .. **D'Angelo,** Michl D '07 %Schulte R&Z LLP -919 3rd Av -NY 10022
(212) 652-3890 .. **D'Angelo,** Michl J '01 %Pitta & G LLP -120 Bway -NY 10271
(212) 525-6447 .. **D'Angelo,** Mireya Calderin '94 HSBC Bank USA -452 5th Av -NY 10018
(718) 259-4280 .. **D'Angelo,** Ronald James '66 -8735 Bay Pkwy -Brklyn 11214 **Fx:**259-4280
(212) 341-6514 .. **D'Angelo,** Victor J '86 %Liquidation Bur -123 William -NY 10038 **Fx:**608-3398
(716) 250-1800 .. **D'Angelo,** Victoria L '79 (Jaeckle F&M,LLP) -400 Essjay Rd -Amherst 14221
(315) 781-6897 .. **Dangl,** John R Jr. '92 -409 S Main Bx1072 -Geneva 14456 **Fx:**781-6841
(212) 450-2543 .. **Danias,** Anastasia T '99 %NFL -280 Park Av -NY 10017 **Fx:**681-7599
(212) 836-8000 .. **Danias,** Peter G '84 %Kaye S LLP -425 Park Av -NY 10022
(212) 974-7474 .. **Daniel,** Al J Jr. '89 (Cowan DA&S LLP) -41 Mad Av -NY 10010
(585) 546-2500 .. **Daniel,** Edw C III '01 (McConville CC&M,PC) -25 E Main -Rchstr 14614
(212) 998-6281 .. **Daniel,** Elizabeth Barry '96 %Brennan Ctr for Justice -161 Av of Amer -NY 10013
(212) 995-2074 .. **Daniel,** Emily R '86 -69 W 9th -NY 10011
(516) 354-0149 .. **Daniel,** Jacques C '06 %Lubin & S -229 Jericho Tpk -Floral Pk 11001
(212) 806-5400 .. **Daniel,** Jeffrey '08 %Stroock &S&L LLP -180 Maiden Ln -NY 10038
(212) 532-3850 .. **Daniel,** Jill A '99 %Menagh & F,PC -386 Park Av S -NY 10016
(212) 264-8000 .. **Daniel,** Lisa H '84 %HUD -26 Fed Plz -NY 10278
(516) 354-0149 .. **Daniel,** Rommel '01 -229 Jericho Tpk -Floral Pk 11001
(212) 448-0702 .. **Daniel,** Sargon '08 Prospect Capital Corp -10 E 40th -NY 10016
(212) 756-2000 .. **Daniel,** Stacey '08 %Schulte R&Z LLP -919 3rd Av -NY 10022
(212) 247-2500 .. **Daniele,** Anthony R '77 -75 Rckfllr Plz -NY 10019 **Fx:**202-7930
(914) 995-4075 .. **Daniele,** Christopher R '08 %DA -188 Tarrytown Rd -White Plns 10601
(212) 728-8000 .. **Daniele,** Frank A '89 (Willkie F&G LLP) -787 7th Av -NY 10019
(631) 661-2222 .. **Daniele,** Kelly '92 (K Daniele,PC) -181 W Main -Babylon 11702 **Fx:**661-0706
(914) 949-0777 .. **Daniele,** Theresa M '85 -222 Mamaroneck Av -White Plns 10605 **Fx:**949-4411
(718) 613-2460 .. **Daniel-Favors,** Lurie T '06 %Hon S Johnson Jr -225 Cadman Plz E -Brklyn 11201
(212) 530-5000 .. **Danielides,** Philippe N '10 %Milbank TH&M LLP -1 Chase Manh Plz -NY 10005
(212) 393-1000 .. **Danielle,** Carly '90 -233 Bway -NY 10279 **Fx:**267-2110
(212) 819-8200 .. **D'Aniello,** Stefano Z '07 %White & C LLP -1155 Av of Amer -NY 10036
(212) 745-9718 .. **Daniels,** Aaron M '06 Brigade Capital Mgmt LLC -399 Park Av -NY 10022
(212) 225-2000 .. **Daniels,** Benjamin M '09 %Cleary GS&H -1 Lbrty Plz -NY 10006
(315) 735-7993 .. **Daniels,** Bruce F Jr. '92 (B Daniels Jr,PC) -23 Oxford Rd -New Hartfrd 13413 **Fx:**735-7924
(646) 386-4520 .. **Daniels,** Charlene G '83 %Criminal Ct -100 Centre -NY 10013
(518) 379-1213 .. **Daniels,** Christine Carey '82 Cnsl Golub Corp -501 Duanesburg Rd Bx1074 -Schnctdy 12306 **Fx:**379-3536
(212) 728-8000 .. **Daniels,** Colin J '09 %Willkie F&G LLP -787 7th Av -NY 10019
(212) 490-1700 .. **Daniels,** Danl L '88 (Wiggin & D) -450 Lex Av -NY 10017
(845) 855-5900 .. **Daniels,** David E '83 (Daniels & P,LLP) -517 Route 22 -Pawling 12564
(212) 640-5747 .. **Daniels,** Douglas H '84 %Amer Exp -200 Vesey -NY 10285
(212) 607-8160 .. **Daniels,** Edw F '09 %MoloLamken -540 Mad Av -NY 10022 **Fx:**607-8161
(212) 715-9100 .. **Daniels,** Elan M '09 %Kramer LN&F,LLP -1177 Av of Amer -NY 10036
(516) 338-7520 .. **Daniels,** Fred G '76 (Daniels & N,PC) -900 Merchants Cncrs -Westbury 11590
(718) 459-6000 .. **Daniels,** Fred G '76 (Pennisi D&N LLP) -97-77 Qns Blvd -Rego Pk 11374
(973) 315-4424 .. **Daniels,** James B '90 (Budd L) -140 Bway -NY 10005
(718) 858-7571 .. **Daniels,** James Eliot '66 -187 Hicks -Brklyn 11201
(518) 449-3166 .. **Daniels,** James P '86 %UHY Advisors -66 State -Albany 12207 **Fx:**449-5832
(212) 656-8462 .. **Daniels,** Janet Leslie '81 NYSE -20 Broad -NY 10005
(516) 745-5430 .. **Daniels,** Jeffrey C '81 -585 Stewart Av -Gdn Cty 11530 **Fx:**745-8769
(212) 885-5000 .. **Daniels,** Jennifer J '08 (Blank R LLP) -405 Lex Av -NY 10174
(212) 352-3888 .. **Daniels,** Jennifer M '89 Barnes & Noble,Inc -122 5th Av -NY 10011
(716) 856-5140 .. **Daniels,** Joel L '63 -42 Delaware Av -Buffalo 14202 **Fx:**856-3106
(516) 746-7111 .. **Daniels,** John H '54 -114 Old Cntry Rd -Mineola 11501
(212) 446-7000 .. **Daniels,** Jos C '99 %McKinsey & Co -55 E 52nd -NY 10055 **Fx:**688-9521
(212) 751-4300 .. **Daniels,** Jos F '04 (Hodgson R LLP) -1540 Bway -NY 10036
(212) 406-6040 .. **Daniels,** Jos R '99 -225 Bway -NY 10007 **Fx:**406-6043
(212) 767-6921 .. **Daniels,** Katherine J '91 %Hachette Filipacchi -1633 Bway -NY 10019 **Fx:**767-5631
(518) 869-7145 .. **Daniels,** Keith A '94 -1510 Central Av -Albany 12205 **Fx:**869-7205
(914) 725-1557 .. **Daniels,** Laura A '01 -56 Woods Ln -Scarsdale 10583
(516) 596-2116 .. **Daniels,** Lisa '92 -74 Rowe Av -E Rockaway 11518
(516) 746-7111 .. **Daniels,** Marc A '84 -114 Old Cntry Rd -Mineola 11501
(914) 948-1556 .. **Daniels,** Martin P '91 %Danziger & M LLP -123 Main -White Plns 10601
(212) 859-8000 .. **Daniels,** Noah S '08 %Fried FHS&J LLP -1 NY Plz -NY 10004
(516) 338-7520 .. **Daniels & Norelli,PC** -900 Merchants Cncrs -Westbury 11590 **Fx:**338-1063
(607) 723-7435 .. **Daniels,** Peter A '53 -19 Chenango -Bnghmtn 13901 **Fx:**723-7435
(845) 855-5900 .. **Daniels & Porco,LLP** -517 Route 22 -Pawling 12564 **Fx:**855-5945

(518) 462-7770 .. **Daniels & Porco,LLP** -119 Wshngtn Av -Albany 12210 **Fx:**462-3771
(845) 225-8404 .. **Daniels & Porco,LLP** -102 Gleneida Av -Carmel 10512 **Fx:**225-4262
(212) 816-5067 .. **Daniels**, Rona '80 Citigroup -388 Greenwich -NY 10013
(215) 669-2583 .. **Daniels**, Scott M '06 -625 E 14th -NY 10009
(212) 304-3103 .. **Daniels**, Shirley L '78 %Paragon Cable Manh -5120 Bway -NY 10034 **Fx:**304-3111
(212) 759-4888 .. **Daniels**, Tamara A '06 %Phillips L LLP -437 Mad Av -NY 10022
(516) 745-6000 .. **Daniels**, Theo '53 -585 Stewart Av -Gdn Cty 11530 **Fx:**745-6642
(585) 464-9400 .. **Daniels**, Thos W '93 %Wilmorite -1265 Scottsvll Rd -Rchstr 14624 **Fx:**328-1784
(212) 753-7500 .. **Daniels**, Tracey L '00 %Hartman & C LLP -488 Mad Av -NY 10022
(516) 294-5433 .. **Danielsen**, Kenneth B '09 %Ahmuty D&M -200 IU Willets Rd -Albertson 11507
(516) 571-3800 .. **Danielson**, Mishael Ahmad '05 %DA -262 Old Cntry Rd -Mineola 11501 **Fx:**248-9479
(518) 402-1434 .. **Daniels Rivera**, Janine Y '91 Medicaid Inspctr Gen Ofc -800 N Pearl -Albany 12204 **Fx:**408-0536
(716) 852-0400 .. **Danieu**, John P '92 (Roach BM&G,PC) -424 Main -Buffalo 14202
(716) 566-5400 .. **Danieu**, Kimberlee Lupton '92 %Goldberg S LLP -665 Main -Buffalo 14203
(212) 310-8000 .. **Danilow**, Greg A '75 (Weil G&M LLP) -767 5th Av -NY 10153
(212) 758-1626 .. **Danilowitz**, Sorrel A '90 -488 Mad Av -NY 10022 **Fx:**308-8582
(212) 784-5800 .. **Danish**, Keith E '78 Cnsl Hiscock & B,LLP -7 Times Sq -NY 10036
(516) 255-1800 .. **Danisi**, Jason R '04 %Rosenblum & B LLP -100 Merrick Rd -Rockvll Ctr 11570
(718) 286-6000 .. **Dank**, Elizabeth S '06 %DA -125-01 Qns Blvd -Kew Gdns 11415
(516) 660-9453 .. **Dank**, Warren S '05 -62 Belmont Cir -Syosset 11791 **Fx:**364-6308
(212) 967-1114 .. **Dankberg**, Jay S '71 -1220 Bway -NY 10001 **Fx:**967-1112
(718) 761-9300 .. **Danke**, Paul J Jr. '91 (Vaslas LH&D LLP) -201 Edward Curry Av -Staten Isl 10314
(212) 371-3141 .. **Dankin**, Peter A '68 (McPheters & D,PC) -260 Mad Av -NY 10016
(212) 751-8000 .. **Dankner**, Jay W '74 (Dankner & M,PC) -41 E 57th -NY 10022
(212) 751-8000 .. **Dankner & Milstein,PC** -41 E 57th -NY 10022 **Fx:**751-8091
(212) 909-6000 .. **Dankworth**, Courtney M '07 %Debevoise & P LLP -919 3rd Av -NY 10022
(914) 249-5012 .. **Dann**, Diane F '86 %MasterCard Intl -2000 Purchase -Purchase 10577
(212) 902-5481 .. **Dann**, Eric R '97 Goldman Sachs -1 NY Plz -NY 10004
(212) 848-4000 .. **Dann**, Morgan E R '09 %Shearman & S LLP -599 Lex Av -NY 10022
(716) 895-2100 .. **Dann**, Theo E Jr. '90 %Buflovak LLC -750 E Ferry -Buffalo 14211
(516) 539-6770 .. **D'Anna**, Agesilas '55 (Nigro D&U) -215 Uniondale Av -Uniondale 11553
(718) 273-0300 .. **Danna**, Anthony S '94 (Danna & Assoc,PC) -1145 Forest Av -Staten Isl 10310 **Fx:**448-6820
(718) 448-0100 .. **Danna**, Anthony S '94 (Danna & Assoc,PC) -406 Forest Av -Staten Isl 10301 **Fx:**448-0188
(716) 434-4132 .. **Danna**, Mark R '84 (Danna & D) -155 East Av -Lockprt 14094 **Fx:**434-3271
(212) 790-9200 .. **Dannay**, Richd '65 (Cowan L&L,PC) -1133 Av of Amer -NY 10036
(212) 416-8000 .. **Dannelly**, Ashlyn H '05 %Dept of Law -120 Bway -NY 10271
(212) 486-3370 .. **Dannenberg**, Jeffrey C '84 (Kestenbaum D&K,LLP) -104 W 40th -NY 10018
(914) 997-0500 .. **Dannenberg**, Richd B '55 Cnsl Lowey DC&H,PC -1 N Bway -White Plns 10601
(212) 837-6077 .. **Danner**, Amy E '08 %Hughes H&R LLP -1 Bttry Pk Plz -NY 10004
(973) 494-0604 .. **Danner**, Paul S '01 %Mound CW&G -One Bttry Pk Plz -NY 10004
(516) 992-1848 .. **Danner**, Tracee A '99 OfCnsl M Carmen & Assoc,PLLC -1201 RXR Plz -Uniondale 11556 **Fx:**739-0981
(518) 402-0205 .. **Danner-Conboy**, Mary Beth '92 %UIA Bd -Troy Atrium Bx15126 -Albany 12212 **Fx:**402-6208
(212) 698-0773 .. **Dannhauser**, James F '78 %Lepercq de Neuflize -1675 Bway -NY 10019 **Fx:**262-0155
(212) 489-1400 .. **Dannhauser**, Robt F '08 %Bickel & B -767 5th Av -NY 10153
(212) 310-8000 .. **Dannhauser**, Stephen J '76 (Weil G&M LLP) -767 5th Av -NY 10153
(212) 557-4000 .. **Dano**, Ellen M '09 %Grunfeld DLS&K LLP -399 Park Av -NY 10022
(212) 573-6064 .. **Danoff**, Martin A '61 -230 Park Av -NY 10169 **Fx:**573-9031
(212) 752-9700 .. **Danovitch**, David E '88 (Gersten S LLP) -600 Lex Av -NY 10022
(212) 940-8800 .. **Danow**, Bret J '01 (Katten MR LLP) -575 Mad Av -NY 10022
(212) 370-3744 .. **Danow**, Keven '76 (Danow M&P,PC) -275 Mad Av -NY 10016
(212) 953-6000 .. **Danow**, Matthew J '00 (Katsky K LLP) -605 3rd Av -NY 10158
(212) 370-3744 .. **Danow McMullan & Panoff,PC** -275 Mad Av -NY 10016 **Fx:**370-4996
(718) 590-3786 .. **Danow**, Steven '71 %Supreme Ct -851 Grnd Cncrs -Bronx 10451 **Fx:**590-8899
(631) 727-4900 .. **Danowski**, Peter S Jr. '70 -616 Roanoke Av Bx779 -Rvrhead 11901
(212) 272-2563 .. **Danowsky**, Jos F '88 JP Morgan Chase -383 Mad Av -NY 10179 **Fx:**272-5917
(212) 362-7258 .. **Danquah**, Marmaduke K D '98 -401 West End Av -NY 10024
(212) 298-5019 .. **Dan-Salami**, J Olayinka '90 %Leg Aid -49 Thomas -NY 10013 **Fx:**298-5252
(212) 732-2929 .. **Dansker**, Paul D '80 (Dansker & A Assoc) -30 Vesey -NY 10007 **Fx:**732-8795
(212) 536-9526 .. **Dansky**, Ira M '71 Jones Apparel Grp -1411 Bway -NY 10018
(718) 828-8382 .. **Danso Ayesu**, Kwame '91 -1 Metro Oval -Bronx 10462 **Fx:**792-7271
(914) 993-9062 .. **D'Antona**, Gaetano G '75 -399 Knollwood Rd -White Plns 10603 **Fx:**761-9262
(516) 623-1111 .. **D'Antone**, Patricia M '02 %Curtis V PC -2174 Hewlett Av Bx801 -Merrick 11566 **Fx:**623-0758
(516) 572-2000 .. **D'Antonio**, Adam '08 %DA -99 Main -Hempstd 11550 **Fx:**572-2606
(518) 457-4380 .. **D'Antonio**, Carolyn '84 %Dept of Labor -State Campus Bldg 12 -Albany 12240 **Fx:**485-1819
(212) 227-4210 .. **D'Antonio**, Dennis T '82 (Weg & M,PC) -52 Duane -NY 10007
(212) 688-3025 .. **D'Antonio**, Rebekah E '08 Hitchcock & C,LLP -757 3rd Av -NY 10017 **Fx:**688-3040
(585) 454-0700 .. **D'Antonio**, Thos S '83 (Ward GH&R LLP) -300 State -Rchstr 14614
(212) 788-0939 .. **Dantowitz**, Jeffrey S '89 %Law Dept -100 Church -NY 10007 **Fx:**788-0367
(212) 968-2703 .. **D'Antuono**, Christopher C '01 GFI -55 Water -NY 10041
(516) 733-7080 .. **Dantuono**, Mary A '82 %Catholic Charities -90 Cherry Ln -Hicksvll 11801 **Fx:**733-7098
(516) 365-9191 .. **Dantuono**, Michl A '84 %S Friedman -1 Hllw Ln -New Hyde Pk 11042 **Fx:**365-6138
(516) 294-6410 .. **Dantzig**, Susan D '84 %S Cohn -1 Old Cntry Rd -Carle Pl 11514 **Fx:**294-0094
(212) 819-8200 .. **Dantzler**, J Wm Jr. '80 (White & C LLP) -1155 Av of Amer -NY 10036
(212) 389-5000 .. **Dany**, Lawr A III '06 %Sutherland A&B LLP -1114 Av of Amer -NY 10036
(973) 596-4653 .. **Danylchuk**, Rita M '91 Cnsl Gibbons PC -1 Penn Plz -NY 10119 **Fx:**639-6348
(212) 669-7913 .. **Danza**, Cynthia J '82 %Landmarks Pres Comm -1 Centre -NY 10007
(212) 818-9600 .. **Danzer**, Elana L '93 %Greenfield S&S,LLP -600 3rd Av -NY 10016
(516) 228-4226 .. **Danzi**, Robt F '80 -900 Merchants Cncrs -Westbury 11590 **Fx:**228-6569
(631) 648-1354 .. **Danzi**, Vincent G '03 -444 Route 111 -Smithtwn 11787 **Fx:**648-1454
(516) 489-4390 .. **D'Anzica**, Tony L '98 (D'Anzica & Assoc,PC) -Bx57 -Franklin Sq 11010 **Fx:**908-4605
(212) 697-1111 .. **Danzig**, Allen E '83 L-3 Cmmnctns Corp -600 3rd Av -NY 10016 **Fx:**682-7959
(212) 318-3000 .. **Danzig**, Douglas J '75 (Fulbright & J LLP) -666 5th Av -NY 10103
(914) 285-1400 .. **Danzig Fishman & Decea** -1 N Bway -White Plns 10601 **Fx:**285-1401
(212) 616-1566 .. **Danzig Fishman & Decea** -360 Lex Av -NY 10017 **Fx:**(646) 454-4191
(212) 416-8000 .. **Danzig**, Jodi A '93 %Dept of Law -120 Bway -NY 10271
(212) 735-3000 .. **Danzig**, Matthew D '08 %Skadden ASM&F LLP -4 Times Sq -NY 10036
(914) 285-1400 .. **Danzig**, Richd A '79 Cnsl Danzig F&D -1 N Bway -White Plns 10601
(212) 922-1920 .. **Danziger**, Andrea L '95 %West Group -530 5th Av -NY 10036 **Fx:**867-2404
(631) 224-5550 .. **Danziger**, Anne Marie '94 Town Atty -655 Main -Islip 11751 **Fx:**224-5573
(212) 754-7000 .. **Danziger**, Chas T '88 Danziger D&M -405 Park Av -NY 10022 **Fx:**758-0143
(914) 288-8052 .. **Danziger**, Elliot J '09 %Danziger & M LLP -170 Hmltn Av -White Plns 10601 **Fx:**323-0369
(212) 218-7910 .. **Danziger**, Fredk M '65 %Griffin Land & Nurseries Inc -1 Rckfllr Plz -NY 10020
(716) 842-1796 .. **Danziger**, Jack '75 -70 Niagara -Buffalo 14202
(914) 948-1556 .. **Danziger**, Joel '58 (Danziger & M LLP) -123 Main -White Plns 10601
(212) 756-2000 .. **Danziger**, Jonathan '05 %Schulte R&Z LLP -919 3rd Av -NY 10022
(914) 288-8052 .. **Danziger**, Joyce '84 (Danziger & M LLP) -170 Hmltn Av -White Plns 10601 **Fx:**323-0369
(914) 948-1556 .. **Danziger & Markhoff LLP** -123 Main -White Plns 10601 **Fx:**948-1706
(518) 462-5601 .. **Danziger**, Peter L '74 (O'Connell & A) -54 State -Albany 12207
(212) 262-7433 .. **Danziger**, Richd M '64 -720 5th Av -NY 10019
(914) 948-1556 .. **Danziger**, Robt B '88 (Danziger & M LLP) -123 Main -White Plns 10601
(212) 754-7000 .. **Danziger**, Susan V '91 Danziger D&M -405 Park Av -NY 10022 **Fx:**758-0143
(212) 754-7000 .. **Danziger**, Thos C '85 Danziger D&M -405 Park Av -NY 10022 **Fx:**758-0143
(212) 947-4520 .. **Danzis**, Herman '42 -350 5th Av -NY 10118
(212) 878-4099 .. **Danzis**, Saml M '81 Mitsui & Co -200 Park Av -NY 10166 **Fx:**878-4368
(212) 715-9100 .. **Danzo**, Jennifer Raiola '94 %Kramer LN&F,LLP -1177 Av of Amer -NY 10036
(212) 832-1977 .. **Dapello**, Jos J '89 (Schreck RDA&H) -1790 Bway -NY 10019 **Fx:**832-2969
(631) 654-9500 .. **Dapelo**, Robt W '87 (R Dapelo,PC) -110 N Ocean Av -Patchogue 11772 **Fx:**654-4613
(718) 855-5684 .. **D'Apice**, Rosario M '74 (Longo & D) -26 Court -Brklyn 11242
(212) 801-3116 .. **DaProcida**, Jos C '92 %Greenberg T,LLP -200 Park Av -NY 10166
(646) 253-5400 .. **D'Aquino**, Albert J '86 (Goldberg S LLP) -1200 Av of Amer -NY 10036
(716) 566-5400 .. **D'Aquino**, Albert J '86 (Goldberg S LLP) -665 Main -Buffalo 14203
(516) 379-5300 .. **Dara**, Jos M '92 -906 Atl Av -Baldwin 11510 **Fx:**379-5377
(631) 567-7757 .. **Darbee**, Donald H '73 -1213A Main -Oakdale 11769 **Fx:**567-7781
(914) 941-1140 .. **Darby**, Jos M '61 -1402 Eagle Bay Dr Bx248 -Ossining 10562 **Fx:**941-1943
(212) 231-8185 .. **Darby**, Lawr A III '76 -410 Park Av -NY 10022
(631) 777-2020 .. **Darby**, Nicole Ina '02 NI Darby,PC -1111 Route 110 -Farmngdl 11735 **Fx:**777-2030
(212) 925-5040 .. **Darby**, Regina L '77 R Darby -20 Vesey -NY 10007 **Fx:**732-4648
(718) 969-9200 .. **Darby**, Sonja C '04 %C Marshburn,PC -160-29 Union Tpk -Fresh Mdws 11366 **Fx:**969-0707
(212) 971-3175 .. **d'Arcambal**, Michelle J '87 (d'Arcambal L&O LLP) -40 Fulton -NY 10038 **Fx:**971-3176
(212) 558-5500 .. **Darche**, Benjamin A '01 %Weitz & L,PC -700 Bway -NY 10003
(718) 263-7900 .. **Darche**, Gary M '64 -125-10 Qns Blvd -Kew Gdns 11415 **Fx:**793-0782
(718) 286-6000 .. **Darche**, Jonathan A '06 %DA -125-01 Qns Blvd -Kew Gdns 11415
(516) 872-4100 .. **Darcy**, James M '81 -212 Wheeler Av -Vly Stream 11580
(585) 586-8060 .. **Darcy**, John J '51 (Sutton DC&D,PLLC) -359 N Wshngtn -Rchstr 14625
(516) 741-6355 .. **Darcy**, John J '95 %Nicolini PF&S -114 Old Cntry Rd Bx9006 -Mineola 11501
(914) 997-8100 .. **D'Arcy**, Kevin T '99 %Burke LM&G -10 Bank -White Plns 10606
(516) 869-7600 .. **Darcy**, Michele M '03 %Town Atty -220 Plandome Rd -Manhsst 11030 **Fx:**869-7605
(917) 421-4646 .. **Darcy**, Paul L '92 %IRS -33 Maiden Ln -NY 10038
(212) 888-8200 .. **Darcy**, Paul T '96 %Feder K LLP -845 3rd Av -NY 10022

(212) 435-3571 .. **Darcy,** Ryan B '09 Port Auth of NY/NJ -225 Park Av S -NY 10003 **Fx:**435-3555
(845) 343-5141 .. **Darcy,** Thos J '68 -20 Roberts Bx2200 -Middletwn 10940 **Fx:**343-4159
(585) 325-4300 .. **Dardaganis,** Athanasios '97 (Pelton DDD&B) -45 Exchange Blvd -Rchstr 14614 **Fx:**325-6075
(212) 840-3456 .. **Dardashtian,** Tamir '00 %Anchin Block & Anchin -1375 Bway -NY 10018
(212) 837-6000 .. **Darden,** Marisa T '09 %Hughes H&R LLP -1 Bttry Pk Plz -NY 10004
(718) 377-0600 .. **Dardis,** Linda M '99 -2911 Kings Hwy -Brklyn 11229 **Fx:**377-7420
(631) 755-0101 .. **Dargan,** Thos J '97 (Lewis JAA,LLP) -425 Broad Hollow Rd -Melvll 11747
(212) 953-5500 .. **Dargaty,** Doxia '06 %Alter M LLP -90 Park Av -NY 10016
(212) 452-5300 .. **Darger & Errante,LLP** -116 E 27th -NY 10016 **Fx:**452-5301
(212) 452-5300 .. **Darger,** Jennifer Wilcox '89 (Darger & E,LLP) -116 E 27th -NY 10016
(631) 367-3966 .. **Darienzo,** Anthony C '84 -5 Nichols Pl -South Huntington 11746
(212) 736-1940 .. **D'Arienzo,** Felix L Jr. '76 (Davidson D&K LLC) -485 7th Av -NY 10018
(718) 875-8580 .. **Darienzo,** John A Jr. '73 (Halpern B&D) -26 Court -Brklyn 11242
(516) 267-6300 .. **Darienzo,** Lauren J '02 %Bond S&K,PLLC -1399 Franklin Av -Gdn Cty 11530
(212) 728-8000 .. **Darienzo,** Marie B '85 %Willkie F&G LLP -787 7th Av -NY 10019
(212) 599-3303 .. **D'Aries,** Michl C '06 %Helfand & H -350 5th Av -NY 10118 **Fx:**599-3029
(212) 566-4060 .. **Dario,** Ronald A '98 (Dario YS&A) -44 Wall -NY 10005
(212) 566-4060 .. **Dario Yacker Suarez & Albert** -44 Wall -NY 10005 **Fx:**(201) 944-6775
(212) 509-3456 .. **Darish,** Robt W '06 %McGivney & K,PC -80 Broad -NY 10004
(212) 428-2130 .. **Darkeh,** Abena '94 OCA -25 Beaver -NY 10004 **Fx:**428-2192
(212) 218-2100 .. **Darkin,** Fiona E '08 %Fitzpatrick CH&S -1290 Av of Amer -NY 10104
(212) 385-1144 .. **Darko,** Eric Okyere '01 -299 Bway -NY 10007
(516) 741-6565 .. **Darling,** Donnalynn '79 (Meyer SE&K,PC) -990 Stewart Av Bx9194 -Gdn Cty 11530
(212) 648-0349 .. **Darling,** James G '07 JP Morgan Chase & Co -245 Park Av -NY 10167
(518) 464-2273 .. **Darling,** Jennifer R '06 AYCO -1 Wall Bx15073 -Albany 12212
(518) 271-8555 .. **Darling,** John E '72 -297 River Bx988 -Troy 12181 **Fx:**271-8563
(585) 388-5262 .. **Darling,** John F '78 (Ruffo TM&M PC) -145 Sullys Trl -Pittsfrd 14534
(716) 852-5200 .. **Darling,** Karen M '02 %Hamberger & W -700 Main Pl Twr -Buffalo 14202
(212) 903-9000 .. **Darling,** Sterling P Jr. '05 %Linklaters -1345 Av of Amer -NY 10105
(914) 761-3600 .. **Darlington,** Chas F '66 -34 S Bway -White Plns 10601 **Fx:**761-8736
(516) 538-2500 .. **Darlington,** Susan W '85 (Furey FLMW&D,PC) -600 Front -Hempstd 11550
(212) 692-0872 .. **Darmanian,** Denise G '83 Gallo & D -645 5th Av -NY 10022 **Fx:**692-0875
(914) 251-1618 .. **D'Arminio,** Louis L '98 (Price MS&D,PC) -106 Corp Park Dr -White Plns 10604
(212) 968-8300 .. **Darmody,** Thos G '97 %Mintzer SZL&M LLP -39 Bway -NY 10006
(914) 332-0700 .. **Darmofal,** Eric S '01 %M Pollack -150 Wht Plns Rd -Tarrytwn 10591 **Fx:**684-6069
(585) 377-1777 .. **Darnall,** Carl M '73 -53 Pioneer Dr -Fairprt 14450
(631) 444-1422 .. **Darnel,** David H '97 %SUNY Biomed Engineering -Univ Hsptl -Stony Brk 11794
(212) 318-9161 .. **Darnell,** Alana J '05 Scientific Games Corp -750 Lex Av -NY 10022
(516) 794-1100 .. **Darnell,** Glenn H '85 (Russo D&L) -1975 Hempstd Tpk -E Meadow 11554
(212) 455-2000 .. **Da Rocha Barros,** Maria F L '08 %Simpson T&B LLP -425 Lex Av -NY 10017
(212) 969-1431 .. **DaRosa,** Norma L '04 %Alliance Bernstein LP -1345 Av of Amer -NY 10105 **Fx:**554-4639
(212) 261-8000 .. **Darpino,** Erica L '09 %Mendes & M,LLP -750 7th Av -NY 10019
(718) 935-5115 .. **Darpino,** Jessica C '04 Dept of Ed -335 Adams -Brklyn 11201
(585) 262-3490 .. **D'Arpino,** John J '92 -10 Huntsman Way -Webster 14580 **Fx:**546-4749
(212) 825-0900 .. **D'Arpino,** Vincent A '93 Clinton Grp Inc -9 W 57th -NY 10019 **Fx:**825-0079
(516) 571-3056 .. **Darquea,** Michelle '94 -1 West -Mineola 11501 **Fx:**571-6604
(212) 964-6611 .. **Darr,** Jos T '03 %Lester SK&D -120 Bway -NY 10271
(212) 506-3900 .. **Darr,** Kristin M '07 %Steptoe & J LLP -750 7th Av -NY 10019
(631) 852-1650 .. **Darrell,** Cynthia Carew '99 %Leg Aid -300 Center Dr -Rvrhead 11901 **Fx:**852-1655
(212) 558-4000 .. **Darrell,** Norris Jr. '55 SrCnsl Sullivan & C LLP -125 Broad -NY 10004
(631) 324-8778 .. **Darrell,** Trevor M '04 (Fleming & D,PLLC) -10 Gingerbread Ln -E Hampton 11937
(845) 561-2594 .. **Darrigo,** Carl A '96 -67 S Plnk Rd -Newburgh 12550 **Fx:**561-9832
(718) 447-1962 .. **D'Arrigo,** Chas J '54 Cnsl Hall & H,LLP -57 Beach -Staten Isl 10304 **Fx:**447-2761
(212) 416-8759 .. **D'Arrigo,** Jos G '01 %Dept of Law -120 Bway -NY 10271
(518) 487-7600 .. **D'Arrigo,** Leonard J '06 %Whiteman O&H LLP -1 Commerce Plz -Albany 12260
(315) 451-2383 .. **D'Arrigo,** Mario '73 D'Arrigo -7515 Morgan Rd -Liverpool 13090 **Fx:**451-4106
(516) 741-6355 .. **D'Arrigo,** Richd A '72 %Nicolini PF&S -114 Old Cntry Rd Bx9006 -Mineola 11501
(212) 812-3100 .. **Darringer,** Bruce S '95 King St Capital Mgmt -65 E 55th -NY 10022
(212) 839-5300 .. **Darrow,** Duncan N '75 (Sidley A LLP) -787 7th Av -NY 10019
(212) 479-6724 .. **Darrow,** James '07 Macht SA&I LLP -1114 Av of Amer -NY 10036 **Fx:**202-6417
(516) 496-1919 .. **Darrow,** Jessica L '95 %Keller O&W,PC -242 Crsswys Park Dr W -Woodbury 11797
(212) 940-7113 .. **Darrow,** Jill E '79 (Katten MR LLP) -575 Mad Av -NY 10022
(516) 746-4373 .. **Darrow,** Kim L '79 %MHLS -170 Old Cntry Rd -Mineola 11501 **Fx:**746-0598
(212) 225-2000 .. **Darrow,** Peter H '68 SrCnsl Cleary GS&H -1 Lbrty Plz -NY 10006
(212) 335-4500 .. **Darrow,** Peter V '80 (DLA Piper LLP) -1251 Av of Amer -NY 10020
(212) 335-9000 .. **Darrow,** Wm W Jr. '82 %DA -1 Hogan Pl -NY 10013
(631) 761-7116 .. **Darrow-Kleinhaus,** Suzanne D '98 Touro Cllg Law Ctr -225 Eastvw Dr -Central Islip 11722
(516) 921-1948 .. **Darsa,** George J '64 -15 Deer Path Ln -Syosset 11791
(716) 878-4329 .. **Darstein,** Carol A '92 %Buffalo State Cllg -1300 Elmwood -Buffalo 14222
(914) 328-0674 .. **Darts,** Courtney A '09 %Pro Bono Prtnrshp,Inc -237 Mamaroneck Av -White Plns 10605 **Fx:**328-0538
(718) 875-1300 .. **Darvil,** Ben Jr. '04 Appllt Div 2nd Dept -45 Monroe Pl -Brklyn 11201 **Fx:**858-2446
(718) 780-7544 .. **Darvil,** Kathleen N '05 %Bklyn Law Schl -250 Joralemon -Brklyn 11201 **Fx:**780-0393
(516) 504-4200 .. **Darvish,** David '97 -11 Grace Av -Gt Neck 11021 **Fx:**466-3877
(845) 657-2000 .. **Darwak,** John J '71 -3140 State Route 28 Bx240 -Shokan 12481 **Fx:**657-2086
(585) 225-3446 .. **Darweesh,** Jos N '65 (Darweesh LK&V,LLP) -1081 Long Pond Rd -Rchstr 14626
(585) 225-3446 .. **Darweesh Lewis Kelly & Von Dohlen, LLP** -1081 Long Pond Rd -Rchstr 14626 **Fx:**723-0044
(212) 701-3000 .. **Darwin,** Abigail K '09 %Cahill G&R LLP -80 Pine -NY 10005 **Fx:**269-5420
(212) 940-3000 .. **Darwin,** Amanda D '04 (Nixon P LLP) -437 Mad Av -NY 10022
(845) 291-3150 .. **Darwin,** David L '84 %Cnty Atty -255 Main -Goshen 10924 **Fx:**291-3167
(315) 701-0926 .. **Darwish,** Diane E '02 -731 James -Syracuse 13203 **Fx:**410-0095
(914) 670-3788 .. **Daryanani,** April Fredlund '93 GlobeOp Fincl Srvcs -1 South Rd -Harrison 10528
(212) 431-5576 .. **Daryanani,** Protima '99 %Siskind SB -430 W 14th -NY 10014
(212) 998-6467 .. **Das,** Alina '07 NYU Law Schl -245 Sullivan -NY 10012 **Fx:**995-4031
(212) 878-8000 .. **Das,** Anitra '08 %Clifford C LLP -31 W 52nd -NY 10019
(212) 451-6027 .. **Das,** Bal Gopal '96 Kailix Investment Advisors -444 Mad Av -NY 10022
(212) 574-1200 .. **Das,** Kalyan '83 (Seward & K LLP) -1 Bttry Pk Plz -NY 10004
(212) 458-7465 .. **Das,** Devaleena '03 American International Companies -175 Water -NY 10038
(718) 250-2000 .. **Das,** Iris '09 %DA -350 Jay -Brklyn 11201 **Fx:**250-2314
(212) 813-8800 .. **Das,** Nithya B '07 %Goodwin P LLP -620 8th Av -NY 10018
(516) 545-5160 .. **Das,** Reshmi '02 SrCnsl Natl Grid -175 E Old Cntry Rd -Hicksvll 11801 **Fx:**545-5029
(212) 232-2500 .. **D'Ascoli,** Dominic '83 %Torgan & C,PC -17 State -NY 10004
(212) 412-9500 .. **Dase,** Wolfgang A '77 OfCnsl Flemming ZWZ LLP -1 Lbrty Plz -NY 10006
(212) 446-4800 .. **Dasgupta,** Parikshit '06 %Kirkland & E LLP -153 E 53rd -NY 10022
(212) 209-4800 .. **Dash,** Andrew S '83 (Brown R LLP) -7 Times Sq -NY 10036
(716) 854-3400 .. **Dash,** Johanna M '03 (Rupp BPC&C LLC) -1600 Lbrty Bldg -Buffalo 14202
(212) 924-3300 .. **Dash,** Martin '50 %American Artists Grp -Bx544 -NY 10113 **Fx:**924-3300
(516) 466-6050 .. **Dash,** Richd '50 -1010 Nrthrn Blvd -Gt Neck 11021
(516) 931-5668 .. **Dash,** Robt E '94 -6800 Jericho Tpk -Syosset 11791 **Fx:**931-5647
(212) 836-8000 .. **Dashefsky,** Lowell I '98 Cnsl Kaye S LLP -425 Park Av -NY 10022
(631) 361-7981 .. **Dashefsky,** Paul L '80 -317 Middle Cntry Rd -Smithtwn 11787
(212) 393-1424 .. **Dashevsky,** Felix A '03 Five Rings LLC -120 Bway -NY 10271
(914) 271-9499 .. **Dashman,** Danl D '94 -6 Dailey Dr -Croton-On-Hud 10520
(212) 495-0100 .. **Dashow,** Robt A '92 (Gottesman WMF&W,PC) -11 Hanover Sq -NY 10005
(718) 522-3550 .. **Dashow,** Sharon Weintraub '82 -50 Court -Brklyn 11201 **Fx:**852-6086
(212) 238-3000 .. **DaSilva,** Andrew L '94 OfCnsl Emmet M&M,LLP -120 Bway -NY 10271
(914) 941-4344 .. **DaSilva,** Cristina G '05 -95 Main -Ossining 10562 **Fx:**941-2648
(516) 487-3883 .. **DaSilva,** Gary N '79 -7 Kenneth Ct -Kings Pnt 11024 **Fx:**487-3955
(516) 222-0700 .. **DaSilva Hilowitz & McEvily LLP** -585 Stewart Av -Gdn Cty 11530 **Fx:**222-0743
(845) 638-1550 .. **DaSilva Hilowitz & McEvily LLP** -120 N Main -New Cty 10956 **Fx:**638-6951
(718) 579-7900 .. **DaSilva,** Leah '09 %Leg Aid -900 Sheridan Av -Bronx 10451 **Fx:**293-8744
(845) 291-2650 .. **DaSilva,** Linda Pierson '02 %Cnty Atty -285 Main -Goshen 10924 **Fx:**291-3014
(212) 918-3000 .. **DaSilva,** Russell J '80 (Hogan L LLP) -875 3rd Av -NY 10022
(845) 638-1550 .. **DaSilva,** Willard H '49 (DaSilva H&M LLP) -120 N Main -New Cty 10956
(516) 222-0700 .. **DaSilva,** Willard H '49 (DaSilva H&M LLP) -585 Stewart Av -Gdn Cty 11530
(212) 302-2400 .. **Daskal,** Bernard '97 (Lynch DE LLP) -264 W 40th -NY 10018
(212) 261-8000 .. **Daskalakis,** Olympia '91 SrCnsl Mendes & M,LLP -750 7th Av -NY 10019
(212) 572-6325 .. **Daskalakis,** Paris '02 (Daskalakis Law Firm,LLC) -300 Park Av -NY 10022 **Fx:**656-1472
(718) 672-2131 .. **Dass,** Anil '95 -42-27 Gleane -Elmhrst 11373
(631) 224-6621 .. **Dassau,** Ryan W '04 T-Mobile USA,Inc -3500 Sunrise Hwy -Great Rvr 11739
(716) 858-2424 .. **Dassero,** Brian P '07 %DA -25 Delaware Av -Buffalo 14202 **Fx:**858-7425
(212) 225-2000 .. **Dassin,** Lev '91 (Cleary GS&H) -1 Lbrty Plz -NY 10006
(212) 668-1900 .. **Dassori,** Melissa Schatzberg '04 %Brune & R LLP -80 Broad -NY 10004
(212) 627-9898 .. **Dasti,** Jerry L '03 %Sloss Law Ofc,PC -555 W 25th -NY 10001 **Fx:**627-9498
(212) 776-5000 .. **Datlof,** Susan M '79 %NYC Housing Auth -250 Bway -NY 10007 **Fx:**776-5039
(212) 571-0111 .. **Datny,** David B '09 Hardin KM&P,PA -110 William -NY 10038
(516) 488-8811 .. **Dato,** Margaret Lo Giudice '93 %STG Assoc -1010 Nrthrn Blvd -Gt Neck 11021 **Fx:**488-8611
(212) 307-5500 .. **Datoo,** Shaffin A '01 %Venable LLP -1270 Av of Amer -NY 10020
(212) 358-9690 .. **Datta,** Neal R '93 -237 1st Av -NY 10003 **Fx:**358-1916
(516) 742-1212 .. **Datta,** Pranali M '01 %Stein W&R -1 Old Cntry Rd -Carle Pl 11514
(212) 455-2000 .. **Dattner,** Ian R '06 %Simpson T&B LLP -425 Lex Av -NY 10017
(212) 513-3200 .. **Dattola,** Rita C '77 SrCnsl Holland & K LLP -31 W 52nd -NY 10019
(212) 735-3000 .. **Dau,** Nathan M '07 %Skadden ASM&F LLP -4 Times Sq -NY 10036

(516) 542-5900 .. **Daub**, Joshua A '01 %Congdon FORDT&F -333 Earle Ovngton Blvd -Uniondale 11553
(516) 832-7613 .. **Daub**, Tara E '00 %Nixon P LLP -50 Jericho Quadrangle -Jericho 11753
(212) 310-4040 .. **Dauber**, Susan G '86 Instinet Group LLC -3 Times Sq -NY 10036
(212) 986-9700 .. **Dauber**, Wm R '90 Cnsl Eilenberg & K LLP -11 E 44th -NY 10017
(716) 856-4000 .. **Daubert**, Michelle A '08 %Hodgson R LLP -140 Pearl -Buffalo 14202
(607) 733-8866 .. **Daubner**, Susan M '95 %Ziff Law Firm,LLP -303 William -Elmira 14901 **Fx**:732-6062
(212) 408-5100 .. **Daucher**, Eric C '10 %Chadbourne & P LLP -30 Rckfllr Plz -NY 10112
(212) 446-8697 .. **Dauchez**, Christine '94 McKinsey & Co -55 E 52nd -NY 10055
(845) 454-9700 .. **Dauerer**, Louis M '93 %Ouimette G&A -88 Market Bx192 -Poughkeepsie 12601
(212) 619-4444 .. **Dauerty**, Guy P '91 %Marshall CW&B,PC -116 John -NY 10038
(212) 578-5883 .. **Daugherty**, Danielle Cooper '97 MetLife -1095 Av of Amer -NY 10036 **Fx**:743-0611
(212) 750-8700 .. **Daugherty**, Jonathan D '05 %Friedman & W,PC -600 Lex Av -NY 10022
(313) 234-7103 .. **Daugherty**, Patrick D '82 (Foley & L LLP) -90 Park Av -NY 10016
(212) 659-7300 .. **Daughney**, Brian C '87 (Haynes & B,LLP) -1221 Av of Amer -NY 10020
(212) 637-1579 .. **Daughtry**, Emily E '04 %US Atty -86 Chmbrs -NY 10007
(914) 766-4458 .. **Daughtry**, Lloyd '92 IBM -294 Route 100 -Somers 10589
(212) 813-5900 .. **Daum**, Casey M L '07 %Fross ZL&Z,PC -866 UN Plz -NY 10017
(716) 842-4608 .. **Daum**, Evis '04 M&T Bk -1 M & T Plz -Buffalo 14203 **Fx**:842-5376
(212) 992-8837 .. **Daum**, Jeremy L '09 NYU -110 W 3rd -NY 10012
(718) 403-3600 .. **Dauman**, Robt S '86 %Dept of Finance -345 Adams -Brklyn 11201 **Fx**:403-3650
(716) 845-9352 .. **Daumen**, Michl P '75 %Supreme Ct -50 Delaware Av -Buffalo 14202
(212) 294-6700 .. **D'Auria**, Anthony J '61 (Winston & S) -200 Park Av -NY 10166
(212) 541-2000 .. **D'Auria**, Emily R '02 %Bryan C LLP -1290 Av of Amer -NY 10104
(212) 521-5400 .. **D'Auria**, Kelly B '04 %Reed S LLP -599 Lex Av -NY 10022
(585) 467-9360 .. **D'Aurizio**, Franklin '61 -1780 E Ridge Rd -Rchstr 14622 **Fx**:467-0156
(585) 342-9555 .. **D'Aurizio**, John F '89 (J D'Aurizio,PLLC) -1780 E Ridge Rd -Rchstr 14622 **Fx**:342-9557
(212) 676-1003 .. **Daus**, Matthew W '92 Taxi & Limo Comm -40 Rector -NY 10006 **Fx**:676-1100
(518) 455-7700 .. **Dautel**, Susan S '82 %Ct of Appls -20 Eagle -Albany 12207
(518) 473-4596 .. **Dautner**, Richd J '76 %Gov Ofc Emply Rel -Agncy Bldg 2 ESP -Albany 12223
(212) 476-9000 .. **Davalla**, Andrew J '04 %Neuberger Berman,LLC -605 3rd Av -NY 10158 **Fx**:476-9862
(212) 766-1888 .. **Davanzo**, Jeannine M '00 %Morris DA&F -2 Rector -NY 10006
(212) 490-3000 .. **D'Avanzo**, Jos A '83 (Wilson EME&D LLP) -150 E 42nd -NY 10017
(914) 323-7000 .. **D'Avanzo**, Jos A '83 (Wilson EME&D LLP) -3 Gannett Dr -White Plns 10604
(646) 471-3000 .. **D'Avanzo**, Peter A '97 PricewaterhouseCoopers LLP -300 Mad Av -NY 10017
(212) 455-2000 .. **Dave**, Brijesh Pradyuman '02 %Simpson T&B LLP -425 Lex Av -NY 10017
(212) 963-5219 .. **Dave**, Nomita '01 %UN-Dept Economics & Social Affrs -1 UN Plz -NY 10017
(917) 777-4200 .. **Dave**, Priti K '04 %Bingham M LLP -1 Bttry Pk Plz -NY 10004
(212) 859-7285 .. **Dave**, Raj B '00 Fortis Inc -1 Chase Manh Plz -NY 10005
(212) 867-5800 .. **Davé**, Sachin '00 %Osler H&H LLP -620 8th Av -NY 10018
(212) 474-1000 .. **D'Avella**, Joanna H '08 %Cravath S&M LLP -825 8th Av -NY 10019
(212) 697-2062 .. **Davenport**, Carolyn W '81 -11 E 44th -NY 10017
(845) 334-9526 .. **Davenport**, Claudia S '86 -110 Maiden Ln -Kingston 12401 **Fx**:339-2656
(518) 761-6405 .. **Davenport**, Emilee B '06 %DA -Cnty Mncpl Ctr -Lk George 12845
(914) 749-8200 .. **Davenport**, Jonathan W '00 %Boies S&F LLP -333 Main -Armonk 10504
(212) 906-1200 .. **Davenport**, Kirk A II '85 (Latham & W) -885 3rd Av -NY 10022
(212) 909-6000 .. **Davenport**, Margaret Andrews '88 (Debevoise & P LLP) -919 3rd Av -NY 10022
(212) 761-4000 .. **Davenport**, Megan A '03 Morgan Stanley -1221 Av of Amer -NY 10020
(518) 433-2521 .. **Davenport**, Nancy Stover '92 JP Morgan Chase -12 Corp Wds Blvd -Albany 12211
(518) 438-2000 .. **Davenport**, Paul E '91 (Lombardi WWHA&D PC) -III Winners Cir -Albany 12205
(212) 506-5000 .. **D'Aversa**, Raniero Jr. '91 (Orrick H&S LLP) -51 W 52nd -NY 10019
(212) 209-3056 .. **Davey**, Brendan M '94 (Reitler K&R LLC) -885 3rd Av -NY 10022
(516) 248-1200 .. **Davey**, Brian R '87 (Mulholland M&R) -374 Hillside Av -Williston Pk 11596
(212) 770-1768 .. **Davey**, Christopher G '91 %AIG -80 Pine -NY 10005 **Fx**:344-2286
(914) 961-6008 .. **Davey**, Sean J '93 -34 Oak Av -Tuckahoe 10707 **Fx**:961-9220
(607) 277-3198 .. **Davey**, Stephen C '03 Citizens Concrnd for Children-Law Guardian Ofc -121 E Buffalo -Ithaca 14850
(212) 547-5400 .. **Davi**, Chas '10 %McDermott W&E LLP -340 Mad Av -NY 10173
(212) 237-0000 .. **Davi**, Michl S '01 %Vinson & E LLP -666 5th Av -NY 10103
(516) 227-0700 .. **Davi**, Steven N '97 Cnsl Farrell F,PC -1320 RXR Plz -Uniondale 11556
(631) 271-6363 .. **Davicino**, L Michl '87 Cannon & A,LLP -1923 NY Av -Huntngtn Sta 11746 **Fx**:271-7128
(212) 348-7449 .. **Da Victoria Lobo**, Elizabeth M '08 Legal Srvcs -1 W 125th -NY 10027 **Fx**:348-4093
(516) 741-6266 .. **David**, Abraham '07 %McCabe CM&F,LLP -346 Westbury Av Bx9000 -Carle Pl 11514
(212) 587-1100 .. **David**, Allen A '75 -40 Exch Pl -NY 10005 **Fx**:785-1188
(212) 416-8000 .. **David**, Alphonso B '02 %Dept of Law -120 Bway -NY 10271
(212) 788-0602 .. **David**, Anshel '82 %Law Dept -100 Church -NY 10007 **Fx**:788-0367
(212) 369-2530 .. **David**, Bruce H '93 -Bx6095 -NY 10128 **Fx**:732-7091
(718) 493-2293 .. **David**, Chas Peter '93 -822 Clarkson Av -Brklyn 11203
(212) 791-7608 .. **David**, Cheryl R '96 -299 Bway -NY 10007 **Fx**:791-7606
(212) 880-3800 .. **David**, Donald N '73 (Akerman S) -335 Mad Av -NY 10017
(212) 661-3080 .. **David**, Edw '86 (E David & Assoc,LLC) -369 Lex Av -NY 10017 **Fx**:(973) 994-4949
(212) 446-4800 .. **David**, Geoffrey A '07 %Kirkland & E LLP -153 E 53rd -NY 10022
(212) 859-8000 .. **David**, Israel '97 (Fried FHS&J LLP) -1 NY Plz -NY 10004
(212) 362-5869 .. **David**, Jack '67 -210 W 90th -NY 10024
(718) 645-3111 .. **David**, Jacques L '06 Leg Aid Society Ofc for the Aging -111 Lvngstn -Brklyn 11201 **Fx**:260-4722
(212) 732-8700 .. **David**, Jill S '08 %McAloon & F,PC -123 William -NY 10038
(646) 610-5400 .. **David**, Jonathan '88 %NYPD -1 Police Plz -NY 10038
(718) 875-2000 .. **David**, Joyce B '78 -16 Court -Brklyn 11241 **Fx**:852-8716
(212) 506-1700 .. **David**, Kenneth R '00 (Kasowitz BT&F LLP) -1633 Bway -NY 10019
(718) 756-0604 .. **David**, LaFleur A '95 (L David & Assoc) -4906 Church Av -Brklyn 11203
(631) 843-5905 .. **David**, Leonard A '82 Henry Schein,Inc -135 Duryea Rd -Melvll 11747 **Fx**:843-5658
(212) 369-2530 .. **David**, Marvin M '56 Bryer & D -225 Bway -NY 10007 **Fx**:732-7091
(718) 360-9953 .. **David**, Maryellen '98 %RJ Adams Jr,LLC -300 Grdn City Plz -Gdn Cty 11530 **Fx**:360-9953
(212) 363-1997 .. **David**, Michl N '85 -82 Wall -NY 10005 **Fx**:742-9869
(914) 225-5559 .. **David**, Michele C '00 Morgan Stanley -2000 Wstchstr Av -Purchase 10577
(212) 867-4466 .. **David**, Nicholas M '10 %Belkin BW&G,LLP -270 Mad Av -NY 10016
(212) 260-4956 .. **David**, Reuben '69 -30 5th Av -NY 10011
(212) 425-9300 .. **David**, Risa M '07 %Bressler A&R,PC -17 State -NY 10004
(212) 448-9933 .. **David**, Sara R '06 %Finder & C LLP -9 E 38th -NY 10016
(212) 756-2000 .. **David**, Simcha B '09 %Schulte R&Z LLP -919 3rd Av -NY 10022
(212) 210-9491 .. **David**, Todd R '09 (Alston & B LLP) -90 Park Av -NY 10016
(212) 940-8800 .. **Davida**, Bernadette H '88 (Katten MR LLP) -575 Mad Av -NY 10022
(516) 623-5723 .. **David-Gaines**, Wendy '79 %DataPhase -101 Gregory Av -Merrick 11566
(718) 990-6617 .. **Davidian**, John E '76 %St John's Law Schl -8000 Utopia Pkwy -Jamaica 11439 **Fx**:591-1855
(212) 632-1897 .. **Davidian**, Michl E '03 %Lazard Freres -30 Rckfllr Plz -NY 10112 **Fx**:632-6060
(516) 773-7758 .. **Davidoff**, Howard '83 -10 Grace Av -Gt Neck 11021
(212) 265-4900 .. **Davidoff**, Jacob '09 (Turk & D PLLC) -250 W 57th -NY 10019 **Fx**:964-6600
(212) 587-5971 .. **Davidoff**, Jonathan M '99 (Davidoff Law Firm,PLLC) -60 E 42nd -NY 10165 **Fx**:658-9852
(212) 557-7200 .. **Davidoff Malito & Hutcher,LLP** -605 3rd Av -NY 10158 **Fx**:286-1884
(516) 248-6400 .. **Davidoff Malito & Hutcher,LLP** -200 Grdn City Plz -Gdn Cty 11530 **Fx**:248-6422
(845) 794-5000 .. **Davidoff**, Michl '69 (Drew D&E,LLP) -13 Lbrty Drwr1040 -Monticello 12701
(212) 453-5900 .. **Davidoff**, Philip K '92 (Ford & H LLP) -100 Park Av -NY 10017
(212) 682-8383 .. **Davidoff**, Richd S '60 (Kantor DWMT&G,PC) -51 E 42nd -NY 10017
(212) 806-5400 .. **Davidoff**, Sarah R '97 (Stroock &S&L LLP) -180 Maiden Ln -NY 10038
(518) 453-8383 .. **Davidoff**, Scott S '86 -3 Atrium Dr -Albany 12205 **Fx**:453-8385
(212) 557-7200 .. **Davidoff**, Sid '64 (Davidoff M&H,LLP) -605 3rd Av -NY 10158
(718) 793-7000 .. **Davidov**, Ilana F '00 (Davidov & D,PC) -108-18 Qns Blvd -Frst Hlls 11375 **Fx**:793-7222
(718) 793-7000 .. **Davidov**, Michl '06 (Davidov & D,PC) -108-18 Qns Blvd -Frst Hlls 11375 **Fx**:793-7222
(212) 508-6700 .. **Davidovich**, Ricardo W '94 (Tannenbaum HS&H LLP) -900 3rd Av -NY 10022
(212) 966-5020 .. **Davidovitch**, Diane E '06 %Seligson R&R -29 W 30th -NY 10001
(212) 474-1000 .. **Davidovitch**, Jessica L '05 %Cravath S&M LLP -825 8th Av -NY 10019
(516) 785-4040 .. **Davidow**, Binnie A '83 -254 Pettit Av -Bellmore 11710 **Fx**:785-4531
(631) 234-3030 .. **Davidow Davidow Siegel & Stern, LLP** -1601 Vets Mem'l Hwy -Islandia 11749 **Fx**:234-3140
(516) 393-0222 .. **Davidow Davidow Siegel & Stern, LLP** -666 Old Cntry Rd -Gdn Cty 11530 **Fx**:228-6672
(631) 420-4040 .. **Davidow Davidow Siegel & Stern, LLP** -13235 Main Rd Bx344 -Mattituck 11952 **Fx**:761-0370
(347) 744-9340 .. **Davidow**, Jerome Lee '90 -140 Riverside Dr -NY 10024 **Fx**:(636) 216-8944
(212) 788-0524 .. **Davidow**, Judith A '86 %Law Dept -100 Church -NY 10007 **Fx**:788-0367
(631) 234-3030 .. **Davidow**, Lawr E '87 (Davidow DS&S,LLP) -1601 Vets Mem'l Hwy -Islandia 11749
(917) 421-4659 .. **Davidow**, Lawr L '85 %IRS -33 Maiden Ln -NY 10038
(212) 378-2051 .. **Davidowitz**, Craig L '91 -989 Av of Amer -NY 10018 **Fx**:378-2054
(212) 940-8800 .. **Davidowitz**, Ronni G '79 (Katten MR LLP) -575 Mad Av -NY 10022
(212) 456-4552 .. **David-Sinatra**, Tonia H '90 %ABC -47 W 66th -NY 10023
(212) 412-8754 .. **Davidson**, Anthony H '88 %MBS Clearing Corp -55 Water -NY 10041 **Fx**:412-8783
(718) 680-5778 .. **Davidson**, Bernadette M '01 %Caruso C&B, PC -7302 13th Av -Brklyn 11228
(212) 428-2130 .. **Davidson**, Charlotte E '99 OCA -25 Beaver -NY 10004
(212) 736-1940 .. **Davidson**, Clifford M '87 (Davidson D&K LLC) -485 7th Av -NY 10018
(516) 763-6700 .. **Davidson & Cohen,PC** -265 Sunrise Hwy -Rockvll Ctr 11570 **Fx**:763-0567
(516) 671-8187 .. **Davidson**, Dana T '90 (Davidson & Assoc,PC) -15 Glen -Glen Cove 11542 **Fx**:671-2954
(212) 861-8078 .. **Davidson**, Daphne L '89 -171 E 84th -NY 10028
(212) 736-1940 .. **Davidson Davidson & Kappel LLC** -485 7th Av -NY 10018 **Fx**:736-2427
(212) 557-7700 .. **Davidson Dawson & Clark LLP** -60 E 42nd -NY 10165 **Fx**:286-8513
(212) 309-6000 .. **Davidson**, Douglas E '72 (Morgan L&B LLP) -101 Park Av -NY 10178
(914) 698-8255 .. **Davidson**, Edw A '83 -100 Mamaroneck Av Bx546 -Mamaroneck 10543
(212) 577-3339 .. **Davidson**, Ellen B '00 Leg Aid -199 Water -NY 10038
(585) 546-6448 .. **Davidson Fink LLP** -28 E Main -Rchstr 14614 **Fx**:546-8125
(212) 837-6000 .. **Davidson**, George A '67 (Hughes H&R LLP) -1 Bttry Pk Plz -NY 10004

(845) 365-9100 .. **Davidson & Grannum** -30 Ramland Rd -Orangebrg 10962 **Fx**:365-9190
(212) 547-5400 .. **Davidson,** Harold C '08 %McDermott W&E LLP -340 Mad Av -NY 10173
(315) 479-1769 .. **Davidson,** J Alexander '77 (Davidson & Y) -333 E Onondaga -Syracuse 13202 **Fx**:474-4575
(212) 878-8000 .. **Davidson,** James V '10 %Clifford C LLP -31 W 52nd -NY 10019
(212) 867-6000 .. **Davidson,** Jason R '97 (Rosenberg & E,PC) -733 3rd Av -NY 10017
(212) 735-3000 .. **Davidson,** Jeffrey J '10 %Skadden ASM&F LLP -4 Times Sq -NY 10036
(212) 883-4900 .. **Davidson,** Jill P '03 (Cozen O) -277 Park Av -NY 10172
(845) 365-9100 .. **Davidson,** Joel E '76 (Davidson & G) -30 Ramland Rd -Orangebrg 10962
(845) 268-2430 .. **Davidson,** John J '85 -14 Chauncey -Congers 10920
(212) 625-1835 .. **Davidson,** Karie Parker '96 -520 Bway -NY 10012
(315) 734-2000 .. **Davidson,** Kathrine K '90 %Utica Natl Ins -180 Genesee Bx530 -Utica 13502 **Fx**:734-2662
(516) 763-6700 .. **Davidson,** Keith S '82 (Davidson & C,PC) -265 Sunrise Hwy -Rockvll Ctr 11570
(212) 440-4400 .. **Davidson,** Kristi A '05 Cnsl Buchanan I&R PC -620 8th Av -NY 10018
(212) 736-1940 .. **Davidson,** Leslye B '91 (Davidson D&K LLC) -485 7th Av -NY 10018
(212) 848-4000 .. **Davidson,** Margaret J '05 %Shearman & S LLP -599 Lex Av -NY 10022
(212) 756-2000 .. **Davidson,** Marisa J '08 %Schulte R&Z LLP -919 3rd Av -NY 10022
(212) 969-3000 .. **Davidson,** Mark E '78 SrCnsl Proskauer R LLP -1585 Bway -NY 10036
(212) 770-7000 .. **Davidson,** Michelle R '96 AIG -175 Water -NY 10038
(212) 308-4810 .. **Davidson,** Miriam '90 (M Davidson,PC) -156 W 56th -NY 10019 **Fx**:308-4810
(212) 888-5700 .. **Davidson,** Mitchell A '96 Post Capital Ptnrs LLC -805 3rd Av -NY 10022
(212) 756-2000 .. **Davidson,** Nicole Z '10 %Schulte R&Z LLP -919 3rd Av -NY 10022
(607) 733-4635 .. **Davidson & O'Mara,PC** -243 Lk -Elmira 14901 **Fx**:732-1033
(315) 426-2145 .. **Davidson,** Richd E '88 NYS OCFS -333 E Wshngtn -Syracuse 13202
(212) 751-2700 .. **Davidson,** Robt B '73 JAMS -620 8th Av -NY 10018 **Fx**:751-4099
(585) 546-6448 .. **Davidson,** S Gerald '55 (Davidson F LLP) -28 E Main -Rchstr 14614
(212) 556-2100 .. **Davidson,** Scott I '96 Cnsl King & S -1185 Av of Amer -NY 10036
(212) 576-5353 .. **Davidson,** Sheila Kearney '87 %NY Life Ins -51 Mad Av -NY 10010 **Fx**:447-0569
(212) 335-4500 .. **Davidson,** Stephen P '97 (DLA Piper LLP) -1251 Av of Amer -NY 10020
(800) 397-1529 .. **Davidson,** Steven C '90 -2 Gannet Dr -White Plns 10604 **Fx**:(914) 644-6111
(212) 788-0761 .. **Davidson,** Susan R '00 %Law Dept -100 Church -NY 10007 **Fx**:788-0367
(212) 473-0255 .. **Davidson,** Tiffany S '06 %Seedco -915 Bway -NY 10010
(631) 393-9400 .. **Davidson,** Tina B '95 %Forster & G -500 Bi-Cnty Blvd Bx9030 -Farmngdl 11735
(518) 761-6207 .. **Davidson,** Wm F IV '00 Pub Def -1340 State Route 9 -Lk George 12845 **Fx**:761-6208
(212) 267-6364 .. **Davidson,** Zoe L '05 %Kossoff & U -217 Bway -NY 10007
(716) 855-0203 .. **Davidzik,** Brad J '06 %Western NY Law Ctr -237 Main -Buffalo 14203 **Fx**:270-4005
(718) 928-3700 .. **Davie,** Ian M S '08 %LSNYC-Bronx -579 Courtlandt Av -Bronx 10451 **Fx**:402-7586
(718) 923-8400 .. **Davie,** John W '92 Forest City Ratner -1 Metrotech Ctr N -Brklyn 11201 **Fx**:923-8722
(631) 853-4549 .. **Davie,** Linda J '85 %District Ct Law Dept -400 Carleton Av Bx9075 -Central Islip 11722
(315) 474-7571 .. **Davie,** Stephen S '90 (Mackenzie H LLP) -101 S Salina Bx4967 -Syracuse 13221
(212) 610-6300 .. **Davies,** Andrew Rhys '02 (Allen & O) -1221 Av of Amer -NY 10020
(716) 853-9555 .. **Davies,** Barbara J '76 %Leg Aid -237 Main -Buffalo 14203 **Fx**:853-3219
(315) 472-6511 .. **Davies,** Fredk P '86 Davies Law Firm,PC -210 E Fayette -Syracuse 13202 **Fx**:475-9539
(212) 238-4800 .. **Davies,** James E '95 (Landman CB&F,PC) -120 Bway -NY 10271
(518) 798-9556 .. **Davies,** James R '70 -27 Pearl Bx2002 -Glens Fls 12801 **Fx**:798-4031
(315) 671-2027 .. **Davies,** Kathryn Z '78 %Family Ct -401 Mntgmry -Syracuse 13202 **Fx**:671-1173
(518) 457-2070 .. **Davies,** Kileen C '02 %Dept of Tax & Fin -Bldg 9 State Campus -Albany 12227 **Fx**:457-6131
(212) 442-1400 .. **Davies,** Mark L '76 Conflicts of Int Bd -2 Lafayette -NY 10007 **Fx**:442-1407
(212) 407-7700 .. **Davies,** Michl G '84 (Vedder P,PC) -1633 Bway -NY 10019
(212) 282-5186 .. **Davies,** Richd P '98 %Avon Products -1345 Av of Amer -NY 10105
(518) 402-9405 .. **Davies,** Robt K '91 %DEC -625 Bway -Albany 12233 **Fx**:402-9028
(631) 941-4444 .. **Davies,** Ronald C '64 -220 Lk Av -St James 11780 **Fx**:941-3822
(212) 239-4340 .. **Davies,** Susan M '91 Cnsl Shalov SB&R LLP -485 7th Av -NY 10018
(631) 209-1111 .. **Davies,** Timothy R '91 (Davies at Law) -565 Route 25A -Miller Pl 11764 **Fx**:209-1112
(631) 209-1111 .. **Davies,** Victoria L '90 (Davies at Law) -565 Route 25A -Miller Pl 11764 **Fx**:209-1112
(212) 588-5500 .. **Davies Ward Phillips & Vineberg LLP** -625 Mad Av -NY 10022 **Fx**:308-0132
(212) 909-6000 .. **Davies Knechtel,** Kerith '08 %Debevoise & P LLP -919 3rd Av -NY 10022
(518) 465-3484 .. **Davignon,** Luke C '08 %Carter CCBM&L,PC -20 Corp Wds Blvd -Albany 12211
(646) 315-7605 .. **Davila,** Ana L '88 STEPS to End Family Violence -Bx287326 -NY 10128 **Fx**:315-7697
(718) 237-2000 .. **Davila,** Edgar '97 %Leg Aid -111 Lvngstn -Brklyn 11201 **Fx**:237-8737
(212) 909-6000 .. **Davila,** Erica M '09 %Debevoise & P LLP -919 3rd Av -NY 10022
(718) 618-2500 .. **Davila,** Michele '05 %Civil Ct -851 Grnd Cncrs -Bronx 10451 **Fx**:590-7294
(212) 640-1103 .. **Davila,** Michelle B '93 Amer Exp Bk -200 Vesey -NY 10285
(212) 609-1500 .. **Davin,** Denise Moira '79 %VNSNY -107 E 70th -NY 10021 **Fx**:794-6357
(212) 278-1382 .. **D'Avino,** Carey R '85 -1251 Av of Amer -NY 10020 **Fx**:278-1733
(212) 980-9600 .. **Davino,** Margaret Jakacki '85 (Kaufman B&R) -120 Bway -NY 10271
(212) 355-4149 .. **Davis,** Aimee L '08 %Goldweber E LLP -635 Mad Av -NY 10022
(631) 598-0500 .. **Davis,** Alan M '97 -121B W Oak -Amityvll 11701 **Fx**:598-0506
(516) 933-4080 .. **Davis,** Altagracia M '90 (Davis & V) -176 Woodbury Rd -Hicksvll 11801
(212) 484-8000 .. **Davis,** Amanda L '04 %Time Warner -1 Time Warner Ctr -NY 10019
(212) 506-5000 .. **Davis,** Amie B '06 %Orrick H&S LLP -51 W 52nd -NY 10019
(212) 351-4000 .. **Davis,** Amy E '07 Gibson D&C LLP -200 Park Av -NY 10166
(212) 788-2721 .. **Davis,** Andrea Shapiro '86 Ofc of the Mayor -253 Bway -NY 10007 **Fx**:788-7812
(212) 416-6597 .. **Davis,** Andrew P '58 %Dept of Law -120 Bway -NY 10271
(212) 935-1100 .. **Davis,** Anthony E '75 (Hinshaw & C LLP) -780 3rd Av -NY 10017
(212) 972-0786 .. **Davis,** Anthony J '93 (Nicoll D&S LLP) -250 Park Av -NY 10177 **Fx**:953-7201
(212) 471-8500 .. **Davis,** Ari S '08 %Herzfeld & R,PC -125 Broad -NY 10004
(212) 344-3399 .. **Davis,** Arnold '51 -40 Exch Pl -NY 10005 **Fx**:482-1303
(212) 661-5270 .. **Davis,** Bonni G '86 Finlay Fine Jwlry -529 5th Av -NY 10017 **Fx**:808-0349
(516) 797-4076 .. **Davis,** Bradley B '61 -3 Delta Rd -Massapequa 11758
(212) 247-0848 .. **Davis,** Brent M '07 %Bienstock & M,PC -250 W 57th -NY 10107
(516) 542-0249 .. **Davis,** Brian J '84 B Davis,PC -400 Grdn City Plz -Gdn Cty 11530 **Fx**:542-0259
(212) 421-1011 .. **Davis,** Brian T '78 %Major Lindsey & Africa -551 5th Av -NY 10176 **Fx**:421-1042
(212) 416-6493 .. **Davis,** Brooke P '02 %Dept of Law -120 Bway -NY 10271
(718) 590-2000 .. **Davis,** Catherine '88 %DA -198 E 161st -Bronx 10451 **Fx**:590-6477
(845) 634-6633 .. **Davis,** Chas G '69 (Davis and D) -20 Squadron Blvd -New Cty 10956 **Fx**:634-7688
(212) 545-1900 .. **Davis,** Cheryl L '87 (Menaker & H LLP) -10 E 40th -NY 10016
(212) 903-9000 .. **Davis,** Christopher B '09 %Linklaters -1345 Av of Amer -NY 10105
(212) 609-6800 .. **Davis,** Christopher L '74 SpclCnsl McCarter & E,LLP -245 Park Av -NY 10167
(212) 986-6000 .. **Davis,** Christopher P '91 (Kleinberg KW&C,PC) -551 5th Av -NY 10176
(212) 257-6800 .. **Davis,** Christopher Q '02 %Thompson W&G LLP -85 5th Av -NY 10003
(914) 761-1003 .. **Davis,** Clifford L '86 -200 Mamaroneck Av -White Plns 10601 **Fx**:428-5052
(646) 840-5600 .. **Davis,** Clive Jay '57 J Records -745 5th Av -NY 10151
(845) 735-2067 .. **Davis,** Danl J '69 -42 E Nauraushaun Av -Pearl Rvr 10965 **Fx**:735-2067
(631) 543-2900 .. **Davis,** David A '94 (Davis & H,LLP) -1345 Motor Pkwy -Islandia 11749
(716) 852-5200 .. **Davis,** David F '84 (Hamberger & W) -700 Main Pl Twr -Buffalo 14202
(718) 802-1616 .. **Davis,** David M '84 -26 Court -Brklyn 11242
(518) 822-1890 .. **Davis,** Deborah Lynn '74 Deborah Davis Fine Art -Bx332 -Hudson 12534
(212) 489-8230 .. **Davis,** Deirdre E '94 %Davis WT LLP -1633 Bway -NY 10019
(212) 801-6706 .. **Davis,** Diana S '02 OfCnsl Greenberg T,LLP -200 Park Av -NY 10166
(646) 708-8088 .. **Davis,** Donald G '82 Fidelity Natl Law Grp -350 5th Av -NY 10118 **Fx**:(212) 594-8378
(212) 414-4200 .. **Davis,** Douglas J '99 -7 W 22nd -NY 10010
(212) 373-3000 .. **Davis,** Douglas R '80 (Paul WRW&G LLP) -1285 Av of Amer -NY 10019
(404) 572-4791 .. **Davis,** Dwight J '02 (King & S) -1185 Av of Amer -NY 10036 **Fx**:572-5100
(212) 506-2500 .. **Davis,** Edw A '97 (Mayer B LLP) -1675 Bway -NY 10019
(212) 489-8230 .. **Davis,** Edw J '88 (Davis WT LLP) -1633 Bway -NY 10019
(718) 391-6055 .. **Davis,** Elizabeth A '91 DOE-Ofc Student Suspension -28-11 Qns Plz -LIC 11101
(212) 267-0505 .. **Davis,** Ellen S '85 %N Dembin & Assoc,PC -1123 Bway -NY 10010 **Fx**:267-9244
(212) 735-3000 .. **Davis,** Elliott M '08 %Skadden ASM&F LLP -4 Times Sq -NY 10036
(212) 297-6407 .. **Davis,** Eric B '99 Viacom Outdoor -405 Lex Av -NY 10174
(212) 909-6000 .. **Davis,** Eric F '05 %Debevoise & P LLP -919 3rd Av -NY 10022
(212) 721-8000 .. **Davis,** Eric M '92 (Davis & D,LLP) -154 W 18th -NY 10011 **Fx**:721-8321
(212) 225-2000 .. **Davis,** Evan A '70 (Cleary GS&H) -1 Lbrty Plz -NY 10006
(212) 770-5457 .. **Davis,** Florence Ann '80 %Starr Foundation -70 Pine -NY 10270
(718) 471-8898 .. **Davis,** Frank J '91 -1931 Mott Av -Far Rckwy 11691 **Fx**:471-8897
(516) 248-1700 .. **Davis,** Franklin R '87 (Forchelli CDSM&T,LLP) -333 Earle Ovngton Blvd -Uniondale 11553
(212) 230-5500 .. **Davis,** Fred '86 (Davis SLM&H LLP) -689 5th Av -NY 10022
(212) 704-1200 .. **Davis,** Gabrielle V '89 Interpublic Grp -1114 Av of Amer -NY 10036 **Fx**:704-2236
(212) 504-6000 .. **Davis,** George A '91 (Cadwalader W&T LLP) -1 World Fncl Ctr -NY 10281
(212) 323-8255 .. **Davis,** Gilbert H '00 (Sims MK&D LLP) -67 Wall -NY 10005
(212) 468-4800 .. **Davis & Gilbert LLP** -1740 Bway -NY 10019 **Fx**:468-4888
(212) 259-8000 .. **Davis,** Gordon J '73 (Dewey & L LLP) -1301 Av of Amer -NY 10019
(212) 264-0300 .. **Davis,** Gregory B '88 %NLRB -26 Fed Plz -NY 10278 **Fx**:264-8427
(212) 732-3200 .. **Davis,** H Thos Jr. '73 (Carter L&M LLP) -2 Wall -NY 10005
(212) 756-2000 .. **Davis,** Harry S '89 (Schulte R&Z LLP) -919 3rd Av -NY 10022
(518) 455-7700 .. **Davis,** Heather A '02 Ct of Appls -20 Eagle -Albany 12207
(212) 751-5252 .. **Davis,** Henry P '94 Arden Asset Mgmt,LLC -375 Park Av -NY 10152
(631) 543-2900 .. **Davis & Hersh,LLP** -1345 Motor Pkwy -Islandia 11749 **Fx**:543-2987
(212) 655-3500 .. **Davis,** Howard S '07 %Meister S&F LLP -140 E 45th -NY 10017
(716) 842-0483 .. **Davis,** J Glenn '77 -70 Niagara -Buffalo 14202 **Fx**:842-1409
(212) 756-2000 .. **Davis,** Jackson Sidney '09 %Schulte R&Z LLP -919 3rd Av -NY 10022
(212) 756-2000 .. **Davis,** Jaimie C '06 %Schulte R&Z LLP -919 3rd Av -NY 10022

(716) 852-5875 .. **Davis,** James A '10 %Feldman K LLP -110 Pearl -Buffalo 14202
(518) 456-6456 .. **Davis,** James C III '03 Gerstenzang OH&G -210 Great Oaks Blvd -Albany 12203
(631) 324-3710 .. **Davis,** James H '60 -25 Folkstone Dr -E Hampton 11937 **Fx:**324-3710
(212) 957-7600 .. **Davis,** James M '73 OfCnsl Cohen & G LLP -800 3rd Av -NY 10022
(716) 847-2606 .. **Davis,** James P '85 -181 Franklin -Buffalo 14202
(518) 885-2263 .. **Davis,** James R '97 %DA -25 W High -Ballston Spa 12020 **Fx:**884-8627
(212) 794-5382 .. **Davis,** Jane E '93 %CUNY -535 E 80th -NY 10075 **Fx:**794-5426
(516) 222-2880 .. **Davis,** Jay J '74 (J Davis & Assoc) -600 Old Cntry Rd -Gdn Cty 11530 **Fx:**222-0828
(631) 893-7837 .. **Davis,** Jay S '55 -12 Commodore Ln -W Babylon 11704
(718) 780-7534 .. **Davis,** Jean J '90 Brooklyn Law Schl Library -250 Joralemon -Brklyn 11201
(315) 478-1234 .. **Davis,** Jeffrey B '74 -61 Main -Camillus 13031 **Fx:**478-1202
(212) 554-7800 .. **Davis,** Jeffrey M '02 (Moses & S LLP) -405 Lex Av -NY 10174
(212) 223-1100 .. **Davis,** Jeffrey S '04 %Rosen & Assoc,PC -747 3rd Av -NY 10017 **Fx:**223-1102
(212) 715-9100 .. **Davis,** Jeffrey W '88 (Kramer LN&F,LLP) -1177 Av of Amer -NY 10036
(315) 425-2700 .. **Davis,** Jeffrey W '01 OfCnsl Hiscock & B,LLP -One Park Pl -Syracuse 13202
(858) 314-1503 .. **Davis,** Jeffry A '81 (Mintz LCFG&P,PC) -666 3rd Av -NY 10017
(631) 756-4252 .. **Davis,** Jeremy B '06 %State Ins Fund -8 Corp Ctr Dr -Melvll 11747 **Fx:**756-4060
(718) 956-4211 .. **Davis,** Jeremy W '05 %E Kossaris -28-03 43rd -Astoria 11103 **Fx:**626-6553
(212) 906-1200 .. **Davis,** Jessalyn R '10 %Latham & W -885 3rd Av -NY 10022
(212) 784-6303 .. **Davis,** Jessica A '01 %Protege Prtnrs -25 W 53rd -NY 10019
(518) 587-5188 .. **Davis,** Joanna S '06 %Leg Aid -112 Spring -Saratoga Spgs 12866 **Fx:**587-0959
(212) 858-1000 .. **Davis,** John E '97 Cnsl Pillsbury WSP LLP -1540 Bway -NY 10036
(914) 255-5613 .. **Davis,** John P '99 Morgan Stanley -2000 Wstchstr Av -Purchase 10577
(212) 687-5464 .. **Davis,** Jonathan D '83 (JD Davis,PC) -99 Park Av -NY 10016 **Fx:**557-0565
(718) 254-7000 .. **Davis,** Jonathan E '91 %US Atty -271 Cadman Plz E -Brklyn 11201 **Fx:**254-6479
(718) 461-6633 .. **Davis,** Jonathan K '95 Mallilo & G -163-09 Nrthrn Blvd -Flushng 11358
(212) 474-1000 .. **Davis,** Jonathan L '08 %Cravath S&M LLP -825 8th Av -NY 10019
(845) 634-6633 .. **Davis,** Jordon S '97 %Davis and D -20 Squadron Blvd -New Cty 10956 **Fx:**634-7688
(212) 216-8000 .. **Davis,** Jos A II '97 %Tarter K&D LLP -1350 Bway -NY 10018
(212) 218-2100 .. **Davis,** Joshua A '07 %Fitzpatrick CH&S -1290 Av of Amer -NY 10104
(212) 715-9100 .. **Davis,** Joshua E '00 %Kramer LN&F,LLP -1177 Av of Amer -NY 10036
(212) 721-8000 .. **Davis,** Joyce A '92 (Davis & D,LLP) -154 W 18th -NY 10011 **Fx:**721-8321
(212) 442-1400 .. **Davis,** Julia R '87 %Conflicts of Int Bd -2 Lafayette -NY 10007 **Fx:**442-1407
(716) 856-4000 .. **Davis,** Julie M '07 %Hodgson R LLP -140 Pearl -Buffalo 14202
(315) 425-2700 .. **Davis,** Katherine Maguire '07 %Hiscock & B,LLP -One Park Pl -Syracuse 13202
(646) 386-4800 .. **Davis,** Kelvin S '01 %Comm Judicial Cndct -61 Bway -NY 10006 **Fx:**458-0037
(212) 872-1000 .. **Davis,** Kenneth A '96 -One Bryant Park -NY 10036 **Fx:**872-1002
(212) 636-6150 .. **Davis,** Kenneth R '78 %Fordham Grad Schl -113 W 60th -NY 10023
(212) 431-8700 .. **Davis,** Keven J '01 (Garvey SB) -100 Wall -NY 10005
(516) 932-4300 .. **Davis,** Kevin B '01 %Technology Practice Grp LLC -1010 Nrthrn Blvd -Gt Neck 11021
(518) 355-8363 .. **Davis,** Kimberly Anne '97 Underwriters Rating Bd -2932 Curry Rd -Schnctdy 12303
(212) 373-3000 .. **Davis,** Kira Alexis '05 %Paul WRW&G LLP -1285 Av of Amer -NY 10019
(212) 455-2000 .. **Davis,** Kirsten Lu Ann '99 Cnsl Simpson T&B LLP -425 Lex Av -NY 10017
(914) 288-8194 .. **Davis,** Kory K '00 Acadia Realty Trust -1311 Mamaroneck Av -White Plns 10605
(631) 289-1600 .. **Davis,** Larry R '92 (Davis & P,PC) -175 Oak -Patchogue 11772
(212) 613-5000 .. **Davis,** Laura Diamond '91 Leg Assist Grp -450 W 33rd -NY 10001 **Fx:**750-0820
(518) 486-1841 .. **Davis,** Lee A '87 %Dept of Health -Corning Twr 24th Fl -Albany 12237 **Fx:**473-2430
(516) 569-4671 .. **Davis,** Lenore S '90 (L Davis,PC) -125 Linden -Woodmere 11598
(631) 878-8000 .. **Davis,** Leo P '74 -442 Main Bx425 -E Moriches 11940 **Fx:**878-0079
(212) 578-5170 .. **Davis,** Leonard A '75 %MetLife -27-01 Qns Plz N -LIC 11101
(212) 506-1700 .. **Davis,** Libby Skye '01 %Kasowitz BT&F LLP -1633 Bway -NY 10019
(718) 590-2000 .. **Davis,** Lisa A '00 %DA -198 E 161st -Bronx 10451 **Fx:**590-6477
(212) 980-0120 .. **Davis,** Lisa E '86 (Frankfurt KK&S,PC) -488 Mad Av -NY 10022
(212) 483-8266 .. **Davis,** Lisa Waxman '82 OfCnsl G Wright & Assoc,LLC -88 Pine -NY 10005 **Fx:**483-0971
(845) 351-2643 .. **Davis,** Loretta K '83 -Club Hse Rd -Tuxedo Pk 10987
(516) 746-7474 .. **Davis,** Lowell B '82 -1 Old Cntry Rd -Carle Pl 11514 **Fx:**746-1535
(212) 916-4216 .. **Davis,** Lynne M '97 %TIAA-CREF -730 3rd Av -NY 10017
(212) 371-0033 .. **Davis,** Malcolm H '69 (Levy D&M,LLP) -29 Bway -NY 10006
(212) 992-8288 .. **Davis,** Mara L '04 NYU -285 Mercer MC:0625 -NY 10003 **Fx:**995-4392
(212) 249-2136 .. **Davis,** Marc '87 -291 Bway -NY 10007
(212) 986-6470 .. **Davis,** Marc L '90 %Precision Acoustics -501 5th Av -NY 10017
(718) 802-2745 .. **Davis,** Marcia J '02 ACS -330 Jay -Brklyn 11201
(845) 634-6633 .. **Davis,** Marilyn P '82 (Davis and D) -20 Squadron Blvd -New Cty 10956 **Fx:**634-7688
(212) 487-4444 .. **Davis,** Mark A '02 %Dept Cnsmr Affrs -42 Bway -NY 10004 **Fx:**487-4197
(716) 842-2800 .. **Davis,** Mark C '07 %Webster S LLP -1400 Lbrty Bldg -Buffalo 14202
(347) 404-9709 .. **Davis,** Marydene '88 Surrogates Ct -2 Johnson -Brklyn 11201 **Fx:**(718) 643-4743
(212) 554-4272 .. **Davis,** Matthew H '05 Paramount BioCaptl -787 7th Av -NY 10019
(718) 488-2620 .. **Davis,** Maureen C '91 %IRS -625 Fulton -Brklyn 11201
(212) 412-9500 .. **Davis,** Megan P '98 %Flemming ZWZ LLP -1 Lbrty Plz -NY 10006
(315) 428-4093 .. **Davis,** Melissa M '91 %Div of Parole -333 E Wshngtn -Syracuse 13202
(212) 225-2000 .. **Davis,** Micaela '10 %Cleary GS&H -1 Lbrty Plz -NY 10006
(585) 262-8244 .. **Davis,** Michl E '82 Rochester Schl Dist -131 W Broad -Rchstr 14614
(845) 291-2454 .. **Davis,** Michl E '91 %Leg Aid -2 Court Ln Bx328 -Goshen 10924 **Fx:**294-2638
(212) 813-5900 .. **Davis,** Michl I '73 SpclCnsl Fross ZL&Z,PC -866 UN Plz -NY 10017
(212) 450-4000 .. **Davis,** Michl K '00 (Davis P&W LLP) -450 Lex Av -NY 10017
(212) 692-1000 .. **Davis,** Michl P '05 %Duane M LLP -1540 Bway -NY 10036
(212) 223-0400 .. **Davis,** Michl S '73 (Zeichner E&K LLP) -575 Lex Av -NY 10022
(212) 331-5862 .. **Davis,** Millicent D '84 %HRA -180 Water -NY 10038 **Fx:**331-5853
(914) 499-4311 .. **Davis,** Mitzi S '03 IBM -1 New Orchrd Rd -Armonk 10504
(585) 454-2020 .. **Davis,** Nicholas B '06 (Cellino & B,PC) -16 W Main -Rchstr 14614
(518) 436-2840 .. **Davis,** Pamela J '94 %Thruway Auth -200 Southrn Blvd Bx189 -Albany 12201 **Fx:**471-4340
(212) 998-6550 .. **Davis,** Peggy Cooper '69 %NYU Law Schl -245 Sullivan -NY 10012
(212) 628-8644 .. **Davis,** Peter N '87 -301 E 66th -NY 10065
(212) 450-4000 .. **Davis Polk & Wardwell LLP** -450 Lex Av -NY 10017 **Fx:**701-5800
(631) 289-1600 .. **Davis & Prager,PC** -175 Oak -Patchogue 11772 **Fx:**289-1679
(212) 262-9154 .. **Davis,** R Mark '88 (Engel & D LLP) -521 5th Av -NY 10175 **Fx:**262-9321
(212) 456-7777 .. **Davis,** R Townsend Jr. '92 ABC News -77 W 66th -NY 10023
(212) 752-5258 .. **Davis,** Rachel A '01 Cnsl Schwartz SE&C LLC -845 3rd Av -NY 10022
(212) 559-7870 .. **Davis,** Ria A '88 %Citicorp -153 E 53rd -NY 10043
(212) 310-8000 .. **Davis,** Richd J '70 (Weil G&M LLP) -767 5th Av -NY 10153
(212) 708-9334 .. **Davis,** Richd R '66 Bessemer Trst Co -630 5th Av -NY 10111 **Fx:**265-5826
(212) 504-6000 .. **Davis,** Robt A Jr. '92 SpclCnsl Cadwalader W&T LLP -1 World Fncl Ctr -NY 10281
(212) 477-4777 .. **Davis,** Robt B '84 -233 Bway -NY 10279 **Fx:**477-4126
(917) 596-1623 .. **Davis,** Robt B '03 -420 Lex Av -NY 10170 **Fx:**(646) 619-4592
(914) 666-5600 .. **Davis,** Robt F '80 (Shamberg MD&H,PC) -55 Smith Av -Mt Kisco 10549
(607) 637-3602 .. **Davis,** Robt G '77 -142 E Front Bx848 -Hancock 13783 **Fx:**637-9979
(212) 225-2000 .. **Davis,** Robt P '79 (Cleary GS&H) -1 Lbrty Plz -NY 10006
(212) 541-2000 .. **Davis,** Robt S '75 (Bryan C LLP) -1290 Av of Amer -NY 10104
(212) 918-3000 .. **Davis,** Robin M '09 %Hogan L LLP -875 3rd Av -NY 10022
(212) 586-3377 .. **Davis,** Roger H '70 -1650 Bway -NY 10019 **Fx:**262-0208
(212) 812-2672 .. **Davis,** Salamon '05 -39 W 37th -NY 10018
(716) 853-7611 .. **Davis,** Saml P '05 -69 Delaware Av -Buffalo 14202 **Fx:**852-6784
(212) 848-9800 .. **Davis,** Sanford J '85 (Withers B LLP) -430 Park Av -NY 10022
(212) 608-1917 .. **Davis Saperstein & Salomon,PC** -44 Wall -NY 10005 **Fx:**(201) 692-0444
(315) 343-4607 .. **Davis,** Sara E '94 -53 Murray -Oswego 13126
(212) 474-1000 .. **Davis,** Sarah Dunn '09 %Cravath S&M LLP -825 8th Av -NY 10019
(212) 264-3584 .. **Davis,** Saul '73 %US DOJ -26 Fed Plz -NY 10278 **Fx:**264-1916
(212) 777-7710 .. **Davis,** Scott '97 Ballet Tech Schl -890 Bway -NY 10003
(718) 268-2986 .. **Davis,** Scott M '89 (Davis & G) -118-35 Qns Blvd -Frst Hlls 11375 **Fx:**520-8306
(914) 925-0000 .. **Davis,** Seth A '76 Elias Grp -411 Theo Fremd Av -Rye 10580 **Fx:**925-9344
(212) 506-1700 .. **Davis,** Seth B '99 (Kasowitz BT&F LLP) -1633 Bway -NY 10019
(212) 230-5500 .. **Davis Shapiro Lewit Montone & Hayes LLP** -689 5th Av -NY 10022 **Fx:**230-5510
(516) 803-3000 .. **Davis,** Sharon C '81 Rainbow Prog -1111 Stewart Av -Bethpage 11714
(718) 298-8900 .. **Davis,** Sol '08 Leg Aid -153-01 Jamaica Av -Jamaica 11432 **Fx:**657-0537
(518) 457-2070 .. **Davis,** Stafford '88 %Dept of Tax & Fin -Bldg 9 State Campus -Albany 12227 **Fx:**457-6131
(315) 342-5822 .. **Davis,** Stephanie N '91 -118 W Van Buren -Oswego 13126 **Fx:**342-4904
(914) 946-3700 .. **Davis,** Stephen '60 Cnsl McCarthy F LLP -11 Martine Av -White Plns 10606
(212) 292-0456 .. **Davis,** Stephen '63 -67 Wall -NY 10005 **Fx:**292-0463
(212) 813-8800 .. **Davis,** Stephen M '80 (Goodwin P LLP) -620 8th Av -NY 10018
(845) 856-6351 .. **Davis,** Steven G '82 (Jacoby & M,LLP) -1 Cole -Pt Jervis 12771 **Fx:**856-6353
(212) 259-8000 .. **Davis,** Steven H '78 (Dewey & L LLP) -1301 Av of Amer -NY 10019
(212) 338-5467 .. **Davis,** Steven M '91 Loral Spacecom Corp -600 3rd Av -NY 10016
(585) 419-8800 .. **Davis,** Stewart D '66 (Harris B PLLC) -99 Garnsey Rd -Pittsfrd 14534
(516) 541-6200 .. **Davis,** Stuart E '59 (Davis & B) -254 Pettit Av -Bellmore 11710 **Fx:**798-9097
(718) 618-1200 .. **Davis,** Stuart L '78 Supreme Ct -851 Grnd Cncrs -Bronx 10451
(212) 563-4100 .. **Davis,** Susan '82 (Cohen W&S LLP) -330 W 42nd -NY 10036
(212) 996-8700 .. **Davis,** Susan '92 %A Iadevaia -1932 2nd Av -NY 10029 **Fx:**996-4235
(718) 783-6819 .. **Davis,** Tarik A '92 -26 Court -Brklyn 11242
(718) 390-5337 .. **Davis,** Thea K '01 %Law Dept -60 Bay -Staten Isl 10301 **Fx:**390-5338
(718) 789-6789 .. **Davis,** Theo M '97 -172 5th Av PMB 178 -Brklyn 11217 **Fx:**399-7086
(480) 812-0823 .. **Davis,** Thos J '94 -7954 Transit Rd #192 -Williamsvll 14221
(845) 298-2000 .. **Davis,** Thos R '92 (Vergilis SRD&D,LLP) -1136 Route 9 -Wappingers Fls 12590
(585) 428-5210 .. **Davis,** Timothy S '93 %Pub Def -10 N Fitzhugh -Rchstr 14614 **Fx:**428-2234
(212) 223-0400 .. **Davis,** Tracee E '92 OfCnsl Zeichner E&K LLP -575 Lex Av -NY 10022
(212) 510-0500 .. **Davis,** Tracy H '94 %US Trustees Ofc -33 Whitehall -NY 10004 **Fx:**668-2255
(212) 351-4000 .. **Davis,** Travis P '09 Gibson D&C LLP -200 Park Av -NY 10166
(212) 530-5000 .. **Davis,** Trayton M '81 (Milbank TH&M LLP) -1 Chase Manh Plz -NY 10005

(212) 371-1011 .. **Davis,** Tyrone A '95 Rice High School -74 W 124th -NY 10027 **Fx:**421-3693
(718) 585-8773 .. **Davis,** Vincent B Jr. '83 -370 E 149th -Bronx 10455 **Fx:**993-3407
(212) 918-3000 .. **Davis,** W Sidney Jr. '70 OfCnsl Hogan L LLP -875 3rd Av -NY 10022
(518) 789-3636 .. **Davis,** Walter W '38 OfCnsl Davis & T -Millerton Plz Bx481 -Millerton 12546 **Fx:**789-6654
(212) 508-6700 .. **Davis,** Wayne H '85 (Tannenbaum HS&H LLP) -900 3rd Av -NY 10022
(518) 813-4461 .. **Davis,** Wayne M '57 -7 Halfmoon Exec Park Dr -Clifton Pk 12065
(212) 883-4947 .. **Davis,** Wm F '03 (Cozen O) -277 Park Av -NY 10172 **Fx:**672-1147
(212) 688-3200 .. **Davis,** Wm J '70 (Scheichet & D,PC) -767 3rd Av -NY 10017
(212) 489-8230 .. **Davis Wright Tremaine LLP** -1633 Bway -NY 10019 **Fx:**489-8340
(585) 641-8000 .. **Davis Brugg,** Betsy L '93 (Fix SB&G,PC) -295 Woodcliff Dr -Fairprt 14450
(212) 909-6000 .. **Davis-Noll,** Bethany A '07 %Debevoise & P LLP -919 3rd Av -NY 10022
(212) 225-2000 .. **Davison,** Casey J '09 %Cleary GS&H -1 Lbrty Plz -NY 10006
(914) 235-2700 .. **Davison,** Irwin S '67 %Beth El Synagogue -Nrthfld Rd at North Av -New Rchll 10804 **Fx:**235-2718
(516) 542-1000 .. **Davison,** Lindsey A '89 (Geisler & G,LLP) -100 Q Roosevelt Blvd -Gdn Cty 11530
(716) 856-1344 .. **Davison,** Roger T '63 SpclCnsl Bouvier Prtnrshp,LLP -350 Main -Buffalo 14202 **Fx:**856-1369
(718) 222-2308 .. **Davison-March,** Rebecca L '08 %Law Dept -350 Jay -Brklyn 11201 **Fx:**222-2373
(631) 543-2900 .. **Davis Sica,** Allison '92 %Davis & H,LLP -1345 Motor Pkwy -Islandia 11749
(212) 728-2200 .. **Davitz,** Michl A '98 (Axinn V&H LLP) -114 W 47th -NY 10036
(516) 992-8082 .. **Davoli,** Henry W Jr. '82 -342 N Lng Bch Rd -Rockvll Ctr 11570 **Fx:**543-4190
(315) 474-2911 .. **Davoli,** Michelle M '08 %Smith SK&S,PC -250 S Clinton -Syracuse 13202
(315) 474-2943 .. **Davoli,** Stephen A '04 %Sugarman Law Firm,LLP -211 W Jffrsn -Syracuse 13202
(212) 735-3000 .. **D'Avolio,** Lisa R '97 Cnsl Skadden ASM&F LLP -4 Times Sq -NY 10036
(631) 727-2340 .. **DaVolio,** Richd J '87 (Ahmuty D&M) -750 Roanoke Av -Rvrhead 11901
(212) 558-4000 .. **Davy,** Elizabeth T '87 (Sullivan & C LLP) -125 Broad -NY 10004
(212) 558-4000 .. **Davy,** Erez J '06 %Sullivan & C LLP -125 Broad -NY 10004
(212) 310-3229 .. **Davy,** Kathleen J '99 %Colgate-Palmolive -300 Park Av -NY 10022 **Fx:**310-3230
(516) 248-9700 .. **Daw,** James J Jr. '75 %S Levitt & Assoc,PC -2 Hillside Av -Williston Pk 11596 **Fx:**741-9224
(212) 998-2262 .. **Dawe,** Cathleen '90 %NYU Ofc Leg Cnsl -70 Wshngtn Sq S -NY 10012 **Fx:**995-3048
(212) 474-1000 .. **Dawe,** Timothy '10 %Cravath S&M LLP -825 8th Av -NY 10019
(718) 641-5000 .. **Dawes-Janczys,** Nancy '92 Five Star Electric -101-32 101st -Ozone Pk 11416
(212) 416-8118 .. **Dawkins,** Julinda A '02 %Dept of Law -120 Bway -NY 10271
(212) 297-5800 .. **Dawood Azib,** Marian N '05 %Day P LLP -7 Times Sq -NY 10036
(585) 243-4222 .. **Dawson,** Dennis R '79 (Dawson & VW,LLP) -129 Main Bx69 -Geneseo 14454 **Fx:**243-2387
(631) 854-5861 .. **Dawson,** Frances C '91 %Cnty Dept Soc Srvcs -Bx18100 -Hauppauge 11788 **Fx:**854-5876
(212) 442-7530 .. **Dawson,** Herman L '94 %Juvenile Justice -110 William -NY 10038 **Fx:**442-8517
(718) 250-2000 .. **Dawson,** Janesse '10 %DA -350 Jay -Brklyn 11201 **Fx:**250-2314
(516) 248-2131 .. **Dawson,** John B Jr. '57 (J Dawson Jr,PC) -6800 Jericho Tpke -Syosset 11791 **Fx:**822-1974
(212) 762-7100 .. **Dawson,** Melissa J '00 Morgan Stanley -1221 Av of Amer -NY 10020
(914) 251-1525 .. **Dawson,** Peter S '07 %Pollock & M,LLP -106 Corp Park Dr -White Plns 10604
(212) 318-3000 .. **Dawson,** Ralph C '77 (Fulbright & J LLP) -666 5th Av -NY 10103
(917) 551-1300 .. **Dawson,** Rena C '91 %Koehler & I LLP -61 Bway -NY 10006
(212) 785-2929 .. **Dawson,** Richd W '96 (Conway FC&K,PC) -48 Wall -NY 10005
(212) 309-6000 .. **Dawson,** Robt Alec '95 (Morgan L&B LLP) -101 Park Av -NY 10178
(516) 676-4600 .. **Dawson,** Sara E '07 %Humes & W -147 Forest Av Bx546 -Locust Vly 11560
(212) 259-8000 .. **Dawson,** Thos M '81 (Dewey & L LLP) -1301 Av of Amer -NY 10019
(631) 852-2084 .. **Dawydiak,** Walter '94 %Office of Ecology -Cnty Ctr Dr -Rvrhead 11901
(518) 432-1002 .. **Dax,** John W '78 Dax Law,PC -54 State -Albany 12207 **Fx:**432-1028
(518) 736-1946 .. **Day,** Allen R '76 A Day,LLC -148 W Main -Johnstwn 12095
(212) 252-0005 .. **Day,** Amy Carron '92 -230 Park Av -NY 10169
(914) 242-7200 .. **Day,** Amy Carron '92 Ctr for Collbrtv Fmly Law & Divorce Mediatn -241 Lex Av -Mt Kisco 10549 **Fx:**241-8373
(212) 446-6457 .. **Day,** Andrew C '10 %Kirkland & E LLP -153 E 53rd -NY 10022 **Fx:**446-6460
(212) 931-7448 .. **Day,** Bryan J '03 MLB Properties -245 Park Av -NY 10167 **Fx:**949-5697
(315) 443-2524 .. **Day,** Christian C '05 Syracuse Univ Cllg of Law -Wht Hall -Syracuse 13244 **Fx:**443-4213
(516) 236-2604 .. **Day,** David A '99 -11 Grace Av -Gt Neck 11021 **Fx:**466-7736
(212) 447-7070 .. **Day,** Dominique '00 %Whatley D&K LLC -1540 Bway -NY 10036
(716) 566-1300 .. **Day,** Donald S '49 OfCnsl Hiscock & B,LLP -1100 M&T Ctr -Buffalo 14203
(845) 639-7800 .. **Day,** Gary '99 (Mandel K&B,LLP) -210 Route 303 -Vly Cottage 10989
(212) 841-3258 .. **Day,** Grenville Reed '05 BNP Paribas Securities -787 7th Av -NY 10019
(212) 237-0000 .. **Day,** James W '08 %Vinson & E LLP -666 5th Av -NY 10103
(212) 450-4000 .. **Day,** Karin S '88 (Davis P&W LLP) -450 Lex Av -NY 10017
(518) 457-4380 .. **Day,** Marshall H '99 Dept of Labor -State Campus Bldg 12 -Albany 12240 **Fx:**485-1819
(212) 673-0484 .. **Day,** Matthew J '92 -380 Lex Av -NY 10168
(716) 852-3540 .. **Day,** Melissa Ann '97 %Watson BCJ&S -12 Fountain Plz -Buffalo 14202
(518) 478-0663 .. **Day,** Meryl D '99 -80 Brookvw Av -Delmar 12054 **Fx:**478-0663
(212) 506-5000 .. **Day,** Minh '03 %Orrick H&S LLP -51 W 52nd -NY 10019
(212) 297-5800 .. **Day Pitney LLP** -7 Times Sq -NY 10036 **Fx:**916-2940
(716) 566-1300 .. **Day,** Richd J '77 (Hiscock & B,LLP) -1100 M&T Ctr -Buffalo 14203
(516) 466-1700 .. **Day,** Rose M '91 (Day & Assoc,PC) -11 Grace Av -Gt Neck 11021 **Fx:**466-7736
(212) 999-5800 .. **Day,** Selim B '89 (Wilson SG&R) -1301 Av of Americas -NY 10019
(212) 848-4000 .. **Day,** Thos A '02 %Shearman & S LLP -599 Lex Av -NY 10022
(212) 904-1815 .. **Day,** Ursula B '86 -708 3rd Av -NY 10017
(212) 468-4800 .. **Dayal,** Ashima Aggarwal '99 (Davis & G LLP) -1740 Bway -NY 10019
(212) 644-1010 .. **Dayan,** Lisa E '92 %Kauff M&M LLP -950 3rd Av -NY 10022
(212) 225-2000 .. **Dayan,** Michl D '93 (Cleary GS&H) -1 Lbrty Plz -NY 10006
(212) 681-3131 .. **Dayan,** Ronald '01 Fischer Francis Trees & Watts -200 Park Av -NY 10166
(212) 688-5151 .. **Dayan,** Shai E '07 %Gibney A&F,LLP -665 5th Av -NY 10022
(212) 335-9000 .. **Dayananda,** Soumyalatha '02 %DA -1 Hogan Pl -NY 10013
(518) 853-3834 .. **Dayian,** Michl G '95 Pub Def -Cnty Ct Chmbrs Bx1500 -Fonda 12068 **Fx:**853-3596
(212) 944-0900 .. **Dayon,** Jeffery D '86 (Mishaan D&L) -1370 Bway -NY 10018
(845) 877-3737 .. **Dayter,** James W Jr. '00 %MHLS -Taconic DDSO-Wassaic Campus -Wassaic 12592 **Fx:**877-9003
(212) 264-2131 .. **Dayton,** Bryan H '05 %Hon D Pogue -1 Fed Plz -NY 10278
(212) 331-5068 .. **Dayton,** Cynthia D '01 %Dept of Social Srvcs -180 Water -NY 10038
(718) 423-3000 .. **Dayton & D'Amato,PC** -42-40 Bell Blvd -Bayside 11361 **Fx:**631-4808
(516) 746-7660 .. **Dayton,** Erin L '05 %Klemanowicz H&VS,LLP -300 Old Cntry Rd -Mineola 11501 **Fx:**747-7292
(631) 853-5761 .. **Dayton,** Jeffrey '88 %Cnty Atty -400 Carleton Av -Central Islip 11722 **Fx:**853-7788
(607) 758-8566 .. **Dayton,** Keith D '93 -20½ Groton Av -Cortlnd 13045
(212) 541-6222 .. **Dayton,** Lauren M '04 %Kane K,PC -1350 Av of Amer -NY 10019
(631) 654-4900 .. **Dazzo,** George E '97 (Cartier BA&D,PC) -100 Austin -Patchogue 11772
(516) 628-0312 .. **D'Chiutiis,** Patricia B '96 -Bx1341 -Bayvll 11709
(646) 386-5000 .. **De,** Meena Goel '97 %Surrogates Ct -31 Chmbrs -NY 10007
(212) 596-9000 .. **De,** Sona '00 (Ropes & G LLP) -1211 Av of Amer -NY 10036
(212) 213-6996 .. **Deabler,** Justin A '02 %Spears & I LLP -51 Mad Av -NY 10010
(212) 728-8000 .. **Deacon,** Emma-Ann L '09 %Willkie F&G LLP -787 7th Av -NY 10019
(516) 496-1919 .. **Deacy,** Erin L '07 %Keller O&W,PC -242 Crsswys Park Dr W -Woodbury 11797
(917) 373-1580 .. **Deadman,** Robt M '89 -314 W 231st -Bronx 10463
(212) 252-9550 .. **Deak,** Danielle '00 %Freiberg & P -49 W 37th -NY 10018
(631) 843-5944 .. **Deal,** Andrew P '96 Henry Schein,Inc -135 Duryea Rd -Melvll 11747
(716) 849-1333 .. **Deal,** Michl S '01 (Lipsitz GSC LLP) -42 Delaware Av -Buffalo 14202
(212) 698-3500 .. **De Alba,** Claudia L '03 %Dechert LLP -1095 Av of Amer -NY 10036
(212) 858-1000 .. **Dealy,** James D '08 %Pillsbury WSP LLP -1540 Bway -NY 10036
(212) 385-0066 .. **Dealy & Silberstein,LLP** -225 Bway -NY 10007 **Fx:**385-2117
(212) 385-0066 .. **Dealy,** Wm J '71 (Dealy & S,LLP) -225 Bway -NY 10007
(518) 473-8709 .. **DeAmelia,** Victor P '05 Div of Human Rts -ESP -Albany 12205
(607) 334-9194 .. **Dean,** Aaron A '86 (Vitanza D&D,LLP) -15 Maple -Norwich 13815
(212) 450-4000 .. **Dean,** Alan '79 (Davis P&W LLP) -450 Lex Av -NY 10017
(212) 490-1700 .. **Dean,** Andrew B '02 %Wiggin & D -450 Lex Av -NY 10017
(212) 599-5455 .. **Dean,** Andrew W '09 %Simon Lesser,PC -420 Lex Av -NY 10170 **Fx:**599-5459
(212) 613-2025 .. **Dean,** Anthony A '67 Cnsl Gibbons PC -1 Penn Plz -NY 10119 **Fx:**554-9668
(212) 237-1000 .. **Dean,** Christopher E '99 %Windels ML&M,LLP -156 W 56th -NY 10019
(212) 564-3555 .. **Dean,** Christopher R '92 %Bauman & K,PC -14 Penn Plz -NY 10122
(212) 732-9000 .. **Dean,** David J '62 (Sullivan PBM&C PC) -120 Bway -NY 10271
(518) 474-6530 .. **Dean,** Diane T '88 %Dept Pub Srvc -3 ESP -Albany 12223
(718) 250-2000 .. **Dean,** Emily J '09 DA -350 Jay -Brklyn 11201 **Fx:**250-2314
(718) 694-5721 .. **Dean,** Florence '76 %Transit Auth -130 Lvngstn -Brklyn 11201 **Fx:**694-5726
(914) 631-3000 .. **Dean,** Howard '70 H Dean,PC -150 Wht Plns Rd -Tarrytwn 10591 **Fx:**631-0363
(212) 416-8000 .. **Dean,** Janice A '06 %Dept of Law -120 Bway -NY 10271
(212) 661-1100 .. **Dean,** Jay Douglas '89 Pomerantz HG&G LLP -100 Park Av -NY 10017
(212) 509-9400 .. **Dean,** Laura Erb '10 %Cozen O -45 Bway Atrium -NY 10006
(212) 576-8088 .. **Dean,** Mary '85 NY Life Ins -51 Mad Av -NY 10010
(212) 389-5000 .. **Dean,** Peter H '77 (Sutherland A&B LLP) -1114 Av of Amer -NY 10036
(212) 577-2523 .. **Dean,** Robt S '78 %Ctr for Appllt Litigation -74 Trinity Pl -NY 10006 **Fx:**577-2535
(718) 254-0700 .. **Dean,** Stephen '87 %Bklyn Defender Srvcs -177 Lvngstn -Brklyn 11201 **Fx:**254-0897
(718) 780-7939 .. **Dean,** Steven A '00 %Bklyn Law Schl -250 Joralemon -Brklyn 11201 **Fx:**780-0393
(212) 695-6446 .. **Dean,** Thos R '85 %Ressler & R -48 Wall -NY 10005 **Fx:**268-0287
(212) 966-4400 .. **Dean,** Wm J '63 %VOLS -54 Greene -NY 10013 **Fx:**219-8943
(212) 967-1557 .. **de Andrade,** David '89 -358 5th Av -NY 10001 **Fx:**695-4041
(212) 665-0663 .. **DeAndrade,** Luciane S '03 -50 W 97th -NY 10025
(212) 577-3565 .. **Deane,** Jacqueline '86 %Leg Aid -199 Water -NY 10038 **Fx:**577-3520
(718) 261-3047 .. **Deane,** Kenneth B '77 Queens Law Assoc -118-21 Qns Blvd -Frst Hlls 11375 **Fx:**261-0798
(914) 377-6240 .. **DeAngeli,** John A '86 %Law Dept -300 City Hall -Ynkrs 10701 **Fx:**964-0563
(631) 754-4470 .. **DeAngelis,** Dennis '77 -1019 Ft Salonga Rd -Northprt 11768 **Fx:**754-8764
(518) 436-0751 .. **DeAngelis,** Donald D '61 (Hinman S PC) -121 State -Albany 12207
(973) 494-0602 .. **DeAngelis,** Frank J '97 (Mound CW&G) -One Bttry Pk Plz -NY 10004 **Fx:**242-4244
(917) 882-9683 .. **DeAngelis,** Mark E '97 RNK Capital LLC -527 Mad Av -NY 10022
(914) 667-1188 .. **DeAngelis,** Mark S '89 (DeAngelis & H) -22 W 1st -Mt Vernon 10550 **Fx:**667-0836

(212) 318-6390 .. **DeAngelis,** Robt J '77 -75 E 55th -NY 10022
(716) 484-7196 .. **DeAngelo,** Chas S '84 (Fessenden L&D) -81 Forest Av Bx590 -Jamestwn 14702
(518) 371-8888 .. **DeAngelus,** Donald J '65 (DeAngelus & D) -805 Route 146 -Clifton Pk 12065 **Fx:**383-6132
(518) 587-0316 .. **DeAngelus,** Karen L '00 (Herkenham & D,PC) -18 Division -Saratoga Spgs 12866 **Fx:**583-2936
(518) 374-3399 .. **DeAngelus,** Lawr A '00 (Higgins RB&C,PC) -1430 Balltown Rd -Niskayuna 12309
(518) 371-8888 .. **DeAngelus,** Ronald P '60 (DeAngelus & D) -805 Route 146 -Clifton Pk 12065 **Fx:**383-6132
(212) 547-5400 .. **Deans Martell,** Johanna '06 %McDermott W&E LLP -340 Mad Av -NY 10173
(212) 878-8000 .. **Dear,** Eliott '05 %Clifford C LLP -31 W 52nd -NY 10019
(212) 735-3000 .. **Dear,** Mary K '08 %Skadden ASM&F LLP -4 Times Sq -NY 10036
(212) 351-4000 .. **DeArcy,** La Shann M '01 %Gibson D&C LLP -200 Park Av -NY 10166
(212) 980-0404 .. **Dearie,** John C '87 (J Dearie & Assoc) -515 Mad Av -NY 10022 **Fx:**980-0555
(212) 308-4411 .. **Dearie,** John P '79 (Edwards AP&D LLP) -750 Lex Av -NY 10022
(212) 558-4000 .. **Dearman,** Cara E '10 %Sullivan & C LLP -125 Broad -NY 10004
(518) 463-2259 .. **Dearmas,** Justin V '08 %Ackerman W&F -90 State -Albany 12207
(718) 546-0950 .. **de Armas,** Orbein A '88 %Dept of Correction -75-20 Astoria Blvd -E Elmhrst 11370
(518) 465-8085 .. **Dears-Kent,** Elizabeth C '85 %Med Society -1 Commerce Plz -Albany 12210 **Fx:**465-0976
(212) 298-5077 .. **Dearth,** Deborah Hean '89 %Leg Aid -49 Thomas -NY 10013 **Fx:**298-5252
(212) 735-3000 .. **Deas,** Andrew W '06 %Skadden ASM&F LLP -4 Times Sq -NY 10036
(212) 728-8000 .. **Deason,** Paul Joshua '08 %Willkie F&G LLP -787 7th Av -NY 10019
(212) 357-1327 .. **Deaton,** Shane D '05 Goldman Sachs -1 NY Plz -NY 10004
(212) 490-3000 .. **Deaver,** James T H '93 (Wilson EME&D LLP) -150 E 42nd -NY 10017
(516) 222-2299 .. **Deaver,** Jennifer L '04 %J Schecter & Assoc -595 Stewart Av -Gdn Cty 11530 **Fx:**222-2303
(212) 974-7474 .. **DeBaets,** Timothy J '76 (Cowan DA&S LLP) -41 Mad Av -NY 10010
(315) 437-2220 .. **DeBaise,** Ralph R '59 -6756 Myers Rd -E Syracuse 13057
(212) 806-5400 .. **DeBare,** Nicole S '06 %Stroock &S&L LLP -180 Maiden Ln -NY 10038
(212) 715-9100 .. **DeBari,** Vito J '96 (Kramer LN&F,LLP) -1177 Av of Amer -NY 10036
(315) 256-6651 .. **DeBartolo,** Gregg J '83 -Bx160 -Fayettevll 13066
(212) 592-1400 .. **DeBartolo,** Jessica T '10 %Herrick,F LLP -2 Park Av -NY 10016
(212) 644-5300 .. **deBary,** Paul A '72 Marquette deBary Co,Inc -230 Park Av -NY 10169 **Fx:**371-6054
(516) 327-7780 .. **DeBaun,** David J '00 Astoria Fed Savings & Loan -1 Astoria Fed Plz -Lk Success 11042
(212) 839-5300 .. **DeBaun,** Nicholas H '95 (Sidley A LLP) -787 7th Av -NY 10019
(212) 888-3100 .. **Debbas,** Pierre E '06 -820 2nd Av -NY 10017 **Fx:**888-1701
(212) 554-7800 .. **Debel,** Loren M '06 %Moses & S LLP -405 Lex Av -NY 10174
(212) 636-6000 .. **Debelak,** Jamela S '07 Fordham Univ Sch of Law -140 W 62nd -NY 10023 **Fx:**636-6899
(315) 735-6481 .. **DeBella,** Vincent M '90 (Paravati KG&D) -12 Steuben Pk -Utica 13501
(516) 408-9000 .. **DeBellis,** Claudio '95 (Walsh MM&D LLP) -229 Seventh -Gdn Cty 11530
(845) 565-9261 .. **DeBellis,** Julio '84 %B Kulak -484 Temple Hill Rd -New Windsor 12553
(212) 687-4900 .. **DeBellis,** Lauren J '06 %Wormser KG&J LLP -825 3rd Av -NY 10022
(718) 575-4175 .. **DeBellis,** Philip J '78 -98-20 Metro Av -Frst Hlls 11375 **Fx:**(866) 545-7703
(914) 241-8900 .. **DeBellis,** Rosanne M '06 PIA Inc -37 Radio Circle Dr -Mt Kisco 10549
(845) 628-5900 .. **DeBellis,** Rose S '81 %Spain & S -671 Route 6 -Mahopac 10541 **Fx:**628-0694
(646) 610-5400 .. **De Bellis,** Rosemary F '88 %NYPD -1 Police Plz -NY 10038
(212) 809-7074 .. **DeBellis,** Silvana '86 (Armienti DG&R,LLP) -39 Bway -NY 10006
(212) 277-6500 .. **DeBello,** Nicole P '03 %Dickstein S LLP -1633 Bway -NY 10019
(516) 686-8888 .. **DeBenedetto,** Yvonne '92 -145 Merritts Rd -Farmngdl 11735 **Fx:**(631) 957-3834
(845) 602-2126 .. **DeBenedictis,** Karen '86 %Pfizer,Inc -401 N Mddltwn Rd -Pearl Rvr 10965
(631) 582-1776 .. **DeBenedittis,** Mark L '90 -99 Smithtwn Blvd -Smithtwn 11787 **Fx:**582-1804
(718) 237-9400 .. **DeBerardine,** Elaine A '91 (DeBerardine & D) -96 Schermerhorn -Brklyn 11201 **Fx:**237-9407
(718) 237-9400 .. **DeBerardine,** Roger B '54 (DeBerardine & D) -96 Schermerhorn -Brklyn 11201 **Fx:**237-9407
(212) 450-4000 .. **Debergalis,** Sarah L '08 %Davis P&W LLP -450 Lex Av -NY 10017
(212) 487-9701 .. **DeBernardis,** Philip J '88 %Robin HK&F -1 Bttry Pk Plz -NY 10014
(914) 323-7000 .. **DeBernardis,** Stephen A '99 OfCnsl Wilson EME&D LLP -3 Gannett Dr -White Plns 10604
(646) 264-3650 .. **DeBernardo,** Louis D '70 %US Dept of Labor -201 Varick -NY 10014 **Fx:**264-3660
(212) 504-6000 .. **DeBerry,** Jeremiah A '92 Cadwalader W&T LLP -1 World Fncl Ctr -NY 10281
(718) 262-7100 .. **Deberry,** Melissa '01 Civil Ct -89-17 Sutphin Blvd -Jamaica 11435 **Fx:**262-7107
(212) 909-6000 .. **Debevoise & Plimpton LLP** -919 3rd Av -NY 10022 **Fx:**909-6836
(212) 318-6000 .. **Debiak,** Monica L '03 %Paul HJ&W LLP -75 E 55th -NY 10022
(212) 578-9414 .. **DeBiase,** Christine M '96 %MetLife -1095 Av of Amer -NY 10036
(845) 454-1110 .. **DeBiase,** Vincent L '75 (Corbally G and R LLP) -35 Market -Poughkeepsie 12601
(516) 794-5310 .. **DeBisceglia,** Anthony P '98 Abrams GMB,LLP -125 Jericho Tpk -Jericho 11753
(631) 509-0875 .. **DeBlasi,** Kevin '98 -5 Millie Ln -E Setauket 11733
(631) 218-0150 .. **DeBlasio,** John W '91 JW DeBlasio,PC -4175 Vets Mem'l Hwy -Ronkonkoma 11779 **Fx:**389-2478
(212) 732-9000 .. **DeBlasio,** Peter E '55 OfCnsl Sullivan PBM&C PC -120 Bway -NY 10271
(212) 451-2300 .. **Deblinger,** Jonathan H '04 %Olshan GFR&W LLP -65 E 55th -NY 10022
(631) 738-9100 .. **Deblois,** Eryn Y K '09 %Campolo M&M,LLP -3340 Vets Mem'l Hwy -Bohemia 11716 **Fx:**738-0659
(212) 244-9500 .. **DeBoisblanc,** Peter M '05 %White and W LLP -1 Penn Plz -NY 10119
(718) 442-6910 .. **DeBoissiere,** Alexander J '84 -30 Bay -Staten Isl 10301
(718) 442-6910 .. **DeBoissiere,** Robt J '59 -30 Bay -Staten Isl 10301
(585) 454-2181 .. **DeBolt,** Danl P '04 %Trevett CS&A,PC -2 State -Rchstr 14614
(518) 237-1871 .. **DeBonis,** Sharon Couch '82 -406 7th Av -Troy 12182 **Fx:**237-1871
(212) 455-2000 .. **De Bonis,** Theo R '06 %Simpson T&B LLP -425 Lex Av -NY 10017
(845) 627-4700 .. **DeBonis,** Victor M '82 %BOCES -65 Parrott Rd -W Nyack 10994 **Fx:**623-3368
(631) 501-5700 .. **DeBono,** Michl J '06 %Carter DF&S LLP -445 Broadhallow Rd -Melvll 11747
(315) 363-6800 .. **DeBottis,** Michel J '86 (DeBottis & S) -312 Broad -Oneida 13421 **Fx:**363-6801
(716) 604-0660 .. **DeBoy,** Thos J '91 -212 Sterling Av -Buffalo 14216
(212) 421-4100 .. **deBrauwere,** Robt J '94 (Pryor C LLP) -7 Times Sq -NY 10036
(212) 698-3500 .. **deBrito,** Carl A '78 (Dechert LLP) -1095 Av of Amer -NY 10036
(212) 504-6000 .. **Debrito,** Diana R '84 (Cadwalader W&T LLP) -1 World Fncl Ctr -NY 10281
(718) 740-3000 .. **DeBrosse,** James G '92 -211-31 Jamaica Av -Qns Vllg 11428
(718) 658-3000 .. **Debrosse,** Richd A '99 (Debrosse & S,LLP) -182-38 Hillside Av -Jamaica 11432 **Fx:**658-3187
(212) 599-0125 .. **Debrot,** Jacques L '63 -60 E 42nd -NY 10165 **Fx:**826-6136
(212) 819-8200 .. **De Brouckere,** Lien '09 %White & C LLP -1155 Av of Amer -NY 10036
(212) 981-4501 .. **Debrowski,** Mark D '01 Smith A,LLP -90 Broad -NY 10004
(212) 259-4100 .. **DeBruijn,** Julie J M '03 DeBrauw BW PC -650 5th AV -NY 10019
(516) 248-6500 .. **deBruin,** Wm E Jr. '65 (Froehlich M&D) -34 Willis Av -Mineola 11501
(212) 318-3000 .. **deButts,** Robt E L Jr. '87 SrCnsl Fulbright & J LLP -666 5th Av -NY 10103
(315) 252-6240 .. **Dec,** Francis P '96 -7 Westwood Dr -Auburn 13021
(518) 437-9300 .. **DeCaire,** Avis S '00 %Congdon FORDT&F -12 Metro Park Rd -Colonie 12205
(518) 465-3484 .. **Decaire,** Wm J '01 (Carter CCBM&L,PC) -20 Corp Wds Blvd -Albany 12211
(212) 252-0004 .. **de Callies,** Eileen H '95 %Carroll M&K LLC -570 Lex Av -NY 10022
(212) 458-1033 .. **Decaminada,** Jos '88 AIG -175 Water -NY 10038
(914) 347-2600 .. **DeCamp,** Jerri A '03 %Traub LS&S LLP -7 Skyline Dr -Hawthorne 10532
(212) 558-4000 .. **DeCamp,** Justin J '06 %Sullivan & C LLP -125 Broad -NY 10004
(212) 775-0055 .. **DeCamp,** Robt D '04 %Simon G&K LLP -1700 Bway -NY 10019
(212) 758-3500 .. **DeCampo Diamond & Ash** -747 3rd Av -NY 10017 **Fx:**758-1728
(212) 758-3500 .. **DeCampo,** Jos A '76 (DeCampo D&A) -747 3rd Av -NY 10017
(518) 474-6400 .. **DeCandia,** Louise M '93 Dept of Ed -89 Wshngtn Av -Albany 12234 **Fx:**473-2925
(212) 664-7123 .. **De Candia,** Maryanne '97 %NBC -30 Rckfllr Plz -NY 10112
(718) 275-6600 .. **DeCandido,** Wm V '92 W DeCandido,PC -71-50 Austin -Frst Hlls 11375
(845) 354-3212 .. **DeCaprio,** Ronald V '97 -65 W Ramapo Rd -Garnervll 10923 **Fx:**354-3213
(516) 498-1000 .. **DeCapua,** Anthony P '00 %Hollander & S,LLP -40 Cuttermill Rd -Gt Neck 11021
(516) 764-2226 .. **DeCapua,** Gerard A '86 (Solomon & D) -430 Sunrise Hwy Bx1100 -Rockvll Ctr 11570 **Fx:**536-5389
(516) 622-2337 .. **DeCarlo,** Donald T '70 -1979 Marcus Av -Lk Success 11042 **Fx:**622-2338
(212) 801-6729 .. **DeCarlo,** James J '92 (Greenberg T,LLP) -200 Park Av -NY 10166
(631) 351-3042 .. **DeCarlo,** Luciana Marie '89 %Town Atty -100 Main -Huntngtn 11743 **Fx:**351-3032
(212) 683-7100 .. **DeCarlo,** Michl P '81 %Gallo V&K,LLP -90 Broad -NY 10004
(718) 370-7030 .. **DeCarlo,** Paul M '75 (Amabile & E,PC) -1000 South Av -Staten Isl 10314
(631) 669-8600 .. **DeCarlo,** Paul R '89 (DeCarlo & A,PC) -175 W Main -Babylon 11702 **Fx:**669-2150
(212) 318-3000 .. **DeCarmine,** India '88 SrCnsl Fulbright & J LLP -666 5th Av -NY 10103
(718) 293-7574 .. **De Caro,** Francis M '56 -881 Gerard Av -Bronx 10452 **Fx:**293-7655
(914) 250-2400 .. **De Caro,** Loriel R '09 Benchmark Title Agncy LLC -222 Bloomingdale Rd -White Plns 10605
(914) 835-6200 .. **DeCaro,** Philip A '89 (DeCaro & D) -480 Mamaroneck Av -Harrison 10528
(914) 747-4410 .. **De Caro,** Shana '81 (DeCaro & K,LLP) -427 Bedford Rd -Plsntvll 10570
(914) 835-6200 .. **DeCaro,** Thos G '55 (DeCaro & D) -480 Mamaroneck Av -Harrison 10528
(585) 753-4500 .. **De Carolis,** Brian C '06 DA -832 Watts Bldg -Rchstr 14614 **Fx:**753-4576
(212) 861-4180 .. **DeCarolis,** Mary Ann '76 -240 E 82nd -NY 10028 **Fx:**861-4180
(212) 490-2020 .. **Decasseres,** Lesley A '07 %Littman K LLP -655 3rd Av -NY 10017
(212) 812-8910 .. **de Castro,** César '01 %Lankler & C,LLP -845 3rd Av -NY 10022
(716) 282-1242 .. **DeCastro,** Damon A '86 %Roscetti & D -730 Main -Niagara Fls 14301
(716) 439-7085 .. **De Castro,** Heather A '06 %DA -175 Hawley -Lockprt 14094 **Fx:**439-7102
(212) 953-2213 .. **DeCastro,** Jose V P '84 -501 5th Av -NY 10017 **Fx:**953-2215
(212) 964-5364 .. **DeCastro,** Steven M '99 -305 Bway -NY 10007
(212) 250-8501 .. **deCastro,** Tomas Rui '95 %Deutsche Bank -60 Wall -NY 10005
(518) 285-8780 .. **DeCataldo,** Kathleen R '89 Perm Jud Comm on Justice for Children -150 State -Albany 12207
(518) 432-3463 .. **DeCataldo,** Robt T '84 %Ct of Claims -Justice Bldg ESP Bx7344 -Albany 12224 **Fx:**432-3450
(212) 836-8000 .. **Decea,** Nanette E '91 %Kaye S LLP -425 Park Av -NY 10022
(914) 285-1400 .. **Decea,** Thos B '86 (Danzig F&D) -1 N Bway -White Plns 10601
(212) 837-6000 .. **DeCecchis,** Erin E '04 %Hughes H&R LLP -1 Bttry Pk Plz -NY 10004
(212) 554-1234 .. **DeCelie,** Kathleen P '95 AXA Financial Inc -1290 Av of Amer -NY 10104 **Fx:**707-3963
(516) 832-7529 .. **DeCerbo,** David '75 (Nixon P LLP) -50 Jericho Quadrangle -Jericho 11753

(212) 282-2570 .. **DeChabert**, Gisele Francoise '94 %Rockefeller Grp -1221 Av of Amer -NY 10020 **Fx:**282-2005
(718) 206-9595 .. **DeChalus**, Henry P '91 -166-01 144th Av -Jamaica 11434 **Fx:**206-0403
(631) 727-6983 .. **DeChance**, Paul M '88 -224 Griffing Av Bx1626 -Rvrhead 11901 **Fx:**727-6990
(212) 425-9600 .. **DeCharles**, Patrick Michl II '93 Cnsl Vanuatu Maritime Svcs Ltd -39 Bway -NY 10006 **Fx:**425-9652
(212) 701-3000 .. **Dechen**, Julie E '08 %Cahill G&R LLP -80 Pine -NY 10005 **Fx:**269-5420
(212) 698-3500 .. **Dechert LLP** -1095 Av of Amer -NY 10036 **Fx:**698-3599
(212) 294-6700 .. **DeChiara**, Dominick P '92 (Winston & S) -200 Park Av -NY 10166
(212) 682-6800 .. **De Chiara**, Michl K '84 (Zetlin & D LLP) -801 2nd Av -NY 10017
(212) 563-4100 .. **DeChiara**, Peter D '89 (Cohen W&S LLP) -330 W 42nd -NY 10036
(914) 834-4400 .. **DeChiaro**, John F '77 -2001 Palmer Av -Larchmnt 10538 **Fx:**834-6064
(212) 735-3000 .. **De Cholnoky**, Eric S '09 %Skadden ASM&F LLP -4 Times Sq -NY 10036
(212) 661-6800 .. **DeCicco**, Alfonso '01 %Cyruli SH&Z LLP -420 Lex Av -NY 10170
(212) 447-1222 .. **DeCicco**, Danl E '09 %DeCicco G&M,PC -14 E 38th -NY 10016
(212) 233-8100 .. **DeCicco**, Fred A '85 (Pollack Pl&D) -225 Bway -NY 10007
(212) 447-1222 .. **DeCicco Gibbons & McNamara,PC** -14 E 38th -NY 10016 **Fx:**689-0153
(516) 248-2234 .. **DeCicco**, Mark J '95 %Sackstein S&L,LLP -1140 Franklin Av -Gdn Cty 11530
(845) 486-3048 .. **DeCicco**, Mary Ellen '97 %Cnty Atty -60 Market -Poughkeepsie 12601 **Fx:**486-2796
(914) 995-3128 .. **DeCicco**, Nicholas S '04 %Cnty Atty -148 Martine Av -White Plns 10601 **Fx:**995-5858
(212) 447-1222 .. **DeCicco**, Philip A '70 (DeCicco G&M,PC) -14 E 38th -NY 10016
(516) 545-5160 .. **DeCicco**, Philip A Jr. '99 %Natl Grid -175 E Old Cntry Rd -Hicksvll 11801 **Fx:**545-5029
(718) 292-7711 .. **DeCicco**, Philip M '79 -184 E 161st -Bronx 10451 **Fx:**292-7712
(718) 531-4098 .. **DeCicco**, Roy C '83 -2221 E 63rd -Brklyn 11234
(914) 793-8055 .. **DeCintio**, Anthony J '88 -60 Winterhill Rd -Tuckahoe 10707
(516) 921-0800 .. **Deciutiis**, James H '01 %Blumenfeld Dvlpmnt Grp,Ltd -300 Robbins Ln -Syosset 11791
(212) 758-0050 .. **DeCiutiis**, Jos C '87 %Title Assoc -825 3rd Av -NY 10022 **Fx:**758-8223
(516) 869-7216 .. **Deck-Abrescia**, Susan M '99 %Kimco Realty Corp -3333 New Hyde Pk Rd -New Hyde Pk 11042 **Fx:**869-7199
(212) 373-3000 .. **Deckelbaum**, Ariel J '99 (Paul WRW&G LLP) -1285 Av of Amer -NY 10019
(718) 438-0786 .. **Deckelbaum**, Yakov '00 -4203 13th Av -Brklyn 11219 **Fx:**436-5237
(212) 757-1120 .. **Decker**, Alan B '59 -250 W 57th -NY 10107 **Fx:**246-5334
(607) 231-5900 .. **Decker**, Alice D '05 %Leg Aid -30 Fayette -Bnghmtn 13901 **Fx:**724-7211
(607) 433-2220 .. **Decker**, Alice D '05 %Leg Aid -Bx887 -Oneonta 13820 **Fx:**433-1433
(718) 448-1070 .. **Decker**, Arnold '86 -390 Manor Rd -Staten Isl 10314 **Fx:**816-6137
(718) 979-4300 .. **Decker**, Arthur W '73 (Decker DD&I,LLP) -1610 Richmond Rd -Staten Isl 10304
(518) 734-4788 .. **Decker**, Benjamin T '07 %SJ Doolan -5428 Main Bx298 -Windham 12496 **Fx:**734-6917
(212) 909-6000 .. **Decker**, Charlotte W '09 %Debevoise & P LLP -919 3rd Av -NY 10022
(914) 682-3300 .. **Decker**, David E '04 %La Sorsa & B -3 Barker Av -White Plns 10601
(718) 979-4300 .. **Decker Decker Dito & Internicola,LLP** -1610 Richmond Rd -Staten Isl 10304 **Fx:**351-3514
(518) 234-2261 .. **Decker**, Frank A '54 -571 Main Bx28 -Cobleskill 12043
(212) 599-1892 .. **Decker Hubbard LLC** -315 Mad Av -NY 10017 **Fx:**599-2956
(718) 969-2400 .. **Decker**, Jerry M '62 -80-30 164th -Jamaica 11432 **Fx:**969-0994
(212) 225-2000 .. **Decker**, Marla A '08 %Cleary GS&H -1 Lbrty Plz -NY 10006
(212) 210-9449 .. **Decker**, Matthew C '10 %Alston & B LLP -90 Park Av -NY 10016
(518) 487-7600 .. **Decker**, Scott T '01 %Whiteman O&H LLP -1 Commerce Plz -Albany 12260
(718) 979-4300 .. **Decker**, Steven T '91 (Decker DD&I,LLP) -1610 Richmond Rd -Staten Isl 10304
(212) 225-2000 .. **Decker**, Suzanne deVries '07 %Cleary GS&H -1 Lbrty Plz -NY 10006
(212) 369-6596 .. **Deckoff**, Marvin J '67 -1060 Park Av -NY 10128
(212) 918-3000 .. **DeClerck**, Russell '99 %Hogan L LLP -875 3rd Av -NY 10022
(212) 340-0400 .. **Declet**, Rafael A Jr. '98 %Appllt Div 1st Dept -27 Mad Av -NY 10010 **Fx:**889-4412
(607) 967-2211 .. **DeClue**, David A '74 -29 N Main -Bainbrdg 13733 **Fx:**967-5342
(917) 280-1760 .. **DeCola**, Patricia B '03 -Bx26 -Orangebrg 10962
(516) 742-6575 .. **Decolator Cohen & DiPrisco,LLP** -1399 Franklin Av -Gdn Cty 11530 **Fx:**742-6706
(516) 578-8212 .. **Decolator**, John V '94 -39 Verbena Av -N Merrick 11566 **Fx:**747-4567
(516) 742-6575 .. **Decolator**, Jos L '86 (Decolator C&D,LLP) -1399 Franklin Av -Gdn Cty 11530
(212) 684-3900 .. **Decolvenaere**, Frank D '79 %Gottlieb R&R,PC -270 Mad Av -NY 10016
(212) 227-5220 .. **Deconinck**, Magda M '86 (Sanders & D LLP) -225 Bway -NY 10007 **Fx:**227-5221
(212) 742-8700 .. **DeCorato**, Linda J '89 (Garson D&C LLP) -110 Wall -NY 10005
(845) 452-3045 .. **deCordova**, Michl '94 -101 New Hcknsck Rd -Poughkeepsie 12603
(212) 306-7170 .. **DeCosta**, Steven C '75 Cnsl Ofc Cllctv Brgn -40 Rector -NY 10006 **Fx:**306-7167
(212) 727-4555 .. **DeCostanzo**, Donna C '97 NRDC -40 W 20th -NY 10011 **Fx:**727-1773
(212) 285-1200 .. **De Coste**, Wm R '01 -132 Nassau -NY 10038
(212) 292-6331 .. **DeCoteau**, Jenelle J '05 Ziff Bros Invstmts -350 Park Av -NY 10022
(518) 408-2552 .. **DeCotis**, Henry A '74 Ofc of Secretary to Gov -State Cptl -Albany 12224
(518) 399-5400 .. **De Coursey**, Eleanor M '84 (Gordon T&D,LLP) -113 Saratoga Rd -Glenvll 12302
(585) 262-6390 .. **DeCoursey**, Jos P '05 %Hamberger & W -1 S Wshngtn -Rchstr 14614
(212) 466-7700 .. **DeCresce**, Christopher J '02 %Sandler O'Neill & Prtnrs,LP -919 3rd Av -NY 10022 **Fx:**466-7998
(212) 888-4702 .. **DeCrescente**, Justin D '98 -444 Mad Av -NY 10022 **Fx:**888-4705
(212) 506-1700 .. **DeCristofaro**, Courtney Ozer '04 %Kasowitz BT&F LLP -1633 Bway -NY 10019
(212) 269-4900 .. **DeCristofaro**, Elizabeth M '84 (Ford MEW&G,LLP) -Wall Street Plz -NY 10005
(315) 472-6000 .. **De Croce**, Alexander M Jr. '88 (A De Croce Jr,PC) -619 W Genesee -Syracuse 13204 **Fx:**472-6215
(315) 682-2563 .. **DeCrow**, Karen '74 -7599 Brown Gulf Rd -Jamesvll 13078
(516) 671-5880 .. **Decsi**, Henry C Jr. '78 -48 Forest Av -Glen Cove 11542 **Fx:**671-5580
(631) 692-0562 .. **DeCurtis**, Peter D '78 -3 Knndy Ln -Cold Spg Hbr 11724
(516) 433-6677 .. **DeCurtis**, Peter M '04 %Stewart GM&B -6800 Jericho Tpk -Syosset 11791
(518) 842-1414 .. **DeCusatis**, Gerard C '95 -178 Clizbe Av -Amsterdam 12010 **Fx:**842-5802
(212) 971-0111 .. **DeCuzzi**, James '84 Zar Realty -384 5th Av -NY 10018
(212) 407-4000 .. **Dede**, Rochelle A '02 %Loeb & L,LLP -345 Park Av -NY 10154
(585) 325-4300 .. **Dedes**, Wm C '78 (Pelton DDD&B) -45 Exchange Blvd -Rchstr 14614 **Fx:**325-6075
(212) 425-2200 .. **De Dios**, Gilbert '01 %Claugus & M -110 Wall -NY 10005
(212) 425-7200 .. **Deditch**, Aaron C '90 Cnsl Kenyon & K,LLP -1 Bway -NY 10004
(516) 728-4979 .. **DeDona-Friedman**, Natalie M '98 -439 Oak Neck Rd -W Islip 11795
(212) 809-1111 .. **DeDonato**, Jos '90 (Morgan MA) -39 Bway -NY 10006
(212) 451-2300 .. **DeDonato**, Michl D '10 %Olshan GFR&W LLP -65 E 55th -NY 10022
(212) 310-8000 .. **Dedyo**, John J '94 (Weil G&M LLP) -767 5th Av -NY 10153
(516) 357-3700 .. **Dee**, Craig Nathan '04 (Cullen and D LLP) -100 Q Roosevelt Blvd -Gdn Cty 11530
(914) 241-7963 .. **Dee**, Harold '74 (H Dee,PC) -401 Crow Hill Rd -Mt Kisco 10549 **Fx:**244-6346
(716) 834-9181 .. **Dee**, John P '64 (Blair & R,LLP) -2645 Sheridan Dr -Tonawanda 14150
(716) 845-7465 .. **Dee**, Julie Ann '84 %Family Ct -1 Niagara Plz -Buffalo 14202 **Fx:**858-6293
(212) 530-1800 .. **Dee**, Mary Jeanette '94 (Richards K&O LLP) -1 World Fncl Ctr -NY 10281
(212) 259-8000 .. **Dee**, Nathan C '08 %Dewey & L LLP -1301 Av of Amer -NY 10019
(212) 227-3550 .. **Dee**, Peter C '08 %Waesche S&O,PC -111 Bway -NY 10006
(212) 758-9300 .. **Dee-Bilka**, Patricia C '88 OfCnsl Lazare P&G LLP -950 3rd Av -NY 10022
(631) 853-4307 .. **Deedy**, Matthew M '91 %Family Ct -400 Carleton Av -Central Islip 11722
(516) 221-8133 .. **Deedy**, Susan Jonides '91 -3280 Sunrise Hwy -Wantagh 11793
(516) 248-1700 .. **Deegan**, Danl P '89 (Forchelli CDSM&T,LLP) -333 Earle Ovngton Blvd -Uniondale 11553
(516) 486-9400 .. **Deegan**, Donald E '57 Deegan & D,LLP -200 Old Cntry Rd -Mineola 11501 **Fx:**486-8680
(631) 923-0230 .. **Deegan**, James V '87 -4 Polly Pl -Huntngtn 11743
(212) 272-4258 .. **Deegan**, John J '96 %JP Morgan Chase -383 Mad Av -NY 10179
(631) 549-0200 .. **Deegan**, Kenneth A '62 -34 Dewey Bx570 -Huntngtn 11743 **Fx:**271-0656
(516) 317-3893 .. **Deegan**, Michl J '93 -8 McKinley Av -Lynbrk 11563
(516) 747-0720 .. **Deegan**, Patricia A '92 %V Mevorah,PC -100 Grdn City Plz -Gdn Cty 11530 **Fx:**742-4106
(516) 248-1700 .. **Deegan Dickson**, Kathleen A '91 (Forchelli CDSM&T,LLP) -333 Earle Ovngton Blvd -Uniondale 11553
(914) 665-0397 .. **Deem**, Michl A '98 -22 W 1st -Mt Vernon 10550
(212) 298-5334 .. **Deenihan**, Gerard M '04 %Leg Aid -49 Thomas -NY 10013 **Fx:**298-5252
(315) 725-2008 .. **Deep**, Norman P '94 -Bx300 -Clinton 13323
(315) 269-1267 .. **Deep**, Paul M '05 -2103 Genesee -Utica 13501
(212) 367-1325 .. **Deere**, Kelly J '93 %GMHC,Inc -119 W 24th -NY 10011 **Fx:**367-1305
(212) 648-1666 .. **Deering**, Abigail Lowe '06 JP Morgan Chase -245 Park Av -NY 10167
(718) 423-1167 .. **Deerson**, Adele S '46 -271-10 Grnd Cntrl Pkwy -Floral Pk 11005
(315) 724-3164 .. **Deery**, Jos S '72 (Kowalczyk TD&H,LLP) -185 Genesee -Utica 13501
(845) 228-7040 .. **DeEsso**, Frank E '91 -41 Joseph Ct -Carmel 10512 **Fx:**228-7041
(646) 414-6976 .. **DeFalco**, Marie T '99 (Lowenstein S PC) -1251 Av of Amer -NY 10020 **Fx:**(973) 597-6181
(845) 298-2000 .. **DeFazio**, Anthony M '98 Vergilis SRD&D,LLP -1136 Route 9 -Wappingers Fls 12590
(716) 636-7600 .. **DeFazio**, John L '02 %HoganWillig -2410 N Forest Rd -Amherst 14068
(607) 722-3495 .. **DeFazio**, Kimberlee N '09 %Aswad & I -46 Front -Bnghmtn 13905
(518) 402-6996 .. **DeFazio**, Maura Spratt '89 OCFS -52 Wshngtn -Rensselaer 12144
(716) 854-2100 .. **DeFazio**, Sheri N '00 %Lewis & L,PC -37 Franklin -Buffalo 14202 **Fx:**854-0433
(212) 768-1000 .. **De Feis**, Nicholas M '84 (De Feis O&R,PC) -500 5th Av -NY 10110
(212) 768-1000 .. **De Feis O'Connell & Rose,PC** -500 5th Av -NY 10110 **Fx:**768-3511
(212) 465-5000 .. **DeFeis**, Thos G '80 %Parsons Brinckerhoff -1 Penn Plz -NY 10119
(212) 401-4239 .. **DeFelice**, James A '00 (Sarno & D LLC) -235 W 23rd -NY 10011
(718) 261-3358 .. **DeFelice**, Jos F '74 -125-10 Qns Blvd -Kew Gdns 11415 **Fx:**793-5072
(212) 868-0939 .. **Defferrire**, Nancy C '00 Immigrants United Fndtn -580 8th Av -NY 10018
(718) 590-2000 .. **DeFilippi**, Danl P '98 %DA -198 E 161st -Bronx 10451 **Fx:**590-6477
(212) 558-4000 .. **Defilippis**, Andrew J '08 %Sullivan & C LLP -125 Broad -NY 10004
(212) 252-0004 .. **DeFilippis**, John P '98 %Carroll M&K LLC -570 Lex Av -NY 10022
(212) 227-4001 .. **DeFilippis**, Peter '89 (P DeFilippis & Assoc) -262 W 38th -NY 10018 **Fx:**227-4124
(607) 734-8175 .. **DeFilippo**, Gerald E '69 %DeFilippo Law Firm,PLLC -250 E Water -Elmira 14901 **Fx:**733-8037
(607) 734-8175 .. **DeFilippo**, James E '00 (DeFilippo Law Firm,PLLC) -250 E Water -Elmira 14901 **Fx:**733-8037
(718) 667-8700 .. **DeFilippo**, Michl J '99 -37 New Dorp Plz N -Staten Isl 10306
(212) 382-3300 .. **DeFilippo**, Paul R '99 (Wollmuth M&D LLP) -500 5th Av -NY 10110

(718) 474-0111 .. **DeFillipo,** Natalie A '95 %Macron & C, PC -257 Beach 116th -Rckwy Pk 11694
(315) 272-2565 .. **DeFina,** Chad D '00 Cnsl Adirondack Bk -185 Genesee -Utica 13501 **Fx:**798-9479
(212) 880-1200 .. **Defina,** Vincent R '77 %Chicago Title/Ticor -711 3rd Av -NY 10017 **Fx:**880-1400
(315) 488-7339 .. **DeFio,** Danl N '99 (DeFio Law Firm,PLLC) -774½ State Fair Blvd -Syracuse 13209 **Fx:**488-7339
(315) 218-8000 .. **DeFio,** Karen V '99 %Bond S&K,PLLC -1 Lincoln Ctr -Syracuse 13202
(718) 361-7290 .. **De Fiore,** Paul P '81 UTOG 2-Way Radio,Inc -25-20 39th Av -LIC 11101
(845) 735-1615 .. **DeFlora,** Jordan B '83 -420 Route 59 -Airmont 10952
(212) 442-0432 .. **DeFoe,** Elizabeth J '07 Admin Children Srvcs -220 Church -NY 10013
(718) 273-6677 .. **DeFonso,** Teresa K '96 %Leg Aid -60 Bay -Staten Isl 10301 **Fx:**442-2679
(212) 326-2000 .. **deFord,** Ryan K '04 Cnsl O'Melveny & M LLP -7 Times Sq -NY 10036
(212) 788-1340 .. **DeFrancesco,** Deanna '09 %Law Dept -100 Church -NY 10007 **Fx:**788-0367
(212) 425-5566 .. **DeFrancesco,** Roxanne '04 %S Shainwald,PC -200 W 57th -NY 10019 **Fx:**608-5863
(212) 456-6921 .. **DeFrancisco,** James C '02 ABC Inc -77 W 66th -NY 10023
(315) 479-9000 .. **DeFrancisco,** Jeff D '00 (DeFrancisco & F) -121 E Water -Syracuse 13202 **Fx:**479-9300
(315) 479-9000 .. **DeFrancisco,** John A '72 (DeFrancisco & F) -121 E Water -Syracuse 13202 **Fx:**479-9300
(212) 849-7000 .. **DeFranco,** Edw J '87 (Quinn EU&S,LLP) -51 Mad Av -NY 10010
(718) 357-6999 .. **DeFranco,** James P Jr. '68 -43-22 193rd -Flushng 11358 **Fx:**357-6999
(518) 209-3673 .. **De Francqueville,** Christian D '06 -174 Wshngtn Av -Albany 12210 **Fx:**514-1174
(718) 590-2000 .. **DeFrank,** Jose '08 %DA -198 E 161st -Bronx 10451 **Fx:**590-6477
(716) 858-2424 .. **DeFranks,** John J '74 %DA -25 Delaware Av -Buffalo 14202 **Fx:**858-7425
(212) 489-1600 .. **DeFreese,** Jeanine Dore '95 %Deloitte LLP -1633 Bway -NY 10019 **Fx:**492-4201
(212) 474-1000 .. **DeFrehn,** Brandon R '07 %Cravath S&M LLP -825 8th Av -NY 10019
(718) 590-2000 .. **DeFreitas,** Anthony E '09 %DA -198 E 161st -Bronx 10451 **Fx:**590-6477
(845) 325-5122 .. **DeFreitas,** Derek '98 -16 Reynolds Rd -Monroe 10950
(716) 633-6500 .. **deFreitas,** Michl A O '86 %W Moran & Assoc,PC -6500 Main -Williamsvll 14221 **Fx:**633-3370
(212) 683-3636 .. **deFreitas,** Paul C '90 (Krass S&S,PC) -419 Park Av S -NY 10016
(212) 809-2700 .. **deFreitas,** Peachetta S '94 %A Kenny -11 Park Pl -NY 10007
(212) 608-6482 .. **Defren,** Joel '72 -7 Dey -NY 10007
(212) 734-4040 .. **de Fritsch,** Carol R '87 -520 E 76th -NY 10021
(212) 801-6817 .. **DeFunis,** Bension D '03 %Greenberg T,LLP -200 Park Av -NY 10166
(718) 286-6000 .. **DeGaetano,** Frank P '88 %DA -125-01 Qns Blvd -Kew Gdns 11415
(212) 935-7100 .. **DeGaetano,** George A '91 -488 Mad Av -NY 10022 **Fx:**935-7125
(516) 622-0686 .. **DeGaetano,** Jos S '94 JS DeGaetano,PLLC -393 Jericho Tpk -Mineola 11501 **Fx:**280-4999
(212) 935-7100 .. **DeGaetano,** Paul J '04 -488 Mad Av -NY 10022 **Fx:**935-7125
(212) 935-7100 .. **DeGaetano,** Peter F '50 -488 Mad Av -NY 10022 **Fx:**935-7125
(845) 339-6733 .. **DeGasperis,** John Arthur '10 %E Schneider -41 Pearl Bx3936 -Kingston 12402 **Fx:**331-2754
(718) 590-7834 .. **Degatano,** Albert J '79 %Hon B Newman -851 Grnd Cncrs -Bronx 10451
(646) 471-2645 .. **DeGaudenzi,** Robt C '95 %PricewaterhouseCoopers LLP -300 Mad Av -NY 10017
(212) 310-8000 .. **Degeest,** Oliver '10 %Weil G&M LLP -767 5th Av -NY 10153
(212) 294-6700 .. **Degen,** Michele H '06 %Winston & S -200 Park Av -NY 10166
(914) 320-3611 .. **Degen,** Robt P '99 RPD Consulting,LLC -Bx383 -Larchmnt 10538 **Fx:**833-2526
(212) 227-4530 .. **Degen,** Ronald D '70 (O'Rourke & D,PLLC) -225 Bway -NY 10007
(718) 250-2000 .. **De Genaro,** Julie C '06 DA -350 Jay -Brklyn 11201 **Fx:**250-2314
(212) 808-2700 .. **Degener,** Carol M '90 OfCnsl Pepper H LLP -620 8th Av -NY 10018
(212) 632-1885 .. **DeGennaro,** Maxence P '02 %Lazard Freres -30 Rckfllr Plz -NY 10112 **Fx:**632-6060
(212) 806-5400 .. **Degenshein,** Dale J '85 SpclCnsl Stroock &S&L LLP -180 Maiden Ln -NY 10038
(212) 261-8000 .. **DeGeorge,** Steven R '96 (Mendes & M,LLP) -750 7th Av -NY 10019
(914) 693-0473 .. **DeGeorge,** Susan G '89 South Presbyterian Church -343 Bway -Dobbs Ferry 10522
(212) 964-6611 .. **DeGeorge,** Victor N '89 %Lester SK&D -120 Bway -NY 10271
(516) 542-1000 .. **DeGeorges,** Jeffrey P '96 (Geisler & G,LLP) -100 Q Roosevelt Blvd -Gdn Cty 11530
(212) 363-6900 .. **DeGeorgio,** Danielle M '00 %Faust GS&B LLP -2 Rector -NY 10006
(212) 450-4000 .. **De Ghenghi,** Luigi L '86 (Davis P&W LLP) -450 Lex Av -NY 10017
(212) 318-3000 .. **DeGiacomo,** Stephanie E '09 %Fulbright & J LLP -666 5th Av -NY 10103
(516) 767-1231 .. **DeGiorgio,** Dina M '93 -551 Port Wshngtn Blvd -Pt Wash 11050
(212) 406-1855 .. **DeGiulio,** Frank P '93 (Palmer B&H) -140 Bway -NY 10005
(914) 949-2700 .. **DeGiuseppe,** Jos Jr. '78 (Bleakley P&S,LLP) -1 N Lex Av -White Plns 10601
(585) 343-3206 .. **Degnan,** Brian P '05 -81 E Main -Batavia 14020 **Fx:**343-4454
(914) 286-3400 .. **Degnan,** Clare J '90 %Leg Aid -1 N Bway -White Plns 10601 **Fx:**682-4112
(607) 698-2089 .. **Degnan,** Edw J '59 -2 Depot Bx25 -Canisteo 14823 **Fx:**698-2911
(716) 852-3600 .. **Degnan,** Kristen B '05 %Chelus HS&M,PC -438 Main -Buffalo 14202
(914) 769-6900 .. **Degnan,** Mary F '81 %Human Rltns Media -41 Kensico Dr -Mt Kisco 10549
(607) 587-8188 .. **Degnan,** Peter J '89 -35 Glen -Alfred 14802 **Fx:**587-9898
(212) 859-8000 .. **de Govia,** Arianne H '02 %Fried FHS&J LLP -1 NY Plz -NY 10004
(212) 766-1406 .. **De Graaf,** Kai Wm '96 -64 Fulton -NY 10038 **Fx:**766-1408
(917) 748-1370 .. **DeGrado,** Paul '97 -861 Manh Av -Brklyn 11222
(518) 462-5300 .. **DeGraff Foy & Kunz LLP** -90 State -Albany 12207 **Fx:**436-0210
(518) 581-3200 .. **DeGraff Foy & Kunz LLP** -47 W Harrison -Saratoga Spgs 12866 **Fx:**581-9435
(518) 429-4200 .. **DeGraff,** Garrett E '78 (Hiscock & B,LLP) -50 Beaver -Albany 12207
(518) 462-5300 .. **DeGraff,** John T Jr. '56 (DeGraff F&K LLP) -90 State -Albany 12207
(212) 278-0400 .. **Degrasse,** Letitia A '09 %Cooper & D LLP -30 Rckfllr Plz -NY 10112
(718) 876-6435 .. **Degree,** Michl K '94 Hon A Giacobbe -355 Front -Staten Isl 10304
(212) 906-1200 .. **DeGregorio,** Alison '00 %Latham & W -885 3rd Av -NY 10022
(212) 656-4166 .. **DeGregorio,** David '89 SrCnsl NYSE Regulation,Inc -20 Broad -NY 10005 **Fx:**656-5200
(212) 906-1200 .. **Degregorio,** Heather M '08 %Latham & W -885 3rd Av -NY 10022
(631) 757-0017 .. **DeGregorio,** Robt E '78 -14 Bob-O-Link Ln -Northprt 11768 **Fx:**757-3333
(718) 994-0229 .. **DeGregorio,** Thos M '92 -3549 Ropes Av -Bronx 10475 **Fx:**(888) 475-5088
DeGregoris, Albert '96 -370 Old Cntry Rd -Gdn Cty 11530 **Fx:**(516) 294-4860
(516) 877-7900 .. **DeGregoris,** Gerard Jr. '80 -145 Willis Av -Mineola 11501 **Fx:**877-7902
(212) 779-9800 .. **De Grim,** Frank E '84 %Luboja & T,LLP -10 E 40th -NY 10016
(718) 876-7311 .. **de Grimston,** Fay M '88 %Supreme Ct -355 Front -Staten Isl 10304
(845) 429-8316 .. **DeGroat,** Chas W '56 -11 W Railroad Av -W Haverstraw 10993
(607) 865-6507 .. **DeGroat,** Michl P '78 -10 Townsend Bx60 -Walton 13856 **Fx:**865-6509
(212) 360-1411 .. **DeGroat,** Pia Y '03 Dept Parks & Rec -1234 5th Av -NY 10029
(212) 314-3836 .. **DeGroote-Striano,** Maryanne '82 %AXA Financial Inc -1290 Av of Amer -NY 10104 **Fx:**707-1897
(718) 823-2000 .. **DeGuardia,** Jos M '90 -991 Morris Park Av -Bronx 10462 **Fx:**823-6330
(347) 495-7554 .. **DeGuerre,** Anthony M '05 (DeGuerre Law Firm,PC) -Bx140038 -Staten Isl 10314 **Fx:**442-3156
(212) 270-7690 .. **De Guzman,** Elizabeth '01 %JP Morgan Chase -277 Park Av -NY 10172
(212) 619-1946 .. **DeGuzman,** Emiliano T '81 (DeGuzman & Assoc) -319 Bway -NY 10007 **Fx:**732-7443
(212) 587-1167 .. **DeGuzman,** Gregorio T '84 -132 Nassau -NY 10038
(212) 610-6300 .. **De Haan,** Brian A '08 %Allen & O -1221 Av of Amer -NY 10020
(631) 582-1200 .. **DeHaan,** John W '95 %DeHaan B LLP -300 Rabro Dr -Hauppauge 11788
(631) 777-3200 .. **Dehan,** Audra E '92 (Spanton & D,LLP) -425 Broad Hollow Rd -Melvll 11747
(516) 393-2200 .. **de Harder,** Wilhelmina A '99 %Garfunkel W,PC -111 Grt Nck Rd -Gt Neck 11021
(516) 357-3000 .. **DeHaven,** George K '82 (Rivkin R LLP) -926 RXR Plz -Uniondale 11556
(212) 608-6500 .. **DeHeng Chen, LLC** -225 Bway -NY 10007 **Fx:**608-9050
(585) 383-1860 .. **Dehm,** Curtis R '82 -3380 Monroe Av -Rchstr 14618
(203) 425-1519 .. **Dehmel,** Paul R '98 %Fox R LLP -100 Park Av -NY 10017 **Fx:**425-9595
(585) 924-3050 .. **Dehmler,** Michl F '97 Christa Constrctn -119 Victor Heights Pkwy -Victor 14564 **Fx:**924-4320
(212) 370-1843 .. **Dehn,** Francis X '85 (SmithDehn LLP) -381 Park Av S -NY 10016
(585) 295-4400 .. **DeHond,** Wayne F '71 (Hiscock & B,LLP) -2000 HSBC Plz -Rchstr 14604
(212) 558-4000 .. **Dehoney,** David R '08 %Sullivan & C LLP -125 Broad -NY 10004
(973) 596-4573 .. **DeHonney,** Melissa C '03 %Gibbons PC -1 Penn Plz -NY 10119 **Fx:**639-6245
(212) 617-2000 .. **De Iasi,** Christina '03 Bloomberg LP -731 Lex Av -NY 10022 **Fx:**728-8111
(212) 415-8600 .. **Deibert,** Karen S '85 OfCnsl Locke LB&L LLP -3 World Fncl Ctr -NY 10281
(516) 338-7200 .. **Deifik,** Mark G '91 -160 Butler -Westbury 11590 **Fx:**338-4342
(212) 994-0260 .. **Deignan,** Edw F S Jr. '92 %Cornicello T&B-C,LLP -2 Wall -NY 10005
(518) 436-0344 .. **Deily,** Jonathan D '75 (Deily M&G,LLP) -8 Thurlow Ter -Albany 12203
(518) 436-0344 .. **Deily Mooney & Glastetter,LLP** -8 Thurlow Ter -Albany 12203 **Fx:**436-8273
(518) 943-6632 .. **Deily,** Robt J '72 (Deily & S) -1 Brdg Bx489 -Catskill 12414 **Fx:**943-1210
(518) 828-4101 .. **Deily,** Wm E '73 -431 Warren -Hudson 12534 **Fx:**828-2230
(212) 415-9200 .. **Deinard,** Lile H '75 (Dorsey & W LLP) -250 Park Av -NY 10177
(718) 250-2000 .. **DeIngeniis,** Alfred '94 %DA -350 Jay -Brklyn 11201 **Fx:**250-2314
(718) 237-8693 .. **Deinhardt,** Barbara C '84 -52 3rd -Brklyn 11231
(914) 696-5555 .. **Delorio,** Patrick V '93 (Delorio Law Firm,LLP) -800 Wstchstr Av -Rye Brook 10573 **Fx:**696-0450
(914) 696-5555 .. **Delorio,** Vincent A '55 (Delorio Law Firm,LLP) -800 Wstchstr Av -Rye Brook 10573 **Fx:**696-0450
(516) 396-3000 .. **Deitch,** David A '86 Rainbow Media Holdings -200 Jericho Quadrangle -Jericho 11753
(212) 293-9400 .. **Deitelzweig,** Craig M '95 %Lawr Ruben Co -600 Mad Av -NY 10022 **Fx:**293-9401
(212) 679-8080 .. **Deitz,** David L '73 (Wohl LSF&D,PC) -9 E 40th -NY 10016
(518) 285-8450 .. **Deitz,** Laura C '06 Hon M Powers -620 State -Schnctdy 12305 **Fx:**393-1610
(212) 838-2288 .. **Deitz,** Roger M '69 Dispute Resolution -477 Mad Av -NY 10022 **Fx:**838-1064
(631) 351-3501 .. **Dejesu,** Jos C '08 %M Cuthbertson -434 NY Av -Huntngtn 11743 **Fx:**614-4314
(718) 622-0085 .. **DeJesus,** Alma '91 -639 Prsdnt -Brklyn 11215 **Fx:**638-3933
(718) 243-6341 .. **DeJesus,** Jason H '96 %Leg Aid -111 Lvngstn -Brklyn 11201 **Fx:**237-8737
(585) 263-2772 .. **DeJohn,** Timothy W '82 -144 Exchange Blvd -Rchstr 14614 **Fx:**263-2776
(212) 504-6000 .. **Dejoie,** Jessy '95 Cadwalader W&T LLP -1 World Fncl Ctr -NY 10281
(631) 724-8833 .. **deJong,** Jeltje '82 (Devitt SB,LLP) -50 Route 111 -Smithtwn 11787
(212) 315-5575 .. **de Jong,** Remko B '99 -200 Park Av S -NY 10003
(516) 294-7900 .. **DeJoseph,** Andrew J '01 -224 7th -Gdn Cty 11530 **Fx:**248-8670

(315) 422-1152 .. **Dejoseph,** Christina F '07 %Costello C&F,PLLC -500 Plum -Syracuse 13204
(212) 626-4100 .. **DeJoy,** Robt W Jr. '81 (Baker & M LLP) -1114 Av of Amer -NY 10036
(718) 817-3111 .. **DeJulio,** Thos E '78 Fordham Univ -441 E Fordham Rd -Bronx 10458
(585) 454-4060 .. **DeJung,** Trilby E '87 %Empire Justice Ctr -1 W Main -Rchstr 14614 **Fx:**454-4019
(212) 836-8000 .. **Deka,** Soumitra '04 %Kaye S LLP -425 Park Av -NY 10022
(516) 542-9300 .. **Dekajlo,** Oleh N '83 -1900 Hempstd Tpk -E Meadow 11554 **Fx:**542-9303
(516) 542-9300 .. **Dekajlo,** Orest T '90 -1900 Hempstd Tpk -E Meadow 11554 **Fx:**542-9303
(212) 331-7676 .. **Dekki,** Amanda D '04 Berdon LLP -360 Mad Av -NY 10017
(212) 871-1790 .. **de Konkoly-Thege,** Michel M '79 LREI -40 Charlton -NY 10014
(212) 259-8000 .. **DeKraker,** Hailey D '10 %Dewey & L LLP -1301 Av of Amer -NY 10019
(212) 373-3000 .. **de la Bastide,** Thos V III '97 (Paul WRW&G LLP) -1285 Av of Amer -NY 10019
(212) 940-3081 .. **de La Chapelle,** Dominique '77 (Nixon P LLP) -437 Mad Av -NY 10022
(212) 759-9080 .. **de la Chapelle,** Philippe '67 %Hill Thompson -437 Mad Av -NY 10022 **Fx:**759-0299
(914) 761-2257 .. **DeLaCruz,** Basil '58 -67 Chadwick Rd -White Plns 10604
(212) 527-1000 .. **DeLaCruz,** Ivette '00 %Jones HC&B PC -1 Bttry Pk Plz -NY 10004
(914) 253-2443 .. **DeLaCruz,** Marjorie '99 %Pepsico -700 Andrsn Hill Rd -Purchase 10577
(212) 713-2293 .. **De La Cruz,** Nelson '09 UBS -1285 Av of Amer -NY 10019
(212) 554-7800 .. **Delacruz,** Walter S '91 OfCnsl Moses & S LLP -405 Lex Av -NY 10174
(212) 867-3456 .. **Delafield Hope & Linker** -311 E 38th -NY 10016 **Fx:**867-3458
(518) 374-7700 .. **De La Fleur,** Brian G '97 -1334 Union -Schnctdy 12308 **Fx:**374-3466
(212) 286-4471 .. **Delagrammatikas,** Harry J '96 SrCnsl McCormick & O,LLP -9 E 40th -NY 10016 **Fx:**504-9574
(212) 225-2000 .. **Delahaye,** Shannon R '09 %Cleary GS&H -1 Lbrty Plz -NY 10006
(212) 455-2000 .. **De La Huerta,** Ignacio '09 %Simpson T&B LLP -425 Lex Av -NY 10017
(716) 853-3801 .. **Delahunt,** Timothy E '98 (Kenney SL&N,LLP) -14 Lafayette Sq -Buffalo 14203
(518) 371-4599 .. **Delain,** Nancy Baum '04 Delain Law Ofc,PLLC -107 N Cllg -Schnctdy 12305 **Fx:**874-5086
(516) 561-4700 .. **De Laire,** Justin M '06 %Kaplon & M -444 Merrick Rd -Lynbrk 11563 **Fx:**872-1185
(212) 661-5030 .. **Delamater,** John O '64 (Schoeman U&K,LLP) -60 E 42nd -NY 10165
(212) 558-4000 .. **DeLaMater,** Robt G '86 (Sullivan & C LLP) -125 Broad -NY 10004
(212) 791-7621 .. **De La Merced,** Gabriel S '92 -30 Vesey -NY 10007
(212) 640-7136 .. **De La Mota,** Marisol '99 AmerEx Corp Srvcs -200 Vesey -NY 10285 **Fx:**(612) 547-2993
(914) 737-4909 .. **De La Mothe,** Cassandra '97 -100 S Bedford Rd -Mt Kisco 10549
(212) 294-6700 .. **Deland,** Alexander T '83 (Winston & S) -200 Park Av -NY 10166
(212) 832-5570 .. **de Landri,** Adria '87 Cnsl Brief C&K,LLP -805 3rd Av -NY 10022
(845) 896-1106 .. **DeLane-Gurley,** Mia C '05 %L Geraci,PC -21 Old Main -Fishkill 12524 **Fx:**896-1107
(212) 373-3000 .. **Delaney,** Aaron S '05 %Paul WRW&G LLP -1285 Av of Amer -NY 10019
(631) 852-2379 .. **Delaney,** Barbara '82 %Supreme Ct -Center Dr S -Rvrhead 11901 **Fx:**852-2020
(212) 335-4500 .. **Delaney,** Corey E '06 %DLA Piper LLP -1251 Av of Amer -NY 10020
(212) 907-0700 .. **Delaney,** Donald P '02 %Labaton S LLP -140 Bway -NY 10005
(212) 310-8000 .. **Delaney,** Edwin M '04 %Weil G&M LLP -767 5th Av -NY 10153
(914) 244-0029 .. **Delaney,** George T '58 OfCnsl Quaranta & Assoc -121 Smith Av -Mt Kisco 10549 **Fx:**244-0031
(212) 837-6000 .. **Delaney,** James F '85 Cnsl Hughes H&R LLP -1 Bttry Pk Plz -NY 10004
(212) 571-7100 .. **Delaney,** James P '97 %O'Dwyer & B,LLP -52 Duane -NY 10007
(212) 858-1000 .. **Delaney,** Jeffrey J '93 (Pillsbury WSP LLP) -1540 Bway -NY 10036
(716) 675-7495 .. **Delaney,** Jerome P '72 -44 Carmolite Dr -W Seneca 14224
(212) 335-9000 .. **Delaney,** Joan C '92 %DA -1 Hogan Pl -NY 10013
(212) 556-5600 .. **De Laney,** John B '94 %ICM -825 8th Av -NY 10019 **Fx:**556-5665
(212) 468-8000 .. **Delaney,** John F '94 (Morrison & F LLP) -1290 Av of Amer -NY 10104
(315) 476-8450 .. **DeLaney,** John M '72 (DeLaney & O,LLP) -1 Lincoln Ctr -Syracuse 13202
(212) 225-2000 .. **Delaney,** John R '08 %Cleary GS&H -1 Lbrty Plz -NY 10006
(315) 471-3151 .. **DeLaney,** Karin Sloan '96 OfCnsl Hancock & E,LLP -1500 AXA Twr I Bx4976 -Syracuse 13221
(585) 385-6666 .. **Delaney,** Kelee L '00 Paychex Inc -911 Panorama Trl S -Rchstr 14625
(518) 474-1310 .. **Delaney,** Kerry Ann '05 %Gov's Cnsls Ofc -242 State Cptl -Albany 12224
(516) 663-2202 .. **Delaney,** Martin J '84 -15 Russell Rd -Gdn Cty 11530
(212) 479-6000 .. **De Laney,** Mary Kathleen '06 %Cooley LLP -1114 Av of Amer -NY 10036
(212) 483-9490 .. **Delaney,** Michl C '99 %McElroy DM&C,LLP -88 Pine -NY 10005
(518) 456-0271 .. **Delaney,** Michl P '90 -465 New Karner Rd -Albany 12205 **Fx:**862-7185
(914) 683-1112 .. **Delaney,** Montgomery J '98 (Laub D,LLP) -3 Barker Av -White Plns 10601 **Fx:**683-8903
(212) 696-6000 .. **Delaney,** Nancy E '89 (Curtis M-PC&M LLP) -101 Park Av -NY 10178
(315) 476-8450 .. **DeLaney & O'Connor,LLP** -1 Lincoln Ctr -Syracuse 13202 **Fx:**476-8730
(631) 863-0877 .. **Delaney,** Patricia C '86 -100 Motor Pkwy -Hauppauge 11788 **Fx:**863-0879
(212) 450-4000 .. **Delaney,** Patrick X '10 %Davis P&W LLP -450 Lex Av -NY 10017
(212) 420-8541 .. **Delaney,** Paul F '91 -530 E 23rd -NY 10010
(716) 566-5400 .. **Delaney,** Sarah J '00 %Goldberg S LLP -665 Main -Buffalo 14203
(516) 775-7007 .. **Delaney,** Shane '99 (Gutman MB&S,PC) -813 Jericho Tpk -New Hyde Pk 11040
(518) 489-0903 .. **Delaney,** Wm J '00 -14 Home Av -Albany 12208 **Fx:**489-0903
(607) 733-7798 .. **DeLaney,** Wm R '61 -915 Upland Dr -Elmira 14905
(212) 229-1516 .. **Delanney,** Bertrand J '79 (Buttermore ND&F,LLP) -111 Bway -NY 10006
(212) 229-1516 .. **Delanney,** Susana '77 (Buttermore ND&F,LLP) -111 Bway -NY 10006
(212) 735-3000 .. **Delano,** Cindy Chen '05 %Skadden ASM&F LLP -4 Times Sq -NY 10036
(212) 728-8000 .. **Delanoy,** Laura Lee '01 (Willkie F&G LLP) -787 7th Av -NY 10019
(212) 661-2490 .. **Delany,** John J III '00 (Delany & O) -80 Broad -NY 10004
(516) 365-6357 .. **Delany,** John M '67 AFPD -1 Hllw Ln -New Hyde Pk 11042
(914) 591-5969 .. **Delany,** Logan D Jr. '75 %Delany Cptl Mngmnt -41 N Bway -Irvngtn 10533 **Fx:**591-7783
(212) 661-2490 .. **Delany & O'Brien** -80 Broad -NY 10004 **Fx:**661-2491
(212) 219-1800 .. **Delany,** Sean '81 %Lawyers Alliance NY -171 Mad Av -NY 10016 **Fx:**941-7458
(212) 837-6000 .. **Delany,** Teresa A '93 %Hughes H&R LLP -1 Bttry Pk Plz -NY 10004
(212) 803-5100 .. **DeLaPava,** Sergio R '96 %NY Cnty Defender Srvcs -225 Bway -NY 10007 **Fx:**571-6035
(212) 709-8315 .. **Delapava,** Susanna Forsythe '96 -110 Wall -NY 10005
(212) 768-6700 .. **Delarck,** Yuta N '07 %Sonnenschein N&R LLP -2 World Fncl Ctr -NY 10281
(212) 918-3000 .. **DeLarco,** Michl E '01 %Hogan L LLP -875 3rd Av -NY 10022
(212) 626-4100 .. **de Lasa,** Jose M '73 OfCnsl Baker & M LLP -1114 Av of Amer -NY 10036
(212) 941-9090 .. **DeLaTorre,** Monica '95 %The Door -121 Av of Amer -NY 10013 **Fx:**941-0714
(212) 354-6300 .. **DeLaurentis,** Brian M '94 (B DeLaurentis,PC) -36 W 44th -NY 10036 **Fx:**764-6795
(718) 979-3293 .. **Delauro,** James M '87 -430 Adams Av -Staten Isl 10306
(585) 753-1000 .. **DeLaus,** Danl M Jr. '88 Cnty Executive -39 W Main -Rchstr 14614 **Fx:**753-1014
(212) 353-2200 .. **de la Vega,** Fredk C '97 (Turkel F&D LLP) -304 Park Av S -NY 10010
(212) 883-1700 .. **DeLay,** Robt R '09 %Duval & S LLP -101 Park Av -NY 10178
(212) 966-2049 .. **Delbaum,** David S '83 -100 Lafayette -NY 10013 **Fx:**941-9183
(212) 848-4000 .. **Delbaum,** Jessica Kornhauser '02 %Shearman & S LLP -599 Lex Av -NY 10022
(914) 681-0200 .. **DelBello,** Alfred B '60 (DelBello DWW&W,LLP) -1 N Lex Av -White Plns 10601
(914) 681-0200 .. **DelBello Donnellan Weingarten Wise & Wiederkehr,LLP** -1 N Lex Av -White Plns 10601 **Fx:**684-0288
(914) 271-9560 .. **Del Bianco,** Jane '80 -12 Wolf Rd -Croton-On-Hud 10520
(315) 798-5299 .. **Del Buono,** Carl '58 Hon M Dwyer -200 Elizabeth -Utica 13501
(718) 464-4448 .. **DelCarmen,** Tamara Lopez '05 (DelCarmen & M,PC) -8787 F Lewis Blvd -Qns Vllg 11427
(516) 741-6565 .. **Del Casino,** Anne J '78 OfCnsl Meyer SE&K,PC -990 Stewart Av Bx9194 -Gdn Cty 11530
(212) 546-4313 .. **DelCastillo,** Maria L '04 Bristol-Myers Squibb -345 Park Av -NY 10154
(212) 839-5300 .. **Del Chiaro,** Gina M '06 %Sidley A LLP -787 7th Av -NY 10019
(631) 271-4684 .. **Delcol,** Robt J '91 -1038 W Jericho Tpk -Smithtwn 11787 **Fx:**629-4583
(646) 733-3100 .. **DelColliano,** Jean M '04 US Customs & Border Protection -One Penn Plz -NY 10119
(315) 343-9116 .. **DelConte,** Scott J '99 (Bond S&K,PLLC) -130 E 2nd -Oswego 13126
(518) 648-5457 .. **Delcore,** Colleen E '95 -1 W Main Bx273 -Indian Lk 12842 **Fx:**(619) 789-6556
(212) 709-8129 .. **Del Duca,** Anthony J '88 -110 Wall -NY 10005 **Fx:**(732) 909-2626
(212) 530-5000 .. **DelDuca,** Erika N '04 %Milbank TH&M LLP -1 Chase Manh Plz -NY 10005
(315) 422-2763 .. **DelDuchetto,** Ernest A '78 (DelDuchetto & P) -1 Lincoln Ctr -Syracuse 13202
(315) 422-2763 .. **DelDuchetto & Potter** -1 Lincoln Ctr -Syracuse 13202 **Fx:**476-8730
(212) 558-4000 .. **De Leeuw,** Marc '93 (Sullivan & C LLP) -125 Broad -NY 10004
(212) 859-8000 .. **deLeeuw,** Michl B '97 (Fried FHS&J LLP) -1 NY Plz -NY 10004
(518) 481-1544 .. **Delehanty,** John D '77 %DA -Ct Hse -Malone 12953 **Fx:**481-1545
(518) 359-9191 .. **Delehanty,** John D '77 -56 Lake -Tupper Lk 12986 **Fx:**359-7311
(212) 935-3000 .. **Delehanty,** John M '71 (Mintz LCFG&P,PC) -666 3rd Av -NY 10017
(212) 818-9200 .. **Delehanty,** Michl S '08 %Satterlee SB&B LLP -230 Park Av -NY 10169
(585) 265-9144 .. **Deleo,** Dennis M '67 -524 Webster Rd -Webster 14580 **Fx:**265-1415
(212) 510-0153 .. **DeLeo,** Jos M '91 Great Amer Ins Co -65 Bway -NY 10006
(212) 351-0079 .. **DeLeo,** Thos J '85 Sithe Energies -245 Park Av -NY 10167
(212) 336-0954 .. **DeLeo,** Vincenzo A '99 %SEC -3 World Fncl Ctr -NY 10281 **Fx:**336-1323
(212) 747-0200 .. **DeLeon,** Edgar '98 (DeLeon & Assoc,PLLC) -26 Bway -NY 10004 **Fx:**747-0202
(212) 416-8000 .. **De Leon,** Elizabeth '06 %Dept of Law -120 Bway -NY 10271
(718) 590-2000 .. **DeLeon,** Julie C '96 %DA -198 E 161st -Bronx 10451 **Fx:**590-6477
(516) 621-0222 .. **DeLeon,** Julie R '04 GosmanLaw PC -55 Bryant Av -Roslyn 11576 **Fx:**621-3322
(212) 250-4913 .. **DeLeon,** Keith B '93 %Deutsche Bank -60 Wall -NY 10005
(212) 969-1335 .. **De Leon,** Robt S '91 Alliance Bernstein LP -1345 Av of Amer -NY 10105 **Fx:**554-4639
(212) 692-1000 .. **De Leon,** Rowena J A '08 %Duane M LLP -1540 Bway -NY 10036
(516) 873-9696 .. **DeLeonardis,** John C '54 -11 Laurel Dr -Mineola 11501 **Fx:**873-3993
(518) 456-0082 .. **DeLeonardis,** Vincent J '02 %Bailey K&J,PC -5 Pine West Plz -Albany 12205 **Fx:**456-4767
(212) 558-4000 .. **DeLeonardo,** Jennifer M '06 %Sullivan & C LLP -125 Broad -NY 10004
(212) 768-6700 .. **Delfin,** Benito '04 %Sonnenschein N&R LLP -1221 Av of Amer -NY 10020
(212) 916-7800 .. **Delfino,** Brett D '96 Rabobank Nederland -245 Park Av -NY 10167
(516) 357-3700 .. **Delfino,** Jos D '04 %Cullen and D LLP -100 Q Roosevelt Blvd -Gdn Cty 11530
(212) 832-2797 .. **Delforte,** Matthew J '99 (Shebitz B&C,PC) -1325 Av of Amer -NY 10019

(212) 513-3200 ..**DelFranco,** Randolph A '90 (Holland & K LLP) -31 W 52nd -NY 10019
(718) 250-2000 ..**Delfyett,** Karen M '07 %DA -350 Jay -Brklyn 11201 **Fx:**250-2314
(516) 683-0200 ..**Del Gadio,** Robt G '68 -90 Merrick Av -E Meadow 11554 **Fx:**683-0246
(914) 684-1700 ..**Delgado,** Anita '92 (Delgado & D) -300 Martine Av -White Plns 10601 **Fx:**684-1701
(718) 999-2365 ..**Delgado,** Belinda '03 NYFD -9 Metrotech Ctr -Brklyn 11201
(212) 252-9550 ..**Delgado,** Gamaliel B '07 %Freiberg & P -49 W 37th -NY 10018
(212) 786-8240 ..**Delgado,** Glenn '95 Virgin Records Amer,Inc -150 5th Av -NY 10011
(914) 684-1700 ..**Delgado,** Lorenzo F '92 (Delgado & D) -300 Martine Av -White Plns 10601 **Fx:**684-1701
(212) 391-7755 ..**Delgado,** Michelle M '94 (MM Delgado,PC) -555 Mad Av -NY 10022 **Fx:**391-7732
(631) 630-2273 ..**Delgado,** Patrick A '96 -150 Motor Pkwy -Hauppauge 11788 **Fx:**630-9411
(518) 785-1900 ..**Delgado,** Renee L '07 %PEF -1168-70 Troy-Schnctdy Rd Bx12414 -Albany 12212 **Fx:**785-1323
(914) 323-7000 ..**Del Gatto,** Brian T '88 (Wilson EME&D LLP) -3 Gannett Dr -White Plns 10604
(845) 592-7000 ..**Del Gaudio,** Laura M '09 %Donoghue TA&D LLP -2517 Route 52 -Hopewell Junct 12533
(516) 628-2775 ..**Del Giacco,** Jos C R '75 -25 Bayvll Pk Blvd -Bayvll 11709 **Fx:**628-2125
(516) 571-3800 ..**DelGiorno,** Lauren '03 DA -262 Old Cntry Rd -Mineola 11501 **Fx:**248-9479
(516) 393-2200 ..**DelGiorno,** Robt A '03 %Garfunkel W,PC -111 Grt Nck Rd -Gt Neck 11021
(212) 504-6000 ..**Del Giudice,** Anthony J '08 %Cadwalader W&T LLP -1 World Fncl Ctr -NY 10281
(212) 688-5310 ..**DelGreco,** Phylliss Ann '92 %DelGreco & Co -232 E 59th -NY 10022 **Fx:**688-5207
(516) 484-5230 ..**Del Greco,** Vincent J '59 -14 E Horseshoe Dr -Roslyn Hts 11577 **Fx:**484-5230
(716) 855-5715 ..**Delgross,** Barbara J '78 %L Ogden -60 Lakefront Blvd -Buffalo 14202 **Fx:**855-5755
(212) 949-5800 ..**DelGrosso,** John E '99 %Brady K&W,LLP -501 5th Av -NY 10017
(516) 294-3554 ..**Del Grosso,** Robt G '80 -114 Old Cntry Rd -Mineola 11501 **Fx:**741-0912
(646) 833-0900 ..**Delhagen,** Michl R '96 (Tressler LLP) -One Penn Plz -NY 10119
(212) 450-4000 ..**Delia,** Andrew M '08 %Davis P&W LLP -450 Lex Av -NY 10017
(516) 655-1265 ..**D'Elia,** Anne J '97 -125-10 Qns Blvd -Kew Gdns 11415 **Fx:**829-7122
(315) 422-1391 ..**D'Elia,** Anthony J '96 %Green & S,PLLC -One Lincoln Ctr #900 -Syracuse 13202
(212) 406-9686 ..**D'Elia,** Edmund P '59 (E D'Elia,PC) -120 Bway -NY 10271 **Fx:**406-9688
(646) 888-4040 ..**D'Elia,** Elizabeth M '94 %Sloan-Kettering -1275 York Av -NY 10065 **Fx:**888-4047
(516) 944-3838 ..**D'Elia,** Frank A '59 -33 Main -Pt Wash 11050 **Fx:**944-3017
(631) 673-3222 ..**D'Elia,** Jos '78 -464 NY Av -Huntngtn 11743 **Fx:**673-4958
(212) 692-1000 ..**D'Elia,** Justin J '06 %Duane M LLP -1540 Bway -NY 10036
(516) 746-4545 ..**De Lia,** Lesley M '80 %MHLS -170 Old Cntry Rd -Mineola 11501 **Fx:**746-4372
(201) 656-6503 ..**D'Elia,** Vincent J '75 -4901 H Hdsn Pkwy -Bronx 10471
(718) 615-0044 ..**Delianites,** Dean G '92 %Lozner & M -1901 Emmons Av -Brklyn 11235
(212) 486-9494 ..**D'Elia-Wilson,** Robin E '85 -488 Mad Av -NY 10022 **Fx:**486-0701
(914) 337-8080 ..**Delicata,** Alfred A Jr. '94 -484 Wht Plns Rd -Eastchstr 10709 **Fx:**337-3936
(212) 701-3000 ..**Delich-Gould,** Stacey '06 %Cahill G&R LLP -80 Pine -NY 10005 **Fx:**269-5420
(212) 506-1700 ..**D'Elicio,** James E '01 Kasowitz BT&F LLP -1633 Bway -NY 10019
(212) 506-5000 ..**Delikat,** Michl '78 (Orrick H&S LLP) -51 W 52nd -NY 10019
(845) 294-7287 ..**Delile-Abbatine,** Tammy A '88 %MHLS -5 Coates Dr -Goshen 10924 **Fx:**294-6389
(516) 496-5822 ..**DeLillo,** Denise '05 %T Spina -170 Froehlich Farm Blvd -Woodbury 11797 **Fx:**496-5420
(718) 448-2800 ..**DeLillo,** Diane L '93 %Richmond Cnty Savings Bk -1214 Castleton Av -Staten Isl 10310
(212) 971-0111 ..**DeLillo,** Lorenzo V '00 Sapir Org -384 5th Av -NY 10018
(212) 559-6500 ..**DeLillo,** Vivian Pablo '99 %Citigroup Trust -485 Lex Av -NY 10017
(212) 298-5389 ..**Delince,** Christine '07 Leg Aid -49 Thomas -NY 10013
(212) 710-9512 ..**DeLince,** J Patrick '90 DeLince Law PLLC -44 Wall -NY 10005 **Fx:**710-9513
(914) 681-6200 ..**Delince,** Karen '89 NYPA -123 Main -White Plns 10601 **Fx:**390-8038
(212) 363-6900 ..**De Lindsay,** Lisa '02 %Faust GS&B LLP -2 Rector -NY 10006
(914) 241-8900 ..**Delio,** Suzanne Crocifissa '05 Professional Indemnity Agency -37 Radio Circle Dr Bx5000 -Mt Kisco 10549 **Fx:**241-8098
(212) 349-7511 ..**Delio,** Toni Ann '06 %CM Evall,PC -291 Bway -NY 10007
(516) 378-1700 ..**DeLisa,** Lynn H '88 %Chesney & M -2305 Grand Av -Baldwin 11510
(914) 925-1885 ..**D'Elisa,** Thos J '99 Tremont Capital Mgmt -555 Theo Fremd Av -Rye 10580
(973) 228-5700 ..**DeLisi,** Paul M '92 Cnsl Brach E LLC -100 Park Av -NY 10017 **Fx:**228-7852
(631) 370-1177 ..**Delisle,** Christopher J '02 (Puleo D,LLC) -444 Route 111 -Smithtwn 11787 **Fx:**370-1222
(518) 393-2232 ..**Delisle,** Gary P '79 -836 Plymouth Av -Schnctdy 12308 **Fx:**370-3840
(718) 238-3100 ..**Deliso,** Jos A '86 -8004 5th Av -Brklyn 11209 **Fx:**238-3122
(917) 495-8687 ..**Delisser,** Trina E '04 T Delisser PC -168 Park Av -Mt Vernon 10550 **Fx:**(201) 608-7770
(914) 738-5992 ..**DeLitta,** Laurieanne '01 %CH Greene & Assoc -145 Huguenot -New Rchll 10801 **Fx:**738-7197
(212) 684-8282 ..**De Little,** Letti E B '01 %Maxwell-Kates, Inc -9 E 38th -NY 10016
(212) 773-3885 ..**DeLitto,** Sylvester R '92 Ernst & Young LLP -5 Times Sq -NY 10036
(516) 248-3510 ..**Deliyannis,** Theo '85 (Sharit & D) -1 Old Cntry Rd -Carle Pl 11514
(718) 390-8645 ..**DeLizzo,** Peter F '96 Supreme Ct-Special Ref -366 Front -Staten Isl 10304
(212) 547-5400 ..**Del Juidice,** Louis J '02 (McDermott W&E LLP) -340 Mad Av -NY 10173
(914) 642-6519 ..**Delk,** Rodham T III '09 IBM -1133 Wstchstr Av -White Plns 10604
(518) 862-5555 ..**Dell,** Alex C '95 -450 New Karner Rd -Albany 12205 **Fx:**862-5545
(212) 682-2280 ..**Dell,** Carol Giuliano '02 (Holm & O LLP) -3 W 35th -NY 10001
(732) 855-6068 ..**Dell,** Elizabeth Connolly '85 %Wilentz G&S -110 William -NY 10038 **Fx:**726-6687
(212) 490-3000 ..**Dell,** Gregory J '01 (Wilson EME&D LLP) -150 E 42nd -NY 10017
(212) 661-1100 ..**Dell,** Jessica N '10 Pomerantz HG&G LLP -100 Park Av -NY 10017
(631) 913-4444 ..**Dell,** Jos G '92 (Dell LT&V LLP) -5 Orvll Dr -Bohemia 11716
(518) 283-3546 ..**Dell,** Kathryn S '92 -298 N Greenbush Rd -Troy 12180 **Fx:**283-4709
(212) 416-8646 ..**Dell,** Lisa R '82 %Dept of Law -120 Bway -NY 10271
(631) 913-4444 ..**Dell Little Trovato & Vecere LLP** -5 Orvll Dr -Bohemia 11716 **Fx:**913-7777
(212) 715-9100 ..**Dell,** Michl J '79 (Kramer LN&F,LLP) -1177 Av of Amer -NY 10036
(716) 362-1156 ..**Dell,** Paul G '94 -70 Niagara -Buffalo 14202 **Fx:**362-1156
(212) 440-2350 ..**Dell,** Richd '75 %C Siegel -40 Wall -NY 10005 **Fx:**440-2385
(516) 812-4500 ..**DellaChiesa,** Jacqueline M '02 %Stagg TC&W LLP -401 Franklin Av -Gdn Cty 11530
(845) 225-1382 ..**Della Cioppa,** Alfred '82 (Della Cioppa & B) -64 Gleneida Av -Carmel 10512 **Fx:**225-1385
(631) 231-1450 ..**Dellacona,** Candace '03 %Feldman K&M,PC -330 Vndrblt Motor Pkwy -Hauppauge 11788
(212) 446-4800 ..**Della Monica,** Armand A '98 (Kirkland & E LLP) -153 E 53rd -NY 10022
(516) 746-8000 ..**Dell'Amore,** Frank C '06 %Jaspan S LLP -300 Grdn City Plz -Gdn Cty 11530
(516) 921-8600 ..**Dell'Amore,** Rachel N '07 %McAndrew C&P -95 Froehlich Farm Blvd -Woodbury 11797
(718) 405-1500 ..**Della Mura,** Peter '99 (Della Mura & C LLP) -981 Allerton Av -Bronx 10469 **Fx:**405-2500
(212) 490-3000 ..**Dell'Anno,** Nicholas W '09 %Wilson EME&D LLP -150 E 42nd -NY 10017
(607) 797-4330 ..**Dellapenna,** Thos J Jr. '95 %Dellapenna Bros,Inc -86 Olive -Johnson Cty 13790 **Fx:**797-1377
(212) 355-8555 ..**Della Pietra,** Christopher V '93 (Potters & D LLP) -546 5th Av -NY 10036
(718) 459-8605 ..**Della Porta,** Edmond A '47 -88-47 74th Av -Glendale 11385 **Fx:**275-6743
(518) 457-2070 ..**Della Porta,** James J '80 %Dept of Tax & Fin -Bldg 9 State Campus -Albany 12227 **Fx:**457-6131
(212) 692-1000 ..**Dellaportas,** John '95 (Duane M LLP) -1540 Bway -NY 10036
(716) 532-2284 ..**Della Posta,** Frank P '57 (Kysor & D) -95 W Main Bx 270 -Gowanda 14070
(716) 856-1636 ..**Della Posta,** Mark P '84 (Walsh R&G) -14 Lafayette Sq -Buffalo 14203
(718) 579-7900 ..**Dellaquila,** Mark A '09 Leg Aid -900 Sheridan Av -Bronx 10451 **Fx:**293-8744
(516) 694-3650 ..**DellAquila,** Thos Jr. '87 -219 Birch Av -Farmngdl 11735
(516) 621-2676 ..**Della Ratta,** Andrew F J '96 -80 Glen Cove Rd -Greenvale 11548
(518) 372-5467 ..**Della Ratta,** John A '96 %Della Ratta Law Ofc -147 Barrett -Schnctdy 12305 **Fx:**381-4109
(516) 621-2676 ..**Della Ratta,** John P '59 -80 Glen Cove Rd -Greenvale 11548
(516) 621-2676 ..**Della Ratta,** John P Jr. '90 -11 Mtn Cut -Manhsst 11030
(516) 621-2676 ..**Della Ratta,** John P Jr. '90 -80 Glen Cove Rd -Greenvale 11548
(518) 372-5467 ..**Della Ratta,** Richd G '61 -147 Barrett -Schnctdy 12305 **Fx:**381-4109
(516) 764-2983 ..**Della Rocca,** James E '99 CSEA Inc -3 Garet Pl -Commack 11725
(212) 351-1600 ..**Della Rocca,** Steven '98 Vestar Capital Prtnrs -245 Park Av -NY 10167
(212) 430-6341 ..**Della Salla,** Annette Marie '02 (A Della Salla,PLLC) -65 Bway -NY 10006 **Fx:**430-6342
(631) 737-4110 ..**Della Universita,** Michl L '06 %Gruenberg & K,PC -3275 Vets Mem'l Hwy -Ronkonkoma 11779 **Fx:**737-4155
(212) 969-3000 ..**Dellaverson,** Gary J '80 SpclCnsl Proskauer R LLP -1585 Bway -NY 10036
(212) 973-9797 ..**Dellay,** Patrick J '90 (Saretsky KD&G,LLP) -475 Park Av S -NY 10016
(516) 539-0055 ..**Delle,** Paul R '88 -1225 Franklin Av -Gdn Cty 11530 **Fx:**485-2968
(718) 872-0533 ..**Delle Donne,** Frank A '94 SpclCnsl Monaco & M,LLP -7610 13th Av -Brklyn 11228 **Fx:**872-0536
(518) 828-3079 ..**Dellehunt,** David A '87 %Supreme Ct -401 Union -Hudson 12534 **Fx:**828-5534
(518) 473-1403 ..**Dellenbaugh,** Holly T M '99 %Dept of Health -Corning Twr 24th Fl -Albany 12237 **Fx:**473-2019
(212) 552-2670 ..**Deller,** Lindsay B '02 JP Morgan Chase -1 Chase Manh Plz -NY 10081
(212) 577-3688 ..**Dellheim,** Jeffrey I '83 %Leg Aid -199 Water -NY 10038 **Fx:**509-8431
(914) 381-6700 ..**Delli Carpini,** Angelo '98 %Judicial Title Ins -800 Wstchstr Av -Rye Brook 10573
(631) 242-1600 ..**DelliCarpini,** John M '74 (Kujawski & D) -1637 Deer Prk Av -Deer Pk 11729
(845) 638-5001 ..**Dellicarri,** Anthony R '82 %DA -1 S Main -New Cty 10956 **Fx:**638-5070
(212) 244-4890 ..**Dellicato,** Wm M '96 -303 5th Av -NY 10016 **Fx:**629-9656
(914) 766-4403 ..**Delligatti,** Stephen '90 IBM -Route 100 -Somers 10589
(585) 454-4060 ..**Dellinger,** Peter O '83 %Empire Justice Ctr -1 W Main -Rchstr 14614 **Fx:**454-4019
(516) 572-2000 ..**Dellinger,** Stephanie L '09 %DA -99 Main -Hempstd 11550 **Fx:**572-2606
(718) 984-5064 ..**Delli Paoli,** Edw '71 -129 New Dorp Plz -Staten Isl 10306 **Fx:**966-5679
(212) 591-7158 ..**Delli Venneri,** John '86 ASME -3 Park Av -NY 10016
(718) 923-2993 ..**Delloff,** Robt J '90 OTDA Fair Hearings -14 Boerum Pl -Brklyn 11201
(631) 844-9611 ..**Dello-Iacono,** John D '06 %Shapiro D&B,LLP -105 Maxness Rd -Melvll 11747
(212) 776-5042 ..**Dell'Olio,** Andrew J '94 NYC Housing Auth -250 Bway -NY 10007 **Fx:**776-5215
(212) 341-6400 ..**Dell'Orto,** Melissa A '04 %Liquidation Bur -123 William -NY 10038 **Fx:**608-3398

(516) 944-4583 .. **Dellutri,** Eric J '05 Cedar Shopping Ctr,Inc -44 S Bayles Av -Pt Wash 11050
(212) 902-1806 .. **Delman,** Alexandra L '97 %Goldman Sachs -1 NY Plz -NY 10004
(646) 471-4000 .. **Delman,** Mary T Defesi '98 %PricewaterhouseCoopers LLP -300 Mad Av -NY 10017
(718) 442-6364 .. **Delman,** Norman '60 -402 St Marks Pl -Staten Isl 10301 **Fx:**448-3751
(718) 852-8770 .. **Delman,** Peter S '88 (P Delman,PC) -26 Court -Brklyn 11242 **Fx:**852-8846
(212) 279-9500 .. **Delman,** Stephen B '68 -515 Mad Av -NY 10022 **Fx:**279-9595
(917) 412-1261 .. **Delmar,** John D H '79 -630 5th Av -NY 10111 **Fx:**(212) 832-4185
(212) 326-3939 .. **Del Medico,** Jennifer L '06 %Jones D -222 E 41st -NY 10017
(212) 446-4800 .. **DelMonaco,** John P '05 %Kirkland & E LLP -153 E 53rd -NY 10022
(212) 785-2929 .. **Delmond,** Robt S '89 %Conway FC&K,PC -48 Wall -NY 10005
(212) 670-0377 .. **DelMonico,** Jill M '01 Merrill Lynch -222 Bway -NY 10038
(718) 643-1400 .. **Delmont,** Andre M '92 (A Delmont,PC) -26 Court -Brklyn 11242 **Fx:**643-0100
(716) 853-1616 .. **Delmont,** Phillip A '97 (Harter S&E LLP) -12 Fountain Plz -Buffalo 14202
(716) 282-4511 .. **Del Monte,** John J '80 -2706 Pine Av Bx2146NMS -Niagara Fls 14301 **Fx:**285-8279
(914) 681-5108 .. **Del Negro,** Arthur L Jr. '62 -175 Main -White Plns 10601 **Fx:**761-1246
(212) 310-8000 .. **Del Nido,** Erika R '10 %Weil G&M LLP -767 5th Av -NY 10153
(888) 733-5299 .. **DeLoach,** Stacey Peck '03 %Redlich Law Firm -255 Washington Av Ext -Albany 12205 **Fx:**(518) 862-1551
(607) 277-6500 .. **DeLoache,** Abigail L '98 -122 W Court -Ithaca 14850 **Fx:**277-6500
(914) 843-8677 .. **DeLoe,** Ronna L '80 -933 Mamaroneck Av -Mamaroneck 10543
(914) 995-3460 .. **Delohery,** Michl A '88 %DA -111 Martin Luther King Blvd -White Plns 10601 **Fx:**995-3363
(212) 272-0892 .. **Delon,** Marlene '03 %JP Morgan Chase -383 Mad Av -NY 10179
(212) 364-5340 .. **DeLone,** Madeline Hecksher '95 Innocence Project -100 5th Av -NY 10011 **Fx:**364-5341
(518) 884-4795 .. **DeLong,** John '00 %Pub Def -40 McMaster -Ballston Spa 12020 **Fx:**884-4789
(315) 386-7503 .. **DeLong,** Jondavid S '93 SUNY Canton -34 Cornell Dr -Canton 13617
(516) 433-6677 .. **Delorbe,** Jacqueline C '09 %Stewart GM&B -6800 Jericho Tpk -Syosset 11791
(718) 243-2700 .. **DeLorenz,** Steven J '87 (Talisman & D,PC) -409 Fulton -Brklyn 11201
(973) 596-4743 .. **De Lorenzi,** David E '91 (Gibbons PC) -1 Penn Plz -NY 10119 **Fx:**639-6235
(212) 693-0500 .. **DeLorenzo,** Anthony P '82 -220 5th Av -NY 10001 **Fx:**779-7916
(518) 374-8494 .. **DeLorenzo,** Paul E '93 %DeLorenzo Law Firm -201 Nott Ter -Schnctdy 12307 **Fx:**374-5906
(518) 374-8494 .. **DeLorenzo,** Thos E '59 (DeLorenzo Law Firm) -201 Nott Ter -Schnctdy 12307 **Fx:**374-5906
(212) 661-0565 .. **DeLorenzo,** Wm A '65 -420 Lex Av -NY 10170 **Fx:**949-0048
(518) 474-7700 .. **Delorey,** Patricia A '87 %NYS OPWDD -44 Holland Av -Albany 12229 **Fx:**474-7382
(212) 435-3571 .. **de los Reyes,** Maria T '82 %Port Auth of NY/NJ -225 Park Av S -NY 10003 **Fx:**435-3555
(607) 763-9200 .. **Delos Santos,** Lanalee D '10 %Levene G&T,LLP -BxF-1706 -Bnghmtn 13902
(516) 939-2999 .. **Delott,** Jeffrey D '86 -366 N Bway -Jericho 11753 **Fx:**942-4385
(212) 787-4947 .. **Delott,** Jonathan E '84 -98 Riverside Dr -NY 10024
(212) 455-2000 .. **DeLott,** Steven Rand '89 SrCnsl Simpson T&B LLP -425 Lex Av -NY 10017
(212) 404-7069 .. **De Lotto & Fajardo LLP** -44 Wall -NY 10005 **Fx:**(646) 827-3390
(212) 404-7069 .. **De Lotto,** Lauren '88 (De Lotto & F LLP) -44 Wall -NY 10005
(212) 335-9000 .. **Delozier,** Marit A '05 %DA -1 Hogan Pl -NY 10013
(518) 392-4267 .. **Del Peral,** Sonya K '92 -22 Park Row -Chatham 12037 **Fx:**392-4389
(212) 484-3900 .. **DelPercio,** Stephen T '06 %Arent F LLP -1675 Bway -NY 10019
(212) 906-1200 .. **Del Pino,** Antonio '95 (Latham & W) -885 3rd Av -NY 10022
(845) 358-6091 .. **Del Pizzo,** G Nicholas '85 -35 4th Av -Nyack 10960
(212) 335-3636 .. **DelPizzo,** Lisa J '96 %DA -1 Hogan Pl -NY 10013
(212) 973-0572 .. **Del Pizzo,** Nancy A '06 %Wolff & S PC -140 Bway -NY 10005
(845) 486-3048 .. **Delpizzo,** Thos P '88 %Cnty Atty -60 Market -Poughkeepsie 12601 **Fx:**486-2796
(718) 579-7900 .. **Del Plato,** Lina G '01 Leg Aid -900 Sheridan Av -Bronx 10451 **Fx:**293-8744
(585) 344-1050 .. **Del Plato,** Michl A '73 -73 Main -Batavia 14020 **Fx:**344-4165
(631) 754-1217 .. **DelPonte,** John D '94 %All Island Abstract -81 Scudder Av -Northprt 11768 **Fx:**754-1295
(718) 398-1076 .. **Del Prete,** Carl '56 -784 Carroll -Brklyn 11215 **Fx:**398-1076
(845) 638-5180 .. **Del Principio,** Fina '97 %Cnty Atty -Cnty Ofc Bldg -New Cty 10956 **Fx:**638-5676
(917) 778-6500 .. **Del Re,** Andre '87 K Dodson -485 Lex Av -NY 10017
(845) 357-7567 .. **Del Re,** Rose M '85 -22 S Lorna Ln -Monsey 10952
(212) 688-8555 .. **Del Rey,** Alfred J Jr. '71 (Fragomen DB&L LLP) -7 Hanover Sq -NY 10004
(212) 218-5500 .. **Del Rey-Cone,** Christie '03 %Seyfarth S LLP -620 8th Av -NY 10018
(716) 684-8060 .. **DelRio,** Ernesto '02 Ecology & Envrnmnt -368 Plsntvw Dr -Lancaster 14086 **Fx:**684-0844
(646) 251-6904 .. **Del Rio,** Mirta '80 -321 Bway -NY 10007 **Fx:**607-2100
(516) 222-8855 .. **Del Rosso,** Anthony N '51 AN Del Rosso PC -9 Endo Blvd -Gdn Cty 11530 **Fx:**222-8870
(212) 530-5000 .. **DelRosso,** Matthew J '04 %Milbank TH&M LLP -1 Chase Manh Plz -NY 10005
(212) 613-5000 .. **Delruelle,** Antoinette '94 %Leg Assist Grp -450 W 33rd -NY 10001 **Fx:**750-0820
(212) 819-8200 .. **Delsack,** Amy L '91 %White & C LLP -1155 Av of Amer -NY 10036
(212) 688-8944 .. **Delsack,** Craig S '97 (C Delsack,LLC) -600 Mad Av -NY 10022 **Fx:**753-4530
(212) 279-9200 .. **Del Signore,** Louis J Jr. '06 %Abrams FFEGF&E,LLP -630 3rd Av -NY 10017
(518) 793-4900 .. **Del Signore,** Mark S '96 (Borgos & D,PC) -82 Glenwood Av Bx4392 -Queensbury 12804
(212) 813-8800 .. **Delsignore,** Marta E '91 (Goodwin P LLP) -620 8th Av -NY 10018
(212) 269-5600 .. **Delson,** Benjamin R '03 OfCnsl Mandel B LLP -11 Bway -NY 10004 **Fx:**(646) 964-6667
(212) 468-8000 .. **Delson,** Christopher S '02 (Morrison & F LLP) -1290 Av of Amer -NY 10104
(516) 746-0676 .. **Delson,** Robt M '54 -229 7th -Gdn Cty 11530
(212) 513-7788 .. **Del Sordo,** Deborah A '81 (Ahmuty D&M) -123 William -NY 10038
(212) 506-2500 .. **Del Tatto,** Gina L '09 %Mayer B LLP -1675 Bway -NY 10019
(646) 392-9250 .. **Del Toro,** Corwin '83 %M Klein & Assoc -200 Mad Av -NY 10016 **Fx:**(212) 779-1499
(212) 238-4800 .. **Del Toro,** Nadia '05 %Landman CB&F,PC -120 Bway -NY 10271
(914) 864-7054 .. **Del Torto,** Robt L '90 %Parks Dept -25 Moore Av -Mt Kisco 10549
(212) 735-3000 .. **Del Tufo,** Robt J '82 OfCnsl Skadden ASM&F LLP -4 Times Sq -NY 10036
(646) 228-5331 .. **DeLuca,** Adrienne '81 -Bx721 -NY 10021
(718) 855-5684 .. **Deluca,** Anthony E '86 %Longo & D -26 Court -Brklyn 11242
(631) 981-3555 .. **DeLuca,** Danl W '80 -3555 Vets Mem'l Hwy -Ronkonkoma 11779
(585) 272-7007 .. **DeLuca,** David V '68 -2540 Brighton Henrietta TL Rd -Rchstr 14623 **Fx:**272-7011
(518) 374-1200 .. **DeLuca,** Donald W '79 OfCnsl Kouray & K -525 State -Schnctdy 12305 **Fx:**374-7414
(718) 206-4723 .. **DeLuca,** Janet P '95 %Law Dept -89-17 Sutphin Blvd -Jamaica 11435 **Fx:**206-4702
(212) 259-8000 .. **DeLuca,** Mary I '03 %Dewey & L LLP -1301 Av of Amer -NY 10019
(212) 326-3939 .. **DeLuca,** Nicholas D '09 %Jones D -222 E 41st -NY 10017
(631) 501-5700 .. **DeLuca,** Peter '87 (Carter DF&S LLP) -445 Broadhallow Rd -Melvll 11747
(212) 836-8000 .. **DeLuca,** Peter J '54 SpclCnsl Kaye S LLP -425 Park Av -NY 10022
(516) 802-0630 .. **DeLuca,** Sal F '00 (Simmons J,LLP) -115 Eileen Way -Syosset 11791
(718) 852-8888 .. **DeLuca,** Sally '88 %LSNYC-Brooklyn -180 Lvngstn -Brklyn 11201 **Fx:**858-1786
(212) 705-7460 .. **DeLuca,** Stephen M '93 -399 Park Av -NY 10022
(518) 784-2940 .. **DeLuca,** Thos G '81 (DeLuca & F) -45 E Shore Dr -Valatie 12184 **Fx:**(908) 276-6260
(212) 218-2100 .. **De Lucia,** Frank A '00 (Fitzpatrick CH&S) -1290 Av of Amer -NY 10104
(212) 261-8000 .. **DeLucia,** James L '08 %Mendes & M,LLP -750 7th Av -NY 10019
(212) 753-5000 .. **DeLucia,** Louis T '08 (Schiff H LLP) -900 3rd Av -NY 10022
(607) 778-2423 .. **DeLucia,** Peter N '02 %DA -45 Hawley Bx1766 -Bnghmtn 13902 **Fx:**778-8870
(212) 425-7200 .. **DeLucia,** Richd L '79 (Kenyon & K,LLP) -1 Bway -NY 10004
(518) 474-4283 .. **DeLuise,** Jerry '74 %Dept of Health -Corning Twr 24th Fl -Albany 12237 **Fx:**486-1858
(212) 879-5500 .. **Del Valle,** Cristina '91 %Metropolitan Museum -1000 5th Av -NY 10028 **Fx:**570-3850
(718) 258-3096 .. **Del Valle,** Fidel F '77 -1536 Ryder -Brklyn 11234
(212) 898-8401 .. **del Valle,** Manuel '75 Americhoice -7 Hanover Sq -NY 10004 **Fx:**898-7909
(212) 877-0100 .. **Del Valle,** Marguerite '85 (Power D LLP) -233 W 72nd -NY 10023 **Fx:**580-0325
(716) 841-4726 .. **Del Valle,** Michl '96 %Marine Midland Bk -251 Main -Buffalo 14203 **Fx:**841-1207
(212) 447-5599 .. **Del Valle,** Richd H '97 %Agins SR&B,LLP -386 Park Av S -NY 10016
(212) 244-4664 .. **Del Valle,** Sandra '89 %NY Lawyers Pub Intrst -151 W 30th -NY 10001 **Fx:**244-4570
(212) 481-1900 .. **Del Valle,** Telesforo Jr. '84 (Del Valle & Assoc) -445 Park Av -NY 10022 **Fx:**481-4853
(845) 208-7835 .. **DelVecchio,** Amelia T '63 Putnam Cnty Sup Ct -20 Cnty Ctr -Carmel 10512
(212) 238-3000 .. **Delvecchio,** August J '08 Emmet M&M,LLP -120 Bway -NY 10271
(315) 433-9115 .. **DelVecchio,** John F '61 -145 Watertree Dr -E Syracuse 13057
(716) 857-7328 .. **Del Vecchio,** Jos N '97 %Natl Fuel Gas -6363 Main -Williamsvll 14221 **Fx:**857-7614
(212) 286-8585 .. **DelVecchio,** Laura A '04 %Heidell PM&B,LLP -99 Park Av -NY 10016
(914) 686-3700 .. **DelVecchio,** Michl G '09 %Worby GE LLP -11 Martine Av -White Plns 10606
(716) 853-4080 .. **Del Vecchio,** Regina Ann '89 (Colucci & G,PC) -424 Main -Buffalo 14202
(516) 294-5555 .. **Del Vecchio,** Steven M '77 (Del Vecchio & R,LLP) -1100 Franklin Av -Gdn Cty 11530 **Fx:**873-5336
(718) 592-3388 .. **Del Villar,** Angel L '94 (Del Villar & Assoc) -45-14 104th -Corona 11368 **Fx:**592-3775
(212) 371-5478 .. **Del Virginia,** Gabriel '90 -488 Mad Av -NY 10022 **Fx:**371-0460
(212) 571-5700 .. **DeMaggio,** Steven A '73 (DeMaggio & D,LLP) -116 John -NY 10038 **Fx:**571-5706
(212) 306-1196 .. **DeMaio,** Gene G '97 %Amer Stock Exch -86 Trinity Pl -NY 10006
(212) 888-8300 .. **De Maio & Hughes,PC** -330 E 30th -NY 10016
(212) 405-2104 .. **DeMaio,** John P '78 SrCnsl DeMaio & Assoc -75 Maiden Ln -NY 10038 **Fx:**(646) 202-1439
(212) 888-8300 .. **De Maio,** Luigi P '74 (De M&H,PC) -330 E 30th -NY 10016
(631) 261-7778 .. **DeMaio,** Tanya '91 %Brody O&O -7 Bayview Av -Northprt 11768
(718) 590-5263 .. **DeMar,** David J '88 %Supreme Ct -851 Grand Cncrs -Bronx 10451 **Fx:**590-8914
(315) 366-2236 .. **DeMarche,** Douglas M Jr. '98 %DA -Cnty Cthse Bx578 -Wampsville 13163 **Fx:**366-2503
(518) 432-8161 .. **DeMarco,** Andrew V '09 Morgan Stanley -30 S Pearl -Albany 12207
(212) 685-4700 .. **DeMarco,** Enrico '97 -300 Park Av -NY 10022
(716) 838-1515 .. **DeMarco,** James C III '90 -2655 Sheridan Dr -Tonawanda 14150
(212) 878-8000 .. **DeMarco,** Jennifer C '90 (Clifford C LLP) -31 W 52nd -NY 10019
(516) 877-1800 .. **DeMarco,** Jos A '02 (Schlissel OK,PLLC) -200 Grdn City Plz -Gdn Cty 11530
(212) 922-9499 .. **DeMarco,** Jos V '93 (DeVore & D LLP) -99 Park Av -NY 10016 **Fx:**922-1799
(914) 937-2213 .. **DeMarco,** Mario L '93 -1 Gtwy Plz -Pt Chester 10573 **Fx:**937-3066
(718) 239-7070 .. **DeMarco,** Mark S '92 -2027 Wllmsbrdg Rd -Bronx 10461
(516) 742-8930 .. **DeMarco,** Matthew J '92 (Schwarz & D,LLP) -191 Grnd Cntrl Av -Amityvll 11701 **Fx:**742-8937
(914) 946-4777 .. **DeMarco,** Ralph C '94 (Keane & B,PC) -445 Hmltn Av -White Plns 10601
(212) 206-6191 .. **DeMarco,** Raymond M '81 (Kantor & D) -55 5th Av -NY 10003

(646) 471-4000 .. **DeMarco,** Richd J Jr. '87 %PricewaterhouseCoopers LLP -300 Mad Av -NY 10017
(315) 435-2470 .. **DeMarco,** Robt J '02 %DA -505 S State -Syracuse 13202 **Fx:**435-3969
(631) 673-7200 .. **DeMarco Lee,** Mary '91 M DeMarco Lee PLLC -82 Main -Huntngtn 11743 **Fx:**424-1060
(585) 325-2520 .. **De Mareo,** Michelle M '02 %Leg Assistance -1 W Main -Rchstr 14614 **Fx:**325-2559
(212) 262-2390 .. **Demareski,** Craig S '99 %Connell F LLP -888 7th Av -NY 10106
(646) 386-3046 .. **Demarest,** Kathryn E '95 %Supreme Ct Applit Term -60 Centre -NY 10007
(315) 422-0314 .. **DeMari,** Jos E '90 %Germain & G -314 E Fayette -Syracuse 13202 **Fx:**478-6544
(212) 687-7410 .. **DeMaria,** Alfred T '62 (Clifton B&D,LLP) -420 Lex Av -NY 10170
(585) 232-4910 .. **DeMaria,** Jos G '55 -301 Exchange Blvd -Rchstr 14608 **Fx:**232-8840
(212) 449-8240 .. **DeMaria,** Roseanna '82 %Merrill Lynch -250 Vesey -NY 10080
(631) 361-9494 .. **Demaria,** Wm D '82 -732 Smithtwn Bypass -Smithtwn 11787 **Fx:**361-8752
(716) 856-0024 .. **DeMarie,** Anthony J '56 OfCnsl DeMarie & S,PC -800 Convntn Twr -Buffalo 14202
(716) 856-0024 .. **DeMarie,** Jos '63 (DeMarie & S,PC) -800 Convntn Twr -Buffalo 14202
(716) 856-0024 .. **DeMarie & Schoenborn,PC** -800 Convntn Twr -Buffalo 14202 **Fx:**856-6537
(212) 826-8800 .. **DeMarinis,** Dorothy H '00 %Calinoff & K,LLP -245 5th Av -NY 10016
(212) 791-0285 .. **DeMario,** Grace L '05 %Malaby & B,LLC -150 Bway -NY 10038 **Fx:**791-0286
(516) 663-6600 .. **DeMaro,** John A '92 (Ruskin MF,PC) -1425 RXR Plz -Uniondale 11556
(518) 690-4410 .. **Demars,** Sandra Poland '94 %R Croak & Assoc -314 Great Oaks Blvd -Albany 12203 **Fx:**690-4435
(914) 286-3471 .. **de Marte,** Vincent '85 %Leg Aid -1 N Bway -White Plns 10601 **Fx:**682-4112
(516) 294-1333 .. **DeMartini,** Arthur J '89 (DeMartini & Y LLP) -264 Hillside Av -Williston Pk 11596
(212) 951-7147 .. **De Martini,** Francis J '97 %NYS Ed Dept-OLS -475 Park Av S -NY 10016 **Fx:**951-6573
(212) 845-3132 .. **DeMartini,** Nicholas '88 %Fidelity Natl Title Ins -1 Park Av -NY 10016 **Fx:**(646) 424-9380
(516) 294-1333 .. **DeMartini & Yi LLP** -264 Hillside Av -Williston Pk 11596 **Fx:**294-2756
(914) 323-7000 .. **DeMartino,** Chas C '05 %Wilson EME&D LLP -3 Gannett Dr -White Plns 10604
(212) 455-2000 .. **De Martino,** Jeffrey C '06 %Simpson T&B LLP -425 Lex Av -NY 10017
(518) 455-3341 .. **DeMartino,** Michl J III '04 %Sen C Fuschillo Jr -LOB 915 -Albany 12247
(315) 448-4800 .. **DeMartino,** Nicholas J '86 %Dept of Law -615 Erie Blvd W -Syracuse 13204 **Fx:**448-4853
(212) 697-3122 .. **DeMarzo,** Jos L '80 (Martin C&B LLP) -220 E 42nd -NY 10017
(212) 495-0100 .. **Demas,** Richd B '01 %Gottesman WMF&W,PC -11 Hanover Sq -NY 10005
(914) 761-2700 .. **DeMase,** Lauren J '93 %Henderson & B -222 Mamaroneck Av -White Plns 10605
(212) 328-6180 .. **DeMasi,** Juliet M '98 %CMW Lgl Search -845 3rd Av -NY 10022 **Fx:**328-6181
(212) 474-1000 .. **DeMasi,** Karin A '97 (Cravath S&M LLP) -825 8th Av -NY 10019
(212) 756-2000 .. **Demasi,** Lauren '07 %Schulte R&Z LLP -919 3rd Av -NY 10022
(315) 422-3600 .. **De Masi,** Ralph G '04 -201 E Jffrsn -Syracuse 13202 **Fx:**471-5759
(212) 310-8000 .. **DeMasi,** Timothy E '97 (Weil G&M LLP) -767 5th Av -NY 10153
(212) 373-3000 .. **DeMatos,** Anna B C '00 Paul WRW&G LLP -1285 Av of Amer -NY 10019
(212) 474-1000 .. **DeMatteis,** Jared W '09 %Cravath S&M LLP -825 8th Av -NY 10019
(212) 277-6500 .. **DeMatteo,** Bryan N '02 %Dickstein S LLP -1633 Bway -NY 10019
(716) 883-3300 .. **DeMatteo,** James '92 %R Cercone -484 Delaware Av -Buffalo 14202 **Fx:**883-2163
(212) 964-6611 .. **DeMatteo,** John III '93 Cnsl Lester SK&D -120 Bway -NY 10271
(212) 661-1661 .. **DeMatteo,** Jos R '88 (Bernfeld D&B) -600 3rd Av -NY 10016 **Fx:**557-9610
(518) 393-1311 .. **DeMatteo,** Raymond E Jr. '80 DeMatteo D&D -166 Lafayette -Schnctdy 12305 **Fx:**377-5893
(212) 509-3456 .. **DeMattheis,** Nicholas C Jr. '99 %McGivney & K,PC -80 Broad -NY 10004
(914) 563-9223 .. **DeMattio,** Michl F '92 -445 Hmltn Av -White Plns 10601
(212) 973-0572 .. **DeMauro,** Lauren R '09 %Wolff & S PC -140 Bway -NY 10005
(212) 474-1000 .. **Demay,** Brendon T '08 %Cravath S&M LLP -825 8th Av -NY 10019
(212) 490-9100 .. **DeMay,** Jonathan E '99 (Condon & F LLP) -7 Times Sq -NY 10036
(212) 344-7042 .. **DeMay,** Jos F Jr. '79 (Cichanowicz CKV&T,LLP) -61 Bway -NY 10006
(212) 788-6827 .. **DeMayo,** Barbara T '86 %Crim Justice Coordntr -1 Centre -NY 10007
(631) 728-7306 .. **DeMayo,** Thos J '74 -42 Ponquogue Av Bx1334 -Hampton Bays 11946
(888) 835-0006 .. **Demba,** Danl S '07 (Demba W,LLP) -1221 Av of Amer -NY 10020 **Fx:**835-1116
(212) 909-6000 .. **Dembeck,** John '86 Cnsl Debevoise & P LLP -919 3rd Av -NY 10022
(212) 581-5166 .. **Dembeck,** Louise E '66 AIMAC Ctr for ADR -157 E 57th -NY 10022 **Fx:**957-2205
(212) 637-2563 .. **Dember,** Andrew S '80 %US Atty -1 St Andrews Plz -NY 10007
(212) 226-5905 .. **Dembia,** Robt '78 (R Dembia,PC) -350 Bway -NY 10013 **Fx:**226-7859
(212) 526-5842 .. **Dembicer,** Tracy S '83 %Lehman Bros Inc -399 Park Av -NY 10022
(212) 267-0505 .. **Dembin,** Nathan L '72 (N Dembin & Assoc,PC) -1123 Bway -NY 10010 **Fx:**267-9244
(212) 888-4200 .. **Dembitzer,** David H '94 (Dembitzer & D LLP) -100 Wall -NY 10005 **Fx:**230-1090
(212) 944-0588 .. **Dembitzer,** Herbert M '92 -36 W 44th -NY 10036 **Fx:**944-0588
(212) 888-4200 .. **Dembitzer,** Stephen A '89 (Dembitzer & D LLP) -100 Wall -NY 10005 **Fx:**230-1090
(212) 947-1999 .. **Dembling,** Marc L '81 Cnsl Methfessel & W,PC -450 7th Av -NY 10123
(212) 600-9288 .. **Demblowski,** Matthew A '09 Stick Figure Productions -432 W 45th -NY 10036
(516) 486-4640 .. **Dembner,** Scott '87 (Cherry E&K,LLP) -1 Old Cntry Rd -Carle Pl 11514
(516) 679-1431 .. **Dembrosky,** Katherine C '87 -3815 Mill Rd -Seafrd 11783
(212) 801-9260 .. **Dembrow,** Adam C '01 %Greenberg T,LLP -200 Park Av -NY 10166
(212) 701-3000 .. **Dembrow,** Ira J '66 %Cahill G&R LLP -80 Pine -NY 10005 **Fx:**269-5420
(315) 474-7541 .. **Dembs,** Marcy R '86 (Menter R&T,PC) -308 Maltbie -Syracuse 13204
(516) 294-1231 .. **DeMelfi,** Christy M '07 CM DeMelfi,PC -1415 Kellum Pl -Gdn Cty 11530 **Fx:**345-1604
(212) 732-2767 .. **De Mell,** Harry A '78 -225 Bway -NY 10007 **Fx:**566-1033
(212) 909-6000 .. **Demeny,** Rachel R '05 %Debevoise & P LLP -919 3rd Av -NY 10022
(212) 792-7778 .. **De Meo,** Emilia M '88 (DeMeo & F,LLC) -9 E 40th -NY 10016 **Fx:**898-1251
(718) 565-4751 .. **DeMeo,** Karen L '96 Flight Safety Intl Inc -LaGuardia Airport -Flushng 11371
(516) 355-4552 .. **DeMeo,** Peter W '92 -1111 A Marcus Av -Lk Success 11042 **Fx:**344-4652
(516) 938-7072 .. **DeMeo,** Rhonda S '85 -18 Fountain Ln -Jericho 11753
(212) 352-6964 .. **DeMeo,** Teresa A '89 %UIA Bd -Bx29002 -Brklyn 11201 **Fx:**352-6813
(718) 875-1300 .. **DeMeola,** Amanda S '05 %Applt Div 2nd Dept -45 Monroe Pl -Brklyn 11201 **Fx:**858-2446
(716) 853-1616 .. **Demerle,** Angela M '86 Cnsl Harter S&E LLP -12 Fountain Plz -Buffalo 14202
(518) 465-3553 .. **Demers,** Andrea R '07 %Maynard OS&C,LLP -6 Twr Pl -Albany 12203
(516) 294-5433 .. **Demers,** Henri A '74 (Ahmuty D&M) -200 IU Willets Rd -Albertson 11507
(917) 783-9423 .. **Demers,** James P '04 Gotham Patent Srvcs LLC -425 Riverside Dr -NY 10025
(716) 834-2101 .. **Demert,** Jennifer M '94 Buffalo Academy of the Sacred Heart -3860 Main -Buffalo 14226 **Fx:**834-2944
(518) 457-2070 .. **Demeter,** David J '87 %Dept of Tax & Fin -Bldg 9 State Campus -Albany 12227 **Fx:**457-6131
(516) 222-4567 .. **Demetri,** Adam C '92 (Sawyer H&D) -666 Old Cntry Rd -Gdn Cty 11530
(516) 248-0880 .. **Demetriou,** Michl '53 (Demetriou & D,PC) -648 Franklin Av -Gdn Cty 11530 **Fx:**248-2281
(516) 248-0880 .. **Demetriou,** Paul '03 (Demetriou & D,PC) -648 Franklin Av -Gdn Cty 11530 **Fx:**248-2281
(718) 238-1400 .. **DeMeyer,** Suzanne M '01 %Cantor C&S,LLP -8778 Bay Pkwy -Brklyn 11214 **Fx:**238-7642
(718) 250-2000 .. **D'Emic,** Matthew J Jr. '08 %DA -350 Jay -Brklyn 11201 **Fx:**250-2314
(212) 576-4452 .. **DeMicco,** Michl A '85 %NY Life Ins -51 Mad Av -NY 10010 **Fx:**447-0569
(914) 323-7000 .. **DeMicco,** Thos M '02 %Wilson EME&D LLP -3 Gannett Dr -White Plns 10604
(212) 599-3303 .. **D'Emidio,** Michl A '03 %Helfand & H -350 5th Av -NY 10118 **Fx:**599-3029
(212) 627-2874 .. **D'Emilia,** Robt F '78 -181 7th Av -NY 10011
(914) 674-9015 .. **D'Emilio,** Joann '87 -28 Grandvw Av -Ardsley 10502
(212) 863-6300 .. **DeMilt,** Marc S '91 %HPD -100 Gold -NY 10038
(212) 735-3000 .. **Deming,** John G '10 %Skadden ASM&F LLP -4 Times Sq -NY 10036
(315) 788-6700 .. **Deming,** Leslie H '55 OfCnsl Schwerzmann & W,PC -215 Wshngtn Bx704 -Watertwn 13601
(607) 746-7122 .. **Deming,** Nancy K '79 -Bx325 -Delhi 13753 **Fx:**746-6775
(212) 757-0007 .. **Deming,** Rachel E '83 Scarola E LLP -888 7th Av -NY 10106
(212) 867-9500 .. **Demirdjan,** Diana J '03 %Kurzman K&F,LLP -230 Park Av -NY 10169
(212) 558-4000 .. **Demirel Atakan,** Ayse '08 %Sullivan & C LLP -125 Broad -NY 10004
(516) 328-2300 .. **Demiris,** Harry C Jr. '00 (Abrams FFEGF&E,LLP) -1111 Marcus Av -Lk Success 11042
(646) 264-3650 .. **Demitrio,** Suzanne L '98 %US Dept of Labor -201 Varick -NY 10014 **Fx:**264-3660
(516) 463-6190 .. **Demleitner,** Nora V '93 %Hofstra Law Schl -121 Hofstra Univ -Hempstd 11549
(212) 815-1450 .. **Demmings,** Eddie M Jr. '82 %DC 37 Gen Cnsl -125 Barclay -NY 10007 **Fx:**815-1440
(212) 403-1000 .. **Demmo,** Nicholas G '98 (Wachtell LR&K) -51 W 52nd -NY 10019
(718) 875-1300 .. **Demner,** Heather R '07 Applt Div 2nd Dept -45 Monroe Pl -Brklyn 11201 **Fx:**858-2446
(718) 227-1800 .. **DeMonaco,** MaryKim '91 (DeMonaco & S) -114 Seguine Av -Staten Isl 10309 **Fx:**605-5156
(212) 808-2700 .. **Demont,** Valerie '96 (Pepper H LLP) -620 8th Av -NY 10018
(212) 225-2000 .. **De Moor,** Olivier J '09 %Cleary GS&H -1 Lbrty Plz -NY 10006
(716) 845-9376 .. **Demopoulos,** Ann '85 %Supreme Ct -25 Delaware Av -Buffalo 14202 **Fx:**851-3293
(315) 683-5655 .. **DeMore,** Robt S '74 (Perrin & D,PC) -Main -Fabius 13063 **Fx:**683-5479
(315) 677-3117 .. **DeMore,** Robt S '74 (Perrin & D,PC) -6006 Route 20 Bx130 -LaFayette 13084 **Fx:**677-3530
(315) 425-2700 .. **DeMore,** Timothy J '00 (Hiscock & B,LLP) -One Park Pl -Syracuse 13202
(631) 648-0301 .. **Demos,** George G '03 -5 Vllg Plz Dr -Ronkonkoma 11779
(845) 782-5197 .. **Demos,** Katherine A '83 -127 Stage Rd -Monroe 10950 **Fx:**783-1100
(212) 261-8000 .. **Demosthene,** Barbara '99 %Mendes & M,LLP -750 7th Av -NY 10019
(718) 618-2500 .. **Demosthene,** Natasha '04 Civil Ct -851 Grnd Cncrs -Bronx 10451 **Fx:**590-7294
(585) 427-0675 .. **Demo-Vazquez,** Kristine M '04 -1425 Jffrsn Rd -Rchstr 14623 **Fx:**427-0056

(845) 639-4600 .. **deMoya,** Desiree V '93 (deMoya & Assoc,PC) -163 S Main -New Cty 10956 **Fx:**639-4610
(631) 539-0375 .. **DeMoya Coyle,** Magda '09 %Cruser M&N,LLP -175 Pinelawn Rd -Melvll 11747
(518) 463-1177 .. **Dempf,** Louis Jr. '55 (Tobin & D,LLP) -33 Elk -Albany 12207
(518) 463-1177 .. **Dempf,** R Christopher '85 (Tobin & D,LLP) -33 Elk -Albany 12207
(212) 351-4500 .. **Dempsey,** Aime Gessler '91 %Epstein B&G,PC -250 Park Av -NY 10177
(716) 885-8645 .. **Dempsey,** Catherine B '06 %Dempsey & D -561 Franklin -Buffalo 14202 **Fx:**885-8569
(212) 906-1200 .. **Dempsey,** Guy C Jr. '78 Cnsl Latham & W -885 3rd Av -NY 10022
(716) 885-8645 .. **Dempsey,** Helen K '70 (Dempsey & D) -561 Franklin -Buffalo 14202 **Fx:**885-8569
(716) 885-8645 .. **Dempsey,** John M '69 (Dempsey & D) -561 Franklin -Buffalo 14202 **Fx:**885-8569
(718) 447-8841 .. **Dempsey,** Kathleen M '97 %Lahr DMK&P -33 Decker Av -Staten Isl 10302
(914) 737-0030 .. **Dempsey & Langan** -1200 Brown -Peekskill 10566 **Fx:**736-9999
(914) 686-4456 .. **Dempsey,** Laura C '01 %Marsh M&W PLLC -81 Main -White Plns 10601 **Fx:**206-3998
(212) 269-7308 .. **Dempsey,** Michl G '86 %Leahey & J PC -120 Wall -NY 10005
(631) 369-5100 .. **Dempsey,** Patricia A '77 (Ciarelli & D) -737 Roanoke Av -Rvrhead 11901 **Fx:**369-5132
(212) 969-3000 .. **Dempsey,** Patrick J '07 %Proskauer R LLP -1585 Bway -NY 10036
(212) 759-7466 .. **Dempsey,** Ryan E '05 %Raven & K,LLP -126 E 56th -NY 10022
(914) 946-0400 .. **Dempsey,** Terence E '95 %Schiavetti CDW&N,LLP -709 Wstchstr Av -White Plns 10604
(516) 746-0707 .. **Dempsey,** Wade T '79 (Hammill OCDP&K,PC) -6851 Jericho Tpk -Syosset 11791
(516) 571-3800 .. **Dempsey,** Wm J Jr. '78 %DA -262 Old Cntry Rd -Mineola 11501 **Fx:**248-9479
(212) 492-5800 .. **de Muinck Keizer,** Johannes H '91 %Kaplan Educ Ctrs,Inc -888 7th Av -NY 10106 **Fx:**489-2301
(212) 902-4087 .. **DeMunnynck,** Natalie M '02 Goldman Sachs & Co -180 Maiden Ln -NY 10038
(212) 735-3000 .. **Demuth,** Bradley J '00 %Skadden ASM&F LLP -4 Times Sq -NY 10036
(518) 474-6639 .. **Demuth,** Owen W '03 Dept of Law -The Cptl -Albany 12224
(212) 435-3436 .. **Denalli,** Karla D '97 %Port Auth of NY/NJ -225 Park Av S -NY 10003 **Fx:**435-3555
(516) 481-6082 .. **Denaro,** Anthony D '64 A Denaro,PC -62 Nichols Ct -Hempstd 11550 **Fx:**481-6302
(516) 626-0007 .. **Denaro,** Barry '98 %Natl Med Health Card Sys -26 Hrbr Pk Dr -Pt Wash 11050
(718) 370-2900 .. **Denaro,** Kevin '10 %Bonfiglio & A,LLC -900 South Av -Staten Isl 10314 **Fx:**370-2910
(212) 530-5000 .. **Denaro,** Paul E '00 (Milbank TH&M LLP) -1 Chase Manh Plz -NY 10005
(718) 863-6000 .. **Denaro,** Thos M '82 -1726 Edison Av -Bronx 10461 **Fx:**319-1772
(212) 806-5400 .. **DeNatale,** Andrew P '76 (Stroock &S&L LLP) -180 Maiden Ln -NY 10038
(631) 281-2500 .. **De Natale,** Susan A '99 (Hennessey & D) -501 Wm Floyd Pkwy -Shirley 11967 **Fx:**281-2598
(845) 639-1954 .. **Denbeaux,** Marcia '86 (Denbeaux & D) -155 N Main -New Cty 10956 **Fx:**(201) 666-8589
(212) 906-1200 .. **Denberg,** Dara M '02 %Latham & W -885 3rd Av -NY 10022
(212) 683-7100 .. **Denburg,** Stephen A '99 %Gallo V&K,LLP -90 Broad -NY 10004
(631) 724-8833 .. **Denby,** John M '87 (Devitt SB,LLP) -50 Route 111 -Smithtwn 11787
(212) 269-5550 .. **Denby,** Walter A '78 DF King & Co -48 Wall -NY 10005 **Fx:**269-2798
(212) 506-1700 .. **Dender,** Chas F '05 %Kasowitz BT&F LLP -1633 Bway -NY 10019
(516) 433-7999 .. **Dender,** David S '87 (D Dender, PC) -380 N Bway -Jericho 11753 **Fx:**433-9310
(585) 613-4070 .. **Denefrio,** Carey A '06 Hon J Feldman -100 State -Rchstr 14614 **Fx:**613-4075
(631) 360-0100 .. **Denehan,** Stephen P '89 -2 Prescott Ln -Smithtwn 11787 **Fx:**360-0163
(212) 557-7200 .. **Denenberg,** David W '88 (Davidoff M&H,LLP) -605 3rd Av -NY 10158
(212) 490-3000 .. **Denenberg,** Deborah J '91 (Wilson EME&D LLP) -150 E 42nd -NY 10017
(914) 323-7000 .. **Denenberg,** Deborah J '91 (Wilson EME&D LLP) -3 Gannett Dr -White Plns 10604
(917) 351-1335 .. **Denenberg,** Seth E '84 (Sperber D&K,PC) -48 W 37th -NY 10018
(212) 416-8000 .. **Denerstein,** Mylan Lee '94 %Dept of Law -120 Bway -NY 10271
(212) 931-7960 .. **DeNeve,** Alexandra '04 MLB Properties -245 Park Av -NY 10167 **Fx:**949-5697
(631) 390-0010 .. **Denezzo,** Gregory J '09 %Bruno G&S,LLP -445 Broad Hollow Rd -Melvll 11747
(718) 946-0731 .. **Deng,** Chaoping '07 -2562 Cropsey Av -Brklyn 11214
(212) 969-3000 .. **Deng,** Lucia F '06 %Proskauer R LLP -1585 Bway -NY 10036
(212) 450-4000 .. **Deng,** Wei '09 %Davis P&W LLP -450 Lex Av -NY 10017
(212) 596-9000 .. **Deng,** Xin '09 %Ropes & G LLP -1211 Av of Amer -NY 10036
(315) 677-3384 .. **Dengel,** Carl W '48 -2542 Rt 11 Bx126 -LaFayette 13084
(212) 450-4000 .. **Dengel,** Hilary A E '08 %Davis P&W LLP -450 Lex Av -NY 10017
(212) 384-1000 .. **Dengler,** Kurt F '99 %FBI -26 Fed Plz -NY 10278
(212) 732-2422 .. **Dengler,** Norbert '58 -170 Bway -NY 10038
(212) 218-2100 .. **Dengler,** Ralph A '97 %Fitzpatrick CH&S -1290 Av of Amer -NY 10104
(212) 319-5240 .. **Dengler,** Robt N '97 %Flicker G & Assoc,LLP -45 Bway -NY 10006
(212) 239-4215 .. **Denhoffer,** Ira M '60 -450 7th Av -NY 10123 **Fx:**239-4215
(212) 318-6000 .. **Denhup,** Richd S '06 (Paul HJ&W LLP) -75 E 55th -NY 10022
(212) 922-6808 .. **DeNicholas,** Kathleen '00 Dreyfus Corp -200 Park Av -NY 10166 **Fx:**922-6880
(631) 567-1200 .. **DeNicola,** Andrea '91 %E DeNicola -200 Railroad Av Bx68 -Sayvll 11782 **Fx:**567-1287
(212) 373-3000 .. **Denicola,** Christopher P '10 %Paul WRW&G LLP -1285 Av of Amer -NY 10019
(212) 867-4466 .. **DeNicola,** Denise C '93 (Belkin BW&G,LLP) -270 Mad Av -NY 10016
(212) 264-8819 .. **DeNicola,** Donna M '91 %SSA-OHA -26 Fed Plz -NY 10278
(631) 567-1200 .. **DeNicola,** Eugene L '62 -200 Railroad Av Bx68 -Sayvll 11782 **Fx:**567-1287
(212) 449-2916 .. **Denicola,** Robt M '85 Merrill Lynch & Co Inc -250 Vesey -NY 10281
(914) 390-4130 .. **Denig,** Lisa Marie '10 Hon L Smith -300 Quarropas -White Plns 10601
(646) 473-3949 .. **Deninno,** Sherilyn A '01 USPS Law Dept -90 Church -NY 10007
(516) 571-6651 .. **Denion,** Conal '90 %Cnty Atty -1 West -Mineola 11501 **Fx:**571-6604
(212) 940-8800 .. **Denis,** Alessandra '02 %Katten MR LLP -575 Mad Av -NY 10022
(914) 995-3497 .. **Denise,** Stefanie D '09 %DA -111 Martin Luther King Blvd -White Plns 10601 **Fx:**995-3363
(212) 916-6261 .. **Denizé,** Yves P '94 %TIAA-CREF -730 3rd Av -NY 10017 **Fx:**916-6980
(718) 641-2000 .. **Denkberg,** Steven B '84 (Santucci & D) -113-18A Lbrty Av -S Richmond Hll 11419
(718) 997-5725 .. **Denkensohn,** Jane '73 %Queens College -65-30 Kissena Blvd -Flushng 11367 **Fx:**997-5738
(516) 294-7037 .. **Denker,** John L '85 %Spano Abstract Srvc Corp -370 Old Cntry Rd -Gdn Cty 11530 **Fx:**742-9375
(212) 619-5000 .. **Denkin,** Juliette F '83 %EDC -110 William -NY 10038 **Fx:**312-3912
(516) 496-5822 .. **Denkovich,** Courtney B '02 %T Spina -170 Froehlich Farm Blvd -Woodbury 11797 **Fx:**496-5420
(516) 827-0248 .. **Denkovich,** Michl R '01 -46 Knckrbckr Rd -Plainvw 11803 **Fx:**908-3939
(212) 210-9534 .. **Denkowicz,** Stephanie '84 (Alston & B LLP) -90 Park Av -NY 10016
(914) 517-5000 .. **Denlea,** James R '80 (Meiselman DPC&E,PC) -1311 Mamaroneck Av -White Plns 10605
(212) 668-2870 .. **Denman,** Harrison L '06 Hon J Peck -1 Bowling Grn -NY 10004
(315) 798-5492 .. **Denman,** Lisa Procter '06 %Dept Soc Srvcs -800 Park Av -Utica 13501
(607) 723-5341 .. **Denmon,** John D '93 (Hinman H&K,LLP) -80 Exchange Bx5250 -Bnghmtn 13902
(973) 642-1440 .. **Denne,** Edmund C '95 -116 John -NY 10038
(212) 493-6837 .. **Denne-Bolton,** Aileen C '90 %Brown Bros Harriman -140 Bway -NY 10005 **Fx:**493-8206
(212) 508-4578 .. **Denneen,** John E '93 %The Royce Funds -1414 Av of Amer -NY 10019 **Fx:**832-8921
(518) 339-6935 .. **Dennehey,** James R '72 -294 New Scotland Av -Albany 12208
(212) 758-9700 .. **Dennehy,** Edw K '93 %KPMG LLP -345 Park Av -NY 10154
(718) 254-7000 .. **Dennehy,** John J '95 %US Atty -271 Cadman Plz E -Brklyn 11201 **Fx:**254-6479
(212) 643-7000 .. **Dennehy,** Matthew T '02 %Sills C&G PC -One Rckfllr Plz -NY 10020
(718) 250-2000 .. **Dennehy,** Morgan J '94 %DA -350 Jay -Brklyn 11201 **Fx:**250-2314
(212) 974-6100 .. **Dennehy,** Susan S '76 Dennehy Law Firm -250 W 57th -NY 10107 **Fx:**974-6113
(212) 940-3079 .. **Dennery,** Natalie A '03 %Nixon P LLP -437 Mad Av -NY 10022
(516) 504-1400 .. **Dennett,** Richd A '81 -505 Nrthrn Blvd -Gt Neck 11021 **Fx:**214-8095
(718) 875-1300 .. **Dennihy,** Emily L '06 Appllt Div 2nd Dept -45 Monroe Pl -Brklyn 11201 **Fx:**858-2446
(518) 523-2595 .. **Dennin,** Fredk S '48 OfCnsl Dennin & D -2745 Main -Lk Placid 12946 **Fx:**523-4766
(518) 523-2595 .. **Dennin,** Gregory M '86 (Dennin & D) -2745 Main -Lk Placid 12946 **Fx:**523-4766
(718) 928-3700 .. **Dennin,** Kathleen '91 %LSNYC-Bronx -579 Courtlandt Av -Bronx 10451 **Fx:**402-7586
(516) 229-4200 .. **Dennin,** Peter '92 %Mendolia & S -875 Merrick Av -Westbury 11590
(212) 918-3000 .. **Dennin,** Peter J '03 %Hogan L LLP -875 3rd Av -NY 10022
(631) 261-0250 .. **Dennin,** Timothy J '84 (T Dennin,PC) -316 Main -Northprt 11768 **Fx:**261-0395 ***[Securities Law]***
(212) 826-1500 .. **Dennin,** Timothy J '84 (T Dennin,PC) -270 Mad Av -NY 10016 **Fx:**688-6457
(518) 447-7110 .. **Denning,** Craig A '86 %Cnty Atty -112 State -Albany 12207
(212) 268-5136 .. **Denning,** Kristine '94 %Harwood L -350 5th Av -NY 10118
(516) 571-3056 .. **Dennis,** Barry M '75 %Cnty Atty -1 West -Mineola 11501 **Fx:**571-6604
(585) 396-4289 .. **Dennis,** Brian D '87 %DA -27 N Main -Canandaigua 14424 **Fx:**396-4860
(212) 225-2000 .. **Dennis,** Deanna S '07 %Cleary GS&H -1 Lbrty Plz -NY 10006
(518) 562-0600 .. **Dennis,** Heidi '98 (O'Connell & A) -206 W Bay Plz -Plattsbrgh 12901
(212) 804-4200 .. **Dennis,** James M '87 (Mound CW&G) -One Bttry Pk Plz -NY 10004
(212) 862-5512 .. **Dennis,** Jayne M '87 -230 W 135th -NY 10030 **Fx:**862-5324
(518) 465-1425 .. **Dennis,** John H '72 -270 Mt Hope Dr -Albany 12202 **Fx:**465-0364
(212) 980-9600 .. **Dennis,** Kristopher M '02 %Kaufman B&R -120 Bway -NY 10271
(212) 741-1300 .. **Dennis,** M Stephen '85 Thornton Tomasetti -51 Mad Av -NY 10010 **Fx:**645-9236
(212) 681-0600 .. **Dennis,** Manette '81 OfCnsl Ostrager CF&B,PC -570 Lex Av -NY 10022
(212) 668-2894 .. **Dennis,** Neil O '05 %Hon A Gonzalez -One Bowling Grn -NY 10004
(212) 686-7999 .. **Dennis,** Noel '80 -1040 Av of Amer -NY 10018 **Fx:**686-0630
(212) 702-0900 .. **Dennis,** Osman '97 (Axelrod F&D) -260 Mad Av -NY 10016 **Fx:**355-7365
(212) 538-2422 .. **Dennis,** Tracy J '97 Credit Suisse -11 Mad Av -NY 10010
(914) 272-3202 .. **Dennis,** Wm C '95 Entergy Corp -440 Hmltn Av -White Plns 10601
(212) 536-3900 .. **Dennis,** Willie E '90 (K&L Gates LLP) -599 Lex Av -NY 10022
(212) 461-2323 .. **Dennison,** Gregory T '98 %Saiber LLC -44 Wall -NY 10005
(716) 626-1564 .. **Denniston,** Kurt R '10 %Simpson & S PLLC -5555 Main -Williamsvll 14221 **Fx:**626-0366
(212) 425-5566 .. **Denniston,** Lavinia H '93 S Shainwald,PC -200 W 57th -NY 10019 **Fx:**608-5863
(718) 221-5520 .. **Denny,** Jeffrey T '82 -140 Rogers Av -Brklyn 11216
(212) 222-4084 .. **Denny,** Marvina D '04 %R Brewster -356 W 122nd -NY 10027
(914) 323-7000 .. **DeNoia,** Philip J '01 %Wilson EME&D LLP -3 Gannett Dr -White Plns 10604
(516) 739-1100 .. **DeNorscia,** James C '94 (Sonageri & F,LLC) -1461 Franklin Av -Gdn Cty 11530
(631) 665-3400 .. **DeNoto,** Michl P '71 %Siben & S,LLP -90 E Main Bx149P -Bay Shr 11706
(516) 408-1600 .. **DeNoto,** Peter '97 (Heidell PM&B,LLP) -1050 Franklin Av -Gdn Cty 11530

(212) 706-0248 .. **Denowitz,** David C '83 (Hollyer B LLP) -60 E 42nd -NY 10165 **Fx:**(646) 214-0913
(212) 684-6655 .. **deNoyelles,** Griffith G Jr. '76 (Chernofsky & deN) -360 W 22nd -NY 10011 **Fx:**239-4463
(518) 884-9207 .. **Densmore,** James H '82 Family Ct -35 W High -Ballston Spa 12020
(212) 547-5400 .. **Dent,** Rebecca J '10 %McDermott W&E LLP -340 Mad Av -NY 10173
(718) 604-4690 .. **Dent,** Rodney R '93 -254 Decatur -Brklyn 11233 **Fx:**604-8884
(212) 883-2420 .. **Dent,** Valerie Paris '95 %Grand Cntrl Prtnrshp -122 E 42nd -NY 10168
(518) 474-6208 .. **Dentinger,** Jennifer M '97 %Dept of Law -The Cptl -Albany 12224
(585) 263-1000 .. **Dentinger,** Penny A '05 %Nixon P LLP -1100 Clinton Sq -Rchstr 14604
(585) 325-7440 .. **Dentino,** Anthony A '79 (Kaman BMJ&G LLP) -135 Corp Woods -Rchstr 14623
(212) 735-3000 .. **Denton,** Anna B '09 %Skadden ASM&F LLP -4 Times Sq -NY 10036
(212) 906-1200 .. **Denton,** Blake T '09 %Latham & W -885 3rd Av -NY 10022
(607) 734-0661 .. **Denton,** Christopher '78 -311 Lk -Elmira 14901
(516) 775-7007 .. **Denton,** Donna L '89 (Gutman MB&S,PC) -813 Jericho Tpk -New Hyde Pk 11040
(212) 807-8686 .. **Denton,** G Hallett '87 %AFS Intl -71 W 23rd -NY 10010 **Fx:**352-9824
(212) 735-3000 .. **Denton,** J Russel '09 %Skadden ASM&F LLP -4 Times Sq -NY 10036
(315) 336-4700 .. **Denton,** Julie Grow '98 (McMahon & G) -301 N Wshngtn Bx4350 -Rome 13442
(845) 855-1230 .. **Denton,** Kevin A '75 (Denton & M,PC) -One Mem'l Av Bx418 -Pawling 12564 **Fx:**855-0024
(212) 357-3466 .. **Denton,** Maureen B '92 Goldman Sachs -85 Broad -NY 10004
(518) 402-9188 .. **Denue-Hourigan,** Rebecca L '01 %DEC -625 Bway -Albany 12233 **Fx:**402-9018
(212) 226-2800 .. **Denver,** Nicole R '06 %Alterman & B LLP -35 Worth -NY 10013
(212) 506-1700 .. **Denver,** Wm E '96 (Kasowitz BT&F LLP) -1633 Bway -NY 10019
(212) 836-8000 .. **Denvir,** Michl D '08 %Kaye S LLP -425 Park Av -NY 10022
(845) 331-2525 .. **Denvir,** Sean J '82 (Ryan R&R,LLP) -115 Green Bx3153 -Kingston 12402
(212) 265-6888 .. **Denys,** Todd A '00 Cnsl Porzio B&N,PC -156 W 56th -NY 10019
(716) 852-1300 .. **Denz,** Michl D '84 (Amigone S&M,LLP) -350 Main -Buffalo 14202
(646) 386-5700 .. **Deo,** Shalini R '09 Civil Ct -111 Centre -NY 10013
(718) 876-6300 .. **Deodati,** Michl J '83 %DA -130 Styvsnt Pl -Staten Isl 10301
(518) 272-6565 .. **De Oliveira,** Carlo A C '08 %Martin SWD&J -279 River Bx1530 -Troy 12181
(516) 496-5822 .. **DeOliveira,** John '07 %T Spina -170 Froehlich Farm Blvd -Woodbury 11797 **Fx:**496-5420
(212) 909-6000 .. **DeOliveira,** Pedro L '10 %Debevoise & P LLP -919 3rd Av -NY 10022
(718) 876-6300 .. **DeOliveira,** Wanda L '93 DA -130 Styvsnt Pl -Staten Isl 10301
(212) 608-2000 .. **Deonarine,** Barry D '94 -225 Bway -NY 10007 **Fx:**571-6679
(212) 310-8000 .. **Deopersaud,** Savitri A '05 Weil G&M LLP -767 5th Av -NY 10153
(212) 446-4800 .. **Deoras,** Akshay S '09 %Kirkland & E LLP -153 E 53rd -NY 10022
(212) 344-4700 .. **DeOrchis,** Mario E '48 SrCnsl DeOrchis & Prtnrs LLP -61 Bway -NY 10006
(212) 344-4700 .. **DeOrchis & Partners LLP** -61 Bway -NY 10006 **Fx:**422-5299
(212) 344-4700 .. **DeOrchis,** Vincent M '75 (DeOrchis & Prtnrs LLP) -61 Bway -NY 10006
(212) 974-2400 .. **DeOreo,** Matthew G '99 %J Burstein -1790 Bway -NY 10019 **Fx:**974-2944
(845) 357-1555 .. **Deoul,** Gerard '62 -33 Dawn Ln -Suffern 10901 **Fx:**357-1555
(516) 877-5600 .. **DePace,** Gerald '66 %R Tusa -1225 Franklin Av -Gdn Cty 11530 **Fx:**877-5695
(646) 340-1904 .. **DePaiva,** Khadine D '05 Leg Aid -953 Southrn Blvd -Bronx 10459
(212) 636-7813 .. **De Palma,** Annette M '86 %Fordham Univ Sch of Law -140 W 62nd -NY 10023 **Fx:**636-6899
(315) 255-2859 .. **DePalma,** Carl J '03 -17 Cady -Auburn 13021 **Fx:**253-9253
(212) 771-9507 .. **DePalma,** Danielle M '04 %CIT -505 5th Av -NY 10017
(212) 344-5680 .. **DePalma,** Richd A '92 (Thompson H LLP) -335 Mad Av -NY 10017
(718) 987-1717 .. **DePalma,** Robt J '87 -88 New Dorp Plz -Staten Isl 10306 **Fx:**351-4350
(914) 358-1090 .. **DePalma,** Stephen '86 -399 Knollwood Rd -White Plns 10603 **Fx:**358-1091
(212) 972-0786 .. **DePalma,** Steven C '05 Cnsl Nicoll D&S LLP -250 Park Av -NY 10177 **Fx:**953-7201
(718) 351-3748 .. **DePalo,** Anne-Louise '87 -94 Hancock -Staten Isl 10305 **Fx:**351-3792
(212) 872-1000 .. **Depalo,** Laurie E '10 -One Bryant Park -NY 10036 **Fx:**872-1002
(212) 318-6724 .. **DePaola,** Bruce S '92 (Paul HJ&W LLP) -75 E 55th -NY 10022
(212) 484-3734 .. **DePaola,** Dennis P '97 %Orsid Realty Corp -1740 Bway -NY 10019
(718) 281-4000 .. **DePaola,** John R '83 (Papa D&B) -42-40 Bell Blvd -Bayside 11361 **Fx:**281-4030
(845) 656-5415 .. **De Paola,** Jos P '06 -320 Turk Hill Rd -Brewstr 10509 **Fx:**704-0475
(716) 856-1344 .. **DePaolo,** John P '91 SpclCnsl Bouvier Prtnrshp,LLP -350 Main -Buffalo 14202 **Fx:**856-1369
(212) 438-3651 .. **DePaolo,** Jos J '00 Standard & Poor's -55 Water -NY 10041
(518) 377-1562 .. **DePasquale,** Leonard '71 -1150 Millington Rd -Schnctdy 12309
(212) 335-9000 .. **DePasquale,** Lisa '85 %DA -1 Hogan Pl -NY 10013
(716) 858-2424 .. **DePasquale,** Mary Beth '02 %DA -25 Delaware Av -Buffalo 14202 **Fx:**858-7425
(212) 819-8200 .. **De Pasquale,** Megan '07 %White & C LLP -1155 Av of Amer -NY 10036
(718) 923-0690 .. **De Pass,** Aaron C '00 %R Santoriella PC -335 Adams -Brklyn 11201 **Fx:**923-0683
(212) 788-0823 .. **DePaul,** Philip R '09 %Law Dept -100 Church -NY 10007 **Fx:**788-0367
(516) 922-7686 .. **DePaula,** Jos A '77 -600 Pine Hllw Rd -E Norwich 11732
(212) 903-9000 .. **De Paula,** Julia S-C '08 %Linklaters -1345 Av of Amer -NY 10105
(212) 859-8000 .. **Depaz,** Keisha L '08 %Fried FHS&J LLP -1 NY Plz -NY 10004
(917) 592-1744 .. **DePedro,** Mari '93 -78 Bedford -NY 10014
(212) 252-0004 .. **DePekary,** Denise M '94 (Carroll M&K LLC) -570 Lex Av -NY 10022
(718) 816-0005 .. **De Peppo-Malloy,** Valerie M '05 %Angiuli K&G,LLP -60 Bay -Staten Isl 10301
(718) 590-8585 .. **De Peralta,** Caterina '05 %Adm Chldrn Srvcs -900 Sheridan Av -Bronx 10451
(212) 267-3091 .. **DePeralta,** Marcello L '02 %Wilentz G&S -110 William -NY 10038 **Fx:**267-3828
(315) 762-2992 .. **DePerno & Khanzadian** -Bx83 -Sylvan Bch 13157 **Fx:**762-2946
(315) 762-2992 .. **DePerno,** Rocco A '69 (DePerno & K) -Bx83 -Sylvan Bch 13157
(607) 777-9601 .. **DePersis,** Dominic S '99 %F Xlander -520 Columbia Dr -Johnson Cty 13790 **Fx:**777-9609
(516) 248-4840 .. **DePeter,** Edw '74 %Boundary Title Srvc -69 E Jericho Tpk -Mineola 11501 **Fx:**746-1449
(914) 323-7000 .. **Depeter,** Sheilagh M '03 %Wilson EME&D LLP -3 Gannett Dr -White Plns 10604
(716) 853-3801 .. **DePeters,** Alan J '08 %Kenney SL&N,LLP -14 Lafayette Sq -Buffalo 14203
(212) 250-2500 .. **Depetris,** Alexis N '06 %Deutsche Bank -60 Wall -NY 10005
(631) 287-2777 .. **DePetris,** Richd E '70 -21 S Main Bx2297 -Southampton 11969
(212) 557-7747 .. **DePetris,** Ronald E '70 (DePetris & B,LLP) -240 Mad Av -NY 10016 **Fx:**557-3383
(718) 286-6000 .. **Depetro,** Matthew L '07 %DA -125-01 Qns Blvd -Kew Gdns 11415
(516) 594-4944 .. **De Phillips,** Catherine '95 Airway Companies -15 Clinton Av -Rockvll Ctr 11570
(212) 265-6888 .. **DePhillips,** Christopher P '99 (Porzio B&N,PC) -156 W 56th -NY 10019
(212) 259-8000 .. **Dephoure,** Emily A '99 %Dewey & L LLP -1301 Av of Amer -NY 10019
(212) 790-0456 .. **DePierro,** Heather Ann '05 Benj N Cardozo Schl of Law -55 5th Av -NY 10003 **Fx:**790-0448
(631) 249-8200 .. **DePinto,** David J '00 (DePinto N & Assoc,LLP) -445 Broadhllw Rd -Melvll 11747 **Fx:**249-8209
(212) 446-4800 .. **DePippo,** Henry J '86 (Kirkland & E LLP) -153 E 53rd -NY 10022
(212) 335-4500 .. **Depke,** John E '95 (DLA Piper LLP) -1251 Av of Amer -NY 10020
(516) 873-8600 .. **Deplas,** Georgia '94 %Mahon & B -21 Glen -Glen Cove 11542 **Fx:**873-1937
(212) 449-1000 .. **DePoalo,** Sandra L '93 %Merrill Lynch -220 Bway -NY 10038
(518) 828-9444 .. **Depoian,** Carolyn K '10 %Rapport MWS&R,LLP -436 Union -Hudson 12534
(315) 597-6789 .. **De Point,** James I '72 -1706 Palmyra-Marion Rd Bx92 -Palmyra 14522 **Fx:**597-6789
(212) 310-8000 .. **Depowski,** Kristen L '09 %Weil G&M LLP -767 5th Av -NY 10153
(212) 446-2300 .. **DePozsgay,** Stefan '07 %Boies S&F LLP -575 Lex Av -NY 10022
(914) 962-4100 .. **de Prado,** Alfred F M '66 -2014 Crompond Rd Bx173 -Yorktwn Hts 10598 **Fx:**962-4188
(716) 563-2617 .. **DePrima,** Gina M '04 -3380 Sheridan Dr -Buffalo 14226
(516) 733-4905 .. **DePrisco,** Patrick P '95 -114-11 135th Av -Jamaica 11420
(212) 471-3803 .. **DeProfio,** Elizabeth A '01 %Fidelity Natl Title Ins -1 Park Av -NY 10016 **Fx:**481-8747
(845) 294-3361 .. **DeProspo Petrizzo & Longo** -42 Park Pl -Goshen 10924 **Fx:**294-8246
(845) 294-3361 .. **De Prospo,** Wm L '85 (DeProspo P&L) -42 Park Pl -Goshen 10924
(315) 425-2700 .. **Deptula,** George S '67 OfCnsl Hiscock & B,LLP -One Park Pl -Syracuse 13202
(212) 788-0597 .. **Depugh,** David L '99 %Law Dept -100 Church -NY 10007 **Fx:**788-0367
(315) 734-2000 .. **De Pumpo,** Regina A '01 %Utica Natl Ins -180 Genesee Bx530 -Utica 13502 **Fx:**734-2198
(212) 557-7200 .. **Deraco,** Maria C '98 %Davidoff M&H,LLP -605 3rd Av -NY 10158
(845) 562-9100 .. **de Ramon,** Roderick E '88 (Rider W&F,PC) -655 Little Britain Rd -New Windsor 12553
(212) 267-3320 .. **D'Erasmo,** Raymond M '80 (Savona D&H LLC) -111 Bway -NY 10006
(212) 295-6430 .. **Derbes,** Elizabeth Keith '06 (WilmerHale) -399 Park Av -NY 10022
(212) 603-6300 .. **D'Ercole,** John D '86 (Robinson BLGG&G PC) -875 3rd Av -NY 10022
(845) 477-2453 .. **Derderian,** Stephen H '74 -95 Windemere Av Bx66 -Greenwd Lk 10925 **Fx:**477-3983
(212) 309-6000 .. **Dereka,** Jennifer L '03 %Morgan L&B LLP -101 Park Av -NY 10178
(914) 232-8174 .. **Deren Genett & Macreery** -28 Edgemont Rd -Katonah 10536 **Fx:**232-0363
(716) 845-2655 .. **Deren,** Jos V Jr. '81 %City Court -50 Delaware Av -Buffalo 14202
(716) 822-0722 .. **Deren,** Patricia A '85 -24 Cheryl Dr -Lackawanna 14218
(631) 853-4049 .. **Deren-Braddish,** Barbara A '89 %Cnty Atty -Dennison Bldg Bx6100 -Hauppauge 11788 **Fx:**853-5169
(631) 265-0134 .. **Derenze,** James V '90 %Kral CRRP&G,LLP -538 Broadhllw Rd -Melvll 11747 **Fx:**265-4289
(212) 223-4000 .. **DeRenzi,** Bruce D '88 (Crowell & M LLP) -590 Mad Av -NY 10022
(516) 408-1600 .. **Derevlany,** Louise A '85 (Heidell PM&B,LLP) -1050 Franklin Av -Gdn Cty 11530
(518) 283-7496 .. **Derevlany,** Michl J '97 -Bx263 -Wynantskill 12198 **Fx:**283-7496
(212) 836-8000 .. **Derevyanny,** Gerald Y '10 Kaye S LLP -425 Park Av -NY 10022
(212) 697-8100 .. **Derfner,** Donald A '69 (Derfner & G,LLP) -60 E 42nd -NY 10165
(212) 563-6557 .. **Derfner,** Eric B '97 Feil Org -7 Penn Plz -NY 10001
(212) 697-8100 .. **Derfner & Gillett,LLP** -60 E 42nd -NY 10165 **Fx:**681-9122
(212) 563-6557 .. **Derfner,** Justin M '97 Feil Org -7 Penn Plz -NY 10001 **Fx:**563-6657
(516) 766-1619 .. **Dergarabedian,** Michl '90 (Dergarabedian D & Assoc) -11 Clinton Av -Rockvll Ctr 11570 **Fx:**766-6121
(212) 819-8200 .. **Derhalli,** Hazem Y '01 (White & C LLP) -1155 Av of Amer -NY 10036
(718) 641-1795 .. **Deri,** Lynne M '89 -159-20 88th -Howard Bch 11414 **Fx:**323-3124
(718) 250-2000 .. **Derian,** Renee Brooke '89 %DA -350 Jay -Brklyn 11201 **Fx:**250-2314
(914) 694-2150 .. **DeRicco,** Steven P '87 (Whitman BA&M LLC) -99 Court -White Plns 10601
(718) 875-1300 .. **DeRico,** Barbara A '06 %Applt Div 2nd Dept -45 Monroe Pl -Brklyn 11201 **Fx:**858-2446
(212) 431-9700 .. **Derienzo,** Harold '90 %Parodneck Foundation -121 6th Av -NY 10013 **Fx:**431-9783
(516) 799-7380 .. **De Riggi,** Anthony P '61 De Riggi D&D -5788 Merrick Rd -Massapequa 11758 **Fx:**799-7391
(516) 296-7000 .. **De Riggi,** Brendan J '97 (Certilman BA&H,LLP) -90 Merrick Av -E Meadow 11554
(212) 351-4500 .. **DeRight,** Robt E Jr. '68 OfCnsl Epstein B&G,PC -250 Park Av -NY 10177
(212) 406-1700 .. **Derin,** Natalia '08 %Queller FWF&K LLP -233 Bway -NY 10279

(518) 474-7330 .. **Dering,** James E '92 %Dept of Law -The Cptl -Albany 12224
(212) 373-3000 .. **Derish,** Julia A '10 %Paul WRW&G LLP -1285 Av of Amer -NY 10019
(718) 746-7900 .. **De Riso,** Dominick A '68 Dorsey & D -24-44 F Lewis Blvd -Flushng 11357 **Fx:**746-7781
(631) 761-5451 .. **Derkasch,** Paul J '73 CAS -490 Wheeler Rd -Hauppauge 11788 **Fx:**761-5454
(585) 325-2426 .. **Derleth,** Thos J '55 -2200 Rynlds Arcd -Rchstr 14614
(718) 760-8518 .. **Der-Long,** Ma '92 -90-49 53rd Av -Elmhrst 11373 **Fx:**592-4039
(212) 751-3001 .. **Derman,** Andrew B '05 (Thompson & K LLP) -919 3rd Av -NY 10022
(212) 983-3100 .. **Derman,** Bret S '93 %Enhance Fncl Srvcs -335 Mad Av -NY 10017
(212) 575-7900 .. **Dermesropian,** Daniele '02 %Ballon SB&N,PC -729 7th Av -NY 10019
(315) 479-6445 .. **DeRoberts,** Jeffrey '93 -333 E Onondaga -Syracuse 13202 **Fx:**295-2393
(212) 574-1200 .. **DeRoche,** Mandy B '07 %Seward & K LLP -1 Bttry Pk Plz -NY 10004
(718) 816-8411 .. **DeRogatis,** Rosemarie A '85 -315 Demorest Av -Staten Isl 10314 **Fx:**816-8420
(518) 465-6420 .. **DerOhannesian,** Paul II '79 (DerOhannesian & D) -677 Bway -Albany 12207 **Fx:**427-0614
(212) 554-0400 .. **deRosa,** Alisa S '99 %Grubman I&S,PC -152 W 57th -NY 10019
(845) 486-2110 .. **DeRosa,** Anthony J '72 %Cnty Atty -22 Market -Poughkeepsie 12601 **Fx:**486-2002
(718) 544-6800 .. **DeRosa,** Dominick '91 %JA Faraldo -125-10 Qns Blvd -Kew Gdns 11415
(212) 588-0800 .. **DeRosa,** Frank J '75 (Frommer L&H LLP) -745 5th Av -NY 10151
(607) 255-3626 .. **DeRosa,** John R '93 %Cornell Law Schl -Myron Taylor Hall -Ithaca 14853 **Fx:**255-7193
(212) 356-8100 .. **DeRosa,** Ralph '96 %CIR -520 8th Av -NY 10018 **Fx:**356-8111
(914) 631-0913 .. **DeRosa,** Ralph A '84 -54 Main -Tarrytwn 10591 **Fx:**631-0946
(716) 284-8111 .. **DeRosa,** Stephen J '80 -663 Main Bx2261 -Niagara Fls 14302
(516) 872-8580 .. **De Rosa,** Vincent J '60 -Bx037015 -Elmont 11003
(716) 855-0600 .. **de Rosas,** Jorge Santiago '01 %Wolfgang & W -69 Delaware Av -Buffalo 14202 **Fx:**855-1016
(212) 270-2359 .. **DeRose,** Angela J '04 JP Morgan Chase -270 Park Av -NY 10017
(716) 372-2161 .. **DeRose,** Danl A '73 Kehoe & D -613 Community Bk Bldg Bx548 -Olean 14760 **Fx:**372-2163
(718) 286-6000 .. **Derose,** Louisa M '08 %DA -125-01 Qns Blvd -Kew Gdns 11415
(212) 335-9981 .. **Derose,** Mirella A '07 DA -1 Hogan Pl -NY 10013
(718) 279-2000 .. **DeRose,** R James Jr. '75 (DeRose & S) -213-44 38th Av -Bayside 11361
(212) 415-8600 .. **DeRose,** R James J III '04 %Locke LB&L LLP -3 World Fncl Ctr -NY 10281
(718) 875-1300 .. **DeRose,** Richd '78 %Appllt Div 2nd Dept -45 Monroe Pl -Brklyn 11201 **Fx:**858-2446
(718) 279-2000 .. **DeRose & Surico** -213-44 38th Av -Bayside 11361 **Fx:**279-1948
(518) 474-6740 .. **Derosia,** Darrin B '97 Dept of State -41 State -Albany 12231 **Fx:**473-9211
(516) 280-6900 .. **DeRossi,** Mario J '02 (Stern & D,LLP) -1 Old Cntry Rd -Carle Pl 11514 **Fx:**294-0094
(631) 231-1450 .. **DeRosso,** Danl J '94 %Feldman K&M,PC -330 Vndrblt Motor Pkwy -Hauppauge 11788
(212) 759-0707 .. **Derounian,** Paul D '69 P Derounian,PC -900 3rd Av -NY 10022 **Fx:**752-3196
(212) 242-6650 .. **Derr,** Maria St A '78 -80 5th Av -NY 10011 **Fx:**989-7795
(631) 547-4271 .. **Derrick,** Eugene J '92 Nikon Inc -1300 Walt Whitman Rd -Melvll 11747 **Fx:**547-6261
(716) 855-0203 .. **Derrico,** David F '95 Wstrn NY Law Cntr -237 Main -Buffalo 14203
(212) 490-3000 .. **Derrico,** Donald G '91 (Wilson EME&D LLP) -150 E 42nd -NY 10017
(914) 323-7000 .. **Derrico,** Donald G '91 (Wilson EME&D LLP) -3 Gannett Dr -White Plns 10604
(516) 294-0540 .. **D'Errico,** Frank N '75 (D'Errico D,LLP) -1205 Franklin Av -Gdn Cty 11530 **Fx:**280-5301
(631) 501-3142 .. **D'Errico,** Larraine '88 %J Humphreys -3 Huntngtn Quad Bx9028 -Melvll 11747 **Fx:**501-3085
(212) 218-8760 .. **Dersch,** Stephanie H '05 %Hargraves M&C,PC -420 Lex Av -NY 10170
(212) 964-6611 .. **Derschowitz,** Harold J '81 OfCnsl Lester SK&D -120 Bway -NY 10271
(212) 889-4009 .. **Dershowitz Eiger & Adelson,PC** -220 5th Av -NY 10001 **Fx:**889-3595
(212) 407-8015 .. **Dershowitz,** Jamin '89 NBA -645 5th Av -NY 10022
(646) 386-3657 .. **Dershowitz,** Marilyn B '87 Supreme Ct Spcl Referee -60 Centre -NY 10007
(516) 481-0393 .. **Dershowitz,** Morris '42 -434 Walton -W Hempstead 11552
(212) 889-4009 .. **Dershowitz,** Nathan Z '66 (Dershowitz E&A,PC) -220 5th Av -NY 10001
(212) 465-6000 .. **Dershowitz,** Rana K '96 %Madison Sq Grdn,LP -2 Penn Plz -NY 10121 **Fx:**465-6011
(212) 631-3568 .. **Dertinger,** Wm E Jr. '93 Esquire Consultant Grp,Ltd -132 E 43rd -NY 10017
(212) 839-5300 .. **Deru,** Adekunle Adedayo '05 %Sidley A LLP -787 7th Av -NY 10019
(315) 472-2440 .. **DeRue,** Patricia L '89 -731 James -Syracuse 13203 **Fx:**410-0015
(212) 768-6700 .. **DeRuyter,** Kerri M '03 %Sonnenschein N&R LLP -2 World Fncl Ctr -NY 10281
(212) 785-5115 .. **Dervishi,** Fatos '06 (Dervishi L&M,PC) -11 Bway -NY 10004 **Fx:**480-8560
(212) 838-4644 .. **Derzaw,** Richd L '82 -477 Mad Av -NY 10022
(212) 660-3000 .. **Derzie,** Cyril M '04 %Sullivan & W LLP -1290 Av of Amer -NY 10104
(212) 310-8000 .. **Desai,** Anish R '06 %Weil G&M LLP -767 5th Av -NY 10153
(212) 310-8000 .. **Desai,** Kavita C '09 %Weil G&M LLP -767 5th Av -NY 10153
(212) 768-6700 .. **Desai,** Mansi '08 %Sonnenschein N&R LLP -2 World Fncl Ctr -NY 10281
(212) 819-8200 .. **Desai,** Mihir A '07 %White & C LLP -1155 Av of Amer -NY 10036
(212) 728-8000 .. **Desai,** Mili G '10 %Willkie F&G LLP -787 7th Av -NY 10019
(212) 593-6700 .. **Desai,** Neel S '10 %Aaronson RF&D,LLP -757 3rd Av -NY 10017
(212) 588-0800 .. **Desai,** Sam V '06 %Frommer L&H LLP -745 5th Av -NY 10151
(212) 679-2900 .. **Desai,** Samira H '09 %Hoffman & P LLP -260 Mad Av -NY 10016
(718) 739-6400 .. **DeSalvo,** Frank '99 DHCR -92-31 Union Hall -Jamaica 11433 **Fx:**262-7938
(212) 858-5144 .. **DeSalvo,** Frank J Jr. '98 FINRA -1 Lbrty Plz -NY 10006
(212) 922-9700 .. **DeSalvo,** Jos D '75 %1st Amer Title -633 3rd Av -NY 10017 **Fx:**922-0881
(516) 776-2505 .. **DeSalvo,** Karen J '90 -20 Rose -Plainvw 11803
(212) 560-9790 .. **DeSalvo,** Marc C '93 (M DeSalvo PC) -358 5th Av -NY 10001 **Fx:**560-9570
(315) 446-0254 .. **DeSantis,** Angela C '83 -112 Rosewll Meadow -DeWitt 13214
(718) 241-4644 .. **De Santis,** Dominick '99 %Crowe Financial Svcs -2018 Ralph Av -Brklyn 11234
(518) 449-3359 .. **De Santis,** Eugene D '79 (Malkin & R) -80 State -Albany 12207 **Fx:**449-5788
(518) 251-2215 .. **DeSantis,** Frank V '76 (Staples & D,PC) -280 Main Bx66 -N Creek 12853 **Fx:**251-5038
(516) 739-1000 .. **De Santis,** Gerard D '69 -1 Old Cntry Rd -Carle Pl 11514 **Fx:**739-1006
(917) 267-8890 .. **DeSantis,** James J '09 DeSantis Firm,LLC -110 Wall -NY 10005 **Fx:**(201) 490-1783
(212) 701-3000 .. **DeSantis,** Jonathan M '04 %Cahill G&R LLP -80 Pine -NY 10005 **Fx:**269-5420
(516) 739-1000 .. **De Santis,** Marc G '02 %G De Santis -1 Old Cntry Rd -Carle Pl 11514 **Fx:**739-1006
(315) 724-2155 .. **DeSantis,** Michl P '50 (DeSantis & D) -286 Genesee -Utica 13502 **Fx:**724-6876
(315) 724-2155 .. **DeSantis,** Michl V '77 (DeSantis & D) -286 Genesee -Utica 13502 **Fx:**724-6876
(516) 681-1100 .. **DeSantis,** Michl V '94 (Kaufman DV&G,LLP) -135 Crsswys Park Dr -Woodbury 11797
(212) 869-3200 .. **DeSantis,** Salvatore J '86 (Molod S&D,PC) -104 W 40th -NY 10018
(518) 690-7850 .. **DeSantis,** Shauna McMillen '87 Nature Conservancy -195 New Karner Rd -Albany 12205
(212) 444-6461 .. **DeSanto,** Angelique F M '03 %ITG Inc -380 Mad Av -NY 10017
(631) 369-6240 .. **De Santo,** Catherine C '97 -431 Griffing Av -Rvrhead 11901
(212) 326-2000 .. **DeSanto,** Ralph P '87 Cnsl O'Melveny & M LLP -7 Times Sq -NY 10036
(518) 465-3484 .. **Desany,** Jessica A '99 (Carter CCBM&L,PC) -20 Corp Wds Blvd -Albany 12211
(212) 821-2749 .. **DeSaro-Calella,** Jolie Ann '96 UBS Fincl Svcs Inc -299 Park Av -NY 10171
(212) 363-1380 .. **DeScherer,** Nilufer Ozizmir '96 Herten BSCBL&H,LLC -747 3rd Av -NY 10017
(212) 728-8000 .. **DeScherer,** Richd K '70 (Willkie F&G LLP) -787 7th Av -NY 10019
(212) 259-8000 .. **d'Esclapon,** Pierre F '75 OfCnsl Dewey & L LLP -1301 Av of Amer -NY 10019
(212) 610-6300 .. **DeSear,** Edw M '74 (Allen & O) -1221 Av of Amer -NY 10020
(718) 845-4422 .. **De Sena,** Louis A '68 De Sena & D -96-11 101st Av -Ozone Pk 11416 **Fx:**738-6103
(631) 360-7333 .. **De Sena,** Louis J '97 (De Sena & S) -1383 Vets Mem'l Hwy -Hauppauge 11788
(516) 763-1226 .. **DeSena,** Nancy Fox '84 -68 Oxford Rd -Rockvll Ctr 11570 **Fx:**763-1226
(212) 762-4901 .. **DeSena,** Ralph A '95 Morgan Stanley -1221 Av of Amer -NY 10020
(212) 233-7744 .. **DeSena,** Ralph E Jr. '81 (DeSena & Assoc,LLP) -225 Bway -NY 10007 **Fx:**766-2298
(631) 360-7333 .. **De Sena & Sweeney** -1383 Vets Mem'l Hwy -Hauppauge 11788 **Fx:**360-3763
(212) 836-8000 .. **DeSevo,** Richd A '77 Cnsl Kaye S LLP -425 Park Av -NY 10022
(716) 676-2475 .. **Desha,** Michl J '78 -7 Park Sq Bx213 -Franklinvll 14737 **Fx:**676-2499
(212) 860-2423 .. **Deshensky,** George '62 -152 E 94th -NY 10128
(516) 374-2267 .. **DeSibio,** Nicholas '63 -1253 Colonial Rd -Hewlett 11557
(212) 318-6000 .. **Desiderio,** Christopher M '05 %Paul HJ&W LLP -75 E 55th -NY 10022
(212) 557-4000 .. **Desiderio,** Frank J '73 (Grunfeld DLS&K LLP) -399 Park Av -NY 10022
(212) 825-0365 .. **Desiderio,** John M '67 (AL Bailey,PC) -120 Bway -NY 10271 **Fx:**825-0999
(716) 826-3038 .. **Desiderio,** Lawr J '90 -69 Delaware Av -Buffalo 14202 **Fx:**826-3064
(212) 705-7000 .. **Desieno,** Timothy B '04 (Bingham M LLP) -399 Park Av -NY 10022
(212) 458-2868 .. **De Silva,** James T '93 AIG -175 Water -NY 10038
(212) 705-7000 .. **DeSilva,** Joanne '01 OfCnsl Bingham M LLP -399 Park Av -NY 10022
(212) 688-8555 .. **De Silva,** Miwa '06 %Fragomen DB&L LLP -7 Hanover Sq -NY 10004
(315) 345-8845 .. **deSilva,** Raymond J Jr. '57 -127 Hllcrst Rd -Syracuse 13219 **Fx:**468-2618
(516) 942-0244 .. **DeSilva,** Robt '89 %Office oDA&R -375 N Bway -Jericho 11753 **Fx:**942-0353
(518) 486-9567 .. **DeSilva,** Sharon V '97 %OTDA-Fair Hearings -40 N Pearl -Albany 12243 **Fx:**473-6735
(631) 844-7027 .. **DeSilva,** Susan R '91 ADECCO -175 Broadhllw Rd -Melvll 11747
(585) 419-8800 .. **DeSimon,** Thos A '86 (Harris B PLLC) -99 Garnsey Rd -Pittsfrd 14534
(914) 668-9600 .. **DeSimone,** Alphonse E '87 (Miller & P,PC) -175 Main -White Plns 10601
(212) 307-0023 .. **DeSimone Aviles Shorter & Oxamendi LLP** -145 Hudson -NY 10013 **Fx:**307-0187
(212) 265-6888 .. **DeSimone,** C John III '98 Cnsl Porzio B&N,PC -156 W 56th -NY 10019
(516) 822-8900 .. **DeSimone,** Dawn C '93 Fiedelman & M -2 Jericho Plz -Jericho 11753
(212) 691-1201 .. **DeSimone,** Giro '93 -224 W 4th -NY 10014 **Fx:**929-6294
(212) 506-2500 .. **DeSimone,** Jos '96 (Mayer B LLP) -1675 Bway -NY 10019
(212) 300-1100 .. **De Simone,** Jos F '96 %Clair G LLP -555 Mad Av -NY 10022 **Fx:**300-1111
(516) 572-2381 .. **De Simone,** Josephine E '97 %Dist Ct -99 Main -Hempstd 11550
(845) 638-5001 .. **DeSimone,** Maria T '04 %DA -1 S Main -New Cty 10956 **Fx:**638-5070
(212) 210-9537 .. **De Simone,** Michl P '93 Cnsl Alston & B LLP -90 Park Av -NY 10016

(212) 819-8200 .. **Desimone,** Michl P '09 %White & C LLP -1155 Av of Amer -NY 10036
(212) 307-0023 .. **DeSimone,** Ralph '95 (DeSimone AS&O LLP) -145 Hudson -NY 10013
(518) 457-4652 .. **de Simone,** Richd J '83 %Dept Correctional Srvcs -1220 Wshngtn Av -Albany 12226 **Fx:**486-9751
(631) 765-3535 .. **DeSimone,** Scott '92 -41780 Route 25 Bx233 -Peconic 11958 **Fx:**765-5148
(212) 836-8000 .. **DeSimone,** Thos '05 %Kaye S LLP -425 Park Av -NY 10022
(212) 613-2077 .. **DeSimone,** Thos R '06 %Gibbons PC -1 Penn Plz -NY 10119 **Fx:**554-9627
(718) 261-3000 .. **DeSimone,** Toby '92 -118-21 Qns Blvd -Frst Hlls 11375 **Fx:**793-0385
(212) 447-5500 .. **Desimone,** Todd J '06 %Quinn M LLP -274 Mad Av -NY 10016 **Fx:**889-2981
(212) 909-6000 .. **DeSimone,** Vanessa Stich '05 %Debevoise & P LLP -919 3rd Av -NY 10022
(212) 867-6233 .. **Desimone,** Wayne '83 -362 5th Av -NY 10001 **Fx:**(516) 869-3408
(585) 451-9932 .. **Desino,** Frank A '84 -Bx976 -Penfld 14526
(212) 577-3271 .. **Desir,** Robt R Jr. '02 %Leg Aid -199 Water -NY 10038
(212) 728-8000 .. **Desisto,** John M '09 %Willkie F&G LLP -787 7th Av -NY 10019
(516) 620-6360 .. **DeSiver,** David B '94 Rogak & G,LLP -50 Charles Lindburgh Blvd -Uniondale 11553
(212) 474-1000 .. **Des Lauriers,** Stephane P '04 Cravath S&M LLP -825 8th Av -NY 10019
(212) 351-3400 .. **Desmarais,** John M '89 (Desmarais LLP) -230 Park Av -NY 10169 **Fx:**351-3401
(212) 906-1200 .. **Desmarais,** Kimberly A '02 %Latham & W -885 3rd Av -NY 10022
(585) 454-5190 .. **Des Marteau,** George '74 (Des Marteau & B) -370 Rynlds Arcd -Rchstr 14614
(585) 232-6500 .. **Des Marteau,** Leslie E '01 Cnsl Harter S&E LLP -1600 Bausch & Lomb Pl -Rchstr 14604
(212) 818-9200 .. **Desmond,** Carol Spawn '83 Cnsl Satterlee SB&B LLP -230 Park Av -NY 10169
(716) 856-4200 .. **Desmond,** Chas S II '89 (Gibson M&C,LLP) -69 Delaware Av -Buffalo 14202
(212) 506-2500 .. **Desmond,** Christopher J '08 %Mayer B LLP -1675 Bway -NY 10019
(212) 506-1700 .. **Desmond,** Darlene M '93 Kasowitz BT&F LLP -1633 Bway -NY 10019
(631) 264-0303 .. **Desmond,** David S '92 (VanNostrand & M) -53 Bway Bx307 -Amityvll 11701
(212) 326-3939 .. **Desmond,** Mary E '00 Jones D -222 E 41st -NY 10017
(716) 851-7050 .. **Desmond,** Maura C '84 %DEC -270 Mich Av -Buffalo 14203 **Fx:**851-7211
(917) 777-4200 .. **Desmond,** Michl J '08 (Bingham M LLP) -1 Bttry Pk Plz -NY 10004
(212) 801-2193 .. **Desmond,** Scott M '83 OfCnsl Greenberg T,LLP -200 Park Av -NY 10166
(212) 591-9500 .. **Desner,** Steven Z '76 %Pub Srvc Mutual Ins -1 Park Av -NY 10016 **Fx:**591-9600
(518) 402-9706 .. **Desnoyers,** Dale A '90 %DEC -625 Bway -Albany 12233 **Fx:**402-9020
(518) 402-9188 .. **Desnoyers,** Patricia J '90 %DEC -625 Bway -Albany 12233 **Fx:**402-9018
(631) 231-6034 .. **DeSocio,** Jerald J '80 (DeSocio & F,PC) -245 Marcus Blvd -Hauppauge 11788 **Fx:**231-6072
(516) 628-2356 .. **DeSocio,** Jerald J '80 (DeSocio & F,PC) -271 Bayvll Av -Bayvll 11709 **Fx:**628-2770
(212) 472-1870 .. **De Sola,** Isabella M '84 -346 E 76th -NY 10021
(212) 832-4770 .. **DeSola,** Michl J '95 (DeSola Grp) -1 Penn Plz -NY 10119
(212) 428-2515 .. **DeSole,** Lauren P '87 %OCA -25 Beaver -NY 10004 **Fx:**428-2513
(212) 227-5117 .. **DeSorbo,** Louis S '99 -233 Bway -NY 10279
(516) 505-7715 .. **DeSousa,** Frank A '92 -24 Main -Hempstd 11550
(518) 533-3000 .. **DeSoyza,** Sanjeeve K '03 %Bond S&K,PLLC -111 Wshngtn Av -Albany 12210
(212) 527-1000 .. **Despas-Barous,** Katina '98 %Jones HC&B PC -1 Bttry Pk Plz -NY 10004
(212) 318-6000 .. **Despins,** Luc A '86 (Paul HJ&W LLP) -75 E 55th -NY 10022
(212) 284-2300 .. **DeSpirito,** Justin A '03 Jefferies & Co,Inc -520 Mad Av -NY 10022
(914) 591-5400 .. **D'Esposito,** Frank G '86 %D'Ambrosio & D,PC -42 Main -Irvngtn 10533 **Fx:**591-5122
(212) 696-0046 .. **D'Esposito,** James J '80 -330 Mad Av -NY 10017 **Fx:**(646) 495-5009
(914) 997-0500 .. **D'Esposito,** Jeanne F '91 (Lowey DC&H,PC) -1 N Bway -White Plns 10601
(914) 323-7000 .. **Despotakis,** Constantine A '77 (Wilson EME&D LLP) -3 Gannett Dr -White Plns 10604
(212) 966-6700 .. **DesRochers,** Andre '02 (Gray K LLP) -207 W 25th -NY 10001 **Fx:**966-6051
(914) 995-3237 .. **Desrosiers,** Danielle A '02 %Cnty Atty -148 Martine Av -White Plns 10601
(212) 715-1000 .. **Desrosiers,** Kris D '10 %Arnold & P LLP -399 Park Av -NY 10022
(212) 480-5284 .. **Dess,** Susan A '97 %Insurance Dept -25 Beaver -NY 10004 **Fx:**480-5272
(212) 682-2288 .. **Dessberg,** Claudio J '87 (Sankel S&M,LLP) -750 3rd Av -NY 10017
(212) 460-4889 .. **Dessen,** Eric M '89 Con Ed -4 Irving Pl -NY 10003 **Fx:**260-8627
(914) 323-7000 .. **Dessi,** Antonella '02 %Wilson EME&D LLP -3 Gannett Dr -White Plns 10604
(212) 422-0202 .. **Dessi,** Mark A '00 %Sedgwick DM&A LLP -125 Broad -NY 10004
(212) 373-0641 .. **Dessler,** Derek C '97 %Universal Music Grp -1755 Bway -NY 10019 **Fx:**373-0676
(315) 331-0922 .. **De Staffan,** Anthony J '51 OfCnsl De Staffan & S -110 High -Newark 14513
(315) 331-0922 .. **De Staffan & Saracino** -110 High -Newark 14513 **Fx:**331-3813
(516) 487-5800 .. **DeStefano,** Anthony F '01 %Mauro G&L LLP -60 Cuttermill Rd -Gt Neck 11021
(718) 624-6880 .. **DeStefano,** Anthony M '81 %Newsday -225 Cadman Plz -Brklyn 11201
(718) 390-0580 .. **DeStefano,** Chas C '88 -1082 Victory Blvd -Staten Isl 10301 **Fx:**442-3563
(518) 229-2231 .. **De Stefano,** Constantine F '06 C DeStefano,PLLC -48 S Main Bx654 -Mechanicvll 12118 **Fx:**541-2200
(315) 487-0210 .. **DeStefano,** Dennis '83 %Adorante T & Assoc,PC -5111 W Genesee Bx600 -Camillus 13031 **Fx:**487-2990
(845) 638-5180 .. **DeStefano,** Elizabeth Balsamo '83 %Cnty Atty -Cnty Ofc Bldg -New Cty 10956 **Fx:**638-5676
(315) 253-1391 .. **De Stefano,** Heather M '06 %DA -95 Genesee -Auburn 13021 **Fx:**253-1521
(718) 876-6300 .. **DeStefano,** Jennifer L '04 %DA -130 Styvsnt Pl -Staten Isl 10301
(212) 696-6000 .. **De Stefano,** Stefano E IV '08 %Curtis M-PC&M LLP -101 Park Av -NY 10178
(212) 553-0435 .. **Destro,** Franco '03 %Moody's Invstr Srvc -250 Greenwich -NY 10007
(718) 721-6419 .. **Destro,** Sebastian '54 -31-75 29th -LIC 11106
(212) 227-3636 .. **Desvarieux,** Melissa M '06 %Spar & B,PC -225 Bway -NY 10007
(718) 872-5455 .. **Desyatnikova,** Nadia I '01 -1815 Av U -Brklyn 11229 **Fx:**(347) 922-7491
(914) 591-4402 .. **Determan,** Margaret S '91 -15 Lewis Rd -Irvngtn 10533 **Fx:**591-4504
(718) 625-4695 .. **Detherage,** Kimberly L '86 -32 Court -Brklyn 11201
(631) 390-0010 .. **Detherage,** Michele '10 %Bruno G&S,LLP -445 Broad Hollow Rd -Melvll 11747
(914) 967-2114 .. **DeThomas,** Frances A '00 (Tyre & D) -150 Purchase -Rye 10580
(212) 227-8242 .. **Detiere,** Ann L '85 -225 Bway -NY 10007 **Fx:**385-0339
(716) 773-3015 .. **Detig,** Pamela S '87 -3951 E River Rd -Grand Isl 14072 **Fx:**773-0026
(716) 847-0650 .. **DeTine,** Linda J '84 %Leg Srvcs -237 Main -Buffalo 14203 **Fx:**847-0227
(212) 210-9416 .. **Detjen,** David W '81 (Alston & B LLP) -90 Park Av -NY 10016
(212) 962-2220 .. **DeToffol,** David J '95 -30 Broad -NY 10004 **Fx:**962-2221
(914) 686-2111 .. **DeTommasi,** Anthony J Jr. '96 (DiGiacomo & D,LLP) -One Water -White Plns 10601
(845) 452-6100 .. **DeTraglia,** Erica S '05 %Rizzo & K -272 Mill -Poughkeepsie 12601 **Fx:**452-8459
(315) 738-1133 .. **DeTraglia,** Gustave J Jr. '74 G DeTraglia Jr -1425 Genesee -Utica 13501 **Fx:**738-1134
(315) 738-1133 .. **DeTraglia,** Gustave J III '04 G DeTraglia Jr -1425 Genesee -Utica 13501 **Fx:**738-1134
(315) 797-9261 .. **DeTraglia,** Jos A '96 %Getnick LA&P,LLP -258 Genesee -Utica 13502
(315) 738-1133 .. **DeTraglia,** Michele E '06 %G DeTraglia Jr -1425 Genesee -Utica 13501 **Fx:**738-1134
(212) 635-7373 .. **DeTraglia,** Scott M '94 Bank of NY -1 Wall -NY 10005
(609) 818-1047 .. **Detrick,** Herbert H II '98 -133 Mulberry -NY 10013 **Fx:**(805) 499-5908
(914) 323-7000 .. **Detsky,** Adam J '03 %Wilson EME&D LLP -3 Gannett Dr -White Plns 10604
(914) 738-8782 .. **Dettmer,** Fredk R '80 -340 Corlies Av -Pelham 10803 **Fx:**738-8784
(315) 422-1391 .. **Dettor,** Christine Woodcock '97 %Green & S,PLLC -One Lincoln Ctr #900 -Syracuse 13202 **Fx:**423-2819
(212) 902-3874 .. **DeTurris,** Teresa A '94 Goldman Sachs -85 Broad -NY 10004
(716) 858-2424 .. **Deubler,** Robin J '05 %DA -25 Delaware Av -Buffalo 14202 **Fx:**858-7425
(212) 878-8000 .. **De Urioste,** Alejandra '08 %Clifford C LLP -31 W 52nd -NY 10019
(914) 946-9468 .. **De Urso,** Darren '87 -188 E Post Rd -White Plns 10601 **Fx:**948-5287
(716) 674-6913 .. **Deuschle,** Thos A '83 -3557 Seneca -W Seneca 14224 **Fx:**674-0082
(212) 335-4500 .. **Deutch,** Gillian M '04 %DLA Piper LLP -1251 Av of Amer -NY 10020
(212) 704-6000 .. **Deutch,** Paul H '96 %Troutman S LLP -405 Lex Av -NY 10174
(212) 290-8200 .. **Deutch,** Samayla D '94 SrCnsl Open Space Institute,Inc -1350 Bway -NY 10018
(212) 822-1424 .. **Deutch,** Victor A '82 Deutch & Assoc LLC -305 Bway -NY 10007 **Fx:**(732) 636-7395
(212) 751-9800 .. **Deutsch,** Adam E '03 %Morelli R PC -950 3rd Av -NY 10022
(845) 292-3211 .. **Deutsch,** Alan S '76 -Bx407 -Swan Lk 12783
(212) 448-1100 .. **Deutsch,** Alvin '59 (McLaughlin & S,LLP) -260 Mad Av -NY 10016
(212) 335-4500 .. **Deutsch,** Andrew L '78 (DLA Piper LLP) -1251 Av of Amer -NY 10020
(212) 407-8696 .. **Deutsch,** Ayala '89 NBA Properties -645 5th Av -NY 10022
(718) 934-8908 .. **Deutsch,** Barry J '74 -2718 Ocean Av -Brklyn 11229
(212) 973-8000 .. **Deutsch,** Benjamin P '96 %Schnader HS&L LLP -140 Bway -NY 10005
(212) 801-6979 .. **Deutsch,** Bennett I '81 (Greenberg T,LLP) -200 Park Av -NY 10166
(212) 987-4000 .. **Deutsch,** Dennis S '81 (Kaufman BD&L,LLP) -888 7th Av -NY 10106
(212) 408-5100 .. **Deutsch,** Douglas E '97 (Chadbourne & P LLP) -30 Rckfllr Plz -NY 10112
(917) 655-4971 .. **Deutsch,** Elizabeth A '89 OTDA Fair Hearings -14 Boerum Pl -Brklyn 11201
(212) 684-1111 .. **Deutsch,** Herbert I '69 (Deutsch M&D,LLP) -18 East 41st -NY 10017
(516) 294-8899 .. **Deutsch,** Herbert M '83 (Deutsch & L) -1325 Franklin Av -Gdn Cty 11530
(516) 482-0666 .. **Deutsch,** Ilana L '05 -11 Middle Nck Rd -Gt Neck 11021 **Fx:**482-0644
(212) 832-3939 .. **Deutsch,** Ilene Siegel '97 %R Felder & Prtnrs,PC -437 Mad Av -NY 10022 **Fx:**838-1103
(212) 639-9131 .. **Deutsch,** Irwin F '58 -870 5th Av -NY 10065 **Fx:**639-9131
(212) 558-4000 .. **Deutsch,** Ivan D '97 (Sullivan & C LLP) -125 Broad -NY 10004
(212) 977-9700 .. **Deutsch,** Jeffrey '03 %Phillips N LLP -666 5th Av -NY 10103
(212) 684-1111 .. **Deutsch,** Jeremy E '94 (Deutsch M&D,LLP) -18 East 41st -NY 10017
(212) 766-4000 .. **Deutsch,** Jeremy J '84 (Deutsch TW&W,PC) -120 Bway -NY 10271
(845) 638-4717 .. **Deutsch,** Jos '68 -155 N Main -New Cty 10956 **Fx:**638-4753
(718) 417-1700 .. **Deutsch,** Joshua '88 (Deutsch & S LLP) -79-37 Myrtle Av -Glendale 11385
(212) 593-6700 .. **Deutsch,** Joshua A '07 %Aaronson RF&D,LLP -757 3rd Av -NY 10017
(212) 414-8200 .. **Deutsch,** Laurence M '88 (Deutsch Law Firm,PC) -363 7th Av -NY 10001 **Fx:**239-6571
(516) 745-3050 .. **Deutsch,** Lee K '79 %JP Morgan Chase -900 Stewart Av -Gdn Cty 11530 **Fx:**745-3220
(516) 294-8899 .. **Deutsch & Lipner** -1325 Franklin Av -Gdn Cty 11530

(212) 684-1111 .. **Deutsch Metz & Deutsch,LLP** -18 East 41st -NY 10017 **Fx:**684-1113
(212) 490-9366 .. **Deutsch,** Michl C '93 Impact Sports Mgmt Intl -331 Mad Av -NY 10017 **Fx:**682-7718
(518) 445-2311 .. **Deutsch,** Norman T '84 Albany Law Schl -80 New Scotland Av -Albany 12208 **Fx:**445-2315
(212) 593-4702 .. **Deutsch,** Paul A '82 -235 E 49th -NY 10017 **Fx:**593-4788
(212) 593-6700 .. **Deutsch,** Robt S '74 (Aaronson RF&D,LLP) -757 3rd Av -NY 10017
(212) 872-1000 .. **Deutsch,** Ron E '03 -One Bryant Park -NY 10036 **Fx:**872-1002
(212) 382-3300 .. **Deutsch,** Rory M '88 (Wollmuth M&D LLP) -500 5th Av -NY 10110
(718) 417-1700 .. **Deutsch & Schneider LLP** -79-37 Myrtle Av -Glendale 11385 **Fx:**417-3095
(212) 949-8433 .. **Deutsch,** Stephen H '65 (Beerman & D LLP) -122 E 42nd -NY 10168
(212) 766-4000 .. **Deutsch Tane Waterman & Wurtzel,PC** -120 Bway -NY 10271 **Fx:**766-4022
(212) 333-6418 .. **Deutsch,** Tessa B '03 Glocap Search,LLC -156 W 56th -NY 10019
(212) 791-3900 .. **Deutschmeister,** Gary P '87 -111 Bway -NY 10006 **Fx:**791-4072
(212) 791-3900 .. **Deutschmeister,** Jason S '86 (Breier DU&F PC) -111 Bway -NY 10006
(516) 794-2800 .. **Devack,** Mitchell J '76 -90 Merrick Av -E Meadow 11554 **Fx:**794-2900
(212) 559-5099 .. **Devadason,** Sneha '91 Citi Alternative Invstmnts -399 Park Av -NY 10022 **Fx:**793-3368
(315) 483-6931 .. **DeValk Power & Lair, PC** -6 E Main -Sodus 14551 **Fx:**483-4239
(315) 483-6931 .. **DeValk,** Richd L '76 (DeValk P&L,PC) -6 E Main -Sodus 14551
(518) 584-8521 .. **DeVall,** David F '78 (DeVall & D) -59 Franklin -Saratoga Spgs 12866
(518) 584-8521 .. **DeVall,** Richd F '85 (DeVall & D) -59 Franklin -Saratoga Spgs 12866
(518) 475-9845 .. **Devane,** Brian W '90 -636 Delaware Av -Delmar 12054 **Fx:**475-9846
(516) 248-8090 .. **Devane,** Christopher '92 (Devane & G) -114 Old Cntry Rd -Mineola 11501 **Fx:**248-8089
(518) 462-2200 .. **Devane,** Paul T '68 -112 State -Albany 12207 **Fx:**462-2883
(212) 877-8594 .. **Devane,** Timothy P '96 -204 W 84th -NY 10024
(212) 735-3000 .. **Devaney,** Brenna K '03 %Skadden ASM&F LLP -4 Times Sq -NY 10036
(212) 223-6444 .. **Devaney,** Deirdre A '99 Scott +S,LLP -500 5th Av -NY 10110 **Fx:**223-6334
(212) 849-7000 .. **Devaney,** Elizabeth McKee '09 %Quinn EU&S,LLP -51 Mad Av -NY 10010
(631) 757-2092 .. **Devaney,** Hubert J '65 -30 Pine Hllw Ln -Greenlawn 11740
(518) 456-7200 .. **Devaney,** Linda Crane '89 %Solomon & S,PC -5 Columbia Cir Bx15019 -Albany 12212
(607) 737-2923 .. **Devaney,** Stephanie L '04 %Hon J Hayden -Bx588 -Elmira 14902
(212) 969-3000 .. **Devaney,** Stephen A '99 SrCnsl Proskauer R LLP -1585 Bway -NY 10036
(212) 468-8000 .. **Devaney,** Thos M '99 (Morrison & F LLP) -1290 Av of Amer -NY 10104
(212) 307-5500 .. **Devaney,** Wm H '92 (Venable LLP) -1270 Av of Amer -NY 10020
(212) 483-2323 .. **Devanney,** Patrick A '89 %JP Morgan Chase -345 Park Av -NY 10154
(516) 512-6590 .. **Devany,** Eugene P '87 %Pieret & Assoc -400 Grdn City Plz -Gdn Cty 11530 **Fx:**742-4116
(518) 462-7770 .. **Devaprasad,** S David '93 (Daniels & P,LLP) -119 Wshngtn Av -Albany 12210
(516) 227-0700 .. **DeVarso,** James F '74 Cnsl Farrell F,PC -1320 RXR Plz -Uniondale 11556
(917) 551-1300 .. **Devasia,** Cynthia '03 %Koehler & I LLP -61 Bway -NY 10006
(646) 563-6306 .. **Deveau,** Nora E '04 Arch Ins Grp -1 Lbrty Plz -NY 10006
(212) 262-2390 .. **Deveau,** Wm D '06 %Connell F LLP -888 7th Av -NY 10106
(718) 539-4111 .. **DeVelasco,** Gustavo E '94 -136-14B Nrthrn Blvd -Flushng 11354 **Fx:**539-5336
(516) 328-2300 .. **De Vellis,** Claudio '98 (Abrams FFEGF&E,LLP) -1111 Marcus Av -Lk Success 11042
(516) 742-8340 .. **Devendorf,** Alfred E '73 OfCnsl Pacifico D&P -136 Willis Av -Mineola 11501
(315) 425-2700 .. **Devendorf,** Jon P '91 (Hiscock & B,LLP) -One Park Pl -Syracuse 13202
(631) 777-2330 .. **Deveney,** Brian T '80 (O'Connor OH&D,LLP) -1 Huntngtn Quad -Melvll 11747
(212) 889-2121 .. **Deveney,** John P '78 (Chehebar D&P LLP) -470 Park Av S -NY 10016 **Fx:**684-6224
(212) 705-7000 .. **Deveno,** Mark W '03 (Bingham M LLP) -399 Park Av -NY 10022
(718) 423-6800 .. **De Venuti,** Jennifer L '06 %MacKay W&B LLP -40-26 235th -Douglastn 11363
(212) 336-0058 .. **Dever,** Jos P Jr. '00 %SEC -3 World Fncl Ctr -NY 10281 **Fx:**336-1323
(212) 644-1710 .. **Dever,** Martin J Jr. '77 (Winne BH&B,PC) -286 Mad Av -NY 10017
(585) 262-7693 .. **Dever,** Richd W '85 -16 E Main -Rchstr 14614
(212) 941-1552 .. **Devereaux & Lubitz,PC** -277 Bway -NY 10007
(212) 785-5959 .. **Devereaux,** Michl J '88 (Devereaux B) -39 Bway -NY 10006 **Fx:**785-4487
(212) 941-1552 .. **Devereaux,** Philip J '79 (Devereaux & L,PC) -277 Bway -NY 10007
(631) 232-0200 .. **DeVerna,** James R '10 %Fumuso KDSS&F,LLP -110 Marcus Blvd -Hauppauge 11788
(718) 250-2000 .. **DeVerna,** John P '09 %DA -350 Jay -Brklyn 11201 **Fx:**250-2314
(631) 232-0200 .. **DeVerna,** Robt W '76 (Fumuso KDSS&F,LLP) -110 Marcus Blvd -Hauppauge 11788
(212) 533-2279 .. **Devers,** Peter Dix '65 -Bx2295 -NY 10009
(212) 655-5000 .. **DeVerteuil,** Steve M '96 %Gannon R&M -120 Bway -NY 10271
(516) 327-6000 .. **Devery,** Brian S '03 AmeriTrust -1981 Marcus Av -Lk Success 11042
(212) 407-4000 .. **DeVesta,** Jos J '04 %Loeb & L,LLP -345 Park Av -NY 10154
(914) 701-0774 .. **DeVincenzo,** Anthony J '95 -205 Mead -Waccabuc 10597
(212) 813-8800 .. **DeVincenzo,** Michl S '01 %Goodwin P LLP -620 8th Av -NY 10018
(631) 289-0303 .. **Devine,** Alfred E '91 (Devine & M) -Bx580 -Manorvll 11949
(212) 745-3565 .. **Devine,** Ariel S '97 IBM Corp -590 Mad Av -NY 10022
(212) 885-5000 .. **Devine,** Brian P '98 (Blank R LLP) -405 Lex Av -NY 10174
(845) 638-5081 .. **Devine,** Edw F '90 Cnty Drainage Agency -23 New Hempstd Rd -New Cty 10956
(516) 431-9200 .. **Devine,** Gene P '95 %Dept Cnsrvtn Hmpstd -Lido Blvd BxJ -Point Lookout 11569
(212) 460-4493 .. **Devine,** Gerard P '96 ConEd -4 Irving Pl -NY 10003
(631) 761-0800 .. **Devine,** James E '96 (Lazer AR&Y,PC) -225 Old Cntry Rd -Melvll 11747
(212) 336-2000 .. **Devine,** Jesse A '07 %Patterson BW&T LLP -1133 Av of Amer -NY 10036
(718) 768-5335 .. **Devine,** Joanne C '89 -10 Fuller Pl -Brklyn 11215 **Fx:**768-5335
(518) 463-6155 .. **Devine,** John M '74 -600 Bway -Albany 12207
(518) 464-0640 .. **Devine Markovits & Snyder LLP** -52 Corp Cir -Albany 12203 **Fx:**464-0200
(631) 289-0303 .. **Devine & McCormick** -Bx580 -Manorvll 11949
(212) 490-4949 .. **Devine,** Michl C '66 (Kieffer & H LLP) -230 Park Av -NY 10169
(631) 474-5400 .. **Devine,** Michl V '92 -1000 Main -Pt Jffrsn 11777 **Fx:**474-3772
(516) 281-9800 .. **Devine,** Paul S '80 (Goldberg S LLP) -200 Old Cntry Rd -Mineola 11501
(516) 326-2400 .. **Devine,** Robt '64 (Ivone D&J,LLP) -2001 Marcus Av -Lk Success 11042
(518) 464-0640 .. **Devine,** Terence J '77 (Devine M&S LLP) -52 Corp Cir -Albany 12203
(516) 747-1010 .. **Devins,** Alicia B '87 %Dollinger G&G -1 Old Cntry Rd -Carle Pl 11514
(212) 613-5000 .. **Devins,** Elissa '02 %Leg Assist Grp -450 W 33rd -NY 10001 **Fx:**750-0820
(212) 483-9490 .. **Devins,** Michl B '99 (McElroy DM&C,LLP) -88 Pine -NY 10005
(212) 909-6000 .. **Devins,** Michl D '02 Cnsl Debevoise & P LLP -919 3rd Av -NY 10022
(516) 622-7575 .. **DeVita,** Danl F '83 -377 Oak -Gdn Cty 11530 **Fx:**622-7577
(212) 766-1888 .. **DeVita,** Diane L '91 %Morris DA&F -2 Rector -NY 10006
(631) 543-7667 .. **DeVita,** Gerard '88 (Carner & D) -350 Vets Mem'l Hwy -Commack 11725 **Fx:**543-7901
(212) 661-5030 .. **DeVita,** James R '75 (Schoeman U&K,LLP) -60 E 42nd -NY 10165
(212) 251-9840 .. **DeVita,** M Christine '81 Wallace Foundation -5 Penn Plz -NY 10001
(212) 772-8900 .. **DeVita,** Peter J '95 Intl Mgmt Grp -420 W 45th -NY 10036 **Fx:**772-2617
(212) 735-3000 .. **DeVito,** Danl A '87 (Skadden ASM&F LLP) -4 Times Sq -NY 10036
(800) 291-0677 .. **DeVito,** Felix R '81 -50 Main -White Plns 10606 **Fx:**(845) 278-5213
(212) 501-7899 .. **DeVito,** Francis J '82 -150 Bway -NY 10038
(845) 638-5001 .. **DeVito,** Joanna Marie '02 %DA -1 S Main -New Cty 10956 **Fx:**638-5070
(516) 355-5900 .. **DeVito,** Jos '00 DeVito & Assoc PC -30 S Central Av -Vly Stream 11580 **Fx:**355-5915
(212) 450-4000 .. **DeVito,** Laura M '03 %Davis P&W LLP -450 Lex Av -NY 10017
(631) 249-8200 .. **DeVito,** Louis '05 %DePinto N & Assoc,LLP -445 Broadhllw Rd -Melvll 11747 **Fx:**249-8209
(914) 470-0001 .. **Devito,** Marisa C '07 %Babchik & Y,LLP -200 E Post Rd -White Plns 10601
(516) 747-4000 .. **DeVito,** Michl A '97 -226 7th -Gdn Cty 11530
(718) 391-6526 .. **DeVito,** Michl I '90 Dept of Ed -28-11 Qns Plz N -LIC 11101
(631) 393-6220 .. **DeVito,** Ronald J '62 -445 Broadhllw Rd -Melvll 11747 **Fx:**393-6229
(631) 853-5212 .. **DeVito,** Steven L '05 %Leg Aid -400 Carleton Av Bx9082 -Central Islip 11722 **Fx:**853-7798
(718) 494-2555 .. **DeVito,** Thos J '73 -2043 Richmond Av -Staten Isl 10314 **Fx:**370-7394
(718) 494-2555 .. **DeVito,** Thos J Jr. '99 %T DeVito -2043 Richmond Av -Staten Isl 10314 **Fx:**370-7394
(718) 250-1100 .. **DeVito,** Wm N '94 E Garfinkel -12 Metrotech Ctr -Brklyn 11201 **Fx:**250-1168
(212) 338-2615 .. **DeVito,** Wm P '94 Kaye Grp -1065 Av of Amer -NY 10018
(631) 724-8833 .. **Devitt Spellman Barrett,LLP** -50 Route 111 -Smithtwn 11787 **Fx:**724-8010
(212) 715-9100 .. **DeVivo,** Dana A '08 %Kramer LN&F,LLP -1177 Av of Amer -NY 10036
(212) 269-2353 .. **DeVivo,** Edw Chas '79 (DeVivo & Co,PC) -61 Bway -NY 10006
(212) 344-7042 .. **DeVivo,** Jessica A '02 %Cichanowicz CKV&T,LLP -61 Bway -NY 10006
(516) 571-2624 .. **DeVivo,** Thos G Jr. '79 -262 Old Cntry Rd -Mineola 11501
(212) 286-8585 .. **Devlin,** Austa S '82 (Heidell PM&B,LLP) -99 Park Av -NY 10016
(585) 422-0980 .. **Devlin,** Denise A '95 %Xerox -800 Phillips Rd -Webster 14580
(212) 546-9255 .. **Devlin,** Kathleen J '02 Cnsl Scarinci H -107 Grand -NY 10013
(315) 479-3900 .. **Devlin,** Michl W '91 %SSA-ODAR -300 S State -Syracuse 13202 **Fx:**479-3933
(212) 530-1800 .. **Devlin,** Paul J '05 %Richards K&O LLP -1 World Fncl Ctr -NY 10281
(212) 450-4000 .. **Devlin,** Peter E '09 %Davis P&W LLP -450 Lex Av -NY 10017
(631) 755-0101 .. **Devlin,** Rebecca K '07 %Lewis JAA,LLP -425 Broad Hollow Rd -Melvll 11747
(212) 801-6997 .. **Devlin,** Roderick N '98 %Greenberg T,LLP -200 Park Av -NY 10166
(212) 637-2506 .. **Devlin-Brown,** Arlo '01 US Atty -1 St Andrews Plz -NY 10007
(516) 877-2525 .. **De Voe,** Daniele D '06 %Weinstein K&C,PC -1325 Franklin Av -Gdn Cty 11530
(212) 788-0825 .. **Devoe,** Margaret A '09 Law Dept -100 Church -NY 10007 **Fx:**788-0367
(518) 371-8888 .. **Devoe,** Susan A '91 %Ianniello A&R,PC -805 Route 146 -Clifton Pk 12065
(585) 641-8000 .. **De Voesick,** Jeffrey F '01 (Fix SB&G,PC) -295 Woodcliff Dr -Fairprt 14450
(212) 964-0046 .. **Devolpi,** Pietro M Jr. '09 %Schoengold & S,PC -19 Fulton -NY 10038
(212) 374-1969 .. **Devor,** James W '85 -305 Bway -NY 10007
(718) 967-1600 .. **Devora,** Glen '01 %J D'Agostino & Assoc -3309 Richmond Av -Staten Isl 10312 **Fx:**967-8677
(212) 922-9499 .. **DeVore,** Andrew C '97 (DeVore & D LLP) -99 Park Av -NY 10016 **Fx:**922-1799
(631) 853-4104 .. **DeVore,** Wm A '74 %DA -400 Carleton Av Bx9082 -Central Islip 11722 **Fx:**853-7838
(212) 907-7300 .. **Devorkin,** Michl S '71 (Golenbock EAB&P) -437 Mad Av -NY 10022
(315) 422-6600 .. **Devorsetz,** Sidney '60 (S Devorsetz,PLLC) -307 S Townsend -Syracuse 13202 **Fx:**422-4228
(212) 857-8813 .. **De Vos,** Christian M '08 US Ct Appls -40 Foley -NY 10007
(212) 786-1000 .. **DeVos,** Lloyd '75 (DeVos & Co,PLLC) -1230 Av of Amer -NY 10020 **Fx:**(800) 223-1273

(212) 277-6500 .. **DeVries,** Christina J '04 %Dickstein S LLP -1633 Bway -NY 10019
(212) 227-0780 .. **DeVries,** Keith '83 -42 Bway -NY 10004 **Fx:**349-6564
(212) 551-4000 .. **Dew,** Kevin W '89 %Sanofi-Synthelabo -90 Park Av -NY 10016 **Fx:**551-4919
(646) 557-8458 .. **DeWaal,** Gary Alan '81 Newedge USA,LLC -630 5th Av -NY 10111 **Fx:**557-8519
(914) 253-2215 .. **DeWalt,** Stacy L '06 %Pepsico -700 Andrsn Hill Rd -Purchase 10577
(347) 643-5815 .. **Dewan,** Debra Siedman '80 Transit Adjudication Bur -505 Fulton -Brklyn 11201
(718) 923-6300 .. **DeWan,** Mark F '83 %Atty Grievance Comm -335 Adams -Brklyn 11201 **Fx:**624-2978
(516) 741-6355 .. **DeWan,** Mary Reed '92 %Nicolini PF&S -114 Old Cntry Rd Bx9006 -Mineola 11501
(631) 882-4669 .. **Dewan,** Naresh K '02 -11865 Metro Av -Kew Gdns 11415
(646) 315-7300 .. **Dewan,** Sonya '05 %FINRA -14 Wall -NY 10005 **Fx:**315-7440
(212) 839-5300 .. **Dewan,** Vijay '09 %Sidley A LLP -787 7th Av -NY 10019
(914) 946-0400 .. **Dewar,** Keith A J '03 %Schiavetti CDW&N,LLP -709 Wstchstr Av -White Plns 10604
(585) 546-8426 .. **Dewart,** Wm F Jr. '77 (Branch D&W) -45 Exchange Blvd -Rchstr 14614
(845) 228-2800 .. **Dewbury,** Stamatia Kampitsis '97 (Dewbury & Assoc,PC) -1787 Route 6 -Carmel 10512
(212) 425-7200 .. **DeWeerd,** Willem F C '05 %Kenyon & K,LLP -1 Bway -NY 10004
(914) 633-4251 .. **Dewey,** David W '81 -481 Main -New Rchll 10801 **Fx:**633-4175
(212) 728-8000 .. **Dewey,** Ericka '96 Willkie F&G LLP -787 7th Av -NY 10019
(212) 259-8000 .. **Dewey & LeBoeuf LLP** -1301 Av of Amer -NY 10019 **Fx:**259-6333
(518) 626-9000 .. **Dewey & LeBoeuf LLP** -99 Wshngtn Av -Albany 12210 **Fx:**626-9010
(212) 943-9000 .. **Dewey Pegno & Kramarsky LLP** -220 E 42nd -NY 10017 **Fx:**943-4325
(914) 923-6401 .. **Dewey,** Stephen P '03 -Bx2511 -Briarclff Mnr 10510 **Fx:**923-6403
(212) 943-9000 .. **Dewey,** Thos E L '92 (Dewey P&K LLP) -220 E 42nd -NY 10017
(212) 999-5800 .. **De Wied,** Warren S '88 (Wilson SG&R) -1301 Av of Americas -NY 10019
(607) 778-2117 .. **De Wind,** Peter J '01 %Cnty Atty -Cnty Ofc Bldg Bx1766 -Bnghmtn 13902 **Fx:**778-6122
(607) 797-4839 .. **DeWind,** Wendy Ann K '96 (Hogan SLS&D,LLP) -Bx660 -Bnghmtn 13902
(516) 676-3679 .. **DeWitt & Higgins** -26 Robnsn Av -Glen Cove 11542 **Fx:**676-5198
(914) 921-4700 .. **Dewitt,** Patricia A '88 -222A Purchase -Rye 10580
(516) 746-5599 .. **DeWitt,** Wm C '01 %Bee RFH&D,LLP -170 Old Cntry Rd -Mineola 11501
(212) 259-4100 .. **de Witt Wijnen,** H Rutger '99 (De Brauw BW PC) -650 5th Av -NY 10019
(212) 906-1200 .. **Dewitz,** Matthew C '09 %Latham & W -885 3rd Av -NY 10022
(212) 935-3000 .. **DeWolf,** Danl I '83 (Mintz LCFG&P,PC) -666 3rd Av -NY 10017
(518) 213-6000 .. **DeWolf,** Gerard J '76 %NYSUT -800 Troy-Schnctdy Rd -Latham 12110 **Fx:**213-6488
(212) 884-2113 .. **DeWolf,** John E '80 Lerner New York,Inc -450 W 33rd -NY 10001
(585) 377-2724 .. **DeWolff,** Lynette I '84 -23 Cambray Dr -Fairprt 14450
(516) 482-4436 .. **Dewoski,** John F '96 (Gleich S&F) -36 S Station Plz -Gt Neck 11021
(212) 421-1300 .. **Dexter,** Cecily '77 Jack Resnick & Sons -110 E 59th -NY 10022
(212) 446-4800 .. **Dexter,** Matthew F '05 %Kirkland & E LLP -153 E 53rd -NY 10022
(315) 366-2585 .. **Dexter,** Todd D '01 -N Court Bx312 -Wampsville 13163 **Fx:**366-2816
(718) 261-7700 .. **Dey-Chao,** Milan '99 %Rappaport HC&R,PC -118-35 Qns Blvd -Frst Hlls 11375
(518) 462-3000 .. **Deyo,** Michl W '08 %Iseman CR&H,LLP -9 Thurlow Ter -Albany 12203
(518) 474-4661 .. **Deyoe,** Stephanie J '04 NYS Education Dept -89 Wshngtn Av -Albany 12234
(212) 903-9000 .. **Deyong,** Michl A '06 %Linklaters -1345 Av of Amer -NY 10105
(212) 490-9550 .. **DeYoung,** Neal A '87 -16 W 46th -NY 10036 **Fx:**986-0158
(914) 784-0001 .. **DeYoung,** Steven E '78 -22 Saw Mill Rvr Rd -Hawthorne 10532
(718) 263-2760 .. **Dezelic,** Dennis V '97 (Dezelic & K,LLC) -108-18 Qns Blvd -Frst Hlls 11375 **Fx:**228-5558
(516) 437-4385 .. **Deziel,** Christopher J L '87 (Vishnick MM LLP) -3000 Marcus Av -Lk Success 11042
(518) 745-1400 .. **Dezik,** Michl D '05 %FitzGerald MBF -16 Pearl Bx2017 -Glens Fls 12801
(718) 262-7100 .. **Dezlo,** Anne-Marie '85 %Civil Ct -89-17 Sutphin Blvd -Jamaica 11435 **Fx:**262-7107
(718) 217-3719 .. **DeZorett,** Michl J '77 -75-24 Bell Blvd -Oakland Gdns 11364
(212) 819-8200 .. **Dezotti-Hallake,** Flavia '98 %White & C LLP -1155 Av of Amer -NY 10036
(212) 345-2785 .. **Dhandapani,** Murugan '98 %Marsh & McLennan Cos -1166 Av of Amer -NY 10036
(212) 949-8700 .. **Dhar,** Aninda '04 Eisner LLP -750 3rd Av -NY 10017 **Fx:**891-4100
(212) 891-9100 .. **Dharia,** Bindi R '04 %Goldfarb & F LLP -345 Park Av -NY 10154
(212) 819-8200 .. **Dharia,** Binoy A '08 %White & C LLP -1155 Av of Amer -NY 10036
(718) 613-2220 .. **Dharia,** Kruti '07 %Hon A Carter -225 Cadman Plz E -Brklyn 11201 **Fx:**613-2330
(212) 819-8200 .. **Dhume,** Mangesh '10 %White & C LLP -1155 Av of Amer -NY 10036
(212) 629-5590 .. **Dhungana,** Galab B '01 (SJ Smith,PC) -45 W 34th -NY 10001 **Fx:**629-5591
(212) 846-6544 .. **Diab,** Waleed S '05 %MTV Networks -1515 Bway -NY 10036 **Fx:**258-8358
(212) 715-9100 .. **Diaba,** Franciscus Ladejola '01 %Kramer LN&F,LLP -1177 Av of Amer -NY 10036
(212) 225-2000 .. **Diaba,** Liliane S '10 %Cleary GS&H -1 Lbrty Plz -NY 10006
(212) 733-9000 .. **Diaco,** Michl '01 Pfizer Inc-Legal Div -235 E 42nd -NY 10017 **Fx:**(646) 792-4147
(914) 949-2700 .. **Diaconis,** John S '81 (Bleakley P&S,LLP) -1 N Lex Av -White Plns 10601
(212) 335-9000 .. **Diacosavvas,** Savvas S '02 %DA -1 Hogan Pl -NY 10013
(212) 536-3900 .. **Diakos,** Joanna A '00 (K&L Gates LLP) -599 Lex Av -NY 10022
(212) 770-2884 .. **Diakow,** Nicholas T '67 %AIG -80 Pine -NY 10005
(718) 972-6207 .. **Dial,** Ashram '86 -540 E 5th -Brklyn 11218
(212) 355-9500 .. **Diamand,** Nicholas R '03 OfCnsl Lieff CH&B,LLP -250 Hudson -NY 10013
(212) 859-8000 .. **Diamant,** Aviva F '73 (Fried FHS&J LLP) -1 NY Plz -NY 10004
(212) 455-2000 .. **Diamant,** Jillian P '08 %Simpson T&B LLP -425 Lex Av -NY 10017
(516) 569-0284 .. **Diamant,** June '82 -229 Linwood Av -Cedarhrst 11516 **Fx:**569-4856
(212) 852-6394 .. **Diamant,** Violet '84 CIFG -825 3rd Av -NY 10022
(212) 806-5400 .. **Diamante,** Jos '80 (Stroock &S&L LLP) -180 Maiden Ln -NY 10038
(718) 237-5500 .. **Diamanti,** Anna Maria '01 %Leg Srvcs -105 Court -Brklyn 11201 **Fx:**855-0733
(212) 839-5300 .. **Diamantis,** Christina E '03 %Sidley A LLP -787 7th Av -NY 10019
(516) 712-4000 .. **Diamantis,** Nikolaos E '02 %Milber MP&S LLP -1000 Woodbury Rd -Woodbury 11797
(718) 590-3632 .. **Diamantis,** Panagiota '97 %Hon M Gross -851 Grnd Cncrs -Bronx 10451
(914) 997-1346 .. **Diamantopoulos,** George '91 %Seham SM&P,LLP -445 Hmltn Av -White Plns 10601
(212) 785-3041 .. **Diamantstein,** Saml '05 D Carlebach -40 Exch Pl -NY 10005 **Fx:**785-3618
(212) 768-6700 .. **Diament,** Matthew R '10 %Sonnenschein N&R LLP -1221 Av of Amer -NY 10020
(914) 946-0045 .. **Diament,** Wm M '64 -173 Woodbrook Rd -White Plns 10605
(212) 801-6958 .. **Diamond,** Aaron M '08 %Greenberg T,LLP -200 Park Av -NY 10166
(516) 932-1571 .. **Diamond,** Aileen '02 -36 Holiday Pond Rd -Jericho 11753
(212) 436-1137 .. **Diamond,** Alice Knapp '87 IRS -290 Bway -NY 10007
(212) 973-8000 .. **Diamond,** Alizah Z '08 %Schnader HS&L LLP -140 Bway -NY 10005
(212) 966-5020 .. **Diamond,** Alyne I '83 %Seligson R&R -29 W 30th -NY 10001
(212) 964-5570 .. **Diamond,** Andrew R '86 Sacks & S -150 Bway -NY 10038 **Fx:**349-2141
(212) 521-3500 .. **Diamond,** Ann C '78 OfCnsl Aronson M&S, LLP -485 Lex Av -NY 10017
(212) 715-7288 .. **Diamond,** Bernard R '73 %Trump Orgn -725 5th Av -NY 10022 **Fx:**935-0141
(646) 943-5912 .. **Diamond,** Beth D '95 Beazley-Lloyds -1270 Av of Amer -NY 10020 **Fx:**378-4039
(212) 683-3800 .. **Diamond,** Beth M '98 %Dinkes & S,PC -112 Mad Av -NY 10016
(212) 806-5400 .. **Diamond,** Brian '83 (Stroock &S&L LLP) -180 Maiden Ln -NY 10038
(631) 694-2300 .. **Diamond,** Chumi R '05 %Lamb & B,LLP -534 Broadhllw Rd Bx9034 -Melvll 11747
(212) 819-8200 .. **Diamond,** Colin J '00 (White & C LLP) -1155 Av of Amer -NY 10036
(212) 785-4100 .. **Diamond,** Cyrus M '58 OfCnsl Fensterstock & Prtnrs LLP -30 Wall -NY 10005
(518) 486-6303 .. **Diamond,** David A '87 %DHCR -38-40 State -Albany 12207
(646) 278-4280 .. **Diamond,** David B '01 -260 Mad Av -NY 10016 **Fx:**278-4281
(212) 969-3000 .. **Diamond,** David H '73 (Proskauer R LLP) -1585 Bway -NY 10036
(646) 282-5841 .. **Diamond,** Efram I '02 Davidson Kempner Cptl Mgmt LLC -65 E 55th -NY 10022
(212) 446-4800 .. **Diamond,** Evan D '08 %Kirkland & E LLP -153 E 53rd -NY 10022
(212) 776-5256 .. **Diamond,** Harley D '88 NYC Housing Auth -250 Bway -NY 10007 **Fx:**776-5008
(212) 445-8202 .. **Diamond,** Harris '84 %BSMG Worldwide -919 3rd Av -NY 10022 **Fx:**445-8295
(212) 661-9100 .. **Diamond,** Harris J '02 %Otterbourg SH&R,PC -230 Park Av -NY 10169
(212) 947-6600 .. **Diamond,** Helene Levy '89 %Peak Cnsl Inc -25 W 31st -NY 10001
(718) 588-2660 .. **Diamond,** Ivan M '96 -888 Granc Cncrs -Bronx 10451
(631) 342-5224 .. **Diamond,** Jay H '80 %CA,Inc -1 CA Plz -Islandia 11749 **Fx:**342-4866
(212) 755-7500 .. **Diamond,** Jeffrey M '79 (Marcus R&D LLP) -488 Mad Av -NY 10022
(718) 579-7900 .. **Diamond,** Jesse '09 Leg Aid -900 Sheridan Av -Bronx 10451 **Fx:**293-8744
(718) 896-9600 .. **Diamond,** Joel B '74 %Algin Mgt -64-35 Yllwstn Blvd -Frst Hlls 11375
(518) 842-1900 .. **Diamond,** Julieann '99 St Mary's Hospital-Amsterdam -427 Guy Park Av -Amsterdam 12010
(212) 227-3377 .. **Diamond,** Kenneth '87 (Diamond & D LLC) -111 John -NY 10038 **Fx:**227-5684
(516) 482-8039 .. **Diamond,** Lauren Heiden '83 -18 Mitchell Dr -Gt Neck 11024
(518) 736-5517 .. **Diamond,** Lorraine C '02 Fulton Cnty DSS -4 Daisy Ln -Johnstwn 12095
(718) 448-4800 .. **Diamond,** Louis E '73 -88 New Dorp Plz S -Staten Isl 10306
(516) 228-0820 .. **Diamond,** Marilyn '82 (Diamond Law Ofcs) -600 Old Cntry Rd -Gdn Cty 11530
(212) 227-3377 .. **Diamond,** Mark '86 (Diamond & D LLC) -111 John -NY 10038 **Fx:**227-5684
(212) 668-2870 .. **Diamond,** Mark E '81 %US Bankruptcy Ct-SDNY -1 Bowling Grn -NY 10004
(212) 809-2663 .. **Diamond,** Marni '02 Bondholder Comm Grp -30 Broad -NY 10004
(212) 430-5400 .. **Diamond McCarthy LLP** -620 8th Av -NY 10018 **Fx:**430-5499
(212) 210-9579 .. **Diamond,** Meryl P '99 (Alston & B LLP) -90 Park Av -NY 10016
(516) 663-5151 .. **Diamond,** Mitchell L '99 (Diamond Law Grp) -244 Mineola Blvd -Mineola 11501 **Fx:**663-5152
(718) 531-1921 .. **Diamond,** Murray J '50 -267 Whitman Dr -Brklyn 11234 **Fx:**763-4440
(914) 273-4545 .. **Diamond,** Patrick '07 MBIA -113 King -Armonk 10504
(212) 661-8000 .. **Diamond,** Paul '04 %Lucas & M,LLP -475 Park Av S -NY 10016
(212) 728-2000 .. **Diamond,** Richd H '95 %Athletes & Artists -220 W 42nd -NY 10036
(516) 794-5255 .. **Diamond,** Richd L '81 -1900 Hempstd Tpke -E Meadow 11554
(212) 819-8200 .. **Diamond,** S Lynne '07 %White & C LLP -1155 Av of Amer -NY 10036
(212) 313-9188 .. **Diamond,** Sara G '85 Amer Lawyer Media -120 Bway -NY 10271
(212) 224-4415 .. **Diamond,** Scott L '05 Sumitomo Mitsui Banking Corp -277 Park Av -NY 10172
(917) 778-6600 .. **Diamond,** Stanley A '78 %J Toomey -485 Lex Av -NY 10017 **Fx:**778-7048
(845) 677-2101 .. **Diamond,** Stephen C '71 OfCnsl Teahan & C -41 Front Bx1181 -Millbrook 12545
(845) 298-2000 .. **Diamond,** Stephen E '84 (Vergilis SRD&D,LLP) -1136 Route 9 -Wappingers Fls 12590
(718) 422-1150 .. **Diamond,** Stewart J '96 -26 Court -Brklyn 11242 **Fx:**422-1159

(212) 227-3377 .. **Diamond,** Stuart '85 (Diamond & D LLC) -111 John -NY 10038 **Fx:**227-5684
(212) 964-7990 .. **Diamond,** Syma F '06 %Mallow K&N,PC -321 Bway -NY 10007
(585) 234-2604 .. **Diamond,** Tamra M '94 -Bx822 -Fairprt 14450
(212) 223-8409 .. **Diamond,** Tara M '05 -150 E 58th -NY 10155 **Fx:**317-2946
(212) 894-8589 .. **Diamond,** Wm C '80 CT Corp System -111 8th Av -NY 10011
(212) 758-3500 .. **Diamond,** Wm H '82 (DeCampo D&A) -747 3rd Av -NY 10017
(718) 833-9006 .. **Diamond,** Yitzchok S '02 -7206 5th Av -Brklyn 11209
(516) 294-8844 .. **Diamondstein,** Alison A '05 %L'Abbate BC&C,LLP -1001 Franklin Av -Gdn Cty 11530
(212) 506-2500 .. **Diana,** Anthony J '95 (Mayer B LLP) -1675 Bway -NY 10019
(212) 715-9100 .. **Diana,** Jennifer '07 %Kramer LN&F,LLP -1177 Av of Amer -NY 10036
(212) 218-2100 .. **Diana,** Leonard P '79 (Fitzpatrick CH&S) -1290 Av of Amer -NY 10104
(212) 259-8000 .. **DiAngelo,** Christopher J '85 (Dewey & L LLP) -1301 Av of Amer -NY 10019
(212) 860-7089 .. **Dias,** Christine M '95 -160 E 88th -NY 10128
(518) 452-5600 .. **Dias,** Kathy Smith '96 %Heslin RF&M PC -5 Columbia Cir -Albany 12203
(212) 546-9255 .. **Dias,** Sean D '92 Cnsl Scarinci H -107 Grand -NY 10013
(212) 770-1732 .. **Diaso,** Janet L '97 %AIG -80 Pine -NY 10005
(212) 214-0121 .. **Diaso,** Victor H '96 %Capmark Securities Inc -485 Mad Av -NY 10022
(212) 661-8780 .. **Diawuo-Amankonah,** Peter K '99 %Adam Law Ofc,PC -275 Mad Av -NY 10016
(646) 610-5400 .. **Diaz,** Arthur '97 NYPD -1 Police Plz -NY 10038
(212) 259-8000 .. **Diaz,** Bozena M '06 %Dewey & L LLP -1301 Av of Amer -NY 10019
(212) 450-4000 .. **Diaz,** Cristina '05 %Davis P&W LLP -450 Lex Av -NY 10017
(212) 808-7800 .. **Diaz,** Damaris M '08 %Kelley D&W LLP -101 Park Av -NY 10178
(212) 872-1000 .. **Diaz,** Estela '09 -One Bryant Park -NY 10036 **Fx:**872-1002
(212) 431-8905 .. **Diaz,** Henry N '95 -Bx824 -W Hempstead 11552 **Fx:**625-1046
(212) 770-2765 .. **Diaz,** Ileana '01 Transatlantic Reinsurance Co -80 Pine -NY 10005
(914) 993-9393 .. **Diaz,** Jennifer M '06 Stewart Title Ins -707 Wstchstr Av -White Plns 10604 **Fx:**997-1698
(631) 234-0800 .. **Diaz,** Jennifer R '99 -1 Suffolk Sq -Islandia 11749
(347) 387-7286 .. **Diaz,** John A '06 -15301 Jamaica Av -Jamaica 11432
(212) 226-3649 .. **Diaz,** John M '03 -141 Mulberry -NY 10013
(212) 506-1966 .. **Diaz,** Jorge A '01 Kasowitz BT&F LLP -1633 Bway -NY 10019
(212) 416-8006 .. **Diaz,** Kathryn E '96 %Dept of Law -120 Bway -NY 10271
(212) 966-6420 .. **Diaz,** Linda M '91 %Lwyrs For Children -110 Lafayette -NY 10013 **Fx:**966-0531
(212) 942-6400 .. **Diaz,** Luis O '96 -710 W 190th -NY 10040
(718) 388-5454 .. **Diaz,** Luisa M '96 -11-29 Catherine -Brklyn 11211 **Fx:**486-5982
(212) 969-1722 .. **Diaz,** Maria A '09 Venro Petroleum -630 5th Av -NY 10111
(646) 223-4200 .. **Diaz,** Maria B '90 %Reuters -3 Times Sq -NY 10036 **Fx:**223-4250
(917) 463-3691 .. **Diaz,** Maritza '96 Amer Immgrtn Ntwrk -333 W 39th -NY 10018 **Fx:**(646) 349-5468
(718) 478-1507 .. **Diaz,** Nestor H '90 -12510 Qns Blvd -Kew Gdns 11415
(718) 286-6000 .. **Diaz,** Patricia A '06 DA -125-01 Qns Blvd -Kew Gdns 11415
(212) 237-8900 .. **Diaz,** Robt E '79 %John Jay College -899 10th Av -NY 10019
(212) 813-8800 .. **Diaz,** Silvia C '09 %Goodwin P LLP -620 8th Av -NY 10018
(718) 286-6000 .. **Diaz,** Soledad V '07 %DA -125-01 Qns Blvd -Kew Gdns 11415
(212) 701-3000 .. **Diaz-Albertini,** Antonio L '08 %Cahill G&R LLP -80 Pine -NY 10005 **Fx:**269-5420
(212) 415-9200 .. **Diaz-Cruz,** Mario III '71 (Dorsey & W LLP) -250 Park Av -NY 10177
(212) 734-9770 .. **Diaz-Espino,** Ovidio E '89 -197 E 76th -NY 10021
(212) 716-5790 .. **Diaz-Matos,** Alexander G '08 %Cohen Lgl Grp,LLC -230 Park Av -NY 10169
(845) 433-5583 .. **Diaz-Matos,** Andrew B '99 IBM -2455 South Rd -Poughkeepsie 12601
(212) 947-9779 .. **Diaz-Pedrosa,** Lilliana '00 %Advocates for Chldrn of NY -151 W 30th -NY 10001
(718) 967-1600 .. **DiBari,** Frank J '97 %J D'Agostino & Assoc -3309 Richmond Av -Staten Isl 10312 **Fx:**967-8677
(518) 474-2721 .. **Di Bari,** John J Jr. '83 %OTDA -40 N Pearl -Albany 12243 **Fx:**474-9389
(212) 294-6700 .. **DiBari,** John M '04 %Winston & S -200 Park Av -NY 10166
(914) 763-6362 .. **DiBari,** Mary Ann C '91 -105 Cross Pond Rd -Pound Rdg 10576 **Fx:**763-6989
(914) 948-8316 .. **DiBart,** Jos R '46 -300C Hgh Pnt Dr -Hartsdale 10530
(914) 965-1011 .. **Dibbini,** James G '98 -570 Ynkrs Av -Ynkrs 10704 **Fx:**965-0019
(212) 613-5000 .. **Dibble,** Ann E '89 %Leg Assist Grp -450 W 33rd -NY 10001 **Fx:**750-0820
(585) 271-1500 .. **Dibble,** Gerald W '72 (Dibble & M,PC) -55 Canterbury Rd -Rchstr 14607
(212) 770-7000 .. **Dibble,** Kevin M '99 AIG -175 Water -NY 10038
(585) 271-1500 .. **Dibble & Miller,PC** -55 Canterbury Rd -Rchstr 14607 **Fx:**271-0118
(718) 767-1606 .. **DiBella,** Carolyn R '82 -24-44 F Lewis Blvd -Flushng 11357
(212) 969-3000 .. **Di Bella,** Dolores F '07 %Proskauer R LLP -1585 Bway -NY 10036
(212) 869-1119 .. **DiBella,** John B '76 (JB DiBella,PC) -1500 Bway -NY 10036 **Fx:**869-7234
(631) 730-2200 .. **DiBella,** Mia G '08 Hain Celestial Inc -58 S Srvc Rd -Melvll 11747
(631) 843-5847 .. **DiBello,** Michl '03 Henry Schein,Inc -135 Duryea Rd -Melvll 11747
(212) 613-2033 .. **DiBenedetto,** Brian '02 %Gibbons PC -1 Penn Plz -NY 10119 **Fx:**554-9671
(315) 422-1152 .. **DiBenedetto,** Donald S '84 (Costello C&F,PLLC) -500 Plum -Syracuse 13204
(718) 224-7771 .. **DiBenedetto,** Jos '92 -38-08 Bell Blvd -Bayside 11361 **Fx:**281-2590
(212) 227-4700 .. **DiBenedetto,** Jos '02 %JR Benfante -225 Bway -NY 10007 **Fx:**406-6890
(212) 294-6700 .. **DiBenedetto,** Jos A '71 (Winston & S) -200 Park Av -NY 10166
(914) 995-3419 .. **DiBenedetto,** Jos A '89 %DA -111 Martin Luther King Blvd -White Plns 10601 **Fx:**995-3363
(718) 250-2000 .. **DiBenedetto,** Jos A '97 %DA -350 Jay -Brklyn 11201 **Fx:**250-2314
(914) 423-1222 .. **DiBenedetto,** Jos C '76 -1 Alxndr -Ynkrs 10701
(718) 721-4333 .. **DiBenedetto,** Jos J '91 -35-01 30th Av -Astoria 11103
(917) 583-8132 .. **DiBenedetto,** Michelle C '02 Spa Chakra,Inc -22907 56th Av -Oakland Gdns 11364
(315) 422-1152 .. **DiBenedetto,** Shelly L '97 SpclCnsl Costello C&F,PLLC -500 Plum -Syracuse 13204
(212) 373-3000 .. **DiBenedetto,** Tara J '10 %Paul WRW&G LLP -1285 Av of Amer -NY 10019
(516) 466-6030 .. **DiBerardino,** Arthur J '92 %Mirkin & G,PC -98 Cuttermill Rd -Gt Neck 11021
(212) 363-3100 .. **Di Berardino,** Elio M '98 (Bivona & C,PC) -88 Pine -NY 10005
(212) 238-4800 .. **DiBerardino,** Philip J '99 (Landman CB&F,PC) -120 Bway -NY 10271
(212) 806-5400 .. **DiBernardo,** Ian G '96 (Stroock &S&L LLP) -180 Maiden Ln -NY 10038
(718) 230-1517 .. **Dibia,** Ikechukwu P '98 -767 Franklin Av -Brklyn 11238
(212) 428-2130 .. **DiBiase,** Bruna L '85 %OCA -25 Beaver -NY 10004 **Fx:**428-2192
(718) 722-3100 .. **DiBiase,** Emily '02 %Leg Aid -111 Lvngstn -Brklyn 11201 **Fx:**722-3093
(716) 839-0354 .. **DiBlasi,** Frank A '87 -4721 Main -Amherst 14226 **Fx:**839-1907
(212) 558-4000 .. **DiBlasi,** Gandolfo V '79 (Sullivan & C LLP) -125 Broad -NY 10004
(716) 633-3700 .. **DiBlasi,** Jill Lynch '86 %Devere Cptl Corp -5400 Bway -Lancaster 14086
(800) 358-2550 .. **Di Blasi,** John P '81 NAM -122 E 42nd -NY 10168
(212) 310-8000 .. **DiBlasi,** Kelly '05 %Weil G&M LLP -767 5th Av -NY 10153
(212) 506-1700 .. **DiBlasi,** Matthew R '04 %Kasowitz BT&F LLP -1633 Bway -NY 10019
(718) 492-4455 .. **DiBona,** Peter D '88 -436 Bay Ridge Pkwy -Brklyn 11209 **Fx:**238-6999
(718) 858-5110 .. **DiBrienza,** Stephen '80 -93 Minna -Brklyn 11218
(212) 532-2211 .. **DiBrita,** Anthony J Jr. '93 DeSimone Cnsltng Engineers -18 W 18th -NY 10011
(516) 607-1018 .. **DiBrizzi,** Michl A '99 -47 Windmill Ln -Levittwn 11756
(716) 282-2341 .. **DiCamillo,** Margrit M '98 %DiCamillo Baking Co Inc -811 Linwood Av -Niagara Fls 14305
(212) 735-3000 .. **DiCamillo,** Veronica M '08 %Skadden ASM&F LLP -4 Times Sq -NY 10036
(212) 521-5400 .. **Dicanio,** Michl '07 %Reed S LLP -599 Lex Av -NY 10022
(212) 449-0360 .. **DiCapua,** Jos P '03 Merrill Lynch -4 World Fncl Ctr -NY 10080
(718) 546-0950 .. **DiCarlo,** Carl D '81 %Dept of Correction -75-20 Astoria Blvd -E Elmhrst 11370
(212) 506-1700 .. **DiCarlo,** Frank S '09 %Kasowitz BT&F LLP -1633 Bway -NY 10019
(914) 995-4300 .. **DiCarlo,** Louis '75 %Hon P Rosato -111 Martin Luther King Blvd -White Plns 10601
(516) 568-7566 .. **DiCarlo,** Mary E '88 -110 N Cottage -Vly Stream 11580
(585) 247-9000 .. **DiCaro,** John A '82 (Shapiro D&B,LLP) -250 Mile Xing Blvd -Rchstr 14624
(212) 308-4411 .. **Di Ceglie,** Nicholas J Jr. '07 %Edwards AP&D LLP -750 Lex Av -NY 10022
(845) 451-4065 .. **DiCerbo,** Lynn M '83 Law Dept -62 Civic Ctr Plz -Poughkeepsie 12601 **Fx:**451-4070
(716) 373-2165 .. **DiCerbo,** Nicholas A '74 (DiCerbo & P) -201 N Union -Olean 14760
(716) 373-2165 .. **DiCerbo,** Nicholas A Jr. '00 %DiCerbo & P -201 N Union -Olean 14760
(716) 373-2165 .. **DiCerbo & Palumbo** -201 N Union -Olean 14760 **Fx:**373-5180
(212) 688-5151 .. **Di Cesare,** Jos '87 (Gibney A&F,LLP) -665 5th Av -NY 10022
(716) 566-1300 .. **DiCesare,** Nicholas J '05 %Hiscock & B,LLP -1100 M&T Ctr -Buffalo 14203
(212) 837-6000 .. **DiCesare,** Steven S '04 %Hughes H&R LLP -1 Bttry Pk Plz -NY 10004
(212) 679-1958 .. **DiChiara,** Gerald J '76 -404 Park Av S -NY 10016 **Fx:**689-3315
(212) 679-1958 .. **DiChiara,** Laura '89 %GJ DiChiara -404 Park Av S -NY 10016 **Fx:**689-3315
(718) 590-2000 .. **Di Chiara,** Lauren '07 %DA -198 E 161st -Bronx 10451 **Fx:**590-6477
(914) 390-4088 .. **Dichiara,** Laurie '98 %Hon G Yanthis -300 Quarropas -White Plns 10601 **Fx:**390-4095
(212) 358-6581 .. **DiChiara,** Lucia V '89 %Hayes & M -315 Park Av S -NY 10010
(212) 930-9700 .. **DiChiara,** Peter '98 Cnsl Sichenzia RFF LLP -61 Bway -NY 10006
(845) 368-9797 .. **DiChiaro,** Michl A '89 M DiChiaro,PC -1 Exec Blvd -Suffern 10901
(212) 228-7727 .. **Dichner,** Ellen '83 (Gladstein R&M,LLP) -817 Bway -NY 10003
(212) 521-2000 .. **Dichter,** Anita '80 %Loews Corp -667 Mad Av -NY 10065 **Fx:**521-2997
(212) 597-8305 .. **Dichter,** Gloria Sonen '95 %Westdeutsche Landesbank -1211 Av of Amer -NY 10036
(212) 593-4202 .. **Dichter,** Joel R '79 (Dichter Law,LLC) -488 Mad Av -NY 10022 **Fx:**994-5394
(212) 953-6060 .. **DiCicco,** Bruce M '86 -99 Park Av -NY 10016 **Fx:**972-6569
(212) 705-7000 .. **DiCicco,** Susan Felice '93 (Bingham M LLP) -399 Park Av -NY 10022
(212) 935-3000 .. **Dicioccio,** Jos M '08 %Mintz LCFG&P,PC -666 3rd Av -NY 10017
(212) 759-4888 .. **DiCioccio,** Stephen J '85 SpclCnsl Phillips L LLP -437 Mad Av -NY 10022
(212) 897-7660 .. **Dick,** Alexander W '06 Forex Cptl Mrkts -32 Old Slip -NY 10005 **Fx:**897-7669
(212) 351-4000 .. **Dick,** Andrew A '09 Gibson D&C LLP -200 Park Av -NY 10166
(212) 492-3763 .. **Dick,** David L '89 Deloitte Consulting LLP -1633 Bway -NY 10019
(518) 486-7009 .. **Dick,** Kathleen R '77 DHCR -38-40 State -Albany 12207 **Fx:**473-8206
(607) 277-1441 .. **Dick,** Michl J '85 %Supreme Ct -Cnty Cthse Bx70 -Ithaca 14851 **Fx:**272-0690
(212) 957-7600 .. **Dick,** Stephen Gale '99 %Cohen & G LLP -800 3rd Av -NY 10022
(877) 222-1814 .. **Dickens,** Amanda '07 B Rothenberg -100 Duffy Av -Hicksvll 11801 **Fx:**(866) 894-2182
(585) 987-2800 .. **Dickens,** Gordon S '82 (Woods OG LLP) -2 State -Rchstr 14614
(212) 420-5800 .. **Dickens,** Jeremy W '99 Houghton Mifflin Riverdeep Grp -215 Park Av S -NY 10003
(518) 435-1040 .. **Dicker,** Arthur F III '84 -26 Parkwyn Dr -Delmar 12054
(212) 310-8000 .. **Dicker,** Howard B '90 (Weil G&M LLP) -767 5th Av -NY 10153
(516) 569-8922 .. **Dicker,** James W '84 -370 Felter Av -Hewlett 11557 **Fx:**569-8922
(212) 425-7200 .. **Dicker,** Jeffrey K '09 %Kenyon & K,LLP -1 Bway -NY 10004
(516) 478-5451 .. **Dicker,** Joshua '88 (Getty Realty Corp) -125 Jericho Tpk -Jericho 11753 **Fx:**478-5490
(212) 290-4700 .. **Dicker,** Richd '89 %Human Rights Watch -350 5th Av -NY 10118 **Fx:**736-1300
(212) 245-7633 .. **Dickerman,** Stephen G '70 %Dickerman Grp -1 Penn Plz -NY 10019 **Fx:**582-5128

(212) 446-4800 .. **Dickerson,** Allen J '06 %Kirkland & E LLP -153 E 53rd -NY 10022
(212) 752-1000 .. **Dickerson,** Chad M '00 Eiseman LL&K,PC -805 3rd Av -NY 10022
(212) 644-6006 .. **Dickerson Tomaselli & Mullen** -600 Mad Av -NY 10022 **Fx:**486-3032
(212) 558-4000 .. **Dickey,** John W '55 SrCnsl Sullivan & C LLP -125 Broad -NY 10004
(212) 351-4000 .. **Dickey,** Jonathan C '08 (Gibson D&C LLP) -200 Park Av -NY 10166
(212) 309-6000 .. **Dickey,** Robt W '99 (Morgan L&B LLP) -101 Park Av -NY 10178
(212) 609-6800 .. **Dickey,** Sydney E '01 %McCarter & E,LLP -245 Park Av -NY 10167
(914) 253-2950 .. **Dickie,** Lawr F '73 %Pepsico -700 Andrsn Hill Rd -Purchase 10577
(518) 455-2711 .. **Dickinson,** Christina L '03 Minority Cnsl's Ofc -316 The Cptl -Albany 12247
(315) 782-5650 .. **Dickinson,** Danl S III '79 -20889 Weaver Rd -Watertwn 13601 **Fx:**782-5652
(716) 847-8400 .. **Dickinson,** Joanna '03 %Phillips L LLP -3400 HSBC Ctr -Buffalo 14203
(212) 962-2000 .. **Dickler,** Richd '80 (Dickler & R,LLP) -19 Fulton -NY 10038 **Fx:**962-3222
(212) 953-2375 .. **Dickman,** Barry '62 -605 3rd Av -NY 10158
(718) 254-6022 .. **Dickman,** Mary M '91 %US Atty -271 Cadman Plz E -Brklyn 11201 **Fx:**254-6479
(845) 294-9447 .. **Dickover Donnelly Donovan & Biagi LLP** -28 Bruen Pl Bx610 -Goshen 10924 **Fx:**294-6553
(845) 294-9447 .. **Dickover,** Robt J '80 (Dickover DD&B LLP) -28 Bruen Pl Bx610 -Goshen 10924
(212) 351-4000 .. **Dicks,** Caroline Spector '03 %Gibson D&C LLP -200 Park Av -NY 10166
(718) 442-2828 .. **Dicks,** Maryellen '86 %Zachary & Z,PC -75 Little Clove Rd -Staten Isl 10301 **Fx:**720-5935
(212) 735-3000 .. **Dickson,** Ben '07 %Skadden ASM&F LLP -4 Times Sq -NY 10036
(212) 436-6041 .. **Dickson,** Clifford S '83 Deloitte & Touche,LLP -2 World Fncl Ctr -NY 10281
(646) 452-9700 .. **Dickson,** Emma M '06 Man Invstmnts Inc -1 Rckfllr Plz -NY 10020
(718) 250-0400 .. **Dickson,** Graham '92 %R Tusa -1 MetroTech Ctr -Brklyn 11201 **Fx:**250-0591
(516) 505-7001 .. **Dickson,** Mark F '75 (M Dickson & Assoc) -215 Uniondale Av -Uniondale 11553 **Fx:**505-5120
(212) 816-2434 .. **Dickson,** Mary Ann '01 Citigrp Glbl Mkts -388 Greenwich -NY 10013
(718) 442-1500 .. **Dickson,** Matthew A '01 -698 Forest Av -Staten Isl 10310
(212) 450-4000 .. **Dickson,** Robt A III '10 %Davis P&W LLP -450 Lex Av -NY 10017
(212) 661-2023 .. **Dickson,** Theo F '61 -192 Lex Av -NY 10016 **Fx:**661-4813
(212) 536-3900 .. **Dickstein,** David Y '00 (K&L Gates LLP) -599 Lex Av -NY 10022
(516) 581-0398 .. **Dickstein,** Jerry I '62 -95 Estate Dr -Jericho 11753
(212) 277-6500 .. **Dickstein Shapiro LLP** -1633 Bway -NY 10019 **Fx:**277-6501
(212) 407-4000 .. **Dickstein,** Tal E '05 %Loeb & L,LLP -345 Park Av -NY 10154
(212) 754-1010 .. **DiCola,** Annemarie G '84 Trepp, LLC -477 Mad Av -NY 10022 **Fx:**832-6738
(718) 590-6174 .. **DiCola,** Gia R '04 %Law Dept -198 E 161st -Bronx 10451 **Fx:**590-2686
(212) 682-4940 .. **DiConza,** Gerard '95 (DiConza Law,PC) -630 3rd Av -NY 10017 **Fx:**682-4942
(718) 238-6800 .. **DiConza Larocca DiCunto & Kaplin** -478 Bay Ridge Pkwy -Brklyn 11209 **Fx:**680-2294
(212) 801-9278 .. **DiConza,** Maria J '98 (Greenberg T,LLP) -200 Park Av -NY 10166
(212) 813-5900 .. **DiConza,** Nancy '00 Cnsl Fross ZL&Z,PC -866 UN Plz -NY 10017
(518) 387-6131 .. **Di Conza,** Paul J '06 %GE Co -1 Rsrch Cir -Niskayuna 12309
(516) 365-9281 .. **DiConza,** Peter J Jr. '75 -1295 Nrthrn Blvd -Manhsst 11030
(718) 238-6800 .. **DiConza,** Peter J Jr. '75 %DiConza LD&K -478 Bay Ridge Pkwy -Brklyn 11209
(212) 735-3000 .. **Di Conza,** Peter J III '06 %Skadden ASM&F LLP -4 Times Sq -NY 10036
(516) 624-0866 .. **DiConza,** Wm A '86 -5 Audrey Av Bx457 -Oyster Bay 11771 **Fx:**624-7735
(518) 408-0469 .. **DiCostanzo,** Maria '98 %Workers Comp Bd -20 Park -Albany 12207
(914) 337-4419 .. **DiCostanzo,** Nicholas M '58 -4 Mdlnd Gdns -Bronxvll 10708
(914) 995-3497 .. **DiCostanzo,** Nicholas W '08 %DA -111 Martin Luther King Blvd -White Plns 10601 **Fx:**995-3363
(914) 834-3500 .. **DiCostanzo,** Salvatore M '01 (McMillan CM&P LLP) -2180 Bstn Post Rd -Larchmnt 10538
(516) 470-1379 .. **DiCrescio,** Jacqueline '91 (DiCrescio & T,LLP) -400 Jericho Tpk -Jericho 11753 **Fx:**470-1382
(585) 232-6500 .. **Didas,** Michl J '07 %Harter S&E LLP -1600 Bausch & Lomb Pl -Rchstr 14604
(518) 487-7600 .. **Diddel,** Heather D '84 (Whiteman O&H LLP) -1 Commerce Plz -Albany 12260
(212) 403-1000 .. **Didden,** Damian G '03 (Wachtell LR&K) -51 W 52nd -NY 10019
(212) 850-1267 .. **Didden,** James M Jr. '96 %J&W Seligman -100 Park Av -NY 10017 **Fx:**922-0738
(718) 461-1219 .. **Didero,** Frank J '60 -47-14 158th -Flushng 11358 **Fx:**445-9828
(212) 382-2573 .. **Didia,** Victor E '70 -22 W 38th -NY 10018 **Fx:**764-3269
(914) 356-8647 .. **Didio,** Mildred C '90 Hudson Vlly Abstract Srvcs,Inc -181 S Bway -Sleepy Hollow 10591
(718) 575-5145 .. **DiDio,** Robt D '87 -80-02 Kew Grdns Rd -Kew Gdns 11415 **Fx:**793-0165
(518) 664-7338 .. **DiDomenico,** Andrea J '90 -One Vosburgh Rd -Mechanicvll 12118 **Fx:**664-2090
(212) 801-2127 .. **Di Domenico,** Timothy E '96 OfCnsl Greenberg T,LLP -200 Park Av -NY 10166
(516) 496-0730 .. **DiDonato,** Brenda M '89 -242 Crsswys Park Dr W -Woodbury 11797
(212) 506-2500 .. **DiDonato,** Matthew J '98 Cnsl Mayer B LLP -1675 Bway -NY 10019
(914) 347-2600 .. **Didonato,** Michl A '07 %Traub LS&S LLP -7 Skyline Dr -Hawthorne 10532
(518) 477-8771 .. **DiDonato,** Susan McGettrick '81 Questar III -10 Empire State Blvd -Castleton On Hudson 12033
(716) 854-3400 .. **DiDone,** Kyle C '08 %Rupp BPC&C LLC -1600 Lbrty Bldg -Buffalo 14202
(845) 336-6417 .. **DiDonna,** Louis A '51 -Bx3567 -Kingston 12402
(516) 663-6600 .. **Didora,** Matthew F '05 %Ruskin MF,PC -1425 RXR Plz -Uniondale 11556
(212) 259-8000 .. **Didriksen,** Michl W E '98 (Dewey & L LLP) -1301 Av of Amer -NY 10019
(518) 285-8380 .. **Diebel,** Beth Ann '02 Cnty Ct -16 Eagle -Albany 12207
(212) 704-6000 .. **Diebner,** Gerard F '84 OfCnsl Troutman S LLP -405 Lex Av -NY 10174
(716) 853-8190 .. **Diebold,** Richd J '64 -14 Lafayette Sq -Buffalo 14203 **Fx:**853-8197
(845) 942-0795 .. **Diederich,** Michl D Jr. '81 -361 Route 210 -Stony Pnt 10980 **Fx:**942-0796
(914) 946-0400 .. **DiEdwards,** Gerald D '89 (Schiavetti CDW&N,LLP) -709 Wstchstr Av -White Plns 10604
(212) 981-2233 .. **Diefenbach,** Gordon '87 (Diefenbach Law Firm,PLLC) -55 Broad -NY 10004 **Fx:**425-5443
(516) 683-1717 .. **Diefenbach,** Shirley Meiler '04 %V Russo & Assoc,PC -1600 Stewart Av -Westbury 11590 **Fx:**683-9393
(917) 452-5144 .. **Dieffenbach,** John J '93 Accenture -1345 Av of Amer -NY 10105
(914) 245-7402 .. **Diehl,** Barbara R '82 -2074 Crompond Rd -Yorktwn Hts 10598 **Fx:**245-7403
(212) 872-1000 .. **Diehl,** Jamison A '01 -One Bryant Park -NY 10036 **Fx:**872-1002
(718) 286-6000 .. **Diehl,** Jeanine R '07 %DA -125-01 Qns Blvd -Kew Gdns 11415
(646) 505-2071 .. **Diehl,** John J '82 Pheonix House -164 W 74th -NY 10023
(518) 464-2032 .. **Diehl,** Roy M '93 %AYCO -1 Wall -Albany 12205
(212) 589-6200 .. **Diemand,** Kelly S '00 MF Global Inc -717 5th Av -NY 10022
(212) 704-6000 .. **Diener,** Jason I '03 %Troutman S LLP -405 Lex Av -NY 10174
(718) 590-2000 .. **Diener,** Tara L '09 %DA -198 E 161st -Bronx 10451 **Fx:**590-6477
(718) 618-2500 .. **Diennor,** Martin '74 Civil Ct -851 Grnd Cncrs -Bronx 10451 **Fx:**590-7294
(212) 384-0201 .. **Dienst,** Richd A '65 -20 Vesey -NY 10007 **Fx:**608-1035
(212) 715-9100 .. **Dienstag,** Abbe L '83 (Kramer LN&F,LLP) -1177 Av of Amer -NY 10036
(212) 837-3056 .. **Dienstag,** Glenn '87 %AIG -160 Water -NY 10038
(516) 773-3382 .. **Dienstag,** Robt V '78 -11 Grace Av -Gt Neck 11021 **Fx:**482-5112
(631) 587-5100 .. **Diesa,** Elizabeth L '03 (Tabat CB&Y,LLP) -500 Montauk Hwy -W Islip 11795
(516) 816-0093 .. **Dietchweiler,** Danl O '89 -3 Mahan Rd -Old Bethpage 11804 **Fx:**908-7707
(212) 558-4000 .. **Dietderich,** Andrew G '97 (Sullivan & C LLP) -125 Broad -NY 10004
(212) 326-2000 .. **Dieter,** Brian S '10 %O'Melveny & M LLP -7 Times Sq -NY 10036
(914) 524-5600 .. **Dieter,** George R '82 %L Fishman -303 S Bway -Tarrytwn 10591 **Fx:**524-5742
(914) 248-0561 .. **Dieter,** Lois May '82 -2 Alyce Ct -Somers 10589 **Fx:**248-0561
(212) 373-3000 .. **Dieterich,** Amy P '09 %Paul WRW&G LLP -1285 Av of Amer -NY 10019
(914) 701-8327 .. **Dietrich,** John W '00 %Atlas Air,Inc -2000 Wstchstr Av -Purchase 10577
(716) 839-3939 .. **Dietrich,** Jos E III '96 Dietrich Law,PC -1323 N Forest Rd -Buffalo 14221 **Fx:**408-8888
(212) 261-8000 .. **Dietrich,** Wm J '99 (Mendes & M,LLP) -750 7th Av -NY 10019
(212) 813-8800 .. **Dietrick,** Heather L '08 %Goodwin P LLP -620 8th Av -NY 10018
(518) 295-8640 .. **Dietz,** Darrin M '95 %Hon D Lamont -Schoharie Cnty Cthse Bx369 -Schoharie 12157 **Fx:**295-8638
(212) 918-3000 .. **Dietz,** Eva L '04 %Hogan L LLP -875 3rd Av -NY 10022
(516) 933-2720 .. **Dietz,** John R '85 -Bx283 -Old Westbury 11568 **Fx:**822-8494
(212) 998-6596 .. **Dietz,** Mary K '93 NYU Law Schl -40 Wshngtn Sq S -NY 10012
(845) 452-4000 .. **Dietz,** Robt B '68 -2 Cannon -Poughkeepsie 12601 **Fx:**454-4966
(716) 636-7600 .. **Dietz,** Steven B '98 %HoganWillig -2410 N Forest Rd -Amherst 14068
(845) 452-4000 .. **Dietz,** Thos E '94 -2 Cannon -Poughkeepsie 12601 **Fx:**454-4966
(212) 940-3000 .. **Dietzgen,** Chas A Jr. '78 (Nixon P LLP) -437 Mad Av -NY 10022
(516) 542-5900 .. **Dieudonne,** Henry C Jr. '03 %Congdon FORDT&F -333 Earle Ovngton Blvd -Uniondale 11553
(212) 696-6000 .. **Diez-Hidalgo,** Ricardo J '84 (Curtis M-PC&M LLP) -101 Park Av -NY 10178
(518) 459-1000 .. **DiFabio,** E Michl '57 DiFabio Law Firm,PC -4 Automation Ln -Albany 12205 **Fx:**459-1038
(518) 459-1000 .. **DiFabio,** Michl D '90 DiFabio Law Firm,PC -4 Automation Ln -Albany 12205 **Fx:**459-1038
(212) 980-1900 .. **DiFalco,** Christophe L '02 Cnsl Donovan & G,LLP -261 Mad Av -NY 10016
(718) 935-5849 .. **DiFava,** Marco R '04 NYC Dept of Ed -65 Court -Brklyn 11201
(631) 421-9051 .. **DiFazio,** S Russ '85 (Goldstein RG&D,PC) -18 W Carver -Huntngtn 11743
(914) 476-1159 .. **DiFede,** M Victor '56 -711 Ynkrs Av -Ynkrs 10704 **Fx:**476-1205
(212) 558-4000 .. **Diffee,** Christopher M '09 %Sullivan & C LLP -125 Broad -NY 10004
(718) 746-9777 .. **Diffley,** John F '06 -1255 150th -Whitestone 11357 **Fx:**746-9778
(212) 294-6700 .. **DiFiglia,** Catherine A '96 (Winston & S) -200 Park Av -NY 10166
(212) 949-9022 .. **DiFilippi,** Anthony J '95 %Abelman F&S -666 3rd Av -NY 10017
(716) 652-9600 .. **DiFilippo,** Anthony III '63 (DiFilippo & F) -382 Main -E Aurora 14052
(716) 652-9560 .. **DiFilippo,** Anthony IV '88 (Bennett D&K,LLP) -681 Main -E Aurora 14052
(716) 652-9600 .. **DiFilippo & Flaherty** -382 Main -E Aurora 14052 **Fx:**655-7777
(914) 997-0555 .. **DiFiore,** Anthony '97 %Quinn & M,LLP -399 Knollwood Rd -White Plns 10603
(212) 676-0055 .. **DiFiore,** Barbara A '85 Assigned Council Plan -253 Bway 200 -NY 10007
(516) 747-4343 .. **DiFiore,** Elizabeth Ann '84 %JP DiMascio & Assoc,LLP -300 Grdn City Plz -Gdn Cty 11530 **Fx:**747-0204
(212) 521-5400 .. **DiFiore,** Gerard S '89 (Reed S LLP) -599 Lex Av -NY 10022
(914) 995-3408 .. **DiFiore,** Janet M '82 (DA) -111 Martin Luther King Blvd -White Plns 10601 **Fx:**995-3363
(718) 828-6407 .. **DiFiore,** Julius C '85 -3231 Ampere Av -Bronx 10465
(212) 294-6700 .. **Difiore,** Michl G '10 %Winston & S -200 Park Av -NY 10166
(646) 386-3873 .. **Di Flumeri,** Jos '98 %Hon D Conviser-Supreme Ct -111 Centre -NY 10013
(212) 732-8700 .. **Di Folco,** Gina Bernardi '96 (McAloon & F,PC) -123 William -NY 10038
(516) 463-5934 .. **DiFonzo,** J Herbie '97 %Hofstra Law Schl -121 Hofstra Univ -Hempstd 11549

(212) 435-3516 .. **DiFrancesco,** Marci A '99 Port Auth of NY/NJ -225 Park Av S -NY 10003 **Fx:**435-3555
(585) 546-7830 .. **DiFranco,** Amy L '00 %Culley MT&P,LLP -36 W Main -Rchstr 14614
(585) 428-6990 .. **DiGaetano,** Michele '69 %Law Dept -30 Church -Rchstr 14614 **Fx:**428-6950
(718) 849-8900 .. **DiGangi,** Angelo A '91 -101-05 Lefferts Blvd -S Richmond Hll 11419 **Fx:**849-6210
(212) 571-1980 .. **DiGangi,** Roberta L '84 -233 Bway -NY 10279 **Fx:**571-1981
(212) 969-3000 .. **DiGasper,** Sheila K '07 %Proskauer R LLP -1585 Bway -NY 10036
(718) 238-9555 .. **DiGaudio,** Gina M '04 %Gullo & Assoc,LLP -520 86th -Brklyn 11209 **Fx:**238-9552
(212) 327-8557 .. **DiGennaro,** Gloria C '86 Rockefeller Univ -1230 York Av -NY 10065
(516) 357-3000 .. **DiGennaro,** Janice J '84 (Rivkin R LLP) -926 RXR Plz -Uniondale 11556
(718) 242-0429 .. **DiGennaro,** Jos E '84 %Chase Manhattan Bk -4 Metrotech Ctr -Brklyn 11245
(212) 974-7474 .. **Digernes,** Lisa K '03 %Cowan DA&S LLP -41 Mad Av -NY 10010
(212) 450-4000 .. **Diggs,** Jamila A '10 %Davis P&W LLP -450 Lex Av -NY 10017
(212) 824-5700 .. **Dighton,** Mark D '97 %Practising Law Inst -810 7th Av -NY 10019
(718) 248-2968 .. **DiGia,** Allegra H '93 %Citibank -1 Court Sq -LIC 11101
(212) 351-4500 .. **DiGia,** Kenneth W '89 (Epstein B&G,PC) -250 Park Av -NY 10177
(212) 980-9600 .. **DiGiacinto,** Christopher E '95 (Kaufman B&R) -120 Bway -NY 10271
(914) 428-8500 .. **DiGiacinto,** Jos W '72 -235 Main -White Plns 10601 **Fx:**428-8737
(315) 472-5201 .. **DiGiacomo,** Albert D '86 (Mackay C&C,PC) -103 E Water -Syracuse 13202
(212) 655-6000 .. **DiGiacomo,** Anthony M '92 (Chapman & C LLP) -330 Mad Av -NY 10017
(914) 686-2111 .. **DiGiacomo & DeTommasi,LLP** -One Water -White Plns 10601 **Fx:**686-3567
(716) 843-5885 .. **Di Giacomo,** Michl '94 %US Atty -138 Delaware Av -Buffalo 14202 **Fx:**551-3052
(914) 686-2111 .. **DiGiacomo,** Paul D '96 (DiGiacomo & D,LLP) -One Water -White Plns 10601
(716) 688-3800 .. **DiGiacomo,** Richd F '77 (Nesper F&D,LLP) -501 JJ Audobon Pkwy -Amherst 14228
(212) 819-8200 .. **Di Giacomo,** Vincent E '07 White & C LLP -1155 Av of Amer -NY 10036
(718) 822-0707 .. **DiGiansante,** Lawr '91 -984 Morris Park Av -Bronx 10462 **Fx:**904-1030
(212) 536-3994 .. **DiGiglio,** Angela '95 %K&L Gates LLP -599 Lex Av -NY 10022
(516) 742-4343 .. **DiGiglio,** Frank S '83 (Scully SM&P PC) -400 Grdn City Plz -Gdn Cty 11530
(845) 454-1171 .. **Digilio,** Craig T '75 Feldman & J -94 Market -Poughkeepsie 12601
(212) 329-8477 .. **DiGioia,** Gina R '97 %Alloy Inc -151 W 26th -NY 10001
(212) 599-3322 .. **DiGioia,** Victor J '78 (Becker P,LLP) -45 Bway -NY 10006
(212) 967-1800 .. **Digiore,** Trisha A '07 %Bryant BJ&R LLP -140 Bway -NY 10005
(718) 330-7861 .. **DiGiorgio,** Clara S '95 %ODAR-SSA -111 Lvngstn -Brklyn 11201 **Fx:**330-2009
(315) 738-7101 .. **DiGiorgio,** Peter J '88 -2103 Genesee -Utica 13501
(518) 459-2100 .. **DiGiorgio,** Philip A Jr. '91 %Pierro Law Grp,LLC -20 Corp Wds Blvd -Albany 12211 **Fx:**459-2200
(631) 979-1960 .. **DiGiovanna,** John C '69 -Bx639 -St James 11780 **Fx:**797-1961
(718) 238-6900 .. **DiGiovanna,** Lawr F '77 -357 Bay Ridge Pkwy -Brklyn 11209 **Fx:**921-0753
(212) 232-0706 .. **DiGiovanna,** Margaret M '86 Dept Probation -33 Beaver -NY 10004 **Fx:**232-0718
(609) 919-6364 .. **DiGiovanna,** Michl D '66 -217 Bway -NY 10007 **Fx:**452-9473
(518) 474-6740 .. **DiGiovanna,** Richd '82 %Dept of State -41 State -Albany 12231 **Fx:**473-9211
(718) 590-2000 .. **DiGiovanni,** Agata A '06 %DA -198 E 161st -Bronx 10451 **Fx:**590-6477
(718) 289-2240 .. **DiGiovanni,** Louis '96 %Parker Jewish Inst -271-11 76th Av -New Hyde Pk 11040 **Fx:**289-2323
(516) 942-6005 .. **DiGirolamo,** Donna J '83 NY Community Bk -1 Jericho Plz -Jericho 11753 **Fx:**942-6907
(212) 340-0400 .. **DiGirolamo,** Mauro J '85 %Appllt Div 1st Dept -27 Mad Av -NY 10010 **Fx:**889-4412
(908) 757-7800 .. **Digirolamo,** V Anthony '80 (DiFrancesco BCYKD&L,PC) -88 Pine -NY 10005 **Fx:**757-8039
(516) 396-0354 .. **DiGirolomo,** Alfred C Jr. '91 (DiGirolomo & D,PC) -595 Stewart Av -Gdn Cty 11530
(718) 793-2111 .. **DiGirolomo,** Lucille S '81 -118-21 Qns Blvd -Frst Hlls 11375 **Fx:**793-2101
(516) 396-0354 .. **DiGirolomo,** Renee M '98 (DiGirolomo & D,PC) -595 Stewart Av -Gdn Cty 11530
(646) 386-4520 .. **DiGiulio,** Albert L '95 %Criminal Ct -100 Centre -NY 10013
(212) 514-7800 .. **DiGiulio,** Christopher P '80 -111 John -NY 10038 **Fx:**514-7838
(212) 483-9490 .. **Digiulio,** James J '07 %McElroy DM&C,LLP -88 Pine -NY 10005
(716) 635-4943 .. **DiGiulio,** Lawr C '93 Independent Hlth -511 Farber Lks Dr -Buffalo 14221 **Fx:**635-3838
(516) 248-2425 .. **Diglio,** Maria Campese '89 %MJ Conroy & Assoc -350 Old Cntry Rd -Gdn Cty 11530 **Fx:**248-2427
(212) 773-2980 .. **Dignam,** Rhea Kemble '73 Ernst & Young LLP -5 Times Sq -NY 10036
(212) 259-8000 .. **Dignan,** Brendan O '09 %Dewey & L LLP -1301 Av of Amer -NY 10019
(212) 310-8000 .. **Digon,** Rocio I '09 %Weil G&M LLP -767 5th Av -NY 10153
(718) 615-2060 .. **DiGrazia,** Jos N '83 -2108 E 19th -Brklyn 11229 **Fx:**615-2097
(516) 571-3800 .. **DiGregorio,** Andrea M '87 %DA -262 Old Cntry Rd -Mineola 11501 **Fx:**248-9479
(212) 232-1300 .. **DiGregorio,** Jos '03 %Lewis BB&S LLP -77 Water -NY 10005
(718) 286-6256 .. **Digregorio,** Tara A '07 %DA -125-01 Qns Blvd -Kew Gdns 11415 **Fx:**286-6255
(212) 264-3650 .. **DiGrigoli,** Tomasina '84 %SSA Ofc Genl Cnsl -26 Fed Plz -NY 10278 **Fx:**264-6372
(718) 274-1600 .. **Digrugilliers,** Renee '88 -31-10 37th Av -LIC 11101 **Fx:**204-7100
(718) 694-5615 .. **di Guida,** Jamileh-Sofia '88 %Transit Auth -130 Lvngstn -Brklyn 11201 **Fx:**694-5726
(516) 663-0780 .. **Dilorio,** Nicholas '98 %D Green -175 Pinelawn Rd -Melvll 11747 **Fx:**740-9731
(212) 339-2440 .. **Dilorio,** Peter '90 Allen & Co LLC -711 5th Av -NY 10022
(212) 344-7000 .. **Di Joseph,** Arnold E III '84 (A Di Joseph,PC) -50 Bway -NY 10004
(212) 909-6000 .. **Diké,** Chinelo E '08 %Debevoise & P LLP -919 3rd Av -NY 10022
(516) 354-2526 .. **Dikman,** David S '87 (Dikman & D) -5 Dakota Dr -Lk Success 11042 **Fx:**354-2528
(516) 354-2526 .. **Dikman,** Michl '61 (Dikman & D) -5 Dakota Dr -Lk Success 11042 **Fx:**354-2528
(516) 431-8900 .. **Dikranis,** Frank D '87 -1009 W Beech -Long Bch 11561 **Fx:**431-8352
(212) 440-3513 .. **DiLallo,** Laura M '92 %CNA Ins Co -40 Wall -NY 10005
(315) 476-7615 .. **DiLauro,** John P '73 -472 S Salina -Syracuse 13202 **Fx:**476-7645
(718) 522-3333 .. **Dildine,** Barbara H '75 %Children's Law Ctr -44 Court -Brklyn 11201 **Fx:**522-7376
(212) 326-2000 .. **DiLello,** Anthony '08 %O'Melveny & M LLP -7 Times Sq -NY 10036
(845) 765-0090 .. **Di Lello,** Dario '94 -939 Route 376 -Wappingers Fls 12590
(212) 687-2770 .. **DiLello,** Edw V '94 %Cohen PL&P -551 5th Av -NY 10176
(212) 972-1000 .. **DiLena,** Joshua A '09 %London F LLP -59 Maiden Ln -NY 10038
(516) 742-1444 .. **DiLeo,** Diana D'Alessio '94 %Wagner D&L,PC -227 Mineola Blvd -Mineola 11501
(516) 535-3824 .. **DiLeo,** Michl J '95 -59 Hilton Av -Gdn Cty 11530 **Fx:**742-6935
(718) 544-1478 .. **DiLeonardo,** Gary C '75 -118-35 Qns Blvd -Frst Hlls 11375 **Fx:**520-8544
(212) 806-5400 .. **Dileonardo,** Lauren V '09 %Stroock &S&L LLP -180 Maiden Ln -NY 10038
(718) 454-9600 .. **Diliberto,** Salvatore A '71 -21548 Jamaica Av -Qns Vllg 11428 **Fx:**454-7999
(516) 869-1111 .. **Dilimetin,** Laura May '91 (Dilimetin & D) -47 Plandome Rd -Manhsst 11030 **Fx:**869-1133
(212) 553-0300 .. **Dill,** Alexander C '87 %Moody's Invstr Srvc -250 Greenwich -NY 10007
(212) 577-3688 .. **Dille,** Ellen '86 %Leg Aid -199 Water -NY 10038 **Fx:**509-8431
(718) 935-1111 .. **Dillenberger,** Cassandra E '96 %ABRA Construction -320 Dean -Brklyn 11217
(212) 684-3000 .. **Diller,** Mark N '86 Shatzkin & M,PC -1776 Bway -NY 10019 **Fx:**684-5333
(212) 790-0200 .. **Diller,** Matthew '87 Benj N Cardozo Schl of Law -55 5th Av -NY 10003 **Fx:**790-0345
(212) 992-8635 .. **Diller,** Rebekah R '98 Brennan Ctr for Justice -161 Av of Amer -NY 10013
(212) 878-8000 .. **Dillingham,** Analisa '08 %Clifford C LLP -31 W 52nd -NY 10019
(914) 698-3216 .. **Dillon,** Alan E '00 -100 Mamaroneck Av -Mamaroneck 10543
(518) 842-7690 .. **Dillon,** Carol M '88 -3 Hibbard -Amsterdam 12010 **Fx:**842-7691
(212) 354-3800 .. **Dillon,** Christopher H '83 (Burke & P) -100 Park Av -NY 10017
(212) 846-7360 .. **Dillon,** Danl H '08 MTV Networks -1515 Bway -NY 10036
(516) 889-0200 .. **Dillon,** Danl J '68 -57 Cheltenham -Lido Bch 11561 **Fx:**889-0230
(845) 228-4200 .. **Dillon,** Debora J '94 %W Sayegh,PC -65 Gleneida Av -Carmel 10512 **Fx:**228-4832
(845) 638-3938 .. **Dillon,** Dennis M '79 -20 Squadron Blvd -New Cty 10956 **Fx:**638-3915
(716) 858-2424 .. **Dillon,** Emily A '10 %DA -25 Delaware Av -Buffalo 14202 **Fx:**858-7425
(315) 793-2225 .. **Dillon,** G Lawr '85 %Dept of Law -207 Genesee -Utica 13501 **Fx:**793-2228
(516) 676-2733 .. **Dillon,** Herbert J '65 (Dillon H&D) -Bx382 -Glen Head 11545 **Fx:**676-2732
(212) 248-4900 .. **Dillon Horowitz & Goldstein LLP** -11 Hanover Sq -NY 10005 **Fx:**248-2848
(914) 631-1611 .. **Dillon,** Irene '85 %Health Source -303 S Bway -Tarrytwn 10591
(212) 558-4000 .. **Dillon,** James R '04 %Sullivan & C LLP -125 Broad -NY 10004
(212) 422-0202 .. **Dillon,** Jeffrey W '05 %Sedgwick DM&A LLP -125 Broad -NY 10004
(716) 662-9808 .. **Dillon,** Jennifer M '91 J Dillon,PC -4513 S Buffalo -Orchard Pk 14127 **Fx:**662-9546
(914) 698-6392 .. **Dillon,** John M '87 (Caruso & D) -100 Mamaroneck Av -Mamaroneck 10543 **Fx:**698-2038
(315) 735-3535 .. **Dillon,** John W '95 -23 Oxford Rd -New Hartfrd 13413 **Fx:**735-7924
(212) 506-2500 .. **Dillon,** Justin M '09 %Mayer B LLP -1675 Bway -NY 10019
(631) 501-3100 .. **Dillon,** Kathleen M '97 %J Humphreys -3 Huntngtn Quad Bx9028 -Melvll 11747 **Fx:**501-3085
(716) 854-6140 .. **Dillon,** Lauren E '06 %Baxter S&S,PC -182 Dwyer -W Seneca 14224
(212) 521-5400 .. **Dillon,** Lee Ann '84 (Reed S LLP) -599 Lex Av -NY 10022
(315) 797-8839 .. **Dillon,** Linda '82 -1 Phelps Av -New Hartfrd 13413 **Fx:**797-5320
(914) 766-4259 .. **Dillon,** Marian J '97 IBM -294 Route 100 -Somers 10589
(212) 547-5400 .. **Dillon,** Michl J '06 %McDermott W&E LLP -340 Mad Av -NY 10173
(212) 474-1000 .. **Dillon,** Nina M '92 Cravath S&M LLP -825 8th Av -NY 10019
(631) 673-7555 .. **Dillon,** Noel C '97 -191 NY Av -Huntngtn 11743 **Fx:**425-7030
(914) 997-8100 .. **Dillon,** Philip J '93 %Burke LM&G -10 Bank -White Plns 10606
(212) 821-6030 .. **Dillon,** Sean P '04 UBS Securities LLC -299 Park Av -NY 10171
(212) 248-4900 .. **Dillon,** Thos '91 (Dillon H&G LLP) -11 Hanover Sq -NY 10005
(212) 924-6639 .. **Dillport,** Donald B '72 -200 W 54th -NY 10019
(516) 379-9370 .. **Dillworth,** Richd S '92 Dillworth & Assoc,PC -389 S Main -Freeprt 11520 **Fx:**379-8965
(646) 375-2269 .. **Dilmaghani,** Alireza '97 RML -116 W 23rd -NY 10011
(631) 232-6130 .. **DiLonardo,** Anna M '90 (Weiner L LLP) -888 Vets Mem'l Hwy -Hauppauge 11788
(212) 906-1200 .. **Diloné,** Isorys A '07 %Latham & W -885 3rd Av -NY 10022
(631) 390-0010 .. **DiLorenzo,** Chantelle N '10 %Bruno G&S,LLP -445 Broad Hollow Rd -Melvll 11747
(718) 537-9885 .. **DiLorenzo,** Chris M '92 (DiLorenzo & R) -944 Gerard Av -Bronx 10452
(518) 272-6565 .. **DiLorenzo,** Kirby W '74 (Martin SWD&J) -279 River Bx1530 -Troy 12181
(914) 769-7970 .. **DiLorenzo,** Lillian '92 -64 Eastvw Dr -Valhalla 10595
(646) 253-2300 .. **DiLorenzo,** Louis P '77 (Bond S&K,PLLC) -330 Mad Av -NY 10017
(315) 218-8000 .. **DiLorenzo,** Louis P '77 (Bond S&K,PLLC) -1 Lincoln Ctr -Syracuse 13202
(212) 578-0399 .. **DiLorenzo,** Robt F '88 %MetLife -1095 Av of Amer -NY 10036
(716) 686-0418 .. **DiLorenzo,** Rosario J '63 -1 Clermont Ct -Lancaster 14086
(718) 537-9885 .. **DiLorenzo & Rush** -944 Gerard Av -Bronx 10452 **Fx:**293-0870

(716) 858-2424 .. **DiLorenzo,** Stephen J '03 %DA -25 Delaware Av -Buffalo 14202 **Fx:**858-7425
(212) 868-0420 .. **DiLorenzo,** Stephen L '89 -350 5th Av -NY 10118 **Fx:**868-0513
(718) 990-6092 .. **DiLorenzo,** Vincent '79 %St John's Law Schl -8000 Utopia Pkwy -Jamaica 11439 **Fx:**591-1855
(718) 250-1400 .. **Dilos,** Demetrios T '88 %BZ Green -12 MetroTech Ctr -Brklyn 11201 **Fx:**250-1401
(914) 323-7000 .. **DiLuca,** Tara R '05 %Wilson EME&D LLP -3 Gannett Dr -White Plns 10604
(516) 409-6200 .. **DiLuccio,** Jeffrey M '92 (Furey KWM&C,PC) -2174 Jackson Av -Seafrd 11783
(516) 561-5300 .. **DiLuccio,** Patrick M '88 (Silverman & D) -41B W Merrick Rd -Vly Stream 11580 **Fx:**561-5379
(212) 475-4120 .. **DiLucia,** Gilbert A '58 -11 5th Av -NY 10003
(212) 903-9000 .. **DiLuigi,** Brenda D '00 %Linklaters -1345 Av of Amer -NY 10105
(516) 496-5822 .. **Di Lullo,** Nico '06 %T Spina -170 Froehlich Farm Blvd -Woodbury 11797 **Fx:**496-5420
(516) 248-8930 .. **DiLuzio,** Adrian L '80 -200 Old Cntry Rd -Mineola 11501 **Fx:**248-8281
(212) 696-9494 .. **DiLuzio,** Louis M '89 %Park WC&N,LLP -15 E 32nd -NY 10016 **Fx:**447-0968
(516) 228-8484 .. **Dilworth & Barrese, LLP** -1000 Woodbury Rd -Woodbury 11797 **Fx:**228-8516
(516) 228-8484 .. **Dilworth,** Peter G '70 (Dilworth & B,LLP) -1000 Woodbury Rd -Woodbury 11797
(212) 733-4563 .. **Dilworth,** Theresa K '86 Pfizer Inc -150 E 42nd -NY 10017 **Fx:**573-2298
(212) 566-6212 .. **DiMaggio,** Chas M '97 (Fasulo S&D) -225 Bway -NY 10007
(718) 590-2000 .. **DiMaggio,** Dominick J Jr. '98 %DA -198 E 161st -Bronx 10451 **Fx:**590-6477
(516) 294-0300 .. **Di Maggio,** Michl J '07 %Collins M&G -138 Mineola Blvd -Mineola 11501
(212) 697-3122 .. **DiMaio,** Nicholas G '05 %Martin C&B LLP -220 E 42nd -NY 10017
(718) 260-8700 .. **DiMango,** Anthony J '87 %Admin Children's Srvcs -345 Adams -Brklyn 11201
(212) 598-8000 .. **DiManni,** Margherita L '89 %Guardian Life Ins -7 Hanover Sq -NY 10004 **Fx:**919-2693
(212) 736-1940 .. **DiMarco,** Benjamin S '04 %Davidson D&K LLC -485 7th Av -NY 10018
(315) 428-4374 .. **DiMarco,** Carla A '97 Dept Tax & Finance -333 E Wshngtn -Syracuse 13202 **Fx:**428-4968
(718) 816-5991 .. **DiMarco,** Cynthia A '85 -981 Bay -Staten Isl 10305
(585) 987-2800 .. **DiMarco,** David C '98 (Woods OG LLP) -2 State -Rchstr 14614
(212) 490-3000 .. **DiMarco,** Erik C '98 (Wilson EME&D LLP) -150 E 42nd -NY 10017
(914) 633-5330 .. **DiMarco,** Frank P '71 -20 Cedar -New Rchll 10801 **Fx:**633-5332
(585) 232-2550 .. **DiMarco,** Gerard D '72 -2 State -Rchstr 14614 **Fx:**232-6138
(212) 935-3000 .. **DiMarco,** Jennifer '00 %Mintz LCFG&P,PC -666 3rd Av -NY 10017
(718) 248-5286 .. **DiMarco,** Jos S '98 Citicorp Invstmnt Srvcs -1 Court Sq -LIC 11120 **Fx:**248-1406
(845) 225-1100 .. **DiMaria,** Anthony G '99 %E Sumber,PC -18 Fair -Carmel 10512 **Fx:**225-1187
(212) 269-5900 .. **DiMaria,** Dana Marie '05 Regal Title Agency -90 Broad -NY 10004
(347) 296-1674 .. **DiMaria,** Wm P '76 %Supreme Ct Law Dept -360 Adams -Brklyn 11201 **Fx:**643-6114
(516) 794-2800 .. **Dimarinis,** Peter J '08 %M Devack,PLLC -90 Merrick Av -E Meadow 11554 **Fx:**794-2900
(518) 487-7600 .. **DiMarino,** Jason M '01 %Whiteman O&H LLP -1 Commerce Plz -Albany 12260
(212) 576-6419 .. **DiMartini,** Carol Anne '96 NY Life Ins -51 Mad Av -NY 10010 **Fx:**447-0569
(212) 553-8300 .. **DiMartini,** Michl V '87 %Cohen K & Assoc -2 Park Av -NY 10016 **Fx:**553-8721
(212) 867-9595 .. **Di Martini,** Stuart C '87 %Vogel & R -630 Third Av -NY 10017
(315) 341-5815 .. **DiMartino,** Anthony J Jr. '91 -193 W 1st -Oswego 13126 **Fx:**341-7008
(716) 856-8200 .. **DiMartino,** Janelle M '05 %Williams & W -43 Court -Buffalo 14202 **Fx:**856-0559
(212) 728-8000 .. **DiMartino,** Rose F '82 (Willkie F&G LLP) -787 7th Av -NY 10019
(212) 593-6700 .. **DiMartino,** Theresa M '98 (Aaronson RF&D,LLP) -757 3rd Av -NY 10017
(516) 747-4343 .. **DiMascio,** John P '84 -300 Grdn City Plz -Gdn Cty 11530 **Fx:**747-0204
(516) 747-4343 .. **DiMascio,** John P Jr. '98 -300 Grdn City Plz -Gdn Cty 11530 **Fx:**747-0204
(212) 335-9000 .. **DiMase,** Christopher J '05 %DA -1 Hogan Pl -NY 10013
(585) 546-5510 .. **Dimassimo,** James D '84 -263 S Plymouth Av -Rchstr 14608
(716) 856-1600 .. **DiMatteo,** Anne C '86 (Hurwitz & D) -424 Main -Buffalo 14202
(585) 343-2770 .. **DiMatteo,** Danl M '79 -39 Ellicott -Batavia 14020
(585) 786-2110 .. **DiMatteo,** David '90 DiMatteo Law Ofc -87 N Main Bx190 -Warsaw 14569 **Fx:**786-0126
(212) 728-8000 .. **DiMatteo,** John M '89 (Willkie F&G LLP) -787 7th Av -NY 10019
(716) 693-7907 .. **DiMatteo,** Larry A '83 -3060 Niagara Flls Blvd -N Tonawanda 14120 **Fx:**693-6751
(518) 843-2002 .. **Di Matteo,** Richd A '98 -245 W Main -Amsterdam 12010 **Fx:**843-2111
(212) 548-2100 .. **Di Mattia,** Michl J '79 (McGuire W LLP) -1345 Av of Amer -NY 10105
(718) 351-7747 .. **DiMauro,** Michl A '96 -159 New Dorp Plz -Staten Isl 10306 **Fx:**351-7754
(631) 547-9401 .. **DiMeglio,** Saml J Jr. '87 -191 E Main -Huntngtn 11743 **Fx:**547-1072
(212) 261-8000 .. **Dimian,** Sandy A '06 %Mendes & M,LLP -750 7th Av -NY 10019
(212) 468-4800 .. **DiMiceli,** Jos A '96 (Davis & G LLP) -1740 Bway -NY 10019
(631) 390-0010 .. **Dimiceli,** Megan C '09 %Bruno G&S,LLP -445 Broad Hollow Rd -Melvll 11747
(212) 449-3539 .. **Dimich,** Katarina V '92 %Merrill Lynch -220 Bway -NY 10038
(212) 806-5400 .. **DiMichele,** Elizabeth E '97 SpclCnsl Stroock &S&L LLP -180 Maiden Ln -NY 10038
(718) 261-7800 .. **DiMichele & Franzese** -118-21 Qns Blvd -Frst Hlls 11375 **Fx:**261-4264
(718) 261-7800 .. **DiMichele,** James '88 (DiMichele & F) -118-21 Qns Blvd -Frst Hlls 11375
(845) 638-5180 .. **Dimick,** Thos N '92 %Cnty Atty -Cnty Ofc Bldg -New Cty 10956 **Fx:**638-5676
(212) 837-1353 .. **Dimig,** Theo F '02 JP Morgan Fleming Asset Mgmt -522 5th Av -NY 10036
(716) 434-9177 .. **DiMillo,** A Angelo '81 (Muscato D&V) -107 East Av -Lockprt 14094
(631) 715-7800 .. **Dimino,** Alfred M '80 %US Trustees Ofc -560 Fed Plz -Central Islip 11722 **Fx:**715-7777
(212) 381-7000 .. **DiMino,** Robt L '90 (Sabin B&G LLP) -4 Times Sq -NY 10036
(212) 723-3319 .. **Dimitrievich,** Donald R '99 City Group Global Corp Invstmnt Bank -250 West -NY 10013 **Fx:**723-2980
(718) 760-0311 .. **Dimitris,** Ariane '99 -61-15 97th -Rego Pk 11374
(716) 847-8400 .. **Dimitroff,** Douglas W '90 (Phillips L LLP) -3400 HSBC Ctr -Buffalo 14203
(518) 472-1224 .. **Dimitroff,** Douglas W '90 (Phillips L LLP) -30 S Pearl -Albany 12207
(212) 351-4000 .. **Dimitrov,** Delyan M '09 Gibson D&C LLP -200 Park Av -NY 10166
(716) 373-0004 .. **Dimmer,** James S '95 Pub Def -175 N Union -Olean 14760 **Fx:**373-3462
(716) 853-8100 .. **Dimoh,** Paul E '09 %Nixon P LLP -40 Fountain Plz -Buffalo 14202
(212) 450-4000 .. **Dimon,** Saml J '95 (Davis P&W LLP) -450 Lex Av -NY 10017
(212) 220-3000 .. **DiMona,** Jos J '87 %Broadcast Music Inc -250 Greenwich -NY 10007
(914) 472-4242 .. **Dimopoulos,** Constance G '01 (Maniatis D&L,LLP) -700 Wht Plns Rd -Scarsdale 10583 **Fx:**472-5074
(914) 905-6351 .. **Dimos,** Bill '05 IBM Credit -N Castleton Dr -Armonk 10504
(212) 858-1000 .. **Dimos,** Gianni Cadre '05 %Pillsbury WSP LLP -1540 Bway -NY 10036
(212) 774-8802 .. **D'Imperio,** Anthony M '05 IMG Media -420 W 45th -NY 10036
(315) 451-3810 .. **D'Imperio,** Dominic S '09 %O'Hara O&C,PC -7207 E Genesee -Fayettevll 13066
(212) 878-7212 .. **Din,** Naeem Y '86 %MTA Ofc Of Civil Rights -347 Mad Av -NY 10017
(212) 998-0100 .. **Dinallo,** Eric R '91 NYU Stern Schl of Business -44 W 4th -NY 10012
(212) 836-8000 .. **DiNapoli,** Danl P '90 (Kaye S LLP) -425 Park Av -NY 10022
(212) 345-5540 .. **DiNapoli,** Leonard F '70 %Marsh USA -1166 Av of Amer -NY 10036 **Fx:**345-4808
(646) 485-3131 .. **Di Nardo,** Bruno '69 (Di Nardo & Co,PC) -633 3rd Av -NY 10017 **Fx:**485-3132
(716) 204-9001 .. **DiNardo,** Emil R '83 (DiNardo & M,PC) -2813 Wehrle Dr -Williamsvll 14221
(716) 204-9001 .. **DiNardo & Metschl, PC** -2813 Wehrle Dr -Williamsvll 14221 **Fx:**204-9016
(845) 778-2121 .. **DiNardo,** Robt E '70 (Jacobowitz & G,LLP) -158 Orange Av Bx367 -Walden 12586
(212) 834-0600 .. **Dince,** David M '79 (Gordon & S,PC) -355 Lex Av -NY 10017
(914) 285-8500 .. **Dinces,** Neil B '76 %TK Moore -701 Wstchstr Av -White Plns 10604 **Fx:**285-8510
(212) 574-1200 .. **Dine,** Jeffrey M '96 %Seward & K LLP -1 Bttry Pk Plz -NY 10004
(212) 858-1000 .. **Dine,** Karen B '94 (Pillsbury WSP LLP) -1540 Bway -NY 10036
(518) 427-6310 .. **Dineen,** Deirdre M '78 -61 Rockrose Dr -E Greenbush 12061
(212) 532-8100 .. **Dineen,** Elizabeth A '05 %Stern & M,LLP -115 Bway -NY 10006
(516) 512-8968 .. **Dineen,** Jos P '81 -1225 Franklin Av -Gdn Cty 11530
(212) 244-9500 .. **Dineen,** Matthew G '82 Cnsl White and W LLP -1 Penn Plz -NY 10119
(914) 245-4098 .. **Dineen,** Patricia C Wilkens '88 (Dineen & P,PC) -1335 Wht Hill Rd -Yorktwn Hts 10598
(212) 294-6700 .. **Dineen,** Patricia M '90 (Winston & S) -200 Park Av -NY 10166
(914) 245-4098 .. **Dineen & Pratt,PC** -1335 Wht Hill Rd -Yorktwn Hts 10598
(212) 848-8012 .. **Dineen,** Robt E Jr. '66 OfCnsl Shearman & S LLP -599 Lex Av -NY 10022
(212) 770-5884 .. **Dinella,** Roger W '92 %AIG -70 Pine -NY 10270 **Fx:**785-1468
(212) 267-7575 .. **Dinerman,** Barry M '85 (Dinerman B&D) -170 Bway -NY 10038 **Fx:**571-7475
(212) 626-4100 .. **Dinerman,** Isabelle A '09 %Baker & M LLP -1114 Av of Amer -NY 10036
(631) 462-1226 .. **Dinerstein,** Robt Jay '73 RJ Dinerstein,PC -16 Cross Bow Ln -Commack 11725 **Fx:**462-1236
(716) 852-4400 .. **Dines,** Maria LoTempio '88 Roberts-Gordon LLC -1250 William Bx44 -Buffalo 14206
(212) 951-6417 .. **Ding,** George M '79 %Dept of Education -475 Park Av S -NY 10016 **Fx:**951-6465
(212) 578-2211 .. **Ding,** Wm K '94 %MetLife -27-01 Qns Plz N -LIC 11101
(716) 854-6140 .. **Dingeldey,** Louis B Jr. '03 %Baxter S&S,PC -182 Dwyer -W Seneca 14224
(212) 312-6000 .. **Dinger,** Angela B '99 William H Sadlier Inc -9 Pine -NY 10005
(212) 676-7906 .. **Dingledy,** Mary Jane '84 %Admin Children's Srvcs -220 Church -NY 10013
(518) 371-1151 .. **Dingley,** Albert F '81 -68 Droms Rd -Rexfrd 12148 **Fx:**371-1151
(914) 428-4233 .. **Dingott,** Marvin M '61 -4 Macy Av -White Plns 10605
(516) 678-3500 .. **Dinhofer,** Philip J '83 PJ Dinhofer,LLC -77 N Centre Av -Rockvll Ctr 11570 **Fx:**678-4235
(212) 408-5100 .. **DiNicola,** Annemarie S '10 %Chadbourne & P LLP -30 Rckfllr Plz -NY 10112
(315) 923-2281 .. **DiNieri,** Robt A '79 -47 Glasgow -Clyde 14433 **Fx:**923-2291
(212) 709-3540 .. **Dinin,** John R '74 Banking Dept -1 State -NY 10004 **Fx:**709-1655
(646) 485-3131 .. **Dinkelmeyer,** Kurt '71 %Di Nardo & Co,PC -633 3rd Av -NY 10017 **Fx:**485-3132
(877) 829-3750 .. **Dinkes,** Michl '76 -390 McDermott Rd -Rockvll Ctr 11570 **Fx:**(516) 764-6223
(212) 683-3800 .. **Dinkes & Schwitzer, PC** -112 Mad Av -NY 10016 **Fx:**685-2356
(716) 542-5413 .. **Dinki,** Edw J '76 Nicholas PSB&Z -12364 Main Rd Bx176 -Akron 14001
(212) 854-4253 .. **Dinkins,** David N '56 Columbia Univ-SIPA -420 W 118th -NY 10027
(212) 310-6771 .. **Dinkoff,** Allan David '81 Cnsl Weil G&M LLP -767 5th Av -NY 10153
(212) 626-4100 .. **Dinlenc,** Ata '98 (Baker & M LLP) -1114 Av of Amer -NY 10036
(516) 832-7645 .. **Dinneen,** Kerry A '05 %Nixon P LLP -50 Jericho Quadrangle -Jericho 11753
(212) 261-8000 .. **Dinneen,** Molly E '04 %Mendes & M,LLP -750 7th Av -NY 10019
(212) 349-6009 .. **Dinnerstein,** Julie E '96 %Sanctuary for Families -110 Wall -NY 10005 **Fx:**566-0344

(212) 925-0793 .. **Dinnerstein,** Mitchell '77 -350 Bway -NY 10013 **Fx:**625-3939
(212) 486-6060 .. **Dinnocenzo,** Eric J '06 %Trief & O -150 E 58th -NY 10155
(516) 496-5822 .. **Dinolfo,** Joanna J '04 T Spina -170 Froehlich Farm Blvd -Woodbury 11797 **Fx:**496-5420
(585) 241-3414 .. **Dinolfo,** Jos F '94 -649 Park Av -Rchstr 14607
(585) 428-5200 .. **Dinolfo,** Vincent M '85 %Surrogates Ct -541 Hall of Justice -Rchstr 14614
(212) 765-9000 .. **Dinoso,** David '10 %Gazes,LLC -32 Av of Amer -NY 10013 **Fx:**765-9675
(716) 688-6152 .. **DiNoto,** John C '64 -701 Schoelles Rd -Amherst 14228
(718) 591-0341 .. **Dinovitser,** Esther G '99 -80-37 Utopia Pkwy -Jamaica 11432
(518) 462-5601 .. **DiNovo,** Thos J '88 (O'Connell & A) -54 State -Albany 12207
(212) 999-5800 .. **Dinow,** Adam M '97 (Wilson SG&R) -1301 Av of Americas -NY 10019
(718) 796-5345 .. **Dinowitz,** Jeffrey E '80 -3107 Kngsbrdg Av -Bronx 10463
(212) 370-1300 .. **Dinowitz,** Michl A '87 (Ellenoff G&S LLP) -150 E 42nd -NY 10017
(212) 458-1073 .. **Dinowitz,** Wendy '93 %AIG -175 Water -NY 10038
(212) 735-3000 .. **Dinsmore,** Courtney Ann '93 %Skadden ASM&F LLP -4 Times Sq -NY 10036
(877) 222-1814 .. **Dinstell,** Scott R '97 B Rothenberg -100 Duffy Av -Hicksvll 11801 **Fx:**(866) 894-2182
(716) 853-5100 .. **Dintino,** Anne N '05 %Lippes MWF LLP -665 Main -Buffalo 14203
(631) 331-1900 .. **DiNunzio,** Edw J '74 -1031 Main -Pt Jffrsn 11777 **Fx:**331-1925
(315) 724-5140 .. **Diodati,** David R '90 -23 Genesee -New Hartfrd 13413 **Fx:**724-0338
(516) 479-6300 .. **Dioguardi,** Rachael E '07 %Silverman A LLP -100 Jericho Quad -Jericho 11753
(212) 733-0949 .. **Diomande,** Dara J '02 Pfizer Inc -235 E 42nd -NY 10017
(212) 857-8230 .. **Diomede,** Vito S '92 %Baker MM&M,PC -330 W 34th -NY 10001
(212) 676-0932 .. **Dion,** Norman M '89 NYC Health & Hospitals Corp -160 Water -NY 10038
(914) 514-6106 .. **DiOrio,** Anthony J '81 (Jackson L LLP) -1 N Bway -White Plns 10601
(516) 663-6628 .. **DiOrio,** Michl A '03 -1425 RXR Plz -Uniondale 11556
(212) 940-3145 .. **Diorio,** Thos F '03 Cnsl Nixon P LLP -437 Mad Av -NY 10022
(212) 773-3603 .. **Dios,** Anthony M '87 Ernst & Young LLP -5 Times Sq -NY 10036
(518) 408-1495 .. **DiPace,** Denise M '01 Dept of Health -Corning Twr 24th Fl -Albany 12237 **Fx:**486-4834
(585) 454-6480 .. **DiPalma,** Jeffrey P '96 %Osborn R&B,LLP -45 Exchange Blvd -Rchstr 14614
(631) 321-4069 .. **DiPalma,** John T '61 -2 Elena Ct -W Islip 11795 **Fx:**321-6661
(845) 457-5332 .. **DiPalma,** Maryellen '00 OfCnsl Johnson & F,PC -15 Scotts Crnrs Dr Bx664 -Montgmry 12549 **Fx:**457-5931
(646) 386-4800 .. **Di Palo,** Melissa R '01 %Comm Judicial Cndct -61 Bway -NY 10006 **Fx:**458-0037
(518) 487-7600 .. **DiPaola,** Kathleen Copps '10 %Whiteman O&H LLP -1 Commerce Plz -Albany 12260
(212) 759-4530 .. **DiPaola,** Robt B '55 (Rubin D&D) -405 Park Av -NY 10022
(212) 759-4530 .. **DiPaola,** Thos S '83 %Rubin D&D -405 Park Av -NY 10022
(718) 989-8800 .. **DiPaolo,** Anthony '98 A DiPaolo PC -235-07 Braddock Av -Qns Vllg 11428 **Fx:**740-2975
(212) 400-6900 .. **DiPaolo,** Barrett S '90 Cnsl Gottbetter & Prtnrs -488 Mad Av -NY 10022 **Fx:**400-6901
(212) 323-7070 .. **DiPaolo,** Claudio J '07 OfCnsl Rawle & H LLP -14 Wall -NY 10005
(914) 592-1919 .. **DiPaolo,** Jean A '04 %FG Cottrell -5 W Main -Elmsfrd 10523 **Fx:**592-2987
(718) 556-9600 .. **DiPaolo,** Lori A '00 Leventhal & K,LLP -60 Bay -Staten Isl 10301
(212) 513-3200 .. **DiPaolo,** Michl G '97 SrCnsl Holland & K LLP -31 W 52nd -NY 10019
(646) 536-8153 .. **DiPaolo,** Robt E '95 -Bx2242 -NY 10185
(716) 854-6522 .. **DiPasquale,** Chas G '81 -49 Forestglen Cir -Buffalo 14221
(585) 419-8800 .. **DiPasquale,** Christopher A '88 (Harris B PLLC) -99 Garnsey Rd -Pittsfrd 14534
(518) 725-0655 .. **DiPasquale,** James D '05 (Gifford D LLP) -13 W Fulton -Gloversvll 12078 **Fx:**725-9884
(716) 854-5311 .. **Di Pasquale,** Jason R '08 Carney Law Ofcs -43 Court -Buffalo 14202
(716) 882-5532 .. **DiPasquale,** Linda M '90 -1 Niagara Sq -Buffalo 14202
(585) 454-0700 .. **DiPasquale,** Meghan McManus '93 (Ward GH&R LLP) -300 State -Rchstr 14614
(212) 785-6410 .. **Dipchand,** Elizabeth S '06 McCarthy T LLP -1 NY Plz -NY 10004
(212) 735-3000 .. **Dipchand,** June S '07 %Skadden ASM&F LLP -4 Times Sq -NY 10036
(718) 356-8869 .. **DiPerna,** Jos M '93 -131 Woehrle Av -Staten Isl 10312
(212) 692-1000 .. **DiPerna,** Meghan M '08 %Duane M LLP -1540 Bway -NY 10036
(315) 637-4870 .. **DiPiazza,** Barbara '89 -202 3rd -Fayettevll 13066
(718) 286-6000 .. **Di Piazza,** Frank T '07 %DA -125-01 Qns Blvd -Kew Gdns 11415
(585) 987-2800 .. **DiPiazza,** Thos M Jr. '78 (Woods OG LLP) -2 State -Rchstr 14614
(212) 233-3600 .. **DiPietro,** Anthony T '99 -233 Bway -NY 10279 **Fx:**202-7575
(212) 509-5050 .. **Di Pietro,** Francesco Amalio '98 (Wuersch & G LLP) -100 Wall -NY 10005
(718) 875-4207 .. **DiPietro,** James J '80 (Aronne & D) -186 Joralemon -Brklyn 11201 **Fx:**855-1112
(914) 337-3221 .. **DiPietro,** Mary Lynne '92 -428 New Rochelle Rd -Bronxvll 10708 **Fx:**632-7723
(315) 446-2384 .. **DiPilato,** Dean J '00 %Pinsky & S -5790 Widewaters Pkwy -Syracuse 13214
(516) 739-3278 .. **DiPippo,** Maria A '84 (DiPippo & Assoc) -236 Mineola Blvd -Mineola 11501 **Fx:**739-2673
(718) 721-5740 .. **DiPippo,** Philip A '88 (Latos L&D,PC) -22-15 31st -Astoria 11105 **Fx:**721-9645
(716) 636-7600 .. **DiPirro,** Elizabeth M '89 %HoganWillig -2410 N Forest Rd -Amherst 14068
(585) 530-8515 .. **DiPonzio,** Jason S '95 JS DiPonzio,PC -16 E Main -Rchstr 14614
(718) 229-1505 .. **Dippel,** George H '81 -38-50 Bell Blvd -Bayside 11361 **Fx:**425-0615
(914) 286-2813 .. **Dippert,** Wm H '76 (Eckert SC&M,LLC) -10 Bank -White Plns 10606
(212) 277-5822 .. **Dippold,** Karen '86 (Beldock L&H LLP) -99 Park Av -NY 10016
(631) 853-5212 .. **Dipresso,** Michl E '04 Leg Aid -400 Carleton Av Bx9082 -Central Islip 11722 **Fx:**853-7798
(516) 873-6334 .. **DiPreta,** Laurie Ann '87 %Ohrenstein & B,LLP -1010 Franklin Av Bx9243 -Gdn Cty 11530
(212) 563-4100 .. **DiPreta,** Manlio C '85 (Cohen W&S LLP) -330 W 42nd -NY 10036
(212) 728-8000 .. **Diprete,** Julia C '10 %Willkie F&G LLP -787 7th Av -NY 10019
(585) 797-7926 .. **DiPrima,** Michl '73 -40 Humboldt -Rchstr 14609 **Fx:**292-5580
(212) 403-1000 .. **DiPrima,** Stephen R '97 (Wachtell LR&K) -51 W 52nd -NY 10019
(516) 364-9200 .. **DiPrimo,** Marie '86 Rothbard & D -59 Schl Hse Ln -Syosset 11791
(516) 742-6575 .. **DiPrisco,** Dominic '81 (Decolator C&D,LLP) -1399 Franklin Av -Gdn Cty 11530
(585) 865-5750 .. **DiRaddo,** Raymond S '78 (Burgess D&C) -2725 Dewey Av -Rchstr 14616
(516) 485-0400 .. **DiRaimo,** Jos '88 (Muscarella & D) -42 Nassau Blvd -Gdn Cty 11530
(212) 688-8555 .. **DiRaimondo,** Dana A '10 %Fragomen DB&L LLP -7 Hanover Sq -NY 10004
(631) 777-5557 .. **DiRaimondo,** Michl P '81 (DiRaimondo & M,LLP) -445 Broadhllw Rd -Melvll 11747 **Fx:**777-5114
(212) 587-0550 .. **DiRaimondo,** Michl P '81 (DiRaimondo & M,LLP) -120 Bway -NY 10271 **Fx:**587-0545
(212) 376-5666 .. **Dircks,** Richd J '98 (Getnick & G) -620 5th Av -NY 10020 **Fx:**292-3942
(718) 260-8771 .. **Dircks,** Tara Jean '98 %Admin Children's Srvcs -345 Adams -Brklyn 11201
(718) 815-3300 .. **DiRe,** Mario J '86 -Bx10052 -Staten Isl 10301 **Fx:**815-6468
(212) 756-2000 .. **Director,** Brett S '96 SpclCnsl Schulte R&Z LLP -919 3rd Av -NY 10022
(212) 918-8000 .. **Director,** Jonathan '68 Traxys NA,Inc -825 3rd Av -NY 10022
(212) 837-6033 .. **Director,** Justin J '09 %Hughes H&R LLP -1 Bttry Pk Plz -NY 10004
(516) 228-9090 .. **Director,** Michl C '72 -600 Old Cntry Rd -Gdn Cty 11530 **Fx:**228-4278
(212) 385-8000 .. **Director,** Sara Alta '03 %Barasch MS&P -11 Park Pl -NY 10007
(585) 295-4400 .. **Direnzo,** Erica M '08 %Hiscock & B,LLP -2000 HSBC Plz -Rchstr 14604
(516) 431-5000 .. **DiResta,** Timothy D '96 (Odery & D,PC) -945 W Beech -Long Bch 11561
(516) 933-9760 .. **DiRienzo,** Dino R '96 -64 Division Av -Levittwn 11756
(718) 442-6060 .. **DiRinaldi,** Roseann Scotto '04 -136 Bay -Staten Isl 10301 **Fx:**815-1872
(212) 259-8000 .. **DiRisio,** Matthew L '04 %Dewey & L LLP -1301 Av of Amer -NY 10019
(718) 596-3185 .. **Dirks,** Jos H '78 -60 2nd -Brklyn 11231
(914) 928-9400 .. **DiRusso,** Elizabeth A '00 (Wallman & D,LLC) -81 Main -White Plns 10601
(646) 471-5926 .. **DiRuzzo,** Jos A III '06 PricewaterhouseCoopers LLP -300 Mad Av -NY 10017
(914) 946-0056 .. **DiSalvo,** Allan A '74 -9 Bryant Crescent -White Plns 10605
(914) 337-6300 .. **DiSalvo,** Jos A '77 (Nobile M&D,LLP) -111 Kraft Av -Bronxvll 10708
(718) 746-0087 .. **DiSalvo,** Jos R '98 Energy Brands Inc -1720 Whitestone Expy -Whitestone 11357
(516) 294-5200 .. **Disalvo,** Jos S '08 %Picciano & S -900 Merchants Cncrs -Westbury 11590
(212) 728-8000 .. **Disalvo,** Nina E '08 %Willkie F&G LLP -787 7th Av -NY 10019
(914) 390-4157 .. **DiSalvo,** Rosemary '93 %US Bankruptcy Ct -300 Quarropas -White Plns 10601
(585) 231-6117 .. **DiSalvo,** Saml C '85 %Price Waterhouse -1100 Bausch & Lomb Pl -Rchstr 14604
(585) 787-6920 .. **DiSalvo,** Thos J '83 (TJ DiSalvo,PC) -672 Ridge Rd -Webster 14580 **Fx:**787-6922
(212) 766-2466 .. **Di Santo,** Beth A '00 (DiSanto LLP) -15 Maiden Ln -NY 10038 **Fx:**(866) 746-0504
(914) 235-2300 .. **DiSanto,** Michl A '94 -510 North Av -New Rchll 10801 **Fx:**235-2557
(516) 328-1499 .. **DiSanza,** Frank A '62 -5 Nassau -Floral Pk 11001
(716) 856-5500 .. **Disare,** Melinda G '81 (Damon M LLP) -200 Delaware Av -Buffalo 14202
(716) 645-3696 .. **Disare,** Thos F '81 SUNY Buffalo Lw Schl -O'Brian Hall -Buffalo 14260 **Fx:**645-5968
(631) 712-5720 .. **Disbrow,** Sandra J '88 Hon W Wall -824 Fed Plz Bx9014 -Central Islip 11722
(315) 424-8944 .. **Discenza,** Michl A '08 %Shulman CG&R,PC -250 S Clinton -Syracuse 13202
(212) 458-3548 .. **Discepolo,** Tracey A '01 AIG -175 Water -NY 10038
(212) 596-9000 .. **Dische,** Isabel Reichardt '08 %Ropes & G LLP -1211 Av of Amer -NY 10036
(212) 422-1020 .. **Discioarro,** Michl S '03 (M Discioarro,LLC) -40 Exch Pl -NY 10005 **Fx:**422-1069
(718) 370-7030 .. **Discipio,** Frank A '10 %Amabile & E,PC -1000 South Av -Staten Isl 10314
(914) 694-3300 .. **DiSciullo,** Robt J '87 (DiSciullo & Assoc) -2975 Wstchstr Av -Purchase 10577 **Fx:**694-2244
(914) 684-0090 .. **Diserio Martin O'Connor & Castiglioni LLP** -50 Main -White Plns 10606 **Fx:**684-0590
(212) 269-4900 .. **D'Isernia,** Alfred L '01 %Ford MEW&G,LLP -Wall Street Plz -NY 10005
(914) 701-7625 .. **DiSiena,** Robt F '02 Smith Barney -4 Manhattanvll Rd -Purchase 10577 **Fx:**701-7676
(212) 422-1200 .. **DiSiervi,** Steven '99 (Abrams GF&J,PC) -1 Bttry Pk Plz -NY 10004
(516) 868-3000 .. **DiSimone,** Damon C '01 P Scalamandre & Sons -157 Albany Av -Freeprt 11520 **Fx:**868-3342
(212) 336-2000 .. **Diskant,** Gregory L '75 (Patterson BW&T LLP) -1133 Av of Amer -NY 10036
(646) 386-3038 .. **Diskint,** Peter G '81 %Supreme Ct Appllt Term -60 Centre -NY 10007
(212) 461-2323 .. **DiSomma,** Jennine '86 (Saiber LLC) -44 Wall -NY 10005
(718) 680-3331 .. **DiSomma,** Ralph F '85 -7608 11th Av -Brklyn 11228
(718) 628-5363 .. **Dispenza,** Maria R '91 -69-06 Myrtle Av -Glendale 11385 **Fx:**628-5419
(585) 586-6600 .. **Dispenza,** Saml A Jr. '66 -349 W Cmmrcial -E Rchstr 14445 **Fx:**586-9644
(212) 909-6000 .. **Dissinger,** Suzanne M '03 %Debevoise & P LLP -919 3rd Av -NY 10022
(845) 691-7292 .. **DiStasi,** Lewis C Jr. '65 (DiStasi M&M PLLC) -400 Uppr North Rd Bx915 -Highlnd 12528
(845) 691-7292 .. **DiStasi Moriello & Murphy Law PLLC** -400 Uppr North Rd Bx915 -Highlnd 12528 **Fx:**691-2710

(212) 578-3713 .. **DiStasio,** Lynne E '77 %MetLife -27-01 Qns Plz N -LIC 11101 **Fx:**578-3916
(212) 416-6349 .. **Distefano,** Carl L '79 %Dept of Law -120 Bway -NY 10271
(607) 334-9194 .. **DiStefano,** Diane M '01 (Vitanza D&D,LLP) -15 Maple -Norwich 13815
(212) 909-6000 .. **DiStefano,** Emily C '00 Cnsl Debevoise & P LLP -919 3rd Av -NY 10022
(716) 204-9480 .. **DiStefano,** Henry P '95 %SJ Baum,PC -900 Merchants Cncrs -Westbury 11590 **Fx:**204-9680
(518) 457-2411 .. **DiStefano,** Jo Anne W '90 Cnsl DOT -50 Wolf Rd -Albany 12232 **Fx:**457-4021
(212) 788-7104 .. **DiStefano,** Matthew E '91 %NYC Council -City Hall Room 5 -NY 10007
(212) 885-5000 .. **DiStefano,** Richd '83 (Blank R LLP) -405 Lex Av -NY 10174
(518) 446-1696 .. **DiStefano,** Richd T '86 (DiStefano & D) -40 Colvin Av -Albany 12206 **Fx:**689-5392
(212) 938-5000 .. **Distell,** Gary N '00 Cantor Fitzgerald -110 E 59th -NY 10022
(516) 932-4300 .. **DiStephan,** Michl F '01 Technology Practice Grp LLC -1010 Nrthrn Blvd -Gt Neck 11021
(718) 499-7333 .. **Distinti,** Anthony J Jr. '73 -679 10th -Brklyn 11215
(212) 735-3000 .. **Distinti,** Anthony J IV '08 %Skadden ASM&F LLP -4 Times Sq -NY 10036
(212) 564-3311 .. **Distler,** M David '59 -60 Gramercy Park N -NY 10010 **Fx:**(646) 416-6700
(212) 486-1400 .. **Distler,** Thos R '84 (Brooks & D) -110 E 59th -NY 10022
(718) 243-6854 .. **Disu,** Femi B '07 Leg Aid -111 Lvngstn -Brklyn 11201
(631) 369-1700 .. **DiTalia,** Carmela M '96 (Esseks H&A,LLP) -108 E Main Bx279 -Rvrhead 11901
(718) 901-6600 .. **DiTata,** Barbara A '76 %Schl Cnstrctn Auth -188 W 230th -Bronx 10463 **Fx:**901-6649
(718) 390-5383 .. **DiTata,** Jerry A '74 %Supreme Ct Law Dept -18 Richmond Ter -Staten Isl 10301
(516) 747-3200 .. **DiTata,** Maureen Rothschild '79 (Berwitz & D LLP) -310 Old Cntry Rd -Gdn Cty 11530
(212) 450-4000 .. **Ditchfield,** Andrew '08 %Davis P&W LLP -450 Lex Av -NY 10017
(212) 661-6400 .. **Ditchik,** Alan '57 (Ditchik & D,LLP) -230 Park Av -NY 10169
(212) 661-6400 .. **Ditchik & Ditchik,LLP** -230 Park Av -NY 10169 **Fx:**661-9473
(212) 661-6400 .. **Ditchik,** Joel '93 (Ditchik & D,LLP) -230 Park Av -NY 10169
(718) 979-4300 .. **Dito,** Frank J Jr. '98 (Decker DD&I,LLP) -1610 Richmond Rd -Staten Isl 10304
(914) 907-7074 .. **DiTomaso,** Marc A '00 -1385 Bstn Post Rd -Larchmnt 10538 **Fx:**833-7733
(212) 619-3380 .. **DiTomasso,** Edw A '91 OfCnsl DiTomasso & D -20 Vesey -NY 10007
(212) 619-3380 .. **DiTomasso,** Edw T '62 (DiTomasso & D) -20 Vesey -NY 10007
(516) 741-8222 .. **Di Tomasso,** Melissa A '06 %Flanzig & F LLP -323 Willis Av Bx669 -Mineola 11501 **Fx:**741-8889
(212) 619-3380 .. **DiTomasso,** Michl N '83 OfCnsl DiTomasso & D -20 Vesey -NY 10007
(212) 267-3320 .. **DiTomasso,** Michl N '83 %Savona D&H LLC -111 Bway -NY 10006
(212) 619-3380 .. **DiTomasso,** Michl R '54 OfCnsl DiTomasso & D -20 Vesey -NY 10007
(914) 666-3800 .. **DiTomasso,** Michl R '54 (M DiTomasso,PC) -45 Main -Bedfrd Hlls 10507 **Fx:**666-4303
(212) 619-3380 .. **DiTomasso,** Peter C '85 OfCnsl DiTomasso & D -20 Vesey -NY 10007
(914) 666-3800 .. **DiTomasso,** Susan A '95 (M DiTomasso,PC) -45 Main -Bedfrd Hlls 10507 **Fx:**666-4303
(914) 251-1900 .. **DiTrapani,** Matthew J '03 %G Febbraio,PC -110 Corp Park Dr -White Plns 10604 **Fx:**251-1490
(212) 925-4475 .. **Dittenhoefer,** Marc M '77 (Blank G&D) -111 John -NY 10038
(212) 318-6000 .. **Dittmann,** Eric W '01 %Paul HJ&W LLP -75 E 55th -NY 10022
(718) 298-0959 .. **Ditto,** Robbin A '95 %Criminal Ct -125-01 Qns Blvd -Kew Gdns 11415
(212) 326-3939 .. **Dittus,** Erin L '09 %Jones D -222 E 41st -NY 10017
(212) 574-1200 .. **Dittus,** Jaime G '10 %Seward & K LLP -1 Bttry Pk Plz -NY 10004
(845) 331-1603 .. **Dittus,** Kathleen H '03 -286 Clinton Av Bx3883 -Kingston 12402
(212) 308-4411 .. **DiUbaldo,** Robt W '05 %Edwards AP&D LLP -750 Lex Av -NY 10022
(845) 794-1248 .. **Diuguid,** John M '86 %Hon F LaBuda -414 Bway -Monticello 12701 **Fx:**794-6208
(718) 722-6086 .. **Diulio,** Jeanne M '92 %Catholic Charities -191 Joralemon -Brklyn 11201
(212) 478-7200 .. **Divack,** Joshua I '88 (Hahn & H LLP) -488 Mad Av -NY 10022
(212) 853-6000 .. **Divak,** Jodi E '93 Geller & Co -800 3rd Av -NY 10022
(212) 554-1234 .. **Divak,** Russell A '93 %AXA Financial Inc -1290 Av of Amer -NY 10104 **Fx:**707-3963
(516) 489-8330 .. **Divaris,** Angela '95 %Carecen -91 N Franklin -Hempstd 11550 **Fx:**489-8308
(212) 297-5800 .. **Diver,** Colleen R '09 %Day P LLP -7 Times Sq -NY 10036
(718) 667-1301 .. **DiVernieri,** Roseann F '81 (DiVernieri D&C) -361 Edison -Staten Isl 10306 **Fx:**667-9413
(631) 348-1668 .. **Divers,** Michl D '99 %Brecher FPWT&Z,PC -868 Church -Bohemia 11716
(212) 335-4500 .. **Diviaio,** Danielle A '08 %DLA Piper LLP -1251 Av of Amer -NY 10020
(212) 218-2100 .. **Divinagracia,** Jos B '02 %Fitzpatrick CH&S -1290 Av of Amer -NY 10104
(631) 852-2500 .. **DiVincenzo,** Grazia Romano '00 %DA -200 Center Dr -Rvrhead 11901 **Fx:**852-1769
(212) 455-2000 .. **Divine,** Charlie L '03 %Simpson T&B LLP -425 Lex Av -NY 10017
(315) 471-3151 .. **Diviney,** Catherine A '89 (Hancock & E,LLP) -1500 AXA Twr I Bx4976 -Syracuse 13221
(516) 746-7371 .. **Diviney,** James F '88 %Burns RT&R,LLP -390 Old Cntry Rd -Gdn Cty 11530
(516) 357-3000 .. **Diviney,** John K '86 (Rivkin R LLP) -926 RXR Plz -Uniondale 11556
(212) 883-4909 .. **Divino,** Amy F '92 (Cozen O) -277 Park Av -NY 10172 **Fx:**672-1109
(845) 201-8090 .. **Diviny,** Thos F '99 (Diviny & M,PC) -39 E Central Av -Pearl Rvr 10965 **Fx:**201-8092
(212) 925-8756 .. **Divis,** Gary E '72 -99 Hudson -NY 10013 **Fx:**925-8774
(631) 738-3405 .. **DiVita,** Bartholomew J '03 Motorola Inc -1 Motorola Plz -Holtsvll 11742
(212) 573-0370 .. **Divito,** Amy B '98 Rodale Inc -733 3rd Av -NY 10017
(914) 524-8500 .. **Divney,** Brian J '02 %Housman & Assoc,PC -150 Wht Plns Rd -Tarrytwn 10591
(516) 294-8015 .. **Divone,** Mary Ellen '90 -515 Hrrcks Rd -New Hyde Pk 11040 **Fx:**294-8016
(518) 402-6757 .. **Dix,** Kathleen '88 %Workers Comp Bd -20 Park -Albany 12207
(212) 447-6202 .. **Dix,** Mitchell A '81 (M Dix & Assoc) -185 Mad Av -NY 10016 **Fx:**447-6204
(212) 474-1000 .. **Dixler,** Scott P '09 %Cravath S&M LLP -825 8th Av -NY 10019
(212) 909-6000 .. **Dixon,** Adiya A '09 %Debevoise & P LLP -919 3rd Av -NY 10022
(718) 694-3875 .. **Dixon,** Angele F '97 %Transit Auth -130 Lvngstn -Brklyn 11201 **Fx:**694-5726
(914) 328-8679 .. **Dixon,** C Douglas '74 OfCnsl Adorno & Y LLC -399 Knollwood Rd -White Plns 10603 **Fx:**328-1074
(212) 809-5700 .. **Dixon,** C Douglas '74 OfCnsl Adorno & Y LLP -350 5th Av -NY 10118
(585) 263-1000 .. **Dixon,** Cressida A '97 (Nixon P LLP) -1100 Clinton Sq -Rchstr 14604
(212) 417-5940 .. **Dixon,** Diana '99 NYS Dept of Health -90 Church -NY 10007
(212) 709-3591 .. **Dixon,** Dianne E '83 %Banking Dept -1 State -NY 10004 **Fx:**709-1655
(212) 474-1000 .. **Dixon,** Douglas J '06 %Cravath S&M LLP -825 8th Av -NY 10019
(917) 696-2442 .. **Dixon,** Eric T '95 E Dixon & Assoc -116 W 23rd -NY 10011
(212) 735-3000 .. **Dixon,** Felicia A '08 %Skadden ASM&F LLP -4 Times Sq -NY 10036
(516) 355-7901 .. **Dixon,** Francis J '62 %Paganini GCC&F -1979 Marcus Av -Lk Success 11042
(718) 363-2100 .. **Dixon,** Glenda M '93 -1141 Eastern Pkwy -Brklyn 11213
(716) 639-4006 .. **Dixon & Hamilton,LLP** -2350 N Forest Rd -Getzvll 14068 **Fx:**639-4926
(716) 639-4006 .. **Dixon,** Harry T Jr. '87 (Dixon & H,LLP) -2350 N Forest Rd -Getzvll 14068
(212) 614-6423 .. **Dixon,** J Wells '03 Ctr Cnstnl Rights -666 Bway -NY 10012 **Fx:**614-6499
(914) 286-7085 .. **Dixon,** James J '90 Con Ed Solutions -100 Summit Lk Dr -Valhalla 10595
(518) 381-6011 .. **Dixon,** James L III '89 -1765 Rugby Rd -Schnctdy 12309
(212) 474-1000 .. **Dixon,** Jennifer A '10 %Cravath S&M LLP -825 8th Av -NY 10019
(212) 661-1010 .. **Dixon,** Marianne '94 (Ogihara & Assoc,PLLC) -122 E 42nd -NY 10168 **Fx:**661-6116
(716) 639-4006 .. **Dixon,** Michl B '86 (Dixon & H,LLP) -2350 N Forest Rd -Getzvll 14068
(518) 487-7600 .. **Dixon,** Philip H '81 (Whiteman O&H LLP) -1 Commerce Plz -Albany 12260
(631) 852-1650 .. **Dixon,** Sean M '07 %Leg Aid -300 Center Dr -Rvrhead 11901 **Fx:**852-1655
(212) 770-7000 .. **Dixon,** Steven M '85 %AIG -70 Pine -NY 10270
(212) 816-2675 .. **Dixon,** Wm S '98 Citigroup Global Mrkts -388 Greenwich -NY 10013
(718) 286-6000 .. **Dixon-Gordon,** Stephen M '89 %DA -125-01 Qns Blvd -Kew Gdns 11415
(607) 687-8253 .. **Dixson,** Mark A '88 (Cnty Atty) -56 Main -Owego 13827 **Fx:**223-7003
(212) 225-2000 .. **Dixter,** David J '03 %Cleary GS&H -1 Lbrty Plz -NY 10006
(212) 909-6000 .. **Diz,** Michl A '05 %Debevoise & P LLP -919 3rd Av -NY 10022
(212) 872-1000 .. **Dizengoff,** Ira S '93 -One Bryant Park -NY 10036 **Fx:**872-1002
(718) 261-2647 .. **DiZozza,** Nicholas F '54 -69-56 Exeter -Frst Hlls 11375
(718) 361-8080 .. **Dizozza,** Peter W '87 %J Werlin -45-10 Court Sq -LIC 11101 **Fx:**361-0344
(212) 596-9000 .. **Djaha,** David C '89 (Ropes & G LLP) -1211 Av of Amer -NY 10036
(212) 566-7188 .. **D'jamoos,** Alexander L '06 %Genova B&G -115 Bway -NY 10006
(631) 247-0404 .. **Djata,** Jessie M '97 (Jackson L LLP) -58 S Srvc Rd -Melvll 11747
(718) 286-1500 .. **Djemal,** Rami '08 Leg Srvcs -97-77 Qns Blvd -Rego Pk 11374 **Fx:**275-5352
(914) 723-2032 .. **Djonovic,** Valentin '99 -670 Wht Plns Rd -Scarsdale 10583 **Fx:**725-7724
(212) 902-9444 .. **Djurasovic,** George '97 Cnsl Goldman Sachs -1 NY Plz -NY 10004
(212) 335-4500 .. **DLA Piper LLP (US)** -1251 Av of Amer -NY 10020 **Fx:**335-4501
(718) 590-3867 .. **Dlabola,** Mary L W '81 %Supreme Ct -851 Grnd Cncrs -Bronx 10451
(212) 254-6470 .. **Dlugacz,** Henry A '93 -488 Mad Av -NY 10022
(212) 309-6000 .. **Dlutowski,** Christopher J '94 OfCnsl Morgan L&B LLP -101 Park Av -NY 10178
(718) 856-8800 .. **D'Meza,** Bob '99 (R Martian,PC) -105 Court -Brklyn 11201
(607) 723-9511 .. **Dmitriev,** Anna '08 Coughlin & G,LLP -19 Chenango Bx2039 -Bnghmtn 13902
(212) 259-8000 .. **Dmitronow,** Tanya J '02 %Dewey & L LLP -1301 Av of Amer -NY 10019
(718) 939-4444 .. **Dmoch,** Gary J '77 (GJ Dmoch & Assoc) -171-22 Nrthrn Blvd -Flushng 11358 **Fx:**445-2520
(718) 286-6000 .. **Dmochowski,** Katherine A '06 %DA -125-01 Qns Blvd -Kew Gdns 11415
(212) 582-8900 .. **Dnistrian,** Barrie A '01 Weinstein Law Firm PLLC -521 5th Av -NY 10175 **Fx:**582-8989
(212) 310-8000 .. **Do,** Danielle D '00 (Weil G&M LLP) -767 5th Av -NY 10153
(212) 530-1800 .. **Do,** Thao Huu Van '95 %Richards K&O LLP -1 World Fncl Ctr -NY 10281
(212) 895-1800 .. **Doak,** James L '03 %Miller Buckfire & Co -153 E 53rd -NY 10022
(212) 355-9500 .. **do Amaral,** Pauline '97 (Lieff CH&B,LLP) -250 Hudson -NY 10013
(212) 619-3730 .. **Doar,** John '75 OfCnsl Doar RK&M -217 Bway -NY 10007
(212) 619-3730 .. **Doar Rieck Kaley & Mack** -217 Bway -NY 10007 **Fx:**962-5037
(631) 712-5742 .. **Dobbin,** Deborah L '96 %Hon S Bernstein -290 Fed Plz -Central Islip 11722
(212) 336-2000 .. **Dobbins,** David F '57 OfCnsl Patterson BW&T LLP -1133 Av of Amer -NY 10036
(212) 953-6000 .. **Dobbs,** Elan R '05 %Katsky K LLP -605 3rd Av -NY 10158
(212) 367-6627 .. **Dobbs,** Lon E '97 Thomson Reuters -195 Bway -NY 10007
(212) 940-8800 .. **Dobbs,** Marcia N '09 %Katten MR LLP -575 Mad Av -NY 10022
(212) 966-1091 .. **Dobbs,** Wm K '84 -Prince St Sta Bx7 -NY 10012
(914) 249-4707 .. **Dobbyn,** Colm J '85 %MasterCard Intl -2000 Purchase -Purchase 10577
(518) 474-7469 .. **Dobiel,** Maryrita '84 %OCA -Agncy Bldg 4 ESP -Albany 12223 **Fx:**473-5514

(212) 964-1890 .. **Dobies,** Mark M '84 %Hoffman & R,LLP -505 8th Av -NY 10018
(212) 593-3310 .. **Dobis,** James S '84 (Dobis R&P,PC) -7 Elk PMB 159 -NY 10007 **Fx:**(973) 740-2484
(631) 878-5959 .. **Dobise,** John J Jr. '75 -Bx256 -Eastport 11941 **Fx:**878-3884
(917) 202-2761 .. **Dobish,** Aaron J '07 -223 Carroll -Brklyn 11231
(718) 836-2900 .. **Dobkin,** Chas H '69 -77-03 5th Av -Brklyn 11209 **Fx:**745-6567
(212) 587-2400 .. **Dobkin,** Stephen G '72 (Collins D&M,LLP) -277 Bway -NY 10007
(718) 279-8700 .. **Doblin,** Debra L '89 (Doblin & D) -42-40 Bell Blvd -Bayside 11361 **Fx:**428-3981
(718) 279-8700 .. **Doblin,** Marvin H '53 (Doblin & D) -42-40 Bell Blvd -Bayside 11361 **Fx:**428-3981
(212) 449-7406 .. **Dobosh,** Laurence D '86 %Merrill Lynch -220 Bway -NY 10038
(716) 810-9220 .. **Dobosiewicz,** Elizabeth J '94 (Saccone & D LLP) -300 Intl Dr -Williamsvll 14221
(716) 852-6905 .. **Dobozin,** Carl H '62 -70 Niagara -Buffalo 14202 **Fx:**854-2780
(212) 450-4000 .. **Dobrev,** Dessislav '08 %Davis P&W LLP -450 Lex Av -NY 10017
(212) 532-4000 .. **Dobrish,** Robt Z '65 (Dobrish ZG LLP) -757 3rd Av -NY 10017
(212) 532-4000 .. **Dobrish Zeif Gross LLP** -757 3rd Av -NY 10017 **Fx:**532-3153
(212) 227-3636 .. **Dobroshi,** Nita '02 %Spar & B,PC -225 Bway -NY 10007
(315) 253-0326 .. **Dobrovosky,** Janet Egert '96 (Boyle & A,PC) -110 Genesee -Auburn 13021
(212) 769-3809 .. **Dobrow,** Lawr M '96 -250 W 93rd -NY 10025 **Fx:**753-2456
(212) 344-0900 .. **Dobshinsky,** Neal S '75 (N Dobshinsky,LLC) -61 Bway -NY 10006
(716) 633-1500 .. **Dobson,** Arthur F Jr. '73 (Michalak & D) -6225 Sheridan Dr -Williamsvll 14221
(212) 705-7000 .. **Dobson,** Katherine M '09 %Bingham M LLP -399 Park Av -NY 10022
(212) 701-3000 .. **Dobson,** Katie J '09 %Cahill G&R LLP -80 Pine -NY 10005 **Fx:**269-5420
(631) 247-0404 .. **Dobson,** Kimberly N '09 %Jackson L LLP -58 S Srvc Rd -Melvll 11747
(212) 863-8359 .. **Dobson,** Maurice W '99 %HPD -100 Gold -NY 10038
(212) 704-1350 .. **Dobson,** Robt J '97 %Interpublic Grp -1114 Av of Amer -NY 10036 **Fx:**704-1201
(212) 701-3000 .. **Dobson,** Stephen L '09 %Cahill G&R LLP -80 Pine -NY 10005 **Fx:**269-5420
(718) 675-8758 .. **D'Oca,** Robt R '78 NYS Unified Ct System -130 Styvsnt Pl -Staten Isl 10301
(718) 745-3239 .. **DoCampo,** James A '83 -942 80th -Brklyn 11228
(518) 464-9075 .. **Dochat,** Lisa Kenneally '03 OfCnsl Meyers & M,LLP -1734 Wstrn Av -Albany 12203 **Fx:**464-9078
(914) 995-4075 .. **Docherty,** Robt F Jr. '81 %DA -188 Tarrytown Rd -White Plns 10601
(516) 365-5100 .. **Dochter,** Ivan M '58 (Excel Rlty Advsrs LP) -333 Earle Ovngton Blvd -Uniondale 11553 **Fx:**365-5266
(212) 859-8000 .. **Dock,** Bradley M '08 %Fried FHS&J LLP -1 NY Plz -NY 10004
(212) 909-6000 .. **Dockery,** John C '05 %Debevoise & P LLP -919 3rd Av -NY 10022
(212) 238-3000 .. **Dockery,** Katharine F '09 %Emmet M&M,LLP -120 Bway -NY 10271
(212) 588-0022 .. **Dockery,** Timothy L '01 Cnsl Sanders OV&R -501 Mad Av -NY 10022
(212) 425-6150 .. **Dockery,** Wm J '70 -17 Battery Pl -NY 10004 **Fx:**422-5360
(212) 705-7000 .. **Dockray,** Jaimie Fried '96 Bingham M LLP -399 Park Av -NY 10022
(212) 836-8000 .. **Dockwell,** Brett D '05 %Kaye S LLP -425 Park Av -NY 10022
(315) 445-2499 .. **Docter,** Karen J '92 -7000 E Genesee -Fayettevll 13066 **Fx:**445-2495
(212) 617-0000 .. **Doctoroff,** Danl L '85 Bloomberg LP -731 Lex Av -NY 10022
(212) 819-8200 .. **Dodd,** Allison M '08 %White & C LLP -1155 Av of Amer -NY 10036
(315) 349-3200 .. **Dodd,** Donald H '85 (DA) -Pub Safety Ctr -Oswego 13126 **Fx:**349-3212
(212) 335-9000 .. **Dodd,** Meggan K '77 %DA -1 Hogan Pl -NY 10013
(315) 437-7600 .. **Dodd,** Michl L '94 (Ferrara FLB&R,PC) -5010 Campuswood Dr -E Syracuse 13057
(315) 472-4481 .. **Dodd,** P Douglas '86 (Ali P&C) -614 James -Syracuse 13203
(516) 794-3737 .. **Doddato,** Frank A '74 -666 Old Cntry Rd -Gdn Cty 11530 **Fx:**683-8410
(516) 571-3800 .. **Doddato,** Lauren M '06 %DA -262 Old Cntry Rd -Mineola 11501 **Fx:**248-9479
(914) 640-6422 .. **Dodderidge,** Nancy M '92 %Jones Apparel Grp -1129 Wstchstr Av -White Plns 10604
(718) 590-2508 .. **Dodds,** Donna M '88 %Dept Probation -215 E 161st -Bronx 10451 **Fx:**293-3319
(212) 698-3500 .. **Dodds,** Wm K '84 (Dechert LLP) -1095 Av of Amer -NY 10036
(212) 640-2000 .. **Dodds-Brown,** Sarah C '99 %Amer Exp -200 Vesey -NY 10285
(516) 248-6000 .. **Dodds-Marshall,** Belinda '97 %Kaufman B&R -1205 Franklin Av -Gdn Cty 11530
(212) 889-2021 .. **Dodeja,** Himanshu '09 %Rele & B LLC -1178 Bway -NY 10001 **Fx:**(646) 390-8000
(212) 306-7100 .. **Dodell,** Sue Ellen '79 %Campaign Finance Bd -40 Rector -NY 10006 **Fx:**306-7143
(212) 538-3948 .. **Dodes,** Ivy B '88 Credit Suisse -11 Mad Av -NY 10010
(212) 727-0016 .. **Dodes,** Jeffrey L '04 Zomba Recording -137-139 W 25th -NY 10001
(315) 336-8330 .. **Dodge,** Andrea T '82 Tyler & D -400 N Wshngtn Bx208 -Rome 13442 **Fx:**339-3794
(212) 425-7200 .. **Dodge,** Jonathan E '10 %Kenyon & K,LLP -1 Bway -NY 10004
(631) 844-9555 .. **Dodge,** Peter X '91 (Dodge & M,PC) -175 Pinelawn Rd -Melvll 11747 **Fx:**844-9666
(315) 479-5190 .. **Dodge,** Ralph E '78 -531 Oak -Syracuse 13203
(212) 702-3281 .. **Dodge,** S Regina '97 %WP Stewart & Co,Inc -527 Mad Av -NY 10022
(212) 490-3000 .. **Dodge,** Stephanie A '09 %Wilson EME&D LLP -150 E 42nd -NY 10017
(212) 532-0171 .. **Dodge,** Wm E '85 (Dodge & Assoc PC) -205 Lex Av -NY 10016 **Fx:**532-2040
(631) 928-8440 .. **Dodorico,** Paul A '89 -34 Samuels Path -Miller Pl 11764
(212) 839-7000 .. **Dodson,** Ella W '85 Cnsl Hill B&N LLP -200 Lbrty -NY 10281
(631) 577-7720 .. **Dodson,** Karen C '95 -100 Baylis Rd -Melvll 11747 **Fx:**577-7199
(212) 504-6000 .. **Dodson,** Peter M '84 (Cadwalader W&T LLP) -1 World Fncl Ctr -NY 10281
(716) 883-1900 .. **Doebler,** Anne Elizabeth '91 %Intl Inst of Buffalo -864 Delaware Av -Buffalo 14209 **Fx:**883-9529
(212) 735-3000 .. **D'Oench,** Russell G III '93 (Skadden ASM&F LLP) -4 Times Sq -NY 10036
(646) 610-5400 .. **Doepfner,** Thos P '84 %NYPD -1 Police Plz -NY 10038
(718) 250-2000 .. **Doerfler,** Elizabeth S '01 %DA -350 Jay -Brklyn 11201 **Fx:**250-2314
(646) 378-2021 .. **Doerfler,** Robt D '03 %SVP Worldwide -5 Penn Plz -NY 10001
(516) 249-3450 .. **Doering,** Christopher G '08 Carman C&I,LLP -266 Main -Farmngdl 11735
(716) 852-5200 .. **Doering,** Kevin R '05 %Hamberger & W -700 Main Pl Twr -Buffalo 14202
(518) 581-8441 .. **Doern,** James E D '92 (Rodriguez & D,PLLC) -100 West Av -Saratoga Spgs 12866
(212) 471-8535 .. **Doerner-Fogel,** Maureen '85 (Herzfeld & R,PC) -125 Broad -NY 10004
(315) 432-9171 .. **Doerr,** Donald C '89 Cnsl POMCO Grp -2425 James -Syracuse 13206 **Fx:**703-4884
(716) 847-3449 .. **Doerr,** Jean '82 %PERB -535 Wshngtn -Buffalo 14203 **Fx:**847-3690
(212) 837-6842 .. **Doeschner,** Danl C '07 %Hughes H&R LLP -1 Bttry Pk Plz -NY 10004
(212) 421-5550 .. **Doft,** Jonathan A '95 %Doft & Co -55 E 59th -NY 10022
(212) 416-8000 .. **Doft,** Rachel A '01 %Dept of Law -120 Bway -NY 10271
(212) 688-5151 .. **Dogan,** Irem '09 %Gibney A&F,LLP -665 5th Av -NY 10022
(212) 755-1550 .. **Dogan,** Mel '79 Dogan & Assoc -145 E 57th -NY 10022 **Fx:**755-1575
(212) 455-2000 .. **Dogramaci,** Ihsan '06 %Simpson T&B LLP -425 Lex Av -NY 10017
(212) 279-6200 .. **Doherty,** Brian J '95 %McGovern & Assoc -16 W 32nd -NY 10001
(518) 432-1523 .. **Doherty,** Danl L '87 -90 State -Albany 12207 **Fx:**426-7708
(315) 472-4481 .. **Doherty,** David P '88 (Ali P&C) -614 James -Syracuse 13203
(800) 219-9423 .. **Doherty,** Eileen P '92 (E Doherty,PC) -715 160th -Whitestone 11357
(716) 983-3742 .. **Doherty,** Eric P '91 -6094 Versailles Rd -Lk View 14085 **Fx:**983-3217
(212) 417-8700 .. **Doherty,** Fiona M '01 Fed Def of NY Inc -52 Duane -NY 10007 **Fx:**571-0392
(518) 447-3200 .. **Doherty,** Glen P '90 (McNamee LT&W,PC) -677 Bway -Albany 12207
(212) 599-0777 .. **Doherty,** James E '94 %Eisenberg T&L -675 3rd Av -NY 10017
(212) 755-5510 .. **Doherty,** John C '97 %Loeb B & Prtnrs -505 Park Av -NY 10022
(518) 237-5921 .. **Doherty,** John J Jr. '72 -94 Remsen -Cohoes 12047 **Fx:**237-5974
(212) 210-1282 .. **Doherty,** John P '97 (Alston & B LLP) -90 Park Av -NY 10016
(914) 949-2826 .. **Doherty,** John T '94 (Robinowitz CD&D,LLP) -199 Main -White Plns 10601
(516) 747-4301 .. **Doherty,** Kathleen M '95 -200 Old Cntry Rd -Mineola 11501 **Fx:**747-5956
(845) 638-1943 .. **Doherty,** Kevin M '96 (Greenwald D LLP) -30 Ramland Rd -Orangebrg 10962
(212) 885-5000 .. **Doherty,** Kevin R '09 %Blank R LLP -405 Lex Av -NY 10174
(315) 448-8400 .. **Doherty,** Mary Anne '01 %Law Dept -233 E Wshngtn -Syracuse 13202 **Fx:**448-8381
(212) 250-5548 .. **Doherty,** Mary E '00 Mortgageit Holdings,Inc -60 Wall -NY 10005
(212) 468-8000 .. **Doherty,** Michl A '85 (Morrison & F LLP) -1290 Av of Amer -NY 10104
(212) 596-9000 .. **Doherty,** Michl G '98 (Ropes & G LLP) -1211 Av of Amer -NY 10036
(718) 495-2579 .. **Doherty,** Moira A '94 -6900 Jericho Tpk -Syosset 11791 **Fx:**495-2738
(212) 799-9638 .. **Doherty,** Molly '01 West Side SRO Law Proj -647 Columbus Av -NY 10025
(212) 326-2000 .. **Doherty,** Patrick F '08 Cnsl O'Melveny & M LLP -7 Times Sq -NY 10036
(212) 335-9000 .. **Doherty,** Patrick J '10 %DA -1 Hogan Pl -NY 10013
(212) 669-2651 .. **Doherty,** Patrick W '85 %NYC Comptroller -1 Centre -NY 10007 **Fx:**669-4072
(914) 512-7453 .. **Doherty,** Sharon Ann '88 (SA Doherty,PC) -976 McLean Av -Ynkrs 10704
(646) 386-5137 .. **Doherty,** Susan M '90 %Family Ct -60 Lafayette -NY 10013
(212) 601-2680 .. **Doherty,** Susan Mikes '77 SpclCnsl Gonzalez S&H LLP -350 5th Av -NY 10118
(212) 371-8855 .. **Doherty,** Terence W '02 %Stikeman E LLP -445 Park Av -NY 10022
(212) 592-1400 .. **Doherty,** Therese M '89 (Herrick,F LLP) -2 Park Av -NY 10016
(716) 945-3060 .. **Dohl,** Bert R '56 (Congdon PD&R) -107 Main -Salamanca 14779
(914) 472-7700 .. **Dohn,** Robt P '76 (Bertine HHZD&D,LLP) -700 Wht Plns Rd -Scarsdale 10583
(212) 682-7474 .. **Doi,** Etsuo '98 (Foley & L LLP) -90 Park Av -NY 10016
(914) 640-8100 .. **Dojlidko,** Michl T '99 Starwood Hotels & Resorts -1111 Wstchstr Av -White Plns 10604 **Fx:**640-8250
(212) 310-8000 .. **Dokos,** Danl S '87 (Weil G&M LLP) -767 5th Av -NY 10153
(631) 673-9600 .. **Doktofsky,** Andrew M '98 -191 NY Av -Huntngtn 11743
(212) 310-8000 .. **Doktor,** Christine M '08 %Weil G&M LLP -767 5th Av -NY 10153
(315) 443-2524 .. **Dolak,** Lisa A '89 %Syracuse Univ Cllg of Law -Wht Hall -Syracuse 13244 **Fx:**443-4213
(718) 590-2000 .. **Dolan,** Adam R '07 %DA -198 E 161st -Bronx 10451 **Fx:**590-6477
(212) 809-2663 .. **Dolan,** Alyssandra Y '02 Bondholder Comm Grp -30 Broad -NY 10004
(516) 877-0016 .. **Dolan,** Christine '94 -190 Willis Av -Mineola 11501 **Fx:**877-2743
(212) 449-1260 .. **Dolan,** Danl A Jr. '61 %Merrill Lynch -220 Bway -NY 10038
(212) 865-5879 .. **Dolan,** Dorothy V '92 -49 W 96th -NY 10025
(212) 698-3500 .. **Dolan,** Elise M '03 %Dechert LLP -1095 Av of Amer -NY 10036
(585) 454-2181 .. **Dolan,** Eric M '03 %Trevett CS&A,PC -2 State -Rchstr 14614
(212) 449-5828 .. **Dolan,** Gary C '81 %Merrill Lynch -220 Bway -NY 10038
(516) 797-1769 .. **Dolan,** Gary E '78 -4110 Merrick Rd -Massapequa 11758 **Fx:**(866) 518-7845
(212) 285-3300 .. **Dolan,** Glenn P '91 (Lipsig SM&M,PC) -40 Fulton -NY 10038
(585) 325-4300 .. **Dolan,** Gregory L '81 (Pelton DDD&B) -45 Exchange Blvd -Rchstr 14614 **Fx:**325-6075
(212) 698-3500 .. **Dolan,** James A '91 %Dechert LLP -1095 Av of Amer -NY 10036
(973) 596-4801 .. **Dolan,** John T '81 (Gibbons PC) -1 Penn Plz -NY 10119 **Fx:**639-6275
(212) 250-2500 .. **Dolan,** Kavita Natarajan '00 Deutsche Bank -60 Wall -NY 10005
(718) 250-2000 .. **Dolan,** Keith '87 %DA -350 Jay -Brklyn 11201 **Fx:**250-2314

(212) 332-8825 .. **Dolan,** Kent B '95 %Lifflander & R LLP -1221 Av of Amer -NY 10020
(212) 858-6032 .. **Dolan,** Kimberly R '01 RBC Cptl Mkts -1 Lbrty Plz -NY 10006
(518) 862-9292 .. **Dolan,** Mark J '95 %Napierski V&N,LLP -296 Wshngtn Av Ext -Albany 12203
(607) 762-7743 .. **Dolan,** Mark V '85 -Bx5224 -Bnghmtn 13902
(212) 504-6000 .. **Dolan,** Michl G '75 SrCnsl Cadwalader W&T LLP -1 World Fncl Ctr -NY 10281
(212) 871-2000 .. **Dolan,** Michl H II '00 Duff & Phelps LLC -55 E 52nd -NY 10055
(212) 698-3500 .. **Dolan,** Patrick D '88 (Dechert LLP) -1095 Av of Amer -NY 10036
(315) 478-3138 .. **Dolan,** Paul J '77 (Harrigan & D) -2 Clinton Sq -Syracuse 13202
(212) 344-5400 .. **Dolan,** Richd H '77 (Schlam S&D LLP) -26 Bway -NY 10004
(212) 589-4200 .. **Dolatly,** George C '94 (Baker & H LLP) -45 Rckfllr Plz -NY 10111
(718) 548-3019 .. **Dolber,** Fredk A '50 -4560 H Hdsn Pkwy -Bronx 10471 **Fx:**548-8988
(716) 852-1888 .. **Dolce,** Frank J '80 (Cantor LD&P,PC) -350 Main -Buffalo 14202
(212) 310-4126 .. **Dolce,** Jared C '00 %Click IQ -3 Times Sq -NY 10036
(212) 408-4203 .. **Dolce,** Rosa Maria '96 Bank of NY -1290 Av of Amer -NY 10104
(212) 762-5198 .. **Doldo,** Joanne '95 Morgan Stanley -1221 Av of Amer -NY 10020
(315) 782-5898 .. **Doldo,** Todd J '94 (Doldo & N,PC) -230 Franklin -Watertwn 13601 **Fx:**782-5482
(716) 209-6313 .. **Dole,** Jennifer E '98 Orchard Park High School -4040 Baker Rd -Orchard Pk 14127
(315) 218-8000 .. **Dole,** Jos C '89 SrCnsl Bond S&K,PLLC -1 Lincoln Ctr -Syracuse 13202
(212) 460-3366 .. **Dole,** Vivian '85 Con Ed -4 Irving Pl -NY 10003
(212) 626-4100 .. **Dolenz,** Nicole '01 %Baker & M LLP -1114 Av of Amer -NY 10036
(212) 878-8000 .. **Doley,** Kimberly M '09 %Clifford C LLP -31 W 52nd -NY 10019
(212) 820-9421 .. **Dolfman,** Jessica B '08 %Hawkins D&W LLP -One Chase Manh Plz -NY 10005
(212) 848-9800 .. **Dolgenas,** Ilyse S '96 %Withers B LLP -430 Park Av -NY 10022
(212) 925-2800 .. **Dolgenos Newman & Cronin LLP** -271 Mad Av -NY 10016 **Fx:**925-0690
(845) 225-1100 .. **Dolgetta,** John '99 %E Sumber,PC -18 Fair -Carmel 10512 **Fx:**225-1187
(212) 427-2798 .. **Dolgin,** Brynn S '98 %Bd of Education Lower Lab School -1700 3rd Av -NY 10128
(516) 463-5873 .. **Dolgin,** Janet L '82 %Hofstra Law Schl -121 Hofstra Univ -Hempstd 11549
(718) 388-7700 .. **Dolgin,** Kalmon '67 -101 Richardson -Brklyn 11211 **Fx:**782-3755
(914) 995-2673 .. **Dolgin-Kmetz,** Stacey '85 %Cnty Atty -148 Martine Av -White Plns 10601 **Fx:**995-5858
(716) 626-3030 .. **Dolgoff,** Barry S '92 -300 Intl Dr -Williamsvll 14221 **Fx:**639-7645
(212) 907-0700 .. **Dolgoff,** Mindy S '05 %Labaton S LLP -140 Bway -NY 10005
(212) 310-8000 .. **Dolgonos,** Boris '96 (Weil G&M LLP) -767 5th Av -NY 10153
(212) 788-1065 .. **Dolgow,** Pamela S '78 %Law Dept -100 Church -NY 10007 **Fx:**788-0367
(212) 318-3000 .. **Dolido,** Edw '89 (Fulbright & J LLP) -666 5th Av -NY 10103
(585) 272-0540 .. **Dolin,** Lonny H '84 OfCnsl Thomas & S LLP -693 East Av -Rchstr 14607
(518) 474-9833 .. **Dolin,** Susanne H '00 OTDA -40 N Pearl -Albany 12243 **Fx:**474-9389
(518) 765-4085 .. **Dolin,** Thos E '64 -32 Swift Rd -Voorheesvll 12186
(518) 262-3828 .. **Dolin,** Thos E Jr. '00 %Albany Med Ctr -43 New Scotland Av -Albany 12208 **Fx:**262-4184
(212) 837-8001 .. **Dolinar,** Sarah J '87 %Dept of Sanitation -44 Beaver -NY 10004 **Fx:**785-3952
(212) 696-6000 .. **Doline,** Bradley H '07 %Curtis M-PC&M LLP -101 Park Av -NY 10178
(518) 527-1758 .. **Doling,** Richd E '69 -105 S Lake Av -Albany 12208
(516) 921-8600 .. **Dolinger,** Craig M '97 (McAndrew C&P) -95 Froehlich Farm Blvd -Woodbury 11797
(212) 909-6000 .. **Doll,** Catherine M '05 %Debevoise & P LLP -919 3rd Av -NY 10022
(716) 875-6970 .. **Doll,** David A '51 -321 Orchrd Dr -Buffalo 14223
(718) 983-8000 .. **Dollard,** James A '76 (Marrazzo & D) -1265 Richmond Av -Staten Isl 10314
(212) 788-0861 .. **Dollin,** Elizabeth Wizeman '96 %Law Dept -100 Church -NY 10007 **Fx:**788-0367
(718) 875-1300 .. **Dollin,** James A '78 %Appllt Div 2nd Dept -45 Monroe Pl -Brklyn 11201 **Fx:**858-2446
(585) 424-3270 .. **Dollinger,** David M '86 (Dollinger & Assoc,PC) -777 Canal Vw Blvd -Rchstr 14623
(845) 294-2771 .. **Dollinger,** Douglas R '90 -40 Matthews -Goshen 10924
(914) 467-7823 .. **Dollinger,** Edmund '58 -520 Wht Plns Rd -Tarrytwn 10591 **Fx:**467-7801
(516) 747-1010 .. **Dollinger Gonski & Grossman** -1 Old Cntry Rd -Carle Pl 11514 **Fx:**747-2494
(631) 491-7470 .. **Dollinger,** Jay L '89 -5 Threepence Dr -Melvll 11747 **Fx:**643-4331
(516) 747-1010 .. **Dollinger,** Joyce S '00 OfCnsl Dollinger G&G -1 Old Cntry Rd -Carle Pl 11514
(516) 747-1010 .. **Dollinger,** Matthew '69 (Dollinger G&G) -1 Old Cntry Rd -Carle Pl 11514
(212) 504-6000 .. **Dollinger,** Maureen M '09 %Cadwalader W&T LLP -1 World Fncl Ctr -NY 10281
(585) 753-4500 .. **Dollinger,** Michl L '08 DA -832 Watts Bldg -Rchstr 14614 **Fx:**753-4576
(631) 243-3709 .. **Dollinger,** Steven D '87 -Bx369 -Huntngtn Sta 11746 **Fx:**643-4331
(212) 969-3000 .. **Dollinger,** Thos W '79 (Proskauer R LLP) -1585 Bway -NY 10036
(516) 365-6690 .. **Dolman,** Gerald '67 PRI -1800 Nrthrn Blvd -Roslyn 11576
(718) 625-2805 .. **Dolman,** Tina M '05 %Leopold G&S,PC -16 Court -Brklyn 11241
(516) 681-1100 .. **Dolowich,** Ivan J '93 (Kaufman DV&G,LLP) -135 Crsswys Park Dr -Woodbury 11797
(212) 286-8585 .. **Dolsky,** Robin R '81 (Heidell PM&B,LLP) -99 Park Av -NY 10016
(315) 423-3328 .. **Dolson,** Steven R '04 -500 S Salina -Syracuse 13202 **Fx:**423-3330
(315) 476-9494 .. **Domachowski,** Jeffrey A '95 -201 E Jffrsn -Syracuse 13202
(716) 566-1300 .. **Domagalski,** James P '91 (Hiscock & B,LLP) -1100 M&T Ctr -Buffalo 14203
(516) 742-1444 .. **Doman,** Danl F '82 (Wagner D&L,PC) -227 Mineola Blvd -Mineola 11501
(212) 458-3498 .. **Domanico,** Gene T '86 AIG Tech Srvcs -175 Water -NY 10038
(718) 720-9255 .. **Domanski,** Angela C '94 -90 McClean Av -Staten Isl 10305 **Fx:**720-1627
(212) 285-3800 .. **Domashitsky,** Asya '06 Subin Assoc LLP -150 Bway -NY 10007
(212) 880-3800 .. **Domb,** Martin '79 (Akerman S) -335 Mad Av -NY 10017
(866) 331-3271 .. **Dombeck,** James E '70 %SSA-ODAR -100 State -Rchstr 14614 **Fx:**(585) 263-5792
(800) 299-1930 .. **Domber,** Matthew J '51 -2500 Johnson Av -Bronx 10463
(212) 612-9550 .. **Dombroff & Gilmore,PC** -40 Broad -NY 10004 **Fx:**785-2274
(212) 705-7000 .. **Dombroff,** Robt M '02 (Bingham M LLP) -399 Park Av -NY 10022
(212) 790-4500 .. **Dombroski,** Matthew A '06 %Manatt P&P,LLP -7 Times Sq -NY 10036
(631) 265-1200 .. **Dombrow,** Lawr A '94 %Lawfinders Assoc,LLC -50 Karl Av -Smithtwn 11787
(212) 374-6746 .. **Dombrow,** Susan L '94 %NYC Dept Educ-OLS -52 Chmbrs -NY 10007 **Fx:**374-5596
(212) 218-2100 .. **Dombrowski,** Damien N '09 %Fitzpatrick CH&S -1290 Av of Amer -NY 10104
(518) 429-4200 .. **Dombrowski,** Thais M '06 %Hiscock & B,LLP -50 Beaver -Albany 12207
(718) 875-1300 .. **Dome,** Lauren G '97 %Appllt Div 2nd Dept -45 Monroe Pl -Brklyn 11201 **Fx:**858-2446
(212) 804-4200 .. **Dome,** Leonard S '59 OfCnsl Mound CW&G -One Bttry Pk Plz -NY 10004
(718) 579-7907 .. **Domena,** Michelle L '05 %Leg Aid -900 Sheridan Av -Bronx 10451 **Fx:**293-8744
(212) 949-8989 .. **Domenech,** Justin A '07 %Lifshutz & L,PC -501 5th Av -NY 10017 **Fx:**922-9620
(646) 862-3416 .. **Domercq,** Courtney P '03 Weinstein Co -345 Hudson -NY 10014
(212) 940-8800 .. **Domina,** Daren R '92 (Katten MR LLP) -575 Mad Av -NY 10022
(631) 784-7880 .. **Domina,** Dino J '95 -775 Park Av -Huntngtn 11743
(315) 793-7000 .. **Domingue-Hendrickson,** Cindy '01 %Leg Aid -255 Genesee -Utica 13501 **Fx:**732-3202
(212) 458-1027 .. **Domingues,** Albina R '97 Natl Union Fire Ins Co -175 Water -NY 10038
(212) 521-5400 .. **Dominguez,** Heather '08 %Reed S LLP -599 Lex Av -NY 10022
(212) 388-3600 .. **Dominguez,** Humberto S '89 %32B-J Leg Srvcs -101 Av of Amer -NY 10013 **Fx:**388-3061
(212) 504-5725 .. **Dominguez,** Ivan J '96 -1 World Fncl Ctr -NY 10281 **Fx:**504-6666
(212) 455-2000 .. **Dominguez,** Katherine Q '09 %Simpson T&B LLP -425 Lex Av -NY 10017
(914) 423-4000 .. **Dominguez,** Peter A '83 -72 Belvedere Dr -Ynkrs 10705 **Fx:**423-3515
(713) 890-5155 .. **Dominguez-Sotomayor,** Rodrigo '08 Morgan L&B LLP -101 Park Av -NY 10178 **Fx:**890-5001
(212) 527-1000 .. **Domini,** James A '98 (Jones HC&B PC) -1 Bttry Pk Plz -NY 10004
(212) 318-6000 .. **Dominique,** Elvita '08 %Paul HJ&W LLP -75 E 55th -NY 10022
(212) 455-2000 .. **Dominique,** Rachel J '10 %Simpson T&B LLP -425 Lex Av -NY 10017
(212) 474-1000 .. **Dominitz,** Meir '09 %Cravath S&M LLP -825 8th Av -NY 10019
(315) 829-8900 .. **Dominski,** Paul J '06 Oneida Indian Nation -2037 Dream Catcher Plz -Oneida 13421
(212) 845-2000 .. **Dominus,** Andrew R '92 KBC Fncl Hldngs -140 E 45th -NY 10017
(718) 658-0234 .. **Domnitch,** Harold '51 -85-15 Main -Briarwd 11435
(914) 378-3900 .. **Domoto,** Jeffrey A '99 %Kaplan & M -1 Exec Blvd -Ynkrs 10701
(212) 272-4286 .. **Domow,** Penny P '82 %JP Morgan Chase -383 Mad Av -NY 10179
(516) 571-3800 .. **Dompkowski,** Jos P '86 %DA -262 Old Cntry Rd -Mineola 11501 **Fx:**248-9479
(585) 381-3150 .. **Domres,** Debra A '80 -10 Tobey Vllg Ofc Park -Pittsfrd 14534
(212) 980-9600 .. **Domsky,** Douglas J '03 %Kaufman B&R -120 Bway -NY 10271
(315) 448-0507 .. **Domurad,** John M '94 %US Dist Ct -100 S Clinton Bx7367 -Syracuse 13261
(716) 501-2288 .. **Domzalski,** James R '00 Seneca Gaming Corp -310 4th -Niagara Fls 14303
(718) 645-7004 .. **Don,** James S '96 OfCnsl GG Giuliano -355 Av X -Brklyn 11223 **Fx:**998-9853
(718) 227-5147 .. **Don,** Michl D '99 -205 Noel -Staten Isl 10312 **Fx:**227-5145
(315) 379-2282 .. **Dona,** Amy L '04 %Pub Def -Cnty Cthse -Canton 13617 **Fx:**379-2300
(315) 379-2282 .. **Dona,** Heather A '06 %Pub Def -Cnty Cthse -Canton 13617 **Fx:**386-8241
(212) 393-1000 .. **Donadio,** Christopher J '08 %Burns & H -233 Bway -NY 10279
(718) 374-5093 .. **Donado,** Valmiro L '00 V Donado,PC -7707 Parsons Blvd -Fresh Mdws 11366 **Fx:**785-9580
(212) 264-3650 .. **Donaghy,** Margaret A '01 %SSA Ofc Genl Cnsl -26 Fed Plz -NY 10278 **Fx:**264-6372
(212) 318-6000 .. **Donaher,** Matthew M '93 Paul HJ&W LLP -75 E 55th -NY 10022
(585) 428-5210 .. **Donaher,** Timothy P '94 (Pub Def) -10 N Fitzhugh -Rchstr 14614 **Fx:**428-2234
(212) 259-8000 .. **Donahue,** Brendan R '06 %Dewey & L LLP -1301 Av of Amer -NY 10019
(516) 294-1333 .. **Donahue,** Caitlin C '09 %DeMartini & Y LLP -264 Hillside Av -Williston Pk 11596
(212) 813-5900 .. **Donahue,** David '00 (Fross ZL&Z,PC) -866 UN Plz -NY 10017
(212) 504-6000 .. **Donahue,** Douglas J '05 %Cadwalader W&T LLP -1 World Fncl Ctr -NY 10281
(212) 762-2077 .. **Donahue,** Edw J Jr. '94 %Morgan Stanley -750 7th Av -NY 10019
(212) 504-6000 .. **Donahue,** Kevin C '09 %Cadwalader W&T LLP -1 World Fncl Ctr -NY 10281
(212) 788-0892 .. **Donahue,** Linda '90 %Law Dept -100 Church -NY 10007 **Fx:**788-0367
(212) 841-1000 .. **Donahue,** Meghann E '06 %Covington & B LLP -620 8th Av -NY 10018
(718) 442-1212 .. **Donahue,** Robt M '56 -358 St Marks Pl -Staten Isl 10301 **Fx:**442-4988
(212) 736-5300 .. **Donahue,** S Jos '98 %Block O&M LLP -1 Penn Plz -NY 10119
(516) 571-2042 .. **Donahue,** Sally M '91 %Surrogate's Ct -262 Old Cntry Rd -Mineola 11501 **Fx:**571-3864
(212) 571-0111 .. **Donahue,** Stephen J '96 %Hardin KM&P,PA -110 William -NY 10038
(718) 875-1300 .. **Donahue,** Vincent R Jr. '99 %Appllt Div 2nd Dept -45 Monroe Pl -Brklyn 11201 **Fx:**858-2446
(212) 458-7014 .. **Donahue-Aguilar,** Kathleen '99 AIG -175 Water -NY 10038
(212) 344-5680 .. **Donaker,** Jennifer '09 %Thompson H LLP -335 Mad Av -NY 10017
(631) 242-1600 .. **Donald,** Henry F '78 %Kujawski & D -1637 Deer Prk Av -Deer Pk 11729
(718) 643-7141 .. **Donaldson,** Chas W '93 -203A Bergen -Brklyn 11217

(212) 416-7334 .. **Donaldson,** Charlie '71 %Dept of Law -120 Bway -NY 10271
(212) 722-4900 .. **Donaldson Chilliest & McDaniel,LLP** -1825 Park Av -NY 10035 **Fx:**722-4966
(212) 819-8200 .. **Donaldson,** Katharine '08 %White & C LLP -1155 Av of Amer -NY 10036
(914) 631-6200 .. **Donaldson,** Mary N '85 %Gibralter Mngmnt -150 Wht Plns Rd -Tarrytwn 10591 **Fx:**631-6243
(518) 233-0637 .. **Donaldson,** Robt E '05 -Bx4122 -Clifton Pk 12065
(212) 465-2529 .. **Donaldson,** Thos B '05 -342 Bway -NY 10013
(212) 722-4900 .. **Donaldson,** Xavier R '95 (Donaldson C&M,LLP) -1825 Park Av -NY 10035
(212) 558-4000 .. **Don Angelo,** Francesca '07 %Sullivan & C LLP -125 Broad -NY 10004
(203) 255-5669 .. **Donas,** George N '58 -4 W Red Oak Ln -White Plns 10604
(212) 632-6000 .. **Donat,** Gregory S '98 Lazard Freres & Co -30 Rckfllr Plz -NY 10112
(212) 471-8463 .. **Donat,** Jos E '75 (Herzfeld & R,PC) -125 Broad -NY 10004
(914) 640-8424 .. **Donat,** Marshall J '81 %Starwood Hotels & Resorts -1111 Wstchstr Av -White Plns 10604 **Fx:**640-8250
(516) 767-9500 .. **Donatelli,** Danl D '84 -31 S Bayles Av -Pt Wash 11050 **Fx:**883-0718
(516) 921-5300 .. **Donatelli,** Jason T '02 %Donatelli & D,LLP -6800 Jericho Tpk -Syosset 11791 **Fx:**921-2221
(718) 302-2697 .. **Donatelli,** Jos J '99 -325 Manh Av -Brklyn 11211 **Fx:**302-2699
(212) 344-7042 .. **Donatelli,** Randolph H '89 (Cichanowicz CKV&T,LLP) -61 Bway -NY 10006
(516) 921-5300 .. **Donatelli,** Robt A '66 (Donatelli & D,LLP) -6800 Jericho Tpk -Syosset 11791 **Fx:**921-2221
(716) 439-7085 .. **Donatello,** Elizabeth R '97 %DA -175 Hawley -Lockprt 14094 **Fx:**439-7102
(212) 483-0105 .. **Donath,** Jonathan F '06 %Coughlin D LLP -88 Pine-Wall St Plz -NY 10005
(212) 757-5000 .. **Donath,** Sheree R '02 %Sklover D&F,LLC -10 Rckfllr Plz -NY 10020 **Fx:**757-5002
(716) 847-8400 .. **Donathen,** James D '79 (Phillips L LLP) -3400 HSBC Ctr -Buffalo 14203
(212) 839-5300 .. **Donato,** Elaine '86 Sidley A LLP -787 7th Av -NY 10019
(631) 588-5000 .. **Donato,** Jeffrey M '02 %AN Guzzone & Assoc,PC -2450 Middle Cntry Rd -Centereach 11720 **Fx:**588-5001
(631) 654-9008 .. **Donato,** Jodi Ann '93 JA Donato,LLC -136 E Main -E Islip 11730 **Fx:**654-0337
(631) 982-0130 .. **Donato,** Linda '02 -180 E Main -Smithtwn 11787 **Fx:**982-0086
(845) 562-8262 .. **Donato,** Stephanie '90 -162 S Robnsn Av -Newburgh 12550 **Fx:**565-0677
(315) 218-8000 .. **Donato,** Stephen A '84 (Bond S&K,PLLC) -1 Lincoln Ctr -Syracuse 13202
(212) 298-5210 .. **Donchak,** Lisa M '88 %Leg Aid -49 Thomas -NY 10013 **Fx:**298-5252
(212) 907-0700 .. **Donders,** Lloyd M '02 %Labaton S LLP -140 Bway -NY 10005
(212) 834-0600 .. **Dondes,** Edw M '95 (Gordon & S,PC) -355 Lex Av -NY 10017
(518) 274-2114 .. **Dondes,** Yvie J '87 -Bx1468 -Troy 12181
(212) 836-8000 .. **Donefer,** Chas A P '09 %Kaye S LLP -425 Park Av -NY 10022
(212) 307-1122 .. **Donegan,** James M '79 %Novartis Pharmaceuticals Corp -608 5th Av -NY 10020
(212) 546-9255 .. **Donegan,** Jos M '93 (Scarinci H) -107 Grand -NY 10013
(518) 485-2346 .. **Donegan,** Michl F '85 %Comm of Correction -80 Wolf Rd -Albany 12205 **Fx:**485-2467
(315) 482-1008 .. **Donegan,** Patrick M '95 %Vision Development,Inc -23590 Iroquois Isl Shore Rd Bx802 -Alexandria Bay 13607 **Fx:**482-1025
(212) 909-6000 .. **Donehower,** R Weston '04 %Debevoise & P LLP -919 3rd Av -NY 10022
(914) 946-3700 .. **Donelli,** Kathleen '86 (McCarthy F LLP) -11 Martine Av -White Plns 10606
(718) 969-8744 .. **Dong,** David '88 -166-16 Union Tpk -Flushng 11366 **Fx:**969-8744
(212) 625-0300 .. **Dong,** David B '90 %Kee & L-K,PLLC -354 Broome -NY 10013
(718) 250-2000 .. **Donhauser,** Caroline Rathbun '90 %DA -350 Jay -Brklyn 11201 **Fx:**250-2314
(315) 479-8660 .. **Donigan,** James L '99 %Alexander & C,LLC -115 E Jffrsn -Syracuse 13202
(914) 750-5933 .. **Donigan,** Thos M '09 %Kissel H&W LLP -580 Wht Plns Rd -Tarrytwn 10591
(212) 879-3438 .. **Doniger,** Alan F '53 -150 E 69th -NY 10021
(631) 262-7400 .. **Doniger,** Wende A '86 (Doniger & E) -12 Bayview Av -Northprt 11768
(212) 697-3122 .. **Donihue,** Ryan M '00 (Martin C&B LLP) -220 E 42nd -NY 10017
(212) 370-1300 .. **Donikyan,** Tamar '06 %Ellenoff G&S LLP -150 E 42nd -NY 10017
(212) 909-6000 .. **Doninger,** Jaime E '07 %Debevoise & P LLP -919 3rd Av -NY 10022
(212) 925-3456 .. **Donini,** Lisa M '98 %Sedlmayr & Assoc -200 Park Av S -NY 10003 **Fx:**925-0554
(607) 723-5341 .. **Donlan,** Jennifer M '09 %Hinman H&K,LLP -80 Exchange Bx5250 -Bnghmtn 13902
(212) 735-2449 .. **Donlan,** Katy H '09 %Skadden ASM&F LLP -4 Times Sq -NY 10036 **Fx:**(917) 777-2449
(718) 463-5422 .. **Donlevy,** Andrew P '72 -35-21 153rd -Flushng 11354
(212) 698-3500 .. **Donley,** Jos F '78 (Dechert LLP) -1095 Av of Amer -NY 10036
(212) 859-5035 .. **Donlon,** Edw '98 -110 Wall -NY 10005
(516) 542-5900 .. **Donlon,** Edw J '68 (Congdon FORDT&F) -333 Earle Ovngton Blvd -Uniondale 11553
(516) 222-0248 .. **Donlon,** Elizabeth P '79 (Donlon & H) -350 Old Cntry Rd -Gdn Cty 11530
(718) 273-2099 .. **Donlon,** James F '74 -25 Manor Rd -Staten Isl 10310 **Fx:**273-2777
(212) 525-4724 .. **Donlon,** Jos P '02 %WTAS -452 5th Av -NY 10018
(518) 761-6405 .. **Donlon,** Kevin P '02 %DA -Cnty Mncpl Ctr -Lk George 12845
(716) 856-0600 .. **Donlon,** Michl C '00 (Jaeckle F&M,LLP) -12 Fountain Plz -Buffalo 14202
(516) 229-4363 .. **Donlon,** Thos S '03 GEICO -875 Merrick Av -Westbury 11590
(212) 693-0085 .. **Donn,** Anthony Alexander '07 Appellate Advocates -2 Rector -NY 10006 **Fx:**693-0878
(212) 219-9866 .. **Donnard,** Brian '84 (Plunkett & D) -401 Bway -NY 10013
(516) 832-7777 .. **Donnel,** Judith A '88 %Silberstein A&M,PC -600 Old Cntry Rd -Gdn Cty 11530
(212) 294-6700 .. **Donnell,** James '06 (Winston & S) -200 Park Av -NY 10166
(914) 681-0200 .. **Donnellan,** Alfred E '82 (DelBello DWW&W,LLP) -1 N Lex Av -White Plns 10601
(212) 272-2555 .. **Donnellan,** Andrew B Jr. '78 %JP Morgan Chase -383 Mad Av -NY 10179
(212) 630-5617 .. **Donnellan,** Christopher P '97 Conde Nast Publications -750 3rd Av -NY 10017
(631) 585-4872 .. **Donnellan,** Edw P '69 -56 Brandy Ln -Lk Grove 11755
(212) 649-2051 .. **Donnellan,** Jonathan R '92 SrCnsl Hearst Corp -300 W 57th -NY 10019 **Fx:**649-2035
(212) 480-5284 .. **Donnellan,** Susan Skaling '95 %Insurance Dept -25 Beaver -NY 10004 **Fx:**480-5272
(518) 884-0200 .. **Donnellan,** Teresa G '92 (Donnellan & K,PLLC) -20 Prospect -Ballston Spa 12020 **Fx:**884-0343
(516) 571-3800 .. **Donnelly,** Anne T '90 %DA -262 Old Cntry Rd -Mineola 11501 **Fx:**248-9479
(212) 683-8775 .. **Donnelly,** Bob E '74 -133 W 25th -NY 10001 **Fx:**414-0525
(212) 513-7788 .. **Donnelly,** Brian J '86 (Ahmuty D&M) -123 William -NY 10038
(845) 424-3877 .. **Donnelly,** Danl '60 -94 Frazier Rd Bx253 -Garrison 10524 **Fx:**424-3968
(718) 590-2000 .. **Donnelly,** Danl M '09 %DA -198 E 161st -Bronx 10451 **Fx:**590-6477
(212) 661-1400 .. **Donnelly,** Diane '86 (Von Maltitz DKJ&G) -60 E 42nd -NY 10017
(516) 931-1800 .. **Donnelly,** Emmet D '10 %Catalano G&P LLP -100 Jericho Quadrangle -Jericho 11753
(631) 851-9700 .. **Donnelly,** Gerard J '99 G Donnelly,PC -490 Wheeler Rd -Hauppauge 11788 **Fx:**851-9701
(718) 935-2182 .. **Donnelly,** Heather E '06 %NYC Dept Educ -65 Court -Brklyn 11201
(516) 328-1100 .. **Donnelly,** John M '96 (Ryan B&D LLP) -131 Tulip Av -Floral Pk 11001
(212) 363-3100 .. **Donnelly,** Kevin J '87 %Bivona & C,PC -88 Pine -NY 10005
(718) 410-0583 .. **Donnelly,** Lauren J '98 Legal Aid-Civil Div -1118 Grnd Cncrs -Bronx 10456
(516) 712-4000 .. **Donnelly,** Lorin A '91 (Milber MP&S LLP) -1000 Woodbury Rd -Woodbury 11797
(518) 477-6230 .. **Donnelly,** Margaret E '01 -728 A Columbia Tpk -E Greenbush 12061 **Fx:**477-8994
(315) 445-4432 .. **Donnelly,** Mary Ann Abend '62 %Lemoyne Cllg -1419 Salt Sprngs Rd -Syracuse 13214
(212) 682-0020 .. **Donnelly,** Mary Ellen '92 (Putney TH&H LLP) -521 5th Av -NY 10175
(518) 462-6714 .. **Donnelly,** Mary Pat '98 %City Ct-Crim Part -Morton Av at Broad -Albany 12202 **Fx:**447-8778
(315) 424-7209 .. **Donnelly,** Michl G '75 SrCnsl T Puleo -441 S Salina -Syracuse 13202 **Fx:**424-5553
(845) 294-9447 .. **Donnelly,** Michl H '79 (Dickover DD&B LLP) -28 Bruen Pl Bx610 -Goshen 10924
(212) 949-9100 .. **Donnelly,** Michl H '83 -2 Park Av -NY 10016
(212) 735-3000 .. **Donnelly,** Paul D '07 %Skadden ASM&F LLP -4 Times Sq -NY 10036
(718) 945-0794 .. **Donnelly,** Robt J '84 -84 216th -Rckwy Pnt 11697
(646) 855-0775 .. **Donnelly,** Sarah '02 Bank of America -1 Bryant Pk -NY 10036
(631) 577-2400 .. **Donnelly,** Stephen J Jr. '93 %Tromello M&K -25 Melvll Park Rd Bx9038 -Melvll 11747
(516) 627-9414 .. **Donnelly,** Warren E '60 -131 Exec Dr -New Hyde Pk 11040 **Fx:**365-5789
(518) 402-6092 .. **Donnelly-Heg,** Martin E '00 %Workers Comp Bd -20 Park -Albany 12207
(917) 262-1193 .. **Donnenfeld,** Gregg R '96 Marc Ecko Entrprs -40 W 23rd -NY 10010
(631) 427-0101 .. **Donnenfeld,** Judith '03 %M Stern,PC -17 Cardiff Ct -Huntngtn Sta 11746 **Fx:**427-0196
(212) 577-3688 .. **Donner,** Amy I '87 %Leg Aid -199 Water -NY 10038 **Fx:**509-8431
(212) 806-5400 .. **Donner,** Irah H '92 (Stroock &S&L LLP) -180 Maiden Ln -NY 10038
(212) 432-9180 .. **Donner,** Jeffrey A '74 (Stryker T&D LLP) -2 Penn Plz -NY 10121
(716) 631-7835 .. **Donner,** John J '01 %Sierra Research -485 Cayuga Rd -Buffalo 14225
(631) 269-5516 .. **Donner,** Lorraine Ricca '83 -98 Cuttermill Rd -Gt Neck 11021 **Fx:**269-5518
(516) 797-9797 .. **Donofrio,** Anthony C '90 -5518 Merrick Rd -Massapequa 11758 **Fx:**977-6700
(917) 885-3545 .. **D'Onofrio,** Chas V III '05 -Bx1369 -Patchogue 11772 **Fx:**(631) 343-4817
(212) 918-3000 .. **Donofrio,** Douglas A '87 Cnsl Hogan L LLP -875 3rd Av -NY 10022
(914) 725-9666 .. **D'Onofrio,** Frank T Jr. '68 -142 Garth Rd -Scarsdale 10583 **Fx:**725-9676
(585) 546-6448 .. **Donofrio,** Laurie Ann '92 %Davidson F LLP -28 E Main -Rchstr 14614
(212) 297-2419 .. **D'Onofrio,** Linda L '82 OfCnsl Day P LLP -7 Times Sq -NY 10036
(631) 367-9696 .. **D'Onofrio,** Maria C '94 %Kean Development, Inc -5 Main -Cold Spg Hbr 11724
(914) 632-7209 .. **D'Onofrio,** Paul N '79 -50 Wht Oak -New Rchll 10801
(914) 683-0505 .. **D'Onofrio,** Raymond A '92 H Stern -3 Barker Av -White Plns 10601 **Fx:**683-0508
(212) 349-3000 .. **Donoghue,** Elizabeth '85 (Himmelstein MGD&J) -15 Maiden Ln -NY 10038
(845) 592-7000 .. **Donoghue,** John M '68 (Donoghue TA&D LLP) -2517 Route 52 -Hopewell Junct 12533
(516) 393-2200 .. **Donoghue,** Kevin G '00 %Garfunkel W,PC -111 Grt Nck Rd -Gt Neck 11021
(212) 448-4964 .. **Donoghue,** Marie P '92 ESPN Internet Grp -19 E 34th -NY 10016
(212) 770-9014 .. **Donoghue,** Mary P '97 AIG-Amer Genl -70 Pine -NY 10270 **Fx:**770-8020
(716) 885-9700 .. **Donoghue,** Patrick J '98 (Collins C&D) -267 North -Buffalo 14201 **Fx:**885-9770
(631) 715-7900 .. **Donoghue,** Richd P '92 %US Atty -610 Fed Plz -Central Islip 11722
(845) 592-7000 .. **Donoghue Thomas Auslander & Drohan LLP** -2517 Route 52 -Hopewell Junct 12533 **Fx:**592-7020
(914) 725-7893 .. **Donoghue Thomas Auslander & Drohan LLP** -700 Wht Plns Rd -Scarsdale 10583
(212) 918-3000 .. **Donoho,** Christopher R III '97 (Hogan L LLP) -875 3rd Av -NY 10022
(212) 689-1600 .. **Donohoe,** Margaret M '97 (Marsh V&D LLP) -500 5th Av -NY 10110 **Fx:**689-0210

(516) 746-8000 .. **Donohue,** Antonia M '85 (Jaspan S LLP) -300 Grdn City Plz -Gdn Cty 11530
(212) 742-3390 .. **Donohue,** Barry J '75 Lindabury ME&C,PC -26 Bway -NY 10004
(716) 693-3244 .. **Donohue,** Barry J '90 %JF Donohue -77 Broad -Tonawanda 14150 **Fx:**693-1158
(518) 272-2300 .. **Donohue,** Brian E '84 -68 2nd -Troy 12180 **Fx:**272-0540
(212) 623-5179 .. **Donohue,** Catherine F '93 JP Morgan Chase & Co -4 NY Plz -NY 10004
(716) 693-4218 .. **Donohue,** David C '94 %JF Donohue -77 Broad -Tonawanda 14150 **Fx:**693-1158
(212) 692-9030 .. **Donohue,** James P Jr. '76 (Crystal & D) -708 3rd Av -NY 10017
(212) 335-9000 .. **Donohue,** Jean M '04 %DA -1 Hogan Pl -NY 10013
(716) 693-3244 .. **Donohue,** John F '60 -77 Broad -Tonawanda 14150 **Fx:**693-1158
(914) 241-1720 .. **Donohue,** John J '65 -84 Smith Av -Mt Kisco 10549 **Fx:**666-0556
(516) 869-6900 .. **Donohue,** John J Jr. '85 %Nicolosi & N,LLP -111 Plandome Rd -Manhsst 11030 **Fx:**869-6500
(646) 610-5390 .. **Donohue,** John K '04 %NYPD -1 Police Plz -NY 10038
(212) 269-2330 .. **Donohue,** John P '73 (Donohue and D) -26 Bway -NY 10004 **Fx:**269-5016
(212) 269-2330 .. **Donohue,** Jos F Jr. '70 (Donohue and D) -26 Bway -NY 10004 **Fx:**269-5016
(845) 986-9596 .. **Donohue,** Jos M '05 (Donohue & N LLP) -11 Oaklnd Av -Warwick 10990 **Fx:**986-9479
(585) 658-2832 .. **Donohue,** Kelly J '93 %J Putney -63 Main Bx307 -Mt Morris 14510 **Fx:**658-4098
(631) 957-2000 .. **Donohue Kretz & Garabrant** -36 E Montauk Hwy -Lindenhrst 11757 **Fx:**957-3443
(212) 373-5937 .. **Donohue,** Marc F '97 Mizuho Trust & Banking Co -135 W 50th -NY 10020
(518) 463-5400 .. **Donohue,** Mark P '84 SpclCnsl Goldberg S LLP -8 Southwoods Blvd -Albany 12211
(212) 770-7000 .. **Donohue,** Matthew P '96 %AIG -160 Water -NY 10038
(516) 681-3100 .. **Donohue McGahan Catalano & Belitsis** -555 N Bway Bx350 -Jericho 11753 **Fx:**681-5357
(516) 681-3100 .. **Donohue,** Nicholas J '76 (Donohue MC&B) -555 N Bway Bx350 -Jericho 11753
(212) 261-8000 .. **Donohue,** Patrick J '95 (Mendes & M,LLP) -750 7th Av -NY 10019
(718) 222-2040 .. **Donohue,** Rachel '07 %Law Dept -350 Jay -Brklyn 11201 **Fx:**222-2088
(631) 665-0609 .. **Donohue,** Richd W '95 (Sherman FS&L LLP) -8 E Main -Bay Shr 11706
(212) 972-5252 .. **Donohue,** Robt D '92 (Donohue & Prtnrs,PC) -90 Broad -NY 10004 **Fx:**697-2737
(212) 872-1000 .. **Donohue,** Ryan J '07 -One Bryant Park -NY 10036 **Fx:**872-1002
(518) 458-8922 .. **Donohue Sabo Varley & Huttner,LLP** -24 Aviation Rd -Albany 12205 **Fx:**438-4349
(516) 445-9681 .. **Donohue,** Scott J '94 -235 Brompton Rd S -Gdn Cty 11530
(845) 623-2345 .. **Donohue,** Stephen D '86 (S Donohue,PC) -365 Route 304 -Bardonia 10954 **Fx:**623-2303
(518) 474-6750 .. **Donohue,** Thos J '86 %Liquor Auth -80 S Swan -Albany 12210 **Fx:**402-2304
(212) 940-3033 .. **Donohue,** Victoria C '03 %Nixon P LLP -437 Mad Av -NY 10022
(718) 590-3715 .. **Donohue,** Wm F '95 %Supreme Ct Civil -851 Grnd Cncrs -Bronx 10451 **Fx:**590-8914
(212) 801-2195 .. **Donoian,** James H '88 (Greenberg T,LLP) -200 Park Av -NY 10166
(212) 583-9600 .. **Donovan,** Amy S '06 %Littler M,PC -900 3rd Av -NY 10022
(212) 430-8020 .. **Donovan,** Andrew H '85 (LeClairRyan,PC) -830 3rd Av -NY 10022
(631) 929-4700 .. **Donovan,** Annamarie '94 The Donovan Law Firm,LLC -1530 N Cntry Rd -Wading Rvr 11792 **Fx:**929-0728
(212) 846-7872 .. **Donovan,** Anne P '92 %MTV Networks -1515 Bway -NY 10036 **Fx:**258-8358
(212) 839-5300 .. **Donovan,** Bindu '99 (Sidley A LLP) -787 7th Av -NY 10019
(718) 624-0081 .. **Donovan,** Brian K '66 -204 Columbia Hts -Brklyn 11201
(973) 642-8680 .. **Donovan,** C Steven '77 (Hawkins D&W LLP) -One Chase Manh Plz -NY 10005 **Fx:**642-6773
(914) 232-9570 .. **Donovan,** Caroline '81 -215 Katonah Av -Katonah 10536 **Fx:**232-6984
(212) 297-5800 .. **Donovan,** Colleen R '88 (Day P LLP) -7 Times Sq -NY 10036
(212) 897-5818 .. **Donovan,** Craig T '99 -305 Bway -NY 10007 **Fx:**897-5819
(914) 969-6500 .. **Donovan,** Danl J '71 %Precision Valve -700 Nepperhan Av Bx309 -Ynkrs 10702
(718) 876-6300 .. **Donovan,** Danl M Jr. '89 (DA) -130 Styvsnt Pl -Staten Isl 10301
(845) 294-9447 .. **Donovan,** David A '87 (Dickover DD&B LLP) -28 Bruen Pl Bx610 -Goshen 10924
(212) 909-6000 .. **Donovan,** Donald F '83 (Debevoise & P LLP) -919 3rd Av -NY 10022
(212) 785-2929 .. **Donovan,** Eileen '94 %Conway FC&K,PC -48 Wall -NY 10005
(914) 723-2456 .. **Donovan,** Eileen Cotter '93 -62 Tunstall Rd -Scarsdale 10583
(516) 938-1717 .. **Donovan,** Francis J '42 %Donovan & D,PC -90 Newbrdg Rd -Hicksvll 11801 **Fx:**938-1730
(212) 980-1900 .. **Donovan & Giannuzzi, LLP** -261 Mad Av -NY 10016 **Fx:**223-0966
(212) 244-3333 .. **Donovan Hatem LLP** -1350 Bway -NY 10018 **Fx:**244-5697
(212) 221-5700 .. **Donovan,** J Ted '81 %Goldberg WFG LLP -1501 Bway -NY 10036
(516) 229-4200 .. **Donovan,** James N '94 %Mendolia & S -875 Merrick Av -Westbury 11590
(914) 323-7000 .. **Donovan,** James P '70 (Wilson EME&D LLP) -3 Gannett Dr -White Plns 10604
(212) 490-3000 .. **Donovan,** James P '70 (Wilson EME&D LLP) -150 E 42nd -NY 10017
(716) 847-8400 .. **Donovan,** John F '60 OfCnsl Phillips L LLP -3400 HSBC Ctr -Buffalo 14203
(718) 351-2758 .. **Donovan,** John M '73 -17 Holly Pl -Staten Isl 10306
(212) 819-8200 .. **Donovan,** John M '84 (White & C LLP) -1155 Av of Amer -NY 10036
(516) 822-1222 .. **Donovan,** Jos D '76 -211 Newbrdg Rd -Hicksvll 11801
(212) 425-9300 .. **Donovan,** Jos K '94 Cnsl Bressler A&R,PC -17 State -NY 10004
(212) 635-3150 .. **Donovan,** Kelly L '95 %Ofc Inspector Genl -61 Bway -NY 10006 **Fx:**809-6287
(518) 474-7330 .. **Donovan,** Kevin P '90 %Dept of Law -The Cptl -Albany 12224
(914) 961-1555 .. **Donovan,** Lawr '79 (Donovan & V) -80 Palmer Av -Bronxvll 10708
(518) 383-4000 .. **Donovan,** Linda L '91 (Overton RD&D,LLP) -19 Halfmoon Exec Park Dr Bx437 -Clifton Pk 12065
(718) 390-5321 .. **Donovan,** Lisa M '04 %Law Dept -60 Bay -Staten Isl 10301 **Fx:**390-5338
(631) 952-7422 .. **Donovan,** Martha M '05 NYS Dept of Educ -250 Vets Mem'l Hwy -Hauppauge 11788 **Fx:**952-1029
(212) 226-7700 .. **Donovan,** Mary A '82 (Donovan & Y LLP) -161 Av of Amer -NY 10013
(718) 619-9641 .. **Donovan,** Mary F '88 -155 Sycamore -Staten Isl 10308 **Fx:**356-2320
(212) 687-1230 .. **Donovan,** Matthew D '06 %Farrell F,PC -370 Lex Av -NY 10017
(516) 938-1717 .. **Donovan,** Matthew T '79 (Donovan & D,PC) -90 Newbrdg Rd -Hicksvll 11801 **Fx:**938-1730
(212) 819-8200 .. **Donovan,** Maureen D '66 (White & C LLP) -1155 Av of Amer -NY 10036
(718) 222-2363 .. **Donovan,** Meredith G '01 %Law Dept -350 Jay -Brklyn 11201 **Fx:**222-2373
(212) 259-8000 .. **Donovan,** Molly Murphy '06 %Dewey & L LLP -1301 Av of Amer -NY 10019
(212) 735-3000 .. **Donovan,** Nancy L '04 %Skadden ASM&F LLP -4 Times Sq -NY 10036
(212) 980-1900 .. **Donovan,** Nicholas T '92 (Donovan & G,LLP) -261 Mad Av -NY 10016
(516) 248-9595 .. **Donovan,** Noreen Cooney '87 OfCnsl Palmieri C & Assoc,PC -250 Mineola Blvd -Mineola 11501
(212) 808-7800 .. **Donovan,** Richd E '78 (Kelley D&W LLP) -101 Park Av -NY 10178
(518) 436-1661 .. **Donovan,** Ryan T '02 (Harris C&D,PLLC) -5 Clinton Sq -Albany 12207
(212) 431-9076 .. **Donovan,** Sherri F '86 S Donovan & Assoc,PC -225 Bway -NY 10007 **Fx:**431-9596
(631) 969-1322 .. **Donovan,** Timothy M '78 Netsmart Technologies -3500 Sunrise Hwy -Great Rvr 11739 **Fx:**968-2123
(646) 610-5140 .. **Donovan,** Timothy P '92 %NYPD -1 Police Plz -NY 10038
(212) 969-3000 .. **Donovan,** Timothy W '01 %Proskauer R LLP -1585 Bway -NY 10036
(212) 326-3939 .. **Donovan,** Traci M '08 %Jones D -222 E 41st -NY 10017
(518) 486-1841 .. **Donovan,** Valerie B '93 %Dept of Health -Corning Twr 24th Fl -Albany 12237 **Fx:**473-2430
(631) 232-2224 .. **Donovan,** Wayne J '92 %Perini & H -1770 Motor Pkwy -Hauppauge 11788 **Fx:**232-2344
(914) 946-3700 .. **Donovan,** Wm A '51 OfCnsl McCarthy F LLP -11 Martine Av -White Plns 10606
(212) 226-7700 .. **Donovan & Yee LLP** -161 Av of Amer -NY 10013 **Fx:**226-1995
(212) 289-6650 .. **Donovan-Estades,** Erika '97 East Harlem Cncl for Human Srvcs -2253 3rd Av -NY 10035 **Fx:**360-6149
(607) 264-9988 .. **Donovan Laughlin,** Tracy A '95 Tracys Law Ofc -77 Alden Bx217 -Cherry Vly 13320 **Fx:**264-9094
(212) 750-8700 .. **Dontzin,** Mary Hillyer '96 (Friedman & W,PC) -600 Lex Av -NY 10022
(212) 717-2900 .. **Dontzin,** Matthew S '84 (Dontzin Law Firm) -6 E 81st -NY 10028 **Fx:**717-8088
(212) 751-2700 .. **Dontzin,** Michl J '52 %JAMS -620 8th Av -NY 10018 **Fx:**751-4099
(516) 741-5252 .. **Donuk,** Aybike '10 %Sanders SBWV&G,PC -100 Hrrcks Rd -Mineola 11501
(212) 570-4499 .. **Donziger,** Steven R '97 -245 W 104th -NY 10025 **Fx:**570-9944
(718) 938-9284 .. **Doobay,** Sedesh '02 -211-41 Jamaica Av -Qns Vllg 11428 **Fx:**468-6291
(315) 475-3127 .. **Doody,** Crystal M '06 %Leg Srvcs -472 S Salina -Syracuse 13202 **Fx:**475-2706
(212) 952-0100 .. **Doody,** Dennis J '75 %USAU -199 Water -NY 10038
(914) 323-7000 .. **Doody,** Jacqueline '06 %Wilson EME&D LLP -3 Gannett Dr -White Plns 10604
(212) 232-1300 .. **Doody,** John J '93 (Lewis BB&S LLP) -77 Water -NY 10005
(212) 610-6300 .. **Doody,** Stephen '83 SrCnsl Allen & O -1221 Av of Amer -NY 10020
(718) 522-3333 .. **Doogan,** Debra Katz '95 %Children's Law Ctr -44 Court -Brklyn 11201 **Fx:**522-7376
(212) 450-4000 .. **Doolan,** Angela T '07 %Davis P&W LLP -450 Lex Av -NY 10017
(516) 592-6800 .. **Doolan,** Catherine C '07 %Spellman RSGM&P,LLP -229 Seventh -Gdn Cty 11530
(516) 355-7901 .. **Doolan,** Robt J '97 %Paganini GCC&F -1979 Marcus Av -Lk Success 11042
(518) 734-4788 .. **Doolan,** Sean J '94 -5428 Main Bx298 -Windham 12496 **Fx:**734-6917
(518) 436-0751 .. **Doolan,** Sean M '88 (Hinman S PC) -121 State -Albany 12207
(212) 839-5300 .. **Dooley,** Chrystie A '04 %Sidley A LLP -787 7th Av -NY 10019
(518) 459-1000 .. **Dooley,** Colleen A '07 %DiFabio Law Firm,PC -4 Automation Ln -Albany 12205 **Fx:**459-1038
(631) 351-8734 .. **Dooley,** Edw W '81 -6 Welder Ct -Huntngtn Sta 11746 **Fx:**351-8734
(212) 506-1700 .. **Dooley,** Kevin J '93 SpclCnsl Kasowitz BT&F LLP -1633 Bway -NY 10019
(607) 773-2887 .. **Dooley,** Kevin P '81 %US Atty -15 Henry -Bnghmtn 13901 **Fx:**773-2901
(516) 571-9041 .. **Dooley,** Patricia M '04 %Cnty Atty -1200 Old Cntry Rd -Westbury 11590
(212) 872-1000 .. **Dooley,** Patrick J '83 -One Bryant Park -NY 10036 **Fx:**872-1002
(516) 869-7181 .. **Dooley,** Paul C '02 Kimco Realty Corp -3333 New Hyde Pk Rd -New Hyde Pk 11042 **Fx:**869-7199
(212) 756-2000 .. **Dooley,** Rosemary '00 %Schulte R&Z LLP -919 3rd Av -NY 10022
(212) 460-3192 .. **Dooley,** Sylvia Vadi '89 Con Ed -4 Irving Pl -NY 10003 **Fx:**260-8627
(315) 475-5452 .. **Doolittle,** James A '74 Alliance Bk NA -120 Madison -Syracuse 13202 **Fx:**475-5459
(585) 724-1932 .. **Doolittle,** Kenneth K '74 %Eastman Kodak -343 State -Rchstr 14650
(716) 853-1887 .. **Doolittle,** Laura C '84 %E Tenney -5 Niagara Sq -Buffalo 14202 **Fx:**853-1893
(518) 465-3553 .. **Doolity,** Crystal Ann '05 %Maynard OS&C,LLP -6 Twr Pl -Albany 12203
(718) 652-6307 .. **Doonan,** Wm '82 -1135 Pelham Pkwy -Bronx 10469
(585) 753-4500 .. **Doorley,** Sandra '89 %DA -832 Watts Bldg -Rchstr 14614 **Fx:**753-4576
(212) 244-2999 .. **Dopf,** Glenn W '80 (Kopff N&D LLP) -440 9th Av -NY 10001

(646) 386-4800 .. **Dopico,** Jorge '80 %Comm Judicial Cndct -61 Bway -NY 10006 **Fx:**458-0037
(716) 856-4000 .. **Dopkins,** Richd B '59 (Hodgson R LLP) -140 Pearl -Buffalo 14202
(518) 792-1461 .. **Dopman,** Kara Mackey '94 -Bx663 -Glens Fls 12801 **Fx:**761-0365
(646) 654-5036 .. **Doppelt,** Earl H '78 VNU Inc -770 Bway -NY 10003 **Fx:**654-5060
(212) 573-5000 .. **Doppstadt,** Eric W '85 Ford Fndtn -320 E 43rd -NY 10017
(212) 468-8000 .. **Dopsch,** Peter C '87 (Morrison & F LLP) -1290 Av of Amer -NY 10104
(212) 635-1643 .. **Dorado,** Raymond J '84 Bk of NY Mellon -1 Wall -NY 10286
(212) 803-3100 .. **Dorado,** Richd M '83 %Empire State Dvlmnt Corp -633 3rd Av -NY 10017
(212) 445-1982 .. **Doran,** Brian F '85 %Banco Popular NA -7 W 51st -NY 10019 **Fx:**977-5739
(518) 474-7700 .. **Doran,** Christine M '78 %NYS OPWDD -44 Holland Av -Albany 12229 **Fx:**474-7382
(914) 238-3837 .. **Doran,** Danl A III '65 -9 Hunts Ln Bx479 -Chappaqua 10514
(716) 592-2323 .. **Doran,** John E '59 -10509 Pratham Rd -Glenwd 14069 **Fx:**592-2323
(914) 472-8069 .. **Doran,** John E '01 %S Lubowitz -700 Wht Plns Rd -Scarsdale 10583 **Fx:**725-6160
(516) 746-7799 .. **Doran,** Lisa K '97 %Reisman P&R LLP -1305 Franklin Av -Gdn Cty 11530
(518) 523-9588 .. **Doran,** Margaret E '75 -30 Fawn Ridge Rd Bx830 -Lk Placid 12946 **Fx:**523-9589
(315) 435-2470 .. **Doran,** Matthew J '94 %DA -505 S State -Syracuse 13202 **Fx:**435-3969
(585) 428-5210 .. **Doran,** Michl R '89 %Pub Def -10 N Fitzhugh -Rchstr 14614 **Fx:**428-2234
(716) 884-2000 .. **Doran & Murphy** -1234 Delaware Av -Buffalo 14209 **Fx:**884-2146
(914) 237-7393 .. **Doran,** Peter M '97 -832 McLean Av -Ynkrs 10704 **Fx:**237-7394
(518) 464-6770 .. **Doran,** Robt F '57 OfCnsl Thorn GT&B,LLP -5 Wembley Ct Bx15054 -Albany 12212
(718) 968-6228 .. **Dorancy,** Rubain J '06 %NYC Dept Educ -5619 Flatlands Av -Brklyn 11234
(212) 608-5300 .. **D'Orazio,** Bernard '86 -100 Lafayette -NY 10013 **Fx:**608-5398
(518) 487-7600 .. **D'Orazio,** Giovanna '07 %Whiteman O&H LLP -1 Commerce Plz -Albany 12260
(845) 331-2300 .. **D'Orazio,** Marino '87 -4687 Atwood Rd -Stone Rdg 12484 **Fx:**657-1457
(718) 243-6250 .. **D'Orazio,** Nicole M '03 Leg Aid -111 Lvngstn -Brklyn 11201 **Fx:**237-8737
(212) 788-0842 .. **D'Orazio,** Vincent '86 %Law Dept -100 Church -NY 10007 **Fx:**788-0367
(516) 365-9802 .. **Dorchak,** Fredk J '80 (Collard & R,PC) -1077 Nrthrn Blvd -Roslyn 11576
(212) 705-7000 .. **Dorchak,** Joshua '01 (Bingham M LLP) -399 Park Av -NY 10022
(212) 977-9700 .. **Dore,** David M '05 Phillips N LLP -666 5th Av -NY 10103
(516) 465-8090 .. **Dore,** Elizabeth A '98 %North Shore-LIJ Hlth Systm -145 Community Dr -Gt Neck 11021 **Fx:**465-8013
(212) 450-4000 .. **Dore,** Thos Patrick Jr. '80 (Davis P&W LLP) -450 Lex Av -NY 10017
(716) 566-2800 .. **Doren,** Robt A '76 (Bond S&K,PLLC) -40 Fountian Plz -Buffalo 14202
(516) 374-6600 .. **Doret,** Peter '73 OfCnsl Hein W&K -825 E Gate Blvd -Gdn Cty 11530
(716) 763-7023 .. **Dorey,** Thos A '77 -Bx247 -Lakewd 14750 **Fx:**(800) 450-4176
(914) 381-7600 .. **Dorf,** Jon A '91 (Dorf Law Firm,LLP) -740 W Bstn Post Rd -Mamaroneck 10543 **Fx:**381-7608
(212) 264-8056 .. **Dorf,** Robt C '73 SSA-OHA -26 Fed Plz -NY 10278 **Fx:**264-8633
(516) 877-1845 .. **Dorf,** Sheryll Borsuk '84 -114 Old Cntry Rd -Mineola 11501 **Fx:**678-0777
(718) 875-6060 .. **Dorfman,** Alfred '53 (Kuslansky & D) -26 Court -Brklyn 11242
(516) 379-0500 .. **Dorfman,** Alvin '58 (Dorfman & D) -72 Guy Lombardo Av -Freeprt 11520 **Fx:**378-4929
(845) 290-9596 .. **Dorfman,** Anne L '00 -55 Old Tpk Rd -Nanuet 10954
(212) 951-6558 .. **Dorfman,** Barry '73 %NYS Ed Dept-OLS -475 Park Av S -NY 10016 **Fx:**951-6573
(212) 545-1921 .. **Dorfman,** Bernard '39 OfCnsl Fischer PT&R,PC -250 W 57th -NY 10107
(646) 366-4863 .. **Dorfman,** Beth Charney '86 Bk of America -50 Rckfllr Plz -NY 10020
(845) 353-3500 .. **Dorfman,** Burton I '79 (Dorfman K&C LLP) -51 N Bway -Nyack 10960
(212) 596-9000 .. **Dorfman,** Howard L '76 Cnsl Ropes & G LLP -1211 Av of Amer -NY 10036
(516) 379-0500 .. **Dorfman,** Isaac '98 (Dorfman & D) -72 Guy Lombardo Av -Freeprt 11520 **Fx:**378-4929
(914) 834-2775 .. **Dorfman,** Jerold W '63 -1328 Bstn Post Rd -Larchmnt 10538 **Fx:**834-4503
(518) 474-4453 .. **Dorfman,** John E '71 %MHLS -40 Steuben -Albany 12207 **Fx:**473-5849
(845) 353-3500 .. **Dorfman Knoebel & Conway LLP** -51 N Bway -Nyack 10960 **Fx:**353-3529
(516) 334-4500 .. **Dorfman,** Leo '09 %Sokoloff S LLP -355 Post Av -Westbury 11590 **Fx:**334-4501
(516) 802-0878 .. **Dorfman,** Martin S '70 -100 Crsswys Park W -Woodbury 11797 **Fx:**802-0838
(845) 215-9183 .. **Dorfman,** Michl N '70 -55 Old Tpk Rd -Nanuet 10954
(518) 431-0247 .. **Dorfman,** Nathaniel J '03 %US Atty -445 Bway -Albany 12207 **Fx:**431-0249
(646) 522-0011 .. **Dorfman,** Rina J '04 -383 Grand -NY 10002
(518) 447-3200 .. **Dorfman,** Robt L '54 OfCnsl McNamee LT&W,PC -677 Bway -Albany 12207
(212) 732-5800 .. **Dorfman,** Steven B '97 %Friedman & M LLP -233 Bway -NY 10279
(212) 326-3939 .. **Dorfman,** Victoria '08 %Jones D -222 E 41st -NY 10017
(212) 458-3206 .. **Dorgan,** Susan M '89 AIG -175 Water -NY 10038
(212) 906-1200 .. **Dorian,** J Christopher '80 %Latham & W -885 3rd Av -NY 10022
(212) 733-1898 .. **Dorigo,** Andrea '02 Pfizer, Inc -150 E 42nd -NY 10017
(212) 552-5181 .. **Dorin,** Jeremy S '06 JP Morgan Chase Bk,NA -1 Chase Manh Plz -NY 10005
(212) 962-2450 .. **Doris,** Lawr A '81 (Flynn G&D) -80 Maiden Ln -NY 10038
(773) 969-6265 .. **Dorish,** Sterling M '06 Sunterra Horiculture (US) Inc -666 Greenwich -NY 10014
(212) 922-1800 .. **Dorkey,** Chas E III '75 (McKenna L&A) -230 Park Av -NY 10169
(518) 457-2070 .. **Dorman,** Arnold '75 %Dept of Tax & Fin -Bldg 9 State Campus -Albany 12227 **Fx:**457-6131
(718) 792-0444 .. **Dorman,** Beverly J '74 %MHLS -1500 Waters Pl -Bronx 10461 **Fx:**597-7385
(212) 759-4888 .. **Dorman,** Christopher G '91 (Phillips L LLP) -437 Mad Av -NY 10022
(518) 452-0584 .. **Dorman,** Deborah Landau '81 Eastern NY Coalition of Auto Retailers,Inc -4 Pine West Plz -Albany 12205
(212) 541-2000 .. **Dorman,** Jay M '82 (Bryan C LLP) -1290 Av of Amer -NY 10104
(718) 274-2700 .. **Dorman,** Larry '80 (L Dorman,PC) -25-28 Bway -Astoria 11106 **Fx:**204-5565
(914) 235-0703 .. **Dorman,** Lisa Boslow '83 -29 Rolling Way -New Rchll 10804
(212) 715-9100 .. **Dorman,** Madelyn R '09 %Kramer LN&F,LLP -1177 Av of Amer -NY 10036
(646) 230-7444 .. **Dorman,** Mary D '75 -134 W 26th -NY 10001
(212) 753-7500 .. **Dorman,** Neal T '72 (Hartman & C LLP) -488 Mad Av -NY 10022
(212) 455-2000 .. **Dorment,** Genevieve M '09 %Simpson T&B LLP -425 Lex Av -NY 10017
(212) 601-2680 .. **Dorn,** Angela K '99 (Gonzalez S&H LLP) -350 5th Av -NY 10118
(212) 969-3000 .. **Dorn,** Jacqueline M '07 %Proskauer R LLP -1585 Bway -NY 10036
(716) 688-3800 .. **Dorn,** John W '72 OfCnsl Nesper F&D,LLP -501 JJ Audobon Pkwy -Amherst 14228
(212) 627-8100 .. **Dorn,** Richd L '60 (Levy R,PC) -80 8th Av -NY 10011
(718) 539-8448 .. **Dorn,** Sheldon P '87 %DMV -30-56 Whitestone Expwy -Flushng 11354
(315) 472-8533 .. **Dorn,** Tricia M '10 Finocchio & E -430 E Genesee -Syracuse 13202
(607) 255-2796 .. **Dorn,** Valerie C '91 %Cornell Univ -300 CCC Bldg-Grdn Av -Ithaca 14853 **Fx:**255-2794
(718) 670-3224 .. **Dornagon,** Mandares M '94 -78-48 223rd -Oakland Gdns 11364
(718) 707-9997 .. **Dornan,** Eamonn S '97 (Dornan & Assoc,PLLC) -10-40 Jackson Av -LIC 11101 **Fx:**228-5940
(516) 357-3700 .. **Dornbaum,** Michl L '86 (Cullen and D LLP) -100 Q Roosevelt Blvd -Gdn Cty 11530
(212) 759-3300 .. **Dornbush,** Darwin C '54 (Dornbush SS&V,LLP) -747 3rd Av -NY 10017
(212) 759-3300 .. **Dornbush,** Jerold P '85 (Dornbush SS&V,LLP) -747 3rd Av -NY 10017
(212) 759-3300 .. **Dornbush Schaeffer Strongin & Venaglia,LLP** -747 3rd Av -NY 10017 **Fx:**753-7673
(518) 966-4412 .. **Dorner,** Dale '74 -E Main Bx70 -Greenvll 12083 **Fx:**966-8258
(516) 746-6064 .. **Dorney,** Colin '74 -141 Park Av -Williston Pk 11596
(718) 238-6500 .. **Dorney,** Edw R '77 %Connors & S,PC -7408 5th Av -Brklyn 11209
(631) 236-9877 .. **Dornfeld,** Danl S '94 (Dornfeld & N,LLP) -145 Marcus Blvd -Hauppauge 11788
(212) 740-4004 .. **Dornfeld,** Glenn E '83 -156 Pinehurst Av -NY 10033
(631) 236-9877 .. **Dornfeld & Nasis, LLP** -145 Marcus Blvd -Hauppauge 11788 **Fx:**236-9871
(212) 683-7100 .. **D'Oro,** Attilio A '01 %Gallo V&K,LLP -90 Broad -NY 10004
(212) 813-8800 .. **Doron,** Danl J '03 %Goodwin P LLP -620 8th Av -NY 10018
(212) 776-5034 .. **Doron,** Oren D '02 %NYC Housing Auth -250 Bway -NY 10007 **Fx:**776-5039
(212) 521-5400 .. **Doron,** Uri '01 (Reed S LLP) -599 Lex Av -NY 10022
(212) 374-3445 .. **Dorosin,** Aimee W '01 %NYC Dept Educ-OLS -52 Chmbrs -NY 10007 **Fx:**374-5939
(212) 558-6668 .. **Dorr,** Kevin W '01 %Foley SO&W -100 William -NY 10038
(315) 793-2370 .. **Dorr,** Megan E '05 %MHLS -207 Genesee -Utica 13501 **Fx:**793-2371
(516) 486-4640 .. **Dorr,** Shayne L '00 %Cherry E&K,LLP -1 Old Cntry Rd -Carle Pl 11514
(315) 671-6706 .. **Dorr,** Wm L '65 Excellus Blue Cross Blue Shield -344 S Warren -Syracuse 13202 **Fx:**671-6700
(347) 534-3728 .. **Dorra,** Michl A '00 US Probation Dept -75 Clinton -Brklyn 11201
(516) 742-5363 .. **Dorris,** Howard S '52 -377 Oak -Gdn Cty 11530 **Fx:**742-0908
(212) 698-3500 .. **Dorris,** Malcolm S '81 (Dechert LLP) -1095 Av of Amer -NY 10036
(585) 232-6500 .. **Dorritie,** Megan K '04 %Harter S&E LLP -1600 Bausch & Lomb Pl -Rchstr 14604
(212) 867-7579 .. **Dorros,** Torin A '02 -600 3rd Av -NY 10016
(516) 623-1111 .. **Dorry,** Michl J '93 -2174 Hewlett Av Bx801 -Merrick 11566 **Fx:**623-0758
(845) 358-9700 .. **Dorsainvil,** Laurie A '00 %D Bertolino -407 N Highland Av -Upper Nyack 10960 **Fx:**358-9707
(212) 676-6219 .. **Dorsch,** Eric M '99 Business Integrity Commission -100 Church -NY 10007 **Fx:**676-6204
(212) 998-6233 .. **Dorsen,** Norman '53 %NYU Law Schl -40 Wshngtn Sq S -NY 10012 **Fx:**995-4030
(212) 208-4200 .. **Dorsett,** Brenda K '97 Liberty Int'l Underwriters -55 Water -NY 10041
(212) 368-9885 .. **Dorsett,** Janine D '95 -Bx230385 -NY 10023 **Fx:**898-1140
(212) 309-1000 .. **Dorsey,** Dee A '04 (Hunton & W) -200 Park Av -NY 10166
(518) 583-0500 .. **Dorsey,** James B '53 -5 S Collins Ter -Saratoga Spgs 12866 **Fx:**583-9853
(518) 583-0500 .. **Dorsey,** James B Jr. '95 -42 Saratoga Cir -Saratoga Spgs 12866 **Fx:**583-9853
(315) 676-7314 .. **Dorsey,** Lonnie M '06 %Sheats & Assoc,PC -9650 Brewertn Rd Bx820 -Brewertn 13029 **Fx:**676-7189
(518) 584-5205 .. **Dorsey,** Matthew J '97 OfCnsl O'Connell & A -1 Court -Saratoga Spgs 12866 **Fx:**584-5441
(212) 474-1000 .. **Dorsey,** Nicholas A '10 %Cravath S&M LLP -825 8th Av -NY 10019
(585) 546-5530 .. **Dorsey,** Philip A '82 %Thomson West -50 E Broad -Rchstr 14694
(518) 884-4770 .. **Dorsey,** Stephen M '87 %Cnty Atty -Cnty Mncpl Ctr -Ballston Spa 12020 **Fx:**884-4720
(914) 761-7190 .. **Dorsey,** Thos P '56 %ODAR-SSA -75 S Bway -White Plns 10601 **Fx:**682-7006
(212) 415-9200 .. **Dorsey & Whitney LLP** -250 Park Av -NY 10177 **Fx:**953-7201
(973) 596-4673 .. **Dorsi,** Carla N '03 %Gibbons PC -1 Penn Plz -NY 10119 **Fx:**639-8312
(212) 869-3222 .. **Dorsky,** Adam B '01 -1103 45th Av -LIC 11101
(516) 227-3541 .. **Dorsky,** Michl H '77 %DMV -801 Axinn Av -Gdn Cty 11530
(212) 723-6275 .. **Dorsky,** Risa I '96 Citigroup Global Mrkts -390 Greenwich -NY 10013
(212) 436-3155 .. **Dorsky,** Stuart '79 %Deloitte & Touche LLP -2 World Fncl Ctr -NY 10281

(518) 218-1200 .. **Dorsman**, Abraham B III '80 Dorsman & D -7 Exec Centre Dr -Albany 12203
(518) 218-1200 .. **Dorsman & Dorsman** -7 Exec Centre Dr -Albany 12203 **Fx:**456-6709
(212) 371-8300 .. **Dorton**, Katina J '88 Needham & Co -445 Park Av -NY 10022 **Fx:**751-1450
(212) 735-3000 .. **Dorum**, Michl D '92 (Skadden ASM&F LLP) -4 Times Sq -NY 10036
(212) 262-2390 .. **Dory**, Nicole B '07 %Connell F LLP -888 7th Av -NY 10106
(315) 474-7447 .. **Dosa**, Jos D '78 -333 E Onondaga -Syracuse 13202 **Fx:**474-0425
(518) 474-7330 .. **Dosanjh**, Rajit S '01 %Dept of Law -The Cptl -Albany 12224
(716) 858-2424 .. **Doscher**, John C '78 %DA -25 Delaware Av -Buffalo 14202 **Fx:**858-7425
(914) 698-8432 .. **Doses**, Michelle D '95 -953 W Bstn Post Rd -Mamaroneck 10543
(212) 297-5800 .. **Doshi**, Amish R '98 SrCnsl Day P LLP -7 Times Sq -NY 10036
(212) 880-3800 .. **Doshi**, Amy J '09 %Akerman S -335 Mad Av -NY 10017
(212) 849-7000 .. **Doshi**, Hetal J '09 %Quinn EU&S,LLP -51 Mad Av -NY 10010
(212) 621-7287 .. **Doshi**, Priti H '04 Assoc Press -450 W 33rd -NY 10001
(607) 754-3615 .. **Doshi**, Purnima '87 -505 African Rd -Vestal 13850 **Fx:**754-6010
(212) 886-3000 .. **Dosik**, Jill L '95 %GTFH-Public Relations -114 5th Av -NY 10011
(212) 788-1330 .. **Doskow**, Ellen '76 %Law Dept -100 Church -NY 10007 **Fx:**788-0367
(212) 848-4000 .. **Dosman**, E Alexandra '06 %Shearman & S LLP -599 Lex Av -NY 10022
(914) 699-7230 .. **Dos Santos**, Peter I '00 Mt Vernon Urban Renewal -City Hall-Roosevelt Sq -Mt Vernon 10550 **Fx:**699-1435
(914) 376-3757 .. **Dos Santos**, Sandra M '09 %Leg Srvcs -30 S Bway -Ynkrs 10701 **Fx:**376-8739
(631) 232-2400 .. **Dosso**, Maria '88 %Nassau/Sfflk Law Srv -1757 Vets Hwy -Islandia 11749 **Fx:**232-2489
(212) 450-4000 .. **Dostal**, Derek '07 %Davis P&W LLP -450 Lex Av -NY 10017
(212) 480-6786 .. **Doti**, Maria I '89 %DHCR -25 Beaver -NY 10004 **Fx:**480-7416
(212) 752-5258 .. **Dotoli**, Nicholas J '07 %Schwartz SE&C LLC -845 3rd Av -NY 10022
(212) 483-0105 .. **Dotro**, Lorna A '98 OfCnsl Coughlin D LLP -88 Pine-Wall St Plz -NY 10005
(716) 828-0745 .. **Dotterweich**, Jos J '96 Ficel Transport,Inc -310 Lk Av -Blasdell 14219
(212) 265-7200 .. **Dotts**, Brianne N '09 %Mayerson & Assoc -330 W 38th -NY 10018 **Fx:**265-1735
(212) 980-9600 .. **Doty**, Carol S '00 (Kaufman B&R) -120 Bway -NY 10271
(212) 848-4000 .. **Doty**, Curtis A '97 Cnsl Shearman & S LLP -599 Lex Av -NY 10022
(631) 734-6648 .. **Doty**, Deborah '85 -West Crk Av Bx1181 -Cutchogue 11935
(212) 818-9200 .. **Doty**, James I '07 %Satterlee SB&B LLP -230 Park Av -NY 10169
(212) 770-7015 .. **Doty**, Virginia M '77 %AIG -70 Pine -NY 10270
(315) 425-2700 .. **Dotzler**, Anne B '08 %Hiscock & B,LLP -One Park Pl -Syracuse 13202
(315) 435-2470 .. **Dotzler**, Matthew D '08 %DA -505 S State -Syracuse 13202 **Fx:**435-3969
(212) 610-6300 .. **Double**, Stephen J '99 Cnsl Allen & O -1221 Av of Amer -NY 10020
(212) 264-8566 .. **Douchy**, Evalyn P '96 US DHS -26 Fed Plz -NY 10278
(212) 735-3000 .. **Doud**, Randall H '82 (Skadden ASM&F LLP) -4 Times Sq -NY 10036
(516) 742-8058 .. **Doud**, Robt H '89 %Abamont & Assoc -200 Grdn City Plz Bx9250 -Gdn Cty 11530 **Fx:**742-7308
(212) 924-3191 .. **Doudna**, Patricia E '88 -103 5th Av -NY 10003
(212) 610-6300 .. **Doueck**, Morris '07 %Allen & O -1221 Av of Amer -NY 10020
(212) 832-5455 .. **Douenias**, Steven '92 -485 Mad Av -NY 10022
(212) 858-7576 .. **Dougall**, Keir N '92 -140 Bway -NY 10005
(212) 770-3891 .. **Dougall**, Wendy M '94 AIG -72 Wall -NY 10005
(212) 858-1000 .. **Dougan**, Hugh M '61 (Pillsbury WSP LLP) -1540 Bway -NY 10036
(212) 335-9000 .. **Dougan-Akuoku**, Angela '05 %DA -1 Hogan Pl -NY 10013
(212) 216-8000 .. **Dougherty**, Anthony '91 (Tarter K&D LLP) -1350 Bway -NY 10018
(212) 940-8758 .. **Dougherty**, C Michl '91 %Katten MR LLP -575 Mad Av -NY 10022
(718) 286-1500 .. **Dougherty**, Donna B '87 %Leg Srvcs -97-77 Qns Blvd -Rego Pk 11374 **Fx:**275-5352
(212) 610-6300 .. **Dougherty**, Edw J '09 %Allen & O -1221 Av of Amer -NY 10020
(212) 994-9963 .. **Dougherty**, Ellen M '03 OfCnsl Federman S LLP -220 E 42nd -NY 10017 **Fx:**685-5199
(914) 263-7955 .. **Dougherty**, Eugene R '91 -1 Water -White Plns 10601 **Fx:**591-8235
(585) 546-5530 .. **Dougherty**, Francis M '76 %Thomson West -50 E Broad -Rchstr 14694
(212) 548-2100 .. **Dougherty**, J Kevin '91 (McGuire W LLP) -1345 Av of Amer -NY 10105
(212) 238-4800 .. **Dougherty**, James T '09 %Landman CB&F,PC -120 Bway -NY 10271
(516) 248-2424 .. **Dougherty**, James W '72 JW Dougherty,PC -1122 Franklin Av -Gdn Cty 11530 **Fx:**248-1302
(716) 847-8400 .. **Dougherty**, Jennifer '05 %Phillips L LLP -3400 HSBC Ctr -Buffalo 14203
(212) 816-4464 .. **Dougherty**, John A '83 Citigroup -388 Greenwich -NY 10013
(518) 436-0751 .. **Dougherty**, Jos M '07 %Hinman S PC -121 State -Albany 12207
(315) 435-2170 .. **Dougherty**, Kathleen M '85 %Cnty Atty -421 Mntgmry -Syracuse 13202 **Fx:**435-5729
(212) 571-0068 .. **Dougherty**, Linda M '08 %Ullman S&U,LLP -299 Bway -NY 10007
(212) 530-5000 .. **Dougherty**, Marcus J '01 (Milbank TH&M LLP) -1 Chase Manh Plz -NY 10005
(518) 465-0400 .. **Dougherty**, Margaret E '09 %O'Connor OB&F,PC -20 Corp Wds Blvd -Albany 12211
(212) 326-3939 .. **Dougherty**, Marguerite S '01 %Jones D -222 E 41st -NY 10017
(516) 248-4817 .. **Dougherty**, Maureen '86 (Comerford & D,LLP) -1122 Franklin Av -Gdn Cty 11530
(212) 335-4500 .. **Dougherty**, Meghan K '09 %DLA Piper LLP -1251 Av of Amer -NY 10020
(212) 888-3033 .. **Dougherty**, Michl J '76 (Becker GM&M LLP) -299 Park Av -NY 10171
(212) 504-6000 .. **Dougherty**, Michl P '86 SpclCnsl Cadwalader W&T LLP -1 World Fncl Ctr -NY 10281
(212) 335-9000 .. **Dougherty**, Michl T '99 %DA -1 Hogan Pl -NY 10013
(212) 889-2300 .. **Dougherty Ryan Giuffra Zambito & Hession** -131 E 38th -NY 10016 **Fx:**889-1288
(516) 223-2621 .. **Dougherty & Schneider** -625 W Merrick Rd -Baldwin 11510 **Fx:**868-3870
(516) 223-2621 .. **Dougherty**, Thos P '61 (Dougherty & S) -625 W Merrick Rd -Baldwin 11510
(516) 223-2621 .. **Dougherty**, Timothy M '82 (Dougherty & S) -625 W Merrick Rd -Baldwin 11510
(212) 354-3800 .. **Dougherty**, Wm F '81 (Burke & P) -100 Park Av -NY 10017
(518) 465-3345 .. **Dougherty**, Wm J '63 -61 Patroon Pl -Loudonvll 12211
(212) 455-2000 .. **Dougherty**, Wm R '88 (Simpson T&B LLP) -425 Lex Av -NY 10017
(845) 938-3724 .. **Doughty**, Lori L '94 %US Military Academy -OSJA Bldg 606 -West Pnt 10996
(212) 570-9885 .. **Doughty**, Tatyana '74 -225 E 73rd -NY 10021 **Fx:**570-9885
(845) 876-4047 .. **Douglas**, Angela M '06 %J Martin -187 E Market Bx649 -Rhinebeck 12572 **Fx:**876-3906
(646) 610-6288 .. **Douglas**, Beth T '97 NYPD -1 Police Plz -NY 10038
(212) 248-2217 .. **Douglas**, Blair H '05 Gotham Realty Holdings -30 Broad -NY 10004
(716) 439-4444 .. **Douglas**, David C '76 (Douglas & S) -260 East Av -Lockprt 14094 **Fx:**439-4452
(212) 935-3131 .. **Douglas**, David S '86 (Gallet D&B,LLP) -845 3rd Av -NY 10022
(212) 815-1818 .. **Douglas**, Dietrich L '06 DC 37 MELS -125 Barclay -NY 10007 **Fx:**815-1343
(718) 455-3072 .. **Douglas**, Donna M '92 Family Srvc Ntwrk of NY -1420 Bushwick Av -Brklyn 11207 **Fx:**455-3036
(518) 434-8337 .. **Douglas**, Edw M '81 OfCnsl Rice & J -111 Wshngtn Av -Albany 12210
(914) 948-4500 .. **Douglas**, Elizabeth A '08 %O'Connor MCD&O -1 Barker Av -White Plns 10601
(212) 865-5249 .. **Douglas**, Franklin '89 -945 W End Av -NY 10025
(212) 566-7500 .. **Douglas**, Gary J '89 (Douglas & L) -111 John -NY 10038
(718) 451-4900 .. **Douglas**, Gerald P '98 (Douglas & Assoc,PC) -4517 Av D -Brklyn 11203 **Fx:**451-1660
(516) 745-0777 .. **Douglas**, James J '83 J Douglas,PC -585 Stewart Av -Gdn Cty 11530 **Fx:**745-0004
(212) 735-3000 .. **Douglas**, James M '82 (Skadden ASM&F LLP) -4 Times Sq -NY 10036
(212) 673-2895 .. **Douglas**, Jo Ann '85 -170 2nd Av -NY 10003 **Fx:**673-0945
(212) 450-4000 .. **Douglas**, John L '09 (Davis P&W LLP) -450 Lex Av -NY 10017
(516) 357-3700 .. **Douglas**, Kathleen L '86 (Cullen and D LLP) -100 Q Roosevelt Blvd -Gdn Cty 11530
(212) 566-7500 .. **Douglas & London** -111 John -NY 10038 **Fx:**566-7501
(212) 407-4000 .. **Douglas**, Mark A '10 %Loeb & L,LLP -345 Park Av -NY 10154
(212) 668-2304 .. **Douglas**, Mark G '89 %Hon S Bernstein -1 Bowling Grn -NY 10004
(914) 725-5123 .. **Douglas**, Paul A '61 -670 Wht Plns Rd -Scarsdale 10583 **Fx:**725-7724
(212) 612-4000 .. **Douglas**, Paul P '85 %Chubb Grp -55 Water -NY 10041
(212) 450-4000 .. **Douglas**, Peter R '76 (Davis P&W LLP) -450 Lex Av -NY 10017
(212) 326-3939 .. **Douglas**, Philip Le B '76 (Jones D) -222 E 41st -NY 10017
(212) 406-1600 .. **Douglas**, Preston J '78 (Gurfein D LLP) -11 Park Pl -NY 10007
(914) 745-4000 .. **Douglas**, Stephen A '98 %Towers Watson -100 Summit Lk Dr -Valhalla 10595
(646) 541-4225 .. **Douglas**, Stephen H '94 Barclays Capital -200 Park Av -NY 10166
(646) 442-3100 .. **Douglas**, Tanya M '94 %Legal Srvcs -90 John -NY 10038 **Fx:**(212) 227-9798
(516) 357-3700 .. **Douglas**, Thos J Jr. '78 (Cullen and D LLP) -100 Q Roosevelt Blvd -Gdn Cty 11530
(212) 876-5500 .. **Douglas**, Traci L '98 %Neighborhood Def Srv -317 Lenox Av -NY 10027 **Fx:**876-5586
(212) 641-3813 .. **Douglas-Hamilton**, Margaret H '81 Schroder US Holding Inc -875 3rd Av -NY 10022 **Fx:**641-3801
(212) 508-6700 .. **Douglas-Heck**, Shahkira '04 %Tannenbaum HS&H LLP -900 3rd Av -NY 10022
(212) 335-4500 .. **Douglass**, Brandon L '09 %DLA Piper LLP -1251 Av of Amer -NY 10020
(212) 695-3800 .. **Douglass**, Catherine J '77 %inMotion,Inc -70 W 36th -NY 10018 **Fx:**695-9519
(585) 272-0540 .. **Douglass**, Cristina A '06 %Thomas & S LLP -693 East Av -Rchstr 14607
(212) 554-7800 .. **Douglass**, Lori A '88 (Moses & S LLP) -405 Lex Av -NY 10174
(212) 813-5900 .. **Douglass**, Susan U '81 (Fross ZL&Z,PC) -866 UN Plz -NY 10017
(212) 672-6659 .. **Douglass**, Wm F '03 Headway Corp Resrcs Inc -317 Mad Av -NY 10017 **Fx:**672-6699
(212) 310-8000 .. **Dougnac**, Rachel L '09 %Weil G&M LLP -767 5th Av -NY 10153
(516) 355-9600 .. **Doukas**, Barbara '98 %Friedman HK&P -3000 Marcus Av -Lk Success 11042
(212) 450-4000 .. **Doulamis**, John K '05 %Davis P&W LLP -450 Lex Av -NY 10017
(212) 336-2000 .. **Doumar**, Dahlia Balsam '94 Cnsl Patterson BW&T LLP -1133 Av of Amer -NY 10036
(845) 340-3232 .. **Dourdeville**, Denise Y '78 %Pub Def -18 Lucas Av Bx1800 -Kingston 12402 **Fx:**340-3744
(518) 565-4770 .. **Douthat**, Jaime A '05 %DA -137 Margaret -Plattsbrgh 12901 **Fx:**565-4777
(518) 566-0833 .. **Douthat**, Matthew E '04 -187 Margaret -Plattsbrgh 12901 **Fx:**314-1544
(212) 837-6000 .. **Douvas**, George S '01 Cnsl Hughes H&R LLP -1 Bttry Pk Plz -NY 10004
(212) 637-2327 .. **Douvas**, Maria E '99 %US Atty -1 St Andrews Plz -NY 10007
(315) 474-7541 .. **Dove**, Jeffrey A '85 (Menter R&T,PC) -308 Maltbie -Syracuse 13204
(212) 594-5300 .. **Dover**, Anna C '06 (Milberg LLP) -1 Penn Plz -NY 10119
(607) 737-2940 .. **Dovi**, Brian '83 %Hon P Buckley -Cnty Cthse -Elmira 14901 **Fx:**732-3343
(585) 263-1000 .. **Dovi**, Danl F '10 %Nixon P LLP -1100 Clinton Sq -Rchstr 14604
(845) 291-2050 .. **Dovico**, Jessica M '06 %DA -255-275 Main -Goshen 10924 **Fx:**291-2085
(212) 312-2260 .. **Dow**, Erin E '07 Leg Aid -60 Lafayette -NY 10013 **Fx:**349-0874
(518) 474-7330 .. **Dow**, Francis V '53 %Dept of Law -The Cptl -Albany 12224
(212) 836-8000 .. **Dow**, Karen R '00 %Kaye S LLP -425 Park Av -NY 10022
(518) 455-2681 .. **Dow**, Kenneth J '09 NYS Ofc of Majority Cnsl -The Cptl -Albany 12247
(212) 490-9100 .. **Dow**, Mary K '10 %Condon & F LLP -7 Times Sq -NY 10036
(845) 357-2660 .. **Dow**, Scott A '89 (Kornfeld RN&S) -46 Wshngtn Av Bx177 -Suffern 10901
(212) 407-4000 .. **Dowd**, Angela M '89 (Loeb & L,LLP) -345 Park Av -NY 10154
(914) 289-2324 .. **Dowd**, Barbara C '83 %Ct of Claims -140 Grand -White Plns 10601

(212) 813-8800 .. **Dowd,** Betsy Kingsbury '03 %Goodwin P LLP -620 8th Av -NY 10018
(646) 855-0790 .. **Dowd,** Brendan '00 Bank of America -1 Bryant Park -NY 10036
(631) 265-7200 .. **Dowd,** Colleen F '02 %Russo KW&C -400 Townline Rd -Hauppauge 11788
(212) 903-9000 .. **Dowd,** Elizabeth M '08 %Linklaters -1345 Av of Amer -NY 10105
(516) 741-0657 .. **Dowd,** James L '75 -180 Concord -E Williston 11596
(212) 713-3892 .. **Dowd,** James P '78 UBS -1285 Av of Amer -NY 10019
(212) 820-7700 .. **Dowd,** Jennifer A '03 %Boundas SW&B,LLC -1 Bttry Pk Plz -NY 10004
(718) 268-6963 .. **Dowd,** Joanne '81 -67-84 Dartmth -Frst Hlls 11375
(516) 921-1144 .. **Dowd,** John A '58 (Dowd & D) -63 Cherry Ln -Syosset 11791 **Fx:**921-5987
(845) 298-2870 .. **Dowd,** John F '93 Jacoby & M,LLP -1778 South Rd -Wappingers Fls 12590 **Fx:**298-1476
(607) 723-5341 .. **Dowd,** John G '80 (Hinman H&K,LLP) -80 Exchange Bx5250 -Bnghmtn 13902
(518) 463-7784 .. **Dowd,** John J '98 %Dreyer B LLP -75 Columbia -Albany 12210
(516) 921-1144 .. **Dowd,** Karen M '88 (Dowd & D) -63 Cherry Ln -Syosset 11791 **Fx:**921-5987
(212) 609-6800 .. **Dowd,** Martin F '85 (McCarter & E,LLP) -245 Park Av -NY 10167
(212) 751-1640 .. **Dowd,** Michl G '67 -112 Mad Av -NY 10016 **Fx:**398-2693
(716) 754-7865 .. **Dowd,** Michl J '89 -920 Center Bx1238 -Lewiston 14092
(516) 470-6000 .. **Dowd,** Patricia A '94 %Briarcliff College -1055 Stewart Av -Bethpage 11714
(212) 455-2000 .. **Dowd,** Patrick M '07 %Simpson T&B LLP -425 Lex Av -NY 10017
(212) 682-8811 .. **Dowd,** Raymond J '93 (Dunnington B&M LLP) -1359 Bway -NY 10018
(716) 847-3004 .. **Dowd,** Susan E '84 %OTDA -295 Main -Buffalo 14203 **Fx:**847-3699
(718) 590-2000 .. **Dowdy,** Michl L '02 %DA -198 E 161st -Bronx 10451 **Fx:**590-6477
(212) 771-9356 .. **Dowe,** Steven R '95 CIT Grp Inc -505 5th Av -NY 10017
(516) 764-1100 .. **Dower,** Barbara Ann Marra '99 Signature Grp -950 Franklin Av -Gdn Cty 11530
(315) 422-7000 .. **Dower,** Gary L '78 %Pyramid -4 Clinton Sq -Syracuse 13202 **Fx:**422-2717
(212) 856-6668 .. **Dowicz,** Christopher '90 CIBC -425 Lex Av -NY 10080
(631) 360-3056 .. **Dowis,** Lenore '88 -33 Beverly Rd -Smithtwn 11787
(212) 558-4000 .. **Dowling,** Chas T '94 (Sullivan & C LLP) -125 Broad -NY 10004
(212) 819-8200 .. **Dowling,** Donald C Jr. '06 Cnsl White & C LLP -1155 Av of Amer -NY 10036
(518) 533-3000 .. **Dowling,** Joanmarie M '03 %Bond S&K,PLLC -111 Wshngtn Av -Albany 12210
(718) 250-2000 .. **Dowling,** Joel J '08 %DA -350 Jay -Brklyn 11201 **Fx:**250-2314
(518) 474-6522 .. **Dowling,** Jos '07 %Dept Pub Srvc -3 ESP -Albany 12223
(212) 839-5300 .. **Dowling,** Madeleine J '94 (Sidley A LLP) -787 7th Av -NY 10019
(315) 671-2042 .. **Dowling,** Wm F '72 Family Ct -401 Mntgmry -Syracuse 13202 **Fx:**671-1169
(212) 909-9500 .. **Dowling,** Wm F '74 OfCnsl Wachtel & M,LLP -885 2nd Av -NY 10017
(914) 337-3838 .. **Dowling,** Wm J '63 -141 Pkwy Rd -Bronxvll 10708 **Fx:**337-3257
(212) 319-0304 .. **Downer,** Morgan E '06 %M Kramer & Assoc -150 E 58th -NY 10155 **Fx:**319-0545
(212) 571-7100 .. **Downes,** Christopher F '86 (O'Dwyer & B,LLP) -52 Duane -NY 10007
(631) 725-3630 .. **Downes,** Dennis E '72 -207 Main Bx1229 -Sag Hbr 11963 **Fx:**725-8272
(914) 681-0444 .. **Downes,** James J '69 (Rende R&D,LLP) -202 Mamaroneck Av -White Plns 10601
(212) 548-2100 .. **Downes,** Kevin P '91 (McGuire W LLP) -1345 Av of Amer -NY 10105
(212) 227-5937 .. **Downes,** Lawr C '83 Friends of Sinn Féin -45 Bway -NY 10006
(212) 558-4000 .. **Downes,** Robt W '92 (Sullivan & C LLP) -125 Broad -NY 10004
(212) 248-3232 .. **Downes,** Sean '86 -11 Hanover Sq -NY 10005
(212) 759-3300 .. **Downes,** Wm Patrick '04 %Dornbush SS&V,LLP -747 3rd Av -NY 10017
(716) 941-5423 .. **Downey,** Anne F '86 (Downey & D) -8999 Rockwood Rd -Boston 14025 **Fx:**941-6382
(716) 712-0039 .. **Downey,** Brian W '86 (Downey & D) -976-A Union Rd -W Seneca 14224 **Fx:**674-1005
(718) 741-8402 .. **Downey,** Caroline J '78 %Div of Human Rights -1 Fordham Plz -Bronx 10458 **Fx:**741-8102
(518) 862-7341 .. **Downey,** Edw B '81 Travelers -900 Watervliet Shaker Rd -Albany 12205 **Fx:**(866) 422-8263
(518) 789-4442 .. **Downey,** Edw E '74 (Downey H&M PLLC) -1 John BxZ -Millerton 12546
(518) 789-4442 .. **Downey Haab & Murphy PLLC** -1 John BxZ -Millerton 12546 **Fx:**789-3968
(607) 334-6646 .. **Downey,** James E '77 J Downey,PC -24 Fair -Norwich 13815 **Fx:**334-4132
(212) 841-7806 .. **Downey,** James S '84 %Cushman & Wakefield -51 W 52nd -NY 10019 **Fx:**698-2663
(716) 856-4000 .. **Downey,** Mariely L '04 -140 Pearl -Buffalo 14202 **Fx:**849-0349
(212) 576-7000 .. **Downey,** Richd J '09 NY Life Ins -51 Mad Av -NY 10010 **Fx:**447-0569
(212) 244-9500 .. **Downey,** Sarah D '05 %White and W LLP -1 Penn Plz -NY 10119
(212) 250-2500 .. **Downie,** David C Jr. '94 Deutsche Bank AG -60 Wall -NY 10005
(212) 506-5000 .. **Downie,** Sarah E '00 OfCnsl Orrick H&S LLP -51 W 52nd -NY 10019
(212) 872-9800 .. **Downing,** Allison L '99 %Squire S&D LLP -30 Rckfllr Plz -NY 10112
(212) 735-3000 .. **Downing,** Caitlin M '08 %Skadden ASM&F LLP -4 Times Sq -NY 10036
(212) 223-4000 .. **Downing,** Dickerson M '78 (Crowell & M LLP) -590 Mad Av -NY 10022
(716) 854-2100 .. **Downing,** Emily S '97 %Lewis & L,PC -37 Franklin -Buffalo 14202 **Fx:**854-0433
(212) 514-9190 .. **Downing,** John M '62 (Downing & P,PC) -17 Battery Pl -NY 10004
(212) 514-9190 .. **Downing,** John M Jr. '89 (Downing & P,PC) -17 Battery Pl -NY 10004
(212) 613-0300 .. **Downing,** Nancy J '02 Covenant Hse -460 W 41st -NY 10036 **Fx:**629-3756
(212) 514-9190 .. **Downing & Peck,PC** -17 Battery Pl -NY 10004 **Fx:**514-9241
(212) 701-3000 .. **Downing,** Stuart G '01 (Cahill G&R LLP) -80 Pine -NY 10005 **Fx:**269-5420
(718) 250-2000 .. **Downing,** Tracey K '06 DA -350 Jay -Brklyn 11201 **Fx:**250-2314
(914) 428-2100 .. **Downs,** Adam W '06 %Welby B&G,LLP -11 Martine Av -White Plns 10606
(212) 326-3939 .. **Downs,** Paul D '78 (Jones D) -222 E 41st -NY 10017
(716) 847-8400 .. **Doxey,** Deborah A '88 (Phillips L LLP) -3400 HSBC Ctr -Buffalo 14203
(718) 488-7500 .. **Doyaga,** David J '81 (Doyaga & S) -26 Court -Brklyn 11242 **Fx:**488-7505
(914) 699-5500 .. **Doyaga,** David J '05 -6 Gramatan Av -Mt Vernon 10550
(212) 715-1000 .. **Doyle,** A Patrick '76 (Arnold & P LLP) -399 Park Av -NY 10022
(631) 537-3100 .. **Doyle,** Brian C '01 Cnsl Farrell F,PC -2488 Montauk Hwy Bx1980 -Brdghmptn 11932
(212) 765-5070 .. **Doyle,** Brian J '08 %Fish & R,PC -153 E 53rd -NY 10022
(212) 574-1200 .. **Doyle,** Brian M '09 %Seward & K LLP -1 Bttry Pk Plz -NY 10004
(718) 796-2210 .. **Doyle & Broumand,LLP** -3152 Albany Crescent -Bronx 10463 **Fx:**884-1630
(607) 723-5341 .. **Doyle,** Casey Egan '00 %Hinman H&K,LLP -80 Exchange Bx5250 -Bnghmtn 13902
(212) 916-6492 .. **Doyle,** Christine '86 %TIAA-CREF -730 3rd Av -NY 10017
(212) 806-5400 .. **Doyle,** Christopher J '97 (Stroock &S&L LLP) -180 Maiden Ln -NY 10038
(716) 856-4000 .. **Doyle,** Christopher L '88 (Hodgson R LLP) -140 Pearl -Buffalo 14202
(212) 859-8000 .. **Doyle,** Crystal L '10 %Fried FHS&J LLP -1 NY Plz -NY 10004
(914) 948-4500 .. **Doyle,** Dennis T '68 (O'Connor MCD&O) -1 Barker Av -White Plns 10601
(518) 279-1212 .. **Doyle Doyle & Spain** -317 Brick Church Rd -Troy 12180 **Fx:**279-4153
(914) 737-0020 .. **Doyle,** Edw W '74 E Doyle -1010 Park Bx150 -Peekskill 10566 **Fx:**737-2679
(212) 723-3812 .. **Doyle,** Jacqueline R '94 Citigroup -250 West -NY 10013
(212) 455-2000 .. **Doyle,** James '09 %Simpson T&B LLP -425 Lex Av -NY 10017
(607) 776-9631 .. **Doyle,** James B III '79 %Cnty Atty -3 E Pulteney Sq -Bath 14810 **Fx:**776-4930
(212) 762-4892 .. **Doyle,** James F '96 Morgan Stanley -1221 Av of Amer -NY 10020
(518) 583-1559 .. **Doyle,** James G '98 -175 Church -Saratoga Spgs 12866 **Fx:**584-1209
(212) 728-2200 .. **Doyle,** James P '95 (Axinn V&H LLP) -114 W 47th -NY 10036
(212) 521-5400 .. **Doyle,** John H III '63 (Reed S LLP) -599 Lex Av -NY 10022
(516) 938-5250 .. **Doyle,** Jos P '50 -102 Morton Blvd -Plainvw 11803
(315) 448-8400 .. **Doyle,** Jos R H '04 %Law Dept -233 E Wshngtn -Syracuse 13202 **Fx:**448-8381
(516) 616-7770 .. **Doyle,** Josephine A '88 (J Doyle,LLC) -2001 Marcus Av -Lk Success 11042 **Fx:**437-7292
(212) 532-1886 .. **Doyle,** Joyce Ann '73 -235 E 22nd -NY 10010
(585) 546-5530 .. **Doyle,** Julie E '04 Thompson West -50 Broad E -Rchstr 14694
(585) 263-1000 .. **Doyle,** Justin P '75 SrCnsl Nixon P LLP -1100 Clinton Sq -Rchstr 14604
(212) 676-8517 .. **Doyle,** Karen L '94 %Law Dept -100 Church -NY 10007 **Fx:**788-0367
(212) 335-9000 .. **Doyle,** Kathleen V '84 %DA -1 Hogan Pl -NY 10013
(212) 208-3283 .. **Doyle,** Kevin J '88 %Ambac Assurance -1 State Street Plz -NY 10004 **Fx:**785-1178
(845) 353-2000 .. **Doyle,** Kevin M '83 OfCnsl Feerick LM PLLC -96 S Bway -Nyack 10960
(716) 845-3650 .. **Doyle,** Kevin S '92 %MHLS -438 Main -Buffalo 14202 **Fx:**874-7794
(212) 790-9200 .. **Doyle,** Kieran G '96 %Cowan L&L,PC -1133 Av of Amer -NY 10036
(518) 279-1212 .. **Doyle,** Marcia J '92 (Doyle D&S) -317 Brick Church Rd -Troy 12180
(212) 308-6100 .. **Doyle,** Mary Ann '88 Cnsl Levi L&F LLP -1185 Av of Amer -NY 10036
(585) 530-3207 .. **Doyle,** Mary H '85 %Appllt Div 4th Dept -50 East Av Ste 200 -Rchstr 14604 **Fx:**530-3247
(845) 534-0400 .. **Doyle,** Meaghan E '08 %Calhelha & D,LLC -2640 Route 9W -Cornwall 12518
(718) 796-2210 .. **Doyle,** Michl B '75 (Doyle & B,LLP) -3152 Albany Crescent -Bronx 10463
(845) 534-0400 .. **Doyle,** Michl J '80 (Calhelha & D,LLC) -2640 Route 9W -Cornwall 12518
(212) 681-0600 .. **Doyle,** Michl J '80 OfCnsl Ostrager CF&B,PC -570 Lex Av -NY 10022
(212) 803-5100 .. **Doyle,** Michl J '88 %NY Cnty Defender Srvcs -225 Bway -NY 10007 **Fx:**571-6035
(212) 859-5020 .. **Doyle,** Michl J '89 -110 Wall -NY 10005 **Fx:**898-1196
(718) 520-3745 .. **Doyle,** Myra J '77 %Hon N Berke -89-17 Sutphin Blvd -Jamaica 11435
(646) 386-3653 .. **Doyle,** Nicholas '78 Supreme Ct Spcl Referee -60 Centre -NY 10007
(212) 340-0400 .. **Doyle,** Patricia '97 %Appllt Div 1st Dept -27 Mad Av -NY 10010 **Fx:**889-4412
(516) 571-9038 .. **Doyle,** Patricia E '84 Family Ct -1200 Old Cntry Rd -Westbury 11590 **Fx:**571-9335
(212) 808-7800 .. **Doyle,** Paul F Jr. '75 (Kelley D&W LLP) -101 Park Av -NY 10178
(212) 446-4800 .. **Doyle,** Peter D '94 (Kirkland & E LLP) -153 E 53rd -NY 10022
(212) 972-6161 .. **Doyle,** Peter M Jr. '08 Cassin & C LLP -711 3rd Av -NY 10017
(646) 562-4546 .. **Doyle,** Rani E '96 Och-Ziff Capital Mgt Grp -9 W 57th -NY 10019
(631) 589-3754 .. **Doyle,** Raymond S '02 (Byrnes & D) -284 W Main -Sayvll 11782 **Fx:**589-3907
(315) 946-5459 .. **Doyle,** Richd M '79 Wayne Cnty -54 Broad -Lyons 14489 **Fx:**946-5456
(718) 520-7125 .. **Doyle,** Robt D '06 -11940 Union Tpk -Kew Gdns 11415
(631) 755-0101 .. **Doyle,** Robt W Jr. '96 (Lewis JAA,LLP) -425 Broad Hollow Rd -Melvll 11747
(212) 553-8300 .. **Doyle,** Roberta E '00 %Cohen K & Assoc -2 Park Av -NY 10016 **Fx:**553-8721
(716) 853-3801 .. **Doyle,** Rodger P Jr. '92 %Kenney SL&N,LLP -14 Lafayette Sq -Buffalo 14203
(212) 559-2820 .. **Doyle,** Rodney T '98 %Citibank -399 Park Av -NY 10022
(212) 735-3000 .. **Doyle,** Sean C '94 (Skadden ASM&F LLP) -4 Times Sq -NY 10036
(914) 641-2122 .. **Doyle,** Valerie M '91 %ITT Industries -4 W Red Oak Ln -White Plns 10604
(212) 859-8000 .. **Doyle,** Victoria J B '95 %Fried FHS&J LLP -1 NY Plz -NY 10004

(716) 852-5533 .. **Doyle,** Vincent E III '90 (Connors & V,LLP) -1000 Lbrty Bldg -Buffalo 14202
(518) 279-1212 .. **Doyle,** Wm J Jr. '58 OfCnsl Doyle D&S -317 Brick Church Rd -Troy 12180
(518) 279-1212 .. **Doyle,** Wm J III '85 (Doyle D&S) -317 Brick Church Rd -Troy 12180
(845) 354-8648 .. **Doynow,** Irving '55 -36 Plsnt Rdg Rd -Spg Vly 10977
(718) 250-2000 .. **Dozier,** Crystal E '09 %DA -350 Jay -Brklyn 11201 **Fx:**250-2314
(212) 980-9600 .. **Dozis,** Dennis J '05 %Kaufman B&R -120 Bway -NY 10271
(315) 785-2239 .. **Drabicki,** Judy '82 %DEC -317 Wshngtn -Watertwn 13601 **Fx:**785-2242
(212) 554-0400 .. **Drabkin,** Jess H '83 (Grubman I&S,PC) -152 W 57th -NY 10019
(212) 964-3400 .. **Drabkin & Margulies** -120 Bway -NY 10271 **Fx:**732-4064
(212) 964-3400 .. **Drabkin,** Ralph J '63 (Drabkin & M) -120 Bway -NY 10271
(212) 223-3900 .. **Drachler,** Dan '88 OfCnsl Zwerling S&Z,LLP -41 Mad Av -NY 10010
(914) 713-0305 .. **Drachman & Helfman** -175 Thornbury Rd -Scarsdale 10583 **Fx:**713-0198
(212) 882-5819 .. **Drachman,** Steven S '94 UBS -51 W 52nd -NY 10019
(212) 455-2000 .. **Draganovic,** Ana-Claudia B '10 %Simpson T&B LLP -425 Lex Av -NY 10017
(212) 625-9949 .. **Dragazis,** Florendia '97 %Joseph & S,LLC -2 Rector -NY 10006
(212) 436-6890 .. **Drager,** Michl J '03 Deloitte Tax LLP -2 World Fncl Ctr -NY 10281
(212) 259-8000 .. **Draghi,** John D '71 SrCnsl Dewey & L LLP -1301 Av of Amer -NY 10019
(516) 622-9200 .. **Draghi,** Thos A '90 (Westerman BEM&S,LLP) -1201 RXR Plz -Uniondale 11553
(212) 858-7710 .. **Drago,** Alexander J '82 Cnsl Nowell AKB,PA -140 Bway PMB 46028 -NY 10005
(518) 487-5460 .. **Drago,** Kelly K '07 %DA -6 Lodge -Albany 12207 **Fx:**487-5093
(212) 351-4500 .. **Drago,** Scott M '93 (Epstein B&G,PC) -250 Park Av -NY 10177
(212) 465-1500 .. **Dragovic,** Aleksandra '02 %I Gonzalez & Assoc,PC -53 W 36th -NY 10018
(212) 848-4000 .. **Dragulev,** Irina '02 Shearman & S LLP -599 Lex Av -NY 10022
(973) 596-4609 .. **Draikiwicz,** John D '83 (Gibbons PC) -1 Penn Plz -NY 10119 **Fx:**639-6269
(212) 756-2000 .. **Draim,** Ida Wurczinger '82 (Schulte R&Z LLP) -919 3rd Av -NY 10022
(585) 258-0101 .. **Drake,** Christopher D '96 Garrison Lit Mgmt Grp Ltd -120 East Av -Rchstr 14604
(585) 530-3180 .. **Drake,** Danl A '88 %Atty Grievance Comm -50 East Av -Rchstr 14604 **Fx:**530-3191
(212) 450-4000 .. **Drake,** Hannine '09 %Davis P&W LLP -450 Lex Av -NY 10017
(212) 627-0090 .. **Drake,** James W Jr. '92 %MHLS -75 Morton -NY 10014 **Fx:**645-0753
(607) 776-9631 .. **Drake,** Jessica M '04 %Cnty Atty -3 E Pulteney Sq -Bath 14810 **Fx:**776-4930
(631) 912-1222 .. **Drake,** John J '90 (J Drake,PC) -44 Woody Crest Dr -Northprt 11768 **Fx:**261-0788
(212) 225-2000 .. **Drake,** Juliet Anne '95 %Cleary GS&H -1 Lbrty Plz -NY 10006
(845) 561-0550 .. **Drake Loeb Heller Kennedy Gogerty Gaba & Rodd PLLC** -555 Hudson Valley Av -New Windsor 12553 **Fx:**561-1235
(518) 474-1331 .. **Drake,** Margaret M '87 %Ofc Mntl Health -44 Holland Av -Albany 12229 **Fx:**473-7863
(845) 561-0550 .. **Drake,** Richd J '59 (Drake LHKGG&R PLLC) -555 Hudson Valley Av -New Windsor 12553
(607) 562-3358 .. **Drake,** Robt P '81 -53 Hammond Bx113 -Big Flats 14814 **Fx:**562-3372
(212) 696-0011 .. **Drakeford,** Kevin A '99 (Drakeford Grp LLC) -114 W 47th -NY 10036 **Fx:**696-0070
(212) 486-6561 .. **Drakotos,** Markos L '97 %M&N Management Corp -5056 Bway -NY 10034 **Fx:**567-2280
(516) 876-0720 .. **Dramer,** Kenneth H '94 -99 Jericho Tpk -Jericho 11753 **Fx:**908-4613
(212) 594-0468 .. **Drangel,** Alfred '55 -317 Mad Av -NY 10017 **Fx:**874-4507
(212) 292-5390 .. **Drangel,** Jason M '93 (Epstein DB&J,LLP) -60 E 42nd -NY 10165
(845) 677-5145 .. **Dranginis,** Eileen M '76 -94 Verbank Vllg Rd -Verbank 12585
(914) 749-8536 .. **Dranginis,** Peter J Jr. '76 USI Holdings Corp -555 Plsntvll Rd -Briarclff Mnr 10510 **Fx:**(610) 537-4588
(212) 855-9156 .. **Dranikoff,** Joanna L '93 Goldman Sachs & Co -180 Maiden Ln -NY 10038
(212) 446-7000 .. **Dranikoff,** Lee P '93 %McKinsey & Co -55 E 52nd -NY 10055 **Fx:**688-9521
(631) 475-0200 .. **Dranitzke Lechtrecker Trabold & Johnson** -73 N Ocean Av Bx510 -Patchogue 11772
(212) 973-9797 .. **Dranoff,** Eric '85 (Saretsky KD&G,LLP) -475 Park Av S -NY 10016
(212) 697-0888 .. **Dranoff,** Peter D '96 Preferred Placement -370 Lex -NY 10017
(845) 398-3030 .. **Dranoff,** Sanford S '55 (Saretsky KD&G,LLP) -450 Piermont Av -Piermont 10968
(718) 237-5500 .. **Dranoff,** Sarah E '93 %Leg Srvcs -105 Court -Brklyn 11201 **Fx:**855-0733
(212) 619-5700 .. **Dranove,** Joel K '73 -225 Bway -NY 10007
(516) 286-2980 .. **Dranow,** Mitchell T '90 -114 Old Cntry Rd -Mineola 11501
(516) 921-6645 .. **Drantch,** Dawn Davidson '93 %A Pearl & Assoc,PC -6800 Jericho Tpk -Syosset 11791 **Fx:**921-6774
(718) 590-2000 .. **Drantch,** Todd A '09 %DA -198 E 161st -Bronx 10451 **Fx:**590-6477
(631) 398-1324 .. **Drapala,** Steven M '92 -1155 Little Neck Av -Bellmore 11710
(212) 883-4900 .. **Drapeau,** Kathleen A '85 (Cozen O) -277 Park Av -NY 10172
(212) 836-8000 .. **Draper,** David N '10 Kaye S LLP -425 Park Av -NY 10022
(718) 802-2763 .. **Draper,** Laura B '05 ACS-DLS -330 Jay -Brklyn 11201
(212) 295-6360 .. **Draper,** Matthew E '05 Cnsl WilmerHale -399 Park Av -NY 10022
(212) 839-5300 .. **Draper,** Robt C '08 %Sidley A LLP -787 7th Av -NY 10019
(212) 686-7700 .. **Draper,** Thos G Jr. '68 (Mazur CR&S PC) -1250 Bway -NY 10001
(212) 318-2000 .. **Drapey,** Marina '04 Bloomberg LLP -731 Lex Av -NY 10022
(212) 632-6000 .. **Drapkin,** Donald G '72 Lazard Freres -30 Rckfllr Plz -NY 10112 **Fx:**632-6060
(212) 331-5048 .. **Drapkin,** Robt T '83 %HRA-OLA -180 Water -NY 10038
(212) 775-9002 .. **Drasco,** Dennis J '82 (Lum D&P,LLC) -325 Bway -NY 10007
(212) 681-0117 .. **Drasheff,** Barbara '98 %Starr GD&R -530 5th Av -NY 10036
(212) 571-1808 .. **Dratch,** Adam D '04 %Franzblau D,PC -233 Bway -NY 10279
(212) 571-1808 .. **Dratch,** Brian M '01 %Franzblau D,PC -233 Bway -NY 10279
(212) 571-1808 .. **Dratch,** Stephen N '81 (Franzblau D,PC) -233 Bway -NY 10279
(212) 732-0707 .. **Dratel,** Joshua L '82 -2 Wall -NY 10005 **Fx:**571-3792
(212) 980-4200 .. **Drath,** Lawr I '65 (Levy HP&D,LLP) -950 3rd Av -NY 10022
(518) 465-9500 .. **Dratler,** Eric N '90 %Tabner R&K,LLP -18 Corp Wds Blvd -Albany 12211
(212) 805-3900 .. **Draucikas,** Maria L '06 %Clausen M PC -1 Chase Manh Plz -NY 10005
(716) 851-7200 .. **Draves,** Karen J '95 DEC -270 Mich Av -Buffalo 14203 **Fx:**851-7211
(631) 853-4311 .. **Draycott,** Thos E '78 %Family Ct -400 Carlton Av -Central Islip 11722
(716) 673-1381 .. **Drayo,** John D '08 %Drayo Law Ofc -31 W Main Bx345 -Fredonia 14063 **Fx:**679-0860
(716) 673-1381 .. **Drayo,** Saml L Jr. '66 Drayo Law Ofc -31 W Main Bx345 -Fredonia 14063 **Fx:**679-0860
(212) 836-8000 .. **Drayton,** Jos M '98 Cnsl Kaye S LLP -425 Park Av -NY 10022
(607) 723-9494 .. **Drazen,** Douglas W '89 -2-8 Hawley -Bnghmtn 13901 **Fx:**723-1927
(607) 723-9494 .. **Drazen,** Stanton M '62 -20 Hawley -Bnghmtn 13901 **Fx:**723-1927
(212) 940-3091 .. **Drebsky,** Dennis J '71 (Nixon P LLP) -437 Mad Av -NY 10022
(212) 953-8890 .. **Drechsler,** Beatrice K '88 (Drechsler & D LLP) -60 E 42nd -NY 10165 **Fx:**953-8899
(212) 953-8890 .. **Drechsler,** Robt H '89 (Drechsler & D LLP) -60 E 42nd -NY 10165 **Fx:**953-8899
(516) 683-8880 .. **Dredger,** Elena S '92 %Massimo & P,PC -99 Q Roosevelt Blvd -Gdn Cty 11530
(516) 656-5300 .. **Dredger,** Thos A Jr. '84 (Mullooly JR&F LLP) -6851 Jericho Tpk Bx9036 -Syosset 11791
(516) 294-0540 .. **Dreeben,** Nancy J '97 (D'Errico D,LLP) -1205 Franklin Av -Gdn Cty 11530 **Fx:**280-5301
(631) 486-6080 .. **Dreher,** Rachel Lee '04 -239 Laurel Rd Bx162 -E Northprt 11731 **Fx:**498-1159
(718) 590-2000 .. **Dreher,** Robt L '74 %DA -198 E 161st -Bronx 10451 **Fx:**590-6477
(212) 349-3366 .. **Dreiblatt,** Dean '91 %Rose & R -291 Bway -NY 10007 **Fx:**349-2292
(212) 819-8200 .. **Dreier,** David H '95 (White & C LLP) -1155 Av of Amer -NY 10036
(212) 835-1514 .. **Dreifuss Bonacci & Parker,LLP** -1 Penn Plz -NY 10019 **Fx:**(973) 514-5959
(212) 264-8000 .. **Dreifuss,** Janet B '87 %HUD -26 Fed Plz -NY 10278
(212) 297-1053 .. **Dreilinger,** Evan M '99 Gramercy Capital Corp -420 Lex Av -NY 10170
(718) 935-1877 .. **Dreises,** Howard I '90 -155 Henry -Brklyn 11201
(718) 793-5555 .. **Dreishpoon,** Michl '91 -118-35 Qns Blvd -Frst Hlls 11375 **Fx:**520-8306
(845) 452-3434 .. **Dreispiel,** Mariel '08 %Handel & C,LLP -112 Delafld -Poughkeepsie 12601 **Fx:**471-0105
(212) 819-8200 .. **Dreizen,** Alison M '78 (White & C LLP) -1155 Av of Amer -NY 10036
(212) 545-4784 .. **Dreizen,** Jonathan L '07 %Wolf HAF&H LLP -270 Mad Av -NY 10016
(212) 558-5500 .. **Dreksler,** Adam S '10 %Weitz & L,PC -700 Bway -NY 10003
(212) 684-3630 .. **Drelich,** Gloria '67 %D Horowitz,PC -276 5th Av -NY 10001 **Fx:**685-8617
(718) 279-7555 .. **Drelich,** Steven B '88 B Montague & Prtnrs -212-45 26th Av -Bayside 11360 **Fx:**279-8154
(212) 218-5500 .. **Dremluk,** Robt W '79 (Seyfarth S LLP) -620 8th Av -NY 10018
(716) 856-4000 .. **Drenning,** John B Jr. '65 (Hodgson R LLP) -140 Pearl -Buffalo 14202
(518) 257-3000 .. **Drescher,** Debra Pulenskey '84 %Dormitory Auth -515 Bway -Albany 12207 **Fx:**257-3101
(718) 482-4963 .. **Drescher,** Udo M '92 %DEC -1 Hunters Pnt Plz -LIC 11101 **Fx:**482-4962
(914) 576-0578 .. **Dresdner,** Irwin '90 -205 Rogers Dr -Scarsdale 10583
(585) 395-5532 .. **Dresnack,** Wm H '98 %SUNY Brockport -Hartwell Hall -Brockprt 14420
(212) 692-1000 .. **Dresner,** Arthur '69 OfCnsl Duane M LLP -1540 Bway -NY 10036
(212) 679-6240 .. **Dresner,** Byron '52 (Dresner & D) -276 5th Av -NY 10001
(212) 679-6240 .. **Dresner,** Cheryl F '86 (Dresner & D) -276 5th Av -NY 10001
(212) 679-6240 .. **Dresner & Dresner** -276 5th Av -NY 10001 **Fx:**481-9569
(212) 980-0202 .. **Dressel & Hatab,PC** -6 E 45th -NY 10017 **Fx:**980-4297
(212) 408-2500 .. **Dresser,** G Brayton '97 (Baker B,LLP) -30 Rckfllr Plz -NY 10112
(212) 815-7530 .. **Dressler,** Bennett L '83 %PELS -125 Barclay -NY 10007 **Fx:**815-7534
(212) 878-4000 .. **Dressler,** David A '87 %Mitsui & Co -200 Park Av -NY 10166 **Fx:**878-4800
(212) 566-7766 .. **Dressler,** Jordan M '00 %R Gottlieb -111 Bway -NY 10006 **Fx:**374-1506
(212) 558-4000 .. **Dressner,** Adam B '09 %Sullivan & C LLP -125 Broad -NY 10004
(212) 578-5288 .. **Dressner,** Robt G '75 %MetLife -27-01 Qns Plz N -LIC 11101
(585) 473-3100 .. **Dreste,** John W '85 (Ernstrom & D,LLP) -180 Canal Vw Blvd -Rchstr 14623
(845) 794-5000 .. **Drew Davidoff & Edwards,LLP** -13 Lbrty Drwr1040 -Monticello 12701 **Fx:**794-5606
(716) 885-1150 .. **Drew,** Dean A '53 (Drew & D,LLP) -159 Linwood Av -Buffalo 14209 **Fx:**884-3707
(716) 885-1150 .. **Drew,** Dean M '78 (Drew & D,LLP) -159 Linwood Av -Buffalo 14209 **Fx:**884-3707
(212) 696-6000 .. **Drew,** James V '02 %Curtis M-PC&M LLP -101 Park Av -NY 10178
(716) 877-8500 .. **Drew,** Theresa A '88 -522 Amherst -Buffalo 14207 **Fx:**877-1024
(212) 728-8000 .. **Drewes,** David C '02 %Willkie F&G LLP -787 7th Av -NY 10019
(212) 808-7800 .. **Drewes,** W Christian '76 (Kelley D&W LLP) -101 Park Av -NY 10178
(212) 228-0402 .. **Drewes,** Wm H '83 -7 Lex Av -NY 10010 **Fx:**228-0402
(516) 502-2620 .. **Drewitz,** Richd H '84 %Thomas & G LLP -1983 Marcus Av -Lk Success 11042
(212) 221-6900 .. **Drewniak,** Erik W '99 %Winget S&S,LLP -45 Bway -NY 10006
(212) 490-3000 .. **Drews,** Denise L '03 %Wilson EME&D LLP -150 E 42nd -NY 10017
(212) 689-1113 .. **Drews,** Michl D '03 %Garbarini & S,PC -432 Park Av S -NY 10016
(866) 781-6101 .. **Drexel,** Allen A '01 (Drexel G LLC) -220 E 42nd -NY 10007
(716) 875-7552 .. **Drexelius,** John R Jr. '80 -390 Stillwell Av -Kenmore 14217
(212) 213-8844 .. **Drexler,** Adam M '04 Allyn & F LLP -200 Mad Av -NY 10016
(631) 777-2330 .. **Drexler,** Aimee D '95 %O'Connor OH&D,LLP -1 Huntngtn Quad -Melvll 11747
(518) 474-6530 .. **Drexler,** David G '00 %Dept Pub Srvc -3 ESP -Albany 12223
(516) 764-2800 .. **Drexler,** Eugene '50 OfCnsl Goldberg & C -66 N Vllg Av -Rockvll Ctr 11570

(607) 334-9744 .. **Drexler,** Henry J '74 -39 Sheldon -Norwich 13815
(212) 474-1000 .. **Drexler,** Kimberley S '99 Cravath S&M LLP -825 8th Av -NY 10019
(585) 546-7650 .. **Drexler,** Mark '80 -30 W Broad -Rchstr 14614 **Fx:**546-7667
(315) 477-0100 .. **Drexler,** Wm F '75 (Baldwin & S,LLP) -126 N Salina -Syracuse 13202
(212) 735-3000 .. **Dreyer,** Anthony J '99 (Skadden ASM&F LLP) -4 Times Sq -NY 10036
(518) 463-7784 .. **Dreyer Boyajian LLP** -75 Columbia -Albany 12210 **Fx:**463-4039
(845) 522-8910 .. **Dreyer,** Darryl J '94 Dreyer Law Ofc,PLLC -5419 Route 9 W -Newburgh 12550 **Fx:**522-8981
(212) 716-3444 .. **Dreyer,** Douglas P '91 Amer Benefits & Comp Systems -99 Park Av -NY 10016
(212) 606-7259 .. **Dreyer,** Elyse M '05 Sotheby's,Inc -1334 York Av -NY 10021 **Fx:**606-7574
(212) 599-1515 .. **Dreyer,** Ivan W '80 (Stein RM,LLP) -405 Lex Av -NY 10174
(212) 998-1212 .. **Dreyer,** Laurence M '02 NYU Stern Schl Bus -44 W 4th -NY 10012
(212) 935-3131 .. **Dreyer,** Stanley B '51 OfCnsl Gallet D&B,LLP -845 3rd Av -NY 10022
(212) 484-3900 .. **Dreyer,** Steven D '72 (Arent F LLP) -1675 Bway -NY 10019
(518) 463-7784 .. **Dreyer,** Wm J '69 (Dreyer B LLP) -75 Columbia -Albany 12210
(914) 428-0940 .. **Dreyfus,** Eric M '63 -1 N Bway -White Plns 10601 **Fx:**428-2808
(212) 318-3000 .. **Dreyfus,** James K '74 (Fulbright & J LLP) -666 5th Av -NY 10103
(718) 694-3894 .. **Dreyfus,** Richd I '68 %Transit Auth -130 Lvngstn -Brklyn 11201 **Fx:**694-5726
(212) 721-6133 .. **Dreyfuss,** David M '87 (Wyndham Partners,LP) -61 W 74th -NY 10023 **Fx:**721-6740
(212) 982-2080 .. **Dreyfuss,** Goldie S '97 %H reininger -55 Av A -NY 10009
(212) 331-5878 .. **Dreyfuss,** Richd H '92 %HRA -180 Water -NY 10038 **Fx:**331-5853
(212) 967-1800 .. **Dreyspool,** Anthony A '71 OfCnsl Bryant BJ&R LLP -140 Bway -NY 10005
(212) 737-3501 .. **Dreyspool,** Phyllis C '70 -710 Park Av -NY 10021
(718) 624-5553 .. **Drezin,** Alan '65 -26 Court -Brklyn 11242 **Fx:**624-7849
(718) 823-7211 .. **Drezin,** Michl '78 -25 Wstchstr Sq -Bronx 10461 **Fx:**822-1022
(845) 291-2650 .. **Drian,** Allan H Y '77 %Cnty Atty -285 Main -Goshen 10924 **Fx:**291-3014
(518) 436-1662 .. **Dribusch,** Christian H '94 -5 Clinton Sq -Albany 12207 **Fx:**432-1996
(518) 436-8495 .. **Dribusch,** Elizabeth C '97 NY Farm Bureau -159 Wolf Rd Bx5330 -Albany 12205 **Fx:**431-5656
(212) 878-8000 .. **Drichta,** Jeffrey H '98 Cnsl Clifford C LLP -31 W 52nd -NY 10019
(212) 404-4073 .. **Driesen,** Danl T '96 NYU Langone Medical Ctr -3 Park Av -NY 10016
(718) 743-2746 .. **Driesman,** Danl L '60 -2650 Ocean Pkwy -Brklyn 11235 **Fx:**743-2746
(516) 877-5600 .. **Driggs,** Hamilton I III '85 %R Tusa -1225 Franklin Av -Gdn Cty 11530 **Fx:**877-5695
(516) 683-4583 .. **Drillich,** Lisa G '82 NY Cmmnty Bancorp,Inc -615 Merrick Av -Westbury 11590
(845) 791-1728 .. **Drillings,** Jay M '90 -10 Prince Bx1442 -Monticello 12701
(845) 794-3344 .. **Drillings,** Joey Z '94 %DA -414 Bway -Monticello 12701 **Fx:**794-3646
(212) 880-3800 .. **Drillings,** Robt M '80 OfCnsl Akerman S -335 Mad Av -NY 10017
(315) 472-4331 .. **Drimer,** Jeffrey L '76 -217 Mntgmry -Syracuse 13202 **Fx:**425-5990
(718) 694-3892 .. **Drinan,** Robt K '80 Transit Auth -130 Lvngstn -Brklyn 11201 **Fx:**694-5726
(212) 940-3000 .. **Drinkard,** Michelle C '10 %Nixon P LLP -437 Mad Av -NY 10022
(212) 248-3140 .. **Drinker Biddle & Reath LLP** -140 Bway -NY 10005 **Fx:**248-3141
(518) 452-8787 .. **Drinker Biddle & Reath LLP** -321 Great Oaks Blvd -Albany 12203 **Fx:**452-8767
(607) 734-2271 .. **Drinkwater-Lunn,** Clover M '82 (Sayles & E) -1 W Church -Elmira 14901
(212) 819-8200 .. **Driscoll,** Brendan M '08 %White & C LLP -1155 Av of Amer -NY 10036
(347) 418-4250 .. **Driscoll,** Danl L '92 %British Airways -75-20 Astoria Blvd -Jcksn Hts 11370 **Fx:**418-4204
(631) 665-3400 .. **Driscoll,** Danl T '93 %Siben & S,LLP -90 E Main Bx149P -Bay Shr 11706
(716) 375-5130 .. **Driscoll,** Gerald M '95 (Driscoll & B) -2646 W State -Olean 14760 **Fx:**375-5131
(212) 922-0450 .. **Driscoll,** Jeanine C '93 %Kaplan M&A,LLC -70 E 55th -NY 10022
(646) 471-4000 .. **Driscoll,** Jennifer L S '06 %PricewaterhouseCoopers LLP -300 Mad Av -NY 10017
(631) 351-3501 .. **Driscoll,** Jessica P '08 %M Cuthbertson -434 NY Av -Huntngtn 11743 **Fx:**614-4314
(516) 625-0621 .. **Driscoll,** John C '83 -34 Wagon Rd -East Hills 11577
(212) 964-7500 .. **Driscoll,** John F '79 %Captains Endowment Assn -233 Bway -NY 10279 **Fx:**406-3105
(212) 237-1000 .. **Driscoll,** John J '77 (Windels ML&M,LLP) -156 W 56th -NY 10019
(212) 278-5491 .. **Driscoll,** John M '99 %Societe Generale -1221 Av of Amer -NY 10020
(212) 599-9000 .. **Driscoll,** John T '65 (JT Driscoll,PC) -300 E 42nd -NY 10017 **Fx:**972-9609
(212) 566-4600 .. **Driscoll,** Justin E '81 (Brown & W PLLC) -233 Bway -NY 10279
(315) 422-1946 .. **Driscoll,** Margaret M '02 -327 W Fayette -Syracuse 13202
(212) 331-5132 .. **Driscoll,** Matthew J '99 HRA -180 Water -NY 10038
(212) 223-2100 .. **Driscoll,** Melissa K '05 %Menz B&K LLP -444 Mad Av -NY 10022
(716) 842-4611 .. **Driscoll,** Michl C '94 %M&T Bk -1 M & T Plz -Buffalo 14203 **Fx:**842-5376
(212) 286-8585 .. **Driscoll,** Michl J '08 %Heidell PM&B,LLP -99 Park Av -NY 10016
(315) 258-9977 .. **Driscoll,** Michele R '92 -21 Lincoln -Auburn 13021
(212) 986-4030 .. **Driscoll,** Peter J '70 (Driscoll & R) -521 5th Av -NY 10175 **Fx:**986-4050
(212) 489-8230 .. **Driscoll,** Robt J '97 (Davis WT LLP) -1633 Bway -NY 10019
(585) 325-8123 .. **Driscoll,** Sheila J '80 %Baden St Settlement -585 Joseph Av -Rchstr 14605
(516) 873-2000 .. **Driscoll,** Theresa A '01 %Moritt HH&H LLP -400 Grdn City Plz -Gdn Cty 11530
(718) 965-6623 .. **Driscoll,** Timothy B '85 -619 8th Av -Brklyn 11215
(315) 471-2627 .. **Driscoll,** Timothy T '93 %NEC -241 W Fayette -Syracuse 13202
(212) 230-8800 .. **Dritz,** Melanie J '06 %WilmerHale -399 Park Av -NY 10022
(212) 819-8200 .. **Drivas,** Dimitrios T '85 (White & C LLP) -1155 Av of Amer -NY 10036
(518) 449-3125 .. **Driver,** Jennifer C '03 %Stockli GS&P,LLP -90 State -Albany 12207
(631) 501-3100 .. **Driver,** Scott W '95 %J Humphreys -3 Huntngtn Quad Bx9028 -Melvll 11747 **Fx:**501-3085
(716) 858-2424 .. **Drmacich,** G Michl '87 %DA -25 Delaware Av -Buffalo 14202 **Fx:**858-7425
(212) 506-2500 .. **Drnek,** John C Jr. '04 %Mayer B LLP -1675 Bway -NY 10019
(718) 797-3030 .. **Drobenare,** Michl A '78 -50 Court -Brklyn 11201 **Fx:**852-8428
(718) 721-2000 .. **Drobenko,** Walter '90 (Drobenko & Assoc,PC) -25-84 Steinway -Astoria 11103 **Fx:**721-8812
(518) 783-3843 .. **Drobny,** Cathy L '00 %Hacker & M,LLP -7 Airport Park Blvd -Latham 12110
(212) 612-4000 .. **Droesch,** Jennifer A '93 %Chubb Grp -55 Water -NY 10041
(631) 331-6464 .. **Droge,** Robt J '79 -36 Winside Ln -Coram 11727
(212) 589-4200 .. **Drogen,** Andrew M '83 (Baker & H LLP) -45 Rckfllr Plz -NY 10111
(646) 458-6811 .. **Drogin,** David E '06 Ace USA -140 Bway -NY 10005
(212) 216-8000 .. **Drogin,** Ira '59 OfCnsl Tarter K&D LLP -1350 Bway -NY 10018
(212) 216-8000 .. **Drogin,** Laurent S '91 (Tarter K&D LLP) -1350 Bway -NY 10018
(212) 925-0730 .. **Drogin,** Louis J '94 Brandgenuity LLC -205 Hudson -NY 10013 **Fx:**924-9060
(315) 349-3270 .. **Drohan,** Alan S '82 %Hon N Seiter Jr -25 E Oneida -Oswego 13126
(845) 592-7000 .. **Drohan,** James P '83 (Donoghue TA&D LLP) -2517 Route 52 -Hopewell Junct 12533
(212) 710-0000 .. **Drohan,** John P III '91 (Drohan L,LLP) -489 5th Av -NY 10017
(212) 710-0000 .. **Drohan Lee, LLP** -489 5th Av -NY 10017 **Fx:**710-0003
(212) 732-3200 .. **Drohan,** Margaret M '00 %Carter L&M LLP -2 Wall -NY 10005
(212) 710-0000 .. **Drohan,** Vivian Rivera '90 (Drohan L,LLP) -489 5th Av -NY 10017
(516) 674-8935 .. **Droogan,** Cornelius J Jr. '76 -Bx750 -Mineola 11501 **Fx:**674-4151
(212) 613-5000 .. **Drook,** Helen '85 %Leg Assist Grp -450 W 33rd -NY 10001 **Fx:**750-0820
(212) 969-3000 .. **Dropkin,** Chas E '78 (Proskauer R LLP) -1585 Bway -NY 10036
(914) 328-0404 .. **Dropkin,** Keith A '05 %Jackson L LLP -1 N Bway -White Plns 10601
(315) 798-2023 .. **Dropkin,** Robt F '85 %Special Metals Corp -Middle Settlmnt Rd -New Hartfrd 13413
(212) 793-7396 .. **Dropkin,** Shelley J '89 %Citigroup -425 Park Av -NY 10022
(718) 347-6445 .. **Dror,** Asaf '96 (A Dror,PC) -1 Holland Av -Floral Pk 11001 **Fx:**(516) 775-2085
(646) 200-6300 .. **Dror,** Eyal '08 %Park & J LLP -630 3rd Av -NY 10017 **Fx:**200-6301
(212) 479-6724 .. **Drori,** Danna '01 Macht SA&I LLP -1114 Av of Amer -NY 10036 **Fx:**202-6417
(845) 987-1311 .. **Drosdowich,** George M '99 Iberdrola Renewables Inc -488 Old Dutch Hllw Rd -Monroe 10950
(212) 250-6828 .. **Droskoski,** Matthew J '02 %Deutsche Bank -60 Wall -NY 10005
(212) 655-5000 .. **Drossman,** David A '99 %Gannon R&M -120 Bway -NY 10271
(516) 708-1970 .. **Drossman,** Jennifer L '98 (Drossman & Assoc) -23 Vllg Sq -Glen Cove 11542 **Fx:**385-1817
(718) 387-7882 .. **Drossman,** Leslie J '61 -111 Graham Av -Brklyn 11206 **Fx:**387-1310
(212) 852-1977 .. **Drossman,** Mitchell A '92 US Trust Co of NY -114 W 47th -NY 10036 **Fx:**852-1930
(914) 765-0429 .. **Drossman,** Valerie L '92 -12 Yale Pl -Armonk 10504 **Fx:**765-0431
(516) 223-5500 .. **Drost,** Matthew R '09 %R Nelson -2249 Derby Rd -Baldwin 11510 **Fx:**223-5505
(212) 809-7074 .. **Drotzer,** Karen S '84 (Armienti DG&R,LLP) -39 Bway -NY 10006
(212) 682-7050 .. **Drouin,** Aimee A '07 %Geringer & D -5 Hanover Sq -NY 10004
(212) 982-4370 .. **Drouzas,** Pari '93 -237 1st Av -NY 10003
(518) 563-3769 .. **Drown,** Curtis P '96 -30 Clinton Bx1818 -Plattsbrgh 12901 **Fx:**561-1443
(212) 310-8000 .. **Drozda,** Brian C '09 %Weil G&M LLP -767 5th Av -NY 10153
(212) 859-8000 .. **Drozdetski,** Eugene '09 %Fried FHS&J LLP -1 NY Plz -NY 10004
(516) 367-5010 .. **Drozdoff,** Vladimir V '99 %CSHL -1 Bungtown Rd -Cold Spg Hbr 11724
(212) 736-2121 .. **Drubner & Hartley,LLC** -1540 Bway -NY 10036 **Fx:**736-2122
(516) 488-7808 .. **Druck,** Marilyn A '77 -828 Hempstd Tpk -Franklin Sq 11010 **Fx:**488-7808
(718) 458-2312 .. **Drucker,** Arnold W '82 -37-06 82nd -Jcksn Hts 11372 **Fx:**639-1854
(718) 458-1489 .. **Drucker,** Danl S '03 -37-06 82nd -Jcksn Hts 11372
(212) 335-9224 .. **Drucker,** David G '76 %DA -1 Hogan Pl -NY 10013
(914) 378-2644 .. **Drucker,** Douglas R Jr. '96 Consumers Union -101 Truman Av -Ynkrs 10703
(212) 239-4999 .. **Drucker,** Emily J '98 OfCnsl Meyer SE&K,PC -1350 Bway Bx822 -NY 10018
(212) 688-3819 .. **Drucker,** Jacquelin F '92 -432 E 58th -NY 10022 **Fx:**935-1870
(212) 422-0488 .. **Drucker,** Joel A '77 OfCnsl Rick SF&B,LLP -90 Broad -NY 10004
(212) 752-8000 .. **Drucker,** John H '79 (Cole SMF&L,PA) -900 3rd Av -NY 10022
(212) 935-4990 .. **Drucker,** Jonathan D '86 %Veronis Suhler & Assoc Inc -350 Park Av -NY 10022 **Fx:**486-3091
(212) 277-6500 .. **Drucker,** Lawr C '89 (Dickstein S LLP) -1633 Bway -NY 10019
(212) 556-7602 .. **Drucker,** Margo R '91 %The NY Times Co -620 8th Av -NY 10018 **Fx:**556-4634
(718) 458-1489 .. **Drucker,** Mark S '75 -37-06 82nd -Jcksn Hts 11372
(631) 582-6555 .. **Drucker,** Mitchell S '95 -51 E Main -Smithtwn 11787 **Fx:**582-6556
(914) 333-7460 .. **Drucker,** Peter A '89 %Akzo Nobel -120 Wht Plns Rd -Tarrytwn 10591
(212) 450-4000 .. **Drucker,** Richd A '78 (Davis P&W LLP) -450 Lex Av -NY 10017
(718) 458-1973 .. **Drucker,** Richd M '76 -37-06 82nd -Jcksn Hts 11372 **Fx:**639-1854
(212) 382-0909 .. **Drucker,** Robt A '81 (Peckar & A,PC) -41 Mad Av -NY 10154
(212) 697-3122 .. **Drucker,** Robt M '02 %Martin C&B LLP -220 E 42nd -NY 10017
(516) 487-3720 .. **Drucker,** Susan J '83 -4 E Mill Dr -Gt Neck 11021 **Fx:**487-3720
(631) 543-0003 .. **Drucker-Albert,** Ellen R '86 OfCnsl PG Albert -356 Vets Mem'l Hwy -Commack 11725 **Fx:**864-3786
(718) 538-8800 .. **Druckman,** David J '86 -910 Grnd Cncrs -Bronx 10451 **Fx:**538-1877
(212) 557-7200 .. **Druckman,** Howard E '71 (Davidoff M&H,LLP) -605 3rd Av -NY 10158
(212) 689-2960 .. **Druckman,** James P '73 -200 Lex Av -NY 10016 **Fx:**685-1807
(516) 876-0800 .. **Druckman,** Stuart L '88 (Druckman Law Grp PLLC) -242 Drexel Av -Westbury 11590 **Fx:**876-0888
(212) 819-8200 .. **Druehl,** Claudette R '99 %White & C LLP -1155 Av of Amer -NY 10036
(212) 698-3500 .. **Druehl,** Craig P '99 (Dechert LLP) -1095 Av of Amer -NY 10036

(212) 608-4400 .. **Druker,** David W '85 (Wilson GD&N) -233 Bway -NY 10279
(212) 278-1475 .. **Druker,** Isaac E '66 (Anderson K&O,PC) -1251 Av of Amer -NY 10020
(516) 746-4300 .. **Druker,** James O '74 (Kase & D) -1325 Franklin Av -Gdn Cty 11530
(212) 663-8353 .. **Drum,** Sydney M '91 -138 W 120th -NY 10027 **Fx:**663-8353
(718) 928-3700 .. **Drumm,** Kristen E '07 %LSNYC-Bronx -579 Courtlandt Av -Bronx 10451 **Fx:**402-7586
(716) 681-7190 .. **Drumm,** Michl R '85 %Brown C LLP -5775 Bway -Lancaster 14086
(212) 994-0260 .. **Drummer,** Todd R '93 %Cornicello T&B-C,LLP -2 Wall -NY 10005
(718) 776-0001 .. **Drummond & Crawford PC** -221-10 Jamaica Av -Qns Vllg 11428 **Fx:**776-1557
(914) 948-1522 .. **Drummond,** J Gregory '82 -244 Wstchstr Av -White Plns 10604 **Fx:**948-1524
(212) 872-1000 .. **Drummond,** Renuka Sriyani '06 -One Bryant Park -NY 10036 **Fx:**872-1002
(718) 776-0001 .. **Drummond,** Stephen L '97 (Drummond & C PC) -221-10 Jamaica Av -Qns Vllg 11428
(914) 472-7700 .. **Drummond,** Wm H '73 (Bertine HHZD&D,LLP) -700 Wht Plns Rd -Scarsdale 10583
(347) 853-1859 .. **Drury,** James J '88 -624 Bard Av -Staten Isl 10310 **Fx:**(718) 720-0575
(716) 856-5500 .. **Drury,** Thos J '81 (Damon M LLP) -200 Delaware Av -Buffalo 14202
(212) 210-9456 .. **Drutman,** Evan M '90 (Alston & B LLP) -90 Park Av -NY 10016
(212) 279-5577 .. **Druyan,** B Martin '78 (M Druyan) -450 7th Av -NY 10123
(718) 250-2000 .. **Druyan,** Lauren A '09 %DA -350 Jay -Brklyn 11201 **Fx:**250-2314
(518) 828-9411 .. **Dryer,** Katrina L '06 Cnty Dept Socl Srvcs -25 Railroad Av Bx458 -Hudson 12534 **Fx:**828-9412
(914) 636-5657 .. **Dryer,** Rhoda K '66 (Dryer D&W) -271 North Av -New Rchll 10801 **Fx:**636-5890
(212) 803-5100 .. **Drysdale,** Althea E M '88 %NY Cnty Defender Srvcs -225 Bway -NY 10007 **Fx:**571-6035
(718) 452-6804 .. **Drysdale,** Suzanne '94 Drysdale & Assoc,PC -428 Decatur -Brklyn 11233
(212) 272-3464 .. **D'Sidocky,** James C '00 %JP Morgan Chase -383 Mad Av -NY 10179
(212) 703-8702 .. **Du,** John '99 -630 5th Av -NY 10111 **Fx:**703-8720
(212) 775-8700 .. **Du,** Na '07 %Kilpatrick S,LLP -31 W 52nd -NY 10019
(212) 949-6720 .. **Duane,** John F '79 (Leavitt K&D) -228 E 45th -NY 10017
(212) 692-1000 .. **Duane Morris LLP** -1540 Bway -NY 10036 **Fx:**692-1020
(718) 352-2764 .. **Duarte,** Alfonso '58 -199-14 24th Rd -Whitestone 11357 **Fx:**767-0261
(212) 682-4001 .. **Duarte,** Katerina I '06 %Lynch R LLP -630 3rd Av -NY 10017
(212) 295-6825 .. **Dub,** Peter A '01 WilmerHale -399 Park Av -NY 10022
(631) 218-7326 .. **Duban,** Michl C '60 -90 Orvll Dr -Bohemia 11716
(212) 267-3700 .. **Dubanevich,** Wm J '03 %Napoli BR LLP -350 5th Av -NY 10118
(845) 634-4455 .. **Dubbs,** Seymour '64 -5 Landsdale Rd -New Cty 10956 **Fx:**638-0592
(212) 907-0871 .. **Dubbs,** Thos A '76 (Labaton S LLP) -140 Bway -NY 10005
(718) 857-3721 .. **Dube,** Jill M '82 (Dube & W) -295 St Johns Pl -Brklyn 11238 **Fx:**857-3748
(212) 326-3939 .. **Dubeck,** Leslie B '08 %Jones D -222 E 41st -NY 10017
(607) 734-1647 .. **Dubel,** Thos S '70 %Leg Srvcs -215 E Church -Elmira 14901 **Fx:**734-1018
(212) 355-6800 .. **Duberstein,** Gary K '80 %Greenway Partners -150 E 57th -NY 10022 **Fx:**207-3901
(212) 450-1200 .. **Duberstein,** Jennifer D '03 MLS/Soccer United Mrktng -420 5th Av -NY 10018
(631) 234-9240 .. **Dubey,** Zachary D '07 %H Besunder -1 Suffolk Sq -Islandia 11749 **Fx:**234-9278
(631) 499-3030 .. **Dubi,** Richd A '90 (Dubi B,PC) -9 Cedar Ridge Ln -Dix Hlls 11746 **Fx:**462-4976
(212) 238-2420 .. **Dubiac,** Diane L '69 UIA Bd -59 Maiden Ln -NY 10038 **Fx:**238-2451
(212) 554-7800 .. **Dubin,** Arlene G '80 (Moses & S LLP) -405 Lex Av -NY 10174
(718) 252-0888 .. **Dubin,** Avrohom P '88 -1140 E 19th -Brklyn 11230 **Fx:**253-5327
(631) 727-2180 .. **Dubin,** David M '83 (Twomey LSKD&Q,LLP) -33 W 2nd Bx9398 -Rvrhead 11901
(718) 871-6300 .. **Dubin,** Harry '40 -1258 Prospect Av -Brklyn 11218
(212) 373-3000 .. **Dubin,** James M '75 (Paul WRW&G LLP) -1285 Av of Amer -NY 10019
(718) 657-1855 .. **Dubin,** Janette E '92 -84-32 Avon -Jamaica 11432
(631) 351-0300 .. **Dubin,** Jeffrey S '68 -464 NY Av -Huntngtn 11743 **Fx:**351-1900
(212) 431-9380 .. **Dubin,** Lawr A '67 (Goldberger & D,PC) -401 Bway -NY 10013
(716) 853-1283 .. **Dubin,** Marvin T '62 OfCnsl Dubin & D,LLP -14 Lafayette Sq -Buffalo 14203 **Fx:**847-1980
(212) 859-8000 .. **Dubin,** Michelle L '99 Fried FHS&J LLP -1 NY Plz -NY 10004
(212) 506-5000 .. **Dubin,** Morton D '97 (Orrick H&S LLP) -51 W 52nd -NY 10019
(716) 853-1283 .. **Dubin,** Robt J '93 Cnsl Dubin & D,LLP -14 Lafayette Sq -Buffalo 14203 **Fx:**847-1980
(212) 772-0136 .. **Dubin,** Roger E M '83 %Val-Pak Of Manhattan -236 E 75th -NY 10021 **Fx:**734-4337
(212) 318-6000 .. **Dubin,** Sandi F '01 %Paul HJ&W LLP -75 E 55th -NY 10022
(212) 818-9200 .. **Dubin,** Seth H '57 Cnsl Satterlee SB&B LLP -230 Park Av -NY 10169
(212) 576-4575 .. **Dubin,** Vivian L '86 %NYLIM -51 Mad Av -NY 10010
(212) 287-8282 .. **Dubiner,** Jay L '93 Warnaco Inc -501 7th Av -NY 10018
(516) 333-8300 .. **Dubinsky,** Donna Dikman '90 (Dubinsky Assoc) -1400 Old Cntry Rd -Westbury 11590 **Fx:**333-5696
(516) 333-8300 .. **Dubinsky,** Eric '88 (Dubinsky Assoc) -1400 Old Cntry Rd -Westbury 11590 **Fx:**333-5696
(212) 233-4354 .. **Dubinsky,** Melvin '62 -170 Bway -NY 10038 **Fx:**233-1150
(212) 872-1000 .. **Dublin,** Philip C '99 -One Bryant Park -NY 10036 **Fx:**872-1002
(212) 902-1000 .. **Dubner,** David P '03 Goldman Sachs -1 NY Plz -NY 10004
(631) 694-8100 .. **Dubner,** Wendy B '96 %Global Pottery Dist -140 Half Hllw Rd -Dix Hlls 11746
(212) 319-5351 .. **Dubno,** Erica T '95 %HP Fahringer PLLC -120 E 56th -NY 10022 **Fx:**319-6657
(718) 789-7777 .. **Dubno,** Robt C '76 -823 Prsdnt -Brklyn 11215 **Fx:**789-1940
(315) 435-2957 .. **Dubnoff,** Ira S '76 %Dept Soc Srvcs -421 Mntgmry -Syracuse 13202 **Fx:**435-3590
(212) 909-6000 .. **Dubnoff,** Neil A '06 %Debevoise & P LLP -919 3rd Av -NY 10022
(646) 264-3650 .. **Dubnoff,** Stephen D '69 %US Dept of Labor -201 Varick -NY 10014 **Fx:**264-3660
(212) 687-3860 .. **Du Boff,** Michl H '71 (Snow BK,PC) -605 3rd Av -NY 10158
(212) 269-4900 .. **DuBoff,** Rebecca A '07 %Ford MEW&G,LLP -Wall Street Plz -NY 10005
(212) 977-9700 .. **DuBoff,** Sandra J '82 (Phillips N LLP) -666 5th Av -NY 10103
(845) 796-2100 .. **DuBois,** D Christopher '75 Frontier Ins Co -195 Lk Louise Marie Rd Bx8000 -Rck Hll 12775 **Fx:**796-1506
(716) 881-3010 .. **DuBois,** Danl J '00 %Cohen & L,PC -343 Elmwood Av Bx5204 -Buffalo 14213
(212) 859-7000 .. **DuBois,** Heidi S '00 Assurant,Inc -1 Chase Manh Plz -NY 10005
(718) 643-4680 .. **Dubois,** Paul E '82 %Hon J DeLury -120 Schermerhorn -Brklyn 11201
(917) 881-8003 .. **Du Bois,** Sylvia '97 -22 Nordica Dr -Croton-On-Hud 10520 **Fx:**(914) 271-1142
(212) 966-3970 .. **DuBoulay,** Donald D '78 -401 Bway -NY 10013
(914) 949-2826 .. **Dubow,** Alan M '81 (Robinowitz CD&D,LLP) -199 Main -White Plns 10601
(607) 273-6841 .. **Dubow,** David A '77 (Barney GDM&O,LLP) -119 E Seneca -Ithaca 14850
(631) 390-5000 .. **Dubow,** Howard I '69 (Genser DG&C,LLP) -445 Broad Hollow Rd -Melvll 11747
(718) 402-1990 .. **DuBow,** Michl '62 (Dubow & S) -860 Grnd Cncrs -Bronx 10451
(212) 916-5791 .. **Dubow,** Rachel L '96 %TIAA-CREF -730 3rd Av -NY 10017
(212) 856-5800 .. **Dubow,** Robt M '60 (Samson F&D) -10 E 40th -NY 10016
(718) 423-3600 .. **Dubowski,** Jos '69 -247-30 Nrthrn Blvd -Douglastn 11362
(914) 220-1900 .. **Dubowsky,** Scott M '98 (Nelson Law Firm,LLC) -1 N Bway -White Plns 10601
(585) 428-5210 .. **DuBrin,** Drew R '87 %Pub Def -10 N Fitzhugh -Rchstr 14614 **Fx:**428-2234
(914) 761-1300 .. **DuBroff,** Kenneth '65 (Cuddy & F LLP) -445 Hmltn Av -White Plns 10601
(212) 836-8000 .. **DuBroff,** Roger '62 Cnsl Kaye S LLP -425 Park Av -NY 10022
(212) 848-4000 .. **Dubrovsky,** David '08 %Shearman & S LLP -599 Lex Av -NY 10022
(212) 977-9700 .. **Dubrow,** David L '83 (Phillips N LLP) -666 5th Av -NY 10103
(212) 484-3900 .. **Dubrow,** David L '87 (Arent F LLP) -1675 Bway -NY 10019
(212) 661-2885 .. **Dubrow,** Phyllis E '91 -230 Park Av -NY 10169 **Fx:**409-8682
(212) 806-5400 .. **Dubrowski,** Maria '09 %Stroock &S&L LLP -180 Maiden Ln -NY 10038
(212) 885-5000 .. **Du Brul,** Karen '79 (Blank R LLP) -405 Lex Av -NY 10174
(914) 241-6740 .. **Dubs,** Howard F '80 -71 Smith Av -Mt Kisco 10549 **Fx:**241-6741
(716) 854-2050 .. **Dubs,** Joshua E '09 -485 Mich Av -Buffalo 14203 **Fx:**852-0560
(518) 465-7591 .. **Dubuc,** John M '00 %Miller & D,PC -14 Corp Wds Blvd -Albany 12211
(212) 682-2280 .. **Dubuss,** Jessica L '10 %Holm & O LLP -3 W 35th -NY 10001
(212) 335-9000 .. **Ducao,** Ayn Brigoli '03 %DA -1 Hogan Pl -NY 10013
(518) 563-1588 .. **Ducharme,** Danny J '83 -323 Pellerin Rd -Plattsbrgh 12901
(315) 386-8544 .. **Ducharme,** Gerald J '80 (Conboy MB&K,LLP) -2 Judson -Canton 13617
(518) 373-1482 .. **DuCharme Harp & Clark,LLP** -10 Maxwell Dr -Clifton Pk 12065 **Fx:**373-8758
(518) 373-1482 .. **Ducharme,** John B '88 (DuCharme H&C,LLP) -10 Maxwell Dr -Clifton Pk 12065
(718) 254-7000 .. **DuCharme,** Seth D '04 %US Atty -271 Cadman Plz E -Brklyn 11201 **Fx:**254-6479
(718) 987-1234 .. **Duchene,** Helen M '93 A Very Special Place -1429 Hylan Blvd -Staten Isl 10305
(212) 318-6000 .. **Duchesne,** Alexandra C '09 %Paul HJ&W LLP -75 E 55th -NY 10022
(212) 872-1000 .. **DuChez,** Neil F '09 -One Bryant Park -NY 10036 **Fx:**872-1002
(845) 724-4432 .. **Duckham,** James A '04 -146 Gold Rd -Poughquag 12570
(585) 753-4500 .. **Duckles,** Perry M '03 %DA -832 Watts Bldg -Rchstr 14614 **Fx:**753-4576
(212) 883-9111 .. **Duckworth,** R Demarest III '77 (Meaders D&M) -551 5th Av -NY 10176
(585) 272-8558 .. **Duclos,** Marc A '99 -1425 Jffrsn Rd -Rchstr 14623 **Fx:**272-8559
(212) 610-6300 .. **Duclos,** Nicole R '03 %Allen & O -1221 Av of Amer -NY 10020
(212) 872-1000 .. **Duda,** Monica T '09 -One Bryant Park -NY 10036 **Fx:**872-1002
(315) 435-2585 .. **Duda,** Paul E '71 %Dept Social Srvcs -421 Mntgmry -Syracuse 13202
(212) 728-8000 .. **Dudanowicz,** Jennifer L '08 %Willkie F&G LLP -787 7th Av -NY 10019
(718) 286-6103 .. **Duddy,** Kevin M '86 %DA -125-01 Qns Blvd -Kew Gdns 11415
(718) 855-5100 .. **Dudelson,** Alexander M '04 -26 Court -Brklyn 11242 **Fx:**624-9552
(212) 533-6300 .. **Dudich,** Neil J '02 %NYSUT -52 Bway -NY 10004 **Fx:**995-2347
(212) 294-6700 .. **Dudine,** Wm F III '88 (Winston & S) -200 Park Av -NY 10166
(718) 250-2000 .. **Dudis,** Frank R '01 %DA -350 Jay -Brklyn 11201 **Fx:**250-2314
(313) 225-7070 .. **Dudley,** Arthur II '78 (Butzel L,PC) -380 Mad Av -NY 10017 **Fx:**225-7080
(212) 297-5800 .. **Dudley,** B Dane '03 (Day P LLP) -7 Times Sq -NY 10036
(518) 436-6202 .. **Dudley,** David R '70 OfCnsl Ostroff Hiffa & Assoc,Inc -12 Sheridan Av -Albany 12207 **Fx:**436-1956
(718) 292-9600 .. **Dudley,** Edw R Jr. '68 -602 Grnd Cncrs -Bronx 10451
(716) 855-3200 .. **Dudley,** Patrick A '94 %Zdarsky S&A -298 Main -Buffalo 14202
(718) 341-1023 .. **Dudley,** Yvette V '93 YV Dudley,PC -217-01 Merrick Blvd -Sprngfld Gdns 11413 **Fx:**341-1023
(212) 297-5800 .. **Duelks,** Erika L '08 %Day P LLP -7 Times Sq -NY 10036
(516) 505-3800 .. **Duenas,** Gene '86 (G Duenas,PC) -92 Front -Hempstd 11550 **Fx:**505-3833
(212) 541-2000 .. **Duer,** John B '94 OfCnsl Bryan C LLP -1290 Av of Amer -NY 10104
(516) 294-5200 .. **Duer,** Paul '99 %Picciano & S -900 Merchants Cncrs -Westbury 11590
(716) 693-1588 .. **Duerr,** Robt K '55 -150 Payne Av Bx159 -N Tonawanda 14120 **Fx:**693-1589
(518) 402-6757 .. **Duerr Burke,** Cherie '92 %Workers Comp Bd -20 Park -Albany 12207
(212) 233-3079 .. **Duesel,** Kristen Ann '96 %Maloof LC&O,PA -299 Bway -NY 10007
(518) 464-2402 .. **Duesterdick,** P Scott '80 AYCO -1 Wall Bx15073 -Albany 12212
(212) 578-2211 .. **Duff,** Danl V '98 %MetLife -27-01 Qns Plz N -LIC 11101
(212) 530-1800 .. **Duff,** Kathleen P '07 %Richards K&O LLP -1 World Fncl Ctr -NY 10281

(914) 723-4300 .. **Duff,** Renee L '99 OfCnsl Lackenbach S LLP -1 Chase Rd -Scarsdale 10583
(212) 940-8800 .. **Duff,** Wm B '83 (Katten MR LLP) -575 Mad Av -NY 10022
(212) 269-0927 .. **Duffalo,** Jan Hudson '91 (D'Amato & L,LLP) -2 World Fncl Ctr -NY 10281
(212) 506-2500 .. **Duffee,** David K '85 (Mayer B LLP) -1675 Bway -NY 10019
(212) 785-0157 .. **Duffett,** Kathleen '92 %NYS Nurses Assn -120 Wall -NY 10005 **Fx:**785-0429
(212) 815-1818 .. **Duffett,** Liam P '06 DC 37 MELS -125 Barclay -NY 10007 **Fx:**815-1343
(212) 765-2100 .. **Duffey,** Denis P Jr. '04 %Spivak L LLP -1700 Bway -NY 10019
(212) 286-8585 .. **Dufficy,** Doreen '06 %Heidell PM&B,LLP -99 Park Av -NY 10016
(212) 715-9100 .. **Duffield,** Carl D '09 %Kramer LN&F,LLP -1177 Av of Amer -NY 10036
(212) 859-8000 .. **Duffine,** Alexander S '09 %Fried FHS&J LLP -1 NY Plz -NY 10004
(212) 408-5100 .. **Duffy,** Adrienne M '09 %Chadbourne & P LLP -30 Rckfllr Plz -NY 10112
(212) 446-2300 .. **Duffy,** Christopher E '02 (Boies S&F LLP) -575 Lex Av -NY 10022
(718) 520-3556 .. **Duffy,** Cornelia H '81 %Hon J Rosenzweig -125-01 Qns Blvd -Kew Gdns 11415
(212) 859-8000 .. **Duffy,** Dawn M '09 %Fried FHS&J LLP -1 NY Plz -NY 10004
(914) 964-6806 .. **Duffy,** Diana M '97 OfCnsl J Marra -909 Mdlnd Av -Ynkrs 10704 **Fx:**964-0137
(516) 766-7600 .. **Duffy,** Doris Rios '83 -55 Maple Av -Rockvll Ctr 11570 **Fx:**766-6630
(516) 394-4200 .. **Duffy & Duffy** -1370 RXR Plz -Uniondale 11556 **Fx:**394-4229
(212) 735-3000 .. **Duffy,** Edmund C '67 OfCnsl Skadden ASM&F LLP -4 Times Sq -NY 10036
(212) 752-1000 .. **Duffy,** Edw F '85 %Eiseman LL&K,PC -805 3rd Av -NY 10022
(212) 415-1407 .. **Duffy,** Elizabeth C '02 McKinsey & Co -55 E 52nd -NY 10055 **Fx:**446-8575
(516) 747-7500 .. **Duffy,** Garrett '83 (Fogarty D,PC) -185 Willis Av -Mineola 11501
(845) 278-6935 .. **Duffy,** Gerard J '91 -12 Irby Rd -Patterson 12563 **Fx:**278-6935
(518) 374-3373 .. **Duffy,** James E '89 (Silverman S&S) -527 State -Schnctdy 12305
(212) 916-9608 .. **Duffy,** James M '96 %Natl Australia Bk -245 Park Av -NY 10167
(212) 508-6700 .. **Duffy,** James P III '68 SrCnsl Tannenbaum HS&H LLP -900 3rd Av -NY 10022
(212) 335-4500 .. **Duffy,** James P IV '03 %DLA Piper LLP -1251 Av of Amer -NY 10020
(516) 394-4200 .. **Duffy,** James R '66 (Duffy & D) -1370 RXR Plz -Uniondale 11556
(212) 474-1000 .. **Duffy,** John C '10 %Cravath S&M LLP -825 8th Av -NY 10019
(845) 359-1915 .. **Duffy,** John F '63 -121 Moehring Dr -Blauvelt 10913
(212) 766-1888 .. **Duffy,** John J '57 Cnsl Morris DA&F -2 Rector -NY 10006
(212) 416-8610 .. **Duffy,** June '87 %Dept of Law -120 Bway -NY 10271
(212) 420-5013 .. **Duffy,** Justin F '00 %MetLife Housing Invstmnts -317 Av C -NY 10009
(516) 229-4400 .. **Duffy,** Kelly Anne '95 %Kay & G -875 Merrick Av -Westbury 11590
(631) 853-4094 .. **Duffy,** Kevin J '78 %Budget Review Ofc -725 Vets Mem'l Hwy -Smithtwn 11787
(914) 682-1400 .. **Duffy,** M Sean '96 %Scarcella Law Ofc -44 Church -White Plns 10601 **Fx:**948-2255
(646) 885-5003 .. **Duffy,** Marcia A '82 %Dept of Sanitation -125 Worth -NY 10013 **Fx:**(212) 442-9090
(516) 394-4200 .. **Duffy,** Mary Ellen '01 (Duffy & D) -1370 RXR Plz -Uniondale 11556
(212) 455-2000 .. **Duffy,** Meredith C '09 %Simpson T&B LLP -425 Lex Av -NY 10017
(516) 394-4200 .. **Duffy,** Michl E '95 (Duffy & D) -1370 RXR Plz -Uniondale 11556
(585) 232-7510 .. **Duffy,** Michl J '59 OfCnsl Duffy & T -45 Exchange -Rchstr 14614 **Fx:**232-9110
(646) 654-5095 .. **Duffy,** Michl J '98 VNU,Inc -770 Bway -NY 10003
(914) 949-2544 .. **Duffy,** Michl Kevin '04 MK Duffy,PC -2 William -White Plns 10601 **Fx:**949-2644
(518) 745-5030 .. **Duffy,** Monica A '88 (Judge & D) -1 Broad Street Plz Bx2850 -Glens Fls 12801
(516) 767-3600 .. **Duffy,** Owen F '90 (Chalos O&D) -366 Main -Pt Wash 11050
(516) 248-1200 .. **Duffy,** Paul M '78 (Mulholland M&R) -374 Hillside Av -Williston Pk 11596
(212) 977-9700 .. **Duffy,** Richd J '73 (Phillips N LLP) -666 5th Av -NY 10103
(212) 961-8255 .. **Duffy,** Rita A '81 %OTDA -40 N Pearl -Albany 12243 **Fx:**(518) 474-9389
(516) 394-4200 .. **Duffy,** Sean M '97 %Duffy & D -1370 RXR Plz -Uniondale 11556
(315) 422-8191 .. **Duffy,** Shirley K '00 %Leg Aid -351 S Warren -Syracuse 13202 **Fx:**472-2819
(716) 852-5200 .. **Duffy,** Susan R '85 (Hamberger & W) -700 Main Pl Twr -Buffalo 14202
(212) 259-8000 .. **Duffy,** Susann C '06 %Dewey & L LLP -1301 Av of Amer -NY 10019
(212) 922-0700 .. **Duffy,** Thos A '66 -71 Vndrblt Av -NY 10169 **Fx:**922-1697
(212) 278-1000 .. **Duffy,** Todd E '00 (Anderson K&O,PC) -1251 Av of Amer -NY 10020
(212) 701-3000 .. **Duffy,** W Leslie '64 SrCnsl Cahill G&R LLP -80 Pine -NY 10005 **Fx:**269-5420
(914) 779-2935 .. **Duffy,** Walter T Jr. '81 -163 Manh Av -Tuckahoe 10707
(212) 826-0100 .. **Duffy,** Wm B III '93 %FSA -31 W 52nd -NY 10019 **Fx:**893-2710
(631) 447-8100 .. **Duffy,** Wm M '02 -475 E Main -Patchogue 11772
(212) 903-9000 .. **Dufner,** Danl G Jr. '96 (Linklaters) -1345 Av of Amer -NY 10105
(914) 684-0090 .. **Dufort,** David L '91 (Diserio MO&C LLP) -50 Main -White Plns 10606
(212) 947-3793 .. **Dufresne,** Chas H Jr. '03 OfCnsl Sadis & G LLP -551 5th Av -NY 10176
(212) 682-6935 .. **Dufresne,** Denis A '96 (Lombardo D LLP) -275 Mad Av -NY 10016 **Fx:**619-1028
(914) 579-2200 .. **Dugan,** Brian M '97 (Dugan & D,PC) -245 Saw Mill Rvr Rd -Hawthorne 10532 **Fx:**579-2201
(646) 252-7000 .. **Dugan,** Cindy '79 %TBTA -2 Bway -NY 10004
(212) 973-0572 .. **Dugan,** David M '03 %Wolff & S PC -140 Bway -NY 10005
(718) 387-2879 .. **Dugan,** Dawn M '96 %Bd of Educ -850 Grand -Brklyn 11211
(518) 474-0871 .. **Dugan,** Deborah V '85 %DMV -6 ESP -Albany 12228 **Fx:**486-4485
(718) 442-2889 .. **Dugan,** Eleanor M '87 -424 Davis Av -Staten Isl 10310
(212) 728-8000 .. **Dugan,** James C '94 (Willkie F&G LLP) -787 7th Av -NY 10019
(646) 312-3320 .. **Dugan,** John R Jr. '78 Baruch College -1 Bernard Baruch Way -NY 10010 **Fx:**312-3321
(212) 850-6220 .. **Dugan,** Kevin M '70 Lathrop & G LC -230 Park Av -NY 10169
(212) 335-9000 .. **Dugan,** Patrick J '75 %DA -1 Hogan Pl -NY 10013
(212) 935-6020 .. **Dugan,** Peter J '05 %Klein ZR LLP -485 Mad Av -NY 10022
(212) 558-4000 .. **Dugan,** Rachael M '07 %Sullivan & C LLP -125 Broad -NY 10004
(212) 697-3122 .. **Dugan,** Sean F X '78 (Martin C&B LLP) -220 E 42nd -NY 10017
(646) 298-7306 .. **Dugan,** Sheila '89 -110 Wall -NY 10005
(631) 563-3055 .. **Dugan,** Stacey Rose '94 SR Dugan PC -231 Middle Rd -Blue Pnt 11715 **Fx:**363-8226
(518) 486-3501 .. **Dugan,** Suzanne M '90 State Comptroller -110 State -Albany 12236 **Fx:**473-9104
(212) 309-6000 .. **Dugan,** Terrence L '85 (Morgan L&B LLP) -101 Park Av -NY 10178
(607) 754-9181 .. **Dugan,** Terrence R '72 -515 E Main -Endicott 13760 **Fx:**754-6826
(914) 579-2200 .. **Dugan,** Valerie G '94 (Dugan & D,PC) -245 Saw Mill Rvr Rd -Hawthorne 10532 **Fx:**579-2201
(212) 696-6000 .. **Duggal,** Kabir A N '10 %Curtis M-PC&M LLP -101 Park Av -NY 10178
(212) 935-3000 .. **Duggal,** Raoul '06 %Mintz LCFG&P,PC -666 3rd Av -NY 10017
(631) 807-3027 .. **Duggan,** Brian R '06 -14 Cottage Ct -Huntngtn Sta 11746
(212) 264-8819 .. **Duggan,** Catherine F '88 OHA/SSA -26 Fed Plz -NY 10278
(212) 450-4000 .. **Duggan,** Chas S '97 (Davis P&W LLP) -450 Lex Av -NY 10017
(212) 687-0077 .. **Duggan,** David N '90 -420 Lex Av #300 -NY 10170 **Fx:**338-9229
(716) 853-3801 .. **Duggan,** James J '79 (Kenney SL&N,LLP) -14 Lafayette Sq -Buffalo 14203
(716) 833-1931 .. **Duggan,** James T '40 -2971 Delaware Av -Buffalo 14217
(212) 701-3000 .. **Duggan,** Kathleen G '92 %Cahill G&R LLP -80 Pine -NY 10005 **Fx:**269-5420
(716) 854-4705 .. **Duggan,** Matthew J '92 Lippman O -300 Pearl -Buffalo 14202
(845) 562-9100 .. **Duggan,** Stephen P III '65 Cnsl Rider W&F,PC -655 Little Britain Rd -New Windsor 12553
(212) 770-1204 .. **Duggan,** Thos P '00 AIGTS -80 Pine -NY 10005
(718) 254-7000 .. **Dugger,** Christina B '95 %US Atty -271 Cadman Plz E -Brklyn 11201 **Fx:**254-6479
(585) 232-5756 .. **Duguay,** David M '93 Comm Judicial Cndct -400 Andrews -Rchstr 14604 **Fx:**232-7834
(212) 553-5523 .. **Duguay,** Jaime '07 Zurich Fncl Srvcs -1 Lbrty Plz -NY 10006 **Fx:**(866) 255-2962
(585) 428-5210 .. **Duguay,** Kimberly Fox '93 %Pub Def -10 N Fitzhugh -Rchstr 14614 **Fx:**428-2234
(718) 575-5550 .. **Duhan,** David E '92 -118-35 Qns Blvd -Frst Hlls 11375 **Fx:**(888) 270-0557
(212) 349-1611 .. **Duignan,** Richd M '62 R Duignan & Assoc -233 Bway -NY 10279 **Fx:**349-0197
(631) 853-5761 .. **Dujmic,** Jos S Jr. '10 %Cnty Atty -400 Carleton Av -Central Islip 11722 **Fx:**853-7788
(212) 382-0700 .. **Dujmich,** Louis C '82 (Ostrolenk FG&S,LLP) -1180 Av of Amer -NY 10036
(315) 442-0100 .. **Dujnic,** Melissa J '06 %Gilberti SH&S,PC -555 E Genesee -Syracuse 13202
(212) 788-1011 .. **Duke,** Brandon W '09 Law Dept -100 Church -NY 10007 **Fx:**788-0367
(212) 969-3000 .. **Duke,** Catherine A '90 %Proskauer R LLP -1585 Bway -NY 10036
(516) 562-6782 .. **Duke,** Deirdre J '91 %St Francis Hsptl -100 Port Wshngtn Blvd -Roslyn 11576
(212) 588-8868 .. **Duke,** George C D '03 %Gilberti SH&S,PC -885 3rd Av -NY 10022
(716) 855-1111 .. **Duke Holzman Photiadis & Gresens LLP** -350 Main -Buffalo 14202 **Fx:**855-0327
(716) 894-4340 .. **Duke,** Kenneth A '80 -95 Ludington -Buffalo 14206
(212) 530-5000 .. **Duke,** Laurie N '05 %Milbank TH&M LLP -1 Chase Manh Plz -NY 10005
(212) 525-3153 .. **Duke,** Mary K '91 %HSBC Bank -452 5th Av -NY 10018
(212) 841-1000 .. **Duke,** P Benjamin '94 (Covington & B LLP) -620 8th Av -NY 10018
(585) 346-3220 .. **Duke,** Susan K '96 (Duke Law Firm,PC) -3407 Rochester Rd Bx609 -Lakeville 14480 **Fx:**346-6850
(914) 997-0981 .. **Duker,** Naomi R '79 (Gold & D) -470 Mamaroneck Av -White Plns 10605
(212) 412-2536 .. **Duke-Richardet,** Iain C L '06 %Barclays Capital Inc -1271 Av of Amer -NY 10020
(212) 859-8000 .. **Duke-Richardet,** Kristen '02 Fried FHS&J LLP -1 NY Plz -NY 10004
(518) 272-5917 .. **Dukes,** Heather L '05 %Unity Hse Law Projct -504 Bway -Troy 12180
(212) 687-5100 .. **Dukes,** Tanya D '02 Elite Taveler Magazine -801 Second Av -NY 10017
(212) 864-4695 .. **Dukess,** Laura F '88 -225 W 106th -NY 10025
(212) 867-4100 .. **Dukette,** Lynn M '06 %Furman K&B LLP -61 Bway -NY 10006
(646) 556-5989 .. **Dukhan,** Helen M '07 -26 Court -Brklyn 11242 **Fx:**558-0231
(718) 579-3036 .. **Dula,** Monica D '01 %Leg Aid -1020 Grnd Cncrs -Bronx 10451 **Fx:**588-2611
(212) 607-2814 .. **Dulabon,** David W '08 %FTC -1 Bowling Grn -NY 10004 **Fx:**607-2822
(212) 730-1770 .. **Dulaney,** Samantha '95 Cnsl IATSE -1430 Bway -NY 10018 **Fx:**730-7809
(212) 449-7475 .. **Dulberg,** Andrea L '86 %Merrill Lynch -220 Bway -NY 10038
(718) 639-5678 .. **Dulberg,** Matthew S '85 -37-06 82nd -Jcksn Hts 11372 **Fx:**639-4861
(718) 681-5400 .. **Dulberg,** Sam '70 -903B Sheridan Av -Bronx 10451
(518) 447-5532 .. **Dulin,** Thos N '77 Conflict Defender -112 State -Albany 12207 **Fx:**447-7416
(212) 813-8800 .. **Dulka,** Mary K '90 %Goodwin P LLP -620 8th Av -NY 10018
(516) 227-0800 .. **Dull,** Edw F '77 SrCnsl Natl Land Tenure Co LLC -1122 Franklin Av -Gdn Cty 11530 **Fx:**227-1160
(212) 753-3737 .. **D'Ull,** Walter '54 -223 E 62nd -NY 10065
(212) 969-3000 .. **Dullaghan,** Alice G '05 %Proskauer R LLP -1585 Bway -NY 10036
(212) 487-9700 .. **Dultz,** Alisa '91 OfCnsl White F&F,LLP -61 Bway -NY 10006
(212) 336-2000 .. **Dumain,** Ian M '05 %Patterson BW&T LLP -1133 Av of Amer -NY 10036
(212) 788-0838 .. **Dumain,** Rita D '84 %Law Dept -100 Church -NY 10007 **Fx:**788-0367
(212) 594-5300 .. **Dumain,** Sanford P '82 (Milberg LLP) -1 Penn Plz -NY 10119
(518) 474-4552 .. **Dumar,** Peter A Jr. '98 %Insurance Dept -99 Wshngtn Av -Albany 12257 **Fx:**473-4600
(212) 373-3000 .. **Dumas,** Brandilyn Y '09 %Paul WRW&G LLP -1285 Av of Amer -NY 10019
(518) 433-8800 .. **Dumas,** Chas B '83 (Lemery G LLC) -50 Beaver -Albany 12207

(516) 719-9838 .. **Dumas,** Edw M '97 LI Power Auth -333 Earle Ovngton Blvd -Uniondale 11553
(518) 285-8462 .. **Dumas,** Elizabeth M '82 Hon B Kramer -612 State -Schnctdy 12305
(518) 483-8800 .. **Dumas,** Peter A '00 -453 E Main -Malone 12953 **Fx:**483-5666
(212) 839-5300 .. **Dummett,** Lynn Ann '86 (Sidley A LLP) -787 7th Av -NY 10019
(212) 323-7070 .. **Dumont,** Jon M '99 (Rawle & H LLP) -14 Wall -NY 10005
(212) 464-2402 .. **Dumont,** Judith I '81 JP Morgan Chase & Co -345 Park Av -NY 10154
(607) 723-9511 .. **Dumont,** Katelyn Reid '10 %Coughlin & G,LLP -19 Chenango Bx2039 -Bnghmtn 13902
(631) 748-1100 .. **Dumont,** Kathleen M '91 Sedgwick Claims -300 Broadhllw Rd -Melvll 11747 **Fx:**454-2700
(212) 558-4000 .. **Dumont,** Nicolas H R '07 %Sullivan & C LLP -125 Broad -NY 10004
(845) 486-2280 .. **Dumser,** August J '05 Pub Def -22 Market -Poughkeepsie 12601 **Fx:**486-2266
(212) 878-8000 .. **Dunaevsky,** Yelena '03 %Clifford C LLP -31 W 52nd -NY 10019
(212) 687-7410 .. **Dunaway,** Carlyle M Jr. '70 (Clifton B&D,LLP) -420 Lex Av -NY 10170
(518) 886-4360 .. **Dunbar,** Jacqueline '92 AYCO -321 Bway Bx860 -Saratoga Spgs 12866
(716) 856-5500 .. **Dunbar,** Jos W '87 (Damon M LLP) -200 Delaware Av -Buffalo 14202
(631) 224-1345 .. **Dunbar,** Kelly A '94 Threshold Land Inc -584 Main -Islip 11751 **Fx:**224-5129
(202) 739-3000 .. **Dunbar,** Mary M '06 OfCnsl Morgan L&B LLP -101 Park Av -NY 10178 **Fx:**739-3001
(212) 423-2363 .. **Duncan,** Blair M '95 %North General Hptl -1879 Mad Av -NY 10035
(516) 376-9569 .. **Duncan,** Brian M '06 %McGlew & T -1 Scarboro Station Plz -Scarboro 10510 **Fx:**(914) 941-5855
(518) 463-2196 .. **Duncan,** E David '58 (Duncan and D) -112 State -Albany 12207 **Fx:**432-4847
(212) 588-5500 .. **Duncan,** Erica N '06 %Davies WP&V LLP -625 Mad Av -NY 10022
(631) 689-8001 .. **Duncan Fish & Vogel** -317 Middle Cntry Rd -Smithtwn 11787 **Fx:**724-5163
(631) 361-5360 .. **Duncan,** George H '95 (Keahon FD&F) -1393 Vets Mem'l Hwy -Hauppauge 11788 **Fx:**361-5365
(212) 225-2000 .. **Duncan,** James A '80 (Cleary GS&H) -1 Lbrty Plz -NY 10006
(315) 448-0672 .. **Duncan,** John G '76 %US Atty -100 S Clinton Bx7198 -Syracuse 13261 **Fx:**448-0689
(212) 451-2300 .. **Duncan,** Johnathan C '03 %Olshan GFR&W LLP -65 E 55th -NY 10022
(212) 230-8800 .. **Duncan,** Malene Kesi '05 %WilmerHale -399 Park Av -NY 10022
(212) 489-1600 .. **Duncan,** Nicole '96 %Deloitte LLP -1633 Bway -NY 10019 **Fx:**492-4201
(800) 742-9696 .. **Duncan,** Robin L '04 %Binder & B,PC -33-00 Nrthrn Blvd -LIC 11101 **Fx:**(718) 512-2424
(518) 463-2196 .. **Duncan,** Sara A '02 (Duncan and D) -112 State -Albany 12207 **Fx:**432-4847
(212) 560-7543 .. **Duncan,** Sharyn M '90 -1100 Lincoln Pl -Brklyn 11213
(516) 229-4400 .. **Duncan,** Susan G '81 %Kay & G -875 Merrick Av -Westbury 11590
(212) 620-4746 .. **Duncan,** Terrence '99 DOL-Ofc of Solicitor -201 Varick -NY 10014
(212) 382-6600 .. **Duncan,** Vivienne '91 %NYC Bar -42 W 44th -NY 10036 **Fx:**398-6634
(212) 701-3000 .. **Duncanson,** John C '04 %Cahill G&R LLP -80 Pine -NY 10005 **Fx:**269-5420
(315) 435-2470 .. **Duncanson,** Robt A '91 %DA -505 S State -Syracuse 13202 **Fx:**435-3969
(716) 483-3233 .. **Duncanson,** Wm F Jr. '85 -501 W 3rd -Jamestwn 14701
(315) 376-6565 .. **Dunckel,** Earl B '68 (Dunckel & K LLP) -5423 Shady Av Bx473 -Lowvll 13367 **Fx:**376-8418
(518) 295-7515 .. **Duncombe,** Raynor B '72 -283 Main Bx490 -Schoharie 12157 **Fx:**295-7519
(212) 372-2186 .. **Dundas,** Lorette H '05 SrCnsl Newmark Knight Frank -125 Park Av -NY 10017 **Fx:**372-2386
(212) 474-1000 .. **Dundon,** Mark E '08 %Cravath S&M LLP -825 8th Av -NY 10019
(212) 370-0040 .. **Dundon,** Matthew J '99 Miller Tabak Roberts Securities -331 Mad Av -NY 10017
(212) 848-9800 .. **Dunefsky,** Brian '93 (Withers B LLP) -430 Park Av -NY 10022
(212) 384-1000 .. **Duner,** James M '89 %FBI -26 Fed Plz -NY 10278
(212) 506-2500 .. **Dunetz,** Jeffrey L '84 (Mayer B LLP) -1675 Bway -NY 10019
(718) 591-9255 .. **Dunfee,** Lorraine R '80 -150-56 78th Av -Flushng 11367
(212) 356-8195 .. **Dunham,** Carol Gibbons '87 CIR -520 8th Av -NY 10018 **Fx:**356-8111
(518) 462-5601 .. **Dunham,** Chas C IV '09 %O'Connell & A -54 State -Albany 12207
(212) 278-0400 .. **Dunham,** Christopher C '61 OfCnsl Cooper & D LLP -30 Rckfllr Plz -NY 10112
(212) 735-3000 .. **Dunham,** Douglas W '88 Cnsl Skadden ASM&F LLP -4 Times Sq -NY 10036
(212) 832-1977 .. **Dunham,** Isaac P '05 %Schreck RDA&H -1790 Bway -NY 10019 **Fx:**832-2969
(585) 753-4500 .. **Dunham,** Matthew R '06 DA -832 Watts Bldg -Rchstr 14614 **Fx:**753-4576
(212) 859-8000 .. **Dunham,** Molly M B '07 %Fried FHS&J LLP -1 NY Plz -NY 10004
(315) 492-1666 .. **Dunham,** Philip M '04 %Sargent & G,LLP -892 E Brighton Av -Syracuse 13205
(518) 455-3171 .. **Dunham,** Thos K '04 Sen D Skelos -503 State Cptl -Albany 12247
(212) 909-6000 .. **Dunham,** Wolcott B Jr. '69 (Debevoise & P LLP) -919 3rd Av -NY 10022
(212) 613-2021 .. **Dunican,** Patrick C Jr. '92 (Gibbons PC) -1 Penn Plz -NY 10119 **Fx:**(973) 639-6320
(516) 571-0440 .. **Dunkel,** Jason A '03 Cnty Labor Relations Ofc -400 Cnty Seat Dr -Mineola 11501
(212) 655-6592 .. **Dunkin,** Ellen R '83 %Risk & Ins Mgmt Soc -1065 Av of Amer -NY 10018
(212) 446-4800 .. **Dunlap,** Andrew R '03 (Kirkland & E LLP) -153 E 53rd -NY 10022
(212) 682-8811 .. **Dunlap,** John T '86 (Dunnington B&M LLP) -1359 Bway -NY 10018
(845) 638-5001 .. **Dunlap,** Kevin M '07 %DA -1 S Main -New Cty 10956 **Fx:**638-5070
(914) 701-8000 .. **Dunlay,** Christian J '95 Atlas Air,Inc -2000 Wstchstr Av -Purchase 10577
(518) 434-7371 .. **Dunlea,** Mark A '80 %Hunger Action Ntwrk -275 State -Albany 12210
(212) 431-2366 .. **Dunleavy,** April Z '87 NY Law Schl -57 Worth -NY 10013
(516) 741-2585 .. **Dunleavy,** Barbara I '97 %Rosicki R & Assoc,PC -51 E Bethpage Rd -Plainvw 11803 **Fx:**741-4748
(212) 226-6662 .. **Dunleavy,** Denise M '78 (Kramer & D) -350 Bway -NY 10013
(914) 682-3300 .. **Dunleavy,** Michelle '97 %La Sorsa & B -3 Barker Av -White Plns 10601
(212) 816-6187 .. **Dunleavy,** Patrick S '88 Salomon Smith Barney -388 Greenwich -NY 10013
(212) 848-4000 .. **Dunlop,** Lisl Joanne '98 Cnsl Shearman & S LLP -599 Lex Av -NY 10022
(212) 973-8000 .. **Dunlop,** Wm R '69 Cnsl Schnader HS&L LLP -140 Bway -NY 10005
(718) 237-5500 .. **Dunlop-German,** Allison A '99 %Leg Srvcs -105 Court -Brklyn 11201 **Fx:**855-0733
(716) 845-8717 .. **Dunn,** Amy '03 Roswell Park Cancer Inst -Elm & Carlton -Buffalo 14263
(518) 266-9355 .. **Dunn,** Arthur G '97 -17 1st -Troy 12180
(631) 321-1969 .. **Dunn Browne,LLC** -500 Bicounty Blvd -Farmngdl 11735
(845) 562-9100 .. **Dunn,** Bruce C Sr. '77 Cnsl Rider W&F,PC -655 Little Britain Rd -New Windsor 12553
(315) 363-4690 .. **Dunn Bruno & St Leger LLP** -1507 Uppr Lenox Av -Oneida 13421 **Fx:**363-4195
(315) 824-3430 .. **Dunn Bruno & St Leger LLP** -13 Payne -Hamilton 13346
(516) 622-0099 .. **Dunn,** Christine A '01 %Carlinsky D&P,PLLC -8 Duffy Av -Hicksvll 11801
(212) 607-3300 .. **Dunn,** Christopher T '97 NYCLU -125 Broad -NY 10004 **Fx:**607-3318
(212) 841-1000 .. **Dunn,** Damion R '09 %Covington & B LLP -620 8th Av -NY 10018
(212) 698-3500 .. **Dunn,** Danl M '93 (Dechert LLP) -1095 Av of Amer -NY 10036
(212) 918-3000 .. **Dunn,** David '79 (Hogan L LLP) -875 3rd Av -NY 10022
(212) 218-5500 .. **Dunn,** Donald R Jr. '06 %Seyfarth S LLP -620 8th Av -NY 10018
(212) 595-4036 .. **Dunn,** Douglas K '85 -277 West End Av -NY 10023
(315) 474-4648 .. **Dunn,** Edw P '90 Dunn Law Ofc -333 E Onondaga -Syracuse 13202 **Fx:**474-4623
(212) 259-8000 .. **Dunn,** Ellen M '93 (Dewey & L LLP) -1301 Av of Amer -NY 10019
(516) 248-9388 .. **Dunn,** Gary S '80 -1225 Franklin Av -Gdn Cty 11530
(212) 506-1766 .. **Dunn,** Gary W '90 %Kasowitz BT&F LLP -1633 Bway -NY 10019
(202) 474-0503 .. **Dunn,** Jason M '02 %Global Crossing -225 Kenneth Dr -Rchstr 14623 **Fx:**(877) 769-9844
(212) 756-2000 .. **Dunn,** Jennifer '03 %Schulte R&Z LLP -919 3rd Av -NY 10022
(518) 694-8380 .. **Dunn,** Jill A '94 Dunn Law Firm PLLC -99 Pine -Albany 12207 **Fx:**935-9353
(212) 676-0972 .. **Dunn,** Kelley A '96 %Law Dept -60 Lafayette -NY 10013 **Fx:**442-6865
(212) 756-2000 .. **Dunn,** Kelly V '05 %Schulte R&Z LLP -919 3rd Av -NY 10022
(212) 224-4000 .. **Dunn,** Lawr A '96 %Sumitomo Mitsui -277 Park Av -NY 10172 **Fx:**593-9522
(212) 225-2000 .. **Dunn,** Lindsay Colbert '08 %Cleary GS&H -1 Lbrty Plz -NY 10006
(518) 456-5249 .. **Dunn,** Louise E '84 %MA Bjork -500 New Karner Rd -Albany 12205 **Fx:**456-1288
(315) 449-2616 .. **Dunn,** Mark L '87 Martin GBM&C,PC -5790 Widewaters Pkwy -DeWitt 13214
(212) 732-3200 .. **Dunn,** Matthew D '04 %Carter L&M LLP -2 Wall -NY 10005
(518) 285-8382 .. **Dunn,** Matthew R '01 Hon V Graffeo -20 Eagle -Albany 12207 **Fx:**487-5337
(315) 408-0788 .. **Dunn,** Matthew R '02 -1207-7 Faichney Dr -Watertwn 13601
(212) 715-9100 .. **Dunn,** Matthew S '94 (Kramer LN&F,LLP) -1177 Av of Amer -NY 10036
(845) 331-0396 .. **Dunn,** Matthew T '05 %Klein & K,PC -70 Maiden Ln Bx3158 -Kingston 12402 **Fx:**331-1482
(516) 622-0099 .. **Dunn,** Michl C '00 (Carlinsky D&P,PLLC) -8 Duffy Av -Hicksvll 11801
(212) 653-8700 .. **Dunn,** Michl K '09 %Sheppard MR&H LLP -30 Rckfllr Plz -NY 10112
(716) 626-1564 .. **Dunn,** Michl L '73 OfCnsl Simpson & S PLLC -5555 Main -Williamsvll 14221 **Fx:**626-0366
(212) 218-5500 .. **Dunn,** Michl T '03 %Seyfarth S LLP -620 8th Av -NY 10018
(212) 617-8169 .. **Dunn,** Michl W '06 %Bloomberg LLP -731 Lex Av -NY 10022
(607) 274-6504 .. **Dunn,** Patricia '88 %City Atty -108 E Green -Ithaca 14850 **Fx:**274-6507
(718) 590-7802 .. **Dunn,** Patrick A '06 %ACS -900 Sheridan Av -Bronx 10451 **Fx:**992-0084
(315) 422-9538 .. **Dunn,** Peter A '91 Central NY Community Fndtn -500 S Salina -Syracuse 13202
(631) 586-1550 .. **Dunn,** Peter J '92 -2137 Deer Prk Av -Deer Pk 11729 **Fx:**667-1030
(315) 363-4690 .. **Dunn,** Peter M '61 (Dunn B&S LLP) -1507 Uppr Lenox Av -Oneida 13421
(631) 321-1969 .. **Dunn,** Philip M '81 (Dunn B,LLC) -500 Bicounty Blvd -Farmngdl 11735
(718) 471-3670 .. **Dunn,** Raymond A '00 -1225 Norton Dr -Far Rckwy 11691 **Fx:**337-3003
(212) 296-6075 .. **Dunn,** Robt A '87 Morgan Stanley -522 5th Av -NY 10036
(212) 735-3000 .. **Dunn,** Robt L '08 %Skadden ASM&F LLP -4 Times Sq -NY 10036
(212) 964-6611 .. **Dunn,** Robt N '89 (Lester SK&D) -120 Bway -NY 10271
(518) 432-7511 .. **Dunn,** Ronald G '81 (Gleason DW&O) -40 Beaver -Albany 12207
(212) 455-2000 .. **Dunn,** Sarah L '04 %Simpson T&B LLP -425 Lex Av -NY 10017
(718) 254-7000 .. **Dunn,** Scott '85 %US Atty -271 Cadman Plz E -Brklyn 11201 **Fx:**254-6479
(718) 796-0837 .. **Dunn,** Susan M '91 -630 W 246th -Bronx 10471 **Fx:**796-3473
(212) 336-0060 .. **Dunn,** Susannah M '02 %SEC -3 World Fncl Ctr -NY 10281 **Fx:**336-1323
(212) 391-9500 .. **Dunn,** Terrence M '84 (Einbinder & D,PC) -104 W 40th -NY 10018
(718) 703-6176 .. **Dunn,** Theresa '84 -276 Stratford Rd -Brklyn 11218 **Fx:**703-6177
(212) 474-1000 .. **Dunn,** Thos E '93 (Cravath S&M LLP) -825 8th Av -NY 10019
(212) 940-9940 .. **Dunn,** Thos F X '81 -7 Dey -NY 10007
(631) 321-1969 .. **Dunn,** Timothy J II '80 (Dunn B,LLC) -500 Bicounty Blvd -Farmngdl 11735
(631) 249-6600 .. **Dunn,** Timothy J III '97 %Rebore T&P PC -500 Bi-Cnty Blvd -Farmngdl 11735 **Fx:**249-8190
(646) 386-5700 .. **Dunn,** Tracey A '04 %Civil Ct -111 Centre -NY 10013
(212) 408-5100 .. **Dunn,** Vincent '90 (Chadbourne & P LLP) -30 Rckfllr Plz -NY 10112
(212) 460-4418 .. **Dunne,** Barbara M '99 ConEd -4 Irving Pl -NY 10003
(518) 455-7723 .. **Dunne,** Brian J '08 Hon S Read -20 Eagle -Albany 12207

(212) 450-4000 .. **Dunne,** Carey R '85 (Davis P&W LLP) -450 Lex Av -NY 10017
(646) 640-5114 .. **Dunne,** Chas G '03 NYPD -1 Police Plz -NY 10038
(212) 558-4000 .. **Dunne,** Christopher J '06 %Sullivan & C LLP -125 Broad -NY 10004
(212) 530-5000 .. **Dunne,** Dennis F '91 (Milbank TH&M LLP) -1 Chase Manh Plz -NY 10005
(212) 645-2410 .. **Dunne,** Gerard F '75 -156 5th Av -NY 10010 **Fx:**645-2435
(516) 671-2700 .. **Dunne,** James L '69 (Dunne & H) -215 Glen Cove Av -Sea Cliff 11579 **Fx:**671-2696
(518) 452-1800 .. **Dunne,** John D '10 %Towne R & Prtnrs,PC -450 New Karner Rd Bx15072 -Albany 12212
(518) 487-7600 .. **Dunne,** John R '55 SrCnsl Whiteman O&H LLP -1 Commerce Plz -Albany 12260
(516) 742-6200 .. **Dunne,** John W '94 (Lynn G&D,LLP) -330 Old Cntry Rd -Mineola 11501 **Fx:**742-5294
(212) 766-1888 .. **Dunne,** Jos F '86 %Morris DA&F -2 Rector -NY 10006
(631) 878-4171 .. **Dunne,** Karen Lee '85 -32 Gtwy Ln -Manorvll 11949 **Fx:**874-5058
(845) 306-1000 .. **Dunne,** Keturah A '06 %Watchtower -100 Watchtower Dr -Patterson 12563 **Fx:**306-0709
(914) 946-1452 .. **Dunne,** Michl P '00 %Markhoff & M PC -14 Mamaroneck Av -White Plns 10601
(718) 520-4737 .. **Dunne,** Peter '79 %Hon J Clabby -125-01 Qns Blvd -Kew Gdns 11415
(518) 436-0751 .. **Dunne,** Philip T '76 (Hinman S PC) -121 State -Albany 12207
(631) 853-4049 .. **Dunne,** Richd T '87 %Cnty Atty -Dennison Bldg Bx6100 -Hauppauge 11788 **Fx:**853-5169
(212) 551-1750 .. **Dunne,** Robt D '02 R Dunne,LLC -230 Park Av -NY 10169 **Fx:**808-3020
(212) 395-6315 .. **Dunne,** Thos A '78 Verizon -1095 Av of Amer -NY 10036
(212) 332-8300 .. **Dunnegan,** Wm '81 (Dunnegan LLC) -350 5th Av -NY 10118 **Fx:**332-8301
(917) 421-4673 .. **Dunnigan,** Abigail K '00 IRS -33 Maiden Ln -NY 10038
(212) 336-0061 .. **Dunnigan,** Christopher J '00 %SEC -3 World Fncl Ctr -NY 10281 **Fx:**336-1323
(212) 751-3001 .. **Dunning,** Brian C '91 (Thompson & K LLP) -919 3rd Av -NY 10022
(516) 708-9500 .. **Dunning,** Carol Ann '95 CA Dunning,PC -46 George -Manhsst 11030 **Fx:**708-9501
(212) 809-7074 .. **Dunning,** James J '01 %Armienti DG&R,LLP -39 Bway -NY 10006
(212) 351-4000 .. **Dunning,** Mary Kay '05 %Gibson D&C LLP -200 Park Av -NY 10166
(212) 682-8811 .. **Dunnington Bartholow & Miller LLP** -1359 Bway -NY 10018 **Fx:**661-7769
(212) 455-2000 .. **Dunogue,** Agnes '05 %Simpson T&B LLP -425 Lex Av -NY 10017
(212) 742-8700 .. **Dunphy,** Brian M '03 %Garson D&C LLP -110 Wall -NY 10005
(212) 801-6850 .. **Dunphy,** Burke A '08 %Greenberg T,LLP -200 Park Av -NY 10166
(914) 377-6240 .. **Dunphy,** Edw P '78 Law Dept -300 City Hall -Ynkrs 10701 **Fx:**964-0563
(607) 272-1283 .. **Dunphy,** Robt E '02 -401 E State -Ithaca 14850
(607) 337-1745 .. **Dunshee,** Stephen M '91 %DA -5 Court -Norwich 13815 **Fx:**337-1746
(212) 558-4000 .. **Dunson,** Danl '73 (Sullivan & C LLP) -125 Broad -NY 10004
(212) 808-7800 .. **Dunst,** Adam H '06 %Kelley D&W LLP -101 Park Av -NY 10178
(212) 351-4000 .. **Dunst,** Lee G '93 (Gibson D&C LLP) -200 Park Av -NY 10166
(212) 819-8200 .. **Dunstan,** Shanan D '10 %White & C LLP -1155 Av of Amer -NY 10036
(212) 688-5151 .. **Dunworth,** Gerald J Jr. '79 (Gibney A&F,LLP) -665 5th Av -NY 10022
(212) 421-4100 .. **Dunworth,** Michl P '89 (Pryor C LLP) -7 Times Sq -NY 10036
(631) 951-3700 .. **Duoba,** Valdas C '70 V Duoba,PC -2025 Brentwd Rd -Brentwd 11717 **Fx:**617-5563
(347) 404-9920 .. **Duong,** Jaime Nhu '05 %MHLS -120 Schermerhorn -Brklyn 11201 **Fx:**(718) 243-2410
(212) 788-0627 .. **Duong,** Karen '10 %Law Dept -100 Church -NY 10007 **Fx:**788-0367
(845) 294-8900 .. **Dupee,** Jon C Jr. '90 (Dupee & M,PC) -211 Main Bx470 -Goshen 10924
(845) 294-8900 .. **Dupee & Monroe,PC** -211 Main Bx470 -Goshen 10924 **Fx:**294-3619
(212) 318-6000 .. **Dupill,** Emily '08 %Paul HJ&W LLP -75 E 55th -NY 10022
(212) 688-5151 .. **Dupler,** Jeffrey E '92 SrCnsl Gibney A&F,LLP -665 5th Av -NY 10022
(212) 508-6700 .. **du Pont,** George F '02 %Tannenbaum HS&H LLP -900 3rd Av -NY 10022
(212) 836-8000 .. **du Pont,** Julie K '02 %Kaye S LLP -425 Park Av -NY 10022
(212) 231-8132 .. **DuPont,** Olivier L '05 %Sacks & M LLC -410 Park Av -NY 10022
(518) 238-4339 .. **Dupree,** Brendon D '07 %OCA -187 Wolf Rd -Albany 12205 **Fx:**438-3518
(914) 238-1000 .. **DuPree,** Clifford H R '76 Reader's Digest -Readers Digest Rd -Plsntvll 10570 **Fx:**241-5644
(315) 386-4583 .. **Duprey,** Mathew P '00 (Lekki HF&D,PC) -21 Court Bx469 -Canton 13617
(718) 298-8900 .. **Duprey,** Michelle R '09 Leg Aid -153-01 Jamaica Av -Jamaica 11432 **Fx:**657-0537
(516) 714-7336 .. **Dupuy,** John L '02 %T Spina -170 Froehlich Farm Blvd -Woodbury 11797 **Fx:**496-5420
(212) 931-7814 .. **Dupuy,** Robt A '01 %MLB -245 Park Av -NY 10167 **Fx:**949-5657
(212) 903-9000 .. **Duque,** Francisco H '02 %Linklaters -1345 Av of Amer -NY 10105
(631) 226-2255 .. **Duque,** Guillermo '04 G Duque PLLC -411 S 1st -Lindenhrst 11757 **Fx:**412-3831
(845) 778-2121 .. **Duquette,** Wm E Jr. '03 %Jacobowitz & G,LLP -158 Orange Av Bx367 -Walden 12586
(716) 849-8900 .. **Duquin,** Scott M '03 %Hurwitz & F,PC -1300 Lbrty Bldg -Buffalo 14202
(212) 756-2000 .. **Durand,** Nancy '09 %Schulte R&Z LLP -919 3rd Av -NY 10022
(212) 455-2000 .. **Duran Giral,** Ismael '06 %Simpson T&B LLP -425 Lex Av -NY 10017
(212) 710-5160 .. **Durant,** L Marc '91 OfCnsl Gallion & S -75 Rckfllr Plz -NY 10019 **Fx:**428-6777
(585) 263-1000 .. **Durant,** Peter H '80 (Nixon P LLP) -1100 Clinton Sq -Rchstr 14604
(212) 819-1414 .. **Durant,** Sandra B '74 (Durant & Assoc) -509 W 110th -NY 10025
(914) 245-6060 .. **Durante,** Albert J '03 (Durante B&T,PLLC) -2000 Maple Hill -Yorktwn Hts 10598
(914) 245-6060 .. **Durante Bock & Tota,PLLC** -2000 Maple Hill -Yorktwn Hts 10598 **Fx:**245-6844
(516) 496-5822 .. **Durante,** Kathleen H '02 %T Spina -170 Froehlich Farm Blvd -Woodbury 11797 **Fx:**496-5420
(212) 335-9000 .. **Durastanti,** Armand '80 %DA -1 Hogan Pl -NY 10013
(212) 969-3000 .. **Durba,** Erin C '06 %Proskauer R LLP -1585 Bway -NY 10036
(800) 237-8834 .. **Durben,** Richd H '01 Fidelity Personal Trust Co -980 Mad Av -NY 10075
(212) 558-4000 .. **Durbin,** Erik W '10 %Sullivan & C LLP -125 Broad -NY 10004
(212) 704-4400 .. **Durbin,** Paul D '09 (Miller CP&S,PLLC) -500 5th Av -NY 10110
(212) 416-8653 .. **Durden,** Rebecca A '89 %Dept of Law -120 Bway -NY 10271
(518) 474-1331 .. **Durfee,** Peter A '82 %Ofc Mntl Health -44 Holland Av -Albany 12229 **Fx:**473-7863
(315) 253-3263 .. **Durgala,** Milan M '63 -144 Genesee -Auburn 13021 **Fx:**255-2262
(516) 249-1342 .. **Durgana,** James V '09 %Grey & G,LLP -360 Main -Farmngdl 11735
(718) 645-3111 .. **Durham,** Bernard '63 %Leg Aid Society Ofc for the Aging -111 Lvngstn -Brklyn 11201 **Fx:**260-4722
(631) 715-7851 .. **Durham,** John J '02 US Atty-EDNY -610 Fed Plz -Central Islip 11722
(212) 801-6923 .. **Durham,** Sylvie A '86 (Greenberg T,LLP) -200 Park Av -NY 10166
(212) 384-1000 .. **Durkan,** Eileen F '99 %FBI -26 Fed Plz -NY 10278
(212) 225-2000 .. **Durkee,** Melissa J '08 %Cleary GS&H -1 Lbrty Plz -NY 10006
(212) 337-2646 .. **Durkin,** James M '91 Dept of Labor -201 Varick -NY 10014
(518) 257-3000 .. **Durkin,** Jos F '83 %Dormitory Auth -515 Bway -Albany 12207 **Fx:**257-3101
(914) 699-3550 .. **Durkin,** Patrick J '96 (Durkin Law Ofc) -71 Vernon Pl -Mt Vernon 10552 **Fx:**699-6418
(212) 349-8173 .. **Durkin,** Thos E III '84 (Durkin & D) -111 Bway -NY 10006 **Fx:**285-1968
(585) 454-3616 .. **Durkin,** Thos P '86 %MA Bjork -2 State -Rchstr 14614 **Fx:**454-3664
(516) 799-5253 .. **Durnin,** Douglas A '76 -5355 Merrick Rd -Massapequa 11758 **Fx:**795-0468
(718) 291-6390 .. **Duroseau,** Alix Jr. '86 -89-00 Sutphin Blvd -Jamaica 11435 **Fx:**291-6392
(315) 475-1202 .. **Durr,** Robt A '88 -103 E Water -Syracuse 13202 **Fx:**474-8867
(718) 558-3549 .. **Durrant-Mayo,** Annette L '86 -93-59 183rd -Hollis 11423
(212) 586-2435 .. **Durrow,** Heidi W '96 -61 W 62nd -NY 10023
(212) 506-2500 .. **Durschlag,** Danl B '08 %Mayer B LLP -1675 Bway -NY 10019
(212) 407-4766 .. **Dursht,** Kenneth A '99 Gam USA Inc -330 Mad Av -NY 10017
(212) 872-1000 .. **D'Urso,** David J '97 -One Bryant Park -NY 10036 **Fx:**872-1002
(212) 916-9216 .. **Durso,** Edwin M '83 %ESPN -605 3rd Av -NY 10158
(212) 243-7000 .. **D'Urso,** Gary A '91 %Clarendon Mgmt -435 W 23rd -NY 10011
(212) 927-2655 .. **D'Urso,** Jos D '89 -92 Pinehurst Av -NY 10033
(845) 708-7600 .. **Durso,** Michele C '06 Cnty Dept Weights & Measures -18 New Hampstead Rd -New Cty 10956
(212) 964-1000 .. **Durst,** John E Jr. '81 (Durst Law Firm,PC) -319 Bway -NY 10007 **Fx:**964-1400
(212) 285-4900 .. **Durst,** Keith E '94 Wagging Tail/Doggie Day Care Inc -77 Worth -NY 10013
(516) 867-3333 .. **Durst,** Sanford J '67 -106 Woodcleft Av -Freeprt 11520 **Fx:**867-3397
(631) 423-4494 .. **Durst-Blair,** Ellen '04 -250 Mineola Blvd -Mineola 11501 **Fx:**423-4493
(718) 575-9330 .. **Duru,** Okechukwu A '96 (Duru Assoc,PLLC) -123-60 83rd Av -Kew Gdns 11415
(212) 986-6840 .. **Dus,** Melinda M '01 %N Brickman -317 Mad Av -NY 10017 **Fx:**986-7691
(845) 562-0203 .. **DuSault,** Marie M '95 %Finkelstein & Prtnrs,LLP -1279 Route 300 Bx1111 -Newburgh 12550
(212) 735-3000 .. **Dusek,** Danl '01 (Skadden ASM&F LLP) -4 Times Sq -NY 10036
(718) 897-2700 .. **Dusek,** Laurie D '94 -63-52 Saunders -Rego Pk 11374 **Fx:**897-2703
(518) 761-6463 .. **Dusek,** Paul B '82 Cnty Atty -1340 State Route 9 -Lk George 12845
(718) 625-1777 .. **Dusenberry,** Harry A '76 -125 Lvngstn -Brklyn 11201 **Fx:**625-0135
(518) 477-2303 .. **Dush,** George H '70 -77 Troy Rd -E Greenbush 12061 **Fx:**477-6851
(631) 435-1053 .. **Dushaj,** Anthony J '01 -330 Vndrblt Motor Pkwy -Hauppauge 11788 **Fx:**952-5600
(914) 995-4172 .. **Dushaj,** Kristina '04 %DA -111 Martin Luther King Blvd -White Plns 10601 **Fx:**995-3363
(718) 855-5684 .. **Dushas,** Marina '75 %Longo & D -26 Court -Brklyn 11242
(718) 981-6200 .. **Duskin,** Jay S '86 (Duskin & C) -1688 Victory Blvd -Staten Isl 10314 **Fx:**981-0433
(212) 571-9196 .. **Dussek,** Philippe R '88 -111 Bway -NY 10006 **Fx:**346-4665
(718) 250-2000 .. **Dussek,** Viviane '10 %DA -350 Jay -Brklyn 11201 **Fx:**250-2314
(914) 522-2391 .. **Dussol,** Patrick J '96 %Tamat Advsrs -Bx1909 -NY 10156
(212) 833-5098 .. **Dustman,** Ann Elizabeth '95 Sony Corp of America -550 Mad Av -NY 10022
(917) 696-7487 .. **Duswalt,** Geraldene Sherr '88 -2600 Netherland Av -Bronx 10463
(212) 344-3100 .. **Duszak,** M Diane '92 (Frenkel LWW&G,LLP) -1 Whitehall -NY 10004
(716) 843-5700 .. **Duszkiewicz,** Thos S '78 %US Atty -138 Delaware Av -Buffalo 14202 **Fx:**551-3052
(585) 256-0090 .. **Dutcher,** B Andrew '76 (Dutcher & Z) -1399 Monroe Av -Rchstr 14618
(845) 247-0220 .. **Dutcher,** Desmond J '05 -132 Glasco Tpk Bx145 -Glasco 12432 **Fx:**247-0330
(585) 454-7545 .. **Dutcher & Sidoti** -183 E Main -Rchstr 14604 **Fx:**232-7455
(585) 256-0090 .. **Dutcher & Zatkowsky** -1399 Monroe Av -Rchstr 14618 **Fx:**256-0783
(716) 859-1305 .. **Duthe,** Lorraine M '07 Kaleida Health -100 High -Buffalo 14203
(718) 591-1134 .. **Duthely,** Ralph '88 -9050 Parsons Blvd -Jamaica 11432
(845) 988-0453 .. **Duthie,** Danl P '77 -Bx8 -Bellvale 10912
(212) 310-8000 .. **Dutka,** Paul I '79 (Weil G&M LLP) -767 5th Av -NY 10153
(212) 345-5525 .. **Dutt,** John R '81 %Marsh USA -1166 Av of Amer -NY 10036 **Fx:**345-4808
(716) 856-4000 .. **Dutta,** Reetuparna '09 %Hodgson R LLP -140 Pearl -Buffalo 14202
(212) 450-4000 .. **Dutta,** Sapna '07 %Davis P&W LLP -450 Lex Av -NY 10017
(212) 298-5205 .. **Dutta,** Suvra '90 %Leg Aid -49 Thomas -NY 10013 **Fx:**298-5252

(917) 536-5940 .. **Dutton,** Andrew '03 A Dutton,PC -1076 Davis -Franklin Sq 11010 **Fx:**(516) 706-0531
(516) 249-1342 .. **Dutton,** Danl A '98 (Grey & G,LLP) -360 Main -Farmngdl 11735
(212) 790-4500 .. **Dutton,** Melinda J '93 (Manatt P&P,LLP) -7 Times Sq -NY 10036
(212) 701-3000 .. **Dutton,** Richd L '77 %Cahill G&R LLP -80 Pine -NY 10005 **Fx:**269-5420
(516) 535-1700 .. **Duval,** Christopher J '87 %Horing W&R,PC -11 Hillside Av -Williston Pk 11596
(212) 292-6580 .. **Duval,** Jacqueline '93 %ZBI -350 Park Av -NY 10022
(212) 323-2291 .. **Duval,** Joelle N '00 NYC Health & Hospital Corp -346 Bway -NY 10013
(718) 608-0200 .. **Duval,** Leo V III '87 -885 Annadale Rd -Staten Isl 10312
(212) 883-1700 .. **Duval,** Patrick W '89 (Duval & S LLP) -101 Park Av -NY 10178
(212) 883-1700 .. **Duval & Stachenfeld LLP** -101 Park Av -NY 10178 **Fx:**883-8883
(516) 944-4440 .. **DuVal,** Wally '88 -201 Cow Neck Rd -Pt Wash 11050 **Fx:**944-5335
(845) 486-6800 .. **DuVall,** Richd R '86 (McCabe & M LLP) -63 Wshngtn Bx509 -Poughkeepsie 12602
(212) 756-2000 .. **Duvanel,** Fonda '97 SpclCnsl Schulte R&Z LLP -919 3rd Av -NY 10022
(212) 335-4500 .. **Duvdevani,** Tamar Y '03 %DLA Piper LLP -1251 Av of Amer -NY 10020
(315) 379-2225 .. **Duvé,** Nicole M '91 DA -48 Court -Canton 13617 **Fx:**379-2301
(212) 407-4000 .. **Duver,** Theo F '94 SrCnsl Loeb & L,LLP -345 Park Av -NY 10154
(607) 273-0633 .. **Duvernoy,** Austin A '84 -Bx7001 -Ithaca 14851 **Fx:**273-0633
(212) 434-0100 .. **Dvorkin,** Michl K '93 %Litchfield C LLP -420 Lex Av -NY 10170
(212) 277-6500 .. **Dvorkin,** Stephen A '74 (Dickstein S LLP) -1633 Bway -NY 10019
(631) 738-5768 .. **Dvorkis,** Ariela '93 %Symbol Tech -1 Symbol Plz -Holtsvll 11742
(212) 558-4000 .. **Dvorkis,** Taly '10 %Sullivan & C LLP -125 Broad -NY 10004
(212) 403-1000 .. **Dvornic,** Tijana J '10 %Wachtell LR&K -51 W 52nd -NY 10019
(631) 539-0375 .. **Dvoskin,** Gary E '94 %Cruser M&N,LLP -175 Pinelawn Rd -Melvll 11747
(516) 937-5900 .. **Dvoskin,** Lisa R '09 %Moomjian WW&C LLP -100 Jericho Quad -Jericho 11753
(716) 683-0300 .. **Dwan,** Timothy J '70 -5647 Bway -Lancaster 14086 **Fx:**683-7473
(585) 343-4577 .. **Dwanicki,** Don B '64 -43 Jackson -Batavia 14020
(212) 766-1888 .. **Dweck,** Amelia '98 %Morris DA&F -2 Rector -NY 10006
(212) 909-9500 .. **Dweck,** Eli D '00 (Wachtel & M,LLP) -885 2nd Av -NY 10017
(212) 687-8200 .. **Dweck,** H P Sean '96 (Dweck Law Firm,LLP) -75 Rckfllr Plz -NY 10019 **Fx:**697-2521
(212) 610-6300 .. **Dweck,** Isaac E '02 %Allen & O -1221 Av of Amer -NY 10020
(212) 687-8200 .. **Dweck,** Jack S '61 (Dweck Law Firm,LLP) -75 Rckfllr Plz -NY 10019 **Fx:**697-2521
(212) 502-6150 .. **Dweck,** Jeffrey S '97 (J Dweck,PC) -100 W 33rd -NY 10001 **Fx:**502-2010
(914) 273-7341 .. **Dweck,** Shoshana R '93 -14 Patriots Farm Pl -Armonk 10504
(914) 682-6824 .. **Dweck,** Stuart M '92 -50 Main -White Plns 10606 **Fx:**682-7784
(718) 250-2000 .. **Dwimoh,** Stephanie-Ama E '90 %DA -350 Jay -Brklyn 11201 **Fx:**250-2314
(212) 522-7673 .. **Dwin,** Dasha Smith '99 %Time Inc -1271 Av of Amer -NY 10020 **Fx:**522-0437
(718) 474-6004 .. **Dworetsky,** David H '76 -127-20 Cronston Av -Belle Hbr 11694
(845) 352-5652 .. **Dworetsky,** Saml H '79 -6 Dana Rd -Monsey 10952
(212) 867-6000 .. **Dwork,** Neil C '99 (Rosenberg & E,PC) -733 3rd Av -NY 10017
(212) 701-3000 .. **Dworkin,** Adam M '96 (Cahill G&R LLP) -80 Pine -NY 10005 **Fx:**269-5420
(212) 710-5220 .. **Dworkin,** Andrew L '87 (Vedanta Captial,LP) -540 Mad Av -NY 10022 **Fx:**710-5221
(212) 599-0020 .. **Dworkin,** Bernard '64 -750 3rd Av -NY 10017 **Fx:**599-0346
(212) 388-3600 .. **Dworkin,** Brian M '91 %32B-J Leg Srvcs -101 Av of Amer -NY 10013 **Fx:**388-3061
(518) 452-5442 .. **Dworkin,** Carl G '73 -44 Bentwood Ct -Albany 12203 **Fx:**452-5520
(718) 438-2525 .. **Dworkin,** Eva D '07 NC Caller,PC -4309 13th Av -Brklyn 11219 **Fx:**972-4154
(718) 722-4200 .. **Dworkin,** Howard S '88 %Dept of Law -55 Hanson Pl -Brklyn 11217 **Fx:**722-2846
(212) 835-2400 .. **Dworkin,** Jason A '04 Olnick Org -110 E 59th -NY 10022
(212) 450-4000 .. **Dworkin,** Meyer C '06 %Davis P&W LLP -450 Lex Av -NY 10017
(585) 244-3575 .. **Dworkin,** Wendy L '00 %LLD Ent -415 Park Av -Rchstr 14607
(212) 581-9000 .. **Dworman,** Todd '89 -65 W 55th -NY 10019 **Fx:**333-3191
(212) 210-2100 .. **Dwoskin,** Peter M '92 %Daily News,LP -450 W 33rd -NY 10001 **Fx:**643-7855
(518) 434-0600 .. **Dwyer,** Angus W '07 %Boies S&F LLP -10 N Pearl -Albany 12207
(716) 853-8100 .. **Dwyer,** Benjamin R '97 %Nixon P LLP -40 Fountain Plz -Buffalo 14202
(716) 373-1920 .. **Dwyer Black & Lyle,LLP** -1616 W State Bx648 -Olean 14760 **Fx:**373-3110
(212) 571-4067 .. **Dwyer & Brennan** -7 Dey -NY 10007 **Fx:**587-0227
(212) 326-2000 .. **Dwyer,** Christopher A Jr. '09 %O'Melveny & M LLP -7 Times Sq -NY 10036
(212) 259-8000 .. **Dwyer,** Daisy Hilse '87 Cnsl Dewey & L LLP -1301 Av of Amer -NY 10019
(631) 283-9503 .. **Dwyer,** Danl C '92 -169 Bridles Path -Southampton 11968
(212) 459-7894 .. **Dwyer,** Deborah J '78 %Dept of Tax & Fin -1740 Bway -NY 10019 **Fx:**459-7897
(212) 227-6000 .. **Dwyer,** Gary J '84 (Dwyer & T) -111 John -NY 10038
(518) 895-2420 .. **Dwyer,** Gerald A '78 -4958 Wstrn Tpk Bx39 -Duanesbrg 12056 **Fx:**895-9069
(518) 388-4364 .. **Dwyer,** Gerald A '78 %DA -612 State -Schnctdy 12305 **Fx:**388-4569
(212) 571-4067 .. **Dwyer,** Gerald P '68 (Dwyer & B) -7 Dey -NY 10007
(212) 451-2900 .. **Dwyer,** Gerald P Jr. '00 (Robinson & C LLP) -885 3rd Av -NY 10022
(212) 882-5819 .. **Dwyer,** James J '94 UBS Fncl Srvcs -51 W 52nd -NY 10019
(212) 233-0591 .. **Dwyer,** Joanne M '81 -225 Bway -NY 10007 **Fx:**732-8167
(716) 373-1920 .. **Dwyer,** Jos C '53 (Dwyer B&L,LLP) -1616 W State Bx648 -Olean 14760
(716) 858-2424 .. **Dwyer,** Liam A '09 DA -25 Delaware Av -Buffalo 14202 **Fx:**858-7425
(212) 317-1411 .. **Dwyer,** Martha M '79 -875 3rd Av -NY 10022 **Fx:**317-1611
(631) 728-6700 .. **Dwyer,** Matthew R Jr. '75 -42 Ponquogue Av -Hampton Bays 11946 **Fx:**728-5691
(212) 308-4440 .. **Dwyer,** Meghan E '09 %Ferrante,PLLC -5 W 19th -NY 10011 **Fx:**888-3839
(716) 835-4100 .. **Dwyer,** Michl G Jr. '85 -2431 Eggert Rd -Tonawanda 14150
(716) 929-0440 .. **Dwyer,** Michl G '94 -336 Harris Hill Rd -Williamsvll 14221
(718) 390-5157 .. **Dwyer,** Michl T '91 %Hon S Rooney -18 Richmond Ter -Staten Isl 10301
(914) 835-1628 .. **Dwyer,** Pamela S '73 -5 Indn Trl -Harrison 10528
(609) 734-6186 .. **Dwyer,** Patrick J '81 (Smith SWH&B,LLP) -100 Park Av -NY 10017
(518) 432-5988 .. **Dwyer,** Paul F '81 -350 Nrthrn Blvd -Albany 12204 **Fx:**432-5980
(212) 374-9287 .. **Dwyer,** Philip J '84 PJD Corp Realty Inc -900 W 190th -NY 10040
(212) 446-2300 .. **Dwyer,** Robt J '73 (Boies S&F LLP) -575 Lex Av -NY 10022
(212) 415-9200 .. **Dwyer,** Robt J Jr. '86 (Dorsey & W LLP) -250 Park Av -NY 10177
(315) 474-2943 .. **Dwyer,** Robt P '82 (Sugarman Law Firm,LLP) -211 W Jffrsn -Syracuse 13202
(914) 363-3334 .. **Dwyer,** Sandra E A '96 -60 Broad W -Mt Vernon 10552
(516) 471-1900 .. **Dwyer,** Sean P '88 (Havkins RR&V,LLP) -114 Old Cntry Rd -Mineola 11501
(212) 592-1400 .. **Dwyer,** Susan T '79 (Herrick,F LLP) -2 Park Av -NY 10016
(212) 227-6000 .. **Dwyer & Taglia** -111 John -NY 10038 **Fx:**227-6050
(518) 943-7775 .. **Dwyer,** Terrence P '92 (Jordan & D) -277 Main -Catskill 12414 **Fx:**943-7177
(212) 765-9100 .. **Dyas,** Julie D '03 %Halperin BR,LLP -555 Mad Av -NY 10022
(212) 940-8800 .. **Dybner,** Ariel M '99 (Katten MR LLP) -575 Mad Av -NY 10022
(212) 471-1888 .. **Dyce,** Jamie R '06 %Duane M LLP -1540 Bway -NY 10036 **Fx:**202-7790
(516) 877-2900 .. **Dyckman,** Deborah Anne '88 (Bartlett MB&M,LLP) -300 Old Cntry Rd -Mineola 11501
(212) 903-8785 .. **Dyckman,** Ezra '92 (Roberts & H,LLP) -825 8th Av -NY 10019
(212) 661-7100 .. **Dyckman,** Jacob M '64 (Salon MDN&B,LLP) -292 Mad Av -NY 10017
(212) 546-4000 .. **Dyckman,** Joshua S '01 Bristol-Myers Squibb -345 Park Av -NY 10154 **Fx:**546-9562
(212) 335-4500 .. **Dydek,** David C '09 %DLA Piper LLP -1251 Av of Amer -NY 10020
(212) 259-8000 .. **Dye,** Alexander M '83 (Dewey & L LLP) -1301 Av of Amer -NY 10019
(212) 408-5100 .. **Dye,** Bonnie E '09 %Chadbourne & P LLP -30 Rckfllr Plz -NY 10112
(212) 793-8121 .. **Dye,** John R '87 -425 Park Av -NY 10022
(212) 728-8000 .. **Dye,** Wm N '88 (Willkie F&G LLP) -787 7th Av -NY 10019
(315) 479-8660 .. **Dyer,** Danl E '93 %Alexander & C,LLC -115 E Jffrsn -Syracuse 13202
(518) 793-9276 .. **Dyer,** Deborah '94 -82 Glenwood Av -Queensbury 12804
(212) 455-2000 .. **Dyer,** J Scott '81 SrCnsl Simpson T&B LLP -425 Lex Av -NY 10017
(212) 599-2396 .. **Dyer,** Kevin M '85 (Dyer Law Firm PLLC) -80 Maiden Ln -NY 10038 **Fx:**214-0927
(212) 692-1000 .. **Dyer,** Richd P '79 (Duane M LLP) -1540 Bway -NY 10036
(607) 763-9200 .. **Dyer,** Sharon L '79 (Levene G&T,LLP) -BxF-1706 -Bnghmtn 13902
(212) 225-2000 .. **Dyer,** Tenisha C '09 %Cleary GS&H -1 Lbrty Plz -NY 10006
(212) 310-8000 .. **Dyer-LaRoche,** Chrystal '04 %Weil G&M LLP -767 5th Av -NY 10153
(212) 477-1846 .. **Dyett,** John F '93 OfCnsl McLaughlin & W,PC -276 5th Av -NY 10001 **Fx:**477-1731
(718) 933-6700 .. **Dykes,** Diana '88 Monroe College -1 Monroe Cllg Way -Bronx 10468 **Fx:**933-8820
(212) 336-2000 .. **Dykhouse,** David W '76 (Patterson BW&T LLP) -1133 Av of Amer -NY 10036
(212) 644-4420 .. **Dyki,** Steven R '06 %Fabiani C&H,LLP -570 Lex Av -NY 10022
(212) 819-8200 .. **Dylan,** Andrew '09 %White & C LLP -1155 Av of Amer -NY 10036
(518) 884-9388 .. **Dylis,** David P '76 -72 W High Bx177 -Ballston Spa 12020 **Fx:**884-0513
(212) 698-3500 .. **Dylke,** Elizabeth K '09 %Dechert LLP -1095 Av of Amer -NY 10036
(212) 278-0400 .. **Dym,** Hindy '07 %Cooper & D LLP -30 Rckfllr Plz -NY 10112
(212) 532-5700 .. **Dym,** Michl A '89 -80 Maiden Ln -NY 10038 **Fx:**566-7406
(646) 366-5500 .. **Dymbort,** Jason E '06 1st Solar,Inc -620 8th Av -NY 10018
(212) 566-7188 .. **Dymond,** Jisha V '04 %Genova B&G -115 Bway -NY 10006
(518) 431-4125 .. **Dymond,** Kenneth '76 Cnsl Fed Hwy Admin -719 O'Brien Fed Bldg -Albany 12207 **Fx:**431-4121
(212) 681-1575 .. **Dymond,** Seth A '04 %Belluck & F LLP -546 5th Av -NY 10036
(585) 753-4500 .. **Dys,** David P '05 %DA -832 Watts Bldg -Rchstr 14614 **Fx:**753-4576
(585) 346-0511 .. **Dys,** James M '94 -5 Wshngtn Bx41 -Livonia 14487 **Fx:**346-0589
(212) 213-6996 .. **Dysard,** Christopher W '99 (Spears & I LLP) -51 Mad Av -NY 10010
(212) 446-4800 .. **Dysart,** Matthew S '09 %Kirkland & E LLP -153 E 53rd -NY 10022
(718) 730-9497 .. **Dzhamgarova,** Ilona '07 Dzhamgarova & Assoc,PC -603 Brighton Beach Av -Brklyn 11235
(315) 724-6175 .. **Dziekan,** Carl S '86 (Steates RS&D) -408 Lomond Pl -Utica 13502
(866) 931-6092 .. **Dziepak,** Anthony L '99 %SSA-ODAR -155-10 Jamaica Av Bx319300 -Jamaica 11431 **Fx:**(718) 557-6575
(212) 458-3695 .. **Dzierzawski,** Robyn A '00 Natl Union Fire Ins Co -175 Water -NY 10038
(315) 785-3053 .. **Dziuba,** Patricia L '01 %DA -175 Arsenal -Watertwn 13601 **Fx:**785-3371
(212) 715-1000 .. **Dziubek,** Kerry Ann '98 Cnsl Arnold & P LLP -399 Park Av -NY 10022
(315) 793-7000 .. **Dziwis,** Gregory J '84 %Leg Aid -255 Genesee -Utica 13501 **Fx:**732-3202
(516) 869-7600 .. **Dzwilewski,** Peter A '09 Ofc of Town Atty -220 Plandome Rd Bx3000 -Manhsst 11030 **Fx:**869-7605
(212) 969-3000 .. **Ead,** Michl A '06 %Proskauer R LLP -1585 Bway -NY 10036
(212) 508-6700 .. **Ead,** Oreen M '06 %Tannenbaum HS&H LLP -900 3rd Av -NY 10022
(212) 455-2000 .. **Eadan,** Batsheva '09 %Simpson T&B LLP -425 Lex Av -NY 10017
(212) 649-2000 .. **Eaddy,** Carolene S '97 %Hearst Corp -300 W 57th -NY 10019 **Fx:**649-2035
(718) 246-2500 .. **Eaddy,** Danielle V '92 -26 Court -Brklyn 11242
(607) 974-4019 .. **Eade,** Katherine A '02 Corning -1 Rvrfrnt Plz -Corning 14831 **Fx:**974-6135
(631) 878-2282 .. **Eaderesto,** Annette '83 (A Eaderesto,LLC) -18 Railroad Av -Ctr Moriches 11934 **Fx:**878-6803
(315) 789-8010 .. **Eades,** Martin E '73 Cnsl Housing Auth -41 Lewis Bx153 -Geneva 14456 **Fx:**789-8024
(716) 672-2164 .. **Eades & Militello, PC** -11 E Main Bx149 -Fredonia 14063 **Fx:**672-7979

(716) 672-2164 .. **Eades,** R Timothy '85 (Eades & M,PC) -11 E Main Bx149 -Fredonia 14063
(631) 324-5909 .. **Eagan,** David E '83 (MacLachlan & E LLP) -241 Pantigo Rd -E Hampton 11937
(718) 237-5500 .. **Eagan,** Emilie A '07 %Leg Srvcs -105 Court -Brklyn 11201 **Fx:**855-0733
(716) 645-8138 .. **Eagan,** Esther Garvey '05 -1576 Sweet Home Rd -Buffalo 14228
(716) 856-0600 .. **Eagan,** Gayle L '86 (Jaeckle F&M,LLP) -12 Fountain Plz -Buffalo 14202
(212) 541-2000 .. **Eagan,** J Christopher '78 (Bryan C LLP) -1290 Av of Amer -NY 10104
(716) 852-5875 .. **Eagan,** James E '98 (Feldman K LLP) -110 Pearl -Buffalo 14202
(212) 373-3000 .. **Eagan,** Kathleen A '10 %Paul WRW&G LLP -1285 Av of Amer -NY 10019
(718) 442-7171 .. **Eagan,** Kelly Marie '99 (Columbo & E,PC) -207 Forest Av -Staten Isl 10301 **Fx:**273-9526
(212) 773-4457 .. **Eagan,** Michl J '00 Ernst & Young LLP -5 Times Sq -NY 10036
(212) 338-0700 .. **Eagan,** Robt A '85 (Hoffman P&F PLLC) -220 E 42nd -NY 10017
(716) 845-3630 .. **Eagan,** Susan Etu '97 %Atty Grievance Comm -438 Main -Buffalo 14202 **Fx:**856-2701
(914) 921-1200 .. **Eagan,** Thos M '83 (Maloof B&E LLC) -411 Theo Fremd Av -Rye 10580 **Fx:**921-1023
(212) 308-5858 .. **Eagel,** Lawr P '84 (Bragar WE&S,PC) -885 3rd Av -NY 10022
(315) 425-2700 .. **Eagen,** Ellen K '08 %Hiscock & B,LLP -One Park Pl -Syracuse 13202
(914) 946-8900 .. **Eagen,** Sarah J '03 %Clark G&M -99 Court -White Plns 10601
(585) 428-5210 .. **Eaggleston,** V Christopher '07 Pub Def -10 N Fitzhugh -Rchstr 14614 **Fx:**428-2234
(516) 357-3000 .. **Eagle,** Alan C '87 (Rivkin R LLP) -926 RXR Plz -Uniondale 11556
(212) 586-0052 .. **Eagle,** Bart J '81 B Eagle,PLLC -250 W 57th -NY 10107 **Fx:**586-5491
(317) 726-1714 .. **Eagle,** Brian A '91 OfCnsl Eagle & S -303 5th Av -NY 10016 **Fx:**475-1270
(516) 484-9276 .. **Eagle,** Denis A '67 -40 Ash Dr -Roslyn 11576
(212) 801-3760 .. **Eagle,** Marcia R '84 Michael L&R LLP -60 Columbus Cir -NY 10023
(212) 685-8456 .. **Eagle & Selden** -303 5th Av -NY 10016 **Fx:**629-9656
(212) 685-8456 .. **Eagle,** Sidney '63 OfCnsl Eagle & S -303 5th Av -NY 10016
(718) 222-8880 .. **Eagleton,** Irma J '99 (Jones JO) -45 Main -Brklyn 11201
(212) 595-7640 .. **Eaken,** Bruce W Jr. '65 -316 W 79th -NY 10024 **Fx:**595-2143
(212) 867-8280 .. **Eakins,** Wm S Jr. '78 (Patton ELM&S) -420 Lex Av -NY 10170 **Fx:**370-5637
(585) 454-2181 .. **Ealy,** David H '86 (Trevett CS&A,PC) -2 State -Rchstr 14614
(315) 376-5347 .. **Eannace,** Paula J '86 %Hon J Parker -Cnty Cthse -Lowvll 13367 **Fx:**376-4145
(212) 343-1771 .. **Eanni,** Rekha S '06 ROC of NY -275 7th Av -NY 10001
(212) 809-1111 .. **Eapen,** Shaji M '02 %Morgan MA -39 Bway -NY 10006
(212) 878-8000 .. **Eardley,** Frances '09 %Clifford C LLP -31 W 52nd -NY 10019
(718) 262-7100 .. **Eardley,** Kevin C '93 %Civil Ct -89-17 Sutphin Blvd -Jamaica 11435 **Fx:**262-7107
(518) 869-6227 .. **Earing,** Amy L '08 %Lavelle & F,LLP -29 British Amer Blvd -Latham 12110
(646) 442-3100 .. **Earisman,** Peggy '93 Legal Srvcs -90 John -NY 10038 **Fx:**(212) 227-9798
(716) 853-1887 .. **Earl,** Boyd L '90 E Tenney -5 Niagara Sq -Buffalo 14202 **Fx:**853-1893
(315) 853-4436 .. **Earl,** Edw D '66 (Felt E,LLP) -4-6 N Park Row -Clinton 13323
(585) 343-6320 .. **Earl,** Kevin D '78 (Oshlag S&E) -216 E Main -Batavia 14020
(315) 474-5533 .. **Earl,** Robt A '77 -506 E Wshngtn -Syracuse 13202
(212) 918-3000 .. **Earl,** Scott T '01 %Hogan L LLP -875 3rd Av -NY 10022
(212) 279-5979 .. **Earle,** Matthew Z '05 %Kates NRE&F,LLP -845 3rd Av -NY 10022
(718) 990-8735 .. **Earle-Dei,** Beatrice '85 -1 Cross Isl Plz -Rosedale 11422
(516) 229-6000 .. **Earle-Gargan,** Jessica G '02 %R Lau & Assoc -300 Jericho Quad Bx9040 -Jericho 11753 **Fx:**229-6167
(646) 853-0757 .. **Earley,** Anthony L '82 -Wllmsbrg Station Bx110449 -Brklyn 11211
(212) 935-3000 .. **Earley,** Francis J '99 (Mintz LCFG&P,PC) -666 3rd Av -NY 10017
(212) 986-2233 .. **Early,** Brian F '01 (Early & S LLC) -360 Lex Av Bx3601 -NY 10163
(212) 986-2233 .. **Early,** Ethan J '00 (Early & S LLC) -360 Lex Av Bx3601 -NY 10163
(212) 989-5744 .. **Early,** Lawr G '86 -352 W 11th -NY 10014
(212) 298-2091 .. **Early,** Shawna A '99 %IRS -290 Bway -NY 10007
(212) 986-2233 .. **Early & Strauss LLC** -360 Lex Av Bx3601 -NY 10163 **Fx:**986-2255
(917) 570-0012 .. **Early,** Tracey Cahill '05 Girls on the Run -315 Bleecker -NY 10014
(212) 858-1000 .. **Early-Hubelbank,** David E '93 Cnsl Pillsbury WSP LLP -1540 Bway -NY 10036
(516) 333-7799 .. **Early-Hubelbank,** Latonia '93 %Steinberg & E-H PLLC -1400 Old Cntry Rd -Westbury 11590
(716) 684-9000 .. **Earne,** Richd M '70 -6495 Transit Rd -Bowmansville 14026 **Fx:**684-9098
(212) 474-1000 .. **Earnhardt,** Joe W '05 %Cravath S&M LLP -825 8th Av -NY 10019
(212) 593-6900 .. **Earthy,** Carolyn Janiak '05 Avista Capital Partners -65 E 55th -NY 10022 **Fx:**593-6901
(516) 873-0600 .. **Easa,** Easa '55 (Easa & E) -1000 Franklin Av -Gdn Cty 11530 **Fx:**473-7814
(516) 873-0600 .. **Easa,** Jack '58 (Easa & E) -1000 Franklin Av -Gdn Cty 11530 **Fx:**473-7814
(212) 788-5010 .. **Eason,** Eric '09 Dept Hlth -125 Worth CN-30 -NY 10013 **Fx:**788-4300
(718) 250-0400 .. **Eason,** Etta L '06 %R Tusa -1 MetroTech Ctr -Brklyn 11201 **Fx:**250-0591
(212) 504-6000 .. **Eason,** Nicole M '10 %Cadwalader W&T LLP -1 World Fncl Ctr -NY 10281
(718) 741-8403 .. **East,** Sara T '54 %Div of Human Rights -1 Fordham Plz -Bronx 10458 **Fx:**741-8102
(212) 770-7506 .. **East,** Thos '85 %AIG -70 Pine -NY 10270 **Fx:**809-5722
(845) 338-7267 .. **Easter,** Leonard D '77 -Bx1853 -Kingston 12402
(315) 379-2214 .. **Easter,** Stephen J '74 St Lawr Cnty Ct -48 Court -Canton 13617 **Fx:**379-9934
(212) 246-5757 .. **Eastman,** John L '65 (Eastman & E) -39 W 54th -NY 10019 **Fx:**977-8408
(716) 883-4931 .. **Eastman,** Kathryn Morgan '05 -55 Cottage -Buffalo 14201
(212) 246-5757 .. **Eastman,** Lee V '98 (Eastman & E) -39 W 54th -NY 10019 **Fx:**977-8408
(516) 292-8100 .. **Easton,** Philip '01 %Nassau/Sfflk Law Srv -1 Helen Keller Way -Hempstd 11550 **Fx:**292-6529
(212) 551-1420 .. **Easton,** Reed W '86 (RW Easton,PC) -230 Park Av -NY 10169 **Fx:**(908) 879-5618
(212) 295-8000 .. **Easton,** Robt H '98 Integro -1 State St Plz -NY 10004
(212) 288-2270 .. **Easton,** Robin D '97 -45 E 89th -NY 10128
(518) 434-0127 .. **Easton,** Stephen W '74 %Sneeringer MPR -50 Chapel -Albany 12207
(585) 272-7007 .. **Easton,** Wm E '51 -250 Mill -Rchstr 14614 **Fx:**272-7011
(585) 423-8290 .. **Easton,** Wm T '85 (Easton TKS,LLP) -16 W Main -Rchstr 14614 **Fx:**423-0890
(518) 747-4197 .. **Eastwood,** Thos I '72 -24 Maple Bx142 -Hudson Fls 12839
(212) 373-3000 .. **Eaton,** Alice Belisle '00 (Paul WRW&G LLP) -1285 Av of Amer -NY 10019
(718) 332-7766 .. **Eaton,** Craig A '86 (Eaton & T,LLP) -1662 Sheepshead Bay Rd -Brklyn 11235 **Fx:**332-5898
(212) 373-3000 .. **Eaton,** Elizabeth M '03 %Paul WRW&G LLP -1285 Av of Amer -NY 10019
(607) 563-3565 .. **Eaton & Griffith** -76 Main Bx270 -Sidney 13838 **Fx:**563-3568
(212) 301-8303 .. **Eaton,** Joshua P '98 Dune Capital Mgmt -623 5th Av -NY 10022
(585) 232-3730 .. **Eaton,** K Wade '72 (Chamberlain D LLP) -1600 Crssrds Bldg -Rchstr 14614
(914) 948-7000 .. **Eaton,** Lori A '99 %Keidel W&C LLP -925 Wstchstr Av -White Plns 10604
(315) 445-9405 .. **Eaton,** Marcie P '09 Special Funds Conservation Committee -5789 Widewaters Pkwy -Syracuse 13214
(212) 728-8000 .. **Eaton,** Mary J '97 (Willkie F&G LLP) -787 7th Av -NY 10019
(845) 638-5001 .. **Eaton,** Michl W '86 %DA -1 S Main -New Cty 10956 **Fx:**638-5070
(607) 563-3565 .. **Eaton,** Paul F Jr. '73 (Eaton & G) -76 Main Bx270 -Sidney 13838
(631) 444-5776 .. **Eaton,** Robt G '99 SUNY Stony Brook -3 Tech Dr -E Setauket 11733 **Fx:**444-5791
(212) 756-2000 .. **Eaton,** Robyn '05 %Schulte R&Z LLP -919 3rd Av -NY 10022
(212) 345-5618 .. **Eaton,** Shelly R '00 %Marsh USA -1166 Av of Amer -NY 10036 **Fx:**345-4808
(212) 779-9910 .. **Eaton & Van Winkle LLP** -3 Park Av -NY 10016 **Fx:**779-9928
(646) 386-3992 .. **Eaton,** Wendy C '80 -269 Bowery -NY 10002
(212) 766-4411 .. **Ebanks,** Alberto A '94 (Ebanks & S,LLP) -20 Vesey -NY 10007 **Fx:**766-5899
(212) 458-1359 .. **Ebba,** Wosenyelesh Tura '03 AIG -175 Water -NY 10038
(718) 934-2961 .. **Ebbin,** Steven H '98 -2401 Av U -Brklyn 11229 **Fx:**615-2185
(212) 759-3300 .. **Ebbs,** Cynthia L '02 %Dornbush SS&V,LLP -747 3rd Av -NY 10017
(212) 541-2000 .. **Ebel,** Eileen M '93 Cnsl Bryan C LLP -1290 Av of Amer -NY 10104
(631) 725-8800 .. **Ebel,** John J '03 -17 Main Bx1740 -Sag Hbr 11963
(212) 909-6000 .. **Ebel,** Oran M '09 %Debevoise & P LLP -919 3rd Av -NY 10022
(212) 504-6000 .. **Ebeling,** Douglas W '01 Cadwalader W&T LLP -1 World Fncl Ctr -NY 10281
(845) 528-0910 .. **Ebeling,** Richd C '80 -8 Wdrdg -Putnam Vly 10579 **Fx:**528-0912
(914) 725-2257 .. **Ebenstein,** Barbara J '90 -14 Harwood Ct -Scarsdale 10583 **Fx:**725-1790
(212) 336-8000 .. **Ebenstein,** Danl S '67 (Amster R&E) -90 Park Av -NY 10016
(212) 821-3000 .. **Eber,** Louis R '84 USB AG -299 Park Av -NY 10171
(914) 674-2000 .. **Eber,** Robt I '69 -828 S Bway -Tarrytwn 10591
(212) 317-1300 .. **Eber,** Saml '87 -100 Park Av -NY 10017 **Fx:**326-8815
(212) 408-5100 .. **Eberhardt,** Robt W III '07 %Chadbourne & P LLP -30 Rckfllr Plz -NY 10112
(212) 431-1300 .. **Eberight,** Wm J '79 (Borah GAN&G PC) -377 Bway -NY 10013
(716) 856-4000 .. **Eberl,** Catherine B '07 %Hodgson R LLP -140 Pearl -Buffalo 14202
(845) 426-2525 .. **Eberle,** Geoffrey D '92 -747 Chestnut Rdg Rd -Chestnut Rdg 10977 **Fx:**(201) 962-2236
(212) 233-4185 .. **Eberle,** Mark J '97 (Augustine & E,LLP) -90 Broad -NY 10004 **Fx:**792-6580
(716) 849-6500 .. **Eberle,** Susan Anne '84 (Brown & T,LLC) -14 Lafayette Sq -Buffalo 14203
(716) 852-1888 .. **Ebersole,** Gary R '73 %Cantor LD&P,PC -350 Main -Buffalo 14202
(212) 534-0149 .. **Eberstein,** Conrad J '76 -1619 3rd Av -NY 10128
(212) 907-9600 .. **Ebert,** David G '87 (Ingram YGC&B,LLP) -250 Park Av -NY 10177
(212) 466-7700 .. **Ebert,** Rebecca F '03 %Sandler O'Neill & Prtnrs,LP -919 3rd Av -NY 10022 **Fx:**466-7998
(212) 290-4000 .. **Ebert,** Steven R '01 (Ebert & Assoc,LLC) -110 E 30th -NY 10016 **Fx:**290-1717
(212) 508-6100 .. **Ebert,** Wm H '09 %Bracewell & G,LLP -1251 Av of Amer -NY 10020
(607) 778-2156 .. **Eberz,** Robt J '77 %Family Ct -Cnty Justice Bldg 5 Fl -Bnghmtn 13901 **Fx:**778-2439
(914) 766-3551 .. **Ebetino,** James M '82 IBM -294 Route 100 -Somers 10589
(212) 833-1100 .. **Ebie,** Kenneth N '07 %Friedman KS&A LLP -1633 Bway -NY 10019
(212) 310-8000 .. **Ebin,** Jacob B '08 %Weil G&M LLP -767 5th Av -NY 10153
(212) 632-5500 .. **Ebin,** Robt F '65 Cnsl Salans LLP -620 5th Av -NY 10020
(516) 683-1717 .. **Eble,** Deanna M '01 %V Russo & Assoc,PC -1600 Stewart Av -Westbury 11590 **Fx:**683-9393
(212) 504-6000 .. **Ebling,** Taylor A '09 %Cadwalader W&T LLP -1 World Fncl Ctr -NY 10281
(516) 677-0300 .. **Ebrahimi,** Reza '06 %CF Weil -35 Roosevelt Av -Syosset 11791 **Fx:**496-9047
(718) 643-5482 .. **Ebrahimoff,** Rosalyn Joan '87 %Family Ct -283 Adams -Brklyn 11201 **Fx:**643-5103
(212) 566-4769 .. **Ebright,** Peter I '99 NYC Dept of Bldgs -280 Bway -NY 10007
(315) 342-1773 .. **Eby,** James K '76 -91 W 3rd -Oswego 13126 **Fx:**342-1700
(212) 964-7400 .. **Eccher,** Ann P '99 Smith MDWY&Y,PC -111 John -NY 10038
(212) 208-8893 .. **Eccles,** Peter R '91 %Standard & Poor's -55 Water -NY 10041
(212) 264-8000 .. **Eccleston,** Marie A '79 %HUD -26 Fed Plz -NY 10278
(212) 355-6182 .. **Echelman,** Amy Schehr '83 %EP Dine Inc -115 E 57th -NY 10022 **Fx:**755-8486
(212) 310-8000 .. **Echemendia,** Kristen M '09 %Weil G&M LLP -767 5th Av -NY 10153
(917) 286-1532 .. **Echenberg,** Heather Lynne '03 Childrens Aid Society -105 E 22nd -NY 10010
(212) 637-2597 .. **Echenberg,** Janis M '04 %US Atty -1 St Andrews Plz -NY 10007
(914) 686-4800 .. **Echenthal,** Evan H '00 %Harrington O&M,LLP -81 Main -White Plns 10601
(212) 720-3700 .. **Echer,** Joy D '88 %Foot Locker,Inc -112 W 34th -NY 10120 **Fx:**720-4116

(212) 286-9499 .. **Echevarria,** Daisy '09 %M Nolfo -275 Mad Av -NY 10016 **Fx:**286-8881
(914) 923-3600 .. **Echevarria,** George W '80 -100 Exec Blvd -Ossining 10562
(845) 294-4080 .. **Echevarria,** Jennifer S '09 %Burke M&G -40 Matthews Bx216 -Goshen 10924
(212) 668-2894 .. **Echevarria,** Lorraine M '77 %US Bankruptcy Ct -1 Bowling Grn -NY 10004
(201) 386-7095 .. **Echevarria,** Margarita '90 HSBC Bank -452 5th Av -NY 10018
(718) 476-2700 .. **Echeverria,** Luis F '80 -50-60 69th -Woodside 11377 **Fx:**476-0341
(212) 373-2381 .. **Echeveste,** Colleen '04 -1285 Av of Amer -NY 10019
(212) 506-5000 .. **Echtman,** Elyse D '94 OfCnsl Orrick H&S LLP -51 W 52nd -NY 10019
(212) 757-2310 .. **Echtman,** Irwin M '61 (Echtman & E,LLP) -250 W 57th -NY 10107 **Fx:**757-2366
(845) 340-8500 .. **Eck,** Franklin Jr. '91 -668 Aaron Ct Bx4205 -Kingston 12402 **Fx:**340-1515
(212) 788-0425 .. **Eck,** Ilana A '05 Law Dept -100 Church -NY 10007 **Fx:**788-0367
(212) 408-5100 .. **Eck,** Peter K '82 Cnsl Chadbourne & P LLP -30 Rckfllr Plz -NY 10112
(212) 705-7000 .. **Eckas,** Scott E '90 (Bingham M LLP) -399 Park Av -NY 10022
(607) 272-0674 .. **Eckel,** Timothy C '80 Hon R Mulvey -320 N Tioga Bx70 -Ithaca 14851 **Fx:**272-0691
(718) 595-6535 .. **Eckels,** Marcella R '98 DEP -59-17 Junction Blvd -Flushng 11373 **Fx:**595-6543
(212) 225-2000 .. **Eckenrod,** Russell D '10 %Cleary GS&H -1 Lbrty Plz -NY 10006
(212) 831-5677 .. **Ecker,** Allan B '54 -420 E 61st -NY 10065 **Fx:**831-6285
(914) 347-2600 .. **Ecker,** Danl G '97 (Traub LS&S LLP) -7 Skyline Dr -Hawthorne 10532
(212) 431-1300 .. **Ecker,** Jennifer Ann '98 (Borah GAN&G PC) -377 Bway -NY 10013 **Fx:**965-2657
(914) 333-9618 .. **Ecker,** Kevin C '00 Philips Intellectual -Bx3001 -Briarclff Mnr 10510
(914) 965-4288 .. **Ecker,** Louis A '63 (L Ecker,PLLC) -1250 Cntrl Pk Av -Ynkrs 10704 **Fx:**968-0918
(914) 273-0777 .. **Ecker,** Robt L '83 (Ecker E & Assoc LLP) -80 Business Park Dr -Armonk 10504 **Fx:**273-1787
(646) 579-2456 .. **Eckerle,** Bettina '96 Focus Fncl Prtnrs -462 7th Av -NY 10018 **Fx:**475-3927
(914) 286-2912 .. **Eckers,** Randy S '00 %Greenberg T,LLP -445 Hmltn Av -White Plns 10601
(212) 922-0450 .. **Eckert,** Anthony W III '90 (Kaplan M&A,LLC) -70 E 55th -NY 10022
(845) 565-9261 .. **Eckert,** Claudia M '99 B Kulak -484 Temple Hill Rd -New Windsor 12553
(212) 227-0347 .. **Eckert,** Danl T '90 %Weiss W&W,PC -25 Park Pl -NY 10007
(585) 428-5210 .. **Eckert,** James G '84 %Pub Def -10 N Fitzhugh -Rchstr 14614 **Fx:**428-2234
(607) 337-1585 .. **Eckert,** Jody P '93 Dept of Social Srvcs -Bx590 -Norwich 13815 **Fx:**334-8768
(646) 746-9700 .. **Eckert,** Lawr T '00 US CFTC -140 Bway -NY 10005 **Fx:**746-9938
(212) 232-1300 .. **Eckert,** Louis F '99 (Lewis BB&S LLP) -77 Water -NY 10005
(914) 949-2909 .. **Eckert Seamans Cherin & Mellott, LLC** -10 Bank -White Plns 10606 **Fx:**949-5424
(718) 390-5464 .. **Eckhardt,** Nancy J '89 %Family Ct -100 Richmond Ter -Staten Isl 10301
(516) 223-3841 .. **Eckhardt & Sutton** -2020 Grand Av -Baldwin 11510
(518) 402-9521 .. **Eckhaus,** Larry S '03 DEC -625 Bway -Albany 12233 **Fx:**402-9018
(212) 940-8800 .. **Eckhaus,** Steven G '77 (Katten MR LLP) -575 Mad Av -NY 10022
(212) 813-8800 .. **Eckhoff,** Erin M '08 %Goodwin P LLP -620 8th Av -NY 10018
(212) 627-9898 .. **Eckhouse,** Jacqueline G '97 -555 W 25th -NY 10001 **Fx:**627-9498
(516) 822-1600 .. **Eckl,** Andrea D '80 %Russo & P -16 E Old Cntry Rd -Hicksvll 11801
(518) 402-9512 .. **Eckl,** James H '76 %DEC -625 Bway -Albany 12233 **Fx:**402-9018
(212) 858-1000 .. **Eckland,** Todd W '87 (Pillsbury WSP LLP) -1540 Bway -NY 10036
(212) 735-3000 .. **Eckles,** Paul M '03 (Skadden ASM&F LLP) -4 Times Sq -NY 10036
(607) 433-0090 .. **Eckmair,** Kelley M '91 -526 Main -Oneonta 13820 **Fx:**433-2828
(585) 338-6889 .. **Eckman,** Brian C '99 %Bausch & Lomb -One Bausch & Lomb Pl -Rchstr 14604 **Fx:**338-8706
(631) 390-0010 .. **Eckman,** Laura K '10 %Bruno G&S,LLP -445 Broad Hollow Rd -Melvll 11747
(516) 571-2480 .. **Eckman,** Rose '84 %Hon J Lockman -100 Supreme Ct Dr -Mineola 11501
(212) 554-7800 .. **Eckstein,** Amyt M '02 %Moses & S LLP -405 Lex Av -NY 10174
(212) 885-5000 .. **Eckstein,** Andrew B '86 (Blank R LLP) -405 Lex Av -NY 10174
(516) 334-1111 .. **Eckstein,** Barbara P '84 -220 Westbury Av -Carle Pl 11514 **Fx:**334-5611
(518) 285-8682 .. **Eckstein,** Brenda Kaplan '94 %Family Ct -30 Clinton Av -Albany 12207 **Fx:**462-4164
(212) 521-5400 .. **Eckstein,** Gail M '04 %Reed S LLP -599 Lex Av -NY 10022
(646) 386-3755 .. **Eckstein,** Gary '88 Supreme Ct -80 Centre -NY 10013
(917) 939-2115 .. **Eckstein,** Jos M '92 NYC Taxi & Limo Commission Licensing -3202 Qns Blvd -LIC 11101
(212) 715-9100 .. **Eckstein,** Kenneth H '80 (Kramer LN&F,LLP) -1177 Av of Amer -NY 10036
(212) 728-8000 .. **Eckstut,** S F Burr '09 %Willkie F&G LLP -787 7th Av -NY 10019
(518) 474-7330 .. **Economides,** James A '75 %Dept of Law -The Cptl -Albany 12224
(212) 422-0488 .. **Economon,** Ariane C '91 %Rick SF&B,LLP -90 Broad -NY 10004
(212) 607-2004 .. **Economou,** Andoni '93 MetTel -55 Water -NY 10041
(516) 682-0010 .. **Economou,** Anna M '02 Economou & E -485 Underhill Blvd -Syosset 11791 **Fx:**682-0011
(516) 682-0010 .. **Economou,** Chris '02 (Economou & E) -485 Underhill Blvd -Syosset 11791 **Fx:**682-0011
(845) 471-2160 .. **Economou,** Jack '60 -11 Market -Poughkeepsie 12601
(212) 736-1940 .. **Economou,** John S '99 Davidson D&K LLC -485 7th Av -NY 10018
(212) 541-4477 .. **Economou,** John T '96 AJ Clarke Real Estate Corp -1881 Bway -NY 10023 **Fx:**541-4881
(516) 682-0010 .. **Economou,** Theo '94 (Economou & E) -485 Underhill Blvd -Syosset 11791 **Fx:**682-0011
(212) 863-6300 .. **Eddison,** Sarah C '87 %HPD -100 Gold -NY 10038 **Fx:**863-8201
(212) 346-1356 .. **Edds,** Elizabeth Ann '89 Pace Univ-Planned Giving -156 William -NY 10038
(518) 479-0729 .. **Eddy,** Teresa A '81 -4119 US Route 20 -Nassau 12123
(914) 949-0109 .. **Eddy,** W David Jr. '84 (Owen & E) -1 Water -White Plns 10601 **Fx:**949-9223
(212) 335-9000 .. **Edel,** Christopher C '92 %DA -1 Hogan Pl -NY 10013
(212) 336-3500 .. **Edel,** Martin D '76 (Miller & W,PC) -570 Lex Av -NY 10022
(716) 856-8200 .. **Edel,** Roger J '77 (Williams & W) -43 Court -Buffalo 14202 **Fx:**856-0559
(212) 858-7710 .. **Edelberg,** David '84 (Nowell AKB,PA) -140 Bway PMB 46028 -NY 10005
(212) 227-0430 .. **Edelman,** A Sheldon '60 (Moskowitz P&E) -225 Bway -NY 10007
(212) 592-1400 .. **Edelman,** Alexandra E '06 %Herrick,F LLP -2 Park Av -NY 10016
(518) 783-2704 .. **Edelman,** Allegra R '09 Colonie Town Atty -Mem'l Town Hall Bx508 -Newtonville 12128 **Fx:**786-7324
(212) 209-3023 .. **Edelman,** Amos S '96 (Reitler K&R LLC) -885 3rd Av -NY 10022
(212) 715-9100 .. **Edelman,** Ari '06 %Kramer LN&F,LLP -1177 Av of Amer -NY 10036
(212) 935-3000 .. **Edelman,** Charlotte '99 (Mintz LCFG&P,PC) -666 3rd Av -NY 10017
(212) 223-4000 .. **Edelman,** Danl D '93 (Crowell & M LLP) -590 Mad Av -NY 10022
(212) 349-7330 .. **Edelman,** David '57 (D Edelman,PC) -160 Bway -NY 10038 **Fx:**732-1425
(516) 354-2800 .. **Edelman,** Glen S '85 (Mandell MO&E,LLP) -3000 Marcus Av -Lk Success 11042
(516) 739-8801 .. **Edelman,** Herbert M '60 -100 E Old Cntry Rd -Mineola 11501 **Fx:**739-8803
(516) 764-4316 .. **Edelman,** Howard C '83 -119 Andvr Rd -Rockvll Ctr 11570
(212) 986-1910 .. **Edelman,** Jeffrey E '96 (Edelman Law Ofcs,LLC) -60 E 42nd -NY 10165 **Fx:**(973) 299-9220
(516) 681-6363 .. **Edelman,** Jos '54 (Edelman & N) -265 Foxhunt Crescent -Syosset 11791
(516) 742-9200 .. **Edelman Krasin & Jaye PLLC** -1 Old Cntry Rd -Carle Pl 11514 **Fx:**742-7622
(212) 852-1000 .. **Edelman,** Laurence D '81 %US Trust Co,NA -114 W 47th -NY 10036 **Fx:**852-1310
(716) 843-5700 .. **Edelman,** Lynn S '80 %US Atty -138 Delaware Av -Buffalo 14202 **Fx:**551-3052
(516) 729-4383 .. **Edelman,** Marc L '04 -20 Vesey -NY 10007
(212) 888-0658 .. **Edelman,** Marsha '64 -400 E 56th -NY 10022 **Fx:**888-0695
(212) 318-6000 .. **Edelman,** Martin L '66 SpclCnsl Paul HJ&W LLP -75 E 55th -NY 10022
(212) 943-1200 .. **Edelman,** Martin W '78 (Edelman & E,PC) -61 Bway -NY 10006 **Fx:**943-0001
(718) 549-6056 .. **Edelman,** Meredith A '89 -4941 Arlngtn Av -Bronx 10471
(212) 407-7700 .. **Edelman,** Michl J '91 (Vedder P,PC) -1633 Bway -NY 10019
(212) 661-7300 .. **Edelman,** Michl L '05 %Malapero & P LLP -295 Mad Av -NY 10017
(914) 686-3700 .. **Edelman,** Michl R '73 (Worby GE LLP) -11 Martine Av -White Plns 10606
(718) 549-6056 .. **Edelman,** Minna J '56 -4941 Arlngtn Av -Bronx 10471 **Fx:**543-7632
(516) 681-6363 .. **Edelman & Ness** -265 Foxhunt Crescent -Syosset 11791 **Fx:**681-3512
(516) 742-9200 .. **Edelman,** Paul B '82 (Edelman K&J PLLC) -1 Old Cntry Rd -Carle Pl 11514
(212) 687-8181 .. **Edelman,** Paul S '51 OfCnsl Kreindler & K -750 3rd Av -NY 10017
(212) 267-5225 .. **Edelman,** Peri B '97 -225 Bway -NY 10007 **Fx:**766-2298
(212) 838-8282 .. **Edelman,** Peter F '72 -110 E 59th -NY 10022 **Fx:**223-4912
(585) 262-5140 .. **Edelman,** Robt J '51 -2 State -Rchstr 14614 **Fx:**232-3164
(212) 415-9200 .. **Edelman,** Sandra '82 (Dorsey & W LLP) -250 Park Av -NY 10177
(212) 468-4800 .. **Edelman,** Sara Lynn '94 (Davis & G LLP) -1740 Bway -NY 10019
(212) 530-5000 .. **Edelman,** Scott A '89 (Milbank TH&M LLP) -1 Chase Manh Plz -NY 10005
(212) 553-3200 .. **Edelman,** Scott R '93 (Marulli LE&T,LLP) -5 Hanover Sq -NY 10004
(212) 558-4000 .. **Edelman,** Theo '84 (Sullivan & C LLP) -125 Broad -NY 10004
(914) 552-7214 .. **Edelman,** Wendi M '99 -41 Glen Wood Rd -Millwd 10546
(212) 449-1683 .. **Edelmann,** Pauline C '06 Merrill Lynch -4 World Fncl Ctr -NY 10281
(845) 291-2050 .. **Edelman-Reyes,** Karen D '00 %DA -255-275 Main -Goshen 10924 **Fx:**291-2085
(212) 940-8800 .. **Edelson,** Danl A '03 %Katten MR LLP -575 Mad Av -NY 10022
(212) 940-7070 .. **Edelson,** Gilbert S '55 Cnsl Katten MR LLP -575 Mad Av -NY 10022
(212) 953-4100 .. **Edelson,** James I '81 OSG Ship Mgmt -666 3rd Av -NY 10017 **Fx:**578-1832
(212) 980-1900 .. **Edelson,** Lee D '06 %Donovan & G,LLP -261 Mad Av -NY 10016
(212) 522-0143 .. **Edelson,** Maurice F '94 Time Inc -1271 Av of Amer -NY 10020 **Fx:**522-0437
(914) 323-3400 .. **Edelson,** Neal H '85 Benefitmall -1133 Wstchstr Av -White Plns 10604
(914) 946-2524 .. **Edelson,** Wm A '91 %Met Life -399 Knollwood Rd -White Plns 10603 **Fx:**946-5732
(212) 425-1999 .. **Edelstein,** Adam J '92 (Edelsteins F&B,LLP) -61 Bway -NY 10006
(914) 939-3606 .. **Edelstein,** Bernard A '78 -315 Wstchstr Av -Pt Chester 10573
(212) 986-6000 .. **Edelstein,** Darren J '07 %Kleinberg KW&C,PC -551 5th Av -NY 10176
(212) 599-1717 .. **Edelstein,** Edw '78 (Barnett EGK&L,PC) -122 E 42nd -NY 10168
(845) 638-0610 .. **Edelstein,** Harry '51 -43 Jffrsn Ln -New Cty 10956 **Fx:**638-0707
(212) 521-4488 .. **Edelstein,** Howard S '74 -590 Mad Av -NY 10022
(914) 375-0100 .. **Edelstein,** I Scott '73 (Novick ELRW&L,PC) -733 Ynkrs Av -Ynkrs 10704
(212) 790-4500 .. **Edelstein,** Jeffrey S '73 (Manatt P&P,LLP) -7 Times Sq -NY 10036
(212) 504-6000 .. **Edelstein,** Keith J '04 %Cadwalader W&T LLP -1 World Fncl Ctr -NY 10281
(516) 228-3355 .. **Edelstein,** Lewis C '74 -300 Grdn City Plz -Gdn Cty 11530 **Fx:**228-3356
(212) 401-0800 .. **Edelstein,** Mady J '75 %Disciplinary Comm -61 Bway -NY 10006 **Fx:**287-1045
(212) 468-8000 .. **Edelstein,** Mark S '83 (Morrison & F LLP) -1290 Av of Amer -NY 10104
(212) 330-6080 .. **Edelstein,** Martin A '81 -2 Penn Plz -NY 10121 **Fx:**643-1951
(212) 425-1999 .. **Edelstein,** Paul J '95 (Edelsteins F&B,LLP) -61 Bway -NY 10006
(914) 773-1818 .. **Edelstein,** Peter M '66 (Edelstein & L LLP) -343 Manvll Rd -Plsntvll 10570
(212) 425-1999 .. **Edelstein,** Saul '61 Edelsteins F&B,LLP -61 Bway -NY 10006
(212) 798-6100 .. **Edelstein,** Shimon B '02 Fortress Invsmnt Grp,LLC -1345 Av of Amer -NY 10105
(212) 349-5618 .. **Edelstein,** Stephanie D '06 %Chaves & P LLP -116 John -NY 10038

(718) 243-6351 .. **Edelstein,** Susan B '03 Leg Aid -111 Lvngstn -Brklyn 11201 **Fx:**237-8737
(718) 250-2000 .. **Edelstein,** Tamara '00 %DA -350 Jay -Brklyn 11201 **Fx:**250-2314
(212) 759-1200 .. **Edelstein,** Walter '85 (Lefkowitz & E) -444 Mad Av -NY 10022 **Fx:**317-8717
(914) 824-5790 .. **Edelstein-Alegria,** Jayni '95 %Hon J Hubert -111 Dr ML King Jr Blvd -White Plns 10601
(212) 425-1999 .. **The Edelsteins Faegenburg & Browne, LLP** -61 Bway -NY 10006 **Fx:**425-5430
(212) 947-6030 .. **Eden,** Edw N '78 -314 5th Av -NY 10001
(718) 248-0578 .. **Eden,** Rosemary S '80 Citigroup -1 Court Sq -LIC 11101
(718) 923-6312 .. **Eder,** Joana C '98 Sup Crt App 2nd Div -335 Adams -Brklyn 11201
(212) 651-7500 .. **Eder,** Theo M '99 (Segal MS&M) -850 3rd Av -NY 10022
(516) 622-9200 .. **Ederer,** Alan C '87 (Westerman BEM&S,LLP) -1201 RXR Plz -Uniondale 11553
(212) 232-1300 .. **Ederer,** Jason L '09 %Lewis BB&S LLP -77 Water -NY 10005
(212) 715-1000 .. **Ederer,** Louis S '79 (Arnold & P LLP) -399 Park Av -NY 10022
(212) 625-8700 .. **Eder-Kaufman,** Terry L '00 Cnsl Gene Kaufman Architect,PC -525 Bway -NY 10012 **Fx:**625-8867
(212) 481-7770 .. **Edgar,** Chad L '02 %D Cardi & Assoc -2 Park Av -NY 10016 **Fx:**684-3008
(212) 427-5977 .. **Edgar,** Harold S H '68 -1158 5th Av -NY 10029
(212) 455-2000 .. **Edgar,** Kenneth C Jr. '74 OfCnsl Simpson T&B LLP -425 Lex Av -NY 10017
(212) 556-2100 .. **Edgemon,** Joshua T '09 %King & S -1185 Av of Amer -NY 10036
(516) 481-0513 .. **Edgerton,** Charlene E '94 (Edgerton & H) -299 Roxbury Rd S -Gdn Cty 11530
(212) 798-6100 .. **Edinburg,** Barry M '95 %Fortress Invstmt Grp -1345 Av of Amer -NY 10105
(212) 471-8529 .. **Edinburgh,** Howard S '79 (Herzfeld & R,PC) -125 Broad -NY 10004
(212) 953-4441 .. **Edip-Walden,** Derin '96 (Guadagno & E,LLP) -420 Lex Av -NY 10170 **Fx:**953-6079
(718) 423-1926 .. **Edley,** Adrienne R '82 -54-40 Little Neck Pkwy -Little Neck 11362
(212) 801-6528 .. **Edlin,** Richd A '86 (Greenberg T,LLP) -200 Park Av -NY 10166
(212) 294-6700 .. **Edmonds,** Colette Bonnard '93 OfCnsl Winston & S -200 Park Av -NY 10166
(212) 349-5150 .. **Edmonds,** Kyle S '01 %Galvano & X,PC -150 Bway -NY 10038
(212) 473-0255 .. **Edmonds,** Leila Finucane '98 %Seedco -915 Bway -NY 10010
(212) 670-0213 .. **Edmonds,** Philip T '00 Merrill Lynch -222 Bway -NY 10038
(212) 819-0089 .. **Edmonds,** Robt C '73 (Edmonds & Co,PC) -112 Mad Av -NY 10016 **Fx:**819-0189
(212) 238-3000 .. **Edmonds,** Robt Scott '78 (Emmet M&M,LLP) -120 Bway -NY 10271
(212) 891-1600 .. **Edmondson,** Elizabeth A '09 %Jenner & B LLP -919 3rd Av -NY 10022
(212) 578-6310 .. **Edmondson,** Timothy H '90 %MetLife -27-01 Qns Plz N -LIC 11101
(631) 547-6418 .. **Edmonson,** Barbara M '72 -191 NY Av -Huntngtn 11743 **Fx:**427-5871
(212) 801-6786 .. **Edmunds,** Leah '07 %Greenberg T,LLP -200 Park Av -NY 10166
(212) 704-6000 .. **Edmundson,** Danl C '72 (Troutman S LLP) -405 Lex Av -NY 10174
(212) 590-2414 .. **Edozie,** John '91 (Madu E&M,PC) -304 Park Av S -NY 10010
(212) 446-4800 .. **Edsall,** Michl T '04 (Kirkland & E LLP) -153 E 53rd -NY 10022
(212) 224-1600 .. **Edson,** Elizabeth E '05 Mutual of America -320 Park Av -NY 10022
(718) 466-3000 .. **Edusei,** Rosemary '96 %Civil Ct -1118 Grnd Cncrs -Bronx 10456 **Fx:**466-3006
(646) 386-3652 .. **Edwards,** Alison '93 %Supreme Ct-Law Dept -60 Centre -NY 10007
(212) 308-4411 .. **Edwards Angell Palmer & Dodge LLP** -750 Lex Av -NY 10022 **Fx:**308-4844
(718) 469-8555 .. **Edwards,** Arthur A '97 -572A Flatbush Av -Brklyn 11225 **Fx:**469-2733
(585) 263-1000 .. **Edwards,** Ashley E '10 %Nixon P LLP -1100 Clinton Sq -Rchstr 14604
(212) 848-4000 .. **Edwards,** Barbara Ann '97 Cnsl Shearman & S LLP -599 Lex Av -NY 10022
(212) 735-3000 .. **Edwards,** Benjamin P '09 %Skadden ASM&F LLP -4 Times Sq -NY 10036
(917) 421-4730 .. **Edwards,** Bonnie '79 %IRS -33 Maiden Ln -NY 10038 **Fx:**421-3946
(845) 794-5000 .. **Edwards,** Brian T '83 (Drew D&E,LLP) -13 Lbrty Drwr1040 -Monticello 12701
(212) 670-0232 .. **Edwards,** Bryna L '90 Merrill Lynch -222 Bway -NY 10038 **Fx:**670-4503
(212) 501-9000 .. **Edwards,** Caitlin M '03 %Brower P,PC -488 Mad Av -NY 10022 **Fx:**501-0300
(212) 455-2000 .. **Edwards,** Caleb J '09 %Simpson T&B LLP -425 Lex Av -NY 10017
(212) 335-4500 .. **Edwards,** Cara D '04 %DLA Piper LLP -1251 Av of Amer -NY 10020
(315) 637-0108 .. **Edwards,** Chas S '63 -904 S Manlius -Fayettevll 13066 **Fx:**637-0108
(347) 296-1053 .. **Edwards,** Christine S '96 Supreme Ct -320 Jay -Brklyn 11201 **Fx:**296-1367
(212) 209-3072 .. **Edwards,** Christopher S '01 %Reitler K&R LLC -885 3rd Av -NY 10022
(718) 671-4910 .. **Edwards,** Christopher W '00 -3049 Eastchstr Rd -Bronx 10469
(212) 704-1352 .. **Edwards,** Dana '98 %Interpublic Grp -1114 Av of Amer -NY 10036 **Fx:**704-1201
(718) 739-1529 .. **Edwards,** Darwin L '91 Edwards & Co,PC -175-20 Wexford Ter -Jamaica 11432 **Fx:**739-1583
(585) 419-8800 .. **Edwards,** David J '94 (Harris B PLLC) -99 Garnsey Rd -Pittsfrd 14534
(718) 624-6263 .. **Edwards,** Ellen E '89 (Edwards & Assoc) -188 Montague -Brklyn 11201 **Fx:**858-0411
(212) 722-4900 .. **Edwards,** Erika McDaniel '94 (Donaldson C&M,LLP) -1825 Park Av -NY 10035
(212) 364-5340 .. **Edwards,** Ezekiel R '03 %Innocence Project -100 5th Av -NY 10011 **Fx:**364-5341
(212) 785-3344 .. **Edwards,** Flora '96 -115 Bway -NY 10006 **Fx:**577-2865
(718) 694-4825 .. **Edwards,** Franklyn E '97 %Transit Auth -130 Lvngstn -Brklyn 11201 **Fx:**694-5726
(212) 262-8632 .. **Edwards,** Gerald T '94 -250 W 57th -NY 10107
(212) 282-5000 .. **Edwards,** Ginny '03 %Avon Products -1345 Av of Amer -NY 10105
(212) 818-9200 .. **Edwards,** Glenn C '01 (Satterlee SB&B LLP) -230 Park Av -NY 10169
(716) 753-4211 .. **Edwards,** Gregory J '88 County Exec -3 N Erie -Mayvll 14757 **Fx:**753-4756
(516) 379-1323 .. **Edwards,** Harrison J Jr. '77 (Edwards & E) -336 S Ocean Av Bx191 -Freeprt 11520 **Fx:**546-0384
(516) 379-1323 .. **Edwards,** Harrison J IV '04 %Edwards & E -336 S Ocean Av Bx191 -Freeprt 11520 **Fx:**546-0384
(631) 577-3276 .. **Edwards,** Indira T '05 %Capital One,NA -265 Broadhllw Rd -Melvll 11747 **Fx:**577-2836
(212) 715-9100 .. **Edwards,** Jacqueline S '01 %Kramer LN&F,LLP -1177 Av of Amer -NY 10036
(212) 225-2000 .. **Edwards,** Jaime A '03 %Cleary GS&H -1 Lbrty Plz -NY 10006
(212) 513-7788 .. **Edwards,** James A '88 (Ahmuty D&M) -123 William -NY 10038
(212) 558-4000 .. **Edwards,** Jane H '10 %Sullivan & C LLP -125 Broad -NY 10004
(914) 499-4478 .. **Edwards,** Jane Papaccio '00 IBM Corp -1 New Orchrd Rd -Armonk 10504
(718) 596-2834 .. **Edwards,** Jasmine '03 -45 Main -Brklyn 11201
(631) 859-3911 .. **Edwards,** John H '94 -86 W Main -E Islip 11730 **Fx:**859-3916
(914) 251-1618 .. **Edwards,** John R Jr. '96 (Price MS&D,PC) -106 Corp Park Dr -White Plns 10604
(845) 634-6404 .. **Edwards,** John S '79 -317 Little Tor Rd S -New Cty 10956 **Fx:**634-6538
(516) 379-1323 .. **Edwards,** Jonathan E '88 (Edwards & E) -336 S Ocean Av Bx191 -Freeprt 11520 **Fx:**546-0384
(212) 273-5095 .. **Edwards,** Kay M '91 %Dormitory Auth -515 Bway -Albany 12207 **Fx:**(518) 257-3101
(212) 766-5222 .. **Edwards,** Lennon C '97 %Leav & S LLP -120 Bway -NY 10271 **Fx:**693-2377
(212) 722-2000 .. **Edwards,** Lisa R '91 %Leg Aid -230 E 106th -NY 10029 **Fx:**876-5365
(212) 267-9222 .. **Edwards,** Mark H '82 %Gorayeb & Assoc,PC -100 William -NY 10038 **Fx:**962-5418
(646) 312-3580 .. **Edwards,** Matthew A '94 Baruch Cllg CUNY Law Dept -1 Bernard Baruch Way Bx B9/225 -NY 10010 **Fx:**312-3571
(212) 903-9000 .. **Edwards,** Natalie K '02 %Linklaters -1345 Av of Amer -NY 10105
(212) 468-4800 .. **Edwards,** Nordia '08 %Davis & G LLP -1740 Bway -NY 10019
(212) 513-3200 .. **Edwards,** Oliver '76 (Holland & K LLP) -31 W 52nd -NY 10019
(718) 340-4200 .. **Edwards,** Pamela '92 %CUNY Law Schl -65-21 Main -Flushng 11367 **Fx:**340-4482
(518) 462-2200 .. **Edwards,** Paul R '91 -112 State -Albany 12207 **Fx:**462-2883
(516) 869-2586 .. **Edwards,** Raymond A '93 %Kimco Realty Corp -3333 New Hyde Pk Rd -New Hyde Pk 11042 **Fx:**869-7199
(518) 483-5531 .. **Edwards,** Richd H '77 Walsh & E -346 W Main -Malone 12953 **Fx:**483-5572
(212) 615-9171 .. **Edwards,** Robt W '97 %Salomon Smith Barney -333 W 34th -NY 10001
(718) 858-4350 .. **Edwards,** S Anderson '96 -907 Fulton -Brklyn 11238
(212) 404-5777 .. **Edwards,** Sarah J '03 (Littleton JUP&K LLP) -39 Bway -NY 10006
(212) 225-7700 .. **Edwards,** Sean O '01 %Cartafalsa ST&L -165 Bway -NY 10006
(212) 837-6036 .. **Edwards,** Steven G '07 %Hughes H&R LLP -1 Bttry Pk Plz -NY 10004
(212) 918-3000 .. **Edwards,** Steven M '73 (Hogan L LLP) -875 3rd Av -NY 10022
(716) 826-7000 .. **Edwards,** Susan Davis '95 %Mercy Hsptl -565 Abbott Rd -Buffalo 14220
(914) 997-1346 .. **Edwards,** Susan T '05 %Seham SM&P,LLP -445 Hmltn Av -White Plns 10601
(212) 669-4692 .. **Edwards,** Tanisha S '05 Cnsl NYC Comptrollers Ofc -1 Centre -NY 10007
(585) 753-3481 .. **Edwards,** Tynise Y '91 Monroe Cnty Conflict Defenders Ofc -30 W Broad -Rchstr 14614
(516) 328-2300 .. **Edwards,** Wayne G '78 (Abrams FFEGF&E,LLP) -1111 Marcus Av -Lk Success 11042
(585) 753-4500 .. **Edwards-Morrison,** Caroline '04 %DA -832 Watts Bldg -Rchstr 14614 **Fx:**753-4576
(516) 485-2578 .. **Edwards Neumann,** Christine Y '74 -71 Long Dr -Hempstd 11550 **Fx:**505-7608
(212) 833-8721 .. **Edwin,** Gail I '77 Sony BMG Music Entrtnmnt -550 Mad Av -NY 10022 **Fx:**833-8406
(212) 619-4444 .. **Edwins,** Wm J '02 %Marshall CW&B,PC -116 John -NY 10038
(212) 261-8000 .. **Efaplomatidis,** Maria '02 %Mendes & M,LLP -750 7th Av -NY 10019
(718) 565-4116 .. **Eff,** Thos A '83 %FlightSafety Intl Inc -Marine Air Trmnl-LaGuardia Airport -Flushng 11371 **Fx:**565-4134
(914) 948-4500 .. **Effinger,** Montgomery L '92 (O'Connor MCD&O) -1 Barker Av -White Plns 10601
(914) 305-1649 .. **Effler,** Stephen Corry '74 -274 N Ridge -Rye Brook 10573
(518) 457-4951 .. **Effman,** Jason D '98 %Dept Correctional Srvcs -1220 Wshngtn Av -Albany 12226 **Fx:**457-7555
(585) 786-8450 .. **Effman,** Norman P '69 -18 Linwood Av -Warsaw 14569 **Fx:**786-8478
(585) 721-6859 .. **Effman,** Norman P '69 -42 Delaware Av -Buffalo 14202
(212) 922-1177 .. **Effrain,** Craig H '94 %Stursberg & V -1500 Bway -NY 10036
(212) 334-1082 .. **Effron,** Alan S '90 (Pelosi WE&S LLP) -233 Bway -NY 10279 **Fx:**965-1488
(518) 439-0733 .. **Effron,** Joshua J '60 -425 Kenwood Av -Delmar 12054
(718) 780-7933 .. **Effron,** Robin J '05 %Bklyn Law Schl -250 Joralemon -Brklyn 11201 **Fx:**780-0393
(212) 935-3000 .. **Effron,** Saml A '07 %Mintz LCFG&P,PC -666 3rd Av -NY 10017
(516) 466-6050 .. **Effros,** Erik A '87 American Star Abstract,LLC -1010 Nrthrn Blvd -Gt Neck 11021
(212) 701-3000 .. **Efimova,** Anastasia Yurievna '97 Cnsl Cahill G&R LLP -80 Pine -NY 10005 **Fx:**269-5420
(212) 848-4000 .. **Efland,** Erin R '09 %Shearman & S LLP -599 Lex Av -NY 10022
(212) 548-7432 .. **Efrati,** Stefanie Vines '00 %West Group -530 5th Av -NY 10036 **Fx:**867-2404
(212) 902-0900 .. **Efremov,** Yavor P '01 Goldman Sachs -85 Broad -NY 10004 **Fx:**902-3876
(212) 756-2000 .. **Efron,** David J '94 (Schulte R&Z LLP) -919 3rd Av -NY 10022
(212) 867-1067 .. **Efron,** Steve S '79 -237 W 35th -NY 10001 **Fx:**682-5958
(646) 682-7299 .. **Efros,** Nicole K '92 -285 Cntrl Pk W -NY 10024

(212) 685-9800 .. **Efroymson,** Sarah E '91 %Counsel Press,LLC -520 8th Av -NY 10018 **Fx:**213-4273
(212) 326-2000 .. **Eftekhari,** Shiva '04 Cnsl O'Melveny & M LLP -7 Times Sq -NY 10036
(607) 974-9000 .. **Efthimiou,** Marcus P '93 %Corning -1 Rvrfrnt Plz -Corning 14831 **Fx:**974-6135
(212) 637-2205 .. **Egal,** Loyaan A '03 US Atty -1 St Andrews Plz -NY 10007
(212) 506-5000 .. **Egal,** Zahra M '09 %Orrick H&S LLP -51 W 52nd -NY 10019
(212) 852-3552 .. **Egan,** Ann Marie '92 US Trust Co,NA -114 W 47th -NY 10036 **Fx:**852-1310
(212) 373-3000 .. **Egan,** Brian P '05 %Paul WRW&G LLP -1285 Av of Amer -NY 10019
(631) 447-8100 .. **Egan,** Brian T '99 (Egan & G,LLP) -96 S Ocean Av -Patchogue 11772 **Fx:**447-8181
(631) 853-4104 .. **Egan,** Carla A '07 %DA -400 Carleton Av Bx9082 -Central Islip 11722 **Fx:**853-7838
(212) 382-4060 .. **Egan,** Catherine C '00 Lloyds America,Inc -25 W 53rd -NY 10019 **Fx:**382-4070
(212) 335-4500 .. **Egan,** Danl G '08 %DLA Piper LLP -1251 Av of Amer -NY 10020
(212) 852-3572 .. **Egan,** Deirdre A '97 %US Trust Co,NA -114 W 47th -NY 10036 **Fx:**852-3525
(716) 856-3500 .. **Egan,** Donald J '66 OfCnsl Magavern MG LLP -1100 Rand Bldg -Buffalo 14203
(914) 366-3335 .. **Egan,** Eileen E '04 Phelps Mem Hosp Ctr -701 N Bway -Sleepy Hollow 10591
(718) 590-5944 .. **Egan,** Grace F '99 %ACS-DLS -900 Sheridan Av -Bronx 10451
(585) 753-4500 .. **Egan,** James C '07 DA -832 Watts Bldg -Rchstr 14614 **Fx:**753-4576
(315) 701-0080 .. **Egan,** James P '08 %Fed Pub Def -4 Clinton Sq -Syracuse 13202 **Fx:**701-0081
(212) 739-7081 .. **Egan,** Jeffrey R '97 Fishman Constructn -666 5th Av -NY 10103
(716) 856-3087 .. **Egan,** John Lloyd Jr. '85 -43 Court -Buffalo 14202 **Fx:**856-3091
(516) 357-3000 .. **Egan,** John W '07 %Rivkin R LLP -926 RXR Plz -Uniondale 11556
(631) 265-2077 .. **Egan,** Kathleen M '08 %Castrovinci & M -1 Edgewood Av -Smithtwn 11787 **Fx:**265-0627
(212) 670-0425 .. **Egan,** Lawr M Jr. '92 %Merrill Lynch -222 Bway -NY 10038
(212) 455-0541 .. **Egan,** Lorraine White '91 Runyon Cancer Rsrch Fndtn -1 Exch Plz -NY 10006
(914) 941-0494 .. **Egan,** Michl S '92 (Egan & Assoc,LLC) -78 N State Rd -Briarclff Mnr 10510
(212) 335-4396 .. **Egan,** Patrick B R '06 %DA-Spcl Narcotics Pros -80 Centre -NY 10013
(212) 309-6000 .. **Egan,** Patrick J '03 %Morgan L&B LLP -101 Park Av -NY 10178
(585) 546-4097 .. **Egan,** Patrick S '53 -45 Exchange -Rchstr 14614
(516) 832-7500 .. **Egan,** Peter A '99 (Nixon P LLP) -50 Jericho Quadrangle -Jericho 11753
(212) 552-7791 .. **Egan,** Robt J '62 JP Morgan Chase -1 Chase Manh Plz -NY 10081
(607) 272-5891 .. **Egan,** Sara Campbell '00 -3226 Wilkins Rd -Ithaca 14850
(212) 450-4000 .. **Egan,** Sarah McDonald '06 %Davis P&W LLP -450 Lex Av -NY 10017
(607) 255-5124 .. **Egan,** Shirley K '74 %Cornell Univ -300 CCC Bldg-Grdn Av -Ithaca 14853 **Fx:**255-2794
(212) 619-8456 .. **Egan,** Susan B '76 -112 Mad Av -NY 10016 **Fx:**819-0189
(212) 264-5916 .. **Egan,** Susan Mary '79 %DHS -26 Fed Plz -NY 10278
(518) 474-0871 .. **Egan,** Theresa L '87 %DMV -6 ESP -Albany 12228 **Fx:**486-4485
(212) 412-9500 .. **Egan,** Thos A '85 OfCnsl Flemming ZWZ LLP -1 Lbrty Plz -NY 10006
(845) 782-5474 .. **Egan,** Thos J '59 -101 Stage Rd -Monroe 10950 **Fx:**782-5485
(212) 224-2720 .. **Egan,** Thos J '05 (Egan Law Grp,LLC) -481 8th Av -NY 10001 **Fx:**244-2721
(585) 427-5400 .. **Egan,** Wayne J '00 %Xerox -100 Clinton Av S -Rchstr 14644
(212) 837-6000 .. **Egbert,** Walter M III '95 (Hughes H&R LLP) -1 Bttry Pk Plz -NY 10004
(518) 485-2312 .. **Egel,** Deborah M '06 %OASAS -1450 Wstrn Av -Albany 12203 **Fx:**485-2335
(718) 544-6363 .. **Egelfeld,** Madaleine S '81 -125-10 Qns Blvd -Kew Gdns 11415
(212) 450-4000 .. **Egelhof,** Richd J '08 %Davis P&W LLP -450 Lex Av -NY 10017
(914) 995-3000 .. **Egenhauser,** Barbara '80 %DA -111 Martin Luther King Blvd -White Plns 10601 **Fx:**995-3363
(212) 657-2055 .. **Egeonu-Egbuchulam,** Theodora '99 Citigroup -77 Water -NY 10005
(516) 877-5600 .. **Egers,** Ronald R '64 %R Tusa -1225 Franklin Av -Gdn Cty 11530 **Fx:**877-5695
(212) 227-2009 .. **Egert,** Bruce '80 -86-25 Lefferts Blvd -Richmnd Hll 11418 **Fx:**227-2021
(212) 334-6858 .. **Egert,** Leonard D '92 -165 W 91st -NY 10024 **Fx:**579-7315
(212) 223-4000 .. **Egert,** Mark A '88 (Crowell & M LLP) -590 Mad Av -NY 10022
(585) 325-4545 .. **Egger,** Jan P '76 (Egger & L) -144 Exchange Blvd -Rchstr 14614 **Fx:**325-6716
(212) 577-3562 .. **Egger,** Marcia '80 %Leg Aid -199 Water -NY 10038 **Fx:**577-3520
(212) 715-9100 .. **Eggermann,** Danl M '03 %Kramer LN&F,LLP -1177 Av of Amer -NY 10036
(631) 853-4161 .. **Eggers,** Melissa L '03 %DA -N Cnty Cmplx Bldg 77 -Hauppauge 11788 **Fx:**853-4192
(212) 969-3000 .. **Eggers,** Scott A '89 SrCnsl Proskauer R LLP -1585 Bway -NY 10036
(585) 263-1000 .. **Eggers,** Wm D '70 SrCnsl Nixon P LLP -1100 Clinton Sq -Rchstr 14604
(516) 327-3000 .. **Eggleston,** Alan P '78 %Astoria Fed Svngs & Loan -1 Astoria Fed Plz -Lk Success 11042 **Fx:**327-7421
(518) 587-1060 .. **Eggleston,** John D '83 -77 Crescent -Saratoga Spgs 12866 **Fx:**587-1070
(315) 797-9261 .. **Eghigian,** David A '04 %Getnick LA&P,LLP -258 Genesee -Utica 13502
(631) 265-0599 .. **Eghrari,** Carolyn Kian '97 %MS Eghrari & Assoc -50 Karl Av -Smithtwn 11787 **Fx:**265-0754
(631) 265-0599 .. **Eghrari,** Mark S '88 (MS Eghrari & Assoc) -50 Karl Av -Smithtwn 11787 **Fx:**265-0754
(212) 635-1560 .. **Egidi,** David J '92 Bk of NY Mellon -1 Wall -NY 10286
(212) 336-1758 .. **Egilinsky,** Sharon R '91 Deutsche Bk -345 Park Av -NY 10154
(845) 454-2200 .. **Egitto,** Jos A '86 (Wolfson G&E PC) -11 Market -Poughkeepsie 12601
(315) 471-8111 .. **Egitton,** Amy B '95 (Scolaro SCF&B,PC) -507 Plum -Syracuse 13204 **Fx:**425-3617
(212) 858-1000 .. **Egler,** Wm D '89 Pillsbury WSP LLP -1540 Bway -NY 10036
(212) 872-1000 .. **Egleson,** Christopher M '06 -One Bryant Park -NY 10036 **Fx:**872-1002
(716) 876-7458 .. **Egloff,** Carol S '87 -398 Knowlton Av -Kenmore 14217
(716) 845-2560 .. **Egloff,** Susan J '81 %Surrogates Ct -92 Franklin -Buffalo 14202 **Fx:**853-3741
(212) 455-2000 .. **Egnal,** Mark G '05 %Simpson T&B LLP -425 Lex Av -NY 10017
(518) 447-7360 .. **Egner,** Laura J '93 %Dept of Social Srvcs -112 State -Albany 12207 **Fx:**447-7388
(516) 357-3000 .. **Egor,** Glenn H '95 (Rivkin R LLP) -926 RXR Plz -Uniondale 11556
(212) 272-3271 .. **Egorova,** Olga '00 %JP Morgan Chase -383 Mad Av -NY 10179
(212) 728-8000 .. **Eguchi,** Weston Taichiro '06 %Willkie F&G LLP -787 7th Av -NY 10019
(516) 393-2200 .. **Ehle,** Theresa '07 %Garfunkel W,PC -111 Grt Nck Rd -Gt Neck 11021
(631) 369-1155 .. **Ehlers,** Richd A '80 -456 Griffing Av -Rvrhead 11901
(845) 454-3250 .. **Ehlers,** Stephen E '68 (Gellert & K,PC) -75 Wshngtn -Poughkeepsie 12601
(716) 853-8100 .. **Ehlers,** Tracey B '05 %Nixon P LLP -40 Fountain Plz -Buffalo 14202
(212) 574-1200 .. **Ehlke,** Erin M '10 %Seward & K LLP -1 Bttry Pk Plz -NY 10004
(716) 856-1344 .. **Ehman,** Dale A '76 (Bouvier Prtnrshp,LLP) -350 Main -Buffalo 14202 **Fx:**856-1369
(716) 849-8900 .. **Ehman,** Jennifer A '10 %Hurwitz & F,PC -1300 Lbrty Bldg -Buffalo 14202
(212) 297-5800 .. **Ehnert,** Jesse C '08 %Day P LLP -7 Times Sq -NY 10036
(914) 594-4495 .. **Ehren,** Judith A '03 NY Medical Cllg - Registrars Ofc -Sunshine Cottage -Valhalla 10595
(212) 808-7800 .. **Ehrenbard,** Robt '51 (Kelley D&W LLP) -101 Park Av -NY 10178
(716) 645-2444 .. **Ehrenberg,** Kenneth M '99 SUNY at Buffalo -135 Park Hall -Buffalo 14260
(212) 730-0200 .. **Ehrenberg,** Lance '76 -122 E 42nd -NY 10168 **Fx:**730-1099
(646) 414-6815 .. **Ehrenberg,** Peter H '08 (Lowenstein S PC) -1251 Av of Amer -NY 10020 **Fx:**(973) 597-2351
(212) 558-4000 .. **Ehrenberg,** Stephen '03 %Sullivan & C LLP -125 Broad -NY 10004
(212) 577-2220 .. **Ehrenburg,** Dina '06 %H Wang -277 Bway -NY 10007 **Fx:**577-2259
(718) 596-9000 .. **Ehrenfeld,** Robt '72 (Cohen HEP&T) -25 Chapel -Brklyn 11201
(212) 751-5959 .. **Ehrenkranz,** Joel S '61 (Ehrenkranz & E,LLP) -375 Park Av -NY 10152 **Fx:**754-1905
(212) 403-1000 .. **Ehrenkranz,** Pamela '84 Cnsl Wachtell LR&K -51 W 52nd -NY 10019
(212) 751-5959 .. **Ehrenkranz,** Sanford B '64 (Ehrenkranz & E,LLP) -375 Park Av -NY 10152 **Fx:**754-1905
(212) 506-1700 .. **Ehrenpreis,** Rachel Feuer '06 %Kasowitz BT&F LLP -1633 Bway -NY 10019
(212) 233-8100 .. **Ehrens,** L Batya Schwartz '07 %Pollack Pl&D -225 Bway -NY 10007
(845) 724-3233 .. **Ehrenzweig,** Hugh B '98 -Bx743 -Poughquag 12570
(315) 703-6500 .. **Ehresman,** Kenneth B '06 Leg Srvcs -472 S Salina -Syracuse 13202 **Fx:**475-2706
(315) 793-7000 .. **Ehrhard,** Brian J '09 %Leg Aid -255 Genesee -Utica 13501 **Fx:**732-3202
(212) 455-2000 .. **Ehrhard,** Kenneth C '04 %Simpson T&B LLP -425 Lex Av -NY 10017
(631) 390-0010 .. **Ehrhardt,** James T '84 (Bruno G&S,LLP) -445 Broad Hollow Rd -Melvll 11747
(631) 271-9195 .. **Ehrhart,** John R '96 -33 Walt Whitman Rd -Huntngtn Sta 11746 **Fx:**271-9196
(518) 439-9999 .. **Ehring,** Danl A '92 -Bx1457 -Albany 12201 **Fx:**439-9253
(518) 455-7927 .. **Ehrlich,** A Joshua '84 (Spec Cnsl to Minority Leader) -500 F The Cptl -Albany 12247 **Fx:**465-2070
(212) 643-2503 .. **Ehrlich,** Alan '76 (Levy E&P,PC) -555 5th Av -NY 10017
(212) 373-3000 .. **Ehrlich,** Andrew J '03 (Paul WRW&G LLP) -1285 Av of Amer -NY 10019
(518) 272-2110 .. **Ehrlich & Arcodia** -64 2nd -Troy 12180 **Fx:**272-2345
(646) 228-7871 .. **Ehrlich,** Dan '03 -29 Bway -NY 10006 **Fx:**(212) 869-4907
(646) 473-7565 .. **Ehrlich,** David M '87 D Ehrlich & Assoc -237 W 35th -NY 10001
(631) 247-0404 .. **Ehrlich,** David Ross '00 %Jackson L LLP -58 S Srvc Rd -Melvll 11747
(212) 813-5900 .. **Ehrlich,** David W '78 (Fross ZL&Z,PC) -866 UN Plz -NY 10017
(212) 655-5000 .. **Ehrlich,** Edw B '82 %Gannon R&M -120 Bway -NY 10271
(212) 558-4000 .. **Ehrlich,** Elizabeth '07 %Sullivan & C LLP -125 Broad -NY 10004
(212) 768-4343 .. **Ehrlich,** Gary S '90 %Cantor E&M,LLP -49 W 37th -NY 10018
(212) 701-3000 .. **Ehrlich,** Ilana R Friedman '08 %Cahill G&R LLP -80 Pine -NY 10005 **Fx:**269-5420
(516) 624-6150 .. **Ehrlich,** Jeffrey H '78 %Town Atty -Town Hall -Oyster Bay 11771 **Fx:**624-6196
(516) 931-3525 .. **Ehrlich,** Jeffrey S '83 -575 Jericho Tpk -Jericho 11753
(516) 742-9500 .. **Ehrlich,** Jerome H '62 J Ehrlich,PLLC -200 Grdn City Plz -Gdn Cty 11530
(212) 351-4500 .. **Ehrlich,** Jerrold I '58 Epstein B&G,PC -250 Park Av -NY 10177
(212) 554-0400 .. **Ehrlich,** Jonathan '81 (Grubman I&S,PC) -152 W 57th -NY 10019
(212) 566-7012 .. **Ehrlich,** Jos '98 Owens Grp -183 Mad Av -NY 10016
(212) 221-5999 .. **Ehrlich,** Jos L '84 (Antin E&E,LLP) -49 W 37th -NY 10018
(914) 785-5300 .. **Ehrlich,** Julian D '90 %A Lamer -555 Taxter Rd -Elmsfrd 10523 **Fx:**347-4269
(516) 627-5411 .. **Ehrlich,** Louise '86 -45 Woodlnd Way -Manhsst 11030
(845) 892-0845 .. **Ehrlich,** Marc A '95 IBM -2070 Route 52 -Hopewell Junct 12533
(518) 272-2110 .. **Ehrlich,** Marc S '84 (Ehrlich & A) -64 2nd -Troy 12180
(212) 269-0927 .. **Ehrlich,** Maria T '95 %D'Amato & L,LLP -2 World Fncl Ctr -NY 10281
(212) 867-2240 .. **Ehrlich,** Matthew H '02 (MH Ehrlich,LLP) -122 E 42nd -NY 10168 **Fx:**370-4812
(212) 340-0655 .. **Ehrlich,** Michl C '76 Counsel Press,LLC -520 8th Av -NY 10018 **Fx:**447-1621
(212) 918-3000 .. **Ehrlich,** Philip H '87 Cnsl Hogan L LLP -875 3rd Av -NY 10022
(212) 827-0555 .. **Ehrlich,** Rachel '95 -200 Park Av S -NY 10003 **Fx:**827-0999
(212) 532-0500 .. **Ehrlich,** Robt C '95 (Heiberger & Assoc,PC) -205 Lex Av -NY 10016 **Fx:**532-2040

(518) 473-1416 .. **Ehrlich**, Ronald S '98 Employee Relations -2 ESP -Albany 12223
(718) 694-3865 .. **Ehrlich**, Sherri '86 %Transit Auth -130 Lvngstn -Brklyn 11201 **Fx**:694-5726
(212) 872-5951 .. **Ehrlich**, Stephen E '96 %KPMG LLP -345 Park Av -NY 10154
(212) 410-2600 .. **Ehrlich**, Steven G '83 -100 Park Av -NY 10017
(212) 264-8819 .. **Ehrman**, David M '95 %ODAR-SSA -26 Fed Plz -NY 10278
(516) 810-4150 .. **Ehrman**, Kevin S '97 -Bx648 -Huntngtn 11743
(212) 759-4433 .. **Ehrmann**, Danl J '96 Alvarez & Marsal -101 E 52nd -NY 10022
(718) 222-2506 .. **Ehrmann**, Louise M '94 Two Trees Mgmt Co LLC -45 Main -Brklyn 11201 **Fx**:222-2501
(718) 237-2000 .. **Eibel**, Andrew H '77 %Leg Aid -111 Lvngstn -Brklyn 11201 **Fx**:237-8737
(516) 466-7600 .. **Eiber**, Bruce '81 B Eiber,PC -99 Powerhse Rd -Roslyn Hts 11577 **Fx**:466-2557
(212) 687-0100 .. **Eichel**, Jessica Saunders '07 %Harris B PLLC -100 Wall -NY 10005
(914) 948-9031 .. **Eichel**, Roger M '74 -60 Brook Hills Cir -White Plns 10605 **Fx**:949-3532
(212) 223-4000 .. **Eichel**, Steven B '89 Cnsl Crowell & M LLP -590 Mad Av -NY 10022
(212) 836-8000 .. **Eichel**, Steven R '97 Cnsl Kaye S LLP -425 Park Av -NY 10022
(914) 682-9750 .. **Eichen**, Linda A '83 (Fuchs & E) -550 Mamaroneck Av -Harrison 10528 **Fx**:682-9723
(212) 607-2800 .. **Eichen**, Robin E '82 %FTC -1 Bowling Grn -NY 10004 **Fx**:607-2822
(212) 788-0885 .. **Eichenholtz**, Eric J '03 %Law Dept -100 Church -NY 10007 **Fx**:788-0367
(718) 254-7000 .. **Eichenholtz**, Seth D '02 %US Atty -271 Cadman Plz E -Brklyn 11201 **Fx**:254-6479
(518) 474-8494 .. **Eichenlaub**, Eric D '95 %Gov's Cnsls Ofc -242 State Cptl -Albany 12224
(212) 788-1052 .. **Eichinger**, Bridget T '07 %Law Dept -100 Church -NY 10007 **Fx**:788-0367
(631) 234-1666 .. **Eichinger**, Chas G '67 (C Eichinger & Assoc,PC) -1601 Vets Hwy -Islandia 11749 **Fx**:234-1776
(212) 735-3000 .. **Eichinger**, Jamie B '07 %Skadden ASM&F LLP -4 Times Sq -NY 10036
(212) 220-3830 .. **Eichler**, Nathaniel L '09 %Nicoletti H&S -88 Pine -NY 10005
(212) 805-0222 .. **Eichner**, James A '97 %Hon J Koeltl -500 Pearl -NY 10007
(585) 428-6810 .. **Eichner**, Jeffrey P '77 %Law Dept -30 Church -Rchstr 14614 **Fx**:428-6950
(212) 983-1199 .. **Eichner**, Stacie B '03 %Cutler M&A,LLP -708 3rd Av -NY 10017
(718) 222-2363 .. **Eicholtz**, Carrie A '09 %Law Dept -350 Jay -Brklyn 11201 **Fx**:222-2373
(212) 407-7700 .. **Eickemeyer**, John H '81 (Vedder P,PC) -1633 Bway -NY 10019
(718) 590-2000 .. **Eida**, Marc I '08 %DA -198 E 161st -Bronx 10451 **Fx**:590-6477
(212) 345-6257 .. **Eidenberg**, Judith N '96 %Marsh USA Inc -1166 Av of Amer -NY 10036 **Fx**:345-4665
(518) 831-1733 .. **Eidens**, Michl C '76 -Bx2767 -Glenvll 12325
(518) 402-9185 .. **Eidle**, Timothy E '94 %DEC -625 Bway -Albany 12233 **Fx**:402-9018
(516) 935-1100 .. **Eidler**, Alan D '79 %Spiegel Assoc -375 N Bway -Jericho 11753
(212) 385-9190 .. **Eidlisz**, Mark '98 (Finkelstein M&E) -11 Park Pl -NY 10007
(212) 489-0500 .. **Eidman**, Michl K '80 -1500 Bway -NY 10036 **Fx**:(201) 503-1336
(212) 265-5666 .. **Eidman**, Seymour H '56 -1500 Bway -NY 10036 **Fx**:(201) 503-1336
(516) 663-6600 .. **Eig**, Allison D '08 %Ruskin MF,PC -1425 RXR Plz -Uniondale 11556
(718) 225-3233 .. **Eiger**, Arnold '65 -218-14 Nrthrn Blvd -Bayside 11361 **Fx**:225-5730
(212) 889-4009 .. **Eiger**, Victoria B '81 (Dershowitz E&A,PC) -220 5th Av -NY 10001
(212) 468-8000 .. **Eiger**, Ze'-Ev D '03 %Morrison & F LLP -1290 Av of Amer -NY 10104
(212) 213-6866 .. **Eigerman**, Danl A '81 -260 Mad Av -NY 10016 **Fx**:532-6400
(212) 766-6300 .. **Eiges**, Kenneth A '76 (Eiges G&B,LLP) -225 Bway -NY 10007 **Fx**:233-5633
(212) 233-2020 .. **Eiges**, Kenneth A '76 (Eiges & E) -225 Bway -NY 10007 **Fx**:233-5633
(212) 233-2020 .. **Eiges**, Linda J '79 (Eiges & E) -225 Bway -NY 10007 **Fx**:233-5633
(518) 473-7051 .. **Eihacker**, Orrie '84 %OTDA-Fair Hearings -40 N Pearl -Albany 12243 **Fx**:473-6735
(212) 385-1050 .. **Eikenberry**, Peter G '65 (P Eikenberry) -74 Trinity Pl -NY 10006 **Fx**:385-1017
(845) 634-3627 .. **Eilbaum**, Harvey A '76 %Leg Aid -2 Congers Rd -New Cty 10956 **Fx**:634-8505
(212) 696-6000 .. **Eilbott**, Cindi '07 %Curtis M-PC&M LLP -101 Park Av -NY 10178
(516) 222-0888 .. **Eilen**, Howard S '80 (Lehman & E LLP) -50 Chas Lindbergh Blvd -Uniondale 11553
(212) 986-9700 .. **Eilenberg**, Adam D '82 (Eilenberg & K LLP) -11 E 44th -NY 10017
(212) 986-9700 .. **Eilenberg & Krause LLP** -11 E 44th -NY 10017 **Fx**:986-2399
(212) 251-5718 .. **Eilenberg**, Matthew '84 Towers Watson -875 3rd Av -NY 10022 **Fx**:644-6483
(212) 344-5400 .. **Eilender**, Jeffrey M '92 (Schlam S&D LLP) -26 Bway -NY 10004
(212) 331-5047 .. **Einbender**, Paula D '02 HRA Ofc Lgl Affrs -180 Water -NY 10038
(212) 391-9500 .. **Einbinder & Dunn,PC** -104 W 40th -NY 10018 **Fx**:391-9025
(212) 766-5300 .. **Einbinder**, Howard '68 -150 Bway -NY 10038 **Fx**:766-3399
(212) 455-2000 .. **Einbinder**, Matthew P '08 %Simpson T&B LLP -425 Lex Av -NY 10017
(212) 391-9500 .. **Einbinder**, Michl '81 (Einbinder & D,PC) -104 W 40th -NY 10018
(347) 448-4135 .. **Einbinder**, Robin Stone '84 -153-01 Jamaica Av -Jamaica 11432 **Fx**:(718) 228-8598
(212) 589-4200 .. **Einhorn**, David A '87 (Baker & H LLP) -45 Rckfllr Plz -NY 10111
(212) 403-1000 .. **Einhorn**, David M '77 (Wachtell LR&K) -51 W 52nd -NY 10019
(212) 349-6775 .. **Einhorn**, Jaymie L '84 (Peltz & W) -222 Bway -NY 10038
(212) 566-7188 .. **Einhorn**, Kathleen Barnett '93 (Genova B&G) -115 Bway -NY 10006
(646) 386-3649 .. **Einhorn**, Marcy '80 %Supreme Ct-Law Dept -60 Centre -NY 10007
(718) 383-5100 .. **Einhorn**, Steven '77 -449 Graham Av -Brklyn 11211
(212) 969-3000 .. **Einhorn**, Steven D '09 %Proskauer R LLP -1585 Bway -NY 10036
(718) 256-2000 .. **Einhorn**, Sylvia '88 OfCnsl M Zilberberg & Assoc,PC -6619 13th Av -Brklyn 11219 **Fx**:256-7900
(212) 983-8866 .. **Einig & Bush** -420 Lex Av -NY 10170 **Fx**:983-1050
(212) 983-8866 .. **Einig**, Steven L '83 (Einig & B) -420 Lex Av -NY 10170
(212) 279-9200 .. **Einiger**, Scott I '88 (Abrams FFEGF&E,LLP) -630 3rd Av -NY 10017
(315) 789-9869 .. **Einset**, Peter O '84 -42 Castle Bx307 -Geneva 14456 **Fx**:789-9869
(212) 907-0843 .. **Einstein**, Jos H '60 OfCnsl Labaton S LLP -140 Bway -NY 10005
(212) 578-8203 .. **Einstein**, Robt '82 %MetLife -27-01 Qns Plz N -LIC 11101
(212) 267-3550 .. **Einstein**, Stephen '81 (S Einstein & Assoc,PC) -20 Vesey -NY 10007 **Fx**:267-3803
(646) 471-4000 .. **Einstein**, Steven H '85 %PricewaterhouseCoopers LLP -300 Mad Av -NY 10017
(212) 766-2466 .. **Einwohner**, Stewart G '04 (DiSanto LLP) -15 Maiden Ln -NY 10038 **Fx**:(866) 746-0504
(212) 227-0347 .. **Einziger**, Ronald S '72 %Weiss W&W,PC -25 Park Pl -NY 10007
(212) 608-3500 .. **Eisberg**, James S '66 OfCnsl Beckman L&B LLP -116 John -NY 10038
(212) 643-0044 .. **Eisbrouch**, David L '01 (Eisbrouch & M,PC) -950 3rd Av -NY 10022 **Fx**:(201) 342-3211
(516) 931-1425 .. **Eisbruck**, Stuart H '67 -104 Cedar Dr -Plainvw 11803 **Fx**:937-6110
(607) 589-6261 .. **Eischen**, Dana E '75 -Bx730 -Spencer 14883
(212) 907-7300 .. **Eiseman**, David J '78 (Golenbock EAB&P) -437 Mad Av -NY 10022
(212) 428-2150 .. **Eiseman**, John P '76 %OCA -25 Beaver -NY 10004 **Fx**:428-2155
(212) 752-1000 .. **Eiseman**, Jonathan R '83 (Eiseman LL&K,PC) -805 3rd Av -NY 10022
(212) 752-1000 .. **Eiseman Levine Lehrhaupt & Kakoyiannis,PC** -805 3rd Av -NY 10022 **Fx**:355-4608
(212) 695-8100 .. **Eiseman**, Neal M '82 (Goetz F,LLP) -1 Penn Plz -NY 10119
(212) 752-1000 .. **Eiseman**, Robin J '88 OfCnsl Eiseman LL&K,PC -805 3rd Av -NY 10022
(914) 763-6444 .. **Eisemann**, Alexander E '84 -282 Katonah Av -Katonah 10536
(914) 737-8816 .. **Eisen**, Brian A '86 -4 Crestvw Av -Cortlandt Manor 10567 **Fx**:737-6805
(212) 832-4000 .. **Eisen**, Edwin Roy '58 (Eisen & S,LLP) -18 E 48th -NY 10017
(212) 248-8800 .. **Eisen**, Faye N '07 %Callan KB&B LLP -1 Whitehall -NY 10004
(212) 668-2301 .. **Eisen**, Jamie M '04 Hon S Chapman US Bankruptcy Ct -1 Bowling Grn -NY 10004
(516) 393-2200 .. **Eisen**, Judith A '87 (Garfunkel W,PC) -111 Grt Nck Rd -Gt Neck 11021
(212) 408-5100 .. **Eisen**, Karen Heiss '86 -30 Rckfllr Plz -NY 10112 **Fx**:541-5369
(212) 474-1000 .. **Eisen**, Lizabethann R '98 (Cravath S&M LLP) -825 8th Av -NY 10019
(914) 428-3313 .. **Eisen**, Robt J '99 Curan AF&N,LLP -14 Mamaroneck Av -White Plns 10601 **Fx**:949-5800
(212) 626-4100 .. **Eisen**, Robt L '71 (Baker & M LLP) -1114 Av of Amer -NY 10036
(212) 832-4000 .. **Eisen & Schulman, LLP** -18 E 48th -NY 10017 **Fx**:832-4092
(212) 685-7600 .. **Eisenberg**, Allen M '93 %Heller H&F,PC -292 Mad Av -NY 10017
(845) 735-7000 .. **Eisenberg**, Amy M '04 %Johnson & C,LLP -1 Blue Hill Plz -Pearl Rvr 10965
(718) 508-3414 .. **Eisenberg**, Anne L '09 Bronx Defenders -860 Courtlandt Av -Bronx 10451
(212) 607-3300 .. **Eisenberg**, Arthur N '71 %NYCLU -125 Broad -NY 10004
(212) 209-8161 .. **Eisenberg**, Barbara K '71 %J Crew Group Inc -770 Bway -NY 10003
(212) 695-8100 .. **Eisenberg**, Barry R '74 (Goetz F,LLP) -1 Penn Plz -NY 10119
(914) 946-7735 .. **Eisenberg**, Barry R '74 (Goetz F,LLP) -1 N Bway -White Plns 10601
(516) 222-1331 .. **Eisenberg**, Carol S '75 -666 Old Cntry Rd -Gdn Cty 11530 **Fx**:222-1713
(845) 426-3790 .. **Eisenberg**, Chana R '97 %CCH Inc -42 Melnick Dr -Monsey 10952
(212) 388-3600 .. **Eisenberg**, Cindy B '85 %32B-J Leg Srvcs -101 Av of Amer -NY 10013 **Fx**:388-3061
(212) 455-2000 .. **Eisenberg**, David M '79 (Simpson T&B LLP) -425 Lex Av -NY 10017
(212) 353-8700 .. **Eisenberg**, Douglas A '84 (Simon E&B LLP) -24 Union Sq E -NY 10003 **Fx**:353-1708
(212) 406-2554 .. **Eisenberg**, Elizaveta '06 -17 State -NY 10004
(212) 278-0400 .. **Eisenberg**, Eric M '09 %Cooper & D LLP -30 Rckfllr Plz -NY 10112
(212) 806-5400 .. **Eisenberg**, Gary D '02 %Stroock &S&L LLP -180 Maiden Ln -NY 10038
(845) 634-0135 .. **Eisenberg**, Gary E '85 -10 Esquire Rd -New Cty 10956
(212) 592-1400 .. **Eisenberg**, Gary F '90 (Herrick,F LLP) -2 Park Av -NY 10016
(516) 294-9400 .. **Eisenberg**, Gerald '64 (Eisenberg & M,LLP) -100 Q Roosevelt Blvd -Gdn Cty 11530 **Fx**:294-5877
(212) 326-2000 .. **Eisenberg**, Harvey M '92 (O'Melveny & M LLP) -7 Times Sq -NY 10036
(212) 966-8900 .. **Eisenberg**, Herbert '84 (Eisenberg & S,LLP) -233 Bway -NY 10279
(585) 232-6500 .. **Eisenberg**, Jack D '73 (Harter S&E LLP) -1600 Bausch & Lomb Pl -Rchstr 14604
(716) 853-1616 .. **Eisenberg**, Jack D '73 (Harter S&E LLP) -12 Fountain Plz -Buffalo 14202
(212) 412-9500 .. **Eisenberg**, James B '78 OfCnsl Flemming ZWZ LLP -1 Lbrty Plz -NY 10006
(718) 923-4206 .. **Eisenberg**, Janet P '92 %OTDA Fair Hearings -14 Boerum Pl -Brklyn 11201
(212) 219-3041 .. **Eisenberg**, Jeffrey S '85 -401 Bway -NY 10013 **Fx**:966-1801
(718) 838-7878 .. **Eisenberg**, Jennifer M '08 Bronx Defenders -860 Crtlandt Av -Bronx 10451 **Fx**:665-0100
(718) 658-0500 .. **Eisenberg**, Jolie R '90 %Law Dept -151-20 Jamaica Av -Jamaica 11432 **Fx**:658-4025
(212) 578-5170 .. **Eisenberg**, Kenneth A '86 %MetLife -27-01 Qns Plz N -LIC 11101
(212) 407-4000 .. **Eisenberg**, Kevin M '99 (Loeb & L,LLP) -345 Park Av -NY 10154
(845) 292-4412 .. **Eisenberg & Kirsch** -25 Darbee Ln Bx715 -Liberty 12754 **Fx**:292-1636
(212) 248-3140 .. **Eisenberg**, Lance T '00 %Drinker B&R LLP -140 Bway -NY 10005
(212) 940-8800 .. **Eisenberg**, Lawr D '68 OfCnsl Katten MR LLP -575 Mad Av -NY 10022
(914) 761-0716 .. **Eisenberg**, Lawr J '78 (L Eisenberg,LLC) -11 Martine Av -White Plns 10606 **Fx**:761-0929
(212) 484-3900 .. **Eisenberg**, Leah M '01 (Arent F LLP) -1675 Bway -NY 10019
(212) 907-7300 .. **Eisenberg**, Leonard '60 (Golenbock EAB&P) -437 Mad Av -NY 10022
(212) 417-4357 .. **Eisenberg**, Leslie A '93 %Dept of Health -90 Church -NY 10007 **Fx**:417-4392
(212) 373-3000 .. **Eisenberg**, Lisa Krausz '10 %Paul WRW&G LLP -1285 Av of Amer -NY 10019
(516) 221-3700 .. **Eisenberg**, Lloyd M '89 (Eisenberg & C) -2631 Merrick Rd -Bellmore 11710 **Fx**:977-3337

(212) 983-4800 .. **Eisenberg,** Marcia R '79 %JCRC -70 W 36th -NY 10018 **Fx:**983-4084
(212) 833-5392 .. **Eisenberg,** Mark R '89 Sony BMG Music Entrtnmnt -550 Mad Av -NY 10022 **Fx:**833-4873
(212) 592-1400 .. **Eisenberg,** Michl A '07 Herrick,F LLP -2 Park Av -NY 10016
(212) 310-8000 .. **Eisenberg,** Michl B '01 Cnsl Weil G&M LLP -767 5th Av -NY 10153
(516) 683-6100 .. **Eisenberg,** Michl M '93 Chernoff Diamond & Co -990 Stewart Av -Gdn Cty 11530
(212) 407-4000 .. **Eisenberg,** Nicole D '05 %Loeb & L,LLP -345 Park Av -NY 10154
(315) 448-8400 .. **Eisenberg,** Pamela R '85 %Law Dept -233 E Wshngtn -Syracuse 13202 **Fx:**448-8381
(212) 541-2000 .. **Eisenberg,** Peter A '60 OfCnsl Bryan C LLP -1290 Av of Amer -NY 10104
(212) 816-8145 .. **Eisenberg,** Philip J '85 Citigroup -388 Greenwich -NY 10013
(212) 336-8000 .. **Eisenberg,** Rebecca R '05 %Amster R&E -90 Park Av -NY 10016
(212) 373-3000 .. **Eisenberg,** Richd B '09 Paul WRW&G LLP -1285 Av of Amer -NY 10019
(212) 599-0777 .. **Eisenberg,** Richd D '76 (Eisenberg T&L) -675 3rd Av -NY 10017
(516) 741-6565 .. **Eisenberg,** Richd J '77 OfCnsl Meyer SE&K,PC -990 Stewart Av Bx9194 -Gdn Cty 11530
(516) 295-2949 .. **Eisenberg,** Ronald L '77 -888 Woodmere Pl -Woodmere 11598 **Fx:**374-5713
(914) 285-9800 .. **Eisenberg,** Sam '39 (Kurzman EC&L,LLP) -1 N Bway -White Plns 10601
(631) 666-6915 .. **Eisenberg,** Saul '76 -111 Wohseepee Dr -Bay Shr 11706
(212) 966-8900 .. **Eisenberg & Schnell, LLP** -233 Bway -NY 10279 **Fx:**966-2505
(212) 683-1668 .. **Eisenberg,** Scott C '99 -280 Mad Av -NY 10016 **Fx:**(646) 292-5110
(631) 755-0101 .. **Eisenberg,** Scott P '07 %Lewis JAA,LLP -425 Broad Hollow Rd -Melvll 11747
(607) 773-2892 .. **Eisenberg,** Seth F '96 %US Dist Ct -15 Henry -Bnghmtn 13901
(518) 789-4953 .. **Eisenberg,** Stephen J '70 -237 Silver Mtn Rd -Millerton 12546 **Fx:**(866) 884-7492
(212) 909-6000 .. **Eisenberg,** Svetlana M '05 %Debevoise & P LLP -919 3rd Av -NY 10022
(212) 599-0777 .. **Eisenberg Tanchum & Levy** -675 3rd Av -NY 10017 **Fx:**599-0770
(607) 255-6477 .. **Eisenberg,** Theo '72 -203 The Pkwy -Ithaca 14850
(212) 512-1000 .. **Eisenberg,** Viviane '77 %HBO -1100 Av of Amer -NY 10036 **Fx:**512-1986
(212) 406-2811 .. **Eisenberger,** Benjamin P '79 -321 Bway -NY 10007 **Fx:**349-4037
(212) 521-2864 .. **Eisenberger,** Jeffrey M '88 %Loews Corp -667 Mad Av -NY 10065
(845) 426-3400 .. **Eisenberger,** Seth '95 -108 Airport Exec Park -Nanuet 10954 **Fx:**426-3401
(212) 422-3843 .. **Eisenberger,** Sheldon '74 -30 Broad -NY 10004 **Fx:**422-3844
(212) 465-5000 .. **Eisenberg Peled,** Yifat '05 %Parsons Brinckerhoff -1 Penn Plz -NY 10119
(212) 705-7000 .. **Eisenbiegler,** Fredk F '05 (Bingham M LLP) -399 Park Av -NY 10022
(631) 493-9800 .. **Eisenbud,** Fredk '76 -6165 Jericho Tpk -Commack 11725 **Fx:**493-9806
(212) 335-4500 .. **Eisenegger,** Erich P '02 %DLA Piper LLP -1251 Av of Amer -NY 10020
(718) 626-7730 .. **Eisenfeld,** Jason S '08 %Pyrros & S LLP -31-01 Bway -LIC 11106
(716) 854-2100 .. **Eisenhauer,** Peter J '99 %Lewis & L,PC -37 Franklin -Buffalo 14202 **Fx:**854-0433
(646) 722-8500 .. **Eisenhofer,** Jay W '06 (Grant & E,PA) -485 Lex Av -NY 10017
(315) 724-7523 .. **Eisenhut,** Keith A '81 -1602 Sunset Av -Utica 13502 **Fx:**797-1519
(212) 838-7797 .. **Eisenkraft,** Michl B '05 %Cohen MS&T,PLLC -88 Pine -NY 10005
(212) 735-3000 .. **Eisenlord,** Heather A '04 %Skadden ASM&F LLP -4 Times Sq -NY 10036
(585) 428-5755 .. **Eisenman,** Carol L '86 %Cnty Atty -50 W Main -Rchstr 14614 **Fx:**428-2031
(212) 679-0400 .. **Eisenman,** Corissa L '06 %Miller & E,LLP -450 7th Av -NY 10123
(212) 474-1000 .. **Eisenman,** Gary R '86 %Cravath S&M LLP -825 8th Av -NY 10019
(212) 679-0400 .. **Eisenman,** Michl P '86 (Miller & E,LLP) -450 7th Av -NY 10123
(212) 931-7532 .. **Eisenman,** Nicholas H '06 %MLB Properties -245 Park Av -NY 10167 **Fx:**949-5697
(516) 357-3000 .. **Eisenmesser,** Scott A '88 (Rivkin R LLP) -926 RXR Plz -Uniondale 11556
(914) 834-7169 .. **Eisenpress,** Brad '82 -45 Linwood Rd -New Rchll 10804
(212) 753-2424 .. **Eisenpress,** Sherri Lee '90 (Reiss E LLP) -425 Mad Av -NY 10017
(212) 859-8000 .. **Eisensmith,** Randy C '06 %Fried FHS&J LLP -1 NY Plz -NY 10004
(917) 373-8113 .. **Eisenstadt,** Herzl S '59 -1206 E 21st -Brklyn 11210 **Fx:**(718) 252-3453
(212) 272-6707 .. **Eisenstadt,** Neil B '88 %JP Morgan Chase -383 Mad Av -NY 10179
(212) 427-5000 .. **Eisenstat,** Saml '63 -45 E 89th -NY 10128
(212) 252-0004 .. **Eisenstein,** Douglas K '96 OfCnsl Carroll M&K LLC -570 Lex Av -NY 10022
(212) 458-1530 .. **Eisenstein,** Erik J '95 %AIG -175 Water -NY 10038 **Fx:**458-1475
(212) 803-3100 .. **Eisenstein,** Fredrick C '82 %Empire State Dvlmnt Corp -633 3rd Av -NY 10017
(518) 213-6000 .. **Eisenstein,** Harold '87 %NYSUT -800 Troy-Schnctdy Rd -Latham 12110 **Fx:**213-6488
(212) 577-6500 .. **Eisenstein,** Jethro M '68 (Profeta & E) -14 Wall -NY 10005 **Fx:**577-6702
(212) 773-9052 .. **Eisenstein,** Keith D '97 Ernst & Young LLP -5 Times Sq -NY 10036
(516) 496-2828 .. **Eisenstein,** Paul '64 -7600 Jericho Tpk -Woodbury 11797
(212) 775-9002 .. **Eisenstein,** Steven J '85 (Lum D&P,LLC) -325 Bway -NY 10007
(212) 536-3900 .. **Eisert,** Edw G '74 (K&L Gates LLP) -599 Lex Av -NY 10022
(212) 468-4800 .. **Eisert,** Richd S '93 (Davis & G LLP) -1740 Bway -NY 10019
(212) 422-9424 .. **Eisig,** Eyal S '04 %Gogick B&O,LLP -11 Bway -NY 10004
(914) 949-6400 .. **Eisland,** Evan M '88 (McCullough G&S,LLP) -1311 Mamaroneck Av -White Plns 10605
(212) 837-6170 .. **Eisler,** Nathan M '84 (Hughes H&R LLP) -1 Bttry Pk Plz -NY 10004
(212) 838-7797 .. **Eisler,** Robt G '00 (Cohen MS&T,PLLC) -88 Pine -NY 10005
(212) 683-9550 .. **Eisman,** Clyde J '95 -450 7th Av -NY 10123
(212) 902-2432 .. **Eisman,** David P '96 %Goldman Sachs -1 NY Plz -NY 10004
(914) 251-1115 .. **Eisman,** Frederic B '93 %Walsh & A LLP -2900 Wstchstr Av -Purchase 10577
(212) 459-7894 .. **Eisman,** Robt B '94 %Dept of Tax & Fin -1740 Bway -NY 10019 **Fx:**459-7897
(631) 393-5158 .. **Eisman,** Russell K '80 -200 Broadhllw Rd -Melvll 11747 **Fx:**673-0631
(516) 328-2300 .. **Eisman,** Steven J '80 (Abrams FFEGF&E,LLP) -1111 Marcus Av -Lk Success 11042
(718) 261-2300 .. **Eisner,** Alyssa '02 %Sager & G -118-35 Qns Blvd -Frst Hlls 11375
(718) 403-3600 .. **Eisner,** Andrew B '77 Dept of Finance -345 Adams -Brklyn 11201 **Fx:**403-3650
(212) 969-3000 .. **Eisner,** Danl J '01 (Proskauer R LLP) -1585 Bway -NY 10036
(718) 250-2000 .. **Eisner,** Diane R '75 %DA -350 Jay -Brklyn 11201 **Fx:**250-2314
(212) 473-8700 .. **Eisner,** Eugene G '61 (Eisner & M,PC) -113 Univ Pl -NY 10003 **Fx:**473-8705
(212) 735-3000 .. **Eisner,** Imri '06 %Skadden ASM&F LLP -4 Times Sq -NY 10036
(212) 230-1210 .. **Eisner,** Jamie R '99 Cnsl Golden Arc Cptl -110 E 55th -NY 10022
(212) 662-4503 .. **Eisner,** Kenneth J '75 -235 W 108th -NY 10025
(212) 349-6009 .. **Eisner,** Laurel Weinstein '86 Sanctuary for Families -110 Wall -NY 10005 **Fx:**566-0344
(212) 506-2500 .. **Eisner,** Nancy K '81 Cnsl Mayer B LLP -1675 Bway -NY 10019
(212) 705-6213 .. **Eisner,** Oren '02 QVT Fncl LP -1177 Av of Amer -NY 10036
(212) 788-6775 .. **Eisner,** Susan B '99 %Law Dept -100 Church -NY 10007 **Fx:**788-0367
(845) 567-5779 .. **Eisner,** Susan R '88 PRG -539 Temple Hill Rd -New Windsor 12553
(212) 883-1700 .. **Eisner,** Todd R '96 (Duval & S LLP) -101 Park Av -NY 10178
(212) 788-1240 .. **Eison,** Howard '75 %Law Dept -100 Church -NY 10007 **Fx:**788-0367
(716) 633-9300 .. **Eiss,** James D '89 -19 Limestone Dr -Buffalo 14221 **Fx:**633-0492
(212) 455-2000 .. **Eissler,** Ralph G D '08 %Simpson T&B LLP -425 Lex Av -NY 10017
(212) 442-4553 .. **Eiss-Proctor,** Megan E '06 Dept Probation -100 Centre -NY 10013
(212) 558-4000 .. **Eitel,** Mitchell S '88 (Sullivan & C LLP) -125 Broad -NY 10004
(212) 407-4000 .. **Eizenman,** David B '65 (Loeb & L,LLP) -345 Park Av -NY 10154
(212) 430-8020 .. **Ekblom,** Neil H '86 (LeClairRyan,PC) -830 3rd Av -NY 10022
(212) 839-5300 .. **Ekeland,** Tor B '07 %Sidley A LLP -787 7th Av -NY 10019
(212) 545-4000 .. **Ekelman,** Felice B '86 (Jackson L LLP) -666 3rd Av -NY 10017
(212) 687-6444 .. **Ekenberg,** Anetta V '93 OfCnsl J Cannistraci -58 Twin Ridges Rd -Ossining 10562
(718) 852-8300 .. **Eke-Nweke,** Vincent I '95 (V Eke-Nweke,PC) -498 Atl Av -Brklyn 11217 **Fx:**852-7361
(212) 571-1213 .. **Ekici,** Yasemin '07 -20 Vesey -NY 10007 **Fx:**571-1214
(212) 210-9503 .. **Eklund,** David J '06 %Alston & B LLP -90 Park Av -NY 10016
(212) 648-0354 .. **Ekman,** Gershon '84 JP Morgan Chase -245 Park Av -NY 10167
(212) 816-1707 .. **Ekman,** Patricia '82 Citibank NA -388 Greenwich -NY 10013
(212) 389-1547 .. **Ekman,** Ulrika '91 Greenhill & Co -300 Park Av -NY 10022
(212) 554-1234 .. **Ekpe,** Bolanle A '04 %AXA Financial Inc -1290 Av of Amer -NY 10104 **Fx:**707-3963
(212) 773-2374 .. **Elacqua,** Amelia E '09 Ernst & Young LLP -5 Times Sq -NY 10036
(518) 382-5239 .. **Elacqua,** Angela M '79 NY-UCS City Ct -105 Jay -Schnctdy 12305
(518) 473-4146 .. **Elacqua,** Jamie L '89 State Comptroller -110 State -Albany 12236 **Fx:**473-9104
(212) 619-0261 .. **Elan,** Kenneth A '78 -217 Bway -NY 10007 **Fx:**385-2707
(212) 962-1224 .. **Elan,** Robt I '75 -217 Bway -NY 10007 **Fx:**271-4230
(631) 351-3042 .. **Elan Mangano,** Cindy '83 %Town Atty -100 Main -Huntngtn 11743 **Fx:**351-3032
(716) 847-0662 .. **Elardo,** Robt M '82 %Volunteer Lwyrs Prjt -237 Main -Buffalo 14203 **Fx:**847-0307
(315) 474-2943 .. **Elbadawi,** Esam A '92 (Sugarman Law Firm,LLP) -211 W Jffrsn -Syracuse 13202
(716) 853-9555 .. **El-Bahtity,** Laura '99 %Leg Aid -237 Main -Buffalo 14203 **Fx:**853-3219
(212) 867-4300 .. **Elbaum,** Brian J '95 -111 John -NY 10038
(212) 668-1900 .. **Elbaum,** David '96 Brune & R LLP -80 Broad -NY 10004
(914) 997-2500 .. **Elbaum,** David '01 %Bodnar & M LLP -140 Grand -White Plns 10601 **Fx:**997-8155
(516) 248-1700 .. **Elbaum,** Eli '05 %Forchelli CDSM&T,LLP -333 Earle Ovngton Blvd -Uniondale 11553
(212) 969-3000 .. **Elbaum,** Lawr S '06 %Proskauer R LLP -1585 Bway -NY 10036
(212) 596-9000 .. **Elbaum,** Michl J '10 %Ropes & G LLP -1211 Av of Amer -NY 10036
(212) 608-4088 .. **Elbaz,** Michl M '00 -20 Vesey -NY 10007
(718) 852-3113 .. **Elber,** Myles R '78 (Siegel & E) -16 Court -Brklyn 11241 **Fx:**852-0285
(212) 430-5400 .. **Elberg,** Amos B '04 %Diamond M LLP -620 8th Av -NY 10018
(212) 578-7697 .. **Elberg,** Mitchell '78 %MetLife -27-01 Qns Plz N -LIC 11101 **Fx:**578-3916
(212) 735-3000 .. **Elberg,** Shana A '02 %Skadden ASM&F LLP -4 Times Sq -NY 10036
(212) 326-3939 .. **Elbert,** Maya '09 %Jones D -222 E 41st -NY 10017
(516) 294-2978 .. **Elbert,** Michl D '99 (Elbert & E,LLP) -221 Mineola Blvd -Mineola 11501 **Fx:**294-2979
(212) 576-2670 .. **Elbert,** Richd L '95 R Elbert,LLC -841 Bway -NY 10003
(212) 938-1213 .. **Elbogen,** Israel D '07 %Levitin & Assoc,PC -1430 Bway -NY 10018
(718) 338-3727 .. **Elbogen,** Wm '86 -1069 E 24th -Brklyn 11210 **Fx:**692-3626
(212) 482-0001 .. **Elci,** Huseyin Devrim '09 %Russo K&T LLP -33 Whitehall -NY 10004
(212) 599-8200 .. **Eldada,** Zena '07 %Shaub AC&S,LLP -655 3rd Av -NY 10017
(212) 460-6856 .. **Elder,** Crystal R '02 Con Ed -4 Irving Pl -NY 10003
(212) 267-9222 .. **Elder,** Mark J '76 OfCnsl Gorayeb & Assoc,PC -100 William -NY 10038 **Fx:**962-5418
(518) 862-2737 .. **Elder,** Michl S '86 %GE -319 Great Oaks Blvd -Albany 12203
(212) 695-2724 .. **Elder,** Robt S '74 OR Elder Inc -58 W 40th -NY 10018 **Fx:**643-9894
(212) 858-1000 .. **Elder,** Roger C '08 %Pillsbury WSP LLP -1540 Bway -NY 10036
(914) 703-6300 .. **Elder,** Wm A '96 %Pillinger MT,LLP -570 Taxter Rd -Elmsfrd 10523
(212) 474-1000 .. **Elders,** Christopher C '09 %Cravath S&M LLP -825 8th Av -NY 10019
(212) 735-3000 .. **Eldor,** Avi Y '07 %Skadden ASM&F LLP -4 Times Sq -NY 10036
(315) 479-3900 .. **Eldred,** Jeremy G '97 %SSA-ODAR -300 S State -Syracuse 13202 **Fx:**479-3933
(518) 475-0393 .. **Eldridge,** Douglas A '72 -9 Pinedale Av -Delmar 12054
(631) 360-9000 .. **Eldridge,** J David '98 Damianos Realty Grp -222 Middle Cntry Rd -Smithtwn 11787
(716) 843-4100 .. **Eldridge,** Kathleen Ann '93 %US SBA -130 S Elmwood Av -Buffalo 14202
(212) 836-8000 .. **Elefano,** Antonio C Jr. '06 %Kaye S LLP -425 Park Av -NY 10022

(212) 480-3030 .. **Elefant,** Marc '98 M Pressman -125 Maiden Ln -NY 10038 **Fx:**480-2590
(212) 318-3000 .. **Elefant,** Sheldon '03 %Fulbright & J LLP -666 5th Av -NY 10103
(315) 792-2262 .. **Elefante,** Angela M '61 City Schl Dist -1115 Mohawk -Utica 13501 **Fx:**792-5210
(914) 961-4400 .. **Elefante & Persanis,LLP** -141 Hillside Pl -Eastchstr 10709 **Fx:**961-4402
(914) 961-4400 .. **Elefante,** Ralph J '80 (Elefante & P,LLP) -141 Hillside Pl -Eastchstr 10709
(631) 582-4000 .. **Elefante-Link,** Rose M '97 Cnsl Tsunis G&L,LLP -2929 Express Dr N -Islandia 11749
(718) 802-1616 .. **Elefterakis,** John '10 %Avanzino & M,PC -26 Court -Brklyn 11242 **Fx:**802-0189
(212) 553-0300 .. **Elepano,** Aurora '02 %Moody's Invstr Srvc -250 Greenwich -NY 10007
(516) 869-0383 .. **Eletto,** Lisa Gervais '95 -60 Old Pine Dr -Manhsst 11030
(212) 309-6000 .. **Eley,** Claud V S '04 (Morgan L&B LLP) -101 Park Av -NY 10178
(212) 674-5151 .. **Elf,** Michl W '88 %Macmillan -175 5th Av -NY 10010 **Fx:**529-0594
(212) 819-8200 .. **Elfand,** Ross E '06 %White & C LLP -1155 Av of Amer -NY 10036
(516) 295-5023 .. **Elfenbein,** Arthur '55 -891 Wstmnstr Rd Bx118 -Woodmere 11598 **Fx:**295-3316
(212) 679-5400 .. **Elfenbein,** Randall M '90 %D Taback,PC -470 Park Av S -NY 10016 **Fx:**679-1033
(212) 837-6052 .. **Elfenbein,** Tina I '09 %Hughes H&R LLP -1 Bttry Pk Plz -NY 10004
(718) 390-5405 .. **Elford,** Kevin M '80 Richmond Cnty Surrogates Ct -18 Richmond Ter -Staten Isl 10301
(212) 966-6420 .. **Elgabry,** Myra '05 Lwyrs For Children -110 Lafayette -NY 10013 **Fx:**966-0531
(212) 245-1320 .. **Elgabry,** Reda Abd Elsalam '01 -250 W 57th -NY 10107
(212) 577-3688 .. **Elgarten,** Kerry M '84 %Leg Aid -199 Water -NY 10038 **Fx:**509-8431
(802) 272-4629 .. **El Gawhary,** Muhammad S '10 -90 Meyer Rd -Amherst 14226
(212) 375-1155 .. **Elghanayan,** H Henry '66 -290 Park Av S -NY 10010
(631) 444-0260 .. **Elgut,** Craig L '94 DEC -SUNY Campus 50 Circle Rd -Stony Brk 11790 **Fx:**444-0348
(212) 244-4111 .. **Elhadad-Chemtob,** Lilach '04 OfCnsl Shiboleth YR&Z,LLP -1 Penn Plz -NY 10119
(212) 969-1800 .. **Elhai,** Hymie J '03 NY Jets -50 W 57th -NY 10019
(718) 833-2100 .. **Elhilow,** Jos M '75 (Elhilow & Assoc) -259 86th -Brklyn 11209 **Fx:**833-0476
(718) 854-2361 .. **Elia,** Anthony N III '01 AN Elia,PC -185 Prospect Pk SW -Brklyn 11218 **Fx:**854-1025
(716) 759-2060 .. **Elia,** David A '81 -4950 Strickler Rd -Clarence 14031
(631) 844-1000 .. **Elia,** Nancy A '95 Nrth Fork Bnk -275 Broadhllw Rd -Melvll 11747
(212) 503-8800 .. **Eliach,** Steven J '86 %Marks Paneth & Shron LLP -622 3rd Av -NY 10017
(212) 947-7077 .. **Eliades,** Costas M '98 (C Eliades, PC) -405 Lex Av-26th Fl -NY 10174 **Fx:**658-9730
(212) 618-1791 .. **Elias,** Alicia N '06 %V Williams & Assoc -14 Wall -NY 10005
(212) 326-2000 .. **Elias,** Brad M '08 %O'Melveny & M LLP -7 Times Sq -NY 10036
(914) 925-0000 .. **Elias,** Dan '86 (Elias Grp) -411 Theo Fremd Av -Rye 10580 **Fx:**925-9344
(914) 946-1452 .. **Elias,** Danl S '86 (Markhoff & M PC) -14 Mamaroneck Av -White Plns 10601
(718) 448-6655 .. **Elias,** Danielle Leventhal '99 -60 Bay -Staten Isl 10301
(646) 218-4447 .. **Elias,** Dov B '98 Le Marquis -12 E 31st -NY 10016
(212) 585-4407 .. **Elias,** Gary I '79 -201 E 83rd -NY 10028
(973) 596-4517 .. **Elias,** Joshua R '05 %Gibbons PC -1 Penn Plz -NY 10119 **Fx:**639-6351
(516) 627-5807 .. **Elias,** Platon '77 -74 Woodedge Rd -Plandome 11030 **Fx:**627-5807
(212) 242-6615 .. **Elias,** Steven '66 -49 W 24th -NY 10010 **Fx:**645-7322
(212) 687-0100 .. **Eliasberg Fuchs,** Abbie L '91 (Harris B PLLC) -100 Wall -NY 10005
(212) 832-4540 .. **Eliav,** Arthur G '07 Roosevelt Island Operating Corp -591 Main -NY 10044
(716) 854-4300 .. **Elibol,** David H '96 (Gross SB&G,PC) -465 Main -Buffalo 14203
(516) 227-2300 .. **Elicks,** Gerard P '87 Wright Risk Mgmt -333 Earle Ovngton Blvd -Uniondale 11553
(212) 867-5800 .. **Elie,** Danl E '02 %Osler H&H LLP -620 8th Av -NY 10018
(212) 596-9000 .. **Elihu,** David M '10 %Ropes & G LLP -1211 Av of Amer -NY 10036
(212) 430-6239 .. **Elimelekh,** Ron '05 FSI Captl LLC -150 E 52nd -NY 10022 **Fx:**430-6219
(212) 407-4000 .. **Elimelekh,** Shelly '07 %Loeb & L,LLP -345 Park Av -NY 10154
(212) 801-2148 .. **Elings,** G Roxanne '87 (Greenberg T,LLP) -200 Park Av -NY 10166
(212) 490-9000 .. **Elinski,** Karen M '89 %TIAA-CREF -730 3rd Av -NY 10017
(212) 547-5400 .. **Eliopoulos,** Elias '96 (McDermott W&E LLP) -340 Mad Av -NY 10173
(212) 537-7000 .. **Eliopoulos,** Peter J '99 %MS Gray -251 W 93rd -NY 10025 **Fx:**537-8800
(212) 224-4557 .. **Eliopulos,** Linda Sohrer '01 %Sumitomo Mitsui -277 Park Av -NY 10172 **Fx:**593-9522
(212) 317-1717 .. **Eliot,** Andrew M '01 %Chemtob MF&T LLP -3 E 54th -NY 10022
(212) 356-8100 .. **Eliot,** Anita S '95 %CIR -520 8th Av -NY 10018 **Fx:**356-8111
(516) 227-2662 .. **Elis,** Alan M '92 %Rubin & L,PC -591 Stewart Av -Gdn Cty 11530
(516) 433-5017 .. **Eliseo,** Michl A '58 -53 MacArthur Av -Plainvw 11803
(718) 852-1700 .. **Elisofon,** Barry '73 -26 Court -Brklyn 11242
(212) 592-1400 .. **Elisofon,** Howard R '74 (Herrick,F LLP) -2 Park Av -NY 10016
(718) 852-1700 .. **Elisofon,** Pamela A '93 -26 Court -Brklyn 11242 **Fx:**852-2468
(212) 386-8359 .. **Elisseou,** Elaine '88 %HPD -100 Gold -NY 10038
(212) 577-3615 .. **Elitcher,** Anthony J '92 %Leg Aid -199 Water -NY 10038
(607) 547-5261 .. **Elkan,** Paul W '73 -43 Pioneer Bx207 -Cooperstwn 13326
(212) 474-1000 .. **Elken,** Andrew C '09 %Cravath S&M LLP -825 8th Av -NY 10019
(212) 556-2100 .. **Elkhouly,** Ahmad M '08 %King & S -1185 Av of Amer -NY 10036
(845) 732-8988 .. **Elkin,** Dayna L '96 %Active Media Srvcs -1 Blue Hill Plz -Pearl Rvr 10965 **Fx:**735-2342
(212) 682-2596 .. **Elkin,** Edw '83 -333 E 38th -NY 10016 **Fx:**481-8209
(212) 294-6700 .. **Elkin,** Jeffrey H '71 (Winston & S) -200 Park Av -NY 10166
(212) 659-7300 .. **Elkin,** Judith '04 (Haynes & B,LLP) -1221 Av of Amer -NY 10020
(212) 468-8000 .. **Elkin,** Marjorie S '76 OfCnsl Morrison & F LLP -1290 Av of Amer -NY 10104
(212) 294-6700 .. **Elkin,** Michl S '85 (Winston & S) -200 Park Av -NY 10166
(212) 596-9000 .. **Elkind,** David S '76 (Ropes & G LLP) -1211 Av of Amer -NY 10036
(212) 474-1000 .. **Elkind,** Diana '08 %Cravath S&M LLP -825 8th Av -NY 10019
(212) 797-3544 .. **Elkind,** Jenna E '08 %French & C,LLP -29 Bway -NY 10006
(607) 535-7143 .. **Elkins,** Wm C '49 -4335 State Route 414 -Burdett 14818
(212) 225-2000 .. **El Koury,** Jaime A '81 (Cleary GS&H) -1 Lbrty Plz -NY 10006
(518) 431-5000 .. **Elkovitch,** April A '01 Farm Family Ins -Bx656 -Albany 12201 **Fx:**431-5979
(315) 252-1389 .. **Elkovitch,** David P '78 -199 Genesee -Auburn 13021
(212) 310-9500 .. **Elkowitz,** Robin S '93 Instinet Corp -3 Times Sq -NY 10036
(212) 735-3000 .. **Ellberger,** Ruven '09 %Skadden ASM&F LLP -4 Times Sq -NY 10036
(212) 309-6000 .. **Ellegaard,** Peter K '08 %Morgan L&B LLP -101 Park Av -NY 10178
(315) 218-8000 .. **Elleman,** John B '88 (Bond S&K,PLLC) -1 Lincoln Ctr -Syracuse 13202
(212) 834-4718 .. **Ellenberg,** Ari I '06 -270 Park Av -NY 10017
(212) 629-8585 .. **Ellenberg,** Michl A '77 (Ellenberg & Prtnrs LLP) -575 8th Av -NY 10018
(212) 629-8585 .. **Ellenberg & Partners LLP** -575 8th Av -NY 10018 **Fx:**629-6017
(212) 964-3290 .. **Ellenberg,** Robt L '75 %Levidow L&O -299 Bway -NY 10007
(212) 336-0062 .. **Ellenbogen,** Bennett '91 %SEC -3 World Fncl Ctr -NY 10281 **Fx:**336-1323
(212) 576-1400 .. **Ellenbogen,** Bernard '57 -440 Park Av S -NY 10016 **Fx:**576-1414
(212) 522-1361 .. **Ellenbogen,** Marc A '95 Time Inc -1271 Av of Amer -NY 10020 **Fx:**522-0437
(212) 715-9100 .. **Ellenbogen,** Philip M '10 %Kramer LN&F,LLP -1177 Av of Amer -NY 10036
(212) 310-8000 .. **Ellenbogen,** Richd I '85 SpclCnsl Weil G&M LLP -767 5th Av -NY 10153
(516) 759-2722 .. **Ellenbogen,** Wayne L '98 Cnsl Ryan M&L,LLP -90 Forest Av -Locust Vly 11560
(212) 416-6388 .. **Ellenhorn,** David N '62 %Dept of Law -120 Bway -NY 10271
(212) 370-1300 .. **Ellenoff,** Douglas S '88 (Ellenoff G&S LLP) -150 E 42nd -NY 10017
(212) 370-1300 .. **Ellenoff Grossman & Schole LLP** -150 E 42nd -NY 10017 **Fx:**370-7889
(212) 786-1000 .. **Ellenzweig,** Sherry '99 (DeVos & Co,PLLC) -1230 Av of Amer -NY 10020 **Fx:**(800) 223-1273
(212) 210-9424 .. **Ellerin,** Betty Weinberg '53 SrCnsl Alston & B LLP -90 Park Av -NY 10016
(845) 342-2245 .. **Ellerin,** Michele P '84 (M Ellerin,LLP) -528 E Main -Middletwn 10940 **Fx:**344-5970
(518) 443-5400 .. **Ellermann,** Marti Anne '79 %SUNY Univ Cnsl -S333 SUNY Plz -Albany 12246 **Fx:**443-5409
(212) 969-3000 .. **Ellert,** Wanda L '77 SrCnsl Proskauer R LLP -1585 Bway -NY 10036
(212) 813-1600 .. **Ellett,** J David Jr. '78 %Kalow & S -488 Mad Av -NY 10022
(212) 986-1000 .. **Ellexson,** Brian L '09 %Goldberg C&G,LLP -331 Mad Av -NY 10017 **Fx:**986-8039
(212) 209-4800 .. **Ellias,** Jared A '09 %Brown R LLP -7 Times Sq -NY 10036
(212) 806-5400 .. **Ellice,** Christine E '08 %Stroock &S&L LLP -180 Maiden Ln -NY 10038
(914) 323-7000 .. **Ellick,** Ross J '89 (Wilson EME&D LLP) -3 Gannett Dr -White Plns 10604
(212) 735-3000 .. **Ellin,** Howard L '91 (Skadden ASM&F LLP) -4 Times Sq -NY 10036
(212) 918-4868 .. **Ellington,** Michl L II '04 (Cobos EM&M,LLC) -48 Wall -NY 10005 **Fx:**918-4801
(212) 450-4000 .. **Ellins,** Howard A '77 SrCnsl Davis P&W LLP -450 Lex Av -NY 10017
(718) 254-7000 .. **Elliot,** Cameron R '05 US Atty -271 Cadman Plz E -Brklyn 11201 **Fx:**254-6479
(212) 546-4000 .. **Elliot,** Carrie L '97 %Bristol-Myers Squibb -345 Park Av -NY 10154 **Fx:**546-9562
(212) 725-0200 .. **Elliot,** David O'Melia '61 OfCnsl Barnes R&C -475 Park Av S -NY 10016
(212) 506-5000 .. **Elliot,** Lauren J '94 (Orrick H&S LLP) -51 W 52nd -NY 10019
(518) 283-6992 .. **Elliot,** Raymond J III '73 -225 N Greenbush Rd -Troy 12180 **Fx:**283-6992
(516) 741-3060 .. **Elliot,** Thos A '93 (Moran B&E) -300 Grdn City Plz -Gdn Cty 11530
(718) 436-4330 .. **Elliott,** A Irene '79 -41 Schermerhorn -Brklyn 11201 **Fx:**438-5310
(212) 889-4009 .. **Elliott,** Daniela Klare '94 %Dershowitz E&A,PC -220 5th Av -NY 10001
(716) 852-2500 .. **Elliott,** Danielle K '02 %Augello & M LLP -17 Court -Buffalo 14202
(212) 818-1110 .. **Elliott,** Donald H '58 Cnsl Butzel L,PC -380 Mad Av -NY 10017
(212) 277-6500 .. **Elliott,** Jessica E '07 %Dickstein S LLP -1633 Bway -NY 10019
(716) 652-1122 .. **Elliott,** John B '60 -673 Main -E Aurora 14052 **Fx:**652-2350
(212) 801-2234 .. **Elliott,** John J '06 %Greenberg T,LLP -200 Park Av -NY 10166
(585) 232-4724 .. **Elliott,** Karen M '93 %Elliott S&C,LLP -1 E Main -Rchstr 14614
(212) 808-7800 .. **Elliott,** Kristin S '04 %Kelley D&W LLP -101 Park Av -NY 10178
(212) 766-4800 .. **Elliott,** Marc E '88 (ME Elliott, PC) -233 Bway -NY 10279 **Fx:**406-2222
(212) 490-3000 .. **Elliott,** Margaret J '08 %Wilson EME&D LLP -150 E 42nd -NY 10017
(212) 705-7000 .. **Elliott,** Mark M '91 (Bingham M LLP) -399 Park Av -NY 10022
(315) 422-1391 .. **Elliott,** Marri Tussing '05 Green & S,PLLC -One Lincoln Ctr #900 -Syracuse 13202
(212) 425-1900 .. **Elliott,** Michl C '06 %Freehill H&M LLP -80 Pine -NY 10005
(212) 259-8000 .. **Elliott,** Michl S '10 %Dewey & L LLP -1301 Av of Amer -NY 10019
(212) 455-2000 .. **Elliott,** Nakia M '07 %Simpson T&B LLP -425 Lex Av -NY 10017
(315) 422-3030 .. **Elliott,** Peter L Sr. '88 (Messenger & E) -441 S Salina -Syracuse 13202 **Fx:**422-4554
(914) 345-3020 .. **Elliott,** Peter L Sr. '88 (Knuckles K&E,LLP) -565 Taxter Rd -Elmsfrd 10523
(212) 361-1885 .. **Elliott,** Randi '81 %Envrnmntl Cntrl Brd -66 John -NY 10038 **Fx:**361-1900
(585) 232-4724 .. **Elliott,** Richd J '59 (Elliott S&C,LLP) -1 E Main -Rchstr 14614
(516) 877-2900 .. **Elliott,** Robt F '89 (Bartlett MB&M,LLP) -300 Old Cntry Rd -Mineola 11501
(212) 552-1325 .. **Elliott,** Robt R '77 JP Morgan Chase & Co -1 Chase Manh Plz -NY 10081 **Fx:**552-1295
(716) 854-3400 .. **Elliott,** Stephanie G '04 %Rupp BPC&C LLC -1600 Lbrty Bldg -Buffalo 14202
(212) 836-8000 .. **Elliott,** Stephen J '96 Cnsl Kaye S LLP -425 Park Av -NY 10022

(585) 232-4724 .. **Elliott Stern & Calabrese, LLP** -1 E Main -Rchstr 14614 **Fx:**232-6674
(212) 584-0700 .. **Elliott**, Susan J '05 %Seeger W LLP -1 William -NY 10004
(518) 218-1750 .. **Elliott**, Timothy J '93 -8 Airline Dr -Albany 12205 **Fx:**218-1754
(718) 596-1308 .. **Ellis**, Adrian A '95 -26 Court -Brklyn 11242
(212) 478-7200 .. **Ellis**, Anthony P '06 %Hahn & H LLP -488 Mad Av -NY 10022
(212) 425-9300 .. **Ellis**, Brian J '09 %Bressler A&R,PC -17 State -NY 10004
(212) 417-5300 .. **Ellis**, Carolyn T '75 %Medicaid Fraud Cntrl -120 Bway -NY 10271 **Fx:**417-5274
(212) 980-2248 .. **Ellis**, Caryl '86 -110 E 57th -NY 10022 **Fx:**308-2928
(212) 533-9415 .. **Ellis**, David J '70 -25 5th Av -NY 10003
(212) 998-6668 .. **Ellis**, Deborah A '83 NYU Pub Interest Law Ctr -245 Sullivan -NY 10012
(845) 462-2700 .. **Ellis**, Dennis Gerard '83 -2076 South Rd -Poughkeepsie 12601 **Fx:**462-4895
(914) 739-1022 .. **Ellis**, Donna '85 -7 Elena Dr -Cortlandt Manor 10567 **Fx:**739-1022
(718) 287-0059 .. **Ellis**, Edw D '95 -2809 Church Av -Brklyn 11226 **Fx:**693-3346
(212) 259-8000 .. **Ellis**, Emmett N IV '79 (Dewey & L LLP) -1301 Av of Amer -NY 10019
(212) 583-9600 .. **Ellis**, H Reed '71 (Littler M,PC) -900 3rd Av -NY 10022
(800) 218-4658 .. **Ellis**, Herbert I '89 -116 John -NY 10038 **Fx:**(732) 577-0100
(212) 319-1000 .. **Ellis**, Jeffrey J '79 (Quirk & B,PC) -845 3rd Av -NY 10022
(212) 887-1673 .. **Ellis**, Jesse A '09 Citadel Broadcasting Corp -142 W 57th -NY 10019
(212) 556-2100 .. **Ellis**, Kana A '08 %King & S -1185 Av of Amer -NY 10036
(315) 785-3343 .. **Ellis**, Keith E '86 %Jefferson County Dept of Soc Srvcs -250 Arsenal -Watertwn 13601
(212) 259-8000 .. **Ellis**, Krista M '05 %Dewey & L LLP -1301 Av of Amer -NY 10019
(516) 433-1555 .. **Ellis**, Laura A '92 OfCnsl S Schneider -117 Bway -Hicksvll 11801 **Fx:**433-1511
(212) 416-6025 .. **Ellis**, Lauren Popper '08 %Dept of Law -120 Bway -NY 10271
(212) 728-8000 .. **Ellis**, Mia C '10 %Willkie F&G LLP -787 7th Av -NY 10019
(212) 416-6232 .. **Ellis**, Michl C '09 Dept of Law -120 Bway -NY 10271
(212) 969-3000 .. **Ellis**, Michl E '07 %Proskauer R LLP -1585 Bway -NY 10036
(212) 757-0007 .. **Ellis**, Paul S '96 (Scarola E LLP) -888 7th Av -NY 10106
(212) 330-1000 .. **Ellis**, Pauline O '86 %Buck Consultants -1 Penn Plz -NY 10119 **Fx:**695-4184
(212) 371-3933 .. **Ellis**, Richd I '73 -515 Mad Av -NY 10022 **Fx:**371-4519
(212) 317-5400 .. **Ellis**, Robt D '91 %Swiss Re New Markets -55 E 52nd -NY 10055
(212) 922-1800 .. **Ellis**, Wm L Jr. '65 SrCnsl McKenna L&A -230 Park Av -NY 10169
(212) 867-8280 .. **Ellis**, Wm S '55 (Patton ELM&S) -420 Lex Av -NY 10170
(646) 252-2747 .. **Ellis**, Winston D '82 %Transit Auth -2 Bway -NY 10004 **Fx:**252-5559
(646) 450-2520 .. **Ellisen**, Hays '00 (Shahmoon & E LLP) -1036 Park Av -NY 10028 **Fx:**(917) 591-3064
(914) 428-6340 .. **Ellison**, Eddie '85 -21 Pine Wood Dr -White Plns 10603
(917) 673-0554 .. **Ellison**, Jo Ann '85 -1 Irving Pl -NY 10003
(212) 969-3000 .. **Ellison**, Jonathan G '10 %Proskauer R LLP -1585 Bway -NY 10036
(212) 563-4100 .. **Ellison**, Joshua J '05 %Cohen W&S LLP -330 W 42nd -NY 10036
(212) 732-8700 .. **Ellison**, Kenneth G '92 %McAloon & F,PC -123 William -NY 10038
(212) 927-1420 .. **Ellison**, Marjorie '84 -282 Cabrini Blvd -NY 10040
(315) 443-3654 .. **Ellison**, Richd A '66 %Syracuse Univ Cllg of Law -Wht Hall -Syracuse 13244 **Fx:**443-4213
(212) 451-6218 .. **Ellison**, Tamar Sadeh '89 %Hadassah -50 W 58th -NY 10019
(212) 907-0700 .. **Ellman**, Alan I '05 %Labaton S LLP -140 Bway -NY 10005
(212) 938-0801 .. **Ellman**, Avi '03 Tribecka,LLC -1369 Bway -NY 10018
(212) 656-2092 .. **Ellman**, Craig T '04 NYSE Regulation Div of Enforcement -14 Wall -NY 10005
(646) 833-0900 .. **Ellman**, Jill A '07 %Tressler LLP -One Penn Plz -NY 10119
(718) 694-3910 .. **Ellman**, Joyce R '80 %Transit Auth -130 Lvngstn -Brklyn 11201 **Fx:**694-5726
(212) 490-3000 .. **Ellman**, Linda S '93 OfCnsl Wilson EME&D LLP -150 E 42nd -NY 10017
(212) 538-8218 .. **Ellman**, Mark A '84 Credit Suisse -11 Mad Av -NY 10010
(516) 560-6400 .. **Ellman**, Richd P '70 %Leg Aid -1 Helen Keller Way -Hempstd 11550 **Fx:**565-3694
(212) 223-0400 .. **Ellman**, Stephen F '75 (Zeichner E&K LLP) -575 Lex Av -NY 10022
(212) 431-2392 .. **Ellmann**, Stephen J '87 %NY Law Schl -185 W Bway -NY 10013 **Fx:**431-1804
(516) 741-9455 .. **Ellmer**, Raymond J '52 (Ellmer & E) -300 Old Cntry Rd -Mineola 11501 **Fx:**747-7292
(516) 741-9455 .. **Ellmer**, Raymond Jude '86 (Ellmer & E) -300 Old Cntry Rd -Mineola 11501 **Fx:**747-7292
(212) 374-6684 .. **Ellner**, Brian V '96 NY Dept of Ed -52 Chmbrs -NY 10007
(845) 353-3500 .. **Ellner**, David J '05 %Dorfman K&C LLP -51 N Bway -Nyack 10960
(212) 839-5300 .. **Elloie**, Christian N '09 %Sidley A LLP -787 7th Av -NY 10019
(718) 590-5436 .. **Elloras**, Alicea '00 ACS-Div Lgl Srvcs -900 Sheridan Av -Bronx 10451
(212) 840-6585 .. **Ells**, Theo F '68 -551 5th Av -NY 10176 **Fx:**(203) 643-2265
(631) 271-5000 .. **Ellsworth**, Andrew C '93 (Craco & E,LLP) -7 High -Huntngtn 11743
(212) 688-8555 .. **Ellsworth**, Chad R '03 %Fragomen DB&L LLP -7 Hanover Sq -NY 10004
(718) 590-2000 .. **Ellsworth**, Jennifer B '08 %DA -198 E 161st -Bronx 10451 **Fx:**590-6477
(212) 755-0100 .. **Ellsworth**, Kathryn C '91 (Grais & E LLP) -40 E 52nd -NY 10022
(845) 357-2744 .. **Ellsworth**, Richd M '95 (Balsamo BC&E) -16 Chestnut Bx209 -Suffern 10901
(212) 201-8787 .. **Ellwood**, Stephen C '99 Quattro Global Capital LLC -546 5th Av -NY 10036
(212) 340-0400 .. **Elm**, Joanna '06 Applt Div 1st Dept -27 Mad Av -NY 10010 **Fx:**889-4412
(212) 233-2100 .. **Elmaleh-Schoenman**, Sharon '97 %Oshman & M,LLP -42 Bway -NY 10004
(212) 859-5175 .. **Elman**, Andrew A '89 ZenithOptimedia Grp -299 W Houston -NY 10014
(646) 722-8500 .. **Elman**, Deborah A '05 %Grant & E,PA -485 Lex Av -NY 10017
(212) 244-9000 .. **Elman**, Howard I '93 (Matalon SE) -450 7th Av -NY 10123 **Fx:**244-4615
(212) 370-9090 .. **Elman**, Leonard S '58 -150 E 42nd -NY 10017 **Fx:**370-0207
(718) 843-2300 .. **Elman**, Mitchell C '88 (M Elman,PC) -6901 Jericho Tpke -Syosset 11791
(718) 923-8400 .. **Elman**, Susan '86 %Forest City Ratner -1 Metrotech Ctr N -Brklyn 11201 **Fx:**923-8722
(212) 813-8800 .. **Elman**, Victoria A '10 Goodwin P LLP -620 8th Av -NY 10018
(518) 745-1400 .. **Elmen**, Lawr Jr. '95 (FitzGerald MBF) -16 Pearl Bx2017 -Glens Fls 12801
(212) 696-1629 .. **Elmlinger**, Marye L '80 -10 Waterside Plz -NY 10010
(716) 681-7190 .. **Elmore**, John V '85 SrCnsl Brown C LLP -69 Delaware Av -Buffalo 14202
(212) 424-8256 .. **Elmore**, Leonard J '88 Pivor Productions -247 W 87th -NY 10024
(516) 741-2585 .. **Elmore-Sue**, Stephanie I '97 %Rosicki R & Assoc,PC -51 E Bethpage Rd -Plainvw 11803 **Fx:**741-4748
(516) 437-4385 .. **Elnadav**, Saul '07 %Vishnick MM LLP -3000 Marcus Av -Lk Success 11042
(212) 302-1257 .. **Elo**, Elliot M '01 -42 W 48th -NY 10036 **Fx:**302-1648
(646) 315-7300 .. **Elovic**, Suzanne R '92 %FINRA -14 Wall -NY 10005 **Fx:**315-7440
(516) 432-6263 .. **Elovich & Adell** -164 W Park Av -Long Bch 11561 **Fx:**432-4897
(516) 432-6263 .. **Elovich**, Lawr E '61 (Elovich & A) -164 W Park Av -Long Bch 11561
(518) 474-6022 .. **Elovich**, Lisa B '00 NYS OCFS -52 Wshngtn -Rensselaer 12144
(212) 756-2000 .. **Elovitz**, Marc E '91 (Schulte R&Z LLP) -919 3rd Av -NY 10022
(212) 916-3454 .. **Elphick**, Kevin J '90 %Lexis/Nexis -125 Park Av -NY 10017 **Fx:**309-8187
(212) 935-3000 .. **Elrifi**, Ivor R '91 (Mintz LCFG&P,PC) -666 3rd Av -NY 10017
(212) 566-7188 .. **Elrom**, Jordana S '05 %Genova B&G -115 Bway -NY 10006
(716) 759-6841 .. **Elsaesser & O'Connell** -10646 Main -Clarence 14031 **Fx:**759-6978
(212) 735-3000 .. **Elsas**, Jordan '09 %Skadden ASM&F LLP -4 Times Sq -NY 10036
(212) 710-3914 .. **Elsasser**, Deborah A '89 Clyde & Co US LLP -405 Lex Av -NY 10174 **Fx:**710-3950
(212) 849-7000 .. **Elsberg**, David L '97 (Quinn EU&S,LLP) -51 Mad Av -NY 10010
(518) 462-5601 .. **Elsen**, Robyn B '05 %O'Connell & A -54 State -Albany 12207
(212) 586-2211 .. **Elsen**, Sheldon H '59 (Orans EL&B LLP) -875 3rd Av -NY 10022
(212) 325-0471 .. **ElShaer**, Amr A '95 Credit Suisse -11 Mad Av -NY 10010
(212) 619-2446 .. **Elshawi**, Ahmed Z '85 -160 Bway -NY 10038
(718) 875-5199 .. **El Sherbini**, Judith A '98 %Composto & C -142 Joralemon -Brklyn 11201 **Fx:**639-7586
(585) 325-4600 .. **Elsner**, Erin M '08 %Fero & I -183 E Main -Rchstr 14604 **Fx:**325-1525
(212) 373-3000 .. **Elson**, Alexander S '10 %Paul WRW&G LLP -1285 Av of Amer -NY 10019
(212) 857-2420 .. **Elstein**, Melissa L '98 %Hon S Sotomayor -40 Foley Sq -NY 10007
(631) 864-5636 .. **Elston**, A Roger '64 -18 Cherry Ln -Huntngtn 11743 **Fx:**864-6151
(585) 475-1100 .. **Elston**, Alecia L '88 %Segar & S -400 Meridian Centre -Rchstr 14618
(212) 922-1177 .. **Elstroth**, Bettina C '02 %Stursberg & V -1500 Bway -NY 10036
(212) 626-4582 .. **Elt**, Leonid Y '99 -1114 Av of Amer -NY 10036 **Fx:**626-4120
(516) 498-1700 .. **Elterman**, Warren B '69 -80 Cuttermill Rd -Gt Neck 11021 **Fx:**829-8801
(718) 875-1300 .. **Elting**, Robt P '09 %Applt Div 2nd Dept -45 Monroe Pl -Brklyn 11201 **Fx:**858-2446
(212) 440-3028 .. **Eltman**, Alyson J '00 CNA Global Spclty Lines -40 Wall -NY 10005
(212) 660-3100 .. **Eltman Eltman & Cooper,PC** -140 Bway -NY 10005 **Fx:**660-3101
(516) 593-1362 .. **Eltman**, Marc M '75 -34 Davison Av -E Rockaway 11518
(212) 837-6000 .. **Elul**, Hagit M '04 %Hughes H&R LLP -1 Bttry Pk Plz -NY 10004
(212) 415-8600 .. **Elum**, J Edgar A '05 %Locke LB&L LLP -3 World Fncl Ctr -NY 10281
(718) 694-3902 .. **Eluto**, Lawr G '72 %Transit Auth -130 Lvngstn -Brklyn 11201 **Fx:**694-5726
(212) 676-1135 .. **Eluto**, Sherryl A '89 %Taxi & Limo Comm -40 Rector -NY 10006
(718) 382-7231 .. **Eluto**, Steven Elliot '87 -1333 E 18th -Brklyn 11230
(212) 737-6754 .. **Elvin**, Francine '82 -308 E 79th -NY 10075
(212) 521-4300 .. **Elvin**, George M '67 -205 W 57th -NY 10019
(718) 768-3113 .. **Elvir**, Tomas '95 -57 Prospect Park SW -Brklyn 11215 **Fx:**768-4343
(718) 590-2000 .. **Elwell**, Shannon C '10 %DA -198 E 161st -Bronx 10451 **Fx:**590-6477
(212) 805-0184 .. **Elwick**, Jasmine '06 US Dist Ct -500 Pearl -NY 10007
(607) 637-4791 .. **Elwood**, George H '53 (Elwood & E) -38 W Main -Hancock 13783 **Fx:**637-4701
(212) 450-4000 .. **Elworth**, James E '04 %Davis P&W LLP -450 Lex Av -NY 10017
(212) 558-4000 .. **Elworth**, Jennifer P '04 %Sullivan & C LLP -125 Broad -NY 10004
(212) 728-8000 .. **Elwyn**, Morgan D '99 (Willkie F&G LLP) -787 7th Av -NY 10019
(212) 637-2214 .. **Ely**, Amie N '06 US Atty -1 St Andrews Plz -NY 10007
(212) 238-8900 .. **Ely**, Robt D '88 %Melito & A,PC -233 Bway -NY 10279
(518) 436-0786 .. **Ely**, Scott J '96 %Featherstonhaugh W&C,LLP -99 Pine -Albany 12207
(212) 852-6196 .. **Emami**, Shirin '84 Westdeutsche Landesbank -1211 Av of Amer -NY 10036
(516) 227-3777 .. **Emanuel**, Anthony J '88 (Bornstein & E,PC) -200 Grdn City Plz -Gdn Cty 11530
(646) 264-1306 .. **Emanuel**, Claudia '84 %Leg Aid -49 Thomas -NY 10013 **Fx:**(212) 298-5252
(845) 634-0888 .. **Emanuel**, Ira M '81 OfCnsl Freeman & L RLLP -4 Laurel Rd -New Cty 10956
(973) 641-6445 .. **Emanuel**, Lance C '08 (Gotcoders) -135 Grand -NY 10013
(914) 834-0098 .. **Emanuel**, Lazar '48 %NYPRR -1328 Bstn Post Rd -Larchmnt 10538 **Fx:**833-9392
(718) 390-5422 .. **Emanuel**, Maria Colonna '93 %Civil Ct -927 Castleton Av -Staten Isl 10310 **Fx:**390-8108
(212) 483-7000 .. **Emanuel**, Michl S '96 %Loeb Prtnrs Corp -61 Bway -NY 10006
(212) 541-2000 .. **Emanuel**, Ronald B '93 (Bryan C LLP) -1290 Av of Amer -NY 10104
(914) 834-0118 .. **Emanuel**, Steven L '77 %NYPRR -1328 Bstn Post Rd -Larchmnt 10538 **Fx:**833-9392
(516) 746-3878 .. **Emanuele**, Edw J '83 -300 Old Cntry Rd -Mineola 11501 **Fx:**746-5109
(212) 225-2000 .. **Emberger**, Kathleen M '01 Cnsl Cleary GS&H -1 Lbrty Plz -NY 10006
(585) 624-5030 .. **Emborsky**, Andrew F '05 %Kruk & C -7312 E Main Bx30-A -Lima 14485 **Fx:**624-3972
(212) 238-4800 .. **Embry**, Rebecca W '00 (Landman CB&F,PC) -120 Bway -NY 10271

(585) 593-1090 .. **Embser,** J Timothy '61 (Embser & W,PC) -164 N Main -Wellsvll 14895
(585) 593-1090 .. **Embser & Woltag, PC** -164 N Main -Wellsvll 14895 **Fx:**593-6540
(718) 403-3600 .. **Emdin,** Alan C '84 %Dept of Finance -345 Adams -Brklyn 11201 **Fx:**403-3650
(212) 683-3995 .. **Emdin,** Jeffrey L '87 (Emdin & R,LLP) -286 Mad Av -NY 10016 **Fx:**683-4032
(718) 624-5001 .. **Emefieh,** John O '00 -310 Atl Av -Brklyn 11201
(212) 408-5100 .. **Emehelu,** Ikenna P '03 %Chadbourne & P LLP -30 Rckfllr Plz -NY 10112
(212) 909-6000 .. **Emehelu,** Shirley U '04 %Debevoise & P LLP -919 3rd Av -NY 10022
(718) 379-3500 .. **Emelumadu,** Uchenna '92 (Madu E&M,PC) -3007 Eastchstr Rd -Bronx 10469
(212) 306-1482 .. **Emen,** Michl S '75 %Amer Stock Exch -86 Trinity Pl -NY 10006
(212) 854-8879 .. **Emens,** Elizabeth F '03 %Columbia Law Schl -435 W 116th -NY 10027 **Fx:**854-7946
(315) 471-0420 .. **Emerson,** Amy A '00 Fair Housing Cncl of Cntrl NY -327 W Fayette -Syracuse 13202
(212) 613-5000 .. **Emerson,** Anya M P '08 %Leg Assist Grp -450 W 33rd -NY 10001 **Fx:**750-0820
(716) 853-3801 .. **Emerson,** Laura J '07 %Kenney SL&N,LLP -14 Lafayette Sq -Buffalo 14203
(212) 408-2500 .. **Emerson,** Lauren B '08 %Baker B,LLP -30 Rckfllr Plz -NY 10112
(212) 325-2676 .. **Emerson,** Michl W '85 %CSFP Cptl -11 Mad Av -NY 10010
(212) 596-9000 .. **Emerson,** Robt C '09 %Ropes & G LLP -1211 Av of Amer -NY 10036
(607) 334-2247 .. **Emerson,** Thos C '74 (Lee & E) -35 W Main Bx711 -Norwich 13815
(585) 268-5800 .. **Emerson,** Warren M '78 %Cnty Ct -Cnty Cthouse 7 Court -Belmont 14813 **Fx:**268-7090
(212) 816-5984 .. **Emert,** John P '71 Citigroup -388 Greenwich -NY 10013
(212) 436-1051 .. **Emert,** Laurence T '98 IRS Chief Cnsl Ofc -290 Bway -NY 10007
(212) 763-5000 .. **Emery Celli Brinckerhoff & Abady LLP** -75 Rckfllr Plz -NY 10019 **Fx:**763-5001
(585) 232-6500 .. **Emery,** R Clinton '55 Harter S&E LLP -1600 Bausch & Lomb Pl -Rchstr 14604
(212) 763-5000 .. **Emery,** Richd D '71 (Emery CB&A LLP) -75 Rckfllr Plz -NY 10019
(315) 474-7571 .. **Emery,** Ryan T '07 %Mackenzie H LLP -101 S Salina Bx4967 -Syracuse 13221
(212) 302-2400 .. **Emery,** Scott R '98 (Lynch DE LLP) -264 W 40th -NY 10018
(212) 298-5034 .. **Emhoff,** Jeanne M '05 %Leg Aid -49 Thomas -NY 10013 **Fx:**298-5252
(718) 232-3001 .. **Emma,** Chas L '73 -8008 20th Av -Brklyn 11214 **Fx:**232-2330
(718) 748-0254 .. **Emma,** Karen M '92 -1245 72nd -Brklyn 11228 **Fx:**748-0975
(212) 209-3020 .. **Emmanuel,** Gary M '05 %Reitler K&R LLC -885 3rd Av -NY 10022
(718) 992-8042 .. **Emmanuelli,** Dean '83 (Emmanuelli & P) -1188-A Grnd Cncrs -Bronx 10456 **Fx:**992-8419
(718) 466-3000 .. **Emmanuelli,** Robin Zeikowitz '88 %Civil Ct -1118 Grnd Cncrs -Bronx 10456 **Fx:**466-3006
(212) 310-8000 .. **Emmel,** Heather L '05 Cnsl Weil G&M LLP -767 5th Av -NY 10153
(585) 454-5650 .. **Emmens,** Terrance W '92 (Lacy K LLP) -130 E Main -Rchstr 14604
(212) 610-6300 .. **Emmer,** Laurie B '04 %Allen & O -1221 Av of Amer -NY 10020
(212) 403-1000 .. **Emmerich,** Adam O '87 (Wachtell LR&K) -51 W 52nd -NY 10019
(212) 721-7265 .. **Emmerich,** Pamela A N '85 -171 W 71st -NY 10023 **Fx:**721-7271
(716) 250-1800 .. **Emmerling,** Patrick L '94 (Jaeckle F&M,LLP) -400 Essjay Rd -Amherst 14221
(212) 940-8800 .. **Emmerman,** Todd J '91 (Katten MR LLP) -575 Mad Av -NY 10022
(212) 238-3000 .. **Emmet Marvin & Martin,LLP** -120 Bway -NY 10271 **Fx:**238-3100
(212) 474-1000 .. **Emmi,** Peter A '05 Cravath S&M LLP -825 8th Av -NY 10019
(518) 435-8092 .. **Emminger,** Michl M '77 %Finkelstein & Prtnrs,LLP -80 Wolf Rd -Albany 12205
(212) 577-3688 .. **Emmons,** Elizabeth B '85 %Leg Aid -199 Water -NY 10038 **Fx:**509-8431
(516) 571-3800 .. **Emmons,** Robt '81 %DA -262 Old Cntry Rd -Mineola 11501 **Fx:**248-9479
(718) 262-7100 .. **Emory,** James E Jr. '88 %Civil Ct -89-17 Sutphin Blvd -Jamaica 11435 **Fx:**262-7107
(516) 482-4436 .. **Emouna,** Lara Pouratian '98 %Gleich S&F -36 S Station Plz -Gt Neck 11021
(516) 877-9111 .. **Emouna,** Matin '96 -110 Old Cntry Rd -Mineola 11501 **Fx:**877-9112
(516) 822-3550 .. **Emr,** Lauren T '01 %Hoffmann & B LLP -6900 Jericho Tpk -Syosset 11791 **Fx:**822-3582
(212) 848-4000 .. **Emrich,** Edmund M '82 Cnsl Shearman & S LLP -599 Lex Av -NY 10022
(212) 481-1411 .. **Emrich,** Michl E '84 Donlin Recano Co -419 Park Av S -NY 10016
(718) 422-4836 .. **Emrich,** Patricia '07 NYC OEM -165 Cadman Plz E -Brklyn 11201
(212) 285-3025 .. **Emsellem,** Maurice '89 %NELP -75 Maiden Ln -NY 10038 **Fx:**285-3044
(516) 374-7430 .. **Emsellem-Lewisohn,** Carol J '88 -483 Chestnut -Cedarhrst 11516 **Fx:**374-7293
(212) 735-3000 .. **Ena,** Michl '10 %Skadden ASM&F LLP -4 Times Sq -NY 10036
(212) 310-8000 .. **Enayati,** Robt P '10 %Weil G&M LLP -767 5th Av -NY 10153
(917) 937-3000 .. **Encarnacion,** Vivian D '01 %Guy Carpenter & Co,Inc -1166 Av of Amer -NY 10036
(212) 949-0100 .. **Ende,** Donald C '84 %Cmmnwlth Land Title -140 E 45th -NY 10017 **Fx:**983-8430
(631) 979-8315 .. **Ende,** Howard S '75 -37 Apple Tree Dr -Hauppauge 11788
(718) 286-2000 .. **Ende,** James I '73 %Leg Aid -120-46 Qns Blvd -Kew Gdns 11415 **Fx:**286-2286
(516) 463-5871 .. **Ende,** Michl J '90 Hofstra Univ Law Schl -108 Hofstra Univ -Hempstd 11549
(212) 762-4907 .. **Ender,** Michelle '04 -1221 6th Av -NY 10020
(845) 485-7530 .. **Enderley,** Kelley M '05 -201 South Av -Poughkeepsie 12601
(518) 402-6757 .. **Enders,** Camille Siano '95 %Workers Comp Bd -20 Park -Albany 12207
(315) 853-8691 .. **Enders,** Richd D '66 -Bx257 -Clinton 13323 **Fx:**853-3966
(914) 576-7601 .. **Endervelt,** Jeffrey K '71 Blimpie of Calif -145 Huguenot -New Rchll 10801
(212) 735-3159 .. **Endick,** Adam M '98 (Skadden ASM&F LLP) -4 Times Sq -NY 10036
(212) 804-4200 .. **Endick,** Danl J '99 %Mound CW&G -One Bttry Pk Plz -NY 10004
(212) 490-3000 .. **Endick,** Marshal S '71 (Wilson EME&D LLP) -150 E 42nd -NY 10017
(315) 487-9458 .. **Endieveri,** Anthony F '67 -5016 W Genesee -Camillus 13031 **Fx:**487-2871
(518) 434-0600 .. **Endler,** Michl I '98 (Boies S&F LLP) -10 N Pearl -Albany 12207
(212) 268-6900 .. **Endlich,** Matthew E '01 %Winograd & W PC -450 7th Av -NY 10123 **Fx:**629-5825
(212) 735-3000 .. **Endreny,** Pamela Lawr '95 (Skadden ASM&F LLP) -4 Times Sq -NY 10036
(716) 856-4000 .. **Endres,** Jos N '06 %Hodgson R LLP -140 Pearl -Buffalo 14202
(212) 449-4985 .. **Endres,** Karen '03 Merrill Lynch -4 Wrld Fncl Ctr -NY 10080
(212) 302-8989 .. **Endres,** Martin P '91 (Hedman & C,PC) -1185 Av of Amer -NY 10036
(212) 972-1000 .. **Endres,** Richd S '90 (London F LLP) -59 Maiden Ln -NY 10038
(516) 542-5900 .. **Endrizzi,** Laura A '88 %Congdon FORDT&F -333 Earle Ovngton Blvd -Uniondale 11553
(212) 636-7157 .. **Endrizzi,** Suzanne M '97 %Fordham Univ Sch of Law -140 W 62nd -NY 10023 **Fx:**636-6899
(646) 254-7519 .. **Endy,** Karin '94 Cnsl French Culinary Inst -462 Bway -NY 10013 **Fx:**254-1219
(212) 728-8000 .. **Endzweig,** Jennifer K '10 %Willkie F&G LLP -787 7th Av -NY 10019
(516) 482-8500 .. **Endzweig,** Jos M '78 (Samanowitz & E) -98 Cutter Mill Rd -Gt Neck 11021 **Fx:**482-8655
(914) 948-1500 .. **Enea,** Anthony J '86 (Enea S&S LLP) -245 Main -White Plns 10601
(718) 254-6169 .. **Enea,** Dione M '98 %US Atty -271 Cadman Plz E -Brklyn 11201 **Fx:**254-6479
(914) 948-1500 .. **Enea Scanlan & Sirignano LLP** -245 Main -White Plns 10601
(212) 906-1200 .. **Enendu,** Obianuju A '08 %Latham & W -885 3rd Av -NY 10022
(212) 310-8000 .. **Eng,** Diana M '04 %Weil G&M LLP -767 5th Av -NY 10153
(212) 608-1939 .. **Eng,** Donald '78 -217 Park Row -NY 10038 **Fx:**608-1948
(212) 909-6000 .. **Eng,** Gordon '05 %Debevoise & P LLP -919 3rd Av -NY 10022
(212) 431-1760 .. **Eng,** Irving '81 -101 Mott -NY 10013 **Fx:**226-6983
(212) 379-6988 .. **Eng,** Jane T '75 (Chas B Wang Hlth Ctr) -268 Canal -NY 10013 **Fx:**379-6936
(212) 558-4000 .. **Eng,** Jillian Danielle '05 %Sullivan & C LLP -125 Broad -NY 10004
(516) 227-2300 .. **Eng,** John '95 %Wright Risk Mgmt -333 Earle Ovngton Blvd -Uniondale 11553
(212) 556-2100 .. **Eng,** Jos D Jr. '08 %King & S -1185 Av of Amer -NY 10036
(718) 923-3331 .. **Eng,** Judy M '87 OTDA Fair Hearings -14 Boerum Pl -Brklyn 11201
(212) 962-0747 .. **Eng,** Keith R '00 %CHM Abstract Inc -17 Oliver -NY 10038
(212) 578-2789 .. **Eng,** Michl J '84 %MetLife -27-01 Qns Plz N -LIC 11101
(212) 834-9289 .. **Eng,** Mimi '95 JP Morgan Sec -270 Park Av -NY 10017
(212) 627-2227 .. **Eng,** Norman '00 NY Immigration Coalition -137139 W 25th -NY 10001
(212) 941-0906 .. **Eng,** Richd K '88 -100 Lafayette -NY 10013
(212) 940-8800 .. **Engel,** Adam '03 %Katten MR LLP -575 Mad Av -NY 10022
(718) 802-2768 .. **Engel,** Aura M '06 %ACS -330 Jay -Brklyn 11201
(212) 523-2162 .. **Engel,** David '84 %Beth Israel Med Ctr -555 W 57th -NY 10019
(518) 449-3300 .. **Engel,** David A '76 OfCnsl Nolan & H,LLP -39 N Pearl -Albany 12207
(516) 248-5757 .. **Engel,** Denis A '94 (Colleran O&M,LLP) -1225 Franklin Av -Gdn Cty 11530
(212) 613-5039 .. **Engel,** Elizabeth B '04 Leg Assist Grp -450 W 33rd -NY 10001 **Fx:**750-0820
(845) 679-7378 .. **Engel,** Franklyn J '72 -21 Tinker -Woodstock 12498 **Fx:**679-7094
(516) 741-1250 .. **Engel & Gutsin,LLP** -198 Miller Pl -Hicksvll 11801 **Fx:**742-4908
(518) 455-7700 .. **Engel,** Hope B '87 %Ct of Appls -20 Eagle -Albany 12207
(212) 547-5400 .. **Engel,** John J '09 %McDermott W&E LLP -340 Mad Av -NY 10173
(212) 262-9154 .. **Engel,** John P '76 (Engel & D LLP) -521 5th Av -NY 10175 **Fx:**262-9321
(212) 866-2600 .. **Engel,** Jonathan P '84 Heritage Hlth & Housing,Inc -416 W 127th -NY 10027
(212) 801-6872 .. **Engel,** Julia A '08 %Greenberg T,LLP -200 Park Av -NY 10166
(518) 477-1018 .. **Engel,** Kevin J '77 K Engel,PC -738 Columbia Tpk -E Greenbush 12061 **Fx:**477-1021
(212) 723-6717 .. **Engel,** Marcy '84 Citigroup Global Mrkts -388 Greenwich -NY 10013
(516) 937-5262 .. **Engel,** Mark B '02 Campers World -48511 S Bway -Hicksvll 11801
(516) 741-1250 .. **Engel,** Mona C '76 (Engel & G,LLP) -198 Miller Pl -Hicksvll 11801
(212) 768-6700 .. **Engel,** Ralph M '68 (Sonnenschein N&R LLP) -1221 Av of Amer -NY 10020
(212) 924-2000 .. **Engel,** Rebecca J '04 Loc 237 Teamsters -216 W 14th -NY 10011
(315) 474-7571 .. **Engel,** Richd C '90 (Mackenzie H LLP) -101 S Salina Bx4967 -Syracuse 13221
(212) 402-9400 .. **Engel,** Thos E '72 (McKool S,PC) -1 Bryant Park -NY 10036
(315) 295-1450 .. **Engel,** Todd S '98 -214 N State -Syracuse 13203
(631) 462-1930 .. **Engelberg,** Judith B '83 -5 Stony Run Ct -Dix Hlls 11746
(516) 576-1600 .. **Engelberg,** Richd A '68 -54 Sunnyside Blvd -Plainvw 11803 **Fx:**576-0565
(315) 339-1037 .. **Engelbrecht,** Chas W '81 -211 N George -Rome 13440
(516) 357-3000 .. **Engeldrum,** Joanne M '97 %Rivkin R LLP -926 RXR Plz -Uniondale 11556
(212) 403-7300 .. **Engelhard,** Sheldon '61 (Vladeck WE&E,PC) -1501 Bway -NY 10036
(212) 909-6000 .. **Engelhardt,** Jane '98 Cnsl Debevoise & P LLP -919 3rd Av -NY 10022
(212) 336-2000 .. **Engelhardt,** Jordan M '10 %Patterson BW&T LLP -1133 Av of Amer -NY 10036
(212) 902-1000 .. **Engelhardt,** Laura A '01 Goldman Sachs -1 NY Plz -NY 10004
(914) 428-0505 .. **Engelhardt,** Martin B Jr. '66 -200 E Post Rd -White Plns 10601 **Fx:**428-0519
(212) 468-8000 .. **Engelhardt,** Stefan W '90 (Morrison & F LLP) -1290 Av of Amer -NY 10104
(212) 335-4500 .. **Engell,** Catherine B '08 %DLA Piper LLP -1251 Av of Amer -NY 10020
(212) 244-4664 .. **Engelman Lado,** Marianne L '88 Cnsl NY Lawyers Pub Intrst -151 W 30th -NY 10001 **Fx:**244-4570
(212) 813-5900 .. **Engelmann,** Mark D '86 (Fross ZL&Z,PC) -866 UN Plz -NY 10017
(212) 230-8820 .. **Engelmayer,** Paul A '88 (WilmerHale) -399 Park Av -NY 10022
(212) 837-6638 .. **Engels,** Andrea '09 %Hughes H&R LLP -1 Bttry Pk Plz -NY 10004
(718) 892-0400 .. **Engelsher,** David L '88 %W Gallina -1180 Morris Park Av -Bronx 10461 **Fx:**892-0033

(718) 250-2000 .. **Engelsohn,** Leslie G '06 DA -350 Jay -Brklyn 11201 **Fx:**250-2314
(212) 504-6000 .. **Engelson,** Erika B '06 %Cadwalader W&T LLP -1 World Fncl Ctr -NY 10281
(212) 627-8100 .. **Engelstein,** Danl '80 (Levy R,PC) -80 8th Av -NY 10011
(212) 388-2128 .. **Engelstein,** Larry '99 %Local 32B-32J SEIU -101 Av of Amer -NY 10013
(212) 592-1400 .. **Engelstein,** Rachel C '04 %Herrick,F LLP -2 Park Av -NY 10016
(718) 779-3493 .. **Engineer,** Bipin '92 -37-19 83rd -Jcksn Hts 11372 **Fx:**779-3493
(631) 588-0250 .. **England,** Catherine T '40 (England & E,PC) -2556 Middle Cntry Rd -Centereach 11720 **Fx:**588-0329
(212) 596-9000 .. **England,** Christopher R '10 %Ropes & G LLP -1211 Av of Amer -NY 10036
(631) 588-0250 .. **England,** Donna '87 (England & E,PC) -2556 Middle Cntry Rd -Centereach 11720 **Fx:**588-0329
(631) 588-0250 .. **England,** Louis C '69 (England & E,PC) -2556 Middle Cntry Rd -Centereach 11720 **Fx:**588-0329
(212) 278-1483 .. **England,** Phillip C '75 (Anderson K&O,PC) -1251 Av of Amer -NY 10020
(914) 747-1319 .. **England,** Rimfa '78 -67 Sunnyside Av -Plsntvll 10570 **Fx:**747-1319
(212) 867-4466 .. **Englander,** Alexa L '06 %Belkin BW&G,LLP -270 Mad Av -NY 10016
(212) 474-1000 .. **Englander,** Andrew M '10 %Cravath S&M LLP -825 8th Av -NY 10019
(845) 398-3427 .. **Englander,** David A '70 -1 Kings Hwy -Tappan 10983 **Fx:**398-3439
(212) 245-4519 .. **Englander,** David A '70 -250 W 57th -NY 10107 **Fx:**(845) 398-3439
(212) 735-8720 .. **Englander,** Jeffrey P '76 (Morrison C LLP) -909 3rd Av -NY 10022
(516) 487-0175 .. **Englander,** Michelle '83 %E Schwartz -343 Grt Nck Rd -Gt Neck 11021 **Fx:**773-7706
(212) 617-6126 .. **Englander,** Tara S '01 Bloomberg LP -731 Lex Av -NY 10022
(516) 334-0088 .. **Englander,** Wm H '52 -300 Grdn City Plz -Gdn Cty 11530
(212) 370-1300 .. **Englard,** Joshua N '01 %Ellenoff G&S LLP -150 E 42nd -NY 10017
(646) 442-3100 .. **Englard,** Rubin '72 %Legal Srvcs -90 John -NY 10038 **Fx:**(212) 227-9798
(917) 439-6774 .. **Engle,** Howard R '83 -111 Bway -NY 10006
(914) 251-0920 .. **Engle,** Lawr D '83 -2900 Wstchstr Av -Purchase 10577 **Fx:**696-3833
(516) 496-1919 .. **Engle,** Patrick J '89 %Keller O&W,PC -242 Crsswys Park Dr W -Woodbury 11797
(212) 458-7028 .. **Englehardt,** Gregg E '99 AIG -175 Water -NY 10038
(212) 297-5800 .. **Engler,** Florice E '09 %Day P LLP -7 Times Sq -NY 10036
(212) 790-0200 .. **Engler,** Mitchell L '91 %Benj N Cardozo Schl of Law -55 5th Av -NY 10003 **Fx:**790-0345
(212) 977-9700 .. **Engler,** Monte '66 (Phillips N LLP) -666 5th Av -NY 10103
(518) 370-4645 .. **Englert Coffey McHugh & Fantauzzi, LLP** -224 State Bx1092 -Schnctdy 12301 **Fx:**370-4979
(518) 370-4645 .. **Englert,** Dennis M '64 (Englert CM&F,LLP) -224 State Bx1092 -Schnctdy 12301
(518) 584-5455 .. **Englert,** Michl J '86 -52 Franklin -Saratoga Spgs 12866
(212) 980-9892 .. **Englis,** Wm V '78 -535 Mad Av -NY 10022
(212) 430-0800 .. **English,** Craig S '78 (Kennedy LS&E) -75 Maiden Ln -NY 10038
(607) 776-9631 .. **English,** David F '78 %Cnty Atty -3 E Pulteney Sq -Bath 14810 **Fx:**776-4930
(212) 349-3366 .. **English,** James A '03 Rose & R -291 Bway -NY 10007 **Fx:**349-2292
(718) 466-3000 .. **English,** Kamella D '04 %Civil Ct -1118 Grnd Cncrs -Bronx 10456 **Fx:**466-3006
(716) 847-8400 .. **English,** Kevin J '85 (Phillips L LLP) -3400 HSBC Ctr -Buffalo 14203
(518) 893-2421 .. **English,** Mark D '84 -16 Pine Robin Rd -Greenfld Ctr 12833
(315) 472-8533 .. **English,** Mark J '88 (Finocchio & E) -430 E Genesee -Syracuse 13202
(212) 637-2594 .. **English,** Michl Q '01 US Atty -1 St Andrews Plz -NY 10007
(607) 687-0567 .. **English,** Susan L '90 (Coughlin & G,LLP) -27-29 Lk Bx250 -Owego 13827
(607) 723-9511 .. **English,** Susan L '90 (Coughlin & G,LLP) -19 Chenango Bx2039 -Bnghmtn 13902
(212) 576-6973 .. **English,** Thos F '00 %NY Life Ins -51 Mad Av -NY 10010 **Fx:**447-0569
(212) 506-5000 .. **Englund,** Alyssa Dawan '02 %Orrick H&S LLP -51 W 52nd -NY 10019
(212) 326-3939 .. **Engman,** Richd H '97 (Jones D) -222 E 41st -NY 10017
(212) 309-6000 .. **Engros,** Chas E Jr. '79 (Morgan L&B LLP) -101 Park Av -NY 10178
(518) 279-9136 .. **Engster,** Paul R '78 -777 Hoosick Rd -Troy 12180 **Fx:**279-9179
(631) 262-7400 .. **Engstrand,** D Danl Jr. '86 (Doniger & E) -12 Bayview Av -Northprt 11768
(212) 964-6611 .. **Eniclerico,** Richd '74 (Lester SK&D) -120 Bway -NY 10271
(518) 434-0600 .. **Enison,** Randi M '05 Boies S&F LLP -10 N Pearl -Albany 12207 **Fx:**434-0665
(212) 416-8910 .. **Enloe,** Chas E '09 %Dept of Law -120 Bway -NY 10271
(646) 471-4000 .. **Enloe,** Margaret '82 %PricewaterhouseCoopers LLP -300 Mad Av -NY 10017
(516) 561-7161 .. **Ennis,** Evette C '04 -430 W Merrick Rd -Vly Stream 11580
(212) 603-6300 .. **Ennis,** Felicia S '93 (Robinson BLGG&G PC) -875 3rd Av -NY 10022
(212) 686-0666 .. **Ennis,** Nancy '70 (Quijano & E,PC) -381 Park Av S -NY 10016
(914) 428-9330 .. **Ennis,** Wm J '61 (Oestreicher ED&D,LLP) -235 Mamaroneck Av -White Plns 10605
(212) 558-4000 .. **Enniss,** Brittany D '10 %Sullivan & C LLP -125 Broad -NY 10004
(800) 877-1373 .. **Enobakhare,** Lucky Osagie '96 Workers Comp Bd -168-46 91st Av -Jamaica 11432
(914) 285-0700 .. **Enoch,** Lisa Ann '84 SpclCnsl Renzulli Law Firm,LLP -81 Main -White Plns 10601 **Fx:**285-1213
(914) 693-6363 .. **Enochs,** Elizabeth M '59 -52 Cedar -Dobbs Ferry 10522 **Fx:**693-0376
(516) 465-9141 .. **Enoksen,** Nancy P '05 -366 N Bway -Jericho 11753 **Fx:**465-9145
(585) 546-3393 .. **Enos,** Christopher J '74 (Enos & E) -400 State -Rchstr 14608 **Fx:**546-3426
(585) 546-3393 .. **Enos,** Gregory E '80 (Enos & E) -400 State -Rchstr 14608 **Fx:**546-3426
(212) 474-1000 .. **Enright,** Anthony J '07 %Cravath S&M LLP -825 8th Av -NY 10019
(212) 490-2020 .. **Enright,** Martin W '86 (Littman K LLP) -655 3rd Av -NY 10017
(212) 872-1000 .. **Enright,** Terence K '07 -One Bryant Park -NY 10036 **Fx:**872-1002
(212) 449-6692 .. **Enriquez,** J David '02 Merrill Lynch & Co -4 World Fncl Ctr -NY 10080
(516) 248-2222 .. **Enteen,** Laura Z '86 %LI Advocacy Ctr -999 Hrrcks Rd -New Hyde Pk 11040 **Fx:**248-2290
(212) 405-4782 .. **Enteman,** John H F '76 GenSpring Family Ofcs,LLC -13 W 54th -NY 10019 **Fx:**405-4799
(718) 828-3070 .. **Entes,** Harold S '67 -1978 Wllmsbrdg Rd -Bronx 10461 **Fx:**828-3118
(212) 894-7200 .. **Entwistle,** Andrew J '85 (Entwistle & C LLP) -280 Park Av -NY 10017 **Fx:**894-7251
(212) 894-7200 .. **Entwistle & Cappucci LLP** -280 Park Av -NY 10017 **Fx:**894-7272
(914) 730-3200 .. **Entwistle & Cappucci LLP** -200 Business Park Dr -Armonk 10504 **Fx:**730-3206
(212) 688-8555 .. **Enu,** Haseena J '96 %Fragomen DB&L LLP -7 Hanover Sq -NY 10004
(212) 373-3000 .. **Enzer,** Samson A '08 %Paul WRW&G LLP -1285 Av of Amer -NY 10019
(518) 235-3040 .. **Enzien,** Peter J '61 -566 2nd Av -Troy 12182 **Fx:**235-3043
(518) 388-4293 .. **Enzinna,** Diane D '91 %Surrogates Ct -612 State -Schnctdy 12305
(716) 885-2889 .. **Eoannou Lana & D'Amico** -484 Delaware Av -Buffalo 14202 **Fx:**883-2163
(716) 885-2889 .. **Eoannou,** Thos '83 (Eoannou L&D) -484 Delaware Av -Buffalo 14202
(212) 526-4058 .. **Epes,** Christopher R '92 Cnsl 1 William St Capital Mgmt -1271 Av of Amer -NY 10020
(212) 648-3498 .. **Epes,** Travis F '85 %JP Morgan Chase & Co -270 Park Av -NY 10017
(212) 619-5400 .. **Ephron-Mandel,** Melissa G '85 OfCnsl Newman F LLP -1250 Bway -NY 10001
(212) 450-4000 .. **Epifantseva,** Yuliya Y '09 %Davis P&W LLP -450 Lex Av -NY 10017
(212) 599-1515 .. **Epilone,** Alison L '09 %Stein RM,LLP -405 Lex Av -NY 10174
(212) 725-5554 .. **Episcopio,** Jos A '04 -232 Madison -NY 10016
(518) 432-4501 .. **Epler-Carl,** Penny L '04 Taconic Title Agency -40 Beaver -Albany 12207
(212) 858-1000 .. **Epling,** Richd L '88 (Pillsbury WSP LLP) -1540 Bway -NY 10036
(212) 999-5800 .. **Epner,** Mitchell E '96 OfCnsl Wilson SG&R -1301 Av of Americas -NY 10019
(212) 679-6000 .. **Eppenstein & Eppenstein** -48 Wall -NY 10005 **Fx:**759-3122
(212) 679-6000 .. **Eppenstein,** Madelaine '80 (Eppenstein & E) -48 Wall -NY 10005
(212) 679-6000 .. **Eppenstein,** Theo G '74 (Eppenstein & E) -48 Wall -NY 10005
(716) 854-2620 .. **Eppers,** Donald B '70 (Brown & K,LLP) -1500 Lbrty Bldg -Buffalo 14202
(718) 286-6000 .. **Epperson,** Dietrich P '06 %DA -125-01 Qns Blvd -Kew Gdns 11415
(631) 587-8778 .. **Eppig,** Wm J '74 -1175 Montauk Hwy -W Islip 11795 **Fx:**587-5030
(914) 833-0500 .. **Eppinger Reingold & Korder** -131 Larchmnt Av Bx868 -Larchmnt 10538 **Fx:**833-0511
(914) 833-0500 .. **Eppinger,** Ronald M '87 (Eppinger R&K) -131 Larchmnt Av Bx868 -Larchmnt 10538
(914) 833-0500 .. **Eppinger,** Theo F '54 (Eppinger R&K) -131 Larchmnt Av Bx868 -Larchmnt 10538
(212) 757-1544 .. **Eppler,** David M '86 CEW Prtnrs -780 3rd Av -NY 10017
(212) 969-3000 .. **Eppler,** Klaus '56 (Proskauer R LLP) -1585 Bway -NY 10036
(315) 363-3440 .. **Eppolito,** Anthony P '79 (Nemeti ME&H) -112 Farrier Av -Oneida 13421
(516) 345-0309 .. **Epstein,** Adam E '87 Wall & William Fncl Srvcs Grp -100 N Centre -Rockvll Ctr 11570 **Fx:**596-6777
(212) 819-1130 .. **Epstein,** Alan I '85 (Hirschen S&E) -902 Bway -NY 10010
(212) 609-6800 .. **Epstein,** Alan M '75 SpclCnsl McCarter & E,LLP -245 Park Av -NY 10167
(212) 697-5353 .. **Epstein,** Alan S '84 Epstein Engineering,PC -317 Mad Av -NY 10017
(212) 878-8000 .. **Epstein,** Andrew S '93 (Clifford C LLP) -31 W 52nd -NY 10019
(212) 647-6787 .. **Epstein,** Arlen Tobias '92 Bloomberg LP -731 Lex Av -NY 10022
(732) 855-6121 .. **Epstein,** Barry M '82 (Wilentz G&S) -110 William -NY 10038 **Fx:**726-6543
(212) 351-4500 .. **Epstein Becker & Green,PC** -250 Park Av -NY 10177 **Fx:**878-8600
(718) 336-6658 .. **Epstein,** Benjamin Z '99 -2394 Nostrand Av -Brklyn 11210 **Fx:**336-4115
(212) 684-1230 .. **Epstein,** Bennett '69 -100 Lafayette -NY 10013
(212) 382-2121 .. **Epstein,** Bernard S '57 -36 W 44th -NY 10036 **Fx:**764-6795
(631) 698-3900 .. **Epstein,** Brian T '92 -1305 Middle Cntry Rd -Selden 11784 **Fx:**698-3968
(212) 867-4466 .. **Epstein,** Brian Y '99 (Belkin BW&G,LLP) -270 Mad Av -NY 10016
(212) 859-8000 .. **Epstein,** Carol M '91 SpclCnsl Fried FHS&J LLP -1 NY Plz -NY 10004
(718) 380-7233 .. **Epstein,** Chas I '79 -150-15 79th Av -Flushng 11367 **Fx:**(201) 489-2128
(212) 570-2440 .. **Epstein,** Chloe E '02 Stribling & Assoc -924 Mad Av -NY 10021
(212) 233-8300 .. **Epstein & Cresci** -7 Dey -NY 10007 **Fx:**233-8325
(212) 947-3793 .. **Epstein,** Danielle E '99 (Sadis & G LLP) -551 5th Av -NY 10176
(845) 634-3775 .. **Epstein,** Darren J '94 (Fellows H&E,PC) -254 S Main -New Cty 10956
(212) 373-3000 .. **Epstein,** David '08 %Paul WRW&G LLP -1285 Av of Amer -NY 10019
(718) 852-6763 .. **Epstein,** David B '90 (Epstein & C) -410 Myrtle Av -Brklyn 11205 **Fx:**834-7631
(212) 431-2100 .. **Epstein,** David M '76 %NY Law Schl -185 W Bway -NY 10013 **Fx:**343-1860
(516) 656-0324 .. **Epstein,** Dina E '88 -Bx293 -Sea Cliff 11579 **Fx:**656-0325
(212) 822-1000 .. **Epstein,** Douglas A '94 %Modells Sporting Gds -498 7th Av -NY 10018 **Fx:**822-1090
(212) 292-5390 .. **Epstein Drangel Bazerman & James,LLP** -60 E 42nd -NY 10165 **Fx:**252-5391
(718) 205-3100 .. **Epstein,** Eric B '95 (Epstein & Assoc) -6527 Roosevelt Av -Woodside 11377 **Fx:**205-3101
(212) 415-9200 .. **Epstein,** Eric B '04 %Dorsey & W LLP -250 Park Av -NY 10177
(516) 364-7900 .. **Epstein Frankini & Grammatico** -45 Crsswys Park Dr W -Woodbury 11797 **Fx:**364-7930
(914) 472-5067 .. **Epstein,** Fred L '73 -35M Rockldg Rd -Hartsdale 10530 **Fx:**472-1630

(845) 732-7500 .. **Epstein,** Gilbert '67 %Medicaid Fraud Cntrl -1 Blue Hill Plz Bx1557 -Pearl Rvr 10965 **Fx:**732-7555
(212) 705-7000 .. **Epstein,** Gillian I '05 %Bingham M LLP -399 Park Av -NY 10022
(631) 265-9191 .. **Epstein & Grammatico** -1393 Vets Mem'l Hwy -Hauppauge 11788 **Fx:**265-9258
(212) 248-9100 .. **Epstein Harms & McDonald** -1 Whitehall -NY 10004 **Fx:**510-9258
(845) 831-1710 .. **Epstein,** Harold D '73 -Bx2 -Beacon 12508
(315) 461-0091 .. **Epstein & Hartford** -110 Elwood-Davis Rd -N Syracuse 13212 **Fx:**453-3576
(646) 459-3002 .. **Epstein,** Harvey D '95 Urban Justice Ctr -123 William -NY 10038 **Fx:**(212) 533-4598
(516) 357-3000 .. **Epstein,** Harvey S '87 (Rivkin R LLP) -926 RXR Plz -Uniondale 11556
(516) 825-4837 .. **Epstein,** Herbert '40 -16 Lynwood Dr -Vly Stream 11580
(212) 626-1187 .. **Epstein,** Howard '86 %Bank Leumi USA -562 5th Av -NY 10036 **Fx:**626-1195
(212) 756-2000 .. **Epstein,** Howard B '80 (Schulte R&Z LLP) -919 3rd Av -NY 10022
(212) 764-6444 .. **Epstein,** Jason E '96 (Epstein & L,LLP) -450 7th Av -NY 10123 **Fx:**764-6445
(212) 790-9200 .. **Epstein,** Jeffrey H '87 (Cowan L&L,PC) -1133 Av of Amer -NY 10036
(212) 836-8000 .. **Epstein,** Jeffrey M '66 (Kaye S LLP) -425 Park Av -NY 10022
(212) 371-5400 .. **Epstein,** Jesse A '67 %Weisman CS&M PC -445 Park Av -NY 10022
(347) 404-9133 .. **Epstein,** Jill R '84 %Civil Ct -141 Lvngstn -Brklyn 11201 **Fx:**(718) 643-3733
(516) 328-3500 .. **Epstein,** Joel D '74 %McDonnell & A,PC -401 Franklin Av -Gdn Cty 11530
(646) 252-7620 .. **Epstein,** John G '84 %TBTA -2 Bway -NY 10004
(718) 291-3400 .. **Epstein,** Jon F '88 %Shaevitz & S -148-55 Hillside Av -Jamaica 11435 **Fx:**739-5654
(516) 671-8187 .. **Epstein,** Joshua G '08 Davidson & Assoc,PC -15 Glen -Glen Cove 11542 **Fx:**671-2954
(212) 618-6352 .. **Epstein,** Joshua H '89 (Sorin RC LLC) -1230 Av of Amer -NY 10020
(631) 390-0010 .. **Epstein,** Joshua L '10 %Bruno G&S,LLP -445 Broad Hollow Rd -Melvll 11747
(516) 745-1325 .. **Epstein,** Jules A '78 -600 Old Cntry Rd -Gdn Cty 11530 **Fx:**222-1499
(914) 422-4069 .. **Epstein,** Laurie C '86 Pace Womens Justice Ctr -78 N Bway -White Plns 10603
(212) 233-1050 .. **Epstein,** Lawr '62 (Newman O&E,LLC) -217 Bway -NY 10007
(212) 268-7111 .. **Epstein,** Lee M '87 (Fried & E LLP) -350 5th Av -NY 10118
(212) 319-3900 .. **Epstein,** Leonard '62 -437 Mad Av -NY 10022 **Fx:**319-3070
(212) 732-4888 .. **Epstein,** Lloyd '79 (Epstein & W) -225 Bway -NY 10007 **Fx:**732-6703
(212) 885-5000 .. **Epstein,** Lora M '10 %Blank R LLP -405 Lex Av -NY 10174
(212) 223-3200 .. **Epstein,** Louis '83 Transammonia,Inc -350 Park Av -NY 10022 **Fx:**759-1410
(212) 735-3000 .. **Epstein,** M Oren '04 %Skadden ASM&F LLP -4 Times Sq -NY 10036
(212) 227-1212 .. **Epstein,** Mark J '89 (Pazer E&J,PC) -20 Vesey -NY 10007
(914) 358-3288 .. **Epstein,** Martin B '65 M Epstein PLLC -445 Hmltn Av -White Plns 10601 **Fx:**358-3287
(212) 821-5116 .. **Epstein,** Matthew '95 UBS Warburg -299 Park Av -NY 10171
(845) 639-7800 .. **Epstein,** Matthew J '90 (Mandel K&B,LLP) -210 Route 303 -Vly Cottage 10989
(212) 248-9100 .. **Epstein McDonald & McCarthy** -1 Whitehall -NY 10004 **Fx:**510-9258
(212) 806-5400 .. **Epstein,** Melvin '63 OfCnsl Stroock &S&L LLP -180 Maiden Ln -NY 10038
(212) 310-8000 .. **Epstein,** Michl A '80 (Weil G&M LLP) -767 5th Av -NY 10153
(516) 741-5252 .. **Epstein,** Michl S '10 %Sanders SBWV&G,PC -100 Hrrcks Rd -Mineola 11501
(212) 696-0001 .. **Epstein,** Michelle I '91 -251 5th Av -NY 10016 **Fx:**686-4489
(212) 355-4149 .. **Epstein,** Nina S '73 (Goldweber E LLP) -635 Mad Av -NY 10022
(212) 278-7119 .. **Epstein,** Patricia N '83 %Societe Generale -1221 Av of Amer -NY 10020 **Fx:**278-7595
(845) 831-1710 .. **Epstein,** Paul J '69 -Bx2 -Beacon 12508
(212) 909-6000 .. **Epstein,** Paul J '00 %Debevoise & P LLP -919 3rd Av -NY 10022
(212) 644-1394 .. **Epstein,** Philip A '85 %Belfer Investments -767 5th Av -NY 10153 **Fx:**644-2230
(212) 506-1700 .. **Epstein,** R Tali '94 (Kasowitz BT&F LLP) -1633 Bway -NY 10019
(518) 474-6530 .. **Epstein,** Rafael '83 %Dept Pub Srvc -3 ESP -Albany 12223
(518) 783-4406 .. **Epstein & Rayhill** -950 New Loudon Rd -Latham 12110 **Fx:**783-2207
(914) 347-6360 .. **Epstein & Rayhill** -565 Taxter Rd -Elmsfrd 10523 **Fx:**347-7017
(212) 612-4200 .. **Epstein,** Rhonda L '84 (Hoey KT&E) -55 Water -NY 10041
(631) 853-2007 .. **Epstein,** Richd A '86 %Dept of Social Srvcs -415 Oser Av Bx18030 -Hauppauge 11788 **Fx:**853-2129
(212) 619-5400 .. **Epstein,** Robt C '90 OfCnsl Newman F LLP -1250 Bway -NY 10001
(718) 590-3781 .. **Epstein,** Robt E '81 %Hon D Boyle -851 Grnd Cncrs -Bronx 10451
(212) 277-5895 .. **Epstein,** Robt J '69 OfCnsl Beldock L&H LLP -99 Park Av -NY 10016
(718) 237-0900 .. **Epstein,** Robt J '86 -32 Court -Brklyn 11201 **Fx:**254-9242
(212) 240-9470 .. **Epstein,** Robt J '94 -One Whitehall -NY 10004
(212) 307-1499 .. **Epstein,** Robt J '94 OfCnsl Lissner & L LLP -250 W 57th -NY 10107 **Fx:**757-1825
(212) 292-5390 .. **Epstein,** Robt L '72 (Epstein DB&J,LLP) -60 E 42nd -NY 10165
(516) 652-2109 .. **Epstein,** Ronald '70 -143 E Park Av -Long Bch 11561
(516) 249-1342 .. **Epstein,** Ronald L '83 %Grey & G,LLP -360 Main -Farmngdl 11735
(516) 719-9819 .. **Epstein,** Roni F '02 %LI Power Auth -333 Earle Ovngton Blvd -Uniondale 11553 **Fx:**222-9137
(212) 834-5327 .. **Epstein,** Roy A '91 %Chase Writes Inc -270 Park Av -NY 10017
(212) 768-4343 .. **Epstein,** Scott W '84 (Cantor E&M,LLP) -49 W 37th -NY 10018
(212) 221-5999 .. **Epstein,** Scott W '84 (Antin E&E,LLP) -49 W 37th -NY 10018
(212) 218-5500 .. **Epstein,** Stephen G '76 (Seyfarth S LLP) -620 8th Av -NY 10018
(516) 746-8000 .. **Epstein,** Stephen P '79 (Jaspan S LLP) -300 Grdn City Plz -Gdn Cty 11530
(212) 859-8000 .. **Epstein,** Steven '99 (Fried FHS&J LLP) -1 NY Plz -NY 10004
(212) 248-7800 .. **Epstein,** Steven A '84 (Figman & E,LLP) -11 Bway -NY 10004
(516) 292-2700 .. **Epstein,** Steven B '93 -215 Hilton Av Bx1200 -Hempstd 11551 **Fx:**292-2702
(212) 536-3900 .. **Epstein,** Steven H '87 (K&L Gates LLP) -599 Lex Av -NY 10022
(212) 317-8500 .. **Epstein,** Stewart J '83 (Snitow KH&M,LLP) -575 Lex Av -NY 10022
(212) 577-3688 .. **Epstein,** Susan T '90 %Leg Aid -199 Water -NY 10038 **Fx:**509-8431
(631) 265-9191 .. **Epstein,** Tracey J '85 Epstein & G -1393 Vets Mem'l Hwy -Hauppauge 11788
(212) 468-4800 .. **Epstein,** Walter M '66 (Davis & G LLP) -1740 Bway -NY 10019
(914) 761-9167 .. **Epstein,** Warren W '63 -12 Adrienne Pl -White Plns 10605
(718) 361-2556 .. **Epstein,** Wendy J '99 1st Spice Mixing -3333 Greenpoint Av -LIC 11101
(646) 386-3654 .. **Epstein,** Wm A '93 %Supreme Ct-Law Dept -60 Centre -NY 10007
(607) 737-2762 .. **Eraca-Cornish,** Nancy M '90 -150 Lk -Elmira 14901 **Fx:**767-0177
(212) 576-7000 .. **Eracleous,** Elena '01 NY Life Ins -51 Mad Av -NY 10010 **Fx:**447-0569
(631) 273-7121 .. **Erale,** Alexander B '49 -5 Wicks Rd -Brentwd 11717
(631) 273-7121 .. **Erale,** Francesca V '83 %AB Erale -5 Wicks Rd -Brentwd 11717
(718) 875-9264 .. **Eras,** Ira L '88 OfCnsl Warren & W,PC -185 Montague -Brklyn 11201 **Fx:**852-3069
(212) 962-5550 .. **Erazo,** Estelle M Cabrera '82 (Erazo & E) -53 E 124th -NY 10035 **Fx:**876-7670
(212) 962-5550 .. **Erazo,** Jos R '60 (Erazo & E) -53 E 124th -NY 10035 **Fx:**876-7670
(716) 847-7632 .. **Erazo,** Martin M Jr. '94 %Div of Human Rights -65 Court -Buffalo 14202 **Fx:**847-7625
(516) 621-5296 .. **Erb,** Karen E '84 -77 Magnolia Ln -East Hills 11577
(516) 294-5432 .. **Erbaio,** Ralph A Jr. '81 SrCnsl Kern AC&S,PC -1325 Franklin Av -Gdn Cty 11530
(212) 335-4500 .. **Erbsen,** Diana L '93 (DLA Piper LLP) -1251 Av of Amer -NY 10020
(212) 756-2000 .. **Erbst,** Lauren Gitlitz '06 %Schulte R&Z LLP -919 3rd Av -NY 10022
(212) 632-3560 .. **Ercklentz,** Enno W Jr. '58 -620 5th Av -NY 10020
(212) 728-8000 .. **Ercole,** Christian L '07 %Willkie F&G LLP -787 7th Av -NY 10019
(212) 679-1007 .. **Ercole,** Donald J '72 Poole & Assoc -60 E 42nd -NY 10165
(646) 315-7300 .. **Ercolino,** Gino F '03 %FINRA -14 Wall -NY 10005 **Fx:**315-7440
(212) 286-1666 .. **Erda,** Susan M '80 -276 5th Av -NY 10001 **Fx:**286-1616
(212) 839-5300 .. **Erdmann,** Andrew P '06 %Sidley A LLP -787 7th Av -NY 10019
(718) 375-7766 .. **Erdos,** Jacques '99 -1552 E 5th -Brklyn 11230 **Fx:**375-6465
(914) 287-7711 .. **Erdreich,** Ryan L '08 %Pisciotti M&B,PC -445 Hmltn Av -White Plns 10601 **Fx:**287-7715
(516) 627-5417 .. **Eredics,** Rita '63 -103 Plandome Rd -Manhsst 11030 **Fx:**627-5852
(212) 259-8000 .. **Eren,** Burcin '09 %Dewey & L LLP -1301 Av of Amer -NY 10019
(212) 504-6000 .. **Erenburg,** Anna '95 Cadwalader W&T LLP -1 World Fncl Ctr -NY 10281
(212) 869-5030 .. **Erenburg,** Aram L '98 %Kucker & B,LLP -747 3rd Av -NY 10017
(212) 264-2880 .. **Eres,** Tatjana A '05 %Hon T Stanceu -1 Fed Plz -NY 10278
(646) 386-5404 .. **Erez,** Donna '07 Unified Ct Sys -60 Lafayette -NY 10013
(212) 450-4000 .. **Erez,** Joshua '08 %Davis P&W LLP -450 Lex Av -NY 10017
(718) 250-2000 .. **Eribo,** Christopher Eyakiniovo '99 %DA -350 Jay -Brklyn 11201 **Fx:**250-2314
(212) 553-3200 .. **Erichsen,** Francesca M '97 (Marulli LE&T,LLP) -5 Hanover Sq -NY 10004
(646) 312-8233 .. **Erichson,** Howard M '91 Fordham Law Schl -140 W 62nd -NY 10023
(212) 790-9200 .. **Erickson,** Clarence John III '88 Cowan L&L,PC -1133 Av of Amer -NY 10036
(516) 877-1800 .. **Erickson,** Elizabeth E '07 %Schlissel OK,PLLC -200 Grdn City Plz -Gdn Cty 11530
(212) 949-6490 .. **Erickson,** Helena T '87 CPR Inst -575 Lex Av -NY 10022 **Fx:**949-8859
(315) 637-6861 .. **Erickson,** Jean V '77 -304 Southfld Dr -Fayettevll 13066
(585) 786-8183 .. **Erickson,** Jeffrey E '75 -189 N Main Bx270 -Warsaw 14569 **Fx:**786-8222
(718) 398-2601 .. **Erickson,** Nancy S '74 -172 5th Av -Brklyn 11217
(516) 684-2900 .. **Erickson,** Stephen E '79 (Pegalis & E,LLC) -1 Hllw Ln -Lk Success 11042
(716) 488-1178 .. **Erickson Webb Scolton & Hajdu** -414 E Fairmount Av Bx414 -Lakewd 14750 **Fx:**488-1448
(212) 455-2000 .. **Ericson,** John C '99 (Simpson T&B LLP) -425 Lex Av -NY 10017
(516) 688-1700 .. **Ericson,** Mark A '90 %IRS -1600 Stewart Av -Westbury 11590 **Fx:**688-1750
(212) 294-6700 .. **Ericson,** Robt W '92 (Winston & S) -200 Park Av -NY 10166
(845) 291-2050 .. **Eriksen,** Neal E '08 %DA -255-275 Main -Goshen 10924 **Fx:**291-2085
(845) 778-2121 .. **Eriksen,** Peter R '74 (Jacobowitz & G,LLP) -158 Orange Av Bx367 -Walden 12586
(518) 766-0613 .. **Erikson,** Phyllis A '81 -25 Cnty Route 7 -Nassau 12123
(212) 848-4000 .. **Erker,** Ferdinand J '96 Cnsl Shearman & S LLP -599 Lex Av -NY 10022
(212) 309-6584 .. **Erlandsen,** Jodi A '05 %ING Asset Mngt -230 Park Av -NY 10169
(212) 686-8045 .. **Erlanger,** Robt K '86 Erlanger Law Firm PLLC -122 E 42nd -NY 10168 **Fx:**986-1379
(212) 858-1000 .. **Erlich,** Margot P '98 %Pillsbury WSP LLP -1540 Bway -NY 10036
(718) 793-2553 .. **Erlich,** Nathan '91 (N Erlich,PC) -108-18 Qns Blvd -Frst Hlls 11375 **Fx:**793-1627
(212) 508-6100 .. **Erlichman,** Ron I '06 (Bracewell & G,LLP) -1251 Av of Amer -NY 10020
(212) 507-9700 .. **Erlinger,** Michl J '05 Embassy Row -325 Hudson -NY 10013
(718) 934-9000 .. **Erlitz,** Gail M '90 (Erlitz & E) -2623 E 16th -Brklyn 11235 **Fx:**648-7181
(718) 934-9000 .. **Erlitz,** Stephen N '63 (Erlitz & E) -2623 E 16th -Brklyn 11235 **Fx:**648-7181
(718) 370-7030 .. **Erman,** Carl M '71 (Amabile & E,PC) -1000 South Av -Staten Isl 10314
(718) 370-7030 .. **Erman,** Jonathan S '99 (Amabile & E,PC) -1000 South Av -Staten Isl 10314
(607) 563-8910 .. **Ermeti,** Jos A '92 -9 Division -Sidney 13838 **Fx:**563-1128
(518) 432-3468 .. **Ermides,** Lea A '00 %Ct of Claims -Justice Bldg ESP Bx7344 -Albany 12224 **Fx:**432-3450
(212) 490-3000 .. **Ermogenous,** Irene M '07 %Wilson EME&D LLP -150 E 42nd -NY 10017
(845) 565-1100 .. **Ernenwein,** Paul S '96 (Tarshis CLM&M,PLLC) -One Corwin Ct -Newburgh 12550
(212) 819-8200 .. **Ernst,** David J '99 Cnsl White & C LLP -1155 Av of Amer -NY 10036

(516) 771-9102 .. **Ernst,** Gerald '55 -1841 Stanley Dr -Merrick 11566
(212) 488-1710 .. **Ernst,** Marcus A '96 (Ernst & L,LLC) -17 Battery Pl -NY 10004 **Fx:**488-1667
(212) 230-8800 .. **Ernst,** Matthew '97 Cnsl WilmerHale -399 Park Av -NY 10022
(518) 474-4096 .. **Ernst,** Richd '82 %Dept of Law -The Cptl -Albany 12224
(212) 285-2969 .. **Ernst,** Robt G '89 (Ernst & Assoc) -49 Clinton -NY 10002 **Fx:**577-2321
(212) 553-0300 .. **Ernst,** Yaron '96 %Moody's Invstr Srvc -250 Greenwich -NY 10007
(585) 473-3100 .. **Ernstrom & Dreste,LLP** -180 Canal Vw Blvd -Rchstr 14623 **Fx:**473-3113
(585) 473-3100 .. **Ernstrom,** J Wm '72 OfCnsl Ernstrom & D,LLP -180 Canal Vw Blvd -Rchstr 14623
(315) 218-8000 .. **Eron,** Thos G '88 (Bond S&K,PLLC) -1 Lincoln Ctr -Syracuse 13202
(212) 452-5300 .. **Errante,** Vincent A '00 (Darger & E,LLP) -116 E 27th -NY 10016
(212) 715-9100 .. **Errea,** Julia B '07 %Kramer LN&F,LLP -1177 Av of Amer -NY 10036
(212) 903-8700 .. **Erreich,** Allen '89 (Roberts & H,LLP) -825 8th Av -NY 10019
(212) 376-0900 .. **Erreich,** Harry J '76 %Royal Abstract -500 5th Av -NY 10110 **Fx:**376-0911
(516) 739-0000 .. **Errera,** James '07 Martyn T&M -330 Old Cntry Rd -Mineola 11501
(845) 294-4141 .. **Errichetti,** Janis L '89 -55 Main Bx864 -Goshen 10924 **Fx:**294-6372
(212) 248-3140 .. **Errico,** Mark C '00 Cnsl Drinker B&R LLP -140 Bway -NY 10005
(631) 587-1468 .. **Erroll,** David C '02 -15 Brookdale Ct -Sayvll 11782
(718) 250-2000 .. **Erskine,** Joan '02 %DA -350 Jay -Brklyn 11201 **Fx:**250-2314
(212) 238-8704 .. **Erskine,** Robt S Jr. '62 -2 Wall -NY 10005 **Fx:**732-3232
(516) 364-8933 .. **Erstein,** Howard S '72 -485 Underhill Blvd -Syosset 11791
(716) 858-2424 .. **Ertel,** Gary M '07 %DA -25 Delaware Av -Buffalo 14202 **Fx:**858-7425
(212) 728-8000 .. **Ertel,** Jason R '07 %Willkie F&G LLP -787 7th Av -NY 10019
(516) 992-3483 .. **Ertel,** Richd C '95 -1225 Franklin Av -Gdn Cty 11530
(914) 762-5018 .. **Ertischek,** Rodney H '73 -20 Fuller Rd -Briarclff Mnr 10510 **Fx:**762-5330
(212) 596-9000 .. **Ertman,** John C '93 (Ropes & G LLP) -1211 Av of Amer -NY 10036
(718) 286-2000 .. **Ertrachter,** Jana Greene '90 %Leg Aid -120-46 Qns Blvd -Kew Gdns 11415 **Fx:**286-2286
(516) 481-8009 .. **Ervin,** Howard '84 -409 Uniondale Av -Uniondale 11553 **Fx:**489-6798
(212) 858-1000 .. **Ervine,** Meredith L '09 %Pillsbury WSP LLP -1540 Bway -NY 10036
(212) 766-1888 .. **Ervolina,** Anna J '96 %Morris DA&F -2 Rector -NY 10006
(212) 931-5500 .. **Erwin,** Gianna A '09 %McCue S&Z,PC -521 5th Av -NY 10175
(212) 682-3366 .. **Erwin,** John S '72 (Hill U&E,LLP) -825 3rd Av -NY 10022
(518) 449-2245 .. **Erwin,** Thos C '81 (Erwin M&D) -23 Elk -Albany 12207 **Fx:**449-7890
(212) 849-7000 .. **Erwine,** Richd W '96 (Quinn EU&S,LLP) -51 Mad Av -NY 10010
(212) 340-0400 .. **Esakoff,** Sharon R '86 %Appllt Div 1st Dept -27 Mad Av -NY 10010 **Fx:**889-4412
(914) 722-1118 .. **Esannason,** Wayne D '95 Village Atty -1001 Post Rd -Scarsdale 10583 **Fx:**722-1119
(212) 953-6000 .. **Esanu,** Warren H '70 SrCnsl Katsky K LLP -605 3rd Av -NY 10158
(516) 742-4343 .. **Esatto,** Paul J Jr. '84 (Scully SM&P PC) -400 Grdn City Plz -Gdn Cty 11530
(845) 634-7909 .. **Esbin,** Scott L '90 (Esbin & A,LLP) -497 S Main -New Cty 10956 **Fx:**634-4160
(212) 363-1380 .. **Escala,** Gerald C '89 SpclCnsl Herten BSCBL&H,LLC -747 3rd Av -NY 10017
(914) 993-9393 .. **Escalera,** Alexandra Y '06 %Stewart Title Ins -707 Wstchstr Av -White Plns 10604 **Fx:**997-1698
(212) 636-6000 .. **Escalera,** Nitza Milagros '91 %Fordham Univ Sch of Law -140 W 62nd -NY 10023 **Fx:**636-6899
(212) 461-2323 .. **Escanlar,** Katherine A '08 %Saiber LLC -44 Wall -NY 10005
(315) 431-0736 .. **Esce,** Susan N '88 (Esce & M) -10 Adler Dr -E Syracuse 13057 **Fx:**437-9462
(516) 496-8555 .. **Eschen,** Seth A '82 -485 Underhill Blvd -Syosset 11791 **Fx:**921-7785
(212) 539-4090 .. **Eschenasy,** Aveeram E '92 %October Films -65 Bleecker -NY 10012
(212) 513-7788 .. **Eschmann,** Paul A '00 (Ahmuty D&M) -123 William -NY 10038
(212) 225-2000 .. **Escobar,** Angela M '09 %Cleary GS&H -1 Lbrty Plz -NY 10006
(212) 969-3000 .. **Escobar,** Jeffrey R '05 %Proskauer R LLP -1585 Bway -NY 10036
(212) 458-1586 .. **Escobar,** Louis Jr. '80 %AIG Professional Liability -175 Water -NY 10038 **Fx:**458-1259
(212) 808-7800 .. **Escobar,** Wm A '82 (Kelley D&W LLP) -101 Park Av -NY 10178
(516) 620-1199 .. **Escoffery,** David S '01 Nemean Cptl,LLC -666 Old Cntry Rd -Gdn Cty 11530
(212) 468-8000 .. **Escuder,** Diana L '09 %Morrison & F LLP -1290 Av of Amer -NY 10104
(212) 492-4381 .. **Escuder,** Jeffrey M '05 %Deloitte LLP -1633 Bway -NY 10019 **Fx:**653-3250
(212) 558-4000 .. **Escue,** Michl T '99 (Sullivan & C LLP) -125 Broad -NY 10004
(716) 204-2400 .. **Esdinsky,** Patricia M '07 %SJ Baum,PC -220 Nrthpnte Pkwy Bx1291 -Buffalo 14240 **Fx:**204-4600
(212) 351-4000 .. **Esdorn,** Joerg H '98 (Gibson D&C LLP) -200 Park Av -NY 10166
(914) 969-4136 .. **Esehak,** Kenneth G '90 -Bx703 -Ynkrs 10703 **Fx:**969-4136
(315) 785-3088 .. **Eseltine,** Polly S '89 Cnty Atty -175 Arsenal -Watertwn 13601 **Fx:**785-5178
(516) 248-7000 .. **Esernio,** George P '69 OfCnsl Albanese & A LLP -1050 Franklin Av -Gdn Cty 11530
(212) 733-3860 .. **Esguerra-Agcaoili,** Maria C '07 Pfizer Inc -235 E 42nd -NY 10017
(646) 935-1090 .. **Eshaghian,** Sabrina V '02 Somerset Mgmt -215 Lex Av -NY 10016
(212) 294-6700 .. **Eshaghpour,** Nicole S '10 %Winston & S -200 Park Av -NY 10166
(212) 872-1000 .. **Eshanov,** Dinmukhamed T '09 -One Bryant Park -NY 10036 **Fx:**872-1002
(212) 637-2758 .. **Eshkenazi,** Lara K '96 %US Atty -86 Chmbrs -NY 10007
(212) 668-8400 .. **Eskenasi,** Leigh D '06 %L Grandelli,PC -90 Broad -NY 10004 **Fx:**483-0918
(212) 728-8000 .. **Eskenazi,** Lisa J '05 %Willkie F&G LLP -787 7th Av -NY 10019
(718) 250-2000 .. **Eskenazi,** Michl E '07 %DA -350 Jay -Brklyn 11201 **Fx:**250-2314
(212) 967-1134 .. **Eskesen,** Frank N '00 (Marder E&N) -450 7th Av -NY 10123
(212) 806-5400 .. **Eskew,** Richd '00 SpclCnsl Stroock &S&L LLP -180 Maiden Ln -NY 10038
(718) 402-5204 .. **Eskin,** David J '93 (Eskin & E,PC) -903F Sheridan Av -Bronx 10451 **Fx:**(347) 577-6628
(718) 402-5204 .. **Eskin,** Monica S '94 (Eskin & E,PC) -903F Sheridan Av -Bronx 10451 **Fx:**(347) 577-6628
(518) 456-0082 .. **Eskin-Colon,** Dinna '07 %Bailey K&J,PC -5 Pine West Plz -Albany 12205 **Fx:**456-4767
(212) 839-5300 .. **Esko,** Stephen B '84 (Sidley A LLP) -787 7th Av -NY 10019
(510) 874-1000 .. **Eskovitz,** Katherine A '96 OfCnsl Boies S&F LLP -333 Main -Armonk 10504
(212) 490-9100 .. **Eskridge,** Timothy H '04 %Condon & F LLP -7 Times Sq -NY 10036
(212) 858-1000 .. **Esmaili,** Ranah L '07 %Pillsbury WSP LLP -1540 Bway -NY 10036
(212) 918-3000 .. **Esmay,** John J '08 %Hogan L LLP -875 3rd Av -NY 10022
(212) 331-6167 .. **Esnard,** Roy A '91 HRA Ofc of Legal Affrs -180 Water -NY 10038
(212) 953-2381 .. **Eson,** Jason B '07 %Rubin F&F,LLP -292 Mad Av -NY 10017
(631) 725-7600 .. **Espach,** Robt W '57 OfCnsl S Grossman & Assoc -17 Main Bx1949 -Sag Hbr 11963 **Fx:**725-5618
(718) 983-8800 .. **Espada,** Ainissa '07 %Lee & A,LLP -260 Christopher Ln -Staten Isl 10314
(212) 506-2500 .. **Espana,** Mauricio A '05 %Mayer B LLP -1675 Bway -NY 10019
(845) 635-2690 .. **Espejo,** Barbara Gordon '81 -124 Carter Rd -Plsnt Vlly 12569 **Fx:**635-5174
(315) 781-6311 .. **Espenscheid,** Alaine T '78 -9 Genesee Park Pl -Geneva 14456 **Fx:**781-5476
(212) 815-1301 .. **Esperon,** Rosaria '81 %DC 37 Hlth & Scrty Plan -125 Barclay -NY 10007
(516) 873-2000 .. **Espey,** Michelle E '04 %Moritt HH&H LLP -400 Grdn City Plz -Gdn Cty 11530
(212) 768-6700 .. **Espinal,** George L '02 %Sonnenschein N&R LLP -2 World Fncl Ctr -NY 10281
(718) 286-6000 .. **Espinal,** Keshia J '01 %DA -125-01 Qns Blvd -Kew Gdns 11415
(631) 273-8444 .. **Espinosa,** Ana C '04 Cnsl Collado C&F,PLLC -14 Wshngtn Av -Brentwd 11717
(212) 916-2000 .. **Espinosa,** Charisse '02 UBS Intl -101 Park Av -NY 10178
(212) 269-2091 .. **Espinosa & Espinosa, LLP** -61 Bway -NY 10006 **Fx:**269-7866
(716) 856-4000 .. **Espinosa,** Kevin J '10 %Hodgson R LLP -140 Pearl -Buffalo 14202
(212) 696-1999 .. **Espinosa,** Sandra P '05 %Lax & N LLP -1412 Bway -NY 10018
(212) 909-6000 .. **Espinoza,** Cheryl Testa '10 %Debevoise & P LLP -919 3rd Av -NY 10022
(718) 274-3370 .. **Espinoza,** Jeannette '92 -25-84 Steinway -Astoria 11103 **Fx:**721-8812
(212) 259-8000 .. **Espinoza,** Michl E '08 %Dewey & L LLP -1301 Av of Amer -NY 10019
(718) 767-2201 .. **Esposito,** Anthony '90 -11-01 154th -Whitestone 11357 **Fx:**767-2958
(718) 698-3666 .. **Esposito,** Anthony R '00 -4308 Richmond Av -Staten Isl 10312
(516) 877-1878 .. **Esposito,** Anthony S '91 A Esposito,PC -623 Stewart Av -Gdn Cty 11530 **Fx:**877-1890
(718) 286-7452 .. **Esposito,** Carmine A '99 FBI -80-02 Kew Grdn Rd -Kew Gdns 11415
(631) 393-5009 .. **Esposito,** Carmine E '89 -200 Broad Hollow Rd -Melvll 11747 **Fx:**393-5102
(516) 742-1444 .. **Esposito,** Carol Lynn '86 %Wagner D&L,PC -227 Mineola Blvd -Mineola 11501
(212) 966-6570 .. **Esposito,** Chas J '79 Press of Fremont Payne,Inc -55 Broad -NY 10004
(718) 796-6454 .. **Esposito,** Christopher L '89 -269 W 231st -Bronx 10463 **Fx:**796-4412
(718) 722-6364 .. **Esposito,** Eileen D '04 -195 Montague -Brklyn 11201
(212) 530-5000 .. **Esposito,** George A Jr. '09 %Milbank TH&M LLP -1 Chase Manh Plz -NY 10005
(212) 468-8000 .. **Esposito,** Grant J '93 (Morrison & F LLP) -1290 Av of Amer -NY 10104
(516) 739-5100 .. **Esposito,** James '87 OfCnsl Farber B&Z LLP -51 Charles -Mineola 11501
(718) 855-6103 .. **Esposito,** John C '81 -385½ Union -Brklyn 11231 **Fx:**855-6261
(212) 587-7840 .. **Esposito,** John S '85 -321 Bway -NY 10007 **Fx:**587-7862
(212) 264-0300 .. **Esposito,** Lauren Ann '94 %NLRB -26 Fed Plz -NY 10278 **Fx:**264-8427
(212) 824-5700 .. **Esposito,** Lauren J '05 Practising Law Inst -810 7th Av -NY 10019
(518) 581-8405 .. **Esposito,** Licia A '93 -137 Circular -Saratoga Spgs 12866
(212) 681-1380 .. **Esposito,** Liliana M '07 Mercury Public Affairs -137 5th Av -NY 10010
(212) 728-8710 .. **Esposito,** Margaret '91 -787 7th Av -NY 10019
(212) 632-1882 .. **Esposito,** Marisa A '97 Lazard Asset Mgmt LLC -30 Rckfllr Plz -NY 10112
(212) 310-8000 .. **Esposito,** Michl J '09 %Weil G&M LLP -767 5th Av -NY 10153
(516) 571-3056 .. **Esposito,** Nicholas A '94 %Cnty Atty -1 West -Mineola 11501 **Fx:**571-6604
(631) 604-1593 .. **Esposito,** Ralph J '05 -300 Pantigo Pl -E Hampton 11937
(914) 682-9773 .. **Esposito,** Roger L '77 -399 Knollwood Rd -White Plns 10603 **Fx:**682-1512
(914) 769-6040 .. **Esposito,** Stanley E '64 -390 Bedford Rd -Plsntvll 10570 **Fx:**741-2736
(718) 263-3059 .. **Esposito,** Thos '70 -70-25 Yllwstn Blvd -Frst Hlls 11375
(212) 269-4900 .. **Esposito,** Thos R '68 (Ford MEW&G,LLP) -Wall Street Plz -NY 10005
(631) 271-7254 .. **Esposito,** Vincent M '72 -7 Ponds Edge Ct -Huntngtn Sta 11746 **Fx:**421-4611
(914) 681-6200 .. **Esposito,** Vincent P Jr. '90 %NYPA -123 Main -White Plns 10601 **Fx:**390-8038
(631) 300-4960 .. **Esposito,** Wayne P '80 %Bello & L -150 Motor Pkwy -Hauppauge 11788
(315) 379-2225 .. **Esposito-Shea,** Victoria M '07 DA -48 Court -Canton 13617 **Fx:**379-2301
(518) 402-0205 .. **Esrick,** Deborah '84 %UIA Bd -Troy Atrium Bx15126 -Albany 12212 **Fx:**402-6208
(718) 667-3954 .. **Esrick,** Edw E '77 %JTD Land Srvcs -1911 Richmond Ab -Staten Isl 10314 **Fx:**667-4049
(518) 392-2223 .. **Esrick,** Kenneth L '84 -32 Main -Chatham 12037 **Fx:**392-9650
(914) 683-8277 .. **Essayan,** Gregory J '82 -7 Platt Pl -White Plns 10605
(914) 632-4700 .. **Essed,** Salihah R '05 %McDonough Law Firm, LLP -145 Huguenot -New Rchll 10801

(212) 610-6300 .. **Esseks,** David C '92 (Allen & O) -1221 Av of Amer -NY 10020
(631) 369-1700 .. **Esseks Hefter & Angel, LLP** -108 E Main Bx279 -Rvrhead 11901 **Fx:**369-2065
(212) 549-2627 .. **Esseks,** James D '94 %ACLU -125 Broad -NY 10004 **Fx:**549-2651
(631) 369-1700 .. **Esseks,** Wm W '59 (Esseks H&A,LLP) -108 E Main Bx279 -Rvrhead 11901
(518) 402-0205 .. **Essepian,** Chas H '90 %UIA Bd -Troy Atrium Bx15126 -Albany 12212 **Fx:**402-6208
(518) 785-1197 .. **Essepian,** Chas H '90 -180 Old Loudon Rd -Latham 12110 **Fx:**783-4519
(212) 589-4200 .. **Esser,** Brian K '06 %Baker & H LLP -45 Rckfllr Plz -NY 10111
(212) 214-5600 .. **Esser,** Darren J '95 Wachovia Securities -375 Park Av -NY 10152
(212) 532-6555 .. **Esses,** Eli '73 -458 Av T -Brklyn 11223
(212) 586-5800 .. **Esses,** Leo L '00 SrCnsl Cohen TS&W PC -420 Lex Av -NY 10170
(212) 351-4500 .. **Essig,** Beth R '79 (Epstein B&G,PC) -250 Park Av -NY 10177
(631) 360-7800 .. **Essig,** Gerald '64 OfCnsl Spada A&S,PLLC -64 Smithtwn Blvd -Smithtwn 11787
(315) 422-1152 .. **Essig,** Robt D '76 Costello C&F,PLLC -500 Plum -Syracuse 13204
(585) 641-8000 .. **Essler,** Karl S '80 (Fix SB&G,PC) -295 Woodcliff Dr -Fairprt 14450
(585) 428-5755 .. **Essley,** Peter A '96 %Cnty Atty -50 W Main -Rchstr 14614 **Fx:**428-2031
(518) 622-9910 .. **Esslie,** Denise Frenia '99 (Esslie & F) -Bx1121 -Cairo 12413 **Fx:**622-9778
(212) 944-2200 .. **Essner,** Allen P '74 (Ferber CE&C,LLP) -530 5th Av -NY 10036
(212) 750-4949 .. **Essner,** Allison S '90 OfCnsl Shearer & E,LLP -50 Bway -NY 10004
(212) 750-4949 .. **Essner,** Howard '90 (Shearer & E,LLP) -50 Bway -NY 10004
(212) 345-0413 .. **Essoff,** Patricia A '94 %Marsh USA -1166 Av of Amer -NY 10036 **Fx:**345-4808
(718) 250-2000 .. **Esswein,** Craig '82 %DA -350 Jay -Brklyn 11201 **Fx:**250-2314
(212) 508-6332 .. **Estabil,** Mary I '93 %Zesiger Capital Grp -320 Park Av -NY 10022
(845) 796-2300 .. **Estabrook,** James M Jr. '70 %Frontier Ins -195 Lk Louise Marie Rd -Rck Hll 12775 **Fx:**791-5053
(212) 306-7200 .. **Estacio,** Jazmine A '98 %Mayors Ofc Labor Rel -40 Rector -NY 10006 **Fx:**306-7223
(212) 335-9000 .. **Estacio,** Peter F '08 DA -1 Hogan Pl -NY 10013
(212) 450-4000 .. **Estacio,** Richd A '10 %Davis P&W LLP -450 Lex Av -NY 10017
(212) 715-1000 .. **Estaver,** Aron J '06 %Arnold & P LLP -399 Park Av -NY 10022
(212) 335-9000 .. **Estela,** Emilio '87 %DA -1 Hogan Pl -NY 10013
(516) 747-0300 .. **Esterces,** Howard M '63 (Meltzer LG&B,LLP) -190 Willis Av -Mineola 11501
(212) 354-5650 .. **Esterhay,** Susan E '96 OfCnsl Graham C PC -36 W 44th -NY 10036
(718) 923-8400 .. **Esterman,** David N '99 %Forest City Ratner -1 Metrotech Ctr N -Brklyn 11201 **Fx:**923-8722
(212) 972-5560 .. **Esterman,** Lester '49 Cnsl Zichello & M,LLP -60 E 42nd -NY 10165
(212) 527-4000 .. **Esterman,** Marc R '97 Revlon Consumer Products Corp -237 Park Av -NY 10017
(212) 421-2150 .. **Esterman,** Pamela R '84 (Sive P&R,PC) -460 Park Av -NY 10022
(585) 727-4219 .. **Estes,** J Montieth '70 -219 S Fitzhugh -Rchstr 14608
(212) 558-4000 .. **Estes,** John E '95 (Sullivan & C LLP) -125 Broad -NY 10004
(914) 249-2000 .. **Estes,** Judy Kang '00 %MasterCard Intl -2000 Purchase -Purchase 10577
(518) 436-2840 .. **Estes,** Wm J '99 %Thruway Auth -200 Southrn Blvd Bx189 -Albany 12201 **Fx:**471-4340
(212) 788-0541 .. **Estess,** Alison E '96 %Law Dept -100 Church -NY 10007 **Fx:**788-0367
(973) 596-4717 .. **Esteves,** Elvin '94 Cnsl Gibbons PC -1 Penn Plz -NY 10119 **Fx:**639-6489
(212) 735-3000 .. **Esteves,** Jose A '98 (Skadden ASM&F LLP) -4 Times Sq -NY 10036
(845) 291-3150 .. **Estevez,** Judith M '06 %Cnty Atty -255 Main -Goshen 10924 **Fx:**291-3167
(516) 571-3800 .. **Estevez,** Olgarina M '06 %DA -262 Old Cntry Rd -Mineola 11501 **Fx:**248-9479
(516) 496-5822 .. **Estevez,** P Stephanie '01 %T Spina -170 Froehlich Farm Blvd -Woodbury 11797 **Fx:**496-5420
(212) 530-5000 .. **Estevez,** Roland '05 %Milbank TH&M LLP -1 Chase Manh Plz -NY 10005
(212) 867-6000 .. **Estis,** Warren A '74 (Rosenberg & E,PC) -733 3rd Av -NY 10017
(212) 660-5000 .. **Estline,** Yair '01 %Zysman A&G LLP -1290 Av of Amer -NY 10104
(212) 687-7410 .. **Estock,** Howard G '74 (Clifton B&D,LLP) -420 Lex Av -NY 10170
(716) 854-1002 .. **Estoff,** Jonathan D '72 (Miserendino CS&E,PC) -295 Main -Buffalo 14203
(212) 863-6300 .. **Estrada,** Cesar A Jr. '87 %HPD -100 Gold -NY 10038 **Fx:**863-8201
(718) 507-8153 .. **Estrada,** Diego '00 -10603 Corona Av -Corona 11368 **Fx:**507-8156
(212) 521-5400 .. **Estrada,** Edw J '98 (Reed S LLP) -599 Lex Av -NY 10022
(718) 250-4521 .. **Estrada,** Rudolph '05 Leg Aid -111 Lvngstn -Brklyn 11201
(212) 230-8885 .. **Estrada,** Steven A '09 WilmerHale -399 Park Av -NY 10022
(212) 599-0291 .. **Estreich,** Sonia S '87 -248 E 31st -NY 10016
(718) 339-3330 .. **Estreicher,** Alan B '81 %Meyers S&C -3620 Quentin Rd -Brklyn 11234
(212) 479-6000 .. **Estreicher,** Michl S '06 %Cooley LLP -1114 Av of Amer -NY 10036
(212) 326-3939 .. **Estreicher,** Saml '76 OfCnsl Jones D -222 E 41st -NY 10017
(212) 998-6226 .. **Estreicher,** Saml '76 %NYU Law Schl -40 Wshngtn Sq S -NY 10012 **Fx:**995-4341
(516) 334-6727 .. **Estrella,** Richd F '94 %Fidelity Natl Title Ins -900 Merchants Cncrs -Westbury 11590 **Fx:**334-7459
(718) 741-8263 .. **Estrella-Castillo,** Lilliana M '96 %Div of Human Rights -1 Fordham Plz -Bronx 10458 **Fx:**741-8104
(212) 564-9800 .. **Estren,** Brooke N '07 D'Agostino L&L,LLP -345 7th Av -NY 10001
(914) 422-4343 .. **Estrin,** Danl E '94 SpclCnsl Envrnmtl Lit Clinic -78 N Bway -White Plns 10603 **Fx:**422-4437
(212) 962-0800 .. **Estrin,** Melvyn J '68 (Estrin B&L) -225 Bway -NY 10007 **Fx:**732-1408
(607) 624-6658 .. **Esworthy,** Jos W '84 -2613 Rustic Ridge Rd -Endicott 13760
(516) 478-4160 .. **Etah,** Lawr N '04 -250 Fulton Av -Hempstd 11550 **Fx:**478-4158
(845) 368-3310 .. **Etelson,** Arnold '62 (Etelson & F) -1 Exec Blvd -Suffern 10901
(845) 368-3310 .. **Etelson & Fassberg** -1 Exec Blvd -Suffern 10901 **Fx:**368-3392
(212) 237-1000 .. **Etheridge,** Derek R '04 %Windels ML&M,LLP -156 W 56th -NY 10019
(646) 610-5400 .. **Etheridge,** Jeffrey W Jr. '95 %NYPD -1 Police Plz -NY 10038
(212) 308-4411 .. **Etherington,** Geoffrey III '98 (Edwards AP&D LLP) -750 Lex Av -NY 10022
(518) 435-1919 .. **Ethier,** Mederic J III '93 (Stockton B&M,LLP) -2 Twr Pl -Albany 12203
(212) 888-7500 .. **Etkin,** Wm D '83 %Etkin & Co -14 E 60th -NY 10022
(212) 757-2310 .. **Etkind,** David A '89 (Echtman & E,LLP) -250 W 57th -NY 10107 **Fx:**757-2366
(212) 788-3300 .. **Etkind,** Elizabeth Ann '91 %Hlth & Hsptl Corp -125 Worth -NY 10013 **Fx:**267-6905
(607) 732-6646 .. **Etkind & Golos** -150 Lk -Elmira 14901 **Fx:**732-4262
(212) 947-3793 .. **Etkind,** Steven M '87 (Sadis & G LLP) -551 5th Av -NY 10176
(518) 402-3424 .. **Etlinger,** Laura '96 %OCFS -52 Wshngtn -Rensselaer 12144 **Fx:**486-6361
(212) 592-1400 .. **Etna,** Danl A '87 (Herrick,F LLP) -2 Park Av -NY 10016
(315) 424-8944 .. **Etoll,** Stephen G '94 (Shulman CG&R,PC) -250 S Clinton -Syracuse 13202
(212) 829-5565 .. **Etra,** Aaron '66 OfCnsl Indeva -445 Park Av -NY 10022 **Fx:**(917) 322-2105
(212) 315-7386 .. **Etra,** Adam B '03 Eastdil Secured -40 W 57th -NY 10019
(212) 728-8000 .. **Etra,** Jessica S '03 %Willkie F&G LLP -787 7th Av -NY 10019
(212) 373-3000 .. **Etra,** Jos D '05 %Paul WRW&G LLP -1285 Av of Amer -NY 10019
(212) 903-8700 .. **Etra,** Lionel '68 OfCnsl Roberts & H,LLP -825 8th Av -NY 10019
(212) 983-0800 .. **Etra,** Marshall I '71 -331 Mad Av -NY 10017 **Fx:**682-7718
(212) 672-4718 .. **Etra,** Michl S '01 Witkoff Grp LLC -220 E 42nd -NY 10017
(212) 472-7270 .. **Etra,** Susan '79 (Yoeli G&E LLP) -260 Mad Av -NY 10016
(212) 785-9100 .. **Etre,** Alicia '07 %Paduano & W LLP -1251 Av of Amer -NY 10020
(914) 654-1040 .. **Etre,** Saml R '07 ELQ Industries,Ltd -567 5th Av -New Rchll 10801
(516) 486-1408 .. **Etro,** Thos A '82 -833 Rutgers Rd -Franklin Sq 11010
(212) 735-3000 .. **Ettannani,** Michl M '09 %Skadden ASM&F LLP -4 Times Sq -NY 10036
(212) 715-9100 .. **Ettari,** Samantha V '06 %Kramer LN&F,LLP -1177 Av of Amer -NY 10036
(516) 227-6300 .. **Ettelman,** Gary '82 (Ettelman & H,PC) -100 Q Roosevelt Blvd -Gdn Cty 11530
(516) 227-6300 .. **Ettelman & Hochheiser,PC** -100 Q Roosevelt Blvd -Gdn Cty 11530 **Fx:**227-6307
(516) 681-1100 .. **Ettenger,** Jeffrey S '97 OfCnsl Kaufman DV&G,LLP -135 Crsswys Park Dr -Woodbury 11797
(516) 487-5800 .. **Ettenger,** Jennifer B '99 OfCnsl Mauro G&L LLP -60 Cuttermill Rd -Gt Neck 11021
(212) 575-0055 .. **Ettinger,** Arthur D '98 (Rottenstreich & E LLP) -150 E 58th -NY 10155 **Fx:**575-0046
(212) 547-5400 .. **Ettinger,** Heather Morehouse '07 %McDermott W&E LLP -340 Mad Av -NY 10173
(212) 450-4000 .. **Ettinger,** John R '79 (Davis P&W LLP) -450 Lex Av -NY 10017
(845) 692-8700 .. **Ettinger,** Michl '80 (Ettinger,PC) -75 Crystal Run Rd -Middletwn 10941 **Fx:**692-8708
(518) 459-2700 .. **Ettinger,** Michl '80 (Ettinger,PC) -125 Wolf Rd -Albany 12205 **Fx:**459-2714
(718) 477-2700 .. **Ettinger,** Michl '80 (Ettinger,PC) -900 South Av -Staten Isl 10314 **Fx:**568-3550
(845) 897-4700 .. **Ettinger,** Michl '80 (Ettinger,PC) -200 Westage Bus Ctr -Fishkill 12524 **Fx:**897-4747
(518) 581-9200 .. **Ettinger,** Michl '80 (Ettinger,PC) -340 Bway -Saratoga Spgs 12866 **Fx:**581-9220
(845) 353-9555 .. **Ettinger,** Michl '80 (Ettinger,PC) -99 Main -Nyack 10960 **Fx:**353-2090
(914) 684-6100 .. **Ettinger,** Michl '80 (Ettinger,PC) -150 Grand -White Plns 10601 **Fx:**684-6188
(845) 876-6266 .. **Ettinger,** Michl '80 (Ettinger,PC) -6369 Mill -Rhinebeck 12572 **Fx:**876-6268
(631) 843-5500 .. **Ettinger,** Michl S '86 Henry Schein,Inc -135 Duryea Rd -Melvll 11747
(212) 282-5250 .. **Ettinger,** Patrice S '88 Avon Products Inc -1345 Av of Amer -NY 10105
(585) 295-5775 .. **Ettinger,** Tonia M '04 Leg Aid -1 W Main -Rchstr 14614
(212) 526-8203 .. **Ettlinger,** Michl B '85 Barclays Cptl Inc -745 7th Av -NY 10019
(212) 973-0572 .. **Ettman,** Bruce D '84 Cnsl Wolff & S PC -140 Bway -NY 10005
(315) 568-8199 .. **Ettman,** David K '90 -115 Fall Bx805 -Seneca Fls 13148 **Fx:**568-8299
(516) 229-4501 .. **Ettus,** Deirdre '94 %Russo A&T -875 Merrick Av -Westbury 11590
(212) 207-4527 .. **Etufugh,** Alozie N '02 -325 Bway -NY 10007
(718) 848-8700 .. **Etwaroo,** Baljit '94 -119-02 Lbrty Av -S Richmond Hll 11419 **Fx:**848-9292
(716) 851-3469 .. **Etzel,** Thos P '98 State Ins Fund -225 Oak -Buffalo 14203 **Fx:**851-2138
(212) 725-7111 .. **Etzrodt,** Michl T Jr. '97 %Bender RI&R LLP -451 Park Av S -NY 10016
(718) 722-3949 .. **Eubank,** Matthew S '04 %Dept of Law -55 Hanson Pl -Brklyn 11217 **Fx:**722-3951
(212) 331-4995 .. **Eubanks,** Clinton F Jr. '85 HRA-Ofc Lgl Affrs -180 Water -NY 10038 **Fx:**331-4465
(516) 570-0685 .. **Eubanks,** Eric B '04 A Faber LLC -80 Cutter Mill Rd -Gt Neck 11021 **Fx:**908-4170
(212) 574-1200 .. **Eubanks,** Renee '96 Cnsl Seward & K LLP -1 Bttry Pk Plz -NY 10004
(212) 806-5400 .. **Eubanks,** Robin B '07 %Stroock &S&L LLP -180 Maiden Ln -NY 10038
(716) 759-9759 .. **Eugeni,** Anthony L '92 (Damon M LLP) -9276 Main -Clarence 14031
(212) 815-1818 .. **Eulau,** Lisa M '98 DC 37 MELS -125 Barclay -NY 10007 **Fx:**815-1343
(212) 506-5000 .. **Eum,** Julie '06 %Orrick H&S LLP -51 W 52nd -NY 10019
(212) 460-4285 .. **Eure,** Geraldine R '79 Con Ed -4 Irving Pl -NY 10003 **Fx:**260-8627
(212) 374-6888 .. **Europe,** Theresa Ann '95 %NYC Dept Educ-OLS -52 Chmbrs -NY 10007 **Fx:**374-5596
(212) 344-3100 .. **Eusanio,** Eric M '01 (Frenkel LWW&G,LLP) -1 Whitehall -NY 10004
(914) 989-6650 .. **Eustace,** Edw M '86 (Eustace & M) -1133 Wstchstr Av -White Plns 10604
(914) 989-6650 .. **Eustace & Marquez** -1133 Wstchstr Av -White Plns 10604 **Fx:**989-6638

(212) 479-6000 .. **Eustice,** James E '59 OfCnsl Cooley LLP -1114 Av of Amer -NY 10036
(212) 836-8000 .. **Eustice,** Larissa A '08 %Kaye S LLP -425 Park Av -NY 10022
(212) 820-9450 .. **Eustis,** James R Jr. '73 (Hawkins D&W LLP) -One Chase Manh Plz -NY 10005
(212) 334-9002 .. **Eustis,** Polly '76 -351 Bway -NY 10013
(315) 474-1511 .. **Euto,** Jeremy J '95 %National Grid -300 Erie Blvd W -Syracuse 13202 **Fx:**428-6149
(212) 349-7511 .. **Evall,** Clay M '86 (CM Evall,PC) -291 Bway -NY 10007
(212) 506-5000 .. **Evall,** Jos '91 (Orrick H&S LLP) -51 W 52nd -NY 10019
(212) 557-4000 .. **Evan,** David J '94 (Grunfeld DLS&K LLP) -399 Park Av -NY 10022
(914) 730-5800 .. **Evan,** Lior '90 Parallel Asset Mgmt LLC -84 Business Park Dr -Armonk 10504 **Fx:**730-5805
(212) 838-1177 .. **Evan,** Sagit A '99 %Morse ZR&L LLP -405 Park Av -NY 10022
(212) 558-4000 .. **Evangelakos,** John '87 (Sullivan & C LLP) -125 Broad -NY 10004
(631) 692-0978 .. **Evangelist,** Frank J '58 -5 Woodvale Ln -Huntngtn 11743 **Fx:**271-7620
(631) 470-0526 .. **Evangelist,** Gregg R '91 -272 Taylor -Centerprt 11721
(212) 527-1000 .. **Evangelista,** Angela M '92 (Jones HC&B PC) -1 Bttry Pk Plz -NY 10004
(212) 425-9300 .. **Evangelista,** Dominick F '93 (Bressler A&R,PC) -17 State -NY 10004
(212) 480-4200 .. **Evangelista,** Laura E '93 Cnsl Naush Hogan & Murray,Inc -180 Maiden Ln -NY 10038 **Fx:**480-2920
(845) 942-4226 .. **Evangelista,** Margret Jonsson '97 -54 Wilderness Dr -Stony Pnt 10980
(518) 436-1850 .. **Evangelista,** Paul J '95 %Fed Pub Def -39 N Pearl -Albany 12207 **Fx:**436-1780
(718) 923-4206 .. **Evangelista,** Peter '88 %OTDA Fair Hearings -14 Boerum Pl -Brklyn 11201
(516) 742-1444 .. **Evangelou,** Evelyn M '05 %Wagner D&L,PC -227 Mineola Blvd -Mineola 11501
(718) 286-6000 .. **Evangelou,** James W '81 %DA -125-01 Qns Blvd -Kew Gdns 11415
(716) 849-8900 .. **Evanko,** Ann E '80 (Hurwitz & F,PC) -1300 Lbrty Bldg -Buffalo 14202
(631) 734-7600 .. **Evanko,** Linda A '82 -3870 Stillwtr Av -Cutchogue 11935
(212) 593-6700 .. **Evans,** Amelia R '09 %Aaronson RF&D,LLP -757 3rd Av -NY 10017
(716) 856-5500 .. **Evans,** Anne C '86 (Damon M LLP) -200 Delaware Av -Buffalo 14202
(212) 622-5593 .. **Evans,** Arnold B '98 JP Morgan Chase & Co -277 Park Av -NY 10172
(212) 715-9100 .. **Evans,** Barry '65 Cnsl Kramer LN&F,LLP -1177 Av of Amer -NY 10036
(212) 527-8400 .. **Evans,** Chandler B '05 Cnsl Oak Hill Cptl Ptnrs -65 E 55th -NY 10022 **Fx:**527-8450
(212) 318-6000 .. **Evans,** Christopher M '03 %Paul HJ&W LLP -75 E 55th -NY 10022
(212) 218-5500 .. **Evans,** Danl J '03 %Seyfarth S LLP -620 8th Av -NY 10018
(212) 367-1000 .. **Evans,** Danl L '05 GMHC,Inc -119 W 24th -NY 10011 **Fx:**367-1305
(518) 272-6565 .. **Evans,** David L '79 Martin SWD&J -279 River Bx1530 -Troy 12181
(716) 822-7978 .. **Evans,** David P '56 -2732 Seneca Bx527 -W Seneca 14224 **Fx:**823-0006
(212) 558-4000 .. **Evans,** Douglas H '76 SpclCnsl Sullivan & C LLP -125 Broad -NY 10004
(315) 472-6511 .. **Evans,** Elizabeth A '09 %Davies Law Firm,PC -210 E Fayette -Syracuse 13202 **Fx:**475-9539
(212) 326-3939 .. **Evans,** Elizabeth H '91 (Jones D) -222 E 41st -NY 10017
(212) 586-8286 .. **Evans,** Elliot L '69 -462 7th Av -NY 10018 **Fx:**697-4512
(585) 241-5999 .. **Evans & Fox LLP** -95 Allens Crk Rd -Rchstr 14618 **Fx:**241-5989
(212) 513-7788 .. **Evans,** George S Jr. '89 %Ahmuty D&M -123 William -NY 10038
(518) 346-6211 .. **Evans,** Gerald J '69 %Community Cllg -78 Wshngtn Av -Schnctdy 12305 **Fx:**346-0379
(212) 752-5200 .. **Evans,** Hilary '92 %Greene Levin Snyder LLC -150 E 58th -NY 10155
(917) 699-5033 .. **Evans,** Iona M '05 -509 E 12th -NY 10009
(516) 487-4459 .. **Evans,** Jack '92 -46 Grace Av -Gt Neck 11021 **Fx:**829-1782
(516) 292-8100 .. **Evans,** Jack B Jr. '09 %Nassau/Sfflk Law Srv -1 Helen Keller Way -Hempstd 11550 **Fx:**292-6529
(315) 474-6077 .. **Evans,** James F III '81 %R Rothman PC -120 E Wshngtn -Syracuse 13202 **Fx:**474-0126
(315) 425-2700 .. **Evans,** James P '96 (Hiscock & B,LLP) -One Park Pl -Syracuse 13202
(716) 630-0555 .. **Evans,** Jason J '98 JJ Evans,PC -5355 Main -Williamsvll 14221 **Fx:**630-0553
(212) 326-2000 .. **Evans,** Jennifer Merzon '03 Cnsl O'Melveny & M LLP -7 Times Sq -NY 10036
(718) 250-0400 .. **Evans,** Joel S '00 %R Tusa -1 MetroTech Ctr -Brklyn 11201 **Fx:**250-0591
(212) 238-3361 .. **Evans,** John J '96 %Mncpl Crdt Union -22 Crtlandt -NY 10007 **Fx:**479-2975
(212) 344-3900 .. **Evans,** John T '74 (Belair & E LLP) -61 Bway -NY 10006
(212) 259-8000 .. **Evans,** Jonathan D S '10 %Dewey & L LLP -1301 Av of Amer -NY 10019
(212) 490-3000 .. **Evans,** Julie R '87 (Wilson EME&D LLP) -150 E 42nd -NY 10017
(212) 613-2000 .. **Evans,** Kevin S '09 Cnsl Gibbons PC -1 Penn Plz -NY 10119
(212) 903-9000 .. **Evans,** Kimberly A '04 %Linklaters -1345 Av of Amer -NY 10105
(718) 262-7100 .. **Evans,** Lance P '84 %Civil Ct -89-17 Sutphin Blvd -Jamaica 11435 **Fx:**262-7107
(718) 442-4516 .. **Evans,** Leslie S '80 -56 DeHart Av -Staten Isl 10303
(212) 428-2150 .. **Evans,** Lisa M '86 %OCA -25 Beaver -NY 10004 **Fx:**428-2155
(212) 592-1400 .. **Evans,** Louis A '81 Cnsl Herrick,F LLP -2 Park Av -NY 10016
(631) 788-7101 .. **Evans,** Louisa P '85 -Bx546 -Fishers Isl 06390
(716) 679-7200 .. **Evans,** Lydia Vaughn '94 (Evans & E) -131 Temple -Fredonia 14063
(212) 471-8543 .. **Evans,** Martin '49 OfCnsl Herzfeld & R,PC -125 Broad -NY 10004
(212) 909-6000 .. **Evans,** Martin F '73 (Debevoise & P LLP) -919 3rd Av -NY 10022
(718) 875-2191 .. **Evans,** Matthew J '62 -26 Court -Brklyn 11242 **Fx:**797-0558
(212) 465-6000 .. **Evans,** Mechelle '94 %Madison Sq Grdn,LP -2 Penn Plz -NY 10121 **Fx:**465-6011
(212) 815-1120 .. **Evans,** Michele E '90 %DC 37 MELS -125 Barclay -NY 10007 **Fx:**815-1343
(212) 468-8000 .. **Evans,** Nilene R '80 OfCnsl Morrison & F LLP -1290 Av of Amer -NY 10104
(212) 755-7500 .. **Evans,** Pamela D '98 %Marcus R&D LLP -488 Mad Av -NY 10022
(315) 782-3600 .. **Evans,** Patrick L '75 (Evans Law Firm) -531 Wshngtn -Watertwn 13601 **Fx:**782-4854
(212) 504-6000 .. **Evans,** Patrick R '10 %Cadwalader W&T LLP -1 World Fncl Ctr -NY 10281
(212) 292-4412 .. **Evans,** Patti E '87 (Isaacs & E,LLP) -521 5th Av -NY 10175
(212) 593-1700 .. **Evans,** Paul C '07 %Kaplan L LLP -1065 Av of Amer -NY 10018
(315) 853-4436 .. **Evans,** Philip L '53 (Felt E,LLP) -4-6 N Park Row -Clinton 13323
(585) 241-5999 .. **Evans,** Richd J '73 (Evans & F LLP) -95 Allens Crk Rd -Rchstr 14618
(585) 238-2000 .. **Evans,** Richd J Jr. '87 %Phillips L LLP -1400 First Fed Plz -Rchstr 14614
(212) 848-8830 .. **Evans,** Robt III '91 (Shearman & S LLP) -599 Lex Av -NY 10022
(212) 234-6804 .. **Evans,** Robt A Jr. '04 (RA Evans Jr PC) -32 Edgecombe Av -NY 10030 **Fx:**(646) 514-0755
(315) 474-3986 .. **Evans,** Robt G Jr. '61 -135 Dewitt -Syracuse 13203
(718) 834-0087 .. **Evans,** Robt S '75 -26 Court -Brklyn 11242
(212) 541-7800 .. **Evans,** Roger K '74 %Planned Parenthood -434 W 33rd -NY 10001 **Fx:**868-4677
(646) 257-4751 .. **Evans,** Samantha H '07 %Bowles C&C LLP -54 W 21st -NY 10010 **Fx:**(866) 844-8305
(212) 599-0900 .. **Evans,** Sarah B '05 %Bower & L,PC -261 Mad Av -NY 10016
(212) 753-2500 .. **Evans,** Sebastian '02 Hoyos Inc -10 E 53rd -NY 10022
(631) 761-7000 .. **Evans,** Stacy J '92 %Touro Cllg Law Ctr -225 Eastvw Dr -Central Islip 11722
(716) 679-7200 .. **Evans,** Sue Montgomery '85 (Evans & E) -131 Temple -Fredonia 14063
(212) 484-1755 .. **Evans,** Suzan I '82 %Rock & Roll Hll Fame -1290 Av of Amer -NY 10104
(716) 853-9555 .. **Evans,** Tara S '08 Cntr for Community Alternatives -115 E Jffrsn -Syracuse 13202 **Fx:**853-3219
(718) 260-8700 .. **Evans,** Terrell C '84 %Admin Children's Srvcs -345 Adams -Brklyn 11201
(516) 542-5900 .. **Evans,** Thos M '88 (Congdon FORDT&F) -333 Earle Ovngton Blvd -Uniondale 11553
(315) 218-8000 .. **Evans,** Thos S '71 (Bond S&K,PLLC) -1 Lincoln Ctr -Syracuse 13202
(315) 425-9000 .. **Evans,** Timothy D '04 %Marjama MB&S LLP -250 S Clinton -Syracuse 13202
(646) 386-5330 .. **Evans,** Vanessa M '94 %Family Ct -60 Lafayette -NY 10013
(716) 487-2657 .. **Evans,** Wm A '72 %Sthrn Tier/Pizza Hut -4th &Pine Bldg -Jamestwn 14701 **Fx:**664-1849
(212) 708-1800 .. **Evans,** Wm R '75 (Ladas & P) -26 W 61st -NY 10023
(212) 592-1400 .. **Evansburg,** Amanda R '03 %Herrick,F LLP -2 Park Av -NY 10016
(212) 374-5110 .. **Evans Srinivasan,** LaVerne '90 %NYC Dept Educ -52 Chmbrs -NY 10007
(212) 806-5400 .. **Evanusa,** Michel S '79 (Stroock &S&L LLP) -180 Maiden Ln -NY 10038
(212) 858-1000 .. **Evarts,** Wm M Jr. '53 SrCnsl Pillsbury WSP LLP -1540 Bway -NY 10036
(212) 264-0300 .. **Eveillard,** Audrey '95 %NLRB -26 Fed Plz -NY 10278 **Fx:**264-8427
(212) 474-1000 .. **Even,** Yonatan '05 %Cravath S&M LLP -825 8th Av -NY 10019
(212) 489-6800 .. **Evenhaim,** Hagit '00 DAG Media,Inc -192 Lex Av -NY 10016
(212) 659-7300 .. **Even-Shoshan,** Avital E '10 %Haynes & B,LLP -1221 Av of Amer -NY 10020
(212) 254-1111 .. **Evenson,** Debra M '77 OfCnsl Rabinowitz BSK&L,PC -111 Bway -NY 10006
(212) 637-2556 .. **Everdell,** Christian R '02 %US Atty -1 St Andrews Plz -NY 10007
(212) 577-2523 .. **Everett,** Abigail C '80 %Ctr for Applt Litigation -74 Trinity Pl -NY 10006 **Fx:**577-2535
(212) 664-2540 .. **Everett,** Alicia Glekas '94 %NBC -30 Rckfllr Plz -NY 10112
(212) 530-5000 .. **Everett,** Andrew H II '09 %Milbank TH&M LLP -1 Chase Manh Plz -NY 10005
(516) 294-5433 .. **Everett,** Catherine Ruggieri '03 %Ahmuty D&M -200 IU Willets Rd -Albertson 11507
(914) 777-1400 .. **Everett,** David F '77 (D Everett,PC) -100 Mamaroneck Av -Mamaroneck 10543
(518) 487-7600 .. **Everett,** David R '92 (Whiteman O&H LLP) -1 Commerce Plz -Albany 12260
(212) 480-5284 .. **Everett,** James W Jr. '85 %Insurance Dept -25 Beaver -NY 10004 **Fx:**480-5272
(212) 434-0100 .. **Everett,** Mark A '83 (Litchfield C LLP) -420 Lex Av -NY 10170
(518) 793-6611 .. **Everhart,** Leah A '04 (Miller MS&H,LLC) -451 Glen Bx765 -Glens Fls 12801
(716) 856-4000 .. **Everhart,** Ryan L '99 (Hodgson R LLP) -140 Pearl -Buffalo 14202
(518) 591-5232 .. **Everitt,** Gayle Ann '90 %NYS ORPTS -WA Harriman State Campus -Albany 12227 **Fx:**474-3657
(212) 344-5680 .. **Evers,** Garrett D '05 (Thompson H LLP) -335 Mad Av -NY 10017
(212) 554-1234 .. **Evers,** Wm J '03 AXA Financial Inc -1290 Av of Amer -NY 10104 **Fx:**707-3963
(212) 678-7064 .. **Eversley,** Thos W '68 -382 Cntrl Pk W -NY 10025
(212) 888-7500 .. **Every,** Glenn R '87 %Etkin & Co -14 E 60th -NY 10022
(212) 436-1108 .. **Evola,** Maura J '84 %IRS -290 Bway -NY 10007
(718) 875-0903 .. **Evseroff,** Jacob R '49 (Evseroff & S) -186 Joralemon -Brklyn 11201
(718) 875-0903 .. **Evseroff & Sonenshine** -186 Joralemon -Brklyn 11201
(212) 506-5000 .. **Ewald,** John L '04 %Orrick H&S LLP -51 W 52nd -NY 10019
(212) 761-4584 .. **Ewald,** Katharine W '98 Morgan Stanley -1585 Bway -NY 10036 **Fx:**761-0086
(631) 852-2500 .. **Ewald,** Robt F '80 %DA -200 Center Dr -Rvrhead 11901 **Fx:**852-1769
(631) 547-1500 .. **Ewall,** Laura E '89 %Ewall & E -946 Park Av -Huntngtn 11743 **Fx:**424-6435
(631) 547-1500 .. **Ewall,** Steven B '84 (Ewall & E) -946 Park Av -Huntngtn 11743 **Fx:**424-6435
(212) 859-8000 .. **Ewan,** Christopher '00 (Fried FHS&J LLP) -1 NY Plz -NY 10004
(212) 728-8000 .. **Ewen,** Sean M '05 %Willkie F&G LLP -787 7th Av -NY 10019
(212) 838-8400 .. **Ewenstein,** Jacqueline D '00 Andrew W Mellon Fndtn -140 E 62nd -NY 10065
(212) 669-0600 .. **Ewig,** Caspar F '68 %Hill R LLP -45 Bway -NY 10006

(212) 792-4327 .. **Ewing,** Anthony P '96 Logos Consulting Grp -245 Park Av -NY 10167
(212) 415-9200 .. **Ewing,** Bruce R '93 (Dorsey & W LLP) -250 Park Av -NY 10177
(716) 645-2770 .. **Ewing,** Chas P '84 %SUNY Buffalo Lw Schl -O'Brian Hall -Buffalo 14260 **Fx:**645-5968
(315) 443-9582 .. **Ewing,** Gregory P '06 %Syracuse Univ Cllg of Law -Wht Hall -Syracuse 13244 **Fx:**443-4213
(212) 878-4082 .. **Ewing,** Keith F '79 Mitsui & Co -200 Park Av -NY 10166
(212) 693-9464 .. **Ewing,** Wm J '83 (WJ Ewing,PC) -1650 Bway -NY 10019
(212) 458-1481 .. **Exelbert,** Robt P '89 %AIG -175 Water -NY 10038 **Fx:**458-1600
(315) 379-0857 .. **Exoo,** Diane J '90 -36 State Bx397 -Canton 13617 **Fx:**379-9741
(718) 487-1300 .. **Exter,** Hillary J '80 %Leg Srvcs Corp A -80 Jamaica Av -Brklyn 11207 **Fx:**342-1780
(631) 232-2580 .. **Exum,** Curtis R '94 -1770 Motor Pkwy -Hauppauge 11749
(716) 856-4000 .. **Eydt,** George J '97 (Hodgson R LLP) -140 Pearl -Buffalo 14202
(646) 808-4200 .. **Eydt,** Madeline M '97 NY Mediate LLC -PO Bx 20179 -NY 10014
(212) 921-0069 .. **Eyerman,** John R '90 -225 Bway -NY 10007 **Fx:**354-0611
(212) 819-8200 .. **Eyers,** Patrick J '06 %White & C LLP -1155 Av of Amer -NY 10036
(212) 792-8484 .. **Eyland,** Jessica '96 %Stern T&B LLP -380 Lex Av -NY 10168
(315) 386-4586 .. **Eyler,** Cynthia A '88 %Leg Aid -17 Hodskin Bx648 -Canton 13617 **Fx:**386-2868
(212) 655-1043 .. **Eylward,** Susan M '07 Tower Grp Co -120 Bway -NY 10271
(877) 222-1814 .. **Eyma,** Leslie A Jr. '04 %B Rothenberg -100 Duffy Av -Hicksvll 11801 **Fx:**(866) 894-2182
(315) 673-3933 .. **Eysman,** Harvey A '64 -4547 NW Townline Rd -Marcellus 13108 **Fx:**673-0103
(212) 691-1309 .. **Eyster,** Deametrice '00 -332 Bleecker -NY 10014 **Fx:**691-8361
(718) 780-7936 .. **Eyster,** Mary Jo '79 %Bklyn Law Schl -250 Joralemon -Brklyn 11201 **Fx:**780-0393
(607) 778-2685 .. **Eytina,** Kuredin V '89 %Dept Soc Srvcs -36-42 Main -Bnghmtn 13905 **Fx:**778-2710
(914) 834-5116 .. **Ezbitski,** Deborah A '84 -208 Mulberry Ln -Larchmnt 10538 **Fx:**833-1778
(212) 735-8600 .. **Ezcurra,** Joaquin J '02 %Morrison C LLP -909 3rd Av -NY 10022
(718) 643-8800 .. **Eze,** Chidi A '03 -255 Lvngstn Av -Brklyn 11217
(212) 312-7214 .. **Eze,** Uzoma A '06 -11 Bway -NY 10004
(631) 232-2400 .. **Ezechi,** Antonia U '95 %Nassau/Sfflk Law Srv -1757 Vets Hwy -Islandia 11749 **Fx:**232-2489
(718) 923-4206 .. **Ezediaro,** Angel Uche '98 %OTDA Fair Hearings -14 Boerum Pl -Brklyn 11201
(718) 441-2000 .. **Ezekiel,** Jillian B '01 New Homestead Home for Adults -8245 Grenfell -Kew Gdns 11415
(212) 548-0659 .. **Ezer,** Tamar G '02 Open Society Institute -400 W 59th -NY 10019
(917) 216-2446 .. **Ezersky,** Wm M '79 -125-10 Qns Blvd -Kew Gdns 11415
(518) 434-9807 .. **Ezick,** Randall J '75 OfCnsl D'Agostino KM&C,PC -16 Sage Estate -Menands 12204
(631) 761-7000 .. **Ezor,** Jonathan I '93 Touro Cllg Law Ctr -225 Eastvw Dr -Central Islip 11722
(516) 536-6290 .. **Ezra,** Joel S '69 -95 Seaman Av -Rockvll Ctr 11570 **Fx:**(888) 285-4129
(516) 747-5566 .. **Ezratty Ezratty & Levine** -80 E Old Cntry Rd -Mineola 11501 **Fx:**873-1451
(516) 747-5566 .. **Ezratty,** Ira S '85 (Ezratty E&L) -80 E Old Cntry Rd -Mineola 11501
(516) 747-5566 .. **Ezratty,** Jaime D '89 (Ezratty E&L) -80 E Old Cntry Rd -Mineola 11501
(212) 737-1247 .. **Ezri,** Sandra '04 Alternative Advisory Srvcs -900 Park Av -NY 10075
(212) 326-2000 .. **Ezring,** Gregory A '91 (O'Melveny & M LLP) -7 Times Sq -NY 10036
(212) 906-1200 .. **Ezring,** Jennifer Buczek '99 (Latham & W) -885 3rd Av -NY 10022
(212) 440-2553 .. **Faas,** Jennifer A '00 CNA -40 Wall -NY 10005
(212) 957-9600 .. **Fabbri,** Roberta '05 %Gianni OG & Prtnrs -75 Rckfllr Plz -NY 10019
(212) 351-4000 .. **Fabens,** Andrew L IV '01 (Gibson D&C LLP) -200 Park Av -NY 10166
(516) 570-0685 .. **Faber,** Adam E '98 -80 Cutter Mill Rd -Gt Neck 11021 **Fx:**908-4170
(631) 665-3400 .. **Faber,** Alan G '80 %Siben & S,LLP -90 E Main Bx149P -Bay Shr 11706
(516) 486-4640 .. **Faber,** David W '93 (Cherry E&K,LLP) -1 Old Cntry Rd -Carle Pl 11514
(516) 677-9660 .. **Faber,** Glen S '88 %Faber & T -180 Froehlich Farm Blvd -Woodbury 11797
(516) 484-4311 .. **Faber,** Janet R '86 -18 Oak Ln -Roslyn Hts 11577
(914) 241-3680 .. **Faber,** Jill F '06 (Frishman & F) -83 S Bedford Rd -Mt Kisco 10549 **Fx:**241-3681
(212) 455-2000 .. **Faber,** Joshua J '09 %Simpson T&B LLP -425 Lex Av -NY 10017
(585) 427-5400 .. **Faber,** Louis '78 %Xerox -100 Clinton Av S -Rchstr 14644
(212) 999-5800 .. **Faber,** Michl R '09 (Wilson SG&R) -1301 Av of Americas -NY 10019
(516) 526-2456 .. **Faber,** Nan Geist '81 (NG Faber,PC) -996 Dartmth Ln -Woodmere 11598 **Fx:**295-2974
(212) 521-4350 .. **Faber,** Norman L '67 -590 Mad Av -NY 10022 **Fx:**489-8167
(212) 547-5400 .. **Faber,** Peter L '64 (McDermott W&E LLP) -340 Mad Av -NY 10173
(212) 382-0700 .. **Faber,** Robt C '66 (Ostrolenk FG&S,LLP) -1180 Av of Amer -NY 10036
(516) 677-9660 .. **Faber & Troy** -180 Froehlich Farm Blvd -Woodbury 11797
(718) 250-2000 .. **Fabi,** Teresa '86 %DA -350 Jay -Brklyn 11201 **Fx:**250-2314
(917) 640-1654 .. **Fabian,** Andrew B '01 Sorcery -79 5th Av -NY 10003
(212) 264-6104 .. **Fabian,** Elaine A '98 DHS -26 Fed Plz -NY 10278
(212) 940-3071 .. **Fabian,** James '79 (Nixon P LLP) -437 Mad Av -NY 10022
(212) 644-8096 .. **Fabian,** Lawr E '70 -437 5th Av -NY 10016 **Fx:**644-4217
(718) 397-7700 .. **Fabian,** Manuel '83 -37-31 76th -Jcksn Hts 11372
(212) 362-8769 .. **Fabian,** Marie E '02 Rodeph Sholom Schl -10 W 84th -NY 10024
(212) 265-6888 .. **Fabian,** Marie-Laurence '87 OfCnsl Porzio B&N,PC -156 W 56th -NY 10019
(212) 788-0906 .. **Fabian,** Shawn D '07 %Law Dept -100 Church -NY 10007 **Fx:**788-0367
(212) 788-0079 .. **Fabian,** Sosimo J '05 %Law Dept -100 Church -NY 10007 **Fx:**788-0367
(212) 644-4420 .. **Fabiani Cohen & Hall, LLP** -570 Lex Av -NY 10022 **Fx:**207-8182
(347) 410-5332 .. **Fabiani,** John F '08 (Segarra & F) -540 Prsdnt -Brklyn 11215 **Fx:**(562) 286-5202
(212) 644-4420 .. **Fabiani,** John V Jr. '77 (Fabiani C&H,LLP) -570 Lex Av -NY 10022
(212) 906-1200 .. **Fabiani,** Jos S '08 %Latham & W -885 3rd Av -NY 10022
(516) 741-3900 .. **Fabiano,** Angela '93 -170 Old Cntry Rd -Mineola 11501 **Fx:**741-3383
(212) 577-3688 .. **Fabiano,** Denise M '94 %Leg Aid -199 Water -NY 10038 **Fx:**509-8431
(315) 453-9535 .. **Fabiano,** Francesco '88 Fabiano & Assoc,PC -1035 7th N -Liverpool 13088 **Fx:**461-4711
(914) 323-7000 .. **Fabiaschi,** Meredith L '09 %Wilson EME&D LLP -3 Gannett Dr -White Plns 10604
(315) 428-2231 .. **Fabic,** M Margaret '82 United Way-Central NY,Inc -Bx2129 -Syracuse 13220
(914) 241-2400 .. **Fabriani,** Sylvia '82 (Novenstern F&G) -69 S Bedford Rd -Mt Kisco 10549
(212) 277-6500 .. **Fabricant,** Alfred R '81 (Dickstein S LLP) -1633 Bway -NY 10019
(516) 621-9000 .. **Fabricant,** Kenneth L '95 Fabricant & Fabricant,Inc -1251 Old Nrthrn Blvd -Roslyn 11576
(845) 294-7944 .. **Fabricant Lipman & Frishberg, PLLC** -1 Harriman Sq Bx60 -Goshen 10924 **Fx:**294-7889
(718) 838-7878 .. **Fabricant,** M Chris '98 Bronx Defenders -860 Crtlandt Av -Bronx 10451 **Fx:**665-0100
(212) 997-7776 .. **Fabricant,** Peter J '69 -36 W 44th -NY 10036 **Fx:**704-9992
(212) 679-8080 .. **Fabricant,** Richd '54 (Wohl LSF&D,PC) -9 E 40th -NY 10016
(516) 621-9000 .. **Fabricant,** Robt S '95 Fabricant & Fabricant,Inc -1251 Old Nrthrn Blvd -Roslyn 11576
(212) 412-9500 .. **Fabrikant,** Erica '06 %Flemming ZWZ LLP -1 Lbrty Plz -NY 10006
(212) 697-8601 .. **Fabrikant,** Stacey G '87 %Kipp-Stawski Mgt Grp -565 5th Av -NY 10017 **Fx:**697-9439
(845) 359-0606 .. **Fabrizio,** Emily R '94 MHLS -140 Old Orangebrg Rd -Orangebrg 10962 **Fx:**365-1773
(607) 771-1984 .. **Fabrizio,** Jo A '84 -84 Court -Bnghmtn 13901 **Fx:**722-2842
(212) 703-3910 .. **Fabrizio,** Wm R '70 Wells Fargo Trade Cptl Srvcs,Inc -119 W 40th -NY 10018 **Fx:**703-3520
(212) 836-8000 .. **Faccini,** Kathleen M '78 Cnsl Kaye S LLP -425 Park Av -NY 10022
(718) 990-1832 .. **Facciolo,** Francis J III '84 %St John's Law Schl -8000 Utopia Pkwy -Jamaica 11439 **Fx:**591-1855
(212) 637-2522 .. **Facciponti,** Jos P '02 US Atty -1 St Andrews Plz -NY 10007
(212) 609-6800 .. **Faccone,** Alitia '98 (McCarter & E,LLP) -245 Park Av -NY 10167
(716) 633-6500 .. **Facer-Kreidler,** Susan J '88 %W Moran & Assoc,PC -6500 Main -Williamsvll 14221 **Fx:**633-3370
(212) 598-5900 .. **Facher,** Catania T '04 %Alonso A&K PC -920 Bway -NY 10010
(212) 504-6000 .. **Facher,** Jared L '05 %Cadwalader W&T LLP -1 World Fncl Ctr -NY 10281
(718) 658-0500 .. **Facio-Lince,** Vanessa M '07 %Law Dept -151-20 Jamaica Av -Jamaica 11432 **Fx:**658-4025
(212) 632-1524 .. **Fackler,** Benjamin D '99 %Lazard Freres -30 Rckfllr Plz -NY 10112 **Fx:**632-6060
(212) 351-4000 .. **Fackler,** Stephen W '04 (Gibson D&C LLP) -200 Park Av -NY 10166
(718) 494-6096 .. **Factor,** Harlene Lachman '94 -514 Golfvw Ct -Staten Isl 10314 **Fx:**370-1302
(212) 225-2000 .. **Factor,** Jason R '98 (Cleary GS&H) -1 Lbrty Plz -NY 10006
(212) 267-9090 .. **Factor,** Jonathan D '77 %S Salles -225 Bway -NY 10007 **Fx:**267-9175
(631) 493-9800 .. **Factor,** Lilia '04 %F Eisenbud -6165 Jericho Tpk -Commack 11725 **Fx:**493-9806
(212) 878-8000 .. **Fad,** Regan D '03 %Clifford C LLP -31 W 52nd -NY 10019
(516) 997-5553 .. **Faden,** Mark S '76 (Faden & G) -576 Salisbury Pk Dr -Westbury 11590
(212) 790-4500 .. **Faden,** Neil S '95 (Manatt P&P,LLP) -7 Times Sq -NY 10036
(212) 969-3000 .. **Fader,** Bruce E '75 (Proskauer R LLP) -1585 Bway -NY 10036
(212) 308-4411 .. **Fader,** Eric D '84 Cnsl Edwards AP&D LLP -750 Lex Av -NY 10022
(212) 259-6336 .. **Fader,** Marc '02 James Mintz Grp -32 Av of Amer -NY 10013
(516) 437-9500 .. **Fader,** Robt S '81 (R Fader,PC) -99 Tulip Av -Floral Pk 11001 **Fx:**437-9534
(212) 455-2000 .. **Fadil,** Adeeb R '86 SrCnsl Simpson T&B LLP -425 Lex Av -NY 10017
(212) 425-1999 .. **Faegenburg,** Glenn '92 (Edelsteins F&B,LLP) -61 Bway -NY 10006
(845) 627-3990 .. **Faerber,** Jos '71 -55 Old Tpk Rd -Nanuet 10954
(212) 728-8000 .. **Faerstein,** Brian R '06 %Willkie F&G LLP -787 7th Av -NY 10019
(718) 364-4000 .. **Fafinski,** Donna Ann '89 (MacAluso & F,PC) -1 Fordham Plz -Bronx 10458 **Fx:**364-6330
(315) 797-6990 .. **Faga,** Antonio J '77 -23 Oxford Rd -New Hartfrd 13413 **Fx:**735-7924
(585) 987-2800 .. **Faga,** Enzo A '59 OfCnsl Woods OG LLP -2 State -Rchstr 14614
(914) 592-0601 .. **Faga,** Kevin B '94 (Faga S LLP) -399 Knollwood Rd -White Plns 10603
(914) 592-0601 .. **Faga Savino LLP** -399 Knollwood Rd -White Plns 10603 **Fx:**358-1381
(716) 664-5614 .. **Fagan,** Chas E '74 -606 Htl Jmstwn Ofc Bldg -Jamestwn 14701 **Fx:**664-2338
(631) 853-6322 .. **Fagan,** James F Jr. '85 Hon H Berler -Bx9070 -Central Islip 11722 **Fx:**853-6320
(845) 225-8404 .. **Fagan,** Mary K '98 (Daniels & P,LLP) -102 Gleneida Av -Carmel 10512
(718) 351-1837 .. **Fagan,** Michl F '93 -251 Titus Av -Staten Isl 10306
(585) 232-3730 .. **Fagan,** Michelle L '06 %Chamberlain D LLP -1600 Crssrds Bldg -Rchstr 14614
(212) 458-1461 .. **Fagan,** Terri Green '85 %AIG -175 Water -NY 10038
(315) 866-2855 .. **Fagan-Polidori,** Cissy '80 -109 Park Av Bx745 -Herkimer 13350 **Fx:**866-2994
(315) 474-1273 .. **Fagelman,** Elissa Katz '99 %Ticor Title Insurance -201 E Jffrsn -Syracuse 13202 **Fx:**474-4281
(212) 736-8977 .. **Fagen,** Brian T '03 Prestige Toy -240 W 35th -NY 10001
(212) 373-3000 .. **Fagen,** Leslie G '75 (Paul WRW&G LLP) -1285 Av of Amer -NY 10019
(212) 603-6300 .. **Fagen,** Shari J '93 (Robinson BLGG&G PC) -875 3rd Av -NY 10022
(212) 268-2128 .. **Fagenson,** Lawr M '77 (Fagenson & P) -450 7th Av -NY 10123
(212) 268-2128 .. **Fagenson & Puglisi** -450 7th Av -NY 10123 **Fx:**268-2127
(516) 794-7340 .. **Fager & Amsler, LLP** -90 Merrick Av -E Meadow 11554 **Fx:**794-8114

(518) 786-2880 .. **Fager & Amsler, LLP** -8 British Amer Blvd -Latham 12110 **Fx:**782-7445
(315) 428-1380 .. **Fager & Amsler, LLP** -2 Clinton Sq -Syracuse 13202 **Fx:**428-0082
(212) 889-2498 .. **Fager & Amsler, LLP** -2 Park Av -NY 10016 **Fx:**779-4782
(212) 889-2498 .. **Fager,** Donald J '56 (Fager & A,LLP) -2 Park Av -NY 10016
(212) 918-3000 .. **Fagerstrom,** Donna G '90 Hogan L LLP -875 3rd Av -NY 10022
(212) 935-7800 .. **Fagerstrom,** Karen R '84 Babcock & Brown,Inc -600 Lex Av -NY 10022 **Fx:**935-8949
(212) 969-3000 .. **Fagin,** Allen I '76 (Proskauer R LLP) -1585 Bway -NY 10036
(212) 421-9630 .. **Fagin,** Marc J '02 Smythe Masterson & Judd -230 Park Av -NY 10169 **Fx:**421-9665
(212) 735-3000 .. **Fagin,** Matthew B '04 %Skadden ASM&F LLP -4 Times Sq -NY 10036
(914) 684-0090 .. **Fagin,** Saml S '04 %Diserio MO&C LLP -50 Main -White Plns 10606
(212) 848-4000 .. **Fagiola,** Robt W '78 Cnsl Shearman & S LLP -599 Lex Av -NY 10022
(845) 638-6495 .. **Faherty,** M Teresa A '89 -20 S Main -New Cty 10956 **Fx:**634-4637
(718) 399-5920 .. **Fahey,** Annmarie '95 %Diocese Pension Ofc -75 Greene Av -Brklyn 11238
(716) 849-6500 .. **Fahey,** Colleen P '90 (Brown & T,LLC) -14 Lafayette Sq -Buffalo 14203
(716) 839-5480 .. **Fahey,** Jos P '92 -232 Lorfld Dr -Amherst 14226
(917) 454-1100 .. **Fahey,** Kathleen E '06 Police Dept -2 Lafayette -NY 10007
(315) 445-1500 .. **Fahey,** Lisa M '95 %TK Fahey -6519 Towpath Rd -E Syracuse 13057 **Fx:**445-1516
(212) 693-0085 .. **Fahey,** Lynn W L '71 %Appellate Advocates -2 Rector -NY 10006 **Fx:**693-0878
(315) 472-3522 .. **Fahey,** Mary J '82 -4736 Onondaga Blvd PMB 228 -Syracuse 13219
(914) 681-7175 .. **Fahey,** Michl '92 %Bartels & F LLP -925 Wstchstr Av -White Plns 10604
(212) 259-8000 .. **Fahey,** Ryan D '07 %Dewey & L LLP -1301 Av of Amer -NY 10019
(212) 969-3000 .. **Fahey,** Stacey O'Haire '89 %Proskauer R LLP -1585 Bway -NY 10036
(315) 445-1500 .. **Fahey,** T Kevin '72 TK Fahey -6519 Towpath Rd -E Syracuse 13057 **Fx:**445-1516
(212) 676-2800 .. **Fahie,** Lois E '92 Dept Hlth & Mental Hygiene -40 Worth -NY 10013
(914) 328-0366 .. **Fahrbach,** Cristina A '03 %Sapir & F LLP -399 Knollwood Rd -White Plns 10603
(607) 723-5341 .. **Fahrenz,** Richd E '71 SpclCnsl Hinman H&K,LLP -80 Exchange Bx5250 -Bnghmtn 13902
(212) 319-5351 .. **Fahringer,** Herald P '57 OfCnsl HP Fahringer PLLC -120 E 56th -NY 10022 **Fx:**319-6657
(212) 783-3991 .. **Fahs,** Jeffrey J '98 Citigroup Global Mrkts,Inc -485 Lex Av -NY 10017
(716) 631-0610 .. **Fahs,** Randy C '89 Northrop Grumman Corp -1740 Wehrle Dr -Williamsvll 14221 **Fx:**633-5190
(212) 732-2000 .. **Fahy,** Margaret H '98 (Cullen and D LLP) -44 Wall -NY 10005
(914) 633-7199 .. **Faier,** Joan '81 -1011 North Av -New Rchll 10804
(212) 388-3203 .. **Faige,** Jessica A '04 SEIU Local 32BJ -101 Av of Amer -NY 10013
(212) 310-8000 .. **Fail,** Garrett A '04 %Weil G&M LLP -767 5th Av -NY 10153
(212) 969-3000 .. **Failla,** John E '88 (Proskauer R LLP) -1585 Bway -NY 10036
(914) 946-1400 .. **Failla,** Jos B '99 %Vouté LM&C,LLP -170 Hmltn Av -White Plns 10601
(212) 637-2324 .. **Failla,** Katherine P '94 %US Atty -1 St Andrews Plz -NY 10007
(212) 309-1000 .. **Failla,** Susan S '96 (Hunton & W) -200 Park Av -NY 10166
(212) 732-8700 .. **Faillace,** Chas K '82 (McAloon & F,PC) -123 William -NY 10038
(212) 317-1200 .. **Faillace,** Michl A '84 (M Faillace & Assoc,PC) -110 E 59th -NY 10022
(631) 777-2330 .. **Faillace-Dillon,** Dawn C '01 %O'Connor OH&D,LLP -1 Huntngtn Quad -Melvll 11747
(315) 472-6388 .. **Failmezger & Liegel** -202 N Townsend -Syracuse 13203 **Fx:**472-6380
(315) 472-6388 .. **Failmezger,** Robt C '54 (Failmezger & L) -202 N Townsend -Syracuse 13203
(212) 310-8000 .. **Fain,** Courtney P '09 %Weil G&M LLP -767 5th Av -NY 10153
(212) 403-1000 .. **Fain,** Sebastian L '09 %Wachtell LR&K -51 W 52nd -NY 10019
(212) 456-6391 .. **Fain,** T Scott '84 %ABC -77 W 66th -NY 10023 **Fx:**456-6202
(212) 484-3900 .. **Fainberg,** Michl '06 %Arent F LLP -1675 Bway -NY 10019
(212) 756-2000 .. **Fainé,** Lindsay M '08 %Schulte R&Z LLP -919 3rd Av -NY 10022
(718) 840-5860 .. **Fainkich,** David '96 -407 Smith -Brklyn 11231 **Fx:**840-5863
(212) 412-7594 .. **Fainman,** Jessica L '04 Barclays Capital Inc -200 Park Av -NY 10166
(914) 253-8600 .. **Fair,** Andrew J '73 (Fair F&H,PC) -110 Corp Park Dr -White Plns 10604
(212) 966-6704 .. **Fair,** Andrew L '80 -401 Bway -NY 10013 **Fx:**343-0938
(631) 283-7551 .. **Fair,** Barbara M '83 -180 Towd Pnt Rd -Southampton 11968 **Fx:**283-5456
(914) 253-8600 .. **Fair,** David J '99 %Fair F&H,PC -110 Corp Park Dr -White Plns 10604
(914) 253-8600 .. **Fair Fitzgerald & Hershaft,PC** -110 Corp Park Dr -White Plns 10604 **Fx:**253-8610
(914) 995-3000 .. **Fair,** Jamie E '06 %DA -111 Martin Luther King Blvd -White Plns 10601 **Fx:**995-3363
(212) 596-9000 .. **Fairall,** Cameron S '03 %Ropes & G LLP -1211 Av of Amer -NY 10036
(212) 878-8000 .. **Fairbairn,** Daryl W '01 %Clifford C LLP -31 W 52nd -NY 10019
(845) 586-2070 .. **Fairbairn,** John R III '07 %Metnick,PC -835 Main Bx1011 -Margaretvll 12455 **Fx:**586-2815
(845) 338-0510 .. **Fairbanks,** Jonathan '78 (Zwiebel & F,LLP) -72 Maiden Ln Bx3907 -Kingston 12402
(518) 581-8600 .. **Fairbanks-Fletcher,** Elizabeth L '05 (Fairbanks-Fletcher,PLLC) -78 Church -Saratoga Spgs 12866 **Fx:**(888) 859-8140
(631) 321-5540 .. **Fairbrother,** Deborah Buttacy '90 -120 Beach Dr -W Islip 11795
(716) 373-4701 .. **Fairchild,** Kelly A '04 %Leg Srvcs -103 S Barry -Olean 14760 **Fx:**373-7771
(212) 238-2420 .. **Fairchild,** Lois M '94 UIA Bd -59 Maiden Ln -NY 10038 **Fx:**238-2451
(212) 407-4000 .. **Fairchild,** Steven R '06 %Loeb & L,LLP -345 Park Av -NY 10154
(718) 379-1937 .. **Fairclough,** Pamela M '94 -4239 Byron Av -Bronx 10466
(631) 853-4161 .. **Fairgrieve,** Tara A '06 %DA -N Cnty Cmplx Bldg 77 -Hauppauge 11788 **Fx:**853-4192
(212) 415-9200 .. **Fairhurst,** Douglas C '68 OfCnsl Dorsey & W LLP -250 Park Av -NY 10177
(212) 509-3456 .. **Fairley,** Matthew T '06 %McGivney & K,PC -80 Broad -NY 10004
(845) 562-9100 .. **Fairlie,** Darren H '06 Rider W&F,PC -655 Little Britain Rd -New Windsor 12553
(212) 592-1400 .. **Fairman,** Darlene B '90 Cnsl Herrick,F LLP -2 Park Av -NY 10016
(212) 849-7000 .. **Fairneny,** Laura L '09 %Quinn EU&S,LLP -51 Mad Av -NY 10010
(914) 285-9800 .. **Fairstein,** Guy R '70 -1 N Bway -White Plns 10601 **Fx:**285-9855
(212) 458-5663 .. **Fairweather,** Andrene V '09 Chartis -175 Water -NY 10038
(718) 629-5766 .. **Fairweather,** Julian N '98 (JN Fairweather & Assoc,PC) -114-12 178th Pl -Jamaica 11434
(646) 386-4520 .. **Faison,** Pamela D '90 %Criminal Ct -100 Centre -NY 10013
(518) 432-0599 .. **Faist,** Thos W '81 (Faist Govt Affrs Grp,LLC) -54 Willett -Albany 12210 **Fx:**449-2294
(312) 984-0000 .. **Fait,** Mary Jane '80 (Wolf HAF&H LLP) -270 Mad Av -NY 10016
(212) 619-3100 .. **Faizakoff,** Danl B '97 (D Faizakoff,PC) -750 3rd Av -NY 10017 **Fx:**(800) 728-3768
(716) 566-1300 .. **Faizer,** M Akram '01 %Hiscock & B,LLP -1100 M&T Ctr -Buffalo 14203
(212) 788-0970 .. **Fajans,** Anita '83 %Law Dept -100 Church -NY 10007 **Fx:**788-0367
(212) 635-6613 .. **Fajardo,** Aielleen P P '02 Bk of NY Mellon -1 Wall -NY 10286
(212) 404-7069 .. **Fajardo,** Eduardo A '98 (De Lotto & F LLP) -44 Wall -NY 10005
(212) 637-3132 .. **Fajardo,** Juan M '95 %EPA -290 Bway -NY 10007 **Fx:**637-3096
(718) 875-1300 .. **Fajardo,** Rossiya B '01 %Appllt Div 2nd Dept -45 Monroe Pl -Brklyn 11201 **Fx:**858-2446
(212) 880-6000 .. **Fajt,** Miroslav M '81 (Torys LLP) -237 Park Av -NY 10017
(845) 486-2110 .. **Fakhoury,** Linda D '05 %Cnty Atty -22 Market -Poughkeepsie 12601 **Fx:**486-2002
(845) 896-5200 .. **Fakhoury,** Michl A '99 MA Fakhoury,PC -804 US Hwy 9 -Fishkill 12524 **Fx:**896-4016
(212) 484-3900 .. **Fakler,** Paul M '99 (Arent F LLP) -1675 Bway -NY 10019
(516) 485-9025 .. **Fakuade,** Olugbenga A '98 (Fakuade & Assoc,PC) -510 Front -Hempstd 11550
(212) 310-8000 .. **Falabella,** Pablo '09 %Weil G&M LLP -767 5th Av -NY 10153
(516) 783-3176 .. **Falabella-Reich,** Laura A '98 -2101 Beech -Wantagh 11793 **Fx:**783-0229
(212) 262-2390 .. **Falanga,** Stephen V '01 (Connell F LLP) -888 7th Av -NY 10106
(516) 409-6200 .. **Falasco,** Gerilynn Fedrich '05 %Furey KWM&C,PC -2174 Jackson Av -Seafrd 11783
(631) 969-3100 .. **Falasco,** Todd C '05 %Frenkel LWW&G,LLP -20 W Main -Bay Shr 11706
(518) 452-5600 .. **Falati,** Shahrokh '09 %Heslin RF&M PC -5 Columbia Cir -Albany 12203
(212) 473-3000 .. **Falber,** Mitchell '81 ABC Carpet & Home -888 Bway -NY 10003 **Fx:**533-6359
(516) 794-4666 .. **Falbo,** Jos Jr. '79 -666 Old Cntry Rd -Gdn Cty 11530
(716) 565-2000 .. **Falbo,** Renee M '07 %Freid & K -17 Beresford Ct -Williamsvll 14221 **Fx:**565-2002
(914) 949-6996 .. **Falch,** Douglas W '96 (Penino & M,LLP) -180 E Post Rd -White Plns 10601
(212) 916-3445 .. **Falcigno,** Nisha Antony '91 %Lexis/Nexis -125 Park Av -NY 10017 **Fx:**309-8187
(718) 630-4549 .. **Falcigno,** Pat M '83 %Army Corps of Engineers -405 Gen Lee Av -Brklyn 11252
(212) 345-4343 .. **Falcinelli,** Carol A '92 %Marsh Inc -1166 Av of the America -NY 10036
(212) 566-4844 .. **Falco,** Dawn E '01 Dept of Bldgs -280 Bway -NY 10007
(914) 835-4862 .. **Falco,** Gerard A '82 -480 Mamaroneck Av -Harrison 10528 **Fx:**835-6800
(718) 353-9730 .. **Falco,** Lorraine P '92 (L Falco,PC) -42-40 Bell Blvd -Bayside 11361 **Fx:**661-3198
(315) 876-2265 .. **Falco,** Mark J '84 -5860 Bowman Rd -E Syracuse 13057
(718) 458-0085 .. **Falco,** Michl J '79 -69-64 Grand Av -Maspeth 11378 **Fx:**478-0609
(845) 298-2000 .. **Falcon,** Angel I '05 %Vergilis SRD&D,LLP -1136 Route 9 -Wappingers Fls 12590
(718) 694-3965 .. **Falcon,** Elias S '98 Transit Auth -130 Lvngstn -Brklyn 11201 **Fx:**694-5726
(914) 723-3919 .. **Falcon,** Raymond J Jr. '79 (Falcon & S PC) -14 Harwood Ct -Scarsdale 10583
(914) 723-3919 .. **Falcon & Singer PC** -14 Harwood Ct -Scarsdale 10583 **Fx:**723-1951
(516) 280-1325 .. **Falcone,** Anthony V '06 (A Falcone & Assoc,PC) -1225 Franklin Av -Gdn Cty 11530
(914) 592-1575 .. **Falcone,** Carl A '69 -399 Knollwood Rd -White Plns 10603
(212) 261-8000 .. **Falcone,** John P '90 (Mendes & M,LLP) -750 7th Av -NY 10019
(212) 408-5100 .. **Falcone,** Jos G '94 (Chadbourne & P LLP) -30 Rckfllr Plz -NY 10112
(516) 292-1717 .. **Falcone,** Leonard J '87 -58 Hilton Av -Hempstd 11550 **Fx:**489-1940
(212) 532-3850 .. **Falcone,** Lucille '76 (Menagh & F,PC) -386 Park Av S -NY 10016
(212) 373-3000 .. **Falcone,** Marc C '96 (Paul WRW&G LLP) -1285 Av of Amer -NY 10019
(718) 370-7030 .. **Falcone,** Marc J '98 %Amabile & E,PC -1000 South Av -Staten Isl 10314
(212) 818-9200 .. **Falcone,** Monica J '07 %Satterlee SB&B LLP -230 Park Av -NY 10169
(212) 758-0050 .. **Falcone,** Neil A '86 %Title Assoc -825 3rd Av -NY 10022 **Fx:**758-8223
(716) 845-6446 .. **Falcone,** Wm R '90 (Gleichenhaus M&F,PC) -43 Court -Buffalo 14202 **Fx:**845-6475
(516) 328-2300 .. **Falcone-Macleod,** Shannon '04 %Abrams FFEGF&E,LLP -1111 Marcus Av -Lk Success 11042
(212) 733-4330 .. **Falconer,** Kelly A '01 %Pfizer Inc -235 E 42nd -NY 10017
(516) 249-1342 .. **Falconetti,** Christopher M '03 %Grey & G,LLP -360 Main -Farmngdl 11735
(718) 260-8777 .. **Falda,** Nathaniel N '02 ACS -345 Adams -Brklyn 11201 **Fx:**260-8773
(631) 249-8200 .. **Faldetta,** Bridget T '05 %DePinto N & Assoc,LLP -445 Broadhllw Rd -Melvll 11747 **Fx:**249-8209
(718) 250-2000 .. **Faldich,** Mary '89 %DA -350 Jay -Brklyn 11201 **Fx:**250-2314
(718) 590-2000 .. **Faldman,** Nikki D '07 DA -198 E 161st -Bronx 10451 **Fx:**590-6477

(347) 401-9580 .. **Faleck,** Victor S '80 %Applt Term -141 Lvngstn -Brklyn 11201 **Fx:**(718) 643-7889
(212) 351-4000 .. **Falek,** Richd L '97 %Gibson D&C LLP -200 Park Av -NY 10166
(212) 859-8000 .. **Falevich,** Andrew '05 %Fried FHS&J LLP -1 NY Plz -NY 10004
(516) 294-8844 .. **Faley,** Joan M '84 OfCnsl L'Abbate BC&C,LLP -1001 Franklin Av -Gdn Cty 11530
(212) 766-1888 .. **Faley,** Kevin G '84 (Morris DA&F) -2 Rector -NY 10006
(315) 461-4277 .. **Falge,** Danl J '94 (Falge & M,PC) -3300 Vickery Rd -N Syracuse 13212
(315) 488-2018 .. **Falge,** John J '87 -1086 State Fair Blvd -Syracuse 13209
(315) 461-4277 .. **Falge & McLean,PC** -3300 Vickery Rd -N Syracuse 13212 **Fx:**461-4298
(212) 672-5781 .. **Falger,** Gabrielle U '86 %Bayerische Hypo & Vereinsbank Inc -150 E 42nd -NY 10017
(212) 422-0202 .. **Falgiani,** Jos F '90 SpclCnsl Sedgwick DM&A LLP -125 Broad -NY 10004
(315) 479-9000 .. **Falgiatano,** Chas L '02 (DeFrancisco & F) -121 E Water -Syracuse 13202 **Fx:**479-9300
(212) 721-0682 .. **Falick,** James '82 -136 W 75th -NY 10023
(212) 903-1789 .. **Falick,** Paul '69 %ICC -460 Park Av -NY 10022
(212) 373-3000 .. **Falik,** Reuven B '04 %Paul WRW&G LLP -1285 Av of Amer -NY 10019
(212) 269-1400 .. **Falis,** Melvyn J '65 (Gusrae KB&N PLLC) -120 Wall -NY 10005
(914) 629-4089 .. **Falk,** Andrew I '95 -21 Carolyn Way -Patterson 12563 **Fx:**(845) 878-3352
(212) 425-9300 .. **Falk,** Bennett '69 (Bressler A&R,PC) -17 State -NY 10004
(716) 284-7891 .. **Falk,** Clifford '86 (Falk & F) -445 3rd -Niagara Fls 14301
(716) 284-7891 .. **Falk,** Cynthia A '78 (Falk & F) -445 3rd -Niagara Fls 14301
(212) 381-7000 .. **Falk,** Edw '80 (Sabin B&G LLP) -4 Times Sq -NY 10036
(212) 977-9700 .. **Falk,** Elliot E '78 (Phillips N LLP) -666 5th Av -NY 10103
(212) 262-2390 .. **Falk,** Jason D '09 %Connell F LLP -888 7th Av -NY 10106
(516) 564-4200 .. **Falk,** Jeffrey P '85 (Falk & K,PC) -392 Woodfld Rd -W Hempstead 11552
(585) 325-5150 .. **Falk,** John A '91 (Faraci L,LLP) -28 E Main -Rchstr 14614
(212) 428-2150 .. **Falk,** Kenneth A '78 %OCA -25 Beaver -NY 10004 **Fx:**428-2155
(212) 319-7332 .. **Falk,** Kenneth B '63 (Falk & Assoc,LLC) -30 Broad -NY 10004 **Fx:**(732) 636-3575
(212) 267-9082 .. **Falk,** Kenneth L '68 -233 Bway -NY 10279
(516) 564-4200 .. **Falk & Klebanoff,PC** -392 Woodfld Rd -W Hempstead 11552 **Fx:**564-8163
(212) 436-1116 .. **Falk,** Lawr '91 %IRS -290 Bway -NY 10007
(914) 833-0558 .. **Falk,** Linda Levy '86 -1 Cedar Isl -Larchmnt 10538 **Fx:**833-0339
(718) 780-7920 .. **Falk,** Mary R '81 %Bklyn Law Schl -250 Joralemon -Brklyn 11201 **Fx:**780-0393
(516) 571-2949 .. **Falk,** Milton Philip '63 %Hon A DiPaola -100 Supreme Ct Dr -Mineola 11501
(212) 907-0700 .. **Falk,** Morissa R '07 %Labaton S LLP -140 Bway -NY 10005
(212) 416-8000 .. **Falk,** Noah L '06 %Dept of Law -120 Bway -NY 10271
(212) 515-3214 .. **Falk,** Robt H '64 Apollo Mgmt -9 W 57th -NY 10019
(716) 631-9981 .. **Falk,** Terrance A Jr. '94 %Labin & B -531 Farber Lks Dr -Williamsvll 14221
(212) 292-5057 .. **Falkenberg,** Christopher E '99 -2 Penn Plz -NY 10121
(212) 620-2329 .. **Falkenberg,** Kai B '00 Forbes Inc -60 5th Av -NY 10011
(212) 335-4500 .. **Falkenberry,** Eric M '96 (DLA Piper LLP) -1251 Av of Amer -NY 10020
(212) 228-4168 .. **Falkenstein,** Alice R '95 -5 Styvsnt Oval -NY 10009
(716) 852-3540 .. **Falkides,** A Nicholas '94 %Watson BCJ&S -12 Fountain Plz -Buffalo 14202
(631) 451-6500 .. **Falkner,** David V '95 Town Attys Ofc -1 Indpndnc Hill -Farmngvll 11738
(718) 439-4211 .. **Falkner,** Mary '02 NYPD -333 65th -Brklyn 11220
(212) 697-9280 .. **Falkoff,** Steven C '85 (Rosenberg MF&W) -122 E 42nd -NY 10168
(516) 466-6500 .. **Falkowitz,** Gary P '06 %Parker WA LLP -6 Hrbr Park Dr S -Pt Wash 11050
(607) 255-4680 .. **Falkson,** Linda Bearse '90 Cornell Univ -500 Day Hall -Ithaca 14853
(315) 435-2470 .. **Fall,** Janet M '05 %DA -505 S State -Syracuse 13202 **Fx:**435-3969
(212) 345-5538 .. **Fall,** Kenneth G '97 %Marsh USA -1166 Av of Amer -NY 10036 **Fx:**345-4808
(516) 877-5600 .. **Fallarino,** Ralph A Jr. '87 %R Tusa -1225 Franklin Av -Gdn Cty 11530 **Fx:**877-5695
(516) 684-2900 .. **Fallarino,** Robt V '87 %Pegalis & E,LLC -1 Hllw Ln -Lk Success 11042
(518) 465-9500 .. **Fallati,** Thos R '96 (Tabner R&K,LLP) -18 Corp Wds Blvd -Albany 12211
(212) 577-3688 .. **Fallek,** Allen L '89 %Leg Aid -199 Water -NY 10038 **Fx:**509-8431
(212) 797-4700 .. **Fallek,** Andrew M '82 OfCnsl J Fallek,PC -110 Wall -NY 10005 **Fx:**797-1550
(212) 282-2129 .. **Fallek,** Dana M '85 %Rockefeller Grp -1221 Av of Amer -NY 10020 **Fx:**282-2005
(212) 797-4700 .. **Fallek,** Jos '52 -110 Wall -NY 10005 **Fx:**797-1550
(212) 857-8532 .. **Fallek,** Joy '02 2nd Circ Ct of Appeals -40 Foley Sq -NY 10007
(212) 797-4700 .. **Fallek,** Lawr L '85 %J Fallek,PC -110 Wall -NY 10005 **Fx:**797-1550
(212) 687-2770 .. **Faller,** F Brice '89 %Cohen PL&P -551 5th Av -NY 10176
(212) 922-0050 .. **Faller,** Julie M '98 Cnsl Stewart Title Ins Co -300 E 42nd -NY 10017 **Fx:**499-4253
(516) 742-2500 .. **Faller,** Robt A '77 (Gallagher & F) -1050 Franklin Av -Gdn Cty 11530
(914) 946-2822 .. **Faller,** Robt J Jr. '94 (O'Kelley & F,PC) -445 Hmltn Av -White Plns 10601
(631) 293-2350 .. **Fallis,** Harvey D '67 -555 Broadhllw Rd -Melvll 11747
(212) 681-6500 .. **Fallis,** Stephen J '67 OfCnsl Stempel BC&H,PC -675 3rd Av -NY 10017
(212) 688-8555 .. **Fallon,** Amy E '04 %Fragomen DB&L LLP -7 Hanover Sq -NY 10004
(518) 449-5400 .. **Fallon,** Charlene S '95 (Linnan & F,LLP) -61 Columbia #300 -Albany 12210
(631) 567-0340 .. **Fallon,** David P '87 (Fallon & F) -53 Main -Sayvll 11782 **Fx:**567-0353
(212) 558-4000 .. **Fallon,** Fiona M '09 %Sullivan & C LLP -125 Broad -NY 10004
(716) 778-7456 .. **Fallon,** Gerald P '89 -Bx1 -Appleton 14008
(631) 567-0340 .. **Fallon,** James V '39 (Fallon & F) -53 Main -Sayvll 11782 **Fx:**567-0353
(631) 567-0340 .. **Fallon,** James V Jr. '72 (Fallon & F) -53 Main -Sayvll 11782 **Fx:**567-0353
(518) 487-7600 .. **Fallon,** Janis E '97 OfCnsl Whiteman O&H LLP -1 Commerce Plz -Albany 12260
(845) 778-7588 .. **Fallon,** John J '68 (McAdam & F,PC) -90 Scofld Bx500 -Walden 12586
(212) 259-8000 .. **Fallon,** John R Jr. '82 (Dewey & L LLP) -1301 Av of Amer -NY 10019
(212) 264-2727 .. **Fallon,** Jos R '81 %DOJ-Ins -26 Fed Plz -NY 10278
(212) 492-4023 .. **Fallon,** Kathleen '90 %Deloitte LLP -1633 Bway -NY 10019 **Fx:**492-4201
(315) 475-4410 .. **Fallon,** Megan M '94 (Fallon F&B) -501 E Wshngtn -Syracuse 13202 **Fx:**475-0759
(518) 436-0751 .. **Fallon,** Michl C '93 (Hinman S PC) -121 State -Albany 12207
(315) 422-8614 .. **Fallon,** Patrick T '97 -5298 Terry Rd -Syracuse 13219
(212) 415-8600 .. **Fallon,** Peter J '02 %Locke LB&L LLP -3 World Fncl Ctr -NY 10281
(716) 845-3650 .. **Fallon,** Sarah M '94 %MHLS -438 Main -Buffalo 14202 **Fx:**874-7794
(315) 475-4410 .. **Fallon,** Sheila M '90 (Fallon F&B) -501 E Wshngtn -Syracuse 13202 **Fx:**475-0759
(718) 590-8584 .. **Fallon,** Tara B '04 ACS DLA -900 Sheridan Av -Bronx 10451
(914) 285-8500 .. **Fallon,** Walter J Jr. '84 %TK Moore -701 Wstchstr Av -White Plns 10604 **Fx:**285-8510
(516) 515-9744 .. **Fallon,** Wm J '02 (Newfeld & F,PLLC) -1900 Hempstd Tpk -E Meadow 11554 **Fx:**222-7722
(212) 808-0700 .. **Falls,** Mia D '97 %Norris M&M,PA -875 3rd Av -NY 10022
(518) 388-4364 .. **Falotico,** Carl G '10 %DA -612 State -Schnctdy 12305 **Fx:**388-4569
(914) 713-0001 .. **Falow,** Lance H '85 -774 Post Rd -Scarsdale 10583
(716) 885-1834 .. **Falsone,** Gioacchino Jack '96 -484 Delaware Av -Buffalo 14202
(212) 506-1700 .. **Falstrault,** Jennifer A '99 (Kasowitz BT&F LLP) -1633 Bway -NY 10019
(631) 730-2210 .. **Faltischek,** Denise A '01 Hain Celestrial Grp -58 S Srvc Rd -Melvll 11747
(516) 605-6652 .. **Faltischek,** Kenneth D '01 Sandata Technologies -26 Hrbr Park Dr -Pt Wash 11050
(516) 663-6600 .. **Faltischek,** Michl L '74 (Ruskin MF,PC) -1425 RXR Plz -Uniondale 11556
(718) 361-9150 .. **Falussy,** Rosemarie C '90 %Stan Deutsch Assoc -31-30 Hunters Pnt Av -LIC 11101
(212) 839-5300 .. **Falvey,** Anne Meade '88 (Sidley A LLP) -787 7th Av -NY 10019
(212) 326-3939 .. **Falvey,** Eileen E '02 (Jones D) -222 E 41st -NY 10017
(716) 847-6779 .. **Falvey,** Julie '91 -424 Main -Buffalo 14202 **Fx:**854-1419
(585) 394-3410 .. **Falvey,** Scott P '95 -66 N Main -Canandaigua 14424 **Fx:**394-3427
(914) 261-6812 .. **Falvey,** Stephen P '86 -2027 Wllmsbrdg Rd -Bronx 10461
(518) 459-2495 .. **Falzani,** Nisar A '07 OfCnsl Summers Law Firm,PC -125 Wolf Rd -Albany 12205 **Fx:**459-2571
(212) 525-8096 .. **Falzon,** Jos K '98 HSBC Securities -452 5th Av -NY 10018
(718) 250-0400 .. **Falzone,** Frank C '79 %R Tusa -1 MetroTech Ctr -Brklyn 11201 **Fx:**250-0591
(585) 292-6007 .. **Fama,** Andrew J '83 AJ Fama Asset Mgmt,LLC -3445 Winton Pl -Rchstr 14623 **Fx:**427-0218
(585) 458-0310 .. **Fama,** Anthony '87 -1347 Lyell Av -Rchstr 14606
(212) 790-0200 .. **Fama,** Arthur F Jr. '87 Benj N Cardozo Schl of Law -55 5th Av -NY 10003 **Fx:**790-0345
(718) 852-1919 .. **Fama,** Christina J '08 RBA,Inc -45 Main -Brklyn 11201
(718) 934-5732 .. **Fama,** Peter J '00 -2328 E 28th -Brklyn 11229 **Fx:**934-5761
(212) 509-9400 .. **Fama,** Richd '94 (Cozen O) -45 Bway Atrium -NY 10006
(585) 232-3197 .. **Fame,** Michl A '86 -1000 Rynlds Arcd -Rchstr 14614 **Fx:**232-3198
(516) 571-3056 .. **Famighetti,** Peter J '01 %Cnty Atty -1 West -Mineola 11501 **Fx:**571-6604
(212) 408-2500 .. **Familant,** Scott B '91 (Baker B,LLP) -30 Rckfllr Plz -NY 10112
(718) 777-7010 .. **Fampritsis,** Leonidas '99 -31-53 Steinway -Astoria 11103
(718) 748-3333 .. **Famulari,** Dominic J '97 %J Famulari -6741 3rd Av -Brklyn 11220 **Fx:**748-3368
(212) 788-8875 .. **Famulari,** Gianna M '02 %Law Dept -100 Church -NY 10007 **Fx:**788-0367
(718) 748-3333 .. **Famulari,** John D '76 -6741 3rd Av -Brklyn 11220 **Fx:**748-3368
(718) 298-8900 .. **Famularo,** Tara A '02 Leg Aid -153-01 Jamaica Av -Jamaica 11432 **Fx:**657-0537
(718) 647-6767 .. **Famuyide,** Jos Rotimi '96 -2750 Atl Av -Brklyn 11207 **Fx:**647-6777
(212) 503-2184 .. **Fan,** George I '96 GSO Fncl Prtnrs -280 Park Av -NY 10017
(212) 669-7952 .. **Fan,** Lily I '89 %Landmarks Preservation Cmmssn -1 Centre -NY 10007
(973) 228-5700 .. **Fanburg,** John D '84 (Brach E LLC) -100 Park Av -NY 10017 **Fx:**228-7852
(212) 713-2000 .. **Fanciullo,** Anthony A '99 UBS Invstmnt Bk -1285 Av of Amer -NY 10019
(518) 427-8261 .. **Fanciullo,** Wm P '80 -61 Columbia -Albany 12210 **Fx:**436-0097
(212) 440-3981 .. **Fandrey,** Kimberly A '00 CNA -40 Wall -NY 10005
(718) 630-2746 .. **Fanelli,** Anna '89 -7703 5th Av -Brklyn 11209
(212) 806-5400 .. **Fanelli,** Cecelia L '02 (Stroock &S&L LLP) -180 Maiden Ln -NY 10038
(212) 558-5500 .. **Fanelli,** Michl P '04 %Weitz & L,PC -700 Bway -NY 10003
(914) 696-7500 .. **Fanelli,** Robt C '67 %DCI -2900 Wstchstr Av -Purchase 10577 **Fx:**696-7505
(212) 832-8000 .. **Fanelli,** Rosemary '90 Allen & Co -711 5th Av -NY 10022
(914) 948-8700 .. **Fanelli,** Thos F Jr. '76 -470 Mamaroneck -White Plns 10605 **Fx:**948-8796
(212) 373-3000 .. **Fanelly,** James '10 %Paul WRW&G LLP -1285 Av of Amer -NY 10019
(212) 554-7800 .. **Fang,** Catherine '08 %Moses & S LLP -405 Lex Av -NY 10174
(212) 836-8000 .. **Fang,** Guanyu '09 %Kaye S LLP -425 Park Av -NY 10022
(212) 504-6000 .. **Fang,** James Z '10 %Cadwalader W&T LLP -1 World Fncl Ctr -NY 10281
(212) 728-8000 .. **Fang,** Jeffrey '07 %Willkie F&G LLP -787 7th Av -NY 10019
(212) 906-1200 .. **Fang,** Leah R '04 %Latham & W -885 3rd Av -NY 10022
(212) 225-2000 .. **Fang,** Lian '08 %Cleary GS&H -1 Lbrty Plz -NY 10006
(212) 856-9600 .. **Fang,** Linda '07 %Morvillo AGIA&B,PC -565 5th Av -NY 10017
(212) 661-5655 .. **Fang,** Mark C '95 -50 E 42nd -NY 10017
(516) 620-8585 .. **Fang,** Neil B '94 (Schwartz & F,PC) -3000 Marcus Av -Lk Success 11042 **Fx:**488-1238

(212) 705-7000 .. **Fang,** Patrick S '09 %Bingham M LLP -399 Park Av -NY 10022
(212) 219-8869 .. **Fang,** Peng '99 (P Fang,PC) -350 Bway -NY 10013 **Fx:**219-8867
(212) 264-6014 .. **Fang,** Rita M '98 %Army Corps Engrs -26 Fed Plz -NY 10278 **Fx:**264-8171
(212) 683-0088 .. **Fang,** Seymour H '61 -225 W 83rd -NY 10024
(212) 415-9200 .. **Fang,** Steven S '01 %Dorsey & W LLP -250 Park Av -NY 10177
(718) 466-3000 .. **Fang,** Vanessa '10 %Civil Ct -1118 Grnd Cncrs -Bronx 10456 **Fx:**466-3006
(315) 472-7832 .. **Fangio,** Mary Lannon '81 (Whitelaw & F) -247-259 W Fayette -Syracuse 13202 **Fx:**472-7816
(212) 651-6500 .. **Fani,** Susan A '00 Arch Ins Grp -1 Lbrty Plz -NY 10006
(516) 586-6036 .. **Fanizza,** Joanne '07 J Fanizza,PA -111 Conklin -Farmngdl 11735
(212) 318-3000 .. **Fankhanel,** K Jane '73 (Fulbright & J LLP) -666 5th Av -NY 10103
(212) 826-0808 .. **Fannell,** Jeffery B '97 %MLB Players Assn -12 E 49th -NY 10017 **Fx:**752-3649
(518) 783-0200 .. **Fanniff,** Kimberly A '00 %NYS Schl Bds Assn -24 Century Hill Dr -Latham 12110
(718) 261-3290 .. **Fanning,** Christopher S '97 (Fanning & H,PLLC) -108-18 Qns Blvd -Frst Hlls 11375
(516) 942-3600 .. **Fanning,** Douglas J '92 -500 N Bway -Jericho 11753
(212) 609-6800 .. **Fanning,** Edw J Jr. '95 (McCarter & E,LLP) -245 Park Av -NY 10167
(718) 261-3290 .. **Fanning & Hughes, PLLC** -108-18 Qns Blvd -Frst Hlls 11375 **Fx:**228-2422
(716) 566-1300 .. **Fanning,** James S '58 OfCnsl Hiscock & B,LLP -1100 M&T Ctr -Buffalo 14203
(718) 855-9000 .. **Fanning,** John J '82 (Cullen and D LLP) -177 Montague -Brklyn 11201
(212) 308-1790 .. **Fannon,** David T '97 Screen Media Ventures -757 3rd Av -NY 10017
(518) 474-6036 .. **Fanshawe,** Helen M '79 %State Comptroller -110 State -Albany 12236 **Fx:**473-9104
(518) 473-5174 .. **Fantauzzi,** Gretchen E '93 %Dept of Health -Corning Twr 24th Fl -Albany 12237 **Fx:**486-1858
(518) 370-4645 .. **Fantauzzi,** John A '96 (Englert CM&F,LLP) -224 State Bx1092 -Schnctdy 12301
(914) 242-8646 .. **Fantauzzi-Singer,** Leticia M '95 (Singer & F) -40 W Main -Mt Kisco 10549 **Fx:**242-1672
(631) 962-9600 .. **Fante,** Peter D '95 Verint Systems -330 S Srvc Rd -Melvll 11747
(212) 755-7503 .. **Fantechi,** Massimo '88 -590 Mad Av -NY 10022
(585) 753-4500 .. **Fantigrossi,** Nicole M '04 DA -832 Watts Bldg -Rchstr 14614 **Fx:**753-4576
(914) 777-5451 .. **Fantino,** Lisa M '98 -424 Mamaroneck Av -Mamaroneck 10543
(718) 780-7566 .. **Fanto,** James A '00 %Bklyn Law Schl -250 Joralemon -Brklyn 11201 **Fx:**780-0393
(212) 891-6150 .. **Fantozzi,** Stephen J '00 Natixis Cptl Mkts Inc -9 W 57th -NY 10019 **Fx:**891-6288
(212) 227-0347 .. **Fantulin,** Kristofor T '92 %Weiss W&W,PC -25 Park Pl -NY 10007
(212) 294-6700 .. **Fanucci,** Allan A '83 (Winston & S) -200 Park Av -NY 10166
(914) 682-2636 .. **Fappiano,** Tara C '99 (Havkins RR&V,LLP) -50 Main -White Plns 10606
(585) 263-1000 .. **Farace,** Thos M '80 (Nixon P LLP) -1100 Clinton Sq -Rchstr 14604
(585) 325-5150 .. **Faraci,** Angelo G '57 (Faraci L,LLP) -28 E Main -Rchstr 14614
(585) 325-5150 .. **Faraci Lange,LLP** -28 E Main -Rchstr 14614 **Fx:**325-3285
(516) 571-3931 .. **Faraci,** Michelle M '04 %Cnty Atty -1 West -Mineola 11501 **Fx:**571-6604
(212) 408-2500 .. **Faragi,** Eric J '05 %Baker B,LLP -30 Rckfllr Plz -NY 10112
(917) 709-4331 .. **Farago,** Lisa Marie '99 -1756 Brnxdale Av -Bronx 10462
(212) 373-3000 .. **Farah,** Ehab '09 %Paul WRW&G LLP -1285 Av of Amer -NY 10019
(212) 878-8000 .. **Farah,** Omar A '08 %Clifford C LLP -31 W 52nd -NY 10019
(212) 552-7544 .. **Farahnakian,** Lilly '00 JP Morgan Chase & Co -1 Chase Manh Plz -NY 10081 **Fx:**552-5856
(212) 766-5665 .. **Faraldo,** Carla V '05 %Lefkowicz & G -150 Bway -NY 10038 **Fx:**608-5201
(718) 544-6800 .. **Faraldo,** Jos A '70 -125-10 Qns Blvd -Kew Gdns 11415
(212) 859-8000 .. **Farano,** Jos P '08 %Fried FHS&J LLP -1 NY Plz -NY 10004
(212) 294-7733 .. **Farbanish,** Glen R '04 Cantor Fitzgerald -110 E 59th -NY 10022
(212) 813-8800 .. **Farbenblum,** Michl '06 %Goodwin P LLP -620 8th Av -NY 10018
(212) 331-5136 .. **Farber,** Allyn Ann '84 %HRA -180 Water -NY 10038
(212) 228-7000 .. **Farber,** Andrew B '89 Best Case Scenario LLC -648 Bway -NY 10012 **Fx:**228-7017
(718) 875-7584 .. **Farber,** Arthur I '60 -105 Court -Brklyn 11201 **Fx:**875-3488
(518) 472-1224 .. **Farber,** Benjamin M '00 %Phillips L LLP -30 S Pearl -Albany 12207
(516) 739-5100 .. **Farber,** Braden H '95 (Farber B&Z LLP) -51 Charles -Mineola 11501
(516) 739-5100 .. **Farber Brocks & Zane LLP** -51 Charles -Mineola 11501 **Fx:**739-5103
(212) 855-9607 .. **Farber,** Craig R '97 Goldman Sachs & Co -180 Maiden Ln -NY 10038
(212) 334-4466 .. **Farber,** Curtis J '86 -350 Bway -NY 10013 **Fx:**226-3224
(212) 554-7800 .. **Farber,** Danielle S '05 %Moses & S LLP -405 Lex Av -NY 10174
(212) 513-6432 .. **Farber,** David I '95 Dept of Small Bus Srvcs -110 William -NY 10038
(315) 946-7521 .. **Farber,** Deborah Gerber '77 Hall of Justice -54 Broad -Lyons 14489 **Fx:**946-5456
(212) 861-2325 .. **Farber,** Donald C '50 -14 E 75th -NY 10021
(914) 761-9400 .. **Farber,** Eugene I '74 (Farber P&C) -200 E Post Rd -White Plns 10601
(212) 521-5400 .. **Farber,** Evan K '05 %Reed S LLP -599 Lex Av -NY 10022
(718) 995-4700 .. **Farber,** Felice S '90 %Green Bus Lines -165-25 147th -Jamaica 11434
(914) 761-9400 .. **Farber,** Hinda Keller '92 %Farber P&C -200 E Post Rd -White Plns 10601
(914) 946-5100 .. **Farber,** Irving O '68 (Bashian & F,LLP) -235 Main -White Plns 10601
(212) 619-1811 .. **Farber,** Joanne '79 -225 Bway -NY 10007 **Fx:**766-2298
(718) 459-5400 .. **Farber,** Jos '69 (Farber R&K PC) -97-77 Qns Blvd -Rego Pk 11374
(212) 449-6352 .. **Farber,** Luke '90 %Merrill Lynch -220 Bway -NY 10038
(716) 635-4379 .. **Farber,** Mark Brian '98 Merrill Lynch -6245D Sheridan Dr -Buffalo 14221
(716) 688-0773 .. **Farber,** Martin B '71 -235 Ranch Trl W -Williamsvll 14221 **Fx:**689-3059
(212) 859-8000 .. **Farber,** Menachem M '06 %Fried FHS&J LLP -1 NY Plz -NY 10004
(212) 450-4000 .. **Farber,** Michl S '95 (Davis P&W LLP) -450 Lex Av -NY 10017
(212) 336-2000 .. **Farber,** Nina P '92 Patterson BW&T LLP -1133 Av of Amer -NY 10036
(914) 761-9400 .. **Farber Pappalardo & Carbonari** -200 E Post Rd -White Plns 10601 **Fx:**761-0747
(212) 715-9100 .. **Farber,** Peggy J '05 %Kramer LN&F,LLP -1177 Av of Amer -NY 10036
(718) 459-5400 .. **Farber Rosen & Kaufman PC** -97-77 Qns Blvd -Rego Pk 11374
(212) 521-1788 .. **Farber,** Sandra R '86 ICC Industries -460 Park Av -NY 10022
(212) 259-8000 .. **Farber,** Seth C '90 (Dewey & L LLP) -1301 Av of Amer -NY 10019
(212) 416-8029 .. **Farber,** Seth J '87 %Dept of Law -120 Bway -NY 10271
(212) 956-0881 .. **Farber,** Sheldon '61 -162 W 54th -NY 10019 **Fx:**956-0103
(585) 428-5788 .. **Farber,** Sidney T '74 7th Judicial Dist -1985 Baird Rd -Penfld 14526
(212) 922-9700 .. **Farber,** Stephen R '91 %1st Amer Title -633 3rd Av -NY 10017 **Fx:**922-0881
(212) 490-3113 .. **Farber,** Walter V '59 -5 W 37th -NY 10018 **Fx:**986-3679
(212) 207-0700 .. **Farberman,** Lewis E '98 Sumitomo Corp -600 3rd Av -NY 10016
(347) 825-2369 .. **Farberov,** Arthur '08 Kushel & F -299 Bway -NY 10007 **Fx:**(212) 994-9470
(212) 637-1587 .. **Farbiarz,** Michl E '00 %US Atty -1 St Andrews Plz -NY 10007
(212) 223-6700 .. **Farbman,** David M '74 (Zukerman GB&C,LLP) -875 3rd Av -NY 10022
(516) 571-2949 .. **Farbman,** Lawr S '75 %Hon UW Lally -Supreme Ct Bldg -Mineola 11501
(212) 474-1000 .. **Farbood,** Mina M '08 %Cravath S&M LLP -825 8th Av -NY 10019
(212) 431-1300 .. **Farca,** Jos I '96 (Borah GAN&G PC) -377 Bway -NY 10013
(518) 453-4600 .. **Farcher,** Chas F '08 %Comm Judicial Cndct -ESP -Albany 12223 **Fx:**486-1850
(315) 475-9334 .. **Farchione,** Mark D '86 (Farchione & B LLP) -217 Mntgmry -Syracuse 13202 **Fx:**475-9655
(212) 415-8600 .. **Farco,** Jos A '09 %Locke LB&L LLP -3 World Fncl Ctr -NY 10281
(718) 935-2599 .. **Fardella,** Jess Thos '93 Ofc of Auditor Genl -65 Court -Brklyn 11201 **Fx:**935-5458
(631) 424-0747 .. **Fardella,** Robt '67 -33 Walt Whitman Rd -Huntngtn Sta 11746 **Fx:**423-0732
(914) 824-5392 .. **Farella,** Alfred A '84 Hon LJ Lubell -111 Dr Martin Luther King Blvd -White Plns 10601
(212) 652-3890 .. **Farelli,** Jos F '95 (Pitta & G LLP) -120 Bway -NY 10271
(212) 964-3453 .. **Farensbach,** Jan V '98 -277 Bway -NY 10007 **Fx:**571-0276
(518) 785-1111 .. **Farer,** Steven D '75 (Farer & S,PC) -12 Century Hill Dr -Latham 12110 **Fx:**785-4325
(212) 574-1200 .. **Farez,** Nordin M '08 %Seward & K LLP -1 Bttry Pk Plz -NY 10004
(212) 474-1000 .. **Fargo,** Christopher K '07 %Cravath S&M LLP -825 8th Av -NY 10019
(212) 888-1040 .. **Farhadian,** Leeor F '03 EnTrust Captl -717 5th Av -NY 10022 **Fx:**888-0751
(212) 732-3200 .. **Farhangian,** Jasmin J '05 %Carter L&M LLP -2 Wall -NY 10005
(800) 742-9696 .. **Farhi,** Jacques M '93 %Binder & B,PC -33-00 Nrthrn Blvd -LIC 11101 **Fx:**(718) 512-2424
(212) 279-5979 .. **Farhi,** Michl '85 (Kates NRE&F,LLP) -845 3rd Av -NY 10022
(212) 949-5000 .. **Farhi,** Nancy Miller '96 Tarragon Corp -192 Lex Av -NY 10016
(516) 741-1110 .. **Faria,** Jos A '94 (Foley GJ&F,LLP) -666 Old Cntry Rd -Gdn Cty 11530
(917) 663-2199 .. **Faria,** Mary I '86 Altria Grp,Inc -120 Park Av -NY 10017
(212) 732-7922 .. **Faria,** Vanessa '96 (Rosenbaum F,LLP) -11 Penn Plz -NY 10001 **Fx:**937-2155
(212) 309-6000 .. **Farid,** Amani '08 %Morgan L&B LLP -101 Park Av -NY 10178
(212) 376-3131 .. **Farid,** Elizabeth A '00 %Vera Inst of Justice -233 Bway -NY 10279 **Fx:**941-9407
(718) 262-3422 .. **Farid,** Riham M '02 ACS -92-31 Union Hall -Jamaica 11433
(212) 336-2000 .. **Faridi,** Muhammad U '08 %Patterson BW&T LLP -1133 Av of Amer -NY 10036
(212) 825-3330 .. **Fariello,** Vittoria M '03 Bldgs Special Investigations Unit -83 Maiden Ln -NY 10038
(212) 751-3001 .. **Farina,** Gabrielle E '06 %Thompson & K LLP -919 3rd Av -NY 10022
(212) 841-1000 .. **Farina,** Jennifer Overbeck '06 %Covington & B LLP -620 8th Av -NY 10018
(516) 997-0999 .. **Farina,** Michl A '91 %Pryor & M,LLP -675 Old Cntry Rd -Westbury 11590
(845) 986-5375 .. **Farina,** Richd D '69 -17 Dunning Rd -Warwick 10990
(607) 547-8500 .. **Farina,** Summer J '04 %Trosset Grp -31 Pioneer Bx28 -Cooperstwn 13326
(516) 746-5599 .. **Farinacci,** Donald J '69 (Bee RFH&D,LLP) -170 Old Cntry Rd -Mineola 11501
(516) 746-8000 .. **Farinacci,** John G '98 (Jaspan S LLP) -300 Grdn City Plz -Gdn Cty 11530
(212) 962-8020 .. **Farinella,** Dawn M '97 (Farinella & F,LLC) -1 Whitehall -NY 10038 **Fx:**(908) 791-2833
(718) 899-1400 .. **Farinella,** Gus Michl '95 -242-11 Braddock Av -Bellerose 11426 **Fx:**899-8844
(212) 675-6161 .. **Farinella,** Gus Michl '95 SrCnsl GM Farinella PC -15 Park Av -NY 10016 **Fx:**675-4367
(212) 768-6700 .. **Farinella,** Jacqueline D '09 %Sonnenschein N&R LLP -2 World Fncl Ctr -NY 10281
(212) 962-8020 .. **Farinella,** John T Jr. '96 (Farinella & F,LLC) -1 Whitehall -NY 10038 **Fx:**(908) 791-2833
(917) 806-7053 .. **Farinella,** Thos A '02 -275 Mad Av -NY 10016
(212) 815-0424 .. **Farinha,** Nigel I '96 %DA -1 Hogan Pl -NY 10013
(516) 496-5822 .. **Faris,** John M '08 T Spina -170 Froehlich Farm Blvd -Woodbury 11797 **Fx:**496-5420
(212) 735-3000 .. **Farjad,** Nasim '09 %Skadden ASM&F LLP -4 Times Sq -NY 10036
(347) 581-4648 .. **Farkas,** Aaron '05 -56 Maple Av -Cedarhrst 11516
(917) 778-6500 .. **Farkas,** Allison H '06 %K Dodson -485 Lex Av -NY 10017
(718) 250-2000 .. **Farkas,** Ari '05 %DA -350 Jay -Brklyn 11201 **Fx:**250-2314
(845) 732-8956 .. **Farkas,** Cheryl Schechter '07 Active Media Servcs,Inc -Bx1705 -Pearl Rvr 10965
(212) 225-2000 .. **Farkas,** Esther '07 %Cleary GS&H -1 Lbrty Plz -NY 10006
(718) 625-2500 .. **Farkas,** George A '73 -32 Court -Brklyn 11201 **Fx:**625-6837
(212) 421-4100 .. **Farkas,** Ilene S '94 (Pryor C LLP) -7 Times Sq -NY 10036
(718) 459-8080 .. **Farkas,** Jeffrey A '87 SrCnsl Wolfson F&G,PC -104-18 Metro Av -Frst Hlls 11375 **Fx:**268-3739

(718) 645-5600 .. **Farkas,** Joshua '96 (Stein F&S LLP) -1639 E 13th -Brklyn 11229
(516) 482-4436 .. **Farkas,** Lawr W '89 (Gleich S&F) -36 S Station Plz -Gt Neck 11021
(212) 779-8600 .. **Farkas,** Michl C '95 (Silverman SS&B PLLC) -381 Park Av S -NY 10016
(212) 723-3869 .. **Farkas,** Nancy E '87 %Salomon Bros -250 West -NY 10013
(212) 506-2500 .. **Farkas,** Susan Butler '03 %Mayer B LLP -1675 Bway -NY 10019
(212) 848-9800 .. **Farkas-DiNardo,** Eva '03 %Withers B LLP -430 Park Av -NY 10022
(718) 591-0703 .. **Farkash,** Lawr '75 -67-19 183rd -Fresh Mdws 11365 **Fx:**591-6268
(212) 461-2323 .. **Farkouh,** David M '05 %Saiber LLC -44 Wall -NY 10005
(212) 298-5103 .. **Farley,** Anthony J '71 %Leg Aid -49 Thomas -NY 10013 **Fx:**298-5252
(518) 436-9370 .. **Farley,** Brian P '80 -36 S Pearl -Albany 12207 **Fx:**436-8233
(212) 609-6800 .. **Farley,** Clement J '95 (McCarter & E,LLP) -245 Park Av -NY 10167
(607) 762-7750 .. **Farley,** Danl W '84 %Electric & Gas Corp -4500 Vestal Pkwy E -Bnghmtn 13902 **Fx:**762-8564
(516) 746-0232 .. **Farley Glockner & Halpern, LLP** -200 Old Cntry Rd -Mineola 11501 **Fx:**746-1054
(516) 746-0232 .. **Farley,** Graceann '73 %Farley G&H,LLP -200 Old Cntry Rd -Mineola 11501
(518) 455-2181 .. **Farley,** Hugh T '75 SrCnsl Senate -412 LOB -Albany 12247 **Fx:**455-2271
(518) 399-9769 .. **Farley,** Hugh T '75 (Farley & F) -7 Glenwood Dr -Scotia 12302
(212) 609-1500 .. **Farley,** Joan R '76 %VNSNY -107 E 70th -NY 10021 **Fx:**794-6357
(917) 637-0438 .. **Farley,** Joel S '86 -130 W 57th -NY 10019 **Fx:**(212) 307-5944
(516) 433-4220 .. **Farley & Kessler,PC** -55 Jericho Tpk -Jericho 11753 **Fx:**939-9839
(518) 399-9769 .. **Farley,** Marilyn E '87 (Farley & F) -7 Glenwood Dr -Scotia 12302
(212) 382-0700 .. **Farley,** Mark A '86 OfCnsl Ostrolenk FG&S,LLP -1180 Av of Amer -NY 10036
(315) 379-0326 .. **Farley,** Mary M '93 Hon D Demarest -48 Court -Canton 13617 **Fx:**379-2311
(212) 248-3150 .. **Farley,** Matthew '74 (Drinker B&R LLP) -140 Bway -NY 10005
(845) 896-7077 .. **Farley,** Michl P '94 -1092 Main -Fishkill 12524 **Fx:**896-7079
(718) 428-8360 .. **Farley,** Richd C Jr. '94 -28-28 216th -Bayside 11360
(212) 701-3000 .. **Farley,** Richd E '92 (Cahill G&R LLP) -80 Pine -NY 10005 **Fx:**269-5420
(516) 433-4220 .. **Farley,** Richd L '83 (Farley & K,PC) -55 Jericho Tpk -Jericho 11753
(212) 661-4600 .. **Farley,** Robt D '71 %Dyson-Kissner-Moran -565 5th Av -NY 10017 **Fx:**599-5105
(212) 536-3900 .. **Farley,** Robt F '08 %K&L Gates LLP -599 Lex Av -NY 10022
(516) 746-0232 .. **Farley,** Robt J '78 (Farley G&H,LLP) -200 Old Cntry Rd -Mineola 11501
(518) 455-3111 .. **Farley,** Robt T '88 %Sen V Leibell -802 LOB -Albany 12247 **Fx:**426-6977
(518) 399-9769 .. **Farley,** Robt T '88 (Farley & F) -7 Glenwood Dr -Scotia 12302
(212) 589-4200 .. **Farley,** Ryan P '99 Cnsl Baker & H LLP -45 Rckfllr Plz -NY 10111
(518) 452-5600 .. **Farley,** Susan E '86 (Heslin RF&M PC) -5 Columbia Cir -Albany 12203
(716) 947-7671 .. **Farley,** Thos C Jr. '88 -7008 Erie Rd -Derby 14047
(914) 328-7000 .. **Farley,** Thos F '75 (T Farley PC) -50 Main -White Plns 10606 **Fx:**206-3944
(315) 493-9373 .. **Farley,** Timothy A '87 T Farley,PC -514 State -Carthage 13619 **Fx:**493-9390
(716) 856-3646 .. **Farley,** Victor N '58 -37 Franklin -Buffalo 14202 **Fx:**854-2531
(212) 512-3625 .. **Farley,** Wm P '82 %McGraw-Hill -1221 Av of Amer -NY 10020 **Fx:**512-4827
(718) 292-8600 .. **Farman,** David C '84 -888 Grnd Cncrs -Bronx 10451 **Fx:**742-2058
(212) 563-1710 .. **Farman,** Edw '64 OfCnsl Schindel FLG&R LLP -14 Penn Plz -NY 10122
(212) 770-5820 .. **Farman-Farmaian,** Afsar '97 AIG Global Invstmnt -70 Pine -NY 10270
(716) 856-4000 .. **Farmelo,** David A '79 (Hodgson R LLP) -140 Pearl -Buffalo 14202
(212) 775-3060 .. **Farmer,** Jeffrey R '04 Cnsl LimeWire LLC -45 Howard -NY 10013
(212) 318-3000 .. **Farmer,** Richd M '75 (Fulbright & J LLP) -666 5th Av -NY 10103
(212) 787-6566 .. **Farmer,** Shirley Stewart '63 -1 Lincoln Plz -NY 10023 **Fx:**787-6567
(516) 741-2121 .. **Farmer,** Steven T J '87 %N Kanzer -1325 Franklin Av -Gdn Cty 11530 **Fx:**741-3930
(212) 925-5901 .. **Farnen,** Clare M '02 Sligo Tribeca Assoc,Inc -35 Worth -NY 10013 **Fx:**226-5904
(716) 852-0202 .. **Farner,** Wm C '64 (Farner & F) -808 Main Seneca Bldg -Buffalo 14203 **Fx:**852-0271
(718) 769-2007 .. **Farnes,** Milagros '89 -14 Kay Ct -Brklyn 11229
(607) 763-9200 .. **Farneti,** Gary W '91 (Levene G&T,LLP) -BxF-1706 -Bnghmtn 13902
(718) 590-2000 .. **Farnham,** Jordan A '09 %DA -198 E 161st -Bronx 10451 **Fx:**590-6477
(212) 684-1880 .. **Farnolo,** Nicholas R '08 %Rheingold VRS&M LLP -113 E 37th -NY 10016
(212) 735-3000 .. **Farnsworth,** Joyce P '92 Cnsl Skadden ASM&F LLP -4 Times Sq -NY 10036
(212) 598-8000 .. **Farnsworth Einsidler,** Karen L '84 %Guardian Life Ins -7 Hanover Sq -NY 10004 **Fx:**919-2693
(516) 997-5118 .. **Farnung Klein,** Jutta '86 -807 Hmptn Ct -Westbury 11590
(718) 460-9500 .. **Faro,** James J '78 -159-18 Nrthrn Blvd -Flushng 11358 **Fx:**461-5651
(516) 355-7901 .. **Farole,** Gary A '88 (Paganini GCC&F) -1979 Marcus Av -Lk Success 11042
(212) 461-5606 .. **Farooq,** Umar '03 %CIT -11 W 42nd -NY 10036
(212) 819-8200 .. **Farooqi,** Ayesha Khan '01 Cnsl White & C LLP -1155 Av of Amer -NY 10036
(718) 896-3061 .. **Farooqi,** Mufti Showkat A '02 -110-51 64th Rd -Frst Hlls 11375
(212) 446-4800 .. **Farouki,** Shiva S '99 (Kirkland & E LLP) -153 E 53rd -NY 10022
(516) 334-2500 .. **Farquharson,** Bruce W '87 (Feldman RK&F,PC) -410 Jericho Tpk -Jericho 11753
(212) 878-3302 .. **Farquharson,** Jacob A '03 %Clifford C LLP -31 W 52nd -NY 10019
(315) 425-2700 .. **Farr,** Jan R '63 OfCnsl Hiscock & B,LLP -One Park Pl -Syracuse 13202
(212) 450-4000 .. **Farr,** Lucy W '96 (Davis P&W LLP) -450 Lex Av -NY 10017
(631) 588-4000 .. **Farr,** Ronald A '69 (Farr & B) -3100 Vets Mem'l Hwy -Bohemia 11716 **Fx:**588-0276
(585) 423-0003 .. **Farr,** Wm H '80 -1 E Main -Rchstr 14614
(212) 922-6755 .. **Farragher,** Janette '92 Dreyfus -200 Park Av -NY 10166
(212) 808-7800 .. **Farrah,** James E '09 %Kelley D&W LLP -101 Park Av -NY 10178
(212) 839-7000 .. **Farrar,** Boriana '07 %Hill B&N LLP -200 Lbrty -NY 10281
(212) 341-0797 .. **Farrar,** Brian J '10 %Law Dept -100 Church -NY 10007 **Fx:**788-0367
(716) 636-7600 .. **Farrar,** Carol A '06 %HoganWillig -2410 N Forest Rd -Amherst 14068
(212) 558-4000 .. **Farrar,** Wm G '93 (Sullivan & C LLP) -125 Broad -NY 10004
(212) 705-0123 .. **Farrara,** Kathryn L '09 National Advertising Div -70 W 36th -NY 10018
(914) 423-8880 .. **Farrauto Berman & Slater** -1250 Cntrl Pk Av -Ynkrs 10704 **Fx:**423-8964
(914) 423-8880 .. **Farrauto,** John P '64 (Farrauto B&S) -1250 Cntrl Pk Av -Ynkrs 10704
(585) 546-1280 .. **Farrell,** Barbara '87 -16 Main -Rchstr 14614 **Fx:**546-6006
(212) 264-0483 .. **Farrell,** Beverly A '02 US DOJ-Civil Div -26 Fed Plz -NY 10278
(914) 378-1010 .. **Farrell,** Brian J '92 OfCnsl Fitzgerald & F -538 Riverdale Av -Ynkrs 10705
(212) 416-8515 .. **Farrell,** Bridget E '79 Dept of Law -120 Bway -NY 10271
(212) 709-1640 .. **Farrell,** Bryan J '85 %Banking Dept -1 State -NY 10004 **Fx:**709-1655
(315) 635-3222 .. **Farrell,** Chas '76 (Farrell M&B) -44 Oswego Bx199 -Baldwinsvll 13027
(631) 853-5761 .. **Farrell,** Christina E '04 %Cnty Atty -400 Carleton Av -Central Islip 11722 **Fx:**853-7788
(315) 671-1135 .. **Farrell,** Colleen M '98 Hon J Centra -401 Mntgmry -Syracuse 13202 **Fx:**671-1182
(212) 259-8000 .. **Farrell,** Danl P '05 %Dewey & L LLP -1301 Av of Amer -NY 10019
(914) 347-2600 .. **Farrell,** Denis M '01 %Traub LS&S LLP -7 Skyline Dr -Hawthorne 10532
(631) 724-8833 .. **Farrell,** Diane K '80 (Devitt SB,LLP) -50 Route 111 -Smithtwn 11787
(516) 741-6611 .. **Farrell,** Edmond D '90 OfCnsl Farrell F&B -212 Station Plaza N -Mineola 11501
(212) 216-8000 .. **Farrell,** Edw J '90 %Tarter K&D LLP -1350 Bway -NY 10018
(516) 222-2434 .. **Farrell,** Eileen L '88 %White Q&S -377 Oak Bx9304 -Gdn Cty 11530
(212) 396-4742 .. **Farrell,** Ellen M '83 -305 E 72nd -NY 10021
(516) 741-6611 .. **Farrell Farrell & Burke** -212 Station Plaza N -Mineola 11501 **Fx:**741-6682
(518) 583-7272 .. **Farrell,** Fiona S '98 Full Circle Farm -184 Lohnes Rd -Stillwtr 12170 **Fx:**583-7272
(516) 227-0700 .. **Farrell Fritz,PC** -1320 RXR Plz -Uniondale 11556 **Fx:**227-0777
(212) 687-1230 .. **Farrell Fritz,PC** -370 Lex Av -NY 10017 **Fx:**687-2175
(631) 547-8400 .. **Farrell Fritz,PC** -290 Broad Hollow Rd -Melvll 11747 **Fx:**547-0501
(631) 537-3100 .. **Farrell Fritz,PC** -2488 Montauk Hwy Bx1980 -Brdghmptn 11932 **Fx:**537-0560
(212) 681-2195 .. **Farrell,** Gary '87 -305 Bway -NY 10007
(631) 537-3100 .. **Farrell,** George J Jr. '58 (Farrell F,PC) -2488 Montauk Hwy Bx1980 -Brdghmptn 11932
(212) 837-6037 .. **Farrell,** Gregory C '09 %Hughes H&R LLP -1 Bttry Pk Plz -NY 10004 **Fx:**299-6037
(212) 446-8080 .. **Farrell,** James E Jr. '77 %McKinsey & Co -55 E 52nd -NY 10055 **Fx:**688-9521
(631) 232-0200 .. **Farrell,** James F Jr. '80 (Fumuso KDSS&F,LLP) -110 Marcus Blvd -Hauppauge 11788
(631) 874-7360 .. **Farrell,** James P Jr. '84 -Bx237 -Eastport 11941
(845) 794-3344 .. **Farrell,** James R '95 %DA -414 Bway -Monticello 12701 **Fx:**794-3646
(212) 521-5400 .. **Farrell,** Jean M '90 (Reed S LLP) -599 Lex Av -NY 10022
(716) 648-2810 .. **Farrell,** Jennifer S '03 (Farrell & F) -5872 Camp Rd -Hambrg 14075 **Fx:**648-2510
(516) 228-1300 .. **Farrell,** John C '01 %Sahn WC&B,PLLC -333 Earle Ovngton Blvd -Uniondale 11553
(917) 322-2222 .. **Farrell,** John F Jr. '63 %Automatic Srvc Co -445 Park Av -NY 10022 **Fx:**322-2223
(516) 829-6900 .. **Farrell,** John M Jr. '57 OfCnsl Ackerman LCB&L,LLP -1010 Nrthrn Blvd -Gt Neck 11021
(516) 747-0300 .. **Farrell,** Jonathan D '93 (Meltzer LG&B,LLP) -190 Willis Av -Mineola 11501
(212) 801-6911 .. **Farrell,** Jos D '94 (Greenberg T,LLP) -200 Park Av -NY 10166
(212) 785-2929 .. **Farrell,** Jos H '61 (Conway FC&K,PC) -48 Wall -NY 10005
(212) 629-9690 .. **Farrell,** Jos P III '02 %P Merani -298 5th Av -NY 10001 **Fx:**629-9664
(518) 285-8949 .. **Farrell,** Joshua L '03 Hon J Teresi -16 Eagle -Albany 12207
(716) 648-2810 .. **Farrell,** Kenneth J '90 (Farrell & F) -5872 Camp Rd -Hambrg 14075 **Fx:**648-2510
(718) 901-6600 .. **Farrell,** Lynn P '79 %Schl Cnstrctn Auth -188 W 230th -Bronx 10463 **Fx:**901-6649
(914) 666-4000 .. **Farrell,** Mark F '82 -84 Smith Av Bx387 -Mt Kisco 10549 **Fx:**666-0556
(716) 689-4250 .. **Farrell,** Mark G '72 Amherst Town Justice -400 John James Audubon -Amherst 14228
(315) 635-3222 .. **Farrell Martin & Barnell** -44 Oswego Bx199 -Baldwinsvll 13027 **Fx:**635-4636
(585) 344-7908 .. **Farrell,** Michl J '88 Genesee Vlly BOCES -80 Munson -Le Roy 14482
(212) 442-8678 .. **Farrell,** Odile Maun '06 %Law Dept -100 Church -NY 10007 **Fx:**788-0367
(585) 753-4500 .. **Farrell,** Patrick B '04 %DA -832 Watts Bldg -Rchstr 14614 **Fx:**753-4576
(516) 228-3565 .. **Farrell,** Paul J '87 (Farrell Law Firm,PC) -290 Broadhllw Rd -Melvll 11747
(212) 442-4687 .. **Farrell,** Peter G '91 %Law Dept -100 Church -NY 10007 **Fx:**788-0367
(631) 501-5700 .. **Farrell,** Raymond E '90 (Carter DF&S LLP) -445 Broadhallow Rd -Melvll 11747
(718) 250-2000 .. **Farrell,** Richd K '93 %DA -350 Jay -Brklyn 11201 **Fx:**250-2314
(718) 780-7930 .. **Farrell,** Richd T '64 %Bklyn Law Schl -250 Joralemon -Brklyn 11201 **Fx:**780-0393
(212) 458-1596 .. **Farrell,** Robt '97 %AIG -175 Water -NY 10038
(914) 766-4034 .. **Farrell,** Robt G Jr. '88 %IBM -Route 100 Bldg 4 -Somers 10589
(518) 439-7744 .. **Farrell,** Robt J '61 -75 Dumbarton Dr -Delmar 12054 **Fx:**439-7744
(518) 623-2020 .. **Farrell,** Robt T '75 -38 Oak -Warrensburg 12885 **Fx:**623-2317

(315) 431-6127 .. **Farrell**, Sarah C '97 Peerless Ins -5062 Brittonfld Pkwy -E Syracuse 13057
(212) 545-4668 .. **Farrell**, Scott J '00 %Wolf HAF&H LLP -270 Mad Av -NY 10016
(212) 530-5000 .. **Farrell**, Sean M '08 %Milbank TH&M LLP -1 Chase Manh Plz -NY 10005
(212) 309-6000 .. **Farrell**, Stephen P '72 (Morgan L&B LLP) -101 Park Av -NY 10178
(518) 462-1015 .. **Farrell**, Terence '83 %OHA-SSA -76 N Pearl -Albany 12207
(607) 723-5341 .. **Farrell**, Thos F '66 SpclCnsl Hinman H&K,LLP -80 Exchange Bx5250 -Bnghmtn 13902
(845) 343-2155 .. **Farrell**, Thos G '69 -41 Dolson Av -Middletwn 10940
(516) 741-6611 .. **Farrell**, Vincent D '69 (Farrell F&B) -212 Station Plaza N -Mineola 11501
(631) 727-2800 .. **Farrell**, Wm F '83 -214 Roanoke Av -Rvrhead 11901 **Fx:**727-8262
(212) 684-8700 .. **Farrelly**, Kevin J '81 -270 Mad Av -NY 10016 **Fx:**686-1706
(914) 995-4725 .. **Farrelly**, Raymond P '67 %Hon K Rudolph -111 Martin Luther King Blvd -White Plns 10601
(212) 762-5065 .. **Farrelly**, Tara A '97 Morgan Stanley Invsmnt Mgmt -1221 Av of Amer -NY 10020
(212) 321-8327 .. **Farrelly**, Thos J '75 Verizon -140 West -NY 10007
(212) 701-3000 .. **Farren**, Patricia '74 (Cahill G&R LLP) -80 Pine -NY 10005 **Fx:**269-5420
(212) 448-1100 .. **Farren**, Richd L '72 (McLaughlin & S,LLP) -260 Mad Av -NY 10016
(212) 530-5000 .. **Farren**, Victoria '10 %Milbank TH&M LLP -1 Chase Manh Plz -NY 10005
(212) 435-3417 .. **Farrington**, Christine '85 %Port Auth of NY/NJ -225 Park Av S -NY 10003 **Fx:**435-5241
(212) 335-9574 .. **Farrington**, Mary C '85 %DA -1 Hogan Pl -NY 10013
(914) 397-7500 .. **Farrington**, Robt B '95 GRP Fincl Srvcs Corp -445 Hmltn Av -White Plns 10601 **Fx:**397-7550
(212) 504-6000 .. **Farris**, Marsena M '84 Cadwalader W&T LLP -1 World Fncl Ctr -NY 10281
(212) 415-9200 .. **Farris**, Theo N '78 (Dorsey & W LLP) -250 Park Av -NY 10177
(212) 558-4000 .. **Farris**, Wm L '79 SpclCnsl Sullivan & C LLP -125 Broad -NY 10004
(914) 245-2487 .. **Farron**, Lucien G '58 -79 Stonewall Ct -Yorktwn Hts 10598
(585) 232-6500 .. **Farrow**, Brett E '05 %Harter S&E LLP -1600 Bausch & Lomb Pl -Rchstr 14604
(212) 578-5030 .. **Farrow**, James R '05 %MetLife -27-01 Qns Plz N -LIC 11101
(646) 458-6969 .. **Farrow**, Lee W '96 Ace Medical Risk -140 Bway -NY 10005
(716) 433-5962 .. **Farrugia**, David J '79 -131 East Av -Lockprt 14094 **Fx:**439-5941
(718) 286-6000 .. **Farrugia**, George J '96 %DA -125-01 Qns Blvd -Kew Gdns 11415
(212) 250-2825 .. **Farry**, John L '93 %Deutsche Bank -60 Wall -NY 10005
(716) 433-1991 .. **Farugia**, Johannah M '84 UAW GM Leg Srvcs -90 Prof Pkwy -Lockprt 14094 **Fx:**433-4888
(212) 983-9330 .. **Faruqi**, Lubna M '88 (Faruqi & F,LLP) -369 Lex Av -NY 10017 **Fx:**983-9331
(212) 983-9330 .. **Faruqi**, Nadeem '88 (Faruqi & F,LLP) -369 Lex Av -NY 10017 **Fx:**983-9331
(716) 849-2121 .. **Fasanello**, Sebastian W '92 %Merrill Lynch -50 Fountain Plz -Buffalo 14202
(212) 973-9273 .. **Fasano**, Craig M '00 Sontag Advisory LLC -261 Mad Av -NY 10016
(212) 791-7791 .. **Fasano**, H Raymond '96 (Madeo & F) -299 Bway -NY 10007 **Fx:**791-9706
(212) 490-3000 .. **Fasano**, Louise '98 %Wilson EME&D LLP -150 E 42nd -NY 10017
(718) 966-4400 .. **Fasano**, Raymond A '86 -885 Annadale Rd -Staten Isl 10312 **Fx:**966-5352
(212) 964-3290 .. **Fasano**, Tara L '04 %Levidow L&O -299 Bway -NY 10007
(718) 658-5999 .. **Fasanya**, Ade O '92 (Cheng & F,LLP) -246-11 F Lewis Blvd -Rosedale 11422 **Fx:**528-5708
(212) 310-8000 .. **Fasbender**, Jordan R '09 %Weil G&M LLP -767 5th Av -NY 10153
(518) 486-1841 .. **Fascia**, Cindy '83 %Dept of Health -Corning Twr 24th Fl -Albany 12237 **Fx:**473-2430
(212) 405-1691 .. **Fasciano**, Matthew J '03 Posse Fndtn -14 Wall -NY 10005
(212) 947-3793 .. **Fasciano**, Paul D '98 (Sadis & G LLP) -551 5th Av -NY 10176
(212) 735-3000 .. **Fashakin**, Deborah O '10 %Skadden ASM&F LLP -4 Times Sq -NY 10036
(718) 805-2522 .. **Fashakin**, Janet O '01 -105-22 Jamaica Av -Richmnd Hll 11418
(212) 947-0151 .. **Fashing**, Jos '84 -347 W 39th -NY 10018
(212) 309-6000 .. **Fasman**, Igor '09 %Morgan L&B LLP -101 Park Av -NY 10178
(212) 572-8600 .. **Fasman**, Steven L '88 %MacAndrews & Forbes -35 E 62nd -NY 10065
(212) 318-6000 .. **Fasman**, Zachary D '01 (Paul HJ&W LLP) -75 E 55th -NY 10022
(716) 284-6513 .. **Faso**, James J Jr. '95 %Mark Grossman -710 4th -Niagara Fls 14302
(212) 790-4500 .. **Faso**, John J '81 (Manatt P&P,LLP) -7 Times Sq -NY 10036
(518) 431-6700 .. **Faso**, John J '81 (Manatt P&P,LLP) -30 S Pearl -Albany 12207
(212) 385-8247 .. **Fasone**, John M '90 %HRA -60 Lafayette -NY 10013
(212) 903-9000 .. **Fasoro**, Patrick '10 %Linklaters -1345 Av of Amer -NY 10105
(914) 287-6466 .. **Fass**, Danl A '78 (Klapper & F) -170 Hmltn Av -White Plns 10601 **Fx:**287-6422
(516) 742-8111 .. **Fass**, Florence M '80 (Fass & G,LLP) -1225 Franklin Av -Gdn Cty 11530 **Fx:**742-8999
(212) 484-3900 .. **Fass**, Lauren Tabak '05 %Arent F LLP -1675 Bway -NY 10019
(212) 746-6500 .. **Fass**, Maxine '81 %NY Presbyterian Hsptl -525 E 68th Bx88 -NY 10065 **Fx:**746-8603
(212) 969-3445 .. **Fass**, Peter M '62 (Proskauer R LLP) -1585 Bway -NY 10036
(516) 569-3100 .. **Fass**, Steven S '74 -112 Spruce -Cedarhrst 11516
(516) 741-4799 .. **Fass**, Todd E '01 (Baker SBGFM&N,LLC) -100 Grdn City Plz -Gdn Cty 11530
(516) 622-0606 .. **Fassberg**, Bruce P '85 %P Rizzuto,PC -1 Old Cntry Rd -Carle Pl 11514 **Fx:**622-2112
(518) 356-0436 .. **Fassett**, Edw C Jr. '81 -4662 Duanesbrg Rd -Duanesbrg 12056 **Fx:**(866) 812-1851
(914) 793-2146 .. **Fassler**, Allen L '99 -206 Longvue Ter -Ynkrs 10710
(212) 691-0950 .. **Fassler**, Elizabeth L '99 Ctr for Family Representation -116 John -NY 10038 **Fx:**691-0951
(212) 748-4084 .. **Fassler**, Jill S '74 %Bd of Trade -1 North End Av -NY 10282
(914) 697-7667 .. **Fassler**, Norman '59 Convergence -800 Wstchstr Av -Pt Chester 10573
(845) 457-7501 .. **Fassnacht**, Tina M '00 (Fassnacht & R LLP) -201 Ward -Montgmry 12549 **Fx:**457-7503
(914) 948-5152 .. **Fassuliotis**, Karen '01 OfCnsl E Atnally -99 Court -White Plns 10601 **Fx:**948-5401
(212) 416-6250 .. **Fast**, Carolyn M '03 %Dept of Law -120 Bway -NY 10271
(212) 788-0785 .. **Fastenberg**, Andrea '95 %Law Dept -100 Church -NY 10007 **Fx:**788-0367
(212) 697-2112 .. **Fastenberg**, Arthur '40 -60 E 42nd -NY 10165
(212) 697-0024 .. **Fastenberg & Birnant** -60 E 42nd -NY 10165
(212) 692-1000 .. **Fastenberg**, Chas '76 SpclCnsl Duane M LLP -1540 Bway -NY 10036
(212) 697-0024 .. **Fastenberg**, Marvin '54 (Fastenberg & B) -60 E 42nd -NY 10165
(212) 396-8698 .. **Fastert**, Michl R '05 Tiedemann Invstmnt Grp -535 Mad Av -NY 10022
(212) 701-3000 .. **Fastiggi**, Jos M '08 %Cahill G&R LLP -80 Pine -NY 10005 **Fx:**269-5420
(516) 437-7300 .. **Fastman**, Harley S '95 -2001 Marcus Av -New Hyde Pk 11042 **Fx:**437-7292
(718) 447-1962 .. **Fastman**, Lainie R '82 (Hall & H,LLP) -57 Beach -Staten Isl 10304 **Fx:**447-2761
(212) 376-6400 .. **Fastman**, Tammy '08 %Marshall DWC&G -88 Pine -NY 10005
(212) 435-3571 .. **Fastow**, Fredric S '93 %Port Auth of NY/NJ -225 Park Av S -NY 10003 **Fx:**435-3555
(212) 277-6500 .. **Fastow**, Jay N '78 (Dickstein S LLP) -1633 Bway -NY 10019
(212) 566-6212 .. **Fasulo**, Louis V '84 (Fasulo S&D) -225 Bway -NY 10007
(718) 722-6472 .. **Fasulo**, Maria T '96 Appllt Div 2nd Dept -45 Monroe Pl -Brklyn 11201 **Fx:**858-2446
(212) 566-6212 .. **Fasulo Shalley & DiMaggio** -225 Bway -NY 10007 **Fx:**566-8165
(212) 859-8000 .. **Fatale**, Alfred L III '08 %Fried FHS&J LLP -1 NY Plz -NY 10004
(315) 792-0171 .. **Fatata**, Linda Sullivan '84 %Law Dept -1 Knndy Plz -Utica 13502 **Fx:**792-0175
(315) 422-1152 .. **Fatcheric**, Maureen G '89 (Costello C&F,PLLC) -500 Plum -Syracuse 13204
(631) 654-2303 .. **Fath**, John N '71 -629 Route 112 -Patchogue 11772
(212) 686-7800 .. **Fatoullah**, Ellice '70 (Fatoullah Assoc) -2 Park Av -NY 10016
(516) 466-4422 .. **Fatoullah**, Ronald A '77 R Fatoullah & Assoc -425 Nrthrn Blvd -Gt Neck 11021 **Fx:**466-2219 ***[Estate Planning & Administration] [Elder Law]***
(212) 751-7600 .. **Fatoullah**, Ronald A '77 R Fatoullah & Assoc -475 Park Av S -NY 10016
(718) 621-5300 .. **Fatoullah**, Ronald A '77 R Fatoullah & Assoc -1861 86th -Brklyn 11214
(718) 261-1700 .. **Fatoullah**, Ronald A '77 R Fatoullah & Assoc -100-15 Qns Blvd -Frst Hlls 11375 **Fx:**504-7849
(845) 446-4886 .. **Fatsis**, Konstantinos G '00 Fatsis & Assoc,PLLC -239 Main Bx258 -Highlnd Fls 10928 **Fx:**(775) 255-4891
(516) 488-3300 .. **Fatsis**, Kyriakoula '02 %Shaub AC&S,LLP -1983 Marcus Av -Lk Success 11042
(716) 856-4000 .. **Fattey**, Christofer C '07 %Hodgson R LLP -140 Pearl -Buffalo 14202
(518) 487-5593 .. **Fattorusso**, Leslie A '95 NYS Bar Assn -1 Elk -Albany 12207 **Fx:**463-8844
(212) 309-3104 .. **Faucetta**, Danl A '92 %UBS Financial Srvcs Inc -200 Park Av -NY 10166
(518) 476-2001 .. **Faucher**, Gregory D '87 (Gilberti SH&S,PC) -111 Wshngtn Av -Albany 12210
(212) 486-2400 .. **Faucher**, Mary D '78 OfCnsl Leader & B LLP -630 3rd Av -NY 10017
(516) 496-5822 .. **Fauci**, Bryan P '07 %T Spina -170 Froehlich Farm Blvd -Woodbury 11797 **Fx:**496-5420
(518) 885-5011 .. **Fauci**, James A '96 -30 Remsen -Malta 12020 **Fx:**885-5298
(607) 754-0711 .. **Fauci**, Michl S '94 (Fauci & F) -43 Wshngtn Av Bx7 -Endicott 13761 **Fx:**786-5869
(607) 754-0711 .. **Fauci**, Salvatore A '59 OfCnsl Fauci & F -43 Wshngtn Av Bx7 -Endicott 13761 **Fx:**786-5869
(516) 759-1212 .. **Faughnan**, Elizabeth Ann '94 Cnsl Mohen & T LLP -186 Birch Hill Rd -Locust Vly 11560
(607) 723-5341 .. **Faughnan**, Eugene D '91 (Hinman H&K,LLP) -80 Exchange Bx5250 -Bnghmtn 13902
(718) 254-6146 .. **Faughnan**, Richd T '84 %US Atty -271 Cadman Plz E -Brklyn 11201 **Fx:**254-6481
(516) 357-3000 .. **Faul**, Regina E '89 (Rivkin R LLP) -926 RXR Plz -Uniondale 11556
(212) 406-9710 .. **Faulkner**, Amara S '02 Kral CRRP&G,LLP -170 Bway -NY 10038
(212) 735-3000 .. **Faulkner**, Andrew M '86 (Skadden ASM&F LLP) -4 Times Sq -NY 10036
(212) 816-1141 .. **Faulkner**, Benjamin M '04 Citigrp Glbl Mkts -388 Greenwich -NY 10013
(212) 306-7470 .. **Faulkner**, Joan Simon '82 %Comm on Human Rights -40 Rector -NY 10006 **Fx:**306-7414
(212) 762-4921 .. **Faulkner**, John H '86 Morgan Stanley -1221 Av of Amer -NY 10020
(518) 843-1728 .. **Faulkner**, John R '83 -279 Guy Park Av -Amsterdam 12010 **Fx:**843-1728
(518) 447-9664 .. **Faulkner**, Laureen F '84 %MHLS -75 New Scotland Av -Albany 12208 **Fx:**447-9697
(914) 428-8330 .. **Faulkner**, Lawr '74 Westchester ARC -265 Saw Mill Rvr Rd -Hawthorne 10532 **Fx:**428-0322
(212) 449-7016 .. **Faulkner**, Robin '85 %Merrill Lynch -220 Bway -NY 10038
(518) 374-7731 .. **Faulkner**, Roland L '64 Faulkner & M -38 N Ferry -Schnctdy 12305 **Fx:**374-7475
(845) 486-4300 .. **Faulkner**, Sharon M '02 (Ostertag OB&F) -17 Cllgvw Av -Poughkeepsie 12603
(212) 808-7800 .. **Faulkner**, Walter T '56 (Kelley D&W LLP) -101 Park Av -NY 10178
(212) 751-7700 .. **Faust**, David I '65 (Faust & O,LLP) -488 Mad Av -NY 10022
(716) 884-8882 .. **Faust**, Francis S '48 -23 Highland Av -Buffalo 14222
(716) 856-5608 .. **Faust**, George R '89 -14 Lafayette Sq -Buffalo 14203
(212) 363-6900 .. **Faust Goetz Schenker & Blee LLP** -2 Rector -NY 10006 **Fx:**363-1090
(212) 922-9700 .. **Faust**, Gregory S '00 %1st Amer Title -633 3rd Av -NY 10017 **Fx:**922-0881
(212) 940-8639 .. **Faust**, Jonathan J '94 (Katten MR LLP) -575 Mad Av -NY 10022
(914) 686-8383 .. **Faust**, Marilyn S '85 -4 Cntry Clb Dr -Larchmnt 10538 **Fx:**834-1437
(212) 425-7200 .. **Faust**, Matthew J '07 %Kenyon & K,LLP -1 Bway -NY 10004
(212) 751-7700 .. **Faust & Oppenheim,LLP** -488 Mad Av -NY 10022 **Fx:**371-8410
(212) 363-6900 .. **Faust**, Randy S '90 (Faust GS&B LLP) -2 Rector -NY 10006
(315) 532-6900 .. **Faust**, Susan M '01 %Leg Aid -108 W Brdg -Oswego 13126 **Fx:**342-1891
(212) 450-4000 .. **Fausten**, Marcel R '08 %Davis P&W LLP -450 Lex Av -NY 10017

(212) 398-9366 .. **Faux,** David H '06 %Dramatists Guild of America,Inc -1501 Bway -NY 10036 **Fx:**944-0420
(718) 237-5500 .. **Faux,** Meghan '00 %Leg Srvcs -105 Court -Brklyn 11201 **Fx:**855-0733
(212) 318-6000 .. **Fava,** Palmina M '98 (Paul HJ&W LLP) -75 E 55th -NY 10022
(516) 742-9090 .. **Favale,** G Michl '96 (Terino K&F) -Bx1185 -Syosset 11791
(631) 424-6100 .. **Favara,** Christine Anne '05 %Advantage Title -410 NY Av -Huntngtn 11743 **Fx:**424-6049
(716) 856-1700 .. **Favaro,** Timmon M '06 (Cannon H&W,LLP) -726 Exchange -Buffalo 14210
(914) 428-2143 .. **Favata,** Chas J '93 -445 Hmltn Av -White Plns 10601 **Fx:**428-1660
(315) 473-0899 .. **Favata,** Jos D '07 %Anelli X,PC -441 S Salina -Syracuse 13202 **Fx:**473-0530
(212) 837-6105 .. **Favata,** Richd D '05 %Hughes H&R LLP -1 Bttry Pk Plz -NY 10004
(516) 742-9494 .. **Favata,** Robt F '77 (Favata & W,LLP) -229 7th -Gdn Cty 11530
(516) 742-9494 .. **Favata & Wallace, LLP** -229 7th -Gdn Cty 11530 **Fx:**742-7088
(212) 867-4466 .. **Favilukis,** Vladimir '07 %Belkin BW&G,LLP -270 Mad Av -NY 10016
(212) 610-6300 .. **Favour,** Anna R '09 %Allen & O -1221 Av of Amer -NY 10020
(212) 326-2000 .. **Favre,** Emily G '08 %O'Melveny & M LLP -7 Times Sq -NY 10036
(518) 474-6530 .. **Favreau,** John Laurent '95 %Dept Pub Srvc -3 ESP -Albany 12223
(518) 562-0600 .. **Favreau,** Wm A '84 (O'Connell & A) -206 W Bay Plz -Plattsbrgh 12901
(212) 446-2300 .. **Favretto,** Michl P '07 %Boies S&F LLP -575 Lex Av -NY 10022
(518) 474-1697 .. **Favretto,** Peter G '77 %Dept of Law -The Cptl -Albany 12224
(518) 561-1100 .. **Favro,** Gary L '77 -46 Court Bx924 -Plattsbrgh 12901 **Fx:**562-5667
(212) 295-6483 .. **Fawcett,** James T '03 WilmerHale -399 Park Av -NY 10022
(212) 301-8450 .. **Fawer,** David S '94 Dune Cptl -623 5th Av -NY 10022
(212) 277-6500 .. **Fawer,** Mark S '87 (Dickstein S LLP) -1633 Bway -NY 10019
(718) 250-2000 .. **Fay,** Christina P '06 DA -350 Jay -Brklyn 11201 **Fx:**250-2314
(212) 227-7878 .. **Fay,** Donald J '81 (Waters MM) -233 Bway -NY 10279
(716) 636-7600 .. **Fay,** Jennifer L '08 %HoganWillig -2410 N Forest Rd -Amherst 14068
(212) 788-8699 .. **Fay,** Joshua R '03 Law Dept -100 Church -NY 10007 **Fx:**788-0367
(212) 506-1700 .. **Fay,** Michl M '88 (Kasowitz BT&F LLP) -1633 Bway -NY 10019
(716) 636-7600 .. **Fay,** Patricia A '10 %HoganWillig -2410 N Forest Rd -Amherst 14068
(212) 619-6000 .. **Fay,** Patrick J '91 (Fay K&M,LLP) -150 Bway -NY 10038 **Fx:**208-6879
(212) 617-2516 .. **Fayad,** Nihal M '04 Bloomberg LP -731 Lex Av -NY 10022
(212) 655-3500 .. **Fayenson,** Inna '90 Cnsl Meister S&F LLP -140 E 45th -NY 10017
(212) 218-2100 .. **Fayer,** Aleksandra '09 %Fitzpatrick CH&S -1290 Av of Amer -NY 10104
(914) 761-9093 .. **Fayer,** Eric M '92 (Jacoby & M) -175 Main -White Plns 10601 **Fx:**761-9160
(914) 220-1089 .. **Fayer,** Russell A '73 -111 Church -White Plns 10601
(212) 643-2800 .. **Fayer,** Zlata '08 %JTK Cohen,PC -1350 Bway -NY 10018 **Fx:**643-4386
(212) 878-7900 .. **Fayerberg,** Roman '07 %Fox R LLP -100 Park Av -NY 10017
(212) 632-5500 .. **Fayman,** Irina '09 %Salans LLP -620 5th Av -NY 10020
(585) 454-2020 .. **Fazili,** Sareer Ahmed '98 (Cellino & B,PC) -16 W Main -Rchstr 14614
(212) 509-9595 .. **Fazio,** Alfred M '84 (Capuder FG LLP) -90 Broad -NY 10004
(212) 942-6011 .. **Fazio,** Cataldo F '87 (C Fazio,LLC) -305 Mad Av -NY 10165 **Fx:**942-6014
(212) 732-3200 .. **Fazio,** Christine A '00 (Carter L&M LLP) -2 Wall -NY 10005
(212) 265-6888 .. **Fazio,** Frank '90 (Porzio B&N,PC) -156 W 56th -NY 10019
(585) 325-7440 .. **Fazio,** Jennifer L '95 (Kaman BMJ&G LLP) -135 Corp Woods -Rchstr 14623
(914) 729-6319 .. **Fazio,** Jos A '03 (Fazio & K,PLLC) -10 Bank -White Plns 10606
(212) 593-6700 .. **Fazio,** Peter J '01 (Aaronson RF&D,LLP) -757 3rd Av -NY 10017
(516) 280-7105 .. **Fazio,** Thos R '86 (Blodnick F & Assoc,PC) -1325 Franklin Av -Gdn Cty 11530 **Fx:**280-7102
(212) 940-3120 .. **Fazlibegu,** Dino '95 (Nixon P LLP) -437 Mad Av -NY 10022
(212) 687-2770 .. **Fazzari,** Vincent M '75 %Cohen PL&P -551 5th Av -NY 10176
(607) 535-8383 .. **Fazzary,** Jos G '93 (DA) -105 9th -Watkins Glen 14891
(631) 547-8989 .. **Fazzini,** John '93 -33 Walt Whitman Rd -Huntngtn Sta 11746 **Fx:**427-1516
(212) 836-4862 .. **Fazzio,** John P III '06 -445 Park Av -NY 10022 **Fx:**(917) 322-2105
(212) 233-0130 .. **Fazzolari,** Diane '06 %Nelson Ld&H -120 Bway -NY 10271
(212) 553-5476 .. **Fazzolari,** Maria '97 Zurich NA -1 Lbrty Plz -NY 10006
(518) 372-3300 .. **Fazzone,** A Jos '57 (Fazzone F&C,PLLC) -1536 Union -Schnctdy 12309 **Fx:**372-7400
(518) 372-3300 .. **Fazzone,** Anthony A '92 (Fazzone F&C,PLLC) -1536 Union -Schnctdy 12309 **Fx:**372-7400
(518) 432-3423 .. **Fazzone,** Eileen Fitzpatrick '93 %Ct of Claims -Justice Bldg ESP Bx7344 -Albany 12224 **Fx:**432-3450
(716) 847-0662 .. **Feal,** Sophie I '89 %Volunteer Lwyrs Prjt -237 Main -Buffalo 14203 **Fx:**847-0307
(518) 457-8334 .. **Feane,** Tyler L '08 %Dept of Tax & Fin -Bldg 9 State Campus -Albany 12227 **Fx:**457-6131
(914) 997-2435 .. **Fear,** Alexander M '96 -280 N Cntrl Pk Av -Hartsdale 10530
(212) 713-2841 .. **Fearey,** John L '82 UBS -1285 Av of Amer -NY 10019
(212) 977-9700 .. **Fearon,** George R '71 (Phillips N LLP) -666 5th Av -NY 10103
(212) 490-9100 .. **Fearon,** Stephen J '64 OfCnsl Condon & F LLP -7 Times Sq -NY 10036
(212) 421-6492 .. **Fearon,** Stephen J Jr. '91 (Squitieri & F,LLP) -32 E 57th -NY 10022 **Fx:**421-6553
(212) 450-4000 .. **Fears,** Derek T '08 %Davis P&W LLP -450 Lex Av -NY 10017
(516) 745-9000 .. **Feather,** David S '94 -666 Old Cntry Rd -Gdn Cty 11530 **Fx:**228-8349
(212) 859-8000 .. **Featherman,** Scott J '05 %Fried FHS&J LLP -1 NY Plz -NY 10004
(518) 691-0088 .. **Feathers,** Cynthia '88 -48 Union Av Bx4818 -Saratoga Spgs 12866 **Fx:**587-0128
(212) 779-8600 .. **Featherstone,** Shamus F '09 %Silverman SS&B PLLC -381 Park Av S -NY 10016
(518) 436-0786 .. **Featherstonhaugh,** James D '69 (Featherstonhaugh W&C,LLP) -99 Pine -Albany 12207
(518) 436-0786 .. **Featherstonhaugh Wiley & Clyne, LLP** -99 Pine -Albany 12207 **Fx:**427-0452
(914) 251-1900 .. **Febbraio,** Gregg M '87 (G Febbraio,PC) -110 Corp Park Dr -White Plns 10604 **Fx:**251-1490
(212) 983-7080 .. **Febbraro,** Lawr E '88 -110 Wall -NY 10005
(212) 751-1700 .. **Fechner,** Lawr '74 (Jaffe R&L LLP) -880 3rd Av -NY 10022
(212) 609-6800 .. **Fechter,** Gary H '91 (McCarter & E,LLP) -245 Park Av -NY 10167
(716) 856-4000 .. **Fechter,** Wendy K '83 %Hodgson R LLP -140 Pearl -Buffalo 14202
(914) 683-1333 .. **Fecko,** Christine M '98 Cnsl My Sisters Pl,Inc -1 Water -White Plns 10601
(914) 285-9500 .. **Fecteau,** Denyse M '04 %Beck LP,PC -399 Knollwood Rd -White Plns 10603
(212) 259-8000 .. **Fedder,** Andrew S '09 %Dewey & L LLP -1301 Av of Amer -NY 10019
(718) 630-2900 .. **Fede,** Maryann '01 %VA -800 Poly Pl -Brklyn 11209 **Fx:**630-2917
(718) 250-4219 .. **Fedele,** Briana '07 Leg Aid -111 Lvngstn -Brklyn 11201 **Fx:**250-4243
(518) 439-1516 .. **Fedele,** Kathleen M '90 -52 Font Grove Rd -Slingerlnds 12159
(518) 462-5601 .. **Fedele,** Sara B '08 %O'Connell & A -54 State -Albany 12207
(212) 736-4430 .. **Fedele,** Thos D '77 (Blecher M&F) -1501 Bway -NY 10036
(718) 625-1111 .. **Feder,** Adam B '96 %Feder & R,PLLC -105 Court -Brklyn 11201 **Fx:**875-1860
(212) 888-8200 .. **Feder,** Alvin M '56 (Feder K LLP) -845 3rd Av -NY 10022
(212) 808-7800 .. **Feder,** Benjamin D '86 SpclCnsl Kelley D&W LLP -101 Park Av -NY 10178
(212) 949-0100 .. **Feder,** Craig S '88 %Cmmnwlth Land Title -140 E 45th -NY 10017 **Fx:**949-2438
(212) 909-6000 .. **Feder,** David W '08 %Debevoise & P LLP -919 3rd Av -NY 10022
(212) 493-8350 .. **Feder,** Florian A '07 Brown Bros Harriman -140 Bway -NY 10005 **Fx:**493-8206
(718) 625-1111 .. **Feder,** Fredk '59 (Feder & R,PLLC) -105 Court -Brklyn 11201 **Fx:**875-1860
(212) 521-5400 .. **Feder,** Gil '90 (Reed S LLP) -599 Lex Av -NY 10022
(212) 981-4500 .. **Feder,** Gwen L '83 PeterSan Grp -1450 Bway -NY 10018 **Fx:**981-4560
(212) 888-8200 .. **Feder Kaszovitz LLP** -845 3rd Av -NY 10022 **Fx:**888-7776
(212) 326-3939 .. **Feder,** Meir '91 (Jones D) -222 E 41st -NY 10017
(718) 729-6970 .. **Feder,** Melvin '74 -34-11 35th Av -Astoria 11106 **Fx:**729-6295
(212) 619-1910 .. **Feder,** Michl E '02 Regosin ES&F -225 Bway -NY 10007
(516) 229-6000 .. **Feder,** Mitchell S '01 %R Lau & Assoc -300 Jericho Quad Bx9040 -Jericho 11753 **Fx:**229-6167
(516) 294-8844 .. **Feder,** Nicole '02 %L'Abbate BC&C,LLP -1001 Franklin Av -Gdn Cty 11530
(718) 618-2500 .. **Feder,** Paul T '82 %Civil Ct -851 Grnd Cncrs -Bronx 10451 **Fx:**590-7294
(585) 473-1180 .. **Feder,** R Eric '85 -1580 Elmwood Av -Rchstr 14620
(631) 465-0058 .. **Feder,** Rebecca A '03 %S Schwaber & Assoc -6 Corp Ctr Dr -Melvll 11747 **Fx:**465-0057
(914) 761-1300 .. **Feder,** Robt '53 (Cuddy & F LLP) -445 Hmltn Av -White Plns 10601
(212) 619-1910 .. **Feder,** Saul E '69 (Regosin ES&F) -225 Bway -NY 10007
(516) 572-7774 .. **Feder,** Sharon I '80 Nassau Comm Cllg -1 Educ Dr -Gdn Cty 11530
(212) 455-2000 .. **Feder,** Stephan J '82 (Simpson T&B LLP) -425 Lex Av -NY 10017
(718) 268-9040 .. **Feder,** Stephen I '83 -116-55 Qns Blvd -Frst Hlls 11375 **Fx:**268-3894
(585) 544-7090 .. **Feder,** Steven E '87 (Pirrello MP&F) -2040 E Ridge Rd -Rchstr 14622
(212) 909-8459 .. **Feder,** Warren H '80 Carl Marks Capital Advisors -900 3rd Av -NY 10022
(212) 603-7843 .. **Federbusch,** Stephen J '01 %Universal Music Grp -825 8th Av -NY 10019
(212) 969-3000 .. **Federbush,** Alan '92 %Proskauer R LLP -1585 Bway -NY 10036
(212) 446-7000 .. **Federbush,** Judith G '96 %McKinsey & Co -55 E 52nd -NY 10055 **Fx:**688-9521
(212) 613-2035 .. **Federgreen,** Shepard A '81 (Gibbons PC) -1 Penn Plz -NY 10119 **Fx:**554-9679
(716) 854-3455 .. **Federice,** John R '97 (Gielowski F&C,LLP) -135 Delaware Av -Buffalo 14202 **Fx:**854-2797
(212) 953-2381 .. **Federici,** Jos R '05 %Rubin F&F,LLP -292 Mad Av -NY 10017
(212) 692-9666 .. **Federici,** Nicholas E '07 %Gilbride TL&S LLC -708 3rd Av -NY 10017
(212) 742-8700 .. **Federico,** Danl G '91 (Garson D&C LLP) -110 Wall -NY 10005
(718) 268-3900 .. **Federman,** Allen '69 (Federman & M) -118-21 Qns Blvd -Frst Hlls 11375 **Fx:**268-3963
(646) 855-0889 .. **Federman,** Harvey L '03 Bank of Amer -1 Bryant Pk -NY 10036
(518) 436-0751 .. **Federman,** Jonathan '95 (Hinman S PC) -121 State -Albany 12207
(718) 768-2388 .. **Federman,** Mark I '69 -508 First -Brklyn 11215
(212) 994-9963 .. **Federman,** Michl K '97 (Federman S LLP) -220 E 42nd -NY 10017 **Fx:**685-5199
(631) 665-0609 .. **Federman,** Paul R '87 (Sherman FS&L LLP) -8 E Main -Bay Shr 11706
(845) 339-5656 .. **Federoff,** Michl S '67 M Federoff PC -110 Maiden Ln -Kingston 12401 **Fx:**339-2656
(212) 225-2000 .. **Fedida,** Meyer H '04 %Cleary GS&H -1 Lbrty Plz -NY 10006
(212) 248-3140 .. **Fedor,** Matthew J '03 %Drinker B&R LLP -140 Bway -NY 10005
(845) 486-2110 .. **Fedorchak,** James M '74 Cnty Atty -22 Market -Poughkeepsie 12601 **Fx:**486-2002
(315) 772-6628 .. **Fedorko,** Jos A '02 US Army OSJA -141 Lewis Av -Fort Drum 13602
(212) 573-3953 .. **Fedowich,** Valerie '87 %Pfizer Inc -150 E 42nd -NY 10017
(718) 721-7600 .. **Fedrizzi,** Linda A F '87 -25-84 Steinway -Astoria 11103 **Fx:**721-9892
(212) 363-3100 .. **Fedrow,** Richd M '75 (Bivona & C,PC) -88 Pine -NY 10005
(212) 896-6500 .. **Fedun,** John A '05 %Howrey LLP -601 Lex Av -NY 10022
(212) 583-0100 .. **Fedus,** Ronald C '87 %Enzo Biochem -527 Mad Av -NY 10022 **Fx:**583-0150
(212) 238-4800 .. **Fedyna,** Laura C '08 %Landman CB&F,PC -120 Bway -NY 10271
(212) 558-4000 .. **Fee,** Anna H '08 %Sullivan & C LLP -125 Broad -NY 10004
(212) 223-8409 .. **Fee,** Elizabeth J '85 -150 E 58th -NY 10155 **Fx:**317-2946
(212) 418-8600 .. **Fee,** Kevin J '85 (Kornstein VW&P,LLP) -757 3rd Av -NY 10017
(607) 786-7777 .. **Fee,** Peter '84 -222 Front -Vestal 13850
(518) 473-7194 .. **Feedore,** Jeremy R '84 %Dept of Law -The Cptl -Albany 12224 **Fx:**473-1635
(212) 612-4200 .. **Feehan,** David P '92 %Hoey KT&E -55 Water -NY 10041
(212) 773-5334 .. **Feehan,** Jos R '03 Ernst & Young LLP -5 Times Sq -NY 10036
(516) 571-3800 .. **Feehan,** Kathleen C '03 %DA -262 Old Cntry Rd -Mineola 11501 **Fx:**248-9479

(516) 229-6000 .. **Feehan**, Thos G '93 %R Lau & Assoc -300 Jericho Quad Bx9040 -Jericho 11753 **Fx**:229-6167
(212) 309-6000 .. **Feeley**, Kristen L '08 %Morgan L&B LLP -101 Park Av -NY 10178
(716) 854-3400 .. **Feeley**, Michl T '93 (Rupp BPC&C LLC) -1600 Lbrty Bldg -Buffalo 14202
(212) 415-9200 .. **Feeley**, Patrick J '89 (Dorsey & W LLP) -250 Park Av -NY 10177
(212) 765-2100 .. **Feeley**, Thos M Jr. '07 %Spivak L LLP -1700 Bway -NY 10019
(212) 858-7931 .. **Feeley-Calvin**, Lynda D '92 IPC Info Systems -1 State -NY 10004
(646) 471-0515 .. **Feeman**, Amanda G '04 PricewaterhouseCoopers LLP -300 Mad Av -NY 10017
(516) 741-2121 .. **Feen**, David R '79 %N Kanzer -1325 Franklin Av -Gdn Cty 11530 **Fx**:741-3930
(212) 918-3000 .. **Feeney**, Adam R '10 %Hogan L LLP -875 3rd Av -NY 10022
(212) 425-5005 .. **Feeney**, Caroline L '94 %Clemente M&T,PA -14 Wall -NY 10005
(518) 452-3710 .. **Feeney Centi & Mackey** -116 Great Oaks Blvd -Albany 12203 **Fx**:452-3925
(212) 504-6000 .. **Feeney**, David W '63 (Cadwalader W&T LLP) -1 World Fncl Ctr -NY 10281
(607) 697-0066 .. **Feeney**, David W II '90 -950 Danby Rd -Ithaca 14850 **Fx**:697-0059
(518) 452-3710 .. **Feeney**, Dennis A '87 (Feeney C&M) -116 Great Oaks Blvd -Albany 12203
(212) 705-7000 .. **Feeney**, Elizabeth E '04 Cnsl Bingham M LLP -399 Park Av -NY 10022
(718) 875-1300 .. **Feeney**, Elizabeth S '00 %Appllt Div 2nd Dept -45 Monroe Pl -Brklyn 11201 **Fx**:858-2446
(315) 339-7670 .. **Feeney**, Gerard F '05 Corp Cnsl -City Hall 198 N Wshngtn -Rome 13440 **Fx**:838-1166
(845) 638-0200 .. **Feeney**, James M '70 (J Feeney,PC) -254 S Main -New Cty 10956
(212) 661-9100 .. **Feeney**, Jennifer S '98 %Otterbourg SH&R,PC -230 Park Av -NY 10169
(212) 859-5053 .. **Feeney**, Paul A '00 -110 Wall -NY 10005 **Fx**:943-2300
(631) 366-3300 .. **Feeney**, Rosa M '92 -503 Route 111 -Hauppauge 11788 **Fx**:366-0632
(212) 609-6800 .. **Feeney**, Susan A '82 (McCarter & E,LLP) -245 Park Av -NY 10167
(212) 310-8000 .. **Feeney**, Thos E '05 %Weil G&M LLP -767 5th Av -NY 10153
(845) 857-4135 .. **Feeney**, Thos E '06 -7509 N Bway -Red Hook 12571
(718) 448-6053 .. **Feeney**, Thos R '78 -590 Hanover Av -Staten Isl 10304
(212) 788-9137 .. **Feerick**, Deirdre A '96 NYC Cncl-Admin Srvcs -250 Bway -NY 10007
(845) 353-2000 .. **Feerick**, Donald J Jr. '91 (Feerick LM PLLC) -96 S Bway -Nyack 10960
(845) 353-2000 .. **Feerick**, Jennifer M '99 %Feerick LM PLLC -96 S Bway -Nyack 10960
(212) 636-6873 .. **Feerick**, John D '61 Fordham Univ Sch of Law -140 W 62nd -NY 10023 **Fx**:(646) 312-8238
(212) 736-2624 .. **Feerick**, Kevin P '83 -236 W 26th -NY 10001
(845) 353-2000 .. **Feerick Lynch MacCartney PLLC** -96 S Bway -Nyack 10960 **Fx**:353-2789
(212) 360-5005 .. **Feerick**, Mary Elizabeth '91 MHLS -600 E 125th -NY 10035
(718) 384-9111 .. **Feerst**, Alex J '10 -236 Bway -Brklyn 11211
(212) 697-1900 .. **Feezell**, James T '94 %Booz Allen Hamilton -101 Park Av -NY 10178
(212) 687-3860 .. **Feffer**, Bruce M '84 (Snow BK,PC) -605 3rd Av -NY 10158
(212) 272-2000 .. **Feffer**, Bruce R '89 JP Morgan Chase -1 Metrotech Ctr N -Brklyn 11201
(212) 318-3000 .. **Feffer**, Jaclyn G '04 %Fulbright & J LLP -666 5th Av -NY 10103
(212) 935-7400 .. **Feffer**, Joel C '70 (Harwood F LLP) -488 Mad Av -NY 10022
(516) 620-6360 .. **Feffer**, Louise Hartstein '82 %Rogak & G,LLP -50 Charles Lindburgh Blvd -Uniondale 11553
(212) 682-7755 .. **Feffer**, Nicholas W O '97 Custom F/X Inc -216 E 45th -NY 10017
(212) 885-8017 .. **Fefferman**, Michelle G '97 %BDO USA,LLP -330 Mad Av -NY 10017 **Fx**:697-1299
(917) 262-1002 .. **Fefferman**, Stephen A '03 Mark Ecko Enterprises -40 W 23rd -NY 10010
(212) 312-2269 .. **Fegan**, Carol A '88 %Leg Aid -60 Lafayette -NY 10013 **Fx**:349-0874
(718) 855-9000 .. **Fegan**, Jeffrey C '05 %Cullen and D LLP -177 Montague -Brklyn 11201
(718) 855-9000 .. **Fegan**, Jos C '76 (Cullen and D LLP) -177 Montague -Brklyn 11201
(845) 365-3828 .. **Feggans**, Linda '91 -12 Woodlnd Ter -Orangebrg 10962
(212) 259-8000 .. **Feher**, David '85 (Dewey & L LLP) -1301 Av of Amer -NY 10019
(212) 826-0808 .. **Fehr**, Donald M '78 %MLB Players Assn -12 E 49th -NY 10017 **Fx**:752-3649
(607) 741-6023 .. **Fehrer**, James J '85 %State Ins Fund -2001 Perimeter Rd E -Endicott 13760 **Fx**:741-5029
(716) 845-3650 .. **Fehrer**, Keith M '85 %MHLS -438 Main -Buffalo 14202 **Fx**:874-7794
(631) 231-1199 .. **Fehringer**, Michl E '06 %Reynolds CGHL&Q,LLP -35 Arkay Dr -Hauppauge 11788
(212) 725-6422 .. **Fei**, Michelle T '05 %Immigrant Defense Proj -3 W 29th -NY 10001 **Fx**:(800) 391-5713
(845) 735-8500 .. **Feiden**, Larraine S '87 %S Feiden -1 Blue Hill Plz Bx1629 -Pearl Rvr 10965 **Fx**:735-7045
(845) 735-8500 .. **Feiden**, Scott B '88 -1 Blue Hill Plz Bx1629 -Pearl Rvr 10965 **Fx**:735-7045
(212) 854-6182 .. **Feierman**, Michl S '86 %Barnard College -3009 Bway -NY 10027 **Fx**:749-6531
(973) 274-3281 .. **Feiertag**, Tzvia '03 %Proskauer R LLP -1585 Bway -NY 10036 **Fx**:274-3299
(516) 746-8000 .. **Feifer**, Leslie '95 (Jaspan S LLP) -300 Grdn City Plz -Gdn Cty 11530
(212) 255-5556 .. **Feifer**, Scott E '96 (Feifer & G LLP) -27 Union Sq W -NY 10003
(212) 909-5344 .. **Feig**, Edw S '89 KPMG LLP -757 3rd Av -NY 10017
(212) 504-6000 .. **Feig**, Matthew S '00 %Cadwalader W&T LLP -1 World Fncl Ctr -NY 10281
(212) 551-9415 .. **Feigelson**, Jeff B '87 1st Amer Title Ins -633 3rd Av -NY 10017
(212) 909-6000 .. **Feigelson**, Jeremy P '93 (Debevoise & P LLP) -919 3rd Av -NY 10022
(212) 490-9000 .. **Feigelson**, Jonathan E '95 %TIAA-CREF -730 3rd Av -NY 10017
(516) 357-3000 .. **Feigen**, Bernard '52 (Rivkin R LLP) -926 RXR Plz -Uniondale 11556
(212) 474-1000 .. **Feigenbaum**, Aaron J '08 %Cravath S&M LLP -825 8th Av -NY 10019
(212) 506-1700 .. **Feigenbaum**, Alan R '04 %Kasowitz BT&F LLP -1633 Bway -NY 10019
(212) 763-1897 .. **Feigenbaum**, Danl M '02 Alvarez & Marsal Holdings,LLC -600 Lex Av -NY 10022 **Fx**:759-5532
(516) 420-6900 .. **Feigenbaum**, I Leonard '59 -1670 Old Cntry Rd -Plainvw 11803 **Fx**:420-8444
(516) 433-3000 .. **Feigenbaum**, Jay L '77 (Finz & F,PC) -410 E Jericho Tpk -Mineola 11501 **Fx**:433-3001
(212) 416-8844 .. **Feigenbaum**, Joy '81 %Dept of Law -120 Bway -NY 10271
(212) 949-9555 .. **Feigenbaum**, Matthew '80 %Cohn B&S PC -110 Wall -NY 10005
(516) 663-6600 .. **Feigenbaum**, Michl K '66 (Ruskin MF,PC) -1425 RXR Plz -Uniondale 11556
(518) 452-0941 .. **Feigenbaum**, Paul A '71 OfCnsl Segel GM&S,PC -9 Wshngtn Sq -Albany 12205
(518) 452-0941 .. **Feigenbaum**, Polly J '84 %Segel GM&S,PC -9 Wshngtn Sq -Albany 12205
(212) 308-6100 .. **Feigenbaum**, Steven B '86 (Levi L&F LLP) -1185 Av of Amer -NY 10036
(716) 849-1333 .. **Feigenbaum**, Wm M '75 (Lipsitz GSC LLP) -42 Delaware Av -Buffalo 14202
(212) 558-4000 .. **Feiger**, Jared A B '10 %Sullivan & C LLP -125 Broad -NY 10004
(914) 766-4273 .. **Feighan**, Patricia Blank '95 IBM -294 Route 100 -Somers 10589
(212) 792-7778 .. **Feigin**, Cynthia A '82 (DeMeo & F,LLC) -9 E 40th -NY 10016 **Fx**:898-1251
(212) 788-6810 .. **Feigin**, Matthew A '02 %Mayor's Crim Justice Coordinator -1 Centre -NY 10007 **Fx**:788-6815
(212) 592-6700 .. **Feigin**, Michl M '86 %Bovis Lend Lease Hldngs -200 Park Av -NY 10166 **Fx**:592-6997
(718) 459-5400 .. **Feijoo**, John '93 %Farber R&K PC -97-77 Qns Blvd -Rego Pk 11374
(212) 563-6557 .. **Feil**, Jeffrey J '74 -370 7th Av -NY 10001 **Fx**:563-6657
(212) 643-7000 .. **Feil**, Joanne '79 (Sills C&G PC) -One Rckfllr Plz -NY 10020
(212) 756-2000 .. **Feiler**, Jonathan H '08 %Schulte R&Z LLP -919 3rd Av -NY 10022
(212) 854-5795 .. **Feiler**, Michl E '73 OfCnsl Columbia Univ -535 W 116th 412 Low Mem'l Library -NY 10027
(212) 415-8600 .. **Feiler**, Wm S '75 (Locke LB&L LLP) -3 World Fncl Ctr -NY 10281
(516) 596-0066 .. **Feilich**, Burt F '78 -65 Rhame Av -E Rockaway 11518
(212) 715-9100 .. **Feiman**, Ronald M '78 (Kramer LN&F,LLP) -1177 Av of Amer -NY 10036
(212) 659-7300 .. **Feimer**, Adam D '09 %Haynes & B,LLP -1221 Av of Amer -NY 10020
(845) 369-1000 .. **Fein**, Alan H '88 -2 Exec Blvd -Suffern 10901 **Fx**:369-0998
(845) 369-1000 .. **Fein**, Arthur S '63 -2 Exec Blvd -Suffern 10901 **Fx**:369-0998
(212) 436-4416 .. **Fein**, Bradley A '91 Deloitte & Touche,LLP -2 World Fncl Ctr -NY 10281
(315) 479-3900 .. **Fein**, Bruce S '88 SSA-ODAR -300 S State -Syracuse 13202 **Fx**:479-3933
(845) 371-4700 .. **Fein**, Henry H '81 (Fein SK&S,PC) -747 Chestnut Rdg Rd -Spg Vly 10977
(212) 732-9290 .. **Fein**, Iris W '89 (Fein & J) -233 Bway -NY 10279 **Fx**:227-6479
(212) 732-9290 .. **Fein**, Irving W '60 (Fein & J) -233 Bway -NY 10279 **Fx**:227-6479
(212) 532-8686 .. **Fein**, Jarett S '00 Kensington Vanguard Ntl Land Srvcs LLC -39 W 37th -NY 10018
(845) 638-5001 .. **Fein**, Jessica A '08 %DA -1 S Main -New Cty 10956 **Fx**:638-5070
(516) 792-9119 .. **Fein**, Jos M '94 -1175 W Bway -Hewlett 11557 **Fx**:792-2977
(212) 859-8000 .. **Fein**, Joshua H '03 %Fried FHS&J LLP -1 NY Plz -NY 10004
(917) 741-0065 .. **Fein**, Lori F '98 -5 Greenway -Roslyn 11576
(718) 339-2260 .. **Fein**, Marc M '99 -624 Av M -Brklyn 11230 **Fx**:339-2324
(718) 364-2102 .. **Fein**, Marc S '77 -2388 Valentine Av -Bronx 10458
(212) 227-1212 .. **Fein**, Matthew J '97 %Pazer E&J,PC -20 Vesey -NY 10007
(212) 922-2200 .. **Fein**, Michl S '94 (Watson F&W LLP) -1133 Av of Amer -NY 10036
(646) 837-0100 .. **Fein**, Robt E '92 (Wenick & F,PC) -28 E 28th -NY 10016
(845) 628-2734 .. **Fein**, Scott E '83 -747 Union Valley Rd -Carmel 10512
(518) 487-7600 .. **Fein**, Scott N '76 (Whiteman O&H LLP) -1 Commerce Plz -Albany 12260
(914) 788-5000 .. **Fein**, Spencer M '02 %Goldblatt & Assoc,PC -1846 E Main -Mohegan Lk 10547 **Fx**:526-7800
(718) 261-1100 .. **Fein**, Stephen J '78 (Fein & B,LLP) -80-02 Kew Grdns Rd -Kew Gdns 11415 **Fx**:575-9842
(845) 371-4700 .. **Fein Such Kahn & Shepard,PC** -747 Chestnut Rdg Rd -Spg Vly 10977 **Fx**:371-4747
(718) 339-7224 .. **Feinberg**, Aaron M '85 -1777 E 10th -Brklyn 11223
(212) 674-5151 .. **Feinberg**, Audrey Sue '82 Macmillan -175 5th Av -NY 10010 **Fx**:529-0594
(212) 859-8000 .. **Feinberg**, Avi D '03 %Fried FHS&J LLP -1 NY Plz -NY 10004
(516) 239-3375 .. **Feinberg**, Cheryl H '88 -75 Merrall Dr -Lawrence 11559
(212) 644-8200 .. **Feinberg**, David H '68 -126 E 56th -NY 10022 **Fx**:644-9097
(212) 206-6070 .. **Feinberg**, David R '00 Time Equities Inc -55 5th Av -NY 10003 **Fx**:727-0563
(516) 484-9532 .. **Feinberg**, Donna M '92 -16 Entrance Rd -East Hills 11577 **Fx**:484-9532
(518) 475-9088 .. **Feinberg**, Edw R '78 -1 Juniper Dr -Delmar 12054 **Fx**:439-8803
(845) 634-3627 .. **Feinberg**, Eric '87 Leg Aid -2 Congers Rd -New Cty 10956 **Fx**:634-8505
(917) 204-1856 .. **Feinberg**, Evan S '97 -305 Bway -NY 10007
(347) 296-1501 .. **Feinberg**, Felicia A '97 %Hon D Schmidt-Supreme Ct -360 Adams -Brklyn 11201
(914) 946-4343 .. **Feinberg**, Gerry E '78 G Feinberg,PC -11 Martine Av -White Plns 10606 **Fx**:682-9188
(914) 323-7000 .. **Feinberg**, Glen S '78 (Wilson EME&D LLP) -3 Gannett Dr -White Plns 10604
(212) 490-3000 .. **Feinberg**, Glen S '78 (Wilson EME&D LLP) -150 E 42nd -NY 10017
(914) 479-0712 .. **Feinberg**, H Robt '56 -27 Springhurst Park Dr -Dobbs Ferry 10522 **Fx**:479-0713
(585) 325-8000 .. **Feinberg**, Heidi M '03 %Wolford Law LLP -16 E Main -Rchstr 14614 **Fx**:325-8009
(518) 474-8211 .. **Feinberg**, Ira Bruce '75 %Law Reporting Bur -1 Commerce Plz -Albany 12210 **Fx**:463-6869
(212) 918-3000 .. **Feinberg**, Ira M '74 (Hogan L LLP) -875 3rd Av -NY 10022
(607) 724-8865 .. **Feinberg**, Jeffrey N '79 -201 Robnsn -Bnghmtn 13904 **Fx**:722-6665
(212) 428-2547 .. **Feinberg**, Jeremy R '96 %OCA -25 Beaver -NY 10004

(518) 474-6530 .. **Feinberg,** Jonathan D '81 %Dept Pub Srvc -3 ESP -Albany 12223
(212) 527-9600 .. **Feinberg,** Kenneth R '71 (Feinberg R,LLP) -780 3rd Av -NY 10017 **Fx:**527-9611
(646) 386-3356 .. **Feinberg,** Lindsay N '84 Hon L Drager Supreme Ct -71 Thomas -NY 10013
(718) 357-2431 .. **Feinberg,** Lindsay R '01 Classical Learning Universe -305 W Bway -NY 10013
(718) 855-0009 .. **Feinberg,** Mark E '84 -142 Joralemon -Brklyn 11201 **Fx:**855-2507
(212) 451-2300 .. **Feinberg,** Martin J '91 (Olshan GFR&W LLP) -65 E 55th -NY 10022
(212) 937-7415 .. **Feinberg,** Michl L '04 Cnsl WilmerHale -399 Park Av -NY 10022
(585) 454-5050 .. **Feinberg,** R Andrew '02 %Brown & H -2 State -Rchstr 14614
(212) 715-9100 .. **Feinberg,** Rachel L '10 %Kramer LN&F,LLP -1177 Av of Amer -NY 10036
(845) 634-7007 .. **Feinberg,** Richd J '69 -254 S Main -New Cty 10956 **Fx:**634-2625
(212) 560-6981 .. **Feinberg,** Robt A '88 WNET.ORG -450 W 33rd -NY 10001 **Fx:**560-4946
(212) 773-3488 .. **Feinberg,** Robt B '82 Ernst & Young LLP -5 Times Sq -NY 10036
(631) 451-4820 .. **Feinberg,** Ronald A '87 %Sfflk Cnty Comm Cllg -533 Cllg Rd -Selden 11784 **Fx:**451-4681
(212) 661-7100 .. **Feinberg,** Stephen J '64 OfCnsl Salon MDN&B,LLP -292 Mad Av -NY 10017
(516) 997-9797 .. **Feinberg,** Steven M '89 (S Feinberg,LLC) -50 Jericho Tpk -Jericho 11753 **Fx:**338-9693
(212) 838-9300 .. **Feinberg,** Susan Kramer '05 -9 Oak Hill Rd -Chappaqua 10514
(845) 354-5600 .. **Feinberg,** Wayne R '70 -1593 Rt 202 Bx3100 -Pomona 10970 **Fx:**354-8193
(212) 705-7000 .. **Feinberg,** Zoe F '04 %Bingham M LLP -399 Park Av -NY 10022
(212) 788-6810 .. **Feinblatt,** John A '79 (Criminal Justice Coordinator) -1 Centre -NY 10007 **Fx:**788-6847
(212) 279-5299 .. **Feinbloom Bertisch LLP** -40 Worth -NY 10013 **Fx:**643-8182
(631) 293-7800 .. **Feinbloom,** Chas R '68 -445 Broad Hollow Rd -Melvll 11747 **Fx:**293-7886
(516) 868-6087 .. **Feinbloom,** Irwin '55 -2052 Blanche Ln -Merrick 11566
(212) 279-5299 .. **Feinbloom,** Jeffrey A '96 (Feinbloom B LLP) -40 Worth -NY 10013
(585) 385-3532 .. **Feindt,** Mary E '91 -100 French Rd -Rchstr 14618
(212) 850-2800 .. **Feiner,** Andrew D '83 (Andrews K LLP) -450 Lex Av -NY 10017
(718) 871-1200 .. **Feiner,** Jacob A '08 %E Rubin -4915 12th Av -Brklyn 11219 **Fx:**972-0246
(212) 416-8479 .. **Feiner,** Lisa '80 %Dept of Law -120 Bway -NY 10271
(516) 622-4780 .. **Feiner,** Michl I '97 -500 N Bway -Jericho 11753
(914) 993-1540 .. **Feiner,** Paul J '82 (Town Supervisor) -Greenburgh Town Hall Bx205 -Elmsfrd 10523 **Fx:**993-1541
(212) 779-8600 .. **Feiner,** Richd I '81 (Silverman SS&B PLLC) -381 Park Av S -NY 10016
(212) 230-1300 .. **Feiner,** Ronald E '68 (Beigelman F&F,PC) -100 Wall -NY 10005 **Fx:**230-1090
(516) 674-4617 .. **Feiner,** Stephen H '02 -21 Maple Av -Sea Cliff 11579
(212) 244-2999 .. **Feinglass,** Susan B '96 (Kopff N&D LLP) -440 9th Av -NY 10001
(212) 582-8000 .. **Feingold & Alpert,LLP** -1330 Av of Amer -NY 10019 **Fx:**582-8080
(212) 878-8000 .. **Feingold,** Anton '08 %Clifford C LLP -31 W 52nd -NY 10019
(718) 376-0900 .. **Feingold,** Cora Sue '79 -1600 Ocean Pkwy -Brklyn 11230
(212) 582-8000 .. **Feingold,** Fred '70 (Feingold & A,LLP) -1330 Av of Amer -NY 10019
(516) 571-3560 .. **Feingold,** Jennifer L '87 Hon M Berkowitz -262 Old Cntry Rd -Mineola 11501
(212) 918-3000 .. **Feingold,** Jessica Pesce '02 %Hogan L LLP -875 3rd Av -NY 10022
(516) 678-2362 .. **Feingold,** Leon A '99 -591 Watervw Rd -Oceanside 11572 **Fx:**678-1339
(212) 682-4426 .. **Feingold,** Marc D '96 %O'Shea Prtnrs LLP -521 5th Av -NY 10175 **Fx:**682-4437
(212) 264-8844 .. **Feingold,** Margo R '94 %ODAR-SSA -26 Fed Plz -NY 10278
(212) 935-4400 .. **Feingold,** Ronald B '76 (LePatner & Assoc LLP) -600 Lex Av -NY 10022 **Fx:**935-4404
(718) 855-7955 .. **Feingold,** Sarah M '06 Etsy,Inc -55 Washington -Brklyn 11201
(212) 775-8700 .. **Feingold,** Stephen W '86 (Kilpatrick S,LLP) -31 W 52nd -NY 10019
(212) 786-8110 .. **Feingold,** Susan '92 %EMI Music NA -150 5th Av -NY 10011 **Fx:**786-8103
(212) 259-8000 .. **Feingold,** Yaakov B '06 %Dewey & L LLP -1301 Av of Amer -NY 10019
(212) 637-2436 .. **Feingold,** Zachary A '02 US Atty -1 St Andrews Plz -NY 10007
(718) 923-4206 .. **Feinman,** Carol '78 %OTDA Fair Hearings -14 Boerum Pl -Brklyn 11201
(516) 746-2300 .. **Feinman,** Justin C '08 %A Capetola -2C Hillside Av -Williston Pk 11596 **Fx:**746-2318
(718) 250-4238 .. **Feinman,** Martin '84 %Leg Aid -111 Lvngstn -Brklyn 11201 **Fx:**250-4243
(212) 506-1700 .. **Feinman,** Matthew T '09 %Kasowitz BT&F LLP -1633 Bway -NY 10019
(212) 885-5000 .. **Feinman,** Michl J '81 (Blank R LLP) -405 Lex Av -NY 10174
(212) 953-1100 .. **Feinman,** Paul S '83 -551 5th Av -NY 10176
(914) 949-8214 .. **Feinman,** Steven N '87 (Feinman & G,PC) -19 Court Plz -White Plns 10601 **Fx:**949-0379
(212) 361-1094 .. **Feinman,** Sylvia J '80 DOH -66 John -NY 10038
(212) 790-4500 .. **Feinrider,** Nancy K '86 (Manatt P&P,LLP) -7 Times Sq -NY 10036
(212) 279-1069 .. **Feinsilver,** David '82 (Feinsilver Law Grp,PC) -26 Court -Brklyn 11242 **Fx:**(973) 376-4405
(212) 693-5806 .. **Feinsilver,** Jonathan S '97 -111 John -NY 10038
(516) 873-6330 .. **Feinsilver,** Richd S '84 (Feinsilver & C,LLC) -1 Old Cntry Rd -Carle Pl 11514
(516) 333-6100 .. **Feinsod,** George I '68 -131 Jericho Tpk -Jericho 11753 **Fx:**633-6846
(212) 995-8300 .. **Feinsod,** Michl R '97 %Mark Boyar & Co -35 E 21st -NY 10010
(212) 663-5059 .. **Feinson,** Richd J '91 -740 West End Av -NY 10025
(718) 595-5595 .. **Feinstein,** Aaron J '06 DEP -59-17 Junction Blvd -Flushng 11373 **Fx:**595-6543
(212) 526-7000 .. **Feinstein,** Alex D '07 Barclays Capital -745 7th Av -NY 10019
(718) 250-2000 .. **Feinstein,** Amy P '81 %DA -350 Jay -Brklyn 11201 **Fx:**250-2314
(718) 590-3730 .. **Feinstein,** Barbara K '84 Supreme Ct -851 Grnd Cncrs -Bronx 10451
(212) 647-1900 .. **Feinstein,** Barry L '61 -275 7th Av -NY 10001
(516) 742-6444 .. **Feinstein,** Brian R '97 (Sunshine & F,LLP) -666 Old Cntry Rd -Gdn Cty 11530 **Fx:**794-0463
(718) 570-8100 .. **Feinstein,** Bruce I '98 (B Feinstein,PC) -86-66 110th -Richmnd Hll 11418
(212) 363-3000 .. **Feinstein,** Chas '88 (Feinstein & F) -61 Bway -NY 10006 **Fx:**363-8202
(212) 265-1535 .. **Feinstein,** Chas A '61 (Feinstein & F) -228 W 47th -NY 10036 **Fx:**944-9028
(212) 468-4800 .. **Feinstein,** Danl A '97 (Davis & G LLP) -1740 Bway -NY 10019
(212) 351-4000 .. **Feinstein,** Diana M '08 %Gibson D&C LLP -200 Park Av -NY 10166
(212) 363-3000 .. **Feinstein,** Jerome '52 (Feinstein & F) -61 Bway -NY 10006 **Fx:**363-8202
(212) 832-3600 .. **Feinstein,** Joan L '78 Cnsl Wertheimer F,LLC -230 Park Av -NY 10169
(716) 856-4000 .. **Feinstein,** Joshua I '02 %Hodgson R LLP -140 Pearl -Buffalo 14202
(212) 593-6700 .. **Feinstein,** Mark B '73 (Aaronson RF&D,LLP) -757 3rd Av -NY 10017
(212) 867-6000 .. **Feinstein,** Michl E '91 (Rosenberg & E,PC) -733 3rd Av -NY 10017
(718) 631-0800 .. **Feinstein & Nisnewitz,PC** -42-40 Bell Blvd -Bayside 11361 **Fx:**279-8584
(914) 375-3613 .. **Feinstein,** Paul D '68 PD Feinstein,PC -102 Sunnyside Dr -Ynkrs 10705 **Fx:**375-3629
(212) 561-7700 .. **Feinstein,** Robt '82 (Pachulski SZ&J) -780 3rd Av -NY 10017
(212) 265-1535 .. **Feinstein,** Sharon '86 (Feinstein & F) -228 W 47th -NY 10036 **Fx:**944-9028
(718) 631-0800 .. **Feinstein,** Sheldon '61 Cnsl Feinstein & N,PC -42-40 Bell Blvd -Bayside 11361
(914) 939-0002 .. **Feinstein,** Steven D '86 (Gallo F&N,LLP) -211 S Ridge -Rye Brook 10573
(201) 788-6458 .. **Feinstein,** Steven Jay '91 -275 7th Av -NY 10001 **Fx:**217-6778
(607) 292-3952 .. **Feinstein,** Wm A '78 Ventura Devlpmnt -13321 Route 54 -Hammondsprt 14840
(585) 454-2433 .. **Feinstock,** Carl L '65 -1 Main E -Rchstr 14614
(212) 308-4411 .. **Feintuch,** Harvey A '79 (Edwards AP&D LLP) -750 Lex Av -NY 10022
(718) 377-7800 .. **Feinzeig,** Jacob S '84 -1386 Coney Isl Av -Brklyn 11230 **Fx:**258-7659
(845) 628-5900 .. **Feinzig,** Bonnie N '88 %Spain & S -671 Route 6 -Mahopac 10541 **Fx:**628-0694
(914) 993-1912 .. **Feinzig,** Margery B '90 %US Atty -300 Quarropas -White Plns 10601 **Fx:**993-9036
(212) 361-8255 .. **Feiring,** Eric D '79 Dept of Finance -66 John -NY 10038
(212) 839-5300 .. **Feiring,** Marshall D '79 (Sidley A LLP) -787 7th Av -NY 10019
(212) 687-8700 .. **Feirman,** Jack K '72 Cnsl Malkin Hldngs,LLC -60 E 42nd -NY 10165 **Fx:**986-7679
(212) 735-3000 .. **Feirman,** Jordan A '08 %Skadden ASM&F LLP -4 Times Sq -NY 10036
(212) 403-1000 .. **Feirstein,** David B '07 %Wachtell LR&K -51 W 52nd -NY 10019
(212) 628-1035 .. **Feirstein,** Michl A '67 -178 E 70th -NY 10021
(518) 465-3052 .. **Feirstein,** Richd P '77 -1658 New Scotland Rd -Slingerlnds 12159 **Fx:**465-3659
(646) 536-2842 .. **Feist,** Gena A '00 Take Two -622 Bway -NY 10012
(212) 310-8000 .. **Feit,** Adam J '09 %Weil G&M LLP -767 5th Av -NY 10153
(212) 357-9447 .. **Feit,** Danl Y '93 Goldman Sachs -1 NY Plz -NY 10004
(212) 608-1445 .. **Feit,** David J '89 -22 Crtlandt -NY 10007 **Fx:**608-1803
(212) 685-7600 .. **Feit,** Eli '73 (Heller H&F,PC) -292 Mad Av -NY 10017
(516) 249-1342 .. **Feit,** Elliot M '66 %Grey & G,LLP -360 Main -Farmngdl 11735
(212) 969-3000 .. **Feit,** Glenn M '58 (Proskauer R LLP) -1585 Bway -NY 10036
(516) 822-3550 .. **Feit,** Irving N '80 (Hoffmann & B LLP) -6900 Jericho Tpk -Syosset 11791 **Fx:**822-3582
(212) 455-2000 .. **Feit,** Jos J '71 OfCnsl Simpson T&B LLP -425 Lex Av -NY 10017
(516) 535-1550 .. **Feit,** Kenneth R '78 (Tell C&B) -320 Old Cntry Rd -Gdn Cty 11530
(518) 434-2306 .. **Feit,** Michl A '66 -383 Clinton Av -Albany 12206 **Fx:**434-2217
(212) 295-6358 .. **Feit,** Nicole E '07 %WilmerHale -399 Park Av -NY 10022
(212) 902-7507 .. **Feit,** Norman '82 %Goldman Sachs -1 NY Plz -NY 10004
(212) 838-8400 .. **Feit,** Rebecca N '03 Andrew W Mellon Fndtn -140 E 62nd -NY 10065 **Fx:**500-2302
(212) 571-5710 .. **Feitell,** Bennett M '98 %L Feitell -225 Bway -NY 10007 **Fx:**571-5711
(212) 571-5710 .. **Feitell,** Lawr K '53 -225 Bway -NY 10007 **Fx:**571-5711
(914) 524-9000 .. **Feitelson,** Robt J '63 -660 Wht Plns Rd -Tarrytwn 10591 **Fx:**524-9185
(212) 872-1000 .. **Feivelson,** Neal K '97 -One Bryant Park -NY 10036 **Fx:**872-1002
(212) 506-1700 .. **Feiwus,** Leonard A '94 (Kasowitz BT&F LLP) -1633 Bway -NY 10019
(212) 388-3600 .. **Fekert,** James D '90 %32B-J Leg Srvcs -101 Av of Amer -NY 10013 **Fx:**388-3061
(516) 485-4221 .. **Fekett,** Warren J '78 (Foley SO&W) -175 Fulton Av -Hempstd 11550
(315) 598-8552 .. **Felasco,** Mary A '85 -163 S 1st -Fulton 13069 **Fx:**598-1830
(212) 757-5000 .. **Felber,** Danl '83 (Sklover D&F,LLC) -10 Rckfllr Plz -NY 10020 **Fx:**757-5002
(718) 579-3126 .. **Felber,** Elizabeth Sack '87 %Leg Aid -1020 Grnd Cncrs -Bronx 10451 **Fx:**588-2611
(516) 877-1500 .. **Felber,** Gregory J '04 (Ackerman & F) -6901 Jericho Tpk -Syosset 11791
(212) 355-4449 .. **Felber,** Jennifer D '01 %Joele Frank Wilkinson Brimmer Katcher -140 E 45th -NY 10017
(631) 864-0800 .. **Felberbaum Halbridge & Wirth** -357 Vets Mem'l Hwy -Commack 11725
(631) 864-0800 .. **Felberbaum,** Saml E '81 (Felberbaum H&W) -357 Vets Mem'l Hwy -Commack 11725
(212) 686-4600 .. **Felcher,** Howard B '80 -347 5th Av -NY 10016 **Fx:**686-4686
(212) 373-3000 .. **Felcher,** Peter L '64 OfCnsl Paul WRW&G LLP -1285 Av of Amer -NY 10019
(212) 695-7800 .. **Felcher,** Scott A '84 (Felcher & F,LLP) -358 5th Av -NY 10001 **Fx:**695-4041
(914) 946-3800 .. **Felcher Leavitt,** Benjamin L '04 -5 Waller Av -White Plns 10601
(212) 225-2000 .. **Feld,** Alan J '08 %Cleary GS&H -1 Lbrty Plz -NY 10006
(212) 807-2191 .. **Feld,** Danl E '75 %Thomson Reuters/RIA -195 Bway -NY 10007

(212) 964-4100 .. **Feld,** David L '82 (Feld Law Firm PC) -150 Bway -NY 10038 **Fx:**964-4295
(516) 746-4373 .. **Feld,** Dennis B '71 %MHLS -170 Old Cntry Rd -Mineola 11501 **Fx:**746-0598
(212) 819-8200 .. **Feld,** Elizabeth '01 %White & C LLP -1155 Av of Amer -NY 10036
(212) 989-8900 .. **Feld,** Fredric E '86 (Bevmax Painting Corp) -75 Rckfllr Plz -NY 10019 **Fx:**989-9546
(631) 493-9464 .. **Feld,** Joann '82 -44 Seward Dr -Dix Hills 11746 **Fx:**493-9477
(212) 742-1610 .. **Feld,** Lawr S '67 -260 Mad Av -NY 10016 **Fx:**742-1637
(516) 938-4228 .. **Feld,** Leonard B '87 -243 Halsey Av -Jericho 11753 **Fx:**939-9238
(914) 273-6490 .. **Feld,** Lloyd D '63 -Bx663 -Armonk 10504 **Fx:**273-4729
(212) 735-3000 .. **Feld,** Stephanie R '84 Cnsl Skadden ASM&F LLP -4 Times Sq -NY 10036
(718) 250-2000 .. **Feldberg,** Howard L '10 %DA -350 Jay -Brklyn 11201 **Fx:**250-2314
(212) 610-6300 .. **Feldberg,** Michl S '78 (Allen & O) -1221 Av of Amer -NY 10020
(212) 773-3000 .. **Feldberg,** Yisacher '04 Ernst & Young,LLP -5 Times Sq -NY 10036
(212) 682-7474 .. **Felder,** Barry G '78 (Foley & L LLP) -90 Park Av -NY 10016
(212) 752-3668 .. **Felder,** Myrna '71 (R Felder & Prtnrs,PC) -437 Mad Av -NY 10022 **Fx:**838-1103
(212) 832-3939 .. **Felder,** Raoul L '59 (R Felder & Prtnrs,PC) -437 Mad Av -NY 10022 **Fx:**838-1103
(212) 935-3000 .. **Felder,** Sara L '08 %Mintz LCFG&P,PC -666 3rd Av -NY 10017
(212) 859-8000 .. **Feldhamer,** Marc '06 %Fried FHS&J LLP -1 NY Plz -NY 10004
(212) 682-0020 .. **Feldheim,** Randi B '08 %Putney TH&H LLP -521 5th Av -NY 10175
(516) 222-2626 .. **Feldherr,** Craig E '91 (Feldherr & F) -900 Merchnts Cncrs -Westbury 11590 **Fx:**222-2651
(516) 222-2626 .. **Feldherr,** Norman J '63 (Feldherr & F) -900 Merchnts Cncrs -Westbury 11590 **Fx:**222-2651
(718) 891-2900 .. **Feldman,** Aaron M '03 %Goldfarb & G -2774 Coney Isl Av -Brklyn 11235 **Fx:**891-2950
(212) 244-4422 .. **Feldman,** Adam J '96 (Feldman R) -19 W 34th -NY 10001
(716) 852-5875 .. **Feldman,** Andrew '69 (Feldman K LLP) -110 Pearl -Buffalo 14202
(516) 747-2828 .. **Feldman,** Andrew L '87 (A Feldman,PC) -263 Mineola Blvd -Mineola 11501 **Fx:**747-7223
(212) 829-9200 .. **Feldman,** Anna '01 %Janoff & G,LLP -216 E 49th -NY 10017
(516) 227-0700 .. **Feldman,** Arthur K '87 (Farrell F,PC) -1320 RXR Plz -Uniondale 11556
(516) 522-2828 .. **Feldman,** Arza Rayches '86 (Feldman & F) -626 RXR Plz -Uniondale 11556 **Fx:**522-2844
(516) 248-1700 .. **Feldman,** Barry C '75 Cnsl Forchelli CDSM&T,LLP -333 Earle Ovngton Blvd -Uniondale 11553
(631) 287-8700 .. **Feldman,** Barry H '75 -27 Bowden Sq -Southampton 11968 **Fx:**287-5547
(347) 702-4867 .. **Feldman,** Barry R '01 -1413 Av J -Brklyn 11230
(212) 230-1300 .. **Feldman,** Benjamin C '98 (Beigelman F&F,PC) -100 Wall -NY 10005 **Fx:**230-1090
(516) 829-3800 .. **Feldman,** Bernard S '70 -80 Cuttermill Rd -Gt Neck 11021
(212) 508-8900 .. **Feldman,** Brian M '99 AM Investment Prtnrs LLC -1 Lbrty Plz -NY 10006
(212) 637-2777 .. **Feldman,** Brian M '04 US Atty -86 Chmbrs -NY 10007
(212) 897-5808 .. **Feldman,** Bruce A '85 -305 Bway -NY 10007 **Fx:**897-5837
(518) 457-2411 .. **Feldman,** Bruce D '79 %DOT -50 Wolf Rd -Albany 12232 **Fx:**457-4021
(212) 351-4000 .. **Feldman,** Chas F '68 (Gibson D&C LLP) -200 Park Av -NY 10166
(518) 429-4200 .. **Feldman,** Chas Z '05 %Hiscock & B,LLP -50 Beaver -Albany 12207
(914) 683-1200 .. **Feldman,** Christopher H '08 %Harris B PLLC -445 Hmltn Av -White Plns 10601
(212) 644-4420 .. **Feldman,** Courtney B '02 %Fabiani C&H,LLP -570 Lex Av -NY 10022
(212) 681-6069 .. **Feldman,** Danl L '75 State Comptroller -59 Maiden Ln -NY 10038 **Fx:**383-3901
(718) 886-4000 .. **Feldman,** Danl L '88 -41-46 Main -Flushng 11355
(212) 940-3013 .. **Feldman,** David A '96 (Nixon P LLP) -437 Mad Av -NY 10022
(646) 253-2300 .. **Feldman,** David B '84 (Bond S&K,PLLC) -330 Mad Av -NY 10017
(212) 395-6362 .. **Feldman,** David M '91 %Verizon -140 West -NY 10007
(212) 351-4000 .. **Feldman,** David M '94 (Gibson D&C LLP) -200 Park Av -NY 10166
(212) 869-7000 .. **Feldman,** David N '86 (Feldman W&S LLP) -420 Lex Av -NY 10170
(716) 845-5300 .. **Feldman,** David P '51 -69 Delaware Av -Buffalo 14202 **Fx:**852-6784
(516) 334-2500 .. **Feldman,** Donald J '74 (Feldman RK&F,PC) -410 Jericho Tpk -Jericho 11753
(718) 258-5100 .. **Feldman,** Edw '92 Sovereign Motor Cars -1800 Shore Pkwy -Brklyn 11214
(212) 685-2277 .. **Feldman,** Edw S '75 (Feldman & Assoc,PLLC) -33 E 33rd -NY 10016 **Fx:**725-2798
(212) 354-4500 .. **Feldman,** Elise Simon '01 %Friedman & W -1500 Bway -NY 10036
(212) 918-3000 .. **Feldman,** Eric N '09 %Hogan L LLP -875 3rd Av -NY 10022
(212) 785-9120 .. **Feldman,** Eugene '53 -736 Carroll -Brklyn 11215 **Fx:**(718) 499-5042
(212) 687-3440 .. **Feldman,** Eugene H '55 %Goldstick WF&G,PC -7 Penn Plz -NY 10001
(212) 318-9800 .. **Feldman,** Greg S '84 Wellspring Capital Mgmt LLC -390 Park Av -NY 10022
(212) 730-8133 .. **Feldman,** Gregory S '06 %Gunderson DSVF&H,LLP -220 W 42nd -NY 10036
(212) 670-0190 .. **Feldman,** H Leigh '92 Merrill Lynch -222 Bway -NY 10038
(914) 993-1289 .. **Feldman,** Hadley E '87 Abovenet Comm -360 Hmltn Av -White Plns 10601
(212) 312-7887 .. **Feldman,** Howard A '80 %State Ins Fund -199 Church -NY 10007 **Fx:**385-9199
(212) 226-3232 .. **Feldman,** I Ronald '63 %R Feldman Fine Arts -31 Mercer -NY 10013 **Fx:**941-1536
(212) 687-0044 .. **Feldman,** Ivan S '66 -475 Park Av S -NY 10016 **Fx:**(646) 437-1010
(212) 576-7000 .. **Feldman,** J Steven '86 %NY Life Ins -51 Mad Av -NY 10010 **Fx:**447-0569
(516) 742-7777 .. **Feldman,** Jacob S '77 (Frazer & F,LLP) -1415 Kellum Pl -Gdn Cty 11530
(845) 454-1171 .. **Feldman & Jacobson** -94 Market -Poughkeepsie 12601 **Fx:**454-3720
(212) 713-4932 .. **Feldman,** James C '02 UBS Securities LLC -1285 Av of Amer -NY 10019
(212) 805-0192 .. **Feldman,** James M '97 %Hon S Stein -500 Pearl -NY 10007
(732) 855-6058 .. **Feldman,** Jay B '06 %Wilentz G&S -110 William -NY 10038 **Fx:**726-6694
(212) 474-1000 .. **Feldman,** Jed F '08 %Cravath S&M LLP -825 8th Av -NY 10019
(212) 632-6900 .. **Feldman,** Jeffrey B '82 Colonnade Properties LLC -380 Lex Av -NY 10168 **Fx:**632-6919
(212) 267-1650 .. **Feldman,** Jeffrey B '93 (Fine O&A,LLP) -39 Bway -NY 10006
(845) 897-5199 .. **Feldman,** Jeffrey M '78 (Feldman K&C,LLP) -995 Main BxA -Fishkill 12524
(718) 250-2000 .. **Feldman,** Jennifer L '07 %DA -350 Jay -Brklyn 11201 **Fx:**250-2314
(212) 837-6000 .. **Feldman,** Jessica A '04 %Hughes H&R LLP -1 Bttry Pk Plz -NY 10004
(914) 949-6400 .. **Feldman,** Joanna C '03 %McCullough G&S,LLP -1311 Mamaroneck Av -White Plns 10605
(631) 979-1200 .. **Feldman,** Jodi P '99 (Feldman & F,LLP) -811 W Jericho Tpk -Smithtwn 11787 **Fx:**979-1264
(212) 735-8600 .. **Feldman,** Joel A '69 OfCnsl Morrison C LLP -909 3rd Av -NY 10022
(585) 454-4060 .. **Feldman,** Jonathan '94 %Empire Justice Ctr -1 W Main -Rchstr 14614 **Fx:**454-4019
(212) 277-6500 .. **Feldman,** Jordana H '01 %Dickstein S LLP -1633 Bway -NY 10019
(212) 812-3132 .. **Feldman,** Joshua J '97 King Street Capital Mgmt -65 E 55th -NY 10022
(716) 652-2820 .. **Feldman,** Joy A '92 The Park Assoc,Inc -300 Gleed Av -E Aurora 14052 **Fx:**652-4245
(718) 260-8700 .. **Feldman,** Julie Ann '94 %Admin Children's Srvcs -345 Adams -Brklyn 11201 **Fx:**260-8710
(718) 969-9723 .. **Feldman,** Julius '53 -7150 169th -Flushng 11365 **Fx:**969-9723
(212) 820-9526 .. **Feldman,** Justin L '07 %Hawkins D&W LLP -One Chase Manh Plz -NY 10005
(212) 479-6000 .. **Feldman,** Justin N '42 OfCnsl Cooley LLP -1114 Av of Amer -NY 10036
(212) 532-8585 .. **Feldman,** Kenneth S '87 %S Feldman -12 E 41st -NY 10017 **Fx:**532-8598
(716) 852-5875 .. **Feldman Kieffer LLP** -110 Pearl -Buffalo 14202 **Fx:**852-4253
(845) 897-5199 .. **Feldman Kleidman & Coffey,LLP** -995 Main BxA -Fishkill 12524 **Fx:**897-5945
(631) 231-1450 .. **Feldman Kramer & Monaco,PC** -330 Vndrblt Motor Pkwy -Hauppauge 11788 **Fx:**231-4732
(212) 425-0230 .. **Feldman Kronfeld & Beatty** -42 Bway -NY 10004 **Fx:**809-6174
(516) 482-2282 .. **Feldman Kronfeld & Beatty** -45 N Station Plz -Gt Neck 11021
(212) 804-4200 .. **Feldman,** Labe C '01 %Mound CW&G -One Bttry Pk Plz -NY 10004
(212) 728-8915 .. **Feldman,** Laura Gottlieb '98 -787 7th Av -NY 10019 **Fx:**728-9915
(516) 935-2280 .. **Feldman,** Lee H '02 National Commerce Exchange -400 Jericho Tpk -Jericho 11753
(631) 979-1200 .. **Feldman,** Leonard B '69 (Feldman & F,LLP) -811 W Jericho Tpk -Smithtwn 11787 **Fx:**979-1264
(212) 233-5688 .. **Feldman,** Leslie C '68 L Feldman,PC -277 Bway -NY 10007 **Fx:**385-4960
(718) 780-7929 .. **Feldman,** Linda B '83 %Bklyn Law Schl -250 Joralemon -Brklyn 11201 **Fx:**780-0393
(212) 869-9555 .. **Feldman,** Linda I '94 %J Palatin Diamond Co -11 W 47th -NY 10036 **Fx:**(203) 232-2575
(212) 594-5300 .. **Feldman,** Lori G '91 (Milberg LLP) -1 Penn Plz -NY 10119
(212) 345-6000 .. **Feldman,** Lorraine Jablowsky '97 %Marsh USA -1166 Av of Amer -NY 10036 **Fx:**345-4808
(718) 627-7900 .. **Feldman,** Mark A '77 -1717 E 18th -Brklyn 11229 **Fx:**627-1525
(212) 885-8000 .. **Feldman,** Mark E '76 %BDO USA,LLP -330 Mad Av -NY 10017 **Fx:**697-1299
(516) 746-4111 .. **Feldman,** Mark H '77 -1 Old Cntry Rd -Carle Pl 11514 **Fx:**746-4768
(646) 328-0850 .. **Feldman,** Mark J '95 %Outside Cnsl Solutns LLP -1430 Bway -NY 10018 **Fx:**360-5000
(914) 723-4300 .. **Feldman,** Marvin '70 (Lackenbach S LLP) -1 Chase Rd -Scarsdale 10583
(212) 728-8000 .. **Feldman,** Matthew A '92 (Willkie F&G LLP) -787 7th Av -NY 10019
(718) 281-0550 .. **Feldman,** Matthew J '95 Douglaston Devlpmnt -42-09 235th -Douglastn 11363 **Fx:**(212) 400-9294
(716) 636-7600 .. **Feldman,** Matthew S '10 %HoganWillig -2410 N Forest Rd -Amherst 14068
(718) 250-2000 .. **Feldman,** Melissa J '08 %DA -350 Jay -Brklyn 11201 **Fx:**250-2314
(212) 969-3000 .. **Feldman,** Michl E '69 (Proskauer R LLP) -1585 Bway -NY 10036
(845) 352-9240 .. **Feldman,** Michl S '84 (Jacoby & M,LLP) -296 Main -Spg Vly 10977 **Fx:**344-2090
(631) 694-2300 .. **Feldman,** Michelle S '84 (Lamb & B,LLP) -534 Broadhllw Rd Bx9034 -Melvll 11747
(516) 747-7640 .. **Feldman,** Morris S '40 -18 Peppermill Rd -Roslyn 11576
(845) 598-5043 .. **Feldman,** Patricia Lulov '84 -2 Neva Ct -Suffern 10901 **Fx:**362-4794
(212) 267-2600 .. **Feldman,** Paul '96 (Gould & F,LLP) -61 Bway -NY 10006
(212) 422-1500 .. **Feldman,** Paul K '67 (Meyers TF&G LLP) -14 Wall -NY 10005
(212) 661-9100 .. **Feldman,** Peter L '80 (Otterbourg SH&R,PC) -230 Park Av -NY 10169
(212) 682-3454 .. **Feldman,** Richd B '81 (Rosenberg FS LLP) -551 5th Av -NY 10176
(212) 245-6754 .. **Feldman,** Richd E '73 (Sonnenschein S&D,LLP) -7 Penn Plz -NY 10001
(516) 357-3000 .. **Feldman,** Richd S '77 (Rivkin R LLP) -926 RXR Plz -Uniondale 11556
(914) 995-3650 .. **Feldman,** Ricki A '80 %Cnty Atty -148 Martine Av -White Plns 10601 **Fx:**995-5858
(914) 723-6217 .. **Feldman,** Robt '62 -4 Copper Beech Ln -Scarsdale 10583 **Fx:**941-7704
(585) 454-0700 .. **Feldman,** Robt A '54 Cnsl Ward GH&R LLP -300 State -Rchstr 14614
(845) 454-1171 .. **Feldman,** Robt A '65 (Feldman & J) -94 Market -Poughkeepsie 12601
(716) 854-4300 .. **Feldman,** Robt J '77 (Gross SB&G,PC) -465 Main -Buffalo 14203
(585) 218-8620 .. **Feldman,** Roberta Kirsch '81 (Gray & F,LLP) -625 Panorama Trl -Rchstr 14625
(516) 334-2500 .. **Feldman Rudy Kirby & Farquharson,PC** -410 Jericho Tpk -Jericho 11753 **Fx:**334-2532
(585) 424-4760 .. **Feldman,** Sammy '74 (Silver & F) -3445 Winton Pl -Rchstr 14623
(212) 941-7272 .. **Feldman,** Saml M '88 -350 Bway -NY 10013 **Fx:**226-3224
(212) 894-8599 .. **Feldman,** Sandra B '84 CT Corp System -111 8th Av -NY 10011

(212) 536-3900 .. **Feldman,** Sandy K '80 (K&L Gates LLP) -599 Lex Av -NY 10022
(212) 695-0910 .. **Feldman,** Sara B '03 %Sullivan Law Grp,LLP -1350 Bway -NY 10018 **Fx:**695-0915
(212) 832-3160 .. **Feldman,** Sharon D '84 (A Lawler,PC) -641 Lex Av -NY 10022 **Fx:**832-3158
(212) 335-9000 .. **Feldman,** Sheryl G '87 %DA -1 Hogan Pl -NY 10013
(212) 732-6652 .. **Feldman,** Sidney P '75 -225 Bway -NY 10007
(212) 801-9221 .. **Feldman,** Spencer G '88 (Greenberg T,LLP) -200 Park Av -NY 10166
(212) 267-6364 .. **Feldman,** Stacie Bryce '86 %Kossoff & U -217 Bway -NY 10007
(212) 685-2277 .. **Feldman,** Stephanie R '02 Feldman & Assoc,PLLC -33 E 33rd -NY 10016
(631) 549-3770 .. **Feldman,** Stephen E '63 -120 Main -Huntngtn 11743
(212) 532-8585 .. **Feldman,** Stephen E '63 -12 E 41st -NY 10017 **Fx:**532-8598
(516) 812-6045 .. **Feldman,** Stephen J '66 (Spector & F,LLP) -360 Merrick Rd -Lynbrk 11563
(212) 468-8000 .. **Feldman,** Stephen L '82 (Morrison & F LLP) -1290 Av of Amer -NY 10104
(516) 522-2828 .. **Feldman,** Steven A '87 (Feldman & F) -626 RXR Plz -Uniondale 11556 **Fx:**522-2844
(212) 592-1400 .. **Feldman,** Steven D '99 (Herrick,F LLP) -2 Park Av -NY 10016
(212) 902-1000 .. **Feldman,** Steven M '88 %Goldman Sachs -1 NY Plz -NY 10004
(516) 255-0200 .. **Feldman,** Steven Mitchell '82 -1225 Franklin Av -Gdn Cty 11530
(212) 450-4000 .. **Feldman,** Steven N '09 %Davis P&W LLP -450 Lex Av -NY 10017
(212) 371-1492 .. **Feldman,** Theo F '69 (Raymond & F) -110 E 59th -NY 10022
(631) 231-1450 .. **Feldman,** Warren B '77 (Feldman K&M,PC) -330 Vndrblt Motor Pkwy -Hauppauge 11788
(212) 735-3000 .. **Feldman,** Warren L '84 (Skadden ASM&F LLP) -4 Times Sq -NY 10036
(212) 869-7000 .. **Feldman Weinstein & Smith LLP** -420 Lex Av -NY 10170 **Fx:**997-4242
(914) 834-0879 .. **Feldman-Gordon,** Susan '82 -46 Woodbine Av -Larchmnt 10538
(718) 537-4958 .. **Feldmeier,** Arlene Garbett '91 %ODAR-SSA -226 E 161st -Bronx 10451 **Fx:**590-1673
(212) 232-1300 .. **Feldscher,** Jennifer H '02 %Lewis BB&S LLP -77 Water -NY 10005
(212) 880-3800 .. **Feldschreiber,** Harvey '74 (Akerman S) -335 Mad Av -NY 10017
(212) 508-6100 .. **Feldsher,** Jennifer '01 (Bracewell & G,LLP) -1251 Av of Amer -NY 10020
(917) 374-1711 .. **Feldshon,** Lee Adhemar G '95 (Feldshon & S,LLP) -457 W 57th -NY 10019 **Fx:**(212) 898-0357
(585) 232-5300 .. **Feldstein,** Alan R '70 (Boylan BCV&W,LLP) -2400 Chase Sq -Rchstr 14604
(212) 290-4700 .. **Feldstein,** Alan S '96 Cnsl Human Rights Watch -350 5th Av -NY 10118
(212) 648-9970 .. **Feldstein,** Andrew T '92 JP Morgan Chase & Co -270 Park Av -NY 10017
(212) 687-8500 .. **Feldstein,** David H '06 %Liddle & R,LLP -800 3rd Av -NY 10022
(212) 733-5105 .. **Feldstein,** Federico A '02 %Pfizer Inc -235 E 42nd -NY 10017
(212) 982-3847 .. **Feldstein,** Helen S '87 -28 E 10th -NY 10003
(646) 344-8845 .. **Feldstein,** Miriam L K '87 NPXL -420 Lex Av -NY 10170
(212) 318-3000 .. **Felfe,** Peter F '65 (Fulbright & J LLP) -666 5th Av -NY 10103
(212) 735-3000 .. **Felfe,** Tess C '09 %Skadden ASM&F LLP -4 Times Sq -NY 10036
(347) 226-4232 .. **Feliberty,** Melba '98 -4303 Junction Blvd -Corona 11368
(212) 806-5400 .. **Felice,** Frances L '02 %Stroock &S&L LLP -180 Maiden Ln -NY 10038
(212) 867-2700 .. **Felice,** Jon B '87 (J Felice & Assoc,PC) -11 E 44th -NY 10017 **Fx:**867-2783
(315) 471-5773 .. **Felice,** Michele R '78 -232 Whitestone Cir -Syracuse 13215
(631) 893-3900 .. **Felice,** Phil W '99 -333 Sunrise Hwy -W Islip 11795 **Fx:**893-5300
(212) 336-2000 .. **Felicello,** Rosanne E '07 %Patterson BW&T LLP -1133 Av of Amer -NY 10036
(716) 858-2424 .. **Felicetta,** Michl P '07 %DA -25 Delaware Av -Buffalo 14202 **Fx:**858-7425
(516) 747-8668 .. **Felicetti,** Brian P '97 -226 7th -Gdn Cty 11530
(631) 806-7347 .. **Felicetti,** Scott A '89 -226 7th -Gdn Cty 11530
(212) 947-7800 .. **Feliciano,** Carol '94 First Quality Maintenance -70 W 36th -NY 10018
(718) 461-6633 .. **Feliciano,** Dennis J '03 %Mallilo & G -163-09 Nrthrn Blvd -Flushng 11358
(212) 448-2727 .. **Feliciano,** Joel '92 Applied Discovery -125 Park Av S -NY 10017 **Fx:**448-2703
(212) 433-0997 .. **Feliciano,** Luis D '94 %Sheriff's Ofc -31 Chmbrs -NY 10007
(716) 837-7455 .. **Feliciano,** Michl J '94 -521 Highgate Av -Buffalo 14215
(212) 341-6400 .. **Felicione,** Lauren M '85 %Liquidation Bur -123 William -NY 10038 **Fx:**608-3398
(631) 360-7333 .. **Felicione,** Paul J '88 %De Sena & S -1383 Vets Mem'l Hwy -Hauppauge 11788
(845) 774-3333 .. **Felicissimo,** Lisa J '90 -107 Stage Rd -Monroe 10950 **Fx:**782-9458
(914) 765-4203 .. **Felicissimo,** Mark A '97 IBM -1 New Orchrd Rd -Armonk 10504 **Fx:**765-7533
(212) 335-9000 .. **Felig,** Elliot M '94 %DA -1 Hogan Pl -NY 10013
(212) 763-6800 .. **Feliu,** Alfred G '82 (Vandenberg & F,LLP) -60 E 42nd -NY 10165
(212) 357-5884 .. **Felix,** Genevieve Ann '95 Goldman Sachs & Co -180 Maiden Ln -NY 10038
(212) 461-7190 .. **Felix,** Isabelle S '05 %Fishman M,PC -44 Wall -NY 10005
(212) 419-1492 .. **Felix,** James M '81 (Kilhenny & F) -350 7th Av -NY 10001 **Fx:**419-1499
(212) 884-6227 .. **Felix,** Kevin A '95 Guggenheim Prtnrs -135 E 57th -NY 10022 **Fx:**644-2947
(516) 872-8827 .. **Felix,** Richd '87 -108 S Franklin Av -Vly Stream 11580
(212) 747-1433 .. **Felix,** Robt N '76 -11 Bway -NY 10004 **Fx:**943-1238
(212) 422-0488 .. **Fell,** Alan '75 (Rick SF&B,LLP) -90 Broad -NY 10004
(631) 737-4110 .. **Fella,** Matthew T '03 %Gruenberg & K,PC -3275 Vets Mem'l Hwy -Ronkonkoma 11779 **Fx:**737-4155
(212) 837-6000 .. **Fellas,** John N '89 (Hughes H&R LLP) -1 Bttry Pk Plz -NY 10004
(716) 505-2700 .. **Felle,** Wayne C '94 (Felle S&M,LLC) -6024 Main -Williamsvll 14221 **Fx:**506-2727
(845) 794-3000 .. **Felleman,** Frank '64 Surrogates Ct -Govt Ctr -Monticello 12701 **Fx:**791-6252
(212) 489-8888 .. **Felleman,** George P '68 (Pollet & F,LLP) -1700 Bway -NY 10019
(212) 986-4848 .. **Fellenbaum,** Neal '78 (Zegen & F) -261 Mad Av -NY 10016 **Fx:**808-9808
(845) 342-1808 .. **Fellenzer,** Joy A '84 -11 Starhaven Av -Middletwn 10940
(212) 264-6426 .. **Feller,** Adam P '92 %DHS -26 Fed Plz -NY 10278
(845) 621-8640 .. **Feller,** Alan D '02 (Sloan & F) -880 S Lk Blvd -Mahopac 10541 **Fx:**621-8639
(212) 788-9555 .. **Feller,** Andrea B '82 %Law Dept -100 Church -NY 10007 **Fx:**788-0367
(212) 852-3233 .. **Feller,** Deena K '94 US Trust Co of NY -114 W 47th -NY 10036
(212) 284-2266 .. **Feller,** Lloyd H '67 Jeffries & Co -520 Mad Av -NY 10022
(212) 780-2057 .. **Feller,** Marcy E '80 Multiplan Inc -115 5th Av -NY 10003 **Fx:**843-3513
(212) 308-0600 .. **Feller,** Mitchell S '97 (Sobel & F LLP) -444 Mad Av -NY 10022 **Fx:**308-0611
(212) 573-4747 .. **Feller,** Nancy '76 Ford Fndtn -320 E 43rd -NY 10017
(516) 239-8800 .. **Feller,** Nathaniel D '92 -50 Bway -Lawrence 11559 **Fx:**239-6800
(518) 533-3000 .. **Feller,** Robt H '78 SrCnsl Bond S&K,PLLC -111 Wshngtn Av -Albany 12210
(516) 229-4587 .. **Feller,** Sharon T '95 %G Lauzon -875 Merrick Av -Westbury 11590
(212) 237-1000 .. **Fellerman,** Michl J '03 %Windels ML&M,LLP -156 W 56th -NY 10019
(212) 461-7142 .. **Fellheimer,** Alan S '07 (Fellheimer & E LLP) -44 Wall -NY 10005 **Fx:**461-2223
(212) 461-7142 .. **Fellheimer,** Judith E '08 (Fellheimer & E LLP) -44 Wall -NY 10005 **Fx:**461-2223
(516) 538-1111 .. **Fellin,** Paul J '07 %Mahon MK&O,LLC -254 Nassau Blvd -Garden City South 11530
(212) 688-1010 .. **Fellinger,** John G '79 -110 E 59th -NY 10022 **Fx:**223-4911
(212) 265-6888 .. **Fellner,** Gary M '92 (Porzio B&N,PC) -156 W 56th -NY 10019
(845) 634-3775 .. **Fellows Hymowitz & Epstein,PC** -254 S Main -New Cty 10956 **Fx:**634-3598
(315) 218-8000 .. **Fellows,** Jonathan B '87 (Bond S&K,PLLC) -1 Lincoln Ctr -Syracuse 13202
(845) 634-3775 .. **Fellows,** Robt L '76 (Fellows H&E,PC) -254 S Main -New Cty 10956
(718) 236-2457 .. **Fellus,** Saul '90 -25 Bay 7th -Brklyn 11228
(212) 902-0300 .. **Felman,** David S '07 Goldman Sachs & Co -85 Broad -NY 10004
(619) 384-7263 .. **Felmar,** Michl S '94 -225 Bennett Av -NY 10040
(716) 852-3540 .. **Felmet,** Aaron J '09 %Watson BCJ&S -12 Fountain Plz -Buffalo 14202
(212) 559-7050 .. **Felner,** Andrew M '91 %Citigroup Inc -399 Park Av -NY 10022
(631) 247-0404 .. **Felsberg,** Eric J '99 (Jackson L LLP) -58 S Srvc Rd -Melvll 11747
(516) 328-8899 .. **Felsen,** Jamie S '05 %Milman L Law Grp PLLC -3000 Marcus Av -Lk Success 11042 **Fx:**328-0082
(212) 553-5549 .. **Felsen,** Marnie A '04 Zurich NA -1 Lbrty Plz -NY 10006
(212) 850-2800 .. **Felsenfeld,** Arthur D '76 (Andrews K LLP) -450 Lex Av -NY 10017
(212) 636-6000 .. **Felsenfeld,** Carl '54 %Fordham Univ Sch of Law -140 W 62nd -NY 10023 **Fx:**636-6899
(914) 271-2100 .. **Felsenfeld,** Steven '96 -75 S Riverside Av -Croton-On-Hud 10520 **Fx:**271-2141
(212) 935-3131 .. **Felsenstein,** Adam M '08 %Gallet D&B,LLP -845 3rd Av -NY 10022
(212) 878-8000 .. **Felsenthal,** David L '86 (Clifford C LLP) -31 W 52nd -NY 10019
(212) 332-7300 .. **Felsenthal,** Steven M '97 Millburn Corp -1270 Av of Amer -NY 10020
(212) 610-9000 .. **Felsher,** Celia A '80 %Reservoir Cptl Grp -650 Mad Av -NY 10022 **Fx:**610-9001
(212) 308-8505 .. **Felsher,** David P '85 OfCnsl Akabas & S -488 Mad Av -NY 10022
(212) 489-8230 .. **Felsten,** Nancy J '87 (Davis WT LLP) -1633 Bway -NY 10019
(315) 853-4436 .. **Felt Evans,LLP** -4-6 N Park Row -Clinton 13323 **Fx:**853-4511
(212) 735-3000 .. **Feltenstein,** Martha '82 (Skadden ASM&F LLP) -4 Times Sq -NY 10036
(315) 234-8570 .. **Felter,** Karen Guyder '93 %Hon N Mordue -100 S Clinton Bx7367 -Syracuse 13261 **Fx:**234-8571
(212) 310-8000 .. **Feltham,** Timothy S '89 Cnsl Weil G&M LLP -767 5th Av -NY 10153
(516) 437-3300 .. **Feltman,** Arthur A '93 %Comforce Corp -415 Crsswys Park Dr Bx9006 -Woodbury 11797
(212) 403-1000 .. **Feltman,** Joshua A '03 (Wachtell LR&K) -51 W 52nd -NY 10019
(518) 873-3335 .. **Felton,** Brian W '05 DA -Cthse -Elizabethtwn 12932 **Fx:**873-3788
(516) 746-5711 .. **Felton,** Cheryl J '87 (Felton & F) -1527 Franklin -Mineola 11501 **Fx:**746-5717
(718) 273-9600 .. **Felton,** Duane C '81 -805 Castleton Av -Staten Isl 10310 **Fx:**273-7456
(516) 746-5711 .. **Felton,** Leslie G '97 (Felton & F) -1527 Franklin -Mineola 11501 **Fx:**746-5717
(212) 657-1153 .. **Felton,** Nicole L '90 Citigroup Global Mrkts -77 Water -NY 10005
(718) 622-1100 .. **Felton,** Regina '78 (Felton & Assoc) -1371 Fulton -Brklyn 11216 **Fx:**783-0327
(212) 259-8000 .. **Felz,** Kevin C '03 %Dewey & L LLP -1301 Av of Amer -NY 10019
(212) 751-5822 .. **Felzen,** Paul '64 -641 Lex Av -NY 10022 **Fx:**888-7711
(718) 237-2000 .. **Feman,** Danielle '05 Leg Aid -111 Lvngstn -Brklyn 11201 **Fx:**237-8737
(516) 560-6400 .. **Feman,** Tammy '98 %Leg Aid -1 Helen Keller Way -Hempstd 11550 **Fx:**565-3694
(845) 371-4700 .. **Femano,** Richd D '98 %Fein SK&S,PC -747 Chestnut Rdg Rd -Spg Vly 10977
(212) 612-2496 .. **Femia,** Andrew M '00 Chubb Grp -55 Water -NY 10041
(212) 833-7292 .. **Femia,** Robt T '06 Cnsl Sony BMG Music Entertainment -550 Mad Av -NY 10022 **Fx:**833-7843
(516) 222-6200 .. **Fenchel,** Saul R '72 (Berkman HPP&F,PC) -100 Grdn City Plz -Gdn Cty 11530
(212) 388-0092 .. **Fendelman,** Burton M '75 B Fendelman & Assoc -60 Gramercy Park N -NY 10010 **Fx:**473-5436
(212) 449-7541 .. **Fendo,** Julie '02 Merrill Lynch -4 World Fncl Ctr -NY 10080
(914) 948-2299 .. **Fendt,** Eric G '04 %JB Cherico & Assoc -308 Battle Av -White Plns 10606 **Fx:**948-4248
(718) 875-5199 .. **Fendt,** John L '04 %Composto & C -142 Joralemon -Brklyn 11201 **Fx:**639-7586
(212) 629-9690 .. **Fenelon,** Mark J '02 %P Merani -298 5th Av -NY 10001 **Fx:**629-9664
(212) 848-4000 .. **Feng,** Andrew S '08 %Shearman & S LLP -599 Lex Av -NY 10022
(212) 903-9000 .. **Feng,** Dan '09 %Linklaters -1345 Av of Amer -NY 10105
(212) 965-1899 .. **Feng,** David Xiaoming '99 The Feng Law Firm,PC -401 Bway -NY 10013 **Fx:**965-1852

(917) 777-4200 .. **Fenge,** Jennifer Kang '02 Cnsl Bingham M LLP -1 Bttry Pk Plz -NY 10004
(516) 742-8058 .. **Fengos,** Nicholas J '88 %Abamont & Assoc -200 Grdn City Plz Bx9250 -Gdn Cty 11530 **Fx:**742-7308
(646) 458-6835 .. **Fenice,** Michele L '94 ACE USA -140 Bway -NY 10005
(212) 839-6519 .. **Fenichel,** David A '91 NYDOT -55 Water -NY 10041
(212) 585-3425 .. **Fenichel,** Roy S '05 %B Kishner & Assoc -420 Lex Av -NY 10170 **Fx:**752-1810
(212) 581-3508 .. **Fenig,** Steven M '93 -75 West End Av -NY 10023 **Fx:**957-9295
(212) 571-0111 .. **Fenley,** Jason P '07 %Hardin KM&P,PA -110 William -NY 10038
(518) 434-0600 .. **Fenlon,** Christopher V '10 %Boies S&F LLP -10 N Pearl -Albany 12207
(212) 906-1200 .. **Fenn,** Chas Timothy '08 (Latham & W) -885 3rd Av -NY 10022
(718) 286-6000 .. **Fenn,** Danielle S '05 %DA -125-01 Qns Blvd -Kew Gdns 11415
(516) 367-5010 .. **Fenn,** Edw A '04 Cold Spring Harbor Lab -1 Bungtown Rd -Cold Spg Hbr 11724
(212) 931-5140 .. **Fenn,** Lucy A '04 Prince Street Capital Mgmt -152 W 57th -NY 10019
(212) 872-1000 .. **Fenn,** Patrick B '83 -One Bryant Park -NY 10036 **Fx:**872-1002
(212) 310-8000 .. **Fennell,** Gregory '04 %Weil G&M LLP -767 5th Av -NY 10153
(212) 696-6000 .. **Fennell,** Louisa A '08 %Curtis M-PC&M LLP -101 Park Av -NY 10178
(315) 343-6363 .. **Fennell,** Timothy J '84 (Amdursky PF&W,PC) -26 E Oneida -Oswego 13126
(212) 220-3830 .. **Fennell,** Wm M '01 %Nicoletti H&S -88 Pine -NY 10005
(212) 940-3732 .. **Fennelly,** Meghan C '08 %Nixon P LLP -437 Mad Av -NY 10022
(518) 463-1269 .. **Fennelly,** Wm E '99 %Walsh & H -18 Corp Wds Blvd -Albany 12211
(718) 250-0400 .. **Fenner,** Braxton F '91 %R Tusa -1 MetroTech Ctr -Brklyn 11201 **Fx:**250-0591
(212) 848-4000 .. **Fennessey,** Susan A '01 Cnsl Shearman & S LLP -599 Lex Av -NY 10022
(212) 593-6700 .. **Fenno,** Craig P '82 (Aaronson RF&D,LLP) -757 3rd Av -NY 10017
(607) 547-2555 .. **Fenno,** Nathan R '83 %Delaware Otsego Corp -1 Railroad Av -Cooperstwn 13326 **Fx:**547-2555
(212) 210-9477 .. **Fenoglio,** Catherine R '04 %Alston & B LLP -90 Park Av -NY 10016
(212) 636-7533 .. **Fenrich,** Jeanmarie K '99 Fordham Univ -33 W 60th -NY 10023
(212) 450-4000 .. **Fenrich,** Wm J '99 (Davis P&W LLP) -450 Lex Av -NY 10017
(315) 456-3598 .. **Fenske,** Sandra Lee '94 %Lockheed Martin -Bldg 7 Bx4840 -Syracuse 13221 **Fx:**456-2178
(212) 836-8000 .. **Fenster,** Albert M '77 (Kaye S LLP) -425 Park Av -NY 10022
(212) 474-1000 .. **Fenster,** Amanda R '10 %Cravath S&M LLP -825 8th Av -NY 10019
(716) 685-4167 .. **Fenster,** David D '87 (Fenster & L,LLC) -5460 Bway -Lancaster 14086 **Fx:**685-2664
(212) 351-4500 .. **Fenster,** Hylan B '06 %Epstein B&G,PC -250 Park Av -NY 10177
(914) 948-1556 .. **Fenster,** Jay '81 (Danziger & M LLP) -123 Main -White Plns 10601
(518) 408-0469 .. **Fenster,** Jeffrey R '08 Workers Comp Bd -20 Park -Albany 12207
(212) 425-9300 .. **Fenster,** Lawr E '77 (Bressler A&R,PC) -17 State -NY 10004
(212) 436-1069 .. **Fenster,** Madeleine J '87 IRS -290 Bway -NY 10007
(212) 801-2155 .. **Fenster,** Matthew S '99 (Greenberg T,LLP) -200 Park Av -NY 10166
(212) 954-2075 .. **Fenster,** Rachel A '06 KPMG LLP -345 Park Av -NY 10154
(845) 638-4700 .. **Fenster,** Robt D '74 (Fenster & K LLP) -337 N Main -New Cty 10956 **Fx:**638-4767
(718) 423-5066 .. **Fenster,** Simon A '80 -64-51 210th -Oakland Gdns 11364 **Fx:**423-5066
(914) 366-8400 .. **Fensterheim,** Asher '51 (A Fensterheim,PLLC) -660 Wht Plns Rd -Tarrytwn 10591 **Fx:**366-9626
(845) 638-1368 .. **Fensterheim,** Robin G '84 -39 Windgate Dr -New Cty 10956 **Fx:**638-1389
(212) 572-6297 .. **Fenstermaker,** Scott L '93 -300 Park Av -NY 10022 **Fx:**572-6499
(516) 328-2300 .. **Fensterman,** Howard '80 (Abrams FFEGF&E,LLP) -1111 Marcus Av -Lk Success 11042
(516) 328-2300 .. **Fensterman,** Jordan S '09 %Abrams FFEGF&E,LLP -1111 Marcus Av -Lk Success 11042
(212) 619-5000 .. **Fensterman,** Judy Ellen '85 %EDC -110 William -NY 10038 **Fx:**312-3912
(516) 328-2300 .. **Fensterman,** Robt G '85 (Abrams FFEGF&E,LLP) -1111 Marcus Av -Lk Success 11042
(212) 785-4100 .. **Fensterstock,** Blair C '76 (Fensterstock & Prtnrs LLP) -30 Wall -NY 10005
(212) 527-7575 .. **Fensterstock,** David '95 (Grover & F,PC) -750 3rd Av -NY 10017
(212) 506-1700 .. **Fensterstock,** Evan S '10 %Kasowitz BT&F LLP -1633 Bway -NY 10019
(212) 751-5444 .. **Fensterstock,** Joshua G '04 %Isaacs & Assoc,PLLC -260 Mad Av -NY 10016 **Fx:**532-6400
(212) 785-4100 .. **Fensterstock & Partners LLP** -30 Wall -NY 10005 **Fx:**785-4040
(914) 422-4422 .. **Fentiman,** Linda C '95 Pace Law Schl -78 N Bway -White Plns 10603 **Fx:**422-4229
(914) 428-6565 .. **Fentin,** Barry H '67 (Fentin & G,LLP) -44 S Bway -White Plns 10601
(914) 428-6565 .. **Fentin & Goldman,LLP** -44 S Bway -White Plns 10601 **Fx:**428-4455
(212) 918-4840 .. **Fenton,** Bruce '77 -48 Wall -NY 10005
(212) 848-4000 .. **Fenton,** Christopher R '04 %Shearman & S LLP -599 Lex Av -NY 10022
(718) 960-8283 .. **Fenton,** Denise R '99 %Lehman Cllg -250 Bedford Park Blvd W -Bronx 10468
(212) 801-2144 .. **Fenton,** Loring I '85 (Greenberg T,LLP) -200 Park Av -NY 10166
(845) 676-3188 .. **Fenton,** Mary L '65 -Bx245 -Andes 13731
(212) 791-8400 .. **Fenton,** Michl '09 %Mait W&S -110 Wall -NY 10005
(212) 704-6000 .. **Fenton,** Mitchell '70 (Troutman S LLP) -405 Lex Av -NY 10174
(718) 286-6000 .. **Fenton,** Neil P '97 DA -125-01 Qns Blvd -Kew Gdns 11415
(212) 801-6977 .. **Fenton,** Nicole L '94 (Greenberg T,LLP) -200 Park Av -NY 10166
(646) 391-1144 .. **Fenton,** Paula B '73 -260 Mad Av -NY 10016 **Fx:**(212) 253-4262
(716) 853-2050 .. **Fenton,** Russell J '09 %Sliwa & L -237 Main -Buffalo 14203
(212) 891-9100 .. **Fenton,** Steven M '07 %Goldfarb & F LLP -345 Park Av -NY 10154
(914) 237-4300 .. **Fenwick,** John B '72 J Fenwick PLLC -849 McLean Av -Ynkrs 10704 **Fx:**237-4380
(212) 866-8364 .. **Fenwick,** Lila A '58 -317 W 108th -NY 10025
(212) 480-3030 .. **Fenyes,** Eric S '88 %M Pressman -125 Maiden Ln -NY 10038 **Fx:**480-2590
(212) 455-2000 .. **Fenyes,** Richd A '96 (Simpson T&B LLP) -425 Lex Av -NY 10017
(212) 446-7000 .. **Fenyo,** Kenneth M '94 %McKinsey & Co -55 E 52nd -NY 10055 **Fx:**688-9521
(914) 495-3050 .. **Feo,** Christina M '07 %Reisman R&M,LLP -151 Bway -Hawthorne 10532 **Fx:**495-3051
(716) 204-2400 .. **Feor,** Sarah '08 %SJ Baum,PC -220 Nrthpnte Pkwy Bx1291 -Buffalo 14240 **Fx:**204-4600
(718) 590-6167 .. **Fequiere-Pierre,** Karlyne '00 %Law Dept -198 E 161st -Bronx 10451 **Fx:**590-2686
(212) 468-0489 .. **Ferando,** Elizabeth L '91 %TD Securities -31 W 52nd -NY 10019
(516) 535-3333 .. **Feraru,** Kenneth S '95 KS Feraru,PC -200 Old Cntry Rd -Mineola 11501 **Fx:**535-4090
(212) 450-2357 .. **Ferazani,** Lawr P Jr. '96 %NFL -280 Park Av -NY 10017 **Fx:**681-7599
(212) 944-2200 .. **Ferber Chan Essner & Coller, LLP** -530 5th Av -NY 10036 **Fx:**944-7630
(212) 944-2200 .. **Ferber,** David I '67 (Ferber CE&C,LLP) -530 5th Av -NY 10036
(716) 688-3800 .. **Ferber,** Gabriel J '77 (Nesper F&D,LLP) -501 JJ Audobon Pkwy -Amherst 14228
(212) 902-5746 .. **Ferber,** Laurie R '81 Goldman Sachs -85 Broad -NY 10004
(631) 234-2222 .. **Ferber,** Steven B '79 (Siben & F) -1455 Vets Mem'l Hwy -Hauppauge 11749
(212) 326-0194 .. **Ferber,** Tom J '83 (Pryor C LLP) -7 Times Sq -NY 10036
(212) 956-1313 .. **Ferch,** Michl L '95 -130 W 57th -NY 10019 **Fx:**956-4596
(631) 232-2400 .. **Ferdenzi,** Giovanna M '00 Nassau/Sfflk Law Srv -1757 Vets Hwy -Islandia 11749 **Fx:**232-2489
(718) 590-2000 .. **Ferdenzi,** Jos '79 %DA -198 E 161st -Bronx 10451 **Fx:**590-6477
(516) 742-0067 .. **Ferdinand,** Deborah M '94 -233 7th -Gdn Cty 11530 **Fx:**742-0696
(212) 335-9000 .. **Ferdinand,** Rhonda '84 %DA -1 Hogan Pl -NY 10013
(716) 566-1300 .. **Ferdman,** Michl E '80 (Hiscock & B,LLP) -1100 M&T Ctr -Buffalo 14203
(212) 318-3000 .. **Ferdon,** Robt E '58 OfCnsl Fulbright & J LLP -666 5th Av -NY 10103
(212) 930-9700 .. **Ference,** Michl H '96 (Sichenzia RFF LLP) -61 Bway -NY 10006
(516) 489-5000 .. **Ferencik,** Eugene Kirby '73 %Town Atty -Town Hall -Hempstd 11550 **Fx:**489-5150
(914) 225-4779 .. **Ferencz,** Cynthia D '99 Morgan Stanley Inc -2000 Wstchstr Av -Purchase 10577
(914) 784-4800 .. **Ferencz,** Donald M '84 Crompton Corp -771 Old Saw Mill Rvr Rd -Tarrytwn 10591
(845) 454-0500 .. **Ferenz,** David G '69 -2 Cannon -Poughkeepsie 12601
(212) 530-3900 .. **Feretic,** James J '76 (Hannum FP&M, LLC) -55 Bway -NY 10006
(646) 313-8126 .. **Fergerson,** Ranada R '89 Bank of Amer Securities -1 Bryant Pk -NY 10036
(212) 834-0600 .. **Fergus,** Thos M '96 %Gordon & S,PC -355 Lex Av -NY 10017
(212) 374-2986 .. **Ferguson,** Alexandra D '95 %NYC Dept Educ -52 Chmbrs -NY 10007
(212) 552-9047 .. **Ferguson,** Beverley B '96 %Chase Manhattan Bk -270 Park Av -NY 10017
(212) 558-5500 .. **Ferguson,** Chas M '88 %Weitz & L,PC -700 Bway -NY 10003
(212) 808-8100 .. **Ferguson,** Christopher M '00 %Kostelanetz & F,LLP -7 Wrld Trd Ctr -NY 10007
(212) 219-1001 .. **Ferguson,** David R '77 -401 Bway -NY 10013
(212) 314-7334 .. **Ferguson,** Edw T III '82 IAC Interactive -555 W 18th -NY 10011
(212) 589-4200 .. **Ferguson,** Gerald J '89 (Baker & H LLP) -45 Rckfllr Plz -NY 10111
(212) 577-3548 .. **Ferguson,** Harold V Jr. '85 %Leg Aid -199 Water -NY 10038 **Fx:**577-3525
(212) 306-1403 .. **Ferguson,** J B '72 %Amer Stock Exch -86 Trinity Pl -NY 10006
(212) 736-9924 .. **Ferguson,** James B Jr. '93 Bd of Parole -119 W 31st -NY 10001
(718) 250-2000 .. **Ferguson,** Jeffrey L '83 %DA -350 Jay -Brklyn 11201 **Fx:**250-2314
(914) 397-2400 .. **Ferguson,** John J '66 (Ferguson C,LLP) -1 N Lex Av -White Plns 10601 **Fx:**683-6956
(212) 813-8800 .. **Ferguson,** John M '99 (Goodwin P LLP) -620 8th Av -NY 10018
(518) 436-8421 .. **Ferguson,** Lisa N '92 Nigro Companies -20 Corp Wds Blvd -Albany 12211 **Fx:**436-8429
(212) 450-4000 .. **Ferguson,** M Carr Jr. '54 SrCnsl Davis P&W LLP -450 Lex Av -NY 10017
(212) 425-7500 .. **Ferguson,** Marie D '94 Argus Research Grp -61 Bway -NY 10006
(914) 741-6100 .. **Ferguson,** Matthew M '06 %Kaufman B&R -200 Summit Lk Dr -Valhalla 10595
(516) 571-3056 .. **Ferguson,** Michl J '78 Cnty Atty -1 West -Mineola 11501 **Fx:**571-6604
(212) 788-2342 .. **Ferguson,** Nikisha L '07 ACS -220 Church -NY 10013
(516) 626-3636 .. **Ferguson,** Randall S '78 -99 Powerhse Rd -Roslyn Hts 11577 **Fx:**626-3565
(585) 232-1260 .. **Ferguson,** Richd C '89 -45 Exchange Blvd -Rchstr 14614 **Fx:**232-1280
(212) 490-9000 .. **Ferguson,** Roger W Jr. '83 %TIAA-CREF -730 3rd Av -NY 10017
(646) 386-5700 .. **Ferguson,** Sharon M '06 %Civil Ct -111 Centre -NY 10013
(212) 306-7701 .. **Ferguson-Woods,** Alison V '07 Comm on Human Rights -40 Rector -NY 10006 **Fx:**306-7414
(718) 692-0055 .. **Ferington,** Karen J D '87 -2124 Kimball -Brklyn 11234 **Fx:**692-0556
(718) 286-6000 .. **Ferino,** Robt J '93 %DA -125-01 Qns Blvd -Kew Gdns 11415
(212) 351-4500 .. **Ferko,** Sharon L '92 OfCnsl Epstein B&G,PC -250 Park Av -NY 10177
(212) 805-3900 .. **Ferland,** Paul C '06 %Clausen M PC -1 Chase Manh Plz -NY 10005
(212) 496-1848 .. **Ferlanti,** Wm J '80 -66 W 82nd -NY 10024
(212) 269-4900 .. **Ferlazzo,** Matthew C '05 %Ford MEW&G,LLP -Wall Street Plz -NY 10005
(518) 462-0300 .. **Ferlazzo,** Salvatore D '81 (Girvin & F,PC) -20 Corp Wds Blvd -Albany 12211
(212) 416-8629 .. **Ferleger,** Deborah E '96 %Dept of Law -120 Bway -NY 10271
(585) 325-3860 .. **Ferlicca,** John J '89 -1411 Chili Av -Rchstr 14624 **Fx:**546-4749
(718) 963-1600 .. **Ferlisi,** Michl J '60 -85 Kngslnd Av -Brklyn 11222
(631) 225-5960 .. **Ferlito,** Angelo G '90 (A Ferlito,PC) -1355A Merrick Rd -Copiague 11726 **Fx:**225-5965
(845) 567-7776 .. **Fermanian,** Silvia A '01 %Finkelstein & Prtnrs,LLP -103 Exec Dr -New Windsor 12553
(212) 687-0100 .. **Fern,** Fredk H '81 (Harris B PLLC) -100 Wall -NY 10005

(718) 520-2259 .. **Fern,** Ilene P '89 %Hon M Schulman -125-01 Qns Blvd -Kew Gdns 11415
(914) 559-8010 .. **Fern,** Robt E '87 -72 N Bway -Irvngtn 10533
(845) 677-0046 .. **Fernald,** Louann T '01 -Bx1008 -Millbrook 12545
(631) 283-3510 .. **Fernan,** Richd S '76 -592 Hmptn Rd Bx1283 -Southampton 11969 **Fx:**283-3001
(212) 419-1600 .. **Fernand,** Jaime A '05 Edison Schls Inc -485 Lex Av -NY 10017
(212) 839-5300 .. **Fernand,** Matthew E '04 %Sidley A LLP -787 7th Av -NY 10019
(631) 667-5911 .. **Fernandes,** Thos '66 -191 Oakfld Av -Dix Hlls 11746
(212) 732-3200 .. **Fernandes,** Zara Falbel '05 %Carter L&M LLP -2 Wall -NY 10005
(212) 558-4000 .. **Fernandez,** Angel D '07 %Sullivan & C LLP -125 Broad -NY 10004
(212) 773-0237 .. **Fernandez,** Catherina M '05 Ernst & Young,LLP -5 Times Sq -NY 10036
(212) 348-3334 .. **Fernandez,** Cesar A '97 -2298 1st Av -NY 10035 **Fx:**348-3449
(212) 689-1113 .. **Fernandez,** Christine E '96 (Garbarini & S,PC) -432 Park Av S -NY 10016
(212) 335-9000 .. **Fernandez,** Consuelo L '76 %DA -1 Hogan Pl -NY 10013
(212) 340-0400 .. **Fernandez,** Cristina L '04 %Appllt Div 1st Dept -27 Mad Av -NY 10010 **Fx:**889-4412
(212) 732-3200 .. **Fernández,** David J '93 (Carter L&M LLP) -2 Wall -NY 10005
(718) 286-6000 .. **Fernandez,** Franchesca '07 %DA -125-01 Qns Blvd -Kew Gdns 11415
(212) 820-9416 .. **Fernandez,** Gerard Jr. '50 OfCnsl Hawkins D&W LLP -One Chase Manh Plz -NY 10005
(518) 533-3000 .. **Fernandez,** Hermes '82 (Bond S&K,PLLC) -111 Wshngtn Av -Albany 12210
(212) 867-4466 .. **Fernandez,** Jordi '03 %Belkin BW&G,LLP -270 Mad Av -NY 10016
(212) 458-1605 .. **Fernandez,** Katherine Nuqui '02 %AIG -175 Water -NY 10038
(212) 878-8000 .. **Fernández,** Kevin D '09 %Clifford C LLP -31 W 52nd -NY 10019
(718) 260-2523 .. **Fernandez,** Laura A '03 Hon J Weinstein -225 Cadman Plz E -Brklyn 11201
(212) 417-5300 .. **Fernandez,** Lissette G '04 %Medicaid Fraud Cntrl -120 Bway -NY 10271 **Fx:**417-5274
(212) 225-2000 .. **Fernandez,** Melissa '08 %Cleary GS&H -1 Lbrty Plz -NY 10006
(212) 425-1900 .. **Fernandez,** Michl '91 (Freehill H&M LLP) -80 Pine -NY 10005
(212) 687-5154 .. **Fernandez,** Paola Lorena '99 Atco Prop & Mgmt Inc -555 5th Av -NY 10017
(718) 590-3664 .. **Fernandez,** Patricia M Kleczka '93 NYS Unified Ct Sys -851 Grnd Cncrs -Bronx 10451
(914) 428-8288 .. **Fernandez,** Paul J '98 %L Shaw -75 S Bway -White Plns 10601 **Fx:**428-8181
(212) 940-8800 .. **Fernandez,** Pedro C '97 %Katten MR LLP -575 Mad Av -NY 10022
(718) 522-2401 .. **Fernandez,** Ricardo E '86 -16 Court -Brklyn 11241
(518) 356-6000 .. **Fernandez,** Robt E '85 NY Indpndnt System Operator -10 Krey Blvd -Rensselaer 12144
(646) 429-7500 .. **Fernandez,** Santiago A '05 %Macys,Inc -11 Penn Plz -NY 10001 **Fx:**429-7521
(212) 577-3688 .. **Fernandez,** Sheilah '93 %Leg Aid -199 Water -NY 10038 **Fx:**509-8431
(212) 264-3650 .. **Fernandez,** Sistina '97 %SSA Ofc Genl Cnsl -26 Fed Plz -NY 10278 **Fx:**264-6372
(518) 402-3966 .. **Fernandez,** Thania '86 %OTDA -40 N Pearl -Albany 12243 **Fx:**474-9389
(607) 723-5341 .. **Fernandez,** Tina '04 %Hinman H&K,LLP -80 Exchange Bx5250 -Bnghmtn 13902
(914) 287-0888 .. **Fernandez Harswick,** Giovanna '07 %J Sena Jr -55 Church -White Plns 10601 **Fx:**997-1204
(914) 761-8131 .. **Fernandez-Herrera,** Pablo E '99 -82 E Post Rd -White Plns 10601 **Fx:**761-8132
(716) 842-1379 .. **Fernandez-Hiltz,** Noemi '97 N Fernandez,PLLC -69 Delaware Av -Buffalo 14202 **Fx:**854-3821
(212) 849-7000 .. **Fernands,** Anastasia M '05 %Quinn EU&S,LLP -51 Mad Av -NY 10010
(212) 508-9477 .. **Fernbach,** Jason D '01 Zephyr Mgmt LP -320 Park Av -NY 10022
(212) 264-0300 .. **Fernbach,** Karen Pastalove '78 %NLRB -26 Fed Plz -NY 10278 **Fx:**264-8427
(516) 873-2000 .. **Fernbach,** Rachel A '99 %Moritt HH&H LLP -400 Grdn City Plz -Gdn Cty 11530
(347) 422-5321 .. **Ferng,** Joan H '09 Leg Aid -60 Bay -Staten Isl 10301 **Fx:**(718) 981-6623
(212) 446-2346 .. **Fernich,** Marc A '92 -152 W 57th -NY 10019 **Fx:**446-2299
(212) 735-3000 .. **Fernicola,** Gregory A '86 (Skadden ASM&F LLP) -4 Times Sq -NY 10036
(585) 325-4600 .. **Fero,** Dean J '56 (Fero & I) -183 E Main -Rchstr 14604 **Fx:**325-1525
(585) 325-4600 .. **Fero,** Matthew J '04 %Fero & I -183 E Main -Rchstr 14604 **Fx:**325-1525
(585) 753-1380 .. **Fero Giess,** Shela K '00 %Cnty Atty -307 Cnty Ofc Bldg -Rchstr 14614 **Fx:**753-1331
(716) 854-0700 .. **Feroleto,** John P '83 -438 Main -Buffalo 14202 **Fx:**854-0265
(716) 858-2424 .. **Feroleto,** John Patrick '08 %DA -25 Delaware Av -Buffalo 14202 **Fx:**858-7425
(716) 854-1111 .. **Feron,** Kelly A '90 %Spadafora & V -2 Symphony Cir -Buffalo 14201
(716) 851-2711 .. **Feron,** Thos P '90 %UIA Bd -290 Main -Buffalo 14202 **Fx:**851-2795
(914) 961-3636 .. **Ferone,** Jos J Jr. '61 Ferone & F -484 Wht Plns Rd -Eastchstr 10709 **Fx:**961-4440
(914) 949-1305 .. **Ferone,** Mary Grace '93 %Leg Srvcs -90 Maple Av -White Plns 10601 **Fx:**949-6213
(518) 587-0080 .. **Ferradino,** Stephanie W '97 (Jones F) -68 West Av Bx4400 -Saratoga Spgs 12866
(212) 641-8606 .. **Ferragamo,** Michl P '97 AXA Private Equity -1370 Av of Amer -NY 10019
(212) 233-4824 .. **Ferraiuolo,** Peter P '95 (P Ferraiuolo,PLLC) -160 Bway -NY 10038 **Fx:**267-7571
(631) 765-9888 .. **Ferraiuolo,** Thos J '91 -350 Richmond Ln -Peconic 11958
(212) 661-0279 .. **Ferrall,** Wm J '89 Smith & K,LLP -122 E 42nd -NY 10168
(716) 852-5875 .. **Ferrandino,** Adam C '94 (Feldman K LLP) -110 Pearl -Buffalo 14202
(646) 253-2300 .. **Ferrandino,** Margo G '03 %Bond S&K,PLLC -330 Mad Av -NY 10017
(631) 470-5000 .. **Ferrante,** Angela '01 Garden City Crp Inc -105 Maxess Rd -Melvll 11747
(516) 747-3222 .. **Ferrante,** Anthony A '07 %Levine & W,PLLC -259 Mineola Blvd -Mineola 11501
(212) 308-4440 .. **Ferrante,** Frank Jr. '95 (Ferrante,PLLC) -5 W 19th -NY 10011 **Fx:**888-3839
(631) 361-5360 .. **Ferrante,** Jos '06 (Keahon FD&F) -1393 Vets Mem'l Hwy -Hauppauge 11788 **Fx:**361-5365
(631) 249-0505 .. **Ferrante,** Michl A '86 %Comax Manu Corp -130 Baylis Rd -Melvll 11747 **Fx:**249-9255
(315) 435-2470 .. **Ferrante,** Michl E '89 %DA -505 S State -Syracuse 13202 **Fx:**435-3969
(212) 751-3001 .. **Ferrante,** Pablo C '05 %Thompson & K LLP -919 3rd Av -NY 10022
(212) 735-3000 .. **Ferrante,** Rebecca M '05 %Skadden ASM&F LLP -4 Times Sq -NY 10036
(914) 997-1777 .. **Ferrante,** Richd L '93 -399 Knollwood Rd -White Plns 10603 **Fx:**997-1778
(212) 363-6900 .. **Ferrante,** Vito J '79 (Faust GS&B LLP) -2 Rector -NY 10006
(631) 390-5000 .. **Ferranti,** Diana L '10 %Genser DG&C,LLP -445 Broad Hollow Rd -Melvll 11747
(212) 848-4000 .. **Ferranti,** Kristopher T '10 Shearman & S LLP -599 Lex Av -NY 10022
(212) 538-8040 .. **Ferranti,** Neil J '90 Credit Suisse -11 Mad Av -NY 10010
(718) 317-9777 .. **Ferranti,** Thos Jr. '95 -99 Pitney Av -Staten Isl 10309 **Fx:**317-5294
(516) 294-5555 .. **Ferrar,** Nicholas J '80 OfCnsl Del Vecchio & R,LLP -1100 Franklin Av -Gdn Cty 11530 **Fx:**873-5336
(315) 437-7600 .. **Ferrara,** Benjamin J '74 (Ferrara FLB&R,PC) -5010 Campuswood Dr -E Syracuse 13057
(212) 269-7308 .. **Ferrara,** Bryan J '09 %Leahey & J PC -120 Wall -NY 10005
(212) 216-8000 .. **Ferrara,** Catherine M '01 %Tarter K&D LLP -1350 Bway -NY 10018
(212) 656-4684 .. **Ferrara,** Christopher P '08 NYSE Regulation -11 Wall -NY 10005
(315) 218-8000 .. **Ferrara,** David M '88 (Bond S&K,PLLC) -1 Lincoln Ctr -Syracuse 13202
(315) 437-7600 .. **Ferrara Fiorenza Larrison Barrett & Reitz,PC** -5010 Campuswood Dr -E Syracuse 13057 **Fx:**437-7744
(212) 577-0504 .. **Ferrara,** Geraldine '86 %Criminal Justice Agncy -52 Duane -NY 10007 **Fx:**577-0586
(212) 637-3233 .. **Ferrara,** Helen S '83 %EPA -290 Bway -NY 10007 **Fx:**637-3032
(845) 291-2050 .. **Ferrara,** Jamie T '07 %DA -255-275 Main -Goshen 10924 **Fx:**291-2085
(845) 794-1303 .. **Ferrara,** John '84 (Ferrara & S) -34 North Bx785 -Monticello 12701 **Fx:**794-1305
(212) 593-1766 .. **Ferrara,** Jos J '83 -375 Park Av -NY 10152 **Fx:**593-1872
(718) 939-3030 .. **Ferrara,** Jos J '87 -120-05 31st Av -Flushng 11354 **Fx:**539-1998
(518) 584-3900 .. **Ferrara,** Keith M '78 OfCnsl Ferrara & N,PLLC -358 Bway -Saratoga Spgs 12866
(518) 584-9007 .. **Ferrara,** Keith M '78 Bonacio Cnstrctn -18 Division -Saratoga Spgs 12866
(212) 619-5400 .. **Ferrara,** Lucas A '85 (Newman F LLP) -1250 Bway -NY 10001
(518) 457-4951 .. **Ferrara,** Lucia Anne '97 Dept Correctional Srvcs -1220 Wshngtn Av -Albany 12226 **Fx:**457-7555
(212) 245-7300 .. **Ferrara,** Nicholas '87 (Serling R&F,LLP) -119 5th Av -NY 10003
(518) 584-3900 .. **Ferrara & Nigro,PLLC** -358 Bway -Saratoga Spgs 12866 **Fx:**587-2926
(212) 210-3867 .. **Ferrara,** Paul A '04 %Alston & B LLP -90 Park Av -NY 10016
(315) 422-1152 .. **Ferrara,** Paul G '88 (Costello C&F,PLLC) -500 Plum -Syracuse 13204
(212) 765-5070 .. **Ferrara,** Richd P '76 OfCnsl Fish & R,PC -153 E 53rd -NY 10022
(718) 590-2000 .. **Ferrara,** Robt J '92 %DA -198 E 161st -Bronx 10451 **Fx:**590-6477
(516) 328-2300 .. **Ferrara,** Saml J '95 (Abrams FFEGF&E,LLP) -1111 Marcus Av -Lk Success 11042
(212) 233-2122 .. **Ferrara Turitz Harraka & Goldberg** -711 3rd Av -NY 10017 **Fx:**(201) 489-0880
(646) 722-8500 .. **Ferrarese,** Lydia '05 %Grant & E,PA -485 Lex Av -NY 10017
(607) 336-2554 .. **Ferrarese,** Michl D '00 -19 Eaton Av -Norwich 13815
(914) 779-2600 .. **Ferrari,** Anthony O '82 (Ball & F,PC) -2066 Cntrl Pk Av -Ynkrs 10710 **Fx:**779-2690
(607) 547-1865 .. **Ferrari,** James P '99 -Bx1047 -Cooperstwn 13326
(212) 535-5759 .. **Ferrari,** Jill E '91 -1365 York Av -NY 10021 **Fx:**535-5742
(631) 547-9646 .. **Ferrari,** Joan '84 (Ferrari & W,LLP) -290 Broadhllw Rd -Melvll 11747
(212) 687-2770 .. **Ferrari,** Lisa Ann '91 (Cohen PL&P) -551 5th Av -NY 10176
(718) 250-2000 .. **Ferrari,** Michl F '05 DA -350 Jay -Brklyn 11201 **Fx:**250-2314
(212) 878-7900 .. **Ferrari,** Patricia '76 (Fox R LLP) -100 Park Av -NY 10017
(212) 335-9000 .. **Ferrari,** Rachel A '03 %DA -1 Hogan Pl -NY 10013
(212) 335-9000 .. **Ferrari,** Robt D '99 %DA -1 Hogan Pl -NY 10013
(212) 972-7040 .. **Ferrari,** Robt V '61 -630 3rd Av -NY 10017 **Fx:**922-1939
(516) 627-9325 .. **Ferrari & Rosenthal** -100 Jericho Quad -Jericho 11753 **Fx:**931-8101
(631) 547-9646 .. **Ferrari & Wallace,LLP** -290 Broadhllw Rd -Melvll 11747 **Fx:**391-9655
(212) 693-1000 .. **Ferrario,** Remy J '74 %Golub & G,LLP -225 Bway -NY 10007 **Fx:**693-0090
(845) 638-5001 .. **Ferraro,** Arthur J '65 %DA -1 S Main -New Cty 10956 **Fx:**638-5070
(212) 797-9035 .. **Ferraro,** Frances P '86 -41 Mad Av -NY 10010
(914) 684-2088 .. **Ferraro,** Frank '01 -75 S Bway -White Plns 10601 **Fx:**(201) 767-4223
(212) 788-6783 .. **Ferraro,** Janine '86 Mayors Ofc-Crim Justice -1 Centre -NY 10007
(212) 728-8000 .. **Ferraro,** Johanna L '06 %Willkie F&G LLP -787 7th Av -NY 10019
(212) 446-2300 .. **Ferraro,** Jos A '03 %Boies S&F LLP -575 Lex Av -NY 10022
(212) 897-0229 .. **Ferraro,** Jos W III '98 Intl Sec Exchg -60 Broad -NY 10004 **Fx:**509-3955
(212) 813-5900 .. **Ferraro,** Joyce M '89 Cnsl Fross ZL&Z,PC -866 UN Plz -NY 10017
(212) 341-6486 .. **Ferraro,** Lori A '01 %Liquidation Bur -123 William -NY 10038 **Fx:**608-3398
(212) 310-8000 .. **Ferraro,** Marisa L '03 %Weil G&M LLP -767 5th Av -NY 10153
(845) 291-2050 .. **Ferraro,** Melissa Gilbon '00 %DA -255-275 Main -Goshen 10924 **Fx:**291-2085
(845) 534-8700 .. **Ferraro,** Michl A '01 M Ferraro,PC -318 Main -Cornwall 12518 **Fx:**534-3003
(631) 289-8100 .. **Ferraro,** Mitchell P '97 -629 Route 112 -Patchogue 11772 **Fx:**289-8116

(201) 437-7300 .. **Ferraro,** Susan '98 -154 E Bstn Post Rd -Mamaroneck 10543 **Fx:**437-8552
(716) 853-3087 .. **Ferraro-Zaffram,** Helen J '89 Leg Srvcs -237 Main -Buffalo 14203 **Fx:**856-5317
(607) 962-3194 .. **Ferratella,** Christopher J '06 %Yorio & R -145 W High -Painted Post 14870
(607) 739-7529 .. **Ferratella,** James P '05 -2854 Wstnghse Rd -Horseheads 14845 **Fx:**733-1640
(914) 766-2710 .. **Ferrauiola,** Scott E '92 IBM -294 Route 100 -Somers 10589
(212) 696-6000 .. **Ferré,** Hermann '00 (Curtis M-PC&M LLP) -101 Park Av -NY 10178
(212) 735-3000 .. **Ferree,** Thos A '03 %Skadden ASM&F LLP -4 Times Sq -NY 10036
(212) 709-8219 .. **Ferreira,** Danl '93 -110 Wall -NY 10005 **Fx:**943-2300
(646) 386-3196 .. **Ferreira,** Lissett Costa '05 Hon L Visitacion-Lewis -60 Centre -NY 10007
(718) 590-2533 .. **Ferreiro,** Cari E '86 %DA -198 E 161st -Bronx 10451 **Fx:**590-6477
(718) 590-2133 .. **Ferreiro,** Nestor A '82 %DA -198 E 161st -Bronx 10451 **Fx:**590-6477
(718) 921-0338 .. **Ferreiro,** Vivian E '95 -1261 74th -Brklyn 11228 **Fx:**921-2686
(212) 848-4000 .. **Ferrell,** Erin L '08 Shearman & S LLP -599 Lex Av -NY 10022
(212) 450-4000 .. **Ferrell,** Kathleen L '98 (Davis P&W LLP) -450 Lex Av -NY 10017
(718) 250-2000 .. **Ferrell,** Monique D '90 %DA -350 Jay -Brklyn 11201 **Fx:**250-2314
(212) 640-4036 .. **Ferrell,** Raymond R '93 %Amer Exp -200 Vesey -NY 10285 **Fx:**619-8755
(518) 402-6969 .. **Ferrentino,** Carl T '83 %Envrnmtl Facilities -625 Bway -Albany 12207 **Fx:**402-6972
(212) 991-6726 .. **Ferrer,** Alfred III '76 -61 Bway -NY 10006
(212) 218-5500 .. **Ferrer,** Esteban A III '76 (Seyfarth S LLP) -620 8th Av -NY 10018
(212) 205-7000 .. **Ferrer,** Eugene Y '93 Ashurst LLP -7 Times Sq -NY 10036
(212) 509-9400 .. **Ferrer,** Geoffrey D '82 (Cozen O) -45 Bway Atrium -NY 10006
(212) 835-9470 .. **Ferrer,** Gilbert C '80 -1 Lbrty Plz -NY 10006
(212) 455-2000 .. **Ferrer,** Nicholas E '08 %Simpson T&B LLP -425 Lex Av -NY 10017
(718) 429-1770 .. **Ferrera,** Bernard F '79 -104-14 Roosevelt Av -Corona 11368
(718) 999-2040 .. **Ferrera,** Elena '87 %Fire Dept Bureau Leg Afrs -9 Metrotech Ctr -Brklyn 11201
(212) 309-6000 .. **Ferreri,** Michelle N '09 %Morgan L&B LLP -101 Park Av -NY 10178
(212) 815-1510 .. **Ferreri,** Richd J '71 DC 37 AFSCME AFL-CIO -125 Barclay -NY 10007
(212) 513-7788 .. **Ferreri,** Robt J '08 %Ahmuty D&M -123 William -NY 10038
(631) 843-5500 .. **Ferrero,** Jennifer '98 Henry Schein,Inc -135 Duryea Rd -Melvll 11747
(585) 546-6448 .. **Ferrero,** Vincent M '03 (Davidson F LLP) -28 E Main -Rchstr 14614
(212) 793-7904 .. **Ferrette,** Chelsea P '02 Citigroup -425 Park Av -NY 10022
(212) 344-3900 .. **Ferrette,** Jos Francis '88 %Belair & E LLP -61 Bway -NY 10006
(212) 925-3456 .. **Ferretti,** Adeline B '84 %Sedlmayr & Assoc -200 Park Av S -NY 10003 **Fx:**925-0554
(718) 447-4442 .. **Ferretti,** Eugene V P '52 -358 St Marks Pl -Staten Isl 10301
(518) 792-4828 .. **Ferretti,** Joan M '84 (Lustberg & F) -5 Garrison Rd -Queensbury 12804 **Fx:**792-4896
(516) 228-4226 .. **Ferretti,** Joan M '84 OfCnsl R Danzi -900 Merchants Cncrs -Westbury 11590 **Fx:**228-6569
(516) 741-6355 .. **Ferretti,** John R '84 (Nicolini PF&S) -114 Old Cntry Rd Bx9006 -Mineola 11501
(718) 377-2300 .. **Ferretti,** John S '91 -5122 Av N -Brklyn 11234 **Fx:**377-0771
(212) 474-1000 .. **Ferretti,** Scott J '91 Cravath S&M LLP -825 8th Av -NY 10019
(516) 280-5620 .. **Ferri,** Jos P Jr. '89 J Ferri,PC -666 Old Cntry Rd -Gdn Cty 11530 **Fx:**280-5621
(212) 506-2500 .. **Ferri,** Lisa M '88 (Mayer B LLP) -1675 Bway -NY 10019
(212) 265-6888 .. **Ferri,** Robt '75 (Porzio B&N,PC) -156 W 56th -NY 10019
(607) 778-2423 .. **Ferri,** Stephen D '97 %DA -45 Hawley Bx1766 -Bnghmtn 13902 **Fx:**778-8870
(212) 821-5124 .. **Ferri,** Wm J '93 UBS -299 Park Av -NY 10171
(212) 262-1103 .. **Ferriabough,** Alicia D '04 %R Celestin -250 W 57th -NY 10107 **Fx:**262-1173
(716) 875-4981 .. **Ferrick,** Arlene A '79 -245 Crosby Av -Kenmore 14217
(718) 259-4500 .. **Ferrier,** Michl A '96 OfCnsl Vanchieri & F -1724 86th -Brklyn 11214
(718) 259-4500 .. **Ferrier,** Raymond L '67 (Vanchieri & F) -1724 86th -Brklyn 11214
(212) 480-4800 .. **Ferriere,** Patrick L '78 (Fox H&C LLP) -825 3rd Av -NY 10022
(516) 248-7000 .. **Ferriggi,** Richd H '84 (Albanese & A LLP) -1050 Franklin Av -Gdn Cty 11530
(845) 790-0945 .. **Ferrigno,** Jos A '01 JA Ferrigno,PC -25 Market -Poughkeepsie 12601 **Fx:**790-1223
(212) 269-0927 .. **Ferrigno,** Richd F '98 (D'Amato & L,LLP) -2 World Fncl Ctr -NY 10281
(845) 496-0732 .. **Ferrigno-Ohm,** Rebecca '02 -79 E Main Bx177 -Washingtnvll 10992 **Fx:**496-3801
(212) 310-8000 .. **Ferrillo,** Paul A '89 Cnsl Weil G&M LLP -767 5th Av -NY 10153
(718) 286-2000 .. **Ferrin,** Ana Maria '96 %Leg Aid -120-46 Qns Blvd -Kew Gdns 11415 **Fx:**286-2286
(212) 766-4300 .. **Ferrini,** Alexander F '95 (A Ferrini,PC) -200 Park Av S -NY 10003 **Fx:**(646) 390-8314
(518) 455-4265 .. **Ferrini,** NancyLynn '92 Ofc of Minority Consl -440 The Cptl -Albany 12248
(212) 259-8000 .. **Ferris,** Anya Jenkins '10 %Dewey & L LLP -1301 Av of Amer -NY 10019
(585) 232-6500 .. **Ferris,** David R '77 (Harter S&E LLP) -1600 Bausch & Lomb Pl -Rchstr 14604
(212) 651-1014 .. **Ferris,** Deborah J '71 Bessemer Trust Co -630 5th Av -NY 10111
(585) 586-6280 .. **Ferris,** Frank H III '65 -349 W Cmmrcial -E Rchstr 14445 **Fx:**586-2023
(315) 488-2659 .. **Ferris,** John E '60 -110 Brentwood Dr -Syracuse 13219
(315) 724-3464 .. **Ferris,** Richd P '81 -239 Genesee -Utica 13501
(212) 406-4755 .. **Ferris,** Spiro '81 -225 Bway -NY 10007 **Fx:**964-4360
(516) 512-6590 .. **Ferris,** Thos B '90 %Pieret & Assoc -400 Grdn City Plz -Gdn Cty 11530 **Fx:**742-4116
(585) 262-2667 .. **Ferris,** Thos F '97 (Connors & F,LLP) -3445 Winton Pl -Rchstr 14623
(631) 234-8585 .. **Ferris,** Wm T III '77 Cnsl Bracken & M,LLP -1 Suffolk Sq -Islandia 11749
(212) 836-8000 .. **Ferriso,** Amanda M '04 %Kaye S LLP -425 Park Av -NY 10022
(212) 480-5683 .. **Ferrity,** Edw J '98 Cnsl Insurance Dept -25 Beaver -NY 10004 **Fx:**480-6066
(315) 458-5040 .. **Ferro,** Andrea M '09 %Karp -428 S Main -N Syracuse 13212 **Fx:**458-4321
(212) 966-7775 .. **Ferro & Cuccia** -100 Lafayette -NY 10013 **Fx:**966-0338
(845) 795-5533 .. **Ferro,** Francis E '72 -80 Old Indn Rd -Milton 12547 **Fx:**795-5269
(516) 292-8100 .. **Ferro,** John J '04 %Nassau/Sfflk Law Srv -1 Helen Keller Way -Hempstd 11550 **Fx:**292-6529
(212) 244-7676 .. **Ferro Kuba Mangano Sklyar,PC** -424 W 33rd -NY 10001 **Fx:**244-9393
(631) 581-9494 .. **Ferro Kuba Mangano Sklyar,PC** -350 Motor Pkwy -Hauppauge 11788 **Fx:**581-9393
(914) 358-4934 .. **Ferro Labella & Zucker LLC** -1025 Wstchstr Av -White Plns 10604 **Fx:**358-4935
(516) 229-4200 .. **Ferro,** Michl A '03 %Mendolia & S -875 Merrick Av -Westbury 11590
(516) 832-3200 .. **Ferro,** Vincent J '84 %1st Amer Title -333 Earle Ovngton Blvd -Uniondale 11553 **Fx:**832-3299
(212) 244-7676 .. **Ferro,** Wm V '88 (Ferro KMS,PC) -424 W 33rd -NY 10001
(212) 586-4900 .. **Ferrone,** Diane '02 %Sercarz & R,LLP -152 W 57th -NY 10019
(212) 434-0100 .. **Ferrone,** Erin M '04 %Litchfield C LLP -420 Lex Av -NY 10170
(518) 372-1500 .. **Ferrucci,** Albie S '51 (Ferrucci & C) -835 Union -Schnctdy 12308
(516) 294-5200 .. **Ferrucci,** Andrea E '05 %Picciano & S -900 Merchants Cncrs -Westbury 11590
(518) 372-1500 .. **Ferrucci,** Brian Corrigan '86 (Ferrucci & C) -835 Union -Schnctdy 12308
(518) 372-1500 .. **Ferrucci & Corrigan** -835 Union -Schnctdy 12308
(518) 372-1500 .. **Ferrucci,** Sheila Corrigan '91 %Ferrucci & C -835 Union -Schnctdy 12308
(212) 609-6800 .. **Ferruggia,** Frank E '89 (McCarter & E,LLP) -245 Park Av -NY 10167
(631) 232-0030 .. **Ferruggia,** Michl A '94 (Ferruggia & C,LLP) -150 Motor Pkwy -Hauppauge 11788 **Fx:**232-2330
(212) 788-9188 .. **Ferrugia,** Thos S '00 City Cncl -250 Bway -NY 10007
(516) 742-7777 .. **Ferrugiari,** Laura Ann '95 (Frazer & F,LLP) -1415 Kellum Pl -Gdn Cty 11530
(718) 488-5710 .. **Ferruzzi,** Kenneth A '82 DMV Traffic Violations Bur -696 E Fordham Rd -Bronx 10458
(212) 791-7610 .. **Ferry,** Arnold B '89 -30 Vesey -NY 10007
(212) 422-2660 .. **Fersch,** Patricia Ann '94 (Family Law Ctr) -11 Bway -NY 10004 **Fx:**422-2666
(718) 333-2394 .. **Fershteyn,** Inna '99 (I Fershteyn & Assoc,PC) -8622 Bay Pkwy -Brklyn 11214
(718) 256-6794 .. **Fersko,** Marie A '97 -72 Bay 7th -Brklyn 11228
(212) 661-8770 .. **Fersko,** Raymond S '73 Ferskos LLC -221 E 31st -NY 10016 **Fx:**661-9251
(212) 683-8055 .. **Ferst,** Nathan M '80 -350 5th Av -NY 10118 **Fx:**683-8354
(212) 213-1233 .. **Ferstendig,** David L '82 -292 Mad Av -NY 10017 **Fx:**213-1221
(212) 213-1233 .. **Ferstendig,** Michl L '99 %D Ferstendig,LLC -292 Mad Av -NY 10017 **Fx:**213-1221
(212) 331-5044 .. **Ferster,** Alan '83 %HRA-Legal -180 Water -NY 10038
(914) 235-9258 .. **Ferster,** Bernard A '62 -125 Ramona Ct -New Rchll 10804 **Fx:**235-9258
(212) 973-0572 .. **Ferszt,** Stephen L '86 (Wolff & S PC) -140 Bway -NY 10005
(212) 455-2000 .. **Fert,** Igor '01 %Simpson T&B LLP -425 Lex Av -NY 10017
(914) 740-4346 .. **Fertel,** Barry R '78 -270 North Av -New Rchll 10801 **Fx:**632-7706
(718) 835-1100 .. **Fertig,** Adam J '92 (Fertig & F) -108-14 Crossbay Blvd -Ozone Pk 11417 **Fx:**323-0270
(718) 835-1100 .. **Fertig,** Bret A '90 (Fertig & F) -108-14 Crossbay Blvd -Ozone Pk 11417 **Fx:**323-0270
(212) 310-8000 .. **Fertig,** David R '98 (Weil G&M LLP) -767 5th Av -NY 10153
(212) 783-4033 .. **Fertig,** Harper D '05 Smith Barney -485 Lex Av -NY 10017
(212) 788-6875 .. **Fertig,** Harvey N '67 %City Cncl Spkrs Ofc -City Hall -NY 10007 **Fx:**788-7207
(607) 656-4101 .. **Fertig,** James H '77 -14 N Chenango Bx189 -Greene 13778 **Fx:**656-4004
(212) 526-2411 .. **Fertig,** Jason S '97 %Barclays Capital Inc -745 7th Av -NY 10019
(516) 227-6300 .. **Fertig,** Suzanne Brooks '96 %Ettelman & H,PC -100 Q Roosevelt Blvd -Gdn Cty 11530
(212) 728-8000 .. **Fertman,** Jared N '07 %Willkie F&G LLP -787 7th Av -NY 10019
(716) 847-6500 .. **Ferullo,** Michl K '05 %Steiner & B -300 Delaware Av -Buffalo 14202
(646) 328-0850 .. **Ferziger,** Meira Schulman '97 %Outside Cnsl Solutns LLP -1430 Bway -NY 10018 **Fx:**360-5000
(212) 490-8585 .. **Ferziger,** Rubin '75 -708 3rd Av -NY 10017 **Fx:**697-5207
(516) 333-2006 .. **Ferzola,** Chas '86 -1400 Old Cntry Rd -Westbury 11590
(518) 474-3219 .. **Fesel,** Donna A '00 %NYSHESC -99 Wshngtn Av -Albany 12255 **Fx:**486-6515
(212) 735-3000 .. **Fesenmyer,** Timothy M '00 Cnsl Skadden ASM&F LLP -4 Times Sq -NY 10036
(212) 977-4660 .. **Feser,** Matthew P '03 Salisbury & R LLP -1325 Av of Amer -NY 10019
(914) 738-7411 .. **Fesjian,** Robt A '80 -101 Secor Ln Bx8369 -Pelham 10803 **Fx:**738-7521
(212) 504-6000 .. **Fesnak,** Heather L '05 %Cadwalader W&T LLP -1 World Fncl Ctr -NY 10281
(631) 344-8629 .. **Fess,** Gregory H '00 Brookhaven Natl Lab -40 Brookhvn Av Bx500 -Upton 11973
(716) 204-3570 .. **Fessard,** Louis C '79 Acquest Holdings Inc -80 Curtwright Dr -Buffalo 14221
(212) 666-4600 .. **Fessel,** Mark N '82 %James Development -780 W End Av -NY 10025
(212) 430-5968 .. **Fessel,** Moshe '02 -80 Maiden Ln -NY 10038
(212) 558-4000 .. **Fessel,** Robin D '90 (Sullivan & C LLP) -125 Broad -NY 10004
(716) 484-7196 .. **Fessenden Laumer & DeAngelo** -81 Forest Av Bx590 -Jamestwn 14702 **Fx:**488-9146
(716) 484-7196 .. **Fessenden,** Richd H '74 (Fessenden L&D) -81 Forest Av Bx590 -Jamestwn 14702
(212) 930-9700 .. **Fessler,** Jeffrey J '92 (Sichenzia RFF LLP) -61 Bway -NY 10006
(212) 775-9002 .. **Fessler,** Walter J '81 (Lum D&P,LLC) -325 Bway -NY 10007
(212) 788-5017 .. **Festa,** Michele '92 Dept Hlth -125 Worth CN-30 -NY 10013 **Fx:**788-4300
(212) 218-3916 .. **Festekjian,** Taline '07 Lyon Ross Cptl Mgmt LLC -150 E 52nd -NY 10022
(315) 735-7900 .. **Festine,** Armond J '81 -258 Genesee -Utica 13502 **Fx:**735-9002
(212) 297-5800 .. **Fetner,** Howard '99 Cnsl Day P LLP -7 Times Sq -NY 10036

(212) 788-8343 .. **Fett**, Baree Nichole '99 %Law Dept -100 Church -NY 10007 **Fx**:788-0367
(212) 310-8000 .. **Fett**, Rebecca E '08 %Weil G&M LLP -767 5th Av -NY 10153
(585) 546-5530 .. **Fetter**, Carol L '94 %Thomson West -50 E Broad -Rchstr 14694
(315) 471-8111 .. **Fetter**, Jeffrey M '84 (Scolaro SCF&B,PC) -507 Plum -Syracuse 13204
(212) 836-8000 .. **Fetter**, Joanna R '09 %Kaye S LLP -425 Park Av -NY 10022
(212) 506-1700 .. **Fetterman**, Danl J '89 (Kasowitz BT&F LLP) -1633 Bway -NY 10019
(212) 558-4000 .. **Fettman**, Robt M '06 %Sullivan & C LLP -125 Broad -NY 10004
(212) 648-0044 .. **Fetzer**, Gary S '86 %JP Morgan Chase -245 Park Av -NY 10167
(718) 263-9874 .. **Feuer**, Albert '79 -110-45 71st Rd -Frst Hlls 11375
(212) 633-3245 .. **Feuer**, Bradley A '95 %Barnes & Noble -122 5th Av -NY 10011
(914) 323-7000 .. **Feuer**, Chas M '70 (Wilson EME&D LLP) -3 Gannett Dr -White Plns 10604
(212) 225-2000 .. **Feuer**, Elana S '09 %Cleary GS&H -1 Lbrty Plz -NY 10006
(718) 330-2148 .. **Feuer**, Elias '78 %NLRB -2 Metrotech Ctr -Brklyn 11201 **Fx**:330-7579
(917) 339-1768 .. **Feuer**, Joshua D '01 NYC Educ Dept -333 7th Av -NY 10001
(631) 447-1600 .. **Feuer**, Lloyd A '52 Cnsl Feuer & F -124 Medford Av -Patchogue 11772 **Fx**:447-2609
(516) 489-2322 .. **Feuer**, Marcia Z '91 %Mental Hlth Assn -16 Main -Hempstd 11550 **Fx**:489-2784
(212) 715-9100 .. **Feuer**, Michl I '06 Kramer LN&F,LLP -1177 Av of Amer -NY 10036
(631) 447-1600 .. **Feuer**, Paul R '82 (Feuer & F) -124 Medford Av -Patchogue 11772 **Fx**:447-2609
(631) 761-0800 .. **Feuer**, Scott L '94 (Lazer AR&Y,PC) -225 Old Cntry Rd -Melvll 11747
(607) 432-0108 .. **Feuer**, Steven Z '85 -23 Ford Av -Oneonta 13820 **Fx**:432-0965
(212) 896-9150 .. **Feuer**, Yitzchok I '02 Greystone Mutli-Unit Finance -152 W 57th -NY 10019
(716) 856-9704 .. **Feuerstein**, Alan R '78 (Feuerstein & S,LLP) -17 St Louis Pl -Buffalo 14202 **Fx**:856-9707
(516) 579-3700 .. **Feuerstein**, Albert I '62 -775 Wantagh Av -Wantagh 11793 **Fx**:579-3877
(212) 592-1400 .. **Feuerstein**, David T '02 %Herrick,F LLP -2 Park Av -NY 10016
(212) 351-4000 .. **Feuerstein**, Eric M '97 (Gibson D&C LLP) -200 Park Av -NY 10166
(212) 592-1400 .. **Feuerstein**, Harvey S '63 (Herrick,F LLP) -2 Park Av -NY 10016
(212) 679-1222 .. **Feuerstein**, Henry I '78 Cohen & Co Inc -9 E 40th -NY 10016 **Fx**:679-1533
(212) 661-2900 .. **Feuerstein**, Jerold C '94 (Kriss & F LLP) -360 Lex Av -NY 10017
(716) 551-4931 .. **Feuerstein**, Jesse S '07 NLRB -130 S Elmwood Av -Buffalo 14202 **Fx**:551-4972
(212) 461-5507 .. **Feuerstein**, Randy L '91 CIT Grp Inc -11 W 42nd -NY 10036
(212) 417-2103 .. **Feuerstein**, Robt A '75 %Racing & Wagering Bd -86 Chmbrs -NY 10007 **Fx**:417-2160
(914) 681-7175 .. **Feureisen**, David '86 (Bartels & F LLP) -925 Wstchstr Av -White Plns 10604
(212) 779-9910 .. **Fewell**, Chas K Jr. '68 (Eaton & V LLP) -3 Park Av -NY 10016
(718) 739-6400 .. **Fewer**, Gregory C '85 %DHCR -92-31 Union Hall -Jamaica 11433 **Fx**:262-7938
(516) 571-3800 .. **Fexas**, Kristen M '97 %DA -262 Old Cntry Rd -Mineola 11501 **Fx**:248-9479
(212) 596-9000 .. **Fey**, Albert E '59 OfCnsl Ropes & G LLP -1211 Av of Amer -NY 10036
(631) 351-9090 .. **Feyler**, Heidi '97 -1160 E Jericho Tpke -Huntngtn 11743
(914) 381-7400 .. **Feynman**, Erica R '03 %Rattet P&G,LLP -550 Mamaroneck Av -Harrison 10528
(518) 689-1485 .. **Feyrer**, Emily P '05 %Greenberg T,LLP -54 State -Albany 12207
(212) 888-8922 .. **Fiabane**, Louis C '86 -947 2nd Av -NY 10022
(212) 732-4992 .. **Fiala**, Robt M '91 %Arye L&S,PC -20 Vesey -NY 10007
(914) 422-4069 .. **Fialk**, Rebecca J '98 Pace Womens Justice Ctr -78 N Bway -White Plns 10603
(212) 554-7800 .. **Fialkoff**, Jay R '77 (Moses & S LLP) -405 Lex Av -NY 10174
(212) 906-1200 .. **Fialkovskiy**, Eugene J '07 %Latham & W -885 3rd Av -NY 10022
(585) 244-8910 .. **Fiandach**, Edw L '79 (Fiandach & F) -100 Allens Crk Rd -Rchstr 14618 **Fx**:244-4863
(347) 621-2221 .. **Fiano**, Astrid R '05 -Bx323 -Bronx 10461
(631) 237-4917 .. **Ficara**, Anthony J '03 (Ficara & Assoc,PC) -510 Broadhllw Rd -Melvll 11747 **Fx**:237-4776
(212) 687-3000 .. **Ficarra**, Debra '05 %Jaffe & A,LLP -600 3rd Av -NY 10016
(845) 620-1012 .. **Ficarra**, John S '88 -37 Mtnvw Av -Pearl Rvr 10965
(212) 644-4420 .. **Ficarra**, Michele V '98 %Fabiani C&H,LLP -570 Lex Av -NY 10022
(718) 788-4100 .. **Ficchi**, Michl J '80 -706 5th Av -Brklyn 11215
(718) 797-5700 .. **Ficchi**, Michl J Jr. '07 %Wenig S LLP -26 Court -Brklyn 11242
(212) 461-2323 .. **Fichera**, Christina L '99 %Saiber LLC -44 Wall -NY 10005
(845) 452-7400 .. **Fichera**, Cynthia K '86 (Spiegel BF&C,LLP) -272 Mill -Poughkeepsie 12601
(845) 473-7568 .. **Fichera**, Linda R '97 -96 Mahoney Rd -Milton 12547
(212) 480-3030 .. **Fichtelberg**, Tod S '88 %M Pressman -125 Maiden Ln -NY 10038 **Fx**:480-2590
(516) 623-5253 .. **Fichtenbaum**, Mark A '79 -1916 Leonard Ln -Merrick 11566
(516) 357-3000 .. **Fichtl**, Christhoper J '89 %Rivkin R LLP -926 RXR Plz -Uniondale 11556
(585) 383-3216 .. **Fici**, Amy Levine '98 Paychex Inc -911 Panorama Trl S -Rchstr 14625 **Fx**:383-3441
(716) 565-1100 .. **Fickess**, Edw D '89 Andreozzi F LLP -9145 Main -Clarence 14031
(914) 995-2676 .. **Fico**, John A '87 %Cnty Atty -148 Martine Av -White Plns 10601 **Fx**:995-5858
(718) 286-6000 .. **Fidel**, Gary S '80 %DA -125-01 Qns Blvd -Kew Gdns 11415
(212) 587-9006 .. **Fidel**, Stanley J '83 -42 Bway -NY 10004
(914) 934-1725 .. **Fidelibus**, Agnes H '94 -3 Rye Ridge Plz -Rye Brook 10573 **Fx**:934-1725
(914) 428-3313 .. **Fiden**, Joan L '85 (Curan AF&N,LLP) -14 Mamaroneck Av -White Plns 10601 **Fx**:949-5800
(718) 875-0605 .. **Fidler**, Lewis A '79 (Roberts & F,PC) -26 Court -Brklyn 11242 **Fx**:875-0608
(212) 530-5000 .. **Fidler**, Nicole L '09 %Milbank TH&M LLP -1 Chase Manh Plz -NY 10005
(212) 455-2000 .. **Fiebig**, Chantale '07 %Simpson T&B LLP -425 Lex Av -NY 10017
(212) 237-1000 .. **Fiechter**, Elizabeth '06 %Windels ML&M,LLP -156 W 56th -NY 10019
(516) 571-1090 .. **Fiechter**, Rene P '75 %DA -262 Old Cntry Rd -Mineola 11501 **Fx**:571-1633
(212) 833-7464 .. **Fiedel**, Barry J '87 Sony BMG Music Entrtnmnt -550 Mad Av -NY 10022 **Fx**:833-4421
(516) 822-8900 .. **Fiedelman & McGaw** -2 Jericho Plz -Jericho 11753 **Fx**:822-8919
(516) 822-8900 .. **Fiedelman**, Robt I '75 (Fiedelman & M) -2 Jericho Plz -Jericho 11753
(212) 753-5000 .. **Fiedler**, Alyson M '01 Cnsl Schiff H LLP -900 3rd Av -NY 10022
(914) 993-0393 .. **Fiedler**, Duane M '79 -81 Main -White Plns 10601 **Fx**:993-0394
(212) 312-9608 .. **Fiedler**, James S '79 %State Ins Fund -199 Church -NY 10007 **Fx**:385-9199
(212) 580-1363 .. **Fiedler**, Norman D '50 -2373 Bway -NY 10024
(212) 225-2000 .. **Fiege**, Carsten J '04 %Cleary GS&H -1 Lbrty Plz -NY 10006
(716) 847-7696 .. **Fiegl-Bock**, Kay E '01 OTDA-Ofc of Admin Hearings -295 Main Bx #574 -Buffalo 14203
(845) 634-8500 .. **Fiel**, Martin E '72 -369 S Main -New Cty 10956 **Fx**:634-8930
(212) 735-8600 .. **Fiel**, Wendy M '03 %Morrison C LLP -909 3rd Av -NY 10022
(716) 837-8858 .. **Field**, A Scott '78 -71 E Northrup Pl -Buffalo 14214
(646) 386-3235 .. **Field**, Andrea S '87 %Hon J Goodman -60 Centre -NY 10007 **Fx**:(212) 374-0664
(212) 688-5801 .. **Field**, Arthur Norman '59 Field Consulting Srvcs LLC -35 Sutton Pl -NY 10022
(212) 370-2100 .. **Field**, David A '58 (Field L,PC) -122 E 42nd -NY 10168
(315) 422-0420 .. **Field**, Deborah K '80 (Field & C) -4933 Jamesvll Rd -Jamesvll 13078
(516) 482-4480 .. **Field**, Ernest R '55 -5A Foxwood Rd -Gt Neck 11024 **Fx**:482-4439
(631) 351-8787 .. **Field**, Gary P '80 -425 NY Av -Huntngtn 11743 **Fx**:351-1080
(914) 997-7400 .. **Field**, Joel '56 -50 Main -White Plns 10606 **Fx**:997-9642
(585) 263-6760 .. **Field**, John J III '96 %US Atty -620 Fed Bldg -Rchstr 14614 **Fx**:263-6226
(212) 848-9800 .. **Field**, Jos A '04 (Withers B LLP) -430 Park Av -NY 10022
(212) 583-9600 .. **Field**, Jos E '89 Cnsl Littler M,PC -900 3rd Av -NY 10022
(212) 370-2100 .. **Field Lomenzo,PC** -122 E 42nd -NY 10168 **Fx**:370-4812
(516) 627-8444 .. **Field**, Marcia K '76 (Field & F) -36 Maple Pl -Manhsst 11030
(212) 689-1113 .. **Field**, Pamela D '02 %Garbarini & S,PC -432 Park Av S -NY 10016
(212) 370-2100 .. **Field**, Robt S '63 OfCnsl Field L,PC -122 E 42nd -NY 10168
(718) 741-8415 .. **Field**, Sharon J '91 %Div of Human Rights -1 Fordham Plz -Bronx 10458 **Fx**:741-8102
(212) 332-6050 .. **Field**, Stephen R '64 -620 5th Av -NY 10020
(212) 806-5400 .. **Field**, Thos '53 OfCnsl Stroock &S&L LLP -180 Maiden Ln -NY 10038
(212) 677-8222 .. **Fielden**, Leslie C '84 -28 E 10th -NY 10003
(631) 361-9494 .. **Fielder**, Karen A '03 %A Vardaro,PC -732 Smithtwn Bypass -Smithtwn 11787 **Fx**:361-8752
(718) 286-2450 .. **Fielding**, Craig E '94 %Leg Aid -120-46 Qns Blvd -Kew Gdns 11415 **Fx**:263-4234
(212) 373-3000 .. **Fielding**, Elizabeth T '05 %Paul WRW&G LLP -1285 Av of Amer -NY 10019
(516) 728-7451 .. **Fielding**, Jonathan P '05 -129 3rd -Mineola 11501 **Fx**:(917) 522-9592
(212) 421-7100 .. **Fielding**, Lewette '81 -41 E 57th -NY 10022 **Fx**:593-8833
(716) 856-5500 .. **Fielding**, Pamela J '87 SpclCnsl Damon M LLP -200 Delaware Av -Buffalo 14202
(516) 872-7400 .. **Fielding**, Wm J '96 %Minerva & D -107 S Central Av -Vly Stream 11580
(347) 404-9612 .. **Fieldman**, Eric S '94 %Criminal Ct -120 Schermerhorn -Brklyn 11201 **Fx**:(718) 643-3538
(212) 828-1545 .. **Fieldman**, Gale Z '77 -315 E 86th -NY 10028 **Fx**:828-1535
(718) 630-2900 .. **Fields**, Aaron J '75 %VA -800 Poly Pl -Brklyn 11209 **Fx**:630-2917
(212) 420-9160 .. **Fields**, Adrienne R '05 Artists Rights Society -536 Bway -NY 10012
(631) 853-4102 .. **Fields**, Aletha Victoria '89 %Family Ct -400 Carleton Av Bx9077 -Central Islip 11722
(212) 335-9000 .. **Fields**, Brian J '98 %DA -1 Hogan Pl -NY 10013
(212) 468-8193 .. **Fields**, Craig B '90 (Morrison & F LLP) -1290 Av of Amer -NY 10104
(212) 417-8700 .. **Fields**, Darrell '82 %Fed Def of NY Inc -52 Duane -NY 10007 **Fx**:571-0392
(718) 246-7103 .. **Fields**, Darren S '00 -26 Court -Brklyn 11242
(718) 340-4200 .. **Fields**, Dave '80 %CUNY Law Schl -65-21 Main -Flushng 11367 **Fx**:340-4482
(212) 249-4700 .. **Fields**, David H '94 -888 Park Av -NY 10075 **Fx**:249-5688
(212) 902-1000 .. **Fields**, Eileen M '88 %Goldman Sachs -1 NY Plz -NY 10004
(212) 905-9217 .. **Fields**, Eric B '99 Waterfront Comm -39 Bway -NY 10006 **Fx**:480-0587
(212) 509-3456 .. **Fields**, Eric J '96 %McGivney & K,PC -80 Broad -NY 10004
(585) 255-1432 .. **Fields**, Francis J III '86 %Global Crossing -225 Kenneth Dr -Rchstr 14623 **Fx**:(877) 769-9844
(212) 593-4900 .. **Fields**, Gary I '85 -425 Mad Av -NY 10017
(212) 318-6000 .. **Fields**, Gerald J '66 (Paul HJ&W LLP) -75 E 55th -NY 10022
(212) 371-0033 .. **Fields**, Harmon L '03 %Levy D&M,LLP -29 Bway -NY 10006
(718) 939-9400 .. **Fields**, Helene '92 (Fields & A,LLP) -167-20 Nrthrn Blvd -Flushng 11358
(845) 291-2650 .. **Fields**, Howard A '91 %Cnty Atty -285 Main -Goshen 10924 **Fx**:291-3014
(914) 478-5129 .. **Fields**, Ian M '99 (Quinlan & F) -245 Saw Mill Rvr Rd -Hawthorne 10532 **Fx**:478-0817
(516) 328-5122 .. **Fields**, Jeffrey D '78 Canon USA -1 Canon Plz -Lk Success 11042
(212) 254-8652 .. **Fields**, John C '81 -647 E 14th -NY 10009
(212) 460-3990 .. **Fields**, Jonathan A '81 Con Ed -4 Irving Pl -NY 10003
(212) 639-1617 .. **Fields**, Jonathan S '93 %Adventure Fitness Tours -1202 Lex Av -NY 10028
(212) 277-6500 .. **Fields**, Jos F '87 Cnsl Dickstein S LLP -1633 Bway -NY 10019
(212) 705-7000 .. **Fields**, Kimiko T '90 Bingham M LLP -399 Park Av -NY 10022
(718) 286-2000 .. **Fields**, Leanne M '00 %Leg Aid -120-46 Qns Blvd -Kew Gdns 11415 **Fx**:286-2286
(917) 320-2500 .. **Fields**, Lorraine S '85 %FDIC -350 5th Av -NY 10118 **Fx**:320-2917
(212) 277-5845 .. **Fields**, Marjory D '71 SpclCnsl Beldock L&H LLP -99 Park Av -NY 10016
(518) 447-9664 .. **Fields**, Michl J '87 %MHLS -75 New Scotland Av -Albany 12208 **Fx**:447-9697
(914) 288-0022 .. **Fields**, Paul '62 OfCnsl Leason E LLP -81 Main -White Plns 10601

(212) 448-1800 .. **Fields,** Peter A '91 (Roberts RLSC&F LLP) -235 Park Av S -NY 10003
(917) 388-3055 .. **Fields,** Richd W '05 (Fields SS PLLC) -65 E 55th -NY 10022 **Fx:**388-3094
(585) 381-3142 .. **Fields,** Roger A '64 -8 Rustic Pines -Pittsfrd 14534
(631) 661-0672 .. **Fields,** Seth I '02 (Fields & L LLP) -112 Route 109 -W Babylon 11704 **Fx:**661-0676
(212) 248-2220 .. **Fields,** Shannon J '07 %Kennedy JG LLC -99 Wall -NY 10005 **Fx:**248-0170
(212) 609-6803 .. **Fields,** Stephen M '66 (McCarter & E,LLP) -245 Park Av -NY 10167
(212) 692-5554 .. **Fields,** Steven W '07 %Duval & S LLP -101 Park Av -NY 10178
(718) 838-7878 .. **Fields,** Walter Levi '06 %Bronx Defenders -860 Crtlandt Av -Bronx 10451 **Fx:**665-0100
(646) 315-7336 .. **Fieldstein,** Jill G '99 FINRA -14 Wall -NY 10005
(212) 450-4000 .. **Fieldston,** Brett D '10 %Davis P&W LLP -450 Lex Av -NY 10017
(212) 403-1000 .. **Fieldston,** Ross A '06 %Wachtell LR&K -51 W 52nd -NY 10019
(212) 298-5209 .. **Fiellman,** Jennifer M '98 Leg Aid -49 Thomas -NY 10013
(914) 272-4000 .. **Fier,** David J '81 Gerber Life Ins Co -1311 Mamaroneck Av -White Plns 10605
(212) 349-6000 .. **Fier,** Jonathan A '97 %R Flaster,PC -225 Bway -NY 10007 **Fx:**349-1146
(631) 585-4343 .. **Fier,** Michl H '85 Fier Law Ofc,PC -160-2 Remngtn Blvd -Ronkonkoma 11779 **Fx:**585-0004
(347) 296-1740 .. **Fier,** Noreen Soto '95 Supreme Ct Law Dept -360 Adams -Brklyn 11201 **Fx:**643-6114
(212) 969-3231 .. **Fier,** Seth D '07 %Proskauer R LLP -1585 Bway -NY 10036
(718) 557-6576 .. **Fier,** Seymour '54 OHA-SSA -Bx319300 -Jamaica 11431
(212) 736-4500 .. **Fierman,** Robt '80 OfCnsl Nesenoff & M,LLP -363 7th Av -NY 10001
(516) 561-2090 .. **Fiero,** Anthony W '41 -15 Sylvan Pl -Vly Stream 11581
(347) 226-5666 .. **Fierro,** Anthony '94 -260 W 21st -NY 10011
(516) 448-1854 .. **Fierro,** Christopher P '94 Weisbach Greenfield Felderman Katz Fierro,LLP -55 Nrthrn Blvd -Gt Neck 11021 **Fx:**708-1924
(212) 839-5300 .. **Fierro,** Edw A '07 %Sidley A LLP -787 7th Av -NY 10019
(607) 737-5450 .. **Fierro,** Scott N '02 %Chemung Cnty DSS -425 Penn Av Bx588 -Elmira 14902
(212) 223-4000 .. **Fierst,** Timothy J '91 Cnsl Crowell & M LLP -590 Mad Av -NY 10022
(212) 241-4400 .. **Fierstein,** Ronald K '79 RF Entertainment Inc -29 Haines Rd -Bedfrd Hlls 10507
(315) 823-2350 .. **Fiesinger,** G Gerald Jr. '72 -572 E Main Bx218 -Little Fls 13365
(212) 916-2862 .. **Fiestal,** David H '01 UBS Intl -101 Park Av -NY 10178
(718) 390-5396 .. **Fietkau,** Carol Dimino '68 %Cnty Clerk -18 Richmond Ter -Staten Isl 10301
(212) 772-3570 .. **Fieve,** Vanessa A '98 Fieve Clinical Srvcs -952 5th Av -NY 10075
(212) 310-8318 .. **Fife,** Lori '84 (Weil G&M LLP) -767 5th Av -NY 10153
(631) 727-2180 .. **Fife,** Patrick B '04 %Twomey LSKD&Q,LLP -33 W 2nd Bx9398 -Rvrhead 11901
(212) 594-9190 .. **Fifer,** Howard '83 (Sonkin & F) -1350 Bway -NY 10018
(718) 254-6788 .. **Fig,** Geoffrey '99 US Atty -271 Cadman Plz E -Brklyn 11201 **Fx:**254-6479
(631) 419-6111 .. **Fig,** Heather A '99 -982 Montauk Hwy -Bayport 11705 **Fx:**363-6569
(212) 632-5500 .. **Figdor,** Peter '70 (Salans LLP) -620 5th Av -NY 10020
(585) 203-3400 .. **Figer,** Jeannie Yim '06 SpclCnsl Littler M,PC -400 Linden Oaks -Rchstr 14625
(718) 834-0190 .. **Figeroux,** Brian '95 -26 Court -Brklyn 11242 **Fx:**222-3153
(718) 797-7425 .. **Figeroux,** Davina J '04 Hon S Townes -225 Cadman Plz E -Brklyn 11201
(212) 859-3487 .. **Figgins,** Montell '04 -110 Wall -NY 10005 **Fx:**943-2300
(518) 474-8211 .. **FiggsGanter,** Amanda I '06 Law Reporting Bur -1 Commerce Plz -Albany 12210 **Fx:**463-6869
(518) 434-1022 .. **FiggsGanter,** Michl P '06 %Sullivan KO&V, LLP -152 Central Av -Albany 12206
(212) 709-8836 .. **Fightmaster,** Sarah E '08 Lovell Safety Mgmt Co,LLC -110 William -NY 10038
(212) 349-6009 .. **Figlewski,** Brett M '02 %Sanctuary for Families -110 Wall -NY 10005 **Fx:**566-0344
(212) 587-5765 .. **Figliolo,** Jos V Jr. '76 -80 Gold -NY 10038 **Fx:**587-5765
(212) 248-7800 .. **Figman,** Alan H '83 (Figman & E,LLP) -11 Bway -NY 10004
(212) 248-7800 .. **Figman & Epstein,LLP** -11 Bway -NY 10004 **Fx:**248-2960
(212) 799-2833 .. **Figman,** Lynne M '85 -40 W 72nd -NY 10023
(212) 969-3000 .. **Figueira,** Elizabeth A '07 %Proskauer R LLP -1585 Bway -NY 10036
(718) 424-2839 .. **Figueredo,** Maximo A '75 -37-31 76th -Jcksn Hts 11372 **Fx:**335-4198
(212) 805-6325 .. **Figueredo,** Valerie '07 Hon C McMahon -500 Pearl -NY 10007
(212) 509-3456 .. **Figueroa,** Carl '96 %McGivney & K,PC -80 Broad -NY 10004
(718) 722-3100 .. **Figueroa,** Edna E '90 %Leg Aid -111 Lvngstn -Brklyn 11201 **Fx:**722-3093
(212) 431-1300 .. **Figueroa,** Lester J '84 (Borah GAN&G PC) -377 Bway -NY 10013
(212) 869-7000 .. **Figueroa,** Melanie '09 %Feldman W&S LLP -420 Lex Av -NY 10170
(212) 416-8421 .. **Figueroa,** Nevillia A '82 %Dept of Law -120 Bway -NY 10271
(516) 466-3100 .. **Figueroa,** Richd M '96 %Gould Investors -60 Cuttermill Rd -Gt Neck 11021 **Fx:**466-3132
(212) 723-3884 .. **Figueroa,** Roberto L '03 Citigroup Global Mrkts -250 West -NY 10013
(718) 447-2800 .. **Figueroa,** Saml '03 -1578 Forest Av -Staten Isl 10302
(914) 345-8537 .. **Figueroa-Morgade,** Maria I '95 -19 Orchrd Ln -Elmsfrd 10523
(212) 973-8000 .. **Fihma,** Allison N '05 %Schnader HS&L LLP -140 Bway -NY 10005
(716) 849-8900 .. **Fijal,** Katherine Ann '89 (Hurwitz & F,PC) -1300 Lbrty Bldg -Buffalo 14202
(212) 720-5909 .. **Filabi,** Azish E '06 %Fed Reserve Bk -33 Lbrty -NY 10045 **Fx:**785-5748
(212) 809-7800 .. **Filacouris,** Nick '96 OfCnsl Jaffe & K,LLP -40 Wall -NY 10005
(718) 723-5954 .. **Filandro,** Dolores V '95 %DOJ INS -1 Cross Isl Plz -Rosedale 11422 **Fx:**723-1121
(914) 725-9600 .. **Filannino,** Nicole Apuzzo '93 (Filannino & T,LLP) -188 Summerfld -Scarsdale 10583 **Fx:**725-9604
(212) 735-3000 .. **Filardi,** Edw V '68 (Skadden ASM&F LLP) -4 Times Sq -NY 10036
(516) 365-6066 .. **Filardi,** Jos J '62 J Filardi,PC -565 Plandome Rd #334 -Manhsst 11030 **Fx:**365-1766
(212) 687-3860 .. **Filardo,** Thos '03 Snow BK,PC -605 3rd Av -NY 10158
(212) 612-3270 .. **Filardo,** Vincent Jr. '99 %Mishcon de R NY LLP -200 Park Av -NY 10166
(914) 683-2500 .. **Filasto,** Rachel J '01 %Harold SS&S -81 Main -White Plns 10601
(212) 225-2000 .. **Filauro,** Denise '09 %Cleary GS&H -1 Lbrty Plz -NY 10006
(716) 853-9555 .. **Filbert,** Shannon E '08 Leg Aid -237 Main -Buffalo 14203 **Fx:**853-3219
(212) 373-3000 .. **Filburn,** Christopher L '10 %Paul WRW&G LLP -1285 Av of Amer -NY 10019
(716) 856-1344 .. **Fildes,** Joan M '99 Bouvier Prtnrshp,LLP -350 Main -Buffalo 14202 **Fx:**856-1369
(718) 494-8800 .. **File,** Howard M '78 -260 Christopher Ln -Staten Isl 10314 **Fx:**494-1776
(914) 789-8100 .. **File,** Jonathan E '84 Fuji Photo -200 Summit Lk Dr -Valhalla 10595 **Fx:**789-8514
(718) 982-1573 .. **Fileccia,** Robt J '92 -496 Wllwbrk Rd -Staten Isl 10314
(212) 233-4069 .. **Filemyr,** Edw J IV '85 -11 Park Pl -NY 10007
(212) 335-9000 .. **Filer,** David L '03 %DA -1 Hogan Pl -NY 10013
(585) 232-6500 .. **Fileri,** Philip R '78 (Harter S&E LLP) -1600 Bausch & Lomb Pl -Rchstr 14604
(607) 723-6665 .. **Filetto,** Frank J '76 -122 State -Bnghmtn 13901 **Fx:**723-0192
(718) 579-3040 .. **Filiaci,** Japel M '96 Legal Aid -1020 Grnd Cncrs -Bronx 10451
(212) 269-7308 .. **Filiberti,** Joanne '04 %Leahey & J PC -120 Wall -NY 10005
(631) 509-1820 .. **Filiberto,** Erin L '04 -Bx229 -Mt Sinai 11766 **Fx:**509-1821
(631) 439-1720 .. **Filiberto,** Richd L '92 MHLS -320 Carleton Av -Central Islip 11722 **Fx:**951-2562
(718) 286-6000 .. **Filingeri,** Marilyn A '07 %DA -125-01 Qns Blvd -Kew Gdns 11415
(518) 798-9643 .. **Filion,** David R '87 -27 Pearl Bx2002 -Glens Fls 12801 **Fx:**798-4031
(516) 478-5451 .. **Filip,** Randi Young '86 %Getty Realty Corp -125 Jericho Tpk -Jericho 11753 **Fx:**478-5490
(212) 859-8000 .. **Filipink,** Jeffrey M '08 %Fried FHS&J LLP -1 NY Plz -NY 10004
(212) 715-9100 .. **Filipovic,** Jill N '09 %Kramer LN&F,LLP -1177 Av of Amer -NY 10036
(212) 449-1000 .. **Filipowicz,** Arlena B '91 %Merrill Lynch -220 Bway -NY 10038
(718) 590-2000 .. **Filipowski,** Eliza R '05 %DA -198 E 161st -Bronx 10451 **Fx:**590-6477
(914) 949-0109 .. **Filipowski,** Francis L '72 OfCnsl Owen & E -1 Water -White Plns 10601 **Fx:**949-9223
(212) 847-7211 .. **Filippa,** Alejandro D '04 -234 5th Av -NY 10001
(212) 682-2400 .. **Filippatos,** Parisis G '92 Filippatos PLLC -303 Park Av S -NY 10010 **Fx:**682-0091
(212) 547-5400 .. **Filippazzo,** Jennifer L '03 McDermott W&E LLP -340 Mad Av -NY 10173
(718) 855-1350 .. **Filippazzo,** Stefano A '01 (S Filippazzo,PC) -16 Court -Brklyn 11241 **Fx:**855-2191
(212) 880-1317 .. **Filippelli,** Maria C '89 Fidelity Natl Title Grp -711 3rd Av -NY 10017 **Fx:**880-9606
(585) 385-0090 .. **Filippetti,** Paolo '04 Blasland Bouck & Lee Inc -295 Woodcliff Dr -Fairprt 14450
(718) 320-3326 .. **Filizzola,** Annemarie '91 %Riverbay Corp -2049 Bartow Av -Bronx 10475 **Fx:**320-3397
(212) 415-8600 .. **Fill,** Peter N '94 (Locke LB&L LLP) -3 World Fncl Ctr -NY 10281
(718) 746-3440 .. **Fillas,** Elias N '01 (Sacco & F,LLP) -141-07 20th Av -Whitestone 11357
(212) 431-2812 .. **Filler,** Ronald H '93 %NY Law Schl -185 W Bway -NY 10013 **Fx:**406-0103
(914) 332-4114 .. **Filler,** Stephen C '89 -303 S Bway -Tarrytwn 10591
(716) 858-2424 .. **Filocamo,** Sarah A '05 %DA -25 Delaware Av -Buffalo 14202 **Fx:**858-7425
(212) 637-2726 .. **Filor,** Danl P '01 %US Atty -86 Chmbrs -NY 10007
(516) 228-6666 .. **Filosa,** Anthony R '08 %Rosenberg F&L,LLP -666 Old Cntry Rd -Gdn Cty 11530
(212) 257-6800 .. **Filosa,** Gregory N '08 %Thompson W&G LLP -85 5th Av -NY 10003
(516) 877-5700 .. **Filosa,** Linda '04 Allstate Ins -1225 Franklin Av -Gdn Cty 11530
(631) 853-5761 .. **Filosa,** Mary A '04 %Cnty Atty -400 Carleton Av -Central Islip 11722 **Fx:**853-7788
(631) 231-3775 .. **Filosa,** Michele '02 Atty Grievance Comm -150 Motor Pkwy -Hauppauge 11788
(516) 294-5775 .. **Filpi,** Andrea E '07 %Klee & W,LLP -350 Willis Av -Mineola 11501
(212) 260-0311 .. **Filson,** Marguerite B '71 -808 Bway -NY 10003 **Fx:**305-6205
(212) 701-3000 .. **Filter,** Alicia M '09 %Cahill G&R LLP -80 Pine -NY 10005 **Fx:**269-5420
(212) 506-1700 .. **Filusch,** Edw E '07 %Kasowitz BT&F LLP -1633 Bway -NY 10019
(631) 543-3334 .. **Finamore,** Michl A '97 %Gemini Pharmaceuticals -87 Modular Av -Commack 11725
(516) 365-9380 .. **Finamore,** Richd J '73 -500 Plandome Rd -Manhsst 11030 **Fx:**365-9382
(718) 863-2897 .. **Finan,** Maureen T '99 %M Varrichio & Assoc -3144 Wstchstr Av -Bronx 10461 **Fx:**863-3136
(585) 546-5530 .. **Finan,** Wm J Jr. '81 %Thomson West -50 E Broad -Rchstr 14694
(212) 784-8802 .. **Finatti,** Mauro A M '01 MMSO,LLC -110 E 55th -NY 10022 **Fx:**758-1028
(845) 639-3245 .. **Finch,** Amy L '98 -20 S Main -New Cty 10956 **Fx:**818-3581
(212) 373-3000 .. **Finch,** Andrew C '06 (Paul WRW&G LLP) -1285 Av of Amer -NY 10019
(646) 348-4328 .. **Finch,** Caroline C '02 Deloitte Consulting LLP -1633 Bway -NY 10019
(718) 767-2600 .. **Finch,** David E '96 Skanska USA Civil NE Inc -16-16 Whitestone Expy -Whitestone 11357 **Fx:**767-2624
(212) 327-0493 .. **Finch,** Edw R Jr. '48 -862 Park Av -NY 10075 **Fx:**327-0593
(212) 237-1000 .. **Finch,** Katharine M '00 %Windels ML&M,LLP -156 W 56th -NY 10019
(212) 450-4000 .. **Finch,** Lindsey A '08 %Davis P&W LLP -450 Lex Av -NY 10017
(212) 941-9090 .. **Finck,** Kara Ryan '02 The Door -121 Av of Amer -NY 10013 **Fx:**941-0714
(212) 594-5300 .. **Findeis,** Alastair J M '04 %Milberg LLP -1 Penn Plz -NY 10119
(212) 448-9933 .. **Finder & Cuomo LLP** -9 E 38th -NY 10016 **Fx:**448-9943
(631) 424-3888 .. **Finder & Cuomo LLP** -150 Broadhllw Rd -Melvll 11747 **Fx:**424-4494
(212) 480-4240 .. **Finder,** Iris C '63 %Fuchsberg & F -29 Bway -NY 10006
(212) 382-0700 .. **Finder,** James A '81 (Ostrolenk FG&S,LLP) -1180 Av of Amer -NY 10036

(212) 448-9933 .. **Finder,** Kenneth A '81 (Finder & C LLP) -9 E 38th -NY 10016
(212) 989-9100 .. **Finder,** Michl '81 (Finder NK LLP) -276 Park Av S -NY 10010
(212) 989-9100 .. **Finder Novick Kerrigan LLP** -276 Park Av S -NY 10010 **Fx:**505-2839
(845) 339-6860 .. **Findholt,** Brian L '73 (Findholt & J) -204 Fair Bx4120 -Kingston 12402 **Fx:**339-7063
(212) 649-2000 .. **Findikyan,** Kristina Lutz '00 %Hearst Corp -300 W 57th -NY 10019 **Fx:**649-2035
(516) 522-2725 .. **Findlay,** Deborah Hewitt '93 -626 Reckson Plz -Uniondale 11556
(631) 255-2000 .. **Findlay,** Randolph S '99 -5 Jackson Av -Centereach 11720 **Fx:**963-3221
(212) 816-3660 .. **Findley,** Silas J '07 Citigroup Global Mrkts Inc -388 Greenwich -NY 10013
(631) 831-1954 .. **Findley,** Susan W '94 -150 Broadhllw Rd -Melvll 11747 **Fx:**351-8236
(585) 428-5210 .. **Fine,** Adele M '90 %Pub Def -10 N Fitzhugh -Rchstr 14614 **Fx:**428-2234
(212) 549-2500 .. **Fine,** Aden '05 %ACLU -125 Broad -NY 10004 **Fx:**549-2651
(914) 250-2400 .. **Fine,** Alan D '82 Benchmark Title Agency,LLC -222 Bloomingdale Av -White Plns 10605 **Fx:**422-1500
(516) 487-4800 .. **Fine,** Alexander '73 (Fine & B) -316 Grt Nck Rd -Gt Neck 11021
(212) 577-3688 .. **Fine,** Andrew C '75 %Leg Aid -199 Water -NY 10038 **Fx:**509-8431
(631) 351-2100 .. **Fine,** Barry K '91 (Fine F&B) -445 Broadhllw Rd -Melvll 11747 **Fx:**773-6766
(516) 487-4800 .. **Fine & Bassik** -316 Grt Nck Rd -Gt Neck 11021 **Fx:**829-7110
(212) 949-9696 .. **Fine,** Burton M '58 -60 E 42nd -NY 10165 **Fx:**949-6241
(212) 354-0966 .. **Fine,** Chas J '56 -1501 Bway -NY 10036 **Fx:**354-0968
(718) 351-5190 .. **Fine,** Craig A '06 (CA Fine,PC) -159 New Dorp Plz -Staten Isl 10306 **Fx:**351-5845
(845) 292-2000 .. **Fine,** Craig S '90 OfCnsl B Rourke,PC -3 Maple Bx71 -Liberty 12754 **Fx:**292-0385
(212) 336-1100 .. **Fine,** David J '01 US SEC -233 Bway -NY 10279
(212) 556-2100 .. **Fine,** David M '00 (King & S) -1185 Av of Amer -NY 10036
(212) 530-5000 .. **Fine,** Drew S '88 (Milbank TH&M LLP) -1 Chase Manh Plz -NY 10005
(212) 839-5300 .. **Fine,** Edw J '84 (Sidley A LLP) -787 7th Av -NY 10019
(212) 719-0200 .. **Fine,** Erica B '83 %BAR/BRI -1500 Bway -NY 10036 **Fx:**719-1421
(718) 520-3511 .. **Fine,** Gerald L '69 %Supreme Ct -125-01 Qns Blvd -Kew Gdns 11415
(914) 245-6250 .. **Fine,** Gordon B '86 -1500 Front -Yorktwn Hts 10598 **Fx:**245-6249
(212) 859-8000 .. **Fine,** Howard A '92 SpclCnsl Fried FHS&J LLP -1 NY Plz -NY 10004
(914) 824-5421 .. **Fine,** James G '67 %Hon J Lefkowitz -111 Dr MLK Jr Blvd -White Plns 10601 **Fx:**995-4184
(212) 819-8200 .. **Fine,** Johanna B '08 %White & C LLP -1155 Av of Amer -NY 10036
(914) 725-0655 .. **Fine,** John C '67 -150 Puitan Dr -Scarsdale 10583 **Fx:**725-0655
(212) 458-1065 .. **Fine,** Lawr M '90 %AIG -175 Water -NY 10038
(718) 222-9858 .. **Fine,** Lee A '92 -26 Court -Brklyn 11242 **Fx:**222-9865
(631) 361-9600 .. **Fine,** Lisa S '97 LS Fine.PC -900 Wheeler Rd -Hauppauge 11788 **Fx:**361-9601
(646) 825-9080 .. **Fine,** Michelle F '95 Avalon Business Sys -110 Wall -NY 10005
(212) 578-0423 .. **Fine,** Miriam Gottesfeld '94 %MetLife -27-01 Qns Plz N -LIC 11101
(212) 267-1650 .. **Fine Olin & Anderman,LLP** -39 Bway -NY 10006 **Fx:**962-5619
(888) 909-4362 .. **Fine Olin & Anderman,LLP** -537 James -Syracuse 13203 **Fx:**(315) 422-6793
(518) 435-8092 .. **Fine Olin & Anderman,LLP** -80 Wolf Rd -Albany 12205 **Fx:**435-9984
(516) 542-1295 .. **Fine Olin & Anderman,LLP** -600 Old Cntry Rd -Gdn Cty 11530 **Fx:**542-4722
(716) 856-8004 .. **Fine Olin & Anderman,LLP** -69 Delaware Av -Buffalo 14202
(212) 341-2758 .. **Fine,** Rachel L '92 %Admin Children's Srvcs -150 William -NY 10038
(212) 277-6300 .. **Fine,** Rebecca L '94 (Schindler C&H LLP) -100 Wall -NY 10005
(716) 849-8900 .. **Fine,** Robt P '68 (Hurwitz & F,PC) -1300 Lbrty Bldg -Buffalo 14202
(631) 351-2100 .. **Fine,** Scott J '98 (Fine F&B) -445 Broadhllw Rd -Melvll 11747 **Fx:**773-6766
(212) 698-3500 .. **Fine,** Sheryl Cohen '99 %Dechert LLP -1095 Av of Amer -NY 10036
(646) 315-7337 .. **Fine,** Stephanie B '80 %FINRA -14 Wall -NY 10005 **Fx:**315-7440
(212) 224-0343 .. **Fine,** Susan E '80 Fisher Bros -299 Park Av -NY 10171
(631) 261-8834 .. **Fine,** Susan E '89 %Ingerman S LLP -150 Motor Pkwy -Hauppauge 11788
(315) 435-2470 .. **Fineberg,** Alison B '98 %DA -505 S State -Syracuse 13202 **Fx:**435-3969
(716) 886-0211 .. **Fineberg,** Lawr J '91 %Benderson Dvlpmnt -570 Delaware Av -Buffalo 14202 **Fx:**886-2269
(315) 474-4283 .. **Fineberg,** Lewis H '63 -Bx41 -Syracuse 13214 **Fx:**474-2051
(212) 282-4963 .. **Fineberg,** Martin I '90 Mizuho Corp -1251 Av of Amer -NY 10020
(914) 945-3212 .. **Finegan,** Neil C '91 IBM -Bx218 -Yorktwn Hts 10598
(212) 315-1338 .. **Finegan,** Patrick T '85 (Finegan & Co LLC) -200 Cntrl Pk S -NY 10019 **Fx:**861-6811
(212) 695-8100 .. **Finegan,** Thos S '75 (Goetz F,LLP) -1 Penn Plz -NY 10119
(212) 906-1200 .. **Finegold,** Loren Nathan '99 (Latham & W) -885 3rd Av -NY 10022
(212) 709-8136 .. **Finell,** Steven '72 (S Finell LLC) -110 Wall -NY 10005
(212) 869-2050 .. **Finelli,** Chas E '94 -112 Mad Av -NY 10016
(518) 486-5950 .. **Finelli,** Debra S '94 %Dept of Law -The Cptl -Albany 12224 **Fx:**408-2102
(212) 859-8000 .. **Finelli,** Jon '08 %Fried FHS&J LLP -1 NY Plz -NY 10004
(212) 897-5823 .. **Fineman,** Michl '02 -305 Bway -NY 10007
(212) 454-4104 .. **Fineman,** Phyllis M '75 %Deutsche Bk -280 Park Av -NY 10017
(212) 355-9500 .. **Fineman,** Steven E '97 (Lieff CH&B,LLP) -250 Hudson -NY 10013
(607) 274-5603 .. **Fineman-Sowers,** Martha A '97 Cnty Dept Soc Srvcs -320 W State -Ithaca 14850
(516) 747-1136 .. **Fineo,** Francis G '86 (Steinberg FB&F,PC) -40 Crsswys Park Dr -Woodbury 11797
(315) 724-7800 .. **Finer,** Stuart E '72 (Finer & G-M) -2615 Genesee -Utica 13501
(212) 451-2300 .. **Finerman,** Adam W '92 (Olshan GFR&W LLP) -65 E 55th -NY 10022
(212) 523-1570 .. **Finerman,** Ralph '60 -1185 Av of Amer -NY 10036 **Fx:**523-1235
(212) 376-5666 .. **Finerty,** Margaret J '79 (Getnick & G) -620 5th Av -NY 10020 **Fx:**292-3942
(212) 337-2228 .. **Finesmith,** Madeline S '95 %US Dept Labor -201 Varick -NY 10014
(212) 849-7000 .. **Finestone,** Benjamin I '05 %Quinn EU&S,LLP -51 Mad Av -NY 10010
(212) 245-4580 .. **Finestone,** Jason A '01 %Shukat AHW&H,LLP -111 W 57th -NY 10019
(585) 637-1912 .. **Fingar,** Melissa A '97 Brockport Cntrl Schl Dist -40 Allen -Brockprt 14420
(212) 808-2307 .. **Finger,** Adam G '97 Balyasny Asset Mgmt -135 E 57th -NY 10022
(646) 837-0100 .. **Finger,** Barbara S '80 (Wenick & F,PC) -28 E 28th -NY 10016
(914) 949-0308 .. **Finger,** Carl L '94 (Finger & F,PC) -158 Grand -White Plns 10601 **Fx:**949-3608
(718) 824-5800 .. **Finger,** Christopher E '77 C Finger,PC -778 Castle Hill Av -Bronx 10473 **Fx:**430-9230
(914) 949-0308 .. **Finger,** Danl S '00 (Finger & F,PC) -158 Grand -White Plns 10601 **Fx:**949-3608
(914) 949-0308 .. **Finger,** Dorothy M '81 (Finger & F,PC) -158 Grand -White Plns 10601 **Fx:**949-3608
(212) 583-9600 .. **Finger,** Joel L '74 (Littler M,PC) -900 3rd Av -NY 10022
(914) 949-0308 .. **Finger,** Kenneth J '64 (Finger & F,PC) -158 Grand -White Plns 10601 **Fx:**949-3608
(212) 547-5400 .. **Finger,** Todd A '98 (McDermott W&E LLP) -340 Mad Av -NY 10173
(212) 715-9100 .. **Finger,** Toni L '00 %Kramer LN&F,LLP -1177 Av of Amer -NY 10036
(212) 756-2000 .. **Finger,** Wallis K '10 %Schulte R&Z LLP -919 3rd Av -NY 10022
(212) 906-1200 .. **Fingeret,** Kevin T '94 (Latham & W) -885 3rd Av -NY 10022
(212) 458-3476 .. **Fingerhut,** Dana M '02 AIG -175 Water -NY 10038
(212) 702-0900 .. **Fingerhut,** David L '86 (Axelrod F&D) -260 Mad Av -NY 10016 **Fx:**355-7365
(212) 249-7700 .. **Fingerit,** Irwin K '57 (Fingerit W&F,LLP) -75 East End Av -NY 10028 **Fx:**249-7706
(212) 249-7700 .. **Fingerit,** Michl J '86 (Fingerit W&F,LLP) -75 East End Av -NY 10028 **Fx:**249-7706
(212) 374-3436 .. **Fingerle,** Susan A '05 %NYC Dept Educ-OLS -52 Chmbrs -NY 10007 **Fx:**374-5939
(212) 819-8200 .. **Finguerra-Ducharme,** Dyan M '97 Cnsl White & C LLP -1155 Av of Amer -NY 10036
(212) 504-6000 .. **Fini,** Tom M '94 (Cadwalader W&T LLP) -1 World Fncl Ctr -NY 10281
(845) 469-2777 .. **Finiello,** Philip J '77 (P Finiello,PC) -1222 Whsprng Hills Dr -Chester 10918 **Fx:**469-2101
(212) 687-3000 .. **Fink,** Alexander R '01 %Jaffe & A,LLP -600 3rd Av -NY 10016
(212) 373-3000 .. **Fink,** Alexis A '10 %Paul WRW&G LLP -1285 Av of Amer -NY 10019
(212) 813-9201 .. **Fink,** Andrew A '95 Trevi Health Ventures -110 E 59th -NY 10022
(212) 762-7975 .. **Fink,** Barry '80 Morgan Stanley -1221 Av of Amer -NY 10020
(917) 575-8604 .. **Fink,** Danl H '05 -475 FDR Dr -NY 10002
(212) 309-1260 .. **Fink,** David '74 -200 Park Av -NY 10166 **Fx:**309-1100
(212) 673-0288 .. **Fink,** Eleanor '79 -8 Gramercy Park S -NY 10003
(718) 783-3682 .. **Fink,** Elizabeth M '74 -36 Plz St E -Brklyn 11238 **Fx:**783-5853
(914) 470-0001 .. **Fink,** Ephraim Jacob '00 %Babchik & Y,LLP -200 E Post Rd -White Plns 10601
(518) 424-1765 .. **Fink,** Fredk M '07 -Bx621 -Long Lk 12847 **Fx:**382-0873
(718) 286-1500 .. **Fink,** Ita '95 %Leg Srvcs -97-77 Qns Blvd -Rego Pk 11374 **Fx:**275-5352
(212) 428-2150 .. **Fink,** Janet R '75 %OCA -25 Beaver -NY 10004 **Fx:**428-2155
(646) 648-3027 .. **Fink,** Jason B '04 -205 E 78th -NY 10075
(212) 649-5732 .. **Fink,** Jeffrey D '72 %Rockefeller & Co,Inc -30 Rckfllr Plz -NY 10112 **Fx:**649-5977
(212) 504-6000 .. **Fink,** Jessica L '01 SpclCnsl Cadwalader W&T LLP -1 World Fncl Ctr -NY 10281
(212) 385-1373 .. **Fink,** Jonathan A '93 (Fink & K,PLLC) -40 Exch Pl -NY 10005
(212) 856-5800 .. **Fink,** Jonathan J '78 (Samson F&D) -10 E 40th -NY 10016
(212) 373-3000 .. **Fink,** Julie E '06 %Paul WRW&G LLP -1285 Av of Amer -NY 10019
(212) 808-8100 .. **Fink,** Juliet L '08 %Kostelanetz & F,LLP -7 Wrld Trd Ctr -NY 10007
(212) 385-1373 .. **Fink & Katz,PLLC** -40 Exch Pl -NY 10005
(212) 285-4100 .. **Fink,** Kenneth S '92 (Cheriff & F,PC) -2 Rector -NY 10006
(212) 878-8000 .. **Fink,** Kristina V '02 %Clifford C LLP -31 W 52nd -NY 10019
(212) 732-8700 .. **Fink,** Linda A '08 %McAloon & F,PC -123 William -NY 10038
(585) 427-5400 .. **Fink,** Michl I '71 %Xerox -100 Clinton Av S -Rchstr 14644
(718) 377-7600 .. **Fink,** Neil '03 (Adler & F PC) -3006 Av M -Brklyn 11201 **Fx:**377-7603
(718) 237-1800 .. **Fink,** Paul '56 (P Fink,LLC) -32 Court -Brklyn 11201 **Fx:**855-1940
(516) 280-5516 .. **Fink & Platz** -1325 Franklin Av -Gdn Cty 11530 **Fx:**280-5520
(212) 530-5000 .. **Fink,** Rachel A '09 %Milbank TH&M LLP -1 Chase Manh Plz -NY 10005
(716) 853-1616 .. **Fink,** Raymond L '78 (Harter S&E LLP) -12 Fountain Plz -Buffalo 14202
(212) 335-4500 .. **Fink,** Robt F '71 (DLA Piper LLP) -1251 Av of Amer -NY 10020
(212) 808-8100 .. **Fink,** Robt S '69 (Kostelanetz & F,LLP) -7 Wrld Trd Ctr -NY 10007
(845) 294-9721 .. **Fink,** Robt W '72 -110 Murray Av Bx900 -Goshen 10924 **Fx:**294-3131
(516) 944-5722 .. **Fink,** Ronald R '73 Tono-Bungay Consulting,Inc -82 Orchrd Beach Blvd -Pt Wash 11050 **Fx:**944-5572
(212) 753-5599 .. **Fink,** Rosalind S '73 OfCnsl Brill & M -845 3rd Av -NY 10022
(212) 801-6955 .. **Fink,** Scott E '01 %Greenberg T,LLP -200 Park Av -NY 10166
(718) 261-5550 .. **Fink,** Stephen D '77 -118-35 Qns Blvd -Frst Hlls 11375 **Fx:**520-8544
(212) 506-5000 .. **Fink,** Steven J '95 (Orrick H&S LLP) -51 W 52nd -NY 10019
(516) 280-5516 .. **Fink,** Steven M '86 (Fink & P) -1325 Franklin Av -Gdn Cty 11530
(631) 390-0010 .. **Fink,** Stewart C '82 (Bruno G&S,LLP) -445 Broad Hollow Rd -Melvll 11747
(212) 307-7876 .. **Fink,** Stewart R '72 -445 Park Av -NY 10022 **Fx:**307-7951
(585) 546-6448 .. **Fink,** Thos A '59 (Davidson F LLP) -28 E Main -Rchstr 14614
(631) 462-4911 .. **Finkel,** Alan L '85 (Bianco B&F,LLP) -5036 Jericho Tpk Bx49 -Commack 11725
(718) 459-3300 .. **Finkel,** Bernard '50 (Argiriou & F) -110-11 Qns Blvd -Frst Hlls 11375
(718) 625-3398 .. **Finkel,** Fern J '85 -41 Pierrepont -Brklyn 11201 **Fx:**625-2785
(718) 463-7209 .. **Finkel,** Leonard '74 -68-17 Fresh Meadow Ln -Fresh Mdws 11365 **Fx:**463-7262

(914) 694-9500 .. **Finkel,** Melanie F '89 OfCnsl Trokie L LLP -1133 Wstchstr Av -White Plns 10604
(718) 298-8921 .. **Finkel,** Oscar '69 %Leg Aid -153-01 Jamaica Av -Jamaica 11432 **Fx:**657-0537
(212) 689-8600 .. **Finkel,** Richd A '77 (Meissner K&F,LLP) -275 Mad Av -NY 10016
(516) 869-7600 .. **Finkel,** Richd S '88 (Town Atty) -220 Plandome Rd -Manhsst 11030 **Fx:**869-7605
(212) 759-4600 .. **Finkel,** Robt C '82 (Wolf P LLP) -845 3rd Av -NY 10022
(212) 530-5000 .. **Finkel,** Robt M '88 (Milbank TH&M LLP) -1 Chase Manh Plz -NY 10005
(518) 272-2300 .. **Finkel,** Sanford N '75 -68 2nd -Troy 12180 **Fx:**272-0540
(212) 688-8555 .. **Finkel,** Sharon '02 %Fragomen DB&L LLP -7 Hanover Sq -NY 10004
(212) 336-0068 .. **Finkel,** Wm '02 SEC -3 World Fncl Ctr -NY 10281 **Fx:**336-1323
(518) 221-0725 .. **Finkell,** Gregory C '83 -425 Kenwood Av -Delmar 12054
(518) 581-8800 .. **Finkell,** Seth D '02 Lemery G LLC -60 Railroad Pl -Saratoga Spgs 12866
(718) 286-2138 .. **Finkelman,** Kenneth L '89 %Leg Aid -120-46 Qns Blvd -Kew Gdns 11415 **Fx:**286-2286
(212) 669-2048 .. **Finkelman,** Lewis S '87 %Comptroller -1 Centre -NY 10007 **Fx:**669-2884
(718) 645-7770 .. **Finkelshteyn,** Ilona '04 -2305 65th -Brklyn 11204 **Fx:**382-6982
(212) 474-1000 .. **Finkelson,** Allen '72 (Cravath S&M LLP) -825 8th Av -NY 10019
(212) 461-5506 .. **Finkelson,** Ira '67 CIT Leasing Corp -11 W 42nd -NY 10036 **Fx:**461-5402
(212) 252-0300 .. **Finkelstein,** Adam D '95 (Kagan LLLG&C,LLP) -200 Mad Av -NY 10016
(212) 922-9250 .. **Finkelstein,** Allen L '68 (Ganfer & S LLP) -360 Lex Av -NY 10017
(845) 562-0203 .. **Finkelstein,** Andrew G '92 (Finkelstein & Prtnrs,LLP) -1279 Route 300 Bx1111 -Newburgh 12550
(914) 949-1305 .. **Finkelstein,** Barbara D '79 %Leg Srvcs -90 Maple Av -White Plns 10601 **Fx:**949-6213
(845) 947-1100 .. **Finkelstein,** Beth B '94 %Phillips & M,LLP -148 Route 9W -Stony Pnt 10980
(212) 326-2000 .. **Finkelstein,** Brad J '98 (O'Melveny & M LLP) -7 Times Sq -NY 10036
(718) 852-6560 .. **Finkelstein,** Chas '91 -26 Court -Brklyn 11242
(212) 323-2250 .. **Finkelstein,** Cori M '98 %HHC-OLA-Medical Litigation -346 Bway -NY 10013 **Fx:**323-2251
(516) 747-1136 .. **Finkelstein,** Dana J '91 OfCnsl Steinberg FB&F,PC -40 Crsswys Park Dr -Woodbury 11797
(212) 619-5400 .. **Finkelstein,** Danl '56 (Newman F LLP) -1250 Bway -NY 10001
(212) 239-9087 .. **Finkelstein,** Danielle E '96 Clean Us -98 Cuttermill Rd -Gt Neck 11021
(631) 425-7070 .. **Finkelstein,** Darin '04 F Giachetti -18 Fairvw -Huntngtn 11743 **Fx:**425-1872
(212) 474-1000 .. **Finkelstein,** David S '99 (Cravath S&M LLP) -825 8th Av -NY 10019
(212) 216-8000 .. **Finkelstein,** Edw R '89 Cnsl Tarter K&D LLP -1350 Bway -NY 10018
(212) 799-3100 .. **Finkelstein,** Evelyn M '73 Metropolitan Opera -Lincoln Ctr -NY 10023 **Fx:**870-7681
(516) 539-6208 .. **Finkelstein,** Harold J '65 %IRS -50 Clinton -Hempstd 11550
(212) 661-4480 .. **Finkelstein,** Herbert L '57 Jaffin C&F -19 Eldrdg Av -Ossining 10562 **Fx:**599-2957
(631) 727-4100 .. **Finkelstein,** Howard M '53 (Smith FLI&Y) -456 Griffing Av Bx389 -Rvrhead 11901
(845) 562-0203 .. **Finkelstein,** Howard S '59 (Finkelstein & Prtnrs,LLP) -1279 Route 300 Bx1111 -Newburgh 12550
(212) 599-7575 .. **Finkelstein,** Ira A '74 (Harnik & F LLP) -645 5th Av -NY 10022 **Fx:**867-8120
(212) 385-9190 .. **Finkelstein,** Irving '58 (Finkelstein M&E) -11 Park Pl -NY 10007
(914) 640-8212 .. **Finkelstein,** Jared T '85 Starwoods Hotels & Resorts -1111 Wstchstr Av -White Plns 10604
(845) 344-4855 .. **Finkelstein,** Joel S '86 (Finkelstein & Prtnrs,LLP) -726 E Main -Middletwn 10940
(516) 746-3500 .. **Finkelstein,** Kenneth '88 Brand G&B,PC -600 Old Cntry Rd -Gdn Cty 11530
(212) 538-0318 .. **Finkelstein,** Marc H '00 Credit Suisse -1 Mad Av -NY 10010
(631) 694-2300 .. **Finkelstein,** Marcia L '87 (Lamb & B,LLP) -534 Broadhllw Rd Bx9034 -Melvll 11747
(212) 972-1000 .. **Finkelstein,** Matthew K '98 %London F LLP -59 Maiden Ln -NY 10038
(212) 484-3900 .. **Finkelstein,** Matthew L '05 %Arent F LLP -1675 Bway -NY 10019
(631) 727-4100 .. **Finkelstein,** Matthew M '93 %Smith FLI&Y -456 Griffing Av Bx389 -Rvrhead 11901
(212) 318-3000 .. **Finkelstein,** Meryl Grossman '91 SrCnsl Fulbright & J LLP -666 5th Av -NY 10103
(212) 876-1715 .. **Finkelstein,** Michl O '59 -2628 Bway -NY 10025
(212) 756-2000 .. **Finkelstein,** Nancy R '79 (Schulte R&Z LLP) -919 3rd Av -NY 10022
(845) 562-0203 .. **Finkelstein & Partners,LLP** -1279 Route 300 Bx1111 -Newburgh 12550 **Fx:**562-3492
(315) 453-3053 .. **Finkelstein & Partners,LLP** -716 7th N -Liverpool 13088 **Fx:**453-3605
(845) 339-5815 .. **Finkelstein & Partners,LLP** -785 Bway -Kingston 12401 **Fx:**339-5825
(518) 435-8092 .. **Finkelstein & Partners,LLP** -80 Wolf Rd -Albany 12205 **Fx:**435-9984
(518) 270-1911 .. **Finkelstein & Partners,LLP** -759 Hoosick Rd -Troy 12180 **Fx:**270-0915
(845) 856-6351 .. **Finkelstein & Partners,LLP** -1 Cole -Pt Jervis 12771 **Fx:**856-6353
(845) 344-4855 .. **Finkelstein & Partners,LLP** -726 E Main -Middletwn 10940 **Fx:**344-2090
(845) 567-7776 .. **Finkelstein & Partners,LLP** -103 Exec Dr -New Windsor 12553 **Fx:**567-9996
(845) 298-2870 .. **Finkelstein & Partners,LLP** -1778 South Rd -Wappingers Fls 12590 **Fx:**298-1476
(845) 352-9240 .. **Finkelstein & Partners,LLP** -296 Main -Spg Vly 10977 **Fx:**344-2090
(914) 375-0100 .. **Finkelstein,** Paul '91 %Novick ELRW&L,PC -733 Ynkrs Av -Ynkrs 10704
(212) 273-0030 .. **Finkelstein,** Richd G '72 Ofc of Prog Integrity -330 W 34th -NY 10001
(212) 759-2929 .. **Finkelstein,** Richd Lee '81 -655 Mad Av -NY 10065 **Fx:**832-2434
(212) 964-8700 .. **Finkelstein,** Robt '89 (Finkelstein Firm,LLP) -11 Park Pl -NY 10007
(914) 761-3800 .. **Finkelstein,** Robt A '80 -101 Vllg Sq -Somers 10589 **Fx:**761-0737
(212) 571-0550 .. **Finkelstein,** Robt F '02 %Allegaert B&V LLP -111 Bway -NY 10006
(631) 414-4000 .. **Finkelstein,** Ronald M '87 Marcum & Kliegman LLP -10 Melvll Park Rd -Melvll 11747 **Fx:**414-4001
(212) 869-7000 .. **Finkelstein,** Saul H '82 (Feldman W&S LLP) -420 Lex Av -NY 10170
(516) 571-3800 .. **Finkelstein,** Silvia P '83 %DA -262 Old Cntry Rd -Mineola 11501 **Fx:**248-9479
(212) 532-0008 .. **Finkelstein,** Stephen H '67 -369 Lex Av -NY 10017 **Fx:**695-6007
(718) 447-6300 .. **Finkelstein,** Steven J '85 -1164 Victory Blvd -Staten Isl 10301 **Fx:**447-9908
(212) 363-2500 .. **Finkelstein,** Steven R '82 (Finkelstein & V PC) -90 Broad -NY 10004
(212) 735-2841 .. **Finkelstein,** Stuart M '86 (Skadden ASM&F LLP) -4 Times Sq -NY 10036
(212) 340-0400 .. **Finkelstein,** Tamar '95 Applt Div 1st Dept -27 Mad Av -NY 10010 **Fx:**889-4412
(845) 485-5278 .. **Finkelstein,** Ted H '79 Gilman Ciocia,Inc -11 Raymnd Av -Poughkeepsie 12603
(212) 363-2500 .. **Finkelstein & Virga PC** -90 Broad -NY 10004 **Fx:**363-2723
(212) 490-3000 .. **Finkelstein,** Wendy J '01 OfCnsl Wilson EME&D LLP -150 E 42nd -NY 10017
(212) 635-1270 .. **Finkenberg,** Lincoln S '99 Bk of NY Mellon -1 Wall -NY 10286
(315) 422-7111 .. **Finkenberg,** Susan J '86 %Blitman & K LLP -443 N Franklin -Syracuse 13204
(718) 261-0090 .. **Finkin,** Bob M '54 (Finkin & F) -118-21 Qns Blvd -Frst Hlls 11375 **Fx:**261-0352
(718) 261-0090 .. **Finkin,** Steven D '86 (Finkin & F) -118-21 Qns Blvd -Frst Hlls 11375 **Fx:**261-0352
(718) 546-0310 .. **Finkle,** Florence L '88 %Dept of Correction -75-20 Astoria Blvd -E Elmhrst 11370
(212) 675-3520 .. **Finkler,** David J '87 (D Finkler,PC) -9 E 38th -NY 10016 **Fx:**448-9943
(212) 471-8533 .. **Finkston,** Neil R '92 (Herzfeld & R,PC) -125 Broad -NY 10004
(315) 474-7541 .. **Finlay,** J Scott '76 (Menter R&T,PC) -308 Maltbie -Syracuse 13204
(607) 277-7286 .. **Finlay,** Marcie Ann '97 (Blumkin F&B) -401 E State -Ithaca 14850
(607) 565-2321 .. **Finlayson,** Mary H '90 %Frederick & F -HSBC Bk Bldg -Waverly 14892 **Fx:**565-3064
(212) 230-5500 .. **Finley,** Alison K '99 %Davis SLM&H LLP -689 5th Av -NY 10022
(212) 859-8000 .. **Finley,** Danl W '05 %Fried FHS&J LLP -1 NY Plz -NY 10004
(718) 520-3842 .. **Finley,** Deirdre A '99 Supreme Ct -188-15 Sutphin Blvd -Jamaica 11435
(212) 483-2323 .. **Finley,** Edw J II '92 %JP Morgan Chase -345 Park Av -NY 10154
(718) 828-4888 .. **Finley,** Glenn '79 (G Finley & Assoc) -2024 Wllmsbrdg Rd -Bronx 10461 **Fx:**828-8181
(718) 461-6633 .. **Finley,** Jawan N '02 %Mallilo & G -163-09 Nrthrn Blvd -Flushng 11358
(716) 841-2637 .. **Finley,** John D '95 %Marine Mdland Bk -1 Marine Mdlnd Ctr -Buffalo 14203
(212) 583-5000 .. **Finley,** John G '82 Blackstone Group -345 Park Av -NY 10154 **Fx:**583-5749
(212) 697-2700 .. **Finley,** John J '72 (Stairs DF) -200 Park Av S -NY 10003
(212) 848-4000 .. **Finley,** John W III '99 Shearman & S LLP -599 Lex Av -NY 10022
(212) 633-2373 .. **Finley,** Myron G '83 (Finley F&P LLP) -19 Vestry -NY 10013 **Fx:**633-9865
(212) 782-7349 .. **Finley,** Patrick J '78 Moore Capital Mgmt,Inc -1251 Av of Amer -NY 10020
(516) 572-2000 .. **Finley,** Patrick J '09 %DA -99 Main -Hempstd 11550 **Fx:**572-2606
(212) 556-2100 .. **Finley,** Robt S '77 (King & S) -1185 Av of Amer -NY 10036
(212) 593-6700 .. **Finley,** Stacey D '02 %Aaronson RF&D,LLP -757 3rd Av -NY 10017
(212) 351-4000 .. **Finley,** Steven R '74 (Gibson D&C LLP) -200 Park Av -NY 10166
(516) 357-3700 .. **Finmann,** Victor M '76 (Cullen and D LLP) -100 Q Roosevelt Blvd -Gdn Cty 11530
(212) 558-4000 .. **Finn,** Andrew J '09 %Sullivan & C LLP -125 Broad -NY 10004
(212) 695-5670 .. **Finn,** Christine M '07 %Goldfinger & L LLP -750 3rd Av -NY 10017
(212) 850-2800 .. **Finn,** Erika N '04 %Andrews K LLP -450 Lex Av -NY 10017
(516) 741-6266 .. **Finn,** James R '07 %McCabe CM&F,LLP -346 Westbury Av Bx9000 -Carle Pl 11514
(516) 483-6480 .. **Finn,** Kevin P '85 Finn & F -500 Front -Hempstd 11550
(716) 631-8310 .. **Finn,** Lynne Marie '80 %Superior Design -250 Intl Dr Bx 9057 -Williamsvll 14221 **Fx:**631-0274
(518) 869-6227 .. **Finn,** Martin S '84 (Lavelle & F,LLP) -29 British Amer Blvd -Latham 12110
(607) 432-3333 .. **Finn,** Martin S '84 (Lavelle & F,LLP) -22-26 Watkins Av -Oneonta 13820 **Fx:**(518) 869-0572
(212) 788-7990 .. **Finn,** Maureen M '84 Dept Sanitation-Ofc of Dept Advocate -51 Chmbrs -NY 10007
(585) 593-3341 .. **Finn,** Michl B '05 (Hutter & F) -22 W State Bx1137 -Wellsvll 14895 **Fx:**593-3782
(845) 875-4393 .. **Finn,** Patricia A '03 -450 Piermont Av -Piermont 10968
(212) 857-8230 .. **Finn,** Patrick M '90 %Baker MM&M,PC -330 W 34th -NY 10001
(212) 889-4100 .. **Finn,** Peter M '84 %Realty Advisory Bd -292 Mad Av -NY 10017 **Fx:**889-4105
(716) 856-4200 .. **Finn,** R Donald '70 (Gibson M&C,LLP) -69 Delaware Av -Buffalo 14202
(212) 968-1001 .. **Finn,** Robt J '87 %Gwertzman LBS&M -80 Broad -NY 10004
(212) 261-7000 .. **Finn,** Ronald N '70 %Calyon -1301 Av of Amer -NY 10019
(518) 533-3000 .. **Finn,** Ryan M '06 %Bond S&K,PLLC -111 Wshngtn Av -Albany 12210
(718) 275-1008 .. **Finn,** Thos J '03 -6712 Yllwstn Blvd -Frst Hlls 11375
(212) 559-5026 .. **Finn,** Thos P Jr. '65 %Citibank NA -153 E 53rd -NY 10043
(212) 474-1000 .. **Finn,** Wm J '09 %Cravath S&M LLP -825 8th Av -NY 10019
(212) 855-3283 .. **Finnegan,** Allison M '98 Depository Trust -55 Water -NY 10041 **Fx:**855-3279
(212) 326-2000 .. **Finnegan,** Brian P '02 Cnsl O'Melveny & M LLP -7 Times Sq -NY 10036
(212) 458-3345 .. **Finnegan,** Colleen Ann '96 AIG -175 Water -NY 10038
(212) 361-8240 .. **Finnegan,** David '79 -625 Main -NY 10044

(315) 682-3808 .. **Finnegan**, Diane Van Epps '94 -8390 Turnberry Dr -Manlius 13104 **Fx**:682-3868
(212) 660-3000 .. **Finnegan**, Hugh P '84 (Sullivan & W LLP) -1290 Av of Amer -NY 10104
(516) 393-2200 .. **Finnegan**, Jacqueline H '02 Garfunkel W,PC -111 Grt Nck Rd -Gt Neck 11021
(212) 408-4906 .. **Finnegan**, James P '79 %BNY Leasing -1290 Av of Amer -NY 10104 **Fx**:246-1803
(212) 592-1400 .. **Finnegan**, Jennifer R '96 (Herrick,F LLP) -2 Park Av -NY 10016
(845) 634-7010 .. **Finnegan**, John E '85 (Montalbano C&F,PC) -67 N Main Bx1070 -New Cty 10956
(212) 408-5100 .. **Finnegan**, John F '83 (Chadbourne & P LLP) -30 Rckfllr Plz -NY 10112
(718) 298-1219 .. **Finnegan**, Kerian Aideen '96 %Hon J Lebowitz -88-11 Sutphin Blvd -Jamaica 11435
(212) 627-8100 .. **Finnegan**, Kevin A '87 (Levy R,PC) -80 8th Av -NY 10011
(212) 578-4391 .. **Finnegan**, Kevin S '82 %MetLife -27-01 Qns Plz N -LIC 11101 **Fx**:578-3916
(631) 765-1939 .. **Finnegan**, Martin D '00 Town Atty -Bx1179 -Southold 11971 **Fx**:765-6639
(212) 648-7806 .. **Finnegan**, Michl C '90 %JP Morgan Chase -60 Wall -NY 10260
(631) 765-1939 .. **Finnegan**, Patricia A '01 Town of Southold -Bx1179 -Southold 11971
(845) 627-8423 .. **Finnegan**, Patrick J '55 -4 Short -W Nyack 10994 **Fx**:627-8431
(518) 464-3127 .. **Finnegan**, Patrick T '98 %AIG -1 Park Pl -Albany 12205
(646) 471-1176 .. **Finnegan**, Thos M '87 PricewaterhouseCoopers LLP -300 Mad Av -NY 10017
(212) 524-5000 .. **Finnegan**, Timothy M '68 (Jacob M&F) -1270 Av of Amer -NY 10020
(516) 227-2260 .. **Finnegan**, Vincent D '94 (Callan KB&B LLP) -333 Earle Ovngton Blvd -Uniondale 11553
(585) 344-2550 .. **Finnell**, Kevin T '87 %DA -1 W Main -Batavia 14020 **Fx**:344-8544
(212) 609-6800 .. **Finnell**, Lawr J '06 %McCarter & E,LLP -245 Park Av -NY 10167
(516) 542-5900 .. **Finnell**, Warren J '58 -333 Earle Ovngton Blvd -Uniondale 11553 **Fx**:542-5912
(212) 223-0400 .. **Finneran**, B J Phoenix '88 OfCnsl Zeichner E&K LLP -575 Lex Av -NY 10022
(212) 721-9588 .. **Finneran**, Ethan V '83 -221 W 82nd -NY 10024 **Fx**:721-9865
(212) 385-0066 .. **Finneran**, Patricia L '10 %Dealy & S,LLP -225 Bway -NY 10007
(516) 502-2620 .. **Finneran**, Wm F '89 %Thomas & G LLP -1983 Marcus Av -Lk Success 11042
(716) 854-6424 .. **Finnerty**, Betsy '06 %K Ricotta -350 Main -Buffalo 14202 **Fx**:854-6425
(212) 813-1801 .. **Finnerty Canda & Drisgula,PC** -488 Mad Av -NY 10022 **Fx**:(201) 845-6799
(718) 286-6000 .. **Finnerty**, Courtney A '08 %DA -125-01 Qns Blvd -Kew Gdns 11415
(518) 523-3006 .. **Finnerty**, Edw P '77 -307 Main Bx308 -Lk Placid 12946 **Fx**:523-4298
(516) 628-2268 .. **Finnerty**, Frank A '63 -40 Dickerson Av -Bayvll 11709
(631) 665-8060 .. **Finnerty**, John P '75 -21 Maple Av Bx151P -Bay Shr 11706 **Fx**:665-8086
(212) 335-4500 .. **Finnerty**, Jos G III '88 (DLA Piper LLP) -1251 Av of Amer -NY 10020
(716) 566-1300 .. **Finnerty**, Jos M '82 (Hiscock & B,LLP) -1100 M&T Ctr -Buffalo 14203
(607) 734-0990 .. **Finnerty**, Peter F '00 Keyser M&W LLP -150 Lk -Elmira 14901
(315) 379-2225 .. **Finnerty**, Thos C Jr. '99 DA -48 Court -Canton 13617 **Fx**:379-2301
(716) 858-2424 .. **Finnerty**, Thos M '93 %DA -25 Delaware Av -Buffalo 14202 **Fx**:858-7425
(518) 473-2998 .. **Finnessey**, Saml J Jr. '01 Educ Dept OSPRA Lgl & Invstgtn Unit -89 Wshngtn Av -Albany 12234 **Fx**:402-5940
(212) 816-5730 .. **Finnigan**, Helen M '78 Salomon Smith Barney -388 Greenwich -NY 10013
(845) 359-0300 .. **Finning**, Richd C '89 -566 Route 303 -Blauvelt 10913
(718) 855-2335 .. **Finno**, Ralph B '73 (Scheinberg F&S,PC) -16 Court -Brklyn 11241
(212) 487-9700 .. **Fino**, Paul A Jr. '70 (White F&F,LLP) -61 Bway -NY 10006
(315) 697-3331 .. **Finocchiaro**, Peter M '95 -Bx90 -Canastota 13032 **Fx**:697-5287
(212) 686-0800 .. **Finocchio**, Carol R '86 -419 Park Av S -NY 10016 **Fx**:481-1285
(315) 472-8533 .. **Finocchio & English** -430 E Genesee -Syracuse 13202 **Fx**:474-8990
(585) 753-4500 .. **Finocchio**, Julie M '99 %DA -832 Watts Bldg -Rchstr 14614 **Fx**:753-4576
(315) 472-8533 .. **Finocchio**, Vincent J Jr. '75 (Finocchio & E) -430 E Genesee -Syracuse 13202
(212) 965-2200 .. **Fins**, Deborah '79 %NAACP/LDF -99 Hudson -NY 10013 **Fx**:226-7592
(212) 308-4411 .. **Finsness**, Mary H '10 %Edwards AP&D LLP -750 Lex Av -NY 10022
(212) 315-5575 .. **Finster**, Evelyn '95 %Muchnick G&G,PC -200 Park Av S -NY 10003
(212) 707-6306 .. **Finster**, Margaret C '04 Jefferies & Co,Inc -520 Mad Av -NY 10022
(914) 949-7800 .. **Finsterwald**, Lori '84 (Schillinger & F,LLP) -81 Main -White Plns 10601 **Fx**:206-3870
(315) 424-8252 .. **Fintel**, Edw J '85 (E Fintel & Assoc) -430 E Genesee -Syracuse 13202 **Fx**:424-7990
(518) 463-2259 .. **Finton**, Stewart M '81 (Ackerman W&F) -90 State -Albany 12207
(518) 756-3121 .. **Finton**, Stewart M '81 (Ackerman W&F) -Bx177 -Ravena 12143
(718) 852-2400 .. **Fintz**, Alan S '81 -26 Court -Brklyn 11242 **Fx**:852-4386
(718) 852-2400 .. **Fintz**, Bernard '52 -26 Court -Brklyn 11242 **Fx**:852-4386
(585) 586-0220 .. **Finucane & Hartzell,LLP** -6 N Main -Pittsfrd 14534 **Fx**:586-5131
(585) 586-0220 .. **Finucane**, Leo G '83 (Finucane & H,LLP) -6 N Main -Pittsfrd 14534
(212) 373-3000 .. **Finucane**, Mark T '10 %Paul WRW&G LLP -1285 Av of Amer -NY 10019
(518) 873-6351 .. **Finucane**, Wm M '82 -103 Hand Av BxD-1 -Elizabethtwn 12932 **Fx**:873-2038
(516) 433-3000 .. **Finz**, Leonard L '53 (Finz & F,PC) -410 E Jericho Tpk -Mineola 11501 **Fx**:433-3001
Finz, Michl S '77 -383 Holmes -Levittwn 11756
(516) 433-3000 .. **Finz**, Stuart L '88 (Finz & F,PC) -410 E Jericho Tpk -Mineola 11501 **Fx**:433-3001
(212) 373-3000 .. **Finzi**, Roberto '95 (Paul WRW&G LLP) -1285 Av of Amer -NY 10019
(212) 468-8000 .. **Fioccola**, David J '01 (Morrison & F LLP) -1290 Av of Amer -NY 10104
(718) 254-0700 .. **Fiol**, Juan R '92 %Bklyn Defender Srvcs -177 Lvngstn -Brklyn 11201 **Fx**:254-0897
(212) 580-1160 .. **Fioramonti**, Frank R '69 -315 W End Av -NY 10023 **Fx**:580-1160
(585) 428-4533 .. **Fioravanti**, Lori C '97 %Hon E Bellini -545 Hall of Justice -Rchstr 14614
(585) 325-2350 .. **Fioravanti**, Paul M '96 -1 E Main -Rchstr 14614 **Fx**:262-2610
(716) 831-0188 .. **Fiordaliso**, Robt A '86 (Kadish & F) -3517 Genesee -Buffalo 14225 **Fx**:831-0177
(212) 294-6700 .. **Fiore**, Alexandra L '09 %Winston & S -200 Park Av -NY 10166
(631) 273-8444 .. **Fiore**, Andrew J '91 (Collado C&F,PLLC) -14 Wshngtn Av -Brentwd 11717
(212) 285-2290 .. **Fiore**, Chas G '80 (Lewis & F) -225 Bway -NY 10007
(212) 808-3905 .. **Fiore**, Joan V '84 %Furman Selz Inc -237 Park Av -NY 10017
(516) 564-7791 .. **Fiore**, John J '98 %Sherman FS&L LLP -175 Fulton Av -Hempstd 11550
(631) 761-0800 .. **Fiore**, Louis H '99 (Lazer AR&Y,PC) -225 Old Cntry Rd -Melvll 11747
(718) 351-3000 .. **Fiore**, Marguerite A '92 (Fiore & W,PC) -623 N Railroad Av -Staten Isl 10304 **Fx**:351-6513
(212) 310-8000 .. **Fiore**, Mark J '03 %Weil G&M LLP -767 5th Av -NY 10153
(914) 764-4474 .. **Fiore**, Nick '86 -Uppr Shad Rd -Pound Rdg 10576
(518) 783-2600 .. **Fiore**, Patrick C '94 (Zappone & F) -6 Century Hill Dr -Latham 12110 **Fx**:783-2607
(212) 310-8000 .. **Fiore**, Susan L '08 %Weil G&M LLP -767 5th Av -NY 10153
(914) 964-6806 .. **Fiore**, Vincent P '95 %J Marra -909 Mdlnd Av -Ynkrs 10704 **Fx**:964-0137
(914) 249-6609 .. **Fiorella**, Abby C '89 %MasterCard Intl -2000 Purchase -Purchase 10577
(716) 882-3333 .. **Fiorella**, John C '96 %PJ Fiorella -155 Summer -Buffalo 14222 **Fx**:882-4998
(212) 953-2381 .. **Fiorella**, Kenneth S '78 (Rubin F&F,LLP) -292 Mad Av -NY 10017
(716) 882-3333 .. **Fiorella**, Peter J Jr. '65 -155 Summer -Buffalo 14222 **Fx**:882-4998
(716) 881-1800 .. **Fiorella**, Peter J III '94 (Fiorella & S,LLP) -155 Summer -Buffalo 14222 **Fx**:881-1897
(516) 826-6500 .. **Fiorelli**, Donna M '02 OfCnsl LaMonica H&M LLP -3305 Jerusalem Av -Wantagh 11793
(212) 326-0533 .. **Fiorelli**, Elizabeth A '10 Sumitomo Trust & Banking Ltd -527 Mad Av -NY 10022
(516) 794-7500 .. **Fiorello**, Carolyn Kearney '04 %Westermann SKS&A,LLP -333 Earle Ovngton Blvd -Uniondale 11553
(716) 483-7540 .. **Fiore-Nieves**, Marilyn L '89 Corp Cnsl -200 E 3rd -Jamestwn 14701
(718) 894-1109 .. **Fiorenza**, Dorothy '92 -66-64 Plsntvw -Middl Vllg 11379
(315) 435-2470 .. **Fiorenza**, Laura Ann '94 %DA -505 S State -Syracuse 13202 **Fx**:435-3969
(315) 437-7600 .. **Fiorenza**, Nicholas J '80 (Ferrara FLB&R,PC) -5010 Campuswood Dr -E Syracuse 13057
(631) 751-3094 .. **Fiore-Rosenfeld**, Steven '96 %Asemblyman S Englebright -149 Main -Setauket 11733 **Fx**:751-3082
(516) 229-6000 .. **Fioretti**, Kathleen E '91 %R Lau & Assoc -300 Jericho Quad Bx9040 -Jericho 11753 **Fx**:229-6167
(845) 486-2300 .. **Fiorile**, Richd W '86 %DA -236 Main -Poughkeepsie 12601 **Fx**:486-2324
(212) 480-4800 .. **Fiorilla di Santa Croce**, Annie Borello '99 Cnsl Fox H&C LLP -825 3rd Av -NY 10022
(212) 661-6222 .. **Fiorilla di Santa Croce**, John L '91 Triptych Holdings Inc -44 E 65th -NY 10065
(212) 661-9100 .. **Fiorillo**, Danl F '98 %Otterbourg SH&R,PC -230 Park Av -NY 10169
(516) 746-5599 .. **Fiorillo**, James N '09 %Bee RFH&D,LLP -170 Old Cntry Rd -Mineola 11501
(212) 558-4000 .. **Fiorini**, Judith R '98 SpclCnsl Sullivan & C LLP -125 Broad -NY 10004
(212) 682-6800 .. **Fiorito**, Michelle '99 Zetlin & D LLP -801 2nd Av -NY 10017
(646) 392-9250 .. **Fippinger**, Jeffrey D '97 %M Klein & Assoc -200 Mad Av -NY 10016 **Fx**:(212) 779-1499
(212) 506-5000 .. **Fippinger**, Robt A '74 (Orrick H&S LLP) -51 W 52nd -NY 10019
(212) 766-2200 .. **Fireman**, Wm D '66 OfCnsl Meiselman & G,LLP -80 Maiden Ln -NY 10038
(516) 572-1934 .. **Firenze**, Laurice '87 Cnty OHIA -40 Main -Hempstd 11550
(516) 227-2662 .. **Firestein**, Jason S '93 %Rubin & L,PC -591 Stewart Av -Gdn Cty 11530
(212) 417-4357 .. **Firestein**, Rose E '85 Dept of Health -90 Church -NY 10007 **Fx**:417-4392
(718) 522-5800 .. **Firestone**, Alan J '71 (Firestone & H) -32 Court -Brklyn 11201
(631) 543-3700 .. **Firestone**, Arnold B '60 Cnsl A Firestone,PC -612 Vets Mem'l Hwy -Hauppauge 11788 **Fx**:543-3737
(212) 541-2000 .. **Firestone**, David E '08 %Bryan C LLP -1290 Av of Amer -NY 10104
(718) 298-5455 .. **Firestone**, Eric C '95 -138-44 Qns Blvd -Jamaica 11435
(718) 522-5800 .. **Firestone & Harris** -32 Court -Brklyn 11201 **Fx**:522-1768
(212) 980-3500 .. **Firestone**, John R '86 (Pavia & H LLP) -600 Mad Av -NY 10022
(212) 931-2700 .. **Firestone**, Louise '86 SrCnsl Moet Hennessy Louis Vuitton Inc -19 E 57th -NY 10022 **Fx**:931-2729
(212) 310-8000 .. **Firestone**, Michl J '04 %Weil G&M LLP -767 5th Av -NY 10153
(212) 669-2070 .. **Firestone**, Robt J '91 %Tax Appls Tribunal -1 Centre -NY 10007 **Fx**:669-2211
(866) 931-4494 .. **Firestone**, Scott C '89 SSA-ODAR -375 Bway -Jericho 11753 **Fx**:(516) 942-0353
(718) 254-7000 .. **Firestone**, Thos A '94 %US Atty -271 Cadman Plz E -Brklyn 11201 **Fx**:254-6479
(212) 209-4800 .. **Firestone**, Zach A '10 Brown R LLP -7 Times Sq -NY 10036
(516) 845-8087 .. **Firetog**, Theo W '80 -111 Thomas Powell Blvd -Farmngdl 11735 **Fx**:845-8031
(212) 458-3775 .. **Firnau**, Gregory M '03 AIG,Inc -175 Water -NY 10038
(914) 767-6391 .. **Firooznia**, Farzin '02 Cnsl Pepsi Beverages Co -1 Pepsi Way -Somers 10589
(212) 692-1000 .. **Firriolo**, Robt P '91 (Duane M LLP) -1540 Bway -NY 10036
(212) 937-6323 .. **Firsenbaum**, Ross E '06 %WilmerHale -399 Park Av -NY 10022
(518) 465-0400 .. **First**, Dennis A '79 (O'Connor OB&F,PC) -20 Corp Wds Blvd -Albany 12211

(212) 962-6338 .. **First,** Harry '49 (First & F) -233 Bway -NY 10279 **Fx:**962-2024
(212) 998-6211 .. **First,** Harry '79 NYU Law Schl -40 Wshngtn Sq S -NY 10012
(212) 449-4264 .. **First,** Lawr A '89 Merrill Lynch -4 World Fncl Ctr -NY 10080
(212) 962-6338 .. **First,** Lee B '55 (First & F) -233 Bway -NY 10279 **Fx:**962-2024
(212) 689-0642 .. **First,** Marie-Eleana '99 -270 Mad Av -NY 10016 **Fx:**297-0527
(212) 962-6338 .. **First,** Mitchell M '83 (First & F) -233 Bway -NY 10279 **Fx:**962-2024
(212) 430-6303 .. **Firtell,** Leslie A '97 Tower Legal Staffing -65 Bway -NY 10006
(518) 455-9952 .. **Firth,** Wm C '06 %Thuillez FGB&Y,LLP -20 Corp Wds Blvd -Albany 12211
(516) 739-8000 .. **Fiscella,** James B '90 (Schrier F&S) -825 E Gate Blvd -Gdn Cty 11530
(718) 250-2000 .. **Fisch,** Alec M '09 %DA -350 Jay -Brklyn 11201 **Fx:**250-2314
(914) 478-7432 .. **Fisch,** Annette '87 -Bx85 -Hastings-On-Hud 10706
(212) 661-8900 .. **Fisch,** Jerome '51 Rosenberg & W LLP -100 Park Av -NY 10017
(212) 636-6000 .. **Fisch,** Jill E '85 %Fordham Univ Sch of Law -140 W 62nd -NY 10023 **Fx:**636-6899
(212) 752-8000 .. **Fisch,** Jordan '06 (Cole SMF&L,PA) -900 3rd Av -NY 10022
(212) 635-3150 .. **Fisch,** Jos '58 Ofc Inspector Genl -61 Bway -NY 10006 **Fx:**809-6287
(212) 889-3700 .. **Fisch,** Karin E '93 (Abbey SR&A LLP) -212 E 39th -NY 10016
(718) 694-3854 .. **Fisch,** Marla '88 %Transit Auth -130 Lvngstn -Brklyn 11201 **Fx:**694-5726
(212) 373-3000 .. **Fisch,** Peter E '90 (Paul WRW&G LLP) -1285 Av of Amer -NY 10019
(914) 668-4027 .. **Fischbach,** Robt C '97 -539 New Rochelle Rd -Mt Vernon 10552
(212) 486-3000 .. **Fischbein,** Beth W '95 %M Bodner,PC -470 Park Av S -NY 10016 **Fx:**(646) 514-0888
(212) 752-3374 .. **Fischbein,** Lewis S '76 L Fischbein,PC -6 E 39th -NY 10016 **Fx:**(914) 738-7412
(212) 346-0045 .. **Fischbein,** Michl A '99 %P Weitz & Assoc,PC -233 Bway -NY 10279 **Fx:**346-0876
(212) 784-5800 .. **Fischbein,** Richd S '71 (Hiscock & B,LLP) -7 Times Sq -NY 10036
(212) 681-4466 .. **Fischel,** Richd S '98 %NYS Comptrollers Ofc -633 3rd Av -NY 10017
(212) 512-1351 .. **Fischel,** Shelley D '78 HBO -1100 Av of Amer -NY 10036
(718) 497-6090 .. **Fischel-Wolovick,** Lisa '89 Coalition Hispanic Fam Srvcs -315 Wyckoff Av -Brklyn 11237
(212) 223-0200 .. **Fischer,** Alison L '08 %Stillman F&S,PC -425 Park Av -NY 10022
(914) 242-4900 .. **Fischer,** Allison Guthrie '98 (Casper & F,LLP) -38 Smith Av -Mt Kisco 10549 **Fx:**242-4902
(212) 451-2300 .. **Fischer,** Andrea '91 (Olshan GFR&W LLP) -65 E 55th -NY 10022
(212) 626-4100 .. **Fischer,** Anjele B '95 %Baker & M LLP -1114 Av of Amer -NY 10036
(212) 596-0580 .. **Fischer,** Annabelle '06 Levine S,LLP -130 W 42nd -NY 10036
(212) 336-2000 .. **Fischer,** Aron R '07 %Patterson BW&T LLP -1133 Av of Amer -NY 10036
(212) 840-9300 .. **Fischer,** Barry R '67 (B Fischer LLC) -550 5th Av -NY 10036 **Fx:**840-9323
(718) 225-0986 .. **Fischer,** Benjamin J '97 -213-37 39th Av -Bayside 11361
(212) 880-9585 .. **Fischer,** Benjamin S '03 %Morvillo AGIA&B,PC -565 5th Av -NY 10017
(518) 481-5000 .. **Fischer Bessette & Muldowney** -Cntry Clb Rd Bx420 -Malone 12953 **Fx:**481-5203
(212) 335-9000 .. **Fischer,** Brenda L '97 %DA -1 Hogan Pl -NY 10013
(212) 891-1600 .. **Fischer,** Brian J '03 (Jenner & B LLP) -919 3rd Av -NY 10022
(516) 829-1900 .. **Fischer & Burstein,PC** -98 Cuttermill Rd -Gt Neck 11021 **Fx:**829-5973
(718) 544-1600 .. **Fischer & Burstein,PC** -80-02 Kew Grdns Rd -Kew Gdns 11415 **Fx:**544-1658
(212) 268-7900 .. **Fischer & Burstein,PC** -888 7th Av -NY 10106 **Fx:**268-0913
(212) 416-8014 .. **Fischer,** Carol M '88 %Dept of Law -120 Bway -NY 10271
(718) 250-2000 .. **Fischer,** Cary S '00 %DA -350 Jay -Brklyn 11201 **Fx:**250-2314
(212) 439-6462 .. **Fischer,** Chas '56 -300 E 85th -NY 10028
(212) 351-4000 .. **Fischer,** Christian '07 %Gibson D&C LLP -200 Park Av -NY 10166
(212) 506-2500 .. **Fischer,** Christopher B '05 %Mayer B LLP -1675 Bway -NY 10019
(212) 973-8000 .. **Fischer,** Cynthia G '76 (Schnader HS&L LLP) -140 Bway -NY 10005
(315) 472-6676 .. **Fischer,** D Christian '94 Alario & Assoc,PC -500 S Salina -Syracuse 13202
(212) 972-1000 .. **Fischer,** Damian F '07 %London F LLP -59 Maiden Ln -NY 10038
(212) 407-4000 .. **Fischer,** David C '78 (Loeb & L,LLP) -345 Park Av -NY 10154
(516) 829-1900 .. **Fischer,** David S '06 %Fischer & B,PC -98 Cuttermill Rd -Gt Neck 11021
(516) 921-4466 .. **Fischer,** Debra Farrell '95 Amer Land Srvcs -6800 Jericho Tpk -Syosset 11791
(212) 679-2900 .. **Fischer,** Diane '07 %Hoffman & P LLP -260 Mad Av -NY 10016
(212) 770-2409 .. **Fischer,** Donna R '92 %AIG Tech Srvcs -80 Pine -NY 10005
(212) 504-6000 .. **Fischer,** Douglas H '09 %Cadwalader W&T LLP -1 World Fncl Ctr -NY 10281
(212) 637-3180 .. **Fischer,** Douglas L '91 %EPA -290 Bway -NY 10007 **Fx:**637-3096
(914) 684-6800 .. **Fischer,** Efrem Zevi '97 %Collier HNN&B,LLP -1 N Lex Av -White Plns 10601
(212) 323-2250 .. **Fischer,** Elisabeth Hirsch '05 HHC-OLA-Medical Litigation -346 Bway -NY 10013 **Fx:**323-2251
(212) 596-9000 .. **Fischer,** Erica M '08 %Ropes & G LLP -1211 Av of Amer -NY 10036
(646) 840-3397 .. **Fischer,** Eugene B '64 -18 E 48th -NY 10017
(212) 682-8383 .. **Fischer,** Gerald D '61 -51 E 42nd -NY 10017 **Fx:**949-5206
(212) 721-3700 .. **Fischer,** Harriet Z '90 -20 W 72nd -NY 10023 **Fx:**787-1475
(212) 336-0589 .. **Fischer,** Howard A '94 SEC -3 World Fncl Ctr -NY 10281 **Fx:**336-1323
(212) 338-2616 .. **Fischer,** Ivy S '83 Hub Intl NE Ltd -1065 Av of Amer -NY 10018
(631) 329-0421 .. **Fischer,** James H '92 -68 N Main -E Hampton 11937 **Fx:**329-4977
(212) 248-3140 .. **Fischer,** James M '02 %Drinker B&R LLP -140 Bway -NY 10005
(212) 545-1921 .. **Fischer,** Jay D '55 (Fischer PT&R,PC) -250 W 57th -NY 10107
(212) 480-4800 .. **Fischer,** Jennifer A '09 %Fox H&C LLP -825 3rd Av -NY 10022
(212) 506-1769 .. **Fischer,** Julie '81 Kasowitz BT&F LLP -1633 Bway -NY 10019
(607) 772-6104 .. **Fischer,** Kelly E '87 -142 Front -Bnghmtn 13905 **Fx:**772-6243
(212) 538-2589 .. **Fischer,** Lauren E '97 Credit Suisse -1 Mad Av -NY 10010
(631) 465-0044 .. **Fischer,** Leonard M '90 -48 S Srvc Rd -Melvll 11747
(212) 530-3900 .. **Fischer,** Leslie V '10 %Hannum FP&M, LLC -55 Bway -NY 10006
(212) 734-7555 .. **Fischer,** Marilyn A '75 -215 E 68th -NY 10065 **Fx:**734-7555
(212) 381-3509 .. **Fischer,** Mark D '88 %Phillips-Van Heusen Corp -200 Mad Av -NY 10016 **Fx:**381-3950
(212) 472-8662 .. **Fischer,** Martin A '64 -254 E 68th -NY 10065 **Fx:**472-8663
(212) 867-5800 .. **Fischer,** Medard T '09 %Osler H&H LLP -620 8th Av -NY 10018
(212) 393-1510 .. **Fischer,** Michl A '00 (Fischer Law Firm,PLLC) -233 Bway -NY 10279
(212) 822-9723 .. **Fischer,** Michl R '01 Ospraie Mgmt,LLC -320 Park Av -NY 10022
(212) 838-7380 .. **Fischer,** Miles P '67 %Wohabe -405 Lex Av -NY 10174 **Fx:**838-7463
(212) 515-7156 .. **Fischer,** N Alexandra '98 Dexia Global -445 Park Av -NY 10022
(646) 264-3650 .. **Fischer,** Noelle B '98 %US Dept of Labor -201 Varick -NY 10014 **Fx:**264-3660
(585) 654-9485 .. **Fischer,** Paul A '75 -127 Empire Blvd -Rchstr 14609
(212) 545-1921 .. **Fischer Porter Thomas & Reinfeld,PC** -250 W 57th -NY 10107 **Fx:**545-9102
(212) 841-2239 .. **Fischer,** Renee E '02 BNP Paribas -787 7th Av -NY 10019
(212) 883-4901 .. **Fischer,** Robt E '55 OfCnsl Cozen O -277 Park Av -NY 10172
(212) 218-2100 .. **Fischer,** Robt H '80 (Fitzpatrick CH&S) -1290 Av of Amer -NY 10104
(212) 407-4000 .. **Fischer,** Ronit V '80 SrCnsl Loeb & L,LLP -345 Park Av -NY 10154
(315) 475-0000 .. **Fischer,** Seth A '85 (Hill & F,PC) -1117 E Genesee -Syracuse 13210 **Fx:**475-8498
(516) 829-1900 .. **Fischer,** Stanley H '68 (Fischer & B,PC) -98 Cuttermill Rd -Gt Neck 11021
(212) 268-7900 .. **Fischer,** Stanley H '68 (Fischer & B,PC) -888 7th Av -NY 10106
(914) 289-1600 .. **Fischer,** Stephen F '79 -202 Mamaroneck Av -White Plns 10601
(212) 836-8000 .. **Fischer,** Thekla B '01 %Kaye S LLP -425 Park Av -NY 10022
(631) 283-9696 .. **Fischette,** Robt M '05 %Bennett & R -212 Windmill Ln -Southampton 11968
(516) 873-1511 .. **Fischetti,** Anthony M '83 (Fischetti & P) -310 Old Cntry Rd -Gdn Cty 11530
(516) 873-1511 .. **Fischetti & Pesce** -310 Old Cntry Rd -Gdn Cty 11530 **Fx:**741-7414
(212) 848-4000 .. **Fischetti,** Richd C '08 %Shearman & S LLP -599 Lex Av -NY 10022
(212) 593-7100 .. **Fischetti,** Ronald P '62 (Fischetti & M LLP) -747 3rd Av -NY 10017 **Fx:**758-2809
(212) 381-7000 .. **Fischgrund,** Stacy B '06 %Sabin B&G LLP -4 Times Sq -NY 10036
(212) 732-8700 .. **Fischkelta,** Adam J '98 %McAloon & F,PC -123 William -NY 10038
(212) 859-8000 .. **Fischkin,** Brian H '10 %Fried FHS&J LLP -1 NY Plz -NY 10004
(516) 487-6002 .. **Fischl,** Alan J '56 -10 Crk Rd -Gt Neck 11024 **Fx:**487-5327
(516) 739-6060 .. **Fischl,** Robt K '83 -100 Ring Rd W -Gdn Cty 11530 **Fx:**739-5959
(516) 374-6256 .. **Fischler,** Jaclyn A '84 -162 Hanse Av -Freeprt 11520
(212) 480-3030 .. **Fischler,** Robt H '76 -125 Maiden Ln -NY 10038 **Fx:**480-2590
(212) 596-9000 .. **Fischler,** Robt S '81 (Ropes & G LLP) -1211 Av of Amer -NY 10036
(212) 715-9100 .. **Fischman,** Charlotte M '67 (Kramer LN&F,LLP) -1177 Av of Amer -NY 10036
(212) 403-1000 .. **Fischman,** David '06 %Wachtell LR&K -51 W 52nd -NY 10019
(718) 505-9800 .. **Fischman,** David J '85 -8003 Roosevelt Av -Jcksn Hts 11372
(212) 274-0555 .. **Fischman,** Doreen J '76 (Fischman & F) -335 Bway -NY 10013 **Fx:**274-0603
(914) 725-2625 .. **Fischman,** Edw S '93 -12 Whig Rd -Scarsdale 10583
(212) 696-5252 .. **Fischman,** Harold '61 -410 E 57th -NY 10022
(212) 637-2305 .. **Fischman,** Harris M '06 %US Atty -1 St Andrews Plz -NY 10007
(212) 808-0202 .. **Fischman,** Herbert W '63 H Fischman,PC -230 Park Av -NY 10169 **Fx:**661-2153
(212) 274-0555 .. **Fischman,** Lon Paul '73 (Fischman & F) -335 Bway -NY 10013 **Fx:**274-0603
(212) 977-9700 .. **Fischman,** Michl S '89 (Phillips N LLP) -666 5th Av -NY 10103
(516) 742-4343 .. **Fischman,** Steven '93 (Scully SM&P PC) -400 Grdn City Plz -Gdn Cty 11530
(212) 735-3000 .. **Fischmann,** Kristy L '08 %Skadden ASM&F LLP -4 Times Sq -NY 10036
(516) 747-1136 .. **Fischoff,** Gary C '84 (Steinberg FB&F,PC) -40 Crsswys Park Dr -Woodbury 11797
(718) 694-3850 .. **Fischthal,** Bennett S '97 %Transit Auth -130 Lvngstn -Brklyn 11201 **Fx:**694-5726
(516) 248-2234 .. **Fiscus,** Joshua I '10 %Sackstein S&L,LLP -1140 Franklin Av -Gdn Cty 11530
(718) 645-5600 .. **Fish,** Benjamin '03 %Stein F&S LLP -1639 E 13th -Brklyn 11229
(212) 728-8000 .. **Fish,** Chantalle N R '09 %Willkie F&G LLP -787 7th Av -NY 10019
(212) 408-5100 .. **Fish,** Chas M '93 Cnsl Chadbourne & P LLP -30 Rckfllr Plz -NY 10112
(212) 448-6224 .. **Fish,** Danl G '81 (D Fish,LLC) -260 Mad Av -NY 10016 **Fx:**448-6227
(212) 340-0400 .. **Fish,** Danl J '89 %Appllt Div 1st Dept -27 Mad Av -NY 10010 **Fx:**889-4412
(212) 869-1040 .. **Fish,** David M '96 -3 Park Av -NY 10016 **Fx:**(646) 964-6538
(716) 372-3933 .. **Fish,** Donald T '61 -608 Community Bk Bldg Bx394 -Olean 14760 **Fx:**372-3934
(212) 589-4200 .. **Fish,** Eric R '09 %Baker & H LLP -45 Rckfllr Plz -NY 10111
(212) 964-5100 .. **Fish,** Gary S '89 -15 Maiden Ln -NY 10038 **Fx:**349-1887
(212) 732-8700 .. **Fish,** Ilene Rubin '95 %McAloon & F,PC -123 William -NY 10038
(607) 723-5341 .. **Fish,** John C '66 (Hinman H&K,LLP) -80 Exchange Bx5250 -Bnghmtn 13902
(212) 799-0584 .. **Fish,** Kenneth D '58 -60 Riverside Dr -NY 10024 **Fx:**799-0584
(315) 471-3151 .. **Fish,** Marion Hancock '81 (Hancock & E,LLP) -1500 AXA Twr I Bx4976 -Syracuse 13221
(212) 393-1390 .. **Fish,** Mark N '83 (M Fish & Assoc) -299 Bway -NY 10007
(631) 689-8001 .. **Fish,** Richd E '72 (Duncan F&V) -317 Middle Cntry Rd -Smithtwn 11787
(212) 765-5070 .. **Fish & Richardson,PC** -153 E 53rd -NY 10022 **Fx:**258-2291
(718) 263-5500 .. **Fish,** Sima R '01 %Ezra Academy -11945 Union Tpk -Frst Hlls 11375
(212) 752-4433 .. **Fishbach & Hertan** -767 3rd Av -NY 10017 **Fx:**593-2441
(212) 752-4433 .. **Fishbach,** Myron '65 (Fishbach & H) -767 3rd Av -NY 10017
(212) 804-4200 .. **Fishbein,** Aaron F '85 %Mound CW&G -One Bttry Pk Plz -NY 10004
(516) 791-4400 .. **Fishbein,** Adam J '94 (A Fishbein,PC) -483 Chestnut -Cedarhrst 11516 **Fx:**791-4411
(212) 233-9555 .. **Fishbein,** Harvey '73 -61 Bway -NY 10006

(518) 439-1480 .. **Fishbein,** Jonathan S '92 -35 Fairway Av Bx10 -Delmar 12054
(212) 909-6000 .. **Fishbein,** Matthew E '80 (Debevoise & P LLP) -919 3rd Av -NY 10022
(212) 836-8000 .. **Fishbein,** Peter M '59 SpclCnsl Kaye S LLP -425 Park Av -NY 10022
(516) 746-5599 .. **Fishbein,** Peter M '96 (Bee RFH&D,LLP) -170 Old Cntry Rd -Mineola 11501
(518) 598-1700 .. **Fishbein,** Richd J '04 Hanson & F -725 Bway -Albany 12207 **Fx:**449-7823
(212) 309-8100 .. **Fishbein,** Stacey B '01 Lexis Nexis -125 Park Av -NY 10017
(212) 848-4000 .. **Fishbein,** Stephen R '88 (Shearman & S LLP) -599 Lex Av -NY 10022
(516) 357-3700 .. **Fishberg,** Gerard '72 (Cullen and D LLP) -100 Q Roosevelt Blvd -Gdn Cty 11530
(212) 608-7778 .. **Fishbeyn,** Alexander '92 (Fishbeyn & B,PC) -225 Bway -NY 10007 **Fx:**608-7779
(212) 819-8200 .. **Fishburn,** C Randolph '90 (White & C LLP) -1155 Av of Amer -NY 10036
(212) 245-1000 .. **Fishel,** Allegra '87 OfCnsl Outten & G LLP -3 Park Av -NY 10016
(631) 669-0894 .. **Fishel,** Gustave III '56 -107 Cooper -Babylon 11702 **Fx:**669-0260
(718) 875-1300 .. **Fishel,** Shannon K '08 Appllt Div 2nd Dept -45 Monroe Pl -Brklyn 11201 **Fx:**858-2446
(212) 248-9100 .. **Fisher,** Alexander D '04 %Epstein M&M -1 Whitehall -NY 10004
(212) 872-9800 .. **Fisher,** Andrea K '93 Squire S&D LLP -30 Rckfllr Plz -NY 10112
(212) 514-8888 .. **Fisher,** Andrew S '66 (Fisher & F) -New Dorp Station Bx61060 -Staten Isl 10306 **Fx:**514-9016
(212) 558-4000 .. **Fisher,** Ann Bailen '77 (Sullivan & C LLP) -125 Broad -NY 10004
(516) 336-2005 .. **Fisher,** Arthur S '89 (Abrams GMB,LLP) -2-12 W Park Av -Long Bch 11561
(516) 280-5065 .. **Fisher,** Barry J '83 -600 Old Cntry Rd -Gdn Cty 11530
(518) 473-9521 .. **Fisher,** Barry J '97 %Capital Defender Ofc -Corning Twr Bx2113 -Albany 12220 **Fx:**473-9438
(212) 541-2000 .. **Fisher,** Bartley F '72 (Bryan C LLP) -1290 Av of Amer -NY 10104
(914) 285-8500 .. **Fisher,** Bonnie L '74 %TK Moore -701 Wstchstr Av -White Plns 10604 **Fx:**285-8510
(516) 228-0033 .. **Fisher,** Chas J Jr. '96 (Pollack C&F,PC) -5372 Merrick Rd -Massapequa 11758 **Fx:**797-1227
(518) 474-3219 .. **Fisher,** Cheryl B '90 %NYSHESC -99 Wshngtn Av -Albany 12255 **Fx:**486-6515
(716) 856-3500 .. **Fisher,** Cheryl Smith '77 (Magavern MG LLP) -1100 Rand Bldg -Buffalo 14203
(914) 761-1300 .. **Fisher,** Christopher B '95 (Cuddy & F LLP) -445 Hmltn Av -White Plns 10601
(212) 784-6400 .. **Fisher,** Clinton B '84 (Hanly CBSF&H LLP) -112 Mad Av -NY 10016
(212) 965-2328 .. **Fisher,** Craig A '96 Capital Z Mgmt -230 Park Av S -NY 10003 **Fx:**343-5128
(212) 344-0606 .. **Fisher,** Cynthia D '92 -40 Rector -NY 10006
(212) 872-1000 .. **Fisher,** Danl H '06 -One Bryant Park -NY 10036 **Fx:**872-1002
(212) 541-2000 .. **Fisher,** David E '97 (Bryan C LLP) -1290 Av of Amer -NY 10104
(212) 715-9100 .. **Fisher,** David J '85 (Kramer LN&F,LLP) -1177 Av of Amer -NY 10036
(212) 468-4800 .. **Fisher,** David J '07 %Davis & G LLP -1740 Bway -NY 10019
(212) 709-8261 .. **Fisher,** David N '06 (Fisher & B,PLLC) -110 Wall -NY 10005 **Fx:**943-2300
(212) 925-6286 .. **Fisher,** Deanna '90 -401 Bway -NY 10013
(518) 456-7200 .. **Fisher,** Douglas M '87 %Solomon & S,PC -5 Columbia Cir Bx15019 -Albany 12212
(212) 818-1110 .. **Fisher,** Eric B '96 (Butzel L,PC) -380 Mad Av -NY 10017
(212) 489-1600 .. **Fisher,** Eric H '77 %Deloitte LLP -1633 Bway -NY 10019 **Fx:**492-4201
(516) 676-4600 .. **Fisher,** Eric M '05 %Humes & W -147 Forest Av Bx546 -Locust Vly 11560
(718) 286-6000 .. **Fisher,** Erin M '06 %DA -125-01 Qns Blvd -Kew Gdns 11415
(212) 593-1400 .. **Fisher Fallon PC** -30 Vesey -NY 10007 **Fx:**753-4776
(212) 872-1500 .. **Fisher,** Felicia K '96 %Lacher & L-T -460 Park Av -NY 10022
(631) 204-0073 .. **Fisher,** Fred '82 -135 Straight Path -Southampton 11968 **Fx:**204-0343
(212) 317-5095 .. **Fisher,** Gerald F '70 %Swiss Re New Markets -55 E 52nd -NY 10055
(212) 732-8700 .. **Fisher,** Gillian Anne '96 (McAloon & F,PC) -123 William -NY 10038
(212) 458-5688 .. **Fisher,** Helene S '94 %AIG -175 Water -NY 10038
(212) 396-9292 .. **Fisher,** Herbert F '59 -23 E 73rd -NY 10021
(212) 521-1622 .. **Fisher,** Irene '91 Big Flower Holdings -345 Park Av -NY 10154 **Fx:**521-1640
(845) 338-1120 .. **Fisher,** James H '62 -261 Fair Bx3069 -Kingston 12402 **Fx:**338-2554
(212) 572-7298 .. **Fisher,** James R '86 Vivendi Universal -800 3rd Av -NY 10022
(212) 225-2000 .. **Fisher,** Janet '85 (Cleary GS&H) -1 Lbrty Plz -NY 10006
(212) 609-1856 .. **Fisher,** Jennifer K '03 Partners in Care -1250 Bway -NY 10001
(212) 969-3000 .. **Fisher,** Jessica P '10 %Proskauer R LLP -1585 Bway -NY 10036
(212) 719-5930 .. **Fisher,** John C '74 (Hamburger W&F) -36 W 44th -NY 10036
(845) 331-9434 .. **Fisher,** John H '92 Mainetti M&O,PC -303 Clinton Av Bx3058 -Kingston 12402
(212) 759-1200 .. **Fisher,** Jonathan B '91 -444 Mad Av -NY 10022
(516) 222-4544 .. **Fisher,** Jos A '84 -585 Stewart Av -Gdn Cty 11530 **Fx:**222-0583
(212) 980-9600 .. **Fisher,** Judith M '94 (Kaufman B&R) -120 Bway -NY 10271
(212) 607-8630 .. **Fisher,** Julie B '98 US Dept of Labor -33 Whitehall -NY 10004
(212) 331-5041 .. **Fisher,** Kahlia E '97 HRA Ofc Legal Affrs -180 Water -NY 10038
(212) 883-4962 .. **Fisher,** Kenneth K '77 (Cozen O) -277 Park Av -NY 10172 **Fx:**672-1162
(212) 367-1051 .. **Fisher,** Kevin A '85 AVAC -101 W 23rd -NY 10011
(212) 226-5700 .. **Fisher,** Lawr M '89 -350 Bway -NY 10013 **Fx:**226-3224
(845) 338-1120 .. **Fisher,** Lisa Marie '94 %J Fisher,PC -261 Fair Bx3069 -Kingston 12402 **Fx:**338-2554
(212) 425-9300 .. **Fisher,** Logan S '10 %Bressler A&R,PC -17 State -NY 10004
(585) 454-4060 .. **Fisher,** Lynda J '01 %Empire Justice Ctr -1 W Main -Rchstr 14614 **Fx:**454-4019
(212) 836-8000 .. **Fisher,** Lynn Toby '74 (Kaye S LLP) -425 Park Av -NY 10022
(718) 286-6000 .. **Fisher,** Marjory D '84 %DA -125-01 Qns Blvd -Kew Gdns 11415
(845) 343-2444 .. **Fisher,** Mark A '75 (M Fisher,PLLC) -41 Dolson Av -Middletwn 10940 **Fx:**343-0233
(212) 940-8877 .. **Fisher,** Mark I '67 (Katten MR LLP) -575 Mad Av -NY 10022
(212) 858-3600 .. **Fisher,** Mark J '80 %Reliance Ins -75 Broad -NY 10004
(212) 587-9802 .. **Fisher,** Martin C '75 -63 E 9th -NY 10003 **Fx:**587-9803
(914) 762-3081 .. **Fisher,** Martin L '74 -5 Ganung Dr -Ossining 10562
(585) 232-5300 .. **Fisher,** Mary V '80 OfCnsl Boylan BCV&W,LLP -2400 Chase Sq -Rchstr 14604
(212) 713-2412 .. **Fisher,** Maryann S '04 UBS -1285 Av of Amer -NY 10019
(212) 558-4000 .. **Fisher,** Melissa F '06 %Sullivan & C LLP -125 Broad -NY 10004
(212) 478-0875 .. **Fisher,** Michelle S '95 DE Shaw & Co -120 W 45th -NY 10036 **Fx:**478-0100
(212) 720-5003 .. **Fisher,** Peter R '86 %Fed Reserve Bk -33 Lbrty -NY 10045 **Fx:**720-8892
(212) 903-9000 .. **Fisher,** Raymond J '91 (Linklaters) -1345 Av of Amer -NY 10105
(212) 619-5000 .. **Fisher,** Robt G Jr. '84 %EDC -110 William -NY 10038 **Fx:**312-3912
(212) 940-8800 .. **Fisher,** Robt I '64 (Katten MR LLP) -575 Mad Av -NY 10022
(212) 803-5100 .. **Fisher,** Robt J '82 %NY Cnty Defender Srvcs -225 Bway -NY 10007 **Fx:**571-6035
(845) 339-2289 .. **Fisher,** Robt J '96 -261 Fair -Kingston 12401 **Fx:**338-3126
(212) 226-5700 .. **Fisher,** Robt M '49 -350 Bway -NY 10013 **Fx:**226-3224
(718) 487-2300 .. **Fisher,** Robyn D '89 %Leg Srvcs Corp -256-260 Bway -Brklyn 11211 **Fx:**782-6790
(212) 395-2121 .. **Fisher,** Saul '69 %Verizon -140 West -NY 10007
(716) 852-8020 .. **Fisher,** Scot D '94 -341 Delaware Av -Buffalo 14202
(516) 746-8000 .. **Fisher,** Scott B '91 (Jaspan S LLP) -300 Grdn City Plz -Gdn Cty 11530
(212) 504-6000 .. **Fisher,** Scott D '00 %Cadwalader W&T LLP -1 World Fncl Ctr -NY 10281
(516) 829-0363 .. **Fisher,** Scott H '95 %Israel I&P,LLP -11 Grace Av -Gt Neck 11021 **Fx:**829-0366
(212) 398-0055 .. **Fisher,** Scott W '83 (Garwin G&F,LLP) -1501 Bway -NY 10036
(212) 788-1083 .. **Fisher,** Spencer A '87 %Law Dept -100 Church -NY 10007 **Fx:**788-0367
(212) 248-0800 .. **Fisher,** Stephan A '04 %Martinez & R,PC -67 Wall -NY 10005
(212) 758-6022 .. **Fisher,** Stuart B '71 Tourneau Inc -3 E 54th -NY 10022 **Fx:**758-3375
(212) 683-4224 .. **Fisher,** Timothy P '74 (T Fisher,PC) -10 E 40th -NY 10016 **Fx:**683-2184
(212) 340-0658 .. **Fisher,** Tina A '92 %Counsel Press,LLC -520 8th Av -NY 10018 **Fx:**213-6574
(212) 272-4011 .. **Fisher,** Victoria Austin '03 %JP Morgan Chase -383 Mad Av -NY 10179
(212) 458-3498 .. **Fisher,** Zachary W '94 AIGTS -175 Water -NY 10038
(917) 763-3266 .. **Fishkin,** Alexander '92 -366 Amstrdm Av -NY 10024
(212) 308-4411 .. **Fishkin,** Andrew P '88 (Edwards AP&D LLP) -750 Lex Av -NY 10022
(212) 977-9700 .. **Fishkin,** Barry H '66 (Phillips N LLP) -666 5th Av -NY 10103
(516) 437-6095 .. **Fishkin,** Brian '76 -1055 Franklin Av -Gdn Cty 11530
(631) 952-6505 .. **Fishkin,** Craig M '87 %UIA Bd -NYS Ofc Bldg -Hauppauge 11788 **Fx:**952-3385
(212) 687-3860 .. **Fishkin,** David R '94 (Snow BK,PC) -605 3rd Av -NY 10158
(516) 826-6325 .. **Fishkin,** Howard '66 -2619 Phyllis Dr -N Bellmore 11710
(212) 619-2859 .. **Fishkin,** Ilya '07 %Gell & G -299 Bway -NY 10007 **Fx:**964-9485
(877) 222-1814 .. **Fishkin,** Robt A '90 %B Rothenberg -100 Duffy Av -Hicksvll 11801 **Fx:**(866) 894-2182
(516) 766-0088 .. **Fishkind,** Robt B '55 -111 N Vllg Av -Rockvll Ctr 11570
(212) 906-1200 .. **Fishkoff,** Andrew R '06 %Latham & W -885 3rd Av -NY 10022
(212) 506-1700 .. **Fishkoff,** Lauren Charme '05 %Kasowitz BT&F LLP -1633 Bway -NY 10019
(718) 983-9400 .. **Fishler,** Robt M '86 (Gaines & F LLP) -2555 Richmond Av -Staten Isl 10314 **Fx:**494-4192
(212) 736-8000 .. **Fishlin,** Lewis H '69 (Fishlin & F,PLLC) -7 Penn Plz -NY 10001 **Fx:**202-4720
(212) 736-8000 .. **Fishlin,** Todd A '10 (Fishlin & F,PLLC) -7 Penn Plz -NY 10001 **Fx:**202-4720
(516) 542-5900 .. **Fishlinger,** Wm J '88 (Congdon FORDT&F) -333 Earle Ovngton Blvd -Uniondale 11553
(646) 495-7347 .. **Fishman,** Andrew M '76 Horizon Asset Mgmt Inc -470 Park Av S -NY 10016 **Fx:**495-7354
(212) 922-9191 .. **Fishman,** Bernard H '58 -230 Park Av -NY 10169 **Fx:**599-1759
(212) 335-9000 .. **Fishman,** Charlotte Eugénie '05 %DA -1 Hogan Pl -NY 10013
(212) 474-1000 .. **Fishman,** David L '08 %Cravath S&M LLP -825 8th Av -NY 10019
(212) 697-3122 .. **Fishman,** Ellen B '79 (Martin C&B LLP) -220 E 42nd -NY 10017
(212) 478-7200 .. **Fishman,** Emily M '07 %Hahn & H LLP -488 Mad Av -NY 10022
(212) 513-3200 .. **Fishman,** Eric '77 (Holland & K LLP) -31 W 52nd -NY 10019
(212) 858-1000 .. **Fishman,** Eric '94 (Pillsbury WSP LLP) -1540 Bway -NY 10036
(212) 421-4100 .. **Fishman,** Eric M '06 %Pryor C LLP -7 Times Sq -NY 10036
(212) 335-9000 .. **Fishman,** Gary T '96 %DA -1 Hogan Pl -NY 10013
(212) 261-1863 .. **Fishman,** Gregg R '90 -888 7th Av -NY 10106 **Fx:**(646) 349-1455
(212) 797-4362 .. **Fishman,** Howard K '87 %Rafter & Assoc,PLLC -29 Bway -NY 10006 **Fx:**797-4363
(212) 897-5840 .. **Fishman,** James B '80 (Fishman & N) -305 Bway -NY 10007 **Fx:**897-5841
(914) 422-4222 .. **Fishman,** James J '69 %Pace Law Schl -78 N Bway -White Plns 10603 **Fx:**422-4039
(212) 558-4000 .. **Fishman,** Jared M '06 %Sullivan & C LLP -125 Broad -NY 10004
(212) 599-3700 .. **Fishman,** Jeffrey '84 RKF -521 5th Av -NY 10175
(516) 379-9806 .. **Fishman,** John '81 (Fishman & T) -2174 Hewlett Av -Merrick 11566
(212) 341-7900 .. **Fishman,** Jordana L '05 %Brecher FPWT&Z,PC -233 Bway -NY 10279
(212) 869-0085 .. **Fishman,** Joshua E '77 %A Fishman & Son -580 5th Av -NY 10036 **Fx:**302-2548
(212) 479-6173 .. **Fishman,** Lauren R '06 Cooley LLP -1114 Av of Amer -NY 10036
(914) 524-5600 .. **Fishman,** Lori D '91 -303 S Bway -Tarrytwn 10591 **Fx:**524-5742
(212) 277-4000 .. **Fishman,** Marshall H '81 (Freshfields BD LLP) -520 Mad Av -NY 10022
(212) 719-5734 .. **Fishman,** Martin '70 %Northwestern Mutual Life Ins -245 Park Av -NY 10167 **Fx:**819-9716
(201) 933-9015 .. **Fishman,** Martin S '77 -5 Sunderland Pl -Suffern 10901 **Fx:**933-9018
(212) 461-7190 .. **Fishman McIntyre, PC** -44 Wall -NY 10005 **Fx:**(845) 369-0673
(516) 746-1982 .. **Fishman,** Michl L '74 -194 Old Cntry Rd -Mineola 11501

(516) 280-4600 .. **Fishman,** Michl N '03 (Monteiro & F LLP) -91 N Franklin -Hempstd 11550 **Fx:**280-4530
(212) 323-8309 .. **Fishman,** Renée M '01 Credix Inc -875 3rd Av -NY 10022
(212) 373-3000 .. **Fishman,** Robt A '09 %Paul WRW&G LLP -1285 Av of Amer -NY 10019
(516) 742-3636 .. **Fishman,** Robt J '64 (Brecher FPWT&Z,PC) -1325 Franklin Av -Gdn Cty 11530
(212) 341-7900 .. **Fishman,** Robt J '64 (Brecher FPWT&Z,PC) -233 Bway -NY 10279
(212) 616-1566 .. **Fishman,** Ronald A '86 (Danzig F&D) -360 Lex Av -NY 10017
(718) 403-3617 .. **Fishman,** Saul T '82 Dept of Finance -345 Adams -Brklyn 11201 **Fx:**403-3650
(212) 259-8000 .. **Fishman,** Scot H '04 Dewey & L LLP -1301 Av of Amer -NY 10019
(212) 461-7190 .. **Fishman,** Stanley P '81 (Fishman M,PC) -44 Wall -NY 10005
(212) 969-3000 .. **Fishman,** Steven A '77 SrCnsl Proskauer R LLP -1585 Bway -NY 10036
(212) 648-0359 .. **Fishman,** Stuart D '84 JP Morgan Chase -245 Park Av -NY 10167
(212) 610-6300 .. **Fishman,** Todd S '96 (Allen & O) -1221 Av of Amer -NY 10020
(516) 379-9806 .. **Fishman & Tynan** -2174 Hewlett Av -Merrick 11566
(212) 608-5487 .. **Fishman,** Yehuda M '86 -2109 Bway -NY 10023
(212) 244-4630 .. **Fishman,** Zachary M '09 %Katz & M,PC -1350 Av of Amer -NY 10019 **Fx:**(646) 219-5717
(212) 872-3873 .. **Fishner,** Steven M '79 KPMG LLP -345 Park Av -NY 10154
(585) 425-3219 .. **Fisk,** John R '68 -7 Sheffiled Post -Fairprt 14450 **Fx:**425-1764
(212) 450-4000 .. **Fiske,** Robt B Jr. '56 (Davis P&W LLP) -450 Lex Av -NY 10017
(718) 898-0088 .. **Fiss,** Deborah G '82 -37-06 82nd -Jcksn Hts 11372 **Fx:**898-9843
(718) 793-6400 .. **Fistel,** Andrew S '93 -118-35 Qns Blvd -Frst Hlls 11375
(212) 335-9000 .. **Fistel,** Michl K '90 %DA -1 Hogan Pl -NY 10013
(212) 264-3650 .. **Fiszer,** Karen G '92 %SSA Ofc Genl Cnsl -26 Fed Plz -NY 10278 **Fx:**264-6372
(516) 357-3000 .. **Fitapelli,** Carlie '04 %Rivkin R LLP -926 RXR Plz -Uniondale 11556
(212) 300-0375 .. **Fitapelli,** Jos A '02 (Fitapelli & S,LLP) -1250 Bway -NY 10001 **Fx:**564-5468
(212) 613-2169 .. **Fitapelli,** Marc D '08 %Gibbons PC -1 Penn Plz -NY 10119 **Fx:**554-9693
(716) 856-4000 .. **Fitch,** Amy J '97 (Hodgson R LLP) -140 Pearl -Buffalo 14202
(585) 258-2800 .. **Fitch,** David H '98 SrCnsl Underberg & K LLP -300 Bausch & Lomb Pl -Rchstr 14604
(212) 374-9115 .. **Fitch,** Joshua P '05 (Cohen & F LLP) -225 Bway -NY 10007 **Fx:**406-6890
(585) 546-2960 .. **Fitch,** Julian M '49 -19 W Main -Rchstr 14614
(212) 323-7070 .. **Fitch,** Robt A '74 (Rawle & H LLP) -14 Wall -NY 10005
(716) 855-3200 .. **Fitch,** Thos P '94 %Zdarsky S&A -298 Main -Buffalo 14202
(212) 858-1000 .. **Fitch,** Valerie L '89 Pillsbury WSP LLP -1540 Bway -NY 10036
(212) 586-4700 .. **Fitelson Lasky Aslan & Couture** -551 5th Av -NY 10176 **Fx:**949-6746
(716) 845-8682 .. **Fitt,** Benjamin J '81 Atty Gen -Elm & Carlton -Buffalo 14263 **Fx:**845-8792
(631) 689-6770 .. **Fitterman,** Perri Carol '83 -39 Old Coach Rd -E Setauket 11733 **Fx:**689-6821
(914) 428-6306 .. **Fitton,** John P '85 -21 Burling Av -White Plns 10605
(212) 841-3966 .. **Fitton,** Pamela J '85 BNP Paribas -787 7th Av -NY 10019
(607) 753-3036 .. **Fitts,** Calvert A '73 Fitts & F -24 Clinton Av Bx826 -Cortlnd 13045 **Fx:**753-3036
(212) 403-1000 .. **Fitts,** Nelson O '01 (Wachtell LR&K) -51 W 52nd -NY 10019
(212) 909-6251 .. **Fitts,** Sarah Anne Watkins '91 (Debevoise & P LLP) -919 3rd Av -NY 10022
(212) 318-2000 .. **Fitz,** Andrea '00 Bloomberg LP -731 Lex Av -NY 10022
(518) 471-4805 .. **Fitz,** Paula P '87 %Appllt Div 3rd Dept -Capitol Station Bx7288 -Albany 12224 **Fx:**471-4750
(212) 446-2300 .. **Fitzdam,** Justin D '06 %Boies S&F LLP -575 Lex Av -NY 10022
(315) 446-1162 .. **Fitzer,** Donald N '57 -211 Eden Roc Cir -Syracuse 13214
(718) 237-2000 .. **Fitzer,** Katherine Barton '95 %Leg Aid -111 Lvngstn -Brklyn 11201 **Fx:**237-8737
(914) 378-1010 .. **Fitzgerald,** Annette M '71 (Fitzgerald & F) -538 Riverdale Av -Ynkrs 10705
(212) 696-6000 .. **Fitzgerald,** Anthony W '62 OfCnsl Curtis M-PC&M LLP -101 Park Av -NY 10178
(914) 995-3420 .. **Fitzgerald,** Brian F '07 %DA -111 Martin Luther King Blvd -White Plns 10601 **Fx:**995-3363
(516) 227-0800 .. **Fitzgerald,** Brian J '00 Cnsl Natl Land Tenure Co LLC -1122 Franklin Av -Gdn Cty 11530 **Fx:**227-1160
(716) 852-2000 .. **Fitzgerald,** Brian P '75 (B Fitzgerald,PC) -509 Lbrty Bldg -Buffalo 14202 **Fx:**852-2002
(631) 439-4200 .. **Fitzgerald,** Brian T '88 %R Tusa -898 Vets Mem'l Hwy -Hauppauge 11788 **Fx:**439-4292
(518) 626-9000 .. **FitzGerald,** Brian T '91 (Dewey & L LLP) -99 Wshngtn Av -Albany 12210
(516) 742-3636 .. **Fitzgerald,** Catherine M '09 %Brecher FPWT&Z,PC -1325 Franklin Av -Gdn Cty 11530
(212) 837-6000 .. **Fitzgerald,** Christine M '01 %Hughes H&R LLP -1 Bttry Pk Plz -NY 10004
(212) 425-1900 .. **Fitzgerald,** Danl J '01 %Freehill H&M LLP -80 Pine -NY 10005
(516) 571-3323 .. **Fitzgerald,** David J '99 %Health Dept -240 Old Cntry Rd -Mineola 11501
(914) 923-8499 .. **Fitzgerald,** Dennis M '75 (Chadbourne OTW&F) -Bx701 -Sleepy Hollow 10591
(212) 450-4000 .. **FitzGerald,** Edmond T '92 (Davis P&W LLP) -450 Lex Av -NY 10017
(914) 378-1010 .. **Fitzgerald & Fitzgerald** -538 Riverdale Av -Ynkrs 10705 **Fx:**378-1092
(212) 906-1200 .. **Fitzgerald,** Ian P '05 %Latham & W -885 3rd Av -NY 10022
(631) 852-2500 .. **Fitzgerald,** Ian T '05 %DA -200 Center Dr -Rvrhead 11901 **Fx:**852-1769
(716) 434-9131 .. **Fitzgerald,** J Michl '73 (Pusateri & F,LLP) -135 Main Bx850 -Lockprt 14095
(212) 903-2800 .. **Fitzgerald,** James E '02 Clarium Capital Mgmt LLC -1114 Av of Amer -NY 10036
(914) 378-1010 .. **Fitzgerald,** John E '70 (Fitzgerald & F) -538 Riverdale Av -Ynkrs 10705
(518) 792-1174 .. **Fitzgerald,** John E Jr. '86 (McPhillips F&C,LLP) -288 Glen Bx299 -Glens Fls 12801
(212) 644-0214 .. **Fitzgerald,** John S '00 -110 E 59th -NY 10022
(585) 263-1000 .. **Fitzgerald,** John T Jr. '73 (Nixon P LLP) -1100 Clinton Sq -Rchstr 14604
(212) 837-2300 .. **Fitzgerald,** John T '01 JP Morgan Asset Mgmt -522 5th Av -NY 10036
(631) 666-6200 .. **Fitzgerald,** Jos F '96 %PF Adams,PC -49 5th Av Bx1089M -Bay Shr 11706 **Fx:**665-6739
(607) 723-5341 .. **Fitzgerald,** Katherine A '81 (Hinman H&K,LLP) -80 Exchange Bx5250 -Bnghmtn 13902
(914) 995-3356 .. **Fitzgerald,** Katherine S '95 %DA -111 Martin Luther King Blvd -White Plns 10601 **Fx:**995-3363
(631) 501-3100 .. **Fitzgerald,** Kathleen T '92 %J Humphreys -3 Huntngtn Quad Bx9028 -Melvll 11747 **Fx:**501-3085
(585) 753-4500 .. **Fitzgerald,** Kevin D '07 DA -832 Watts Bldg -Rchstr 14614 **Fx:**753-4576
(631) 360-7272 .. **Fitzgerald,** Kevin J '87 -186 W Main -Smithtwn 11787
(914) 347-2600 .. **Fitzgerald,** Lisa Marie '08 %Traub LS&S LLP -7 Skyline Dr -Hawthorne 10532
(212) 336-0069 .. **Fitzgerald,** Lucas M '02 SEC -3 World Fncl Ctr -NY 10281 **Fx:**336-1323
(716) 847-3449 .. **Fitzgerald,** M Lynn '90 %PERB -535 Wshngtn -Buffalo 14203 **Fx:**847-3690
(212) 558-4000 .. **Fitzgerald,** Maureen A '07 %Sullivan & C LLP -125 Broad -NY 10004
(516) 826-6500 .. **FitzGerald,** Melanie A '91 %LaMonica H&M LLP -3305 Jerusalem Av -Wantagh 11793
(718) 273-7900 .. **Fitzgerald,** Michl D '02 %Sgarlato & S,PLLC -1444 Clove Rd -Staten Isl 10301 **Fx:**273-9629
(212) 687-1230 .. **Fitzgerald,** Michl F '67 Cnsl Farrell F,PC -370 Lex Av -NY 10017
(212) 939-7281 .. **Fitzgerald,** Michl F '84 -410 Park Av -NY 10022
(716) 885-3500 .. **Fitzgerald,** Michl J '69 -329 Elmwood Av -Buffalo 14222 **Fx:**885-3505
(212) 530-5000 .. **Fitzgerald,** Michl L '80 (Milbank TH&M LLP) -1 Chase Manh Plz -NY 10005
(212) 788-3672 .. **Fitzgerald,** Moira E '07 Cnsl Hlth & Hsptl Corp -125 Worth -NY 10013 **Fx:**267-6905
(518) 745-1400 .. **FitzGerald Morris Baker Firth** -16 Pearl Bx2017 -Glens Fls 12801 **Fx:**745-1576
(800) 828-7763 .. **Fitzgerald,** Nicholas '84 (Fitzgerald & Assoc) -41 Mad Av -NY 10010 **Fx:**(212) 385-1916
(212) 819-0555 .. **Fitzgerald,** Nicole C '08 %Parmet & G,LLC -60 E 42nd -NY 10165 **Fx:**840-2288
(518) 462-0300 .. **Fitzgerald,** Patrick J III '01 (Girvin & F,PC) -20 Corp Wds Blvd -Albany 12211
(212) 384-3138 .. **Fitzgerald,** Peter D '96 FBI -26 Fed Plz -NY 10278 **Fx:**384-2177
(212) 615-2200 .. **Fitzgerald,** Raymond L '73 (Butler FF&M,PC) -36 W 44th -NY 10036
(914) 686-1640 .. **Fitzgerald,** Robt A '87 R Fitzgerald,PC -Bx498 -White Plns 10602 **Fx:**670-0829
(716) 856-1010 .. **Fitzgerald,** Sean A '91 S Collesano,LLC -69 Delaware Av -Buffalo 14202
(516) 365-1919 .. **Fitzgerald,** Shawn P '86 -205 Circle Dr -Manhsst 11030
(212) 286-8585 .. **Fitzgerald,** Sheree L '06 %Heidell PM&B,LLP -99 Park Av -NY 10016
(212) 455-2000 .. **Fitzgerald,** Steven S '04 %Simpson T&B LLP -425 Lex Av -NY 10017
(631) 751-4300 .. **Fitzgerald,** Susan M '99 Stafford Capital -1 Romeo Dr -Smithtwn 11787
(914) 253-8600 .. **FitzGerald,** Thos A '67 (Fair F&H,PC) -110 Corp Park Dr -White Plns 10604
(516) 229-6000 .. **FitzGerald,** Thos J '72 %R Lau & Assoc -300 Jericho Quad Bx9040 -Jericho 11753 **Fx:**229-6167
(212) 850-6220 .. **Fitzgerald,** Thos J '05 %Lathrop & G LC -230 Park Av -NY 10169
(585) 295-4400 .. **FitzGerald,** Thos R '73 (Hiscock & B,LLP) -2000 HSBC Plz -Rchstr 14604
(585) 362-4700 .. **Fitzgerald,** Timothy M '94 (Bond S&K,PLLC) -350 Linden Oaks -Rchstr 14625
(315) 798-5766 .. **Fitzgerald,** Timothy P '75 %DA -800 Park Av -Utica 13501 **Fx:**798-5582
(212) 447-1222 .. **Fitzgerald,** Wm A '84 %DeCicco G&M,PC -14 E 38th -NY 10016
(518) 792-1174 .. **Fitzgerald,** Wm E '75 (McPhillips F&C,LLP) -288 Glen Bx299 -Glens Fls 12801
Fitzgerald, Wm P '00 -Bx283 -Farmngvll 11738
(516) 542-1000 .. **Fitzgibbon,** Elizabeth Ann '93 (Geisler & G,LLP) -100 Q Roosevelt Blvd -Gdn Cty 11530
(212) 944-5104 .. **Fitzhenry,** David S '06 %MC Bielesz -500 5th Av -NY 10110 **Fx:**944-8720
(212) 848-4000 .. **Fitzmaurice,** Kristen M '02 %Shearman & S LLP -599 Lex Av -NY 10022
(914) 437-9057 .. **Fitzmaurice,** Mark J '92 (Fitzmaurice & W,LLP) -15 Chester Av -White Plns 10601
(212) 768-6700 .. **Fitzmaurice,** Patrick E '02 %Sonnenschein N&R LLP -1221 Av of Amer -NY 10020
(516) 542-1000 .. **Fitzmaurice,** Stacy '92 (Geisler & G,LLP) -100 Q Roosevelt Blvd -Gdn Cty 11530
(212) 335-9000 .. **Fitzmaurice,** Theresa A '03 %DA -1 Hogan Pl -NY 10013
(914) 741-6100 .. **Fitzmorris,** Douglas J '85 (Kaufman B&R) -200 Summit Lk Dr -Valhalla 10595
(315) 638-0089 .. **Fitzmorris,** E Lynne '75 -3658 Doyle Rd -Baldwinsvll 13027
(212) 468-4800 .. **Fitzpatrick,** Allison '02 %Davis & G LLP -1740 Bway -NY 10019
(516) 294-5433 .. **Fitzpatrick,** Brendan T '96 (Ahmuty D&M) -200 IU Willets Rd -Albertson 11507
(212) 681-1575 .. **Fitzpatrick,** Brian T '87 OfCnsl Belluck & F LLP -546 5th Av -NY 10036
(212) 649-2059 .. **Fitzpatrick,** Bridgette '92 %Hearst Corp -300 W 57th -NY 10019 **Fx:**649-2035
(212) 218-2100 .. **Fitzpatrick Cella Harper & Scinto** -1290 Av of Amer -NY 10104 **Fx:**218-2200
(212) 907-9700 .. **FitzPatrick,** Christopher G '77 Cnsl Smith G&R,LLP -250 Park Av -NY 10177
(718) 442-4600 .. **Fitzpatrick,** Christopher J '95 (Jacobi SBP&F,PC) -235 Forest Av -Staten Isl 10301
(914) 315-6618 .. **Fitzpatrick,** Christopher M '97 -746 Mamaroneck Av -Mamaroneck 10543

(914) 225-5554 .. **Fitzpatrick,** Danl J '86 Morgan Stanley -2000 Wstchstr Av -Purchase 10577
(631) 755-0101 .. **Fitzpatrick,** Elizabeth A '91 Cnsl Lewis JAA,LLP -425 Broad Hollow Rd -Melvll 11747
(212) 937-4000 .. **Fitzpatrick,** Garrett J '74 (Fitzpatrick & HTCPA,LLP) -12 E 49th -NY 10017
(212) 937-4000 .. **Fitzpatrick & Hunt Tucker Collier Pagano Aubert, LLP** -12 E 49th -NY 10017 **Fx:**937-4050
(212) 259-8000 .. **FitzPatrick,** James A Jr. '75 (Dewey & L LLP) -1301 Av of Amer -NY 10019
(212) 837-6000 .. **Fitzpatrick,** James C '97 (Hughes H&R LLP) -1 Bttry Pk Plz -NY 10004
(516) 229-4501 .. **Fitzpatrick,** James E '98 %Russo A&T -875 Merrick Av -Westbury 11590
(212) 435-3571 .. **Fitzpatrick,** John B '75 %Port Auth of NY/NJ -225 Park Av S -NY 10003 **Fx:**435-3555
(516) 671-4900 .. **Fitzpatrick,** John G '93 %First Natl Bk of LI -10 Glen Head Rd -Glen Head 11545 **Fx:**671-4918
(212) 218-2100 .. **Fitzpatrick,** Jos M '55 OfCnsl Fitzpatrick CH&S -1290 Av of Amer -NY 10104
(212) 230-8800 .. **Fitzpatrick,** Kate M '06 %WilmerHale -399 Park Av -NY 10022
(212) 859-8000 .. **Fitzpatrick,** Kathleen R '10 %Fried FHS&J LLP -1 NY Plz -NY 10004
(212) 421-2800 .. **Fitzpatrick,** Kelly A '10 %Lanier Law Firm,PLLC -126 E 56th -NY 10022 **Fx:**421-2878
(516) 747-8000 .. **Fitzpatrick,** Kevin P '93 (Marschhausen & F,PC) -835 Old Cntry Rd -Westbury 11590 **Fx:**747-6439
(914) 946-1400 .. **Fitzpatrick,** Kevin P '93 %Vouté LM&C,LLP -170 Hmltn Av -White Plns 10601
(212) 596-9000 .. **FitzPatrick,** Laurel '91 (Ropes & G LLP) -1211 Av of Amer -NY 10036
(914) 632-9300 .. **Fitzpatrick,** Margaret M '83 (McGovern C&D) -145 Huguenot -New Rchll 10801
(212) 213-5577 .. **Fitzpatrick,** Mary W '01 %Litman & J -1133 Bway -NY 10010
(646) 562-3405 .. **Fitzpatrick,** Melanie Arad '01 %PLC -747 3rd Av -NY 10017
(212) 858-5167 .. **Fitzpatrick,** Michl '08 FINRA -1 Lbrty Plz -NY 10006
(212) 259-8000 .. **Fitzpatrick,** Michl F Jr. '91 (Dewey & L LLP) -1301 Av of Amer -NY 10019
(212) 962-1020 .. **Fitzpatrick,** Michl J '98 %M Lamonsoff -80 Maiden Ln -NY 10038 **Fx:**962-3078
(212) 657-3971 .. **Fitzpatrick,** Patricia A '89 Citigroup Global Mrkts Inc -77 Water -NY 10005
(212) 480-4200 .. **Fitzpatrick,** Paul J '92 Nausch Hogan & Murray -180 Maiden Ln -NY 10038
(212) 484-3900 .. **Fitzpatrick,** Peter J '85 (Arent F LLP) -1675 Bway -NY 10019
(718) 273-2233 .. **Fitzpatrick,** Philip J '62 (P Fitzpatrick,PC) -1 Edgewtr -Staten Isl 10305 **Fx:**273-0874
(718) 273-2233 .. **Fitzpatrick,** Philip J IV '89 -1 Edgewtr -Staten Isl 10305 **Fx:**273-0874
(845) 331-9434 .. **Fitzpatrick,** Regina A '00 %Mainetti M&O,PC -303 Clinton Av Bx3058 -Kingston 12402
(212) 909-6000 .. **Fitzpatrick,** Robt K '07 %Debevoise & P LLP -919 3rd Av -NY 10022
(607) 337-1545 .. **Fitzpatrick,** Sarah C '97 Dept of Social Srvcs -5 Court Bx590 -Norwich 13815 **Fx:**334-8768
(212) 596-9000 .. **Fitzpatrick,** Simon A '03 %Ropes & G LLP -1211 Av of Amer -NY 10036
(631) 751-5173 .. **Fitzpatrick,** Susan '92 -5 Brookvw Ct -Stony Brk 11790 **Fx:**751-5173
(518) 452-1961 .. **Fitzpatrick,** Susan A '03 %Burke & C,PC -255 Washington Av Ext -Albany 12205
(212) 930-1290 .. **Fitzpatrick,** Thos '66 -500 5th Av -NY 10110 **Fx:**730-9690
(212) 530-5000 .. **Fitzpatrick,** Timothy D '09 %Milbank TH&M LLP -1 Chase Manh Plz -NY 10005
(212) 819-8200 .. **FitzPatrick,** Vincent R Jr. '70 (White & C LLP) -1155 Av of Amer -NY 10036
(212) 224-1555 .. **Fitzpatrick,** Vincent R III '03 Mutual of America -320 Park Av -NY 10022
(516) 294-3500 .. **Fitzpatrick,** Ward W '87 Fitpatrick & F -238 Mineola Blvd -Mineola 11501 **Fx:**294-8711
(315) 435-2470 .. **Fitzpatrick,** Wm J '77 (DA) -505 S State -Syracuse 13202 **Fx:**435-3969
(516) 281-9800 .. **Fitzpatrick,** Wm J '83 (Goldberg S LLP) -200 Old Cntry Rd -Mineola 11501
(212) 223-4000 .. **Fitzrandolph,** Caitlin D '08 %Crowell & M LLP -590 Mad Av -NY 10022
(716) 856-4000 .. **Fitzsimmons,** Carol A '88 (Hodgson R LLP) -140 Pearl -Buffalo 14202
(607) 535-8932 .. **Fitzsimmons,** Danl J '96 (Fitzsimmons Law Firm) -221 N Franklin -Watkins Glen 14891 **Fx:**535-5403
(585) 546-5270 .. **Fitzsimmons,** James B '61 (Fitzsimmons NF&P,LLP) -16 E Main -Rchstr 14614
(212) 759-3300 .. **Fitzsimmons,** James Cody '92 (Dornbush SS&V,LLP) -747 3rd Av -NY 10017
(631) 751-0806 .. **Fitzsimmons,** James J '67 -2 Blueberry Rdg Rd -E Setauket 11733
(585) 546-5270 .. **Fitzsimmons,** John B '91 (Fitzsimmons NF&P,LLP) -16 E Main -Rchstr 14614
(212) 373-3000 .. **Fitzsimmons,** Meagan L '08 %Paul WRW&G LLP -1285 Av of Amer -NY 10019
(585) 546-5270 .. **Fitzsimmons Nunn Fitzsimmons & Plukas,LLP** -16 E Main -Rchstr 14614 **Fx:**546-8129
(212) 596-9000 .. **Fitzsimmons,** Patrick E '10 %Ropes & G LLP -1211 Av of Amer -NY 10036
(518) 758-2333 .. **Fitzsimmons,** Robt J '99 (Fitzsimmons & M,PC) -3223 Church Bx310 -Valatie 12184 **Fx:**758-2330
(914) 949-2700 .. **Fitzsimmons,** Sally '86 OfCnsl Bleakley P&S,LLP -1 N Lex Av -White Plns 10601
(518) 884-4753 .. **Fitzsimmons,** Susan Marie '88 %County Court -30 McMaster -Ballston Spa 12020
(212) 841-3293 .. **Fitzsimons,** Eileen P '06 BNP Paribas -787 7th Av -NY 10019
(212) 465-8840 .. **Fitzsimons,** James G '80 Cnsl Hofmann & S -360 W 31st -NY 10001 **Fx:**465-8849
(212) 661-4600 .. **Fitzsimons,** John '74 %Dyson-Kissner-Moran -565 5th Av -NY 10017 **Fx:**599-5105
(212) 269-0927 .. **FitzSimons,** John H '84 (D'Amato & L,LLP) -2 World Fncl Ctr -NY 10281
(212) 557-7700 .. **Fitzsimons,** Louise M '91 OfCnsl Davidson D&C LLP -60 E 42nd -NY 10165
(212) 333-0200 .. **Fitzwater,** Elizabeth A '03 %Arkin KR LLP -590 Mad Av -NY 10022
(212) 558-4000 .. **Fitzwater,** Matthew S '02 %Sullivan & C LLP -125 Broad -NY 10004
(212) 506-1700 .. **Fiumano,** Karen L '03 Kasowitz BT&F LLP -1633 Bway -NY 10019
(585) 419-8800 .. **Fiumara,** Anthony '99 %Harris B PLLC -99 Garnsey Rd -Pittsfrd 14534
(347) 296-1680 .. **Fiumara,** John G '90 %Supreme Ct Law Dept -360 Adams -Brklyn 11201 **Fx:**643-6114
(212) 474-1000 .. **Fiumara,** Raffael M '10 %Cravath S&M LLP -825 8th Av -NY 10019
(212) 615-2200 .. **Fiveson,** David K '78 (Butler FF&M,PC) -36 W 44th -NY 10036
(315) 343-8287 .. **Fix,** Robt H '91 Fix Law Firm -157 W Brdg Bx336 -Oswego 13126 **Fx:**343-9513
(585) 641-8000 .. **Fix Spindelman Brovitz & Goldman,PC** -295 Woodcliff Dr -Fairprt 14450 **Fx:**641-8080
(585) 232-5756 .. **Fix,** Stephanie A '97 %Comm Judicial Cndct -400 Andrews -Rchstr 14604 **Fx:**232-7834
(718) 382-5454 .. **Fixler,** Eli S '97 -1507 Av M -Brklyn 11230 **Fx:**732-4542
(914) 418-9004 .. **Fixler,** Elliot H '71 Fixler & Assoc,LLP -530 Saw Mill Rvr Rd -Elmsfrd 10523 **Fx:**418-9003
(212) 297-2670 .. **Fixler,** Herbert B '69 (Cozen O) -277 Park Av -NY 10172 **Fx:**672-1180
(212) 785-9800 .. **Fixler,** Jason L '99 (Fixler & L) -61 Bway -NY 10006
(212) 785-9800 .. **Fixler & LaGattuta** -61 Bway -NY 10006
(914) 824-5070 .. **Fixler-Fuchs,** Fredda S '96 %Atty Grievance Comm -399 Knollwood Rd -White Plns 10603 **Fx:**949-0997
(718) 967-5131 .. **Fizzarotti,** Ronald V '88 -1441 Arden Av -Staten Isl 10312
(585) 546-6448 .. **Fjermedal,** Glenn M '90 (Davidson F LLP) -28 E Main -Rchstr 14614
(212) 269-3444 .. **Flach,** Eleanor N '77 (Capriano L&F,LLP) -80 Wall -NY 10005
(212) 545-4632 .. **Flachner,** Mitchell J '00 %Wolf HAF&H LLP -270 Mad Av -NY 10016
(718) 237-3100 .. **Flad,** Kiera K '09 Leg Aid -111 Lvngstn -Brklyn 11201 **Fx:**250-4243
(212) 732-3200 .. **Flägel,** Peter G '00 Cnsl Carter L&M LLP -2 Wall -NY 10005
(845) 454-9460 .. **Flagello,** Genoveffa '80 %MHLS -One Civic Ctr Plz -Poughkeepsie 12601 **Fx:**471-9308
(212) 816-8335 .. **Flagg,** Edw R '01 Citigroup Global Mrkts -388 Greenwich -NY 10013
(716) 856-5500 .. **Flaherty,** Amy Archer '92 (Damon M LLP) -200 Delaware Av -Buffalo 14202
(516) 294-9076 .. **Flaherty,** B Frank '59 -109 Wickham Rd -Gdn Cty 11530
(716) 652-9600 .. **Flaherty,** Carol A '89 (DiFilippo & F) -382 Main -E Aurora 14052
(914) 636-7100 .. **Flaherty,** Dennis M '74 (Novick & K) -56 Harrison -New Rchll 10801
(212) 681-0600 .. **Flaherty,** Dennis M '85 (Ostrager CF&B,PC) -570 Lex Av -NY 10022
(646) 610-5400 .. **Flaherty,** Eileen G '02 NYPD -1 Police Plz -NY 10038
(845) 626-3540 .. **Flaherty,** Jeremiah M '78 -6123 Route 209 -Kerhonkson 12446 **Fx:**626-3611
(212) 455-2000 .. **Flaherty,** Joan E '10 %Simpson T&B LLP -425 Lex Av -NY 10017
(212) 609-6800 .. **Flaherty,** John E '89 (McCarter & E,LLP) -245 Park Av -NY 10167
(212) 688-5151 .. **Flaherty,** John F '62 (Gibney A&F,LLP) -665 5th Av -NY 10022
(716) 204-0301 .. **Flaherty,** John J '86 -5500 Main -Williamsvll 14221
(516) 542-5900 .. **Flaherty,** John P '73 (Congdon FORDT&F) -333 Earle Ovngton Blvd -Uniondale 11553
(607) 273-2283 .. **Flaherty,** Krin '04 %Prisoners' Leg Srvcs -114 Prospect -Ithaca 14850 **Fx:**272-9122
(212) 541-2000 .. **Flaherty,** Kyle P '95 (Bryan C LLP) -1290 Av of Amer -NY 10104
(212) 715-9100 .. **Flaherty,** Mary B '99 %Kramer LN&F,LLP -1177 Av of Amer -NY 10036
(716) 885-3500 .. **Flaherty,** Michl J '65 (Flaherty & S) -329 Elmwood Av -Buffalo 14222 **Fx:**885-3505
(716) 885-3500 .. **Flaherty,** Michl J Jr. '91 %Flaherty & S -329 Elmwood Av -Buffalo 14222 **Fx:**885-3505
(212) 885-5000 .. **Flaherty,** Pamela E '80 (Blank R LLP) -405 Lex Av -NY 10174
(518) 485-2312 .. **Flaherty,** Patricia '97 OASAS -1450 Wstrn Av -Albany 12203 **Fx:**485-2335
(516) 352-3187 .. **Flaherty,** Rita A '88 -1031 N 2nd -New Hyde Pk 11040
(518) 459-1819 .. **Flaherty,** Shawn D '82 -21 Everett Rd Ext -Albany 12205 **Fx:**459-1827
(212) 841-1000 .. **Flahive Wu,** Laura M '09 %Covington & B LLP -620 8th Av -NY 10018
(914) 428-1438 .. **Flake,** Michl A '03 %T Bona,PC -123 Main -White Plns 10601 **Fx:**428-1413
(212) 967-8500 .. **Flaks,** Michl '82 (Ross LRZ&F,LLP) -450 7th Av -NY 10123
(516) 328-3500 .. **Flamen,** Stuart M '97 (McDonnell & A,PC) -401 Franklin Av -Gdn Cty 11530
(212) 416-6376 .. **Flamenbaum,** Hannah K '74 %Dept of Law -120 Bway -NY 10271
(718) 334-1856 .. **Flamenbaum,** Israel '86 %MHLS -79-01 Bway -Elmhrst 11373 **Fx:**334-2353
(917) 821-0936 .. **Flamenbaum,** Judith A '96 -219 E 72nd -NY 10021
(212) 318-3000 .. **Flamenbaum,** Michl '92 (Fulbright & J LLP) -666 5th Av -NY 10103
(646) 365-3419 .. **Flamenbaum,** Miles J '94 Soms Technologies LLC -6 Hissarlik Way -Bedfrd 10506
(212) 773-2421 .. **Flament,** Benjamin F '09 Ernst & Young LLP -5 Times Sq -NY 10036
(212) 586-5570 .. **Flamhaft,** Jonathan P '93 -310 W 47th -NY 10036 **Fx:**586-0808
(718) 237-1900 .. **Flamhaft Levy Hirsch & Rendeiro** -16 Court -Brklyn 11241 **Fx:**624-5626
(516) 248-5522 .. **Flamhaft Levy Hirsch & Rendeiro** -170 Old Cntry Rd -Mineola 11501 **Fx:**742-4105
(718) 237-1900 .. **Flamhaft,** Stephen '66 (Flamhaft LH&R) -16 Court -Brklyn 11241
(212) 752-3380 .. **Flamm,** Leonard N '70 -880 3rd Av -NY 10022 **Fx:**755-1670
(718) 797-3117 .. **Flamm,** Matthew S '88 -26 Court -Brklyn 11242 **Fx:**522-2026
(646) 471-4643 .. **Flamm,** Rachel Phillips '03 %PricewaterhouseCoopers LLP -300 Mad Av -NY 10017
(516) 466-7900 .. **Flanagan,** Andrew J '10 %Kiley K&K,PLLC -107 Nrthrn Blvd -Gt Neck 11021
(585) 263-1000 .. **Flanagan,** Brian G '83 (Nixon P LLP) -1100 Clinton Sq -Rchstr 14604
(518) 785-4431 .. **Flanagan,** Chas F '67 -17 Spring Street Rd -Loudonvll 12211

(607) 763-9200 .. **Flanagan,** Donald M '57 OfCnsl Levene G&T,LLP -BxF-1706 -Bnghmtn 13902
(212) 790-9200 .. **Flanagan,** Eugene L III '76 (Cowan L&L,PC) -1133 Av of Amer -NY 10036
(631) 283-0046 .. **Flanagan,** Gilbert G '79 (Bourke F&A PC) -21 S Main -Southampton 11968
(516) 302-5647 .. **Flanagan,** James R '87 -19 Park Av -Manhsst 11030 **Fx:**365-6922
(516) 248-1700 .. **Flanagan,** John J '91 Cnsl Forchelli CDSM&T,LLP -333 Earle Ovngton Blvd -Uniondale 11553
(212) 318-6000 .. **Flanagan,** John P '04 %Paul HJ&W LLP -75 E 55th -NY 10022
(212) 394-4745 .. **Flanagan,** Julia A '01 %PricewaterhouseCoopers LLP -300 Mad Av -NY 10017 **Fx:**(813) 375-7474
(718) 990-7612 .. **Flanagan,** Leslie G '08 St John's Law Schl -8000 Utopia Pkwy -Jamaica 11439 **Fx:**591-1855
(212) 570-0854 .. **Flanagan,** Linda C '95 -1100 Mad Av -NY 10028
(516) 931-1800 .. **Flanagan,** Matthew K '93 (Catalano G&P LLP) -100 Jericho Quadrangle -Jericho 11753
(716) 856-4000 .. **Flanagan,** Michl J '06 %Hodgson R LLP -140 Pearl -Buffalo 14202
(607) 334-9323 .. **Flanagan,** Patrick J '94 (Nelson & F) -42 S Broad -Norwich 13815
(212) 530-5000 .. **Flanagan,** Patrick J '99 (Milbank TH&M LLP) -1 Chase Manh Plz -NY 10005
(212) 578-8683 .. **Flanagan,** Peter J '90 %MetLife -27-01 Qns Plz N -LIC 11101 **Fx:**578-3916
(212) 626-4100 .. **Flanagan,** Pia D '97 (Baker & M LLP) -1114 Av of Amer -NY 10036
(212) 637-3136 .. **Flanagan,** Sarah P '92 %EPA -290 Bway -NY 10007 **Fx:**637-3096
(212) 808-7800 .. **Flanagan,** Sean R '03 %Kelley D&W LLP -101 Park Av -NY 10178
(631) 396-0150 .. **Flanagan,** Susan A '81 -80 Orvll Dr -Bohemia 11716 **Fx:**979-8119
(631) 864-5575 .. **Flanagan,** Suzanne C '94 (Kelly G&F,LLP) -901A Motor Pkwy -Hauppauge 11788
(212) 278-7608 .. **Flanagan,** Tara E '00 SG Cowen Securities -1221 Av of Amer -NY 10020
(516) 357-3700 .. **Flanagan,** Timothy J '79 (Cullen and D LLP) -100 Q Roosevelt Blvd -Gdn Cty 11530
(212) 885-8427 .. **Flanagan,** Vincent J '01 BDO USA,LLP -330 Mad Av -NY 10017 **Fx:**697-1299
(631) 578-1888 .. **Flanary,** Walker G III '90 (Margolis & F,LLP) -41 Natcon Dr -Shirley 11967 **Fx:**410-1937
(212) 858-1000 .. **Flanders,** Edw '89 (Pillsbury WSP LLP) -1540 Bway -NY 10036
(212) 883-4915 .. **Flanders,** Martha J '77 (Cozen O) -277 Park Av -NY 10172 **Fx:**672-1115
(212) 573-8040 .. **Flanders,** Steven M '92 Seeds of Peace -370 Lex Av -NY 10017 **Fx:**573-8047
(212) 218-2100 .. **Flanders,** Susanne L '10 %Fitzpatrick CH&S -1290 Av of Amer -NY 10104
(212) 684-0199 .. **Flanigan,** Danl J '04 (Polsinelli S PC) -7 Penn Plz -NY 10001
(212) 309-6000 .. **Flannery,** Anne C '77 (Morgan L&B LLP) -101 Park Av -NY 10178
(212) 449-1263 .. **Flannery,** Francis X '65 %Merrill Lynch -220 Bway -NY 10038
(716) 856-5500 .. **Flannery,** Jennifer G '07 %Damon M LLP -200 Delaware Av -Buffalo 14202
(212) 490-3000 .. **Flannery,** John M '92 (Wilson EME&D LLP) -150 E 42nd -NY 10017
(914) 323-7000 .. **Flannery,** John M '92 (Wilson EME&D LLP) -3 Gannett Dr -White Plns 10604
(716) 842-5855 .. **Flannery,** John M '99 %M&T Bk -1 M & T Plz -Buffalo 14203 **Fx:**842-5376
(914) 220-0038 .. **Flannery,** Martin J Jr. '82 (Pattison & F) -1 N Lex Av -White Plns 10601
(212) 261-8000 .. **Flannery,** Robt M '84 (Mendes & M,LLP) -750 7th Av -NY 10019
(212) 578-2211 .. **Flannery,** Susan Nanovic '95 %MetLife -27-01 Qns Plz N -LIC 11101
(585) 238-2000 .. **Flansburg,** Chad W '03 %Phillips L LLP -1400 First Fed Plz -Rchstr 14614
(518) 474-8211 .. **Flansburg,** Kelli J '93 %Law Reporting Bur -1 Commerce Plz -Albany 12210 **Fx:**463-6869
(516) 741-8222 .. **Flanzig,** Cathy Sue '87 (Flanzig & F LLP) -323 Willis Av Bx669 -Mineola 11501 **Fx:**741-8889
(516) 741-8222 .. **Flanzig,** Danl '95 (Flanzig & F LLP) -323 Willis Av Bx669 -Mineola 11501 **Fx:**741-8889
(716) 566-5400 .. **Flascher,** Troy S '01 %Goldberg S LLP -665 Main -Buffalo 14203
(607) 273-4200 .. **Flash,** Elena Salerno '85 (Miller M,LLP) -202 E State -Ithaca 14850
(212) 947-7650 .. **Flashner,** Barrish K '70 -450 7th Av -NY 10123 **Fx:**695-6090
(212) 302-6868 .. **Flaster,** Alan S '76 (Flaster & W,PC) -36 W 44th -NY 10036
(212) 349-6000 .. **Flaster,** Robt A '81 (R Flaster,PC) -225 Bway -NY 10007 **Fx:**349-1146
(212) 302-6868 .. **Flaster & Willis,PC** -36 W 44th -NY 10036 **Fx:**944-6883
(212) 274-6716 .. **Flateau,** Gabrielle M '03 Admin Children's Srvcs -220 Church -NY 10013
(212) 840-6050 .. **Flateman,** Bernard I '88 (B Flateman,LLC) -500 5th Av -NY 10110 **Fx:**840-2345
(516) 365-2240 .. **Flaton,** Bernard '66 -36 Maple Pl -Manhsst 11030
(516) 365-2240 .. **Flaton,** Lloyd '88 B Flaton -36 Maple Pl -Manhsst 11030
(516) 365-2240 .. **Flaton,** Robin A '87 %B Flaton -36 Maple Pl -Manhsst 11030
(212) 687-1600 .. **Flatow,** Jay M '83 (Lurie & F PC) -420 Lex Av -NY 10170
(212) 297-5800 .. **Flatt,** Kelly E P '00 Cnsl Day P LLP -7 Times Sq -NY 10036
(718) 544-2767 .. **Flatt,** Saml D '99 -147-26 Hillside Av -Jamaica 11435 **Fx:**544-4590
(212) 290-4700 .. **Flattau,** Isaac H '03 Human Rights Watch -350 5th Av -NY 10118 **Fx:**736-1300
(212) 254-9692 .. **Flattau,** John W '66 -714 Bway -NY 10003
(212) 593-6700 .. **Flattery,** Benjamin P '04 %Aaronson RF&D,LLP -757 3rd Av -NY 10017
(212) 446-4800 .. **Flattmann,** Gerald J Jr. '93 (Kirkland & E LLP) -153 E 53rd -NY 10022
(718) 262-7100 .. **Flatts,** Barbara A '84 Civil Ct -89-17 Sutphin Blvd -Jamaica 11435 **Fx:**262-7107
(212) 859-8000 .. **Flaum,** Douglas H '87 (Fried FHS&J LLP) -1 NY Plz -NY 10004
(212) 509-7400 .. **Flaum,** Neil R '76 N Flaum,PC -369 Lex Av -NY 10017 **Fx:**509-0740
(631) 750-2638 .. **Flaumenhaft,** Steven P '96 -93 Main -W Sayvll 11796 **Fx:**750-2639
(212) 723-3878 .. **Flaute,** Jon E '01 Citigroup Global Mrkts -250 West -NY 10013
(877) 230-1031 .. **Flavin,** Marie C '94 Invstmnt Proprty Exchng Srvcs -245 Main -White Plns 10601 **Fx:**(888) 310-1868
(212) 248-2200 .. **Flavin,** Mark C '78 -67 Wall -NY 10005
(212) 724-6263 .. **Flax,** Robt H '78 -70 Riverside Dr -NY 10024
(212) 907-7300 .. **Flaxer,** Jonathan L '80 (Golenbock EAB&P) -437 Mad Av -NY 10022
(212) 356-0936 .. **Flaxman,** David '64 Rosenthal & Rosenthal, Inc -1370 Bway -NY 10018 **Fx:**356-0989
(631) 273-1212 .. **Flaxman,** Stephen A '67 -330 Motor Pkwy -Hauppauge 11788
(914) 422-6265 .. **Flecha,** Danl R '08 %DA -77 S Lex Av -White Plns 10601
(516) 742-5200 .. **Fleck,** Edw A '83 %Fleck F&F -1205 Franklin Av -Gdn Cty 11530 **Fx:**248-1085
(212) 530-5000 .. **Fleck,** Evan R '02 (Milbank TH&M LLP) -1 Chase Manh Plz -NY 10005
(212) 373-3000 .. **Fleck,** Leah C '08 %Paul WRW&G LLP -1285 Av of Amer -NY 10019
(516) 742-5200 .. **Fleck,** Patricia A '86 %Fleck F&F -1205 Franklin Av -Gdn Cty 11530 **Fx:**248-1085
(516) 742-5200 .. **Fleck,** Raymond A Jr. '71 (Fleck F&F) -1205 Franklin Av -Gdn Cty 11530 **Fx:**248-1085
(315) 475-3012 .. **Fleckenstein,** James '78 -1 S State -Syracuse 13202 **Fx:**475-4225
(516) 496-5822 .. **Flecker,** Anthony A '07 %T Spina -170 Froehlich Farm Blvd -Woodbury 11797 **Fx:**496-5420
(212) 683-3800 .. **Fleckner,** Steven M '97 %Dinkes & S,PC -112 Mad Av -NY 10016
(212) 373-3000 .. **Fleder,** Robt C '77 (Paul WRW&G LLP) -1285 Av of Amer -NY 10019
(212) 755-5510 .. **Fleenor,** Shane M '07 %Loeb B & Prtnrs -505 Park Av -NY 10022
(212) 554-7800 .. **Fleesler,** Gregory J '97 (Moses & S LLP) -405 Lex Av -NY 10174
(914) 235-1555 .. **Fleischer,** Arnold D '68 -246 Coligni Av -New Rchll 10801
(212) 859-8000 .. **Fleischer,** Arthur Jr. '59 (Fried FHS&J LLP) -1 NY Plz -NY 10004
(631) 361-5360 .. **Fleischer,** Craig J '02 (Keahon FD&F) -1393 Vets Mem'l Hwy -Hauppauge 11788 **Fx:**361-5365
(212) 659-7300 .. **Fleischer,** David '73 (Haynes & B,LLP) -1221 Av of Amer -NY 10020
(516) 571-3800 .. **Fleischer,** Ilisa T '91 DA -262 Old Cntry Rd -Mineola 11501 **Fx:**248-9479
(914) 417-1715 .. **Fleischer,** L Melissa '84 HR Learning Ctr -222 Purchase -Rye 10580 **Fx:**417-1715
(212) 966-5897 .. **Fleischer,** Lawr M '77 OfCnsl Gotlin & J -100 Lafayette -NY 10013 **Fx:**941-9183
(518) 473-1707 .. **Fleischer,** Mark D '95 %Dept of Health -Corning Twr 24th Fl -Albany 12237 **Fx:**486-1858
(516) 747-8830 .. **Fleischer,** Matthew L '99 %Jaghab & J -176 Mineola Blvd -Mineola 11501 **Fx:**747-8770
(212) 272-6249 .. **Fleischer,** Michl A '97 %JP Morgan Chase -383 Mad Av -NY 10179
(518) 436-2900 .. **Fleischer,** Michl R '07 Thruway Auth -200 Southrn Blvd Bx189 -Albany 12201 **Fx:**471-4340
(212) 421-4100 .. **Fleischer,** Robt M '93 OfCnsl Pryor C LLP -7 Times Sq -NY 10036
(212) 407-7700 .. **Fleischman,** Brandon J '10 %Vedder P,PC -1633 Bway -NY 10019
(212) 906-1200 .. **Fleischman,** Dana G '90 (Latham & W) -885 3rd Av -NY 10022
(212) 903-9000 .. **Fleischman,** Edw H '59 SrCnsl Linklaters -1345 Av of Amer -NY 10105
(212) 570-0602 .. **Fleischman,** Gail R '85 -333 E 79th -NY 10075
(718) 894-4111 .. **Fleischman,** Gerald M '75 -75-30 Metro Av -Middl Vllg 11379 **Fx:**894-2444
(212) 298-5097 .. **Fleischman,** Golda M '05 %Leg Aid -49 Thomas -NY 10013 **Fx:**298-5252
(516) 883-8792 .. **Fleischman,** Grace S '81 -8 Seagull Ln -Pt Wash 11050 **Fx:**883-3774
(516) 867-3100 .. **Fleischman,** Herman I '77 -1758 Bedford Av -Merrick 11566 **Fx:**867-3255
(516) 829-3449 .. **Fleischman,** Howard S '65 -60 Cuttermill Rd -Gt Neck 11021
(212) 785-1136 .. **Fleischman,** Jay S '95 (Fleischman Law,PC) -315 Flatbush Av -Brklyn 11217 **Fx:**785-1137
(516) 747-0300 .. **Fleischman,** Jeffrey A '94 OfCnsl Meltzer LG&B,LLP -190 Willis Av -Mineola 11501
(516) 432-4911 .. **Fleischman,** Jerome B '57 -20 W Park Av -Long Bch 11561 **Fx:**889-1619
(646) 722-8500 .. **Fleischman,** Keith M '85 (Grant & E,PA) -485 Lex Av -NY 10017
(212) 512-1000 .. **Fleischman,** Lisa '89 HBO -1100 Av of Amer -NY 10036 **Fx:**512-1986
(212) 973-0572 .. **Fleischman,** Michl D '10 %Wolff & S PC -140 Bway -NY 10005
(212) 725-2800 .. **Fleischman,** Peter N '90 -205 E 22nd -NY 10010 **Fx:**725-6823
(516) 432-5023 .. **Fleischman,** Robt P '86 -241 W Olive -Long Bch 11561 **Fx:**889-1619
(212) 541-2000 .. **Fleischmann,** Dennis C '76 (Bryan C LLP) -1290 Av of Amer -NY 10104
(646) 657-9623 .. **Fleischmann,** Jeffrey '08 -347 5th Av -NY 10016 **Fx:**351-0694
(212) 416-8802 .. **Fleischmann,** Lisa '93 %Dept of Law -120 Bway -NY 10271
(212) 343-8353 .. **Fleischmann,** Stefanie C '02 Bicent Power LLC -575 Bway -NY 10012
(212) 848-7527 .. **Fleischmann,** Stuart K '83 (Shearman & S LLP) -599 Lex Av -NY 10022
(212) 487-9700 .. **Fleischner,** Benjamin A '79 (White F&F,LLP) -61 Bway -NY 10006
(212) 307-5500 .. **Fleischner,** Laura Reiter '09 %Venable LLP -1270 Av of Amer -NY 10020
(212) 362-6945 .. **Fleischner,** Robin A '81 -11 Riverside Dr -NY 10023
(516) 869-2511 .. **Fleishaker,** Aaron J '88 Kimco Rlty Corp -3333 New Hyde Pk Rd -New Hyde Pk 11042
(212) 686-6611 .. **Fleishaker,** Donald J '52 -120 E 37th -NY 10016 **Fx:**683-7007
(212) 972-1355 .. **Fleishell,** Thos S '81 T Fleishell & Assoc PC -561 7th Av -NY 10018 **Fx:**972-1356
(212) 225-2000 .. **Fleisher,** Adam E '01 (Cleary GS&H) -1 Lbrty Plz -NY 10006
(914) 946-6300 .. **Fleisher,** David M '80 (D Fleisher,PC) -399 Knollwood Rd -White Plns 10603 **Fx:**428-7164
(212) 595-0595 .. **Fleisher,** Marc '80 -98 Riverside Dr -NY 10024 **Fx:**595-0760
(212) 767-7307 .. **Fleisher,** Martin E '85 -880 3rd Av -NY 10022 **Fx:**504-8256
(212) 508-6100 .. **Fleishman,** Craig B '03 %Bracewell & G,LLP -1251 Av of Amer -NY 10020
(212) 695-8100 .. **Fleishman,** Michl R '87 (Goetz F,LLP) -1 Penn Plz -NY 10119
(212) 216-8000 .. **Fleishman,** Rachel S '93 OfCnsl Tarter K&D LLP -1350 Bway -NY 10018
(718) 520-3238 .. **Fleishman,** Randi L '86 %Hon R Hanophy -125-01 Qns Blvd -Kew Gdns 11415
(212) 564-6900 .. **Fleishman,** Sheldon '86 -352 7th Av -NY 10001

(212) 355-9500 .. **Fleishman,** Wendy R '92 (Lieff CH&B,LLP) -250 Hudson -NY 10013
(718) 263-7763 .. **Fleisig,** Vina M '93 -67-69 Groton -Frst Hlls 11375 **Fx:**793-2937
(212) 259-8000 .. **Fleiss,** Michl E '89 Cnsl Dewey & L LLP -1301 Av of Amer -NY 10019
(212) 717-2900 .. **Fleissig,** David A '92 (Dontzin Law Firm) -6 E 81st -NY 10028 **Fx:**717-8088
(212) 319-1000 .. **Fleissig,** Liza R '95 (Quirk & B,PC) -845 3rd Av -NY 10022
(716) 648-3030 .. **Fleming,** Andrew P '86 (Chiacchia & F,LLP) -5113 S Park Av -Hambrg 14075
(718) 237-5500 .. **Fleming,** Anne C '06 %Leg Srvcs -105 Court -Brklyn 11201 **Fx:**855-0733
(212) 351-4000 .. **Fleming,** Brendon S '10 Gibson D&C LLP -200 Park Av -NY 10166
(212) 751-4300 .. **Fleming,** Cathy '80 (Hodgson R LLP) -1540 Bway -NY 10036
(212) 643-9668 .. **Fleming,** Danl C '99 (Wong F,PC) -350 5th Av -NY 10118
(212) 506-1700 .. **Fleming,** Danl J '05 Kasowitz BT&F LLP -1633 Bway -NY 10019
(212) 697-9660 .. **Fleming,** David E '81 Cnsl Warren Resources,Inc -1114 Av of Amer -NY 10036 **Fx:**697-9466
(646) 502-7196 .. **Fleming,** David E '98 Cnsl Omni NY LLC -885 2nd Av -NY 10017
(212) 735-3000 .. **Fleming,** Douglas E III '95 Cnsl Skadden ASM&F LLP -4 Times Sq -NY 10036
(716) 816-3743 .. **Fleming,** Eileen S '95 Buffalo Bd of Ed -65 Niagara -Buffalo 14202
(212) 687-8181 .. **Fleming,** Francis G Jr. '74 OfCnsl Kreindler & K -750 3rd Av -NY 10017
(631) 425-4100 .. **Fleming,** Jacalyn R '02 %Ré NH&C,LLP -36 N NY Av -Huntngtn 11743
(212) 687-6262 .. **Fleming,** Jennifer A '09 %Barton B&P,LLP -420 Lex Av -NY 10170
(212) 385-8036 .. **Fleming,** Jos '77 (J Fleming,PC) -22 Crtlandt -NY 10007 **Fx:**406-2045
(716) 843-5700 .. **Fleming,** Mary E '86 %US Atty -138 Delaware Av -Buffalo 14202 **Fx:**551-3052
(212) 210-9547 .. **Fleming,** Matthew K '04 %Alston & B LLP -90 Park Av -NY 10016
(718) 391-8219 .. **Fleming,** Matthew R '96 NYC Dept Educ Integrated Srvcs Ctr -2811 Qns Plz N -LIC 11101
(212) 421-4100 .. **Fleming,** Melissa L '06 %Pryor C LLP -7 Times Sq -NY 10036
(212) 261-8000 .. **Fleming,** Michl A '99 (Mendes & M,LLP) -750 7th Av -NY 10019
(212) 840-1781 .. **Fleming,** Michl F '02 Furgueson Cptl Mgmt -19 W 44th -NY 10036
(516) 365-7827 .. **Fleming,** Michl J '72 -11 Wedgewood Ct -Manhsst 11030
(516) 692-9610 .. **Fleming,** Michl J '85 -3 Elizabeth Dr -Laurel Hollow 11791
(212) 266-5892 .. **Fleming,** Michl Jos '02 %BZ Green -12 MetroTech Ctr -Brklyn 11201 **Fx:**(718) 250-1401
(212) 455-2000 .. **Fleming,** Paige E '08 %Simpson T&B LLP -425 Lex Av -NY 10017
(212) 588-0800 .. **Fleming,** Porter F '86 (Frommer L&H LLP) -745 5th Av -NY 10151
(718) 286-6000 .. **Fleming,** Quynda L '06 %DA -125-01 Qns Blvd -Kew Gdns 11415
(716) 856-4000 .. **Fleming,** Robt B Jr. '79 (Hodgson R LLP) -140 Pearl -Buffalo 14202
(212) 858-1000 .. **Fleming,** Ronald A Jr. '92 (Pillsbury WSP LLP) -1540 Bway -NY 10036
(716) 853-3801 .. **Fleming,** Ryon D '02 %Kenney SL&N,LLP -14 Lafayette Sq -Buffalo 14203
(516) 833-5034 .. **Fleming,** Stephen M '03 -403 Merrick Av -E Meadow 11554
(212) 836-8000 .. **Fleming,** Thos F '87 (Kaye S LLP) -425 Park Av -NY 10022
(212) 451-2300 .. **Fleming,** Thos J Jr. '79 (Olshan GFR&W LLP) -65 E 55th -NY 10022
(516) 712-4000 .. **Fleming,** Thos M II '03 %Milber MP&S LLP -1000 Woodbury Rd -Woodbury 11797
(914) 696-7510 .. **Fleming,** Thos P '89 -2900 Wstchstr Av -Purchase 10577
(212) 819-8200 .. **Fleming,** Travis '07 %White & C LLP -1155 Av of Amer -NY 10036
(212) 768-4900 .. **Fleming,** Wm B '92 (Gage S&F) -410 Park Av -NY 10022
(631) 324-8778 .. **Fleming,** Wm J '79 (Fleming & D,PLLC) -10 Gingerbread Ln -E Hampton 11937
(212) 225-2000 .. **Fleming-Delacruz,** Megan J '09 %Cleary GS&H -1 Lbrty Plz -NY 10006
(212) 468-8000 .. **Fleming Nolan,** Natalie A '07 %Morrison & F LLP -1290 Av of Amer -NY 10104
(718) 250-2000 .. **Fleming-Warren,** Terence E '08 %DA -350 Jay -Brklyn 11201 **Fx:**250-2314
(212) 937-9894 .. **Flemma,** G John '94 J Flemma,PC -11 Bway -NY 10004 **Fx:**(646) 839-4856
(315) 793-2370 .. **Flemma,** Jason D '04 %MHLS -207 Genesee -Utica 13501 **Fx:**793-2371
(315) 724-7563 .. **Flemma,** John E '52 -25 Hopper -Utica 13501 **Fx:**724-2501
(212) 339-3429 .. **Flemming,** Gregory J '85 %FSA -31 W 52nd -NY 10019 **Fx:**893-2710
(212) 412-9500 .. **Flemming Zulack Williamson Zauderer LLP** -1 Lbrty Plz -NY 10006 **Fx:**964-9200
(212) 929-5397 .. **Flesher,** Alexander D '93 %MacKenzie Partners -105 Mad Av -NY 10016 **Fx:**929-0308
(212) 788-0772 .. **Flesher,** Elizabeth A '08 %Law Dept -100 Church -NY 10007 **Fx:**788-0367
(212) 450-4000 .. **Flesher,** Gail A '89 (Davis P&W LLP) -450 Lex Av -NY 10017
(212) 676-8203 .. **Fleshman,** Karen K '04 Youth & Comm Devlpmnt -156 William -NY 10038
(716) 852-0441 .. **Flessa,** Brian '90 -534 Delaware Av -Buffalo 14202 **Fx:**332-7177
(212) 770-7000 .. **Fletcher,** Andrew J '92 %AIG -70 Pine -NY 10270
(212) 765-5070 .. **Fletcher,** Anthony L '63 SrCnsl Fish & R,PC -153 E 53rd -NY 10022
(212) 865-0800 .. **Fletcher,** Anthony Q '97 -31 Tiemann -NY 10027
(518) 274-3510 .. **Fletcher,** Bellanca J '94 %Bartle MD&J,LLP -251 River Bx448 -Troy 12181
(212) 770-1783 .. **Fletcher,** Bettieann A '94 %AIG -80 Pine -NY 10005 **Fx:**344-0972
(212) 455-9255 .. **Fletcher,** Christina J '08 %Rao & T LLP -90 Park Av -NY 10016 **Fx:**297-0005
(315) 422-1152 .. **Fletcher,** Danl P '89 (Costello C&F,PLLC) -500 Plum -Syracuse 13204
(646) 253-6422 .. **Fletcher,** Jason S '02 XE Capital Mgmt LLC -24 W 40th -NY 10018
(585) 271-8142 .. **Fletcher,** Jere B '79 -Bx10632 -Rchstr 14610
(212) 619-3900 .. **Fletcher,** Lancelot L '05 -225 Bway -NY 10007 **Fx:**406-6890
(212) 468-8000 .. **Fletcher,** Leah C '09 %Morrison & F LLP -1290 Av of Amer -NY 10104
(315) 448-0672 .. **Fletcher,** Lisa M '90 %US Atty -100 S Clinton Bx7198 -Syracuse 13261 **Fx:**448-0689
(315) 253-0361 .. **Fletcher,** Matthew R '78 -1879 W Genesee St Rd -Auburn 13021
(212) 633-2373 .. **Fletcher,** Robt E '91 (Finley F&P LLP) -19 Vestry -NY 10013 **Fx:**633-9865
(845) 810-0421 .. **Fletcher,** Sharon Capra '90 (SC Fletcher,PLLC) -89 N Front -Kingston 12401 **Fx:**810-0201
(585) 546-6448 .. **Fletcher,** Wm P '85 (Davidson F LLP) -28 E Main -Rchstr 14614
(716) 847-8400 .. **Fleury,** Joshua '07 %Phillips L LLP -3400 HSBC Ctr -Buffalo 14203
(518) 474-5220 .. **Fleury,** Robt J '83 %Dept of Law -The Cptl -Albany 12224
(347) 404-9133 .. **Flexer,** Alan '87 %Civil Ct -141 Lvngstn -Brklyn 11201 **Fx:**(718) 643-3733
(212) 446-2300 .. **Flexner,** Donald L '67 (Boies S&F LLP) -575 Lex Av -NY 10022
(212) 703-5097 .. **Flick,** Charlene B '93 US Cnsl for Intl Business -1212 Av of Amer -NY 10036
(212) 885-5000 .. **Flick,** Lawr F II '06 (Blank R LLP) -405 Lex Av -NY 10174
(212) 319-5240 .. **Flicker Garelick & Associates,LLP** -45 Bway -NY 10006 **Fx:**888-5271
(212) 319-5240 .. **Flicker,** Keith L '79 (Flicker G & Assoc,LLP) -45 Bway -NY 10006
(212) 859-8000 .. **Flicker,** Omri Y '08 %Fried FHS&J LLP -1 NY Plz -NY 10004
(212) 767-6918 .. **Flickinger,** Catherine R '77 %Hachette Filipacchi -1633 Bway -NY 10019 **Fx:**767-5631
(914) 345-3020 .. **Flickinger,** Kenneth J '05 %Knuckles K&E,LLP -565 Taxter Rd -Elmsfrd 10523
(212) 903-9000 .. **Flics,** Martin N '80 (Linklaters) -1345 Av of Amer -NY 10105
(212) 573-1430 .. **Fliederbaum,** Merrill '82 %Pfizer Inc -235 E 42nd -NY 10017
(718) 250-2000 .. **Fliedner,** Marc J '89 %DA -350 Jay -Brklyn 11201 **Fx:**250-2314
(212) 233-0350 .. **Fliegel,** L Barry '56 Sobel RF&S,LLP -150 Bway -NY 10038
(212) 506-1700 .. **Fliman,** Danl A '04 %Kasowitz BT&F LLP -1633 Bway -NY 10019
(518) 786-1800 .. **Flink,** Edw B '78 (Flink S LLC) -23 British Amer Blvd -Latham 12110 **Fx:**786-1969
(631) 852-1650 .. **Flink,** Robt A '05 %Leg Aid -300 Center Dr -Rvrhead 11901 **Fx:**852-1655
(212) 377-2062 .. **Flink,** Robt H '90 (Flink & Assoc) -555 5th Av -NY 10017 **Fx:**986-5316
(914) 793-1010 .. **Flink,** Stephen K '66 (Morgan B&P) -274 Wht Plns Rd -Eastchstr 10707
(212) 835-2424 .. **Flinn,** Heidi M '03 Olnick Orgnztn,Inc -110 E 59th -NY 10022
(212) 558-4000 .. **Flinn,** Irvine D '64 SrCnsl Sullivan & C LLP -125 Broad -NY 10004
(212) 400-7177 .. **Flinn,** Thos '82 (Garrity GMG&F) -40 Wall -NY 10005
(518) 862-7181 .. **Flint,** Christopher P '86 (Flint & G) -465 New Karner Rd -Albany 12205 **Fx:**862-7185
(516) 479-6300 .. **Flint,** Edw M '83 (Silverman A LLP) -100 Jericho Quad -Jericho 11753
(518) 392-2555 .. **Flint,** Keith G '65 -75 Main Bx363 -Chatham 12037 **Fx:**392-2578
(914) 422-4333 .. **Flint,** Margaret Mitchell '84 %John Jay Lgl Srvcs -80 N Bway -White Plns 10603 **Fx:**422-4391
(518) 392-2555 .. **Flint,** Paul G '04 Flint Law Firm LLC -75 Main Bx363 -Chatham 12037 **Fx:**392-2578
(212) 565-2189 .. **Flippen,** John A '09 Google Inc -76 9th Av -NY 10011
(212) 735-3000 .. **Flis,** Edw W '98 %Skadden ASM&F LLP -4 Times Sq -NY 10036
(631) 277-1510 .. **Flis,** James S '69 -149 E Main Bx2 -E Islip 11730
(212) 867-6000 .. **Flitt,** Norman '76 (Rosenberg & E,PC) -733 3rd Av -NY 10017
(212) 425-7200 .. **Flock,** John '81 (Kenyon & K,LLP) -1 Bway -NY 10004
(212) 536-3900 .. **Flocos,** Peter N '91 (K&L Gates LLP) -599 Lex Av -NY 10022
(212) 750-4806 .. **Flohr,** Arlene '80 -575 Lex Av -NY 10022 **Fx:**750-4809
(212) 318-3000 .. **Flom,** Beret L '10 %Fulbright & J LLP -666 5th Av -NY 10103
(212) 603-1801 .. **Flom,** Jonathan S '83 -1619 Bway -NY 10019
(212) 735-3000 .. **Flom,** Jos H '49 (Skadden ASM&F LLP) -4 Times Sq -NY 10036
(212) 310-2231 .. **Floman Fishbone,** Betsy '96 %Colgate-Palmolive -300 Park Av -NY 10022 **Fx:**310-3230
(212) 482-0001 .. **Flomenhaft,** Fern '85 (Russo K&T LLP) -33 Whitehall -NY 10004
(800) 890-3090 .. **Flomenhaft,** Michl '81 (Jacoby & M,LLP) -39 Bway -NY 10002 **Fx:**(212) 344-9400
(212) 594-2400 .. **Flood,** Edw P '83 (Lyons & F) -65 W 36th -NY 10018
(516) 795-8480 .. **Flood,** James E Jr. '80 -670 Bway -Massapequa 11758 **Fx:**541-0307
(212) 699-0730 .. **Flood,** Kevin Patrick '68 -4 E 1st -NY 10003 **Fx:**(800) 728-9619
(212) 408-2500 .. **Flood,** Kristin E '09 %Baker B,LLP -30 Rckfllr Plz -NY 10112
(212) 267-6646 .. **Flood,** Marilyn J '91 NY Cnty Lwyrs Assn -14 Vesey -NY 10007 **Fx:**406-9252
(212) 578-2211 .. **Flood,** Nora K '04 %MetLife -27-01 Qns Plz N -LIC 11101
(845) 758-1388 .. **Flood-Myers,** Kelly '91 (Trezza & F,PLLC) -17 St John -Red Hook 12571 **Fx:**876-1239
(718) 590-2000 .. **Flook,** Lindsey D '09 %DA -198 E 161st -Bronx 10451 **Fx:**590-6477
(212) 701-3000 .. **Flora,** Lindsay K '09 %Cahill G&R LLP -80 Pine -NY 10005 **Fx:**269-5420
(212) 450-4000 .. **Florack,** James A '88 (Davis P&W LLP) -450 Lex Av -NY 10017
(716) 566-5400 .. **Floreale,** Christopher G '98 (Goldberg S LLP) -665 Main -Buffalo 14203
(347) 404-9133 .. **Florek,** Anna E '08 Civil Ct -141 Lvngstn -Brklyn 11201 **Fx:**(718) 643-3733
(212) 302-8989 .. **Florek,** Kenneth F '87 (Hedman & C,PC) -1185 Av of Amer -NY 10036
(716) 839-3628 .. **Florek,** Susan Bembia '80 -4685 Main -Snyder 14226
(914) 631-6200 .. **Florence,** Anne Laird '94 Gibraltar Mgt -150 Wht Plns Rd -Tarrytwn 10591
(212) 335-4008 .. **Florence,** Diana J '97 %DA -1 Hogan Pl -NY 10013
(914) 737-7001 .. **Florence,** Wm J Jr. '65 -1 Park Pl -Peekskill 10566 **Fx:**737-7077
(212) 883-1700 .. **Florendo,** Alan B '07 %Duval & S LLP -101 Park Av -NY 10178
(631) 666-8500 .. **Florentino,** Gregory '62 -111 Ocean Av -Bay Shr 11706 **Fx:**666-4272
(212) 758-7600 .. **Florentino,** Tonianne '87 (Collazo C&M) -747 3rd Av -NY 10017
(718) 340-4306 .. **Flores,** Claudia M '03 Main St Leg Srvcs -65-21 Main -Flushng 11367
(212) 490-3000 .. **Flores,** Danl F '91 (Wilson EME&D LLP) -150 E 42nd -NY 10017
(212) 373-3000 .. **Flores,** Daniele D '03 Paul WRW&G LLP -1285 Av of Amer -NY 10019
(212) 854-2675 .. **Flores,** Danielle A '09 Columbia Law Schl -435 W 116th -NY 10027 **Fx:**854-7946
(212) 266-0400 .. **Flores,** Edw A '84 (Krez & F,LLP) -225 Bway -NY 10007
(718) 229-4160 .. **Flores,** Estelle '03 -42-40 Bell Blvd -Bayside 11361
(315) 682-3590 .. **Flores,** Irene Aurora '01 -Bx433 -Manlius 13104 **Fx:**478-4352
(516) 229-4200 .. **Flores,** John C '01 Mendolia & S -875 Merrick Av -Westbury 11590

(718) 286-2468 .. **Flores,** Josephine C '94 %Leg Aid -120-46 Qns Blvd -Kew Gdns 11415 **Fx:**286-2286
(518) 623-4845 .. **Flores,** Marcy I '83 -Bx373 -Warrensburg 12885 **Fx:**623-4845
(212) 331-5137 .. **Flores,** Ramon E '06 %NYC HRA -180 Water -NY 10038 **Fx:**331-4465
(203) 330-2264 .. **Flores,** Raul G '09 %Pullman & C,LLC -50 Main -White Plns 10606
(212) 594-5000 .. **Flores,** Steven S '00 %Togut S&S LLP -1 Penn Plz -NY 10119
(212) 627-8100 .. **Flores,** Vanessa '09 %Levy R,PC -80 8th Av -NY 10011
(718) 898-6000 .. **Flores,** Vanessa M '03 -82-11 37th Av -Jcksn Hts 11372
(212) 885-5000 .. **Florescue,** Leonard G '73 (Blank R LLP) -405 Lex Av -NY 10174
(646) 375-2132 .. **Florestal,** Marcel '01 -116 W 23rd -NY 10011
(718) 685-0073 .. **Florez,** Milton H '97 -40-06 Warren -Elmhrst 11373 **Fx:**685-0077
(516) 799-8697 .. **Floriani,** Denise '81 -558 Ocean Av -Massapequa 11758 **Fx:**541-6260
(212) 732-9000 .. **Floriani,** Frank V '78 (Sullivan PBM&C PC) -120 Bway -NY 10271
(212) 653-8827 .. **Floriani,** Jos '02 Mara Grp,LLC -909 3rd Av -NY 10022
(212) 816-6115 .. **Florin,** Aimee B '96 Citigroup -388 Greenwich -NY 10013
(212) 407-4000 .. **Florin,** Kenneth R '93 (Loeb & L,LLP) -345 Park Av -NY 10154
(914) 997-1212 .. **Florio,** Danl F Jr. '96 (Jasne & F,LLP) -30 Glenn -White Plns 10603
(212) 939-9539 .. **Florio,** Dawn M '89 (DM Florio Law Firm PLLC) -3604 Bway -NY 10031 **Fx:**939-9533
(212) 500-3123 .. **Florio,** Gregory L '96 Marathon Asset Mgt -1 Bryant Pk -NY 10036
(914) 934-8877 .. **Florio,** John L '81 %Talbots -211 S Ridge -Rye Brook 10573 **Fx:**934-9136
(914) 761-7190 .. **Florio,** Josephine '94 %ODAR-SSA -75 S Bway -White Plns 10601 **Fx:**682-7006
(516) 627-4404 .. **Florio,** Lawr B '58 -11 Willets Ln -Plandome 11030 **Fx:**627-0209
(914) 997-1212 .. **Florio,** Lisa C '93 %Jasne & F,LLP -30 Glenn -White Plns 10603
(212) 344-1600 .. **Florio Perrucci Steinhardt & Fader** -80 Wall -NY 10005
(716) 856-0875 .. **Florkowski,** Jill Z '08 D Archilla -170 Franklin -Buffalo 14202 **Fx:**853-1897
(212) 940-8800 .. **Florman,** David A '81 SpclCnsl Katten MR LLP -575 Mad Av -NY 10022
(516) 829-6900 .. **Florman,** Donald '68 (Ackerman LCB&L,LLP) -1010 Nrthrn Blvd -Gt Neck 11021
(585) 263-1000 .. **Floro,** Allan E '84 Cnsl Nixon P LLP -1100 Clinton Sq -Rchstr 14604
(516) 674-0060 .. **Floroff,** Olga '90 -84 Plymouth Dr N -Glen Head 11545 **Fx:**674-0400
(518) 279-1143 .. **Florsch,** John C '08 %Fowler Law Ofc,PLLC -1011 Hoosick Rd -Troy 12180 **Fx:**279-4320
(212) 779-4046 .. **Florsheim,** Robt '64 -253 5th Av -NY 10016 **Fx:**378-4972
(518) 449-1421 .. **Flory,** Judith A '86 %R D'Alessandro -69 Columbia -Albany 12210 **Fx:**449-3193
(212) 319-7332 .. **Flotteron,** Kim M '07 %Falk & Assoc,LLC -30 Broad -NY 10004 **Fx:**(732) 636-3575
(516) 537-1130 .. **Floumanhaft,** Philip S '83 (Glinkenhouse F&Q) -116 Spruce -Cedarhrst 11516
(212) 225-2000 .. **Flow,** Sandra L '97 (Cleary GS&H) -1 Lbrty Plz -NY 10006
(631) 968-7600 .. **Flower,** Edw '56 Cnsl Flower M&M -24 E Main -Bay Shr 11706
(518) 792-1582 .. **Flower,** Kristine K '03 (Caffry & F) -100 Bay -Glens Fls 12801
(631) 968-7600 .. **Flower Medalie & Markowitz** -24 E Main -Bay Shr 11706 **Fx:**665-4293
(914) 779-6299 .. **Flower Cox,** Roberta A '99 -66 Palmer Av -Bronxvll 10708
(516) 328-2300 .. **Flowers,** Ellen L '93 (Abrams FFEGF&E,LLP) -1111 Marcus Av -Lk Success 11042
(212) 410-6446 .. **Flowers,** Horace '77 -Morningside Sta Bx876 -NY 10026
(718) 527-5229 .. **Flowers,** Joan E '88 (J Flowers & Assoc) -219-10 S Conduit Av -Sprngfld Gdns 11413 **Fx:**949-8280
(631) 271-6596 .. **Flowers,** Larry E '05 %C Cassar,PC -13 E Carver -Huntngtn 11743
(212) 522-5771 .. **Flowers,** Shawn G '94 %Time Inc -1271 Av of Amer -NY 10020 **Fx:**522-0437
(716) 664-5210 .. **Flowers,** Thos I '74 (Price FM&W) -400 Key Bk Bldg Bx1219 -Jamestwn 14702
(212) 248-9100 .. **Floyd,** Cecil E '89 %Epstein H&M -1 Whitehall -NY 10004
(716) 847-8400 .. **Floyd,** David K '60 OfCnsl Phillips L LLP -3400 HSBC Ctr -Buffalo 14203
(212) 779-9910 .. **Floyd,** Edw W '06 %Eaton & V LLP -3 Park Av -NY 10016
(212) 867-6000 .. **Floyd,** Jeanine '08 %Rosenberg & E,PC -733 3rd Av -NY 10017
(212) 440-4300 .. **Floyd-Mayers,** Yvonne T '92 %Leg Aid -199 Water -NY 10038
(518) 477-2269 .. **Fluery,** Mark A '97 -3509 Route 150 -E Greenbush 12061 **Fx:**477-2938
(516) 612-7034 .. **Flug,** Ita R '04 -877 N Corona Av -Vly Stream 11580
(212) 676-0061 .. **Flug,** Jacqueline P '02 Assgnd Cnsl Plan -253 Bway -NY 10007
(212) 562-4961 .. **Flug,** Margo S '04 MHLS -Bellevue Hsptl 27th & 1st Av -NY 10016
(212) 766-4700 .. **Fluger,** Andrew N '03 %Katz & R -116 John -NY 10038 **Fx:**766-4705
(212) 446-4800 .. **Flugman,** David S '07 %Kirkland & E LLP -153 E 53rd -NY 10022
(212) 326-3939 .. **Fluhr,** Michl J '07 %Jones D -222 E 41st -NY 10017
(212) 313-3600 .. **Fluitt,** Shawnette A '03 %Barry M&M -2 Rector -NY 10006
(718) 435-7214 .. **Fluk,** Gershon H '95 -5302 15th Av -Brklyn 11219 **Fx:**436-2052
(212) 373-3000 .. **Flumenbaum,** Martin '75 (Paul WRW&G LLP) -1285 Av of Amer -NY 10019
(716) 856-4000 .. **Fluskey,** Robt J Jr. '04 %Hodgson R LLP -140 Pearl -Buffalo 14202
(718) 232-7990 .. **Flyer,** Morris '52 -1406 W 5th -Brklyn 11204 **Fx:**256-2108
(212) 885-4735 .. **Flyer,** Steven A '92 %CIBC World Markets -425 Lex Av -NY 10017
(212) 533-6300 .. **Flynes,** Pamela Patton '92 NYSUT -52 Bway -NY 10004 **Fx:**995-2347
(212) 381-9700 .. **Flynn,** Ann Marie '83 %Lambos Firm,LLP -303 S Bway -Tarrytwn 10591 **Fx:**797-9213
(212) 770-1705 .. **Flynn,** Brian E '95 %AIG -70 Pine -NY 10270
(631) 277-7714 .. **Flynn,** Brian M '88 -74 Carleton Av -E Islip 11730 **Fx:**277-7750
(212) 308-0888 .. **Flynn,** Brian P '89 %Widowski & S LLP -425 Mad Av -NY 10017
(518) 487-7600 .. **Flynn,** Carrie E '03 %Whiteman O&H LLP -1 Commerce Plz -Albany 12260
(212) 312-7806 .. **Flynn,** Charlotte '78 %State Ins Fund -199 Church -NY 10007 **Fx:**385-9199
(914) 524-5600 .. **Flynn,** Danl D '93 %L Fishman -303 S Bway -Tarrytwn 10591 **Fx:**524-5742
(518) 371-8621 .. **Flynn,** Danl G '87 -15 Beechwd Dr -Clifton Pk 12065
(716) 847-8400 .. **Flynn,** David P '88 (Phillips L LLP) -3400 HSBC Ctr -Buffalo 14203
(212) 759-4888 .. **Flynn,** David P '88 (Phillips L LLP) -437 Mad Av -NY 10022
(585) 758-7617 .. **Flynn,** Deirdre M '96 %Univ of Rochester Med Ctr -Bx278979 -Rchstr 14627 **Fx:**272-9311
(914) 381-5041 .. **Flynn,** Edw E '93 -1014 Keeler Av -Mamaroneck 10543
(914) 390-8014 .. **Flynn,** Eileen P '98 %NYPA -123 Main -White Plns 10601 **Fx:**390-8038
(212) 861-1631 .. **Flynn,** Gayle Montague '85 -435 E 79th -NY 10075
(631) 689-9203 .. **Flynn,** Gerald M Jr. '69 -42 Hastings Dr -Stony Brk 11790 **Fx:**941-1404
(516) 656-5300 .. **Flynn,** Gerald W '69 (Mullooly JR&F LLP) -6851 Jericho Tpk Bx9036 -Syosset 11791
(212) 962-2450 .. **Flynn Gibbons & Dowd** -80 Maiden Ln -NY 10038 **Fx:**233-6483
(315) 422-8191 .. **Flynn,** Gregory B '82 %Leg Aid -351 S Warren -Syracuse 13202 **Fx:**472-2819
(212) 935-7400 .. **Flynn,** James G '89 (Harwood F LLP) -488 Mad Av -NY 10022
(212) 206-2433 .. **Flynn,** John J III '61 -49 E 41st -NY 10165 **Fx:**(732) 577-0734
(716) 839-7777 .. **Flynn,** John J Jr. '96 %O'Brien B PC -40 N Forest Rd -Williamsvll 14221
(212) 330-1000 .. **Flynn,** John T '71 Buck Consultants -1 Penn Plz -NY 10119 **Fx:**695-4184
(646) 610-6645 .. **Flynn,** Jos A '78 NYPD -1 Police Plz -NY 10038
(516) 656-5300 .. **Flynn,** Kerri S '08 %Mullooly JR&F LLP -6851 Jericho Tpk Bx9036 -Syosset 11791
(212) 357-4378 .. **Flynn,** Kerry E '04 %Goldman Sachs -1 NY Plz -NY 10004
(212) 261-8000 .. **Flynn,** Kevin G '90 (Mendes & M,LLP) -750 7th Av -NY 10019
(212) 808-8100 .. **Flynn,** Kevin M '90 (Kostelanetz & F,LLP) -7 Wrld Trd Ctr -NY 10007
(607) 732-8990 .. **Flynn,** Kevin P '94 -463 W Church -Elmira 14901 **Fx:**732-8999
(914) 963-3600 .. **Flynn,** Kristen N '99 Cnsl Ecco III Enterprises -201 Saw Mill Rvr Rd -Ynkrs 10701 **Fx:**476-8705
(212) 495-0100 .. **Flynn,** Lawr L '80 (Gottesman WMF&W,PC) -11 Hanover Sq -NY 10005 **Fx:**480-9797
(716) 662-1585 .. **Flynn,** Louise M '02 -60 Wshngtn Av -Orchard Pk 14127
(212) 735-8631 .. **Flynn,** Mary E '89 (Morrison C LLP) -909 3rd Av -NY 10022
(718) 945-1000 .. **Flynn,** Mary P '89 (Flynn & F) -114-12 Beach Channel Dr -Rckwy Pk 11694 **Fx:**318-6162
(516) 877-1234 .. **Flynn,** Michl '79 M Flynn,PLLC -1205 Franklin Av -Gdn Cty 11530 **Fx:**877-1177
(212) 946-2720 .. **Flynn,** Michl D '72 (Feren & F) -11 Penn Plz -NY 10001
(212) 318-3000 .. **Flynn,** Michl R '95 (Fulbright & J LLP) -666 5th Av -NY 10103
(212) 450-4000 .. **Flynn,** Michl S '94 (Davis P&W LLP) -450 Lex Av -NY 10017
(212) 336-2000 .. **Flynn,** Michl S '08 %Patterson BW&T LLP -1133 Av of Amer -NY 10036
(516) 535-5555 .. **Flynn,** Neil '97 %P Ajlouny & Assoc PC -320 Old Cntry Rd -Gdn Cty 11530 **Fx:**535-5556
(718) 875-1300 .. **Flynn,** Penelope J '01 %Applt Div 2nd Dept -45 Monroe Pl -Brklyn 11201 **Fx:**858-2446
(212) 987-3202 .. **Flynn,** Rebecca M '90 -108 E 91st -NY 10128
(716) 854-4705 .. **Flynn,** Robt H '97 Lippman O -300 Pearl -Buffalo 14202
(212) 483-9490 .. **Flynn,** Scott S '05 OfCnsl McElroy DM&C,LLP -88 Pine -NY 10005
(631) 853-4049 .. **Flynn,** Susan A '86 %Cnty Atty -Dennison Bldg Bx6100 -Hauppauge 11788 **Fx:**853-5169
(845) 486-2522 .. **Flynn,** Susan Liess '87 Hon J Posner -50 Market -Poughkeepsie 12601
(212) 574-1200 .. **Flynn,** Tara K '04 %Seward & K LLP -1 Bttry Pk Plz -NY 10004
(716) 200-5050 .. **Flynn,** Terrance P '89 (Harris B PLLC) -726 Exchange -Buffalo 14210
(718) 945-1000 .. **Flynn,** Terrence R Jr. '87 (Flynn & F) -114-12 Beach Channel Dr -Rckwy Pk 11694 **Fx:**318-6162
(716) 854-2211 .. **Flynn,** Timothy J '93 %E Cosgrove -525 Delaware Av -Buffalo 14202 **Fx:**854-8122
(212) 248-7200 .. **Flynn,** Wm B '75 (McCabe & F,LLP) -1 Whitehall -NY 10004
(518) 427-9700 .. **Flynn,** Wm M '92 (Harris B PLLC) -677 Bway -Albany 12207
(845) 569-9110 .. **Flynn,** Wm T '01 %Leg Srvcs -123 Grand -Newburgh 12550 **Fx:**569-9120
(716) 649-4747 .. **Flynt,** W Rogers '77 -170 Union -Hambrg 14075
(212) 237-0000 .. **Foarde,** Timothy F '00 (Vinson & E LLP) -666 5th Av -NY 10103
(914) 286-3400 .. **Focarile,** Allan '75 %Leg Aid -1 N Bway -White Plns 10601 **Fx:**682-4112
(631) 321-1111 .. **Focarile,** Anthony N '04 -324 Farmngdl Rd -W Babylon 11704 **Fx:**321-0010
(917) 202-3434 .. **Foda,** Rasha B '07 -302 Seaver Av -Staten Isl 10305 **Fx:**(718) 667-3918
(212) 999-5800 .. **Fodeman,** Morris J '98 OfCnsl Wilson SG&R -1301 Av of Americas -NY 10019
(212) 287-4420 .. **Fodera,** Baldo '99 %Bank of Amer -590 Mad Av -NY 10022 **Fx:**230-8441
(718) 745-3338 .. **Fodera,** L Richd '52 (Fodera Law Firm) -87 81st -Brklyn 11209 **Fx:**748-0111
(212) 487-9701 .. **Fodera,** Richd J '89 (Robin HK&F) -1 Bttry Pk Plz -NY 10014
(917) 454-1100 .. **Fodera,** Robt F '96 %Police Dept -2 Lafayette -NY 10007
(718) 454-8603 .. **Fodera,** Theo G '93 -67-18F 195th Ln -Fresh Mdws 11365 **Fx:**264-2839
(315) 394-1111 .. **Fodor,** Nicholas E '84 -315 State -Ogdensbrg 13669 **Fx:**394-7920
(212) 326-3939 .. **Fodor,** Susanna S '74 (Jones D) -222 E 41st -NY 10017
(585) 464-9400 .. **Foerster,** Mark R '81 %Wilmorite -1265 Scottsvll Rd -Rchstr 14624 **Fx:**328-1784
(212) 244-2999 .. **Foertsch,** Ralph A '92 %Kopff N&D LLP -440 9th Av -NY 10001
(518) 473-1124 .. **Fogarty,** Andrew C '05 NYS Dept Health -1441 Corning Twr -Albany 12237
(607) 369-3000 .. **Fogarty,** Dolores G '88 -183 Main Bx727 -Unadilla 13849 **Fx:**369-4814
(516) 747-7500 .. **Fogarty Duffy,PC** -185 Willis Av -Mineola 11501 **Fx:**747-7543
(212) 434-0100 .. **Fogarty,** Edw Jr. '85 (Litchfield C LLP) -420 Lex Av -NY 10170
(212) 969-3000 .. **Fogarty,** Erin L '10 %Proskauer R LLP -1585 Bway -NY 10036
(212) 335-9000 .. **Fogarty,** Frank '80 %DA -1 Hogan Pl -NY 10013
(212) 819-8200 .. **Fogarty,** James M '10 %White & C LLP -1155 Av of Amer -NY 10036
(212) 364-8464 .. **Fogarty,** John E '76 Time Warner Cable -60 Columbus Av -NY 10023 **Fx:**364-8460
(845) 291-3141 .. **Fogarty,** Jos P '81 %Hon J McGuirk -255-275 Main -Goshen 10924
(718) 286-6000 .. **Fogarty,** Kevin P '81 %DA -125-01 Qns Blvd -Kew Gdns 11415

(914) 249-3986 .. **Fogarty,** Marianne '91 MasterCard Intl -2000 Purchase -Purchase 10577
(585) 268-7603 .. **Fogarty,** Patricia K '75 (Serra & F,PC) -25 Schuyler -Belmont 14813 **Fx:**268-5750
(516) 747-7500 .. **Fogarty,** Patrick J '54 (Fogarty D,PC) -185 Willis Av -Mineola 11501
(516) 357-0056 .. **Fogarty,** Thos E '09 %LaReddola L & Assoc,LLP -600 Old Cntry Rd -Gdn Cty 11530
(631) 231-1450 .. **Fogel,** Allan E '90 %Feldman K&M,PC -330 Vndrblt Motor Pkwy -Hauppauge 11788
(718) 953-6480 .. **Fogel,** Alter S '96 -32 Court -Brklyn 11201 **Fx:**221-0950
(914) 682-2018 .. **Fogel,** Alter S '96 -50 Main -White Plns 10606 **Fx:**682-7784
(315) 474-2943 .. **Fogel,** Danielle M '05 %Sugarman Law Firm,LLP -211 W Jffrsn -Syracuse 13202
(212) 373-3000 .. **Fogel,** Dorian S '03 %Paul WRW&G LLP -1285 Av of Amer -NY 10019
(212) 292-6534 .. **Fogel,** Fredk H '86 Ziff Bros Invstmnts -153 E 53rd -NY 10022
(718) 855-4792 .. **Fogel,** Jacob T '97 -32 Court -Brklyn 11201 **Fx:**228-9278
(718) 876-6300 .. **Fogel,** Jonathan K '05 %DA -130 Styvsnt Pl -Staten Isl 10301
(212) 962-1190 .. **Fogel,** Joshua '06 %Sanocki N&T,LLP -225 Bway -NY 10007
(212) 481-4801 .. **Fogel,** Joshua L '02 %B Silberzweig -271 Mad Av -NY 10016 **Fx:**481-4971
(212) 944-1580 .. **Fogel,** Louis I '84 (Fogel & W PC) -420 5th Av -NY 10018 **Fx:**944-1869
(212) 451-3698 .. **Fogel,** Meredith D '01 Saks & Co -12 E 49th -NY 10017 **Fx:**888-9063
(315) 442-0100 .. **Fogel,** Michl A '05 %Gilberti SH&S,PC -555 E Genesee -Syracuse 13202
(212) 385-1122 .. **Fogel,** Nussin S '87 -299 Bway -NY 10007 **Fx:**964-2292
(845) 639-3080 .. **Fogel,** Philip B '63 -369 S Main -New Cty 10956 **Fx:**639-3077
(516) 721-7161 .. **Fogel,** Richd A '88 RA Fogel,PC -389 Cedar Av -Islip 11751 **Fx:**(631) 650-5254
(516) 374-8400 .. **Fogel,** Usher '77 -557 Central Av -Cedarhrst 11516
(212) 962-1200 .. **Fogelgaren,** Eric I '74 (Fogelgaren F&B,LLP) -277 Bway -NY 10007
(212) 962-1200 .. **Fogelgaren Forman & Bergman,LLP** -277 Bway -NY 10007 **Fx:**608-5935
(212) 233-5252 .. **Fogelgaren,** Ira F '80 -277 Bway -NY 10007 **Fx:**608-5935
(212) 637-2719 .. **Fogelman,** Lawr H '00 %US Atty -86 Chmbrs -NY 10007
(212) 370-1530 .. **Fogelman,** Leonard M '76 -305 Mad Av -NY 10165 **Fx:**370-2851
(631) 427-9175 .. **Fogelman,** Martin '50 Fordham Law Schl -21 Brookside Dr -Huntngtn 11743 **Fx:**427-0678
(212) 532-7250 .. **Fogelman,** Sheldon '53 -10 E 40th -NY 10016 **Fx:**685-8939
(917) 287-1338 .. **Fogelnest,** Robt C '87 -20 Vesey -NY 10007
(212) 969-2700 .. **Fogelson,** Robt A '94 Wasserstein & Co -1301 Av of Amer -NY 10019
(212) 891-1600 .. **Fogerty,** Melissa C '09 %Jenner & B LLP -919 3rd Av -NY 10022
(212) 735-3000 .. **Fogg,** Blaine V '66 OfCnsl Skadden ASM&F LLP -4 Times Sq -NY 10036
(716) 852-6781 .. **Fogg,** Robt R '02 -69 Delaware Av -Buffalo 14202 **Fx:**852-6784
(212) 474-1000 .. **Fogg,** Wm V '92 (Cravath S&M LLP) -825 8th Av -NY 10019
(212) 635-3150 .. **Foglia,** Philip F '81 Ofc Inspector Genl -61 Bway -NY 10006 **Fx:**809-2992
(212) 344-4700 .. **Foglietta,** Maria Jorgelina '09 %DeOrchis & Prtnrs LLP -61 Bway -NY 10006
(518) 383-8706 .. **Foglietta,** Sheila M '94 -21 Twilight Dr -Clifton Pk 12065
(631) 852-2500 .. **Fohrkolb,** Mary-Kathleen '01 %DA -200 Center Dr -Rvrhead 11901 **Fx:**852-1769
(212) 306-7160 .. **Fois,** Michl T '92 %Ofc Cllctv Brgn -40 Rector -NY 10006 **Fx:**306-7167
(716) 213-0910 .. **Foit,** C Kenneth '81 -1540 Ellicott Crk Rd -Tonawanda 14150 **Fx:**213-0911
(212) 407-4000 .. **Fojas,** Martin O C '10 %Loeb & L,LLP -345 Park Av -NY 10154
(212) 589-4200 .. **Fokas,** Jimmy '01 (Baker & H LLP) -45 Rckfllr Plz -NY 10111
(212) 732-9867 .. **Fokas,** Marcia E '81 -370 Lex Av -NY 10017 **Fx:**732-2953
(212) 715-9100 .. **Folb,** Kerri B '01 %Kramer LN&F,LLP -1177 Av of Amer -NY 10036
(845) 225-1900 .. **Folchetti,** Gregory L '96 (Costello & F,LLP) -1875 Route 6 -Carmel 10512
(914) 683-8792 .. **Folchetti,** Robt W '87 (Klein & F) -1849 Route 6 -Carmel 10512 **Fx:**683-8790
(914) 934-8792 .. **Folchetti,** Robt W '87 (Klein & F) -219 Wstchstr Av -Pt Chester 10573 **Fx:**934-8793
(212) 558-4000 .. **Foldenauer,** Aaron S '06 %Sullivan & C LLP -125 Broad -NY 10004
(212) 373-3000 .. **Foley,** Andrew J '94 (Paul WRW&G LLP) -1285 Av of Amer -NY 10019
(315) 597-6611 .. **Foley,** Ann Firestine '81 (Foley & F) -235 E Main Bx211 -Palmyra 14522
(212) 335-9000 .. **Foley,** Brian D '82 %DA -1 Hogan Pl -NY 10013
(914) 964-9700 .. **Foley,** Brian T '76 (B Foley & Company Inc) -1 N Bway -White Plns 10601
(212) 867-4100 .. **Foley,** Bryan J '08 %Furman K&B LLP -61 Bway -NY 10006
(212) 489-8230 .. **Foley,** Carolyn K '92 (Davis WT LLP) -1633 Bway -NY 10019
(716) 852-1000 .. **Foley,** Catherine Beltz '89 %PW Beltz,PC -36 Church -Buffalo 14202 **Fx:**852-5887
(914) 301-5925 .. **Foley,** Christopher P '93 CP Foley,LLC -51 Bedford Rd -Katonah 10536 **Fx:**301-5924
(845) 291-2454 .. **Foley,** Colleen '96 %Leg Aid -2 Court Ln Bx328 -Goshen 10924 **Fx:**294-2638
(518) 851-9094 .. **Foley,** David R '74 -Bx657 -Claverack 12513
(716) 753-4241 .. **Foley,** David W '93 (DA) -Cnty Cthse -Mayvll 14757 **Fx:**753-4628
(212) 788-0781 .. **Foley,** Eamonn F '95 Law Dept -100 Church -NY 10007
(845) 775-4868 .. **Foley,** Fiona A '05 F Foley,PC -39 North -Middletwn 10940 **Fx:**775-4145
(716) 366-3677 .. **Foley Foley & Passafaro** -93-95 E 4th Bx50 -Dunkirk 14048 **Fx:**366-3691
(716) 847-8400 .. **Foley,** Gabrielle S '10 %Phillips L LLP -3400 HSBC Ctr -Buffalo 14203
(516) 741-1110 .. **Foley Griffin Jacobson & Faria,LLP** -666 Old Cntry Rd -Gdn Cty 11530 **Fx:**741-9171
(212) 596-9000 .. **Foley,** Hope Drury '00 %Ropes & G LLP -1211 Av of Amer -NY 10036
(212) 318-3000 .. **Foley,** J Colin '99 Cnsl Fulbright & J LLP -666 5th Av -NY 10103
(212) 709-8025 .. **Foley,** J Garth '90 -110 Wall -NY 10005
(315) 597-6611 .. **Foley,** James F '74 (Foley & F) -235 E Main Bx211 -Palmyra 14522
(212) 310-8000 .. **Foley,** Jared B '09 %Weil G&M LLP -767 5th Av -NY 10153
(212) 506-1700 .. **Foley,** Jenifer J '01 %Kasowitz BT&F LLP -1633 Bway -NY 10019
(516) 795-7752 .. **Foley,** Karen Anne '94 -666 Old Cntry Rd -Gdn Cty 11530
(516) 542-5900 .. **Foley,** Kathleen D '93 %Congdon FORDT&F -333 Earle Ovngton Blvd -Uniondale 11553
(212) 506-5000 .. **Foley,** Kathleen E '07 %Orrick H&S LLP -51 W 52nd -NY 10019
(212) 391-6464 .. **Foley,** Kerry C '97 %Shapiro Firm,LLP -500 5th Av -NY 10110 **Fx:**719-1616
(845) 457-5332 .. **Foley,** Kevin '99 %Johnson & F,PC -15 Scotts Crnrs Dr Bx664 -Montgmry 12549 **Fx:**457-5931
(212) 483-8266 .. **Foley,** Kevin '99 OfCnsl G Wright & Assoc,LLC -88 Pine -NY 10005 **Fx:**483-0971
(212) 464-1373 .. **Foley,** Kevin J '78 %JP Morgan Chase -345 Park Av -NY 10154
(212) 682-7474 .. **Foley & Lardner LLP** -90 Park Av -NY 10016 **Fx:**687-2329
(212) 872-1000 .. **Foley,** Miriam F '97 -One Bryant Park -NY 10036 **Fx:**872-1002
(212) 474-1000 .. **Foley,** Nicholas M '10 %Cravath S&M LLP -825 8th Av -NY 10019
(212) 715-9100 .. **Foley,** Nicole D '09 %Kramer LN&F,LLP -1177 Av of Amer -NY 10036
(914) 301-5925 .. **Foley,** Patrick F '65 (McCormick D&F) -51 Bedford Rd -Katonah 10536
(212) 416-8565 .. **Foley,** Raymond J '75 %Dept of Law -120 Bway -NY 10271
(518) 583-5330 .. **Foley,** Robt J '85 %Ct of Claims -65 S Bway -Saratoga Spgs 12866 **Fx:**583-5335
(516) 683-0020 .. **Foley,** Robt M '63 -900 Merchants Cncrs -Westbury 11590 **Fx:**683-1160
(212) 251-9379 .. **Foley,** Shioban M '95 Structure Tone Inc -770 Bway -NY 10003
(212) 558-6668 .. **Foley Smit O'Boyle & Weisman** -100 William -NY 10038 **Fx:**482-0272
(516) 485-4221 .. **Foley Smit O'Boyle & Weisman** -175 Fulton Av -Hempstd 11550
(212) 468-4800 .. **Foley,** Stephen P '83 OfCnsl Davis & G LLP -1740 Bway -NY 10019
(716) 852-1000 .. **Foley,** Stephen R '91 %PW Beltz,PC -36 Church -Buffalo 14202 **Fx:**852-5887
(212) 398-9238 .. **Foley,** Thos '02 %D Guerin -315 Mad Av -NY 10017 **Fx:**869-0944
(212) 574-1200 .. **Foley,** Thos B '09 %Seward & K LLP -1 Bttry Pk Plz -NY 10004
(516) 741-1110 .. **Foley,** Thos J '94 (Foley GJ&F,LLP) -666 Old Cntry Rd -Gdn Cty 11530
(315) 369-3544 .. **Foley,** Timothy D '85 (Frye F&C) -2973 State Route 28 Bx291 -Old Forge 13420
(315) 733-7549 .. **Foley,** Timothy D '85 (Frye F&C) -2219 Genesee -Utica 13501
(212) 318-3000 .. **Foley,** Veronica Hincapie '06 %Fulbright & J LLP -666 5th Av -NY 10103
(212) 513-3200 .. **Foley,** Vincent J '97 (Holland & K LLP) -31 W 52nd -NY 10019
(212) 415-8600 .. **Foley,** Wm D '08 %Locke LB&L LLP -3 World Fncl Ctr -NY 10281
(212) 504-6000 .. **Foley,** Wm J '10 %Cadwalader W&T LLP -1 World Fncl Ctr -NY 10281
(212) 697-6464 .. **Folger,** Jeffrey S '01 (Folger & F) -521 5th Av -NY 10175
(212) 697-6464 .. **Folger,** Oscar D '72 (Folger & F) -521 5th Av -NY 10175
(212) 878-8000 .. **Folkemer,** Nathaniel T W '10 %Clifford C LLP -31 W 52nd -NY 10019
(212) 757-0400 .. **Folkenflik,** Max '76 (Folkenflik & M) -1500 Bway -NY 10036 **Fx:**757-2010
(212) 223-4000 .. **Folkinshteyn,** Benjamin J '07 %Crowell & M LLP -590 Mad Av -NY 10022
(631) 586-9444 .. **Folkman,** Jos M '92 VMI -365 Bay Shore Rd -Deer Pk 11729
(631) 845-1900 .. **Folks,** Robt L '73 (RL Folks & Assoc,LLP) -510 Broadhllw Rd -Melvll 11747 **Fx:**845-8779
(646) 471-4741 .. **Follana,** Gilles '97 %PricewaterhouseCoopers LLP -300 Mad Av -NY 10017
(516) 825-5356 .. **Follender,** James '99 -215 E Merrick Rd -Vly Stream 11580 **Fx:**825-5297
(845) 586-2307 .. **Follender,** Jonathan S '85 J Follender,PC -42838 Hwy 28 Bx511 -Arkvll 12406 **Fx:**586-2302
(631) 549-1938 .. **Follick & Bessich,PC** -33 Walt Whitman Rd -Huntngtn Sta 11746 **Fx:**549-2189
(631) 734-6807 .. **Folts,** Mary Lou '94 (Lark & F) -Main Rd Bx973 -Cutchogue 11935
(585) 454-5650 .. **Folts,** Robin L '10 %Lacy K LLP -130 E Main -Rchstr 14604
(212) 229-1516 .. **Foltz,** David B '87 (Buttermore ND&F,LLP) -111 Bway -NY 10006
(212) 218-7155 .. **Foltz,** Michl R '04 Special Cnsl Inc -60 E 42nd -NY 10165
(716) 433-5921 .. **Foltz,** R Jos '72 (Smith SF&M) -131 East Av Bx540 -Lockprt 14095
(212) 335-9000 .. **Foncello,** Martin J '06 %DA -1 Hogan Pl -NY 10013
(212) 381-4194 .. **Foncillas,** Ignacio M '93 -135 E 57th -NY 10022
(585) 396-7600 .. **Fondiller,** Ronald C '79 Canandaigua Wine Co -235 N Blmfld Rd -Canandaigua 14424 **Fx:**396-7831
(646) 386-3229 .. **Fondriest,** Irene '05 Hon C Ramos -60 Centre -NY 10007
(212) 906-1200 .. **Fondufe,** Clement N '02 (Latham & W) -885 3rd Av -NY 10022
(631) 852-2156 .. **Fondulis,** Colleen McManus '99 Supreme Ct -210 Centre Dr -Rvrhead 11901
(631) 878-4847 .. **Fondulis,** Steve '78 -503 Main -Pt Jffrsn 11777 **Fx:**473-9330
(212) 318-6000 .. **Fong,** Christopher '08 %Paul HJ&W LLP -75 E 55th -NY 10022
(212) 406-1774 .. **Fong,** Dean K '84 -212 Canal -NY 10013 **Fx:**406-2172
(212) 941-8800 .. **Fong,** Edmond J '84 (Fong & W,PC) -254 Canal -NY 10013
(212) 385-0034 .. **Fong,** Henry Lee '88 -11E Bway -NY 10038 **Fx:**571-4807
(845) 639-7800 .. **Fong,** Joan Chung Yin '93 (Mandel K&B,LLP) -210 Route 303 -Vly Cottage 10989
(212) 807-2896 .. **Fong,** Samantha A '95 Thomson Reuters -195 Bway -NY 10007
(212) 908-0500 .. **Fong,** Viola '90 Fitch,Inc -1 State Street Plz -NY 10004 **Fx:**480-4438
(212) 966-6668 .. **Fong & Wong,PC** -254 Canal -NY 10013 **Fx:**334-6759
(516) 741-0040 .. **Fonseca,** Anthony '84 -100 E Old Cntry Rd -Mineola 11501
(212) 553-5400 .. **Fonseca,** Gina M '99 %Zurich NA -1 Lbrty Plz -NY 10006
(845) 225-9254 .. **Fonseca,** Jos J '91 -37 Fair -Carmel 10512 **Fx:**225-7423
(212) 736-0500 .. **Fonseca,** M David '05 %Mitofsky SN&H LLP -152 Mad Av -NY 10016
(212) 440-7324 .. **Fonseca,** Sharon '02 CNA -40 Wall -NY 10005
(212) 947-1999 .. **Fonseca,** Timothy J '07 %Methfessel & W,PC -450 7th Av -NY 10123
(212) 839-5300 .. **Fonstein,** Cliff H '94 (Sidley A LLP) -787 7th Av -NY 10019
(585) 419-8800 .. **Fontaine,** Alyssa Hochberg '07 %Harris B PLLC -99 Garnsey Rd -Pittsfrd 14534

(718) 855-2894 .. **Fontaine,** Anne E '81 -91 Columbia Hts -Brklyn 11201
(718) 625-8940 .. **Fontaine,** Christine '93 %B Lawrence -15 Metrotech Ctr N -Brklyn 11201 **Fx:**624-5756
(212) 880-6000 .. **Fontaine,** Jared J '09 %Torys LLP -237 Park Av -NY 10017
(212) 836-8000 .. **Fontaine,** R Nadine '95 %Kaye S LLP -425 Park Av -NY 10022
(718) 928-3700 .. **Fontaine,** Sienna M F '08 %LSNYC-Bronx -579 Courtlandt Av -Bronx 10451 **Fx:**402-7586
(212) 486-2400 .. **Fontak,** Jos I '92 OfCnsl Leader & B LLP -630 3rd Av -NY 10017
(212) 374-6888 .. **Fontana,** Emily Jordan '05 NYC Dept of Ed -52 Chmbrs -NY 10007
(516) 802-0630 .. **Fontana,** George C Jr. '05 %Simmons J,LLP -115 Eileen Way -Syosset 11791
(718) 435-0203 .. **Fontana,** Louis D '72 -925 McDonald Av -Brklyn 11218
(914) 946-8900 .. **Fontana,** Lucille A '81 (Clark G&M) -99 Court -White Plns 10601
(212) 839-5300 .. **Fontana,** Pietro '08 %Sidley A LLP -787 7th Av -NY 10019
(914) 423-8880 .. **Fontana,** Richd G '70 -1250 Cntrl Pk Av -Ynkrs 10704 **Fx:**423-6117
(516) 640-4505 .. **Fontana,** Vincent R '65 (V Fontana,PC) -1010 Franklin Av -Gdn Cty 11530 **Fx:**640-4983
(718) 875-4444 .. **Fontanelli,** Robt C '99 R Fontanelli,PC -32 Court -Brklyn 11201 **Fx:**852-4780
(212) 602-0854 .. **Fontanetta,** Peter '05 Trinity Real Estate -74 Trinity Pl -NY 10006
(718) 720-4949 .. **Fonte,** Mark J '86 -60 Bay -Staten Isl 10301 **Fx:**448-8685
(212) 839-5300 .. **Fontecilla,** Adrian '10 %Sidley A LLP -787 7th Av -NY 10019
(212) 450-4000 .. **Fonte Harsch,** Mutya D '99 %Davis P&W LLP -450 Lex Av -NY 10017
(718) 263-6219 .. **Fontek,** Paul '86 -996 E 19th -Brklyn 11230
(845) 602-3144 .. **Fontenot,** James D '02 Pfizer,Inc -401 N Mddltwn Rd -Pearl Rvr 10965
(212) 935-5700 .. **Fontenot,** Mary G '00 %Colucci & U -218 E 50th -NY 10022
(718) 837-0677 .. **Fonti,** Gregg X '78 (Fonti & F) -8516 23rd Av -Brklyn 11214 **Fx:**234-3359
(212) 907-0700 .. **Fonti,** Jos A '00 (Labaton S LLP) -140 Bway -NY 10005
(718) 837-0677 .. **Fonti,** Maureen P '93 (Fonti & F) -8516 23rd Av -Brklyn 11214 **Fx:**234-3359
(212) 707-6500 .. **Fonti,** Melissa R '07 Burberry Limited,USA -1350 Av of Amer -NY 10019
(212) 732-0707 .. **Fontier,** Alice L '08 J Dratel,PC -2 Wall -NY 10005 **Fx:**571-3792
(212) 340-0400 .. **Foodim,** Lauren A '86 %Appllt Div 1st Dept -27 Mad Av -NY 10010 **Fx:**889-4412
(516) 747-1010 .. **Foodim,** Leslie A '82 %Dollinger G&G -1 Old Cntry Rd -Carle Pl 11514
(518) 473-0345 .. **Foody,** Diane DeFurio '76 %State Comptroller -110 State -Albany 12236 **Fx:**473-9104
(315) 696-8702 .. **Foody,** James T '72 -1684 Dutch Hill Rd -Tully 13159
(212) 458-1340 .. **Fooksman,** Alex '01 AIGTS -175 Water -NY 10038
(718) 505-6650 .. **Fooksman,** Alex '07 Kaplan & M -75-20 Astoria Blvd -E Elmhrst 11370
(212) 686-3838 .. **Fooksman,** Marina '04 %Barst M&K LLP -2 Park Av -NY 10016
(212) 446-2300 .. **Foote,** Amy R '00 %Boies S&F LLP -575 Lex Av -NY 10022
(212) 237-1000 .. **Foote,** Carrie E '02 %Windels ML&M,LLP -156 W 56th -NY 10019
(518) 822-9309 .. **Foote,** Chas F '71 -414 Union -Hudson 12534 **Fx:**822-8639
(212) 504-6000 .. **Foote,** Robt III '07 %Cadwalader W&T LLP -1 World Fncl Ctr -NY 10281
(585) 468-2010 .. **Foote,** Theron A '70 -21 S State Bx400 -Nunda 14517 **Fx:**468-2009
(585) 786-2727 .. **Foote,** Theron A '70 -23 W Court Bx72 -Warsaw 14569 **Fx:**786-9904
(716) 845-7465 .. **Foote-Beavers,** Lenora B '99 Family Ct -1 Niagara Plz -Buffalo 14202 **Fx:**858-6293
(212) 973-0572 .. **Forand,** Mark A '01 %Wolff & S PC -140 Bway -NY 10005
(212) 272-6162 .. **Forastiere,** Michl A III '71 JP Morgan Chase -383 Mad Av -NY 10179
(914) 948-7000 .. **Forbes,** April L '00 %Keidel W&C LLP -925 Wstchstr Av -White Plns 10604
(212) 776-5108 .. **Forbes,** Jacqueline C '01 NYC Housing Auth -250 Bway -NY 10007 **Fx:**776-5039
(212) 859-8000 .. **Forbes,** Jessica '89 (Fried FHS&J LLP) -1 NY Plz -NY 10004
(845) 291-3104 .. **Forbes,** Joanne M '93 Hon W Giacomo -255-285 Main -Goshen 10924 **Fx:**291-2595
(914) 995-3460 .. **Forbes,** Laura A '01 %DA -111 Martin Luther King Blvd -White Plns 10601 **Fx:**995-3363
(845) 565-1744 .. **Forbes,** Richd D '94 -372 Fullerton Av -Newburgh 12550 **Fx:**839-2805
(212) 969-3000 .. **Forbes,** Robt D '08 %Proskauer R LLP -1585 Bway -NY 10036
(212) 486-4300 .. **Forbes & Sommers** -150 E 58th -NY 10155 **Fx:**317-2946
(718) 791-8444 .. **Forbes,** Steven P '95 -153-01 Jamaica Av -Jamaica 11432
(917) 224-3886 .. **Forbin,** Claudeth V '98 -3811 Barnes Av -Bronx 10467
(212) 425-7200 .. **Force,** Alan P '94 %Kenyon & K,LLP -1 Bway -NY 10004
(888) 524-1320 .. **Force,** Thos J '95 Financial Medical Systems -55 Knndy Dr -Hauppauge 11788
(212) 701-3939 .. **Forcellon,** Mary C '74 -80 Pine -NY 10005
(718) 278-6117 .. **Forchelli,** Chas N '73 Forchelli & F -32-02 30th Av -LIC 11102 **Fx:**726-8449
(516) 248-1700 .. **Forchelli Curto Deegan Schwartz Mineo & Terrana, LLP** -333 Earle Ovngton Blvd -Uniondale 11553 **Fx:**248-1729
(516) 248-1700 .. **Forchelli,** Jeffrey D '69 (Forchelli CDSM&T,LLP) -333 Earle Ovngton Blvd -Uniondale 11553
(718) 250-2000 .. **Forchelli,** Nicole S '08 %DA -350 Jay -Brklyn 11201 **Fx:**250-2314
(212) 325-2000 .. **Forchheimer,** Adam I '03 %Credit Suisse -11 Mad Av -NY 10010
(212) 836-8000 .. **Forchheimer,** Danl E '06 %Kaye S LLP -425 Park Av -NY 10022
(212) 820-9522 .. **Forcht,** Lisa A '94 Cnsl Hawkins D&W LLP -One Chase Manh Plz -NY 10005
(518) 566-6726 .. **Forcier,** Gerald R Jr. '94 Cnsl Westelcom Communications -23 Durkee -Plattsbrgh 12901 **Fx:**566-6420
(315) 785-3928 .. **Forcier,** Michl R '84 Westelcom Comm Inc -130 Park Pl -Watertwn 13601 **Fx:**786-8498
(718) 357-1216 .. **Forcina,** Elio '03 (Forcina & M PC) -148-29 Cross Isl Pkwy -Whitestone 11357 **Fx:**357-1219
(212) 715-9100 .. **Ford,** Adam C '03 %Kramer LN&F,LLP -1177 Av of Amer -NY 10036
(212) 335-4500 .. **Ford,** Ann K '87 (DLA Piper LLP) -1251 Av of Amer -NY 10020
(718) 250-3841 .. **Ford,** Anthony J '09 DA -350 Jay -Brklyn 11201
(516) 502-4080 .. **Ford,** Barbara L '99 (BL Ford,PC) -99 Tulip Av -Floral Pk 11001 **Fx:**502-4082
(516) 572-2000 .. **Ford,** Bernadette K '86 %DA -99 Main -Hempstd 11550 **Fx:**572-2606
(516) 364-6006 .. **Ford,** Charis M '04 %Cohen & S,LLP -199 Crsswys Park Dr Bx9004 -Woodbury 11797
(212) 478-7200 .. **Ford,** Danl M '01 (Hahn & H LLP) -488 Mad Av -NY 10022
(212) 788-0838 .. **Ford,** David K '73 SpclCnsl Law Dept -100 Church -NY 10007 **Fx:**788-0367
(585) 423-8305 .. **Ford,** David P '88 %Xerox -100 Clinton Av S -Rchstr 14644
(518) 455-9952 .. **Ford,** Donald P Jr. '76 (Thuillez FGB&Y,LLP) -20 Corp Wds Blvd -Albany 12211
(845) 353-0250 .. **Ford,** Edw L '83 -10 Gail Dr -Nyack 10960
(212) 902-6385 .. **Ford,** Elizabeth J '88 Goldman Sachs & Co -85 Broad -NY 10004
(716) 841-4262 .. **Ford,** Georgiana '90 %HSBC Bank -1 HSBC Ctr -Buffalo 14203 **Fx:**841-5087
(212) 474-1000 .. **Ford,** Gerald A '82 Cravath S&M LLP -825 8th Av -NY 10019
(212) 238-4800 .. **Ford,** Gerald T '80 (Landman CB&F,PC) -120 Bway -NY 10271
(212) 453-5900 .. **Ford & Harrison LLP** -100 Park Av -NY 10017 **Fx:**453-5959
(212) 610-6300 .. **Ford,** Heather J '07 %Allen & O -1221 Av of Amer -NY 10020
(631) 224-5550 .. **Ford,** Janet '93 %Town Atty -655 Main -Islip 11751 **Fx:**224-5573
(212) 487-9700 .. **Ford,** Janet P '98 OfCnsl White F&F,LLP -61 Bway -NY 10006
(212) 225-2000 .. **Ford,** Jason C '10 %Cleary GS&H -1 Lbrty Plz -NY 10006
(212) 326-3939 .. **Ford,** John F '08 %Jones D -222 E 41st -NY 10017
(212) 878-8000 .. **Ford,** John L '07 %Clifford C LLP -31 W 52nd -NY 10019
(716) 856-5500 .. **Ford,** John P '05 %Damon M LLP -200 Delaware Av -Buffalo 14202
(212) 909-6000 .. **Ford,** Joshua Q '08 %Debevoise & P LLP -919 3rd Av -NY 10022
(212) 687-6262 .. **Ford,** Kaleen S '08 %Barton B&P,LLP -420 Lex Av -NY 10170
(212) 558-4000 .. **Ford,** Kathryn E '93 (Sullivan & C LLP) -125 Broad -NY 10004
(516) 229-6000 .. **Ford,** Keith E '94 %R Lau & Assoc -300 Jericho Quad Bx9040 -Jericho 11753 **Fx:**229-6167
(212) 357-1759 .. **Ford,** Kevin J '83 Goldman Sachs -85 Broad -NY 10004
(212) 335-9000 .. **Ford,** Linda L '89 %DA -1 Hogan Pl -NY 10013
(212) 269-4900 .. **Ford Marrin Esposito Witmeyer & Gleser,LLP** -Wall Street Plz -NY 10005 **Fx:**344-4294
(212) 701-3000 .. **Ford,** Matthew A '09 %Cahill G&R LLP -80 Pine -NY 10005 **Fx:**269-5420
(718) 590-2000 .. **Ford,** Michl A '10 %DA -198 E 161st -Bronx 10451 **Fx:**590-6477
(914) 925-0707 .. **Ford,** Patrick A '95 (PA Ford,LLC) -2 Seneca -Rye 10580
(212) 455-2000 .. **Ford,** Paul B Jr. '68 OfCnsl Simpson T&B LLP -425 Lex Av -NY 10017
(518) 426-2955 .. **Ford,** Peter G '83 -161 Southrn Blvd -Albany 12209
(516) 222-0200 .. **Ford,** Richd P '94 (Keith S&F) -666 Old Cntry Rd -Gdn Cty 11530
(212) 837-6819 .. **Ford,** Robt T '10 %Hughes H&R LLP -1 Bttry Pk Plz -NY 10004 **Fx:**299-6819
(212) 715-9100 .. **Ford,** Samantha McQuaid '09 Kramer LN&F,LLP -1177 Av of Amer -NY 10036
(646) 428-7028 .. **Ford,** Stefan P '86 GE -299 Park Av -NY 10171
(315) 477-9108 .. **Ford,** Steven J '86 %Carlisle Companies Inc -250 S Clinton -Syracuse 13202 **Fx:**474-2008
(212) 905-2882 .. **Ford,** Valerie J '09 Avenue Capital Grp -535 Mad Av -NY 10022
(212) 259-8000 .. **Forde,** Bianca M '09 %Dewey & L LLP -1301 Av of Amer -NY 10019
(212) 425-5750 .. **Forde,** Hugh A '96 Gard (NA) Inc -30 Broad -NY 10004
(212) 839-7000 .. **Forde,** James E '93 (Hill B&N LLP) -200 Lbrty -NY 10281
(212) 921-5200 .. **Forde,** James L '84 %Rappaport GG&L LLP -733 3rd Av -NY 10017
(718) 250-0400 .. **Forde,** Kevin T '92 %R Tusa -1 MetroTech Ctr -Brklyn 11201 **Fx:**250-0591
(516) 512-6590 .. **Forde,** Michl E '81 %Pieret & Assoc -400 Grdn City Plz -Gdn Cty 11530 **Fx:**742-4116
(914) 422-8755 .. **Forde,** Shelley A '90 %Dept of Law -101 E Post Rd -White Plns 10601 **Fx:**422-8706
(212) 310-8000 .. **Forde-Chandler,** Tanya B '09 %Weil G&M LLP -767 5th Av -NY 10153
(212) 690-2510 .. **Fordham,** Edw F '79 -2286 Adam Clayton Powell Jr Blvd -NY 10030 **Fx:**690-2511
(212) 270-6000 .. **Fordham,** Michl R Jr. '97 JP Morgan Chase -270 Park Av -NY 10017
(212) 997-1500 .. **Fordin,** Candice D '06 Value Line Inc -220 E 42nd -NY 10017
(212) 935-8880 .. **Foreht Last Landau & Katz,LLP** -228 E 45th -NY 10017 **Fx:**935-5554
(212) 935-8880 .. **Foreht,** Stephen R '86 (Foreht LL&K,LLP) -228 E 45th -NY 10017
(212) 455-2000 .. **Forelle,** John M '71 OfCnsl Simpson T&B LLP -425 Lex Av -NY 10017
(718) 590-2000 .. **Foreman,** Joshlyn A '97 %DA -198 E 161st -Bronx 10451 **Fx:**590-6477
(718) 658-0500 .. **Foreman,** Judith '88 %Law Dept -151-20 Jamaica Av -Jamaica 11432 **Fx:**658-4025
(631) 232-4444 .. **Foreman,** Kevin J '88 %A Presberg,PC -100 Corp Plz -Islandia 11749 **Fx:**232-2603
(212) 267-6659 .. **Foreman-Harris,** Mary E '89 -305 Bway -NY 10007 **Fx:**732-2191
(914) 533-6858 .. **Forese,** Angela Vizzini '90 -18 Wakeman Rd -S Salem 10590 **Fx:**533-6858
(845) 621-9868 .. **Forest,** Lester Jr. '82 L Forest Jr,PC -299 Route 6 N -Mahopac 10541 **Fx:**621-4548
(212) 506-5000 .. **Foresta,** Stephen G '88 (Orrick H&S LLP) -51 W 52nd -NY 10019
(212) 278-6133 .. **Foret-Geary,** Sandrine A '06 Societe Generale -1221 Av of Amer -NY 10020
(212) 938-0500 .. **Forgang,** Chas S '82 -530 5th Av -NY 10036 **Fx:**938-0502
(631) 249-8200 .. **Forgas-Gartland,** Melissa L '03 %DePinto N & Assoc,LLP -445 Broadhllw Rd -Melvll 11747 **Fx:**249-8209
(212) 957-4162 .. **Forger,** Alexander D '51 Oak Spring Farms,LLC -160 Cntrl Pk S -NY 10019
(212) 286-8585 .. **Forgione,** Anthony P '04 %Heidell PM&B,LLP -99 Park Av -NY 10016
(718) 482-1400 .. **Forgione,** Frances M '05 Forgione Fincl Srvcs -395 Graham Av -Brklyn 11211
(212) 824-5700 .. **Forgione,** Meghan '07 Practising Law Inst -810 7th Av -NY 10019
(212) 261-8000 .. **Forgione,** Traysia M '06 %Mendes & M,LLP -750 7th Av -NY 10019
(518) 731-6118 .. **Fori,** Thos J '68 Curtis W&F -46 Reed -Coxsackie 12051
(518) 449-0751 .. **Forkeutis,** Paul M '95 -20 Fairlawn Av -Rensselaer 12144 **Fx:**449-0751

(212) 328-0555 .. **Forlano,** Lori J '99 Lightyear Captl -375 Park Av -NY 10152 **Fx:**328-0516
(212) 310-8000 .. **Forlenza,** Justin D '08 %Weil G&M LLP -767 5th Av -NY 10153
(212) 421-2111 .. **Forlenza,** Lee A '83 (Granoff W&F,PC) -747 3rd Av -NY 10017
(212) 336-2000 .. **Forlenza,** Philip R '67 (Patterson BW&T LLP) -1133 Av of Amer -NY 10036
(212) 607-8317 .. **Form,** David A '06 ROC Capital Mgmt LP -650 5th Av -NY 10019
(516) 803-2300 .. **Forma,** Chas A '77 %Cablevision Sys -1111 Stewart Av -Bethpage 11714
(212) 327-8058 .. **Forman,** Adam P '03 Rockefeller Univ -1230 York Av -NY 10065
(718) 268-2616 .. **Forman,** Arthur H '81 -98-20 Metro Av -Frst Hlls 11375 **Fx:**575-1600
(212) 872-1000 .. **Forman,** Brian R '05 -One Bryant Park -NY 10036 **Fx:**872-1002
(212) 766-9111 .. **Forman,** Cory E '01 (Cohen & F,LLP) -40 Fulton -NY 10038 **Fx:**766-9166
(212) 728-8000 .. **Forman,** Danl I '10 %Willkie F&G LLP -787 7th Av -NY 10019
(212) 859-8000 .. **Forman,** Danl L '09 %Fried FHS&J LLP -1 NY Plz -NY 10004
(212) 761-5563 .. **Forman,** Donald M '00 Morgan Stanley -1585 Bway -NY 10036
(646) 386-5206 .. **Forman,** Douglas R '87 %Family Ct -60 Lafayette -NY 10013
(212) 450-2800 .. **Forman,** Edw S '93 Duff & Phelps LLC -55 E 52nd -NY 10055
(212) 416-8538 .. **Forman,** Elizabeth A '87 %Dept of Law -120 Bway -NY 10271
(212) 541-2000 .. **Forman,** Erica R '80 (Bryan C LLP) -1290 Av of Amer -NY 10104
(716) 754-2224 .. **Forman,** George H '64 -4744 Lwr River Rd -Lewiston 14092
(518) 437-6962 .. **Forman,** Glenn M '81 %State Ins Fund -15 Computer Dr W -Albany 12205 **Fx:**485-8761
(212) 353-2200 .. **Forman,** Howard M '77 (Turkel F&D LLP) -304 Park Av S -NY 10010
(212) 619-4350 .. **Forman,** Ian B '97 %Newman MKGH,PC -14 Wall -NY 10005
(718) 935-1586 .. **Forman,** Ira J '80 -26 Court -Brklyn 11242 **Fx:**625-4176
(212) 461-2143 .. **Forman,** Jamie A '01 (Bedell & F LLP) -44 Wall -NY 10005 **Fx:**(646) 219-7441
(212) 407-7700 .. **Forman,** Joel S '74 Vedder P,PC -1633 Bway -NY 10019
(212) 859-8000 .. **Forman,** Jonathan A '07 %Fried FHS&J LLP -1 NY Plz -NY 10004
(212) 962-1200 .. **Forman,** Jonathan E '75 (Fogelgaren F&B,LLP) -277 Bway -NY 10007
(212) 317-1717 .. **Forman,** Joshua T '99 (Chemtob MF&T LLP) -3 E 54th -NY 10022
(212) 225-2000 .. **Forman,** Laura J '05 %Cleary GS&H -1 Lbrty Plz -NY 10006
(718) 596-0504 .. **Forman,** Lauren H '04 Clocktower Properties -325 Gold -Brklyn 11201 **Fx:**596-6443
(914) 693-8033 .. **Forman,** Laurie A '83 -17 Westway -Hartsdale 10530
(212) 953-2381 .. **Forman,** Mandie R '05 %Rubin F&F,LLP -292 Mad Av -NY 10017
(212) 696-6000 .. **Forman,** Martin L '86 (Curtis M-PC&M LLP) -101 Park Av -NY 10178
(718) 625-4423 .. **Forman,** Neal B '67 -26 Court -Brklyn 11242
(212) 479-2145 .. **Forman,** Perry S '93 %Eurohypo -1114 Av of Amer -NY 10036
(914) 962-1241 .. **Forman,** Robt M '83 -40 Triangle Ctr -Yorktwn Hts 10598 **Fx:**962-1197
(212) 972-4900 .. **Forman,** Robt W '80 (Shapiro FA&S LLP) -380 Mad Av -NY 10017
(212) 582-0900 .. **Forman,** Sandra M '02 Harris & Harris Grp,Inc -1450 Bway -NY 10018
(212) 759-3300 .. **Forman,** Shira '05 %Dornbush SS&V,LLP -747 3rd Av -NY 10017
(212) 244-0110 .. **Forman,** Stuart A '69 -450 7th Av -NY 10123 **Fx:**244-3686
(845) 434-4777 .. **Forman,** Terry S '98 (Kalter KZ&F) -6166 State Rte 42 Bx30 -Woodbourne 12788
(845) 647-4110 .. **Forman,** Terry S '98 (Kalter KZ&F) -47 N Main Bx186 -Ellenvll 12428
(518) 526-3556 .. **Forman,** Walter J '89 -68 Simmons Av -Cohoes 12047 **Fx:**237-3281
(212) 791-5500 .. **Forman,** Warren L '69 (Forman Assoc,PC) -156 William -NY 10038 **Fx:**791-5544
(516) 328-2300 .. **Formato,** Patrick '94 (Abrams FFEGF&E,LLP) -1111 Marcus Av -Lk Success 11042
(718) 250-0400 .. **Formica,** Judith Anselmo '83 %R Tusa -1 MetroTech Ctr -Brklyn 11201 **Fx:**250-0591
(212) 480-6341 .. **Formichelli,** Michl S '93 %Insurance Dept -25 Beaver -NY 10004 **Fx:**480-5272
(516) 571-3800 .. **Formichelli,** Robt P '91 DA -262 Old Cntry Rd -Mineola 11501 **Fx:**248-9479
(212) 233-7195 .. **Formicola,** Carl A '81 %Lewis JAA,LLP -61 Bway -NY 10006
(631) 737-8200 .. **Formisano,** Bianca '06 %T Campagna -4949 Express Dr N -Ronkonkoma 11779 **Fx:**737-8687
(212) 752-9700 .. **Fornari,** James D '69 (Gersten S LLP) -600 Lex Av -NY 10022
(212) 474-1000 .. **Fornarotto,** Lauren L '10 %Cravath S&M LLP -825 8th Av -NY 10019
(212) 526-7000 .. **Fornasar,** Gregory C '94 Lehman Bros -399 Park Av -NY 10022
(212) 594-5300 .. **Fornecker,** Anne K '03 %Milberg LLP -1 Penn Plz -NY 10119
(914) 238-8727 .. **Forni,** Fred L '56 -106 Marcourt Dr -Chappaqua 10514
(212) 231-1000 .. **Forni,** Fredk P '92 MacQuarie Securities -125 W 55th -NY 10019
(212) 637-2740 .. **Fornos,** Carolina A '01 %US Atty -86 Chmbrs -NY 10007
(516) 536-0094 .. **Foronjy,** Richd P '60 -87 Windsor Av -Rockvll Ctr 11570 **Fx:**764-2294
(212) 349-5890 .. **Forrest,** Alan M '82 NYS Trial Lawyers Assn -132 Nassau -NY 10038
(716) 854-4300 .. **Forrest,** Harry J '00 (Gross SB&G,PC) -465 Main -Buffalo 14203
(212) 474-1000 .. **Forrest,** Katherine B '91 (Cravath S&M LLP) -825 8th Av -NY 10019
(212) 403-1000 .. **Forrest,** Kenneth B '77 (Wachtell LR&K) -51 W 52nd -NY 10019
(212) 513-3200 .. **Forrest,** Loren L Jr. '99 %Holland & K LLP -31 W 52nd -NY 10019
(212) 213-6261 .. **Forrest,** Michl I '97 Forrest Prtnrs LLC -133 Ludlow -NY 10002 **Fx:**(646) 390-1224
(212) 446-7044 .. **Forrest,** Michelle R '01 %McKinsey & Co -55 E 52nd -NY 10055 **Fx:**688-9521
(212) 225-2000 .. **Forrest,** Neil P '81 Cleary GS&H -1 Lbrty Plz -NY 10006
(607) 737-5681 .. **Forrest,** Steven W '81 Elmira City Ct -317 E Church -Elmira 14901
(518) 251-2215 .. **Forrest,** Thos J '67 OfCnsl Staples & D,PC -280 Main Bx66 -N Creek 12853 **Fx:**251-5038
(212) 776-5000 .. **Forrest,** Tracy L '89 %NYC Housing Auth -250 Bway -NY 10007 **Fx:**776-5039
(716) 542-4144 .. **Forrestel,** Richd E '50 -11 Mad Av -Akron 14001 **Fx:**542-4944
(718) 637-6560 .. **Forrester,** Janet '04 Osborne Assoc -175 Remsen -Brklyn 11201
(718) 658-3200 .. **Forrester,** Joan C '84 -145-11 Jamaica Av -Jamaica 11435
(212) 308-4411 .. **Forrester,** Joe E '74 Cnsl Edwards AP&D LLP -750 Lex Av -NY 10022
(718) 523-1111 .. **Forrester,** Jomo C '04 %Gildin Z&S,PC -138-44 Qns Blvd -Briarwd 11435
(845) 562-9020 .. **Forrester,** Michl H '68 (Silver FS&L) -3250 Route 9W -New Windsor 12553
(212) 233-5500 .. **Forrester,** Stephen P '84 %SPCC -161 William -NY 10038 **Fx:**791-2821
(646) 345-0586 .. **Forry,** John I '98 -50 Sutton Pl -NY 10022
(212) 521-5400 .. **Forsberg,** Lars '79 (Reed S LLP) -599 Lex Av -NY 10022
(718) 855-4529 .. **Forschein,** Scott L '92 -625 Atl Av -Brklyn 11217
(212) 504-6000 .. **Forsh,** David S '08 %Cadwalader W&T LLP -1 World Fncl Ctr -NY 10281
(212) 455-2000 .. **Forshaw,** Mary Beth '90 (Simpson T&B LLP) -425 Lex Av -NY 10017
(518) 474-1310 .. **Forshaw,** Robin A '88 %Gov's Cnsls Ofc -242 State Cptl -Albany 12224
(212) 232-1300 .. **Forshner,** Ian M '07 %Lewis BB&S LLP -77 Water -NY 10005
(718) 399-6868 .. **Forson,** Frank K '91 -639 Carlton Av -Brklyn 11238
(212) 545-1921 .. **Forst,** Reena '93 OfCnsl Fischer PT&R,PC -250 W 57th -NY 10107
(315) 446-1865 .. **Forstadt,** Clifford '74 -5788 Widewaters Pkwy -DeWitt 13214 **Fx:**446-1208
(212) 340-0400 .. **Forstadt,** Jonathan H '95 Appllt Div 1st Dept -27 Mad Av -NY 10010 **Fx:**889-4412
(212) 806-5400 .. **Forstadt,** Jos L '65 (Stroock &S&L LLP) -180 Maiden Ln -NY 10038
(914) 347-2290 .. **Forstbauer,** Kristine Ann '97 -47 Nepperhan Av -Elmsfrd 10523
(212) 345-5629 .. **Forstenzer,** Andrew P '84 %Marsh USA -1166 Av of Amer -NY 10036 **Fx:**345-4808
(212) 586-4700 .. **Forster,** Clifford '39 OfCnsl Fitelson LA&C -551 5th Av -NY 10176
(212) 808-3060 .. **Forster,** Denis '85 -230 Park Av -NY 10169 **Fx:**599-2339
(631) 393-9400 .. **Forster & Garbus** -500 Bi-Cnty Blvd Bx9030 -Farmngdl 11735 **Fx:**393-9490
(518) 784-2940 .. **Forster,** James F '82 OfCnsl DeLuca & F -45 E Shore Dr -Valatie 12184 **Fx:**(908) 276-6260
(718) 631-2500 .. **Forster,** Jeanne Ellen '99 OfCnsl Bailey & S,PC -42-21 Douglstn Pkwy -Douglastn 11363
(718) 667-1948 .. **Forster,** Paul S '77 -82 Ross Av Bx61240 -Staten Isl 10306 **Fx:**987-2547
(212) 449-3180 .. **Forster,** Robt S Jr. '03 Merrill Lynch -4 World Fncl Ctr -NY 10080
(631) 393-9400 .. **Forster,** Ronald '69 (Forster & G) -500 Bi-Cnty Blvd Bx9030 -Farmngdl 11735
(914) 948-0405 .. **Forster,** Sandra A '80 -8 Beechwd Rd -Hartsdale 10530 **Fx:**761-7915
(212) 558-4000 .. **Forster,** Stephen '07 %Sullivan & C LLP -125 Broad -NY 10004
(212) 355-5656 .. **Forstmann,** Theo J '66 %Forstmann Little -767 5th Av -NY 10153
(516) 746-7799 .. **Forstner,** Glenn S '95 %Reisman P&R LLP -1305 Franklin Av -Gdn Cty 11530
(212) 768-6700 .. **Forstot,** Jonathan D '89 (Sonnenschein N&R LLP) -1221 Av of Amer -NY 10020
(585) 325-7515 .. **Forsyth,** C Benn '50 (Forsyth HOK&M,PC) -1 Chase Sq -Rchstr 14604
(716) 566-2800 .. **Forsyth,** Danl P '82 (Bond S&K,PLLC) -40 Fountian Plz -Buffalo 14202
(585) 262-3400 .. **Forsyth,** Donald A '49 (Forsyth & F) -16 W Main -Rchstr 14614
(585) 262-3400 .. **Forsyth,** George K '79 (Forsyth & F) -16 W Main -Rchstr 14614
(585) 325-7515 .. **Forsyth Howe O'Dwyer Kalb & Murphy, PC** -1 Chase Sq -Rchstr 14604 **Fx:**325-6407
(315) 637-3673 .. **Forsyth,** J Michl '81 -519 E Genesee -Fayettevll 13066 **Fx:**637-3672
(646) 915-0025 .. **Forsyth,** Priscilla J '07 Lighthouse Academies -1001 Intervale Av -Bronx 10459 **Fx:**915-0037
(585) 262-3400 .. **Forsyth,** Scott A '77 (Forsyth & F) -16 W Main -Rchstr 14614
(212) 788-1091 .. **Forsyth,** Susan Grossi '69 %Law Dept -100 Church -NY 10007 **Fx:**788-0367
(718) 981-1072 .. **Forsyth,** Timothy '88 -195 Crystal Av -Staten Isl 10302 **Fx:**720-5009
(212) 708-9335 .. **Forsyth,** Wm H Jr. '71 Bessemer Trst Co -630 5th Av -NY 10111 **Fx:**265-5826
(646) 871-8773 .. **Forsythe,** Warren '57 -36 E 20th -NY 10003 **Fx:**(212) 624-0236
(212) 804-4200 .. **Fort,** Andrea L '05 %Mound CW&G -One Bttry Pk Plz -NY 10004
(212) 682-1818 .. **Fort,** Olga E '05 %Murray F&S LLP -275 Mad Av -NY 10016
(646) 610-5400 .. **Fortain,** Renee T '92 %NYPD -1 Police Plz -NY 10038
(516) 437-5800 .. **Fortanasce,** Frank T '84 -608 Jericho Tpk -New Hyde Pk 11040 **Fx:**328-0864
(914) 592-4275 .. **Forte,** Alejandro A '00 %MHLS -100 Clearbrook Rd -Elmsfrd 10523 **Fx:**592-2634
(212) 425-3100 .. **Forte,** Ann Marie '89 (McManus C&R,PC) -48 Wall -NY 10005
(914) 390-4126 .. **Forte,** Chris E '81 %Hon M Fox -300 Quarropas -White Plns 10601
(914) 949-9075 .. **Forte,** Denise A '96 (Trivella & F LLP) -1311 Mamaroneck Av -White Plns 10605 **Fx:**949-4752
(516) 466-6030 .. **Forte,** E Lisa '87 %Mirkin & G,PC -98 Cuttermill Rd -Gt Neck 11021
(718) 698-0569 .. **Forte,** Jennifer '04 (Cutrona & F,PC) -41 Kell Av -Staten Isl 10314
(631) 234-1154 .. **Forte,** John N '08 S Mishkin,PC -1 Suffolk Sq -Islandia 11749 **Fx:**234-5048
(212) 210-9513 .. **Forte,** Jos P '74 (Alston & B LLP) -90 Park Av -NY 10016
(212) 735-3000 .. **Forte,** Julia E '06 %Skadden ASM&F LLP -4 Times Sq -NY 10036
(212) 577-3915 .. **Forte,** Kimberly '00 %Leg Aid -199 Water -NY 10038 **Fx:**577-3520
(914) 785-2483 .. **Forte,** Michelle F '85 %Ciba Corp -540 Wht Plns Rd -Tarrytwn 10591 **Fx:**785-4831
(212) 495-0100 .. **Forte,** Rachael '03 %Gottesman WMF&W,PC -11 Hanover Sq -NY 10005
(845) 357-0036 .. **Forte,** Stephen M '09 %Lexow B&A,PC -56 Park Av Bx239 -Suffern 10901
(718) 334-2351 .. **Forte,** Tessa J '04 %MHLS -79-01 Bway -Elmhrst 11373 **Fx:**334-2353
(718) 277-5004 .. **Forteau,** Clement '97 -Bx170241 -Jamaica 11417 **Fx:**277-5200
(212) 596-3379 .. **Fortenbaugh,** Saml B III '61 -630 5th Av -NY 10111 **Fx:**596-3391
(212) 776-5000 .. **Fortgang,** Anna S '82 %NYC Housing Auth -250 Bway -NY 10007 **Fx:**776-5039
(212) 362-2506 .. **Fortgang,** Brauna E '74 -90 Riverside Dr -NY 10024 **Fx:**362-5306

(212) 984-7896 .. **Fortgang**, Marvin J '74 (Warshaw BCS&K,LLP) -555 5th Av -NY 10017
(585) 987-2800 .. **Forth**, Gordon E '88 (Woods OG LLP) -2 State -Rchstr 14614
(585) 232-8314 .. **Forth**, Lynn A '87 (Buckner & K) -1 S Wshngtn -Rchstr 14614
(718) 237-2323 .. **Forth**, Michl C '86 -326 Atl Av -Brklyn 11201 **Fx:**237-2904
(716) 684-8060 .. **Forti**, Jos '83 %Ecology & Envrnmnt -368 Plsntvw Dr -Lancaster 14086 **Fx:**684-0844
(212) 566-3230 .. **Fortier**, Edw J '01 %Dept of Bldgs -280 Bway -NY 10007
(646) 557-5100 .. **Fortin**, Robt Jay '85 (Patton B LLP) -1185 Av of Amer -NY 10036
(315) 793-2370 .. **Fortino**, Elizabeth S '01 %MHLS -207 Genesee -Utica 13501 **Fx:**793-2371
(212) 909-6000 .. **Fortino**, Philip A '06 %Debevoise & P LLP -919 3rd Av -NY 10022
(315) 637-5151 .. **Fortino**, Philip G '00 %F Josef,PC -519 E Genesee -Fayettevll 13066 **Fx:**637-3436
(212) 848-4000 .. **Fortinsky**, Jerome S '88 (Shearman & S LLP) -599 Lex Av -NY 10022
(315) 853-2120 .. **Fortnam**, Steven R '80 -Bx323 -Westmoreland 13490
(212) 351-4000 .. **Fortney**, Jonathan D '10 Gibson D&C LLP -200 Park Av -NY 10166
(631) 581-9494 .. **Fortney**, Rebecca J '96 %Ferro KMS,PC -350 Motor Pkwy -Hauppauge 11788
(716) 855-2626 .. **Forton**, Gerard F '90 (Forton & F) -361 Delaware Av -Buffalo 14202
(716) 855-2626 .. **Forton**, James F '58 (Forton & F) -361 Delaware Av -Buffalo 14202
(516) 228-6666 .. **Fortuna**, John A '93 (Rosenberg F&L,LLP) -666 Old Cntry Rd -Gdn Cty 11530
(212) 213-8844 .. **Fortuna**, Nicholas J '87 (Allyn & F LLP) -200 Mad Av -NY 10016
(718) 858-4366 .. **Fortunato**, Annamarie '97 (Fortunato & F,PLLC) -26 Court -Brklyn 11242 **Fx:**852-6432
(718) 858-4366 .. **Fortunato**, Camille '03 (Fortunato & F,PLLC) -26 Court -Brklyn 11242 **Fx:**852-6432
(631) 673-6670 .. **Fortunato**, Gina M '94 %Speyer & P,LLP -115 Broadhllw Rd -Melvll 11747
(845) 735-0088 .. **Fortunato**, Jeffrey J '85 -275 N Mddltwn Rd -Pearl Rvr 10965 **Fx:**735-7660
(845) 638-5180 .. **Fortunato**, Jeffrey J '85 %Cnty Atty -Cnty Ofc Bldg -New Cty 10956 **Fx:**638-5676
(212) 524-5000 .. **Fortunato**, John E '65 OfCnsl Jacob M&F -1270 Av of Amer -NY 10020
(212) 735-2577 .. **Fortunato**, Richd S '86 (Skadden ASM&F LLP) -4 Times Sq -NY 10036
(516) 496-3500 .. **Fortunato**, Theo Jr. '93 -6800 Jericho Tpk -Syosset 11791 **Fx:**496-3530
(212) 453-8988 .. **Fortune**, Brian H '97 Hunter Global Investors LP -485 Mad Av -NY 10022
(212) 239-5715 .. **Fortune**, Brigitte L '88 %Div Of Parole -314 W 40th -NY 10018 **Fx:**239-6160
(718) 298-8900 .. **Fortune**, Natasha M '09 %Leg Aid -153-01 Jamaica Av -Jamaica 11432 **Fx:**657-0537
(315) 677-9777 .. **Forward**, Stephen A '76 (Jacobs & F) -Route 11 Maher Bldg Bx184 -LaFayette 13084 **Fx:**677-4652
(914) 965-1011 .. **Forzaglia**, Anthony '10 %JG Dibbini -570 Ynkrs Av -Ynkrs 10704 **Fx:**965-0019
(718) 372-1397 .. **Forzano**, Michl A '77 -271 Av U -Brklyn 11223 **Fx:**372-6999
(516) 484-5400 .. **Forzano**, Michl J '85 %Pall Corp -25 Hrbr Park Dr -Pt Wash 11050
(347) 249-0504 .. **Fosbinder**, Jane L '89 -123 7th Av -Brklyn 11215
(212) 450-4000 .. **Foschi**, Jessica K '08 %Davis P&W LLP -450 Lex Av -NY 10017
(716) 853-3801 .. **Foscolo**, Jessica L '09 %Kenney SL&N,LLP -14 Lafayette Sq -Buffalo 14203
(212) 416-6150 .. **Foshee**, Dawn A '92 %Dept of Law -120 Bway -NY 10271 **Fx:**416-6147
(516) 572-0200 .. **Foskey**, Carnell T '81 Cnty Parks Commissioner -Esnhwr Park -E Meadow 11554
(212) 449-8452 .. **Foskey**, Tiffany M '06 Merrill Lynch -4 World Fncl Ctr -NY 10081
(585) 419-8800 .. **Foss**, Douglas A '80 (Harris B PLLC) -99 Garnsey Rd -Pittsfrd 14534
(212) 664-4444 .. **Fossett**, Andrew G '90 %NBC -30 Rckfllr Plz -NY 10112
(212) 803-5100 .. **Foster**, Bradley E '96 %NY Cnty Defender Srvcs -225 Bway -NY 10007 **Fx:**571-6035
(212) 504-6000 .. **Foster**, Brian D '05 %Cadwalader W&T LLP -1 World Fncl Ctr -NY 10281
(212) 480-7418 .. **Foster**, Carl M '94 %DHCR -25 Beaver -NY 10004 **Fx:**480-7416
(212) 685-5545 .. **Foster**, Cheryl I '06 %J Barnett -260 Mad Av -NY 10016 **Fx:**685-5695
(212) 335-9000 .. **Foster**, Christopher J '02 %DA -1 Hogan Pl -NY 10013
(585) 530-3142 .. **Foster**, David A '88 %Appllt Div 4th Dept -50 East Av Ste 200 -Rchstr 14604 **Fx:**530-3247
(315) 781-0138 .. **Foster**, David Lee '79 -438 Exchange Bx143 -Geneva 14456 **Fx:**781-3299
(315) 946-7463 .. **Foster**, David Lee '79 %Leg Aid -9 Pearl -Lyons 14489 **Fx:**946-5964
(914) 995-2576 .. **Foster**, Dawn Marie '02 %Cnty Atty -148 Martine Av -White Plns 10601 **Fx:**995-2495
(516) 877-5600 .. **Foster**, Denise E '92 %R Tusa -1225 Franklin Av -Gdn Cty 11530 **Fx:**877-5695
(585) 352-5556 .. **Foster**, Edwin A '53 (Foster F&Z) -5500 W Ridge Rd -Spencerprt 14559
(212) 403-1000 .. **Foster**, Edwin J '09 %Wachtell LR&K -51 W 52nd -NY 10019
(646) 557-5100 .. **Foster**, Eric L '91 (Patton B LLP) -1185 Av of Amer -NY 10036
(631) 727-7731 .. **Foster**, Frederic C '79 (Foster & V,LLP) -220 Roanoke Av -Rvrhead 11901
(845) 255-6020 .. **Foster**, Gale L '80 (GL Foster,PC) -5 Paradies Ln -New Paltz 12561 **Fx:**255-6044
(585) 352-5556 .. **Foster**, John J '76 (Foster F&Z) -5500 W Ridge Rd -Spencerprt 14559
(516) 681-8210 .. **Foster**, John P '86 -420 Jericho Tpk -Jericho 11753 **Fx:**935-0238
(212) 227-3550 .. **Foster**, John R '78 (Waesche S&O,PC) -111 Bway -NY 10006
(516) 577-2642 .. **Foster**, Joshua P '01 Honeywell Intl,Inc -2 Corp Ctr Dr -Melvll 11747 **Fx:**(631) 351-6658
(516) 227-6363 .. **Foster**, Kerry Anne '98 %Amato & Assoc,PC -666 Old Cntry Rd -Gdn Cty 11530 **Fx:**227-6367
(718) 241-6493 .. **Foster**, Kharl A '85 -105-74 Av N -Brklyn 11236 **Fx:**241-6495
(212) 309-6000 .. **Foster**, Laurie E '78 (Morgan L&B LLP) -101 Park Av -NY 10178
(212) 651-7500 .. **Foster**, Lindsey Tylus '10 %Segal MS&M -850 3rd Av -NY 10022
(212) 474-1000 .. **Foster**, Nicole F '04 %Cravath S&M LLP -825 8th Av -NY 10019
(212) 869-8500 .. **Foster**, Pamela O'Kane '03 Rockefeller Foundation -420 5th Av -NY 10018
(585) 383-1300 .. **Foster**, Patricia C '80 %OppenheimerFunds,Inc -350 Linden Oaks -Rchstr 14625
(516) 746-5599 .. **Foster**, Patrick K '06 %Bee RFH&D,LLP -170 Old Cntry Rd -Mineola 11501
(212) 691-2313 .. **Foster**, Peter B '84 (Foster & W,PC) -80 5th Av -NY 10011 **Fx:**691-2459
(718) 260-8860 .. **Foster**, Rachel E '95 -96 Pierrepont -Brklyn 11201
(315) 536-2500 .. **Foster**, Robt C '77 -305 Lbrty -Penn Yan 14527 **Fx:**536-4951
(315) 424-0205 .. **Foster**, Susan M '84 %Eljay Abstract -1010 James -Syracuse 13203
(516) 393-6116 .. **Foster**, Tanya S '03 %S Rubin -999 Stewart Av -Bethpage 11714 **Fx:**393-6150
(347) 592-2200 .. **Foster**, Tara J '91 %Leg Srvcs -89-00 Sutphin Blvd -Jamaica 11435 **Fx:**(718) 937-5350
(212) 479-6000 .. **Foster**, Timothy L '09 %Cooley LLP -1114 Av of Amer -NY 10036
(917) 442-9580 .. **Foster**, Tina Monshipour '01 Intl Justice Network -Bx610119 -Bayside 11361
(718) 243-6369 .. **Foster**, Tosha Yvette '98 %Leg Aid -111 Lvngstn -Brklyn 11201 **Fx:**237-8737
(212) 705-9439 .. **Foster**, Tyreta E '00 %BBC Worldwide Americas -747 3rd Av -NY 10017
(631) 727-7731 .. **Foster & Vandenburgh,LLP** -220 Roanoke Av -Rvrhead 11901 **Fx:**727-7741
(212) 530-5000 .. **Foster**, Wilbur F Jr. '82 (Milbank TH&M LLP) -1 Chase Manh Plz -NY 10005
(518) 429-4200 .. **Foster**, Wm C '89 (Hiscock & B,LLP) -50 Beaver -Albany 12207
(914) 834-3500 .. **Foster**, Wm J IV '73 (McMillan CM&P LLP) -2180 Bstn Post Rd -Larchmnt 10538
(315) 437-7255 .. **Foster**, Wm L '84 -232 Shotwell Park -Syracuse 13206 **Fx:**471-6290
(212) 858-1000 .. **Foti**, Anthony D '07 %Pillsbury WSP LLP -1540 Bway -NY 10036
(212) 880-9530 .. **Foti**, Catherine M '86 (Morvillo AGIA&B,PC) -565 5th Av -NY 10017
(212) 965-0442 .. **Foti**, Franco G '80 %Foti & Lazo, Inc -39 Bway -NY 10006 **Fx:**965-0631
(716) 853-3801 .. **Foti**, Melissa A '04 %Kenney SL&N,LLP -14 Lafayette Sq -Buffalo 14203
(212) 446-4800 .. **Fotiades**, Adam L '08 %Kirkland & E LLP -153 E 53rd -NY 10022
(212) 781-2111 .. **Fotopoulos**, Alexander D '92 %Fotopoulos R&G -4160 Bway -NY 10033
(212) 781-2111 .. **Fotopoulos**, Constantine D '00 %Fotopoulos R&G -4160 Bway -NY 10033
(212) 781-2111 .. **Fotopoulos**, Dimitrios C '61 (Fotopoulos R&G) -4160 Bway -NY 10033
(212) 781-2111 .. **Fotopoulos Rosenblatt & Green** -4160 Bway -NY 10033 **Fx:**795-0423
(631) 638-4012 .. **Fouassier**, James G '82 Stony Brook Univ Hsptl Med Ctr -188 Belle Mead Rd -E Setauket 11733 **Fx:**638-4075
(212) 635-2244 .. **Foudy**, John P '94 %Rosner N&R LLP -110 Wall -NY 10005
(212) 696-6000 .. **Foudy**, Theresa Ann '94 (Curtis M-PC&M LLP) -101 Park Av -NY 10178
(212) 450-4000 .. **Fouhey**, John '74 SrCnsl Davis P&W LLP -450 Lex Av -NY 10017
(646) 392-9250 .. **Fouhy**, Kevin P '80 %M Klein & Assoc -200 Mad Av -NY 10016 **Fx:**(212) 779-1499
(212) 837-6000 .. **Foukas**, Savvas A '02 %Hughes H&R LLP -1 Bttry Pk Plz -NY 10004
(607) 778-2473 .. **Foulk**, Stephen D '80 %Hon R Rose -203 Cnty Cthse Bx1766 -Bnghmtn 13902 **Fx:**772-8331
(315) 255-1655 .. **Foulke**, E Kenton '94 (Foulke Law Firm) -5 Court Bx797 -Auburn 13021 **Fx:**253-1391
(845) 294-4308 .. **Foulke**, Evan M '91 -1997 Route 17 M -Goshen 10924 **Fx:**294-4309
(607) 778-8990 .. **Foulke**, Melissa G '95 %Probation Dept -Bx1766 -Bnghmtn 13902
(518) 583-0523 .. **Foulke**, Sarah B '84 -229 Wshngtn -Saratoga Spgs 12866 **Fx:**583-0783
(315) 255-1655 .. **Foulke**, Walter C '61 -5 Court Bx797 -Auburn 13021
(212) 541-2000 .. **Foulkes**, Richd B '07 %Bryan C LLP -1290 Av of Amer -NY 10104
(212) 833-1190 .. **Fourmaux**, Jeffrey C '00 %Friedman KS&A LLP -1633 Bway -NY 10019 **Fx:**373-7990
(212) 664-4444 .. **Fournier**, Chas W '83 %NBC -30 Rckfllr Plz -NY 10112
(212) 246-8045 .. **Fournier**, Clotilde '90 %Bureau FL -101 Park Av -NY 10178 **Fx:**246-2951
(212) 506-5000 .. **Fournier**, Kristen R '06 %Orrick H&S LLP -51 W 52nd -NY 10019
(212) 538-4353 .. **Fouron**, Seendy G '99 Credit Suisse -1 Mad Av -NY 10010
(212) 277-4000 .. **Fourteau**, Timothy G '08 %Freshfields BD LLP -520 Mad Av -NY 10022
(716) 204-2400 .. **Fourtner**, Tracy M '06 %SJ Baum,PC -220 Nrthpnte Pkwy Bx1291 -Buffalo 14240 **Fx:**204-4600
(917) 922-2891 .. **Fourton**, Leslie E '96 -314 W 92nd -NY 10025 **Fx:**(212) 593-3224
(212) 661-5030 .. **Foust**, Jonathan E '06 %Schoeman U&K,LLP -60 E 42nd -NY 10165
(212) 450-4000 .. **Foust**, Joshua T '09 %Davis P&W LLP -450 Lex Av -NY 10017
(212) 949-0924 .. **Fouts**, Julius P '58 -300 E 40th -NY 10016
(212) 545-1900 .. **Fouts**, Stephanie D '04 %Menaker & H LLP -10 E 40th -NY 10016
(718) 590-2000 .. **Fouz**, Yahya A '07 %DA -198 E 161st -Bronx 10451 **Fx:**590-6477
(718) 254-7450 .. **Fowle**, Linda I '91 %US Probation Dept -75 Clinton -Brklyn 11201 **Fx:**254-7461
(212) 297-2420 .. **Fowler**, Andrew F '99 (Gray H LLP) -7 Times Sq -NY 10036 **Fx:**916-2940
(212) 277-0403 .. **Fowler**, Anthony J '91 Hartford Fncl -2 Park Av -NY 10016
(518) 487-5460 .. **Fowler**, Cheryl K '93 %DA -6 Lodge -Albany 12207 **Fx:**487-5093
(516) 741-6266 .. **Fowler**, David T '81 (McCabe CM&F,LLP) -346 Westbury Av Bx9000 -Carle Pl 11514
(212) 836-8000 .. **Fowler**, Ericka J A '09 %Kaye S LLP -425 Park Av -NY 10022
(518) 279-1143 .. **Fowler**, Fredk L '75 -1011 Hoosick Rd -Troy 12180 **Fx:**279-4320
(315) 479-3380 .. **Fowler**, Herbert C '89 %UIA Bd -450 S Salina -Syracuse 13202 **Fx:**479-3418
(914) 946-3700 .. **Fowler**, John A '68 (McCarthy F LLP) -11 Martine Av -White Plns 10606
(212) 250-3398 .. **Fowler**, John D Jr. '87 Deutsche Bk Sec -60 Wall -NY 10005 **Fx:**797-0058

(607) 763-9200 .. **Fowler,** Margaret J '91 (Levene G&T,LLP) -BxF-1706 -Bnghmtn 13902
(212) 818-9200 .. **Fowler,** Mark A '86 (Satterlee SB&B LLP) -230 Park Av -NY 10169
(518) 457-5472 .. **Fowler,** Paul K '97 NYS Police -State Campus Plz Bldg 24 -Albany 12201
(716) 681-7380 .. **Fowler,** Thos E '76 -5441 Bway -Lancaster 14086
(718) 237-2000 .. **Fowlkes,** Wm O '00 %Leg Aid -111 Lvngstn -Brklyn 11201 **Fx:**237-8737
(716) 440-7218 .. **Fowlston,** Tamara R '93 -170 Cmmnwlth Av -Buffalo 14216 **Fx:**874-3870
(212) 698-3500 .. **Fox,** Adam M '92 (Dechert LLP) -1095 Av of Amer -NY 10036
(212) 646-1132 .. **Fox,** Aileen J '86 %Taxi & Limo Comm -40 Rector -NY 10006
(212) 451-2900 .. **Fox,** Alan D '76 Cnsl Robinson & C LLP -885 3rd Av -NY 10022
(212) 609-6800 .. **Fox,** Alan H '91 (McCarter & E,LLP) -245 Park Av -NY 10167
(646) 471-1131 .. **Fox,** Alan S '84 PricewaterhouseCoopers LLP -300 Mad Av -NY 10017
(718) 334-0687 .. **Fox,** Alexander F '98 -4036 Junction Blvd -Corona 11368
(212) 956-0101 .. **Fox,** Andrew J '92 -1626 Bway -NY 10019 **Fx:**391-6917
(212) 906-1200 .. **Fox,** Ariel A '98 OfCnsl Latham & W -885 3rd Av -NY 10022
(212) 225-2000 .. **Fox,** Barry M '71 (Cleary GS&H) -1 Lbrty Plz -NY 10006
(212) 768-7900 .. **Fox,** Barry P '72 -1500 Bway -NY 10036 **Fx:**302-6715
(212) 746-1744 .. **Fox,** Caroline L '00 %NY Presbyterian Hsptl -525 E 68th Bx88 -NY 10065 **Fx:**746-8603
(518) 474-0411 .. **Fox,** Chas G '92 Executive Chamber -State Cptl -Albany 12224 **Fx:**473-7619
(914) 509-5943 .. **Fox,** Chas M '84 Fox Professional Devel LLC -360 Hmltn Av -White Plns 10601 **Fx:**509-6134
(212) 687-1980 .. **Fox,** Christine M '95 %Kaplan F&K LLP -850 3rd Av -NY 10022
(315) 449-6431 .. **Fox,** Christopher W '79 %Agway,Inc -Bx4933 -Syracuse 13221 **Fx:**449-6253
(203) 775-7008 .. **Fox,** Cynthia D '90 -375 Bailey Rd -Montgmry 12549
(212) 964-6611 .. **Fox,** Danl J '02 Cnsl Lester SK&D -120 Bway -NY 10271
(914) 766-1394 .. **Fox,** Danl P '02 IBM -294 Route 100 -Somers 10589
(212) 446-4800 .. **Fox,** David '84 (Kirkland & E LLP) -153 E 53rd -NY 10022
(212) 907-9700 .. **Fox,** David L '67 Cnsl Smith G&R,LLP -250 Park Av -NY 10177
(212) 474-1000 .. **Fox,** Deborah M L '08 %Cravath S&M LLP -825 8th Av -NY 10019
(914) 948-4555 .. **Fox,** Dennis M '66 -286 Horseshoe Cir -Ossining 10562 **Fx:**682-7032
(212) 243-1313 .. **Fox,** Diedra I '07 Leg Action Ctr -225 Varick -NY 10014 **Fx:**675-0286
(585) 241-5999 .. **Fox,** Donald R '75 (Evans & F LLP) -95 Allens Crk Rd -Rchstr 14618
(315) 986-3980 .. **Fox,** Donald R '75 -2687 Hance Rd -Macedon 14502
(212) 480-4800 .. **Fox,** Donald T '57 (Fox H&C LLP) -825 3rd Av -NY 10022
(212) 509-9400 .. **Fox,** Douglas B '97 (Cozen O) -45 Bway Atrium -NY 10006
(631) 724-7980 .. **Fox,** Edw J '92 -400 Townline Rd -Hauppauge 11788
(212) 536-3900 .. **Fox,** Edw M '86 (K&L Gates LLP) -599 Lex Av -NY 10022
(212) 998-6171 .. **Fox,** Eleanor M '61 %NYU Law Schl -40 Wshngtn Sq S -NY 10012 **Fx:**995-4341
(212) 867-9123 .. **Fox,** Elizabeth A '06 %Berkman BN&R,LLP -521 5th Av -NY 10175
(212) 449-0227 .. **Fox,** Eric C '97 Merrill Lynch -4 World Fncl Ctr -NY 10080
(516) 222-0505 .. **Fox,** Ernest L '84 (Fox & L,LLP) -666 Old Cntry Rd -Gdn Cty 11530 **Fx:**228-8990
(212) 687-1980 .. **Fox,** Frederic S '85 (Kaplan F&K LLP) -850 3rd Av -NY 10022
(212) 210-9544 .. **Fox,** Glenn G '91 (Alston & B LLP) -90 Park Av -NY 10016
(212) 833-1177 .. **Fox,** Gregory W '07 %Friedman KS&A LLP -1633 Bway -NY 10019 **Fx:**373-7977
(212) 715-1000 .. **Fox,** Hanna M '04 %Arnold & P LLP -399 Park Av -NY 10022
(516) 248-1180 .. **Fox,** Harvey '80 -1 Old Cntry Rd -Carle Pl 11514 **Fx:**248-7596
(212) 458-1034 .. **Fox,** Heather M '95 %AIG -175 Water -NY 10038 **Fx:**458-1043
(212) 480-4800 .. **Fox Horan & Camerini LLP** -825 3rd Av -NY 10022 **Fx:**269-2383
(716) 662-5563 .. **Fox,** Jack M '85 -4329 S Buffalo -Orchard Pk 14127 **Fx:**662-5788
(718) 643-4968 .. **Fox,** James J '83 %Criminal Ct -120 Schermerhorn -Brklyn 11201
(212) 237-0000 .. **Fox,** James J '01 (Vinson & E LLP) -666 5th Av -NY 10103
(716) 434-6392 .. **Fox,** James L '73 -556 S Transit -Lockprt 14094 **Fx:**434-5269
(212) 319-0600 .. **Fox,** Jay '55 OfCnsl O'Donnell & F,PC -29 Bway -NY 10006
(212) 730-8133 .. **Fox,** Jeffrey A '04 %Gunderson DSVF&H,LLP -220 W 42nd -NY 10036
(518) 463-1269 .. **Fox,** Jeffrey M '93 (Walsh & H) -18 Corp Wds Blvd -Albany 12211
(212) 481-1220 .. **Fox,** Jesse J '09 %Markowitz & C LLP -271 Mad Av -NY 10016 **Fx:**481-1221
(212) 460-1149 .. **Fox,** John M '93 Con Ed -4 Irving Pl -NY 10003
(212) 553-5522 .. **Fox,** John R '95 Zurich NA -1 Lbrty Plz -NY 10006
(315) 422-1311 .. **Fox,** Jonathan E '68 (Melvin & M,PLLC) -217 S Salina -Syracuse 13202
(212) 306-7422 .. **Fox,** Jonathan M '06 Comm on Human Rights -40 Rector -NY 10006
(212) 681-1575 .. **Fox,** Jordan C '85 (Belluck & F LLP) -546 5th Av -NY 10036
(212) 859-8000 .. **Fox,** Jos E '07 %Fried FHS&J LLP -1 NY Plz -NY 10004
(212) 949-8300 .. **Fox,** Jos L '84 -60 E 42nd -NY 10165 **Fx:**684-1428
(516) 747-0300 .. **Fox,** Kamini '03 %Meltzer LG&B,LLP -190 Willis Av -Mineola 11501
(516) 496-0730 .. **Fox,** Kathleen M '88 (Fratello & F,PC) -242 Crsswys Park Dr W -Woodbury 11797 **Fx:**496-9791
(212) 732-8700 .. **Fox,** Kenneth A '97 (McAloon & F,PC) -123 William -NY 10038
(212) 418-8721 .. **Fox,** Kerri L '95 Fortis Cptl Corp -520 Mad Av -NY 10022
(914) 245-1454 .. **Fox,** Kevin G '77 -186 Long Hill Dr -Yorktwn Hts 10598
(631) 656-8537 .. **Fox,** Kevin M '78 KM Fox,PLLC -400 Townline Rd -Hauppauge 11788 **Fx:**656-8563
(518) 383-0200 .. **Fox & Kowalewski, LLP** -4 Old Route 146 Bx958 -Clifton Pk 12065 **Fx:**383-1510
(212) 838-3100 .. **Fox,** Kraig G '94 %Sillerman Companies -650 Mad Av -NY 10022
(646) 610-5483 .. **Fox,** Lauren '83 %NYPD -1 Police Plz -NY 10038 **Fx:**610-2995
(518) 383-0200 .. **Fox,** Laurence I '73 (Fox & K,LLP) -4 Old Route 146 Bx958 -Clifton Pk 12065
(212) 418-8600 .. **Fox,** Lawr C '83 (Kornstein VW&P,LLP) -757 3rd Av -NY 10017
(212) 547-5400 .. **Fox,** Lawr I '78 (McDermott W&E LLP) -340 Mad Av -NY 10173
(212) 867-9595 .. **Fox,** Leo '77 -630 3rd Av -NY 10017 **Fx:**949-1857
(518) 474-0571 .. **Fox,** Lisa K '85 Ofc Gnl Srvcs -Corning Twr ESP -Albany 12242 **Fx:**473-4973
(212) 685-5015 .. **Fox,** Mark J '76 -111 E 35th -NY 10016 **Fx:**685-5041
(212) 367-1312 .. **Fox,** Mary Ellen '98 %GMHC,Inc -119 W 24th -NY 10011 **Fx:**367-1305
(212) 336-8000 .. **Fox,** Matthew A '04 %Amster R&E -90 Park Av -NY 10016
(212) 474-1000 .. **Fox,** Matthew B '08 %Cravath S&M LLP -825 8th Av -NY 10019
(212) 530-5000 .. **Fox,** Melanie J '09 %Milbank TH&M LLP -1 Chase Manh Plz -NY 10005
(845) 778-2121 .. **Fox,** Michl L '04 Jacobowitz & G,LLP -158 Orange Av Bx367 -Walden 12586
(212) 451-2300 .. **Fox,** Michl S '83 (Olshan GFR&W LLP) -65 E 55th -NY 10022
(212) 577-3688 .. **Fox,** Michelle M '86 %Leg Aid -199 Water -NY 10038 **Fx:**509-8431
(212) 545-4755 .. **Fox,** Paulette S '02 %Wolf HAF&H LLP -270 Mad Av -NY 10016
(212) 701-3000 .. **Fox,** Peter R '10 %Cahill G&R LLP -80 Pine -NY 10005 **Fx:**269-5420
(212) 995-8440 .. **Fox,** Rachel H '94 -808 Bway -NY 10003 **Fx:**253-2074
(212) 417-5300 .. **Fox,** Randall M '92 %Medicaid Fraud Cntrl -120 Bway -NY 10271 **Fx:**417-5274
(212) 773-4911 .. **Fox,** Richd D '86 %Ernst & Young LLP -5 Times Sq -NY 10036
(212) 984-9129 .. **Fox,** Richd K '04 Radian Asset Assurance Inc -335 Mad Av -NY 10017
(212) 867-9595 .. **Fox,** Robt M '07 -630 3rd Av -NY 10017 **Fx:**949-1857
(516) 671-3807 .. **Fox,** Roberta '85 -34 Hrbr Way -Sea Cliff 11579 **Fx:**671-3922
(212) 688-5151 .. **Fox,** Rosanna M '07 %Gibney A&F,LLP -665 5th Av -NY 10022
(212) 878-7900 .. **Fox Rothschild LLP** -100 Park Av -NY 10017 **Fx:**692-0940
(716) 853-9555 .. **Fox,** Russell E '94 %Leg Aid -237 Main -Buffalo 14203 **Fx:**853-3219
(518) 273-0000 .. **Fox,** Seymour '50 -219 River Bx869 -Troy 12181 **Fx:**273-2030
(212) 548-2100 .. **Fox,** Shawn R '03 %McGuire W LLP -1345 Av of Amer -NY 10105
(212) 582-5200 .. **Fox,** Sigmund '60 S Fox,PC -370 Lex Av -NY 10017 **Fx:**586-9683
(212) 592-1400 .. **Fox,** Stephen E '97 (Herrick,F LLP) -2 Park Av -NY 10016
(516) 248-1180 .. **Fox,** Steven A '10 %H Fox -1 Old Cntry Rd -Carle Pl 11514 **Fx:**248-7596
(212) 351-4500 .. **Fox,** Steven E '87 (Epstein B&G,PC) -250 Park Av -NY 10177
(212) 421-8100 .. **Fox,** Steven I '99 (Wrobel & S LLP) -1040 Av of Amer -NY 10018
(716) 852-3800 .. **Fox,** Steven S '87 -122 Deerhurst Park Plvd -Buffalo 14217
(516) 573-7210 .. **Fox,** Tatum J '03 Nassau Cnty Police-Legal -1490 Franklin Av -Mineola 11501
(212) 735-3000 .. **Fox,** Thos E '84 Cnsl Skadden ASM&F LLP -4 Times Sq -NY 10036
(718) 281-3425 .. **Fox,** Thos E Jr. '89 %NYC Dept Educ-OLS -52 Chmbrs -NY 10007 **Fx:**(212) 374-5596
(518) 455-3039 .. **Fox,** Thos J Jr. '79 %Assembly -12th Fl Agncy Bldg 4 ESP -Albany 12248
(315) 483-6733 .. **Fox,** Tracey L '93 -29 W Main Bx249 -Sodus 14551 **Fx:**483-2073
(518) 477-7553 .. **Fox,** Wm L '76 -4 Springhurst Dr -E Greenbush 12061 **Fx:**477-7599
(718) 570-5871 .. **Foxman,** Noah Y '80 Digital Publishing Intl,Ltd -1125 E 10th -Brklyn 11230
(718) 520-2259 .. **Fox-McDonough,** Elizabeth M '88 Hon B Kron -125-01 Qns Blvd -Kew Gdns 11415
(585) 530-3146 .. **Fox-Solomon,** Elizabeth M '07 Appellate Div -50 East Av -Rchstr 14604
(212) 709-8230 .. **Foy,** Jason E '96 (Foy & F,LLC) -110 Wall -NY 10005
(212) 815-1818 .. **Foy,** Joan Altagracia '84 %DC 37 MELS -125 Barclay -NY 10007 **Fx:**815-1343
(646) 471-4000 .. **Foy,** Jos J '91 %PricewaterhouseCoopers LLP -300 Mad Av -NY 10017
(212) 709-8230 .. **Foy,** Karla Y '93 (Foy & F,LLC) -110 Wall -NY 10005
(631) 471-2500 .. **Foy,** Peggy A '92 -622 Hawkins Av -Ronkonkoma 11779 **Fx:**467-1930
(631) 467-4600 .. **Foy,** Thos F '72 -2701 Middle Cntry Rd -Lk Grove 11755 **Fx:**467-4603
(718) 590-3299 .. **Foyer,** Steven I '78 %Law Dept -198 E 161st -Bronx 10451 **Fx:**590-2686
(212) 352-8098 .. **Foytlin,** Stephen C '04 Cnsl Spa Week Media Grp -89 5th Av -NY 10003
(212) 486-2500 .. **Fraade,** Alan P '76 (Mintz & F,PC) -488 Mad Av -NY 10022
(585) 288-4200 .. **Fracassi,** Frank J '73 -2289 Clifford Av Bx90851 -Rchstr 14609 **Fx:**288-1720
(914) 287-8061 .. **Fraccio,** Patrice '06 %Pearson Educ -10 Bank -White Plns 10606
(212) 326-2000 .. **Frackman,** Andrew J '82 (O'Melveny & M LLP) -7 Times Sq -NY 10036
(212) 243-5894 .. **Frackman,** Jeffrey '71 -400 Chmbrs -NY 10282 **Fx:**243-5936
(212) 943-9079 .. **Frade,** Manny A '02 (Mastropietro & F,LLC) -111 Bway -NY 10006 **Fx:**943-9218
(212) 674-5151 .. **Fradin,** Alice L '92 Macmillan -175 5th Av -NY 10010 **Fx:**529-0594
(917) 237-2900 .. **Fradin-Rhodes,** Jill M '96 Axiom Law -75 Spring -NY 10012
(212) 891-1600 .. **Fradkin,** Ilya '08 %Jenner & B LLP -919 3rd Av -NY 10022
(212) 696-6000 .. **Fraenkel,** Orietta M '99 %Curtis M-PC&M LLP -101 Park Av -NY 10178
(212) 788-1247 .. **Fraenkel,** Wm S J '91 %Law Dept -100 Church -NY 10007 **Fx:**788-0367
(718) 590-2000 .. **Fraggetta,** Michl J '08 %DA -198 E 161st -Bronx 10451 **Fx:**590-6477
(212) 461-6804 .. **Fragin,** Gregory S '03 Silar Advisors -333 7th Av -NY 10001
(212) 852-7886 .. **Fragola,** Cristiana V '97 News Corp -1211 Av of Amer -NY 10036 **Fx:**852-7147
(212) 688-8555 .. **Fragomen,** Austin T Jr. '73 (Fragomen DB&L LLP) -7 Hanover Sq -NY 10004
(212) 688-8555 .. **Fragomen Del Rey Bernsen & Loewy LLP** -7 Hanover Sq -NY 10004 **Fx:**480-9930
(516) 829-0363 .. **Fraiberg,** Andra G '06 %Israel I&P,LLP -11 Grace Av -Gt Neck 11021 **Fx:**829-0366
(212) 294-6700 .. **Fraid,** Lauren N '09 %Winston & S -200 Park Av -NY 10166
(718) 993-9911 .. **Fraiden,** David A '02 %Fraiden & P -327 E 149th -Bronx 10451
(718) 993-9911 .. **Fraiden,** Norman '67 (Fraiden & P) -327 E 149th -Bronx 10451
(718) 993-9911 .. **Fraiden & Palen** -327 E 149th -Bronx 10451 **Fx:**401-3328
(212) 407-1200 .. **Fraidin,** Saml N '06 %Joseph Law Ofcs LLC -485 Lex Av -NY 10017 **Fx:**407-1299
(212) 446-4800 .. **Fraidin,** Stephen '65 (Kirkland & E LLP) -153 E 53rd -NY 10022
(718) 802-2767 .. **Fraidstern,** Danl M '06 %ACS -330 Jay -Brklyn 11201
(716) 566-5400 .. **Frain,** Toni L '00 %Goldberg S LLP -665 Main -Buffalo 14203
(212) 804-4200 .. **Fraley,** Amy J '06 %Mound CW&G -One Bttry Pk Plz -NY 10004
(315) 218-8000 .. **Frame,** Kristy B '10 %Bond S&K,PLLC -1 Lincoln Ctr -Syracuse 13202

(212) 558-4000 .. **Frame,** Nuri G '08 %Sullivan & C LLP -125 Broad -NY 10004
(845) 454-1110 .. **Frame,** Wm W '05 Corbally G and R LLP -35 Market -Poughkeepsie 12601
(518) 674-2922 .. **Frament,** Danl '84 Frament & F -104 Lawson Rd -Sand Lake 12153
(518) 869-9094 .. **Frament,** Jason A '01 %Wein & F -951 Albany Shaker Rd -Latham 12110
(212) 819-8200 .. **Frampton,** Christopher P '89 (White & C LLP) -1155 Av of Amer -NY 10036
(212) 841-1000 .. **Frampton,** George T Jr. '70 SrCnsl Covington & B LLP -620 8th Av -NY 10018
(631) 234-5678 .. **Frampton,** Robt H '93 %Wallace WF&V,PC -600 Suffolk Av -Brentwd 11717
(212) 909-6000 .. **Franca Pereira,** Mariana T '06 %Debevoise & P LLP -919 3rd Av -NY 10022
(212) 599-0900 .. **France,** Edw A III '99 %Bower & L,PC -261 Mad Av -NY 10016
(718) 884-0477 .. **France,** Michelle J '84 -5700 Arlngtn Av -Bronx 10471
(718) 706-1111 .. **France,** Robt G '98 %Telebeam Telephone Sys Inc -36-40 37th -LIC 11101
(212) 860-2481 .. **France,** Willa N '78 -318 E 120th -NY 10035
(845) 247-3775 .. **Francello,** Robt '69 -34 W Brdg Bx89 -Saugerties 12477 **Fx:**246-3657
(845) 246-3655 .. **Francello & Van Benschoten** -34 W Brdg Bx359 -Saugerties 12477 **Fx:**246-3657
(518) 587-6670 .. **Frances,** Julie M '07 D Harper -480 Bway -Saratoga Spgs 12866 **Fx:**587-6672
(212) 765-5070 .. **Francescani,** David R '68 (Fish & R,PC) -153 E 53rd -NY 10022
(212) 341-6400 .. **Franceschetti,** Jack '87 %Liquidation Bur -123 William -NY 10038 **Fx:**608-3398
(718) 205-6667 .. **Franceschini,** Edw D '99 -212-05 82nd Av -Qns Vllg 11427
(646) 855-0803 .. **Francese,** Gerald A '01 Bank of America -1 Bryant Pk -NY 10036
(212) 345-3273 .. **Franceski,** Jos A '85 Marsh Aviation -1166 Av of Amer -NY 10036
(315) 894-9976 .. **Franchi,** James J '82 (Getman F&A,LLP) -38 Morgan Bx477 -Ilion 13357
(516) 877-7500 .. **Franchina,** Emily F '90 (Franchina & G,PC) -1100 Franklin Av -Gdn Cty 11530
(516) 877-7500 .. **Franchina & Giordano,PC** -1100 Franklin Av -Gdn Cty 11530 **Fx:**877-7743
(516) 229-4200 .. **Franchina,** Marijana Bolanca '99 %Mendolia & S -875 Merrick Av -Westbury 11590
(315) 428-8100 .. **Franchini,** Eugene J '96 OfCnsl Wittenburg Law Firm,LLC -920 Univ Bldg -Syracuse 13202 **Fx:**426-8102
(212) 733-5141 .. **Franchini,** Indrani M '99 %Pfizer Inc -235 E 42nd -NY 10017
(212) 530-5000 .. **Franchini,** John D '96 (Milbank TH&M LLP) -1 Chase Manh Plz -NY 10005
(212) 335-9000 .. **Franchini,** Lisa M '09 %DA -1 Hogan Pl -NY 10013
(212) 530-5000 .. **Francini,** Mark B '02 %Milbank TH&M LLP -1 Chase Manh Plz -NY 10005
(631) 665-3400 .. **Francino,** Andrew P '75 %Siben & S,LLP -90 E Main Bx149P -Bay Shr 11706
(212) 918-3000 .. **Franciose,** Christopher N '08 %Hogan L LLP -875 3rd Av -NY 10022
(718) 493-2293 .. **Francis,** Clement A '00 -822 Clarkson Av -Brklyn 11203
(212) 815-1818 .. **Francis,** Jacqueline D '96 %DC 37 MELS -125 Barclay -NY 10007 **Fx:**815-1343
(212) 715-1000 .. **Francis,** Jonathan '03 %Arnold & P LLP -399 Park Av -NY 10022
(212) 363-6900 .. **Francis,** Kirl Carl '00 %Faust GS&B LLP -2 Rector -NY 10006
(516) 505-5600 .. **Francis,** Leslie L '93 -250 Fulton Av -Hempstd 11550 **Fx:**505-5617
(212) 556-2100 .. **Francis,** Mark H '07 %King & S -1185 Av of Amer -NY 10036
(212) 506-2500 .. **Francis,** Melissa B '07 %Mayer B LLP -1675 Bway -NY 10019
(516) 229-6000 .. **Francis,** Michl A '93 %R Lau & Assoc -300 Jericho Quad Bx9040 -Jericho 11753 **Fx:**229-6167
(518) 486-9871 .. **Francis,** Paul E '81 %Governors Ofc -207 State Cptl -Albany 12224
(212) 279-6536 .. **Francis,** Ronald '89 -350 5th Av -NY 10118 **Fx:**244-6784
(212) 969-3000 .. **Francis,** Stephen M '05 %Proskauer R LLP -1585 Bway -NY 10036
(718) 286-6000 .. **Francis,** Yvonne '89 %DA -125-01 Qns Blvd -Kew Gdns 11415
(212) 967-2262 .. **Francisco,** Aris '91 (Francisco & P) -421 7th Av -NY 10001
(518) 843-3300 .. **Francisco,** Jeffrey '90 Francisco Law Firm -17 Market -Amsterdam 12010 **Fx:**843-3305
(212) 852-1000 .. **Franciscovich,** Linda R '83 %US Trust Co,NA -114 W 47th -NY 10036 **Fx:**852-1310
(212) 696-6000 .. **Francke,** Albert III '62 OfCnsl Curtis M-PC&M LLP -101 Park Av -NY 10178
(516) 621-9399 .. **Franckel,** Philip L '82 (1-800-HURT-911) -42 Davis Ln -Roslyn 11576
(212) 878-8000 .. **Franco,** Alanna L '09 %Clifford C LLP -31 W 52nd -NY 10019
(212) 270-5026 .. **Franco,** Beatriz R J '00 JP MorganChase -270 Park Av -NY 10017
(516) 357-3700 .. **Franco,** Deborah M '94 (Cullen and D LLP) -100 Q Roosevelt Blvd -Gdn Cty 11530
(212) 417-5800 .. **Franco,** Dolores '98 Dept of State -123 William -NY 10038
(212) 975-5575 .. **Franco,** Laura S '88 %CBS Inc -51 W 52nd -NY 10019 **Fx:**975-3930
(716) 849-8900 .. **Franco,** Lawr C '77 (Hurwitz & F,PC) -1300 Lbrty Bldg -Buffalo 14202
(917) 573-3378 .. **Franco,** Lidelfo A '02 -50 Manh Av -NY 10025 **Fx:**(212) 866-1130
(212) 655-3597 .. **Franco,** Lorrie B '86 (Freiman F PC) -140 E 45th -NY 10017 **Fx:**655-3529
(718) 250-2000 .. **Franco,** Melissa '97 %DA -350 Jay -Brklyn 11201 **Fx:**250-2314
(212) 686-5700 .. **Franco,** Michl J '95 M Franco,PC -15 W 81st -NY 10024 **Fx:**230-8001
(716) 854-7888 .. **Franco,** Nicole J '03 %Venzon B,LLP -300 Delaware Av -Buffalo 14202 **Fx:**854-0294
(212) 768-6700 .. **Franco,** Salvatore O '99 (Sonnenschein N&R LLP) -2 World Fncl Ctr -NY 10281
(212) 468-4800 .. **Franco,** Shira '02 %Davis & G LLP -1740 Bway -NY 10019
(914) 821-8828 .. **Franco,** Stephanie '06 Lukemia & Lymphoma Society -1311 Mamaroneck Av -White Plns 10605
(212) 490-3000 .. **Francoeur,** Jos L '99 (Wilson EME&D LLP) -150 E 42nd -NY 10017
(212) 225-2000 .. **Francois,** Daphney '10 %Cleary GS&H -1 Lbrty Plz -NY 10006
(212) 335-9000 .. **Francois,** Lucrece '03 %DA -1 Hogan Pl -NY 10013
(914) 789-7943 .. **Francois,** Marie A '00 %Fujifilm Holdings -200 Summit Lk Dr -Valhalla 10595 **Fx:**789-8514
(212) 563-2200 .. **Francois,** Michaelle '03 %Brandt S&L LLP -386 Park Av S -NY 10016
(631) 728-1403 .. **Francolini,** E R '58 -42 Ponquogue Av -Hampton Bays 11946
(212) 788-0988 .. **Francolla,** Brian C '08 %Law Dept -100 Church -NY 10007 **Fx:**788-0367
(212) 578-2211 .. **Francolla,** Stacy Laine '00 %MetLife -27-01 Qns Plz N -LIC 11101
(212) 610-6300 .. **Frandina,** Michl M '09 %Allen & O -1221 Av of Amer -NY 10020
(212) 906-1200 .. **Franek,** Melinda C '06 %Latham & W -885 3rd Av -NY 10022
(212) 250-2694 .. **Frangenberg,** Gunter '01 %Deutsche Bk Sec -60 Wall -NY 10005
(212) 788-1184 .. **Frangiose,** Mario G '91 %Law Dept -100 Church -NY 10007 **Fx:**788-0367
(845) 473-2040 .. **Frangk,** Stanley A '85 (Levine H&F) -316 Main -Poughkeepsie 12601
(718) 631-5699 .. **Frangopoulos,** Constantine '95 -47-01 Bell Blvd -Bayside 11361 **Fx:**631-2002
(646) 428-3831 .. **Frangos,** Emily '02 US Dept of Ed -32 Old Slip -NY 10005
(315) 474-7740 .. **Frani,** Elizabeth C '98 -333 E Onondaga -Syracuse 13202 **Fx:**474-0425
(212) 272-1543 .. **Frank,** Adam L '94 %JP Morgan Chase -383 Mad Av -NY 10179
(212) 416-8271 .. **Frank,** Andrew G '98 %Dept of Law -120 Bway -NY 10271
(631) 265-9191 .. **Frank,** Andrew J '93 Epstein & G -1393 Vets Mem'l Hwy -Hauppauge 11788
(646) 562-4505 .. **Frank,** Andrew J '04 OCH-ZIFF Cap Mgmt Grp -9 W 57th -NY 10019
(212) 661-3381 .. **Frank,** Arthur L '59 -100 Park Av -NY 10017
(212) 345-6000 .. **Frank,** Barbara H '77 %Marsh USA -1166 Av of Amer -NY 10036 **Fx:**345-4808
(212) 310-8000 .. **Frank,** Barry '67 (Weil G&M LLP) -767 5th Av -NY 10153
(516) 506-6771 .. **Frank,** David '94 RexCorp Realty LLC -625 RXR Plz -Uniondale 11556
(646) 392-9250 .. **Frank,** David R '94 %M Klein & Assoc -200 Mad Av -NY 10016 **Fx:**(212) 779-1499
(212) 885-5000 .. **Frank,** Donald '69 (Blank R LLP) -405 Lex Av -NY 10174
(631) 859-0300 .. **Frank,** Edw J '85 %Zaklukiewicz P&M,LLP -2701 Sunrise Hwy Bx389 -Islip Terr 11752
(212) 756-2000 .. **Frank,** Erica '08 %Schulte R&Z LLP -919 3rd Av -NY 10022
(212) 686-0100 .. **Frank Frank Goldstein & Nager,LLP** -1430 Bway -NY 10018 **Fx:**686-6726
(914) 528-5450 .. **Frank,** Gary '80 -3475 Lakeside Dr -Mohegan Lk 10547
(212) 278-1853 .. **Frank,** Gloria J '84 (Anderson K&O,PC) -1251 Av of Amer -NY 10020
(212) 682-1818 .. **Frank,** Gregory A '08 %Murray F&S LLP -275 Mad Av -NY 10016
(716) 858-6599 .. **Frank,** Howard B '74 %Dept Soc Srvcs -95 Franklin -Buffalo 14202 **Fx:**858-8072
(212) 351-4500 .. **Frank,** James S '75 (Epstein B&G,PC) -250 Park Av -NY 10177
(516) 908-6658 .. **Frank,** Jamie E '78 -8 Haven Ln -Levittwn 11756 **Fx:**706-1114
(315) 793-2370 .. **Frank,** Janine E '01 %MHLS -207 Genesee -Utica 13501 **Fx:**793-2371
(212) 259-8000 .. **Frank,** Jason P '03 %Dewey & L LLP -1301 Av of Amer -NY 10019
(212) 230-8800 .. **Frank,** Jason S '03 Cnsl WilmerHale -399 Park Av -NY 10022
(315) 786-7950 .. **Frank,** Jennifer K '97 %Menter R&T,PC -120 Wshngtn -Watertwn 13601
(212) 421-2233 .. **Frank,** Joel I '82 (Wilk A LLP) -675 3rd Av -NY 10017
(631) 694-0033 .. **Frank,** John R '88 %Lawrence WR&B,PC -425 Broadhllw Rd -Melvll 11747
(212) 735-3000 .. **Frank,** Jonathan L '84 (Skadden ASM&F LLP) -4 Times Sq -NY 10036
(646) 471-4000 .. **Frank,** Jonny J '81 %PricewaterhouseCoopers LLP -300 Mad Av -NY 10017
(516) 798-1043 .. **Frank,** Jos F '84 (Sapienza & F) -5550 Merrick Rd -Massapequa 11758 **Fx:**798-3566
(212) 506-5000 .. **Frank,** Jos J '01 (Orrick H&S LLP) -51 W 52nd -NY 10019
(518) 447-7110 .. **Frank,** Kara M '08 Cnty Atty -112 State -Albany 12207
(516) 745-8310 .. **Frank,** Keith J '90 (Perez & V) -333 Earle Ovngton Blvd Bx9372 -Uniondale 11553
(607) 772-7013 .. **Frank,** Kenneth J '84 Law Dept -City Hall 38 Hawley -Bnghmtn 13901 **Fx:**723-6164
(212) 790-0364 .. **Frank,** Kerry A '04 %Benj N Cardozo Schl of Law -55 5th Av -NY 10003 **Fx:**790-0345
(212) 755-6200 .. **Frank,** Lance M '88 -18 E 48th -NY 10017
(212) 326-2000 .. **Frank,** Lauren M '07 %O'Melveny & M LLP -7 Times Sq -NY 10036
(716) 853-8582 .. **Frank,** Laurie A '87 %Medicaid Fraud Cntrl -350 Main Pl Twr -Buffalo 14202 **Fx:**853-8525
(212) 425-7200 .. **Frank,** Lawr H '02 %Kenyon & K,LLP -1 Bway -NY 10004
(212) 254-1111 .. **Frank,** Lindsey '07 %Rabinowitz BSK&L,PC -111 Bway -NY 10006
(516) 229-4501 .. **Frank,** Lisa '92 %Russo A&T -875 Merrick Av -Westbury 11590
(212) 704-6000 .. **Frank,** Lloyd '50 SrCnsl Troutman S LLP -405 Lex Av -NY 10174
(212) 724-5973 .. **Frank,** Louis L '63 -201 W 74th -NY 10023
(212) 788-9188 .. **Frank,** Lyle E '98 NYC Council Infrastructure Div -250 Bway -NY 10007
(914) 962-5802 .. **Frank,** Maria J '83 -2648 Windmill Dr -Yorktwn Hts 10598
(212) 682-1818 .. **Frank,** Marvin L '91 (Murray F&S LLP) -275 Mad Av -NY 10016
(607) 427-5387 .. **Frank,** Maryclaire Donovan '84 SpclCnsl NYS-OCA 7th Jud Dist -19 E Pulteney Sq -Bath 14810 **Fx:**776-7790
(516) 255-4160 .. **Frank,** Matthew M '03 %Kardisch L & Assoc PC -80 E Old Cntry Rd -Mineola 11501 **Fx:**255-4163
(212) 773-3000 .. **Frank,** Michl B '78 %Ernst & Young,LLP -5 Times Sq -NY 10036
(212) 599-1515 .. **Frank,** Michelle H '98 OfCnsl Stein RM,LLP -405 Lex Av -NY 10174
(212) 692-1000 .. **Frank,** Mitchell A '76 SpclCnsl Duane M LLP -1540 Bway -NY 10036
(516) 466-8855 .. **Frank,** Murray '47 -111 Grt Nck Rd -Gt Neck 11021 **Fx:**829-1008
(646) 386-3648 .. **Frank,** Neil A '73 Supreme Ct-Condemnation Certiorari -60 Centre -NY 10007
(631) 756-0400 .. **Frank,** Neil M '63 (Frank & Assoc,PC) -500 Bi-Cnty Blvd -Farmngdl 11735 **Fx:**756-0547
(212) 751-4300 .. **Frank,** Paul M '63 (Hodgson R LLP) -1540 Bway -NY 10036
(315) 785-3001 .. **Frank,** Paul V '87 -175 Arsenal -Watertwn 13601
(845) 331-9373 .. **Frank,** Peter M '72 Leg Srvcs -101 Hurley Av -Kingston 12401 **Fx:**331-4813
(212) 788-0893 .. **Frank,** Philip S '08 %Law Dept -100 Church -NY 10007 **Fx:**788-0367
(212) 697-0500 .. **Frank,** Philip T '95 Constellation Wealth Advisors -505 5th Av -NY 10017

(212) 355-3900 .. **Frank**, Richd '56 R Frank,PC -110 E 59th -NY 10022 **Fx:**355-3936
(718) 544-2444 .. **Frank**, Robt G '89 -98-20 Metro Av -Frst Hlls 11375 **Fx:**575-1600
(516) 295-2955 .. **Frank**, Robyn M '84 (Atlantis Persnl Training) -1433 Bway -Hewlett 11557
(914) 997-7990 .. **Frank**, Stephen D '74 -30 Glenn -White Plns 10603 **Fx:**997-7992
(718) 254-7000 .. **Frank**, Stephen E '05 US Atty-EDNY -271 Cadman Plz E -Brklyn 11201
(212) 224-4415 .. **Frank**, Stephen I '89 %Sumitomo Mitsui -277 Park Av -NY 10172 **Fx:**593-9522
(315) 637-5350 .. **Frank**, Susan Scuderi '92 -5300 MacClenthen Rd -Manlius 13104
(212) 589-2708 .. **Frank**, Terri J '83 Weight Watchers -11 Mad Av -NY 10010
(845) 634-7010 .. **Frank**, Wm '66 (Montalbano C&F,PC) -67 N Main Bx1070 -New Cty 10956
(845) 888-2456 .. **Frank**, Wm A '89 -138 Sullivan Bx266 -Wurtsboro 12790 **Fx:**888-5606
(212) 735-3000 .. **Frank**, Wm P '67 (Skadden ASM&F LLP) -4 Times Sq -NY 10036
(212) 219-3781 .. **Frank**, Wm S '67 -181 Hudson -NY 10013 **Fx:**941-0619
(631) 421-1145 .. **Franke**, George L '98 %T Casey -6 Red Deer Ln -Huntngtn 11743 **Fx:**421-3855
(212) 715-9100 .. **Frankel**, Aaron M '02 %Kramer LN&F,LLP -1177 Av of Amer -NY 10036
(212) 661-5000 .. **Frankel & Abrams** -230 Park Av -NY 10169 **Fx:**661-5007
(212) 857-3100 .. **Frankel**, Adam B '94 Evercore Prtnrs -55 E 52nd -NY 10055 **Fx:**857-3101
(212) 455-2000 .. **Frankel**, Andrew T '91 (Simpson T&B LLP) -425 Lex Av -NY 10017
(212) 421-3417 .. **Frankel**, Arthur I '69 (A Frankel,PC) -14 E 60th -NY 10022 **Fx:**759-2525
(718) 793-1133 .. **Frankel**, Audrey R '98 %B Seidel & Assoc -88-03 69th Av -Frst Hlls 11375 **Fx:**263-8811
(212) 808-7800 .. **Frankel**, B Harrison '54 (Kelley D&W LLP) -101 Park Av -NY 10178
(718) 258-1110 .. **Frankel**, Benzion '99 -1716 Coney Isl Av -Brklyn 11230 **Fx:**258-5566
(718) 591-5579 .. **Frankel**, Brian '97 -168-07 Jewel Av -Flushng 11365
(212) 554-7800 .. **Frankel**, Cathy J '84 (Moses & S LLP) -405 Lex Av -NY 10174
(845) 562-9100 .. **Frankel**, Chas E '81 (Rider W&F,PC) -655 Little Britain Rd -New Windsor 12553
(718) 590-2000 .. **Frankel**, Daphna '00 %DA -198 E 161st -Bronx 10451 **Fx:**590-6477
(212) 831-6811 .. **Frankel**, David A '81 -200 E 90th -NY 10128
(914) 460-1640 .. **Frankel**, David L '90 MIM Corp -100 Clearbrook Rd -Elmsfrd 10523
(212) 715-9100 .. **Frankel**, David S '84 (Kramer LN&F,LLP) -1177 Av of Amer -NY 10036
(516) 596-9800 .. **Frankel**, David S '91 -870 Franklin Av -Vly Stream 11580
(845) 357-0547 .. **Frankel**, Ira F '75 -19 Riverside Dr -Suffern 10901
(212) 484-3900 .. **Frankel**, James E '74 (Arent F LLP) -1675 Bway -NY 10019
(212) 852-1000 .. **Frankel**, Jay N '86 %US Trust Co,NA -114 W 47th -NY 10036 **Fx:**852-1310
(212) 661-5000 .. **Frankel**, Jennifer P '03 %Frankel & A -230 Park Av -NY 10169
(212) 701-3000 .. **Frankel**, Joan M '73 (Cahill G&R LLP) -80 Pine -NY 10005 **Fx:**269-5420
(212) 701-3000 .. **Frankel**, Jonathan J '00 (Cahill G&R LLP) -80 Pine -NY 10005 **Fx:**269-5420
(516) 222-1600 .. **Frankel**, Justin C '97 (Frankel & N,PC) -585 Stewart Av -Gdn Cty 11530
(212) 373-3000 .. **Frankel**, Kevin B '08 %Paul WRW&G LLP -1285 Av of Amer -NY 10019
(212) 889-7990 .. **Frankel**, Lawr D '88 %Thomas & W -104 W 27th -NY 10001
(212) 593-1100 .. **Frankel**, Mark '84 (Backenroth F&K,LLP) -489 5th Av -NY 10017
(914) 276-4221 .. **Frankel**, Melvin '52 -378D Heritage Hills -Somers 10589 **Fx:**276-2403
(914) 328-0404 .. **Frankel**, Michl A '04 %Jackson L LLP -1 N Bway -White Plns 10601
(212) 309-5447 .. **Frankel**, Michl E S '96 LexisNexis -125 Park Av -NY 10017
(212) 732-3200 .. **Frankel**, Michl I '73 (Carter L&M LLP) -2 Wall -NY 10005
(212) 888-5100 .. **Frankel**, Michl Stewart '77 -275 Mad Av -NY 10016 **Fx:**202-9630
(212) 563-6557 .. **Frankel**, Michelle '07 Feil Org -7 Penn Plz -NY 10001
(212) 421-6060 .. **Frankel**, Miri Keren '05 Beanstalk Grp,LLC -28 E 28th -NY 10016
(212) 688-8895 .. **Frankel**, Mitchell D '91 (Sussman & F,LLP) -805 3rd Av -NY 10022 **Fx:**688-4252
(516) 222-1600 .. **Frankel & Newfield,PC** -585 Stewart Av -Gdn Cty 11530 **Fx:**248-8711
(212) 468-8034 .. **Frankel**, Paul H '83 (Morrison & F LLP) -1290 Av of Amer -NY 10104
(212) 587-0400 .. **Frankel**, Peter A '77 -225 Bway -NY 10007 **Fx:**587-0755
(212) 732-0002 .. **Frankel**, Peter M '89 (Cohen F&R,LLP) -20 Vesey -NY 10007
(315) 218-8000 .. **Frankel**, Philip I '79 (Bond S&K,PLLC) -1 Lincoln Ctr -Syracuse 13202
(518) 462-3000 .. **Frankel**, Richd A '84 (Iseman CR&H,LLP) -9 Thurlow Ter -Albany 12203
(212) 384-1000 .. **Frankel**, Richd M '90 %FBI -26 Fed Plz -NY 10278
(212) 684-1919 .. **Frankel**, Robt S '94 (Cohen & F) -286 Mad Av -NY 10017 **Fx:**686-8367
(718) 579-3000 .. **Frankel**, Robin C '88 %Leg Aid -1020 Grnd Cncrs -Bronx 10451 **Fx:**588-2611
(212) 661-5000 .. **Frankel**, Sandor '67 (Frankel & A) -230 Park Av -NY 10169
(212) 527-1000 .. **Frankel**, Seth A '06 %Jones HC&B PC -1 Bttry Pk Plz -NY 10004
(516) 742-0400 .. **Frankel**, Stephen H '89 -368 Willis Av -Mineola 11501 **Fx:**742-0499
(212) 833-1178 .. **Frankel**, Steven E '05 %Friedman KS&A LLP -1633 Bway -NY 10019 **Fx:**373-7978
(212) 732-0001 .. **Frankel**, Steven K '73 -319 Bway -NY 10007 **Fx:**732-8460
(212) 818-9200 .. **Frankel**, Steven R '64 (Satterlee SB&B LLP) -230 Park Av -NY 10169
(516) 739-5100 .. **Frankel**, Tracy L '00 %Farber B&Z LLP -51 Charles -Mineola 11501
(718) 464-3200 .. **Frankenberg**, Alvin '52 -205-07 Hillside Av -Jamaica 11423 **Fx:**464-3808
(212) 836-8000 .. **Frankenburg**, Victoria H '94 Cnsl Kaye S LLP -425 Park Av -NY 10022
(718) 286-6000 .. **Frankenstein**, Barry M '09 DA -125-01 Qns Blvd -Kew Gdns 11415
(212) 269-4310 .. **Frankenthaler Kohn Schneider & Katz** -420 Lex Av -NY 10170
(212) 818-8892 .. **Frankenthaler**, Marci J '95 Fredericks of Hollywood Grp Inc -1115 Bway -NY 10010
(631) 242-7815 .. **Frankfort**, Robt D '65 (Frankfort & K) -2061 Deer Prk Av -Deer Pk 11729 **Fx:**586-6029
(914) 636-7100 .. **Frankfurt**, Barbara J '84 %Novick & K -56 Harrison -New Rchll 10801
(212) 980-0120 .. **Frankfurt Kurnit Klein & Selz,PC** -488 Mad Av -NY 10022 **Fx:**593-9175
(212) 980-0120 .. **Frankfurt**, Michl P '60 (Frankfurt KK&S,PC) -488 Mad Av -NY 10022
(718) 225-1409 .. **Frankfurt**, Morton A '61 -27110 Grnd Cntrl Pkwy -Floral Pk 11005 **Fx:**224-6745
(516) 742-6590 .. **Frankie**, James G '81 (Frankie & G,PC) -1527 Franklin Av -Mineola 11501 **Fx:**742-6875
(585) 340-5400 .. **Frankiewich**, Bruce T '89 American Fiber Systems Inc -100 Meridian Ctr -Rchstr 14618 **Fx:**756-1966
(516) 364-7900 .. **Frankini**, James '87 Epstein F&G -45 Crsswys Park Dr W -Woodbury 11797
(212) 989-2990 .. **Frankino**, Sean A '07 5th Av Ctr -50 W 23rd -NY 10010
(212) 682-9200 .. **Frankl**, Arianna '00 (Ostrow K&F LLP) -405 Lex Av -NY 10174
(631) 267-7971 .. **Frankl**, Jeanne Silver '56 -Bx1396 -Amagansett 11930
(631) 267-7971 .. **Frankl**, Kenneth R '51 -Bx1396 -Amagansett 11930
(212) 250-7514 .. **Frankle**, Matthew G '00 %Deutsche Bank -60 Wall -NY 10005
(212) 468-2789 .. **Franklin**, Alan M '74 A Franklin,PC -115 E 87th -NY 10128 **Fx:**722-3952
Franklin, Allyson '08 -133 Rutland Rd -Brklyn 11225
(212) 475-1630 .. **Franklin**, Annemarie '90 -Bx1024 -NY 10276
(212) 326-2000 .. **Franklin**, Danl J '09 %O'Melveny & M LLP -7 Times Sq -NY 10036
(212) 479-6000 .. **Franklin**, David R '01 %Cooley LLP -1114 Av of Amer -NY 10036
(212) 382-0909 .. **Franklin**, Douglas A '79 %Peckar & A,PC -41 Mad Av -NY 10154
(516) 228-3131 .. **Franklin**, Glenn J '78 (Franklin G&C,PC) -666 Old Cntry Rd -Gdn Cty 11530
(585) 442-0540 .. **Franklin**, Gregory A '85 (Ashcraft FY&P,LLP) -150 Allens Crk Rd -Rchstr 14618
(516) 228-3131 .. **Franklin Gringer & Cohen,PC** -666 Old Cntry Rd -Gdn Cty 11530 **Fx:**228-3136
(212) 725-3131 .. **Franklin Gringer & Cohen,PC** -150 E 58th -NY 10155 **Fx:**725-3268
(212) 356-8100 .. **Franklin**, Harry M '81 %CIR -520 8th Av -NY 10018 **Fx:**356-8111
(212) 909-6000 .. **Franklin**, James E III '04 %Debevoise & P LLP -919 3rd Av -NY 10022
(212) 455-2000 .. **Franklin**, Jennifer L '99 Cnsl Simpson T&B LLP -425 Lex Av -NY 10017
(212) 614-6445 .. **Franklin**, Karl F '99 -666 Bway -NY 10012
(212) 431-2353 .. **Franklin**, Kristine Lee '93 %NY Law Schl -185 W Bway -NY 10013 **Fx:**431-8193
(212) 821-4885 .. **Franklin**, Patricia M '92 UBS Invstmnt -299 Park Av -NY 10171
(718) 590-3771 .. **Franklin**, Raymond P '86 %Hon D Massaro -851 Cncrs -Bronx 10451 **Fx:**590-3986
(212) 612-4000 .. **Franklin**, Renee L '78 Chubb & Co -55 Water -NY 10041
(315) 422-3322 .. **Franklin**, Richd A '73 -201 E Jffrsn -Syracuse 13202 **Fx:**471-5759
(212) 415-9200 .. **Franklin**, Robt S '66 OfCnsl Dorsey & W LLP -250 Park Av -NY 10177
(212) 969-3000 .. **Franklin**, Ron D '94 (Proskauer R LLP) -1585 Bway -NY 10036
(212) 446-2300 .. **Franklin**, Russell M '08 %Boies S&F LLP -575 Lex Av -NY 10022
(212) 848-4000 .. **Franklin**, Timothy E '09 %Shearman & S LLP -599 Lex Av -NY 10022
(212) 460-4600 .. **Franklin**, Vanessa Moreno '02 Con Ed -4 Irving Pl -NY 10003
(212) 935-5500 .. **Franklin Weinrib Rudell & Vassallo** -488 Mad Av -NY 10022 **Fx:**308-0642
(607) 756-3440 .. **Franklin**, Wendy Lee '93 Cnty Dept Social Srvcs -60 Central Av -Cortlnd 13045
(212) 326-3939 .. **Franklyn**, Sashay N '10 %Jones D -222 E 41st -NY 10017
(718) 237-3100 .. **Frank-Meltzer**, Molly N '08 %Leg Aid -111 Lvngstn -Brklyn 11201 **Fx:**250-4243
(212) 233-7195 .. **Frankola**, Jennifer M '10 %Lewis JAA,LLP -61 Bway -NY 10006
(212) 880-6000 .. **Franks**, Matthew E '01 %Torys LLP -237 Park Av -NY 10017
(212) 588-0800 .. **Franks**, Vicki M '05 %Frommer L&H LLP -745 5th Av -NY 10151
(516) 714-7131 .. **Frankson**, Duane '05 Geico Ins Co -750 Woodbury Rd -Woodbury 11797
(212) 578-2211 .. **Franqui**, Elizabeth '98 %MetLife -27-01 Qns Plz N -LIC 11101
(315) 451-3810 .. **Franta**, Thos J '07 %O'Hara O&C,PC -7207 E Genesee -Fayettevll 13066
(212) 506-2500 .. **Frantz**, Gregory A '01 %Mayer B LLP -1675 Bway -NY 10019
(914) 323-7000 .. **Frantz**, Judith Zuckerman '95 OfCnsl Wilson EME&D LLP -3 Gannett Dr -White Plns 10604
(607) 687-0467 .. **Franz**, Emy Lore '82 %Family Ct -Cnty Cthse Annx Bx10 -Owego 13827
(212) 355-2200 .. **Franz**, Eric P '94 -747 3rd Av -NY 10017 **Fx:**937-2217
(607) 723-5341 .. **Franz**, James R '82 (Hinman H&K,LLP) -80 Exchange Bx5250 -Bnghmtn 13902
(212) 885-5000 .. **Franzblau**, Deborah Ann '82 (Blank R LLP) -405 Lex Av -NY 10174
(212) 571-1808 .. **Franzblau Dratch,PC** -233 Bway -NY 10279 **Fx:**732-1339
(718) 655-2900 .. **Franzblau**, Mitchell '86 (Belovin & F) -2311 Wht Plns Rd -Bronx 10467
(212) 351-4000 .. **Franzel**, Joanne '83 OfCnsl Gibson D&C LLP -200 Park Av -NY 10166
(631) 761-0800 .. **Franzella**, Giuseppe '07 %Lazer AR&Y,PC -225 Old Cntry Rd -Melvll 11747
(212) 557-5485 .. **Franzese**, Bruce J '74 %Verizon -245 Park Av -NY 10167
(212) 574-1200 .. **Franzese**, Debra A '09 %Seward & K LLP -1 Bttry Pk Plz -NY 10004
(516) 877-5600 .. **Franzese**, Laura M '92 %R Tusa -1225 Franklin Av -Gdn Cty 11530 **Fx:**877-5695
(212) 940-8800 .. **Franzese**, Marla G '89 Cnsl Katten MR LLP -575 Mad Av -NY 10022
(516) 746-2400 .. **Franzese**, Michl R '91 -114 Old Cntry Rd -Mineola 11501
(718) 261-7800 .. **Franzese**, Paul N '89 (DiMichele & F) -118-21 Qns Blvd -Frst Hlls 11375
(212) 684-3630 .. **Franzetti**, James J '04 %D Horowitz,PC -276 5th Av -NY 10001 **Fx:**685-8617
(212) 697-2700 .. **Franzino**, Frank J Jr. '71 OfCnsl Stairs DF -200 Park Av S -NY 10003
(212) 759-9770 .. **Franzino**, Frank J Jr. '71 (Meier F&S,LLP) -570 Lex Av -NY 10022

(212) 541-6222 .. **Franzitta,** Niki J '98 %Kane K,PC -1350 Av of Amer -NY 10019
(845) 331-3258 .. **Franzman,** Stephen '85 -24 John Bx3900 -Kingston 12402 **Fx:**331-7648
(212) 759-9770 .. **Franzoni,** Tinamarie '03 %Meier F&S,LLP -570 Lex Av -NY 10022
(212) 809-4800 .. **Frare,** Suzanne C '96 %N Kanzer -30 Broad -NY 10004 **Fx:**363-3097
(585) 455-0477 .. **Frarey,** Kimberlee Ann '93 -108 Nrthmbrlnd Rd -Rchstr 14618
(518) 452-0802 .. **Frary,** Keith M '96 %Taylor & Assoc -1 Columbia Cir -Albany 12203 **Fx:**452-1863
(914) 232-2242 .. **Frasca,** Giulia '08 %PD Hoffman,PC -200 Katonah Av -Katonah 10536 **Fx:**232-2245
(212) 544-8892 .. **Frasciello,** Giulio S '77 (Rosenblatt F&K-D,LLC) -4791 Bway -NY 10034
(212) 225-2000 .. **Frasco,** Jason B '08 %Cleary GS&H -1 Lbrty Plz -NY 10006
(716) 854-1300 .. **Frascogna,** Frank J '81 Rosenthal S&M,LLP -300 Main -Buffalo 14202
(212) 637-2329 .. **Frase,** Sharon E '01 US Atty -1 St Andrews Plz -NY 10007
(212) 259-8000 .. **Fraser,** Alexander G '88 (Dewey & L LLP) -1301 Av of Amer -NY 10019
(212) 530-5000 .. **Fraser,** Alison S '08 %Milbank TH&M LLP -1 Chase Manh Plz -NY 10005
(212) 530-1800 .. **Fraser,** Brian S '85 (Richards K&O LLP) -1 World Fncl Ctr -NY 10281
(212) 566-4479 .. **Fraser,** Chas R '82 %Dept of Bldgs -280 Bway -NY 10007
(212) 649-2158 .. **Fraser,** Christopher A '90 %Hearst Corp -300 W 57th -NY 10019 **Fx:**649-2035
(718) 694-3909 .. **Fraser,** Denise '83 %Transit Auth -130 Lvngstn -Brklyn 11201 **Fx:**694-5726
(212) 759-4888 .. **Fraser,** Dionne A '05 %Phillips L LLP -437 Mad Av -NY 10022
(718) 625-7766 .. **Fraser,** Donald G '85 (Fraser & F) -142 Joralemon -Brklyn 11201 **Fx:**858-3036
(718) 625-7766 .. **Fraser,** Duncan A Jr. '52 (Fraser & F) -142 Joralemon -Brklyn 11201 **Fx:**858-3036
(607) 273-4200 .. **Fraser,** Hilary T '92 (Miller M,LLP) -202 E State -Ithaca 14850
(718) 250-2000 .. **Fraser,** Jennifer '10 %DA -350 Jay -Brklyn 11201 **Fx:**250-2314
(518) 474-3219 .. **Fraser,** John W '89 %NYSHESC -99 Wshngtn Av -Albany 12255 **Fx:**486-6515
(718) 286-6000 .. **Fraser,** Kristin J '02 %DA -125-01 Qns Blvd -Kew Gdns 11415
(212) 717-6381 .. **Fraser,** Linda '77 -245 E 80th -NY 10075
(212) 594-5300 .. **Fraser,** Neil R '02 (Milberg LLP) -1 Penn Plz -NY 10119
(212) 269-0927 .. **Fraser,** Robt S '79 (D'Amato & L,LLP) -2 World Fncl Ctr -NY 10281
(212) 248-3140 .. **Fraser,** Timothy J '03 %Drinker B&R LLP -140 Bway -NY 10005
(212) 859-8000 .. **Frastai,** Eddie E '03 %Fried FHS&J LLP -1 NY Plz -NY 10004
(212) 310-8000 .. **Frastai,** Robt H '97 (Weil G&M LLP) -767 5th Av -NY 10153
(212) 836-8000 .. **Fratangelo,** Peter '04 Cnsl Kaye S LLP -425 Park Av -NY 10022
(516) 496-0730 .. **Fratello,** Cheryl L '05 %Fratello & F,PC -242 Crsswys Park Dr W -Woodbury 11797 **Fx:**496-9791
(516) 496-0730 .. **Fratello,** Thos J '81 (Fratello & F,PC) -242 Crsswys Park Dr W -Woodbury 11797 **Fx:**496-9791
(212) 922-0050 .. **Frates,** John A '91 %Stewart Title Ins -300 E 42nd -NY 10017 **Fx:**983-1133
(315) 423-7100 .. **Frateschi,** Timothy A '99 (Harris B PLLC) -300 S State -Syracuse 13202
(212) 848-8560 .. **Fratianni,** Constance A '86 (Shearman & S LLP) -599 Lex Av -NY 10022
(914) 701-8067 .. **Frattini,** Jennifer L '02 SrCnsl Atlas Air,Inc -2000 Wstchstr Av -Purchase 10577 **Fx:**701-8333
(212) 839-5300 .. **Fratto,** Patricia C '06 %Sidley A LLP -787 7th Av -NY 10019
(718) 579-3000 .. **Frau,** Angel G '91 %Leg Aid -1020 Grnd Cncrs -Bronx 10451 **Fx:**588-2611
(212) 848-4000 .. **Frautschi,** Schuyler H '03 %Shearman & S LLP -599 Lex Av -NY 10022
(212) 558-4000 .. **Frawley,** Brian T '94 (Sullivan & C LLP) -125 Broad -NY 10004
(607) 733-7750 .. **Frawley,** John D '49 -820 W Water -Elmira 14905
(212) 506-1700 .. **Frawley,** Kelly A '05 %Kasowitz BT&F LLP -1633 Bway -NY 10019
(212) 238-3000 .. **Frayer,** Elizabeth A '07 %Emmet M&M,LLP -120 Bway -NY 10271
(212) 771-0853 .. **Frayman,** Susan '80 CCH Tax & Acctng -111 8th Av -NY 10011 **Fx:**771-0771
(631) 585-2644 .. **Frayne,** James J '63 -1820 Middle Cntry Rd -Centereach 11720 **Fx:**585-5063
(212) 335-9000 .. **Frazer,** Allen J '68 %DA -1 Hogan Pl -NY 10013
(212) 285-1300 .. **Frazer,** David E '86 -15 Maiden Ln -NY 10038 **Fx:**587-0744
(516) 742-7777 .. **Frazer & Feldman, LLP** -1415 Kellum Pl -Gdn Cty 11530 **Fx:**742-7868
(516) 742-7777 .. **Frazer,** Florence T '78 (Frazer & F,LLP) -1415 Kellum Pl -Gdn Cty 11530
(212) 335-9000 .. **Frazer,** Leroy Jr. '82 %DA -1 Hogan Pl -NY 10013
(212) 421-4100 .. **Frazer,** Richd S '88 (Pryor C LLP) -7 Times Sq -NY 10036
(212) 312-2326 .. **Frazier,** Demetra D '95 %Leg Aid -60 Lafayette -NY 10013 **Fx:**349-0874
(518) 434-9000 .. **Frazier,** Diane E '97 %Bogdan L&K LLC -111 Wshngtn Av -Albany 12210 **Fx:**434-2510
(212) 385-3959 .. **Frazier,** Donald '00 -233 Bway -NY 10279
(212) 504-6000 .. **Frazier,** James S '01 (Cadwalader W&T LLP) -1 World Fncl Ctr -NY 10281
(716) 433-1344 .. **Frazier,** Jos G '90 -280 East Av Bx464 -Lockprt 14095
(518) 465-0400 .. **Frazier,** Shannon D '01 %O'Connor OB&F,PC -20 Corp Wds Blvd -Albany 12211
(212) 336-2000 .. **Frazza,** George '59 OfCnsl Patterson BW&T LLP -1133 Av of Amer -NY 10036
(631) 368-2128 .. **Frazzetto,** Stephen L '84 -5 Lipson Ct -E Northprt 11731
(212) 732-8700 .. **Frazzetto,** Susan E '06 %McAloon & F,PC -123 William -NY 10038
(716) 854-1007 .. **Frech,** David H Jr. '07 Prisoners' Leg Srvcs -107 Delaware Av -Buffalo 14202 **Fx:**854-1008
(212) 506-1700 .. **Frechette-Moulter,** Alexander '09 %Kasowitz BT&F LLP -1633 Bway -NY 10019
(212) 685-6400 .. **Frechter,** Harold Z '94 %Smith & S -116 E 27th -NY 10016
(212) 580-7402 .. **Frechtman,** A Bernard '52 -305 Bway -NY 10007 **Fx:**(317) 536-3512
(212) 764-4222 .. **Frecker,** Eva '04 %S Jeffries & Assoc -1560 Bway -NY 10036 **Fx:**764-4229
(585) 987-2800 .. **Freckleton,** Stacyann S '10 %Woods OG LLP -2 State -Rchstr 14614
(212) 841-7838 .. **Freda,** Frank A '78 %Cushman & Wakefield -51 W 52nd -NY 10019
(212) 277-4000 .. **Freda,** Giacomo '07 %Freshfields BD LLP -520 Mad Av -NY 10022
(212) 310-8000 .. **Freda,** Lucia '08 %Weil G&M LLP -767 5th Av -NY 10153
(212) 813-5900 .. **Fredbeck,** Andrew N '90 (Fross ZL&Z,PC) -866 UN Plz -NY 10017
(212) 458-3964 .. **Frede,** Jodi S '06 AIG -175 Water -NY 10038 **Fx:**(866) 638-9085
(917) 821-9779 .. **Fredella,** Lawr J '95 L Fredella,PC -110 Wall -NY 10005 **Fx:**(646) 596-7810
(212) 530-5000 .. **Frederick,** Alyssa Adams '10 %Milbank TH&M LLP -1 Chase Manh Plz -NY 10005
(212) 574-1200 .. **Frederick,** Carolyn '09 %Seward & K LLP -1 Bttry Pk Plz -NY 10004
(718) 237-2000 .. **Frederick,** Dale I '99 %Leg Aid -111 Lvngstn -Brklyn 11201 **Fx:**237-8737
(212) 450-4000 .. **Frederick,** Dharma Betancourt '07 %Davis P&W LLP -450 Lex Av -NY 10017
(607) 565-2321 .. **Frederick,** Donald B '51 (Frederick & F) -HSBC Bk Bldg -Waverly 14892 **Fx:**565-3064
(212) 354-6800 .. **Frederick,** Howard G '91 (Silbowitz GSS&F,LLP) -25 W 43rd -NY 10036
(212) 471-8500 .. **Frederick,** Keith A '01 %Herzfeld & R,PC -125 Broad -NY 10004
(716) 883-8601 .. **Frederick,** Sarah A '03 %Heritage Ctrs -2643 Main -Buffalo 14214
(518) 745-4343 .. **Frederick,** Stacy M '02 %Stanclift L&M,PC -3 Warren Bx358 -Glens Fls 12801 **Fx:**745-4344
(716) 842-5352 .. **Frederick,** Thos K '03 M&T Bk -One M&T Plz -Buffalo 14203
(212) 506-5000 .. **Frederick,** Toi '08 %Orrick H&S LLP -51 W 52nd -NY 10019
(212) 715-9100 .. **Fredericks,** Albert G '79 SpclCnsl Kramer LN&F,LLP -1177 Av of Amer -NY 10036
(212) 586-5042 .. **Fredericks,** Barry I '61 -230 Park Av 23rd Fl -NY 10169
(212) 688-5640 .. **Fredericks,** Brian P '07 %Joseph & H LLP -757 3rd Av -NY 10017
(646) 733-5709 .. **Fredericks,** Carla F '02 (Milberg LLP) -1 Penn Plz -NY 10119 **Fx:**(212) 208-2544
(212) 261-8000 .. **Fredericks,** Christopher J '05 %Mendes & M,LLP -750 7th Av -NY 10019
(516) 221-8502 .. **Fredericks,** Jos A Jr. '79 -Bx713 -N Bellmore 11710 **Fx:**221-8512
(212) 813-8834 .. **Fredericks,** Wesley C Jr. '94 (Goodwin P LLP) -620 8th Av -NY 10018
(212) 554-1400 .. **Fredericks,** Wm C '90 (Bernstein LB&G LLP) -1285 Av of Amer -NY 10019
(914) 997-9070 .. **Fredman Baken & Kosan LLP** -333 Wstchstr Av -White Plns 10604 **Fx:**997-9038
(212) 506-1700 .. **Fredman,** Martha W '84 Kasowitz BT&F LLP -1633 Bway -NY 10019
(212) 832-3600 .. **Fredman,** Michele Wertheimer '77 (Wertheimer F,LLC) -230 Park Av -NY 10169
(914) 997-9070 .. **Fredman,** Neil A '78 (Fredman B&K LLP) -333 Wstchstr Av -White Plns 10604
(914) 323-7000 .. **Fredman,** Saml G '49 OfCnsl Wilson EME&D LLP -3 Gannett Dr -White Plns 10604
(212) 756-2000 .. **Fredman,** Steven J '81 (Schulte R&Z LLP) -919 3rd Av -NY 10022
(516) 463-1800 .. **Fredrich,** Dolores '81 Hofstra Univ -101 Hofstra Univ -Hempstd 11549
(585) 225-2250 .. **Fredrick,** Robt P '93 -970 Vintage Way -Rchstr 14626 **Fx:**225-3034
(716) 962-3825 .. **Fredrickson,** Hope L '83 -11 Jamestwn Bx430 -Sinclairvll 14782 **Fx:**962-5901
(212) 858-1000 .. **Fredston,** Arthur H '54 SrCnsl Pillsbury WSP LLP -1540 Bway -NY 10036
(212) 757-8064 .. **Fredston,** Dale C '79 Sterling Natl Bank -650 5th Av -NY 10019
(212) 225-2000 .. **Free,** Ayana N '08 %Cleary GS&H -1 Lbrty Plz -NY 10006
(212) 922-2200 .. **Freeberg Sarma,** Jane '93 %Watson F&W LLP -1133 Av of Amer -NY 10036
(212) 692-9666 .. **Freeburg,** Dorothy Matthews '85 (Gilbride TL&S LLC) -708 3rd Av -NY 10017
(212) 918-3000 .. **Freed,** Amy Bowerman '08 (Hogan L LLP) -875 3rd Av -NY 10022
(718) 855-0070 .. **Freed,** David A '74 -189 Montague -Brklyn 11201 **Fx:**875-6797
(516) 922-9300 .. **Freed,** Helaine B '88 -Bx275 -E Norwich 11732 **Fx:**922-9301
(212) 558-4000 .. **Freed,** Janna '08 %Sullivan & C LLP -125 Broad -NY 10004
(212) 684-7776 .. **Freed & Lerner** -12 E 33rd -NY 10016 **Fx:**447-7073
(212) 863-6300 .. **Freed,** Michl '76 %HPD -100 Gold -NY 10038 **Fx:**863-8201
(212) 889-7184 .. **Freed,** Myra L '81 -521 5th Av -NY 10175 **Fx:**983-8526
(212) 566-7188 .. **Freed,** Rebecca Moll '02 Cnsl Genova B&G -115 Bway -NY 10006
(516) 227-0733 .. **Freed,** Saml B '65 Cnsl Farrell F,PC -1320 RXR Plz -Uniondale 11556
(212) 735-3000 .. **Freed,** Todd E '98 (Skadden ASM&F LLP) -4 Times Sq -NY 10036
(212) 878-7900 .. **Freedberg,** Eli Z '03 %Fox R LLP -100 Park Av -NY 10017
(646) 253-5400 .. **Freedenberg,** John P '85 (Goldberg S LLP) -1200 Av of Amer -NY 10036
(716) 566-5400 .. **Freedenberg,** John P '85 (Goldberg S LLP) -665 Main -Buffalo 14203
(718) 833-0500 .. **Freedhand,** Justin J '98 Freedhand & F,LLP -8118 13th Av -Brklyn 11228 **Fx:**945-9369
(718) 833-0500 .. **Freedhand,** Lorraine E '99 Freedhand & F,LLP -8118 13th Av -Brklyn 11228 **Fx:**945-9369
(718) 833-0500 .. **Freedhand,** Martin '70 Freedhand & F,LLP -8118 13th Av -Brklyn 11228 **Fx:**945-9369
(212) 687-7770 .. **Freedland,** Andrew B '04 %Rosen L&C LLP -275 Mad Av -NY 10016
(212) 335-4500 .. **Freedlander,** John E '06 %DLA Piper LLP -1251 Av of Amer -NY 10020
(212) 619-0775 .. **Freedman,** Adam D '92 -233 Bway -NY 10279 **Fx:**227-6534
(212) 715-9100 .. **Freedman,** Alexander J '06 %Kramer LN&F,LLP -1177 Av of Amer -NY 10036
(212) 765-9528 .. **Freedman,** Allan R '69 -450 7th Av -NY 10123
(212) 318-3244 .. **Freedman,** Andrew C '69 (Fulbright & J LLP) -666 5th Av -NY 10103
(315) 437-7600 .. **Freedman,** Andrew J '97 (Ferrara FLB&R,PC) -5010 Campuswood Dr -E Syracuse 13057
(212) 451-2300 .. **Freedman,** Andrew M '06 %Olshan GFR&W LLP -65 E 55th -NY 10022
(914) 478-8244 .. **Freedman,** Andrew S '76 -2279 Dalton Dr -Cortlandt Manor 10567
(914) 723-6388 .. **Freedman,** Bernard '59 -111 Hilburn Rd -Scarsdale 10583 **Fx:**725-7070
(315) 437-7600 .. **Freedman,** Bernard B '64 (Ferrara FLB&R,PC) -5010 Campuswood Dr -E Syracuse 13057

(718) 923-0690 .. **Freedman,** Bethany E '07 %R Santoriella PC -335 Adams -Brklyn 11201 **Fx:**923-0683

(716) 845-2754 .. **Freedman,** Brenda M '90 Family Ct -1 Niagara Plz -Buffalo 14202 **Fx:**858-4739

(315) 448-0672 .. **Freedman,** Carla B '89 US Atty -100 S Clinton Bx7198 -Syracuse 13261 **Fx:**448-0689

(516) 364-8989 .. **Freedman,** Danl E '94 %Berman & F -6900 Jericho Tpk -Syosset 11791

(212) 626-4100 .. **Freedman,** David F '87 (Baker & M LLP) -1114 Av of Amer -NY 10036

(518) 434-3183 .. **Freedman,** David M '81 -100 State -Albany 12207 **Fx:**434-3194

(516) 364-8989 .. **Freedman,** Donald E '68 (Berman & F) -6900 Jericho Tpk -Syosset 11791

(516) 365-9802 .. **Freedman,** Edw R '71 SrCnsl Collard & R,PC -1077 Nrthrn Blvd -Roslyn 11576

(212) 788-1026 .. **Freedman,** Elizabeth I '83 %Law Dept -100 Church -NY 10007 **Fx:**788-0367

(212) 665-2713 .. **Freedman,** Eric M '80 -250 W 94th -NY 10025 **Fx:**665-2714

(516) 463-5167 .. **Freedman,** Eric M '80 Hofstra Law Schl -121 Hofstra Univ -Hempstd 11549

(212) 708-0826 .. **Freedman,** Gregg M '03 Milstein Bros Cptl Prtnrs,LLC -335 Mad Av -NY 10017

(212) 633-6967 .. **Freedman,** Henry A '66 %Natl Ctr Law & Economic Justice -275 7th Av -NY 10001 **Fx:**633-6371

(212) 876-6800 .. **Freedman,** Herbert D '64 %Marion Scott Real Estate -2104 1st Av -NY 10029

(716) 856-7091 .. **Freedman,** Jeffrey M '77 (J Freedman) -424 Main -Buffalo 14202 **Fx:**856-7097

(914) 948-1200 .. **Freedman,** Jennifer R '97 %Cerussi & S,PC -1 N Lex Av -White Plns 10601

(212) 869-4646 .. **Freedman,** Jeremy S '08 Kraus & Z LLP -500 5th Av -NY 10110

(212) 259-8000 .. **Freedman,** Jill K '07 %Dewey & L LLP -1301 Av of Amer -NY 10019

(212) 373-3098 .. **Freedman,** Jonathan J '88 %Paul WRW&G LLP -1285 Av of Amer -NY 10019

(212) 839-5300 .. **Freedman,** Jonathan L '82 (Sidley A LLP) -787 7th Av -NY 10019

(914) 251-0001 .. **Freedman,** Jonathan P '95 OfCnsl Lane S&L LLP -106 Corp Park Dr -White Plns 10604

(212) 966-6420 .. **Freedman,** Karen J '81 %Lwyrs For Children -110 Lafayette -NY 10013 **Fx:**966-0531

(585) 238-8300 .. **Freedman,** Keith D '90 %Workers Comp Bd -130 W Main -Rchstr 14614

(212) 758-3388 .. **Freedman,** Lawr '73 Verdura -745 5th Av -NY 10151

(516) 248-1180 .. **Freedman,** Lee B '59 %Continental Abstrct -1 Old Cntry Rd -Carle Pl 11514 **Fx:**873-6602

(212) 312-2332 .. **Freedman,** Lisa B '99 %Leg Aid -60 Lafayette -NY 10013 **Fx:**349-0874

(212) 304-5281 .. **Freedman,** Lynn P '82 %Columbia Univ -60 Haven Av -NY 10032

(845) 359-0367 .. **Freedman,** Martin '51 -144 Lbrty Rd -Tappan 10983

(716) 881-3010 .. **Freedman,** Maryann Saccomando '59 OfCnsl Cohen & L,PC -343 Elmwood Av Bx5204 -Buffalo 14213

(212) 644-4420 .. **Freedman,** Melissa L '95 %Fabiani C&H,LLP -570 Lex Av -NY 10022

(212) 421-6492 .. **Freedman,** Michl G '07 %Squitieri & F,LLP -32 E 57th -NY 10022 **Fx:**421-6553

(516) 767-1697 .. **Freedman,** Michl H '91 M Freedman PLLC -394 Wht Birch Ln -Jericho 11753

(516) 463-5858 .. **Freedman,** Monroe H '78 %Hofstra Law Schl -121 Hofstra Univ -Hempstd 11549

(914) 289-0040 .. **Freedman,** Perry D '84 -10 Bank -White Plns 10606 **Fx:**289-0054

(212) 440-2809 .. **Freedman,** Rachel L '97 CNA Ins -40 Wall -NY 10005

(212) 974-7474 .. **Freedman,** Robt I '67 OfCnsl Cowan DA&S LLP -41 Mad Av -NY 10010

(212) 480-5284 .. **Freedman,** Robt I '84 %Insurance Dept -25 Beaver -NY 10004 **Fx:**480-5272

(212) 686-7700 .. **Freedman,** Robt M '81 (Mazur CR&S PC) -1250 Bway -NY 10001

(212) 848-4000 .. **Freedman,** Robt N '97 (Shearman & S LLP) -599 Lex Av -NY 10022

(516) 763-3200 .. **Freedman,** Sol '59 -255 Merrick Rd -Rockvll Ctr 11570 **Fx:**763-3243

(212) 447-5599 .. **Freedman,** Solomon J '52 OfCnsl Agins SR&B,LLP -386 Park Av S -NY 10016

(212) 416-8000 .. **Freedman,** Spencer B '01 %Dept of Law -120 Bway -NY 10271

(516) 822-1446 .. **Freedman,** Steven L '82 -109 Birchwood Park Dr -Syosset 11791 **Fx:**822-1446

(212) 756-2000 .. **Freedman,** Stuart D '80 (Schulte R&Z LLP) -919 3rd Av -NY 10022

(914) 948-1400 .. **Freedman,** Susan '79 -399 Knollwood Rd -White Plns 10603 **Fx:**948-9656

(212) 446-4934 .. **Freedman,** Theo L '92 (Kirkland & E LLP) -153 E 53rd -NY 10022

(212) 226-2376 .. **Freedman,** Thos '99 %Oved & O LLP -101 Av of Amer -NY 10013 **Fx:**226-7555

(845) 638-1400 .. **Freedman Wagner Tabakman & Weiss** -130 N Main -New Cty 10956 **Fx:**638-0548

(212) 664-2893 .. **Freedman,** Wendy L '82 %NBC -30 Rckfllr Plz -NY 10112

(212) 704-6000 .. **Freedman,** Wm D '80 (Troutman S LLP) -405 Lex Av -NY 10174

(212) 896-6512 .. **Freeh,** Louis J '80 (Freeh S&S LLP) -601 Lex Av -NY 10022

(212) 425-1900 .. **Freehill,** George B '60 (Freehill H&M LLP) -80 Pine -NY 10005

(212) 425-1900 .. **Freehill Hogan & Mahar LLP** -80 Pine -NY 10005 **Fx:**425-1901

(212) 832-0400 .. **Freel,** Michl G '95 Berdon LLP -360 Mad Av -NY 10017

(212) 728-8000 .. **Freeland,** Christopher R '06 %Willkie F&G LLP -787 7th Av -NY 10019

(516) 746-8100 .. **Freeley,** Mark T '89 (D Buttafuoco & Assoc) -144 Woodbury Rd -Woodbury 11797 **Fx:**746-6473

(718) 855-9141 .. **Freeman,** Aldric '96 -386 Tompkins Av -Brklyn 11216

(212) 872-1000 .. **Freeman,** Alexis '03 -One Bryant Park -NY 10036 **Fx:**872-1002

(212) 819-8200 .. **Freeman,** Brandon C '09 %White & C LLP -1155 Av of Amer -NY 10036

(585) 454-2321 .. **Freeman,** Bruce F '84 %Redmond & P,LLP -36 W Main -Rchstr 14614

(212) 504-6470 .. **Freeman,** Claudia M '92 -1 World Fncl Ctr -NY 10281 **Fx:**504-6666

(212) 210-9591 .. **Freeman,** Craig E '93 (Alston & B LLP) -90 Park Av -NY 10016

(212) 310-8000 .. **Freeman,** Danek A '99 Cnsl Weil G&M LLP -767 5th Av -NY 10153

(212) 865-2663 .. **Freeman,** Danl A '90 -80 LaSalle -NY 10027

(914) 484-1614 .. **Freeman,** David J '69 -45 Knollwood Rd -Elmsfrd 10523

(212) 318-6000 .. **Freeman,** David J '82 (Paul HJ&W LLP) -75 E 55th -NY 10022

(212) 960-0051 .. **Freeman,** Debbie '04 %Yeshiva Univ -500 W 185th -NY 10033 **Fx:**960-5346

(212) 210-6957 .. **Freeman,** Debra Ann '91 %J Walter Thompson -466 Lex Av -NY 10017

(212) 556-1558 .. **Freeman,** George H '77 %The NY Times Co -620 8th Av -NY 10018 **Fx:**556-4634

(212) 369-9250 .. **Freeman,** Harvey I '62 -137 E 94th -NY 10128

(212) 977-9700 .. **Freeman,** Helene M '75 (Phillips N LLP) -666 5th Av -NY 10103

(516) 741-6565 .. **Freeman,** Howard A '05 %Meyer SE&K,PC -990 Stewart Av Bx9194 -Gdn Cty 11530

(914) 948-4700 .. **Freeman,** James C '90 (Kent HWCV&F,LLP) -111 Church -White Plns 10601

(845) 634-0888 .. **Freeman,** James J Jr. '64 (Freeman & L RLLP) -4 Laurel Rd -New Cty 10956

(212) 980-4050 .. **Freeman,** Jennifer '80 (Freeman L LLP) -228 E 45th -NY 10017

(212) 548-2100 .. **Freeman,** Jeremy '03 (McGuire W LLP) -1345 Av of Amer -NY 10105

(718) 693-3384 .. **Freeman,** Jo '83 -410 E 8th -Brklyn 11218

(212) 488-1365 .. **Freeman,** John F '90 Palmetto Mgmt,LLC -Pier 62 Chelsea Piers -NY 10011

(212) 407-4000 .. **Freeman,** Kenneth D '81 (Loeb & L,LLP) -345 Park Av -NY 10154

(718) 238-8999 .. **Freeman,** Kenneth S '96 Massey Knakal Realty -205 Montague -Brklyn 11201 **Fx:**238-6091

(212) 512-1000 .. **Freeman,** Lesley G '07 HBO -1100 Av of Amer -NY 10036 **Fx:**512-1986

(212) 980-4050 .. **Freeman Lewis LLP** -228 E 45th -NY 10017 **Fx:**980-4055

(212) 577-3530 .. **Freeman,** Lisa A '90 %Leg Aid -199 Water -NY 10038 **Fx:**425-2465

(212) 455-2000 .. **Freeman,** Lisa A '08 %Simpson T&B LLP -425 Lex Av -NY 10017

(845) 634-0888 .. **Freeman & Loftus, RLLP** -4 Laurel Rd -New Cty 10956 **Fx:**634-9312

(212) 608-0808 .. **Freeman,** Louis M '74 (Freeman N&G) -30 Vesey -NY 10007 **Fx:**962-9696

(212) 204-3525 .. **Freeman,** M E '77 (Ragan & F LLP) -11 E 44th -NY 10017 **Fx:**204-3515

(212) 838-3121 .. **Freeman,** Michl A '91 (Greenberg F LLP) -110 E 59th -NY 10022 **Fx:**838-5032

(212) 889-3900 .. **Freeman,** Michl M '73 (Hymowitz & F) -404 Park Av S -NY 10016

(212) 431-7129 .. **Freeman,** Neil M '93 (Purrington MW LLP) -320 W 13th -NY 10014

(212) 259-8000 .. **Freeman,** Paul C '99 %Dewey & L LLP -1301 Av of Amer -NY 10019

(518) 828-2021 .. **Freeman,** Paul M '89 (Freeman H,PC) -441 E Allen Bx1328 -Hudson 12534 **Fx:**828-2420

(718) 855-9000 .. **Freeman,** Richd H '74 (Cullen and D LLP) -177 Montague -Brklyn 11201

(212) 969-3000 .. **Freeman,** Robt E '94 (Proskauer R LLP) -1585 Bway -NY 10036

(518) 474-6740 .. **Freeman,** Robt J '74 %Dept of State -41 State -Albany 12231 **Fx:**473-9211

(212) 839-5300 .. **Freeman,** Scott M '85 (Sidley A LLP) -787 7th Av -NY 10019

(516) 869-7600 .. **Freeman,** Simone M '08 Town Atty -220 Plandome Rd -Manhsst 11030 **Fx:**869-7605

(212) 490-3000 .. **Freeman,** Stephanie F '05 %Wilson EME&D LLP -150 E 42nd -NY 10017

(212) 490-2525 .. **Freeman,** Steven M '81 %ADL -605 3rd Av -NY 10158 **Fx:**867-0779

(212) 422-0202 .. **Freeman,** Timothy R '07 %Sedgwick DM&A LLP -125 Broad -NY 10004

(212) 656-6096 .. **Freeman,** Wm M Jr. '75 NYSE -20 Broad -NY 10005

(212) 735-3000 .. **Freeman-Fisher,** Berit '91 Cnsl Skadden ASM&F LLP -4 Times Sq -NY 10036

(845) 849-0610 .. **Freer,** Edw L '03 -3 Mitchell Av -Poughkeepsie 12603 **Fx:**625-1523

(914) 332-9777 .. **Frees,** Barbara S '76 -282 Katonah Av -Katonah 10536 **Fx:**(203) 761-9949

(518) 383-5300 .. **Freestone,** Dianne N '86 (Pentkowski P&F) -646 Plnk Rd -Clifton Pk 12065

(212) 233-7195 .. **Freeze,** Lawr J '98 %Lewis JAA,LLP -61 Bway -NY 10006

(718) 836-0960 .. **Freeze,** Mary C '91 -64 74th -Brklyn 11209 **Fx:**921-4959

(516) 742-7600 .. **Fregosi,** Edw A Jr. '88 %Raiser & K,PC -1517 Franklin Av -Mineola 11501

(212) 252-9550 .. **Freiberg,** Craig J '96 (Freiberg & P) -49 W 37th -NY 10018

(212) 940-8800 .. **Freiberg,** Jay W '94 (Katten MR LLP) -575 Mad Av -NY 10022

(845) 759-4041 .. **Freiberg,** Margaret B G '76 %IBM -300 Long Mdw Rd -Sterling Frst 10979

(212) 252-9550 .. **Freiberg & Peck** -49 W 37th -NY 10018 **Fx:**252-9552

(914) 517-5000 .. **Freiberg,** Peter N '90 OfCnsl Meiselman DPC&E,PC -1311 Mamaroneck Av -White Plns 10605

(212) 455-2000 .. **Freiberg,** Wm M '07 %Simpson T&B LLP -425 Lex Av -NY 10017

(516) 482-4436 .. **Freiberger,** Jonathan H '90 (Gleich S&F) -36 S Station Plz -Gt Neck 11021

(212) 337-4143 .. **Freid,** David C '81 %Thomson Reuters/RIA -195 Bway -NY 10007

(716) 565-2000 .. **Freid,** Wayne I '72 (Freid & K) -17 Beresford Ct -Williamsvll 14221 **Fx:**565-2002

(631) 271-7221 .. **Freidel,** Melvin D '50 -2 Sequoia Ln -Dix Hlls 11746 **Fx:**271-3013

(516) 222-8500 .. **Freidlin,** Danl L '03 (Martin C&B LLP) -90 Merrick Av -E Meadow 11554

(212) 244-6553 .. **Freidman,** Evgeny A '97 Taxi Club Mgmt -313 10th Av -NY 10001 **Fx:**244-6554

(212) 818-9600 .. **Freidman,** Gary B '79 (Greenfield S&S,LLP) -600 3rd Av -NY 10016

(212) 219-3144 .. **Freidson,** Jane B '79 -110 William -NY 10038

(212) 373-3064 .. **Freidus,** Harris B '90 (Paul WRW&G LLP) -1285 Av of Amer -NY 10019

(212) 634-3112 .. **Freier,** Ilene D '94 GT Systems -295 Mad Av -NY 10017

(718) 259-4525 .. **Freier,** Rachel E '06 -1716 56th -Brklyn 11204 **Fx:**259-4039

(631) 752-4040 .. **Freier,** Robin '04 %Weiner & B,LLP -555 Broadhllw Rd -Melvll 11747 **Fx:**752-4049

(212) 332-1616 .. **Freierman,** Arthur P '81 Southbridge Fncl Corp -45 Rckfllr Plz -NY 10111

(212) 240-9406 .. **Freifeld,** Andrew '90 -30 Vesey -NY 10007 **Fx:**385-0662

(212) 695-7800 .. **Freifeld,** Evan L '96 (Felcher & F,LLP) -358 5th Av -NY 10001 **Fx:**695-4041

(718) 338-1971 .. **Freifeld,** Harry '80 -1318 Av J -Brklyn 11230

(212) 265-6600 .. **Freifeld**, Lisa M '00 RD Mgmt LLC -810 7th Av -NY 10019 **Fx**:492-8458
(212) 697-3122 .. **Freilich**, Caroline M '07 %Martin C&B LLP -220 E 42nd -NY 10017
(718) 590-2000 .. **Freilich**, Hannah H '87 %DA -198 E 161st -Bronx 10451 **Fx**:590-6477
(212) 238-8668 .. **Freilich**, Joshua D '94 %John Jay Cllg -899 10th Av -NY 10019
(212) 891-4188 .. **Freilich**, Paul A '88 Eisner LLP -750 3rd Av -NY 10017
(212) 872-5738 .. **Freilich**, Peter E '99 KPMG LLP -757 3rd Av -NY 10017
(631) 396-2222 .. **Freilich**, Richd T '87 -1805 5th Av -Bay Shr 11706 **Fx**:435-2967
(212) 661-3080 .. **Freilich**, Robt A '05 %Rottenberg LR,PC -369 Lex Av -NY 10017
(212) 272-6808 .. **Freilich**, Wm H '83 %JP Morgan Chase -383 Mad Av -NY 10179
(212) 977-9700 .. **Freilicher**, Morton '57 Cnsl Phillips N LLP -666 5th Av -NY 10103
(212) 556-2100 .. **Freiman**, Adam M '99 (King & S) -1185 Av of Amer -NY 10036
(212) 450-4000 .. **Freiman**, Jennifer L '09 %Davis P&W LLP -450 Lex Av -NY 10017
(212) 319-1000 .. **Freiman**, Richd M '84 (Quirk & B,PC) -845 3rd Av -NY 10022
(212) 655-3566 .. **Freiman**, Robt W '70 (Freiman F PC) -140 E 45th -NY 10017 **Fx**:655-3529
(914) 428-4140 .. **Freimann**, Robin Persky '00 -30 Glenn -White Plns 10603
(212) 309-1000 .. **Freimuth**, Matthew S '02 (Hunton & W) -200 Park Av -NY 10166
(212) 468-8000 .. **Freimuth**, Renee L '05 %Morrison & F LLP -1290 Av of Amer -NY 10104
(212) 683-2210 .. **Frei-Pearson**, Jeremiah L '04 %Childrens Rts Inc -330 7th Av -NY 10001 **Fx**:683-4015
(212) 527-1000 .. **Freire**, James '84 (Jones HC&B PC) -1 Bttry Pk Plz -NY 10004
(212) 612-4200 .. **Freire**, Richd J '98 %Hoey KT&E -55 Water -NY 10041
(212) 430-6040 .. **Freireich**, Donna L '78 Wasser & R LLP -80 Maiden Ln -NY 10038 **Fx**:430-6041
(914) 967-9235 .. **Freis**, Jeffrey B '71 (J Freis,PC) -9 Rigene Rd -Harrison 10528 **Fx**:(248) 281-0844
(516) 364-3333 .. **Freiser**, Munro I '67 %Mass Mutual -1000 Woodbury Rd -Woodbury 11797 **Fx**:364-3647
(212) 715-9100 .. **Frejka**, Elise Scherr '91 SpclCnsl Kramer LN&F,LLP -1177 Av of Amer -NY 10036
(718) 331-7700 .. **Frekhtman**, Arkady '99 (Frekhtman & Assoc) -60 Bay 26th -Brklyn 11214
(212) 837-6000 .. **Frelinghuysen**, Anson B '08 %Hughes H&R LLP -1 Bttry Pk Plz -NY 10004
(212) 695-8100 .. **Fremer**, Christina M '93 %Goetz F,LLP -1 Penn Plz -NY 10119
(646) 386-5700 .. **Fremmer**, Rachel J '00 %Civil Ct -111 Centre -NY 10013
(914) 833-0500 .. **Fremont**, Stanley '51 Cnsl Eppinger R&K -131 Larchmnt Av Bx868 -Larchmnt 10538
(212) 797-3544 .. **French & Casey,LLP** -29 Bway -NY 10006 **Fx**:797-3545
(718) 428-5292 .. **French & Casey,LLP** -42-24 235th -Douglastn 11363 **Fx**:352-5706
(212) 842-6033 .. **French**, Christopher J '88 -40 Wall -NY 10005
(315) 413-4050 .. **French**, Danl J '96 (French-Alcott) -One Park Pl -Syracuse 13202 **Fx**:413-4055
(212) 603-5700 .. **French**, Jamil O '02 Sandell Asset Mgt -40 W 57th -NY 10019
(212) 585-3123 .. **French**, John III '59 (Tudor Assoc LLC) -33 E 70th -NY 10021 **Fx**:879-1610
(212) 797-3544 .. **French**, Jos A '84 (French & C,LLP) -29 Bway -NY 10006
(914) 333-0670 .. **French**, Richd H Jr. '02 -660 Wht Plns Rd -Tarrytwn 10591 **Fx**:333-0676
(212) 264-9271 .. **French**, Sheryl A '82 %US Customs -26 Fed Plz -NY 10278
(212) 728-8000 .. **French**, Thos H '94 (Willkie F&G LLP) -787 7th Av -NY 10019
(212) 237-0000 .. **French**, Tina S '06 %Vinson & E LLP -666 5th Av -NY 10103
(585) 586-3649 .. **French**, Wm T '61 -4 Knobb Hill Dr -Pittsfrd 14534
(212) 849-7000 .. **French-Brown**, Wanda D '09 %Quinn EU&S,LLP -51 Mad Av -NY 10010
(212) 688-5151 .. **Frenchman**, Beth M '90 SrCnsl Gibney A&F,LLP -665 5th Av -NY 10022
(212) 506-1700 .. **Frenchman**, Kenneth H '00 (Kasowitz BT&F LLP) -1633 Bway -NY 10019
(212) 508-6100 .. **Frenchman**, Robt S '94 (Bracewell & G,LLP) -1251 Av of Amer -NY 10020
(845) 634-7701 .. **Frendel**, Scott D '97 (Braunfotel & F LLC) -49 Maple Av -New Cty 10956 **Fx**:634-7710
(212) 474-1000 .. **Frenkel**, Dana '07 %Cravath S&M LLP -825 8th Av -NY 10019
(212) 679-4666 .. **Frenkel**, David '73 (Frenkel H&S LLP) -16 E 34th -NY 10016
(631) 969-7777 .. **Frenkel**, David L '92 (Frenkel LWW&G,LLP) -20 W Main -Bay Shr 11706 **Fx**:206-0540
(212) 679-4666 .. **Frenkel**, Donny '99 %Frenkel H&S LLP -16 E 34th -NY 10016
(516) 620-4230 .. **Frenkel**, Ephraim Z '89 Land Title Assoc -214-20 41st Av -Bayside 11361 **Fx**:(646) 253-1275
(212) 679-4666 .. **Frenkel Hershkowitz & Shafran LLP** -16 E 34th -NY 10016 **Fx**:889-5072
(212) 693-1355 .. **Frenkel**, Kenneth K '93 -20 Broad -NY 10005 **Fx**:385-0506
(212) 344-3100 .. **Frenkel Lambert Weiss Weisman & Gordon, LLP** -1 Whitehall -NY 10004 **Fx**:422-4047
(631) 969-3100 .. **Frenkel Lambert Weiss Weisman & Gordon, LLP** -20 W Main -Bay Shr 11706 **Fx**:969-3101
(212) 446-2300 .. **Frenkel**, Lidia '09 %Boies S&F LLP -575 Lex Av -NY 10022
(718) 601-5260 .. **Frenkel**, Sylvia H '81 -271 Mad Av -NY 10016
(212) 292-4470 .. **Frenkel**, Wm G '88 -521 5th Av -NY 10175 **Fx**:(914) 739-2666
(212) 425-7200 .. **Freno**, Michl J '02 %Kenyon & K,LLP -1 Bway -NY 10004
(716) 773-2442 .. **Frentzel**, Mark J '85 M Frentzel -1763 Baseline Rd -Grand Isl 14072 **Fx**:773-4750
(845) 782-3032 .. **Frerichs**, Mike '81 -Bx5 -Harriman 10926
(518) 474-6750 .. **Frering**, Mark D '87 Liquor Auth -80 S Swan -Albany 12210 **Fx**:402-2304
(212) 277-4000 .. **Freshfields Bruckhaus Deringer LLP** -520 Mad Av -NY 10022 **Fx**:277-4001
(631) 366-2300 .. **Fresolone**, Ralph '78 (Tartamella T&F) -235 Brooksite Dr -Hauppauge 11788
(212) 440-4400 .. **Fretel**, Anna Nguyen '05 %Buchanan I&R PC -620 8th Av -NY 10018
(212) 238-4800 .. **Fretel**, Christopher G '05 %Landman CB&F,PC -120 Bway -NY 10271
(914) 686-4800 .. **Freudenberg**, Michl W '02 %Harrington O&M,LLP -81 Main -White Plns 10601
(212) 388-3600 .. **Freudenberger**, Michelle '85 %32B-J Leg Srvcs -101 Av of Amer -NY 10013 **Fx**:388-3061
(718) 665-0220 .. **Freund**, Andrea L '82 (Irom WFB&S,PC) -349 E 149th -Bronx 10451
(212) 336-2000 .. **Freund**, Hugh J '71 (Patterson BW&T LLP) -1133 Av of Amer -NY 10036
(212) 735-3000 .. **Freund**, James C '62 OfCnsl Skadden ASM&F LLP -4 Times Sq -NY 10036
(212) 285-3300 .. **Freund**, Marc E '06 %Lipsig SM&M,PC -40 Fulton -NY 10038
(212) 962-3362 .. **Freund**, Meir '77 (Katz LGW&F) -277 Bway -NY 10007
(516) 393-2200 .. **Freundlich**, Jordan M '00 %Garfunkel W,PC -111 Grt Nck Rd -Gt Neck 11021
(212) 921-8399 .. **Freundlich**, Lauren C '99 %Lankler S&W LLP -500 5th Av -NY 10110
(212) 878-7219 .. **Freundlich**, Lester G '70 %MTA -347 Mad Av -NY 10017
(718) 851-8552 .. **Freundlich**, Margaret '57 -1624 53rd -Brklyn 11204
(516) 295-2237 .. **Freundlich**, Samson M '99 Per Diem Srvcs -675 Ibsen -Woodmere 11598
(212) 832-0400 .. **Freundlich**, Stanley H '69 Berdon LLP -360 Mad Av -NY 10017
(212) 513-3200 .. **Frevola**, Michl J '96 (Holland & K LLP) -31 W 52nd -NY 10019
(718) 447-8300 .. **Frew**, Wm J Jr. '76 -791 Jewett Av Bx179 -Staten Isl 10314 **Fx**:727-8985
(212) 275-8478 .. **Frey**, Andrea C '09 CNN -1 Time Warner Ctr -NY 10019
(212) 506-2500 .. **Frey**, Andrew L '62 (Mayer B LLP) -1675 Bway -NY 10019
(212) 637-2270 .. **Frey**, Christopher D '04 US Atty -1 St Andrews Plz -NY 10007
(718) 876-6300 .. **Frey**, David '93 %DA -130 Styvsnt Pl -Staten Isl 10301
(212) 210-9550 .. **Frey**, Donald G '03 %Alston & B LLP -90 Park Av -NY 10016
(914) 684-0333 .. **Frey**, Edw A '75 %J Maria -301 Old Tarrytown Rd -White Plns 10603 **Fx**:684-9772
(718) 522-3333 .. **Frey**, Gina M '04 Children's Law Ctr -44 Court -Brklyn 11201 **Fx**:522-7376
(212) 608-4040 .. **Frey**, Jaclyn M '08 %Silverstein & B -217 Bway -NY 10007
(914) 767-3602 .. **Frey**, Jeanne M '97 -247 Route 100 -Somers 10589
(212) 953-2626 .. **Frey**, Lisa A '84 %Kelly & H -380 Lex Av -NY 10168 **Fx**:983-5271
(212) 373-3000 .. **Frey**, Manuel S '00 (Paul WRW&G LLP) -1285 Av of Amer -NY 10019
(212) 684-3929 .. **Frey**, Mark S '82 -119 5th Av -NY 10003 **Fx**:586-5175
(646) 610-5400 .. **Frey**, Mary Lynne '02 NYPD -1 Police Plz -NY 10038
(845) 557-8000 .. **Frey**, Michl '82 -Bx190 -Barryvll 12719
(716) 626-5200 .. **Frey**, Stephen S '68 (Sarles F&J) -5800 Main -Williamsvll 14221
(718) 605-2772 .. **Frey**, Steven '60 -25 Scarsdale -Staten Isl 10308 **Fx**:605-6914
(212) 754-9200 .. **Freyberg**, Mark L '82 -950 3rd Av -NY 10022 **Fx**:888-4792
(516) 857-9681 .. **Freydin**, Michl S '98 -135 E Olive -Long Bch 11561
(518) 373-8200 .. **Freyer**, Sharon P '93 -1 Halfmoon Exec Park -Clifton Pk 12065 **Fx**:373-2100
(212) 373-3000 .. **Friar**, David J '05 %Paul WRW&G LLP -1285 Av of Amer -NY 10019
(212) 374-6754 .. **Frias-Colon**, Patria Yudelka '95 %NYC Dept Educ-OLS -52 Chmbrs -NY 10007
(212) 258-6070 .. **Fricklas**, Michl D '93 %Viacom -1515 Bway -NY 10036
(718) 986-6315 .. **Frid**, Chana L '05 -137-57 70th Av -Flushng 11367
(212) 728-8000 .. **Friday**, Marjorie J '01 %Willkie F&G LLP -787 7th Av -NY 10019
(212) 754-4050 .. **Fridegotto**, Linda '03 %L Zack & Assoc -405 Park Av -NY 10022 **Fx**:759-8890
(212) 697-3122 .. **Fridel**, Alexandra '08 %Martin C&B LLP -220 E 42nd -NY 10017
(212) 218-5500 .. **Frider**, Yonatan-Yoni '08 %Seyfarth S LLP -620 8th Av -NY 10018
(718) 998-1800 .. **Fridman**, Eduard '04 (Fridman S,LLP) -1795 Coney Isl Av -Brklyn 11230 **Fx**:998-1881
(212) 261-7315 .. **Fridman**, Felicity '98 Calyon -1301 Av of Amer -NY 10019
(212) 620-0935 .. **Fridman**, Iliya M '99 (Fridman Law Grp PLLC) -287 Spring -NY 10013 **Fx**:(646) 304-1030
(718) 543-8100 .. **Frieary**, Paul W '82 (PW Frieary,PLLC) -6001A Riverdale Av -Bronx 10471 **Fx**:543-8110
(212) 326-3939 .. **Friebel**, Thos E '82 (Jones D) -222 E 41st -NY 10017
(646) 230-8380 .. **Frieber**, Laury Mercedes '83 NY Festival of Song -307 7th Av -NY 10001
(718) 330-7861 .. **Frieberger**, Joanne Giorgio '95 %ODAR-SSA -111 Lvngstn -Brklyn 11201 **Fx**:330-2009
(212) 682-2900 .. **Fried**, Alan C '76 (Braverman & Assoc,PC) -331 Mad Av -NY 10017 **Fx**:682-7718
(212) 808-7800 .. **Fried**, Amanda Carton '06 %Kelley D&W LLP -101 Park Av -NY 10178
(718) 937-0330 .. **Fried**, Armand '82 -43-31 194th -Flushng 11358
(718) 226-8662 .. **Fried**, Arthur J '76 Staten Isl Univ Hosp -475 Seaview Av -Staten Isl 10305
(212) 949-0100 .. **Fried**, Asher R '76 %Cmmnwlth Land Title -140 E 45th -NY 10017 **Fx**:949-2438
(212) 407-4000 .. **Fried**, Dana Scott '84 (Loeb & L,LLP) -345 Park Av -NY 10154
(212) 779-1414 .. **Fried**, Danl '05 %Bernstein L LLP -10 E 40th -NY 10016
(212) 620-7788 .. **Fried**, Danl A '78 -80 Maiden Ln -NY 10038 **Fx**:620-4144
(212) 473-9173 .. **Fried**, Darren M '00 Razor & Tie Direct,LLC -214 Sullivan -NY 10012
(845) 638-5728 .. **Fried**, David '06 -55 New Hempstd Rd -New Cty 10956 **Fx**:638-5035
(914) 993-1546 .. **Fried**, David R '86 %Town Atty -177 Hillside Av -Greenburgh 10607 **Fx**:993-1656
(212) 309-1000 .. **Fried**, Donald D '59 SrCnsl Hunton & W -200 Park Av -NY 10166
(212) 408-5100 .. **Fried**, Douglas M '87 (Chadbourne & P LLP) -30 Rckfllr Plz -NY 10112
(212) 732-0076 .. **Fried**, Ellen H '81 %CASES -346 Bway -NY 10013 **Fx**:571-0292
(212) 416-8000 .. **Fried**, Ellen J '78 %Dept of Law -120 Bway -NY 10271
(212) 268-7111 .. **Fried & Epstein LLP** -350 5th Av -NY 10118 **Fx**:268-3110
(212) 859-8000 .. **Fried Frank Harris Shriver & Jacobson LLP** -1 NY Plz -NY 10004 **Fx**:859-4000
(212) 264-3436 .. **Fried**, Ginnine B '05 US DHS -26 Fed Plz -NY 10278
(212) 651-7500 .. **Fried**, Howard A '84 (Segal MS&M) -850 3rd Av -NY 10022
(212) 643-0000 .. **Fried**, Israel '99 (Fried & R,LLP) -247-249 W 36th -NY 10018 **Fx**:643-0035
(212) 421-5333 .. **Fried**, J Michl '75 %Related Capital -625 Mad Av -NY 10022 **Fx**:593-6131
(212) 819-9140 .. **Fried**, Jeffrey M '87 -500 5th Av -NY 10110
(631) 853-5394 .. **Fried**, Jeffrey R '84 %District Ct Law Dept -400 Carleton Av Bx9075 -Central Islip 11722
(212) 801-6752 .. **Fried**, Jeffrey R '90 (Greenberg T,LLP) -200 Park Av -NY 10166
(212) 407-4000 .. **Fried**, Jeffrey S '96 (Loeb & L,LLP) -345 Park Av -NY 10154
(212) 331-5925 .. **Fried**, Jennifer E '02 HRA -180 Water -NY 10038

(212) 268-7111 .. **Fried,** John W '72 (Fried & E LLP) -350 5th Av -NY 10118
(212) 715-9100 .. **Fried,** Jonathan L '98 %Kramer LN&F,LLP -1177 Av of Amer -NY 10036
(212) 596-9000 .. **Fried,** Kerith L '92 %Ropes & G LLP -1211 Av of Amer -NY 10036
(212) 918-3000 .. **Fried,** Lisa Jean '03 %Hogan L LLP -875 3rd Av -NY 10022
(212) 706-3030 .. **Fried,** Marc L '91 Metro Loft Mgmt LLC -20 Exch Pl -NY 10005
(315) 471-3151 .. **Fried,** Martin L '59 OfCnsl Hancock & E,LLP -1500 AXA Twr I Bx4976 -Syracuse 13221
(315) 443-4236 .. **Fried,** Martin L '59 (Syracuse Univ Cllg of Law) -Wht Hall -Syracuse 13244 **Fx:**443-4213
(646) 855-4347 .. **Fried,** Meredith J '02 Bnk of Amer -1 Bryant Pk -NY 10036
(732) 855-6072 .. **Fried,** Michl F '95 %Wilentz G&S -110 William -NY 10038 **Fx:**726-6536
(516) 222-1350 .. **Fried,** Michl L '97 (Barrocas & R) -100 Q Roosevelt Blvd -Gdn Cty 11530
(646) 458-6992 .. **Fried,** Michl P '85 Ace USA Ins Co -140 Bway -NY 10005
(646) 471-4788 .. **Fried,** Philip E '91 %PricewaterhouseCoopers LLP -300 Mad Av -NY 10017
(212) 806-5400 .. **Fried,** Richd L '84 (Stroock &S&L LLP) -180 Maiden Ln -NY 10038
(212) 964-5777 .. **Fried,** Robin C '93 -18 E 41st -NY 10017 **Fx:**385-8699
(718) 466-3000 .. **Fried,** Rochelle G '79 %Civil Ct -1118 Grnd Cncrs -Bronx 10456 **Fx:**466-3006
(516) 484-1248 .. **Fried,** Ronald '70 -62 Laurel Ln -Roslyn Hts 11577
(516) 829-7270 .. **Fried,** Samantha '94 %M Weinberger,PC -50 Merrick Rd -Rockvll Ctr 11570 **Fx:**829-0102
(347) 436-8446 .. **Fried,** Shana R '08 (Higgins & F LLP) -110 W 71st -NY 10023 **Fx:**436-8447
(212) 350-3694 .. **Fried,** Sheldon '60 %Banco Cntrl NY -45 E 53rd -NY 10022
(212) 705-7000 .. **Fried,** Sima G '09 %Bingham M LLP -399 Park Av -NY 10022
(212) 964-5777 .. **Fried,** Steven I '93 (S Fried,PC) -18 E 41st -NY 10017 **Fx:**385-8699
(212) 805-3900 .. **Fried,** Steven J '91 (Clausen M PC) -1 Chase Manh Plz -NY 10005
(212) 554-0400 .. **Fried,** Stuart '92 (Grubman I&S,PC) -152 W 57th -NY 10019
(212) 640-2585 .. **Fried,** Tammy D '96 American Express -200 Vesey -NY 10285
(914) 428-8300 .. **Fried,** Vivian A '86 %Sacks,PC -707 Wstchstr Av -White Plns 10604 **Fx:**682-1707
(212) 592-1400 .. **Fried,** Wm R '88 (Herrick,F LLP) -2 Park Av -NY 10016
(914) 323-7000 .. **Friedberg,** Alan B '78 (Wilson EME&D LLP) -3 Gannett Dr -White Plns 10604
(212) 401-0800 .. **Friedberg,** Alan W '73 %Disciplinary Comm -61 Bway -NY 10006 **Fx:**287-1045
(212) 972-2929 .. **Friedberg,** Barry J '88 (Trachtenberg R&F LLP) -545 5th Av -NY 10017 **Fx:**972-7581
(212) 829-9090 .. **Friedberg,** Bruce D '84 (Friedberg CC&P,LLP) -767 3rd Av -NY 10017
(212) 829-9090 .. **Friedberg Cohen Coleman & Pinkas, LLP** -767 3rd Av -NY 10017 **Fx:**829-0999
(212) 947-7291 .. **Friedberg,** David S '66 -521 5th Av -NY 10175
(212) 981-6540 .. **Friedberg,** Eric '84 (Stroz Friedberg LLC) -32 Av of Amer -NY 10013 **Fx:**981-6545
(518) 370-2676 .. **Friedberg,** Frances L '88 -3012 E Old State Rd -Schnctdy 12303 **Fx:**370-3514
(212) 867-0755 .. **Friedberg,** Harry J '62 -551 5th Av -NY 10176 **Fx:**986-6607
(914) 615-2121 .. **Friedberg,** Joel M '80 Jade Assets LLC -245 Main -White Plns 10601 **Fx:**948-2477
(212) 422-0700 .. **Friedberg,** Micah I '09 %Gerspach S LLP -59 Maiden Ln -NY 10038 **Fx:**422-0701
(212) 244-9500 .. **Friedberg,** Randy M '86 Cnsl White and W LLP -1 Penn Plz -NY 10119
(212) 750-0990 .. **Friedberg,** Rosalie D '78 -110 E 59th -NY 10022
(212) 935-3000 .. **Friedberg,** Stephen E '77 (Mintz LCFG&P,PC) -666 3rd Av -NY 10017
(212) 581-5383 .. **Friedberg,** Stephen M '60 -205 W 57th -NY 10019 **Fx:**(646) 349-2580
(212) 759-1110 .. **Friedberg,** Steven G '86 (S Friedberg & Assoc) -400 E 56th -NY 10022
(212) 458-3736 .. **Friedberg,** Suzan Barott '88 %AIU -175 Water -NY 10038
(845) 562-0203 .. **Fried-DeRosa,** Elyssa M '88 (Finkelstein & Prtnrs,LLP) -1279 Route 300 Bx1111 -Newburgh 12550
(212) 468-4800 .. **Friedel,** Stuart L '72 (Davis & G LLP) -1740 Bway -NY 10019
(914) 834-5492 .. **Frieden,** Nancy Mandelker '85 -3 Douglas Ln -Larchmnt 10538
(718) 261-3047 .. **Friedenberg,** Debra J '83 Cnsl Queens Law Assoc -118-21 Qns Blvd -Frst Hlls 11375 **Fx:**261-0798
(212) 837-6000 .. **Friedenberg,** Ellen S '82 (Hughes H&R LLP) -1 Bttry Pk Plz -NY 10004
(516) 222-6200 .. **Friedenberg,** Gary H '65 (Berkman HPP&F,PC) -100 Grdn City Plz -Gdn Cty 11530
(845) 362-0123 .. **Friedenberg,** Isidor D '84 -2 Cara Dr -Suffern 10901 **Fx:**362-7718
(212) 849-7000 .. **Friedenberg,** Marc A '10 %Quinn EU&S,LLP -51 Mad Av -NY 10010
(516) 626-0734 .. **Friedenberg,** Stanley '50 -80 Wheatley Rd -Old Westbury 11568 **Fx:**484-7290
(718) 590-2000 .. **Friedenthal,** Edw '75 %DA -198 E 161st -Bronx 10451 **Fx:**590-6477
(718) 991-4600 .. **Frieder,** Helen M '91 %Leg Aid -953 Southrn Blvd -Bronx 10459 **Fx:**842-2867
(718) 520-3990 .. **Friederwitzer,** Lisa J '92 %Family Ct -89-14 Parsons Blvd -Jamaica 11432 **Fx:**520-5085
(212) 969-3000 .. **Friedfel,** Susan Deegan '03 %Proskauer R LLP -1585 Bway -NY 10036
(631) 787-1500 .. **Friedfeld,** David K '84 %Clear Vision Optical -425 Rabro Dr -Hauppauge 11788 **Fx:**787-1510
(212) 616-5020 .. **Friedfeld,** Eddy W '87 -300 E 71st -NY 10021
(646) 290-9296 .. **Friedfeld,** Elyce H '92 OfCnsl Imke R,PLLC -140 Bway -NY 10005 **Fx:**290-5965
(716) 853-8400 .. **Friedfertig,** Richd B '78 %Dept of Law -350 Main Pl Twr -Buffalo 14202 **Fx:**853-8571
(716) 847-3984 .. **Friedfertig,** Sandra '03 %Medicaid Inspctr Genl -584 Delaware Av -Buffalo 14202
(973) 992-4800 .. **Fried-Grodin,** Lisa I '02 %Fox R LLP -100 Park Av -NY 10017 **Fx:**992-9125
(716) 542-5413 .. **Friedhaber,** Eric D '03 %Nicholas PSB&Z -12364 Main Rd Bx176 -Akron 14001
(718) 286-2450 .. **Friedheim,** Oda C '98 %Leg Aid -120-46 Qns Blvd -Kew Gdns 11415 **Fx:**263-4234
(212) 839-5300 .. **Friedhoff,** Jason A '07 %Sidley A LLP -787 7th Av -NY 10019
(212) 574-1200 .. **Friedhoff,** Jessica Mazzaro '07 %Seward & K LLP -1 Bttry Pk Plz -NY 10004
(212) 340-0400 .. **Friedkin,** Neil '81 %Appllt Div 1st Dept -27 Mad Av -NY 10010 **Fx:**889-4412
(212) 849-7000 .. **Friedland,** Amos E '10 %Quinn EU&S,LLP -51 Mad Av -NY 10010
(718) 741-8309 .. **Friedland,** Edw A '01 Div of Human Rights -1 Fordham Plz -Bronx 10458
(212) 450-4000 .. **Friedland,** Elyssa N '08 %Davis P&W LLP -450 Lex Av -NY 10017
(845) 354-6440 .. **Friedland,** Gerald B '60 -6 Elyise Rd -Monsey 10952
(212) 369-2030 .. **Friedland,** Kenneth S '72 -250 W 49th -NY 10019 **Fx:**586-8872
(212) 344-1400 .. **Friedland Laifer & Robbins,LLP** -62 William -NY 10005 **Fx:**344-2301
(212) 331-5143 .. **Friedland,** Lauren B '02 HRA-OLA -180 Water -NY 10038
(212) 451-2300 .. **Friedland,** Lawr N '49 Cnsl Olshan GFR&W LLP -65 E 55th -NY 10022
(212) 580-2932 .. **Friedland,** Lesley A '86 -37 W 72nd -NY 10023
(516) 741-1040 .. **Friedland,** Lloyd M '74 (Librett F&L,LLP) -1325 Franklin Av -Gdn Cty 11530
(212) 657-1349 .. **Friedland,** Marcie S '84 Citigroup -77 Water -NY 10005
(212) 436-3448 .. **Friedland,** Michl H '02 Deloitte & Touche LLP -2 World Fncl Ctr -NY 10281
(212) 819-8200 .. **Friedland,** Paul D '81 (White & C LLP) -1155 Av of Amer -NY 10036
(212) 344-1400 .. **Friedland,** Seth D '79 (Friedland L&R,LLP) -62 William -NY 10005
(212) 472-7440 .. **Friedland,** Sharon L '78 -203 E 74th -NY 10021 **Fx:**472-7443
(646) 722-8500 .. **Friedland,** Shelly L '98 %Grant & E,PA -485 Lex Av -NY 10017
(212) 505-0142 .. **Friedland,** Susan G '91 -325 Bway -NY 10007 **Fx:**249-0489
(607) 272-5590 .. **Friedlander,** Betty D '59 (Friedlander & F,PC) -103 W Seneca Bx6577 -Ithaca 14851 **Fx:**272-5594
(607) 565-8155 .. **Friedlander,** Betty D '59 (Friedlander & F,PC) -425 Park Av Bx109 -Waverly 14892 **Fx:**565-8485
(212) 302-5252 .. **Friedlander,** David H '96 (Lazarus & H LLP) -561 7th Av -NY 10018 **Fx:**302-8181
(212) 788-0700 .. **Friedlander,** Jeffrey D '71 %Law Dept -100 Church -NY 10007 **Fx:**788-0367
(516) 349-2802 .. **Friedlander,** Joel L '77 JL Friedlander,PC -54 Sunnyside Blvd -Plainvw 11803 **Fx:**576-1039
(631) 424-2600 .. **Friedlander,** L Keith '83 -18 Prospect -Huntngtn 11743
(212) 962-2877 .. **Friedlander,** Mark S '75 -15 Maiden Ln -NY 10038 **Fx:**571-4613
(888) 472-4425 .. **Friedlander,** Michl '95 Schick Tech,Inc -30-00 47th Av -LIC 11101
(212) 637-2211 .. **Friedlander,** Nicole W '02 US Atty -1 St Andrews Plz -NY 10007
(917) 921-5674 .. **Friedlander,** Robt S '95 MetLife -1095 Av of Amer -NY 10036
(914) 420-2656 .. **Friedlander,** Saml D '89 -20 Babbitt Rd Bx354 -Bedfrd Hlls 10507
(518) 457-1260 .. **Friedlander,** Valerie '80 %DCJS -4 Twr Pl -Albany 12203 **Fx:**457-3089
(607) 565-8155 .. **Friedlander,** Wm S '75 (Friedlander & F,PC) -425 Park Av Bx109 -Waverly 14892 **Fx:**565-8485
(607) 272-5590 .. **Friedlander,** Wm S '75 (Friedlander & F,PC) -103 W Seneca Bx6577 -Ithaca 14851 **Fx:**272-5594
(212) 744-3300 .. **Friedland Meyer,** Elizabeth '00 %Friedland Prop -22 E 65th -NY 10065
(212) 830-5377 .. **Friedland-Wechsler,** Naomi '72 Reich & Tang Asset Mgmt,LLC -600 5th Av -NY 10020 **Fx:**265-9040
(212) 947-3793 .. **Friedler,** Lance S '98 (Sadis & G LLP) -551 5th Av -NY 10176
(212) 232-1300 .. **Friedler,** Meredith Ross '98 OfCnsl Lewis BB&S LLP -77 Water -NY 10005
(212) 692-9091 .. **Friedlich,** Leo '84 -230 Park Av -NY 10169
(212) 268-9878 .. **Friedman,** Aaron A '86 (A Friedman,LLC) -450 7th Av -NY 10123
(212) 619-4350 .. **Friedman,** Abraham A '80 %Newman MKGH,PC -14 Wall -NY 10005
(212) 451-2300 .. **Friedman,** Adam H '94 (Olshan GFR&W LLP) -65 E 55th -NY 10022
(212) 973-0572 .. **Friedman,** Adam P '92 (Wolff & S PC) -140 Bway -NY 10005
(212) 787-4177 .. **Friedman,** Alan H '64 -252 W 85th -NY 10024
(212) 679-5554 .. **Friedman,** Alan L '72 (A Friedman,PC) -355 Lex Av -NY 10017 **Fx:**679-1080
(212) 889-2121 .. **Friedman,** Alan M '84 (Kellner HG&F) -470 Park Av S -NY 10016
(212) 267-0380 .. **Friedman,** Alan M '86 (Friedman FC&G) -2 Rector -NY 10006
(212) 715-9100 .. **Friedman,** Alan R '77 (Kramer LN&F,LLP) -1177 Av of Amer -NY 10036
(212) 940-8800 .. **Friedman,** Alan R '82 (Katten MR LLP) -575 Mad Av -NY 10022
(212) 244-5424 .. **Friedman,** Alan S '92 -875 Av of Amer -NY 10001
(212) 686-5681 .. **Friedman,** Alfred S '62 Rhodes Bldg Mgmt Inc -286 Mad Av -NY 10017
(585) 546-1980 .. **Friedman,** Allen D '92 (Fulton F&G LLP) -28 E Main -Rchstr 14614
(212) 552-1039 .. **Friedman,** Allen R '84 JP Morgan Chase -1 Chase Manh Plz -NY 10081
(212) 373-3000 .. **Friedman,** Allison J '08 %Paul WRW&G LLP -1285 Av of Amer -NY 10019
(212) 626-4202 .. **Friedman,** Andre H '85 (Nagy & T) -1114 Av of Amer -NY 10036
(516) 222-1030 .. **Friedman,** Andrea B '09 %S Friedman,PC -666 Old Cntry Rd -Gdn Cty 11530 **Fx:**222-1053
(212) 725-6530 .. **Friedman,** Andrea D '06 Global Justice Ctr -25 E 21st -NY 10010 **Fx:**725-6536
(212) 450-4000 .. **Friedman,** Andrew C '09 %Davis P&W LLP -450 Lex Av -NY 10017
(212) 308-6300 .. **Friedman,** Andrew D '86 OfCnsl Glancy B &G,LLP -430 Park Av -NY 10022 **Fx:**308-6570
(718) 418-7690 .. **Friedman,** Andrew D '99 Make the Rd by Walking -301 Grove -Brklyn 11237
(718) 422-0567 .. **Friedman,** Andrew G '86 -50 Court -Brklyn 11201
(914) 725-7200 .. **Friedman,** Andrew H '07 Madison Abstract Inc -670 Wht Plns Rd -Scarsdale 10583
(212) 242-5903 .. **Friedman,** Andrew L '91 -164 W 25th -NY 10001
(718) 797-2488 .. **Friedman,** Andrew M '91 (Friedman K&S,LLP) -16 Court -Brklyn 11241 **Fx:**797-4304
(212) 689-0288 .. **Friedman,** Arthur '66 -280 Mad Av -NY 10016
(718) 241-9174 .. **Friedman,** Arthur J '85 %Rickly Corp -6932 Av L -Brklyn 11234 **Fx:**241-8905
(212) 986-1144 .. **Friedman,** Arthur S '69 -275 Mad Av -NY 10016 **Fx:**686-0252

(212) 541-2000 .. **Friedman,** Arthur S '81 Cnsl Bryan C LLP -1290 Av of Amer -NY 10104
(212) 799-3087 .. **Friedman,** Barbara S '87 -205 West End Av -NY 10023
(212) 576-7000 .. **Friedman,** Barbara T '85 %NYLIM -51 Mad Av -NY 10010
(212) 371-1171 .. **Friedman,** Barbara W '79 -400 E 56th -NY 10022 **Fx:**(646) 448-4330
(212) 362-0025 .. **Friedman,** Barrie L '88 %Beacway Operating Corp -2130 Bway -NY 10023 **Fx:**787-8119
(212) 998-6293 .. **Friedman,** Barry E '02 NYU Law Schl -40 Wshngtn Sq S -NY 10012
(845) 471-7600 .. **Friedman,** Barry H '73 -224 Church -Poughkeepsie 12601 **Fx:**471-7662
(212) 701-3000 .. **Friedman,** Bart '70 (Cahill G&R LLP) -80 Pine -NY 10005 **Fx:**269-5420
(212) 592-1400 .. **Friedman,** Benjamin A '10 %Herrick,F LLP -2 Park Av -NY 10016
(212) 336-2000 .. **Friedman,** Benjamin D '06 %Patterson BW&T LLP -1133 Av of Amer -NY 10036
(518) 689-1488 .. **Friedman,** Benjamin M '08 Greenberg T,LLP -54 State -Albany 12207
(212) 233-9385 .. **Friedman,** Bernard D '77 (Friedman J&B LLP) -132 Nassau -NY 10038
(212) 594-5300 .. **Friedman,** Brad N '87 (Milberg LLP) -1 Penn Plz -NY 10119
(212) 735-3000 .. **Friedman,** Bradley M '07 %Skadden ASM&F LLP -4 Times Sq -NY 10036
(646) 562-1923 .. **Friedman,** Bradley R '03 Cowen & Co -1221 Av of Amer -NY 10020
(212) 530-5000 .. **Friedman,** Bradley S '10 %Milbank TH&M LLP -1 Chase Manh Plz -NY 10005
(212) 596-9000 .. **Friedman,** Brett R '08 %Ropes & G LLP -1211 Av of Amer -NY 10036
(212) 969-3000 .. **Friedman,** Brian L '00 %Proskauer R LLP -1585 Bway -NY 10036
(212) 450-4000 .. **Friedman,** Brian L '10 %Davis P&W LLP -450 Lex Av -NY 10017
(212) 298-5065 .. **Friedman,** Bruce '85 %Leg Aid -49 Thomas -NY 10013 **Fx:**298-5252
(212) 953-2381 .. **Friedman,** Bruce M '75 (Rubin F&F,LLP) -292 Mad Av -NY 10017
(212) 474-1000 .. **Friedman,** Bryan C '10 %Cravath S&M LLP -825 8th Av -NY 10019
(212) 455-2000 .. **Friedman,** Bryce L '98 (Simpson T&B LLP) -425 Lex Av -NY 10017
(914) 417-3400 .. **Friedman,** Bryon L '87 (Littleton JUP&K LLP) -1 Manhattanvll Rd -Purchase 10577
(718) 263-0400 .. **Friedman,** Burton A '58 -110-50 71st Rd -Frst Hlls 11375 **Fx:**263-2638
(718) 698-6272 .. **Friedman,** Carl A '58 -294 Sheraden Av -Staten Isl 10314 **Fx:**761-7324
(646) 386-5402 .. **Friedman,** Catherine J '89 Family Ct -60 Lafayette -NY 10013
(212) 730-7700 .. **Friedman,** Chas B '86 (Michelman & R,LLP) -114 W 47th -NY 10036
(212) 337-2228 .. **Friedman,** Clifford C '96 %US Dept Labor -201 Varick -NY 10014
(212) 879-9751 .. **Friedman,** Cory E '83 -123 E 75th -NY 10021 **Fx:**879-2595
(518) 597-3672 .. **Friedman,** Cory E '83 -328 Hogan Hill Rd -Crown Point 12928 **Fx:**597-3671
(212) 326-3939 .. **Friedman,** Craig S '06 %Jones D -222 E 41st -NY 10017
(212) 964-6622 .. **Friedman,** Dana B '86 Kleinberg & F -217 Bway -NY 10007 **Fx:**385-2558
(212) 302-9400 .. **Friedman,** Danl '82 OfCnsl Goldburd M LLP -42 W 38th -NY 10018 **Fx:**302-8973
(516) 721-0412 .. **Friedman,** Danl B '92 -114 Old Cntry Rd -Mineola 11501
(212) 634-7373 .. **Friedman,** Danl E '02 Corbin Capital Prtnrs,LP -590 Mad Av -NY 10022
(212) 267-0380 .. **Friedman,** Danl J '55 (Friedman FC&G) -2 Rector -NY 10006
(212) 502-7900 .. **Friedman,** Danl J '92 Railworks Corp -5 Penn Plz -NY 10001
(212) 723-5534 .. **Friedman,** David E '89 Citlgroup Global Mrkts -390 Greenwich -NY 10013
(646) 242-6783 .. **Friedman,** David G '68 DG Friedman PLLC -67-86 Selfrdg -Frst Hlls 11375 **Fx:**(718) 793-1571
(212) 735-3000 .. **Friedman,** David J '80 (Skadden ASM&F LLP) -4 Times Sq -NY 10036
(718) 286-2000 .. **Friedman,** David L '70 %Leg Aid -120-46 Qns Blvd -Kew Gdns 11415 **Fx:**286-2286
(646) 315-7300 .. **Friedman,** David L '05 FINRA -14 Wall -NY 10005 **Fx:**315-7440
(212) 506-1700 .. **Friedman,** David M '82 (Kasowitz BT&F LLP) -1633 Bway -NY 10019
(212) 351-4000 .. **Friedman,** Dennis J '70 (Gibson D&C LLP) -200 Park Av -NY 10166
(631) 650-2306 .. **Friedman,** Donald J '76 %Empire Justice Ctr -225 Eastvw Dr -Central Islip 11722 **Fx:**348-3571
(212) 554-0400 .. **Friedman,** Donald R '78 (Grubman I&S,PC) -152 W 57th -NY 10019
(914) 997-6363 .. **Friedman,** Doris T '71 -291 S Bway -Tarrytwn 10591 **Fx:**682-5377
(212) 264-0663 .. **Friedman,** Edw '68 %US DOJ Antitrust Div -26 Fed Plz Ste 3630 -NY 10278
(914) 375-0100 .. **Friedman,** Edw A '75 (Novick ELRW&L,PC) -733 Ynkrs Av -Ynkrs 10704
(212) 833-1102 .. **Friedman,** Edw A '75 (Friedman KS&A LLP) -1633 Bway -NY 10019 **Fx:**373-7902
(516) 932-0400 .. **Friedman,** Edw D '85 (Friedman & S) -333 Jericho Tpk -Jericho 11753 **Fx:**932-0455
(718) 852-8849 .. **Friedman,** Edw David '85 -26 Court -Brklyn 11242 **Fx:**852-1489
(212) 592-1400 .. **Friedman,** Efram '05 %Herrick,F LLP -2 Park Av -NY 10016
(212) 577-2523 .. **Friedman,** Elaine E '83 %Ctr for Applt Litigation -74 Trinity Pl -NY 10006 **Fx:**577-2535
(212) 687-6380 .. **Friedman,** Elaine F '47 -60 E 42nd -NY 10165 **Fx:**687-2727
(516) 487-4800 .. **Friedman,** Elaine R '77 %Fine & B -316 Grt Nck Rd -Gt Neck 11021
(212) 326-2000 .. **Friedman,** Elizabeth L '10 %O'Melveny & M LLP -7 Times Sq -NY 10036
(212) 940-3053 .. **Friedman,** Ellen S '90 (Nixon P LLP) -437 Mad Av -NY 10022
(212) 277-4000 .. **Friedman,** Elliot '06 %Freshfields BD LLP -520 Mad Av -NY 10022
(212) 310-8000 .. **Friedman,** Emily E '06 %Weil G&M LLP -767 5th Av -NY 10153
(212) 735-3000 .. **Friedman,** Eric J '90 (Skadden ASM&F LLP) -4 Times Sq -NY 10036
(212) 354-4500 .. **Friedman,** Eugene S '65 (Friedman & W) -1500 Bway -NY 10036
(212) 661-9100 .. **Friedman,** Evan M '99 %Otterbourg SH&R,PC -230 Park Av -NY 10169
(212) 737-0400 .. **Friedman,** Faith A '99 %G Lefcourt,PC -148 E 78th -NY 10075 **Fx:**988-6192
(516) 379-8388 .. **Friedman,** Fredk A '98 (Friedman & F PC) -2116 Merrick Av -Merrick 11566
(212) 267-0380 .. **Friedman Friedman Chiaravalloti & Giannini** -2 Rector -NY 10006 **Fx:**962-1199
(516) 379-8388 .. **Friedman & Funk PC** -2116 Merrick Av -Merrick 11566
(212) 921-8399 .. **Friedman,** Gabrielle S '01 %Lankler S&W LLP -500 5th Av -NY 10110
(914) 765-0351 .. **Friedman,** Gary A '86 (G Friedman,PC) -80 Business Park Dr -Armonk 10504 **Fx:**765-0356
(212) 680-5150 .. **Friedman,** Gary B '88 (Friedman Law Grp LLP) -270 Lafayette -NY 10012
(212) 833-1105 .. **Friedman,** Gary D '77 (Friedman KS&A LLP) -1633 Bway -NY 10019 **Fx:**373-7905
(516) 775-7007 .. **Friedman,** Gary D '86 (Gutman MB&S,PC) -813 Jericho Tpk -New Hyde Pk 11040
(212) 310-8000 .. **Friedman,** Gary D '89 (Weil G&M LLP) -767 5th Av -NY 10153
(212) 909-6000 .. **Friedman,** Gary M '84 (Debevoise & P LLP) -919 3rd Av -NY 10022
(212) 687-1700 .. **Friedman,** Gary S '80 (Kaufman FP&G,LLP) -300 E 42nd -NY 10017
(212) 490-3000 .. **Friedman,** George '60 OfCnsl Wilson EME&D LLP -150 E 42nd -NY 10017
(212) 858-4488 .. **Friedman,** George H '82 %FINRA -1 Lbrty Plz -NY 10006
(561) 498-7680 .. **Friedman,** Gerald I '59 -90 E Main -Bay Shr 11706
(516) 624-7527 .. **Friedman,** Geri '83 -6 Anchorage Ln -Oyster Bay 11771 **Fx:**624-7527
(212) 720-3223 .. **Friedman,** Glenn E '96 %Dept City Planning -22 Reade -NY 10007 **Fx:**720-3219
(212) 925-4545 .. **Friedman & Gotbaum,LLP** -568 Bway -NY 10012 **Fx:**925-5199
(646) 563-8928 .. **Friedman,** Greg A '03 %Cole SMF&L,PA -900 3rd Av -NY 10022 **Fx:**521-2028
(212) 312-9629 .. **Friedman,** Hal M '95 %State Ins Fund -199 Church -NY 10007 **Fx:**312-9859
(516) 355-9600 .. **Friedman Harfenist Kraut & Perlstein** -3000 Marcus Av -Lk Success 11042 **Fx:**355-9601
(914) 701-0800 .. **Friedman Harfenist Kraut & Perlstein** -2975 Wstchstr Av -Purchase 10577 **Fx:**701-0808
(518) 457-2070 .. **Friedman,** Herbert M Jr. '95 %Dept of Tax & Fin -Bldg 9 State Campus -Albany 12227 **Fx:**457-6131
(518) 377-2225 .. **Friedman Hirschen & Miller, LLP** -100 Great Oaks Blvd Bx38279 -Albany 12203 **Fx:**377-2247
(212) 788-0727 .. **Friedman,** Howard B '86 %Law Dept -100 Church -NY 10007 **Fx:**788-0367
(212) 578-3381 .. **Friedman,** Ira '73 %MetLife -27-01 Qns Plz N -LIC 11101
(516) 338-4237 .. **Friedman,** Jack B '70 -393 Old Cntry Rd -Carle Pl 11514 **Fx:**338-5798
(518) 220-1850 .. **Friedman,** Jack P '99 %Schmeiser O&W -22 Century Hill Dr -Latham 12110
(212) 969-3000 .. **Friedman,** Jacob I '76 (Proskauer R LLP) -1585 Bway -NY 10036
(212) 233-9385 .. **Friedman James & Buchsbaum LLP** -132 Nassau -NY 10038 **Fx:**619-2340
(646) 855-0804 .. **Friedman,** Jami L '01 Banc of Amer Sec -1 Bryant Pk -NY 10036
(212) 986-2022 .. **Friedman,** Jason D '97 (Smiley & S LLP) -60 E 42nd -NY 10165
(212) 336-0554 .. **Friedman,** Jason E '03 %SEC -3 World Fncl Ctr -NY 10281 **Fx:**336-1323
(212) 455-2000 .. **Friedman,** Jason S '08 %Simpson T&B LLP -425 Lex Av -NY 10017
(212) 788-1328 .. **Friedman,** Jason W '07 %Law Dept -100 Church -NY 10007 **Fx:**788-0367
(212) 969-3000 .. **Friedman,** Jed W '08 %Proskauer R LLP -1585 Bway -NY 10036
(212) 940-7035 .. **Friedman,** Jeff J '82 (Katten MR LLP) -575 Mad Av -NY 10022
(212) 922-6000 .. **Friedman,** Jeffrey F '85 Dreyfus -200 Park Av -NY 10166
(212) 425-9300 .. **Friedman,** Jeffrey L '86 (Bressler A&R,PC) -17 State -NY 10004
(212) 310-8000 .. **Friedman,** Jeffrey R '09 %Weil G&M LLP -767 5th Av -NY 10153
(516) 208-5120 .. **Friedman,** Jeffrey S '94 -9 Marlboro Ct -Rockvll Ctr 11570
(914) 422-4128 .. **Friedman,** Jennifer C '00 %Pace Law Schl -78 N Bway -White Plns 10603 **Fx:**422-4039
(716) 883-7272 .. **Friedman,** Jennifer L '98 %McGee & G -200 Summer -Buffalo 14222
(718) 838-7878 .. **Friedman,** Jennifer T '08 Bronx Defenders -860 Crtlandt Av -Bronx 10451 **Fx:**665-0100
(212) 554-1400 .. **Friedman,** Jeremy S '08 %Bernstein LB&G LLP -1285 Av of Amer -NY 10019
(212) 220-0900 .. **Friedman,** Jessica R '85 OfCnsl Winslett SM&B LLP -6 E 39th -NY 10016 **Fx:**973-9101
(212) 708-7195 .. **Friedman,** Jodie Simon '90 %Intl Flavors & Fragrances -521 W 57th -NY 10019
(212) 702-0950 .. **Friedman,** John H '79 Easton Cptl Grp -767 3rd Av -NY 10017
(212) 366-1324 .. **Friedman,** John K '96 -111 John -NY 10038
(212) 682-7474 .. **Friedman,** Jonathan H '06 %Foley & L LLP -90 Park Av -NY 10016
(718) 482-2163 .. **Friedman,** Jonathan I '96 Sirona Dental Systems,Inc -3030 47th Av -LIC 11101
(516) 623-5518 .. **Friedman,** Jos '61 -756 S Lng Bch Av -Freeprt 11520
(646) 416-7143 .. **Friedman,** Jos N '58 Regal Title Agency -90 Broad -NY 10004 **Fx:**(212) 344-2133
(212) 813-8800 .. **Friedman,** Joshua A '06 %Goodwin P LLP -620 8th Av -NY 10018
(212) 223-0200 .. **Friedman,** Julian W '69 (Stillman F&S,PC) -425 Park Av -NY 10022
(518) 447-9664 .. **Friedman,** Julie B '94 %MHLS -75 New Scotland Av -Albany 12208 **Fx:**447-9697
(212) 833-1100 .. **Friedman Kaplan Seiler & Adelman LLP** -1633 Bway -NY 10019 **Fx:**833-1250
(212) 859-8000 .. **Friedman,** Kara R '06 %Fried FHS&J LLP -1 NY Plz -NY 10004
(212) 213-2145 .. **Friedman,** Karen A '84 -404 Park Av S -NY 10016 **Fx:**779-3289
(718) 286-6000 .. **Friedman,** Karen J '95 %DA -125-01 Qns Blvd -Kew Gdns 11415
(716) 856-3500 .. **Friedman,** Kathryn B '99 SpclCnsl Magavern MG LLP -1100 Rand Bldg -Buffalo 14203
(212) 830-7184 .. **Friedman,** Kenneth D '94 Cnsl Manatt P&P,LLP -7 Times Sq -NY 10036 **Fx:**830-3012
(212) 659-7300 .. **Friedman,** Kenneth J '83 (Haynes & B,LLP) -1221 Av of Amer -NY 10020
(716) 856-4000 .. **Friedman,** Kenneth P '85 (Hodgson R LLP) -140 Pearl -Buffalo 14202

(212) 267-3091 .. **Friedman,** Keven H '99 %Wilentz G&S -110 William -NY 10038 **Fx:**(732) 726-6553
(631) 423-4390 .. **Friedman,** Kimberly D '01 %Mincone & M,PC -110 Walt Whitman Rd -South Huntington 11746 **Fx:**423-1411
(212) 715-9100 .. **Friedman,** Kimberly E '10 Kramer LN&F LLP -1177 Av of Amer -NY 10036 **Fx:**715-8000
(212) 224-5067 .. **Friedman,** Lauren D '06 SMBC Cptl Mkts -277 Park Av -NY 10172
(212) 557-4000 .. **Friedman,** Laurence M '87 (Grunfeld DLS&K LLP) -399 Park Av -NY 10022
(585) 344-2550 .. **Friedman,** Lawr '82 (DA) -1 W Main -Batavia 14020 **Fx:**344-8544
(212) 225-2000 .. **Friedman,** Lawr B '83 (Cleary GS&H) -1 Lbrty Plz -NY 10006
(212) 587-5876 .. **Friedman,** Lawr L '84 %State Ins Fund -199 Church -NY 10007 **Fx:**385-9199
(212) 474-1000 .. **Friedman,** Leah '09 %Cravath S&M LLP -825 8th Av -NY 10019
(212) 682-2288 .. **Friedman,** Lee M '06 %Sankel S&M,LLP -750 3rd Av -NY 10017
(516) 377-7100 .. **Friedman,** Leon '53 %S Bilkis & Assoc -805 Smith -Baldwin 11510 **Fx:**377-7327
(516) 463-5889 .. **Friedman,** Leon '61 %Hofstra Law Schl -121 Hofstra Univ -Hempstd 11549
(212) 307-5800 .. **Friedman Levy Goldfarb & Green, PC** -250 W 57th -NY 10107 **Fx:**262-6128
(212) 873-3366 .. **Friedman,** Lewis '59 -201 W 91st -NY 10024
(212) 953-1200 .. **Friedman,** Lisa Klee '83 -232 Mad Av -NY 10016 **Fx:**986-5994
(212) 768-6700 .. **Friedman,** Marc S '80 (Sonnenschein N&R LLP) -1221 Av of Amer -NY 10020
(212) 508-6100 .. **Friedman,** Marcus '08 %Bracewell & G,LLP -1251 Av of Amer -NY 10020
(718) 858-3333 .. **Friedman,** Mark '91 -70 Remsen -Brklyn 11201
(516) 479-6300 .. **Friedman,** Mark J '02 %Silverman A LLP -100 Jericho Quad -Jericho 11753
(212) 285-0510 .. **Friedman,** Mark L '76 (Wilkofsky FK&C) -299 Bway -NY 10007
(212) 909-6000 .. **Friedman,** Mark W '93 (Debevoise & P LLP) -919 3rd Av -NY 10022
(212) 448-1100 .. **Friedman,** Martin J '70 (McLaughlin & S,LLP) -260 Mad Av -NY 10016
(212) 245-6754 .. **Friedman,** Martin J '84 (Sonnenschein S&D,LLP) -7 Penn Plz -NY 10001
(718) 236-2323 .. **Friedman,** Martin R '68 OfCnsl Held H&H -6920 Bay Pkwy -Brklyn 11204 **Fx:**234-1678
(212) 608-1040 .. **Friedman,** Matthew A '00 %Susquehanna Prtnrs -40 Wall -NY 10005
(212) 728-8000 .. **Friedman,** Matthew B '09 %Willkie F&G LLP -787 7th Av -NY 10019
(212) 878-5124 .. **Friedman,** Max '79 (Goulston & S,PC) -750 3rd Av -NY 10017
(212) 525-3923 .. **Friedman,** Meredith L '97 HSBC Bank -452 5th Av -NY 10018 **Fx:**(917) 229-5276
(212) 530-1800 .. **Friedman,** Michl '92 %Richards K&O LLP -1 World Fncl Ctr -NY 10281
(212) 244-4111 .. **Friedman,** Michl D '74 OfCnsl Shiboleth YR&Z,LLP -1 Penn Plz -NY 10119
(212) 704-6000 .. **Friedman,** Michl D '80 (Troutman S LLP) -405 Lex Av -NY 10174
(212) 506-1700 .. **Friedman,** Michl E '93 Kasowitz BT&F LLP -1633 Bway -NY 10019
(914) 285-9800 .. **Friedman,** Michl H '91 (Kurzman EC&L,LLP) -1 N Bway -White Plns 10601
(212) 294-6700 .. **Friedman,** Michl J '00 (Winston & S) -200 Park Av -NY 10166
(212) 848-0600 .. **Friedman,** Michl L '59 (First NY Sec) -90 Park Av -NY 10016 **Fx:**848-0799
(518) 439-0375 .. **Friedman,** Michl P '77 (Friedman & M,PC) -2 Normanskill Blvd Bx69 -Delmar 12054
(212) 732-5800 .. **Friedman,** Mitchell R '69 (Friedman & M LLP) -233 Bway -NY 10279
(212) 764-2550 .. **Friedman,** Mitchell R '87 (M Friedman PC) -67 Wall -NY 10005 **Fx:**(973) 669-3733
(212) 578-3417 .. **Friedman,** Mitchell R '92 %MetLife -1 Mad Av -NY 10010
(718) 518-2927 .. **Friedman,** Mitchell S '82 -7 Lawrence -New Hyde Pk 11040
(518) 439-0375 .. **Friedman & Molinsek,PC** -2 Normanskill Blvd Bx69 -Delmar 12054 **Fx:**439-0521
(212) 732-5800 .. **Friedman & Moses LLP** -233 Bway -NY 10279 **Fx:**608-3280
(718) 871-1200 .. **Friedman,** Moshe I '95 %E Rubin -4915 12th Av -Brklyn 11219 **Fx:**972-0246
(845) 292-2000 .. **Friedman,** Myron M '49 (B Rourke,PC) -3 Maple Bx71 -Liberty 12754 **Fx:**292-0385
(212) 580-9230 .. **Friedman,** Nansi '81 -225 W 83rd -NY 10024 **Fx:**580-0310
(516) 487-2252 .. **Friedman,** Neal S '90 Rothkrug R&S,LLP -55 Watermill Ln -Gt Neck 11021
(212) 836-8000 .. **Friedman,** Nicholas C '08 %Kaye S LLP -425 Park Av -NY 10022
(415) 722-4160 .. **Friedman,** Paul A '07 Kenneth Cole Productions -603 W 50th -NY 10019
(212) 885-5000 .. **Friedman,** Paul A '08 (Blank R LLP) -405 Lex Av -NY 10174
(212) 872-1000 .. **Friedman,** Peter M '07 -One Bryant Park -NY 10036 **Fx:**872-1002
(716) 542-5444 .. **Friedman & Ranzenhofer,PC** -74 Main Bx31 -Akron 14001 **Fx:**542-4090
(212) 930-9700 .. **Friedman,** Richd A '88 (Sichenzia RFF LLP) -61 Bway -NY 10006
(212) 922-1800 .. **Friedman,** Richd B '83 (McKenna L&A) -230 Park Av -NY 10169
(212) 486-6667 .. **Friedman,** Richd E '68 -110 E 59th -NY 10022 **Fx:**753-2694
(212) 789-5947 .. **Friedman,** Richd G '89 %Chase Private Banking -1211 Av of Amer -NY 10036 **Fx:**944-0959
(212) 483-0875 .. **Friedman,** Richd I '89 OfCnsl JF McHugh -6 Water -NY 10004 **Fx:**483-0876
(212) 435-7000 .. **Friedman,** Richd P '87 Port Auth of NY/NJ -225 Park Av S -NY 10003
(518) 464-2000 .. **Friedman,** Richd W '77 AYCO -1 Wall Bx15073 -Albany 12212
(516) 428-3978 .. **Friedman,** Ricki S '98 -125 E Bway -Long Bch 11561
(716) 542-5444 .. **Friedman,** Robt '79 (Friedman & R,PC) -74 Main Bx31 -Akron 14001
(212) 872-1000 .. **Friedman,** Robt '09 -One Bryant Park -NY 10036 **Fx:**872-1002
(212) 704-6000 .. **Friedman,** Robt A '99 (Troutman S LLP) -405 Lex Av -NY 10174
(212) 940-8744 .. **Friedman,** Robt E '76 Cnsl Katten MR LLP -575 Mad Av -NY 10022
(212) 744-9675 .. **Friedman,** Robt G '71 -510 E 80th -NY 10075 **Fx:**744-2126
(212) 451-2300 .. **Friedman,** Robt H '84 (Olshan GFR&W LLP) -65 E 55th -NY 10022
(914) 949-7940 .. **Friedman,** Robt J '50 OfCnsl Holden Bros,PC -124 Court -White Plns 10601
(212) 513-3200 .. **Friedman,** Robt J '81 (Holland & K LLP) -31 W 52nd -NY 10019
(212) 583-5000 .. **Friedman,** Robt L '68 %The Blackstone Grp -345 Park Av -NY 10154
(212) 698-3500 .. **Friedman,** Robt M '85 (Dechert LLP) -1095 Av of Amer -NY 10036
(212) 653-8700 .. **Friedman,** Robt S '90 (Sheppard MR&H LLP) -30 Rckfllr Plz -NY 10112
(516) 479-6300 .. **Friedman,** Ronald J '97 (Silverman A LLP) -100 Jericho Quad -Jericho 11753
(845) 897-4001 .. **Friedman,** Ronald K '78 R Friedman,PLLC -1073 Main -Fishkill 12524 **Fx:**897-4485
(914) 631-6200 .. **Friedman,** Ronald S '68 -150 Wht Plns Rd -Tarrytwn 10591
(516) 355-9600 .. **Friedman,** Russell C '84 (Friedman HK&P) -3000 Marcus Av -Lk Success 11042
(914) 962-7678 .. **Friedman,** S Wm '53 -40 Triangle Ctr -Yorktwn Hts 10598 **Fx:**962-7901
(212) 243-1313 .. **Friedman,** Sally B '92 %Leg Action Ctr -225 Varick -NY 10014 **Fx:**675-0286
(212) 267-2900 .. **Friedman,** Saml '88 -225 Bway -NY 10007
(212) 535-4108 .. **Friedman,** Sandra F '77 -35 E 75th -NY 10021
(212) 725-0200 .. **Friedman,** Sandra Liss '80 (Barnes R&C) -475 Park Av S -NY 10016
(212) 981-4500 .. **Friedman,** Sandrea '85 PeterSan Grp -1450 Bway -NY 10018 **Fx:**981-4560
(212) 278-9374 .. **Friedman,** Sari J '02 Invesco Inst -1166 Av of Amer -NY 10036
(516) 222-1030 .. **Friedman,** Sari M '81 -666 Old Cntry Rd -Gdn Cty 11530 **Fx:**222-1053
(212) 918-3000 .. **Friedman,** Scott '86 (Hogan L LLP) -875 3rd Av -NY 10022
(716) 853-5100 .. **Friedman,** Scott E '84 (Lippes MWF LLP) -665 Main -Buffalo 14203
(212) 326-3939 .. **Friedman,** Scott J '98 Cnsl Jones D -222 E 41st -NY 10017
(212) 909-5387 .. **Friedman,** Seth L '00 KPMG LLP -757 3rd Av -NY 10017
(212) 295-6361 .. **Friedman,** Shauna K '07 %WilmerHale -399 Park Av -NY 10022
(718) 694-5715 .. **Friedman,** Shawn M '99 %Transit Auth -130 Lvngstn -Brklyn 11201 **Fx:**694-5726
(212) 925-4545 .. **Friedman,** Shelly S '82 (Friedman & G,LLP) -568 Bway -NY 10012
(718) 232-8476 .. **Friedman,** Sholem '76 -5417 18th Av -Brklyn 11204
(845) 639-7800 .. **Friedman,** Sidney '04 %Mandel K&B,LLP -210 Route 303 -Vly Cottage 10989
(212) 554-7800 .. **Friedman,** Solomon P '61 (Moses & S LLP) -405 Lex Av -NY 10174
(212) 558-4000 .. **Friedman,** Stacey R '98 (Sullivan & C LLP) -125 Broad -NY 10004
(718) 250-8598 .. **Friedman,** Stacy A '97 Bklyn Hospital Ctr -121 Dekalb Av -Brklyn 11201
(212) 732-8700 .. **Friedman,** Stanley D '55 (McAloon & F,PC) -123 William -NY 10038
(585) 232-3730 .. **Friedman,** Stanley M '54 OfCnsl Chamberlain D LLP -1600 Crssrds Bldg -Rchstr 14614
(212) 554-1716 .. **Friedman,** Stefanie M '03 Monarch Alternative Capital LP -535 Mad Av -NY 10022
(212) 907-9700 .. **Friedman,** Stephen S '89 (Smith G&R,LLP) -250 Park Av -NY 10177
(212) 533-6300 .. **Friedman,** Steven A '86 %NYSUT -52 Bway -NY 10004 **Fx:**995-2347
(212) 821-6220 .. **Friedman,** Steven A '97 UBS -299 Park Av -NY 10171
(212) 583-9600 .. **Friedman,** Steven J '86 (Littler M,PC) -900 3rd Av -NY 10022
(212) 832-5804 .. **Friedman,** Steven M '84 (Eos Partners) -320 Park Av -NY 10022 **Fx:**832-5805
(516) 365-9191 .. **Friedman,** Stewart '75 -1 Hllw Ln -New Hyde Pk 11042 **Fx:**365-6138
(212) 750-8700 .. **Friedman,** Stuart I '77 (Friedman & W,PC) -600 Lex Av -NY 10022
(516) 295-5705 .. **Friedman,** Stuart R '83 -225 Narrow Ln -Woodmere 11598
(212) 345-6000 .. **Friedman,** Susan F '94 Marsh USA -1166 Av of Amer -NY 10036 **Fx:**345-4808
(212) 696-2666 .. **Friedman,** Terry K '77 (Weisberg F&K) -261 5th Av -NY 10016
(212) 655-3500 .. **Friedman,** Thos L '90 (Meister S&F LLP) -140 E 45th -NY 10017
(212) 446-4800 .. **Friedman,** Todd M '99 (Kirkland & E LLP) -153 E 53rd -NY 10022
(212) 558-4000 .. **Friedman,** Tyler J '07 %Sullivan & C LLP -125 Broad -NY 10004
(718) 537-7233 .. **Friedman,** Valerie B '01 %DA -198 E 161st -Bronx 10451 **Fx:**590-6477
(212) 859-8000 .. **Friedman,** Victor S '58 OfCnsl Fried FHS&J LLP -1 NY Plz -NY 10004
(516) 222-6200 .. **Friedman,** Vinson J '76 (Berkman HPP&F,PC) -100 Grdn City Plz -Gdn Cty 11530
(212) 361-1400 .. **Friedman,** Vivian Rivkin '79 Envrnmntl Cntrl Brd -66 John -NY 10038 **Fx:**361-1900
(212) 724-1997 .. **Friedman,** Vivian Rivkin '79 -333 West End Av -NY 10023 **Fx:**724-1328
(212) 969-3986 .. **Friedman,** Wilbur H '31 (Proskauer R LLP) -1585 Bway -NY 10036
(212) 302-0100 .. **Friedman,** Wilfred T '58 -60 E 42nd -NY 10165 **Fx:**302-1119
(212) 248-2936 .. **Friedman,** Wm A '09 %Kirsch GH LLP -11 Penn Plz -NY 10001
(516) 538-5462 .. **Friedman,** Wm D '64 -507 Fulton Av -Hempstd 11550 **Fx:**538-5549
(212) 756-2000 .. **Friedman,** Wm I '02 %Schulte R&Z LLP -919 3rd Av -NY 10022
(973) 228-5700 .. **Friedman,** Wm J '77 (Brach E LLC) -100 Park Av -NY 10017 **Fx:**228-7852
(516) 292-8100 .. **Friedman,** Wm J '08 Nassau/Sfflk Law Srv -1 Helen Keller Way -Hempstd 11550 **Fx:**292-6529
(212) 949-5000 .. **Friedman,** Wm S '71 %Tarragon Rlty Advsr -160 Varick -NY 10013
(212) 750-8700 .. **Friedman & Wittenstein,PC** -600 Lex Av -NY 10022 **Fx:**223-8391
(212) 354-4500 .. **Friedman & Wolf** -1500 Bway -NY 10036 **Fx:**719-9072
(347) 401-9580 .. **Friedman,** Zara G '06 %Appllt Term -141 Lvngstn -Brklyn 11201 **Fx:**(718) 643-7889
(212) 335-9000 .. **Friedman Agnifilo,** Karen P '93 %DA -1 Hogan Pl -NY 10013
(516) 513-0815 .. **Friedmann,** Alan R '83 Envision Title Srvcs,LLC -333 Earle Ovngton Blvd -Uniondale 11553 **Fx:**208-2088
(212) 878-8000 .. **Friedmann,** Chas '09 %Clifford C LLP -31 W 52nd -NY 10019
(212) 310-8000 .. **Friedmann,** Jared R '04 %Weil G&M LLP -767 5th Av -NY 10153
(212) 561-5559 .. **Friedmann,** Kevin '07 (Richardson & P,LLP) -750 3rd Av -NY 10017
(212) 526-3435 .. **Friedmann,** Rachel L '03 %Barclays Capital Inc -745 7th Av -NY 10019
(212) 557-7440 .. **Friedner,** Howard '86 %Garrison Bradford & Assoc -122 E 42nd -NY 10168 **Fx:**557-8008
(212) 308-0210 .. **Friedrich,** Bruce R '87 -110 E 59th -NY 10022 **Fx:**308-0213

(631) 261-7778 .. **Friedrich,** Jennifer C '03 Cnsl Brody O&O -7 Bayview Av -Northprt 11768
(212) 848-4000 .. **Friedrich,** Laura S '97 (Shearman & S LLP) -599 Lex Av -NY 10022
(646) 672-4350 .. **Friedrich,** Lya T '92 -6 E 87th -NY 10128 **Fx:**672-4353
(212) 407-8484 .. **Friedrich,** Robt B '96 NBA -645 5th Av -NY 10022
(914) 249-2000 .. **Friedrichs,** Natasha I '04 %MasterCard Intl -2000 Purchase -Purchase 10577
(518) 436-9711 .. **Friedricks,** David '65 %Chicago Title Ins Co -80 State -Albany 12207 **Fx:**436-0891
(212) 335-9000 .. **Friel,** Lisa Mendelson '84 %DA -1 Hogan Pl -NY 10013
(914) 666-2328 .. **Friel,** M Alison '76 -23 Bretton Ridge Rd -Mt Kisco 10549 **Fx:**666-3076
(212) 432-3800 .. **Frieland,** Harry '72 (Levitan & F,PC) -111 E 35th -NY 10016
(212) 792-8484 .. **Frieman,** Karen S '85 SpclCnsl Stern T&B LLP -380 Lex Av -NY 10168
(212) 576-2670 .. **Friend,** James H '82 OfCnsl J Osborn,PC -841 Bway -NY 10003 **Fx:**686-4023
(212) 695-0060 .. **Friend,** Lauren M '06 %Wilens & B,PC -450 7th Av -NY 10123
(212) 441-6822 .. **Friend,** Paul S '87 Cnsl Fed Home Loan Bk -101 Park Av -NY 10178 **Fx:**949-2007
(212) 587-1960 .. **Friend & Reiskind PLLC** -100 William -NY 10038 **Fx:**587-1957
(516) 487-8559 .. **Friend,** Solomon H '48 -58 Grace Av -Gt Neck 11021 **Fx:**(561) 241-0911
(212) 259-8000 .. **Friend,** Steven C '02 (Dewey & L LLP) -1301 Av of Amer -NY 10019
(212) 732-6640 .. **Frier,** Ronald H '82 -7 Dey -NY 10007
(212) 455-2000 .. **Frierson,** Crystal L '08 %Simpson T&B LLP -425 Lex Av -NY 10017
(516) 379-3940 .. **Frierson-Davis,** Renaire '87 -164 Moore Av -Freeprt 11520 **Fx:**379-6639
(716) 565-2000 .. **Fries,** Donald N '66 -17 Beresford Ct -Williamsvll 14221
(607) 778-2156 .. **Fries,** Margaret M '89 Family Ct -65 Hawley Bx1766 -Bnghmtn 13902 **Fx:**778-2439
(212) 756-2000 .. **Fries,** Marisa N '08 %Schulte R&Z LLP -919 3rd Av -NY 10022
(212) 705-7000 .. **Fries,** Richd S '78 (Bingham M LLP) -399 Park Av -NY 10022
(845) 358-0074 .. **Friesen,** Catherine Harries '95 %MacCartney MK&M -13 N Bway Bx350 -Nyack 10960
(212) 839-5300 .. **Friesen,** Connie M '80 (Sidley A LLP) -787 7th Av -NY 10019
(212) 223-6700 .. **Friesen,** Jeffrey L '95 %Zukerman GB&C,LLP -875 3rd Av -NY 10022
(212) 756-2000 .. **Friess,** Marc '02 %Schulte R&Z LLP -919 3rd Av -NY 10022
(212) 558-4000 .. **Friestedt,** Matthew M '98 (Sullivan & C LLP) -125 Broad -NY 10004
(212) 788-0649 .. **Friesz,** Mark I '08 %Law Dept -100 Church -NY 10007 **Fx:**788-0367
(212) 401-0800 .. **Friman,** Paul L '90 Disciplinary Comm -61 Bway -NY 10006 **Fx:**287-1045
(516) 222-2230 .. **Frimet,** Ian J '09 %Burkhart W&H,LLP -585 Stewart Av -Gdn Cty 11530
(212) 922-6296 .. **Frimet,** Marc B '93 Bk of NY Mellon -200 Park Av -NY 10166
(212) 513-1075 .. **Frimet,** Michl J '99 (Stalker VB&F, LLP) -80 Broad -NY 10004
(212) 290-2247 .. **Frimet,** Rhett A '93 (R Frimet,PC) -10 E 40th -NY 10016
(516) 328-2300 .. **Frimmel,** Mark '89 %Abrams FFEGF&E,LLP -1111 Marcus Av -Lk Success 11042
(212) 259-8000 .. **Frimmer,** Scott E '07 %Dewey & L LLP -1301 Av of Amer -NY 10019
(212) 909-6000 .. **Frimpong,** Naana Abenaa '05 %Debevoise & P LLP -919 3rd Av -NY 10022
(518) 402-9184 .. **Frinks-Dixon,** Cindylou '87 DEC -625 Bway -Albany 12233 **Fx:**402-9018
(347) 401-9580 .. **Frisa,** Danielle B '09 %Appllt Term -141 Lvngstn -Brklyn 11201 **Fx:**(718) 643-7889
(212) 310-8000 .. **Frisby,** Alanna J '09 %Weil G&M LLP -767 5th Av -NY 10153
(212) 784-2413 .. **Frisch,** Andrew J '85 -950 3rd Av -NY 10022
(212) 670-0375 .. **Frisch,** Harry D '81 Merrill Lynch -222 Bway -NY 10038 **Fx:**670-0729
(212) 436-1757 .. **Frisch,** Jill A '85 %IRS -290 Bway -NY 10007
(212) 732-3200 .. **Frisch,** Kelly M '08 %Carter L&M LLP -2 Wall -NY 10005
(212) 245-4580 .. **Frisch,** Michl B '04 %Shukat AHW&H,LLP -111 W 57th -NY 10019
(212) 969-3000 .. **Frischer,** Harry '80 (Proskauer R LLP) -1585 Bway -NY 10036
(212) 701-3000 .. **Frischer,** Lindsey F '10 %Cahill G&R LLP -80 Pine -NY 10005 **Fx:**269-5420
(212) 257-6960 .. **Frischknecht,** Andreas A '03 %Chaffetz L LLP -1350 Av of Amer -NY 10019
(631) 390-0010 .. **Frischling,** Allison B '04 %Bruno G&S,LLP -445 Broad Hollow Rd -Melvll 11747
(212) 715-9100 .. **Frischling,** Carl '63 (Kramer LN&F,LLP) -1177 Av of Amer -NY 10036
(212) 909-6000 .. **Frischtak,** Ana L '07 %Debevoise & P LLP -919 3rd Av -NY 10022
(718) 442-9000 .. **Friscia,** John S '84 (Ameduri G&F) -471 Bement Av -Staten Isl 10310
(212) 609-6800 .. **Friscia,** Michl R '90 (McCarter & E,LLP) -245 Park Av -NY 10167
(718) 292-2200 .. **Frisco,** Nick M '88 -184 E 161st -Bronx 10451 **Fx:**292-1610
(914) 946-8900 .. **Frisenda,** Robt J '77 (Clark G&M) -99 Court -White Plns 10601
(212) 319-4900 .. **Frishauf Holtz Goodman & Chick** -220 5th Av -NY 10001 **Fx:**319-5101
(212) 740-4544 .. **Frishberg,** Aaron D '87 OfCnsl Stevens H&W,PC -116 W 111th -NY 10026
(310) 776-7320 .. **Frishberg,** Michl J '04 Kurtzman Carson Cnsltnts -1230 Av of Amer -NY 10020
(845) 294-7944 .. **Frishberg,** Neal D '85 (Fabricant L&F,PLLC) -1 Harriman Sq Bx60 -Goshen 10924
(212) 735-3000 .. **Frishman,** Lawr D '89 (Skadden ASM&F LLP) -4 Times Sq -NY 10036
(914) 241-3680 .. **Frishman,** Sheryl R '97 (Frishman & F) -83 S Bedford Rd -Mt Kisco 10549 **Fx:**241-3681
(631) 390-4343 .. **Frisoni,** Robt J '89 (Frisoni H & Assoc,PC) -527 Townline Rd -Hauppauge 11788 **Fx:**390-4344
(585) 232-6760 .. **Fritsch,** Jos G Jr. '76 -45 Exchange -Rchstr 14614
(212) 558-4000 .. **Fritsch,** Joshua J '06 %Sullivan & C LLP -125 Broad -NY 10004
(212) 888-5500 .. **Fritsch,** Thos X '98 Smith Mgmt LLC -885 3rd Av -NY 10022
(212) 504-6000 .. **Fritts,** John F '60 SrCnsl Cadwalader W&T LLP -1 World Fncl Ctr -NY 10281
(518) 471-4726 .. **Fritts,** Roger M '66 %Appllt Div 3rd Dept -Capitol Station Bx7288 -Albany 12224 **Fx:**471-4750
(718) 250-2000 .. **Fritts,** Stephanie M '06 DA -350 Jay -Brklyn 11201 **Fx:**250-2314
(914) 286-4765 .. **Fritz,** Allison J '96 %Heineken USA Inc -360 Hmltn Av -White Plns 10601
(212) 640-1137 .. **Fritz,** Brooke A '01 Amer Exp -200 Vesey -NY 10285
(212) 336-2000 .. **Fritz,** Dana '02 %Patterson BW&T LLP -1133 Av of Amer -NY 10036
(212) 223-6700 .. **Fritz,** David R '75 OfCnsl Zukerman GB&C,LLP -875 3rd Av -NY 10022
(718) 353-9091 .. **Fritz,** Howard C '86 -40-16 149th Pl -Flushng 11354
(516) 747-8348 .. **Fritz,** Howard P '53 -15 Roslyn Rd -Mineola 11501 **Fx:**294-1335
(212) 297-5800 .. **Fritz,** Jeffrey A '04 %Day P LLP -7 Times Sq -NY 10036
(585) 262-6390 .. **Fritz,** John E '08 %Hamberger & W -1 S Wshngtn -Rchstr 14614
(631) 277-5600 .. **Fritz,** Jos L '73 -135 W Main -E Islip 11730 **Fx:**277-0092
(212) 655-3500 .. **Fritz,** Kevin A '03 %Meister S&R LLP -140 E 45th -NY 10017
(212) 471-6202 .. **Fritz,** Maranda E '83 (Hinshaw & C LLP) -780 3rd Av -NY 10017
(212) 558-4000 .. **Fritz,** Michl J '07 %Sullivan & C LLP -125 Broad -NY 10004
(212) 335-9000 .. **Fritz,** Steven '01 %DA -1 Hogan Pl -NY 10013
(212) 259-8000 .. **Fritzinger,** John G Jr. '62 OfCnsl Dewey & L LLP -1301 Av of Amer -NY 10019
(607) 722-5106 .. **Fritzsch,** Craig R '84 -34 Chenango Bx561 -Bnghmtn 13902 **Fx:**231-8630
(212) 848-4000 .. **Frizzley,** Jill K '02 %Shearman & S LLP -599 Lex Av -NY 10022
(212) 357-9588 .. **Froberg,** Andrew D '98 %Goldman Sachs & Co -180 Maiden Ln -NY 10038
(516) 944-5062 .. **Froccaro,** James R '88 -20 Vanderventer Av -Pt Wash 11050 **Fx:**944-5064
(212) 553-4149 .. **Froeba,** Mark N '97 %Moody's Invstr Srvc -250 Greenwich -NY 10007
(212) 687-2770 .. **Froebrich,** Alfred W '94 (Cohen PL&P) -551 5th Av -NY 10176
(212) 415-8600 .. **Froehlich,** Jos N '97 (Locke LB&L LLP) -3 World Fncl Ctr -NY 10281
(516) 248-6500 .. **Froehlich Mahony & deBruin** -34 Willis Av -Mineola 11501 **Fx:**248-7555
(212) 227-7435 .. **Froehlich,** Richd M '89 HDC -110 William -NY 10038 **Fx:**227-6865
(516) 921-1465 .. **Froehlich,** Robt A '69 -102 Sterling Ct -Syosset 11791
(516) 538-2500 .. **Froehlich,** Valerie '98 (Furey FLMW&D,PC) -600 Front -Hempstd 11550
(212) 326-3939 .. **Froelich,** Christopher G '06 %Jones D -222 E 41st -NY 10017
(212) 940-8800 .. **Froelich,** Louis J '09 %Katten MR LLP -575 Mad Av -NY 10022
(212) 859-8000 .. **Froes,** Stephanie '08 %Fried FHS&J LLP -1 NY Plz -NY 10004
(212) 513-3200 .. **Froessel,** Timothy B '92 SrCnsl Holland & K LLP -31 W 52nd -NY 10019
(212) 819-8200 .. **Frogel,** Judah I '06 %White & C LLP -1155 Av of Amer -NY 10036
(914) 684-1613 .. **Frohlinger,** Kim A '83 K Frohlinger LLC -135 Lakevw Av -Hartsdale 10530 **Fx:**946-9720
(212) 808-7800 .. **Frohman,** Jacob J '00 (Kelley D&W LLP) -101 Park Av -NY 10178
(212) 883-1300 .. **Frohman,** Morgan L '05 %Sandler T&R,PA -551 5th Av -NY 10176
(212) 751-8899 .. **Frohman,** Paul '51 (Alfieri F&P,LLP) -460 Park Av -NY 10022
(845) 225-4362 .. **Frohne,** Wm J '77 -103 Church Hill Rd -Carmel 10512
(718) 590-2000 .. **From,** Beth R '03 %DA -198 E 161st -Bronx 10451 **Fx:**590-6477
(718) 855-7675 .. **Fromartz,** D Bunji '88 (Fromartz Law Ofc) -32 Court -Brklyn 11201
(212) 909-6000 .. **Fromberg,** Eliza Sporn '02 %Debevoise & P LLP -919 3rd Av -NY 10022
(718) 422-4960 .. **Frome,** Jacqueline A '99 %US Trustees Ofc -271 Cadman Plz E -Brklyn 11201 **Fx:**422-4990
(516) 248-6444 .. **Frome,** Paula Schwartz '75 -1325 Franklin Av -Gdn Cty 11530 **Fx:**742-9416
(212) 977-5050 .. **Frome,** Richd M '67 -880 3rd Av -NY 10022 **Fx:**751-2235
(212) 451-2300 .. **Frome,** Robt L '62 (Olshan GFR&W LLP) -65 E 55th -NY 10022
(716) 855-1222 .. **Fromen,** John J '67 -350 Main -Buffalo 14202
(716) 855-1222 .. **Fromen,** John J Jr. '87 %JJ Fromen -350 Main -Buffalo 14202
(212) 636-6000 .. **Fromer,** Jeanne C '03 %Fordham Univ Sch of Law -140 W 62nd -NY 10023 **Fx:**636-6899
(516) 741-6565 .. **Fromewick,** Richd G '73 (Meyer SE&K,PC) -990 Stewart Av Bx9194 -Gdn Cty 11530
(212) 838-6333 .. **Fromkin,** David H '59 -20 Beekman Pl -NY 10022
(212) 983-8500 .. **Fromm,** David H '79 (Brown G&F LLP) -355 Lex Av -NY 10017
(212) 878-7214 .. **Fromm,** Helene '76 MTA -347 Mad Av -NY 10017
(212) 686-3838 .. **Fromm,** Isaac '73 (Barst M&K LLP) -2 Park Av -NY 10016
(212) 415-9200 .. **Fromm,** Jeffrey A '88 (Dorsey & W LLP) -250 Park Av -NY 10177
(212) 791-1409 .. **Fromme,** Douglas L '84 (D Fromme,PC) -462 7th Av -NY 10018 **Fx:**(516) 745-1381
(212) 791-3900 .. **Fromme,** Eric F '82 (Breier DU&F PC) -111 Bway -NY 10006
(212) 687-1230 .. **Frommer,** Hillary A '01 %Farrell F,PC -370 Lex Av -NY 10017
(212) 588-0800 .. **Frommer Lawrence & Haug LLP** -745 5th Av -NY 10151 **Fx:**588-0500
(718) 767-3333 .. **Frommer,** Robt W '95 %Borchert GL&L,PC -19-02 Whitestone Expy -Whitestone 11357
(516) 742-7900 .. **Frommer,** Stephen G '76 (Frommer & C,LLP) -42 Nassau Blvd Bx8134 -Gdn Cty 11530 **Fx:**742-7999
(212) 588-0800 .. **Frommer,** Wm S '70 (Frommer L&H LLP) -745 5th Av -NY 10151
(845) 339-5815 .. **Fromson,** Kenneth B '95 (Finkelstein & Prtnrs,LLP) -785 Bway -Kingston 12401
(845) 356-3334 .. **Fromson,** Stephen M '77 (Greenberg W&F) -150 Airport Exec Park -Nanuet 10954
(212) 422-1200 .. **Fronce,** John O '94 %Abrams GF&J,PC -1 Bttry Pk Plz -NY 10004
(212) 270-3615 .. **Froom,** Ilene Katinka '97 JP Morgan Chase & Co -270 Park Av -NY 10017
(212) 446-2380 .. **Froot,** Steven I '86 (Boies S&F LLP) -575 Lex Av -NY 10022
(914) 946-4777 .. **Frosco,** Donna E '93 (Keane & B,PC) -445 Hmltn Av -White Plns 10601
(212) 813-5900 .. **Fross Zelnick Lehrman & Zissu,PC** -866 UN Plz -NY 10017 **Fx:**813-5901
(518) 283-3000 .. **Frost,** Arthur R '96 (Frost & K,PC) -287 N Greenbush Rd -Troy 12180 **Fx:**283-8060
(212) 336-2000 .. **Frost,** Claire D '08 %Patterson BW&T LLP -1133 Av of Amer -NY 10036
(212) 837-6038 .. **Frost,** Danl N '09 %Hughes H&R LLP -1 Bttry Pk Plz -NY 10004
(212) 674-5151 .. **Frost,** Diana R '86 Macmillan -175 5th Av -NY 10010 **Fx:**529-0594
(212) 248-3140 .. **Frost,** Jack N Jr. '06 %Drinker B&R LLP -140 Bway -NY 10005

(845) 471-0058 .. **Frost,** Jacqueline A '84 %Leg Srvcs -29 N Hmltn -Poughkeepsie 12601 **Fx:**471-0244
(212) 557-7700 .. **Frost,** Louis B '67 (Davidson D&C LLP) -60 E 42nd -NY 10165
(212) 541-2000 .. **Frost,** Renee E '85 Cnsl Bryan C LLP -1290 Av of Amer -NY 10104
(518) 473-5809 .. **Frost,** Teneka E '03 NYS Dept of Civil Srvc -80 S Swan -Albany 12239
(845) 897-1600 .. **Frost,** Thos C '02 %Rosicki R & Assoc,PC -2 Summit Ct -Fishkill 12524 **Fx:**897-2648
(212) 697-2677 .. **Frost,** Wm L '51 -60 E 42nd -NY 10165
(718) 268-2722 .. **Frost,** Wm P '66 -67-50 Kessel -Frst Hlls 11375
(212) 370-1300 .. **Froum,** Holly R '06 %Ellenoff G&S LLP -150 E 42nd -NY 10017
(212) 668-0059 .. **Frowley,** Norman E '73 %Zalman & S -61 Bway -NY 10006
(212) 968-8300 .. **Frucchione,** Peter A '98 %Mintzer SZL&M LLP -39 Bway -NY 10006
(914) 997-7100 .. **Frucco,** John P '68 (Berman BF&G pc) -123 Main -White Plns 10601
(212) 947-9779 .. **Frucher,** Kathryn I '02 Advocates for Chldrn of NY -151 W 30th -NY 10001
(212) 223-4000 .. **Frucht,** Robt G '98 (Crowell & M LLP) -590 Mad Av -NY 10022
(518) 473-5095 .. **Fruchter,** David '76 %Dept of Law -The Cptl -Albany 12224
(212) 279-5050 .. **Fruchter,** Jack G '93 (Abraham F&T LLP) -1 Penn Plz -NY 10119
(631) 232-0178 .. **Fruchter,** Jos B '92 -140 Fell Ct -Hauppauge 11788 **Fx:**232-0176
(212) 790-9200 .. **Fruchter,** Lynn S '76 OfCnsl Cowan L&L,PC -1133 Av of Amer -NY 10036
(212) 421-4100 .. **Fruchter,** Michl Y '02 %Pryor C LLP -7 Times Sq -NY 10036
(212) 770-7000 .. **Fruchter,** Raquel M '09 AIG -175 Water -NY 10038
(845) 473-8100 .. **Fruchtman,** Elliot N '09 %Iseman CR&H,LLP -2649 South Rd -Poughkeepsie 12601
(212) 837-6000 .. **Fruchtman,** Joshua A '07 %Hughes H&R LLP -1 Bttry Pk Plz -NY 10004
(212) 895-4431 .. **Fruchtman,** Lawr D '72 Amalgamated Bank -275 7th Av -NY 10001 **Fx:**895-4726
(516) 682-0667 .. **Fruchtman,** Steven R '93 Integrated Risk Srvcs -Bx85 -Syosset 11791 **Fx:**682-0668
(914) 592-4275 .. **Fruendt,** Debra A '00 %MHLS -100 Clearbrook Rd -Elmsfrd 10523 **Fx:**592-9404
(212) 385-4410 .. **Fruhling,** Michl A '92 (Gersowitz L&K,PC) -111 Bway -NY 10006
(212) 264-1647 .. **Fruitman,** Irina '95 %ODAR-SSA -26 Fed Plz -NY 10278
(914) 347-5522 .. **Frum,** Donald L '79 -565 Taxter Rd -Elmsfrd 10523 **Fx:**347-8760
(212) 783-3183 .. **Frumento,** Aegis J '80 Citigroup Inc -787 7th Av -NY 10019
(718) 389-0240 .. **Frumin,** Lucille L '88 (Piazza D&F) -824 Manh Av -Brklyn 11222
(212) 494-0070 .. **Frumkin,** Jacob '96 -65 W 36th -NY 10018 **Fx:**494-0088
(212) 558-4000 .. **Frumkin,** Jos B '86 (Sullivan & C LLP) -125 Broad -NY 10004
(914) 328-0366 .. **Frumkin,** Wm D '87 (Sapir & F LLP) -399 Knollwood Rd -White Plns 10603
(212) 756-2000 .. **Frunzi,** Susan C '84 (Schulte R&Z LLP) -919 3rd Av -NY 10022
(716) 645-2907 .. **Fruscione,** Melissa A '03 SUNY Buffalo Lw Schl -O'Brian Hall -Buffalo 14260 **Fx:**645-5968
(716) 627-1221 .. **Fruth,** Michl H '97 -5624 Truscott Ter -Lk View 14085
(212) 478-0756 .. **Fry,** Bertrand C '94 DE Shaw & Co -120 W 45th -NY 10036 **Fx:**478-0100
(212) 661-0011 .. **Fry,** Christina M '01 %Speiser KN&G -140 E 45th -NY 10017
(212) 858-1000 .. **Fry,** Elizabeth H W '78 (Pillsbury WSP LLP) -1540 Bway -NY 10036
(718) 243-6804 .. **Fry,** Julie N '05 %Leg Aid -111 Lvngstn -Brklyn 11201 **Fx:**237-8737
(914) 629-0855 .. **Fryburg,** Marc H '82 -15 Harper -Lk Peekskill 10537
(516) 222-8500 .. **Frycek,** Scott O '99 (Martin C&B LLP) -90 Merrick Av -E Meadow 11554
(212) 431-6530 .. **Fryd,** Paul A '80 (P Fryd,LLC) -361 Greenwich -NY 10013 **Fx:**431-8079
(212) 984-7855 .. **Fryd,** Robt '78 (Warshaw BCS&K,LLP) -555 5th Av -NY 10017
(718) 882-1500 .. **Frydman,** Abraham '61 -352 Ft Hill Rd -Scarsdale 10583
(212) 355-9100 .. **Frydman,** David S '92 (Frydman LLC) -18 E 48th -NY 10017 **Fx:**355-8988
(347) 809-0763 .. **Frydman,** Jeffrey '89 -352 Ft Hill Rd -Scarsdale 10583
(315) 733-7549 .. **Frye Foley & Carbone** -2219 Genesee -Utica 13501 **Fx:**733-4471
(315) 369-3544 .. **Frye Foley & Carbone** -2973 State Route 28 Bx291 -Old Forge 13420 **Fx:**369-6433
(315) 369-3544 .. **Frye,** Richd A '58 (Frye F&C) -2973 State Route 28 Bx291 -Old Forge 13420
(315) 733-7549 .. **Frye,** Richd A '58 (Frye F&C) -2219 Genesee -Utica 13501
(516) 355-9600 .. **Fryer,** Angelina L '09 %Friedman HK&P -3000 Marcus Av -Lk Success 11042
(518) 238-4339 .. **Fryer,** David W '91 OCA -187 Wolf Rd -Albany 12205 **Fx:**438-3518
(212) 455-2000 .. **Fryer,** Gibbs P '10 %Simpson T&B LLP -425 Lex Av -NY 10017
(212) 801-9330 .. **Fryer,** Judith D '76 (Greenberg T,LLP) -200 Park Av -NY 10166
(212) 286-0099 .. **Fryer & Ross LLP** -551 5th Av -NY 10176 **Fx:**286-0495
(516) 794-7500 .. **Fryman,** Robt J '90 (Westermann SKS&A,LLP) -333 Earle Ovngton Blvd -Uniondale 11553
(212) 735-3000 .. **Fu,** Grace E '10 %Skadden ASM&F LLP -4 Times Sq -NY 10036
(212) 530-1800 .. **Fu,** Jingwei Lu '99 %Richards K&O LLP -1 World Fncl Ctr -NY 10281
(718) 559-3153 .. **Fu,** Joyce L '07 NY Mets -12301 Roosevelt Av -Flushng 11368
(212) 836-8000 .. **Fu,** Tzung-Lin '07 %Kaye S LLP -425 Park Av -NY 10022
(212) 715-1000 .. **Fucci,** Fredk R '88 (Arnold & P LLP) -399 Park Av -NY 10022
(212) 839-6537 .. **Fuccillo,** Jos P '04 Dept of Transportation -55 Water -NY 10041
(212) 739-3222 .. **Fuccillo,** Thos J '97 Allianz Global Invstrs of Amer LP -1345 Av of Amer -NY 10105 **Fx:**739-3948
(631) 231-6034 .. **Fuccio,** James B '88 (DeSocio & F,PC) -245 Marcus Blvd -Hauppauge 11788 **Fx:**231-6072
(516) 628-2356 .. **Fuccio,** James B '88 (DeSocio & F,PC) -271 Bayvll Av -Bayvll 11709 **Fx:**628-2770
(212) 259-8000 .. **Fuchs,** Ariella S '10 %Dewey & L LLP -1301 Av of Amer -NY 10019
(914) 682-9750 .. **Fuchs,** Charna L '78 (Fuchs & E) -550 Mamaroneck Av -Harrison 10528 **Fx:**682-9723
(212) 267-1900 .. **Fuchs,** Cheryl D '06 %Wade CM -111 Bway -NY 10006
(212) 406-1700 .. **Fuchs,** Dallin M '91 (Queller FWF&K LLP) -233 Bway -NY 10279
(212) 962-5065 .. **Fuchs,** Fredk N '91 %Harnick & H -305 Bway -NY 10007 **Fx:**962-6232
(212) 726-0772 .. **Fuchs,** Harvey '89 Midtown Equities LLC -417 5th Av -NY 10016
(718) 788-5052 .. **Fuchs,** Jonathan A '91 %Icelandair -Trmnl 7 JFK Airport -Jamaica 11430 **Fx:**965-4017
(718) 788-5052 .. **Fuchs,** Jonathan A '91 %Hagan C & Assoc -908 4th Av -Brklyn 11232
(212) 778-6387 .. **Fuchs,** Kenneth '78 %Prudential Sec -One NY Plz -NY 10004
(631) 231-3775 .. **Fuchs,** Michl '85 %Atty Grievance Comm -150 Motor Pkwy -Hauppauge 11788
(212) 836-8000 .. **Fuchs,** Nancy E '82 (Kaye S LLP) -425 Park Av -NY 10022
(718) 390-5157 .. **Fuchs,** Richd L '67 %Hon C Kuffner, Jr -18 Richmond -Staten Isl 10301 **Fx:**390-5230
(631) 666-7612 .. **Fuchs,** Robt T '87 -256C Orinoco Dr Bx322 -Brightwtrs 11718 **Fx:**666-0411
(516) 832-9600 .. **Fuchs,** Shaye J '00 %Zwerling S&Z,LLP -990 Stewart Av -Gdn Cty 11530
(516) 766-8977 .. **Fuchs,** Sidney P '76 -324 Jordan -Oceanside 11572
(212) 583-9600 .. **Fuchs,** Stephen A '92 OfCnsl Littler M,PC -900 3rd Av -NY 10022
(212) 373-3000 .. **Fuchs,** Yael '07 %Paul WRW&G LLP -1285 Av of Amer -NY 10019
(212) 869-3500 .. **Fuchsberg,** Alan L '80 (J Fuchsberg Law Firm,LLP) -500 5th Av -NY 10110 **Fx:**398-1532
(212) 480-5284 .. **Fuchsberg,** Lawr M '80 %Insurance Dept -25 Beaver -NY 10004 **Fx:**480-5272
(315) 474-7541 .. **Fucillo,** Thos J '85 (Menter R&T,PC) -308 Maltbie -Syracuse 13204
(914) 750-5933 .. **Fuda,** Daniela '06 %Kissel H&W LLP -580 Wht Plns Rd -Tarrytwn 10591
(212) 907-7300 .. **Fudem,** Tammy '99 %Golenbock EAB&P -437 Mad Av -NY 10022
(212) 880-3800 .. **Fudim,** Elissa P '08 %Akerman S -335 Mad Av -NY 10017
(718) 542-9300 .. **Fuentes,** Alisa Rodriguez '98 OfCnsl Rodriguez & F -644 Soundvw Av -Bronx 10473
(212) 309-6000 .. **Fuentes,** Heather E '08 %Morgan L&B LLP -101 Park Av -NY 10178
(212) 318-6000 .. **Fuentes,** Ingrid M '08 %Paul HJ&W LLP -75 E 55th -NY 10022
(718) 261-9460 .. **Fuentes,** Veronica A '02 %Pearlman AFS&S,LLP -80-02 Kew Grdns Rd -Kew Gdns 11415
(212) 506-1700 .. **Fuentes Skinner,** Olga L '02 %Kasowitz BT&F LLP -1633 Bway -NY 10019
(212) 335-4500 .. **Fuerch,** Jennifer A '08 %DLA Piper LLP -1251 Av of Amer -NY 10020
(716) 774-0091 .. **Fuerle,** Richd D '98 US Patent Applications -1711 W River Rd -Grand Isl 14072
(212) 337-4152 .. **Fuerst,** Cornell R '81 %Thomson Reuters/RIA -195 Bway -NY 10007
(212) 258-6000 .. **Fuerst,** Jane R '81 %Viacom -1515 Bway -NY 10036
(518) 374-3399 .. **Fuerst,** Richd A '01 (Higgins RB&C,PC) -1430 Balltown Rd -Niskayuna 12309
(212) 490-3000 .. **Fuerth,** Glenn J '79 (Wilson EME&D LLP) -150 E 42nd -NY 10017
(212) 687-4900 .. **Fuerth,** Thos L '81 (Wormser KG&J LLP) -825 3rd Av -NY 10022
(914) 761-9200 .. **Fufidio,** George E '83 (Mancuso R&F) -1 N Bway -White Plns 10601
(914) 873-5222 .. **Fugaro,** Maritza '04 Family Ct -420 North Av -New Rchll 10801
(516) 584-1642 .. **Fugazy,** Amanda M '99 (Fugazy & R LLP) -126 Glen -Glen Cove 11542 **Fx:**(484) 805-7022
(516) 496-5822 .. **Fugazzi,** Tina M '98 %T Spina -170 Froehlich Farm Blvd -Woodbury 11797 **Fx:**496-5420
(631) 755-0101 .. **Fugelsang,** Erica K '07 %Lewis JAA,LLP -425 Broad Hollow Rd -Melvll 11747
(631) 694-0033 .. **Fugelsang,** Kathleen A '86 (Lawrence WR&B,PC) -425 Broadhllw Rd -Melvll 11747
(212) 681-7888 .. **Fuhrer,** Neil L '58 (N Fuhrer & Assoc,LLP) -750 3rd Av -NY 10017
(718) 881-5600 .. **Fuhrman,** Jason K '93 %Lazarus L&W -3699 Bainbrdg Av -Bronx 10467 **Fx:**881-5666
(212) 456-3256 .. **Fuhrman,** Jeffrey P '02 Valley Crest Productions Ltd -30 W 67th -NY 10023
(212) 941-3800 .. **Fuhrman,** Jonathan D '01 %Weinstein Co -375 Greenwich -NY 10013
(973) 228-5700 .. **Fuhrman,** Lauren D '06 %Brach E LLC -100 Park Av -NY 10017 **Fx:**228-7852
(212) 250-2500 .. **Fuhrman,** Marc H '85 Deutsche Bank -60 Wall -NY 10005
(718) 293-0980 .. **Fuhrman,** Marvin D '85 (Wolf & F) -1453 Webster Av -Bronx 10456
(212) 858-1000 .. **Fuhrman,** Shane D '07 %Pillsbury WSP LLP -1540 Bway -NY 10036
(212) 455-2000 .. **Fuhrman,** Steven M '86 (Simpson T&B LLP) -425 Lex Av -NY 10017
(718) 701-5449 .. **Fuiaxis,** George K '01 -30-39 48th -Astoria 11103 **Fx:**576-2390
(585) 288-4832 .. **Fuierer,** Alana M '96 %Heslin RF&M PC -100 Meridian Centre -Rchstr 14618
(212) 571-7100 .. **Fuiman,** Jason S '03 %O'Dwyer & B,LLP -52 Duane -NY 10007
(212) 836-8000 .. **Fuisz,** Jeffrey A '92 (Kaye S LLP) -425 Park Av -NY 10022
(212) 332-7592 .. **Fujimaki,** Yoriko '99 %Breitenecker & Assoc -45 Rckfllr Plz -NY 10111 **Fx:**332-7597
(212) 735-3000 .. **Fujimoto,** Kenji '98 %Skadden ASM&F LLP -4 Times Sq -NY 10036
(212) 605-2125 .. **Fujimura,** Takehiro '98 Mitsubishi Intl Corp -655 3rd Av -NY 10017
(917) 637-3600 .. **Fujimura-Fanselow,** Aya D '06 %Ctr for Reproductive Rts -120 Wall -NY 10005 **Fx:**637-3666
(718) 590-2000 .. **Fujiwara,** Akane C '07 %DA -198 E 161st -Bronx 10451 **Fx:**590-6477
(212) 478-0954 .. **Fuks,** Igor '07 DE Shaw & Co,LP -120 W 45th -NY 10036
(212) 594-5300 .. **Fuks,** Sara E '05 %Milberg LLP -1 Penn Plz -NY 10119
(516) 571-3800 .. **Fukuda,** Andrew '04 DA -262 Old Cntry Rd -Mineola 11501 **Fx:**248-9479
(212) 596-9000 .. **Fukuda,** Ching-Lee '98 (Ropes & G LLP) -1211 Av of Amer -NY 10036
(212) 906-7814 .. **Fukushima,** Izumi '00 RaboBank Intl -245 Park Av -NY 10167
(212) 318-3000 .. **Fulbright & Jaworski LLP** -666 5th Av -NY 10103 **Fx:**318-3400
(212) 661-7100 .. **Fulco,** John Paul '81 (Salon MDN&B,LLP) -292 Mad Av -NY 10017
(718) 410-4111 .. **Fuld,** Elliot H '83 -930 Grnd Cncrs -Bronx 10451 **Fx:**410-4884
(212) 595-4046 .. **Fuld,** Fred S '88 -46 W 87th -NY 10024
(212) 714-0421 .. **Fuld,** Moshe D '93 (M Fuld,PC) -38 W 32nd -NY 10001 **Fx:**714-0436
(914) 968-1299 .. **Fulfree,** Richd W '60 -115 Bennett Av -Ynkrs 10701 **Fx:**968-1299
(914) 933-5714 .. **Fulgieri,** Maria A '82 %Parsons & Whittemore -4 Intl Dr -Rye Brook 10573
(212) 762-4955 .. **Fullam,** John J '06 Morgan Stanley -1585 Bway -NY 10036

(631) 423-0483 .. **Fullam,** Vincent F '75 %Seminary Immaculate Cncptn -440 West Neck Rd -Huntngtn 11743
(518) 782-0600 .. **Fullem,** Robt T '99 School Admin Assn NYS -8 Airport Park Blvd -Latham 12110 **Fx:**782-9552
(212) 735-3000 .. **Fuller,** Barbara Campbell '08 %Skadden ASM&F LLP -4 Times Sq -NY 10036
(914) 337-3626 .. **Fuller,** David O Jr. '67 Bosworth G&F -116 Kraft Av -Bronxvll 10708
(585) 232-3240 .. **Fuller,** Diantha L '02 %V Criscuolo Jr -16 E Main -Rchstr 14614
(718) 261-6200 .. **Fuller,** Jade L '05 %Giaimo & Assoc,LLP -80-02 Kew Grdns Rd -Kew Gdns 11415 **Fx:**261-0316
(212) 317-0700 .. **Fuller,** Lee M Jr. '67 (Fuller & F) -845 3rd Av -NY 10022 **Fx:**317-8833
(518) 745-1400 .. **Fuller,** Matthew F '01 %FitzGerald MBF -16 Pearl Bx2017 -Glens Fls 12801
(212) 715-9100 .. **Fuller,** Megan '10 %Kramer LN&F,LLP -1177 Av of Amer -NY 10036
(845) 343-3323 .. **Fuller,** Melissa Eisenberg '90 -125 Wickham Av -Middletwn 10940
(585) 753-1380 .. **Fuller,** Paul D '87 %Cnty Atty -307 Cnty Ofc Bldg -Rchstr 14614 **Fx:**753-1331
(718) 739-6400 .. **Fuller,** Paul K '80 %DHCR -92-31 Union Hall -Jamaica 11433 **Fx:**262-7938
(212) 317-0700 .. **Fuller,** Scott R '91 (Fuller & F) -845 3rd Av -NY 10022 **Fx:**317-8833
(518) 213-6000 .. **Fuller,** Susan Whiteley '82 NYSUT -800 Troy-Schnctdy Rd -Latham 12110 **Fx:**213-6488
(212) 980-9600 .. **Fullerton,** Eileen R '02 %Kaufman B&R -120 Bway -NY 10271
(212) 558-4000 .. **Fullerton,** John F III '95 SpclCnsl Sullivan & C LLP -125 Broad -NY 10004
(718) 780-7925 .. **Fullerton,** Maryellen '86 %Bklyn Law Schl -250 Joralemon -Brklyn 11201 **Fx:**780-0393
(212) 592-1400 .. **Fullington,** Kevin E '99 Cnsl Herrick,F LLP -2 Park Av -NY 10016
(646) 447-6260 .. **Fullwood,** Michl D '73 HIP -55 Water -NY 10041
(585) 381-1988 .. **Fulmer,** Danl C '97 %TD Cook -7 State -Pittsfrd 14534
(914) 948-0945 .. **Fulop,** Candi J '81 -470 Mamaroneck Av -White Plns 10605 **Fx:**428-4317
(212) 506-1700 .. **Fulop,** Joshua D '08 %Kasowitz BT&F LLP -1633 Bway -NY 10019
(917) 322-2573 .. **Fulrath,** Logan Jr. '73 -445 Park Av -NY 10022 **Fx:**(732) 583-0286
(585) 546-1980 .. **Fulton Friedman & Gullace LLP** -28 E Main -Rchstr 14614 **Fx:**546-4241
(212) 808-7800 .. **Fulton,** Karyn E '98 (Kelley D&W LLP) -101 Park Av -NY 10178
(212) 586-0700 .. **Fulton Rowe & Hart, LLP** -1 Rckfllr Plz -NY 10020 **Fx:**245-1863
(518) 789-3939 .. **Fulton Rowe & Hart, LLP** -63 Main Bx374 -Millerton 12546 **Fx:**789-3940
(212) 417-3700 .. **Fulton,** Sara J '00 %MFY Legal Srvcs -299 Bway -NY 10007 **Fx:**417-3890
(212) 382-0909 .. **Fultz,** David A '03 %Peckar & A,PC -41 Mad Av -NY 10154
(212) 344-4700 .. **Fulweiler,** John K '98 (DeOrchis & Prtnrs LLP) -61 Bway -NY 10006
(212) 224-4000 .. **Fulweiler,** Marie-Louise '77 %Sumitomo Mitsui -277 Park Av -NY 10172 **Fx:**593-9522
(212) 698-3500 .. **Fumai,** Allison M '03 %Dechert LLP -1095 Av of Amer -NY 10036
(212) 878-8000 .. **Fumai,** Kevin M '03 %Clifford C LLP -31 W 52nd -NY 10019
(716) 854-1205 .. **Fumerelle,** Anthony L '94 -346 S Elmwood Av -Buffalo 14201 **Fx:**995-5344
(212) 735-3000 .. **Fumerton,** Robt A '05 %Skadden ASM&F LLP -4 Times Sq -NY 10036
(585) 753-1380 .. **Fumia,** James A '98 %Cnty Atty -307 Cnty Ofc Bldg -Rchstr 14614 **Fx:**753-1331
(917) 778-6600 .. **Fumo,** Robt P '92 %J Toomey -485 Lex Av -NY 10017 **Fx:**778-7048
(631) 232-0200 .. **Fumuso,** Alan J '77 (Fumuso KDSS&F,LLP) -110 Marcus Blvd -Hauppauge 11788
(631) 232-0200 .. **Fumuso,** Christian A '08 %Fumuso KDSS&F,LLP -110 Marcus Blvd -Hauppauge 11788
(631) 232-0200 .. **Fumuso Kelly DeVerna Snyder Swart & Farrell,LLP** -110 Marcus Blvd -Hauppauge 11788 **Fx:**232-1305
(718) 321-7000 .. **Fung,** Alison Geewai '90 (Shih & F) -136-20 38th Av -Flushng 11354 **Fx:**762-7679
(718) 286-6000 .. **Fung,** Anna K '08 %DA -125-01 Qns Blvd -Kew Gdns 11415
(212) 966-5932 .. **Fung,** Margaret '79 %AALDEF -99 Hudson -NY 10013 **Fx:**966-4303
(212) 859-3529 .. **Fung,** Mark T '95 -110 Wall -NY 10005 **Fx:**943-2300
(718) 793-8934 .. **Fung,** Mary Kuk-Lin '88 -7025 Yllwstn Blvd -Flushng 11375
(718) 661-3838 .. **Fung,** Stephen G '92 Franklin Land Srvcs,Inc -136-20 38th Av -Flushng 11354 **Fx:**460-8900
(516) 933-4080 .. **Funk,** Amy M '04 %Davis & V -176 Woodbury Rd -Hicksvll 11801
(212) 964-7400 .. **Funk,** Andrew J '91 Smith MDWY&Y,PC -111 John -NY 10038
(212) 265-4304 .. **Funk,** Debra S '81 Accurate Copy Srvc -250 W 57th -NY 10107
(212) 838-7461 .. **Funk,** Harlan J '55 -845 UN Plz -NY 10017 **Fx:**319-4906
(212) 431-1228 .. **Funk,** Karen M '86 (Cohen & F,PC) -145 Hudson -NY 10013 **Fx:**307-0187
(585) 325-4080 .. **Funk,** Mark D '96 -144 Exchange Blvd -Rchstr 14614 **Fx:**325-3839
(718) 222-9800 .. **Funk,** Matthew A '99 (Brecher FPWT&Z,PC) -118-21 Qns Blvd -Frst Hlls 11375
(585) 546-5530 .. **Funk,** Melissa Kirby '97 %Thomson West -50 E Broad -Rchstr 14694
(212) 692-1000 .. **Funk,** Peter V K Jr. '74 (Duane M LLP) -1540 Bway -NY 10036
(516) 379-8388 .. **Funk,** Wendy L '95 (Friedman & F PC) -2116 Merrick Av -Merrick 11566
(646) 471-7075 .. **Funk,** Wm M '00 %PricewaterhouseCoopers LLP -300 Mad Av -NY 10017
(212) 891-1136 .. **Funt,** Barry M '91 %CDC Mortg Capital -9 W 57th -NY 10019
(914) 995-2115 .. **Funt,** Syma B '90 %Cnty Atty -148 Martine Av -White Plns 10601 **Fx:**995-5858
(585) 466-3004 .. **Fuoco,** J Thos '97 -7980 Cnty Road 15 -Angelica 14709 **Fx:**466-3435
(212) 483-9490 .. **Fuoco,** Jos G '05 %McElroy DM&C,LLP -88 Pine -NY 10005
(718) 381-3311 .. **Fuoco,** Tina A '91 -65-09 Fresh Pond Rd -Rdgwd 11385
(212) 909-6000 .. **Furci,** Peter A '96 (Debevoise & P LLP) -919 3rd Av -NY 10022
(212) 221-6666 .. **Furer,** Keith S '95 Apple Mortgage Corp -19 W 44th -NY 10036
(718) 590-2000 .. **Furey,** Christine E '09 %DA -198 E 161st -Bronx 10451 **Fx:**590-6477
(516) 538-2500 .. **Furey Furey Leverage Manzione Williams & Darlington,PC** -600 Front -Hempstd 11550 **Fx:**489-5056
(516) 887-1898 .. **Furey,** James F '74 -54 Parkvw Pl -Malverne 11565
(516) 538-2500 .. **Furey,** James M '57 (Furey FLMW&D,PC) -600 Front -Hempstd 11550
(516) 538-2500 .. **Furey,** James M Jr. '86 (Furey FLMW&D,PC) -600 Front -Hempstd 11550
(212) 308-4411 .. **Furey,** Kathleen M '90 (Edwards AP&D LLP) -750 Lex Av -NY 10022
(516) 409-6200 .. **Furey Kerley Walsh Matera & Cinquemani,PC** -2174 Jackson Av -Seafrd 11783 **Fx:**409-8288
(516) 409-6200 .. **Furey,** Raymond J Jr. '72 (Furey KWM&C,PC) -2174 Jackson Av -Seafrd 11783
(212) 735-3000 .. **Furfaro,** John P '81 (Skadden ASM&F LLP) -4 Times Sq -NY 10036
(914) 633-3103 .. **Furfero,** Arlene Joyce '97 -82 Vaughn Av -New Rchll 10801 **Fx:**(419) 844-7053
(914) 428-5300 .. **Furgang,** Philip '66 (Furgang & A,LLP) -11 Martine Av -White Plns 10606 **Fx:**428-0226
(845) 353-1818 .. **Furgang,** Philip '66 (Furgang & A,LLP) -2 Crosfld Av -W Nyack 10994 **Fx:**353-1996
(212) 725-1818 .. **Furgang,** Philip '66 (Furgang & A,LLP) -1325 Av of Amer -NY 10019 **Fx:**941-9711
(212) 591-9595 .. **Furgatch,** Andrew L '86 %Pub Srvc Mutual Ins -1 Park Av -NY 10016 **Fx:**591-9600
(212) 859-8000 .. **Furka,** Christen M '09 %Fried FHS&J LLP -1 NY Plz -NY 10004
(516) 747-0117 .. **Furlong,** Claire Smith '82 -165 Oxford Blvd -Gdn Cty 11530
(716) 849-8900 .. **Furlong,** Danl J '84 OfCnsl Hurwitz & F,PC -1300 Lbrty Bldg -Buffalo 14202
(718) 657-5757 .. **Furlong,** Jos D '80 (O'Leary & O) -88-14 Sutphin Blvd -Jamaica 11435
(716) 849-1333 .. **Furlong,** Richd D Jr. '85 SpclCnsl Lipsitz GSC LLP -42 Delaware Av -Buffalo 14202
(631) 581-6700 .. **Furlow,** Harold G '02 -260 Montauk Hwy -Bay Shr 11706
(212) 867-4100 .. **Furman,** A Michl '90 (Furman K&B LLP) -61 Bway -NY 10006
(212) 684-9400 .. **Furman,** Allison M '99 -120 E 37th -NY 10016
(516) 746-8000 .. **Furman,** Blake J '08 %Jaspan S LLP -300 Grdn City Plz -Gdn Cty 11530
(212) 351-4000 .. **Furman,** David J '87 (Gibson D&C LLP) -200 Park Av -NY 10166
(914) 478-3407 .. **Furman,** Denise W '94 -50 Fenwick Rd -Hastings-On-Hud 10706 **Fx:**478-3012
(914) 377-6963 .. **Furman,** Esther R '81 %City Ct -100 S Bway -Ynkrs 10701 **Fx:**377-6395
(212) 637-2475 .. **Furman,** Jesse M '99 %US Atty -1 St Andrews Plz -NY 10007
(631) 289-6128 .. **Furman,** Joel M '83 -10 S Ocean Av Bx349 -Patchogue 11772 **Fx:**475-0328
(212) 351-4000 .. **Furman,** Joshua R '08 %Gibson D&C LLP -200 Park Av -NY 10166
(212) 867-4100 .. **Furman Kornfeld & Brennan LLP** -61 Bway -NY 10006 **Fx:**867-4118
(212) 772-0688 .. **Furman,** Leonard D '66 (Levine & F,LLC) -645 5th Av -NY 10022 **Fx:**(732) 238-6055
(212) 427-1356 .. **Furman,** Mark A '83 -50 Fenwick Rd -Hastings-On-Hud 10706 **Fx:**(914) 478-3012
(212) 338-0700 .. **Furman,** Mark L '80 (Hoffman P&F PLLC) -220 E 42nd -NY 10017
(917) 778-6828 .. **Furman,** Matthew S '95 Travelers Cos -485 Lex Av -NY 10017
(212) 318-6000 .. **Furman,** Natalie Grunfeld '10 %Paul HJ&W LLP -75 E 55th -NY 10022
(212) 252-0004 .. **Furman,** Richd L '70 (Carroll M&K LLC) -570 Lex Av -NY 10022
(212) 508-6700 .. **Furman,** Scott E '86 (Tannenbaum HS&H LLP) -900 3rd Av -NY 10022
(212) 480-8800 .. **Furnari,** Stephen T '99 (Furnari L LLP) -11 Bway -NY 10004 **Fx:**480-4208
(518) 533-1050 .. **Furnish,** Kimberly Boucher '98 Conway & K LLP -9 Cornell Rd -Latham 12110
(518) 455-2452 .. **Furnish,** Mark W '98 %Sen T Duane -NYS Senate -Albany 12247 **Fx:**426-6846
(607) 273-5555 .. **Furniss,** Wm E Jr. '97 -122 S Cayuga -Ithaca 14850
(315) 266-6100 .. **Furno,** Frank J '89 %Pub Def -235 Elizabeth -Utica 13501 **Fx:**266-6105
(914) 730-3400 .. **Furrer,** Urs Broderick '92 (Harriton & F,LLP) -84 Business Park Dr -Armonk 10504 **Fx:**730-3405
(212) 857-8809 .. **Furrie,** Kristin M '06 US Ct of Appls-2nd Cir -40 Foley Sq -NY 10007
(212) 218-2100 .. **Furrow,** Michl E '08 %Fitzpatrick CH&S -1290 Av of Amer -NY 10104
(631) 244-4519 .. **Furshpan,** Danl E '10 -1563 Montauk Hwy -Oakdale 11769
(212) 345-5515 .. **Furst,** Barry W '73 %Marsh USA -1166 Av of Amer -NY 10036 **Fx:**345-4808
(212) 532-8100 .. **Furst,** Danl S '01 %Stern & M,LLP -115 Bway -NY 10006
(845) 896-2229 .. **Furst,** John W '00 %Cuddy & F LLP -300 Westage Business Ctr -Fishkill 12524
(212) 756-2000 .. **Furst,** Jos III '01 %Schulte R&Z LLP -919 3rd Av -NY 10022
(718) 575-1244 .. **Furst,** Michl L '84 (Furst & T) -71-21 Austin -Frst Hlls 11375 **Fx:**575-1544
(212) 240-5444 .. **Fürst,** Roland F '95 GFK Holding Inc -75 9th Av -NY 10011
(212) 837-6000 .. **Furst,** Thos '85 %Hughes H&R LLP -1 Bttry Pk Plz -NY 10004
(914) 846-7000 .. **Furtado,** Chas F '03 NY Life Ins -1 Rockwood Rd -Sleepy Hollow 10591 **Fx:**846-4755
(212) 373-3000 .. **Furtado,** D Branch '08 %Paul WRW&G LLP -1285 Av of Amer -NY 10019
(212) 907-7300 .. **Furth,** Douglas L '87 (Golenbock EAB&P) -437 Mad Av -NY 10022
(212) 868-1010 .. **Furth,** Thos M '89 %Kudman TA LLP -350 5th Av -NY 10118
(212) 530-4116 .. **Furtivo,** Eugene P '74 %Risk Ent Mgmt -59 Maiden Ln -NY 10038
(914) 827-3988 .. **Furtzaig,** Lawr M '86 -7 Park Av -Croton-On-Hud 10520 **Fx:**271-0256
(212) 373-3000 .. **Furukawa,** Takuyo '10 %Paul WRW&G LLP -1285 Av of Amer -NY 10019
(845) 735-4300 .. **Fury Kennedy & Griffin** -5 E Central Av -Pearl Rvr 10965 **Fx:**735-6312
(845) 735-4300 .. **Fury,** Michl H '52 (Fury K&G) -5 E Central Av -Pearl Rvr 10965
(845) 735-4300 .. **Fury,** Michl J '91 %Fury K&G -5 E Central Av -Pearl Rvr 10965
(212) 238-4800 .. **Fusaro,** Cristi L '03 %Landman CB&F,PC -120 Bway -NY 10271
(212) 599-8200 .. **Fusaro,** Scott M '08 %Shaub AC&S,LLP -655 3rd Av -NY 10017
(315) 255-4176 .. **Fusco,** Andrew S '79 Corp Cnsl -24 South -Auburn 13021 **Fx:**255-4735

(315) 253-5555 .. **Fusco,** Andrew S '79 -52 South -Auburn 13021 **Fx:**253-5565
(800) 416-5454 .. **Fusco Brandenstein & Rada** -180 Froehlich Farm Blvd -Woodbury 11797 **Fx:**(516) 921-3078
(800) 416-5454 .. **Fusco Brandenstein & Rada** -2116 Wllmsbrdg Rd -Bronx 10461 **Fx:**(516) 921-3078
(800) 416-5454 .. **Fusco Brandenstein & Rada** -80-02 Kew Grdns Rd -Kew Gdns 11415 **Fx:**(516) 921-3078
(800) 416-5454 .. **Fusco Brandenstein & Rada** -353 Vets Mem'l Hwy -Commack 11725 **Fx:**(516) 921-3078
(800) 416-5454 .. **Fusco Brandenstein & Rada** -3253 Route 112 -Medfrd 11763 **Fx:**(516) 921-3078
(800) 416-5454 .. **Fusco Brandenstein & Rada** -9207 Flatlands Av -Brklyn 11236 **Fx:**(718) 717-7161
(800) 416-5454 .. **Fusco Brandenstein & Rada** -11 Penn Plz -NY 10001 **Fx:**(516) 921-3078
(800) 416-5454 .. **Fusco Brandenstein & Rada** -626 RXR Plz -Uniondale 11553 **Fx:**(516) 921-3078
(516) 942-3900 .. **Fusco,** Carlo M '05 (Manners & Assoc,LLP) -950 Jericho Tpk -Westbury 11590 **Fx:**942-4330
(212) 448-9570 .. **Fusco,** Christopher G '93 (Callahan & F,LLC) -40 Exch Pl -NY 10005
(516) 741-8585 .. **Fusco,** Desiree L '04 %Bondi & I -1055 Franklin Av -Gdn Cty 11530
(718) 788-3333 .. **Fusco,** Edw D '78 -310 7th Av -Brklyn 11215 **Fx:**965-1094
(212) 308-4626 .. **Fusco,** Eileen Skevin '82 %Twenty-First Securities Corp -780 3rd Av -NY 10017
(212) 593-6700 .. **Fusco,** Jos P '08 %Aaronson RF&D,LLP -757 3rd Av -NY 10017
(212) 585-4440 .. **Fusco,** Louis Jr. '47 -900 Park Av -NY 10075
(585) 232-3730 .. **Fusco,** Matthew J '87 (Chamberlain D LLP) -1600 Crssrds Bldg -Rchstr 14614
(518) 533-3000 .. **Fusco,** Nicholas A '10 %Bond S&K,PLLC -111 Wshngtn Av -Albany 12210
(585) 232-5300 .. **Fusco,** Paul S '07 %Boylan BCV&W,LLP -2400 Chase Sq -Rchstr 14604
(315) 724-3115 .. **Fusco,** Ralph W '71 -2311 Genesee -Utica 13501
(914) 681-6006 .. **Fusco,** Sandra M '07 %Goldschmidt & G,LLP -1 N Lex Av -White Plns 10601
(716) 847-7618 .. **Fusco,** Thos '90 %Insurance Dept -99 Wshngtn Av -Albany 12257 **Fx:**847-7925
(800) 416-5454 .. **Fusco,** Victor '76 (Fusco B&R) -180 Froehlich Farm Blvd -Woodbury 11797
(800) 416-5454 .. **Fusco,** Victor '76 (Fusco B&R) -353 Vets Mem'l Hwy -Commack 11725
(845) 503-5350 .. **Fuselier,** Francis A '96 Gateway Energy Srvcs Corp -400 Rella Blvd -Montebello 10901 **Fx:**503-5588
(212) 388-0840 .. **Fusfeld,** Steven R '79 -19 E 9th Bx1025 -NY 10276 **Fx:**388-0843
(516) 571-3518 .. **Fusillo,** Matthew R '80 %Supreme Ct -100 Supreme Ct Dr -Mineola 11501
(212) 820-9440 .. **Fuss,** Danl N '87 (Hawkins D&W LLP) -One Chase Manh Plz -NY 10005
(212) 542-7845 .. **Fussa,** Glenda Luz '88 HUD -26 Fed Plz -NY 10278
(585) 768-2240 .. **Fussell,** E Robt '72 (ER Fussell,PC) -46 Wolcott -Le Roy 14482 **Fx:**768-2662
(347) 642-4486 .. **Fuster,** A David II '99 -3316 70th -Jcksn Hts 11372
(212) 532-0800 .. **Fuster,** Peter '83 %AFTRA -260 Mad Av -NY 10016 **Fx:**545-1238
(212) 554-2664 .. **Fusto,** John F '87 Daylight Forensic -1 Rckfllr Plz -NY 10020
(212) 684-8400 .. **Futerfas,** Alan S '88 -260 Mad Av -NY 10016 **Fx:**684-5259
(914) 682-2171 .. **Futerfas,** Neal D '91 -50 Main -White Plns 10606 **Fx:**428-0963
(845) 331-0100 .. **Futerfas,** Rod P '74 (Wapner K&F,PLLC) -239 Wall Bx3268 -Kingston 12402
(845) 679-7207 .. **Futerfas,** Rod P '74 (Wapner K&F,PLLC) -45 Mill Hill Rd Bx572 -Woodstock 12498
(212) 412-4750 .. **Futoran,** Herbert S '67 (Wollerstein & F) -59 Maiden Ln -NY 10038
(212) 412-4750 .. **Futoran,** Jeffrey A '93 %Wollerstein & F -59 Maiden Ln -NY 10038
(718) 579-3000 .. **Futral,** Mark '89 %Leg Aid -1020 Grnd Cncrs -Bronx 10451 **Fx:**588-2611
(212) 769-5997 .. **Futter,** Ellen V '75 %Amer Museum Natural Hist -Cntrl Pk W & 79th -NY 10024 **Fx:**769-5018
(212) 460-3933 .. **Futter,** Jeffrey L '71 Con Ed -4 Irving Pl -NY 10003 **Fx:**677-0601
(631) 979-4300 .. **Futterman,** Aaron E '99 (Futterman & L,LLP) -222 E Main -Smithtwn 11787 **Fx:**979-9546
(646) 855-0807 .. **Futterman,** David H '95 Bank of Amer -1 Bryant Pk -NY 10036
(212) 809-4050 .. **Futterman,** Hans '98 (DeepBridge) -1 Lbrty Plz -NY 10006
(718) 261-9460 .. **Futterman,** Ira H '68 (Pearlman AFS&S,LLP) -80-02 Kew Grdns Rd -Kew Gdns 11415
(212) 593-6700 .. **Futterman,** Michl M '74 (Aaronson RF&D,LLP) -757 3rd Av -NY 10017
(212) 308-0070 .. **Futterman,** Michl R '05 %McCusker AR&C,PC -805 3rd Av -NY 10022
(212) 267-4177 .. **Futterman,** Robt M '76 %Kramer DL&M -217 Bway -NY 10007
(646) 682-7041 .. **Futterman,** Stanley N '66 -153 E 87th -NY 10128 **Fx:**(212) 722-5937
(716) 849-8429 .. **Fuzak,** Mark J '80 -295 Main -Buffalo 14203 **Fx:**849-8463
(212) 445-4479 .. **Fuzesi,** Stephen Jr. '75 %Newsweek -395 Hudson -NY 10014
(914) 949-2700 .. **Fyfe,** Hugh D Jr. '73 (Bleakley P&S,LLP) -1 N Lex Av -White Plns 10601
(646) 205-7864 .. **Fyffe,** Felicia A '05 MVAIC -110 William -NY 10038
(212) 759-7466 .. **Fyffe-Gauntlett,** Sheryl S '10 %Raven & K,LLP -126 E 56th -NY 10022
(516) 357-3000 .. **Fyman,** Avigael Cymrot '06 %Rivkin R LLP -926 RXR Plz -Uniondale 11556
(315) 218-8000 .. **Gaal,** John '78 (Bond S&K,PLLC) -1 Lincoln Ctr -Syracuse 13202
(631) 853-4161 .. **Gaash,** Shiry '04 %DA -N Cnty Cmplx Bldg 77 -Hauppauge 11788 **Fx:**853-4192
(212) 349-6000 .. **Gaba,** Jos '98 %R Flaster,PC -225 Bway -NY 10007 **Fx:**349-1146
(518) 329-0242 .. **Gaba,** Richd M '56 -1114 Cnty Route 3 Bx25 -Ancramdale 12503 **Fx:**329-7525
(845) 561-0550 .. **Gaba,** Stephen J '88 (Drake LHKGG&R PLLC) -555 Hudson Valley Av -New Windsor 12553
(212) 326-3939 .. **Gabai,** Amanda L '07 %Jones D -222 E 41st -NY 10017
(631) 244-1612 .. **Gabay,** David A '96 -4250 Vets Mem'l Hwy -Holbrook 11741 **Fx:**244-1631
(212) 806-5400 .. **Gabay,** Donald D '62 OfCnsl Stroock &S&L LLP -180 Maiden Ln -NY 10038
(914) 824-5754 .. **Gabay,** Sheila D '84 Cnsl Hon W Edwards -111 Dr Martin Luther King Jr Blvd -White Plns 10601 **Fx:**995-4490
(212) 941-5025 .. **Gabay-Rafiy,** Sari '01 (Gabay-Rafiy & B LLP) -299 Bway -NY 10007 **Fx:**202-3883
(212) 489-1600 .. **Gabbai,** David E '97 %Deloitte LLP -1633 Bway -NY 10019 **Fx:**492-4201
(212) 245-2050 .. **Gabbard,** Jason D '02 AFC Realty Capital -111 W 57th -NY 10019
(212) 836-8000 .. **Gabbay,** Edmond '86 (Kaye S LLP) -425 Park Av -NY 10022
(201) 390-2835 .. **Gabbay,** Ronen '96 -240 W Beech -Long Bch 11561
(718) 250-2000 .. **Gabbidon,** Joan B '77 %DA -350 Jay -Brklyn 11201 **Fx:**250-2314
(212) 371-5700 .. **Gabe,** Lawr M '74 (Jankoff & G,PC) -575 Lex Av -NY 10022
(212) 227-8865 .. **Gabel,** Clifford D '93 %Breadbar G&S -11 Park Pl -NY 10007
(845) 471-5300 .. **Gabel,** Edw A III '78 -15 Davis Av Bx3007 -Poughkeepsie 12603 **Fx:**471-5353
(716) 856-4000 .. **Gabel,** Janet N '85 (Hodgson R LLP) -140 Pearl -Buffalo 14202
(516) 897-4444 .. **Gabel,** Jeffrey '75 -4315 Austin Blvd -Isl Pk 11558
(212) 695-2877 .. **Gabel,** Jeffrey '80 -286 Mad Av -NY 10017 **Fx:**213-2393
(212) 830-4370 .. **Gabel,** Joan E '82 Air France -125 W 55th -NY 10019 **Fx:**830-4141
(212) 318-3000 .. **Gabel,** Johannes K '83 (Fulbright & J LLP) -666 5th Av -NY 10103
(914) 941-2150 .. **Gabel,** Wayne '84 -75 S Highland Av -Ossining 10562 **Fx:**762-6614
(212) 455-2000 .. **Gabel Silverman,** Alison J '99 Cnsl Simpson T&B LLP -425 Lex Av -NY 10017
(845) 471-2447 .. **Gabiger,** Pamela J '99 -9 Vassar -Poughkeepsie 12601
(646) 840-5000 .. **Gabin,** Matthew G '03 Allianz Risk Transfer Inc -350 Park Av -NY 10022
(716) 858-2424 .. **Gable,** Colleen Curtin '93 %DA -25 Delaware Av -Buffalo 14202 **Fx:**858-7425
(212) 768-6700 .. **Gable,** Elizabeth A '06 %Sonnenschein N&R LLP -2 World Fncl Ctr -NY 10281
(518) 432-1200 .. **Gable,** John J '89 OfCnsl McGlinchey S PLLC -194 Wshngtn Av -Albany 12210
(212) 250-8681 .. **Gable,** Melissa G '03 Deutsche Bank -60 Wall -NY 10005
(212) 790-9200 .. **Gable,** R Lewis '69 OfCnsl Cowan L&L,PC -1133 Av of Amer -NY 10036
(212) 829-0454 .. **Gabler,** Lisa H '95 (Gabler & M LLP) -209 E 56th -NY 10022 **Fx:**829-0455
(845) 221-3876 .. **Gabler,** Robt J '48 -21 Arthursburg Rd -LaGrangevll 12540
(212) 704-0515 .. **Gabo,** Irene H '05 %G Peck -350 5th Av -NY 10118 **Fx:**704-0945
(561) 243-8253 .. **Gabor,** Arthur M '70 -1878 Victory Blvd -Staten Isl 10314 **Fx:**278-6209
(516) 248-2525 .. **Gabor,** David G '88 (Gabor & G) -400 Grdn City Plz -Gdn Cty 11530 **Fx:**248-4468
(516) 248-2525 .. **Gabor,** Hope Senzer '85 (Gabor & G) -400 Grdn City Plz -Gdn Cty 11530 **Fx:**248-4468
(212) 268-1188 .. **Gabor,** Jaime H '07 %B Somerstein & Assoc,PC -370 7th Av -NY 10001 **Fx:**268-2688
(718) 390-0555 .. **Gabor and Marotta LLC** -1878 Victory Blvd -Staten Isl 10314 **Fx:**390-9886
(212) 349-1200 .. **Gabor and Marotta LLC** -277 Bway -NY 10007
(718) 390-0555 .. **Gabor,** Richd M '80 (Gabor & M LLC) -1878 Victory Blvd -Staten Isl 10314
(212) 403-1000 .. **Gabor,** Stephanie I '09 %Wachtell LR&K -51 W 52nd -NY 10019
(212) 575-5766 .. **Gabor,** Steven M '84 -209 W 38th -NY 10018
(516) 569-8100 .. **Gabor,** Todd A '85 OfCnsl Rosenfeld & M -132 Spruce -Cedarhrst 11516
(315) 366-2236 .. **Gabor,** Wm G '85 DA -Cnty Cthse Bx578 -Wampsville 13163 **Fx:**366-2503
(914) 381-7600 .. **Gaboury,** Ralph N '00 %Dorf Law Firm,LLP -740 W Bstn Post Rd -Mamaroneck 10543 **Fx:**381-7608
(212) 728-8000 .. **Gabriel,** Christopher P '10 %Willkie F&G LLP -787 7th Av -NY 10019
(718) 260-4750 .. **Gabriel,** George '86 %Leg Aid -111 Lvngstn -Brklyn 11201 **Fx:**260-4744
(914) 232-7531 .. **Gabriel,** Harold J '79 Andron Cnstrctn -21 Andrsn Ln -Goldens Bridge 10526 **Fx:**232-4185
(607) 869-9646 .. **Gabriel,** James A '73 Franklin & G -7185 Main Bx449 -Ovid 14521 **Fx:**869-3042
(212) 247-1010 .. **Gabriel,** Manfred J '03 FTI -3 Times Sq -NY 10036 **Fx:**841-9350
(212) 530-5000 .. **Gabriel,** Meghan C '10 %Milbank TH&M LLP -1 Chase Manh Plz -NY 10005
(212) 697-6262 .. **Gabriel,** Michl G '05 %Ward & O -380 Mad Av -NY 10017
(631) 231-3775 .. **Gabriel,** Nancy B '87 %Atty Grievance Comm -150 Motor Pkwy -Hauppauge 11788
(212) 371-8888 .. **Gabriel,** Susan R '85 JRT Realty Inc -780 3rd Av -NY 10017 **Fx:**371-8075
(212) 218-2100 .. **Gabriel,** Thos S '06 %Fitzpatrick CH&S -1290 Av of Amer -NY 10104
(516) 542-1000 .. **Gabriele,** Guido '80 (Geisler & G,LLP) -100 Q Roosevelt Blvd -Gdn Cty 11530
(516) 571-3800 .. **Gabriele,** Guido III '06 %DA -262 Old Cntry Rd -Mineola 11501 **Fx:**248-9479
(212) 294-6700 .. **Gabriele,** Jos F '10 %Winston & S -200 Park Av -NY 10166
(716) 285-1535 .. **Gabriele,** Mark J '89 (Harris B PLLC) -800 Main Bx712 -Niagara Fls 14302
(631) 265-9880 .. **Gabriele,** Nicholas A '83 (N Gabriele,PC) -191 Terry Rd -Smithtwn 11787 **Fx:**265-6273
(516) 622-9200 .. **Gabriele,** Richd '74 Cnsl Westerman BEM&S,LLP -1201 RXR Plz -Uniondale 11553
(718) 708-5322 .. **Gabrielli,** Michl J '00 -2426 Eastchstr Rd -Bronx 10469
(518) 459-2667 .. **Gabriels,** Catherine B '84 (Welt G&S LLP) -4 Exec Park Dr Bx3716 -Albany 12203
(518) 482-3056 .. **Gabriels,** Jeffrey K '93 -469 Albany-Shaker Rd -Loudonvll 12211 **Fx:**482-3396
(518) 463-1069 .. **Gabriels,** Thos J '86 -99 Pine -Albany 12207 **Fx:**463-9813
(212) 676-7934 .. **Gabrielski,** Julie A '06 %HRA Ofc Leg Affrs -220 Church -NY 10013
(212) 326-3939 .. **Gabuzda,** Lawr R '06 %Jones D -222 E 41st -NY 10017
(516) 872-8880 .. **Gaccione,** Louis J Jr. '92 -906 Atl Av -Baldwin 11510 **Fx:**872-1343
(518) 464-7634 .. **Gach,** Karen Georgenson '96 NY Indep Sys Oper,Inc -10 Krey Blvd -Rensselaer 12144
(845) 353-3500 .. **Gach,** Michl A '07 %Dorfman K&C LLP -51 N Bway -Nyack 10960

(518) 487-7600 .. **Gach,** Robt M '97 (Whiteman O&H LLP) -1 Commerce Plz -Albany 12260
(607) 772-9262 .. **Gacioch,** James C '75 (O'Connor GL&C,LLP) -84 Court -Bnghmtn 13901
(631) 543-5400 .. **Gacovino,** Steven D '93 (Gacovino L & Assoc,PC) -270 W Main -Sayvll 11782 **Fx:**543-5450
(631) 581-9494 .. **Gacovino,** Steven D '93 OfCnsl Ferro KMS,PC -350 Motor Pkwy -Hauppauge 11788
(212) 675-3710 .. **Gadaleta,** Frank '96 (Glassman G&G) -49 W 24th -NY 10010 **Fx:**633-9013
(585) 295-4400 .. **Gaddis,** Sheila A '82 (Hiscock & B,LLP) -2000 HSBC Plz -Rchstr 14604
(585) 232-3051 .. **Gaddis,** Sheila A '82 %Legal Srvcs -1 W Main -Rchstr 14614 **Fx:**232-5103
(212) 335-9000 .. **Gadlin,** Alan B '87 %DA -1 Hogan Pl -NY 10013
(516) 741-7676 .. **Gadon,** Nir M '08 %Miranda SSSV LLP -240 Mineola Blvd -Mineola 11501
(212) 732-3200 .. **Gadsden,** James '75 (Carter L&M LLP) -2 Wall -NY 10005
(212) 558-4000 .. **Gadwood,** James R '09 %Sullivan & C LLP -125 Broad -NY 10004
(516) 248-1700 .. **Gaebler,** Steven G '83 (Forchelli CDSM&T,LLP) -333 Earle Ovngton Blvd -Uniondale 11553
(212) 267-4876 .. **Gaeckle,** Richd W '03 %Hoagland LMD&D,LLP -1501 Bway -NY 10036
(607) 277-7527 .. **Gaenslen,** J Anthony '67 OfCnsl Littman & B -308 N Tioga -Ithaca 14850 **Fx:**275-9141
(585) 419-8800 .. **Gaenzle,** Russell E '98 (Harris B PLLC) -99 Garnsey Rd -Pittsfrd 14534
(212) 949-9696 .. **Gaer,** Eugene A '78 -420 Lex Av -NY 10170 **Fx:**949-6241
(516) 358-5690 .. **Gaeta,** Christine Ann '96 %V Toomey -3000 Marcus Av -Lk Success 11042 **Fx:**775-0237
(212) 246-0069 .. **Gaeta,** Gillian R F '07 Wylie Agency -250 W 57th -NY 10107 **Fx:**586-8953
(347) 273-1381 .. **Gaeta,** Kasey Lynn '03 -1110 South Av -Staten Isl 10314 **Fx:**273-1481
(516) 572-2000 .. **Gaeta,** Nicole R '08 %DA -99 Main -Hempstd 11550 **Fx:**572-2606
(914) 286-3416 .. **Gaetani,** Salvatore A '83 %Leg Aid -1 N Bway -White Plns 10601 **Fx:**682-4112
(716) 852-1300 .. **Gaetanos,** Christ '80 (Amigone S&M,LLP) -350 Main -Buffalo 14202
(212) 458-1034 .. **Gafar,** Shakira '94 %AIG -70 Pine -NY 10270
(315) 471-3151 .. **Gaffey,** Meghan S '09 %Hancock & E,LLP -1500 AXA Twr I Bx4976 -Syracuse 13221
(718) 261-3047 .. **Gaffey,** Michl J '87 Queens Law Assoc -118-21 Qns Blvd -Frst Hlls 11375 **Fx:**261-0798
(212) 326-3939 .. **Gaffey,** Robt W '83 (Jones D) -222 E 41st -NY 10017
(631) 712-6500 .. **Gaffey,** Tracey Eadie '88 %Fed Def of NY Inc -770 Fed Plz -Central Islip 11722 **Fx:**712-6505
(212) 962-5757 .. **Gaffin,** Dudley J '53 (Gaffin & M,PC) -225 Bway -NY 10007
(212) 455-2000 .. **Gaffin,** Julia F '10 %Simpson T&B LLP -425 Lex Av -NY 10017
(212) 962-5757 .. **Gaffin & Mayo,PC** -225 Bway -NY 10007 **Fx:**406-3548
(516) 829-8140 .. **Gaffner,** David L '80 (Marsh & G,PC) -350 Nrthrn Blvd -Gt Neck 11021 **Fx:**829-7431
(845) 338-9571 .. **Gaffney,** Danl J '73 Gaffney & G -23 Crown -Kingston 12401 **Fx:**853-7332
(845) 638-5983 .. **Gaffney,** Edw J Jr. '83 %Hon M Garvey -1 S Main -New Cty 10956
(212) 483-9600 .. **Gaffney,** Fredk N '76 (Costello S&G LLP) -44 Wall -NY 10005
(716) 854-1002 .. **Gaffney,** Gary R '82 OfCnsl Miserendino CS&E,PC -295 Main -Buffalo 14203
(212) 353-8700 .. **Gaffney,** Harry J '88 Simon E&B LLP -24 Union Sq E -NY 10003 **Fx:**353-1708
(212) 335-9000 .. **Gaffney,** Jennifer '99 %DA -1 Hogan Pl -NY 10013
(646) 366-5500 .. **Gaffney,** John T '87 1st Solar,Inc -620 8th Av -NY 10018
(518) 474-6400 .. **Gaffney,** Katherine J '93 %Dept of Ed -89 Wshngtn Av -Albany 12234 **Fx:**473-2925
(914) 381-7600 .. **Gaffney,** Laura Alcott '94 %Dorf Law Firm,LLP -740 W Bstn Post Rd -Mamaroneck 10543 **Fx:**381-7608
(516) 873-3000 .. **Gaffney,** Mark W '82 -200 Old Cntry Rd -Mineola 11501
(718) 815-6400 .. **Gaffney,** Michl J '80 -1164 Victory Blvd -Staten Isl 10301 **Fx:**447-9908
(212) 545-1900 .. **Gaffney,** Nicholas F '07 %Menaker & H LLP -10 E 40th -NY 10016
(646) 723-2756 .. **Gaffney,** Patrick '88 -11 Bway -NY 10004 **Fx:**(212) 943-1238
(516) 294-7037 .. **Gaffney,** Thos E '83 -370 Old Cntry Rd -Gdn Cty 11530 **Fx:**742-9375
(716) 852-1102 .. **Gaffney,** Thos J '68 -80 W Huron -Buffalo 14202
(716) 853-5100 .. **Gaffney,** Thos J '05 %Lippes MWF LLP -665 Main -Buffalo 14203
(607) 274-5461 .. **Gafford,** Linda E '92 %DA -320 N Tioga -Ithaca 14850 **Fx:**274-5429
(518) 474-9963 .. **Gagan,** Kevin T '90 %Dept of Law -The Cptl -Albany 12224
(212) 962-1190 .. **Gagasoules,** Maria '06 %Sanocki N&T,LLP -225 Bway -NY 10007
(212) 538-9137 .. **Gage,** Allen S '94 Credit Suisse -1 Mad Av -NY 10010
(212) 768-4900 .. **Gage,** G Robt Jr. '83 (Gage S&F) -410 Park Av -NY 10022
(212) 903-9000 .. **Gage,** Robt D Jr. '95 (Linklaters) -1345 Av of Amer -NY 10105
(212) 768-4900 .. **Gage Spencer & Fleming** -410 Park Av -NY 10022 **Fx:**768-3629
(315) 789-4770 .. **Gage,** Walter C '66 (Gage G&B) -33 Seneca Bx1187 -Geneva 14456 **Fx:**781-1663
(518) 828-5554 .. **Gagen,** Robt J '77 -424 Warren -Hudson 12534 **Fx:**828-2685
(212) 655-6000 .. **Gagion,** Leo '85 (Chapman & C LLP) -330 Mad Av -NY 10017
(518) 473-7051 .. **Gagliano,** Joselle G '79 %OTDA-Fair Hearings -40 N Pearl -Albany 12243 **Fx:**473-6735
(212) 640-2000 .. **Gagliano,** Jos A '93 %Amer Exp -200 Vesey -NY 10285
(646) 530-8411 .. **Gagliano,** Jos R Jr. '86 -575 Mad Av -NY 10022 **Fx:**560-8413
(212) 947-0007 .. **Gagliano,** Thos D '82 %Safeguard Realty -138 W 25th -NY 10001
(212) 237-1000 .. **Gagliano,** Tina J '94 (Windels ML&M,LLP) -156 W 56th -NY 10019
(914) 747-0274 .. **Gagliardi,** Danl F '98 -370 Elwood Av -Hawthorne 10532
(914) 592-5745 .. **Gagliardi,** Roseann '86 -45 Knollwood -Elmsfrd 10523 **Fx:**592-0087
(212) 455-2000 .. **Gagliardi,** Salvatore J '08 %Simpson T&B LLP -425 Lex Av -NY 10017
(716) 856-1344 .. **Gagliardi,** Victor J '66 SpclCnsl Bouvier Prtnrshp,LLP -350 Main -Buffalo 14202 **Fx:**856-1369
(212) 815-1818 .. **Gagliardi,** Vincent '73 %DC 37 MELS -125 Barclay -NY 10007 **Fx:**815-1343
(212) 576-7000 .. **Gagliardo,** Jos Bart '84 %NY Life Ins -51 Mad Av -NY 10010 **Fx:**447-0569
(212) 578-2211 .. **Gagliardo,** Michele M '97 %MetLife -27-01 Qns Plz N -LIC 11101
(212) 728-2200 .. **Gaglio,** Nicholas E O '02 (Axinn V&H LLP) -114 W 47th -NY 10036
(716) 566-1300 .. **Gaglione,** Frank T '70 OfCnsl Hiscock & B,LLP -1100 M&T Ctr -Buffalo 14203
(212) 558-4000 .. **Gagne,** Jean-Frederic '09 %Sullivan & C LLP -125 Broad -NY 10004
(518) 359-5036 .. **Gagnier,** Kirk A '99 -44 Park -Tupper Lk 12986 **Fx:**(888) 632-9547
(212) 576-7000 .. **Gagnon,** Dennis T '81 %NY Life Ins -51 Mad Av -NY 10010 **Fx:**447-0569
(646) 471-4000 .. **Gagnon,** Laura E '09 %PricewaterhouseCoopers LLP -300 Mad Av -NY 10017
(212) 756-2000 .. **Gagnon,** Matthew J '04 %Schulte R&Z LLP -919 3rd Av -NY 10022
(716) 681-3355 .. **Gagola,** Thos L '88 (Wojtan V&G) -2956 Union Rd -Cheektowaga 14227
(718) 592-3724 .. **Gagui,** Jesus F '84 -92-31 57th Av -Elmhrst 11373
(914) 251-0010 .. **Gahagan,** Peter T '72 (Gahagan & L,LLP) -2900 Wstchstr Av -Purchase 10577 **Fx:**251-0020
(212) 819-8200 .. **Gahtan,** Adam R '97 (White & C LLP) -1155 Av of Amer -NY 10036
(212) 221-6900 .. **Gaico,** Michl R '09 %Winget S&S,LLP -45 Bway -NY 10006
(212) 373-3000 .. **Gaier,** Danielle L '10 %Paul WRW&G LLP -1285 Av of Amer -NY 10019
(212) 267-3745 .. **Gaier,** Jos '61 -450 7th Av -NY 10123 **Fx:**(201) 894-5842
(212) 267-4177 .. **Gaier,** Matthew M '88 (Kramer DL&M) -217 Bway -NY 10007
(516) 489-6100 .. **Gaier,** Phyllis Luster '86 (Posner & G) -215 Hilton Av Bx1200 -Hempstd 11551
(315) 865-4952 .. **Gaige,** Peter O '84 (P Gaige,PC) -9537 Main Bx304 -Holland Patent 13354 **Fx:**865-4464
(845) 778-2121 .. **Gailey,** J Benjamin '83 (Jacobowitz & G,LLP) -158 Orange Av Bx367 -Walden 12586
(914) 235-3654 .. **Gailhard,** Judith '86 (Pogostin & G) -305 North Av -New Rchll 10801 **Fx:**633-3894
(212) 733-2323 .. **Gaillard,** Andrew P '86 %Pfizer Inc -235 E 42nd -NY 10017
(917) 778-6500 .. **Gaillard,** Keisha M '03 %K Dodson -485 Lex Av -NY 10017
(518) 462-6765 .. **Gailliard,** Glinnesa D '08 %Leg Aid -55 Colvin Av -Albany 12206 **Fx:**427-8352
(845) 434-3000 .. **Gaiman & Krutman** -5214 Main Bx366 -S Fallsbrg 12779 **Fx:**434-3001
(845) 791-4700 .. **Gaiman,** Robt S '79 -11 Rosen Rd -Monticello 12701 **Fx:**791-1642
(212) 907-9600 .. **Gainen,** Larry F '75 (Ingram YGC&B,LLP) -250 Park Av -NY 10177
(845) 225-8403 .. **Gainer,** Ben S '96 -101 Carolan Rd E -Carmel 10512
(718) 983-8400 .. **Gaines,** Alan R '62 -2555 Richmond Av -Staten Isl 10314 **Fx:**494-4192
(212) 310-8000 .. **Gaines,** Andrew L '87 (Weil G&M LLP) -767 5th Av -NY 10153
(212) 306-7230 .. **Gaines,** Deborah M '93 %Mayors Ofc Labor Rel -40 Rector -NY 10006 **Fx:**306-7223
(914) 288-9595 .. **Gaines Gruner Ponzini & Novick,LLP** -1 N Bway -White Plns 10601 **Fx:**288-0850
(212) 554-1234 .. **Gaines,** Jonathan E '67 %AXA Financial Inc -1290 Av of Amer -NY 10104 **Fx:**707-3963
(718) 983-9400 .. **Gaines,** Jonathan S '90 -2555 Richmond Av -Staten Isl 10314
(716) 297-9786 .. **Gaines,** Kathleen E '85 -4701 Military Rd -Niagara Fls 14305 **Fx:**297-9534
(718) 983-9400 .. **Gaines,** Spencer H '59 (Gaines & F LLP) -2555 Richmond Av -Staten Isl 10314 **Fx:**494-4192
(914) 495-3515 .. **Gaines,** Stephen M '84 OfCnsl Ginsburg & R,PC -245 Saw Mill Rvr Rd -Hawthorne 10532 **Fx:**495-3520
(914) 288-9595 .. **Gaines,** Steven H '76 (Gaines GP&N,LLP) -1 N Bway -White Plns 10601
(212) 983-1300 .. **Gainey,** Barry J '85 (Gainey & M) -295 Mad Av -NY 10017
(212) 983-1300 .. **Gainey & McKenna** -295 Mad Av -NY 10017 **Fx:**983-0383
(212) 674-5151 .. **Gainsburg,** Roy '57 Holtzbrinck Publishers -175 5th Av -NY 10010
(516) 829-6900 .. **Gaioni,** John M '82 (Ackerman LCB&L,LLP) -1010 Nrthrn Blvd -Gt Neck 11021
(212) 943-1090 .. **Gair,** Anthony H '80 (Gair GCSMB&R) -80 Pine -NY 10005
(212) 943-1090 .. **Gair Gair Conason Steigman Mackauf Bloom & Rubinowitz** -80 Pine -NY 10005 **Fx:**425-7513
(718) 451-1200 .. **Gairy,** Trevor T '85 -4304 Av D -Brklyn 11203 **Fx:**451-1753
(315) 701-2939 .. **Gaiser,** Christopher S '87 -109 S Warren -Syracuse 13202 **Fx:**701-2938
(212) 593-7600 .. **Gaisi,** Matthew '03 S Harris & Assoc -110 E 59th -NY 10022
(516) 208-8599 .. **Gaissert,** Lawr R '96 -330 Sunrise Hwy -Rockvll Ctr 11570 **Fx:**536-5720
(212) 530-1800 .. **Gaither,** H Rowan IV '96 %Richards K&O LLP -1 World Fncl Ctr -NY 10281
(516) 522-2730 .. **Gaitman,** Steven J '96 -165 EAB Plz -Uniondale 11556 **Fx:**522-2675
(212) 863-8806 .. **Gajadharsingh,** Shalini '08 HPD -100 Gold -NY 10038
(718) 918-3835 .. **Gajdjis,** Philip K '94 %Bronx Mun Hsptl -Pelham Pkwy S & Eastchstr Rd -Bronx 10461
(631) 447-1200 .. **Gajdos,** Michl A '98 (Russo & G) -31 W Main -Patchogue 11772
(212) 768-6700 .. **Gajer,** Paul A '80 (Sonnenschein N&R LLP) -1221 Av of Amer -NY 10020
(212) 691-3383 .. **Gajewski,** Paul '86 -15 Sheridan Sq -NY 10014
(607) 772-0803 .. **Gaji,** Feyi O '95 -36 Oak -Bnghmtn 13905 **Fx:**723-4059
(212) 421-1300 .. **Gajjar,** Kalpana '93 Jack Resnick & Sons,Inc -110 E 59th -NY 10022 **Fx:**758-2948
(718) 762-2953 .. **Gajo,** Sofronio G '76 -39-01 Main -Flushng 11354
(212) 980-0408 .. **Gal,** Dov '01 (Pusch & G) -31 W 31st -NY 10001 **Fx:**980-7055
(212) 819-8200 .. **Gal,** Elodie '07 %White & C LLP -1155 Av of Amer -NY 10036
(212) 805-6115 .. **Galacatos,** Theodora '97 %Hon M Pollack -40 Foley Sq -NY 10007
(718) 646-4715 .. **Galak,** Juliean '04 (J Galak,PC) -3105 Brighton 3rd -Brklyn 11235 **Fx:**(516) 908-3975
(212) 869-7000 .. **Galalis,** David J '05 %Feldman W&S LLP -420 Lex Av -NY 10170
(347) 350-6592 .. **Galan,** Jos A '08 -1580 74th -Brklyn 11228
(347) 350-6592 .. **Galan,** Thos J '02 (Galan Law Firm,PC) -1580 74th -Brklyn 11228 **Fx:**312-5183
(212) 995-8153 .. **Galanes,** Philip '92 -Bx4285 -E Hampton 11937
(212) 370-1300 .. **Galano,** Anthony III '96 %Ellenoff G&S LLP -150 E 42nd -NY 10017
(631) 757-7108 .. **Galano,** Donald J '73 -52 Senne Rd -Northprt 11768

(212) 318-3000 .. **Galant,** Felice B '92 SrCnsl Fulbright & J LLP -666 5th Av -NY 10103
(212) 218-5500 .. **Galant,** Gloria '04 %Seyfarth S LLP -620 8th Av -NY 10018
(516) 747-0300 .. **Galant,** Jeffrey A '65 Cnsl Meltzer LG&B,LLP -190 Willis Av -Mineola 11501
(718) 442-9000 .. **Galante,** Anthony L '81 (Ameduri G&F) -471 Bement Av -Staten Isl 10310
(212) 775-8700 .. **Galante,** Joshua G '05 %Kilpatrick S,LLP -31 W 52nd -NY 10019
(518) 272-3311 .. **Galante,** Joyce M '66 -53 2nd Bx605 -Troy 12181 **Fx:**272-1250
(212) 259-8000 .. **Galante,** Michl V '08 %Dewey & L LLP -1301 Av of Amer -NY 10019
(212) 468-8000 .. **Galante,** Paul A '02 %Morrison & F LLP -1290 Av of Amer -NY 10104
(973) 491-3364 .. **Galante,** Todd M '87 (LeClairRyan,PC) -830 3rd Av -NY 10022 **Fx:**491-3555
(212) 221-5700 .. **Galanter,** David '86 OfCnsl Goldberg WFG LLP -1501 Bway -NY 10036
(914) 668-9600 .. **Galarce,** Carl J '86 (Miller & P,PC) -175 Main -White Plns 10601
(518) 487-5460 .. **Galarneau,** Eric M '98 %DA -6 Lodge -Albany 12207 **Fx:**487-5093
(845) 369-0980 .. **Galarneau,** Judith J '93 -169 S Main -New Cty 10956 **Fx:**369-7554
(212) 857-8230 .. **Galarza,** Jennifer A '04 %Baker MM&M,PC -330 W 34th -NY 10001
(516) 797-1600 .. **Galarza,** Julio Ceasar '95 -5020 Sunrise Hwy -Massapequa Pk 11762 **Fx:**798-8300
(516) 873-1600 .. **Galassi,** Nancy K '89 -300 Grdn City Plz -Gdn Cty 11530
(716) 633-6986 .. **Galasso,** Christopher D '88 -17 Limestone Dr -Williamsvll 14221 **Fx:**631-1906
(516) 222-6500 .. **Galasso Langione Catterson & LoFrumento, LLP** -377 Oak -Gdn Cty 11530 **Fx:**222-1094
(516) 222-6500 .. **Galasso,** Peter J '82 (Galasso LC&L,LLP) -377 Oak -Gdn Cty 11530
(516) 279-5139 .. **Galatan,** Albert J '92 %Picciano & S -900 Merchants Cncrs -Westbury 11590
(845) 567-9635 .. **Galati,** Gary A '73 -263 Rte 17K -Newburgh 12550 **Fx:**567-9378
(212) 326-3939 .. **Galati,** Richd J '10 %Jones D -222 E 41st -NY 10017
(212) 574-1200 .. **Galban,** John J '85 Cnsl Seward & K LLP -1 Bttry Pk Plz -NY 10004
(315) 253-6219 .. **Galbato,** Riccardo T '95 (Karpinski SG&T) -110 Genesee -Auburn 13021
(315) 218-8000 .. **Galbato,** Suzanne O '99 (Bond S&K,PLLC) -1 Lincoln Ctr -Syracuse 13202
(914) 834-2141 .. **Galbo,** Andrea '88 -2065 Bstn Post Rd -Larchmnt 10538
(716) 332-0151 .. **Galbo,** Richd A '85 (Galbo & Assoc) -420 Main -Buffalo 14202 **Fx:**332-0153
(716) 634-5525 .. **Galbo,** Thos S '79 (Ralabate & G) -5792 Main -Buffalo 14221
(585) 396-1930 .. **Galbraith,** Anne S '78 -Bx363 -Canandaigua 14424 **Fx:**396-9678
(607) 273-5475 .. **Galbraith,** Dirk A '72 (Holmberg GV&M) -200 E Buffalo -Ithaca 14850
(212) 425-7200 .. **Galbraith,** James '77 (Kenyon & K,LLP) -1 Bway -NY 10004
(212) 906-1200 .. **Galbraith,** Jason R '08 %Latham & W -885 3rd Av -NY 10022
(212) 742-1414 .. **Galbraith,** Kevin D '03 %Zamansky & Assoc LLC -50 Bway -NY 10005 **Fx:**742-1177
(585) 546-6448 .. **Galbraith,** Robt L Jr. '87 (Davidson F LLP) -28 E Main -Rchstr 14614
(607) 255-4196 .. **Galbreath,** Glenn G '88 %Leg Aid -Myron Taylor Hall -Ithaca 14853 **Fx:**255-3269
(718) 229-2628 .. **Galchus,** Frank M '82 (Galchus & G) -38-50 Bell Blvd -Bayside 11361
(212) 450-4000 .. **Galdos,** Michelle B '10 %Davis P&W LLP -450 Lex Av -NY 10017
(212) 388-3391 .. **Galdri,** Alberta L '04 Local 32B-J Bldg Srvc -101 Av of Amer -NY 10013
(212) 408-5100 .. **Gale,** Adam D '94 Cnsl Chadbourne & P LLP -30 Rckfllr Plz -NY 10112
(954) 531-3499 .. **Gale,** Ashley I '10 -300 Mercer -NY 10003
(212) 848-4000 .. **Gale,** Caitlyn B '10 Shearman & S LLP -599 Lex Av -NY 10022
(315) 637-3663 .. **Gale,** Catherine A '79 (Gale & D,LLC) -Bx6527 -Syracuse 13217
(315) 637-3663 .. **Gale & Dancks,LLC** -Bx6527 -Syracuse 13217 **Fx:**637-3667
(315) 637-3663 .. **Gale,** Max D '98 (Gale & D,LLC) -Bx6527 -Syracuse 13217
(516) 767-1200 .. **Gale,** Peter L '79 (B Clark & Assoc,PC) -22 S Bayles Av -Pt Wash 11050 **Fx:**767-1702
(518) 782-7700 .. **Galeano,** Ana-Maria '94 Plug Power Inc -968 Albany-Shaker Rd -Latham 12110
(212) 468-8000 .. **Galeazzi,** Marc Alain '07 %Morrison & F LLP -1290 Av of Amer -NY 10104
(914) 995-3419 .. **Galef,** Gwendolyn '97 %DA -111 Martin Luther King Blvd -White Plns 10601 **Fx:**995-3363
(914) 739-8293 .. **Galella,** Jos P '82 Kenneth Pregno Agy -2 S Division -Peekskill 10566 **Fx:**739-0832
(212) 858-1000 .. **Galeno,** Maria T '82 (Pillsbury WSP LLP) -1540 Bway -NY 10036
(718) 848-5286 .. **Galeno,** Michl L '87 -159-31 78th -Howard Bch 11414 **Fx:**323-2786
(212) 403-1000 .. **Galeon,** Jennifer R '07 %Wachtell LR&K -51 W 52nd -NY 10019
(212) 446-4800 .. **Galese,** Martin A '09 %Kirkland & E LLP -153 E 53rd -NY 10022
(718) 680-6008 .. **Galette,** Helen Z '96 (Villani & G,PC) -8212 3rd Av -Brklyn 11209 **Fx:**238-8212
(585) 419-8800 .. **Galewski,** Roy R '03 (Harris B PLLC) -99 Garnsey Rd -Pittsfrd 14534
(716) 856-1010 .. **Galeziowski,** John A Jr. '81 -69 Delaware Av -Buffalo 14202
(212) 227-0347 .. **Galfunt,** Heather A '97 %Weiss W&W,PC -25 Park Pl -NY 10007
(914) 428-2323 .. **Galgano,** George W '00 (Galgano & Assoc) -399 Knollwood Rd -White Plns 10603 **Fx:**428-3298
(914) 674-7864 .. **Galgano,** John L '04 Mercy College -555 Bway -Dobbs Ferry 10522 **Fx:**674-7395
(516) 248-2500 .. **Galgano,** Kathleen M '87 (Redmond P&C, LLP) -1461 Franklin Av -Gdn Cty 11530
(914) 761-4313 .. **Galgano,** Louis J III '80 -303 Old Tarrytown Rd -White Plns 10603
(516) 431-1177 .. **Galgano,** Thos M '75 (Galgano & Assoc,PLLC) -20 W Park Av -Long Bch 11561
(518) 797-9289 .. **Galgay,** Aline D Gioffre '88 -44 Cnty Route 1 -Westerlo 12193 **Fx:**797-9541
(718) 260-8752 .. **Galia,** Joanna C '02 ACS -345 Adams -Brklyn 11201
(212) 986-5900 .. **Galiardo,** Christopher D '92 (Myers S&G) -299 Bway -NY 10007 **Fx:**986-6250
(212) 739-7511 .. **Galib,** M Salome '99 Puerto Rican Legal Defense & Educ Fund -99 Hudson -NY 10013
(212) 530-5000 .. **Galicia,** Melissa A '09 %Milbank TH&M LLP -1 Chase Manh Plz -NY 10005
(212) 351-4000 .. **Galil,** Yair Yehuda '05 %Gibson D&C LLP -200 Park Av -NY 10166
(212) 450-4000 .. **Galin,** Ross B '02 %Davis P&W LLP -450 Lex Av -NY 10017
(516) 739-8222 .. **Galina,** Michl R '89 (Rabinowitz & G) -94 Willis Av -Mineola 11501
(718) 237-5500 .. **Galinsky,** Shira Y '06 %Leg Srvcs -105 Court -Brklyn 11201 **Fx:**855-0733
(516) 729-6507 .. **Galioto,** Anthony J '96 -166 Euston Rd -Gdn Cty 11530
(718) 931-7382 .. **Galioto,** Laurie '94 Galioto Law Ofc -3342 Agar Pl -Bronx 10465
(212) 227-4072 .. **Galis-Menendez,** Isabel V '86 Law Dept -100 Church -NY 10007 **Fx:**788-0367
(516) 742-0370 .. **Galison,** David P '97 (Galison & G) -1539 Franklin Av -Mineola 11501 **Fx:**742-6477
(516) 742-0370 .. **Galison,** Edw '69 (Galison & G) -1539 Franklin Av -Mineola 11501 **Fx:**742-6477
(212) 728-2098 .. **Galkin,** Lee D '98 SFX Sports Grp -220 W 42nd -NY 10036 **Fx:**(917) 421-5386
(315) 798-5224 .. **Gall,** Erin Pelnik '97 %Hon B Donalty -200 Elizabeth -Utica 13501
(212) 504-6000 .. **Gall,** Maria A '08 %Cadwalader W&T LLP -1 World Fncl Ctr -NY 10281
(212) 479-6000 .. **Gall,** Phillip J '95 (Cooley LLP) -1114 Av of Amer -NY 10036
(212) 269-0927 .. **Galla,** Deeanna M '92 (D'Amato & L,LLP) -2 World Fncl Ctr -NY 10281
(212) 543-1770 .. **Gallacher,** Dominique F '01 -116 Pinehurst Av -NY 10033
(212) 875-6576 .. **Gallacher,** John M '04 Sesame Workshop -1 Lincoln Plz -NY 10023
(212) 903-9000 .. **Gallagher,** Amanda J '95 (Linklaters) -1345 Av of Amer -NY 10105
(718) 590-5400 .. **Gallagher,** Arthur L '96 %M Ridge -910 Grnd Cncrs -Bronx 10451 **Fx:**681-0285
(212) 451-2300 .. **Gallagher,** Brad M '07 %Olshan GFR&W LLP -65 E 55th -NY 10022
(212) 758-9700 .. **Gallagher,** Brian G '01 %KPMG LLP -345 Park Av -NY 10154
(212) 479-6000 .. **Gallagher,** Brian J '65 SrCnsl Cooley LLP -1114 Av of Amer -NY 10036
(212) 983-9700 .. **Gallagher,** Brian K '87 (Gallagher H&L LLP) -380 Lex Av -NY 10168
(212) 697-8500 .. **Gallagher,** Brian P '85 (Konner T&G) -462 7th Av -NY 10018
(212) 468-4800 .. **Gallagher,** Brian R '82 (Davis & G LLP) -1740 Bway -NY 10019
(607) 729-1539 .. **Gallagher,** Brian R '97 (Cenesky AS&G) -251 Main -Johnson Cty 13790
(212) 318-6000 .. **Gallagher,** Bryan W '08 %Paul HJ&W LLP -75 E 55th -NY 10022
(212) 282-4739 .. **Gallagher,** Candice S '02 Mizuho Alternative Invstmnts LLC -1251 Av of Amer -NY 10020
(845) 726-3227 .. **Gallagher,** Carole L '89 (Gallagher & G) -225 Route 284 Bx333 -Unionvll 10988 **Fx:**726-3954
(212) 825-1565 .. **Gallagher,** Cathy Ann '84 Ptashnik & Assoc -45 Bway -NY 10006 **Fx:**825-1559
(914) 683-5300 .. **Gallagher,** Claire M '91 %Silverman B&S,LLP -81 Main -White Plns 10601
(518) 402-6757 .. **Gallagher,** Craig '91 %Workers Comp Bd -20 Park -Albany 12207
(212) 693-2222 .. **Gallagher,** Danl C '83 (D Gallagher,PC) -150 Bway -NY 10038 **Fx:**608-5977
(315) 637-0489 .. **Gallagher,** Danl J '87 -506 S Manlius -Fayettevll 13066
(518) 743-9000 .. **Gallagher,** Danl J '94 (Toomey & G) -1 South Wstrn Plz Bx2144 -Glens Fls 12801 **Fx:**743-9023
(845) 340-3315 .. **Gallagher,** Dylan S '10 %DA -285 Wall -Kingston 12401 **Fx:**340-3185
(518) 387-6383 .. **Gallagher,** Eileen W '08 GE Global Research -1 Rsrch Cir -Schnctdy 12309
(212) 303-1839 .. **Gallagher,** Elizabeth A '08 Rosen Seymour Shapss Martin & Co LLP -757 3rd Av -NY 10017
(914) 899-3100 .. **Gallagher,** Eugene G '86 (Mead HC&G) -109 Spencer Pl -Mamaroneck 10543
(516) 742-2500 .. **Gallagher & Faller** -1050 Franklin Av -Gdn Cty 11530 **Fx:**742-2516
(212) 577-3688 .. **Gallagher,** Frances A '79 %Leg Aid -199 Water -NY 10038 **Fx:**509-8431
(516) 248-2002 .. **Gallagher,** Gerard M '79 (Gallagher WB&P) -98 Willis Av -Mineola 11501
(212) 983-9700 .. **Gallagher Harnett & Lagalante LLP** -380 Lex Av -NY 10168 **Fx:**983-9701
(516) 489-5000 .. **Gallagher,** Herbert F '72 %Town Atty -Town Hall -Hempstd 11550 **Fx:**489-5150
(518) 474-6750 .. **Gallagher,** Jaime L '03 Liquor Auth -80 S Swan -Albany 12210 **Fx:**402-2304
(516) 742-2500 .. **Gallagher,** James A Jr. '70 (Gallagher & F) -1050 Franklin Av -Gdn Cty 11530
(516) 742-2500 .. **Gallagher,** James F '03 %Gallagher & F -1050 Franklin Av -Gdn Cty 11530
(212) 429-2294 .. **Gallagher,** James M '76 -75 Wall -NY 10005
(516) 223-0993 .. **Gallagher,** James M '81 -2249 Derby Rd -Baldwin 11510 **Fx:**223-5505
(516) 571-3056 .. **Gallagher,** James N '70 %Cnty Atty -1 West -Mineola 11501 **Fx:**571-6604
(585) 544-5442 .. **Gallagher,** John B Jr. '95 -26 Chelsea Rd -Rchstr 14617
(212) 521-5400 .. **Gallagher,** John C III '05 Cnsl Reed S LLP -599 Lex Av -NY 10022
(516) 228-8484 .. **Gallagher,** John F III '95 %Dilworth & B,LLP -1000 Woodbury Rd -Woodbury 11797
(516) 766-5965 .. **Gallagher,** John J '85 -15 Devon Rd -Rockvll Ctr 11570
(212) 277-6500 .. **Gallagher,** John T '89 (Dickstein S LLP) -1633 Bway -NY 10019
(212) 450-4000 .. **Gallagher,** Jos T '09 %Davis P&W LLP -450 Lex Av -NY 10017
(212) 656-2973 .. **Gallagher,** Kathleen A '85 NYSE -20 Broad -NY 10005
(212) 687-1101 .. **Gallagher,** Kevin M '95 (Portnoy & G,PC) -260 Mad Av -NY 10016 **Fx:**949-9835
(212) 252-0004 .. **Gallagher,** Kristin V '96 %Carroll M&K LLC -570 Lex Av -NY 10022
(914) 323-7000 .. **Gallagher,** Lorraine E J '00 (Wilson EME&D LLP) -3 Gannett Dr -White Plns 10604
(914) 995-2660 .. **Gallagher,** Makaria L '85 %Cnty Atty -148 Martine Av -White Plns 10601 **Fx:**995-5858
(212) 785-2929 .. **Gallagher,** Margo O'Donnell '07 %Conway FC&K,PC -48 Wall -NY 10005
(212) 245-2392 .. **Gallagher,** Mark S '80 -504 W 55th -NY 10019 **Fx:**957-0745

(212) 669-2070 .. **Gallagher,** Mary E '84 %Tax Appls Tribunal -1 Centre -NY 10007 **Fx:**669-2211
(212) 696-6000 .. **Gallagher,** Maryann '88 Cnsl Curtis M-PC&M LLP -101 Park Av -NY 10178
(914) 995-3588 .. **Gallagher,** Matthew I '98 %Cnty Atty -148 Martine Av -White Plns 10601 **Fx:**995-5858
(516) 571-3800 .. **Gallagher,** Megan A '86 %DA -262 Old Cntry Rd -Mineola 11501 **Fx:**248-9479
(212) 940-8800 .. **Gallagher,** Michl F '93 SpclCnsl Katten MR LLP -575 Mad Av -NY 10022
(716) 858-5000 .. **Gallagher,** Michl J '85 Delaware North -40 Fountain Plz -Buffalo 14202 **Fx:**858-5056
(212) 819-8200 .. **Gallagher,** Michl J '94 (White & C LLP) -1155 Av of Amer -NY 10036
(212) 878-1700 .. **Gallagher,** Michl P '06 %Marshall DWC&G -140 Bway -NY 10005
(212) 935-3131 .. **Gallagher,** Pamela L '09 %Gallet D&B,LLP -845 3rd Av -NY 10022
(212) 446-4800 .. **Gallagher,** Patrick C '89 (Kirkland & E LLP) -153 E 53rd -NY 10022
(646) 610-5140 .. **Gallagher,** Paul J '85 %NYPD -1 Police Plz -NY 10038
(315) 841-3370 .. **Gallagher,** Paul M '92 -7723 State Route 20 Bx57 -Sangerfield 13455 **Fx:**841-3202
(212) 248-2220 .. **Gallagher,** Peter J '93 (Kennedy JG LLC) -99 Wall -NY 10005 **Fx:**248-0170
(212) 265-6888 .. **Gallagher,** Peter J '03 %Porzio B&N,PC -156 W 56th -NY 10019
(718) 523-1111 .. **Gallagher,** Rachel E '08 %Gildin Z&S,PC -138-44 Qns Blvd -Briarwd 11435
(212) 609-6800 .. **Gallagher,** Renee A '02 %McCarter & E,LLP -245 Park Av -NY 10167
(716) 853-4600 .. **Gallagher,** Robt E Jr. '93 Morenus CG&B -37 Franklin -Buffalo 14202 **Fx:**853-4610
(212) 269-5900 .. **Gallagher,** Rose M '95 Cnsl Regal Title Agency -90 Broad -NY 10004 **Fx:**937-3376
(212) 557-5055 .. **Gallagher,** Shannon P '90 %Semetis Law Firm -286 Mad Av -NY 10017 **Fx:**557-5051
(631) 864-4460 .. **Gallagher,** Susan I '94 %Primary Land Srvcs LLC -368 Vets Mem'l Hwy -Commack 11725
(212) 863-8061 .. **Gallagher,** Ted W '03 %HPD -100 Gold -NY 10038
(914) 472-2300 .. **Gallagher,** Terence J III '94 (Jones G,LLP) -670 Wht Plns Rd -Scarsdale 10583
(607) 723-5341 .. **Gallagher,** Terence P '98 (Hinman H&K,LLP) -80 Exchange Bx5250 -Bnghmtn 13902
(607) 498-5800 .. **Gallagher,** Thos E '06 -Bx426 -Roscoe 12776
(212) 415-9200 .. **Gallagher,** Thos S '87 (Dorsey & W LLP) -250 Park Av -NY 10177
(212) 747-1230 .. **Gallagher,** Timothy D '91 (McMahon M&G LLP) -55 Washington -Brklyn 11201
(212) 701-3000 .. **Gallagher,** Timothy G '04 %Cahill G&R LLP -80 Pine -NY 10005 **Fx:**269-5420
(516) 248-2002 .. **Gallagher Walker Bianco & Plastaras** -98 Willis Av -Mineola 11501 **Fx:**248-2394
(212) 747-1230 .. **Gallagher,** Wm D '58 (McMahon M&G LLP) -55 Washington -Brklyn 11201
(516) 488-9860 .. **Gallagher-Gaffney,** Bernadette '90 -77 Landau Av -Floral Pk 11001
(212) 277-6500 .. **Gallagher-Whitman,** Mikaela C '09 %Dickstein S LLP -1633 Bway -NY 10019
(716) 853-4080 .. **Gallaher,** Dennis P '95 (Colucci & G,PC) -424 Main -Buffalo 14202
(212) 408-5100 .. **Gallai,** David '00 (Chadbourne & P LLP) -30 Rckfllr Plz -NY 10112
(212) 878-0128 .. **Gallan,** Michl A '97 %MTA -347 Mad Av -NY 10017 **Fx:**878-0162
(212) 704-6000 .. **Gallancy-Wininger,** Jean E '74 (Troutman S LLP) -405 Lex Av -NY 10174
(212) 359-4212 .. **Gallant,** Antje L '04 -122 W 27th -NY 10001
(212) 648-2091 .. **Gallant,** Bruce D '82 JP Morgan Chase -245 Park Av -NY 10167
(212) 818-8800 .. **Gallant,** Jeffrey M '00 (Graubard M) -405 Lex Av -NY 10174
(585) 232-5768 .. **Gallant,** Kenneth '78 (Christiano G&C) -16 E Main -Rchstr 14614
(518) 585-6737 .. **Gallant,** Kevin A '79 %Hon D Viscardi -15 Father Joques Pl -Ticonderoga 12883
(518) 873-3380 .. **Gallant,** Michl J '72 %Cnty Atty -7551 Court Bx217 -Elizabethtwn 12932 **Fx:**873-3854
(516) 639-5949 .. **Gallanter,** Peter '87 -56 Sintsink Dr E -Pt Wash 11050
(212) 682-8383 .. **Gallanty,** Alan T '83 (Kantor DWMT&G,PC) -51 E 42nd -NY 10017
(212) 532-7171 .. **Gallardo,** Diana '04 Kiwi Partners,Inc -381 Park Av -NY 10016
(516) 931-1800 .. **Gallardo,** Domingo R '90 (Catalano G&P LLP) -100 Jericho Quadrangle -Jericho 11753
(212) 351-4000 .. **Gallardo,** Eduardo '00 (Gibson D&C LLP) -200 Park Av -NY 10166
(212) 867-4466 .. **Gallaudet,** Lisa M '08 %Belkin BW&G,LLP -270 Mad Av -NY 10016
(212) 771-0829 .. **Gallaway,** Matthew L '96 Aspen Publishers -76 9th Av -NY 10011
(212) 788-8884 .. **Gallay,** Elizabeth Glener '93 %Law Dept -100 Church -NY 10007 **Fx:**788-0367
(212) 697-3122 .. **Gallay,** Michl E '93 (Martin C&B LLP) -220 E 42nd -NY 10017
(914) 241-6346 .. **Gallay,** Paul A '85 Westchester Land Trust -403 Harris Rd -Bedfrd Hlls 10507
(518) 765-2056 .. **Galle,** Katherine Hammond '96 Hammond Tours -34 Wedgewood Ln -Voorheesvll 12186
(212) 756-2000 .. **Gallego,** Dominique Padilla '02 (Schulte R&Z LLP) -919 3rd Av -NY 10022
(212) 768-6700 .. **Gallegos,** Jody L '02 %Sonnenschein N&R LLP -2 World Fncl Ctr -NY 10281
(212) 541-2000 .. **Gallent,** Judith M '90 (Bryan C LLP) -1290 Av of Amer -NY 10104
(516) 463-5895 .. **Galler,** Linda '83 %Hofstra Law Schl -121 Hofstra Univ -Hempstd 11549
(212) 977-9700 .. **Galler,** Perry S '72 (Phillips N LLP) -666 5th Av -NY 10103
(212) 689-8808 .. **Galler,** Sheryl B '94 (Hoguet NR&K,LLP) -10 E 40th -NY 10016
(212) 355-5575 .. **Gallerizzo,** Angela M '07 %Smith & N,LLP -363 7th Av -NY 10001 **Fx:**486-3150
(212) 430-6526 .. **Gallers,** Jackie '71 -65 Bway -NY 10006
(718) 326-6200 .. **Galleshaw,** James J '00 (Sullivan & G) -73-42 68th Av -Middl Vllg 11379 **Fx:**228-7010
(212) 935-3131 .. **Gallet Dreyer & Berkey,LLP** -845 3rd Av -NY 10022 **Fx:**935-4514
(212) 779-1414 .. **Galletti,** Gabriel G '05 %Bernstein L LLP -10 E 40th -NY 10016
(212) 909-2621 .. **Galley,** H Johannes '75 -60 E 42nd -NY 10165
(212) 457-0382 .. **Galli,** Mary Ann '93 %Aetna US Hlthcare -99 Park Av -NY 10016
(718) 838-7878 .. **Gallicchio,** Amy '99 %Bronx Defenders -860 Crtlandt Av -Bronx 10451 **Fx:**665-0100
(716) 566-1300 .. **Gallick,** Lawr J '64 OfCnsl Hiscock & B,LLP -1100 M&T Ctr -Buffalo 14203
(212) 558-4000 .. **Gallien,** Monique Marie '06 %Sullivan & C LLP -125 Broad -NY 10004
(914) 761-1300 .. **Galligan,** Brian P '06 %Cuddy & F LLP -445 Hmltn Av -White Plns 10601
(518) 408-2374 .. **Galligan,** Colleen D '99 %Dept of Law -The Cptl -Albany 12224
(212) 509-9400 .. **Galligan,** John B '97 (Cozen O) -45 Bway Atrium -NY 10006
(212) 449-5133 .. **Galligan,** Kelly M '03 Merrill Lynch Mortgage Lending -4 World Fncl Ctr -NY 10080
(518) 436-2840 .. **Galligan,** Linda M '07 %Thruway Auth -200 Southrn Blvd Bx189 -Albany 12201 **Fx:**471-4340
(845) 794-3344 .. **Galligan,** Meagan K '07 %DA -414 Bway -Monticello 12701 **Fx:**794-3646
(914) 766-2296 .. **Galligan,** Michl R '02 IBM -294 Route 100 -Somers 10589
(212) 977-9700 .. **Galligan,** Michl W '86 (Phillips N LLP) -666 5th Av -NY 10103
(212) 218-5500 .. **Galligan,** Paul H '91 (Seyfarth S LLP) -620 8th Av -NY 10018
(212) 756-2000 .. **Galligan,** Susan R '89 SpclCnsl Schulte R&Z LLP -919 3rd Av -NY 10022
(518) 266-3000 .. **Galliher,** Dennis M '82 %Div Tax Appls -500 Fed -Troy 12180 **Fx:**272-5178
(917) 301-2041 .. **Galliker,** Lauren E '97 -165 W 66th -NY 10023
(516) 832-7500 .. **Gallin,** Alexander E '06 %Nixon P LLP -50 Jericho Quadrangle -Jericho 11753
(631) 231-1450 .. **Gallin,** Deborah S '78 OfCnsl Feldman K&M,PC -330 Vndrblt Motor Pkwy -Hauppauge 11788
(212) 947-1999 .. **Gallin,** Fredric P '82 (Methfessel & W,PC) -450 7th Av -NY 10123
(212) 537-9000 .. **Gallin,** Marisa E '08 %Cohen G&S,LLP -850 3rd Av -NY 10022
(718) 585-3512 .. **Gallin,** Martin '49 (Gallin & N) -860 Grnd Cncrs -Bronx 10451 **Fx:**993-3712
(516) 328-8448 .. **Gallin,** Steven L '73 -1 Holland Av -Floral Pk 11001 **Fx:**775-2085
(585) 325-3120 .. **Gallina,** Fred S '79 -1 Monterey Dr -Pittsfrd 14534 **Fx:**325-2635
(212) 751-2700 .. **Gallina,** Ronnie Bernon '78 JAMS -620 8th Av -NY 10018 **Fx:**751-4099
(212) 474-1000 .. **Gallina,** Stephanie R '09 %Cravath S&M LLP -825 8th Av -NY 10019
(718) 892-0400 .. **Gallina,** Wm A '67 -1180 Morris Park Av -Bronx 10461 **Fx:**892-0033
(718) 226-9990 .. **Gallinari,** Karen L Illuzzi '88 SIUH-Legal & Reg Affrs -475 Seaview Av -Staten Isl 10305 **Fx:**226-8255
(212) 710-5160 .. **Gallion,** Edw R '87 (Gallion & S) -75 Rckfllr Plz -NY 10019 **Fx:**428-6777
(516) 747-2010 .. **Gallipoli,** Marianne J '94 -235 Emory Rd -Mineola 11501
(914) 220-1086 .. **Gallivan,** Danl F '74 (Gallivan & G) -111 Church -White Plns 10601 **Fx:**948-4721
(718) 237-2000 .. **Gallivan,** Molly Jack '02 %Leg Aid -111 Lvngstn -Brklyn 11201 **Fx:**237-8737
(914) 220-1086 .. **Gallivan,** Thos L '05 (Gallivan & G) -111 Church -White Plns 10601 **Fx:**948-4721
(631) 499-2773 .. **Gallo,** Anthony J '97 -6080 Jericho Tpk -Commack 11725
(631) 499-2555 .. **Gallo,** Anthony P '58 A Gallo,PC -6080 Jericho Tpk -Commack 11725 **Fx:**499-4318
(718) 360-1424 .. **Gallo,** Dana C '83 -89 Sterling Pl -Brklyn 11217
(212) 335-9000 .. **Gallo,** Daniela T '02 %DA -1 Hogan Pl -NY 10013
(718) 459-9000 .. **Gallo,** David A '81 (Sweeney GR&B,LLP) -95-25 Qns Blvd -Rego Pk 11374
(914) 939-0002 .. **Gallo,** David G '79 (Gallo F&N,LLP) -211 S Ridge -Rye Brook 10573
(585) 815-0288 .. **Gallo,** Deborah M '95 %Rosicki R & Assoc,PC -26 Harvester Av -Batavia 14020 **Fx:**815-0299
(845) 831-7333 .. **Gallo,** Donald J '87 -28 S Walnut -Beacon 12508
(212) 697-3122 .. **Gallo,** Enrico N '10 %Martin C&B LLP -220 E 42nd -NY 10017
(914) 939-0002 .. **Gallo Feinstein & Naishtut,LLP** -211 S Ridge -Rye Brook 10573 **Fx:**939-4253
(212) 940-8800 .. **Gallo,** Ferdinand J III '07 (Katten MR LLP) -575 Mad Av -NY 10022
(585) 454-7145 .. **Gallo & Iacovangelo,LLP** -39 State -Rchstr 14614 **Fx:**454-2476
(516) 746-5647 .. **Gallo,** Joan A '90 -215 Raff Av -Mineola 11501
(516) 572-2381 .. **Gallo,** Joan D '89 Dist Ct Law Dept -99 Main -Hempstd 11550
(516) 229-6000 .. **Gallo,** Jos G '94 %R Lau & Assoc -300 Jericho Quad Bx9040 -Jericho 11753 **Fx:**229-6167
(914) 559-3100 .. **Gallo,** Kathleen '98 OfCnsl Heidell PM&B,LLP -81 Main -White Plns 10601
(718) 746-0933 .. **Gallo,** Kathleen Clifford '86 -95-25 Qns Blvd -Rego Pk 11374
(518) 745-1400 .. **Gallo,** Kimberly J '08 FitzGerald MBF -16 Pearl Bx2017 -Glens Fls 12801
(845) 278-8710 .. **Gallo,** Laurie A '00 %Jowdy & J -1454 Route 22 -Brewstr 10509
(518) 471-4721 .. **Gallo,** Linda Vellis '84 %Appllt Div 3rd Dept -Capitol Station Bx7288 -Albany 12224 **Fx:**471-4750
(718) 761-6464 .. **Gallo,** Mark '94 -2300 Victory Blvd -Staten Isl 10314 **Fx:**761-7632
(585) 295-4400 .. **Gallo,** Nicholas J '09 %Hiscock & B,LLP -2000 HSBC Plz -Rchstr 14604
(914) 765-4355 .. **Gallo,** Nicole J '91 %IBM -North Castle Dr -Armonk 10504
(631) 853-4921 .. **Gallo,** Philip '91 %District Ct Law Dept -400 Carleton Av Bx9075 -Central Islip 11722
(212) 336-1746 .. **Gallo,** Philip W '88 Deutsche Asset Mgmt -345 Park Av -NY 10154
(212) 683-7100 .. **Gallo,** Richd J '93 (Gallo V&K,LLP) -90 Broad -NY 10004
(631) 563-7755 .. **Gallo,** Robt D '87 -116 Greene Av -Sayvll 11782 **Fx:**563-7475
(516) 745-6700 .. **Gallo,** Robt T '90 -825 E Gate Blvd -Gdn Cty 11530 **Fx:**745-6705
(212) 767-7800 .. **Gallo,** Ruth '88 %Writers Guild -250 Hudson -NY 10013 **Fx:**582-1909
(845) 331-1000 .. **Gallo,** Shayne R '96 OfCnsl G Redder -243 Wall Bx3100 -Kingston 12402 **Fx:**331-1009
(914) 703-6300 .. **Gallo,** Stephanie M '95 %Pillinger MT,LLP -570 Taxter Rd -Elmsfrd 10523
(718) 727-7900 .. **Gallo,** Stephen A '72 -1860 Clove Rd -Staten Isl 10304
(631) 979-1029 .. **Gallo,** Thos M '94 -11 Thide Ct -Smithtwn 11787 **Fx:**979-2580
(212) 732-3200 .. **Gallo,** Victor J '95 %Carter L&M LLP -2 Wall -NY 10005
(718) 273-1699 .. **Gallo,** Vincent J '82 -706 Forest Av -Staten Isl 10310 **Fx:**273-3101
(212) 286-8585 .. **Gallo,** Vincent L Jr. '93 (Heidell PM&B,LLP) -99 Park Av -NY 10016
(212) 683-7100 .. **Gallo Vittucci & Klar,LLP** -90 Broad -NY 10004 **Fx:**683-5555
(718) 491-5999 .. **Gallogly,** Barry A '81 -7004 Louise Ter -Brklyn 11209

(212) 360-3097 .. **Gallo-Kotcher,** Sharon '86 %TBTA -Randalls Isl -NY 10035 **Fx:**860-1596
(212) 474-1000 .. **Galloway,** Carrie B '09 %Cravath S&M LLP -825 8th Av -NY 10019
(914) 723-2404 .. **Galloway,** Frances C '67 (Cunningham G&M) -220 Harwood Bldg -Scarsdale 10583
(212) 837-6000 .. **Galloway,** Jeff H '82 (Hughes H&R LLP) -1 Bttry Pk Plz -NY 10004
(914) 723-2404 .. **Galloway,** John H III '66 (Cunningham G&M) -220 Harwood Bldg -Scarsdale 10583
(212) 708-1800 .. **Galloway,** Peter D '79 (Ladas & P) -26 W 61st -NY 10023
(212) 318-6000 .. **Galloway-Scimone,** Meagan S '05 %Paul HJ&W LLP -75 E 55th -NY 10022
(212) 471-8536 .. **Gallub,** Michl B '87 (Herzfeld & R,PC) -125 Broad -NY 10004
(585) 340-4328 .. **Gallucci,** Francis V '02 Fujifilm E-Systems -155 Bellwood Dr -Rchstr 14606
(845) 359-4379 .. **Gallucci,** John A Jr. '78 -830 Piermont Av -Piermont 10968 **Fx:**365-2149
(718) 273-9000 .. **Gallucci,** Mario F '91 (Helbock N&G) -2550 Victory Blvd -Staten Isl 10314 **Fx:**816-0718
(212) 609-6800 .. **Galluccio,** John V '99 (McCarter & E,LLP) -245 Park Av -NY 10167
(212) 530-5000 .. **Gallup,** Joy K '91 (Milbank TH&M LLP) -1 Chase Manh Plz -NY 10005
(212) 576-8570 .. **Galluzzi,** David D '00 Marvel Entertainment Inc -417 5th Av -NY 10016
(212) 964-9640 .. **Galluzzi,** Michl J '91 (Cascione P&G,PC) -20 Vesey -NY 10007
(212) 506-1700 .. **Galluzzo,** David J '07 %Kasowitz BT&F LLP -1633 Bway -NY 10019
(631) 390-0010 .. **Galluzzo,** Dianne M '97 %Bruno G&S,LLP -445 Broad Hollow Rd -Melvll 11747
(212) 918-4661 .. **Galluzzo,** Matthew J '02 (Galluzzo & J LLP) -48 Wall -NY 10005
(914) 475-1276 .. **Galos,** Jodie-Beth '77 Galos & Assoc,LLC -Bx362 -Millerton 12546
(212) 998-6430 .. **Galowitz,** Paula '77 %NYU Law Schl -245 Sullivan -NY 10012 **Fx:**995-4031
(914) 428-3427 .. **Galowitz,** Sam W '60 -10 City Pl -White Plns 10601 **Fx:**428-3428
(212) 335-9000 .. **Galperin,** Gary J '81 %DA -1 Hogan Pl -NY 10013
(914) 934-2627 .. **Galperin,** Jeffrey '80 -189 N Main -Pt Chester 10573 **Fx:**937-9407
(212) 230-0223 .. **Galpern,** Danl H '97 CurtCo Media Labs -1359 Bway -NY 10018
(212) 450-2121 .. **Galst,** Jonathan R '93 %NFL -280 Park Av -NY 10017 **Fx:**681-7599
(718) 260-2490 .. **Galston,** Katharine J '04 Hon R Raggi -225 Cadman Plz E -Brklyn 11201
(518) 641-5571 .. **Galt,** Fredk B '88 Cptl Dist Physicians Hlth Plan,Inc -500 Patroon Crk Blvd -Albany 12206 **Fx:**641-5505
(516) 741-6565 .. **Galteri,** Patricia '84 (Meyer SE&K,PC) -990 Stewart Av Bx9194 -Gdn Cty 11530
(631) 360-7570 .. **Galteri,** Stephanie C '88 %Town Atty -99 W Main -Smithtwn 11787 **Fx:**360-7719
(212) 687-3000 .. **Galterio,** Gregory E '87 (Jaffe & A,LLP) -600 3rd Av -NY 10016
(212) 595-4598 .. **Galub,** Arthur L '55 -205 West End Av -NY 10023 **Fx:**595-4348
(212) 885-8174 .. **Galuppo,** Christopher J '93 %BDO USA,LLP -330 Mad Av -NY 10017 **Fx:**697-1299
(646) 386-5700 .. **Galvan,** Elba-Rose '96 %Civil Ct -111 Centre -NY 10013
(212) 209-4800 .. **Galvan,** Emilio A '93 (Brown R LLP) -7 Times Sq -NY 10036
(212) 705-7000 .. **Galvan,** Rafael I '99 OfCnsl Bingham M LLP -399 Park Av -NY 10022
(914) 749-8200 .. **Galvani,** Ann M '77 (Boies S&F LLP) -333 Main -Armonk 10504
(212) 596-9000 .. **Galvani,** Paul B '65 (Ropes & G LLP) -1211 Av of Amer -NY 10036
(716) 692-5821 .. **Galvano,** Douglas F '91 -7173 Winbert Dr -N Tonawanda 14120
(212) 349-5150 .. **Galvano,** Jos '85 (Galvano & X,PC) -150 Bway -NY 10038
(212) 883-1700 .. **Galvano,** Jos J '04 %Duval & S LLP -101 Park Av -NY 10178
(212) 349-5150 .. **Galvano & Xanthakis,PC** -150 Bway -NY 10038 **Fx:**349-5298
(914) 997-7980 .. **Galvao,** Antonio '93 %OCA -140 Grand -White Plns 10601 **Fx:**997-7781
(914) 949-2700 .. **Galvao,** Susan E '94 (Bleakley P&S,LLP) -1 N Lex Av -White Plns 10601
(516) 747-2200 .. **Galvez,** Alexander J '00 %M Alter -200 Old Cntry Rd -Mineola 11501 **Fx:**747-2200
(718) 982-2355 .. **Galvez,** Kathleen E F '72 CUNY-SI -2800 Victory Blvd -Staten Isl 10314
(212) 715-1000 .. **Galvez,** Lorena '08 %Arnold & P LLP -399 Park Av -NY 10022
(212) 839-5300 .. **Galvez,** Michelle M '08 %Sidley A LLP -787 7th Av -NY 10019
(518) 474-7700 .. **Galvin,** Christine M '83 NYS OPWDD -44 Holland Av -Albany 12229 **Fx:**474-7382
(212) 221-5700 .. **Galvin,** Dorothy A '05 %Goldberg WFG LLP -1501 Bway -NY 10036
(716) 856-4000 .. **Galvin,** Jodyann '99 (Hodgson R LLP) -140 Pearl -Buffalo 14202
(212) 679-1500 .. **Galvin,** John J '79 (Galvin & M) -470 Park Av S -NY 10016
(212) 903-9000 .. **Galvin,** Joni Forster '06 %Linklaters -1345 Av of Amer -NY 10105
(516) 357-3700 .. **Galvin,** Kerry A '07 %Cullen and D LLP -100 Q Roosevelt Blvd -Gdn Cty 11530
(212) 483-9490 .. **Galvin,** Kevin P '89 (McElroy DM&C,LLP) -88 Pine -NY 10005
(518) 439-7734 .. **Galvin,** Madeline S '74 (Galvin & M) -217 Delaware Av -Delmar 12054
(212) 972-6161 .. **Galvin,** Mari J '96 OfCnsl Cassin & C LLP -711 3rd Av -NY 10017
(718) 665-1800 .. **Galvin,** Martin '75 -903B Sheridan Av -Bronx 10451
(212) 918-3000 .. **Galvin,** Matthew J '06 %Hogan L LLP -875 3rd Av -NY 10022
(212) 679-1500 .. **Galvin & Mlawski** -470 Park Av S -NY 10016
(518) 439-7734 .. **Galvin & Morgan** -217 Delaware Av -Delmar 12054 **Fx:**475-1810
(914) 965-4600 .. **Galvin,** Pauline M '92 -1 Exec Blvd -Ynkrs 10701 **Fx:**965-4618
(315) 379-2282 .. **Galvin,** Wm J '98 %Pub Def -Cnty Cthse -Canton 13617 **Fx:**379-2300
(212) 225-2000 .. **Galvis,** Sandra Jordan '96 Cleary GS&H -1 Lbrty Plz -NY 10006
(212) 558-4000 .. **Galvis,** Sergio J '84 (Sullivan & C LLP) -125 Broad -NY 10004
(212) 837-6099 .. **Galynker,** Benjamin M '08 %Hughes H&R LLP -1 Bttry Pk Plz -NY 10004 **Fx:**299-6099
(516) 792-3175 .. **Gamache,** Eugene R '97 -95 West Blvd -E Rockaway 11518 **Fx:**792-3178
(845) 634-3344 .. **Gamache,** Julie A '78 %Family Shelter -9 Johnsons Ln -New Cty 10956
(212) 504-6000 .. **Gamadia,** Tushna '01 %Cadwalader W&T LLP -1 World Fncl Ctr -NY 10281
(516) 357-3000 .. **Gambardella,** Anthony R '80 (Rivkin R LLP) -926 RXR Plz -Uniondale 11556
(212) 758-0050 .. **Gambardella,** Gelsomina A '04 %Title Assoc -825 3rd Av -NY 10022 **Fx:**758-8223
(914) 747-4455 .. **Gambardella,** Joni '04 D'Agostino,PC -427 Bedford Rd -Plsntvll 10570 **Fx:**747-3626
(914) 323-7000 .. **Gambardella,** Thos M '80 (Wilson EME&D LLP) -3 Gannett Dr -White Plns 10604
(212) 490-3000 .. **Gambardella,** Thos M '80 (Wilson EME&D LLP) -150 E 42nd -NY 10017
(212) 490-0705 .. **Gambari,** Omar B '00 Thorgood Law Firm -100 Park Av -NY 10017
(212) 533-6300 .. **Gambella,** Ariana A '07 NYSUT -52 Bway -NY 10004 **Fx:**995-2347
(718) 579-7900 .. **Gambella-Dexter,** Debra A '09 %Leg Aid -900 Sheridan Av -Bronx 10451 **Fx:**293-8744
(516) 739-3916 .. **Gamber,** Mark E '85 -3 Kilburn Rd -Gdn Cty 11530
(718) 739-6400 .. **Gamberg,** Anthony D '91 %DHCR -92-31 Union Hall -Jamaica 11433 **Fx:**262-7938
(516) 355-7901 .. **Gambeski,** George P '83 (Paganini GCC&F) -1979 Marcus Av -Lk Success 11042
(716) 856-4200 .. **Gambino,** Angelo S '08 %Gibson M&C,LLP -69 Delaware Av -Buffalo 14202
(212) 250-7332 .. **Gambino,** Calogero(Charlie) '98 %Deutsche Bank -60 Wall -NY 10005
(716) 856-3646 .. **Gambino,** Jerry A '84 (Cole SHH&G,PC) -37 Franklin -Buffalo 14202
(518) 486-5156 .. **Gambino,** Lawr F '82 %DHCR -38-40 State -Albany 12207 **Fx:**473-8206
(518) 584-1991 .. **Gambino,** Louis Jr. '02 (Cahill/Wink LLP) -60 Railroad Pl -Saratoga Spgs 12866
(516) 229-6000 .. **Gambino,** Peter D '73 %R Lau & Assoc -300 Jericho Quad Bx9040 -Jericho 11753 **Fx:**229-6167
(914) 694-3300 .. **Gambino,** Philip '04 %DiSciullo & Assoc -2975 Wstchstr Av -Purchase 10577 **Fx:**694-2244
(718) 923-4206 .. **Gamble,** Chandar '92 %OTDA Fair Hearings -14 Boerum Pl -Brklyn 11201
(212) 455-2000 .. **Gamble,** James G '95 (Simpson T&B LLP) -425 Lex Av -NY 10017
(914) 995-3460 .. **Gamble,** Nicole Y '96 %DA -111 Martin Luther King Blvd -White Plns 10601 **Fx:**995-3363
(718) 298-0929 .. **Gamble,** Paul M '84 %Criminal Ct -125-01 Qns Blvd -Kew Gdns 11415
(646) 251-7298 .. **Gambol,** Melissa J '07 Downtownbox LLC -216 Grand -Brklyn 11211
(212) 701-3000 .. **Gamboni,** Ciro A '65 (Cahill G&R LLP) -80 Pine -NY 10005 **Fx:**269-5420
(212) 504-6000 .. **Gambro,** Michl S '81 (Cadwalader W&T LLP) -1 World Fncl Ctr -NY 10281
(516) 240-8900 .. **Gamell,** Mark S '80 (Torre LGG&R,LLP) -100 Jericho Quad -Jericho 11753
(212) 755-1254 .. **Gamet-Pol,** Francoise J '93 -340 E 64th -NY 10065 **Fx:**813-1922
(212) 932-1058 .. **Gamils,** Jeffrey H '05 NYC Educ Dept -209 W 125th -NY 10027
(212) 298-5224 .. **Gamliel,** Alyssa L '04 %Leg Aid -49 Thomas -NY 10013 **Fx:**298-5252
(212) 922-1215 .. **Gamliel,** Martin N '73 (MN Gamliel,PC) -300 E 42nd -NY 10017 **Fx:**(914) 793-8983
(718) 667-8686 .. **Gammarano,** Paul J '94 -465 New Dorp Ln -Staten Isl 10306 **Fx:**987-4889
(212) 547-5400 .. **Gammel,** Robt P '06 %McDermott W&E LLP -340 Mad Av -NY 10173
(516) 921-5600 .. **Gammerman,** Danl '81 -6800 Jericho Tpk -Syosset 11791 **Fx:**921-5666
(212) 692-9666 .. **Gammill,** Kenneth M Jr. '96 (Gilbride TL&S LLC) -708 3rd Av -NY 10017
(212) 272-2000 .. **Gammon,** Donald A '05 %JP Morgan Chase -383 Mad Av -NY 10179
(212) 514-5007 .. **Gammons,** Matthew T '03 %Rosenbaum & R,PC -110 Wall -NY 10005 **Fx:**514-9178
(212) 807-8686 .. **Gamper,** Anouk Dutruit '05 %AFS Intercultural Prgms -71 W 23rd -NY 10010
(631) 501-3100 .. **Gamrat,** Christopher G '88 %J Humphreys -3 Huntngtn Quad Bx9028 -Melvll 11747 **Fx:**501-3085
(212) 541-6222 .. **Gamss,** Ari M '04 %Kane K,PC -1350 Av of Amer -NY 10019
(212) 554-7800 .. **Gamza,** Alan E '86 (Moses & S LLP) -405 Lex Av -NY 10174
(516) 796-9777 .. **Gamzo,** Leor E '99 L Gamzo,PC -272 Jericho Tpk -Mineola 11501 **Fx:**796-5222
(212) 308-2210 .. **Ganani,** Rachel J '09 %Eviction Intrvntn Srvcs -1233 2nd Av -NY 10065 **Fx:**888-7140
(212) 819-8200 .. **Ganani,** Tal '09 %White & C LLP -1155 Av of Amer -NY 10036
(212) 986-6000 .. **Ganapathy,** Sandhya '08 %Kleinberg KW&C,PC -551 5th Av -NY 10176
(212) 478-7200 .. **Ganatra,** Avinash Velji '95 (Hahn & H LLP) -488 Mad Av -NY 10022
(212) 683-6699 .. **Ganchrow,** Ari Dov '01 (Raab SG&G,LLP) -317 Mad Av -NY 10017
(212) 310-8000 .. **Ganchrow,** Elliot D '01 %Weil G&M LLP -767 5th Av -NY 10153
(212) 688-8555 .. **Gandarez,** Maria Fernanda '89 %Fragomen DB&L LLP -7 Hanover Sq -NY 10004
(212) 289-0709 .. **Gandel,** Jeffrey B '97 -1623 3rd Av -NY 10128
(212) 819-8200 .. **Gandesha,** Raj S '06 %White & C LLP -1155 Av of Amer -NY 10036
(212) 310-8000 .. **Gandhi,** Ashish D '02 %Weil G&M LLP -767 5th Av -NY 10153
(212) 541-2000 .. **Gandhi,** Gita '03 %Bryan C LLP -1290 Av of Amer -NY 10104
(212) 973-0572 .. **Gandhi,** Rohini C '09 %Wolff & S PC -140 Bway -NY 10005
(212) 839-5300 .. **Gandhi,** Samir A '94 (Sidley A LLP) -787 7th Av -NY 10019
(212) 446-8123 .. **Gandhi,** Sanjay Kumar '01 %McKinsey & Co -55 E 52nd -NY 10055 **Fx:**688-9521
(516) 377-5692 .. **Gandhi,** Smita '84 -92 Main -Freeprt 11520 **Fx:**377-6336
(718) 237-2000 .. **Gandin,** David M '99 %Leg Aid -111 Lvngstn -Brklyn 11201 **Fx:**237-8737
(212) 698-3500 .. **Gandoak,** Parveet Singh '07 %Dechert LLP -1095 Av of Amer -NY 10036
(914) 332-0505 .. **Gandolfo,** Janet A '77 -174 Webber Av -Tarrytwn 10591
(516) 221-0231 .. **Gandolfo,** Thos M '86 -2202 Bellmore Av -Bellmore 11710
(212) 726-1069 .. **Gandy,** Cheryl M '95 -244 5th Av -NY 10001 **Fx:**726-3069
(212) 815-0192 .. **Gandy,** Margaret E '06 %Ofc Special Narcotics -80 Centre -NY 10013
(212) 859-8179 .. **Ganek,** JoAnne D '76 -1 NY Plz 27th Fl -NY 10004 **Fx:**859-4000
(718) 250-2000 .. **Ganeles,** Alan '81 %DA -350 Jay -Brklyn 11201 **Fx:**250-2314

(212) 880-1212 .. **Ganfer,** Jason A '06 %Fidelity Natl Title Ins -711 3rd Av -NY 10017
(212) 922-9250 .. **Ganfer & Shore LLP** -360 Lex Av -NY 10017 **Fx:**922-9335
(212) 922-9250 .. **Ganfer,** Steven R '74 (Ganfer & S LLP) -360 Lex Av -NY 10017
(212) 931-2744 .. **Gang,** Adam S '05 Moet Hennessy Louis Vuitton Inc -19 E 57th -NY 10022
(212) 924-5977 .. **Gang,** Effie S '69 -340 W 28th -NY 10001
(718) 850-1555 .. **Gangadeen,** Michl L '95 Gangadeen & Assoc -12415 101st Av -S Richmond Hll 11419 **Fx:**850-1105
(585) 225-6890 .. **Gangarosa,** Edw C '93 -2250 W Ridge Rd -Rchstr 14626 **Fx:**225-6847
(212) 337-0200 .. **Gangat,** Maherin Y '98 Media Law Resource Ctr -520 8th Av -NY 10018 **Fx:**337-9893
(212) 422-9424 .. **Gangel,** Elaine C '85 %Gogick B&O,LLP -11 Bway -NY 10004
(212) 797-4600 .. **Gangemi,** Jeffrey A '99 (Coritsidis & L,PLLC) -46 Trinity Pl -NY 10006
(718) 234-2244 .. **Gangemi,** John F '64 -1432 86th -Brklyn 11228 **Fx:**234-1938
(212) 425-1401 .. **Gangemi,** Salvatore G '94 OfCnsl O'Hare P LLP -82 Wall -NY 10005 **Fx:**425-1421
(718) 238-8855 .. **Gangemi,** Ursula A '91 (U Gangemi,PLLC) -7820 3rd Av -Brklyn 11209
(646) 205-7880 .. **Gangi,** Ann '89 Cruz & G & Assoc -110 William -NY 10038 **Fx:**(212) 233-9848
(716) 854-1446 .. **Gangi,** Jeffrey D '94 (Losi & G) -170 Franklin -Buffalo 14202
(516) 935-8747 .. **Gangi,** Jos F '98 (Jurissolutions.com) -550 Old Cntry Rd -Hicksvll 11803 **Fx:**935-8748
(212) 725-1633 .. **Gangi,** Russell R E '63 -185 Mad Av -NY 10016 **Fx:**779-7370
(212) 801-9200 .. **Gangitano,** Jos C '10 %Greenberg T,LLP -200 Park Av -NY 10166
(212) 969-2155 .. **Gangolf,** Andrew L '85 %Alliance Bernstein LP -1345 Av of Amer -NY 10105 **Fx:**554-4639
(212) 790-4500 .. **Gangsei,** Paul A '75 (Manatt P&P,LLP) -7 Times Sq -NY 10036
(585) 753-4544 .. **Ganguly,** Avik K '05 %DA -832 Watts Bldg -Rchstr 14614 **Fx:**753-4557
(212) 566-1000 .. **Ganguly,** Tara B '07 %Sullivan & B LLP -115 Bway -NY 10006 **Fx:**566-1068
(516) 735-6552 .. **Ganiaris,** Thos N '85 -900 Mayer Dr -Wantagh 11793
(212) 557-1144 .. **Ganiaris Detroyer,** Chryssanthe '96 Wachovia Securities -280 Park Av -NY 10017
(212) 841-7500 .. **Ganiere,** Cynthia R '09 %Cushman & Wakefield -1290 Av of Amer -NY 10104
(516) 248-1700 .. **Ganio,** Janet '85 Cnsl Forchelli CDSM&T,LLP -333 Earle Ovngton Blvd -Uniondale 11553
(212) 969-3000 .. **Ganitsky,** Danl I '01 SrCnsl Proskauer R LLP -1585 Bway -NY 10036
(212) 355-0755 .. **Ganjaei,** Ali '87 %HBI Inc -535 Mad Av -NY 10022
(518) 437-9000 .. **Ganje,** David L '90 -Two Twr Pl -Albany 12203 **Fx:**437-9115
(585) 344-2550 .. **Gann,** David E '76 %DA -1 W Main -Batavia 14020 **Fx:**344-8544
(516) 294-0300 .. **Gann,** Marc '85 (Collins M&G) -138 Mineola Blvd -Mineola 11501
(212) 779-1980 .. **Gannes,** Margo L '06 (Gannes & M,LLP) -325 Bway -NY 10007 **Fx:**779-1981
(212) 701-3000 .. **Gannett,** Wm B '86 (Cahill G&R LLP) -80 Pine -NY 10005 **Fx:**269-5420
(212) 651-7500 .. **Gannon,** Christian H '90 (Segal MS&M) -850 3rd Av -NY 10022
(212) 262-2390 .. **Gannon,** Christine I '04 %Connell F LLP -888 7th Av -NY 10106
(212) 629-8585 .. **Gannon,** David A '93 (Ellenberg & Prtnrs LLP) -575 8th Av -NY 10018
(518) 486-6304 .. **Gannon,** Frank M '86 %DHCR -38-40 State -Albany 12207 **Fx:**473-8206
(716) 856-4091 .. **Gannon Gannon & Sullivan,LLP** -618 Brisbane Bldg -Buffalo 14203 **Fx:**856-0621
(716) 856-4091 .. **Gannon,** Gordon Jr. '62 (Gannon G&S,LLP) -618 Brisbane Bldg -Buffalo 14203
(212) 906-9470 .. **Gannon,** James P '00 %Koeppel Tener -575 Lex Av -NY 10022
(716) 693-9600 .. **Gannon,** Jos T '96 %McKenna B&L -126 Broad -Tonawanda 14150 **Fx:**693-0024
(212) 819-8200 .. **Gannon,** Lawr J '73 (White & C LLP) -1155 Av of Amer -NY 10036
(914) 965-1011 .. **Gannon,** Marie J '09 %JG Dibbini -570 Ynkrs Av -Ynkrs 10704 **Fx:**965-0019
(212) 526-2718 .. **Gannon,** Pamela N '89 Barclays Capital Inc -1271 Av of Amer -NY 10020
(212) 655-5000 .. **Gannon,** Peter J '93 (Gannon R&M) -120 Bway -NY 10271
(716) 693-9600 .. **Gannon,** Robt F '97 %McKenna B&L -126 Broad -Tonawanda 14150 **Fx:**693-0024
(716) 835-5305 .. **Gannon,** Robt I '74 -61 Delaney Av -Buffalo 14216
(212) 655-5000 .. **Gannon Rosenfarb & Moskowitz** -120 Bway -NY 10271 **Fx:**655-5039
(212) 742-9700 .. **Gannon,** Thos M '93 %Godosky & G,PC -61 Bway -NY 10006
(212) 652-3779 .. **Gannon,** Thos P Jr. '83 (Schlesinger G&L LLP) -535 Mad Av -NY 10022
(212) 599-5799 .. **Gannon,** Veronica '00 %Rutherford & C LLP -369 Lex Av -NY 10017
(315) 428-1380 .. **Ganotis,** James G '78 %Fager & A,LLP -2 Clinton Sq -Syracuse 13202
(315) 449-2616 .. **Ganotis,** John '66 Martin GBM&C,PC -5790 Widewaters Pkwy -DeWitt 13214
(917) 750-2932 .. **Gans,** Jeremy A '00 JDJ Cptl Prtnrs -575 Mad Av -NY 10022
(212) 335-4500 .. **Gans,** Kiera S '02 %DLA Piper LLP -1251 Av of Amer -NY 10020
(212) 249-3776 .. **Gans,** Michl J '90 -860 5th Av -NY 10065 **Fx:**861-6320
(516) 747-8877 .. **Gans,** Mitchell M '75 OfCnsl Spizz & C,LLP -114 Old Cntry Rd -Mineola 11501
(516) 463-5858 .. **Gans,** Mitchell M '75 %Hofstra Law Schl -121 Hofstra Univ -Hempstd 11549
(212) 340-3043 .. **Gans,** Richd L '88 %Metro-North -347 Mad Av -NY 10017 **Fx:**697-9079
(212) 928-8768 .. **Gans,** Susan L '82 -Bx314 -NY 10040
(212) 319-7010 .. **Gans,** Walter G '61 -425 Park Av -NY 10022
(518) 427-2650 .. **Gansberg,** Andrew '72 (Nixon P LLP) -677 Bway -Albany 12207
(718) 447-3700 .. **Gansberg,** Eric M '84 -36 Richmond Ter -Staten Isl 10301 **Fx:**447-4328
(212) 366-1093 .. **Gansell,** Ralph E '76 -27 Union Sq W -NY 10003
(516) 802-0501 .. **Gansl,** Evan C '89 E Gansl,PLLC -6800 Jericho Tpk -Syosset 11791 **Fx:**558-1117
(212) 819-8200 .. **Gant,** Bryan D '05 %White & C LLP -1155 Av of Amer -NY 10036
(212) 358-1500 .. **Gant,** Christopher G '06 %Kennedy J&M,PC -113 Univ Pl -NY 10003
(516) 897-6145 .. **Gant,** Robin R '94 -536 W Penn -Long Bch 11561
(212) 834-5748 .. **Ganti,** Rishi '01 %JP Morgan Chase & Co -270 Park Av -NY 10017
(212) 577-3688 .. **Gantt,** Adrienne M '85 %Leg Aid -199 Water -NY 10038 **Fx:**509-8431
(845) 639-3470 .. **Gantt,** Larry '96 -151 S Main -New Cty 10956
(212) 788-0908 .. **Gantz,** Toni L '07 %Law Dept -100 Church -NY 10007 **Fx:**788-0367
(718) 261-3000 .. **Ganun,** Francis '63 -118-21 Qns Blvd -Frst Hlls 11375
(212) 382-3300 .. **Gany,** Alicia M '78 (Wollmuth M&D LLP) -500 5th Av -NY 10110
(212) 517-5500 .. **Ganz,** David L '77 (Ganz & H,PC) -1394 3rd Av -NY 10075
(212) 880-3003 .. **Ganz,** Elliot '81 Loan Syndctn & Trading Assn -366 Mad Av -NY 10017
(212) 517-5500 .. **Ganz & Hollinger,PC** -1394 3rd Av -NY 10075 **Fx:**772-2720
(212) 969-3000 .. **Ganz,** Howard L '66 (Proskauer R LLP) -1585 Bway -NY 10036
(212) 309-8100 .. **Ganz,** Jacqueline D '06 %Lexis/Nexis -125 Park Av -NY 10017 **Fx:**309-8187
(516) 393-8400 .. **Ganz,** Jennifer H '00 Skyline Mgmt Corp -600 Old Cntry Rd -Gdn Cty 11530
(212) 389-1561 .. **Ganz,** Jodi B '99 (GCP Capital Prtnrs) -300 Park Av -NY 10022 **Fx:**389-1761
(516) 822-4400 .. **Ganz,** Michl D '98 %Tunstead & S -500 N Bway -Jericho 11753
(212) 938-5000 .. **Ganz,** Nicholas T '90 Cantor Fitzgerald -110 E 59th -NY 10022
(518) 869-9500 .. **Ganz,** Robt E '76 (Ganz W&S,LLP) -1 Columbia Cir -Albany 12203
(518) 869-9500 .. **Ganz Wolkenbreit & Siegfeld,LLP** -1 Columbia Cir -Albany 12203 **Fx:**869-9556
(212) 984-1070 .. **Ganz Wolkenbreit & Siegfeld,LLP** -230 Park Av -NY 10169 **Fx:**984-1071
(212) 596-9000 .. **Gao,** Ethan '07 %Ropes & G LLP -1211 Av of Amer -NY 10036
(212) 687-2770 .. **Gao,** Hua Helene '04 %Cohen PL&P -551 5th Av -NY 10176
(212) 325-7102 .. **Gao,** J Kevin '99 Credit Suisse Asset Mgmt -11 Mad Av -NY 10010
(212) 848-4000 .. **Gao,** Jason S '09 %Shearman & S LLP -599 Lex Av -NY 10022
(212) 250-5763 .. **Gao,** Nicholas N '02 %Deutsche Bank -60 Wall -NY 10005
(212) 558-4000 .. **Gao,** Qian Allison '07 %Sullivan & C LLP -125 Broad -NY 10004
(212) 735-3000 .. **Gao,** Shan '05 %Skadden ASM&F LLP -4 Times Sq -NY 10036
(212) 526-7000 .. **Gao,** Weining '09 Barclays Capital -745 7th Av -NY 10019
(607) 821-1913 .. **Gao,** Xibai '03 -4208 Woods Rd -Vestal 13850 **Fx:**(866) 513-7035
(212) 878-8000 .. **Gao,** Yile '05 %Clifford C LLP -31 W 52nd -NY 10019
(631) 608-1100 .. **Gapinski,** Laurie M '03 %Charron & Assoc -534 Broadhllw Rd -Melvll 11747 **Fx:**608-1114
(631) 712-5650 .. **Gapinski,** Michele '82 US Dist Ct EDNY -934 Fed Plz -Central Islip 11722
(315) 671-1050 .. **Garabedian,** Lisa '90 %Hon J Fahey -401 Mntgmry -Syracuse 13202
(631) 297-8360 .. **Garabedian,** Michl '86 (Rayano & G,PC) -267 Carleton Av -Central Islip 11722
(631) 957-2000 .. **Garabrant,** Mark R '84 (Donohue K&G) -36 E Montauk Hwy -Lindenhrst 11757
(212) 354-6800 .. **Garafola,** George J '76 (Silbowitz GSS&F,LLP) -25 W 43rd -NY 10036
(914) 946-7796 .. **Garafola,** Jos S '89 -399 Knollwood Rd -White Plns 10603 **Fx:**682-2966
(212) 460-2985 .. **Garam,** Peter P '70 Con Ed -4 Irving Pl -NY 10003
(212) 637-3238 .. **Garamone,** Matthew D '99 %US EPA -290 Bway -NY 10007 **Fx:**637-3202
(631) 928-5500 .. **Garant,** Margot J '01 MJ Garant,Inc -220 E Main -Pt Jffrsn 11777 **Fx:**928-7640
(716) 842-6200 .. **Garas,** John C '86 -465 Main -Buffalo 14203
(516) 742-8058 .. **Garavito,** Tulia '93 %Abamont & Assoc -200 Grdn City Plz Bx9250 -Gdn Cty 11530 **Fx:**742-7308
(516) 741-6565 .. **Garay,** Erica B '79 (Meyer SE&K,PC) -990 Stewart Av Bx9194 -Gdn Cty 11530
(212) 225-2000 .. **Garay,** Francisco J '10 %Cleary GS&H -1 Lbrty Plz -NY 10006
(212) 735-3000 .. **Garb,** Sharon '95 %Skadden ASM&F LLP -4 Times Sq -NY 10036
(212) 574-1200 .. **Garbaccio,** Justin M '01 %Seward & K LLP -1 Bttry Pk Plz -NY 10004
(718) 739-6400 .. **Garbanzos,** Francis '86 %DHCR -92-31 Union Hall -Jamaica 11433 **Fx:**262-4749
(516) 822-1749 .. **Garbanzos,** Francis '86 St Joseph -Bx575 -Hicksvll 11802 **Fx:**(718) 262-4749
(516) 826-0400 .. **Garbar,** Harvey O '66 (Goldstein & G PC) -1800 Bellmore Av -Bellmore 11710
(212) 689-1113 .. **Garbarini & Scher,PC** -432 Park Av S -NY 10016 **Fx:**725-9630
(516) 571-3800 .. **Garbarino,** Andrew T '03 %DA -262 Old Cntry Rd -Mineola 11501 **Fx:**248-9479
(212) 484-8000 .. **Garbarino,** Erin K '98 Time Warner -1 Time Warner Ctr -NY 10019
(631) 563-4411 .. **Garbarino,** Wm R '72 -40 Main Bx717 -Sayvll 11782 **Fx:**563-4435
(212) 840-0097 .. **Garbell,** Jason I '00 Novozymes NA,Inc -500 5th Av -NY 10110
(212) 267-6130 .. **Garber,** Calvin D '73 (Garber & G) -225 Bway -NY 10007 **Fx:**385-2689
(315) 361-8687 .. **Garber,** David M '71 Oneida Indian Nation Enterprises -5218 Patrick Rd -Verona 13478 **Fx:**361-8009
(718) 250-2000 .. **Garber,** Diana E '09 %DA -350 Jay -Brklyn 11201 **Fx:**250-2314
(212) 267-6130 .. **Garber,** Fern S '79 (Garber & G) -225 Bway -NY 10007 **Fx:**385-2689
(212) 965-9370 .. **Garber,** Glenn A '90 (G Garber,PC) -350 Bway -NY 10013 **Fx:**965-9375
(212) 779-2740 .. **Garber,** Greg '04 -60 Mad Av -NY 10010
(516) 248-1122 .. **Garber,** Jeffrey B '70 -990 Stewart Av -Gdn Cty 11530 **Fx:**248-1183
(212) 401-0800 .. **Garber,** Jeremy S '86 %Disciplinary Comm -61 Bway -NY 10006 **Fx:**287-1045
(516) 227-7770 .. **Garber,** Karen R '04 Dept Soc Srvcs -60 Chas Lindbergh Blvd -Uniondale 11553
(718) 238-3693 .. **Garber,** Michl D '87 -9201 4th Av -Brklyn 11209 **Fx:**921-4526
(212) 918-3000 .. **Garber,** Michl I '10 %Hogan L LLP -875 3rd Av -NY 10022
(212) 964-8038 .. **Garber,** Mitchell S '81 -111 John -NY 10038
(516) 560-6400 .. **Garber,** Nancy E '80 %Leg Aid -1 Helen Keller Way -Hempstd 11550 **Fx:**565-3694
(212) 506-1700 .. **Garber,** Rachel L '05 %Kasowitz BT&F LLP -1633 Bway -NY 10019
(516) 222-2255 .. **Garber,** Stephan '75 -600 Old Cntry Rd -Gdn Cty 11530 **Fx:**393-9769

(914) 997-0500 .. **Garber,** Todd S '03 %Lowey DC&H,PC -1 N Bway -White Plns 10601
(845) 634-5124 .. **Garbett,** Yvonne F '02 Amer Combustible Corp -192 Strawtown Rd -New Cty 10956
(718) 643-5195 .. **Garbow,** Mitchell J '93 %Hon F Rivera -360 Adams -Brklyn 11201
(212) 278-1169 .. **Garbowski,** Mark E '88 (Anderson K&O,PC) -1251 Av of Amer -NY 10020
(631) 393-9400 .. **Garbus,** Glenn S '97 (Forster & G) -500 Bi-Cnty Blvd Bx9030 -Farmngdl 11735
(516) 741-6565 .. **Garbus,** James D '89 (Meyer SE&K,PC) -990 Stewart Av Bx9194 -Gdn Cty 11530
(516) 390-9595 .. **Garbus,** Leland N '82 %Maimone & Assoc,PLLC -170 Old Cntry Rd -Mineola 11501 **Fx:**877-0321
(631) 393-9400 .. **Garbus,** Mark A '68 (Forster & G) -500 Bi-Cnty Blvd Bx9030 -Farmngdl 11735
(212) 779-9910 .. **Garbus,** Martin '60 (Eaton & V LLP) -3 Park Av -NY 10016
(212) 309-6000 .. **Garbutt,** Bernard J III '91 (Morgan L&B LLP) -101 Park Av -NY 10178
(212) 867-9140 .. **Garbuz,** Lawr I '96 (Lewis & G,PC) -60 E 42nd -NY 10165 **Fx:**867-9143
(212) 756-2000 .. **Garces,** John C '95 SpclCnsl Schulte R&Z LLP -919 3rd Av -NY 10022
(212) 487-4444 .. **Garcia,** Alina A '03 %Dept Cnsmr Affrs -42 Bway -NY 10004 **Fx:**487-4197
(212) 261-7000 .. **Garcia,** Allan L '96 %Calyon -1301 Av of Amer -NY 10019
(212) 551-4000 .. **Garcia,** Anamaria '87 %Sanofi-Synthelabo -90 Park Av -NY 10016 **Fx:**551-4919
(914) 428-9200 .. **Garcia,** Anieska J '00 %M Cooper,PC -245 Main -White Plns 10601 **Fx:**428-4126
(516) 997-7330 .. **Garcia,** Anne Marie LaDia M '02 %Baxter S&S,PC -99 N Bway -Hicksvll 11801
(718) 991-4758 .. **Garcia,** Belkys '07 Leg Aid -953 Southrn Blvd -Bronx 10459
(631) 436-5589 .. **Garcia,** Carlos G '76 -66 2nd Av -Brentwd 11717 **Fx:**436-5643
(516) 933-0325 .. **Garcia,** Christopher J '99 XO Communications,Inc -176 Cntrl Pk Rd -Plainvw 11803
(212) 637-1022 .. **Garcia,** Christopher L '01 %US Atty -1 St Andrews Plz -NY 10007
(718) 585-6551 .. **Garcia,** Claire M '95 Pena & K,PLLC -1200 Waters Pl -Bronx 10461 **Fx:**585-6618
(718) 590-2000 .. **Garcia,** Cory M '03 %DA -198 E 161st -Bronx 10451 **Fx:**590-6477
(212) 225-2000 .. **Garcia,** Dalmau '02 %Cleary GS&H -1 Lbrty Plz -NY 10006
(914) 788-4126 .. **Garcia,** David A '00 D Garcia,PLLC -2117 Crompond Rd -Cortlandt Manor 10567 **Fx:**788-5741
(212) 684-3933 .. **Garcia,** Diana Y '03 %Hantman & Assoc -1515 Bway -NY 10036 **Fx:**520-4301
(646) 386-3726 .. **Garcia,** Eider G '97 Hon K Payne - Supreme Ct -80 Centre -NY 10013
(917) 335-4803 .. **Garcia,** Elizabeth M '88 -Bx684 -Bronx 10461 **Fx:**(718) 822-4224
(212) 564-9800 .. **Garcia,** Eric R '08 D'Agostino L&L,LLP -345 7th Av -NY 10001
(212) 969-3000 .. **Garcia,** Fredelina E '08 %Proskauer R LLP -1585 Bway -NY 10036
(212) 335-9000 .. **Garcia,** Gloria '07 DA -1 Hogan Pl -NY 10013
(212) 224-7158 .. **Garcia,** Iciar P '06 Forest Laboratories -909 3rd Av -NY 10022
(646) 239-4330 .. **Garcia,** Izabel Olszowa '90 -26 Court -Brklyn 11242
(917) 698-6928 .. **Garcia,** James S '95 -51 E 90th -NY 10128
(646) 386-4520 .. **Garcia,** Jeffrey '96 %Criminal Ct -100 Centre -NY 10013
(718) 268-8111 .. **Garcia,** Jennifer '07 %D Mastrodomenico -107-19 71st Av -Frst Hlls 11375 **Fx:**268-7382
(631) 249-6644 .. **Garcia,** Jos F '61 (Garcia & S) -2076 Deer Prk Av -Deer Pk 11729
(631) 249-6644 .. **Garcia,** Jos T '00 (Garcia & S) -2076 Deer Prk Av -Deer Pk 11729
(212) 622-5532 .. **Garcia,** Juan A '01 JP Morgan -277 Park Av -NY 10172
(212) 836-8000 .. **Garcia,** Juan C '09 %Kaye S LLP -425 Park Av -NY 10022
(631) 864-2443 .. **Garcia,** Judith C '96 -732 Smithtwn Bypass -Smithtwn 11787 **Fx:**864-2993
(518) 962-2200 .. **Garcia,** Julie A '00 -Bx352 -Westport 12993
(718) 993-2100 .. **Garcia,** Justino '89 -384 E 149th -Bronx 10455 **Fx:**665-5066
(212) 557-0055 .. **Garcia,** Justino '89 (J Garcia & Assoc,PC) -60 E 42nd -NY 10165 **Fx:**557-9119
(212) 916-3477 .. **Garcia,** Kelly E '96 %Lexis/Nexis -125 Park Av -NY 10017 **Fx:**309-8187
(917) 778-6500 .. **Garcia,** Lesly A '09 K Dodson -485 Lex Av -NY 10017
(718) 579-4487 .. **Garcia,** Manuel '09 NY Yankees -1 E 161st -Bronx 10451
(914) 231-2422 .. **Garcia,** Margarita J '93 Family Ct -53 S Bway -Ynkrs 10701
(212) 227-3636 .. **Garcia,** Mariana '99 %Spar & B,PC -225 Bway -NY 10007
(212) 940-3094 .. **Garcia,** Michl '09 %Nixon P LLP -437 Mad Av -NY 10022
(212) 446-4800 .. **Garcia,** Michl J '90 (Kirkland & E LLP) -153 E 53rd -NY 10022
(212) 841-1000 .. **Garcia,** Michelle '08 %Covington & B LLP -620 8th Av -NY 10018
(212) 274-6694 .. **Garcia,** Myra J '89 ACS-Legal Dept -220 Church -NY 10013
(212) 238-4800 .. **Garcia,** Natalie '02 (Landman CB&F,PC) -120 Bway -NY 10271
(631) 689-5577 .. **Garcia,** Peter R '97 P Garcia,PC -38 Cedar -Stony Brk 11790 **Fx:**689-5588
(212) 274-7500 .. **Garcia,** Ramon P '92 %Roadrunner Records -902 Bway -NY 10010 **Fx:**505-7469
(212) 571-7100 .. **Garcia,** Raul '00 %O'Dwyer & B,LLP -52 Duane -NY 10007
(212) 918-3000 .. **Garcia,** Renee M '09 %Hogan L LLP -875 3rd Av -NY 10022
(212) 696-6000 .. **Garcia,** Robt B '02 %Curtis M-PC&M LLP -101 Park Av -NY 10178
(631) 667-3757 .. **Garcia,** Robt M '93 -320 Carleton Av -Central Islip 11722
(212) 696-6000 .. **Garcia,** Roberto Alejandro '01 %Curtis M-PC&M LLP -101 Park Av -NY 10178
(631) 249-6644 .. **Garcia & Stallone** -2076 Deer Prk Av -Deer Pk 11729 **Fx:**249-6686
(212) 632-3020 .. **Garcia,** Susan Ann '75 Fiduciary Trust Co Intl -600 5th Av -NY 10020 **Fx:**632-3002
(212) 664-4444 .. **Garcia,** Susan Mary '99 %NBC -30 Rckfllr Plz -NY 10112
(914) 428-1100 .. **Garcia,** Suzanne M '00 Cnsl Westcor Land Title Ins Co -701 Wstchstr Av -White Plns 10604 **Fx:**428-1110
(716) 485-6521 .. **Garcia,** Vivian '84 -38 Pettit Pl -Cassadaga 14718 **Fx:**673-3397
(212) 942-1166 .. **Garcia,** Wm A '95 Garcia & K,PC -710 W 190th -NY 10040 **Fx:**942-4949
(212) 649-5600 .. **Garcia,** Yvette M '96 %Rockefeller & Co,Inc -30 Rckfllr Plz -NY 10112 **Fx:**649-5977
(212) 569-0290 .. **Garcia-Badillo,** Rosa M '89 Amistad Schl -4862 Bway -NY 10034
(212) 450-4000 .. **Garciadiaz,** Manuel '98 (Davis P&W LLP) -450 Lex Av -NY 10017
(845) 634-3627 .. **Garcia McSweeney,** Angela '02 Leg Aid -2 Congers Rd -New Cty 10956 **Fx:**634-8505
(718) 274-6900 .. **Garcia-Miret,** Norma T '96 OfCnsl G Miret -31-17 Ditmars Blvd -Astoria 11105 **Fx:**274-7500
(212) 676-1309 .. **Garcia-Tuduri,** Jorge A '81 %Law Dept -100 Church -NY 10007 **Fx:**788-0367
(212) 852-3156 .. **Garcia-Tufro,** Valeria A '04 US Trust -114 W 47th -NY 10036
(716) 867-7543 .. **Gard,** Danl C '05 -93 E 4th -Dunkirk 14048
(914) 472-7700 .. **Gardella,** Richd M '73 OfCnsl Bertine HHZD&D,LLP -700 Wht Plns Rd -Scarsdale 10583
(631) 761-0800 .. **Gardella,** Todd M '07 %Lazer AR&Y,PC -225 Old Cntry Rd -Melvll 11747
(212) 578-2211 .. **Gardella,** Wm P '80 %MetLife -27-01 Qns Plz N -LIC 11101
(718) 451-5768 .. **Gardener,** Yvonne E '97 (Y Gardener,PC) -261 E 57th -Brklyn 11203 **Fx:**451-5769
(212) 969-3000 .. **Gardephe,** Christopher H '00 Proskauer R LLP -1585 Bway -NY 10036
(212) 326-3939 .. **Gardere,** M R Annabelle '10 %Jones D -222 E 41st -NY 10017
(212) 450-2000 .. **Gardi,** T David '97 %NFL -280 Park Av -NY 10017 **Fx:**681-7599
(212) 728-8000 .. **Gardiner,** Aimee N '97 %Willkie F&G LLP -787 7th Av -NY 10019
(212) 587-2020 .. **Gardiner,** Barry L '67 -292 Mad Av -NY 10017
(212) 450-2000 .. **Gardiner,** Brook F '04 NFL -280 Park Av -NY 10017 **Fx:**681-7599
(518) 266-3036 .. **Gardiner,** Donna M '91 %Tax Appls Tribunal -500 Fed -Troy 12180 **Fx:**271-0886
(212) 735-2442 .. **Gardiner,** John '88 (Skadden ASM&F LLP) -4 Times Sq -NY 10036
(212) 721-5355 .. **Gardiner,** Kay '85 -115 Cntrl Pk W -NY 10023
(212) 756-2000 .. **Gardiner,** Marguerite '08 %Schulte R&Z LLP -919 3rd Av -NY 10022
(914) 995-3652 .. **Gardiner,** Thos G '88 %Cnty Atty -148 Martine Av -White Plns 10601 **Fx:**995-5858
(718) 858-7440 .. **Gardiner,** Wm A '73 (Gardiner & N) -142 Joralemon -Brklyn 11201 **Fx:**624-2455
(212) 807-0909 .. **Gardini,** Marisa '94 -59 W 12th -NY 10011
(212) 836-8000 .. **Gardner,** Aaron R '06 %Kaye S LLP -425 Park Av -NY 10022
(212) 227-1700 .. **Gardner,** Alan J '66 -225 Bway -NY 10007 **Fx:**766-2628
(212) 965-9112 .. **Gardner,** Alan M '87 -350 Bway -NY 10013 **Fx:**965-9375
(212) 406-9710 .. **Gardner,** Alana N '06 %Kral CRRP&G,LLP -170 Bway -NY 10038
(212) 696-4848 .. **Gardner,** Alexander H '93 Mintz & G LLP -470 Park Av S -NY 10016
(646) 386-3751 .. **Gardner,** Ann '79 Hon J Stackhouse -80 Centre -NY 10013
(716) 845-6000 .. **Gardner,** Arnold B '54 (Kavinoky C LLP) -726 Exchange -Buffalo 14210
(212) 672-2232 .. **Gardner,** Brandon W '03 Serengeti Asset Mgt -632 Bway -NY 10012
(212) 687-5900 .. **Gardner,** Brian L '91 (Sullivan & G,LLP) -475 Park Av S -NY 10016 **Fx:**687-4060
(212) 530-5000 .. **Gardner,** Bruce T '78 OfCnsl Milbank TH&M LLP -1 Chase Manh Plz -NY 10005
(516) 867-7237 .. **Gardner,** Carol Ann '81 -2837 Whaleneck Dr -Merrick 11566
(212) 312-3000 .. **Gardner,** Carolanne '89 %FGIC -125 Park Av -NY 10017 **Fx:**312-3221
(212) 997-2002 .. **Gardner,** Cecilia L '78 %Jewelers Vigilance Comm -25 W 45th -NY 10036 **Fx:**997-9148
(315) 287-4955 .. **Gardner,** Chas A '77 -123 E Main Bx369 -Gouverneur 13642 **Fx:**287-1790
(518) 388-4276 .. **Gardner,** Christopher H '82 Cnty Atty -620 State -Schnctdy 12305 **Fx:**388-4493
(212) 425-7200 .. **Gardner,** Elizabeth A '92 (Kenyon & K,LLP) -1 Bway -NY 10004
(212) 250-0017 .. **Gardner,** Ellen S '01 %Deutsche Bk -60 Wall -NY 10005
(212) 490-3000 .. **Gardner,** Gary A '95 (Wilson EME&D LLP) -150 E 42nd -NY 10017
(212) 852-1000 .. **Gardner,** Grant S '89 %US Trust Co,NA -114 W 47th -NY 10036 **Fx:**852-1310
(212) 277-6500 .. **Gardner,** Hillary R '10 %Dickstein S LLP -1633 Bway -NY 10019
(212) 308-7697 .. **Gardner,** Howard A '88 OfCnsl Butterman & K,LLP -425 Park Av -NY 10022
(716) 645-3607 .. **Gardner,** James '85 SUNY Buffalo -514 O'Brian Hall, N Campus -Buffalo 14260 **Fx:**645-2064
(716) 858-2424 .. **Gardner,** James R '10 %DA -25 Delaware Av -Buffalo 14202 **Fx:**858-7425
(212) 563-1710 .. **Gardner,** Jean M '86 (Schindel FLG&R LLP) -14 Penn Plz -NY 10122 **Fx:**695-6602
(845) 371-1299 .. **Gardner,** John '59 -395 Avalon Grdns Dr -Nanuet 10954
(914) 967-2200 .. **Gardner,** John P '87 Lambden & G -16 Elm Pl -Rye 10580 **Fx:**967-2325
(212) 907-0839 .. **Gardner,** Jonathan '91 (Labaton S LLP) -140 Bway -NY 10005
(716) 845-6000 .. **Gardner,** Jonathan H '93 (Kavinoky C LLP) -726 Exchange -Buffalo 14210
(518) 346-8090 .. **Gardner,** Jos D '90 -1528 Union -Schnctdy 12309 **Fx:**346-8103
(212) 907-0600 .. **Gardner,** Kenneth H '82 (Gardner W&R LLP) -270 Mad Av -NY 10016
(518) 734-4344 .. **Gardner,** Larry F '79 -5364 Main Bx279 -Windham 12496 **Fx:**734-5162
(212) 270-5872 .. **Gardner,** Leslie K '84 JP Morgan Chase & Co -270 Park Av -NY 10017
(212) 343-0800 .. **Gardner,** Luke G '99 Cnsl Interieurs -228 E 58th -NY 10013
(914) 749-8516 .. **Gardner,** Mark '86 USI Holdings Corp -555 Plsntvll Rd -Briarclff Mnr 10510 **Fx:**747-6399
(212) 238-9366 .. **Gardner,** Molly E '03 Platinum Admin Srvcs Inc -2 World Fncl Ctr -NY 10281
(646) 223-4200 .. **Gardner,** Nancy '84 %Reuters -3 Times Sq -NY 10036 **Fx:**223-4250
(718) 596-2600 .. **Gardner,** Naomi C '87 (N Gardner,PC) -142 Joralemon -Brklyn 11201 **Fx:**596-0619
(315) 331-6621 .. **Gardner,** Pamela J '81 -330 East Av -Newark 14513 **Fx:**331-6802
(212) 309-6000 .. **Gardner,** Richd N '52 SrCnsl Morgan L&B LLP -101 Park Av -NY 10178
(315) 379-2115 .. **Gardner,** Richd R '75 Pub Def -Cnty Cthse -Canton 13617 **Fx:**386-8241
(718) 410-0333 .. **Gardner,** Robt I '76 -903-F Sheridan Av -Bronx 10451 **Fx:**(347) 577-6628
(212) 636-7231 .. **Gardner,** Romaine L '80 Fordham Law Schl -33 W 60th -NY 10023

(212) 850-7519 .. **Gardner,** Sonia E '87 %Ave Cptl Grp -535 Mad Av -NY 10022 **Fx:**850-7598
(212) 479-6000 .. **Gardner,** Stephen D '67 (Cooley LLP) -1114 Av of Amer -NY 10036
(212) 294-6700 .. **Gardner,** Stephen M '10 %Winston & S -200 Park Av -NY 10166
(716) 845-6000 .. **Gardner,** Sue S '77 (Kavinoky C LLP) -726 Exchange -Buffalo 14210
(212) 294-6700 .. **Gardner,** Thos B '10 %Winston & S -200 Park Av -NY 10166
(212) 735-3000 .. **Gardner,** Tracy C '09 %Skadden ASM&F LLP -4 Times Sq -NY 10036
(315) 536-2851 .. **Gardner,** Valerie G '95 -215 Main -Penn Yan 14527 **Fx:**536-2837
(212) 907-0600 .. **Gardner Weiss & Rosenblum LLP** -270 Mad Av -NY 10016 **Fx:**907-0610
(212) 244-4187 .. **Gardner,** Wm D '78 -350 5th Av -NY 10118
(716) 881-0681 .. **Gardner,** Wm H '59 -1141 Delaware Av -Buffalo 14209
(516) 249-1342 .. **Gardos,** Alissa Paige '97 %Grey & G,LLP -360 Main -Farmngdl 11735
(631) 439-2450 .. **Gardos,** Howard A '97 %Leg Aid -320 Carleton Av -Central Islip 11722 **Fx:**439-2453
(718) 279-7555 .. **Gardy,** Craig I '95 %B Montague & Prtnrs -212-45 26th Av -Bayside 11360 **Fx:**279-8154
(518) 455-5462 .. **Gareeb,** Nadia K '01 NYS Assembly -831 LOB -Albany 12248
(212) 222-9271 .. **Gareen,** Paul Shelomo '44 -245 W 104th -NY 10025
(212) 416-6118 .. **Garelick,** Jason P '01 %Dept of Law -120 Bway -NY 10271
(212) 218-2100 .. **Garelick,** Joanna L '04 %Fitzpatrick CH&S -1290 Av of Amer -NY 10104
(212) 577-3688 .. **Garelick,** Jonathan '90 %Leg Aid -199 Water -NY 10038 **Fx:**509-8431
(516) 944-4736 .. **Garelick,** Kimberly B '09 Publishers Clearing House -382 Channel Dr -Pt Wash 11050
(212) 319-5240 .. **Garelick,** Richd L '87 (Flicker G & Assoc,LLP) -45 Bway -NY 10006
(212) 315-8257 .. **Garelick,** Shari K '98 Kenneth Cole Prdctns -603 W 50th -NY 10019
(212) 557-2900 .. **Garelik,** David M '62 (Schwartzman GW&T,PC) -355 Lex Av -NY 10017
(631) 673-6670 .. **Garelle,** Marie E '02 %Speyer & P,LLP -115 Broadhllw Rd -Melvll 11747
(212) 922-9700 .. **Garelli,** Theresa A '98 %1st Amer Title -633 3rd Av -NY 10017 **Fx:**922-0881
(212) 258-4000 .. **Garfein,** Mary C '89 %Siemens Corp -153 E 53rd -NY 10022 **Fx:**767-0580
(914) 253-2000 .. **Garfield,** H Douglas '87 %Pepsico -700 Andrsn Hill Rd -Purchase 10577
(212) 801-2241 .. **Garfield,** Heidi S '05 %Greenberg T,LLP -200 Park Av -NY 10166
(718) 634-9800 .. **Garfield,** Jack C '52 -169 Beach 133rd -Rckwy Pk 11694 **Fx:**634-3700
(212) 592-1400 .. **Garfield,** Jacquelyne D '10 %Herrick,F LLP -2 Park Av -NY 10016
(914) 422-4308 .. **Garfield,** Leslie Y '86 %Pace Law Schl -78 N Bway -White Plns 10603 **Fx:**422-4039
(212) 227-8865 .. **Garfield,** Martin R '65 (Breadbar G&S) -11 Park Pl -NY 10007
(212) 756-2000 .. **Garfield,** Max '05 %Schulte R&Z LLP -919 3rd Av -NY 10022
(212) 478-0768 .. **Garfield,** Robinne A '01 DE Shaw & Co -120 W 45th -NY 10036
(212) 953-2381 .. **Garfield,** Wendy A '03 %Rubin F&F,LLP -292 Mad Av -NY 10017
(212) 735-2500 .. **Garfinkel,** Barry H '55 OfCnsl Skadden ASM&F LLP -4 Times Sq -NY 10036 **Fx:**(917) 777-2500
(718) 250-1100 .. **Garfinkel,** Edw A '82 -12 Metrotech Ctr -Brklyn 11201 **Fx:**250-1168
(212) 323-2298 .. **Garfinkel,** Frances L '92 %HHC-OLA-Medical Litigation -346 Bway -NY 10013 **Fx:**323-2251
(914) 779-2211 .. **Garfinkel,** Howard I '83 (Lauterbach GD&H LLP) -35 E Grassy Sprain Rd -Ynkrs 10710
(212) 715-9100 .. **Garfinkel,** Jill B '88 %Kramer LN&F,LLP -1177 Av of Amer -NY 10036
(212) 201-1170 .. **Garfinkel,** Neil B '90 (Abrams GMB,LLP) -237 W 35th -NY 10001
(212) 373-3703 .. **Garfinkel,** Paul C '99 -1285 Av of Amer -NY 10019 **Fx:**757-3990
(212) 605-0340 .. **Garfinkel,** Wendy W '95 Mestel & Co -575 Mad Av -NY 10022 **Fx:**969-2900
(914) 358-0041 .. **Garfinkle,** Eric J '04 %Mahadeva,PLLC -445 Hmltn Av -White Plns 10601
(718) 739-6400 .. **Garfinkle,** Gerald L '75 %DHCR -92-31 Union Hall -Jamaica 11433 **Fx:**262-7938
(516) 294-5100 .. **Garfinkle,** Robt L '76 %Murphy B&O,LLP -22 Jericho Tpk -Mineola 11501
(212) 888-7300 .. **Garfunkel,** Alan J '72 -444 Mad Av -NY 10022 **Fx:**888-7306
(516) 393-2200 .. **Garfunkel,** George M '64 OfCnsl Garfunkel W,PC -111 Grt Nck Rd -Gt Neck 11021
(516) 741-6565 .. **Garfunkel,** Sylvan Z '06 %Meyer SE&K,PC -990 Stewart Av Bx9194 -Gdn Cty 11530
(516) 393-2200 .. **Garfunkel Wild, PC** -111 Grt Nck Rd -Gt Neck 11021 **Fx:**466-5964
(718) 286-6000 .. **Garg,** Anjula '04 %DA -125-01 Qns Blvd -Kew Gdns 11415
(718) 250-2000 .. **Garg,** Rajeev '09 %DA -350 Jay -Brklyn 11201 **Fx:**250-2314
(212) 839-7000 .. **Gargan,** Terence '69 Cnsl Hill B&N LLP -200 Lbrty -NY 10281
(585) 753-4500 .. **Gargan,** Wm T '98 %DA -832 Watts Bldg -Rchstr 14614 **Fx:**753-4576
(212) 643-6400 .. **Garganigo,** Albert '67 (Garganigo G&W) -14 Penn Plz -NY 10122
(212) 643-6400 .. **Garganigo Goldsmith & Weiss** -14 Penn Plz -NY 10122 **Fx:**643-6549
(845) 892-5097 .. **Gargano,** Anthony C '91 IBM -2070 Route 52 -Hopewell Junct 12533
(315) 449-2616 .. **Gargano,** Brian M '06 Martin GBM&C,PC -5790 Widewaters Pkwy -DeWitt 13214
(201) 653-6166 .. **Gargano,** Christopher P '93 (Coughlin & G) -360 Sunrise Hwy -W Babylon 11704 **Fx:**653-9352
(914) 686-5600 .. **Gargano,** Dennis V '00 %All NY Title Agency -180 E Post Rd -White Plns 10601 **Fx:**686-1440
(718) 748-9892 .. **Gargano,** Jos R '86 -Bx940095 -Rckwy Pk 11694 **Fx:**748-3262
(212) 326-1000 .. **Gargano,** Michl D '86 %Julien J Studley,Inc -300 Park Av -NY 10022 **Fx:**753-6413
(212) 292-8700 .. **Garger,** Andrew J '93 Cnsl Water Quality Ins Syndicate -80 Broad -NY 10004 **Fx:**292-8716
(646) 746-9730 .. **Gargiulo,** Janine M '91 US CFTC -140 Bway -NY 10005
(212) 416-8274 .. **Gargiulo,** Linda J '80 %Dept of Law -120 Bway -NY 10271
(914) 421-0905 .. **Gargiulo,** Paul G '91 -235 Main -White Plns 10601 **Fx:**328-3472
(631) 777-3900 .. **Gargiulo,** Stephen A '03 %Guttman & G -1 Huntngtn Quad -Melvll 11747 **Fx:**777-3907
(631) 439-1720 .. **Garguilo,** Anthony '80 MHLS -320 Carleton Av -Central Islip 11722 **Fx:**951-2562
(914) 333-6256 .. **Garguilo,** Raymond Jr. '06 Bayer HlthCare LLC -555 Wht Plns Rd -Tarrytwn 10591
(718) 497-9142 .. **Garibaldi,** Deborah M '89 -67-04 Myrtle Av -Glendale 11385 **Fx:**497-9159
(212) 618-4163 .. **Garick,** Jason A '96 Deloitte Consulting LLP -144 E 22nd -NY 10010
(845) 796-1010 .. **Garigliano,** Barbara A '81 -449 Bway Drwr1069 -Monticello 12701 **Fx:**796-1040
(845) 796-1010 .. **Garigliano,** Walter F '80 -449 Bway Drwr1069 -Monticello 12701 **Fx:**796-1040
(516) 354-1570 .. **Garil,** Herbert '51 OfCnsl Meyerson & L,LLP -1040 Hempstd Tpk -Franklin Sq 11010 **Fx:**358-9673
(516) 481-1220 .. **Garille,** Timothy D '93 -119 Jackson -Hempstd 11550
(212) 968-0120 .. **Garin,** Alexia N '01 %Marans & W,LLC -29 Bway -NY 10006 **Fx:**785-1618
(845) 485-3900 .. **Garin,** G Nicholas '75 %Dept of Law -235 Main -Poughkeepsie 12601 **Fx:**452-3303
(212) 813-8800 .. **Garipoli,** Kerri E '97 %Goodwin P LLP -620 8th Av -NY 10018
(212) 351-4500 .. **Garland,** David W '95 (Epstein B&G,PC) -250 Park Av -NY 10177
(631) 269-5161 .. **Garland,** Dawn B '95 -13 Balboa Dr -Kings Pk 11754
(212) 685-6629 .. **Garland,** Gary B '92 -425 Mad Av -NY 10017
(315) 379-2282 .. **Garland,** Jane S '00 %Pub Def -Cnty Cthse -Canton 13617 **Fx:**379-2300
(212) 213-1812 .. **Garland,** Jos P '82 -275 Mad Av -NY 10016 **Fx:**213-1816
(212) 977-3900 .. **Garland,** Paul B '76 -250 W 57th -NY 10107 **Fx:**977-7035
(212) 613-2003 .. **Garley,** R Scott '82 (Gibbons PC) -1 Penn Plz -NY 10119 **Fx:**554-9680
(518) 402-9003 .. **Garlick,** P Nicholas '90 %DEC -625 Bway -Albany 12233 **Fx:**402-9018
(518) 402-9223 .. **Garlick,** Sandra A '93 %DEC -625 Bway -Albany 12233 **Fx:**402-9018
(716) 856-8200 .. **Garlipp,** Jared L '01 %Williams & W -43 Court -Buffalo 14202 **Fx:**856-0559
(212) 261-8000 .. **Garlock,** Emily A '09 %Mendes & M,LLP -750 7th Av -NY 10019
(212) 815-0423 .. **Garment,** Lawr S '76 Special Narcotics -80 Centre -NY 10013
(212) 878-8000 .. **Garment,** Suzanne R '04 %Clifford C LLP -31 W 52nd -NY 10019
(631) 476-4384 .. **Garmhausen,** Chas F '96 -116 Wedgewood Dr -Coram 11727 **Fx:**476-4384
(516) 228-6500 .. **Garmise,** Jason B '99 Ivy Asset Mgnt Corp -1 Jericho Plz -Jericho 11753
(631) 962-9570 .. **Garmise,** Jessica A '01 Verint Systems Inc -330 S Srvc Rd -Melvll 11747 **Fx:**962-9623
(212) 644-3335 .. **Garmise,** Richd E '89 %J Harris -240 W 44th -NY 10036 **Fx:**644-3343
(845) 796-7480 .. **Garn,** K C '78 -34 North -Monticello 12701
(914) 472-2300 .. **Garneau,** Gregg P '94 (Jones G,LLP) -670 Wht Plns Rd -Scarsdale 10583
(212) 450-4000 .. **Garner,** Albert '09 %Davis P&W LLP -450 Lex Av -NY 10017
(212) 468-8000 .. **Garner,** Joi L '08 %Morrison & F LLP -1290 Av of Amer -NY 10104
(914) 288-0022 .. **Garner,** Melvin C '74 (Leason E LLP) -81 Main -White Plns 10601
(516) 496-5825 .. **Garner,** Michl '93 Cnsl J Bilello & Assoc -875 Merrick Av -Westbury 11590
(212) 964-1004 .. **Garner,** Paul C '72 -319 Bway -NY 10007 **Fx:**964-1400
(212) 489-1400 .. **Garner,** Robt L '00 Cnsl Bickel & B -767 5th Av -NY 10153
(212) 815-1818 .. **Garner,** Robt W '88 %DC 37 MELS -125 Barclay -NY 10007 **Fx:**815-1343
(518) 827-6707 .. **Garner,** Thos F '93 OfCnsl D Ross -338 Main Bx990 -Middleburgh 12122 **Fx:**827-6750
(914) 630-3095 .. **Garner,** Tiffany F '01 Harrison High Schl -255 Union Av -Harrison 10528
(212) 483-1818 .. **Garnett,** Craig H '96 Brown Brothers Harriman & Co -140 Bway -NY 10005
(516) 285-8867 .. **Garnett,** Edw J '81 (Riconda & G,LLP) -753 W Merrick Rd -Vly Stream 11580
(212) 637-2520 .. **Garnett,** Margaret M '01 US Atty -1 St Andrews Plz -NY 10007
(516) 371-4598 .. **Garnett,** Miles '54 -66 Wayne Av -Atlantic Bch 11509
(212) 756-2000 .. **Garnett,** Peter S '10 %Schulte R&Z LLP -919 3rd Av -NY 10022
(212) 587-5159 .. **Garnett,** Ronald L '73 -299 Bway -NY 10007 **Fx:**587-3867
(646) 312-3591 .. **Garnica,** Gabriel B '92 %Baruch College -17 Lex Av Bx 316 -NY 10010
(516) 877-9574 .. **Garnice,** Victor Abel '85 -2171 Jericho Tpk -Commack 11725 **Fx:**877-9579
(212) 869-3500 .. **Garnsey,** Robt F '94 %J Fuchsberg Law Firm,LLP -500 5th Av -NY 10110 **Fx:**398-1532
(845) 486-2280 .. **Garo,** Nancy B '90 %Pub Def -22 Market -Poughkeepsie 12601 **Fx:**486-2266
(212) 788-7393 .. **Garodnick,** Danl R '01 NYC Council -250 Bway -NY 10007 **Fx:**442-1457
(718) 788-1567 .. **Garofallou,** George D '50 -388 9th -Brklyn 11215
(518) 584-1557 .. **Garofalo,** Gregory P '91 -376 Bway -Saratoga Spgs 12866
(212) 806-5400 .. **Garofalo,** Matthew G '07 %Stroock &S&L LLP -180 Maiden Ln -NY 10038
(516) 705-3706 .. **Garofalo,** Patricia Ann '93 Catholic Health Srvcs of LI -992 N Vllg Av -Rockvll Ctr 11570 **Fx:**705-3728
(914) 828-8945 .. **Garofalo,** Wm S '81 %Swiss Re America -175 King -Armonk 10504 **Fx:**828-7000
(212) 488-1200 .. **Garofola,** Michl J '07 %Kobre & K,LLP -800 3rd Av -NY 10022
(516) 739-0400 .. **Garone,** Peter D '82 %Kelly R&K,LLP -330 Old Cntry Rd -Mineola 11501
(212) 697-3122 .. **Garoon,** Kimberly B '10 %Martin C&B LLP -220 E 42nd -NY 10017
(718) 761-5156 .. **Garpestad,** Christopher '95 -965 Manor Rd -Staten Isl 10314 **Fx:**761-6581
(212) 986-9193 .. **Garr,** Andrew '68 -228 E 45th -NY 10017
(212) 750-1333 .. **Garr,** Ira E '76 I Garr,PC -777 3rd Av -NY 10017 **Fx:**486-2978
(845) 565-1165 .. **Garrabrant,** Torey Alan '96 -442 Strawrdg Rd -Wallkill 12589
(315) 798-5766 .. **Garramone,** Grant J '95 %DA -800 Park Av -Utica 13501 **Fx:**798-5582
(315) 734-2926 .. **Garramone,** Laura Shea '96 %Utica Natl Ins -180 Genesee Bx530 -Utica 13502 **Fx:**734-2198
(516) 483-4112 .. **Garrastegui,** Vivian '87 (Schneider & G PLLC) -4230 Hempstd Tpk -Bethpage 11714 **Fx:**485-4363

(212) 808-7800 .. **Garraty,** John A Jr. '76 (Kelley D&W LLP) -101 Park Av -NY 10178
(212) 265-7000 .. **Garren,** Brent '88 %UNITE HERE -275 7th Av -NY 10001 **Fx:**307-6904
(516) 228-9350 .. **Garret,** Keith S '08 %Solomon & S -50 Chas Lindbergh Blvd -Uniondale 11553
(212) 765-5070 .. **Garretson,** John D '93 (Fish & R,PC) -153 E 53rd -NY 10022
(718) 590-2000 .. **Garretson,** Nicole M '02 %DA -198 E 161st -Bronx 10451 **Fx:**590-6477
(585) 454-7943 .. **Garretson,** Scott A '84 -30 Westway -Rchstr 14624
(212) 598-8000 .. **Garrett,** Elizabeth M '02 %Guardian Life Ins -7 Hanover Sq -NY 10004 **Fx:**919-2693
(212) 965-2200 .. **Garrett,** Jenigh J '04 %NAACP/LDF -99 Hudson -NY 10013 **Fx:**226-7592
(212) 940-8800 .. **Garrett,** Jessica M '09 %Katten MR LLP -575 Mad Av -NY 10022
(518) 474-8816 .. **Garrett,** Jevon L '96 Comm Prof Standrds -40 Steuben -Albany 12207 **Fx:**474-0389
(845) 298-2000 .. **Garrett,** Joan F '88 (Vergilis SRD&D,LLP) -1136 Route 9 -Wappingers Fls 12590
(585) 263-1000 .. **Garrett,** John L '79 (Nixon P LLP) -1100 Clinton Sq -Rchstr 14604
(212) 877-3400 .. **Garrett,** Michl '71 Exec Coaching Grp,Inc -132 W 78th -NY 10024
(914) 995-3497 .. **Garretto,** Mark A '79 %DA -111 Martin Luther King Blvd -White Plns 10601 **Fx:**995-3363
(718) 979-0632 .. **Garrigan,** Kathleen M '91 -1475 Hylan Blvd -Staten Isl 10305 **Fx:**979-4548
(212) 385-3624 .. **Garrin,** Stephen H '89 -225 Bway -NY 10007
(212) 878-8000 .. **Garrison,** Kirsten '08 %Clifford C LLP -31 W 52nd -NY 10019
(718) 780-7947 .. **Garrison,** Marsha '77 %Bklyn Law Schl -250 Joralemon -Brklyn 11201 **Fx:**780-0393
(516) 229-4400 .. **Garrison,** Michelle L '01 %Kay & G -875 Merrick Av -Westbury 11590
(212) 719-6174 .. **Garrison,** Philip R '76 IRS -110 W 44th -NY 10036
(585) 454-2263 .. **Garrison,** Wm A '78 %4 Corners Abstract -370 East Av -Rchstr 14604 **Fx:**454-6163
(212) 400-7177 .. **Garrity Graham Murphy Garofalo & Flinn** -40 Wall -NY 10005 **Fx:**(973) 509-0414
(212) 848-4000 .. **Garrity,** James L Jr. '81 (Shearman & S LLP) -599 Lex Av -NY 10022
(716) 838-1118 .. **Garrity,** John M '58 (Garrity & G) -1773 Hertel Av -Buffalo 14216
(716) 838-1118 .. **Garrity,** Patrick T '96 (Garrity & G) -1773 Hertel Av -Buffalo 14216
(212) 653-8700 .. **Garrity,** Paul W '96 (Sheppard MR&H LLP) -30 Rckfllr Plz -NY 10112
(212) 836-8000 .. **Garrod,** Danielle J '07 %Kaye S LLP -425 Park Av -NY 10022
(917) 749-4212 .. **Garrod,** David J '96 -12 Main -Brewstr 10509
(212) 940-8800 .. **Garrod,** Jacqueline '02 %Katten MR LLP -575 Mad Av -NY 10022
(516) 746-3500 .. **Garron,** Michl E '97 %Brand G&B,PC -600 Old Cntry Rd -Gdn Cty 11530
(212) 609-6800 .. **Garrone,** Kelly J '01 %McCarter & E,LLP -245 Park Av -NY 10167
(518) 457-4380 .. **Garry,** Benjamin T '87 Dept of Labor -State Campus Bldg 12 -Albany 12240 **Fx:**485-1819
(212) 728-8000 .. **Garry,** Chandra E '05 %Willkie F&G LLP -787 7th Av -NY 10019
(212) 839-5300 .. **Garry,** Colin J '08 %Sidley A LLP -787 7th Av -NY 10019
(212) 406-1919 .. **Garry,** Danl J '09 %Gennet KA&R,PC -140 Bway -NY 10005
(212) 834-3668 .. **Garry,** Karen Anne '93 JP Morgan Chase -270 Park Av -NY 10017
(518) 465-3680 .. **Garry,** Michl J '76 (Garry & G,PLLC) -600 Bway -Albany 12207 **Fx:**465-9355
(212) 483-9600 .. **Garry,** Steven E '80 (Costello S&G LLP) -44 Wall -NY 10005
(516) 880-8484 .. **Garry,** Thos J '95 (Harris B PLLC) -333 Earle Ovngton Blvd -Uniondale 11553
(516) 880-8484 .. **Garry,** Wm J '84 (Harris B PLLC) -333 Earle Ovngton Blvd -Uniondale 11553
(212) 318-6000 .. **Garshelis,** Daren S '09 %Paul HJ&W LLP -75 E 55th -NY 10022
(212) 742-8700 .. **Garson,** Andrew S '79 (Garson D&C LLP) -110 Wall -NY 10005
(212) 506-1700 .. **Garson,** Burt M '00 %Kasowitz BT&F LLP -1633 Bway -NY 10019
(212) 742-8700 .. **Garson DeCorato & Cohen LLP** -110 Wall -NY 10005 **Fx:**742-1471
(212) 521-2000 .. **Garson,** Gary W '71 %Loews Corp -667 Mad Av -NY 10065 **Fx:**521-2997
(212) 833-0584 .. **Garson,** Heather E '97 %Jennison Assoc LLC -466 Lex Av -NY 10017
(914) 779-2858 .. **Garson,** Jeffrey '84 -1180 Mdlnd Av -Bronxvll 10708
(212) 626-4100 .. **Garsson,** Frederic M '94 %Baker & M LLP -1114 Av of Amer -NY 10036
(516) 294-8844 .. **Gart,** Paula M '80 (L'Abbate BC&C,LLP) -1001 Franklin Av -Gdn Cty 11530
(607) 637-4791 .. **Gartell,** Edw M '69 -38 W Main -Hancock 13783
(212) 755-0500 .. **Garten,** F Lloyd '89 %Maidman and M,LLP -70 E 55th -NY 10022
(631) 293-0200 .. **Garten,** Laurence I '92 %Daley-Hodkin Corp -68 S Srvc Rd -Melvll 11747
(212) 230-2000 .. **Garten,** Steven M '91 Poten & Prtnrs -805 3rd Av -NY 10022 **Fx:**355-0295
(516) 688-1702 .. **Gartenbaum,** Peggy J '86 IRS -1600 Stewart Av -Westbury 11590
(212) 248-2936 .. **Gartenberg,** Amie '82 (Kirsch GH LLP) -11 Penn Plz -NY 10001
(212) 868-0929 .. **Gartenberg,** Caryn S '84 -350 5th Av -NY 10118 **Fx:**465-8519
(212) 530-5000 .. **Gartenberg,** Karen '06 %Milbank TH&M LLP -1 Chase Manh Plz -NY 10005
(607) 724-8529 .. **Gartenman,** Eric H '04 (Battisti G&T) -19 Chenango -Bnghmtn 13901
(718) 643-8032 .. **Gartenstein,** Danl '92 %Family Ct -283 Adams -Brklyn 11201
(718) 769-7000 .. **Gartenstein,** David M '92 %V Gartenstein,PC -3711 Shore Pkwy Bx350179 -Brklyn 11235 **Fx:**769-4302
(718) 520-2993 .. **Gartenstein,** Stanley '55 Supreme Ct -88-11 Sutphin Blvd -Jamaica 11435 **Fx:**758-9834
(718) 769-7000 .. **Gartenstein,** Victor '64 (V Gartenstein,PC) -3711 Shore Pkwy Bx350179 -Brklyn 11235 **Fx:**769-4302
(845) 454-1110 .. **Gartland,** Michl G '74 (Corbally G and R LLP) -35 Market -Poughkeepsie 12601
(212) 837-6000 .. **Gartland,** Patrick T '00 (Hughes H&R LLP) -1 Bttry Pk Plz -NY 10004
(631) 761-0800 .. **Gartland,** Wm A '02 %Lazer AR&Y,PC -225 Old Cntry Rd -Melvll 11747
(212) 944-0500 .. **Gartlir,** Bernard '42 (Hofheimer G&G,LLP) -530 5th Av -NY 10036 **Fx:**869-4930
(212) 679-1076 .. **Gartlir,** Lois I '85 -136 E 36th -NY 10016
(212) 837-6350 .. **Gartman,** Christopher C '08 %Hughes H&R LLP -1 Bttry Pk Plz -NY 10004 **Fx:**299-6350
(212) 759-5800 .. **Gartner + Bloom, PC** -801 2nd Av -NY 10017 **Fx:**759-5842
(212) 541-7800 .. **Gartner,** Eve C '90 %Planned Parenthood -434 W 33rd -NY 10001 **Fx:**868-4677
(212) 836-8000 .. **Gartner,** Gary J '84 (Kaye S LLP) -425 Park Av -NY 10022
(716) 849-0021 .. **Gartner,** Henry D '85 -135 Delaware Av -Buffalo 14202 **Fx:**849-0708
(716) 433-0143 .. **Gartner,** John M '96 %HW Schmidt Jr -8 W Main -Lockprt 14094 **Fx:**433-4526
(516) 431-0737 .. **Gartner,** Jon H '84 -210 Shore Rd -Long Bch 11561
(212) 318-6000 .. **Gartner,** Keith C '10 %Paul HJ&W LLP -75 E 55th -NY 10022
(516) 742-6200 .. **Gartner,** Kenneth L '79 (Lynn G&D,LLP) -330 Old Cntry Rd -Mineola 11501 **Fx:**742-5294
(212) 428-2100 .. **Gartner,** Michele Lippa '81 OCA -25 Beaver -NY 10004
(212) 575-0825 .. **Gartner,** Paul M '64 -555 5th Av -NY 10017 **Fx:**575-5979
(212) 728-8000 .. **Gartner,** Steven J '85 (Willkie F&G LLP) -787 7th Av -NY 10019
(212) 759-5800 .. **Gartner,** Stuart F '71 (Gartner + B,PC) -801 2nd Av -NY 10017
(718) 466-3000 .. **Gartner,** Wm C III '99 %Civil Ct -1118 Grnd Cncrs -Bronx 10456 **Fx:**466-3006
(607) 722-5000 .. **Garufi,** Carman M '89 C Garufi -68 Oak -Bnghmtn 13905 **Fx:**722-5626
(516) 746-6020 .. **Garufi,** Carmelo '84 -100 Grdn City Plz -Gdn Cty 11530 **Fx:**742-4106
(212) 804-4200 .. **Garufi,** Francis A '99 %Mound CW&G -One Bttry Pk Plz -NY 10004
(607) 778-2015 .. **Garufy,** Sandra J '89 %Cnty Ct -65 Hawley -Bnghmtn 13901
(212) 735-8600 .. **Garvelink,** Todd K '96 (Morrison C LLP) -909 3rd Av -NY 10022
(516) 873-2000 .. **Garver,** Brett P '00 %Moritt HH&H LLP -400 Grdn City Plz -Gdn Cty 11530
(212) 579-8400 .. **Garver,** John A '70 -160 W 66th -NY 10023
(212) 458-5752 .. **Garvey,** Althea E '87 AIG -175 Water -NY 10038
(518) 408-2649 .. **Garvey,** Brian C '06 %Insurance Dept -99 Wshngtn Av -Albany 12257 **Fx:**473-4600
(212) 637-3181 .. **Garvey,** Carl P '97 %EPA -290 Bway -NY 10007 **Fx:**637-3096
(315) 435-2470 .. **Garvey,** Christine M '95 %DA -505 S State -Syracuse 13202 **Fx:**435-3969
(212) 461-2323 .. **Garvey,** Christle R '09 %Saiber LLC -44 Wall -NY 10005
(516) 365-9802 .. **Garvey,** Christopher B '82 OfCnsl Collard & R,PC -1077 Nrthrn Blvd -Roslyn 11576
(516) 365-9802 .. **Garvey,** Christopher B '82 (Nolte N&H) -1077 Nrthrn Blvd -Roslyn 11576
(212) 813-8800 .. **Garvey,** Christopher J '93 (Goodwin P LLP) -620 8th Av -NY 10018
(518) 828-3303 .. **Garvey,** Clarissa D '00 %Cnty Atty -401 State -Hudson 12534 **Fx:**828-9535
(212) 474-1000 .. **Garvey,** Craig J '10 %Cravath S&M LLP -825 8th Av -NY 10019
(518) 272-6565 .. **Garvey,** David T '67 (Martin SWD&J) -279 River Bx1530 -Troy 12181
(716) 854-4800 .. **Garvey,** Dennis J '84 (Garvey & G) -416 Pearl -Buffalo 14202 **Fx:**854-2843
(914) 472-8680 .. **Garvey,** James A III '84 -145 Brwstr Rd -Scarsdale 10583 **Fx:**472-1509
(631) 360-8300 .. **Garvey,** John P '88 -180 E Main -Smithtwn 11787 **Fx:**360-8178
(212) 836-8000 .. **Garvey,** Karin E '99 Cnsl Kaye S LLP -425 Park Av -NY 10022
(914) 524-9400 .. **Garvey,** Lawr A '02 (Cushner & G LLP) -155 Wht Plns Rd -Tarrytwn 10591 **Fx:**524-0422
(716) 854-4800 .. **Garvey,** Matthew J '85 (Garvey & G) -416 Pearl -Buffalo 14202 **Fx:**854-2843
(585) 955-6111 .. **Garvey,** Maureen '90 Cnsl Frontier Abstract -30 W Broad -Rchstr 14614 **Fx:**295-1211
(212) 455-2000 .. **Garvey,** Michl J '99 (Simpson T&B LLP) -425 Lex Av -NY 10017
(716) 853-2050 .. **Garvey,** Michl J '09 %Sliwa & L -237 Main -Buffalo 14203
(716) 854-4800 .. **Garvey,** Neil E '84 OfCnsl Garvey & G -416 Pearl -Buffalo 14202 **Fx:**854-2843
(212) 455-2000 .. **Garvey,** Richd A '76 OfCnsl Simpson T&B LLP -425 Lex Av -NY 10017
(212) 431-8700 .. **Garvey Schubert Barer** -100 Wall -NY 10005 **Fx:**334-1278
(212) 870-3325 .. **Garvey,** Sheila M '87 Columbia Univ-Emp & Labor -1220 Interchurch -NY 10115
(607) 255-8589 .. **Garvey,** Stephen P '93 Cornell Law Schl -Myron Taylor Hall -Ithaca 14850
(212) 693-0085 .. **Garvin,** Jonathan F '99 %Appellate Advocates -2 Rector -NY 10006 **Fx:**693-0878
(631) 287-3065 .. **Garvin,** Kathryn V '96 %Town Atty -116 Hmptn Rd -Southampton 11968 **Fx:**287-3662
(212) 589-4200 .. **Garvin,** Naima J '07 %Baker & H LLP -45 Rckfllr Plz -NY 10111
(914) 213-4541 .. **Garvin,** Wm J '01 (Garvin & G,LLP) -450 Bway -Newburgh 12550 **Fx:**(845) 561-6095
(212) 398-0055 .. **Garwin Gerstein & Fisher,LLP** -1501 Bway -NY 10036 **Fx:**764-6620
(315) 682-8514 .. **Garwood,** David B '97 -101 Sherbrooke Rd -Manlius 13104
(585) 325-6325 .. **Garwood,** Fredk '80 -245 Stafford Way -Rchstr 14626 **Fx:**325-6784
(631) 501-3100 .. **Gary,** David S '74 %J Humphreys -3 Huntngtn Quad Bx9028 -Melvll 11747 **Fx:**501-3085
(914) 682-4495 .. **Gary,** Ernest '02 -2 William -White Plns 10601 **Fx:**682-4498
(212) 813-8800 .. **Gary,** Jessica A '08 %Goodwin P LLP -620 8th Av -NY 10018
(516) 240-8900 .. **Gary,** Kevin M '92 (Torre LGG&R,LLP) -100 Jericho Quad -Jericho 11753
(212) 267-5333 .. **Gary,** Wendy '95 (Lieber & G) -11 Park Pl -NY 10007
(212) 641-2081 .. **Garza,** Melissa '99 Westwood One,Inc -1166 Av of Amer -NY 10036
(212) 830-2522 .. **Garza,** Richd A '99 %Broadcast Music Inc -250 Greenwich -NY 10007
(315) 673-4602 .. **Garzia,** Raymond A '88 -3828 Rockwell Rd -Marcellus 13108
(607) 778-2423 .. **Garzo,** Michl A Jr. '03 %DA -45 Hawley Bx1766 -Bnghmtn 13902 **Fx:**778-8870
(718) 433-1331 .. **Garzon,** John J '89 J Garzon,PC -46-12 Qns Blvd -Sunnyside 11104 **Fx:**433-1330
(212) 640-5193 .. **Garzon,** Paula E '85 %Amer Exp -200 Vesey -NY 10285
(212) 956-9595 .. **Gasarch,** Mark '67 -150 E 58th -NY 10155 **Fx:**956-7216
(718) 875-1300 .. **Gasbarro,** Jeffrey W H '09 %Appllt Div 2nd Dept -45 Monroe Pl -Brklyn 11201 **Fx:**858-2446

(212) 819-8200 .. **Gasbarro,** Nicholas M '09 %White & C LLP -1155 Av of Amer -NY 10036
(212) 912-0520 .. **Gaschler,** Michl '90 (Gaschler & B) -375 South End Av -NY 10280 **Fx:**(917) 591-6322
(315) 422-1152 .. **Gascon,** James J '87 (Costello C&F,PLLC) -500 Plum -Syracuse 13204
(212) 486-2400 .. **Gase,** Stephanie L '08 %Leader & B LLP -630 3rd Av -NY 10017
(914) 328-8800 .. **Gash,** Gary M '83 (Gash & Assoc,PC) -235 Main -White Plns 10601 **Fx:**328-3503
(212) 968-8300 .. **Gash,** Richd A '76 (Mintzer SZL&M LLP) -39 Bway -NY 10006
(646) 404-1978 .. **Gasi,** Michl '09 -82-05 25th Av -E Elmhrst 11370 **Fx:**(203) 738-1595
(212) 416-8570 .. **Gasior,** John P '88 %Dept of Law -120 Bway -NY 10271
(212) 336-2000 .. **Gaske,** Wm F '91 Cnsl Patterson BW&T LLP -1133 Av of Amer -NY 10036
(212) 455-2000 .. **Gaskill,** Christopher B '09 %Simpson T&B LLP -425 Lex Av -NY 10017
(212) 695-6012 .. **Gasman,** Gerald B '70 -10 Park Av -NY 10016 **Fx:**563-2765
(212) 788-5759 .. **Gasner,** M Rose '84 %NYC Dept of Hlth -125 Worth -NY 10013
(212) 530-5000 .. **Gaspar,** Christopher J '98 %Milbank TH&M LLP -1 Chase Manh Plz -NY 10005
(212) 578-8182 .. **Gaspard,** Marie C '06 Cnsl MetLife -1095 Av of Amer -NY 10036 **Fx:**251-1667
(212) 558-4000 .. **Gaspard,** Nicholas A '09 %Sullivan & C LLP -125 Broad -NY 10004
(718) 266-3009 .. **Gaspari,** Eva M '04 -2300 W 7th -Brklyn 11223
(516) 938-5476 .. **Gaspari,** James W '01 %Liro Group -6 Aerial Way -Syosset 11791
(212) 510-0500 .. **Gasparini,** Elisabetta G M '02 %US Trustees Ofc -33 Whitehall -NY 10004 **Fx:**668-2255
(914) 304-4353 .. **Gasparini,** Louis U '03 (Lynch S, PLLC) -75 S Bway -White Plns 10601 **Fx:**304-4378
(315) 471-1835 .. **Gasparini,** Mary E '92 SrCnsl Atty Grievance Comm-5th Jud Dist -224 Harrison -Syracuse 13202 **Fx:**479-0123
(631) 582-4000 .. **Gasparis,** Maria '97 (Tsunis G&L,LLP) -2929 Express Dr N -Islandia 11749
(212) 626-4100 .. **Gasparo,** Frank M '99 (Baker & M LLP) -1114 Av of Amer -NY 10036
(212) 384-1000 .. **Gasper,** Frank Walter '91 %FBI -26 Fed Plz -NY 10278
(212) 878-8000 .. **Gasper,** Jos T II '07 %Clifford C LLP -31 W 52nd -NY 10019
(718) 286-6000 .. **Gasper,** Kateri A '83 %DA -125-01 Qns Blvd -Kew Gdns 11415
(212) 688-1196 .. **Gasperetti,** Jos E '81 -115 Bway -NY 10006
(212) 998-6730 .. **Gass,** Jonathan J '97 Brennan Ctr for Justice -161 Av of Amer -NY 10013
(718) 246-2700 .. **Gass,** Thos E '83 -125 Lvngstn -Brklyn 11201
(212) 351-4500 .. **Gassel,** Philip M '73 (Epstein B&G,PC) -250 Park Av -NY 10177
(516) 542-5900 .. **Gasser,** Christine '88 (Congdon FORDT&F) -333 Earle Ovngton Blvd -Uniondale 11553
(718) 263-8025 .. **Gasser & Hayes** -106-19 Metro Av -Frst Hlls 11375 **Fx:**263-8031
(516) 466-5291 .. **Gassler,** Chas P '95 (Gassler & O,PC) -1 Nrthrn Blvd -Gt Neck 11021 **Fx:**466-5290
(516) 228-9181 .. **Gassman Baiamonte Betts & Tannenbaum, PC** -666 Old Cntry Rd -Gdn Cty 11530 **Fx:**745-6712
(212) 858-1000 .. **Gassman,** Barry K '72 (Pillsbury WSP LLP) -1540 Bway -NY 10036
(212) 838-7797 .. **Gassman,** Seth R '04 %Cohen MS&T,PLLC -88 Pine -NY 10005
(516) 228-9181 .. **Gassman,** Stephen '72 (Gassman BB&T,PC) -666 Old Cntry Rd -Gdn Cty 11530
(212) 416-8250 .. **Gassmann,** Kayla R '09 %Dept of Law -120 Bway -NY 10271
(585) 232-7361 .. **Gastel,** Bernard '52 -450 Rynlds Arcd -Rchstr 14614
(212) 876-4077 .. **Gaster,** Jeffrey N '78 -1675 York Av -NY 10128 **Fx:**410-2424
(212) 715-9100 .. **Gasthalter,** Adam B '08 %Kramer LN&F,LLP -1177 Av of Amer -NY 10036
(212) 829-9818 .. **Gasthalter,** Edw '67 -445 Park Av -NY 10022 **Fx:**371-5407
(716) 845-3650 .. **Gastle,** Diane S '84 %MHLS -438 Main -Buffalo 14202 **Fx:**874-7794
(212) 267-9222 .. **Gastman,** Gregory S '99 %Gorayeb & Assoc,PC -100 William -NY 10038 **Fx:**962-5418
(716) 878-4618 .. **Gaston-Marsh,** Latonia '94 Buffalo State Cllg -1300 Elmwood Av -Buffalo 14222
(516) 747-0300 .. **Gastwirth,** Loretta M '84 (Meltzer LG&B,LLP) -190 Willis Av -Mineola 11501
(516) 931-0700 .. **Gastwirth & Mirsky,LLP** -479 S Oyster Bay Rd -Plainvw 11803 **Fx:**932-0220
(631) 259-8500 .. **Gastwirth & Mirsky,LLP** -295 N Sea Rd -Southampton 11968 **Fx:**932-0220
(516) 931-0700 .. **Gastwirth,** Stuart L '63 (Gastwirth & M,LLP) -479 S Oyster Bay Rd -Plainvw 11803
(212) 248-3140 .. **Gately,** Matthew F '10 %Drinker B&R LLP -140 Bway -NY 10005
(585) 232-6900 .. **Gates & Adams,PC** -28 E Main -Rchstr 14614 **Fx:**232-8463
(585) 232-6900 .. **Gates,** Douglas S '68 (Gates & A,PC) -28 E Main -Rchstr 14614
(607) 723-1990 .. **Gates,** Gregory A '79 (Hickey S&G) -160 Hawley Bx2124 -Bnghmtn 13902
(212) 788-7100 .. **Gates,** Harold '01 NYC Council -250 Bway -NY 10007
(212) 756-2000 .. **Gates,** Jessica '09 %Schulte R&Z LLP -919 3rd Av -NY 10022
(212) 297-5800 .. **Gates,** Jonathan E '08 %Day P LLP -7 Times Sq -NY 10036
(718) 931-6300 .. **Gates,** Laurie Rabine '94 -993 Morris Park Av -Bronx 10462 **Fx:**792-4253
(212) 593-3000 .. **Gates,** Linda Mandel '82 %Platzer SKLG&J,LLP -1065 Av of Amer -NY 10018
(716) 852-1544 .. **Gates,** Lynn D '77 (Smith M&S,LLC) -786 Ellicott Sq Bldg -Buffalo 14203
(716) 693-4550 .. **Gates,** Nancy E '91 %Washington Mills -1000 E Niagara -Tonawanda 14150
(212) 732-3200 .. **Gates,** Peter P Mc N '63 Cnsl Carter L&M LLP -2 Wall -NY 10005
(516) 294-3111 .. **Gates,** Richd M '64 (Gates & G LLP) -600 Old Cntry Rd -Gdn Cty 11530 **Fx:**294-3225
(212) 416-8564 .. **Gatewood,** Diane Ridley '90 %Dept of Law -120 Bway -NY 10271 **Fx:**416-8816
(518) 474-6740 .. **Gathen,** Kari L '03 %Dept of State -41 State -Albany 12231 **Fx:**473-9211
(631) 423-7777 .. **Gathman,** J Edw Jr. '86 (Gathman & B,LLP) -191 NY Av -Huntngtn 11743 **Fx:**423-7784
(914) 332-0222 .. **Gathman,** Laurie E '93 %Philips Electronics -345 Scarborough Rd Bx3001 -Briarclff Mnr 10510 **Fx:**332-0615
(212) 506-5000 .. **Gatimu,** Njoki Elizabeth '10 %Orrick H&S LLP -51 W 52nd -NY 10019
(212) 306-7450 .. **Gatling,** Patricia L '84 %Comm on Human Rights -40 Rector -NY 10006 **Fx:**306-7414
(516) 338-8500 .. **Gatoff,** Eric '95 Nathans Famous Inc -1 Jericho Plz -Jericho 11753
(212) 728-8000 .. **Gatsik,** Jonathan H '03 %Willkie F&G LLP -787 7th Av -NY 10019
(212) 325-1884 .. **Gatsos,** John D '84 %CSFP Capital -11 Mad Av -NY 10010 **Fx:**325-8282
(718) 254-7000 .. **Gatta,** James D '03 US Atty -271 Cadman Plz E -Brklyn 11201 **Fx:**254-6479
(212) 250-2500 .. **Gatter,** Shaun '05 %Deutsche Bank -60 Wall -NY 10005
(718) 637-7607 .. **Gatti,** John J '06 -540 62nd -Brklyn 11220
(718) 589-9000 .. **Gatti,** Jos J '95 John Civetta Construction Corp -1123 Brnx Rvr Av -Bronx 10472
(212) 225-2000 .. **Gatti,** Matteo '08 %Cleary GS&H -1 Lbrty Plz -NY 10006
(212) 922-0891 .. **Gatti,** Patrick D '94 %Segal & L -501 5th Av -NY 10017
(631) 853-4049 .. **Gatto,** Christopher M '02 %Cnty Atty -Dennison Bldg Bx6100 -Hauppauge 11788 **Fx:**853-5169
(718) 590-2000 .. **Gatto,** Diane M '96 %DA -198 E 161st -Bronx 10451 **Fx:**590-6477
(212) 417-8700 .. **Gatto,** Julia '01 %Fed Def of NY Inc -52 Duane -NY 10007 **Fx:**571-0392
(646) 386-3668 .. **Gatto,** Robt W '02 %Supreme Ct-Law Dept -60 Centre -NY 10007
(518) 463-0300 .. **Gatto,** Salvatore Anthony '02 NYS Assn of Realtors -130 Wshngtn Av -Albany 12210
(315) 451-3810 .. **Gattuso,** Frank S '99 %O'Hara O&C,PC -7207 E Genesee -Fayettevll 13066
(212) 728-8000 .. **Gattuso,** Maria R '95 (Willkie F&G LLP) -787 7th Av -NY 10019
(212) 225-2000 .. **Gauchier,** Neslihan M '09 %Cleary GS&H -1 Lbrty Plz -NY 10006
(718) 268-4343 .. **Gaudelli,** Albert A '68 -16 Tennis Pl -Frst Hlls 11375 **Fx:**268-8761
(914) 241-2400 .. **Gaudio,** Alicia A '00 (Novenstern F&G) -69 S Bedford Rd -Mt Kisco 10549
(212) 943-0110 .. **Gaudio,** Nathan C '05 %Poles TS&G, LLP -46 Trinity Pl -NY 10006
(914) 333-0700 .. **Gaudioso,** Robt D '96 (Snyder & S) -94 Wht Plns Rd -Tarrytwn 10591 **Fx:**333-0743
(212) 521-5400 .. **Gaudreau,** Russell A III '00 (Reed S LLP) -599 Lex Av -NY 10022
(518) 445-2200 .. **Gaug,** Jos M '90 Albany Intl Corp -Bx1907 -Albany 12201
(212) 326-2000 .. **Gaughan,** Chelsea D '09 %O'Melveny & M LLP -7 Times Sq -NY 10036
(716) 648-8000 .. **Gaughan,** Dennis C '84 -6161 S Park Av -Hambrg 14075 **Fx:**648-8000
(212) 628-2647 .. **Gaughan,** Eugene F '04 -164 E 72nd -NY 10021 **Fx:**628-0291
(716) 566-1300 .. **Gaughan,** John P '01 %Hiscock & B,LLP -1100 M&T Ctr -Buffalo 14203
(716) 551-4301 .. **Gaughan,** Mollie B '82 (US SBA) -140 S Elmwood -Buffalo 14202 **Fx:**551-4418
(716) 648-8000 .. **Gaughan,** Vincent M Jr. '79 -6161 S Park Av -Hambrg 14075
(631) 754-0461 .. **Gaughran,** James F '84 -113 Eatons Neck Rd -Northprt 11768 **Fx:**262-1906
(914) 232-0934 .. **Gaughran,** Julie E '95 (Asher G LLP) -223 Katonah Av -Katonah 10536 **Fx:**232-1144
(914) 949-5300 .. **Gaujean,** Max G '92 (Brown & T,LLC) -1 N Bway -White Plns 10601
(585) 258-4538 .. **Gaul,** Annette '97 %UIA Bd -109 S Union -Rchstr 14607 **Fx:**258-4539
(315) 422-2800 .. **Gaul,** James F '67 -201 E Jffrsn -Syracuse 13202
(212) 480-2305 .. **Gaul,** Matthew J '99 %Insurance Dept -25 Beaver -NY 10004 **Fx:**480-5272
(212) 582-9400 .. **Gaulin,** Robt V '77 (Gaulin Grp PLLC) -590 Mad Av -NY 10022 **Fx:**582-9440
(845) 753-2241 .. **Gauntlett,** Bridget A '88 Solid Waste Mgmt Authority -420 Torne Valley Rd -Hillburn 10931 **Fx:**753-2284
(518) 449-3375 .. **Gauthier,** Geraldine M '05 Pub Util Law Proj -194 Wshngtn Av -Albany 12210 **Fx:**449-1769
(716) 852-2086 .. **Gauthier,** James D '75 -Bx526 -Buffalo 14217 **Fx:**877-7631
(585) 723-2376 .. **Gauthier,** John F '90 Town of Greece -647 Long Pond Rd -Rchstr 14612
(212) 848-4000 .. **Gautier,** Matthew B '10 Shearman & S LLP -599 Lex Av -NY 10022
(315) 435-2170 .. **Gauzza,** Michl J '90 %Cnty Atty -421 Mntgmry -Syracuse 13202 **Fx:**435-5729
(516) 688-1700 .. **Gavagan,** Peter J '79 %IRS -1600 Stewart Av -Westbury 11590 **Fx:**688-1750
(516) 746-1515 .. **Gavalas,** George M '92 -200 Old Cntry Rd -Mineola 11501
(212) 537-1879 .. **Gavalis,** Albert T '02 Morgan Stanley -1633 Bway -NY 10019
(212) 407-4000 .. **Gavaris,** Helen '88 (Loeb & L,LLP) -345 Park Av -NY 10154
(212) 608-1717 .. **Gaven,** Danl F '72 (Palmeri & G) -80 Maiden Ln -NY 10038
(212) 852-7024 .. **Gavenchak,** Eugenie C '80 News Corp -1211 Av of Amer -NY 10036 **Fx:**852-7214
(585) 589-8033 .. **Gavenda,** John C '83 -27 N Platt -Albion 14411
(315) 437-7600 .. **Gavett,** Katherine E '04 %Ferrara FLB&R,PC -5010 Campuswood Dr -E Syracuse 13057
(212) 957-7600 .. **Gavigan,** Robt J '98 Cnsl Cohen & G LLP -800 3rd Av -NY 10022
(212) 272-0598 .. **Gavilan,** David '97 %JP Morgan Chase -383 Mad Av -NY 10179
(315) 425-2700 .. **Gavilondo,** Carlos A '08 OfCnsl Hiscock & B,LLP -One Park Pl -Syracuse 13202
(518) 462-6765 .. **Gavin,** Elizabeth A '09 %Leg Aid -55 Colvin Av -Albany 12206 **Fx:**427-8352
(518) 473-0279 .. **Gavin,** Ellen C '88 %Public Srvc Comm -3 ESP -Albany 12223
(212) 799-0549 .. **Gavin,** Gayle A '74 -35 W 90th -NY 10024 **Fx:**712-9868
(516) 739-8182 .. **Gavin,** James '90 -24 Meadow Dr -Pt Wash 11050
(212) 218-2100 .. **Gavin,** Kimberley A '07 %Fitzpatrick CH&S -1290 Av of Amer -NY 10104
(516) 671-6481 .. **Gavin,** Paul J '59 -3 Dixon Ct -Sea Cliff 11579
(914) 946-8738 .. **Gavin,** Paul M '63 -333 Mamaroneck Av PMB 209 -White Plns 10605 **Fx:**946-6452
(212) 455-2000 .. **Gavin,** Ryan M '07 %Simpson T&B LLP -425 Lex Av -NY 10017
(212) 315-3755 .. **Gaviola,** David A '07 %C Juntikka & Assoc,LLP -350 5th Av -NY 10118 **Fx:**315-9032
(845) 624-2525 .. **Gavioli,** Wayne A '77 -101 N Mddltwn Rd -Nanuet 10954 **Fx:**623-1051
(718) 793-0199 .. **Gavriel,** Julia '01 -72-40 Main -Flushng 11367
(518) 474-6400 .. **Gavrilik,** Joan S '96 %Dept of Ed -89 Wshngtn Av -Albany 12234 **Fx:**473-2925

(212) 421-1845 .. **Gavrilov,** Julia '07 %Brown & W,PC -711 3rd Av -NY 10017 **Fx:**421-8418
(212) 593-6700 .. **Gaw,** Heather J '09 %Aaronson RF&D,LLP -757 3rd Av -NY 10017
(914) 225-5510 .. **Gawley,** Christopher J '03 Morgan Stanley -2000 Wstchstr Av -Purchase 10577
(212) 333-8534 .. **Gawley,** Steven '91 Island Def Jam Music Grp -825 8th Av -NY 10019
(716) 846-8257 .. **Gawlik,** Stephen F '98 Empire State Devlpmnt Corp -95 Perry -Buffalo 14203 **Fx:**846-8260
(585) 454-5050 .. **Gawlowicz,** Jos A '07 %Brown & H -2 State -Rchstr 14614
(212) 906-1200 .. **Gawlowski,** Rafal '01 (Latham & W) -885 3rd Av -NY 10022
(212) 863-6300 .. **Gawron,** Robt A '85 %HPD -100 Gold -NY 10038 **Fx:**863-8201
(716) 845-9370 .. **Gawronski,** Evelyn '88 %Supreme Ct -25 Delaware Av -Buffalo 14202 **Fx:**851-3293
(716) 854-6800 .. **Gawronski,** Fredk J '96 (Cook & G,PC) -300 Pearl -Buffalo 14202 **Fx:**854-3020
(212) 484-3900 .. **Gay,** Darrell S '80 (Arent F LLP) -1675 Bway -NY 10019
(718) 832-2669 .. **Gay,** Elaine '85 -177 7th Av -Brklyn 11215 **Fx:**768-3892
(212) 849-7000 .. **Gay,** Faith E '87 (Quinn EU&S,LLP) -51 Mad Av -NY 10010
(212) 571-5910 .. **Gayanilo,** Percy Diego '04 -160 Bway -NY 10038 **Fx:**571-5912
(718) 273-0248 .. **Gayathrinath,** Radhika '93 %S Gayathrinath -40 Cedar Ter -Staten Isl 10304 **Fx:**273-1195
(718) 273-0248 .. **Gayathrinath,** Subramaniam '89 -40 Cedar Ter -Staten Isl 10304 **Fx:**273-1195
(212) 408-5100 .. **Gayda,** Robt J '05 %Chadbourne & P LLP -30 Rckfllr Plz -NY 10112
(631) 761-0800 .. **Gayer,** Alexander M '99 (Lazer AR&Y,PC) -225 Old Cntry Rd -Melvll 11747
(212) 596-9000 .. **Gayer,** Lee S '84 Cnsl Ropes & G LLP -1211 Av of Amer -NY 10036
(212) 446-4800 .. **Gayle,** Aisha D '09 %Kirkland & E LLP -153 E 53rd -NY 10022
(800) 460-1382 .. **Gayle,** Armena D '93 -903 Blake Av -Brklyn 11207 **Fx:**(718) 208-4151
(718) 237-2000 .. **Gayle,** Cedric C '82 Leg Aid -111 Lvngstn -Brklyn 11201 **Fx:**237-8737
(212) 966-6420 .. **Gayle,** Doneth N '02 Lwyrs For Children -110 Lafayette -NY 10013 **Fx:**966-0531
(718) 724-1111 .. **Gayle,** E Dennis '91 -2915 Glenwood Rd -Brklyn 11210
(347) 663-6982 .. **Gayle,** Nadeen R '06 -467 Dekalb Av -Brklyn 11205
(917) 601-0827 .. **Gayle,** Robt K '85 -26 Court -Brklyn 11242
(516) 512-8300 .. **Gaylor,** C Wm III '07 (Gaylor & W LLP) -7 Atl Av -Lynbrk 11563 **Fx:**512-8301
(212) 715-1000 .. **Gaylor,** Monique Anne '05 %Arnold & P LLP -399 Park Av -NY 10022
(212) 232-1300 .. **Gaylord,** Jeffrey R '90 (Lewis BB&S LLP) -77 Water -NY 10005
(212) 598-8000 .. **Gaylord,** Jennifer K '98 %Guardian Life Ins -7 Hanover Sq -NY 10004 **Fx:**919-2693
(518) 347-2300 .. **Gaylord,** Mark J '94 -514 State -Schnctdy 12305
(585) 427-5400 .. **Gaylord,** Wm O '80 %Xerox -100 Clinton Av S -Rchstr 14644
(212) 233-3079 .. **Gayner,** Chas J '92 %Maloof LC&O,PA -299 Bway -NY 10007
(212) 867-2133 .. **Gaynier,** Rhonda L '90 -1250 Bway -NY 10001 **Fx:**564-5468
(212) 692-1000 .. **Gaynin,** Jonathan S '66 OfCnsl Duane M LLP -1540 Bway -NY 10036
(212) 490-3000 .. **Gaynor,** Alan S '95 (Wilson EME&D LLP) -150 E 42nd -NY 10017
(212) 704-6000 .. **Gaynor,** Amanda R '07 %Troutman S LLP -405 Lex Av -NY 10174
(347) 296-1588 .. **Gaynor,** Ian J '05 Hon H Kramer -360 Adams -Brklyn 11201
(631) 342-6065 .. **Gaynor,** Laurie Ann '92 %CA,Inc -1 CA Plz -Islandia 11749 **Fx:**342-4866
(914) 949-3624 .. **Gaynor,** Magdalen '79 -10 Bank -White Plns 10606 **Fx:**949-7199
(212) 581-0216 .. **Gaynor,** Magdalen '79 -333 W 57th #207 -NY 10019 **Fx:**(914) 949-7199
(518) 474-8816 .. **Gaynor,** Michl G '93 %Comm Prof Standrds -40 Steuben -Albany 12207 **Fx:**474-0389
(212) 661-5667 .. **Gaynor,** Philip M '77 -245 Park Av -NY 10167 **Fx:**(914) 472-2561
(212) 268-6100 .. **Gaynor,** Robt L '77 OfCnsl Lusthaus & L,PLLC -330 7th Av -NY 10001 **Fx:**268-6106
(212) 381-7000 .. **Gaynor,** Steven A '07 %Sabin B&G LLP -4 Times Sq -NY 10036
(516) 822-3550 .. **Gayoso,** Tony A '96 %Hoffmann & B LLP -6900 Jericho Tpk -Syosset 11791 **Fx:**822-3582
(914) 347-2600 .. **Gaza,** Copernicus T '97 (Traub LS&S LLP) -7 Skyline Dr -Hawthorne 10532
(212) 401-5560 .. **Gaza,** Mary Kathleen Foynes '96 %The Reserve Fund -1250 Bway -NY 10001 **Fx:**401-5950
(518) 373-2222 .. **Gazda,** Karen M '85 -6 Chelsea Pl -Clifton Pk 12065 **Fx:**373-8817
(212) 268-2665 .. **Gazer,** Raymond E '06 %Sinel & Assoc,PLLC -7 Penn Plz -NY 10001 **Fx:**268-6250
(212) 765-9000 .. **Gazes,** Ian J '85 (Gazes,LLC) -32 Av of Amer -NY 10013 **Fx:**765-9675
(212) 942-6192 .. **Gazetas,** George A '79 -17 Ft George Hl -NY 10040
(212) 972-0688 .. **Gazianis,** Thos L '78 -230 Park Av -NY 10169 **Fx:**661-2153
(212) 373-3000 .. **Gazibara,** Danijela '10 %Paul WRW&G LLP -1285 Av of Amer -NY 10019
(212) 248-8800 .. **Gazis,** James A '09 %Callan KB&B LLP -1 Whitehall -NY 10004
(212) 489-1600 .. **Gazit,** Ophir '98 %Deloitte LLP -1633 Bway -NY 10019 **Fx:**492-4201
(914) 428-1438 .. **Gaztambide,** Elliot Jr. '95 %T Bona,PC -123 Main -White Plns 10601 **Fx:**428-1413
(631) 653-5766 .. **Gazza,** Jos Fredk '77 -5 Ogden Ln Bx969 -Quogue 11959 **Fx:**694-1646
(917) 777-4200 .. **Gazzaway,** Kenneth M '08 %Bingham M LLP -1 Bttry Pk Plz -NY 10004
(716) 204-2400 .. **Gazzo,** Nicole C '04 %SJ Baum,PC -220 Nrthpnte Pkwy Bx1291 -Buffalo 14240 **Fx:**204-4600
(212) 980-3500 .. **Gazzola,** Mario '88 (Pavia & H LLP) -600 Mad Av -NY 10022
(516) 431-4222 .. **Gdanian,** Garyn I '88 (A'Hearn & G) -161 Monroe Blvd -Long Bch 11561
(212) 216-8000 .. **Gdanski,** Abraham S '09 %Tarter K&D LLP -1350 Bway -NY 10018
(845) 362-5238 .. **Gdanski,** Jeffrey I '97 (Gdanski & G,LLP) -25 Sherwood Ridge Rd -Pomona 10970 **Fx:**818-3656
(845) 362-4800 .. **Gdanski,** Sam Z '73 OfCnsl Gdanski & G,LLP -3 Rockwood Ln -Suffern 10901 **Fx:**362-4700
(845) 362-5238 .. **Gdanski,** Scott H '97 (Gdanski & G,LLP) -25 Sherwood Ridge Rd -Pomona 10970 **Fx:**818-3656
(212) 310-8000 .. **Geagan,** Martin C '00 %Weil G&M LLP -767 5th Av -NY 10153
(631) 537-4434 .. **Geaney,** David M '06 Sokolin LLC -Bx1206 -Brdghmptn 11932
(212) 921-8399 .. **Geanuleas,** Gabriella M '08 %Lankler S&W LLP -500 5th Av -NY 10110
(212) 532-1973 .. **Gear,** James E '88 %Krinsky & M -274 Mad Av -NY 10016 **Fx:**545-7211
(212) 705-7000 .. **Gearns,** Mary Gail '86 (Bingham M LLP) -399 Park Av -NY 10022
(518) 431-5000 .. **Gearon,** Jamie H '77 %Farm Family Ins -Bx656 -Albany 12201 **Fx:**431-5979
(718) 250-2000 .. **Gearon,** Timothy D '04 DA -350 Jay -Brklyn 11201 **Fx:**250-2314
(631) 852-1650 .. **Gearrity,** Kathleen '04 %Leg Aid -300 Center Dr -Rvrhead 11901 **Fx:**852-1655
(631) 630-0818 .. **Gearty,** Wm M '84 -168 Smithtown Blvd -Nesconset 11767
(585) 334-9600 .. **Geary,** Brian J '90 Cnsl Bloch Industries LLC -140 Commerce Dr -Rchstr 14623 **Fx:**334-9636
(845) 340-7561 .. **Geary,** Linda A '91 %Law Dept -100 Church -NY 10007 **Fx:**340-7564
(718) 250-2000 .. **Geary,** Robt G '07 DA -350 Jay -Brklyn 11201 **Fx:**250-2314
(718) 768-3500 .. **Geary,** Robt J '78 Harvey-Geary Assoc -387 6th Av -Brklyn 11215 **Fx:**768-2550
(212) 819-8200 .. **Geary,** Sean J '75 (White & C LLP) -1155 Av of Amer -NY 10036
(631) 298-8353 .. **Geasa,** Janet '84 (Wickham BG&G,PC) -13015 Main Rd Bx1424 -Mattituck 11952
(718) 222-8880 .. **Geasor,** Howard J Jr. '84 OfCnsl Jones JO -45 Main -Brklyn 11201
(212) 732-0800 .. **Geballe,** Jonathan L '91 -11 Bway -NY 10004 **Fx:**480-8560
(718) 237-5500 .. **Geballe,** Rachel Dinerstein '08 %Leg Srvcs -105 Court -Brklyn 11201 **Fx:**855-0733
(212) 788-6818 .. **Gebauer,** Frederico '98 Mayors Ofc-Crim Justice -1 Centre -NY 10007
(914) 631-6200 .. **Gebbia,** Tammy F '00 Gibraltar Mgt -150 Wht Plns Rd -Tarrytwn 10591 **Fx:**631-6243
(212) 541-2000 .. **Gebert,** Kathryn E '04 %Bryan C LLP -1290 Av of Amer -NY 10104
(518) 280-3081 .. **Gebert,** Kent J '88 -1054 Baker Av -Schnctdy 12309
(631) 864-4460 .. **Gebert,** Thos A '87 Primary Land Srvcs LLC -368 Vets Mem'l Hwy -Commack 11725 **Fx:**864-4436
(516) 326-2400 .. **Gebhard,** Robt E '06 Ivone D&J,LLP -2001 Marcus Av -Lk Success 11042
(914) 946-3700 .. **Gebhardt,** Dolores '85 (McCarthy F LLP) -11 Martine Av -White Plns 10606
(516) 739-0000 .. **Gebhardt,** Thos M '89 %Martyn T&M -330 Old Cntry Rd -Mineola 11501
(914) 798-9905 .. **Gebicki,** Amanda Bishop '96 Grant McCarthy Grp,LLC -777 Wstchstr Av -White Plns 10604
(212) 272-6580 .. **Gebman,** Rebecca Marrero '04 JP Morgan Chase -383 Mad Av -NY 10179
(315) 788-5900 .. **Gebo,** Mark G '78 (Hrabchak G&L,PC) -216 Wshngtn -Watertwn 13601
(315) 788-5100 .. **Gebo,** Stephen W '77 (Conboy MB&K,LLP) -407 Sherman -Watertwn 13601
(212) 972-3000 .. **Gebrael,** Samir '08 %Klestadt & W,LLP -292 Mad Av -NY 10017
(212) 925-0017 .. **Geck,** Ronald J '97 RMTS Assoc,LLC -6 Harrison -NY 10013
(718) 543-3300 .. **Gedan,** Barry S '75 -555 W 235th -Bronx 10463
(718) 254-7000 .. **Geddes,** Elizabeth A '05 %US Atty -271 Cadman Plz E -Brklyn 11201 **Fx:**254-6479
(212) 858-1000 .. **Geddish,** Wm J '10 %Pillsbury WSP LLP -1540 Bway -NY 10036
(212) 859-8000 .. **Gede-Lange,** Andrea '07 %Fried FHS&J LLP -1 NY Plz -NY 10004
(212) 732-1776 .. **Geduldig,** Albert J '50 OfCnsl A Geduldig & Assoc,PLLC -150 Bway -NY 10038 **Fx:**240-0365
(516) 794-1219 .. **Geduldig,** Martin '67 -600 Old Cntry Rd -Gdn Cty 11530 **Fx:**228-3559
(212) 732-1776 .. **Geduldig,** Richd A '91 -150 Bway -NY 10038 **Fx:**566-1033
(607) 733-8866 .. **Gee,** Adam M '97 %Ziff Law Firm,LLP -303 William -Elmira 14901 **Fx:**732-6062
(212) 833-1171 .. **Gee,** Betty W '07 %Friedman KS&A LLP -1633 Bway -NY 10019 **Fx:**373-7971
(212) 407-7700 .. **Gee,** Cameron A '06 (Vedder P,PC) -1633 Bway -NY 10019
(518) 463-0770 .. **Gee,** Eric R '05 %P Scagnelli -48 Columbia -Albany 12207
(212) 751-3001 .. **Gee,** Irene R '03 %Thompson & K LLP -919 3rd Av -NY 10022
(212) 455-2000 .. **Gee,** Lauren A '09 %Simpson T&B LLP -425 Lex Av -NY 10017
(607) 733-4635 .. **Gee,** Pamela Doyle '97 %Davidson & O,PC -243 Lk -Elmira 14901
(212) 350-9322 .. **Gee,** Richd '03 -110 E 57th -NY 10022 **Fx:**350-9327
(212) 819-8200 .. **Gee,** Steven C '09 %White & C LLP -1155 Av of Amer -NY 10036
(212) 334-8838 .. **Gee,** Steven T '92 -123 Chrystie -NY 10002 **Fx:**732-1043
(212) 836-8000 .. **Geelan,** John D '91 (Kaye S LLP) -425 Park Av -NY 10022
(212) 423-3503 .. **Geelan,** Sara '98 Solomon R Guggenheim Fndtn -345 Hudson -NY 10014 **Fx:**(917) 386-1403
(212) 210-9471 .. **Geercken,** Karl '93 (Alston & B LLP) -90 Park Av -NY 10016
(212) 863-5608 .. **Geevarghese,** Susan '03 HPD -100 Gold -NY 10038
(212) 201-1170 .. **Gefell,** Andrew W '05 %Abrams GMB,LLP -237 W 35th -NY 10001
(516) 437-4385 .. **Gefen,** Avrohom Y '04 %Vishnick MM LLP -3000 Marcus Av -Lk Success 11042
(212) 815-1140 .. **Gefen,** Sheera '02 %DC 37 MELS -125 Barclay -NY 10007 **Fx:**815-7520
(516) 536-0900 .. **Geffen,** Richd S '82 %Jacobson & S -510 Merrick Rd Bx46 -Rockvll Ctr 11571
(516) 294-6666 .. **Geffner,** Alisa J '03 %Samuelson H&S -300 Grdn City Plz -Gdn Cty 11530
(212) 620-0340 .. **Geffner,** Edw I '76 %Project Renewal Inc -200 Varick -NY 10014 **Fx:**633-9044
(212) 765-2100 .. **Geffner,** Michl '79 -1700 Bway -NY 10019
(212) 947-3793 .. **Geffner,** Ron '92 (Sadis & G LLP) -551 5th Av -NY 10176
(212) 846-5385 .. **Geftman,** Hayley N '01 MTV Networks -1515 Bway -NY 10036
(315) 432-8800 .. **Gegan,** Edmund J '94 Cnsl RESCUECOM Corp -2560 Burnet Av -Syracuse 13206 **Fx:**433-5228
(516) 248-1700 .. **Gegwich,** Christopher G '00 (Forchelli CDSM&T,LLP) -333 Earle Ovngton Blvd -Uniondale 11553
(718) 273-6677 .. **Geha,** Nada Alees '03 %Leg Aid -60 Bay -Staten Isl 10301 **Fx:**442-2679
(718) 263-5999 .. **Gehi,** Naresh M '01 -118-21 Qns Blvd -Frst Hlls 11375
(212) 337-8550 .. **Gehi,** Pooja S '05 %S Rivera Law Prjct -322 8th Av -NY 10001
(212) 259-8000 .. **Gehl,** Matthew T '10 %Dewey & L LLP -1301 Av of Amer -NY 10019
(212) 269-1400 .. **Gehn,** David A '93 (Gusrae KB&N PLLC) -120 Wall -NY 10005

(516) 608-7020 .. **Gehnrich,** Donna E '90 Systemax Inc -11 Hrbr Park Dr -Pt Wash 11050
(212) 698-3500 .. **Gehrie,** Adam I '05 %Dechert LLP -1095 Av of Amer -NY 10036
(212) 689-1113 .. **Gehrig,** Lauren E '08 %Garbarini & S,PC -432 Park Av S -NY 10016
(212) 450-4000 .. **Gehring,** Andrew S '10 %Davis P&W LLP -450 Lex Av -NY 10017
(212) 400-7428 .. **Gehring,** Jos E Jr. '97 (Gehring & S LLC) -370 Lex Av -NY 10017
(212) 692-1000 .. **Gehring,** Kathrine A '07 %Duane M LLP -1540 Bway -NY 10036
(212) 400-7420 .. **Gehring & Satriale LLC** -370 Lex Av -NY 10017 **Fx:**400-7440
(212) 736-1940 .. **Gehris,** Wm C '93 (Davidson D&K LLC) -485 7th Av -NY 10018
(315) 663-6485 .. **Gehron,** Linda '81 -109 S Warren -Syracuse 13202
(845) 291-2050 .. **Geidel,** John M '90 %DA -255-275 Main -Goshen 10924 **Fx:**291-2085
(516) 571-3800 .. **Geier,** Christine M '07 %DA -262 Old Cntry Rd -Mineola 11501 **Fx:**248-9479
(212) 735-3000 .. **Geier,** Jeffrey S '03 %Skadden ASM&F LLP -4 Times Sq -NY 10036
(585) 232-1946 .. **Geiger,** Alexander '76 (Geiger & R,LLP) -45 Exchange -Rchstr 14614
(212) 946-2854 .. **Geiger,** Andrew J '04 Capital Mrkts Advsrs,LLC -11 Penn Plz -NY 10001
(212) 768-6700 .. **Geiger,** Brit L '72 (Sonnenschein N&R LLP) -1221 Av of Amer -NY 10020
(212) 310-8000 .. **Geiger,** Caroline P '07 %Weil G&M LLP -767 5th Av -NY 10153
(516) 431-1000 .. **Geiger,** Chas M '94 Corp Cnsl -1 W Chester -Long Bch 11561 **Fx:**431-1016
(516) 409-6200 .. **Geiger,** Christine M '05 %Furey KWM&C,PC -2174 Jackson Av -Seafrd 11783
(718) 625-5860 .. **Geiger,** E Marvin '55 (Williams & G) -26 Court -Brklyn 11242
(516) 538-2500 .. **Geiger,** Elizabeth T '84 %Furey FLMW&D,PC -600 Front -Hempstd 11550
(212) 285-2505 .. **Geiger,** Emily '85 -225 Bway -NY 10007 **Fx:**964-4506
(212) 701-3000 .. **Geiger,** Jay '96 Cnsl Cahill G&R LLP -80 Pine -NY 10005 **Fx:**269-5420
(877) 222-1814 .. **Geiger,** Kathleen McGonigle '94 %B Rothenberg -100 Duffy Av -Hicksvll 11801 **Fx:**(866) 894-2182
(212) 820-9406 .. **Geiger,** Martin A '74 (Hawkins D&W LLP) -One Chase Manh Plz -NY 10005
(212) 493-2351 .. **Geiger,** Michele '03 IBM -33 Maiden Ln -NY 10038
(516) 662-2559 .. **Geiger,** Noelle Traina '97 -222 E Montauk Hwy -Lindenhrst 11757
(585) 232-1946 .. **Geiger & Rothenberg,LLP** -45 Exchange -Rchstr 14614 **Fx:**232-4746
(212) 225-2000 .. **Geiger,** Theo '09 %Cleary GS&H -1 Lbrty Plz -NY 10006
(914) 422-3900 .. **Geiger,** Thos '71 (Oxman TKW&G LLP) -120 Bloomingdale Rd -White Plns 10605
(585) 724-5129 .. **Geil,** Norman H '76 Eastman Kodak -343 State -Rchstr 14650 **Fx:**724-5515
(843) 689-6242 .. **Geis,** David P '73 -445 Hmltn Av -White Plns 10601 **Fx:**689-6282
(631) 665-3400 .. **Geis,** John L '75 %Siben & S,LLP -90 E Main Bx149P -Bay Shr 11706
(212) 883-4900 .. **Geis,** Peter G '96 (Cozen O) -277 Park Av -NY 10172
(631) 234-4400 .. **Geisel,** Amy Boyle '89 OfCnsl Pinks A&N -140 Fell Ct -Hauppauge 11788
(917) 478-8579 .. **Geisel,** Matthew J '03 -949 West End Av -NY 10025
(212) 480-5284 .. **Geisel,** Sally A '91 %Insurance Dept -25 Beaver -NY 10004 **Fx:**480-5272
(518) 629-7125 .. **Geisendorfer,** Ann B '95 %Hudson Valley Comm Cllg -80 Vandenburgh Av -Troy 12180 **Fx:**629-7542
(212) 752-8000 .. **Geisenheimer,** Jill B '09 %Cole SMF&L,PA -900 3rd Av -NY 10022
(914) 723-2121 .. **Geisinger,** Lawr S '79 -455 Cntrl Pk Av -Scarsdale 10583
(516) 542-1000 .. **Geisler & Gabriele,LLP** -100 Q Roosevelt Blvd -Gdn Cty 11530 **Fx:**542-1226
(631) 476-7577 .. **Geisler & Gabriele,LLP** -417 E Main -Pt Jffrsn 11777 **Fx:**476-5744
(212) 421-4000 .. **Geisler,** Mark W '83 Hoffinger S&R,LLP -150 E 58th -NY 10155
(212) 556-2100 .. **Geisler,** Mordechai L '03 %King & S -1185 Av of Amer -NY 10036
(516) 542-1000 .. **Geisler,** Stephen B '71 (Geisler & G,LLP) -100 Q Roosevelt Blvd -Gdn Cty 11530
(718) 422-1180 .. **Geiss,** Virginia '79 -26 Court -Brklyn 11242 **Fx:**246-2863
(718) 354-3200 .. **Geisser,** Mark '88 %Battiste A&S,Inc -60 Bay -Staten Isl 10301
(212) 599-8000 .. **Geisser,** Troy H '86 %Fincl Fed Credit Inc -730 3rd Av -NY 10017 **Fx:**286-5885
(914) 428-2880 .. **Geist,** Alan R '55 -237 Mamaroneck Av -White Plns 10605 **Fx:**428-2881
(212) 326-2000 .. **Geist,** Andrew J '88 (O'Melveny & M LLP) -7 Times Sq -NY 10036
(212) 408-2500 .. **Geist,** Bradley B '70 OfCnsl Baker B,LLP -30 Rckfllr Plz -NY 10112
(212) 557-7700 .. **Geist,** Carol Berg '76 (Davidson D&C LLP) -60 E 42nd -NY 10165
(914) 644-8300 .. **Geist,** Gerald K '80 (Schuman S&G) -1 N Lex Av -White Plns 10601
(914) 428-2880 .. **Geist,** Herman S '51 -235 Mamaroneck Av -White Plns 10605
(212) 998-6683 .. **Geistfeld,** Mark A '90 %NYU Law Schl -40 Wshngtn Sq S -NY 10012 **Fx:**995-4341
(516) 873-2000 .. **Geizhals,** Benjamin '75 OfCnsl Moritt HH&H LLP -400 Grdn City Plz -Gdn Cty 11530
(516) 294-0250 .. **Gekhman,** Leonid '01 %M Haskel -167 Willis Av -Mineola 11501 **Fx:**294-0854
(212) 450-4000 .. **Gelardi,** Adam J '10 %Davis P&W LLP -450 Lex Av -NY 10017
(914) 946-0400 .. **Gelardi,** Marili D'Emilia '83 %Schiavetti CDW&N,LLP -709 Wstchstr Av -White Plns 10604
(914) 251-0603 .. **Gelardi,** Vincent '83 (Gelardi & R,LLP) -800 Wstchstr Av -Rye Brook 10573 **Fx:**253-0909
(212) 527-1000 .. **Gelb,** Alan M '63 (Jones HC&B PC) -1 Bttry Pk Plz -NY 10004
(718) 590-5944 .. **Gelb,** Harry '81 %Admin Children's Srvcs -900 Sheridan Av -Bronx 10451 **Fx:**992-0084
(718) 858-8675 .. **Gelb,** James I '81 (Gelb & B) -26 Court -Brklyn 11201 **Fx:**858-7342
(845) 727-7010 .. **Gelb,** Jonas M '71 -31 Vllg Gate Way -Nyack 10960 **Fx:**727-7010
(212) 310-8000 .. **Gelb,** Jos W '64 (Weil G&M LLP) -767 5th Av -NY 10153
(212) 571-0550 .. **Gelb,** Judith A '59 OfCnsl Allegaert B&V LLP -111 Bway -NY 10006
(585) 232-3730 .. **Gelb,** Sandra Wolk '93 %Chamberlain D LLP -1600 Crssrds Bldg -Rchstr 14614
(914) 833-7602 .. **Gelband,** Jos F '54 (JF Gelband,PC) -45 Pine Rdg Rd -Larchmnt 10538 **Fx:**834-0888
(516) 358-0505 .. **Gelbard,** Bernard '50 %Intracoastal Abstract -5 Carriage Dr -Old Westbury 11568 **Fx:**358-0394
(516) 358-0505 .. **Gelbard,** David J '93 %Intracoastal Abstract -5 Carriage Dr -Old Westbury 11568 **Fx:**358-0394
(212) 984-7785 .. **Gelbard,** Paul E '53 OfCnsl Warshaw BCS&K,LLP -555 5th Av -NY 10017
(212) 878-8000 .. **Gelber,** Avrohom C '97 (Clifford C LLP) -31 W 52nd -NY 10019
(212) 866-9306 .. **Gelber,** Blanche L '80 -215 W 98th -NY 10025 **Fx:**866-9306
(732) 855-6006 .. **Gelber,** Darren M '93 (Wilentz G&S) -110 William -NY 10038 **Fx:**726-6571
(716) 633-5050 .. **Gelber,** Herschel '83 (Gelber & O,LLC) -6512 Main -Amherst 14221 **Fx:**633-9052
(718) 638-2383 .. **Gelber,** Lawr R '82 Vanderbilt Plz -34 Plz W -Brklyn 11238
(212) 756-2000 .. **Gelber,** Lawr V '93 (Schulte R&Z LLP) -919 3rd Av -NY 10022
(212) 661-9400 .. **Gelber,** Martin H '82 %Klein & S LLP -275 Mad Av -NY 10016
(914) 941-5668 .. **Gelber,** Oren '07 %Collen IP -80 S Highland Av -Ossining 10562 **Fx:**941-6091
(212) 530-1800 .. **Gelber,** R Zachary '02 %Richards K&O LLP -1 World Fncl Ctr -NY 10281
(716) 633-5050 .. **Gelber,** Stephanie S '84 %Gelber & O,LLC -6512 Main -Amherst 14221 **Fx:**633-9052
(516) 228-4280 .. **Gelberg,** Stuart P '81 -600 Old Cntry Rd -Gdn Cty 11530 **Fx:**228-4278 ***[Bankruptcy Law]***
(212) 310-8921 .. **Gelbfish,** Larry J '88 (Weil G&M LLP) -767 5th Av -NY 10153
(212) 436-1074 .. **Gelbfish,** Sharon F '89 IRS -290 Bway -NY 10007
(212) 407-4000 .. **Gelblum,** Seth D '83 (Loeb & L,LLP) -345 Park Av -NY 10154
(718) 375-0463 .. **Gelbstein,** Alan D '76 -1510 E 7th -Brklyn 11230
(718) 645-5600 .. **Gelbstein,** Yehoshua '08 %Stein F&S LLP -1639 E 13th -Brklyn 11229
(212) 370-0704 .. **Gelburd,** Robin C '85 Fair Health Inc -330 Mad Av -NY 10017
(607) 273-2272 .. **Geldenhuys,** Mariette '89 -401 E State -Ithaca 14850
(212) 558-4000 .. **Geldzahler,** Janet Thiele '80 OfCnsl Sullivan & C LLP -125 Broad -NY 10004
(718) 312-4100 .. **Gelein,** Kelly K '01 %Empire Blue Cross -15 MetroTech Ctr -Brklyn 11201 **Fx:**312-6010
(212) 504-6000 .. **Gelernt,** Karen B '90 (Cadwalader W&T LLP) -1 World Fncl Ctr -NY 10281
(212) 549-2500 .. **Gelernt,** Lee '91 %ACLU -125 Broad -NY 10004 **Fx:**549-2651
(718) 330-1200 .. **Gelernt,** Michelle A '96 %Fed Def of NY Inc -1 Pierrepont Plz -Brklyn 11201 **Fx:**855-0760
(212) 336-2000 .. **Gelernter,** Eugene '78 (Patterson BW&T LLP) -1133 Av of Amer -NY 10036
(716) 645-5540 .. **Gelernter,** Lise G '85 Univ at Buffalo Law Schl -O'Brian Hall -Buffalo 14260 **Fx:**645-2064
(212) 788-1150 .. **Gelfand,** Andrew '91 %Law Dept -100 Church -NY 10007 **Fx:**788-0367
(212) 558-4000 .. **Gelfand,** Andrew E '07 %Sullivan & C LLP -125 Broad -NY 10004
(914) 285-9800 .. **Gelfand,** Bertram R '53 OfCnsl Kurzman EC&L,LLP -1 N Bway -White Plns 10601
(212) 225-2000 .. **Gelfand,** Boris '10 %Cleary GS&H -1 Lbrty Plz -NY 10006
(646) 386-3641 .. **Gelfand,** Boris L '05 Supreme Ct-Law Dept -60 Centre -NY 10007
(718) 624-2036 .. **Gelfand,** Burton '62 -26 Court -Brklyn 11242 **Fx:**624-5979
(212) 530-5000 .. **Gelfand,** David R '88 (Milbank TH&M LLP) -1 Chase Manh Plz -NY 10005
(718) 624-2036 .. **Gelfand,** Jacob N '94 -26 Court -Brklyn 11242 **Fx:**624-5979
(212) 310-8000 .. **Gelfand,** Joshua S '07 %Weil G&M LLP -767 5th Av -NY 10153
(516) 937-2222 .. **Gelfand,** Mark E '83 Diagnostic Imaging Grp,LLC -560 S Bway -Hicksvll 11801 **Fx:**977-1451
(631) 661-0006 .. **Gelfand,** Mark E '83 OfCnsl E Young & Assoc -112 Route 109 -W Babylon 11704 **Fx:**661-0226
(718) 624-2036 .. **Gelfand,** Matisyahu '01 %B Gelfand -26 Court -Brklyn 11242 **Fx:**624-5979
(516) 622-9200 .. **Gelfand,** Michl J '05 %Westerman BEM&S,LLP -1201 RXR Plz -Uniondale 11553
(516) 371-3419 .. **Gelfand,** Seymour '50 -360 Central Av -Lawrence 11559 **Fx:**371-7727
(631) 470-5300 .. **Gelfand,** Stephen P '70 (S Gelfand,PC) -548 W Jericho Tpk -Smithtwn 11787 **Fx:**470-5302
(212) 867-4488 .. **Gelfarb,** David B '87 %Moss & K -122 E 42nd -NY 10168
(718) 261-9460 .. **Gelfman,** Marianne C '97 %Pearlman AFS&S,LLP -80-02 Kew Grdns Rd -Kew Gdns 11415
(914) 461-1274 .. **Gelfman,** Peter T '89 WHX Corp -1133 Wstchstr Av -White Plns 10604 **Fx:**696-8684
(212) 859-8000 .. **Gelfond,** Stuart H '87 (Fried FHS&J LLP) -1 NY Plz -NY 10004
(212) 450-4000 .. **Geli,** Lisa M '05 -450 Lex Av -NY 10017 **Fx:**450-3800
(212) 551-1755 .. **Geliebter,** Darren M '97 (Lombard & G LLP) -230 Park Av -NY 10169 **Fx:**(646) 349-5567
(212) 442-6652 .. **Geliebter,** Rachel E '06 %Admin Child Svcs -220 Church -NY 10013
(212) 801-2191 .. **Gelin,** D Scott '97 (Greenberg T,LLP) -200 Park Av -NY 10166
(212) 839-5365 .. **Gelinas,** A J Alexis '75 (Sidley A LLP) -787 7th Av -NY 10019
(212) 768-6700 .. **Gelinas,** Chas A '02 %Sonnenschein N&R LLP -2 World Fncl Ctr -NY 10281
(212) 619-2859 .. **Gell,** Amy Nussbaum '88 (Gell & G) -299 Bway -NY 10007 **Fx:**964-9485
(212) 619-2859 .. **Gell,** Roland M '86 (Gell & G) -299 Bway -NY 10007 **Fx:**964-9485
(845) 425-0990 .. **Geller,** Aaron W '93 %Accredited Aides-Plus -305A Airport Exec Pk -Nanuet 10954
(212) 246-1212 .. **Geller,** Alfred '56 Geller Media Mgmt,Inc -250 W 57th -NY 10107 **Fx:**541-6712
(914) 328-9529 .. **Geller,** Alvin '62 -175 Main -White Plns 10601 **Fx:**328-6384
(212) 284-2300 .. **Geller,** Ashley B '04 Jefferies & Co -520 Mad Av -NY 10022
(212) 788-2952 .. **Geller,** Brian H '05 Mayors Ofc -253 Bway -NY 10007
(718) 250-2000 .. **Geller,** Courtney E '06 DA -350 Jay -Brklyn 11201 **Fx:**250-2314
(631) 853-5212 .. **Geller,** David M '06 %Leg Aid -400 Carleton Av Bx9082 -Central Islip 11722 **Fx:**853-7798
(914) 473-6783 .. **Geller,** Edw B '80 -1053 Saw Mill Rvr Rd -Ardsley 10502 **Fx:**738-0999
(212) 557-4000 .. **Geller,** Halie F '08 %Grunfeld DLS&K LLP -399 Park Av -NY 10022
(845) 339-4848 .. **Geller,** James A '63 -31 River Rd -Ulster Pk 12487 **Fx:**339-4188
(212) 732-1188 .. **Geller,** Jan '80 (Altschul G&G) -17 Battery Place -NY 10004 **Fx:**732-1001

(718) 366-3600 .. **Geller**, Jos '89 (Geller & G) -69-03 Fresh Pond Rd -Glendale 11385 **Fx:**628-5437
(212) 997-7595 .. **Geller**, Joshua R '05 %Hafetz N&R -500 5th Av -NY 10110
(212) 696-6000 .. **Geller**, Joshua S '06 %Curtis M-PC&M LLP -101 Park Av -NY 10178
(212) 756-2000 .. **Geller**, Kenneth F '10 %Schulte R&Z LLP -919 3rd Av -NY 10022
(516) 371-0967 .. **Geller**, Kenneth L '73 K Geller,PC -372 Doughty Blvd -Inwood 11096 **Fx:**371-1579
(212) 455-2000 .. **Geller**, Marcy G '98 (Simpson T&B LLP) -425 Lex Av -NY 10017
(718) 382-8700 .. **Geller**, Mark '84 (M Geller & Assoc,PC) -1639 E 13th -Brklyn 11229 **Fx:**377-3624
(718) 999-0415 .. **Geller**, Matthew J '02 Fire Dept Invstgtns & Trials -9 Metrotech Ctr -Brklyn 11201
(212) 259-8000 .. **Geller**, Melissa S '08 %Dewey & L LLP -1301 Av of Amer -NY 10019
(212) 513-3200 .. **Geller**, Mitchell J '79 (Holland & K LLP) -31 W 52nd -NY 10019
(718) 401-2559 .. **Geller**, Moishe '84 (M Geller & Assoc) -840 Grnd Cncrs -Bronx 10451
(718) 544-5350 .. **Geller**, Nathaniel '59 -144-45 Melbourne Av -Flushng 11367
(212) 259-8000 .. **Geller**, Nicholas L '07 %Dewey & L LLP -1301 Av of Amer -NY 10019
(212) 532-0532 .. **Geller**, Richd E '88 (Geller & S,LLP) -419 Park Av S -NY 10016 **Fx:**532-1871
(914) 946-6600 .. **Geller**, Richd L '95 -280 N Central Av -Hartsdale 10530 **Fx:**614-7109
(212) 824-5700 .. **Geller**, Sandra R '76 %Practising Law Inst -810 7th Av -NY 10019
(212) 268-5700 .. **Geller**, Sheldon M '85 -462 7th Av -NY 10018 **Fx:**268-5707
(212) 838-0887 .. **Geller**, Stanley '47 -909 3rd Av -NY 10022 **Fx:**588-1080
(212) 425-3100 .. **Geller**, Stephen L '02 %McManus C&R,PC -48 Wall -NY 10005
(212) 244-4704 .. **Geller**, Tatyana S '96 -362 5th Av -NY 10001 **Fx:**549-6098
(914) 421-1942 .. **Geller**, Thos '74 -53 Club Pnte Dr -White Plns 10605
(212) 825-0365 .. **Geller**, Wm J '95 %AL Bailey,PC -120 Bway -NY 10271 **Fx:**825-0999
(718) 797-3737 .. **Gellerman**, Kenneth J '85 -26 Court -Brklyn 11242 **Fx:**797-2208
(718) 261-2300 .. **Gellerman**, Steven L '78 (Sager & G) -118-35 Qns Blvd -Frst Hlls 11375
(845) 454-3250 .. **Gellert**, Arthur L '66 (Gellert & K,PC) -75 Wshngtn -Poughkeepsie 12601
(212) 661-9100 .. **Gellert**, Donald N '63 OfCnsl Otterbourg SH&R,PC -230 Park Av -NY 10169
(212) 698-3500 .. **Gellert**, Erika '08 %Dechert LLP -1095 Av of Amer -NY 10036
(845) 454-3250 .. **Gellert & Klein,PC** -75 Wshngtn -Poughkeepsie 12601 **Fx:**454-4652
(914) 249-0100 .. **Gellert & Klein,PC** -3010 Wstchstr Av -Purchase 10577 **Fx:**249-0111
(212) 232-1300 .. **Gellert**, Robyn J '00 (Lewis BB&S LLP) -77 Water -NY 10005
(212) 475-1594 .. **Gellert**, Sharman Nina '94 -104 E 17th -NY 10003
(212) 687-3747 .. **Gelles**, Walter R '55 (Tuchman KWL&G,LLP) -6 E 45th -NY 10017
(518) 447-3200 .. **Gellhaus**, Kenneth L '87 (McNamee LT&W,PC) -677 Bway -Albany 12207
(212) 418-5200 .. **Gellis**, George A '98 RPM Asset Man -505 Park Av -NY 10022
(212) 460-5757 .. **Gellis**, Jan Ira '75 (Gellis & M,LLP) -137 5th Av -NY 10010
(212) 460-5757 .. **Gellis & Melinger,LLP** -137 5th Av -NY 10010 **Fx:**353-0831
(716) 833-4986 .. **Gellman**, George I '74 %Benchmark Grp -4053 Maple Rd -Buffalo 14226 **Fx:**833-2954
(718) 793-1300 .. **Gellman**, Jay L '95 -118-35 Qns Blvd -Frst Hlls 11375
(212) 383-2523 .. **Gellman**, Jonathan S '78 State Comptroller -59 Maiden Ln -NY 10038 **Fx:**383-3901
(212) 490-3331 .. **Gellman**, Lance K '73 (Parilla & G,PC) -60 E 42nd -NY 10165 **Fx:**986-4269
(516) 599-8822 .. **Gellman & Mandell** -29 Bway -Lynbrk 11563 **Fx:**599-6611
(516) 873-1511 .. **Gellman**, Michelle A '00 %Fischetti & P -310 Old Cntry Rd -Gdn Cty 11530
(212) 416-8404 .. **Gellman**, Paula '86 %Dept of Law -120 Bway -NY 10271
(716) 853-4080 .. **Gellman**, Ryan L '94 %Colucci & G,PC -424 Main -Buffalo 14202
(212) 403-1000 .. **Gellman**, Stephen G '83 (Wachtell LR&K) -51 W 52nd -NY 10019
(212) 688-6262 .. **Gellman**, Wendy Rosenthal '85 Sen K Gillibrand -780 3rd Av -NY 10017 **Fx:**223-8496
(212) 446-4800 .. **Gellner**, Noah J '07 %Kirkland & E LLP -153 E 53rd -NY 10022
(212) 573-0370 .. **Gelman**, Andrew B '91 Rodale,Inc -733 3rd Av -NY 10017
(718) 615-4024 .. **Gelman**, Elena R '99 Gelman & Assoc -1610 Sheepshead Bay Rd -Brklyn 11235 **Fx:**615-4027
(212) 332-2345 .. **Gelman**, Ernest H '63 E Gelman -350 5th Av -NY 10118 **Fx:**332-8301
(212) 548-2100 .. **Gelman**, James '96 (McGuire W LLP) -1345 Av of Amer -NY 10105
(212) 559-4271 .. **Gelman**, Jane A '89 %Citibank -909 3rd Av -NY 10043
(212) 872-1000 .. **Gelman**, Jason L '06 -One Bryant Park -NY 10036 **Fx:**872-1002
(212) 848-4000 .. **Gelman**, Mark J '02 %Shearman & S LLP -599 Lex Av -NY 10022
(212) 557-0559 .. **Gelman**, Phyllis '76 P Gelman & Assoc,LLC -60 E 42nd -NY 10165 **Fx:**297-0536
(718) 380-8980 .. **Gelman**, Robt D '85 -180-34 Union Tpk -Fresh Mdws 11366 **Fx:**380-8981
(716) 883-7272 .. **Gelman**, Warren B '71 (McGee & G) -200 Summer -Buffalo 14222
(718) 875-1300 .. **Gelnick**, Kenneth S '82 %Applt Div 2nd Dept -45 Monroe Pl -Brklyn 11201 **Fx:**858-2446
(585) 327-3218 .. **Gelormini**, James L '76 %Dept of Law -144 Exchange Blvd -Rchstr 14614 **Fx:**546-7514
(718) 273-9000 .. **Gelormino**, Louis '09 %Helbock N&G -2550 Victory Blvd -Staten Isl 10314 **Fx:**816-0718
(212) 559-9158 .. **Gelper**, Alyssa E '92 Citigroup Private Bk -153 E 53rd -NY 10022
(718) 935-0724 .. **Gelpi**, Rafael J '93 -186 Joralemon -Brklyn 11201
(212) 474-1000 .. **Gelston**, Philip A '79 (Cravath S&M LLP) -825 8th Av -NY 10019
(212) 455-2000 .. **Geltman**, Susannah S '07 %Simpson T&B LLP -425 Lex Av -NY 10017
(212) 428-2105 .. **Geltzer**, Elise A '74 %OCA -25 Beaver -NY 10004 **Fx:**428-2974
(212) 410-0100 .. **Geltzer**, Robt L '69 -1556 3rd Av -NY 10128 **Fx:**410-0400
(212) 715-1000 .. **Geluz**, Raymond R '06 Arnold & P LLP -399 Park Av -NY 10022
(212) 355-9500 .. **Geman**, Rachel J '98 (Lieff CH&B,LLP) -250 Hudson -NY 10013
(518) 473-8708 .. **Gemellaro**, Peter J '94 NYS Div Human Rights -ESP Bx2049 -Albany 12220
(718) 261-2323 .. **Gemelli**, John A '85 (J Gemelli,PC) -105-15 Metro Av -Frst Hlls 11375 **Fx:**520-1669
(845) 454-6920 .. **Gemmati**, Jos T '97 -30 Mnchstr Rd -Poughkeepsie 12603 **Fx:**454-3179
(631) 369-1577 .. **Gemmelli**, Richd P '57 -47 Triangle Ln -Baiting Hollow 11933
(518) 370-4187 .. **Gemmette**, Elizabeth Villiers '90 (Gemmette & G) -19 Front -Schnctdy 12305 **Fx:**370-3937
(212) 693-0085 .. **Gemmill**, John W '85 %Appellate Advocates -2 Rector -NY 10006 **Fx:**693-0878
(518) 487-7600 .. **Gemmiti**, Nicole S '10 %Whiteman O&H LLP -1 Commerce Plz -Albany 12260
(212) 554-1234 .. **Gemski**, Kristin M '03 AXA Financial Inc -1290 Av of Amer -NY 10104 **Fx:**707-3963
(212) 712-6113 .. **Genack**, Ahuva '78 Extell Development -805 3rd Av -NY 10022
(315) 963-7296 .. **Genant**, Robt E '74 -3306 Main Bx480 -Mexico 13114 **Fx:**963-8274
(646) 929-9750 .. **Genasci**, Matthew R '01 %Revenue Watch Inst -1700 Bway -NY 10019
(716) 853-5100 .. **Genau**, Eric C '02 %Lippes MWF LLP -665 Main -Buffalo 14203
(212) 837-6707 .. **Genauer**, Gabrielle K '08 %Hughes H&R LLP -1 Bttry Pk Plz -NY 10004 **Fx:**299-6707
(212) 999-5800 .. **Gencarelli**, Gina R '06 %Wilson SG&R -1301 Av of Americas -NY 10019
(212) 836-8000 .. **Genchi**, Jaclyn M '10 Kaye S LLP -425 Park Av -NY 10022
(914) 683-1002 .. **Gendal**, Steven K '00 %Whippoorwill Assoc,Inc -11 Martine Av -White Plns 10606
(212) 421-4100 .. **Gendel**, Andrea R '99 OfCnsl Pryor C LLP -7 Times Sq -NY 10036
(646) 429-1800 .. **Gendel**, Mitchell S '91 Cnsl MDC Partners -950 3rd Av -NY 10022
(212) 274-6202 .. **Gendell**, Stephanie J '99 %Admin Children's Srvcs -150 William -NY 10038
(212) 867-1050 .. **Gendelman**, David H '74 -16 E 34th -NY 10016 **Fx:**949-8828
(718) 616-1414 .. **Gendelman**, Tanya '96 -3033 Brighton 3rd -Brklyn 11235
(212) 768-6700 .. **Gendloff**, Elie H '03 OfCnsl Sonnenschein N&R LLP -1221 Av of Amer -NY 10020
(212) 326-3939 .. **Gendzier**, Alexander A '99 (Jones D) -222 E 41st -NY 10017
(212) 872-9800 .. **Genecin**, Victor '82 OfCnsl Squire S&D LLP -30 Rckfllr Plz -NY 10112
(585) 546-5530 .. **Generalow**, Alex '00 %Thomson West -50 E Broad -Rchstr 14694
(845) 365-9100 .. **Generelli**, Jos F '79 %Davidson & G -30 Ramland Rd -Orangebrg 10962
(516) 620-1408 .. **Generosa**, Danl T '97 (Lexpath Technologies) -132 E 43rd -NY 10017
(585) 670-9583 .. **Genese**, Chas J '74 -Bx688 -Webster 14580 **Fx:**670-0664
(973) 596-4647 .. **Geneslaw**, Howard D '95 (Gibbons PC) -1 Penn Plz -NY 10119 **Fx:**639-6256
(212) 403-1000 .. **Genet**, Daniella '10 %Wachtell LR&K -51 W 52nd -NY 10019
(212) 336-0182 .. **Genet**, Megan R '05 SEC -3 World Fncl Ctr -NY 10281 **Fx:**336-1323
(516) 535-1700 .. **Genetin Tate**, Debra '90 %Horing W&R,PC -11 Hillside Av -Williston Pk 11596
(914) 232-8174 .. **Genett**, Richd A '84 (Deren G&M) -28 Edgemont Rd -Katonah 10536
(212) 450-4000 .. **Geneve**, Joanna E '10 %Davis P&W LLP -450 Lex Av -NY 10017
(212) 906-1200 .. **Gengel**, Gerhard P '03 (Latham & W) -885 3rd Av -NY 10022
(212) 902-2000 .. **Genger**, Todd W '02 Goldman Sachs -85 Broad -NY 10004
(718) 261-1541 .. **Gengo**, Paul J '81 -118-21 Qns Blvd -Frst Hlls 11375 **Fx:**261-1548
(212) 719-6200 .. **Genin**, Andrew F '70 %IRS -290 Bway -NY 10007
(212) 526-2614 .. **Genirs**, Kevin R '87 Barclays Capital Inc -745 7th Av -NY 10019
(718) 561-4444 .. **Genis**, Robt J '83 (Sonin & G) -1 Fordham Plz -Bronx 10458 **Fx:**561-2162
(718) 862-5140 .. **Genkin**, Michl A '86 MHLS -41 Mad Av -NY 10010
(212) 636-5400 .. **Genkins**, Amy E '82 %DC Comics -1700 Bway -NY 10019 **Fx:**636-5595
(212) 891-1600 .. **Genn**, Elisabeth '07 %Jenner & B LLP -919 3rd Av -NY 10022
(845) 562-0203 .. **Genna**, Andrew J '74 (Finkelstein & Prtnrs,LLP) -1279 Route 300 Bx1111 -Newburgh 12550
(212) 858-8123 .. **Genna**, Frank R '04 1st Investors Corp -110 Wall -NY 10005
(518) 474-0871 .. **Genna**, Russell J '84 %DMV -6 ESP -Albany 12228 **Fx:**486-4485
(212) 918-3000 .. **Gennardo**, Patrick J '94 (Hogan L LLP) -875 3rd Av -NY 10022
(212) 267-1950 .. **Gennarelli**, Gregory S '00 %Salenger SSK&B,LLP -233 Bway -NY 10279
(212) 406-1919 .. **Gennet Kallmann Antin & Robinson,PC** -140 Bway -NY 10005 **Fx:**(973) 285-1177
(631) 854-1133 .. **Gennosa**, Muriel L '86 Appllt Div 2nd Dept -30 E Hoffman Av -Lindenhrst 11757
(212) 867-3345 .. **Gennusa**, Susanne '96 -100 Park Av -NY 10017 **Fx:**867-2994
(212) 752-9700 .. **Gennuso**, Peter J '99 (Gersten S LLP) -600 Lex Av -NY 10022
(516) 759-7940 .. **Genoa**, Marilyn Kalenscher '90 (Genoa & Assoc,PC) -12 Jaegger Dr -Old Brookvll 11545 **Fx:**674-9425
(212) 566-7188 .. **Genova**, Angelo J '79 (Genova B&G) -115 Bway -NY 10006
(212) 566-7188 .. **Genova Burns & Giantomasi** -115 Bway -NY 10006 **Fx:**566-7116
(212) 648-0268 .. **Genova**, Diane '76 JP Morgan Chase -245 Park Av -NY 10167
(212) 773-0438 .. **Genova**, John J '07 Ernst & Young LLP -5 Times Sq -NY 10036
(212) 819-8200 .. **Genova**, John M '85 OfCnsl White & C LLP -1155 Av of Amer -NY 10036
(212) 530-5000 .. **Genova**, Jos S '78 (Milbank TH&M LLP) -1 Chase Manh Plz -NY 10005
(516) 624-6350 .. **Genova**, Leonard '90 %Town Supervisor -54 Audrey Av -Oyster Bay 11771 **Fx:**624-6362
(845) 298-1600 .. **Genova**, Thos '82 (Genova & M) -1136 Route 9 -Wappingers Fls 12590 **Fx:**298-1265
(914) 220-5476 .. **Genova**, Thos J '78 -445 Hmltn Av -White Plns 10601
(914) 347-6360 .. **Genovese**, Danl J '81 %Epstein & R -565 Taxter Rd -Elmsfrd 10523
(914) 681-6006 .. **Genovese**, Donna M '89 (Goldschmidt & G,LLP) -1 N Lex Av -White Plns 10601
(716) 885-1834 .. **Genovese**, Giovanni '90 -484 Deleware Av -Buffalo 14202
(718) 250-2000 .. **Genovese**, John A '94 DA -350 Jay -Brklyn 11201 **Fx:**250-2314
(212) 578-2211 .. **Genovese**, John T '90 %MetLife -27-01 Qns Plz N -LIC 11101
(516) 873-2284 .. **Genovese**, Marta '86 AAA NY -1415 Kellum Pl -Gdn Cty 11530 **Fx:**873-2355
(516) 623-6499 .. **Genovese**, Michl V '96 (Coville & G,PC) -2174 Hewlett Av -Merrick 11566 **Fx:**623-5365

(718) 767-3333 .. **Genovesi,** Anthony J '89 (Borchert GL&L,PC) -19-02 Whitestone Expy -Whitestone 11357
(718) 643-7084 .. **Genovesi,** Lara J '98 NYS Supreme Ct -360 Adams -Brklyn 11201
(716) 833-4447 .. **Genrich,** Willard A Jr. '74 -4949 Main -Amherst 14226
(212) 446-4800 .. **Genser,** Andrew M '95 (Kirkland & E LLP) -153 E 53rd -NY 10022
(631) 390-5000 .. **Genser,** David S '68 (Genser DG&C,LLP) -445 Broad Hollow Rd -Melvll 11747
(631) 390-5000 .. **Genser Dubow Genser & Cona,LLP** -445 Broad Hollow Rd -Melvll 11747 **Fx:**390-5001
(631) 390-5000 .. **Genser,** Jack H '95 (Genser DG&C,LLP) -445 Broad Hollow Rd -Melvll 11747
(315) 234-8600 .. **Gensini,** Gioia A '83 Hon A Baxter -100 S Clinton Bx7396 -Syracuse 13261 **Fx:**234-8601
(716) 856-5012 .. **Gensler,** Kimberly D '02 %Anspach ME,LLP -2400 Main Pl Twr -Buffalo 14202
(718) 590-2000 .. **Gensler,** Terry H '95 %DA -198 E 161st -Bronx 10451 **Fx:**590-6477
(718) 233-6472 .. **Gentes,** Jeffrey S '04 Leg Srvcs for NY -36 Richmond Ter -Staten Isl 10301
(212) 406-4848 .. **Genthner,** Robt G '09 %G Pillersdorf & Assoc,PC -225 Bway -NY 10007 **Fx:**406-5884
(516) 229-4300 .. **Gentile,** Andrew J '97 %J Bilello & Assoc -875 Merrick Av -Westbury 11590
(718) 816-0005 .. **Gentile,** Annamarie Gulino '83 (Angiuli K&G,LLP) -60 Bay -Staten Isl 10301
(212) 742-9700 .. **Gentile,** Anthony P '72 (Godosky & G,PC) -61 Bway -NY 10006
(718) 492-1444 .. **Gentile,** Anthony V '99 -6648 Ridge Blvd -Brklyn 11220 **Fx:**492-9441
(716) 851-4343 .. **Gentile,** Carmen J '83 %Law Dept -65 Niagara Sq -Buffalo 14202 **Fx:**851-4105
(212) 636-7898 .. **Gentile,** Caroline M '95 Fordham Univ Sch of Law -140 W 62nd -NY 10023 **Fx:**636-6899
(212) 686-6112 .. **Gentile,** Carolyn D '68 -451 Park Av S -NY 10016 **Fx:**686-6614
(516) 571-3800 .. **Gentile,** Connie M '84 %DA -262 Old Cntry Rd -Mineola 11501 **Fx:**248-9479
(212) 264-2920 .. **Gentile,** Dominic A '09 US Ct of International Trade -1 Fed Plz -NY 10278
(631) 473-3999 .. **Gentile,** Gladys N '81 (G Gentile LLC) -Bx316 -Pt Jffrsn 11777 **Fx:**473-3999
(631) 421-4488 .. **Gentile,** Janine L '01 %Serpe A&K -149 Main Bx165 -Huntngtn 11743
(212) 474-1000 .. **Gentile,** Joanne M '80 Cravath S&M LLP -825 8th Av -NY 10019
(516) 873-3000 .. **Gentile,** John G '88 (Bellavia G & Assoc,LLP) -200 Old Cntry Rd -Mineola 11501 **Fx:**873-9032
(516) 742-6590 .. **Gentile,** Jos '80 (Frankie & G,PC) -1527 Franklin Av -Mineola 11501 **Fx:**742-6875
(212) 868-3610 .. **Gentile,** Jos '04 (Sarraf G LLP) -116 John -NY 10038 **Fx:**918-7967
(718) 726-1252 .. **Gentile,** Jos J '53 -21-41 46th -LIC 11105
(212) 689-6009 .. **Gentile,** Laura E '88 (Gentile & Assoc) -233 5th Av -NY 10016 **Fx:**213-1093
(212) 907-6453 .. **Gentile,** Michl A '72 -405 Lex Av -NY 10174
(212) 619-2700 .. **Gentile,** Paul T '69 P Gentile PC -261 Mad Av -NY 10016 **Fx:**619-3626
(212) 675-6161 .. **Gentile,** Ryan L '08 %GM Farinella PC -15 Park Av -NY 10016 **Fx:**675-4367
(212) 835-1572 .. **Gentile,** Thos A '96 (Lampf LP&P) -5 Penn Plz 19th Fl -NY 10119
(718) 748-5200 .. **Gentile,** Vincent J '86 NYC Council -7005 7th Av -Brklyn 11228
(212) 742-9700 .. **Gentile,** Wm A '07 %Godosky & G,PC -61 Bway -NY 10006
(212) 325-2000 .. **Gentin,** Pierre M '93 Credit Suisse -1 Mad Av -NY 10010 **Fx:**325-8222
(212) 732-2000 .. **Gentner,** Edw F Jr. '68 (Cullen and D LLP) -44 Wall -NY 10005
(212) 370-4220 .. **Gentry,** Edgar C Jr. '80 OfCnsl CR Clark,PLLC -570 Lex Av -NY 10022 **Fx:**370-4270
(212) 663-8726 .. **Genty,** Philip M '81 %Columbia Law Schl -435 W 116th -NY 10027 **Fx:**854-7946
(315) 422-1311 .. **Genung,** Elizabeth A '99 %Melvin & M,PLLC -217 S Salina -Syracuse 13202
(914) 481-5800 .. **Genzano,** Jos L '90 Alfred Weissman RE,Inc -120 Old Post Rd -Rye 10580
(516) 741-2405 .. **Geoghan Cohen & Bongiorno LLC** -250 Mineola Blvd -Mineola 11501 **Fx:**(212) 753-0960
(718) 250-2000 .. **Geoghan,** Dennis P '80 %DA -350 Jay -Brklyn 11201 **Fx:**250-2314
(718) 762-8104 .. **Geoghan,** Dennis P '85 -155-19 Delaware Av -Flushng 11355
(516) 739-0400 .. **Geoghan,** Donna E '02 %Kelly R&K,LLP -330 Old Cntry Rd -Mineola 11501
(212) 596-6099 .. **Geoghan,** Paul V '83 %Amer Inst of CPA's -1211 Av of Amer -NY 10036 **Fx:**596-6104
(914) 249-0100 .. **Geoghegan,** John A '68 (Gellert & K,PC) -3010 Wstchstr Av -Purchase 10577
(718) 833-8365 .. **Geoly,** Frank T '59 -8118 13th Av -Brklyn 11228 **Fx:**921-3292
(718) 238-2400 .. **Georgaklis,** George P '96 (Georgaklis & M) -9118 5th Av -Brklyn 11209 **Fx:**238-2116
(212) 412-1146 .. **Georgalas,** Andy J '03 Barclays Capital -200 Park Av -NY 10166
(800) 877-1373 .. **Georgalos,** Peter '93 %Workers Comp Bd -168-46 91st Av -Jamaica 11432
(212) 335-9000 .. **George,** Abraham M '04 %DA -1 Hogan Pl -NY 10013
(518) 429-4200 .. **George,** Alexandra M '07 %Hiscock & B,LLP -50 Beaver -Albany 12207
(212) 825-5926 .. **George,** Alicia Gillian '05 %Dept of Bldgs -280 Bway -NY 10007
(212) 918-3000 .. **George,** Alison E '07 %Hogan L LLP -875 3rd Av -NY 10022
(716) 893-1840 .. **George,** Alyssa M '09 Saving Grace Ministries,Inc -Bx1013 -Williamsvll 14231
(212) 407-8330 .. **George,** Anil V '02 NBA Properties -645 5th Av -NY 10022
(518) 377-2225 .. **George,** Carolyn B '79 %Friedman H&M,LLP -100 Great Oaks Blvd Bx38279 -Albany 12203
(631) 376-0716 .. **George,** Cynthia J '98 -78 Capts Dr -W Babylon 11704
(212) 605-6200 .. **George,** Danielle '93 %Levy P&K,LLP -800 3rd Av -NY 10022
(718) 206-4709 .. **George,** Erene K '92 %Law Dept -89-17 Sutphin Blvd -Jamaica 11435 **Fx:**206-4702
(212) 434-2010 .. **George,** Gladys J '74 %Lenox Hill Hsptl -100 E 77th -NY 10075 **Fx:**434-2002
(718) 778-2994 .. **George,** Glenroy M '94 -822 Clarkson Av -Brklyn 11203
(718) 694-3970 .. **George,** Gregory C '04 Transit Auth -130 Lvngstn -Brklyn 11201 **Fx:**694-5726
(212) 967-2011 .. **George,** Habib G '97 (Anreder & G) -143 W 29th -NY 10001 **Fx:**967-2013
(516) 826-5500 .. **George,** Harry F '86 -2631 Merrick Rd -Bellmore 11710 **Fx:**826-2720
(518) 886-4221 .. **George,** Jesse O '07 AYCO -321 Bway Bx860 -Saratoga Spgs 12866
(914) 995-3413 .. **George,** John M '78 %DA -111 Martin Luther King Blvd -White Plns 10601 **Fx:**995-3363
(914) 995-3000 .. **George,** Joyce V '06 %DA -111 Martin Luther King Blvd -White Plns 10601 **Fx:**995-3363
(212) 336-8000 .. **George,** Kenneth P '81 (Amster R&E) -90 Park Av -NY 10016
(212) 308-4411 .. **George,** Kevin C '92 Cnsl Edwards AP&D LLP -750 Lex Av -NY 10022
(212) 806-5400 .. **George,** Laura Goldbard '83 (Stroock &S&L LLP) -180 Maiden Ln -NY 10038
(516) 826-5500 .. **George,** Lisa Raizin '86 -2631 Merrick Rd Av -Bellmore 11710
(212) 373-3000 .. **George,** Marie-Amelie P '09 %Paul WRW&G LLP -1285 Av of Amer -NY 10019
(212) 450-4000 .. **George,** Nicholas N '09 %Davis P&W LLP -450 Lex Av -NY 10017
(212) 326-3939 .. **George,** Nikolaos C '99 (Jones D) -222 E 41st -NY 10017
(716) 434-6641 .. **George,** Patricia A '91 -37 East Av Bx456 -Lockprt 14095 **Fx:**434-1443
(212) 232-1300 .. **George,** Richd '72 (Lewis BB&S LLP) -77 Water -NY 10005
(315) 699-4293 .. **George,** Robt D '92 (R George,PC) -113 N Main -N Syracuse 13212
(716) 854-3400 .. **Georger,** Kimberly A '09 %Rupp BPC&C LLC -1600 Lbrty Bldg -Buffalo 14202
(212) 788-0819 .. **Georges,** Jasmine M '08 %Law Dept -100 Church -NY 10007 **Fx:**788-0367
(212) 340-0400 .. **Georges,** Margaret R '99 Applt Div 1st Dept -27 Mad Av -NY 10010 **Fx:**889-4412
(212) 980-0120 .. **Georges,** Melissa '93 OfCnsl Frankfurt KK&S,PC -488 Mad Av -NY 10022
(212) 689-5292 .. **Georgetti,** Kevin M '88 BNB Bk -250 5th Av -NY 10001 **Fx:**(646) 304-1404
(516) 802-0700 .. **Georgetti,** Vincent L '08 %Braunstein T LLP -7600 Jericho Tpk -Woodbury 11797
(212) 883-4934 .. **Georghiades,** Aaron P '05 %Cozen O -277 Park Av -NY 10172
(315) 234-9900 .. **Georgiady,** Bryan N '10 %F Miller -6575 Kirkvll Rd -E Syracuse 13057 **Fx:**234-9908
(212) 230-8800 .. **Georgieva,** Bilyana P '10 %WilmerHale -399 Park Av -NY 10022
(212) 770-8080 .. **Georgini,** Jenevra '96 %AIG -70 Pine -NY 10270
(914) 793-6144 .. **Georgiopoulos,** Constantine P '64 -775 Scarsdale Rd -Tuckahoe 10707
(914) 997-0900 .. **Georgiou,** Anna L '99 %Wormser KG&J LLP -399 Knollwood Rd -White Plns 10603
(516) 229-4300 .. **Georgiou,** Paraskevi '99 %J Bilello & Assoc -875 Merrick Av -Westbury 11590
(718) 270-1132 .. **Georgis,** Helene '90 %SUNY Hlth Science Ctr -450 Clarkson Av Bx 113 -Brklyn 11203 **Fx:**270-3342
(212) 363-3100 .. **Georgitsis,** A Peter '97 %Bivona & C,PC -88 Pine -NY 10005
(718) 875-1300 .. **Georgopoulos,** Aurelia A '90 %Appllt Div 2nd Dept -45 Monroe Pl -Brklyn 11201 **Fx:**858-2446
(212) 425-7854 .. **Georgoulis,** Chris '80 (Georgoulis & Assoc PLLC) -45 Bway -NY 10006 **Fx:**422-5360
(315) 735-7509 .. **Gerace,** Donald R '80 -2613 Genesee -Utica 13501 **Fx:**735-1485
(716) 839-2652 .. **Gerace,** Gary A '70 (Gerace & H,PC) -3960 Harlem Rd -Snyder 14226
(716) 839-2652 .. **Gerace & Harman,PC** -3960 Harlem Rd -Snyder 14226 **Fx:**839-2825
(585) 262-5140 .. **Gerace,** Vincent J '59 -2 State -Rchstr 14614 **Fx:**232-3164
(315) 536-8953 .. **Geraci,** Anthony J '55 -9 Hllcrst Dr -Penn Yan 14527
(631) 755-0101 .. **Geraci,** Christina L '08 %Lewis JAA,LLP -425 Broad Hollow Rd -Melvll 11747
(212) 295-6380 .. **Geraci,** Justina L '06 %WilmerHale -399 Park Av -NY 10022
(516) 228-3553 .. **Geraci,** Katherine '84 %Thaler & G,LLP -90 Merrick Av -E Meadow 11554
(212) 458-1266 .. **Geraci,** Leonard J '86 %AIG -175 Water -NY 10038 **Fx:**458-1659
(845) 896-1106 .. **Geraci,** Linda Ann '94 -21 Old Main -Fishkill 12524 **Fx:**896-1107
(212) 836-8000 .. **Geraci,** Phillip A '80 (Kaye S LLP) -425 Park Av -NY 10022
(516) 484-3800 .. **Geraci,** Stefania R '00 Luxottica Grp -44 Hrbr Park Dr -Pt Wash 11050
(718) 709-3524 .. **Geraghty,** Joanna L '98 JetBlue Airways -118-29 Qns Blvd -Frst Hlls 11375
(212) 432-9180 .. **Geraghty,** Lisa Besson '97 %Stryker T&D LLP -2 Penn Plz -NY 10121
(212) 557-7200 .. **Geraghty,** Mark D '61 (Davidoff M&H,LLP) -605 3rd Av -NY 10158
(518) 725-8075 .. **Geraghty,** Michl F '51 -12 Saratoga Blvd -Gloversvll 12078 **Fx:**725-8156
(212) 461-2323 .. **Geraghty,** Michl J '88 (Saiber LLC) -44 Wall -NY 10005
(914) 323-7000 .. **Geraghty,** Patrick D '96 (Wilson EME&D LLP) -3 Gannett Dr -White Plns 10604
(212) 490-3000 .. **Geraghty,** Patrick D '96 (Wilson EME&D LLP) -150 E 42nd -NY 10017
(212) 929-2000 .. **Geraigery,** Janine D '04 (JD Geraigery,PC) -1133 Bway -NY 10010 **Fx:**813-3255
(212) 278-1000 .. **Gerard,** Christopher C '94 (Anderson K&O,PC) -1251 Av of Amer -NY 10020
(212) 839-5300 .. **Gerard,** Danl A '87 (Sidley A LLP) -787 7th Av -NY 10019
(212) 255-7300 .. **Gerard,** Ian A '96 %Gen Art -133 W 25th -NY 10001
(212) 766-1120 .. **Gerard,** Kenneth G '84 -225 Bway -NY 10007 **Fx:**766-9035
(212) 473-5077 .. **Gerard,** Lucille '85 -60 E 8th -NY 10003
(585) 263-5750 .. **Gerard,** Mark A '91 %Hon D Larimer -100 State -Rchstr 14614
(212) 468-8000 .. **Gerard,** Michl '06 %Morrison & F LLP -1290 Av of Amer -NY 10104
(607) 732-3793 .. **Gerard,** Richd A '72 -104 Demarest Pkwy -Elmira 14905 **Fx:**732-3181
(212) 605-0179 .. **Gerard,** Roy F '90 -575 Mad Av -NY 10022
(212) 408-5265 .. **Gerard,** Whitney I '64 (Chadbourne & P LLP) -30 Rckfllr Plz -NY 10112
(845) 365-3121 .. **Gerard,** Wm A '83 -71 Woods Rd Bx717 -Palisades 10964 **Fx:**365-4036
(631) 864-6501 .. **Gerardi,** James T '85 -58 Rofay Dr -E Northprt 11731 **Fx:**864-6502

(315) 663-2100 .. **Gerardi,** Jos B '87 %COR Dvlpmt Co -540 Towne Dr -Fayettevll 13066 **Fx:**663-2109
(212) 906-1812 .. **Gerardi,** Melissa C '97 -885 3rd Av -NY 10022 **Fx:**751-4864
(914) 667-6654 .. **Gerardi,** Theresa M '90 -22 W 1st -Mt Vernon 10550 **Fx:**667-6692
(516) 739-0301 .. **Gerardi,** Vincent M '90 (VM Gerardi & Assoc) -1539 Franklin Av -Mineola 11501
(212) 801-9219 .. **Gerasimovich,** Kenneth A '88 (Greenberg T,LLP) -200 Park Av -NY 10166
(212) 310-8000 .. **Gerba,** John R '07 %Weil G&M LLP -767 5th Av -NY 10153
(212) 775-8700 .. **Gerber,** Andrew I '04 %Kilpatrick S,LLP -31 W 52nd -NY 10019
(914) 479-1330 .. **Gerber,** Andrew J '57 -2 Clinton Av -Dobbs Ferry 10522
(212) 667-8300 .. **Gerber,** Chas W '81 %CIBC World Mkts -425 Lex Av -NY 10017 **Fx:**667-8361
(716) 566-5400 .. **Gerber,** Danl W '96 (Goldberg S LLP) -665 Main -Buffalo 14203
(718) 834-4850 .. **Gerber,** Ethan B '89 (Gerber & G LLP) -26 Court -Brklyn 11242 **Fx:**858-8119
(201) 646-1234 .. **Gerber,** Harold '93 -35 E 75th -NY 10021
(914) 421-1693 .. **Gerber,** Howard '83 -5 Old Rd -Elmsfrd 10523 **Fx:**(845) 624-3586
(845) 624-1234 .. **Gerber,** Howard '83 -154 S Mddltwn Rd -Nanuet 10954 **Fx:**624-3586
(212) 225-2000 .. **Gerber,** Jared M '08 %Cleary GS&H -1 Lbrty Plz -NY 10006
(212) 918-3000 .. **Gerber,** Jay E '65 OfCnsl Hogan L LLP -875 3rd Av -NY 10022
(212) 683-6634 .. **Gerber,** Jody N '82 -245 5th Av -NY 10016 **Fx:**684-0646
(716) 853-9555 .. **Gerber,** Judith M '86 Leg Aid -237 Main -Buffalo 14203 **Fx:**853-3219
(212) 969-3000 .. **Gerber,** Kathleen E '10 %Proskauer R LLP -1585 Bway -NY 10036
(212) 788-0473 .. **Gerber,** Louis B '07 %Law Dept -100 Church -NY 10007 **Fx:**788-0367
(516) 466-6050 .. **Gerber,** Marc J '84 %N Shore Abstrct -1010 Nrthrn Blvd -Gt Neck 11021 **Fx:**466-6011
(212) 403-1000 .. **Gerber,** Michl '07 %Wachtell LR&K -51 W 52nd -NY 10019
(718) 780-7923 .. **Gerber,** Michl A '78 %Bklyn Law Schl -250 Joralemon -Brklyn 11201 **Fx:**780-0393
(516) 775-7007 .. **Gerber,** Oren J '09 Gutman MB&S,PC -813 Jericho Tpk -New Hyde Pk 11040
(516) 872-7400 .. **Gerber,** Ross M '87 %Minerva & D -107 S Central Av -Vly Stream 11580
(516) 869-7104 .. **Gerber,** Scott M '94 %Kimco Realty Corp -3333 New Hyde Pk Rd -New Hyde Pk 11042 **Fx:**869-7199
(212) 601-2680 .. **Gerber,** Steven '79 (Gonzalez S&H LLP) -350 5th Av -NY 10118
(212) 974-5444 .. **Gerber,** Steven M '77 -666 5th Av -NY 10103 **Fx:**245-2255
(914) 763-6381 .. **Gerber,** Wendy B '84 Intl Consulting Grp -110 N Salem Rd -Cross Rvr 10518 **Fx:**763-5209
(212) 725-1400 .. **Gerber,** Wm A '77 -260 Mad Av -NY 10016
(518) 591-5232 .. **Gerberg,** Jos K '79 %NYS ORPTS -WA Harriman State Campus -Albany 12227 **Fx:**474-3657
(518) 487-7600 .. **Gerbini,** Jean F '86 OfCnsl Whiteman O&H LLP -1 Commerce Plz -Albany 12260
(845) 371-4700 .. **Gerbino,** Richd A Jr. '86 %Fein SK&S,PC -747 Chestnut Rdg Rd -Spg Vly 10977
(631) 390-0010 .. **Gerbino,** Vincent F '88 (Bruno G&S,LLP) -445 Broad Hollow Rd -Melvll 11747
(585) 425-5210 .. **Gerbush,** Lloyd F '94 Maximus Fed Srvcs -50 Square Dr -Victor 14564
(212) 813-5900 .. **Gercas,** Anna '07 %Fross ZL&Z,PC -866 UN Plz -NY 10017
(212) 423-9237 .. **Gerchik,** Julie R '02 Inst for Democracy Studies -177 E 87th -NY 10128
(516) 741-5252 .. **Gerdes,** Jennifer M '03 %Sanders SBWV&G,PC -100 Hrrcks Rd -Mineola 11501
(718) 250-2000 .. **Gerdes,** Lindsay K '08 %DA -350 Jay -Brklyn 11201 **Fx:**250-2314
(631) 539-0375 .. **Gereg,** Beth S '93 %Cruser M&N,LLP -175 Pinelawn Rd -Melvll 11747
(212) 326-3939 .. **Geremia,** Todd R '99 (Jones D) -222 E 41st -NY 10017
(718) 618-1460 .. **Gerez,** Alicia M '97 Bronx Cnty Supreme Ct -851 Grnd Cncrs -Bronx 10451
(212) 732-2000 .. **Gergel,** Chas F '92 (Cullen and D LLP) -44 Wall -NY 10005
(212) 751-7700 .. **Gergoudis,** Paul L '87 %Faust & O,LLP -488 Mad Av -NY 10022
(212) 474-1000 .. **Gerhard,** John '77 Cravath S&M LLP -825 8th Av -NY 10019
(518) 427-9700 .. **Gerhardt,** Douglas E '93 (Harris B PLLC) -677 Bway -Albany 12207
(212) 554-1234 .. **Geribon,** Hector D '97 AXA Financial Inc -1290 Av of Amer -NY 10104 **Fx:**707-3963
(212) 509-5050 .. **Gering,** Travis L '95 (Wuersch & G LLP) -100 Wall -NY 10005
(212) 682-7050 .. **Geringer & Dolan** -5 Hanover Sq -NY 10004 **Fx:**867-5987
(212) 280-7322 .. **Geringer,** Geoffrey D '88 -1060 Park Av -NY 10128
(212) 682-7050 .. **Geringer,** Harold I '57 (Geringer & D) -5 Hanover Sq -NY 10004
(212) 297-5800 .. **Gerity,** Patrick M '93 SrCnsl Day P LLP -7 Times Sq -NY 10036
(716) 858-2424 .. **Gerken,** John P Jr. '07 %DA -25 Delaware Av -Buffalo 14202 **Fx:**858-7425
(212) 608-1900 .. **Gerkens,** Fredk W '95 (Lovell SH LLP) -61 Bway -NY 10006
(212) 969-3000 .. **Gerkis,** James P '84 (Proskauer R LLP) -1585 Bway -NY 10036
(212) 558-4000 .. **Gerlach,** C Andrew '03 %Sullivan & C LLP -125 Broad -NY 10004
(212) 632-5500 .. **Gerlach,** Deric S '08 %Salans LLP -620 5th Av -NY 10020
(212) 969-8918 .. **Gerling,** Enid K '52 -60 E 8th -NY 10003
(212) 541-2000 .. **Germain,** Christopher R '04 Cnsl Bryan C LLP -1290 Av of Amer -NY 10104
(315) 422-0314 .. **Germain,** Neil G '90 (Germain & G) -314 E Fayette -Syracuse 13202 **Fx:**478-6544
(315) 422-0314 .. **Germain,** Paul A '62 (Germain & G) -314 E Fayette -Syracuse 13202 **Fx:**478-6544
(315) 422-0314 .. **Germain,** Robt M '88 (Germain & G) -314 E Fayette -Syracuse 13202 **Fx:**478-6544
(315) 422-0314 .. **Germain,** Stanley G '58 OfCnsl Germain & G -314 E Fayette -Syracuse 13202 **Fx:**478-6544
(315) 422-0314 .. **Germain,** Stanley R '81 (Germain & G) -314 E Fayette -Syracuse 13202 **Fx:**478-6544
(212) 871-1541 .. **Germain,** Steven D '84 ZGA US Ltd -105 E 17th -NY 10003
(516) 733-1810 .. **German,** Asaf A '04 A German,PC -77 Newbrdg Rd -Hicksvll 11801 **Fx:**620-6826
(518) 892-6688 .. **German,** Galina '03 -191 Bway -Menands 12204 **Fx:**453-1505
(315) 682-8860 .. **German,** George G '81 -4902 Palmer -Manlius 13104 **Fx:**682-8860
(631) 271-8711 .. **German,** June Resnick '68 -150 Main -Huntngtn 11743 **Fx:**424-7732
(212) 715-1000 .. **German,** Michl C '10 %Arnold & P LLP -399 Park Av -NY 10022
(212) 849-7000 .. **German,** Nicole R '09 %Quinn EU&S,LLP -51 Mad Av -NY 10010
(212) 986-6776 .. **German,** Stanislao A '96 -299 Bway -NY 10007 **Fx:**986-6250
(212) 403-1000 .. **Germana,** Ben M '92 (Wachtell LR&K) -51 W 52nd -NY 10019
(516) 248-0202 .. **Germanakos,** Patricia '94 %S Marchelos -87 Mineola Blvd -Mineola 11501 **Fx:**248-0282
(212) 326-2000 .. **Germann,** Mark S '03 Cnsl O'Melveny & M LLP -7 Times Sq -NY 10036
(631) 588-8778 .. **Germano & Cahill,PC** -4250 Vets Mem'l Hwy -Holbrook 11741 **Fx:**588-2550
(516) 489-6959 .. **Germano,** G Wm Jr. '09 %F Brewington -556 Peninsula Blvd -Hempstd 11550 **Fx:**489-6958
(631) 588-8778 .. **Germano,** Guy W '75 (Germano & C,PC) -4250 Vets Mem'l Hwy -Holbrook 11741
(631) 852-2325 .. **Germano,** Lawr J III '00 %MHLS -One Court -Rvrhead 11901 **Fx:**852-3132
(914) 345-3701 .. **Germano,** Michl F '08 %Marks OO&C,PC -530 Saw Mill Rvr Rd -Elmsfrd 10523
(631) 360-9396 .. **Germano,** Stacy L '97 Bk of Smithtown -1 E Main Bx456 -Smithtwn 11787 **Fx:**360-9332
(212) 533-1800 .. **Germansky,** Steven P '76 -302 5th Av -NY 10001
(516) 338-3431 .. **Germany,** Dorion S '97 %Dreyfus Corp -144 Glenn Curtiss Blvd -Uniondale 11556
(212) 681-0117 .. **Gern,** Amos '71 (Starr GD&R) -530 5th Av -NY 10036
(212) 509-3456 .. **Gernant,** Eric M II '06 %McGivney & K,PC -80 Broad -NY 10004
(718) 643-0700 .. **Gerner,** Susan A '76 -60 John -Brklyn 11201 **Fx:**875-2651
(646) 305-9055 .. **Gerney,** Arkadi M '03 CGL Group -33 1st -Brklyn 11231
(212) 474-1000 .. **Gerold,** Kenneth S '10 %Cravath S&M LLP -825 8th Av -NY 10019
(212) 728-8000 .. **Geron,** Anthony '08 %Willkie F&G LLP -787 7th Av -NY 10019
(212) 768-6700 .. **Geron,** Jeffrey S '93 (Sonnenschein N&R LLP) -1221 Av of Amer -NY 10020
(212) 878-7900 .. **Geron,** Yann '89 (Fox R LLP) -100 Park Av -NY 10017
(212) 751-2700 .. **Geronemus,** David '83 %JAMS -620 8th Av -NY 10018 **Fx:**751-4099
(201) 512-4400 .. **Geronimo,** Carole Ann '83 -617 Little Britain Rd -New Windsor 12553 **Fx:**512-4403
(212) 386-7629 .. **Gerontianos,** Elisa P '03 (Weinberg & G,PC) -116 W 23rd -NY 10011
(212) 696-4848 .. **Gerontis,** V Lilly '99 %Mintz & G LLP -470 Park Av S -NY 10016
(845) 225-6686 .. **Gerosa,** Nina Berry '85 -770 Farmers Mills Rd -Carmel 10512
(212) 448-1100 .. **Gerrald,** Jacqueline C '01 %McLaughlin & S,LLP -260 Mad Av -NY 10016
(914) 238-5817 .. **Gerrard,** Barbara S '77 -11 Grdn Ridge Rd -Chappaqua 10514 **Fx:**238-0117
(212) 599-0900 .. **Gerrard,** Jennine A '95 %Bower & L,PC -261 Mad Av -NY 10016
(212) 715-1190 .. **Gerrard,** Michl B '79 OfCnsl Arnold & P LLP -399 Park Av -NY 10022
(718) 260-4717 .. **Gerressu,** Debbora Tabor '06 Legal Aid-Bklyn Ofc for Aging -111 Lvngstn -Brklyn 11201
(212) 506-5000 .. **Gerrish,** Amy S '05 Orrick H&S LLP -51 W 52nd -NY 10019
(212) 735-3000 .. **Gerry,** Kurt '09 %Skadden ASM&F LLP -4 Times Sq -NY 10036
(914) 995-2922 .. **Gerry,** Susan F '93 Cnty Exec Ofc -148 Martine Av -White Plns 10601
(718) 250-2000 .. **Gerschel,** Philippe J '10 %DA -350 Jay -Brklyn 11201 **Fx:**250-2314
(212) 468-8000 .. **Gerschwer,** Lawr '95 (Morrison & F LLP) -1290 Av of Amer -NY 10104
(212) 683-6383 .. **Gersen Blakeman & Ackert LLP** -270 Mad Av -NY 10016 **Fx:**686-2040
(212) 683-6383 .. **Gersen,** Danl '41 (Gersen B&A LLP) -270 Mad Av -NY 10016
(212) 512-1000 .. **Gersen,** Michelle S '79 %HBO -1100 Av of Amer -NY 10036 **Fx:**512-1986
(212) 209-3366 .. **Gersh,** Lewis D '97 (Gersh Venture Ptnrs,LLC) -450 Park Av S -NY 10016
(212) 682-6717 .. **Gersh,** Steven T '82 (Berkowitz T&T,LLC) -275 Mad Av -NY 10016
(212) 385-2121 .. **Gershbaum,** Chas '91 (Gershbaum & W PC) -192 Lex Av -NY 10016 **Fx:**532-3801
(718) 493-4441 .. **Gershbein,** Steven L '87 %MHLS -606 Wnthrp -Brklyn 11203
(607) 746-3906 .. **Gershberg,** Lawr L '86 OfCnsl M Greenberg -130 Main -Delhi 13753 **Fx:**746-3902
(718) 989-0765 .. **Gershburg,** Danl '07 D Gershburg,PC -1400 Av Z -Brklyn 11235 **Fx:**228-8748
(212) 798-6083 .. **Gershenfeld,** Kenneth K '86 Fortress Invstmnt Grp -1345 Av of Amer -NY 10105
(212) 969-3000 .. **Gershengorn,** Brian J '04 %Proskauer R LLP -1585 Bway -NY 10036
(516) 357-3000 .. **Gershenoff,** Max S '07 %Rivkin R LLP -926 RXR Plz -Uniondale 11556
(212) 509-3100 .. **Gershfeld,** Arthur '01 (A Gershfeld & Assoc,PLLC) -140 Bway -NY 10005 **Fx:**858-7760
(212) 768-9500 .. **Gershfeld,** Michelle G '90 (Kittay & G,PC) -1 Exch Plz 55 Bway -NY 10016
(914) 332-8000 .. **Gershfeld,** Michelle G '90 (Kittay & G,PC) -100 Wht Plns Rd -Tarrytwn 10591
(212) 278-0400 .. **Gershik,** Gary J '97 (Cooper & D LLP) -30 Rckfllr Plz -NY 10112
(914) 422-4255 .. **Gershman,** Bennett L '66 %Pace Law Schl -78 N Bway -White Plns 10603 **Fx:**422-4039
(212) 506-1700 .. **Gershman,** Jos A '97 (Kasowitz BT&F LLP) -1633 Bway -NY 10019
(212) 578-2211 .. **Gershman,** Julie Kara '96 %MetLife -27-01 Qns Plz N -LIC 11101
(516) 279-6981 .. **Gershman,** Marc P '87 -263 Mineola Blvd -Mineola 11501 **Fx:**747-7188
(516) 746-3033 .. **Gershman,** Richd S '72 R Gershman & Assoc,PC -3000 Marcus Av -Lk Success 11042 **Fx:**746-3408
(212) 688-0782 .. **Gershon,** A Arnold '64 (Barrack R&B) -1350 Bway -NY 10018
(212) 416-8474 .. **Gershon,** Andrew J '87 %Dept of Law -120 Bway -NY 10271
(212) 267-4459 .. **Gershon,** Martin '67 -233 Bway -NY 10279 **Fx:**966-2505
(212) 509-5050 .. **Gershon,** Michl D '00 %Wuersch & G LLP -100 Wall -NY 10005
(718) 625-3977 .. **Gershon,** Robt S '92 -142 Joralemon -Brklyn 11201 **Fx:**855-2507
(516) 248-1700 .. **Gershonowitz,** Aaron '81 (Forchelli CDSM&T,LLP) -333 Earle Ovngton Blvd -Uniondale 11553
(212) 848-4000 .. **Gershony,** Yarden D '09 %Shearman & S LLP -599 Lex Av -NY 10022
(212) 310-8000 .. **Gershowitz,** Gabriel J '10 %Weil G&M LLP -767 5th Av -NY 10153
(212) 449-0659 .. **Gershowitz,** Lisa N '92 %Merrill Lynch -220 Bway -NY 10038

(516) 367-2278 .. **Gershowitz**, Robin Ann '92 -8 Fox Meadow Ct -Woodbury 11797 **Fx:**367-4073
(212) 268-3222 .. **Gershowitz**, Steven M '94 %Raphaelson & L,PC -14 Penn Plz -NY 10122 **Fx:**268-3313
(212) 935-3000 .. **Gershtenman**, Merav '03 %Mintz LCFG&P,PC -666 3rd Av -NY 10017
(212) 670-0200 .. **Gershuny**, Donald '69 %Merrill Lynch -222 Bway -NY 10038
(845) 462-3609 .. **Gershuny**, Edw S '68 -12 Round Hill Rd -Poughkeepsie 12603
(212) 566-7188 .. **Gershuny**, Lauren W '04 %Genova B&G -115 Bway -NY 10006
(212) 655-4000 .. **Gershweir**, Max W '94 -120 Bway -NY 10271 **Fx:**655-5039
(718) 279-7555 .. **Gerson**, Alan '88 %B Montague & Prtnrs -212-45 26th Av -Bayside 11360 **Fx:**279-8154
(212) 788-7722 .. **Gerson**, Alan J '83 (NYC Council) -51 Chmbrs -NY 10007 **Fx:**788-7727
(212) 521-5400 .. **Gerson**, Brett D '09 %Reed S LLP -599 Lex Av -NY 10022
(212) 446-4800 .. **Gerson**, Christopher M '08 %Kirkland & E LLP -153 E 53rd -NY 10022
(516) 741-2000 .. **Gerson**, Danl S '01 %Carway & F -194 Old Cntry Rd -Mineola 11501
(212) 773-1901 .. **Gerson**, David '70 Ernst & Young LLP -5 Times Sq -NY 10036
(212) 373-3000 .. **Gerson**, Gayle S '06 %Paul WRW&G LLP -1285 Av of Amer -NY 10019
(516) 248-6000 .. **Gerson**, Jeffrey C '91 (Kaufman B&R) -1205 Franklin Av -Gdn Cty 11530
(212) 803-3100 .. **Gerson**, Lawr M '74 %Empire State Dvlmnt Corp -633 3rd Av -NY 10017
(212) 547-5400 .. **Gerson**, Lisa A '07 %McDermott W&E LLP -340 Mad Av -NY 10173
(212) 476-9000 .. **Gerson**, Maxine L '83 %Neuberger Berman,LLC -605 3rd Av -NY 10158 **Fx:**476-9862
(212) 402-4100 .. **Gerson**, Risa B '85 %Ofc Applt Def -11 Park Pl -NY 10007 **Fx:**402-4199
(212) 790-9200 .. **Gerson**, Simon '75 (Cowan L&L,PC) -1133 Av of Amer -NY 10036
(212) 385-4410 .. **Gersowitz**, Edw H '81 (Gersowitz L&K,PC) -111 Bway -NY 10006
(212) 836-8000 .. **Gersowitz**, Erica M '08 %Kaye S LLP -425 Park Av -NY 10022
(212) 385-4410 .. **Gersowitz Libo & Korek,PC** -111 Bway -NY 10006 **Fx:**385-4417
(518) 474-9502 .. **Gersowitz**, Robt S '80 %OTDA -40 N Pearl -Albany 12243 **Fx:**474-9389
(212) 422-8498 .. **Gersowitz**, Stephen H '70 -14 Wall -NY 10005 **Fx:**422-1650
(212) 422-0700 .. **Gerspach**, Thos J '88 (Gerspach S LLP) -59 Maiden Ln -NY 10038 **Fx:**545-4095
(212) 276-2676 .. **Gerspacher**, Aude '03 %Cozen O -277 Park Av -NY 10172
(212) 398-0055 .. **Gerstein**, Bruce E '78 (Garwin G&F,LLP) -1501 Bway -NY 10036
(516) 367-7482 .. **Gerstein**, Caryn R '85 -119 Plainvw Rd -Woodbury 11797
(212) 779-9910 .. **Gerstein**, David M '58 (Eaton & V LLP) -3 Park Av -NY 10016
(212) 969-3000 .. **Gerstein**, Jason D '08 Proskauer R LLP -1585 Bway -NY 10036
(212) 398-7900 .. **Gerstein**, Jonathan H '07 %Gerstein S&R LLP -57 W 38th -NY 10018
(212) 398-0055 .. **Gerstein**, Jonathan M '08 Garwin G&F,LLP -1501 Bway -NY 10036
(212) 756-2000 .. **Gerstein**, Kenneth S '76 (Schulte R&Z LLP) -919 3rd Av -NY 10022
Gerstein, Marc H '77 -3445 83rd -Jcksn Hts 11372
(212) 351-4000 .. **Gerstein**, Moshe '03 %Gibson D&C LLP -200 Park Av -NY 10166
(212) 872-1000 .. **Gerstein**, Rachel Lasky '01 -One Bryant Park -NY 10036 **Fx:**872-1002
(212) 398-7900 .. **Gerstein Strauss & Rinaldi LLP** -57 W 38th -NY 10018 **Fx:**575-2387
(518) 473-3950 .. **Gerstein**, Terri E '01 Dept of Labor -State Campus Bldg 12 -Albany 12240 **Fx:**457-1164
(212) 398-7900 .. **Gerstein**, Victor R '75 (Gerstein S&R LLP) -57 W 38th -NY 10018
(212) 762-7546 .. **Gerstel**, Alice J '00 Morgan Stanley -1221 Av of Amer -NY 10020
(212) 278-1388 .. **Gerstel**, Linda '87 OfCnsl Anderson K&O,PC -1251 Av of Amer -NY 10020
(212) 436-6791 .. **Gersten**, Allison J '08 Deloitte Tax LLP -2 World Fncl Ctr -NY 10281
(212) 532-9736 .. **Gersten**, Diana K '03 %R Skyer & Assoc,LLP -276 5th Av -NY 10001 **Fx:**532-9846
(212) 570-2440 .. **Gersten**, Jennifer Sloane '91 %Stribling & Assoc -924 Mad Av -NY 10021
(631) 361-9494 .. **Gersten**, Marc A '93 -732 Smithtwn Bypass -Smithtwn 11787 **Fx:**361-8752
(212) 752-9700 .. **Gersten Savage LLP** -600 Lex Av -NY 10022 **Fx:**980-5192
(716) 845-9333 .. **Gersten**, Wm A '77 Supreme Ct -25 Delaware Av -Buffalo 14202 **Fx:**851-3293
(516) 747-8830 .. **Gerstenfeld**, Erik J '97 %Jaghab & J -176 Mineola Blvd -Mineola 11501 **Fx:**747-8770
(212) 788-0710 .. **Gerstenfeld**, Holly R '04 %Law Dept -100 Church -NY 10007 **Fx:**788-0367
(518) 456-6456 .. **Gerstenzang**, Karen O '81 (Gerstenzang OH&G) -210 Great Oaks Blvd -Albany 12203
(212) 225-2000 .. **Gerstenzang**, Michl A '90 (Cleary GS&H) -1 Lbrty Plz -NY 10006
(518) 456-6456 .. **Gerstenzang O'Hern Hickey & Gerstenzang** -210 Great Oaks Blvd -Albany 12203 **Fx:**456-6056
(518) 456-6456 .. **Gerstenzang**, Peter '72 (Gerstenzang OH&G) -210 Great Oaks Blvd -Albany 12203
(914) 962-6216 .. **Gerstenzang**, Wm C '78 (Yorktown Ct Justice) -2295 Crompond Rd -Yorktwn Hts 10598
(212) 808-0700 .. **Gerstenzang**, Wm C '78 (Norris M&M,PA) -875 3rd Av -NY 10022
(212) 510-9261 .. **Gerstl**, Carol L '79 United Fed of Teachers -52 Bway -NY 10004
(716) 851-4343 .. **Gerstman**, Alan P D '78 Law Dept -65 Niagara Sq -Buffalo 14202 **Fx:**851-4105
(845) 434-5563 .. **Gerstman**, Alfred M '54 -18 Overlook Dr Bx263 -Mtn Dale 12763
(212) 422-0202 .. **Gerstman**, Barry L '94 SpclCnsl Sedgwick DM&A LLP -125 Broad -NY 10004
(516) 880-8170 .. **Gerstman**, Bradley L '94 (Gerstman S LLP) -1044 Nrthrn Blvd -Roslyn 11576 **Fx:**880-8171
(646) 386-4427 .. **Gerstman**, Carol L '77 %Hon B Wittner -100 Centre -NY 10013
(516) 227-2400 .. **Gerstman**, Louis '66 OfCnsl R Ungar,PC -200 Grdn City Plz -Gdn Cty 11530 **Fx:**227-2406
(716) 845-9475 .. **Gerstman**, Sharon S '81 %Supreme Ct -775 3rd -Niagara Fls 14302
(212) 661-0009 .. **Gerstmann Powell**, Wendy E '95 SpclCnsl Krantz & B LLP -747 3rd Av -NY 10017 **Fx:**355-5009
(212) 846-3033 .. **Gerstner**, Jos P '77 CBS -1515 Bway -NY 10036
(718) 522-4533 .. **Gerstner**, Paul '62 -32 Court -Brklyn 11201 **Fx:**875-4500
(585) 258-2800 .. **Gersz**, Steven R '83 (Underberg & K LLP) -300 Bausch & Lomb Pl -Rchstr 14604
(212) 222-0780 .. **Gertel**, Barbara P '76 -820 West End Av -NY 10025
(718) 258-8080 .. **Gertel**, Irving '72 (Kagan & G) -1575 E 19th -Brklyn 11230
(516) 593-4434 .. **Gertler**, Jos B '72 -197 Merrick Rd -Lynbrk 11563 **Fx:**593-3347
(212) 532-2450 .. **Gertler**, Marc '85 -295 Mad Av -NY 10017 **Fx:**532-0117
(516) 228-3553 .. **Gertler**, Richd G '86 (Thaler & G,LLP) -90 Merrick Av -E Meadow 11554
(212) 859-8000 .. **Gertner**, Oren '05 %Fried FHS&J LLP -1 NY Plz -NY 10004
(732) 636-8000 .. **Gertsberg**, Deniza Gitlin '06 %Wilentz G&S -110 William -NY 10038 **Fx:**726-6631
(718) 253-5943 .. **Gertz**, Aaron S '74 -1419 E 27th -Brklyn 11210
(212) 996-6299 .. **Gertz**, Benjamin I '63 -1075 Park Av -NY 10128
(646) 386-3416 .. **Gertz**, Elizabeth J '90 Supreme Ct Law Dept -60 Centre -NY 10007
(212) 788-0786 .. **Gertzer**, Michl K '97 %Law Dept -100 Church -NY 10007 **Fx:**788-0367
(212) 373-3000 .. **Gertzman**, Michl E '89 (Paul WRW&G LLP) -1285 Av of Amer -NY 10019
(212) 450-2000 .. **Gertzog**, Gary M '84 %NFL -280 Park Av -NY 10017 **Fx:**681-7599
(518) 561-1980 .. **Gervais**, David S '07 %Niles P&B -46-48 Cornelia Bx2729 -Plattsbrgh 12901
(516) 228-6658 .. **Gervase**, Barbara A '85 (Gervase & V,PC) -377 Oak -Gdn Cty 11530
(716) 819-1118 .. **Gervase**, Jos F Jr. '64 -43 Court -Buffalo 14202
(212) 935-3000 .. **Gervase**, Richd G Jr. '90 (Mintz LCFG&P,PC) -666 3rd Av -NY 10017
(516) 228-6658 .. **Gervase & Vallone,PC** -377 Oak -Gdn Cty 11530 **Fx:**228-1293
(718) 442-0900 .. **Gervasi**, Michl V '03 %Russo S&D,PC -1010 Forest Av -Staten Isl 10310
(917) 992-6171 .. **Gerver**, Kenneth W '85 -244 5th Av -NY 10001 **Fx:**(212) 591-6583
(212) 227-2084 .. **Gervis**, Michl '94 %Reade Broadway Assoc -305 Bway -NY 10007
(315) 788-6700 .. **Gerviss**, Lucy M '09 %Schwerzmann & W,PC -215 Wshngtn Bx704 -Watertwn 13601
(607) 962-2479 .. **Gerwig**, Danl P '86 -135 Cedar -Corning 14830 **Fx:**962-2470
(212) 486-0543 .. **Gerwin**, Arthur '53 -445 Park Av -NY 10022 **Fx:**486-1378
(631) 563-8894 .. **Gery**, Eleanor '91 -94 Easy -W Sayvll 11796
(212) 227-4242 .. **Gerzog**, Ira D '90 (Goldfarb & G) -233 Bway -NY 10007
(212) 351-4500 .. **Gerzog**, Jay E '86 (Epstein B&G,PC) -250 Park Av -NY 10177
(212) 712-6000 .. **Gerzon**, Anna '96 %Extell Dvlpmnt -805 3rd Av -NY 10022
(718) 590-7911 .. **Gesell**, Melina '99 Admin Childrens Srvcs -900 Sheridan Av -Bronx 10451
(212) 613-2017 .. **Gesinsky**, Loren M '95 (Gibbons PC) -1 Penn Plz -NY 10119 **Fx:**554-9606
(212) 964-4273 .. **Geslani**, Orlando P '83 -132 Nassau -NY 10038
(212) 735-3000 .. **Geslevich**, Nizan '08 %Skadden ASM&F LLP -4 Times Sq -NY 10036
(212) 267-7767 .. **Gess**, Eric A '91 (Gess G&S,PC) -30 Vesey -NY 10007
(212) 267-7767 .. **Gess Gess & Scanlon,PC** -30 Vesey -NY 10007
(212) 563-3370 .. **Gess**, Jonathan S '04 OfCnsl B Moldovsky,LLC -110 Wall -NY 10005 **Fx:**563-3371
(845) 735-0088 .. **Gess**, Marvin R '61 (Ross & G,PC) -275 N Mddltwn Rd -Pearl Rvr 10965
(212) 267-7767 .. **Gess**, Richd B '94 (Gess G&S,PC) -30 Vesey -NY 10007
(914) 948-1556 .. **Gesser**, David P '86 OfCnsl Danziger & M LLP -123 Main -White Plns 10601
(516) 622-4770 .. **Gest**, Maureen A '00 -2 Center Ct -Bethpage 11714 **Fx:**433-4077
(631) 224-4801 .. **Gesualdi**, James F '89 -58 Wingam Dr -Islip 11751 **Fx:**224-1678
(718) 725-4420 .. **Gesualdo**, Lauri '96 -90-50 Parsons Blvd -Jamaica 11432 **Fx:**725-4420
(212) 728-8000 .. **Getachew**, A Mark '03 (Willkie F&G LLP) -787 7th Av -NY 10019
(212) 728-8000 .. **Getachew**, Adanech '06 %Willkie F&G LLP -787 7th Av -NY 10019
(718) 694-9434 .. **Getachew**, Genet '93 -26 Court -Brklyn 11242 **Fx:**246-9186
(212) 878-8000 .. **Getahun**, Yemeserach '08 %Clifford C LLP -31 W 52nd -NY 10019
(585) 232-5600 .. **Getaz**, Christopher P '06 %Blitman & K LLP -16 W Main -Rchstr 14614
(914) 993-5550 .. **Getler**, Janine A '91 HRH Cons LLC -50 Main -White Plns 10606 **Fx:**993-5902
(212) 272-2767 .. **Getler**, Melissa S '02 %JP Morgan Chase -383 Mad Av -NY 10179
(212) 613-4297 .. **Getler**, Shimon '02 Navigators Mgmt -1 Penn Plz -NY 10119
(315) 798-8700 .. **Getman**, Anne Marie '91 -239 Genesee -Utica 13501 **Fx:**896-6594
(716) 853-4340 .. **Getman & Biryla** -800 Rand Bldg -Buffalo 14203 **Fx:**853-4349
(845) 255-9370 .. **Getman**, Danl C '85 -9 Paradies Ln -New Paltz 12561 **Fx:**943-6412
(315) 894-9976 .. **Getman Franchi & Applegate,LLP** -38 Morgan Bx477 -Ilion 13357 **Fx:**894-5984
(315) 894-9976 .. **Getman**, George H '48 OfCnsl Getman F&A,LLP -38 Morgan Bx477 -Ilion 13357
(716) 853-4340 .. **Getman**, Jack L '58 (Getman & B) -800 Rand Bldg -Buffalo 14203
(607) 432-3530 .. **Getman**, Michl F '91 (Getman Law Firm) -16 Dietz Bx613 -Oneonta 13820 **Fx:**432-3571
(914) 220-5475 .. **Getman**, Michl K '89 -445 Hmltn Av -White Plns 10601
(607) 547-1369 .. **Getman**, Nathaniel P '04 Cnty Law Guardian -21 Railroad Av -Cooperstwn 13326
(315) 539-1989 .. **Getman**, Steven J '92 (Cnty Atty) -1 DiPronio Dr -Waterloo 13165 **Fx:**539-1657
(315) 894-9976 .. **Getman**, Willard E '85 -38 Morgan Bx477 -Ilion 13357
(315) 841-8021 .. **Getman**, Wm H '77 (Woodman & G) -130 E Main -Waterville 13480 **Fx:**841-4472
(315) 797-9261 .. **Getnick Livingston Atkinson & Priore, LLP** -258 Genesee -Utica 13502 **Fx:**732-0755
(315) 797-9261 .. **Getnick**, Michl E '70 (Getnick LA&P,LLP) -258 Genesee -Utica 13502
(212) 376-5666 .. **Getnick**, Neil V '79 (Getnick & G) -620 5th Av -NY 10020 **Fx:**292-3942
(212) 509-6888 .. **Getreu**, Joel L '89 -132 Nassau -NY 10038
(516) 437-7049 .. **Getschel**, Milton H '59 -154 Tulip Ln -Floral Pk 11001
(212) 455-2000 .. **Getsin**, Jennie '01 %Simpson T&B LLP -425 Lex Av -NY 10017
(212) 833-1187 .. **Getson**, Lisa Swedenborg '05 %Friedman KS&A LLP -1633 Bway -NY 10019 **Fx:**373-7987
(212) 735-3000 .. **Gette**, Christopher R '79 Cnsl Skadden ASM&F LLP -4 Times Sq -NY 10036

(212) 336-0076 .. **Gettinger**, Jason R '68 %SEC -3 World Fncl Ctr -NY 10281 **Fx**:336-1323
(914) 666-8033 .. **Gettinger**, John H '80 (Banks SG&W,LLP) -118 N Bedford Rd Bx320 -Mt Kisco 10549
(212) 935-0884 .. **Gettler**, Thos D '86 -950 3rd Av -NY 10022 **Fx**:935-6949
(212) 403-1000 .. **Gettles-Atwa**, Kathryn J '02 %Wachtell LR&K -51 W 52nd -NY 10019
(315) 769-3898 .. **Gettmann**, Virginia A '01 %Pease & G -40 Main -Massena 13662 **Fx**:769-5018
(315) 336-3900 .. **Getty**, Chas R Jr. '78 -220 W Court Bx950 -Rome 13442 **Fx**:336-3902
(212) 889-2121 .. **Getty**, Eugene F '90 (Kellner HG&F) -470 Park Av S -NY 10016
(212) 683-2233 .. **Getz**, Alan M '78 %Vanguard Investors, Ltd -224 5th Av -NY 10001 **Fx**:683-0374
(718) 993-3000 .. **Getz & Braverman,PC** -172 E 161st -Bronx 10451 **Fx**:402-5183
(212) 260-7400 .. **Getz**, Danl B '96 Musicvision -636 Bway -NY 10012
(212) 635-0400 .. **Getz**, Gregory '81 (Leitner & G LLP) -65 Bway -NY 10006
(718) 993-3000 .. **Getz**, Howard I '64 (Getz & B,PC) -172 E 161st -Bronx 10451
(585) 262-5130 .. **Getz**, Jon P '93 (Muldoon & G) -144 Exchange Blvd -Rchstr 14614
(518) 348-0175 .. **Getz**, Michl I '91 -930 Route 146 Bx378 -Clifton Pk 12065 **Fx**:373-9042
(718) 237-2000 .. **Getz**, Saml A '98 %Leg Aid -111 Lvngstn -Brklyn 11201 **Fx**:237-8737
(212) 997-4400 .. **Getzels**, Paul D '88 Cnsl Teitler & T,LLP -1114 Av of Amer -NY 10036 **Fx**:997-4949
(718) 875-1300 .. **Getzler**, Howard '83 %Applt Div 2nd Dept -45 Monroe Pl -Brklyn 11201 **Fx**:858-2446
(212) 869-3200 .. **Getzler**, Lawr '85 %Molod S&D,PC -104 W 40th -NY 10018
(516) 745-3223 .. **Getzler**, Michl J '87 %JP Morgan Chase -900 Stewart Av -Gdn Cty 11530 **Fx**:745-3220
(212) 964-6611 .. **Getzoff**, Steven B '83 (Lester SK&D) -120 Bway -NY 10271
(315) 788-5100 .. **Geurtsen**, David B '93 (Conboy MB&K,LLP) -407 Sherman -Watertwn 13601
(212) 244-4111 .. **Geva**, Liraz '03 (Shiboleth YR&Z,LLP) -1 Penn Plz -NY 10119
(212) 218-5500 .. **Gevanter**, Alexis N '09 %Seyfarth S LLP -620 8th Av -NY 10018
(516) 935-9053 .. **Gevanter**, David '89 -95 Old Cntry Rd -Hicksvll 11801 **Fx**:797-0419
(212) 840-3456 .. **Gevertzman**, Paul '86 %Anchin Block & Anchin -1375 Bway -NY 10018
(212) 538-3594 .. **Gewanter**, Danl S '96 Credit Suisse First Boston -11 Mad Av -NY 10010
(212) 233-2100 .. **Gewanter**, Stanley M '64 (Oshman & M,LLP) -42 Bway -NY 10004
(212) 403-1000 .. **Gewertz**, Theo '62 (Wachtell LR&K) -51 W 52nd -NY 10019
(914) 422-4606 .. **Gewirtz**, Amy Ellen '83 Pace Law Schl -78 N Bway -White Plns 10603 **Fx**:422-4039
(212) 538-1521 .. **Gewirtz**, Danl S '94 Credit Suisse -11 Mad Av -NY 10010
(718) 739-6400 .. **Gewirtz**, Edw D '73 %DHCR -92-31 Union Hall -Jamaica 11433 **Fx**:262-7938
(212) 697-6484 .. **Gewirtz**, Edw N '96 (Bronstein G&G,LLC) -60 E 42nd -NY 10165 **Fx**:697-0877
(212) 530-5000 .. **Gewirtz**, Elliot '73 (Milbank TH&M LLP) -1 Chase Manh Plz -NY 10005
(516) 364-1095 .. **Gewirtz**, Evan '92 (McBreen & K) -500 N Bway -Jericho 11753
(212) 848-4000 .. **Gewirtz**, Gregory F '09 %Shearman & S LLP -599 Lex Av -NY 10022
(212) 732-7090 .. **Gewirtz**, Seymour '64 -225 Bway -NY 10007 **Fx**:732-4157
(212) 431-2134 .. **Gewirtzman**, Doni N '99 NY Law Schl -185 W Bway -NY 10013 **Fx**:431-1864
(212) 450-4000 .. **Gewolb**, Barry J '10 %Davis P&W LLP -450 Lex Av -NY 10017
(585) 232-6500 .. **Gewolb**, Joshua E '07 %Harter S&E LLP -1600 Bausch & Lomb Pl -Rchstr 14604
(516) 228-5500 .. **Gewurz**, Bennett J '90 (Gewurz & Z,PC) -50 Chas Lindbergh Blvd -Uniondale 11553 **Fx**:228-8390
(516) 678-2428 .. **Gewurz**, Eric '52 (Gewurz & G) -3536 Knight -Oceanside 11572
(315) 423-4400 .. **Geyer**, Robt E Jr. '00 %Wolff G&G,LLP -217 Mntgmry -Syracuse 13202
(212) 558-4000 .. **Geykhman**, Julia '07 %Sullivan & C LLP -125 Broad -NY 10004
(212) 701-3000 .. **Gez**, Orly '10 %Cahill G&R LLP -80 Pine -NY 10005 **Fx**:269-5420
(718) 359-5552 .. **Gezelter**, Bertram '56 -162-27 Depot Rd Bx580125 -Flushng 11358 **Fx**:359-5553
(212) 697-2700 .. **Ghafari**, Antoine G '93 OfCnsl Stairs DF -200 Park Av S -NY 10003
(315) 858-0595 .. **Ghaleb**, Jhilmil '91 -42 E Main Bx1298 -Richfld Spgs 13439
(315) 568-1400 .. **Ghaly**, Said S '76 (S Ghaly,PC) -2457 Lwr Lk Rd -Seneca Fls 13148 **Fx**:568-8587
(718) 591-8800 .. **Ghaly**, Said S '76 (S Ghaly,PC) -221-21 Union Tpk -Flushng 11364 **Fx**:591-8987
(212) 651-7500 .. **Gharabeigie**, Arlene '06 %Segal MS&M -850 3rd Av -NY 10022
(212) 468-8000 .. **Gharagozlou**, Armin M '08 %Morrison & F LLP -1290 Av of Amer -NY 10104
(845) 485-3900 .. **Ghartey**, Mbiabah Lisa '95 Dept of Law -235 Main -Poughkeepsie 12601 **Fx**:452-3303
(212) 947-1079 .. **Gharti-Chhetry**, Khagendra '88 (Chhetry & Assoc) -363 7th Av -NY 10001 **Fx**:947-1081
(212) 478-7200 .. **Ghatage**, Padma '03 %Hahn & H LLP -488 Mad Av -NY 10022
(212) 918-3000 .. **Ghavi**, Amir R '07 %Hogan L LLP -875 3rd Av -NY 10022
(516) 484-4400 .. **Ghaytanchi**, Keyvan '04 Sandata Tech,Inc -26 Hrbr Park Dr -Pt Wash 11050
(212) 962-1000 .. **Gheith**, Sebastian Y '04 Spiegel & U,PA -1 Maiden Ln -NY 10038 **Fx**:964-5600
(607) 974-3322 .. **Gheorghiu**, Anca C '99 %Corning Inc -1 Rvrfrnt Plz -Corning 14831
(845) 331-6615 .. **Gheorghiu**, Valeria A '09 Workers Rts Law Ctr -101 Hurley Av -Kingston 12401
(646) 328-0850 .. **Gherman**, Craig L '01 %Outside Cnsl Solutns LLP -1430 Bway -NY 10018 **Fx**:360-5000
(212) 941-0767 .. **Gherman**, Ingrid '84 -225 Bway -NY 10007
(516) 670-8185 .. **Ghezzi**, Frank C '96 -230 W Bway -Long Bch 11561 **Fx**:670-8185
(212) 715-1000 .. **Ghilain**, Katherine E '09 %Arnold & P LLP -399 Park Av -NY 10022
(212) 246-3030 .. **Ghile**, Daniela M '07 Sierchio G&G,LLP -110 E 59th -NY 10022
(212) 532-1770 .. **Ghim**, Susan '02 -1261 Bway -NY 10001
(212) 906-1200 .. **Ghista**, Anamika D '09 %Latham & W -885 3rd Av -NY 10022
(212) 902-0093 .. **Ghodsi**, Tamilla Fatemeh '95 %Goldman Sachs -1 NY Plz -NY 10004
(212) 969-3000 .. **Ghorra**, Theo J '06 %Proskauer R LLP -1585 Bway -NY 10036
(212) 310-8000 .. **Ghose**, Dev A '09 %Weil G&M LLP -767 5th Av -NY 10153
(516) 741-4799 .. **Ghosh**, Sougoto '08 %Baker SBGFM&N,LLC -100 Grdn City Plz -Gdn Cty 11530
(212) 728-2200 .. **Ghosh**, Suchira '08 %Axinn V&H LLP -114 W 47th -NY 10036
(212) 370-4220 .. **Ghosh**, Sukanya '08 %CR Clark,PLLC -570 Lex Av -NY 10022 **Fx**:370-4270
(718) 206-0111 .. **Ghunney**, Albert '99 -171-08 Jamaica Av -Jamaica 11432 **Fx**:206-0777
(212) 848-9800 .. **Giabourani**, Anna '99 OfCnsl Withers B LLP -430 Park Av -NY 10022
(716) 687-1902 .. **Giacalone**, Arthur J '76 -140 Knox Rd Bx63 -E Aurora 14052 **Fx**:687-1903
(212) 425-7200 .. **Giaccio**, Anthony '92 (Kenyon & K,LLP) -1 Bway -NY 10004
(212) 245-7300 .. **Giacco**, Nicole L '01 %Serling R&F,LLP -119 5th Av -NY 10003
(631) 425-7070 .. **Giachetti**, Fredk J '92 -18 Fairvw -Huntngtn 11743 **Fx**:425-1872
(212) 223-0400 .. **Giacobbe**, Anthony I Jr. '95 OfCnsl Zeichner E&K LLP -575 Lex Av -NY 10022
(914) 997-1380 .. **Giacobbe**, John A '09 %Marino & C,PC -1 Barker Av -White Plns 10601
(716) 895-4210 .. **Giacobbe**, Mario A '92 %D Jaworski -2988 William -Cheektowaga 14227 **Fx**:895-2516
(212) 546-9255 .. **Giacobbe**, Matthew J '96 (Scarinci H) -107 Grand -NY 10013
(212) 509-9595 .. **Giacoia**, Jos D '88 (Capuder FG LLP) -90 Broad -NY 10004
(914) 377-9000 .. **Giacomini**, Laura K '05 %Wieder & W,PC -35 E Grassy Sprain Rd -Ynkrs 10710 **Fx**:377-1007
(914) 273-0822 .. **Giacomo**, M Theresa '83 -5 MacDonald Av -Armonk 10504 **Fx**:273-0823
(212) 486-0200 .. **Giacomo**, Paul J Jr. '79 -405 Lex Av -NY 10174
(315) 255-1122 .. **Giacona**, Saml P '84 -9 Court -Auburn 13021 **Fx**:255-3027
(914) 750-5933 .. **Giacopelli**, Mark P '05 Kissel H&W LLP -580 Wht Plns Rd -Tarrytwn 10591
(631) 425-7070 .. **Giacoppi**, John R '98 %F Giachetti -18 Fairvw -Huntngtn 11743 **Fx**:425-1872
(212) 758-9300 .. **Giacovas**, Robt '88 (Lazare P&G LLP) -950 3rd Av -NY 10022
(718) 261-6200 .. **Giaimo**, Jos O '61 (Giaimo & Assoc,LLP) -80-02 Kew Grdns Rd -Kew Gdns 11415 **Fx**:261-0316
(212) 757-8888 .. **Giaimo**, Peter '67 Giaimo & G -643 10th Av -NY 10036 **Fx**:262-8905
(212) 458-3152 .. **Gialleonardo**, Simrun '00 %AIG -175 Water -NY 10038
(212) 248-9100 .. **Gialleonardo**, Victor J Jr. '89 %Epstein H&M -1 Whitehall -NY 10004
(631) 393-6220 .. **Giambalvo**, Christine M '91 -445 Broadhllw Rd -Melvll 11747 **Fx**:393-6229
(845) 371-4700 .. **Giambalvo**, Francis J '10 %Fein SK&S,PC -747 Chestnut Rdg Rd -Spg Vly 10977
(212) 408-9461 .. **Giamboi**, Jos J '87 Cnsl The Zucker Org -101 W 55th -NY 10019 **Fx**:408-9461
(212) 732-9000 .. **Giamboi**, Jos N '55 OfCnsl Sullivan PBM&C PC -120 Bway -NY 10271
(516) 741-7300 .. **Giambona**, Paula '03 Griesmeyer & Assoc -1305 Franklin Av -Gdn Cty 11530
(716) 881-4900 .. **Giambra**, Heather A '04 %Schröder J & Assoc -766 Ellicott -Buffalo 14203
(716) 842-1004 .. **Giambrone**, James P Jr. '92 -534 Delaware Av -Buffalo 14202
(212) 788-1204 .. **Giambrone**, Jessica '06 %Law Dept -100 Church -NY 10007 **Fx**:788-0367
(631) 665-3400 .. **Giambrone**, Michl A '01 Siben & S,LLP -90 E Main Bx149P -Bay Shr 11706
(212) 699-7030 .. **Giambusso**, Ann M '81 Charmer Sunbelt Grp -60 E 42nd -NY 10165
(516) 364-6006 .. **Giametta**, Stephen C '03 %Cohen & S,LLP -199 Crsswys Park Dr Bx9004 -Woodbury 11797
(516) 624-6150 .. **Giammalvo**, Gregory J '75 %Town Atty -Town Hall -Oyster Bay 11771 **Fx**:624-6196
(212) 935-4743 .. **Giammarco**, Jacqueline M '98 Man Financial,Inc -717 5th Av -NY 10022
(718) 665-7700 .. **Giampa**, Richd L '76 (R Giampa,PC) -860 Grnd Cncrs -Bronx 10451
(212) 709-8267 .. **Giampaolo**, Jos '75 -110 Wall -NY 10005
(212) 756-2000 .. **Giampapa**, Christopher Hyde '01 %Schulte R&Z LLP -919 3rd Av -NY 10022
(212) 733-8471 .. **Giampetruzzi**, Gary F '94 %Pfizer Inc -150 E 42nd -NY 10017
(212) 878-9219 .. **Giampetruzzi**, Lora '06 %Warburg Pincus LLC -450 Lex Av -NY 10017
(212) 483-9490 .. **Giampiccolo**, Salvatore A '96 (McElroy DM&C,LLP) -88 Pine -NY 10005
(212) 574-1200 .. **Giampietro**, Kimberly A '09 %Seward & K LLP -1 Bttry Pk Plz -NY 10004
(516) 739-5838 .. **Giampilis**, Michl P '03 -94 Willis Av -Mineola 11501 **Fx**:739-8225
(212) 661-9100 .. **Giampolo**, John D '05 %Otterbourg SH&R,PC -230 Park Av -NY 10169
(845) 454-3421 .. **Giamportone**, Philip '97 -Bx3176 -Poughkeepsie 12603
(631) 300-4960 .. **Giamundo**, John P '04 %Bello & L -150 Motor Pkwy -Hauppauge 11788
(516) 248-7000 .. **Gianakos**, Nancy E '93 OfCnsl Albanese & A LLP -1050 Franklin Av -Gdn Cty 11530
(212) 689-1113 .. **Gianaris**, Bill '88 (Garbarini & S,PC) -432 Park Av S -NY 10016
(718) 956-8477 .. **Gianaris**, Michl L '94 -21-70 42nd -Astoria 11105
(212) 848-4000 .. **Gianatasio**, Jared '07 %Shearman & S LLP -599 Lex Av -NY 10022
(212) 340-3347 .. **Gianazza**, Sara M '01 %Metro North Railroad -347 Mad Av -NY 10017
(212) 770-1632 .. **Giancarlo**, Deana L '98 %AIG -80 Pine -NY 10005
(716) 845-3630 .. **Giancarlo**, Guy C '95 %Atty Grievance Comm -438 Main -Buffalo 14202 **Fx**:856-2701
(212) 968-4100 .. **Giancarlo**, James C '85 GFI Group Inc -55 Water -NY 10041
(631) 231-1199 .. **Gianelli**, Paul '71 (Reynolds CGHL&Q,LLP) -35 Arkay Dr -Hauppauge 11788
(585) 546-7830 .. **Gianforti**, Gary J '77 (Culley MT&P,LLP) -36 W Main -Rchstr 14614
(516) 281-8550 .. **Gianfortune**, John P '91 (Gianfortune & M,PC) -231 Mineola Blvd -Mineola 11501 **Fx**:281-8552

(914) 995-3497 .. **Gianfrancesco,** Raffaelina '98 %DA -111 Martin Luther King Blvd -White Plns 10601 **Fx:**995-3363
(212) 708-9329 .. **Giangolano,** Marie A '84 Bessemer Trust Co -630 5th Av -NY 10111
(212) 850-0661 .. **Giangrande,** Thos M '98 1st Amer Title -633 3rd Av -NY 10017 **Fx:**(646) 487-1347
(716) 852-1500 .. **Giangreco,** Mark G '89 -443 Delaware Av -Buffalo 14202
(516) 741-0302 .. **Giannakos,** Constantine C '00 C Giannakos,PC -128 Front -Mineola 11501 **Fx:**741-0271
(718) 646-1955 .. **Giannakouros,** James G '91 -120 Bay Ridge Av -Brklyn 11220 **Fx:**769-8264
(212) 819-8200 .. **Giannandrea,** Heather A Hayes '07 %White & C LLP -1155 Av of Amer -NY 10036
(914) 220-0216 .. **Giannasca,** Michl A '00 -220 Ferris Av -White Plns 10603 **Fx:**220-0217
(212) 885-5000 .. **Giannasca,** Nicholas A '88 (Blank R LLP) -405 Lex Av -NY 10174
(516) 798-6400 .. **Giannattasio,** Camillo R '76 -686 Bway -Massapequa 11758
(516) 798-6400 .. **Giannattasio,** Edw M '80 -686 Bway -Massapequa 11758
(212) 723-3812 .. **Giannattasio,** Linda R '83 Citigroup Global Mrkts -250 West -NY 10013
(631) 421-8780 .. **Giannelli,** Robt H '04 (Sorel G,LLP) -196 E Main -Huntngtn 11743 **Fx:**421-8786
(914) 323-7000 .. **Giannetta,** Cathleen A '82 (Wilson EME&D LLP) -3 Gannett Dr -White Plns 10604
(845) 568-0755 .. **Giannetta,** Jaime Ann '90 -Bx119 -Wappingers Fls 12590
(518) 843-0043 .. **Giannetti,** Jos D '92 (Horigan H&L,PC) -49 E Main Bx520 -Amsterdam 12010
(518) 452-0633 .. **Giannetti,** Paul D '93 -3 Wshngtn Sq -Albany 12205
(212) 326-3939 .. **Giannetti,** Thos L '77 (Jones D) -222 E 41st -NY 10017
(914) 449-1020 .. **Giannettino,** Mario C '03 %Kaufman B&R -200 Summit Lk Dr -Valhalla 10595
(212) 957-9600 .. **Gianni,** Francesco '79 (Gianni OG & Prtnrs) -75 Rckfllr Plz -NY 10019
(212) 957-9600 .. **Gianni Origoni Grippo & Partners** -75 Rckfllr Plz -NY 10019 **Fx:**957-9608
(845) 357-5100 .. **Giannico Conklin,** Anita '88 %Ramapo Town Atty -237 Route 59 -Suffern 10901 **Fx:**357-2936
(212) 267-0380 .. **Giannini,** A Jos '79 (Friedman FC&G) -2 Rector -NY 10006
(914) 946-8900 .. **Giannini,** Angela Morcone '89 (Clark G&M) -99 Court -White Plns 10601
(631) 267-6666 .. **Giannini,** Jos '74 -Bx1958 -Amagansett 11930 **Fx:**329-6368
(212) 408-5100 .. **Giannini,** Jos F '04 %Chadbourne & P LLP -30 Rckfllr Plz -NY 10112
(212) 461-2323 .. **Gianninoto,** James H '85 (Saiber LLC) -44 Wall -NY 10005
(212) 521-5400 .. **Giannone,** Kristen '07 %Reed S LLP -599 Lex Av -NY 10022
(212) 761-4000 .. **Giannone,** Tara M '03 Morgan Stanley -1633 Bway -NY 10019
(212) 713-2000 .. **Giannopulos,** Bessie T '99 UBS Securities LLC -1285 Av of Amer -NY 10019
(718) 250-2000 .. **Giannotti,** John Jr. '96 %DA -350 Jay -Brklyn 11201 **Fx:**250-2314
(718) 728-3442 .. **Giano,** Steve '72 S Giano -3187 Steinway -Astoria 11103
(212) 841-2000 .. **Gianoukakis,** Evangelo '01 BNP Paribas -787 7th Av -NY 10019 **Fx:**841-2146
(212) 407-1200 .. **Giansanti-Cag,** Madeleine '02 %Joseph Law Ofcs LLC -485 Lex Av -NY 10017 **Fx:**407-1299
(212) 506-5000 .. **Giansello,** John D III '88 OfCnsl Orrick H&S LLP -51 W 52nd -NY 10019
(212) 566-7188 .. **Giantomasi,** Francis J '89 (Genova B&G) -115 Bway -NY 10006
(212) 566-7188 .. **Giantomasi,** Gemma M '06 %Genova B&G -115 Bway -NY 10006
(888) 805-8282 .. **Gianturco,** Diana C '88 -Bx419 -Long Bch 11561 **Fx:**(516) 706-1275
(212) 657-1172 .. **Giappone,** Paul '85 Citigroup Global Mrkts -77 Water -NY 10005
(212) 702-3546 .. **Giaquinto,** Gregg R '96 Rochdale Invstmnt Mgmt -570 Lex Av -NY 10022
(212) 679-8889 .. **Giaramita,** Jonathan P '05 Quarry Tile -132 Lex Av -NY 10016
(718) 748-4440 .. **Giaramita,** Jos Jr. '84 -8215 5th Av -Brklyn 11209
(917) 778-6600 .. **Giard,** Robt J '83 %J Toomey -485 Lex Av -NY 10017 **Fx:**778-7048
(716) 891-5800 .. **Giardina,** James S '05 Giardina Law,PA -461Ellicott -Buffalo 14203
(518) 789-3636 .. **Giardina,** Jeffrey A '70 -Millerton Plz Bx481 -Millerton 12546 **Fx:**789-6654
(646) 865-1590 .. **Giardina,** Jerry '83 (Carlucci & G,LLP) -11 E 44th -NY 10017
(718) 238-7300 .. **Giardina,** Lawr P '79 -8212 3rd Av -Brklyn 11209 **Fx:**238-8212
(315) 437-3321 .. **Giardina,** Nancy L '95 %Kall & R -3522 James -Syracuse 13206 **Fx:**437-0091
(212) 759-4888 .. **Giardino,** John J '83 SpclCnsl Phillips L LLP -437 Mad Av -NY 10022
(716) 847-8400 .. **Giardino,** John J '83 SpclCnsl Phillips L LLP -3400 HSBC Ctr -Buffalo 14203
(914) 241-1113 .. **Gibaldi,** Laurel '89 (Hirsch & G,LLP) -103 S Bedford Rd -Mt Kisco 10549 **Fx:**241-1122
(914) 934-7950 .. **Gibaldi,** Steven '90 Port Chester High Schl -1 Tamarack Rd -Pt Chester 10573
(212) 559-0245 .. **Gibau-Heyman,** Sharyn '90 Citigroup Inc -909 3rd Av -NY 10043 **Fx:**793-6027
(212) 478-0620 .. **Gibber,** Louis '03 DE Shaw & Co -120 W 45th -NY 10036 **Fx:**478-0100
(716) 592-7452 .. **Gibbin,** Leslie J '03 -15 Mechanic Bx43 -Sprngvll 14141 **Fx:**592-7479
(212) 225-2000 .. **Gibbon,** Brendan H '06 %Cleary GS&H -1 Lbrty Plz -NY 10006
(212) 609-6800 .. **Gibbon,** E Johanna '93 %McCarter & E,LLP -245 Park Av -NY 10167
(716) 851-3466 .. **Gibbon,** John R Jr. '98 %State Ins Fund -225 Oak -Buffalo 14203
(315) 946-5842 .. **Gibbon,** John W II '80 %Cnty Atty -26 Church -Lyons 14489 **Fx:**946-5942
(212) 755-4700 .. **Gibbons,** Adam C '95 Latash Inc -950 3rd Av -NY 10022 **Fx:**755-1300
(212) 267-1900 .. **Gibbons,** Brian '04 %Wade CM -111 Bway -NY 10006
(516) 832-7567 .. **Gibbons,** Danl C '06 %Nixon P LLP -50 Jericho Quadrangle -Jericho 11753
(516) 620-6360 .. **Gibbons,** Florence B '87 (Rogak & G,LLP) -50 Charles Lindburgh Blvd -Uniondale 11553
(718) 286-2000 .. **Gibbons,** Francis B '88 %Leg Aid -120-46 Qns Blvd -Kew Gdns 11415 **Fx:**286-2286
(212) 808-7800 .. **Gibbons,** John F '69 (Kelley D&W LLP) -101 Park Av -NY 10178
(516) 592-6800 .. **Gibbons,** John P Jr. '91 (Spellman RSGM&P,LLP) -229 Seventh -Gdn Cty 11530
(631) 298-9676 .. **Gibbons,** Jos H '71 -1380 Grathwohl Rd -New Suffolk 11956
(212) 447-1222 .. **Gibbons,** Jos T '80 (DeCicco G&M,PC) -14 E 38th -NY 10016
(716) 856-4400 .. **Gibbons,** Kenneth W '90 (Gibbons SG&K,PC) -181 Franklin -Buffalo 14202
(518) 372-5097 .. **Gibbons,** Kenneth W '93 -309 Mohawk Av -Scotia 12302 **Fx:**377-3972
(716) 856-4400 .. **Gibbons,** Kevin C '90 (Gibbons SG&K,PC) -181 Franklin -Buffalo 14202
(516) 571-3800 .. **Gibbons,** Laurie K '04 %DA -262 Old Cntry Rd -Mineola 11501 **Fx:**248-9479
(212) 770-8093 .. **Gibbons,** Lisa M '91 AIG -70 Pine -NY 10270
(212) 506-2500 .. **Gibbons,** Michele Lew '99 (Mayer B LLP) -1675 Bway -NY 10019
(585) 753-4267 .. **Gibbons,** Patricia A '01 Pub Def -10 N Fitzhugh -Rchstr 14614 **Fx:**428-2234
(212) 613-2000 .. **Gibbons PC** -1 Penn Plz -NY 10119 **Fx:**290-2018
(516) 620-6360 .. **Gibbons,** Rachel K '95 %Rogak & G,LLP -50 Charles Lindburgh Blvd -Uniondale 11553
(212) 790-4500 .. **Gibbons,** Robt G '90 (Manatt P&P,LLP) -7 Times Sq -NY 10036
(212) 909-6000 .. **Gibbons,** Robt J '70 (Debevoise & P LLP) -919 3rd Av -NY 10022
(716) 856-4400 .. **Gibbons Stadler Gibbons & Kullman,PC** -181 Franklin -Buffalo 14202 **Fx:**856-1200
(518) 487-7600 .. **Gibbons,** Theresa M '90 OfCnsl Whiteman O&H LLP -1 Commerce Plz -Albany 12260
(516) 625-9850 .. **Gibbons,** Timothy K '89 %Shapiro U&M,PC -Expwy Plz 1-#120 -Roslyn Hts 11577
(212) 708-4753 .. **Gibbons,** Trevor B '07 Millennium Mgmt LLC -666 5th Av -NY 10103
(718) 237-6282 .. **Gibbons,** Victoria Anne '83 %HRA -283 Adams -Brklyn 11201
(607) 965-8432 .. **Gibbons,** Wm John '72 -36 North Bx83 -Edmeston 13335
(718) 261-8200 .. **Gibbons,** Wyatt N '88 W Gibbons,PC -125-10 Qns Blvd -Kew Gdns 11415 **Fx:**263-1705
(516) 561-4700 .. **Gibbons Clement,** Catherine M '97 %Kaplon & M -444 Merrick Rd -Lynbrk 11563 **Fx:**872-1185
(212) 382-0700 .. **Gibbs,** A Gregory '03 %Ostrolenk FG&S,LLP -1180 Av of Amer -NY 10036
(518) 474-4567 .. **Gibbs,** Brenda M '96 Insurance Dept -99 Wshngtn Av -Albany 12257 **Fx:**473-4600
(212) 787-2828 .. **Gibbs,** Bud H '55 (Gibbs & Assoc) -146 Cntrl Pk W -NY 10023
(212) 513-3200 .. **Gibbs,** Chas F '63 (Holland & K LLP) -31 W 52nd -NY 10019
(212) 554-1234 .. **Gibbs,** Darryl W '01 AXA Financial Inc -1290 Av of Amer -NY 10104 **Fx:**707-3963
(212) 423-5646 .. **Gibbs,** Derrick W '82 -110 Wall -NY 10005
(646) 610-5400 .. **Gibbs,** Edmund E '88 %NYPD -1 Police Plz -NY 10038
(718) 270-6412 .. **Gibbs,** Jo A '84 %Medgar Evers College Ctr for Law & Social Justice -1150 Carroll -Brklyn 11225
(718) 804-8893 .. **Gibbs,** Joan P '86 %Ctr Law & Social Jus -1150 Carroll -Brklyn 11225 **Fx:**804-8833
(518) 402-9184 .. **Gibbs,** Khai H '03 DEC -625 Bway -Albany 12233 **Fx:**402-9018
(585) 243-2950 .. **Gibbs,** Linda F '76 -4341 Huston Rd -Geneseo 14454
(585) 396-8832 .. **Gibbs,** Linda I '86 %Family Ct -Cnty Cthse -Canandaigua 14424 **Fx:**396-4576
(212) 326-3939 .. **Gibbs,** Michl C '87 Cnsl Jones D -222 E 41st -NY 10017
(212) 508-6700 .. **Gibbs,** Michele K '99 (Tannenbaum HS&H LLP) -900 3rd Av -NY 10022
(212) 222-7005 .. **Gibbs,** Spencer C '01 (Rawlins & G,LLP) -103 E 125th -NY 10035 **Fx:**222-7187
(212) 270-5877 .. **Gibbs,** Wm I '06 JP Morgan Chase -270 Park Av -NY 10017
(212) 293-0770 .. **Gibgot,** Debra S '00 %Burly Bear Ntwk -1619 Bway -NY 10019
(516) 281-9800 .. **Giblin,** Annmarie '07 %Goldberg S LLP -200 Old Cntry Rd -Mineola 11501
(631) 249-5090 .. **Giblin,** John W Jr. '69 -1 Huntngtn Quadrangle -Melvll 11747 **Fx:**249-5514
(212) 227-4762 .. **Giblin,** Thos J '78 (Giblin & L) -225 Bway -NY 10007 **Fx:**732-6703
(212) 906-1200 .. **Giblin,** Thos J '10 %Latham & W -885 3rd Av -NY 10022
(212) 309-6000 .. **Giblin,** Thos P Jr. '98 (Morgan L&B LLP) -101 Park Av -NY 10178
(212) 652-3890 .. **Giblin,** Vincent M '08 (Pitta & G LLP) -120 Bway -NY 10271
(212) 688-5151 .. **Gibney Anthony & Flaherty, LLP** -665 5th Av -NY 10022 **Fx:**688-8315
(212) 938-5518 .. **Gibney,** Jos '90 -200 Rector Pl -NY 10280
(212) 577-3419 .. **Gibney,** Wm D '79 Leg Aid -199 Water -NY 10038
(212) 628-3519 .. **Gibofsky,** Allan '86 -425 E 79th -NY 10075 **Fx:**522-0703
(212) 593-6700 .. **Gibralter,** Danl H '08 %Aaronson RF&D,LLP -757 3rd Av -NY 10017
(914) 472-7700 .. **Gibralter,** Susan F '77 (Bertine HHZD&D,LLP) -700 Wht Plns Rd -Scarsdale 10583
(212) 310-8000 .. **Gibson,** B Keith '03 %Weil G&M LLP -767 5th Av -NY 10153
(212) 609-2634 .. **Gibson & Behman,PC** -14 Wall -NY 10005 **Fx:**609-2943
(212) 909-6000 .. **Gibson,** Caitlin E '09 %Debevoise & P LLP -919 3rd Av -NY 10022
(716) 856-4200 .. **Gibson,** Carol White '75 SpclCnsl Gibson M&C,LLP -69 Delaware Av -Buffalo 14202
(631) 537-1020 .. **Gibson,** Craig '85 (Birtwhistle & G,PC) -2322 Main Bx980 -Brdghmptn 11932 **Fx:**537-1029
(212) 530-5000 .. **Gibson,** Craig A '10 %Milbank TH&M LLP -1 Chase Manh Plz -NY 10005
(212) 500-2500 .. **Gibson,** Danl Barnaby '98 Itahaka Harbors -161 E 61st -NY 10065
(212) 351-4000 .. **Gibson Dunn & Crutcher LLP** -200 Park Av -NY 10166 **Fx:**351-4035
(914) 323-7000 .. **Gibson,** Elaine C '07 %Wilson EME&D LLP -3 Gannett Dr -White Plns 10604
(646) 536-3026 .. **Gibson,** Gregory C '98 Take-Two -622 Bway -NY 10012
(212) 226-5054 .. **Gibson,** James M '94 (Powley & G,PC) -304 Hudson -NY 10013 **Fx:**266-5085
(212) 783-4697 .. **Gibson,** John C '00 Citigroup -485 Lex Av -NY 10017
(585) 258-2800 .. **Gibson,** Kayla D '09 %Underberg & K LLP -300 Bausch & Lomb Pl -Rchstr 14604
(212) 735-3000 .. **Gibson,** Marie L '97 (Skadden ASM&F LLP) -4 Times Sq -NY 10036
(518) 486-3000 .. **Gibson,** Marin E '94 %Dept of Law -The Cptl -Albany 12224 **Fx:**474-4290
(516) 571-5896 .. **Gibson,** Marston C D '89 %Supreme Ct -100 Supreme Ct Dr -Mineola 11501 **Fx:**571-3518

(716) 856-4200 .. **Gibson McAskill & Crosby, LLP** -69 Delaware Av -Buffalo 14202 **Fx:**856-4013
(212) 818-9200 .. **Gibson**, Michl H '05 %Satterlee SB&B LLP -230 Park Av -NY 10169
(718) 802-2790 .. **Gibson**, Nicola J '07 ACS -330 Jay -Brklyn 11201
(718) 250-2000 .. **Gibson**, Rebecca L '98 %DA -350 Jay -Brklyn 11201 **Fx:**250-2314
(914) 559-3100 .. **Gibson**, Robt B '96 (Heidell PM&B,LLP) -81 Main -White Plns 10601
(212) 697-3581 .. **Gibson**, Scott M '82 -60 E 42nd -NY 10165 **Fx:**599-7902
(631) 261-8834 .. **Gibson**, Susan M '00 (Ingerman S LLP) -150 Motor Pkwy -Hauppauge 11788
(212) 872-6814 .. **Gibson**, Virginia M '96 %KPMG LLP -345 Park Av -NY 10154
(607) 778-2117 .. **Gibson**, Wm L Jr. '81 %Cnty Atty -Cnty Ofc Bldg Bx1766 -Bnghmtn 13902 **Fx:**778-6122
(718) 286-2450 .. **Gibson-O'Gara**, Susan E '83 %Leg Aid -120-46 Qns Blvd -Kew Gdns 11415 **Fx:**263-4234
(212) 670-3025 .. **Gicas**, Leonard H '02 Bk of America -222 Bway -NY 10038 **Fx:**670-4524
(212) 622-0426 .. **Gidden**, Christopher W '05 JP Morgan Securities -277 Park Av -NY 10172
(212) 837-6000 .. **Giddens**, James W '67 (Hughes H&R LLP) -1 Bttry Pk Plz -NY 10004
(646) 386-5131 .. **Giddens**, Virginia M '82 %Family Ct -60 Lafayette -NY 10013
(212) 848-4000 .. **Giddings**, Andrew F T '06 %Shearman & S LLP -599 Lex Av -NY 10022
(516) 668-1382 .. **Giddings**, Geoffrey F '70 -126 Park Av -New Hyde Pk 11040
(212) 573-6703 .. **Giddins**, Paul M '84 (Giddins & C LLP) -675 3rd Av -NY 10017 **Fx:**949-1923
(212) 326-2000 .. **Giddon**, Sloane J '09 %O'Melveny & M LLP -7 Times Sq -NY 10036
(212) 403-6700 .. **Gide Loyrette Nouel LLP** -120 W 45th -NY 10036 **Fx:**403-6740
(212) 878-8000 .. **Gidel**, Rebecca L '10 %Clifford C LLP -31 W 52nd -NY 10019
(315) 671-1100 .. **Gideon**, David S '84 %Hon J Tormey III -401 Mntgmry -Syracuse 13202 **Fx:**671-1183
(212) 879-5500 .. **Gideon**, Rebecca S '03 %Metropolitan Museum -1000 5th Av -NY 10028 **Fx:**570-3850
(845) 477-0791 .. **Gidro**, Michl R '87 -Bx1347 -Greenwd Lk 10925 **Fx:**477-7132
(212) 867-3456 .. **Gidseg**, Barry '79 OfCnsl Delafield H&L -311 E 38th -NY 10016
(212) 583-9600 .. **Gidseg**, Randy S '01 (Littler M,PC) -900 3rd Av -NY 10022
(212) 547-5400 .. **Giegerich**, Thos W '81 (McDermott W&E LLP) -340 Mad Av -NY 10173
(212) 278-1000 .. **Giehl**, Brian M '07 %Anderson K&O,PC -1251 Av of Amer -NY 10020
(914) 461-4658 .. **Giel**, Fredk G '96 Combe Inc -1101 Wstchstr Av -West Harrison 10604
(212) 363-1380 .. **Gielchinsky**, Danl Y '02 %Herten BSCBL&H,LLC -747 3rd Av -NY 10017
(212) 267-7342 .. **Gielchinsky**, Dina Z '03 OfCnsl Neiger LLP -317 Mad Av -NY 10017 **Fx:**406-3677
(716) 854-3455 .. **Gielowski**, Stephen M '83 (Gielowski F&C,LLP) -135 Delaware Av -Buffalo 14202 **Fx:**854-2797
(718) 324-2500 .. **Gierer**, Michl R '95 -4348 Katonah Av -Bronx 10470 **Fx:**994-0101
(631) 724-6666 .. **Gierer**, Peter B '79 -400 Town Line Rd Bx5296 -Hauppauge 11788 **Fx:**724-6602
(212) 335-9000 .. **Gieri**, Michelle C '98 %DA -1 Hogan Pl -NY 10013
(212) 223-0400 .. **Giesselman**, Janel B '07 %Zeichner E&K LLP -575 Lex Av -NY 10022
(212) 735-3000 .. **Giesselman**, Nathan W '07 %Skadden ASM&F LLP -4 Times Sq -NY 10036
(716) 856-1700 .. **Giessert**, Constance C '08 %Cannon H&W,LLP -726 Exchange -Buffalo 14210
(212) 351-4500 .. **Giesting**, Sarah K '07 %Epstein B&G,PC -250 Park Av -NY 10177
(212) 310-8000 .. **Gietz**, Raymond O '82 (Weil G&M LLP) -767 5th Av -NY 10153
(845) 677-2101 .. **Gifford**, Ann '70 OfCnsl Teahan & C -41 Front Bx1181 -Millbrook 12545
(585) 272-0540 .. **Gifford**, Annette M '03 Thomas & S LLP -693 East Av -Rchstr 14607
(518) 725-0655 .. **Gifford**, Heidi A '05 (Gifford D LLP) -13 W Fulton -Gloversvll 12078 **Fx:**725-9884
(845) 452-5900 .. **Gifford**, John K '71 (Van DeWater & V,LLP) -85 Civic Ctr Plz Bx112 -Poughkeepsie 12602
(212) 225-2000 .. **Gifford**, Jonathan D W '09 %Cleary GS&H -1 Lbrty Plz -NY 10006
(212) 720-5026 .. **Gifford**, Karen E '90 %Fed Reserve Bk -33 Lbrty -NY 10045 **Fx:**785-5748
(718) 858-7571 .. **Gifford**, Martha E '77 -93 Montague #220 -Brklyn 11201
(212) 483-9490 .. **Gifford**, Robt W '96 (McElroy DM&C,LLP) -88 Pine -NY 10005
(212) 450-4000 .. **Gifford**, Wm C '76 SrCnsl Davis P&W LLP -450 Lex Av -NY 10017
(516) 355-0780 .. **Giffords**, Norma '81 (Randazzo & G PC) -3000 Marcus Av -Lk Success 11042
(212) 366-2959 .. **Gigante**, Alexander '71 %Penguin Putnam Inc -375 Hudson -NY 10014 **Fx:**366-2867
(212) 969-3000 .. **Gigante**, Evandro C '04 %Proskauer R LLP -1585 Bway -NY 10036
(212) 381-7000 .. **Gigante**, John D '99 %Sabin B&G LLP -4 Times Sq -NY 10036
(212) 825-5900 .. **Gigante**, Robt A '01 Dept of Invstgtn -80 Maiden Ln -NY 10038 **Fx:**825-2860
(212) 902-4605 .. **Gigantes**, Jacqueline C '01 Goldman Sachs -1 NY Plz -NY 10004
(212) 705-4824 .. **Giger**, Matthew H '00 (Rosenberg & G PC) -488 Mad Av -NY 10022 **Fx:**593-9175
(212) 695-0060 .. **Gigler**, Claudia '07 %Wilens & B,PC -450 7th Av -NY 10123
(315) 797-2854 .. **Giglio**, David M '99 -231 Elizabeth -Utica 13501 **Fx:**797-2854
(718) 990-6600 .. **Giglio**, Frank '08 %St Johns Univ -8000 Utopia Pkwy -Jamaica 11439 **Fx:**591-1855
(212) 460-2941 .. **Giglio**, Richd J '83 Con Ed -4 Irving Pl -NY 10003
(212) 841-7615 .. **Giglio**, Robt J '91 %Cushman & Wakefield -1290 Av of Amer -NY 10104
(315) 733-6530 .. **Giglio**, Thos J '90 -Bx8090 -Utica 13505
(315) 471-1835 .. **Gigliotti**, Anthony J '73 Atty Grievance Comm -224 Harrison -Syracuse 13202 **Fx:**479-0123
(212) 984-4177 .. **Gigliotti**, Lisa M '88 Loreal USA -575 5th Av -NY 10017
(845) 226-7472 .. **Gigliotti**, Lisa M '93 -2537 Route 52 -Hopewell Junct 12533 **Fx:**226-2397
(212) 697-2715 .. **Gikow**, David H '78 (Lehman & G,PC) -52 Vndrblt Av -NY 10017 **Fx:**697-2773
(212) 715-9100 .. **Gil**, Alexandra '09 %Kramer LN&F,LLP -1177 Av of Amer -NY 10036
(718) 590-2000 .. **Gil**, Andres D '07 %DA -198 E 161st -Bronx 10451 **Fx:**590-6477
(212) 450-4000 .. **Gil**, Andres V '82 (Davis P&W LLP) -450 Lex Av -NY 10017
(212) 506-1700 .. **Gil**, Angela M '06 Kasowitz BT&F LLP -1633 Bway -NY 10019
(212) 891-0700 .. **Gil**, Doritte '89 FOJP Srvc Corp -28 E 28th -NY 10016 **Fx:**308-3911
(845) 473-8100 .. **Gil**, Omer '08 %Iseman CR&H,LLP -2649 South Rd -Poughkeepsie 12601
(212) 561-5522 .. **Gil**, Raphael '06 (Gil Y&C) -636 Bway -NY 10012
(212) 453-5900 .. **Gilaad**, Elana '99 SrCnsl Ford & H LLP -100 Park Av -NY 10017
(212) 806-5400 .. **Gilad**, Erez E '01 (Stroock &S&L LLP) -180 Maiden Ln -NY 10038
(212) 709-8097 .. **Gilberg**, Danl H '91 -110 Wall -NY 10005
(212) 558-4000 .. **Gilberg**, David J '90 (Sullivan & C LLP) -125 Broad -NY 10004
(718) 546-0950 .. **Gilberg**, Jeanne N '89 %Dept of Correction -75-20 Astoria Blvd -E Elmhrst 11370
(914) 632-5710 .. **Gilberg**, Jos B '52 -201 Wolfs Ln -Pelham 10803 **Fx:**632-8560
(212) 822-1440 .. **Gilberg**, Leo '59 -100 Park Av -NY 10017 **Fx:**880-6499
(212) 239-4999 .. **Gilberg**, Richd N '78 (Meyer SE&K,PC) -1350 Bway Bx822 -NY 10018
(212) 940-3004 .. **Gilbert**, Adam B '79 (Nixon P LLP) -437 Mad Av -NY 10022
(718) 286-6000 .. **Gilbert**, Alexander B '07 %DA -125-01 Qns Blvd -Kew Gdns 11415
(518) 474-6530 .. **Gilbert**, Alyce M '05 %Dept Pub Srvc -3 ESP -Albany 12223
(212) 446-2300 .. **Gilbert**, Avery P '08 %Boies S&F LLP -575 Lex Av -NY 10022
(631) 447-6500 .. **Gilbert Blaszcyk & Milburn,LLP** -440 Waverly Av -Patchogue 11772 **Fx:**447-6596
(631) 761-7031 .. **Gilbert**, Brett D '87 %Touro Cllg Law Ctr -225 Eastvw Dr -Central Islip 11722 **Fx:**761-7039
(845) 342-1155 .. **Gilbert**, David B '80 -45-47 Wickham Av -Middletwn 10940
(212) 487-9701 .. **Gilbert**, Dawn K '98 %Robin HK&F -1 Bttry Pk Plz -NY 10014
(646) 878-0800 .. **Gilbert**, Douglas J '82 (Pearl CZL,LLP) -1500 Bway -NY 10036
(212) 345-6000 .. **Gilbert**, E Scott '81 %Marsh USA -1166 Av of Amer -NY 10036 **Fx:**345-4808
(212) 735-8675 .. **Gilbert**, Edw P '94 (Morrison C LLP) -909 3rd Av -NY 10022
(212) 286-8503 .. **Gilbert**, Elisa T '93 (Gilbert & G,LLC) -325 E 57th -NY 10022
(212) 574-1200 .. **Gilbert**, Evan M '09 %Seward & K LLP -1 Bttry Pk Plz -NY 10004
(718) 590-2865 .. **Gilbert**, Fredk R '90 %Criminal Ct -265 E 161st -Bronx 10451
(917) 817-4819 .. **Gilbert**, George T '85 -74 W 68th -NY 10023
(212) 326-2000 .. **Gilbert**, Gregory A '93 (O'Melveny & M LLP) -7 Times Sq -NY 10036
(315) 343-6363 .. **Gilbert**, Gregory R '92 (Amdursky PF&W,PC) -26 E Oneida -Oswego 13126
(631) 630-0100 .. **Gilbert**, Howard E '81 -1233 Walt Whitman Rd -Melvll 11747 **Fx:**630-0101
(518) 402-9223 .. **Gilbert**, Ilse Gruber '87 %DEC -625 Bway -Albany 12233 **Fx:**402-9018
(212) 373-3000 .. **Gilbert**, Ira J '88 Cnsl Paul WRW&G LLP -1285 Av of Amer -NY 10019
(212) 335-9000 .. **Gilbert**, Janine M '98 %DA -1 Hogan Pl -NY 10013
(718) 250-2000 .. **Gilbert**, Jennifer L '05 %DA -350 Jay -Brklyn 11201 **Fx:**250-2314
(518) 794-7348 .. **Gilbert**, Jerrold '62 -Frog Alley Bx106 -Old Chatham 12136 **Fx:**794-6381
(585) 394-7970 .. **Gilbert**, John J '80 (Scott & G,LLP) -28 S Main -Canandaigua 14424
(917) 572-6863 .. **Gilbert**, Karen Stone '89 -30 Illinois Av -Bronxvll 10708
(212) 876-5500 .. **Gilbert**, Kenneth E '95 %Neighborhood Def Srv -317 Lenox Av -NY 10027 **Fx:**876-5586
(914) 833-5297 .. **Gilbert**, Lonya A '02 %Hyman & G -1843 Palmer Av -Larchmnt 10538
(212) 576-7000 .. **Gilbert**, Louis P '82 %NY Life Ins -51 Mad Av -NY 10010 **Fx:**447-0569
(845) 359-7048 .. **Gilbert**, Marshall S '61 -15 Iroquois Av RD 1 Bx 95 -Palisades 10964
(212) 432-9180 .. **Gilbert**, Martin G '85 (Stryker T&D LLP) -2 Penn Plz -NY 10121
(631) 588-4040 .. **Gilbert**, Michl A '00 %M Zwaik & Assoc,PC -3900 Vets Mem'l Hwy -Bohemia 11716 **Fx:**588-7175
(212) 698-3500 .. **Gilbert**, Michl J '96 (Dechert LLP) -1095 Av of Amer -NY 10036
(631) 447-6500 .. **Gilbert**, Michl S '89 (Gilbert B&M,LLP) -440 Waverly Av -Patchogue 11772
(212) 237-1000 .. **Gilbert**, Mitchell A '76 (Windels ML&M,LLP) -156 W 56th -NY 10019
(212) 564-1900 .. **Gilbert**, Paula R '07 %Cohen & K -450 7th Av -NY 10123
(212) 309-7852 .. **Gilbert**, Rachel B '04 %Lexis/Nexis -125 Park Av -NY 10017 **Fx:**309-8187
(516) 535-1700 .. **Gilbert**, Randi B '89 Horing W&R,PC -11 Hillside Av -Williston Pk 11596
(212) 506-5000 .. **Gilbert**, Richd A '78 (Orrick H&S LLP) -51 W 52nd -NY 10019
(212) 645-1990 .. **Gilbert**, Richd A '85 (Levine & G) -115 Christopher -NY 10014
(914) 833-5297 .. **Gilbert**, Rita K '80 (Hyman & G) -1843 Palmer Av -Larchmnt 10538
(212) 506-2500 .. **Gilbert**, Robt D '05 (Mayer B LLP) -1675 Bway -NY 10019
(914) 946-6995 .. **Gilbert**, Saml J '66 -280 N Central Av -Hartsdale 10530 **Fx:**946-0803
(212) 478-7200 .. **Gilbert**, Sarah M '08 %Hahn & H LLP -488 Mad Av -NY 10022
(212) 849-7000 .. **Gilbert**, Sarah M '08 Quinn EU&S,LLP -51 Mad Av -NY 10010
(212) 670-0250 .. **Gilbert**, Scott M '91 %Merrill Lynch -222 Bway -NY 10038
(212) 471-8610 .. **Gilbert**, Stanley Leon '65 (SL Gilbert,PC) -733 3rd Av -NY 10017 **Fx:**972-4350
(212) 541-2000 .. **Gilbert**, Stephen P '76 (Bryan C LLP) -1290 Av of Amer -NY 10104
Gilbert, Theo '51 -500 N Bway -Jericho 11753
(212) 286-8503 .. **Gilbert**, Vivienne '78 (Gilbert & G,LLC) -325 E 57th -NY 10022
(315) 442-0100 .. **Gilberti Stinziano Heintz & Smith,PC** -555 E Genesee -Syracuse 13202 **Fx:**442-0106
(518) 476-2001 .. **Gilberti Stinziano Heintz & Smith,PC** -111 Wshngtn Av -Albany 12210 **Fx:**476-9649
(212) 588-8868 .. **Gilberti Stinziano Heintz & Smith,PC** -885 3rd Av -NY 10022 **Fx:**588-8894
(585) 899-6030 .. **Gilberti Stinziano Heintz & Smith,PC** -1173 Pttsfrd-Vctr Rd -Pittsfrd 14534 **Fx:**248-5638
(315) 442-0100 .. **Gilberti**, Wm J Jr. '79 (Gilberti SH&S,PC) -555 E Genesee -Syracuse 13202
(212) 661-7300 .. **Gilberto**, Paul V '86 %Malapero & P LLP -295 Mad Av -NY 10017

(212) 824-5700 .. **Gilbertson,** Laurie B '93 %Practising Law Inst -810 7th Av -NY 10019
(518) 474-6400 .. **Gilboord,** Seth D '02 %Dept of Ed -89 Wshngtn Av -Albany 12234 **Fx:**473-2925
(212) 692-9666 .. **Gilbride,** Frank J II '68 (Gilbride TL&S LLC) -708 3rd Av -NY 10017
(914) 584-9934 .. **Gilbride,** Gerard A Jr. '78 (Ahmuty D&M) -55 Church -White Plns 10601
(212) 980-9600 .. **Gilbride,** Joan M '88 (Kaufman B&R) -120 Bway -NY 10271
(718) 549-9200 .. **Gilbride,** Kathleen M '86 Sisters of Charity -6301 Riverdale Av -Bronx 10471
(716) 856-4000 .. **Gilbride,** Terrence M '89 (Hodgson R LLP) -140 Pearl -Buffalo 14202
(212) 692-9666 .. **Gilbride Tusa Last & Spellane LLC** -708 3rd Av -NY 10017 **Fx:**661-6328
(518) 463-3990 .. **Gilchrist,** Andrew W '89 (Tuczinski CG&C,PC) -54 State -Albany 12207
(212) 722-4220 .. **Gilday,** Amy M '09 Hunter College -695 Park Av -NY 10065
(845) 331-3200 .. **Gilday,** Andrew J '74 -111 Green Bx3512 -Kingston 12402 **Fx:**331-6873
(718) 258-7494 .. **Gilde,** Anne O '88 -1065 E 18th -Brklyn 11230 **Fx:**951-9039
(212) 841-1000 .. **Gildea,** Andrea J '06 %Covington & B LLP -620 8th Av -NY 10018
(914) 961-1298 .. **Gildea,** John T '87 (Gildea & Assoc,PC) -24 Hllywd Av -Eastchstr 10707 **Fx:**961-1398
(212) 715-9100 .. **Gilden,** Richd H '72 (Kramer LN&F,LLP) -1177 Av of Amer -NY 10036
(212) 474-1000 .. **Gildersleeve,** John M '09 %Cravath S&M LLP -825 8th Av -NY 10019
(212) 849-7000 .. **Gildin,** Benjamin J '09 %Quinn EU&S,LLP -51 Mad Av -NY 10010
(212) 755-3100 .. **Gildin,** Danl '78 (Kaufmann GR&O LLP) -777 3rd Av -NY 10017
(718) 523-1111 .. **Gildin,** Steven '96 (Gildin Z&S,PC) -138-44 Qns Blvd -Briarwd 11435
(631) 623-6456 .. **Gildin,** Wendy L '97 -Bx393 -Deer Pk 11729
(718) 523-1111 .. **Gildin Zelenitz & Shapiro,PC** -138-44 Qns Blvd -Briarwd 11435 **Fx:**725-9606
(315) 428-1268 .. **Gilels,** Lisa A '96 -333 E Onondaga -Syracuse 13202
(914) 766-2684 .. **Giler Mann,** Desiree C '02 IBM -294 Route 100 -Somers 10589
(718) 636-1155 .. **Giles,** Debra A '91 %Leg Srvcs -1368 Fulton -Brklyn 11216 **Fx:**398-6414
(845) 368-3405 .. **Giles,** Irwin F '77 -402 Pawnee Ct -Suffern 10901
(212) 385-0111 .. **Giles,** Kenneth M '95 %R Zweig -325 Bway -NY 10007 **Fx:**571-7476
(212) 267-4177 .. **Giles,** Patricia '83 %Kramer DL&M -217 Bway -NY 10007
(212) 363-3100 .. **Gilfillan,** Curtis B '97 %Bivona & C,PC -88 Pine -NY 10005
(212) 752-5258 .. **Gilfillan,** Katherine A '98 Cnsl Schwartz SE&C LLC -845 3rd Av -NY 10022
(212) 307-1459 .. **Gilford,** Tia L '96 %West Entertainment Srvcs -1790 Bway -NY 10019
(718) 595-4168 .. **Gilgore,** Alison K '01 NYC DEP -59-17 Junction Blvd -Flushng 11373
(212) 504-6000 .. **Gilheany,** Terence F '64 SrCnsl Cadwalader W&T LLP -1 World Fncl Ctr -NY 10281
(631) 465-3600 .. **Gilhuley,** Stephen E '69 Park Electrochemical -48 S Srvc Rd -Melvll 11747 **Fx:**465-3100
(516) 357-3000 .. **Giliberti,** Frank J '82 (Rivkin R LLP) -926 RXR Plz -Uniondale 11556
(518) 474-6530 .. **Giliberto,** Donna M Ciaccio '85 %Dept Pub Srvc -3 ESP -Albany 12223
(212) 278-1513 .. **Gilinsky,** Marshall N '96 (Anderson K&O,PC) -1251 Av of Amer -NY 10020
(212) 696-6000 .. **Gilioli,** Eric L '84 (Curtis M-PC&M LLP) -101 Park Av -NY 10178
(718) 737-6950 .. **Gill,** Annette Hicks '03 -100-31 Bellaire Pl -Qns Vllg 11429
(212) 335-4500 .. **Gill,** Anthony D '05 %DLA Piper LLP -1251 Av of Amer -NY 10020
(212) 486-8500 .. **Gill,** E Ann '77 Balmer Parc LLC -445 Park Av -NY 10022 **Fx:**644-4121
(516) 825-6000 .. **Gill,** Elizabeth '87 (E Gill,PC) -71 S Central Av -Vly Stream 11580 **Fx:**825-2752
(716) 683-7057 .. **Gill,** Gerald J Jr. '95 -5580 Bway -Lancaster 14086 **Fx:**684-1454
(212) 541-2000 .. **Gill,** James F '56 (Bryan C LLP) -1290 Av of Amer -NY 10104
(914) 779-7314 .. **Gill,** John P '60 -230 Penn Av -Tuckahoe 10707
(631) 656-9220 .. **Gill,** Jonathan O'Neill '89 (Creedon & G,PC) -24 Woodbine Av -Northprt 11768 **Fx:**686-6718
(212) 508-6100 .. **Gill,** Jonathan P '00 (Bracewell & G,LLP) -1251 Av of Amer -NY 10020
(914) 654-2120 .. **Gill,** Kathleen E '94 %Law Dept -515 North Av -New Rchll 10801 **Fx:**654-2345
(914) 234-6363 .. **Gill,** Maria Divina '91 %Kuntz S&M,PC -444 Old Post Rd -Bedfrd 10506 **Fx:**234-6249
(212) 962-1020 .. **Gill,** Nicole M '01 %M Lamonsoff -80 Maiden Ln -NY 10038 **Fx:**962-3078
(212) 944-7333 .. **Gill,** Patrick D '68 (Rode & Q) -55 W 39th -NY 10018
(212) 837-3684 .. **Gill,** Peter J '84 %JP Morgan Chase -530 5th Av -NY 10036
(212) 238-8900 .. **Gill,** Rippi '02 %Melito & A,PC -233 Bway -NY 10279
(212) 450-4000 .. **Gill,** Sartaj S '00 (Davis P&W LLP) -450 Lex Av -NY 10017
(212) 335-4500 .. **Gill,** Tanya Singh '01 DLA Piper LLP -1251 Av of Amer -NY 10020
(631) 539-0100 .. **Gillam,** Bradley '92 -560 Broadhllw Rd -Melvll 11747 **Fx:**608-1242
(518) 641-5571 .. **Gillan,** Paul A Jr. '96 Cptl Dist Physicians Hlth Plan,Inc -500 Patroon Crk Blvd -Albany 12206 **Fx:**641-5505
(212) 554-1400 .. **Gillane,** Patricia Solan '90 %Bernstein LB&G LLP -1285 Av of Amer -NY 10019
(631) 878-3352 .. **Gillard,** Patricia '88 -250 Montauk Hwy -E Moriches 11940 **Fx:**878-5685
(518) 867-3001 .. **Gillberg,** Gustaf G Jr. '05 %Sciocchetti & Assoc,PLLC -12 Century Hill Dr -Latham 12110 **Fx:**867-3017
(845) 735-4119 .. **Gilleece,** Anne '91 -8 Craftwood Dr -Chestnut Rdg 10977 **Fx:**732-8143
(845) 638-5001 .. **Gilleece,** Kevin P '68 DA -1 S Main -New Cty 10956 **Fx:**638-5070
(212) 719-0200 .. **Gillen,** Carl G '05 %BAR/BRI -1500 Bway -NY 10036 **Fx:**719-1421
(516) 622-9200 .. **Gillen,** Laura A '01 %Westerman BEM&S,LLP -1201 RXR Plz -Uniondale 11553
(516) 794-6500 .. **Gillen,** Megan T '99 (Kennedy & G) -1050 Franklin Av -Gdn Cty 11530 **Fx:**794-5171
(716) 855-1111 .. **Gillen,** Patricia '87 (Duke HP&G LLP) -350 Main -Buffalo 14202
(212) 916-4653 .. **Giller,** Evan '79 %TIAA-CREF -730 3rd Av -NY 10017 **Fx:**907-2473
(212) 269-5500 .. **Giller,** Ronald A '97 (Gordon & R LLP) -90 Broad -NY 10004
(212) 998-6264 .. **Gillers,** Stephen '68 %NYU Law Schl -40 Wshngtn Sq S -NY 10012 **Fx:**995-4658
(212) 790-0200 .. **Gilles,** Myriam E '97 Benj N Cardozo Schl of Law -55 5th Av -NY 10003 **Fx:**790-0345
(212) 268-7535 .. **Gillespie,** Alexander H '87 (Bonner KT&C,LLP) -350 5th Av -NY 10118
(718) 250-2000 .. **Gillespie,** Camille O '85 %DA -350 Jay -Brklyn 11201 **Fx:**250-2314
(212) 318-3000 .. **Gillespie,** David A '85 (Fulbright & J LLP) -666 5th Av -NY 10103
(516) 867-7222 .. **Gillespie,** Eugenie E '48 -284 Lena Av -Freeprt 11520
(212) 474-1000 .. **Gillespie,** George J III '57 SpclCnsl Cravath S&M LLP -825 8th Av -NY 10019
(212) 513-7788 .. **Gillespie,** John F '99 %Ahmuty D&M -123 William -NY 10038
(516) 742-8171 .. **Gillespie,** Marie Turro '49 -94 3rd -Gdn Cty 11530
(718) 286-6000 .. **Gillespie,** Marissa B '05 %DA -125-01 Qns Blvd -Kew Gdns 11415
(212) 755-5510 .. **Gillespie,** Melissa S '03 %Loeb B & Prtnrs -505 Park Av -NY 10022
(212) 909-6000 .. **Gillespie,** Michl J '87 (Debevoise & P LLP) -919 3rd Av -NY 10022
(212) 450-4000 .. **Gillespie,** S Hazard '37 SrCnsl Davis P&W LLP -450 Lex Av -NY 10017
(516) 794-7500 .. **Gillespie,** Stephen J '99 (Westermann SKS&A,LLP) -333 Earle Ovngton Blvd -Uniondale 11553
(212) 697-8100 .. **Gillett,** David P '93 (Derfner & G,LLP) -60 E 42nd -NY 10165
(212) 335-9000 .. **Gillett,** Om '03 %DA -1 Hogan Pl -NY 10013
(718) 574-7606 .. **Gillett,** Trecia A '03 -1128 Halsey -Brklyn 11207
(212) 479-1580 .. **Gillette,** Alexander P '03 Fortress Investment Grp -1345 Av of Amer -NY 10105
(718) 468-0500 .. **Gillette,** Jos '90 %Ginsburg & M -215-48 Jamaica Av -Qns Vllg 11428
(315) 474-2943 .. **Gillette,** Joshua M '08 %Sugarman Law Firm,LLP -211 W Jffrsn -Syracuse 13202
(212) 816-5679 .. **Gilliam,** Fatimah A '02 Citi -388 Greenwich -NY 10013
(212) 307-5500 .. **Gilliam,** Gregory W '04 %Venable LLP -1270 Av of Amer -NY 10020
(631) 722-8074 .. **Gilliam,** Harriet A '86 -1 Union Sq Bx1485 -Rvrhead 11901
(212) 905-0516 .. **Gilliam,** Ryan S '06 Goldman Sachs -1 NY Plz -NY 10004
(212) 552-0947 .. **Gilliam,** Tracey Cushing '95 JP Morgan Chase -1 Chase Manh Plz -NY 10081
(212) 350-2700 .. **Gilliar,** Rachel Rosenblatt '05 %Constantine C,PC -450 Lex Av -NY 10017
(212) 481-1312 .. **Gilliatt,** David R '76 %Gulotta Law Grp PLLC -271 Mad Av -NY 10016 **Fx:**481-1316
(212) 425-7200 .. **Gillick,** John B Jr. '08 %Kenyon & K,LLP -1 Bway -NY 10004
(212) 277-4000 .. **Gillie,** Jeff B '09 %Freshfields BD LLP -520 Mad Av -NY 10022
(845) 291-2454 .. **Gillies,** Donalda J '91 %Leg Aid -2 Court Ln Bx328 -Goshen 10924 **Fx:**294-2638
(212) 530-5000 .. **Gilligan,** Grace M '05 %Milbank TH&M LLP -1 Chase Manh Plz -NY 10005
(315) 422-1152 .. **Gilligan,** Kevin M '80 (Costello C&F,PLLC) -500 Plum -Syracuse 13204
(212) 610-6300 .. **Gilligan,** Michl '98 (Allen & O) -1221 Av of Amer -NY 10020
(585) 753-4500 .. **Gilligan,** Nancy Ann '91 %DA -832 Watts Bldg -Rchstr 14614 **Fx:**753-4576
(212) 446-7000 .. **Gilligan,** Nellie D '95 %McKinsey & Co -55 E 52nd -NY 10055 **Fx:**688-9521
(212) 683-8583 .. **Gillikin,** Virginia '83 (V Gillikin,PC) -200 E 27th -NY 10016 **Fx:**725-2770
(212) 949-9022 .. **Gilliland,** Alan D '76 OfCnsl Abelman F&S -666 3rd Av -NY 10017
(716) 662-0612 .. **Gilliland,** Jennifer Anne '96 -15 Midway Dr -Orchard Pk 14127
(631) 696-2544 .. **Gillin,** Donna L '97 %CMOR -5507-10 Nesconset Hwy #147 -Mt Sinai 11766 **Fx:**696-2372
(212) 310-6790 .. **Gillis,** Christian D '97 Weil G&M LLP -767 5th Av -NY 10153
(212) 648-0362 .. **Gillis,** David K F '99 JP Morgan Chase -245 Park Av -NY 10167
(518) 487-7600 .. **Gillis,** Margaret J '82 (Whiteman O&H LLP) -1 Commerce Plz -Albany 12260
(212) 896-6500 .. **Gillis,** Theresa M '75 (Howrey LLP) -601 Lex Av -NY 10022
(212) 660-3000 .. **Gillispie,** Robt J '69 (Sullivan & W LLP) -1290 Av of Amer -NY 10104
(212) 310-2235 .. **Gillman,** Nina D '84 %Colgate-Palmolive -300 Park Av -NY 10022 **Fx:**310-3230
(212) 813-8800 .. **Gillman,** Ross D '86 (Goodwin P LLP) -620 8th Av -NY 10018
(516) 869-7600 .. **Gillman,** Wm J '54 %Town Atty -220 Plandome Rd -Manhsst 11030 **Fx:**869-7605
(716) 843-5700 .. **Gillmeister,** Wm J '85 %US Atty -138 Delaware Av -Buffalo 14202 **Fx:**551-3052
(914) 238-1000 .. **Gillow,** Paul L '88 Reader's Digest -Readers Digest Rd -Plsntvll 10570 **Fx:**241-5644
(212) 257-6800 .. **Gilly,** Scott B '99 (Thompson W&G LLP) -85 5th Av -NY 10003
(212) 318-6000 .. **Gilman,** Amanda Burrell '07 %Paul HJ&W LLP -75 E 55th -NY 10022
(212) 701-3000 .. **Gilman,** Chas A '75 (Cahill G&R LLP) -80 Pine -NY 10005 **Fx:**269-5420
(646) 512-5730 .. **Gilman,** David '65 (Gilman & S) -40 Wall -NY 10005 **Fx:**512-5734
(716) 841-6616 .. **Gilman,** Elyse Lubin '82 HSBC Bank -1 HSBC Ctr -Buffalo 14203 **Fx:**841-5087
(212) 909-6000 .. **Gilman,** Felix John '04 %Debevoise & P LLP -919 3rd Av -NY 10022
(212) 468-4800 .. **Gilman,** Gregg A '89 (Davis & G LLP) -1740 Bway -NY 10019
(212) 261-8000 .. **Gilman,** Jennifer A '07 %Mendes & M,LLP -750 7th Av -NY 10019
(718) 459-6200 .. **Gilman,** Keith A '94 (Simon & G) -91-31 Qns Blvd -Elmhrst 11373
(585) 425-5211 .. **Gilman,** Kelly A '06 Maximus Inc -50 Square Dr -Victor 14564
(212) 930-2321 .. **Gilman,** Kimberly A '02 West Point Home,Inc -28 E 28th -NY 10016
(212) 753-5000 .. **Gilman,** Marc G '08 %Schiff H LLP -900 3rd Av -NY 10022
(212) 455-2000 .. **Gilman,** Peter H '05 %Simpson T&B LLP -425 Lex Av -NY 10017
(585) 987-2800 .. **Gilman,** R Thompson '77 (Woods OG LLP) -2 State -Rchstr 14614
(212) 922-0050 .. **Gilman,** Robt '91 Stewart Title Ins Co -300 E 42nd -NY 10017
(212) 558-4000 .. **Gilman,** Roderick M Jr. '08 %Sullivan & C LLP -125 Broad -NY 10004
(212) 599-9999 .. **Gilman,** Scott '89 -380 Lex Av -NY 10168 **Fx:**599-4499
(212) 446-4800 .. **Gilman,** Timothy K '04 %Kirkland & E LLP -153 E 53rd -NY 10022
(212) 282-5000 .. **Gilman,** Timothy M '96 %Avon Products -1251 Av of Amer -NY 10020

(631) 283-0200 .. **Gilmartin & Bregman** -320 Hmptn Rd Bx5071 -Southampton 11969 **Fx:**283-0362
(631) 283-0200 .. **Gilmartin,** David J '64 (Gilmartin & B) -320 Hmptn Rd Bx5071 -Southampton 11969
(631) 283-0200 .. **Gilmartin,** David J Jr. '96 (Gilmartin & B) -320 Hmptn Rd Bx5071 -Southampton 11969
(212) 403-1000 .. **Gilmartin,** James R '06 %Wachtell LR&K -51 W 52nd -NY 10019
(631) 283-1800 .. **Gilmartin,** Martin R '70 -25 Bowden Sq Bx1281 -Southampton 11969 **Fx:**283-1834
(212) 259-8000 .. **Gilmartin,** Matthew R '07 %Dewey & L LLP -1301 Av of Amer -NY 10019
(212) 425-3220 .. **Gilmartin,** Patrick J '59 (Gilmartin P&S LLP) -845 Third Av -NY 10022
(212) 425-3220 .. **Gilmartin Poster & Shafto LLP** -845 Third Av -NY 10022 **Fx:**425-3130
(212) 858-6319 .. **Gilmartin,** Ralph B '80 %Reliance Ins -75 Broad -NY 10004
(212) 422-0202 .. **Gilmartin,** Robt M Jr. '99 %Sedgwick DM&A LLP -125 Broad -NY 10004
(212) 284-1756 .. **Gilmartin,** Sean T '04 Jefferies & Co -520 Mad Av -NY 10022
(516) 484-3460 .. **Gilmartin,** Sharon A '93 Port Washington Dialysis Ctr -50 Seaview Blvd -Pt Wash 11050
(631) 852-3040 .. **Gilmartin,** Timothy M '00 -210 Center Dr -Rvrhead 11901
(315) 435-2170 .. **Gilmore,** Catherine Z '87 %Cnty Atty -421 Mntgmry -Syracuse 13202 **Fx:**435-5729
(212) 558-4000 .. **Gilmore,** Emma '04 %Sullivan & C LLP -125 Broad -NY 10004
(212) 785-5585 .. **Gilmore,** Eugenie '92 -11 Bway -NY 10004
(212) 601-2680 .. **Gilmore,** Gregory B '01 %Gonzalez S&H LLP -350 5th Av -NY 10118
(212) 558-4000 .. **Gilmore,** Kelly A '09 %Sullivan & C LLP -125 Broad -NY 10004
(212) 805-4851 .. **Gilmore,** Martin E '08 US Dist Ct -500 Pearl -NY 10007
(516) 739-9009 .. **Gilmore,** Michl P '88 (Sims MK&D LLP) -129 3rd -Mineola 11501
(212) 538-3495 .. **Gilmore,** Paul A '95 Credit Suisse -11 Mad Av -NY 10010
(914) 682-3300 .. **Gilmore,** Robt '01 %La Sorsa & B -3 Barker Av -White Plns 10601
(516) 798-2712 .. **Gilmore,** Scott J '84 -1000 Park Blvd -Massapequa Pk 11762 **Fx:**798-7732
(315) 492-1666 .. **Gilmore,** Tamara M '96 (Sargent & G,LLP) -892 E Brighton Av -Syracuse 13205
(212) 657-0107 .. **Gilmore,** Winifred G '85 Citigroup -77 Water -NY 10005
(845) 298-7075 .. **Gilmore-Morris,** Lori J '89 -6 Daisy Ln -Wappingers Fls 12590 **Fx:**296-1710
(585) 454-4060 .. **Gilmour,** Sarah J '93 %Empire Justice Ctr -1 W Main -Rchstr 14614 **Fx:**454-4019
(516) 214-0343 .. **Gilot,** Annilus J '03 Gilot & Assoc,PC -950 Jericho Tpk -Westbury 11590 **Fx:**214-0446
(203) 327-1800 .. **Gilpatrick,** Bruce F '81 (Heidell PM&B,LLP) -99 Park Av -NY 10016 **Fx:**353-1892
(718) 590-6212 .. **Gilpin,** Tahesha C '09 %Law Dept -198 E 161st -Bronx 10451 **Fx:**590-2686
(718) 981-8181 .. **Gilroy,** Felix T '65 -60 Bay -Staten Isl 10301 **Fx:**981-5147
(718) 423-6800 .. **Gilroy,** James '79 MacKay W&B LLP -40-26 235th -Douglastn 11363
(718) 658-0500 .. **Gilroy,** Jennifer M '93 %Law Dept -151-20 Jamaica Av -Jamaica 11432 **Fx:**658-4025
(212) 268-5136 .. **Gilroy,** Marcy A '99 %Harwood L -350 5th Av -NY 10118
(212) 310-8000 .. **Gilroy,** Matthew J '00 (Weil G&M LLP) -767 5th Av -NY 10153
(212) 837-6000 .. **Gilroy,** N Thos Jr. '53 SrCnsl Hughes H&R LLP -1 Bttry Pk Plz -NY 10004
(212) 580-2832 .. **Gilroy,** Patricia E '85 -50 Riverside Dr -NY 10024
(212) 848-4000 .. **Gilroy,** Terence P '07 %Shearman & S LLP -599 Lex Av -NY 10022
(212) 617-3117 .. **Giltman,** Leonard J '03 Bloomberg LP -731 Lex Av -NY 10022
(212) 906-1200 .. **Giltner,** Rebecca S '05 %Latham & W -885 3rd Av -NY 10022
(631) 871-2252 .. **Gilvary,** Kevin J '93 -17 Old Cntry Rd -E Quogue 11942
(718) 556-7011 .. **Gim,** Joseb S '04 DA -130 Styvsnt Pl -Staten Isl 10301
(212) 841-1000 .. **Gimbel,** Mark P '99 (Covington & B LLP) -620 8th Av -NY 10018
(212) 836-8000 .. **Gimbel,** Megan E '06 %Kaye S LLP -425 Park Av -NY 10022
(212) 318-6000 .. **Gimenez-Hubbard,** Alicia M '06 %Paul HJ&W LLP -75 E 55th -NY 10022
(516) 822-8900 .. **Gimeno,** Ernesto O '86 Fiedelman & M -2 Jericho Plz -Jericho 11753
(212) 806-5400 .. **Giminaro,** Jos B '84 SplCnsl Stroock &S&L LLP -180 Maiden Ln -NY 10038
(212) 209-3100 .. **Gimm,** Anne Shin '00 Taconic Capital Advisors,LLC -450 Park Av -NY 10022
(212) 506-2500 .. **Gimm,** Edith G '05 %Mayer B LLP -1675 Bway -NY 10019
(212) 705-7000 .. **Gimmel,** Danl '03 Cnsl Bingham M LLP -399 Park Av -NY 10022
(212) 878-8000 .. **Gimpel,** Jeffrey '99 Cnsl Clifford C LLP -31 W 52nd -NY 10019
(212) 803-1314 .. **Gimpel,** Mark S '90 -260 Mad Av -NY 10016 **Fx:**803-1319
(212) 867-7900 .. **Ginach,** Yoram '81 Y Ginach,PC -1 Penn Plz -NY 10119 **Fx:**370-5982
(212) 601-9700 .. **Ginarte O'Dwyer Gonzalez Gallardo & Winograd,LLP** -225 Bway -NY 10007 **Fx:**267-4262
(212) 336-0151 .. **Ginde,** Ashok A '02 %SEC -3 World Fncl Ctr -NY 10281 **Fx:**336-1323
(212) 545-4691 .. **Ginder,** Adam B '06 %Wolf HAF&H LLP -270 Mad Av -NY 10016
(516) 794-5310 .. **Gindi,** Corey M '95 (Abrams GMB,LLP) -125 Jericho Tpk -Jericho 11753
(516) 465-8090 .. **Gindi,** Harry E '66 %North Shore-LIJ Hlth Systm -145 Community Dr -Gt Neck 11021 **Fx:**465-8013
(212) 225-2000 .. **Gindi,** Maurice R '10 %Cleary GS&H -1 Lbrty Plz -NY 10006
(718) 336-5614 .. **Gindi,** Morris '81 -805 Av P -Brklyn 11223
(212) 227-9092 .. **Gindi,** Raymond A '93 %Century 21 -22 Crtlandt -NY 10007
(212) 480-4800 .. **Ginebra,** Rafael A '85 (Fox H&C LLP) -825 3rd Av -NY 10022
(716) 694-5400 .. **Ginestre,** Vincent R '72 -248 Meadow Dr -N Tonawanda 14120 **Fx:**743-1644
(212) 277-6500 .. **Gingher,** Robt G '02 %Dickstein S LLP -1633 Bway -NY 10019
(212) 351-4000 .. **Gingold,** Brian M '01 %Gibson D&C LLP -200 Park Av -NY 10166
(212) 504-6000 .. **Gingold,** David S '99 SplCnsl Cadwalader W&T LLP -1 World Fncl Ctr -NY 10281
(212) 213-1220 .. **Gingold,** Douglas A '91 %Weiner MM&B,LLC -220 5th Av -NY 10001
(212) 286-8585 .. **Gingold,** Eric D '03 %Heidell PM&B,LLP -99 Park Av -NY 10016
(315) 422-2255 .. **Gingold,** Harlan B '71 (Macht B&G) -510 State Twr Bldg -Syracuse 13202
(315) 474-6519 .. **Gingold,** Lawr H '60 -1012 State Twr Bldg -Syracuse 13202
(315) 445-0060 .. **Gingold,** Neil M '71 -5178 Winterton Dr -Fayettevll 13066 **Fx:**445-9222
(718) 250-2000 .. **Gingold,** Rebecca N '04 DA -350 Jay -Brklyn 11201 **Fx:**250-2314
(518) 583-1515 .. **Ginley,** Michl P '94 (Ginley & G,PC) -96 Ballston Av -Saratoga Spgs 12866 **Fx:**226-0187
(315) 676-2094 .. **Ginnelly,** Paul J '66 -6321 Muskrat Bay Rd -Brewertn 13029
(516) 433-1554 .. **Ginnis,** Katherina '98 -720 Parkside Dr -Jericho 11753 **Fx:**433-1662
(212) 246-2400 .. **Ginns,** Jane Yanovsky '08 %Balber PM&VDT,PC -1370 Av of Amer -NY 10019
(212) 403-1000 .. **Ginott,** Jamie H '10 %Wachtell LR&K -51 W 52nd -NY 10019
(212) 674-3805 .. **Ginsberg,** Alan W '74 -300 Mercer -NY 10003
(518) 408-3976 .. **Ginsberg,** Barry '87 %NYS Comm Pub Integrity -540 Bway -Albany 12207
(212) 732-1200 .. **Ginsberg Becker & Weaver** -26 Bway -NY 10004 **Fx:**732-5877
(212) 577-3530 .. **Ginsberg,** Betsy R '03 %Leg Aid -199 Water -NY 10038 **Fx:**425-2465
(212) 841-1000 .. **Ginsberg,** Brian D '08 %Covington & B LLP -620 8th Av -NY 10018
(212) 468-4800 .. **Ginsberg,** Bruce M '79 (Davis & G LLP) -1740 Bway -NY 10019
(212) 320-6000 .. **Ginsberg,** Cynthia L '99 %Barclays Capital Inc -1301 Av of Amer -NY 10019
(212) 806-5400 .. **Ginsberg,** Danl P '97 SplCnsl Stroock &S&L LLP -180 Maiden Ln -NY 10038
(212) 655-0224 .. **Ginsberg,** Deborah J '04 Capital Trust,Inc -410 Park Av -NY 10022
(516) 746-9307 .. **Ginsberg,** Eugene S '55 -300 Grdn City Plz -Gdn Cty 11530 **Fx:**393-8282
(212) 852-7016 .. **Ginsberg,** Gary '88 News Corp -1211 Av of Americas -NY 10036
(518) 432-1200 .. **Ginsberg,** George S '71 OfCnsl McGlinchey S PLLC -194 Wshngtn Av -Albany 12210
(516) 505-3971 .. **Ginsberg,** Harvey B '69 -661 Bellmore Av -E Meadow 11554 **Fx:**483-5021
(718) 852-8888 .. **Ginsberg,** Irene '01 %LSNYC-Brooklyn -180 Lvngstn -Brklyn 11201 **Fx:**858-1786
(212) 490-7900 .. **Ginsberg,** Jeffrey I '86 -420 Lex Av -NY 10170 **Fx:**983-1050
(212) 425-7200 .. **Ginsberg,** Jeffrey S '94 (Kenyon & K,LLP) -1 Bway -NY 10004
(212) 248-2199 .. **Ginsberg,** Jonathan '91 J Ginsberg,LLC -160 Pearl -NY 10005 **Fx:**248-2155
(212) 732-7922 .. **Ginsberg,** Jonathan E '10 OfCnsl Rosenbaum F LLP -11 Penn Plz -NY 10001
(212) 872-1000 .. **Ginsberg,** Jos '89 -One Bryant Park -NY 10036 **Fx:**872-1002
(718) 591-6900 .. **Ginsberg & Katsorhis** -77-53 Main -Flushng 11367 **Fx:**380-8039
(518) 266-1000 .. **Ginsberg,** Lambert L '57 (Pattison SG&G,PC) -22 1st Bx208 -Troy 12181
(718) 896-9600 .. **Ginsberg,** Laurence T '83 %Plaza Rlty Invstrs -64-35 Yllwstn Blvd -Frst Hlls 11375
(212) 986-2277 .. **Ginsberg,** Lawr J '77 Harland Fncl Svc -60 E 42nd -NY 10165
(212) 608-0808 .. **Ginsberg,** Lee A '73 (Freeman N&G) -30 Vesey -NY 10007 **Fx:**962-9696
(212) 421-9630 .. **Ginsberg,** Linda Anne '90 Smythe Masterson & Judd -230 Park Av -NY 10169 **Fx:**421-9665
(516) 625-0105 .. **Ginsberg,** Louis '88 -1613 Nrthrn Blvd -Roslyn 11576 **Fx:**625-0106
(518) 436-0751 .. **Ginsberg,** Mara B '84 (Hinman S PC) -121 State -Albany 12207
(212) 218-5500 .. **Ginsberg,** Mark H '09 %Seyfarth S LLP -620 8th Av -NY 10018
(718) 805-2300 .. **Ginsberg,** Martin L '81 (M Ginsberg,PC) -80-59 Lefferts Blvd -Kew Gdns 11415 **Fx:**805-2201
(518) 266-1000 .. **Ginsberg,** Michl E '93 (Pattison SG&G,PC) -22 1st Bx208 -Troy 12181
(212) 373-3000 .. **Ginsberg,** Paul D '88 (Paul WRW&G LLP) -1285 Av of Amer -NY 10019
(646) 374-0029 .. **Ginsberg,** Peter R '82 (Ginsberg & B,PLLC) -12 E 49th -NY 10017 **Fx:**355-0202
(516) 742-7747 .. **Ginsberg,** Peter R '00 (Ginsberg & B) -114 Old Cntry Rd -Mineola 11501 **Fx:**742-7748
(212) 655-0220 .. **Ginsberg,** Peter S '89 Capital Trust -410 Park Av -NY 10022
(212) 227-0640 .. **Ginsberg,** Robt M '61 (Ginsberg & W,PC) -225 Bway -NY 10007
(212) 319-0304 .. **Ginsberg,** Rubin J '98 %M Kramer & Assoc -150 E 58th -NY 10155 **Fx:**319-0545
(212) 532-8100 .. **Ginsberg,** Scott A '04 %Stern & M,LLP -115 Bway -NY 10006 **Fx:**532-7271
(212) 983-6000 .. **Ginsberg,** Seth R '94 -250 Park Av -NY 10177 **Fx:**983-6008
(646) 435-0300 .. **Ginsberg,** Simon H '97 (McCullough GM&P,LLP) -320 E 53rd -NY 10022
(516) 873-2000 .. **Ginsberg,** Stephen J '06 %Moritt HH&H LLP -400 Grdn City Plz -Gdn Cty 11530
(718) 522-4772 .. **Ginsberg,** Steven E '82 -26 Court -Brklyn 11242
(212) 227-0640 .. **Ginsberg & Wolf,PC** -225 Bway -NY 10007 **Fx:**227-4228
(518) 402-6757 .. **Ginsburg,** Alan B '89 %Workers Comp Bd -20 Park -Albany 12207
(718) 468-0500 .. **Ginsburg,** Hal R '84 (Ginsburg & M) -215-48 Jamaica Av -Qns Vllg 11428
(716) 874-2111 .. **Ginsburg,** Herman J '56 OfCnsl Hawthorne & S PLLC -3080 Delaware Av -Buffalo 14217
(212) 599-3303 .. **Ginsburg,** Jacob '98 OfCnsl Helfand & H -350 5th Av -NY 10118 **Fx:**599-3029
(212) 854-3325 .. **Ginsburg,** Jane C '82 %Columbia Law Schl -435 W 116th -NY 10027 **Fx:**854-7946
(212) 554-7800 .. **Ginsburg,** Lawr L '74 (Moses & S LLP) -405 Lex Av -NY 10174
(315) 852-9761 .. **Ginsburg,** Lawr M '57 -438 W Lake Rd -De Ruyter 13052 **Fx:**(770) 270-5789
(518) 473-0620 .. **Ginsburg,** Lev A '04 %Governor's Ofc Reg Reform -ESP Bx2107 -Albany 12220 **Fx:**473-9962
(914) 495-3515 .. **Ginsburg,** Mark D '87 (Ginsburg & R,PC) -245 Saw Mill Rvr Rd -Hawthorne 10532 **Fx:**495-3520
(212) 949-7300 .. **Ginsburg,** Mel B '74 (Vernon & G,LLP) -261 Mad Av -NY 10016
(718) 468-0500 .. **Ginsburg & Misk** -215-48 Jamaica Av -Qns Vllg 11428 **Fx:**468-0592
(212) 298-5190 .. **Ginsburg,** Nancy L '92 %Leg Aid -49 Thomas -NY 10013 **Fx:**587-3179
(212) 735-3000 .. **Ginsburg,** Nehemiah E '04 %Skadden ASM&F LLP -4 Times Sq -NY 10036
(212) 382-0700 .. **Ginsburg,** Paul H '77 OfCnsl Ostrolenk FG&S,LLP -1180 Av of Amer -NY 10036

(212) 310-8000 .. **Ginsburg,** Richd A '01 (Weil G&M LLP) -767 5th Av -NY 10153
(631) 852-1650 .. **Ginty,** Danl P '02 %Leg Aid -300 Center Dr -Rvrhead 11901 **Fx:**852-1655
(212) 655-3520 .. **Ginzberg,** Robt A '86 (Roe & K,LLP) -440 Park Av S -NY 10016
(212) 836-8000 .. **Ginzburg,** Margarita Y '99 Cnsl Kaye S LLP -425 Park Av -NY 10022
(212) 446-4800 .. **Ginzburg,** Maria '98 (Kirkland & E LLP) -153 E 53rd -NY 10022
(212) 786-7549 .. **Gioconda,** Jos C '98 (Gioconda Law Grp) -One Penn Plz -NY 10119 **Fx:**(888) 697-9665
(631) 853-4104 .. **Gioe,** Christopher M '07 DA -400 Carleton Av Bx9082 -Central Islip 11722 **Fx:**853-7838
(212) 701-3000 .. **Gioello,** Peter J Jr. '09 %Cahill G&R LLP -80 Pine -NY 10005 **Fx:**269-5420
(914) 761-1300 .. **Gioffre,** Anthony B III '95 (Cuddy & F LLP) -445 Hmltn Av -White Plns 10601
(914) 696-3800 .. **Gioffre,** B J '59 Cnsl Gioffre & G -2900 Wstchstr Av -Purchase 10577 **Fx:**696-3833
(914) 997-0555 .. **Gioffre,** Bruno V '99 %Quinn & M,LLP -399 Knollwood Rd -White Plns 10603
(212) 449-5893 .. **Gioia,** Angela Anne '97 %Merrill Lynch -4 World Fncl Ctr -NY 10080
(716) 854-3400 .. **Gioia,** Horace A '81 (Rupp BPC&C LLC) -1600 Lbrty Bldg -Buffalo 14202
(516) 496-0600 .. **Gioia,** Lisa M '86 Grace Ventures -21 Yukon Dr -Woodbury 11797
(212) 238-4800 .. **Gioia,** Michl L '87 (Landman CB&F,PC) -120 Bway -NY 10271
(518) 626-9000 .. **Gioia,** Paul L '66 OfCnsl Dewey & L LLP -99 Wshngtn Av -Albany 12210
(212) 809-4500 .. **Gioiella,** Russell M '80 (Litman A&G,LLP) -140 Bway -NY 10005
(516) 571-4161 .. **Gioino,** Jos '99 Cnty Indstrl Devlpmnt Agncy -400 Cnty Seat Dr -Mineola 11501
(516) 296-7000 .. **Gionis,** John H '83 (Certilman BA&H,LLP) -90 Merrick Av -E Meadow 11554
(845) 638-0500 .. **Gionta,** Barbara L '95 -107 N Main -New Cty 10956 **Fx:**818-4149
(212) 790-9200 .. **Giordanella,** Robt J '86 (Cowan L&L,PC) -1133 Av of Amer -NY 10036
(914) 761-1144 .. **Giordano,** A Robt '64 -235 Mamaroneck Av -White Plns 10605 **Fx:**761-8465
(212) 230-2083 .. **Giordano,** Andrea M '01 %Poten & Prtnrs Inc -885 3rd Av -NY 10022
(718) 266-2700 .. **Giordano,** Angelo A '74 -64 Av U -Brklyn 11223 **Fx:**266-2992
(914) 923-7746 .. **Giordano,** Anthony '83 -100 Exec Blvd -Ossining 10562
(212) 406-9466 .. **Giordano,** Carmen S '86 -225 Bway -NY 10007
(212) 335-4500 .. **Giordano,** Christopher P '93 (DLA Piper LLP) -1251 Av of Amer -NY 10020
(212) 536-3900 .. **Giordano,** Frederic J '96 (K&L Gates LLP) -599 Lex Av -NY 10022
(718) 286-6729 .. **Giordano,** Gail '63 %DA -125-01 Qns Blvd -Kew Gdns 11415
(212) 983-6000 .. **Giordano,** Germana F '03 %D Savatta -250 Park Av -NY 10177
(212) 770-1931 .. **Giordano,** Jeanmarie '94 %AIG -80 Pine -NY 10005
(212) 953-0551 .. **Giordano,** John M '84 -111 Bway -NY 10006 **Fx:**962-5050
(631) 875-4524 .. **Giordano,** Justin A '92 -94 E 24th -Huntngtn Sta 11746
(585) 327-4100 .. **Giordano,** Laurie Ann '97 (Leclair KGC,LLP) -150 State -Rchstr 14614 **Fx:**327-4200
(212) 384-1000 .. **Giordano,** Laurie Anne '95 %FBI -26 Fed Plz -NY 10278
(212) 269-2353 .. **Giordano,** Louis P '94 (Gruvman G&G,LLP) -61 Bway -NY 10006
(212) 415-7887 .. **Giordano,** Mark V '85 %Merrill Lynch -717 5th Av -NY 10022 **Fx:**415-7579
(516) 877-7500 .. **Giordano,** Mary Gold '82 (Franchina & G,PC) -1100 Franklin Av -Gdn Cty 11530
(845) 709-6322 .. **Giordano,** Michl C '88 -572 Route 303 -Blauvelt 10913 **Fx:**(866) 709-1679
(516) 328-3500 .. **Giordano,** Michl J '05 %McDonnell & A,PC -401 Franklin Av -Gdn Cty 11530
(212) 264-0390 .. **Giordano,** Ralph T '62 %US DOJ Antitrust Div -26 Fed Plz Ste 3630 -NY 10278
(718) 286-6000 .. **Giordano,** Richd J '06 %DA -125-01 Qns Blvd -Kew Gdns 11415
(516) 739-0177 .. **Giordano,** Robt '95 (Willoughby & G) -245 Hillside Av -Williston Pk 11596
(212) 407-4000 .. **Giordano,** Scott J '88 (Loeb & L,LLP) -345 Park Av -NY 10154
(212) 557-0020 .. **Giordano,** Steven P '02 Vlock & Assoc,PC -230 Park Av -NY 10169 **Fx:**557-7283
(212) 440-3984 .. **Giordano,** Suzanne M '97 CNA Ins -40 Wall -NY 10005
(212) 973-8000 .. **Giordano,** Thos F '96 Cnsl Schnader HS&L LLP -140 Bway -NY 10005
(212) 592-6700 .. **Giordano,** Thos V '96 Bovis Lend Lease -200 Park Av -NY 10166
(212) 318-2000 .. **Giordano,** Timothy K '02 %Bloomberg LP -731 Lex Av -NY 10022
(212) 661-1400 .. **Giordano,** Vito T '55 (Von Maltitz DKJ&G) -60 E 42nd -NY 10017
(585) 458-5368 .. **Giorgi,** Jos A '69 -315 Seneca Pkwy -Rchstr 14613 **Fx:**327-5050
(631) 957-9600 .. **Giorgini,** Arthur J '63 -326 S Wellwood Av Bx501 -Lindenhrst 11757 **Fx:**957-5020
(631) 243-4012 .. **Giorgini,** Gino L III '91 -1793 Deer Prk Av -Deer Pk 11729 **Fx:**242-4911
(631) 957-9600 .. **Giorgini,** Renee L '95 %A Giorgini -326 S Wellwood Av Bx501 -Lindenhrst 11757 **Fx:**957-5020
(516) 921-7120 .. **Giorgio dePoto & Principe,LLP** -115 Eileen Way -Syosset 11791 **Fx:**921-4253
(516) 921-7120 .. **Giorgio,** Frank Jr. '60 OfCnsl Giorgio deP&P,LLP -115 Eileen Way -Syosset 11791
(516) 622-9200 .. **Giorgio,** Jacqueline L '91 (Westerman BEM&S,LLP) -1201 RXR Plz -Uniondale 11553
(212) 416-6355 .. **Giorno,** Sandra S '98 %Dept of Law -120 Bway -NY 10271
(212) 906-1200 .. **Giouroukakis,** John '98 (Latham & W) -885 3rd Av -NY 10022
(516) 931-1800 .. **Giovacco,** Katherine A '06 %Catalano G&P LLP -100 Jericho Quadrangle -Jericho 11753
(212) 213-6222 .. **Giovannelli,** Christine A '03 %Bull & L,LLP -18 E 41st -NY 10017
(212) 701-3000 .. **Giovannelli,** Justin M '05 %Cahill G&R LLP -80 Pine -NY 10005 **Fx:**269-5420
(212) 805-0689 .. **Giovanni,** Jonathan J '02 %US Dist Ct -500 Pearl -NY 10007
(212) 409-2544 .. **Giovanniello,** Jos Jr. '84 Ladenburg Thalmann & Co,Inc -520 Mad Av -NY 10022 **Fx:**409-2575
(914) 220-1900 .. **Giovannone,** Danielle '07 %Nelson Law Firm,LLC -1 N Bway -White Plns 10601
(212) 373-3000 .. **Giovanola,** Anouck C '07 %Paul WRW&G LLP -1285 Av of Amer -NY 10019
(212) 588-0800 .. **Giove,** Nicholas F '07 %Frommer L&H LLP -745 5th Av -NY 10151
(716) 298-9730 .. **Giove,** Rodney A '02 (Giove Law Ofc,PC) -727 Main -Niagara Fls 14301
(212) 848-7325 .. **Giove,** Stephen T '86 (Shearman & S LLP) -599 Lex Av -NY 10022
(516) 294-5200 .. **Giovinazzi,** Robt E '01 %Picciano & S -900 Merchants Cncrs -Westbury 11590
(212) 455-2000 .. **Giovinazzo,** Frank T '09 %Simpson T&B LLP -425 Lex Av -NY 10017
(212) 228-1331 .. **Giovinazzo,** Lisa E '94 (Kuharski L&G) -176 Hart Blvd -Staten Isl 10301
(212) 760-2222 .. **Giovinco,** Danielle E '06 %Kolenovsky & S,LLP -135 W 29th -NY 10001
(631) 447-8100 .. **Gippetti,** Michl P '10 %Egan & G,LLP -96 S Ocean Av -Patchogue 11772 **Fx:**447-8181
(212) 412-9500 .. **Gipson,** Lissa Carey '99 (Flemming ZWZ LLP) -1 Lbrty Plz -NY 10006
(516) 296-7000 .. **Girace,** Michl V '01 %Certilman BA&H,LLP -90 Merrick Av -E Meadow 11554
(212) 225-2000 .. **Giraldez,** Juan G '99 (Cleary GS&H) -1 Lbrty Plz -NY 10006
(212) 687-3000 .. **Girard,** Gregg '98 %Jaffe & A,LLP -600 3rd Av -NY 10016
(518) 783-2082 .. **Girard,** Julianne '02 -Bx224 -Newtonville 12128 **Fx:**783-2083
(516) 680-4262 .. **Girardi,** Grace Dumelle '90 -1968 Central Dr N -E Meadow 11554 **Fx:**483-9228
(914) 937-6030 .. **Girardi,** John M '92 -12 Rockland Av -Pt Chester 10573
(516) 593-6040 .. **Girardi,** Jos B '85 -877 N Corona Av -N Vly Strm 11580 **Fx:**256-1803
(212) 819-8200 .. **Girdhari,** Anita M '07 %White & C LLP -1155 Av of Amer -NY 10036
(646) 386-5700 .. **Girdharrie,** Sunita '97 %Civil Ct -111 Centre -NY 10013
(716) 836-9000 .. **Girdler,** Bradley R '04 -1152 Brighton Rd -Tonawanda 14150
(718) 590-2000 .. **Girese,** Anthony J '72 %DA -198 E 161st -Bronx 10451 **Fx:**590-6477
(718) 832-7646 .. **Giresi,** Maria T '90 (Giresi & Assoc, LLC) -401 3rd -Brklyn 11215
(212) 906-1200 .. **Girgenti,** Carrie M '99 %Latham & W -885 3rd Av -NY 10022
(212) 331-3030 .. **Girgenti,** Jeanine M '04 %Dept of Invstgtn -180 Water -NY 10038 **Fx:**331-3060
(212) 872-6953 .. **Girgenti,** Richd H '75 KPMG LLP -345 Park Av -NY 10154 **Fx:**872-7701
(212) 812-2146 .. **Girges,** Hany '07 (Girges Law PLLC) -75 Maiden Ln -NY 10038 **Fx:**(888) 858-5840
(212) 305-5368 .. **Girillo,** James A '88 %NY Presbyterian Hsptl -525 E 68th Bx88 -NY 10065 **Fx:**746-8603
(914) 681-0200 .. **Giris,** Janet J '94 (DelBello DWW&W,LLP) -1 N Lex Av -White Plns 10601
(914) 323-7000 .. **Girolamo,** Lorraine M '03 %Wilson EME&D LLP -3 Gannett Dr -White Plns 10604
(631) 451-1906 .. **Girolamo,** Teresa '90 -19 Jonah Rd -Miller Pl 11764 **Fx:**451-1907
(914) 684-6800 .. **Girolamo,** Theresa A '02 %Collier HNN&B,LLP -1 N Lex Av -White Plns 10601 **Fx:**684-8860
(845) 565-5770 .. **Gironda,** Emilio D Jr. '83 -158 N Plnk Rd -Newburgh 12550
(914) 737-3405 .. **Gironda,** Linda A '02 NYS United Crt -2 Nelson Av -Peekskill 10566
(914) 686-9010 .. **Gironda,** Robt J '02 %Wilson BCC&C,PC -2 William -White Plns 10601
(315) 334-5368 .. **Girouard,** Theresa M '98 -225 N Wshngtn Bx4632 -Rome 13442 **Fx:**336-2389
(716) 854-0007 .. **Giroux,** E Jos Jr. '77 (Creighton PJ&G) -295 Main -Buffalo 14203 **Fx:**854-0004
(212) 759-4580 .. **Giroux,** Leigh A '87 -415 Mad Av -NY 10017 **Fx:**(914) 967-8418
(716) 992-2022 .. **Giroux,** Wm L '88 HR Advisors -Bx185 -Eden 14057
(718) 461-6633 .. **Girsch,** Beth J '96 %Mallilo & G -163-09 Nrthrn Blvd -Flushng 11358
(212) 964-5000 .. **Girsh,** Larisa '00 (Peisner GS&S) -225 Bway -NY 10007
(212) 545-4000 .. **Girshon,** Todd H '94 (Jackson L LLP) -666 3rd Av -NY 10017
(516) 466-6911 .. **Girtz,** Eial '99 -15 Grt Nck Rd -Gt Neck 11021
(315) 733-0471 .. **Giruzzi,** F Christopher '96 -301 Bleecker -Utica 13501 **Fx:**724-2950
(315) 733-0471 .. **Giruzzi,** Frank J '59 -301 Bleecker -Utica 13501 **Fx:**724-2950
(315) 733-0471 .. **Giruzzi,** Jos P '92 -301 Bleecker -Utica 13501 **Fx:**724-2950
(518) 402-9254 .. **Giruzzi,** Wm F '96 NY DEC -625 Bway -Albany 12207
(315) 724-7800 .. **Giruzzi-Mosca,** Julie L '01 (Finer & G-M) -2615 Genesee -Utica 13501
(516) 742-3470 .. **Girvan,** James J '80 (Kral CRRP&G,LLP) -538 Broadhllw Rd -Melvll 11747
(718) 206-4687 .. **Girvan,** Paulita M '99 %Law Dept -89-17 Sutphin Blvd -Jamaica 11435 **Fx:**206-4702
(518) 462-0300 .. **Girvin & Ferlazzo,PC** -20 Corp Wds Blvd -Albany 12211 **Fx:**462-5037
(518) 462-0300 .. **Girvin,** James E '81 (Girvin & F,PC) -20 Corp Wds Blvd -Albany 12211
(212) 410-4545 .. **Giscombe,** Shirley F '83 -1825 Park Av -NY 10035 **Fx:**410-7293
(212) 728-8000 .. **Gise,** David I '07 %Willkie F&G LLP -787 7th Av -NY 10019
(716) 878-8000 .. **Gisel,** Wm G Jr. '79 %Rich Products -1 Robert Rich Way -Buffalo 14213 **Fx:**878-8767
(212) 425-1900 .. **Gisholt,** Jan P '06 %Freehill H&M LLP -80 Pine -NY 10005
(212) 847-8315 .. **Giskan,** Oren S '93 (Giskan S&A) -11 Bway -NY 10004 **Fx:**(646) 520-3235
(914) 995-3359 .. **Gismondi,** Alfred N '85 %DA -111 Martin Luther King Blvd -White Plns 10601 **Fx:**995-3363
(212) 310-8000 .. **Gismondi,** Christopher M '10 %Weil G&M LLP -767 5th Av -NY 10153
(716) 636-7600 .. **Gismondi,** Geffrey M W '08 %HoganWillig -2410 N Forest Rd -Amherst 14068
(212) 326-3939 .. **Gisolfi,** Ann L '84 OfCnsl Jones D -222 E 41st -NY 10017
(212) 381-7000 .. **Gisolfi,** Eric E '96 (Sabin B&G LLP) -4 Times Sq -NY 10036
(212) 655-5000 .. **Gisonda,** Nicholas '01 %Gannon R&M -120 Bway -NY 10271
(718) 823-8434 .. **Gisondi,** James B '96 -2312 DeMeyer -Bronx 10469
(516) 921-7773 .. **Gisonni,** Eve-Lynn '97 (Gisonni & H LLP) -20 Crossway Park N -Woodbury 11797 **Fx:**364-3717
(914) 745-4000 .. **Gisonny,** Richd '86 %Towers Watson -100 Summit Lk Dr -Valhalla 10595
(718) 615-4550 .. **Gisser,** Laura L '04 -1803 Gravesend Neck Rd -Brklyn 11229 **Fx:**615-4557

(212) 259-8000 .. **Gissin**, Valentina '05 %Dewey & L LLP -1301 Av of Amer -NY 10019
(212) 683-7050 .. **Gitelson**, Lisa '95 %JM Abramson -375 5th Av -NY 10016 **Fx:**683-7076
(585) 387-0700 .. **Githler**, Chas H II '61 -25 E Main -Rchstr 14614 **Fx:**387-0783
(212) 468-4800 .. **Gitig**, Oriyan '03 %Davis & G LLP -1740 Bway -NY 10019
(718) 286-6000 .. **Gitin**, Neil F '82 %DA -125-01 Qns Blvd -Kew Gdns 11415
(518) 487-7600 .. **Gitlen**, Philip H '73 (Whiteman O&H LLP) -1 Commerce Plz -Albany 12260
(212) 514-5437 .. **Gitlin**, Bruce J '81 B Gitlin,PC -250 W 57th -NY 10107 **Fx:**757-7042
(585) 325-5343 .. **Gitlin**, Robt B '75 -16 E Main -Rchstr 14614
(212) 848-4000 .. **Gitlitz**, Amy B '98 %Shearman & S LLP -599 Lex Av -NY 10022
(212) 885-5000 .. **Gitlitz Courtney**, Michelle G '05 %Blank R LLP -405 Lex Av -NY 10174
(212) 921-8399 .. **Gitner**, Danl M '96 (Lankler S&W LLP) -500 5th Av -NY 10110
(212) 805-3900 .. **Gitnik**, Brian S '01 (Clausen M PC) -1 Chase Manh Plz -NY 10005
(212) 332-8820 .. **Gitnik**, Roman E '04 %Lifflander & R LLP -1221 Av of Amer -NY 10020
(914) 741-6100 .. **Gitnik**, Stephanie B '03 %Kaufman B&R -200 Summit Lk Dr -Valhalla 10595
(212) 209-3810 .. **Gittelman**, Diana B '89 -420 Lex Av -NY 10170
(845) 357-5100 .. **Gittelman**, Janice '86 Ramapo Town Atty -237 Route 59 -Suffern 10901 **Fx:**357-2936
(845) 562-0203 .. **Gittelsohn**, Michl O '66 OfCnsl Finkelstein & Prtnrs,LLP -1279 Route 300 Bx1111 -Newburgh 12550
(631) 231-2412 .. **Gitter**, Alan W '75 %Dept of Law -300 Motor Pkwy -Hauppauge 11788 **Fx:**231-2405
(718) 817-2537 .. **Gitter**, Donna M '95 Fordham Univ-Bus Schl -441 E Fordham Rd -Bronx 10458
(631) 265-0010 .. **Gitter**, Evan M '02 %Cohen & W,PC -80 Maple Av Bx768 -Smithtwn 11787
(212) 225-2000 .. **Gitter**, Max '69 SrCnsl Cleary GS&H -1 Lbrty Plz -NY 10006
(212) 664-3115 .. **Gitter**, Richd P '67 %NBC -30 Rckfllr Plz -NY 10112
(212) 826-2405 .. **Gitter**, Ronald H '77 -110 E 59th -NY 10022 **Fx:**826-2908
(631) 852-2500 .. **Gitter**, Sharyn H '06 %DA -200 Center Dr -Rvrhead 11901 **Fx:**852-1769
(516) 229-4400 .. **Gitter**, Wm '73 %Kay & G -875 Merrick Av -Westbury 11590
(212) 969-3000 .. **Gitterman**, Noah S '05 %Proskauer R LLP -1585 Bway -NY 10036
(212) 735-3000 .. **Gittes**, Franklin M '75 (Skadden ASM&F LLP) -4 Times Sq -NY 10036
(212) 935-3000 .. **Gittes**, Marvin S '68 (Mintz LCFG&P,PC) -666 3rd Av -NY 10017
(914) 378-1010 .. **Gittin**, Mitchell '81 %Fitzgerald & F -538 Riverdale Av -Ynkrs 10705
(212) 848-7317 .. **Gittleman**, Chas S '69 Cnsl Shearman & S LLP -599 Lex Av -NY 10022
(212) 657-1182 .. **Gittlen**, Steve K '98 Salomon Smith Barney -77 Water -NY 10005
(716) 862-3727 .. **Gittler**, Jean E '81 %Vet Admin -120 LeBrun -Buffalo 14215
(212) 458-1570 .. **Gittler**, Jeremy H '99 AIG Domestic Claims -175 Water -NY 10038
(212) 836-8000 .. **Gittlitz**, Sheryl M '92 (Kaye S LLP) -425 Park Av -NY 10022
(607) 723-0600 .. **Gitto**, Donald R '83 (Gitto & N,LLP) -71 State -Bnghmtn 13901 **Fx:**723-0634
(212) 318-6000 .. **Gitto**, Jos M '01 %Paul HJ&W LLP -75 E 55th -NY 10022
(518) 476-2001 .. **Giuda**, Alita J '07 %Gilberti SH&S,PC -111 Wshngtn Av -Albany 12210
(718) 672-2500 .. **Giudice**, Piero G '05 -66-66 Grand Av -Maspeth 11378 **Fx:**672-2513
(212) 889-2300 .. **Giuffra**, Robt J '54 (Dougherty RGZ&H) -131 E 38th -NY 10016
(212) 558-4000 .. **Giuffra**, Robt J Jr. '89 (Sullivan & C LLP) -125 Broad -NY 10004
(212) 687-6262 .. **Giuffra**, Thos P '95 (Barton B&P,LLP) -420 Lex Av -NY 10170
(516) 358-5300 .. **Giuffre**, John J '88 -99 Tulip Av -Floral Pk 11001 **Fx:**358-0400
(516) 877-5600 .. **Giuffre**, Josephine E '96 %R Tusa -1225 Franklin Av -Gdn Cty 11530 **Fx:**877-5695
(516) 364-1095 .. **Giugliano**, Margaret '84 (McBreen & K) -500 N Bway -Jericho 11753
(212) 808-7800 .. **Giuliana**, Antonia F '99 (Kelley D&W LLP) -101 Park Av -NY 10178
(212) 558-4000 .. **Giuliani**, Esterina '07 %Sullivan & C LLP -125 Broad -NY 10004
(800) 597-0318 .. **Giuliani**, Roger A '96 -105 Maxess Rd -Melvll 11747
(212) 508-6100 .. **Giuliani**, Rudolph W '69 (Bracewell & G,LLP) -1251 Av of Amer -NY 10020
(212) 277-4000 .. **Giuliano**, Adam M '06 %Freshfields BD LLP -520 Mad Av -NY 10022
(516) 997-0999 .. **Giuliano**, Anthony F '95 (Pryor & M,LLP) -675 Old Cntry Rd -Westbury 11590
(212) 226-2610 .. **Giuliano**, Edw T '99 -401 Bway -NY 10013
(718) 645-7004 .. **Giuliano**, Guy G '85 -355 Av X -Brklyn 11223 **Fx:**998-9853
(212) 682-9200 .. **Giuliano**, Jeanpierre J '05 %Ostrow K&F LLP -405 Lex Av -NY 10174
(212) 408-5100 .. **Giuliano**, Kimberly A '05 %Chadbourne & P LLP -30 Rckfllr Plz -NY 10112
(646) 328-0120 .. **Giuliano**, Nicholas P '81 (Bennett GM&P,LLP) -494 8th Av -NY 10001
(212) 725-5411 .. **Giulini**, Chas A Jr. '65 (Giulini & G) -274 Mad Av -NY 10016 **Fx:**545-7211
(212) 725-5411 .. **Giulini**, Christine '89 (Giulini & G) -274 Mad Av -NY 10016 **Fx:**545-7211
(212) 874-4389 .. **Giumarra**, Gina Ann '90 -146 W 88th -NY 10024 **Fx:**874-5456
(718) 590-2000 .. **Giunta**, Adrienne A '02 %DA -198 E 161st -Bronx 10451 **Fx:**590-6477
(212) 425-7200 .. **Giunta**, Peter L '05 %Kenyon & K,LLP -1 Bway -NY 10004
(718) 613-3500 .. **Giunta**, Stephen J '95 %UIA Bd -Bx29002 -Brklyn 11201 **Fx:**613-3566
(914) 949-5505 .. **Giuntini**, E Robt '51 -175 Main -White Plns 10601
(212) 267-6456 .. **Giusio**, Kathryn K '02 Fischer Bros -217 Bway -NY 10007 **Fx:**267-6468
(718) 224-5431 .. **Giusti**, Katie E '10 %R Giusti & Assoc, PLLC -42-40 Bell Blvd -Bayside 11361 **Fx:**224-2938
(718) 575-8588 .. **Giusti**, Noreen M '83 -123-35 82nd Rd -Kew Gdns 11415
(718) 224-5431 .. **Giusti**, Robt F '81 (R Giusti & Assoc, PLLC) -42-40 Bell Blvd -Bayside 11361 **Fx:**224-2938
(212) 408-2500 .. **Giusti**, Wm R '75 (Baker B,LLP) -30 Rckfllr Plz -NY 10112
(516) 742-6546 .. **Giustino**, Anthony P '91 %L Stober Jr,LLC -350 Old Cntry Rd -Gdn Cty 11530 **Fx:**742-8603
(212) 986-0999 .. **Giusto**, Michl J '06 %Neufeld & O -230 Park Av -NY 10169
(631) 277-7086 .. **Giusto**, Raymond A '86 -136 E Main -E Islip 11730 **Fx:**277-7641
(212) 687-3320 .. **Givant**, Leonard '61 -60 E 42nd -NY 10165
(315) 472-4481 .. **Givas**, Thos P '83 (Ali P&C) -614 James -Syracuse 13203
(212) 474-1000 .. **Givens**, Alexandra Reeve '09 %Cravath S&M LLP -825 8th Av -NY 10019
(212) 209-2504 .. **Givens**, Alice G '08 J Crew Grp,Inc -2 Penn Plz -NY 10121
(516) 572-2375 .. **Givens**, Chas R '95 Nassau Cty District Ct -99 Main -Hempstd 11550
(212) 848-4000 .. **Givertz**, Adam M '01 (Shearman & S LLP) -599 Lex Av -NY 10022
(212) 474-1000 .. **Giwa**, Femi H '08 %Cravath S&M LLP -825 8th Av -NY 10019
(212) 698-3500 .. **Giwa**, Tayo M '09 %Dechert LLP -1095 Av of Amer -NY 10036
(212) 834-0600 .. **Giwner**, Jerika D '99 %Gordon & S,PC -355 Lex Av -NY 10017
(718) 787-9500 .. **Giyaur**, Kristina '08 %Khenkin & S,PC -9712 3rd Av -Brklyn 11209 **Fx:**787-9502
(212) 344-3900 .. **Gizunterman**, John '06 %Belair & E LLP -61 Bway -NY 10006
(212) 964-6611 .. **Gizzarelli**, Peggy E '05 %Lester SK&D -120 Bway -NY 10271
(212) 728-8000 .. **Gizzi**, Edw J '03 %Willkie F&G LLP -787 7th Av -NY 10019
(212) 558-4000 .. **Gizzi**, Lauren F '10 %Sullivan & C LLP -125 Broad -NY 10004
(212) 336-0077 .. **Gizzi**, Paul G '92 %SEC -3 World Fncl Ctr -NY 10281 **Fx:**336-1323
(914) 323-7000 .. **Gizzo**, Alexander '02 %Wilson EME&D LLP -3 Gannett Dr -White Plns 10604
(914) 761-0030 .. **Gizzo**, Gaetano Antonio '99 -173 Underhill Av -West Harrison 10604 **Fx:**761-0034
(516) 488-3300 .. **Gizzo**, Kathleen McGinty '92 %Shaub AC&S,LLP -1983 Marcus Av -Lk Success 11042
(212) 736-5300 .. **Gjelaj**, Nikolla '02 %Block O&M LLP -1 Penn Plz -NY 10119
(914) 472-6202 .. **Gjertsen**, Gary R '91 (Clair & G) -720 Wht Plns Rd -Scarsdale 10583 **Fx:**472-1936
(212) 888-2422 .. **Gjertsen**, Gerard '89 (Gjertsen & G) -845 3rd Av -NY 10022 **Fx:**888-3459
(914) 472-6202 .. **Gjertsen**, Gerard '89 OfCnsl Clair & G -720 Wht Plns Rd -Scarsdale 10583 **Fx:**472-1936
(212) 809-7074 .. **Gjoni**, Gencian '08 %Armienti DG&R,LLP -39 Bway -NY 10006
(212) 625-8333 .. **Gjoni**, Sam '97 -401 Bway -NY 10013 **Fx:**625-0152
(212) 474-1000 .. **Gkarametsis**, Vasileios '08 %Cravath S&M LLP -825 8th Av -NY 10019
(718) 250-2000 .. **Glachman**, Lori '93 DA -350 Jay -Brklyn 11201 **Fx:**250-2314
(516) 747-4082 .. **Glacken**, Claudia C '79 (Montfort HM&S LLP) -1140 Franklin Av Bx7677 -Gdn Cty 11530
(516) 733-7100 .. **Glackin**, Edw J III '87 %King Kullen -185 Central Av -Bethpage 11714
(631) 427-7843 .. **Glackin**, Maureen A '86 -30 Bay Dr W -Huntngtn 11743
(212) 521-5400 .. **Gladbach**, Eric F '99 (Reed S LLP) -599 Lex Av -NY 10022
(516) 796-9700 .. **Gladd**, Christopher P '93 %Latronica Law Firm,PC -64 Division Av -Levittwn 11756 **Fx:**796-9702
(212) 272-2000 .. **Gladden**, Beate P '04 %JP Morgan Chase -383 Mad Av -NY 10179
(212) 858-1000 .. **Gladden**, Timothy M '04 %Pillsbury WSP LLP -1540 Bway -NY 10036
(212) 809-4800 .. **Glade**, Alfred '97 %N Kanzer -30 Broad -NY 10004 **Fx:**363-3097
(212) 558-4000 .. **Gladin**, Andrew R '01 (Sullivan & C LLP) -125 Broad -NY 10004
(646) 557-5100 .. **Gladis**, Jay '75 (Patton B LLP) -1185 Av of Amer -NY 10036
(212) 871-5413 .. **Gladney**, Kim McLeod '08 Ambridge Ptnrs LLC -520 8th Av -NY 10018 **Fx:**947-1838
(212) 506-2500 .. **Gladney**, Zachry T '08 %Mayer B LLP -1675 Bway -NY 10019
(212) 228-7727 .. **Gladstein**, Amy N '75 (Gladstein R&M,LLP) -817 Bway -NY 10003
(212) 952-1111 .. **Gladstein**, Harvey '57 (H Gladstein & Prtnrs LLC) -110 Wall -NY 10005 **Fx:**943-7427
(718) 793-7800 .. **Gladstein**, Jack '65 (Gladstein & M) -118-21 Qns Blvd -Frst Hlls 11375 **Fx:**793-0524
(212) 228-7727 .. **Gladstein Reif & Meginniss,LLP** -817 Bway -NY 10003 **Fx:**228-7654
(631) 234-1600 .. **Gladston**, Howard R '72 -1737 Vets Hwy -Islandia 11749
(212) 709-8160 .. **Gladston**, Lewis F '87 -110 Wall -NY 10005
(212) 460-6119 .. **Gladstone**, Amy J '91 Con Ed -4 Irving Pl -NY 10003 **Fx:**614-1227
(212) 869-5300 .. **Gladstone**, Andrea D '00 CPC -28 E 28th -NY 10016 **Fx:**683-2909
(914) 328-9666 .. **Gladstone**, David M '81 D Gladstone -1 Barker Av -White Plns 10601 **Fx:**328-7842
(212) 891-9100 .. **Gladstone**, Douglas H '96 (Goldfarb & F LLP) -345 Park Av -NY 10154
(212) 440-4400 .. **Gladstone**, Holly '99 Cnsl Buchanan I&R PC -620 8th Av -NY 10018
(718) 222-5354 .. **Gladstone**, Jessica L '95 -26 Court -Brklyn 11242 **Fx:**222-5698
(516) 227-0700 .. **Gladstone**, Jodi L '88 Cnsl Farrell F,PC -1320 RXR Plz -Uniondale 11556
(973) 228-5700 .. **Gladstone**, Stuart M '82 (Brach E LLC) -100 Park Av -NY 10017 **Fx:**228-7852
(212) 687-0100 .. **Gladstone**, Wayne L '00 %Harris B PLLC -100 Wall -NY 10005
(718) 262-7100 .. **Gladwin**, Sonya Fierro '90 %Civil Ct -89-17 Sutphin Blvd -Jamaica 11435 **Fx:**262-7107
(212) 783-3968 .. **Glaessner**, Ellen P '06 Smith Barney -485 Lex Av -NY 10017
(212) 819-8200 .. **Glancy**, Christopher J '96 (White & C LLP) -1155 Av of Amer -NY 10036
(516) 742-9099 .. **Glanda**, Virginia '00 %S Gross -151 Willis Av -Mineola 11501 **Fx:**742-9199
(518) 457-2070 .. **Glannon**, Michl J '81 %Dept of Tax & Fin -Bldg 9 State Campus -Albany 12227 **Fx:**457-6131
(212) 370-5100 .. **Glanstein**, David M '98 %O'Donnell SG&L,LLP -60 E 42nd -NY 10165
(212) 370-5106 .. **Glanstein**, Eleanor E '76 -305 Mad Av -NY 10165 **Fx:**697-6299
(212) 370-5100 .. **Glanstein**, Joel C '67 (O'Donnell SG&L,LLP) -60 E 42nd -NY 10165
(212) 836-8000 .. **Glantz**, Alan K '00 Cnsl Kaye S LLP -425 Park Av -NY 10022
(212) 452-5300 .. **Glantz**, Craig M '00 Cnsl Darger & E,LLP -116 E 27th -NY 10016
(212) 770-3371 .. **Glantz**, Danl J '06 %AIG -70 Pine -NY 10270
(914) 997-9077 .. **Glantz**, Jeremy T '94 -3 Kitchel Rd -Mt Kisco 10549
Glantz, Miles M '61 -8 Linda Rd -Pt Wash 11050
(716) 847-8400 .. **Glanville**, Robt E '77 (Phillips L LLP) -3400 HSBC Ctr -Buffalo 14203
(212) 237-1000 .. **Glanz**, David L '80 (Windels ML&M,LLP) -156 W 56th -NY 10019
(914) 946-3700 .. **Glanz**, Reine Hope '99 %McCarthy F LLP -11 Martine Av -White Plns 10606

(212) 604-9000 .. **Glanzberg,** Michl G '07 Sinvin Realty -170 Varick -NY 10013 **Fx:**604-9006
(212) 609-6800 .. **Glas,** Eduardo J '97 (McCarter & E,LLP) -245 Park Av -NY 10167
(212) 689-5213 .. **Glascock,** J Scott '79 -Bx1625 Murray Hill Sta -NY 10156
(516) 248-1700 .. **Glascock,** Thos D '96 %Forchelli CDSM&T,LLP -333 Earle Ovngton Blvd -Uniondale 11553
(716) 566-5400 .. **Glascott,** Dennis P '86 (Goldberg S LLP) -665 Main -Buffalo 14203
(716) 566-5400 .. **Glascott,** Michl T '90 (Goldberg S LLP) -665 Main -Buffalo 14203
(716) 858-2424 .. **Glascott,** Paul J '99 %DA -25 Delaware Av -Buffalo 14202 **Fx:**858-7425
(518) 429-4200 .. **Glasel,** David P '70 (Hiscock & B,LLP) -50 Beaver -Albany 12207
(516) 688-1700 .. **Glasel,** Donald A '85 %IRS -1600 Stewart Av -Westbury 11590 **Fx:**688-1750
(516) 496-8300 .. **Glaser,** Adam L '05 Santemma & D,LLC -575 Underhill Blvd -Syosset 11791 **Fx:**496-8303
(585) 232-4080 .. **Glaser,** Alan L '94 -450 Rynlds Arcd Bldg -Rchstr 14614 **Fx:**232-2802
(716) 689-9195 .. **Glaser,** Danl M '86 -Bx546 -Williamsvll 14231
(518) 229-4663 .. **Glaser,** Danl S '05 -9 Corp Dr -Clifton Pk 12065
(212) 336-2000 .. **Glaser,** David M '81 (Patterson BW&T LLP) -1133 Av of Amer -NY 10036
(718) 590-3662 .. **Glaser,** Edith '84 %Hon E Davidowitz -851 Grnd Cncrs -Bronx 10451 **Fx:**590-8914
(212) 239-7323 .. **Glaser,** Ezra B '98 -481 8th Av -NY 10001 **Fx:**239-8353
(212) 335-9000 .. **Glaser,** Frank M '85 %DA -1 Hogan Pl -NY 10013
(212) 218-5500 .. **Glaser,** Gary H '94 (Seyfarth S LLP) -620 8th Av -NY 10018
(212) 431-2309 .. **Glaser,** I Cathy '78 %NY Law Schl -185 W Bway -NY 10013 **Fx:**431-1860
(212) 750-1200 .. **Glaser,** Jack '61 (Trolman G&L,PC) -777 3rd Av -NY 10017
(212) 750-1200 .. **Glaser,** Joel A '02 %Trolman G&L,PC -777 3rd Av -NY 10017
(212) 973-9797 .. **Glaser,** Jonathan E '84 %Saretsky KD&G,LLP -475 Park Av S -NY 10016
(212) 978-1105 .. **Glaser,** Jonathan S '96 %Prudential Securities -1 Lbrty Plz -NY 10006
(212) 371-7230 .. **Glaser,** Leon '50 Butler Fndtn -825 3rd Av -NY 10022 **Fx:**888-4117
(212) 436-1151 .. **Glaser,** Maria Chow '90 IRS -290 Bway -NY 10007
(518) 689-1413 .. **Glaser,** Mark F '77 (Greenberg T,LLP) -54 State -Albany 12207
(212) 373-3000 .. **Glaser,** Miriam Litvac '10 %Paul WRW&G LLP -1285 Av of Amer -NY 10019
(212) 730-7750 .. **Glaser,** Pauline E '94 %Nicoletti GS&O,LLP -555 5th Av -NY 10017
(516) 466-0212 .. **Glaser,** Risa B '88 -88 Cuttermill Rd -Gt Neck 11021
(516) 304-5858 .. **Glaser,** Roni E '82 (Glaser & W,LLP) -175 E Shore Rd -Gt Neck 11023 **Fx:**304-5855
(212) 596-9000 .. **Glaser,** Sabrina C '07 %Ropes & G LLP -1211 Av of Amer -NY 10036
(212) 554-7800 .. **Glaser,** Steven J '77 (Moses & S LLP) -405 Lex Av -NY 10174
(718) 222-2110 .. **Glaser,** Steven P '09 %Law Dept -350 Jay -Brklyn 11201 **Fx:**222-2393
(212) 735-3000 .. **Glaser,** Steven R '96 (Skadden ASM&F LLP) -4 Times Sq -NY 10036
(718) 261-7700 .. **Glasgold,** Kerry S '01 %Rappaport HC&R,PC -118-35 Qns Blvd -Frst Hlls 11375
(212) 319-8736 .. **Glasgow,** Donna '78 (D Glasgow,PC) -110 E 59th -NY 10022 **Fx:**355-6900
(212) 801-9230 .. **Glasgow,** Elizabeth R '09 %Greenberg T,LLP -200 Park Av -NY 10166
(212) 858-4355 .. **Glasgow,** Rachel D '95 %FINRA -1 Lbrty Plz -NY 10006
(212) 969-3000 .. **Glasgow,** Virginia A '06 %Proskauer R LLP -1585 Bway -NY 10036
(718) 694-3854 .. **Glasgow,** Wayne A '94 %Transit Auth -130 Lvngstn -Brklyn 11201 **Fx:**694-5726
(518) 429-4200 .. **Glasheen,** Kevin P '75 (Hiscock & B,LLP) -50 Beaver -Albany 12207
(518) 272-6565 .. **Glasheen,** Sean K '09 %Martin SWD&J -279 River Bx1530 -Troy 12181
(212) 340-0400 .. **Glasman,** Paula '72 %Appllt Div 1st Dept -27 Mad Av -NY 10010 **Fx:**889-4412
(212) 686-4401 .. **Glass,** Adina Tzipora '07 %Abramson Law Grp PLLC -570 Lex Av -NY 10022 **Fx:**686-6515
(845) 735-1700 .. **Glass,** Andrew '01 Active Int'l -1 Blue Hill Plz -Pearl Rvr 10965
(518) 270-4040 .. **Glass,** Arthur F Jr. '84 DA -80 2nd -Troy 12180 **Fx:**270-4025
(914) 931-1386 .. **Glass,** Bryan D '96 (Glass K LLP) -20 Bway -Valhalla 10595 **Fx:**(845) 510-2219
(212) 730-8133 .. **Glass,** Chas F Jr. '05 %Gunderson DSVF&H,LLP -220 W 42nd -NY 10036
(212) 339-5134 .. **Glass,** Corrine Jo '09 Harbinger Capital Prtnrs -450 Park Av -NY 10022
(518) 861-5970 .. **Glass,** David G '96 -19 Sunset Dr -Altamont 12009
(212) 484-3900 .. **Glass,** David L '80 Cnsl Arent F LLP -1675 Bway -NY 10019
(212) 557-7505 .. **Glass,** Elliott M '85 Radin Glass & Co -360 Lex Av -NY 10017
(212) 967-4024 .. **Glass,** Fredric J '88 -1841 Bway -NY 10023 **Fx:**967-4148
(631) 321-1400 .. **Glass,** Gerard J '85 (Glass & G) -72 E Main -Babylon 11702 **Fx:**321-1491
(516) 822-9554 .. **Glass,** James D '62 -327 Doral Ct -Jericho 11753
(212) 849-7000 .. **Glass,** James M '99 (Quinn EU&S,LLP) -51 Mad Av -NY 10010
(212) 705-7000 .. **Glass,** Jason E '09 %Bingham M LLP -399 Park Av -NY 10022
(212) 715-9100 .. **Glass,** Jessica J '05 %Kramer LN&F,LLP -1177 Av of Amer -NY 10036
(212) 973-9797 .. **Glass,** Joel '68 (Saretsky KD&G,LLP) -475 Park Av S -NY 10016
(914) 831-3087 .. **Glass,** Jordan D '95 (J Glass,PC) -7-11 Legion Dr -Valhalla 10595
(212) 578-2508 .. **Glass,** Lisa '87 %MetLife -27-01 Qns Plz N -LIC 11101
(212) 813-8800 .. **Glass,** Martin C '99 (Goodwin P LLP) -620 8th Av -NY 10018
(631) 234-3030 .. **Glass,** Martin S '96 %Davidow DS&S,LLP -1601 Vets Mem'l Hwy -Islandia 11749
(631) 321-1400 .. **Glass,** Maureen A '82 (Glass & G) -72 E Main -Babylon 11702 **Fx:**321-1491
(212) 450-4000 .. **Glass,** Melissa A '09 %Davis P&W LLP -450 Lex Av -NY 10017
(631) 293-2300 .. **Glass,** Michl G '82 (Rappaport GG&L LLP) -1355 Motor Pkwy -Hauppauge 11749
(212) 532-1000 .. **Glass,** Peter '01 Euro RSCG Life LM&P -200 Mad Av -NY 10016 **Fx:**213-0449
(516) 364-1200 .. **Glass,** Peter V '02 CLK Mgmt Corp -135 Crsswys Park Dr -Woodbury 11797
(516) 481-7617 .. **Glass,** Saml I '76 -62 Nichols Ct -Hempstd 11550 **Fx:**481-0477
(914) 682-0257 .. **Glass,** Saul L '85 -1 Barker Av -White Plns 10601 **Fx:**682-0689
(718) 445-9700 .. **Glass,** Sheldon '57 -39-01 Main -Flushng 11354
(212) 964-6611 .. **Glass,** Stuart G '98 Cnsl Lester SK&D -120 Bway -NY 10271
(212) 243-0253 .. **Glass,** Stuart M '66 -64 W 15th -NY 10011 **Fx:**414-8263
(631) 476-6147 .. **Glass,** Wm F Jr. '84 -503 Main -Pt Jffrsn 11777 **Fx:**473-9330
(518) 457-4951 .. **Glassanos,** George A '77 %Dept Correctional Srvcs -1220 Wshngtn Av -Albany 12226 **Fx:**457-7555
(212) 783-4081 .. **Glassberg,** Bruce A '08 Citigroup Global Mrkts,Inc -485 Lex Av -NY 10017
(516) 747-8181 .. **Glassberg,** Michl A '86 -259 Mineola Blvd -Mineola 11501 **Fx:**873-5166
(212) 608-6726 .. **Glassberg,** Steven H '03 (Glassberg & Assoc,LLC) -1375 Bway -NY 10018 **Fx:**(646) 349-1977
(516) 568-2912 .. **Glasser,** Alvin M '60 -99 W Hawthorne Av -Vly Stream 11580
(212) 318-2000 .. **Glasser,** Chas J Jr. '99 Bloomberg LP -731 Lex Av -NY 10022
(914) 946-4777 .. **Glasser,** David '78 (Keane & B,PC) -445 Hmltn Av -White Plns 10601
(212) 867-3636 .. **Glasser,** David G '85 (Levin & G,PC) -420 Lex Av -NY 10170
(718) 526-8100 .. **Glasser,** Jack L '82 -88-28 Sutphin Blvd -Jamaica 11435
(212) 987-9505 .. **Glasser,** Jeanne A '80 -1636 3rd Av -NY 10128 **Fx:**(201) 696-3946
(212) 906-1200 .. **Glasser,** Jennifer E '10 %Latham & W -885 3rd Av -NY 10022
(212) 474-1000 .. **Glasser,** Julie '10 %Cravath S&M LLP -825 8th Av -NY 10019
(718) 250-2037 .. **Glasser,** Kenneth S '04 %DA -350 Jay -Brklyn 11201 **Fx:**250-2314
(212) 335-9000 .. **Glasser,** Larry A '03 %DA -1 Hogan Pl -NY 10013
(212) 279-7300 .. **Glasser,** Martin J '65 (Sachs S&G,PC) -450 7th Av -NY 10123
(212) 589-4200 .. **Glasser,** Michl P '05 %Baker & H LLP -45 Rckfllr Plz -NY 10111
(212) 969-3000 .. **Glasser,** Nathaniel M '05 %Proskauer R LLP -1585 Bway -NY 10036
(516) 694-3000 .. **Glasser,** Randa P '82 (Guercio & G,LLP) -77 Conklin -Farmngdl 11735 **Fx:**694-4738
(212) 344-5680 .. **Glasser,** Robt J '75 (Thompson H LLP) -335 Mad Av -NY 10017
(516) 358-5588 .. **Glasser,** Stanley M '64 -3000 Marcus Av -Lk Success 11042 **Fx:**(718) 229-4128
(212) 732-9000 .. **Glasser,** Stephen C '77 OfCnsl Sullivan PBM&C PC -120 Bway -NY 10271
(516) 823-1800 .. **Glassman,** Adam D '95 Glassman Law Grp -34 Atl Av -Lynbrk 11563 **Fx:**823-4496
(516) 823-1800 .. **Glassman,** Alan C '62 (Glassman Law Grp) -34 Atl Av -Lynbrk 11563 **Fx:**823-4496
(212) 675-3710 .. **Glassman,** Brad B '96 (Glassman G&G) -49 W 24th -NY 10010 **Fx:**633-9013
(914) 686-0108 .. **Glassman & Brown** -99 Court -White Plns 10601 **Fx:**288-9291
(914) 686-0108 .. **Glassman,** Carla '86 (Glassman & B) -99 Court -White Plns 10601
(212) 675-3710 .. **Glassman,** David S '66 (Glassman G&G) -49 W 24th -NY 10010 **Fx:**633-9013
(212) 506-3900 .. **Glassman,** Evan '94 (Steptoe & J LLP) -750 7th Av -NY 10019
(212) 906-1200 .. **Glassman,** Fredric D '06 %Latham & W -885 3rd Av -NY 10022
(212) 381-7000 .. **Glassman,** Jonathan M '96 (Sabin B&G LLP) -4 Times Sq -NY 10036
(212) 213-2510 .. **Glassman,** Kenneth J '81 -475 Park Av S -NY 10016 **Fx:**213-2523
(914) 946-9225 .. **Glassman,** Loren I '76 -99 Court -White Plns 10601 **Fx:**288-9291
(631) 331-8071 .. **Glassman,** Matthew A '87 -1227 Main -Pt Jffrsn 11777 **Fx:**331-8627
(518) 446-0356 .. **Glassman,** Peter S '86 Mediation Matters -10 N Russell Rd -Albany 12206 **Fx:**446-0379
(212) 213-2510 .. **Glassman,** Saul '52 -475 Park Av S -NY 10016 **Fx:**213-2523
(718) 547-0400 .. **Glassman,** Sheldon '81 -770 Allerton Av -Bronx 10467 **Fx:**547-5755
(212) 836-8000 .. **Glassman,** Steven J '70 (Kaye S LLP) -425 Park Av -NY 10022
(212) 267-7868 .. **Glassmith,** Stuart M '02 %L Krause -11 Park Pl -NY 10007 **Fx:**267-7579
(518) 436-0344 .. **Glastetter,** Mark D '89 (Deily M&G,LLP) -8 Thurlow Ter -Albany 12203
(212) 556-1234 .. **Glater,** Jonathan D '00 %The NY Times Co -620 8th Av -NY 10018
(212) 487-9700 .. **Glatstein,** Jos M '80 OfCnsl White F&F,LLP -61 Bway -NY 10006
(914) 723-4333 .. **Glatt,** Adam J '99 %Pirrotti Law Firm LLC -2 Overhill Rd -Scarsdale 10583 **Fx:**723-4838
(212) 417-5300 .. **Glatt,** Debra M '92 %Medicaid Fraud Cntrl -120 Bway -NY 10271 **Fx:**417-5274
(212) 808-7800 .. **Glatt,** Elana B '04 %Kelley D&W LLP -101 Park Av -NY 10178
(212) 515-3450 .. **Glatt,** Jos D '99 Apollo Invstmnt Corp -9 W 57th -NY 10019
(516) 837-6101 .. **Glatt,** Marjorie R '85 Sutton Alliance -515 Rockaway Av -Vly Stream 11581
(718) 590-7793 .. **Glatt,** Michelle Blaire '04 -900 Sheridan Av -Bronx 10451
(212) 272-8391 .. **Glatter,** Danl E '00 %JP Morgan Chase -383 Mad Av -NY 10179
(212) 571-2000 .. **Glatter,** Denise Rubin '97 %Ottinger Firm,PC -19 Fulton -NY 10038 **Fx:**571-0505
(212) 506-5000 .. **Glatter,** Heather A '05 %Orrick H&S LLP -51 W 52nd -NY 10019
(914) 949-2700 .. **Glatthaar,** James W '80 (Bleakley P&S,LLP) -1 N Lex Av -White Plns 10601
(914) 949-2700 .. **Glatthaar,** Jos B '56 (Bleakley P&S,LLP) -1 N Lex Av -White Plns 10601
(212) 481-5858 .. **Glatthaar,** Thos A '89 %Fidelity Natl Title Ins -1 Park Av -NY 10016 **Fx:**481-8747
(718) 858-6400 .. **Glattstein,** Brian F '92 %Greenpark Care Ctr -140 St Edwards -Brklyn 11201
(212) 521-5400 .. **Glatzer,** Jeffrey L '69 (Reed S LLP) -599 Lex Av -NY 10022
(914) 725-8700 .. **Glatzer,** Sanford B '61 -670 Post Rd -Scarsdale 10583 **Fx:**725-8708
(212) 687-3000 .. **Glauber,** Ira N '80 (Jaffe & A,LLP) -600 3rd Av -NY 10016
(212) 302-2666 .. **Glauberman,** Alex J '42 -262 W 38th -NY 10018 **Fx:**302-6637
(212) 557-7700 .. **Glauberman,** Carol R '79 OfCnsl Davidson D&C LLP -60 E 42nd -NY 10165
(212) 599-3322 .. **Glauberman,** Steven L '78 Cnsl Becker P,LLP -45 Bway -NY 10006
(212) 804-4200 .. **Glaubinger,** Wayne R '84 (Mound CW&G) -One Bttry Pk Plz -NY 10004
(212) 274-2553 .. **Glaves-Morgan,** Sandra D '82 %HRA -250 Church -NY 10013
(518) 237-5505 .. **Glavin,** A Rita Chandellier '61 (Glavin & G) -69 2nd Bx40 -Waterfrd 12188 **Fx:**237-1990
(518) 237-5505 .. **Glavin,** James C '00 (Glavin & G) -69 2nd Bx40 -Waterfrd 12188 **Fx:**237-1990

(518) 237-5505 .. **Glavin,** James H III '56 (Glavin & G) -69 2nd Bx40 -Waterfrd 12188 **Fx:**237-1990
(212) 687-7230 .. **Glavin,** James H IV '04 Stull S&B -6 E 45th -NY 10017
(585) 325-4953 .. **Glavin,** John W '61 (Robinson & G) -16 E Main -Rchstr 14614
(212) 944-0500 .. **Glavin,** Marina Ivolgina '05 %Hofheimer G&G,LLP -530 5th Av -NY 10036 **Fx:**897-4997
(212) 237-0000 .. **Glavin,** Rita M '97 (Vinson & E LLP) -666 5th Av -NY 10103
(585) 383-5357 .. **Glavin,** Thos M '88 -70 Linden Oaks -Rchstr 14625
(212) 269-2353 .. **Glaws,** Chas T '92 (Gruvman G&G,LLP) -61 Bway -NY 10006
(716) 856-4200 .. **Glazer,** Aaron F '06 %Gibson M&C,LLP -69 Delaware Av -Buffalo 14202
(718) 875-1300 .. **Glazer,** Adam J '06 Applt Div 2nd Dept -45 Monroe Pl -Brklyn 11201 **Fx:**858-2446
(516) 877-7100 .. **Glazer,** Alyssa C '92 %Bank T&B,PC -400 Post Av -Westbury 11590
(585) 359-3000 .. **Glazer,** Avram A '86 %First Allied -270 Commerce Dr -Rchstr 14623
(212) 336-2000 .. **Glazer,** Danl C '00 Cnsl Patterson BW&T LLP -1133 Av of Amer -NY 10036
(212) 267-0011 .. **Glazer,** David A '96 (Shafer G,LLP) -90 John -NY 10038
(212) 450-4000 .. **Glazer,** Dennis E '80 (Davis P&W LLP) -450 Lex Av -NY 10017
(212) 696-6000 .. **Glazer,** Douglas I '06 %Curtis M-PC&M LLP -101 Park Av -NY 10178
(516) 463-5874 .. **Glazer,** Elizabeth M '05 %Hofstra Law Schl -121 Hofstra Univ -Hempstd 11549
(212) 450-4000 .. **Glazer,** Elyse B '10 %Davis P&W LLP -450 Lex Av -NY 10017
(866) 348-5819 .. **Glazer,** Eric L '73 %SSA-ODAR -50 Fountain Plz -Buffalo 14202 **Fx:**(716) 551-4078
(212) 661-4422 .. **Glazer & Gottlieb** -2 Tudor City Pl -NY 10017 **Fx:**682-7674
(212) 325-2756 .. **Glazer,** John M '94 %Credit Suisse First Boston -11 Mad Av -NY 10010
(518) 434-0439 .. **Glazer,** Jos A '90 Mental Hlth Assn in NYS -194 Wshngtn Av -Albany 12210 **Fx:**427-8676
(845) 359-8258 .. **Glazer & Kamel** -21 Valenza Ln -Blauvelt 10913
(845) 359-8258 .. **Glazer,** Martin M '78 (Glazer & K) -21 Valenza Ln -Blauvelt 10913
(212) 661-4422 .. **Glazer,** May '68 (Glazer & G) -2 Tudor City Pl -NY 10017
(212) 269-0927 .. **Glazer,** Neal M '76 (D'Amato & L,LLP) -2 World Fncl Ctr -NY 10281
(212) 751-3001 .. **Glazer,** Rachelle H '07 (Thompson & K LLP) -919 3rd Av -NY 10022
(212) 325-3165 .. **Glazer,** Ruth Karfiol '93 Credit Suisse -1 Mad Av -NY 10010
(212) 644-4420 .. **Glazer,** Scott L '03 %Fabiani C&H,LLP -570 Lex Av -NY 10022
(646) 386-4418 .. **Glazer,** Sharon S '97 Hon A Goldberg -25 Beaver -NY 10004
(212) 310-8806 .. **Glazer,** Steven D '80 (Weil G&M LLP) -767 5th Av -NY 10153 **Fx:**310-8007
(212) 758-9300 .. **Glazer,** Yale H '98 (Lazare P&G LLP) -950 3rd Av -NY 10022
(212) 685-7100 .. **Glazier,** Faith J '80 OfCnsl C Wisotsky -112 Mad Av -NY 10016 **Fx:**689-9680
(518) 432-7511 .. **Gleason Dunn Walsh & O'Shea** -40 Beaver -Albany 12207 **Fx:**432-5221
(518) 869-9200 .. **Gleason,** G Christopher '01 (Rose Law Firm,PLLC) -501 New Karner Rd -Albany 12205 **Fx:**869-3334
(212) 326-2000 .. **Gleason,** H Scott '07 %O'Melveny & M LLP -7 Times Sq -NY 10036
(607) 723-5341 .. **Gleason,** James S '78 (Hinman H&K,LLP) -80 Exchange Bx5250 -Bnghmtn 13902
(212) 351-4500 .. **Gleason,** John F Jr. '74 (Epstein B&G,PC) -250 Park Av -NY 10177
(212) 986-1544 .. **Gleason,** John P '82 (Gleason & K,LLP) -122 E 42nd -NY 10169 **Fx:**986-1379
(212) 578-2211 .. **Gleason,** Mary C '94 %MetLife -27-01 Qns Plz N -LIC 11101
(212) 232-2500 .. **Gleason,** Megan K '07 %Torgan & C,PC -17 State -NY 10004
(212) 759-7466 .. **Gleason,** Michl T '06 %Raven & K,LLP -126 E 56th -NY 10022
(212) 431-5030 .. **Gleason,** Peter J '04 PJ Gleason PC -53 N Moore -NY 10013
(516) 358-7200 .. **Gleason,** Peter J '09 %Mavrides M & Assoc,LLP -3000 Marcus Av -Lk Success 11042 **Fx:**358-7250
(212) 788-2912 .. **Gleason,** Scot C '87 Law Dept -100 Church -NY 10007 **Fx:**788-0367
(585) 987-4212 .. **Gleason,** Sean E '90 %Ct of Claims -144 Exchange Blvd -Rchstr 14614 **Fx:**262-3019
(518) 432-7511 .. **Gleason,** Thos F '79 (Gleason DW&O) -40 Beaver -Albany 12207
(716) 649-7711 .. **Gleba,** Gary J '87 West Herr Automtv Grp,Inc -Bx1998 -Blasdell 14219
(212) 651-7500 .. **Gleber,** Erich J '96 (Segal MS&M) -850 3rd Av -NY 10022
(718) 250-2000 .. **Gleeson,** Janet L '93 %DA -350 Jay -Brklyn 11201 **Fx:**250-2314
(518) 456-4300 .. **Gleeson,** Kathleen A '95 (Kerker & G PC) -286 Wshngtn Av Ext -Albany 12203 **Fx:**456-5700
(914) 995-4894 .. **Gleeson,** Martin G '90 %Cnty Atty -148 Martine Av -White Plns 10601 **Fx:**995-5858
(516) 482-4436 .. **Gleich Siegel & Farkas** -36 S Station Plz -Gt Neck 11021 **Fx:**482-8916
(516) 482-4436 .. **Gleich,** Stephan B '74 (Gleich S&F) -36 S Station Plz -Gt Neck 11021
(716) 845-6446 .. **Gleichenhaus,** Robt B '81 (Gleichenhaus M&F,PC) -43 Court -Buffalo 14202 **Fx:**845-6475
(212) 267-1900 .. **Gleicher,** Lora H '07 %Wade CM -111 Bway -NY 10006
(212) 451-2300 .. **Gleicher,** Warren R '77 (Olshan GFR&W LLP) -65 E 55th -NY 10022
(212) 559-3625 .. **Gleit,** Diane M '01 Citigroup Trust -485 Lex Av -NY 10017
(212) 506-1700 .. **Gleit,** Jeffrey R '01 (Kasowitz BT&F LLP) -1633 Bway -NY 10019
(718) 742-0200 .. **Gleit,** Jonathan L '91 -888 Grnd Cncrs -Bronx 10451 **Fx:**742-2058
(914) 946-3700 .. **Gleit,** Milton R '62 OfCnsl McCarthy F LLP -11 Martine Av -White Plns 10606
(212) 966-6704 .. **Gleit,** Stephen P '77 -401 Bway -NY 10013 **Fx:**343-0938
(212) 735-3000 .. **Glekel,** Jeffrey '73 (Skadden ASM&F LLP) -4 Times Sq -NY 10036
(212) 837-6351 .. **Glemann,** Gabrielle '07 %Hughes H&R LLP -1 Bttry Pk Plz -NY 10004
(212) 805-0256 .. **Glen,** Andrea A '08 Hon RJ Holwell -500 Pearl -NY 10007
(212) 278-1009 .. **Glen,** Jeffrey E '65 (Anderson K&O,PC) -1251 Av of Amer -NY 10020
(518) 474-7287 .. **Glendinning-Johnson,** Jane C '80 %Dept of Law -The Cptl -Albany 12224
(212) 492-6318 .. **Glener,** Gordon S '97 %Smith Barney -787 7th Av -NY 10019
(212) 243-1069 .. **Glener,** Lyla '83 -61 Horatio -NY 10014
(718) 579-3062 .. **Glenn,** Andrea S '95 -1020 Grnd Cncrs -Bronx 10451
(212) 506-1700 .. **Glenn,** Andrew K '96 (Kasowitz BT&F LLP) -1633 Bway -NY 10019
(914) 793-1700 .. **Glenn,** Arnold B '49 -575 Wht Plns Rd -Eastchstr 10709 **Fx:**793-0516
(716) 853-9555 .. **Glenn,** David M '62 %Leg Aid -237 Main -Buffalo 14203 **Fx:**853-3219
(212) 742-1414 .. **Glenn,** Edw H Jr. '94 %Zamansky & Assoc LLC -50 Bway -NY 10005 **Fx:**742-1177
(212) 732-5250 .. **Glenn,** Gary F '79 -225 Bway -NY 10007
(718) 875-1300 .. **Glenn,** Jonathan S '05 Applt Div 2nd Dept -45 Monroe Pl -Brklyn 11201 **Fx:**858-2446
(516) 294-8844 .. **Glenn,** Kimberly Johnson '95 OfCnsl L'Abbate BC&C,LLP -1001 Franklin Av -Gdn Cty 11530
(212) 530-5000 .. **Glenn,** Sarah N '06 %Milbank TH&M LLP -1 Chase Manh Plz -NY 10005
(845) 561-1951 .. **Glenn,** Stewart P '75 (Glenn & B PLLC) -372 S Plnk Rd -Newburgh 12550 **Fx:**561-5651
(631) 249-6565 .. **Glennon,** Marty G '97 (Archer BG&L,LLP) -425 Broadhllw Rd -Melvll 11747
(518) 562-3288 .. **Glennon,** Robt C '71 %Dept of Law -43 Durkee -Plattsbrgh 12901 **Fx:**562-3294
(646) 315-7300 .. **Glenn-Palmer,** Stephanie D '91 %FINRA -14 Wall -NY 10005 **Fx:**315-7440
(212) 689-6153 .. **Glenns,** Barbara J '84 -30 Waterside Plz -NY 10010 **Fx:**689-6578
(718) 250-2000 .. **Gliatta,** Paul '95 %DA -350 Jay -Brklyn 11201 **Fx:**250-2314
(212) 836-8000 .. **Gliatta,** Stephen '84 (Kaye S LLP) -425 Park Av -NY 10022
(516) 342-0931 .. **Glibowski,** Walter J '03 -12510 Qns Blvd -Kew Gdns 11415
(212) 504-6000 .. **Glick,** Anna H '83 (Cadwalader W&T LLP) -1 World Fncl Ctr -NY 10281
(212) 636-6000 .. **Glick,** Brian '67 %Fordham Univ Sch of Law -140 W 62nd -NY 10023 **Fx:**636-6899
(516) 296-7000 .. **Glick,** Carol A '90 Cnsl Certilman BA&H,LLP -90 Merrick Av -E Meadow 11554
(516) 775-2438 .. **Glick,** David M '67 -31 Stewart -Floral Pk 11001 **Fx:**775-2719
(516) 498-3384 .. **Glick,** Harry '79 Merrill Lynch -1010 Nrthrn Blvd -Gt Neck 11021 **Fx:**498-3187
(516) 797-6686 .. **Glick,** Ira J '90 -112 Southgate Cir -Massapequa Pk 11762 **Fx:**797-6686
(718) 261-3047 .. **Glick,** Joshua '89 %Queens Law Assoc -118-21 Qns Blvd -Frst Hlls 11375 **Fx:**261-0798
(212) 715-9100 .. **Glick,** Joshua D '04 %Kramer LN&F,LLP -1177 Av of Amer -NY 10036
(212) 841-7500 .. **Glick,** Joshua L '01 %Cushman & Wakefield -1290 Av of Amer -NY 10104
(212) 944-1501 .. **Glick,** Marc H '82 (Glick & W) -1501 Bway -NY 10036 **Fx:**768-0785
(845) 838-5030 .. **Glick,** Mark H '84 %City Ct -1 Mncpl Plz -Beacon 12508 **Fx:**838-5041
(212) 735-3000 .. **Glick,** Matthew A '09 %Skadden ASM&F LLP -4 Times Sq -NY 10036
(347) 404-9400 .. **Glick,** Peter '78 %Criminal Ct -120 Schermerhorn -Brklyn 11201 **Fx:**(718) 643-3538
(516) 746-3500 .. **Glick,** Robt A '90 (Brand G&B,PC) -600 Old Cntry Rd -Gdn Cty 11530
(646) 328-0850 .. **Glick,** Shanah D '98 %Outside Cnsl Solutns LLP -1430 Bway -NY 10018 **Fx:**360-5000
(914) 333-9618 .. **Glickberg,** Yan '04 %Philips Electronics -345 Scarborough Rd Bx3001 -Briarclff Mnr 10510 **Fx:**332-0615
(845) 353-4300 .. **Glickel,** Richd A '75 -2 Crosfld Av -W Nyack 10994 **Fx:**353-6221
(212) 588-5500 .. **Glicklich,** Peter A '82 (Davies WP&V LLP) -625 Mad Av -NY 10022
(212) 756-2000 .. **Glickman,** Alan R '81 (Schulte R&Z LLP) -919 3rd Av -NY 10022
(212) 735-3000 .. **Glickman,** Andrew M '10 %Skadden ASM&F LLP -4 Times Sq -NY 10036
(516) 621-7876 .. **Glickman,** Arthur '48 -2 Lydia Ct -Albertson 11507
(212) 223-0400 .. **Glickman,** Barry J '84 (Zeichner RF&K LLP) -575 Lex Av -NY 10022
(212) 233-0350 .. **Glickman,** Bruce W '85 (Sobel RF&S,LLP) -150 Bway -NY 10038
(212) 232-1300 .. **Glickman,** Gregory S '06 %Lewis BB&S LLP -77 Water -NY 10005
(212) 335-9000 .. **Glickman,** Jeremy B '03 %DA -1 Hogan Pl -NY 10013
(718) 852-3710 .. **Glickman,** Leo '96 (Stoll G&B) -71 Nevins -Brklyn 11217 **Fx:**852-3586
(585) 325-2746 .. **Glickman,** Philip S '75 -450 Rynlds Arcd Bldg -Rchstr 14614
(212) 406-2886 .. **Glicksman & Cardoso** -150 Bway -NY 10038 **Fx:**732-9154
(212) 406-2886 .. **Glicksman,** Eugene J '80 (Glicksman & C) -150 Bway -NY 10038
(631) 277-2062 .. **Glicksman,** Mitchell S '84 (Polon & G) -Bx373 -Islip Terr 11752
(203) 674-7935 .. **Glickson,** Andrew A '76 (Pullman & C,LLC) -50 Main -White Plns 10606
(631) 761-7000 .. **Glickstein,** Howard A '54 %Touro Cllg Law Ctr -225 Eastvw Dr -Central Islip 11722
(914) 472-9158 .. **Glickstein,** Richd '80 -29 Scarsdale Farm Rd -Scarsdale 10583
(212) 836-8000 .. **Glickstein,** Steven J '77 (Kaye S LLP) -425 Park Av -NY 10022
(845) 634-5694 .. **Glidden,** Michl J '07 (Myerowitz J&G) -132 Buena Vista Rd -New Cty 10956 **Fx:**634-0917
(212) 458-6272 .. **Glidewell,** Gail '03 AIG,Inc -175 Water -NY 10038
(212) 278-1036 .. **Gliedman,** Diana Shafter '01 (Anderson K&O,PC) -1251 Av of Amer -NY 10020
(718) 523-4343 .. **Gliedman,** Gregory L '01 -153-01 Jamaica Av -Jamaica 11432
(212) 330-1000 .. **Gliedman,** John A '92 %Buck Consultants -1 Penn Plz -NY 10119 **Fx:**695-4184
(212) 867-7750 .. **Gliedman,** Kenneth R '73 (Lichter GO PC) -551 5th Av -NY 10176
(212) 566-3332 .. **Glikin,** Deborah R '92 Dept of Buildings -280 Bway -NY 10007
(212) 244-4111 .. **Glikman,** Joshua '79 OfCnsl Shiboleth YR&Z,LLP -1 Penn Plz -NY 10119
(212) 335-9000 .. **Gliner,** Susan H '80 %DA -1 Hogan Pl -NY 10013
(212) 448-1100 .. **Glinert,** David J '51 OfCnsl McLaughlin & S,LLP -260 Mad Av -NY 10016
(212) 598-2275 .. **Glinert,** Kate A '00 Razor & Tie Direct,LLC -214 Sullivan -NY 10012
(212) 259-8000 .. **Glinets,** Margarita '06 %Dewey & L LLP -1301 Av of Amer -NY 10019
(516) 537-1130 .. **Glinkenhouse,** Alan C '76 (Glinkenhouse F&Q) -116 Spruce -Cedarhrst 11516
(516) 537-1130 .. **Glinkenhouse Floumanhaft & Queen** -116 Spruce -Cedarhrst 11516 **Fx:**374-4550
(212) 594-2770 .. **Glinsky,** Frank J '87 F Glinsky,PC -1350 Bway -NY 10018 **Fx:**594-3820

(716) 854-6424 .. **Gliosca,** Brett P '09 %K Ricotta -350 Main -Buffalo 14202 **Fx:**854-6425
(516) 560-6400 .. **Gliponeo Leventhal,** Martha '07 Leg Aid -1 Helen Keller Way -Hempstd 11550 **Fx:**565-3694
(212) 350-2700 .. **Glist,** A Owen '02 %Constantine C,PC -450 Lex Av -NY 10017
(516) 463-5858 .. **Gloade,** Astrid B '92 %Hofstra Law Schl -121 Hofstra Univ -Hempstd 11549
(516) 465-8090 .. **Gloade,** Mark A '91 %North Shore-LIJ Hlth Systm -145 Community Dr -Gt Neck 11021 **Fx:**465-8105
(631) 273-0900 .. **Globus,** Kenneth H '83 %United Guardian -230 Marcus Blvd Bx18050 -Hauppauge 11788 **Fx:**273-0858
(646) 223-4000 .. **Glocer,** Thos H '85 %Reuters -3 Times Sq -NY 10036
(516) 746-0232 .. **Glockner,** Daryl R '78 (Farley G&H,LLP) -200 Old Cntry Rd -Mineola 11501
(212) 848-4000 .. **Gloger,** Christian K '10 Shearman & S LLP -599 Lex Av -NY 10022
(212) 267-4876 .. **Glogower,** April M '05 %Hoagland LMD&D,LLP -1501 Bway -NY 10036
(716) 566-1300 .. **Glose,** Herbert J '83 (Hiscock & B,LLP) -1100 M&T Ctr -Buffalo 14203
(718) 248-6727 .. **Glotzer,** David L '93 CitiCorp Invstmnt Srvcs -1 Court Sq -LIC 11120
(212) 587-8884 .. **Glotzer,** Gilbert S '65 -225 Bway -NY 10007 **Fx:**577-9715
(212) 225-2000 .. **Glotzer,** Paul E '91 (Cleary GS&H) -1 Lbrty Plz -NY 10006
(212) 788-1370 .. **Glotzer,** Scott B '08 %Law Dept -100 Church -NY 10007 **Fx:**788-0367
(516) 873-6200 .. **Gloumis,** Ioannis P '06 %R Macchia & Assoc -98 Front -Mineola 11501 **Fx:**873-1611
(212) 728-8000 .. **Glover,** Carly R '08 %Willkie F&G LLP -787 7th Av -NY 10019
(516) 496-5822 .. **Glover,** Caroline A '99 %T Spina -170 Froehlich Farm Blvd -Woodbury 11797 **Fx:**496-5420
(212) 458-3763 .. **Glover,** Catherine D '92 AIGTS -175 Water -NY 10038
(718) 224-9700 .. **Glover,** Catherine R '79 -221-29 Hartland Av -Qns Vllg 11427 **Fx:**224-0542
(516) 384-2457 .. **Glover,** Dorian R '98 -600 Franklin Av Bx8089 -Gdn Cty 11530
(315) 671-2000 .. **Glover,** Gina M '99 Family Ct -401 Mntgmry -Syracuse 13202
(212) 408-5100 .. **Glover,** Marjorie M '89 (Chadbourne & P LLP) -30 Rckfllr Plz -NY 10112
(718) 261-3047 .. **Glover,** Melody '87 %Queens Law Assoc -118-21 Qns Blvd -Frst Hlls 11375 **Fx:**261-0798
(315) 734-2916 .. **Glover,** Saml J '97 Utica Natl Ins Grp -180 Genesee -New Hartfrd 13413
(212) 238-4800 .. **Glover-Frey,** Erin E '07 %Landman CB&F,PC -120 Bway -NY 10271
(718) 222-2362 .. **Glover-Thomas,** Charessa L '07 %Law Dept -350 Jay -Brklyn 11201 **Fx:**222-2373
(212) 732-5272 .. **Glovin,** Richd A '72 -20 Vesey -NY 10007 **Fx:**732-5091
(212) 530-5000 .. **Glowitz,** Danl A '10 %Milbank TH&M LLP -1 Chase Manh Plz -NY 10005
(212) 695-0060 .. **Glubin,** Bruce A '75 %Wilens & B,PC -450 7th Av -NY 10123
(716) 856-4000 .. **Gluc,** Kevin K '97 (Hodgson R LLP) -140 Pearl -Buffalo 14202
(212) 455-2000 .. **Gluck,** Brian M '07 %Simpson T&B LLP -425 Lex Av -NY 10017
(212) 775-0055 .. **Gluck,** Danl J '86 (Simon G&K LLP) -1700 Bway -NY 10019
(212) 400-7223 .. **Gluck,** Danl T '07 %Zaremba B&B PLLC -40 Wall -NY 10005 **Fx:**(646) 512-5607
(212) 728-8000 .. **Gluck,** Elliot J '05 %Willkie F&G LLP -787 7th Av -NY 10019
(212) 874-6700 .. **Gluck,** Freema '76 %Peter Max Studio -37 W 65th -NY 10023 **Fx:**877-1146
(914) 761-1205 .. **Gluck,** George '81 -199 Main -White Plns 10601
(212) 233-4401 .. **Gluck,** Irving '82 -225 Bway -NY 10007 **Fx:**608-3785
(718) 596-8886 .. **Gluck,** Joel M '82 -80 Lvngstn -Brklyn 11201
(212) 393-1006 .. **Gluck,** Laurence '78 (Gluck & K) -156 William -NY 10038 **Fx:**267-7695
(212) 603-6300 .. **Gluck,** Marshall J '68 (Robinson BLGG&G PC) -875 3rd Av -NY 10022
(212) 594-5300 .. **Gluck,** Matthew '67 (Milberg LLP) -1 Penn Plz -NY 10119
(631) 451-7900 .. **Gluck,** Michl B '83 (Rosenberg & G,LLP) -1176 Portion Rd -Holtsvll 11742
(212) 551-9420 .. **Gluck,** Mitchell A '84 1st Amer Title -633 3rd Av -NY 10017
(212) 907-8000 .. **Gluck,** Paul '81 Loring Ward Intl -61 Bway -NY 10006 **Fx:**907-8098
(212) 425-5750 .. **Gluck,** Sandra R M '80 GARD (NA) Inc -30 Broad -NY 10004 **Fx:**425-8147
(212) 278-8900 .. **Gluck,** Simon B '62 S Gluck,PC -36 W 44th -NY 10036 **Fx:**221-0999
(516) 374-5818 .. **Gluck,** Simon B '62 S Gluck,PC -19 Copper Beech Ln -Lawrence 11559 **Fx:**569-4590
(516) 374-5818 .. **Gluck,** Simon B '62 S Gluck,PC -575 Chestnut -Cedarhrst 11516 **Fx:**569-4590
(212) 513-3200 .. **Gluck,** Warren E '09 %Holland & K LLP -31 W 52nd -NY 10019
(914) 682-1923 .. **Gluck-Acosta,** Selma M '77 -115 Ogden Av -White Plns 10605
(718) 250-2000 .. **Gluckman,** Adina M '08 %DA -350 Jay -Brklyn 11201 **Fx:**250-2314
(845) 695-2600 .. **Gluckman,** Bruce '91 Mediacom Communications Corp -100 Crystal Run Rd -Middletwn 10941 **Fx:**695-2749
(212) 530-5000 .. **Gluckman,** Derek A '09 %Milbank TH&M LLP -1 Chase Manh Plz -NY 10005
(212) 819-8200 .. **Gluckman,** Todd A '06 %White & C LLP -1155 Av of Amer -NY 10036
(212) 455-2000 .. **Gluckow,** Paul C '96 (Simpson T&B LLP) -425 Lex Av -NY 10017
(212) 596-9000 .. **Gluckselig,** Richd '05 %Ropes & G LLP -1211 Av of Amer -NY 10036
(212) 841-2397 .. **Glucksman,** Adam W '96 BNP Paribas -787 7th Av -NY 10019
(914) 381-7400 .. **Glucksman,** James B '83 %Rattet P&G,LLP -550 Mamaroneck Av -Harrison 10528
(718) 590-2129 .. **Glucksman,** Jeffrey '86 %DA -198 E 161st -Bronx 10451 **Fx:**590-6477
(212) 546-9255 .. **Glucksman,** Joel R '84 (Scarinci H) -107 Grand -NY 10013
(917) 846-7756 .. **Glucksman,** Myron S '86 -36 Stephen Halsey Path -Water Mill 11976
(973) 228-5700 .. **Gluckstern,** Henry A '74 Cnsl Brach E LLC -100 Park Av -NY 10017 **Fx:**228-7852
(212) 940-3000 .. **Glucroft,** Douglas S '86 (Nixon P LLP) -437 Mad Av -NY 10022
(212) 558-4000 .. **Glueckstein,** Brian D '04 %Sullivan & C LLP -125 Broad -NY 10004
(212) 849-7000 .. **Glunt,** Robt A '09 %Quinn EU&S,LLP -51 Mad Av -NY 10010
(212) 732-3200 .. **Glusband,** Steven J '74 (Carter L&M LLP) -2 Wall -NY 10005
(631) 244-9110 .. **Glushakoff,** Martin '73 -15 Aron Dr -Bohemia 11716
(212) 205-7000 .. **Glushko,** Thos N '97 (Ashurst LLP) -7 Times Sq -NY 10036
(212) 858-7000 .. **Glusker,** Danl J '99 %RBC Dominion Sec -165 Bway -NY 10006
(212) 705-7000 .. **Glusky,** Shon E '99 (Bingham M LLP) -399 Park Av -NY 10022
(516) 937-1300 .. **Gluszak,** Richd F '78 -400 S Oyster Bay Rd -Hicksvll 11801 **Fx:**937-1456
(516) 918-7034 .. **Glynn,** Alan C '96 Deloitte & Touche LLP -2 Jericho Plz -Jericho 11753
(212) 303-1800 .. **Glynn,** Carolyn M '92 Rsoen Seymour Shapss Martin & Co LLP -757 3rd Av -NY 10017 **Fx:**755-5600
(212) 425-7200 .. **Glynn,** Christopher W '06 %Kenyon & K,LLP -1 Bway -NY 10004
(212) 259-8000 .. **Glynn,** Dawn E '92 %Dewey & L LLP -1301 Av of Amer -NY 10019
(718) 792-6773 .. **Glynn,** James M '93 -291 William Av -Bronx 10464
(212) 504-6000 .. **Glynn,** Jos P '94 SpclCnsl Cadwalader W&T LLP -1 World Fncl Ctr -NY 10281
(212) 857-8230 .. **Glynn,** Jos T '88 %Baker MM&M,PC -330 W 34th -NY 10001
(212) 858-4776 .. **Glynn,** Julie K '95 FINRA -1 Lbrty Plz -NY 10006 **Fx:**858-4389
(212) 451-2900 .. **Glynn,** Katherine C '99 Cnsl Robinson & C LLP -885 3rd Av -NY 10022
(212) 506-2500 .. **Glynn,** Kelly M '10 Mayer B LLP -1675 Bway -NY 10019
(718) 495-2579 .. **Glynn,** Kevin R '03 %M Doherty,PC -6900 Jericho Tpk -Syosset 11791 **Fx:**495-2738
(718) 570-3338 .. **Glynn,** Lawr C '97 Caruso Glynn,LLC -5304 193rd -Fresh Mdws 11365 **Fx:**767-2474
(914) 761-0404 .. **Glynn,** Lawr J '73 -200 Mamaroneck Av -White Plns 10601 **Fx:**761-9280
(631) 751-5757 .. **Glynn Mercep & Purcell,LLP** -57 North Cntry Rd Bx712 -Stony Brk 11790
(212) 962-1020 .. **Glynn,** Michl E '95 %M Lamonsoff -80 Maiden Ln -NY 10038 **Fx:**962-3078
(518) 399-2626 .. **Glynn,** Robt R '01 -104 Woodhvn Dr -Scotia 12302 **Fx:**399-2626
(716) 854-1446 .. **Glynn,** Thos G '01 %Losi & G -170 Franklin -Buffalo 14202
(212) 558-6668 .. **Glynn,** Thos J '94 %Foley SO&W -100 William -NY 10038
(631) 751-5757 .. **Glynn,** Timothy B '76 (Glynn M&P,LLP) -57 North Cntry Rd Bx712 -Stony Brk 11790
(212) 704-1356 .. **Gmora,** Barbara S '81 Interpublic Grp -1114 Av of Amer -NY 10036 **Fx:**704-2236
(212) 859-8000 .. **Gnall,** Gregory P '79 SpclCnsl Fried FHS&J LLP -1 NY Plz -NY 10004
(212) 655-6000 .. **Gnazzo,** Melanie J '86 (Chapman & C LLP) -330 Mad Av -NY 10017
(212) 431-3000 .. **Gnesin,** Ross L '85 -11 Beach -NY 10013
(212) 909-6000 .. **Gnessin,** Sharon H '07 %Debevoise & P LLP -919 3rd Av -NY 10022
(917) 534-4900 .. **Go,** Elizabeth C '96 Zurich Capital Mrkts -105 E 17th -NY 10003
(212) 788-1145 .. **Goad,** Amanda C '06 %Law Dept -100 Church -NY 10007 **Fx:**788-0367
(212) 558-4000 .. **Goal,** Florence J '08 %Sullivan & C LLP -125 Broad -NY 10004
(914) 241-8900 .. **Goanos,** Larry A '87 Professional Indemnity Agency -37 Radio Circle Dr Bx5000 -Mt Kisco 10549
(212) 819-1130 .. **Gobeille,** Rebecca L '06 %Hirschen S&E -902 Bway -NY 10010
(212) 813-5900 .. **Gobena,** Lydia T '97 (Fross ZL&Z,PC) -866 UN Plz -NY 10017
(718) 738-5252 .. **Goberdhan,** Cheddi B '93 (C Goderdhan,PC) -131-09 Rockaway Blvd -S Ozone Pk 11420 **Fx:**738-5353
(718) 738-5252 .. **Goberdhan,** Janelle V '06 %C Goderdhan,PC -131-09 Rockaway Blvd -S Ozone Pk 11420 **Fx:**738-5353
(914) 713-8900 .. **Gobes,** Frank J '90 -1 N Lex Av -White Plns 10601
(631) 584-4500 .. **Gobetz,** Danl L '92 -960 Middle Cntry Rd -St James 11780 **Fx:**584-4348
(845) 368-1710 .. **Gobetz,** Kenneth C '85 (Wichler & G,PC) -400 Rella Blvd -Suffern 10901 **Fx:**368-1470
(212) 233-3330 .. **Goble,** Maryellen '80 (Hanley & G LLP) -233 Bway -NY 10279
(214) 259-0955 .. **Goch,** Jonathan M '07 %Sonnenschein N&R LLP -1221 Av of Amer -NY 10020
(914) 337-4924 .. **Goche,** Jeannine Padula '90 -575 Wht Plns Rd -Eastchstr 10709
(917) 755-4686 .. **Gochfeld,** Robt '80 -1312 Ditmas Av -Brklyn 11226 **Fx:**(718) 941-8342
(212) 455-2000 .. **Gochman,** Janet Anne '94 %Simpson T&B LLP -425 Lex Av -NY 10017
(914) 271-6236 .. **Gochman,** John J '60 -36 Oneida Av Bx7 -Croton-On-Hud 10520 **Fx:**271-6195
(585) 454-2181 .. **Gocker,** James C '74 (Trevett CS&A,PC) -2 State -Rchstr 14614
(212) 554-1400 .. **Gocyk-Farber,** Beata '98 (Bernstein LB&G LLP) -1285 Av of Amer -NY 10019
(518) 449-1063 .. **Godambe,** Meghana G '02 NYS Cncl of Schl Superintendents -7 Elk -Albany 12207 **Fx:**426-2229
(718) 643-3032 .. **Godby,** Natasha L '03 %Cnty Public Admin -360 Adams -Brklyn 11201
(718) 868-2401 .. **Goddard,** Colvin C '01 (C Goddard & Assoc PC) -Bx901250 -Far Rckwy 11690 **Fx:**337-3185
(212) 716-5790 .. **Goddard,** F Holt '96 %Cohen Lgl Grp,LLC -230 Park Av -NY 10169
(212) 657-1195 .. **Goddard,** James S '85 Citigroup -77 Water -NY 10005
(212) 836-8000 .. **Goddard,** Joan M '06 %Kaye S LLP -425 Park Av -NY 10022
(212) 736-4500 .. **Goddard,** Megan S '04 %Nesenoff & M,LLP -363 7th Av -NY 10001
(212) 815-0157 .. **Goddeyne,** Matthieu S '09 DA -80 Centre -NY 10013
(315) 797-8300 .. **Godemann,** James P '89 (Kernan and K,PC) -258 Genesee -Utica 13502 **Fx:**797-6467
(718) 991-4600 .. **Godeski,** Steven '87 %Leg Aid -953 Southrn Blvd -Bronx 10459 **Fx:**842-2867
(212) 326-2000 .. **Godesky,** Leah '10 %O'Melveny & M LLP -7 Times Sq -NY 10036
(315) 471-3151 .. **Godfread-Brown,** Andrea '02 Hancock & E,LLP -1500 AXA Twr I Bx4976 -Syracuse 13221
(718) 286-2274 .. **Godfrey,** Keisha A '07 %Leg Aid -120-46 Qns Blvd -Kew Gdns 11415 **Fx:**286-2286
(212) 248-3140 .. **Godfrey,** Lauren D '03 %Drinker B&R LLP -140 Bway -NY 10005
(845) 340-3315 .. **Godfrey,** Lisa Marie '09 %DA -285 Wall -Kingston 12401 **Fx:**340-3185
(212) 221-6900 .. **Godfrey,** Maureen B '00 %Winget S&S,LLP -45 Bway -NY 10006
(716) 856-4000 .. **Godfrey,** Peter C '97 (Hodgson R LLP) -140 Pearl -Buffalo 14202
(212) 310-8000 .. **Godhard,** Peter R J '09 %Weil G&M LLP -767 5th Av -NY 10153

(212) 272-2561 .. **Godin**, Laurence S '92 %JP Morgan Chase -383 Mad Av -NY 10179
(212) 695-5281 .. **Godinez**, Cristina A '05 %R Seguritan -450 7th Av -NY 10123 **Fx:**563-2664
(212) 366-4141 .. **Godinez**, Paul E '02 The Reindeer Co -30 Vandam -NY 10013
(917) 660-1379 .. **Godinger**, Isaac '74 -245 E 25th -NY 10010 **Fx:**(866) 435-2962
(315) 724-7523 .. **Godkin**, Scott T '99 %K Eisenhut -1602 Sunset Av -Utica 13502 **Fx:**797-1519
(212) 836-8000 .. **Godler**, Mark D '83 Cnsl Kaye S LLP -425 Park Av -NY 10022
(212) 425-7200 .. **Godlewski**, Kevin T '99 Cnsl Kenyon & K,LLP -1 Bway -NY 10004
(212) 309-6000 .. **Godlewski**, Walter J III '94 (Morgan L&B LLP) -101 Park Av -NY 10178
(212) 599-1744 .. **Godlin**, Paul M '63 (Opton H&F,LLP) -295 Mad Av -NY 10017
(212) 715-9100 .. **Godman**, James P '91 (Kramer LN&F,LLP) -1177 Av of Amer -NY 10036
(212) 756-2000 .. **Godnick**, Howard O '86 (Schulte R&Z LLP) -919 3rd Av -NY 10022
(212) 742-9700 .. **Godosky & Gentile,PC** -61 Bway -NY 10006 **Fx:**742-9706
(212) 742-9700 .. **Godosky**, Richd '58 (Godosky & G,PC) -61 Bway -NY 10006
(212) 742-9700 .. **Godosky**, Robt E '89 %Godosky & G,PC -61 Bway -NY 10006
(212) 375-2980 .. **Godoy**, Brenda Y '05 Guidepoint Global -730 3rd Av -NY 10017 **Fx:**838-9175
(631) 694-2300 .. **Godsberg**, Steven '67 (Lamb & B,LLP) -534 Broadhllw Rd Bx9034 -Melvll 11747
(917) 452-2443 .. **Godsell**, Gloria J '97 %Accenture -1345 6th Av -NY 10105
(718) 625-2200 .. **Godsoe**, Cynthia M '01 Bklyn Law Schl -250 Joralemon -Brklyn 11201 **Fx:**780-0393
(716) 566-2800 .. **Godsoe**, John C '01 (Bond S&K,PLLC) -40 Fountian Plz -Buffalo 14202
(716) 852-1544 .. **Godson**, Frank G '51 (Smith M&S,LLC) -786 Ellicott Sq Bldg -Buffalo 14203
(212) 839-5300 .. **Godwin**, Howard G Jr. '70 (Sidley A LLP) -787 7th Av -NY 10019
(716) 856-4000 .. **Godwin**, John M '08 %Hodgson R LLP -140 Pearl -Buffalo 14202
(212) 915-7855 .. **Godwin**, Marisa A '03 Willis Executive Risks -200 Lbrty -NY 10281
(212) 848-4000 .. **Godwin**, Melissa J '07 %Shearman & S LLP -599 Lex Av -NY 10022
(716) 626-0404 .. **Godwin**, Robt W '99 (Kantor & G,PLLC) -5800 Main -Williamsvll 14221 **Fx:**626-0412
(212) 558-4000 .. **Godzeno**, Robt M '10 %Sullivan & C LLP -125 Broad -NY 10004
(716) 893-1088 .. **Godzuk**, John S '86 -4630 Chapman Pkwy -Hambrg 14075
(212) 922-9700 .. **Goebel**, Jason A '95 %1st Amer Title -633 3rd Av -NY 10017 **Fx:**922-0881
(914) 725-5243 .. **Goebel**, Robt B '83 -14 Walworth Av -Scarsdale 10583
(212) 636-6844 .. **Goebel**, Roger '61 %Fordham Univ Sch of Law -140 W 62nd -NY 10023 **Fx:**636-6899
(516) 921-3425 .. **Goebel**, Wm H '66 -16 Lilac Dr -Syosset 11791
(212) 444-6327 .. **Goebels**, P Mats '92 ITG Inc -380 Mad Av -NY 10017 **Fx:**444-6494
(607) 753-5010 .. **Goehler**, Edw '84 %Hon W Ames -46 Greenbush -Cortlnd 13045
(212) 205-7000 .. **Goehring**, Amanda Buck '01 %Ashurst LLP -7 Times Sq -NY 10036
(646) 273-3608 .. **Goel**, Madhu R '04 AMC Co,LLC -11 Penn Plz -NY 10001
(212) 839-5300 .. **Goel**, Ran '08 %Sidley A LLP -787 7th Av -NY 10019
(585) 385-1511 .. **Goel**, Vinita '90 -5 Torwood Cir -Pittsfrd 14534
(212) 264-9230 .. **Goell**, Geoffrey G '09 %US DOJ -26 Fed Plz -NY 10278 **Fx:**264-1916
(212) 417-3700 .. **Goeman**, Robin N '06 %MFY Legal Srvcs -299 Bway -NY 10007 **Fx:**417-3890
(212) 351-4000 .. **Goergen**, Elizabeth Haynes '09 %Gibson D&C LLP -200 Park Av -NY 10166
(716) 845-2101 .. **Goergen**, Erik A '06 %Hon E Pigott Jr -50 Delaware Av -Buffalo 14202
(716) 626-3540 .. **Goergen**, Jos G II '90 (Damelio G&M) -300 Intl Dr -Williamsvll 14221 **Fx:**626-3542
(212) 653-8700 .. **Goering**, Kevin W '82 (Sheppard MR&H LLP) -30 Rckfllr Plz -NY 10112
(646) 315-7342 .. **Goerke**, Robt J '94 FINRA -14 Wall -NY 10005 **Fx:**315-7440
(516) 355-7901 .. **Goerlich**, Valerie I '87 Paganini GCC&F -1979 Marcus Av -Lk Success 11042
(716) 856-4000 .. **Goerss**, Amy L '10 %Hodgson R LLP -140 Pearl -Buffalo 14202
(716) 858-2424 .. **Goerss**, Douglas A '08 %DA -25 Delaware Av -Buffalo 14202 **Fx:**858-7425
(914) 995-4211 .. **Goethals**, Patricia A '91 %Law Dept Supreme & County Cts -111 Martin Luther King Blvd -White Plns 10601
(212) 415-8600 .. **Goethals**, Robt K '91 (Locke LB&L LLP) -3 World Fncl Ctr -NY 10281
(315) 785-2444 .. **Goettel**, Matthew A '02 %Atty Gen -317 Wshngtn -Watertwn 13601 **Fx:**785-2294
(212) 407-7700 .. **Goettig**, Michl J '08 %Vedder P,PC -1633 Bway -NY 10019
(631) 549-7738 .. **Goetz**, Christian Lee '96 -141 E Main -Huntngtn 11743 **Fx:**754-5844
(212) 489-8230 .. **Goetz**, Claude P '86 (Davis WT LLP) -1633 Bway -NY 10019
(917) 637-3600 .. **Goetz**, Ellen K '90 %Ctr for Reproductive Rts -120 Wall -NY 10005 **Fx:**637-3666
(516) 296-7000 .. **Goetz**, Ernest A Jr. '75 (Certilman BA&H,LLP) -90 Merrick Av -E Meadow 11554
(212) 695-8100 .. **Goetz Fitzpatrick,LLP** -1 Penn Plz -NY 10119 **Fx:**629-4013
(914) 946-7735 .. **Goetz Fitzpatrick,LLP** -1 N Bway -White Plns 10601 **Fx:**946-0098
(516) 741-2162 .. **Goetz Fitzpatrick,LLP** -170 Old Cntry Rd -Mineola 11501 **Fx:**746-1024
(212) 627-8220 .. **Goetz**, Jane '93 Polo Electric Corp -497 Canal -NY 10013
(212) 765-5070 .. **Goetz**, John S '05 %Fish & R,PC -153 E 53rd -NY 10022
(212) 363-6900 .. **Goetz**, Marisa V '83 (Faust GS&B LLP) -2 Rector -NY 10006
(212) 785-2929 .. **Goetz**, Mary T '89 %Conway FC&K,PC -48 Wall -NY 10005
(212) 940-7030 .. **Goetz**, Maurice H '51 Cnsl Katten MR LLP -575 Mad Av -NY 10022
(631) 277-8731 .. **Goetz**, Michele R '88 -81 W Bayberry Rd -Islip 11751
(212) 788-1174 .. **Goetz**, Paul A '96 %Law Dept -100 Church -NY 10007 **Fx:**788-0367
(212) 695-8100 .. **Goetz**, Peter '60 (Goetz F,LLP) -1 Penn Plz -NY 10119
(518) 457-4951 .. **Goetz**, Thos J '84 %Dept Correctional Srvcs -1220 Wshngtn Av -Albany 12226 **Fx:**457-7555
(585) 546-3013 .. **Goewey**, R Brian '80 -44 Exchange Blvd -Rchstr 14614 **Fx:**546-3032
(212) 480-3400 .. **Gofer**, Alexander '05 %Tamir Law Grp -55 Broad -NY 10004
(212) 705-7000 .. **Goff**, Bryan P '08 %Bingham M LLP -399 Park Av -NY 10022
(212) 207-7000 .. **Goff**, Christopher L '79 %HarperCollins Pub -10 E 53rd -NY 10022 **Fx:**207-7552
(212) 695-0060 .. **Goffer**, Jill M '03 %Wilens & B,PC -450 7th Av -NY 10123
(631) 547-2260 .. **Goffin**, Cory M '98 Auto One Ins -Bx9027 -Melvll 11747
(212) 267-2600 .. **Goffin**, Marcia J '83 -61 Bway -NY 10006 **Fx:**267-3024
(212) 530-4836 .. **Goffman**, Florence R '86 %LaRocca HRG&B LLP -40 Wall -NY 10005
(212) 735-3000 .. **Goffman**, Jay M '84 (Skadden ASM&F LLP) -4 Times Sq -NY 10036
(718) 515-0700 .. **Goffney**, Tara R '84 -Bx1014 -Bronx 10469
(716) 204-2400 .. **Gogan**, Jos F '95 %SJ Baum,PC -220 Nrthpnte Pkwy Bx1291 -Buffalo 14240 **Fx:**204-4600
(718) 760-7410 .. **Gogel**, Barry R '94 B Gogel,PC -6120 Grnd Cntrl Pkwy -Frst Hlls 11375 **Fx:**760-7411
(212) 407-5200 .. **Gogel**, Donald Jay '77 %ClaytonDubilier&Rice -375 Park Av -NY 10152 **Fx:**893-7061
(631) 853-7735 .. **Gogel**, Janet Lynn '77 %Hon J Cannavo -400 Carleton Av Bx9070 -Central Islip 11722
(212) 233-9500 .. **Gogel**, Wm A '68 (Agulnick & G,LLC) -305 Bway -NY 10007 **Fx:**693-1666
(845) 561-0550 .. **Gogerty**, Gary J '95 (Drake LHKGG&R PLLC) -555 Hudson Valley Av -New Windsor 12553
(212) 903-9000 .. **Goggan**, Rachel E '09 %Linklaters -1345 Av of Amer -NY 10105
(516) 571-6183 .. **Goggin**, Eileen J '89 %Cnty Atty -1 West -Mineola 11501 **Fx:**571-6604
(212) 613-5000 .. **Goggin**, Virginia M '09 %Leg Assist Grp -450 W 33rd -NY 10001 **Fx:**750-0820
(212) 725-0200 .. **Goggins**, Alan '91 %Barnes R&C -475 Park Av S -NY 10016
(212) 318-6000 .. **Goggins**, B Justin '08 %Paul HJ&W LLP -75 E 55th -NY 10022
(212) 553-0300 .. **Goggins**, John J III '86 %Moody's Invstr Srvc -250 Greenwich -NY 10007
(631) 298-4200 .. **Goggins**, Wm C '90 (Goggins & P) -13105 Main Rd Bx65 -Mattituck 11952 **Fx:**298-4214
(212) 422-9424 .. **Gogick Byrne & O'Neill,LLP** -11 Bway -NY 10004 **Fx:**422-9429
(212) 422-9424 .. **Gogick**, Robt J '75 (Gogick B&O,LLP) -11 Bway -NY 10004
(631) 360-7570 .. **Goglas**, Philip '88 %Town Atty -99 W Main -Smithtwn 11787 **Fx:**360-7719
(518) 474-7330 .. **Goglia**, Douglas J '91 %Dept of Law -The Cptl -Albany 12224
(516) 764-4467 .. **Goglio**, Barbara A '90 -500 Merrick Rd -Rockvll Ctr 11570
(212) 373-3000 .. **Gogliormella**, Salvatore '03 %Paul WRW&G LLP -1285 Av of Amer -NY 10019
(212) 403-1000 .. **Gogolak**, Adam M '05 %Wachtell LR&K -51 W 52nd -NY 10019
(212) 909-6000 .. **Gogolak**, Leonora R '08 %Debevoise & P LLP -919 3rd Av -NY 10022
(212) 965-2200 .. **Gohara**, Miriam Sabry '98 %NAACP/LDF -99 Hudson -NY 10013 **Fx:**226-7592
(212) 715-1000 .. **Gohlke**, Kathleen E '08 %Arnold & P LLP -399 Park Av -NY 10022
(212) 431-1300 .. **Goidel**, Eric M '83 (Borah GAN&G PC) -377 Bway -NY 10013
(212) 840-3737 .. **Goidel**, Jonathan M '86 (Goidel & SL LLP) -122 E 42nd -NY 10168 **Fx:**840-3793
(631) 265-1700 .. **Goidel**, Wendy Kaufmann '88 (Kenney GW&S,LLP) -50 Route 111 -Smithtwn 11787
(516) 683-0001 .. **Goidell**, Mark E '83 -377 Oak -Gdn Cty 11530
(516) 213-2091 .. **Going**, Dorothy M '91 -600 Old Cntry Rd -Gdn Cty 11530 **Fx:**558-1112
(631) 288-6763 .. **Going**, James P '85 -22 Oneck Rd -Westhmptn Bch 11978 **Fx:**288-5152
(845) 565-1100 .. **Goings-Perrot**, Julia C '98 %Tarshis CLM&M,PLLC -One Corwin Ct -Newburgh 12550
(212) 751-2742 .. **Goins**, Charlynn W '77 -30 Beekman Pl -NY 10022
(212) 805-0177 .. **Goins**, Dawnmarie '94 %USDC -500 Pearl -NY 10007
(212) 820-9378 .. **Goins**, Patricia '83 (Hawkins D&W LLP) -One Chase Manh Plz -NY 10005
(212) 326-3939 .. **Goitom**, Haben '09 %Jones D -222 E 41st -NY 10017
(516) 873-6200 .. **Gokce**, Mehmet F '04 %R Macchia & Assoc -98 Front -Mineola 11501 **Fx:**873-1611
(212) 735-3000 .. **Gokcebay**, Nazmiye A '07 %Skadden ASM&F LLP -4 Times Sq -NY 10036
(518) 483-0379 .. **Gokey**, Joy L '94 -Bx526 -Malone 12953
(212) 310-8000 .. **Gokhale**, Ajit V '10 %Weil G&M LLP -767 5th Av -NY 10153
(212) 556-2100 .. **Gokhale**, Anuradha V '09 %King & S -1185 Av of Amer -NY 10036
(585) 429-5182 .. **Gokhale**, Neelima Vijay '91 -101 Westmar Dr -Rchstr 14624 **Fx:**429-5182
(212) 487-4444 .. **Gokhale**, Vedant A '03 %Dept Cnsmr Affrs -42 Bway -NY 10004 **Fx:**487-4197
(212) 363-6900 .. **Gokhulsingh**, Lisa L '99 %Faust GS&B LLP -2 Rector -NY 10006
(212) 223-0400 .. **Golab**, Mark '02 %Zeichner E&K LLP -575 Lex Av -NY 10022
(212) 325-2175 .. **Golan**, Gil '04 Credit Suisse -11 Mad Av -NY 10010
(212) 662-1025 .. **Golan**, Lea M '86 -310 W 106th -NY 10025
(516) 873-0795 .. **Golan**, Robt '87 (Golan & M,LLP) -200 Willis Av -Mineola 11501 **Fx:**873-6686
(518) 457-6137 .. **Goland**, Lois '81 %State Police -1220 Wshngtn Av -Albany 12226 **Fx:**485-1164
(212) 705-7000 .. **Goland**, Marina '91 %Bingham M LLP -399 Park Av -NY 10022
(718) 250-2000 .. **Golani**, Shoshana '05 %DA -350 Jay -Brklyn 11201 **Fx:**250-2314
(212) 558-5500 .. **Golanski**, Alani '88 %Weitz & L,PC -700 Bway -NY 10003
(212) 506-2500 .. **Golant**, Ilana D '08 %Mayer B LLP -1675 Bway -NY 10019
(212) 435-3571 .. **Golar**, Martha L '79 %Port Auth of NY/NJ -225 Park Av S -NY 10003 **Fx:**435-3555
(917) 716-5737 .. **Golat**, Stephen J '85 -54 Hunton -Staten Isl 10304 **Fx:**(718) 980-0065
(212) 859-8000 .. **Golay**, David C '78 (Fried FHS&J LLP) -1 NY Plz -NY 10004
(212) 832-0400 .. **Golbert**, Maury D '93 Berdon LLP -360 Mad Av -NY 10017
(212) 746-1387 .. **Golbey**, Anita R '81 %NY Presbyterian Hsptl -525 E 68th Bx88 -NY 10065 **Fx:**746-8603
(212) 247-1347 .. **Golby**, Jonathan D '77 -261 5th Av -NY 10016 **Fx:**247-1343
(718) 784-2105 .. **Gold**, Adam D '99 %Karp Assoc Inc -54-54 43rd -Maspeth 11378
(646) 885-5001 .. **Gold**, Alan '74 %Dept of Sanitation -125 Worth -NY 10013 **Fx:**(212) 442-9090
(516) 678-0800 .. **Gold**, Allen S '95 -450 Mariners Way -Copiague 11726 **Fx:**536-1909

(212) 964-6611 .. **Gold,** Amanda H '07 %Lester SK&D -120 Bway -NY 10271
(212) 373-3000 .. **Gold,** Amy E '07 %Paul WRW&G LLP -1285 Av of Amer -NY 10019
(212) 592-1400 .. **Gold,** Andrew C '81 (Herrick,F LLP) -2 Park Av -NY 10016
(212) 659-8105 .. **Gold,** Avitai '03 %Mt Sinai Med Ctr -1 Gustave L Levy Pl Bx 1099 -NY 10029 **Fx:**348-2230
(212) 825-9811 .. **Gold,** Barry S '85 (Krebsbach & S,PC) -55 Bway -NY 10006
(716) 285-2267 .. **Gold,** Benjamin '41 -256 3rd -Niagara Fls 14303 **Fx:**285-3922
(718) 579-8908 .. **Gold,** Benjamin D '07 Leg Aid -1020 Grnd Cncrs -Bronx 10451 **Fx:**588-2611
(212) 969-3000 .. **Gold,** Bernard D '55 (Proskauer R LLP) -1585 Bway -NY 10036
(212) 872-2911 .. **Gold,** Brett L '81 %KPMG LLP -345 Park Av -NY 10154
(212) 563-9435 .. **Gold,** Bruce F '89 -110 W 34th -NY 10001 **Fx:**594-1611
(518) 886-4000 .. **Gold,** Darryl M '97 %AYCO -321 Bway Bx860 -Saratoga Spgs 12866
(516) 622-9200 .. **Gold,** David A '93 (Westerman BEM&S,LLP) -1201 RXR Plz -Uniondale 11553
(212) 245-7300 .. **Gold,** David D '92 %Serling R&F,LLP -119 5th Av -NY 10003
(212) 962-2910 .. **Gold,** David J '86 (D Gold,PC) -800 2nd Av -NY 10017 **Fx:**962-2919
(718) 491-8552 .. **Gold,** David J '94 -573 76th -Brklyn 11209
(718) 585-2511 .. **Gold,** David Lawr '67 (Gold & R) -840 Grnd Cncrs -Bronx 10451
(516) 792-9510 .. **Gold,** Denise R '90 D Gold,PC -1253 Colonial Rd -Hewlett 11557 **Fx:**792-9501
(518) 464-1300 .. **Gold,** Elayne G '87 (Roemer WG&M LLP) -13 Columbia Cir -Albany 12203
(631) 435-0781 .. **Gold,** Elliot J '85 (Borda KA&G,LLP) -1805 5th Av -Bay Shr 11706
(212) 223-3400 .. **Gold,** Emanuel R '59 -108-18 Qns Blvd -Frst Hlls 11375
(212) 310-8000 .. **Gold,** Emily L '06 %Weil G&M LLP -767 5th Av -NY 10153
(631) 689-5105 .. **Gold,** Fern T '88 -12 Shaker Hllw Rd -Setauket 11733 **Fx:**689-5105
(212) 244-2740 .. **Gold,** Fredric M '83 (FM Gold PC) -450 7th Av -NY 10123 **Fx:**244-2258
(212) 417-5300 .. **Gold,** Gerri Ann '93 %Medicaid Fraud Cntrl -120 Bway -NY 10271 **Fx:**417-5274
(718) 339-1323 .. **Gold,** Hadley W '57 -1998 E 22nd -Brklyn 11229 **Fx:**382-1161
(212) 975-3045 .. **Gold,** Helen M '83 %CBS News -51 W 52nd -NY 10019 **Fx:**975-7292
(212) 773-3849 .. **Gold,** Howard '97 Ernst & Young LLP -5 Times Sq -NY 10036
(212) 308-9191 .. **Gold,** Ira J '91 (Rubin & G) -488 Mad Av -NY 10022 **Fx:**308-1347
(718) 403-3628 .. **Gold,** Jacqueline '91 %Dept of Finance -345 Adams -Brklyn 11201 **Fx:**403-3650
(914) 591-7856 .. **Gold,** Janet Schiller '75 -50 Deertrack Ln -Irvngtn 10533
(516) 512-6333 .. **Gold,** Jeffrey B '88 (Gold SKB LLP) -1025 Old Cntry Rd -Westbury 11590
(212) 563-6557 .. **Gold,** Jeffrey M '81 %Thefeil Organization -7 Penn Plz -NY 10001 **Fx:**563-6657
(518) 474-7330 .. **Gold,** Jeffrey S '80 %HANYS -1 Empire Dr -Rensselaer 12144
(212) 974-7474 .. **Gold,** Jerrold B '71 OfCnsl Cowan DA&S LLP -41 Mad Av -NY 10010
(212) 768-6700 .. **Gold,** Jessica H '04 %Sonnenschein N&R LLP -2 World Fncl Ctr -NY 10281
(212) 521-5400 .. **Gold,** Jessica L '09 %Reed S LLP -599 Lex Av -NY 10022
(212) 539-4000 .. **Gold,** Joanna H '02 %Focus Features -65 Bleecker -NY 10012
(212) 278-1886 .. **Gold,** Joshua '95 (Anderson K&O,PC) -1251 Av of Amer -NY 10020
(212) 484-3900 .. **Gold,** Kimberly J '09 %Arent F LLP -1675 Bway -NY 10019
(212) 969-3000 .. **Gold,** Leon Phillip '64 (Proskauer R LLP) -1585 Bway -NY 10036
(718) 923-8400 .. **Gold,** Leonard S '79 Forest City Ratner -1 Metrotech Ctr N -Brklyn 11201 **Fx:**923-8722
(212) 373-3000 .. **Gold,** Leslie M '09 %Paul WRW&G LLP -1285 Av of Amer -NY 10019
(607) 273-7037 .. **Gold,** Lucy '91 -415 N Tioga -Ithaca 14850
(845) 338-7494 .. **Gold,** Majer H '83 -72 Maiden Ln Bx4116 -Kingston 12402 **Fx:**338-7497
(518) 758-2100 .. **Gold,** Marc I '69 -12 Hudson Bx510 -Kinderhook 12106 **Fx:**758-2101
(212) 759-8995 .. **Gold,** Mark I '98 Metcom Excess -400 E 56th -NY 10022 **Fx:**759-9667
(212) 306-7160 .. **Gold,** Marlene '79 %Ofc Cllctv Brgn -40 Rector -NY 10006 **Fx:**306-7167
(212) 888-6068 .. **Gold,** Martha G '82 -420 Lex Av -NY 10170
(212) 397-3859 .. **Gold,** Martin '49 -200 Cntrl Pk S -NY 10019
(212) 839-5300 .. **Gold,** Martin E '72 (Sidley A LLP) -787 7th Av -NY 10019
(212) 447-4700 .. **Gold,** Martin I '83 -350 5th Av -NY 10118
(212) 768-6700 .. **Gold,** Martin R '61 (Sonnenschein N&R LLP) -1221 Av of Amer -NY 10020
(212) 643-5445 .. **Gold,** Matthew A '96 Argo Prtnrs -12 W 37th -NY 10018 **Fx:**643-6401
(212) 552-0932 .. **Gold,** Melissa Raff '94 JP Morgan Chase -1 Chase Manh Plz -NY 10081
(716) 285-2267 .. **Gold,** Michl A '74 -256 3rd -Niagara Fls 14303 **Fx:**285-3922
(212) 789-2723 .. **Gold,** Michl H '01 %NHL Enterprises,LP -1185 Av of Amer -NY 10036 **Fx:**789-2020
(718) 246-4653 .. **Gold,** Michl S '02 (MS Gold,PC) -435 Hmltn Av -Brklyn 11232 **Fx:**(212) 202-5310
(212) 969-3000 .. **Gold,** Morgan L '09 %Proskauer R LLP -1585 Bway -NY 10036
(212) 318-3000 .. **Gold,** Neil D '73 (Fulbright & J LLP) -666 5th Av -NY 10103
(212) 373-3000 .. **Gold,** Noah A '10 %Paul WRW&G LLP -1285 Av of Amer -NY 10019
(212) 416-8000 .. **Gold,** Rachel Demarest '97 %Dept of Law -120 Bway -NY 10271
(212) 972-1100 .. **Gold,** Richd L '77 (Morelli & G,LLP) -380 Lex Av -NY 10168
(631) 588-6587 .. **Gold,** Richd M '71 -3100 Vets Mem'l Hwy -Bohemia 11716 **Fx:**588-0276
(212) 340-0400 .. **Gold,** Risa I '89 %Applt Div 1st Dept -27 Mad Av -NY 10010 **Fx:**889-4412
(516) 536-5200 .. **Gold,** Robt '64 -100 N Centre -Rockvll Ctr 11570
(212) 999-5800 .. **Gold,** Robt '72 (Wilson SG&R) -1301 Av of Americas -NY 10019
(212) 254-1444 .. **Gold,** Robt B '85 (Gold SM PLLC) -134 Spring -NY 10012 **Fx:**966-2322
(914) 478-5523 .. **Gold,** Robt N '65 -31 Scenic Dr -Hastings-On-Hud 10706
(212) 484-8000 .. **Gold,** Roger H '97 %Warner Music Grp -75 Rckfllr Plz -NY 10019 **Fx:**489-3342
(212) 252-0300 .. **Gold,** Ronald Jay '75 (Kagan LLLG&C,LLP) -200 Mad Av -NY 10016
(718) 585-2511 .. **Gold & Rosenblatt** -840 Grnd Cncrs -Bronx 10451
(212) 834-0600 .. **Gold,** Sanford '77 (Gordon & S,PC) -355 Lex Av -NY 10017
(518) 785-7800 .. **Gold,** Sarah E '07 %Kieselstein PLLC -1187 Troy Schenectady Rd -Latham 12110
(212) 969-3000 .. **Gold,** Sarah S '75 (Proskauer R LLP) -1585 Bway -NY 10036
(212) 756-2000 .. **Gold,** Scott A '94 SpclCnsl Schulte R&Z LLP -919 3rd Av -NY 10022
(845) 340-3226 .. **Gold,** Shari S '84 Hon C Cahill -285 Wall -Kingston 12401
(212) 310-8000 .. **Gold,** Simeon '74 (Weil G&M LLP) -767 5th Av -NY 10153
(845) 229-5914 .. **Gold,** Stephan Jay '67 -46 Terwilliger Rd -Hyde Pk 12538 **Fx:**229-5914
(212) 691-2451 .. **Gold,** Stephanie S '98 Thomas Card Photography -508 W 26th -NY 10001
(914) 997-0981 .. **Gold,** Stephen Paul '79 (Gold & D) -470 Mamaroneck Av -White Plns 10605
(212) 346-0045 .. **Gold,** Steven '94 %P Weitz & Assoc,PC -233 Bway -NY 10279 **Fx:**346-0876
(212) 696-4848 .. **Gold,** Steven W '89 (Mintz & G LLP) -470 Park Av S -NY 10016
(516) 512-6333 .. **Gold Stewart Kravatz Benes LLP** -1025 Old Cntry Rd -Westbury 11590 **Fx:**512-6334
(212) 474-1000 .. **Gold,** Stuart W '73 (Cravath S&M LLP) -825 8th Av -NY 10019
(518) 457-4380 .. **Gold,** Tsvi J '01 %Dept of Labor -State Campus Bldg 12 -Albany 12240 **Fx:**485-1819
(212) 637-3234 .. **Gold,** Wayne M '77 EPA -290 Bway -NY 10007 **Fx:**637-3096
(516) 484-9878 .. **Goldaber,** Robt D '90 -140 Poplar Dr -Roslyn 11576
(212) 945-1713 .. **Goldart,** Ivar '72 -375 South End Av -NY 10280
(914) 499-4876 .. **Goldbach,** Aline B '03 IBM -New Orchrd Rd MD 327 -Armonk 10504
(212) 788-0545 .. **Goldbach,** Nancy A '91 %Law Dept -100 Church -NY 10007 **Fx:**788-0367
(212) 503-0427 .. **Goldban,** David R '96 Rohman Development LLC -555 5th Av -NY 10017
(718) 923-8400 .. **Goldban,** Michl A '96 Forest City Ratner -1 Metrotech Ctr N -Brklyn 11201
(718) 254-7000 .. **Goldbarg,** Andrea '02 %US Atty -271 Cadman Plz E -Brklyn 11201 **Fx:**254-6479
(315) 724-2248 .. **Goldbas,** David G '89 -185 Genesee -Utica 13501 **Fx:**724-2064
(516) 829-4620 .. **Goldbas,** Esther R '91 %D Tanenbaum -1 Channel Dr -Pt Wash 11050 **Fx:**829-1008
(212) 373-3000 .. **Goldbaum,** Robt D '95 (Paul WRW&G LLP) -1285 Av of Amer -NY 10019
(516) 355-7901 .. **Goldbaum,** Vivien Biss '83 %Paganini GCC&F -1979 Marcus Av -Lk Success 11042
(845) 679-8561 .. **Goldbeck,** David M '68 -Bx87 -Woodstock 12498 **Fx:**679-5573
(212) 513-3200 .. **Goldberg,** Aaron N '06 %Holland & K LLP -31 W 52nd -NY 10019
(212) 906-1200 .. **Goldberg,** Adam J '07 %Latham & W -885 3rd Av -NY 10022
(212) 575-4400 .. **Goldberg,** Adam L '87 %Utility Wrkrs Union of Amer -5 W 37th -NY 10018
(646) 253-2300 .. **Goldberg,** Adin C '85 (Bond S&K,PLLC) -330 Mad Av -NY 10017
(315) 474-2943 .. **Goldberg,** Alan J '53 OfCnsl Sugarman Law Firm,LLP -211 W Jffrsn -Syracuse 13202
(212) 921-1600 .. **Goldberg,** Alan J '80 (Goldberg SL&B,PC) -45 W 45th -NY 10036
(718) 263-8700 .. **Goldberg,** Alan J '80 (Haimowitz & G,PLLC) -104-07 Metro Av -Frst Hlls 11375
(518) 487-7600 .. **Goldberg,** Alan J '95 (Whiteman O&H LLP) -1 Commerce Plz -Albany 12260
(212) 687-7770 .. **Goldberg,** Alan M '80 SpclCnsl Rosen L&C LLP -275 Mad Av -NY 10016
(718) 275-3300 .. **Goldberg,** Allen J '96 (Bergman BG&L,LLP) -108-18 Qns Blvd -Frst Hlls 11375
(212) 417-3700 .. **Goldberg,** Andrew '85 %MFY Legal Srvcs -299 Bway -NY 10007 **Fx:**417-3890
(212) 351-4000 .. **Goldberg,** Andrew C '03 %Gibson D&C LLP -200 Park Av -NY 10166
(516) 741-2585 .. **Goldberg,** Andrew D '99 %Rosicki R & Assoc,PC -51 E Bethpage Rd -Plainvw 11803 **Fx:**741-4748
(718) 591-2100 .. **Goldberg,** Andrew P '92 (Goldberg & A LLC) -77-07 Parsons Blvd -Fresh Mdws 11366 **Fx:**591-2102
(212) 233-2122 .. **Goldberg,** Arthur I '68 (Ferrara TH&G) -711 3rd Av -NY 10017
(212) 595-5810 .. **Goldberg,** Audrey L '59 %Phoenix House -164 W 74th -NY 10023 **Fx:**496-6035
(631) 293-6060 .. **Goldberg,** Avraham Y '03 (Cellino & B,PC) -445 Broad Hollow Rd -Melvll 11747
(516) 487-5800 .. **Goldberg,** Barbara Decrow '80 (Mauro G&L LLP) -60 Cuttermill Rd -Gt Neck 11021
(212) 787-2500 .. **Goldberg,** Barry D '84 Melohn Properties -1995 Bway -NY 10023 **Fx:**787-3500
(212) 269-2363 .. **Goldberg,** Barry R '91 (Goldberg & K) -11 Park Pl -NY 10007
(212) 451-2900 .. **Goldberg,** Benjamin D '08 %Robinson & C LLP -885 3rd Av -NY 10022
(212) 732-8700 .. **Goldberg,** Benjamin J '02 %McAloon & F,PC -123 William -NY 10038
(212) 813-9797 .. **Goldberg,** Bernard '57 -667 Mad Av -NY 10065 **Fx:**813-9876
(516) 227-0700 .. **Goldberg,** Bob G '81 Cnsl Farrell F,PC -1320 RXR Plz -Uniondale 11556
(516) 889-1107 .. **Goldberg & Bokor,LLP** -138 E Park Av -Long Bch 11561 **Fx:**813-0997
(212) 455-2000 .. **Goldberg,** Bradley P '02 %Simpson T&B LLP -425 Lex Av -NY 10017
(212) 269-7308 .. **Goldberg,** Brian D '07 %Leahey & J PC -120 Wall -NY 10005
(212) 574-1200 .. **Goldberg,** Brian D '09 %Seward & K LLP -1 Bttry Pk Plz -NY 10004
(212) 277-6500 .. **Goldberg,** Brian E '01 Cnsl Dickstein S LLP -1633 Bway -NY 10019
(718) 417-1700 .. **Goldberg,** Brian M '00 %Deutsch & S LLP -79-37 Myrtle Av -Glendale 11385
(212) 521-5400 .. **Goldberg,** Brian S '09 %Reed S LLP -599 Lex Av -NY 10022
(718) 585-6144 .. **Goldberg,** Bruce H '93 %ME Goldberg -272 E 149th -Bronx 10451 **Fx:**585-0048
(718) 875-2400 .. **Goldberg & Cohn LLP** -16 Court -Brklyn 11241 **Fx:**858-2101

(516) 764-2800 .. **Goldberg & Connolly** -66 N Vllg Av -Rockvll Ctr 11570 **Fx:**764-2827
(212) 730-8133 .. **Goldberg,** Danl A '07 %Gunderson DSVF&H,LLP -220 W 42nd -NY 10036
(212) 335-4500 .. **Goldberg,** Danl I '96 (DLA Piper LLP) -1251 Av of Amer -NY 10020
(212) 661-7100 .. **Goldberg,** Danl Ian '96 (Salon MDN&B,LLP) -292 Mad Av -NY 10017
(516) 222-2330 .. **Goldberg,** Danl M '94 (Jacobson G&K,LLP) -585 Stewart Av -Gdn Cty 11530
(212) 506-1700 .. **Goldberg,** Danl P '96 (Kasowitz BT&F LLP) -1633 Bway -NY 10019
(516) 560-6400 .. **Goldberg,** Darlene R '94 %Leg Aid -1 Helen Keller Way -Hempstd 11550 **Fx:**565-3694
(212) 882-5705 .. **Goldberg,** David L '90 UBS Paine Webber -51 W 52nd -NY 10019
(845) 373-8196 .. **Goldberg,** David M '81 -Bx254 -Amenia 12501 **Fx:**373-8196
(914) 421-7680 .. **Goldberg,** David M '93 Abovenet Comm -360 Hmltn Av -White Plns 10601
(212) 755-5510 .. **Goldberg,** David R '83 (Loeb B & Prtnrs) -505 Park Av -NY 10022
(212) 334-8813 .. **Goldberg,** David T '93 -99 Hudson -NY 10013
(914) 428-8300 .. **Goldberg,** Dawn E '94 %Sacks,PC -707 Wstchstr Av -White Plns 10604 **Fx:**682-1707
(212) 791-1881 .. **Goldberg,** Deborah '87 Earthjustice -156 William -NY 10038 **Fx:**918-1556
(212) 259-8000 .. **Goldberg,** Debra P '88 SrCnsl Dewey & L LLP -1301 Av of Amer -NY 10019
(718) 826-3760 .. **Goldberg,** Donald Drew '75 (Goldberg & L) -215 Marlboro Rd -Brklyn 11226 **Fx:**826-3760
(516) 336-2558 .. **Goldberg,** Doretta Katzter '80 Cnsl College Directions,LLC -1010 Nrthrn Blvd -Gt Neck 11021 **Fx:**336-2559
(212) 340-0400 .. **Goldberg,** Elena M '07 %Appllt Div 1st Dept -27 Mad Av -NY 10010 **Fx:**889-4412
(212) 541-2000 .. **Goldberg,** Elizabeth J '97 %Bryan C LLP -1290 Av of Amer -NY 10104
(212) 687-5066 .. **Goldberg,** Eric A '04 (Kahn & G,LLP) -708 3rd Av -NY 10017 **Fx:**983-8415
(212) 451-2300 .. **Goldberg,** Eric L '79 (Olshan GFR&W LLP) -65 E 55th -NY 10022
(516) 294-8844 .. **Goldberg,** Eugene H '75 OfCnsl L'Abbate BC&C,LLP -1001 Franklin Av -Gdn Cty 11530
(212) 750-1200 .. **Goldberg,** Evan M '89 (Trolman G&L,PC) -777 3rd Av -NY 10017
(212) 983-1077 .. **Goldberg & Fliegel LLP** -60 E 42nd -NY 10165 **Fx:**973-9577
(212) 488-1200 .. **Goldberg,** Geoffrey L '01 Kobre & K,LLP -800 3rd Av -NY 10022
(212) 592-1413 .. **Goldberg,** Geoffrey R '95 Herrick,F LLP -2 Park Av -NY 10016
(516) 742-2100 .. **Goldberg,** Gerald '79 -1000 Franklin Av -Gdn Cty 11530
(315) 677-9252 .. **Goldberg,** Gerald A '63 -2950 Eager Rd -LaFayette 13084
(212) 446-7000 .. **Goldberg,** Guy J '03 %McKinsey & Co -55 E 52nd -NY 10055 **Fx:**688-9521
(315) 637-4372 .. **Goldberg,** Harold P '63 -201 Summerhaven S -E Syracuse 13057
(201) 236-3420 .. **Goldberg,** Harriet L '80 Pearson Edu,Inc -1330 Av of Amer -NY 10019 **Fx:**818-8749
(212) 733-7400 .. **Goldberg,** Heather C '02 %Pfizer Inc -235 E 42nd -NY 10017
(516) 764-2800 .. **Goldberg,** Henry L '75 (Goldberg & C) -66 N Vllg Av -Rockvll Ctr 11570
(718) 270-3741 .. **Goldberg,** Herbert '86 SUNY Hlth Science Ctr -450 Clarkson Av -Brklyn 11203
(215) 981-4955 .. **Goldberg,** Howard S '01 (Pepper H LLP) -620 8th Av -NY 10018 **Fx:**981-4750
(212) 272-2762 .. **Goldberg,** I Ira '96 %JP Morgan Chase -383 Mad Av -NY 10179
(516) 735-3100 .. **Goldberg,** Ira Lawr '96 (IL Goldberg,PC) -125 Jerusalem Av -Hicksvll 11801 **Fx:**735-3105
(212) 697-3250 .. **Goldberg,** Israel '82 (Goldberg & R PLLC) -115 Bway -NY 10006 **Fx:**227-4533
(212) 227-1900 .. **Goldberg,** Jack G '67 (J Goldberg & Assoc) -225 Bway -NY 10007 **Fx:**227-2736
(212) 416-6133 .. **Goldberg,** Jane R '01 %Dept of Law -120 Bway -NY 10271
(516) 277-7700 .. **Goldberg,** Janet Ann '90 %North Shore School Dist -112 Franklin Av -Sea Cliff 11579
(212) 859-8000 .. **Goldberg,** Janice I '07 %Fried FHS&J LLP -1 NY Plz -NY 10004
(212) 776-5000 .. **Goldberg,** Jason E '01 %NYC Housing Auth -250 Bway -NY 10007 **Fx:**776-5039
(516) 222-0422 .. **Goldberg,** Jason S '93 (Goldberg & G,PC) -20 Crsswys Park N -Woodbury 11797 **Fx:**222-2773
(212) 983-6000 .. **Goldberg,** Jay '57 J Goldberg,PC -250 Park Av -NY 10177 **Fx:**983-6008
(212) 344-1048 .. **Goldberg,** Jay Arthur '67 -42 Bway -NY 10004
(212) 766-3366 .. **Goldberg,** Jay K '83 (Goldberg & A) -49 W 37th -NY 10018 **Fx:**221-6867
(718) 254-7000 .. **Goldberg,** Jeffrey A '99 %US Atty -271 Cadman Plz E -Brklyn 11201 **Fx:**254-6479
(212) 947-3793 .. **Goldberg,** Jeffrey C '95 (Sadis & G LLP) -551 5th Av -NY 10176
(516) 775-9400 .. **Goldberg,** Jeffrey L '75 (Jeffrey Goldberg,PC) -2001 Marcus Av -Lk Success 11042 **Fx:**775-4477
(914) 682-2175 .. **Goldberg,** Jeffrey S '78 -50 Main -White Plns 10606 **Fx:**769-0198
(516) 560-6400 .. **Goldberg,** Jeremy L '88 %Leg Aid -1 Helen Keller Way -Hempstd 11550 **Fx:**565-3694
(212) 801-9209 .. **Goldberg,** Jerrold F '80 (Greenberg T,LLP) -200 Park Av -NY 10166
(212) 806-5400 .. **Goldberg,** Joel H '71 (Stroock &S&L LLP) -180 Maiden Ln -NY 10038
(212) 773-3813 .. **Goldberg,** Joli K '96 Ernst & Young LLP -5 Times Sq -NY 10036
(212) 218-5500 .. **Goldberg,** Jonathan E '96 (Seyfarth S LLP) -620 8th Av -NY 10018
(917) 637-3600 .. **Goldberg,** Jordan R '08 %Ctr for Reproductive Rts -120 Wall -NY 10005 **Fx:**637-3666
(212) 751-4300 .. **Goldberg,** Jos P '92 (Hodgson R LLP) -1540 Bway -NY 10036
(212) 336-2000 .. **Goldberg,** Joshua A '98 Cnsl Patterson BW&T LLP -1133 Av of Amer -NY 10036
(212) 260-6717 .. **Goldberg,** Joshua Rabb '85 -305 2nd Av -NY 10003
(516) 621-0311 .. **Goldberg,** Judith P '00 -86 The Serpentine -Roslyn 11576
(212) 692-1000 .. **Goldberg,** Jules E '71 (Duane M LLP) -1540 Bway -NY 10036
(212) 372-1340 .. **Goldberg,** Karen L '93 RSM McGladrey -1185 Av of Amer -NY 10036
(212) 742-8700 .. **Goldberg,** Katherine R '05 %Garson D&C LLP -110 Wall -NY 10005
(212) 983-1077 .. **Goldberg,** Kenneth A '92 (Goldberg & F LLP) -60 E 42nd -NY 10165
(516) 498-2438 .. **Goldberg,** Kenneth B '93 %1st Quality Enterprises -80 Cuttermill Rd -Gt Neck 11021
(212) 968-2300 .. **Goldberg,** Kenneth D '75 -39 Bway -NY 10006 **Fx:**968-2400
(716) 853-9555 .. **Goldberg,** Kenneth L '85 %Leg Aid -237 Main -Buffalo 14203 **Fx:**853-3219
(212) 661-5306 .. **Goldberg,** Lauren '00 OfCnsl I Wallace,PLLC -501 5th Av -NY 10017
(212) 637-1040 .. **Goldberg,** Lauren R '95 %US Atty -1 St Andrews Plz -NY 10007
(718) 722-6450 .. **Goldberg,** Lawr A '84 %Appllt Div 2nd Dept -45 Monroe Pl -Brklyn 11201 **Fx:**855-3293
(212) 252-8300 .. **Goldberg,** Lawr B '67 -220 5th Av -NY 10001 **Fx:**252-8866
(212) 756-2000 .. **Goldberg,** Lawr S '80 (Schulte R&Z LLP) -919 3rd Av -NY 10022
(646) 878-0800 .. **Goldberg,** Lee '91 (Pearl CZL,LLP) -1500 Bway -NY 10036
(212) 310-8000 .. **Goldberg,** Lee J '09 %Weil G&M LLP -767 5th Av -NY 10153
(212) 464-1255 .. **Goldberg,** Lesley E '79 JP Morgan Chase & Co -345 Park Av -NY 10154
(212) 867-9595 .. **Goldberg,** Lewis S '85 (Goldberg and W) -630 3rd Av -NY 10017
(845) 291-2050 .. **Goldberg,** Lorri Beth '99 %DA -255-275 Main -Goshen 10924 **Fx:**291-2085
(212) 592-1400 .. **Goldberg,** Louis '91 (Herrick,F LLP) -2 Park Av -NY 10016
(212) 450-4000 .. **Goldberg,** Louis L '91 (Davis P&W LLP) -450 Lex Av -NY 10017
(212) 615-8719 .. **Goldberg,** Louis M '97 %Citigroup -333 W 34th -NY 10001
(516) 496-5822 .. **Goldberg,** Marc D '02 %T Spina -170 Froehlich Farm Blvd -Woodbury 11797 **Fx:**496-5420
(518) 472-1224 .. **Goldberg,** Marc H '88 %Phillips L LLP -30 S Pearl -Albany 12207
(914) 949-5400 .. **Goldberg,** Marc Stuart '75 (MS Goldberg,LLC) -81 Main -White Plns 10601 **Fx:**683-1279
(914) 690-0800 .. **Goldberg,** Mark E '84 -130 N Main -Pt Chester 10573 **Fx:**937-1386
(914) 468-0829 .. **Goldberg,** Mark H '70 (Goldberg & P) -600 Mamaroneck Av -Harrison 10528 **Fx:**468-0870
(212) 407-4000 .. **Goldberg,** Mark J '93 (Loeb & L,LLP) -345 Park Av -NY 10154
(212) 244-9500 .. **Goldberg,** Marlene R '90 %White and W LLP -1 Penn Plz -NY 10119
(516) 328-9500 .. **Goldberg,** Martin B '79 (Bruno G&V) -99 Tulip Av -Floral Pk 11001 **Fx:**775-8326
(516) 292-0380 .. **Goldberg,** Martin G '75 -672 Dogwood Av -Franklin Sq 11010 **Fx:**292-0380
(212) 300-1391 .. **Goldberg,** Martin M '97 York Capital Mgmt -767 5th Av -NY 10153 **Fx:**300-1301
(845) 343-5131 .. **Goldberg,** Martin R '70 -225 Dolson Av Bx2083 -Middletwn 10940 **Fx:**344-5547
(718) 585-6144 .. **Goldberg,** Marvin E '62 -272 E 149th -Bronx 10451 **Fx:**585-0048
(212) 416-8296 .. **Goldberg,** Melvin L '80 Dept of Law -120 Bway -NY 10271
(212) 751-3939 .. **Goldberg,** Michl B '74 %Kelso & Co -320 Park Av -NY 10022 **Fx:**223-2379
(212) 421-4100 .. **Goldberg,** Michl G '94 (Pryor C LLP) -7 Times Sq -NY 10036
(212) 424-0100 .. **Goldberg,** Michl H '67 %Natl Media Grp -535 5th Av -NY 10017 **Fx:**867-1116
(212) 481-0011 .. **Goldberg,** Michl M '95 (M Goldberg,PC) -31 E 32nd -NY 10016 **Fx:**481-4144
(718) 858-4250 .. **Goldberg,** Michl P '80 (Goldberg & L) -188 Montague -Brklyn 11201 **Fx:**522-2645
(212) 983-1077 .. **Goldberg,** Michele L '90 (Goldberg & F LLP) -60 E 42nd -NY 10165
(212) 983-1221 .. **Goldberg,** Mitchell D '89 (Ochs & G,LLP) -60 E 42nd -NY 10165
(914) 375-0100 .. **Goldberg,** Morton '78 %Novick ELRW&L,PC -733 Ynkrs Av -Ynkrs 10704
(212) 790-9200 .. **Goldberg,** Morton D '55 OfCnsl Cowan L&L,PC -1133 Av of Amer -NY 10036
(212) 660-3000 .. **Goldberg,** Nathan A '00 (Sullivan & W LLP) -1290 Av of Amer -NY 10104
(518) 446-0104 .. **Goldberg,** Nathan M '49 -175 Tampa Av -Albany 12208 **Fx:**482-6874
(716) 566-5400 .. **Goldberg,** Neil A '74 (Goldberg S LLP) -665 Main -Buffalo 14203
(646) 253-5400 .. **Goldberg,** Neil A '74 (Goldberg S LLP) -1200 Av of Amer -NY 10036
(212) 357-2713 .. **Goldberg,** Noah C '02 Goldman Sachs -1 NY Plz -NY 10004
(212) 969-3000 .. **Goldberg,** Nolan M '01 %Proskauer R LLP -1585 Bway -NY 10036
(516) 354-3600 .. **Goldberg,** Peter D '81 -249-02 Jericho Tpk -Floral Pk 11001
(845) 638-5328 .. **Goldberg,** Phyllis J '97 %Hon L Christopher -1 S Main -New Cty 10956
(718) 270-3768 .. **Goldberg,** Rachel W '86 SUNY Downstate Med Ctr -440 Lenox Rd DMC Bx 117 -Brklyn 11203
(585) 262-5100 .. **Goldberg,** Richd A '79 -1 E Main -Rchstr 14614
(212) 698-3500 .. **Goldberg,** Richd A '79 (Dechert LLP) -1095 Av of Amer -NY 10036
(516) 248-1700 .. **Goldberg,** Richd C '78 Cnsl Forchelli CDSM&T,LLP -333 Earle Ovngton Blvd -Uniondale 11553
(212) 969-3000 .. **Goldberg,** Richd L '60 (Proskauer R LLP) -1585 Bway -NY 10036
(718) 596-7800 .. **Goldberg,** Richd L '85 (Peters BK&G,PC) -26 Court -Brklyn 11242
(718) 875-2400 .. **Goldberg,** Richd S '68 (Goldberg & C LLP) -16 Court -Brklyn 11241
(212) 801-6848 .. **Goldberg,** Robt '08 %Greenberg T,LLP -200 Park Av -NY 10166
(914) 253-2366 .. **Goldberg,** Robt D '84 %Pepsico -700 Andrsn Hill Rd -Purchase 10577
(212) 425-9300 .. **Goldberg,** Robt E '78 (Bressler A&R,PC) -17 State -NY 10004
(212) 683-9559 .. **Goldberg,** Robt H '75 (Goldberg & C,PLLC) -31 E 32nd -NY 10016 **Fx:**683-7901
(212) 921-1600 .. **Goldberg,** Robt H '81 Goldberg SL&B,PC -45 W 45th -NY 10036
(212) 805-1683 .. **Goldberg,** Robt R '79 %Wells Fargo -530 5th Av -NY 10036
(516) 357-3000 .. **Goldberg,** Ryan C '05 %Rivkin R LLP -926 RXR Plz -Uniondale 11556
(212) 872-1000 .. **Goldberg,** Sagi '06 -One Bryant Park -NY 10036 **Fx:**872-1002
(212) 682-8070 .. **Goldberg,** Sanford B '63 -286 Mad Av (21 E 40th) -NY 10017 **Fx:**532-3454
(212) 903-8745 .. **Goldberg,** Sanford H '57 OfCnsl Roberts & H,LLP -825 8th Av -NY 10019
(516) 889-1107 .. **Goldberg,** Scott '91 (Goldberg & B,LLP) -138 E Park Av -Long Bch 11561
(212) 921-1600 .. **Goldberg Scudieri Lindenberg & Block,PC** -45 W 45th -NY 10036 **Fx:**840-3941
(716) 566-5400 .. **Goldberg Segalla LLP** -665 Main -Buffalo 14203 **Fx:**566-5401
(315) 413-5400 .. **Goldberg Segalla LLP** -5789 Widewaters Pkwy -Syracuse 13214 **Fx:**413-5401
(646) 253-5400 .. **Goldberg Segalla LLP** -1200 Av of Amer -NY 10036 **Fx:**253-5500

(585) 295-5400 .. **Goldberg Segalla LLP** -2 State -Rchstr 14614 **Fx:**295-8300
(914) 798-5400 .. **Goldberg Segalla LLP** -11 Martine Av -White Plns 10606 **Fx:**798-5401
(518) 463-5400 .. **Goldberg Segalla LLP** -8 Southwoods Blvd -Albany 12211 **Fx:**463-5420
(516) 281-9800 .. **Goldberg Segalla LLP** -200 Old Cntry Rd -Mineola 11501 **Fx:**281-9801
(212) 269-4900 .. **Goldberg,** Seth B '07 %Ford MEW&G,LLP -Wall Street Plz -NY 10005
(212) 532-0222 .. **Goldberg,** Seth J '06 %L Berger -200 Mad Av -NY 10016 **Fx:**532-0224
(212) 867-1200 .. **Goldberg,** Seth Z '96 %D Buchwald & Assoc -10 E 44th -NY 10017
(516) 222-0422 .. **Goldberg,** Seymour '66 (Goldberg & G,PC) -20 Crsswys Park N -Woodbury 11797 **Fx:**222-2773
(212) 337-2100 .. **Goldberg,** Stacy M '04 US Dept Labor-Solicitors Ofc -201 Varick -NY 10014
(212) 593-3000 .. **Goldberg,** Stan L '79 (Platzer SKLG&J,LLP) -1065 Av of Amer -NY 10018
(718) 649-6000 .. **Goldberg,** Stanley J '61 -8623 Flatlands Av -Brklyn 11236
(212) 248-9100 .. **Goldberg,** Stephen I '53 %Epstein M&M -1 Whitehall -NY 10004
(212) 573-6100 .. **Goldberg,** Steven D '95 Sitrick & Co -655 3rd Av -NY 10017
(845) 291-2050 .. **Goldberg,** Steven E '01 %DA -255-275 Main -Goshen 10924 **Fx:**291-2085
(212) 589-4200 .. **Goldberg,** Steven H '91 (Baker & H LLP) -45 Rckfllr Plz -NY 10111
(914) 422-4439 .. **Goldberg,** Steven H '91 %Pace Law Schl -78 N Bway -White Plns 10603 **Fx:**422-4039
(212) 845-5100 .. **Goldberg,** Steven R '84 -1 North End Av -NY 10282 **Fx:**845-5102
(212) 819-8200 .. **Goldberg,** Steven R '06 %White & C LLP -1155 Av of Amer -NY 10036
(212) 426-9444 .. **Goldberg,** Susan A '73 -200 E 89th -NY 10128 **Fx:**426-9445
(212) 854-0411 .. **Goldberg,** Suzanne B '91 %Columbia Law Schl -435 W 116th -NY 10027 **Fx:**854-7946
(646) 855-0812 .. **Goldberg,** Tamira M '03 Bank of America -1 Bryant Park -NY 10036
(212) 297-5800 .. **Goldberg,** Thos D '80 (Day P LLP) -7 Times Sq -NY 10036
(917) 454-1100 .. **Goldberg,** Todd M '96 %Police Dept -2 Lafayette -NY 10007
(212) 867-9595 .. **Goldberg and Weinberger** -630 3rd Av -NY 10017 **Fx:**949-1857
(212) 558-4000 .. **Goldberg,** Wendy M '02 SpclCnsl Sullivan & C LLP -125 Broad -NY 10004
(212) 221-5700 .. **Goldberg Weprin Finkel Goldstein LLP** -1501 Bway -NY 10036 **Fx:**730-4518
(212) 986-1000 .. **Goldberg,** Zachary S '85 (Goldberg C&G,LLP) -331 Mad Av -NY 10017 **Fx:**986-8039
(212) 788-0758 .. **Goldberg-Cahn,** Michele L '01 %Law Dept -100 Church -NY 10007 **Fx:**788-0367
(518) 393-3688 .. **Goldberger,** Alfred L '58 -224 State -Schnctdy 12305 **Fx:**831-9038
(518) 382-5073 .. **Goldberger,** Alfred L '58 (Law Dept) -201 City Hall -Schnctdy 12305 **Fx:**382-5074
(212) 756-2000 .. **Goldberger,** Alon M '08 %Schulte R&Z LLP -919 3rd Av -NY 10022
(212) 837-6000 .. **Goldberger,** Bruce N '97 Cnsl Hughes H&R LLP -1 Bttry Pk Plz -NY 10004
(518) 436-8313 .. **Goldberger,** Bryan J '85 (Goldberger & K) -39 N Pearl -Albany 12207 **Fx:**436-8316
(914) 949-6400 .. **Goldberger,** Chas A '64 (McCullough G&S,LLP) -1311 Mamaroneck Av -White Plns 10605
(212) 479-6000 .. **Goldberger,** Danl A '94 SpclCnsl Cooley LLP -1114 Av of Amer -NY 10036
(212) 969-3000 .. **Goldberger,** Danl P '08 %Proskauer R LLP -1585 Bway -NY 10036
(914) 949-6400 .. **Goldberger,** Deborah A '02 %McCullough G&S,LLP -1311 Mamaroneck Av -White Plns 10605
(212) 431-9380 .. **Goldberger & Dubin, PC** -401 Bway -NY 10013 **Fx:**966-0588
(518) 434-1300 .. **Goldberger,** Franklin H '72 (Jackson L LLP) -18 Corp Wds Blvd -Albany 12211
(516) 222-6200 .. **Goldberger,** Gena '06 %Berkman HPP&F,PC -100 Grdn City Plz -Gdn Cty 11530
(518) 402-9003 .. **Goldberger,** Helene G '83 DEC -625 Bway -Albany 12233 **Fx:**402-9016
(718) 254-7000 .. **Goldberger,** Michl J '88 %US Atty -271 Cadman Plz E -Brklyn 11201 **Fx:**254-6479
(212) 431-9380 .. **Goldberger,** Paul A '66 (Goldberger & D,PC) -401 Bway -NY 10013
(718) 513-3620 .. **Goldberger,** Peter '07 %W Schneider & Assoc,PC -1400 Av Z -Brklyn 11235
(212) 909-6000 .. **Goldberger,** Richd J '09 %Debevoise & P LLP -919 3rd Av -NY 10022
(212) 681-9101 .. **Goldbergh,** Theo A '82 (T Goldbergh,PC) -305 Bway -NY 10007 **Fx:**822-1407
(212) 756-2000 .. **Goldberg Mintzer,** Jill '03 %Schulte R&Z LLP -919 3rd Av -NY 10022
(212) 816-3176 .. **Goldblat,** Harris C '96 %Citigroup -388 Greenwich -NY 10013
(212) 975-3596 .. **Goldblatt,** Grace R '78 CBS Inc -51 W 52nd -NY 10019 **Fx:**975-3930
(212) 373-3000 .. **Goldblatt,** Hallie S '06 %Paul WRW&G LLP -1285 Av of Amer -NY 10019
(212) 974-7474 .. **Goldblatt,** Hayden M '09 OfCnsl Cowan DA&S LLP -41 Mad Av -NY 10010
(212) 436-2236 .. **Goldblatt,** Jonathan M '98 Deloitte & Touche,LLP -2 World Fncl Ctr -NY 10281
(212) 635-1575 .. **Goldblatt,** Jonathan R '94 Bk of NY Mellon -1 Wall -NY 10286
(718) 993-9999 .. **Goldblatt,** Joshua '07 %J Oresky & Assoc,PLLC -155 E 149th -Bronx 10451 **Fx:**993-0142
(212) 450-4000 .. **Goldblatt,** Justin '06 %Davis P&W LLP -450 Lex Av -NY 10017
(914) 788-5000 .. **Goldblatt,** Kenneth B '89 (Goldblatt & Assoc,PC) -1846 E Main -Mohegan Lk 10547 **Fx:**526-7800
(716) 853-8100 .. **Goldblatt,** Saml '78 (Nixon P LLP) -40 Fountain Plz -Buffalo 14202
(718) 797-4311 .. **Goldblatt,** Stephen '91 (S Goldblatt,PC) -26 Court -Brklyn 11242 **Fx:**797-9080
(718) 898-7459 .. **Goldblum,** A Paul '51 -34-21 80th -Jcksn Hts 11372 **Fx:**898-7459
(212) 766-6300 .. **Goldblum,** Victor '91 (Eiges G&B,LLP) -225 Bway -NY 10007 **Fx:**233-5633
(718) 590-2000 .. **Goldbrenner,** Barry A '08 DA -198 E 161st -Bronx 10451 **Fx:**590-6477
(212) 225-2000 .. **Goldbrenner,** Rachel A '09 %Cleary GS&H -1 Lbrty Plz -NY 10006
(212) 358-1996 .. **Goldbrenner,** Ronald S '66 -104 Pierrepont -Brklyn 11201 **Fx:**(413) 254-6134
(212) 302-9400 .. **Goldburd,** Jos '76 (Goldburd M LLP) -42 W 38th -NY 10018 **Fx:**302-8973
(212) 302-9400 .. **Goldburd,** Steven '07 (Goldburd M LLP) -42 W 38th -NY 10018 **Fx:**302-8973
(212) 577-3688 .. **Goldburg,** Bonnie B '90 %Leg Aid -199 Water -NY 10038 **Fx:**509-8431
(516) 571-3295 .. **Goldburg,** Chas R '76 %Supreme Ct -100 Supreme Ct Dr -Mineola 11501
(845) 306-1000 .. **Golde,** Karli R '04 %Watchtower -100 Watchtower Dr -Patterson 12563 **Fx:**306-0709
(212) 474-1000 .. **Golden,** Aaron M '09 %Cravath S&M LLP -825 8th Av -NY 10019
(212) 836-8000 .. **Golden,** Adam H '91 (Kaye S LLP) -425 Park Av -NY 10022
(212) 245-1000 .. **Golden,** Anne '79 (Outten & G LLP) -3 Park Av -NY 10016
(212) 450-4000 .. **Golden,** Arthur F '70 (Davis P&W LLP) -450 Lex Av -NY 10017
(212) 661-5123 .. **Golden,** Audrey S '68 %Audrey Golden Assoc -633 3rd Av -NY 10017 **Fx:**867-8068
(212) 536-3900 .. **Golden,** Beth L '98 (K&L Gates LLP) -599 Lex Av -NY 10022
(212) 949-9022 .. **Golden,** Constance '54 OfCnsl Abelman F&S -666 3rd Av -NY 10017
(212) 872-1000 .. **Golden,** Danl '78 -One Bryant Park -NY 10036 **Fx:**872-1002
(212) 949-6300 .. **Golden,** David K '88 %Golden & M,LLP -122 E 42nd -NY 10168
(212) 260-3636 .. **Golden,** Denise '90 Standard Realty -117 Waverly Pl -NY 10011
(585) 359-4859 .. **Golden,** Donna J '86 -118 Grdn Pkwy -Henrietta 14467
(212) 682-2300 .. **Golden,** Howard I '81 (H Golden,PC) -305 Mad Av -NY 10165 **Fx:**922-1353
(212) 345-4561 .. **Golden,** Howard J '75 %Mercer HR Cnsltng -1166 Av of Amer -NY 10036
(212) 825-1212 .. **Golden,** Jacquelyn L '07 %Morrison M LLP -17 State -NY 10004
(212) 669-4298 .. **Golden,** Jane F '89 %Pub Advocate's Ofc -1 Centre -NY 10007 **Fx:**669-4701
(212) 758-7288 .. **Golden,** Joanna L '82 -155 E 56th -NY 10022 **Fx:**826-3276
(212) 634-3326 .. **Golden,** John A '69 -12 E 49th -NY 10017
(212) 949-6300 .. **Golden,** Jonathan K '79 (Golden & M,LLP) -122 E 42nd -NY 10168
(631) 329-2828 .. **Golden,** Karen '96 (Egan & G,LLP) -393 Montauk Hwy Bx338 -Wainscott 11975 **Fx:**324-2472
(212) 345-6707 .. **Golden,** Kathleen M '89 Marsh Inc -1166 Av of Amer -NY 10036
(212) 983-3930 .. **Golden,** Keith M '93 MR Beal & Co -110 Wall -NY 10005 **Fx:**983-4539
(718) 739-2000 .. **Golden,** Kenneth E '87 -148-55 Hillside Av -Jamaica 11435 **Fx:**739-2426
(518) 457-4380 .. **Golden,** Kenneth L '77 Dept of Labor -State Campus Bldg 12 -Albany 12240 **Fx:**485-1819
(315) 732-5134 .. **Golden,** Lawr W '70 (Golden Law Firm) -1412 Genesee -Utica 13502 **Fx:**732-5161
(914) 241-1392 .. **Golden,** Leon S '70 -6 Height -Mt Kisco 10549
(516) 746-8000 .. **Golden,** Lisa M '93 (Jaspan S LLP) -300 Grdn City Plz -Gdn Cty 11530
(212) 949-6300 .. **Golden & Mandel, LLP** -122 E 42nd -NY 10168 **Fx:**949-6305
(917) 322-2382 .. **Golden,** Marc A '81 -445 Park Av -NY 10022
(914) 694-4444 .. **Golden,** Marc L '78 %Natl Rlty & Dvlpmnt -3 Manhattanvll Rd -Purchase 10577 **Fx:**694-5448
(212) 376-3052 .. **Golden,** Megan R '93 %Vera Inst of Justice -233 Bway -NY 10279 **Fx:**941-9407
(212) 451-2900 .. **Golden,** Michl B '77 (Robinson & C LLP) -885 3rd Av -NY 10022
(516) 747-6390 .. **Golden,** Patricia Bruno '91 -25 Downing -E Williston 11596 **Fx:**747-5143
(718) 788-5052 .. **Golden,** Paul R '95 %Hagan C & Assoc -908 4th Av -Brklyn 11232
(212) 859-8000 .. **Golden,** Peter S '81 (Fried FHS&J LLP) -1 NY Plz -NY 10004
(845) 294-4080 .. **Golden,** Richd B '81 (Burke M&G) -40 Matthews Bx216 -Goshen 10924
(718) 261-2600 .. **Golden,** Richd N '76 -118-35 Qns Blvd -Frst Hlls 11375 **Fx:**520-8544
(212) 262-5600 .. **Golden,** Richd N '87 Baltic Capital Mgmt -29 W 56th -NY 10019
(914) 723-4300 .. **Golden,** Robt B '93 %Lackenbach S LLP -1 Chase Rd -Scarsdale 10583
(212) 964-0120 .. **Golden Rothschild Spagnola Lundell Boylan & Garubo, PC** -111 John -NY 10038
(631) 694-2300 .. **Golden,** Saml H '66 OfCnsl Lamb & B,LLP -534 Broadhllw Rd Bx9034 -Melvll 11747
(212) 918-3000 .. **Golden,** Scott A '93 (Hogan L LLP) -875 3rd Av -NY 10022
(516) 292-8408 .. **Golden,** Stacey M '79 -165 Oak -W Hempstead 11552
(914) 422-4128 .. **Golden,** Stephanie A '02 %Pace Law Schl -78 N Bway -White Plns 10603 **Fx:**422-4039
(212) 298-5006 .. **Golden,** Steven I '70 %Leg Aid -49 Thomas -NY 10013 **Fx:**298-5252
(212) 668-5637 .. **Golden,** Susan D '88 %Hon P Abram -1 Bowling Grn -NY 10004
(212) 259-8000 .. **Golden,** Susan E '93 Cnsl Dewey & L LLP -1301 Av of Amer -NY 10019
(212) 728-8000 .. **Golden,** Thos H '92 (Willkie F&G LLP) -787 7th Av -NY 10019
(516) 745-6830 .. **Golden Wexler & Buatti PC** -900 Merchants Cncrs -Westbury 11590 **Fx:**745-6844
(212) 808-7992 .. **Golden,** Wm R Jr. '75 (Kelley D&W LLP) -101 Park Av -NY 10178
(212) 455-2000 .. **Golden,** Wm R '09 %Simpson T&B LLP -425 Lex Av -NY 10017
(212) 788-1275 .. **Goldenberg,** Abigail L '02 %Law Dept -100 Church -NY 10007 **Fx:**788-0367
(212) 819-8200 .. **Goldenberg,** Avi '02 %White & C LLP -1155 Av of Amer -NY 10036
(212) 408-4274 .. **Goldenberg,** Brandi M '99 Bnk of NY -1290 Av of Amer -NY 10104
(646) 557-8958 .. **Goldenberg,** C Martin '68 NewEdge USA,LLC -630 5th Av -NY 10111
(315) 345-0999 .. **Goldenberg,** Elizabeth M '84 -719 E Genesee -Syracuse 13210
(212) 545-8611 .. **Goldenberg,** Gloria E '92 OfCnsl Solomon & B -351 Bway -NY 10013
(914) 997-0999 .. **Goldenberg,** Ira S '81 -399 Knollwood Rd -White Plns 10603 **Fx:**682-1512
(212) 331-5140 .. **Goldenberg,** Jan '85 HRA-OLA -180 Water -NY 10038
(212) 656-2587 .. **Goldenberg,** Kendra P '06 NYSE Euronext -11 Wall -NY 10005
(212) 768-9790 .. **Goldenberg,** Robt S '89 (Haberman & G LLP) -1212 Av of Amer -NY 10036 **Fx:**768-9819
(212) 346-0600 .. **Goldenberg,** Stephen M '72 -277 Bway -NY 10007 **Fx:**964-8688

(718) 819-0740 .. **Goldenberg,** Steven P '73 -42-40 Bell Blvd -Bayside 11361 **Fx:**281-0850
(212) 909-5676 .. **Goldenstein,** Joanna '99 KPMG LLP -757 3rd Av -NY 10017
(646) 502-7001 .. **Goldenzweig,** Stephen W '10 %JSBarkats PLLC -100 Church -NY 10007 **Fx:**607-5544
(516) 944-5691 .. **Golder,** Arthur J III '87 (O'Connor & G) -24 N Wshngtn -Pt Wash 11050 **Fx:**944-5692
(516) 229-4400 .. **Golder,** Lynn '98 Cnsl Kay & G -875 Merrick Av -Westbury 11590
(518) 462-0110 .. **Golderman,** Wm P '88 (Sheehan GCG&J LLP) -54 State -Albany 12207
(212) 788-7000 .. **Goldey,** Mark H '97 City Cncl Leg Div -250 Bway -NY 10007 **Fx:**788-7034
(212) 385-4410 .. **Goldfaden,** Brielle C '09 %Gersowitz L&K,PC -111 Bway -NY 10006
(212) 977-9700 .. **Goldfaden,** Raymond W '63 Phillips N LLP -666 5th Av -NY 10103
(212) 387-8400 .. **Goldfarb Abrandt Salzman & Kutzin LLP** -350 5th Av -NY 10118 **Fx:**387-8404
(212) 259-8000 .. **Goldfarb,** Akiva M '07 %Dewey & L LLP -1301 Av of Amer -NY 10019
(212) 248-3977 .. **Goldfarb,** Bruce H '91 Georgeson Shareholder -17 State -NY 10004
(718) 250-2000 .. **Goldfarb,** Carolea '86 %DA -350 Jay -Brklyn 11201 **Fx:**250-2314
(212) 807-0820 .. **Goldfarb,** Carolyn S '80 -20 W 20th -NY 10011 **Fx:**807-0920
(718) 891-2900 .. **Goldfarb,** Chas '66 (Goldfarb & G) -2774 Coney Isl Av -Brklyn 11235 **Fx:**891-2950
(917) 778-6600 .. **Goldfarb,** Danl M '71 %J Toomey -485 Lex Av -NY 10017 **Fx:**778-7048
(212) 387-8400 .. **Goldfarb,** David '73 (Goldfarb AS&K LLP) -350 5th Av -NY 10118
(646) 610-5400 .. **Goldfarb,** David G '05 NYPD -1 Police Plz -NY 10038
(415) 675-3412 .. **Goldfarb,** Deborah Anne '05 %Bryan C LLP -1290 Av of Amer -NY 10104 **Fx:**675-3612
(212) 891-9100 .. **Goldfarb & Fleece LLP** -345 Park Av -NY 10154 **Fx:**751-3738
(212) 883-4900 .. **Goldfarb,** Gail '04 %Cozen O -277 Park Av -NY 10172
(212) 227-4242 .. **Goldfarb & Gerzog** -233 Bway -NY 10007 **Fx:**227-4233
(212) 307-5800 .. **Goldfarb,** Ira H '79 (Friedman LG&G,PC) -250 W 57th -NY 10107
(212) 326-3939 .. **Goldfarb,** James K '00 %Jones D -222 E 41st -NY 10017
(914) 328-8500 .. **Goldfarb,** Jason C '04 %Brecher FPWT&Z,PC -1 N Bway -White Plns 10601
(718) 497-4431 .. **Goldfarb,** Jason R '95 %Cooper Tank Corp -215 Moore -Brklyn 11206
(212) 403-0615 .. **Goldfarb,** Jeffrey D '03 G III Apparel Grp -512 7th Av -NY 10018
(845) 342-2207 .. **Goldfarb,** Jeffrey M '92 -138 W Main -Middletwn 10940
(212) 728-8000 .. **Goldfarb,** Jeffrey M '02 %Willkie F&G LLP -787 7th Av -NY 10019
(212) 475-0099 .. **Goldfarb,** Jessica E '90 -207 W 25th -NY 10001
(718) 740-4455 .. **Goldfarb,** Keith M '91 Parts Authority -211-10 Hillside Av -Qns Vllg 11427
(212) 483-9490 .. **Goldfarb,** Lewis H '01 OfCnsl McElroy DM&C,LLP -88 Pine -NY 10005
(561) 445-4066 .. **Goldfarb,** Lynda J '89 -111 Circle Dr -Roslyn Hts 11577
(631) 421-3107 .. **Goldfarb,** Marci S '89 (M Goldfarb,PC) -713 Walt Whitman Rd -Melvll 11747 **Fx:**614-5107
(212) 984-1850 .. **Goldfarb,** Mark J '78 -100 Park Av -NY 10017 **Fx:**(914) 271-5949
(212) 702-4361 .. **Goldfarb,** Matthew '98 Icahn Assoc Corp -767 5th Av -NY 10153
(212) 962-2626 .. **Goldfarb,** Michl J '93 M Seitelman -111 Bway -NY 10006 **Fx:**962-5050
(212) 859-8000 .. **Goldfarb,** Murray J '01 (Fried FHS&J LLP) -1 NY Plz -NY 10004
(212) 588-5500 .. **Goldfarb,** Pamela L '01 %Davies WP&V LLP -625 Mad Av -NY 10022
(718) 448-7400 .. **Goldfarb,** Randy A '80 -1267 Forest Av -Staten Isl 10302 **Fx:**448-1141
(518) 473-6053 .. **Goldfarb,** Robt M '93 %Dept of Law -The Cptl -Albany 12224 **Fx:**486-3176
(212) 760-2222 .. **Goldfarb,** Robyn S '98 %Kolenovsky & S,LLP -135 W 29th -NY 10001
(212) 219-9614 .. **Goldfarb,** Scott A '86 -366 W Bway -NY 10013
(914) 241-2470 .. **Goldfarb,** Shara H '98 -487 E Main -Mt Kisco 10549 **Fx:**470-1099
(212) 227-4242 .. **Goldfarb,** Steven M '86 (Goldfarb & G) -233 Bway -NY 10007
(212) 506-5000 .. **Goldfarb,** Stuart R '99 Orrick H&S LLP -51 W 52nd -NY 10019
(212) 806-5400 .. **Goldfeder,** Jerry H '80 SpclCnsl Stroock &S&L LLP -180 Maiden Ln -NY 10038
(718) 520-3804 .. **Goldfeder,** Pamela S '92 Probation Dept -125-01A Qns Blvd -Kew Gdns 11415
(212) 885-5000 .. **Goldfeder,** Steven W '91 (Blank R LLP) -405 Lex Av -NY 10174
(516) 739-7110 .. **Goldfeder,** Yoel '99 Natl Info Resrcs -1044 Nrthrn Blvd -Roslyn 11576
(212) 440-4300 .. **Goldfein,** Joshua E '94 Leg Aid -199 Water -NY 10292
(212) 891-4067 .. **Goldfein,** Laurence '60 (Eisner LLP) -750 3rd Av -NY 10017 **Fx:**891-4100
(212) 461-2323 .. **Goldfein,** Morton J '82 OfCnsl Saiber LLC -44 Wall -NY 10005
(212) 909-6000 .. **Goldfein,** Sarah Y '10 %Debevoise & P LLP -919 3rd Av -NY 10022
(212) 735-3000 .. **Goldfein,** Shepard '76 (Skadden ASM&F LLP) -4 Times Sq -NY 10036
(212) 818-1110 .. **Goldfeld,** Orlee '00 %Butzel L,PC -380 Mad Av -NY 10017
(212) 403-1000 .. **Goldfeld,** Victor '04 %Wachtell LR&K -51 W 52nd -NY 10019
(212) 969-3000 .. **Goldfield,** Herschel '95 SrCnsl Proskauer R LLP -1585 Bway -NY 10036
(212) 813-8800 .. **Goldfine,** Emily R '08 %Goodwin P LLP -620 8th Av -NY 10018
(212) 764-4222 .. **Goldfinger,** Desiree '98 %S Jeffries & Assoc -1560 Bway -NY 10036 **Fx:**764-4229
(212) 261-7000 .. **Goldfinger,** Dina '91 %Calyon -1301 Av of Amer -NY 10019
(212) 617-2984 .. **Goldfinger,** Elizabeth M '09 %Bloomberg LLP -731 Lex Av -NY 10022
(212) 695-5670 .. **Goldfinger & Lassar LLP** -750 3rd Av -NY 10017 **Fx:**485-5501
(212) 227-4530 .. **Goldfinger,** Scott G '93 %O'Rourke & D,PLLC -225 Bway -NY 10007
(212) 436-3610 .. **Goldfischer,** Stephanie A '96 Deloitte & Touche LLP -2 World Fncl Ctr -NY 10281
(212) 299-2000 .. **Goldfisher,** Danl M '99 NYMEX -1 North End Av -NY 10282 **Fx:**301-4700
(212) 250-0240 .. **Goldfrank,** Arthur L '94 %Deutsche Bk Sec -60 Wall -NY 10005
(212) 670-2271 .. **Goldfried,** Danl A '04 Merrill Lynch -222 Bway -NY 10038
(718) 768-3046 .. **Goldhaber,** Oren L '08 %N Kupferman -459 6th Av -Brklyn 11215 **Fx:**768-7645
(631) 979-8500 .. **Goldhaber,** Richd F '67 OfCnsl Rosenthal & G,PC -1393 Vets Mem'l Hwy -Hauppauge 11788
(631) 979-8500 .. **Goldhaber,** Robt D '92 (Rosenthal & G,PC) -1393 Vets Mem'l Hwy -Hauppauge 11788
(212) 226-6624 .. **Goldhaber,** Robt M '86 (Goldhaber W&G) -305 Bway -NY 10007 **Fx:**226-7956
(212) 226-6624 .. **Goldhaber,** Stanley '53 (Goldhaber W&G) -305 Bway -NY 10007 **Fx:**226-7956
(845) 356-2570 .. **Goldhamer,** Paul B '75 (Kantrowitz G&G,PC) -747 Chestnut Rdg Rd -Chestnut Rdg 10977
(845) 624-2727 .. **Goldheim,** Laurie B '91 -55 Old Tpk Rd -Nanuet 10954
(718) 233-6480 .. **Goldhill,** Nancy '81 Leg Srvcs for NYC -36 Richmond Ter -Staten Isl 10301 **Fx:**448-2264
(212) 558-5500 .. **Goldhirsch,** Lawr B '70 OfCnsl Weitz & L,PC -700 Bway -NY 10003
(212) 818-9200 .. **Goldie,** Robt H '70 (Satterlee SB&B LLP) -230 Park Av -NY 10169
(315) 386-8544 .. **Goldie,** Scott B '91 (Conboy MB&K,LLP) -2 Judson -Canton 13617
(212) 571-7111 .. **Goldin,** Alexander '96 (Goldin & R LLC) -225 Bway -NY 10007 **Fx:**571-3211
(518) 626-0347 .. **Goldin,** David N '73 -39 N Pearl -Albany 12207 **Fx:**432-6248
(212) 593-2255 .. **Goldin,** Harrison '61 %Goldin Assoc -350 5th Av -NY 10118 **Fx:**888-2841
(347) 528-0300 .. **Goldin,** Jonathan D '09 -2605 Av R -Brklyn 11229
(212) 403-1000 .. **Goldin,** Jonathan E '05 %Wachtell LR&K -51 W 52nd -NY 10019
(212) 751-2600 .. **Goldin,** Laura A '92 %Random House -1745 Bway -NY 10019
(212) 455-2000 .. **Goldin,** Nicholas S '00 Cnsl Simpson T&B LLP -425 Lex Av -NY 10017
(516) 248-0318 .. **Goldin,** Stefani '94 -120 Front Bx30 -Mineola 11501 **Fx:**742-3987
(212) 440-4300 .. **Goldiner,** Judith '89 %Leg Aid -199 Water -NY 10038
(212) 448-4802 .. **Golding,** Frank J '94 %ESPN,Inc -19 E34th -NY 10016 **Fx:**448-4809
(212) 385-2417 .. **Golding,** Kevin S '99 (Golding & Assoc,PLLC) -299 Bway -NY 10007 **Fx:**385-2418
(212) 559-6608 .. **Golding,** Paul W '01 Citi Alternative Invstmnts -731 Lex Av -NY 10022
(718) 227-5260 .. **Golding,** Wm J '06 -1110 South Av -Staten Isl 10314
(516) 227-3344 .. **Goldinger,** Cary Scott '81 -400 Grdn City Plz -Gdn Cty 11530 **Fx:**227-3351
(212) 230-8800 .. **Goldis,** Michelle A '07 %WilmerHale -399 Park Av -NY 10022
(516) 877-5600 .. **Goldklang,** Beth Ann '93 %R Tusa -1225 Franklin Av -Gdn Cty 11530 **Fx:**877-5695
(914) 997-0500 .. **Goldklang,** Michl D '09 %Lowey DC&H,PC -1 N Bway -White Plns 10601
(914) 381-6700 .. **Goldklang,** Sheldon '74 Cnsl Judicial Title -800 Wstchstr Av -Rye Brook 10573
(212) 558-6668 .. **Goldkrand,** Betsy Baron '98 %Foley SO&W -100 William -NY 10038
(516) 997-5553 .. **Goldmacher,** Beth J '76 (Faden & G) -576 Salisbury Pk Dr -Westbury 11590
(718) 590-3771 .. **Goldman,** Adam L '00 NYS Sup Ct-Bronx Cnty -851 Grnd Cncrs -Bronx 10451 **Fx:**590-8914
(516) 354-0257 .. **Goldman,** Alan B '84 -444 Merrick Rd -Lynbrk 11563 **Fx:**354-0837
(212) 628-5968 .. **Goldman,** Alan V '83 -301 E 64th Apt 6H -NY 10065
(212) 768-6700 .. **Goldman,** Alvin J '71 (Sonnenschein N&R LLP) -2 World Fncl Ctr -NY 10281
(212) 230-8836 .. **Goldman,** Andrew N '93 (WilmerHale) -399 Park Av -NY 10022
(646) 872-9601 .. **Goldman,** Andrew P '02 Mr G Productions LLC -546 E 11th -NY 10009
(212) 701-3000 .. **Goldman,** Ariel '09 %Cahill G&R LLP -80 Pine -NY 10005 **Fx:**269-5420
(585) 244-4998 .. **Goldman,** Arnold J '56 -3 Leeward Ln -Rchstr 14618 **Fx:**442-5544
(212) 218-5500 .. **Goldman,** Arren S '99 %Seyfarth S LLP -620 8th Av -NY 10018
(914) 963-2799 .. **Goldman,** Arthur '60 -57 Wellesley Av -Ynkrs 10705
(914) 332-9770 .. **Goldman,** Bernard P '94 Liberty Mutual Ins Co -520 Wht Plns Rd -Tarrytwn 10591
(212) 637-2732 .. **Goldman,** Beth E '89 %US Atty -86 Chmbrs -NY 10007
(212) 617-5621 .. **Goldman,** Betsy A '09 Bloomberg LP -731 Lex Av -NY 10022
(516) 773-8585 .. **Goldman,** Brian S '86 (Goldman & M,LLP) -475 Nrthrn Blvd -Gt Neck 11021
(585) 753-4500 .. **Goldman,** Bruce H '73 %DA -832 Watts Bldg -Rchstr 14614 **Fx:**753-4576
(212) 547-5400 .. **Goldman,** C David '97 (McDermott W&E LLP) -340 Mad Av -NY 10173
(212) 370-1344 .. **Goldman,** Carmen Fernandez '89 -386 Park Av S -NY 10016 **Fx:**370-1435
(212) 836-1755 .. **Goldman,** Chas Ben '79 UJA-Federation -130 E 59th -NY 10022 **Fx:**888-7538
(212) 534-4038 .. **Goldman,** Chas N '56 -139 E 94th -NY 10128 **Fx:**534-3291
(212) 848-4000 .. **Goldman,** Curt E '06 %Shearman & S LLP -599 Lex Av -NY 10022
(212) 318-6000 .. **Goldman,** Danl B '88 (Paul HJ&W LLP) -75 E 55th -NY 10022
(845) 215-9430 .. **Goldman,** Danl R '68 (Krakower & G) -55 Old Tpk Rd -Nanuet 10954
(212) 637-2289 .. **Goldman,** Danl S '06 US Atty -1 St Andrews Plz -NY 10007
(212) 715-9100 .. **Goldman,** Darius J '07 %Kramer LN&F,LLP -1177 Av of Amer -NY 10036
(518) 449-0044 .. **Goldman,** David C '92 Cnsl Hoffman W&D LLC -75 State -Albany 12207 **Fx:**449-0047
(212) 798-6079 .. **Goldman,** David M '92 Fortress Invest Grp -1345 Av of Americas -NY 10105
(631) 549-4677 .. **Goldman,** David M '96 %Sobel K&S,PC -464 NY Av -Huntngtn 11743
(212) 735-3000 .. **Goldman,** David R '09 %Skadden ASM&F LLP -4 Times Sq -NY 10036
(516) 294-5775 .. **Goldman,** Davin '04 %Klee & W,LLP -350 Willis Av -Mineola 11501
(516) 622-2230 .. **Goldman,** Deborah L '93 D Goldman,PLLC -1979 Marcus Av -Lk Success 11042 **Fx:**706-0887
(516) 935-1144 .. **Goldman,** Donald H '68 (Snowe & G) -382 S Oyster Bay Rd -Hicksvll 11801 **Fx:**935-8193
(518) 454-9353 .. **Goldman,** Douglas L '96 -18 Corp Wds Blvd -Albany 12211 **Fx:**514-1259

(212) 684-3030 .. **Goldman,** Dov '97 Everest Abstract Srvcs LLC -152 Mad Av -NY 10016
(212) 791-1275 .. **Goldman,** Eleanor R '78 (Goldman & G) -401 1st Av -NY 10010
(212) 867-7600 .. **Goldman,** Eliot '84 -501 5th Av -NY 10017 **Fx:**682-5511
(212) 790-0200 .. **Goldman,** Elizabeth '92 Benj N Cardozo Schl of Law -55 5th Av -NY 10003 **Fx:**790-0345
(212) 374-2995 .. **Goldman,** Emily R '03 Bd of Ed-OLS -52 Chmbrs -NY 10007
(718) 250-2000 .. **Goldman,** Eric C '08 %DA -350 Jay -Brklyn 11201 **Fx:**250-2314
(212) 840-6400 .. **Goldman,** Eric S '91 %Sendroff & B,LLP -1500 Bway -NY 10036 **Fx:**840-6401
(212) 450-4000 .. **Goldman,** Ethan R '09 %Davis P&W LLP -450 Lex Av -NY 10017
(914) 428-6565 .. **Goldman,** Gary D '89 (Fentin & G,LLP) -44 S Bway -White Plns 10601
(212) 848-4000 .. **Goldman,** Geoffrey B '97 (Shearman & S LLP) -599 Lex Av -NY 10022
(212) 644-1710 .. **Goldman,** Gerald '87 (Winne BH&B,PC) -286 Mad Av -NY 10017
(212) 980-6777 .. **Goldman,** Gilbert M '62 -515 Mad Av -NY 10022
(212) 953-9500 .. **Goldman & Greenbaum,PC** -60 E 42nd -NY 10165 **Fx:**953-9660
(212) 791-1275 .. **Goldman & Grossman** -401 1st Av -NY 10010 **Fx:**587-1532
(516) 228-0348 .. **Goldman Horowitz & Cherno,LLP** -47 Post Av -Westbury 11590 **Fx:**228-0347
(212) 935-1622 .. **Goldman,** Howard J '77 (Goldman H LLC) -475 Park Av S -NY 10016 **Fx:**935-2651
(212) 388-1112 .. **Goldman,** Jacob J '99 -563 Grand -NY 10002 **Fx:**388-1114
(516) 873-8587 .. **Goldman,** Jan D '82 (Goldman & Assoc) -100 Ring Rd W -Gdn Cty 11530 **Fx:**873-8535
(718) 466-3000 .. **Goldman,** Janet L '85 %Civil Ct -1118 Grnd Cncrs -Bronx 10456 **Fx:**466-3006
(212) 222-0872 .. **Goldman,** Jean R '70 -400 Cntrl Pk W -NY 10025 **Fx:**222-0872
(212) 983-8999 .. **Goldman,** Jeffrey E '99 -501 5th Av -NY 10017 **Fx:**949-5085
(212) 867-4466 .. **Goldman,** Jeffrey L '84 (Belkin BW&G,LLP) -270 Mad Av -NY 10016
(212) 265-2171 .. **Goldman,** Jeffrey M '79 %Solil Mgmt -640 5th Av -NY 10019 **Fx:**265-1669
(914) 995-3639 .. **Goldman,** Jeffrey P '94 %Cnty Atty -148 Martine Av -White Plns 10601 **Fx:**995-5858
(212) 980-0120 .. **Goldman,** Jeremy S '06 %Frankfurt KK&S,PC -488 Mad Av -NY 10022
(585) 641-8000 .. **Goldman,** Jerry A '80 (Fix SB&G,PC) -295 Woodcliff Dr -Fairprt 14450
(212) 278-1000 .. **Goldman,** Jerry S '77 (Anderson K&O,PC) -1251 Av of Amer -NY 10020
(914) 670-0030 .. **Goldman,** Jodi L '83 (Alter & G) -550 Mamaroneck Av -Harrison 10528
(212) 539-2976 .. **Goldman,** Jodi P '95 SEIU Local 3285 -101 Av of Amer -NY 10013
(212) 592-1400 .. **Goldman,** John R '89 (Herrick,F LLP) -2 Park Av -NY 10016
(212) 310-8000 .. **Goldman,** John T '03 %Weil G&M LLP -767 5th Av -NY 10153
(212) 344-6500 .. **Goldman,** Karen E '89 %E Sarzin,PC -40 Exch Pl -NY 10005 **Fx:**344-0794
(212) 416-8392 .. **Goldman,** Karin K '77 %Dept of Law -120 Bway -NY 10271
(315) 423-4400 .. **Goldman,** Kenneth S '84 (Wolff G&G,LLP) -217 Mntgmry -Syracuse 13202
(212) 506-2500 .. **Goldman,** Lauren Rosenblum '99 (Mayer B LLP) -1675 Bway -NY 10019
(914) 686-4616 .. **Goldman,** Lawr '66 (Malman & G) -645 5th Av -NY 10022
(973) 596-4645 .. **Goldman,** Lawr A '85 (Gibbons PC) -1 Penn Plz -NY 10119 **Fx:**639-6283
(212) 997-7499 .. **Goldman,** Lawr S '66 -500 5th Av -NY 10110 **Fx:**997-7707
(212) 576-1400 .. **Goldman,** Lewis A '56 (Ere LLP) -440 Park Av S -NY 10016 **Fx:**576-1414
(914) 422-0042 .. **Goldman,** Lisa '99 -199 Main -White Plns 10601 **Fx:**422-5707
(718) 520-1418 .. **Goldman,** Martin '72 -140-04 69th Av -Flushng 11367 **Fx:**520-0976
(212) 656-2032 .. **Goldman,** Martin E '61 FINRA -20 Broad -NY 10005
(212) 953-9500 .. **Goldman,** Martin Wm '61 (Goldman & G,PC) -60 E 42nd -NY 10165
(212) 735-3000 .. **Goldman,** Mateo A '08 %Skadden ASM&F LLP -4 Times Sq -NY 10036
(516) 773-8585 .. **Goldman & Maurer,LLP** -475 Nrthrn Blvd -Gt Neck 11021 **Fx:**773-6190
(212) 541-2000 .. **Goldman,** Melanie P '89 Bryan C LLP -1290 Av of Amer -NY 10104
(212) 576-1400 .. **Goldman,** Melissa '90 (Ere LLP) -440 Park Av S -NY 10016 **Fx:**576-1414
(212) 587-0400 .. **Goldman,** Meta S '81 -225 Bway -NY 10007 **Fx:**587-0755
(718) 262-7100 .. **Goldman,** Michl H '01 %Civil Ct -89-17 Sutphin Blvd -Jamaica 11435 **Fx:**262-7107
(585) 263-1000 .. **Goldman,** Michl L '91 (Nixon P LLP) -1100 Clinton Sq -Rchstr 14604
(631) 344-3324 .. **Goldman,** Michl M '70 Brookhaven Science Assoc -40 Brookhvn Av -Upton 11973
(212) 301-4054 .. **Goldman,** Michl N '98 Natl Financial Prtnrs Corp -340 Mad Av -NY 10173
(212) 474-1000 .. **Goldman,** Michl S '88 (Cravath S&M LLP) -825 8th Av -NY 10019
(212) 698-3500 .. **Goldman,** Michl Z '05 %Dechert LLP -1095 Av of Amer -NY 10036
(212) 619-4220 .. **Goldman,** Michelle J '96 %American E&S -40 Fulton -NY 10038
(212) 831-6594 .. **Goldman,** Morris '49 -155 E 93rd -NY 10128
(212) 696-4848 .. **Goldman,** Neal M '66 OfCnsl Mintz & G LLP -470 Park Av S -NY 10016
(212) 373-3000 .. **Goldman,** Neil A '03 %Paul WRW&G LLP -1285 Av of Amer -NY 10019
(212) 878-5125 .. **Goldman,** Pamela R '06 %Goulston & S,PC -750 3rd Av -NY 10017
(518) 452-0941 .. **Goldman,** Paul J '86 (Segel GM&S,PC) -9 Wshngtn Sq -Albany 12205
(914) 937-6857 .. **Goldman,** Peter A '73 -12 Fairlawn Pkwy -Pt Chester 10573
(716) 483-2801 .. **Goldman,** R Michl '76 -507 Htl Jmstwn -Jamestwn 14701 **Fx:**483-2808
(212) 508-6100 .. **Goldman,** Rachel B '98 (Bracewell & G,LLP) -1251 Av of Amer -NY 10020
(914) 376-3757 .. **Goldman,** Rebecca E '06 %Leg Srvcs -30 S Bway -Ynkrs 10701 **Fx:**376-8739
(212) 701-3000 .. **Goldman,** Richd B '09 %Cahill G&R LLP -80 Pine -NY 10005 **Fx:**269-5420
(518) 449-3107 .. **Goldman,** Richd M '07 %Buckley M&C,PC -29 Wards Ln -Albany 12204
(212) 446-4800 .. **Goldman,** Richd M '08 %Kirkland & E LLP -153 E 53rd -NY 10022
Goldman, Robt E '59 (Goldman & W,PC) -20 E 9th -NY 10003
(631) 499-7500 .. **Goldman,** Robt I '93 -283 Commack Rd -Commack 11725 **Fx:**499-0534
(631) 563-8100 .. **Goldman,** Robt I '93 -1207 Montauk Hwy -Oakdale 11769 **Fx:**218-3525
(212) 513-6426 .. **Goldman,** Robt N '90 Dept Business Srvcs -110 William -NY 10038 **Fx:**618-8989
(518) 474-1331 .. **Goldman,** Robin A '80 %Ofc Mntl Health -44 Holland Av -Albany 12229 **Fx:**473-7863
(212) 751-5509 .. **Goldman,** Roger A '69 (Ehrenkranz & E,LLP) -375 Park Av -NY 10152 **Fx:**891-8652
(631) 738-2400 .. **Goldman,** Ron '90 %Symbol Tech -1 Symbol Plz -Holtsvll 11742
(516) 295-5159 .. **Goldman,** Ronald '75 -575 Chestnut -Cedarhrst 11516
(516) 228-4321 .. **Goldman,** Ronald G '85 Goldman & Assoc,LLP -666 Old Cntry Rd -Gdn Cty 11530 **Fx:**228-8349
(585) 546-7410 .. **Goldman,** Ronald S '88 -45 Exchange -Rchstr 14614 **Fx:**546-7451
(212) 318-3000 .. **Goldman,** Roy L '81 (Fulbright & J LLP) -666 5th Av -NY 10103
(212) 725-1400 .. **Goldman,** Saml '73 (S Goldman & Assoc) -100 Park Av -NY 10017 **Fx:**725-0805
(212) 421-4100 .. **Goldman,** Sanford M '67 (Pryor C LLP) -7 Times Sq -NY 10036
(518) 383-9400 .. **Goldman,** Sarah I '09 %Pennock B&N -1407 Route 9 -Clifton Pk 12065
(718) 828-8646 .. **Goldman,** Scott '90 -2704 E Tremont Av -Bronx 10461
(212) 585-3425 .. **Goldman,** Scott '04 %B Kishner & Assoc -420 Lex Av -NY 10170 **Fx:**752-1810
(718) 250-2000 .. **Goldman,** Seth M '04 %DA -350 Jay -Brklyn 11201 **Fx:**250-2314
(212) 935-3000 .. **Goldman,** Seth R '97 (Mintz LCFG&P,PC) -666 3rd Av -NY 10017
(516) 683-1144 .. **Goldman,** Sheryl S '92 -120 Hicksvll Rd -Bethpage 11714 **Fx:**683-1447
(518) 432-7861 .. **Goldman,** Simeon L '87 %Disability Advocates,Inc -5 Clinton Sq -Albany 12207 **Fx:**427-6561
(516) 222-1030 .. **Goldman,** Steven '09 S Friedman,PC -666 Old Cntry Rd -Gdn Cty 11530 **Fx:**222-1053
(212) 458-1955 .. **Goldman,** Steven F '99 AIG -175 Water -NY 10038
(718) 538-5743 .. **Goldman,** Steven H '89 -190 E 161st -Bronx 10451 **Fx:**588-9599
(914) 285-9800 .. **Goldman,** Steven M '68 (Kurzman EC&L,LLP) -1 N Bway -White Plns 10601
(212) 715-9100 .. **Goldman,** Steven M '88 (Kramer LN&F,LLP) -1177 Av of Amer -NY 10036
(212) 956-3838 .. **Goldman,** Stuart B '61 -1185 Park Av -NY 10128 **Fx:**977-3849
(212) 732-2056 .. **Goldman,** Theo S '61 T Goldman,PC -277 Bway -NY 10007 **Fx:**571-0468
(718) 694-3906 .. **Goldman,** Wendy E '84 %Transit Auth -130 Lvngstn -Brklyn 11201 **Fx:**694-5726
(585) 428-3140 .. **Goldman,** Wm J '68 %City Ct -Rm 15 Hall of Justice -Rchstr 14614 **Fx:**428-3156
(212) 335-4500 .. **Goldman,** Wm M '74 (DLA Piper LLP) -1251 Av of Amer -NY 10020
(212) 318-3000 .. **Goldmark,** Jena B '07 %Fulbright & J LLP -666 5th Av -NY 10103
(914) 422-4126 .. **Goldmark,** Leila C '02 Riverkeeper,Inc -78 N Bway -White Plns 10603
(212) 696-4555 .. **Goldner,** Abraham B '61 -440 Park Av S -NY 10016 **Fx:**685-7277
(212) 381-5336 .. **Goldner,** Andrew M '99 Double Click Inc -111 8th Av -NY 10011
(212) 735-3000 .. **Goldner,** Bruce J '93 (Skadden ASM&F LLP) -4 Times Sq -NY 10036
(212) 259-8000 .. **Goldner,** Saren R '95 %Dewey & L LLP -1301 Av of Amer -NY 10019
(732) 625-9100 .. **Goldner,** Wendy S '83 %Post Resources Inc -363 E 76th -NY 10021
(212) 880-6000 .. **Goldrich,** Ian M '01 %Torys LLP -237 Park Av -NY 10017
(516) 783-7474 .. **Goldrick,** Wm M '86 -1873 Wantagh Av -Wantagh 11793 **Fx:**783-0487
(516) 569-5001 .. **Goldring,** Aliza '97 (Schonfeld & G,LLP) -112 Spruce -Cedarhrst 11516
(212) 310-8312 .. **Goldring,** Stuart J '84 (Weil G&M LLP) -767 5th Av -NY 10153
(212) 547-5400 .. **Goldsamt,** Seth T '96 (McDermott W&E LLP) -340 Mad Av -NY 10173
(845) 278-2000 .. **Goldsand,** Richd I '70 (Goldsand & C) -864 Route 22 -Brewstr 10509 **Fx:**278-9650
(914) 739-2700 .. **Goldsand,** Ronald '51 %RG Agency -1000 N Division Bx431 -Peekskill 10566 **Fx:**739-2808
(212) 986-6840 .. **Goldsborough,** Judith L '84 %N Brickman -317 Mad Av -NY 10017 **Fx:**986-7691
(718) 340-4200 .. **Goldscheid,** Julie '92 %CUNY Law Schl -65-21 Main -Flushng 11367 **Fx:**340-4482
(212) 231-1823 .. **Goldschein,** Geoffrey F '03 Macquarie Capital Funds Inc -125 W 55th -NY 10019
(212) 854-2654 .. **Goldschmid,** Harvey J '65 %Columbia Law Schl -435 W 116th -NY 10027 **Fx:**854-2368
(212) 310-8000 .. **Goldschmid,** Harvey J '65 SrCnsl Weil G&M LLP -767 5th Av -NY 10153
(212) 735-3574 .. **Goldschmidt,** David J '88 (Skadden ASM&F LLP) -4 Times Sq -NY 10036
(212) 661-1344 .. **Goldschmidt,** Deborah N '86 %Newfield & B -60 E 42nd -NY 10165 **Fx:**661-2385
(914) 681-6006 .. **Goldschmidt & Genovese,LLP** -1 N Lex Av -White Plns 10601 **Fx:**686-8728
(212) 838-8269 .. **Goldschmidt,** Joel J '83 (Morse ZR&L LLP) -405 Park Av -NY 10022
(212) 838-2424 .. **Goldschmidt,** Lawr E '67 Goldschmidt & G -641 Lex Av -NY 10022 **Fx:**980-6826
(212) 596-9000 .. **Goldschmidt,** Steven S '02 %Ropes & G LLP -1211 Av of Amer -NY 10036
(914) 681-6006 .. **Goldschmidt,** Sylvia '83 (Goldschmidt & G,LLP) -1 N Lex Av -White Plns 10601
(212) 342-4135 .. **Goldsheft,** David A '09 %Columbia Univ -630 W 168th -NY 10032
(914) 779-1100 .. **Goldshteyn,** Renata '09 %Veneruso CS&C,LLP -35 E Grassy Sprain Rd -Ynkrs 10710
(516) 829-0363 .. **Goldshteyn,** Vadim '01 %Israel I&P,LLP -11 Grace Av -Gt Neck 11021 **Fx:**829-0366

(212) 566-6212 .. **Goldsmith,** Aaron M '03 %Fasulo S&D -225 Bway -NY 10007
(212) 732-8700 .. **Goldsmith,** Adam R '89 (McAloon & F,PC) -123 William -NY 10038
(212) 684-3900 .. **Goldsmith,** Amy B '86 (Gottlieb R&R,PC) -270 Mad Av -NY 10016
(212) 373-3000 .. **Goldsmith,** Andree J '10 %Paul WRW&G LLP -1285 Av of Amer -NY 10019
(718) 254-7000 .. **Goldsmith,** Andrew E '05 US Atty-EDNY -271 Cadman Plz E -Brklyn 11201
(212) 679-0202 .. **Goldsmith,** Andrew S '95 %One Israel Fund -136 E 39th -NY 10016
(212) 643-6400 .. **Goldsmith,** Chas '70 (Garganigo G&W) -14 Penn Plz -NY 10122
(718) 590-2865 .. **Goldsmith,** Chas A '79 %Criminal Ct -265 E 161st -Bronx 10451
(718) 852-0001 .. **Goldsmith,** Craig S '97 -1829 E 19th -Brklyn 11229
(212) 421-5500 .. **Goldsmith Ctorides & Rodriguez, LLP** -747 3rd Av -NY 10017 **Fx:**421-5185
(212) 969-3000 .. **Goldsmith,** Danl S '97 Proskauer R LLP -1585 Bway -NY 10036
(516) 433-6677 .. **Goldsmith,** David J '86 (Stewart GM&B) -6800 Jericho Tpk -Syosset 11791
(212) 907-0879 .. **Goldsmith,** David J '97 (Labaton S LLP) -140 Bway -NY 10005
(212) 513-3200 .. **Goldsmith,** Donald A '68 (Holland & K LLP) -31 W 52nd -NY 10019
(518) 436-2840 .. **Goldsmith,** Edna R '84 %Thruway Auth -200 Southrn Blvd Bx189 -Albany 12201 **Fx:**471-4340
(631) 725-4566 .. **Goldsmith,** Gerald Philip '59 -110 Redwood Rd -Sag Hbr 11963
(212) 227-8525 .. **Goldsmith,** Gerald Philip '59 (GP Goldsmith,PC) -20 Vesey -NY 10007
(212) 969-3000 .. **Goldsmith,** Herman L '88 (Proskauer R LLP) -1585 Bway -NY 10036
(914) 227-5979 .. **Goldsmith,** Irene J '01 -123 Main -White Plns 10601 **Fx:**736-9625
(212) 909-5000 .. **Goldsmith,** James D '86 %KPMG LLP -280 Park Av -NY 10017
(212) 872-1000 .. **Goldsmith,** Jason L '08 -One Bryant Park -NY 10036 **Fx:**872-1002
(212) 298-9716 .. **Goldsmith,** Jeffrey K '97 Skidmore Owings & Merrill LLP -14 Wall -NY 10005
(914) 285-9800 .. **Goldsmith,** Jessica Galligan '86 (Kurzman EC&L,LLP) -1 N Bway -White Plns 10601
(845) 291-3116 .. **Goldsmith,** John W '89 %Hon R Freehill -Govt Ctr -Goshen 10924
(212) 267-6364 .. **Goldsmith,** Jos S '04 %Kossoff & U -217 Bway -NY 10007
(212) 485-8785 .. **Goldsmith,** Lee M '00 MLB Advanced Media LP -75 9th Av -NY 10011
(212) 421-5500 .. **Goldsmith,** Lee S '68 (Goldsmith C&R,LLP) -747 3rd Av -NY 10017
(914) 925-0000 .. **Goldsmith,** Lois S '81 Elias Grp -411 Theo Fremd Av -Rye 10580
(212) 704-6000 .. **Goldsmith,** Mark A '82 (Troutman S LLP) -405 Lex Av -NY 10174
(631) 360-0400 .. **Goldsmith,** Mark J '84 (Jakubowski RMG&T) -969 Jericho Tpk -St James 11780 **Fx:**360-0408
(212) 643-6400 .. **Goldsmith,** Matthew D '06 %Garganigo G&W -14 Penn Plz -NY 10122
(212) 298-5201 .. **Goldsmith,** Matthew H '04 %Leg Aid -49 Thomas -NY 10013 **Fx:**298-5252
(516) 433-3300 .. **Goldsmith,** Michl '87 (Scheich & G,PC) -109 Newbrdg Rd -Hicksvll 11801
(718) 843-7200 .. **Goldsmith,** Michl '87 (Scheich & G,PC) -103-42 Lefferts Blvd -S Richmond Hll 11419
(212) 643-7000 .. **Goldsmith,** Michl B '75 (Sills C&G PC) -One Rckfllr Plz -NY 10020
(212) 525-4753 .. **Goldsmith,** Michl H '92 Advisory Srvcs -452 5th Av -NY 10018
(718) 618-3610 .. **Goldsmith,** Pamela A '92 %Hon A Lorenzo -265 E 161st -Bronx 10451
(212) 687-0100 .. **Goldsmith,** Pamela B '89 (Harris B PLLC) -100 Wall -NY 10005
(516) 766-2237 .. **Goldsmith,** Robt L '85 -3699 Oceanside Rd E -Oceanside 11572
(212) 644-6200 .. **Goldsmith,** Scott E '96 %Titan Outdoor LLC -850 3rd Av -NY 10022
(212) 490-0900 .. **Goldsmith,** Scott R '00 OfCnsl Margolis Law Firm -11 E 44th -NY 10017
(212) 326-3939 .. **Goldsmith,** Shari M '01 %Jones D -222 E 41st -NY 10017
(631) 864-6800 .. **Goldsmith,** Steven B '91 (Goldsmith & T) -2067 Jericho Tpk -Commack 11725
(212) 643-6400 .. **Goldsmith,** Tara J '99 %Garganigo G&W -14 Penn Plz -NY 10122
(212) 770-7218 .. **Goldsmith,** Wm G '86 AIG -70 Pine -NY 10270
(212) 326-3939 .. **Goldsmith,** Willis J '73 (Jones D) -222 E 41st -NY 10017
(631) 236-4105 .. **Goldson,** Howard W '58 (Goldson NC,PC) -145 Marcus Blvd -Hauppauge 11788 **Fx:**236-4110
(212) 612-4000 .. **Goldstein,** Aaron '90 %Chubb Grp -55 Water -NY 10041
(718) 544-7701 .. **Goldstein,** Abbey F '71 (Goldstein & G,LLP) -118-35 Qns Blvd -Frst Hlls 11375
(718) 298-1192 .. **Goldstein,** Abby C '84 %Hon PO Flug -88-11 Sutphin Blvd -Jamaica 11435
(716) 362-1533 .. **Goldstein Ackerhalt & Pletcher,LLP** -70 Niagara -Buffalo 14202
(212) 455-2000 .. **Goldstein,** Aimee H '92 (Simpson T&B LLP) -425 Lex Av -NY 10017
(845) 708-7219 .. **Goldstein,** Alan E '73 %Hon R Berliner -1 S Main -New Cty 10956
(516) 921-8881 .. **Goldstein,** Allan D '78 (Cohn & G,PC) -100 Crsswys Park W -Woodbury 11797
(212) 687-5180 .. **Goldstein,** Allen J '57 -333 E 38th -NY 10016 **Fx:**687-5182
(212) 382-0909 .. **Goldstein,** Alvin '53 (Peckar & A,PC) -41 Mad Av -NY 10154
(845) 469-2020 .. **Goldstein,** Alvin '61 -11 High Bx491 -Chester 10918 **Fx:**469-4841
(212) 966-5253 .. **Goldstein,** Amir J '02 -591 Bway -NY 10012 **Fx:**941-8566
(716) 858-2424 .. **Goldstein,** Amy J '86 %DA -25 Delaware Av -Buffalo 14202 **Fx:**858-7425
(212) 867-8998 .. **Goldstein,** Amy S '94 Grayson Allen Inc -308 E 38th -NY 10016
(212) 373-3000 .. **Goldstein,** Andrew D '08 %Paul WRW&G LLP -1285 Av of Amer -NY 10019
(212) 977-9700 .. **Goldstein,** Andrew E '75 Cnsl Phillips N LLP -666 5th Av -NY 10103
(718) 981-0219 .. **Goldstein,** Ariella G '09 Leg Aid -60 Bay -Staten Isl 10301 **Fx:**981-6623
(718) 756-9898 .. **Goldstein,** Arnold J '55 (Goldstein & G,PC) -26 Court -Brklyn 11242 **Fx:**855-7337
(212) 686-0100 .. **Goldstein,** Arnold V '64 (Frank FG&N,LLP) -1430 Bway -NY 10018
(631) 421-9051 .. **Goldstein,** Arthur '56 (Goldstein RG&D,PC) -18 W Carver -Huntngtn 11743
(212) 557-7200 .. **Goldstein,** Arthur '87 (Davidoff M&H,LLP) -605 3rd Av -NY 10158
(212) 754-9400 .. **Goldstein,** Arthur I '77 (Todtman NS&J,PC) -425 Park Av -NY 10022
(212) 973-0572 .. **Goldstein,** Arthur S '82 (Wolff & S PC) -140 Bway -NY 10005
(516) 677-9400 .. **Goldstein & Avrutine** -575 Underhill Blvd -Syosset 11791 **Fx:**677-9405
(860) 946-4855 .. **Goldstein,** Barrie L '81 -340 E 52nd -NY 10022 **Fx:**868-0303
(914) 225-9286 .. **Goldstein,** Barry H '90 Morgan Stanley -2000 Wstchstr Av -Purchase 10577
(718) 544-7100 .. **Goldstein,** Barry M '75 -125-10 Qns Blvd -Kew Gdns 11415
(212) 527-4000 .. **Goldstein,** Bart S '97 %Revlon -237 Park Av -NY 10017 **Fx:**527-5299
(516) 222-4000 .. **Goldstein & Bashner** -1778 Hempstd Tpk -E Meadow 11554 **Fx:**222-0034
(516) 486-1810 .. **Goldstein,** Bernard '56 -72 Main -Hempstd 11550 **Fx:**486-1804
(212) 619-2270 .. **Goldstein,** Bohunka '97 -299 Bway -NY 10007 **Fx:**619-2271
(716) 854-2020 .. **Goldstein,** Brian A '96 (Cellino & B,PC) -350 Main -Buffalo 14202
(518) 434-1300 .. **Goldstein,** Brian P '90 (Jackson L LLP) -18 Corp Wds Blvd -Albany 12211
(212) 692-1000 .. **Goldstein,** Brian S '65 OfCnsl Duane M LLP -1540 Bway -NY 10036
(877) 385-3864 .. **Goldstein,** Brian T '01 (Fettmann T&M,PC) -40 Exch Pl -NY 10005
(718) 852-1800 .. **Goldstein,** Bruce '90 -26 Court -Brklyn 11242
(716) 362-1533 .. **Goldstein,** Bruce A '73 (Goldstein A&P,LLP) -70 Niagara -Buffalo 14202
(212) 422-1200 .. **Goldstein,** Bryan '00 %Abrams GF&J,PC -1 Bttry Pk Plz -NY 10004
(212) 294-6700 .. **Goldstein,** Bryan C '01 (Winston & S) -200 Park Av -NY 10166
(718) 250-4533 .. **Goldstein,** Byron R '08 %Leg Aid -111 Lvngstn -Brklyn 11201 **Fx:**250-4243
(516) 812-4500 .. **Goldstein,** Cara M '92 %Stagg TC&W LLP -401 Franklin Av -Gdn Cty 11530
(845) 567-0100 .. **Goldstein,** Carol S '80 -843 Union Av -New Windsor 12553 **Fx:**567-0139
(516) 496-5822 .. **Goldstein,** Caryn E '04 %T Spina -170 Froehlich Farm Blvd -Woodbury 11797 **Fx:**496-5420
(718) 579-7917 .. **Goldstein,** Cathy N '80 %Leg Aid -900 Sheridan Av -Bronx 10451 **Fx:**293-8744
(212) 592-1400 .. **Goldstein,** Chas A '62 Cnsl Herrick,F LLP -2 Park Av -NY 10016
(516) 229-2298 .. **Goldstein,** Chas B '92 %Strategic Placement -50 Chas Lindbergh Blvd -Uniondale 11553
(516) 355-7901 .. **Goldstein,** Chas M '84 %Paganini GCC&F -1979 Marcus Av -Lk Success 11042
(718) 923-4206 .. **Goldstein,** Craig M '94 %OTDA Fair Hearings -14 Boerum Pl -Brklyn 11201
(914) 698-9696 .. **Goldstein,** Cynthia '83 -1066 Seahaven Dr -Mamaroneck 10543
(212) 870-2974 .. **Goldstein,** Cynthia M '04 %Columbia Univ Emplyee & Lbr Rltns -1220 Interchurch Ctr -NY 10015
(917) 886-1920 .. **Goldstein,** David A '60 -200 E 78th -NY 10075
(212) 406-9600 .. **Goldstein,** David A '87 -305 Bway -NY 10007
(212) 461-2338 .. **Goldstein,** David A '92 (Goldstein H) -44 Wall -NY 10005 **Fx:**(646) 219-2450
(212) 819-8200 .. **Goldstein,** David A '94 (White & C LLP) -1155 Av of Amer -NY 10036
(516) 296-7000 .. **Goldstein,** David A '96 OfCnsl Certilman BA&H,LLP -90 Merrick Av -E Meadow 11554
(212) 254-1111 .. **Goldstein,** David B '86 (Rabinowitz BSK&L,PC) -111 Bway -NY 10006
(845) 356-4600 .. **Goldstein,** David I '80 -747 Chestnut Rdg Rd -Chestnut Rdg 10977
(718) 665-9000 .. **Goldstein,** David J '74 (Goldstein & W) -888 Grnd Cncrs -Bronx 10451 **Fx:**665-9147
(516) 829-0363 .. **Goldstein,** David M '05 %Israel I&P,LLP -11 Grace Av -Gt Neck 11021 **Fx:**829-0366
(212) 594-6030 .. **Goldstein,** David P '83 (Goldstein & G) -1 Penn Plz -NY 10119 **Fx:**268-6516
(212) 735-8600 .. **Goldstein,** David S '00 (Morrison C LLP) -909 3rd Av -NY 10022
(212) 940-8800 .. **Goldstein,** David S '10 %Katten MR LLP -575 Mad Av -NY 10022
(212) 294-6700 .. **Goldstein,** Deborah J '90 (Winston & S) -200 Park Av -NY 10166
(646) 386-5304 .. **Goldstein,** Deborah L '95 City Ct -111 Centre -NY 10013
(212) 259-8000 .. **Goldstein,** Doron S '99 %Dewey & L LLP -1301 Av of Amer -NY 10019
(516) 536-2317 .. **Goldstein,** Edw L '68 -3466 Park Av -Oceanside 11572 **Fx:**536-7743
(212) 613-5000 .. **Goldstein,** Elena S '04 Leg Assist Grp -450 W 33rd -NY 10001 **Fx:**750-0820
(212) 340-0400 .. **Goldstein,** Ellen Dale '81 %Appllt Div 1st Dept -27 Mad Av -NY 10010 **Fx:**889-4412
(212) 727-2700 .. **Goldstein,** Eric A '76 %NRDC -40 W 20th -NY 10011 **Fx:**727-1773
(212) 728-8000 .. **Goldstein,** Eric C '06 %Willkie F&G LLP -787 7th Av -NY 10019
(212) 582-9700 .. **Goldstein,** Eric M '00 Burton Goldstein & Co -215 Park Av S -NY 10003
(212) 594-1991 .. **Goldstein,** Eric S '84 %M Kay,PC -7 Penn Plz -NY 10001 **Fx:**847-8220
(212) 373-3000 .. **Goldstein,** Eric S '84 (Paul WRW&G LLP) -1285 Av of Amer -NY 10019
(212) 374-1544 .. **Goldstein,** Eugene '71 -150 Bway -NY 10038
(516) 873-7684 .. **Goldstein,** Evelyn '96 -194 Old Cntry Rd -Mineola 11501 **Fx:**739-0428
(212) 826-0808 .. **Goldstein,** Evie C '85 %MLB Players Assn -12 E 49th -NY 10017 **Fx:**752-3649
(212) 595-5810 .. **Goldstein,** Fredric H '83 %Phoenix House -164 W 74th -NY 10023 **Fx:**496-6035
(516) 826-0400 .. **Goldstein & Garbar PC** -1800 Bellmore Av -Bellmore 11710 **Fx:**826-0466
(631) 243-2445 .. **Goldstein,** Garson K '75 -796 Deer Prk Av -N Babylon 11703
(516) 826-0400 .. **Goldstein,** Gary '65 (Goldstein & G PC) -1800 Bellmore Av -Bellmore 11710
(845) 469-8630 .. **Goldstein,** Gary S '92 -13 High Bx591 -Chester 10918
(516) 747-5566 .. **Goldstein,** Gerald '66 -80 E Old Cntry Rd -Mineola 11501 **Fx:**873-1451
(914) 390-8090 .. **Goldstein,** Gerald C '69 %NYPA -123 Main -White Plns 10601 **Fx:**390-8038
(212) 421-5333 .. **Goldstein,** Glenn A '92 %Related Company -625 Mad Av -NY 10022
(212) 537-9000 .. **Goldstein,** Glenn S '81 (Cohen G&S,LLP) -850 3rd Av -NY 10022
(212) 751-2700 .. **Goldstein,** Gloria '56 %JAMS -620 8th Av -NY 10018 **Fx:**751-4099

(718) 544-7701 .. **Goldstein & Greenlaw,LLP** -118-35 Qns Blvd -Frst Hlls 11375 **Fx:**520-1213
(212) 640-6676 .. **Goldstein,** Greg R '98 Amer Exp -200 Vesey -NY 10285
(212) 221-5700 .. **Goldstein,** Harvey L '57 (Goldberg WFG LLP) -1501 Bway -NY 10036
(631) 758-0303 .. **Goldstein,** Harvey M '63 -1719 N Ocean Av -Medfrd 11763 **Fx:**758-0309
(212) 265-2266 .. **Goldstein,** Harvey N '63 (Schneider GB LLP) -90 Broad -NY 10004
(347) 578-1236 .. **Goldstein,** Heath J '09 ACS -350 St Marks Pl -Staten Isl 10301
(212) 376-0528 .. **Goldstein,** Heather R '99 Topps Co,Inc -1 Whitehall -NY 10004
(212) 987-4000 .. **Goldstein,** Heather W '96 %Kaufman BD&L,LLP -888 7th Av -NY 10106
(212) 735-3000 .. **Goldstein,** Heidi B '85 Cnsl Skadden ASM&F LLP -4 Times Sq -NY 10036
(212) 587-3434 .. **Goldstein,** Helen E '54 Raskin & K LLP -160 Bway -NY 10038
(212) 310-8000 .. **Goldstein,** Helyn S '82 (Weil G&M LLP) -767 5th Av -NY 10153
(212) 541-2000 .. **Goldstein,** Hope Sarah '98 (Bryan C LLP) -1290 Av of Amer -NY 10104
(212) 278-9627 .. **Goldstein,** Howard E '84 %Chancellor Cptl Mngt -1166 Av of Amer -NY 10036
(212) 797-5400 .. **Goldstein,** Howard S '78 (Cohen & G,LLP) -32 Bway -NY 10004 **Fx:**943-3295
(212) 859-8000 .. **Goldstein,** Howard W '74 (Fried FHS&J LLP) -1 NY Plz -NY 10004
(718) 788-2900 .. **Goldstein,** Ilan '91 -342 7th Av -Brklyn 11215 **Fx:**832-0335
(631) 777-2330 .. **Goldstein,** Ira E '03 %O'Connor OH&D,LLP -1 Huntngtn Quad -Melvll 11747
(718) 237-2008 .. **Goldstein,** Ira H '72 -350 Lvngstn -Brklyn 11217
(212) 421-4100 .. **Goldstein,** Ira J '56 SrCnsl Pryor C LLP -7 Times Sq -NY 10036
(212) 676-1135 .. **Goldstein,** Ira J '93 Taxi & Limo Comm -40 Rector -NY 10006
(212) 259-8000 .. **Goldstein,** Irena M '91 (Dewey & L LLP) -1301 Av of Amer -NY 10019
(212) 435-3571 .. **Goldstein,** Iris L '09 Port Auth of NY/NJ -225 Park Av S -NY 10003 **Fx:**435-3555
(212) 267-0700 .. **Goldstein,** Jack '59 Goldstein & W -233 Bway -NY 10279 **Fx:**227-6534
(212) 353-8700 .. **Goldstein,** James A '63 OfCnsl Simon E&B LLP -24 Union Sq E -NY 10003 **Fx:**353-1708
(718) 261-7700 .. **Goldstein,** Janet '89 Rappaport HC&R,PC -118-35 Qns Blvd -Frst Hlls 11375
(212) 335-4500 .. **Goldstein,** Jason R '98 (DLA Piper LLP) -1251 Av of Amer -NY 10020
(914) 253-8484 .. **Goldstein,** Jay H '78 -2900 Wstchstr Av -Purchase 10577 **Fx:**253-8087
(212) 806-5400 .. **Goldstein,** Jayme T '03 %Stroock &S&L LLP -180 Maiden Ln -NY 10038
(646) 502-7001 .. **Goldstein,** Jeffrey M '97 (JSBarkats PLLC) -100 Church -NY 10007 **Fx:**607-5544
(914) 738-2692 .. **Goldstein,** Jeffrey S '75 -9 The Hamlet -Pelham 10803 **Fx:**738-4110
(212) 754-5543 .. **Goldstein,** Jennifer L '00 BlackRock -40 E 52nd -NY 10022
(212) 403-1000 .. **Goldstein,** Jeremy L '01 (Wachtell LR&K) -51 W 52nd -NY 10019
(516) 498-8800 .. **Goldstein,** Jonah L '61 Spectrum Fncl Cnsltnts,Inc -Bx299 -Ynkrs 10704 **Fx:**498-9435
(212) 294-6700 .. **Goldstein,** Jonathan '69 (Winston & S) -200 Park Av -NY 10166
(212) 455-2000 .. **Goldstein,** Jonathan A '04 %Simpson T&B LLP -425 Lex Av -NY 10017
(212) 530-5000 .. **Goldstein,** Jonathan C '04 %Milbank TH&M LLP -1 Chase Manh Plz -NY 10005
(917) 777-4200 .. **Goldstein,** Jonathan C '07 %Bingham M LLP -1 Bttry Pk Plz -NY 10004
(212) 849-7000 .. **Goldstein,** Jordan A '03 %Quinn EU&S,LLP -51 Mad Av -NY 10010
(212) 594-6030 .. **Goldstein,** Jos '42 (Goldstein & G) -1 Penn Plz -NY 10119 **Fx:**268-6516
(516) 747-1010 .. **Goldstein,** Jos '55 Cnsl Dollinger G&G -1 Old Cntry Rd -Carle Pl 11514
(212) 455-9164 .. **Goldstein,** Josh D '97 1st Manh Consulting Grp -90 Park Av -NY 10016
(212) 735-3000 .. **Goldstein,** Joshua B '97 Cnsl Skadden ASM&F LLP -4 Times Sq -NY 10036
(212) 205-7000 .. **Goldstein,** Joshua J '08 %Ashurst LLP -7 Times Sq -NY 10036
(212) 422-2400 .. **Goldstein,** Joyce M '80 (Altschul G&G) -17 Battery Place -NY 10004 **Fx:**732-1001
(212) 376-3144 .. **Goldstein,** Karen '77 %Vera Inst of Justice -233 Bway -NY 10279 **Fx:**941-9407
(518) 869-6227 .. **Goldstein,** Keith M '99 %Lavelle & F,LLP -29 British Amer Blvd -Latham 12110
(914) 834-0027 .. **Goldstein,** Kenneth R '72 -2 Homer Av -Larchmnt 10538
(212) 841-7500 .. **Goldstein,** Kenneth R '88 %Cushman & Wakefield -1290 Av of Amer -NY 10104
(516) 294-3111 .. **Goldstein,** Kim Gates '98 (Gates & G LLP) -600 Old Cntry Rd -Gdn Cty 11530 **Fx:**294-3225
(585) 325-4110 .. **Goldstein & LaBue** -45 Exchange Blvd -Rchstr 14614 **Fx:**325-5536
(917) 454-1100 .. **Goldstein,** Laurence S '94 %Police Dept -2 Lafayette -NY 10007
(212) 431-1300 .. **Goldstein,** Lawr E '87 %Borah GAN&G PC -377 Bway -NY 10013
(585) 325-4110 .. **Goldstein,** Lawr I '60 (Goldstein & L) -45 Exchange Blvd -Rchstr 14614
(516) 483-4300 .. **Goldstein,** Lawr J '50 (Goldstein & R,LLP) -129 Hilton Av -Hempstd 11550 **Fx:**564-9363
(212) 842-5724 .. **Goldstein,** Lawr W '78 North Channel LLC -780 3rd Av -NY 10017 **Fx:**842-5721
(718) 789-2480 .. **Goldstein,** Leon '76 -35 Prospect Pk W -Brklyn 11215
(516) 850-2393 .. **Goldstein,** Libby '02 -172 Westvw Ln -Hewlett 11557 **Fx:**569-0550
(212) 790-4500 .. **Goldstein,** Linda A '79 (Manatt P&P,LLP) -7 Times Sq -NY 10036
(212) 841-1000 .. **Goldstein,** Linda C '87 (Covington & B LLP) -620 8th Av -NY 10018
(212) 474-1000 .. **Goldstein,** Lindsay '07 %Cravath S&M LLP -825 8th Av -NY 10019
(212) 596-9000 .. **Goldstein,** Lindsey R '09 %Ropes & G LLP -1211 Av of Amer -NY 10036
(212) 732-8700 .. **Goldstein,** Lisa B '85 (McAloon & F,PC) -123 William -NY 10038
(212) 871-0821 .. **Goldstein,** Lloyd F '87 -30 Vesey -NY 10007 **Fx:**871-0826
(212) 594-4115 .. **Goldstein,** Lori H '86 -470 Park Av S -NY 10016
(212) 422-4000 .. **Goldstein,** M Robt '49 (Goldstein R&R) -80 Pine -NY 10005
(917) 551-1300 .. **Goldstein,** Malcolm A '72 %Koehler & I LLP -61 Bway -NY 10006
(212) 799-8605 .. **Goldstein,** Marc J '81 -1230 Av of Amer -NY 10020 **Fx:**658-9151
(212) 758-9300 .. **Goldstein,** Marci D '01 %Lazare P&G LLP -950 3rd Av -NY 10022
(212) 702-9825 .. **Goldstein,** Marcia C '67 -110 E 59th -NY 10022
(212) 310-8000 .. **Goldstein,** Marcia L '76 (Weil G&M LLP) -767 5th Av -NY 10153
(212) 450-4000 .. **Goldstein,** Marcie A '89 Cnsl Davis P&W LLP -450 Lex Av -NY 10017
(212) 698-3101 .. **Goldstein,** Mark D '90 Arnhold & S Bleichroeder Advisers,LLC -1345 Av of Amer -NY 10105
(718) 756-9898 .. **Goldstein,** Mark I '83 (Goldstein & G,PC) -26 Court -Brklyn 11242 **Fx:**855-7337
(212) 553-9245 .. **Goldstein,** Mark S '83 -233 Bway -NY 10279
(914) 946-3331 .. **Goldstein,** Marshall L '68 -399 Knollwood Rd -White Plns 10603
(212) 806-5400 .. **Goldstein,** Marvin J '77 (Stroock &S&L LLP) -180 Maiden Ln -NY 10038
(212) 969-3000 .. **Goldstein,** Marvin M '70 (Proskauer R LLP) -1585 Bway -NY 10036
(212) 504-6000 .. **Goldstein,** Mathew '09 %Cadwalader W&T LLP -1 World Fncl Ctr -NY 10281
(212) 318-6000 .. **Goldstein,** Matthew B '08 %Paul HJ&W LLP -75 E 55th -NY 10022
(212) 321-5000 .. **Goldstein,** Matthew T '94 TheStreet.com, Inc -14 Wall -NY 10005 **Fx:**321-5016
(212) 805-0192 .. **Goldstein,** Melissa M '96 %Hon S Stein -500 Pearl -NY 10007
(212) 423-6077 .. **Goldstein,** Merrill J '78 %MHLS -1901 1st Av -NY 10029
(845) 473-7000 .. **Goldstein & Metzger,LLP** -40 Grdn -Poughkeepsie 12601 **Fx:**454-4783
(212) 248-4900 .. **Goldstein,** Michl '80 (Dillon H&G LLP) -11 Hanover Sq -NY 10005
(212) 599-3322 .. **Goldstein,** Michl A '95 (Becker P,LLP) -45 Bway -NY 10006
(212) 804-4200 .. **Goldstein,** Michl H '80 (Mound CW&G) -One Bttry Pk Plz -NY 10004
(914) 939-1111 .. **Goldstein,** Michl S '82 -62 Bowman Av -Rye Brook 10573 **Fx:**939-2369
(212) 279-9200 .. **Goldstein,** Michl T '07 OfCnsl Abrams FFEGF&E,LLP -630 3rd Av -NY 10017
(212) 571-6848 .. **Goldstein,** Michl W '79 -299 Bway -NY 10007 **Fx:**619-6743
(718) 286-6000 .. **Goldstein,** Michelle '84 %DA -125-01 Qns Blvd -Kew Gdns 11415
(718) 875-1300 .. **Goldstein,** Miriam L '84 %Appllt Div 2nd Dept -45 Monroe Pl -Brklyn 11201 **Fx:**858-2446
(646) 929-6856 .. **Goldstein,** Mordecai P '03 Gilt Groupe,Inc -40 W 20th -NY 10011
(212) 401-0800 .. **Goldstein,** Naomi Freyda '90 %Disciplinary Comm -61 Bway -NY 10006 **Fx:**287-1045
(516) 222-4000 .. **Goldstein,** Neal A '90 (Goldstein & B) -1778 Hempstd Tpk -E Meadow 11554
(212) 603-6300 .. **Goldstein,** Neil S '68 (Robinson BLGG&G PC) -875 3rd Av -NY 10022
(212) 548-2100 .. **Goldstein,** Pamela N '96 %McGuire W LLP -1345 Av of Amer -NY 10105
(516) 621-6254 .. **Goldstein,** Patricia DeCicco '82 -151 Westwood Cir -Roslyn Hts 11577
(212) 576-6946 .. **Goldstein,** Paul '83 %NY Life Ins -51 Mad Av -NY 10010 **Fx:**447-0569
(845) 473-7000 .. **Goldstein,** Paul J '76 (Goldstein & M,LLP) -40 Grdn -Poughkeepsie 12601
(585) 325-6202 .. **Goldstein,** Paul L '69 (Relin G&C LLP) -28 E Main -Rchstr 14614
(718) 526-0094 .. **Goldstein,** Paul S '59 -148-03 Hillside Av -Jamaica 11435 **Fx:**739-3303
(914) 921-5069 .. **Goldstein,** Peter D '81 %Gabelli Funds Inc -I Corp Ctr -Rye 10580 **Fx:**921-5384
(212) 548-2100 .. **Goldstein,** Philip '88 (McGuire W LLP) -1345 Av of Amer -NY 10105
(212) 548-2100 .. **Goldstein,** Philip A '02 %McGuire W LLP -1345 Av of Amer -NY 10105
(718) 756-9898 .. **Goldstein,** Rena Septee '85 %Goldstein & G,PC -26 Court -Brklyn 11242 **Fx:**855-7337
(212) 641-5018 .. **Goldstein,** Richd D '77 %Alpine Capital Grp -1285 Av of Amer -NY 10019
(212) 969-3000 .. **Goldstein,** Richd M '75 (Proskauer R LLP) -1585 Bway -NY 10036
(212) 957-0500 .. **Goldstein,** Richd S '74 -145 W 57th -NY 10019 **Fx:**957-2020
(212) 506-5000 .. **Goldstein,** Richd S '95 (Orrick H&S LLP) -51 W 52nd -NY 10019
(212) 232-2410 .. **Goldstein,** Richd W '93 (Goldstein J LLP) -110 Wall -NY 10005 **Fx:**232-2412
(718) 701-0700 .. **Goldstein,** Richd W '95 -34 Dumont Av -Staten Isl 10305 **Fx:**(866) 243-8109
(212) 422-4000 .. **Goldstein Rikon & Rikon** -80 Pine -NY 10005 **Fx:**422-4687
(212) 756-2000 .. **Goldstein,** Robt '00 (Schulte R&Z LLP) -919 3rd Av -NY 10022
(212) 227-1010 .. **Goldstein,** Robt A '78 OfCnsl Berger & K -225 Bway -NY 10007
(212) 431-1300 .. **Goldstein,** Robt D '75 (Borah GAN&G PC) -377 Bway -NY 10013
(212) 351-4500 .. **Goldstein,** Robt D '90 (Epstein B&G,PC) -250 Park Av -NY 10177
(212) 417-5300 .. **Goldstein,** Robt J '88 %Medicaid Fraud Cntrl -120 Bway -NY 10271 **Fx:**417-5274
(212) 595-6480 .. **Goldstein,** Robt L '85 -405 E 54th -NY 10022 **Fx:**995-1215
(718) 625-2805 .. **Goldstein,** Robt M '68 %Leopold G&S,PC -16 Court -Brklyn 11241
(716) 856-2700 .. **Goldstein,** Robt M '72 -20 Court -Buffalo 14202
(516) 742-7430 .. **Goldstein,** Robt N '74 OfCnsl Schroder & S LLP -114 Old Cntry Rd -Mineola 11501 **Fx:**742-7433
(914) 253-2603 .. **Goldstein,** Roberta Russo '96 %Pepsico -700 Andrsn Hill Rd -Purchase 10577
(212) 824-5700 .. **Goldstein,** Robin D '06 Practising Law Inst -810 7th Av -NY 10019
(631) 421-9051 .. **Goldstein,** Ronald L '83 (Goldstein RG&D,PC) -18 W Carver -Huntngtn 11743
(212) 458-2883 .. **Goldstein,** Ross D '99 AIGTS -175 Water -NY 10038
(631) 421-9051 .. **Goldstein Rubinton Goldstein & DiFazio,PC** -18 W Carver -Huntngtn 11743 **Fx:**421-9122
(718) 239-0239 .. **Goldstein,** Ryan S '99 R Goldstein,PLLC -43 Wstchstr Sq -Bronx 10461 **Fx:**239-0237
(212) 474-1000 .. **Goldstein,** Sandra C '88 (Cravath S&M LLP) -825 8th Av -NY 10019
(212) 809-4220 .. **Goldstein,** Scott H '92 (Goldstein Law Grp,PC) -61 Bway -NY 10006 **Fx:**809-4228
(212) 268-7535 .. **Goldstein,** Scott H '96 OfCnsl Bonner KT&C,LLP -350 5th Av -NY 10118

(845) 342-2272 .. **Goldstein,** Scott R '95 %Ouimette G&A -402 E Main Bx548 -Middletwn 10940
(718) 520-0722 .. **Goldstein,** Seth Michl '77 -125-10 Qns Blvd -Kew Gdns 11415 **Fx:**793-1526
(212) 906-1200 .. **Goldstein,** Seth R '06 %Latham & W -885 3rd Av -NY 10022
(212) 960-5262 .. **Goldstein,** Seth S '06 Yeshiva Univ -500 W 185th -NY 10033
(212) 809-4220 .. **Goldstein,** Sheldon E '65 (Goldstein Law Grp,PC) -61 Bway -NY 10006 **Fx:**809-4228
(516) 747-0300 .. **Goldstein,** Sheldon M '70 (Meltzer LG&B,LLP) -190 Willis Av -Mineola 11501
(212) 397-3050 .. **Goldstein,** Sheryl '98 Ctr for Ct Innovatn -520 8th Av -NY 10018
(212) 609-6800 .. **Goldstein,** Sidney S '58 (McCarter & E,LLP) -245 Park Av -NY 10167
(516) 227-2662 .. **Goldstein,** Sonna Foxman '88 OfCnsl Rubin & L,PC -591 Stewart Av -Gdn Cty 11530
(518) 348-1000 .. **Goldstein,** Stacey L '99 %Block CS&P,LLP -9 Exec Park Dr -Clifton Pk 12065
(212) 909-6000 .. **Goldstein,** Stacy Posner '07 %Debevoise & P LLP -919 3rd Av -NY 10022
(914) 925-0682 .. **Goldstein,** Stanley '43 -20 James Rd -Harrison 10528
(212) 599-3322 .. **Goldstein,** Stanley R '61 (Becker P,LLP) -45 Bway -NY 10006
(212) 859-8000 .. **Goldstein,** Stephanie J '93 (Fried FHS&J LLP) -1 NY Plz -NY 10004
(212) 878-4078 .. **Goldstein,** Stephen M '85 %Mitsui & Co -200 Park Av -NY 10166 **Fx:**878-4800
(212) 632-6972 .. **Goldstein,** Stephen R '96 Lazard Ltd -30 Rckfllr Plz -NY 10112
(516) 873-0011 .. **Goldstein,** Steven F '86 (S Goldstein,LLP) -1 Old Cntry Rd -Carle Pl 11514 **Fx:**873-0120
(516) 733-1810 .. **Goldstein,** Steven J '87 -77 Newbrdg Rd -Hicksvll 11801 **Fx:**620-0751
(212) 374-3447 .. **Goldstein,** Steven L '96 %NYC Dept Educ -52 Chmbrs -NY 10007
(212) 335-9000 .. **Goldstein,** Steven M '88 %DA -1 Hogan Pl -NY 10013
(914) 698-7772 .. **Goldstein,** Steven R '83 -1066 Seahaven Dr -Mamaroneck 10543
(516) 677-9400 .. **Goldstein,** Steven R '83 (Goldstein & A) -575 Underhill Blvd -Syosset 11791
(516) 488-3300 .. **Goldstein,** Steven R '89 (Shaub AC&S,LLP) -1983 Marcus Av -Lk Success 11042
(212) 679-1330 .. **Goldstein,** Steven T '93 (Goldstein & H,LLP) -280 Mad Av -NY 10016 **Fx:**779-2469
(212) 664-6143 .. **Goldstein,** Stuart J '01 NBC Universal -30 Rckfllr Plz -NY 10112 **Fx:**664-5290
(212) 504-6000 .. **Goldstein,** Stuart N '97 (Cadwalader W&T LLP) -1 World Fncl Ctr -NY 10281
(718) 418-4200 .. **Goldstein,** Stuart R '78 -5703 Catalpa Av -Rdgwd 11385
(212) 245-6565 .. **Goldstein,** Stuart W '79 Cnsl Levine P&M,LLP -1740 Bway -NY 10019
(212) 632-6000 .. **Goldstein,** Tamar '05 %Lazard Freres -30 Rckfllr Plz -NY 10112 **Fx:**632-6060
(212) 351-4500 .. **Goldstein,** Wendy C '96 (Epstein B&G,PC) -250 Park Av -NY 10177
(845) 454-9700 .. **Goldstein,** Wm '57 (Ouimette G&A) -88 Market Bx192 -Poughkeepsie 12601
(212) 483-9600 .. **Goldstein,** Wm A '80 (Costello S&G LLP) -44 Wall -NY 10005
(718) 222-2026 .. **Goldstein,** Yair S '86 %Law Dept -350 Jay -Brklyn 11201 **Fx:**222-2088
(212) 408-2500 .. **Goldstein,** Zachary N '09 %Baker B,LLP -30 Rckfllr Plz -NY 10112
(845) 371-5441 .. **Goldstein,** Zev '84 -Bx952 -Monsey 10952 **Fx:**352-5117
(212) 587-7798 .. **Goldstern,** Vladimir '87 -277 Bway -NY 10007 **Fx:**587-1594
(212) 687-3440 .. **Goldstick,** David T '58 OfCnsl Goldstick WF&G,PC -7 Penn Plz -NY 10001
(212) 687-3440 .. **Goldstick Weinberger Feldman & Grossman,PC** -7 Penn Plz -NY 10001 **Fx:**818-0625
(718) 590-2940 .. **Goldstock,** Bruce A '69 -215 E 161st -Bronx 10451
(212) 742-9280 .. **Goldstock,** Ronald '69 Waterfront Comm -39 Bway -NY 10006 **Fx:**480-0587
(914) 472-5193 .. **Goldston,** Alan M '73 -164 White Rd -Scarsdale 10583 **Fx:**725-7499
(516) 465-8090 .. **Goldston,** Stacey L '02 %North Shore-LIJ Hlth Systm -145 Community Dr -Gt Neck 11021 **Fx:**465-8013
(212) 554-0400 .. **Goldstone,** Andrew A '07 %Grubman I&S,PC -152 W 57th -NY 10019
(212) 962-2800 .. **Goldstone,** Bruce H '58 (Schwartz G&C,LLP) -90 Broad -NY 10004
(212) 363-6900 .. **Goldstone,** Danielle M '06 %Faust GS&B LLP -2 Rector -NY 10006
(716) 551-4965 .. **Goldstone,** Doren G '77 %NLRB -130 S Elmwood Av -Buffalo 14202 **Fx:**551-4972
(212) 687-6642 .. **Goldstone,** Maro A '64 (Newman & Co.PC) -501 Mad Av -NY 10022
(718) 591-5457 .. **Goldstone,** Stephanie S '83 -76-23 171st -Flushng 11366
(212) 962-2800 .. **Goldstone,** Terri J '99 %Schwartz G&C,LLP -90 Broad -NY 10004
(212) 448-1100 .. **Goldvaser,** Amalia '10 %McLaughlin & S,LLP -260 Mad Av -NY 10016
(212) 407-7700 .. **Goldwasser,** Dan L '66 (Vedder P,PC) -1633 Bway -NY 10019
(212) 696-6000 .. **Goldwasser,** Howard M '92 (Curtis M-PC&M LLP) -101 Park Av -NY 10178
(646) 873-6020 .. **Goldwasser,** Peter N '08 Transportation Alternatives -127 W 26th -NY 10001
(212) 833-1106 .. **Goldwater,** Andrew W '83 (Friedman KS&A LLP) -1633 Bway -NY 10019 **Fx:**373-7906
(718) 990-6248 .. **Goldweber,** Ann Leslie '84 %St John's Law Schl -8000 Utopia Pkwy -Jamaica 11439 **Fx:**591-1855
(212) 355-4149 .. **Goldweber,** Elyse S '73 (Goldweber E LLP) -635 Mad Av -NY 10022
(212) 355-4149 .. **Goldweber Epstein LLP** -635 Mad Av -NY 10022 **Fx:**308-9559
(516) 334-1925 .. **Goldweber,** Max '47 (M Goldweber & Assoc) -2056 Stratford Dr -Westbury 11590
(212) 309-5484 .. **Goldweitz,** Julie A '93 Reed Elsevier Inc -125 Park Av -NY 10017
(516) 466-8005 .. **Goldwyn,** Martin M '78 (Tashlik KG&C PC) -40 Cuttermill Rd -Gt Neck 11021
(646) 746-8909 .. **Gold-Zafra,** Pamela R '05 %Wilentz G&S -110 William -NY 10038 **Fx:**(732) 726-6636
(212) 460-3196 .. **Goldzweig,** Sharon G '91 Con Ed -4 Irving Pl -NY 10003
(516) 688-1700 .. **Gole,** Rose E '86 %IRS -1600 Stewart Av -Westbury 11590 **Fx:**688-1750
(212) 947-2900 .. **Golemi,** Ingrid '06 %Kazlow & K -237 W 35th -NY 10001
(212) 907-7300 .. **Golenbock Eiseman Assor Bell & Peskoe** -437 Mad Av -NY 10022 **Fx:**754-0330
(212) 907-7300 .. **Golenbock,** Jeffrey T '77 (Golenbock EAB&P) -437 Mad Av -NY 10022
(212) 403-1000 .. **Golenbock,** Scott W '06 %Wachtell LR&K -51 W 52nd -NY 10019
(914) 764-4680 .. **Golenbock,** Susan A '77 -28 Twin Fawn Ln -Pound Rdg 10576 **Fx:**764-8036
(212) 676-0053 .. **Golfinopoulos,** George '69 Assigned Cnsl Plan -253 Bway -NY 10007 **Fx:**676-0089
(718) 267-9744 .. **Golfinopoulos,** Kostas '91 -3116 Bway -Astoria 11106 **Fx:**267-9746
(718) 298-0500 .. **Golia,** Donna-Marie E '97 %Surrogate's Ct -88-11 Sutphin Blvd -Jamaica 11435 **Fx:**520-5048
(212) 506-2500 .. **Golianopoulos,** Antonia '03 %Mayer B LLP -1675 Bway -NY 10019
(516) 742-4699 .. **Golia-Paladin,** David E '78 -Bx 66 -Mineola 11501
(212) 790-0240 .. **Golick,** Toby '69 %Benj N Cardozo Schl of Law -55 5th Av -NY 10003 **Fx:**790-0345
(212) 315-5575 .. **Golieb,** Abner J '50 Cnsl Muchnick G&G,PC -200 Park Av S -NY 10003
(212) 315-5575 .. **Golieb,** John A '80 (Muchnick G&G,PC) -200 Park Av S -NY 10003
(631) 737-8200 .. **Golightly,** Laura Casale '02 %T Campagna -4949 Express Dr N -Ronkonkoma 11779 **Fx:**737-8687
(914) 672-8047 .. **Golimbu,** Alexander N '95 -81 Pondfld Rd -Bronxvll 10708
(212) 355-5353 .. **Golin,** Chas D '93 -260 Mad Av -NY 10016 **Fx:**448-0066
(212) 403-1000 .. **Golin,** Elaine P '98 Cnsl Wachtell LR&K -51 W 52nd -NY 10019
(607) 277-7286 .. **Golinker,** Lewis '80 -225 Rdgdl Rd -Ithaca 14850
(212) 344-9300 .. **Golino,** Lorraine '87 OfCnsl S Golino -46 Trinity Pl -NY 10006 **Fx:**363-9444
(212) 344-9300 .. **Golino,** Santo '88 -46 Trinity Pl -NY 10006 **Fx:**363-9444
(212) 230-1300 .. **Golinski,** Pamela M '89 (Beigelman F&F,PC) -100 Wall -NY 10005 **Fx:**230-1090
(718) 855-9000 .. **Golinski,** Paul A '64 (Cullen and D LLP) -177 Montague -Brklyn 11201
(914) 249-5978 .. **Golinsky,** Jodi B '99 %MasterCard Intl -2000 Purchase -Purchase 10577
(516) 572-3865 .. **Golio,** Michl R '02 Sheriff's Dept -100 Carman Av -E Meadow 11554 **Fx:**572-3862
(914) 304-4320 .. **Golio,** Richd I '04 -75 S Bway -White Plns 10601
(212) 809-7600 .. **Golisano,** Brent S '02 %Cheven K&H -40 Wall -NY 10005
(212) 393-1200 .. **Golkin,** Jeffrey '84 -150 Bway -NY 10038 **Fx:**393-1201
(212) 750-8300 .. **Golkin,** Perry '79 %KKR -9 W 57th -NY 10019 **Fx:**750-0003
(914) 785-5300 .. **Gollihue,** Lisa L '87 %A Lamer -555 Taxter Rd -Elmsfrd 10523 **Fx:**347-4269
(518) 474-6625 .. **Gollop,** Scott W '84 %Insurance Dept -1 Commerce Plz -Albany 12260
(212) 619-4444 .. **Gollub,** Michl S '95 (Marshall CW&B,PC) -116 John -NY 10038
(212) 371-5400 .. **Golodner,** Scott M '97 %Weisman CS&M PC -445 Park Av -NY 10022
(631) 425-3099 .. **Golomb,** Alan E '69 -707 Walt Whitman Rd -Melvll 11747 **Fx:**923-1447
(212) 661-9000 .. **Golomb,** David B '75 -230 Park Av -NY 10169 **Fx:**661-6181
(212) 859-8000 .. **Golomb,** Tal J '03 %Fried FHS&J LLP -1 NY Plz -NY 10004
(718) 284-3505 .. **Golombeck,** Abraham Zev '84 -960 Franklin Av -Brklyn 11225 **Fx:**693-1941
(516) 334-2120 .. **Golombek,** Lori '83 -400 Post Av -Westbury 11590 **Fx:**334-6605
(718) 590-7781 .. **Golombek,** Sarah L '04 %ACS -900 Sheridan Av -Bronx 10451
(914) 323-7000 .. **Golonka,** Paula J '09 %Wilson EME&D LLP -3 Gannett Dr -White Plns 10604
(607) 732-6646 .. **Golos,** Abraham '55 (Etkind & G) -150 Lk -Elmira 14901
(718) 250-3441 .. **Golowa,** Dvora I '99 %DA -350 Jay -Brklyn 11201 **Fx:**250-2314
(212) 310-8000 .. **Goltser,** Lyuba A '02 %Weil G&M LLP -767 5th Av -NY 10153
(212) 805-3900 .. **Goltsman,** Mara '99 %Clausen M PC -1 Chase Manh Plz -NY 10005
(212) 608-1260 .. **Goltzer,** George R '73 -200 W 57th -NY 10019 **Fx:**980-2968
(212) 838-4811 .. **Golub,** Aaron Richd '72 (AR Golub,PC) -42 E 64th -NY 10065 **Fx:**838-4869
(212) 619-4444 .. **Golub,** Adam J '10 %Marshall CW&B,PC -116 John -NY 10038
(212) 686-4300 .. **Golub,** Benjamin J '66 -10 E 40th -NY 10016 **Fx:**689-2079
(212) 476-9000 .. **Golub,** Carolyn S '90 %Neuberger Berman,LLC -605 3rd Av -NY 10158 **Fx:**476-9862
(212) 542-9860 .. **Golub,** Danl A '75 %Grant Thornton LLP -666 3rd Av -NY 10017 **Fx:**370-4520
(212) 969-3000 .. **Golub,** Ira M '83 (Proskauer R LLP) -1585 Bway -NY 10036
(212) 508-6700 .. **Golub,** Jonathan A '07 %Tannenbaum HS&H LLP -900 3rd Av -NY 10022
(212) 693-1000 .. **Golub,** Mitchell A '79 (Golub & G,LLP) -225 Bway -NY 10007 **Fx:**693-0090
(212) 619-4444 .. **Golub,** Norman J '82 (Marshall CW&B,PC) -116 John -NY 10038
(646) 386-3631 .. **Golub,** Robt '65 %Supreme Ct-Law Dept -60 Centre -NY 10007
(212) 839-5300 .. **Golub,** Robt L '87 (Sidley A LLP) -787 7th Av -NY 10019
(212) 693-1000 .. **Golub,** Steven M '87 (Golub & G,LLP) -225 Bway -NY 10007 **Fx:**693-0090
(212) 617-1395 .. **Golubock,** Janis M '06 %Bloomberg LP -731 Lex Av -NY 10022
(914) 286-4782 .. **Golubock,** Rhona S '95 Heineken USA Inc -360 Hmltn Av -White Plns 10601
(914) 725-8099 .. **Goluboff,** Nicole Belson '91 -31 Lawrence Rd -Scarsdale 10583 **Fx:**725-4010
(212) 446-4800 .. **Golubov,** Oleg '08 %Kirkland & E LLP -153 E 53rd -NY 10022
(212) 221-5700 .. **Golubtchik,** Doran '92 %Goldberg WFG LLP -1501 Bway -NY 10036
(212) 688-4500 .. **Gomberg,** Ira A '70 -444 Mad Av -NY 10022 **Fx:**888-5025
(516) 248-9700 .. **Gomberg,** Trevor M '10 %S Levitt & Assoc,PC -2 Hillside Av -Williston Pk 11596 **Fx:**741-9224
(212) 417-8700 .. **Gombiner,** Mark B '78 %Fed Def of NY Inc -52 Duane -NY 10007 **Fx:**571-0392
(212) 669-4501 .. **Gombinski,** Steven J '80 %Tax Appls Tribunal -1 Centre -NY 10007 **Fx:**669-4503

(718) 613-2164 .. **Gombos,** Carrie L '05 %Hon S Townes USDC -225 Cadman Plz E -Brklyn 11201
(212) 806-5400 .. **Gomelskaya,** Irina '03 %Stroock &S&L LLP -180 Maiden Ln -NY 10038
(718) 715-4699 .. **Gomelsky,** Victor '93 -1330 Vian Av -Hewlett 11557 **Fx:**879-6420
(212) 457-1280 .. **Gomer,** Lisa '92 UN Ofc for Project Srvcs -405 Lex Av -NY 10174
(631) 549-1111 .. **Gomerman,** Adam C '91 -807 E Jericho Tpk -Huntngtn Sta 11746 **Fx:**549-7384
(631) 549-1777 .. **Gomerman,** Jan '02 -807 E Jericho Tpk -Huntngtn Sta 11746 **Fx:**549-7384
(718) 286-2000 .. **Gomes,** Chandra '85 %Leg Aid -120-46 Qns Blvd -Kew Gdns 11415 **Fx:**286-2286
(212) 490-3000 .. **Gomes,** Elefteria M '07 %Wilson EME&D LLP -150 E 42nd -NY 10017
(212) 745-2018 .. **Gomes,** Jannine M '03 IBM Corp -590 Mad Av -NY 10022
(516) 742-3636 .. **Gomes,** Jason I '05 %Brecher FPWT&Z,PC -1325 Franklin Av -Gdn Cty 11530
(212) 450-4000 .. **Gomes,** Juelle J '10 %Davis P&W LLP -450 Lex Av -NY 10017
(845) 278-7272 .. **Gomes,** Linda J '04 Cnsl Putnam ARC -31 Intl Dr -Brewstr 10509
(212) 326-3939 .. **Gomes Williams,** Nadine '05 %Jones D -222 E 41st -NY 10017
(646) 386-4041 .. **Gomez,** Alma M '93 Hon J Yates -100 Centre -NY 10013
(315) 218-8000 .. **Gomez,** Candace J '08 %Bond S&K,PLLC -1 Lincoln Ctr -Syracuse 13202
(212) 883-9268 .. **Gomez,** Danl T '01 %Verizon -240 E 38th -NY 10016
(212) 458-5953 .. **Gomez,** Fabio M '01 AIG -175 Water -NY 10038 **Fx:**458-2263
(212) 340-0400 .. **Gomez,** Fidel E '00 %Appllt Div 1st Dept -27 Mad Av -NY 10010 **Fx:**889-4412
(212) 395-6405 .. **Gomez,** Gayton P '96 Verizon -1095 Av of Amer -NY 10036
(212) 992-8932 .. **Gomez,** Jennifer M '09 Institute for Policy Integrity -139 MacDougal -NY 10012 **Fx:**995-4592
(516) 759-1212 .. **Gomez,** John B '93 Cnsl Mohen & T LLP -186 Birch Hill Rd -Locust Vly 11560
(212) 487-9701 .. **Gomez,** Jose M '08 %Robin HK&F -1 Bttry Pk Plz -NY 10014
(212) 791-0285 .. **Gomez,** Julissa A '01 %Malaby & B,LLC -150 Bway -NY 10038 **Fx:**791-0286
(212) 953-3500 .. **Gomez,** Kenneth V '84 -600 3rd Av -NY 10016 **Fx:**953-3506
(845) 321-5116 .. **Gomez,** Kevin '01 -930 Grnd Cncrs -Bronx 10451 **Fx:**(718) 410-7776
(212) 563-4100 .. **Gomez,** Lisa M '95 (Cohen W&S LLP) -330 W 42nd -NY 10036
(212) 221-7005 .. **Gomez,** Lourdes P '89 -275 Mad Av -NY 10016 **Fx:**730-0485
(212) 382-6600 .. **Gomez,** Maureen Suyapa '96 %NYC Bar -42 W 44th -NY 10036 **Fx:**398-6634
(716) 857-4688 .. **Gomez,** Megan A '06 Univera Healthcare -205 Park Club Ln -Buffalo 14221
(716) 856-1344 .. **Gomez,** Rafael O '01 (Bouvier Prtnrshp,LLP) -350 Main -Buffalo 14202 **Fx:**856-1369
(212) 681-0600 .. **Gomez,** Roberto L '92 %Ostrager CF&B,PC -570 Lex Av -NY 10022
(212) 788-0522 .. **Gomez,** Sheila L '94 %Law Dept -100 Church -NY 10007 **Fx:**788-0367
(718) 505-6650 .. **Gomez,** Vanessa A '00 %Kaplan & M -75-20 Astoria Blvd -E Elmhrst 11370
(845) 452-5900 .. **Gomez Anderson,** Janis M '98 OfCnsl Van DeWater & V,LLP -85 Civic Ctr Plz Bx112 -Poughkeepsie 12602
(212) 788-0883 .. **Gomez-Sanchez,** Danl S '09 %Law Dept -100 Church -NY 10007 **Fx:**788-0367
(212) 688-8555 .. **Gomez-Trochez,** Jonathan '09 %Fragomen DB&L LLP -7 Hanover Sq -NY 10004
(718) 340-4200 .. **Gomez-Velez,** Natalie '90 %CUNY Law Schl -65-21 Main -Flushng 11367 **Fx:**340-4482
(516) 599-1759 .. **Gomoka,** Christopher N '05 -877 N Corona Av -Vly Stream 11580
(212) 351-4500 .. **Gomprecht,** Diana Costantino '02 %Epstein B&G,PC -250 Park Av -NY 10177
(516) 739-2229 .. **Goncalves,** Ana M '07 %M Pollack -114 Old Cntry Rd -Mineola 11501
(212) 588-0800 .. **Goncalves,** Brian S '07 %Frommer L&H LLP -745 5th Av -NY 10151
(212) 962-1020 .. **Goncalves,** Carmine J '00 %M Lamonsoff -80 Maiden Ln -NY 10038 **Fx:**962-3078
(212) 431-7129 .. **Goncalves,** Jessica M '08 %Purrington MW LLP -320 W 13th -NY 10014
(212) 376-5588 .. **Gonchar,** Eric P '89 -757 3rd Av -NY 10017
(212) 804-4200 .. **Gondiosa,** Tania A '98 %Mound CW&G -One Bttry Pk Plz -NY 10004
(716) 668-0001 .. **Gondree,** Howard F '70 -2448 Union Rd -Cheektowaga 14227
(212) 468-8000 .. **Gondrez,** Marisa S '04 %Morrison & F LLP -1290 Av of Amer -NY 10104
(949) 399-7000 .. **Gonell,** Carrie Anne '00 %Morgan L&B LLP -101 Park Av -NY 10178 **Fx:**399-7001
(212) 735-3000 .. **Gonen,** Danl M '08 %Skadden ASM&F LLP -4 Times Sq -NY 10036
(516) 358-8825 .. **Goner,** Robt D '93 (Bunting G & Assoc PC) -60 E 42nd -NY 10165 **Fx:**450-3510
(212) 259-8000 .. **Gong,** Chang-Do '02 (Dewey & L LLP) -1301 Av of Amer -NY 10019
(212) 682-2288 .. **Gong,** Eileen L '99 %Sankel S&M,LLP -750 3rd Av -NY 10017
(718) 888-8880 .. **Gongsun,** Dawei '04 %Dai & Assoc,PC -136-20 38th Av -Flushng 11354 **Fx:**888-9270
(518) 370-4793 .. **Gonick,** Denise V '92 MVP Health Care -625 State -Schnctdy 12305 **Fx:**370-0852
(212) 983-9330 .. **Gonnelli,** Adam R '98 %Faruqi & F,LLP -369 Lex Av -NY 10017 **Fx:**983-9331
(212) 894-7200 .. **Gonnello,** Richd W '00 (Entwistle & C LLP) -280 Park Av -NY 10017
(585) 288-4832 .. **Gonsalves,** Andrew K '98 %Heslin RF&M PC -100 Meridian Centre -Rchstr 14618
(718) 270-5190 .. **Gonsalves,** Emmanuel E '97 %Medgar Evers Cllg -1650 Bedford Av -Brklyn 11225
(518) 377-2225 .. **Gonsalves Lloyd,** Jeanne M '89 (Friedman H&M,LLP) -100 Great Oaks Blvd Bx38279 -Albany 12203
(718) 246-5708 .. **Gonshorek,** Eliot D '87 (Gonshorek & P) -50 Court -Brklyn 11201
(718) 246-5708 .. **Gonshorek & Pludwin** -50 Court -Brklyn 11201 **Fx:**852-6086
(516) 747-1010 .. **Gonski,** Dennis M '75 (Dollinger G&G) -1 Old Cntry Rd -Carle Pl 11514
(212) 730-7750 .. **Gonson,** Benjamin N '87 (Nicoletti GS&O,LLP) -555 5th Av -NY 10017
(518) 474-3219 .. **Gonsowski,** Margaret Mary '84 %NYSHESC -99 Wshngtn Av -Albany 12255 **Fx:**486-6515
(716) 373-0004 .. **Gonzales,** Bronwyn E '08 %Pub Def -175 N Union -Olean 14760 **Fx:**373-3462
(212) 455-2000 .. **Gonzales,** Jessica L '07 %Simpson T&B LLP -425 Lex Av -NY 10017
(914) 738-3632 .. **Gonzales,** Michl P '90 -1329 Manor Cir -Pelham Mnr 10803
(212) 698-3500 .. **Gonzales,** Robt S '04 Dechert LLP -1095 Av of Amer -NY 10036
(914) 366-5700 .. **Gonzales,** Rosellen '06 %MA Bjork -660 Wht Plns Rd -Tarrytwn 10591 **Fx:**366-5759
(631) 665-5884 .. **Gonzales,** Victor R '99 -220 5th Av -Bay Shr 11706
(212) 751-9800 .. **Gonzales-Frisbie,** Jennifer T '08 %Morelli R PC -950 3rd Av -NY 10022
(212) 836-8000 .. **Gonzalez,** Adrienne '02 %Kaye S LLP -425 Park Av -NY 10022
(212) 259-8000 .. **Gonzalez,** Albert A '05 %Dewey & L LLP -1301 Av of Amer -NY 10019
(914) 725-7893 .. **Gonzalez,** Ana I '94 %Donoghue TA&D LLP -700 Wht Plns Rd -Scarsdale 10583
(212) 587-7977 .. **Gonzalez,** Andrew A '92 (Gonzalez O&H LLP) -841 Bway -NY 10013
(914) 681-8700 .. **Gonzalez,** Antonio A '07 %Milber MP&S LLP -3 Barker Av -White Plns 10601
(212) 883-1700 .. **Gonzalez,** Carolina R '08 %Duval & S LLP -101 Park Av -NY 10178
(718) 292-3154 .. **Gonzalez,** Cesar Jr. '89 -840 Grnd Cncrs -Bronx 10451
(516) 560-6400 .. **Gonzalez,** Connie '02 %Leg Aid -1 Helen Keller Way -Hempstd 11550 **Fx:**565-3694
(646) 610-5400 .. **Gonzalez,** Danl '03 NYPD -1 Police Plz -NY 10038
(518) 275-4720 .. **Gonzalez,** David A '00 %DA -6 Lodge -Albany 12207 **Fx:**487-5093
(718) 871-5560 .. **Gonzalez,** Dwight M '95 -453 4th Av -Brklyn 11215 **Fx:**871-8024
(212) 735-3000 .. **Gonzalez,** Edw E '80 (Skadden ASM&F LLP) -4 Times Sq -NY 10036
(212) 451-2300 .. **Gonzalez,** Elizabeth R '05 %Olshan GFR&W LLP -65 E 55th -NY 10022
(718) 250-2000 .. **Gonzalez,** Eric '96 %DA -350 Jay -Brklyn 11201 **Fx:**250-2314
(212) 295-1223 .. **Gonzalez,** Felix A '01 KDDI -825 3rd Av -NY 10022
(718) 845-4444 .. **Gonzalez,** Frank '82 (Aliazzo M&G) -94-03 101st Av -Ozone Pk 11416
(718) 391-6035 .. **Gonzalez,** George '02 Dept of Ed -28-11 Qns Plz N -LIC 11101
(212) 317-5436 .. **Gonzalez,** Gloria G '00 Swiss Re New Markets -55 E 52nd -NY 10055
(212) 468-4800 .. **Gonzalez,** Gustavo M '07 %Davis & G LLP -1740 Bway -NY 10019
(212) 506-2500 .. **Gonzalez,** Hector '88 (Mayer B LLP) -1675 Bway -NY 10019
(212) 465-1500 .. **Gonzalez,** Ismael '90 (I Gonzalez & Assoc,PC) -53 W 36th -NY 10018
(631) 271-9500 .. **Gonzalez,** John J '92 -175 Deer Prk Rd W -Dix Hlls 11746 **Fx:**271-9528
(212) 275-1563 .. **Gonzalez,** Jorge L '97 TAG Assoc LLC -75 Rckfllr Plz -NY 10019 **Fx:**275-1510
(718) 472-4493 .. **Gonzalez,** Jose A '88 -82-11 37th Av -Jcksn Hts 11372
(212) 770-5508 .. **Gonzalez,** Jose R '96 %AIG -70 Pine -NY 10270
(914) 249-3846 .. **Gonzalez,** Juan C '02 %MasterCard Intl -2000 Purchase -Purchase 10577
(212) 599-8200 .. **Gonzalez,** Juan C '07 %Shaub AC&S,LLP -655 3rd Av -NY 10017
(516) 877-5600 .. **Gonzalez,** Juan S '98 %R Tusa -1225 Franklin Av -Gdn Cty 11530 **Fx:**877-5695
(212) 419-1500 .. **Gonzalez,** Julian J '05 %Lewis C&N,PC -350 7th Av -NY 10001
(315) 433-4582 .. **Gonzalez,** Kelly B '02 Syracuse Univ Cllg of Law -306 MacNaughton Hall -Syracuse 13244
(718) 698-2200 .. **Gonzalez,** Kenneth A '94 (Merlino & G) -1259 Richmond Av -Staten Isl 10314 **Fx:**698-0024
(212) 783-4440 .. **Gonzalez,** Laura C '97 Citigroup Global Mgmt -485 Lex Av -NY 10017
(212) 533-6300 .. **Gonzalez,** Maria Elena V '89 %NYSUT -52 Bway -NY 10004 **Fx:**995-2347
(718) 526-2746 .. **Gonzalez,** Maria Ines '95 -185-01 Hillside Av -Jamaica 11432 **Fx:**297-4613
(718) 850-6969 .. **Gonzalez,** Marianne '94 -95-07 Jamaica Av -Woodhvn 11421 **Fx:**850-6967
(718) 643-0411 .. **Gonzalez,** Maricel '88 Family Ct -283 Adams -Brklyn 11201
(212) 966-6420 .. **Gonzalez,** Marly '99 Lwyrs For Children -110 Lafayette -NY 10013 **Fx:**966-0531
(212) 968-2300 .. **Gonzalez,** Matthew L '03 -39 Bway -NY 10006 **Fx:**968-2400
(212) 326-2000 .. **Gonzalez,** Mia N '09 %O'Melveny & M LLP -7 Times Sq -NY 10036
(212) 361-1099 .. **Gonzalez,** Miguel A '73 DOH -66 John -NY 10038
(917) 533-0707 .. **Gonzalez,** Miriam M '97 (Gonzalez & Prtnr) -1 Plymouth Dr S -Glen Head 11545 **Fx:**(516) 671-6280
(212) 669-7778 .. **Gonzalez,** Miriam M '00 %Comptroller -1 Centre -NY 10007 **Fx:**669-2884
(516) 741-2170 .. **Gonzalez,** Myrka A '83 -221 Mineola Blvd -Mineola 11501
(212) 587-7977 .. **Gonzalez Oberlander & Holohan LLP** -841 Bway -NY 10013 **Fx:**587-7955
(212) 297-5800 .. **Gonzalez,** Rachel A '07 %Day P LLP -7 Times Sq -NY 10036
(212) 225-2000 .. **Gonzalez,** Rachel L '10 %Cleary GS&H -1 Lbrty Plz -NY 10006
(212) 697-7383 .. **Gonzalez,** Rafael '88 %Mandel Law Firm -370 Lex Av -NY 10017 **Fx:**681-6157
(212) 770-3817 .. **Gonzalez,** Ralph R '87 ALICO -277 Park Av -NY 10017
(212) 953-2381 .. **Gonzalez,** Richd '09 %Rubin F&F,LLP -292 Mad Av -NY 10017
(212) 943-0110 .. **Gonzalez,** Rodrigo A '91 (Poles TS&G, LLP) -46 Trinity Pl -NY 10006
(212) 564-3625 .. **Gonzalez,** Ronnie '96 -600 W 111th -NY 10025
(212) 601-2680 .. **Gonzalez Saggio & Harlan LLP** -350 5th Av -NY 10118 **Fx:**601-2681
(212) 902-1000 .. **Gonzalez,** Steven A '03 %Goldman Sachs -1 NY Plz -NY 10004
(212) 931-7800 .. **Gonzalez,** Steven P '03 Ofc of Commsnr of Baseball -245 Park Av -NY 10167
(212) 768-6700 .. **Gonzalez,** Susana K '03 %Sonnenschein N&R LLP -2 World Fncl Ctr -NY 10281
(212) 557-4000 .. **Gonzalez,** Tracey Topper '04 %Grunfeld DLS&K LLP -399 Park Av -NY 10022

(212) 225-2000 .. **Gonzalez,** Vanessa M '07 %Cleary GS&H -1 Lbrty Plz -NY 10006
(212) 297-5800 .. **Gonzalez,** Veronica M '10 %Day P LLP -7 Times Sq -NY 10036
(212) 341-7946 .. **Gonzalez,** Vincent L '89 (Brecher FPWT&Z,PC) -233 Bway -NY 10279
(518) 457-4951 .. **Gonzalez,** Wm M '78 %Dept Correctional Srvcs -1220 Wshngtn Av -Albany 12226 **Fx:**457-7555
(212) 575-7900 .. **Gonzalez,** Yasmin T '06 %Ballon SB&N,PC -729 7th Av -NY 10019
(718) 898-6000 .. **Gonzalez,** Zoraida E '00 -82-11 37th Av -Jcksn Hts 11372
(516) 775-7007 .. **Gonzalez-Abreu,** Arianna M '09 %Gutman MB&S,PC -813 Jericho Tpk -New Hyde Pk 11040
(718) 273-0300 .. **Gonzalez-Acaron,** Sara '06 %Danna & Assoc,PC -1145 Forest Av -Staten Isl 10310 **Fx:**448-6820
(631) 712-6314 .. **Gonzalez-Dotzler,** Ana Maria '96 US Probation Dept -202 Fed Plz -Central Islip 11722
(718) 590-6563 .. **Gonzalez-Harris,** Adilia '00 %Law Dept -198 E 161st -Bronx 10451 **Fx:**590-2686
(212) 735-3000 .. **Gonzalez Lazzeri,** Alejandro '09 %Skadden ASM&F LLP -4 Times Sq -NY 10036
(212) 489-1600 .. **Gonzalez-Padron,** Melissa L '07 %Deloitte LLP -1633 Bway -NY 10019 **Fx:**492-4201
(646) 223-4200 .. **Gonzalez-Roth,** Beatriz '96 %Reuters -3 Times Sq -NY 10036 **Fx:**223-4250
(646) 610-6325 .. **Gonzalez-Taylor,** Yadhira '03 Police Dept -1 Police Plz -NY 10038 **Fx:**610-8938
(718) 875-1300 .. **Gonzo,** Barbara D '78 %Appllt Div 2nd Dept -45 Monroe Pl -Brklyn 11201 **Fx:**858-2446
(914) 682-2068 .. **Gooby,** Steven F '96 (Ansa A,LLP) -50 Main -White Plns 10606
(212) 225-2000 .. **Gooch,** Anthony C '63 (Cleary GS&H) -1 Lbrty Plz -NY 10006
(212) 836-8000 .. **Gooch,** Kyle D '10 Kaye S LLP -425 Park Av -NY 10022
(718) 782-4200 .. **Good,** Adam E '01 Gaseteria Oil Corp -364 Maspeth Av -Brklyn 11211
(212) 735-3000 .. **Good,** Andrew M '07 %Skadden ASM&F LLP -4 Times Sq -NY 10036
(212) 340-3813 .. **Good,** David H '84 Credit Sights,Inc -470 Park Av S -NY 10016
(516) 663-6600 .. **Good,** Douglas J '72 (Ruskin MF,PC) -1425 RXR Plz -Uniondale 11556
(518) 447-8788 .. **Good,** Gerald S '96 (Lynch S, PLLC) -99 Pine -Albany 12207 **Fx:**320-8244
(716) 836-2397 .. **Good,** Marie S '53 -426 Woodward Av -Buffalo 14214
(718) 852-4612 .. **Good,** Michl J '85 -26 Court -Brklyn 11242 **Fx:**852-0092
(212) 391-6464 .. **Good,** Natalia Porcelli '01 %Shapiro Firm,LLP -500 5th Av -NY 10110 **Fx:**719-1616
(631) 727-2180 .. **Goodale,** Anne Marie '96 (Twomey LSKD&Q,LLP) -33 W 2nd Bx9398 -Rvrhead 11901
(212) 326-2000 .. **Goodall,** Catherine L '07 %O'Melveny & M LLP -7 Times Sq -NY 10036
(212) 310-8000 .. **Goodchild,** Seth '87 Cnsl Weil G&M LLP -767 5th Av -NY 10153
(607) 734-5004 .. **Goode,** James D '96 (Hamm R&G) -523 W Church -Elmira 14905 **Fx:**733-0277
(631) 231-1450 .. **Goode,** Wm G '00 Feldman K&M,PC -330 Vndrblt Motor Pkwy -Hauppauge 11788
(718) 222-2006 .. **Goode,** Y Gail '87 %Law Dept -350 Jay -Brklyn 11201 **Fx:**222-2088
(212) 486-2400 .. **Goodearl,** David J '02 %Leader & B LLP -630 3rd Av -NY 10017
(716) 664-4705 .. **Goodell,** Andrew W '82 (Goodell & G) -617 Wshngtn -Jamestwn 14701 **Fx:**483-6481
(607) 656-2311 .. **Goodell,** Arthur A '97 Raymond Corp -20 S Canal Bx130 -Greene 13778 **Fx:**656-9005
(212) 403-7300 .. **Goodell,** Maia B '05 %Vladeck WE&E,PC -1501 Bway -NY 10036
(518) 395-5400 .. **Goodell,** Rick '84 Racing & Wagering Bd -1 Bway Ctr -Schnctdy 12305 **Fx:**347-1250
(212) 536-8004 .. **Goodell,** Timothy B '85 Hess Corp -1185 Av of Amer -NY 10036
(212) 813-1600 .. **Gooden,** Shadaia M '09 %Kalow & S -488 Mad Av -NY 10022
(607) 734-1647 .. **Gooderum,** Karen '84 %Leg Srvcs -215 E Church -Elmira 14901 **Fx:**734-1018
(212) 788-8681 .. **Goode-Trufant,** Muriel L '93 %Law Dept -100 Church -NY 10007 **Fx:**788-0367
(914) 428-3400 .. **Goodfarb,** Adam D '80 (Goodfarb & S,LLP) -235 Main -White Plns 10601 **Fx:**428-8737
(212) 506-5000 .. **Goodfriend,** Douglas E '86 (Orrick H&S LLP) -51 W 52nd -NY 10019
(845) 369-3800 .. **Goodfriend,** Mark F '75 (Goodfriend S&G) -4 Exec Blvd -Suffern 10901
(845) 369-3800 .. **Goodfriend Saltzman & Goodfriend** -4 Exec Blvd -Suffern 10901 **Fx:**369-6356
(212) 715-0300 .. **Goodgold,** Christine M '88 %Tishman Speyer Prop -45 Rckfllr Plz -NY 10111 **Fx:**332-6603
(212) 318-6000 .. **Goodhouse,** Brendan M '09 %Paul HJ&W LLP -75 E 55th -NY 10022
(212) 909-6000 .. **Gooding,** Gregory V '89 (Debevoise & P LLP) -919 3rd Av -NY 10022
(212) 373-3000 .. **Goodison,** Eric S '88 (Paul WRW&G LLP) -1285 Av of Amer -NY 10019
(212) 421-4100 .. **Goodkind,** E Robt '59 (Pryor C LLP) -7 Times Sq -NY 10036
(212) 735-3000 .. **Goodlatte,** Jennifer F '10 %Skadden ASM&F LLP -4 Times Sq -NY 10036
(212) 984-7194 .. **Goodloe,** Wanda N '86 CB Richard Ellis -200 Park Av -NY 10166
(212) 715-9100 .. **Goodman,** Alissa R '03 %Kramer LN&F,LLP -1177 Av of Amer -NY 10036
(212) 431-8700 .. **Goodman,** Andrew J '78 (Garvey SB) -100 Wall -NY 10005
(212) 964-9755 .. **Goodman,** Ari M '94 -225 Bway -NY 10007
(212) 873-4806 .. **Goodman,** Arnold P '60 -500 West End Av -NY 10024 **Fx:**580-3278
(212) 739-0700 .. **Goodman,** Benjamin A '08 %Guggenheim Ptnrs -135 E 57th -NY 10022
(631) 421-2569 .. **Goodman,** Bonnie Sue '90 -Bx225 -Woodbury 11797
(212) 704-6000 .. **Goodman,** Brett D '07 %Troutman S LLP -405 Lex Av -NY 10174
(212) 664-3275 .. **Goodman,** Brett T '96 %NBC Olympics -30 Rckfllr Plz -NY 10112
(212) 223-0400 .. **Goodman,** Bruce S '04 %Zeichner E&K LLP -575 Lex Av -NY 10022
(212) 592-1400 .. **Goodman,** Carol M '91 (Herrick,F LLP) -2 Park Av -NY 10016
(212) 225-2000 .. **Goodman,** Corey M '08 %Cleary GS&H -1 Lbrty Plz -NY 10006
(516) 249-3450 .. **Goodman,** Dara C '08 Carman C&I,LLP -266 Main -Farmngdl 11735
(716) 854-2020 .. **Goodman,** David M '92 (Cellino & B,PC) -350 Main -Buffalo 14202
(845) 486-2280 .. **Goodman,** David S '68 Pub Def -22 Market -Poughkeepsie 12601 **Fx:**486-2266
(212) 907-9600 .. **Goodman,** Edw '85 (Ingram YGC&B,LLP) -250 Park Av -NY 10177
(212) 233-5000 .. **Goodman,** Edw S '95 (Simonson HL&G,PC) -15 Maiden Ln -NY 10038
(212) 808-0700 .. **Goodman,** Ezra N '68 (Norris M&M,PA) -875 3rd Av -NY 10022
(516) 624-6150 .. **Goodman,** Fern Susan '85 %Town Atty -Town Hall -Oyster Bay 11771 **Fx:**624-6196
(718) 888-7884 .. **Goodman,** Francine B '94 (FB Goodman,PC) -20-35 Parsons Blvd -Whitestone 11357
(518) 388-4276 .. **Goodman,** Fred L '84 %Cnty Atty -620 State -Schnctdy 12305 **Fx:**388-4493
(212) 661-1151 .. **Goodman,** Fredric B '89 (Marin G LLP) -40 Wall -NY 10005
(212) 768-6700 .. **Goodman,** Gary A '74 (Sonnenschein N&R LLP) -2 World Fncl Ctr -NY 10281
(212) 980-9697 .. **Goodman,** George S '87 Brady & Assoc -48 Wall -NY 10005
(631) 427-7790 .. **Goodman,** Gregory A '03 (Lewin GB,LLP) -900 Walt Whitman Rd -Melvll 11747
(631) 331-6182 .. **Goodman,** Gregory Scott '95 (Goodman & G) -45 Jesse Way -Mt Sinai 11766
(212) 319-1000 .. **Goodman,** H Nicholas '85 (Quirk & B,PC) -845 3rd Av -NY 10022
(212) 563-2866 .. **Goodman,** Herbert '65 -450 7th Av -NY 10123 **Fx:**268-6968
(212) 319-4900 .. **Goodman,** Herbert H '53 (Frishauf HG&C) -220 5th Av -NY 10001
(718) 250-2000 .. **Goodman,** Howard B '82 %DA -350 Jay -Brklyn 11201 **Fx:**250-2314
(212) 951-6566 .. **Goodman,** Howard J '82 %NYS Ed Dept-OLS -475 Park Av S -NY 10016 **Fx:**951-6573
(914) 277-3746 .. **Goodman,** Jacob '49 -27B Heritage Hills -Somers 10589
(212) 385-1191 .. **Goodman & Jacobs LLP** -75 Broad -NY 10004 **Fx:**385-1770
(212) 770-6019 .. **Goodman,** James B '87 %AIG -70 Pine -NY 10270 **Fx:**422-8198
(914) 664-4616 .. **Goodman,** Jane E '84 (Goodman & S) -22 W 1st -Mt Vernon 10550 **Fx:**664-4006
(212) 869-1940 .. **Goodman,** Janice '72 -275 7th Av -NY 10001 **Fx:**419-1510
(716) 856-4200 .. **Goodman,** Jason A '09 %Gibson M&C,LLP -69 Delaware Av -Buffalo 14202
(516) 466-1155 .. **Goodman,** Jay S '54 -6 Ridgeway -Gt Neck 11024 **Fx:**466-1156
(631) 261-5500 .. **Goodman,** Jeffrey L '00 J Goodman PC -115 Harrison Dr -Centerprt 11721
(212) 678-8881 .. **Goodman,** Jeffrey M '91 %Natl Ramah Commission -3080 Bway -NY 10027
(212) 428-2794 .. **Goodman,** Jill L '76 %Judicial Comm Women In Cts -25 Beaver -NY 10004
(914) 428-8300 .. **Goodman,** John A '87 OfCnsl Sacks,PC -707 Wstchstr Av -White Plns 10604 **Fx:**682-1707
(518) 692-7123 .. **Goodman,** John J Jr. '99 -8 Meader Rd -Greenwich 12834 **Fx:**692-7173
(212) 612-6272 .. **Goodman,** Joshua D '98 %Daiwa Cptl Mkts Amer,Inc -32 Old Slip -NY 10005 **Fx:**612-8433
(212) 848-4000 .. **Goodman,** Joshua M '09 %Shearman & S LLP -599 Lex Av -NY 10022
(716) 501-2078 .. **Goodman,** Joy '08 Cnsl Seneca Gaming Corp -310 4th -Niagara Fls 14303
(212) 755-5770 .. **Goodman,** Joyce P '89 %World Jewish Cong -501 Mad Av -NY 10022 **Fx:**755-5883
(212) 385-1191 .. **Goodman,** Judith F '80 (Goodman & J LLP) -75 Broad -NY 10004
(212) 250-2063 .. **Goodman,** Jules S '76 %Deutsche Bk -60 Wall -NY 10005
(516) 222-0500 .. **Goodman Jurist & Pandolfo,LLP** -1103 Stewart Av -Gdn Cty 11530 **Fx:**222-2462
(914) 381-7400 .. **Goodman,** Kendra M '05 %Rattet P&G,LLP -550 Mamaroneck Av -Harrison 10528
(516) 487-3690 .. **Goodman,** Kevin L '96 -59 Valley Vw Rd -Gt Neck 11021
(212) 940-8800 .. **Goodman,** Lauren M '06 %Katten MR LLP -575 Mad Av -NY 10022
(212) 696-6000 .. **Goodman,** Lawr '89 (Curtis M-PC&M LLP) -101 Park Av -NY 10178
(212) 725-5305 .. **Goodman,** Lawr B '95 -419 Park Av S -NY 10016 **Fx:**725-5321
(212) 949-8700 .. **Goodman,** Lawr G '61 (Eisner LLP) -750 3rd Av -NY 10017 **Fx:**891-4100
(914) 232-1800 .. **Goodman,** Lawr I '76 -247 Route 100 Bx431 -Somers 10589 **Fx:**470-1860
(212) 474-1000 .. **Goodman,** Lori Diamond '04 %Cravath S&M LLP -825 8th Av -NY 10019
(212) 442-1503 .. **Goodman,** Lorna B '76 %Law Dept -100 Church -NY 10007 **Fx:**788-0367
(212) 312-7125 .. **Goodman,** Lynn '89 State Ins Fund -199 Church -NY 10007 **Fx:**385-9199
(718) 464-7978 .. **Goodman,** Lynn C '85 -82-38 190th -Hollis 11423 **Fx:**464-7978
(914) 286-6803 .. **Goodman,** Marc A '87 5th St Capital -10 Bank -White Plns 10606
(212) 909-6000 .. **Goodman,** Mark P '88 (Debevoise & P LLP) -919 3rd Av -NY 10022
(518) 449-7777 .. **Goodman,** Martin J '73 Goodman Law Ofcs -784 Hmpshr Seat -Niskayuna 12309 **Fx:**391-2669
(212) 652-3782 .. **Goodman,** Martin R '94 (Schlesinger G&L LLP) -535 Mad Av -NY 10022
(212) 310-8000 .. **Goodman,** Max A '04 %Weil G&M LLP -767 5th Av -NY 10153
(212) 549-2622 .. **Goodman,** Melissa A '04 %ACLU -125 Broad -NY 10004 **Fx:**549-2651
(212) 895-2202 .. **Goodman,** Micah J '97 Ladder Capital Finance LLC -600 Lex Av -NY 10022
(212) 967-8001 .. **Goodman,** Michl S '68 (Goodman & L LLP) -460 Park Av -NY 10022
(516) 229-6000 .. **Goodman,** Nancy Steiger '89 %R Lau & Assoc -300 Jericho Quad Bx9040 -Jericho 11753 **Fx:**229-6167
(646) 386-5959 .. **Goodman,** Norman '50 (Cnty Clerk) -60 Centre -NY 10007
(212) 788-1088 .. **Goodman,** Olivia T '76 %Law Dept -100 Church -NY 10007 **Fx:**788-0367
(212) 753-7500 .. **Goodman,** Peter G '88 (Hartman & C LLP) -488 Mad Av -NY 10022
(631) 756-6050 .. **Goodman,** Peter J '96 Goodman Law Firm -535 Broadhllw Rd -Melvll 11747
(212) 402-9400 .. **Goodman,** Peter S '87 (McKool S,PC) -1 Bryant Park -NY 10036

(914) 375-0100 .. **Goodman,** Ramona L '86 (Novick ELRW&L,PC) -733 Ynkrs Av -Ynkrs 10704
(212) 578-1924 .. **Goodman,** Richd B '96 OSG Ship Mgmt -666 3rd Av -NY 10017
(917) 543-7630 .. **Goodman,** Richd J '77 -1482 1st Av -NY 10075
(212) 909-6000 .. **Goodman,** Robt D '89 (Debevoise & P LLP) -919 3rd Av -NY 10022
(212) 564-8883 .. **Goodman,** Robt G '68 R Goodman,PC -3 W 35th -NY 10001 **Fx:**594-0019
(914) 935-0015 .. **Goodman,** Robt I '91 -6 Legendary Cir -Rye Brook 10573 **Fx:**935-1061
(917) 601-1713 .. **Goodman,** Robt M '96 Environmental Control Bd -66 John -NY 10038
(212) 804-4200 .. **Goodman,** Robt S '71 (Mound CW&G) -One Bttry Pk Plz -NY 10004
(914) 391-8783 .. **Goodman,** Roberta S '82 -55 Whitetail Rd -Irvngtn 10533
(212) 766-1888 .. **Goodman,** Robyn B '05 %Morris DA&F -2 Rector -NY 10006
(212) 603-6300 .. **Goodman,** Ronald B '72 (Robinson BLGG&G PC) -875 3rd Av -NY 10022
(516) 227-2100 .. **Goodman & Saperstein** -100 Grdn City Plz -Gdn Cty 11530 **Fx:**227-2108
(631) 247-0404 .. **Goodman,** Scott A '08 %Jackson L LLP -58 S Srvc Rd -Melvll 11747
(212) 297-5800 .. **Goodman,** Scott Warren '98 (Day P LLP) -7 Times Sq -NY 10036
(212) 372-1000 .. **Goodman,** Sharon H '78 %Goldstein Golub Kessler -1185 Av of Amer -NY 10036 **Fx:**372-1001
(212) 306-8657 .. **Goodman,** Shelley '79 %Housing Auth -250 Bway -NY 10007
(973) 992-4800 .. **Goodman,** Stanley L '78 (Fox R LLP) -100 Park Av -NY 10017 **Fx:**992-9125
(516) 227-2100 .. **Goodman,** Stanley R '56 (Goodman & S) -100 Grdn City Plz -Gdn Cty 11530
(212) 431-7500 .. **Goodman,** Stephanie H '91 United Amer Land,LLC -430 W Bway -NY 10012
(518) 426-4600 .. **Goodman,** Stephen J '08 %Couch W,LLP -540 Bway Bx22222 -Albany 12201
(212) 421-4100 .. **Goodman,** Stephen M '78 (Pryor C LLP) -7 Times Sq -NY 10036
(212) 776-5000 .. **Goodman,** Stephen W '89 %NYC Housing Auth -250 Bway -NY 10007 **Fx:**776-5039
(631) 247-0404 .. **Goodman,** Steven S '80 (Jackson L LLP) -58 S Srvc Rd -Melvll 11747
(631) 331-6182 .. **Goodman,** Suzanne Napolitano '90 (Goodman & G) -45 Jesse Way -Mt Sinai 11766
(516) 466-3434 .. **Goodman,** Wm '84 -330 Grt Nck Rd -Gt Neck 11021 **Fx:**466-3490
(718) 488-7764 .. **Goodman,** Zerline L '89 -15 Clark -Brklyn 11201 **Fx:**596-0355
(212) 756-2000 .. **Goodman Binick,** Emily H '05 %Schulte R&Z LLP -919 3rd Av -NY 10022
(212) 972-1000 .. **Goodman Futterman,** Virginia L '83 (London F LLP) -59 Maiden Ln -NY 10038
(516) 240-8900 .. **Goodnough,** Roger A '72 OfCnsl Torre LGG&R,LLP -100 Jericho Quad -Jericho 11753
(516) 536-0900 .. **Goodovitch,** Paul '72 (Jacobson & S) -510 Merrick Rd Bx46 -Rockvll Ctr 11571
(914) 683-8484 .. **Goodrich & Bendish** -5 Old Rd -Elmsfrd 10523 **Fx:**683-6770
(518) 474-6530 .. **Goodrich,** Brandon F '09 %Dept Pub Srvc -3 ESP -Albany 12223
(315) 423-4400 .. **Goodrich,** Dennis K '82 (Wolff G&G,LLP) -217 Mntgmry -Syracuse 13202
(212) 250-7636 .. **Goodrich,** Ernest C Jr. '78 %Deutsche Bank -60 Wall -NY 10005
(914) 683-8484 .. **Goodrich,** Peter T '72 (Goodrich & B) -5 Old Rd -Elmsfrd 10523
(212) 973-8000 .. **Goodridge,** Allan D '60 (Schnader HS&L LLP) -140 Bway -NY 10005
(716) 839-1196 .. **Goods,** Robt R '90 -5140 Main -Williamsvll 14221
(516) 328-3254 .. **Goodsell,** Patricia A '80 (Baron & G) -608 Jericho Tpk -New Hyde Pk 11040
(518) 761-6405 .. **Goodspeed,** Sterling T '88 -Bx11 -N Creek 12853
(212) 257-6800 .. **Goodstadt,** Andrew S '98 (Thompson W&G LLP) -85 5th Av -NY 10003
(631) 712-5730 .. **Goodstein,** Alyce H '98 USDC-EDNY -814 Fed Plz -Central Islip 11722
(212) 259-8000 .. **Goodstein,** Barbara '77 (Dewey & L LLP) -1301 Av of Amer -NY 10019
(914) 997-1346 .. **Goodstein,** Carol '85 Seham SM&P,LLP -445 Hmltn Av -White Plns 10601
(212) 594-5300 .. **Goodstein,** Clifford S '96 (Milberg LLP) -1 Penn Plz -NY 10119
(212) 735-3000 .. **Goodstein,** Erica J '00 %Skadden ASM&F LLP -4 Times Sq -NY 10036
(212) 867-1100 .. **Goodstein,** Jason Y '99 %Tratner & M -551 5th Av -NY 10176
(516) 571-2613 .. **Goodstein,** Jeffrey A '98 %Hon K Davis -100 Supreme Ct Dr -Mineola 11501
(516) 681-9757 .. **Goodstein,** Judy '82 (Verill & G) -2 Robbins Ln -Jericho 11753 **Fx:**681-9766
(914) 253-8400 .. **Goodstein,** Peter H '78 PRM Benefits Corp -2500 Wstchstr Av -Purchase 10577
(914) 632-8382 .. **Goodstein,** Robt D '76 (Goodstein & Assoc) -270 North Av -New Rchll 10801 **Fx:**632-1833
(212) 317-9224 .. **Goodstein,** Ruth S '85 Central Park Grp,LLC -12 E 49th -NY 10017 **Fx:**813-1543
(212) 336-2000 .. **Goodstine,** Sarah Levin '08 %Patterson BW&T LLP -1133 Av of Amer -NY 10036
(212) 819-8200 .. **Goodwillie,** Eugene Jr. '67 (White & C LLP) -1155 Av of Amer -NY 10036
(518) 445-6050 .. **Goodwin,** Dianna M '00 %Prisoners' Leg Srvcs -41 State -Albany 12207 **Fx:**445-6053
(212) 210-9447 .. **Goodwin,** Ellen M '90 (Alston & B LLP) -90 Park Av -NY 10016
(212) 536-4003 .. **Goodwin,** Ernest V '07 %K&L Gates LLP -599 Lex Av -NY 10022
(212) 412-3530 .. **Goodwin,** Jeffrey B '96 Barclays Capital Inc -200 Park Av -NY 10166
(718) 590-2000 .. **Goodwin,** Jessica '08 %DA -198 E 161st -Bronx 10451 **Fx:**590-6477
(212) 655-3500 .. **Goodwin,** Kenneth S '81 SpclCnsl Meister S&F LLP -140 E 45th -NY 10017
(212) 506-1700 .. **Goodwin,** Lawr B '82 (Kasowitz BT&F LLP) -1633 Bway -NY 10019
(212) 714-3524 .. **Goodwin,** Mark D '94 M Goodwin -292 5th Av -NY 10001
(908) 277-4100 .. **Goodwin,** Meghan C '03 %Clyde & Co US LLP -405 Lex Av -NY 10174 **Fx:**277-4110
(212) 813-8800 .. **Goodwin Procter LLP** -620 8th Av -NY 10018 **Fx:**355-3333
(212) 609-6800 .. **Goodwin,** Thos J '82 (McCarter & E,LLP) -245 Park Av -NY 10167
(315) 493-0311 .. **Goodwin,** Thos P '67 Goodwin Law Ofc -255 State -Carthage 13619 **Fx:**493-1097
(917) 778-6233 .. **Goodwine-Pittman,** Cheryl '96 %Travelers -485 Lex Av -NY 10017 **Fx:**778-7001
(212) 574-1200 .. **Goodwyn,** Lauri K '91 %Seward & K LLP -1 Bttry Pk Plz -NY 10004
(631) 462-3434 .. **Goody,** Jennifer H '98 (Wand P&G) -1776 E Jericho Tpk -Huntngtn 11743 **Fx:**462-3939
(212) 209-4800 .. **Goodyear,** Chiara Masciandaro '01 %Brown R LLP -7 Times Sq -NY 10036
(212) 450-4000 .. **Goodyear,** Justin '05 %Davis P&W LLP -450 Lex Av -NY 10017
(212) 373-3000 .. **Googe,** Chas H Jr. '88 (Paul WRW&G LLP) -1285 Av of Amer -NY 10019
(212) 754-9400 .. **Googel,** Jody Litt '99 %Todtman NS&J,PC -425 Park Av -NY 10022
(212) 566-5000 .. **Goold,** Adam M '04 Dept of Bldgs -280 Bway -NY 10007
(212) 925-4475 .. **Goolnick,** Steven B '81 (Blank G&D) -111 John -NY 10038
(718) 848-3759 .. **Goolsarran,** Jaipersaud '92 -119-02 Lbrty Av -S Richmond Hll 11419 **Fx:**848-4279
(212) 687-3860 .. **Goorevitch,** Jillian L '08 %Snow BK,PC -605 3rd Av -NY 10158
(516) 803-3000 .. **Goorin,** Kenneth H '82 Rainbow Prog -1111 Stewart Av -Bethpage 11714 **Fx:**803-4824
(212) 687-0100 .. **Goos,** Stanley '93 (Harris B PLLC) -100 Wall -NY 10005
(212) 336-0081 .. **Goot,** Elisabeth A Love '91 %SEC -3 World Fncl Ctr -NY 10281 **Fx:**336-1323
(914) 469-1672 .. **Gootzeit,** Elias S '94 -351 Bedford Av -Mt Vernon 10553
(718) 923-8225 .. **Gopee,** Karen '98 Red Hook Comm Justice Ctr -88 Visitation Pl -Brklyn 11231 **Fx:**923-8248
(212) 805-0194 .. **Gopstein,** David N '09 Hon NR Buchwald -500 Pearl -NY 10007 **Fx:**805-7927
(212) 363-2400 .. **Gopstein,** Sheldon H '83 -275 Mad Av -NY 10016 **Fx:**363-3313
(718) 780-7926 .. **Gora,** Joel M '67 %Bklyn Law Schl -250 Joralemon -Brklyn 11201 **Fx:**780-0393
(732) 855-6459 .. **Gorab,** Lisa Ann '91 (Wilentz G&S) -110 William -NY 10038 **Fx:**726-6580
(516) 921-2525 .. **Goralski,** Theo F Jr. '92 %McHenry H&L,PC -6800 Jericho Tpk -Syosset 11791
(212) 267-9222 .. **Gorayeb,** Christopher J '86 (Gorayeb & Assoc,PC) -100 William -NY 10038 **Fx:**962-5418
(212) 676-1817 .. **Gorayeb,** Danl E '06 %Law Dept -100 Church -NY 10007 **Fx:**788-0367
(212) 267-9222 .. **Gorayeb,** Jos G '58 (Gorayeb & Assoc,PC) -100 William -NY 10038 **Fx:**962-5418
(516) 869-5700 .. **Gorbaty,** Dmitry '02 Astra Grp,Inc -1129 Nrthrn Blvd -Manhsst 11030 **Fx:**869-5600
(212) 977-7033 .. **Gorczyca,** Jos E '09 %Perecman Firm PLLC -250 W 57th -NY 10107
(631) 851-9394 .. **Gorczynski,** Peter R '80 -38 Kings Hwy -Hauppauge 11788 **Fx:**348-0269
(212) 309-6000 .. **Gordan,** John D III '69 (Morgan L&B LLP) -101 Park Av -NY 10178
(212) 848-4000 .. **Gordano,** Alejandro A '06 %Shearman & S LLP -599 Lex Av -NY 10022
(718) 855-5123 .. **Gordet,** Rona '92 (Levine & G) -32 Court -Brklyn 11201 **Fx:**522-0432
(212) 613-8240 .. **Gordimer,** Andrew '97 %Orthodox Union -11 Bway -NY 10004
(718) 491-6006 .. **Gordina,** Yelena '99 (Brodsky & G,PC) -539 86th -Brklyn 11209
(607) 843-8221 .. **Gordon,** Alan E '81 -16 Lafayette Park Bx549 -Oxfrd 13830 **Fx:**843-7618
(718) 286-2000 .. **Gordon,** Alan R '85 %Leg Aid -120-46 Qns Blvd -Kew Gdns 11415 **Fx:**286-2286
(917) 343-1846 .. **Gordon,** Alexander N '97 Goldman Sachs -1 NY Plz -NY 10004
(212) 766-2200 .. **Gordon,** Alvin C '92 (Meiselman & G,LLP) -80 Maiden Ln -NY 10038
(718) 243-6817 .. **Gordon,** Andrea '06 Leg Aid -111 Lvngstn -Brklyn 11201 **Fx:**237-8737
(212) 373-3000 .. **Gordon,** Andrew G '95 (Paul WRW&G LLP) -1285 Av of Amer -NY 10019
(212) 504-6000 .. **Gordon,** Ariel V '07 %Cadwalader W&T LLP -1 World Fncl Ctr -NY 10281
(212) 766-2200 .. **Gordon,** Ava M '95 %Meiselman & G,LLP -80 Maiden Ln -NY 10038
(212) 422-1212 .. **Gordon,** Ayana Z '02 QBEIC -88 Pine -NY 10005 **Fx:**422-1313
(914) 406-7000 .. **Gordon,** Bernard S '77 (Rand RR&G LLP) -50 Main -White Plns 10606
(212) 312-2513 .. **Gordon,** Bernice F '80 %Folksamerica Reinsurance -1 Lbrty Plz -NY 10006 **Fx:**385-3723
(516) 741-7676 .. **Gordon,** Brian L '03 %Miranda SSSV LLP -240 Mineola Blvd -Mineola 11501
(516) 791-5400 .. **Gordon,** Bryan '91 (Gordon J&S) -51 Valley Ln E -N Woodmere 11581 **Fx:**791-4406
(212) 834-0600 .. **Gordon,** Burton '56 OfCnsl Gordon & S,PC -355 Lex Av -NY 10017
(718) 858-7645 .. **Gordon,** Carlton J '91 -Peck Slip Station Bx54 -NY 10038
(212) 566-7766 .. **Gordon,** Celia A '98 -111 Bway -NY 10006 **Fx:**374-1506
(516) 433-5065 .. **Gordon,** Chas Eric '80 -Bx514 -Plainvw 11803
(212) 686-3477 .. **Gordon,** Chas Eric '80 -370 7th Av -NY 10001
(631) 957-3029 .. **Gordon,** Chelley A '96 %Babylon Town Atty -200 E Sunrise Hwy -Lindenhrst 11757 **Fx:**957-3146
(845) 452-2022 .. **Gordon,** Chester H '70 (Brenner G&L) -219 Church -Poughkeepsie 12601
(212) 839-6525 .. **Gordon,** Chevenne G '06 %Dept of Transportation -55 Water -NY 10041
(585) 325-6320 .. **Gordon,** Christine Diachishin '78 -500 Exec Ofc Bldg -Rchstr 14614 **Fx:**325-6323
(845) 794-4043 .. **Gordon,** Cliff '76 -541 Bway Bx803 -Monticello 12701 **Fx:**794-7229
(718) 298-1200 .. **Gordon,** Danl S '02 %Supreme Ct -88-11 Sutphin Blvd -Jamaica 11435
(646) 878-0800 .. **Gordon,** Danielle A '04 %Pearl CZL,LLP -1500 Bway -NY 10036
(914) 238-7702 .. **Gordon,** David '68 (Gordon & H) -480 Mamaroneck Av -Harrison 10528
(212) 863-6300 .. **Gordon,** David '75 %HPD -100 Gold -NY 10038 **Fx:**863-8201
(631) 582-4423 .. **Gordon,** David '00 -Bx231 -Highmount 12441 **Fx:**348-0351
(212) 906-1200 .. **Gordon,** David A '95 (Latham & W) -885 3rd Av -NY 10022

(646) 755-7315 .. **Gordon,** David B '93 (Richardson & P,LLP) -750 3rd Av -NY 10017 **Fx:**(917) 591-3479
(914) 381-4848 .. **Gordon,** David E '90 (Gordon & H) -480 Mamaroneck Av -Harrison 10528 **Fx:**777-8605
(914) 921-5504 .. **Gordon,** David L '06 Gordon Asset Mgmt LLC -411 Theo Fremd Av -Rye 10580
(212) 297-5800 .. **Gordon,** Davidson T '80 Cnsl Day P LLP -7 Times Sq -NY 10036
(315) 724-2194 .. **Gordon,** Dean L '76 (Levitt & G) -91 Genesee Bx97 -New Hartfrd 13413 **Fx:**724-2261
(212) 259-8000 .. **Gordon,** Donna L '98 (Dewey & L LLP) -1301 Av of Amer -NY 10019
(914) 946-4777 .. **Gordon,** Eric L '94 (Keane & B,PC) -445 Hmltn Av -White Plns 10601
(917) 693-2919 .. **Gordon,** Eric T '98 -301 E 80th -NY 10075 **Fx:**(212) 628-1403
(212) 762-4977 .. **Gordon,** Erica H '05 Morgan Stanley -1221 Av of Amer -NY 10020
(212) 648-0363 .. **Gordon,** Evan J '98 JP Morgan Chase -245 Park Av -NY 10167
(212) 681-0625 .. **Gordon,** Evan L '66 -150 E 58th -NY 10155 **Fx:**317-8909
(212) 963-0099 .. **Gordon,** Felicia S '96 UNMISET -Bx4758 -NY 10163
(212) 810-5300 .. **Gordon,** Frank D '95 %BlackRock -40 E 52nd -NY 10022
(516) 484-5400 .. **Gordon,** Gail R '75 Pall Corp -25 Hrbr Park Dr -Pt Wash 11050
(212) 277-0709 .. **Gordon,** Garry '99 Hartford Fincl Products -2 Park Av -NY 10016
(212) 371-5400 .. **Gordon,** Gerald '65 %Weisman CS&M PC -445 Park Av -NY 10022
(212) 909-1432 .. **Gordon,** Greg D '98 Cerberus Capital Mgmt LP -299 Park Av -NY 10171 **Fx:**891-1540
(212) 732-5812 .. **Gordon,** Harold '55 (Kahn GT&R,PC) -20 Vesey -NY 10007
(518) 426-4600 .. **Gordon,** Harold D '76 (Couch W,LLP) -540 Bway Bx22222 -Albany 12201
(212) 326-3939 .. **Gordon,** Harold K '89 (Jones D) -222 E 41st -NY 10017
(212) 532-8360 .. **Gordon,** Harold L '61 -200 Lex Av -NY 10016
(718) 935-4268 .. **Gordon,** Harvey A '96 NYC Bd of Ed-Retirement Systm -65 Court -Brklyn 11201 **Fx:**935-4856
(212) 272-8972 .. **Gordon,** Heather A '01 %JP Morgan Chase -383 Mad Av -NY 10179
(212) 690-2990 .. **Gordon,** Helen A '50 -304 W 138th -NY 10030
(212) 986-1200 .. **Gordon Herlands Randolph & Cox LLP** -355 Lex Av -NY 10017 **Fx:**983-0772
(212) 986-1200 .. **Gordon,** Hiram D '73 (Gordon HR&C LLP) -355 Lex Av -NY 10017
(631) 941-4887 .. **Gordon,** Howard J '85 Cnsl Swartz Organization,LLC -1239 Route 25A -Stony Brk 11790 **Fx:**689-8084
(212) 688-8555 .. **Gordon,** Howard W '09 (Fragomen DB&L LLP) -7 Hanover Sq -NY 10004
(914) 631-3131 .. **Gordon,** Howland R '02 DLC Mgmt Corp -580 Wht Plns Rd -Tarrytwn 10591 **Fx:**206-3587
(718) 338-3000 .. **Gordon,** Ira B '94 %Weser & W,PC -1392 Coney Isl Av -Brklyn 11230 **Fx:**377-6915
(212) 421-4300 .. **Gordon,** Jack A '86 (Kent B&G,LLP) -425 Park Av -NY 10022
(212) 998-6082 .. **Gordon,** Jamie N '06 NYU-Law -245 Sullivan -NY 10012 **Fx:**995-4076
(212) 788-1043 .. **Gordon,** Jane L '86 %Law Dept -100 Church -NY 10007 **Fx:**788-0367
(646) 386-3620 .. **Gordon,** Janet A M '92 %Supreme Ct-Law Dept -60 Centre -NY 10007
(212) 710-5504 .. **Gordon,** Jason M '99 Fidelity Natl Title Ins -711 3rd Av -NY 10017
(516) 371-9337 .. **Gordon,** Jay F '49 -269 Central Av -Lawrence 11559 **Fx:**371-5291
(718) 681-0800 .. **Gordon,** Jeffrey '82 (Gordon & G) -187 E 163rd -Bronx 10451
(212) 854-2675 .. **Gordon,** Jeffrey N '77 %Columbia Law Schl -435 W 116th -NY 10027 **Fx:**854-7946
(212) 408-2500 .. **Gordon,** Jennifer '86 (Baker B,LLP) -30 Rckfllr Plz -NY 10112
(212) 902-9450 .. **Gordon,** Jennifer Kruer '01 Goldman Sachs & Co -85 Broad -NY 10004
(212) 636-6000 .. **Gordon,** Jennifer L '92 %Fordham Univ Sch of Law -140 W 62nd -NY 10023 **Fx:**636-6899
(212) 609-7888 .. **Gordon,** Jennifer S '99 Visting Nurse Srvc -1250 Bway -NY 10001
(212) 765-8600 .. **Gordon,** Jesse E '00 (Costello & G LLP) -1790 Bway -NY 10019
(516) 437-4385 .. **Gordon,** John P '05 %Vishnick MM LLP -3000 Marcus Av -Lk Success 11042
(212) 588-0800 .. **Gordon,** Jon E '96 %Frommer L&H LLP -745 5th Av -NY 10151
(212) 408-2500 .. **Gordon,** Jonathan '98 (Baker B,LLP) -30 Rckfllr Plz -NY 10112
(212) 403-1000 .. **Gordon,** Jonathan H '03 %Wachtell LR&K -51 W 52nd -NY 10019
(585) 381-1400 .. **Gordon,** Jos H '76 -1699 Crk Bx25083 -Rchstr 14625 **Fx:**381-4944
(646) 471-4000 .. **Gordon,** Joshua A '06 %PricewaterhouseCoopers LLP -300 Mad Av -NY 10017
(631) 738-0505 .. **Gordon & Juengst,PC** -1785 Express Dr N -Hauppauge 11788
(585) 428-1791 .. **Gordon,** Julie Anne '87 Family Ct -252 Hall of Justice -Rchstr 14614 **Fx:**428-2597
(914) 997-8100 .. **Gordon,** Kathleen E '84 (Burke LM&G) -10 Bank -White Plns 10606
(212) 536-3900 .. **Gordon,** Kay A '98 (K&L Gates LLP) -599 Lex Av -NY 10022
(212) 335-4500 .. **Gordon,** Keara O'Donnell '94 (DLA Piper LLP) -1251 Av of Amer -NY 10020
(212) 416-8320 .. **Gordon,** Keith H '85 %Dept of Law -120 Bway -NY 10271
(212) 408-5100 .. **Gordon,** Keith Lee '08 %Chadbourne & P LLP -30 Rckfllr Plz -NY 10112
(212) 880-3800 .. **Gordon,** Kenneth '68 (Akerman S) -335 Mad Av -NY 10017
(212) 355-3200 .. **Gordon,** Kenneth E '76 (Gordon G&S,PC) -437 Mad Av -NY 10022 **Fx:**355-3292
(585) 244-1070 .. **Gordon,** Kenneth W '87 (Gordon & S,LLP) -1039 Monroe Av -Rchstr 14620 **Fx:**244-1085
(631) 427-5700 .. **Gordon Kushnick & Gordon** -780 NY Av -Huntngtn 11743 **Fx:**427-5724
(518) 399-5400 .. **Gordon,** Lawr M '67 (Gordon T&D,LLP) -113 Saratoga Rd -Glenvll 12302
(516) 333-5000 .. **Gordon,** Lawr M '74 (Gordon S&I PC) -400 Grdn City Plz -Gdn Cty 11530 **Fx:**333-3260
(212) 274-6177 .. **Gordon,** Lee A '92 %NYC Ofc of Leg Affrs -220 Church -NY 10013
(518) 439-6900 .. **Gordon,** Lisa '85 Albany Mediation Ctr -278 Delaware Av -Delmar 12054 **Fx:**439-6900
(631) 969-3100 .. **Gordon,** Lisa K '94 (Frenkel LWW&G,LLP) -20 W Main -Bay Shr 11706
(914) 937-7093 .. **Gordon,** Lois A '93 -202 Ivy Hill Cres -Rye Brook 10573
(631) 249-9480 .. **Gordon,** Lynne M '72 (Wickham BG&G,PC) -275 Broad Hollow Rd -Melvll 11747
(917) 656-3376 .. **Gordon,** Maple A '91 -26-20 23rd Av -Astoria 11105 **Fx:**(718) 278-2928
(212) 272-0072 .. **Gordon,** Marcy Jane '88 %JP Morgan Chase -383 Mad Av -NY 10179
(845) 454-9460 .. **Gordon,** Marga L '04 %MHLS -One Civic Ctr Plz -Poughkeepsie 12601 **Fx:**471-9308
(516) 873-0303 .. **Gordon,** Maris R '92 (Gordon & G) -199 Willis Av -Mineola 11501
(718) 544-7070 .. **Gordon,** Maris R '92 (Gordon & G) -108-18 Qns Blvd -Frst Hlls 11375 **Fx:**544-0994
(914) 765-4258 .. **Gordon,** Marji L '94 IBM -N Castle Dr -Armonk 10504
(212) 403-1000 .. **Gordon,** Mark '95 (Wachtell LR&K) -51 W 52nd -NY 10019
(845) 294-7505 .. **Gordon,** Mark J '88 -Bx111 -Goshen 10924 **Fx:**294-8115
(212) 418-8600 .. **Gordon,** Marla Meg '78 OfCnsl Kornstein VW&P,LLP -757 3rd Av -NY 10017
(917) 309-3523 .. **Gordon,** Matthew B '98 Sightpoint Prtnrs -51 Warren -Hastings-On-Hud 10706
(914) 375-0100 .. **Gordon,** Matthew L '86 %Novick ELRW&L,PC -733 Ynkrs Av -Ynkrs 10704
(212) 533-6300 .. **Gordon,** Melinda G '87 %NYSUT -52 Bway -NY 10004 **Fx:**995-2347
(212) 728-8000 .. **Gordon,** Meredith B '04 %Willkie F&G LLP -787 7th Av -NY 10019
(516) 803-3189 .. **Gordon,** Merryl '94 Cablevision -1111 Stewart Av -Bethpage 11714
(212) 733-1197 .. **Gordon,** Michl A '05 %Friedman KS&A LLP -1633 Bway -NY 10019 **Fx:**373-7997
(212) 973-0572 .. **Gordon,** Michl G '10 %Wolff & S PC -140 Bway -NY 10005
(212) 536-3900 .. **Gordon,** Michl R '86 (K&L Gates LLP) -599 Lex Av -NY 10022
(212) 940-8800 .. **Gordon,** Michl S '93 (Katten MR LLP) -575 Mad Av -NY 10022
(516) 294-8844 .. **Gordon,** Michelle L '10 %L'Abbate BC&C,LLP -1001 Franklin Av -Gdn Cty 11530
(212) 773-1912 .. **Gordon,** Mitchell H '96 Ernst & Young,LLP -5 Times Sq -NY 10036
(212) 685-7600 .. **Gordon,** Nahum L '60 OfCnsl Heller H&F,PC -292 Mad Av -NY 10017
(212) 398-3505 .. **Gordon,** Naomi '81 -49 W 37th -NY 10018
(212) 753-0111 .. **Gordon,** Neal '67 %Cartier Intl -2 E 52nd -NY 10022 **Fx:**223-3582
(212) 935-5500 .. **Gordon,** Nicholas '72 (Franklin WR&V) -488 Mad Av -NY 10022
(212) 880-9488 .. **Gordon,** Patrick J '05 %Morvillo AGIA&B,PC -565 5th Av -NY 10017
(212) 944-4433 .. **Gordon,** Paul R '76 (Raich Ende Malter & Co LLP) -1375 Bway -NY 10018 **Fx:**944-5404
(212) 312-7521 .. **Gordon,** Paula Cohen '81 %State Ins Fund -199 Church -NY 10007 **Fx:**385-9199
(212) 403-1000 .. **Gordon,** Paula N '98 %Wachtell LR&K -51 W 52nd -NY 10019
(212) 836-8000 .. **Gordon,** Peta '04 %Kaye S LLP -425 Park Av -NY 10022
(212) 455-2000 .. **Gordon,** Peter J '81 (Simpson T&B LLP) -425 Lex Av -NY 10017
(718) 544-7070 .. **Gordon,** Peter S '89 (Gordon & G) -108-18 Qns Blvd -Frst Hlls 11375 **Fx:**544-0994
(516) 873-0303 .. **Gordon,** Peter S '89 (Gordon & G) -199 Willis Av -Mineola 11501
(718) 783-1393 .. **Gordon,** Randi E '80 -143 St Marks Av -Brklyn 11238
(212) 269-5500 .. **Gordon & Rees LLP** -90 Broad -NY 10004 **Fx:**269-5505
(212) 909-6000 .. **Gordon,** Rhea F '06 %Debevoise & P LLP -919 3rd Av -NY 10022
(212) 284-3756 .. **Gordon,** Richd C '78 -45 Bway -NY 10006
(315) 701-9998 .. **Gordon,** Richd E '56 -1 Lincoln Ctr -Syracuse 13202
(716) 873-1326 .. **Gordon,** Richd H '61 -309 Lincoln Pkwy -Buffalo 14216
(631) 427-5700 .. **Gordon,** Richd M '74 (Gordon K&G) -780 NY Av -Huntngtn 11743
(516) 801-6338 .. **Gordon,** Richd M '03 (RM Gordon,PC) -1 Plz Rd -Greenvale 11548
(212) 527-1000 .. **Gordon,** Rita W '89 OfCnsl Jones HC&B PC -1 Bttry Pk Plz -NY 10004
(212) 481-9011 .. **Gordon,** Robt H '85 %Shaw & B -9 E 40th -NY 10016
(212) 558-5500 .. **Gordon,** Robt J '87 (Weitz & L,PC) -700 Bway -NY 10003
(718) 267-9513 .. **Gordon,** Robt L '87 -21 Swan -Palisades 10964 **Fx:**267-9551
(212) 857-2310 .. **Gordon,** Robt M '99 %Hon P Leval -40 Foley Sq -NY 10007
(212) 788-1205 .. **Gordon,** Robt W '05 %Law Dept -100 Church -NY 10007 **Fx:**788-0367
(212) 541-2000 .. **Gordon,** Roberta G '87 Cnsl Bryan C LLP -1290 Av of Amer -NY 10104
(718) 229-2628 .. **Gordon,** Ronna H '88 (Galchus & G) -38-50 Bell Blvd -Bayside 11361
(914) 332-4144 .. **Gordon,** Rosemarie N '85 -55 S Bway -Tarrytwn 10591 **Fx:**332-4147
(516) 747-0377 .. **Gordon,** Roy C '97 (Costella & G,LLP) -7 12th -Gdn Cty 11530 **Fx:**248-0023
(845) 357-2550 .. **Gordon,** S Martin '69 -222 Route 59 -Suffern 10901 **Fx:**357-2566
(212) 442-8462 .. **Gordon,** Sandra C '97 Juvenile Justice -110 William -NY 10038 **Fx:**442-8517
(212) 309-6000 .. **Gordon,** Sara M '06 %Morgan L&B LLP -101 Park Av -NY 10178
(631) 300-2425 .. **Gordon,** Scott I '95 -775 Park Av -Huntngtn 11743 **Fx:**300-2409
(212) 446-4800 .. **Gordon,** Scott J '94 (Kirkland & E LLP) -153 E 53rd -NY 10022
(845) 756-3400 .. **Gordon,** Scott L '83 -43 Blackberry Hill Rd -Red Hook 12571
(914) 962-2722 .. **Gordon,** Shari R '86 -40 Triangle Ctr -Yorktwn Hts 10598
(516) 781-7988 .. **Gordon,** Sherwood '53 -2225 Brody Ln Bx1103 -Bellmore 11710 **Fx:**781-8992
(212) 834-0600 .. **Gordon & Silber,PC** -355 Lex Av -NY 10017 **Fx:**490-0035
(914) 682-2097 .. **Gordon & Silber,PC** -50 Main -White Plns 10606
(516) 621-0900 .. **Gordon,** Stacey Natiss '89 (Natiss & G,PC) -277 Willis Av -Roslyn Hts 11577
(585) 987-2897 .. **Gordon,** Stanley A '64 OfCnsl Woods OG LLP -2 State -Rchstr 14614 **Fx:**987-2997
(212) 436-1082 .. **Gordon,** Stephen A '73 IRS -290 Bway -NY 10007
(516) 466-6030 .. **Gordon,** Stephen F '63 (Mirkin & G,PC) -98 Cuttermill Rd -Gt Neck 11021
(914) 684-6840 .. **Gordon,** Stephen G '79 -333 Wstchstr Av -West Harrison 10604 **Fx:**684-6973
(212) 701-3000 .. **Gordon,** Stephen J '94 Cnsl Cahill G&R LLP -80 Pine -NY 10005 **Fx:**269-5420
(212) 702-5400 .. **Gordon,** Stephen L '72 (Beveridge & D,PC) -477 Mad Av -NY 10022
(212) 474-1000 .. **Gordon,** Stephen L '82 (Cravath S&M LLP) -825 8th Av -NY 10019
Gordon, Steven B '96 -Bx524072 -Bronx 10452
(212) 308-6000 .. **Gordon,** Steven N '93 -400 Mad Av -NY 10017 **Fx:**308-3900
(212) 541-2000 .. **Gordon,** Stuart A '65 (Bryan C LLP) -1290 Av of Amer -NY 10104

(516) 357-3000 .. **Gordon,** Stuart I '83 (Rivkin R LLP) -926 RXR Plz -Uniondale 11556
(914) 723-1462 .. **Gordon,** Susan E H '76 -154 Brwstr Rd -Scarsdale 10583
(212) 458-7023 .. **Gordon,** Susan L '97 AIG,Inc -175 Water -NY 10038
(518) 483-1950 .. **Gordon,** Tammy Lee V '88 -63 E Main Bx95 -Malone 12953
(518) 399-5400 .. **Gordon Tepper & DeCoursey,LLP** -113 Saratoga Rd -Glenvll 12302 **Fx:**399-5951
(518) 270-3761 .. **Gordon,** Thos '84 Family Ct -1504 5th Av -Troy 12180 **Fx:**272-6573
(716) 854-4300 .. **Gordon,** Thos M '06 %Gross SB&G,PC -465 Main -Buffalo 14203
(631) 738-0505 .. **Gordon,** Todd A '90 (Gordon & J,PC) -1785 Express Dr N -Hauppauge 11788
(914) 591-4465 .. **Gordon,** Todd I '80 -53 Jaffray Ct -Irvngtn 10533
(212) 269-7308 .. **Gordon,** Wm J '89 (Leahey & J PC) -120 Wall -NY 10005
(716) 633-8059 .. **Gordon,** Wm S '56 -100 W Maplemere -Williamsvll 14221 **Fx:**633-7280
(718) 479-9133 .. **Gordon,** Winston A '88 -104-13 Farmers Blvd -Jamaica 11412
(212) 431-2110 .. **Gordon-Reed,** Annette '85 %NY Law Schl -185 W Bway -NY 10013 **Fx:**406-0103
(718) 250-2000 .. **Gordon-Somers,** Kimathi K '98 %DA -350 Jay -Brklyn 11201 **Fx:**250-2314
(212) 335-4500 .. **Gore,** Kiran N '10 %DLA Piper LLP -1251 Av of Amer -NY 10020
(212) 885-5000 .. **Gore,** Michl J '09 %Blank R LLP -405 Lex Av -NY 10174
(212) 223-6700 .. **Gore,** Nathaniel S '79 (Zukerman GB&C,LLP) -875 3rd Av -NY 10022
(973) 344-6100 .. **Gore,** Stephen H '71 (Gore & G) -20 Sttlrs Lndng -E Hampton 11937 **Fx:**589-0944
(212) 506-1700 .. **Gorecki,** Maria '98 (Kasowitz BT&F LLP) -1633 Bway -NY 10019
(212) 504-6000 .. **Gorel,** Gennady A '07 %Cadwalader W&T LLP -1 World Fncl Ctr -NY 10281
(212) 753-7500 .. **Gorelick,** Benjamin A '05 %Hartman & C LLP -488 Mad Av -NY 10022
(212) 422-1200 .. **Gorelick,** Michl E '76 (Abrams GF&J,PC) -1 Bttry Pk Plz -NY 10004
(212) 704-6000 .. **Gorell,** Stephen G '80 (Troutman S LLP) -405 Lex Av -NY 10174
(631) 756-4680 .. **Goren,** David '88 -1865 New Hwy -Farmngdl 11735
(212) 326-3939 .. **Goren,** Jonathan H '10 %Jones D -222 E 41st -NY 10017
(212) 310-8000 .. **Goren,** Matthew P '07 %Weil G&M LLP -767 5th Av -NY 10153
(631) 845-2600 .. **Goren,** Thos B '89 (Morenus CG&B) -58 S Srvc Rd -Melvll 11747
(212) 468-8000 .. **Goren,** Todd M '03 %Morrison & F LLP -1290 Av of Amer -NY 10104
(212) 809-8585 .. **Gorenberg,** Hayley J '93 Lambda Leg Def -120 Wall -NY 10005 **Fx:**809-0055
(518) 456-6439 .. **Gorenstein,** Barbara Werlin '84 -3 Bonnie Dr -Guilderlnd 12084 **Fx:**456-6439
(718) 713-9046 .. **Gorfin,** Karina Gradus '96 -1322 Gravesend Neck Rd -Brklyn 11229 **Fx:**713-9051
(212) 525-8248 .. **Gorfinkel,** David B '96 HSBC Bank NA -452 5th Av -NY 10018
(516) 357-3000 .. **Gorfinkel,** M Paul '79 (Rivkin R LLP) -926 RXR Plz -Uniondale 11556
(315) 448-0126 .. **Gorgoni,** Jos P '91 -314 E Fayette -Syracuse 13202 **Fx:**448-0246
(607) 723-9511 .. **Gorgos,** Mark S '81 (Coughlin & G,LLP) -19 Chenango Bx2039 -Bnghmtn 13902
(516) 694-3000 .. **Gorham,** Bonnie Lener '84 %Guercio & G,LLP -77 Conklin -Farmngdl 11735 **Fx:**694-4738
(212) 553-8300 .. **Gorham,** Jonathan D '84 %Cohen K & Assoc -2 Park Av -NY 10016 **Fx:**553-8721
(718) 251-7054 .. **Gorin,** Jos '51 -1248 E 102nd -Brklyn 11236
(212) 225-2000 .. **Gorin,** Wm F '79 (Cleary GS&H) -1 Lbrty Plz -NY 10006
(212) 281-2231 .. **Goring-Piard,** Sophia M '01 -1916 Park Av -NY 10037
(845) 290-0299 .. **Gorinsky,** Gerald '77 (G Gorinsky,PC) -5 Maurice Ln -Suffern 10901
(516) 572-6818 .. **Gorinsky,** Joel I '85 %MHLS -2201 Hempstd Tpk -E Meadow 11554 **Fx:**572-4926
(315) 655-3463 .. **Goris,** Mark D '94 (Mitchell G&S,LLC) -5 Mill Bx312 -Cazenovia 13035
(212) 829-7144 .. **Gorji,** Gita '01 -410 Park Av -NY 10022 **Fx:**(646) 365-3100
(212) 355-5575 .. **Gorka,** Kristine '96 %Smith & N,LLP -363 7th Av -NY 10001 **Fx:**486-3150
(212) 269-2500 .. **Gorlick,** Andrew A '86 OfCnsl Gorlick K&L,PC -17 State -NY 10004
(212) 269-2500 .. **Gorlick Kravitz & Listhaus,PC** -17 State -NY 10004 **Fx:**269-2540
(973) 228-5700 .. **Gormally,** Chas X '90 (Brach E LLC) -100 Park Av -NY 10017 **Fx:**228-7852
(212) 986-7180 .. **Gorman,** Albert H '70 (AH Gorman,PC) -501 5th Av -NY 10017 **Fx:**986-3752
(315) 724-2147 .. **Gorman,** Bartle J '67 (Gorman WG&S) -1508 Genesee -Utica 13502
(212) 885-5000 .. **Gorman,** Bruce M Jr. '05 %Blank R LLP -405 Lex Av -NY 10174
(973) 596-4865 .. **Gorman,** Cheryl A '82 (Gibbons PC) -1 Penn Plz -NY 10119 **Fx:**639-8305
(516) 622-9200 .. **Gorman,** Christopher A '05 %Westerman BEM&S,LLP -1201 RXR Plz -Uniondale 11553
(212) 883-1700 .. **Gorman,** Christopher M '05 %Duval & S LLP -101 Park Av -NY 10178
(607) 798-1094 .. **Gorman,** Danl L '73 -409 Mnchstr Rd -Vestal 13850
(315) 471-3151 .. **Gorman,** Douglas J '08 %Hancock & E,LLP -1500 AXA Twr I Bx4976 -Syracuse 13221
(518) 686-4331 .. **Gorman,** Edw J '95 (Sternberg & G,LLP) -5 Main Bx68 -Hoosick Fls 12090 **Fx:**686-7596
(212) 447-1111 .. **Gorman,** Edw J '06 %Ledy-Gurren B&S -475 Park Av S -NY 10016
(516) 712-4000 .. **Gorman,** Elizabeth Rolande '97 %Milber MP&S LLP -1000 Woodbury Rd -Woodbury 11797
(315) 445-2424 .. **Gorman,** Francis L III '88 Widewaters Grp -5786 Widewaters Pkwy Bx3 -DeWitt 13214
(716) 648-9611 .. **Gorman,** Gerald P '74 -180 Main -Hambrg 14075 **Fx:**648-9614
(212) 848-4000 .. **Gorman,** H Miriam Farber '95 %Shearman & S LLP -599 Lex Av -NY 10022
(212) 815-1450 .. **Gorman,** Idina M '01 %DC 37 Gen Cnsl -125 Barclay -NY 10007 **Fx:**815-1440
(212) 428-2521 .. **Gorman,** James '06 %OCA -25 Beaver -NY 10004
(315) 671-2000 .. **Gorman,** James L '79 Family Ct -401 Mntgmry -Syracuse 13202
(716) 845-2749 .. **Gorman,** Jonathan G '04 %Supreme Ct -25 Delaware Av -Buffalo 14202 **Fx:**851-3293
(518) 833-6000 .. **Gorman,** Jos A '97 Dept Soc Srvcs -127 Bloomingrove Dr -Troy 12180 **Fx:**833-6121
(212) 906-1200 .. **Gorman,** Jude M '06 %Latham & W -885 3rd Av -NY 10022
(518) 786-3900 .. **Gorman,** Keith Robt '80 -17 British Amer Blvd -Latham 12110 **Fx:**786-6446
(212) 267-0033 .. **Gorman,** Kenneth J '01 -111 John -NY 10038 **Fx:**385-4198
(914) 993-0600 .. **Gorman,** Kevin C '06 %Keogh T&M -1 N Bway -White Plns 10601 **Fx:**993-0251
(914) 335-3602 .. **Gorman,** Martin D '73 Kraft Foods,Inc -555 S Bway -Tarrytwn 10591
(315) 435-2470 .. **Gorman,** Mary A '04 %DA -505 S State -Syracuse 13202 **Fx:**435-3969
(718) 358-8807 .. **Gorman,** Michl J '88 -149-31 21st Av -Whitestone 11357
(516) 803-2300 .. **Gorman,** Michl P '85 %Cablevision Sys -1111 Stewart Av -Bethpage 11714
(212) 969-3000 .. **Gorman,** Neill C '09 %Proskauer R LLP -1585 Bway -NY 10036
(516) 798-5304 .. **Gorman,** Patricia A '89 -65 Beach Rd -Massapequa 11758
(718) 858-3000 .. **Gorman,** Raymond A '72 OfCnsl D Rankin & Assoc PC -26 Court -Brklyn 11242 **Fx:**858-9615
(212) 400-1640 .. **Gorman,** Robt S M '96 -315 Mad Av -NY 10017
(585) 637-5645 .. **Gorman,** Shirley A '80 -19 Market Bx629 -Brockprt 14420 **Fx:**637-5644
(518) 363-0011 .. **Gorman,** Stacey L '00 -22 Wshngtn -Ballston Spa 12020 **Fx:**363-0344
(518) 434-2532 .. **Gorman,** Terrence A '03 ALDC -21 Lodge -Albany 12207
(914) 684-1155 .. **Gorman,** Thos E '85 -244 Wstchstr Av -White Plns 10604 **Fx:**684-1150
(212) 474-1000 .. **Gorman,** Thos M '99 Cravath S&M LLP -825 8th Av -NY 10019
(607) 729-0216 .. **Gorman,** Walter T '56 -4 Oak -Bnghmtn 13905
(315) 724-2147 .. **Gorman Waszkiewicz Gorman & Schmitt** -1508 Genesee -Utica 13502 **Fx:**724-1183
(716) 877-5441 .. **Gorman,** Wm H Jr. '56 -840 Colvin Blvd -Kenmore 14217
(845) 638-5337 .. **Gorman-Phelan,** Maureen P '95 %Hon C Bartlett -1 S Main -New Cty 10956
(585) 436-6664 .. **Gormel,** Angela L '94 Omni Group,Inc -1099 Jay -Rchstr 14611 **Fx:**436-3633
(212) 446-7000 .. **Gormezano,** Kammie M '98 %McKinsey & Co -55 E 52nd -NY 10055 **Fx:**688-9521
(716) 845-3650 .. **Gormley,** James N '87 %MHLS -438 Main -Buffalo 14202 **Fx:**874-7794
(716) 856-5500 .. **Gormley,** James W '80 (Damon M LLP) -200 Delaware Av -Buffalo 14202
(315) 877-3340 .. **Gormley,** John W '72 -5485 Ortloff Rd -LaFayette 13084
(212) 415-8600 .. **Gormley,** Kenneth J '95 (Locke LB&L LLP) -3 World Fncl Ctr -NY 10281 **Fx:**812-8373
(631) 277-1800 .. **Gormley,** Marilyn C '91 (Gormley & G,PLLC) -130 W Main -E Islip 11730
(212) 487-4444 .. **Gormley,** Robt C '97 %Dept Cnsmr Affrs -42 Bway -NY 10004 **Fx:**487-4197
(631) 277-1800 .. **Gormley,** Wm F '89 (Gormley & G,PLLC) -130 W Main -E Islip 11730
(212) 259-8000 .. **Gorniak,** Carla '09 %Dewey & L LLP -1301 Av of Amer -NY 10019
(212) 353-6400 .. **Gornitsky,** Rhonda '88 %Intl Masters Pub -225 Park Av S -NY 10003 **Fx:**353-7100
(631) 755-0101 .. **Gorny,** Stacey E '01 %Lewis JAA,LLP -425 Broad Hollow Rd -Melvll 11747
(212) 850-2800 .. **Gorodetsky,** Julia '09 %Andrews K LLP -450 Lex Av -NY 10017
(212) 341-2765 .. **Gorordo-Daly,** Maria A '78 %Admin for Childrens Srvcs -150 William -NY 10038
(518) 891-4050 .. **Goroski,** Mitchell Jr. '72 %Adirondack Pk Agncy -Bx99 -Ray Brk 12977 **Fx:**891-3938
(516) 228-9898 .. **Gorray,** Stephen G '73 (SG Gorray LLC) -900 Merchants Cncrs -Westbury 11590 **Fx:**228-6569
(212) 918-3000 .. **Gorrell,** J Warren Jr. '95 (Hogan L LLP) -875 3rd Av -NY 10022
(973) 228-5700 .. **Gorrell,** Jos M '86 (Brach E LLC) -100 Park Av -NY 10017 **Fx:**228-7852
(212) 909-6000 .. **Gorrin,** Lisa B '06 %Debevoise & P LLP -919 3rd Av -NY 10022
(516) 377-7537 .. **Gorry,** Kevin R '87 -660 Stowe Av -Baldwin 11510 **Fx:**377-7515
(212) 474-1000 .. **Gorsche,** Ryan D '08 %Cravath S&M LLP -825 8th Av -NY 10019
(212) 455-2000 .. **Gorski,** Kara M '10 %Simpson T&B LLP -425 Lex Av -NY 10017
(716) 847-3303 .. **Gorski,** Rachel M '95 SrCnsl OCFS -295 Main -Buffalo 14203
(718) 579-7943 .. **Gorski,** Theresa V '91 %Leg Aid -900 Sheridan Av -Bronx 10451 **Fx:**293-8744
(212) 225-2000 .. **Gorskie,** Jennifer L '05 %Cleary GS&H -1 Lbrty Plz -NY 10006
(845) 457-9283 .. **Gorss,** Fredk G '74 -Bx684 -Montgmry 12549 **Fx:**457-1056
(914) 422-8755 .. **Gorti,** Jyotsna '85 %Dept of Law -101 E Post Rd -White Plns 10601 **Fx:**422-8706
(212) 446-4800 .. **Gorton,** Alexis '03 (Kirkland & E LLP) -153 E 53rd -NY 10022
(212) 906-1200 .. **Gorton,** James C '87 (Latham & W) -885 3rd Av -NY 10022
(516) 742-8466 .. **Gorton,** John T '86 -1539 Franklin Av -Mineola 11501
(607) 754-0500 .. **Gorton,** Peter A '76 (Lachman & G) -1500 E Main Bx89 -Endicott 13761 **Fx:**748-6978
(516) 742-8466 .. **Gorton,** Thos P '81 -1539 Franklin Av -Mineola 11501
(212) 969-3000 .. **Gortz,** Albert W '71 (Proskauer R LLP) -1585 Bway -NY 10036
(212) 849-7000 .. **Gory,** Simona '09 %Quinn EU&S,LLP -51 Mad Av -NY 10010
(718) 250-2000 .. **Goryanina,** Mariya A '07 %DA -350 Jay -Brklyn 11201 **Fx:**250-2314
(212) 381-8759 .. **Gorycki,** Kara L '03 SrCnsl Cohen TS&W PC -420 Lex Av -NY 10170
(718) 428-1770 .. **Gorycki,** Thaddeus S '51 -38-33 Regatta Pl -Douglastn 11363 **Fx:**428-1770
(212) 574-1200 .. **Gorzelany,** Robt J '00 Cnsl Seward & K LLP -1 Bttry Pk Plz -NY 10004
(315) 472-4487 .. **Gosch,** D Jeffrey '74 -120 E Wshngtn -Syracuse 13202 **Fx:**422-2289
(631) 501-3100 .. **Goscilo,** Jozef K '83 %J Humphreys -3 Huntngtn Quad Bx9028 -Melvll 11747 **Fx:**501-3085
(518) 463-5449 .. **Gosdeck,** Thos J '79 (Hill & G) -99 Wshngtn Av -Albany 12210 **Fx:**463-0947
(212) 867-4466 .. **Gosdin,** Allan L '91 %Belkin BW&G,LLP -270 Mad Av -NY 10016
(631) 242-8846 .. **Goshman,** Pamela R '85 -45 Burt Dr Bx765 -Deer Pk 11729 **Fx:**242-5761

(315) 478-5300 .. **Gosier,** James A '87 (J Gosier,PC) -313 E Willow -Syracuse 13203 **Fx:**478-5336
(516) 621-0222 .. **Gosman,** Theo F '87 (GosmanLaw PC) -55 Bryant Av -Roslyn 11576 **Fx:**621-3322
(718) 590-2000 .. **Gosnell,** Wayne E Jr. '06 DA -198 E 161st -Bronx 10451 **Fx:**590-6477
(585) 394-9470 .. **Gosper,** Robt L '90 -66 N Main -Canandaigua 14424
(212) 770-1667 .. **Goss,** Adrian A '03 AIGTS -80 Pine -NY 10005
(518) 372-5400 .. **Goss,** Christine J '02 -7 Droms Rd Ext -Schnctdy 12302 **Fx:**372-5400
(212) 660-3000 .. **Goss,** David C '78 (Sullivan & W LLP) -1290 Av of Amer -NY 10104
(518) 792-8300 .. **Goss-Duerr,** Sheila M '91 -5 Warren -Glens Fls 12801
(212) 922-9250 .. **Gosseen,** Robt I '67 OfCnsl Ganfer & S LLP -360 Lex Av -NY 10017 **Fx:**922-0645
(716) 857-7991 .. **Gossel,** Kenneth M '92 %Natl Fuel Gas -6363 Main -Williamsvll 14221 **Fx:**857-7614
(212) 975-3615 .. **Gosset,** Steven P '95 CBS -524 W 57th -NY 10019
(718) 694-3860 .. **Gossett,** Wallace D '69 %Transit Auth -130 Lvngstn -Brklyn 11201 **Fx:**694-5726
(212) 735-3000 .. **Gostin,** Bryn G '07 %Skadden ASM&F LLP -4 Times Sq -NY 10036
(212) 969-3000 .. **Goswami,** Alak R '03 %Proskauer R LLP -1585 Bway -NY 10036
(212) 925-4545 .. **Gotbaum,** Irving J '82 (Friedman & G,LLP) -568 Bway -NY 10012
(212) 318-3000 .. **Gotbetter,** Susan '80 Cnsl Fulbright & J LLP -666 5th Av -NY 10103
(212) 596-9000 .. **Gotfried,** Gall C '10 %Ropes & G LLP -1211 Av of Amer -NY 10036
(212) 969-3000 .. **Gotfrit,** Shannon Farrah '08 %Proskauer R LLP -1585 Bway -NY 10036
(716) 827-6672 .. **Gotham-Audin,** Kelly L '01 City Ct -714 Ridge Rd -Lackawanna 14218
(516) 437-3915 .. **Gotimer,** Donald F '96 -210 Bellmore -Floral Pk 11001 **Fx:**437-4782
(718) 553-3285 .. **Gotimer,** Jeanine C '92 %FAA -1 Aviation Plz -Jamaica 11434 **Fx:**995-5699
(212) 935-3000 .. **Gotkin,** Jerome '53 (Mintz LCFG&P,PC) -666 3rd Av -NY 10017
(845) 359-1250 .. **Gotkin,** Martin E '59 -43 Horne Tooke Rd Bx74 -Palisades 10964 **Fx:**359-1250
(212) 349-2000 .. **Gotkin,** Michl M '69 %Alpert & K, LLP -233 Bway -NY 10279
(212) 833-1115 .. **Gotko,** Lance J '89 (Friedman KS&A LLP) -1633 Bway -NY 10019 **Fx:**373-7915
(212) 373-3715 .. **Gotler,** Ross M '99 -1285 Av of Amer -NY 10019
(212) 632-6000 .. **Gotlib,** Amir '98 %Lazard Freres -30 Rckfllr Plz -NY 10112 **Fx:**632-6060
(212) 924-1609 .. **Gotlib,** Kerry '81 -80 5th Av -NY 10011 **Fx:**645-0724
(212) 968-8300 .. **Gotlib,** Mayya S '00 %Mintzer SZL&M LLP -39 Bway -NY 10006
(212) 202-2600 .. **Gotlib,** Valerie A '10 %Sher LLP -41 Mad Av -NY 10010 **Fx:**202-4156
(212) 592-1400 .. **Gotlieb,** Danl M '07 %Herrick,F LLP -2 Park Av -NY 10016
(212) 966-5897 .. **Gotlin,** Danl J '70 (Gotlin & J) -100 Lafayette -NY 10013 **Fx:**941-9183
(212) 907-0700 .. **Goto,** Yoko '07 %Labaton S LLP -140 Bway -NY 10005
(212) 361-8296 .. **Gotsopoulis,** Mary '91 -66 John -NY 10038
(212) 400-6900 .. **Gottbetter,** Adam S '93 (Gottbetter & Prtnrs) -488 Mad Av -NY 10022 **Fx:**400-6901
(212) 400-6900 .. **Gottbetter,** Paul B '55 (Gottbetter & Prtnrs) -488 Mad Av -NY 10022 **Fx:**400-6901
(212) 906-1200 .. **Gottdiener,** Ian Scott '91 (Latham & W) -885 3rd Av -NY 10022
(718) 778-1500 .. **Gottesdiener,** Eli '02 (Gottesdiener Law Firm,PLLC) -498 7th -Brklyn 11215 **Fx:**778-1650
(212) 974-7474 .. **Gottesman,** Albert '57 OfCnsl Cowan DA&S LLP -41 Mad Av -NY 10010
(212) 668-5632 .. **Gottesman,** Andrew R '99 Hon J Peck-US Bnkrptcy Ct -1 Bowling Grn -NY 10004
(718) 454-4422 .. **Gottesman,** Baruch S '07 -185-12 Union Tpk -Fresh Mdws 11366 **Fx:**(212) 859-7307
(646) 253-8843 .. **Gottesman,** Chaim '01 CW Capital LLC -1540 Bway -NY 10036
(212) 308-2320 .. **Gottesman,** J Michl '64 -270 Mad Av -NY 10016 **Fx:**308-2323
(888) 375-3060 .. **Gottesman,** Josephine C '91 -11 Penn Plz -NY 10001
(212) 541-2000 .. **Gottesman,** Lawr P '85 (Bryan C LLP) -1290 Av of Amer -NY 10104
(212) 877-7791 .. **Gottesman,** Phyllis R '88 -355 W 85th -NY 10024
(718) 522-0009 .. **Gottesman,** Richd H '85 %D Hernandez & Assoc -26 Court -Brklyn 11242 **Fx:**522-3305
(212) 495-0100 .. **Gottesman Wolgel Malamy Flynn & Weinberg, PC** -11 Hanover Sq -NY 10005 **Fx:**480-9797
(212) 309-6000 .. **Gottfried,** Andrew D '75 (Morgan L&B LLP) -101 Park Av -NY 10178
(516) 935-6338 .. **Gottfried,** Ellen Nadler '76 -48 Sylvia Ln -Plainvw 11803
(212) 766-5665 .. **Gottfried,** Eric J '95 (Lefkowicz & G) -150 Bway -NY 10038 **Fx:**608-5201
(516) 745-0066 .. **Gottfried,** Glenn R '81 %Karol H&S,PC -600 Old Cntry Rd -Gdn Cty 11530
(212) 336-2000 .. **Gottfried,** Jonathan L '04 %Patterson BW&T LLP -1133 Av of Amer -NY 10036
(914) 630-0044 .. **Gottfried,** Michl N '94 (Gottfried & Assoc,PC) -1328 Bstn Post Rd -Larchmnt 10538 **Fx:**630-0043
(212) 336-8000 .. **Gottfried,** Philip H '69 (Amster R&E) -90 Park Av -NY 10016
(718) 643-8768 .. **Gottfried,** Rena R '83 %Family Ct -283 Adams -Brklyn 11201
(212) 661-3535 .. **Gottfried,** Robt N '76 (Hodgson R LLP) -60 E 42nd -NY 10165
(518) 456-9616 .. **Gottheim,** Robt M '77 -465 New Karner Rd -Albany 12205
(212) 367-7350 .. **Gottheim,** Robt M '97 US Rep J Nadler -201 Varick -NY 10014 **Fx:**367-7356
(646) 386-4685 .. **Gotthelf,** Alan '02 Supreme Ct -60 Centre -NY 10007
(212) 521-5400 .. **Gotthoffer,** Lance '75 (Reed S LLP) -599 Lex Av -NY 10022
(212) 237-1000 .. **Gottilla,** Craig D '01 %Windels ML&M,LLP -156 W 56th -NY 10019
(212) 859-8000 .. **Gottlieb,** Adam B '06 %Fried FHS&J LLP -1 NY Plz -NY 10004
(516) 663-6507 .. **Gottlieb,** Adam J '97 OfCnsl Ruskin MF,PC -1425 RXR Plz -Uniondale 11556 **Fx:**663-6707
(212) 619-5400 .. **Gottlieb,** Barry '75 %Newman F LLP -1250 Bway -NY 10001
(845) 623-9330 .. **Gottlieb,** Barry M '73 (B Gottlieb,PC) -404 E Route 59 Bx573 -Nanuet 10954 **Fx:**627-7120
(212) 998-6693 .. **Gottlieb,** Christine E '98 NYU Schl of Law -245 Sullivan -NY 10012
(212) 242-7480 .. **Gottlieb,** David E '06 M Lubelsky & Assoc -123 W 18th -NY 10011
(516) 741-4799 .. **Gottlieb,** David M '05 %Baker SBGFM&N,LLC -100 Grdn City Plz -Gdn Cty 11530
(212) 558-4000 .. **Gottlieb,** David M '10 %Sullivan & C LLP -125 Broad -NY 10004
(718) 262-3408 .. **Gottlieb,** Dorien '02 -89-14 Parsons Blvd -Jamaica 11432
(212) 455-2000 .. **Gottlieb,** Dov M '07 %Simpson T&B LLP -425 Lex Av -NY 10017
(212) 267-2801 .. **Gottlieb,** Emily Mindel '99 Ctr for Justice & Democracy -90 Broad -NY 10004
(212) 794-3778 .. **Gottlieb,** Eric J '98 -110 Wall -NY 10005
(212) 506-5000 .. **Gottlieb,** F Susan '79 OfCnsl Orrick H&S LLP -51 W 52nd -NY 10019
(718) 923-4206 .. **Gottlieb,** Frank F '85 %OTDA Fair Hearings -14 Boerum Pl -Brklyn 11201
(845) 796-3046 .. **Gottlieb,** Gary P '88 %Trading Post -67 Rck Hll Dr Bx310 -Rck Hll 12775 **Fx:**796-3054
(212) 684-3900 .. **Gottlieb,** George '62 (Gottlieb R&R,PC) -270 Mad Av -NY 10016
(718) 260-8737 .. **Gottlieb,** Janet '80 ACS-DCS -345 Adams -Brklyn 11201
(212) 846-6378 .. **Gottlieb,** Jason A '02 MTV Networks -1515 Bway -NY 10036
(212) 696-6000 .. **Gottlieb,** Jason P '02 Cnsl Curtis M-PC&M LLP -101 Park Av -NY 10178
(212) 228-9795 .. **Gottlieb,** Jeffrey M '73 -150 E 18th -NY 10003
(516) 496-8300 .. **Gottlieb,** Jonathan D '06 %Santemma & D,LLC -575 Underhill Blvd -Syosset 11791 **Fx:**496-8303
(212) 839-5300 .. **Gottlieb,** Jos R '09 %Sidley A LLP -787 7th Av -NY 10019
(212) 554-0400 .. **Gottlieb,** Karen J '94 (Grubman I&S,PC) -152 W 57th -NY 10019
(716) 856-4022 .. **Gottlieb,** Krista '80 (Mattar D&G,LLP) -17 Court -Buffalo 14202
(212) 479-6000 .. **Gottlieb,** Lawr C '74 (Cooley LLP) -1114 Av of Amer -NY 10036
(914) 725-2600 .. **Gottlieb,** Lawr M '85 (Hass & G) -670 Wht Plns Rd -Scarsdale 10583 **Fx:**725-7724
(212) 541-2000 .. **Gottlieb,** Leah E '09 %Bryan C LLP -1290 Av of Amer -NY 10104
(212) 907-0872 .. **Gottlieb,** Louis '91 (Labaton S LLP) -140 Bway -NY 10005
(212) 552-0932 .. **Gottlieb,** Manuel W '78 JP Morgan Chase -1 Chase Manh Plz -NY 10081
(646) 961-3210 .. **Gottlieb,** Marc S '90 -61 Bway -NY 10006
(212) 816-8158 .. **Gottlieb,** Mark A '92 Salomon Smith Barney -388 Greenwich -NY 10013
(718) 665-1700 .. **Gottlieb,** Michl H '83 (Gottlieb S&S,LLP) -180 E 162nd -Bronx 10451
(212) 969-3000 .. **Gottlieb,** Neta-Li '07 %Proskauer R LLP -1585 Bway -NY 10036
(212) 951-6400 .. **Gottlieb,** Nina '74 %Dept of Education -475 Park Av S -NY 10016 **Fx:**951-6465
(212) 687-3860 .. **Gottlieb,** Paul '73 (Snow BK,PC) -605 3rd Av -NY 10158
(212) 858-7444 .. **Gottlieb,** Paul M '88 RBC Cptl Mkts -1 Lbrty Plz -NY 10006
(212) 670-0212 .. **Gottlieb,** Paul S '77 Merrill Lynch -222 Bway -NY 10038
(212) 684-3900 .. **Gottlieb Rackman & Reisman,PC** -270 Mad Av -NY 10016 **Fx:**684-3999
(212) 472-7270 .. **Gottlieb,** Richd J '78 (Yoeli G&E LLP) -260 Mad Av -NY 10016
(212) 566-7766 .. **Gottlieb,** Robt C '76 -111 Bway -NY 10006 **Fx:**374-1506
(212) 422-4000 .. **Gottlieb,** Robt S '65 OfCnsl Goldstein R&R -80 Pine -NY 10005
(212) 940-7090 .. **Gottlieb,** Robt W '67 (Katten MR LLP) -575 Mad Av -NY 10022
(607) 724-7700 .. **Gottlieb,** Scott C '78 -29 Riverside Dr -Bnghmtn 13905 **Fx:**724-5370
(212) 661-7100 .. **Gottlieb,** Seth Russell '00 (Salon MDN&B,LLP) -292 Mad Av -NY 10017
(518) 445-2311 .. **Gottlieb,** Stephen E '67 Albany Law Schl -80 New Scotland Av -Albany 12208 **Fx:**445-2315
(845) 339-5556 .. **Gottlieb,** Steven I '92 (Moran & G) -60 Pearl -Kingston 12401 **Fx:**339-5671
(718) 590-2000 .. **Gottlieb,** Theresa A '82 %DA -198 E 161st -Bronx 10451 **Fx:**590-6477
(718) 222-8880 .. **Gottlieb,** Warren S '97 %Jones JO -45 Main -Brklyn 11201
(212) 431-8073 .. **Gottlieb,** Wm P '85 (Axelrod & G) -100 Lafayette -NY 10013 **Fx:**431-8521
(212) 661-4422 .. **Gottlieb,** Wilma P '78 (Glazer & G) -2 Tudor City Pl -NY 10017
(212) 767-8842 .. **Gottlock,** Brian W '01 Comedy Central -345 Hudson -NY 10014
(518) 583-1515 .. **Gottmann,** Steven H '98 (Ginley & G,PC) -96 Ballston Av -Saratoga Spgs 12866 **Fx:**226-0187
(212) 918-3000 .. **Gottridge,** Marc J '79 (Hogan L LLP) -875 3rd Av -NY 10022
(212) 403-1000 .. **Gotts,** Ilene Knable '97 (Wachtell LR&K) -51 W 52nd -NY 10019
(212) 455-2000 .. **Gottschalk,** Caroline B '91 (Simpson T&B LLP) -425 Lex Av -NY 10017
(516) 797-1383 .. **Gottschalk,** Cathy '96 -40 Monroe -Massapequa Pk 11762 **Fx:**541-2185
(212) 446-4800 .. **Gottschalk,** Elizabeth P '01 (Kirkland & E LLP) -153 E 53rd -NY 10022
(212) 702-6500 .. **Gottscho,** Christopher M '90 %Brean Murray & Co -570 Lex Av -NY 10022
(212) 474-1000 .. **Gottshall,** Elizabeth Rush '09 %Cravath S&M LLP -825 8th Av -NY 10019
(914) 664-4829 .. **Goubeaud,** Jos G Jr. '75 -22 W 1st -Mt Vernon 10550 **Fx:**664-4853
(212) 850-1302 .. **Goucher,** Paul B '94 %J&W Seligman & Co -100 Park Av -NY 10017 **Fx:**922-5731
(212) 527-5647 .. **Goudie,** Joy S '01 Revlon -237 Park Av -NY 10017
(212) 848-4000 .. **Goudiss,** Alan S '88 (Shearman & S LLP) -599 Lex Av -NY 10022
(716) 200-5050 .. **Gough,** Colleen Ennis '96 %Harris B PLLC -726 Exchange -Buffalo 14210
(718) 250-2000 .. **Gough,** Timothy G '91 %DA -350 Jay -Brklyn 11201 **Fx:**250-2314
(315) 478-3186 .. **Gould,** A Sheldon '73 -447 E Wshngtn -Syracuse 13202 **Fx:**478-4352
(212) 750-1276 .. **Gould,** Amy L '06 %P Nissman -111 Bway -NY 10006 **Fx:**346-7719
(212) 673-3113 .. **Gould,** Anthony C '96 Gould Family Fndtn -1114 Av of Amer -NY 10036
(914) 669-9087 .. **Gould,** Arnold J '63 -405 B Heritage Hills -Somers 10589 **Fx:**669-0159
(914) 397-1050 .. **Gould & Berg, LLP** -222 Bloomingdale Rd -White Plns 10605 **Fx:**397-1051
(718) 293-7660 .. **Gould,** Bonnie Brooke '87 Pub Admin -851 Grnd Cncrs -Bronx 10451 **Fx:**293-7851
(212) 874-3633 .. **Gould,** Bruce J '54 -40 W 77th -NY 10024 **Fx:**724-4143
(212) 801-9200 .. **Gould,** Danl P '09 %Greenberg T,LLP -200 Park Av -NY 10166
(516) 883-8776 .. **Gould,** David S '73 -76 Reid Av -Pt Wash 11050 **Fx:**883-8776
(212) 425-7775 .. **Gould,** David S '73 OfCnsl SL Salzman,PC -1350 Bway -NY 10018 **Fx:**643-1882

(212) 482-0001 .. **Gould,** David S '92 %Russo K&T LLP -33 Whitehall -NY 10004
(212) 699-8400 .. **Gould,** Dirk S '60 %Van Wagner Comm,LLC -800 3rd Av -NY 10022
(212) 446-4800 .. **Gould,** Douglas R '09 %Kirkland & E LLP -153 E 53rd -NY 10022
(212) 415-9200 .. **Gould,** E Bradley '07 (Dorsey & W LLP) -250 Park Av -NY 10177
(212) 267-2600 .. **Gould & Feldman, LLP** -61 Bway -NY 10006 **Fx:**267-3024
(212) 267-2600 .. **Gould,** Franklyn '56 (Gould & F,LLP) -61 Bway -NY 10006
(973) 596-4613 .. **Gould,** George M '63 Cnsl Gibbons PC -1 Penn Plz -NY 10119 **Fx:**639-6460
(718) 338-2758 .. **Gould,** Geraldine J '73 -1119 Ocean Pkwy -Brklyn 11230
(212) 415-8600 .. **Gould,** James W '81 (Locke LB&L LLP) -3 World Fncl Ctr -NY 10281
(914) 397-1050 .. **Gould,** Jane B '74 (Gould & B,LLP) -222 Bloomingdale Rd -White Plns 10605
(212) 336-2000 .. **Gould,** Jason S '07 %Patterson BW&T LLP -1133 Av of Amer -NY 10036
(631) 477-8607 .. **Gould,** Jennifer B '94 -210 Main Bx177 -Greenprt 11944 **Fx:**477-2601
(585) 232-6500 .. **Gould,** Jo Ann E '80 Cnsl Harter S&E LLP -1600 Bausch & Lomb Pl -Rchstr 14604
(212) 344-5680 .. **Gould,** John E '70 (Thompson H LLP) -335 Mad Av -NY 10017
(212) 531-4852 .. **Gould,** Jonathan S '89 -603 W 115th -NY 10025 **Fx:**531-4854
(914) 683-0090 .. **Gould,** Kenneth J '74 (Marcus G&S,LLP) -222 Bloomingdale Rd -White Plns 10605
(718) 990-2179 .. **Gould,** Keri K '83 %St John's Law Schl -8000 Utopia Pkwy -Jamaica 11439 **Fx:**591-1855
(585) 232-3730 .. **Gould,** Lewis J '57 OfCnsl Chamberlain D LLP -1600 Crssrds Bldg -Rchstr 14614
(212) 805-0588 .. **Gould,** Marissa K '06 Hon A Peck -500 Pearl -NY 10007
(516) 466-3100 .. **Gould,** Matthew J '86 %Gould Investors -60 Cuttermill Rd -Gt Neck 11021 **Fx:**466-3132
(718) 645-3111 .. **Gould,** Maxwell '86 %Leg Aid Society Ofc for the Aging -111 Lvngstn -Brklyn 11201 **Fx:**260-4722
(212) 697-8500 .. **Gould,** Michl A '85 %Konner T&G -462 7th Av -NY 10018
(718) 254-0700 .. **Gould,** Michl K '81 %Bklyn Defender Srvcs -177 Lvngstn -Brklyn 11201 **Fx:**254-0897
(718) 626-7730 .. **Gould,** Michl N '92 %Pyrros & S LLP -31-01 Bway -LIC 11106
(518) 783-0200 .. **Gould,** Patricia H '94 %NYS Schl Bds Assn -24 Century Hill Dr -Latham 12110
(212) 578-8265 .. **Gould,** Peter A '98 %MetLife -27-01 Qns Plz N -LIC 11101
(212) 381-7000 .. **Gould,** Peter C '73 (Sabin B&G LLP) -4 Times Sq -NY 10036
(914) 946-6969 .. **Gould,** Richd A '70 -199 Main -White Plns 10601 **Fx:**761-4672
(917) 670-0151 .. **Gould,** Robt D '60 (R Gould,PC) -646 Main -Margaretvll 12455
(212) 583-9600 .. **Gould,** Theo E '04 %Littler M,PC -900 3rd Av -NY 10022
(516) 624-6530 .. **Gould,** Thos W '06 Oyster Bay-E Norwich Cntrl Schl Dist -1 McCouns Ln -Oyster Bay 11771
(914) 576-2922 .. **Gould,** Warren Morris '79 -271 North Av -New Rchll 10801
(607) 776-4164 .. **Gould,** Wendy Lee '75 -3 Robie -Bath 14810 **Fx:**776-9255
(718) 515-7500 .. **Gouldborne,** Patsy D '95 (McLaughlin G&C) -959 E 233rd -Bronx 10466 **Fx:**515-5557
(212) 788-1087 .. **Goulden,** Steven L '86 %Law Dept -100 Church -NY 10007 **Fx:**788-0367
(607) 763-9200 .. **Gouldin,** David M '66 (Levene G&T,LLP) -BxF-1706 -Bnghmtn 13902
(212) 403-1000 .. **Gouldin,** Lauryn Powers '01 %Wachtell LR&K -51 W 52nd -NY 10019
(607) 433-2088 .. **Gouldin,** Robt A '96 Gouldin Law Ofc -93 Main -Oneonta 13820 **Fx:**433-2054
(585) 325-6942 .. **Gould-Ross,** Bette M '77 (Ross & G-R) -16 E Main -Rchstr 14614 **Fx:**262-6486
(212) 225-2000 .. **Gouldy,** Lisa M '09 %Cleary GS&H -1 Lbrty Plz -NY 10006
(718) 286-6000 .. **Goulet,** Morgan A L '06 %DA -125-01 Qns Blvd -Kew Gdns 11415
(212) 473-5425 .. **Goulian,** Nancy Knauer '83 -130 E 18th -NY 10003
(212) 878-6900 .. **Goulston & Storrs,PC** -750 3rd Av -NY 10017 **Fx:**878-6911
(516) 294-8844 .. **Gounelas,** D James '00 %L'Abbate BC&C,LLP -1001 Franklin Av -Gdn Cty 11530
(212) 351-4500 .. **Gouraige,** Hervé '78 (Epstein B&G,PC) -250 Park Av -NY 10177
(646) 502-7001 .. **Gourari,** Natalia '99 SpclCnsl JSBarkats PLLC -100 Church -NY 10007 **Fx:**607-5544
(212) 841-1000 .. **Gourary,** John P '83 (Covington & B LLP) -620 8th Av -NY 10018
(212) 310-3522 .. **Gourdine,** Amanda J '02 Colgate Palmolive Co -300 Park Av -NY 10022
(212) 806-5400 .. **Gourdine,** Peter C '09 %Stroock &S&L LLP -180 Maiden Ln -NY 10038
(718) 796-8780 .. **Gourdine,** Simon P '66 NYC Civil Srvc Cmmsn -5251 Fieldston Rd -Bronx 10471
(212) 355-1300 .. **Gourevitch,** David U '98 -150 E 58th -NY 10155 **Fx:**355-1531
(212) 872-1000 .. **Goursaud,** Sylvie C '09 -One Bryant Park -NY 10036 **Fx:**872-1002
(516) 378-1700 .. **Goutzounis,** Marie I '93 %Chesney & M -2305 Grand Av -Baldwin 11510
(631) 234-8585 .. **Gouvis,** Olympia '93 OfCnsl Bracken & M,LLP -1 Suffolk Sq -Islandia 11749
(631) 543-3456 .. **Gouvitsas,** Panagiotis '05 %V Trimarco -1038 W Jericho Tpk -Smithtwn 11787
(917) 777-4200 .. **Gouwar,** James A '88 (Bingham M LLP) -1 Bttry Pk Plz -NY 10004
(914) 997-7100 .. **Gouz,** Ronnie '82 (Berman BF&G pc) -123 Main -White Plns 10601
(212) 272-4448 .. **Gouzenko,** Alexander '02 %JP Morgan Chase -383 Mad Av -NY 10179
(845) 469-4900 .. **Gove,** David L '04 %Greenwald Law Ofc -99 Brookside Av -Chester 10918 **Fx:**469-2022
(212) 416-2162 .. **Gove,** Gail C '05 Dow Jones -1211 Av of Amer -NY 10036
(212) 407-4000 .. **Gove,** Steven C '03 %Loeb & L,LLP -345 Park Av -NY 10154
(212) 819-8200 .. **Gover,** Alan S '06 (White & C LLP) -1155 Av of Amer -NY 10036
(718) 590-6228 .. **Gover,** Erin M '09 %Law Dept -900 Sheridan Av -Bronx 10451 **Fx:**590-2699
(212) 940-8800 .. **Governale,** Jack P '81 (Katten MR LLP) -575 Mad Av -NY 10022
(212) 883-1700 .. **Govshtein,** Ella '09 Duval & S LLP -101 Park Av -NY 10178
(212) 430-5400 .. **Gowan,** Sheila M '90 (Diamond M LLP) -620 8th Av -NY 10018
(212) 735-3000 .. **Gowan,** Thos W '92 (Skadden ASM&F LLP) -4 Times Sq -NY 10036
(718) 590-2000 .. **Goward,** James L '95 %DA -198 E 161st -Bronx 10451 **Fx:**590-6477
(212) 682-8811 .. **Gowen,** George W '58 (Dunnington B&M LLP) -1359 Bway -NY 10018
(212) 973-0572 .. **Goydan,** Wm E '89 (Wolff & S PC) -140 Bway -NY 10005
(212) 547-5400 .. **Goyer,** KC '06 %McDermott W&E LLP -340 Mad Av -NY 10173
(212) 616-4100 .. **Goz,** Warren T '99 -154 W 14th -NY 10011 **Fx:**616-4122
(212) 227-1212 .. **Gozenput,** Eugene '06 %Pazer E&J,PC -20 Vesey -NY 10007
(607) 547-2522 .. **Gozigian,** E W Garo '97 (Gozigian W&C) -103 Main Bx431 -Cooperstwn 13326
(607) 547-2522 .. **Gozigian,** Edw '59 (Gozigian W&C) -103 Main Bx431 -Cooperstwn 13326
(607) 547-2522 .. **Gozigian Washburn & Clinton** -103 Main Bx431 -Cooperstwn 13326 **Fx:**547-2845
(516) 227-0400 .. **Gozinsky,** Steven S '94 -99 Q Roosevelt Blvd -Gdn Cty 11530 **Fx:**794-9039
(212) 229-6000 .. **Gozo,** Sara J '90 %Turner Corp -375 Hudson -NY 10014 **Fx:**229-6094
(315) 435-2170 .. **Gozzi,** Joanna '80 %Cnty Atty -421 Mntgmry -Syracuse 13202 **Fx:**435-5729
(212) 225-2000 .. **Grabar,** Nicolas '84 (Cleary GS&H) -1 Lbrty Plz -NY 10006
(212) 264-3650 .. **Grabeel,** Thos A '97 %SSA Ofc Genl Cnsl -26 Fed Plz -NY 10278 **Fx:**264-6372
(212) 446-4800 .. **Grabel,** Drew N '98 (Kirkland & E LLP) -153 E 53rd -NY 10022
(516) 484-2828 .. **Grabel,** Jeffry N '71 Chernoff Diamond & Co -990 Stewart Av -Gdn Cty 11530 **Fx:**484-4755
(646) 471-1447 .. **Graber,** Bruce M '97 %PricewaterhouseCoopers LLP -300 Mad Av -NY 10017
(212) 687-5900 .. **Graber,** Danl A '05 %Sullivan & G,LLP -475 Park Av S -NY 10016 **Fx:**687-4060
(516) 292-8500 .. **Graber,** David W '87 -55 Watermill Ln -Gt Neck 11021 **Fx:**538-1206
(315) 471-1047 .. **Graber,** Donna M '02 -500 S Salina -Syracuse 13202
(716) 856-4000 .. **Graber,** Garry M '79 (Hodgson R LLP) -140 Pearl -Buffalo 14202
(212) 416-8645 .. **Graber,** Joel '78 %Dept of Law -120 Bway -NY 10271
(716) 847-3513 .. **Graber,** Kenneth E '76 %Div of Parole -460 Main -Buffalo 14202 **Fx:**847-3464
(516) 509-5844 .. **Graber,** Peter H '86 -166 E 23rd -Huntngtn Sta 11746 **Fx:**(631) 425-0947
(212) 896-3310 .. **Graber,** Staci A '00 %PS Schram,PC -350 Bway -NY 10013 **Fx:**896-3316
(212) 603-6300 .. **Graber,** Steve R '99 (Robinson BLGG&G PC) -875 3rd Av -NY 10022
(716) 856-4200 .. **Graber,** Timothy J '92 (Gibson M&C,LLP) -69 Delaware Av -Buffalo 14202
(631) 360-5600 .. **Grabie,** Jeanette '02 (Grabie & G,LLP) -162 Terry Rd -Smithtwn 11787 **Fx:**360-3370
(212) 450-4000 .. **Grabill,** Chiara M '09 %Davis P&W LLP -450 Lex Av -NY 10017
(212) 310-8000 .. **Grabill,** Jeremy T '07 %Weil G&M LLP -767 5th Av -NY 10153
(212) 259-8000 .. **Grabill,** Meredith S '07 %Dewey & L LLP -1301 Av of Amer -NY 10019
(212) 344-0200 .. **Grabiner,** Andrew D '06 (Grabiner & Assoc PLLC) -61 Bway -NY 10006 **Fx:**344-0201
(212) 712-0680 .. **Grabino,** Eric '85 -15 W 72nd -NY 10023 **Fx:**712-0681
(212) 506-2500 .. **Grabinska-Marusek,** Kalina '08 Mayer B LLP -1675 Bway -NY 10019
(716) 551-4741 .. **Grable,** James W '66 (US DHS) -130 Delaware Av -Buffalo 14202
(716) 852-5533 .. **Grable,** James W '97 (Connors & V,LLP) -1000 Lbrty Bldg -Buffalo 14202
(212) 478-7200 .. **Grable,** Stephen J '08 %Hahn & H LLP -488 Mad Av -NY 10022
(212) 571-7100 .. **Grabois,** Andrew R '05 %O'Dwyer & B,LLP -52 Duane -NY 10007
(212) 366-7840 .. **GraBois,** Stuart R '68 NYC Dist Cnsl -395 Hudson -NY 10014 **Fx:**366-7841
(212) 265-2266 .. **Grabovich,** Nelly C '05 %Schneider GB LLP -90 Broad -NY 10004
(212) 872-1000 .. **Grabov-Nardini,** Ron '03 -One Bryant Park -NY 10036 **Fx:**872-1002
(212) 541-4477 .. **Grabow,** Michl D '79 (AJ Clarke Real Estate Corp) -1881 Bway -NY 10023 **Fx:**541-4881
(585) 798-5555 .. **Grabowski,** Edw J '98 OfCnsl E Grabowski,PLLC -539A Main Bx426 -Medina 14103 **Fx:**798-5559
(631) 231-3775 .. **Grabowski,** Elizabeth A '97 %Atty Grievance Comm -150 Motor Pkwy -Hauppauge 11788
(212) 269-4900 .. **Grabowski,** Jon R '06 %Ford MEW&G,LLP -Wall Street Plz -NY 10005
(716) 857-6309 .. **Grabowski,** Melinda L '06 Excellus Health Plan,Inc -205 Park Club Ln -Buffalo 14221
(212) 269-4767 .. **Grabowski-Jegorow,** Danuta K '94 -112 Mad Av -NY 10016 **Fx:**685-2356
(212) 370-1300 .. **Grabowski-Shaikh,** Asim '03 %Ellenoff G&S LLP -150 E 42nd -NY 10017
(212) 336-0083 .. **Grace,** Adam S '92 %SEC -3 World Fncl Ctr -NY 10281 **Fx:**336-1323
(212) 668-2170 .. **Grace,** Alicia M '92 %FTA -1 Bowling Grn -NY 10004
(516) 742-8405 .. **Grace,** Barbara M '89 Public Library -60 7th -Gdn Cty 11530
(607) 778-2423 .. **Grace,** Christopher D '00 %DA -45 Hawley Bx1766 -Bnghmtn 13902 **Fx:**778-8870
(518) 388-4121 .. **Grace,** Ellen M '03 GE -1 River Rd -Schnctdy 12345
(212) 486-4100 .. **Grace,** George E '92 %GE Grace & Co,Inc -232 Mad Av -NY 10016 **Fx:**486-4447
(716) 856-1636 .. **Grace,** Gerald Jr. '73 (Walsh R&G) -14 Lafayette Sq -Buffalo 14203
(718) 518-4154 .. **Grace,** Glenda G '91 Hostos Comm Cllg-Labor/Legal Relations -475 Grnd Cncrs -Bronx 10451 **Fx:**518-4198
(212) 233-1100 .. **Grace,** Keith D '01 (Cornell G) -225 Bway -NY 10007 **Fx:**233-1110
(607) 778-2423 .. **Grace,** Mara T '02 DA -45 Hawley Bx1766 -Bnghmtn 13902 **Fx:**778-8870
(914) 962-6100 .. **Grace,** Michl J '85 (Grace & G) -360 Underhill Av -Yorktwn Hts 10598 **Fx:**962-6181
(716) 841-5733 .. **Grace,** Patricia N '86 %HSBC Bank -1 HSBC Ctr -Buffalo 14203 **Fx:**841-5087
(607) 772-1111 .. **Grace,** Richd J '68 -134 Riverside Dr Bx2083 -Bnghmtn 13902 **Fx:**772-8724
(212) 857-8230 .. **Grace,** Robt D '92 %Baker MM&M,PC -330 W 34th -NY 10001
(914) 962-6100 .. **Grace,** Wm J '82 (Grace & G) -360 Underhill Av -Yorktwn Hts 10598 **Fx:**962-6181

(212) 421-2150 .. **Gracer,** Jeffrey B '87 (Sive P&R,PC) -460 Park Av -NY 10022
(716) 852-5200 .. **Graci,** Nicole '00 %Hamberger & W -700 Main Pl Twr -Buffalo 14202
(212) 732-3665 .. **Graci,** Thos A '00 %Harmon L&R -42 Bway -NY 10004
(718) 579-3011 .. **Graci,** Vincent J '00 %Leg Aid -1020 Grnd Cncrs -Bronx 10451 **Fx:**588-2611
(516) 222-0888 .. **Gracin,** Hank '82 (Lehman & E LLP) -50 Chas Lindbergh Blvd -Uniondale 11553
(212) 762-6587 .. **Gracin,** Jay '96 Morgan Stanley -1221 Av of Amer -NY 10020
(518) 561-3088 .. **Graczyk,** Stacy L '03 Prisoners' Leg Srvcs -121 Brdg -Plattsbrgh 12901 **Fx:**561-3262
(212) 732-0400 .. **Grad,** Catharine A '85 (Grad & W,LLP) -305 Bway -NY 10007 **Fx:**571-0831
(212) 854-2685 .. **Grad,** Frank P '49 %Columbia Law Schl -435 W 116th -NY 10027 **Fx:**854-7946
(716) 853-9555 .. **Gradascevic,** Lisa R '97 %Leg Aid -237 Main -Buffalo 14203 **Fx:**853-3219
(347) 404-9133 .. **Graddy,** Lenise R '97 %Civil Ct -141 Lvngstn -Brklyn 11201 **Fx:**(718) 643-3733
(212) 373-3000 .. **Grader,** Scott P '81 Cnsl Paul WRW&G LLP -1285 Av of Amer -NY 10019
(518) 465-3524 .. **Gradess,** Jonathan E '74 %NYS Defenders Assn -194 Wshngtn Av -Albany 12210 **Fx:**465-3249
(718) 590-2000 .. **Gradinger,** Joshua E '05 DA -198 E 161st -Bronx 10451 **Fx:**590-6477
(716) 656-9093 .. **Gradl,** Cindy Algase '86 Cnsl Costanzo's Bakery Inc -30 Innsbruck Dr -Cheektowaga 14227 **Fx:**656-1096
(716) 855-7300 .. **Gradl,** Wayne R '84 NFTA -181 Ellicott -Buffalo 14203 **Fx:**855-7657
(212) 920-2940 .. **Gradman,** Arielle A '99 Cnsl Dahlman Rose & Co -142 W 57th -NY 10019 **Fx:**920-2995
(212) 659-7300 .. **Grados,** Robt J '01 (Haynes & B,LLP) -1221 Av of Amer -NY 10020
(718) 876-6300 .. **Grady,** Anne E '00 %DA -130 Styvsnt Pl -Staten Isl 10301
(718) 465-2230 .. **Grady,** Colleen A '90 %St Joachim & Anne Schl -218-19 105th Av -Qns Vllg 11429
(845) 635-2434 .. **Grady,** Edw J Jr. '80 -757 Traver Rd -Plsnt Vlly 12569
(845) 677-3393 .. **Grady,** Edw J Jr. '80 -160 Church Bx785 -Millbrook 12545 **Fx:**677-3315
(212) 530-1800 .. **Grady,** Jennifer K '00 %Richards K&O LLP -1 World Fncl Ctr -NY 10281
(315) 445-5608 .. **Grady,** Jessica G '04 (Harris-Courage & G PLLC) -225 Greenfld Pkwy -Liverpool 13088 **Fx:**445-0738
(914) 681-0444 .. **Grady,** Michl F '88 (Rende R&D,LLP) -202 Mamaroneck Av -White Plns 10601
(212) 509-3456 .. **Grady,** Michelle D '01 %McGivney & K,PC -80 Broad -NY 10004
(718) 875-3390 .. **Grady,** Richd A '78 -50 Court -Brklyn 11201
(212) 885-5000 .. **Grady,** Shawnda M '08 %Blank R LLP -405 Lex Av -NY 10174
(585) 238-2000 .. **Grady,** Victoria L '96 (Phillips L LLP) -1400 First Fed Plz -Rchstr 14614
(716) 847-8400 .. **Grady,** Victoria L '96 (Phillips L LLP) -3400 HSBC Ctr -Buffalo 14203
(845) 486-2300 .. **Grady,** Wm V '70 (DA) -236 Main -Poughkeepsie 12601 **Fx:**486-2324
(845) 641-1105 .. **Grady-Smith,** Mattie D '95 -Bx383 -Tarrytwn 10591 **Fx:**371-4429
(212) 687-0140 .. **Grae,** Seth H '88 -555 5th Av -NY 10017 **Fx:**986-5316
(212) 968-2300 .. **Grae,** Wm H '95 %Chartwell Law Ofc,LLP -39 Bway -NY 10006 **Fx:**968-2400
(516) 792-0605 .. **Graeber,** Bruce '81 -445 Central Av -Cedarhrst 11516 **Fx:**792-0823
(315) 858-1360 .. **Graepel,** Edw C '90 -3597 US Route 20 -Richfld Spgs 13439
(212) 994-0660 .. **Graev,** Lawr G '70 Glenrock Grp,LLC -767 3rd Av -NY 10017
(212) 201-0860 .. **Graf,** Andrew J '00 Enliven Mrktng Tech Corp -205 W 39th -NY 10018
(212) 807-2194 .. **Graf,** Catherine Anne '91 %Thomson Reuters/RIA -195 Bway -NY 10007
(203) 829-4723 .. **Graf,** Diane Lehman '99 (D Graf,PA,PC) -700 Wht Plns Rd -Scarsdale 10583
(212) 848-4000 .. **Graf,** Ian E '09 %Shearman & S LLP -599 Lex Av -NY 10022
(212) 302-3300 .. **Graf,** Peter G '60 (Graf Repetti & Co) -1114 Av of Amer -NY 10036 **Fx:**302-9662
(585) 232-6500 .. **Graf,** Rebecca E '03 %Harter S&E LLP -1600 Bausch & Lomb Pl -Rchstr 14604
(212) 758-9700 .. **Graf,** Stephanie '97 %KPMG LLP -345 Park Av -NY 10154
(212) 257-6800 .. **Graff,** Ariel Y '07 %Thompson W&G LLP -85 5th Av -NY 10003
(516) 746-5040 .. **Graff,** Austin R '01 %Scher Law Firm,LLP -1 Old Cntry Rd -Carle Pl 11514 **Fx:**747-9100
(212) 455-2000 .. **Graff,** Elisha D '01 (Simpson T&B LLP) -425 Lex Av -NY 10017
(212) 318-6000 .. **Graff,** George L '67 (Paul HJ&W LLP) -75 E 55th -NY 10022
(212) 277-6500 .. **Graff,** Howard '74 (Dickstein S LLP) -1633 Bway -NY 10019
(845) 638-2726 .. **Graff,** Ilene Kim '89 %Thorsen Law Ofc -5 S Little Tor Rd -New Cty 10956 **Fx:**638-1125
(315) 462-3010 .. **Graff,** Jeffrey D '98 %Riley & G -26 E Main Bx604 -Clifton Spgs 14432
(212) 725-9300 .. **Graff,** Jehoshua '73 (Sukenik S&G,PC) -404 5th Av -NY 10018
(212) 474-1000 .. **Graff,** Jennifer R '09 %Cravath S&M LLP -825 8th Av -NY 10019
(716) 852-1000 .. **Graff,** Kevin J '01 PW Beltz,PC -36 Church -Buffalo 14202 **Fx:**852-5887
(845) 338-4993 .. **Graff,** Michl E '98 (Wilkie & G LLC) -78 Main Bx4148 -Kingston 12402
(917) 902-7979 .. **Graff,** Michl P '61 (Graff Law Ofcs) -161 W 61st -NY 10023 **Fx:**(212) 246-6774
(631) 234-5678 .. **Graff,** Peter J '95 %Wallace WF&V,PC -600 Suffolk Av -Brentwd 11717
(716) 439-7140 .. **Graff,** Robt M '78 %Hon S Sperrazza -175 Hawley -Lockprt 14094
(845) 338-4993 .. **Graff,** Sharon Ann '98 %Wilkie & G LLC -78 Main Bx4148 -Kingston 12402
(845) 338-4993 .. **Graff,** Wayne L '71 (Wilkie & G LLC) -78 Main Bx4148 -Kingston 12402
(212) 468-8000 .. **Graffagna,** Michl C '03 (Morrison & F LLP) -1290 Av of Amer -NY 10104
(212) 490-3000 .. **Graffeo,** Allison R '00 (Wilson EME&D LLP) -150 E 42nd -NY 10017
(212) 232-1300 .. **Graffeo,** Brian P '05 %Lewis BB&S LLP -77 Water -NY 10005
(631) 547-0300 .. **Graffeo,** John P '98 %Novick & Assoc,PC -202 E Main -Huntngtn 11743 **Fx:**547-0212
(212) 458-6257 .. **Graffeo,** Michele '94 AIG -175 Water -NY 10038
(516) 292-8100 .. **Graffeo,** Sandra '96 Nassau/Sfflk Law Srv -1 Helen Keller Way -Hempstd 11550 **Fx:**292-6529
(631) 242-7801 .. **Grafstein,** Fred '68 -2061 Deer Prk Av -Deer Pk 11729
(631) 242-7801 .. **Grafstein,** Howard S '77 -2061 Deer Prk Av -Deer Pk 11729 **Fx:**586-6029
(718) 375-3684 .. **Grafstein,** Israel '03 -1760 E 28th -Brklyn 11229
(631) 239-5100 .. **Grafstein-Suarez,** Paula E '99 OfCnsl G Suarez,PC -50 Elm -Huntngtn 11743 **Fx:**421-2110
(212) 290-2630 .. **Grafton,** Joy R '86 %Popper & G -225 W 34th -NY 10122
(212) 290-2630 .. **Grafton,** Saml R '74 (Popper & G) -225 W 34th -NY 10122
(212) 837-6101 .. **Gragg,** Meaghan C '09 %Hughes H&R LLP -1 Bttry Pk Plz -NY 10004
(212) 354-5650 .. **Graham Campaign PC** -36 W 44th -NY 10036 **Fx:**354-6354
(212) 450-4000 .. **Graham,** Christine E '08 %Davis P&W LLP -450 Lex Av -NY 10017
(212) 922-1800 .. **Graham,** Christopher F '83 (McKenna L&A) -230 Park Av -NY 10169
(212) 325-7951 .. **Graham,** Colleen A '92 Credit Suisse -1 Mad Av -NY 10010 **Fx:**325-8220
(718) 579-7961 .. **Graham,** Holly B '02 %Leg Aid -900 Sheridan Av -Bronx 10451 **Fx:**293-8744
(212) 236-6055 .. **Graham,** James A '01 Merrill Lynch & Co,Inc -2 World Fncl Ctr -NY 10281 **Fx:**236-6111
(516) 294-1949 .. **Graham,** James J Jr. '96 (Mangi & G LLP) -1400 Old Cntry Rd -Westbury 11590
(518) 486-9840 .. **Graham,** Janet A '97 %State Comptroller -110 State -Albany 12236 **Fx:**473-9104
(845) 485-8035 .. **Graham,** Jeffrey S '67 (J Graham,PC) -95 Cannon -Poughkeepsie 12601 **Fx:**485-8055
(212) 837-6000 .. **Graham,** Jennifer E '03 %Hughes H&R LLP -1 Bttry Pk Plz -NY 10004
(516) 357-3000 .. **Graham,** Jesse J II '76 (Rivkin R LLP) -926 RXR Plz -Uniondale 11556
(518) 474-6530 .. **Graham,** John C '02 %Dept Pub Srvc -3 ESP -Albany 12223
(212) 878-8000 .. **Graham,** John L '08 (Clifford C LLP) -31 W 52nd -NY 10019
(516) 502-2620 .. **Graham,** John M Jr. '63 (Thomas & G LLP) -1983 Marcus Av -Lk Success 11042
(516) 502-2620 .. **Graham,** John M III '85 (Thomas & G LLP) -1983 Marcus Av -Lk Success 11042
(315) 779-9022 .. **Graham,** John W '86 -120 Wshngtn -Watertwn 13601 **Fx:**779-9022
(212) 340-0400 .. **Graham,** Jul E '79 %Appllt Div 1st Dept -27 Mad Av -NY 10010 **Fx:**889-4412
(516) 357-3000 .. **Graham,** Kelsey D III '92 (Rivkin R LLP) -926 RXR Plz -Uniondale 11556
(315) 473-9414 .. **Graham,** Kevin B '97 %Hinman H&K,LLP -224 Harrison -Syracuse 13202
(914) 238-4000 .. **Graham,** Lawr O '90 -233 S Greeley Av -Chappaqua 10514 **Fx:**238-5011
(212) 815-1818 .. **Graham,** Lynn G '88 %DC 37 MELS -125 Barclay -NY 10007 **Fx:**815-1343
(212) 640-2000 .. **Graham,** Maxine Y '97 %Amer Exp -200 Vesey -NY 10285
(718) 579-3000 .. **Graham,** Maya S '10 Leg Aid -1020 Grnd Cncrs -Bronx 10451 **Fx:**588-2611
(212) 775-8700 .. **Graham,** Michelle M '98 Cnsl Kilpatrick S,LLP -31 W 52nd -NY 10019
(212) 671-1179 .. **Graham Miller Neandross Mullin & Roonan,PC** -2350 Bway -NY 10024 **Fx:**877-4487
(716) 847-8400 .. **Graham,** Morgan G '85 (Phillips L LLP) -3400 HSBC Ctr -Buffalo 14203
(718) 499-0809 .. **Graham,** Nancy R W '80 (Graham & G) -363 6th Av -Brklyn 11215 **Fx:**499-0829
(212) 592-1400 .. **Graham,** Patricia M '88 Cnsl Herrick,F LLP -2 Park Av -NY 10016
(845) 331-1001 .. **Graham,** Peter C '74 -479 Wshngtn Av -Kingston 12401 **Fx:**331-1002
(631) 473-4900 .. **Graham,** Peter J '58 -1523 Main -Pt Jffrsn 11777 **Fx:**473-6748
(516) 333-8230 .. **Graham,** Peter J '96 %E-Z-EM,Inc -1111 Marcus Av -New Hyde Pk 11042
(212) 558-4000 .. **Graham,** Philip L Jr. '71 (Sullivan & C LLP) -125 Broad -NY 10004
(212) 819-8200 .. **Graham,** Richd A '03 %White & C LLP -1155 Av of Amer -NY 10036
(315) 376-5282 .. **Graham,** Richd J '84 -7660 N State -Lowvll 13367 **Fx:**376-3857
(212) 613-2231 .. **Graham,** Sadia N '98 -292 5th Av -NY 10001
(917) 521-3489 .. **Graham,** Shanee M '06 %NYC Dept Homeless Svcs -346 Powers Av -Bronx 10454
(212) 612-9276 .. **Graham,** Sharie K '92 SrCnsl The Clearing House -450 W 33rd -NY 10001 **Fx:**612-9253
(212) 490-3000 .. **Graham,** Shawn C '07 %Wilson EME&D LLP -150 E 42nd -NY 10017
(212) 612-9550 .. **Graham,** Teresa L '95 (Dombroff & G,PC) -40 Broad -NY 10004
(718) 357-4764 .. **Graham,** Thos J '52 -4558 194th -Flushng 11358 **Fx:**747-2302
(212) 922-0450 .. **Graham,** Warren R '81 OfCnsl Kaplan M&A,LLC -70 E 55th -NY 10022
(631) 231-2954 .. **Graham,** Wm J '95 -982 Montauk Hwy -Bayport 11705
(518) 474-0609 .. **Graham,** Wm T '82 %Ofc for the Aging -Bldg 2 ESP -Albany 12223 **Fx:**474-0608
(718) 250-2000 .. **Graham-Brogan,** Diana L '07 %DA -350 Jay -Brklyn 11201 **Fx:**250-2314
(212) 696-6000 .. **Graif,** Michl R '92 (Curtis M-PC&M LLP) -101 Park Av -NY 10178
(212) 269-1400 .. **Graifman,** Brian D '88 Gusrae KB&N PLLC -120 Wall -NY 10005
(845) 356-2570 .. **Graifman,** Gary S '81 (Kantrowitz G&G,PC) -747 Chestnut Rdg Rd -Chestnut Rdg 10977
(914) 949-6400 .. **Grainger,** Edmund C III '77 %McCullough G&S,LLP -1311 Mamaroneck Av -White Plns 10605
(212) 343-0114 .. **Grainger,** Katherine A '04 %NARAL -470 Park Av S -NY 10016 **Fx:**343-0119
(315) 478-9392 .. **Grainger,** Michl P '97 %Rollinson Law Firm -307 S Townsend -Syracuse 13202 **Fx:**478-9521
(212) 755-0100 .. **Grais,** David J '79 (Grais & E LLP) -40 E 52nd -NY 10022
(212) 755-0100 .. **Grais & Ellsworth LLP** -40 E 52nd -NY 10022 **Fx:**755-0052
(646) 386-4000 .. **Grajales,** Ananias '01 Supreme Ct-Crim -111 Centre -NY 10013

(718) 830-3200 .. **Grajales,** Emily C '07 %Rosado C&B,LLP -31-00 47th Av -LIC 11101 **Fx:**830-3534
(212) 455-2000 .. **Grajales,** Jose C '09 %Simpson T&B LLP -425 Lex Av -NY 10017
(718) 435-7260 .. **Grajales,** José M '06 -44-21 5th Av -Brklyn 11220
(212) 504-6000 .. **Grala,** Bronislaw E '72 (Cadwalader W&T LLP) -1 World Fncl Ctr -NY 10281
(914) 472-2900 .. **Gralicer & Kaiser** -455 Cntrl Pk Av -Scarsdale 10583 **Fx:**472-1481
(914) 472-2900 .. **Gralicer,** Richd '52 (Gralicer & K) -455 Cntrl Pk Av -Scarsdale 10583
(212) 593-4683 .. **Gralitzer,** Keith J '03 Schneider Legal Srch -1230 Av of Amer -NY 10020
(607) 763-9200 .. **Grall,** John G '86 (Levene G&T,LLP) -BxF-1706 -Bnghmtn 13902
(212) 980-9600 .. **Gralnick,** Jeffrey A '00 %Kaufman B&R -120 Bway -NY 10271
(716) 373-8043 .. **Gram,** Fredk J '73 %OCA -1701 Lincoln Av -Olean 14760 **Fx:**373-0449
(212) 449-3201 .. **Gramling Lopez,** Jo Willa '73 %Merrill Lynch -220 Bway -NY 10038
(631) 265-9191 .. **Grammatico,** Claude N '82 Epstein & G -1393 Vets Mem'l Hwy -Hauppauge 11788
(516) 364-7900 .. **Grammatico,** Claude N '82 Epstein F&G -45 Crsswys Park Dr W -Woodbury 11797
(212) 728-8000 .. **Granacher,** Amanda L '05 %Willkie F&G LLP -787 7th Av -NY 10019
(718) 784-2240 .. **Granahan,** Sean T '99 Floating Hospital -41-40 27th -LIC 11101 **Fx:**784-0240
(516) 222-2330 .. **Granat,** Jeffrey A '78 %Jacobson G&K,LLP -585 Stewart Av -Gdn Cty 11530
(212) 492-5800 .. **Granat,** Sari B '96 %Kaplan Educ Ctrs,Inc -888 7th Av -NY 10106 **Fx:**489-2301
(212) 558-4000 .. **Granata,** Enrico '06 %Sullivan & C LLP -125 Broad -NY 10004
(212) 331-5946 .. **Granby,** Starr J '08 ACS Collection -180 Water -NY 10038
(212) 534-4179 .. **Grancher,** Carolyn '67 -425 E 86th -NY 10028 **Fx:**534-4179
(212) 584-0700 .. **Grand,** Jeffrey S '03 %Seeger W LLP -1 William -NY 10004
(212) 789-2043 .. **Grand,** Julie Spar '95 %NHL -1251 Av of Amer -NY 10020
(212) 880-9510 .. **Grand,** Paul R '60 (Morvillo AGIA&B,PC) -565 5th Av -NY 10017
(607) 974-8775 .. **Grand,** Yvonne L '97 %Corning Inc -1 Rvrfrnt Plz -Corning 14831
(716) 675-2313 .. **Grande,** Albert '90 -3700 Seneca -Buffalo 14224 **Fx:**675-2315
(212) 668-5927 .. **Grande,** Anthony D '89 (Ropers MK&B) -17 State -NY 10004
(315) 361-7506 .. **Grande,** Ignatius A '00 Oneida Indian Nation -5218 Patrick Rd -Verona 13478
(914) 948-7000 .. **Grande,** Robt J '02 %Keidel W&C LLP -925 Wstchstr Av -White Plns 10604
(866) 781-6101 .. **Grande,** Toni Ann J '01 (Drexel G LLC) -220 E 42nd -NY 10007
(631) 225-0744 .. **Grande,** Vincent J III '00 -248 W Montauk Hwy -Lindenhrst 11757
(212) 449-4385 .. **Grande,** Virginia A '87 %Merrill Lynch -220 Bway -NY 10038
(716) 447-1047 .. **Grande,** Wm E '86 -300 Internatinal Dr PMB 10031 -Buffalo 14221 **Fx:**873-7854
(212) 668-8400 .. **Grandelli,** Louis '91 -90 Broad -NY 10004 **Fx:**483-0918
(212) 407-7700 .. **Grandin,** T Miles '10 %Vedder P,PC -1633 Bway -NY 10019
(516) 248-5317 .. **Grandinette,** Anthony M '87 (Grandinette & S,LLP) -114 Old Cntry Rd -Mineola 11501 **Fx:**294-5348
(212) 225-2000 .. **Grandinetti,** Megan J '09 %Cleary GS&H -1 Lbrty Plz -NY 10006
(212) 907-9600 .. **Grandis,** Michl H '01 (Ingram YGC&B,LLP) -250 Park Av -NY 10177
(914) 767-6745 .. **Grandison,** Diana S '05 %Pepsi Bottling Grp -1 Pepsi Way -Somers 10589
(212) 326-3939 .. **Grandt,** Suzanne C '10 %Jones D -222 E 41st -NY 10017
(718) 852-3000 .. **Grandwetter,** David N '04 Cnsl CSA -16 Court -Brklyn 11241 **Fx:**403-0278
(516) 746-8000 .. **Granelli,** Laura J '98 (Jaspan S LLP) -300 Grdn City Plz -Gdn Cty 11530
(516) 594-0909 .. **Granelli,** Scott P '95 %Polsky S&R,PC -500 Merrick Rd -Rockvll Ctr 11570
(718) 321-8224 .. **Graner,** Garran J '85 -38-11 Ditmars Blvd -Astoria 11105 **Fx:**321-8553
(718) 222-2457 .. **Granet,** Jaclyn S '05 Law Dept -350 Jay -Brklyn 11201 **Fx:**222-2393
(914) 698-3250 .. **Granett,** Solomon '38 -407 Crk Rd -Mamaroneck 10543
(716) 842-2800 .. **Graney,** Chas E '94 (Webster S LLP) -1400 Lbrty Bldg -Buffalo 14202
(585) 768-8420 .. **Graney,** John R '41 -9769 Perry Rd -Le Roy 14482 **Fx:**768-8157
(212) 225-2000 .. **Granfield,** Lindsee P '86 (Cleary GS&H) -1 Lbrty Plz -NY 10006
(212) 387-8400 .. **Granfort,** Mary E '85 (Goldfarb AS&K LLP) -350 5th Av -NY 10118
(315) 458-5040 .. **Granger,** Cindy A '86 %Karp -428 S Main -N Syracuse 13212 **Fx:**458-4321
(518) 445-2328 .. **Granger,** Leslie A '09 %Law Clinic & Justice Ctr -80 New Scotland Av -Albany 12208
(716) 852-5430 .. **Granger,** Patrick E '82 -295 Main -Buffalo 14203 **Fx:**852-5441
(212) 688-1669 .. **Granger,** Raymond R '85 (Granger & Assoc LLC) -40 Fulton -NY 10038 **Fx:**346-9319
(716) 852-5430 .. **Granger,** Terry '89 -295 Main -Buffalo 14203 **Fx:**852-5441
(518) 862-7181 .. **Granich,** Jos A '98 (Flint & G) -465 New Karner Rd -Albany 12205 **Fx:**862-7185
(212) 806-5400 .. **Granik,** Gary L '78 (Stroock &S&L LLP) -180 Maiden Ln -NY 10038
(845) 634-9700 .. **Granirer,** Martus '96 -100 South Mtn Rd -New Cty 10956 **Fx:**634-9700
(607) 255-5141 .. **Granison,** Henry C '99 %Cornell Law Schl -Myron Taylor Hall -Ithaca 14853 **Fx:**255-7193
(212) 661-0011 .. **Granito,** Frank H Jr. '62 OfCnsl Speiser KN&G -140 E 45th -NY 10017
(212) 661-0011 .. **Granito,** Frank H III '87 (Speiser KN&G) -140 E 45th -NY 10017
(315) 451-2387 .. **Granito,** V James Jr. '77 (Granito & S) -890 7th N -Liverpool 13088 **Fx:**451-3981
(917) 375-7955 .. **Granizo-O'Hare,** Marti '89 -16 E 34th -NY 10016 **Fx:**(888) 684-2569
(212) 903-1025 .. **Grannis,** Eric J '95 -620 5th Av -NY 10020
(212) 225-2000 .. **Grannis,** Helena '01 %Cleary GS&H -1 Lbrty Plz -NY 10006
(212) 728-8000 .. **Grannis,** Keith W '08 Willkie F&G LLP -787 7th Av -NY 10019
(914) 632-1698 .. **Grannum,** Colvin W '85 -25 Croft Ter -New Rchll 10804 **Fx:**632-1698
(845) 365-9100 .. **Grannum,** Sandra D '87 (Davidson & G) -30 Ramland Rd -Orangebrg 10962
(212) 416-8920 .. **Grannum,** Sandra Jefferson '87 %Dept of Law -120 Bway -NY 10271
(212) 421-2111 .. **Granoff,** Gary C '73 (Granoff W&F,PC) -747 3rd Av -NY 10017
(212) 277-4000 .. **Granoff,** Ilmi '08 %Freshfields BD LLP -520 Mad Av -NY 10022
(212) 421-2111 .. **Granoff Walker & Forlenza,PC** -747 3rd Av -NY 10017 **Fx:**421-3488
(212) 964-6611 .. **Granofsky,** Richd '79 (Lester SK&D) -120 Bway -NY 10271
(212) 223-4000 .. **Granovsky,** Alexander '04 %Crowell & M LLP -590 Mad Av -NY 10022
(212) 849-7000 .. **Granovsky,** Maria '09 %Quinn EU&S,LLP -51 Mad Av -NY 10010
(212) 756-2000 .. **Granowitz,** Danl E '10 %Schulte R&Z LLP -919 3rd Av -NY 10022
(212) 916-2250 .. **Granski,** Edmund W Jr. '96 UBS AG -101 Park Av -NY 10178
(212) 506-1700 .. **Grant,** Adam K '02 %Kasowitz BT&F LLP -1633 Bway -NY 10019
(212) 643-8249 .. **Grant,** Albert O II '76 -350 5th Av -NY 10118 **Fx:**643-8256
(212) 558-4000 .. **Grant,** Alphonzo A Jr. '99 SpclCnsl Sullivan & C LLP -125 Broad -NY 10004
(718) 994-3420 .. **Grant,** Andrea A '98 -4120 Baychester Av -Bronx 10466 **Fx:**994-8755
(718) 341-2618 .. **Grant,** Andrea S '93 -20547 Linden Blvd -St Albans 11412
(914) 241-0940 .. **Grant,** Anthony J '70 -256 W Main -Mt Kisco 10549
(212) 308-2200 .. **Grant & Appelbaum,PC** -444 Mad Av -NY 10022 **Fx:**308-2223
(212) 450-4000 .. **Grant,** Bernice A '04 %Davis P&W LLP -450 Lex Av -NY 10017
(212) 440-4400 .. **Grant,** Cameron E '08 %Buchanan I&R PC -620 8th Av -NY 10018
(212) 458-1029 .. **Grant,** Carl M '98 AIG -175 Water -NY 10038
(212) 442-9617 .. **Grant,** Collette V '03 NYC Dept of Prob -100 Centre -NY 10013
(212) 455-2000 .. **Grant,** Daeyna M '09 %Simpson T&B LLP -425 Lex Av -NY 10017
(212) 261-8000 .. **Grant,** Danielle A '07 %Mendes & M,LLP -750 7th Av -NY 10019
(518) 781-4567 .. **Grant,** Darlene C '88 Berkshire Farm -13640 State Hwy 22 -Canaan 12029
(212) 629-8585 .. **Grant,** Dawn L '94 (Ellenberg & Prtnrs LLP) -575 8th Av -NY 10018
(212) 848-7959 .. **Grant,** Denise M '90 (Shearman & S LLP) -599 Lex Av -NY 10022
(845) 876-2800 .. **Grant,** Drayton '76 (Grant & L,LLP) -149 Wurtemburg Rd -Rhinebeck 12572
(646) 722-8500 .. **Grant & Eisenhofer, PA** -485 Lex Av -NY 10017 **Fx:**722-8501
(212) 644-6006 .. **Grant,** Ernest F '62 OfCnsl Dickerson T&M -600 Mad Av -NY 10022
(212) 490-0004 .. **Grant,** Gayle D '98 Imperial Capital,LLC -485 Lex Av -NY 10017
(212) 632-5582 .. **Grant,** Gregg S '96 Cnsl Salans LLP -620 5th Av -NY 10020
(212) 682-1800 .. **Grant Herrmann Schwartz & Klinger LLP** -675 3rd Av -NY 10017 **Fx:**682-1850
(631) 761-7000 .. **Grant,** J Kirkland '71 %Touro Cllg Law Ctr -225 Eastvw Dr -Central Islip 11722
(212) 801-2240 .. **Grant,** Jacqueline C '05 Greenberg T,LLP -200 Park Av -NY 10166 **Fx:**801-6400
(212) 728-8000 .. **Grant,** Jill Kaden '09 %Willkie F&G LLP -787 7th Av -NY 10019
(914) 722-9120 .. **Grant,** Joan Salzman '81 -115 Carthage Rd -Scarsdale 10583 **Fx:**722-4179
(212) 501-9000 .. **Grant,** John D '09 %Brower P,PC -488 Mad Av -NY 10022 **Fx:**501-0300
(845) 358-2288 .. **Grant,** John K '88 -3 Main -Nyack 10960
(212) 903-9000 .. **Grant,** Jonathan M '03 %Linklaters -1345 Av of Amer -NY 10105
(516) 739-2077 .. **Grant,** Karen C '91 -137 Willis Av -Mineola 11501 **Fx:**739-2083
(914) 385-6000 .. **Grant,** Leicia '07 %Hodges W&S LLP -55 Church -White Plns 10601 **Fx:**385-6060
(845) 638-5180 .. **Grant,** Linda H '05 Cnty Atty -Cnty Ofc Bldg -New Cty 10956 **Fx:**638-5676
(212) 838-7797 .. **Grant,** Lynda J '83 (Cohen MS&T,PLLC) -88 Pine -NY 10005
(845) 876-2800 .. **Grant & Lyons, LLP** -149 Wurtemburg Rd -Rhinebeck 12572 **Fx:**876-2816
(212) 396-0991 .. **Grant & Lyons, LLP** -1 Rckfllr Plz -NY 10020
(212) 720-5026 .. **Grant,** Martin C '91 %Fed Reserve Bk -33 Lbrty -NY 10045 **Fx:**785-5748
(607) 255-4680 .. **Grant,** Mary E '99 %Cornell Univ -500 Day Hall -Ithaca 14853
(212) 715-1000 .. **Grant,** Matthew D '03 %Arnold & P LLP -399 Park Av -NY 10022
(212) 310-8000 .. **Grant,** Maya M '04 %Weil G&M LLP -767 5th Av -NY 10153
(212) 308-2200 .. **Grant,** Patricia Ann '86 (Grant & A,PC) -444 Mad Av -NY 10022
(585) 258-0103 .. **Grant,** Paul L Jr. '96 %Garrison Litigation -120 East Av -Rchstr 14604 **Fx:**325-7356
(212) 554-0400 .. **Grant,** Peter E '98 (Grubman I&S,PC) -152 W 57th -NY 10019
(212) 512-0515 .. **Grant,** Savyon '93 S Grant & Assoc -1040 Av of Amer -NY 10018 **Fx:**512-0501
(518) 486-7003 .. **Grant,** Selica Y '02 NY Div of Housing & Cmmty Renewal -38-40 State -Albany 12207
(518) 832-1220 .. **Grant,** Sheila E '00 US Benefits,Inc -250 Glen -Glens Fls 12801
(212) 692-1000 .. **Grant,** Stefan C '98 (Duane M LLP) -1540 Bway -NY 10036
(212) 822-1451 .. **Grant,** Steven A '03 -305 Bway -NY 10007 **Fx:**693-1410
(914) 479-5804 .. **Grant,** Steven P '84 (Grant & L,LLP) -377 Ashford Av -Dobbs Ferry 10522 **Fx:**479-5808
(646) 722-8500 .. **Grant,** Stuart M '87 (Grant & E,PA) -485 Lex Av -NY 10017
(718) 261-4501 .. **Grant,** Susan I '78 -110-45 Qns Blvd -Frst Hlls 11375 **Fx:**268-6569
(718) 595-6530 .. **Grant,** Tevin C S '03 %DEP -59-17 Junction Blvd -Flushng 11373 **Fx:**595-6543
(718) 858-3000 .. **Grant,** Tracey A '00 OfCnsl D Rankin & Assoc PC -26 Court -Brklyn 11242 **Fx:**858-9615
(212) 294-6700 .. **Grant,** Wm J Jr. '71 (Winston & S) -200 Park Av -NY 10166
(516) 873-9550 .. **Grant,** Xena P '09 Leeds M&B -1 Old Cntry Rd -Carle Pl 11514
(914) 697-7581 .. **Grant,** Zachary '90 -70 W Red Oak Ln -White Plns 10604
(631) 351-3042 .. **GrantFlynn,** Patricia T '85 Town Atty -100 Main -Huntngtn 11743 **Fx:**351-3032
(212) 701-3000 .. **Granum,** Ajana M '10 %Cahill G&R LLP -80 Pine -NY 10005 **Fx:**269-5420
(585) 753-1380 .. **Granville,** Brett C '93 Cnty Atty -307 Cnty Ofc Bldg -Rchstr 14614 **Fx:**753-1331
(716) 683-3364 .. **Granville,** James F '94 OfCnsl Watson BCJ&S -3521 Union Rd -Cheektowaga 14225
(212) 349-5150 .. **Granville,** Steven F '95 %Galvano & X,PC -150 Bway -NY 10038
(315) 445-1700 .. **Granzow,** Jennifer B '98 %Wladis Law Firm,PC -5795 Widewaters Pkwy -Syracuse 13214 **Fx:**251-1073
(585) 815-0288 .. **Grapensteter,** Virginia C '08 %Rosicki R & Assoc,PC -26 Harvester Av -Batavia 14020 **Fx:**815-0299
(646) 610-5140 .. **Grappone,** John '93 %NYPD -1 Police Plz -NY 10038
(212) 418-8700 .. **Grappotte,** Xavier Philippe '98 Fortis -520 Mad Av -NY 10022
(212) 310-8000 .. **Grapsas,** Rebecca C '05 %Weil G&M LLP -767 5th Av -NY 10153

(631) 277-6543 .. **Graseck,** Arthur V Jr. '64 -1870 Spur Dr S -Islip Terr 11752 **Fx:**277-2227
(516) 873-6200 .. **Grasing,** Raymond R '92 %R Macchia & Assoc -98 Front -Mineola 11501 **Fx:**873-1611
(315) 474-3742 .. **Grasmann,** Edwin J '07 %Stanley Law Ofcs -500 S Salina -Syracuse 13202 **Fx:**471-1536
(716) 842-3100 .. **Grasmick,** Jos C '78 -300 Intl Dr -Williamsvll 14221 **Fx:**842-3105
(914) 762-0261 .. **Grass,** Andrew N Jr. '53 -Bx307 -Scarboro 10510
(212) 836-8000 .. **Grass,** Robt M '92 Cnsl Kaye S LLP -425 Park Av -NY 10022
(845) 291-3126 .. **Grasselena,** Gregory C '83 %Sup Ct -255 Main -Goshen 10924
(716) 847-8400 .. **Grasser,** George R '66 OfCnsl Phillips L LLP -3400 HSBC Ctr -Buffalo 14203
(212) 983-3274 .. **Grassi,** Jos F '74 -100 Park Av -NY 10017 **Fx:**983-0227
(212) 770-0928 .. **Grassi,** Paolo '93 AIG -80 Pine -NY 10005
(516) 328-3500 .. **Grassini,** Carin M '02 %McDonnell & A,PC -401 Franklin Av -Gdn Cty 11530
(212) 922-9225 .. **Grasso,** Alexander A '81 -355 Lex Av -NY 10017 **Fx:**922-2817
(212) 818-9600 .. **Grasso,** Angelo M '03 %Greenfield S&S,LLP -600 3rd Av -NY 10016
(212) 471-8525 .. **Grasso,** Carl T '80 (Herzfeld & R,PC) -125 Broad -NY 10004
(716) 823-3308 .. **Grasso,** Danl P '93 -3652 South Park -Blasdell 14219
(315) 668-2669 .. **Grasso,** David S '93 (Russell R&G,PLLC) -3250 Fulton Av Bx503 -Centrl Sq 13036 **Fx:**668-3333
(212) 753-5000 .. **Grasso,** Fabrizio '07 %Schiff H LLP -900 3rd Av -NY 10022
(585) 343-3090 .. **Grasso,** Jacqueline M '86 (Rybak M&G,LLP) -104 Bank -Batavia 14020
(716) 847-8400 .. **Grasso,** James R '91 (Phillips L LLP) -3400 HSBC Ctr -Buffalo 14203
(212) 490-1700 .. **Grasso,** Jos G '87 (Wiggin & D) -450 Lex Av -NY 10017
(845) 291-2050 .. **Grasso,** Lauren E '08 %DA -255-275 Main -Goshen 10924 **Fx:**291-2085
(212) 592-1400 .. **Grasso,** Laurie A '00 (Herrick,F LLP) -2 Park Av -NY 10016
(646) 386-3639 .. **Grasso,** Lisa M '87 %Supreme Ct-Law Dept -60 Centre -NY 10007
(212) 267-6364 .. **Grasso,** Meredith P '08 %Kossoff & U -217 Bway -NY 10007
(518) 393-8011 .. **Grasso,** Nicholas J '48 (Grasso R&G) -751 State -Schnctdy 12307
(212) 722-6247 .. **Grasso,** Richd D '87 -185 E 85th -NY 10028
(518) 393-8011 .. **Grasso Rodriguez & Grasso** -751 State -Schnctdy 12307 **Fx:**393-7110
(845) 291-2050 .. **Grasso,** Steven L '08 %DA -255-275 Main -Goshen 10924 **Fx:**291-2085
(212) 286-0225 .. **Grasso,** Thos M '98 %Casey & B LLC -65 W 36th -NY 10018 **Fx:**286-0261
(212) 801-6765 .. **Grassotti,** Lauren B '06 %Greenberg T,LLP -200 Park Av -NY 10166
(516) 228-3131 .. **Grasty,** Jesse '07 %Franklin G&C,PC -666 Old Cntry Rd -Gdn Cty 11530
(516) 992-1848 .. **Gratale,** Dominick F '01 OfCnsl M Carmen & Assoc,PLLC -1201 RXR Plz -Uniondale 11556 **Fx:**739-0981
(516) 921-6645 .. **Grath,** Gina Ianne '04 %A Pearl & Assoc,PC -6800 Jericho Tpk -Syosset 11791 **Fx:**921-6774
(718) 963-3339 .. **Gratt,** Kevin D '98 (Gratt & Assoc PC) -2021 Nostrand Av -Brklyn 11210 **Fx:**963-1470
(518) 758-9215 .. **Grattan,** Patrick M '97 -2870 Route 9 Bx718 -Valatie 12184 **Fx:**758-9654
(212) 819-8200 .. **Gratton,** Catherine '05 %White & C LLP -1155 Av of Amer -NY 10036
(718) 250-2000 .. **Gratton,** Wm M '10 %DA -350 Jay -Brklyn 11201 **Fx:**250-2314
(212) 929-5600 .. **Grau,** Kenneth '84 -1201 Bway -NY 10001 **Fx:**929-7050
(718) 859-2444 .. **Grau,** Leonard '60 -770 Rugby Rd -Brklyn 11230 **Fx:**859-6514
(347) 404-9133 .. **Graubard,** Howard J '92 %Civil Ct -141 Lvngstn -Brklyn 11201 **Fx:**(718) 643-3733
(212) 336-0084 .. **Graubard,** John J '68 SEC -3 World Fncl Ctr -NY 10281 **Fx:**336-1323
(212) 681-1600 .. **Graubard,** M David '70 (Kera & G) -240 Mad Av -NY 10016 **Fx:**681-1601
(212) 818-8800 .. **Graubard Miller** -405 Lex Av -NY 10174 **Fx:**818-8881
(212) 288-4645 .. **Graubard,** Myra L '68 -176 E 71st -NY 10021 **Fx:**358-9904
(212) 447-0500 .. **Graubard,** Peter L '94 (Graubard & Assoc,PC) -65 W 36th -NY 10018 **Fx:**447-7505
(212) 326-8614 .. **Graubard,** Robt C '82 Julien J Studley Inc -300 Park Av -NY 10022
(914) 946-1444 .. **Graubart,** Danl '79 (D Graubart,PC) -34 S Bway -White Plns 10601 **Fx:**948-1800 ***[Bankruptcy Law]***
(646) 781-9321 .. **Graubart,** Joshua G '08 J Graubart,PC -6 E 39th -NY 10016 **Fx:**224-8088
(212) 554-7800 .. **Grauberd,** Allan '84 (Moses & S LLP) -405 Lex Av -NY 10174
(914) 946-5480 .. **Grauer,** David I '77 -50 Main -White Plns 10606
(914) 761-1300 .. **Grauer,** Joshua J '81 (Cuddy & F LLP) -445 Hmltn Av -White Plns 10601
(212) 454-7121 .. **Grauer,** Meredith K '00 %Deutsche Bank -60 Wall -NY 10005
(212) 598-8000 .. **Grauer,** Robt D '97 %Guardian Life Ins -7 Hanover Sq -NY 10004 **Fx:**919-2693
(212) 450-4000 .. **Graulich,** Timothy E '95 (Davis P&W LLP) -450 Lex Av -NY 10017
(212) 558-4000 .. **Grauman,** Edw M '04 %Sullivan & C LLP -125 Broad -NY 10004
(212) 626-4100 .. **Grauman,** Robt A '74 (Baker & M LLP) -1114 Av of Amer -NY 10036
(718) 228-1310 .. **Grauman,** Scott A '09 -125-16 Qns Blvd -Kew Gdns 11415
(631) 277-8618 .. **Gravano,** Karen A '04 -499 Islip Av -Islip 11751
(718) 236-3800 .. **Gravante & Looby** -1514 86th -Brklyn 11228 **Fx:**236-2100
(718) 236-4500 .. **Gravante,** Nicholas A '63 -1482 86th -Brklyn 11228
(212) 446-2300 .. **Gravante,** Nicholas A Jr. '86 (Boies S&F LLP) -575 Lex Av -NY 10022
(718) 236-3800 .. **Gravante,** Richd S '87 (Gravante & L) -1514 86th -Brklyn 11228
(212) 859-8000 .. **Gravelle,** David E '10 %Fried FHS&J LLP -1 NY Plz -NY 10004
(607) 687-4344 .. **Graven,** Irene C '85 %DA -20 Court Bx300 -Owego 13827
(607) 687-0827 .. **Graven,** Michl P '84 -Bx428 -Owego 13827
(585) 325-3050 .. **Graver,** Molly L '02 Farmworker Lgl Srvcs -1187 Culver Rd -Rchstr 14609 **Fx:**325-7614
(212) 319-6898 .. **Graver,** Wayne A '97 (Lavin ORC&D) -420 Lex Av -NY 10170
(212) 793-7025 .. **Graves,** Anne M '92 %Citigroup Inc -425 Park Av -NY 10043
(212) 566-7200 .. **Graves,** Chas C II '85 -52 Duane -NY 10007
(212) 374-3445 .. **Graves,** Christina C '05 Dept of Ed -52 Chmbrs -NY 10007
(212) 577-3688 .. **Graves,** Edw S '84 %Leg Aid -199 Water -NY 10038 **Fx:**509-8431
(917) 204-0094 .. **Graves,** Gerald '06 -225 Bway -NY 10007
(212) 886-9523 .. **Graves,** John C '93 %Earl Graves Ltd -130 5th Av -NY 10011 **Fx:**886-9615
(212) 506-2500 .. **Graves,** John C '99 -1675 Bway -NY 10019 **Fx:**262-1910
(315) 699-3095 .. **Graves,** Kelly J '03 %Mafrici Law Ofc -8355 US Route 11 -Cicero 13039 **Fx:**699-3809
(914) 949-8373 .. **Graves,** Kevin G '85 (Doonan G&L) -35 Old Tarrytown Rd -White Plns 10603 **Fx:**948-3848
(212) 532-8100 .. **Graves,** Paige A '95 %Stern & M,LLP -115 Bway -NY 10006
(212) 318-6000 .. **Graves,** Sarah E '93 Paul HJ&W LLP -75 E 55th -NY 10022
(914) 358-0036 .. **Gravett,** Margaretha L '01 (Gravett & G) -100 S Bedford Rd -Mt Kisco 10549 **Fx:**358-0037
(914) 358-0036 .. **Gravett,** Willem H '99 (Gravett & G) -100 S Bedford Rd -Mt Kisco 10549 **Fx:**358-0037
(631) 385-5226 .. **Gravino,** Pat '03 Axa Advisors -155 Pinelawn Rd -Melvll 11747
(212) 715-9100 .. **Gray,** Allison D '06 %Kramer LN&F,LLP -1177 Av of Amer -NY 10036
(212) 258-6000 .. **Gray,** Allison Snider '01 %Viacom -1515 Bway -NY 10036
(212) 267-2555 .. **Gray,** Amanda E '06 %Bretz & C,LLP -305 Bway -NY 10007
(212) 455-2000 .. **Gray,** Andre K '10 %Simpson T&B LLP -425 Lex Av -NY 10017
(212) 813-8800 .. **Gray,** Ashley H '01 %Goodwin P LLP -620 8th Av -NY 10018
(845) 895-5758 .. **Gray,** Billie '86 -56 Bona Ventura Av Bx814 -Wallkill 12589
(518) 388-4364 .. **Gray,** Brian S '10 %DA -612 State -Schnctdy 12305 **Fx:**388-4569
(718) 254-0700 .. **Gray,** Carol A '93 %Bklyn Defender Srvcs -177 Lvngstn -Brklyn 11201 **Fx:**254-0897
(516) 248-1200 .. **Gray,** Catherine M '97 Mulholland M&R -374 Hillside Av -Williston Pk 11596
(516) 571-3056 .. **Gray,** Catherine N '81 %Cnty Atty -1 West -Mineola 11501 **Fx:**571-6604
(212) 720-8407 .. **Gray,** Chas C Jr. '02 %Fed Reserve Bk -33 Lbrty -NY 10045 **Fx:**785-5748
(212) 838-3221 .. **Gray,** Christopher J '97 -460 Park Av -NY 10022 **Fx:**937-3139
(212) 530-5000 .. **Gray,** Christopher N '00 %Milbank TH&M LLP -1 Chase Manh Plz -NY 10005
(212) 868-2222 .. **Gray,** Danl F '96 %True World Grp,Inc -481 8th Av -NY 10001 **Fx:**868-0002
(212) 292-6517 .. **Gray,** David G '96 %Ziff Bros Invstmnts -153 E 53rd -NY 10022
(516) 747-9700 .. **Gray,** Deborah A '98 %Ryan & H,PC -1 Old Cntry Rd -Carle Pl 11514
(212) 984-1058 .. **Gray,** Dian R '00 D Gray -100 Park Av -NY 10017
(212) 486-4284 .. **Gray,** Dorothy F '51 -430 E 57th -NY 10022
(716) 652-2000 .. **Gray,** Eric D '00 Moog Inc -Jamison Rd -E Aurora 14052 **Fx:**687-4457
(212) 366-6100 .. **Gray,** Erik L '01 %Weiss & R,PC -27 Union Sq W -NY 10003
(212) 935-6000 .. **Gray,** Evan W '88 Cnsl Lebow & S LLP -770 Lex Av -NY 10065
(585) 218-8620 .. **Gray & Feldman,LLP** -625 Panorama Trl -Rchstr 14625
(646) 495-6067 .. **Gray,** Gail '87 -770 Bway -NY 10003
(631) 549-2000 .. **Gray,** Garrett L '91 %Weber Law Grp,LLP -290 Broad Hollow Rd -Melvll 11747 **Fx:**549-2015
(585) 218-8620 .. **Gray,** George H '77 (Gray & F,LLP) -625 Panorama Trl -Rchstr 14625
(212) 692-1000 .. **Gray,** Gilson B III '59 OfCnsl Duane M LLP -1540 Bway -NY 10036
(716) 649-6244 .. **Gray,** Harry J '56 -4894 Hickory Rd -Hambrg 14075
(518) 424-3439 .. **Gray,** Heather M '08 -33 Halcyon -Scotia 12302
(212) 735-3000 .. **Gray,** Jason '07 %Skadden ASM&F LLP -4 Times Sq -NY 10036
(212) 813-8800 .. **Gray,** Joanne M '84 (Goodwin P LLP) -620 8th Av -NY 10018
(718) 237-5500 .. **Gray,** John C '69 %Leg Srvcs -105 Court -Brklyn 11201 **Fx:**855-0733
(516) 766-3200 .. **Gray,** John E '85 OfCnsl Murtagh C&B -100 N Park Av -Rockvll Ctr 11570
(973) 315-4481 .. **Gray,** Jonathan B '98 Cnsl Budd L -140 Bway -NY 10005
(212) 966-6700 .. **Gray,** Jonathan W '91 (Gray K LLP) -207 W 25th -NY 10001 **Fx:**966-6051
(212) 735-3000 .. **Gray,** Joshua B '99 %Skadden ASM&F LLP -4 Times Sq -NY 10036
(212) 867-5800 .. **Gray,** Julia N '05 %Osler H&H LLP -620 8th Av -NY 10018
(646) 223-4200 .. **Gray,** Karen A '96 %Reuters -3 Times Sq -NY 10036 **Fx:**223-4250
(212) 969-3000 .. **Gray,** Keisha-Ann G '01 SrCnsl Proskauer R LLP -1585 Bway -NY 10036
(516) 746-5599 .. **Gray,** Kenneth A '94 (Bee RFH&D,LLP) -170 Old Cntry Rd -Mineola 11501
(212) 590-2100 .. **Gray,** Kristen M '00 4Kids Entertainment,Inc -53 W 23rd -NY 10010
(212) 756-2000 .. **Gray,** Lindsay H '10 %Schulte R&Z LLP -919 3rd Av -NY 10022
(718) 286-6000 .. **Gray,** Lisa Ann '05 %DA -125-01 Qns Blvd -Kew Gdns 11415
(212) 537-7000 .. **Gray,** Mark S '96 -251 W 93rd -NY 10025 **Fx:**537-8800
(212) 705-7000 .. **Gray,** Mathew A '06 %Bingham M LLP -399 Park Av -NY 10022
(212) 758-7600 .. **Gray,** Melany R '87 %Collazo C&M -747 3rd Av -NY 10017
(516) 627-6919 .. **Gray,** Meredith L '01 %J Bailey & Assoc -111 Vllg Rd -Manhsst 11030 **Fx:**365-3209
(212) 836-8000 .. **Gray,** Paulette M '05 %Kaye S LLP -425 Park Av -NY 10022
(212) 274-6765 .. **Gray,** Pauline '97 %Admin Children's Srvcs -220 Church -NY 10013
(718) 237-2023 .. **Gray,** Peter G '88 (P Gray,PC) -189 Montague -Brklyn 11201 **Fx:**237-2066
(212) 530-5000 .. **Gray,** Richd M '82 (Milbank TH&M LLP) -1 Chase Manh Plz -NY 10005
(212) 422-1500 .. **Gray,** Richd N '70 (Meyers TF&G LLP) -14 Wall -NY 10005
(585) 436-7720 .. **Gray,** Robt '80 %UAW Leg Srvcs Plan -1200C Scottsvll Rd -Rchstr 14624 **Fx:**436-7741
(212) 858-1000 .. **Gray,** Robt W '65 SrCnsl Pillsbury WSP LLP -1540 Bway -NY 10036
(516) 678-1412 .. **Gray,** Robin A '94 -849 Woodfld Rd -W Hempstead 11552
(212) 906-1200 .. **Gray,** Rosalie Walker '02 (Latham & W) -885 3rd Av -NY 10022
(631) 852-2500 .. **Gray,** Rosalind C '01 %DA -200 Center Dr -Rvrhead 11901 **Fx:**852-1769
(212) 859-8000 .. **Gray,** Sarah S '10 %Fried FHS&J LLP -1 NY Plz -NY 10004
(212) 878-8000 .. **Gray,** Sean M '08 %Clifford C LLP -31 W 52nd -NY 10019
(212) 227-9163 .. **Gray,** Stacy M '99 -55 Broad -NY 10004
(212) 483-2323 .. **Gray,** Stephen E '81 JP Morgan Chase & Co -277 Park Av -NY 10172
(212) 425-1144 .. **Gray,** Stephen H '97 LaBranche & Co -1 Exch Plz -NY 10006
(516) 229-4400 .. **Gray,** Terrance M '78 (Kay & G) -875 Merrick Av -Westbury 11590

(212) 335-9000 .. **Gray,** Thandiwe M '03 %DA -1 Hogan Pl -NY 10013
(212) 705-7000 .. **Gray,** Thos '04 Cnsl Bingham M LLP -399 Park Av -NY 10022
(518) 786-2880 .. **Gray,** Thos R '98 %Fager & A,LLP -8 British Amer Blvd -Latham 12110
(646) 826-5758 .. **Gray,** Timothy W '02 Oz Mgmt -9 W 57th -NY 10019
(718) 231-4285 .. **Gray,** Valerie Ann '92 -3539 Tiemann Av -Bronx 10469 **Fx:**231-4680
(212) 205-7000 .. **Gray,** Wm A '82 (Ashurst LLP) -7 Times Sq -NY 10036
(212) 880-6000 .. **Gray,** Wm F Jr. '81 (Torys LLP) -237 Park Av -NY 10017
(212) 382-0700 .. **Gray,** Wm O III '84 (Ostrolenk FG&S,LLP) -1180 Av of Amer -NY 10036
(212) 940-3076 .. **Graybeal,** David P '88 (Nixon P LLP) -437 Mad Av -NY 10022
(914) 946-0600 .. **Graybow,** Lori F '02 %Pino & Assoc -50 Main -White Plns 10606 **Fx:**946-0650
(212) 362-0125 .. **Grayburn,** Susan T '82 -2109 Bway -NY 10023 **Fx:**362-0126
(212) 474-1000 .. **Grayer,** Elizabeth L '90 (Cravath S&M LLP) -825 8th Av -NY 10019
(212) 715-9100 .. **Grayer,** James A '92 (Kramer LN&F,LLP) -1177 Av of Amer -NY 10036
(914) 948-4434 .. **Gray-Huertas,** April A '89 %DHCR -75 S Bway -White Plns 10601 **Fx:**948-7783
(718) 579-3000 .. **Grayman,** Burt '75 %Leg Aid -1020 Grnd Cncrs -Bronx 10451 **Fx:**588-2611
(631) 439-2905 .. **Graynor,** Louis '53 L Graynor,PC -194 Wind Watch Dr -Hauppauge 11788 **Fx:**582-9608
(212) 578-2211 .. **Grays,** Taa Rasheemah '98 %MetLife -27-01 Qns Plz N -LIC 11101
(212) 624-3986 .. **Grayson,** Anne Roderick '03 %WebMD Inc -111 8th Av -NY 10011
(516) 747-2428 .. **Grayson,** Christopher L '97 -1225 Franklin Av -Gdn Cty 11530
(607) 865-6571 .. **Grayson,** Gary J '76 -91 Townsend -Walton 13856 **Fx:**865-6500
(212) 777-5851 .. **Grayson,** Mark R '76 -6 Peter Cooper Rd -NY 10010 **Fx:**(646) 414-7260
(212) 907-7300 .. **Grayson,** Nina P '89 OfCnsl Golenbock EAB&P -437 Mad Av -NY 10022
(914) 682-0037 .. **Grayson,** Richd E '79 -175 Main -White Plns 10601 **Fx:**684-0646
(516) 562-5000 .. **Grayson,** Sandra L '74 %CMP Media LLC -600 Community Dr -Manhsst 11030 **Fx:**562-7123
(212) 732-3200 .. **Gray-Trefry,** G Christina '03 %Carter L&M LLP -2 Wall -NY 10005
(315) 768-1522 .. **Graziadei,** Carl V '90 -214 Oriskany Blvd -Whitesboro 13492
(212) 785-0885 .. **Graziadei,** Frank M '78 -130 Water -NY 10005 **Fx:**785-2195
(518) 533-1050 .. **Graziane,** Elizabeth A '91 %Conway & K LLP -9 Cornell Rd -Latham 12110
(516) 294-5200 .. **Graziani,** Anthony E '84 %Picciano & S -900 Merchants Cncrs -Westbury 11590
(917) 626-7948 .. **Graziani,** David G '02 Classic Media,Inc -640 Verona Dr -Melvll 11747
(585) 249-5042 .. **Graziano,** Chas '01 -2 Delancy Ct -Pittsfrd 14534
(631) 264-0600 .. **Graziano,** Christopher M '05 (Jacobowitz & G,LLP) -43 Ireland Pl Bx668 -Amityvll 11701
(516) 746-0123 .. **Graziano,** Christopher V '01 -114 Old Cntry Rd -Mineola 11501 **Fx:**746-0021
(212) 336-3620 .. **Graziano,** Louis '86 %EEOC -33 Whitehall -NY 10004
(212) 554-1400 .. **Graziano,** Salvatore J '92 (Bernstein LB&G LLP) -1285 Av of Amer -NY 10019
(716) 834-3899 .. **Graziano,** Sheila G '79 -Bx180 -Buffalo 14207 **Fx:**831-9667
(914) 249-3186 .. **Grazio,** Michl L '07 MasterCard Worldwide -2000 Purchase -Purchase 10577
(914) 793-6412 .. **Grazioli,** Anthony J '73 -107 Lk Av -Tuckahoe 10707
(516) 801-6350 .. **Graziosi,** Anzelmo '98 -126 Glen -Glen Cove 11542 **Fx:**801-6349
(516) 877-5600 .. **Graziosi,** Peter S '85 %R Tusa -1225 Franklin Av -Gdn Cty 11530 **Fx:**877-5695
(212) 297-5800 .. **Grazioso,** Kristy L '07 %Day P LLP -7 Times Sq -NY 10036
(518) 402-6969 .. **Grazulis,** Tahnya Nicole '00 %Envrnmtl Facilities -625 Bway -Albany 12207 **Fx:**402-6972
(212) 816-5046 .. **Grbic,** Susan M '87 Citigroup Global Mrkts -388 Greenwich -NY 10013
(347) 404-9400 .. **Grcevic,** Barbara H '83 %Criminal Ct -120 Schermerhorn -Brklyn 11201 **Fx:**(718) 643-3538
(212) 610-6300 .. **Grdan,** Sara '07 %Allen & O -1221 Av of Amer -NY 10020
(518) 463-5400 .. **Greagan,** Wm J '89 (Goldberg S LLP) -8 Southwoods Blvd -Albany 12211
(212) 455-2000 .. **Grealis,** Catherine S '10 %Simpson T&B LLP -425 Lex Av -NY 10017
(914) 937-2800 .. **Grean & Ward** -222 Grace Church -Pt Chester 10573 **Fx:**937-7404
(212) 351-4000 .. **Greaney,** Edw Michl '99 %Gibson D&C LLP -200 Park Av -NY 10166
(212) 839-5300 .. **Greaney,** Isaac S '00 (Sidley A LLP) -787 7th Av -NY 10019
(716) 636-7600 .. **Grear,** Linda Stravalaci '95 %HoganWillig -2410 N Forest Rd -Amherst 14068
(212) 245-7779 .. **Greason,** Edw W Jr. '92 %F Montgomery -30 Vesey -NY 10007
(212) 408-5100 .. **Greason,** Wm A '88 (Chadbourne & P LLP) -30 Rckfllr Plz -NY 10112
(212) 490-1700 .. **Greathead,** R Scott '74 (Wiggin & D) -450 Lex Av -NY 10017
(212) 430-6466 .. **Greaves,** Valerie D '85 -234 5th Av -NY 10001
(212) 619-4444 .. **Greben,** Brian L '96 %Marshall CW&B,PC -116 John -NY 10038
(718) 234-2345 .. **Greber,** Michl J '84 -251 86th -Brklyn 11209 **Fx:**745-7275
(212) 277-4000 .. **Greber-Raines,** Blair H '03 Freshfields BD LLP -520 Mad Av -NY 10022
(212) 837-6000 .. **Greber-Raines,** Ian '08 %Hughes H&R LLP -1 Bttry Pk Plz -NY 10004
(212) 554-5811 .. **Grebin,** Jason R '92 -767 5th Av -NY 10153 **Fx:**489-7431
(212) 768-6700 .. **Grebinar,** Jonathan S '05 %Sonnenschein N&R LLP -2 World Fncl Ctr -NY 10281
(631) 821-1500 .. **Grecco,** Allan D '76 -131 Route 25A -Rocky Pnt 11778
(212) 355-6182 .. **Grech,** Anthoula '04 %EP Dine Inc -115 E 57th -NY 10022 **Fx:**755-8486
(516) 746-5040 .. **Grech,** David J '05 %Scher Law Firm,LLP -1 Old Cntry Rd -Carle Pl 11514 **Fx:**747-9100
(212) 894-7200 .. **Greco,** Alfred V '61 OfCnsl Entwistle & C LLP -280 Park Av -NY 10017
(212) 246-3030 .. **Greco,** Alfred V '61 (Sierchio G&G,LLP) -110 E 59th -NY 10022
(212) 558-4000 .. **Greco,** Anthony D '08 %Sullivan & C LLP -125 Broad -NY 10004
(518) 762-3103 .. **Greco,** Carmel J '71 (Murphy N&G) -8 S William Bx687 -Johnstwn 12095
(212) 270-5910 .. **Greco,** Christian T '03 JP Morgan Chase & Co -270 Park Av -NY 10017
(212) 446-4800 .. **Greco,** Christopher T '08 %Kirkland & E LLP -153 E 53rd -NY 10022
(212) 670-0187 .. **Greco,** Gloria R '99 %Merrill Lynch -222 Bway -NY 10038
(716) 853-4080 .. **Greco,** James J '92 %Colucci & G,PC -424 Main -Buffalo 14202
(516) 599-3525 .. **Greco,** Jeanne A '82 -363 Hempstd Av -Malverne 11565 **Fx:**599-2066
(212) 297-0050 .. **Greco,** John '88 (Betancourt VHG&K LLC) -46 Trinity Pl -NY 10006
(845) 331-6073 .. **Greco,** John J '84 -1 Albany Av -Kingston 12401 **Fx:**331-1529
(716) 856-5800 .. **Greco,** Josephine Ann '82 (J Greco & Assoc,PLLC) -14 Lafayette Sq -Buffalo 14203 **Fx:**856-5801
(845) 454-2200 .. **Greco,** Kevin R '04 %Wolfson G&E PC -11 Market -Poughkeepsie 12601
(212) 455-9800 .. **Greco,** Lara M '94 %LISC -501 Fashion Av -NY 10018 **Fx:**682-5929
(518) 432-1200 .. **Greco,** Laura M '06 OfCnsl McGlinchey S PLLC -194 Wshngtn Av -Albany 12210
(212) 969-3000 .. **Greco,** Louis '91 %Proskauer R LLP -1585 Bway -NY 10036
(845) 380-9960 .. **Greco,** Maria J '88 -Bx1174 -Hopewell Junct 12533
(518) 465-1500 .. **Greco,** Michl A '84 (Cannon H&W,LLP) -54 State -Albany 12207
(914) 697-4811 .. **Greco,** Michl J '53 -800 Wstchstr Av -Rye Brook 10573 **Fx:**697-4813
(212) 246-3030 .. **Greco,** Paul V '88 (Sierchio G&G,LLP) -110 E 59th -NY 10022
(212) 883-6500 .. **Greco,** Paul V '94 (Podell SS&B,LLP) -605 3rd Av -NY 10158
(212) 986-7353 .. **Greco,** Paula M '88 OfCnsl Wingate R&S -420 Lex Av -NY 10170
(212) 962-9400 .. **Greco,** Philip A '55 Greco & G -233 Bway -NY 10279 **Fx:**732-8486
(212) 836-8000 .. **Greco,** Richd G '75 (Kaye S LLP) -425 Park Av -NY 10022
(516) 747-9006 .. **Greco,** Robt S '90 (Greco & W) -300 Grdn City Plz -Gdn Cty 11530
(845) 357-8977 .. **Greco,** Steven M '92 S Greco & Assoc,PC -One Exec Blvd -Suffern 10901 **Fx:**357-8955
(212) 571-7100 .. **Greco,** Victor '87 (O'Dwyer & B,LLP) -52 Duane -NY 10007
(516) 747-9006 .. **Greco & Wolfe** -300 Grdn City Plz -Gdn Cty 11530 **Fx:**741-3647
(212) 921-8399 .. **Gredd,** Helen A '85 (Lankler S&W LLP) -500 5th Av -NY 10110
(914) 631-5900 .. **Greebel,** Chas R '71 -15 Neperan Rd -Tarrytwn 10591
(212) 940-8800 .. **Greebel,** Evan L '01 (Katten MR LLP) -575 Mad Av -NY 10022
(516) 248-7008 .. **Greebel,** Lawr M '58 (Greebel & G) -170 Old Cntry Rd -Mineola 11501 **Fx:**248-7715
(516) 248-7008 .. **Greebel,** Mitchell A '85 (Greebel & G) -170 Old Cntry Rd -Mineola 11501 **Fx:**248-7715
(212) 371-3000 .. **Greebel,** Robt A '03 Davidson Kempner -65 E 55th -NY 10022
(212) 834-0600 .. **Greebel,** Rory G '08 %Gordon & S,PC -355 Lex Av -NY 10017
(212) 592-1400 .. **Greeley,** Christopher P '05 %Herrick,F LLP -2 Park Av -NY 10016
(212) 859-8000 .. **Greeley,** Patrick T C '08 %Fried FHS&J LLP -1 NY Plz -NY 10004
(212) 440-3755 .. **Greeley,** Todd M '95 CNA Global -410 Wall -NY 10005
(315) 829-8455 .. **Greeley Thompson,** Kristin B '99 %Oneida Indian Nation -1256 Union Bx662 -Oneida 13421 **Fx:**829-8471
(212) 719-4400 .. **Green,** Abbey '00 %Lynn & C,LLP -58 W 40th -NY 10018 **Fx:**719-4440
(212) 751-2400 .. **Green,** Allen '64 (Kalnick K&G,LLP) -767 3rd Av -NY 10017
(212) 644-3707 .. **Green,** Alvin '61 (Seham SM&P,LLP) -145 E 48th -NY 10017
(212) 500-5030 .. **Green,** Andrea '79 OfCnsl Kehl K&S,LLP -317 Mad Av -NY 10017
(516) 542-1000 .. **Green,** Andrew '99 %Geisler & G,LLP -100 Q Roosevelt Blvd -Gdn Cty 11530
(212) 326-3939 .. **Green,** Andrew J '77 OfCnsl Jones D -222 E 41st -NY 10017
(212) 849-7000 .. **Green,** Anne E '06 %Quinn EU&S,LLP -51 Mad Av -NY 10010
(518) 473-8418 .. **Green,** Anne Marguerite '84 %OCFS -52 Wshngtn -Rensselaer 12144 **Fx:**486-6361
(212) 696-0100 .. **Green,** Anthony C '10 Annaly Capital Mgmt,Inc -1211 Av of Amer -NY 10036
(212) 759-4600 .. **Green,** Anthony D '06 %Wolf P LLP -845 3rd Av -NY 10022
(212) 805-0688 .. **Green,** Ariadne K '01 US Dist Ct-Pro Se Ofc -500 Pearl -NY 10007
(845) 356-0634 .. **Green,** Barbara B '90 %Berg & B -71 E Eckerson Rd -Spg Vly 10977
(212) 223-0400 .. **Green,** Benjamin '78 (Zeichner E&K LLP) -575 Lex Av -NY 10022
(516) 357-3000 .. **Green,** Beth E '01 %Rivkin R LLP -926 RXR Plz -Uniondale 11556
(718) 250-1400 .. **Green,** Beth Zaro '83 -12 MetroTech Ctr -Brklyn 11201 **Fx:**250-1401
(631) 853-4104 .. **Green,** Bethany K '09 %DA -400 Carleton Av Bx9082 -Central Islip 11722 **Fx:**853-7838
(845) 294-5573 .. **Green,** Bob '80 -155 Main -Goshen 10924 **Fx:**504-2701
(212) 806-5400 .. **Green,** Bradford A '09 %Stroock &S&L LLP -180 Maiden Ln -NY 10038
(212) 695-5980 .. **Green,** Bradley J '06 %The Rizzo Grp LLP -11 Penn Plz -NY 10001 **Fx:**695-6058
(212) 308-4411 .. **Green,** Brian J '00 %Edwards AP&D LLP -750 Lex Av -NY 10022
(585) 753-4500 .. **Green,** Brian P '08 %DA -832 Watts Bldg -Rchstr 14614 **Fx:**753-4576
(212) 636-6000 .. **Green,** Bruce A '82 %Fordham Univ Sch of Law -140 W 62nd -NY 10023 **Fx:**636-6899
(212) 773-8416 .. **Green,** Candice H '07 Ernst & Young LLP -5 Times Sq -NY 10036
(716) 849-1333 .. **Green,** Carl A '50 OfCnsl Lipsitz GSC LLP -42 Delaware Av -Buffalo 14202
(212) 613-0099 .. **Green,** Carole L '84 -3900 Bailey Av -Bronx 10463
(212) 307-5800 .. **Green,** Chas E '91 (Friedman LG&G,PC) -250 W 57th -NY 10107
(516) 739-5100 .. **Green,** Charlie '99 %Farber B&Z LLP -51 Charles -Mineola 11501
(716) 858-2200 .. **Green,** Cheryl Ann '96 Cnty Atty -95 Franklin -Buffalo 14202 **Fx:**858-2281
(212) 537-6171 .. **Green,** Christopher D '05 (Dissident Indstrs) -1 Penn Plz -NY 10119
(914) 749-8200 .. **Green,** Christopher M '97 (Boies S&F LLP) -333 Main -Armonk 10504
(212) 553-0300 .. **Green,** Claudia Naomi '99 Moody's Invstr Srvc -250 Greenwich -NY 10007
(212) 770-1053 .. **Green,** Cynthia R '93 AIG -80 Pine -NY 10005
(212) 973-0445 .. **Green,** Danl '94 -420 Lex Av -NY 10170 **Fx:**973-0450
(212) 407-7700 .. **Green,** Danl C '04 %Vedder P,PC -1633 Bway -NY 10019
(518) 455-2225 .. **Green,** Darcy Long '03 Sen N Breslin -414 State Cptl Bldg -Albany 12247
(212) 841-7989 .. **Green,** David A '82 Cushman Wakefield -51 W 52nd -NY 10019
(212) 571-6161 .. **Green,** David A '87 -310 Greenwich -NY 10013 **Fx:**964-0334
(212) 351-4500 .. **Green,** David D '07 Cnsl Epstein B&G,PC -250 Park Av -NY 10177

(646) 610-5140 .. **Green,** David H '94 NYPD Advocates Ofc -1 Police Plz -NY 10038
(212) 537-0401 .. **Green,** David M '80 (Stevens & L PC) -485 Mad Av -NY 10022 **Fx:**(610) 371-1221
(516) 663-0780 .. **Green,** David M '89 -175 Pinelawn Rd -Melvll 11747 **Fx:**740-9731
(518) 389-2000 .. **Green,** David R '02 -Bx11177 -Albany 12211 **Fx:**389-2268
(212) 986-8671 .. **Green,** David S '98 (Sydney A&G,PLLC) -122 E 42nd -NY 10168
(212) 457-7717 .. **Green,** Dorothy L '98 Law Journal Press/ALM Media LLC -120 Bway -NY 10271 **Fx:**587-5714
(212) 670-0183 .. **Green,** Douglas M '94 Merrill Lynch -222 Bway -NY 10038 **Fx:**670-4516
(212) 272-4881 .. **Green,** Edith C '98 %JP Morgan Chase -383 Mad Av -NY 10179
(315) 422-1391 .. **Green,** Edw S '61 OfCnsl Green & S,PLLC -One Lincoln Ctr #900 -Syracuse 13202
(212) 407-4000 .. **Green,** Eliot P '89 (Loeb & L,LLP) -345 Park Av -NY 10154
(718) 260-8668 .. **Green,** Elliot '00 -188 Montague -Brklyn 11201
(212) 506-5000 .. **Green,** Emily J '09 %Orrick H&S LLP -51 W 52nd -NY 10019
(212) 532-2450 .. **Green,** Eric H '77 -295 Mad Av -NY 10017 **Fx:**532-0117
(212) 357-1975 .. **Green,** Erica A '08 Goldman Sachs -200 West -NY 10282
(212) 351-4500 .. **Green,** Frances M '87 (Epstein B&G,PC) -250 Park Av -NY 10177
(212) 859-8000 .. **Green,** Franklin L '69 OfCnsl Fried FHS&J LLP -1 NY Plz -NY 10004
(212) 592-1400 .. **Green,** Fred R '85 Cnsl Herrick,F LLP -2 Park Av -NY 10016
(212) 310-8000 .. **Green,** Fredk S '80 (Weil G&M LLP) -767 5th Av -NY 10153
(914) 995-4172 .. **Green,** Fredric I '88 %DA -111 Martin Luther King Blvd -White Plns 10601 **Fx:**995-3363
(516) 561-8580 .. **Green,** Gerald H '59 -479 Merrick Rd -Lynbrk 11563 **Fx:**561-6716
(315) 735-6481 .. **Green,** Gerald J '82 (Paravati KG&D) -12 Steuben Pk -Utica 13501
(631) 852-2500 .. **Green,** Glenn D '87 %DA -200 Center Dr -Rvrhead 11901 **Fx:**852-1769
(516) 873-6300 .. **Green,** Gregory '89 J Lichtenstein,PC -131 Mineola Blvd -Mineola 11501 **Fx:**873-7986
(516) 661-3624 .. **Green,** Henry E '74 -450 7th Av -NY 10123 **Fx:**742-0366
(516) 742-0615 .. **Green,** Henry E '74 -1050 Franklin Av -Gdn Cty 11530 **Fx:**742-0366
(516) 565-4123 .. **Green,** Jack '81 (Newman & G) -230 Hilton Av -Hempstd 11550
(212) 859-8000 .. **Green,** Jaclyn B '09 %Fried FHS&J LLP -1 NY Plz -NY 10004
(518) 447-7295 .. **Green,** James J '93 %Cnty Dept Soc Srvcs -112 State -Albany 12207
(516) 227-2200 .. **Green,** James L '80 -900 Merchants Cncrs -Westbury 11590 **Fx:**227-1135
(212) 831-4400 .. **Green,** Jason '92 (Green & C,PC) -319 E 91st -NY 10128 **Fx:**831-8390
(845) 735-6299 .. **Green,** Jeffrey S '69 -229 Ehrhardt Rd -Pearl Rvr 10965
(212) 688-8555 .. **Green,** Jennifer Asheleigh '96 -515 Mad Av -NY 10022 **Fx:**758-7215
(212) 614-6483 .. **Green,** Jennifer M '92 Ctr Cnstnl Rights -666 Bway -NY 10012 **Fx:**614-6499
(212) 819-8200 .. **Green,** Jesse L '07 %White & C LLP -1155 Av of Amer -NY 10036
(917) 430-2026 .. **Green,** Jonathan '91 -Bx15 -NY 10113
(212) 585-3425 .. **Green,** Jonathan A '09 %B Kishner & Assoc -420 Lex Av -NY 10170 **Fx:**752-1810
(718) 254-7000 .. **Green,** Jonathan E '02 %US Atty -271 Cadman Plz E -Brklyn 11201 **Fx:**254-6479
(212) 530-5000 .. **Green,** Jonathan J '85 (Milbank TH&M LLP) -1 Chase Manh Plz -NY 10005
(212) 455-2000 .. **Green,** Jos M '09 %Simpson T&B LLP -425 Lex Av -NY 10017
(212) 921-8399 .. **Green,** Julia C '04 %Lankler S&W LLP -500 5th Av -NY 10110
(212) 687-8181 .. **Green,** Justin T '96 (Kreindler & K) -750 3rd Av -NY 10017
(631) 853-4049 .. **Green,** Kelly '92 %Cnty Atty -Dennison Bldg Bx6100 -Hauppauge 11788 **Fx:**853-5169
(212) 964-6611 .. **Green,** Lawr R '79 (Lester SK&D) -120 Bway -NY 10271
(914) 319-7769 .. **Green,** Leslie B '83 -115 E Stevens Av -Valhalla 10595
(212) 788-4303 .. **Green,** Lisa R '94 Ofc Mental Hygiene -125 Worth -NY 10013
(212) 661-9100 .. **Green,** Lloyd M '85 OfCnsl Otterbourg SH&R,PC -230 Park Av -NY 10169
(585) 263-1000 .. **Green,** Lori B '85 (Nixon P LLP) -1100 Clinton Sq -Rchstr 14604
(212) 446-2800 .. **Green,** Luke J '09 Boston Consulting Grp -430 Park Av -NY 10022 **Fx:**446-2801
(631) 853-4318 .. **Green,** Lynn A '89 %Family Ct -400 Carleton Av -Central Islip 11722 **Fx:**853-6218
(607) 547-9985 .. **Green,** Lynn E Jr. '71 (Green & G) -50 Main Bx148 -Cooperstwn 13326 **Fx:**547-9160
(212) 436-1409 .. **Green,** Margaret Alicia '98 IRS -290 Bway -NY 10007
(516) 791-9170 .. **Green,** Mark A '97 (Green & H,LLP) -2079 Wantagh Av -Wantagh 11793 **Fx:**345-1616
(212) 733-3966 .. **Green,** Markus '99 Pfizer -150 E 42nd -NY 10017 **Fx:**(646) 441-5604
(718) 991-4600 .. **Green,** Marshall W '75 %Leg Aid -953 Southrn Blvd -Bronx 10459 **Fx:**842-2867
(516) 803-2554 .. **Green,** Marti '80 %Cablevision Sys -1111 Stewart Av -Bethpage 11714
(212) 370-7634 .. **Green,** Michl A '81 UBS PaineWebber -200 Park Av -NY 10166
(718) 923-1111 .. **Green,** Michl B '98 Pencom Systems Inc -152 Remsen -Brklyn 11201
(516) 993-4357 .. **Green,** Michl B '98 -Bx2451 -Seafrd 11783 **Fx:**908-7772
(585) 753-4500 .. **Green,** Michl C '87 (DA) -832 Watts Bldg -Rchstr 14614 **Fx:**753-4576
(212) 681-6400 .. **Green,** Nancy M '92 (Burger Y&G LLP) -60 E 42nd -NY 10165 **Fx:**681-6999
(212) 326-3939 .. **Green,** Paul B '09 %Jones D -222 E 41st -NY 10017
(914) 833-9100 .. **Green,** Paula B '86 Bessemer Venture Prtnrs -1865 Palmer Av -Larchmnt 10538
(845) 820-5091 .. **Green,** Peter W '07 (Garvin & G,LLP) -450 Bway -Newburgh 12550 **Fx:**561-6095
(718) 965-9236 .. **Green,** Rachel F '91 ReSolutions -82 Garfld Pl -Brklyn 11215 **Fx:**965-9236
(718) 886-2259 .. **Green,** Raymond C '52 -33-01 149th Pl -Flushng 11354
(212) 818-1110 .. **Green,** Richd S '81 (Butzel L,PC) -380 Mad Av -NY 10017
(631) 231-3775 .. **Green,** Robt A '76 %Atty Grievance Comm -150 Motor Pkwy -Hauppauge 11788
(212) 788-1155 .. **Green,** Robin '89 %Law Dept -100 Church -NY 10007 **Fx:**788-0367
(212) 458-1269 .. **Green,** Robin T-R '09 Chartis Claims -175 Water -NY 10038
(212) 351-4500 .. **Green,** Ronald M '69 (Epstein B&G,PC) -250 Park Av -NY 10177
(212) 513-3591 .. **Green,** Rudy D '90 -195 Bway -NY 10007 **Fx:**385-9010
(212) 541-2000 .. **Green,** Sandor A '84 (Bryan C LLP) -1290 Av of Amer -NY 10104
(585) 546-4419 .. **Green,** Scott M '85 -36 W Main -Rchstr 14614
(516) 357-3000 .. **Green,** Scott R '07 %Rivkin R LLP -926 RXR Plz -Uniondale 11556
(315) 422-1391 .. **Green & Seifter,PLLC** -One Lincoln Ctr #900 -Syracuse 13202 **Fx:**422-3549
(518) 689-3570 .. **Green & Seifter,PLLC** -194 Wshngtn Av -Albany 12210 **Fx:**689-3571
(212) 837-6930 .. **Green,** Shannon E '06 %Hughes H&R LLP -1 Bttry Pk Plz -NY 10004
(516) 569-3300 .. **Green,** Sheldon E '92 (S Green PC) -566 Sunset Dr -Woodmere 11598 **Fx:**812-9097
(315) 448-0672 .. **Green,** Stephen C '89 %US Atty -100 S Clinton Bx7198 -Syracuse 13261 **Fx:**448-0689
(212) 850-8543 .. **Green,** Stephen H '78 %TBG Srvcs Inc -1350 Av of Amer -NY 10019 **Fx:**850-8503
(516) 537-1130 .. **Green,** Stephen J '84 %Glinkenhouse F&Q -116 Spruce -Cedarhrst 11516
(212) 506-1700 .. **Green,** Susanna B '05 %Kasowitz BT&F LLP -1633 Bway -NY 10019
(845) 634-7010 .. **Green,** Sydell J '83 OfCnsl Montalbano C&F,PC -67 N Main Bx1070 -New Cty 10956
(347) 404-9920 .. **Green,** Taylor L '07 %MHLS -120 Schermerhorn -Brklyn 11201 **Fx:**(718) 243-2410
(914) 948-5656 .. **Green,** Theo S '81 (Green & W) -200 Mamaroneck Av -White Plns 10601
(718) 855-8692 .. **Green,** Thos D '58 -129 Columbia Hts -Brklyn 11201
(914) 683-7900 .. **Green,** Timothy A '02 -81 Main -White Plns 10601 **Fx:**683-1279
(315) 425-2700 .. **Green,** Timothy J '95 OfCnsl Hiscock & B,LLP -One Park Pl -Syracuse 13202
(212) 264-8819 .. **Green,** Tonya N '05 %SSA Ofc Genl Cnsl -26 Fed Plz -NY 10278 **Fx:**264-6372
(631) 853-5212 .. **Green,** Walter J Jr. '89 %Leg Aid -400 Carleton Av Bx9082 -Central Islip 11722 **Fx:**853-7798
(607) 547-9985 .. **Green,** Wm C '03 (Green & G) -50 Main Bx148 -Cooperstwn 13326 **Fx:**547-9160
(516) 944-7234 .. **Green,** Wm H '76 -Laurel Ln -Sands Pnt 11050 **Fx:**944-6872
(718) 613-3500 .. **Green,** Yolanda V '88 %UIA Bd -Bx29002 -Brklyn 11201 **Fx:**613-3566
(585) 428-6990 .. **Green,** Yvette Chancellor '93 %Law Dept -30 Church -Rchstr 14614 **Fx:**428-6950
(212) 909-8270 .. **Green,** Zachary C '96 Infonxx,Inc -655 Mad Av -NY 10065
(716) 675-6111 .. **Greenan,** Gerald J '62 -3755 Seneca Bx188 -W Seneca 14224 **Fx:**674-2597
(716) 200-5050 .. **Greenan,** Gerald J III '89 OfCnsl Harris B PLLC -726 Exchange -Buffalo 14210
(212) 315-6315 .. **Greenan,** Paul '92 Salomon Smith Barney -590 Mad Av -NY 10022
(212) 953-6633 .. **Greenapple,** Lawr '52 L Greenapple,PC -630 3rd Av -NY 10017 **Fx:**949-6943
(914) 422-4092 .. **Greenawalt,** Alexander K A '02 %Pace Law Schl -78 N Bway -White Plns 10603 **Fx:**422-4039
(212) 854-2675 .. **Greenawalt,** R Kent '63 %Columbia Law Schl -435 W 116th -NY 10027 **Fx:**854-7946
(212) 973-8000 .. **Greenawalt,** Robt M '05 %Schnader HS&L LLP -140 Bway -NY 10005
(914) 946-3700 .. **Greenawalt,** Wm Sloan '62 OfCnsl McCarthy F LLP -11 Martine Av -White Plns 10606
(212) 878-3500 .. **Greenbarg,** Todd S '01 Avenue Capital Grp -535 Mad Av -NY 10022
(212) 790-9200 .. **Greenbaum,** Arthur J '56 (Cowan L&L,PC) -1133 Av of Amer -NY 10036
(212) 425-7200 .. **Greenbaum,** Barry M '09 %Kenyon & K,LLP -1 Bway -NY 10004
(516) 379-1010 .. **Greenbaum,** Bernard '52 -2677 Merrick Av -Merrick 11566 **Fx:**379-0633
(718) 250-4237 .. **Greenbaum,** Danl J '84 %Leg Aid -111 Lvngstn -Brklyn 11201 **Fx:**250-4243
(212) 739-1000 .. **Greenbaum,** David '99 Comverse Technology -810 7th Av -NY 10019
(212) 308-4411 .. **Greenbaum,** David I '99 %Edwards AP&D LLP -750 Lex Av -NY 10022
(212) 385-3555 .. **Greenbaum,** Don R '87 (Greenbaum & M) -225 Bway -NY 10007 **Fx:**385-2875
(212) 839-5300 .. **Greenbaum,** Harry P '99 %Sidley A LLP -787 7th Av -NY 10019
(212) 885-5000 .. **Greenbaum,** Jack A '71 (Blank R LLP) -405 Lex Av -NY 10174
(212) 980-0120 .. **Greenbaum,** Jeffrey A '94 (Frankfurt KK&S,PC) -488 Mad Av -NY 10022
(212) 335-9000 .. **Greenbaum,** Joel Wm '77 %DA -1 Hogan Pl -NY 10013
(716) 854-4300 .. **Greenbaum,** Leslie M '74 (Gross SB&G,PC) -465 Main -Buffalo 14203
(212) 468-4800 .. **Greenbaum,** Lisa R '05 %Davis & G LLP -1740 Bway -NY 10019
(914) 995-2601 .. **Greenbaum,** Michelle L '08 %Cnty Atty -148 Martine Av -White Plns 10601 **Fx:**995-2495
(212) 403-1000 .. **Greenbaum,** Nancy B '96 Cnsl Wachtell LR&K -51 W 52nd -NY 10019
(732) 855-6426 .. **Greenbaum,** Peter A '97 (Wilentz G&S) -110 William -NY 10038 **Fx:**726-6589
(212) 799-2983 .. **Greenbaum,** Richd '81 -15 W 84th -NY 10024
(845) 291-2050 .. **Greenbaum,** Ryan A '09 %DA -255-275 Main -Goshen 10924 **Fx:**291-2085
(212) 953-9500 .. **Greenbaum,** Sheldon M '75 (Goldman & G,PC) -60 E 42nd -NY 10165
(973) 422-6766 .. **Greenbaum,** Wm I '77 (Lowenstein S PC) -1251 Av of Amer -NY 10020 **Fx:**422-6767
(914) 686-4800 .. **Greenberg,** Adam G '94 (Harrington O&M,LLP) -81 Main -White Plns 10601
(212) 735-3000 .. **Greenberg,** Adam P '10 %Skadden ASM&F LLP -4 Times Sq -NY 10036
(718) 925-9200 .. **Greenberg,** Alan H '90 (Corozzo & G,PC) -158-01 Cross Bay Blvd -Howard Bch 11414
(212) 972-5656 .. **Greenberg,** Alan M '86 -60 E 42nd -NY 10165 **Fx:**697-3551

(212) 813-5900 .. **Greenberg,** Alexander L '07 %Fross ZL&Z,PC -866 UN Plz -NY 10017
(718) 655-8200 .. **Greenberg,** Alfred I '64 A I Greenberg,PC -4200 Wht Plns Rd -Bronx 10466 **Fx:**655-8267
(212) 967-1980 .. **Greenberg,** Alison G '00 A Greenberg,LLC -14 Penn Plz -NY 10122 **Fx:**(646) 390-2889
(212) 983-2440 .. **Greenberg,** Allan H '78 -60 E 42nd -NY 10165 **Fx:**983-0415
(212) 818-8670 .. **Greenberg,** Allen '55 (Graubard M) -405 Lex Av -NY 10174
(212) 351-4500 .. **Greenberg,** Alyssa B '06 %Epstein B&G,PC -250 Park Av -NY 10177
(212) 869-7878 .. **Greenberg,** Andrew A '80 %Basha Scarves Inc -15 W 37th -NY 10018 **Fx:**869-7905
(212) 258-8638 .. **Greenberg,** Andrew M '80 Viacom -1515 Bway -NY 10036
(212) 504-6000 .. **Greenberg,** Andrew M '10 %Cadwalader W&T LLP -1 World Fncl Ctr -NY 10281
(315) 443-7654 .. **Greenberg,** Andrew S '90 Syracuse Univ Cllg of Law -Wht Hall -Syracuse 13244 **Fx:**443-4213
(212) 421-5600 .. **Greenberg,** Arnold L '55 -244 5th Av -NY 10001
(212) 532-3840 .. **Greenberg,** Arthur R '57 (Greenberg & G) -888 7th Av -NY 10019 **Fx:**532-3829
(518) 828-3336 .. **Greenberg,** Arthur R '57 (Greenberg & G) -4 E Court -Hudson 12534 **Fx:**828-9888
(516) 621-7717 .. **Greenberg,** Barbara F '87 (Greenberg & G) -3 Sierks Ln -Roslyn Harbor 11576 **Fx:**621-9340
(516) 755-2200 .. **Greenberg,** Barry E '81 B Greenberg,PC -109 Greenway Dr -Farmngdl 11735 **Fx:**586-5683
(212) 344-8700 .. **Greenberg,** Barry M '91 Country Wide Ins -40 Wall -NY 10005
(718) 250-1100 .. **Greenberg,** Barry N '93 %E Garfinkel -12 Metrotech Ctr -Brklyn 11201 **Fx:**250-1168
(212) 758-7666 .. **Greenberg,** Brian J '99 4Kids Entertainment -1414 Av of Amer -NY 10019
(973) 315-4405 .. **Greenberg,** Carl '83 (Budd L) -140 Bway -NY 10005
(212) 504-6000 .. **Greenberg,** Carly '07 %Cadwalader W&T LLP -1 World Fncl Ctr -NY 10281
(631) 543-2900 .. **Greenberg,** Cary M '85 %Davis & H,LLP -1345 Motor Pkwy -Islandia 11749
(212) 545-7337 .. **Greenberg,** Clifford L '90 (Greenberg & G,LLP) -363 7th Av -NY 10001 **Fx:**545-7406
(212) 405-9197 .. **Greenberg,** Cory L '95 Alvin Ailey Amer Dance Theater -405 W 55th -NY 10019 **Fx:**405-9003
(631) 261-8834 .. **Greenberg,** Danl '52 (Ingerman S LLP) -150 Motor Pkwy -Hauppauge 11788
(212) 756-2000 .. **Greenberg,** Danl L '69 SpclCnsl Schulte R&Z LLP -919 3rd Av -NY 10022
(212) 833-1145 .. **Greenberg,** Danl R '06 %Friedman KS&A LLP -1633 Bway -NY 10019 **Fx:**373-7965
(212) 801-6545 .. **Greenberg,** David M '94 (Greenberg T,LLP) -200 Park Av -NY 10166
(212) 693-0085 .. **Greenberg,** David P '81 %Appellate Advocates -2 Rector -NY 10006 **Fx:**693-0878
(212) 468-4800 .. **Greenberg,** David S '03 %Davis & G LLP -1740 Bway -NY 10019
(212) 596-9000 .. **Greenberg,** David S '09 %Ropes & G LLP -1211 Av of Amer -NY 10036
(516) 714-1332 .. **Greenberg,** Douglas I '92 Cnsl RJM Acquisitions,LLC -575 Underhill Blvd -Syosset 11791
(516) 679-9804 .. **Greenberg,** E Hope '92 -2650 Merrick Rd -Bellmore 11710 **Fx:**679-2523
(212) 697-8777 .. **Greenberg,** Edw C '79 E Greenberg,PC -570 Lex Av -NY 10022 **Fx:**697-2528
(212) 267-4455 .. **Greenberg,** Edw D '69 (Schwartz & G) -520 8th Av -NY 10018
(516) 742-8111 .. **Greenberg,** Elena L '83 (Fass & G,LLP) -1225 Franklin Av -Gdn Cty 11530 **Fx:**742-8999
(212) 545-4790 .. **Greenberg,** Eli D '85 (Wolf HAF&H LLP) -270 Mad Av -NY 10016
(212) 635-2244 .. **Greenberg,** Eliot L '90 %Rosner N&R LLP -110 Wall -NY 10005
(212) 326-3939 .. **Greenberg,** Elizabeth G '10 %Jones D -222 E 41st -NY 10017
(212) 663-1453 .. **Greenberg,** Ezra T '86 -204 W 98th -NY 10025 **Fx:**663-6711
(212) 661-5600 .. **Greenberg,** Gabriel '98 V Porter -51 E 42nd -NY 10017 **Fx:**681-4508
(212) 298-5069 .. **Greenberg,** Gary '68 %Leg Aid -49 Thomas -NY 10013 **Fx:**298-5252
(212) 765-5770 .. **Greenberg,** Gary H '75 -666 5th Av -NY 10103
(212) 964-0503 .. **Greenberg,** Harlan G '88 -20 Vesey -NY 10007
(212) 599-0777 .. **Greenberg,** Harold '59 OfCnsl Eisenberg T&L -675 3rd Av -NY 10017
(516) 570-4343 .. **Greenberg,** Harry '85 (Greenberg BG PC) -3000 Marcus Av -New Hyde Pk 11042 **Fx:**570-4348
(212) 953-2300 .. **Greenberg,** Harvey L '60 (Greenberg & W LLP) -232 Mad Av -NY 10016
(212) 593-6111 .. **Greenberg,** Hayley R '95 (Greenberg & M) -521 5th Av -NY 10175 **Fx:**(516) 887-1720
(914) 347-1250 .. **Greenberg,** Helene '84 -45 Knollwood Rd -Elmsfrd 10523 **Fx:**345-2114
(518) 474-7330 .. **Greenberg,** Henry M '87 %Dept of Law -The Cptl -Albany 12224
(718) 225-3200 .. **Greenberg & Hofstein,PC** -254-10 Nrthrn Blvd -Little Neck 11362 **Fx:**423-9617
(718) 797-1800 .. **Greenberg,** Howard '92 -86 Court -Brklyn 11201 **Fx:**797-1855
(212) 962-1596 .. **Greenberg,** Howard B '76 (Van Leer V-G&G) -132 Nassau -NY 10038
(516) 248-1180 .. **Greenberg,** Howard C '96 %Continental Abstrct -1 Old Cntry Rd -Carle Pl 11514 **Fx:**873-6602
(631) 982-0080 .. **Greenberg,** Howard E '85 H Greenberg,PC -180 E Main -Smithtwn 11787 **Fx:**982-0087
(212) 308-4411 .. **Greenberg,** Ira G '72 (Edwards AP&D LLP) -750 Lex Av -NY 10022
(718) 456-9492 .. **Greenberg,** Ira R '97 Assemblywoman C Nolan -61-08 Linden -Rdgwd 11385 **Fx:**417-4982
(914) 478-0933 .. **Greenberg,** Irene D '92 -1767 Cntrl Pk Av -Ynkrs 10710 **Fx:**(718) 907-4804
(212) 906-1173 .. **Greenberg,** Irene S '88 3rd Av Mgmt LLC -622 3rd Av -NY 10017
(516) 621-7717 .. **Greenberg,** J Michl '61 (Greenberg & G) -3 Sierks Ln -Roslyn Harbor 11576 **Fx:**621-9340
(212) 545-7337 .. **Greenberg,** James K '91 (Greenberg & G,LLP) -363 7th Av -NY 10001 **Fx:**545-7406
(516) 621-7717 .. **Greenberg,** James M '99 %Greenberg & G -3 Sierks Ln -Roslyn Harbor 11576 **Fx:**621-9340
(212) 351-4000 .. **Greenberg,** Jamie A '06 %Gibson D&C LLP -200 Park Av -NY 10166
(516) 357-3000 .. **Greenberg,** Janice M '99 %Rivkin R LLP -926 RXR Plz -Uniondale 11556
(516) 730-5047 .. **Greenberg,** Jason A '99 -250 Mineola Blvd -Mineola 11501 **Fx:**450-3501
(212) 277-5837 .. **Greenberg,** Jeffrey A '88 (Beldock L&H LLP) -99 Park Av -NY 10016
(212) 612-4200 .. **Greenberg,** Jeffrey D '91 %Hoey KT&E -55 Water -NY 10041
(212) 770-7000 .. **Greenberg,** Jeffrey W '78 %AIG -70 Pine -NY 10270
(914) 422-2500 .. **Greenberg,** Jennifer '94 -81 Main -White Plns 10601 **Fx:**683-1279
(212) 906-1200 .. **Greenberg,** Jennifer '08 %Latham & W -885 3rd Av -NY 10022
(212) 721-3144 .. **Greenberg,** Jeremy M '89 (Freeport Equities) -459 Columbus Av -NY 10024 **Fx:**501-8639
(631) 755-0101 .. **Greenberg,** Jill A '97 %Lewis JAA,LLP -425 Broad Hollow Rd -Melvll 11747
(212) 490-0949 .. **Greenberg,** Joan L '88 JL Greenberg PLLC -60 E 42nd -NY 10165 **Fx:**697-0877
(212) 836-8000 .. **Greenberg,** Joel I '74 (Kaye S LLP) -425 Park Av -NY 10022
(516) 328-2300 .. **Greenberg,** Joel M '80 (Abrams FFEGF&E,LLP) -1111 Marcus Av -Lk Success 11042
(718) 658-0500 .. **Greenberg,** Jos J '67 %Law Dept -151-20 Jamaica Av -Jamaica 11432 **Fx:**658-4025
(212) 245-0105 .. **Greenberg,** Josiah '82 (Greenberg & O) -150 W 51st -NY 10019
(212) 697-8590 .. **Greenberg,** Julia '06 %Rubin M Intl Law,PC -303 5th Av -NY 10016 **Fx:**687-1407
(212) 447-8690 .. **Greenberg,** Julia M '10 %Lamson & C,PC -9 E 40th -NY 10016 **Fx:**447-8691
(212) 815-1818 .. **Greenberg,** Karen E '78 %DC 37 MELS -125 Barclay -NY 10007 **Fx:**815-1343
(212) 613-5000 .. **Greenberg,** Kathryn O '83 %Leg Assist Grp -450 W 33rd -NY 10001 **Fx:**750-0820
(212) 474-1000 .. **Greenberg,** Kristy J '05 %Cravath S&M LLP -825 8th Av -NY 10019
(212) 728-8000 .. **Greenberg,** Laura J '10 %Willkie F&G LLP -787 7th Av -NY 10019
(212) 335-9000 .. **Greenberg,** Laura Sperling '02 %DA -1 Hogan Pl -NY 10013
(212) 608-9000 .. **Greenberg,** Laurence P '92 -299 Bway -NY 10007 **Fx:**732-6972
(212) 791-8933 .. **Greenberg,** Leibert L '69 -30 Vesey -NY 10007
(212) 446-4800 .. **Greenberg,** Leo M '06 %Kirkland & E LLP -153 E 53rd -NY 10022
(845) 638-2211 .. **Greenberg,** Leonard '59 -155 N Main -New Cty 10956
(212) 216-8000 .. **Greenberg,** Lester Alan '64 Cnsl Tarter K&D LLP -1350 Bway -NY 10018
(212) 857-8751 .. **Greenberg,** Lisa J '83 Ct of Appls -40 Foley Sq -NY 10007
(212) 772-5182 .. **Greenberg,** Lynne Ann '91 Hunter Cllg -695 Park Av -NY 10065
(631) 234-5484 .. **Greenberg,** Lynne R '89 %E Levine & Assoc -1455 Vets Mem'l Hwy -Hauppauge 11749 **Fx:**234-5561
(212) 297-0503 .. **Greenberg,** Margery A '84 (Segal & G LLP) -179 Franklin -NY 10013 **Fx:**297-0572
(212) 532-3840 .. **Greenberg,** Mark D '95 (Greenberg & G) -888 7th Av -NY 10019 **Fx:**532-3829
(518) 828-3336 .. **Greenberg,** Mark D '95 (Greenberg & G) -4 E Court -Hudson 12534 **Fx:**828-9888
(212) 349-8100 .. **Greenberg,** Martin R '69 -40 Exch Pl -NY 10005
(212) 255-5556 .. **Greenberg,** Matthew '97 (Feifer & G LLP) -27 Union Sq W -NY 10003
(212) 801-6781 .. **Greenberg,** Matthew N '87 OfCnsl Greenberg T,LLP -200 Park Av -NY 10166
(212) 230-5050 .. **Greenberg,** Maurice R '53 CV Starr & Co,Inc -399 Park Av -NY 10022
(212) 806-5400 .. **Greenberg,** Mayer '90 (Stroock &S&L LLP) -180 Maiden Ln -NY 10038
(607) 746-3906 .. **Greenberg,** Melvin F '85 -130 Main -Delhi 13753 **Fx:**746-3902
(212) 986-1000 .. **Greenberg,** Michl D '71 (Goldberg C&G,LLP) -331 Mad Av -NY 10017 **Fx:**986-8039
(212) 681-8313 .. **Greenberg,** Michl D '99 (Karaahmet L&G LLP) -370 Lex Av -NY 10017 **Fx:**208-2917
(516) 764-7999 .. **Greenberg,** Michl J '90 -55 Maple Av -Rockvll Ctr 11570 **Fx:**764-8999
(347) 468-7792 .. **Greenberg,** Michl J '98 Sun Microsystems,Inc -101 Park Av -NY 10178
(212) 609-4200 .. **Greenberg,** Monica L '95 LivePerson Inc -462 7th Av -NY 10018
(718) 250-2000 .. **Greenberg,** Nancy E '79 %DA -350 Jay -Brklyn 11201 **Fx:**250-2314
(212) 335-9000 .. **Greenberg,** Nancy R '83 %DA -1 Hogan Pl -NY 10013
(212) 490-2277 .. **Greenberg,** Neal L '96 NY Land Srvcs -630 3rd Av -NY 10017 **Fx:**490-8012
(516) 228-5100 .. **Greenberg,** Neil H '82 N Greenberg & Assoc -900 Merchants Cncrs -Westbury 11590 **Fx:**228-5106
(631) 421-0200 .. **Greenberg,** Neil I '65 %Imperial Jewelers -274 NY Av -Huntngtn 11743
(212) 756-2000 .. **Greenberg,** Noam D '06 %Schulte R&Z LLP -919 3rd Av -NY 10022
(212) 245-0105 .. **Greenberg & Oser** -150 W 51st -NY 10019 **Fx:**(973) 783-3653
(212) 334-6880 .. **Greenberg,** Peter E '89 P Greenberg & Assoc -200 Mad Av -NY 10016 **Fx:**334-6895
(212) 279-4550 .. **Greenberg,** Philip A '74 (PA Greenberg,PC) -10 Park Av -NY 10016 **Fx:**279-0466
(212) 335-9000 .. **Greenberg,** Polly '94 %DA -1 Hogan Pl -NY 10013
(516) 867-5100 .. **Greenberg,** Ralph D '77 -106 Woodcleft Av -Freeprt 11520
(718) 838-7878 .. **Greenberg,** Rebecca A '09 %Bronx Defenders -860 Crtlandt Av -Bronx 10451 **Fx:**665-0100
(516) 942-0244 .. **Greenberg,** Rhonda S '88 %Office oDA&R -375 N Bway -Jericho 11753 **Fx:**942-0353
(212) 619-3530 .. **Greenberg,** Richd '74 (Greenberg & S) -9 Murray -NY 10007 **Fx:**732-4443
(212) 308-7900 .. **Greenberg,** Richd A '70 (Newman & G) -950 3rd Av -NY 10022
(212) 657-2087 .. **Greenberg,** Richd D '86 %Citigroup -111 Wall -NY 10043
(732) 636-8800 .. **Greenberg,** Richd H '78 (Greenberg & S) -1600 Stewart Av -Westbury 11590
(212) 545-4000 .. **Greenberg,** Richd I '96 (Jackson L LLP) -666 3rd Av -NY 10017

(212) 402-4100 .. **Greenberg,** Richd M '78 %Ofc Appllt Def -11 Park Pl -NY 10007 **Fx:**402-4199
(718) 225-3200 .. **Greenberg,** Robt B '88 OfCnsl Greenberg & H,PC -254-10 Nrthrn Blvd -Little Neck 11362
(516) 775-4040 .. **Greenberg,** Robt E '73 -3000 Marcus Av -Lk Success 11042
(718) 488-1900 .. **Greenberg,** Roger B '95 %Lazzaro & G,PC -360 Court -Brklyn 11231
(212) 768-6700 .. **Greenberg,** Ronald '61 (Sonnenschein N&R LLP) -2 World Fncl Ctr -NY 10281
(914) 834-7204 .. **Greenberg,** Ronald D '66 -Bx785 -Harrison 10528 **Fx:**834-7204
(212) 715-9100 .. **Greenberg,** Ronald S '88 (Kramer LN&F,LLP) -1177 Av of Amer -NY 10036
(212) 530-4825 .. **Greenberg,** Rose '95 (LaRocca HRG&B LLP) -40 Wall -NY 10005
(631) 324-5120 .. **Greenberg,** Roy E '81 -10 Pantigo Rd Bx731 -E Hampton 11937 **Fx:**324-7494
(212) 838-9738 .. **Greenberg,** Sanford H '91 (Greenberg F LLP) -110 E 59th -NY 10022 **Fx:**838-5032
(212) 754-9400 .. **Greenberg,** Sarah J '08 %Todtman NS&J,PC -425 Park Av -NY 10022
(212) 664-2666 .. **Greenberg,** Sari E '88 %NBC -30 Rckfllr Plz -NY 10112 **Fx:**957-3213
(732) 636-8800 .. **Greenberg & Schulman** -1600 Stewart Av -Westbury 11590 **Fx:**636-8833
(212) 415-8600 .. **Greenberg,** Scott D '83 SrCnsl Locke LB&L LLP -3 World Fncl Ctr -NY 10281
(212) 504-6000 .. **Greenberg,** Scott J '03 SpclCnsl Cadwalader W&T LLP -1 World Fncl Ctr -NY 10281
(516) 570-4343 .. **Greenberg,** Seth H '04 (Greenberg BG PC) -3000 Marcus Av -New Hyde Pk 11042 **Fx:**570-4348
(212) 681-2535 .. **Greenberg,** Seth M '95 (Greenberg & S,PC) -275 Mad Av -NY 10016
(212) 728-8000 .. **Greenberg,** Stacey F '02 %Willkie F&G LLP -787 7th Av -NY 10019
(212) 681-2535 .. **Greenberg & Stein, PC** -275 Mad Av -NY 10016 **Fx:**681-2549
(212) 964-7400 .. **Greenberg,** Steven S '71 Smith MDWY&Y,PC -111 John -NY 10038
(845) 782-5025 .. **Greenberg,** Stuart '74 -106 Stage Rd -Monroe 10950 **Fx:**782-9489
(212) 267-7650 .. **Greenberg,** Stuart J '94 (S Greenberg,PC) -225 Bway -NY 10007 **Fx:**267-7647
(718) 222-2001 .. **Greenberg,** Susan P '03 %Law Dept -350 Jay -Brklyn 11201 **Fx:**222-2088
(212) 250-5947 .. **Greenberg,** Suzanne F '86 %Deutsche Bk -60 Wall -NY 10005
(212) 294-6700 .. **Greenberg,** Tara Lombardi '05 %Winston & S -200 Park Av -NY 10166
(212) 391-5200 .. **Greenberg,** Theo M '52 OfCnsl Locker G&B,PC -420 5th Av -NY 10018
(212) 735-3000 .. **Greenberg,** Thos W '95 (Skadden ASM&F LLP) -4 Times Sq -NY 10036
(718) 268-0400 .. **Greenberg,** Todd D '77 (Addabbo & G) -118-21 Qns Blvd -Frst Hlls 11375
(212) 688-1900 .. **Greenberg Trager & Herbst,LLP** -767 3rd Av -NY 10017 **Fx:**688-3201
(212) 801-9200 .. **Greenberg Traurig,LLP** -200 Park Av -NY 10166 **Fx:**801-6400
(518) 689-1400 .. **Greenberg Traurig,LLP** -54 State -Albany 12207 **Fx:**689-1499
(914) 286-2900 .. **Greenberg Traurig,LLP** -445 Hmltn Av -White Plns 10601 **Fx:**286-2990
(845) 356-3334 .. **Greenberg Wanderman & Fromson** -150 Airport Exec Park -Nanuet 10954
(914) 694-1880 .. **Greenberg,** Wm G '72 (Greenberg & M,LLP) -2929 Purchase -Purchase 10577
(212) 609-6800 .. **Greenberg,** Wm S '84 (McCarter & E,LLP) -245 Park Av -NY 10167
(212) 953-2300 .. **Greenberg & Wilner LLP** -232 Mad Av -NY 10016 **Fx:**986-5994
(718) 250-2000 .. **Greenberger,** Abbie '07 %DA -350 Jay -Brklyn 11201 **Fx:**250-2314
(212) 761-3559 .. **Greenberger,** Abby Rotbart '00 Morgan Stanley -1585 Bway -NY 10036
(212) 687-8500 .. **Greenberger,** David I '00 (Liddle & R,LLP) -800 3rd Av -NY 10022
(212) 763-5000 .. **Greenberger,** Debra L '06 %Emery CB&A LLP -75 Rckfllr Plz -NY 10019
(212) 272-3488 .. **Greenberger,** E Mala '80 %JP Morgan Chase -383 Mad Av -NY 10179
(212) 953-2381 .. **Greenberger,** Gerald A '78 (Rubin F&F,LLP) -292 Mad Av -NY 10017
(212) 998-6221 .. **Greenberger,** Howard L '66 %NYU Law Schl -40 Wshngtn Sq S -NY 10012 **Fx:**995-4692
(212) 554-7800 .. **Greenberger,** Jordan D '08 %Moses & S LLP -405 Lex Av -NY 10174
(212) 757-4001 .. **Greenberger,** Jos '62 -111 E 61st -NY 10065 **Fx:**757-4053
(631) 224-5550 .. **Greenberger,** Melissa B '95 %Town Atty -655 Main -Islip 11751 **Fx:**224-5573
(212) 625-8910 .. **Greenberger,** Michl J '08 %B Kogan & Assoc,PC -277 Bway -NY 10007 **Fx:**219-2728
(516) 222-1525 .. **Greenberger,** Steven L '72 -100 Q Roosevelt Blvd -Gdn Cty 11530 **Fx:**222-0778
(516) 596-1836 .. **Greenberger,** Tomas '73 -195 Rockaway Av -Vly Stream 11580 **Fx:**596-1838
(212) 854-2675 .. **Greenberg-Kobrin,** Michelle A '00 Columbia Law Schl -435 W 116th -NY 10027 **Fx:**854-7946
(212) 308-2200 .. **Greenblatt,** Aaron '07 %Grant & A,PC -444 Mad Av -NY 10022
(516) 352-1366 .. **Greenblatt,** Albert '40 -119 New Hyde Pk Rd -Franklin Sq 11010
(516) 935-4200 .. **Greenblatt,** Amy '81 %America Media -100 Jericho Quad -Jericho 11753
(845) 486-2500 .. **Greenblatt,** Elaine G '81 %Family Ct -50 Market -Poughkeepsie 12601
(212) 819-0555 .. **Greenblatt,** Elysa '01 (Parmet & G,LLC) -60 E 42nd -NY 10165 **Fx:**840-2288
(212) 682-9832 .. **Greenblatt,** Gershon D '94 OfCnsl Greenblatt L LLP -370 Lex Av -NY 10017 **Fx:**867-9319
(212) 832-2000 .. **Greenblatt,** Jason D '93 %Trump Orgn -725 5th Av -NY 10022 **Fx:**935-0141
(212) 593-0909 .. **Greenblatt,** Jeffrey '82 %US Diamond Cutters -579 5th Av -NY 10017 **Fx:**593-1430
(516) 357-3700 .. **Greenblatt,** Jeffrey R '07 %Cullen and D LLP -100 Q Roosevelt Blvd -Gdn Cty 11530
(212) 848-4291 .. **Greenblatt,** Jonathan L '81 (Shearman & S LLP) -599 Lex Av -NY 10022
(212) 506-1700 .. **Greenblatt,** Joshua M '02 (Kasowitz BT&F LLP) -1633 Bway -NY 10019
(212) 682-9832 .. **Greenblatt,** Judah D '85 (Greenblatt L LLP) -370 Lex Av -NY 10017 **Fx:**867-9319
(516) 433-6677 .. **Greenblatt,** Madge E '79 (Stewart GM&B) -6800 Jericho Tpk -Syosset 11791
(518) 457-2070 .. **Greenblatt,** Matthew M '76 %Dept of Tax & Fin -Bldg 9 State Campus -Albany 12227 **Fx:**457-6131
(718) 352-4800 .. **Greenblatt,** Matthew W '02 (Greenblatt & A,PC) -55 Nrthrn Blvd -Gt Neck 11021 **Fx:**732-2110
(914) 428-2100 .. **Greenblatt,** Michl E '91 (Welby B&G,LLP) -11 Martine Av -White Plns 10606
(212) 839-5300 .. **Greenblatt,** Michl H '09 %Sidley A LLP -787 7th Av -NY 10019
(212) 446-4800 .. **Greenblatt,** Nicole L '03 (Kirkland & E LLP) -153 E 53rd -NY 10022
(845) 486-0300 .. **Greenblatt,** Richd '79 Cnsl Rutberg Pl Law -3344 Route 9 N -Poughkeepsie 12601 **Fx:**486-0270
(516) 935-4200 .. **Greenblatt,** Richd R '81 %America Media -100 Jericho Quad -Jericho 11753
(212) 832-1930 .. **Greenblatt,** Sheldon H '94 OfCnsl Breslow & W,LLP -767 3rd Av -NY 10017
(718) 270-3019 .. **Greenblatt,** Steven J '77 %SUNY Hlth Sci Ctr -450 Clarkson Av -Brklyn 11203
(516) 352-1366 .. **Greenblatt,** Steven M '76 -119 New Hyde Pk Rd -Franklin Sq 11010 **Fx:**352-6823
(212) 715-1000 .. **Greenblatt-Harrison,** Andrea I '10 %Arnold & P LLP -399 Park Av -NY 10022
(718) 225-1831 .. **Greenburg,** Ellen J '72 -316 Grt Nck Rd -Gt Neck 11021 **Fx:**225-1831
(631) 399-1706 .. **Greenburg,** Ellen J '72 -Bx446 -Shirley 11967 **Fx:**399-1706
(212) 334-6190 .. **Greenbush,** Eric J '64 -351 Bway -NY 10013
(212) 753-5000 .. **Greendorfer,** Lori D '95 Cnsl Schiff H LLP -900 3rd Av -NY 10022
(212) 603-6300 .. **Greene,** A Mitchell '79 (Robinson BLGG&G PC) -875 3rd Av -NY 10022
(718) 250-2000 .. **Greene,** Abdula B '05 %DA -350 Jay -Brklyn 11201 **Fx:**250-2314
(212) 603-6300 .. **Greene,** Adam J '09 %Robinson BLGG&G PC -875 3rd Av -NY 10022
(212) 902-3895 .. **Greene,** Adam T '99 Goldman Sachs -85 Broad -NY 10004
(212) 530-5000 .. **Greene,** Aisha L '05 %Milbank TH&M LLP -1 Chase Manh Plz -NY 10005
(718) 286-6000 .. **Greene,** Aisha Summersill '06 %DA -125-01 Qns Blvd -Kew Gdns 11415
(516) 248-1180 .. **Greene,** Alan J '78 %Continental Abstrct -1 Old Cntry Rd -Carle Pl 11514 **Fx:**873-6602
(212) 264-4600 .. **Greene,** Alison E '85 %HHS -26 Fed Plz -NY 10278
(716) 847-1414 .. **Greene,** Alvin M '90 -403 Main -Buffalo 14203
(914) 948-4800 .. **Greene,** Andrew '74 (A Greene & Assoc,PC) -202 Mamaroneck Av -White Plns 10601 **Fx:**948-4936
(516) 437-7502 .. **Greene,** Andrew D '84 -3000 Marcus Av -Lk Success 11042
(212) 704-6000 .. **Greene,** Anthony D '06 %Troutman S LLP -405 Lex Av -NY 10174
(212) 373-3000 .. **Greene,** Bernard H '52 OfCnsl Paul WRW&G LLP -1285 Av of Amer -NY 10019
(212) 806-5400 .. **Greene,** Brian I '05 %Stroock &S&L LLP -180 Maiden Ln -NY 10038
(212) 245-1000 .. **Greene,** Cara E '06 %Outten & G LLP -3 Park Av -NY 10016
(718) 694-5208 .. **Greene,** Carolyn Evone '84 %Transit Auth -130 Lvngstn -Brklyn 11201
(716) 856-5500 .. **Greene,** Christopher T '75 (Damon M LLP) -200 Delaware Av -Buffalo 14202
(914) 738-5992 .. **Greene,** Clifford H '94 (CH Greene & Assoc) -145 Huguenot -New Rchll 10801 **Fx:**738-7197
(212) 788-1568 .. **Greene,** Danl P '04 %Law Dept -100 Church -NY 10007 **Fx:**788-0367
(212) 312-2260 .. **Greene,** Danl P '09 Leg Aid -60 Lafayette -NY 10013 **Fx:**349-0874
(212) 425-9300 .. **Greene,** Danielle R '04 %Bressler A&R,PC -17 State -NY 10004
(212) 983-2902 .. **Greene,** David '63 OfCnsl Eisenberg T&L -675 3rd Av -NY 10017
(718) 596-5635 .. **Greene,** David '67 -142 Joralemon -Brklyn 11201 **Fx:**855-6866
(212) 415-8600 .. **Greene,** David G '83 (Locke LB&L LLP) -3 World Fncl Ctr -NY 10281
(212) 259-8000 .. **Greene,** Donald J '61 OfCnsl Dewey & L LLP -1301 Av of Amer -NY 10019
(631) 843-5500 .. **Greene,** Earl A III '03 Henry Schein,Inc -135 Duryea Rd -Melvll 11747
(212) 225-2000 .. **Greene,** Edw F '69 (Cleary GS&H) -1 Lbrty Plz -NY 10006
(518) 462-0110 .. **Greene,** Edw J Jr. '99 (Sheehan GCG&J LLP) -54 State -Albany 12207
(212) 765-2100 .. **Greene,** Eric R '92 (Spivak L LLP) -1700 Bway -NY 10019
(585) 232-6500 .. **Greene,** F Paul '05 %Harter S&E LLP -1600 Bausch & Lomb Pl -Rchstr 14604
(914) 238-5370 .. **Greene,** George I '83 -150 N Bedford Rd -Chappaqua 10514
(315) 422-6154 .. **Greene Hershdorfer & Sharpe** -1 Lincoln Ctr -Syracuse 13202 **Fx:**475-2672
(718) 858-0200 .. **Greene,** Ira H '74 OfCnsl Wenig S LLP -26 Court -Brklyn 11242 **Fx:**237-1393
(212) 918-3000 .. **Greene,** Ira S '72 (Hogan L LLP) -875 3rd Av -NY 10022
(518) 783-7977 .. **Greene,** James R '92 %NYSUT -800 Troy Schenectady Rd -Latham 12110
(212) 682-7474 .. **Greene,** Jeffrey H '97 (Foley & L LLP) -90 Park Av -NY 10016
(914) 686-5091 .. **Greene,** Jeffrey S '89 (JS Greene, PC) -1 Barker Av -White Plns 10601 **Fx:**686-4892
(212) 508-6700 .. **Greene,** John E '03 %Tannenbaum HS&H LLP -900 3rd Av -NY 10022
(212) 264-0650 .. **Greene,** John J '78 %US DOJ Antitrust Div -26 Fed Plz Ste 3630 -NY 10278
(914) 765-6353 .. **Greene,** John W '89 %IBM Credit Corp -N Castle Dr -Armonk 10504
(212) 935-7800 .. **Greene,** Kegan E '04 %Babcock & Brown -600 Lex Av -NY 10022
(914) 736-2250 .. **Greene,** Kenneth J '76 -157 Dogwood Rd -Cortlandt Manor 10567
(516) 465-8090 .. **Greene,** Kim E '80 %North Shore-LIJ Hlth Systm -145 Community Dr -Gt Neck 11021 **Fx:**465-8013

(212) 790-9200 .. **Greene,** Lawr W '98 %Cowan L&L,PC -1133 Av of Amer -NY 10036
(914) 941-5500 .. **Greene Leins & Ryan** -500 Exec Blvd -Ossining 10562
(516) 746-3800 .. **Greene,** Leland L '73 -600 Old Cntry Rd -Gdn Cty 11530 **Fx:**222-6577
(631) 425-0492 .. **Greene,** Leslie C '91 (L Greene,PC) -21 Arrowood Ln -Melvll 11747 **Fx:**425-0024
(917) 210-9923 .. **Greene,** Leslie Whitman '92 S1 Songs America -32 E 31 -NY 10016
(212) 474-1000 .. **Greene,** Mark I '95 (Cravath S&M LLP) -825 8th Av -NY 10019
(914) 251-1618 .. **Greene,** Mark W '99 OfCnsl Price MS&D,PC -106 Corp Park Dr -White Plns 10604
(646) 386-3640 .. **Greene,** Mary Chris '87 %Supreme Ct-Law Dept -60 Centre -NY 10007
(212) 603-6300 .. **Greene,** Michl E '77 (Robinson BLGG&G PC) -875 3rd Av -NY 10022
(631) 293-2300 .. **Greene,** Michl R '71 (Rappaport GG&L LLP) -1355 Motor Pkwy -Hauppauge 11749
(212) 277-4000 .. **Greene,** Michl S '02 %Freshfields BD LLP -520 Mad Av -NY 10022
(212) 975-3949 .. **Greene,** Mindy H '87 %CBS -51 W 52nd -NY 10019
(212) 599-0900 .. **Greene,** Mitchell A '85 (Bower & L,PC) -261 Mad Av -NY 10016
(212) 355-2151 .. **Greene,** Nancy H '88 %EP Dine Inc -115 E 57th -NY 10022 **Fx:**755-8486
(518) 452-0941 .. **Greene,** Nancy M '83 %Segel GM&S,PC -9 Wshngtn Sq -Albany 12205
(212) 848-4000 .. **Greene,** Nathaniel J '00 (Shearman & S LLP) -599 Lex Av -NY 10022
(716) 856-1344 .. **Greene,** Norman E S '65 SplCnsl Bouvier Prtnrshp,LLP -350 Main -Buffalo 14202 **Fx:**856-1369
(212) 661-5030 .. **Greene,** Norman L '75 (Schoeman U&K,LLP) -60 E 42nd -NY 10165
(212) 340-0400 .. **Greene,** Patricia Ryan '93 %Appllt Div 1st Dept -27 Mad Av -NY 10010 **Fx:**889-4412
(212) 382-0909 .. **Greene,** Patrick J Jr. '87 (Peckar & A,PC) -41 Mad Av -NY 10154
(518) 449-3125 .. **Greene,** Patrick K '87 (Stockli GS&P,LLP) -90 State -Albany 12207
(646) 414-6908 .. **Greene,** Peter D '96 (Lowenstein S PC) -1251 Av of Amer -NY 10020 **Fx:**(973) 422-6861
(212) 735-3000 .. **Greene,** Peter E '81 (Skadden ASM&F LLP) -4 Times Sq -NY 10036
(516) 364-7455 .. **Greene,** Philip K '59 (P Greene,PC) -180 Froehlich Farm Blvd -Woodbury 11797 **Fx:**364-7459
(315) 492-9665 .. **Greene & Reid,PLLC** -173 Intrepid Ln -Syracuse 13205 **Fx:**492-9741
(607) 753-3070 .. **Greene & Reid,PLLC** -39 Church -Cortlnd 13045
(315) 331-5633 .. **Greene & Reid,PLLC** -180 E Union -Newark 14513
(315) 786-6600 .. **Greene & Reid,PLLC** -23245 Route 342 -Watertwn 13601
(518) 474-8507 .. **Greene,** Richd G '85 %Dept of Law -The Cptl -Albany 12224 **Fx:**408-2018
(516) 364-7455 .. **Greene,** Richd M '89 -180 Froehlich Farm Blvd -Woodbury 11797
(585) 258-5403 .. **Greene,** Robt G '88 JP Morgan Chase -1 Chase Sq -Rchstr 14643 **Fx:**258-6458
(212) 943-4343 .. **Greene,** Robt L '85 (Storzer & G PLLC) -110 Wall -NY 10005 **Fx:**(202) 315-3996
(716) 847-8400 .. **Greene,** Robt M '70 (Phillips L LLP) -3400 HSBC Ctr -Buffalo 14203
(607) 723-5341 .. **Greene,** Ronald L '93 (Hinman H&K,LLP) -80 Exchange Bx5250 -Bnghmtn 13902
(212) 964-6611 .. **Greene,** Sean P '05 %Lester SK&D -120 Bway -NY 10271
(212) 701-3000 .. **Greene,** Stephen A '65 (Cahill G&R LLP) -80 Pine -NY 10005 **Fx:**269-5420
(315) 342-3191 .. **Greene,** Stephen C '71 S Greene -85 W Brdg -Oswego 13126 **Fx:**342-0732
(315) 342-3191 .. **Greene,** Stephen C Jr. '97 %S Greene -85 W Brdg -Oswego 13126 **Fx:**342-0732
(212) 867-3636 .. **Greene,** Stephen C '01 %Levin & G,PC -420 Lex Av -NY 10170
(212) 837-6000 .. **Greene,** Steven J '88 (Hughes H&R LLP) -1 Bttry Pk Plz -NY 10004
(212) 916-5954 .. **Greene,** Stewart P '84 %TIAA-CREF -730 3rd Av -NY 10017
(212) 786-8119 .. **Greene,** Susan J '94 EMI Music NA -150 5th Av -NY 10011 **Fx:**786-8103
(212) 319-1950 .. **Greene,** Theo J '60 (TJ Greene,PC) -18 E 48th -NY 10017 **Fx:**(203) 358-0687
(718) 584-0132 .. **Greene,** Wm J III '66 -691 E 187th -Bronx 10458
(212) 720-5026 .. **Greene,** Yoon Hi '91 %Fed Reserve Bk -33 Lbrty -NY 10045 **Fx:**785-5748
(516) 357-3000 .. **Greener,** Jeffrey S '88 (Rivkin R LLP) -926 RXR Plz -Uniondale 11556
(615) 479-3900 .. **Greener,** Marie DeMers '90 SSA-OHA -300 S State -Syracuse 13202
(212) 709-8178 .. **Greener,** Robt L '89 -110 Wall -NY 10005
(607) 330-4000 .. **Greener,** Wm '92 (Bond S&K,PLLC) -10 Brown Rd -Ithaca 14850
(212) 888-2005 .. **Greenes,** Steven R '75 (Morgenthau & G,LLP) -575 Lex Av -NY 10022
(212) 878-7900 .. **Greenfader,** Glenn J '86 (Fox R LLP) -100 Park Av -NY 10017
(212) 735-3000 .. **Greenfeld,** Adir E '10 %Skadden ASM&F LLP -4 Times Sq -NY 10036
(646) 878-0835 .. **Greenfeld,** Robt L '97 (Pearl CZL,LLP) -1500 Bway -NY 10036
(516) 621-0271 .. **Greenfest,** Mark W '88 -22 Pchtree Ln -Roslyn Hts 11577
(212) 670-0120 .. **Greenfield,** Adam M '95 Merrill Lynch -222 Bway -NY 10038 **Fx:**670-4527
(212) 688-8555 .. **Greenfield,** Andrew B '03 %Fragomen DB&L LLP -7 Hanover Sq -NY 10004
(212) 801-3099 .. **Greenfield,** Ari D '06 %Greenberg T,LLP -200 Park Av -NY 10166
(212) 788-0872 .. **Greenfield,** Blanche '91 %Law Dept -100 Church -NY 10007 **Fx:**788-0367
(516) 522-2565 .. **Greenfield,** Brian J '83 (Greenfield & R) -626 RXR Plz -Uniondale 11556 **Fx:**522-2566
(212) 351-4000 .. **Greenfield,** Casey C '08 %Gibson D&C LLP -200 Park Av -NY 10166
(516) 746-7371 .. **Greenfield,** Catherine Q '07 Burns RT&R,LLP -390 Old Cntry Rd -Gdn Cty 11530
(516) 277-6900 .. **Greenfield,** Craig B '89 Magna Care Hldngs LLC -825 E Gate Blvd -Gdn Cty 11530
(718) 590-2000 .. **Greenfield,** David E '81 %DA -198 E 161st -Bronx 10451 **Fx:**590-6477
(718) 336-0880 .. **Greenfield,** David G '05 SCF,Inc -485 Kings Hwy -Brklyn 11223
(212) 481-9350 .. **Greenfield,** David S '66 -100 Lafayette -NY 10013 **Fx:**481-6003
(212) 909-6000 .. **Greenfield,** Elliot '06 %Debevoise & P LLP -919 3rd Av -NY 10022
(212) 732-8700 .. **Greenfield,** Gary A '75 (McAloon & F,PC) -123 William -NY 10038
(212) 373-3000 .. **Greenfield,** Jay '61 OfCnsl Paul WRW&G LLP -1285 Av of Amer -NY 10019
(516) 942-3200 .. **Greenfield,** Mace H '99 -420 Jericho Tpk -Jericho 11753 **Fx:**942-3366
(914) 225-4772 .. **Greenfield,** Mark E '95 Morgan Stanley Smith Barney -2000 Wstchstr Av -Purchase 10577
(212) 619-4100 .. **Greenfield,** Paul '69 -225 Bway -NY 10007 **Fx:**406-6890
(718) 875-0308 .. **Greenfield,** Robt J '77 -26 Court -Brklyn 11242 **Fx:**522-4874
(212) 374-2983 .. **Greenfield,** Robin S '86 %NYC Dept Educ-OLS -52 Chmbrs -NY 10007 **Fx:**374-5939
(212) 406-9686 .. **Greenfield,** Ron N '93 %E D'Elia,PC -120 Bway -NY 10271 **Fx:**406-9688
(212) 227-8585 .. **Greenfield,** Scott H '83 -1040 Av of Amer -NY 10018
(212) 818-9600 .. **Greenfield Stein & Senior,LLP** -600 3rd Av -NY 10016 **Fx:**818-1264
(516) 466-2044 .. **Greenfield,** Steven '72 -Bx220429 -Gt Neck 11022
(212) 529-7781 .. **Greenfield-Sanders,** Karin F E '79 -135 E 2nd -NY 10009 **Fx:**473-8073
(212) 804-4200 .. **Greengrass,** Lawr S '77 (Mound CW&G) -One Bttry Pk Plz -NY 10004
(212) 237-1000 .. **Greenhalgh,** James D '74 SplCnsl Windels ML&M,LLP -156 W 56th -NY 10019
(631) 247-0404 .. **Greenhaus,** David S '99 (Jackson L LLP) -58 S Srvc Rd -Melvll 11747
(212) 370-0414 .. **Greenhaus,** Philip Sherwood '68 -60 E 42nd -NY 10165 **Fx:**370-0417
(914) 698-5142 .. **Greenhill,** Ira Judd '48 -8 Sunset Rd -Rye 10580
(212) 287-4956 .. **Greenhill,** Noah D '00 Highbridge Cptl Mgmt LLC -40 W 57th -NY 10019
(212) 661-5533 .. **Greenhill,** Zachary Robb '79 -160 E 65th -NY 10065
(315) 422-8191 .. **Greenhouse,** Andrew A '03 %Leg Aid -351 S Warren -Syracuse 13202 **Fx:**472-2819
(212) 839-5300 .. **Greenhut,** Adam J '06 %Sidley A LLP -787 7th Av -NY 10019
(718) 855-6577 .. **Greenidge,** Edmund A '93 -188 Montague -Brklyn 11201 **Fx:**858-0411
(718) 544-7701 .. **Greenlaw,** Claire H '79 (Goldstein & G,LLP) -118-35 Qns Blvd -Frst Hlls 11375
(518) 370-8100 .. **Greenleaf,** Shari '87 Cnsl Schnectady City Schl Dist -108 Educ Dr -Schnctdy 12303 **Fx:**881-3588
(212) 599-0900 .. **Greenlees,** Margaret J '02 %Bower & L,PC -261 Mad Av -NY 10016
(212) 704-6000 .. **Greenman,** Chas P '75 (Troutman S LLP) -405 Lex Av -NY 10174
(716) 874-8010 .. **Greenman,** Elizabeth Bridge '87 (Bridge & B) -Bx336 -Tonawanda 14223 **Fx:**874-8113
(646) 295-9591 .. **Greenman,** Fredk F Jr. '62 -110 E 59th -NY 10022
(212) 730-7750 .. **Greenman,** Gary R '82 (Nicoletti GS&O,LLP) -555 5th Av -NY 10017
(212) 687-4900 .. **Greenman,** Harlan T '83 (Wormser KG&J LLP) -825 3rd Av -NY 10022
(716) 849-1333 .. **Greenman,** Herbert L '73 (Lipsitz GSC LLP) -42 Delaware Av -Buffalo 14202
(315) 218-8000 .. **Greenman,** Jos A '75 (Bond S&K,PLLC) -1 Lincoln Ctr -Syracuse 13202
(646) 871-4444 .. **Greenman,** Lawr S '89 Natl Jewish Outreach Prog -989 6th Av -NY 10018
(212) 335-9000 .. **Greenman,** Michl C '05 %DA -1 Hogan Pl -NY 10013
(212) 735-3000 .. **Greenman,** Paula S '95 (Skadden ASM&F LLP) -4 Times Sq -NY 10036
(315) 471-4107 .. **Greenough,** Robt K Jr. '83 -4629 Onondaga Blvd -Syracuse 13219 **Fx:**471-6701
(212) 551-3084 .. **Green-Ravenhorst,** Margaret M '90 Intl Rescue Comm -122 E 42nd -NY 10168
(516) 228-8484 .. **Greenseich,** Wendy A '00 %Dilworth & B,LLP -1000 Woodbury Rd -Woodbury 11797
(212) 308-4411 .. **Greenslade,** George A III '88 Cnsl Edwards AP&D LLP -750 Lex Av -NY 10022
(212) 873-0567 .. **Greenspan,** Abraham '50 -210 W 90th -NY 10024
(212) 422-0202 .. **Greenspan,** Alyssa R '09 %Sedgwick DM&A LLP -125 Broad -NY 10004
(212) 530-1800 .. **Greenspan,** Arthur S '90 (Richards K&O LLP) -1 World Fncl Ctr -NY 10281
(212) 756-2000 .. **Greenspan,** Caryn J '07 %Schulte R&Z LLP -919 3rd Av -NY 10022
(516) 465-6500 .. **Greenspan,** Chester H '80 -100 Jericho Quadrangle -Jericho 11753 **Fx:**794-7662
(212) 259-8000 .. **Greenspan,** David L '02 (Dewey & L LLP) -1301 Av of Amer -NY 10019
(212) 973-3043 .. **Greenspan,** Elise R '85 AECOM Tech Corp -605 3rd Av -NY 10158 **Fx:**973-3043
(917) 697-0671 .. **Greenspan,** Justin A '03 -130 E 18th -NY 10003
(716) 858-2424 .. **Greenspan,** Karen M '86 %DA -25 Delaware Av -Buffalo 14202 **Fx:**858-7425
(718) 386-1115 .. **Greenspan,** Lavi Z '99 %IDT Corp -75-17 169th -Flushng 11366 **Fx:**380-0242
(914) 946-2500 .. **Greenspan,** Leon J '59 (Greenspan & G) -150 Grand -White Plns 10601 **Fx:**946-1432
(914) 946-2500 .. **Greenspan,** Michl E '92 (Greenspan & G) -150 Grand -White Plns 10601 **Fx:**946-1432
(516) 222-1112 .. **Greenspan,** Murray H '50 -666 Old Cntry Rd -Gdn Cty 11530 **Fx:**228-6672
(914) 723-4300 .. **Greenspan,** Myron '68 (Lackenbach S LLP) -1 Chase Rd -Scarsdale 10583
(516) 338-5780 .. **Greenspan,** Raphael P '66 (Macri G&M) -393 Old Cntry Rd -Carle Pl 11514
(914) 478-2801 .. **Greenspan,** Richd M '76 (R Greenspan,PC) -220 Heatherdell Rd -Ardsley 10502 **Fx:**478-2913
(212) 779-9800 .. **Greenspan,** Sara '07 %Luboja & T,LLP -10 E 40th -NY 10016

(212) 422-0202 .. **Greenspan,** Scott D '96 (Sedgwick DM&A LLP) -125 Broad -NY 10004
(212) 251-5126 .. **Greenspan,** Steven C '98 Segal Co -1 Park Av -NY 10016 **Fx:**251-5275
(212) 648-2158 .. **Greenspan,** Steven M '86 JP Morgan Investment Mgmt Inc -245 Park Av -NY 10167
(212) 953-2381 .. **Greenspan,** Stewart B '87 %Rubin F&F,LLP -292 Mad Av -NY 10017
(516) 783-3300 .. **Greenspan,** Wm R '73 (Baker G&B) -2099 Bellmore Av -Bellmore 11710
(212) 903-9000 .. **Greenspon,** Colin '05 %Linklaters -1345 Av of Amer -NY 10105
(917) 992-5361 .. **Greenspoon,** David H '94 -28 Bellevue Av -Dobbs Ferry 10522
(212) 963-2850 .. **Greenspoon,** Julie B '04 UN Criminal Tribunal-Rwanda -Pouch Unit 3-B Bx4782 -NY 10163 **Fx:**963-2848
(212) 682-2900 .. **Greenspun,** Scott S '88 (Braverman & Assoc,PC) -331 Mad Av -NY 10017 **Fx:**682-7718
(718) 694-3966 .. **Greenstein,** Adam P '04 Transit Auth -130 Lvngstn -Brklyn 11201 **Fx:**694-5726
(212) 687-3860 .. **Greenstein,** Alisa D '02 Snow BK,PC -605 3rd Av -NY 10158
(212) 685-8500 .. **Greenstein,** Cindy M '00 -1825 Park Av -NY 10035 **Fx:**297-0504
(212) 661-9100 .. **Greenstein,** Danl P '80 %Otterbourg SH&R,PC -230 Park Av -NY 10169
(212) 218-5500 .. **Greenstein,** Dennis H '73 (Seyfarth S LLP) -620 8th Av -NY 10018
(212) 728-8000 .. **Greenstein,** Jaclyn D '09 %Willkie F&G LLP -787 7th Av -NY 10019
(212) 503-3564 .. **Greenstein,** Karen Anne '96 %Ziff-Davis Inc -28 E 28th -NY 10016
(212) 513-3200 .. **Greenstein,** Laura S '89 Holland & K LLP -31 W 52nd -NY 10019
(518) 475-9844 .. **Greenstein,** Lee D '87 -636 Delaware Av -Delmar 12054 **Fx:**475-9846
(518) 475-9844 .. **Greenstein,** Lee D '87 -600 Bway -Albany 12207 **Fx:**475-9846
(516) 596-2800 .. **Greenstein,** Matthew I '04 Fairway Consulting Grp -300 Merrick Rd -Lynbrk 11563
(212) 685-8500 .. **Greenstein & Milbauer,LLP** -1825 Park Av -NY 10035 **Fx:**297-0504
(646) 502-7001 .. **Greenstein,** Neil '99 (JSBarkats PLLC) -100 Church -NY 10007 **Fx:**607-5544
(631) 549-8383 .. **Greenstein,** Paul M '86 -50 Elm -Huntngtn 11743 **Fx:**423-9639
(212) 416-8161 .. **Greenstein,** Rhonda '78 %Dept of Law -120 Bway -NY 10271
(212) 685-8500 .. **Greenstein,** Robt J '94 (Greenstein & M,LLP) -1825 Park Av -NY 10035
(516) 484-9524 .. **Greenstein,** Terry Ann '94 -5 Diana's Trl -Roslyn Estates 11576 **Fx:**621-0349
(212) 228-2108 .. **Greenstone,** Robt Foster '74 -157 E 18th -NY 10003
(518) 427-2650 .. **Greenthal,** John L '74 (Nixon P LLP) -677 Bway -Albany 12207
(212) 862-8700 .. **Greenup,** Jeff L '54 (JL Greenup & Assoc) -205 W 137th -NY 10030 **Fx:**862-2664
(845) 567-4820 .. **Greenwald,** Benjamin A '01 -1229 Route 300 -Newburgh 12550 **Fx:**746-9030
(212) 267-7342 .. **Greenwald,** Brian Y '08 %Neiger LLP -317 Mad Av -NY 10017 **Fx:**406-3677
(212) 201-0190 .. **Greenwald,** Corey R '07 %Nourse & B,LLP -55 Bway -NY 10006
(212) 474-1000 .. **Greenwald,** David N '95 (Cravath S&M LLP) -825 8th Av -NY 10019
(212) 334-5950 .. **Greenwald,** David W '93 (Greenwald & W,LLP) -264 W 40th -NY 10018
(845) 638-1943 .. **Greenwald Doherty LLP** -30 Ramland Rd -Orangebrg 10962 **Fx:**638-2707
(845) 469-4900 .. **Greenwald,** Gary '71 -99 Brookside Av -Chester 10918 **Fx:**469-2022
(914) 793-3700 .. **Greenwald,** Hal B '88 -35 E Grassy Sprain Rd -Ynkrs 10710 **Fx:**793-3737
(315) 701-0080 .. **Greenwald,** James F '79 %Fed Pub Def -4 Clinton Sq -Syracuse 13202 **Fx:**701-0081
(845) 469-4900 .. **Greenwald,** Jamie C '04 %Greenwald Law Ofc -99 Brookside Av -Chester 10918 **Fx:**469-2022
(212) 456-7777 .. **Greenwald,** Jill C '91 %ABC -77 W 66th -NY 10023 **Fx:**456-6202
(845) 469-4900 .. **Greenwald,** Joanna C '00 -99 Brookside Av -Chester 10918 **Fx:**469-2022
(718) 250-2000 .. **Greenwald,** Joel H '07 %DA -350 Jay -Brklyn 11201 **Fx:**250-2314
(845) 638-1943 .. **Greenwald,** Joel J '91 (Greenwald D LLP) -30 Ramland Rd -Orangebrg 10962
(212) 669-4341 .. **Greenwald,** Judith R '64 Tax Commission -1 Centre -NY 10007 **Fx:**669-2003
(212) 806-5400 .. **Greenwald,** Laurence '65 (Stroock &S&L LLP) -180 Maiden Ln -NY 10038
(212) 334-5950 .. **Greenwald,** Leonard '60 OfCnsl Greenwald & W,LLP -264 W 40th -NY 10018
(518) 436-0775 .. **Greenwald,** Marc D '02 %Proskin,PC -423 Loudon Rd -Albany 12211 **Fx:**436-0014
(212) 849-7000 .. **Greenwald,** Marc L '02 (Quinn EU&S,LLP) -51 Mad Av -NY 10010
(212) 925-2332 .. **Greenwald,** Melvin L '57 -401 Bway -NY 10013
(914) 963-6262 .. **Greenwald,** Robt '62 -783 Palisade Av -Ynkrs 10703 **Fx:**963-4247
(718) 252-4200 .. **Greenwald,** Shaul C '08 Riverside Abstract -3839 Flatlands Av -Brklyn 11234 **Fx:**252-4226
(914) 725-6292 .. **Greenwald,** Shelley M '79 -20 Tintern Ln -Scarsdale 10583 **Fx:**472-9550
(212) 343-1234 .. **Greenwald,** Stephen R '78 Metropolitan College of NY -75 Varick -NY 10013
(845) 342-3295 .. **Greenwald,** Stuart M '59 -125 Wickham Av Bx81 -Middletwn 10940 **Fx:**342-1180
(212) 922-8051 .. **Greenwald,** Susan E '85 Bnk of NY Mellon -200 Park Av -NY 10166
(212) 983-1922 .. **Greenwald,** Wayne M '80 W Greenwald,PC -475 Park Av S -NY 10016 **Fx:**983-1965
(516) 466-4400 .. **Greenwald & Weinstock,LLP** -505 Nrthrn Blvd -Gt Neck 11021 **Fx:**466-2643
(212) 334-5950 .. **Greenwald & Weinstock,LLP** -264 W 40th -NY 10018 **Fx:**925-9181
(212) 554-1400 .. **Greenwald Ross,** Hannah E '02 (Bernstein LB&G LLP) -1285 Av of Amer -NY 10019
(212) 596-9000 .. **Greenwood,** Adam D '07 %Ropes & G LLP -1211 Av of Amer -NY 10036
(631) 369-7600 .. **Greenwood,** Brian J '03 %Lewis JAA,LLP -21 E 2nd -Rvrhead 11901
(516) 463-5858 .. **Greenwood,** Danl J H '85 %Hofstra Law Schl -121 Hofstra Univ -Hempstd 11549
(518) 485-9373 .. **Greenwood,** David N '04 NYS Educ Dept -80 Wolf Rd -Albany 12205
(917) 992-8810 .. **Greenwood,** Emma '07 -299 Bway -NY 10007 **Fx:**(212) 619-6743
(914) 640-2681 .. **Greenwood,** Harriet N '02 -1111 Wstchstr Av -White Plns 10604
(212) 231-7100 .. **Greenwood,** Jon S '97 24/7 Real Media Inc -132 W 31st -NY 10001 **Fx:**760-1774
(212) 681-0117 .. **Greenwood,** Kellianne E '98 %Starr GD&R -530 5th Av -NY 10036
(212) 909-6000 .. **Greenwood,** Lee A '10 %Debevoise & P LLP -919 3rd Av -NY 10022
(914) 939-4300 .. **Greenwood,** Richd H '97 %All Souls Parish/The Presbyterian Church -55 Pkwy Dr -Pt Chester 10573
(973) 951-9248 .. **Greenwood,** Robt H '07 -141 Sherman Rd -Kingston 12401 **Fx:**(845) 679-5181
(212) 612-2430 .. **Greenwood,** Susan Meridith '98 %Chubb Grp -55 Water -NY 10041
(716) 856-4000 .. **Greer,** Anita Costello '98 (Hodgson R LLP) -140 Pearl -Buffalo 14202
(212) 455-2000 .. **Greer,** Brandon M '10 %Simpson T&B LLP -425 Lex Av -NY 10017
(212) 698-3536 .. **Greer,** Brian E '99 (Dechert LLP) -1095 Av of Amer -NY 10036
(212) 728-8000 .. **Greer,** Cristopher '96 (Willkie F&G LLP) -787 7th Av -NY 10019
(212) 628-0560 .. **Greer,** Ida Rae '88 Cnsl Merit Operating Corp -351 E 83rd -NY 10028
(845) 454-1200 .. **Greer,** J Scott '85 (Lewis & G,PC) -510 Haight Av Bx2990 -Poughkeepsie 12603
(212) 947-3793 .. **Greer,** Rachel S '09 %Sadis & G LLP -551 5th Av -NY 10176
(212) 705-7000 .. **Greer,** Stefanie J '02 OfCnsl Bingham M LLP -399 Park Av -NY 10022
(718) 793-2553 .. **Gregg,** Heather L '03 %N Erlich,PC -108-18 Qns Blvd -Frst Hlls 11375 **Fx:**793-1627
(315) 422-7138 .. **Gregg,** Hugh C II '67 -120 E Wshngtn -Syracuse 13202 **Fx:**422-5635
(518) 869-9200 .. **Gregg,** Michl J '08 %Rose Law Firm,PLLC -501 New Karner Rd -Albany 12205 **Fx:**869-3334
(718) 568-4505 .. **Gregg,** Ronald A '82 -900 South Av -Staten Isl 10314
(212) 998-7127 .. **Gregoire,** Josiane '93 NYU -726 Bway -NY 10003
(212) 373-3000 .. **Gregor,** Robt N '08 %Paul WRW&G LLP -1285 Av of Amer -NY 10019
(212) 423-5995 .. **Gregorek,** Michl J '89 -1641 3rd Av -NY 10128
(866) 348-5819 .. **Gregori,** Frank L '88 %SSA-ODAR -50 Fountain Plz -Buffalo 14202 **Fx:**(716) 551-4078
(212) 446-4800 .. **Gregory,** Ashley S '00 (Kirkland & E LLP) -153 E 53rd -NY 10022
(516) 812-4500 .. **Gregory,** Danl P '96 (Stagg TC&W LLP) -401 Franklin Av -Gdn Cty 11530
(718) 990-6019 .. **Gregory,** David L '88 %St John's Law Schl -8000 Utopia Pkwy -Jamaica 11439 **Fx:**591-1855
(716) 855-7300 .. **Gregory,** David M '79 %NFTA -181 Ellicott -Buffalo 14203 **Fx:**855-7657
(212) 218-2100 .. **Gregory,** Dennis O '04 %Fitzpatrick CH&S -1290 Av of Amer -NY 10104
(716) 753-4241 .. **Gregory,** Derek Vaughn '94 %DA -Cnty Cthse -Mayvll 14757 **Fx:**753-4628
(585) 263-6760 .. **Gregory,** Douglas E '94 %US Atty -620 Fed Bldg -Rchstr 14614 **Fx:**263-6226
(646) 386-3760 .. **Gregory,** Harvard D '03 Hon M Friedman -80 Centre -NY 10013
(585) 419-8800 .. **Gregory,** Heidi S '94 (Harris B PLLC) -99 Garnsey Rd -Pittsfrd 14534
(212) 310-8000 .. **Gregory,** Holly J '87 (Weil G&M LLP) -767 5th Av -NY 10153
(607) 797-4839 .. **Gregory,** James A '99 (Hogan SLS&D,LLP) -Bx660 -Bnghmtn 13902
(212) 969-3000 .. **Gregory,** James E '89 SrCnsl Proskauer R LLP -1585 Bway -NY 10036
(212) 297-1000 .. **Gregory,** James L III '92 Gramercy Capital -420 Lex Av -NY 10170 **Fx:**297-1090
(212) 819-8200 .. **Gregory,** Jason R '07 %White & C LLP -1155 Av of Amer -NY 10036
(516) 463-5051 .. **Gregory,** John DeWitt '59 %Hofstra Law Schl -121 Hofstra Univ -Hempstd 11549
(718) 953-9221 .. **Gregory,** Jos E '90 J Gregory,LLP -249 NY Av -Brklyn 11216 **Fx:**953-8310
(212) 878-7411 .. **Gregory,** Lauren M '01 %MTA -347 Mad Av -NY 10017
(914) 526-4398 .. **Gregory,** Maura N '88 -1992 Commerce #22 -Yorktwn Hts 10598 **Fx:**526-4398
(845) 562-0203 .. **Gregory,** Melody A '06 %Finkelstein & Prtnrs,LLP -1279 Route 300 Bx1111 -Newburgh 12550
(718) 250-2000 .. **Gregory,** Miss '95 %DA -350 Jay -Brklyn 11201 **Fx:**250-2314
(716) 852-8222 .. **Gregory,** Paul M '96 %Paladino C&Q -295 Main -Buffalo 14203
(212) 608-2629 .. **Gregory & Reed, PC** -111 Bway -NY 10006
(718) 250-2000 .. **Gregory,** Renee V '98 %DA -350 Jay -Brklyn 11201 **Fx:**250-2314
(212) 232-1300 .. **Gregory,** Robin N '82 (Lewis BB&S LLP) -77 Water -NY 10005
(718) 222-2992 .. **Gregory,** Saml '85 -45 Main -Brklyn 11201
(212) 474-1000 .. **Grehan,** Kevin J '84 (Cravath S&M LLP) -825 8th Av -NY 10019
(845) 567-1002 .. **Greher,** Andrew N '01 Greher Law Ofcs PC -1161 Little Britain Rd -New Windsor 12553 **Fx:**567-0025
(845) 567-1002 .. **Greher,** Warren '72 -1161 Little Britain Rd -New Windsor 12553 **Fx:**567-0025
(212) 553-0147 .. **Greif,** Alexandra E '05 Moody's Corp -7 Wrld Trd Ctr -NY 10007
(516) 228-0348 .. **Greif,** Steven D '77 Goldman H&C,LLP -47 Post Av -Westbury 11590
(212) 964-4751 .. **Greifer,** David '60 -233 Bway -NY 10279
(212) 300-1100 .. **Greifer,** Jad B '96 (Clair G LLP) -555 Mad Av -NY 10022 **Fx:**300-1111
(212) 885-8000 .. **Greiff,** Brenda Slawin '94 %BDO USA,LLP -330 Mad Av -NY 10017 **Fx:**697-1299
(718) 992-9600 .. **Greifinger,** Michl '84 -859 Corcord Vllg W -Bronx 10451 **Fx:**293-2891
(212) 735-3000 .. **Greifzu,** James P '09 %Skadden ASM&F LLP -4 Times Sq -NY 10036
(212) 373-3000 .. **Greifzu,** John M Jr. '08 %Paul WRW&G LLP -1285 Av of Amer -NY 10019

(212) 506-2500 .. **Greig**, Andrew W '08 %Mayer B LLP -1675 Bway -NY 10019
(212) 941-0230 .. **Greig**, Arthur W '80 -401 Bway -NY 10013 **Fx**:274-0109
(212) 727-0016 .. **Greilsamer**, Glenn J '03 Zomba Label Grp -137 W 25th -NY 10001
(212) 596-9000 .. **Greilsheimer**, Deborah L '05 %Ropes & G LLP -1211 Av of Amer -NY 10036
(212) 715-9100 .. **Greilsheimer**, James G '63 Cnsl Kramer LN&F,LLP -1177 Av of Amer -NY 10036
(212) 837-6000 .. **Greilsheimer**, Jeffrey M '98 Cnsl Hughes H&R LLP -1 Bttry Pk Plz -NY 10004
(212) 983-3710 .. **Greilsheimer**, Wm H '67 -420 Lex Av -NY 10170 **Fx**:661-2446
(212) 354-6000 .. **Grein**, Mary Lavelle '85 %Daytop Vllg Inc -54 W 40th -NY 10018 **Fx**:382-3899
(212) 306-7200 .. **Greiner**, Melissa '99 %Mayors Ofc Labor Rel -40 Rector -NY 10006 **Fx**:306-7223
(212) 728-8000 .. **Greiner**, Stephen W '69 OfCnsl Willkie F&G LLP -787 7th Av -NY 10019
(716) 626-9993 .. **Greiner**, Terrence A '88 -5687 Main -Williamsvll 14221 **Fx**:(888) 234-4580
(585) 263-1000 .. **Greiner**, Thos C Jr. '80 (Nixon P LLP) -1100 Clinton Sq -Rchstr 14604
(716) 773-7465 .. **Greinert**, Jean Graziani '80 -Bx635 -Grand Isl 14072
(516) 739-5100 .. **Greiper**, Ellen H '86 OfCnsl Farber B&Z LLP -51 Charles -Mineola 11501
(585) 265-3730 .. **Greisberger**, John L '50 (Barrett G LLP) -34 May -Webster 14580
(585) 265-3730 .. **Greisberger**, Mark M '75 (Barrett G LLP) -34 May -Webster 14580
(518) 433-8800 .. **Greisler**, Gretchen M '03 %Lemery G LLC -50 Beaver -Albany 12207
(518) 433-8800 .. **Greisler**, Nicholas J '71 (Lemery G LLC) -50 Beaver -Albany 12207
(212) 762-7293 .. **Greisman**, Beth F '97 Morgan Stanley -1221 Av of Amer -NY 10020
(212) 902-1000 .. **Greisman**, Israel M '04 %Goldman Sachs -180 Maiden Ln -NY 10038
(212) 487-9700 .. **Greisman**, Jared T '99 (White F&F,LLP) -61 Bway -NY 10006
(212) 312-3000 .. **Greiss**, Jill B '81 FGIC -125 Park Av -NY 10017 **Fx**:312-3221
(212) 836-8000 .. **Greiss**, Rory A '81 (Kaye S LLP) -425 Park Av -NY 10022
(212) 819-8200 .. **Greissman**, Scott '95 (White & C LLP) -1155 Av of Amer -NY 10036
(914) 941-8521 .. **Greiter**, Chas L '58 -6 Haymont Ter -Briarclff Mnr 10510
(716) 892-5304 .. **Greitzer**, Deborah '95 VIVE,Inc -50 Wyoming Av -Buffalo 14215
(716) 631-7045 .. **Grelick**, Susan J '87 %Town of Amherst -5583 Main -Williamsvll 14221 **Fx**:631-7152
(646) 471-3000 .. **Grella**, Michl P '97 PricewaterhouseCoopers LLP -300 Mad Av -NY 10017
(212) 566-5600 .. **Greller**, Matthew N '02 %T Burgos & Assoc -115 Bway -NY 10006
(845) 454-2200 .. **Greller**, Stephen L '71 OfCnsl Wolfson G&E PC -11 Market -Poughkeepsie 12601
(516) 742-3470 .. **Gremillot**, Anne M '87 %Kral CRRP&G,LLP -538 Broadhllw Rd -Melvll 11747
(212) 909-5456 .. **Gremminger**, Steven L '97 %KPMG LLP -280 Park Av -NY 10017
(516) 822-8900 .. **Grenci**, Leonard M '88 Fiedelman & M -2 Jericho Plz -Jericho 11753
(631) 737-1962 .. **Grenci**, Salvatore A '85 -10 Richard Ct -Lk Grove 11755
(212) 841-1000 .. **Grendell**, Mary J '05 %Covington & B LLP -620 8th Av -NY 10018
(212) 944-0500 .. **Grendi**, Zachary B '10 Hofheimer G&G,LLP -530 5th Av -NY 10036
(212) 687-8500 .. **Grenert**, Michl E '96 (Liddle & R,LLP) -800 3rd Av -NY 10022
(716) 282-2774 .. **Grenga**, Paul '88 (Bartolomei & G) -335 Buffalo Av -Niagara Fls 14303
(631) 694-2626 .. **Grenier Humes & Nolan LLP** -445 Broadhllw Rd -Melvll 11747 **Fx**:694-2629
(212) 838-5555 .. **Grenier Humes & Nolan LLP** -60 E 42nd -NY 10165 **Fx**:697-4689
(315) 471-7383 .. **Grenis**, Peter S '94 -317 Mntgmry -Syracuse 13202
(212) 446-4800 .. **Grenker**, David M '05 %Kirkland & E LLP -153 E 53rd -NY 10022
(212) 819-8200 .. **Grenley**, Neal F '73 (White & C LLP) -1155 Av of Amer -NY 10036
(212) 918-3000 .. **Grennan**, Elizabeth L '03 %Hogan L LLP -875 3rd Av -NY 10022
(914) 997-0500 .. **Grennan**, Karen R '07 %Lowey DC&H,PC -1 N Bway -White Plns 10601
(516) 745-5490 .. **Grennan**, Kevin T '96 K Grennan,PLLC -1000 Franklin Av -Gdn Cty 11530 **Fx**:745-5453
(716) 549-0810 .. **Grennell**, John C '84 -11 Maple -Angola 14006 **Fx**:549-6581
(518) 464-1700 .. **Grenz**, Eugene Z '72 -113 Great Oaks Ofc Park -Albany 12203 **Fx**:464-0798
(212) 764-8888 .. **Greschler**, Irwin '92 %Arthur Yorkes & Co -520 8th Av -NY 10018 **Fx**:819-1465
(212) 310-8000 .. **Grese**, Frank '09 %Weil G&M LLP -767 5th Av -NY 10153
(716) 855-1111 .. **Gresens**, James W '74 (Duke HP&G LLP) -350 Main -Buffalo 14202
(212) 554-7800 .. **Gresh**, Christopher R '06 %Moses & S LLP -405 Lex Av -NY 10174
(716) 858-2424 .. **Gresham**, Christopher H '95 %DA -25 Delaware Av -Buffalo 14202 **Fx**:858-7425
(212) 244-4664 .. **Gresham**, John A '78 %NY Lawyers Pub Intrst -151 W 30th -NY 10001 **Fx**:244-4570
(914) 989-6650 .. **Gresham**, Kenneth L '89 (Eustace & M) -1133 Wstchstr Av -White Plns 10604
(631) 265-2550 .. **Greshin Ziegler & Amicizia** -199 E Main Bx829 -Smithtwn 11787 **Fx**:265-2832
(718) 846-6380 .. **Gresio**, Richd E '01 (Chand & G LLP) -110-13 Jamaica Av -Richmnd Hll 11418 **Fx**:846-4019
(718) 624-1327 .. **Gress**, Mindy L '04 -44 Court -Brklyn 11201 **Fx**:624-0198
(212) 957-7600 .. **Gresser**, Lawr '62 Cnsl Cohen & G LLP -800 3rd Av -NY 10022
(212) 957-7600 .. **Gresser**, Lawr T '89 (Cohen & G LLP) -800 3rd Av -NY 10022
(212) 859-8000 .. **Gressman**, Christy L '07 %Fried FHS&J LLP -1 NY Plz -NY 10004
(516) 625-1700 .. **Gretah**, Leonard '02 %Salamon GB&S,PC -97 Powerhse Rd -Roslyn Hts 11577
(212) 335-9000 .. **Gretina**, Lauren B '04 %DA -1 Hogan Pl -NY 10013
(914) 272-4037 .. **Gretz**, Albert J '86 Gerber Life Ins Co -1311 Mamaroneck Av -White Plns 10605
(212) 896-6500 .. **Grewal**, Gurbir S '00 OfCnsl Howrey LLP -601 Lex Av -NY 10022
(914) 750-5933 .. **Grewal**, Lissa N '09 %Kissel H&W LLP -580 Wht Plns Rd -Tarrytwn 10591
(212) 683-2210 .. **Grewal-Kok**, Yasmin '01 %Childrens Rts Inc -330 7th Av -NY 10001 **Fx**:683-4015
(718) 556-0737 .. **Grey**, Lisa A '98 -60 Bay -Staten Isl 10301 **Fx**:448-8685
(631) 775-6326 .. **Grey**, Marvin '75 -57 Julia Cir -Middl Isl 11953
(631) 549-5853 .. **Grey**, Robt A '86 Grey Area Dispute Srvcs,Inc -38 Stiles Dr -Melvll 11747
(516) 249-1342 .. **Grey**, Robt E '90 (Grey & G,LLP) -360 Main -Farmngdl 11735
(646) 386-5261 .. **Grey**, Solange Nicole '96 Family Ct -60 Lafayette -NY 10013
(212) 227-7226 .. **Grey**, Wm A '08 %Law Dept -100 Church -NY 10007 **Fx**:788-0367
(212) 818-1110 .. **Greyf**, Jane '99 (Butzel L,PC) -380 Mad Av -NY 10017
(631) 390-0010 .. **Grgas**, Steven '10 %Bruno G&S,LLP -445 Broad Hollow Rd -Melvll 11747
(212) 869-5030 .. **Gribben**, Brandon S '08 %Kucker & B,LLP -747 3rd Av -NY 10017
(585) 987-2800 .. **Gribben**, Gregory W '94 (Woods OG LLP) -2 State -Rchstr 14614
(212) 815-1450 .. **Gribben**, Jesse D '05 %DC 37 Gen Cnsl -125 Barclay -NY 10007 **Fx**:815-1440
(212) 349-3000 .. **Gribben**, Wm '80 (Himmelstein MGD&J) -15 Maiden Ln -NY 10038
(212) 705-7000 .. **Gribetz**, Judah '56 OfCnsl Bingham M LLP -399 Park Av -NY 10022
(845) 634-9500 .. **Gribetz**, Kenneth '68 (Gribetz & L,PLLC) -155 N Main -New Cty 10956 **Fx**:639-9105
(845) 634-9500 .. **Gribetz**, Tamar '95 -155 N Main -New Cty 10956
(914) 949-0100 .. **Gribetz**, Uriel E '89 -19 Court -White Plns 10601
(212) 538-0631 .. **Gribin**, Michl D '97 -1 Mad Av -NY 10010
(631) 293-6060 .. **Gridelli**, George R '75 %Cellino & B,PC -445 Broad Hollow Rd -Melvll 11747
(716) 853-8190 .. **Griebel**, Danl M '86 -14 Lafayette Sq -Buffalo 14203 **Fx**:853-8197
(212) 918-3000 .. **Grieco**, Brian J '02 %Hogan L LLP -875 3rd Av -NY 10022
(716) 856-0600 .. **Grieco**, Chas D '96 (Jaeckle F&M,LLP) -12 Fountain Plz -Buffalo 14202
(212) 532-1200 .. **Grieco**, Lisa L '90 -292 Mad Av -NY 10017 **Fx**:532-6330
(212) 451-2300 .. **Grieco**, Mary L '98 OfCnsl Olshan GFR&W LLP -65 E 55th -NY 10022
(212) 340-0400 .. **Grieco**, Matthew V '95 %Appllt Div 1st Dept -27 Mad Av -NY 10010 **Fx**:889-4412
(212) 523-6568 .. **Grieco**, Michl H '80 -1000 10th Av -NY 10019 **Fx**:523-6704
(845) 331-0650 .. **Grieco**, Robt C '82 (Matthews & G) -Bx3127 -Kingston 12402 **Fx**:331-0747
(212) 530-5000 .. **Griem**, John M Jr. '95 (Milbank TH&M LLP) -1 Chase Manh Plz -NY 10005
(718) 250-2000 .. **Griepp**, Lecia M '08 %DA -350 Jay -Brklyn 11201 **Fx**:250-2314
(212) 627-9898 .. **Grier**, Jos L '88 Sloss Law Ofc,PC -555 W 25th -NY 10001 **Fx**:627-9498
(212) 583-1291 .. **Grier**, Katherine K '02 -445 E 80th -NY 10075
(718) 443-3873 .. **Grier**, Wilmer H '72 -823 Jffrsn Av -Brklyn 11221 **Fx**:453-1276
(212) 848-4000 .. **Grierson**, Damien A '06 %Shearman & S LLP -599 Lex Av -NY 10022
(518) 828-2021 .. **Griesemer**, Matthew J '08 %Freeman H,PC -441 E Allen Bx1328 -Hudson 12534 **Fx**:828-2420
(716) 858-2424 .. **Grieser**, Garrett '06 %DA -25 Delaware Av -Buffalo 14202 **Fx**:858-7425
(212) 852-6104 .. **Griesheimer**, Cornelia '02 WestLB -1211 Av of Amer -NY 10036
(716) 878-8000 .. **Grieshober**, Wm E '89 %Rich Products -1 Robert Rich Way -Buffalo 14213 **Fx**:878-8767
(518) 528-4939 .. **Griesmer**, Terry J '96 Stockade Grp -650 Franklin -Schnctdy 12305
(212) 421-6000 .. **Griesmeyer**, Roger J '05 (LaSasso G Law Grp PLLC) -80 Maiden Ln -NY 10038 **Fx**:421-6006
(212) 373-3000 .. **Grieve**, Brian S '10 %Paul WRW&G LLP -1285 Av of Amer -NY 10019
(914) 253-2000 .. **Griff**, Christine Coakley '94 %Pepsico -700 Andrsn Hill Rd -Purchase 10577
(914) 468-8000 .. **Griff**, David M '98 Endurance Reinsurance -333 Wstchstr Av -White Plns 10604 **Fx**:997-0331
(914) 225-6574 .. **Griff**, Scott H '92 Morgan Stanley -2000 Wstchstr Av -Purchase 10577
(212) 302-6868 .. **Griffel**, Andrew '71 Cnsl Flaster & W,PC -36 W 44th -NY 10036
(212) 756-2000 .. **Griffel**, David S '00 SpclCnsl Schulte R&Z LLP -919 3rd Av -NY 10022
(212) 891-0700 .. **Griffel**, Ellen '92 %FOJP -28 E 28th -NY 10016 **Fx**:684-2132
(607) 723-5341 .. **Griffen**, Fredk A '59 SpclCnsl Hinman H&K,LLP -80 Exchange Bx5250 -Bnghmtn 13902
(518) 476-2001 .. **Griffen**, Thos G '73 %Gilberti SH&S,PC -111 Wshngtn Av -Albany 12210
(518) 452-2552 .. **Grifferty**, James J '54 OfCnsl Tobin & G,PC -678 Troy Schenectady Rd -Latham 12110 **Fx**:452-0175
(518) 452-2552 .. **Grifferty**, Stephen J '88 (Tobin & G,PC) 678 Troy Schenectady Rd -Latham 12110
(212) 709-8059 .. **Grifferty**, Terrence J '88 -110 Wall -NY 10005
(212) 735-3000 .. **Griffin**, Adam C '09 %Skadden ASM&F LLP -4 Times Sq -NY 10036
(212) 916-2132 .. **Griffin**, Alan L '84 UBS AG -101 Park Av -NY 10178
(516) 741-1110 .. **Griffin**, Brian J '93 (Foley GJ&F,LLP) -666 Old Cntry Rd -Gdn Cty 11530
(212) 345-0022 .. **Griffin**, Chas J '83 %Marsh Inc -1166 Av of Amer -NY 10036
(914) 961-1300 .. **Griffin Coogan Blose & Sulzer, PC** -51 Pondfld Rd -Bronxvll 10708 **Fx**:961-1476
(914) 961-1300 .. **Griffin**, Danl J '91 (Griffin CB&S,PC) -51 Pondfld Rd -Bronxvll 10708
(212) 935-6144 .. **Griffin**, David D '67 Ampex Corp -135 E 57th -NY 10022
(718) 250-1100 .. **Griffin**, Elizabeth A '89 %E Garfinkel -12 Metrotech Ctr -Brklyn 11201 **Fx**:250-1168
(212) 788-8430 .. **Griffin**, Ethel J '82 (Public Admnstrtr) -31 Chmbrs -NY 10007 **Fx**:385-0220
(845) 735-4300 .. **Griffin**, F Hollis Jr. '82 (Fury K&G) -5 E Central Av -Pearl Rvr 10965
(518) 266-1000 .. **Griffin**, F Redmond '61 (Pattison SG&G,PC) -22 1st Bx208 -Troy 12181
(631) 728-4525 .. **Griffin**, Gerald M '56 -47 Donellan Rd -Hampton Bays 11946
(212) 732-3200 .. **Griffin**, Gerald W '99 Cnsl Carter L&M LLP -2 Wall -NY 10005
(631) 261-0096 .. **Griffin**, Gerard P Jr. '71 -15 Park Cir -Centerprt 11721
(212) 984-9368 .. **Griffin**, Gilroye A Jr. '66 Korn/Ferry Intl -200 Park Av -NY 10166
(516) 330-6105 .. **Griffin**, James H '03 -4 Clock Twr Ln -Old Westbury 11568
(631) 784-7722 .. **Griffin**, James M '03 OfCnsl N Meyers,PC -55 Elm -Huntngtn 11743 **Fx**:784-5154
(631) 751-5000 .. **Griffin**, John G '74 -46 Route 25A -E Setauket 11733 **Fx**:689-7412
(585) 428-5210 .. **Griffin**, Jon N '03 Pub Def -10 N Fitzhugh -Rchstr 14614 **Fx**:428-2234

(212) 788-0791 .. **Griffin**, Karen M '96 %Law Dept -100 Church -NY 10007 **Fx:**788-0367
(646) 319-5150 .. **Griffin**, Katherine M '04 -206 E 17th -NY 10003
(718) 921-6601 .. **Griffin**, Kelly C '08 %T Beinert -155 Bay Ridge Av -Brklyn 11220 **Fx:**921-6609
(212) 306-7100 .. **Griffin**, Mark P '04 %Campaign Finance Bd -40 Rector -NY 10006 **Fx:**306-7143
(212) 806-5400 .. **Griffin**, Martha J '04 %Stroock &S&L LLP -180 Maiden Ln -NY 10038
(212) 997-5805 .. **Griffin**, Matthew D '00 Kaplan,Inc -1440 Bway -NY 10018
(212) 715-1000 .. **Griffin**, Michl F '81 (Arnold & P LLP) -399 Park Av -NY 10022
(212) 642-4954 .. **Griffin**, Patricia A '86 Amer Natl Standards Inst -25 W 43rd -NY 10036 **Fx:**398-0023
(212) 237-1000 .. **Griffin**, Regina L '93 SpclCnsl Windels ML&M,LLP -156 W 56th -NY 10019
(716) 845-6000 .. **Griffin**, Richd F '57 OfCnsl Kavinoky C LLP -726 Exchange -Buffalo 14210
(212) 906-1200 .. **Griffin**, Sarah K '07 %Latham & W -885 3rd Av -NY 10022
(212) 326-3939 .. **Griffin**, Scott A '08 %Jones D -222 E 41st -NY 10017
(718) 579-3039 .. **Griffin**, Shannon L '08 %Leg Aid -1020 Grnd Cncrs -Bronx 10451 **Fx:**588-2611
(585) 419-8800 .. **Griffin**, Shawn M '90 (Harris B PLLC) -99 Garnsey Rd -Pittsfrd 14534
(914) 761-2252 .. **Griffin**, Sonia R '98 %Boeggeman G&C,PC -1 Water -White Plns 10601
(212) 522-5101 .. **Griffin**, Tara A '93 JP Morgan Chase -1 Chase Manh Plz -NY 10081
(212) 613-2031 .. **Griffin**, Thos M '85 (Gibbons PC) -1 Penn Plz -NY 10119 **Fx:**554-9603
(914) 771-6754 .. **Griffin**, Timothy G '85 -77 Pondfld Rd Bx156 -Bronxvll 10708 **Fx:**771-6752
(518) 523-1409 .. **Griffin**, W Bradney '99 (Wilkins & G,PLLC) -2461 Main -Lk Placid 12946 **Fx:**523-1190
(212) 336-0176 .. **Griffin**, Wendy B '04 %SEC -3 World Fncl Ctr -NY 10281 **Fx:**336-1323
(914) 961-1300 .. **Griffin**, Wm E '59 (Griffin CB&S,PC) -51 Pondfld Rd -Bronxvll 10708
(631) 851-0011 .. **Griffin**, Wm P III '66 -320 Carleton Av -Central Islip 11722 **Fx:**851-0118
(631) 853-5262 .. **Griffin Boivin**, Jennifer '96 %Supreme Ct Law Dept -Bx9080 -Central Islip 11722
(212) 480-4800 .. **Griffing**, Katharine F '02 %Fox H&C LLP -825 3rd Av -NY 10022
(973) 596-4701 .. **Griffinger**, Michl R '64 (Gibbons PC) -1 Penn Plz -NY 10119 **Fx:**639-6294
(212) 219-1001 .. **Griffith**, Beverly A '02 -401 Bway -NY 10013
(607) 563-3565 .. **Griffith**, Carl A '73 (Eaton & G) -76 Main Bx270 -Sidney 13838
(212) 357-7885 .. **Griffith**, Donald E '92 %Goldman Sachs -1 NY Plz -NY 10004
(212) 363-3784 .. **Griffith**, Edw '84 (Bolatti & G) -45 Bway -NY 10006 **Fx:**363-3790
(212) 769-3922 .. **Griffith**, Edw D '74 -235 W 76th -NY 10023 **Fx:**489-9307
(716) 847-8400 .. **Griffith**, Edw M Jr. '61 Cnsl Phillips L LLP -3400 HSBC Ctr -Buffalo 14203
(315) 336-6500 .. **Griffith**, Emlyn I '50 Griffith Law Ofcs -Bx4242 -Rome 13442 **Fx:**336-6628
(212) 296-6984 .. **Griffith**, Eric C '05 Morgan Stanley -522 5th Av -NY 10036 **Fx:**(646) 452-4831
(607) 254-8790 .. **Griffith**, Kati L '05 Cornell Univ -334 Ives Hall E -Ithaca 14853 **Fx:**255-6840
(315) 423-7100 .. **Griffith**, Kelly C '98 %Harris B PLLC -300 S State -Syracuse 13202
(631) 293-4525 .. **Griffith**, Lisa M '05 %Littler M,PC -290 Broadhllw Rd -Melvll 11747
(631) 283-8899 .. **Griffith**, Michl J '73 -Bx796 -Amagansett 11930 **Fx:**267-2462
(212) 384-1000 .. **Griffith**, Michele E '96 %FBI -26 Fed Plz -NY 10278
(212) 298-5269 .. **Griffith**, Pamela J '03 Leg Aid -49 Thomas -NY 10013 **Fx:**298-5252
(516) 228-3565 .. **Griffith**, Robt W '02 %Farrell Law Firm,PC -290 Broadhllw Rd -Melvll 11747
(212) 297-5800 .. **Griffith**, Robt W '08 %Day P LLP -7 Times Sq -NY 10036
(212) 323-7070 .. **Griffith**, Scott F '09 OfCnsl Rawle & H LLP -14 Wall -NY 10005
(212) 636-6000 .. **Griffith**, Sean J '01 %Fordham Univ Sch of Law -140 W 62nd -NY 10023 **Fx:**636-6899
(212) 710-1045 .. **Griffith**, Shondell A '03 Paradigm Legal,LLC -75 Rckfllr Plz -NY 10019
(315) 422-8191 .. **Griffith**, Susan K '86 %Leg Aid -351 S Warren -Syracuse 13202 **Fx:**472-2819
(315) 336-6500 .. **Griffith**, Wm L '90 OfCnsl Griffith Law Ofcs -Bx4242 -Rome 13442 **Fx:**336-6628
(212) 521-5400 .. **Griffith**, Wm R '75 Cnsl Reed S LLP -599 Lex Av -NY 10022
(212) 818-9200 .. **Griffiths**, Alun W '98 Cnsl Satterlee SB&B LLP -230 Park Av -NY 10169
(212) 310-8000 .. **Griffiths**, David N '09 %Weil G&M LLP -767 5th Av -NY 10153
(718) 655-9181 .. **Griffiths**, Donovan L '98 -3958 Brnxwood Av -Bronx 10466 **Fx:**655-9182
(518) 462-6098 .. **Griffiths**, Jos P '96 -352 Hudson Av -Albany 12210
(718) 558-4192 .. **Griffiths**, Patrick A '98 -89-31 161st -Jamaica 11432
(212) 351-4000 .. **Griffiths**, Sean P '93 (Gibson D&C LLP) -200 Park Av -NY 10166
(212) 209-5450 .. **Griffitts**, Robt C '98 (Madama GO LLP) -450 Park Av S -NY 10016 **Fx:**209-5460
(716) 204-2400 .. **Grigg**, Natalie A '03 %SJ Baum,PC -220 Nrthpnte Pkwy Bx1291 -Buffalo 14240 **Fx:**204-4600
(212) 472-8340 .. **Griggs Baldwin & Baldwin** -305 Mad Av -NY 10165 **Fx:**472-8351
(518) 487-5460 .. **Griggs**, Linda M '04 %DA -6 Lodge -Albany 12207 **Fx:**487-5093
(212) 790-4500 .. **Griggs-Pauly**, Leah J '04 %Manatt P&P,LLP -7 Times Sq -NY 10036
(212) 735-3000 .. **Grigoriou**, Steven B '09 %Skadden ASM&F LLP -4 Times Sq -NY 10036
(718) 261-3047 .. **Grigoryan**, Naira '09 Queens Law Assoc -118-21 Qns Blvd -Frst Hlls 11375 **Fx:**261-0798
(212) 373-3000 .. **Grigoryev**, Stanislav '02 %Paul WRW&G LLP -1285 Av of Amer -NY 10019
(212) 431-2100 .. **Grigsby**, Marcey L '07 %NY Law Schl -185 W Bway -NY 10013 **Fx:**406-0103
(212) 839-5300 .. **Grikscheit**, Alyssa A '95 (Sidley A LLP) -787 7th Av -NY 10019
(212) 988-2699 .. **Griliches**, Josef '53 -211 E 79th -NY 10075
(212) 684-0300 .. **Grill**, David M '93 (Bauman K&G LLP) -28 W 44th -NY 10036
(914) 686-1700 .. **Grill**, John P '93 %O'Connor R,LLP -200 Mamaroneck Av -White Plns 10601
(212) 684-0300 .. **Grill**, Jonah C '72 OfCnsl Bauman K&G LLP -28 W 44th -NY 10036
(917) 345-0641 .. **Grill**, Jonathan N '06 Oppenheimer -300 Mad Av -NY 10017
(212) 244-2999 .. **Grill**, Ronnie M '91 (Kopff N&D LLP) -440 9th Av -NY 10001
(212) 657-0135 .. **Grillet-Aubert**, Laura E '85 Salomon Smith Barney -77 Water -NY 10005
(718) 250-2000 .. **Grillo**, Christine M '92 %DA -350 Jay -Brklyn 11201 **Fx:**250-2314
(315) 487-3262 .. **Grillo**, Dana F '82 -5016 W Genesee -Camillus 13031 **Fx:**487-5662
(212) 813-8800 .. **Grillo**, Emanuel C '92 (Goodwin P LLP) -620 8th Av -NY 10018
(212) 252-0004 .. **Grillo**, Emilio F '91 (Carroll M&K LLC) -570 Lex Av -NY 10022
(845) 343-2218 .. **Grillo**, Eugene J '73 -Bx3046 -Middletwn 10940
(716) 634-0500 .. **Grillo**, Thos J Jr. '04 %Ballow Law Firm -8226 Main -Williamsvll 14221 **Fx:**634-9075
(718) 286-6000 .. **Grillo**, Tina '07 DA -125-01 Qns Blvd -Kew Gdns 11415
(718) 298-1219 .. **Grimaldi**, Anna M '95 Hon J Lebowitz -88-11 Sutphin Blvd -Jamaica 11435
(212) 916-4243 .. **Grimaldi**, Anthony L '78 %TIAA-CREF -730 3rd Av -NY 10017
(516) 747-0300 .. **Grimaldi**, Carmelo '89 (Meltzer LG&B,LLP) -190 Willis Av -Mineola 11501
(518) 432-9220 .. **Grimaldi**, Christopher F '95 (Patricia Lynch Assoc Inc) -677 Bway -Albany 12207 **Fx:**432-9186
(212) 408-5100 .. **Grimaldi**, Elizabeth S '08 %Chadbourne & P LLP -30 Rckfllr Plz -NY 10112
(315) 671-2812 .. **Grimaldi**, Frances A '96 City Ct -505 S State -Syracuse 13202
(212) 697-1000 .. **Grimaldi**, James R '83 (Citrin Cooperman & Co,LLP) -529 5th Av -NY 10017 **Fx:**697-9471
(718) 238-6960 .. **Grimaldi**, Judith D '93 (Grimaldi & Y LLP) -9201 4th Av -Brklyn 11209
(845) 849-2596 .. **Grimaldi**, Marion D '93 -18 Old Noxon Rd -Poughkeepsie 12603 **Fx:**485-1971
(718) 828-9288 .. **Grimaldi**, Neil A '74 -2860 Buhre Av -Bronx 10461
(914) 769-1233 .. **Grimaldi**, Phillip A Jr. '89 -245 Saw Mill Rvr Rd -Hawthorne 10532 **Fx:**769-1325
(914) 703-6900 .. **Grimaldi**, Russell W '06 Kinetics Asset Mgmt,Inc -555 Taxter Rd -Elmsfrd 10523 **Fx:**703-6899
(631) 537-1166 .. **Grimaldi**, Stephen D '84 (Burnside & G) -264 Butter Ln Bx1285 -Brdghmptn 11932 **Fx:**537-7348
(718) 238-6960 .. **Grimaldi & Yeung LLP** -9201 4th Av -Brklyn 11209 **Fx:**238-3091
(877) 222-1814 .. **Grimaldo**, Debra J '93 %B Rothenberg -100 Duffy Av -Hicksvll 11801 **Fx:**(866) 894-2182
(212) 349-0450 .. **Grimble & LoGuidice,LLC** -217 Bway -NY 10007 **Fx:**349-0544
(212) 349-0450 .. **Grimble**, Robt '76 (Grimble & L,LLC) -217 Bway -NY 10007
(212) 521-5400 .. **Grimes**, David M '91 (Reed S LLP) -599 Lex Av -NY 10022
(914) 785-5300 .. **Grimes**, Eugene P '89 %A Lamer -555 Taxter Rd -Elmsfrd 10523 **Fx:**347-4269
(718) 948-4555 .. **Grimes**, John F '53 -66 Chelsea -Staten Isl 10307
(212) 570-6375 .. **Grimes**, John J '74 (Grimes & Z) -33 E 70th -NY 10021
(914) 238-1377 .. **Grimes**, John J '74 (Grimes & Z) -16 S Bedford Rd -Chappaqua 10514
(212) 648-1043 .. **Grimes**, John M '94 JP Morgan Chase & Co -245 Park Av -NY 10167
(212) 230-8800 .. **Grimes**, Julia A '09 %WilmerHale -399 Park Av -NY 10022
(212) 839-9345 .. **Grimes**, Julie M '97 -375 S End Av -NY 10280
(212) 956-7168 .. **Grimes**, Robt S '69 -1125 Park Av -NY 10128
(914) 238-1377 .. **Grimes & Zimet** -16 S Bedford Rd -Chappaqua 10514 **Fx:**238-1392
(212) 570-6375 .. **Grimes & Zimet** -33 E 70th -NY 10021 **Fx:**249-9151
(212) 399-2420 .. **Grimm**, David G '94 C2 Media -423 W 55th -NY 10019
(212) 326-3939 .. **Grimm**, I Lewis H '04 %Jones D -222 E 41st -NY 10017
(212) 374-0209 .. **Grimm**, Kathleen '81 NY Dept of Ed -52 Chmbrs -NY 10007
(212) 431-3000 .. **Grimm**, Lawr E '70 -11 Beach -NY 10013
(716) 856-3500 .. **Grimm**, Richd A Jr. '59 (Magavern MG LLP) -1100 Rand Bldg -Buffalo 14203
(716) 856-3500 .. **Grimm**, Richd A III '87 (Magavern MG LLP) -1100 Rand Bldg -Buffalo 14203
(212) 416-8280 .. **Grimm**, Richd E '73 %Dept of Law -120 Bway -NY 10271 **Fx:**416-6015
(716) 856-3500 .. **Grimm**, Robt W Jr. '75 (Magavern MG LLP) -1100 Rand Bldg -Buffalo 14203
(212) 859-8000 .. **Grimm**, Sebastian '06 %Fried FHS&J LLP -1 NY Plz -NY 10004
(845) 291-2050 .. **Grimmer**, Kelle K '98 %DA -255-275 Main -Goshen 10924 **Fx:**291-2085
(518) 271-6170 .. **Grimmick**, Eugene P '78 -52 2nd -Troy 12180
(518) 465-2333 .. **Grimmick**, Noreen De Wire '92 (Hodgson R LLP) -677 Bway -Albany 12207
(212) 541-0600 .. **Grimmig**, Diane M '87 KBC Bk -1177 Av of Amer -NY 10036
(212) 701-3000 .. **Grimshaw**, Wm S '10 %Cahill G&R LLP -80 Pine -NY 10005 **Fx:**269-5420
(602) 364-7117 .. **Grimsley**, J Alexander '92 (Bryan C LLP) -1290 Av of Amer -NY 10104 **Fx:**716-8117
(212) 735-7808 .. **Grinalds**, Maura B '92 (Skadden ASM&F LLP) -4 Times Sq -NY 10036
(212) 504-6000 .. **Grinberg**, Aleksandra '08 %Cadwalader W&T LLP -1 World Fncl Ctr -NY 10281
(212) 202-0342 .. **Grinberg**, Eliza '99 (Grinberg & S,PLLC) -111 Bway -NY 10006 **Fx:**(718) 228-9601
(212) 994-0260 .. **Grinberg**, Kristine L '02 %Cornicello T&B-C,LLP -2 Wall -NY 10005
(212) 858-1000 .. **Grinblat**, Danielle '10 %Pillsbury WSP LLP -1540 Bway -NY 10036
(212) 921-2200 .. **Grinblat**, Michl '03 Update Legal -1140 Av of Amer -NY 10036
(212) 474-1000 .. **Grinceri**, Alan G '09 %Cravath S&M LLP -825 8th Av -NY 10019
(212) 318-6000 .. **Grindlinger**, Glenn S '00 %Paul HJ&W LLP -75 E 55th -NY 10022
(518) 438-1415 .. **Griner**, James J '71 -474 New Scotland Av -Albany 12208
(212) 536-8426 .. **Grinfeld**, Mark '03 Hess Corp -1185 Av of Amer -NY 10036
(516) 228-3131 .. **Gringer**, Martin '76 (Franklin G&C,PC) -666 Old Cntry Rd -Gdn Cty 11530
(315) 475-8893 .. **Grinnals**, R Danl '89 -Bx6066 -Syracuse 13217 **Fx:**475-8897
(585) 546-5530 .. **Grinols**, Elinor I '97 %Thomson West -50 E Broad -Rchstr 14694
(646) 315-7344 .. **Grinsberg**, Howard A '77 %FINRA -14 Wall -NY 10005 **Fx:**315-7440
(718) 237-5500 .. **Grinthal**, Michl '08 %Leg Srvcs -105 Court -Brklyn 11201 **Fx:**855-0733

(212) 701-3000 .. **Grippando,** Elisabeth P '08 %Cahill G&R LLP -80 Pine -NY 10005 **Fx:**269-5420
(516) 571-3056 .. **Grippo,** Danl P '84 %Cnty Atty -1 West -Mineola 11501 **Fx:**571-6604
(212) 216-8000 .. **Grippo,** Jonathan A '08 %Tarter K&D LLP -1350 Bway -NY 10018
(516) 712-4000 .. **Grisafi,** John P '95 (Milber MP&S LLP) -1000 Woodbury Rd -Woodbury 11797
(212) 425-3100 .. **Grisales,** Lisbeth '05 -48 Wall -NY 10005 **Fx:**425-3175
(212) 374-0680 .. **Grisanti,** Anthony M '00 %Rimland & Assoc -225 Bway -NY 10007 **Fx:**374-0681
(716) 843-5818 .. **Grisanti,** Marie P '93 %US Atty -138 Delaware Av -Buffalo 14202 **Fx:**551-3052
(716) 883-0400 .. **Grisanti,** Mark J '93 -577 Niagara -Buffalo 14201 **Fx:**883-0068
(716) 883-0400 .. **Grisanti,** Richd D '57 -577 Niagara -Buffalo 14201 **Fx:**883-0068
(518) 487-7600 .. **Grisaru,** Elizabeth A '89 OfCnsl Whiteman O&H LLP -1 Commerce Plz -Albany 12260
(212) 659-7300 .. **Grishman,** Alexander T '07 %Haynes & B,LLP -1221 Av of Amer -NY 10020
(212) 563-4100 .. **Grisi,** James R '89 (Cohen W&S LLP) -330 W 42nd -NY 10036
(212) 819-8200 .. **Griskonis,** Marius '06 %White & C LLP -1155 Av of Amer -NY 10036
(315) 386-4586 .. **Griskonis,** Susan '07 %Leg Aid -17 Hodskin Bx648 -Canton 13617 **Fx:**386-2868
(212) 446-2300 .. **Grisolia,** Michl S '09 %Boies S&F LLP -575 Lex Av -NY 10022
(212) 455-2000 .. **Griswold,** Andrea M '08 %Simpson T&B LLP -425 Lex Av -NY 10017
(607) 432-9159 .. **Griswold,** Jeffrey C '98 -652 East -Oneonta 13820
(212) 940-8800 .. **Griswold,** Michelle K '09 %Katten MR LLP -575 Mad Av -NY 10022
(212) 449-1329 .. **Griswold,** Zdenka Seiner '92 %Merrill Lynch -220 Bway -NY 10038
(518) 485-2604 .. **Gritsavage,** Wm H '73 Dept of Tax & Fin -WA Harriman Campus -Albany 12227
(212) 223-0400 .. **Griver,** Yoav M '92 (Zeichner E&K LLP) -575 Lex Av -NY 10022
(315) 471-8111 .. **Grizanti,** Anthony J '85 (Scolaro SCF&B,PC) -507 Plum -Syracuse 13204
(516) 766-1619 .. **Grizopoulos,** Gregory '03 %Dergarabedian D & Assoc -11 Clinton Av -Rockvll Ctr 11570 **Fx:**766-6121
(516) 485-1647 .. **Grizzel,** John S '99 -2074 N Jerusalem Rd -N Bellmore 11710 **Fx:**485-1647
(212) 261-8000 .. **Groarke,** Brendan E '04 %Mendes & M,LLP -750 7th Av -NY 10019
(516) 248-5757 .. **Groarke,** Edw J '80 (Colleran O&M,LLP) -1225 Franklin Av -Gdn Cty 11530
(516) 678-7100 .. **Groarke,** Ellen W '02 %G Lisi -55 Front -Rockvll Ctr 11570 **Fx:**536-9548
(212) 504-6000 .. **Groarke,** Gillian P '07 %Cadwalader W&T LLP -1 World Fncl Ctr -NY 10281
(718) 478-0600 .. **Groarke,** John C '58 -69-64 Grand Av -Maspeth 11378 **Fx:**478-0609
(516) 248-5757 .. **Groarke,** John S '02 (Colleran O&M,LLP) -1225 Franklin Av -Gdn Cty 11530
(212) 768-6700 .. **Groarke,** Kevin P '78 (Sonnenschein N&R LLP) -2 World Fncl Ctr -NY 10281
(516) 571-1465 .. **Grob,** A Jeffrey '78 %Supreme Ct -100 Supreme Ct Dr -Mineola 11501
(212) 697-3250 .. **Grob,** Jos A '88 (Goldberg & R PLLC) -115 Bway -NY 10006 **Fx:**227-4533
(718) 250-2000 .. **Grob,** Rhea Turok '89 %DA -350 Jay -Brklyn 11201 **Fx:**250-2314
(212) 351-4500 .. **Groban,** Robt S '75 (Epstein B&G,PC) -250 Park Av -NY 10177
(914) 946-2311 .. **Grobe,** Bruce J '77 G1 Lgl & Cnsltng -43 Winslow Rd -White Plns 10606 **Fx:**946-2311
(631) 751-1111 .. **Grobe,** Christine E '78 (Grobe & W,LP) -1344 Stony Brk Rd -Stony Brk 11790
(631) 751-1111 .. **Grobe & Wenz,LP** -1344 Stony Brk Rd -Stony Brk 11790 **Fx:**689-2318
(315) 428-4633 .. **Groben,** Michl T '85 Div Human Rights -333 E Wshngtn -Syracuse 13202
(718) 858-4880 .. **Groberg,** Susan F '86 -186 Joralemon -Brklyn 11201 **Fx:**858-9570
(212) 903-9000 .. **Grobins,** Mara '07 %Linklaters -1345 Av of Amer -NY 10105
(516) 483-2400 .. **Grobman,** Paul S '88 %Dan's Supreme Supermarkets -474 Fulton Av -Hempstd 11550
(212) 691-9000 .. **Grobman,** Sharyn L '94 Wideband -39 W 29th -NY 10001
(845) 562-2990 .. **Grobstein,** Gene L '83 -10 Little Britain Rd -Newburgh 12550 **Fx:**562-0166
(845) 888-5285 .. **Grobusch,** George H '95 -14 Brook Bx412 -Wurtsboro 12790
(212) 608-4400 .. **Grochow,** Robt A '75 (Wilson GD&N) -233 Bway -NY 10279
(716) 881-6400 .. **Grocott,** Steven H '06 (Moriarty & G) -1109 Delaware Av -Buffalo 14209 **Fx:**881-4861
(212) 869-3200 .. **Grodberg,** Mark S '00 %Molod S&D,PC -104 W 40th -NY 10018
(212) 682-5221 .. **Grodd,** Nancy S '85 First NY Realty -331 Mad Av -NY 10017 **Fx:**682-0151
(212) 986-0933 .. **Grodd,** Robt '01 %RG Tax & Fncl Svcs -FDR Station Bx1008 -NY 10150
(516) 883-2071 .. **Grodensky,** Steven P '01 (Grodensky Law Grp,PLLC) -8 Haven Av -Pt Wash 11050 **Fx:**883-1419
(516) 248-8090 .. **Groder,** Jeffrey S '90 (Devane & G) -114 Old Cntry Rd -Mineola 11501 **Fx:**248-8089
(973) 596-4553 .. **Grodin,** Andrew M '04 %Gibbons PC -1 Penn Plz -NY 10119 **Fx:**639-8355
(212) 221-6556 .. **Grodman,** Ian R '93 (IR Grodman,PC) -116 John -NY 10038 **Fx:**505-8455
(212) 947-9779 .. **Grodner,** Robyn '00 %Advocates for Chldrn of NY -151 W 30th -NY 10001
(718) 222-8880 .. **Grodsky,** Marc A '93 %Jones JO -45 Main -Brklyn 11201
(212) 861-0759 .. **Grody,** Michl J '00 -301 E 75th -NY 10021
(212) 790-4500 .. **Grodzinski,** Ronny '95 %Manatt P&P,LLP -7 Times Sq -NY 10036
(718) 868-8645 .. **Groebner,** Ruth M '00 %ACQC -1600 Central Av -Far Rckwy 11691
(212) 557-7200 .. **Groeneveld,** Maria A '00 %Davidoff M&H,LLP -605 3rd Av -NY 10158
(518) 457-3701 .. **Groenwegen,** Nancy '84 %Dept Civil Srvc -Harriman Campus Bldg 1 -Albany 12239 **Fx:**457-6654
(518) 474-1394 .. **Groenwegen,** Paul '84 %Dept of Law -The Cptl -Albany 12224
(607) 739-3601 .. **Groff,** John G '77 -1 Hanover Sq -Horseheads 14845 **Fx:**739-5317
(212) 805-6140 .. **Groff,** Mari E '04 %Hon J Sprizzo -40 Centre -NY 10007
(607) 739-3602 .. **Groff,** Robt A Jr. '76 -1 Hanover Sq -Horseheads 14845 **Fx:**739-5317
(212) 756-2000 .. **Groff,** Sami '98 %Schulte R&Z LLP -919 3rd Av -NY 10022
(212) 759-2300 .. **Groffman,** Elliot Jay '80 (Carroll G&G,LLP) -1790 Bway -NY 10019
(212) 756-2000 .. **Grofman,** Udi '02 (Schulte R&Z LLP) -919 3rd Av -NY 10022
(716) 845-2113 .. **Grogan,** Bruce D '99 Hon E Pigott Jr - Ct of Appls -438 Main -Buffalo 14202
(212) 770-2480 .. **Grogan,** Dennis W '89 %AIG Tech Srvcs -80 Pine -NY 10005
(518) 664-9200 .. **Grogan,** Edw J '53 -Bx394 -Clifton Pk 12065 **Fx:**664-1207
(518) 431-0247 .. **Grogan,** Edw P '93 %US Atty -445 Bway -Albany 12207 **Fx:**431-0249
(518) 449-8893 .. **Grogan,** Elizabeth J '04 %Wilson EME&D LLP -677 Bway -Albany 12207
(845) 294-6155 .. **Grogan,** Gerard T '71 (Grogan & S,PC) -14 Scotchtown Av Bx330 -Goshen 10924
(212) 455-2000 .. **Grogan,** Gregory T '01 (Simpson T&B LLP) -425 Lex Av -NY 10017
(212) 318-6000 .. **Grogan,** James T '08 %Paul HJ&W LLP -75 E 55th -NY 10022
(716) 834-9181 .. **Grogan,** Julie M '99 %Blair & R,LLP -2645 Sheridan Dr -Tonawanda 14150
(518) 483-4480 .. **Grogan,** Owens D '59 -362 W Main -Malone 12953 **Fx:**483-3625
(718) 680-0585 .. **Grogan,** Sean '89 -549 83rd -Brklyn 11209
(845) 294-6155 .. **Grogan & Souto,PC** -14 Scotchtown Av Bx330 -Goshen 10924 **Fx:**294-3866
(718) 990-2049 .. **Grogan,** Teresa J '90 %St John's Law Schl -8000 Utopia Pkwy -Jamaica 11439 **Fx:**591-1855
(914) 762-2944 .. **Grogan,** Thos F '69 -50 Clinton Av -Ossining 10562
(212) 336-2038 .. **Grogin,** Stephanie L '88 Patterson BW&T LLP -1133 Av of Amer -NY 10036
(914) 934-1700 .. **Groglio,** George M '82 -219 Wstchstr Av -Pt Chester 10573
(516) 827-4300 .. **Groh,** Wm M '97 %Naness C&N LLC -375 N Bway -Jericho 11753
(212) 692-1000 .. **Grohman,** Michl D '84 (Duane M LLP) -1540 Bway -NY 10036
(212) 909-6551 .. **Grohmann,** Noelle Duarte '09 %Debevoise & P LLP -919 3rd Av -NY 10022 **Fx:**521-7551
(716) 326-3700 .. **Grohol,** Mark W '91 -29 Wood -Westfld 14787
(212) 461-2323 .. **Grohs,** Michl J '05 %Saiber LLC -44 Wall -NY 10005
(212) 735-3000 .. **Grohsgal,** James '09 %Skadden ASM&F LLP -4 Times Sq -NY 10036
(212) 259-8000 .. **Groll,** Michl '79 (Dewey & L LLP) -1301 Av of Amer -NY 10019
(212) 225-2000 .. **Groll,** Wm A '84 (Cleary GS&H) -1 Lbrty Plz -NY 10006
(212) 506-1700 .. **Grollman,** Laurin B '97 SpclCnsl Kasowitz BT&F LLP -1633 Bway -NY 10019
(516) 742-4343 .. **Grolz,** Edw W '85 (Scully SM&P PC) -400 Grdn City Plz -Gdn Cty 11530
(718) 852-1196 .. **Groman,** Paul B '98 -188 Montague -Brklyn 11201 **Fx:**852-9678
(516) 248-1700 .. **Groman,** Robt H '65 (Forchelli CDSM&T,LLP) -333 Earle Ovngton Blvd -Uniondale 11553
(212) 697-7220 .. **Groman,** Ronald B '89 %Stein SC&R,LLP -140 E 45th -NY 10017
(516) 626-8750 .. **Groman,** Tod '76 -75 Cedar Dr -Roslyn 11576 **Fx:**626-8752
(518) 424-1779 .. **Gromet,** Roger '83 -Bx1005 -Clifton Pk 12065
(914) 234-6363 .. **Gronbach,** Vanessa '02 Kuntz S&M,PC -444 Old Post Rd -Bedfrd 10506 **Fx:**234-6249
(718) 891-1200 .. **Groner,** Philip M '86 -2115 Av U -Brklyn 11229 **Fx:**891-2274
(212) 859-8000 .. **Groner,** Saml P '07 %Fried FHS&J LLP -1 NY Plz -NY 10004
(914) 686-3700 .. **Groner,** Wm H '81 (Worby GE LLP) -11 Martine Av -White Plns 10606
(631) 805-8436 .. **Gronich,** Kim Bari '94 -78 Bagatelle Rd -Melvll 11747 **Fx:**980-3534
(631) 439-2450 .. **Groom,** Diane B '99 %Leg Aid -320 Carleton Av -Central Islip 11722 **Fx:**439-2453
(212) 310-8000 .. **Groombridge,** Nicholas P '89 (Weil G&M LLP) -767 5th Av -NY 10153
(212) 438-1349 .. **Grooms,** James E '93 Jazz at Lincoln Ctr -33 W 60th -NY 10023
(212) 812-8910 .. **Groopman,** Steven L '10 %Lankler & C,LLP -845 3rd Av -NY 10022
(212) 474-1000 .. **Groot,** Patricia M '10 %Cravath S&M LLP -825 8th Av -NY 10019
(212) 344-5400 .. **Groothuis,** Erik S '98 OfCnsl Schlam S&D LLP -26 Bway -NY 10004
(516) 486-8500 .. **Groothuis,** Mark L '67 -64 Hilton Av -Hempstd 11550 **Fx:**486-8995
(845) 794-1744 .. **Groper,** Eric J '68 -541 Bway Bx980 -Monticello 12701 **Fx:**794-8614
(212) 682-0020 .. **Groppe,** Chas J '59 OfCnsl Putney TH&H LLP -521 5th Av -NY 10175
(718) 590-2000 .. **Groppe,** Jessica S '09 %DA -198 E 161st -Bronx 10451 **Fx:**590-6477
(212) 417-5300 .. **Gropper,** Andrew J '03 %Medicaid Fraud Cntrl -120 Bway -NY 10271 **Fx:**417-5274
(212) 366-4600 .. **Gropper,** Joshua D '92 (Brown & G,LLP) -275 7th Av -NY 10001
(212) 431-2172 .. **Grosberg,** Lawr M '69 %NY Law Schl -185 W Bway -NY 10013 **Fx:**966-2053
(516) 571-9041 .. **Grosch,** Kimberly '03 %Cnty Atty -1200 Old Cntry Rd -Westbury 11590
(585) 987-2800 .. **Groschadl,** Paul S '76 (Woods OG LLP) -2 State -Rchstr 14614
(718) 590-2000 .. **Grosdidier,** Maureen Lee '09 %DA -198 E 161st -Bronx 10451 **Fx:**590-6477
(212) 909-6000 .. **Grosgold,** David '05 %Debevoise & P LLP -919 3rd Av -NY 10022
(518) 373-9891 .. **Grosky,** Mark Brian '96 -634 Plnk Rd -Clifton Pk 12065 **Fx:**373-9892
(585) 473-8810 .. **Grosodonia,** Michl R '79 -233 San Gabriel Dr -Rchstr 14610
(516) 741-4170 .. **Gross,** Aaron C '99 %Bongiorno Law Firm,PLLC -250 Mineola Blvd -Mineola 11501 **Fx:**741-4240
(716) 204-9480 .. **Gross,** Adam L '05 SJ Baum,PC -900 Merchants Cncrs -Westbury 11590 **Fx:**204-9680
(718) 590-3784 .. **Gross,** Alan H '82 %Hon G Friedman -851 Grnd Cncrs -Bronx 10451
(212) 483-1444 .. **Gross,** Allen I '78 -50 Bway -NY 10004 **Fx:**483-1480
(213) 892-5067 .. **Gross,** Amiel S '03 %Sonnenschein N&R LLP -2 World Fncl Ctr -NY 10281
(212) 418-8600 .. **Gross,** Amy C '03 %Kornstein VW&P,LLP -757 3rd Av -NY 10017
(212) 227-8140 .. **Gross,** Anthony G '62 (A Gross,PC) -30 Vesey -NY 10007 **Fx:**385-0662
(347) 866-2274 .. **Gross,** Ari Michl '92 (AM Gross,PC) -47 Oliver Rd -Bedfrd 10506 **Fx:**(914) 205-3416
(718) 447-8006 .. **Gross,** Avery J '64 -30 Bay -Staten Isl 10301

(212) 583-9600 .. **Gross**, Barbara Ann '97 (Littler M,PC) -900 3rd Av -NY 10022
(516) 579-3700 .. **Gross**, Barry J '72 (Parola & G) -775 Wantagh Av -Wantagh 11793
(212) 877-8109 .. **Gross**, Beverly '68 -525 West End Av -NY 10024 **Fx:**877-3364
(212) 768-6700 .. **Gross**, Brett L '00 %Sonnenschein N&R LLP -2 World Fncl Ctr -NY 10281
(585) 232-7870 .. **Gross**, Bryon W '99 -45 Exchange Blvd -Rchstr 14614 **Fx:**232-7618
(845) 352-9240 .. **Gross**, David E '92 (Finkelstein & Prtnrs,LLP) -296 Main -Spg Vly 10977
(212) 720-2356 .. **Gross**, David L '96 Federal Reserve Bk -33 Lbrty -NY 10045
(718) 625-2805 .. **Gross**, David M '51 (Leopold G&S,PC) -16 Court -Brklyn 11241
(631) 368-4244 .. **Gross**, David M '94 -36 Meadowrue Ln -E Northprt 11731
(212) 461-2323 .. **Gross**, David R '82 (Saiber LLC) -44 Wall -NY 10005
(212) 596-9000 .. **Gross**, David Z '06 %Ropes & G LLP -1211 Av of Amer -NY 10036
(646) 315-7300 .. **Gross**, Dorian M '85 %FINRA -14 Wall -NY 10005 **Fx:**315-7440
(212) 944-0500 .. **Gross**, Douglas A '81 (Hofheimer G&G,LLP) -530 5th Av -NY 10036 **Fx:**897-4995
(516) 483-4580 .. **Gross**, Efrom J '88 -713 Wildwood Rd -W Hempstead 11552
(718) 787-0304 .. **Gross**, Efrom J '88 -703 Av U -Brklyn 11223 **Fx:**627-5314
(212) 788-0512 .. **Gross**, Elizabeth Dale '81 %Law Dept -100 Church -NY 10007 **Fx:**788-0367
(516) 536-2900 .. **Gross**, Elliot S '49 (Gross & G LLP) -371 Merrick Rd -Rockvll Ctr 11570 **Fx:**536-2870
(973) 228-5700 .. **Gross**, Eric W '06 %Brach E LLC -100 Park Av -NY 10017 **Fx:**228-7852
(516) 229-6000 .. **Gross**, Faye L '87 %R Lau & Assoc -300 Jericho Quad Bx9040 -Jericho 11753 **Fx:**229-6167
(516) 371-2800 .. **Gross**, Gerald P '92 GP Gross,PC -366 Pearsall Av -Cedarhrst 11516
(716) 854-4300 .. **Gross**, Gordon R '57 (Gross SB&G,PC) -465 Main -Buffalo 14203
(914) 699-1919 .. **Gross**, Hannah S '82 (Gross S&S LLP) -9 W Prospect Av -Mt Vernon 10550 **Fx:**699-6106
(212) 317-1133 .. **Gross**, Henry '79 %Realex Capital -444 Mad Av -NY 10022
(516) 877-2424 .. **Gross**, Howard R '75 (Weinberg G&P LLP) -400 Grdn City Plz -Gdn Cty 11530
(212) 968-2300 .. **Gross**, Jack '87 OfCnsl Chartwell Law Ofc,LLP -39 Bway -NY 10006 **Fx:**968-2400
(516) 571-5079 .. **Gross**, Jackie L '89 %Cnty Atty -100 Cnty Seat Dr -Mineola 11501
(718) 263-9292 .. **Gross**, Jacob '08 %W Slutsky,PC -118-21 Qns Blvd -Frst Hlls 11375 **Fx:**263-4817
(518) 432-1200 .. **Gross**, James E '86 OfCnsl McGlinchey S PLLC -194 Wshngtn Av -Albany 12210
(212) 330-1000 .. **Gross**, Jamie M '94 Buck Consultants -1 Penn Plz -NY 10119 **Fx:**695-4184
(212) 906-1200 .. **Gross**, Jared M '09 %Latham & W -885 3rd Av -NY 10022
(516) 504-1500 .. **Gross**, Jeffrey '82 -111 Grt Nck Rd -Gt Neck 11021
(212) 763-6800 .. **Gross**, Jeffrey E '00 OfCnsl Vandenberg & F,LLP -60 E 42nd -NY 10165
(845) 473-8210 .. **Gross**, Jeffrey J '89 %OMRDD HRPC Brookside -36 Firemans Way -Poughkeepsie 12603
(212) 829-9783 .. **Gross**, Jildy H '85 %J Gross & Assoc,Inc -515 Mad Av -NY 10022
(914) 422-4061 .. **Gross**, Jill I '91 %Pace Law Schl -78 N Bway -White Plns 10603 **Fx:**422-4039
(212) 521-3500 .. **Gross**, Jillian E '04 %Aronson M&S, LLP -485 Lex Av -NY 10017
(212) 415-9200 .. **Gross**, Joan B '83 Dorsey & W LLP -250 Park Av -NY 10177
(212) 969-3000 .. **Gross**, John H '68 (Proskauer R LLP) -1585 Bway -NY 10036
(631) 261-8834 .. **Gross**, John H '72 (Ingerman S LLP) -150 Motor Pkwy -Hauppauge 11788
(212) 682-8552 .. **Gross**, John M '64 -51 E 42nd -NY 10017 **Fx:**983-3228
(315) 443-4582 .. **Gross**, John P '01 Syracuse Univ Cllg of Law -Ofc of Clinical Leg Educ Bx6543 -Syracuse 13217
(212) 335-9000 .. **Gross**, Jonathan L '01 %DA -1 Hogan Pl -NY 10013
(212) 506-5000 .. **Gross**, Jonathan R '99 %Orrick H&S LLP -51 W 52nd -NY 10019
(718) 263-7915 .. **Gross**, Jos A '89 -73-59 Park Dr E -Flushng 11367
(516) 692-8888 .. **Gross**, Jos B '04 %F Chau & Assoc,LLC -130 Woodbury Rd -Woodbury 11797 **Fx:**692-8889
(917) 375-6852 .. **Gross**, Judith E '86 JG Advisory Svcs LLC -200 E 27th -NY 10016
(212) 431-2154 .. **Gross**, Karen '82 %NY Law Schl -185 W Bway -NY 10013 **Fx:**431-1864
(212) 869-3500 .. **Gross**, Keith H '82 %J Fuchsberg Law Firm,LLP -500 5th Av -NY 10110 **Fx:**398-1532
(212) 492-2106 .. **Gross**, Keith J '07 Local 6 Unite Here -709 8th Av -NY 10036
(516) 222-5383 .. **Gross**, Kenneth '91 Pace Prof Srvcs -585 Stewart Av -Gdn Cty 11530
(718) 429-2021 .. **Gross**, Lawr J '63 (Gross & L LLP) -86-26 Qns Blvd -Elmhrst 11373
(516) 488-8811 .. **Gross**, Lawr K '85 Cnsl STG Assoc -1010 Nrthrn Blvd -Gt Neck 11021 **Fx:**488-8611
(212) 741-7009 .. **Gross**, Leigh B '99 Classic Media,Inc -860 Bway -NY 10003
(718) 429-2021 .. **Gross & Levin LLP** -86-26 Qns Blvd -Elmhrst 11373 **Fx:**565-5729
(516) 292-8100 .. **Gross**, Lorraine H '82 %Nassau/Sffk Law Srv -1 Helen Keller Way -Hempstd 11550 **Fx:**292-6529
(212) 267-7580 .. **Gross**, Malcolm '62 OfCnsl Adler & G -155 E 55th -NY 10022 **Fx:**546-9270
(212) 661-1100 .. **Gross**, Marc I '77 (Pomerantz HG&G LLP) -100 Park Av -NY 10017
(212) 709-1640 .. **Gross**, Marjorie E '74 Banking Dept -1 State -NY 10004 **Fx:**709-1655
(212) 599-1717 .. **Gross**, Mark H '85 (Barnett EGK&L,PC) -122 E 42nd -NY 10168
(212) 813-8800 .. **Gross**, Marta E '88 (Goodwin P LLP) -620 8th Av -NY 10018
(516) 536-2900 .. **Gross**, Martin B '77 (Gross & G LLP) -371 Merrick Rd -Rockvll Ctr 11570 **Fx:**536-2870
(212) 558-4000 .. **Gross**, Matthew R '09 %Sullivan & C LLP -125 Broad -NY 10004
(212) 788-0854 .. **Gross**, Melissa L '06 %ACS -220 Church -NY 10013
(212) 708-1800 .. **Gross**, Meyer A '61 OfCnsl Ladas & P -26 W 61st -NY 10023
(631) 281-6440 .. **Gross**, Michl '60 -198 Crestwood Dr -Shirley 11967 **Fx:**281-6493
(516) 612-3678 .. **Gross**, Michl A '89 MA Gross,PC -445 Central Av -Cedarhrst 11516 **Fx:**612-3679
(212) 563-5904 .. **Gross**, Michl S '00 Authors Guild -116 W 23rd -NY 10011
(718) 853-5763 .. **Gross**, Milton J '86 -1381 51st -Brklyn 11219
(212) 872-1000 .. **Gross**, Miriam Yael '07 -One Bryant Park -NY 10036 **Fx:**872-1002
(212) 709-1640 .. **Gross**, Mordechai '10 Banking Dept -1 State -NY 10004 **Fx:**709-1655
(212) 401-4040 .. **Gross**, Morton A '74 %Teplen & Assoc,PLLC -350 5th Av -NY 10118 **Fx:**401-4041
(212) 532-4000 .. **Gross**, Nina S '96 (Dobrish ZG LLP) -757 3rd Av -NY 10017
(212) 944-0500 .. **Gross**, Norman '54 (Hofheimer G&G,LLP) -530 5th Av -NY 10036 **Fx:**869-4930
(315) 437-7600 .. **Gross**, Norman H '74 %Ferrara FLB&R,PC -5010 Campuswood Dr -E Syracuse 13057
(212) 619-4350 .. **Gross**, Olivia M '86 (Newman MKGH,PC) -14 Wall -NY 10005
(212) 474-1000 .. **Gross**, Paget H '92 Cravath S&M LLP -825 8th Av -NY 10019
(718) 625-2805 .. **Gross**, Paul R '84 (Leopold G&S,PC) -16 Court -Brklyn 11241
(212) 836-8000 .. **Gross**, Philip J '09 %Kaye S LLP -425 Park Av -NY 10022
(212) 986-6000 .. **Gross**, Philip S '90 (Kleinberg KW&C,PC) -551 5th Av -NY 10176
(212) 608-3103 .. **Gross**, Richd A '70 (Rubert & G,PC) -150 Bway -NY 10038
(917) 974-6717 .. **Gross**, Richd B '75 Goldenrich Films,LLC -1112 Park Av -NY 10128
(585) 428-5210 .. **Gross**, Richd R '06 %Pub Def -10 N Fitzhugh -Rchstr 14614 **Fx:**428-2234
(212) 779-9910 .. **Gross**, Robt K '82 (Eaton & V LLP) -3 Park Av -NY 10016
(914) 214-8744 .. **Gross**, Robt S '91 OfCnsl GL Vila,PC -1820 Commerce -Yorktwn Hts 10598 **Fx:**214-8737
(914) 761-0010 .. **Gross**, Robin B '78 Wm Paul & Assoc -27 Holland Av -White Plns 10603 **Fx:**761-0508
(212) 326-3939 .. **Gross**, Ronald S '89 (Jones D) -222 E 41st -NY 10017
(516) 569-7730 .. **Gross**, Ronit '85 -53 Cedarhurst Av -Lawrence 11559
(212) 921-7171 .. **Gross**, Ronnie '93 G Holdings Corp -214 W 39th -NY 10018 **Fx:**921-7112
(914) 333-9361 .. **Gross**, Russell I '95 %Philips Electronics -345 Scarborough Rd Bx3001 -Briarclff Mnr 10510 **Fx:**332-0615
(845) 292-4460 .. **Gross**, S Richd '57 (Gross G&G) -9 Maple Bx245 -Liberty 12754 **Fx:**292-3035
(718) 222-2079 .. **Gross**, Sara R '10 %Law Dept -350 Jay -Brklyn 11201 **Fx:**222-2088
(516) 742-9099 .. **Gross**, Scott D '87 -151 Willis Av -Mineola 11501 **Fx:**742-9199
(631) 853-4104 .. **Gross**, Scott E '07 DA -400 Carleton Av Bx9082 -Central Islip 11722 **Fx:**853-7838
(212) 298-5014 .. **Gross**, Seth D '95 %Leg Aid -49 Thomas -NY 10013 **Fx:**298-5252
(212) 300-1100 .. **Gross**, Shprintzy Susan '00 %Clair G LLP -555 Mad Av -NY 10022 **Fx:**300-1111
(716) 854-4300 .. **Gross Shuman Brizdle & Gilfillan, PC** -465 Main -Buffalo 14203 **Fx:**854-2787
(212) 909-6000 .. **Gross**, Steven R '74 (Debevoise & P LLP) -919 3rd Av -NY 10022
(212) 697-9400 .. **Gross**, Stewart F '96 %Cheifetz IM,PC -275 Mad Av -NY 10016
(212) 903-8700 .. **Gross**, Stuart J '83 (Roberts & H,LLP) -825 8th Av -NY 10019
(845) 791-8600 .. **Gross**, Susan L '94 -10 St John -Monticello 12701 **Fx:**791-8602
(415) 544-0200 .. **Gross**, Terry '84 OfCnsl Rabinowitz BSK&L,PC -111 Bway -NY 10006 **Fx:**544-0201
(212) 609-6800 .. **Gross**, Valerie A '07 %McCarter & E,LLP -245 Park Av -NY 10167
(212) 530-5000 .. **Gross**, Wm P '08 %Milbank TH&M LLP -1 Chase Manh Plz -NY 10005
(212) 468-8000 .. **Gross**, Yaacov M '81 (Morrison & F LLP) -1290 Av of Amer -NY 10104
(212) 326-2000 .. **Gross**, Zack H '09 %O'Melveny & M LLP -7 Times Sq -NY 10036
(914) 631-6666 .. **Grossbach**, Candice Sari '02 %M Grossbach,PC -800 Wstchstr Av -Rye Brook 10573 **Fx:**524-7070
(914) 468-0400 .. **Grossbach**, Ira L '92 Ganer Grossbach & Ganer,PC -800 Wstchstr Av -Pt Chester 10573
(914) 631-6666 .. **Grossbach**, Martin '62 (M Grossbach,PC) -800 Wstchstr Av -Rye Brook 10573 **Fx:**524-7070
(212) 474-1000 .. **Grossbard**, Lillian S '98 Cravath S&M LLP -825 8th Av -NY 10019
(914) 949-8214 .. **Grossbard**, Richd R '87 (Feinman & G,PC) -19 Court Plz -White Plns 10601 **Fx:**949-0379
(212) 382-0386 .. **Grossbard**, Stanley M '83 -15 W 47th -NY 10036
(212) 542-8882 .. **Grossbardt**, Jonah A '08 %Roth Law Firm,PLLC -295 Mad Av -NY 10017 **Fx:**542-8883
(845) 429-5607 .. **Grossbarth**, Joel A '94 (Tognino & G,LLP) -50 Route 9W -Stony Pnt 10980 **Fx:**429-2576
(212) 554-0400 .. **Grossberg**, Bruce G '83 OfCnsl Grubman I&S,PC -152 W 57th -NY 10019
(212) 688-6940 .. **Grossberg**, David '51 Cohen & G -770 Lex Av -NY 10065 **Fx:**755-4199
(212) 312-4894 .. **Grossberg**, Henry Gordon '91 -401 E 34th -NY 10016
(212) 751-3001 .. **Grossberg**, Marc E '06 (Thompson & K LLP) -919 3rd Av -NY 10022
(212) 741-7641 .. **Grossberg**, Paul D '03 CMS Inc -19 W 21st -NY 10010
(212) 381-5541 .. **Grossberg**, Robt S '96 %Doubleclick Inc -111 8th Av -NY 10011
(516) 496-8494 .. **Grossblatt**, Dana L '92 -471 N Bway -Jericho 11753
(212) 788-8720 .. **Grossel**, Jeffrey N '73 %Sheriff's Ofc -31 Chmbrs -NY 10007 **Fx:**766-9666
(212) 820-9423 .. **Grosser**, Ronald C '83 (Hawkins D&W LLP) -One Chase Manh Plz -NY 10005
(212) 264-3650 .. **Grossfeld**, Sandra M '82 %SSA Ofc Genl Cnsl -26 Fed Plz -NY 10278 **Fx:**264-6372
(212) 799-8080 .. **Grosshandler**, Arthur J '76 -28 W 88th -NY 10024 **Fx:**799-6999
(212) 225-2000 .. **Grosshandler**, Seth '84 (Cleary GS&H) -1 Lbrty Plz -NY 10006
(212) 318-2000 .. **Grosshans**, Laura S '08 Bloomberg -731 Lex Av -NY 10022
(212) 233-1300 .. **Grosshtern**, Alexei '98 -299 Bway -NY 10007
(845) 298-7290 .. **Grossjung**, Mark S '88 -66 Middlebush Rd -Wappingers Fls 12590 **Fx:**298-7291
(631) 727-4200 .. **Grossman**, Adam B '93 -120 Court Bx155 -Rvrhead 11901 **Fx:**369-4080
(212) 691-8787 .. **Grossman**, Alan '76 -9 Charles -NY 10014 **Fx:**741-9390
(212) 243-2424 .. **Grossman**, Aline S '94 %Schepisi & M,PA -200 Park Av S -NY 10003
(212) 996-6363 .. **Grossman**, Andrew G '93 GGMC Parking,LLC -1651 3rd Av -NY 10128 **Fx:**722-2988
(212) 351-4000 .. **Grossman**, Anya R '10 Gibson D&C LLP -200 Park Av -NY 10166
(212) 715-9100 .. **Grossman**, Aviva L '85 SpclCnsl Kramer LN&F,LLP -1177 Av of Amer -NY 10036
(212) 370-1300 .. **Grossman**, Barry I '86 (Ellenoff G&S LLP) -150 E 42nd -NY 10017
(516) 612-4076 .. **Grossman**, Bea '92 Grossman Law,PLLC -265 Sunrise Hwy -Rockvll Ctr 11570
(212) 326-3939 .. **Grossman**, Benjamin M '07 %Jones D -222 E 41st -NY 10017
(212) 728-8000 .. **Grossman**, Brett J '03 Willkie F&G LLP -787 7th Av -NY 10019

(212) 616-8177 .. **Grossman,** Brett M '04 (Grossman & G,PC) -360 Lex Av -NY 10017
(716) 282-8863 .. **Grossman & Civiletto** -331 Buffalo Av -Niagara Fls 14303 **Fx:**282-2355
(607) 255-8023 .. **Grossman,** Dale Arrison '77 %Cornell Univ -205 Warren Hall -Ithaca 14853 **Fx:**255-9984
(212) 728-8000 .. **Grossman,** Dan S '79 (Willkie F&G LLP) -787 7th Av -NY 10019
(212) 969-3000 .. **Grossman,** Daryn A '94 (Proskauer R LLP) -1585 Bway -NY 10036
(631) 864-5575 .. **Grossman,** David C '95 (Kelly G&F,LLP) -901A Motor Pkwy -Hauppauge 11788
(718) 788-0833 .. **Grossman,** David W '94 -442 5th -Brklyn 11215
(212) 969-3000 .. **Grossman,** Deidre Ann '97 %Proskauer R LLP -1585 Bway -NY 10036
(631) 265-5864 .. **Grossman,** Edw J '86 -135 W Main -Smithtwn 11787 **Fx:**656-9833
(212) 336-3620 .. **Grossman,** Elizabeth Anne '92 %EEOC -33 Whitehall -NY 10004
(212) 788-3431 .. **Grossman,** Ellen B '79 %Hlth & Hsptl Corp -125 Worth -NY 10013 **Fx:**267-6905
(212) 227-6755 .. **Grossman,** Eran '05 -30 Vesey -NY 10007 **Fx:**227-6616
(716) 636-7600 .. **Grossman,** Eric B '85 OfCnsl HoganWillig -2410 N Forest Rd -Amherst 14068
(716) 282-8863 .. **Grossman,** Eric B '85 (Grossman & C) -331 Buffalo Av -Niagara Fls 14303
(212) 537-1340 .. **Grossman,** Eric F '94 Morgan Stanley -1633 Bway -NY 10019
(516) 747-1010 .. **Grossman,** Floyd G '75 (Dollinger G&G) -1 Old Cntry Rd -Carle Pl 11514
(212) 969-3000 .. **Grossman,** Gabriel D '09 %Proskauer R LLP -1585 Bway -NY 10036
(914) 967-2400 .. **Grossman,** George '79 Grossman & Assoc -14 Elm Pl -Rye 10580 **Fx:**967-2443
(212) 328-2124 .. **Grossman,** Gerald J '61 Medallion Business Credit -437 Mad Av -NY 10022
(212) 616-8177 .. **Grossman & Grossman, PC** -360 Lex Av -NY 10017
(516) 745-8000 .. **Grossman,** Harris M '72 (Wolfson & G LLP) -1600 Stewart Av -Westbury 11590
(212) 325-2000 .. **Grossman,** Heather E '04 Credit Suisse -11 Mad Av -NY 10010
(212) 788-0792 .. **Grossman,** Heidi '90 %Law Dept -100 Church -NY 10007 **Fx:**788-0367
(585) 258-6456 .. **Grossman,** Howard J '81 %JP Morgan Chase -1 Chase Sq -Rchstr 14643 **Fx:**258-6458
(212) 687-3440 .. **Grossman,** Howard L '76 (Goldstick WF&G,PC) -7 Penn Plz -NY 10001
(212) 460-4493 .. **Grossman,** Ira J '75 Con Ed -4 Irving Pl -NY 10003
(212) 735-8600 .. **Grossman,** Isaac P '85 (Morrison C LLP) -909 3rd Av -NY 10022
(718) 461-6633 .. **Grossman,** Jack L '88 (Mallilo & G) -163-09 Nrthrn Blvd -Flushng 11358
(585) 295-4400 .. **Grossman,** James S '74 (Hiscock & B,LLP) -2000 HSBC Plz -Rchstr 14604
(212) 791-1275 .. **Grossman,** Jay S '78 (Goldman & G) -401 1st Av -NY 10010
(516) 562-5000 .. **Grossman,** Jeffrey O '98 CMP Media LLC -600 Community Dr -Manhsst 11030
(914) 631-6200 .. **Grossman,** Jeffrey S '98 %Gibraltar Mgt -150 Wht Plns Rd -Tarrytwn 10591 **Fx:**631-6243
(212) 629-3981 .. **Grossman,** Jennifer K '94 Open Space Institute -1350 Bway -NY 10018 **Fx:**244-3441
(516) 463-5858 .. **Grossman,** Joanna L '02 %Hofstra Law Schl -121 Hofstra Univ -Hempstd 11549
(212) 530-5000 .. **Grossman,** Joanna L '09 %Milbank TH&M LLP -1 Chase Manh Plz -NY 10005
(212) 233-2277 .. **Grossman,** Jonah '70 -187-26 Perth Rd -Jamaica 11432 **Fx:**(718) 454-3210
(718) 262-4727 .. **Grossman,** Jonathan '74 %DHCR -92-31 Union Hall -Jamaica 11433 **Fx:**262-7938
(212) 813-8800 .. **Grossman,** Jonathan E '09 %Goodwin P LLP -620 8th Av -NY 10018
(914) 997-8100 .. **Grossman,** Jordan W '85 %Burke LM&G -10 Bank -White Plns 10606
(212) 326-2000 .. **Grossman,** Judd '06 %O'Melveny & M LLP -7 Times Sq -NY 10036
(212) 209-9454 .. **Grossman,** Julie Ann '96 Mizuho Securities USA Inc -1251 Av of Amer -NY 10020
(518) 473-1416 .. **Grossman,** Kevin M '05 Ofc Emp Rltns -Agncy Bldg 2 ESP -Albany 12223
(212) 571-4649 .. **Grossman,** Lance S '87 -233 Bway -NY 10279 **Fx:**227-6534
(516) 487-5413 .. **Grossman,** Laura G '87 -32 Cow Ln -Kings Pnt 11024
(212) 318-3000 .. **Grossman,** Laura L '02 %Fulbright & J LLP -666 5th Av -NY 10103
(212) 813-8800 .. **Grossman,** Liana '07 %Goodwin P LLP -620 8th Av -NY 10018
(516) 292-8100 .. **Grossman,** Lois '90 %Nassau/Sfflk Law Srv -1 Helen Keller Way -Hempstd 11550 **Fx:**292-6529
(516) 741-5252 .. **Grossman,** Marc D '94 (Sanders SBWV&G,PC) -100 Hrrcks Rd -Mineola 11501
(212) 869-4680 .. **Grossman,** Mark '76 -60 E 42nd -NY 10165 **Fx:**869-1674
(716) 284-6513 .. **Grossman,** Mark D '81 -710 4th -Niagara Fls 14302
(718) 286-2000 .. **Grossman,** Marla A '87 %Leg Aid -120-46 Qns Blvd -Kew Gdns 11415 **Fx:**286-2286
(212) 756-2000 .. **Grossman,** Marnie S '95 SpclCnsl Schulte R&Z LLP -919 3rd Av -NY 10022
(212) 964-3855 .. **Grossman,** Martin '88 %R Cardali & Assoc,LLP -39 Bway -NY 10006 **Fx:**634-4856
(718) 393-1732 .. **Grossman,** Marvin '58 -61-20 Grnd Cntrl Pkwy -Frst Hlls 11375 **Fx:**393-1733
(212) 403-1000 .. **Grossman,** Maura R '00 Cnsl Wachtell LR&K -51 W 52nd -NY 10019
(212) 574-1200 .. **Grossman,** Meir R '04 %Seward & K LLP -1 Bttry Pk Plz -NY 10004
(212) 728-8000 .. **Grossman,** Melanie A '08 %Willkie F&G LLP -787 7th Av -NY 10019
(516) 248-7575 .. **Grossman,** Michl B '64 (Levine & G) -114 Old Cntry Rd -Mineola 11501
(212) 616-8177 .. **Grossman,** Michl F '77 (Grossman & G,PC) -360 Lex Av -NY 10017
(212) 514-5121 .. **Grossman,** Michl S '77 -61 Bway -NY 10006 **Fx:**514-7072
(212) 371-5649 .. **Grossman,** Nancy G '71 -211 E 53rd -NY 10022
(212) 697-6484 .. **Grossman,** Neil D '96 (Bronstein G&G,LLC) -60 E 42nd -NY 10165 **Fx:**697-0877
(212) 750-8700 .. **Grossman,** Paul S '93 (Friedman & W,PC) -600 Lex Av -NY 10022
(607) 273-6841 .. **Grossman,** Peter G '77 (Barney GDM&O,LLP) -119 E Seneca -Ithaca 14850
(212) 431-4893 .. **Grossman,** Philip J '81 -168 Mott -NY 10013
(718) 246-5492 .. **Grossman,** Reed S '91 -44 Court -Brklyn 11201
(212) 681-9797 .. **Grossman,** Richd '00 Brahman Capital Corp -655 3rd Av -NY 10017
(212) 735-3000 .. **Grossman,** Richd J '85 (Skadden ASM&F LLP) -4 Times Sq -NY 10036
(718) 520-8722 .. **Grossman & Rinaldo** -108-18 Qns Blvd -Frst Hlls 11375 **Fx:**793-0894
(585) 442-2551 .. **Grossman,** Robt C '72 (Johnson M&B,PC) -1399 Monroe Av -Rchstr 14618
(212) 408-5100 .. **Grossman,** Robt E '06 %Chadbourne & P LLP -30 Rckfllr Plz -NY 10112
(914) 448-2697 .. **Grossman,** Robt M '95 (R Grossman & Assoc,PC) -7 Chesley Rd -White Plns 10605 **Fx:**448-2698
(516) 745-1700 .. **Grossman,** Robt S '96 -585 Stewart Av -Gdn Cty 11530 **Fx:**745-1715
(212) 559-7551 .. **Grossman,** Roberta R '97 %Citicorp -153 E 53rd -NY 10043
(718) 264-0777 .. **Grossman,** Saml '84 -73-48 188th -Fresh Mdws 11366 **Fx:**264-1471
(212) 461-7190 .. **Grossman,** Scott A '01 %Fishman M,PC -44 Wall -NY 10005
(212) 306-7282 .. **Grossman,** Seth A '05 NYC Campaign Finance Bd -40 Rector -NY 10006
(212) 326-2000 .. **Grossman,** Seth A '07 %O'Melveny & M LLP -7 Times Sq -NY 10036
(212) 852-7000 .. **Grossman,** Stacy J '96 News Corp -1211 Av of Amer -NY 10036 **Fx:**852-7147
(212) 661-1100 .. **Grossman,** Stanley M '68 (Pomerantz HG&G LLP) -100 Park Av -NY 10017
(631) 725-7600 .. **Grossman,** Stephen A '66 S Grossman & Assoc -17 Main Bx1949 -Sag Hbr 11963 **Fx:**725-5618
(718) 520-8722 .. **Grossman,** Stuart J '71 (Grossman & R) -108-18 Qns Blvd -Frst Hlls 11375
(516) 228-8484 .. **Grossman,** Victor A '01 %Dilworth & B,LLP -1000 Woodbury Rd -Woodbury 11797
(845) 225-0334 .. **Grossman,** Victor G '79 -9 Fair -Carmel 10512 **Fx:**225-4036
(716) 568-0070 .. **Grossman,** Wm C '88 Counsel Financial -6400 Main -Williamsvll 14221
(212) 310-8000 .. **Grossman,** Y Shukie '95 (Weil G&M LLP) -767 5th Av -NY 10153
(212) 554-1400 .. **Grossmann,** Edw A '74 (Bernstein LB&G LLP) -1285 Av of Amer -NY 10019
(718) 286-6000 .. **Gross-Marks,** Jill '85 %DA -125-01 Qns Blvd -Kew Gdns 11415
(914) 995-2508 .. **Grosso,** Danielle '06 %Cnty Atty -148 Martine Av -White Plns 10601 **Fx:**995-5858
(585) 428-2873 .. **Grosso,** Dawn S '93 Hon D Barry -Hall of Justice -Rchstr 14614
(631) 666-5766 .. **Grosso,** Elizabeth J '05 %Long TBSWJ&S -120 4th Av Bx5591 -Bay Shr 11706
(585) 586-3210 .. **Grosso,** James C '92 -1080 Pttsfrd Victor Rd -Pittsfrd 14534 **Fx:**586-3268
(631) 393-0421 .. **Grosso,** Jos L '77 -500 Bi Cnty Blvd -Farmngdl 11735 **Fx:**393-0424
(212) 858-8121 .. **Grosso,** Robt J '86 SrCnsl First Investors Corp -110 Wall -NY 10005 **Fx:**858-8119
(212) 909-6000 .. **Grosso,** Suzanne M '99 Cnsl Debevoise & P LLP -919 3rd Av -NY 10022
(212) 687-0100 .. **Gross Paris,** Jodie '07 %Harris B PLLC -100 Wall -NY 10005
(212) 209-3068 .. **Grosz,** Edw P '90 SrCnsl Reitler K&R LLC -885 3rd Av -NY 10022
(212) 317-8100 .. **Grosz,** Eleanor '80 -757 3rd Av -NY 10017 **Fx:**679-7426
(212) 909-6000 .. **Grosz,** Erich O '00 Cnsl Debevoise & P LLP -919 3rd Av -NY 10022
(212) 998-6550 .. **Grosz,** Maya L '00 %NYU Law Schl -245 Sullivan -NY 10012
(212) 408-5100 .. **Grosz,** Morton E '68 (Chadbourne & P LLP) -30 Rckfllr Plz -NY 10112
(718) 739-6400 .. **Grotch,** Mitchel D '87 %DHCR -92-31 Union Hall -Jamaica 11433 **Fx:**262-7938
(212) 841-1000 .. **Groth,** Jason L '09 %Covington & B LLP -620 8th Av -NY 10018
(212) 286-8585 .. **Grottalio,** Karen T '93 (Heidell PM&B,LLP) -99 Park Av -NY 10016
(212) 964-6611 .. **Groubert,** Jonathon D '96 Cnsl Lester SK&D -120 Bway -NY 10271
(518) 465-3484 .. **Groudine,** Stephen M '10 %Carter CCBM&L,PC -20 Corp Wds Blvd -Albany 12211
(212) 692-1000 .. **Grouf,** Jon H I '68 (Duane M LLP) -1540 Bway -NY 10036
(212) 805-3900 .. **Group,** David A '02 %Clausen M PC -1 Chase Manh Plz -NY 10005
(212) 474-1000 .. **Grousset,** Kimberly A '96 Cravath S&M LLP -825 8th Av -NY 10019
(516) 803-2300 .. **Groveman,** Amy S '85 %Cablevision Sys -1111 Stewart Av -Bethpage 11714
(516) 741-5252 .. **Groveman,** Liba N '98 %Sanders SBWV&G,PC -100 Hrrcks Rd -Mineola 11501
(212) 527-7575 .. **Grover,** David '95 (Grover & F,PC) -750 3rd Av -NY 10017
(212) 344-5680 .. **Grover,** Douglas E '76 (Thompson H LLP) -335 Mad Av -NY 10017
(212) 527-7575 .. **Grover & Fensterstock,PC** -750 3rd Av -NY 10017 **Fx:**527-7576
(631) 418-1100 .. **Grover & Fensterstock,PC** -10 Newton Pl -Hauppauge 11788 **Fx:**794-2700
(631) 669-1028 .. **Grover,** James R Jr. '50 -1801 Argyle Sq -Babylon 11702
(516) 357-3000 .. **Grover,** Keith S '95 %Rivkin R LLP -926 RXR Plz -Uniondale 11556
(212) 335-9000 .. **Groves,** Courtney R '01 %DA -1 Hogan Pl -NY 10013
(212) 422-0202 .. **Groves,** Edw E '91 SpclCnsl Sedgwick DM&A LLP -125 Broad -NY 10004
(212) 227-3333 .. **Groves,** Tracy L '99 %Smith & L,LLP -291 Bway -NY 10007
(315) 336-4700 .. **Grow,** David C '68 (McMahon & G) -301 N Wshngtn Bx4350 -Rome 13442
(631) 261-5697 .. **Grow,** Gerald L '81 -27 Horse Shoe Dr -Northprt 11768
(315) 589-9693 .. **Grow,** John Lindsay '94 Grow & G -6431 Lk Av -Williamson 14589 **Fx:**589-2021
(315) 336-4700 .. **Grow,** John W '59 OfCnsl McMahon & G -301 N Wshngtn Bx4350 -Rome 13442
(716) 853-1366 .. **Grubea,** Peter D '94 -482 Delaware Av -Buffalo 14202
(516) 623-4130 .. **Grubel,** Henry M '64 H Grubel,PC -37 Prospect -Freeprt 11520 **Fx:**623-1989
(518) 791-2850 .. **Gruben,** Jill A '01 Grubben Law Firm PLLC -12 Hemphill Pl Bx2576 -Malta 12020 **Fx:**708-6370

(212) 474-1000 .. **Gruber,** Aaron M '08 %Cravath S&M LLP -825 8th Av -NY 10019
(212) 618-6352 .. **Gruber,** Alan S '04 %Sorin RC LLC -1230 Av of Amer -NY 10020
(516) 625-1700 .. **Gruber,** Craig M '95 (Salamon GB&S,PC) -97 Powerhse Rd -Roslyn Hts 11577
(716) 566-5400 .. **Gruber,** Damon M '00 (Goldberg S LLP) -665 Main -Buffalo 14203
(516) 625-1700 .. **Gruber,** David '63 (Salamon GB&S,PC) -97 Powerhse Rd -Roslyn Hts 11577
(631) 329-9230 .. **Gruber,** David '79 %Gruber & Co Inc -Bx1180 -E Hampton 11937
(212) 221-8096 .. **Gruber,** David J '86 (Gruber S&P,LLP) -350 5th Av #4022 -NY 10118
(516) 365-1400 .. **Gruber,** Eric H '87 (Cooperman LM LLP) -1129 Nrthrn Blvd -Manhsst 11030
(516) 663-0999 .. **Gruber,** Hermann '84 (Steinberg & G,PC) -300 Grdn City Plz -Gdn Cty 11530
(716) 852-0400 .. **Gruber,** J Mark '80 (Roach BM&G,PC) -424 Main -Buffalo 14202
(212) 733-3223 .. **Gruber,** Jos A '95 %Pfizer Inc -150 E 42nd -NY 10017
(212) 773-1586 .. **Gruber,** Lara C R '07 Ernst & Young -5 Times Sq -NY 10036
(718) 222-9800 .. **Gruber,** Micheal K '96 %Brecher FPWT&Z,PC -335 Adams -Brklyn 11201
(212) 431-1300 .. **Gruber,** Paul N '85 (Borah GAN&G PC) -377 Bway -NY 10013
(212) 689-7606 .. **Gruber,** Rebecca M '07 %RI Gruber,PC -295 Mad Av -NY 10017 **Fx:**447-0948
(212) 689-7606 .. **Gruber,** Robt I '74 (RI Gruber,PC) -295 Mad Av -NY 10017 **Fx:**447-0948
(212) 688-5055 .. **Gruber,** Robin E '92 Chanel Inc -9 W 57th -NY 10019 **Fx:**715-4808
(212) 221-8096 .. **Gruber Schwartz & Posnock,LLP** -350 5th Av #4022 -NY 10118 **Fx:**616-5543
(212) 307-5100 .. **Gruber,** Teresa Ann '98 %McElfish & Assoc,LLC -350 5th Av -NY 10118 **Fx:**307-5200
(516) 845-8088 .. **Gruber,** Vicki S '91 -17 Conklin -Farmngdl 11735
(212) 701-3000 .. **Gruberg,** Stephen P '08 %Cahill G&R LLP -80 Pine -NY 10005 **Fx:**269-5420
(212) 761-5520 .. **Grubert,** Arthur M '99 Morgan Stanley -1585 Bway -NY 10036
(516) 944-0923 .. **Gruber-Truglio,** Danna '88 -95 Radcliff Av -Pt Wash 11050
(212) 754-9400 .. **Grubin,** Janice B '88 (Todtman NS&J,PC) -425 Park Av -NY 10022
(212) 269-8628 .. **Grubin,** Jerome S '56 (Grubin S&T) -60 Broad -NY 10004 **Fx:**809-6185
(212) 581-3320 .. **Grubin,** John F '74 (Wasserman G&R,LLP) -1700 Bway -NY 10019
(212) 601-8000 .. **Grubin,** Scott G '96 (Porter Novelli) -75 Varick -NY 10013 **Fx:**601-8101
(212) 799-3100 .. **Grubin,** Sharon E '74 Metropolitan Opera -Lincoln Ctr -NY 10023 **Fx:**870-7681
(212) 554-0400 .. **Grubman,** Allen J '68 (Grubman I&S,PC) -152 W 57th -NY 10019
(212) 478-7200 .. **Grubman,** Don D '80 (Hahn & H LLP) -488 Mad Av -NY 10022
(212) 554-0400 .. **Grubman Indursky & Shire, PC** -152 W 57th -NY 10019 **Fx:**554-0444
(212) 223-0200 .. **Grudberg,** Michl J '91 (Stillman F&S,PC) -425 Park Av -NY 10022
(212) 278-9821 .. **Gruder,** Benjamin G '01 Invesco Private Capital -1166 Av of Amer -NY 10036
(212) 373-3038 .. **Gruder,** Bruce '91 Cnsl Paul WRW&G LLP -1285 Av of Amer -NY 10019
(631) 784-7717 .. **Gruder,** Fredric J '72 -55 Elm -Huntngtn 11743
(631) 979-3000 .. **Gruder,** Glenn B '86 (Certilman BA&H,LLP) -1393 Vets Mem'l Hwy -Hauppauge 11788
(212) 546-2424 .. **Grudzina,** John J '81 Grey Advertising -777 3rd Av -NY 10017 **Fx:**546-1495
(518) 483-1440 .. **Grue,** Thos A '84 (Poissant NG&V,PC) -367 W Main -Malone 12953
(212) 679-4666 .. **Gruen,** David '00 %Frenkel H&S LLP -16 E 34th -NY 10016
(212) 297-5800 .. **Gruen,** Jeffrey A '10 %Day P LLP -7 Times Sq -NY 10036
(212) 643-7050 .. **Gruen,** Michl S '67 -249 W 34th -NY 10001 **Fx:**643-7051
(518) 274-7252 .. **Gruenberg,** David L '75 -54 2nd -Troy 12180 **Fx:**274-0348
(631) 737-4110 .. **Gruenberg,** Guy C '95 (Gruenberg & K,PC) -3275 Vets Mem'l Hwy -Ronkonkoma 11779 **Fx:**737-4155
(212) 756-2000 .. **Gruenberg,** Matthew J '10 %Schulte R&Z LLP -919 3rd Av -NY 10022
(212) 819-8200 .. **Gruenberg,** Yehuda D '10 %White & C LLP -1155 Av of Amer -NY 10036
(212) 310-8000 .. **Gruenberger,** Peter '61 SrCnsl Weil G&M LLP -767 5th Av -NY 10153
(212) 335-4500 .. **Gruenberger,** Richd L '94 DLA Piper LLP -1251 Av of Amer -NY 10020
(212) 335-4500 .. **Gruendel,** Robt J '83 (DLA Piper LLP) -1251 Av of Amer -NY 10020
(315) 637-5033 .. **Gruenewald,** David J '82 -Bx69 -Manlius 13104 **Fx:**637-2791
(212) 735-3000 .. **Gruenglas,** Michl H '91 (Skadden ASM&F LLP) -4 Times Sq -NY 10036
(212) 330-8151 .. **Gruenhagen,** Stephanie L '09 Brinen & Assoc,LLC -7 Dey -NY 10007 **Fx:**202-5330
(718) 558-4411 .. **Gruenspecht,** Robt '78 -8931 161st -Jamaica 11432
(212) 474-1000 .. **Gruenstein,** Benjamin '01 %Cravath S&M LLP -825 8th Av -NY 10019
(212) 403-1000 .. **Gruenstein,** David '81 (Wachtell LR&K) -51 W 52nd -NY 10019
(718) 928-3700 .. **Gruenwald,** Robt S '91 %LSNYC-Bronx -579 Courtlandt Av -Bronx 10451 **Fx:**402-7586
(516) 487-5400 .. **Gruer,** Sharon Kovacs '86 (SK Gruer,PC) -1010 Nrthrn Blvd -Gt Neck 11021 **Fx:**466-3863
(212) 771-0748 .. **Gruesser,** Susan A '92 WoltersKluwer Law & Business -76 9th Av -NY 10011
(212) 570-5284 .. **Grumbach,** Adam Z '03 -317 E 67th -NY 10065
(212) 336-2000 .. **Grumbach,** Antonia M '71 OfCnsl Patterson BW&T LLP -1133 Av of Amer -NY 10036
(212) 225-2000 .. **Grumbach,** George J Jr. '66 SrCnsl Cleary GS&H -1 Lbrty Plz -NY 10006
(212) 299-7981 .. **Grumet,** Alan M '97 Sandelman Prtnrs -1350 Av of Amer -NY 10019
(212) 308-4411 .. **Grumet,** Andrew M '98 (Edwards AP&D LLP) -750 Lex Av -NY 10022
(212) 788-1355 .. **Grumet,** Lisa Fleming '96 %Law Dept -100 Church -NY 10007 **Fx:**788-0367
(212) 374-1144 .. **Grumet,** Robin '81 -299 Bway -NY 10007 **Fx:**285-0531
(212) 687-1700 .. **Grun,** Howard '85 (Kaufman FP&G,LLP) -300 E 42nd -NY 10017
(631) 727-4100 .. **Grun,** Susan Rogers '81 (Smith FLI&Y) -456 Griffing Av Bx389 -Rvrhead 11901
(212) 839-5300 .. **Grunat,** Joshua G '89 (Sidley A LLP) -787 7th Av -NY 10019
(212) 847-3208 .. **Grunbaum,** Merike '00 -60 Broad -NY 10004
(212) 984-2914 .. **Grunberg,** Danl '01 TRG Mgmt LP -280 Park Av -NY 10017
(212) 425-7200 .. **Grunberger,** Aaron '04 %Kenyon & K,LLP -1 Bway -NY 10004
(973) 274-6021 .. **Grunblatt,** David '78 (Proskauer R LLP) -1585 Bway -NY 10036 **Fx:**274-3299
(845) 331-1191 .. **Grunblatt,** Mark '86 -71 Albany Av -Kingston 12401 **Fx:**331-5515
(631) 724-7600 .. **Grundfast,** Michl K '69 (Grundfast & M) -8 Manor Rd -Smithtwn 11787 **Fx:**724-7812
(631) 751-4444 .. **Grundfast,** Norman J '60 OfCnsl Grundfast Law Firm -207 Hallock Rd -Stony Brk 11790 **Fx:**751-4675
(631) 751-4444 .. **Grundfast,** Robt D '91 Grundfast Law Firm -207 Hallock Rd -Stony Brk 11790 **Fx:**751-4675
(631) 751-4444 .. **Grundfast,** Robt D '91 (Grundfast & H) -207 Hallock Rd -Stony Brk 11790 **Fx:**751-4675
(914) 393-8384 .. **Grundman,** Nancy D '93 -1 Sunset Dr N -Chappaqua 10514
(315) 424-8944 .. **Grundner,** Chas H '79 (Shulman CG&R,PC) -250 S Clinton -Syracuse 13202
(800) 358-2550 .. **Grundstein,** Kenneth '78 NAM -990 Stewart Av -Gdn Cty 11530
(212) 940-8800 .. **Grundstein,** Robt A '93 %Katten MR LLP -575 Mad Av -NY 10022
(212) 770-2604 .. **Grundy,** James R '03 AIG -80 Pine -NY 10005
(212) 909-6000 .. **Gruner,** Brandon C '06 %Debevoise & P LLP -919 3rd Av -NY 10022
(914) 288-9595 .. **Gruner,** Jos H '74 OfCnsl Gaines GP&N,LLP -1 N Bway -White Plns 10601
(914) 288-9595 .. **Gruner,** Jos H '74 (J Gruner,PC) -50 Joyce Rd -Hartsdale 10530 **Fx:**288-0850
(516) 228-9181 .. **Gruner,** Joshua B '01 %Gassman BB&T,PC -666 Old Cntry Rd -Gdn Cty 11530
(631) 755-0100 .. **Gruner,** Katherine R '01 %Smith & D,PA -145 Pinelawn Rd -Melvll 11747
(845) 331-0033 .. **Gruner,** Paul L '74 Gruner Law Ofc -253 Wall Bx4060 -Kingston 12402 **Fx:**331-2948
(516) 496-3500 .. **Grunert,** John J '89 -6800 Jericho Tpk -Syosset 11791 **Fx:**496-3530
(212) 557-4000 .. **Grunfeld Desiderio Lebowitz Silverman & Klestadt LLP** -399 Park Av -NY 10022 **Fx:**557-4415
(212) 557-4000 .. **Grunfeld,** Harold M '73 (Grunfeld DLS&K LLP) -399 Park Av -NY 10022
(718) 284-9500 .. **Grunfeld,** Jason '05 %Grunfeld & Assoc,LLC -15 Ocean Av -Brklyn 11225 **Fx:**284-6102
(212) 986-6000 .. **Grunfeld,** Jason P '02 (Kleinberg KW&C,PC) -551 5th Av -NY 10176
(718) 284-9500 .. **Grunfeld,** Jay E '85 (Grunfeld & Assoc,LLC) -15 Ocean Av -Brklyn 11225 **Fx:**284-6102
(212) 627-8100 .. **Grunfeld,** Nicole D '05 %Levy R,PC -80 8th Av -NY 10011
(212) 732-3200 .. **Grunfeld,** Raphael S '82 (Carter L&M LLP) -2 Wall -NY 10005
(212) 233-2040 .. **Grunfeld,** Thos B '84 %Kahn GT&R,PC -20 Vesey -NY 10007
(212) 627-3000 .. **Grunow,** Christopher A '95 %Bellmarc Realty -16 E 12th -NY 10003
(212) 972-1000 .. **Grunsfeld,** Gerald D '03 %London F LLP -59 Maiden Ln -NY 10038
(212) 704-6000 .. **Grunstein,** Leonard '76 (Troutman S LLP) -405 Lex Av -NY 10174
(516) 248-8889 .. **Grunwald,** Milton '85 (Grunwald & S,PC) -100 Grdn City Plz -Gdn Cty 11530
(516) 248-8889 .. **Grunwald & Seman,PC** -100 Grdn City Plz -Gdn Cty 11530 **Fx:**229-2655
(914) 499-4014 .. **Gruppo,** David M '84 IBM -1 New Orchrd Rd -Armonk 10504
(973) 596-4415 .. **Gruppuso,** Anthony M '02 (Gibbons PC) -1 Penn Plz -NY 10119 **Fx:**639-8333
Grupsmith, George S '76 -67-66 108th -Frst Hlls 11375
(212) 351-4000 .. **Grus,** Karen A '10 Gibson D&C LLP -200 Park Av -NY 10166
(212) 373-3000 .. **Grusauskas,** Caitlin E '10 %Paul WRW&G LLP -1285 Av of Amer -NY 10019
(516) 296-7000 .. **Grusd,** Gavin C '88 (Certilman BA&H,LLP) -90 Merrick Av -E Meadow 11554
(212) 565-8867 .. **Grusd,** Jared E '01 %Google Inc -76 9th Av -NY 10011
(516) 571-7760 .. **Grusenmeyer,** Danl V '06 %DA -1 W Chester -Long Bch 11561 **Fx:**571-7762
(212) 530-5000 .. **Grushkin,** Jay D '91 (Milbank TH&M LLP) -1 Chase Manh Plz -NY 10005
(212) 697-9500 .. **Grushko,** Edw M '81 (Grushko & M,PC) -551 5th Av -NY 10176 **Fx:**697-3575
(212) 310-8000 .. **Gruszczynski,** Christopher R '09 %Weil G&M LLP -767 5th Av -NY 10153
(212) 225-2000 .. **Gruszecki,** Robt '06 %Cleary GS&H -1 Lbrty Plz -NY 10006
(585) 454-3377 .. **Gruttadaro,** Dennis '85 (Brown & T,LLC) -19 Prince -Rchstr 14607
(212) 223-0400 .. **Gruver,** Judy '03 %Zeichner E&K LLP -575 Lex Av -NY 10022
(212) 836-8000 .. **Gruver,** Michl L '07 %Kaye S LLP -425 Park Av -NY 10022
(212) 813-8800 .. **Gruver,** Sean P '03 %Goodwin P LLP -620 8th Av -NY 10018
(212) 269-2353 .. **Gruvman Giordano & Glaws, LLP** -61 Bway -NY 10006 **Fx:**269-2354
(212) 269-2353 .. **Gruvman,** Paul S '90 (Gruvman G&G,LLP) -61 Bway -NY 10006
(631) 549-2000 .. **Gruza,** Sy '86 %Weber Law Grp,LLP -290 Broad Hollow Rd -Melvll 11747 **Fx:**549-2015
(212) 442-3190 .. **Grygiel,** Heidi B '98 %Law Dept -100 Church -NY 10007 **Fx:**788-0367
(518) 689-1406 .. **Grygiel,** Michl J '89 (Greenberg T,LLP) -54 State -Albany 12207
(212) 765-5070 .. **Grygiel,** Sean J '02 (Fish & R,PC) -153 E 53rd -NY 10022
(212) 815-1818 .. **Grynbaum,** Steven '97 %DC 37 MELS -125 Barclay -NY 10007 **Fx:**815-1343
(212) 726-6921 .. **Gsell,** Evan M '90 Infogrames Inc -417 5th Av -NY 10016
(212) 471-8512 .. **Gsovski,** Danl V '70 (Herzfeld & R,PC) -125 Broad -NY 10004
(212) 558-4000 .. **Gu,** Jieni '06 %Sullivan & C LLP -125 Broad -NY 10004
(212) 300-0074 .. **Gu,** Yu '09 Primary Capital LLC -80 Wall -NY 10005
(585) 325-5150 .. **Guadagnino,** Jos S '56 OfCnsl Faraci L,LLP -28 E Main -Rchstr 14614
(212) 709-8099 .. **Guadagnino,** Peter J Jr. '96 -110 Wall -NY 10005 **Fx:**943-2300
(212) 953-4441 .. **Guadagno,** Jo Ann L '94 (Guadagno & E,LLP) -420 Lex Av -NY 10170 **Fx:**953-6079
(631) 224-2796 .. **Guadagno,** John J '86 -136 E Main -E Islip 11730 **Fx:**224-1643

(212) 267-2555 .. **Guadagno,** Matthew L '94 (Bretz & C,LLP) -305 Bway -NY 10007
(516) 357-3000 .. **Guadagnoli,** David '01 %Rivkin R LLP -926 RXR Plz -Uniondale 11556
(212) 833-6059 .. **Guadagnoli,** Donato '07 Sony BMG Music Entertainment -550 Mad Av -NY 10022
(718) 222-2001 .. **Guadagnoli,** Yolanda '91 %Law Dept -350 Jay -Brklyn 11201 **Fx:**222-2088
(212) 541-0704 .. **Guadalupe,** Robt D '99 KBC Group NV -1177 Av of Amer -NY 10036
(212) 880-6000 .. **Guadiana,** James A '66 (Torys LLP) -237 Park Av -NY 10017
(646) 624-5929 .. **Guaglianone,** Victor F '83 Genpact -105 Mad Av -NY 10016 **Fx:**823-0469
(212) 596-9000 .. **Guaragna,** Julia M '06 %Ropes & G LLP -1211 Av of Amer -NY 10036
(631) 753-1056 .. **Guararra,** Mary E '93 Proclaim America -35 Pinelawn Rd -Melvll 11747
(212) 696-9190 .. **Guararra,** Michl J '87 (Guararra & Z) -100 Park Av -NY 10017 **Fx:**681-9189
(716) 651-1900 .. **Guarasci,** Danl J '00 -20 Lawrence Bell Dr -Buffalo 14221
(914) 448-0200 .. **Guardaro,** Edw J Jr. '86 (Bartlett MB&M,LLP) -81 Main -White Plns 10601
(516) 227-0700 .. **Guardino,** Anthony S '92 (Farrell F,PC) -1320 RXR Plz -Uniondale 11556
(718) 648-9312 .. **Guardino,** Anthony V '79 -1649 Sheepshead Bay Rd -Brklyn 11235 **Fx:**769-5445
(212) 852-3562 .. **Guardino,** Christopher S '02 %US Trust Co,NA -114 W 47th -NY 10036 **Fx:**852-1310
(516) 248-7982 .. **Guardino,** Scott F '82 (S Guardino,PLLC) -983 Willis Av -Albertson 11507 **Fx:**248-7984
(718) 262-3400 .. **Guardo,** Christopher '84 %HRA -92-31 Union Hall -Jamaica 11433
(212) 753-7500 .. **Guardo,** Marisa '87 Cnsl Hartman & C LLP -488 Mad Av -NY 10022
(212) 325-0401 .. **Guardo,** Pamela L '91 Credit Suisse -11 Mad Av -NY 10010
(212) 554-0400 .. **Guardo,** Sonya Wheaton '98 (Grubman I&S,PC) -152 W 57th -NY 10019
(212) 609-6800 .. **Guariglia,** Michl A '82 (McCarter & E,LLP) -245 Park Av -NY 10167
(718) 590-2000 .. **Guariglia,** Veronica '00 %DA -198 E 161st -Bronx 10451 **Fx:**590-6477
(718) 618-2044 .. **Guarino,** Annette L '82 Family Ct -900 Sheridan Av -Bronx 10461
(718) 846-6500 .. **Guarino,** Anthony J '48 -87-13 Myrtle Av -Glendale 11385 **Fx:**846-6363
(914) 591-4205 .. **Guarino,** Anthony W '74 -102 Main -Irvngtn 10533
(212) 972-0786 .. **Guarino,** Chas P '96 %Nicoll D&S LLP -250 Park Av -NY 10177 **Fx:**953-7201
(347) 512-7221 .. **Guarino,** Eugene M '00 -21614 Jamaica Av -Qns Vllg 11428
(631) 929-4040 .. **Guarino,** Frank P '77 -N Cnty Rd Bx66 -Wading Rvr 11792
(585) 546-5530 .. **Guarino,** Glenn A '87 %Thomson West -50 E Broad -Rchstr 14694
(631) 617-5240 .. **Guarino,** Jerry C '02 -4 W Main -Bay Shr 11706
(212) 593-6700 .. **Guarino,** Marisa H '08 %Aaronson RF&D,LLP -757 3rd Av -NY 10017
(212) 551-8912 .. **Guarino,** Michl A '83 %Israel Discount Bk -511 5th Av -NY 10017 **Fx:**551-8916
(585) 425-5200 .. **Guarino,** Michl A '97 Maximus Fed Srvcs -50 Square Dr -Victor 14564
(718) 638-2035 .. **Guarna,** Lenae L '92 -51 8th Av -Brklyn 11217 **Fx:**638-0935
(845) 371-4700 .. **Guarneri,** Christina A '10 %Fein SK&S,PC -747 Chestnut Rdg Rd -Spg Vly 10977
(646) 392-9250 .. **Guarneri,** Eugene '72 %M Klein & Assoc -200 Mad Av -NY 10016 **Fx:**(212) 779-1499
(914) 961-1359 .. **Guarneri,** John A '91 (Babaja & G) -35 E Grassy Sprain Rd -Ynkrs 10710 **Fx:**961-1339
(212) 428-2150 .. **Guarneri,** Stephen '75 NYS Ct Admin -25 Beaver -NY 10004
(212) 930-9700 .. **Guarneri-Ferrara,** Tara L '06 %Sichenzia RFF LLP -61 Bway -NY 10006
(718) 590-2000 .. **Guarnieri,** Debra Ann '88 %DA -198 E 161st -Bronx 10451 **Fx:**590-6477
(212) 732-5400 .. **Guarnieri,** Maria T '97 %Raff & B,LLP -470 Park Av S -NY 10016
(718) 876-7400 .. **Guastella,** Maria R '95 -404 Manor Rd -Staten Isl 10314
(212) 239-4999 .. **Guay,** Richd F X '77 (Meyer SE&K,PC) -1350 Bway Bx822 -NY 10018
(646) 658-0500 .. **Guazzo,** Delia M '80 Guazzo & G -711 3rd Av -NY 10017 **Fx:**658-0599
(212) 806-5400 .. **Guazzo,** Robt W '98 (Stroock &S&L LLP) -180 Maiden Ln -NY 10038
(212) 335-4500 .. **Gubar,** Leonard '62 OfCnsl DLA Piper LLP -1251 Av of Amer -NY 10020
(631) 493-5812 .. **Guber,** Deborah A '91 -6268 Jericho Tpk -Commack 11725 **Fx:**980-4133
(631) 755-9400 .. **Guberman,** Harold I '76 -35 Pinelawn Rd -Melvll 11747 **Fx:**755-9402
(212) 575-7900 .. **Guberman,** Harvey C '66 (Ballon SB&N,PC) -729 7th Av -NY 10019
(212) 980-1000 .. **Guberman,** Stephanie C '96 UJA-Federation -130 E 59th -NY 10022 **Fx:**888-7538
(845) 778-2121 .. **Gubits,** David B '67 (Jacobowitz & G,LLP) -158 Orange Av Bx367 -Walden 12586
(631) 262-6911 .. **Gucciardo,** Brian J '94 (Gucciardo Assoc) -256 Main -Northprt 11768
(212) 742-0500 .. **Gucciardo,** Chas S '82 Gucciardo Law Firm -99 Wall -NY 10005 **Fx:**742-0815
(631) 262-6911 .. **Gucciardo,** Glenn E '93 (Gucciardo Assoc) -256 Main -Northprt 11768
(631) 262-6911 .. **Gucciardo,** James T '71 (Gucciardo Assoc) -256 Main -Northprt 11768
(212) 742-0500 .. **Gucciardo,** Maria T '96 %Gucciardo Law Firm -99 Wall -NY 10005 **Fx:**742-0815
(718) 596-4184 .. **Guccione,** Thos P '78 -16 Court -Brklyn 11241 **Fx:**624-2763
(845) 638-5001 .. **Guccione,** Tina L '93 %DA -1 S Main -New Cty 10956 **Fx:**638-5070
(212) 325-2000 .. **Gudaitis,** Arunas E '92 Credit Suisse -11 Mad Av -NY 10010
(212) 770-7876 .. **Gudewicz,** Kristen L '04 AIG Asset Mgmt -70 Pine -NY 10270
(212) 643-2503 .. **Gudin,** Bruce E '90 (Levy E&P,PC) -555 5th Av -NY 10017
(212) 455-2000 .. **Gudis,** Elizabeth A '09 %Simpson T&B LLP -425 Lex Av -NY 10017
(212) 770-6584 .. **Guecia,** Linda Marie '03 AIG -70 Pine -NY 10270 **Fx:**770-3836
(212) 989-8223 .. **Guedry,** James W '66 -79 Charles -NY 10014
(917) 778-6600 .. **Gueldenzopf,** Allen H '80 %J Toomey -485 Lex Av -NY 10017 **Fx:**778-7048
(516) 622-0428 .. **Gueli,** Chas R '99 -100 Crsswys Park W -Woodbury 11797
(212) 848-4000 .. **Gueli,** John '93 (Shearman & S LLP) -599 Lex Av -NY 10022
(716) 845-7482 .. **Guenther,** Theresa M '98 Family Ct -1 Niagara Plz -Buffalo 14202 **Fx:**858-7792
(212) 417-4357 .. **Guenzburger,** Danl I '79 %Dept of Health -90 Church -NY 10007 **Fx:**417-4392
(212) 878-8000 .. **Guerard-Langlois,** Annie '09 %Clifford C LLP -31 W 52nd -NY 10019
(516) 694-3000 .. **Guercio,** Christopher J '01 (Guercio & G,LLP) -77 Conklin -Farmngdl 11735 **Fx:**694-4738
(516) 694-3000 .. **Guercio,** Gregory J '74 (Guercio & G,LLP) -77 Conklin -Farmngdl 11735 **Fx:**694-4738
(212) 728-8000 .. **Guercio,** Matthew J '04 %Willkie F&G LLP -787 7th Av -NY 10019
(516) 694-3000 .. **Guercio,** Richd J '84 (Guercio & G,LLP) -77 Conklin -Farmngdl 11735 **Fx:**694-4738
(212) 788-3300 .. **Guercio,** Susan J '05 %Hlth & Hsptl Corp -125 Worth -NY 10013 **Fx:**267-6905
(212) 398-9238 .. **Guerin,** Denis C '88 -315 Mad Av -NY 10017 **Fx:**869-0944
(845) 247-0065 .. **Guerin,** Erica K F '93 -858 Route 212 -Saugerties 12477 **Fx:**247-0386
(516) 222-2880 .. **Guerin,** Heather L '03 %J Davis & Assoc -600 Old Cntry Rd -Gdn Cty 11530 **Fx:**222-0828
(718) 260-8772 .. **Guerin,** Lisa C '03 ACS -345 Adams -Brklyn 11201
(518) 445-2380 .. **Guernsey,** Thos F '03 %Albany Law Schl -80 New Scotland Av -Albany 12208 **Fx:**445-2315
(212) 633-4310 .. **Gueron,** Nicole L '96 (Clarick GR LLP) -40 W 25th -NY 10010 **Fx:**(646) 478-9484
(212) 272-7133 .. **Guerra,** Ivette '96 %JP Morgan Chase -383 Mad Av -NY 10179
(716) 843-5700 .. **Guerra,** Jos M III '81 %US Atty -138 Delaware Av -Buffalo 14202 **Fx:**551-3052
(516) 858-0219 .. **Guerra,** Karla A '07 -510 S Franklin -Hempstd 11550
(212) 764-4222 .. **Guerra,** Maria I '03 %S Jeffries & Assoc -1560 Bway -NY 10036 **Fx:**764-4229
(516) 512-8924 .. **Guerra,** Mark '99 -1225 Franklin Av -Gdn Cty 11530
(212) 735-3000 .. **Guerrera,** Salvatore Jr. '88 (Skadden ASM&F LLP) -4 Times Sq -NY 10036
(212) 777-7000 .. **Guerrero,** Enrique O Jr. '98 (Guerrero & R) -363 7th Av -NY 10001 **Fx:**505-6681
(631) 273-0202 .. **Guerrero,** Ivan E '98 -1836A 5th Av -Bay Shr 11706
(212) 946-2761 .. **Guerrero,** Luis '98 -11 Penn Plz -NY 10001 **Fx:**(917) 720-9855
(212) 481-2744 .. **Guerrero,** Rio M '99 -404 Park Av S -NY 10016 **Fx:**481-2746
(212) 808-9400 .. **Guerriere,** Terence P '88 Madison Cmmrcl Real Estate Srvcs -757 3rd Av -NY 10017 **Fx:**(646) 519-2564
(585) 753-4500 .. **Guerrieri,** Paul A '07 DA -832 Watts Bldg -Rchstr 14614 **Fx:**753-4576
(212) 981-4501 .. **Guerriero,** John M '00 %Smith A,LLP -90 Broad -NY 10004
(718) 321-1339 .. **Guerriero,** Jos '95 -145-33 24th Av -Whitestone 11357 **Fx:**321-7241
(212) 297-5800 .. **Guerriero,** Michl J '76 (Day P LLP) -7 Times Sq -NY 10036
(845) 344-3770 .. **Guertin,** Richd J '82 -6 North -Middletwn 10940 **Fx:**341-1760
(212) 403-1000 .. **Guest,** Mattthew M '01 (Wachtell LR&K) -51 W 52nd -NY 10019
(212) 512-4563 .. **Guetta,** Danl '86 McGraw-Hill Co,Inc -1221 Av of Amer -NY 10020
(518) 786-1800 .. **Guetti,** Christopher A '02 %Flink S LLC -23 British Amer Blvd -Latham 12110 **Fx:**786-1969
(212) 554-7800 .. **Guevara,** Fabián '04 %Moses & S LLP -405 Lex Av -NY 10174
(518) 827-5533 .. **Guevara,** Henry Douglas '93 -1361 Clauverwie Rd -Middleburgh 12122
(212) 605-2000 .. **Gueye,** Tracy Austin '86 %Mitsubishi Intl -655 3rd Av -NY 10017 **Fx:**605-2129
(212) 506-1700 .. **Gugel,** Alison E '01 Kasowitz BT&F LLP -1633 Bway -NY 10019
(718) 268-2986 .. **Gugerty,** David '88 (Davis & G) -118-35 Qns Blvd -Frst Hlls 11375 **Fx:**520-8306
(516) 921-8600 .. **Gugerty,** Merrill B '85 %McAndrew C&P -95 Froehlich Farm Blvd -Woodbury 11797
(516) 766-7700 .. **Guggenheim,** Jamie L '04 %Kassoff R&L -100 Merrick Rd -Rockvll Ctr 11570
(212) 685-7474 .. **Guggenheim,** Martin '72 OfCnsl Mayerson SA LLP -292 Mad Av -NY 10017
(212) 998-6460 .. **Guggenheim,** Martin '72 %NYU Law Schl -245 Sullivan -NY 10012 **Fx:**995-4031
(212) 219-1800 .. **Guggenheimer,** Elizabeth M '88 Lawyers Alliance NY -171 Mad Av -NY 10016 **Fx:**941-7458
(716) 845-2560 .. **Gugino,** Fredk R '72 %Surrogates Ct -92 Franklin -Buffalo 14202 **Fx:**853-3741
(607) 277-5605 .. **Gugino,** Mark C '97 %Gugino Law Ofc -504 Spencer Rd -Ithaca 14850 **Fx:**256-9961
(716) 833-8455 .. **Gugino,** Randy '80 -2140 Eggert Rd -Amherst 14226 **Fx:**833-8472
(716) 852-1000 .. **Gugino,** Rosanne M '89 %PW Beltz,PC -36 Church -Buffalo 14202 **Fx:**852-5887
(716) 853-9555 .. **Gugino,** Vincent F '88 %Leg Aid -237 Main -Buffalo 14203 **Fx:**853-3219
(212) 744-4517 .. **Guglielmelli,** Jos A '82 %Bonjoe Inc -Bx20735 -NY 10021
(518) 402-9512 .. **Guglielmi,** Andrew O '07 DEC -625 Bway -Albany 12233 **Fx:**402-9018
(716) 856-8200 .. **Guglielmi,** Deborah L '00 %Williams & W -43 Court -Buffalo 14202 **Fx:**856-0559
(716) 856-9704 .. **Guglielmi,** Mark E '00 %Feuerstein & S,LLP -17 St Louis Pl -Buffalo 14202 **Fx:**856-9707
(914) 921-0333 .. **Guglielmo,** Angelo A '93 %A Vitagliano -150 Purchase -Rye 10580 **Fx:**921-0796
(718) 590-2000 .. **Guglielmo,** Dawn E '06 DA -198 E 161st -Bronx 10451 **Fx:**590-6477
(212) 809-7074 .. **Guglielmo,** John '82 (Armienti DG&R,LLP) -39 Bway -NY 10006
(212) 223-6444 .. **Guglielmo,** Jos '96 Scott +S,LLP -500 5th Av -NY 10110 **Fx:**223-6334
(212) 209-4800 .. **Guglielmotti,** Vincent J '06 %Brown R LLP -7 Times Sq -NY 10036
(914) 813-1700 .. **Gugliotta,** John C '97 %Gugliotta & Assoc -145 Huguenot -New Rchll 10801 **Fx:**813-1702

(914) 813-1700 .. **Gugliotta,** Richd G '61 -145 Huguenot -New Rchll 10801 **Fx:**813-1702
(914) 286-3400 .. **Gugliotta,** Theresa M '86 %Leg Aid -1 N Bway -White Plns 10601 **Fx:**682-4112
(718) 590-2000 .. **Gugliucciello,** Bevin-Casey '09 %DA -198 E 161st -Bronx 10451 **Fx:**590-6477
(212) 872-1000 .. **Guha,** Samidh '99 -One Bryant Park -NY 10036 **Fx:**872-1002
(212) 806-5400 .. **Guhin,** Christopher M '09 %Stroock &S&L LLP -180 Maiden Ln -NY 10038
(212) 859-8000 .. **Guhl,** Matthew R '04 %Fried FHS&J LLP -1 NY Plz -NY 10004
(212) 649-2000 .. **Guida,** Carl G '95 %Hearst Corp -300 W 57th -NY 10019 **Fx:**649-2035
(212) 407-4000 .. **Guida,** Thos A '98 (Loeb & L,LLP) -345 Park Av -NY 10154
(518) 270-3707 .. **Guidarelli-Wu,** Jacqueline M '89 %Hon E Spain -2nd & Congress -Troy 12180
(212) 521-5400 .. **Guidea,** Jennifer A '01 %Reed S LLP -599 Lex Av -NY 10022
(212) 408-5100 .. **Guider,** Deborah L '84 Cnsl Chadbourne & P LLP -30 Rckfllr Plz -NY 10112
(631) 283-0046 .. **Guidera,** Kerin R '86 %Bourke F&A PC -21 S Main -Southampton 11968
(212) 536-3900 .. **Guidice,** Richd Jr. '04 %K&L Gates LLP -599 Lex Av -NY 10022
(212) 977-9001 .. **Guido,** Anthony W '76 %RHI Entrtnmnt -1325 Av of Amer -NY 10019 **Fx:**977-9049
(914) 995-3624 .. **Guido,** Catherine M '83 Family Ct -111 Martin Luther King Blvd -White Plns 10601 **Fx:**995-4675
(845) 331-4100 .. **Guido,** Christine H '98 %Rusk WH&M,LLP -255 Fair Bx3356 -Kingston 12402
(212) 732-3320 .. **Guido,** Gregory J '06 Short & B,PC -217 Bway -NY 10007
(212) 558-4000 .. **Guido,** Janine C '02 %Sullivan & C LLP -125 Broad -NY 10004
(212) 759-2300 .. **Guido,** Michl A '81 (Carroll G&G,LLP) -1790 Bway -NY 10019
(631) 854-1130 .. **Guido,** Robt P '79 SpclCnsl Appllt Div 2nd Dept -30 E Hoffman Av -Lindenhrst 11757 **Fx:**854-1135
(516) 746-8000 .. **Guido,** Robt V '75 OfCnsl Jaspan S LLP -300 Grdn City Plz -Gdn Cty 11530
(718) 286-6860 .. **Guido,** Umberto F '88 %DA -125-01 Qns Blvd -Kew Gdns 11415
(516) 393-2800 .. **Guidone,** Dawn Pipek '98 -114 Old Cntry Rd -Mineola 11501 **Fx:**393-2801
(718) 445-7434 .. **Guiducci,** Sandra M '83 -136-89 41st Av -Flushng 11355
(631) 979-0367 .. **Guiffrida,** Grace C '95 -17 Wiigs Rd -Nesconset 11767
(518) 487-7600 .. **Guilbault,** Kristin Koehler '96 (Whiteman O&H LLP) -1 Commerce Plz -Albany 12260
(518) 434-3111 .. **Guilbault,** Matthew F '04 PIA Mgmt Srvcs -25 Chmbrlain Bx997 -Glenmont 12077 **Fx:**434-2342
(516) 747-4020 .. **Guilbert,** Richd J '75 (Brown & G LLP) -320 Old Cntry Rd -Gdn Cty 11530 **Fx:**294-1767
(212) 677-5895 .. **Guild,** Wm K '61 -2 Wshngtn Sq Vllg -NY 10012 **Fx:**677-1072
(212) 826-6251 .. **Guilfoyle,** Jennifer March '01 Catholic Lgl Immigrtn Ntwrk -1011 1st Av -NY 10022
(212) 431-1300 .. **Guiliano,** Anna '05 %Borah GAN&G PC -377 Bway -NY 10013
(212) 695-0910 .. **Guiliano,** Jason J '04 %Sullivan Law Grp,LLP -1350 Bway -NY 10018 **Fx:**695-0915
(212) 596-9000 .. **Guiliano,** Jos M '94 (Ropes & G LLP) -1211 Av of Amer -NY 10036
(917) 421-4639 .. **Guiliano,** Vincent J '81 IRS -33 Maiden Ln -NY 10038
(212) 279-9020 .. **Guillergan,** Eve C '93 -875 Av of Amer -NY 10001 **Fx:**202-5064
(212) 264-8568 .. **Guillod,** Ada '92 DHS -26 Fed Plz -NY 10278
(212) 588-9174 .. **Guillorn,** Brian W '83 -515 Mad Av -NY 10022
(646) 356-0550 .. **Guillotte,** Paul H '99 Hirecounsel -575 Mad Av -NY 10022
(212) 335-9000 .. **Guilmain,** Madeleine L '99 %DA -1 Hogan Pl -NY 10013
(212) 848-9800 .. **Guin,** David S '08 (Withers B LLP) -430 Park Av -NY 10022
(212) 605-6200 .. **Guinan,** John P '04 %Levy P&K,LLP -800 3rd Av -NY 10022
(212) 326-3939 .. **Guindo,** Maxime A '07 Jones D -222 E 41st -NY 10017
(212) 964-6611 .. **Guinee,** James E '05 %Lester SK&D -120 Bway -NY 10271
(212) 336-2000 .. **Guiney,** Brian P '05 %Patterson BW&T LLP -1133 Av of Amer -NY 10036
(646) 386-5300 .. **Guiney,** Cornelius J III '74 OCA-Support Magis -60 Lafayette -NY 10013
(212) 545-4761 .. **Guiney,** Matthew M '03 %Wolf HAF&H LLP -270 Mad Av -NY 10016
(718) 802-2647 .. **Guinn,** Nathaniel W '08 Admin Children's Srvcs -330 Jay -Brklyn 11201
(845) 291-2050 .. **Guinup,** Elizabeth L '08 %DA -255-275 Main -Goshen 10924 **Fx:**291-2085
(212) 318-3000 .. **Guirguis,** Peter '04 %Fulbright & J LLP -666 5th Av -NY 10103
(646) 471-3620 .. **Guiry,** James M '92 PricewaterhouseCoopers LLP -300 Mad Av -NY 10017
(212) 839-5300 .. **Guitar,** Veronica B '08 %Sidley A LLP -787 7th Av -NY 10019
(716) 858-2424 .. **Guite,** Vanessa S '04 %DA -25 Delaware Av -Buffalo 14202 **Fx:**858-7425
(212) 777-1402 .. **Guiton,** John P '83 -27 W 96th -NY 10025
(212) 552-2647 .. **Guja,** Arthur T '77 JP Morgan Chase -1 Chase Manh Plz -NY 10081
(212) 839-5300 .. **Gujadhur,** Santosh K '08 %Sidley A LLP -787 7th Av -NY 10019
(914) 993-1941 .. **Gujarati,** Diane '96 US Atty -300 Quarropas -White Plns 10601 **Fx:**993-9036
(212) 325-5291 .. **Gujral,** Gautam S '98 Credit Suisse -11 Mad Av -NY 10010
(212) 806-3500 .. **Gul,** Eric I '97 %TD Waterhouse -100 Wall -NY 10005
(212) 885-5000 .. **Gulant,** Jos T '86 (Blank R LLP) -405 Lex Av -NY 10174
(516) 742-7127 .. **Gulati,** Reena C '96 -3000 Marcus Av -Lk Success 11042 **Fx:**742-7131
(212) 478-0000 .. **Gulati,** Richa M '06 DE Shaw & Co -120 W 45th -NY 10036
(212) 872-1000 .. **Gulati,** Sunish '04 -One Bryant Park -NY 10036 **Fx:**872-1002
(718) 260-8701 .. **Gulati,** Verita J '04 %ACS -345 Adams -Brklyn 11201
(631) 288-3737 .. **Guldi,** George O '79 -100 Mill Rd -Westhmptn Bch 11978 **Fx:**288-3742
(212) 692-1000 .. **Gulia,** Gregory P '93 (Duane M LLP) -1540 Bway -NY 10036
(516) 393-2200 .. **Gulick,** Stacey L '02 (Garfunkel W,PC) -111 Grt Nck Rd -Gt Neck 11021
(914) 941-5668 .. **Gulick,** Thos P '04 %Collen IP -80 S Highland Av -Ossining 10562 **Fx:**941-6091
(516) 463-5858 .. **Gulino,** Frank '80 Hofstra Law Schl -121 Hofstra Univ -Hempstd 11549
(718) 987-2000 .. **Gulino,** John P '70 (John Gulino,PC) -85 New Dorp Ln -Staten Isl 10306
(212) 730-7750 .. **Gulino,** Jos J '84 (Nicoletti GS&O,LLP) -555 5th Av -NY 10017
(631) 654-9500 .. **Gulino,** Jos S '09 %R Dapelo,PC -110 N Ocean Av -Patchogue 11772 **Fx:**654-4613
(716) 849-6800 .. **Gulisano,** Philip M '97 (Burden G&H,LLC) -403 Main -Buffalo 14203 **Fx:**849-6806
(914) 428-2100 .. **Gulitz,** Lester '77 OfCnsl Welby B&G,LLP -11 Martine Av -White Plns 10606
(631) 756-4186 .. **Gulizia,** Robt R '97 State Ins Fund -8 Corp Ctr Dr -Melvll 11747 **Fx:**756-4060
(631) 451-6370 .. **Gulizio,** Danl J '04 Town of Brookhaven -1 Indpndnc Hill -Farmngvll 11738
(212) 277-6500 .. **Gulkowitz,** Arnold '82 (Dickstein S LLP) -1633 Bway -NY 10019
(516) 759-1212 .. **Gull,** Kathryn N '91 Cnsl Mohen & T LLP -186 Birch Hill Rd -Locust Vly 11560
(585) 546-1980 .. **Gullace,** Dante '61 (Fulton F&G LLP) -28 E Main -Rchstr 14614
(585) 563-9721 .. **Gullace,** Megan E '09 Fulton F&G -500 1st Fed Plz -Rchstr 14614
(212) 446-4800 .. **Gulliford,** Michl J '06 %Kirkland & E LLP -153 E 53rd -NY 10022
(845) 942-4450 .. **Gulliver,** Brigitte M '89 -361 Route 210 -Stony Pnt 10980 **Fx:**942-0796
(516) 294-3550 .. **Gullo,** Benedict S Jr. '67 -114 Old Cntry Rd -Mineola 11501
(718) 238-9555 .. **Gullo,** Dominick '95 (Gullo & Assoc,LLP) -520 86th -Brklyn 11209 **Fx:**238-9552
(516) 692-2744 .. **Gullo,** Elizabeth Lambert '09 %Stefans Law Grp,PC -137 Woodbury Rd -Woodbury 11797 **Fx:**692-2746
(716) 679-0100 .. **Gullo,** John P II '91 -221 Central Av -Fredonia 14063 **Fx:**679-0600
(718) 238-9555 .. **Gullo,** Michl E '95 (Gullo & Assoc,LLP) -520 86th -Brklyn 11209 **Fx:**238-9552
(914) 741-0452 .. **Gullotta,** Susan C '87 -390 Bedford Rd -Plsntvll 10570 **Fx:**741-2736
(716) 484-7196 .. **Gullotti,** Danl T '86 (Fessenden L&D) -81 Forest Av Bx590 -Jamestwn 14702
(212) 949-4700 .. **Gulmi,** Jos E '74 (Bushell SO&G LLP) -60 E 42nd -NY 10165 **Fx:**286-0513
(631) 285-7000 .. **Gulotta,** Anthony J '88 (Tantone & G) -2459 Ocean Av -Ronkonkoma 11779 **Fx:**285-7006
(212) 481-1312 .. **Gulotta,** Christopher J '89 (Gulotta Law Grp PLLC) -271 Mad Av -NY 10016 **Fx:**481-1316
(516) 775-2236 .. **Gulotta,** Franca Maria '81 %Santangelo B&S -1800 Nrthrn Blvd -Roslyn 11576
(212) 935-3000 .. **Gulotta,** Stephen J Jr. '82 (Mintz LCFG&P,PC) -666 3rd Av -NY 10017
(516) 248-7000 .. **Gulotta,** Thos S '69 SpclCnsl Albanese & A LLP -1050 Franklin Av -Gdn Cty 11530
(212) 652-3851 .. **Gulyas,** Winifred Gyongyi '07 %Schlesinger G&L LLP -535 Mad Av -NY 10022
(315) 474-2943 .. **Gumaer,** Matthew D '96 (Sugarman Law Firm,LLP) -211 W Jffrsn -Syracuse 13202
(212) 371-3900 .. **Gumbinger,** Walter '68 -355 Lex Av -NY 10017
(212) 657-1216 .. **Gumbs,** Etta M '89 Citigroup -77 Water -NY 10005
(212) 788-0421 .. **Gumbs,** Robina M '90 %Law Dept -100 Church -NY 10007 **Fx:**788-0367
(212) 964-7400 .. **Gumbs,** Yasmeen K '08 Smith MDWY&Y,PC -111 John -NY 10038
(212) 608-7478 .. **Gumenick,** Robt J '80 RJ Gumenick,PC -260 Mad Av -NY 10016 **Fx:**608-7759
(516) 822-3397 .. **Gumerove,** Saundra M '77 -42 Marian Ln -Jericho 11753 **Fx:**822-3516
(516) 357-3000 .. **Gumersell,** Walter J '80 (Rivkin R LLP) -926 RXR Plz -Uniondale 11556
(585) 724-2803 .. **Gumina,** Gregory J '89 %Eastman Kodak -343 State -Rchstr 14650
(716) 849-1333 .. **Gumkowski,** Jos J '80 (Lipsitz GSC LLP) -42 Delaware Av -Buffalo 14202
(607) 746-3211 .. **Gumo,** Richd L '67 -Bx247 -Delhi 13753
(917) 542-8334 .. **Gump,** Patricia Folan '09 Mass Mutual Financial Grp -340 Mad Av -NY 10173
(212) 858-1000 .. **Gump,** Thos K '07 (Pillsbury WSP LLP) -1540 Bway -NY 10036
(212) 728-8000 .. **Gump,** Wm H '90 (Willkie F&G LLP) -787 7th Av -NY 10019
(631) 501-3100 .. **Gumpert,** Scott Lee '83 %J Humphreys -3 Huntngtn Quad Bx9028 -Melvll 11747 **Fx:**501-3085
(212) 949-9022 .. **Gumport,** Jonathan W '89 (Abelman F&S) -666 3rd Av -NY 10017
(212) 244-2999 .. **Gunasekera,** Priyanthi R '86 %Kopff N&D LLP -440 9th Av -NY 10001
(212) 966-6420 .. **Gundersen,** Krista M '08 Lwyrs For Children -110 Lafayette -NY 10013 **Fx:**966-0531
(212) 554-1400 .. **Gundersheim,** Laura H '05 %Bernstein LB&G LLP -1285 Av of Amer -NY 10019
(917) 639-4157 .. **Gunderson,** Chris G '63 %Universal Express -1230 Av of Amer -NY 10020
(212) 730-8133 .. **Gunderson Dettmer Stough Villeneuve Franklin & Hachigian,LLP** -220 W 42nd -NY 10036
(631) 727-4100 .. **Gunderson,** Jeanmarie '99 %Smith FLI&Y -456 Griffing Av Bx389 -Rvrhead 11901
(315) 253-2288 .. **Gunger,** Richd W '89 -5 Court -Auburn 13021 **Fx:**252-9131
(212) 737-9003 .. **Gunin,** Jeffrey S '75 -301 E 73rd -NY 10021
(631) 286-3500 .. **Gunkel,** Karen E '86 (Gunkel & K,PC) -9 Station Ct -Bellprt 11713 **Fx:**286-6188
(516) 745-1300 .. **Gunn,** Brian R '95 (Cerussi & G,PC) -1325 Franklin Av -Gdn Cty 11530 **Fx:**745-1310
(212) 788-0695 .. **Gunn,** Jos T '86 %Law Dept -100 Church -NY 10007 **Fx:**227-5648
(212) 733-8941 .. **Gunn,** Melissa A '98 %Pfizer Inc -235 E 42nd -NY 10017
(631) 852-2500 .. **Gunn,** Patrick J '05 %DA -200 Center Dr -Rvrhead 11901 **Fx:**852-2762
(212) 981-4501 .. **Gunn,** Robt K '95 SpclCnsl Smith A,LLP -90 Broad -NY 10004
(585) 593-7335 .. **Gunner,** G Wm III '87 -175 N Main -Wellsvll 14895
(212) 596-9000 .. **Gunnison,** Jane Tower '94 (Ropes & G LLP) -1211 Av of Amer -NY 10036
(212) 581-3320 .. **Gunsburg,** Saml A '99 %Wasserman G&R,LLP -1700 Bway -NY 10019
(718) 250-2000 .. **Gunsburg,** Shlomo Z '09 %DA -350 Jay -Brklyn 11201 **Fx:**250-2314
(212) 382-4080 .. **Gunset,** Jos P '82 %Lloyds America,Inc -25 W 53rd -NY 10019
(212) 422-1200 .. **Gunsher,** Jay S '96 %Abrams GF&J,PC -1 Bttry Pk Plz -NY 10004
(914) 241-1094 .. **Gunshor,** Kenneth '72 -100 S Bedford Rd -Mt Kisco 10549
(516) 616-4440 .. **Gunsten,** Glenn G '96 (Brea Y,PC) -35 N Tyson Av -Floral Pk 11001

(212) 735-3000 .. **Gunther,** Christopher J '92 (Skadden ASM&F LLP) -4 Times Sq -NY 10036
(212) 848-4000 .. **Gunther,** Jack D Jr. '66 Cnsl Shearman & S LLP -599 Lex Av -NY 10022
(212) 965-9370 .. **Gunther,** Karen Lee '89 -350 Bway -NY 10013
(212) 632-5500 .. **Gunther,** Paul C '00 %Salans LLP -620 5th Av -NY 10020
(212) 230-8800 .. **Gunther,** Robt J Jr. '85 (WilmerHale) -399 Park Av -NY 10022
(212) 986-6338 .. **Gunther,** Saml P '66 -122 E 42nd -NY 10168
(800) 245-9943 .. **Gunther,** Tess E '01 %Forster & G -500 Bi-Cnty Blvd Bx9030 -Farmngdl 11735
(212) 720-5694 .. **Gunton,** David L '07 Fed Reserve Bk -33 Lbrty -NY 10045 **Fx:**785-5748
(631) 367-7100 .. **Gunyan,** Russell J '96 %Coughlin SGR&R LLP -58 S Srvc Rd -Melvll 11747
(212) 725-8500 .. **Gunzburg,** Michl W '87 (M Gunzburg PC) -275 Mad Av -NY 10016 **Fx:**725-9787
(212) 909-6000 .. **Guo,** Danli '07 %Debevoise & P LLP -919 3rd Av -NY 10022
(718) 888-8720 .. **Guo,** Fengli '02 -3626 Main -Flushng 11354
(212) 225-2000 .. **Guo,** Haini '06 %Cleary GS&H -1 Lbrty Plz -NY 10006
(212) 455-2000 .. **Guo,** Wei '10 %Simpson T&B LLP -425 Lex Av -NY 10017
(212) 885-5000 .. **Guo,** Zhihui '10 %Blank R LLP -405 Lex Av -NY 10174
(718) 260-2300 .. **Gupta,** Anjum '04 %Hon C Sifton -225 Cadman Plz E -Brklyn 11201
(212) 425-7200 .. **Gupta,** Maneesh '09 %Kenyon & K,LLP -1 Bway -NY 10004
(646) 386-5891 .. **Gupta,** Namita '07 MHLS -41 Mad Av -NY 10010
(212) 506-5000 .. **Gupta,** Paul R '75 (Orrick H&S LLP) -51 W 52nd -NY 10019
(212) 819-8818 .. **Gupta,** Poonam '03 -1155 Av of Amer -NY 10036 **Fx:**354-8113
(212) 335-4500 .. **Gupta,** Rachel A '05 %DLA Piper LLP -1251 Av of Amer -NY 10020
(212) 906-1200 .. **Gupta,** Rajani K '03 %Latham & W -885 3rd Av -NY 10022
(212) 909-6000 .. **Gupta,** Rishab '10 %Debevoise & P LLP -919 3rd Av -NY 10022
(212) 739-6400 .. **Gupta,** Rishi '07 Orbimed Advisors -767 3rd Av -NY 10017
(212) 218-2100 .. **Gupta,** Sachin K '09 %Fitzpatrick CH&S -1290 Av of Amer -NY 10104
(212) 551-0963 .. **Gupta,** Sangita '01 Intl Rescue Comm -122 E 42nd -NY 10168
(212) 756-2000 .. **Gupta,** Sonal '07 %Schulte R&Z LLP -919 3rd Av -NY 10022
(212) 965-2200 .. **Gupta,** Vanita '02 %NAACP/LDF -99 Hudson -NY 10013 **Fx:**226-7592
(212) 809-7800 .. **Gupta,** Vijay Kumar Jr. '05 %Jaffe & K,LLP -40 Wall -NY 10005 **Fx:**785-6842
(212) 218-2100 .. **Gupta,** Vishal C '07 %Fitzpatrick CH&S -1290 Av of Amer -NY 10104
(212) 633-2225 .. **Gupta,** Vivek V '03 %M Stumer & Assoc,PC -306 5th Av -NY 10001 **Fx:**691-3642
(212) 527-1000 .. **Gura,** Chas T '97 (Jones HC&B PC) -1 Bttry Pk Plz -NY 10004
(212) 804-4200 .. **Gura,** Lloyd A '91 (Mound CW&G) -One Bttry Pk Plz -NY 10004
(845) 679-7611 .. **Gura,** Rachelle L '89 -10 Evergreen Ln -Woodstock 12498
(516) 539-7900 .. **Gura,** Rona L '87 %Breiter & G,LLP -377 Oak -Gdn Cty 11530
(914) 949-6400 .. **Gurahian,** Patricia W '88 %McCullough G&S,LLP -1311 Mamaroneck Av -White Plns 10605
(516) 541-7872 .. **Guralnick,** Howard R '86 -1045A Park Blvd -Massapequa Pk 11762
(212) 406-4454 .. **Guralnick,** Ilene H '78 -49 W 37th -NY 10018 **Fx:**406-3379
(718) 923-6300 .. **Gur-Arie,** Kathryn Donnelly '90 %Atty Grievance Comm -335 Adams -Brklyn 11201 **Fx:**624-2978
(212) 859-8000 .. **Gurary,** Michl M '06 %Fried FHS&J LLP -1 NY Plz -NY 10004
(716) 652-0828 .. **Gurbacki,** Robt H '81 (Hall RM&G) -471 Main -E Aurora 14052
(347) 721-7090 .. **Gurcan,** Arzu '05 -2619 Emmons Av -Brklyn 11235
(718) 625-8940 .. **Gurcan,** Erol B '90 %B Lawrence -15 Metrotech Ctr N -Brklyn 11201 **Fx:**624-5756
(212) 819-8200 .. **Gurch,** Matthew J '08 %White & C LLP -1155 Av of Amer -NY 10036
(845) 343-2101 .. **Gurda,** Christopher E '02 -41 Dolson Av Bx578 -Middletwn 10940
(845) 343-2101 .. **Gurda,** Michl A Jr. '72 Gurda Law Ofc -41 Dolson Av -Middletwn 10940 **Fx:**343-2120
(212) 310-8000 .. **Gurdian,** Julio C '08 %Weil G&M LLP -767 5th Av -NY 10153
(516) 357-3000 .. **Gurdus,** Jason B '02 %Rivkin R LLP -926 RXR Plz -Uniondale 11556
(212) 218-5500 .. **Gurell,** Marc J '95 (Seyfarth S LLP) -620 8th Av -NY 10018
(518) 237-4673 .. **Guresz,** Caroline '75 -14 Stratford Ct -Cohoes 12047 **Fx:**237-4673
(212) 829-9200 .. **Gurevich,** Alexander J '88 (Janoff & G,LLP) -216 E 49th -NY 10017
(212) 596-9000 .. **Gurevich,** Mark '05 %Ropes & G LLP -1211 Av of Amer -NY 10036
(718) 250-0400 .. **Gurevich,** Michl '01 %R Tusa -1 MetroTech Ctr -Brklyn 11201 **Fx:**250-0591
(516) 767-9862 .. **Gurewitz,** Bruce I '84 -7 Woodlnd Dr -Pt Wash 11050
(212) 818-9200 .. **Gurfein,** Danl G '80 (Satterlee SB&B LLP) -230 Park Av -NY 10169
(212) 406-1600 .. **Gurfein Douglas LLP** -11 Park Pl -NY 10007 **Fx:**406-4779
(212) 406-1600 .. **Gurfein,** Richd A '72 (Gurfein D LLP) -11 Park Pl -NY 10007
(212) 490-9100 .. **Gurfel,** Diana '00 (Condon & F LLP) -7 Times Sq -NY 10036
(347) 404-9133 .. **Gurfinkel,** Stephen J '08 Civil Ct -141 Lvngstn -Brklyn 11201 **Fx:**(718) 643-3733
(718) 250-2587 .. **Guria,** Chas M '87 %DA -350 Jay -Brklyn 11201 **Fx:**250-2314
(212) 346-7600 .. **Gurian,** Craig '84 Anti-Discrim Ctr of Metro NY -233 Bway -NY 10279 **Fx:**242-6126
(646) 822-3663 .. **Gurian,** Jannet L '80 Thomson Fncl Inc -195 Bway -NY 10007
(914) 793-1010 .. **Gurian,** Robt B '74 (Morgan B&P) -274 Wht Plns Rd -Eastchstr 10707
(718) 237-2556 .. **Gurinsky,** Heath '00 New Start,LLC -32 Court -Brklyn 11201 **Fx:**237-4876
(212) 832-5806 .. **Gurion,** Tal '98 %EOS Partners -320 Park Av -NY 10022 **Fx:**832-5815
(212) 385-0285 .. **Gurk,** F S '02 -305 Mad Av -NY 10165 **Fx:**385-0286
(212) 509-0099 .. **Gurkan,** Cicek '07 Haker & O,LLP -29 Bway -NY 10006 **Fx:**506-0488
(212) 430-6040 .. **Gurland,** Robt J '69 Wasser & R LLP -80 Maiden Ln -NY 10038 **Fx:**430-6041
(212) 768-4343 .. **Gurlitz,** Rachael E '08 %Cantor E&M,LLP -49 W 37th -NY 10018
(212) 944-2200 .. **Gurman,** Menahem Z '76 -530 5th Av -NY 10036 **Fx:**944-7630
(516) 883-6050 .. **Gurman,** Rebecca L '92 -40 Sandy Ct -Pt Wash 11050 **Fx:**883-1553
(914) 472-0937 .. **Gurney,** Clark J '64 -12 Sage Cir -Scarsdale 10583
(212) 820-9438 .. **Gurney,** Donald G '71 (Hawkins D&W LLP) -One Chase Manh Plz -NY 10005
(716) 845-7488 .. **Gurney,** Jacquelyn McGuire '98 Family Ct -1 Niagara Plz -Buffalo 14202 **Fx:**858-7756
(212) 758-0050 .. **Gurren,** Jeffrey G '75 %Title Assoc -825 3rd Av -NY 10022 **Fx:**758-8223
(646) 373-2809 .. **Gurrola,** Kenneth W '03 Ernst & Young LLP -5 Times Sq -NY 10036
(718) 261-0300 .. **Gursky,** Robt J '73 -125-10 Qns Blvd -Kew Gdns 11415 **Fx:**793-6564
(212) 741-4445 .. **Gursky,** Ruth M '81 -101 W 12th -NY 10011 **Fx:**243-1434
(212) 451-2385 .. **Gursky,** Steven R '80 (Olshan GFR&W LLP) -65 E 55th -NY 10022
(718) 646-7360 .. **Gursoy,** Umit Mike '00 Gursoy Law Firm,PC -1624 Voorhies Av -Brklyn 11235 **Fx:**646-7321
(212) 937-6461 .. **Gurtman,** Brian N '01 Cnsl WilmerHale -399 Park Av -NY 10022
(631) 617-5595 .. **Gurtman,** Marc H '92 Town Line Veterinary Grp -601 Vets Mem'l Hwy -Hauppauge 11788
(212) 583-9600 .. **Gurtman,** Ronit M '06 %Littler M,PC -900 3rd Av -NY 10022
(212) 964-6611 .. **Gurtman,** Scott '98 %Lester SK&D -120 Bway -NY 10271
(718) 579-3000 .. **Gurwitch,** Laurence A '89 %Leg Aid -1020 Grnd Cncrs -Bronx 10451 **Fx:**588-2611
(212) 402-4100 .. **Gurwitch,** Sara Anne '96 %Ofc Appllt Def -11 Park Pl -NY 10007 **Fx:**402-4199
(212) 859-8000 .. **Guryan,** Peter S '98 (Fried FHS&J LLP) -1 NY Plz -NY 10004
(212) 530-5000 .. **Guseynov,** Emin '08 %Milbank TH&M LLP -1 Chase Manh Plz -NY 10005
(212) 859-8000 .. **Guseynov,** Melissa A '08 %Fried FHS&J LLP -1 NY Plz -NY 10004
(914) 629-6681 .. **Gushner,** Terry J '95 -2 Richbell Rd -Scarsdale 10583 **Fx:**723-7719
(212) 254-7979 .. **Gusick,** Michl S '64 (Gusick Assoc,PC) -648 Bway -NY 10012 **Fx:**995-2341
(212) 496-5333 .. **Gusman,** Jeffrey G '91 -300 Cntrl Pk W -NY 10024
(914) 725-2357 .. **Gusmano,** Jos J '61 -3 Hanfling Rd -Scarsdale 10583
(718) 843-3300 .. **Gusmorino,** Jos D '77 (Gusmorino & M) -104-21 Lefferts Blvd -S Richmond Hll 11419
(718) 843-3300 .. **Gusmorino & Marx** -104-21 Lefferts Blvd -S Richmond Hll 11419 **Fx:**843-4711
(212) 269-1400 .. **Gusrae,** Bert L '62 OfCnsl Gusrae KB&N PLLC -120 Wall -NY 10005
(212) 269-1400 .. **Gusrae Kaplan Bruno & Nusbaum PLLC** -120 Wall -NY 10005 **Fx:**809-5449
(212) 818-9200 .. **Guss,** Amy Jeanne '93 (Satterlee SB&B LLP) -230 Park Av -NY 10169
(212) 779-8600 .. **Guss,** Marc W '94 %Silverman SS&B PLLC -381 Park Av S -NY 10016
(212) 964-1244 .. **Gussin,** Arnold M '61 -9 Murray -NY 10007 **Fx:**732-4443
(212) 756-2000 .. **Gussman,** Wm H '97 (Schulte R&Z LLP) -919 3rd Av -NY 10022
(212) 973-0572 .. **Gussoff,** Jeffrey M '83 (Wolff & S PC) -140 Bway -NY 10005
(315) 769-3898 .. **Gustafson,** Eric J '92 (Pease & G) -40 Main -Massena 13662 **Fx:**769-5018
(212) 819-8200 .. **Gustafson,** Jamie L '08 %White & C LLP -1155 Av of Amer -NY 10036
(716) 636-7600 .. **Gustafson,** Jean Harris '05 %HoganWillig -2410 N Forest Rd -Amherst 14068
(212) 888-3033 .. **Gustafson,** Karin P E '85 %Becker GM&M LLP -299 Park Av -NY 10171
(716) 664-2346 .. **Gustafson,** Kurt D '92 (Lundberg & G,LLP) -202 W 4th -Jamestwn 14701
(585) 454-2000 .. **Gustafson,** Todd W '99 %Brenna B&B,PLLC -31 E Main -Rchstr 14614
(631) 581-3036 .. **Gustavson,** Lawr H '03 -1465 5th Av -Bay Shr 11706
(212) 813-8800 .. **Gustavson,** Steven R '97 Cnsl Goodwin P LLP -620 8th Av -NY 10018
(646) 502-8066 .. **Gusy,** Martin F '03 (Gusy V LLP) -500 5th Av -NY 10110 **Fx:**536-8154
(212) 325-2000 .. **Guszkowski,** Glenn '02 Credit Suisse -11 Mad Av -NY 10010
(914) 422-1241 .. **Gutekunst,** Arthur G '77 %Law Dept -255 Main -White Plns 10601 **Fx:**422-1231
(212) 969-3000 .. **Gutekunst,** Claire P '84 (Proskauer R LLP) -1585 Bway -NY 10036
(607) 273-6841 .. **Gutenberger,** Kristin E '05 %Barney GDM&O,LLP -119 E Seneca -Ithaca 14850
(212) 373-3117 .. **Gutenplan,** Bruce A '86 (Paul WRW&G LLP) -1285 Av of Amer -NY 10019
(914) 761-4488 .. **Guterman,** Mark A '88 %Lehrman & K -199 Main -White Plns 10601
(518) 828-5400 .. **Guterman Shallo & Alford, PLLC** -21 N 7th -Hudson 12534 **Fx:**828-0267
(518) 392-3641 .. **Guterman Shallo & Alford, PLLC** -50-52 Main -Chatham 12037 **Fx:**392-3605
(518) 828-5400 .. **Guterman,** Theo '72 (Guterman S&A,PLLC) -21 N 7th -Hudson 12534
(212) 566-7300 .. **Gutfleisch,** Jeffrey M '91 -220 5th Av -NY 10001
(212) 847-7900 .. **Gutfleisch,** Todd A '95 %Wechsler & C,LLP -17 State -NY 10004
(212) 577-3389 .. **Gutheil,** Karen Fisher '98 %Leg Aid -199 Water -NY 10038 **Fx:**577-3520
(631) 351-3067 .. **Guthman-Abadom,** Jillian Allette '95 Human Svcs Dept-EEO Ofcr -100 Main -Huntngtn 11743 **Fx:**425-0746
(315) 446-0484 .. **Guthmann,** Stephen F '73 -1 Brandon Rd -DeWitt 13214
(718) 237-2000 .. **Guthrie,** Laura Winifred '03 Leg Aid -111 Lvngstn -Brklyn 11201 **Fx:**237-8737
(516) 229-4501 .. **Gutier,** Maria C '00 %Russo A&T -875 Merrick Av -Westbury 11590
(212) 885-5000 .. **Gutierrez,** Carlos E '06 %Blank R LLP -405 Lex Av -NY 10174
(718) 286-6000 .. **Gutierrez,** Carmencita N '89 %DA -125-01 Qns Blvd -Kew Gdns 11415
(212) 813-8800 .. **Gutierrez,** Catalina M '09 %Goodwin P LLP -620 8th Av -NY 10018
(716) 877-4276 .. **Gutierrez,** F Alejandro '02 (A Gutierrez PLLC) -745 Englewood Av -Buffalo 14223 **Fx:**877-4220
(718) 250-2000 .. **Gutierrez,** Gerardo Jr. '09 %DA -350 Jay -Brklyn 11201 **Fx:**250-2314
(212) 614-6464 .. **Gutierrez,** Gitanjali S '03 Ctr Cnstnl Rights -666 Bway -NY 10012 **Fx:**614-6499
(212) 613-4244 .. **Gutierrez,** Jesse F '03 Navigators Ins -1 Penn Plz -NY 10119
(518) 474-9496 .. **Gutierrez,** Malinka K '95 %OTDA -40 N Pearl -Albany 12243 **Fx:**474-9389

(212) 576-5528 .. **Gutierrez,** Maria G '00 NY Life Ins -51 Mad Av -NY 10010
(212) 822-8300 .. **Gutierrez,** Ramon '93 %NMIC -76 Wadsworth Av -NY 10033 **Fx:**740-9645
(718) 520-0663 .. **Gutierrez,** Richd M '83 -118-35 Qns Blvd -Frst Hlls 11375 **Fx:**520-8306
(212) 876-5500 .. **Gutierrez,** Roxanna M '90 Neighborhood Def Srv -317 Lenox Av -NY 10027 **Fx:**876-5586
(212) 351-4000 .. **Gutin,** Danl A '10 Gibson D&C LLP -200 Park Av -NY 10166
(212) 649-9700 .. **Gutkin,** Orit Gila '06 Greystone & Co -152 W 57th -NY 10019
(585) 781-7532 .. **Gutkin,** Paula J '90 Eastman Kodak -343 State -Rchstr 14650
(516) 741-6565 .. **Gutleber,** Edw J '81 (Meyer SE&K,PC) -990 Stewart Av Bx9194 -Gdn Cty 11530
(718) 797-2046 .. **Gutleber,** Jos F Jr. '83 -30 S Oxford -Brklyn 11217 **Fx:**522-0728
(718) 855-6061 .. **Gutleber,** Stephen C '82 -142 Joralemon -Brklyn 11201
(516) 248-0470 .. **Gutman,** Andrew E '87 (Gutman & G LLP) -19 Roslyn Rd -Mineola 11501 **Fx:**746-6997
(718) 259-2100 .. **Gutman,** Arthur '07 (Gutman W,PC) -2276 65th -Brklyn 11204 **Fx:**259-2105
(212) 416-8000 .. **Gutman,** Benjamin N '05 %Dept of Law -120 Bway -NY 10271
(516) 248-0470 .. **Gutman,** Elizabeth A '57 (Gutman & G LLP) -19 Roslyn Rd -Mineola 11501 **Fx:**746-6997
(212) 455-2000 .. **Gutman,** Henry B '77 (Simpson T&B LLP) -425 Lex Av -NY 10017
(212) 644-5200 .. **Gutman,** Jeremy L '81 -233 Bway -NY 10279
(718) 858-4315 .. **Gutman,** Karoly S '84 -13 Pineapple -Brklyn 11201
(516) 248-0470 .. **Gutman,** Lawr C '53 (Gutman & G LLP) -19 Roslyn Rd -Mineola 11501 **Fx:**746-6997
(516) 203-7555 .. **Gutman,** Lisa A '02 -37 Boylston -Gdn Cty 11530 **Fx:**741-1813
(516) 775-7007 .. **Gutman Mintz Baker & Sonnenfeldt,PC** -813 Jericho Tpk -New Hyde Pk 11040 **Fx:**775-7052
(516) 496-5822 .. **Gutman,** Nicole E '08 T Spina -170 Froehlich Farm Blvd -Woodbury 11797 **Fx:**496-5420
(212) 455-2000 .. **Gutman,** Olga '98 (Simpson T&B LLP) -425 Lex Av -NY 10017
(212) 759-2300 .. **Gutman,** Paul S '05 %Carroll G&G,LLP -1790 Bway -NY 10019
(718) 522-0666 .. **Gutman,** Robt '52 (Sanders G&B,PC) -26 Court -Brklyn 11242
(516) 944-0301 .. **Gutman,** S Mac '70 (Gutman & G) -33 Main -Pt Wash 11050 **Fx:**944-0310
(212) 953-2381 .. **Gutman,** Tara K '04 %Rubin F&F,LLP -292 Mad Av -NY 10017
(212) 698-3500 .. **Gutman Mann,** Jillian E '09 %Dechert LLP -1095 Av of Amer -NY 10036
(718) 250-2000 .. **Gutmann,** Anne M '87 %DA -350 Jay -Brklyn 11201 **Fx:**250-2314
(585) 232-3680 .. **Gutmann,** David J '82 %Public Abstract Corp -16 W Main -Rchstr 14614 **Fx:**325-6680
(516) 222-0888 .. **Gutmanstein,** Scott M '06 %Lehman & E LLP -50 Chas Lindbergh Blvd -Uniondale 11553
(212) 499-7700 .. **Gutoff,** Deborah L '80 Eastern Consolidated Properties -355 Lex Av -NY 10017
(212) 310-8000 .. **Gutowitz,** Wm M '82 (Weil G&M LLP) -767 5th Av -NY 10153
(315) 858-9059 .. **Gutowski,** David A '88 -2002 Cnty Hwy 22 -Richfld Spgs 13439
(518) 642-9200 .. **Gutowski,** Gary E '72 -76 Main Bx103 -Granvll 12832 **Fx:**642-9392
(212) 425-1900 .. **Gutowski,** Peter J '82 (Freehill H&M LLP) -80 Pine -NY 10005
(212) 762-1467 .. **Gutowski,** Robt J '00 Morgan Stanley Capital Intl -750 7th Av -NY 10019
(516) 741-1250 .. **Gutsin,** Phillip E '86 (Engel & G,LLP) -198 Miller Pl -Hicksvll 11801
(516) 681-1100 .. **Gutstein,** Keith J '97 (Kaufman DV&G,LLP) -135 Crsswys Park Dr -Woodbury 11797
(212) 922-1983 .. **Gutstein,** Steven I '73 -230 Park Av -NY 10169
(212) 697-3122 .. **Guttell,** Adam G '06 %Martin C&B LLP -220 E 42nd -NY 10017
(516) 616-1155 .. **Guttenplan,** Kenneth S '70 -2001 Marcus Av -Lk Success 11042 **Fx:**616-9797
(516) 616-1155 .. **Guttenplan,** Marra H '07 -2001 Marcus Av -Lk Success 11042 **Fx:**616-9797
(631) 661-5000 .. **Guttentag,** Jeffrey L '94 (Seidner R&G) -403 Deer Prk Av -Babylon 11702
(212) 549-2500 .. **Guttentag,** Lucas '88 %ACLU -125 Broad -NY 10004 **Fx:**549-2651
(516) 803-2596 .. **Gutteridge,** Jessica '98 Cablevision -1111 Stewart Av -Bethpage 11714
(212) 556-4099 .. **Gutterman,** Andrew M '96 %The NY Times Co -620 8th Av -NY 10018
(914) 262-9154 .. **Gutterman,** Barry A '71 -102 Old Army Rd -Scarsdale 10583
(212) 983-1466 .. **Gutterman,** Barry N '87 B Gutterman & Assoc,PC -85 Davids Way -Bedfrd Hlls 10507 **Fx:**983-1229
(914) 683-8998 .. **Gutterman,** Janet J '85 (Gutterman & O) -202 Mamaroneck Av -White Plns 10601 **Fx:**948-1320
(212) 867-4100 .. **Gutterman,** Jennifer Y '02 %Furman K&B LLP -61 Bway -NY 10006
(212) 308-5495 .. **Gutterson,** Scott '84 -515 Mad Av -NY 10022 **Fx:**421-4036
(516) 825-1600 .. **Guttikonda,** Paresh '97 Guttikonda Law,PLLC -195 Rockaway Av -Vly Stream 11580
(212) 766-2466 .. **Guttin,** Matthew S '04 (DiSanto LLP) -15 Maiden Ln -NY 10038 **Fx:**(866) 746-0504
(212) 608-3188 .. **Guttlein,** Jorge D '80 (J Guttlein & Assoc,PC) -291 Bway -NY 10007 **Fx:**385-0231
(212) 261-8000 .. **Guttler,** Chas F '00 (Mendes & M,LLP) -750 7th Av -NY 10019
(631) 777-3900 .. **Guttman,** Bruce H '90 (Guttman & G) -1 Huntngtn Quad -Melvll 11747 **Fx:**777-3907
(607) 272-2102 .. **Guttman,** Chas '76 (Guttman & W) -411 N Tioga -Ithaca 14850 **Fx:**272-2350
(212) 446-4800 .. **Guttman,** Elazar '03 (Kirkland & E LLP) -153 E 53rd -NY 10022
(212) 227-0631 .. **Guttman,** Laurence A '99 -333 Pearl -NY 10038
(212) 788-3349 .. **Guttman,** Leonard B '93 Hlth & Hsptl Corp -125 Worth -NY 10013 **Fx:**267-6905
(212) 506-1700 .. **Guttman,** Matthew A '02 %Kasowitz BT&F LLP -1633 Bway -NY 10019
(631) 777-3900 .. **Guttman,** Robin N '86 (Guttman & G) -1 Huntngtn Quad -Melvll 11747 **Fx:**777-3907
(631) 360-2175 .. **Guttmann,** Danl H '87 (Guttmann & K PC) -25 W Main -Smithtwn 11787 **Fx:**360-3393
(212) 702-5400 .. **Guttmann,** John S Jr. '84 (Beveridge & D,PC) -477 Mad Av -NY 10022
(212) 891-5080 .. **Guttmann,** Mary Louise '84 Wachovia -12 E 49th -NY 10017
(212) 715-9100 .. **Guttmann,** Mindi '10 %Kramer LN&F,LLP -1177 Av of Amer -NY 10036
(212) 223-0400 .. **Guttmann,** Robt '03 %Zeichner E&K LLP -575 Lex Av -NY 10022
(914) 631-6900 .. **Guttridge,** John C '90 (Guttridge & C,PC) -303 S Bway -Tarrytwn 10591 **Fx:**631-6644
(212) 969-3000 .. **Gutwein,** Abraham '81 SrCnsl Proskauer R LLP -1585 Bway -NY 10036
(212) 906-1200 .. **Gutwein,** Lillian E '05 %Latham & W -885 3rd Av -NY 10022
(212) 450-4000 .. **Gutzman,** Lori S '09 %Davis P&W LLP -450 Lex Av -NY 10017
(914) 949-1305 .. **Guven,** Erin N '02 %Leg Srvcs -90 Maple Av -White Plns 10601 **Fx:**949-6213
(315) 488-2933 .. **Guy,** Carl F '58 -850 Fay Rd -Syracuse 13219 **Fx:**488-2934
(516) 741-2585 .. **Guy,** Catherine C '10 %Rosicki R & Assoc,PC -51 E Bethpage Rd -Plainvw 11803 **Fx:**741-4748
(607) 723-9511 .. **Guy,** David H '87 (Coughlin & G,LLP) -19 Chenango Bx2039 -Bnghmtn 13902
(607) 639-2222 .. **Guy,** David H '87 (Coughlin & G,LLP) -190 Main Bx462 -Afton 13730
(315) 263-0100 .. **Guy,** Fredk R '88 -104 Winkworth Pkwy -Syracuse 13215
(607) 723-5341 .. **Guy,** Leslie Prechtl '85 (Hinman H&K,LLP) -80 Exchange Bx5250 -Bnghmtn 13902
(607) 723-0600 .. **Guy,** Patrick B '94 (Gitto & N,LLP) -71 State -Bnghmtn 13901 **Fx:**723-0634
(212) 549-8650 .. **Guy,** Patrick W '78 Scripps Ntwrk -1180 Av of Amer -NY 10036
(212) 370-1300 .. **Guy,** Peter J '99 %Ellenoff G&S LLP -150 E 42nd -NY 10017
(212) 610-6300 .. **Guyder,** Danl J '99 (Allen & O) -1221 Av of Amer -NY 10020
(212) 848-9800 .. **Guyer,** Erica L '05 %Withers B LLP -430 Park Av -NY 10022
(607) 773-0758 .. **Guyette,** Kevin F '88 -136 Court -Bnghmtn 13901 **Fx:**231-4061
(212) 450-4000 .. **Guynn,** Randall D '87 (Davis P&W LLP) -450 Lex Av -NY 10017
(212) 351-4000 .. **Guynn,** Steven D '06 (Gibson D&C LLP) -200 Park Av -NY 10166
(718) 742-6550 .. **Guzman,** Ana J '01 NYC Dept of Ed -501 Courtlandt Av -Bronx 10451
(518) 370-4645 .. **Guzman,** Barbara L '96 %Englert CM&F,LLP -224 State Bx1092 -Schnctdy 12301
(212) 909-2888 .. **Guzman,** Brian F '01 Indus Cptl Ptnrs -152 W 57th -NY 10019
(212) 326-3939 .. **Guzman,** Danl E '09 %Jones D -222 E 41st -NY 10017
(718) 843-1595 .. **Guzman,** Frank H '08 F Guzman,PC -9611 101st Av -Ozone Pk 11416 **Fx:**843-1295
(716) 842-5398 .. **Guzman,** Gina M '97 %M&T Bk -1 M & T Plz -Buffalo 14203 **Fx:**842-5376
(212) 637-3166 .. **Guzman,** Henry A '86 %EPA -290 Bway -NY 10007 **Fx:**637-3096
(212) 227-2900 .. **Guzman,** Jeffrey A '96 (Krentsel & G LLP) -17 Battery Pl -NY 10004 **Fx:**(646) 929-9045
(718) 892-8200 .. **Guzman,** Lauriano Jr. '87 -2565 Frisby Av -Bronx 10461 **Fx:**892-8203
(212) 822-8300 .. **Guzman,** Margarita '03 %NMIC -76 Wadsworth Av -NY 10033 **Fx:**740-9645
(347) 401-9496 .. **Guzman,** Meryl H '96 Family Ct -330 Jay -Brklyn 11201
(516) 222-0099 .. **Guzman,** Stacey Rinaldi '98 (Stanton & G,LLP) -585 Stewart Av -Gdn Cty 11530 **Fx:**222-0079
(845) 562-7747 .. **Guzman,** Victor '97 -Bx4827 -Middletwn 10941 **Fx:**913-7155
(212) 371-8008 .. **Guzov,** Debra J '88 (Guzov O,LLC) -600 Mad Av -NY 10022
(212) 371-8008 .. **Guzov Ofsink,LLC** -600 Mad Av -NY 10022 **Fx:**688-7273
(516) 997-7330 .. **Guzzardo,** Jos M '97 %Baxter S&S,PC -99 N Bway -Hicksvll 11801
(212) 801-6704 .. **Guzzino,** Marlene C '06 %Greenberg T,LLP -200 Park Av -NY 10166
(631) 588-5000 .. **Guzzone,** Amideo N '53 (AN Guzzone & Assoc,PC) -2450 Middle Cntry Rd -Centereach 11720 **Fx:**588-5001
(631) 588-5000 .. **Guzzone,** Roberta K '96 %AN Guzzone & Assoc,PC -2450 Middle Cntry Rd -Centereach 11720 **Fx:**588-5001
(212) 373-3000 .. **Gwathmey,** Gaines III '74 (Paul WRW&G LLP) -1285 Av of Amer -NY 10019
(212) 968-1001 .. **Gwertzman Lefkowitz Burman Smith & Marcus** -80 Broad -NY 10004 **Fx:**344-4140
(212) 595-1278 .. **Gwertzman,** Susan J '79 -215 W 88th -NY 10024 **Fx:**595-5275
(716) 856-5500 .. **Gwitt,** Brian D '99 (Damon M LLP) -200 Delaware Av -Buffalo 14202
(718) 238-6500 .. **Gwozdz,** Joanna '09 Connors & S,PC -7408 5th Av -Brklyn 11209
(631) 847-6333 .. **Gwydir,** Raymond J '73 %Estee Lauder -7 Corp Ctr Dr -Melvll 11747
(212) 691-2457 .. **Gwynne,** James Benjamin '07 -Bx1268 -NY 10113 **Fx:**727-3937
(914) 749-8200 .. **Gwynne,** Peter A '05 %Boies S&F LLP -333 Main -Armonk 10504
(212) 455-2000 .. **Gyasi,** Eric B '10 %Simpson T&B LLP -425 Lex Av -NY 10017
(212) 336-2000 .. **Gyetvan,** Stephanie M '09 %Patterson BW&T LLP -1133 Av of Amer -NY 10036
(718) 967-7733 .. **Gyimesi,** Aladar G '82 -265 Joline Av -Staten Isl 10307 **Fx:**317-2272
(518) 486-9671 .. **Gyory,** Bruce N '80 %Governors Ofc -227 The Cptl -Albany 12224
(212) 504-6000 .. **Gyr,** Peter C '99 SpclCnsl Cadwalader W&T LLP -1 World Fncl Ctr -NY 10281
(212) 474-1000 .. **Gyves,** Michelle A '10 %Cravath S&M LLP -825 8th Av -NY 10019
(212) 894-7200 .. **Gyves,** Wm S '92 (Entwistle & C LLP) -280 Park Av -NY 10017
(212) 537-6971 .. **Ha,** Bryan '01 -799 Bway -NY 10003
(212) 430-6215 .. **Ha,** Quang Jin '98 FSI Capital LLC -150 E 52nd -NY 10022
(212) 530-5000 .. **Ha,** Vina Nguyen '10 %Milbank TH&M LLP -1 Chase Manh Plz -NY 10005
(212) 230-8800 .. **Ha,** Yung-Hoon '09 %WilmerHale -399 Park Av -NY 10022
(315) 422-0314 .. **Haab,** Galen F '99 Germain & G -314 E Fayette -Syracuse 13202 **Fx:**478-6544
(518) 789-3613 .. **Haab,** Michele W '76 (Downey H&M PLLC) -1 John BxZ -Millerton 12546
(212) 468-8000 .. **Haac,** Gunilla N '76 SrCnsl Morrison & F LLP -1290 Av of Amer -NY 10104
(516) 496-5822 .. **Haack,** Kristie L '05 %T Spina -170 Froehlich Farm Blvd -Woodbury 11797 **Fx:**496-5420
(585) 546-5530 .. **Haacker,** Brett J '02 West Group -50 Broad -Rchstr 14694
(212) 351-4500 .. **Haag,** Elizabeth M '04 %Epstein B&G,PC -250 Park Av -NY 10177
(585) 724-4368 .. **Haag,** Joyce P '76 %Eastman Kodak -343 State -Rchstr 14650
(518) 455-4191 .. **Haak,** Brian R '03 %Ofc Cnsl to Majority -448M State Cptl -Albany 12248 **Fx:**455-4103
(716) 881-5966 .. **Haar,** Carol M '88 -1083 Delaware Av -Buffalo 14209
(212) 422-0202 .. **Haarhoff,** Dirk C '05 %Sedgwick DM&A LLP -125 Broad -NY 10004
(212) 218-2100 .. **Haas,** Bruce C '84 (Fitzpatrick CH&S) -1290 Av of Amer -NY 10104
(212) 449-2010 .. **Haas,** Christopher J '92 %Merrill Lynch -220 Bway -NY 10038

(845) 876-6500 .. **Haas,** Edw J '68 -203 Burger Rd Bx88 -Rhinebeck 12572 **Fx:**876-6500
(845) 708-0340 .. **Haas,** Elizabeth A '78 -254 S Main -New Cty 10956 **Fx:**708-5622
(845) 425-3900 .. **Haas,** Emanuel '82 -2 Perlman Dr -Spg Vly 10977 **Fx:**230-8645
(212) 576-2670 .. **Haas,** Eric T '78 OfCnsl J Osborn,PC -841 Bway -NY 10003 **Fx:**686-4023
(212) 336-2000 .. **Haas,** Erik '94 (Patterson BW&T LLP) -1133 Av of Amer -NY 10036
(212) 735-8645 .. **Haas,** G Wm '75 (Morrison C LLP) -909 3rd Av -NY 10022
(716) 847-8400 .. **Haas,** Gerard R '55 OfCnsl Phillips L LLP -3400 HSBC Ctr -Buffalo 14203
(212) 259-8000 .. **Haas,** Heather E '09 %Dewey & L LLP -1301 Av of Amer -NY 10019
(631) 271-0900 .. **Haas,** Herbert L '59 -34 Dewey -Huntngtn 11743 **Fx:**271-0656
(347) 404-9133 .. **Haas,** Holly L '04 %Civil Ct -141 Lvngstn -Brklyn 11201 **Fx:**(718) 643-3733
(212) 431-2340 .. **Haas,** Jeffrey J '89 %NY Law Schl -185 W Bway -NY 10013 **Fx:**431-3295
(631) 853-5761 .. **Haas,** Jennifer J '91 %Cnty Atty -400 Carleton Av -Central Islip 11722 **Fx:**853-7788
(212) 355-2575 .. **Haas,** Jules M '79 -845 3rd Av -NY 10022 **Fx:**751-5911
(212) 302-6511 .. **Haas,** Kenneth R '88 -36 W 44th -NY 10036 **Fx:**278-8935
(212) 509-9400 .. **Haas,** Kevin M '09 (Cozen O) -45 Bway Atrium -NY 10006
(518) 487-5460 .. **Haas,** Kurt W '09 %DA -6 Lodge -Albany 12207 **Fx:**487-5093
(212) 804-4200 .. **Haas,** Marc E '08 %Mound CW&G -One Bttry Pk Plz -NY 10004
(212) 922-9700 .. **Haas,** Mindy B '80 %1st Amer Title -633 3rd Av -NY 10017 **Fx:**922-0881
(516) 364-7900 .. **Haas,** Mona C '87 Epstein F&G -45 Crsswys Park Dr W -Woodbury 11797
(845) 425-3900 .. **Haas,** Stephen '03 %E Haas -2 Perlman Dr -Spg Vly 10977 **Fx:**230-8645
(315) 788-6700 .. **Haas,** Steven C '73 (Schwerzmann & W,PC) -215 Wshngtn Bx704 -Watertwn 13601
(516) 873-3900 .. **Haas,** Stuart '84 %C Connick,PLLC -114 Old Cntry Rd -Mineola 11501 **Fx:**873-3904
(718) 286-2000 .. **Haase,** Donna M '93 %Leg Aid -120-46 Qns Blvd -Kew Gdns 11415 **Fx:**286-2286
(212) 785-2577 .. **Haase,** Heather J '04 Rosner & N -26 Bway -NY 10004 **Fx:**785-5203
(518) 447-3200 .. **Haase,** Wm S '66 (McNamee LT&W,PC) -677 Bway -Albany 12207
(212) 689-1600 .. **Haaz,** Jessica S '03 %Marsh V&D LLP -500 5th Av -NY 10110 **Fx:**689-0210
(914) 749-8200 .. **Haazen,** Olav A '98 Cnsl Boies S&F LLP -333 Main -Armonk 10504
(212) 225-2000 .. **Habachy,** Dora G '08 %Cleary GS&H -1 Lbrty Plz -NY 10006
(845) 359-5400 .. **Habas,** Patricia E '01 Rogers M&H,PC -100 Dutch Hill Rd -Orangebrg 10962 **Fx:**359-5577
(716) 373-1920 .. **Habberfield,** Kevin M '08 %Dwyer B&L,LLP -1616 W State Bx648 -Olean 14760
(212) 878-8000 .. **Habbu,** Ashwini R '10 %Clifford C LLP -31 W 52nd -NY 10019
(518) 449-3900 .. **Habel,** Dennis W '86 %Cooper E&S,LLP -39 N Pearl -Albany 12207
(718) 237-0100 .. **Habel,** Kenneth A '66 -188 Montague -Brklyn 11201 **Fx:**596-1766
(914) 472-1150 .. **Habel,** Kenneth A '66 -42 Mt Joy -Scarsdale 10583
(315) 425-9000 .. **Habelt,** Wm W '99 %Marjama MB&S LLP -250 S Clinton -Syracuse 13202
(212) 233-4411 .. **Haber,** Allan P '85 -111 Bway -NY 10006
(516) 248-7844 .. **Haber,** Amy Cobert '74 (Cobert H&H) -1050 Franklin Av -Gdn Cty 11530
(516) 997-2700 .. **Haber,** Amy M '95 %A Core,PC -173 Schl -Westbury 11590 **Fx:**997-7334
(718) 442-0960 .. **Haber,** Benjamin '02 -36 Richmond Ter -Staten Isl 10301
(212) 302-2600 .. **Haber,** Bernard '75 -22 W 38th -NY 10018 **Fx:**764-3269
(516) 248-7844 .. **Haber,** David C '04 %Cobert H&H -1050 Franklin Av -Gdn Cty 11530
(516) 367-2264 .. **Haber,** David W '99 -137 Woodbury Rd -Woodbury 11797 **Fx:**692-2746
(212) 479-6000 .. **Haber,** Eric J '84 SpclCnsl Cooley LLP -1114 Av of Amer -NY 10036
(212) 599-0900 .. **Haber,** Erica M '04 %Bower & L,PC -261 Mad Av -NY 10016
(212) 867-9500 .. **Haber,** Eugene '59 Cnsl Kurzman K&F,LLP -230 Park Av -NY 10169
(516) 248-7844 .. **Haber,** Eugene F '72 (Cobert H&H) -1050 Franklin Av -Gdn Cty 11530
(978) 750-8400 .. **Haber,** Frederic '84 -430 E 86th -NY 10028 **Fx:**750-4343
(516) 935-0709 .. **Haber,** George '63 (Haber & H) -302 Vista Dr -Jericho 11753
(631) 470-5125 .. **Haber,** Greg E '99 Garden City Grp Inc -105 Maxess Rd -Melvll 11747
(212) 643-7000 .. **Haber,** Harvey T '76 (Sills C&G PC) -One Rckfllr Plz -NY 10020
(718) 291-8581 .. **Haber,** Jacqueline C '76 Workers Comp Bd -168-46 91st Av -Jamaica 11432 **Fx:**291-8940
(914) 347-2500 .. **Haber,** Jarrett B '94 %HP Agency -5 W Main -Elmsfrd 10523
(212) 779-1414 .. **Haber,** Jeffrey M '89 (Bernstein L LLP) -10 E 40th -NY 10016
(631) 465-0058 .. **Haber,** Jeffrey P '99 %S Schwaber & Assoc -6 Corp Ctr Dr -Melvll 11747 **Fx:**465-0057
(212) 878-8000 .. **Haber,** Jessica L '08 %Clifford C LLP -31 W 52nd -NY 10019
(212) 350-2291 .. **Haber,** Kenneth I '73 Douglas Elliman,LLC -575 Mad Av -NY 10022
(516) 762-3117 .. **Haber,** Larry H '86 -6800 Jericho Tpk -Syosset 11791
(516) 742-7277 .. **Haber,** Lisa B '88 (Haber & H,LLP) -1325 Franklin Av -Gdn Cty 11530 **Fx:**742-7054
(315) 234-8620 .. **Haber,** Lisa DiPoala '90 -Bx7345 -Syracuse 13261
(212) 879-1270 .. **Haber,** Martin D '73 -2 East End Av -NY 10075 **Fx:**879-9037
(718) 487-1300 .. **Haber,** Michl L '06 %Leg Srvcs Corp A -80 Jamaica Av -Brklyn 11207 **Fx:**342-1780
(212) 791-6240 .. **Haber,** Michl S '86 -225 Bway -NY 10007 **Fx:**791-7994
(212) 416-8176 .. **Haber,** Nancy J '74 %Dept of Law -120 Bway -NY 10271
(212) 209-3898 .. **Haber,** Neal D '79 %Moss & B -708 3rd Av -NY 10017
(315) 472-5827 .. **Haber,** Patrick J '90 -250 Harrison -Syracuse 13202 **Fx:**476-5350
(212) 536-3900 .. **Haber,** Philip A '88 (K&L Gates LLP) -599 Lex Av -NY 10022
(212) 410-1572 .. **Haber,** Robt Jay '66 -1111 Park Av -NY 10128 **Fx:**831-3011
(212) 768-2100 .. **Haber,** Roger S '80 (Kraditor & H,PC) -75 9th Av -NY 10011
(212) 554-7800 .. **Haber,** Ruth C '80 OfCnsl Moses & S LLP -405 Lex Av -NY 10174
(516) 742-7277 .. **Haber,** Stephen D '87 (Haber & H,LLP) -1325 Franklin Av -Gdn Cty 11530 **Fx:**742-7054
(914) 997-1500 .. **Haber,** Stephen P '84 -445 Hmltn Av -White Plns 10601
(212) 250-8196 .. **Haber,** Steven M '88 %Deutsche Bank -60 Wall -NY 10005
(212) 768-6700 .. **Haber,** Steven Z '05 %Sonnenschein N&R LLP -2 World Fncl Ctr -NY 10281
(646) 386-4200 .. **Haberfeld,** Jacqueline '92 OCA -25 Beaver -NY 10004
(516) 804-6377 .. **Haberlack,** Thos C '92 -600 Old Cntry Rd -Gdn Cty 11530
(718) 334-3696 .. **Haberlin,** Joanne T '91 %Elmhurst Hospital -79-01 Bway -Elmhrst 11373
(212) 867-4466 .. **Haberly,** Brian C '96 (Belkin BW&G,LLP) -270 Mad Av -NY 10016
(212) 768-9790 .. **Haberman,** Alan '65 (Haberman & G LLP) -1212 Av of Amer -NY 10036 **Fx:**768-9819
(845) 638-4294 .. **Haberman,** Barry D '00 -254 S Main -New Cty 10956 **Fx:**638-6080
(212) 873-7575 .. **Haberman,** Brook '87 (Haberman & H) -315 Cntrl Pk W -NY 10025
(212) 349-3366 .. **Haberman,** David P '89 %Rose & R -291 Bway -NY 10007 **Fx:**349-2292
(212) 373-3000 .. **Haberman,** Harley M '02 Paul WRW&G LLP -1285 Av of Amer -NY 10019
(212) 873-7575 .. **Haberman,** Jacob '70 (Haberman & H) -315 Cntrl Pk W -NY 10025
(212) 962-1120 .. **Haberman,** Jay S '79 -150 Bway -NY 10038 **Fx:**964-7919
(212) 788-9122 .. **Haberman,** Jeffrey '76 NYC Council -250 Bway -NY 10007
(631) 581-5890 .. **Haberman,** John R '73 -165 Islip Av -Islip 11751 **Fx:**581-5892
(845) 291-2050 .. **Haberman,** Neal A '79 %DA -255-275 Main -Goshen 10924 **Fx:**291-2085
(212) 310-8000 .. **Haberman,** Noam I '09 %Weil G&M LLP -767 5th Av -NY 10153
(212) 286-8585 .. **Haberman,** Paul S '06 %Heidell PM&B,LLP -99 Park Av -NY 10016
(212) 873-7575 .. **Haberman,** Regina '02 (Haberman & H) -315 Cntrl Pk W -NY 10025
(212) 969-3000 .. **Haberman,** Sharon '04 %Proskauer R LLP -1585 Bway -NY 10036
(212) 873-2900 .. **Haberman,** Simon V '50 (S Haberman,PC) -1 W 85th -NY 10024 **Fx:**724-6200
(212) 873-7575 .. **Haberman,** Sinclair C '86 (Haberman & H) -315 Cntrl Pk W -NY 10025
(212) 728-8000 .. **Habert,** Jack I '97 SpclCnsl Willkie F&G LLP -787 7th Av -NY 10019
(212) 771-9507 .. **Habhab,** Barbara '06 CIT Grp -505 5th Av -NY 10017
(845) 724-4664 .. **Habiague,** Steven '92 -80 Mtn Crk Rd -Poughquag 12570 **Fx:**(866) 724-9383
(212) 697-3122 .. **Habian,** Bruce G '73 (Martin C&B LLP) -220 E 42nd -NY 10017
(917) 783-0632 .. **Habib,** Eric P '98 -459 Columbus Av -NY 10024
(315) 449-0344 .. **Habib,** Fortuna S '92 -119 Doll Pkwy -Syracuse 13214 **Fx:**446-2630
(718) 963-5755 .. **Habib,** Perry M '85 %MHLS -760 Bway -Brklyn 11206
(315) 701-0741 .. **Habib,** Ralph '95 -307 S Clinton -Syracuse 13202 **Fx:**479-8847
(716) 853-5100 .. **Habib Rittling,** Amy M '96 %Lippes MWF LLP -665 Main -Buffalo 14203
(212) 837-6000 .. **Habinsky,** Jason '97 Cnsl Hughes H&R LLP -1 Bttry Pk Plz -NY 10004
(212) 779-0057 .. **Hach,** Gregory S '00 (Hach & R,LLP) -185 Mad Av -NY 10016
(212) 779-0057 .. **Hach & Rose,LLP** -185 Mad Av -NY 10016 **Fx:**779-0028
(212) 509-5050 .. **Hachmeister,** Annamaria '08 %Wuersch & G LLP -100 Wall -NY 10005
(212) 509-9400 .. **Hack,** Ally '05 %Cozen O -45 Bway Atrium -NY 10006
(516) 466-1700 .. **Hack,** Eric S '97 %Day & Assoc,PC -11 Grace Av -Gt Neck 11021 **Fx:**466-7736
(212) 935-3131 .. **Hack,** Jay L '77 (Gallet D&B,LLP) -845 3rd Av -NY 10022
(516) 745-1122 .. **Hack,** Michail Z '00 %Quadrino & S,PC -666 Old Cntry Rd -Gdn Cty 11530
(212) 599-2527 .. **Hack,** Norma '43 N Hack PLLC -60 E 42nd -NY 10165 **Fx:**599-3616
(212) 692-0367 .. **Hack Piro O'Day Merklinger Wallace & McKenna** -600 3rd Av -NY 10016 **Fx:**692-0368
(716) 858-2424 .. **Hackbush,** Gary W '93 %DA -25 Delaware Av -Buffalo 14202 **Fx:**858-7425
(914) 964-7063 .. **Hackeling,** John Christian Jr. '60 (Ronayne H&R) -441 Saw Mill Rvr Rd -Ynkrs 10701
(212) 909-6000 .. **Hackell,** Matthew S '05 %Debevoise & P LLP -919 3rd Av -NY 10022
(212) 735-3000 .. **Hacker,** Gary J '99 Cnsl Skadden ASM&F LLP -4 Times Sq -NY 10036
(516) 248-7000 .. **Hacker,** Hyman '89 (Albanese & A LLP) -1050 Franklin Av -Gdn Cty 11530
(518) 783-3843 .. **Hacker,** James E '85 (Hacker & M,LLP) -7 Airport Park Blvd -Latham 12110
(212) 907-7300 .. **Hacker,** Jonathan S '76 OfCnsl Golenbock EAB&P -437 Mad Av -NY 10022
(718) 628-7800 .. **Hacker,** Kenneth Wayne '95 Network Mortgage,Inc -60-41 Fresh Pond Rd -Maspeth 11378 **Fx:**628-8998
(518) 463-1269 .. **Hacker,** Leo V '74 (Walsh & H) -18 Corp Wds Blvd -Albany 12211
(518) 783-3843 .. **Hacker & Murphy,LLP** -7 Airport Park Blvd -Latham 12110 **Fx:**783-8101
(212) 373-3000 .. **Hacker,** Robt E '95 Paul WRW&G LLP -1285 Av of Amer -NY 10019
(212) 310-8000 .. **Hackett,** Brennan E '08 %Weil G&M LLP -767 5th Av -NY 10153
(212) 972-8935 .. **Hackett,** John J '86 (Harvey & H) -420 Lex Av -NY 10170
(212) 282-2260 .. **Hackett,** Kevin R '75 Rockefeller Grp -1221 Av of Amer -NY 10020
(212) 423-1480 .. **Hackett,** Lisa M '04 North General Hptl -1879 Mad Av -NY 10035
(585) 454-6350 .. **Hackett,** Mark J Jr. '85 -16 E Main -Rchstr 14614
(412) 288-3250 .. **Hackett,** Mary J '08 (Reed S LLP) -599 Lex Av -NY 10022 **Fx:**(212) 521-5400
(516) 248-8877 .. **Hackett,** Patrick J '82 -100 Grdn City Plz -Gdn Cty 11530
(212) 223-2100 .. **Hackman,** Joshua S '09 %Menz B&K LLP -444 Mad Av -NY 10022
(212) 259-8000 .. **Hackney,** Danl C '07 %Dewey & L LLP -1301 Av of Amer -NY 10019
(716) 886-1257 .. **Hackworth,** Pamela A '91 %Perla & P,LLP -367 Linwood Av -Buffalo 14209 **Fx:**886-2720
(212) 788-1165 .. **Hackworth,** Thaddeus J '05 %Law Dept -100 Church -NY 10007 **Fx:**788-0367
(212) 506-5000 .. **Hacohen,** Tal '07 %Orrick H&S LLP -51 W 52nd -NY 10019
(914) 824-5415 .. **Hadala,** Jos S '07 %Hon L Jamieson -111 Dr ML King Jr Blvd -White Plns 10601
(518) 213-6000 .. **Hadam,** Jacquelyn A '09 NYSUT -800 Troy-Schnctdy Rd -Latham 12110 **Fx:**213-6488

(212) 836-8000 .. **Haddad,** A Julia '96 %Kaye S LLP -425 Park Av -NY 10022
(518) 438-8500 .. **Haddad,** Edw S '75 -810 Mad Av -Albany 12208 **Fx:**438-1554
(212) 530-5000 .. **Haddad,** Gabrielle A '07 %Milbank TH&M LLP -1 Chase Manh Plz -NY 10005
(212) 277-6500 .. **Haddad,** Gerard A '96 (Dickstein S LLP) -1633 Bway -NY 10019
(212) 953-2381 .. **Haddad,** James M '94 %Rubin F&F,LLP -292 Mad Av -NY 10017
(315) 474-0736 .. **Haddad,** Laurin R '00 -333 E Onondaga -Syracuse 13202 **Fx:**473-1825
(212) 728-8000 .. **Haddad,** Matthew J '09 %Willkie F&G LLP -787 7th Av -NY 10019
(212) 643-7000 .. **Haddad,** Mitchell D '87 (Sills C&G PC) -One Rckfllr Plz -NY 10020
(718) 876-6300 .. **Haddad,** Rhiannon N '09 %DA -130 Styvsnt Pl -Staten Isl 10301
(212) 661-9100 .. **Haddad,** Richd G '88 (Otterbourg SH&R,PC) -230 Park Av -NY 10169
(212) 969-3000 .. **Haddad,** Richd I '07 %Proskauer R LLP -1585 Bway -NY 10036
(212) 335-4500 .. **Haddad,** Wm N '95 (DLA Piper LLP) -1251 Av of Amer -NY 10020
(212) 270-6000 .. **Haddadin,** Yezan Munther '03 JP Morgan Chase Sec -277 Park Av -NY 10172
(212) 969-3000 .. **Haddock,** Alison M '06 %Proskauer R LLP -1585 Bway -NY 10036
(212) 493-6918 .. **Haddock,** Beth A '94 Brown Bros Harriman -140 Bway -NY 10005
(212) 883-6500 .. **Hade,** Victor '65 SpclCnsl Podell SS&B,LLP -605 3rd Av -NY 10158
(516) 229-4300 .. **Hader,** Annette '06 %J Bilello & Assoc -875 Merrick Av -Westbury 11590
(212) 715-9100 .. **Hader,** Cheryl E '88 (Kramer LN&F,LLP) -1177 Av of Amer -NY 10036
(212) 557-4000 .. **Hadfield,** Frances P '04 %Grunfeld DLS&K LLP -399 Park Av -NY 10022
(212) 218-2100 .. **Hadikusumo,** Sugiarto '08 %Fitzpatrick CH&S -1290 Av of Amer -NY 10104
(212) 259-8000 .. **Hadis,** Vivian K '07 %Dewey & L LLP -1301 Av of Amer -NY 10019
(718) 447-5499 .. **Hadji,** Patricia M '00 Berel & M -358 St Marks Pl -Staten Isl 10301
(212) 809-9100 .. **Hadjikow,** Anna '95 (Brunelle & H,PC) -1 Whitehall -NY 10004 **Fx:**809-3219
(518) 523-3297 .. **Hadjis,** Thos J '68 -Bx48 -Lk Placid 12946 **Fx:**(603) 649-6038
(212) 833-0643 .. **Hadjiyancheva,** Maya G '99 Jennison Assoc LLC/Pru Ins Co -466 Lex Av -NY 10017
(631) 853-7530 .. **Hadler,** John W '84 %Supreme Ct Law Lib -400 Carleton Av -Central Islip 11722
(718) 410-0288 .. **Hadley,** Jason M '04 Leg Aid-Housing Help -1118 Grnd Cncrs -Bronx 10456
(212) 450-4000 .. **Hadley,** Jos P '88 (Davis P&W LLP) -450 Lex Av -NY 10017
(315) 366-2585 .. **Hadley,** Paul '90 Pub Def -Bx576 -Wampsville 13163
(718) 875-1300 .. **Hadley,** Philip J '81 %Appllt Div 2nd Dept -45 Monroe Pl -Brklyn 11201 **Fx:**858-2446
(212) 294-6700 .. **Hadlock,** John M '63 OfCnsl Winston & S -200 Park Av -NY 10166
(212) 609-6800 .. **Hadzismajlovic,** Zlatko '03 %McCarter & E,LLP -245 Park Av -NY 10167
(516) 799-8400 .. **Hadziyianis,** Thos W '96 -4110 Merrick Rd -Massapequa 11758
(212) 805-6374 .. **Haeberle,** Kevin S '06 Hon V Marrero -500 Pearl -NY 10007
(518) 387-5000 .. **Haeckl,** Jenifer '97 GE -1 Rsrch Cir -Niskayuna 12309
(631) 288-4300 .. **Haefeli,** Brette A '06 %R Haefeli -48F Main Bx1112 -Westhmptn Bch 11978 **Fx:**288-5474
(631) 288-4300 .. **Haefeli,** Richd T '69 -48F Main Bx1112 -Westhmptn Bch 11978 **Fx:**288-5474
(212) 349-9100 .. **Haegele,** Gregory P '91 OfCnsl A Chorne -41 Mad Av -NY 10010 **Fx:**(866) 655-8465
(518) 388-4327 .. **Haelen,** Joanne B '89 %Hon V Caruso -612 State -Schnctdy 12305
(631) 531-1195 .. **Haerter,** Martin W '96 %Estee Lauder -125 Pinelawn Rd -Melvll 11747
(631) 367-1485 .. **Haesler,** Gwenn E '94 A Werter -215 E Main -Huntngtn 11743
(516) 877-2900 .. **Haesloop,** E Gordon '72 (Bartlett MB&M,LLP) -300 Old Cntry Rd -Mineola 11501
(516) 571-3310 .. **Haesloop,** Martha V '82 Hon J Dunne -100 Supreme Ct Dr -Mineola 11501
(518) 474-2721 .. **Haettenschwiller,** Inez M '83 %OTDA -40 N Pearl -Albany 12243 **Fx:**474-9389
(212) 245-4580 .. **Hafer,** J Jeffrey '78 (Shukat AHW&H,LLP) -111 W 57th -NY 10019
(212) 997-7595 .. **Hafetz,** Fredk P '64 (Hafetz N&R) -500 5th Av -NY 10110
(212) 998-6289 .. **Hafetz,** Jonathan L '00 %Brennan Ctr for Justice -161 Av of Amer -NY 10013 **Fx:**995-4550
(212) 997-7595 .. **Hafetz Necheles & Rocco** -500 5th Av -NY 10110 **Fx:**997-7646
(212) 969-3000 .. **Haff,** Nicole '08 %Proskauer R LLP -1585 Bway -NY 10036
(212) 801-3135 .. **Haffey,** Bryn K '09 %Greenberg T,LLP -200 Park Av -NY 10166
(718) 631-5678 .. **Haffner,** Steven R '88 (Gordon & H, LLP) -18-15 215th -Bayside 11360 **Fx:**225-5429
(518) 370-0738 .. **Haffner,** Thos E '89 -904 Heather Ln -Schnctdy 12309 **Fx:**370-0738
(212) 944-0600 .. **Hafif,** Steven I '93 (Hafif & Assoc,PLLC) -275 Mad Av -NY 10016 **Fx:**944-7747
(212) 577-3965 .. **Hafiz,** Sameera '02 %Leg Aid -199 Water -NY 10038
(914) 667-1188 .. **Hafiz,** Talay '88 (DeAngelis & H) -22 W 1st -Mt Vernon 10550 **Fx:**667-0836
(516) 593-5656 .. **Hafner,** Bruce R '74 -14 St James Pl -Lynbrk 11563 **Fx:**593-1240
(518) 793-6611 .. **Hafner,** Robt H '93 (Miller MS&H,LLC) -451 Glen Bx765 -Glens Fls 12801
(212) 634-3373 .. **Haft,** Ian D '01 ACI Capital Co,LLC -666 3rd Av -NY 10017 **Fx:**(646) 274-1773
(212) 692-5527 .. **Haft,** Marilyn G '69 (Duval & S LLP) -101 Park Av -NY 10178
(212) 506-5000 .. **Haft,** Wm S '88 (Orrick H&S LLP) -51 W 52nd -NY 10019
(212) 686-3100 .. **Haftel,** Richd E '82 (Haftel & S,PC) -260 Mad Av -NY 10016
(212) 686-3100 .. **Haftel & Silverman, PC** -260 Mad Av -NY 10016 **Fx:**686-3151
(718) 788-5052 .. **Hagan,** Christina '83 OfCnsl Hagan C & Assoc -908 4th Av -Brklyn 11232
(718) 788-5052 .. **Hagan Coury & Associates** -908 4th Av -Brklyn 11232 **Fx:**965-4017
(631) 654-5134 .. **Hagan,** Damon A '04 (Mayer R&H PC) -178 E Main -Patchogue 11772 **Fx:**654-5252
(212) 455-2000 .. **Hagan,** James J '61 OfCnsl Simpson T&B LLP -425 Lex Av -NY 10017
(718) 286-6000 .. **Hagan,** Jennifer '03 %DA -125-01 Qns Blvd -Kew Gdns 11415
(212) 250-3295 .. **Hagan,** Mark E '00 %Deutsche Bank -60 Wall -NY 10005
(212) 344-5680 .. **Hagan,** Michl J '83 (Thompson H LLP) -335 Mad Av -NY 10017
(212) 460-4770 .. **Hagan,** Peter A '73 Con Ed -4 Irving Pl -NY 10003
(718) 788-5052 .. **Hagan,** Saml L '80 (Hagan C & Assoc) -908 4th Av -Brklyn 11232
(212) 819-8200 .. **Hagans,** Brittany G '09 %White & C LLP -1155 Av of Amer -NY 10036
(718) 248-6398 .. **Hagar,** Debra L '92 Citicorp Global Tech,Inc -1 Court Sq -LIC 11120
(212) 468-8000 .. **Hagberg,** Karen L '85 (Morrison & F LLP) -1290 Av of Amer -NY 10104
(518) 434-7045 .. **Hage,** Heather M '07 Research Fndtn SUNY -Bx9 -Albany 12201 **Fx:**434-8352
(315) 797-9850 .. **Hage,** Jos K III '79 Hage & H LLC -283 Genesee -Utica 13501 **Fx:**797-1721
(845) 339-6903 .. **Hagedorn,** Brenda '86 -25 Lucas Av -Kingston 12401 **Fx:**339-6916
(585) 232-5300 .. **Hagelberg,** Frank S '73 OfCnsl Boylan BCV&W,LLP -2400 Chase Sq -Rchstr 14604
(585) 641-2200 .. **Hagelberg,** Michl T '77 -70 Linden Oaks Dr -Rchstr 14625
(718) 649-2000 .. **Hagelin,** Deborah A '87 %V Martorana -9207 Flatlands Av -Brklyn 11236 **Fx:**649-2104
(716) 849-3500 .. **Hagelin,** Michl T '82 (Hagelin & K LLC) -135 Delaware Av -Buffalo 14202 **Fx:**849-3501
(212) 474-1000 .. **Hageman,** Mark R '94 Cnsl Cravath S&M LLP -825 8th Av -NY 10019
(212) 421-4100 .. **Hagemeier,** Luisa Kaye '92 OfCnsl Pryor C LLP -7 Times Sq -NY 10036
(585) 584-8216 .. **Hagen,** Deborah A '00 -Bx446 -Pavilion 14525 **Fx:**(888) 866-4735
(716) 847-7118 .. **Hagen,** Jeffrey J '94 Ofc Inspector Genl -65 Court -Buffalo 14202 **Fx:**847-7156
(212) 284-5537 .. **Hagen,** Marshall C '88 Merrill Lynch -153 E 53rd -NY 10022
(212) 903-8700 .. **Hagen,** Seth A '05 %Roberts & H,LLP -825 8th Av -NY 10019
(716) 851-2711 .. **Hagen,** Suzanne T '83 %UIA Bd -290 Main -Buffalo 14202 **Fx:**851-2795
(212) 506-1700 .. **Hagenson,** Michl E '05 %Kasowitz BT&F LLP -1633 Bway -NY 10019
(212) 506-1700 .. **Hagenson,** Rebecca '07 %Kasowitz BT&F LLP -1633 Bway -NY 10019
(212) 964-7990 .. **Hager,** Benjamin '59 -321 Bway -NY 10007 **Fx:**267-4080
(845) 425-2224 .. **Hager,** Benjamin '59 -9 Kupperman Ln -Monsey 10952 **Fx:**352-0059
(212) 735-3685 .. **Hager,** David '05 %Skadden ASM&F LLP -4 Times Sq -NY 10036 **Fx:**(917) 777-3685
(212) 557-7700 .. **Hager,** Eric W '96 (Davidson D&C LLP) -60 E 42nd -NY 10165
(914) 948-8044 .. **Hager,** Jeremy Ian '98 -200 Mamaroneck Av #304 -White Plns 10601 **Fx:**948-8058
(212) 801-6915 .. **Hager,** Joshua '03 %Greenberg T,LLP -200 Park Av -NY 10166
(212) 252-9550 .. **Hager,** Mark M '09 %Freiberg & P -49 W 37th -NY 10018
(212) 468-8000 .. **Hager,** Melissa Ann '93 OfCnsl Morrison & F LLP -1290 Av of Amer -NY 10104
(212) 973-2940 .. **Hager,** Michl T '04 %AECOM Tech Corp -605 3rd Av -NY 10158 **Fx:**986-4713
(716) 282-2329 .. **Hager,** Rita M '80 -6928 Williams Rd -Niagara Fls 14304 **Fx:**625-1411
(716) 849-6500 .. **Hager,** Tamsin J '98 (Brown & T,LLC) -14 Lafayette Sq -Buffalo 14203
(716) 856-9443 .. **Hagerty & Brady** -69 Delaware Av -Buffalo 14202 **Fx:**856-0511
(716) 856-9443 .. **Hagerty,** James J '51 OfCnsl Hagerty & B -69 Delaware Av -Buffalo 14202
(212) 558-4000 .. **Hagerty,** Terence C '09 %Sullivan & C LLP -125 Broad -NY 10004
(716) 856-9443 .. **Hagerty,** Thos V '77 (Hagerty & B) -69 Delaware Av -Buffalo 14202
(212) 361-8633 .. **Hagevik,** Dan '01 %Dept Homeless Srvcs -33 Beaver -NY 10004
(718) 613-2422 .. **Haggans,** John M '09 Hon F Block USDC -225 Cadman Plz E -Brklyn 11201
(315) 731-3485 .. **Haggas,** Stephen W '78 Family Ct -200 Elizabeth -Utica 13501
(516) 222-0676 .. **Haggerty,** George J '85 (G Haggerty & Assoc,PC) -500 N Bway -Jericho 11753 **Fx:**222-8011
(212) 683-8100 .. **Haggerty,** James F '95 PR Consulting Grp -45 Bway -NY 10006
(516) 227-0800 .. **Haggerty,** James P '91 Cnsl Natl Land Tenure Co LLC -1122 Franklin Av -Gdn Cty 11530 **Fx:**227-1160
(845) 473-1032 .. **Haggerty,** Michel P '78 -310 Mill -Poughkeepsie 12601 **Fx:**473-5227
(845) 876-3300 .. **Haggerty,** Michel P '78 -37 W Market -Rhinebeck 12572 **Fx:**876-3195
(845) 677-4607 .. **Haggerty,** Paul J '04 -55 N Clove Rd -Verbank 12585
(716) 858-2424 .. **Haggerty,** Ryan D '10 %DA -25 Delaware Av -Buffalo 14202 **Fx:**858-7425
(212) 833-1100 .. **Haggerty,** Timothy M '06 %Friedman KS&A LLP -1633 Bway -NY 10019
(212) 735-3000 .. **Hagglund,** Ryan N '08 %Skadden ASM&F LLP -4 Times Sq -NY 10036
(585) 268-9410 .. **Haggstrom,** Leslie J '78 %Cnty Atty -7 Court -Belmont 14813 **Fx:**268-9651
(917) 734-4666 .. **Haghani,** Misha '05 -175 Grt Nck Rd -Gt Neck 11021
(212) 988-0107 .. **Hagler,** Hope Goode '83 -205 E 78th -NY 10075
(212) 238-7330 .. **Hagler,** Mendel R '91 -577 Grand -NY 10002 **Fx:**238-7399
(631) 751-4444 .. **Hagler,** Tzvi Y '09 %Grundfast Law Firm -207 Hallock Rd -Stony Brk 11790 **Fx:**751-4675
(212) 297-5800 .. **Haglund,** Benjamin E '87 (Day P LLP) -7 Times Sq -NY 10036
(315) 732-0779 .. **Haglund,** Heather A '99 -180 Genesee -New Hartfrd 13413
(631) 231-1199 .. **Hagney,** James F '85 (Reynolds CGHL&Q,LLP) -35 Arkay Dr -Hauppauge 11788
(518) 445-2270 .. **Hagoort,** Thos H '59 Albany Intl Corp -Bx1907 -Albany 12201
(212) 788-8024 .. **Hagopian,** Caleb C '05 -100 Church -NY 10007
(212) 424-9024 .. **Hagopian,** Matthew J '91 (Linklaters) -1345 Av of Amer -NY 10105
(212) 626-4100 .. **Hagos,** Lula A '10 %Baker & M LLP -1114 Av of Amer -NY 10036
(845) 485-3633 .. **Hagstrom,** David D '66 %Town Law Dept -1 Overocker Rd -Poughkeepsie 12603 **Fx:**485-3701
(845) 454-1110 .. **Hagstrom,** Karen E '95 %Corbally G and R LLP -35 Market -Poughkeepsie 12601 **Fx:**471-4593
(212) 883-4918 .. **Hahami,** Asaf '01 (Cozen O) -277 Park Av -NY 10172 **Fx:**672-1118
(212) 902-1000 .. **Hahm,** David '07 Goldman Sachs -1 NY Plz -NY 10004
(212) 336-8000 .. **Hahm,** Jung S '01 %Amster R&E -90 Park Av -NY 10016
(212) 373-3000 .. **Hahn,** Adam B '09 %Paul WRW&G LLP -1285 Av of Amer -NY 10019
(212) 468-4800 .. **Hahn,** Alan '96 (Davis & G LLP) -1740 Bway -NY 10019
(212) 218-5500 .. **Hahn,** Andrew T '87 (Seyfarth S LLP) -620 8th Av -NY 10018

(212) 310-8000 .. **Hahn,** Arlene A '02 %Weil G&M LLP -767 5th Av -NY 10153
(845) 558-6773 .. **Hahn,** Chihoe '93 -38 Grandvw Av -Montebello 10901
(516) 747-0300 .. **Hahn,** Christopher M '00 (Meltzer LG&B,LLP) -190 Willis Av -Mineola 11501
(212) 701-3000 .. **Hahn,** David L Jr. '09 %Cahill G&R LLP -80 Pine -NY 10005 **Fx:**269-5420
(631) 423-7750 .. **Hahn,** Edw J '84 -5A Schl Ln -Lloyd Hbr 11743
(212) 477-0351 .. **Hahn,** Erich Leo '00 Judson Mem Church -55 Washington Sq S -NY 10012
(516) 747-4855 .. **Hahn Ford & Hundertmark** -105 Hillside Av -Williston Pk 11596 **Fx:**747-7301
(212) 478-7200 .. **Hahn & Hessen LLP** -488 Mad Av -NY 10022 **Fx:**478-7400
(212) 813-8800 .. **Hahn,** J Todd '98 SrCnsl Goodwin P LLP -620 8th Av -NY 10018
(212) 599-1300 .. **Hahn,** Jasmine '99 %Lex Terrae Ltd -331 Mad Av -NY 10017 **Fx:**983-2791
(212) 848-4000 .. **Hahn,** John '10 Shearman & S LLP -599 Lex Av -NY 10022
(212) 973-0572 .. **Hahn,** Junie '01 (Wolff & S PC) -140 Bway -NY 10005
(212) 629-6890 .. **Hahn,** Kim Sok Chong '81 -330 7th Av -NY 10001 **Fx:**563-6864
(212) 629-6626 .. **Hahn,** Leonard Z '91 -330 7th Av -NY 10001 **Fx:**563-6864
(212) 430-8020 .. **Hahn,** Mary F '05 %LeClairRyan,PC -830 3rd Av -NY 10022
(212) 599-1300 .. **Hahn,** Max '51 %Lex Terrae Ltd -331 Mad Av -NY 10017 **Fx:**983-2791
(212) 907-7300 .. **Hahn,** Paul B '77 (Golenbock EAB&P) -437 Mad Av -NY 10022
(845) 473-8100 .. **Hahn,** Penny M '04 %Iseman CR&H,LLP -2649 South Rd -Poughkeepsie 12601
(585) 546-7430 .. **Hahn,** Reynolds E '74 %Dept of Law -144 Exchange Blvd -Rchstr 14614 **Fx:**546-7514
(212) 826-8200 .. **Hahn,** Richd E '75 (Llorca & H LLP) -845 3rd Av -NY 10022 **Fx:**935-0671
(212) 909-6000 .. **Hahn,** Richd F '85 (Debevoise & P LLP) -919 3rd Av -NY 10022
(212) 626-4100 .. **Hahn,** Sahang-Hee '10 %Baker & M LLP -1114 Av of Amer -NY 10036
(212) 834-0600 .. **Hahn,** Wm L '96 %Gordon & S,PC -355 Lex Av -NY 10017
(212) 818-1110 .. **Hahn,** Zvi '97 (Butzel L,PC) -380 Mad Av -NY 10017
(212) 969-3000 .. **Hahn-Saperstein,** Marcy '95 %Proskauer R LLP -1585 Bway -NY 10036
(212) 428-6580 .. **Hahon,** Nancy E '94 SrCnsl Atlantic Mutual Co -100 Wall -NY 10005 **Fx:**428-6577
(718) 445-9111 .. **Hai,** Ming '01 (M Hai,PC) -36-09 Main -Flushng 11354 **Fx:**445-5424
(212) 848-4000 .. **Haidas,** Michl J '07 %Shearman & S LLP -599 Lex Av -NY 10022
(212) 552-0241 .. **Haider,** Aliya '05 JP Morgan Chase -1 Chase Manh Plz -NY 10005
(212) 573-4656 .. **Haider,** Colette C '02 Ford Fndtn -320 E 43rd -NY 10017
(212) 381-5706 .. **Haies,** Matthew N '99 DoubleClick Inc -111 8th Av -NY 10011
(212) 808-7715 .. **Haig,** Robt L '71 (Kelley D&W LLP) -101 Park Av -NY 10178
(212) 541-6222 .. **Haigian,** Aris '85 (Kane K,PC) -1350 Av of Amer -NY 10019
(212) 557-5590 .. **Haigney,** Dayton P III '88 -350 Bway -NY 10013
(212) 768-0058 .. **Haigney,** Stacy J '73 Burlington Coat Factory -263 W 38th -NY 10018 **Fx:**391-0074
(212) 918-3000 .. **Haigney,** Wm F '83 (Hogan L LLP) -875 3rd Av -NY 10022
(212) 813-8800 .. **Hail,** Brian D '93 (Goodwin P LLP) -620 8th Av -NY 10018
(212) 837-6000 .. **Hail,** Casey J '09 %Hughes H&R LLP -1 Bttry Pk Plz -NY 10004
(646) 386-3621 .. **Haile,** Suzanne W '96 %Supreme Ct-Law Dept -60 Centre -NY 10007
(212) 225-2000 .. **Hailey,** Kara A '99 %Cleary GS&H -1 Lbrty Plz -NY 10006
(212) 506-5000 .. **Haimes,** Burton K '68 (Orrick H&S LLP) -51 W 52nd -NY 10019
(212) 351-4000 .. **Haimo,** Stephan H '84 (Gibson D&C LLP) -200 Park Av -NY 10166
(212) 944-4747 .. **Haimof,** Kamyar '07 Murray Hill Properties LLC -1140 Av of Amer -NY 10036
(212) 490-3000 .. **Haimowitz,** Aaron R '98 (Wilson EME&D LLP) -150 E 42nd -NY 10017
(718) 263-8700 .. **Haimowitz & Goldberg, PLLC** -104-07 Metro Av -Frst Hlls 11375 **Fx:**520-1980
(718) 263-8700 .. **Haimowitz,** Richd '70 (Haimowitz & G,PLLC) -104-07 Metro Av -Frst Hlls 11375
(518) 473-0997 .. **Haimowitz,** Stephan J '87 %Ofc of Mental Hlth -44 Holland Av -Albany 12229
(212) 909-6000 .. **Haims,** Bruce D '68 OfCnsl Debevoise & P LLP -919 3rd Av -NY 10022
(212) 468-8000 .. **Haims,** Joel C '94 (Morrison & F LLP) -1290 Av of Amer -NY 10104
(914) 428-2010 .. **Haines,** Brynne L '78 -142 Greenrdg Av -White Plns 10605 **Fx:**997-2327
(518) 270-4030 .. **Haines,** Cory '97 %Pub Def Ofc -Rensselaer Cnty Cthse -Troy 12180
(914) 637-5331 .. **Haines,** Dennis '00 United Water -2525 Palmer Av -New Rchll 10801
(212) 880-9437 .. **Haines,** Elizabeth '07 %Morvillo AGIA&B,PC -565 5th Av -NY 10017
(718) 991-4600 .. **Haines,** Justin L '06 %Leg Aid -953 Southrn Blvd -Bronx 10459 **Fx:**842-2867
(212) 983-6000 .. **Haines,** Miriam J '75 OfCnsl M Berger -250 Park Av -NY 10177 **Fx:**983-6008
(585) 396-4016 .. **Haining,** Margaret H '01 City Ct -2 N Main -Canandaigua 14424
(718) 243-6831 .. **Hair,** Wm Jr. '02 Leg Aid -111 Lvngstn -Brklyn 11201 **Fx:**237-8737
(212) 714-3528 .. **Hairston,** Joylette R '97 -292 5th Av -NY 10001
(845) 469-9541 .. **Haislip,** Janet M '81 (Chester Town Justice) -1786 Kings Hwy -Chester 10918 **Fx:**469-4657
(845) 291-3115 .. **Haislip,** Janet M '81 %Hon N DeRosa -255 Main - Govt Ctr -Goshen 10924 **Fx:**291-2525
(212) 836-8000 .. **Hait,** Louis J '85 (Kaye S LLP) -425 Park Av -NY 10022
(516) 741-2585 .. **Hajaree-Ramsaran,** Sabita '03 %Rosicki R & Assoc,PC -51 E Bethpage Rd -Plainvw 11803 **Fx:**741-4748
(212) 839-5300 .. **Hajdu,** Istvan Andras '05 %Sidley A LLP -787 7th Av -NY 10019
(716) 488-1178 .. **Hajdu,** Lyle T '97 (Erickson WS&H) -414 E Fairmount Av Bx414 -Lakewd 14750
(716) 488-3090 .. **Hajdu,** Mary Speedy '89 (Burgett & R) -15 E 5th Bx3090 -Jamestwn 14702
(716) 847-8400 .. **Hajduczok,** George '04 SpclCnsl Phillips L LLP -3400 HSBC Ctr -Buffalo 14203
(212) 836-8000 .. **Haje,** Victoria E '05 %Kaye S LLP -425 Park Av -NY 10022
(212) 582-6500 .. **Hajek,** Lynn C '86 (Arshack H&L,PLLC) -1790 Bway -NY 10019
(718) 920-9590 .. **Hajnosz,** Patricia J '85 %Our Lady of Mercy Med Ctr -600 E 233rd -Bronx 10466
(212) 225-2000 .. **Hakala,** Lauren Vida '05 %Cleary GS&H -1 Lbrty Plz -NY 10006
(914) 333-9650 .. **Haken,** Jack E '75 %Philips Electronics -345 Scarborough Rd Bx3001 -Briarclff Mnr 10510 **Fx:**332-0615
(212) 766-2011 .. **Haken,** Stephen B '84 -110 Wall -NY 10005
(212) 509-0099 .. **Haker,** Nusret A '93 (Haker & O,LLP) -29 Bway -NY 10006 **Fx:**506-0488
(212) 957-7600 .. **Haker,** Oliver S '03 %Cohen & G LLP -800 3rd Av -NY 10022
(212) 594-5300 .. **Haker,** Oren B '04 %Milberg LLP -1 Penn Plz -NY 10119
(315) 673-9390 .. **Hakes,** Peter R '05 PR Hakes,LLC -4080 South St Rd Bx41 -Marcellus 13108 **Fx:**673-0925
(212) 506-2500 .. **Hakim,** A David '05 %Mayer B LLP -1675 Bway -NY 10019
(914) 420-8335 .. **Hakim,** Alexandra M '08 %Supreme Ct-Law Dept -60 Centre -NY 10007
(516) 487-5900 .. **Hakim,** Mark A '00 GCP Capital Grp,LLC -60 Cuttermill Rd -Gt Neck 11021
(646) 252-4274 .. **Hakim,** Veronique G '87 MTA Capital Cnstrctn -2 Bway -NY 10004
(212) 848-4000 .. **Hakki,** Adam S '98 (Shearman & S LLP) -599 Lex Av -NY 10022
(212) 868-9688 .. **Hakopian,** Alexander '08 -2 Penn Plz -NY 10121 **Fx:**202-5001
(518) 462-0300 .. **Halaco,** Karen A '07 Girvin & F,PC -20 Corp Wds Blvd -Albany 12211
(212) 819-8200 .. **Haladey,** Diana '07 %White & C LLP -1155 Av of Amer -NY 10036
(631) 665-5139 .. **Halajian,** Dicran '95 (Thorne & H,LLP) -111 W Main -Bay Shr 11706
(212) 756-2000 .. **Halasz,** Peter J '85 (Schulte R&Z LLP) -919 3rd Av -NY 10022
(212) 788-1194 .. **Halatyn,** Susan M '90 %Law Dept -100 Church -NY 10007 **Fx:**788-0367
(212) 698-3500 .. **Halavais,** Jamie L '06 %Dechert LLP -1095 Av of Amer -NY 10036
(212) 313-3600 .. **Halbardier,** Suzanne '84 (Barry M&M) -2 Rector -NY 10006
(212) 953-2381 .. **Halber,** Shelley R '90 (Rubin F&F,LLP) -292 Mad Av -NY 10017
(212) 207-6650 .. **Halberg,** Brian L '00 Bayrock Grp,LLC -160 Varick -NY 10013 **Fx:**207-4667
(718) 627-2490 .. **Halberg,** Saml S '85 -1573 E 18th -Brklyn 11230
(718) 382-4800 .. **Halberstam,** David '62 D Halberstam,PC -1381 E 16th -Brklyn 11230 **Fx:**382-4802
(212) 790-0394 .. **Halberstam,** Malvina '62 %Benj N Cardozo Schl of Law -55 5th Av -NY 10003 **Fx:**790-0345
(718) 377-7337 .. **Halberstam,** Mark '87 -1435 Coney Isl Av -Brklyn 11230 **Fx:**377-8694
(718) 769-7000 .. **Halberstam,** Michl J '73 MJ Halberstam,PC -3711 Shore Pkwy -Brklyn 11235 **Fx:**769-4302
(212) 582-3411 .. **Halberstam,** Saundra R '80 -444 W 50th -NY 10019 **Fx:**582-3411
(516) 546-3773 .. **Halbreich,** Jeffrey W '68 -2152 Grand Av -Baldwin 11510 **Fx:**868-0456
(631) 864-0800 .. **Halbridge,** Bonnie S '86 (Felberbaum H&W) -357 Vets Mem'l Hwy -Commack 11725
(212) 833-6451 .. **Halby,** Karen L '84 %Sony Corp of America -555 Mad Av -NY 10022
(973) 596-4657 .. **Halchak,** Alyce C '02 (Gibbons PC) -1 Penn Plz -NY 10119 **Fx:**639-6221
(212) 474-1000 .. **Halcom,** Kenneth C '07 %Cravath S&M LLP -825 8th Av -NY 10019
(212) 804-4200 .. **Halden,** Ann E '98 %Mound CW&G -One Bttry Pk Plz -NY 10004
(914) 948-4500 .. **Haldenstein,** Kenneth K '06 %O'Connor MCD&O -1 Barker Av -White Plns 10601
(212) 450-4000 .. **Haldin,** James W '05 %Davis P&W LLP -450 Lex Av -NY 10017
(212) 577-3688 .. **Hale,** Adrienne '79 %Leg Aid -199 Water -NY 10038 **Fx:**509-8431
(212) 474-1000 .. **Hale,** Andrew D '10 %Cravath S&M LLP -825 8th Av -NY 10019
(212) 788-0862 .. **Hale,** Ashley J '08 %Law Dept -100 Church -NY 10007 **Fx:**788-0367
(212) 248-3140 .. **Hale,** Audrey A '91 (Drinker B&R LLP) -140 Bway -NY 10005
(518) 523-4671 .. **Hale,** Clayton F '09 %Block CS&P,LLP -2276 Saranac Av -Lk Placid 12946
(315) 474-7571 .. **Hale,** Clayton H Jr. '68 (Mackenzie H LLP) -101 S Salina Bx4967 -Syracuse 13221
(718) 250-2000 .. **Hale,** Mark J '86 %DA -350 Jay -Brklyn 11201 **Fx:**250-2314
(518) 402-6969 .. **Hale,** Michl Patrick '02 %Envrnmtl Facilities -625 Bway -Albany 12207 **Fx:**402-6972
(212) 458-1596 .. **Hale,** Ryan H '05 AIG -175 Water -NY 10038
(212) 696-6000 .. **Hale,** Sarah J '09 %Curtis M-PC&M LLP -101 Park Av -NY 10178
(212) 608-1900 .. **Halebian,** John '78 (Lovell SH LLP) -61 Bway -NY 10006
(212) 931-7401 .. **Halem,** Danl '92 Ofc of Commissioner of Baseball -245 Park Av -NY 10167
(212) 723-3316 .. **Hales,** Shannon J '99 Citigroup Global Mrkts -388 Greenwich -NY 10013
(212) 697-3122 .. **Halesworth,** Kaitlyn M '10 %Martin C&B LLP -220 E 42nd -NY 10017
(212) 715-9100 .. **Haleva,** Aaron '87 %Kramer LN&F,LLP -1177 Av of Amer -NY 10036
(518) 472-5841 .. **Halewood,** Peter H '94 %Albany Law Schl -80 New Scotland Av -Albany 12208 **Fx:**445-2315
(212) 785-4100 .. **Haley,** Brooke K '07 %Fensterstock & Prtnrs LLP -30 Wall -NY 10005
(212) 682-4426 .. **Haley,** Elizabeth A '03 %O'Shea Prtnrs LLP -521 5th Av -NY 10175 **Fx:**682-4437
(212) 859-5001 .. **Haley,** Glen F '05 %Margolis Law Firm,LLC -110 Wall -NY 10005 **Fx:**943-2300
(212) 596-9000 .. **Haley,** James F Jr. '77 (Ropes & G LLP) -1211 Av of Amer -NY 10036
(607) 722-3495 .. **Haley,** James F Jr. '88 (Aswad & I) -46 Front -Bnghmtn 13905
(212) 312-0224 .. **Haley,** John H '76 Folksamerica Re -1 Lbrty Plz -NY 10006
(716) 564-4627 .. **Haley,** Julie Cox '92 ReMarketing Srvc of Amer -6400 Main -Buffalo 14221
(718) 243-0827 .. **Haley,** Reginald W III '92 %Leg Aid -111 Lvngstn -Brklyn 11201 **Fx:**237-8737
(631) 582-5151 .. **Haley,** Richd D Jr. '81 (Haley W&C,LLP) -1601 Vets Mem'l Hwy -Islandia 11749
(212) 558-4000 .. **Haley,** Shannon M '10 %Sullivan & C LLP -125 Broad -NY 10004
(631) 582-5151 .. **Haley Weinblatt & Calcagni,LLP** -1601 Vets Mem'l Hwy -Islandia 11749 **Fx:**234-7108
(212) 873-6000 .. **Halfkenny,** Polly J '96 Local 100 Union Hall -80 W End Av -NY 10023
(212) 848-4000 .. **Halfnight,** Christopher M '08 %Shearman & S LLP -599 Lex Av -NY 10022

(212) 764-0521 .. **Halfon,** Jay R '83 Halfon & Assoc -45 W 36th -NY 10018 **Fx:**428-6769
(518) 851-5297 .. **Halfond,** Ira '84 -1376 Route 23 Bx192 -Craryville 12521 **Fx:**851-2160
(212) 969-3000 .. **Halickman,** Michele E '10 %Proskauer R LLP -1585 Bway -NY 10036
(718) 815-2003 .. **Halk,** Carolyn M '81 -1 Edgewtr Plz -Staten Isl 10305 **Fx:**815-2012
(516) 822-8900 .. **Halka,** Christopher M '90 Fiedelman & M -2 Jericho Plz -Jericho 11753
(914) 833-2681 .. **Halket,** Thos D '79 (Halket & W LLP) -1214 W Bstn Post Rd -Mamaroneck 10543
(914) 833-2681 .. **Halket & Weitz LLP** -1214 W Bstn Post Rd -Mamaroneck 10543 **Fx:**833-2682
(718) 238-7444 .. **Halkias,** John E '03 -455 Bay Ridge Pkwy -Brklyn 11209
(212) 862-8700 .. **Hall,** Adolphus Jr. '06 %JL Greenup & Assoc -205 W 137th -NY 10030 **Fx:**862-2664
(516) 741-6355 .. **Hall,** Barbara L '94 %Nicolini PF&S -114 Old Cntry Rd Bx9006 -Mineola 11501
(888) 299-4633 .. **Hall,** Barry L '00 Hall Firm,LLC -380 Lex Av -NY 10168
(212) 482-0001 .. **Hall,** Brenda R '97 %Russo K&T LLP -33 Whitehall -NY 10004
(212) 732-3200 .. **Hall,** Bryan J '10 %Carter L&M LLP -2 Wall -NY 10005
(212) 649-8106 .. **Hall,** Caroline K '95 UBS Painewebber -1285 Av of Amer -NY 10019
(585) 262-2080 .. **Hall,** Chas A '55 -504 Exec Ofc Bldg -Rchstr 14614 **Fx:**262-2085
(716) 483-0756 .. **Hall,** Chas T '78 (Hall & P) -600 Htl Jmstwn Ofc Bldg -Jamestwn 14702 **Fx:**484-7352
(212) 335-4500 .. **Hall,** Christopher P '83 (DLA Piper LLP) -1251 Av of Amer -NY 10020
(518) 473-6289 .. **Hall,** Christopher W '93 %Dept of Law -The Cptl -Albany 12224
(212) 815-1818 .. **Hall,** Cynthia D '89 %DC 37 MELS -125 Barclay -NY 10007 **Fx:**815-1343
(716) 286-4552 .. **Hall,** Dale '04 %DA -520 Hyde Park Blvd -Niagara Fls 14301
(212) 310-8000 .. **Hall,** Dana J '10 %Weil G&M LLP -767 5th Av -NY 10153
(212) 878-8000 .. **Hall,** Danl J '06 %Clifford C LLP -31 W 52nd -NY 10019
(212) 578-0411 .. **Hall,** Darrell C '98 %MetLife -27-01 Qns Plz N -LIC 11101
(646) 495-2600 .. **Hall,** Darryl H Jr. '06 Tibco Software -120 W 45th -NY 10036
(212) 768-6700 .. **Hall,** David S '95 (Sonnenschein N&R LLP) -2 World Fncl Ctr -NY 10281
(212) 698-3500 .. **Hall,** Davin J '06 %Dechert LLP -1095 Av of Amer -NY 10036
(212) 687-1980 .. **Hall,** Donald R '01 (Kaplan F&K LLP) -850 3rd Av -NY 10022
(914) 697-2962 .. **Hall,** Douglas '82 %Transamerica Leasing, Inc -100 Manhattanvll Rd -Purchase 10577
(914) 831-2200 .. **Hall,** Earl T '04 Schott NA -555 Taxter Rd -Elmsfrd 10523
(212) 655-0880 .. **Hall,** Gary A '99 Cnsl NBPA -310 Lennox Av -NY 10027 **Fx:**655-0881
(914) 941-7000 .. **Hall,** H Glen '64 Daly L&H -500 Exec Blvd -Ossining 10562
(212) 297-1001 .. **Hall,** Hugh F '98 Gramercy Capital Corp -420 Lex Av -NY 10170
(585) 442-1573 .. **Hall,** Ina M '80 -61 Crittenden blvd -Rchstr 14620 **Fx:**473-3704
(212) 701-3000 .. **Hall,** Jason M '05 %Cahill G&R LLP -80 Pine -NY 10005 **Fx:**269-5420
(845) 794-3344 .. **Hall,** Jennifer M '08 %DA -414 Bway -Monticello 12701 **Fx:**794-3646
(718) 447-1962 .. **Hall,** John G '61 (Hall & H,LLP) -57 Beach -Staten Isl 10304 **Fx:**447-2761
(212) 909-6591 .. **Hall,** John H '70 OfCnsl Debevoise & P LLP -919 3rd Av -NY 10022
(516) 997-0999 .. **Hall,** John H Jr. '89 %Pryor & M,LLP -675 Old Cntry Rd -Westbury 11590
(315) 458-5220 .. **Hall,** John M '77 (Hall M&L,PLLC) -111 Church Bx278 -N Syracuse 13212
(212) 622-9731 .. **Hall,** John P III '92 JP Morgan Chase & Co -277 Park Av -NY 10172
(631) 284-2400 .. **Hall,** Johnny D '04 %Chicago Title Ins -901 E Main -Rvrhead 11901
(212) 450-4000 .. **Hall,** Jos A '90 (Davis P&W LLP) -450 Lex Av -NY 10017
(212) 290-4700 .. **Hall,** Julia Anne '99 %Human Rights Watch -350 5th Av -NY 10118 **Fx:**736-1300
(518) 471-4782 .. **Hall,** Julie Thorne '90 %Appllt Div 3rd Dept -Capitol Station Bx7288 -Albany 12224 **Fx:**471-4750
(607) 687-8640 .. **Hall,** Karen A '98 %Cnty Atty -20 Court -Owego 13827 **Fx:**687-6160
(585) 394-5755 .. **Hall & Karz** -6 Gorham -Canandaigua 14424 **Fx:**394-5758
(914) 684-9100 .. **Hall,** Katherine Gavin '02 (Bailly & M,LLP) -244 Wstchstr Av -White Plns 10604
(212) 574-1200 .. **Hall,** Kathryn A '10 %Seward & K LLP -1 Bttry Pk Plz -NY 10004
(914) 937-9009 .. **Hall,** Keith '72 %Parsons & Whittemore -4 Intl Dr -Rye Brook 10573
(212) 521-5400 .. **Hall,** Kevin A '92 (Reed S LLP) -599 Lex Av -NY 10022
(212) 474-1000 .. **Hall,** Laura R '05 %Cravath S&M LLP -825 8th Av -NY 10019
(212) 230-8800 .. **Hall,** Margaux J '09 %WilmerHale -399 Park Av -NY 10022
(212) 809-1111 .. **Hall,** Mark T '08 %Morgan MA -39 Bway -NY 10006
(212) 474-1000 .. **Hall,** Marlene D '91 Cravath S&M LLP -825 8th Av -NY 10019
(315) 458-5220 .. **Hall Martin & Lauri, PLLC** -111 Church Bx278 -N Syracuse 13212 **Fx:**458-4290
(212) 461-2338 .. **Hall,** Matthew B '00 (Goldstein H) -44 Wall -NY 10005 **Fx:**(646) 219-2450
(631) 543-2031 .. **Hall,** Michl '76 -57 Fla Av -Commack 11725 **Fx:**543-2031
(212) 547-5400 .. **Hall,** Michl D '05 %McDermott W&E LLP -340 Mad Av -NY 10173
(518) 447-3200 .. **Hall,** Michl J '91 (McNamee LT&W,PC) -677 Bway -Albany 12207
(212) 227-7200 .. **Hall,** Michl S '84 %Klein W&M -277 Bway -NY 10007
(212) 274-6127 .. **Hall,** Michele Denise '91 %Admin Children's Srvcs -220 Church -NY 10013 **Fx:**274-6109
(212) 474-1000 .. **Hall,** Richd A '89 (Cravath S&M LLP) -825 8th Av -NY 10019
(716) 633-3535 .. **Hall,** Richd A IV '04 %W Mattar,PC -6720 Main -Williamsvll 14221 **Fx:**631-9804
(716) 652-0828 .. **Hall Ricketts Marky & Gurbacki** -471 Main -E Aurora 14052 **Fx:**652-2058
(212) 344-3900 .. **Hall,** Robt C '98 %Belair & E LLP -61 Bway -NY 10006
(516) 622-9200 .. **Hall,** Robt J '55 OfCnsl Westerman BEM&S,LLP -1201 RXR Plz -Uniondale 11553
(914) 745-4277 .. **Hall,** Russell '79 %Towers Watson -100 Summit Lk Dr -Valhalla 10595
(716) 852-5200 .. **Hall,** Russell D '96 (Hamberger & W) -700 Main Pl Twr -Buffalo 14202
(585) 394-5755 .. **Hall,** Saml M '62 (Hall & K) -6 Gorham -Canandaigua 14424
(212) 335-4500 .. **Hall,** Sarah-Jayne '06 %DLA Piper LLP -1251 Av of Amer -NY 10020
(585) 546-3770 .. **Hall,** Stephen E '81 -36 W Main -Rchstr 14614
(631) 983-4337 .. **Hall,** Susan M '00 -50 Hill -Southampton 11968 **Fx:**983-4337
(914) 703-6300 .. **Hall,** Terri S '91 %Pillinger MT,LLP -570 Taxter Rd -Elmsfrd 10523
(212) 436-3218 .. **Hall,** Theresa A '82 Deloitte & Touche,LLP -2 World Fncl Ctr -NY 10281
(518) 279-1040 .. **Hall,** Thos C '78 -1128 Hoosick Rd -Troy 12180
(212) 408-5100 .. **Hall,** Thos J '81 (Chadbourne & P LLP) -30 Rckfllr Plz -NY 10112
(718) 447-1962 .. **Hall,** Thos J '87 (Hall & H,LLP) -57 Beach -Staten Isl 10304 **Fx:**447-2761
(212) 644-4420 .. **Hall,** Thos J '93 (Fabiani C&H,LLP) -570 Lex Av -NY 10022
(914) 848-4648 .. **Hall,** Tiffany M '09 Pernod Ricard USA -100 Manhattanvll Rd -Purchase 10577
(585) 546-5530 .. **Hall,** Timothy M '88 %Thomson West -50 E Broad -Rchstr 14694
(518) 388-4466 .. **Hall,** Ursula E '03 %Dept Soc Srvcs -106 Erie Blvd -Schnctdy 12307 **Fx:**382-1256
(212) 587-2400 .. **Hall,** W Miller '04 %Collins D&M,LLP -277 Bway -NY 10007
(212) 888-5222 .. **Hall,** Willard James '93 Third Ave Mgmt -622 3rd Av -NY 10017
(212) 859-8000 .. **Hall,** Zachary R '09 %Fried FHS&J LLP -1 NY Plz -NY 10004
(914) 642-5561 .. **Hallahan-McAndrew,** Sheila '95 %IBM -1133 Wstchstr Av -White Plns 10604 **Fx:**642-5788
(315) 853-4436 .. **Hallak,** Anthony G '88 (Felt E,LLP) -4-6 N Park Row -Clinton 13323
(212) 751-3001 .. **Hallake,** Marcello '95 (Thompson & K LLP) -919 3rd Av -NY 10022
(212) 908-1317 .. **Hallakorpi,** Mika T '03 Maritime Subrogation Srvcs,LLC -45 Bway -NY 10006
(212) 474-1000 .. **Hallam,** O Keith '08 %Cravath S&M LLP -825 8th Av -NY 10019
(516) 501-0106 .. **Hallas,** Herbert C '90 -64 Woodward Pkwy -Farmngdl 11735
(212) 265-6888 .. **Hallberg,** Justin C '09 %Porzio B&N,PC -156 W 56th -NY 10019
(716) 853-9555 .. **Hallborg,** Robt B Jr. '82 %Leg Aid -237 Main -Buffalo 14203 **Fx:**853-3219
(518) 474-1331 .. **Halleck,** Nancy H '83 Ofc Mntl Health -44 Holland Av -Albany 12229 **Fx:**473-7863
(518) 725-1735 .. **Hallenbeck,** Mark E '80 -536 N Shore Peck Rd -Gloversvll 12078
(518) 486-4508 .. **Hallenbeck,** Peter D '75 %Dept of Law -The Cptl -Albany 12224
(212) 906-1200 .. **Hallenbeck,** Peter W '04 -885 3rd Av -NY 10022 **Fx:**751-4864
(631) 244-3442 .. **Haller,** Bruce L '93 %Dowling Cllg -Idle Hour Blvd -Oakdale 11769
(212) 841-1000 .. **Haller,** David W '89 (Covington & B LLP) -620 8th Av -NY 10018
(718) 821-5577 .. **Haller,** Fred T III '86 Haller & H -62-18 Myrtle Av -Glendale 11385
(800) 656-9529 .. **Haller,** Jason S '07 %Lynch Law Firm,PC -222 Route 59 -Suffern 10901 **Fx:**(888) 271-9726
(212) 458-5690 .. **Haller,** John D '92 %AIG -175 Water -NY 10038
(212) 538-0902 .. **Haller,** Peter E '96 Credit Suisse Securities -1 Mad Av -NY 10010 **Fx:**322-2289
(212) 676-2442 .. **Hallerdin,** Gail I '92 Dept of Health & Mental Hygiene -2 Lafayette -NY 10007
(516) 576-8030 .. **Hallerman,** Andrew '01 %JJ McGuire -131 E Ames Ct -Plainvw 11803
(631) 265-1700 .. **Halleron,** John J III '68 OfCnsl Kenney GW&S,LLP -50 Route 111 -Smithtwn 11787
(212) 218-2100 .. **Hallet,** Margaret A '10 %Fitzpatrick CH&S -1290 Av of Amer -NY 10104
(718) 590-2000 .. **Halley,** Morgan B '08 %DA -198 E 161st -Bronx 10451 **Fx:**590-6477
(845) 452-9120 .. **Halley,** Thos P '76 -80 Wshngtn -Poughkeepsie 12601 **Fx:**452-9192
(518) 433-7300 .. **Halliday,** Andrew W '95 -16 Corp Wds Blvd -Albany 12211
(212) 258-6000 .. **Hallie,** Michelena '84 %Viacom -1515 Bway -NY 10036
(212) 335-9000 .. **Halligan,** Caitlin J '01 %DA -1 Hogan Pl -NY 10013
(212) 371-1000 .. **Halligan,** Claire Quinn '00 %Catholic Home Bureau -1011 1st Av -NY 10022
(212) 792-8484 .. **Halligan,** Rosemary '93 (Stern T&B LLP) -380 Lex Av -NY 10168
(212) 351-4000 .. **Halling,** Patricia A '08 %Gibson D&C LLP -200 Park Av -NY 10166
(212) 788-0960 .. **Hallman,** James L '10 %Law Dept -100 Church -NY 10007 **Fx:**788-0367
(212) 701-3000 .. **Hallman,** Robt M '65 (Cahill G&R LLP) -80 Pine -NY 10005 **Fx:**269-5420
(718) 544-3333 .. **Hallock,** Larry '92 -77-42 164th -Fresh Mdws 11366 **Fx:**544-1341
(516) 248-9595 .. **Halloran,** Danl J '03 OfCnsl Palmieri C & Assoc,PC -250 Mineola Blvd -Mineola 11501
(212) 661-0011 .. **Halloran,** John J Jr. '85 (Speiser KN&G) -140 E 45th -NY 10017
(914) 397-2400 .. **Hallowell,** J Lincoln '72 (Ferguson C,LLP) -1 N Lex Av -White Plns 10601 **Fx:**683-6956
(212) 351-4000 .. **Hallowell,** James L '95 (Gibson D&C LLP) -200 Park Av -NY 10166
(212) 907-0700 .. **Hallowell,** Serena P '04 %Labaton S LLP -140 Bway -NY 10005
(518) 457-6468 .. **Hall Peak,** Sarah R '99 %Agriculture & Mrkts -10B Airline Dr -Albany 12235 **Fx:**457-8842
(212) 788-9100 .. **Halm,** Baaba K '04 NYC Council -250 Bway -NY 10007
(646) 435-0300 .. **Haloulos,** Constantine Dino '00 %McCullough GM&P,LLP -320 E 53rd -NY 10022
(212) 735-3000 .. **Halper,** Adam F '05 %Skadden ASM&F LLP -4 Times Sq -NY 10036
(212) 766-4522 .. **Halper,** Adam J '00 Family Ctr -315 W 36th -NY 10018
(212) 815-1140 .. **Halper,** Barbara M '79 %DC 37 MELS -125 Barclay -NY 10007 **Fx:**815-1343
(516) 625-8300 .. **Halper,** Emanuel B '58 (E Halper,PC) -Bx261 -Greenvale 11548 **Fx:**625-8467
(212) 402-9400 .. **Halper,** Eric B '00 SrCnsl McKool S,PC -1 Bryant Park -NY 10036
(212) 504-6000 .. **Halper,** Jason M '92 (Cadwalader W&T LLP) -1 World Fncl Ctr -NY 10281
(212) 859-8000 .. **Halper,** Loryn B '05 %Fried FHS&J LLP -1 NY Plz -NY 10004
(212) 688-5151 .. **Halper,** Melvyn H '65 (Gibney A&F,LLP) -665 5th Av -NY 10022
(212) 790-9200 .. **Halper,** Robt '65 (Cowan L&L,PC) -1133 Av of Amer -NY 10036
(914) 941-2009 .. **Halper,** Stuart A '87 -105 Whitson Rd Bx295 -Briarclff Mnr 10510
(212) 765-9100 .. **Halperin,** Alan D '91 (Halperin BR,LLP) -555 Mad Av -NY 10022
(212) 373-3000 .. **Halperin,** Alan S '86 (Paul WRW&G LLP) -1285 Av of Amer -NY 10019
(212) 765-9100 .. **Halperin Battaglia Raicht,LLP** -555 Mad Av -NY 10022 **Fx:**765-0964
(212) 458-2866 .. **Halperin,** David B '94 AIG -175 Water -NY 10038
(212) 751-7555 .. **Halperin,** Guy S '85 (Halperin Law Firm,PLLC) -331 Mad Av -NY 10017 **Fx:**371-2131
(516) 747-0300 .. **Halperin,** Ira R '96 (Meltzer LG&B,LLP) -190 Willis Av -Mineola 11501

(914) 993-1933 .. **Halperin**, Jason P W '00 %US Atty -300 Quarropas -White Plns 10601 **Fx:**993-9036
(212) 909-6000 .. **Halperin**, Joanna R '01 %Debevoise & P LLP -919 3rd Av -NY 10022
(212) 526-0170 .. **Halperin**, Joelle L '99 Lehman Bros -1271 Av of Amer -NY 10020
(516) 546-8414 .. **Halperin**, Jonathan '90 %L H Stations Inc -1144 Atl Av -Baldwin 11510 **Fx:**623-5103
(212) 750-2110 .. **Halperin**, Keith G '92 -381 Park Av S -NY 10016
(212) 986-7353 .. **Halperin**, Kenneth J '93 %Wingate R&S -420 Lex Av -NY 10170
(212) 751-7555 .. **Halperin**, Kyle Mallary '91 (Halperin Law Firm,PLLC) -331 Mad Av -NY 10017 **Fx:**371-2131
(212) 530-1800 .. **Halperin**, Larry G '88 (Richards K&O LLP) -1 World Fncl Ctr -NY 10281
(212) 448-1100 .. **Halperin**, Richd E '69 (McLaughlin & S,LLP) -260 Mad Av -NY 10016
(212) 935-2600 .. **Halperin**, Steven T '88 (Halperin & H,PC) -18 E 48th -NY 10017 **Fx:**753-9173
(516) 832-7612 .. **Halpern**, Aaron S '03 %Nixon P LLP -50 Jericho Quadrangle -Jericho 11753
(631) 665-1660 .. **Halpern**, Adam S '85 -256C Orinoco Dr Bx322 -Brightwtrs 11718
(212) 506-1700 .. **Halpern**, Alexandra Stone '10 %Kasowitz BT&F LLP -1633 Bway -NY 10019
(212) 661-9100 .. **Halpern**, Andrew S '86 %Otterbourg SH&R,PC -230 Park Av -NY 10169
(212) 988-9316 .. **Halpern**, Arthur B '56 -325 E 79th -NY 10075 **Fx:**988-2954
(718) 875-8580 .. **Halpern Brown & Darienzo** -26 Court -Brklyn 11242 **Fx:**852-5360
(516) 482-6752 .. **Halpern**, Gerald P '50 -20 Canterbury Rd -Gt Neck 11021
(716) 839-9020 .. **Halpern**, Harold M '58 -3949 Forest Pkwy -N Tonawanda 14120
(212) 825-0365 .. **Halpern**, Jackie '07 %AL Bailey,PC -120 Bway -NY 10271 **Fx:**825-0999
(212) 640-5805 .. **Halpern**, Jason D '97 Amer Exp Travel Related Srvc -200 Vesey -NY 10285
(212) 508-6100 .. **Halpern**, Jonathan N '01 (Bracewell & G,LLP) -1251 Av of Amer -NY 10020
(212) 259-8000 .. **Halpern**, Joshua D '07 %Dewey & L LLP -1301 Av of Amer -NY 10019
(516) 466-3200 .. **Halpern**, Jules Z '78 -525 Nrthrn Blvd -Gt Neck 11021
(516) 746-0232 .. **Halpern**, Karen '88 (Farley G&H,LLP) -200 Old Cntry Rd -Mineola 11501
(516) 222-4567 .. **Halpern**, Kenneth J '69 (Sawyer H&D) -666 Old Cntry Rd -Gdn Cty 11530
(516) 466-3100 .. **Halpern**, Lonnie J '02 BRT Realty Trust -60 Cuttermill Rd -Gt Neck 11021 **Fx:**773-2770
(212) 840-7383 .. **Halpern**, Mark S '85 (Schonbraun McCann Grp,LLP) -750 3rd Av -NY 10017
(212) 426-3022 .. **Halpern**, Marlene '76 Legal Aid -230 E 106th -NY 10029
(516) 354-1414 .. **Halpern**, Meryl L '84 -13915 83rd Av -Jamaica 11435 **Fx:**354-0837
(516) 249-3450 .. **Halpern**, Naftali T '06 Carman C&I,LLP -266 Main -Farmngdl 11735
(914) 684-6800 .. **Halpern**, Philip M '80 (Collier HNN&B,LLP) -1 N Lex Av -White Plns 10601
(716) 856-0600 .. **Halpern**, Ralph L '53 SrCnsl Jaeckle F&M,LLP -12 Fountain Plz -Buffalo 14202
(516) 229-6000 .. **Halpern**, Richd '87 %R Lau & Assoc -300 Jericho Quad Bx9040 -Jericho 11753 **Fx:**229-6167
(516) 221-7400 .. **Halpern**, Richd A '75 -3730 Park Av Bx2900 -Wantagh 11793 **Fx:**221-7991
(518) 445-2311 .. **Halpern**, Sheldon W '59 Albany Law Schl -80 New Scotland Av -Albany 12208 **Fx:**445-2315
(716) 645-2251 .. **Halpern**, Stephen C '84 Univ of Buffalo-Pol Sci -509 Park Hall -Buffalo 14260
(212) 609-6800 .. **Halpern**, Steven E '01 %McCarter & E,LLP -245 Park Av -NY 10167
(212) 418-8448 .. **Halpern**, Susan U '85 -750 3rd Av -NY 10017
(716) 847-8400 .. **Halpern**, Tamar P '83 (Phillips L LLP) -3400 HSBC Ctr -Buffalo 14203
(212) 759-4888 .. **Halpern**, Tamar P '83 (Phillips L LLP) -437 Mad Av -NY 10022
(516) 295-1425 .. **Halpern**, Wilfred J '69 -220 Steven Pl -Woodmere 11598
(718) 590-2000 .. **Halpern**, Wm Dyer '07 %DA -198 E 161st -Bronx 10451 **Fx:**590-6477
(212) 872-3635 .. **Halpert**, Ethan C '96 %KPMG LLP -345 Park Av -NY 10154
(718) 286-2000 .. **Halpert**, Michl T '09 %Leg Aid -120-46 Qns Blvd -Kew Gdns 11415 **Fx:**286-2286
(212) 909-6000 .. **Halpert**, Yehuda Y '01 %Debevoise & P LLP -919 3rd Av -NY 10022
(212) 622-5341 .. **Halpin**, Irene A '90 JP Morgan Chase -277 Park Av -NY 10172
(607) 594-3319 .. **Halpin**, James E '71 Halpin Law Firm,PC -Bx181 -Odessa 14869 **Fx:**594-2426
(212) 944-1121 .. **Halpin**, John E '68 -530 5th Av -NY 10036 **Fx:**944-1145
(315) 735-7566 .. **Halpin**, Mark J '86 %Petrone & P,PC -1624 Genesee -Utica 13502
(212) 504-6000 .. **Halpin**, Peter L '08 %Cadwalader W&T LLP -1 World Fncl Ctr -NY 10281
(607) 594-3786 .. **Halpin**, Robt L '02 -4588 State Route 224 -Montour Fls 14865 **Fx:**594-3788
(212) 998-6074 .. **Halprin**, Jessica Lerner '99 NYU Law Schl -161 Av of Amer -NY 10013
(212) 357-6875 .. **Halsband**, Michl R '90 Goldman Sachs & Co -1 NY Plz -NY 10004
(212) 504-6000 .. **Halski**, John P '07 %Cadwalader W&T LLP -1 World Fncl Ctr -NY 10281
(212) 504-6000 .. **Halstead**, Ellen M '05 %Cadwalader W&T LLP -1 World Fncl Ctr -NY 10281
(516) 294-8844 .. **Halstrom**, Douglas R '91 (L'Abbate BC&C,LLP) -1001 Franklin Av -Gdn Cty 11530
(516) 783-3300 .. **Halstrom**, Robin Rabdell '93 %Baker G&B -2099 Bellmore Av -Bellmore 11710
(212) 687-8500 .. **Halter**, James W '02 %Liddle & R,LLP -800 3rd Av -NY 10022
(212) 351-4000 .. **Halter**, Jennifer Colgan '05 %Gibson D&C LLP -200 Park Av -NY 10166
(914) 686-3850 .. **Halter**, Wm C Jr. '65 -10 Bank -White Plns 10606 **Fx:**993-6303
(212) 259-8000 .. **Haltiwanger**, Nuri L '06 %Dewey & L LLP -1301 Av of Amer -NY 10019
(516) 248-8000 .. **Halton**, John J '91 %Sandback B&M -200 Old Cntry Rd -Mineola 11501
(212) 841-4102 .. **Halustick**, Lisa '96 Millenium Ptnrs LP -666 5th Av -NY 10103
(631) 852-2500 .. **Halverson**, John '06 %DA -200 Center Dr -Rvrhead 11901 **Fx:**852-1769
(212) 906-1200 .. **Halverstam**, Keith L '01 (Latham & W) -885 3rd Av -NY 10022
(716) 853-9555 .. **Halvorsen**, Chas D '73 %Leg Aid -237 Main -Buffalo 14203 **Fx:**853-3219
(631) 486-1200 .. **Halvorsen**, Victoria Ann '91 -115 Broad Hollow Rd -Melvll 11747 **Fx:**486-1202
(631) 283-2400 .. **Ham**, Barbara T '96 (Matthews & H) -38 Nugent -Southampton 11968
(518) 456-0082 .. **Ham**, Catherine P '07 %Bailey K&J,PC -5 Pine West Plz -Albany 12205 **Fx:**456-4767
(631) 283-2400 .. **Ham**, Stephen L III '78 (Matthews & H) -38 Nugent -Southampton 11968
(516) 873-2000 .. **Hamada**, Cindy R '96 %Moritt HH&H LLP -400 Grdn City Plz -Gdn Cty 11530
(212) 351-4000 .. **Hamada**, Dana H '08 %Gibson D&C LLP -200 Park Av -NY 10166
(212) 428-2130 .. **Hamanjian**, Alison M '01 OCA -25 Beaver -NY 10004
(716) 856-1300 .. **Hamberger**, Douglas P '82 %Barth SB -43 Court -Buffalo 14202
(516) 249-1342 .. **Hamberger**, John K '95 %Grey & G,LLP -360 Main -Farmngdl 11735
(716) 852-5200 .. **Hamberger**, Mark W '73 (Hamberger & W) -700 Main Pl Twr -Buffalo 14202
(716) 852-5200 .. **Hamberger & Weiss** -700 Main Pl Twr -Buffalo 14202 **Fx:**852-0003
(585) 262-6390 .. **Hamberger & Weiss** -1 S Wshngtn -Rchstr 14614 **Fx:**262-6399
(212) 577-3500 .. **Hamberlin**, Karen K '99 %Leg Aid -199 Water -NY 10038 **Fx:**809-1370
(212) 506-5000 .. **Hambidge**, Cristin F '08 %Orrick H&S LLP -51 W 52nd -NY 10019
(212) 318-3000 .. **Hambidge**, Todd R '08 %Fulbright & J LLP -666 5th Av -NY 10103
(914) 762-7586 .. **Hamble**, Fredk J '97 Warren Pharm -712 Kitchawan Rd -Ossining 10562
(631) 261-8834 .. **Hamblin**, Antonia L '04 %Ingerman S LLP -150 Motor Pkwy -Hauppauge 11788
(718) 999-2028 .. **Hamblin**, Bridget S '05 %Fire Dept Bureau Leg Afrs -9 Metrotech Ctr -Brklyn 11201
(212) 940-1381 .. **Hambrecht**, Patricia G '79 Phillips de Pury & Co -450 W 15th -NY 10011
(212) 848-4000 .. **Hambrick**, David N '10 Shearman & S LLP -599 Lex Av -NY 10022
(718) 286-2450 .. **Hambrick**, Karen A '87 %Leg Aid -120-46 Qns Blvd -Kew Gdns 11415 **Fx:**263-4234
(347) 296-1860 .. **Hambrock**, Ernest M '97 %Hon J Goldberg -330 Jay -Brklyn 11201
(212) 986-2340 .. **Hamburg**, C Bruce '64 (Jordan & H) -122 E 42nd -NY 10168
(212) 907-7300 .. **Hamburg**, Donald A '64 (Golenbock EAB&P) -437 Mad Av -NY 10022
(202) 220-6993 .. **Hamburg**, Eric '07 %Locke LB&L LLP -3 World Fncl Ctr -NY 10281 **Fx:**220-6945
(212) 808-0700 .. **Hamburg**, Jeanne M '91 (Norris M&M,PA) -875 3rd Av -NY 10022
(917) 885-8275 .. **Hamburg**, Steven D '86 -2736 Indpndnc Av -Bronx 10463 **Fx:**(516) 773-4516
(212) 812-8990 .. **Hamburger**, Bradley G '91 Foa & Son -60 E 42nd -NY 10165 **Fx:**432-1235
(631) 694-2400 .. **Hamburger Maxson Yaffe Knauer & McNally, LLP** -225 Broadhllw Rd -Melvll 11747 **Fx:**694-1376
(212) 819-8200 .. **Hamburger**, Michl E '10 %White & C LLP -1155 Av of Amer -NY 10036
(631) 694-2400 .. **Hamburger**, Richd C '78 (Hamburger MYK&M,LLP) -225 Broadhllw Rd -Melvll 11747
(212) 719-5930 .. **Hamburger Weinschenk & Fisher** -36 W 44th -NY 10036 **Fx:**840-0825
(718) 590-2000 .. **Hamburgh**, Jeremy R '08 %DA -198 E 161st -Bronx 10451 **Fx:**590-6477
(212) 947-0565 .. **Hamburgh**, Mark S '76 -450 7th Av -NY 10123 **Fx:**629-5825
(631) 751-3500 .. **Hamby**, Gerald L '58 -1400 Stony Brk Rd -Stony Brk 11790
(212) 325-4905 .. **Hamdan**, Lawr A '90 %Credit Suisse First Boston -11 Mad Av -NY 10010
(718) 230-0050 .. **Hamed**, Ibrahim '03 %D Akinola,PC -333 Nostrand Av -Brklyn 11216 **Fx:**230-0085
(718) 853-6600 .. **Hamel**, Bernard D '77 -5009 16th Av -Brklyn 11204 **Fx:**851-1737
(212) 683-3800 .. **Hamel**, Wm R '91 %Dinkes & S,PC -112 Mad Av -NY 10016
(315) 798-5766 .. **Hameline**, Christopher D '08 %DA -800 Park Av -Utica 13501 **Fx:**798-5582
(315) 798-5766 .. **Hameline**, Kurt D '75 %DA -800 Park Av -Utica 13501 **Fx:**798-5582
(212) 244-9500 .. **Hamelsky**, Andrew I '97 (White and W LLP) -1 Penn Plz -NY 10119
(212) 909-6000 .. **Hamerman**, Dina L '03 %Debevoise & P LLP -919 3rd Av -NY 10022
(212) 715-9100 .. **Hamerman**, Natan M '02 %Kramer LN&F,LLP -1177 Av of Amer -NY 10036
(718) 330-1020 .. **Hamernick**, Dennis P '83 -26 Court -Brklyn 11242 **Fx:**852-5360
(212) 594-5000 .. **Hamersky**, Michl D '08 Togut S&S LLP -1 Penn Plz -NY 10119
(212) 563-0100 .. **Hames**, Bradley S '00 %A Rothenberg -450 7th Av -NY 10123 **Fx:**629-6813
(516) 877-0777 .. **Hametz**, Ivan W '77 (Taub H&W,PLLC) -190 Willis Av -Mineola 11501
(212) 506-1700 .. **Hametz**, Sheri E '01 %Kasowitz BT&F LLP -1633 Bway -NY 10019
(212) 626-4100 .. **Hamid**, Haroon H '07 %Baker & M LLP -1114 Av of Amer -NY 10036
(212) 909-6000 .. **Hamid**, Jyotin R '99 (Debevoise & P LLP) -919 3rd Av -NY 10022
(212) 776-5000 .. **Hamid**, Stacie R '03 NYC Housing Auth -250 Bway -NY 10007 **Fx:**776-5039
(212) 682-1818 .. **Hamill**, Bridget V '05 %Murray F&S LLP -275 Mad Av -NY 10016
(631) 563-6585 .. **Hamill**, Donald R '87 -40 Main -Sayvll 11782
(212) 373-3000 .. **Hamill**, Justin G '04 %Paul WRW&G LLP -1285 Av of Amer -NY 10019
(845) 634-7430 .. **Hamilla**, Peter Wm '58 -14 Deerfoot Ln -New Cty 10956
(914) 749-8200 .. **Hamill-Green**, Mary '76 Cnsl Boies S&F LLP -333 Main -Armonk 10504
(718) 520-3728 .. **Hamilton**, Arlene A '84 Supreme Ct -89-17 Sutphin Blvd -Jamaica 11435
(212) 558-4000 .. **Hamilton**, Brian E '99 (Sullivan & C LLP) -125 Broad -NY 10004
(516) 297-1338 .. **Hamilton**, Chas F '79 Local 338 RWDSU/UFCW -1505 Kellum Pl -Mineola 11501

(212) 318-6000 .. **Hamilton,** Chas J Jr. '79 (Paul HJ&W LLP) -75 E 55th -NY 10022
(212) 909-6000 .. **Hamilton,** Christopher J '05 %Debevoise & P LLP -919 3rd Av -NY 10022
Hamilton, Courtney A B '73 -17722 Wexford Ter -Jamaica 11432
(718) 739-9400 .. **Hamilton,** Deborah M '02 %RW Hamilton & Assoc -177-22 Wexford Ter -Jamaica 11432 **Fx:**658-3899
(716) 639-4006 .. **Hamilton,** Dennis P '77 (Dixon & H,LLP) -2350 N Forest Rd -Getzvll 14068
(718) 604-4728 .. **Hamilton,** Desiree S '92 -1100 Lincoln Pl -Brklyn 11213
(518) 402-4138 .. **Hamilton,** G Stephen '88 %State Comptroller -110 State -Albany 12236 **Fx:**473-9104
(212) 931-7944 .. **Hamilton,** Jennifer A '99 %MLB Properties -245 Park Av -NY 10167 **Fx:**949-5697
(212) 980-9600 .. **Hamilton,** Jennifer M '06 %Kaufman B&R -120 Bway -NY 10271
(718) 778-8924 .. **Hamilton,** Jesse E '98 -910 Lincoln Pl -Brklyn 11213 **Fx:**778-7301
(212) 728-8000 .. **Hamilton,** John '07 %Willkie F&G LLP -787 7th Av -NY 10019
(516) 794-7500 .. **Hamilton,** John F '85 OfCnsl Westermann SKS&A,LLP -333 Earle Ovngton Blvd -Uniondale 11553
(212) 637-2414 .. **Hamilton,** Julie L '94 US Dept of Jus -1 St Andrews Plz -NY 10007
(212) 353-8280 .. **Hamilton,** Kevin T '97 %ATC Group Srvcs, Inc -104 E 25th -NY 10010 **Fx:**598-4283
(518) 587-8112 .. **Hamilton,** Lawr R '75 (Hamilton W PLLC) -480 Bway -Saratoga Spgs 12866 **Fx:**587-4140
(212) 269-4900 .. **Hamilton,** Lindsay S '07 %Ford MEW&G,LLP -Wall Street Plz -NY 10005
(212) 819-8200 .. **Hamilton,** Mark T '94 (White & C LLP) -1155 Av of Amer -NY 10036
(212) 969-3000 .. **Hamilton,** Martin T '04 %Proskauer R LLP -1585 Bway -NY 10036
(212) 735-3000 .. **Hamilton,** Michl S '09 %Skadden ASM&F LLP -4 Times Sq -NY 10036
(718) 398-2050 .. **Hamilton,** Pamela E '94 %Child Dvlpmnt Support -352-358 Classon Av -Brklyn 11238 **Fx:**398-6883
(718) 739-9400 .. **Hamilton,** Reginald W '91 -177-22 Wexford Ter -Jamaica 11432 **Fx:**658-3899
(646) 840-5736 .. **Hamilton,** Rhea P '02 J Records LLC -745 5th Av -NY 10151
(212) 753-5000 .. **Hamilton,** Russel T '80 (Schiff H LLP) -900 3rd Av -NY 10022
(914) 725-2801 .. **Hamilton,** Sarah Jo '77 (Scalise & H LLP) -670 Wht Plns Rd -Scarsdale 10583 **Fx:**931-2112
(212) 701-3000 .. **Hamilton,** Shana G '05 %Cahill G&R LLP -80 Pine -NY 10005 **Fx:**269-5420
(518) 474-7278 .. **Hamilton,** Stacey A '00 %Dept of Law -The Cptl -Albany 12224 **Fx:**402-2280
(585) 530-3176 .. **Hamilton,** Tracy M '91 %Appllt Div 4th Dept -50 East Av Ste 200 -Rchstr 14604 **Fx:**530-3247
(716) 439-7172 .. **Hamilton,** Wm G Jr. '75 %Family Ct -Cthse -Lockprt 14094 **Fx:**439-7170
(914) 941-7605 .. **Hamilton,** Wm J G '88 Advocates Ofc -26 Pershing Av -Ossining 10562
(718) 694-3854 .. **Hamler,** Sonya Zoe '92 %Transit Auth -130 Lvngstn -Brklyn 11201 **Fx:**694-5726
(585) 394-4260 .. **Hamlin,** George W IV '73 -72 Main -Canandaigua 14424
(315) 797-8300 .. **Hamlin,** Gregory A '74 (Kernan and K,PC) -258 Genesee -Utica 13502 **Fx:**797-6467
(716) 854-2620 .. **Hamlin,** H Ward Jr. '72 (Brown & K,LLP) -1500 Lbrty Bldg -Buffalo 14202
(212) 345-5665 .. **Hamlin,** John W '98 Marsh & McLennen -1166 Av of Amer -NY 10036
(917) 279-6530 .. **Hamlin,** Keith M '99 Hammerline Capital,LLC -46 Wstchstr Av -Pound Rdg 10576 **Fx:**(212) 837-4896
(607) 321-0651 .. **Hamlin,** Linda L '85 Visions Fed Credit Union -24 McKinley Av -Endicott 13760 **Fx:**786-5718
(212) 557-8626 .. **Hamlin,** Richd C '78 OfCnsl Crowe D,LLP -535 5th Av -NY 10017 **Fx:**557-7270
(646) 386-3500 .. **Hamm,** Carol M '93 %OCA -25 Beaver -NY 10004 **Fx:**(212) 514-0158
(212) 471-8542 .. **Hamm,** David B '78 (Herzfeld & R,PC) -125 Broad -NY 10004
(607) 734-5004 .. **Hamm,** Denice A '03 (Hamm R&G) -523 W Church -Elmira 14905 **Fx:**733-0277
(518) 402-9223 .. **Hamm,** Kenneth '77 %DEC -625 Bway -Albany 12233 **Fx:**402-9018
(212) 455-2000 .. **Hamm,** Kimberly A '04 %Simpson T&B LLP -425 Lex Av -NY 10017
(212) 705-7000 .. **Hammack,** Catherine L '09 %Bingham M LLP -399 Park Av -NY 10022
(212) 922-6794 .. **Hammalian,** John B '92 Dreyfus -200 Park Av -NY 10166
(212) 310-8000 .. **Hammalov,** Airi '02 %Weil G&M LLP -767 5th Av -NY 10153
(212) 859-8000 .. **Hammans,** Elijah J '08 %Fried FHS&J LLP -1 NY Plz -NY 10004
(212) 906-1200 .. **Hammel,** Jeff G '97 (Latham & W) -885 3rd Av -NY 10022
(212) 676-6202 .. **Hammel,** Robt '82 %Business Integrity Comm -100 Church -NY 10007 **Fx:**676-6204
(516) 536-5222 .. **Hammel,** Stephen W '92 MacGregor Abstract -500 Rockaway Av -Vly Stream 11581
(973) 228-5700 .. **Hammer,** Alan R '84 (Brach E LLC) -100 Park Av -NY 10017 **Fx:**228-7852
(212) 244-6331 .. **Hammer,** Chas M '79 -37 E 18th -NY 10003 **Fx:**(201) 461-1948
(212) 335-9000 .. **Hammer,** David '96 %DA -1 Hogan Pl -NY 10013
(212) 941-8118 .. **Hammer,** David S '76 -99 Park Av -NY 10016 **Fx:**557-0565
(646) 471-4000 .. **Hammer,** Edw L '91 %PricewaterhouseCoopers LLP -300 Mad Av -NY 10017
(212) 425-5928 .. **Hammer,** Ernest H '59 -26 Bway -NY 10004 **Fx:**425-3664
(718) 548-2500 .. **Hammer,** Gerald J '72 (G Hammer,PC) -Bx1130 -Bronx 10471 **Fx:**548-2590
(212) 752-5258 .. **Hammer,** Ira J '81 Cnsl Schwartz SE&C LLC -845 3rd Av -NY 10022
(914) 923-7707 .. **Hammer,** Jon H '59 -17 Minkel Rd -Ossining 10562 **Fx:**923-7720
(718) 757-7677 .. **Hammer,** Melanie '03 -360 Court -Brklyn 11231
(631) 668-1000 .. **Hammer,** Richd A '97 (Biondo & H LLP) -The Plz Bx5030 -Montauk 11954 **Fx:**668-3971
(718) 598-0485 .. **Hammer,** Scott L '93 SL Hammer & Assoc,PC -160 Bway -NY 10038 **Fx:**(212) 566-4749
(212) 458-2088 .. **Hammer,** Stacey J '98 AIGTS -175 Water -NY 10038
(212) 909-6000 .. **Hammer,** Stuart '93 Cnsl Debevoise & P LLP -919 3rd Av -NY 10022
(914) 925-9695 .. **Hammer,** Todd B '95 %Greenbriar Equity Grp -555 Theo Fremd Av -Rye 10580
(212) 773-3000 .. **Hammer,** Wm P Jr. '82 %Ernst & Young,LLP -5 Times Sq -NY 10036
(212) 408-2500 .. **Hammerbeck,** Rebecca Zahniser '02 %Baker B,LLP -30 Rckfllr Plz -NY 10112
(212) 449-9638 .. **Hammerman,** Chas D '89 %Merrill Lynch -220 Bway -NY 10038 **Fx:**449-9649
(212) 373-3000 .. **Hammerman,** Claudia Lesley '93 (Paul WRW&G LLP) -1285 Av of Amer -NY 10019
(212) 848-9800 .. **Hammerman,** Dara B '04 %Withers B LLP -430 Park Av -NY 10022
(212) 906-1200 .. **Hammerman,** David '07 %Latham & W -885 3rd Av -NY 10022
(877) 381-6519 .. **Hammerman,** Evan C '03 Hammerman Legal Consltnts -228 Montrose Av -Brklyn 11206 **Fx:**(718) 768-4010
(516) 746-3500 .. **Hammerman,** Heather '99 %Brand G&B,PC -600 Old Cntry Rd -Gdn Cty 11530
(212) 980-9600 .. **Hammerman,** Jonathan R '99 %Kaufman B&R -120 Bway -NY 10271
(718) 793-5000 .. **Hammerman,** Michl A '72 (Tarshis & H,LLP) -118-35 Qns Blvd -Frst Hlls 11375
(718) 928-3700 .. **Hammersmith,** Amy S '05 LSNYC-Bronx -579 Courtlandt Av -Bronx 10451 **Fx:**402-7586
(212) 848-4000 .. **Hammes,** Patricia G '94 (Shearman & S LLP) -599 Lex Av -NY 10022
(516) 355-0400 .. **Hammid,** Remo A '98 -99 Tulip Av -Floral Pk 11001 **Fx:**355-0400
(516) 746-0707 .. **Hammill O'Brien Croutier Dempsey Pender & Koehler, PC** -6851 Jericho Tpk -Syosset 11791 **Fx:**677-5475
(718) 358-6400 .. **Hammock,** Edw R '66 (Hammock & S,LLC) -130-30 31st Av -Flushng 11354 **Fx:**358-6424
(718) 358-6400 .. **Hammock,** Jeanne M '80 -130-30 31st Av -Flushng 11354
(212) 521-5400 .. **Hammodi,** Ziad A '03 (Reed S LLP) -599 Lex Av -NY 10022
(212) 819-8200 .. **Hammond,** Andrew W '98 (White & C LLP) -1155 Av of Amer -NY 10036
(212) 770-1383 .. **Hammond,** Chad R '03 AIGTS -80 Pine -NY 10005
(607) 547-9397 .. **Hammond,** Chris '03 %Cnty Atty -Bx815 -Cooperstwn 13326
(212) 449-3073 .. **Hammond,** Craig P '94 Merrill Lynch -4 World Fncl Ctr -NY 10281
(315) 734-2000 .. **Hammond,** Danl J '07 Utica National Ins Grp -Bx530 -New Hartfrd 13413
(212) 761-4811 .. **Hammond,** David H '99 Morgan Stanley -1585 Bway -NY 10036
(212) 301-4050 .. **Hammond,** Douglas W '92 Cnsl Natl Fncl Prtnrs Corp -340 Mad Av -NY 10173 **Fx:**301-4150
(914) 253-2565 .. **Hammond,** Heather A '01 Pepsico -700 Andrsn Hill Rd -Purchase 10577
(212) 849-7000 .. **Hammond,** Jos D '07 %Quinn EU&S,LLP -51 Mad Av -NY 10010
(212) 644-1010 .. **Hammond,** Kristina C '07 %Kauff M&M LLP -950 3rd Av -NY 10022
(212) 314-0400 .. **Hammond,** Michl B '76 %Shattuck Hammond PWCS -630 5th Av -NY 10111
(716) 856-1344 .. **Hammond,** Paul F '88 (Bouvier Prtnrshp,LLP) -350 Main -Buffalo 14202 **Fx:**856-1369
(212) 294-6700 .. **Hammond,** Scott M '03 %Winston & S -200 Park Av -NY 10166
(212) 837-6000 .. **Hammond,** Steven A '80 (Hughes H&R LLP) -1 Bttry Pk Plz -NY 10004
(212) 868-1010 .. **Hammond,** Wm E '91 %Kudman TA LLP -350 5th Av -NY 10118
(646) 855-2922 .. **Hampton,** Gray W III '88 Bank of America -1 Bryant Pk -NY 10036
(516) 873-2000 .. **Hampton,** Nancy A '93 OfCnsl Moritt HH&H LLP -400 Grdn City Plz -Gdn Cty 11530
(212) 836-8000 .. **Hampton,** Neal R '10 Kaye S LLP -425 Park Av -NY 10022
(718) 654-4673 .. **Hampton,** Philip J '91 (Hampton & S,LLC) -4215 Katonah Av -Bronx 10470 **Fx:**654-4675
(516) 873-2000 .. **Hamroff,** Marc L '84 (Moritt HH&H LLP) -400 Grdn City Plz -Gdn Cty 11530
(212) 837-6000 .. **Hamza-Bassey,** Beatrice '99 (Hughes H&R LLP) -1 Bttry Pk Plz -NY 10004
(212) 806-5400 .. **Han,** Benjamin Y J '08 %Stroock &S&L LLP -180 Maiden Ln -NY 10038
(212) 848-4000 .. **Han,** Christopher S '06 %Shearman & S LLP -599 Lex Av -NY 10022
(212) 756-2000 .. **Han,** Eli W '08 %Schulte R&Z LLP -919 3rd Av -NY 10022
(212) 315-3755 .. **Han,** Hae W '07 %C Juntikka & Assoc,LLP -350 5th Av -NY 10118 **Fx:**315-9032
(212) 364-8470 .. **Han,** Jae-Min '03 Time Warner Cable -60 Columbus Av -NY 10023 **Fx:**364-8460
(718) 661-1300 .. **Han,** Janice G '02 FSA & Assoc -36-36 Main -Flushng 11354 **Fx:**661-1700
(212) 836-4704 .. **Han,** Jin Y '94 Han & Assoc,PC -100 Park Av -NY 10017 **Fx:**867-7092
(212) 841-1000 .. **Han,** John '08 %Covington & B LLP -620 8th Av -NY 10018
(212) 474-1000 .. **Han,** Juliana '09 %Cravath S&M LLP -825 8th Av -NY 10019
(212) 335-9000 .. **Han,** Kim '03 %DA -1 Hogan Pl -NY 10013
(631) 843-5500 .. **Han,** Marjorie '94 Henry Schein Inc -135 Duryea Rd -Melvll 11747
(212) 278-5810 .. **Han,** Matthew '04 Societe Generale -1221 Av of Amer -NY 10020
(212) 455-2000 .. **Han,** Paula S '08 %Simpson T&B LLP -425 Lex Av -NY 10017
(212) 284-3433 .. **Han,** Sonia K '96 Equity Derivatives -520 Mad Av -NY 10022
(212) 480-4800 .. **Han,** SooJung '07 %Fox H&C LLP -825 3rd Av -NY 10022
(212) 558-4000 .. **Han,** Suhana S '00 (Sullivan & C LLP) -125 Broad -NY 10004
(212) 351-4000 .. **Han,** Wm T '10 Gibson D&C LLP -200 Park Av -NY 10166
(212) 664-6371 .. **Han,** Yale '05 NBC Universal -30 Rckfllr Plz -NY 10112
(212) 867-9500 .. **Han,** Yoon S '04 %Kurzman K&F,LLP -230 Park Av -NY 10169
(914) 328-0404 .. **Hanagan,** Sean G '96 (Jackson L LLP) -1 N Bway -White Plns 10601
(718) 788-5052 .. **Hanan,** Adam M '08 Hagan C & Assoc -908 4th Av -Brklyn 11232
(973) 992-4800 .. **Hanan,** Michl S '97 (Fox R LLP) -100 Park Av -NY 10017 **Fx:**992-9125
(212) 578-2211 .. **Hanau,** Paul E '86 %MetLife -27-01 Qns Plz N -LIC 11101
(212) 705-7000 .. **Hanawalt,** Cynthia A '08 %Bingham M LLP -399 Park Av -NY 10022
(585) 263-1000 .. **Hancey,** Christian D '99 (Nixon P LLP) -1100 Clinton Sq -Rchstr 14604
(212) 506-2500 .. **Hanchet,** Mark G '89 (Mayer B LLP) -1675 Bway -NY 10019
(212) 408-5100 .. **Hanchuk,** Walter G '93 (Chadbourne & P LLP) -30 Rckfllr Plz -NY 10112

(518) 445-2311 .. **Hancock,** Barbara S '01 Albany Law Schl -80 New Scotland Av -Albany 12208 **Fx:**445-2315
(212) 813-8800 .. **Hancock,** Breck N '06 %Goodwin P LLP -620 8th Av -NY 10018
(631) 232-2400 .. **Hancock,** Diane C '01 %Nassau/Sfflk Law Srv -1757 Vets Hwy -Islandia 11749 **Fx:**232-2489
(315) 471-3151 .. **Hancock & Estabrook,LLP** -1500 AXA Twr I Bx4976 -Syracuse 13221 **Fx:**471-3167
(212) 574-1200 .. **Hancock,** James H '66 (Seward & K LLP) -1 Bttry Pk Plz -NY 10004
(607) 776-9809 .. **Hancock,** James T '60 -10 Gansevoort -Bath 14810
(212) 610-6300 .. **Hancock,** Joanna '10 %Allen & O -1221 Av of Amer -NY 10020
(315) 471-3151 .. **Hancock,** Stewart F Jr. '50 OfCnsl Hancock & E,LLP -1500 AXA Twr I Bx4976 -Syracuse 13221
(212) 670-0147 .. **Hanczor,** Jos A '83 Merrill Lynch -222 Bway -NY 10038
(212) 373-3000 .. **Hand,** Albert P '69 OfCnsl Paul WRW&G LLP -1285 Av of Amer -NY 10019
(718) 243-9323 .. **Hand,** Apryl E '99 (Lewis & H) -45 Main -Brklyn 11201 **Fx:**243-9326
(914) 468-7600 .. **Hand,** Brian M '87 (Nordlicht & H) -800 Wstchstr Av -Rye Brook 10573 **Fx:**468-7608
(212) 956-9500 .. **Hand,** Douglas A '99 (Hand B&A LLP) -8 W 40th -NY 10018 **Fx:**376-6080
(516) 294-5843 .. **Hand,** George F Jr. '85 -1050 Franklin Av -Gdn Cty 11530
(212) 667-4153 .. **Hand,** Pattie L '98 Oppenheimer Asset Mgmt -200 Park Av -NY 10166
(212) 223-2100 .. **Hand,** Rebecca A '09 %Menz B&K LLP -444 Mad Av -NY 10022
(631) 422-4900 .. **Hand,** Richd C '78 (Zumbrunn & H) -1801 Argyle Sq -Babylon 11702 **Fx:**422-4994
(212) 782-4630 .. **Hand,** Robt E '73 %Bk of Tokyo-Mitsubishi -1251 Av of Amer -NY 10020 **Fx:**782-6420
(212) 326-3939 .. **Hand,** S Jos '05 %Jones D -222 E 41st -NY 10017
(518) 457-2070 .. **Hand,** Sheila R '85 %Dept of Tax & Fin -Bldg 9 State Campus -Albany 12227 **Fx:**457-6131
(516) 746-8000 .. **Hand,** Stephen B '68 (Jaspan S LLP) -300 Grdn City Plz -Gdn Cty 11530
(914) 225-5377 .. **Hand,** Todd M '02 Morgan Stanley & Co Inc -2000 Wnchstr Av -Purchase 10577
(212) 344-5680 .. **Handal,** Anthony H '73 (Thompson H LLP) -335 Mad Av -NY 10017
(631) 342-5224 .. **Handal,** Kenneth V '74 %CA,Inc -1 CA Plz -Islandia 11749 **Fx:**342-4866
(212) 627-1000 .. **Handal,** Phillip C '91 -232 Mad Av -NY 10016
(212) 627-1000 .. **Handal,** Virginia M '83 -232 Mad Av -NY 10016
(914) 642-3977 .. **Handel,** Allison R '01 IBM -1133 Wstchstr Av -White Plns 10604 **Fx:**642-5788
(845) 452-3434 .. **Handel,** Evan B '01 (Handel & C,LLP) -112 Delafld -Poughkeepsie 12601 **Fx:**471-0105
(212) 218-5500 .. **Handel,** Joel M '61 (Seyfarth S LLP) -620 8th Av -NY 10018
(212) 547-5400 .. **Handel,** Lauren E '07 (McDermott W&E LLP) -340 Mad Av -NY 10173
(917) 351-1335 .. **Handel-Harbour,** Jacqueline '94 (Sperber D&K,PC) -48 W 37th -NY 10018
(212) 559-3677 .. **Handelman,** Edw I '77 Citigroup Intl -399 Park Av -NY 10022 **Fx:**793-4400
(585) 232-2225 .. **Handelman,** Eric D '97 (Handelman W&L) -410 Rynlds Arcd -Rchstr 14614
(212) 471-6239 .. **Handelman,** Frank '76 -780 3rd Av -NY 10017 **Fx:**935-5012
(212) 980-0120 .. **Handelman,** Marc '89 Frankfurt KK&S,PC -488 Mad Av -NY 10022
(585) 232-2225 .. **Handelman,** Martin S '58 (Handelman W&L) -410 Rynlds Arcd -Rchstr 14614
(212) 696-6000 .. **Handelman,** Thea Dora '08 %Curtis M-PC&M LLP -101 Park Av -NY 10178
(585) 232-2225 .. **Handelman Witkowicz & Levitsky** -410 Rynlds Arcd -Rchstr 14614 **Fx:**232-6327
(914) 238-8310 .. **Handelsman,** Dan G '89 -16 Attitash -Chappaqua 10514
(212) 225-2000 .. **Handelsman,** Lauren K '07 %Cleary GS&H -1 Lbrty Plz -NY 10006
(212) 806-5400 .. **Handelsman,** Lawr M '68 (Stroock &S&L LLP) -180 Maiden Ln -NY 10038
(410) 895-3647 .. **Handera,** Dmitri N '98 %Deutsche Bank -60 Wall -NY 10005
(212) 227-3636 .. **Handler,** Adam S '04 %Spar & B,PC -225 Bway -NY 10007
(212) 804-4200 .. **Handler,** Arthur M '60 SrCnsl Mound CW&G -One Bttry Pk Plz -NY 10004
(212) 735-3000 .. **Handler,** Benjamin J '05 %Skadden ASM&F LLP -4 Times Sq -NY 10036
(212) 759-3300 .. **Handler,** Bruce M '86 (Dornbush SS&V,LLP) -747 3rd Av -NY 10017
(212) 336-2000 .. **Handler,** Carolyn B '89 Cnsl Patterson BW&T LLP -1133 Av of Amer -NY 10036
(516) 741-7676 .. **Handler,** Craig H '03 %Miranda SSSV LLP -240 Mineola Blvd -Mineola 11501
(212) 819-8200 .. **Handler,** Eric J '07 %White & C LLP -1155 Av of Amer -NY 10036
(212) 448-1100 .. **Handler,** Geoffry R '74 (McLaughlin & S,LLP) -260 Mad Av -NY 10016
(212) 455-2000 .. **Handler,** Harold R '61 OfCnsl Simpson T&B LLP -425 Lex Av -NY 10017
(212) 636-6000 .. **Handler,** Janice '71 %Fordham Univ Sch of Law -140 W 62nd -NY 10023 **Fx:**636-6899
(212) 361-7993 .. **Handler,** Jennifer B '00 %Dept Homeless Srvcs -33 Beaver -NY 10004 **Fx:**361-8002
(212) 265-6888 .. **Handler,** Lauren E '84 (Porzio B&N,PC) -156 W 56th -NY 10019
(212) 227-6149 .. **Handler,** Morris '74 -277 Bway -NY 10007 **Fx:**285-9205
(212) 331-5875 .. **Handler,** Peter F '07 HRA -180 Water -NY 10038
(212) 559-8197 .. **Handler,** R Arnold '64 Citigroup -909 3rd Av -NY 10022
(631) 598-1400 .. **Handler,** Richd G '78 -50 Bway Bx427 -Amityvll 11701 **Fx:**598-0952
(212) 758-9129 .. **Handler,** Sharon J '80 -530 Park Av -NY 10065 **Fx:**230-1445
(212) 506-5000 .. **Handley,** Siobhan A '95 (Orrick H&S LLP) -51 W 52nd -NY 10019
(516) 377-7152 .. **Handley,** Wil S '04 -97 Archer -Freeprt 11520
(212) 402-6830 .. **Handlin,** Jos J '77 -75 Maiden Ln -NY 10038 **Fx:**(917) 591-9353
(212) 489-8230 .. **Handman,** Laura R '83 (Davis WT LLP) -1633 Bway -NY 10019
(212) 735-3000 .. **Hands,** Kevin P '06 %Skadden ASM&F LLP -4 Times Sq -NY 10036
(716) 885-8005 .. **Handschu,** Barbara E '67 -155 Summer -Buffalo 14222 **Fx:**882-2880
(212) 750-3636 .. **Handsman,** David S '85 (Handsman & K LLP) -900 3rd Av -NY 10022 **Fx:**750-4699
(518) 439-5027 .. **Handwerger,** Jay R '58 -486 Huron Rd -Delmar 12054
(212) 436-1068 .. **Handwerker,** David J '85 %IRS -290 Bway -NY 10007
(212) 871-5711 .. **Handwerker,** Gavin I '99 (Nissenbaum Law Grp,LLC) -140 Bway -NY 10005 **Fx:**871-5712
(212) 949-8700 .. **Handwerker,** Jay '73 %Eisner LLP -750 3rd Av -NY 10017 **Fx:**891-4100
(212) 476-9000 .. **Handwerker,** Kevin '82 %Neuberger Berman,LLC -605 3rd Av -NY 10158 **Fx:**476-9862
(212) 679-1330 .. **Handwerker,** Michl H '86 (Goldstein & H,LLP) -280 Mad Av -NY 10016 **Fx:**779-2469
(212) 599-2200 .. **Handwerker,** Neil E '85 LucasGroup -52 Vndrblt Av -NY 10017 **Fx:**599-2014
(212) 542-8882 .. **Handwerker,** Stacie '93 Cnsl Roth Law Firm,PLLC -295 Mad Av -NY 10017 **Fx:**542-8883
(212) 819-8200 .. **Handy,** John E '07 %White & C LLP -1155 Av of Amer -NY 10036
(518) 439-8311 .. **Handzel,** Michele V '05 %NYSARC -393 Delaware Av -Delmar 12054
(212) 626-4100 .. **Hanessian,** Grant '86 (Baker & M LLP) -1114 Av of Amer -NY 10036
(212) 859-8000 .. **Hanetz,** Adi '04 %Fried FHS&J LLP -1 NY Plz -NY 10004
(212) 643-9668 .. **Haney,** James K '92 (Wong F,PC) -350 5th Av -NY 10118
(212) 272-0433 .. **Haney,** Jeanne M '01 %JP Morgan Chase -383 Mad Av -NY 10179
(516) 624-6150 .. **Haney,** Lorraine F '02 %Town Atty -Town Hall -Oyster Bay 11771 **Fx:**624-6196
(212) 841-1000 .. **Haney,** Robt P Jr. '84 (Covington & B LLP) -620 8th Av -NY 10018
(212) 848-4000 .. **Haney,** Timothy J '08 %Shearman & S LLP -599 Lex Av -NY 10022
(212) 224-4000 .. **Haney,** Wm D III '72 %Sumitomo Mitsui -277 Park Av -NY 10172 **Fx:**593-9522
(212) 541-6222 .. **Hanft,** James E '94 OfCnsl Kane K,PC -1350 Av of Amer -NY 10019
(631) 231-9800 .. **Hanft,** Julia A '01 Globecomm Systems Inc -45 Oser Av -Hauppauge 11788 **Fx:**231-1557
(914) 249-2000 .. **Hanft,** Noah J '77 %MasterCard Intl -2000 Purchase -Purchase 10577
(212) 406-1919 .. **Hanft,** Wm G '81 %Gennet KA&R,PC -140 Bway -NY 10005
(212) 351-4500 .. **Hang,** Jian '05 %Epstein B&G,PC -250 Park Av -NY 10177
(212) 436-2920 .. **Hanhan,** Alexander N '03 Deloitte & Touche LLP -2 World Fncl Ctr -NY 10281
(212) 940-8800 .. **Hanif,** Jasmine M '00 (Katten MR LLP) -575 Mad Av -NY 10022
(718) 217-6808 .. **Haniff,** Simiyon S '01 (Haniff & O) -216-14 Jamaica Av -Qns Vllg 11428 **Fx:**217-6814
(212) 704-6508 .. **Hanifin,** Jerome L '99 Sojitz Corp of Amer -1211 Av of Amer -NY 10036 **Fx:**704-6947
(716) 566-1300 .. **Hanifin,** Thos J '52 OfCnsl Hiscock & B,LLP -1100 M&T Ctr -Buffalo 14203
(845) 473-1137 .. **Hanig,** C Lynn '71 %Indotronix Intl Corp -331 Main -Poughkeepsie 12601 **Fx:**473-1180
(845) 471-7177 .. **Hanig,** Joel D '71 (Hanig & S,LLP) -22 IBM Rd -Poughkeepsie 12601 **Fx:**790-1212
(212) 506-1700 .. **Hanin,** Michl A '02 (Kasowitz BT&F LLP) -1633 Bway -NY 10019
(212) 813-8800 .. **Hanish,** John P '99 (Goodwin P LLP) -620 8th Av -NY 10018
(212) 935-3000 .. **Hankin,** Alexandra '09 %Mintz LCFG&P,PC -666 3rd Av -NY 10017
(212) 808-7800 .. **Hankin,** Joel A '01 %Kelley D&W LLP -101 Park Av -NY 10178
(212) 488-1513 .. **Hankin,** Lowen K '93 (LK Hankin PC) -444 Mad Av -NY 10022 **Fx:**644-0675
(212) 891-1600 .. **Hankin,** Marc B '94 (Jenner & B LLP) -919 3rd Av -NY 10022
(212) 349-1668 .. **Hankin,** Mark L '84 (Hankin & M,PLLC) -7 Penn Plz -NY 10001
(212) 349-1668 .. **Hankin & Mazel, PLLC** -7 Penn Plz -NY 10001 **Fx:**227-7317
(212) 806-5400 .. **Hankins,** Angie M '99 (Stroock &S&L LLP) -180 Maiden Ln -NY 10038
(212) 909-6000 .. **Hankiss,** Adam '03 %Debevoise & P LLP -919 3rd Av -NY 10022
(212) 962-2600 .. **Hankovszky,** Zoltan '70 -30 Vesey -NY 10007 **Fx:**962-9696
(212) 574-1200 .. **Hanks,** Julia A '10 %Seward & K LLP -1 Bttry Pk Plz -NY 10004
(212) 659-7300 .. **Hanks,** Kendyl T '07 %Haynes & B,LLP -1221 Av of Amer -NY 10020
(585) 546-5960 .. **Hanks,** Robt P '70 (Laverne & H) -36 Main W -Rchstr 14614
(518) 473-7051 .. **Hanks,** Russell J '75 %OTDA-Fair Hearings -40 N Pearl -Albany 12243 **Fx:**473-6735
(212) 878-8000 .. **Hanks,** Sara P '93 %Clifford C LLP -31 W 52nd -NY 10019
(315) 422-1152 .. **Hanley,** Anthony R '89 (Costello C&F,PLLC) -500 Plum -Syracuse 13204
(518) 251-3222 .. **Hanley,** Brendan J '79 -Circle Av Bx54 -N Creek 12853
(212) 804-4200 .. **Hanley,** Catherine S '10 %Mound CW&G -One Bttry Pk Plz -NY 10004
(914) 232-7916 .. **Hanley,** Dianne Braun '97 -121 Katonah Av Bx575 -Katonah 10536 **Fx:**232-7943
(585) 393-5640 .. **Hanley,** Edw T Jr. '55 -70 S Main -Canandaigua 14424 **Fx:**394-3169
(212) 233-3330 .. **Hanley & Goble LLP** -233 Bway -NY 10279 **Fx:**732-1339
(718) 590-2000 .. **Hanley,** James J '09 DA -198 E 161st -Bronx 10451 **Fx:**590-6477
(516) 318-9310 .. **Hanley,** John J '98 -18 Stuart Dr E -Glen Cove 11542 **Fx:**759-5355
(212) 732-3200 .. **Hanley,** John J '02 (Carter L&M LLP) -2 Wall -NY 10005
(845) 225-9254 .. **Hanley,** Kim A '87 OfCnsl J Fonseca -37 Fair -Carmel 10512 **Fx:**225-7423
(716) 845-8717 .. **Hanley,** Marianne E '79 RPCI -Elm & Carlton -Buffalo 14263
(585) 454-4060 .. **Hanley,** Michl L '77 %Empire Justice Ctr -1 W Main -Rchstr 14614 **Fx:**454-4019
(212) 785-2929 .. **Hanley,** Susan K '06 %Conway FC&K,PC -48 Wall -NY 10005
(718) 694-3904 .. **Hanley,** Thos P Jr. '93 %Transit Auth -130 Lvngstn -Brklyn 11201 **Fx:**694-5726
(716) 856-0600 .. **Hanley,** Vincent O '83 (Jaeckle F&M,LLP) -12 Fountain Plz -Buffalo 14202
(212) 233-3330 .. **Hanley,** Vincent P Jr. '74 (Hanley & G LLP) -233 Bway -NY 10279
(212) 425-7200 .. **Hanley,** Walter E Jr. '77 (Kenyon & K,LLP) -1 Bway -NY 10004
(518) 862-3080 .. **Hanlon,** Christine D'Addio '89 (Hanlon V&W) -94 New Karner Rd -Albany 12203
(716) 753-4241 .. **Hanlon,** Grace M '90 %DA -Cnty Cthse -Mayvll 14757 **Fx:**753-4628
(631) 470-9555 .. **Hanlon,** Jessica J '95 J Hanlon,PC -20 Broadhllw Rd Bx1354 -Melvll 11747 **Fx:**470-9557
(516) 822-8900 .. **Hanlon,** Mark J '78 Fiedelman & M -2 Jericho Plz -Jericho 11753

(212) 918-3000 .. **Hanlon,** Maureen Anne '91 (Hogan L LLP) -875 3rd Av -NY 10022
(212) 571-7100 .. **Hanlon,** Nicholas S '05 %O'Dwyer & B,LLP -52 Duane -NY 10007
(518) 474-0571 .. **Hanlon,** Paula Bergmann '98 %Ofc Gnl Srvcs -Corning Twr ESP -Albany 12242 **Fx:**473-4973
(212) 728-8000 .. **Hanlon,** Peter J '80 (Willkie F&G LLP) -787 7th Av -NY 10019
(315) 422-2469 .. **Hanlon,** Richd J P '89 -400 Winkworth Pkwy -Syracuse 13215
(212) 210-9410 .. **Hanlon,** Robt E '91 (Alston & B LLP) -90 Park Av -NY 10016
(212) 483-9490 .. **Hanlon,** Thos W Jr. '83 OfCnsl McElroy DM&C,LLP -88 Pine -NY 10005
(518) 862-3080 .. **Hanlon Veloce & Wilkinson** -94 New Karner Rd -Albany 12203 **Fx:**862-3081
(212) 784-6400 .. **Hanly Conroy Bierstein Sheridan Fisher & Hayes LLP** -112 Mad Av -NY 10016 **Fx:**784-6420
(212) 784-6400 .. **Hanly,** Paul J Jr. '80 (Hanly CBSF&H LLP) -112 Mad Av -NY 10016
(347) 592-2200 .. **Hanmer,** Dorothy A '90 %Leg Srvcs -42-15 Crescent -LIC 11101 **Fx:**(718) 937-5350
(718) 680-8400 .. **Hanna,** Derrick '86 (Hanna & V) -7504 5th Av -Brklyn 11209
(212) 728-8000 .. **Hanna,** Erin M '10 %Willkie F&G LLP -787 7th Av -NY 10019
(212) 455-2000 .. **Hanna,** Fadi G '07 %Simpson T&B LLP -425 Lex Av -NY 10017
(718) 833-8343 .. **Hanna,** Gary Edw '93 -8212 3rd Av -Brklyn 11209
(518) 487-7600 .. **Hanna,** John Jr. '60 (Whiteman O&H LLP) -1 Commerce Plz -Albany 12260
(716) 566-5400 .. **Hanna,** Jos M '06 (Goldberg S LLP) -665 Main -Buffalo 14203
(212) 859-8000 .. **Hanna,** Katherine M '08 %Fried FHS&J LLP -1 NY Plz -NY 10004
(212) 806-5400 .. **Hanna,** Monica '10 %Stroock &S&L LLP -180 Maiden Ln -NY 10038
(212) 891-1600 .. **Hanna,** Peter H '06 %Jenner & B LLP -919 3rd Av -NY 10022
(585) 753-1380 .. **Hanna,** Sean T '88 Cnty Atty -307 Cnty Ofc Bldg -Rchstr 14614 **Fx:**753-1331
(212) 248-3140 .. **Hanna,** Stacey J '02 %Drinker B&R LLP -140 Bway -NY 10005
(718) 680-8400 .. **Hanna & Vlahakis** -7504 5th Av -Brklyn 11209 **Fx:**833-3600
(718) 987-1590 .. **Hannafey,** Dennis P '55 -111 Thomas -Staten Isl 10306
(212) 739-1818 .. **Hannafey,** Mark P '94 Clinton Grp Inc -9 W 57th -NY 10019
(718) 237-5500 .. **Hannaford,** Rachel N '05 %Leg Srvcs -105 Court -Brklyn 11201 **Fx:**855-0733
(212) 867-2856 .. **Hannagan,** Michl E '00 Miller Tabak Roberts Securities,LLC -331 Mad Av -NY 10017
(518) 785-1190 .. **Hannah,** Michl J '78 -11 Sunset Dr -Latham 12110
(212) 344-7400 .. **Hannan,** Christopher P '97 (Kelley JMS&H LLP) -120 Wall -NY 10005 **Fx:**344-7402
(212) 968-8300 .. **Hannan,** Kathleen T '99 %Mintzer SZL&M LLP -39 Bway -NY 10006
(212) 609-6800 .. **Hannan,** Lisa M '03 %McCarter & E,LLP -245 Park Av -NY 10167
(914) 948-2540 .. **Hannaway,** John J '78 -901 N Bway -White Plns 10603
(212) 425-7200 .. **Hannemann,** Mark A '96 (Kenyon & K,LLP) -1 Bway -NY 10004
(212) 450-4000 .. **Hannibal,** Gregory T '06 %Davis P&W LLP -450 Lex Av -NY 10017
(518) 436-2840 .. **Hannibal,** Jon Marc '78 %Thruway Auth -200 Southrn Blvd Bx189 -Albany 12201 **Fx:**471-4340
(845) 651-3190 .. **Hannigan,** David '83 -62 N Main Bx637 -Florida 10921 **Fx:**651-1831
(212) 728-8000 .. **Hannigan,** James P '09 %Willkie F&G LLP -787 7th Av -NY 10019
(914) 949-2700 .. **Hannigan,** John P '78 (Bleakley P&S,LLP) -1 N Lex Av -White Plns 10601
(212) 556-2100 .. **Hannigan,** Michl J '75 (King & S) -1185 Av of Amer -NY 10036
(212) 592-1400 .. **Hannigan,** Raymond N '88 (Herrick,F LLP) -2 Park Av -NY 10016
(518) 465-3484 .. **Hannigan,** Terence S '86 (Carter CCBM&L,PC) -20 Corp Wds Blvd -Albany 12211
(518) 487-5460 .. **Hannigan,** Trevor W '04 %DA -6 Lodge -Albany 12207 **Fx:**487-5093
(631) 582-3700 .. **Hannigan,** Vincent R '99 (Turley RR&R,LLP) -3075 Vets Mem'l Hwy -Ronkonkoma 11779
(212) 626-4100 .. **Hannon,** Gerard V '78 (Baker & M LLP) -1114 Av of Amer -NY 10036
(516) 227-0700 .. **Hannon,** J Kemp '71 SpclCnsl Farrell F,PC -1320 RXR Plz -Uniondale 11556
(212) 589-4200 .. **Hannon,** J Patrick '83 (Baker & H LLP) -45 Rckfllr Plz -NY 10111
(631) 852-2782 .. **Hannon,** Joan Larkin '89 %Hon EH Emerson -210 Center Dr -Rvrhead 11901
(212) 566-7188 .. **Hannon,** Jos M '00 %Genova B&G -115 Bway -NY 10006
(914) 472-2380 .. **Hannon,** Kathleen Murtagh '80 -6 Standish Dr -Scarsdale 10583 **Fx:**472-7861
(212) 479-6000 .. **Hannon,** Maureen E '90 SpclCnsl Cooley LLP -1114 Av of Amer -NY 10036
(845) 639-7800 .. **Hannon,** Tara '92 (Mandel K&B,LLP) -210 Route 303 -Vly Cottage 10989
(516) 564-4973 .. **Hannon,** Timothy J '02 NYS Ofc of Admin & Hearings -50 Clinton -Hempstd 11550
(518) 869-9025 .. **Hannoush,** David E '04 Hannoush Jwlrs -120 Wshngtn Av Ext -Albany 12203
(212) 530-3900 .. **Hannum Feretic Prendergast & Merlino, LLC** -55 Bway -NY 10006 **Fx:**530-3910
(212) 530-3900 .. **Hannum,** John E '86 (Hannum FP&M, LLC) -55 Bway -NY 10006
(718) 641-8441 .. **Hanoman,** Robt H '89 -120-07 Lbrty Av -S Richmond Hll 11419 **Fx:**641-8820
(718) 286-6000 .. **Hanophy,** Christina '91 %DA -125-01 Qns Blvd -Kew Gdns 11415
(718) 286-6000 .. **Hanophy,** Robt J Jr. '91 %DA -125-01 Qns Blvd -Kew Gdns 11415
(212) 822-8888 .. **Hanover,** Lawr J '92 -20 W 20th -NY 10011 **Fx:**822-8865
(212) 472-5776 .. **Hanover,** Richd '89 -320 W 86th -NY 10024
(315) 471-8111 .. **Hanover,** Sarah E '09 %Scolaro SCF&B,PC -507 Plum -Syracuse 13204
(212) 728-8000 .. **Hanrahan,** Andrew T '10 %Willkie F&G LLP -787 7th Av -NY 10019
(607) 273-3339 .. **Hanrahan,** John H III '80 (Williamson C&S) -317 N Tioga Bx126 -Ithaca 14850
(212) 530-5000 .. **Hanrahan,** Lauren A '02 (Milbank TH&M LLP) -1 Chase Manh Plz -NY 10005
(212) 530-5000 .. **Hanrahan,** Marc P '89 (Milbank TH&M LLP) -1 Chase Manh Plz -NY 10005
(914) 738-3400 .. **Hanrahan,** Michl G '75 (Hanrahan & H) -438 5th Av -Pelham 10803 **Fx:**738-4986
(315) 471-3151 .. **Hanrahan,** Paul M '55 OfCnsl Hancock & E,LLP -1500 AXA Twr I Bx4976 -Syracuse 13221
(212) 693-1404 .. **Hanrahan,** Thos J '70 -15 Maiden Ln -NY 10038 **Fx:**(800) 361-9393
(718) 590-2000 .. **Hanratty,** Don '90 %DA -198 E 161st -Bronx 10451 **Fx:**590-6477
(212) 867-1728 .. **Hanratty,** Kevin J '96 NYS Ofc Homeland Security -633 3rd Av -NY 10017
(516) 505-0600 .. **Hanratty,** Michl D '00 %J McCormack,PC -1035 Stewart Av -Gdn Cty 11530 **Fx:**505-0632
(516) 739-6634 .. **Hans,** Alfred J '84 -320 Old Cntry Rd -Gdn Cty 11530 **Fx:**739-6635
(212) 903-8700 .. **Hans,** Howard W '82 %Roberts & H,LLP -825 8th Av -NY 10019
(718) 478-9272 .. **Hans,** Mantaj K '04 %Pitchayan & Assoc PC -72-30 Bway -Jcksn Hts 11372 **Fx:**478-9279
(212) 335-4500 .. **Hans,** Richd F '94 (DLA Piper LLP) -1251 Av of Amer -NY 10020
(718) 275-6700 .. **Hans,** Stephen D '77 (S Hans & Assoc PC) -45-18 Court Sq -LIC 11101 **Fx:**275-6704
(212) 924-6871 .. **Hansbury,** John W '77 -82 Charles -NY 10014 **Fx:**242-5260
(212) 292-6378 .. **Hanschke,** Peter '09 Ziff Brothers Investments -350 Park Av -NY 10022
(212) 338-0700 .. **Hanscom-Bolton,** Christopher J '97 %Hoffman P&F PLLC -220 E 42nd -NY 10017
(518) 436-0786 .. **Hanse,** Stephen B '08 %Featherstonhaugh W&C,LLP -99 Pine -Albany 12207
(212) 915-7825 .. **Hansel,** Elizabeth A '03 Willis -200 Lbrty -NY 10281
(212) 331-6225 .. **Hansell,** David A '84 %Human Resources Admin -180 Water -NY 10038
(917) 237-2907 .. **Hansell,** Jodi L '03 Axiom Legal Solutions -75 Spring -NY 10012
(518) 464-2000 .. **Hanselman,** Sonja L '97 AYCO -1 Wall Bx15073 -Albany 12212
(212) 909-6000 .. **Hansen,** Aric '09 %Debevoise & P LLP -919 3rd Av -NY 10022
(516) 747-4082 .. **Hansen,** Camille L '88 %Montfort HM&S LLP -1140 Franklin Av Bx7677 -Gdn Cty 11530
(212) 454-1312 .. **Hansen,** Christopher F '92 Deutsche Asset Mgmt -280 Park Av -NY 10017
(631) 361-3400 .. **Hansen,** Christopher M '02 (O'Rourke & H,PLLC) -235 Brooksite Dr -Hauppauge 11788 **Fx:**361-7324
(212) 697-3701 .. **Hansen,** Danl J '93 -711 3rd Av -NY 10017
(516) 223-2621 .. **Hansen,** Edw C '84 %Dougherty & S -625 W Merrick Rd -Baldwin 11510
(212) 626-4100 .. **Hansen,** Edw J '91 (Baker & M LLP) -1114 Av of Amer -NY 10036
(212) 756-2000 .. **Hansen,** Emma S '09 %Schulte R&Z LLP -919 3rd Av -NY 10022
(212) 278-1173 .. **Hansen,** Gregory S '03 %Anderson K&O,PC -1251 Av of Amer -NY 10020
(716) 434-6301 .. **Hansen,** Henrik H '61 H Hansen,PLLC -410 Bewley Bldg -Lockprt 14094 **Fx:**434-6302
(212) 636-6854 .. **Hansen,** Hugh C '73 %Fordham Univ Sch of Law -140 W 62nd -NY 10023 **Fx:**636-6899
(516) 873-1902 .. **Hansen,** Janice M '08 %Morici & M -1399 Franklin Av -Gdn Cty 11530 **Fx:**873-3948
(518) 465-3484 .. **Hansen,** Jonathan E '08 %Carter CCBM&L,PC -20 Corp Wds Blvd -Albany 12211
(212) 720-5024 .. **Hansen,** Joyce E '80 %Fed Reserve Bk -33 Lbrty -NY 10045 **Fx:**785-5748
(212) 806-5400 .. **Hansen,** Kristopher M '96 (Stroock &S&L LLP) -180 Maiden Ln -NY 10038
(212) 953-5500 .. **Hansen,** Lawr I '07 %Alter M LLP -90 Park Av -NY 10016
(212) 309-1000 .. **Hansen,** Leslie S '95 Cnsl Hunton & W -200 Park Av -NY 10166
(212) 909-6000 .. **Hansen,** Lisa J '09 %Debevoise & P LLP -919 3rd Av -NY 10022
(212) 473-6740 .. **Hansen,** Lorentz W '61 -624 E 20th -NY 10009 **Fx:**473-6740
(212) 554-1400 .. **Hansen,** Rochelle Feder '80 SrCnsl Bernstein LB&G LLP -1285 Av of Amer -NY 10019
(212) 696-6000 .. **Hansen,** Ryan Christopher '04 %Curtis M-PC&M LLP -101 Park Av -NY 10178
(914) 633-1947 .. **Hansen,** Stephen S '93 -365 North Av Bx566 -New Rchll 10802 **Fx:**632-5937
(516) 571-4929 .. **Hansen,** Steven T '96 Nassau Cty Consumers Affrs -200 Cnty Seat Dr -Mineola 11501
(212) 850-6220 .. **Hansen,** Wm Robt '78 (Lathrop & G LC) -230 Park Av -NY 10169
(718) 250-2000 .. **Hanshaft,** Josh E '95 %DA -350 Jay -Brklyn 11201 **Fx:**250-2314
(631) 563-2426 .. **Hanshe,** Gerard E '07 (Hanshe & H,PLLC) -116 Greene Av -Sayvll 11782
(631) 563-2426 .. **Hanshe,** Jos A '86 (Hanshe & H,PLLC) -116 Greene Av -Sayvll 11782
(212) 841-1000 .. **Hanson,** Alan J '98 Merrill Lynch -4 World Fncl Ctr -NY 10080
(212) 756-2000 .. **Hanson,** Ashley '09 %Schulte R&Z LLP -919 3rd Av -NY 10022
(914) 347-3440 .. **Hanson,** Christine E '98 Calvary Invsmnts -7 Skyline Dr -Hawthorne 10532
(212) 335-3014 .. **Hanson,** Duane E '09 DA -80 Centre -NY 10013
(212) 628-5207 .. **Hanson,** Elizabeth M '04 Doe Fund,Inc -232 E 84th -NY 10028 **Fx:**249-5589
(518) 436-0751 .. **Hanson,** Harold C '67 (Hinman S PC) -121 State -Albany 12207
(212) 336-0087 .. **Hanson,** James K '94 %SEC -3 World Fncl Ctr -NY 10281 **Fx:**336-1323
(212) 530-5000 .. **Hanson,** Jane L '84 OfCnsl Milbank TH&M LLP -1 Chase Manh Plz -NY 10005
(212) 859-8000 .. **Hanson,** Jean E '77 (Fried FHS&J LLP) -1 NY Plz -NY 10004
(212) 688-3025 .. **Hanson,** John W '06 %Hitchcock & C,LLP -757 3rd Av -NY 10017 **Fx:**688-3040
(212) 839-5300 .. **Hanson,** Kersti K '02 %Sidley A LLP -787 7th Av -NY 10019
(518) 355-4525 .. **Hanson,** Kristie H '90 -1801 Altamont Av -Schnctdy 12303 **Fx:**355-4506
(212) 819-8200 .. **Hanson,** Margaret L '09 %White & C LLP -1155 Av of Amer -NY 10036
(212) 318-3000 .. **Hanson,** Norman '83 (Fulbright & J LLP) -666 5th Av -NY 10103
(518) 598-1700 .. **Hanson,** Paul G '95 Hanson & F -725 Bway -Albany 12207 **Fx:**449-7823
(212) 956-9500 .. **Hanson,** Stephen P '97 (Hand B&A LLP) -8 W 40th -NY 10018 **Fx:**376-6080
(212) 848-4000 .. **Hanson,** Timothy W '09 %Shearman & S LLP -599 Lex Av -NY 10022
(212) 468-8000 .. **Hanson,** Vivian L '87 (Morrison & F LLP) -1290 Av of Amer -NY 10104
(212) 318-6000 .. **Hansson,** Kurt W '07 (Paul HJ&W LLP) -75 E 55th -NY 10022
(212) 819-8200 .. **Hanstead,** Alison R '04 %White & C LLP -1155 Av of Amer -NY 10036
(212) 918-3000 .. **Hanswirth,** Dori Ann '87 (Hogan L LLP) -875 3rd Av -NY 10022
(212) 888-8282 .. **Hantgan,** Craig E '94 Esquire Properties,Inc -59 E 54th -NY 10022 **Fx:**888-8204

(212) 425-9300 .. **Hantman**, David I '08 %Bressler A&R,PC -17 State -NY 10004
(212) 684-3933 .. **Hantman**, Robt J '75 (Hantman & Assoc) -1515 Bway -NY 10036 **Fx:**520-4301
(212) 272-6510 .. **Hantz**, Steven A '98 JP Morgan Chase -383 Mad Av -NY 10179
(212) 226-2100 .. **Hanukov**, Milena '09 Caesar & N -350 Bway -NY 10013
(845) 371-4700 .. **Hanusek**, Michl S '04 %Fein SK&S,PC -747 Chestnut Rdg Rd -Spg Vly 10977
(716) 204-2400 .. **Hanzlik-Hexemer**, Dawn A '02 %SJ Baum,PC -220 Nrthpnte Pkwy Bx1291 -Buffalo 14240 **Fx:**204-4600
(212) 237-0000 .. **Hao**, Alex Yong '04 %Vinson & E LLP -666 5th Av -NY 10103
(212) 210-9400 .. **Hao**, Wm '07 %Alston & B LLP -90 Park Av -NY 10016
(716) 855-1050 .. **Hapeman**, Scott R '02 %Personius M LLP -2100 Main Place Twr -Buffalo 14202
(212) 685-7474 .. **Happe**, Judith '98 %Mayerson SA LLP -292 Mad Av -NY 10017
(212) 607-2800 .. **Haq**, Nur-ul '01 %FTC -1 Bowling Grn -NY 10004 **Fx:**607-2822
(212) 278-0341 .. **Haque**, Henna '01 Revman Intl Inc -1211 Av of Amer -NY 10036 **Fx:**840-8446
(212) 558-4000 .. **Haque**, Sameera '10 %Sullivan & C LLP -125 Broad -NY 10004
(212) 608-1917 .. **Haquia**, Luis '90 %Davis S&S,PC -44 Wall -NY 10005
(212) 692-1000 .. **Har**, T Steven '90 (Duane M LLP) -1540 Bway -NY 10036
(212) 541-2000 .. **Haracz**, Stephen M '86 (Bryan C LLP) -1290 Av of Amer -NY 10104
(212) 373-3000 .. **Haraguchi**, Courtney A '10 %Paul WRW&G LLP -1285 Av of Amer -NY 10019
(212) 468-8000 .. **Haraguchi**, Yuichi '06 %Morrison & F LLP -1290 Av of Amer -NY 10104
(212) 710-3900 .. **Harakas**, Andrew J '88 (Clyde & Co US LLP) -405 Lex Av -NY 10174 **Fx:**710-3950
(914) 948-4500 .. **Haralambides**, Heather M '07 %O'Connor MCD&O -1 Barker Av -White Plns 10601
(516) 572-2000 .. **Haran**, Brian J '08 %DA -99 Main -Hempstd 11550 **Fx:**572-2606
(212) 318-6000 .. **Haran**, Sean T '95 OfCnsl Paul HJ&W LLP -75 E 55th -NY 10022
(212) 490-1700 .. **Haranzo**, Mark E '87 (Wiggin & D) -450 Lex Av -NY 10017
(718) 377-4568 .. **Harari**, David '80 -1040 E 10th -Brklyn 11230 **Fx:**377-4491
(212) 832-7400 .. **Harari**, Jack A '94 (Weidenbaum & H,LLP) -708 3rd Av -NY 10017
(718) 923-8400 .. **Harari**, Rachel M '84 Forest City Ratner -1 Metrotech Ctr N -Brklyn 11201 **Fx:**923-8722
(212) 735-8600 .. **Harari Mason**, Randi '04 %Morrison C LLP -909 3rd Av -NY 10022
(516) 506-6000 .. **Harary**, Chas J '03 Reckson Assoc Realty -625 RXR Plz -Uniondale 11556
(212) 213-5353 .. **Harary**, Jared Marc '08 -16 E 34th -NY 10016
(516) 364-1902 .. **Harary**, Jos M '87 Rsrch Frontiers -240 Crsswys Park Dr -Woodbury 11797
(212) 761-4000 .. **Harary**, Leah R '03 Morgan Stanley -1633 Bway -NY 10019
(212) 213-5353 .. **Harary**, Morris '71 -16 E 34th -NY 10016 **Fx:**689-2348
(212) 474-1000 .. **Harasymiak**, Andrei R '95 Cravath S&M LLP -825 8th Av -NY 10019
(212) 894-8062 .. **Harawitz**, Jodi M '99 %Cmmnty Food Resrc Ctr -39 Bway -NY 10006
(212) 704-1339 .. **Haray**, Richd J '88 %Interpublic Grp -1114 Av of Amer -NY 10036 **Fx:**704-1201
(718) 726-6860 .. **Harb**, Rifat A '97 -25-69 Steinway -Astoria 11103 **Fx:**726-6891
(212) 416-6185 .. **Harben**, Jebediah '97 Atty Gen -120 Bway -NY 10271
(212) 699-3965 .. **Harber**, Steven R '93 Discover Ready LLC -55 Bway -NY 10006
(516) 542-1000 .. **Harbert**, Colleen Nugent '95 Cnsl Geisler & G,LLP -100 Q Roosevelt Blvd -Gdn Cty 11530
(516) 663-6600 .. **Harbeson**, Jos R '79 (Ruskin MF,PC) -1425 RXR Plz -Uniondale 11556
(212) 468-8000 .. **Harbin**, Kimberly N '08 %Morrison & F LLP -1290 Av of Amer -NY 10104
(212) 309-6090 .. **Harbison**, James W Jr. '60 Cnsl Morgan L&B LLP -101 Park Av -NY 10178
(212) 848-4000 .. **Harbour**, Grace A '08 %Shearman & S LLP -599 Lex Av -NY 10022
(212) 318-3000 .. **Harbour**, Pamela Jones '85 (Fulbright & J LLP) -666 5th Av -NY 10103
(212) 278-1543 .. **Harckham**, Finley T R '84 (Anderson K&O,PC) -1251 Av of Amer -NY 10020
(212) 504-6000 .. **Harcourt**, Caroline A '87 SpclCnsl Cadwalader W&T LLP -1 World Fncl Ctr -NY 10281
(718) 590-2000 .. **Hard**, Jennifer L '06 DA -198 E 161st -Bronx 10451 **Fx:**590-6477
(212) 403-1000 .. **Hardee**, Catherine A '05 %Wachtell LR&K -51 W 52nd -NY 10019
(212) 676-1130 .. **Hardekopf**, Marc T '01 %Taxi & Limo Comm -40 Rector -NY 10006 **Fx:**676-1206
(212) 309-1000 .. **Harden**, Richd L '73 (Hunton & W) -200 Park Av -NY 10166
(212) 788-0540 .. **Harden**, Zacharie J '10 %Law Dept -100 Church -NY 10007 **Fx:**788-0367
(518) 474-1524 .. **Harder**, Danl C '91 NYS Ed Dept -89 Wshngtn Av -Albany 12234 **Fx:**402-5940
(518) 474-4021 .. **Harder**, Robt G '78 %State Comptroller -110 State -Albany 12236 **Fx:**473-9104
(212) 351-4500 .. **Harders**, Gretchen '98 (Epstein B&G,PC) -250 Park Av -NY 10177
(212) 363-1380 .. **Hardesty**, Leonard J C Jr. '00 OfCnsl Herten BSCBL&H,LLC -747 3rd Av -NY 10017
(718) 852-1502 .. **Hardick**, Danl W '68 -32 Court -Brklyn 11201 **Fx:**875-4500
(585) 338-3430 .. **Hardies**, Robt M '69 -2305 Portlnd Av -Rchstr 14617 **Fx:**338-3642
(212) 558-4000 .. **Hardiman**, John L '83 (Sullivan & C LLP) -125 Broad -NY 10004
(212) 506-1775 .. **Hardiman**, Kevin G '88 %Kasowitz BT&F LLP -1633 Bway -NY 10019
(718) 694-3822 .. **Hardin**, Corey L '04 %Transit Auth -130 Lvngstn -Brklyn 11201 **Fx:**694-5726
(212) 742-3390 .. **Hardin**, David G '90 Lindabury ME&C,PC -26 Bway -NY 10004
(212) 530-5000 .. **Hardin**, Elizabeth Besio '96 (Milbank TH&M LLP) -1 Chase Manh Plz -NY 10005
(212) 571-0111 .. **Hardin**, George R '81 (Hardin KM&P,PA) -110 William -NY 10038
(212) 297-5800 .. **Hardin**, Jane H '79 SrCnsl Day P LLP -7 Times Sq -NY 10036
(212) 571-0111 .. **Hardin Kundla McKeon & Poletto,PA** -110 William -NY 10038 **Fx:**571-1117
(585) 610-7936 .. **Harding**, Annette M '90 -Bx96 -Belmont 14813 **Fx:**268-5780
(518) 384-3400 .. **Harding**, Chas R '77 Harding Law Firm -1343 Balltown Rd -Niskayuna 12309 **Fx:**384-2293
(914) 961-7022 .. **Harding**, Elisabeth S '78 -39 Homesdale Rd -Bronxvll 10708
(315) 457-0506 .. **Harding**, Herman L '62 -201 2nd -Liverpool 13088 **Fx:**641-2673
(718) 805-1500 .. **Harding**, James P '73 (Harding & M) -80-59 Lefferts Blvd -Kew Gdns 11415
(516) 746-0222 .. **Harding**, Kevin J '81 (Harding & H) -1055 Franklin Av -Gdn Cty 11530 **Fx:**746-0519
(315) 443-3677 .. **Harding**, Margaret M '87 %Syracuse Univ Cllg of Law -Wht Hall -Syracuse 13244 **Fx:**443-4213
(718) 354-3200 .. **Harding**, Michl L '91 %Battiste A&S,Inc -60 Bay -Staten Isl 10301
(718) 805-1500 .. **Harding & Moore** -80-59 Lefferts Blvd -Kew Gdns 11415 **Fx:**805-1503
(518) 272-1500 .. **Harding**, Nancy J '98 -53 Second -Troy 12180 **Fx:**272-1250
(718) 590-2000 .. **Harding**, Nikki R '98 %DA -198 E 161st -Bronx 10451 **Fx:**590-6477
(518) 862-1200 .. **Harding**, Paul B Jr. '90 (Martin H&M LLP) -Bx15141 -Albany 12212 **Fx:**724-0440
(212) 801-6750 .. **Harding**, Robt M '83 (Greenberg T,LLP) -200 Park Av -NY 10166
(518) 457-6207 .. **Harding**, Stella Chen '90 %Dept Civil Srvc -Harriman Campus Bldg 1 -Albany 12239 **Fx:**457-6654
(646) 855-3921 .. **Harding**, Thos C '10 Bk of Amer Merrill Lynch -1 Bryant Park -NY 10036
(212) 425-7200 .. **Hardman**, Cynthia L '02 %Kenyon & K,LLP -1 Bway -NY 10004
(718) 604-5789 .. **Hardwick**, Bonita J '97 %Kingsbrook Jewish Med Ctr -585 Schenectady Av -Brklyn 11203
(212) 309-6000 .. **Hardy**, Brettny E '08 %Morgan L&B LLP -101 Park Av -NY 10178
(212) 867-5800 .. **Hardy**, David R '76 (Osler H&H LLP) -620 8th Av -NY 10018
(516) 294-5200 .. **Hardy**, Gilbert J III '01 %Picciano & S -900 Merchants Cncrs -Westbury 11590
(516) 248-4041 .. **Hardy**, Glenn F '95 -226 7th -Gdn Cty 11530 **Fx:**248-4042
(516) 222-7700 .. **Hardy**, Jacqueline '90 LI Power Auth -333 Earle Ovngton Blvd -Uniondale 11553 **Fx:**222-9137
(212) 728-8000 .. **Hardy**, Jennifer J '08 %Willkie F&G LLP -787 7th Av -NY 10019
(212) 940-3000 .. **Hardy**, Kate J '10 %Nixon P LLP -437 Mad Av -NY 10022
(212) 863-5128 .. **Hardy**, Kimberly D '89 HPD-Ofc Cmmnty Prtnrshps -100 Gold -NY 10038 **Fx:**863-8907
(212) 690-3070 .. **Hardy**, Michl A '88 Cnsl Natl Action Network,Inc -106 W 145th -NY 10039 **Fx:**690-3081
(212) 338-9700 .. **Hardy**, Peter A '97 (Shupack & H,LLP) -450 7th Av -NY 10123
(212) 839-5300 .. **Hardy**, Robt P '95 (Sidley A LLP) -787 7th Av -NY 10019
(516) 357-3000 .. **Hardy**, Tamika N '02 %Rivkin R LLP -926 RXR Plz -Uniondale 11556
(716) 633-6500 .. **Hardy**, Wm J '01 %W Moran & Assoc,PC -6500 Main -Williamsvll 14221 **Fx:**633-3370
(212) 442-6841 .. **Hardy**, Zena '91 %Law Dept -60 Lafayette -NY 10013 **Fx:**442-6865
(212) 335-9000 .. **Hare**, Amy S '00 %DA -1 Hogan Pl -NY 10013
(212) 504-6000 .. **Hare**, Jaspal S '08 %Cadwalader W&T LLP -1 World Fncl Ctr -NY 10281
(212) 230-8800 .. **Hare**, Paul A '00 Cnsl WilmerHale -399 Park Av -NY 10022
(212) 735-8600 .. **Harel**, Avital R '06 %Morrison C LLP -909 3rd Av -NY 10022
(212) 402-9400 .. **Harel**, Shahar '08 %McKool S,PC -1 Bryant Park -NY 10036
(914) 358-4934 .. **Harelick**, Maxine E '90 %Ferro L&Z LLC -1025 Wstchstr Av -White Plns 10604
(212) 456-6900 .. **Harewood**, G Francesca D '05 Riverward Productions -147 Columbus Av -NY 10023
(516) 355-9600 .. **Harfenist**, Steven J '90 (Friedman HK&P) -3000 Marcus Av -Lk Success 11042
(315) 448-4800 .. **Harford**, John P '94 %Dept of Law -615 Erie Blvd W -Syracuse 13204 **Fx:**448-4853
(212) 302-2400 .. **Harford**, Scott A '01 %Lynch DE LLP -264 W 40th -NY 10018
(212) 545-4000 .. **Hargadon**, Lisa A '08 %Jackson L LLP -666 3rd Av -NY 10017
(212) 313-3600 .. **Hargas**, Katherine '82 %Barry M&M -2 Rector -NY 10006
(716) 648-4202 .. **Hargesheimer**, Elbert III '70 E Hargeshheimer III,PC -22 Buffalo -Hambrg 14075 **Fx:**648-4206
(212) 742-8700 .. **Hargis**, Erin M '05 %Garson D&C LLP -110 Wall -NY 10005
(212) 401-4040 .. **Hargis**, Jessica '07 %Teplen & Assoc,PLLC -350 5th Av -NY 10118 **Fx:**401-4041
(212) 218-8760 .. **Hargraves**, Danl A '92 (Hargraves M&C,PC) -420 Lex Av -NY 10170
(631) 231-1199 .. **Hargraves**, Dawn L '00 OfCnsl Reynolds CGHL&Q,LLP -35 Arkay Dr -Hauppauge 11788
(212) 218-8760 .. **Hargraves McConnell & Costigan,PC** -420 Lex Av -NY 10170 **Fx:**218-8761
(212) 709-8342 .. **Hargrove**, James K '80 -110 Wall -NY 10005 **Fx:**(973) 580-1740
(212) 793-7533 .. **Hargrove**, Jos J '87 Citigroup -909 3rd Av -NY 10022
(516) 538-2500 .. **Hargrove**, Kenya Sharita '99 %Furey FLMW&D,PC -600 Front -Hempstd 11550
(212) 326-2000 .. **Hargrove**, Sarah Barnes '09 %O'Melveny & M LLP -7 Times Sq -NY 10036
(212) 310-2231 .. **Hargrove Remundo**, Katherine E '93 %Colgate-Palmolive -300 Park Av -NY 10022 **Fx:**310-3230
(212) 250-3914 .. **Hariani**, Sunil '97 %Deutsche Bank -60 Wall -NY 10005
(212) 223-4000 .. **Haridi**, Samaa '00 Cnsl Crowell & M LLP -590 Mad Av -NY 10022
(631) 473-8931 .. **Haring**, J Christopher '83 -4 Snow Crest Ct -Mt Sinai 11766 **Fx:**474-3735
(516) 431-6092 .. **Harinski**, James M '95 %J Petrilli -370 W Park Av -Long Bch 11561 **Fx:**889-8904
(212) 422-9424 .. **Harinstein**, Pamela M '05 %Gogick B&O,LLP -11 Bway -NY 10004
(212) 980-2233 .. **Hariri**, Ronald D '82 (R Hariri & Assoc,PC) -220 E 49th -NY 10017 **Fx:**980-0750
(631) 224-1133 .. **Hariton & D'Angelo, LLP** -3500 Sunrise Hwy -Great Rvr 11739
(212) 558-4000 .. **Hariton**, David P '86 (Sullivan & C LLP) -125 Broad -NY 10004
(914) 674-4373 .. **Hariton**, Frank J '75 -1065 Dobbs Ferry Rd -White Plns 10607 **Fx:**693-2963
(631) 224-1133 .. **Hariton**, Ira M '64 (Hariton & D,LLP) -3500 Sunrise Hwy -Great Rvr 11739
(212) 564-9666 .. **Haritos**, Gus P '80 -450 7th Av -NY 10123 **Fx:**564-6137
(516) 694-3000 .. **Hark**, Nancy M '04 %Guercio & G,LLP -77 Conklin -Farmngdl 11735 **Fx:**694-4738
(212) 949-9696 .. **Harkavy**, Harriet '82 -60 E 42nd -NY 10165 **Fx:**949-6241
(646) 386-5891 .. **Harkavy**, Stephen '81 %MHLS -41 Mad Av -NY 10010
(718) 250-1100 .. **Harkavy**, Steven Jeffrey '86 %E Garfinkel -12 Metrotech Ctr -Brklyn 11201 **Fx:**250-1168
(716) 856-0600 .. **Harkawik**, Dennis P '80 (Jaeckle F&M,LLP) -12 Fountain Plz -Buffalo 14202

(212) 589-4200 .. **Harker,** Francesca M '09 %Baker & H LLP -45 Rckfllr Plz -NY 10111
(518) 583-0639 .. **Harker,** Gary T '00 3H Corporate Srvcs,LLC -6 Clement Av -Saratoga Spgs 12866
(212) 833-1192 .. **Harker,** Mala Ahuja '02 (Friedman KS&A LLP) -1633 Bway -NY 10019 **Fx:**373-7992
(212) 885-5000 .. **Harkiewicz,** Erin O'Brien '08 OfCnsl Blank R LLP -405 Lex Av -NY 10174
(212) 632-6000 .. **Harkin,** David P '05 %Lazard Freres -30 Rckfllr Plz -NY 10112 **Fx:**632-6060
(631) 952-6542 .. **Harkin,** George F '89 %Ct of Claims -NYS Ofc Bldg Vets Mem'l Hwy -Hauppauge 11788 **Fx:**952-6727
(212) 770-7000 .. **Harkins,** Kenneth V '85 %AIG -70 Pine -NY 10270
(212) 416-6551 .. **Harkins,** Kevin R '03 %Dept of Law -120 Bway -NY 10271
(212) 269-5550 .. **Harkins,** Peter C '81 %DF King & Co -48 Wall -NY 10005 **Fx:**952-0137
(212) 670-0106 .. **Harkins,** Susan Gordon '81 Merrill Lynch -222 Bway -NY 10038
(631) 367-1362 .. **Harkins,** Thos S '87 (T Harkins,PC) -24 Glen Way -Cold Spg Hbr 11724 **Fx:**367-1363 ***[Workers' Compensation Law]***
(631) 476-3750 .. **Harkins,** Tracy J '88 -48 Birch Hill Rd -Mt Sinai 11766 **Fx:**476-3750
(212) 558-4000 .. **Harkness,** Kimberly A '10 %Sullivan & C LLP -125 Broad -NY 10004
(212) 715-9100 .. **Harkness,** Timothy P '97 (Kramer LN&F,LLP) -1177 Av of Amer -NY 10036
(212) 728-2200 .. **Harkrider,** John '92 (Axinn V&H LLP) -114 W 47th -NY 10036
(212) 832-8000 .. **Harlan,** Joshua D '02 Allen & Co -711 5th Av -NY 10022
(212) 474-1000 .. **Harlan,** Leigh M '06 %Cravath S&M LLP -825 8th Av -NY 10019
(212) 576-4985 .. **Harland,** David A K '86 %NY Life Ins -51 Mad Av -NY 10010 **Fx:**447-0569
(212) 863-6300 .. **Harlem,** Phyllis R '79 %HPD -100 Gold -NY 10038 **Fx:**863-8201
(607) 432-3611 .. **Harlem,** Richd A '83 (Harlem & J) -493 Chestnut -Oneonta 13820 **Fx:**432-9761
(607) 432-3611 .. **Harlem,** Robt A '53 (Harlem & J) -493 Chestnut -Oneonta 13820 **Fx:**432-9761
(212) 489-1600 .. **Harley,** Alan A '79 %Deloitte LLP -1633 Bway -NY 10019 **Fx:**492-4201
(212) 450-4000 .. **Harley,** Colin E '68 SrCnsl Davis P&W LLP -450 Lex Av -NY 10017
(212) 840-0080 .. **Harley,** Colin K '80 OfCnsl Bierce & K,PC -420 Lex Av -NY 10170
(212) 683-8464 .. **Harley,** Duane M '03 -303 5th Av -NY 10016
(718) 788-7102 .. **Harley,** Emily K '86 -1694 11th Av -Brklyn 11218
(518) 686-4408 .. **Harley,** Gerald A '71 -21176 NY 22 Bx10 -Hoosick Fls 12090 **Fx:**686-4409
(212) 474-1000 .. **Harley,** Nicholas B '10 %Cravath S&M LLP -825 8th Av -NY 10019
(718) 292-2952 .. **Harley,** Nicole M '00 OfCnsl Yalkut & I -865B Walton Av -Bronx 10451
(212) 512-1000 .. **Harley,** Patricia A '03 %HBO -1100 Av of Amer -NY 10036 **Fx:**512-1986
(716) 753-4247 .. **Harley,** Scott F '78 %Cnty Atty -3 N Erie -Mayvll 14757 **Fx:**753-4129
(212) 651-7500 .. **Harlfinger,** Andre E '86 %Segal MS&M -850 3rd Av -NY 10022
(212) 756-2000 .. **Harlow,** Christine '05 %Schulte R&Z LLP -919 3rd Av -NY 10022
(716) 849-0701 .. **Harlow,** Dennis P '07 %Lipsitz & P LLC -135 Delaware Av -Buffalo 14202
(212) 605-0314 .. **Harlow,** Margaret E '88 -575 Mad Av -NY 10022 **Fx:**605-0222
(516) 536-9744 .. **Harlow,** Robt E '67 -47 W Windsor Pkwy -Oceanside 11572 **Fx:**536-9744
(212) 903-9000 .. **Harlow,** Ruth E '88 Cnsl Linklaters -1345 Av of Amer -NY 10105
(212) 578-7647 .. **Harman,** Christine M '99 %MetLife -27-01 Qns Plz N -LIC 11101
(212) 777-6729 .. **Harman,** Lynn '89 -2 5th Av -NY 10011
(716) 839-2652 .. **Harman,** Richd L '73 (Gerace & H,PC) -3960 Harlem Rd -Snyder 14226
(212) 425-2600 .. **Harman,** Walker G Jr. '00 (Harman Firm,PC) -19 Fulton -NY 10038 **Fx:**202-3926
(212) 737-3749 .. **Harman,** Wm R '67 -1 East End Av -NY 10075 **Fx:**861-3830
(212) 382-0777 .. **Harmatz,** Hugo R '99 -280 Mad Av -NY 10016
(631) 234-5222 .. **Harmel,** George M Jr. '73 -33 Wheeler Rd -Central Islip 11722 **Fx:**234-5969
(631) 234-5222 .. **Harmel,** Lara M '96 -33 Wheeler Rd -Central Islip 11722 **Fx:**234-5969
(212) 468-8000 .. **Harmetz,** Lloyd S '94 (Morrison & F LLP) -1290 Av of Amer -NY 10104
(516) 574-6142 .. **Harmitt,** Stafford A '02 %JP Morgan Chase -1985 Marcus Av -New Hyde Pk 11040
(212) 732-3665 .. **Harmon,** David H '46 (Harmon L&R) -42 Bway -NY 10004
(212) 808-0700 .. **Harmon,** David T '87 (Norris M&M,PA) -875 3rd Av -NY 10022
(718) 681-0900 .. **Harmon,** Gregory D '83 -208 E 163rd -Bronx 10451 **Fx:**681-1205
(516) 522-2590 .. **Harmon,** James D '71 -165 EAB Plz -Uniondale 11556
(716) 858-7834 .. **Harmon,** James E '82 Dept Soc Srvcs -95 Franklin -Buffalo 14202
(607) 435-2113 .. **Harmon,** Kara Tobias '91 -47 Sunset Blvd -Oneonta 13820
(212) 474-1000 .. **Harmon,** Kyle C '10 %Cravath S&M LLP -825 8th Av -NY 10019
(212) 732-3665 .. **Harmon Linder & Rogowsky** -42 Bway -NY 10004 **Fx:**732-1462
(212) 751-4300 .. **Harmon,** Mark A '79 (Hodgson R LLP) -1540 Bway -NY 10036
(212) 661-7300 .. **Harmon,** Mary Beth '95 %Malapero & P LLP -295 Mad Av -NY 10017
(212) 563-4100 .. **Harmon,** Richd C '99 %Cohen W&S LLP -330 W 42nd -NY 10036
(212) 373-3000 .. **Harmon,** Robt F Jr. '09 %Paul WRW&G LLP -1285 Av of Amer -NY 10019
(212) 704-6000 .. **Harmon,** Stephen F '68 (Troutman S LLP) -405 Lex Av -NY 10174
Harmon, Susan S '76 -67 S Oxford -Brklyn 11217
(212) 548-2100 .. **Harmon,** Yvette G '69 (McGuire W LLP) -1345 Av of Amer -NY 10105
(212) 248-9100 .. **Harms,** Chas F Jr. '81 (Epstein H&M) -1 Whitehall -NY 10004
(212) 558-4000 .. **Harms,** David B '85 (Sullivan & C LLP) -125 Broad -NY 10004
(516) 921-7773 .. **Harms,** Richd '97 (Gisonni & H LLP) -20 Crossway Park N -Woodbury 11797 **Fx:**364-3717
(518) 486-7815 .. **Harms,** Scott T '03 %Insurance Dept -99 Wshngtn Av -Albany 12257 **Fx:**473-4600
(716) 852-5533 .. **Harned,** Elizabeth B '03 %Connors & V,LLP -1000 Lbrty Bldg -Buffalo 14202
(585) 428-5210 .. **Harned,** Luke V '06 %Pub Def -10 N Fitzhugh -Rchstr 14614 **Fx:**428-2234
(716) 892-3156 .. **Harner,** Timothy R '81 Upstate Farms Cooperative -25 Andrsn Rd -Buffalo 14225 **Fx:**896-8752
(845) 855-1204 .. **Harnes,** Anne Ellis '91 -64 S Quaker Hill Rd -Pawling 12564
(516) 773-6090 .. **Harnes,** Joan Tomic '55 (Chitwood HH LLP) -185 Grt Nck Rd -Gt Neck 11021
(516) 773-6090 .. **Harnes,** John F '82 (Chitwood HH LLP) -185 Grt Nck Rd -Gt Neck 11021
(212) 506-1700 .. **Harness,** Jason E '08 Kasowitz BT&F LLP -1633 Bway -NY 10019
(212) 596-9000 .. **Harnett,** Christopher J '91 (Ropes & G LLP) -1211 Av of Amer -NY 10036
(212) 776-5000 .. **Harnett,** Nancy M '86 %NYC Housing Auth -250 Bway -NY 10007 **Fx:**776-5039
(212) 373-3000 .. **Harnett,** Sarah M '09 Paul WRW&G LLP -1285 Av of Amer -NY 10019
(212) 962-5065 .. **Harnick,** Robt M '88 (Harnick & H) -305 Bway -NY 10007 **Fx:**962-6232
(212) 962-5065 .. **Harnick,** Thos J '99 %Harnick & H -305 Bway -NY 10007 **Fx:**962-6232
(212) 599-7575 .. **Harnik,** Stephen M '79 (Harnik & F LLP) -645 5th Av -NY 10022 **Fx:**867-8120
(212) 668-8000 .. **Harnisch,** Elizabeth Knowles '99 Oppenheimer & Co Inc -125 Broad -NY 10004 **Fx:**668-8081
(646) 315-7300 .. **Harnisch,** Virginia J '91 %FINRA -14 Wall -NY 10005 **Fx:**315-7440
(212) 848-9800 .. **Harnisch,** Wm O' C '67 SrCnsl Withers B LLP -430 Park Av -NY 10022
(212) 756-2000 .. **Harnoy,** Alon '95 %Schulte R&Z LLP -919 3rd Av -NY 10022
(914) 683-2500 .. **Harold,** Christopher P '78 (Harold SS&S) -81 Main -White Plns 10601
(516) 222-0248 .. **Harold,** Patricia A '99 (Donlon & H) -350 Old Cntry Rd -Gdn Cty 11530
(212) 298-5000 .. **Harold,** Robt W '90 %Leg Aid -49 Thomas -NY 10013 **Fx:**298-5252
(914) 683-2500 .. **Harold Salant Strassfield & Spielberg** -81 Main -White Plns 10601 **Fx:**683-1279
(212) 525-8903 .. **Haroldson,** Jeffrey D '82 HSBC Markets USA Inc -452 5th Av -NY 10018
(212) 607-3300 .. **Haroules,** Beth '87 %NYCLU -125 Broad -NY 10004
(212) 697-2800 .. **Haroun,** Robt M '90 (Sofer & H,LLP) -317 Mad Av -NY 10017
(917) 421-5797 .. **Harounian,** Debra D '98 -220 W 42nd -NY 10036
(516) 773-8300 .. **Harounian,** Jacqueline '95 (Wisselman H & Assoc,PC) -1010 Nrthrn Blvd -Gt Neck 11021 **Fx:**773-8304
(212) 575-7900 .. **Haroutunian,** Vano I '03 (Ballon SB&N,PC) -729 7th Av -NY 10019
(518) 371-4836 .. **Harp,** Darrell W '63 -12 Rolling Brook Dr -Clifton Pk 12065 **Fx:**371-9292
(516) 764-2800 .. **Harp,** Darrell W '63 OfCnsl Goldberg & C -66 N Vllg Av -Rockvll Ctr 11570
(845) 255-7200 .. **Harp,** Heather D '01 HD Harp,PC -83 Route 208 Bx400 -New Paltz 12561 **Fx:**255-7218
(845) 340-3315 .. **Harp,** Kevin C '01 DA -285 Wall -Kingston 12401 **Fx:**340-3185
(518) 373-1482 .. **Harp,** Kimberly A '00 (DuCharme H&C,LLP) -10 Maxwell Dr -Clifton Pk 12065
(212) 258-6000 .. **Harp,** Sarah J '01 %Viacom -1515 Bway -NY 10036
(212) 577-3688 .. **Harpaz,** Elon D '90 %Leg Aid -199 Water -NY 10038 **Fx:**509-8431
(212) 363-3500 .. **Harpel,** Joanne L '90 Amrcn Fndtn for Suicide Prvntn -120 Wall -NY 10005
(212) 681-8199 .. **Harper,** Ambia N '07 SrCnsl Common Good -1 Metrotech Ctr -Brklyn 11201 **Fx:**(718) 852-8110
(718) 694-5613 .. **Harper,** Bonnie C '95 %Transit Auth -130 Lvngstn -Brklyn 11201 **Fx:**694-5726
(212) 698-3500 .. **Harper,** Bret M '09 %Dechert LLP -1095 Av of Amer -NY 10036
(914) 747-0828 .. **Harper,** Christa J '04 Northern Westchester Shelter -Bx203 -Plsntvll 10570
(212) 455-2000 .. **Harper,** Conrad K '66 OfCnsl Simpson T&B LLP -425 Lex Av -NY 10017
(518) 587-6670 .. **Harper,** David A '83 -480 Bway -Saratoga Spgs 12866 **Fx:**587-6672
(212) 373-3000 .. **Harper,** Gerard E '80 (Paul WRW&G LLP) -1285 Av of Amer -NY 10019
(212) 406-2606 .. **Harper,** Jake '91 -30 Vesey -NY 10007 **Fx:**732-4923
(315) 594-9488 .. **Harper,** Jeffrey R '79 -Bx7 -Wolcott 14590 **Fx:**594-6414
(212) 644-4141 .. **Harper,** Kathleen D '77 Cerberus Corp -410 E 50th -NY 10022
(212) 446-4800 .. **Harper,** Laura S '98 %Kirkland & E LLP -153 E 53rd -NY 10022
(585) 256-8750 .. **Harper,** Ralph E '74 %Gleason Corp -1000 Univ Av Bx22970 -Rchstr 14692 **Fx:**461-4092
(212) 408-2500 .. **Harper,** Richd B '08 (Baker B,LLP) -30 Rckfllr Plz -NY 10112
(516) 248-1441 .. **Harper,** Robt F '76 -55 Hilton Av -Gdn Cty 11530 **Fx:**248-0630
(516) 227-0700 .. **Harper,** Robt M '08 %Farrell F,PC -1320 RXR Plz -Uniondale 11556
(212) 902-1000 .. **Harper,** Roger C '87 %Goldman Sachs -1 NY Plz -NY 10004
(646) 435-9505 .. **Harper,** Susan L '03 %Baritz & C LLP -233 Bway -NY 10279
(212) 297-0050 .. **Harper,** Virginia A '89 OfCnsl Betancourt VHG&K LLC -46 Trinity Pl -NY 10006
(631) 224-4517 .. **Harper-Iglesias,** Marie T '02 -136 E Main -E Islip 11730
(212) 596-9000 .. **Harper-Smith,** Nicholas D '09 %Ropes & G LLP -1211 Av of Amer -NY 10036
(585) 454-0700 .. **Harradine,** Jeffrey J '05 %Ward GH&R LLP -300 State -Rchstr 14614
(516) 684-3442 .. **Harragan,** Edwin J Jr. '62 (Swiger KH&S) -14 Shore Dr -Plandome 11030
(212) 545-4601 .. **Harrar,** Peter C '85 (Wolf HAF&H LLP) -270 Mad Av -NY 10016
(631) 393-6220 .. **Harras Bloom & Archer LLP** -445 Broad Hollow Rd -Melvll 11747 **Fx:**393-6229
(631) 393-6220 .. **Harras,** John A '82 (Harras B&A LLP) -445 Broad Hollow Rd -Melvll 11747
(315) 428-1967 .. **Harrell,** M Jerald '97 -333 E Onondaga -Syracuse 13202 **Fx:**428-1108
(212) 909-6000 .. **Harrell,** Michl P '86 (Debevoise & P LLP) -919 3rd Av -NY 10022
(518) 464-3901 .. **Harren,** Kevin H '78 Cnsl Capitol Region BOCES -900 Watervliet Shaker Rd -Albany 12205 **Fx:**862-4949
(585) 232-3730 .. **Harren,** Michl T '75 (Chamberlain D LLP) -1600 Crssrds Bldg -Rchstr 14614
(518) 426-7750 .. **Harri,** JoAnn P '87 (Smalline and H) -100 State -Albany 12207
(518) 766-4071 .. **Harri,** JoAnn P '87 (Smalline and H) -Bx80 -N Chatham 12132
(315) 425-2700 .. **Harrigan,** Christopher J '00 (Hiscock & B,LLP) -One Park Pl -Syracuse 13202
(315) 478-3138 .. **Harrigan & Dolan** -2 Clinton Sq -Syracuse 13202 **Fx:**478-3148

(315) 478-3138 .. **Harrigan,** Kevin P '80 (Harrigan & D) -2 Clinton Sq -Syracuse 13202
(585) 753-4500 .. **Harrigan,** Michl J '01 DA -832 Watts Bldg -Rchstr 14614 **Fx:**753-4576
(518) 474-6623 .. **Harrigan,** Patrick M '83 %Insurance Dept -99 Wshngtn Av -Albany 12257 **Fx:**474-5473
(516) 745-1122 .. **Harrigan,** Scott M '00 Cnsl Quadrino & S,PC -666 Old Cntry Rd -Gdn Cty 11530
(212) 259-8000 .. **Harrigan,** Sean M Jr. '08 %Dewey & L LLP -1301 Av of Amer -NY 10019
(212) 483-9490 .. **Harriman,** Chas J '80 (McElroy DM&C,LLP) -88 Pine -NY 10005
(518) 474-1585 .. **Harriman,** Kimberly A '99 Dept Pub Srvc -3 ESP -Albany 12223
(718) 340-4200 .. **Harring,** Sidney L '89 %CUNY Law Schl -65-21 Main -Flushng 11367 **Fx:**340-4482
(212) 728-8000 .. **Harrington,** Ann B '09 %Willkie F&G LLP -787 7th Av -NY 10019
(212) 849-7000 .. **Harrington,** Ben M '10 %Quinn EU&S,LLP -51 Mad Av -NY 10010
(845) 454-3250 .. **Harrington,** Bevin S '98 (Gellert & K,PC) -75 Wshngtn -Poughkeepsie 12601
(212) 335-9000 .. **Harrington,** Brigid A '06 %DA -1 Hogan Pl -NY 10013
(212) 728-8000 .. **Harrington,** Catherine Anne '93 SpclCnsl Willkie F&G LLP -787 7th Av -NY 10019
(212) 909-6000 .. **Harrington,** Christine M '06 %Debevoise & P LLP -919 3rd Av -NY 10022
(212) 490-9100 .. **Harrington,** David J '00 (Condon & F LLP) -7 Times Sq -NY 10036
(212) 766-1888 .. **Harrington,** Edw J '00 %Morris DA&F -2 Rector -NY 10006
(212) 506-1700 .. **Harrington,** Edw M '03 Kasowitz BT&F LLP -1633 Bway -NY 10019
(631) 874-2800 .. **Harrington,** Elizabeth M '86 -442 Main Bx280 -E Moriches 11940 **Fx:**874-3304
(914) 231-7075 .. **Harrington,** Helise '82 Threshold Advisors,LLC -134 High -Hastings-On-Hud 10706
(716) 853-3700 .. **Harrington,** Ian M '10 %Harrington & M -70 Niagara -Buffalo 14202
(516) 822-3550 .. **Harrington,** James F '94 Hoffmann & B LLP -6900 Jericho Tpk -Syosset 11791 **Fx:**822-3582
(212) 370-6716 .. **Harrington,** James J '64 (Harrington H LLP) -305 Mad Av -NY 10165 **Fx:**684-2476
(716) 853-3700 .. **Harrington,** James P '70 (Harrington & M) -70 Niagara -Buffalo 14202
(716) 826-6677 .. **Harrington,** Jane Michalek '98 -300 Center Rd -Buffalo 14224
(845) 346-4059 .. **Harrington,** Jane P '90 %City Ct -2 James -Middletwn 10940 **Fx:**343-5737
(212) 490-3000 .. **Harrington,** Jason A '06 %Wilson EME&D LLP -150 E 42nd -NY 10017
(716) 826-6677 .. **Harrington,** Jeffrey M '99 (Michalek & H) -300 Center Rd -Buffalo 14224
(212) 697-4090 .. **Harrington,** Jillian B '98 %Platzer L&P LLP -61 Bway -NY 10006
(203) 345-6130 .. **Harrington,** John H '97 J Harrington,LLC -555 5th Av -NY 10017 **Fx:**380-9939
(212) 309-6000 .. **Harrington,** John T W '08 %Morgan L&B LLP -101 Park Av -NY 10178
(914) 946-3700 .. **Harrington,** Jos P '72 (McCarthy F LLP) -11 Martine Av -White Plns 10606
(914) 686-4800 .. **Harrington,** Kevin J '82 (Harrington O&M,LLP) -81 Main -White Plns 10601
(716) 853-3700 .. **Harrington & Mahoney** -70 Niagara -Buffalo 14202 **Fx:**853-3710
(315) 474-7571 .. **Harrington,** Mark T '90 (Mackenzie H LLP) -101 S Salina Bx4967 -Syracuse 13221
(315) 637-4438 .. **Harrington,** Mary K '86 -4976 Lakevw Dr -Fayettevll 13066 **Fx:**637-4438
(914) 948-5550 .. **Harrington,** Michl P '07 Cordia Corp -445 Hmltn Av -White Plns 10601
(516) 488-6923 .. **Harrington,** Michl T '70 -104 Fernwood Ter -Stewart Mnr 11530
(518) 457-1260 .. **Harrington,** Michele L '04 %DCJS -4 Twr Pl -Albany 12203 **Fx:**457-3089
(518) 266-1000 .. **Harrington,** Mickki L '91 (Pattison SG&G,PC) -22 1st Bx208 -Troy 12181
(914) 686-4800 .. **Harrington Ocko & Monk,LLP** -81 Main -White Plns 10601 **Fx:**686-4824
(212) 351-7114 .. **Harrington,** Patrick J '86 Monster Worldwide -622 3rd Av -NY 10017
(914) 949-2700 .. **Harrington,** Peter F '95 (Bleakley P&S,LLP) -1 N Lex Av -White Plns 10601
(212) 839-5300 .. **Harrington,** Susan D '74 (Sidley A LLP) -787 7th Av -NY 10019
(516) 766-1189 .. **Harrington,** Wm D '70 -47 Berkshire Rd -Rockvll Ctr 11570
(716) 854-2620 .. **Harrington,** Wm D '79 (Brown & K,LLP) -1500 Lbrty Bldg -Buffalo 14202
(212) 637-2331 .. **Harrington,** Wm J '00 %US Atty -1 St Andrews Plz -NY 10007
(914) 949-2700 .. **Harrington,** Wm P '83 (Bleakley P&S,LLP) -1 N Lex Av -White Plns 10601
(212) 805-6711 .. **Harrington-Steppen,** Suzanne A '06 %Hon K Fox -40 Foley -NY 10007
(212) 756-2000 .. **Harris,** Adam C '87 (Schulte R&Z LLP) -919 3rd Av -NY 10022
(212) 859-8000 .. **Harris,** Adam M '08 %Fried FHS&J LLP -1 NY Plz -NY 10004
(212) 819-1011 .. **Harris,** Adam S '88 -500 7th Av -NY 10018
(212) 558-4000 .. **Harris,** Adrienne A '07 %Sullivan & C LLP -125 Broad -NY 10004
(914) 747-9393 .. **Harris,** Alan J '89 (AJ Harris,PC) -427 Manvll Rd -Plsntvll 10570 **Fx:**747-9394
(585) 232-4090 .. **Harris,** Alan S '77 %Leg Aid -1 W Main -Rchstr 14614 **Fx:**232-2352
(212) 836-8000 .. **Harris,** Alexandra L '06 %Kaye S LLP -425 Park Av -NY 10022
(212) 966-4035 .. **Harris,** Allan M '84 -35 Mercer -NY 10013
(212) 848-4000 .. **Harris,** Allison G '08 %Shearman & S LLP -599 Lex Av -NY 10022
(718) 505-6650 .. **Harris,** Alysia J '96 %Kaplan & M -75-20 Astoria Blvd -E Elmhrst 11370
(212) 805-4772 .. **Harris,** Andrew L '04 %Hon J Koeltl -500 Pearl -NY 10007
(212) 344-5400 .. **Harris,** Andrew S '06 %Schlam S&D LLP -26 Bway -NY 10004
(212) 294-6700 .. **Harris,** Andrew S '09 %Winston & S -200 Park Av -NY 10166
(212) 849-7000 .. **Harris,** Angela L '08 %Quinn EU&S,LLP -51 Mad Av -NY 10010
(212) 599-2396 .. **Harris,** April D '81 (Dyer Law Firm PLLC) -80 Maiden Ln -NY 10038 **Fx:**214-0927
(212) 836-8000 .. **Harris,** Arlene '69 SpclCnsl Kaye S LLP -425 Park Av -NY 10022
(212) 605-0466 .. **Harris,** Asher Anschel '89 -575 Mad Av -NY 10022
(212) 335-4500 .. **Harris,** Barbara J '96 OfCnsl DLA Piper LLP -1251 Av of Amer -NY 10020
(585) 419-8800 .. **Harris Beach PLLC** -99 Garnsey Rd -Pittsfrd 14534 **Fx:**419-8801
(212) 687-0100 .. **Harris Beach PLLC** -100 Wall -NY 10005 **Fx:**687-0659
(516) 880-8484 .. **Harris Beach PLLC** -333 Earle Ovngton Blvd -Uniondale 11553 **Fx:**880-8483
(914) 683-1200 .. **Harris Beach PLLC** -445 Hmltn Av -White Plns 10601 **Fx:**683-1210
(607) 273-6444 .. **Harris Beach PLLC** -119 E Seneca -Ithaca 14850 **Fx:**273-6802
(716) 200-5050 .. **Harris Beach PLLC** -726 Exchange -Buffalo 14210 **Fx:**200-5201
(315) 423-7100 .. **Harris Beach PLLC** -300 S State -Syracuse 13202 **Fx:**422-9331
(518) 427-9700 .. **Harris Beach PLLC** -677 Bway -Albany 12207 **Fx:**427-0235
(716) 285-1535 .. **Harris Beach PLLC** -800 Main Bx712 -Niagara Fls 14302 **Fx:**285-3707
(732) 855-6122 .. **Harris,** Brett R '92 (Wilentz G&S) -110 William -NY 10038 **Fx:**726-6574
(212) 599-2085 .. **Harris,** Brian C '84 (Braff H&S) -305 Bway -NY 10007
(212) 935-1622 .. **Harris,** Caroline G '83 (Goldman H LLC) -475 Park Av S -NY 10016 **Fx:**935-2651
(516) 515-1273 .. **Harris,** Cecily A '03 -99 Tulip Av -Floral Pk 11001
(212) 754-9400 .. **Harris,** Chad I '08 %Todtman NS&J,PC -425 Park Av -NY 10022
(212) 785-7400 .. **Harris,** Cheryl '87 (Harris & M,LLP) -11 Bway -NY 10004
(585) 899-1414 .. **Harris Chesworth O'Brien Johnstone Welch & Leone** -300 Linden Oaks -Rchstr 14625 **Fx:**899-1424
(212) 906-1200 .. **Harris,** Christopher Richd '98 (Latham & W) -885 3rd Av -NY 10022
(718) 590-2000 .. **Harris,** Cicely R '09 %DA -198 E 161st -Bronx 10451 **Fx:**590-6477
(212) 808-7800 .. **Harris,** Conor S '07 %Kelley D&W LLP -101 Park Av -NY 10178
(212) 635-1556 .. **Harris,** Constance S '81 Bk of NY Mellon -1 Wall -NY 10286
(518) 436-1661 .. **Harris Conway & Donovan, PLLC** -5 Clinton Sq -Albany 12207 **Fx:**432-1996
(212) 907-7300 .. **Harris,** Courtney A '06 %Golenbock EAB&P -437 Mad Av -NY 10022
(212) 713-5174 .. **Harris,** Cynthia M '85 -1498 3rd Av -NY 10028
(212) 702-4359 .. **Harris,** Danl J '83 %Lowestloan.com -767 5th Av -NY 10153
(212) 806-5400 .. **Harris,** Danl J '09 %Stroock &S&L LLP -180 Maiden Ln -NY 10038
(845) 808-1150 .. **Harris,** Danielle M '10 Cnty Atty -48 Gleneida Av -Carmel 10512 **Fx:**808-1903
(212) 288-3312 .. **Harris,** Dara D D '82 -444 Cntrl Pk W -NY 10025
(212) 351-4000 .. **Harris,** Darcy C '10 Gibson D&C LLP -200 Park Av -NY 10166
(516) 564-5329 .. **Harris,** Darlene D '89 -275 Pemaco Ln -Uniondale 11553
(212) 373-3000 .. **Harris,** David '03 %Paul WRW&G LLP -1285 Av of Amer -NY 10019
(347) 404-9133 .. **Harris,** David A '96 %Civil Ct -141 Lvngstn -Brklyn 11201 **Fx:**(718) 643-3733
(718) 291-5544 .. **Harris,** David S '96 -88-32 Sutphin Blvd -Jamaica 11435 **Fx:**291-5566
(718) 579-7900 .. **Harris,** Davina N '09 Leg Aid -900 Sheridan Av -Bronx 10451 **Fx:**293-8744
(631) 462-8565 .. **Harris,** Deborah Weksberg '86 -15 Bayard Dr -Dix Hlls 11746
(212) 636-7787 .. **Harris,** Debra J '87 %Fordham Univ -113 W 60th -NY 10023
(212) 264-0159 .. **Harris,** Donald M '87 Army Eng Dist -26 Fed Plz -NY 10278 **Fx:**264-8171
(212) 365-6568 .. **Harris,** Douglas E '76 Promontory Fncl Grp,LLC -280 Park Av -NY 10017
(212) 858-3600 .. **Harris,** Drexel B '86 %Reliance Ins -75 Broad -NY 10004
(212) 883-4900 .. **Harris,** Edw L Jr. '78 (Cozen O) -277 Park Av -NY 10172
(212) 450-4000 .. **Harris,** Elizabeth Ashley '09 %Davis P&W LLP -450 Lex Av -NY 10017
(212) 872-1000 .. **Harris,** Elizabeth E '87 -One Bryant Park -NY 10036 **Fx:**872-1002
(212) 536-3900 .. **Harris,** Elizabeth M '06 %K&L Gates LLP -599 Lex Av -NY 10022
(212) 839-5300 .. **Harris,** Ellen W '78 Cnsl Sidley A LLP -787 7th Av -NY 10019
(704) 444-3694 .. **Harris,** Emily O'Reilly '07 %Mayer B LLP -1675 Bway -NY 10019
(212) 996-7898 .. **Harris,** Eric I '70 -1100 Park Av -NY 10128
(212) 891-1011 .. **Harris,** Eric M '92 -450 7th Av -NY 10123
(845) 565-0999 .. **Harris,** Ernest L '97 -405 Robnsn Av-Rt 9W -Newburgh 12550 **Fx:**565-1281
(212) 406-0998 .. **Harris,** Fitzmore Hezekiah '94 -160 Bway -NY 10038 **Fx:**634-1631
(585) 454-5550 .. **Harris,** Flo Ann '94 %NYSUT -30 N Union -Rchstr 14607
(212) 922-4300 .. **Harris,** Fredk S '80 %Trotwood Corp -200 Park Av -NY 10166 **Fx:**922-4301
(212) 455-2000 .. **Harris,** Gail Block '78 OfCnsl Simpson T&B LLP -425 Lex Av -NY 10017
(212) 688-6400 .. **Harris,** George '53 -270 Mad Av -NY 10016 **Fx:**688-6457
(212) 980-0010 .. **Harris,** George N Jr. '01 (Kozusko HVW LLP) -575 Mad Av -NY 10022 **Fx:**751-0084
Harris, Ginger '89 -6 E 81st -NY 10028
(518) 436-1661 .. **Harris,** Gregory G '80 (Harris C&D,PLLC) -5 Clinton Sq -Albany 12207
(212) 651-7500 .. **Harris,** Gregory N '04 %Segal MS&M -850 3rd Av -NY 10022
(914) 668-4600 .. **Harris,** H Hawthorne '55 -Bx1275 -New Rchll 10802 **Fx:**668-4721
(212) 521-3500 .. **Harris,** Heidi E '91 (Aronson M&S, LLP) -485 Lex Av -NY 10017
(212) 297-5800 .. **Harris,** Helen M '99 (Day P LLP) -7 Times Sq -NY 10036
(212) 682-8383 .. **Harris,** I Robt '57 OfCnsl Kantor DWMT&G,PC -51 E 42nd -NY 10017
(914) 242-8282 .. **Harris,** I Ron '81 -69 S Bedford Rd -Mt Kisco 10549 **Fx:**241-2402
(212) 619-4350 .. **Harris,** Ian F '85 (Newman MKGH,PC) -14 Wall -NY 10005
(212) 228-7346 .. **Harris,** James A '99 -799 Bway -NY 10003
(212) 530-5000 .. **Harris,** James C '08 %Milbank TH&M LLP -1 Chase Manh Plz -NY 10005
(212) 657-0741 .. **Harris,** James L '83 -331 W 57th -NY 10019
(845) 343-3000 .. **Harris,** James P '88 (MacVean LS&M,PC) -34 Grove Bx310 -Middletwn 10940
(212) 849-7000 .. **Harris,** James W '07 Quinn EU&S,LLP -51 Mad Av -NY 10010
(212) 487-9701 .. **Harris,** Jeffrey J '88 (Robin HK&F) -1 Bttry Pk Plz -NY 10014
(212) 530-5000 .. **Harris,** Jennifer P '04 %Milbank TH&M LLP -1 Chase Manh Plz -NY 10005
(212) 858-1000 .. **Harris,** Jeremy R '01 %Pillsbury WSP LLP -1540 Bway -NY 10036
(212) 310-2201 .. **Harris,** Jodi Finder '06 Colgate-Palmolive -300 Park Av -NY 10022 **Fx:**310-3343
(718) 846-1500 .. **Harris,** John '89 -86-56 106th -Richmnd Hll 11418
(212) 223-0200 .. **Harris,** John B '86 (Stillman F&S,PC) -425 Park Av -NY 10022
(518) 427-9700 .. **Harris,** John S '93 (Harris B PLLC) -677 Bway -Albany 12207

(585) 624-3736 .. **Harris,** John T '94 (The Harris Law Firm) -13 N Main -Honeoye Fls 14472 **Fx:**624-1395
(212) 397-3370 .. **Harris,** Jonathan A '90 (Harris CC&H LLP) -111 Bway -NY 10006 **Fx:**202-6206
(212) 526-0457 .. **Harris,** Jonathan C '97 Barclays Capital Inc -1301 Av of Amer -NY 10019
(212) 407-4000 .. **Harris,** Joshua H '05 %Loeb & L,LLP -345 Park Av -NY 10154
(718) 579-7936 .. **Harris,** Judith L '91 %Leg Aid -900 Sheridan Av -Bronx 10451 **Fx:**293-8744
(212) 257-6455 .. **Harris,** Justine A '97 (Colson & H LLP) -10 E 40th -NY 10016 **Fx:**257-6453
(914) 683-0068 .. **Harris,** Katie A '10 %ST Baer -399 Knollwood Rd -White Plns 10603 **Fx:**683-0086
(212) 599-2085 .. **Harris,** Keith '94 (Braff H&S) -305 Bway -NY 10007
(212) 735-3000 .. **Harris,** Kimberly A '07 %Skadden ASM&F LLP -4 Times Sq -NY 10036
(212) 530-5000 .. **Harris,** L Douglas '80 (Milbank TH&M LLP) -1 Chase Manh Plz -NY 10005
(212) 223-0400 .. **Harris,** Lance G '92 (Stein & H) -575 Lex Av -NY 10022 **Fx:**833-0994
(516) 747-7800 .. **Harris,** Laureen C '83 (Cronin C&H,PC) -200 Old Cntry Rd -Mineola 11501
(212) 440-4400 .. **Harris,** Leslie J '95 Cnsl Buchanan I&R PC -620 8th Av -NY 10018
(212) 808-7800 .. **Harris,** Lisa M '08 %Kelley D&W LLP -101 Park Av -NY 10178
(518) 474-3514 .. **Harris,** Lisa R '95 %Consumer Protection Bd -5 ESP -Albany 12223 **Fx:**474-2474
(212) 552-1785 .. **Harris,** Lloyd G '79 JP Morgan Chase -1 Chase Manh Plz -NY 10081
(212) 456-7777 .. **Harris,** Lori '86 %ABC -77 W 66th -NY 10023 **Fx:**456-6202
(212) 756-2000 .. **Harris,** Marcy Ressler '87 (Schulte R&Z LLP) -919 3rd Av -NY 10022
(212) 848-4000 .. **Harris,** Marion R '10 Shearman & S LLP -599 Lex Av -NY 10022
(212) 969-3000 .. **Harris,** Mark D '05 (Proskauer R LLP) -1585 Bway -NY 10036
(212) 232-1300 .. **Harris,** Marsha E '07 %Lewis BB&S LLP -77 Water -NY 10005
(716) 847-8400 .. **Harris,** Martha M '91 (Phillips L LLP) -3400 HSBC Ctr -Buffalo 14203
(212) 909-6000 .. **Harris,** Matthew B '10 %Debevoise & P LLP -919 3rd Av -NY 10022
(718) 622-4104 .. **Harris,** Matthew J '97 -57 Mntgmry Pl -Brklyn 11215
(518) 474-2503 .. **Harris,** Maureen Finnegan '96 %Dept Pub Srvc -3 ESP -Albany 12223 **Fx:**474-2838
(718) 875-1300 .. **Harris,** Mel E '70 %Appllt Div 2nd Dept -45 Monroe Pl -Brklyn 11201 **Fx:**858-2446
(212) 571-4900 .. **Harris,** Mel S '65 -5 Hanover Sq -NY 10004 **Fx:**571-0965
(201) 447-0561 .. **Harris,** Micalyn S '81 Dispute Resolution Srvcs -27 W 44th -NY 10036 **Fx:**447-2547
(914) 798-5400 .. **Harris,** Michl F '89 (Goldberg S LLP) -11 Martine Av -White Plns 10606
(315) 472-1425 .. **Harris,** Michl W '68 (Harris & P) -120 E Wshngtn -Syracuse 13202
(718) 596-4877 .. **Harris,** Monique N '04 %J McMickens & Assoc,PLLC -26 Court -Brklyn 11242 **Fx:**596-5009
(212) 732-6620 .. **Harris,** Nicholas C '82 -20 Vesey -NY 10007
(845) 634-3344 .. **Harris,** Nicole M '01 Family Shelter -9 Johnsons Ln -New Cty 10956
(315) 472-1425 .. **Harris & Panels** -120 E Wshngtn -Syracuse 13202 **Fx:**472-2481
(212) 682-6800 .. **Harris,** Patricia Ann '90 (Zetlin & D LLP) -801 2nd Av -NY 10017
(212) 559-8827 .. **Harris,** Patrick E '84 Citigroup -666 5th Av -NY 10103
(914) 944-9378 .. **Harris,** Paule Apter '88 -51 Random Farms Cir -Chappaqua 10514 **Fx:**944-9378
(212) 735-3000 .. **Harris,** Philip H '86 (Skadden ASM&F LLP) -4 Times Sq -NY 10036
(631) 501-3100 .. **Harris,** Richd A '89 %J Humphreys -3 Huntngtn Quad Bx9028 -Melvll 11747 **Fx:**501-3085
(718) 275-3660 .. **Harris,** Richd T '95 (Harris Law Grp,LLP) -96-14 63rd Dr -Rego Pk 11374 **Fx:**275-3405
(212) 302-5252 .. **Harris,** Robt C '79 (Lazarus & H LLP) -561 7th Av -NY 10018 **Fx:**302-8181
(518) 434-3071 .. **Harris,** Robt E '71 -67 Columbia -Albany 12210
(914) 933-5729 .. **Harris,** Robt L '71 Parsons & Whittemore Inc -4 Intl Dr -Rye Brook 10573
(212) 872-6703 .. **Harris,** Sandra E '85 KPMG LLP -757 3rd Av -NY 10017
(212) 393-1000 .. **Harris,** Seth A '89 (Burns & H) -233 Bway -NY 10279
(212) 431-2826 .. **Harris,** Seth D '91 %NY Law Schl -185 W Bway -NY 10013 **Fx:**406-0103
(212) 530-5000 .. **Harris,** Shemetreal J '10 %Milbank TH&M LLP -1 Chase Manh Plz -NY 10005
(516) 569-2600 .. **Harris,** Sondra I '73 -30 Hempstd Av -Rockvll Ctr 11570 **Fx:**569-6331
(718) 287-0010 .. **Harris,** Stacey-Ann E '00 CAMBA Legal Srvcs -885 Flatbush Av -Brklyn 11226
(212) 593-7600 .. **Harris,** Steven R '81 (S Harris & Assoc) -110 E 59th -NY 10022
(212) 770-0988 .. **Harris,** Steven R '87 AIG -80 Pine -NY 10005
(518) 445-2535 .. **Harris,** Steven W '91 %Cordo & Co LLC -90 State -Albany 12207 **Fx:**445-2539
(212) 448-1100 .. **Harris,** T Randolph '80 (McLaughlin & S,LLP) -260 Mad Av -NY 10016
(212) 710-2758 .. **Harris,** Tamara Monet '06 -1115 Bway -NY 10010
(212) 532-4882 .. **Harris,** Theo '67 -2 Penn Plz -NY 10121 **Fx:**629-4568
(212) 554-0400 .. **Harris,** Theo P '90 (Grubman I&S,PC) -152 W 57th -NY 10019
(212) 490-3000 .. **Harris,** Theresa M '95 (Wilson EME&D LLP) -150 E 42nd -NY 10017
(212) 601-2680 .. **Harris,** Todd R '98 (Gonzalez S&H LLP) -350 5th Av -NY 10118
(212) 326-3939 .. **Harris,** Vandana P '07 %Jones D -222 E 41st -NY 10017
(212) 603-0204 .. **Harris,** Walter L '78 -320 W 57th -NY 10019 **Fx:**262-9470
(917) 778-6600 .. **Harris,** Warren T '81 %J Toomey -485 Lex Av -NY 10017 **Fx:**778-7048
(718) 522-5800 .. **Harris,** Wayne I '76 (Firestone & H) -32 Court -Brklyn 11201
(585) 263-1000 .. **Harris,** Wendell W '08 %Nixon P LLP -1100 Clinton Sq -Rchstr 14604
(212) 530-1800 .. **Harris,** Wendy A '01 Cnsl Richards K&O LLP -1 World Fncl Ctr -NY 10281
(518) 869-6227 .. **Harris,** Wm M '73 SrCnsl Lavelle & F,LLP -29 British Amer Blvd -Latham 12110 **Fx:**869-7024
(718) 590-5944 .. **Harris,** Yolanda '00 ACS-DLS -900 Sheridan Av -Bronx 10451
(315) 445-5608 .. **Harris-Courage,** Laura M '89 (Harris-Courage & G PLLC) -225 Greenfld Pkwy -Liverpool 13088 **Fx:**445-0738
(914) 995-3124 .. **Harrisingh,** F Elaine R '63 %Cnty Clerk -110 Martin Luther King Blvd -White Plns 10601 **Fx:**995-4030
(212) 855-9160 .. **Harrisingh,** John L '90 Goldman Sachs & Co -180 Maiden Ln -NY 10038
(914) 712-1100 .. **Harrison,** Andrew M '77 %Murphy & H,LLP -1 Radisson Plz -New Rchll 10801
(718) 279-8300 .. **Harrison,** Andrew T '83 -25-77 F Lewis Blvd -Flushng 11358 **Fx:**279-8986
(845) 339-4450 .. **Harrison,** Ann E '85 %NYSUT -201 Stockade Dr -Kingston 12401
(516) 483-0450 .. **Harrison,** Ann S '81 -576 Mad Av -W Hempstead 11552 **Fx:**485-9046
(516) 390-0808 .. **Harrison,** Brett J '92 (BJ Harrison,PC) -727 N Bway -Massapequa 11758 **Fx:**390-0810
(212) 259-8000 .. **Harrison,** Brittany L '08 %Dewey & L LLP -1301 Av of Amer -NY 10019
(212) 373-3000 .. **Harrison,** Carrie L '10 %Paul WRW&G LLP -1285 Av of Amer -NY 10019
(212) 756-2000 .. **Harrison,** Christopher S '01 %Schulte R&Z LLP -919 3rd Av -NY 10022
(212) 381-7000 .. **Harrison,** Cody J '05 %Sabin B&G LLP -4 Times Sq -NY 10036
(212) 403-7321 .. **Harrison,** David '05 %Pedowitz & M LLP -1501 Bway -NY 10036 **Fx:**354-6614
(516) 365-9191 .. **Harrison,** David A '74 %S Friedman -1 Hllw Ln -New Hyde Pk 11042 **Fx:**365-6138
(212) 779-1414 .. **Harrison,** David B '08 %Bernstein L LLP -10 E 40th -NY 10016
(914) 997-0500 .. **Harrison,** David C '81 (Lowey DC&H,PC) -1 N Bway -White Plns 10601
(914) 286-6800 .. **Harrison,** David H '99 5th St Capital -10 Bank -White Plns 10606
(718) 243-2109 .. **Harrison,** David M '94 -48 Willoughby -Brklyn 11201
Harrison, Elaine Margret '93 -7 Park Av -NY 10016
(212) 947-1999 .. **Harrison,** Eric L '94 (Methfessel & W,PC) -450 7th Av -NY 10123
(518) 438-2000 .. **Harrison,** Harlan R '62 (Lombardi WWHA&D PC) -III Winners Cir -Albany 12205
(516) 227-0700 .. **Harrison,** Heather P '05 %Farrell F,PC -1320 RXR Plz -Uniondale 11556
(585) 232-4878 .. **Harrison,** James A '94 (Harrison Law Ofc) -69 Cascade Dr -Rchstr 14614 **Fx:**232-8424
(585) 464-9400 .. **Harrison,** John E '87 %Wilmorite -1265 Scottsvll Rd -Rchstr 14624 **Fx:**328-1784
(212) 225-2000 .. **Harrison,** John V '02 %Cleary GS&H -1 Lbrty Plz -NY 10006
(212) 785-9100 .. **Harrison,** Katherine B '88 (Paduano & W LLP) -1251 Av of Amer -NY 10020
(212) 801-2161 .. **Harrison,** Lauren C '09 %Greenberg T,LLP -200 Park Av -NY 10166
(212) 696-4848 .. **Harrison,** Lisabeth '80 %Mintz & G LLP -470 Park Av S -NY 10016
(212) 833-6413 .. **Harrison,** Lori E '04 Sony Corp of America -550 Mad Av -NY 10022
(212) 696-6000 .. **Harrison,** Lynn P 3rd '84 (Curtis M-PC&M LLP) -101 Park Av -NY 10178
(212) 946-2873 .. **Harrison,** Michl III '88 -11 Penn Plz -NY 10001
(212) 773-6343 .. **Harrison,** Nina E '07 Ernst & Young -5 Times Sq -NY 10036
(516) 622-9200 .. **Harrison,** Richd F '82 OfCnsl Westerman BEM&S,LLP -1201 RXR Plz -Uniondale 11553
(212) 949-8700 .. **Harrison,** Robt E '68 %Eisner LLP -750 3rd Av -NY 10017 **Fx:**891-4100
(917) 797-9384 .. **Harrison,** Robt S '82 Clinton Global Initative -1301 Av of Amer -NY 10019
(718) 468-7071 .. **Harrison,** Rohan F '95 -208-07 Hillside Av -Qns Vllg 11427 **Fx:**468-6922
(718) 261-0600 .. **Harrison & Rothbard PC** -105-15 Metro Av -Frst Hlls 11375 **Fx:**261-7516
(212) 687-7770 .. **Harrison,** S David '68 OfCnsl Rosen L&C LLP -275 Mad Av -NY 10016
(212) 837-6000 .. **Harrison,** Spencer L '76 (Hughes H&R LLP) -1 Bttry Pk Plz -NY 10004
(718) 745-1797 .. **Harrison,** Stephen A '75 -544 Bay Ridge Pkwy -Brklyn 11209 **Fx:**745-2786
(518) 591-5232 .. **Harrison,** Stephen J '74 %NYS ORPTS -WA Harriman State Campus -Albany 12227 **Fx:**474-3657
(718) 568-3507 .. **Harrison,** Timothy C '82 -900 South Av -Staten Isl 10314
(646) 557-5125 .. **Harrison,** Todd R '97 Patton B LLP -1185 Av of Amer -NY 10036
(212) 450-4000 .. **Harriss,** Lowell Gordon '72 (Davis P&W LLP) -450 Lex Av -NY 10017
(212) 336-3500 .. **Harrist,** Erin B '08 %Miller & W,PC -570 Lex Av -NY 10022
(914) 730-3400 .. **Harriton,** Keith S '80 (Harriton & F,LLP) -84 Business Park Dr -Armonk 10504 **Fx:**730-3405
(212) 759-4600 .. **Harrod,** James A III '00 (Wolf P LLP) -845 3rd Av -NY 10022
(212) 872-1000 .. **Harrop,** Dawn M '10 -One Bryant Park -NY 10036 **Fx:**872-1002
(866) 348-5819 .. **Harrop,** Grenville W Jr. '72 %SSA-ODAR -50 Fountain Plz -Buffalo 14202 **Fx:**(716) 551-4078
(212) 675-3684 .. **Harrow,** Arthur L '52 -43 Barrow -NY 10014
(718) 487-2300 .. **Harrow,** Beth A '85 %Leg Srvcs Corp -256-260 Bway -Brklyn 11211 **Fx:**782-6790
(212) 754-4800 .. **Harrow,** Howard S '87 (Becker H LLP) -730 3rd Av -NY 10017 **Fx:**253-4198
(518) 474-3032 .. **Harrow,** Richd S '79 %Medicaid Fraud Cntrl -The Cptl -Albany 12223 **Fx:**474-4519
(212) 801-6420 .. **Harsch,** Ryan F '08 %Greenberg T,LLP -200 Park Av -NY 10166
(212) 425-7200 .. **Harsche,** Caryn L '08 %Kenyon & K,LLP -1 Bway -NY 10004
(315) 218-8000 .. **Harshbarger,** Laura H '98 (Bond S&K,PLLC) -1 Lincoln Ctr -Syracuse 13202
(212) 819-8200 .. **Harsu,** Henrikki Juhana '05 %White & C LLP -1155 Av of Amer -NY 10036
(212) 839-5300 .. **Hart,** Andrew D '05 %Sidley A LLP -787 7th Av -NY 10019
(212) 815-7530 .. **Hart,** Anne-Miriam '82 OfCnsl PELS -125 Barclay -NY 10007 **Fx:**815-7534
(212) 661-6800 .. **Hart,** Avely '92 (Cyruli SH&Z LLP) -420 Lex Av -NY 10170
(914) 997-0500 .. **Hart,** Barbara J '93 (Lowey DC&H,PC) -1 N Bway -White Plns 10601
(212) 791-7200 .. **Hart Baxley Daniels & Holton** -90 John -NY 10038 **Fx:**791-7276
(212) 244-2999 .. **Hart,** Caramia R '92 (Kopff N&D LLP) -440 9th Av -NY 10001
(716) 838-8319 .. **Hart,** Chas W '02 -58 Springvll Av -Amherst 14226 **Fx:**837-1199

(516) 281-9800 .. **Hart,** Christopher M '02 %Goldberg S LLP -200 Old Cntry Rd -Mineola 11501
(212) 326-3939 .. **Hart,** Colleen M '00 %Jones D -222 E 41st -NY 10017
(585) 428-2065 .. **Hart,** Constance J '78 %City Ct -Hall of Justice Rm 1 -Rchstr 14614 **Fx:**428-2985
(212) 551-1755 .. **Hart,** Donna M '96 Lombard & G LLP -230 Park Av -NY 10169 **Fx:**(646) 349-5567
(212) 788-0835 .. **Hart,** Edw F X '79 %Law Dept -100 Church -NY 10007 **Fx:**788-0367
(212) 870-2801 .. **Hart,** Ernest F '84 Columbia Univ -475 Riverside Dr -NY 10115
(845) 794-3344 .. **Hart,** Jared K '10 %DA -414 Bway -Monticello 12701 **Fx:**794-3646
(212) 455-2000 .. **Hart,** John C '80 (Simpson T&B LLP) -425 Lex Av -NY 10017
(585) 258-7461 .. **Hart,** John C '84 %JP Morgan Chase -1 Chase Sq -Rchstr 14643 **Fx:**258-6458
(212) 791-7200 .. **Hart,** John J '34 (Hart BD&H) -90 John -NY 10038
(716) 373-1600 .. **Hart,** John M Jr. '71 (Wagner & H) -214 N Barry -Olean 14760
(212) 586-0700 .. **Hart,** Jos T C '62 (Fulton R&H,LLP) -1 Rckfllr Plz -NY 10020
(212) 848-4000 .. **Hart,** Karen S '89 %Shearman & S LLP -599 Lex Av -NY 10022
(212) 264-0652 .. **Hart,** Kevin B '00 %US DOJ Antitrust Div -26 Fed Plz Ste 3630 -NY 10278
(212) 670-0150 .. **Hart,** Lauryn J '96 SrCnsl Merrill Lynch -222 Bway -NY 10038 **Fx:**670-0729
(914) 377-6240 .. **Hart,** Leon P '90 %Law Dept -300 City Hall -Ynkrs 10701 **Fx:**964-0563
(212) 837-6000 .. **Hart,** Lisa J '90 Cnsl Hughes H&R LLP -1 Bttry Pk Plz -NY 10004
(718) 246-8200 .. **Hart,** Lonnie Jr. '99 -44 Court -Brklyn 11201
(212) 356-4794 .. **Hart,** Mary T '98 St Vincent Catholic Med Ctr -450 W 33rd -NY 10001
(716) 662-2611 .. **Hart,** Nancy E '85 -39 Edgewtr Dr -Orchard Pk 14127 **Fx:**662-1039
(212) 351-4000 .. **Hart,** Nancy E '06 %Gibson D&C LLP -200 Park Av -NY 10166
(212) 450-2000 .. **Hart,** Nichol A '06 %NFL -280 Park Av -NY 10017 **Fx:**681-7599
(212) 819-8200 .. **Hart,** Nicole R '06 %White & C LLP -1155 Av of Amer -NY 10036
(607) 738-6138 .. **Hart,** Paul R '78 -460 E Market -Elmira 14901 **Fx:**737-8426
(212) 312-2355 .. **Hart,** Peter '84 %Leg Aid -60 Lafayette -NY 10013 **Fx:**349-0874
(917) 637-3600 .. **Hart,** Rebecca A '09 %Ctr for Reproductive Rts -120 Wall -NY 10005 **Fx:**637-3666
(212) 752-1356 .. **Hart,** Robt M '69 Alleghany Corp -7 Times Sq Twr -NY 10036 **Fx:**759-3295
(212) 766-1443 .. **Hart,** Ronald Paul '86 -225 Bway -NY 10007 **Fx:**766-0943
(212) 508-7272 .. **Hart,** Ronni Lynn '81 %Halstead Mgmt -770 Lex Av -NY 10065
(212) 805-4816 .. **Hart,** Stephanie E '01 %Hon CB Motley -500 Pearl -NY 10007
(917) 232-5800 .. **Hart,** Susan B '92 -61-23 190th -Fresh Mdws 11365 **Fx:**(718) 228-7110
(718) 523-0100 .. **Hart,** Susan E '89 %Newman & N -148-55 Hillside Av -Jamaica 11435 **Fx:**523-9477
(518) 462-5601 .. **Hart,** Timothy S '01 (O'Connell & A) -54 State -Albany 12207
(212) 808-6750 .. **Hart,** Tishawah D '03 NTT America,Inc -101 Park Av -NY 10178
(914) 472-7280 .. **Hart,** Wm '63 -700 Wht Plns Rd -Scarsdale 10583 **Fx:**472-7285
(585) 396-8841 .. **Hart,** Wm J '89 %DA -27 N Main -Canandaigua 14424 **Fx:**396-4860
(212) 969-3000 .. **Hart,** Wm M '82 (Proskauer R LLP) -1585 Bway -NY 10036
(516) 542-0100 .. **Hartell,** Cheryl Ann '97 %MTA/LI Bus -700 Cmmrcial Av -Gdn Cty 11530
(585) 530-3119 .. **Harter,** Jessica L '00 Appllt Div 4th Dept -50 East Av Ste 200 -Rchstr 14604 **Fx:**530-3247
(585) 342-4410 .. **Harter,** Ralph M Peter '81 OfCnsl Burke AH&R,LLP -1800 Hudson Av -Rchstr 14617
(585) 232-6500 .. **Harter Secrest & Emery LLP** -1600 Bausch & Lomb Pl -Rchstr 14604 **Fx:**232-2152
(716) 853-1616 .. **Harter Secrest & Emery LLP** -12 Fountain Plz -Buffalo 14202 **Fx:**853-1617
(518) 434-4377 .. **Harter Secrest & Emery LLP** -111 Wshngtn Av -Albany 12210 **Fx:**449-4025
(347) 462-9900 .. **Hartfield,** Zenobia T '02 %Shapiro & S,LLP -3145 Coney Isl Av -Brklyn 11235
(716) 632-8328 .. **Hartford,** Robt L '87 (Epstein & H) -2350 N Forest Rd -Getzvll 14068 **Fx:**632-3125
(212) 289-4000 .. **Hartig,** Helene W '85 -233 E 86th -NY 10028 **Fx:**289-2020
(718) 343-4450 .. **Hartigan,** Patricia A '93 -80-11 256th -Floral Pk 11004 **Fx:**343-4450
(631) 727-6899 .. **Hartill,** Mary C '99 (Saladino & H,LLP) -431 Griffing Av -Rvrhead 11901
(914) 234-6313 .. **Harting,** Carolyn E '84 -Route 22 Bx218 -Bedfrd 10506 **Fx:**234-9724
(516) 248-8610 .. **Hartlein,** Wm D '86 (Ryan P&H,PC) -200 Old Cntry Rd -Mineola 11501
(888) 543-2788 .. **Hartley,** Gabrielle Mollo '96 -266 Smith -Brklyn 11231
(845) 483-0800 .. **Hartley,** Lisa E '91 L Hartley,PC -66 Forbus -Poughkeepsie 12603 **Fx:**483-0847
(212) 442-2554 .. **Hartley,** Peter A '07 ACS -220 Church -NY 10013
(212) 849-7000 .. **Hartley,** Sarah L '08 %Quinn EU&S,LLP -51 Mad Av -NY 10010
(212) 848-4000 .. **Hartley,** W Fraser '08 %Shearman & S LLP -599 Lex Av -NY 10022
(212) 753-7500 .. **Hartman & Craven LLP** -488 Mad Av -NY 10022 **Fx:**688-2870
(716) 856-9533 .. **Hartman,** Danl J '79 (Hartman & R PC) -403 Main -Buffalo 14203
(212) 986-5576 .. **Hartman,** Danl M '92 -489 5th Av -NY 10017 **Fx:**867-6303
(718) 286-6000 .. **Hartman,** Danielle L '05 %DA -125-01 Qns Blvd -Kew Gdns 11415
(631) 753-0200 .. **Hartman,** Dara M '03 %A Crabtree,PC -225 Broadhllw Rd -Melvll 11747 **Fx:**753-0950
(212) 458-2333 .. **Hartman,** David E '92 GM Asset Mgmt -767 5th Av -NY 10153
(518) 945-1111 .. **Hartman,** Denise '84 %Dept of Law -The Cptl -Albany 12224
(212) 424-2232 .. **Hartman,** Donna H '92 Rémy Cointreau,USA,Inc -1290 Av of Amer -NY 10104
(212) 697-1111 .. **Hartman,** Fagie '95 L-3 Cmmnctns Corp -600 3rd Av -NY 10016 **Fx:**682-7959
(585) 381-3288 .. **Hartman,** James M '54 -15 Oakfld Way -Pittsfrd 14534 **Fx:**218-0071
(607) 763-9200 .. **Hartman,** John H '74 OfCnsl Levene G&T,LLP -BxF-1706 -Bnghmtn 13902
(518) 455-2390 .. **Hartman,** Laura S '95 %NYS Senate -812 LOB -Albany 12247 **Fx:**426-6975
(212) 788-3300 .. **Hartman,** Mark A '77 Cnsl Hlth & Hsptl Corp -125 Worth -NY 10013 **Fx:**267-6905
(212) 869-3500 .. **Hartman,** Melvin C '55 OfCnsl J Fuchsberg Law Firm,LLP -500 5th Av -NY 10110 **Fx:**398-1532
(212) 872-9800 .. **Hartman,** Michl P '07 %Squire S&D LLP -30 Rckfllr Plz -NY 10112
(914) 738-6076 .. **Hartman,** Regina M '98 (Pinto & C,LLP) -210 6th Av -Pelham 10803 **Fx:**712-0647
(716) 856-9533 .. **Hartman & Ridall PC** -403 Main -Buffalo 14203 **Fx:**853-2892
(631) 853-4104 .. **Hartman,** Robbin '88 %DA -400 Carleton Av Bx9082 -Central Islip 11722 **Fx:**853-7838
(212) 437-9110 .. **Hartman,** Robt S '74 (Hartman UR&R,LLP) -305 Bway -NY 10007
(212) 437-9110 .. **Hartman Ule Rose & Ratner,LLP** -305 Bway -NY 10007 **Fx:**571-0831
(607) 741-3930 .. **Hartman,** Wm R '90 State Ins Fund -2001 Perimeter Rd E -Endicott 13760 **Fx:**741-5029
(212) 770-7000 .. **Hartmann,** Gregory A '89 AIG -70 Pine -NY 10270
(607) 746-2152 .. **Hartmann,** James M '75 -Route 10 Bx206 -Delhi 13753 **Fx:**746-6775
(718) 815-1080 .. **Hartmann,** Jean M '90 -345 Bement Av -Staten Isl 10310
(631) 244-1489 .. **Hartmann,** Susan E '02 -80 Orvll Dr -Bohemia 11716 **Fx:**207-8373
(212) 307-5500 .. **Hartmere,** Michl C '02 %Venable LLP -1270 Av of Amer -NY 10020
(845) 624-1966 .. **Hartnagel,** Wm J '91 (Brown B&H,PC) -365 Route 304 -Bardonia 10954
(607) 753-3551 .. **Hartnett,** David S '84 -36 Main Bx866 -Cortlnd 13045 **Fx:**756-8768
(716) 691-0010 .. **Hartnett,** Donna M '97 Ivoclar Vivadent -175 Pinevw Dr -Amherst 14228
(315) 474-7571 .. **Hartnett,** Elizabeth A '75 (Mackenzie H LLP) -101 S Salina Bx4967 -Syracuse 13221
(631) 852-1650 .. **Hartnett,** James P '71 %Leg Aid -300 Center Dr -Rvrhead 11901 **Fx:**852-1655
(518) 783-7977 .. **Hartnett,** Jeffrey S '97 NYSUT -800 Troy-Schnctdy Rd -Latham 12110
(518) 565-3317 .. **Hartnett,** Michl J '07 %Dept Social Srvcs -13 Durkee -Plattsbrgh 12901 **Fx:**565-3626
(212) 964-9282 .. **Hartnett,** Nicole M '06 %N Weinrib & Assoc -305 Bway -NY 10007 **Fx:**964-9525
(315) 471-6265 .. **Hartnett,** Peter M '85 %CJ Billinson & Assoc -342 S Salina -Syracuse 13202 **Fx:**474-3153
(212) 701-3000 .. **Hartnett,** Wm M '80 (Cahill G&R LLP) -80 Pine -NY 10005 **Fx:**269-5420
(212) 949-9022 .. **Hartnick,** Alan J '53 (Abelman F&S) -666 3rd Av -NY 10017
(716) 847-8400 .. **Hart-Nova,** Tara J '98 SpclCnsl Phillips L LLP -3400 HSBC Ctr -Buffalo 14203
(718) 274-0010 .. **Hartofelis,** Michl X '91 -40-12 31st Av -Astoria 11103 **Fx:**274-5955
(212) 416-6295 .. **Hartofilis,** Maria B '95 %Dept of Law -120 Bway -NY 10271
(718) 274-8200 .. **Hartofilis,** Michl J '87 -3117 Ditmars Blvd -Astoria 11105
(212) 687-2770 .. **Hartoonian,** Mher '04 %Cohen PL&P -551 5th Av -NY 10176
(212) 679-4363 .. **Hartsfield,** Joyce Y '79 -381 Park Av S -NY 10016 **Fx:**213-1092
(212) 526-7000 .. **Hartstein,** Danl E '07 Barclays Capital -745 7th Av -NY 10019
(845) 624-2216 .. **Hartstein,** David S '70 (Hartstein & H) -6 Yllwstn Dr -W Nyack 10994
(845) 624-2216 .. **Hartstein,** Saml '75 (Hartstein & H) -6 Yllwstn Dr -W Nyack 10994
(212) 806-3269 .. **Hartung,** David D '97 DBRS -140 Bway -NY 10005
(518) 431-0247 .. **Hartunian,** Richd S '87 %US Atty -445 Bway -Albany 12207 **Fx:**431-0249
(718) 250-2000 .. **Hartwell,** Fredk S '89 %DA -350 Jay -Brklyn 11201 **Fx:**250-2314
(607) 962-9524 .. **Hartwell,** Mark E '97 Corning Cmmnty Cllg -1 Academic Dr -Corning 14830
(315) 798-5870 .. **Hartwell,** Tina L '01 %Pub Def -321 Main -Utica 13501 **Fx:**798-6419
(212) 551-4034 .. **Hart-White,** Susan M '87 Sanofi-Synthelabo Inc -90 Park Av -NY 10016
(212) 609-6800 .. **Harty,** David J '02 %McCarter & E,LLP -245 Park Av -NY 10167
(212) 450-4000 .. **Harty,** Ronan P '87 (Davis P&W LLP) -450 Lex Av -NY 10017
(212) 583-9600 .. **Hartz,** Richd L '74 (Littler M,PC) -900 3rd Av -NY 10022
(518) 449-3300 .. **Hartzell,** John V '99 %Nolan & H,LLP -39 N Pearl -Albany 12207
(585) 586-0220 .. **Hartzell,** Melinda K '92 OfCnsl Finucane & H,LLP -6 N Main -Pittsfrd 14534
(585) 586-5900 .. **Hartzell,** Thos C Sr. '60 OfCnsl Finucane & H,LLP -6 N Main -Pittsfrd 14534
(585) 586-0220 .. **Hartzell,** Thos C Jr. '86 (Finucane & H,LLP) -6 N Main -Pittsfrd 14534
(212) 455-2000 .. **Harunari,** Makiko '08 %Simpson T&B LLP -425 Lex Av -NY 10017
(516) 677-9400 .. **Harutunian,** Tamar '02 %Goldstein & A -575 Underhill Blvd -Syosset 11791
(212) 382-0909 .. **Harvat,** Christian J '08 %Peckar & A,PC -41 Mad Av -NY 10154
(518) 457-4951 .. **Harvey,** Andrew T '82 %Dept Correctional Srvcs -1220 Wshngtn Av -Albany 12226 **Fx:**457-7555
(585) 263-6760 .. **Harvey,** Brett A '96 %US Atty -620 Fed Bldg -Rchstr 14614 **Fx:**263-6226
(212) 813-8800 .. **Harvey,** Brian W '00 (Goodwin P LLP) -620 8th Av -NY 10018
(516) 877-5600 .. **Harvey,** Charmaine Fox '91 %R Tusa -1225 Franklin Av -Gdn Cty 11530 **Fx:**877-5695
(212) 872-1000 .. **Harvey,** Christopher S '91 -One Bryant Park -NY 10036 **Fx:**872-1002
(212) 816-0271 .. **Harvey,** Denise J '85 Citibank NA -388 Greenwich -NY 10013
(212) 532-5000 .. **Harvey,** Francis J Jr. '70 -260 Mad Av -NY 10016
(212) 972-8935 .. **Harvey & Hackett** -420 Lex Av -NY 10170
(212) 541-7800 .. **Harvey,** Hosea H III '02 Planned Parenthood -434 W 33rd -NY 10001 **Fx:**868-4677
(518) 426-4600 .. **Harvey,** Jennifer '10 %Couch W,LLP -540 Bway Bx22222 -Albany 12201
(518) 487-5460 .. **Harvey,** Jennifer E '09 %DA -6 Lodge -Albany 12207 **Fx:**487-5093
(212) 921-8399 .. **Harvey,** Joanne M '99 %Lankler S&W LLP -500 5th Av -NY 10110
(518) 463-4491 .. **Harvey,** Jonathan P '67 (JP Harvey,PLLC) -677 Bway -Albany 12207 **Fx:**463-5665
(631) 694-2300 .. **Harvey,** Mara N '04 %Lamb & B,LLP -534 Broadhllw Rd Bx9034 -Melvll 11747
(212) 360-1393 .. **Harvey,** Nancy S '98 %Dept of Parks & Rec -The Arsenal Cntrl Pk -NY 10065 **Fx:**360-1373
(718) 286-6000 .. **Harvey,** Paul H '89 %DA -125-01 Qns Blvd -Kew Gdns 11415
(212) 682-4900 .. **Harvey Pennington Ltd** -230 Park Av -NY 10169 **Fx:**697-8486
(212) 336-2000 .. **Harvey,** Peter C '84 (Patterson BW&T LLP) -1133 Av of Amer -NY 10036

(212) 224-4136 .. **Harvey,** Peter J '88 %Sumitomo Mitsui -277 Park Av -NY 10172 **Fx:**224-5188
(212) 864-4445 .. **Harvey,** Richd J '82 (Stevens H&W,PC) -116 W 111th -NY 10026
(866) 348-5819 .. **Harvey,** Robt T '79 %SSA-ODAR -50 Fountain Plz -Buffalo 14202 **Fx:**(716) 551-4078
(516) 877-2424 .. **Harvey,** Rosanne '85 Weinberg G&P LLP -400 Grdn City Plz -Gdn Cty 11530
(212) 972-8935 .. **Harvey,** Thos A '91 (Harvey & H) -420 Lex Av -NY 10170
(716) 689-5648 .. **Harvey,** Timothy R '79 %Columbus McKinnon Corp -140 JJ Audobon Pkway -Amherst 14228
(518) 457-5628 .. **Harvin,** Natasha M '03 DCJS -4 Twr Pl -Albany 12203 **Fx:**457-3089
(212) 788-1816 .. **Harvis,** Gabriel P '07 %Law Dept -100 Church -NY 10007 **Fx:**788-0367
(212) 610-6300 .. **Harwich,** A Peter '92 (Allen & O) -1221 Av of Amer -NY 10020
(518) 783-3843 .. **Harwick,** John F '96 %Hacker & M,LLP -7 Airport Park Blvd -Latham 12110
(212) 986-2966 .. **Harwitz,** Jonathan M '93 %Corp Supportive Housing -50 Bway -NY 10004 **Fx:**986-6552
(212) 474-1000 .. **Harwood,** Christopher B '04 %Cravath S&M LLP -825 8th Av -NY 10019
(646) 822-1801 .. **Harwood,** Donald A '88 (Itkowitz & H) -305 Bway -NY 10007 **Fx:**(212) 822-1409
(212) 935-7400 .. **Harwood Feffer LLP** -488 Mad Av -NY 10022 **Fx:**753-3630
(212) 885-5000 .. **Harwood,** Jeremy J O '89 (Blank R LLP) -405 Lex Av -NY 10174
(914) 347-2600 .. **Harwood,** Jonathan '90 (Traub LS&S LLP) -7 Skyline Dr -Hawthorne 10532
(212) 268-5136 .. **Harwood Lloyd** -350 5th Av -NY 10118 **Fx:**564-1135
(212) 506-1700 .. **Harwood,** Michl C '83 (Kasowitz BT&F LLP) -1633 Bway -NY 10019
(212) 696-6000 .. **Harwood,** Miriam K '88 (Curtis M-PC&M LLP) -101 Park Av -NY 10178
(212) 935-7400 .. **Harwood,** Robt I '72 (Harwood F LLP) -488 Mad Av -NY 10022
(212) 363-1380 .. **Harz,** Steven B '77 (Herten BSCBL&H,LLC) -747 3rd Av -NY 10017
(212) 506-3900 .. **Hasan,** Shehzad '97 OfCnsl Steptoe & J LLP -750 7th Av -NY 10019
(212) 227-9192 .. **Hasan,** Syed V '96 (Hasan & Assoc,PLLC) -30 Vesey -NY 10007
(914) 533-3049 .. **Hasapidis,** Annette G '92 -450 Oak Rdg Cmmns -S Salem 10590 **Fx:**533-3051 ***[Appellate Practice]***
(914) 946-5100 .. **Hasapidis,** Annette G '92 OfCnsl Bashian & F,LLP -235 Main -White Plns 10601
(212) 488-0469 .. **Hasday,** Michl J '02 Frenkel & Co,Inc -350 Hudson -NY 10014
(212) 692-1000 .. **Hasday,** Robt J '76 (Duane M LLP) -1540 Bway -NY 10036
(585) 232-6500 .. **Haselbauer,** Eric D '05 %Harter S&E LLP -1600 Bausch & Lomb Pl -Rchstr 14604
(585) 428-5210 .. **Haselbauer,** Karine '05 Pub Def -10 N Fitzhugh -Rchstr 14614 **Fx:**428-2234
(716) 439-8380 .. **Haseley,** Timothy D '89 -556 S Transit -Lockprt 14094
(212) 701-3000 .. **Haselkorn,** Y Aryeh '04 %Cahill G&R LLP -80 Pine -NY 10005 **Fx:**269-5420
(212) 877-8828 .. **Haselnuss,** Solomon '80 -498 West End Av -NY 10024
(212) 698-3500 .. **Hasenauer,** Brooke G '07 %Dechert LLP -1095 Av of Amer -NY 10036
(212) 272-7117 .. **Hasenzahl,** Catherine E '02 %JP Morgan Chase -383 Mad Av -NY 10179
(212) 223-3977 .. **Haserot,** Robt B '67 -60 Sutton Pl S -NY 10022
(650) 704-7261 .. **Hashemi,** Yasamine '10 -628 Hudson -NY 10014
(516) 535-1700 .. **Hasher,** Brian M '06 Horing W&R,PC -11 Hillside Av -Williston Pk 11596
(718) 743-4400 .. **Hasher,** Dennis B '77 %Trump Mngmnt Inc -2611 W 2nd -Brklyn 11223
(212) 715-1000 .. **Hashimoto,** Ken L '04 %Arnold & P LLP -399 Park Av -NY 10022
(718) 805-1271 .. **Hashinsky,** Joel '64 (Hashinsky & A) -101-05 Lefferts Blvd -S Richmond Hll 11419 **Fx:**805-1411
(718) 441-3348 .. **Hashinsky,** Todd D '02 -101-05 Lefferts Blvd -S Richmond Hll 11419
(212) 813-8800 .. **Hashmall,** David M '78 (Goodwin P LLP) -620 8th Av -NY 10018
(914) 761-9111 .. **Hashmall,** Jay B '78 (Bank SS&H) -399 Knollwood Rd -White Plns 10603
(212) 369-7101 .. **Hashmall,** Wendy Harrison '78 -488 Mad Av -NY 10022
(845) 928-1013 .. **Hasin,** David V '93 -5 Corp Dr -Centrl Vly 10917
(845) 928-1013 .. **Hasin,** Marcy Isaacs '93 -Bx332 -Highland Mills 10930
(212) 508-6700 .. **Haskel,** Brian A '91 (Tannenbaum HS&H LLP) -900 3rd Av -NY 10022
(212) 686-7700 .. **Haskel,** Jules J '55 OfCnsl Mazur CR&S PC -1250 Bway -NY 10001
(516) 294-0250 .. **Haskel,** Michl A '76 -167 Willis Av -Mineola 11501 **Fx:**294-0854
(212) 530-1800 .. **Haskel,** Paul B '89 (Richards K&O LLP) -1 World Fncl Ctr -NY 10281
(212) 962-1020 .. **Haskel,** Stacey '92 %M Lamonsoff -80 Maiden Ln -NY 10038 **Fx:**962-3078
(516) 294-0250 .. **Haskel,** Susan '05 %M Haskel -167 Willis Av -Mineola 11501 **Fx:**294-0854
(212) 446-4800 .. **Haskel,** Warren '09 %Kirkland & E LLP -153 E 53rd -NY 10022
(212) 484-8000 .. **Haskell,** Gabrielle Kleinman '99 %Time Warner -1 Time Warner Ctr -NY 10019
(212) 752-5507 .. **Haskell Slaughter Young & Rediker,LLC** -515 Mad Av -NY 10022 **Fx:**935-6424
(518) 447-3200 .. **Haskin,** Michelle Lee '95 (McNamee LT&W,PC) -677 Bway -Albany 12207
(347) 404-9133 .. **Haskin,** Turquoise '07 Civil Ct -141 Lvngstn -Brklyn 11201 **Fx:**(718) 643-3733
(212) 566-1000 .. **Haskins,** Courtney M '08 %Sullivan & B LLP -115 Bway -NY 10006 **Fx:**566-1068
(845) 471-4455 .. **Haskins,** Robt R '85 (Steinberg S&P,LLP) -27 Grdn -Poughkeepsie 12601
(212) 903-9000 .. **Haskins,** Thos G '10 %Linklaters -1345 Av of Amer -NY 10105
(716) 856-3646 .. **Haslinger,** Donna L '91 (Cole SHH&G,PC) -37 Franklin -Buffalo 14202
(716) 854-2907 .. **Haslinger,** John E '75 Chicago Title Ins -424 Main -Buffalo 14202 **Fx:**852-7346
(212) 326-3939 .. **Haspel,** Ahron H '69 OfCnsl Jones D -222 E 41st -NY 10017
(845) 294-8950 .. **Haspel,** Jos J '84 -40 Mathews -Goshen 10924 **Fx:**294-3843
(212) 375-6659 .. **Hass,** Erwin '72 (Hass & H,LLP) -135 W 50th -NY 10020 **Fx:**375-6888
(914) 725-2600 .. **Hass,** Jeffrey K '74 (Hass & G) -670 Wht Plns Rd -Scarsdale 10583 **Fx:**725-7724
(212) 318-6000 .. **Hass,** Lawr J '72 (Paul HJ&W LLP) -75 E 55th -NY 10022
(212) 345-5480 .. **Hass,** Michl A '77 %Marsh USA -1166 Av of Amer -NY 10036 **Fx:**345-4808
(212) 837-6793 .. **Hassan,** Amina '08 %Hughes H&R LLP -1 Bttry Pk Plz -NY 10004 **Fx:**299-6793
(718) 847-3757 .. **Hassan,** Dolly Zulakha '92 Liberty Ctr for Immigrants -125-09 Jamaica Av -Richmnd Hll 11418
(212) 530-5000 .. **Hassan,** Elena H '10 %Milbank TH&M LLP -1 Chase Manh Plz -NY 10005
(212) 504-6000 .. **Hassan,** James S '94 (Cadwalader W&T LLP) -1 World Fncl Ctr -NY 10281
(212) 858-4481 .. **Hassan,** Margo A '87 FINRA -1 Lbrty Plz -NY 10006
(212) 909-9500 .. **Hassan,** Michl S '81 OfCnsl Wachtel & M,LLP -885 2nd Av -NY 10017
(631) 465-5000 .. **Hassan,** Sofia '08 %K Tenenbaum,PC -225 Old Cntry Rd -Melvll 11747 **Fx:**465-5003
(631) 650-2305 .. **Hassberg,** Linda R '92 %Empire Justice Ctr -225 Eastvw Dr -Central Islip 11722 **Fx:**348-3571
(212) 346-8803 .. **Hasselbach,** Richd E '85 %Manhattan Comm Cllg -199 Chmbrs -NY 10007
(315) 493-0030 .. **Hasseler,** Lawr D '75 (Conboy MB&K,LLP) -307 State -Carthage 13619
(914) 663-1869 .. **Hasselman,** Barbara M '99 -216 Rich Av -Mt Vernon 10552
(212) 813-8800 .. **Hassett,** Annemarie '97 (Goodwin P LLP) -620 8th Av -NY 10018
(716) 854-2620 .. **Hassett,** Paul Michl '65 (Brown & K,LLP) -1500 Lbrty Bldg -Buffalo 14202
(516) 794-7340 .. **Hassett,** Wm P '00 %Fager & A,LLP -90 Merrick Av -E Meadow 11554
(914) 769-3942 .. **Hassi,** David G '62 -9 High Ridge Ct -Plsntvll 10570
(212) 326-2000 .. **Hassi,** Ted '96 (O'Melveny & M LLP) -7 Times Sq -NY 10036
(212) 421-4932 .. **Hassid,** Jack '71 -460 Park Av -NY 10022 **Fx:**421-5086
(516) 536-6067 .. **Hassin,** Michl D '84 -330 Sunrise Hwy -Rockvll Ctr 11570 **Fx:**536-3122
(716) 878-9364 .. **Hassinger,** Susan M '86 %Benderson Dvlpmnt -570 Delaware Av -Buffalo 14202 **Fx:**886-2269
(212) 335-9000 .. **Hassler,** Hilary '80 %DA -1 Hogan Pl -NY 10013
(212) 450-4000 .. **Hassman,** Julie '08 %Davis P&W LLP -450 Lex Av -NY 10017
(914) 637-5848 .. **Hasson,** Adam I '03 Sidney Frank Importing Co -20 Cedar -New Rchll 10801
(212) 447-7070 .. **Hasson,** Laurence J '07 %Whatley D&K LLC -1540 Bway -NY 10036
(212) 259-8000 .. **Hassouri,** Parimah '09 %Dewey & L LLP -1301 Av of Amer -NY 10019
(212) 312-2299 .. **Hassuk,** Adam '93 %Leg Aid -199 Water -NY 10038 **Fx:**577-3520
(212) 335-4172 .. **Hast,** Meghan M '07 DA -80 Centre -NY 10013
(914) 597-7800 .. **Hastie,** Colleen E '03 %Lewis S&C,LLC -11 Martine Av -White Plns 10606 **Fx:**597-7801
(585) 454-3030 .. **Hastings,** David M '97 %Merzbach,PC -73 State -Rchstr 14614 **Fx:**454-3044
(518) 463-3826 .. **Hastings,** Donald C '74 -47 Aspinwall Rd -Loudonvll 12211 **Fx:**434-5805
(516) 545-4644 .. **Hastings,** John F '85 %Natl Grid -175 E Old Cntry Rd -Hicksvll 11801 **Fx:**545-5029
(540) 777-3065 .. **Hastings,** Michl E '08 LeClairRyan,PC -830 3rd Av -NY 10022
(212) 768-3878 .. **Hastings,** Thos E '83 (Smith SWH&B,LLP) -100 Park Av -NY 10017
(518) 455-3933 .. **Hata,** Minoru '00 %NYS Assmby Ways & Means -542 The Cptl -Albany 12249
(212) 980-0202 .. **Hatab,** Anthony J '85 (Dressel & H,PC) -6 E 45th -NY 10017
(212) 732-5800 .. **Hatami,** Gina '98 OfCnsl Friedman & M LLP -233 Bway -NY 10279
(516) 742-6546 .. **Hatami,** Sheila S '07 %L Stober Jr,LLC -350 Old Cntry Rd -Gdn Cty 11530 **Fx:**742-8603
(315) 428-6578 .. **Hatch,** David C '76 %National Grid -300 Erie Blvd W -Syracuse 13202 **Fx:**428-6100
(212) 512-1000 .. **Hatch,** Edwin I III '02 %HBO -1100 Av of Amer -NY 10036 **Fx:**512-1986
(212) 756-2000 .. **Hatch,** Emily S '10 %Schulte R&Z LLP -919 3rd Av -NY 10022
(212) 564-6633 .. **Hatch,** Frances Norek '97 %White & M,PC -875 Av of Amer -NY 10001
(315) 234-9900 .. **Hatch,** James Ryan '09 %F Miller -6575 Kirkvll Rd -E Syracuse 13057 **Fx:**234-9908
(212) 336-2000 .. **Hatch,** Jonathan H '07 %Patterson BW&T LLP -1133 Av of Amer -NY 10036
(212) 788-6969 .. **Hatch,** Peter A '02 Councilman B DeBlasio -250 Bway -NY 10007
(212) 455-2000 .. **Hatcher,** Gena R '04 %Simpson T&B LLP -425 Lex Av -NY 10017
(212) 416-8150 .. **Hatcher,** Gwendolyn '80 %Dept of Law -120 Bway -NY 10271
(718) 222-2350 .. **Hatcher,** Jason C '07 %Law Dept -350 Jay -Brklyn 11201 **Fx:**222-2373
(212) 310-8000 .. **Hatcher,** Robyn Todd '09 %Weil G&M LLP -767 5th Av -NY 10153
(212) 972-5430 .. **Hatchett,** Allison N '06 %Rosin SM -801 2nd Av -NY 10017
(212) 973-8000 .. **Hatchett,** Michl E '93 (Schnader HS&L LLP) -140 Bway -NY 10005
(718) 206-4706 .. **Hatcliffe,** Jared J '00 %Law Dept -89-17 Sutphin Blvd -Jamaica 11435 **Fx:**206-4702
(516) 746-0333 .. **Hatcliffe,** Patricia A '99 Kutner & G -300 Old Cntry Rd -Mineola 11501
(914) 686-5700 .. **Hatem,** Albert A '87 -202 Mamaroneck Av -White Plns 10601
(772) 337-3950 .. **Hatem,** Fredk D '61 -5 McKenna Pl -Mamaroneck 10543 **Fx:**337-3951
(914) 995-3000 .. **Hatfield,** Christine E '97 DA -111 Martin Luther King Blvd -White Plns 10601 **Fx:**995-3363
(212) 297-5800 .. **Hatfield,** Wm S '94 (Day P LLP) -7 Times Sq -NY 10036
(718) 236-9400 .. **Hatgipetros,** Catina '05 -8634 18th Av -Brklyn 11214 **Fx:**236-9444
(718) 238-2400 .. **Hatgipetros,** Christina '06 %Georgaklis & M -9118 5th Av -Brklyn 11209 **Fx:**238-2116
(212) 416-8560 .. **Hathaway,** Barbara K '84 %Dept of Law -120 Bway -NY 10271
(212) 583-9600 .. **Hathaway,** Gerald T '83 (Littler M,PC) -900 3rd Av -NY 10022
(212) 468-4800 .. **Hatry,** Patricia '51 (Davis & G LLP) -1740 Bway -NY 10019
(914) 872-7000 .. **Hattar,** Jacqueline '92 (Wilson EME&D LLP) -3 Gannett Dr -White Plns 10604

(212) 554-1234 .. **Hattem,** Dave S '82 %AXA Financial Inc -1290 Av of Amer -NY 10104 **Fx:**707-3963
(516) 746-5599 .. **Hatter,** James R '76 (Bee RFH&D,LLP) -170 Old Cntry Rd -Mineola 11501
(607) 974-9000 .. **Hatton,** Vincent P '82 %Corning -1 Rvrfrnt Plz -Corning 14831 **Fx:**974-6135
(315) 445-1700 .. **Hatz,** Scott R '87 Wladis Law Firm,PC -5795 Widewaters Pkwy -Syracuse 13214 **Fx:**251-1073
(212) 594-5300 .. **Hatzakos,** Stephanie '98 %Milberg LLP -1 Penn Plz -NY 10119
(212) 931-7300 .. **Hatzimemos,** Eric '93 %Giuliani Prtnrs -5 Times Sq -NY 10036
(718) 833-4600 .. **Hatzipetros,** John C '88 -7500 4th Av -Brklyn 11209 **Fx:**238-2494
(212) 809-7600 .. **Hatzis,** Chrisostomos M '85 (Cheven K&H) -40 Wall -NY 10005
(212) 809-7600 .. **Hatzis,** Constantine '98 %Cheven K&H -40 Wall -NY 10005
(212) 773-3800 .. **Hauben,** Ronald B '82 Ernst & Young LLP -5 Times Sq -NY 10036 **Fx:**773-3896
(212) 669-4501 .. **Hauben,** Warren P '75 %Tax Appls Tribunal -1 Centre -NY 10007 **Fx:**669-4503
(716) 566-1300 .. **Hauber,** Vincent P '76 (Hiscock & B,LLP) -1100 M&T Ctr -Buffalo 14203
(516) 571-3800 .. **Hauck,** Khristie A '96 DA -262 Old Cntry Rd -Mineola 11501 **Fx:**248-9479
(212) 808-7800 .. **Hauck,** Stephen G '97 (Kelley D&W LLP) -101 Park Av -NY 10178
(212) 715-1000 .. **Hauck,** Timothy '07 %Arnold & P LLP -399 Park Av -NY 10022
(212) 839-5300 .. **Hauenstein,** Peter R '07 %Sidley A LLP -787 7th Av -NY 10019
(518) 487-5460 .. **Hauf,** Matthew B '09 %DA -6 Lodge -Albany 12207 **Fx:**487-5093
(212) 588-0800 .. **Haug,** Edgar H '79 (Frommer L&H LLP) -745 5th Av -NY 10151
(347) 296-1672 .. **Hauge,** Carol H '96 Supreme Ct Law Dept -360 Adams -Brklyn 11201 **Fx:**643-6114
(973) 596-4471 .. **Hauge,** Paul M '96 %Gibbons PC -1 Penn Plz -NY 10119 **Fx:**639-6215
(516) 572-7809 .. **Haugen,** Donna M '04 Nassau Cmnty Cllg -1 Educ Way -Gdn Cty 11530
(718) 270-3024 .. **Haugh,** Bridget '02 NYC Hlth & Hsptl Corp -1901 1st Av -NY 10029
(718) 984-2841 .. **Haughey,** Hugh F '74 -5753 Amboy Rd -Staten Isl 10309
(845) 794-4094 .. **Haughey,** Patrick J '99 %Leg Aid -11 Bank -Monticello 12701 **Fx:**794-0119
(516) 803-2300 .. **Haughton,** Jamal H '00 Cablevision -1111 Stewart Av -Bethpage 11714
(212) 530-5000 .. **Haugland,** Matthew R '09 %Milbank TH&M LLP -1 Chase Manh Plz -NY 10005
(914) 681-0200 .. **Haupel,** Frank J '83 (DelBello DWW&W,LLP) -1 N Lex Av -White Plns 10601
(212) 561-3527 .. **Hauprich,** Keith C '00 SrCnsl Cherry Lane Music Pblshng Co,Inc -6 E 32nd -NY 10016 **Fx:**683-2040
(646) 386-5700 .. **Hauptman,** Aaron H '89 %Civil Ct -111 Centre -NY 10013
(516) 541-7200 .. **Hauptman,** Arnold J '66 -686 Bway -Massapequa 11758 **Fx:**798-4103
(212) 340-0400 .. **Hauptman,** Lawr M '74 %Applt Div 1st Dept -27 Mad Av -NY 10010 **Fx:**889-4412
(212) 489-1600 .. **Hauptman,** Lisa D '99 %Deloitte LLP -1633 Bway -NY 10019 **Fx:**492-4201
(718) 780-7932 .. **Hauptman,** Martin R '65 %Bklyn Law Schl -250 Joralemon -Brklyn 11201 **Fx:**780-0393
(212) 596-9000 .. **Hauptman,** Naomi '09 %Ropes & G LLP -1211 Av of Amer -NY 10036
(607) 432-6720 .. **Haus,** Ronald R '60 -6 Ford Av -Oneonta 13820 **Fx:**433-1507
(516) 741-2000 .. **Hausch,** Adrienne Flipse '77 (Carway & F) -194 Old Cntry Rd -Mineola 11501
(516) 248-1777 .. **Hausch,** Roger H '66 -194 Old Cntry Rd -Mineola 11501
(516) 294-6666 .. **Hause,** Richd L '80 (Samuelson H&S) -300 Grdn City Plz -Gdn Cty 11530
(607) 974-9000 .. **Hauselt,** Denise A '84 %Corning -1 Rvrfrnt Plz -Corning 14831 **Fx:**974-6135
(585) 593-4050 .. **Hauselt,** Maureen A '89 Hauselt & H -120 N Main Bx603 -Wellsvll 14895
(212) 357-6330 .. **Hausen,** Julie Abraham '95 Goldman Sachs -1 NY Plz -NY 10004
(212) 755-4545 .. **Hausen,** Robt J '79 (R Hausen,PC) -110 E 59th -NY 10022 **Fx:**755-5859
(212) 783-2498 .. **Hauser,** Barbara R '01 Citigroup -787 7th Av -NY 10019
(212) 509-5050 .. **Hauser,** Gregory F '82 (Wuersch & G LLP) -100 Wall -NY 10005
(917) 816-8626 .. **Hauser,** Jesse M '85 -3200 Netherland Av -Riverdale 10463
(518) 462-6765 .. **Hauser,** Joel K '95 %Leg Aid -55 Colvin Av -Albany 12206 **Fx:**427-8352
(212) 966-5253 .. **Hauser,** Lori '88 -591 Bway -NY 10012 **Fx:**941-8566
(212) 603-5874 .. **Hauser,** Mark S '86 Sandell Asset Mgmt -40 W 57th -NY 10019
(212) 354-0099 .. **Hauser,** Michele '87 -1040 Av of Amer -NY 10018 **Fx:**354-0092
(212) 768-6700 .. **Hauser,** Sandra D '92 (Sonnenschein N&R LLP) -1221 Av of Amer -NY 10020
(212) 966-5253 .. **Hauser,** Seth A '87 Hauser & Assoc,PC -591 Bway -NY 10012 **Fx:**941-8566
(212) 336-8000 .. **Hausig,** Matthieu V '02 %Amster R&E -90 Park Av -NY 10016
(212) 577-3506 .. **Hausknecht,** Amy C '95 %Leg Aid -199 Water -NY 10038 **Fx:**577-3520
(585) 263-1000 .. **Hausknecht,** Michl A '82 (Nixon P LLP) -1100 Clinton Sq -Rchstr 14604
(212) 953-6633 .. **Hausler,** Sanford J '88 OfCnsl Cox PS&S LLP -630 3rd Av -NY 10017
(212) 655-3500 .. **Hausman,** James T '97 %Meister S&F LLP -140 E 45th -NY 10017
(914) 946-3344 .. **Hausman,** Jay S '93 J Hausman & Assoc,PC -280 N Central Av -Hartsdale 10530 **Fx:**946-9733
(212) 430-6758 .. **Hausman,** Jos '61 -65 Bway -NY 10006 **Fx:**430-6759
(212) 577-3688 .. **Hausman,** Lawr T '93 %Leg Aid -199 Water -NY 10038 **Fx:**509-8431
(516) 745-0066 .. **Hausman,** Michl J '89 (Karol H&S,PC) -600 Old Cntry Rd -Gdn Cty 11530
(212) 593-5223 .. **Hausner,** Helaine '85 %A Hillman -41 E 57th -NY 10022 **Fx:**593-4633
(646) 375-2109 .. **Hausner & Montanile, PLLC** -116 W 23rd -NY 10011 **Fx:**375-2108
(516) 741-8844 .. **Hausner,** Robt '73 -595 Stewart Av -Gdn Cty 11530
(212) 484-3900 .. **Hausner,** Sanford G '86 (Arent F LLP) -1675 Bway -NY 10019
(516) 292-8500 .. **Hausner-Graber,** Joyce F '90 OfCnsl D Graber -55 Watermill Ln -Gt Neck 11021 **Fx:**538-1206
(212) 558-4000 .. **Hausner-Levine,** Sara '10 %Sullivan & C LLP -125 Broad -NY 10004
(718) 761-9300 .. **Hauss,** Karen S '85 (Vaslas LH&D LLP) -201 Edward Curry Av -Staten Isl 10314
(516) 487-7679 .. **Hausthor,** Brett W '84 -300 Nrthrn Blvd -Gt Neck 11021 **Fx:**487-7663
(212) 746-1334 .. **Hauswald,** Joan M '01 %NY Presbyterian Hsptl -525 E 68th Bx88 -NY 10065 **Fx:**746-8603
(212) 907-7300 .. **Haut,** Lawr R '85 (Golenbock EAB&P) -437 Mad Av -NY 10022
(212) 318-3000 .. **Haut,** Mark C '01 %Fulbright & J LLP -666 5th Av -NY 10103
(845) 794-4094 .. **Havas,** Tim L '89 %Leg Aid -11 Bank -Monticello 12701 **Fx:**794-0119
(212) 816-1726 .. **Havasi,** Evelyn S '86 Citibank -388 Greenwich -NY 10013
(212) 836-8000 .. **Haveles,** H Peter Jr. '81 (Kaye S LLP) -425 Park Av -NY 10022
(518) 436-0876 .. **Haven,** Russ '87 %NYPIRG -107 Wshngtn Av -Albany 12210 **Fx:**432-6178
(347) 296-1671 .. **Havener,** Paula-Jean '81 %Supreme Ct Law Dept -360 Adams -Brklyn 11201 **Fx:**643-6114
(646) 378-7885 .. **Havens,** Jeremy L '09 (Havens & L,PLLC) -1115 Bway -NY 10010
(212) 225-2000 .. **Havens,** Kurt J '08 %Cleary GS&H -1 Lbrty Plz -NY 10006
(585) 889-9659 .. **Havens,** Marcia A '84 -760 Chili Av Ext -Churchville 14428
(315) 394-0520 .. **Havens,** Robt J '73 -78 Pinkerton Rd -Ogdensbrg 13669
(212) 610-6300 .. **Havens,** Sarah E '04 %Allen & O -1221 Av of Amer -NY 10020
(212) 326-3939 .. **Havens,** Thos C '86 (Jones D) -222 E 41st -NY 10017
(212) 733-2225 .. **Havern,** Lindsay A '08 %Pfizer Inc -235 E 42nd -NY 10017
(212) 969-3000 .. **Haverstick,** Amanda D '97 Cnsl Proskauer R LLP -1585 Bway -NY 10036
(212) 692-1000 .. **Haverstick,** Benjamin A '06 %Duane M LLP -1540 Bway -NY 10036
(212) 599-0900 .. **Havia,** Sari '01 %Bower & L,PC -261 Mad Av -NY 10016
(518) 487-7600 .. **Haviland,** Chas R Jr. '90 (Whiteman O&H LLP) -1 Commerce Plz -Albany 12260
(718) 838-7878 .. **Haviland,** Joy F '09 %Bronx Defenders -860 Crtlandt Av -Bronx 10451 **Fx:**665-0100
(212) 683-0015 .. **Haviland,** Mary '97 Connect Inc -Bx20217 -NY 10001
(718) 361-5656 .. **Haviv,** Chas '83 -45-29 47th -Woodside 11377 **Fx:**275-7722
(212) 819-8200 .. **Haviv,** Kimberly A '09 %White & C LLP -1155 Av of Amer -NY 10036
(212) 488-1598 .. **Havkins,** Abraham E '85 (Havkins RR&V,LLP) -11 Penn Plz -NY 10001
(212) 488-1598 .. **Havkins Rosenfeld Ritzert & Varriale,LLP** -11 Penn Plz -NY 10001 **Fx:**564-0203
(914) 682-2636 .. **Havkins Rosenfeld Ritzert & Varriale,LLP** -50 Main -White Plns 10606 **Fx:**560-2245
(516) 471-1900 .. **Havkins Rosenfeld Ritzert & Varriale,LLP** -114 Old Cntry Rd -Mineola 11501 **Fx:**746-0833
(212) 345-5000 .. **Havourd,** Allison R '06 Marsh Inc -1166 Av of Amer -NY 10036
(845) 339-5157 .. **Havranek,** Beatrice '94 -782 Route 213 Bx470 -Rosendale 12472
(212) 953-6633 .. **Hawa,** Laleh '98 OfCnsl Cox PS&S LLP -630 3rd Av -NY 10017
(212) 874-7717 .. **Hawco,** Kenneth B '91 -500 West End Av -NY 10024 **Fx:**874-6784
(212) 636-6000 .. **Hawk,** Barry E '74 Fordham Univ Sch of Law -140 W 62nd -NY 10023 **Fx:**636-6899
(315) 245-1900 .. **Hawkes,** Clarence E '66 -70 Main Bx97 -Camden 13316 **Fx:**245-0672
(607) 741-2110 .. **Hawkes,** Jeffrey J '86 State Ins Fund -2001 Perimeter Rd E -Endicott 13760 **Fx:**741-5029
(212) 702-3551 .. **Hawkesworth,** Kurt A '00 %Rochdale Invstmnt Mgmt -570 Lex Av -NY 10022
(212) 446-4800 .. **Hawkins,** Anne E '08 %Kirkland & E LLP -153 E 53rd -NY 10022
(212) 752-9700 .. **Hawkins,** Ashton '63 OfCnsl Gersten S LLP -600 Lex Av -NY 10022
(917) 551-1300 .. **Hawkins,** Brandi L '03 %Koehler & I LLP -61 Bway -NY 10006
(718) 262-7100 .. **Hawkins,** David M '94 %Civil Ct -89-17 Sutphin Blvd -Jamaica 11435 **Fx:**262-7107
(212) 820-9300 .. **Hawkins Delafield & Wood LLP** -One Chase Manh Plz -NY 10005 **Fx:**514-8425
(212) 541-6741 .. **Hawkins,** Dennis R '75 Fund for Modern Cts -351 W 54th -NY 10019
(845) 677-2101 .. **Hawkins,** Eliot D '60 OfCnsl Teahan & C -41 Front Bx1181 -Millbrook 12545
(212) 310-8000 .. **Hawkins,** Eric C '08 %Weil G&M LLP -767 5th Av -NY 10153
(212) 504-6000 .. **Hawkins,** Howard R Jr. '76 (Cadwalader W&T LLP) -1 World Fncl Ctr -NY 10281
(212) 688-8555 .. **Hawkins,** Janora L '09 Fragomen DB&L LLP -7 Hanover Sq -NY 10004
(212) 314-7230 .. **Hawkins,** Joanne M '86 SrCnsl IAC -555 W 18th -NY 10011 **Fx:**314-7497
(212) 309-1000 .. **Hawkins,** John D '81 (Hunton & W) -200 Park Av -NY 10166
(212) 417-4445 .. **Hawkins,** Katherine A '02 NYS Dept of Health -90 Church -NY 10007 **Fx:**417-4446
(212) 998-6676 .. **Hawkins,** Kimberly Ann '94 -438 8th -Brklyn 11215
(212) 592-1400 .. **Hawkins,** Matthew S '98 Cnsl Herrick,F LLP -2 Park Av -NY 10016
(718) 250-2000 .. **Hawkins,** McCarthy A '06 DA -350 Jay -Brklyn 11201 **Fx:**250-2314
(212) 207-4419 .. **Hawkins,** Oliver L '99 -625 Main -NY 10044 **Fx:**202-6385
(212) 789-2703 .. **Hawkins,** Robt E D '94 NHL Enterprises,LP -1185 Av of Amer -NY 10036
(212) 340-0400 .. **Hawkins,** Susan D '98 Applt Div 1st Dept -27 Mad Av -NY 10010 **Fx:**889-4412
(516) 292-0984 .. **Hawkins,** Valerie A '83 -77 St Pauls Rd N -Hempstd 11550 **Fx:**292-0986
(212) 407-4000 .. **Hawkins,** Wm M '91 (Loeb & L,LLP) -345 Park Av -NY 10154
(212) 749-4274 .. **Hawkins-Greenidge,** Jessica '84 -95 W 95th -NY 10025 **Fx:**749-4274
(315) 735-9414 .. **Hawkridge,** Katherine P '76 -1431 Genesee Bx153 -Utica 13503 **Fx:**734-1976
(212) 649-2000 .. **Hawley,** Robt J '74 %Hearst Corp -300 W 57th -NY 10019 **Fx:**649-2035
(212) 354-3800 .. **Hawley,** Thos J '76 (Burke & P) -100 Park Av -NY 10017
(212) 442-1400 .. **Hawley,** Wayne G '81 %Conflicts of Int Bd -2 Lafayette -NY 10007 **Fx:**442-1407
(845) 486-2300 .. **Hawlk,** Kristine Decker '95 %DA -236 Main -Poughkeepsie 12601 **Fx:**486-2324
(212) 422-0202 .. **Haworth,** Scott L '94 (Sedgwick DM&A LLP) -125 Broad -NY 10004

(212) 526-0857 .. **Hawrylewicz**, Jaroslaw C K '00 Barclays Capital -745 7th Av -NY 10019
(315) 592-5255 .. **Hawthorne**, David H '88 -188 S 3rd -Fulton 13069 **Fx**:592-2251
(315) 592-2800 .. **Hawthorne**, Dennis N Jr. '89 -118 Cayuga -Fulton 13069 **Fx**:592-2836
(212) 909-6000 .. **Hawthorne**, Donald W '92 Cnsl Debevoise & P LLP -919 3rd Av -NY 10022
(718) 665-0050 .. **Hawthorne**, Keith A '94 -594 Grnd Cncrs -Bronx 10451
(212) 336-2000 .. **Hawthorne**, Paul G '03 %Patterson BW&T LLP -1133 Av of Amer -NY 10036
(716) 874-2111 .. **Hawthorne & Siegel PLLC** -3080 Delaware Av -Buffalo 14217 **Fx**:874-0680
(716) 882-2300 .. **Hawthorne**, Tina M '05 %McCready & T -6 N Pearl -Buffalo 14202
(518) 591-5232 .. **Hawver**, Philip J '83 %NYS ORPTS -WA Harriman State Campus -Albany 12227 **Fx**:474-3657
(607) 273-6444 .. **Hay**, Deirdre Gruzaukas '98 OfCnsl Harris B PLLC -119 E Seneca -Ithaca 14850
(212) 722-2000 .. **Hay**, Elizabeth A '76 %Leg Aid -230 E 106th -NY 10029 **Fx**:876-5365
(212) 632-5500 .. **Hay**, John J Jr. '81 (Salans LLP) -620 5th Av -NY 10020
(212) 969-2247 .. **Hay**, Nancy E '99 Alliance Bernstein LP -1345 Av of Amer -NY 10105 **Fx**:554-4639
(212) 723-3037 .. **Hay**, Robt N Jr. '90 Citigroup Global Mrkts -250 West -NY 10013
(518) 474-6400 .. **Hay**, Victoria Hunter '94 %Dept of Ed -89 Wshngtn Av -Albany 12234 **Fx**:473-2925
(212) 450-4000 .. **Hayashi**, Andrew T '09 %Davis P&W LLP -450 Lex Av -NY 10017
(212) 788-1104 .. **Hayat**, Janeen '09 %Law Dept -100 Church -NY 10007 **Fx**:788-0367
(516) 560-6400 .. **Hayat**, Mehreen '09 %Leg Aid -1 Helen Keller Way -Hempstd 11550 **Fx**:565-3694
(212) 225-2000 .. **Hayday**, Caroline F '03 %Cleary GS&H -1 Lbrty Plz -NY 10006
(607) 733-8866 .. **Hayden**, Carl T '70 (Ziff Law Firm,LLP) -303 William -Elmira 14901 **Fx**:732-6062
(585) 334-2578 .. **Hayden**, Chad R '73 -1634 Lehigh Station Rd -Henrietta 14467 **Fx**:334-6235
(716) 635-5029 .. **Hayden**, Debra E '91 -5792 Main -Williamsvll 14221
(518) 785-5340 .. **Hayden**, Derek L '98 Cnsl Shantz & B -26 Century Hill Dr -Latham 12110 **Fx**:785-5470
(212) 513-6300 .. **Hayden**, Donald T '01 %Dept Business Srvcs -110 William -NY 10038 **Fx**:618-8989
(516) 542-5900 .. **Hayden**, Douglas J '89 (Congdon FORDT&F) -333 Earle Ovngton Blvd -Uniondale 11553
(212) 819-8200 .. **Hayden**, James F '85 (White & C LLP) -1155 Av of Amer -NY 10036
(212) 310-2184 .. **Hayden**, Janie R '90 %Colgate-Palmolive -300 Park Av -NY 10022
(315) 425-2700 .. **Hayden**, Kevin M '04 %Hiscock & B,LLP -One Park Pl -Syracuse 13202
(585) 232-8314 .. **Hayden**, Mark J '96 %Buckner & K -1 S Wshngtn -Rchstr 14614
(716) 845-9336 .. **Hayden**, Mary Louise '78 %Supreme Ct -25 Delaware Av -Buffalo 14202 **Fx**:851-3293
(607) 535-8383 .. **Hayden**, Matthew C '02 Schuyler Cty DA -105 9th -Watkins Glen 14891
(212) 548-2100 .. **Hayden**, Patrick L '02 (McGuire W LLP) -1345 Av of Amer -NY 10105
(212) 669-0600 .. **Hayden**, Raymond P '63 OfCnsl Hill R LLP -45 Bway -NY 10006
(212) 922-7203 .. **Hayden**, Robt M '09 Bk of NY Mellon -200 Park Av -NY 10016
(516) 571-3800 .. **Hayden**, Robt T '84 %DA -262 Old Cntry Rd -Mineola 11501 **Fx**:248-9479
(516) 662-2819 .. **Hayden**, Rosemary Cipolla '94 -1 Old Cntry Rd -Carle Pl 11514
(516) 694-3000 .. **Hayden**, Timothy A '06 %Guercio & G,LLP -77 Conklin -Farmngdl 11735 **Fx**:694-4738
(212) 859-8000 .. **Hayek**, Mark S '07 %Fried FHS&J LLP -1 NY Plz -NY 10004
(315) 471-3151 .. **Hayes**, Ashley Duvall '02 (Hancock & E,LLP) -1500 AXA Twr I Bx4976 -Syracuse 13221
(212) 326-2000 .. **Hayes**, Christina J '10 %O'Melveny & M LLP -7 Times Sq -NY 10036
(716) 847-8400 .. **Hayes**, Christopher L '08 %Phillips L LLP -3400 HSBC Ctr -Buffalo 14203
(713) 221-1546 .. **Hayes**, Christopher M '07 %Bracewell & G,LLP -1251 Av of Amer -NY 10020 **Fx**:221-2176
(212) 964-8038 .. **Hayes**, Craig R '00 %Worth L&L,LLP -111 John -NY 10038
(315) 218-8000 .. **Hayes**, David M '69 OfCnsl Bond S&K,PLLC -1 Lincoln Ctr -Syracuse 13202
(716) 332-7863 .. **Hayes**, David R '89 Hon H Scott -68 Court -Buffalo 14202 **Fx**:332-7865
(212) 341-6400 .. **Hayes**, Dennis J '82 %Liquidation Bur -123 William -NY 10038 **Fx**:608-3398
(631) 286-9244 .. **Hayes**, E Anne '77 -16 Station Rd -Bellprt 11713
(212) 655-2087 .. **Hayes**, Edw A '80 Tower Ins Grp -120 Bway -NY 10271 **Fx**:(646) 839-2741
(914) 654-2300 .. **Hayes**, Edw P '02 New Rochelle PD -475 North Av -New Rchll 10801
(212) 644-0303 .. **Hayes**, Edw W '73 (E Hayes,PC) -515 Mad Av -NY 10022
(518) 473-6107 .. **Hayes**, Eileen M '95 %Insurance Dept -99 Wshngtn Av -Albany 12257 **Fx**:474-3397
(212) 277-4000 .. **Hayes**, Ellen L '01 (Freshfields BD LLP) -520 Mad Av -NY 10022
(914) 323-7000 .. **Hayes**, Emily A '02 %Wilson EME&D LLP -3 Gannett Dr -White Plns 10604
(518) 494-7821 .. **Hayes**, Erin E '06 -Bx275 -Brant Lk 12815 **Fx**:494-7831
(212) 626-4100 .. **Hayes**, Gerald J '79 (Baker & M LLP) -1114 Av of Amer -NY 10036
(716) 852-1111 .. **Hayes**, J Michl '76 -69 Delaware Av -Buffalo 14202 **Fx**:852-0711
(518) 842-1128 .. **Hayes**, James C III '78 -131 Maple Av Ext -Amsterdam 12010 **Fx**:842-1203
(516) 741-0896 .. **Hayes**, James E '59 -101 2nd -Gdn Cty 11530
(607) 723-5341 .. **Hayes**, James M '65 (Hinman H&K,LLP) -80 Exchange Bx5250 -Bnghmtn 13902
(631) 777-2330 .. **Hayes**, James M '82 %O'Connor OH&D,LLP -1 Huntngtn Quad -Melvll 11747
(212) 880-9579 .. **Hayes**, James V '03 %Morvillo AGIA&B,PC -565 5th Av -NY 10017
(518) 359-3241 .. **Hayes**, Jeremiah M '74 -64 Park Bx840 -Tupper Lk 12986 **Fx**:359-3432
(914) 912-8388 .. **Hayes**, Jill L '94 -36 Poplar Rd -Briarclff Mnr 10510 **Fx**:762-9292
(212) 479-2662 .. **Hayes**, John C '05 Eurohypo AG -1114 Av of Amer -NY 10036
(607) 594-4890 .. **Hayes**, John C T '86 -101 E Main Bx480 -Odessa 14869 **Fx**:594-4894
(631) 324-2525 .. **Hayes**, Laraine Bellini '80 -Bx1109 -Wainscott 11975
(212) 282-4962 .. **Hayes**, Lisa J '94 Mizuho Corp Bk -1251 Av of Amer -NY 10020
(914) 698-8200 .. **Hayes & LoPresti,PC** -260 Harrison Av -Harrison 10528 **Fx**:698-8248
(212) 891-0813 .. **Hayes**, Louise H '78 -28 E 28th -NY 10016
(585) 546-1980 .. **Hayes**, Margaret O'Reilly '84 OfCnsl Fulton F&G LLP -28 E Main -Rchstr 14614
(914) 698-8200 .. **Hayes**, Martin F IV '78 (Hayes & L,PC) -260 Harrison Av -Harrison 10528
(212) 358-6581 .. **Hayes & Mensching** -315 Park Av S -NY 10010
(845) 486-6800 .. **Hayes**, Michl A Jr. '61 OfCnsl McCabe & M LLP -63 Wshngtn Bx509 -Poughkeepsie 12602
(516) 741-4799 .. **Hayes**, Michl C '03 %Baker SBGFM&N,LLC -100 Grdn City Plz -Gdn Cty 11530
(845) 855-5900 .. **Hayes**, Michl G '95 (Daniels & P,LLP) -517 Route 22 -Pawling 12564
(845) 855-5900 .. **Hayes**, Michele N '98 %Daniels & P,LLP -517 Route 22 -Pawling 12564
(518) 426-4600 .. **Hayes**, N Robt Jr. '74 OfCnsl Couch W,LLP -540 Bway Bx22222 -Albany 12201
(212) 687-8724 .. **Hayes**, Pamela D '86 -200 W 57th -NY 10019 **Fx**:980-2968
(914) 631-6666 .. **Hayes**, Patricia A '78 %M Grossbach,PC -800 Wstchstr Av -Rye Brook 10573 **Fx**:524-7070
(718) 254-6050 .. **Hayes**, Richd K '88 %US Atty -271 Cadman Plz E -Brklyn 11201 **Fx**:254-6479
(716) 853-9555 .. **Hayes**, Roland L W '86 %Leg Aid -237 Main -Buffalo 14203 **Fx**:853-3219
(212) 269-1600 .. **Hayes**, Sara C '09 %Teigland-Hunt LLP -127 W 24th -NY 10011 **Fx**:269-1580
(212) 801-2177 .. **Hayes**, Sean E '99 (Greenberg T,LLP) -200 Park Av -NY 10166
(212) 784-6400 .. **Hayes**, Steven M '74 (Hanly CBSF&H LLP) -112 Mad Av -NY 10016
(212) 657-0362 .. **Hayes**, Steven R '78 %Citibank -111 Wall -NY 10005
(212) 837-6000 .. **Hayes**, Vilia B '81 (Hughes H&R LLP) -1 Bttry Pk Plz -NY 10004
(716) 847-8400 .. **Hayes**, Waldron S Jr. '62 OfCnsl Phillips L LLP -3400 HSBC Ctr -Buffalo 14203
(212) 417-4571 .. **Hayes-Chaffe**, Maura M T '05 Medicaid Insp Gen -217 Bway -NY 10007
(518) 463-1177 .. **Hayford**, Stephen P '03 %Tobin & D,LLP -33 Elk -Albany 12207
(212) 965-2235 .. **Haygood**, Ryan P '02 %NAACP/LDF -99 Hudson -NY 10013 **Fx**:226-7592
(518) 402-0205 .. **Hayko**, Eva Lynn '86 %UIA Bd -Troy Atrium Bx15126 -Albany 12212 **Fx**:402-6208
(518) 452-0144 .. **Hayko**, John F '88 %Mancini and H,PC -2050 Wstrn Av -Guilderlnd 12084
(718) 520-3524 .. **Hayles**, T Anthony '83 Supreme Ct -89-17 Sutphin Blvd -Jamaica 11435
(212) 506-1700 .. **Haylett**, Nicholas F '86 -1301 Av of Amer 36th Fl -NY 10019 **Fx**:506-1800
(212) 363-2900 .. **Hayman**, Alan I '65 OfCnsl Krieger & P LLP -39 Bway -NY 10006
(212) 735-3000 .. **Hayman**, Linda '82 (Skadden ASM&F LLP) -4 Times Sq -NY 10036
(718) 250-2000 .. **Haymandou**, Maria K '06 DA -350 Jay -Brklyn 11201 **Fx**:250-2314
(212) 916-4249 .. **Hayn**, Robt C '77 %TIAA-CREF -730 3rd Av -NY 10017
(516) 747-4301 .. **Hayn**, Thos B '10 %Torino & B,PC -200 Old Cntry Rd -Mineola 11501
(518) 346-4291 .. **Hayner**, Thos B '69 (Moynihan H&M) -704 Union -Schnctdy 12305 **Fx**:346-4292
(212) 533-6300 .. **Haynes**, Alan K '99 %NYSUT -52 Bway -NY 10004 **Fx**:995-2347
(212) 833-8676 .. **Haynes**, Allyson Walker '98 SONY -550 Mad Av -NY 10022
(914) 476-0600 .. **Haynes**, Andre S '09 %Smith B&J,LLP -733 Ynkrs Av -Ynkrs 10704
(212) 627-9898 .. **Haynes**, Bethany M '05 %Sloss Law Ofc,PC -555 W 25th -NY 10001 **Fx**:627-9498
(212) 659-7300 .. **Haynes and Boone,LLP** -1221 Av of Amer -NY 10020 **Fx**:918-8989
(315) 218-8000 .. **Haynes**, Brian K '84 (Bond S&K,PLLC) -1 Lincoln Ctr -Syracuse 13202
(914) 686-4800 .. **Haynes**, Edw C '97 %Harrington O&M,LLP -81 Main -White Plns 10601
(518) 792-2117 .. **Haynes**, Eileen M '97 (Bartlett PS&R,PC) -1 Wshngtn Bx2168 -Glens Fls 12801
(212) 670-0184 .. **Haynes**, Mary M '88 %Merrill Lynch -222 Bway -NY 10038
(716) 645-5539 .. **Haynes**, Nan Lipsitz '93 Buffalo Law Schl -721 O'Brian Hall -Buffalo 14260
(212) 801-2137 .. **Haynes**, Nathan A '99 (Greenberg T,LLP) -200 Park Av -NY 10166
(212) 858-4386 .. **Haynes**, Nicole C '99 %FINRA -1 Lbrty Plz -NY 10006 **Fx**:208-5168
(845) 297-5700 .. **Haynes**, Paul R '77 -2789 W Main -Wappingers Fls 12590
(914) 995-3000 .. **Haynes**, Pauline J '86 %DA -111 Martin Luther King Blvd -White Plns 10601 **Fx**:995-3363
(718) 488-1001 .. **Haynes-Stevens**, Gale A '84 %Long Island Univ -1 Univ Plz -Brklyn 11201 **Fx**:780-4045
(212) 653-8700 .. **Hays**, James R '91 (Sheppard MR&H LLP) -30 Rckfllr Plz -NY 10112
(607) 277-0535 .. **Hays**, M Alan '91 -415 N Tioga -Ithaca 14850
(212) 244-2999 .. **Hays**, Peter B III '01 (Kopff N&D LLP) -440 9th Av -NY 10001
(212) 484-6729 .. **Hays**, Spencer B '74 Time Warner -1 Time Warner Ctr -NY 10019
(845) 294-3596 .. **Haysom**, Simon D '90 (S Haysom LLC) -1 Railroad Av Bx487 -Goshen 10924 **Fx**:294-8495
(631) 393-9439 .. **Hayt Hayt & Landau LLP** -500 Bi-Cnty Blvd -Farmngdl 11735 **Fx**:694-8284
(212) 406-4848 .. **Hayt**, Paul A '91 OfCnsl G Pillersdorf & Assoc,PC -225 Bway -NY 10007 **Fx**:406-5884
(914) 467-1744 .. **Haytaian**, Peter D '95 Oxford Health Plans, Inc -44 S Bway -White Plns 10601 **Fx**:467-4036
(212) 319-3900 .. **Haythe**, Thos M '66 OfCnsl JE Bachelder LLP -437 Mad Av -NY 10022 **Fx**:319-3070
(212) 509-9400 .. **Hayum**, Edw '86 (Cozen O) -45 Bway Atrium -NY 10006
(845) 343-6227 .. **Hayward**, Guy J '75 (Hayward PO&P) -225 Dolson Av Bx929 -Middletwn 10940 **Fx**:343-1927
(212) 906-1200 .. **Haywood**, Amber L '09 %Latham & W -885 3rd Av -NY 10022
(212) 906-1200 .. **Hazan**, Alissa M '08 %Latham & W -885 3rd Av -NY 10022

(212) 788-8084 .. **Hazan,** David M '05 %Law Dept -100 Church -NY 10007 **Fx:**788-0367
(212) 610-5663 .. **Hazan,** Jack '92 Streambank LLC -1913 E 1st -Brklyn 11223
(212) 528-8144 .. **Hazan,** Jeremy B '04 Barclays Capital -745 7th Av -NY 10019
(212) 547-5400 .. **Hazan,** Nava '00 (McDermott W&E LLP) -340 Mad Av -NY 10173
(212) 661-9100 .. **Hazan,** Scott L '74 (Otterbourg SH&R,PC) -230 Park Av -NY 10169
(845) 486-2280 .. **Hazel,** George A '84 %Pub Def -22 Market -Poughkeepsie 12601 **Fx:**486-2266
(716) 551-4711 .. **Hazel,** James M '88 %Social Security Admin -50 Fountain Plz -Buffalo 14202
(718) 999-2110 .. **Hazel,** Rosharna D '03 %Fire Dept Bureau Leg Afrs -9 Metrotech Ctr -Brklyn 11201
(646) 602-5636 .. **Hazeldean,** Susan V '02 %Urban Justice Ctr -123 William -NY 10038 **Fx:**(212) 533-4598
(917) 445-1100 .. **Hazelhurst,** Dawn M '84 -60 E 42nd -NY 10165
(914) 422-4218 .. **Hazell,** Maja D '99 Pace Law Schl -78 N Bway -White Plns 10603 **Fx:**422-4039
(516) 742-7200 .. **Hazelton,** Donald H '91 D Hazelton,PC -245 Hillside Av -Williston Pk 11596 **Fx:**742-4080
(631) 283-6400 .. **Hazelton,** Jean M '82 (JM Hazelton,PC) -176 N Sea Rd Bx5041 -Southampton 11969 **Fx:**283-5385
(516) 496-5822 .. **Hazelton,** Katherine A '01 %T Spina -170 Froehlich Farm Blvd -Woodbury 11797 **Fx:**496-5420
(315) 471-3151 .. **Hazelton,** Lindsey Helmer '98 (Hancock & E,LLP) -1500 AXA Twr I Bx4976 -Syracuse 13221
(914) 761-0381 .. **Hazen,** Andrew E '84 -30 Glenn -White Plns 10603 **Fx:**948-3371
(212) 487-9700 .. **Hazen,** Deanna E '95 (White F&F,LLP) -61 Bway -NY 10006
(646) 221-3698 .. **Hazen,** James M '74 (Kelly & H) -380 Lex Av -NY 10168 **Fx:**(732) 784-2850
(212) 637-3215 .. **Hazen,** Robt G '89 EPA -290 Bway -NY 10007 **Fx:**637-3096
(212) 736-0500 .. **Hazen,** Terry L '88 (Mitofsky SN&H LLP) -152 Mad Av -NY 10016
(212) 551-2614 .. **Hazenberg,** Hein J '86 -450 Lex Av -NY 10017
(212) 554-1234 .. **Hazin,** Karen Field '95 AXA Financial Inc -1290 Av of Amer -NY 10104 **Fx:**707-3963
(212) 984-7810 .. **Hazin,** Slava '92 (Warshaw BCS&K,LLP) -555 5th Av -NY 10017
(212) 455-2000 .. **Hazlett,** Abigail A '06 %Simpson T&B LLP -425 Lex Av -NY 10017
(212) 903-9000 .. **Hazlett,** Katrina E '10 %Linklaters -1345 Av of Amer -NY 10105
(212) 259-8000 .. **Hazlitt,** Arthur V '87 (Dewey & L LLP) -1301 Av of Amer -NY 10019
(607) 535-8121 .. **Hazlitt,** Kristin E '96 %Cnty Atty -105 9th -Watkins Glen 14891
(212) 761-7489 .. **Hazy,** Michl W '01 Morgan Stanley -1585 Bway -NY 10036
(212) 932-8488 .. **Hazzard,** Elaine M '97 -851 West End Av -NY 10025
(516) 292-2669 .. **Hazzard,** Robt S '00 Hazzard & Assoc,PC -62 Nichols Ct -Hempstd 11550
(212) 412-3168 .. **He,** H Ruth '04 Barclays Capital Inc -200 Park Av -NY 10166
(212) 450-4000 .. **He,** Pengyu '08 %Davis P&W LLP -450 Lex Av -NY 10017
(212) 878-8000 .. **He,** Ting '08 %Clifford C LLP -31 W 52nd -NY 10019
(212) 704-6000 .. **He,** Xin '06 OfCnsl Troutman S LLP -405 Lex Av -NY 10174
(212) 226-1198 .. **He,** Yinghui '04 -265 Canal -NY 10013 **Fx:**226-1198
(212) 421-2800 .. **Heacox,** Catherine T '99 %Lanier Law Firm,PLLC -126 E 56th -NY 10022 **Fx:**421-2878
(212) 297-0937 .. **Head,** C J '58 -60 E 42nd -NY 10165 **Fx:**370-5206
(716) 805-2167 .. **Head,** Christopher A '78 Moog Inc -Seneca & Jamison Rd -E Aurora 14052 **Fx:**805-2120
(585) 343-7586 .. **Head,** Colleen Sutherland '83 -5130 Main Street Rd -Batavia 14020
(212) 826-6748 .. **Head,** Elizabeth '58 -300 E 56th -NY 10022 **Fx:**750-0498
(914) 472-7700 .. **Headley,** Frank M Jr. '65 OfCnsl Bertine HHZD&D,LLP -700 Wht Plns Rd -Scarsdale 10583
(718) 693-4056 .. **Headley,** George B '78 -201 Linden Blvd - C16 -Brklyn 11226
(212) 506-1700 .. **Headley,** Kara F '02 %Kasowitz BT&F LLP -1633 Bway -NY 10019
(646) 386-5700 .. **Headley,** Lisa S '02 %Civil Ct -111 Centre -NY 10013
(718) 596-7340 .. **Headley,** Trevor L F '73 -26 Court -Brklyn 11242 **Fx:**596-7577
(212) 879-6404 .. **Heagle,** Khristan A '04 -708 3rd Av -NY 10017
(212) 768-6700 .. **Heald,** Allyn Gregory '94 -1221 Av of Amer -NY 10020
(518) 382-1044 .. **Healey,** Andrew J '07 %F Putorti Jr -1338 Union -Schnctdy 12308 **Fx:**372-3686
(845) 878-6140 .. **Healey,** Francis E Jr. '85 Healey & H -4069 Route 52 -Holmes 12531 **Fx:**878-4316
(914) 422-8755 .. **Healey,** John M '92 %Dept of Law -101 E Post Rd -White Plns 10601 **Fx:**422-8706
(212) 922-9250 .. **Healey,** Matthew D '92 %Ganfer & S LLP -360 Lex Av -NY 10017
(212) 998-6026 .. **Healey,** Megan McKee '03 %NYU Law Schl -40 Wshngtn Sq S -NY 10012 **Fx:**995-4075
(212) 233-8070 .. **Healey,** Michl J '93 %Callan & B -225 Bway -NY 10007
(718) 643-8056 .. **Healey,** Noreen P '90 Hon J Ingram -360 Adams -Brklyn 11201
(516) 624-6150 .. **Healey,** Ralph P '98 %Town Atty -Town Hall -Oyster Bay 11771 **Fx:**624-6196
(212) 943-3520 .. **Healey,** Thos H '58 -17 Battery Pl -NY 10004 **Fx:**943-3525
(973) 228-5700 .. **Healey,** Wm F '08 %Brach E LLC -100 Park Av -NY 10017 **Fx:**228-7852
(212) 739-3230 .. **Healey,** Wm V '79 Allianz Global Investors -1345 Av of ther Americas -NY 10105
(914) 559-3100 .. **Healy,** Brian M '91 %Heidell PM&B,LLP -81 Main -White Plns 10601
(585) 268-9410 .. **Healy,** Carissa M '06 %Cnty Atty -7 Court -Belmont 14813 **Fx:**268-9651
(718) 286-2450 .. **Healy,** Christopher L '09 %Leg Aid -120-46 Qns Blvd -Kew Gdns 11415 **Fx:**263-4234
(212) 521-5400 .. **Healy,** Christopher W '94 (Reed S LLP) -599 Lex Av -NY 10022
(212) 335-3943 .. **Healy,** Daniel K '86 %DA -1 Hogan Pl -NY 10013 **Fx:**335-3974
(212) 819-8200 .. **Healy,** Dwight A '76 (White & C LLP) -1155 Av of Amer -NY 10036
(315) 366-2236 .. **Healy,** Elizabeth S '08 %DA -Cnty Cthse Bx578 -Wampsville 13163 **Fx:**366-2503
(212) 806-5400 .. **Healy,** Francis C '04 %Stroock &S&L LLP -180 Maiden Ln -NY 10038
(845) 279-7432 .. **Healy,** Gary T '03 -2435 Route 6 -Brewstr 10509
(315) 785-3053 .. **Healy,** Harmony A '09 DA -175 Arsenal -Watertwn 13601 **Fx:**785-3371
(212) 541-2000 .. **Healy,** J Kevin '74 (Bryan C LLP) -1290 Av of Amer -NY 10104
(718) 894-4347 .. **Healy,** James F '53 -6462 Dry Hrbr Rd -Middl Vllg 11379
(212) 474-1000 .. **Healy,** Jody A '81 Cravath S&M LLP -825 8th Av -NY 10019
(516) 741-1110 .. **Healy,** John '05 %Foley GJ&F,LLP -666 Old Cntry Rd -Gdn Cty 11530
(212) 878-8281 .. **Healy,** John A '83 (Clifford C LLP) -31 W 52nd -NY 10019
(212) 264-7090 .. **Healy,** John P '95 US Ct of Intl Trade -1 Fed Plz -NY 10278
(518) 388-4364 .. **Healy,** John R '09 DA -612 State -Schnctdy 12305 **Fx:**388-4569
(518) 457-9402 .. **Healy,** Jos R '73 %Dept Civil Srvc -Harriman Campus Bldg 1 -Albany 12239 **Fx:**457-6654
(212) 805-6155 .. **Healy,** Margaret Anne '97 %Hon R Owen -40 Foley Sq -NY 10007
(212) 766-1888 .. **Healy,** Mark A '99 %Morris DA&F -2 Rector -NY 10006
(845) 291-2050 .. **Healy,** Matthew E '98 %DA -255-275 Main -Goshen 10924 **Fx:**291-2085
(516) 248-7000 .. **Healy,** Maureen R '84 (Albanese & A LLP) -1050 Franklin Av -Gdn Cty 11530
(631) 588-8778 .. **Healy,** Meghan C '98 %Germano & C,PC -4250 Vets Mem'l Hwy -Holbrook 11741
(516) 227-0700 .. **Healy,** Michl J '88 Cnsl Farrell F,PC -1320 RXR Plz -Uniondale 11556
(518) 489-1098 .. **Healy,** Miriam C '05 -21 Everett Rd Ext -Albany 12205
(718) 894-4347 .. **Healy,** Patrick J '50 -64-62 Dry Hrbr Rd -Middl Vllg 11379
(212) 554-1234 .. **Healy,** Pauline N '94 AXA Financial Inc -1290 Av of Amer -NY 10104 **Fx:**707-3963
(315) 946-5905 .. **Healy,** Richd M '81 (DA) -54 Broad -Lyons 14489 **Fx:**946-5911
(914) 470-0001 .. **Healy,** Siobhan A '06 %Babchik & Y,LLP -200 E Post Rd -White Plns 10601
(914) 946-0600 .. **Healy,** Thos E '91 (Pino & Assoc) -50 Main -White Plns 10606 **Fx:**946-0650
(212) 708-9228 .. **Healy,** Thos J Jr. '96 Bessemer Trust Co -45 Rckfllr Plz -NY 10111
(516) 482-1411 .. **Heaney,** Arthur '84 -505 Nrthrn Blvd -Gt Neck 11021 **Fx:**482-2497
(212) 226-7098 .. **Heaney,** Ashley '07 %Abramson & M -35 Worth -NY 10013
(212) 583-2166 .. **Heaney,** Gretta J '88 Baron Capital -767 5th Av -NY 10153
(212) 319-1409 .. **Heaney,** Leslie Bathgate '02 -435 E 52nd -NY 10022
(516) 764-1219 .. **Heaney,** Robin Mary '81 -20 Hllywd Ct -Rockvll Ctr 11570 **Fx:**764-1219
(917) 769-5923 .. **Heaney,** Suzanne M '89 NAB -245 Park Av -NY 10167
(212) 307-5500 .. **Heard,** C Stephen Jr. '65 (Venable LLP) -1270 Av of Amer -NY 10020
(212) 964-7770 .. **Heard,** Craig T '77 -135 W 79th -NY 10024
(212) 270-5230 .. **Heard,** Jamette Lonear '03 JP Morgan Chase & Co -270 Park Av -NY 10017
(212) 354-3800 .. **Heard,** Keith W '81 (Burke & P) -100 Park Av -NY 10017
(212) 756-2000 .. **Heard,** Scott A '08 %Schulte R&Z LLP -919 3rd Av -NY 10022
(212) 221-5700 .. **Hearle,** Matthew E '93 (Goldberg WFG LLP) -1501 Bway -NY 10036
(212) 852-1312 .. **Hearn,** Francis J Jr. '90 %US Trust Co,NA -114 W 47th -NY 10036 **Fx:**852-1310
(212) 747-8550 .. **Hearn,** George H '55 %Waterman Steamship -1 Whitehall -NY 10004
(212) 373-2842 .. **Hearn,** John C '85 Paul WRW&G LLP -1285 Av of Amer -NY 10019
(212) 558-4000 .. **Hearn,** Jos A '07 %Sullivan & C LLP -125 Broad -NY 10004
(212) 825-5900 .. **Hearn,** Rose Gill '89 %Dept of Invstgtn -80 Maiden Ln -NY 10038 **Fx:**825-2860
(315) 785-8533 .. **Heary,** James '64 (J Heary,PC) -120 Wshngtn -Watertwn 13601 **Fx:**785-8478
(716) 852-5875 .. **Heary,** Nicole A '98 (Feldman K LLP) -110 Pearl -Buffalo 14202
(716) 566-1300 .. **Heary,** Robt P '92 (Hiscock & B,LLP) -1100 M&T Ctr -Buffalo 14203
(212) 232-1300 .. **Heath,** Andrew D '89 (Lewis BB&S LLP) -77 Water -NY 10005
(212) 417-8000 .. **Heath,** Andrew M III '83 Natl Securities Corp -120 Bway -NY 10271 **Fx:**417-8026
(516) 692-8888 .. **Heath,** David L '00 %F Chau & Assoc,LLC -130 Woodbury Rd -Woodbury 11797 **Fx:**692-8889
(585) 638-6331 .. **Heath,** Douglas M '86 (Heath & M) -66 Vllg Sq Bx200 -Holley 14470 **Fx:**638-7221
(315) 475-2559 .. **Heath,** Jos J '75 -716 E Wshngtn -Syracuse 13210 **Fx:**475-2465
(315) 422-7111 .. **Heath,** Monica Robinson '85 (Blitman & K LLP) -443 N Franklin -Syracuse 13204
(716) 856-4000 .. **Heath,** Richd E '57 (Hodgson R LLP) -140 Pearl -Buffalo 14202
(212) 416-8000 .. **Heatherly,** Gail E '87 %Dept of Law -120 Bway -NY 10271
(315) 789-4549 .. **Heaton,** Eliza G '09 %Heaton & V,LLP -118 Genesee -Geneva 14456 **Fx:**781-2295
(212) 756-2000 .. **Heaton,** Matthew Stephen '09 %Schulte R&Z LLP -919 3rd Av -NY 10022
(315) 789-4549 .. **Heaton,** Murray P '77 (Heaton & V,LLP) -118 Genesee -Geneva 14456 **Fx:**781-2295
(212) 643-7000 .. **Heaton,** Timothy P '02 %Sills C&G PC -One Rckfllr Plz -NY 10020
(516) 481-5235 .. **Heaven,** Paula L '99 (Heaven & Assoc,PLLC) -560 Front -Hempstd 11550 **Fx:**481-5238
(212) 279-9090 .. **Heavey,** James E '08 %Stark & S -One Penn Plz -NY 10119 **Fx:**279-9113
(212) 876-5500 .. **Heavey,** Kristin E '06 %Neighborhood Def Srv -317 Lenox Av -NY 10027 **Fx:**876-5586
(845) 638-5001 .. **Heavner,** Gary L '95 %DA -1 S Main -New Cty 10956 **Fx:**638-5070
(845) 429-4637 .. **Heavner,** Ralph O Jr. '88 -5 Wayne Av -Stony Pnt 10980 **Fx:**429-0343
(212) 624-1280 .. **Hebble,** Robt M '89 -61 Bway -NY 10006
(917) 790-8061 .. **Hebel,** Barbara N '98 Cnsl US Army Corp of Engineers -26 Fed Plz -NY 10278
(516) 873-2000 .. **Heberer,** Wm M III '96 (Moritt HH&H LLP) -400 Grdn City Plz -Gdn Cty 11530
(212) 839-5300 .. **Hebert,** Eric R '01 Cnsl Sidley A LLP -787 7th Av -NY 10019
(212) 872-9800 .. **Heblack,** Alan '76 OfCnsl Squire S&D LLP -30 Rckfllr Plz -NY 10112
(212) 576-5149 .. **Hebron,** Robt J '80 NY Life Ins -51 Mad Av -NY 10010
(212) 588-5500 .. **Heching,** Harry G '79 (Davies WP&V LLP) -625 Mad Av -NY 10022
(212) 816-4430 .. **Heching,** Moshe '95 Citigroup Global Mrkts -388 Greenwich -NY 10013
(516) 294-8844 .. **Hechler,** Eric S '97 %L'Abbate BC&C,LLP -1001 Franklin Av -Gdn Cty 11530
(516) 328-3500 .. **Hechler,** Lisa E '00 %McDonnell & A,PC -401 Franklin Av -Gdn Cty 11530
(718) 263-4512 .. **Hecht,** Abraham '71 -118-21 Qns Blvd -Frst Hlls 11375 **Fx:**793-3076
(212) 683-0220 .. **Hecht,** Allan S '76 (Hecht-Law,LLC) -60 Mad Av -NY 10010 **Fx:**683-2325

(516) 545-5160 .. **Hecht,** Allen M '87 %Natl Grid -175 E Old Cntry Rd -Hicksvll 11801 **Fx:**545-5029
(516) 357-3700 .. **Hecht,** Amy F '88 (Cullen and D LLP) -100 Q Roosevelt Blvd -Gdn Cty 11530
(718) 222-2316 .. **Hecht,** Andrea M '03 %Law Dept -350 Jay -Brklyn 11201 **Fx:**222-2373
(212) 825-5900 .. **Hecht,** Andrea R '94 %Dept of Invstgtn -80 Maiden Ln -NY 10038 **Fx:**825-2860
(718) 892-4000 .. **Hecht,** Barry S '74 -64 Metro Oval -Bronx 10462 **Fx:**824-6171
(212) 490-3232 .. **Hecht,** Chas J '65 (Hecht & Assoc,PC) -275 Mad Av -NY 10016 **Fx:**490-3263
(631) 744-8300 .. **Hecht,** Craig A '93 -127 Route 25A -Rocky Pnt 11778 **Fx:**744-1470
(212) 612-4000 .. **Hecht,** Danl H '92 %Chubb Grp -55 Water -NY 10041 **Fx:**612-4519
(516) 794-7400 .. **Hecht,** Donald S '70 -666 Old Cntry Rd -Gdn Cty 11530 **Fx:**745-0596
(516) 717-1224 .. **Hecht,** Eliezer Z '99 -112 Spruce -Cedarhrst 11516
(914) 899-3100 .. **Hecht,** Elizabeth M '84 (Mead HC&G) -109 Spencer Pl -Mamaroneck 10543
(718) 875-4700 .. **Hecht,** Ephrem '66 (Hecht & H) -26 Court -Brklyn 11242
(516) 942-5010 .. **Hecht,** Ira R '86 -123 Lincoln Rd E -Plainvw 11803
(718) 875-4700 .. **Hecht,** Jacob '32 (Hecht & H) -26 Court -Brklyn 11242
(212) 264-5377 .. **Hecht,** Jay B '74 %Army Corps Engrs -26 Fed Plz -NY 10278 **Fx:**264-8171
(212) 837-6000 .. **Hecht,** Jennifer Alpern '01 %Hughes H&R LLP -1 Bttry Pk Plz -NY 10004
(212) 877-7871 .. **Hecht,** Jesse A '75 -339 W 85th -NY 10024 **Fx:**877-9609
(212) 373-3000 .. **Hecht,** Joanie '98 Paul WRW&G LLP -1285 Av of Amer -NY 10019
(718) 237-2000 .. **Hecht,** John T '92 %Leg Aid -111 Lvngstn -Brklyn 11201 **Fx:**237-8737
(212) 490-5700 .. **Hecht,** Jordan D '95 (Hecht KP&D) -19 W 44th -NY 10036
(516) 747-4343 .. **Hecht,** Joshua B '07 %JP DiMascio & Assoc,LLP -300 Grdn City Plz -Gdn Cty 11530 **Fx:**747-0204
(212) 490-5700 .. **Hecht Kleeger Pintel & Damashek** -19 W 44th -NY 10036 **Fx:**490-4800
(212) 306-7160 .. **Hecht,** Laurie E '99 %Ofc Cllctv Brgn -40 Rector -NY 10006 **Fx:**306-7167
(212) 245-5556 .. **Hecht,** Leonard H '88 OfCnsl T Hecht,PC -1270 Av of Amer -NY 10020 **Fx:**956-7432
(212) 226-2400 .. **Hecht,** Lisa Mendelson '90 (Hecht & H,LLP) -350 Bway -NY 10013 **Fx:**226-6906
(718) 891-9096 .. **Hecht,** Marilyn S '82 (Hecht & Assoc) -728 Av U -Brklyn 11223 **Fx:**891-2555
(212) 226-2400 .. **Hecht,** Michl W '89 (Hecht & H,LLP) -350 Bway -NY 10013 **Fx:**226-6906
(516) 365-6357 .. **Hecht,** Mindi '88 AFPD,Inc -1 Hllw Ln -New Hyde Pk 11042
(646) 471-4737 .. **Hecht,** Nathan '00 %PricewaterhouseCoopers LLP -300 Mad Av -NY 10017
(212) 735-3000 .. **Hecht,** Paul '77 %Skadden ASM&F LLP -4 Times Sq -NY 10036
(914) 995-3496 .. **Hecht,** Richd L '84 %DA -111 Martin Luther King Blvd -White Plns 10601 **Fx:**995-3363
(646) 414-6902 .. **Hecht,** Steven M '93 (Lowenstein S PC) -1251 Av of Amer -NY 10020 **Fx:**(973) 597-2381
(212) 407-6300 .. **Hecht,** Susan G '00 American Society for Technion -55 E 59th -NY 10022
(212) 973-8000 .. **Hecht,** Theo L '80 (Schnader HS&L LLP) -140 Bway -NY 10005
(212) 245-5556 .. **Hecht,** Thos T '58 (T Hecht,PC) -1270 Av of Amer -NY 10020 **Fx:**956-7432
(718) 575-8721 .. **Hecht,** Warren S '86 -118-21 Qns Blvd -Frst Hlls 11375 **Fx:**793-3076
(914) 946-0647 .. **Hecht,** Wm A '83 -901 N Bway -White Plns 10603
(212) 375-6659 .. **Hecht,** Wm D '72 (Hass & H,LLP) -135 W 50th -NY 10020 **Fx:**375-6888
(631) 218-7335 .. **Hechtel,** Lee G '99 %NBTY Inc -2100 Smithtown Av -Ronkonkoma 11779
(212) 689-8808 .. **Hechtkopf,** Helene R '08 %Hoguet NR&K,LLP -10 E 40th -NY 10016
(718) 275-3660 .. **Hechtman,** Saml P '03 %Harris Law Grp,LLP -96-14 63rd Dr -Rego Pk 11374 **Fx:**275-3405
(718) 767-7667 .. **Hechtman,** Sarah Bethel '94 OfCnsl T Ombres LLC -38-39 Bell Blvd -Bayside 11361 **Fx:**767-5488
(845) 807-0654 .. **Heck,** Sandra F '85 %Family Ct -100 North -Monticello 12701 **Fx:**794-8300
(212) 808-7800 .. **Heck,** Wm C '73 (Kelley D&W LLP) -101 Park Av -NY 10178
(212) 450-4000 .. **Heckart,** Robt L '74 (Davis P&W LLP) -450 Lex Av -NY 10017
(212) 836-8000 .. **Heckel,** A Hank '03 %Kaye S LLP -425 Park Av -NY 10022
(212) 763-5000 .. **Hecker,** Eric J '99 (Emery CB&A LLP) -75 Rckfllr Plz -NY 10019
(716) 856-3200 .. **Hecker,** Holly C '87 %Bender & B LLP -68 Niagara -Buffalo 14202 **Fx:**856-3270
(212) 557-9600 .. **Hecker,** Joel L '66 OfCnsl Russo & B -600 3rd Av -NY 10016
(212) 683-7100 .. **Hecker,** Joshua R '07 %Gallo V&K,LLP -90 Broad -NY 10004
(212) 756-2000 .. **Hecker,** Michl J '10 %Schulte R&Z LLP -919 3rd Av -NY 10022
(212) 902-2261 .. **Hecker,** Nicholas E '03 Goldman Sachs -85 Broad -NY 10004
(212) 909-6000 .. **Hecker,** Sean '00 (Debevoise & P LLP) -919 3rd Av -NY 10022
(718) 840-2833 .. **Hecker,** Stuart '70 -666 Carroll -Brklyn 11215 **Fx:**840-2834
(518) 762-0408 .. **Heckler,** Gerard V '86 -8 S William -Johnstwn 12095 **Fx:**762-0412
(716) 853-1616 .. **Heckman,** Carol E '78 (Harter S&E LLP) -12 Fountain Plz -Buffalo 14202
(516) 330-9772 .. **Heckman,** Diane '81 -421 Emerson Pl -Vly Stream 11580
(631) 853-7749 .. **Heckman,** Howard H Jr. '78 %Hon M Tanenbaum -400 Carleton Av -Central Islip 11722
(845) 744-2085 .. **Heckman,** Michl B '72 -44 Main Bx644 -Pine Bush 12566 **Fx:**744-6505
(212) 408-8980 .. **Heckman,** Stanley D '69 Richards Grp -1251 Av of Amer -NY 10020 **Fx:**603-4981
(212) 637-2203 .. **Hector,** Aimee '05 US Atty -1 St Andrews Plz -NY 10007
(718) 254-6212 .. **Hector,** Amanda '05 US Atty - EDNY -271 Cadman Plz E -Brklyn 11201
(845) 339-4444 .. **Hector,** John F '04 -326 Wall -Kingston 12401
(315) 779-0999 .. **Hector,** Lionel Lee '98 Hector Law -One Pub Sq -Watertwn 13601 **Fx:**779-8999
(212) 907-0700 .. **Hector,** Nicholas R '09 %Labaton S LLP -140 Bway -NY 10005
(212) 343-6100 .. **Hedden,** Andrew S '70 Cnsl Scholastic Inc -557 Bway -NY 10012
(718) 254-0700 .. **Hederman,** Robyn S '85 %Bklyn Defender Srvcs -177 Lvngstn -Brklyn 11201 **Fx:**254-0897
(212) 478-0000 .. **Hedge,** Richd A '06 DE Shaw & Co,LP -120 W 45th -NY 10036 **Fx:**478-0100
(518) 573-3108 .. **Hedgeman,** Catherine M '01 -178 Tampa Av -Albany 12208
(716) 852-3600 .. **Hedges,** Katy M '06 %Chelus HS&M,PC -438 Main -Buffalo 14202
(585) 454-2020 .. **Hedges,** Timothy R '06 (Cellino & B,PC) -16 W Main -Rchstr 14614
(315) 363-3440 .. **Hedglon,** Peter F '77 (Nemeti ME&H) -112 Farrier Av -Oneida 13421
(212) 759-8203 .. **Hedinger & Lawless** -110 Wall -NY 10005 **Fx:**751-2984
(212) 759-8203 .. **Hedinger,** Robt '85 (Hedinger & L) -110 Wall -NY 10005
(212) 302-8989 .. **Hedman & Costigan,PC** -1185 Av of Amer -NY 10036 **Fx:**302-8998
(212) 839-5300 .. **Hedrich,** Marc P '09 %Sidley A LLP -787 7th Av -NY 10019
(212) 547-5400 .. **Hedstrom,** Matthew P '08 %McDermott W&E LLP -340 Mad Av -NY 10173
(516) 571-3800 .. **Heegan,** Jessica A '05 DA -262 Old Cntry Rd -Mineola 11501 **Fx:**248-9479
(212) 402-4100 .. **Heeger,** Anastasia Benshoff '05 %Ofc Appllt Def -11 Park Pl -NY 10007 **Fx:**402-4199
(212) 446-4800 .. **Heenan,** Chas H '06 %Kirkland & E LLP -153 E 53rd -NY 10022
(212) 980-9600 .. **Heenan,** Christine '99 (Kaufman B&R) -120 Bway -NY 10271
(212) 697-3122 .. **Heer,** Christopher L '06 %Martin C&B LLP -220 E 42nd -NY 10017
(718) 923-4431 .. **Heer,** Kiranjeet K '90 Dept Taxation & Finance -55 Hanson Pl -Brklyn 11217
(212) 825-1212 .. **Heermance,** Brian P '94 (Morrison M LLP) -17 State -NY 10004
(212) 596-9000 .. **Heesters,** Michl S '10 %Ropes & G LLP -1211 Av of Amer -NY 10036
(212) 682-7474 .. **Heffer,** Douglas S '07 %Foley & L LLP -90 Park Av -NY 10016
(914) 785-2000 .. **Hefferin,** Douglas J '81 %Ciba Corp -540 Wht Plns Rd -Tarrytwn 10591 **Fx:**785-4831
(631) 852-2500 .. **Heffernan,** Andrew J '98 %DA -200 Center Dr -Rvrhead 11901 **Fx:**852-1769
(212) 935-1400 .. **Heffernan,** Deirdre M '09 %Seiden & S,PC -570 Lex Av -NY 10022
(516) 997-7330 .. **Heffernan,** Dennis S '93 (Baxter S&S,PC) -99 N Bway -Hicksvll 11801
(212) 997-8500 .. **Heffernan,** Geoffrey F '02 Hess Corp -1185 6th Av -NY 10036
(212) 446-4800 .. **Heffernan,** Jeanne M '03 (Kirkland & E LLP) -153 E 53rd -NY 10022
(516) 466-6030 .. **Heffernan,** Michl '72 %Mirkin & G,PC -98 Cuttermill Rd -Gt Neck 11021
(716) 856-0600 .. **Heffernan,** Michele O '75 (Jaeckle F&M,LLP) -12 Fountain Plz -Buffalo 14202
(718) 999-2040 .. **Heffernan,** Noel L '09 %Fire Dept Bureau Leg Afrs -9 Metrotech Ctr -Brklyn 11201
(212) 237-8376 .. **Heffernan,** Wm C '79 John Jay Cllg -899 10th Av -NY 10019
(718) 375-5078 .. **Heffez,** Sam N '91 -1502 Kings Hwy -Brklyn 11229
(212) 553-7291 .. **Heffner,** Arthur R '00 %Moody's Invstr Srvc -250 Greenwich -NY 10007
(315) 448-4800 .. **Heffner,** C Andrew '87 %Dept of Law -615 Erie Blvd W -Syracuse 13204 **Fx:**448-4853
(631) 665-5444 .. **Heffner,** Stephen '61 -1 E Main Bx381-P -Bay Shr 11706
(716) 851-4343 .. **Heffron,** John V '86 Law Dept -65 Niagara Sq -Buffalo 14202 **Fx:**851-4105
(212) 599-0777 .. **Hefler,** Elliott D '71 OfCnsl Eisenberg T&L -675 3rd Av -NY 10017
(212) 333-8000 .. **Hefler,** Karen S '90 %Polygram Records -825 8th Av -NY 10019
(212) 504-6000 .. **Hefner,** Gerard A '84 SpclCnsl Cadwalader W&T LLP -1 World Fncl Ctr -NY 10281
(212) 902-9763 .. **Heft,** Adam J '98 %Goldman Sachs -1 NY Plz -NY 10004
(212) 935-8575 .. **Heft,** Carolyn M '66 -60 E 42nd -NY 10165
(212) 226-7700 .. **Heft,** Heather L '98 (Donovan & Y LLP) -161 Av of Amer -NY 10013
(212) 225-2000 .. **Hefta,** Rhys W '06 %Cleary GS&H -1 Lbrty Plz -NY 10006
(516) 376-3737 .. **Hefter,** Eva H '86 -140 Spruce -Cedarhrst 11516 **Fx:**376-3739
(631) 369-1700 .. **Hefter,** Marcia Zipser '67 (Esseks H&A,LLP) -108 E Main Bx279 -Rvrhead 11901
(212) 506-5000 .. **Hefter,** Michl C '92 (Orrick H&S LLP) -51 W 52nd -NY 10019
(585) 255-1474 .. **Heftka,** Robt V '85 %Global Crossing -225 Kenneth Dr -Rchstr 14623 **Fx:**(877) 769-9844
(212) 682-6800 .. **Hegarty,** Timothy F '94 (Zetlin & D LLP) -801 2nd Av -NY 10017
(914) 694-3600 .. **Hegarty,** Wm E '87 %Westfair Publications -3 Gannett Dr -White Plns 10604 **Fx:**694-3680
(646) 313-4580 .. **Hegde,** Satyanarayan S '98 TCS America -101 Park Av -NY 10178
(646) 328-1922 .. **Hegedus,** Nicholas Z '87 -1001 Av of Amer -NY 10018 **Fx:**328-1922
(212) 232-1300 .. **Hegeler,** Jean B B '09 %Lewis BB&S LLP -77 Water -NY 10005
(607) 432-7952 .. **Hegeman,** Thos '78 -50 Dietz -Oneonta 13820 **Fx:**432-7987
(518) 885-2263 .. **Heggen,** Karen A '92 %DA -25 W High -Ballston Spa 12020 **Fx:**884-8627
(516) 739-1462 .. **Hegler,** Jean A '85 (Brosnan & H) -1325 Franklin Av -Gdn Cty 11530
(212) 530-4823 .. **Hegt,** Andrew G '03 %LaRocca HRG&B LLP -40 Wall -NY 10005
(212) 906-1200 .. **Hegt,** Jason C '10 %Latham & W -885 3rd Av -NY 10022
(716) 566-1300 .. **Hehr,** David M '84 OfCnsl Hiscock & B,LLP -1100 M&T Ctr -Buffalo 14203
(212) 400-4550 .. **Heiberger,** Andrew S '94 %Buttonwood Real Estate -45 Horatio -NY 10014
(212) 532-0500 .. **Heiberger-Jacobsen,** Jamie Leigh '94 (Heiberger & Assoc,PC) -205 Lex Av -NY 10016 **Fx:**532-2040
(212) 752-1000 .. **Heichel,** Eric P '89 %Eiseman LL&K,PC -805 3rd Av -NY 10022
(212) 421-4100 .. **Heicklen,** Wayne B '83 (Pryor C LLP) -7 Times Sq -NY 10036
(516) 571-3800 .. **Heid,** Brian '02 DA -262 Old Cntry Rd -Mineola 11501 **Fx:**248-9479
(212) 750-1200 .. **Heide,** Ingrid Hoffman '05 %Trolman G&L,PC -777 3rd Av -NY 10017
(212) 692-1000 .. **Heide,** Nanette C '93 (Duane M LLP) -1540 Bway -NY 10036
(516) 328-8899 .. **Heidecker,** Perry S '76 SrCnsl Milman L Law Grp PLLC -3000 Marcus Av -Lk Success 11042 **Fx:**328-0082
(631) 261-8834 .. **Heidelberger,** Jonathan '74 (Ingerman S LLP) -150 Motor Pkwy -Hauppauge 11788
(212) 286-8585 .. **Heidell Pittoni Murphy & Bach,LLP** -99 Park Av -NY 10016 **Fx:**490-8966
(516) 408-1600 .. **Heidell Pittoni Murphy & Bach,LLP** -1050 Franklin Av -Gdn Cty 11530 **Fx:**408-1601

(914) 559-3100 .. **Heidell Pittoni Murphy & Bach,LLP** -81 Main -White Plns 10601 **Fx**:949-1160
(607) 776-4126 .. **Heidrick**, Ellen R '05 Leg Srvcs -104 E Steuben -Bath 14810 **Fx**:776-4029
(315) 266-6100 .. **Heidt**, James K '83 Pub Def -235 Elizabeth -Utica 13501 **Fx**:266-6105
(914) 328-0404 .. **Heiferman**, Robt '83 (Jackson L LLP) -1 N Bway -White Plns 10601
(212) 849-7000 .. **Heifetz**, Maria '09 %Quinn EU&S,LLP -51 Mad Av -NY 10010
(718) 286-6000 .. **Height**, Rebecca L '02 %DA -125-01 Qns Blvd -Kew Gdns 11415
(212) 225-2000 .. **Heikal**, Hedayat A '10 %Cleary GS&H -1 Lbrty Plz -NY 10006
(212) 272-2000 .. **Heil**, Darren G '01 %JP Morgan Chase -383 Mad Av -NY 10179
(212) 451-2300 .. **Heil**, Jennifer L '03 %Olshan GFR&W LLP -65 E 55th -NY 10022
(212) 318-3207 .. **Heilborn**, Stephanie E '01 (Fulbright & J LLP) -666 5th Av -NY 10103
(914) 237-3348 .. **Heilbraun**, Allison M '89 (A Heilbraun,PC) -1046 McLean Av -Ynkrs 10704
(212) 996-0346 .. **Heilbronn**, Chas G '82 -1115 5th Av -NY 10128
(585) 232-5300 .. **Heilbronner**, Warren H '58 OfCnsl Boylan BCV&W,LLP -2400 Chase Sq -Rchstr 14604
(718) 237-2000 .. **Heilbrun**, Robt '85 %Leg Aid -111 Lvngstn -Brklyn 11201 **Fx**:237-8737
(631) 853-4161 .. **Heilig**, Edw G '87 %DA -N Cnty Cmplx Bldg 77 -Hauppauge 11788 **Fx**:853-4192
(212) 669-0600 .. **Heilig**, Justin M '09 %Hill R LLP -45 Bway -NY 10006
(631) 369-1700 .. **Heilig-Sidor**, Melissa '98 %Esseks H&A,LLP -108 E Main Bx279 -Rvrhead 11901
(585) 263-2790 .. **Heilman**, Alfred J '64 -36 W Main -Rchstr 14614 **Fx**:454-2867
(914) 428-9766 .. **Heilman**, Julia M '86 (Heilman & R) -399 Knollwood Rd -White Plns 10603 **Fx**:285-9769
(716) 856-4000 .. **Heilman**, Pamela D '76 (Hodgson R LLP) -140 Pearl -Buffalo 14202
(718) 858-9658 .. **Heilman**, Rebekah E '07 Ctr for Comm Alternatives,Inc -25 Chapel -Brklyn 11201
(716) 694-2800 .. **Heim**, David Michl '78 DM Heim -3060 Niagara Flls Blvd -N Tonawanda 14120 **Fx**:694-2801
(212) 788-1298 .. **Heim**, Douglas W '07 %Law Dept -100 Church -NY 10007 **Fx**:788-0367
(315) 463-4032 .. **Heim**, Herbert H '53 OfCnsl Koldin Law Ctr -6661 Kirkvll Rd Bx279 -E Syracuse 13057 **Fx**:463-6512
(212) 589-4200 .. **Heim**, Kathryn M '07 %Baker & H LLP -45 Rckfllr Plz -NY 10111
(212) 355-7188 .. **Heim**, Robt G '94 (Meyers & H LLP) -444 Mad Av -NY 10022 **Fx**:355-7190
(716) 849-1333 .. **Heim**, Sharon M '81 (Lipsitz GSC LLP) -42 Delaware Av -Buffalo 14202
(800) 416-5454 .. **Heiman**, Aba '88 (Fusco B&R) -11 Penn Plz -NY 10001
(800) 416-5454 .. **Heiman**, Aba '88 (Fusco B&R) -180 Froehlich Farm Blvd -Woodbury 11797
(212) 735-3000 .. **Heiman**, Laura A '94 %Skadden ASM&F LLP -4 Times Sq -NY 10036
(516) 543-4022 .. **Heiman**, Norman '62 -202 Nelson Ct -Syosset 11791
(212) 244-4111 .. **Heiman**, Oren '98 (Shiboleth YR&Z,LLP) -1 Penn Plz -NY 10119
(845) 334-3063 .. **Heimann**, Judith K '90 Benedictine Hosp -105 Marys Av -Kingston 12401
(212) 265-6888 .. **Heimann**, Matthew B '09 %Porzio B&N,PC -156 W 56th -NY 10019
(212) 355-9500 .. **Heimann**, Richd M '00 (Lieff CH&B,LLP) -250 Hudson -NY 10013
(212) 635-1034 .. **Heimberg**, Eve '96 Bk of NY Mellon -1 Wall -NY 10286
(212) 345-1890 .. **Heimer**, Owen E '79 Marsh Inc -1166 Av of Amer -NY 10036
(716) 200-5050 .. **Heimerl**, Herbert J Jr. '60 (Harris B PLLC) -726 Exchange -Buffalo 14210
(212) 323-7970 .. **Heimerl**, Wolfgang '97 -110 Wall -NY 10005
(212) 686-6650 .. **Heimowitz**, Jonathan I '04 (Langdon Title Agncy LLC) -232 Mad Av -NY 10016 **Fx**:(646) 330-5061
(212) 373-3000 .. **Heimowitz**, Philip A '82 Cnsl Paul WRW&G LLP -1285 Av of Amer -NY 10019
(516) 334-5511 .. **Hein**, Bernard '62 -603 Edgewood Dr -Westbury 11590
(212) 632-6000 .. **Hein**, James G Jr. '04 Lazard Freres -30 Rckfllr Plz -NY 10112 **Fx**:632-6060
(212) 309-1091 .. **Hein**, John R '10 %Hunton & W -200 Park Av -NY 10166
(518) 861-0029 .. **Hein**, Jos '95 -6468 Frenchs Mill Rd -Altamont 12009
(212) 403-1000 .. **Hein**, Peter C '76 (Wachtell LR&K) -51 W 52nd -NY 10019
(516) 374-6600 .. **Hein Waters & Klein** -825 E Gate Blvd -Gdn Cty 11530 **Fx**:374-6615
(212) 963-1254 .. **Heinbecker**, Yasemin '02 Ofc of the President -C176E UN Bldg -NY 10017
(212) 610-6300 .. **Heinberg**, Jack L '90 (Allen & O) -1221 Av of Amer -NY 10020
(914) 493-5667 .. **Heindl**, Deborah M '04 %Cnty Hlthcr Corp -95 Grasslands Rd -Valhalla 10595 **Fx**:493-2321
(914) 241-4335 .. **Heine**, Andrew N '53 -116 Radio Cir Dr -Mt Kisco 10549 **Fx**:241-4319
(516) 489-5000 .. **Heine**, Chas O '85 %Town Atty -Town Hall -Hempstd 11550 **Fx**:489-5150
(212) 640-2000 .. **Heine**, Timothy J '81 %Amer Exp -200 Vesey -NY 10285
(212) 969-3000 .. **Heineman**, Andrew D '53 (Proskauer R LLP) -1585 Bway -NY 10036
(212) 668-5927 .. **Heineman**, Geoffrey W '84 (Ropers MK&B) -17 State -NY 10004
(212) 632-6000 .. **Heineman**, Melvin L '63 %Lazard Freres -30 Rckfllr Plz -NY 10112 **Fx**:632-6060
(212) 278-6465 .. **Heineman**, Steven P '91 %Societe Generale -1221 Av of Amer -NY 10020
(631) 288-1394 .. **Heinkele**, Peggy Anne '72 -153 Oneck Ln Bx282 -Westhmptn Bch 11978 **Fx**:288-6225
(212) 218-2100 .. **Heinle**, Court D '10 %Fitzpatrick CH&S -1290 Av of Amer -NY 10104
(914) 737-2105 .. **Heinlein**, Mary Jane '75 -75 Locust Av -Cortlandt Manor 10567 **Fx**:734-8042
(718) 588-4400 .. **Heinrich**, Benjamin '71 -189 E 163rd -Bronx 10451 **Fx**:588-4716
(315) 437-7600 .. **Heinrich**, Colleen W '94 (Ferrara FLB&R,PC) -5010 Campuswood Dr -E Syracuse 13057
(845) 639-7800 .. **Heinrich**, Jay N '99 %Mandel K&B,LLP -210 Route 303 -Vly Cottage 10989
(212) 566-7766 .. **Heinrich**, Justin F '06 %R Gottlieb -111 Bway -NY 10006 **Fx**:374-1506
(212) 859-8000 .. **Heinrich**, Nowles H '07 %Fried FHS&J LLP -1 NY Plz -NY 10004
(518) 439-8888 .. **Heinrichs**, Donna B '85 Schrade & H -381 Delaware Av -Delmar 12054 **Fx**:439-9486
(315) 448-0420 .. **Heins**, Maurie G '75 %Hon R Pooler -100 S Clinton Bx7395 -Syracuse 13261
(212) 468-8000 .. **Heintz**, Adam J '07 %Morrison & F LLP -1290 Av of Amer -NY 10104
(315) 442-0100 .. **Heintz**, Joshua H '70 (Gilberti SH&S,PC) -555 E Genesee -Syracuse 13202
(212) 877-3663 .. **Heintz**, Madelynn B '85 -200 W 79th -NY 10024 **Fx**:362-4855
(315) 853-2020 .. **Heintz**, Paul B '78 -50 Chenango Av -Clinton 13323 **Fx**:853-1422
(212) 335-9000 .. **Heintz**, Vincent G '92 %DA -1 Hogan Pl -NY 10013
(212) 446-4800 .. **Heinz**, Andrew G '06 %Kirkland & E LLP -153 E 53rd -NY 10022
(518) 797-3783 .. **Heinz**, Kristal M '08 Rensselaerville Institute -63 Huyck Rd -Rensselaervll 12147
(212) 458-1739 .. **Heinz**, Matthew G '04 AIG -175 Water -NY 10038
(212) 343-2662 .. **Heinze**, Mark F '92 (Ofeck & H LLP) -130 Madison -NY 10002 **Fx**:(201) 488-4475
(212) 474-1000 .. **Heinzelman**, Kris F '77 (Cravath S&M LLP) -825 8th Av -NY 10019
(212) 788-3000 .. **Heinzen**, Wm M '99 Cnsl Mayors Ofc -City Hall -NY 10007
(914) 686-5300 .. **Heinzmann**, Jos C Jr. '88 (Speiser & H) -50 Main Bx58 -White Plns 10602 **Fx**:(203) 894-1508
(860) 424-4355 .. **Heiple**, Bonnie L '09 %Pullman & C,LLC -50 Main -White Plns 10606
(212) 772-4220 .. **Heise**, Erika M '00 Hunter Cllg-Legal Affrs Ofc -695 Park Av -NY 10065
(585) 637-3911 .. **Heise**, Roy A '73 (Klafehn & H) -13 Water -Brockprt 14420
(212) 752-1161 .. **Heisenberg**, Christoph C '91 OfCnsl Traiger & H LLP -501 5th Av -NY 10017 **Fx**:937-5229
(914) 934-8024 .. **Heiser**, David M '73 -2 Oriole Pl -Rye Brook 10573 **Fx**:934-2911
(914) 934-8024 .. **Heiser**, Janet L '74 -2 Oriole Pl -Pt Chester 10573
(212) 705-7000 .. **Heiser**, Matthew J '06 %Bingham M LLP -399 Park Av -NY 10022
(631) 853-5761 .. **Heiser**, Michl L '83 %Cnty Atty -400 Carleton Av -Central Islip 11722 **Fx**:853-7788
(212) 333-0200 .. **Heiser**, Stephen T '04 %Arkin KR LLP -590 Mad Av -NY 10022
(646) 723-2947 .. **Heisler**, Jeremy '80 (Sanford W&H,LLP) -1350 Av of Amer -NY 10019
(315) 435-2170 .. **Heisler**, John E Jr. '76 %Cnty Atty -421 Mntgmry -Syracuse 13202 **Fx**:435-5729
(718) 694-3851 .. **Heisler**, Lawr '78 %Transit Auth -130 Lvngstn -Brklyn 11201 **Fx**:694-5726
(212) 889-9041 .. **Heisler**, Stanley D '85 (S Heisler,PC) -330 Mad Av -NY 10017 **Fx**:889-9168
(585) 258-2800 .. **Heisman**, Lewis J '77 (Underberg & K LLP) -300 Bausch & Lomb Pl -Rchstr 14604
(914) 684-3427 .. **Heiss**, Carla Lea '97 Bunge Ltd -50 Main -White Plns 10606
(212) 306-1918 .. **Heiss**, Danl '06 %FINRA -1 Lbrty Plz -NY 10006
(212) 326-2000 .. **Heiss**, Howard E '77 (O'Melveny & M LLP) -7 Times Sq -NY 10036
(212) 867-4466 .. **Heistein**, Martin J '80 (Belkin BW&G,LLP) -270 Mad Av -NY 10016
(212) 477-6600 .. **Heit**, Julia P '66 -142 E 16th -NY 10003 **Fx**:477-1717
(716) 852-5200 .. **Heitger**, Renee E '96 (Hamberger & W) -700 Main Pl Twr -Buffalo 14202
(914) 323-7000 .. **Heitman**, Jennifer S '99 (Wilson EME&D LLP) -3 Gannett Dr -White Plns 10604
(718) 286-6000 .. **Heitmann**, Jacqueline M '99 %DA -125-01 Qns Blvd -Kew Gdns 11415
(718) 816-0044 .. **Heitmann**, Michl '02 -1855 Victory Blvd -Staten Isl 10314 **Fx**:816-0064
(212) 574-1200 .. **Heitmeyer**, Dana L '09 %Seward & K LLP -1 Bttry Pk Plz -NY 10004
(718) 748-8080 .. **Heitner & Breitstein** -26 Court -Brklyn 11242 **Fx**:748-8387
(516) 935-3600 .. **Heitner**, Brian R '93 (Seltzer SH&H LLP) -100 Jericho Quad -Jericho 11753
(914) 701-6292 .. **Heitner**, Carl '81 %State Ins Fund -105 Corp Park Dr -White Plns 10604
(212) 735-3000 .. **Heitner**, Douglas B '07 %Skadden ASM&F LLP -4 Times Sq -NY 10036
(212) 310-8000 .. **Heitner**, Kenneth H '74 (Weil G&M LLP) -767 5th Av -NY 10153
(718) 262-7100 .. **Heitner**, Maureen McHugh '92 Civil Ct -89-17 Sutphin Blvd -Jamaica 11435 **Fx**:262-7107
(212) 592-1400 .. **Heitner**, Michl '65 (Herrick,F LLP) -2 Park Av -NY 10016
(212) 916-4838 .. **Heitz**, Michl G '83 %TIAA-CREF -730 3rd Av -NY 10017
(212) 506-5000 .. **Heitzler**, Eileen B '83 (Orrick H&S LLP) -51 W 52nd -NY 10019
(914) 328-0404 .. **Hekle**, Michl R '02 %Jackson L LLP -1 N Bway -White Plns 10601
(212) 918-3000 .. **Hekmat**, Sina R Jr. '06 (Hogan L LLP) -875 3rd Av -NY 10022
(646) 688-6095 .. **Helbig**, Katherine '01 %Calabro & Assoc,PC -450 7th Av -NY 10123 **Fx**:688-6096
(718) 273-9000 .. **Helbock**, Robt J Jr. '88 (Helbock N&G) -2550 Victory Blvd -Staten Isl 10314 **Fx**:816-0718
(212) 993-9437 .. **Helbraun**, David '02 -28 E 28th -NY 10016
(718) 694-5612 .. **Helco**, Martha L '89 %Transit Auth -130 Lvngstn -Brklyn 11201 **Fx**:694-5726
(718) 236-2323 .. **Held**, Alyssa J '95 Held H&H -6920 Bay Pkwy -Brklyn 11204 **Fx**:234-1678
(212) 417-5300 .. **Held**, Amy '95 %Medicaid Fraud Cntrl -120 Bway -NY 10271 **Fx**:417-5274
(800) 656-9529 .. **Held**, Brian Allan '01 (Lynch Law Firm,PC) -222 Route 59 -Suffern 10901 **Fx**:(888) 271-9726
(716) 842-5955 .. **Held**, Donald J '97 M&T Bank Corp -1 M & T Plz -Buffalo 14203
(718) 236-2323 .. **Held**, Edw '66 (Held H&H) -6920 Bay Pkwy -Brklyn 11204 **Fx**:234-1678
(212) 448-1100 .. **Held**, Huyler C '52 (McLaughlin & S,LLP) -260 Mad Av -NY 10016
(212) 267-4417 .. **Held**, Jeffrey A '83 -277 Bway -NY 10007
(212) 326-2000 .. **Held**, Jeffrey S '82 (O'Melveny & M LLP) -7 Times Sq -NY 10036
(718) 236-2323 .. **Held**, Jennifer R '04 Held H&H -6920 Bay Pkwy -Brklyn 11204 **Fx**:234-1678
(518) 433-4348 .. **Held**, John R '92 %GE -12 Corp Wds Blvd -Albany 12211 **Fx**:433-4361
(212) 505-4985 .. **Held**, Judith E '85 Cnsl STV,Inc -225 Park Av S -NY 10003 **Fx**:780-1577
(212) 361-8290 .. **Held**, Laura '79 NYC Dept of Finance -66 John -NY 10038 **Fx**:361-8233
(516) 626-1587 .. **Held**, Linda '81 -801 Remsens Ln -Oyster Bay 11771 **Fx**:626-1973

(718) 531-9700 .. **Held,** Marc J '97 (Lazarowitz & M,LLP) -2004 Ralph Av -Brklyn 11234
(212) 720-5026 .. **Held,** Michl A '96 %Fed Reserve Bk -33 Lbrty -NY 10045 **Fx:**785-5748
(516) 536-2467 .. **Held,** Rhonda M '87 -37 Rugby Rd -Rockvll Ctr 11570 **Fx:**764-1720
(212) 458-7028 .. **Heldt,** Gisele '00 AIG -175 Water -NY 10038
(212) 813-8800 .. **Heled,** Yaniv '03 %Goodwin P LLP -620 8th Av -NY 10018
(212) 761-4000 .. **Heleniak,** David W '75 Morgan Stanley -1585 Bway -NY 10036
(646) 386-3667 .. **Helewitz,** Jeffrey A '01 %Supreme Ct-Law Dept -60 Centre -NY 10007
(212) 599-3303 .. **Helfand,** Alan J '53 (Helfand & H) -350 5th Av -NY 10118 **Fx:**599-3029
(212) 599-3303 .. **Helfand,** Andrew '84 (Helfand & H) -350 5th Av -NY 10118 **Fx:**599-3029
(212) 775-0055 .. **Helfand,** Neil S '04 %Simon G&K LLP -1700 Bway -NY 10019
(718) 847-5373 .. **Helfant,** David '58 -83-19 141st -Briarwd 11435 **Fx:**846-5110
(212) 661-9100 .. **Helfat,** Jonathan N '72 (Otterbourg SH&R,PC) -230 Park Av -NY 10169
(516) 221-0400 .. **Helfer,** Cheryl M '81 (Helfer & H) -254 Pettit Av -Bellmore 11710 **Fx:**221-0422
(212) 786-8700 .. **Helfer,** David N '94 %EMI Music NA -150 5th Av -NY 10011 **Fx:**786-8103
(212) 244-4630 .. **Helfer,** Jonathan '08 %Katz & M,PC -1350 Av of Amer -NY 10019 **Fx:**(646) 219-5717
(516) 221-0400 .. **Helfer,** Michl '78 (Helfer & H) -254 Pettit Av -Bellmore 11710 **Fx:**221-0422
(212) 559-5152 .. **Helfer,** Michl S '04 Citigroup -399 Park Av -NY 10022
(212) 790-4500 .. **Helferich,** Joanna R '05 %Manatt P&P,LLP -7 Times Sq -NY 10036
(585) 232-6500 .. **Helferich,** Wm H III '69 (Harter S&E LLP) -1600 Bausch & Lomb Pl -Rchstr 14604
(212) 885-5000 .. **Helfgott,** Eliezer M '93 (Blank R LLP) -405 Lex Av -NY 10174
(212) 940-8800 .. **Helfgott,** Gale '81 SpclCnsl Katten MR LLP -575 Mad Av -NY 10022
(212) 940-8800 .. **Helfgott,** Samson '73 (Katten MR LLP) -575 Mad Av -NY 10022
(914) 713-0305 .. **Helfman,** Arthur L '84 (Drachman & H) -175 Thornbury Rd -Scarsdale 10583
(646) 289-3981 .. **Helfman,** Cindy S '89 (Holtzman H,LLP) -350 7th Av -NY 10001 **Fx:**(212) 643-9151
(212) 577-3450 .. **Helfman,** Lester '78 %Leg Aid -199 Water -NY 10038
(914) 683-1800 .. **Helfman,** Richd '67 (Luman H&T) -140 Grand -White Plns 10601
(212) 644-0303 .. **Helfman,** Tara '08 %E Hayes,PC -515 Mad Av -NY 10022 **Fx:**644-4818
(212) 956-8900 .. **Helfrich,** Thos A '77 %League Vol Hosp -555 W 57th -NY 10019
(516) 759-2091 .. **Helfrick,** Jos R '83 -231 Glen Cove Av -Sea Cliff 11579 **Fx:**671-2994
(631) 584-5712 .. **Helfstein,** Lewis B '74 -10 Meadow Gate E -St James 11780
(845) 342-2444 .. **Helhoski,** Ronald E '74 (R Helhoski,PC) -517 E Main Bx3016 -Middletwn 10940 **Fx:**342-2438
(212) 453-3696 .. **Helin,** Chad J '03 Ace INA -1325 Av of Amer -NY 10019
(607) 722-3620 .. **Helisek,** Kenneth P '59 -20 Devon Blvd -Bnghmtn 13903
(212) 354-0808 .. **Helitzer,** Eve F '07 %Moses P&Z,LLP -1065 Av of Amer -NY 10018
(914) 686-4800 .. **Hellberg,** Julie C '07 %Harrington O&M,LLP -81 Main -White Plns 10601
(212) 545-1900 .. **Hellegers,** Paul M '85 (Menaker & H LLP) -10 E 40th -NY 10016
(212) 744-5743 .. **Hellenbrand,** Saml H '42 -177 E 75th -NY 10021
(212) 685-7600 .. **Heller,** Alan A '89 (Heller H&F,PC) -292 Mad Av -NY 10017
(212) 734-2581 .. **Heller,** Allan H '83 -445 E 80th -NY 10075 **Fx:**396-4330
(516) 229-4200 .. **Heller,** Amber E '04 Mendolia & S -875 Merrick Av -Westbury 11590
(212) 310-8000 .. **Heller,** Amy Erenrich '03 %Weil G&M LLP -767 5th Av -NY 10153
(516) 408-1600 .. **Heller,** Anthony M '72 (Heidell PM&B,LLP) -1050 Franklin Av -Gdn Cty 11530
(212) 889-6565 .. **Heller,** Brian A '02 (Schwartz & P LLP) -295 Mad Av -NY 10017
(212) 887-7706 .. **Heller,** Brian W '99 Keefe Bruyette & Woods Inc -787 7th Av -NY 10019
(212) 801-2165 .. **Heller,** Caroline J '01 (Greenberg T,LLP) -200 Park Av -NY 10166
(585) 454-0700 .. **Heller,** Cheryl A '82 (Ward GH&R LLP) -300 State -Rchstr 14614
(516) 512-8898 .. **Heller,** Craig S '87 -1225 Franklin Av -Gdn Cty 11530 **Fx:**873-8881
(718) 520-3501 .. **Heller,** David L '83 %Hon R Dunlop -125-01 Qns Blvd -Kew Gdns 11415
(631) 725-6340 .. **Heller,** David L '86 -3334 Noyac Rd -Sag Hbr 11963 **Fx:**725-6342
(914) 347-6360 .. **Heller,** David M Jr. '88 %Epstein & R -565 Taxter Rd -Elmsfrd 10523
(917) 778-6600 .. **Heller,** David S '74 %J Toomey -485 Lex Av -NY 10017 **Fx:**778-7048
(212) 906-1200 .. **Heller,** David S '09 (Latham & W) -885 3rd Av -NY 10022
(212) 337-0200 .. **Heller,** David V '91 %MLRC -520 8th Av -NY 10018 **Fx:**337-9893
(212) 925-5431 .. **Heller,** Diana '78 -5 White -NY 10013
(212) 592-1400 .. **Heller,** Douglas P '73 (Herrick,F LLP) -2 Park Av -NY 10016
(718) 648-6427 .. **Heller,** Edw Harris '63 -1230 Av Y -Brklyn 11235
(212) 737-4490 .. **Heller,** Elizabeth J '05 (Heller & H) -445 Park Av -NY 10022
(212) 484-8000 .. **Heller,** Eric R '03 %Time Warner -1 Time Warner Ctr -NY 10019
(716) 856-5500 .. **Heller,** Franklin W '74 (Damon M LLP) -200 Delaware Av -Buffalo 14202
(516) 223-0400 .. **Heller,** Fred I '74 -33 Fox Blvd -Merrick 11566 **Fx:**223-0168
(212) 751-4300 .. **Heller,** Gary M '94 %Hodgson R LLP -1540 Bway -NY 10036
(845) 561-0550 .. **Heller,** Glen L '85 (Drake LHKGG&R PLLC) -555 Hudson Valley Av -New Windsor 12553
(212) 685-7600 .. **Heller Horowitz & Feit,PC** -292 Mad Av -NY 10017 **Fx:**696-9459
(845) 634-6570 .. **Heller,** Howard E '75 SpclCnsl Kin Properties,Inc -31 Lady Godiva Way -New Cty 10956 **Fx:**634-6659
(212) 984-7700 .. **Heller,** Hugh M '68 OfCnsl Warshaw BCS&K,LLP -555 5th Av -NY 10017
(212) 685-7600 .. **Heller,** Jacob W '60 (Heller H&F,PC) -292 Mad Av -NY 10017
(212) 416-4176 .. **Heller,** Jamie G '96 Wall St Jrnl -1211 Av of Amer -NY 10036
(212) 715-9100 .. **Heller,** Jared I '06 %Kramer LN&F,LLP -1177 Av of Amer -NY 10036
(646) 840-5734 .. **Heller,** Jason R '04 %RCA Music Grp -745 5th Av -NY 10151
(631) 462-2323 .. **Heller,** Jeffrey T '92 (Somer & H LLP) -2171 Jericho Tpk -Commack 11725 **Fx:**462-2338
(516) 328-5538 .. **Heller,** Jodi Ann '95 %Canon USA -1 Canon Plz -Lk Success 11042
(718) 852-6340 .. **Heller,** Jon '90 -75 Poplar -Brklyn 11201 **Fx:**852-6073
(212) 732-2929 .. **Heller,** Jonathan O '88 %Dansker & A Assoc -30 Vesey -NY 10007 **Fx:**732-8795
(518) 449-3300 .. **Heller,** Justin A '91 (Nolan & H,LLP) -39 N Pearl -Albany 12207
(917) 535-9699 .. **Heller,** Kevin J '02 CNA -40 Wall -NY 10005
(212) 455-2000 .. **Heller,** Laura M '05 %Simpson T&B LLP -425 Lex Av -NY 10017
(212) 735-3000 .. **Heller,** Lauren P '09 %Skadden ASM&F LLP -4 Times Sq -NY 10036
(585) 262-2304 .. **Heller,** Lawr I '73 -1 E Main -Rchstr 14614 **Fx:**454-3595
(516) 835-5550 .. **Heller,** Lewis L '72 -379 Kenrdg Rd -Lawrence 11559 **Fx:**977-6233
(212) 916-5212 .. **Heller,** Lisa J '94 %TIAA-CREF -730 3rd Av -NY 10017
(212) 878-5121 .. **Heller,** Marc B '80 (Goulston & S,PC) -750 3rd Av -NY 10017
(845) 794-3000 .. **Heller,** Marcia '87 %Div of Hlth & Fam Srvcs -Govt Center-100 North -Monticello 12701 **Fx:**807-0507
(516) 775-2111 .. **Heller,** Marilyn '87 -9 Vernon -Floral Pk 11001 **Fx:**775-1859
(212) 737-4490 .. **Heller,** Mark Jay '69 (Heller & H) -445 Park Av -NY 10022
(518) 449-3300 .. **Heller,** Mark L '58 SrCnsl Nolan & H,LLP -39 N Pearl -Albany 12207
(212) 685-7600 .. **Heller,** Maurice W '85 (Heller H&F,PC) -292 Mad Av -NY 10017
(212) 964-3180 .. **Heller,** Melvin S '64 -15 Maiden Ln -NY 10038 **Fx:**233-2608
(212) 737-4490 .. **Heller,** Michl D '02 (Heller & H) -445 Park Av -NY 10022
(631) 694-2300 .. **Heller,** Michl J '92 (Lamb & B,LLP) -534 Broadhllw Rd Bx9034 -Melvll 11747
(631) 853-4104 .. **Heller,** Michelle L '07 %DA -400 Carleton Av Bx9082 -Central Islip 11722 **Fx:**853-7838
(718) 857-2791 .. **Heller,** Mickey Z '92 -315 Flatbush Av PMB 414 -Brklyn 11217 **Fx:**(347) 365-9444
(212) 758-5230 .. **Heller,** Nancy R '85 (Peck & H) -845 3rd Av -NY 10022
(212) 940-8800 .. **Heller,** Noah S '01 (Katten MR LLP) -575 Mad Av -NY 10022
(212) 637-2631 .. **Heller,** Nola B '05 %US Atty -1 St Andrews Plz -NY 10007
(516) 997-5000 .. **Heller,** Norman B '51 -369 Old Cntry Rd -Carle Pl 11514
(631) 390-4343 .. **Heller,** Norman H '94 (Frisoni H & Assoc,PC) -527 Townline Rd -Hauppauge 11788 **Fx:**390-4344
(212) 885-5000 .. **Heller,** Norman S '78 (Blank R LLP) -405 Lex Av -NY 10174
(212) 623-9117 .. **Heller,** Paul '88 %JP Morgan Chase & Co -4 NY Plz -NY 10004
(212) 530-5000 .. **Heller,** Peter B '09 %Milbank TH&M LLP -1 Chase Manh Plz -NY 10005
(212) 935-3131 .. **Heller,** Randy J '80 (Gallet D&B,LLP) -845 3rd Av -NY 10022
(212) 980-0120 .. **Heller,** Richd B '78 (Frankfurt KK&S,PC) -488 Mad Av -NY 10022
(212) 344-5680 .. **Heller,** Richd S '79 (Thompson H LLP) -335 Mad Av -NY 10017
(212) 841-1000 .. **Heller,** Robt B '99 (Covington & B LLP) -620 8th Av -NY 10018
(212) 715-9100 .. **Heller,** Robt M '67 Cnsl Kramer LN&F,LLP -1177 Av of Amer -NY 10036
(315) 424-1743 .. **Heller,** Ruth K '87 %SEIU-Local 1199 -404 Oak Bx6389 -Syracuse 13217 **Fx:**479-6716
(646) 442-3100 .. **Heller,** Simon '87 Legal Srvcs -90 John -NY 10038 **Fx:**(212) 227-9798
(212) 720-5026 .. **Heller,** Stephanie A '92 %Fed Reserve Bk -33 Lbrty -NY 10045 **Fx:**785-5748
(607) 387-4996 .. **Heller,** Stephen P '85 -5208 Buck Hill Rd -Trumansbrg 14886 **Fx:**387-4996
(631) 667-8773 .. **Heller,** Steven B '93 -15 Hastings -Dix Hlls 11746 **Fx:**242-0168
(718) 250-2000 .. **Heller,** Terrence F '08 %DA -350 Jay -Brklyn 11201 **Fx:**250-2314
(212) 686-6373 .. **Heller,** Thos '69 -210 E 36th -NY 10016
(845) 229-2100 .. **Heller,** Todd E '99 Heller Pension Assoc Inc -1363 Route 9G -Hyde Pk 12538 **Fx:**229-2302
(914) 694-4444 .. **Heller,** Wayne E '96 Natl Rlty & Dvlpmnt -3 Manhattanvll Rd -Purchase 10577 **Fx:**694-5448
(212) 858-1000 .. **Hellerer,** Mark R '77 (Pillsbury WSP LLP) -1540 Bway -NY 10036
(716) 839-4001 .. **Hellerer,** Robt J '50 (Hellerer C&O) -4536 Main -Amherst 14226 **Fx:**839-0964
(212) 841-1000 .. **Hellerman,** Eric '81 OfCnsl Covington & B LLP -620 8th Av -NY 10018
(914) 946-6774 .. **Hellerman,** Jeffrey T '91 %Pilkington & L,PC -222 Bloomingdale Rd -White Plns 10605
(718) 780-7954 .. **Hellerstein,** Wm E '64 Bklyn Law Schl -250 Joralemon -Brklyn 11201 **Fx:**780-0375
(212) 421-4100 .. **Hellige,** Eric M '81 (Pryor C LLP) -7 Times Sq -NY 10036
(212) 213-8844 .. **Hellman,** Andrea J '96 (Allyn & F LLP) -200 Mad Av -NY 10016
(212) 258-2555 .. **Hellman,** Chas D '86 -420 Lex Av -NY 10170 **Fx:**(646) 417-4220
(212) 736-2121 .. **Hellman,** Chas S '97 (Drubner & H,LLC) -1540 Bway -NY 10036
(212) 867-6000 .. **Hellman,** Dennis I '75 (Rosenberg & E,PC) -733 3rd Av -NY 10017
(516) 741-7676 .. **Hellman,** H M Todd '95 %Miranda SSSV LLP -240 Mineola Blvd -Mineola 11501
(516) 479-6300 .. **Hellman,** Jay S '95 (Silverman A LLP) -100 Jericho Quad -Jericho 11753
(212) 687-6262 .. **Hellman,** Jeremy A '07 %Barton B&P,LLP -420 Lex Av -NY 10170
(212) 687-3000 .. **Hellman,** Jordan A '10 %Jaffe & A,LLP -600 3rd Av -NY 10016
(212) 479-6000 .. **Hellman,** Jos S '54 OfCnsl Cooley LLP -1114 Av of Amer -NY 10036
(516) 741-7127 .. **Hellman,** Katherine L '87 -115 Willow -Gdn Cty 11530
(212) 839-5300 .. **Hellman,** Reuven '05 %Sidley A LLP -787 7th Av -NY 10019
(718) 428-2500 .. **Hellman,** Ronald B '63 -42-24 Douglstn Pkwy -Douglastn 11363 **Fx:**279-8393
(212) 820-9612 .. **Hellman,** Saml I '69 Cnsl Hawkins D&W LLP -One Chase Manh Plz -NY 10005
(212) 735-3000 .. **Hellmann,** Elizabeth A '99 Cnsl Skadden ASM&F LLP -4 Times Sq -NY 10036
(516) 229-4501 .. **Hellreich,** Steven M '87 %Russo A&T -875 Merrick Av -Westbury 11590
(212) 294-6700 .. **Hellwig,** Jason F '01 (Winston & S) -200 Park Av -NY 10166
(212) 504-6000 .. **Helm,** Anne Marie '03 %Cadwalader W&T LLP -1 World Fncl Ctr -NY 10281
(518) 457-2070 .. **Helm,** Michelle M '00 %Dept of Tax & Fin -Bldg 9 State Campus -Albany 12227 **Fx:**457-6131
(516) 227-6363 .. **Helman,** Eric J '07 %Amato & Assoc,PC -666 Old Cntry Rd -Gdn Cty 11530 **Fx:**227-6367
(845) 365-9100 .. **Helman,** Jamie L '04 %Davidson & G -30 Ramland Rd -Orangebrg 10962
(516) 484-1325 .. **Helman,** Richd K '62 -115 Oakdale Ln -Roslyn Hts 11577 **Fx:**484-1992

(212) 218-2800 .. **Helman,** Stephen A '63 Intervest Natl Bk -1 Rckfllr Plz -NY 10020 **Fx:**218-2808
(315) 732-5121 .. **Helmer Johnson Misiaszek & Kenealy** -405 Court -Utica 13502 **Fx:**792-3979
(973) 848-4049 .. **Helmer,** Kathy Dutton '81 Cnsl K&L Gates LLP -599 Lex Av -NY 10022
(518) 429-4200 .. **Helmer,** Maureen O '83 (Hiscock & B,LLP) -50 Beaver -Albany 12207
(518) 399-5400 .. **Helmer,** Nicole M '04 %Gordon T&D,LLP -113 Saratoga Rd -Glenvll 12302
(315) 474-7571 .. **Helmer,** Stephen T '83 (Mackenzie H LLP) -101 S Salina Bx4967 -Syracuse 13221
(518) 689-3570 .. **Helmer,** Wm S '83 (Green & S,PLLC) -194 Wshngtn Av -Albany 12210
(212) 788-1072 .. **Helmers,** Kristin M '81 %Law Dept -100 Church -NY 10007 **Fx:**788-0367
(212) 246-2400 .. **Helpern,** Martin W '57 SrCnsl Balber PM&VDT,PC -1370 Av of Amer -NY 10019
(212) 508-6700 .. **Helpern,** Robt E '71 (Tannenbaum HS&H LLP) -900 3rd Av -NY 10022
(212) 885-7444 .. **Helprin,** David E '04 BDO Seidman,LLP -330 Mad Av -NY 10017
(516) 393-5810 .. **Helprin,** Deborah G '80 -6800 Jericho Tpk -Syosset 11791 **Fx:**393-5811
(212) 801-6962 .. **Helsel,** Michl D '01 (Greenberg T,LLP) -200 Park Av -NY 10166
(212) 558-4000 .. **Helt,** Kelly '07 %Sullivan & C LLP -125 Broad -NY 10004
(212) 867-5353 .. **Helweil,** Mark S '81 -369 Lex Av -NY 10017 **Fx:**867-1914
(516) 873-7000 .. **Helweil,** Robt H '48 -292 Fulton Av -Hempstd 11550 **Fx:**741-6200
(212) 715-9100 .. **Helwick,** Timothy J '91 SpclCnsl Kramer LN&F,LLP -1177 Av of Amer -NY 10036
(212) 869-5030 .. **Helwig,** Catherine A '87 (Kucker & B,LLP) -747 3rd Av -NY 10017
(914) 834-8758 .. **Helzer,** Anne R '04 -14 Harmony Dr -Larchmnt 10538
(212) 813-8800 .. **Hemani,** Abigail K '02 (Goodwin P LLP) -620 8th Av -NY 10018
(212) 880-9434 .. **Hemani,** Rachel Y '05 %Morvillo AGIA&B,PC -565 5th Av -NY 10017
(212) 676-0966 .. **Hemann,** Katharine V L '08 %Law Dept -60 Lafayette -NY 10013 **Fx:**442-6865
(518) 591-5232 .. **Hembdt,** Philip G '99 %NYS ORPTS -WA Harriman State Campus -Albany 12227 **Fx:**474-3657
(716) 853-1616 .. **Hemenway,** Amy L '02 %Harter S&E LLP -12 Fountain Plz -Buffalo 14202
(212) 687-2770 .. **Hemingway,** Alfred H Jr. '73 %Cohen PL&P -551 5th Av -NY 10176
(212) 848-4000 .. **Hemler,** Kenneth H '08 %Shearman & S LLP -599 Lex Av -NY 10022
(212) 403-1000 .. **Hemli,** Danl E '05 %Wachtell LR&K -51 W 52nd -NY 10019
(212) 310-8000 .. **Hemlock,** Adam C '97 (Weil G&M LLP) -767 5th Av -NY 10153
(212) 841-1000 .. **Hemm,** Robt M '09 %Covington & B LLP -620 8th Av -NY 10018
(716) 854-2211 .. **Hemme,** Deborah L '07 E Cosgrove -525 Delaware Av -Buffalo 14202 **Fx:**854-8122
(212) 687-5154 .. **Hemmerdinger,** Damon J '99 Amenta & Co -555 5th Av -NY 10017 **Fx:**682-7599
(212) 839-5300 .. **Hemmerich,** Steffen G '06 %Sidley A LLP -787 7th Av -NY 10019
(315) 474-7447 .. **Hemmerlein,** Ellen M '02 (Hemmerlein & S,PC) -333 E Onondaga -Syracuse 13202 **Fx:**474-0425
(716) 631-7250 .. **Hemming,** Jennifer A '03 (Hemming & S PC) -336 Harris Hill Rd -Williamsvll 14221 **Fx:**929-3333
(585) 786-8822 .. **Hemming,** Vincent A '01 %DA -147 N Main -Warsaw 14569 **Fx:**786-8842
(212) 747-9560 .. **Hemmings,** Francis Emerson '01 (Hemmings & S LLP) -39 Bway -NY 10006
(212) 468-8000 .. **Hempill,** John R '83 (Morrison & F LLP) -1290 Av of Amer -NY 10104
(646) 862-3496 .. **Hempleman,** Beth M '05 %Weinstein Co -345 Hudson -NY 10014
(212) 921-8399 .. **Hempstead,** Ilizabeth Gonchar '01 %Lankler S&W LLP -500 5th Av -NY 10110
(212) 697-3122 .. **Hemstock,** Jillian R '06 %Martin C&B LLP -220 E 42nd -NY 10017
(718) 875-1300 .. **Henchey,** Terence M '85 %Appllt Div 2nd Dept -45 Monroe Pl -Brklyn 11201 **Fx:**858-2446
(212) 326-3939 .. **Hendee,** Emilie A '08 %Jones D -222 E 41st -NY 10017
(212) 553-9206 .. **Hendele,** Alison B '10 %G Cannata -233 Bway -NY 10279 **Fx:**227-4141
(212) 294-6700 .. **Hendele,** John M IV '08 %Winston & S -200 Park Av -NY 10166
(212) 483-2323 .. **Hendel-McCleary,** Helen M '90 %JP Morgan Chase -345 Park Av -NY 10154
(718) 226-8077 .. **Henderson,** Ann Marie '90 Staten Isl Univ Hosp -475 Seaview Av -Staten Isl 10305 **Fx:**226-8692
(212) 953-2381 .. **Henderson,** Barbara E '04 %Rubin F&F,LLP -292 Mad Av -NY 10017
(914) 761-2700 .. **Henderson & Brennan** -222 Mamaroneck Av -White Plns 10605 **Fx:**761-2708
(914) 761-2700 .. **Henderson,** Brian C '89 (Henderson & B) -222 Mamaroneck Av -White Plns 10605
(347) 401-9127 .. **Henderson,** Charmaine E '82 Supreme Ct Spcl Ref -360 Adams -Brklyn 11201
(212) 416-8000 .. **Henderson,** Cheryl A '88 %Dept of Law -120 Bway -NY 10271
(212) 450-4000 .. **Henderson,** Christina M '10 %Davis P&W LLP -450 Lex Av -NY 10017
(212) 335-9000 .. **Henderson,** Clara E '01 %DA -1 Hogan Pl -NY 10013
(518) 392-3678 .. **Henderson,** Dawnald R '66 -340 Lwr Cady Rd -Old Chatham 12136 **Fx:**392-3307
(518) 392-4202 .. **Henderson,** Deirdre '78 (Henderson & K) -3942 Route 66 -Valatie 12184 **Fx:**392-3673
(212) 484-3900 .. **Henderson,** Dennis J '84 Cnsl Arent F LLP -1675 Bway -NY 10019
(212) 259-8000 .. **Henderson,** Donald B Jr. '83 (Dewey & L LLP) -1301 Av of Amer -NY 10019
(516) 747-9700 .. **Henderson,** Donald W '87 (Ryan & H,PC) -1 Old Cntry Rd -Carle Pl 11514
(646) 386-5172 .. **Henderson,** Dorothy F '76 %Surrogates Ct -31 Chmbrs -NY 10007
(212) 775-8700 .. **Henderson,** Edw J '82 (Kilpatrick S,LLP) -31 W 52nd -NY 10019
(516) 393-2200 .. **Henderson,** Erin L '08 %Garfunkel W,PC -111 Grt Nck Rd -Gt Neck 11021
(212) 310-8000 .. **Henderson,** Gordon D '65 Cnsl Weil G&M LLP -767 5th Av -NY 10153
(212) 695-3800 .. **Henderson,** Heidi Lee '95 %inMotion,Inc -70 W 36th -NY 10018 **Fx:**695-9519
(212) 556-1020 .. **Henderson,** Hilda L '92 %The NY Times Co -620 8th Av -NY 10018
(212) 336-0089 .. **Henderson,** John P '03 %SEC -3 World Fncl Ctr -NY 10281 **Fx:**336-1323
(212) 541-2000 .. **Henderson,** Kenneth L '80 (Bryan C LLP) -1290 Av of Amer -NY 10104
(585) 530-3050 .. **Henderson,** Kristin A '08 %MHLS -50 East Av -Rchstr 14604 **Fx:**530-3079
(718) 694-3880 .. **Henderson,** Lynne Troy '79 Transit Auth -130 Lvngstn -Brklyn 11201 **Fx:**694-5726
(585) 586-5757 .. **Henderson,** Matthew J '99 Sutherland Global Srvcs -1160 Pttsfrd-Vctria Rd -Pittsfrd 14534
(212) 715-1000 .. **Henderson,** Taja-Nia Y '06 %Arnold & P LLP -399 Park Av -NY 10022
(516) 671-4888 .. **Henderson,** Tip '72 -41 Forest Av -Glen Cove 11542
(718) 636-1155 .. **Henderson,** Wm F '91 %Leg Srvcs -1368 Fulton -Brklyn 11216 **Fx:**398-6414
(212) 872-5688 .. **Henderson,** Wm T '86 %KPMG LLP -345 Park Av -NY 10154 **Fx:**872-7701
(212) 530-1800 .. **Hendin,** Jonathan D '95 Richards K&O LLP -1 World Fncl Ctr -NY 10281
(212) 270-5024 .. **Hendler,** Lynne Greenwald '78 JP Morgan Chase -270 Park Av -NY 10017
(212) 596-9000 .. **Hendler,** Pablo D '95 (Ropes & G LLP) -1211 Av of Amer -NY 10036
(212) 998-0057 .. **Hendler,** Richd M '89 %NYU-Stern Schl of Business -40 W 4th -NY 10012 **Fx:**995-4230
(212) 504-6000 .. **Hendler,** Scott M '03 %Cadwalader W&T LLP -1 World Fncl Ctr -NY 10281
(212) 754-9400 .. **Hendler,** Stanley B '49 -425 Park Av -NY 10022 **Fx:**754-6262
(516) 487-6115 .. **Hendon,** Elihu '55 -90 Hmpshr Rd -Gt Neck 11023
(212) 728-8000 .. **Hendon,** Jeremy M '09 %Willkie F&G LLP -787 7th Av -NY 10019
(212) 309-6000 .. **Hendon,** Joanna C '92 (Morgan L&B LLP) -101 Park Av -NY 10178
(212) 446-9314 .. **Hendon,** Seth M '92 %Tinicum -800 3rd Av -NY 10022
(212) 701-3000 .. **Hendrick,** Danl W '10 %Cahill G&R LLP -80 Pine -NY 10005 **Fx:**269-5420
(718) 250-2000 .. **Hendrick,** Michl P J '09 %DA -350 Jay -Brklyn 11201 **Fx:**250-2314
(516) 489-5000 .. **Hendrick,** Wm J '85 %Town Atty -Town Hall -Hempstd 11550 **Fx:**489-5150
(212) 357-0440 .. **Hendricks,** Aime Lebeck '96 %Goldman Sachs & Co -180 Maiden Ln -NY 10038
(585) 428-5001 .. **Hendricks,** James L '76 Sup & Cnty Cts -550 Hall of Justice -Rchstr 14614 **Fx:**428-2190
(212) 351-4000 .. **Hendricks,** Kristen L '07 %Gibson D&C LLP -200 Park Av -NY 10166
(315) 521-3122 .. **Hendricks,** Wm D '79 -7 High -Sodus 14551 **Fx:**483-6756
(212) 735-3000 .. **Hendrickson,** Matthew P '93 (Skadden ASM&F LLP) -4 Times Sq -NY 10036
(212) 489-8230 .. **Hendrickson,** Victor D '06 %Davis WT LLP -1633 Bway -NY 10019
(718) 386-8886 .. **Hendrie,** Jos J '90 -67-04 Myrtle Av -Glendale 11385
(212) 474-1000 .. **Hendrix,** Meredith A '08 %Cravath S&M LLP -825 8th Av -NY 10019
(315) 422-8191 .. **Hendrix,** Sally B '06 %Leg Aid -351 S Warren -Syracuse 13202 **Fx:**472-2819
(212) 310-2231 .. **Hendry,** Andrew D '73 %Colgate-Palmolive -300 Park Av -NY 10022 **Fx:**310-3230
(845) 266-6066 .. **Hendry,** James M III '04 -15 Jersey Av Bx817 -Pt Jervis 12771 **Fx:**363-6301
(516) 741-6565 .. **Hendry,** Melanie D '05 %Meyer SE&K,PC -990 Stewart Av Bx9194 -Gdn Cty 11530
(212) 449-4823 .. **Hendry,** Scott R '87 Merrill Lynch -4 World Fncl Ctr -NY 10080
(212) 310-8000 .. **Hendy,** Amanda M '09 %Weil G&M LLP -767 5th Av -NY 10153
(315) 781-1465 .. **Hendy,** Elizabeth A '89 %Leg Assistance -361 S Main -Geneva 14456 **Fx:**781-2565
(212) 947-6441 .. **Henegan,** Maureen A '82 %Henegan Construction -250 W 30th -NY 10001 **Fx:**643-1053
(212) 906-1200 .. **Henegar,** Matthew L '01 %Latham & W -885 3rd Av -NY 10022
(516) 868-9522 .. **Heneghan,** Francis J '61 -1380 Grand Av -Baldwin 11510
(212) 217-6300 .. **Heneghan,** Michl J '93 CapLease Inc -1065 Av of Amer -NY 10018 **Fx:**217-6301
(716) 882-4890 .. **Heneghan,** Shannon M '99 (Mosey P,LLP) -625 Delaware Av -Buffalo 14202 **Fx:**882-5240
(585) 226-3311 .. **Henehan,** David L '66 (Reynolds & H) -5579 Avon-Lima Rd Bx190 -Avon 14414 **Fx:**226-6740
(212) 836-8000 .. **Henek,** Carly J '02 %Kaye S LLP -425 Park Av -NY 10022
(212) 446-4800 .. **Henes,** Jonathan S '97 (Kirkland & E LLP) -153 E 53rd -NY 10022
(212) 872-1000 .. **Heng,** Sharmaine Tang '07 -One Bryant Park -NY 10036 **Fx:**872-1002
(212) 513-3200 .. **Hengen,** Nancy L '77 (Holland & K LLP) -31 W 52nd -NY 10019
(716) 551-4741 .. **Hengerer,** Carla J '87 %US DHS -130 Delaware Av -Buffalo 14202
(212) 408-2500 .. **Hengl,** Suzanne M '07 %Baker B,LLP -30 Rckfllr Plz -NY 10112
(516) 785-3116 .. **Henig,** Gregory I '88 %J Henig,PC -1598 Bellmore Av Bx1144 -Bellmore 11710 **Fx:**785-1026
(212) 363-6900 .. **Henig,** Jared S '05 %Faust GS&B LLP -2 Rector -NY 10006
(516) 785-3116 .. **Henig,** Jos '54 SrCnsl J Henig,PC -1598 Bellmore Av Bx1144 -Bellmore 11710 **Fx:**785-1026
(516) 791-9170 .. **Henig,** Marc E '99 (Green & H,LLP) -2079 Wantagh Av -Wantagh 11793 **Fx:**345-1616
(917) 521-3488 .. **Henig,** Wm '06 %NYC Dept Homelss Svcs -346 Powers Av -Bronx 10454
(212) 537-2266 .. **Henigan,** Patrick J '00 Morgan Stanley -1633 Bway -NY 10019
(212) 265-7000 .. **Henige,** Zachary R '08 UNITE HERE -275 7th Av -NY 10001 **Fx:**307-6904
(212) 973-0572 .. **Henig-Elona,** Lee '86 Cnsl Wolff & S PC -140 Bway -NY 10005 **Fx:**(973) 530-2378
(718) 286-6000 .. **Henigman,** Laura M '88 %DA -125-01 Qns Blvd -Kew Gdns 11415
(212) 308-4411 .. **Henin,** Larry D '79 (Edwards AP&D LLP) -750 Lex Av -NY 10022
(212) 776-5094 .. **Henits,** Les '86 %NYC Housing Auth -250 Bway -NY 10007 **Fx:**776-5039
(914) 592-1515 .. **Henke,** Dana L '90 %Barnes I&S,LLP -258 Saw Mill Rvr Rd -Elmsfrd 10523

(212) 298-5295 .. **Henken,** Donna M '85 %Leg Aid -49 Thomas -NY 10013 **Fx:**298-5252
(718) 788-1093 .. **Henkin,** Alice P '81 Henkin & H -525 3rd -Brklyn 11215 **Fx:**788-0172
(212) 530-5000 .. **Henkin,** Douglas W '93 (Milbank TH&M LLP) -1 Chase Manh Plz -NY 10005
(212) 804-4200 .. **Henkind,** Hilary M '93 (Mound CW&G) -One Bttry Pk Plz -NY 10004
(914) 694-1533 .. **Henkind,** Lewis '69 -2 Gannett Dr -White Plns 10604
(212) 986-9700 .. **Henkoff,** David M '86 Cnsl Eilenberg & K LLP -11 E 44th -NY 10017
(631) 298-1720 .. **Henle,** Geri C '95 (McGreevy & H,LLP) -455 Lloyds Ln Bx18 -Mattituck 11952 **Fx:**614-4500
(718) 766-9427 .. **Henle,** Heidi J '00 H Henle,PLLC -42-40 Bell Blvd -Bayside 11361
(718) 648-8300 .. **Henle,** Jeff '04 %A Bannìettis -2972 Av X -Brklyn 11235 **Fx:**648-8730
(518) 746-2525 .. **Henley,** Katherine G '97 %DA -383 Bway -Ft Edward 12828 **Fx:**746-2568
(516) 328-3500 .. **Henley,** Martha S '76 (McDonnell & A,PC) -401 Franklin Av -Gdn Cty 11530
(212) 878-7172 .. **Henly,** James B '88 %MTA -347 Mad Av -NY 10017
(212) 788-1024 .. **Henn,** Frances J '81 %Law Dept -100 Church -NY 10007 **Fx:**788-0367
(518) 402-0205 .. **Henn,** Jo Allison '90 %UIA Bd -Troy Atrium Bx15126 -Albany 12212 **Fx:**402-6208
(516) 683-4100 .. **Henneberger,** Craig J '87 NY Community Bank -615 Merrick Av -Westbury 11590
(516) 822-3550 .. **Henneberger,** Glenn T '92 (Hoffmann & B LLP) -6900 Jericho Tpk -Syosset 11791 **Fx:**822-3582
(212) 906-1200 .. **Hennedige,** Althea S '05 %Latham & W -885 3rd Av -NY 10022
(212) 577-3264 .. **Hennen-Anderson,** Mary E '90 Leg Aid -199 Water -NY 10038
(212) 688-8555 .. **Henner,** Janet L '97 %Fragomen DB&L LLP -7 Hanover Sq -NY 10004
(212) 818-8633 .. **Henner,** Lester '78 (Graubard M) -405 Lex Av -NY 10174
(518) 768-8232 .. **Henner,** Peter W '80 -Bx326 -Clarksvll 12041 **Fx:**768-8235
(914) 358-5200 .. **Henner,** Susan B '97 -34 S Bway -White Plns 10601 **Fx:**358-5203
(212) 859-8000 .. **Hennes,** David B '96 (Fried FHS&J LLP) -1 NY Plz -NY 10004
(212) 455-2000 .. **Hennes,** Marc S '08 %Simpson T&B LLP -425 Lex Av -NY 10017
(718) 896-6554 .. **Hennessey,** Brendan J '08 %King & K LLP -27-12 37th Av -LIC 11101
(631) 281-2500 .. **Hennessey,** Edw J '89 (Hennessey & D) -501 Wm Floyd Pkwy -Shirley 11967 **Fx:**281-2598
(212) 297-5800 .. **Hennessey,** James E '07 %Day P LLP -7 Times Sq -NY 10036
(518) 457-3177 .. **Hennessey,** James J Jr. '84 %Dept Civil Srvc -Harriman Campus Bldg 1 -Albany 12239 **Fx:**457-6654
(212) 819-8200 .. **Hennessey,** Logan H '04 %White & C LLP -1155 Av of Amer -NY 10036
(212) 512-0804 .. **Hennessey,** Patricia E '80 (Cohen HB&R,PC) -11 W 42nd -NY 10036
(212) 837-6000 .. **Hennessey,** Wm F 2nd '05 %Hughes H&R LLP -1 Bttry Pk Plz -NY 10004
(518) 641-0507 .. **Hennessey,** Yvonne E '98 (West Firm,PLLC) -677 Bway -Albany 12207 **Fx:**615-1507
(516) 328-3500 .. **Hennessy,** Eileen A '04 %McDonnell & A,PC -401 Franklin Av -Gdn Cty 11530
(212) 720-8195 .. **Hennessy,** James R '93 %Fed Reserve Bk -33 Lbrty -NY 10045
(516) 622-9200 .. **Hennessy,** Mickee M '96 (Westerman BEM&S,LLP) -1201 RXR Plz -Uniondale 11553
(917) 951-5774 .. **Hennessy,** Natalie L '07 Citigroup Inc -425 Park Av -NY 10022
(315) 437-4400 .. **Hennessy,** Richd A Jr. '69 -3333 James -Syracuse 13206 **Fx:**437-1085
(716) 858-2424 .. **Hennessy,** Shawn P '03 %DA -25 Delaware Av -Buffalo 14202 **Fx:**858-7425
(212) 474-1000 .. **Hennessy,** Thos Andrew '08 %Cravath S&M LLP -825 8th Av -NY 10019
(585) 258-0107 .. **Hennessy,** Timothy P '96 %Garrison Litigation -120 East Av -Rchstr 14604 **Fx:**325-7356
(212) 736-0007 .. **Hennessy,** Wm T '07 Weiss I PLLC -462 7th Av -NY 10018
(516) 674-8686 .. **Hennig,** Florence L '95 %J Brady -333 Glen Head Rd -Old Brookvll 11545 **Fx:**674-8118
(315) 422-1152 .. **Hennigan,** Dennis P '82 (Costello C&F,PLLC) -500 Plum -Syracuse 13204
(718) 990-6613 .. **Hennigan,** John P '75 %St John's Law Schl -8000 Utopia Pkwy -Jamaica 11439 **Fx:**591-1855
(212) 236-3130 .. **Hennigan,** Kieran P '01 Merrill Lynch -2 World Fncl Ctr -NY 10281
(315) 435-2470 .. **Hennigan,** Timothy M '85 %DA -505 S State -Syracuse 13202 **Fx:**435-3969
(518) 402-3215 .. **Hennigan-Cohen,** Meghann E '04 %State Comptroller -110 State -Albany 12236 **Fx:**473-9104
(212) 373-3000 .. **Hennigar,** Andrew '07 %Paul WRW&G LLP -1285 Av of Amer -NY 10019
(716) 773-1990 .. **Hennigar,** Wm G Jr. '93 -2025 Whitehaven Rd Bx574 -Grand Isl 14072
(212) 820-9414 .. **Henniger,** R Gregory '93 (Hawkins D&W LLP) -One Chase Manh Plz -NY 10005
(212) 788-5880 .. **Henning,** Marjorie E '84 Ofc Mgmt & Budget -75 Park Pl -NY 10007 **Fx:**788-9197
(212) 804-4200 .. **Henninger,** Gretchen '02 %Mound CW&G -One Bttry Pk Plz -NY 10004
(516) 542-1000 .. **Henninger,** John C '89 (Geisler & G,LLP) -100 Q Roosevelt Blvd -Gdn Cty 11530
(212) 398-0055 .. **Hennings,** Kimberly M '04 %Garwin G&F,LLP -1501 Bway -NY 10036
(631) 694-0033 .. **Hennings,** Paul E '87 %Lawrence WR&B,PC -425 Broadhllw Rd -Melvll 11747
(516) 222-6200 .. **Henoch,** Gilbert '58 (Berkman HPP&F,PC) -100 Grdn City Plz -Gdn Cty 11530
(212) 488-1200 .. **Henoch,** Robt W '94 (Kobre & K,LLP) -800 3rd Av -NY 10022
(212) 371-8855 .. **Henri,** Marie-Josee '00 %Stikeman E LLP -445 Park Av -NY 10022
(716) 856-5500 .. **Henrich,** Christian J '04 %Damon M LLP -200 Delaware Av -Buffalo 14202
(212) 735-3000 .. **Henries,** Elizabeth A '06 %Skadden ASM&F LLP -4 Times Sq -NY 10036
(212) 259-8000 .. **Henrikson,** Matthew B '07 %Dewey & L LLP -1301 Av of Amer -NY 10019
(212) 766-5222 .. **Henriques,** Daniela F '06 %Leav & S LLP -120 Bway -NY 10271 **Fx:**693-2377
(914) 378-1010 .. **Henriquez,** Eloisa '01 %Fitzgerald & F -538 Riverdale Av -Ynkrs 10705
(212) 918-3000 .. **Henriquez,** Luz Maria '09 %Hogan L LLP -875 3rd Av -NY 10022
(212) 344-9022 .. **Henriquez,** Nicole Y '99 %Klein Law Grp,PC -11 Bway -NY 10004 **Fx:**344-0301
(212) 461-7175 .. **Henriquez,** Ronald M '92 -44 Wall -NY 10005
(212) 654-8538 .. **Henriquez,** Ryan S '00 %VH1 -345 Hudson -NY 10014
(212) 909-6000 .. **Henriquez Schmitz,** Carolina '08 %Debevoise & P LLP -919 3rd Av -NY 10022
(914) 665-7971 .. **Henriquez,** Stephan J '81 -117 Esplanade -Mt Vernon 10553
(212) 233-0101 .. **Henriquez-Herrera,** Teodulo A '84 (T Henriquez) -225 Bway -NY 10007
(212) 762-4000 .. **Henry,** A Michl '98 Morgan Stanley -1221 Av of Amer -NY 10020
(212) 723-2112 .. **Henry,** Brian W '98 Citigroup-Capital Mkts -250 West -NY 10013
(716) 854-2620 .. **Henry,** Carolyn M '90 %Brown & K,LLP -1500 Lbrty Bldg -Buffalo 14202
(516) 571-3800 .. **Henry,** Catherine A '07 %DA -262 Old Cntry Rd -Mineola 11501 **Fx:**248-9479
(212) 596-9000 .. **Henry,** Christopher C '04 (Ropes & G LLP) -1211 Av of Amer -NY 10036
(716) 648-0510 .. **Henry,** Danl J Jr. '87 (Villarini & H,LLP) -16 Main -Hambrg 14075 **Fx:**648-1806
(716) 849-1333 .. **Henry,** David G '74 SpclCnsl Lipsitz GSC LLP -42 Delaware Av -Buffalo 14202
(516) 741-5252 .. **Henry,** David S '08 %Sanders SBWV&G,PC -100 Hrrcks Rd -Mineola 11501
(212) 308-4411 .. **Henry,** Deborah H '02 Cnsl Edwards AP&D LLP -750 Lex Av -NY 10022
(914) 946-7403 .. **Henry,** Donald P '90 -99 Church -White Plns 10601
(212) 326-2000 .. **Henry,** Douglas A '06 %O'Melveny & M LLP -7 Times Sq -NY 10036
(212) 566-4807 .. **Henry,** Francia I '91 Dept of Bldgs -280 Bway -NY 10007 **Fx:**566-3015
(607) 898-3209 .. **Henry,** James R '80 -201 E Crtland Bx95 -Groton 13073
(212) 546-9255 .. **Henry,** Jessica V '96 %Scarinci H -107 Grand -NY 10013
(716) 857-7991 .. **Henry,** Joan G '03 %Natl Fuel Gas -6363 Main -Williamsvll 14221 **Fx:**857-7614
(518) 487-7600 .. **Henry,** John J '93 (Whiteman O&H LLP) -1 Commerce Plz -Albany 12260
(914) 948-1450 .. **Henry,** John V '72 (Henry & R) -44 Church -White Plns 10601 **Fx:**948-1439
(212) 373-3000 .. **Henry,** Judd S '05 %Paul WRW&G LLP -1285 Av of Amer -NY 10019
(516) 227-2200 .. **Henry,** Kenneth C Jr. '94 -900 Merchants Cncrs -Westbury 11590 **Fx:**(866) 277-8938
(718) 300-8087 .. **Henry,** Lishomwa D '01 -1 Cross Isl Plz -Rosedale 11422
(516) 877-5600 .. **Henry,** Lucien E '92 %R Tusa -1225 Franklin Av -Gdn Cty 11530 **Fx:**877-5695
(212) 356-0241 .. **Henry,** Marcelle J '01 %Cohen W&S LLP -330 W 42nd -NY 10036
(914) 666-3311 .. **Henry,** Maurice G Jr. '52 -40 W Main -Mt Kisco 10549
(917) 653-4200 .. **Henry,** Michl J '89 -442 7th -Brklyn 11215
(212) 673-7367 .. **Henry,** Nancy Lowe '76 -390 1st Av -NY 10010
(212) 735-3000 .. **Henry,** Oren M '09 %Skadden ASM&F LLP -4 Times Sq -NY 10036
(914) 749-8200 .. **Henry,** Robin Ann '89 (Boies S&F LLP) -333 Main -Armonk 10504
(212) 735-3000 .. **Henry,** Sally M '83 (Skadden ASM&F LLP) -4 Times Sq -NY 10036
(212) 803-5109 .. **Henry,** Sharyn L '97 %NY Cnty Defender Srvcs -225 Bway -NY 10007 **Fx:**571-6035
(518) 462-7770 .. **Henry,** Stephanie A '01 %Daniels & P,LLP -119 Wshngtn Av -Albany 12210
(212) 869-1959 .. **Henry,** Susan '82 %Canaan Foundation -4 W 43rd -NY 10036 **Fx:**869-4268
(212) 758-9700 .. **Henry,** Thos E '87 KPMG LLP -345 Park Av -NY 10154
(212) 728-8000 .. **Henry,** Thos J '00 (Willkie F&G LLP) -787 7th Av -NY 10019
(212) 370-6716 .. **Henry,** Tidal B Jr. '57 (Harrington H LLP) -305 Mad Av -NY 10165 **Fx:**684-2476
(516) 248-2386 .. **Henry,** Veronica M '94 Pharmacon -51 Edgewood Dr -New Hyde Pk 11040
(212) 983-1199 .. **Henry,** Yolanda K '02 %Cutler M&A,LLP -708 3rd Av -NY 10017
(518) 408-3976 .. **Hensel,** Stephen J '78 %NYS Comm Pub Integrity -540 Bway -Albany 12207
(212) 468-8000 .. **Hensler,** Madeleine A '05 %Morrison & F LLP -1290 Av of Amer -NY 10104
(212) 839-5300 .. **Hensley,** Dennis C '01 (Sidley A LLP) -787 7th Av -NY 10019
(212) 373-3000 .. **Hensley,** Judy M '07 %Paul WRW&G LLP -1285 Av of Amer -NY 10019
(212) 425-9300 .. **Hensley,** Michl T '02 %Bressler A&R,PC -17 State -NY 10004
(212) 756-2000 .. **Henslovitz,** Seth R '06 %Schulte R&Z LLP -919 3rd Av -NY 10022
(212) 834-1072 .. **Henson,** Colleen A '85 %GreenPoint Bk -90 Park Av -NY 10016 **Fx:**834-1402
(914) 946-3111 .. **Henson,** James B '92 -149 Grand -White Plns 10601 **Fx:**761-5444
(631) 804-2752 .. **Henthorne,** Danl K '03 -39 Cleveland -Patchogue 11772
(518) 860-1444 .. **Hentnik,** Katherine L '09 %Persing & O,LLP -10 Century Hill Dr -Latham 12110 **Fx:**860-1448
(718) 470-0543 .. **Hentrich,** Wm T '83 -84-12 259th -Floral Pk 11001 **Fx:**343-3942
(212) 326-3939 .. **Henze,** Wm F II '77 (Jones D) -222 E 41st -NY 10017
(585) 258-0105 .. **Henzel,** Brian R '00 Garrison Lit Mgmt Grp Ltd -120 East Av -Rchstr 14604
(212) 455-2000 .. **Hepler,** Erik W '90 %Simpson T&B LLP -425 Lex Av -NY 10017
(212) 373-3000 .. **Hepner,** Lee J '09 %Paul WRW&G LLP -1285 Av of Amer -NY 10019
(212) 627-8100 .. **Hepner,** Suzanne '01 (Levy R,PC) -80 8th Av -NY 10011
(212) 986-7353 .. **Hepner,** Wm P '92 (Wingate R&S) -420 Lex Av -NY 10170
(212) 735-3000 .. **Hepp,** David C '99 (Skadden ASM&F LLP) -4 Times Sq -NY 10036
(212) 770-6445 .. **Heppe,** Rosario E '05 AIG -70 Pine -NY 10270
(845) 331-4100 .. **Heppner,** Danl G '76 (Rusk WH&M,LLP) -255 Fair Bx3356 -Kingston 12402
(212) 973-0839 .. **Heppt,** Jos M '87 -260 Mad Av -NY 10016 **Fx:**973-0891
(212) 446-4800 .. **Heptig,** Katherine A '05 %Kirkland & E LLP -153 E 53rd -NY 10022

(631) 712-5720 .. **Hepworth,** F Judith '88 %Hon W Wall -824 Fed Plz Bx9014 -Central Islip 11722
(212) 545-1199 .. **Hepworth,** Marc S '99 (Hepworth G&R LLC) -192 Lex Av -NY 10016 **Fx:**532-3801
(212) 335-4500 .. **Hepworth,** Michl R '85 OfCnsl DLA Piper LLP -1251 Av of Amer -NY 10020
(212) 726-6927 .. **Her,** Keehwan '06 Atari, Inc -417 5th Av -NY 10016
(716) 873-6765 .. **Herald,** Keith A '88 %Pusatier S&A -2464 Elmwood Av -Kenmore 14217
(518) 862-1200 .. **Heran,** Chas W Jr. '86 %Martin H&M LLP -Bx15141 -Albany 12212
(518) 783-6047 .. **Heran,** Jeanne M '86 -974 Albany Shaker Rd -Latham 12110 **Fx:**783-6009
(914) 681-8700 .. **Heran,** Michl A '95 (Milber MP&S LLP) -3 Barker Av -White Plns 10601
(212) 601-2680 .. **Herasme,** Oscar A '97 OfCnsl Gonzalez S&H LLP -350 5th Av -NY 10118
(716) 858-2424 .. **Heraty,** David A '08 %DA -25 Delaware Av -Buffalo 14202 **Fx:**858-7425
(212) 473-1390 .. **Heraty,** Quinn M '02 (Heraty Law,PLLC) -151 1st Av -NY 10003 **Fx:**202-4020
(718) 270-3780 .. **Herb,** Alice Hoenig '56 %SUNY Hlth Sci Ctr -450 Clarkson Av -Brklyn 11203
(212) 964-7133 .. **Herb,** Peter L '90 -1133 Bway -NY 10010
(212) 425-7200 .. **Herbel,** Elodie S '02 %Kenyon & K,LLP -1 Bway -NY 10004
(718) 852-5223 .. **Herbert,** Harvey A '75 -142 Joralemon -Brklyn 11201 **Fx:**852-6635
(212) 250-7523 .. **Herbert,** Jeffrey L '06 Deutsche Bank AG -60 Wall -NY 10005
(585) 232-6500 .. **Herbert,** John C '79 (Harter S&E LLP) -1600 Bausch & Lomb Pl -Rchstr 14604
(716) 853-1616 .. **Herbert,** John C '79 %Harter S&E LLP -12 Fountain Plz -Buffalo 14202
(212) 556-2100 .. **Herbert,** John S '80 (King & S) -1185 Av of Amer -NY 10036
(212) 248-8800 .. **Herbert,** Jos F III '97 %Callan KB&B LLP -1 Whitehall -NY 10004
(914) 231-2700 .. **Herbert,** Karen D '93 %DA -111 Martin Luther King Blvd -White Plns 10601 **Fx:**995-3363
(212) 980-0120 .. **Herbert,** Lisa A '06 %Frankfurt KK&S,PC -488 Mad Av -NY 10022
(718) 855-0200 .. **Herbert,** R Douglas '95 -26 Court -Brklyn 11242 **Fx:**855-3845
(212) 884-7272 .. **Herbert,** Raymond L '74 GMAC Commercial Finance LLC -1290 Av of Amer -NY 10104 **Fx:**884-7372
(212) 402-4100 .. **Herbert,** Rosemary '97 %Ofc Appllt Def -11 Park Pl -NY 10007 **Fx:**402-4199
(212) 572-4463 .. **Herbert,** Seth E '75 %Estee Lauder -767 5th Av -NY 10153 **Fx:**572-3989
(212) 935-8787 .. **Herbert,** Stephen R '75 (Locke & H,LLP) -1114 Av of Amer -NY 10036 **Fx:**935-5663
(212) 335-9000 .. **Herbert,** Suzanne M '00 %DA -1 Hogan Pl -NY 10013
(518) 457-2614 .. **Herbert,** Wm A '81 PERB -80 Wolf Rd -Albany 12205 **Fx:**457-2664
(212) 553-8738 .. **Herbertson,** Thos C '93 %Cohen K & Assoc -2 Park Av -NY 10016 **Fx:**553-8721
(315) 798-5742 .. **Herbowy,** John A '91 %Dept Soc Srvcs -800 Park Av -Utica 13501
(585) 295-1562 .. **Herbrand,** John S '78 OfCnsl Forsyth HOK&M,PC -1 Chase Sq -Rchstr 14604 **Fx:**325-6287
(212) 245-4580 .. **Herbsman,** Jonas E '91 (Shukat AHW&H,LLP) -111 W 57th -NY 10019
(212) 278-1781 .. **Herbst,** Abbe I '80 (Anderson K&O,PC) -1251 Av of Amer -NY 10020
(516) 826-6500 .. **Herbst,** Gary F '89 (LaMonica H&M LLP) -3305 Jerusalem Av -Wantagh 11793
(212) 689-0996 .. **Herbst,** I Leonard '80 -235 E 22nd -NY 10010
(212) 506-1700 .. **Herbst,** Jason M '05 Kasowitz BT&F LLP -1633 Bway -NY 10019
(631) 424-3597 .. **Herbst,** Jeffrey D '05 %B Salamone & Assoc,PC -8 Ford Pl -Dix Hlls 11746 **Fx:**424-5023
(212) 578-2211 .. **Herbst,** Melinda Socol '78 %MetLife -27-01 Qns Plz N -LIC 11101
(212) 557-1616 .. **Herbst,** Ronald S '78 (Herbst & Assoc) -230 Park Av -NY 10169 **Fx:**661-2153
(212) 688-1900 .. **Herbst,** Todd L '78 (Greenberg T&H,LLP) -767 3rd Av -NY 10017
(718) 382-0303 .. **Herchenroder,** John A '80 (Herchenroder & H) -911 Av U -Brklyn 11223 **Fx:**382-4353
(212) 852-3892 .. **Hercules,** Saml A '94 %US Trust Co,NA -114 W 47th -NY 10036 **Fx:**852-3852
(212) 538-3594 .. **Herczeg,** Larissa F '01 Credit Suisse -11 Mad Av -NY 10010
(646) 386-3375 .. **Herd,** Julia P '96 Hon P Feinman Supreme Ct -60 Centre -NY 10007
(716) 852-3600 .. **Herdzik,** Arthur A '76 (Chelus HS&M,PC) -438 Main -Buffalo 14202
(716) 674-0411 .. **Herdzik,** Matthew B Jr. '80 -3700 Seneca -W Seneca 14224 **Fx:**674-0414
(914) 789-8102 .. **Heredia,** Dolores '00 Fuji Photo Film -200 Summit Lk Dr -Valhalla 10595
(212) 735-3000 .. **Heredia,** Sylvia A '08 %Skadden ASM&F LLP -4 Times Sq -NY 10036
(716) 878-2802 .. **Herer,** David '83 %ABC Companies -1100 Main -Buffalo 14209
(212) 351-4000 .. **Herfort,** John A '75 (Gibson D&C LLP) -200 Park Av -NY 10166
(212) 683-3020 .. **Hering,** Benjamin A '87 -347 5th Av -NY 10016 **Fx:**686-4686
(212) 504-6000 .. **Hering,** Grant B '62 SrCnsl Cadwalader W&T LLP -1 World Fncl Ctr -NY 10281
(718) 625-0987 .. **Hering,** Michele Slochowsky '88 (Slochowsky & S) -26 Court -Brklyn 11242 **Fx:**625-5628
(212) 261-2061 .. **Heringer,** Carl S '77 Computer Generated Solutions,Inc -200 Vesey -NY 10281 **Fx:**261-0830
(315) 422-8769 .. **Herkala,** David W '97 %Cerio Law Ofcs -407 S Warren -Syracuse 13202 **Fx:**476-8002
(845) 355-7830 .. **Herkenham,** James J III '78 -Bx430 -Slate Hll 10973 **Fx:**355-7831
(518) 283-7612 .. **Herkenham,** Mary Dawn '85 SAIC -70 Indn Pipe Dr -Wynantskill 12198
(518) 587-0316 .. **Herkenham,** Thos L '99 (Herkenham & D,PC) -18 Division -Saratoga Spgs 12866 **Fx:**583-2936
(212) 527-1000 .. **Herland,** Warren A '68 (Jones HC&B PC) -1 Bttry Pk Plz -NY 10004
(718) 828-5758 .. **Herland,** Warren C '75 -2210 Manning -Bronx 10462 **Fx:**829-0671
(212) 986-1200 .. **Herlands,** Jonathan '76 (Gordon HR&C LLP) -355 Lex Av -NY 10017
(212) 825-5900 .. **Herlica,** Debra A '03 %Dept of Invstgtn -80 Maiden Ln -NY 10038 **Fx:**825-2860
(212) 227-4716 .. **Herlich,** Theo M '88 -299 Bway -NY 10007 **Fx:**227-4717
(212) 889-2121 .. **Herlihy,** Carol Anne '83 (Kellner HG&F) -470 Park Av S -NY 10016
(212) 403-1000 .. **Herlihy,** Edw D '73 (Wachtell LR&K) -51 W 52nd -NY 10019
(212) 468-8000 .. **Herlihy,** Erin I '10 %Morrison & F LLP -1290 Av of Amer -NY 10104
(518) 487-7600 .. **Herlihy,** Katherine B '09 %Whiteman O&H LLP -1 Commerce Plz -Albany 12260
(516) 678-1800 .. **Herlihy,** Nancy M '06 %S Rubel,PC -100 Merrick Rd -Rockvll Ctr 11570 **Fx:**764-5540
(212) 664-4511 .. **Herlihy,** Timothy P '93 %Saturday Night Live -30 Rckfllr Plz -NY 10112
(914) 644-6400 .. **Herling,** Julius '75 -2 Gannett Dr -White Plns 10604 **Fx:**644-6111
(516) 355-7901 .. **Herling,** Simon '71 (Paganini GCC&F) -1979 Marcus Av -Lk Success 11042
(718) 382-0303 .. **Herman,** Alexander '83 (Herchenroder & H) -911 Av U -Brklyn 11223 **Fx:**382-4353
(516) 565-9600 .. **Herman,** Allen A '05 -614 Hempstd Grdns Dr -W Hempstead 11552
(212) 909-6000 .. **Herman,** Andrew M '10 %Debevoise & P LLP -919 3rd Av -NY 10022
(516) 747-9744 .. **Herman & Beinin** -200 Willis Av -Mineola 11501 **Fx:**747-3799
(914) 666-6999 .. **Herman,** Bertram '54 B Herman,PC -Bx672 -Mt Kisco 10549 **Fx:**666-9499
(718) 645-5840 .. **Herman,** Brett P '84 -2500 65th -Brklyn 11204 **Fx:**336-1389
(212) 309-6000 .. **Herman,** Brian A '99 (Morgan L&B LLP) -101 Park Av -NY 10178
(518) 828-3900 .. **Herman,** Brian J '84 -541 Warren -Hudson 12534 **Fx:**828-3233
(212) 224-6400 .. **Herman,** Bruce '81 %Apple Bk -122 E 42nd -NY 10168
(212) 310-8000 .. **Herman,** David '01 Cnsl Weil G&M LLP -767 5th Av -NY 10153
(212) 588-0800 .. **Herman,** David '05 %Frommer L&H LLP -745 5th Av -NY 10151
(212) 474-1000 .. **Herman,** David A '08 %Cravath S&M LLP -825 8th Av -NY 10019
(212) 903-8700 .. **Herman,** Debra Silverman '00 (Roberts & H,LLP) -825 8th Av -NY 10019
(718) 624-3399 .. **Herman,** Dennis A '78 -16 Court -Brklyn 11241 **Fx:**858-4074
(716) 691-4870 .. **Herman,** Flory G '89 SpclCnsl L Keating -573 Kaymar Dr -Amherst 14228
(212) 269-4200 .. **Herman,** Glenn A '87 (Herman & H,PC) -2440 Bway -NY 10024 **Fx:**269-0030
(516) 374-4378 .. **Herman,** Harold C '55 -1115 Fordham Ln -Woodmere 11598
(845) 233-4329 .. **Herman,** Harold Saml '59 -60 Greentree Dr S -Hyde Pk 12538 **Fx:**299-2118
(212) 833-6140 .. **Herman,** Heidi Ann '96 RCA Music Grp -550 Mad Av -NY 10022
(718) 624-1800 .. **Herman,** Howard J '75 -16 Court -Brklyn 11241
(212) 554-7800 .. **Herman,** Howard R '80 (Moses & S LLP) -405 Lex Av -NY 10174
(212) 751-3001 .. **Herman,** Ira L '83 (Thompson & K LLP) -919 3rd Av -NY 10022
(212) 627-9898 .. **Herman,** Jamie F '06 Sloss Law Ofc,PC -555 W 25th -NY 10001 **Fx:**627-9498
(212) 209-3092 .. **Herman,** Jane E '87 Cnsl Reitler K&R LLC -885 3rd Av -NY 10022
(212) 455-2000 .. **Herman,** Jason A '02 %Simpson T&B LLP -425 Lex Av -NY 10017
(718) 590-2000 .. **Herman,** Jason S '07 %DA -198 E 161st -Bronx 10451 **Fx:**590-6477
(516) 741-1130 .. **Herman,** Jay M '77 (Herman KC&C,LLP) -400 Grdn City Plz -Gdn Cty 11530
(212) 756-2000 .. **Herman,** Jeffrey A '08 %Schulte R&Z LLP -919 3rd Av -NY 10022
(516) 504-0055 .. **Herman,** Jeffrey D '87 J Herman & Assoc,PC -67 Cuttermill Rd -Gt Neck 11021 **Fx:**504-0189
(212) 732-8579 .. **Herman,** Jerald M '65 (Sher HB&T,PC) -277 Bway -NY 10007
(212) 415-9200 .. **Herman,** Jonathan M '74 (Dorsey & W LLP) -250 Park Av -NY 10177 **Fx:**953-7201
(212) 619-6000 .. **Herman,** Joshua M '07 %Fay K&M,LLP -150 Bway -NY 10038 **Fx:**208-6879
(212) 399-3600 .. **Herman,** Judith F '88 Tishman Constrctn Corp -666 5th Av -NY 10103
(631) 232-0200 .. **Herman,** June R '95 %Fumuso KDSS&F,LLP -110 Marcus Blvd -Hauppauge 11788
(516) 741-1130 .. **Herman Katz Cangemi & Clyne, LLP** -400 Grdn City Plz -Gdn Cty 11530 **Fx:**741-1173
(212) 953-5000 .. **Herman Katz Cangemi & Clyne, LLP** -630 3rd Av -NY 10017 **Fx:**953-5001
(212) 596-9000 .. **Herman,** Kenneth B '71 (Ropes & G LLP) -1211 Av of Amer -NY 10036
(212) 425-7200 .. **Herman,** Kent P '05 %Kenyon & K,LLP -1 Bway -NY 10004
(212) 984-8500 .. **Herman,** Laurence R '98 Gerson Lehrman Grp -850 3rd Av -NY 10022
(212) 541-2000 .. **Herman,** Linda R '83 Cnsl Bryan C LLP -1290 Av of Amer -NY 10104
(914) 592-4275 .. **Herman,** Lisa D '97 %MHLS -100 Clearbrook Rd -Elmsfrd 10523 **Fx:**592-9404
(212) 269-0927 .. **Herman,** Lloyd J '86 %D'Amato & L,LLP -2 World Fncl Ctr -NY 10281
(718) 263-5808 .. **Herman,** Manuel '49 -118-35 Qns Blvd -Frst Hlls 11375 **Fx:**261-5013
(516) 747-9744 .. **Herman,** Mark D '70 (Herman & B) -200 Willis Av -Mineola 11501
(212) 277-4000 .. **Herman,** Matthew F '95 (Freshfields BD LLP) -520 Mad Av -NY 10022
(212) 272-5261 .. **Herman,** Matthew I '02 %JP Morgan Chase -383 Mad Av -NY 10179
(212) 972-6161 .. **Herman,** Michl R '03 %Cassin & C LLP -711 3rd Av -NY 10017
(212) 326-3939 .. **Herman,** Michelle F '04 %Jones D -222 E 41st -NY 10017
(212) 309-6000 .. **Herman,** Neil E '86 (Morgan L&B LLP) -101 Park Av -NY 10178
(212) 592-1400 .. **Herman,** Paul R '62 (Herrick,F LLP) -2 Park Av -NY 10016
(212) 563-4100 .. **Herman,** Peter '78 (Cohen W&S LLP) -330 W 42nd -NY 10036
(732) 855-6046 .. **Herman,** Peter R '86 (Wilentz G&S) -110 William -NY 10038 **Fx:**726-6562
(212) 541-6222 .. **Herman,** Peter R '93 OfCnsl Kane K,PC -1350 Av of Amer -NY 10019
(212) 878-6900 .. **Herman,** Philip A '05 (Goulston & S,PC) -750 3rd Av -NY 10017
(716) 858-2424 .. **Herman,** Raymond C '85 %DA -25 Delaware Av -Buffalo 14202 **Fx:**858-7425
(212) 759-6300 .. **Herman,** Richd B '84 RB Herman,LLC -445 Park Av -NY 10022 **Fx:**(917) 322-2105
(212) 269-4200 .. **Herman,** Robin S '89 (Herman & H,PC) -2440 Bway -NY 10024 **Fx:**269-0030
(212) 416-8596 .. **Herman,** Ross N '88 %Dept of Law -120 Bway -NY 10271
(914) 242-1717 .. **Herman,** Ross T '88 %R Candee -116 Radio Cir -Mt Kisco 10549
(516) 487-7401 .. **Herman,** Sonia '91 -74 Meadow Woods Rd -Gt Neck 11020 **Fx:**487-7401

(718) 897-2282 .. **Herman**, Spencer H '79 (S Herman,PC) -80-02 Kew Grdns Rd -Kew Gdns 11415 **Fx:**261-6345
(516) 481-1220 .. **Herman**, Stephen C '76 -119 Jackson -Hempstd 11550 **Fx:**418-1559
(212) 504-6000 .. **Herman**, Steven M '86 (Cadwalader W&T LLP) -1 World Fncl Ctr -NY 10281
(516) 594-2225 .. **Herman**, Steven R '80 -100 N Vllg Av -Rockvll Ctr 11570
(212) 836-8000 .. **Herman**, Stewart B '89 Cnsl Kaye S LLP -425 Park Av -NY 10022
(718) 780-7945 .. **Herman**, Susan N '75 %Bklyn Law Schl -250 Joralemon -Brklyn 11201 **Fx:**780-0393
(212) 790-4500 .. **Herman**, Tara '05 %Manatt P&P,LLP -7 Times Sq -NY 10036
(718) 487-1300 .. **Herman**, Terry '85 %Leg Srvcs Corp A -80 Jamaica Av -Brklyn 11207 **Fx:**342-1780
(631) 462-0368 .. **Herman**, Wendi L '92 -196 Warner Rd -Huntngtn 11743 **Fx:**462-0368
(212) 370-4900 .. **Herman**, Wm C '60 (Rosenthal & H,PC) -420 Lex Av -NY 10170
(718) 834-4850 .. **Herman**, Zelig '55 %Gerber & G LLP -26 Court -Brklyn 11242 **Fx:**858-8119
(212) 373-3000 .. **Hermann**, Brian S '97 (Paul WRW&G LLP) -1285 Av of Amer -NY 10019
(914) 286-3030 .. **Hermann**, Gabriel J '95 (Insler & H LLP) -80 Grasslands Rd -Elmsfrd 10523 **Fx:**372-1392
(516) 676-1610 .. **Hermann**, Martin J '63 -245 Glen Cove Av -Sea Cliff 11579 **Fx:**676-1775
(914) 358-4934 .. **Hermann**, Miriam W '96 (Ferro L&Z LLC) -1025 Wstchstr Av -White Plns 10604
(516) 766-1461 .. **Hermann**, Randi Lana '87 %Oceanside Inst -2525 Lng Bch Rd -Oceanside 11572
(518) 486-3292 .. **Hermann**, Robt H '69 Gov's Ofc of Regulatory Reform -Bx2107 -Albany 12220 **Fx:**473-9962
(212) 683-7373 .. **Hermanowski**, John M '06 %Weiss & Assoc,PC -440 Park Av S -NY 10016 **Fx:**726-0135
(212) 715-9100 .. **Hermawan**, Edwin '10 %Kramer LN&F,LLP -1177 Av of Amer -NY 10036
(631) 582-4000 .. **Hermer**, Susan J '85 Cnsl Tsunis G&L,LLP -2929 Express Dr N -Islandia 11749
(212) 551-5427 .. **Hermida**, Maria C '92 %Royal Alliance Assoc -1 World Fncl Ctr -NY 10281 **Fx:**551-5620
(203) 674-7952 .. **Hernandez**, Alex V '87 (Pullman & C,LLC) -50 Main -White Plns 10606
(212) 663-1525 .. **Hernandez**, Alfredo M '85 -215 W 101st -NY 10025 **Fx:**531-6297
(516) 847-0448 .. **Hernandez**, Angela M '92 -1197 N Bway -Massapequa 11758 **Fx:**753-1207
(718) 357-4333 .. **Hernandez**, Christian M '08 Trop & S -19-02 Whitestone Expy -Whitestone 11357
(212) 506-2500 .. **Hernandez**, Christine M '05 %Mayer B LLP -1675 Bway -NY 10019
(212) 474-1000 .. **Hernandez**, Damaris '08 %Cravath S&M LLP -825 8th Av -NY 10019
(718) 522-0009 .. **Hernandez**, David J '87 (D Hernandez & Assoc) -26 Court -Brklyn 11242 **Fx:**522-3305
(718) 590-2000 .. **Hernandez**, Diego '06 DA -198 E 161st -Bronx 10451 **Fx:**590-6477
(212) 705-7000 .. **Hernandez**, Elsa '09 %Bingham M LLP -399 Park Av -NY 10022
(631) 956-6100 .. **Hernandez**, Francisco J '98 -1732 Grt Nck Rd -Copiague 11726
(718) 590-3793 .. **Hernandez**, Glenda Marie '96 Supreme Ct -851 Grnd Cncrs -Bronx 10451 **Fx:**590-7294
(212) 225-2000 .. **Hernandez**, Ivy L '07 %Cleary GS&H -1 Lbrty Plz -NY 10006
(718) 505-6650 .. **Hernandez**, Jacqueline C '86 %Kaplan & M -75-20 Astoria Blvd -E Elmhrst 11370
(212) 837-6823 .. **Hernandez**, Jaime O '10 %Hughes H&R LLP -1 Bttry Pk Plz -NY 10004 **Fx:**299-6823
(212) 696-6000 .. **Hernandez**, Javier '86 (Curtis M-PC&M LLP) -101 Park Av -NY 10178
(212) 541-5800 .. **Hernandez**, Jessica L '99 Laurus Captl Mgmt -335 Mad Av -NY 10017 **Fx:**541-4434
(718) 590-3850 .. **Hernandez**, Johan A '07 %Law Dept -198 E 161st -Bronx 10451 **Fx:**590-2686
(718) 590-2000 .. **Hernandez**, Johanna '02 %DA -198 E 161st -Bronx 10451 **Fx:**590-6477
(212) 415-9200 .. **Hernandez**, Jose L '09 %Dorsey & W LLP -250 Park Av -NY 10177
(716) 332-7826 .. **Hernandez**, Judy S '97 USDC WDNY -68 Court -Buffalo 14202
(518) 283-4100 .. **Hernandez**, Julio III '90 (Smith H LLC) -105 Jordan Rd -Troy 12180
(646) 610-5400 .. **Hernandez**, Lori B '91 NYPD -1 Police Plz -NY 10038
(718) 237-2000 .. **Hernandez**, Manuela '06 %Leg Aid -111 Lvngstn -Brklyn 11201 **Fx:**237-8737
(516) 572-2000 .. **Hernandez**, Maritza D '07 %DA -99 Main -Hempstd 11550 **Fx:**572-2606
(212) 682-0020 .. **Hernandez**, Mark A '95 (Putney TH&H LLP) -521 5th Av -NY 10175
(718) 522-0009 .. **Hernandez**, Michl R '09 %D Hernandez & Assoc -26 Court -Brklyn 11242 **Fx:**522-3305
(212) 878-8000 .. **Hernandez**, Mirna Sibeles '05 %Clifford C LLP -31 W 52nd -NY 10019
(845) 623-2302 .. **Hernandez**, Nereida Carrasquillo '88 -224 Beekman Av -Tarrytwn 10591
(212) 609-6800 .. **Hernandez**, Richd '03 %McCarter & E,LLP -245 Park Av -NY 10167
(212) 773-3000 .. **Hernandez**, Rita A '84 %Ernst & Young,LLP -5 Times Sq -NY 10036
(212) 967-2388 .. **Hernandez**, Roberto Magnaye '91 -350 5th Av -NY 10118
(212) 766-1888 .. **Hernandez**, Sharon E '03 %Morris DA&F -2 Rector -NY 10006
(212) 393-9000 .. **Hernandez**, Susan '86 (S Hernandez,PC) -233 Bway -NY 10279 **Fx:**385-2530
(212) 370-1600 .. **Hernandez**, Wendy '07 -501 5th Av -NY 10017 **Fx:**370-1606
(516) 224-5652 .. **Hernandez**, Yvonne N '06 CLK Houlihan Parnes -135 Crsswys Park Dr -Woodbury 11797 **Fx:**224-6752
(646) 386-3624 .. **Hernandez-McGibbon**, Lois M '88 %Supreme Ct-Law Dept -60 Centre -NY 10007
(212) 925-1919 .. **Hernández Sánchez**, Desireé C '09 %JA Reiner -291 Bway -NY 10007 **Fx:**941-5975
(212) 779-8600 .. **Herndon**, Thos H Jr. '05 %Silverman SS&B PLLC -381 Park Av S -NY 10016
(518) 358-3581 .. **Herne**, Peter J '99 -Bx685 -Akwesasne 13655
(212) 335-9000 .. **Hernes**, Arlette '81 %DA -1 Hogan Pl -NY 10013
(845) 291-2454 .. **Hernon**, Jean M '90 %Leg Aid -2 Court Ln Bx328 -Goshen 10924 **Fx:**294-2638
(315) 798-5766 .. **Hernon**, Paul J '86 %DA -800 Park Av -Utica 13501 **Fx:**798-5582
(212) 809-2500 .. **Hernstadt**, Edw '92 (Hernstadt A LLP) -11 Bway -NY 10004 **Fx:**214-0307
(845) 628-1100 .. **Herodes**, Jennifer M '94 (Herodes & M,PC) -888 Route 6 -Mahopac 10541 **Fx:**628-1110
(516) 296-7000 .. **Herold**, David E '97 (Certilman BA&H,LLP) -90 Merrick Av -E Meadow 11554
(212) 474-1000 .. **Herold**, Joel F '99 (Cravath S&M LLP) -825 8th Av -NY 10019
(716) 285-6189 .. **Heron**, Michl H A '93 -1625 Buffalo Av -Niagara Fls 14303
(212) 554-7800 .. **Heroux**, Robt O '97 %Moses & S LLP -405 Lex Av -NY 10174
(212) 867-5800 .. **Herr**, Andrew G '00 (Osler H&H LLP) -620 8th Av -NY 10018
(516) 466-6030 .. **Herr**, Brett D M '03 %Mirkin & G,PC -98 Cuttermill Rd -Gt Neck 11021
(212) 314-2765 .. **Herr**, Philip M '81 AXA Equitable -1290 Av of Amer -NY 10104
(516) 579-6200 .. **Herrera**, Danl J '99 %Solomon & H,PLLC -2950 Hempstd Tpk -Levittwn 11756 **Fx:**579-2409
(212) 640-7996 .. **Herrero**, G Reed '08 %Amer Exp -200 Vesey -NY 10285 **Fx:**640-9260
(585) 613-4063 .. **Herrero-Jaarsma**, Maria M '99 %Hon M Telesca-USDC -100 State -Rchstr 14614
(212) 592-1400 .. **Herrick, Feinstein LLP** -2 Park Av -NY 10016 **Fx:**592-1500
(914) 948-2222 .. **Herrick**, Paul R '94 (Rabin P&H) -44 Church -White Plns 10601 **Fx:**948-2255
(212) 326-2000 .. **Herrick**, Peter C '05 %O'Melveny & M LLP -7 Times Sq -NY 10036
(914) 238-6202 .. **Herrick**, Peter J '71 -6 Tanglewild Rd Bx711 -Chappaqua 10514
(518) 218-7100 .. **Herrick**, Steven L '77 Cnsl Tully R,PLLC -441 New Karner Rd -Albany 12205
(212) 695-6465 .. **Herrick**, Timothy G '83 -875 Av of Amer -NY 10001
(212) 659-8105 .. **Herries**, Elizabeth G '88 %Mt Sinai Med Ctr -1 Gustave L Levy Pl Bx 1099 -NY 10029 **Fx:**348-2230
(212) 588-0800 .. **Herriger**, J Niklas '10 %Frommer L&H LLP -745 5th Av -NY 10151
(718) 286-6000 .. **Herring**, Floyd D '84 %DA -125-01 Qns Blvd -Kew Gdns 11415
(212) 490-3000 .. **Herring**, John N '09 %Wilson EME&D LLP -150 E 42nd -NY 10017
(212) 465-6705 .. **Herring**, Kristin '03 MSG Entertainment -2 Penn Plz -NY 10121
(718) 286-6000 .. **Herring**, Mariela Palomino '85 %DA -125-01 Qns Blvd -Kew Gdns 11415
(212) 815-1818 .. **Herring**, Regina P '87 DC 37 MELS -125 Barclay -NY 10007 **Fx:**815-1343
(212) 225-2000 .. **Herrington**, David H '93 Cnsl Cleary GS&H -1 Lbrty Plz -NY 10006
(718) 741-8332 .. **Herrion**, John P '96 %Div of Human Rights -1 Fordham Plz -Bronx 10458 **Fx:**741-8102
(631) 694-0033 .. **Herrman**, Margaret M '84 (Lawrence WR&B,PC) -425 Broadhllw Rd -Melvll 11747
(518) 346-1281 .. **Herrmann**, Diane M '93 %Law Order & Justice Ctr -144 Barrett -Schnctdy 12305
(212) 351-4000 .. **Herrmann**, Gabriel '04 %Gibson D&C LLP -200 Park Av -NY 10166
(212) 922-9093 .. **Herrmann**, Jeffrey M '72 -295 Mad Av -NY 10017 **Fx:**922-9063
(212) 682-1800 .. **Herrmann**, Katherine J '07 %Grant HS&K LLP -675 3rd Av -NY 10017
(718) 779-6630 .. **Herrmann**, Lawr M '66 -37-51 76th -Jcksn Hts 11372 **Fx:**565-7278
(518) 891-3020 .. **Herrmann**, Paul J '80 -115 Main -Saranac Lk 12983 **Fx:**891-8088
(518) 383-1299 .. **Herrmann**, Richd J Jr. '82 -646 Plnk Rd -Clifton Pk 12065 **Fx:**383-0905
(212) 682-1800 .. **Herrmann**, Richd L '68 (Grant HS&K LLP) -675 3rd Av -NY 10017
(212) 545-1900 .. **Herrmann**, Robt F '74 (Menaker & H LLP) -10 E 40th -NY 10016
(212) 969-3000 .. **Herrnson**, Lisa Berkowitz '91 %Proskauer R LLP -1585 Bway -NY 10036
(212) 906-1200 .. **Herron**, Allison M '07 %Latham & W -885 3rd Av -NY 10022
(585) 244-6000 .. **Herron**, Dennis P '92 -2180 Monroe Av -Rchstr 14618 **Fx:**271-4606
(585) 258-4538 .. **Herron**, Scott A '00 %UIA Bd -109 S Union -Rchstr 14607 **Fx:**258-4539
(516) 918-7444 .. **Herron-Hinds**, Aureon '96 Deloitte & Touche,LLP -2 Jericho Plz -Jericho 11753
(716) 852-5875 .. **Herrscher**, Mary Jo '89 (Feldman K LLP) -110 Pearl -Buffalo 14202
(212) 450-4000 .. **Hersch**, Dennis S '71 JP Morgan Chase & Co -277 Park Av -NY 10172 **Fx:**450-3800
(212) 370-4818 .. **Herschberg**, Howard '81 -420 Lex Av -NY 10170
(718) 946-3600 .. **Herschberg**, Joshua G '89 HSBC Bank USA -2301 86th -Brklyn 11214
(631) 342-3298 .. **Herschberg**, Leonard M '01 %CA,Inc -1 CA Plz -Islandia 11749 **Fx:**342-4866
(212) 310-8000 .. **Herschel**, Chas C '08 %Weil G&M LLP -767 5th Av -NY 10153
(212) 722-4167 .. **Herschkorn**, Leon N '90 -111 E 85th -NY 10028
(212) 268-7900 .. **Herschkowitz**, Steven '91 (Fischer & B,PC) -888 7th Av -NY 10106
(516) 829-1900 .. **Herschkowitz**, Steven '91 (Fischer & B,PC) -98 Cuttermill Rd -Gt Neck 11021
(212) 836-8000 .. **Herschlein**, James D '86 (Kaye S LLP) -425 Park Av -NY 10022
(212) 506-1700 .. **Herschmann**, Eric D '87 (Kasowitz BT&F LLP) -1633 Bway -NY 10019
(212) 788-0579 .. **Herscovici**, Jennifer J '99 %Law Dept -100 Church -NY 10007 **Fx:**788-0367
(212) 221-6556 .. **Hersh**, Bruce D '81 (BD Hersh,PC) -116 John -NY 10038 **Fx:**505-8455
(212) 533-6300 .. **Hersh**, Claude I '82 %NYSUT -52 Bway -NY 10004 **Fx:**995-2347
(212) 336-0465 .. **Hersh**, Ellen N '84 %SEC -3 World Fncl Ctr -NY 10281 **Fx:**336-1323
(914) 737-4585 .. **Hersh**, Fredk R '50 -1011 Park Bx527 -Peekskill 10566 **Fx:**737-4587
(631) 543-2900 .. **Hersh**, Harry D '75 (Davis & H,LLP) -1345 Motor Pkwy -Islandia 11749
(718) 886-1100 .. **Hersh**, Jennifer D '94 %F Regan Jr -159-18 Nrthrn Blvd -Flushng 11358 **Fx:**461-5651
(914) 739-4200 .. **Hersh**, John H '82 -1019 Park -Peekskill 10566
(718) 250-2000 .. **Hersh**, Lauren A '03 %DA -350 Jay -Brklyn 11201 **Fx:**250-2314
(212) 969-1000 .. **Hersh**, Leonard H '88 %Alliance Bernstein LP -1345 Av of Amer -NY 10105 **Fx:**554-4639

(212) 218-2100 .. **Hersh,** Lindsay H '09 %Fitzpatrick CH&S -1290 Av of Amer -NY 10104
(845) 292-9345 .. **Hersh,** Martin H '81 -4 Asthalter Rd Bx567 -Liberty 12754 **Fx:**292-9349
(212) 969-3000 .. **Hersh,** Melanie L '03 %Proskauer R LLP -1585 Bway -NY 10036
(914) 428-8288 .. **Hersh,** Michl J '01 %L Shaw -75 S Bway -White Plns 10601 **Fx:**428-8181
(914) 737-5300 .. **Hersh,** Philip '75 -1011 Park Bx105 -Peekskill 10566 **Fx:**737-5739
(914) 737-0270 .. **Hersh,** Robt '77 Hersh & H,PC -2 S Division -Peekskill 10566 **Fx:**737-4718
(914) 737-2500 .. **Hersh,** Scot F '86 -2 S Division -Peekskill 10566 **Fx:**734-7558
(212) 839-6527 .. **Hersh,** Susana Chavez '02 %Dept of Transportation -55 Water -NY 10041
(212) 762-6952 .. **Hersha,** Linda '84 Morgan Stanley -1221 Av of Amer -NY 10020
(914) 253-8600 .. **Hershaft,** Andrew E '92 (Fair F&H,PC) -110 Corp Park Dr -White Plns 10604
(212) 735-8600 .. **Hershberg,** Jared A '00 SrCnsl Morrison C LLP -909 3rd Av -NY 10022
(212) 479-6000 .. **Hershcopf,** Cathy R '89 (Cooley LLP) -1114 Av of Amer -NY 10036
(212) 288-8309 .. **Hershcopf,** Gerald T '49 -737 Park Av -NY 10021 **Fx:**288-8309
(315) 422-6154 .. **Hershdorfer,** Victor J '60 (Greene H&S) -1 Lincoln Ctr -Syracuse 13202
(212) 943-1090 .. **Hershenhorn,** Howard S '89 (Gair GCSMB&R) -80 Pine -NY 10005
(212) 548-0600 .. **Hershenov,** Eileen B '91 %Open Soc Jstc Initiative -400 W 59th -NY 10019 **Fx:**548-4679
(212) 754-1053 .. **Hershenson,** Richd E '71 -30 Broad -NY 10004 **Fx:**363-7171
(516) 571-3800 .. **Hershey,** Joanna '07 %DA -262 Old Cntry Rd -Mineola 11501 **Fx:**248-9479
(516) 424-9111 .. **Hershey,** Laurie S '75 -222 Park Av -Manhsst 11030 **Fx:**365-2216
(212) 349-3000 .. **Hershey-Webb,** David S '00 (Himmelstein MGD&J) -15 Maiden Ln -NY 10038
(212) 998-6285 .. **Hershkoff,** Helen '79 %NYU Law Schl -40 Wshngtn Sq S -NY 10012 **Fx:**995-4760
(212) 512-0831 .. **Hershkovitz,** Orrit '98 %Cohen HB&R,PC -11 W 42nd -NY 10036
(212) 791-0285 .. **Hershkovitz,** Stephanie Yael '01 Malaby & B,LLC -150 Bway -NY 10038 **Fx:**791-0286
(212) 351-4000 .. **Hershkowitz,** Benjamin '94 (Gibson D&C LLP) -200 Park Av -NY 10166
(212) 935-1400 .. **Hershkowitz,** Jason C '07 %Seiden & S,PC -570 Lex Av -NY 10022
(212) 679-4666 .. **Hershkowitz,** Jos M '74 (Frenkel H&S LLP) -16 E 34th -NY 10016
(646) 649-2905 .. **Hershkowitz,** Marcia Berger '53 -170 2nd Av -NY 10003
(212) 458-2028 .. **Hershkowitz,** Robt M '90 AIG -175 Water -NY 10038
(212) 859-3477 .. **Hershkowitz,** Steven A '79 (S Hershkowitz,PC) -118-21 Qns Blvd -Frst Hlls 11375
(212) 416-8590 .. **Hershler,** James M '82 %Dept of Law -120 Bway -NY 10271
(212) 289-6734 .. **Hershman,** Elisabeth A '07 Van Prooyen G LLP -215 E 96th -NY 10128 **Fx:**289-7857
(631) 777-5196 .. **Hershman,** Harold M '56 (Hershman & L,LLP) -425 Broad Hollow Rd -Melvll 11747 **Fx:**777-3204
(212) 705-7000 .. **Hershman,** Jordan D '88 (Bingham M LLP) -399 Park Av -NY 10022
(212) 708-1249 .. **Hershman,** Kenneth N '89 %Showtime Networks Inc -1633 Bway -NY 10019
(212) 391-7721 .. **Hershman,** Richd K '87 (R Hershman PLLC) -49 W 37th -NY 10018 **Fx:**391-7821
(212) 819-8200 .. **Hershman,** Scott E '84 (White & C LLP) -1155 Av of Amer -NY 10036
(212) 867-0124 .. **Hersko,** Geoffrey S '07 -275 Mad Av -NY 10016
(212) 269-1400 .. **Herskovits,** Robt L '97 (Gusrae KB&N PLLC) -120 Wall -NY 10005
(718) 982-2959 .. **Herskovitz,** Paul J '78 %Cllg of Staten Isl -2800 Victory Blvd -Staten Isl 10314
(718) 741-8445 .. **Herskowitz,** Herbert J '61 Div of Human Rights -1 Fordham Plz -Bronx 10458 **Fx:**741-8102
(212) 879-9740 .. **Herskowitz,** Jean E '93 -412 E 78th -NY 10075
(212) 541-2000 .. **Herskowitz,** Jeremy '06 %Bryan C LLP -1290 Av of Amer -NY 10104
(212) 601-2680 .. **Herskowitz,** Michl Scott '07 %Gonzalez S&H LLP -350 5th Av -NY 10118
(718) 338-1571 .. **Herskowitz,** Sol '77 -1125 E 28th -Brklyn 11210 **Fx:**338-1533
(646) 386-3810 .. **Herstein,** Beth L '89 Hon L York Supreme Ct -71 Thomas -NY 10013
(716) 878-8590 .. **Herstek,** Amy Paulson '05 Rich Products -1 Robert Rich Way -Buffalo 14213 **Fx:**878-8767
(716) 853-8100 .. **Herstek,** Jacob J '02 %Nixon P LLP -40 Fountain Plz -Buffalo 14202
(212) 349-5180 .. **Herstic,** Mitchel I '82 -9 Murray -NY 10007 **Fx:**732-4443
(212) 363-1380 .. **Herten Burstein Sheridan Cevasco Bottinelli Litt & Harz,LLC** -747 3rd Av -NY 10017 **Fx:**(201) 342-6611
(212) 363-1380 .. **Herten,** Thos J '85 (Herten BSCBL&H,LLC) -747 3rd Av -NY 10017
(212) 698-3500 .. **Herther-Spiro,** Nicole B '08 Dechert LLP -1095 Av of Amer -NY 10036
(914) 390-4134 .. **Hertwig,** Edw W '06 %Hon L Smith -300 Quarropas -White Plns 10601
(718) 258-4774 .. **Hertz,** Alan B '92 -934 E 19th -Brklyn 11230 **Fx:**258-4994
(212) 782-2000 .. **Hertz,** David N '93 %Bk Hapoalim -1177 Av of Amer -NY 10036 **Fx:**782-2141
(212) 705-7000 .. **Hertz,** Diane C '90 (Bingham M LLP) -399 Park Av -NY 10022
(718) 672-8115 .. **Hertz,** Gerald M '56 (Azam & H LLP) -74-09 37th Av -Jcksn Hts 11372 **Fx:**672-8117
(212) 440-2745 .. **Hertz,** Marian S '83 Colliau EMCK&M -40 Wall -NY 10005
(212) 888-8200 .. **Hertz,** Martin J '54 OfCnsl Feder K LLP -845 3rd Av -NY 10022
(212) 455-2000 .. **Hertz,** Michelle L '08 %Simpson T&B LLP -425 Lex Av -NY 10017
(212) 998-6430 .. **Hertz,** Randy A '86 %NYU Law Schl -245 Sullivan -NY 10012 **Fx:**995-4031
(212) 373-3000 .. **Hertz,** Seymour '56 OfCnsl Paul WRW&G LLP -1285 Av of Amer -NY 10019
(212) 909-6000 .. **Hertz,** Stephen R '87 (Debevoise & P LLP) -919 3rd Av -NY 10022
(718) 261-7700 .. **Hertz,** Steven M '80 (Rappaport HC&R,PC) -118-35 Qns Blvd -Frst Hlls 11375
(212) 696-6000 .. **Hertzberg,** Gabriel '03 %Curtis M-PC&M LLP -101 Park Av -NY 10178
(718) 792-2847 .. **Hertzberg,** Harry '89 H Hertzberg -1526 Wllmsbrdg Rd -Bronx 10461 **Fx:**892-6886
(607) 277-8121 .. **Hertzberg,** Martha Nebelsiek '02 -Bx6596 -Ithaca 14851
(212) 982-9870 .. **Hertzberg,** Michl L '75 -111 Bway -NY 10006 **Fx:**674-4614
(212) 808-2700 .. **Hertzberg,** Robt S '06 (Pepper H LLP) -620 8th Av -NY 10018
(212) 949-9022 .. **Hertzberg,** Steven M '95 %Abelman F&S -666 3rd Av -NY 10017
(212) 715-9100 .. **Hertzberg,** Theordore S '09 %Kramer LN&F,LLP -1177 Av of Amer -NY 10036
(212) 294-6700 .. **Hertzog,** David B '69 OfCnsl Winston & S -200 Park Av -NY 10166
(212) 816-3435 .. **Hertzog,** Matthew O '98 %Salomon Smith Barney -388 Greenwich -NY 10013
(212) 278-1000 .. **Hertzog,** Rene F '08 %Anderson K&O,PC -1251 Av of Amer -NY 10020
(212) 698-3500 .. **Hervey,** Richd M '79 (Dechert LLP) -1095 Av of Amer -NY 10036
(518) 792-5116 .. **Hervieux-Osgood,** Michele C '92 -99 Peggy Ann Rd -Queensbury 12804
(212) 336-2000 .. **Herz,** Andrew L '72 (Patterson BW&T LLP) -1133 Av of Amer -NY 10036
(516) 767-0800 .. **Herz,** Arnold D '92 (A Herz) -14 Vanderventer Av -Pt Wash 11050 **Fx:**706-1416
(631) 993-3000 .. **Herz,** Erik L '01 Sterling Floor Designs,Ltd -82 Modular Av -Commack 11725
(631) 360-0400 .. **Herz,** James J '07 %Jakubowski RMG&T -969 Jericho Tpk -St James 11780 **Fx:**360-0408
(516) 357-3700 .. **Herz,** Jeffrey F '86 (Cullen and D LLP) -100 Q Roosevelt Blvd -Gdn Cty 11530
(212) 801-6926 .. **Herz,** Jos A '92 (Greenberg T,LLP) -200 Park Av -NY 10166
(516) 767-0800 .. **Herz,** Lori G '92 OfCnsl A Herz -14 Vanderventer Av -Pt Wash 11050 **Fx:**706-1416
(212) 790-0307 .. **Herz,** Michl E '86 %Benj N Cardozo Schl of Law -55 5th Av -NY 10003 **Fx:**790-0345
(212) 431-7129 .. **Herz,** Saskia E '06 %Purrington MW LLP -320 W 13th -NY 10014
(212) 541-8641 .. **Herz,** Steven E '91 %RLR Assoc Ltd -7 W 51st -NY 10019 **Fx:**262-7084
(212) 455-2000 .. **Herzbach,** Bryan H '07 %Simpson T&B LLP -425 Lex Av -NY 10017
(516) 296-7000 .. **Herzbach,** Richd '74 (Certilman BA&H,LLP) -90 Merrick Av -E Meadow 11554
(212) 451-2300 .. **Herzberg,** Aliza F '95 (Olshan GFR&W LLP) -65 E 55th -NY 10022
(631) 265-2133 .. **Herzberg,** Jeffrey '80 (Zinker & H,LLP) -278 E Main Bx866 -Smithtwn 11787
(212) 909-6000 .. **Herzberg,** M Uri '08 %Debevoise & P LLP -919 3rd Av -NY 10022
(212) 696-4912 .. **Herzberg,** Steven S '03 (Char & H,LLP) -183 Mad Av -NY 10016
(212) 351-4000 .. **Herzeca,** Lois F '80 (Gibson D&C LLP) -200 Park Av -NY 10166
(347) 296-1670 .. **Herzfeld,** Hildy Levine '86 %Supreme Ct Law Dept -360 Adams -Brklyn 11201 **Fx:**643-6114
(212) 688-5640 .. **Herzfeld,** Oliver J '91 OfCnsl Joseph & H LLP -757 3rd Av -NY 10017
(516) 571-3056 .. **Herzfeld,** Paul '86 %Cnty Atty -1 West -Mineola 11501 **Fx:**571-6604
(212) 818-9019 .. **Herzfeld,** Richd L '78 (Bahn H&M,LLP) -555 5th Av -NY 10017 **Fx:**986-5316
(914) 428-2700 .. **Herzfeld,** Robt '56 -175 Main -White Plns 10601 **Fx:**428-1159
(212) 471-8500 .. **Herzfeld & Rubin,PC** -125 Broad -NY 10004 **Fx:**344-3333
(212) 471-3231 .. **Herzfeld & Rubin,PC** -1225 Franklin Av -Gdn Cty 11530 **Fx:**471-3230
(212) 493-7000 .. **Herzka,** Chas H '81 %Bway Mgmt -80 Broad -NY 10004 **Fx:**493-7032
(607) 737-2923 .. **Herzl-Betz,** Louise '89 Hon J Hayden -203 William Bx588 -Elmira 14902 **Fx:**737-2913
(212) 916-6485 .. **Herzlich,** Gary E '84 %TIAA-CREF -730 3rd Av -NY 10017
(212) 715-9100 .. **Herzog,** Barry Z '92 (Kramer LN&F,LLP) -1177 Av of Amer -NY 10036
(212) 728-8000 .. **Herzog,** Bruce C '06 (Willkie F&G LLP) -787 7th Av -NY 10019
(914) 686-8200 .. **Herzog,** Erin S '08 %Sarcone Law Firm,PLLC -222 Bloomingdale Rd -White Plns 10605 **Fx:**686-8988
(917) 681-2286 .. **Herzog,** Howard '65 -244 Mad Av -NY 10016
(212) 534-1695 .. **Herzog,** Jeanne '87 -40 E 88th -NY 10128
(212) 929-6019 .. **Herzog,** Jonathan C '91 -95 Horatio -NY 10014 **Fx:**229-2545
(631) 853-4104 .. **Herzog,** Keri M '89 %DA -400 Carleton Av Bx9082 -Central Islip 11722 **Fx:**853-7838
(518) 465-7581 .. **Herzog Law Firm, PC** -7 Southwoods Blvd -Albany 12211 **Fx:**462-2743
(718) 376-7635 .. **Herzog,** Lester B '84 -1729 E 15th -Brklyn 11229 **Fx:**382-4430
(315) 443-4105 .. **Herzog,** Peter E '57 %Syracuse Univ Cllg of Law -Wht Hall -Syracuse 13244 **Fx:**443-4213
(212) 725-0001 .. **Herzog,** Robt P '58 -150 E 69th -NY 10021 **Fx:**535-4377
(212) 687-3860 .. **Herzog,** Ronald S '74 (Snow BK,PC) -605 3rd Av -NY 10158
(212) 373-3000 .. **Herzog,** Steven C '88 Cnsl Paul WRW&G LLP -1285 Av of Amer -NY 10019
(516) 877-9653 .. **Hesch,** Jerome M '71 OfCnsl Wolf Law Grp,PC -114 Old Cntry Rd -Mineola 11501 **Fx:**877-9660
(716) 847-8400 .. **Hesch,** Katherine L '02 %Phillips L LLP -3400 HSBC Ctr -Buffalo 14203
(516) 829-6900 .. **Hesekiel,** Todd H '01 %Ackerman LCB&L,LLP -1010 Nrthrn Blvd -Gt Neck 11021
(212) 513-3200 .. **Hesketh,** Robt J '09 %Holland & K LLP -31 W 52nd -NY 10019
(718) 250-2854 .. **Heslin,** David G '85 %DA -350 Jay -Brklyn 11201 **Fx:**250-2314
(845) 454-9460 .. **Heslin,** Eugenia Brennan '83 MHLS -One Civic Ctr Plz -Poughkeepsie 12601 **Fx:**471-9308
(212) 460-4705 .. **Heslin,** Martin F '77 Con Ed -4 Irving Pl -NY 10003
(212) 231-8127 .. **Heslin,** Raymond J '77 West End Financial Advisors LLC -410 Park Av -NY 10022
(518) 452-5600 .. **Heslin,** Robt E '65 (Heslin RF&M PC) -5 Columbia Cir -Albany 12203
(518) 452-5600 .. **Heslin Rothenberg Farley & Mesiti PC** -5 Columbia Cir -Albany 12203 **Fx:**452-5579
(585) 288-4832 .. **Heslin Rothenberg Farley & Mesiti PC** -100 Meridian Centre -Rchstr 14618 **Fx:**288-2010
(212) 331-7479 .. **Heslington,** Monica '07 Berdon LLP -360 Mad Av -NY 10017
(212) 725-2450 .. **Hespos,** Gerald E '81 (Casella & H) -110 W 40th -NY 10018 **Fx:**725-2452

(631) 761-7051 .. **Hespos,** Lauren Chite '01 %Touro Cllg Law Ctr -225 Eastvw Dr -Central Islip 11722
(718) 307-6527 .. **Hess,** Adam J '01 Massey Knakal Realty Srvcs -205 Montague -Brklyn 11201
(607) 722-6417 .. **Hess,** Alan M '90 %J Troy -45 Chenango -Bnghmtn 13901 **Fx:**722-8019
(716) 433-5522 .. **Hess,** Ann Giardina '86 -702 Davison Rd -Lockprt 14094 **Fx:**433-3545
(212) 683-9700 .. **Hess,** David D '97 GNY Mutual Ins -200 Mad Av -NY 10016 **Fx:**843-1962
(914) 289-3036 .. **Hess,** Debra Shaw '91 %Bank of NY -701 Wstchstr Av -West Harrison 10604
(212) 382-0909 .. **Hess,** Frank A '01 %Peckar & A,PC -41 Mad Av -NY 10154
(212) 931-7300 .. **Hess,** Geoffrey N '98 %Giuliani Prtnrs -5 Times Sq -NY 10036
(212) 446-4808 .. **Hess,** Glen E '90 (Kirkland & E LLP) -153 E 53rd -NY 10022
(212) 487-9701 .. **Hess,** Jerry J '01 %Robin HK&F -1 Bttry Pk Plz -NY 10014
(212) 278-1811 .. **Hess,** John J '72 (Anderson K&O,PC) -1251 Av of Amer -NY 10020
(212) 301-3577 .. **Hess,** Kristen R '04 Fox News Ntwrk,LLC -1211 Av of Amer -NY 10036
(212) 225-2000 .. **Hess,** Kristofer W '04 (Cleary GS&H) -1 Lbrty Plz -NY 10006
(716) 204-2400 .. **Hess,** Marc D '07 %SJ Baum,PC -220 Nrthpnte Pkwy Bx1291 -Buffalo 14240 **Fx:**204-4600
(212) 508-6100 .. **Hess,** Michl D '66 (Bracewell & G,LLP) -1251 Av of Amer -NY 10020
(914) 686-1700 .. **Hess,** Michl P '09 %O'Connor R,LLP -200 Mamaroneck Av -White Plns 10601
(212) 805-0359 .. **Hess,** Mirta S '97 %US Dist Ct -500 Pearl -NY 10007
(212) 557-7700 .. **Hess,** P Gregory '72 (Davidson D&C LLP) -60 E 42nd -NY 10165
(518) 438-5364 .. **Hess,** Robt E '93 (Sullivan H&Y,PC) -4 Exec Park Dr -Albany 12203
(212) 866-3064 .. **Hess,** Sigrid A '80 -160 W 97th -NY 10025
(212) 233-5000 .. **Hess,** Steven L '75 (Simonson HL&G,PC) -15 Maiden Ln -NY 10038
(607) 255-1427 .. **Hess,** Suzanne C '05 Cornell Law Schl -Myron Taylor Hall -Ithaca 14853 **Fx:**255-7193
(518) 429-4200 .. **Hessberg,** Albert III '82 (Hiscock & B,LLP) -50 Beaver -Albany 12207
(718) 261-2323 .. **Hesse,** Candace '96 %J Gemelli,PC -105-15 Metro Av -Frst Hlls 11375 **Fx:**520-1669
(212) 750-4991 .. **Hessellund-Jensen,** Peter '76 -521 5th Av -NY 10175
(718) 298-8900 .. **Hesser,** Gwyneth M '09 %Leg Aid -153-01 Jamaica Av -Jamaica 11432 **Fx:**657-0537
(646) 378-2235 .. **Hessinger,** Gregory J '91 (Curley & M LLP) -5 Penn Plz -NY 10001 **Fx:**785-4255
(212) 384-1000 .. **Hessinger,** Stephen B '88 FBI -26 Fed Plz -NY 10278
(516) 408-3666 .. **Hession Bekoff Cooper & Lo Piccolo, LLP** -1103 Stewart Av -Gdn Cty 11530 **Fx:**408-3833
(212) 412-9500 .. **Hession,** Cathi A '81 (Flemming ZWZ LLP) -1 Lbrty Plz -NY 10006
(212) 889-2300 .. **Hession,** John J '81 (Dougherty RGZ&H) -131 E 38th -NY 10016
(212) 762-8498 .. **Hession,** John R '01 Morgan Stanley & Co -1221 Av of Amer -NY 10020
(212) 576-7000 .. **Hession,** Michl '99 %NYLIM -51 Mad Av -NY 10010
(516) 408-3666 .. **Hession,** Thos R '73 (Hession BC&L,LLP) -1103 Stewart Av -Gdn Cty 11530
(212) 903-9000 .. **Hessler,** Paul S '97 (Linklaters) -1345 Av of Amer -NY 10105
(212) 446-4800 .. **Hessler,** Stephen E '08 (Kirkland & E LLP) -153 E 53rd -NY 10022
(212) 318-6000 .. **Hessmiller,** Gannon A '10 %Paul HJ&W LLP -75 E 55th -NY 10022
(518) 274-3510 .. **Hessney,** Wm P Jr. '85 (Bartle MD&J,LLP) -251 River Bx448 -Troy 12181
(212) 318-3000 .. **Hest,** Lionel G '71 (Fulbright & J LLP) -666 5th Av -NY 10103
(212) 688-5640 .. **Hester,** Diane '92 (Joseph & H LLP) -757 3rd Av -NY 10017
(646) 315-7300 .. **Hester,** Felix M '86 %FINRA -14 Wall -NY 10005 **Fx:**315-7440
(212) 401-0800 .. **Hester,** Jos J '78 %Disciplinary Comm -61 Bway -NY 10006 **Fx:**287-1045
(516) 747-0001 .. **Hesterberg,** Gregory X '76 (Hesterberg & K) -1305 Franklin Av -Gdn Cty 11530
(516) 747-0001 .. **Hesterberg & Keller** -1305 Franklin Av -Gdn Cty 11530 **Fx:**741-9213
(585) 454-4060 .. **Hetherington,** Bryan D '76 %Empire Justice Ctr -1 W Main -Rchstr 14614 **Fx:**454-4019
(212) 688-5000 .. **Hetherington,** John W '64 %Westvaco -299 Park Av -NY 10171
(212) 310-8000 .. **Hetherington,** Thos S '05 %Weil G&M LLP -767 5th Av -NY 10153
(518) 463-1252 .. **Hetman,** Stehle '05 (Lynch & H,PLLC) -111 State -Albany 12207 **Fx:**463-1255
(631) 853-4104 .. **Hettiarachchi,** Rashika N '05 %DA -400 Carleton Av Bx9082 -Central Islip 11722 **Fx:**853-7838
(212) 335-9000 .. **Hettleman,** Robt D '97 %DA -1 Hogan Pl -NY 10013
(516) 887-7062 .. **Hettler,** Kenneth R '83 -23 Rhame Av -E Rockaway 11518 **Fx:**593-3894
(716) 875-8664 .. **Hettler,** Michl R '76 (Bartlo H&W) -22 Victoria Blvd -Kenmore 14217
(212) 259-8000 .. **Hetzel,** David G '02 (Dewey & L LLP) -1301 Av of Amer -NY 10019
(718) 417-7800 .. **Hetzer,** Michl J '84 -6017 69th Av -Rdgwd 11385
(845) 331-2525 .. **Heubach,** Jacqueline L '87 (Ryan R&R,LLP) -115 Green Bx3153 -Kingston 12402
(914) 323-7000 .. **Heubel,** Gerard J '80 (Wilson EME&D LLP) -3 Gannett Dr -White Plns 10604
(212) 818-9200 .. **Heubel,** Susanne C '01 %Satterlee SB&B LLP -230 Park Av -NY 10169
(212) 692-1000 .. **Heuer,** Wm C '98 (Duane M LLP) -1540 Bway -NY 10036
(212) 756-2000 .. **Heumann,** Alyssa B '05 %Schulte R&Z LLP -919 3rd Av -NY 10022
(212) 972-3600 .. **Heumann,** Danl M '02 Meridian Cptl Grp -1 Bttry Pk Plz -NY 10004
(518) 873-3320 .. **Heussi,** Jonathan A '81 Family Ct -Bx217 -Elizabethtwn 12932
(212) 692-1000 .. **Hew,** Vanessa C '02 (Duane M LLP) -1540 Bway -NY 10036
(212) 474-1000 .. **Hewitt,** Benjamin C '10 %Cravath S&M LLP -825 8th Av -NY 10019
(718) 923-4206 .. **Hewitt,** Elizabeth L '84 %OTDA Fair Hearings -14 Boerum Pl -Brklyn 11201
(716) 284-9901 .. **Hewitt,** James P III '76 (Phelps G&H) -345 3rd Bx816 -Niagara Fls 14303
(716) 267-4922 .. **Hewitt,** Julie B '89 -Bx61 -Kennedy 14747
(646) 386-3680 .. **Hewitt,** Lancelot B '88 Supreme Ct Spcl Referee -60 Centre -NY 10007
(212) 210-1228 .. **Hewitt,** Martin A '00 Cnsl Alston & B LLP -90 Park Av -NY 10016
(212) 907-9600 .. **Hewitt,** Patricia '91 (Ingram YGC&B,LLP) -250 Park Av -NY 10177
(516) 741-7676 .. **Hewitt,** Robt E B III '03 %Miranda SSSV LLP -240 Mineola Blvd -Mineola 11501
(212) 841-1000 .. **Hewitt,** Ronald A '06 %Covington & B LLP -620 8th Av -NY 10018
(212) 885-5000 .. **Hewitt,** Sarah '83 (Blank R LLP) -405 Lex Av -NY 10174
(718) 488-1988 .. **Hewitt,** Vivienne M '93 -26 Court -Brklyn 11242
(212) 596-9000 .. **Hewitt,** Wm J '65 (Ropes & G LLP) -1211 Av of Amer -NY 10036
(716) 856-3646 .. **Hewner,** Thos F '80 (Cole SHH&G,PC) -37 Franklin -Buffalo 14202
(212) 201-2899 .. **Hewson,** Barbara C '80 New Line Capital Prtnrs -144 E 44th -NY 10017
(800) 416-5454 .. **Hewson,** John '07 %Fusco B&R -180 Froehlich Farm Blvd -Woodbury 11797
(212) 264-9271 .. **Heydrich,** Michl W '03 US Customs -26 Fed Plz -NY 10278
(716) 372-0395 .. **Heyer,** John H II '73 -201 N Union Bx588 -Olean 14760 **Fx:**372-0446
(212) 530-5000 .. **Heyl,** Dorothy '84 OfCnsl Milbank TH&M LLP -1 Chase Manh Plz -NY 10005
(718) 243-6278 .. **Heyman,** Adam S '04 %Leg Aid -111 Lvngstn -Brklyn 11201 **Fx:**237-8737
(914) 723-5500 .. **Heyman,** Danl G '82 -670 Wht Plns Rd -Scarsdale 10583
(212) 922-1495 .. **Heyman,** Danl G '82 -275 Mad Av -NY 10016
(718) 492-4455 .. **Heyman,** Jason M '98 %P DiBona -436 Bay Ridge Pkwy -Brklyn 11209 **Fx:**238-6999
(315) 422-1391 .. **Heyman,** Kim V '96 %Green & S,PLLC -One Lincoln Ctr #900 -Syracuse 13202
(718) 295-1600 .. **Heyman,** Richd S '50 (R Heyman,PC) -2488 Grnd Cncrs -Bronx 10458 **Fx:**295-3171
(585) 325-3283 .. **Heyman,** Sidney '55 -36 W Main -Rchstr 14614
(518) 465-1500 .. **Heyman,** Steven S '76 (Cannon H&W,LLP) -54 State -Albany 12207
(212) 326-3939 .. **Heyman,** Thos V '62 OfCnsl Jones D -222 E 41st -NY 10017
(212) 267-7600 .. **Heymann,** Andrew W '86 (Solomon PBH&S LLP) -40 Wall -NY 10005
(516) 681-3636 .. **Heymann,** David J '90 (Post H&K LLP) -2 Jericho Plz -Jericho 11753
(212) 657-5276 .. **Heyrich,** Michl T '91 %Citigroup -111 Wall -NY 10043
(914) 664-0577 .. **Heyward,** Robt J '89 -139 N Fulton Av -Mt Vernon 10550
(518) 457-4951 .. **Heywood,** Nancy J '83 %Dept Correctional Srvcs -1220 Wshngtn Av -Albany 12226 **Fx:**457-7555
(212) 839-5300 .. **Heyworth,** James O '09 %Sidley A LLP -787 7th Av -NY 10019
(212) 397-3370 .. **Heyworth,** Susannah G '08 Cnsl Harris CC&H LLP -111 Bway -NY 10006 **Fx:**202-6206
(716) 636-2167 .. **Hezel,** George M '74 %SUNY Buffalo Lw Schl -O'Brian Hall -Buffalo 14260 **Fx:**645-5968
(716) 655-1696 .. **Hezel,** Sally C '74 -357 Oakwood Av -E Aurora 14052
(212) 506-1700 .. **Hiatt,** Eric B '05 %Kasowitz BT&F LLP -1633 Bway -NY 10019
(718) 979-8068 .. **Hiatt,** Robt W '96 (R Hiatt,PC) -1819 Richmond Rd -Staten Isl 10306
(845) 791-7700 .. **Hiatt,** Ronald G '81 -10 St John Bx1177 -Monticello 12701 **Fx:**794-1009
(718) 268-4155 .. **Hibbard,** Dale E '78 OfCnsl Barrett L,LLC -109-01 72nd Rd -Frst Hlls 11375
(716) 853-4340 .. **Hibbert,** Seth L '98 %Getman & B -800 Rand Bldg -Buffalo 14203
(718) 254-0700 .. **Hibel,** Miriam J '80 %Bklyn Defender Srvcs -177 Lvngstn -Brklyn 11201 **Fx:**254-0897
(516) 538-7300 .. **Hibner,** John R '78 (Carsey & H PC) -230 Hilton Av -Hempstd 11550 **Fx:**538-7303
(212) 287-4900 .. **Hibri,** Malda N '03 Highbridge Cptl Mgt -9 W 57th -NY 10019
(212) 541-2000 .. **Hibsher,** Wm J '75 (Bryan C LLP) -1290 Av of Amer -NY 10104
(212) 479-6000 .. **Hibshoosh,** Danl M '04 %Cooley LLP -1114 Av of Amer -NY 10036
(585) 750-2512 .. **Hichman,** Donna J '89 -2024 W Henrietta Rd -Rchstr 14623
(212) 574-1200 .. **Hickernell,** Craig Thos '78 (Seward & K LLP) -1 Bttry Pk Plz -NY 10004
(212) 670-0404 .. **Hickerson,** Kristina A K '03 Merrill Lynch -222 Bway -NY 10038
(212) 637-1039 .. **Hickey,** Adam S '03 %US Atty -1 St Andrews Plz -NY 10007
(631) 271-4777 .. **Hickey,** Brian P Jr. '93 %D Kritzer & Assoc,PC -187 E Main -Huntngtn 11743 **Fx:**271-2530
(631) 755-0101 .. **Hickey,** Christine B '94 %Lewis JAA,LLP -425 Broad Hollow Rd -Melvll 11747
(212) 850-4000 .. **Hickey,** Danl C '74 %Emigrant Svngs Bk -5 E 42nd -NY 10017 **Fx:**850-4424
(212) 335-9000 .. **Hickey,** Deborah '86 %DA -1 Hogan Pl -NY 10013
(212) 765-5070 .. **Hickey,** Erin M '07 %Fish & R,PC -153 E 53rd -NY 10022
(607) 273-2039 .. **Hickey,** James R Jr. '80 -102 E State -Ithaca 14850
(716) 849-6800 .. **Hickey,** Jonathan S '02 (Burden G&H,LLC) -403 Main -Buffalo 14203 **Fx:**849-6806
(518) 462-5601 .. **Hickey,** Kevin P '99 %O'Connell & A -54 State -Albany 12207
(845) 452-4100 .. **Hickey,** Leo K '06 CRM USA Holdings Inc -Bx1999 -Poughkeepsie 12601
(315) 781-8492 .. **Hickey,** Leslie Cohen '98 -225 Exchange -Geneva 14456 **Fx:**781-6936
(315) 422-9756 .. **Hickey,** M Christine '86 -120 E Wshngtn -Syracuse 13202
(212) 837-6783 .. **Hickey,** Megan J '03 Hughes H&R LLP -1 Bttry Pk Plz -NY 10004 **Fx:**299-6783
(212) 346-3594 .. **Hickey,** Michl B '06 Goldman Sachs -85 Broad -NY 10004
(585) 263-1000 .. **Hickey,** Michl E '10 %Nixon P LLP -1100 Clinton Sq -Rchstr 14604
(914) 285-8500 .. **Hickey,** Michl J '78 %TK Moore -701 Wstchstr Av -White Plns 10604 **Fx:**285-8510
(212) 773-1506 .. **Hickey,** Michl J '05 Ernst & Young LLP -5 Times Sq -NY 10036
(518) 456-6456 .. **Hickey,** Peter J '91 (Gerstenzang OH&G) -210 Great Oaks Blvd -Albany 12203
(607) 723-1990 .. **Hickey Sheehan & Gates** -160 Hawley Bx2124 -Bnghmtn 13902 **Fx:**723-1967
(212) 730-2000 .. **Hickey,** Susan Garrison '78 MD Sass Investors Srvcs -1185 Av of Amer -NY 10036
(212) 779-9910 .. **Hickey,** Thos A '76 (Eaton & V LLP) -3 Park Av -NY 10016
(212) 340-0400 .. **Hickey,** Thos F '89 %Appllt Div 1st Dept -27 Mad Av -NY 10010 **Fx:**889-4412
(607) 723-1990 .. **Hickey,** Thos J '77 (Hickey S&G) -160 Hawley Bx2124 -Bnghmtn 13902
(718) 579-7900 .. **Hickey,** Vanessa P '06 Leg Aid -900 Sheridan Av -Bronx 10451 **Fx:**293-8744

(212) 417-5300 .. **Hickey-Martin,** Monica J '92 %Medicaid Fraud Cntrl -120 Bway -NY 10271 **Fx:**417-5274
(212) 825-1212 .. **Hickman,** Kevin A '05 %Morrison M LLP -17 State -NY 10004
(212) 803-5100 .. **Hickman,** Stanford E '92 %NY Cnty Defender Srvcs -225 Bway -NY 10007 **Fx:**571-6035
(631) 499-2175 .. **Hickmann,** Chas A '54 -39 Colonial -E Northprt 11731
(646) 610-6299 .. **Hicks,** Eric O '97 %NYPD -1 Police Plz -NY 10038
(212) 655-5944 .. **Hicks,** H Melville Jr. '58 -551 5th Av -NY 10176 **Fx:**867-3185
(914) 834-0801 .. **Hicks,** H Melville Jr. '58 -21 N Chatsworth Av -Larchmnt 10538 **Fx:**630-4805
(212) 858-1000 .. **Hicks,** J Portis '66 SrCnsl Pillsbury WSP LLP -1540 Bway -NY 10036
(518) 463-4441 .. **Hicks,** John P '79 -60 Loudonvll Rd -Albany 12204 **Fx:**463-4468
(212) 728-8000 .. **Hicks,** Jordan C '09 %Willkie F&G LLP -787 7th Av -NY 10019
(212) 371-5400 .. **Hicks,** Kenneth A '77 %Weisman CS&M PC -445 Park Av -NY 10022
(716) 856-9681 .. **Hicks,** Nicholas W '96 -69 Delaware Av -Buffalo 14202 **Fx:**852-6784
(914) 835-5776 .. **Hicks,** Stephen L '84 -17 2nd -Harrison 10528
(212) 946-4768 .. **Hicks,** Wm G '09 -11 Penn Plz -NY 10001
(914) 289-2310 .. **Hickson,** Suzy I '93 %Ct of Claims -140 Grand -White Plns 10601 **Fx:**289-2313
(631) 853-4161 .. **Hicks Pearce,** Emma J '05 DA -N Cnty Cmplx Bldg 77 -Hauppauge 11788 **Fx:**853-4192
(212) 558-4000 .. **Hiden,** Robt B Jr. '61 SrCnsl Sullivan & C LLP -125 Broad -NY 10004
(212) 431-5576 .. **Hidrobo,** Isabel M '03 %Siskind SB -430 W 14th -NY 10014
(516) 564-8000 .. **Hiebler,** James R '77 (J Hiebler & Assoc) -901 Franklin Av -Gdn Cty 11530 **Fx:**564-1714
(212) 468-8000 .. **Hiensch,** Kristin A '07 %Morrison & F LLP -1290 Av of Amer -NY 10104
(914) 666-8033 .. **Higbie,** Brian M '03 %Banks SG&W,LLP -118 N Bedford Rd Bx320 -Mt Kisco 10549
(212) 674-3591 .. **Higer,** Richd P '54 -11 5th Av -NY 10003
(585) 428-3817 .. **Higginbotham,** Sharon L '06 %Supreme Ct -545 Hall of Justice -Rchstr 14614
(212) 863-6300 .. **Higginbotham-Hassan,** Wendi J '77 %HPD -100 Gold -NY 10038 **Fx:**863-8201
(212) 964-7400 .. **Higgins,** Anna Avrasin '03 Smith MDWY&Y,PC -111 John -NY 10038
(516) 393-2200 .. **Higgins,** Brian Scott '02 %Garfunkel W,PC -111 Grt Nck Rd -Gt Neck 11021
(212) 416-8713 .. **Higgins,** C Michl '00 %Dept of Law -120 Bway -NY 10271
(716) 332-0990 .. **Higgins,** Carla E '03 Childrens Lgl Ctr -438 Main -Buffalo 14202
(845) 486-2473 .. **Higgins,** Christopher T '06 %Bd of Elections -47 Cannon -Poughkeepsie 12601
(518) 474-7330 .. **Higgins,** Dean J '74 %Dept of Law -The Cptl -Albany 12224
(516) 921-7050 .. **Higgins,** Edw J '77 -55 Hunters Dr -Syosset 11791
(716) 625-8778 .. **Higgins,** G Peter '60 -5335 Tonawanda Creek Rd -N Tonawanda 14120 **Fx:**625-8766
(212) 345-5935 .. **Higgins,** Gina M '91 %Marsh USA -1166 Av of Amer -NY 10036 **Fx:**345-4808
(516) 365-6414 .. **Higgins,** J Donald Jr. '79 (Higgins H&H) -57 Manhsst Av -Manhsst 11030 **Fx:**365-8520
(518) 438-6739 .. **Higgins,** James P '94 -35 Clifton Way -Slingerlnds 12159
(914) 712-1100 .. **Higgins,** John B '76 (Murphy & H,LLP) -1 Radisson Plz -New Rchll 10801
(518) 427-2650 .. **Higgins,** John E '90 (Nixon P LLP) -677 Bway -Albany 12207
(212) 269-0927 .. **Higgins,** John P '78 (D'Amato & L,LLP) -2 World Fncl Ctr -NY 10281
(845) 892-5020 .. **Higgins,** John T '71 IBM -2070 Route 52 -Hopewell Junct 12533
(516) 357-3000 .. **Higgins,** Karen C '88 %Rivkin R LLP -926 RXR Plz -Uniondale 11556
(718) 422-0053 .. **Higgins,** Kathleen '01 (Weiserbs & H) -270 Jay -Brklyn 11201 **Fx:**422-1459
(347) 436-8446 .. **Higgins,** Kerry E '09 (Higgins & F LLP) -110 W 71st -NY 10023 **Fx:**436-8447
(718) 286-6000 .. **Higgins,** Kevin G '90 %DA -125-01 Qns Blvd -Kew Gdns 11415
(516) 496-5822 .. **Higgins,** Kylie '03 %T Spina -170 Froehlich Farm Blvd -Woodbury 11797 **Fx:**496-5420
(518) 523-9682 .. **Higgins,** Louis H '78 -687 Avryvll Ln -Lk Placid 12946
(845) 331-1500 .. **Higgins,** Melvin T '72 -195 Wall -Kingston 12401 **Fx:**331-1501
(212) 636-6000 .. **Higgins,** Michl E '09 %Fordham Univ Sch of Law -140 W 62nd -NY 10023 **Fx:**636-6899
(718) 243-6867 .. **Higgins,** Michl S '02 Leg Aid -111 Lvngstn -Brklyn 11201 **Fx:**237-8737
(212) 527-1000 .. **Higgins,** Neil E '84 (Jones HC&B PC) -1 Bttry Pk Plz -NY 10004
(607) 724-0337 .. **Higgins,** Norbert A '93 -64 Front -Bnghmtn 13905 **Fx:**772-1014
(518) 465-5995 .. **Higgins,** Patrick J '85 (Powers & S,LLP) -39 N Pearl -Albany 12207
(516) 676-3679 .. **Higgins,** Regina E '85 (DeWitt & H) -26 Robnsn Av -Glen Cove 11542
(716) 847-1098 .. **Higgins,** Richd L '78 %Norstar Dvlpmnt -200 S Division -Buffalo 14204 **Fx:**847-1668
(212) 839-5300 .. **Higgins,** Robt J III '10 %Sidley A LLP -787 7th Av -NY 10019
(518) 374-3399 .. **Higgins Roberts Beyerl & Coan,PC** -1430 Balltown Rd -Niskayuna 12309 **Fx:**374-9416
(212) 292-4412 .. **Higgins,** Sean W '94 %Isaacs & E,LLP -521 5th Av -NY 10175
(212) 277-4000 .. **Higgins,** Susan L A '07 %Freshfields BD LLP -520 Mad Av -NY 10022
(212) 705-7000 .. **Higgins,** Tara A '88 (Bingham M LLP) -399 Park Av -NY 10022
(631) 369-7600 .. **Higgins,** Tara M '91 %Lewis JAA,LLP -21 E 2nd -Rvrhead 11901
(516) 365-6414 .. **Higgins,** Terence M '81 (Higgins H&H) -57 Manhsst Av -Manhsst 11030 **Fx:**365-8520
(716) 362-1158 .. **Higgins,** Terrence P '90 (Higgins K,PC) -70 Niagara -Buffalo 14202 **Fx:**362-1162
(212) 819-8200 .. **Higgins,** Thos P '76 (White & C LLP) -1155 Av of Amer -NY 10036
(518) 474-4096 .. **Higgins,** Thos P '87 %Dept of Law -The Cptl -Albany 12224
(212) 840-8334 .. **Higgins,** Thos P '89 (Higgins & T LLP) -36 W 44th -NY 10036
(518) 465-5995 .. **Higgins,** Timothy J '95 (Powers & S,LLP) -39 N Pearl -Albany 12207
(516) 365-6414 .. **Higgins,** Timothy P '81 (Higgins H&H) -57 Manhsst Av -Manhsst 11030 **Fx:**365-8520
(646) 452-2304 .. **Higgins,** Todd A '02 (Crosby & H LLP) -350 Bway -NY 10013 **Fx:**452-2301
(212) 636-6000 .. **Higgins,** Tracy E '00 %Fordham Univ Sch of Law -140 W 62nd -NY 10023 **Fx:**636-6899
(212) 840-8334 .. **Higgins & Trippett LLP** -36 W 44th -NY 10036 **Fx:**840-8336
(718) 699-8169 .. **Higgins,** Walter P '85 -1225 Franklin Av -Gdn Cty 11530
(212) 891-1600 .. **Higginson,** Carletta F '04 %Jenner & B LLP -919 3rd Av -NY 10022
(914) 309-8189 .. **Higgs,** Andrea Kelli '96 (AK Higgs,LLC) -15 Stewart Pl -White Plns 10603 **Fx:**428-8366
(518) 690-0096 .. **Higgs,** Thos J '03 %Murphy BB&M,LLP -226 Great Oaks Blvd -Albany 12203
(212) 558-4000 .. **High,** Tracy Richelle '00 (Sullivan & C LLP) -125 Broad -NY 10004
(631) 751-4444 .. **Higham,** John P '88 (Grundfast & H) -207 Hallock Rd -Stony Brk 11790 **Fx:**751-4675
(212) 735-3000 .. **Higham,** Thos P '09 %Skadden ASM&F LLP -4 Times Sq -NY 10036
(607) 277-3344 .. **Highland,** Wm D '86 -200 E Buffalo Bx255 -Ithaca 14851 **Fx:**277-6800
(413) 265-3486 .. **Hikry,** Ronete G '10 -100 Maiden Ln -NY 10038
(212) 309-1000 .. **Hilal,** G Shireen '05 %Hunton & W -200 Park Av -NY 10166
(607) 734-2271 .. **Hiland,** Seth T '06 %Sayles & E -1 W Church -Elmira 14901
(917) 368-4050 .. **Hilber,** Albert C '90 Swiss Re Fncl Srvcs -55 E 52nd -NY 10055
(212) 326-3939 .. **Hilbert,** Christopher R '77 (Jones D) -222 E 41st -NY 10017
(866) 348-5819 .. **Hilbert,** John S '89 %SSA-ODAR -50 Fountain Plz -Buffalo 14202 **Fx:**(716) 551-4078
(212) 263-5443 .. **Hilbert,** Timothy P '04 NYU Schl of Medicine -400 E 34th -NY 10016
(212) 573-2386 .. **Hilboldt,** James Jr. '83 %Pfizer Inc -235 E 42nd -NY 10017
(518) 257-1443 .. **Hilburger,** Kara L '08 CSEA,Inc -143 Wshngtn Av Bx7125 -Albany 12224 **Fx:**449-1525
(516) 742-4343 .. **Hild,** Harry A Jr. '03 %Scully SM&P PC -400 Grdn City Plz -Gdn Cty 11530
(516) 747-6300 .. **Hild,** Ryan C '06 %Koeppel M&L,LLP -155 First Bx863 -Mineola 11501
(212) 808-0700 .. **Hildebrand,** Christa '86 (Norris M&M,PA) -875 3rd Av -NY 10022
(212) 373-3000 .. **Hilden,** Zoe '01 %Paul WRW&G LLP -1285 Av of Amer -NY 10019
(347) 688-9529 .. **Hildensperger,** Kristan E '06 KH Law PLLC -379 E 10th -NY 10009
(585) 423-0952 .. **Hilderbrandt,** Randall D '88 %Mangione & Assoc,PC -205 St Paul -Rchstr 14604 **Fx:**546-8355
(212) 847-7900 .. **Hiler,** James F X '82 (Wechsler & C,LLP) -17 State -NY 10004
(212) 951-6400 .. **Hilf,** Michl '80 %Dept of Education -475 Park Av S -NY 10016 **Fx:**951-6465
(212) 349-3420 .. **Hilfer,** Edw J '82 %AM Cass -225 Bway -NY 10007 **Fx:**349-3462
(212) 474-1000 .. **Hilfers,** Eric W '99 (Cravath S&M LLP) -825 8th Av -NY 10019
(212) 238-8900 .. **Hilferty,** Michl P '09 %Melito & A,PC -233 Bway -NY 10279
(585) 385-6090 .. **Hilfiker,** Douglas R '01 Clover Cptl Mgt -400 Meridian Ctr -Rchstr 14618 **Fx:**385-9068
(631) 852-1692 .. **Hilgeman,** John '74 %Supreme Ct -Center Dr S -Rvrhead 11901 **Fx:**852-2020
(212) 523-2162 .. **Hilgeman,** Mary S '74 %Beth Israel Med Ctr -555 W 57th -NY 10019
(631) 298-0106 .. **Hilgendorff,** David N '74 (Hilgendorff & K) -2160 Reeve Rd -Mattituck 11952
(212) 248-3140 .. **Hilgendorff,** Heidi E '01 Cnsl Drinker B&R LLP -140 Bway -NY 10005
(212) 657-0929 .. **Hilgendorff,** Hugo A IV '99 Citigroup -77 Water -NY 10005 **Fx:**657-1453
(212) 728-8000 .. **Hilkin,** Michl J '10 %Willkie F&G LLP -787 7th Av -NY 10019
(607) 723-5341 .. **Hill,** A Edw '53 OfCnsl Hinman H&K,LLP -80 Exchange Bx5250 -Bnghmtn 13902
(212) 759-4888 .. **Hill,** Allan L '02 %Phillips L LLP -437 Mad Av -NY 10022
(718) 624-8923 .. **Hill,** Andrea Merlis '84 (Hill R&T LLC) -26 Court -Brklyn 11242 **Fx:**624-8335
(516) 328-4627 .. **Hill,** Angela M K '00 Canon USA -1 Canon Plz -Lk Success 11042
(718) 855-2324 .. **Hill,** Arthur Warren '78 (Ross & H) -16 Court -Brklyn 11241
(631) 261-4700 .. **Hill,** Barbara Joy '94 -7 Oakwood -Greenlawn 11740
(315) 475-0000 .. **Hill,** Barry R '57 (Hill & F,PC) -1117 E Genesee -Syracuse 13210 **Fx:**475-8498
(212) 839-7000 .. **Hill Betts & Nash LLP** -200 Lbrty -NY 10281 **Fx:**466-0514
(315) 218-8000 .. **Hill,** Camille W '89 (Bond S&K,PLLC) -1 Lincoln Ctr -Syracuse 13202
(516) 822-8900 .. **Hill,** Carolyn A '95 %Fiedelman & M -2 Jericho Plz -Jericho 11753
(518) 487-7600 .. **Hill,** Catherine S '90 OfCnsl Whiteman O&H LLP -1 Commerce Plz -Albany 12260
(607) 746-2271 .. **Hill,** Chas D '80 (Bishop & H) -120 Main Bx191 -Delhi 13753
(516) 739-0000 .. **Hill,** Christine J '95 %Martyn T&M -330 Old Cntry Rd -Mineola 11501
(212) 335-9000 .. **Hill,** Christopher J K '01 %DA -1 Hogan Pl -NY 10013
(212) 203-8099 .. **Hill,** Dana D '99 -304 Park Av S -NY 10010
(212) 474-1000 .. **Hill,** Danton J '10 %Cravath S&M LLP -825 8th Av -NY 10019
(212) 697-6262 .. **Hill,** David M '97 (Ward & O) -380 Mad Av -NY 10017
(718) 875-1300 .. **Hill,** Deborah S '06 Appllt Div 2nd Dept -45 Monroe Pl -Brklyn 11201 **Fx:**858-2446
(518) 445-2311 .. **Hill,** Dorothy E '98 %Albany Law Schl -80 New Scotland Av -Albany 12208 **Fx:**445-2315
(914) 592-4275 .. **Hill,** Eben R '02 %MHLS -100 Clearbrook Rd -Elmsfrd 10523 **Fx:**592-9404
(212) 983-6000 .. **Hill,** Elizabeth T '87 -250 Park Av -NY 10177
(212) 227-1500 .. **Hill,** Erin E '02 One Equity Ptnrs -320 Park Av -NY 10022 **Fx:**227-1533
(212) 697-4455 .. **Hill,** Gadi G '85 (Klein & H) -521 5th Av -NY 10175 **Fx:**697-1958
(585) 641-0790 .. **Hill,** Gregory M '07 %Brown & M,PC -1250 Pttsfrd Victor Rd -Pittsfrd 14534
(212) 918-3000 .. **Hill,** Hugh F '09 %Hogan L LLP -875 3rd Av -NY 10022
(212) 761-4000 .. **Hill,** James J Jr. '92 Morgan Stanley -1585 Bway -NY 10036
(845) 486-2280 .. **Hill,** James W '94 %Pub Def -22 Market -Poughkeepsie 12601 **Fx:**486-2266
(212) 446-2300 .. **Hill,** Jason M '00 (Boies S&F LLP) -575 Lex Av -NY 10022
(518) 463-5449 .. **Hill,** Jeffrey L '75 (Hill & G) -99 Wshngtn Av -Albany 12210 **Fx:**463-0947
(212) 735-3000 .. **Hill,** Jennifer J '07 %Skadden ASM&F LLP -4 Times Sq -NY 10036

(212) 578-2521 .. **Hill,** Jos C '91 MetLife -1095 Av of Amer -NY 10036
(716) 532-4900 .. **Hill,** Jos J '97 %Seneca Nation -1490 Route 438 -Irving 14081
(716) 858-2424 .. **Hill,** Justin M '04 %DA -25 Delaware Av -Buffalo 14202 **Fx:**858-7425
(585) 419-8800 .. **Hill,** Katie L '05 %Harris B PLLC -99 Garnsey Rd -Pittsfrd 14534
(914) 766-4431 .. **Hill,** Kevin M '93 IBM -294 Route 100 -Somers 10589 **Fx:**766-8444
(212) 238-3000 .. **Hill,** Laura Lee '06 %Emmet M&M,LLP -120 Bway -NY 10271
(212) 259-8000 .. **Hill,** Lawr M '85 (Dewey & L LLP) -1301 Av of Amer -NY 10019
(212) 636-7704 .. **Hill,** Leah A '86 %Fordham Univ Sch of Law -140 W 62nd -NY 10023 **Fx:**636-6899
Hill, Lester R Jr. '81 -17 Colgate Ln -Woodbury 11797
(518) 474-5785 .. **Hill,** Mary E '90 %Dept of Law -The Cptl -Albany 12224
(212) 668-6000 .. **Hill,** Melisande '81 (Hill & M LLP) -2 Wall -NY 10005
(518) 793-6611 .. **Hill,** Michl J '00 (Miller MS&H,LLC) -451 Glen Bx765 -Glens Fls 12801
(212) 704-6000 .. **Hill,** Mitchel A '94 (Troutman S LLP) -405 Lex Av -NY 10174
(212) 668-6000 .. **Hill & Moin LLP** -2 Wall -NY 10005 **Fx:**668-6009
(212) 506-2500 .. **Hill,** Monica P '08 %Mayer B LLP -1675 Bway -NY 10019
(315) 386-4583 .. **Hill,** Natasha B '98 (Lekki HF&D,PC) -21 Court Bx469 -Canton 13617
(315) 764-0503 .. **Hill,** Natasha B '98 (Lekki HF&D,PC) -227 E Orvis -Massena 13662
(607) 432-4646 .. **Hill,** Peter W '80 -384 Main Bx823 -Oneonta 13820 **Fx:**432-2711
(914) 725-2187 .. **Hill,** Philip S '53 (Hill U&E,LLP) -700 Wht Plns Post Rd -Scarsdale 10583
(718) 892-8588 .. **Hill,** Renee Corley '93 -2027 Wllmsbrdg Rd -Bronx 10461 **Fx:**518-0674
(212) 264-3650 .. **Hill,** Richd A Jr. '89 %SSA Ofc Genl Cnsl -26 Fed Plz -NY 10278 **Fx:**264-6372
(516) 364-6006 .. **Hill,** Rita '97 %Cohen & S,LLP -199 Crsswys Park Dr Bx9004 -Woodbury 11797
(212) 669-0600 .. **Hill Rivkins LLP** -45 Bway -NY 10006 **Fx:**669-0698
(212) 326-2000 .. **Hill,** Samantha A '08 %O'Melveny & M LLP -7 Times Sq -NY 10036
(212) 371-5205 .. **Hill,** Sandra Ashby J '80 -172 E 61st -NY 10065
(716) 882-8200 .. **Hill,** Sean Dennis '65 -6 N Pearl -Buffalo 14202 **Fx:**884-4455
(516) 248-2474 .. **Hill,** Stephen R '66 (S Hill & Assoc) -41 Hilton Av -Hempstd 11550
(212) 449-8169 .. **Hill,** Suzette '97 %Merrill Lynch -220 Bway -NY 10038
(718) 254-7000 .. **Hill,** Tanya '89 %US Atty -271 Cadman Plz E -Brklyn 11201 **Fx:**254-6479
(631) 650-1200 .. **Hill,** Timothy F '05 %Sinnreich K&M LLP -267 Carleton Av -Central Islip 11722
(718) 286-6000 .. **Hill,** Travis A '06 %DA -125-01 Qns Blvd -Kew Gdns 11415
(212) 682-3366 .. **Hill Ullman & Erwin,LLP** -825 3rd Av -NY 10022 **Fx:**682-3367
(914) 725-2180 .. **Hill Ullman & Erwin,LLP** -700 Wht Plns Post Rd -Scarsdale 10583 **Fx:**725-6160
(212) 819-8200 .. **Hille,** David G '97 (White & C LLP) -1155 Av of Amer -NY 10036
(212) 768-6700 .. **Hillebrandt,** Douglas M '09 %Sonnenschein N&R LLP -2 World Fncl Ctr -NY 10281
(212) 335-4500 .. **Hillebrecht,** John M '90 (DLA Piper LLP) -1251 Av of Amer -NY 10020
(212) 258-6000 .. **Hill-Edgar,** W Keyes '95 %Viacom -1515 Bway -NY 10036
(212) 735-3000 .. **Hillel,** Jonathan '10 %Skadden ASM&F LLP -4 Times Sq -NY 10036
(212) 676-0961 .. **Hillel,** Julia Swire '97 %Law Dept -52 Duane -NY 10007 **Fx:**442-6868
(585) 232-6500 .. **Hiller,** Aaron J '03 %Harter S&E LLP -1600 Bausch & Lomb Pl -Rchstr 14604
(518) 474-6740 .. **Hiller,** Amanda K '02 %Dept of State -41 State -Albany 12231 **Fx:**473-9211
(516) 560-6400 .. **Hiller,** Bryan R '09 %Leg Aid -1 Helen Keller Way -Hempstd 11550 **Fx:**565-3694
(516) 365-3683 .. **Hiller,** Carol B '79 -22 Reni Rd -Manhsst 11030
(212) 770-5197 .. **Hiller,** Carolyn L '01 AIG -70 Pine -NY 10270
(212) 312-7880 .. **Hiller,** Edw L '83 %State Ins Fund -199 Church -NY 10007 **Fx:**385-9199
(212) 290-1849 .. **Hiller,** Gladys '87 %OTDA Fair Hearings -330 W 34th -NY 10001
(516) 571-2777 .. **Hiller,** John L '69 Supreme Ct -100 Supreme Ct Dr -Mineola 11501
(212) 827-0341 .. **Hiller,** Jordan S '04 %Krim & K,PC -114 W 47th -NY 10036 **Fx:**827-0351
(716) 564-3288 .. **Hiller,** Kenneth R '84 -2001 Niagara Flls Blvd -Amherst 14228 **Fx:**564-3291
(718) 641-4700 .. **Hiller,** Lesli P '99 NY Rauge Assoc -Bx90 -Jamaica 11417
(518) 473-5115 .. **Hiller,** Marc D '90 Ofc for Technology -State Cptl ESP Bx2062 -Albany 12220
(212) 319-4000 .. **Hiller,** Michl S '92 (Weiss & H,PC) -600 Mad Av -NY 10022
(212) 245-0808 .. **Hiller,** Richd J '69 (Silbert & H,LLP) -1500 Bway -NY 10036
(914) 276-8424 .. **Hiller,** Roberta L '74 -622-C Heritage Hills Dr -Somers 10589
(212) 962-2009 .. **Hiller,** Roy S '78 -225 Bway -NY 10007 **Fx:**385-0425
(516) 487-4800 .. **Hiller,** Stefanie Fine '99 %Fine & B -316 Grt Nck Rd -Gt Neck 11021
(212) 477-2135 .. **Hiller,** Steven E '78 -172 E 24th -NY 10010
(212) 728-8000 .. **Hiller,** Wm E '78 (Willkie F&G LLP) -787 7th Av -NY 10019
(631) 847-5449 .. **Hillery,** Martin T '94 %Arrow Electronics -50 Marcus Dr -Melvll 11747
(716) 858-2424 .. **Hillery,** Michl J '01 %DA -25 Delaware Av -Buffalo 14202 **Fx:**858-7425
(518) 828-9444 .. **Hilley,** Sheila '84 OfCnsl Rapport MWS&R,LLP -436 Union -Hudson 12534
(212) 250-2500 .. **Hill-Falconer,** Yvonne P '04 %Deutsche Bank -60 Wall -NY 10005
(718) 657-0606 .. **Hillgardner,** Thos J '94 -82-63 170th -Jamaica 11432 **Fx:**657-5692
(212) 279-9090 .. **Hilliard,** Craig S '89 (Stark & S) -One Penn Plz -NY 10119 **Fx:**279-9113
(716) 836-9663 .. **Hilliard,** Warren S '86 -330 Wellngtn Av -Buffalo 14223
(585) 658-5405 .. **Hillier,** Shannon L '05 -18 Chapel Bx277 -Mt Morris 14510 **Fx:**658-5426
(212) 593-5223 .. **Hillman,** Adria S '71 A Hillman -41 E 57th -NY 10022 **Fx:**593-4633
(212) 684-5300 .. **Hillman,** Barbara J '96 (Cornfield & F) -30 E 29th -NY 10016 **Fx:**779-2809
(212) 641-2000 .. **Hillman,** David A '95 %Westwood One,Inc -1166 Av of Amer -NY 10036
(212) 756-2000 .. **Hillman,** David M '96 (Schulte R&Z LLP) -919 3rd Av -NY 10022
(516) 663-6600 .. **Hillman,** Jennifer F '04 %Ruskin MF,PC -1425 RXR Plz -Uniondale 11556
(518) 828-3414 .. **Hillman,** John W '09 %DA -325 Columbia -Hudson 12534 **Fx:**828-8491
(212) 408-5100 .. **Hillman,** Peter N '79 (Chadbourne & P LLP) -30 Rckfllr Plz -NY 10112
(315) 422-1152 .. **Hillman,** Richd D '55 Cnsl Costello C&F,PLLC -500 Plum -Syracuse 13204
(607) 255-4902 .. **Hillman,** Robt A '73 %Cornell Law Schl -Myron Taylor Hall -Ithaca 14853 **Fx:**255-7193
(518) 426-4600 .. **Hillmann,** Donald J '08 %Couch W,LLP -540 Bway Bx22222 -Albany 12201
(516) 466-0090 .. **Hillo,** Aviv '99 %Yerushalmi & Assoc -17 Barstow Rd -Gt Neck 11021 **Fx:**466-8988
(516) 877-2016 .. **Hillowe,** Bruce V '81 (BV Hillowe,PC) -190 Willis Av -Mineola 11501 **Fx:**877-2743
(518) 886-4000 .. **Hills,** Adam L '01 %AYCO -321 Bway Bx860 -Saratoga Spgs 12866
(716) 856-4000 .. **Hills,** Bethany J '06 %Hodgson R LLP -140 Pearl -Buffalo 14202
(315) 452-2440 .. **Hills,** Courtney M '07 %Primo P&K,LLP -7075 Manlius Ctr Rd -E Syracuse 13057
(212) 419-3745 .. **Hills,** Midori '02 Catholic Charities -1011 1st Av -NY 10022
(315) 437-8453 .. **Hillsberg Sharp Corbacio & Vitiello** -346 N Midler Av Bx275 -Syracuse 13206 **Fx:**437-6709
(845) 638-1550 .. **Hilowitz,** Lynne S '81 (DaSilva H&M LLP) -120 N Main -New Cty 10956
(914) 666-5600 .. **Hilpert,** Carrie E '06 %Shamberg MD&H,PC -55 Smith Av -Mt Kisco 10549
(914) 271-2100 .. **Hilpert,** Luke P '04 %R Hilpert -75 S Riverside Av -Croton-On-Hud 10520 **Fx:**271-2141
(212) 415-9200 .. **Hilpert,** Morgan C '08 %Dorsey & W LLP -250 Park Av -NY 10177
(914) 271-2100 .. **Hilpert,** Robt J '75 -75 S Riverside Av -Croton-On-Hud 10520 **Fx:**271-2141
(518) 756-7647 .. **Hilscher,** J Theo '89 (Hilscher & H) -802 Roberts Hill Rd -Hannacroix 12087 **Fx:**943-4877
(518) 943-1060 .. **Hilscher,** J Theo '89 (Hilscher & H) -2 Franklin -Catskill 12414 **Fx:**943-4877
(518) 943-1060 .. **Hilscher,** J Theo '89 (Hilscher & H) -419 Route 27 -Ancram 12502 **Fx:**943-4877
(518) 943-1060 .. **Hilscher,** J Theo '89 (Hilscher & H) -Bx32 -Claverack 12513 **Fx:**943-4877
(518) 943-1060 .. **Hilscher,** Nancy R '89 (Hilscher & H) -2 Franklin -Catskill 12414 **Fx:**943-4877
(518) 943-1060 .. **Hilscher,** Nancy R '89 (Hilscher & H) -419 Route 27 -Ancram 12502 **Fx:**943-4877
(518) 756-7647 .. **Hilscher,** Nancy R '89 (Hilscher & H) -802 Roberts Hill Rd -Hannacroix 12087 **Fx:**943-4877
(518) 943-1060 .. **Hilscher,** Nancy R '89 (Hilscher & H) -Bx32 -Claverack 12513 **Fx:**943-4877
(718) 268-8712 .. **Hilsenrath,** Eugene '56 -136-23 68th Dr -Flushng 11367
(718) 615-4550 .. **Hilsenrath,** Steven I '88 -1803 Gravesend Neck Rd -Brklyn 11229 **Fx:**615-4557
(585) 724-3391 .. **Hilst,** Ronald P '71 %Eastman Kodak Co -343 State -Rchstr 14650 **Fx:**724-9563
(716) 662-2664 .. **Hilton,** Andrew C III '85 (A Hilton) -4063 N Buffalo Rd -Orchard Pk 14127 **Fx:**662-2866
(212) 267-6611 .. **Hilton,** Antony A '04 %J Mainiero -305 Bway -NY 10007 **Fx:**732-0888
(212) 969-3000 .. **Hilton,** Kenneth S '81 (Proskauer R LLP) -1585 Bway -NY 10036
(315) 724-3164 .. **Hilton,** Robt K III '94 (Kowalczyk TD&H,LLP) -185 Genesee -Utica 13501
(212) 558-4000 .. **Hilts,** Craig R '09 %Sullivan & C LLP -125 Broad -NY 10004
(518) 383-1292 .. **Hilts,** Earl T '72 -28 Oakwood Blvd -Clifton Pk 12065 **Fx:**383-1292
(212) 765-3040 .. **Hiltzik,** George J '71 NS Bienstock,Inc -250 W 57th -NY 10107 **Fx:**757-6411
(516) 308-4674 .. **Hiltzik,** Robt C '92 -400 S Oyster Bay Rd -Hicksvll 11801 **Fx:**937-1456
(718) 802-2790 .. **Hiltzik,** Sara L '06 %ACS -330 Jay -Brklyn 11201
(212) 669-3455 .. **Himelewski,** Valerie J '91 NYC Dept of Payroll -1 Centre -NY 10007
(845) 638-1943 .. **Himelstein,** Laura L '97 SrCnsl Greenwald D LLP -30 Ramland Rd -Orangebrg 10962
(646) 282-3000 .. **Himes,** Anne L '77 GXG Mgmt -540 Mad Av -NY 10022
(212) 907-0700 .. **Himes,** Jay L '74 (Labaton S LLP) -140 Bway -NY 10005
(212) 223-0200 .. **Himes,** Scott M '79 (Stillman F&S,PC) -425 Park Av -NY 10022
(212) 631-0200 .. **Himmel,** Andrew D '86 (Himmel & B LLP) -928 Bway -NY 10010
(585) 377-2810 .. **Himmelberg,** John M Jr. '97 %Midwest Fncl -200 Cross Keys Ofc Pk -Fairprt 14450
(914) 682-0040 .. **Himmelfarb,** Norman D '75 (Himmelfarb & S,LLP) -1 N Bway -White Plns 10601
(914) 682-0040 .. **Himmelfarb & Sher,LLP** -1 N Bway -White Plns 10601 **Fx:**682-0387
(212) 986-3663 .. **Himmelman,** Robt F '81 -295 Mad Av -NY 10017 **Fx:**972-8572
(212) 578-1626 .. **Himmelstein,** Alan G '83 Overseas Shipholding Grp,Inc -666 3rd Av -NY 10017 **Fx:**251-1180
(212) 349-3000 .. **Himmelstein McConnell Gribben Donoghue & Joseph** -15 Maiden Ln -NY 10038 **Fx:**587-0744
(212) 349-3000 .. **Himmelstein,** Saml J '80 (Himmelstein MGD&J) -15 Maiden Ln -NY 10038
(516) 621-6500 .. **Himonidis,** Nicholas G '97 NGH Assoc Ltd -30 Jericho Exec Plz -Jericho 11753 **Fx:**621-7345
(607) 273-4200 .. **Hinchcliff,** John Moss '83 (Miller M,LLP) -202 E State -Ithaca 14850
(607) 753-5233 .. **Hinchcliff,** Sarah A '02 Dept of Social Srvcs -60 Central Av -Cortlnd 13045 **Fx:**756-3420
(212) 261-8000 .. **Hinchen,** Michl J '09 %Mendes & M,LLP -750 7th Av -NY 10019
(212) 752-1161 .. **Hinckley,** George R Jr. '88 (Traiger & H LLP) -501 5th Av -NY 10017 **Fx:**937-5229
(518) 464-2319 .. **Hind,** Allison R '09 Ayco Co LP -Bx15073 -Albany 12212
(518) 886-4530 .. **Hind,** Gary '81 AYCO -321 Bway Bx860 -Saratoga Spgs 12866
(212) 727-2717 .. **Hinde,** Georgia J '87 -1133 Bway -NY 10010 **Fx:**727-2627
(212) 732-9450 .. **Hindes,** Alexandra C '04 %N Rosenberg -9 Murray -NY 10007 **Fx:**571-9893
(212) 832-3939 .. **Hindin,** Bettina D '86 (R Felder & Prtnrs,PC) -437 Mad Av -NY 10022 **Fx:**838-1103
(212) 687-3860 .. **Hindin,** Matthew D '07 Snow BK,PC -605 3rd Av -NY 10158

(631) 727-2340 .. **Hindman,** Robt J '75 (Ahmuty D&M) -750 Roanoke Av -Rvrhead 11901
(212) 715-9100 .. **Hindriks,** Inge '97 %Kramer LN&F,LLP -1177 Av of Amer -NY 10036
(518) 474-3494 .. **Hinds,** Donnial K '05 State Comptroller -110 State -Albany 12236 **Fx:**486-3106
(518) 485-9391 .. **Hinds,** James R '79 NYS Education Dept -80 Wolf Rd -Albany 12205
(212) 864-4445 .. **Hinds,** Lennox S '80 (Stevens H&W,PC) -116 W 111th -NY 10026
(718) 801-9416 .. **Hinds,** Terry S '03 -119 Penn Av -Brklyn 11207 **Fx:**228-5003
(718) 748-5000 .. **Hindy,** George V '67 (Hindy & Assoc,PC) -233 87th -Brklyn 11209 **Fx:**748-9695
(212) 609-6800 .. **Hindy,** Gregory J '96 (McCarter & E,LLP) -245 Park Av -NY 10167
(212) 326-3939 .. **Hine,** Wm J '96 (Jones D) -222 E 41st -NY 10017
(631) 689-0290 .. **Hinely,** Susan '85 -8 Maple Rd -Setauket 11733
(212) 309-1000 .. **Hiner,** Thos Y '08 (Hunton & W) -200 Park Av -NY 10166
(718) 298-8900 .. **Hines,** Angela R '08 Leg Aid -153-01 Jamaica Av -Jamaica 11432 **Fx:**657-0537
(212) 818-1110 .. **Hines,** Edw M W '65 (Butzel L,PC) -380 Mad Av -NY 10017
(518) 452-5600 .. **Hines,** Erica M '09 %Heslin RF&M PC -5 Columbia Cir -Albany 12203
(518) 436-0775 .. **Hines,** Jeffry E '01 %Proskin,PC -423 Loudon Rd -Albany 12211 **Fx:**436-0014
(212) 259-8000 .. **Hines,** Jonathan H '81 (Dewey & L LLP) -1301 Av of Amer -NY 10019
(718) 590-5973 .. **Hines,** LeLani E '93 NYC Div Leg Srvcs -900 Sheridan Av -Bronx 10451
(212) 310-8000 .. **Hines,** Nichole '08 %Weil G&M LLP -767 5th Av -NY 10153
(718) 531-9700 .. **Hines,** Philip M '05 %Lazarowitz & M,LLP -2004 Ralph Av -Brklyn 11234
(212) 335-9380 .. **Hines,** Sarah H '76 %DA -1 Hogan Pl -NY 10013
(212) 318-6000 .. **Hiney,** Jesse '03 %Paul HJ&W LLP -75 E 55th -NY 10022
(212) 218-2100 .. **Hiney,** Jessica '02 %Fitzpatrick CH&S -1290 Av of Amer -NY 10104
(212) 696-6000 .. **Hing,** Valarie A '94 (Curtis M-PC&M LLP) -101 Park Av -NY 10178
(212) 318-6000 .. **Hinga,** Karoline J '02 %Paul HJ&W LLP -75 E 55th -NY 10022
(631) 231-2176 .. **Hingerton,** Patricia M '87 %Dept of Law -300 Motor Pkwy -Hauppauge 11788 **Fx:**435-4757
(518) 457-2070 .. **Hink,** Jennifer L '99 %Dept of Tax & Fin -Bldg 9 State Campus -Albany 12227 **Fx:**457-6131
(212) 906-1200 .. **Hinkle,** Casey L '06 %Latham & W -885 3rd Av -NY 10022
(212) 504-6000 .. **Hinkle,** Melissa C '00 (Cadwalader W&T LLP) -1 World Fncl Ctr -NY 10281
(212) 922-1080 .. **Hinkle,** Ramsey '09 %Clayman & R,LLP -305 Mad Av -NY 10165
(716) 856-4000 .. **Hinkle,** Ward B '76 (Hodgson R LLP) -140 Pearl -Buffalo 14202
(607) 723-5341 .. **Hinman Howard & Kattell,LLP** -80 Exchange Bx5250 -Bnghmtn 13902 **Fx:**723-6605
(914) 694-4102 .. **Hinman Howard & Kattell,LLP** -106 Corp Park Dr -White Plns 10604 **Fx:**694-4510
(315) 473-9414 .. **Hinman Howard & Kattell,LLP** -224 Harrison -Syracuse 13202 **Fx:**473-9421
(607) 432-5331 .. **Hinman Howard & Kattell,LLP** -Five Ford Av -Oneonta 13820 **Fx:**432-2683
(212) 840-3017 .. **Hinman Howard & Kattell,LLP** -500 5th Av -NY 10110 **Fx:**840-2345
(315) 342-4092 .. **Hinman Howard & Kattell,LLP** -40 W Cayuga -Oswego 13126
(585) 325-6722 .. **Hinman,** James S '81 J Hinman,PC -16 E Main -Rchstr 14614 **Fx:**325-4496
(212) 269-4900 .. **Hinman,** Nichole M '07 %Ford MEW&G,LLP -Wall Street Plz -NY 10005
(518) 436-0751 .. **Hinman Straub PC** -121 State -Albany 12207 **Fx:**436-4751
(212) 966-6420 .. **Hinojosa,** Maria C '00 %Lwyrs For Children -110 Lafayette -NY 10013 **Fx:**966-0531
(516) 328-2300 .. **Hinrichsen,** Claudia A '91 (Abrams FFEGF&E,LLP) -1111 Marcus Av -Lk Success 11042
(607) 273-4200 .. **Hinrichsen,** Nicolai '00 %Miller M,LLP -202 E State -Ithaca 14850
(212) 471-6200 .. **Hinshaw & Culbertson LLP** -780 3rd Av -NY 10017 **Fx:**935-1166
(212) 449-3231 .. **Hinton,** Brenda I '05 Merrill Lynch -225 Lbrty -NY 10080
(646) 723-3377 .. **Hinton,** Christopher S '03 (Hinton Law Firm) -350 5th Av -NY 10118
(516) 688-1700 .. **Hinton,** Diana P '02 %IRS -1600 Stewart Av -Westbury 11590 **Fx:**688-1750
(631) 390-0010 .. **Hintz,** Alexandra M '09 %Bruno G&S,LLP -445 Broad Hollow Rd -Melvll 11747
(631) 777-2330 .. **Hintz,** Alfred R '85 (O'Connor OH&D,LLP) -1 Huntngtn Quad -Melvll 11747
(518) 457-2411 .. **Hintz,** Donna K '95 %DOT -50 Wolf Rd -Albany 12232 **Fx:**457-4021
(718) 482-6470 .. **Hintz,** Gail M '93 %DEC -1 Hunters Pnt Plz -LIC 11101 **Fx:**482-4962
(212) 408-5100 .. **Hintz,** John M '89 (Chadbourne & P LLP) -30 Rckfllr Plz -NY 10112
(212) 306-8237 .. **Hintz,** Laureen M '00 Housing Auth-Inspector Genl Ofc -250 Bway -NY 10007
(631) 368-9008 .. **Hintze,** Phyllis M '85 %AMPS Inc -37 Holly Dr -E Northprt 11731
(845) 528-4410 .. **Hinz,** Harold W '69 (Bolger H&Z) -Bx8 -Putnam Vly 10579
(212) 699-3960 .. **Hinzmann,** Amy C '06 DiscoverReady LLC -55 Bway -NY 10006 **Fx:**699-3970
(212) 371-8855 .. **Hipsher,** Ralph A '97 %Stikeman E LLP -445 Park Av -NY 10022
(212) 557-4000 .. **Hipshman,** Barry '80 SpclCnsl Grunfeld DLS&K LLP -399 Park Av -NY 10022
(212) 225-2000 .. **Hira,** Ranbir S '07 %Cleary GS&H -1 Lbrty Plz -NY 10006
(212) 266-0400 .. **Hiraoka,** Jos M Jr. '92 %Krez & F,LLP -225 Bway -NY 10007
(212) 282-4598 .. **Hirayama,** Hiromi '99 Mizuho Corp Bank -1251 Av of Amer -NY 10020
(212) 308-0070 .. **Hirce,** Kathleen A '07 %McCusker AR&C,PC -805 3rd Av -NY 10022
(212) 859-8000 .. **Hirce,** Margaret E '09 %Fried FHS&J LLP -1 NY Plz -NY 10004
(212) 321-5535 .. **Hird,** Diana Ida '94 Street.com -14 Wall -NY 10005
(516) 569-8260 .. **Hirmes,** Fran Greenberg '87 -25 Wood Ln -Woodsburgh 11598
(212) 245-1000 .. **Hirose,** Mariko '10 %Outten & G LLP -3 Park Av -NY 10016
(212) 366-2672 .. **Hirose,** Yuki A '96 Penguin Grp(USA)Inc -375 Hudson -NY 10014 **Fx:**366-2867
(212) 756-2000 .. **Hirsch,** Adam Leon '05 %Schulte R&Z LLP -919 3rd Av -NY 10022
(212) 558-4000 .. **Hirsch,** Alison R '86 SpclCnsl Sullivan & C LLP -125 Broad -NY 10004
(914) 696-7237 .. **Hirsch,** Andrea '84 %US Tennis Assn -70 W Red Oak Ln -White Plns 10604
(212) 267-1411 .. **Hirsch,** Andrea G '81 -111 Bway -NY 10006 **Fx:**267-6630
(212) 594-1414 .. **Hirsch,** Andrew S '91 Bernstein Real Estate -150 W 30th -NY 10001
(212) 595-1635 .. **Hirsch,** Arthur I '64 -1 Lincoln Plz -NY 10023 **Fx:**877-7649
(718) 434-5215 .. **Hirsch,** Atara '97 -2800 Kings Hwy -Brklyn 11229 **Fx:**253-6396
(212) 801-3056 .. **Hirsch,** Brian D '08 %Greenberg T,LLP -200 Park Av -NY 10166
(516) 741-1717 .. **Hirsch Britt & Mose** -1225 Franklin Av -Gdn Cty 11530 **Fx:**741-8445
(212) 500-2423 .. **Hirsch,** Cara M '04 ArtStor -151 E 61st -NY 10065
(212) 715-9100 .. **Hirsch,** Dana L '06 %Kramer LN&F,LLP -1177 Av of Amer -NY 10036
(212) 553-5635 .. **Hirsch,** Danl I '92 %Zurich NA -1 Lbrty Plz -NY 10006
(212) 682-8383 .. **Hirsch,** Danl M '61 -51 E 42nd -NY 10017 **Fx:**949-5206
(516) 432-4555 .. **Hirsch,** David A '79 -1019 Atl Av -Baldwin 11510 **Fx:**670-9001
(516) 295-7855 .. **Hirsch,** Debra F '93 -30 Wshngtn Av -Cedarhrst 11516
(212) 947-3793 .. **Hirsch,** Douglas R '91 (Sadis & G LLP) -551 5th Av -NY 10176
(516) 741-1717 .. **Hirsch,** Edgar A III '80 (Hirsch B&M) -1225 Franklin Av -Gdn Cty 11530
(212) 859-8000 .. **Hirsch,** Eric A '99 SpclCnsl Fried FHS&J LLP -1 NY Plz -NY 10004
(718) 590-2000 .. **Hirsch,** Eric W '87 %DA -198 E 161st -Bronx 10451 **Fx:**590-6477
(212) 345-5000 .. **Hirsch,** Gary D '89 Marsh & McLennan Cos -1166 Avnus of the Americas -NY 10036
(845) 368-0330 .. **Hirsch,** Gayle Farb '81 -257 Lafayette Av -Suffern 10901
(518) 583-0430 .. **Hirsch,** Gillian A '97 -3 Thames Way -Saratoga Spgs 12866 **Fx:**583-0430
(718) 322-7308 .. **Hirsch,** Glen D '87 -111-04 Lbrty Av -S Richmond Hll 11419 **Fx:**322-6057
(212) 578-8718 .. **Hirsch,** Gregg P '85 %MetLife -27-01 Qns Plz N -LIC 11101
(212) 801-6868 .. **Hirsch,** Hal M '83 (Greenberg T,LLP) -200 Park Av -NY 10166
(212) 490-3000 .. **Hirsch,** Irving B '79 (Wilson EME&D LLP) -150 E 42nd -NY 10017
(212) 793-4588 .. **Hirsch,** James B '92 Citigroup -425 Park Av -NY 10022
(212) 230-8800 .. **Hirsch,** Jason D '08 %WilmerHale -399 Park Av -NY 10022
(914) 750-5933 .. **Hirsch,** Jeffrey H '87 (Kissel H&W LLP) -580 Wht Plns Rd -Tarrytwn 10591
(516) 295-7855 .. **Hirsch,** Jeffrey L '85 -30 Wshngtn Av -Cedarhrst 11516
(718) 398-3200 .. **Hirsch,** Jeremy B '02 Leviev Boymelgreen -752 Pacific -Brklyn 11238
(212) 735-3000 .. **Hirsch,** Jerome S '75 (Skadden ASM&F LLP) -4 Times Sq -NY 10036
(212) 756-2000 .. **Hirsch,** Jesse M '07 %Schulte R&Z LLP -919 3rd Av -NY 10022
(212) 297-5800 .. **Hirsch,** Jillian B '01 Cnsl Day P LLP -7 Times Sq -NY 10036
(212) 889-4440 .. **Hirsch,** Joel B '77 (Scolari G&W) -475 Park Av S -NY 10016
(212) 968-0120 .. **Hirsch,** Julie Stern '90 Marans & W,LLC -29 Bway -NY 10006 **Fx:**785-1618
(718) 237-2000 .. **Hirsch,** Karen A '94 %Leg Aid -111 Lvngstn -Brklyn 11201 **Fx:**237-8737
(212) 769-4343 .. **Hirsch,** Karen Weiss '84 -142 West End Av -NY 10023 **Fx:**769-4986
(212) 837-6825 .. **Hirsch,** Kari D '10 %Hughes H&R LLP -1 Bttry Pk Plz -NY 10004 **Fx:**299-6825
(718) 410-0940 .. **Hirsch,** Leslie Sirota '95 (Camins & H PLLC) -930 Grnd Cncrs -Bronx 10451
(718) 309-1010 .. **Hirsch,** Margo E K '06 -243 Front -Brklyn 11201 **Fx:**834-9106
(212) 838-1000 .. **Hirsch,** Mark S '79 Trump Grp -404 Park Av S -NY 10016
(914) 669-6706 .. **Hirsch,** Martin '52 -616C Heritage Hills -Somers 10589
(516) 248-5522 .. **Hirsch,** Marvin '69 (Flamhaft LH&R) -170 Old Cntry Rd -Mineola 11501
(516) 486-8500 .. **Hirsch,** Mitchell H '79 (Hirsch & H,LLP) -64 Hilton Av -Hempstd 11550 **Fx:**486-8995
(631) 234-3770 .. **Hirsch,** Nanci '91 -1775 Expwy Dr N -Hauppauge 11788 **Fx:**234-3880
(212) 457-7722 .. **Hirsch,** Neil H '65 %IncisiveMedia /NYLJ -120 Bway -NY 10271
(212) 430-6651 .. **Hirsch,** Paul E '94 -65 Bway -NY 10006
(212) 874-6823 .. **Hirsch,** Peter K '84 %Camp Androscoggin -40 W 86th -NY 10024
(631) 727-2340 .. **Hirsch,** Robt E '68 (Ahmuty D&M) -750 Roanoke Av -Rvrhead 11901
(718) 850-9145 .. **Hirsch,** Robin A '97 Hirsch & Assoc -110-20 Jamaica Av -Richmnd Hll 11418
(212) 592-1400 .. **Hirsch,** Ross L '01 %Herrick,F LLP -2 Park Av -NY 10016
(212) 947-3800 .. **Hirsch,** Saml '73 (S Hirsch & Assoc,PC) -350 5th Av -NY 10118 **Fx:**947-9374
(914) 762-4246 .. **Hirsch,** Sandra C '87 -54 Spring Pond Dr -Ossining 10562
(516) 486-8500 .. **Hirsch,** Scott R '85 (Hirsch & H,LLP) -64 Hilton Av -Hempstd 11550 **Fx:**486-8995
(516) 222-7800 .. **Hirsch,** Stanley '73 (S Hirsch PC) -666 Old Cntry Rd -Gdn Cty 11530 **Fx:**222-0518
(516) 227-1117 .. **Hirsch,** Steven C '86 (Hirsch & G,LLP) -585 Stewart Av -Gdn Cty 11530 **Fx:**227-3387
(212) 489-1600 .. **Hirsch,** Stuart C '98 %Deloitte LLP -1633 Bway -NY 10019 **Fx:**492-4201
(585) 546-2434 .. **Hirsch & Tubiolo PC** -1000 Rynlds Arcd Bldg -Rchstr 14614 **Fx:**546-2511
(212) 906-1655 .. **Hirschberg,** Amanda R '02 -885 3rd Av -NY 10022 **Fx:**751-4864
(585) 641-0790 .. **Hirschberg,** Cynthia J '94 OfCnsl Brown & M,PC -1250 Pttsfrd Victor Rd -Pittsfrd 14534
(516) 222-2230 .. **Hirschberg,** David '78 (Burkhart W&H,LLP) -585 Stewart Av -Gdn Cty 11530
(212) 922-9499 .. **Hirschberg,** David M '09 %DeVore & D LLP -99 Park Av -NY 10016 **Fx:**922-1799
(212) 682-0050 .. **Hirschberg,** Edwin '51 -60 E 42nd -NY 10165 **Fx:**986-2564
(212) 940-8800 .. **Hirschberg,** Michl '74 (Katten MR LLP) -575 Mad Av -NY 10022
(212) 848-7097 .. **Hirschberg,** Wm E '77 (Shearman & S LLP) -599 Lex Av -NY 10022
(212) 227-4210 .. **Hirschel,** Danl E '04 %Weg & M,PC -52 Duane -NY 10007
(212) 819-1130 .. **Hirschen Singer & Epstein** -902 Bway -NY 10010 **Fx:**302-8536
(518) 377-2225 .. **Hirschen,** Thos M '66 (Friedman H&M,LLP) -100 Great Oaks Blvd Bx38279 -Albany 12203

(718) 875-1300 .. **Hirschfeld,** Adam L '05 %Applt Div 2nd Dept -45 Monroe Pl -Brklyn 11201 **Fx:**858-2446
(212) 476-9000 .. **Hirschfeld,** Alan H '86 %Neuberger Berman Trust Co -605 3rd Av -NY 10158 **Fx:**476-9090
(212) 526-7000 .. **Hirschfeld,** Arik '06 Barclays Capital -745 7th Av -NY 10019
(212) 748-4000 .. **Hirschfeld,** Audrey R '80 %Bd of Trade -1 North End Av -NY 10282
(212) 355-3838 .. **Hirschfeld,** Elie '75 (Hirschfeld Properties LLC) -5 E 59th -NY 10022 **Fx:**980-3838
(212) 310-8000 .. **Hirschfeld,** Laura W '92 Cnsl Weil G&M LLP -767 5th Av -NY 10153
(212) 573-5000 .. **Hirschfeld,** Marcy D '91 Ford Fndtn -320 E 43rd -NY 10017
(212) 698-3500 .. **Hirschfeld,** Michl '76 (Dechert LLP) -1095 Av of Amer -NY 10036
(212) 530-5000 .. **Hirschfeld,** Michl L '74 (Milbank TH&M LLP) -1 Chase Manh Plz -NY 10005
(516) 295-4100 .. **Hirschfeld,** N Nat '78 -428 Central Av -Cedarhrst 11516 **Fx:**295-4102
(212) 750-3434 .. **Hirschfeld,** Neil B '63 -805 3rd Av -NY 10022 **Fx:**688-4252
(212) 888-3033 .. **Hirschfeld,** Sarah Schachne '08 %Becker GM&M LLP -299 Park Av -NY 10171
(516) 746-4545 .. **Hirschfeld,** Sidney '74 %MHLS -170 Old Cntry Rd -Mineola 11501 **Fx:**746-4372
(516) 877-7100 .. **Hirschfeld,** Wm '53 OfCnsl Bank T&B,PC -400 Post Av -Westbury 11590
(212) 589-4200 .. **Hirschfield,** Marc E '93 (Baker & H LLP) -45 Rckfllr Plz -NY 10111
(516) 408-3007 .. **Hirschheimer,** Rudy '63 -300 Old Cntry Rd -Mineola 11501 **Fx:**739-2189
(516) 746-8000 .. **Hirschhorn,** Alan K '72 (Jaspan S LLP) -300 Grdn City Plz -Gdn Cty 11530
(718) 528-4424 .. **Hirschhorn,** Andrew '91 -1 Cross Isl Plz -Rosedale 11422 **Fx:**528-6658
(212) 893-6727 .. **Hirschhorn,** Eric S '09 3G Capital Inc -600 3rd Av -NY 10016
(516) 742-8058 .. **Hirschhorn,** Jonathan '85 %Abamont & Assoc -200 Grdn City Plz Bx9250 -Gdn Cty 11530 **Fx:**742-7308
(212) 247-1777 .. **Hirschhorn,** Mark P '76 Northlight Fncl LLC -24 W 40th -NY 10018
(718) 528-4424 .. **Hirschhorn,** Pamela H '87 -1 Cross Isl Plz -Rosedale 11422 **Fx:**528-6658
(212) 440-4400 .. **Hirschhorn,** Philip L '89 Buchanan I&R PC -620 8th Av -NY 10018
(212) 969-3000 .. **Hirschhorn,** Russell L '02 %Proskauer R LLP -1585 Bway -NY 10036
(212) 788-0759 .. **Hirschklau,** Rebecca R '08 %Law Dept -100 Church -NY 10007 **Fx:**788-0367
(212) 221-5700 .. **Hirschler,** Arthur A '84 %Goldberg WFG LLP -1501 Bway -NY 10036
(718) 590-5327 .. **Hirschman,** Jodi E '87 Family Ct -900 Sheridan Av -Bronx 10451
(212) 830-4560 .. **Hirschmann,** Nancy '84 Williams Capital Grp,LP -650 5th Av -NY 10019 **Fx:**830-4561
(631) 427-0100 .. **Hirschmann,** Thos R '74 (Pezold SH&S,LLC) -120 Main -Huntngtn 11743
(212) 825-5900 .. **Hirschorn,** Elyse G '83 %Dept of Invstgtn -80 Maiden Ln -NY 10038 **Fx:**825-2860
(212) 801-9342 .. **Hirschson,** Linda B '65 (Greenberg T,LLP) -200 Park Av -NY 10166
(212) 508-6700 .. **Hirschtritt,** Joel S '71 (Tannenbaum HS&H LLP) -900 3rd Av -NY 10022
(212) 790-7161 .. **Hirsh,** A David '89 -291 Bway -NY 10007
(212) 841-1000 .. **Hirsh,** Jeremy L '09 %Covington & B LLP -620 8th Av -NY 10018
(212) 259-8000 .. **Hirsh,** Lawr S '85 SrCnsl Dewey & L LLP -1301 Av of Amer -NY 10019
(212) 773-1943 .. **Hirsh,** Leonard S '77 Ernst & Young LLP -5 Times Sq -NY 10036
(516) 536-2182 .. **Hirsh,** Lester H '61 -100 Merrick Rd -Rockvll Ctr 11570
(212) 373-3000 .. **Hirsh,** Robt M '78 (Paul WRW&G LLP) -1285 Av of Amer -NY 10019
(212) 484-3900 .. **Hirsh,** Robt M '98 (Arent F LLP) -1675 Bway -NY 10019
(212) 969-3000 .. **Hirshaut,** Tzvi '92 %Proskauer R LLP -1585 Bway -NY 10036
(212) 859-8000 .. **Hirshbein,** Emily Gould '05 %Fried FHS&J LLP -1 NY Plz -NY 10004
(212) 878-8000 .. **Hirshberg,** Brian '07 %Clifford C LLP -31 W 52nd -NY 10019
(917) 501-7814 .. **Hirshberg,** Tal '08 -738 Gilbert Pl -N Woodmere 11581
(845) 638-6761 .. **Hirshfeld,** Felicia S '86 (Hirshfeld & H) -301 N Main -New Cty 10956
(845) 638-6761 .. **Hirshfeld,** Wm A '86 (Hirshfeld & H) -301 N Main -New Cty 10956
(212) 506-1700 .. **Hirshfield,** Adam E '99 -1301 Av of Amer 36th Fl -NY 10019 **Fx:**506-1800
(914) 949-1800 .. **Hirshfield,** Joel A '95 (Hirshfield & C,PC) -62 Waller Av -White Plns 10605 **Fx:**949-5880
(212) 449-1395 .. **Hirshfield,** Matthew S '96 %Merrill Lynch -4 Wrld Fncl Ctr -NY 10080
(646) 827-9362 .. **Hirshfield,** Peter B '71 -1035 Park Av -NY 10028 **Fx:**349-1665
(212) 935-3000 .. **Hirshfield,** Stuart '66 (Mintz LCFG&P,PC) -666 3rd Av -NY 10017
(516) 626-7536 .. **Hirshleifer,** Caryn M '81 -24 Hastings Rd -Old Westbury 11568 **Fx:**626-7536
(718) 855-5066 .. **Hirshman,** Alan L '58 -32 Court -Brklyn 11201 **Fx:**522-0432
(212) 506-3371 .. **Hirshman,** Elisheva M '09 %Kasowitz BT&F LLP -1633 Bway -NY 10019
(212) 373-3000 .. **Hirshman,** Michele S '84 (Paul WRW&G LLP) -1285 Av of Amer -NY 10019
(516) 292-8100 .. **Hirshon,** Judy S '80 %Nassau/Sfflk Law Srv -1 Helen Keller Way -Hempstd 11550 **Fx:**292-6529
(212) 969-3000 .. **Hirshon,** Sheldon I '72 (Proskauer R LLP) -1585 Bway -NY 10036
(518) 265-9284 .. **Hirshorn,** Donald P '61 -860 Hereford Way -Niskayuna 12309 **Fx:**869-0631
(212) 867-9595 .. **Hirshowitz,** Melvin S '63 -630 3rd Av -NY 10017 **Fx:**949-1857
(212) 687-4900 .. **Hirson,** Kevin M '85 (Wormser KG&J LLP) -825 3rd Av -NY 10022
(585) 241-5999 .. **Hirt,** Jared P '05 (Evans & F LLP) -95 Allens Crk Rd -Rchstr 14618
(212) 651-1170 .. **Hirt,** Lance L '93 Lindsay Goldberg LLC -630 5th Av -NY 10111
(631) 537-2618 .. **Hirt,** Maxine '78 -Bx434 -Brdghmptn 11932
(516) 837-6267 .. **Hirth,** Jeffrey Y '03 Sutton Alliance -515 Rockaway Av -Vly Stream 11581
(212) 872-1000 .. **Hirth,** Leon B '98 -One Bryant Park -NY 10036 **Fx:**872-1002
(212) 839-5300 .. **Hirth,** Robt W '79 (Sidley A LLP) -787 7th Av -NY 10019
(315) 425-2700 .. **Hiscock & Barclay,LLP** -One Park Pl -Syracuse 13202 **Fx:**425-2701
(716) 566-1300 .. **Hiscock & Barclay,LLP** -1100 M&T Ctr -Buffalo 14203 **Fx:**566-1301
(212) 784-5800 .. **Hiscock & Barclay,LLP** -7 Times Sq -NY 10036 **Fx:**784-5777
(585) 295-4400 .. **Hiscock & Barclay,LLP** -2000 HSBC Plz -Rchstr 14604 **Fx:**295-4401
(518) 429-4200 .. **Hiscock & Barclay,LLP** -50 Beaver -Albany 12207 **Fx:**429-4201
(212) 336-2000 .. **Hiscock,** Dana W '71 (Patterson BW&T LLP) -1133 Av of Amer -NY 10036
(518) 474-8266 .. **Hiser,** Michl A '83 %Dept of Health -Corning Twr 24th Fl -Albany 12237 **Fx:**473-2430
(516) 873-2000 .. **Hisiger,** Gary C '91 (Moritt HH&H LLP) -400 Grdn City Plz -Gdn Cty 11530
(212) 906-1200 .. **Hisiger,** James Ian '81 (Latham & W) -885 3rd Av -NY 10022
(212) 317-5400 .. **Hissong,** Jos G '90 %Swiss Re New Markets -55 E 52nd -NY 10055
(518) 474-8390 .. **Hitchcock,** Charlotte A '92 Governors Ofd -State Cptl -Albany 12224
(212) 688-3025 .. **Hitchcock,** Christopher B '80 (Hitchcock & C,LLP) -757 3rd Av -NY 10017 **Fx:**688-3040
(518) 689-0966 .. **Hite & Beaumont,PC** -20 Corp Wds Blvd -Albany 12211 **Fx:**689-0962
(518) 457-3177 .. **Hite,** Patricia A '82 %Dept Civil Srvc -Harriman Campus Bldg 1 -Albany 12239 **Fx:**457-6654
(518) 689-0966 .. **Hite,** Robt S '81 (Hite & B,PC) -20 Corp Wds Blvd -Albany 12211
(716) 852-2032 .. **Hites,** Wm R '80 -69 Delaware Av -Buffalo 14202
(914) 592-4167 .. **Hitsman Hoffman & O'Reilly LLC** -220 Wht Plns Rd -Tarrytwn 10591 **Fx:**592-4457
(914) 592-4167 .. **Hitsman,** Michl R '78 (Hitsman H&O LLC) -220 Wht Plns Rd -Tarrytwn 10591
(212) 269-7722 .. **Hitsous,** Kristin N '08 %Rosabianca & Assoc,PLLC -14 Wall -NY 10005 **Fx:**269-7799
(716) 856-5012 .. **Hitzel,** Cheryl L '04 %Anspach ME,LLP -2400 Main Pl Twr -Buffalo 14202
(212) 841-1000 .. **Hives,** Harry G '78 (Covington & B LLP) -620 8th Av -NY 10018
(212) 406-3070 .. **Hivnor,** James O '77 %Karlsson & N,PC -305 Bway -NY 10007
(212) 578-2211 .. **Hixson,** Justin K '84 %MetLife -27-01 Qns Plz N -LIC 11101
(716) 664-5600 .. **Hjort,** Carl A III '06 %Bilicki Law Firm,PC -1285 N Main -Jamestwn 14701 **Fx:**664-5606
(516) 496-0730 .. **Hlady,** Cherie A '07 %Fratello & F,PC -242 Crsswys Park Dr W -Woodbury 11797 **Fx:**496-9791
(212) 735-3000 .. **Hlafter,** Jon A '03 %Skadden ASM&F LLP -4 Times Sq -NY 10036
(914) 824-5454 .. **Hlapatsos,** George Jr. '97 %Hon R Molea -111 Martin Luther King Blvd -White Plns 10601
(212) 222-4711 .. **Hlavaty,** John A '03 (J Hlavaty & Assoc,PLLC) -270 Riverside Dr -NY 10025 **Fx:**666-0092
(914) 595-8200 .. **Hlavaty,** Marie D '92 Visant Holdings -357 Main St -Armonk 10504
(212) 248-3140 .. **Hlavenka,** Kristy M '09 %Drinker B&R LLP -140 Bway -NY 10005
(914) 328-0404 .. **Hlawati,** Ian H '03 %Jackson L LLP -1 N Bway -White Plns 10601
(212) 530-5000 .. **Hlawaty,** Roland '91 (Milbank TH&M LLP) -1 Chase Manh Plz -NY 10005
(718) 709-3030 .. **Hnat,** James G II '97 %JetBlue Airways -118-29 Qns Blvd -Frst Hlls 11375 **Fx:**709-3631
(212) 728-8000 .. **Hnatt,** Kelly M '90 (Willkie F&G LLP) -787 7th Av -NY 10019
(646) 282-5976 .. **Ho,** Alison Honlee '03 Davidson Kempner Cptl Mgmt LLC -65 E 55th -NY 10022
(212) 732-5000 .. **Ho,** Barbara '06 Leg Aid -49 Thomas -NY 10013 **Fx:**298-5252
(212) 335-9000 .. **Ho,** Elson '01 %DA -1 Hogan Pl -NY 10013
(212) 455-2000 .. **Ho,** Emily T '10 %Simpson T&B LLP -425 Lex Av -NY 10017
(212) 526-3582 .. **Ho,** Garrett S '96 %Barclays Capital Inc -399 Park Av -NY 10022
(212) 292-8310 .. **Ho,** Gregory P '78 Spring Mountain Capital -65 E 55th -NY 10022
(212) 906-1200 .. **Ho,** Jenny Yu Chen '06 %Latham & W -885 3rd Av -NY 10022
(212) 269-2500 .. **Ho,** Jocelyn R '09 %Gorlick K&L,PC -17 State -NY 10004
(646) 253-2300 .. **Ho,** John S '98 (Bond S&K,PLLC) -330 Mad Av -NY 10017
(212) 794-5382 .. **Ho,** Marina B '91 CUNY -535 E 80th -NY 10075
(212) 300-1300 .. **Ho,** Nancy N W '00 York Capital Mgmt -767 5th Av -NY 10153
(212) 906-1200 .. **Ho,** Timothy '09 %Latham & W -885 3rd Av -NY 10022
(212) 237-1000 .. **Ho,** Yani Indrajana '06 %Windels ML&M,LLP -156 W 56th -NY 10019
(212) 999-5800 .. **Hoag,** Arthur L '98 (Wilson SG&R) -1301 Av of Americas -NY 10019
(518) 851-7872 .. **Hoag,** Chas Edwin Jr. '73 -218 US Route 9H DrwrC -Claverack 12513 **Fx:**851-7877
(212) 837-6522 .. **Hoag,** Margaret J '06 %Hughes H&R LLP -1 Bttry Pk Plz -NY 10004
(518) 306-6331 .. **Hoag,** Rosemary T '96 -Bx3567 -Saratoga Spgs 12866 **Fx:**306-6531
(212) 267-4876 .. **Hoagland Longo Moran Dunst & Doukas, LLP** -1501 Bway -NY 10036 **Fx:**(732) 545-4579
(646) 386-3676 .. **Hoahng,** Sue Ann '87 Supreme Ct Spcl Referee -60 Centre -NY 10007
(212) 918-3000 .. **Hoang,** Hoa T T '03 %Hogan L LLP -875 3rd Av -NY 10022
(212) 596-9000 .. **Hoang,** Khue Van '03 (Ropes & G LLP) -1211 Av of Amer -NY 10036
(973) 596-4851 .. **Hoang,** Lan '98 (Gibbons PC) -1 Penn Plz -NY 10119 **Fx:**639-8315
(518) 436-0786 .. **Hoare,** Francis G Jr. '86 (Featherstonhaugh W&C,LLP) -99 Pine -Albany 12207
(585) 697-5184 .. **Hoare,** James A '95 Fibertech Ntwrks -300 Meridian Ctr -Rchstr 14618
(315) 624-7777 .. **Hobaica,** Peter M '85 (P Hobaica,LLC) -2045 Genesee -Utica 13501 **Fx:**624-7781
(315) 624-7777 .. **Hobaica,** Peter W '05 %P Hobaica,LLC -2045 Genesee -Utica 13501 **Fx:**624-7781
(212) 848-7847 .. **Hobart,** Susan L '86 Cnsl Shearman & S LLP -599 Lex Av -NY 10022
(631) 953-6901 .. **Hobbes,** John W '68 J Hobbes PLLC -18 1st Bx420 -Rvrhead 11901 **Fx:**953-6923
(518) 581-9797 .. **Hobbs,** Gary C '87 (Poklemba & H,LLC) -2715 State Route 9 -Malta 12020
(212) 688-8555 .. **Hobbs,** Jennifer L '07 Fragomen DB&L LLP -7 Hanover Sq -NY 10004
(212) 455-2000 .. **Hobbs,** Jennifer Lee '00 (Simpson T&B LLP) -425 Lex Av -NY 10017
(845) 634-7010 .. **Hobbs,** Kevin F '80 -67 N Main Bx1070 -New Cty 10956 **Fx:**634-8993

(212) 335-9000 .. **Hobbs,** Lanita K '86 %DA -1 Hogan Pl -NY 10013
(646) 386-5700 .. **Hobbs,** Nancy S '77 %Civil Ct -111 Centre -NY 10013
(212) 649-2131 .. **Hobbs,** Steven A '84 Hearst Business Media -300 W 57th -NY 10019
(516) 741-7676 .. **Hobel,** Kelly C '08 %Miranda SSSV LLP -240 Mineola Blvd -Mineola 11501
(212) 661-2900 .. **Hoberman,** Eric S '99 %Kriss & F LLP -360 Lex Av -NY 10017
(212) 977-9001 .. **Hoberman,** Henry S '99 %RHI Entrtnmnt -1325 Av of Amer -NY 10019 **Fx:**977-9049
(212) 278-6261 .. **Hoberman,** Jason M '02 %Societe Generale -1221 Av of Amer -NY 10020
(212) 408-5100 .. **Hoberman,** Lori S '90 (Chadbourne & P LLP) -30 Rckfllr Plz -NY 10112
(718) 625-1100 .. **Hoberman,** Owen O '62 (Hoberman & T,PC) -2622 E Tremont Av -Bronx 10461
(732) 855-6052 .. **Hoberman,** Stuart A '73 (Wilentz G&S) -110 William -NY 10038 **Fx:**726-6518
(718) 625-1100 .. **Hoberman & Trepp,PC** -2622 E Tremont Av -Bronx 10461 **Fx:**430-1404
(315) 724-1600 .. **Hobika,** Andrew J '96 (Callanen F&H,LLP) -1417 Genesee -Utica 13501
(315) 724-1600 .. **Hobika,** Jos H '56 OfCnsl Callanen F&H,LLP -1417 Genesee -Utica 13501
(315) 792-0171 .. **Hobika,** Jos H '56 (Law Dept) -1 Knndy Plz -Utica 13502 **Fx:**792-0175
(315) 724-1600 .. **Hobika,** Jos H Jr. '86 (Callanen F&H,LLP) -1417 Genesee -Utica 13501
(914) 328-0674 .. **Hobish,** Richd S '83 (Pro Bono Prtnrshp,Inc) -237 Mamaroneck Av -White Plns 10605 **Fx:**328-0538
(212) 704-6000 .. **Hoblin,** Philip J Jr. '57 -405 Lex Av -NY 10174 **Fx:**704-6288
(518) 395-5400 .. **Hoblock,** Michl J Jr. '67 %Racing & Wagering Bd -1 Bway Ctr -Schnctdy 12305 **Fx:**347-1250
(518) 463-2251 .. **Hoblock,** Wm J '61 OfCnsl D'Agostino HF&J,PC -187 Wolf Rd -Albany 12205
(212) 403-1000 .. **Hobson,** Adam S '09 %Wachtell LR&K -51 W 52nd -NY 10019
(212) 841-1000 .. **Hoch,** Benjamin '89 (Covington & B LLP) -620 8th Av -NY 10018
(914) 421-1900 .. **Hoch,** Brian R '85 -3 Barker Av -White Plns 10601 **Fx:**421-1979
(518) 433-4349 .. **Hoch,** Laurence A '91 %GE -12 Corp Wds Blvd -Albany 12211 **Fx:**433-4361
(914) 683-7953 .. **Hoch,** Wm M '88 -96 Ogden Av -White Plns 10605
(718) 855-4800 .. **Hochbaum,** Chas S '77 CS Hochbaum PC -16 Court -Brklyn 11241 **Fx:**855-4877
(516) 227-2111 .. **Hochbaum,** Chas S '77 CS Hochbaum PC -50 Chas Lindbergh Blvd -Uniondale 11553 **Fx:**739-2445
(212) 450-4000 .. **Hochbaum,** Lee E '09 %Davis P&W LLP -450 Lex Av -NY 10017
(718) 298-8970 .. **Hochberg,** Carol J '76 %Leg Aid -153-01 Jamaica Av -Jamaica 11432 **Fx:**657-0537
(212) 833-7670 .. **Hochberg,** Ellen A '03 Sony BMG Music Entrtnmnt -550 Mad Av -NY 10022 **Fx:**833-8406
(212) 788-1241 .. **Hochberg,** Evan D '05 %Law Dept -100 Church -NY 10007 **Fx:**788-0367
(212) 558-4000 .. **Hochberg,** Jeffrey D '96 (Sullivan & C LLP) -125 Broad -NY 10004
(212) 916-2133 .. **Hochberg,** Jennifer E '92 %UBS AG -101 Park Av -NY 10178
(212) 940-6218 .. **Hochberg,** Mitchell C '78 Madden Capital LLC -299 Park Av -NY 10171
(212) 504-6000 .. **Hochberg,** Mitchell E '06 %Cadwalader W&T LLP -1 World Fncl Ctr -NY 10281
(631) 424-5400 .. **Hochberg,** R Mark '83 (Schanker & H) -27 West Neck Rd Bx1905 -Huntngtn 11743
(212) 593-3000 .. **Hochberg,** Ralph R '71 (Platzer SKLG&J,LLP) -1065 Av of Amer -NY 10018
(718) 624-2348 .. **Hochberg,** Stanley J '67 -53 Boerum Pl -Brklyn 11201 **Fx:**(732) 873-5379
(516) 741-7767 .. **Hochberg,** Stanley J '67 OfCnsl Katz & K,LLP -170 Old Cntry Rd -Mineola 11501
(212) 765-2100 .. **Hochberg,** Steven M '67 -1700 Bway -NY 10019 **Fx:**541-5429
(212) 681-6500 .. **Hochberg,** Steven R '87 (Stempel BC&H,PC) -675 3rd Av -NY 10017
(212) 274-5991 .. **Hochberg,** Susan J '90 %Admin Children's Srvcs -220 Church -NY 10013 **Fx:**274-6109
(212) 481-0011 .. **Hochberg,** Thos W '02 %M Goldberg,PC -31 E 32nd -NY 10016 **Fx:**481-4144
(212) 873-9374 .. **Hochberger,** Ruth S '76 -290 West End Av -NY 10023 **Fx:**875-8314
(212) 474-1000 .. **Hochenberg,** Evgeniya E '10 %Cravath S&M LLP -825 8th Av -NY 10019
(212) 558-4000 .. **Hochenberg,** Malcolm S '09 %Sullivan & C LLP -125 Broad -NY 10004
(212) 752-1900 .. **Hochenberg,** Wm S '76 (B Post,LLP) -950 3rd Av -NY 10022 **Fx:**752-1609
(914) 421-1800 .. **Hocherman,** Henry M '71 (Hocherman T&W LLP) -1 N Bway -White Plns 10601
(914) 421-1800 .. **Hocherman Tortorella & Wekstein LLP** -1 N Bway -White Plns 10601 **Fx:**421-1856
(914) 686-0900 .. **Hochfelder,** John M '78 -81 Main -White Plns 10601 **Fx:**686-9048
(716) 845-6000 .. **Hochfield,** Marilyn A '85 SpclCnsl Kavinoky C LLP -726 Exchange -Buffalo 14210
(646) 315-7347 .. **Hochhauser,** Barry M '90 %FINRA -14 Wall -NY 10005 **Fx:**315-7440
(212) 335-9000 .. **Hochhauser,** Rachel L '00 %DA -1 Hogan Pl -NY 10013
(914) 472-7700 .. **Hochhauser,** Stephen '61 OfCnsl Bertine HHZD&D,LLP -700 Wht Plns Rd -Scarsdale 10583
(212) 689-4343 .. **Hochheiser,** Danl A '97 (Hochheiser H&I LLP) -15 Maiden Ln -NY 10038 **Fx:**481-3424
(212) 635-3150 .. **Hochheiser,** Felisa Reinhard '97 Ofc Inspector Genl -61 Bway -NY 10006 **Fx:**809-6287
(516) 227-6300 .. **Hochheiser,** Keith B '91 (Ettelman & H,PC) -100 Q Roosevelt Blvd -Gdn Cty 11530
(914) 995-4172 .. **Hochheiser,** Lana B '98 %DA -111 Martin Luther King Blvd -White Plns 10601 **Fx:**995-3363
(212) 689-4343 .. **Hochheiser,** Lawr '66 (Hochheiser H&I LLP) -15 Maiden Ln -NY 10038 **Fx:**481-3424
(212) 216-9352 .. **Hochheiser,** Leonard '67 -245 5th Av -NY 10016 **Fx:**971-0417
(516) 393-0026 .. **Hochler,** Don L '82 D Hochler,PC -90 Merrick Av -E Meadow 11554 **Fx:**393-0028
(646) 386-5127 .. **Hochman,** Alexandra Ascher '02 Hon J Adams -60 Lafayette -NY 10013
(212) 225-2000 .. **Hochman,** Aliza C '10 %Cleary GS&H -1 Lbrty Plz -NY 10006
(718) 744-5145 .. **Hochman,** Chas M '05 -2214 Av R -Brklyn 11229
(212) 788-1149 .. **Hochman,** Debra A '87 %Law Dept -100 Church -NY 10007 **Fx:**788-0367
(212) 317-4848 .. **Hochman,** Edw S '80 -225 E 57th -NY 10022
(212) 728-8000 .. **Hochman,** Ian K '00 SpclCnsl Willkie F&G LLP -787 7th Av -NY 10019
(212) 728-8000 .. **Hochman,** Jeffrey S '92 (Willkie F&G LLP) -787 7th Av -NY 10019
(212) 277-6300 .. **Hochman,** Jonathan L '89 (Schindler C&H LLP) -100 Wall -NY 10005
(516) 333-0003 .. **Hochman,** Martin M '52 %American Dream Mortgage -400 Post Av -Westbury 11590 **Fx:**333-0655
(516) 393-5903 .. **Hochman,** Richd C '86 -6800 Jericho Tpk -Syosset 11791 **Fx:**393-5923
(212) 566-7081 .. **Hochman,** Robt B '87 (Cohen & H) -80 Maiden Ln -NY 10038
(212) 750-8700 .. **Hochman,** Stephen A '60 -600 Lex Av -NY 10022 **Fx:**223-8391
(212) 768-6700 .. **Hochman,** Susan L '93 %Sonnenschein N&R LLP -1221 Av of Amer -NY 10020
(212) 683-0001 .. **Hochman,** Talia '96 Doubleclick Inc -111 8th Av -NY 10011
(212) 770-5431 .. **Hochman,** Todd S '85 %AIG -70 Pine -NY 10270 **Fx:**809-5722
(212) 310-8000 .. **Hochstadt,** Eric S '04 %Weil G&M LLP -767 5th Av -NY 10153
(212) 580-9930 .. **Hochstadt,** Joy '05 -300 Cntrl Pk W -NY 10024 **Fx:**580-9322
(716) 551-4741 .. **Hochul,** Denise C '87 %US DHS -130 Delaware Av -Buffalo 14202
(716) 843-5700 .. **Hochul,** Wm J Jr. '93 US Atty -138 Delaware Av -Buffalo 14202 **Fx:**551-3052
(716) 847-0650 .. **Hocieniec,** John D '03 %Leg Srvcs -237 Main -Buffalo 14203 **Fx:**847-0227
(516) 873-2000 .. **Hock,** Alan S '82 (Moritt HH&H LLP) -400 Grdn City Plz -Gdn Cty 11530
(516) 877-2900 .. **Hock,** Anna I '08 %Bartlett MB&M,LLP -300 Old Cntry Rd -Mineola 11501
(212) 563-4100 .. **Hock,** David R '03 %Cohen W&S LLP -330 W 42nd -NY 10036
(212) 801-3088 .. **Hockens,** S Nicholas '03 %Greenberg T,LLP -200 Park Av -NY 10166
(212) 752-3380 .. **Hockert,** Lorance T '64 L Hockert LLC -880 3rd Av -NY 10022 **Fx:**(646) 861-4850
(212) 759-8203 .. **Hocking,** Jos J '99 %Hedinger & L -110 Wall -NY 10005
(212) 872-1000 .. **Hodara,** Fred S '82 -One Bryant Park -NY 10036 **Fx:**872-1002
(212) 558-4000 .. **Hodari,** Jamie J '10 %Sullivan & C LLP -125 Broad -NY 10004
(212) 541-2000 .. **Hodarkar,** Nikhil-Pranav J '08 %Bryan C LLP -1290 Av of Amer -NY 10104
(212) 696-6000 .. **Hodeau,** Veronique A '07 %Curtis M-PC&M LLP -101 Park Av -NY 10178
(631) 265-7200 .. **Hodella,** Kristopher M '06 %Russo KW&C -400 Townline Rd -Hauppauge 11788
(518) 402-3683 .. **Hoderath,** Geoffrey T '84 -3840 State -Albany 12207
(631) 589-7242 .. **Hodes,** Andrew D '06 %Zabell & Assoc,LLP -4875 Sunrise Hwy -Bohemia 11716
(212) 732-8700 .. **Hodes,** Hal R '07 %McAloon & F,PC -123 William -NY 10038
(212) 761-8767 .. **Hodes,** Joel '92 Morgan Stanley -1585 Bway -NY 10036
(518) 487-7600 .. **Hodes,** Joel L '72 (Whiteman O&H LLP) -1 Commerce Plz -Albany 12260
(718) 694-1019 .. **Hodes-Urbont,** Lisa '83 %Transit Auth -130 Lvngstn -Brklyn 11201 **Fx:**694-5726
(212) 450-4000 .. **Hodgdon,** Paul D '05 %Davis P&W LLP -450 Lex Av -NY 10017
(212) 916-4270 .. **Hodgdon,** Timothy F '80 %TIAA-CREF -730 3rd Av -NY 10017
(914) 995-3000 .. **Hodge,** Juel L '95 %DA -111 Martin Luther King Blvd -White Plns 10601 **Fx:**995-3363
(716) 753-4241 .. **Hodgens,** Lynn '07 %DA -Cnty Cthse -Mayvll 14757 **Fx:**753-4628
(914) 385-6000 .. **Hodges,** George S '74 (Hodges W&S LLP) -55 Church -White Plns 10601 **Fx:**385-6060
(516) 766-7600 .. **Hodges,** H Wm III '63 -55 Maple Av -Rockvll Ctr 11570 **Fx:**766-6630
(212) 326-2083 .. **Hodgman,** Donald R '85 -153 E 53rd -NY 10022
(212) 661-1100 .. **Hodgson,** R James '04 %Pomerantz HG&G LLP -100 Park Av -NY 10017
(716) 856-4000 .. **Hodgson Russ LLP** -140 Pearl -Buffalo 14202 **Fx:**849-0349
(518) 465-2333 .. **Hodgson Russ LLP** -677 Bway -Albany 12207 **Fx:**465-1567
(212) 751-4300 .. **Hodgson Russ LLP** -1540 Bway -NY 10036 **Fx:**751-0928
(212) 661-3535 .. **Hodgson Russ LLP** -60 E 42nd -NY 10165 **Fx:**972-1677
(518) 736-2900 .. **Hodgson Russ LLP** -55 E Main -Johnstwn 12095 **Fx:**736-8165
(718) 409-1228 .. **Hodinar,** Michl '85 -3158 Schuyler Pl -Bronx 10461
(516) 222-1640 .. **Hodish,** Alan B '89 AB Hodish,LLC -666 Old Cntry Rd -Gdn Cty 11530 **Fx:**393-5556
(631) 439-1720 .. **Hodor,** Wendy '89 %MHLS -320 Carleton Av -Central Islip 11722 **Fx:**951-2562
(212) 986-2233 .. **Hodrinsky,** Jason '07 %Early & S LLC -360 Lex Av Bx3601 -NY 10163
(585) 546-5530 .. **Hodson,** John D '86 %Thomson West -50 E Broad -Rchstr 14694
(914) 736-9700 .. **Hodukavich,** Marie R '85 -1831 Carhart Av -Peekskill 10566 **Fx:**737-2724
(212) 450-4000 .. **Hoeben,** Wendi R F '05 %Davis P&W LLP -450 Lex Av -NY 10017
(516) 676-0333 .. **Hoebich,** Patrick W '96 -1 Schl -Glen Cove 11542 **Fx:**759-5516
(914) 683-5900 .. **Hoechster,** David M '95 Statewide Abstract -202 Mamaroneck Av -White Plns 10601 **Fx:**683-5905
(516) 571-1828 .. **Hoefenkrieg,** Christopher E '95 %Hon I Wexner -262 Old Cntry Rd -Mineola 11501
(718) 931-3131 .. **Hoefer,** Kathryn C '92 %Kravet H&M,PC -1135A Morris Park Av -Bronx 10461
(718) 931-3131 .. **Hoefer,** Kenneth T Jr. '87 (Kravet H&M,PC) -1135A Morris Park Av -Bronx 10461
(718) 931-3131 .. **Hoefer,** Wm '83 %Kravet H&M,PC -1135A Morris Park Av -Bronx 10461
(718) 366-0940 .. **Hoefferle,** Robt J '98 (Kerzner & H,LLC) -74-09 Myrtle Av -Glendale 11385 **Fx:**366-0922
(212) 656-2604 .. **Hoeffner,** Danl N '98 NYSE -14 Wall -NY 10005
(516) 739-0400 .. **Hoefling,** John W '78 (Kelly R&K,LLP) -330 Old Cntry Rd -Mineola 11501

(631) 727-0110 .. **Hoefling,** John W '78 (Kelly R&K,LLP) -218 Griffing -Rvrhead 11901
(212) 687-3000 .. **Hoefs,** Michl J '06 %Jaffe & A,LLP -600 3rd Av -NY 10016
(631) 727-2180 .. **Hoeg,** Karen A '94 OfCnsl Twomey LSKD&Q,LLP -33 W 2nd Bx9398 -Rvrhead 11901
(212) 664-4366 .. **Hoeh,** Jeffrey D '92 %NBC -30 Rckfllr Plz -NY 10112
(212) 310-8000 .. **Hoehne,** Debora A '08 %Weil G&M LLP -767 5th Av -NY 10153
(315) 425-2700 .. **Hoehner,** Holly Johnsen '98 (Hiscock & B,LLP) -One Park Pl -Syracuse 13202
(315) 425-9000 .. **Hoehner,** Thos '08 %Marjama MB&S LLP -250 S Clinton -Syracuse 13202
(718) 739-6910 .. **Hoelldobler,** Frank M '90 %Admin Children's Srvcs -151-20 Jamaica Av -Jamaica 11432
(212) 310-8000 .. **Hoelzer,** Lauren B '09 %Weil G&M LLP -767 5th Av -NY 10153
(212) 768-6700 .. **Hoene,** Mary Joan '82 Cnsl Sonnenschein N&R LLP -2 World Fncl Ctr -NY 10281
(516) 569-4520 .. **Hoenig,** D Bernard '58 Hoenig & H -132 Spruce -Cedarhrst 11516 **Fx:**569-4529
(914) 935-9000 .. **Hoenig,** Kathryn Lee '87 %Hoenig & Co Inc -4 Intl Dr -Rye Brook 10573 **Fx:**935-9296
(212) 310-8146 .. **Hoenig,** Mark '82 (Weil G&M LLP) -767 5th Av -NY 10153
(212) 471-8530 .. **Hoenig,** Michl '66 (Herzfeld & R,PC) -125 Broad -NY 10004
(212) 344-5680 .. **Hoenig,** Michl D '09 %Thompson H LLP -335 Mad Av -NY 10017
(212) 697-6555 .. **Hoenig,** Peter '76 (Biedermann RH&R) -570 Lex Av -NY 10022
(516) 294-8844 .. **Hoenings,** Marie A '86 (L'Abbate BC&C,LLP) -1001 Franklin Av -Gdn Cty 11530
(631) 232-2224 .. **Hoerger,** Maureen S '75 (Perini & H) -1770 Motor Pkwy -Hauppauge 11788 **Fx:**232-2344
(212) 259-8000 .. **Hoernlein,** Michl R '02 %Dewey & L LLP -1301 Av of Amer -NY 10019
(973) 315-4458 .. **Hoerrner,** Mark D '91 (Budd L) -140 Bway -NY 10005
(845) 590-1597 .. **Hoerter,** Jeffrey A '92 -2644 E Main -Wappingers Fls 12590
(212) 766-8040 .. **Hoess,** Sean I '98 Velour Recordings,Inc -26 Dobbin -Brklyn 11222
(518) 453-4600 .. **Hoeth,** Thea '77 %Comm Judicial Cndct -ESP -Albany 12223 **Fx:**486-1850
(212) 335-9429 .. **Hoexter,** Jill A '93 %DA -1 Hogan Pl -NY 10013
(212) 583-9600 .. **Hoey,** Barbara E '85 (Littler M,PC) -900 3rd Av -NY 10022
(716) 683-3364 .. **Hoey,** Benjamin J '72 OfCnsl Watson BCJ&S -3521 Union Rd -Cheektowaga 14225
(212) 670-2764 .. **Hoey,** Bridget D '07 Bk of Amer/Merrill Lynch -222 Bway -NY 10038
(212) 513-3200 .. **Hoey,** Christelette A '04 %Holland & K LLP -31 W 52nd -NY 10019
(212) 612-4200 .. **Hoey King Toker & Epstein** -55 Water -NY 10041 **Fx:**612-4284
(212) 704-1359 .. **Hoey,** Marjorie M '82 %Interpublic Grp -1114 Av of Amer -NY 10036 **Fx:**704-1201
(516) 877-7500 .. **Hoey,** Maureen A '04 %Franchina & G,PC -1100 Franklin Av -Gdn Cty 11530
(212) 612-4200 .. **Hoey,** Patrick T '77 (Hoey KT&E) -55 Water -NY 10041
(212) 735-3000 .. **Hofer,** Jonathan H '09 %Skadden ASM&F LLP -4 Times Sq -NY 10036
(631) 361-9494 .. **Hofer,** Kristen P '06 %A Vardaro,PC -732 Smithtwn Bypass -Smithtwn 11787 **Fx:**361-8752
(212) 554-4300 .. **Hofer,** Timothy M '02 Paramount Capital -787 7th Av -NY 10019
(212) 508-6175 .. **Hoff,** Cheri L '99 (Bracewell & G,LLP) -1251 Av of Amer -NY 10020 **Fx:**938-3875
(212) 504-6000 .. **Hoff,** Jonathan M '82 (Cadwalader W&T LLP) -1 World Fncl Ctr -NY 10281
(718) 254-0700 .. **Hoff,** Linda S '90 %Bklyn Defender Srvcs -177 Lvngstn -Brklyn 11201 **Fx:**254-0897
(518) 285-7424 .. **Hoff,** Matthew P '00 %MapInfo Corp -1 Global Vw -Troy 12180 **Fx:**285-7150
(212) 490-1700 .. **Hoff,** Robt S '00 %Wiggin & D -450 Lex Av -NY 10017
(212) 839-5300 .. **Hoffart,** Benjamin J '09 %Sidley A LLP -787 7th Av -NY 10019
(914) 703-6300 .. **Hoffberg,** David E '93 %Pillinger MT,LLP -570 Taxter Rd -Elmsfrd 10523
(914) 949-3100 .. **Hoffberg,** Steven M '90 -10 Bank -White Plns 10606 **Fx:**949-3416
(212) 732-2929 .. **Hoffer,** Douglas E '94 %Dansker & A Assoc -30 Vesey -NY 10007 **Fx:**732-8795
(914) 723-0511 .. **Hoffer,** Ellen M '83 -670 Wht Plns Rd -Scarsdale 10583 **Fx:**725-7724
(212) 435-7276 .. **Hoffer,** Mark D '77 %Port Auth of NY/NJ -225 Park Av S -NY 10003 **Fx:**435-3555
(516) 868-5842 .. **Hoffer,** Peri '87 -2883 Bay Dr -Merrick 11566
(914) 949-1166 .. **Hoffer-Dashow,** Marjorie G '92 Career Blazers -202 Mamaroneck Av -White Plns 10601
(718) 590-3751 .. **Hoffer-Landsman,** Donna '84 %Hon D Sullivan -851 Grnd Cncrs -Bronx 10451 **Fx:**590-3790
(212) 421-4000 .. **Hoffinger,** Fran R '85 (Hoffinger S&R,LLP) -150 E 58th -NY 10155
(212) 421-4000 .. **Hoffinger,** Jack S '51 (Hoffinger S&R,LLP) -150 E 58th -NY 10155
(212) 421-4000 .. **Hoffinger Stern & Ross,LLP** -150 E 58th -NY 10155 **Fx:**223-3857
(212) 421-4000 .. **Hoffinger,** Susan '90 (Hoffinger S&R,LLP) -150 E 58th -NY 10155
(212) 227-6262 .. **Hofflich,** Richd A '75 (Rosenbloom & H,LLP) -15 Maiden Ln -NY 10038
(212) 777-9400 .. **Hoffmaier,** James C '91 (Hoffmaier & H,PC) -30 Av B -NY 10009 **Fx:**674-1729
(212) 777-9400 .. **Hoffmaier,** Neva M '90 (Hoffmaier & H,PC) -30 Av B -NY 10009 **Fx:**674-1729
(212) 448-1100 .. **Hoffman,** Alan M '60 OfCnsl McLaughlin & S,LLP -260 Mad Av -NY 10016
(716) 884-4700 .. **Hoffman,** Alan S '70 -460 Franklin -Buffalo 14202 **Fx:**886-0057
(212) 294-6700 .. **Hoffman,** Alan S '88 (Winston & S) -200 Park Av -NY 10166
(212) 457-9404 .. **Hoffman,** Allison C '96 %IncisiveMedia /NYLJ -120 Bway -NY 10271
(212) 372-1512 .. **Hoffman,** Arthur S '64 American Express Tax & Bus Srvcs -1185 Av of Amer -NY 10036
(315) 422-7000 .. **Hoffman,** Austin J II '82 SrCnsl Pyramid Mgt Grp,Inc -4 Clinton Sq -Syracuse 13202 **Fx:**472-4035
(212) 762-8802 .. **Hoffman,** B Carole '85 Morgan Stanley -1221 Av of Amer -NY 10020
(212) 873-6200 .. **Hoffman,** Barbara '72 -330 W 72nd -NY 10023 **Fx:**974-7245
(212) 841-1000 .. **Hoffman,** Barbara '92 OfCnsl Covington & B LLP -620 8th Av -NY 10018
(212) 964-1890 .. **Hoffman,** Barry M '78 (Hoffman & R,LLP) -505 8th Av -NY 10018
(516) 746-5360 .. **Hoffman & Behar LLP** -94 Second -Mineola 11501 **Fx:**746-5361
(212) 458-1593 .. **Hoffman,** Bonnie S '88 %AIG -175 Water -NY 10038
(516) 496-8304 .. **Hoffman,** Carol M '77 C Hoffman,PC -575 Underhill Blvd -Syosset 11791 **Fx:**496-8303
(212) 770-2416 .. **Hoffman,** Catherine E '94 %AIG -80 Pine -NY 10005
(917) 686-2314 .. **Hoffman,** Chas D '76 -473 W End Av -NY 10024
(212) 728-2200 .. **Hoffman,** Chas P '06 %Axinn V&H LLP -114 W 47th -NY 10036
(718) 250-2000 .. **Hoffman,** Christiane B '99 %DA -350 Jay -Brklyn 11201 **Fx:**250-2314
(212) 446-4800 .. **Hoffman,** Christopher J '05 %Kirkland & E LLP -153 E 53rd -NY 10022
(917) 952-8519 .. **Hoffman,** Dana B '09 -66 Mad Av -NY 10016
(212) 473-9173 .. **Hoffman,** Danl '87 Razor & Tie Direct LLC -214 Sullivan -NY 10012
(607) 274-6504 .. **Hoffman,** Danl L '94 City Atty -108 E Green -Ithaca 14850 **Fx:**274-6507
(212) 712-2766 .. **Hoffman,** Darnay R '95 -210 W 70th -NY 10023
(212) 608-3230 .. **Hoffman,** David J '02 -132 Nassau -NY 10038
(212) 587-3434 .. **Hoffman,** David M '93 (Raskin & K LLP) -160 Bway -NY 10038
(718) 963-6117 .. **Hoffman,** David N '87 Wyckoff Hts Med Ctr -374 Stockholm -Brklyn 11237
(212) 592-1400 .. **Hoffman,** David R '08 %Herrick,F LLP -2 Park Av -NY 10016
(212) 816-2452 .. **Hoffman,** Douglas J '86 Citigroup -388 Greenwich -NY 10013 **Fx:**816-2467
(212) 673-7809 .. **Hoffman,** Eileen '78 -405 E 14th -NY 10009
(212) 669-2070 .. **Hoffman,** Ellen Emory '78 Tax Appls Tribunal -1 Centre -NY 10007 **Fx:**669-2211
(212) 277-5805 .. **Hoffman,** Elliot L '55 (Beldock L&H LLP) -99 Park Av -NY 10016
(718) 252-1276 .. **Hoffman,** Elliot P '69 (Turchin & H) -976 E 19th -Brklyn 11230
(631) 754-5485 .. **Hoffman,** Elvira N '93 -29 Surryhill Pl -Huntngtn 11743 **Fx:**754-5485
(212) 839-5300 .. **Hoffman,** Eric G '04 %Sidley A LLP -787 7th Av -NY 10019
(212) 949-0100 .. **Hoffman,** Francis M '85 %Cmmnwlth Land Title -140 E 45th -NY 10017 **Fx:**983-8430
(631) 283-5571 .. **Hoffman,** Fredk E '91 -Bx144 -Southampton 11969 **Fx:**283-4303
(631) 666-4444 .. **Hoffman,** G Ronald '77 -250 W Main -Bay Shr 11706 **Fx:**666-1616
(518) 465-0400 .. **Hoffman,** George J Jr. '97 %O'Connor OB&F,PC -20 Corp Wds Blvd -Albany 12211
(315) 474-1273 .. **Hoffman,** Gilbert M '82 Cnsl Chicago Title Ins Co -201 E Jffrsn -Syracuse 13202 **Fx:**474-4281
(212) 479-6000 .. **Hoffman,** Harold M '52 OfCnsl Cooley LLP -1114 Av of Amer -NY 10036
(212) 486-6322 .. **Hoffman,** Harold M '79 -1140 Av of Amer -NY 10036 **Fx:**980-8748
(212) 683-7999 .. **Hoffman,** Henriette D '80 Legal Srvcs for Children Inc -271 Mad Av -NY 10016
(914) 591-5400 .. **Hoffman,** Jacqueline '90 %D'Ambrosio & D,PC -42 Main -Irvngtn 10533 **Fx:**591-5122
(212) 243-5423 .. **Hoffman,** Jane Ellen '85 -55 W 14th -NY 10011 **Fx:**675-4534
(212) 813-5900 .. **Hoffman,** Janet L '83 (Fross ZL&Z,PC) -866 UN Plz -NY 10017
(212) 474-1000 .. **Hoffman,** Jarrett R '08 %Cravath S&M LLP -825 8th Av -NY 10019
(212) 679-2900 .. **Hoffman,** Jeffrey C '67 (Hoffman & P LLP) -260 Mad Av -NY 10016
(212) 698-3500 .. **Hoffman,** Jeffry S '68 (Dechert LLP) -1095 Av of Amer -NY 10036
(212) 850-8500 .. **Hoffman,** Jennifer A '99 %Bruckmann & V,LLP -420 Lex Av -NY 10170
(917) 778-6500 .. **Hoffman,** Jerome F X '88 %K Dodson -485 Lex Av -NY 10017
(518) 449-8893 .. **Hoffman,** Jerry S '79 (Wilson EME&D LLP) -677 Bway -Albany 12207
(212) 558-4000 .. **Hoffman,** Jessica R '02 %Sullivan & C LLP -125 Broad -NY 10004
(212) 922-6119 .. **Hoffman,** Joan E '81 Bk of NY Mellon -200 Park Av -NY 10166
(516) 296-7058 .. **Hoffman,** Jodi S '93 (Certilman BA&H,LLP) -90 Merrick Av -E Meadow 11554
(516) 622-9200 .. **Hoffman,** Jonathan M '83 (Westerman BEM&S,LLP) -1201 RXR Plz -Uniondale 11553
(212) 338-0700 .. **Hoffman,** Jonathan S '90 (Hoffman P&F PLLC) -220 E 42nd -NY 10017
(718) 487-2300 .. **Hoffman,** Joshua D '06 Leg Srvcs Corp -256-260 Bway -Brklyn 11211 **Fx:**782-6790
(212) 455-2000 .. **Hoffman,** Justin F '05 %Simpson T&B LLP -425 Lex Av -NY 10017
(914) 749-8200 .. **Hoffman,** Kelly A '10 %Boies S&F LLP -333 Main -Armonk 10504
(518) 485-2317 .. **Hoffman,** Kenneth S '77 OASAS -1450 Wstrn Av -Albany 12203 **Fx:**485-2335
(516) 712-4000 .. **Hoffman,** Kerri Monyak '91 %Milber MP&S LLP -1000 Woodbury Rd -Woodbury 11797
(212) 757-0007 .. **Hoffman,** Kirk P '02 %Scarola E LLP -888 7th Av -NY 10106
(518) 473-8649 .. **Hoffman,** Kristine J '02 NYS Emergency Mgmt -1220 Wshngtn Av -Albany 12226
(518) 465-3484 .. **Hoffman,** Laura M '06 %Carter CCBM&L,PC -20 Corp Wds Blvd -Albany 12211
(212) 323-2250 .. **Hoffman,** Laurel H '96 %HHC-OLA-Medical Litigation -346 Bway -NY 10013 **Fx:**323-2251
(516) 294-3311 .. **Hoffman,** Lawr M '96 -150 Hrrcks Rd -Mineola 11501
(845) 634-8169 .. **Hoffman,** Lee A Jr. '75 -82 Maple Av -New Cty 10956 **Fx:**634-7963
(518) 436-0344 .. **Hoffman,** Leigh A '98 %Deily M&G,LLP -8 Thurlow Ter -Albany 12203
(718) 625-5430 .. **Hoffman,** Linda J '90 (Stern B&H,PC) -26 Court -Brklyn 11242
(914) 472-2300 .. **Hoffman,** Marianne '97 %Jones G,LLP -670 Wht Plns Rd -Scarsdale 10583
(646) 414-6984 .. **Hoffman,** Mathew B '99 SrCnsl Lowenstein S PC -1251 Av of Amer -NY 10020 **Fx:**(212) 262-7401
(212) 687-6262 .. **Hoffman,** Mathew E '78 OfCnsl Barton B&P,LLP -420 Lex Av -NY 10170
(212) 227-8338 .. **Hoffman,** Melvyn W '04 -80 Univ Pl -NY 10003
(212) 891-9600 .. **Hoffman,** Michl A '01 Stanfield Capital Prtnrs LLC -430 Park Av -NY 10022
(518) 449-0044 .. **Hoffman,** Michl F '96 (Hoffman W&D LLC) -75 State -Albany 12207 **Fx:**449-0047
(212) 735-3000 .. **Hoffman,** Michl K '00 (Skadden ASM&F LLP) -4 Times Sq -NY 10036
(631) 661-2121 .. **Hoffman,** Mikel J '85 M Hoffman,PC -193 E Main -Babylon 11702 **Fx:**661-8854
(518) 257-1443 .. **Hoffman,** Nancy E '74 %CSEA,Inc -143 Wshngtn Av Bx7125 -Albany 12224 **Fx:**449-1525
(212) 293-9416 .. **Hoffman,** Nicholas M W '99 Ruben Co -600 Mad Av -NY 10022

(914) 693-8830 .. **Hoffman,** Patricia Lee '98 -1055 Saw Mill Rvr Rd -Ardsley 10502 **Fx:**693-2597
(914) 232-2242 .. **Hoffman,** Peter D '00 -200 Katonah Av -Katonah 10536 **Fx:**232-2245
(516) 393-2200 .. **Hoffman,** Peter M '92 (Garfunkel W,PC) -111 Grt Nck Rd -Gt Neck 11021
(212) 366-2999 .. **Hoffman,** Philip J '93 %Penguin USA -375 Hudson -NY 10014 **Fx:**366-2995
(212) 594-5544 .. **Hoffman,** Philip Jay '95 -42 W 38th -NY 10018 **Fx:**594-9565
(212) 421-4100 .. **Hoffman,** Philip R '80 (Pryor C LLP) -7 Times Sq -NY 10036
(212) 645-3444 .. **Hoffman,** Piper '03 Partnership for the Homeless -305 7th Av -NY 10001
(212) 338-0700 .. **Hoffman Polland & Furman PLLC** -220 E 42nd -NY 10017 **Fx:**338-0093
(212) 679-2900 .. **Hoffman & Pollok LLP** -260 Mad Av -NY 10016 **Fx:**679-1844
(212) 833-1116 .. **Hoffman,** Richd M '68 (Friedman KS&A LLP) -1633 Bway -NY 10019 **Fx:**373-7916
(914) 245-6060 .. **Hoffman,** Robt A '80 OfCnsl Durante B&T,PLLC -2000 Maple Hill -Yorktwn Hts 10598
(518) 370-4743 .. **Hoffman,** Robt W '79 (Hoffman & N,PLLC) -1802 Eastern Pkwy -Schnctdy 12309 **Fx:**370-4870
(212) 552-1805 .. **Hoffman,** Ronne '80 JP Morgan Chase -1 Chase Manh Plz -NY 10081
(212) 964-1890 .. **Hoffman & Roth,LLP** -505 8th Av -NY 10018 **Fx:**964-4306
(212) 632-6000 .. **Hoffman,** Scott D '88 %Lazard Freres -30 Rckfllr Plz -NY 10112 **Fx:**632-6060
(716) 839-0342 .. **Hoffman,** Sharon Gromer '95 -191 Burbank Dr -Snyder 14226
(212) 248-8800 .. **Hoffman,** Stephen A '98 (Callan KB&B LLP) -1 Whitehall -NY 10004
(212) 421-2233 .. **Hoffman,** Stephen D '69 (Wilk A LLP) -675 3rd Av -NY 10017
(212) 766-1177 .. **Hoffman,** Steven '87 %J Mullen Jr -30 Vesey -NY 10007 **Fx:**766-1131
(631) 666-6800 .. **Hoffman,** T Glenn '93 (TG Hoffman & Assoc) -250 W Main -Bay Shr 11706 **Fx:**666-1616
(212) 841-1000 .. **Hoffman,** Taylor M '03 %Covington & B LLP -620 8th Av -NY 10018
(212) 581-1180 .. **Hoffman,** Thos '72 (T Hoffman,PC) -250 W 57th -NY 10107 **Fx:**581-8002
(212) 907-0700 .. **Hoffman,** Thos G Jr. '05 %Labaton S LLP -140 Bway -NY 10005
(716) 853-8400 .. **Hoffman,** Timothy L '88 %Dept of Law -350 Main Pl Twr -Buffalo 14202 **Fx:**853-8571
(631) 853-4161 .. **Hoffman,** Tracy '88 %DA -N Cnty Cmplx Bldg 77 -Hauppauge 11788 **Fx:**853-4192
(914) 385-4100 .. **Hoffman Wachtell & Rao, LLP** -399 Knollwood Rd -White Plns 10603 **Fx:**682-1512
(516) 746-5360 .. **Hoffman,** Warren S '84 (Hoffman & B LLP) -94 Second -Mineola 11501
(212) 735-3000 .. **Hoffman Lent,** Karen M '00 Cnsl Skadden ASM&F LLP -4 Times Sq -NY 10036
(212) 679-0400 .. **Hoffmann,** Andrew S '85 A Hoffmann & Assoc -450 7th Av -NY 10123 **Fx:**679-1080
(212) 965-9081 .. **Hoffmann,** Anna Benvenutti '06 %Neufeld S&B -99 Hudson -NY 10013
(212) 524-5000 .. **Hoffmann,** Arthur E Jr. '84 (Jacob M&F) -1270 Av of Amer -NY 10020
(212) 878-8000 .. **Hoffmann,** Brian '90 (Clifford C LLP) -31 W 52nd -NY 10019
(607) 273-5787 .. **Hoffmann,** Carolyn R '89 %Crossmore Law Ofc -115 W Green -Ithaca 14850 **Fx:**273-0291
(212) 336-2000 .. **Hoffmann,** Chas D '08 %Patterson BW&T LLP -1133 Av of Amer -NY 10036
(212) 637-3227 .. **Hoffmann,** Chas E '74 %EPA -290 Bway -NY 10007 **Fx:**637-3202
(516) 822-3550 .. **Hoffmann,** Chas R '66 (Hoffmann & B LLP) -6900 Jericho Tpk -Syosset 11791 **Fx:**822-3582
(716) 439-7085 .. **Hoffmann,** Doreen M '01 -175 Hawley -Lockprt 14094
(212) 416-8000 .. **Hoffmann,** Elinor '78 Dept of Law -120 Bway -NY 10271
(518) 402-6757 .. **Hoffmann,** Gary M '83 %Workers Comp Bd -20 Park -Albany 12207
(315) 471-4107 .. **Hoffmann Hubert & Hoffmann,LLP** -4629 Onondaga Blvd -Syracuse 13219 **Fx:**471-6701
(516) 296-7000 .. **Hoffmann,** Kenneth A '94 (Certilman BA&H,LLP) -90 Merrick Av -E Meadow 11554
(607) 763-9200 .. **Hoffmann,** Paul R '81 (Levene G&T,LLP) -BxF-1706 -Bnghmtn 13902
(607) 734-6191 .. **Hoffmann,** Stephen R '01 %Moore & W,LLP -150 Lk -Elmira 14901
(315) 471-4107 .. **Hoffmann,** Terrance J '69 (Hoffmann H&H,LLP) -4629 Onondaga Blvd -Syracuse 13219
(212) 659-7300 .. **Hoffmann,** Trevor R '02 OfCnsl Haynes & B,LLP -1221 Av of Amer -NY 10020
(914) 995-4411 .. **Hoffmeister,** Edw J '81 %Cnty Planning Dept -148 Martine Av -White Plns 10601
(212) 308-4411 .. **Hoffnagle,** Gregory S '07 %Edwards AP&D LLP -750 Lex Av -NY 10022
(212) 698-3500 .. **Hoffner,** David S '90 (Dechert LLP) -1095 Av of Amer -NY 10036
(212) 941-8330 .. **Hoffner,** Steven A '91 -325 Bway -NY 10007
(718) 783-7556 .. **Hofheimer,** Alice J '93 -41 Lincoln Pl -Brklyn 11217
(212) 944-0500 .. **Hofheimer Gartlir & Gross,LLP** -530 5th Av -NY 10036 **Fx:**869-4930
(718) 520-2848 .. **Hofher,** Ira '77 %Hon R Eng -125-01 Qns Blvd -Kew Gdns 11415
(212) 265-2171 .. **Hofherr,** Blair E '02 %Solil Mgmt -640 5th Av -NY 10019 **Fx:**265-1669
(212) 687-3000 .. **Hofherr,** Ross B '08 %Jaffe & A,LLP -600 3rd Av -NY 10016
(631) 588-5000 .. **Hofmann,** Jeffrey T '06 %AN Guzzone & Assoc,PC -2450 Middle Cntry Rd -Centereach 11720 **Fx:**588-5001
(518) 858-0032 .. **Hofmann,** Kathleen M '07 -217 Young Rd -Middl Grv 12850
(212) 465-8840 .. **Hofmann,** Paul T '82 (Hofmann & S) -360 W 31st -NY 10001 **Fx:**465-8849
(212) 449-7738 .. **Hofmann,** Stephen A '03 Merrill Lynch -4 World Fncl Ctr -NY 10080
(212) 312-2260 .. **Hofmeister,** Beth C '07 Leg Aid -60 Lafayette -NY 10013 **Fx:**349-0874
(212) 435-3512 .. **Hofrichter,** Lawr S '72 Port Auth of NY/NJ -225 Park Av S -NY 10003 **Fx:**435-3500
(212) 490-3000 .. **Hofsdal,** Marie Polito '04 OfCnsl Wilson EME&D LLP -150 E 42nd -NY 10017
(718) 225-3200 .. **Hofstein,** Gertrude '55 OfCnsl Greenberg & H,PC -254-10 Nrthrn Blvd -Little Neck 11362
(845) 473-2040 .. **Hofstetter,** Bruce '72 (Levine H&F) -316 Main -Poughkeepsie 12601
(212) 980-0120 .. **Hofstetter,** Richd D '80 (Frankfurt KK&S,PC) -488 Mad Av -NY 10022
(716) 852-1000 .. **Hogan,** Brian R '04 %PW Beltz,PC -36 Church -Buffalo 14202 **Fx:**852-5887
(518) 463-3990 .. **Hogan,** Carla E '89 (Tuczinski CG&C,PC) -54 State -Albany 12207
(212) 836-8000 .. **Hogan,** Christine L '09 Kaye S LLP -425 Park Av -NY 10022
(516) 227-0700 .. **Hogan,** Christine M '09 Farrell F,PC -1320 RXR Plz -Uniondale 11556
(716) 636-7600 .. **Hogan,** Corey J '75 (HoganWillig) -2410 N Forest Rd -Amherst 14068
(212) 728-8000 .. **Hogan,** Curtis W '07 %Willkie F&G LLP -787 7th Av -NY 10019
(518) 792-1174 .. **Hogan,** Danl J '90 (McPhillips F&C,LLP) -288 Glen Bx299 -Glens Fls 12801
(212) 808-0700 .. **Hogan,** Edw A '89 (Norris M&M,PA) -875 3rd Av -NY 10022
(716) 433-5907 .. **Hogan,** F Gerard '75 (Seaman JH&B,LLP) -76 West Av -Lockprt 14094
(718) 250-2000 .. **Hogan,** Grace K '98 %DA -350 Jay -Brklyn 11201 **Fx:**250-2314
(516) 759-4270 .. **Hogan,** Howard T Jr. '70 Hogan & H -108 Forest Av Bx447 -Locust Vly 11560 **Fx:**759-4653
(631) 390-0010 .. **Hogan,** James K '81 %Bruno G&S,LLP -445 Broad Hollow Rd -Melvll 11747
(212) 715-1000 .. **Hogan,** Jennifer L '04 %Arnold & P LLP -399 Park Av -NY 10022
(631) 853-4049 .. **Hogan,** Jessica H '97 %Cnty Atty -Dennison Bldg Bx6100 -Hauppauge 11788 **Fx:**853-5169
(607) 797-4839 .. **Hogan,** John B '54 OfCnsl Hogan SLS&D,LLP -Bx660 -Bnghmtn 13902
(732) 855-6470 .. **Hogan,** John E Jr. '99 (Wilentz G&S) -110 William -NY 10038 **Fx:**726-6629
(845) 279-2986 .. **Hogan,** John J '88 (Hogan & R) -1441 Route 22 -Brewstr 10509
(518) 587-9000 .. **Hogan,** John M Jr. '64 -480 Bway Bx323 -Saratoga Spgs 12866 **Fx:**584-6900
(212) 335-9000 .. **Hogan,** John M '77 %DA -1 Hogan Pl -NY 10013
(518) 587-9000 .. **Hogan,** John M III '90 -480 Bway Bx1041 -Saratoga Spgs 12866 **Fx:**584-6900
(212) 880-6000 .. **Hogan,** Joris M '82 (Torys LLP) -237 Park Av -NY 10017
(518) 761-6405 .. **Hogan,** Kathleen B '89 %DA -Cnty Mncpl Ctr -Lk George 12845
(646) 386-3202 .. **Hogan,** Kellie J '88 %Hon S Crane -60 Centre -NY 10007
(716) 847-8400 .. **Hogan,** Kevin M '92 (Phillips L LLP) -3400 HSBC Ctr -Buffalo 14203
(212) 218-2100 .. **Hogan,** Kristin B '08 %Fitzpatrick CH&S -1290 Av of Amer -NY 10104
(212) 340-0400 .. **Hogan,** Laura '98 %Appllt Div 1st Dept -27 Mad Av -NY 10010 **Fx:**889-4412
(315) 673-7139 .. **Hogan,** Laura A '83 -4241 New Seneca Tpk -Marcellus 13108
(212) 918-3000 .. **Hogan Lovells US LLP** -875 3rd Av -NY 10022 **Fx:**918-3100
(212) 431-2173 .. **Hogan,** Mariana '80 %NY Law Schl -185 W Bway -NY 10013 **Fx:**966-2053
(212) 909-6000 .. **Hogan,** Mary Beth '92 (Debevoise & P LLP) -919 3rd Av -NY 10022
(212) 728-8000 .. **Hogan,** Megan Y '07 %Willkie F&G LLP -787 7th Av -NY 10019
(212) 692-1000 .. **Hogan,** Michl J '82 SpclCnsl Duane M LLP -1540 Bway -NY 10036
(212) 728-2200 .. **Hogan,** Michl P '03 %Axinn V&H LLP -114 W 47th -NY 10036
(212) 504-6000 .. **Hogan,** N Adele '86 SpclCnsl Cadwalader W&T LLP -1 World Fncl Ctr -NY 10281
(315) 218-8000 .. **Hogan,** Peter J '85 (Bond S&K,PLLC) -1 Lincoln Ctr -Syracuse 13202
(315) 474-2943 .. **Hogan,** Rachael M '08 %Sugarman Law Firm,LLP -211 W Jffrsn -Syracuse 13202
(845) 279-2986 .. **Hogan & Rossi** -1441 Route 22 -Brewstr 10509 **Fx:**278-6135
(607) 797-4839 .. **Hogan Sarzynski Lynch Surowka & DeWind,LLP** -Bx660 -Bnghmtn 13902 **Fx:**797-6123
(516) 942-4700 .. **Hogan,** Shaun K '93 (Lefkowitz H&C) -500 N Bway -Jericho 11753
(212) 983-0900 .. **Hogan,** Stephen '76 (Yeskoo H&T LLP) -909 3rd Av -NY 10022
(518) 457-6137 .. **Hogan,** Stephen P '87 %State Police -1220 Wshngtn Av -Albany 12226 **Fx:**485-1164
(716) 662-1638 .. **Hogan,** Susan S '78 -3925 N Buffalo -Orchard Pk 14127
(212) 309-6000 .. **Hogan,** Thos M '07 %Morgan L&B LLP -101 Park Av -NY 10178
(914) 995-2708 .. **Hogan Felix,** Jane E '86 %Cnty Atty -148 Martine Av -White Plns 10601 **Fx:**995-5858
(716) 636-7600 .. **HoganWillig** -2410 N Forest Rd -Amherst 14068 **Fx:**636-7606
(800) 636-5255 .. **HoganWillig** -705 Center -Lewiston 14092
(718) 250-2000 .. **Hogg,** Courtney N '08 %DA -350 Jay -Brklyn 11201 **Fx:**250-2314
(212) 788-0461 .. **Hoggan,** Christina L '04 %Law Dept -100 Church -NY 10007 **Fx:**788-0367
(518) 449-3125 .. **Hoggan,** John D Jr. '01 (Stockli GS&P,LLP) -90 State -Albany 12207
(212) 902-2595 .. **Hoghooghi,** Ida '01 Goldman Sachs -85 Broad -NY 10004
(518) 485-2312 .. **Hogle,** Richd R '83 OASAS -1450 Wstrn Av -Albany 12203 **Fx:**485-2335
(212) 788-1027 .. **Hogrogian,** John '87 %Law Dept -100 Church -NY 10007 **Fx:**788-0367
(315) 781-1465 .. **Hogue,** Jeff L '00 %Leg Assistance -361 S Main -Geneva 14456 **Fx:**781-2565
(212) 689-8808 .. **Hoguet,** Laura Banfield '68 (Hoguet NR&K,LLP) -10 E 40th -NY 10016
(212) 689-8808 .. **Hoguet Newman Regal & Kenney,LLP** -10 E 40th -NY 10016 **Fx:**689-5101
(212) 294-6700 .. **Hoh,** Britt S '04 %Winston & S -200 Park Av -NY 10166
(212) 657-1225 .. **Hohauser,** Wm '86 Citigroup -77 Water -NY 10005
(518) 457-7069 .. **Hohenstein,** Anne Kennedy '92 Dept of Labor -State Campus Bldg 12 -Albany 12240 **Fx:**457-1164
(212) 231-1000 .. **Hohenstein,** Gretchen L '03 Macquarie Hldngs -125 W 55th -NY 10019
(212) 513-3200 .. **Hohenstein,** James H '84 (Holland & K LLP) -31 W 52nd -NY 10019
(212) 446-4800 .. **Hohenthaner,** Jon T '99 (Kirkland & E LLP) -153 E 53rd -NY 10022
(212) 335-9000 .. **Hohenthaner,** Joymarie '99 %DA -1 Hogan Pl -NY 10013
(212) 663-2140 .. **Hohl,** E David '78 -175 W 93rd -NY 10025

(718) 740-2755 .. **Hohn,** Marsha S '00 -87-87 F Lewis Blvd -Jamaica 11427 **Fx:**479-2095
(212) 578-2211 .. **Hoi,** Thos C '84 %MetLife -27-01 Qns Plz N -LIC 11101
(516) 356-7716 .. **Hoil,** Ellen F '98 -Bx221 -S Jamesport 11970
(212) 294-6700 .. **Hojka,** Cory L '08 %Winston & S -200 Park Av -NY 10166
(716) 838-8737 .. **Hojnacki,** Kathleen A '84 %Keycorp Mortgage -3920 Main -Buffalo 14226
(518) 473-7300 .. **Hojraj,** Karina R '97 State Comptroller -110 State -Albany 12236 **Fx:**473-9104
(518) 452-1800 .. **Hoke,** John J '04 %Towne R & Prtnrs,PC -450 New Karner Rd Bx15072 -Albany 12212
(212) 506-1700 .. **Holahan,** David D '05 %Kasowitz BT&F LLP -1633 Bway -NY 10019
(212) 582-0598 .. **Holahan,** Ellen J '91 OfCnsl I Shorin -27 W 55th -NY 10019 **Fx:**489-3303
(212) 483-9490 .. **Holahan,** Frank '85 (McElroy DM&C,LLP) -88 Pine -NY 10005
(585) 362-4700 .. **Holahan,** James C '84 SrCnsl Bond S&K,PLLC -350 Linden Oaks -Rchstr 14625
(212) 397-5516 .. **Holahan,** Richd D Jr. '95 Soros Fund Mgmt LLC -888 7th Av -NY 10106
(516) 333-2640 .. **Holbreich,** Stephen '71 Cnsl Arkwin Industries.Inc -686 Main -Westbury 11590
(518) 862-5555 .. **Holbrook,** Courtney E '04 %A Dell -450 New Karner Rd -Albany 12205 **Fx:**862-5545
(212) 867-8280 .. **Holbrook,** Dean '60 OfCnsl Patton ELM&S -420 Lex Av -NY 10170
(585) 352-1831 .. **Holbrook,** Fredk J '66 -52 Nichols Bx116 -Spencerprt 14559
(518) 686-7324 .. **Holbrook,** George H '61 (Holbrook J&T) -12 Main Bx146 -Hoosick Fls 12090
(516) 487-5800 .. **Holbrook,** Jo-Ellen '98 OfCnsl Mauro G&L LLP -60 Cuttermill Rd -Gt Neck 11021
(518) 686-7324 .. **Holbrook Johnston & Tate** -12 Main Bx146 -Hoosick Fls 12090 **Fx:**686-9597
(716) 841-2784 .. **Holbrook,** Paul K '88 %HSBC Bank -1 HSBC Ctr -Buffalo 14203 **Fx:**841-5087
(607) 674-4770 .. **Holbrook,** Samantha M '91 (Joyce & H) -26 N Main Bx705 -Sherburne 13460 **Fx:**674-5415
(212) 244-9500 .. **Holby,** Wegard D '85 Cnsl White and W LLP -1 Penn Plz -NY 10119
(212) 715-9100 .. **Holcomb,** Megan E '10 %Kramer LN&F,LLP -1177 Av of Amer -NY 10036
(212) 701-3000 .. **Holcomb,** Nathan A '07 %Cahill G&R LLP -80 Pine -NY 10005 **Fx:**269-5420
(315) 686-5572 .. **Holcombe,** Jon K '64 (Carter R&H PLLC) -229 John -Clayton 13624
(585) 262-6250 .. **Holcombe,** P Scott '80 %Crossroads Land Ofc -25 E Main -Rchstr 14614 **Fx:**262-3566
(212) 867-9595 .. **Holczer,** Benjamin P '89 -630 3rd Av -NY 10017 **Fx:**949-1857
(212) 968-9607 .. **Holczer,** Ezra M '03 %M Weisman -45 Bway -NY 10006 **Fx:**968-0296
(212) 484-3900 .. **Hold-Weiss,** Rachel '03 %Arent F LLP -1675 Bway -NY 10019
(914) 949-7940 .. **Holden Brothers,PC** -124 Court -White Plns 10601 **Fx:**949-7321
(716) 856-4000 .. **Holden,** Elizabeth A '05 %Hodgson R LLP -140 Pearl -Buffalo 14202
(914) 949-7940 .. **Holden,** James Jr. '76 (Holden Bros,PC) -124 Court -White Plns 10601
(516) 877-2900 .. **Holden,** Jane E '93 %Bartlett MB&M,LLP -300 Old Cntry Rd -Mineola 11501
(212) 237-1000 .. **Holden,** John D '97 (Windels ML&M,LLP) -156 W 56th -NY 10019
(212) 210-1287 .. **Holden,** Kelly C '09 %Alston & B LLP -90 Park Av -NY 10016
(315) 471-3151 .. **Holden,** Kenneth P '84 (Hancock & E,LLP) -1500 AXA Twr I Bx4976 -Syracuse 13221
(212) 848-9800 .. **Holden,** Mark G '04 (Withers B LLP) -430 Park Av -NY 10022
(212) 788-1444 .. **Holden,** Mary Ann '01 %Law Dept -100 Church -NY 10007 **Fx:**788-0367
(646) 562-3405 .. **Holden,** Matthew L '07 %PLC -747 3rd Av -NY 10017
(516) 353-3210 .. **Holden,** Patricia S '94 -130 Shore Rd -Pt Wash 11050
(718) 472-8220 .. **Holden,** Ross J '87 %Schl Cnstrctn Auth -30-30 Thomson Av -LIC 11101 **Fx:**472-8088
(914) 949-7940 .. **Holden,** Stephen III '65 (Holden Bros,PC) -124 Court -White Plns 10601
(212) 336-0092 .. **Holden,** Stephen B '01 SEC -3 World Fncl Ctr -NY 10281 **Fx:**336-1323
(914) 332-0700 .. **Holden,** Timothy G '01 M Pollack -150 Wht Plns Rd -Tarrytwn 10591 **Fx:**684-6069
(631) 427-4642 .. **Holden,** Wm F '52 -11 Orchrd Pl -Huntngtn 11743
(212) 440-4300 .. **Holder,** Adriene L '95 %Leg Aid -199 Water -NY 10038
(212) 373-3000 .. **Holder,** Aubrey I '85 %Paul WRW&G LLP -1285 Av of Amer -NY 10019
(212) 504-6000 .. **Holder,** Christina T '10 %Cadwalader W&T LLP -1 World Fncl Ctr -NY 10281
(212) 521-2415 .. **Holder,** James B '04 Loews Corp -655 Mad Av -NY 10065
(212) 335-4176 .. **Holderness,** Carolina '07 DA -80 Centre -NY 10013
(212) 848-4000 .. **Holdridge,** Karen D '05 %Shearman & S LLP -599 Lex Av -NY 10022
(716) 856-5500 .. **Holdsworth,** Christina G '10 %Damon M LLP -200 Delaware Av -Buffalo 14202
(212) 504-6000 .. **Holdsworth,** Mark A '95 SpclCnsl Cadwalader W&T LLP -1 World Fncl Ctr -NY 10281
(607) 319-4828 .. **Holdsworth,** Robt J Jr. '82 -200 Cayuga Hghts Rd Bx4107 -Ithaca 14852 **Fx:**319-4829
(315) 218-8000 .. **Hole,** Richd D '76 (Bond S&K,PLLC) -1 Lincoln Ctr -Syracuse 13202
(212) 416-8000 .. **Holgado,** David P '99 %Dept of Law -120 Bway -NY 10271
(718) 222-2022 .. **Holgate,** Denyce M '91 %Law Dept -350 Jay -Brklyn 11201 **Fx:**222-2088
(212) 455-2000 .. **Holick,** Michl T '09 %Simpson T&B LLP -425 Lex Av -NY 10017
(718) 418-4600 .. **Holihan,** Stephen '98 Holihan & Assoc,PC -135-24 Hillside Av -Richmnd Hll 11418 **Fx:**418-4466
(631) 424-8113 .. **Holik,** Ronald W '83 -191 NY Av -Huntngtn 11743
(212) 969-3000 .. **Holinstat,** Steven H '97 %Proskauer R LLP -1585 Bway -NY 10036
(585) 232-6500 .. **Holl,** Diana C '09 %Harter S&E LLP -1600 Bausch & Lomb Pl -Rchstr 14604
(212) 207-8400 .. **Holl,** Jorn A '91 OfCnsl Kavanagh M&O LLP -415 Mad Av -NY 10017
(212) 682-8811 .. **Holladay,** C Randolph '92 (Dunnington B&M LLP) -1359 Bway -NY 10018
(212) 820-2418 .. **Holland,** Andrew R '95 %Amer Intl Cos -160 Water -NY 10038
(718) 590-2000 .. **Holland,** Andrew S '05 %DA -198 E 161st -Bronx 10451 **Fx:**590-6477
(212) 353-5084 .. **Holland,** Arnold J '83 %Lightyear Entertainment -548 W 28th -NY 10001
(212) 259-8000 .. **Holland,** Brian '09 %Dewey & L LLP -1301 Av of Amer -NY 10019
(212) 803-5100 .. **Holland,** Brooks R '95 %NY Cnty Defender Srvcs -225 Bway -NY 10007 **Fx:**571-6035
(516) 396-0800 .. **Holland,** Craig D '83 (Agoglia H&A,PC) -500 N Bway -Jericho 11753
(212) 264-2819 .. **Holland,** Danl R '90 US Ct of Intl Trade -1 Fed Plz -NY 10278
(212) 935-4500 .. **Holland,** David C '96 %M Kennedy -419 Park Av S -NY 10016 **Fx:**980-6881
(631) 501-3100 .. **Holland,** David R '97 %J Humphreys -3 Huntngtn Quad Bx9028 -Melvll 11747 **Fx:**501-3085
(631) 501-1000 .. **Holland,** Diane G '84 (Balfe & H,PC) -135 Pinelawn Rd -Melvll 11747
(212) 425-7200 .. **Holland,** Elizabeth J '89 (Kenyon & K,LLP) -1 Bway -NY 10004
(212) 902-6232 .. **Holland,** Erin E '05 %Goldman Sachs -1 NY Plz -NY 10004
(845) 369-4811 .. **Holland,** Gary L '03 SrCnsl Dress Barn,Inc -30 Dunnigan Dr -Suffern 10901 **Fx:**369-4750
(212) 509-5050 .. **Holland,** Hildegard M '88 (Wuersch & G LLP) -100 Wall -NY 10005
(212) 513-3200 .. **Holland & Knight LLP** -31 W 52nd -NY 10019 **Fx:**385-9010
(212) 756-2000 .. **Holland,** Laura H '08 %Schulte R&Z LLP -919 3rd Av -NY 10022
(212) 813-8800 .. **Holland,** Mark '82 (Goodwin P LLP) -620 8th Av -NY 10018
(212) 490-9100 .. **Holland,** Michl J '73 (Condon & F LLP) -7 Times Sq -NY 10036
(212) 336-1027 .. **Holland,** Michl P '05 SEC -3 World Fncl Ctr -NY 10281 **Fx:**336-1323
(516) 248-2655 .. **Holland,** Michl W '73 -421 Willis Av -Williston Pk 11596 **Fx:**741-0272
(212) 848-4000 .. **Holland,** Monica L '01 (Shearman & S LLP) -599 Lex Av -NY 10022
(212) 867-4466 .. **Holland,** Robt T '91 (Belkin BW&G,LLP) -270 Mad Av -NY 10016
(212) 998-2753 .. **Holland,** S Rebecca '90 NYU Compliance Ofc -285 Mercer -NY 10003 **Fx:**995-4783
(718) 923-4248 .. **Holland,** Sadiqa G '04 Temporary & Disability Assistance -14 Boerum Pl -Brklyn 11201
(212) 487-9700 .. **Holland,** Sheri E '89 (White F&F,LLP) -61 Bway -NY 10006
(516) 356-7810 .. **Holland,** Wendy S '03 -19 Sharon Dr -Patchogue 11772 **Fx:**(631) 289-4728
(212) 259-8000 .. **Hollander,** Adrienne M '09 %Dewey & L LLP -1301 Av of Amer -NY 10019
(631) 390-0010 .. **Hollander,** Allan S '07 %Bruno G&S,LLP -445 Broad Hollow Rd -Melvll 11747
(212) 496-0737 .. **Hollander,** Barry L '81 -155 W 68th -NY 10023
(212) 753-7640 .. **Hollander,** Carl R '69 -909 3rd Av -NY 10022 **Fx:**753-7113
(212) 341-2731 .. **Hollander,** Chas A '69 %Admin Children's Srvcs -150 William -NY 10038 **Fx:**341-2733
(347) 312-2263 .. **Hollander,** David S '76 Evacutech Safety Products LLC -2152 Ralph Av -Brklyn 11234
(212) 819-8200 .. **Hollander,** Evan C '88 (White & C LLP) -1155 Av of Amer -NY 10036
(212) 929-0060 .. **Hollander,** Geoffrey S '89 -113 Jane -NY 10014
(212) 750-0106 .. **Hollander,** Howard '64 -245 E 63rd -NY 10065 **Fx:**750-0106
(212) 506-3804 .. **Hollander,** Jack L '82 %Atlas America Inc -712 5th Av -NY 10019
(212) 476-0352 .. **Hollander,** Jacob '67 %Anvil Knitwear -228 E 45th -NY 10017
(917) 771-5618 .. **Hollander,** Jacqueline K '06 -401 E 80th -NY 10075
(212) 576-1061 .. **Hollander,** Jay '82 (Hollander and Company LLC) -11 Penn Plz -NY 10001 **Fx:**576-1078
(516) 229-6000 .. **Hollander,** Jeffrey J '88 %R Lau & Assoc -300 Jericho Quad Bx9040 -Jericho 11753 **Fx:**229-6167
(212) 302-2600 .. **Hollander,** Jeffry '88 (Lauterbach GD&H LLP) -22 W 38th -NY 10018
(212) 735-3000 .. **Hollander,** Jeremy E '06 %Skadden ASM&F LLP -4 Times Sq -NY 10036
(516) 498-1000 .. **Hollander,** Larry B '84 (Hollander & S,LLP) -40 Cuttermill Rd -Gt Neck 11021
(212) 336-8000 .. **Hollander,** Liel '09 %Amster R&E -90 Park Av -NY 10016
(212) 541-6222 .. **Hollander,** Mitchell D '91 (Kane K,PC) -1350 Av of Amer -NY 10019
(212) 370-4361 .. **Hollander,** Patricia A '64 -330 E 39th -NY 10016
(212) 763-8416 .. **Hollander,** Rachel L '92 (Olasov & H LLP) -1325 Av of Amer -NY 10019 **Fx:**763-8414
(516) 487-0500 .. **Hollander,** Robt S '91 -299 E Shore Rd -Gt Neck 11023
(212) 563-5535 .. **Hollander,** Ronald A '73 -343 E 18th -NY 10003 **Fx:**563-5903
(212) 581-0370 .. **Hollander,** Russell S '89 Directors Guild of Amer -110 W 57th -NY 10019 **Fx:**581-1441
(212) 973-0572 .. **Hollander,** Scott C '10 %Wolff & S PC -140 Bway -NY 10005
(212) 922-2200 .. **Hollander,** Steven J '06 Watson F&W LLP -1133 Av of Amer -NY 10036
(516) 498-1000 .. **Hollander & Strauss,LLP** -40 Cuttermill Rd -Gt Neck 11021 **Fx:**498-2875
(212) 998-6618 .. **Hollander-Blumoff,** Rebecca E '97 NYU Law Schl -137 MacDougal -NY 10012
(212) 816-4493 .. **Hollar,** Kenneth C '09 Citigroup -388 Greenwich -NY 10013
(718) 875-3500 .. **Hollar-Degrasse,** Donna J '81 %Little Flower Children's Srvcs -186 Joralemon -Brklyn 11201
(212) 381-7000 .. **Holleman,** Craig D '73 (Sabin B&G LLP) -4 Times Sq -NY 10036
(212) 483-7047 .. **Holleman,** Vicki Z '73 Loeb Prtnrs Corp -61 Bway -NY 10006
(212) 363-7500 .. **Holleman,** W Scott '08 %Levi & K LLP -30 Broad -NY 10004
(315) 638-8149 .. **Hollembaek,** Richd J '83 -28½ Oswego -Baldwinsvll 13027 **Fx:**638-4602
(212) 530-5000 .. **Hollembeak,** Jeremiah C '07 %Milbank TH&M LLP -1 Chase Manh Plz -NY 10005
(585) 454-7145 .. **Hollenbeck,** Mark S '80 (Gallo & I,LLP) -39 State -Rchstr 14614
(716) 878-0333 .. **Hollenbeck,** Michl D '02 -144 Winston Rd -Buffalo 14216 **Fx:**883-8415
(212) 995-9313 .. **Hollenberg,** Harvard '67 SrCnsl H Hollenberg & Assoc -332 E 22nd -NY 10010

(516) 764-2442 .. **Hollenberg,** Jack E '52 -1321 Surrey Ln -Rockvll Ctr 11570 **Fx:**764-2442
(718) 442-4424 .. **Hollender,** Paul '76 (Corash & H,PC) -1200 South Av -Staten Isl 10314
(212) 735-3000 .. **Hollender,** Victor '98 (Skadden ASM&F LLP) -4 Times Sq -NY 10036
(212) 422-1080 .. **Holler,** John F '97 %D Magee -70 West -NY 10006 **Fx:**422-1090
(212) 547-5400 .. **Holler,** Stephen J '10 %McDermott W&E LLP -340 Mad Av -NY 10173
(212) 667-9334 .. **Hollevoet,** Cecile M '81 Nomura Securities Intl,Inc -2 World Fncl Ctr -NY 10281
(845) 856-5288 .. **Holley,** Henry J '55 HJ Holley,PC -76 E Main Bx3106 -Pt Jervis 12771 **Fx:**858-2787
(914) 767-7296 .. **Holley,** Lynn S '93 %Pepsi Bottling Group,Inc -1 Pepsi Way -Somers 10589
(212) 558-4000 .. **Holley,** Steven L '84 (Sullivan & C LLP) -125 Broad -NY 10004
(585) 546-6988 .. **Holliday,** Billie D '85 -16 W Main -Rchstr 14614 **Fx:**546-5359
(212) 841-9209 .. **Holliday,** Morton '61 Sonnenblick-Goldman -712 5th Av -NY 10019 **Fx:**262-4224
(718) 741-8400 .. **Hollifield,** Toni Ann '04 Div of Human Rights -1 Fordham Plz -Bronx 10458 **Fx:**741-8102
(212) 416-8460 .. **Hollinger,** Jacob E '99 %Dept of Law -120 Bway -NY 10271
(212) 517-5500 .. **Hollinger,** Jerrietta R '75 (Ganz & H,PC) -1394 3rd Av -NY 10075
(212) 940-8800 .. **Hollingsworth,** Ricardo J '96 (Katten MR LLP) -575 Mad Av -NY 10022
(718) 467-4968 .. **Hollingsworth,** Valarie S '99 -100 E 92nd -Brklyn 11212 **Fx:**467-4968
(212) 480-7402 .. **Hollins,** Cecil M '89 %DHCR -25 Beaver -NY 10004 **Fx:**480-7416
(212) 213-8844 .. **Hollis,** A Rebecca '06 %Allyn & F LLP -200 Mad Av -NY 10016
(518) 782-3484 .. **Hollis,** Annette M '08 %J White -582 New Loudon Rd -Latham 12110 **Fx:**782-3478
Hollis, Bernadette M '87 BM Hollis PLLC -Bx645 -Glens Fls 12801
(518) 481-1544 .. **Hollis,** Jennifer M '10 %DA -Ct Hse -Malone 12953 **Fx:**481-1545
(212) 407-4000 .. **Hollis,** Jonathan F '09 %Loeb & L,LLP -345 Park Av -NY 10154
(914) 666-5600 .. **Hollis,** P Danl III '75 (Shamberg MD&H,PC) -55 Smith Av -Mt Kisco 10549
(212) 250-2913 .. **Hollis,** Spring S '00 %Deutsche Bk -60 Wall -NY 10005
(212) 636-6859 .. **Hollister,** Gail '71 Fordham Univ Sch of Law -140 W 62nd -NY 10023 **Fx:**636-6899
(212) 325-3530 .. **Hollister,** Lindsay D '87 Credit Suisse -11 Mad Av -NY 10010
(212) 509-3456 .. **Hollman,** Laura B '03 %McGivney & K,PC -80 Broad -NY 10004
(212) 451-2300 .. **Holloman,** Ellen V '00 %Olshan GFR&W LLP -65 E 55th -NY 10022
(718) 595-6565 .. **Holloway,** Caswell F IV '03 DEP -59-17 Junction Blvd -Flushng 11373 **Fx:**595-3525
(914) 749-8200 .. **Holloway,** Danl E '05 %Boies S&F LLP -333 Main -Armonk 10504
(585) 758-7608 .. **Holloway,** Eileen L '90 %Univ of Rochester Med Ctr -Bx278979 -Rchstr 14627 **Fx:**272-9311
(212) 668-1900 .. **Holloway,** Jessica R '04 %Brune & R LLP -80 Broad -NY 10004
(212) 450-4000 .. **Holloway,** Mark P '08 %Davis P&W LLP -450 Lex Av -NY 10017
(585) 232-6500 .. **Holloway,** Paul W '89 (Harter S&E LLP) -1600 Bausch & Lomb Pl -Rchstr 14604
(212) 670-0234 .. **Hollowell,** T Douglas '92 Merrill Lynch -222 Bway -NY 10038
(212) 589-2700 .. **Hollweg,** Robt W '67 %Weight Watchers -11 Mad Av -NY 10010
(212) 706-0248 .. **Hollyer,** A Rene '68 (Hollyer B LLP) -60 E 42nd -NY 10165 **Fx:**(646) 652-5336
(212) 878-8000 .. **Hollywood,** Meegan F '08 %Clifford C LLP -31 W 52nd -NY 10019
(516) 308-4540 .. **Hollywood,** Rachel M '03 (R Hollywood,PC) -244 Pettit Av -Bellmore 11710 **Fx:**908-4564
(212) 626-4100 .. **Holm,** Klas S D '90 (Baker & M LLP) -1114 Av of Amer -NY 10036
(212) 682-2280 .. **Holm & O'Hara LLP** -3 W 35th -NY 10001 **Fx:**682-2153
(212) 980-4200 .. **Holm,** Steven I '78 (Levy HP&D,LLP) -950 3rd Av -NY 10022
(212) 682-2280 .. **Holm,** Wm P '81 (Holm & O LLP) -3 W 35th -NY 10001
(212) 808-7800 .. **Holman,** Bud George '56 (Kelley D&W LLP) -101 Park Av -NY 10178
(631) 694-2300 .. **Holman,** Gary '55 (Lamb & B,LLP) -534 Broadhllw Rd Bx9034 -Melvll 11747
(718) 834-8092 .. **Holman,** Jonathan H '80 -119 Wyckoff -Brklyn 11201
(212) 227-2780 .. **Holman,** Michelle M '08 Jaroslawicz & J -225 Bway -NY 10007
(212) 300-0345 .. **Holman,** Thos A '73 -1250 Bway -NY 10001
(607) 273-5475 .. **Holmberg,** Anna K '76 (Holmberg GV&M) -200 E Buffalo -Ithaca 14850
(607) 273-5475 .. **Holmberg Galbraith Van Houten & Miller** -200 E Buffalo -Ithaca 14850 **Fx:**272-4140
(212) 687-2770 .. **Holmberg,** Teodor J '97 %Cohen PL&P -551 5th Av -NY 10176
(914) 332-9608 .. **Holmbo,** Todd A '97 Philips Electronics -345 Scarborough Rd Bx3001 -Briarcliff Mnr 10510 **Fx:**332-0615
(212) 474-1000 .. **Holmes,** Aaron B '08 %Cravath S&M LLP -825 8th Av -NY 10019
(718) 741-1446 .. **Holmes,** Alexa A '98 Wildlife Conservation Soc -2300 Southrn Blvd -Bronx 10460
(212) 513-3200 .. **Holmes,** Andrew S '82 (Holland & K LLP) -31 W 52nd -NY 10019
(914) 366-5700 .. **Holmes,** David '76 %MA Bjork -660 Wht Plns Rd -Tarrytwn 10591 **Fx:**366-5759
(718) 775-8005 .. **Holmes,** Davida P '04 -541A Macon -Brklyn 11233
(212) 303-7344 .. **Holmes,** Donna L '87 Tremblant Capital LP -767 5th Av -NY 10153 **Fx:**303-7349
(212) 340-0400 .. **Holmes,** E Lauren '78 %Appllt Div 1st Dept -27 Mad Av -NY 10010 **Fx:**889-4412
(914) 948-4500 .. **Holmes,** Elizabeth '88 %O'Connor MCD&O -1 Barker Av -White Plns 10601
(212) 558-4000 .. **Holmes,** Gavin W '05 %Sullivan & C LLP -125 Broad -NY 10004
(212) 487-9701 .. **Holmes,** Gregory D V '89 %Robin HK&F -1 Bttry Pk Plz -NY 10014
(212) 294-6700 .. **Holmes,** H Sidney III '80 (Winston & S) -200 Park Av -NY 10166
(718) 250-2000 .. **Holmes,** John J '88 %DA -350 Jay -Brklyn 11201 **Fx:**250-2314
(212) 403-1000 .. **Holmes,** Joshua M '00 (Wachtell LR&K) -51 W 52nd -NY 10019
(212) 871-5426 .. **Holmes,** Kelly S '90 Ambridge Prtnrs,LLC -520 8th Av -NY 10018
(718) 722-3100 .. **Holmes,** Linda A '98 %Leg Aid -111 Lvngstn -Brklyn 11201 **Fx:**722-3093
(212) 593-8245 .. **Holmes,** Marguerite '04 %Sloan-Kettering -1275 York Av -NY 10065
(212) 661-9100 .. **Holmes,** Monique E '05 %Otterbourg SH&R,PC -230 Park Av -NY 10169
(212) 599-1717 .. **Holmes,** Naeem V '98 %Barnett EGK&L,PC -122 E 42nd -NY 10168
(212) 606-0391 .. **Holmes,** Nicholas S '04 Whitney Museum -945 Mad Av -NY 10021
(914) 238-6785 .. **Holmes,** Randall D '73 Cnsl Downs R&M,PC -36 Neustadt Ln -Chappaqua 10514
(212) 484-8000 .. **Holmes,** Robt C '87 %Time Warner -1 Time Warner Ctr -NY 10019
(212) 335-9000 .. **Holmes,** Robt S '70 %DA -1 Hogan Pl -NY 10013
(212) 770-6246 .. **Holmes,** Ronald E Jr. '07 AIG -70 Pine -NY 10270
(516) 832-2525 .. **Holmes Schwartz & Gordon** -320 Endo Blvd -Gdn Cty 11530 **Fx:**832-2533
(212) 762-7314 .. **Holmes,** Stephanie A '94 %Morgan Stanley Asset Mgt -1221 Av of Amer -NY 10020 **Fx:**762-7737
(518) 486-5157 .. **Holmes,** Susan L '91 NY Div of Housing & Community Renewal -38-40 State -Albany 12207
(212) 701-3000 .. **Holmes,** Wm E '09 %Cahill G&R LLP -80 Pine -NY 10005 **Fx:**269-5420
(212) 264-5958 .. **Holmes-Simmons,** Theresa '89 %US Immigration Ct -26 Fed Plz -NY 10278
(718) 520-5069 .. **Holmes-Simms,** Maria R '83 %Hon LJ Finnegan Jr -125-01 Qns Blvd -Kew Gdns 11415
(516) 746-7660 .. **Holmquist,** Karen B '83 (Klemanowicz H&VS,LLP) -300 Old Cntry Rd -Mineola 11501 **Fx:**747-7292
(212) 854-5918 .. **Holness,** Vielka V '92 Columbia Univ-Equal Opportunity Ofc -535 W 116th -NY 10027 **Fx:**854-1368
(212) 455-2000 .. **Holo,** Robt E '93 (Simpson T&B LLP) -425 Lex Av -NY 10017
(212) 806-5400 .. **Holob,** Marissa J '01 %Stroock &S&L LLP -180 Maiden Ln -NY 10038
(518) 408-3976 .. **Holohan,** Bridget E '00 %NYS Comm Pub Integrity -540 Bway -Albany 12207
(718) 590-2000 .. **Holohan,** Kellyanne P '09 %DA -198 E 161st -Bronx 10451 **Fx:**590-6477
(212) 587-7977 .. **Holohan,** Kieran P '95 (Gonzalez O&H LLP) -841 Bway -NY 10013
(516) 542-1000 .. **Holohan,** Michl H '81 (Geisler & G,LLP) -100 Q Roosevelt Blvd -Gdn Cty 11530
(516) 739-0000 .. **Holotka,** Jos S '84 %Martyn T&M -330 Old Cntry Rd -Mineola 11501
(212) 218-2100 .. **Holowacz,** Elizabeth F '98 %Fitzpatrick CH&S -1290 Av of Amer -NY 10104
(631) 853-5761 .. **Holownia,** John E '76 %Cnty Atty -400 Carleton Av -Central Islip 11722 **Fx:**853-7788
(212) 446-4800 .. **Holozubiec,** Francis M '86 (Kirkland & E LLP) -153 E 53rd -NY 10022
(212) 684-7676 .. **Holroyd,** Laura A '86 %Atkins & S -220 5th Av -NY 10001
(631) 694-2626 .. **Holsborg,** Janice L '04 %Grenier H&N LLP -445 Broadhllw Rd -Melvll 11747
(212) 219-6000 .. **Holsey,** Laurie E '04 %Tower Rsch Captl LLC -377 Bway -NY 10013 **Fx:**219-6007
(212) 701-3000 .. **Holst,** Mary A '10 %Cahill G&R LLP -80 Pine -NY 10005 **Fx:**269-5420
(212) 537-1712 .. **Holst,** Raymond J '03 Morgan Stanley -1633 Bway -NY 10019
(631) 853-5761 .. **Holst,** Wm G '83 %Cnty Atty -400 Carleton Av -Central Islip 11722 **Fx:**853-7788
(315) 422-1391 .. **Holstein,** David A '76 (Green & S,PLLC) -One Lincoln Ctr #900 -Syracuse 13202
(716) 852-5200 .. **Holstein,** Richd L '94 (Hamberger & W) -700 Main Pl Twr -Buffalo 14202
(516) 747-2330 .. **Holster,** Chas E III '84 -100 E Old Cntry Rd -Mineola 11501
(212) 536-0511 .. **Holt,** Christopher B '99 Phillips Electronics NA -1251 Av of Amer -NY 10020
(212) 363-3100 .. **Holt,** Eugene L '77 (Bivona & C,PC) -88 Pine -NY 10005
(212) 277-4000 .. **Holt,** James J '99 %Freshfields BD LLP -520 Mad Av -NY 10022
(212) 696-6000 .. **Holt,** Joshua R '10 %Curtis M-PC&M LLP -101 Park Av -NY 10178
(212) 951-6416 .. **Holt,** Karen M '94 Educ Dept- Prof Discipline-Pros Div -475 Park Av S -NY 10016
(631) 732-6600 .. **Holt,** Lawr J '60 -910 Middle Cntry Rd -Selden 11784 **Fx:**698-3301
(516) 333-5122 .. **Holt,** Oscar III '82 -114 Old Cntry Rd -Mineola 11501
(518) 274-5820 .. **Holt,** Sarah A '08 %ES Jones -28 2nd -Troy 12181 **Fx:**274-5875
(845) 638-5333 .. **Holt,** Sondra S '85 %Hon R Berliner -1 S Main -New Cty 10956
(607) 974-9000 .. **Holtby,** Nancy T '88 %Corning -1 Rvrfrnt Plz -Corning 14831 **Fx:**974-6135
(585) 924-0540 .. **Holter,** Reid A '84 -117 W Main -Victor 14564 **Fx:**924-0598
(212) 295-6413 .. **Holtmeier,** Jay J '92 (WilmerHale) -399 Park Av -NY 10022
(212) 755-0100 .. **Holton,** Mark B '99 (Grais & E LLP) -40 E 52nd -NY 10022
(212) 715-1000 .. **Holton,** Robt E '95 (Arnold & P LLP) -399 Park Av -NY 10022
(212) 735-8600 .. **Holtz,** Ethan R '02 %Morrison C LLP -909 3rd Av -NY 10022
(212) 319-4900 .. **Holtz,** Leonard '68 (Frishauf HG&C) -220 5th Av -NY 10001
(212) 903-9000 .. **Holtz,** Titia A '04 %Linklaters -1345 Av of Amer -NY 10105
(585) 419-8073 .. **Holtzberg,** Richd H '70 -2526 Browncroft Blvd -Rchstr 14625 **Fx:**385-4199
(212) 578-6158 .. **Holtzer,** David '91 %MetLife -1 Mad Av -NY 10010
(212) 310-8000 .. **Holtzer,** Gary T '91 (Weil G&M LLP) -767 5th Av -NY 10153
(212) 317-8500 .. **Holtzer,** Mark M '86 (Snitow KH&M,LLP) -575 Lex Av -NY 10022
(516) 334-4500 .. **Holtzer,** Melissa L '06 %Sokoloff S LLP -355 Post Av -Westbury 11590 **Fx:**334-4501
(212) 592-1400 .. **Holtzman,** Elizabeth '66 Cnsl Herrick,F LLP -2 Park Av -NY 10016
(845) 627-0127 .. **Holtzman,** Ellen B '83 -101 N Mddltwn Rd -Nanuet 10954 **Fx:**627-1231
(631) 435-8800 .. **Holtzman,** Eric H '73 -330 Vndrblt Motor Pkwy -Hauppauge 11788 **Fx:**435-8253
(646) 289-3981 .. **Holtzman,** Harriet '85 (Holtzman H,LLP) -350 7th Av -NY 10001 **Fx:**(212) 643-9151
(516) 393-4638 .. **Holtzman,** Jill M '95 %Robt Plan Corp of NY -999 Stewart Av -Bethpage 11714 **Fx:**393-4033
(718) 590-2000 .. **Holtzman,** Meredith L '95 %DA -198 E 161st -Bronx 10451 **Fx:**590-6477
(212) 715-9100 .. **Holtzman,** Robt N '93 (Kramer LN&F,LLP) -1177 Av of Amer -NY 10036
(212) 325-2000 .. **Holtzman,** Shari P '00 Credit Suisse -1 Mad Av -NY 10010
(212) 374-2989 .. **Holtzman,** Susan W '83 %NYC Dept Educ-OLS -52 Chmbrs -NY 10007 **Fx:**374-5939
(212) 669-7099 .. **Holtzmann,** Edw M '63 DCAS-DLS -1 Centre -NY 10007 **Fx:**669-8558
(646) 486-9750 .. **Holtzmann,** Howard M '49 -115 E 57th -NY 10022 **Fx:**486-9755

(212) 735-3000 .. **Holtzmuller,** James D '08 %Skadden ASM&F LLP -4 Times Sq -NY 10036
(212) 472-1421 .. **Holtzschue,** Karl B '67 -122 E 82nd -NY 10028 **Fx:**472-6712
(516) 488-3300 .. **Holubnyczyj,** Lena '06 %Shaub AC&S,LLP -1983 Marcus Av -Lk Success 11042
(718) 729-3073 .. **Holz,** Arthur O Jr. '53 -3940 Greenpoint Av -Sunnyside 11104
(212) 292-0456 .. **Holz,** Joy M '58 %S Davis,PC -67 Wall -NY 10005 **Fx:**292-0463
(212) 458-3225 .. **Holzback,** Stephanie M '90 %AIG -175 Water -NY 10038
(212) 391-1139 .. **Holzberg,** David E '82 %E Holzberg & Assoc -1700 Bway -NY 10019 **Fx:**391-8370
(212) 391-1139 .. **Holzberg,** Ernest '53 (E Holzberg & Assoc) -1700 Bway -NY 10019 **Fx:**391-8370
(212) 391-1139 .. **Holzberg,** Richd M '90 %E Holzberg & Assoc -1700 Bway -NY 10019 **Fx:**391-8370
(212) 391-1139 .. **Holzberg,** Suzanne '84 %E Holzberg & Assoc -1700 Bway -NY 10019 **Fx:**391-8370
(212) 833-1183 .. **Holzer,** Benjamin S '10 %Friedman KS&A LLP -1633 Bway -NY 10019 **Fx:**373-7983
(845) 638-5001 .. **Holzer,** Eric M '08 %DA -1 S Main -New Cty 10956 **Fx:**638-5070
(718) 625-2200 .. **Holzer,** Henry M '59 -250 Joralemon -Brklyn 11201
(212) 558-4000 .. **Holzer,** Meg D '07 %Sullivan & C LLP -125 Broad -NY 10004
(212) 691-9500 .. **Holzer,** Stuart J '73 SJH Holdings Inc -142 Law Rd -Briarclff Mnr 10510 **Fx:**265-4189
(315) 428-6341 .. **Holzhauer,** Wm J '87 Cnsl National Grid -300 Erie Blvd W -Syracuse 13202 **Fx:**428-6407
(212) 286-8585 .. **Holzka,** Denise A '97 (Heidell PM&B,LLP) -99 Park Av -NY 10016
(212) 371-8008 .. **Holzman,** Amy '96 OfCnsl Guzov O,LLC -600 Mad Av -NY 10022
(212) 849-7000 .. **Holzman,** Danl S '99 OfCnsl Quinn EU&S,LLP -51 Mad Av -NY 10010
(716) 855-1111 .. **Holzman,** Donald J '55 (Duke HP&G LLP) -350 Main -Buffalo 14202
(212) 210-9553 .. **Holzman,** Lara Anne '93 Cnsl Alston & B LLP -90 Park Av -NY 10016
(718) 424-1400 .. **Holzman,** Ronald S '95 Doshi Diagnostic Imaging Srvcs,PC -37-17 76th -Jcksn Hts 11372
(212) 250-5409 .. **Holzman,** Zev J '06 %Newmark Knight Frank -110 E 42nd -NY 10017
(212) 274-1433 .. **Hom,** Anthony J '95 -401 Bway -NY 10013
(212) 351-7129 .. **Hom,** David J '85 Monster Worldwide,Inc -622 3rd Av -NY 10017
(914) 946-1452 .. **Hom,** David Y '98 %Markhoff & M PC -14 Mamaroneck Av -White Plns 10601
(718) 638-4153 .. **Hom,** Edw S '94 -135 Eastern Pkwy -Brklyn 11238
(212) 328-7921 .. **Hom,** Holly '04 DiMaio Ahmad Capital LLP -277 Park Av -NY 10172
(212) 788-5172 .. **Hom,** Phillip '96 NY City Council -250 Bway -NY 10007
(212) 239-4495 .. **Hom,** Sharon K '81 Human Rights in China -350 5th Av -NY 10118
(212) 527-1000 .. **Hom,** Tony C '96 (Jones HC&B PC) -1 Bttry Pk Plz -NY 10004
(914) 738-9679 .. **Homan,** Maria M '89 -252 Elderwood Av -Pelham 10803
(212) 848-4000 .. **Homan,** Steven A '09 Shearman & S LLP -599 Lex Av -NY 10022
(631) 585-3737 .. **Homayoon,** Steven J '95 -7 Gatelot Av -Ronkonkoma 11779 **Fx:**585-3737
(212) 880-9553 .. **Homberger,** Matthew B '08 %Morvillo AGIA&B,PC -565 5th Av -NY 10017
(914) 592-4275 .. **Home,** Suman S '06 %MHLS -100 Clearbrook Rd -Elmsfrd 10523 **Fx:**592-9404
(212) 559-1000 .. **Homer,** Christine Y '91 Citigroup -399 Park Av -NY 10022
(212) 735-3000 .. **Homison,** Michl J '07 %Skadden ASM&F LLP -4 Times Sq -NY 10036
(631) 859-0300 .. **Hommel,** Douglas E II '09 %Zaklukiewicz P&M,LLP -2701 Sunrise Hwy Bx389 -Islip Terr 11752
(718) 397-6465 .. **Hommel,** Theo E Jr. '78 %Avis -90-20 Grnd Cntrl Pkwy -E Elmhrst 11369 **Fx:**639-5865
(212) 526-0451 .. **Hommel,** Thos '79 Lehman Bros -1271 Av of Amer -NY 10020 **Fx:**526-0940
(845) 562-3262 .. **Hommel Cocchia,** Patricia A '99 (Cocchia & G) -3262 Route 9W -New Windsor 12553 **Fx:**562-6272
(212) 446-7957 .. **Homsany,** Nadim R '03 %McKinsey & Co -55 E 52nd -NY 10055 **Fx:**688-9521
(212) 513-3200 .. **Honan,** Wm J III '70 (Holland & K LLP) -31 W 52nd -NY 10019
(212) 209-3186 .. **Honarvar,** Houdin '02 Taconic Cptl Advsrs LP -450 Park Av -NY 10022
(718) 250-0400 .. **Honculada,** Jehovenn A '90 %R Tusa -1 MetroTech Ctr -Brklyn 11201 **Fx:**250-0591
(914) 793-0194 .. **Hone,** Dawn Kilgallen '94 -211 Read Av -Tuckahoe 10707
(212) 753-5000 .. **Hone,** Graham R '81 (Schiff H LLP) -900 3rd Av -NY 10022
(212) 319-1900 .. **Hone,** Thos E '91 (Berger & W,LLP) -1633 Bway -NY 10019
(212) 829-9890 .. **Honecker,** Ernest '59 -210 E 49th -NY 10017 **Fx:**829-9876
(212) 237-1000 .. **Honecker,** Rodman E '94 SpclCnsl Windels ML&M,LLP -156 W 56th -NY 10019
(518) 472-1224 .. **Honen,** Richd E '86 (Phillips L LLP) -30 S Pearl -Albany 12207
(518) 462-0300 .. **Honeywell,** Jeffrey D '84 (Girvin & F,PC) -20 Corp Wds Blvd -Albany 12211
(212) 536-3900 .. **Honeywell,** Robt T '98 Cnsl K&L Gates LLP -599 Lex Av -NY 10022
(212) 209-8254 .. **Hong,** Arlene S '97 %J Crew Group Inc -770 Bway -NY 10003
(646) 424-6235 .. **Hong,** Bo '99 ING Fncl Srvcs LLC -1325 Av of Amer -NY 10019
(212) 458-1184 .. **Hong,** Chung Woo '95 AIG -175 Water -NY 10038
(212) 902-2983 .. **Hong,** Dana H '05 Goldman Sachs & Co -85 Broad -NY 10004
(212) 812-3117 .. **Hong,** David K '02 King St Capital Mgmt,LP -65 E 55th -NY 10022
(347) 404-9400 .. **Hong,** Gilbert C '92 %Criminal Ct -120 Schermerhorn -Brklyn 11201 **Fx:**(718) 643-3538
(718) 533-1111 .. **Hong,** Hyong Son '95 (Yoon & H) -75-21 Bway -Elmhrst 11373 **Fx:**429-6786
(718) 395-8891 .. **Hong,** James '03 -136-20 38th Av -Flushng 11354 **Fx:**395-8906
(212) 298-5139 .. **Hong,** Janet E '03 Leg Aid -49 Thomas -NY 10013
(212) 373-3000 .. **Hong,** Jeanhee '09 %Paul WRW&G LLP -1285 Av of Amer -NY 10019
(516) 414-6894 .. **Hong,** Jennifer Soonki '98 -600 Old Cntry Rd -Gdn Cty 11530 **Fx:**227-2136
(212) 848-7417 .. **Hong,** Ji Hoon '87 OfCnsl Shearman & S LLP -599 Lex Av -NY 10022
(212) 733-6244 .. **Hong,** John S '05 %Pfizer Inc -150 E 42nd -NY 10017
(212) 530-1800 .. **Hong,** Joon P '92 %Richards K&O LLP -1 World Fncl Ctr -NY 10281
(212) 596-9000 .. **Hong,** Kathryn N '09 %Ropes & G LLP -1211 Av of Amer -NY 10036
(212) 735-3000 .. **Hong,** Michl J '08 %Skadden ASM&F LLP -4 Times Sq -NY 10036
(212) 373-3000 .. **Hong,** Michl Sung-Hyuck '05 %Paul WRW&G LLP -1285 Av of Amer -NY 10019
(212) 458-2328 .. **Hong,** Paul S '97 AIG Capital Prtnrs -175 Water -NY 10038
(212) 455-2000 .. **Hong,** Sarah C '09 %Simpson T&B LLP -425 Lex Av -NY 10017
(212) 532-1770 .. **Hong,** Song Yook '84 -1261 Bway -NY 10001 **Fx:**684-0599
(212) 688-8555 .. **Hong,** Stacy S '05 %Fragomen DB&L LLP -7 Hanover Sq -NY 10004
(718) 366-3880 .. **Hong,** Steve '92 %Koryeo Intl Corp -200 Stewart Av -Brklyn 11237
(212) 625-1001 .. **Hong,** Suk Hwa '00 %M Jeon,PC -401 Bway -NY 10013 **Fx:**625-1202
(212) 446-4800 .. **Hong,** Ye Cecilia '07 %Kirkland & E LLP -153 E 53rd -NY 10022
(212) 416-8000 .. **Hong,** Yu Jin '00 %Dept of Law -120 Bway -NY 10271
(718) 961-0012 .. **Hong,** Yu Mi '93 -38-29 150th -Flushng 11354
(212) 687-3860 .. **Honick,** Eric '77 (Snow BK,PC) -605 3rd Av -NY 10158
(631) 694-0033 .. **Honig,** Jeremy B '05 %Lawrence WR&B,PC -425 Broadhllw Rd -Melvll 11747
(212) 888-8200 .. **Honig,** Jonathan '83 (Feder K LLP) -845 3rd Av -NY 10022
(212) 719-6043 .. **Honig,** Leslie Allan '81 %IRS -110 W 44th -NY 10036
(631) 249-5163 .. **Honig,** Martin '66 -35 Pinelawn Rd -Melvll 11747 **Fx:**777-2293
(516) 466-4460 .. **Honig,** Murray '80 -88 Middle Nck Rd -Gt Neck 11021
(646) 943-5914 .. **Honig,** Robt L '93 Beazley Grp -1270 Av of Amer -NY 10020
(212) 294-6700 .. **Honig,** Ross A '89 (Winston & S) -200 Park Av -NY 10166
(631) 715-8170 .. **Honig,** Sheldon '59 -50 Hauppauge Rd -Commack 11725
(212) 695-8090 .. **Honig,** Steven I '88 %Waterfront NYLP -224 12th Av -NY 10001 **Fx:**629-8768
(212) 267-4000 .. **Honigman,** Allen M '91 %M Rolnik -325 Bway -NY 10007 **Fx:**267-5813
(631) 390-2100 .. **Honigman,** Barry K '82 -225 Old Cntry Rd -Melvll 11747 **Fx:**761-0022
(516) 496-5822 .. **Honkanen,** John R '93 %T Spina -170 Froehlich Farm Blvd -Woodbury 11797 **Fx:**496-5420
(631) 878-0758 .. **Honohan,** Jaime L '98 South Bay Adult Home -Cottontail Run Bx 601 -Ctr Moriches 11934
(212) 735-3000 .. **Honorowski,** Caroline Jacobson '09 %Skadden ASM&F LLP -4 Times Sq -NY 10036
(212) 819-8200 .. **Honsberger,** Kaleb M '07 %White & C LLP -1155 Av of Amer -NY 10036
(212) 530-5000 .. **Hood,** Andrea G '07 %Milbank TH&M LLP -1 Chase Manh Plz -NY 10005
(212) 490-1700 .. **Hood,** Bruce E '85 (Wiggin & D) -450 Lex Av -NY 10017
(212) 259-8000 .. **Hood,** Catherine Carney '88 (Dewey & L LLP) -1301 Av of Amer -NY 10019
(212) 435-3429 .. **Hood,** Dave D '96 Cnsl Port Auth of NY/NJ -225 Park Av S -NY 10003 **Fx:**435-3834
(212) 889-8108 .. **Hood,** Harold L '77 -319 E 24th -NY 10010
(845) 429-6400 .. **Hood,** J Nelson '70 (Hood H&H) -217 Route 9W -Haverstraw 10927 **Fx:**429-6411
(845) 429-6400 .. **Hood,** J Nelson Jr. '96 (Hood H&H) -217 Route 9W -Haverstraw 10927 **Fx:**429-6411
(585) 263-1000 .. **Hood,** John B '70 (Nixon P LLP) -1100 Clinton Sq -Rchstr 14604
(212) 309-6000 .. **Hood,** John T '80 (Morgan L&B LLP) -101 Park Av -NY 10178
(845) 429-6400 .. **Hood,** Kathleen Anne '98 (Hood H&H) -217 Route 9W -Haverstraw 10927 **Fx:**429-6411
(212) 640-2965 .. **Hood,** Nancy E '94 %Amer Exp -200 Vesey -NY 10285
(518) 725-3526 .. **Hood,** Richd H '51 -137 Bleecker -Gloversvll 12078
(212) 326-3939 .. **Hood,** Rory T '07 %Jones D -222 E 41st -NY 10017
(212) 506-2500 .. **Hood,** Thos R '75 (Mayer B LLP) -1675 Bway -NY 10019
(516) 739-7979 .. **Hooghuis,** James J '87 (Hooghuis Grp,LLC) -176 Mineola Blvd -Mineola 11501 **Fx:**739-1862
(212) 659-7300 .. **Hook,** Jonathan '04 %Haynes & B,LLP -1221 Av of Amer -NY 10020
(212) 641-5035 .. **Hook,** Lisa Ann '97 %Alpine Capital Grp -1285 Av of Amer -NY 10019
(212) 335-9000 .. **Hook,** Thos J '09 %DA -1 Hogan Pl -NY 10013
(845) 398-3540 .. **Hooker,** Roger '68 -One Kings Hwy -Tappan 10983 **Fx:**398-3531
(212) 362-2696 .. **Hooker,** Wade S '69 -211 Cntrl Pk W -NY 10024 **Fx:**874-0055
(212) 648-0415 .. **Hooks,** E Randolph '83 JP Morgan Chase -245 Park Av -NY 10167
(607) 273-6444 .. **Hooks,** Edw C '80 (Harris B PLLC) -119 E Seneca -Ithaca 14850
(585) 987-2800 .. **Hooks,** Robt D '87 (Woods OG LLP) -2 State -Rchstr 14614
(518) 474-8211 .. **Hooks,** Wm J '80 %Law Reporting Bur -1 Commerce Plz -Albany 12210 **Fx:**463-6869
(315) 426-2146 .. **Hookway,** Karen A '83 Ofc of Chldrn Fam Srvcs -333 E Wshngtn -Syracuse 13202
(212) 513-3200 .. **Hooper,** Chester D '71 (Holland & K LLP) -31 W 52nd -NY 10019
(212) 466-7700 .. **Hooper,** Christopher S '97 %Sandler O'Neill & Prtnrs,LP -919 3rd Av -NY 10022 **Fx:**466-7998
(212) 521-5400 .. **Hooper,** John P '87 (Reed S LLP) -599 Lex Av -NY 10022
(212) 526-2154 .. **Hooper,** Matthew J '06 Barclays Capital Inc -745 7th Av -NY 10019
(212) 574-1200 .. **Hooper,** Thos R '01 %Seward & K LLP -1 Bttry Pk Plz -NY 10004
(212) 979-3000 .. **Hoot,** W E Scott '86 %Natl Audubon Society -225 Varick -NY 10014
(631) 331-0547 .. **Hooten,** Paul J '89 (PJ Hooten & Assoc,PLLC) -5505 Nesconset Hwy -Mt Sinai 11766 **Fx:**331-2627
(212) 343-0114 .. **Hooton,** Angela D '03 NARAL Pro-Choice -470 Park Av -NY 10022
(716) 566-5400 .. **Hoover,** Bruce W '88 (Goldberg S LLP) -665 Main -Buffalo 14203
(212) 513-7788 .. **Hoover,** Carolee A '08 %Ahmuty D&M -123 William -NY 10038
(716) 821-7097 .. **Hoover,** David A '77 %Erie 1 BOCES -355 Harlem Rd -W Seneca 14224 **Fx:**827-7139
(212) 944-5540 .. **Hoover,** Gilbert C IV '91 Shubert Org -234 W 44th -NY 10036
(845) 496-6100 .. **Hoover,** Gregory G Sr. '80 -Bx28 -Goshen 10924 **Fx:**496-1013
(212) 779-1414 .. **Hoover,** Mary Uebler '93 %Bernstein L LLP -10 E 40th -NY 10016
(518) 474-1010 .. **Hoover,** Patricia R '95 %Ofc Inspector Genl -ESP Agncy Bldg 2 -Albany 12223 **Fx:**486-3745
(716) 847-8400 .. **Hoover,** Timothy W '07 %Phillips L LLP -3400 HSBC Ctr -Buffalo 14203
(845) 469-7577 .. **Hoovler,** David M '98 %Ostrer R,LLP -111 Main Bx509 -Chester 10918

(212) 848-4000 .. **Hope,** Andrew J '05 %Shearman & S LLP -599 Lex Av -NY 10022
(516) 683-5228 .. **Hope,** Christina Walsh '95 %IRS -107 Chas Lindbergh Blvd E -Gdn Cty 11530
(212) 836-8000 .. **Hope,** Danl P '09 %Kaye S LLP -425 Park Av -NY 10022
(315) 474-2911 .. **Hope,** Gabrielle Mardany '00 (Smith SK&S,PC) -250 S Clinton -Syracuse 13202
(718) 963-5774 .. **Hope,** Melanie '08 %MHLS -760 Bway -Brklyn 11206 **Fx:**384-2702
(585) 454-6480 .. **Hopfinger,** Jane B '79 (Osborn R&B,LLP) -45 Exchange Blvd -Rchstr 14614
(516) 294-8844 .. **Hopke,** Debra J '96 (L'Abbate BC&C,LLP) -1001 Franklin Av -Gdn Cty 11530
(212) 313-9776 .. **Hopkins,** Adam R '05 Brencourt Advisors,LLC -600 Lex Av -NY 10022
(212) 935-3000 .. **Hopkins,** Brian P '98 (Mintz LCFG&P,PC) -666 3rd Av -NY 10017
(212) 408-5100 .. **Hopkins,** Dennis C '99 (Chadbourne & P LLP) -30 Rckfllr Plz -NY 10112
(516) 294-5432 .. **Hopkins,** Edw R '89 SrCnsl Kern AC&S,PC -1325 Franklin Av -Gdn Cty 11530
(516) 496-5822 .. **Hopkins,** Eileen M '06 T Spina -170 Froehlich Farm Blvd -Woodbury 11797 **Fx:**496-5420
(212) 416-8000 .. **Hopkins,** Ellen '02 %Dept of Law -120 Bway -NY 10271
(718) 949-9792 .. **Hopkins,** Everett '90 (Hopkins Law Grp,LLC) -186-17 Merrick Blvd -Sprngfld Gdns 11413 **Fx:**949-1352
(516) 741-2585 .. **Hopkins,** Frances E '05 %Rosicki R & Assoc,PC -51 E Bethpage Rd -Plainvw 11803 **Fx:**741-4748
(631) 232-5706 .. **Hopkins,** Garrett P '79 -300 Rabro Dr -Hauppauge 11788
(212) 309-6000 .. **Hopkins,** Heather L '07 %Morgan L&B LLP -101 Park Av -NY 10178
(315) 475-4555 .. **Hopkins,** James C III '79 -217 Mntgmry -Syracuse 13202 **Fx:**424-6826
(212) 551-1835 .. **Hopkins,** John S '03 Westpac Banking Corp -575 5th Av -NY 10017
(212) 576-7780 .. **Hopkins,** Judy E '03 %NY Life Ins -51 Mad Av -NY 10010 **Fx:**447-0569
(516) 571-2684 .. **Hopkins,** Kathryn D '81 %Hon E McCabe -100 Supreme Ct Dr -Mineola 11501 **Fx:**571-3713
(516) 747-4770 .. **Hopkins & Kopilow** -100 Q Roosevelt Blvd -Gdn Cty 11530 **Fx:**747-3928
(212) 841-1000 .. **Hopkins,** Michl B '80 (Covington & B LLP) -620 8th Av -NY 10018
(516) 747-4770 .. **Hopkins,** Michl T '77 (Hopkins & K) -100 Q Roosevelt Blvd -Gdn Cty 11530
(716) 614-8801 .. **Hopkins,** Sean W '95 (Hopkins & S,PLLC) -5500 Main -Williamsvll 14221
(914) 730-3200 .. **Hopkins,** Shannon L '04 %Entwistle & C LLP -200 Business Park Dr -Armonk 10504
(716) 614-8801 .. **Hopkins & Sorgi, PLLC** -5500 Main -Williamsvll 14221
(716) 332-7850 .. **Hopkins,** Therese Anne '95 %Hon L Foschio -68 Court -Buffalo 14202 **Fx:**332-7855
(212) 858-4021 .. **Hopkins,** Thos J '94 FINRA -1 Lbrty Plz -NY 10006
(631) 563-0308 .. **Hopkins,** Timothy J '93 %Suffolk Cnty Water Auth -4060 Sunrise Hwy -Oakdale 11769 **Fx:**563-0370
(631) 234-0909 .. **Hopkins Murray,** Olga '89 (Murray & H) -132 Clyde -W Sayvll 11796 **Fx:**234-2524
(516) 747-4770 .. **Hopkins Murray,** Olga '89 (Murray & H) -100 Q Roosevelt Blvd -Gdn Cty 11530 **Fx:**747-3928
(212) 504-6000 .. **Hopkinson,** R Ronald '89 (Cadwalader W&T LLP) -1 World Fncl Ctr -NY 10281
(212) 577-3688 .. **Hopkirk,** Arthur H '86 %Leg Aid -199 Water -NY 10038 **Fx:**509-8431
(716) 228-7260 .. **Hoppe,** Bernadette M '04 -137 Summer -Buffalo 14222 **Fx:**883-4588
(716) 856-0600 .. **Hoppe,** Bradley A '07 %Jaeckle F&M,LLP -12 Fountain Plz -Buffalo 14202
(212) 682-8383 .. **Hoppe,** Gary D '78 (Kantor DWMT&G,PC) -51 E 42nd -NY 10017
(212) 225-2000 .. **Hoppe,** Jessica S '09 %Cleary GS&H -1 Lbrty Plz -NY 10006
(718) 263-6050 .. **Hoppenfeld,** Marilyn P '52 -109-14 Ascan Av -Frst Hlls 11375
(516) 248-4817 .. **Hopper,** Adrianne '92 %Comerford & D,LLP -1122 Franklin Av -Gdn Cty 11530
(212) 450-4000 .. **Hoppin,** Chas S '64 SrCnsl Davis P&W LLP -450 Lex Av -NY 10017
(718) 265-3287 .. **Hoppmann,** Barbara E '79 -6215 Spencer Ter -Bronx 10471
(212) 374-7839 .. **Hopson,** Frances E '05 %NYC Dept Educ -52 Chmbrs -NY 10007
(914) 328-4100 .. **Hopson,** Seth M '06 N Connelly,PLLC -99 Church -White Plns 10601 **Fx:**684-0401
(914) 345-3701 .. **Hopwood,** John J '03 %Marks OO&C,PC -530 Saw Mill Rvr Rd -Elmsfrd 10523
(212) 309-1000 .. **Hopwood,** Juana C '07 %Hunton & W -200 Park Av -NY 10166
(212) 592-1400 .. **Hoque,** Enam '07 %Herrick,F LLP -2 Park Av -NY 10016
(212) 530-5000 .. **Hora,** Robt C '03 %Milbank TH&M LLP -1 Chase Manh Plz -NY 10005
(315) 685-4558 .. **Horacek,** Chris A '98 Welch Allyn,Inc -4341 State Street Rd -Skaneateles Fls 13153
(212) 270-7122 .. **Horan,** Anthony J '77 JP Morgan Chase -277 Park Av -NY 10172
(845) 469-2027 .. **Horan,** Austin L '95 -302 Sugar Loaf Mt Rd -Chester 10918
(212) 788-1267 .. **Horan,** Brian T '10 %Law Dept -100 Church -NY 10007 **Fx:**788-0367
(518) 402-9512 .. **Horan,** Christopher H '06 %DEC -625 Bway -Albany 12233 **Fx:**402-9018
(716) 847-8400 .. **Horan,** David C '68 OfCnsl Phillips L LLP -3400 HSBC Ctr -Buffalo 14203
(914) 686-7200 .. **Horan,** David F '77 (Horan & H,LLP) -50 Main -White Plns 10606 **Fx:**686-7211
(212) 756-2000 .. **Horan,** Eileen M '93 %Schulte R&Z LLP -919 3rd Av -NY 10022
(516) 921-2525 .. **Horan,** Elizabeth A '81 (McHenry H&L,PC) -6800 Jericho Tpk -Syosset 11791
(518) 402-0748 .. **Horan,** James F '81 %Dept of Health -433 River -Troy 12180 **Fx:**402-0751
(516) 538-2500 .. **Horan,** James M II '01 %Furey FLMW&D,PC -600 Front -Hempstd 11550
(845) 298-2000 .. **Horan,** James P '94 %Vergilis SRD&D,LLP -1136 Route 9 -Wappingers Fls 12590
(212) 233-7195 .. **Horan,** John E '94 %Lewis JAA,LLP -61 Bway -NY 10006
(212) 480-4800 .. **Horan,** John R '66 (Fox H&C LLP) -825 3rd Av -NY 10022
(212) 557-9600 .. **Horan,** Leonard P '69 OfCnsl Russo & B -600 3rd Av -NY 10016
(212) 331-7434 .. **Horan,** Michl J II '02 Berdon LLP -360 Mad Av -NY 10017
(212) 906-1200 .. **Horan,** Michl P '10 %Latham & W -885 3rd Av -NY 10022
(518) 374-0468 .. **Horan,** Michl T '78 -670 Franklin -Schnctdy 12305 **Fx:**374-0791
(914) 686-7200 .. **Horan,** Michele C '84 (Horan & H,LLP) -50 Main -White Plns 10606 **Fx:**686-7211
(212) 931-8569 .. **Horan,** Nina R '04 Cnsl Byrne P LLP -11 Bway -NY 10004 **Fx:**931-8521
(718) 590-6180 .. **Horan,** Pamela M '03 %Law Dept -198 E 161st -Bronx 10451 **Fx:**590-2686
(212) 728-8000 .. **Horan,** Paul W '01 %Willkie F&G LLP -787 7th Av -NY 10019
(631) 249-7662 .. **Horan,** Thos F '79 -104 Copeland Pl -Farmngdl 11735
(315) 682-8171 .. **Horan,** Vincent G '88 -131 W Seneca -Manlius 13104
(631) 482-1433 .. **Horan,** Wm J '78 (Horan & W PC) -366 Vets Mem'l Hwy -Commack 11725 **Fx:**(516) 997-4365
(718) 553-4243 .. **Horan,** Wm K '91 MTA Bus Co -165-25 147th Av -Jamaica 11434
(845) 291-2670 .. **Horaz,** Kristy L '05 %Childrens Rts Society -213 W Main Bx1002 -Goshen 10924 **Fx:**291-2679
(212) 482-0001 .. **Horbatiuk,** Kevin G '82 (Russo K&T LLP) -33 Whitehall -NY 10004
(212) 408-5100 .. **Hord,** Chas E III '76 (Chadbourne & P LLP) -30 Rckfllr Plz -NY 10112
(518) 487-5552 .. **Hordines,** Marsha M '00 NYS Bar Assn -1 Elk -Albany 12207 **Fx:**487-5544
(212) 697-3122 .. **Horenstein,** Geri B '04 (Martin C&B LLP) -220 E 42nd -NY 10017
(212) 490-9100 .. **Horenstein,** John D '95 (Condon & F LLP) -7 Times Sq -NY 10036
(212) 458-2988 .. **Horenstein,** Kenneth P '93 %AIG -175 Water -NY 10038
(631) 368-2122 .. **Horenstein,** Nina '92 -1 Foothill ln -E Northprt 11731 **Fx:**623-6836
(516) 678-2333 .. **Horenstein,** Peter '59 -Bx452 -Rockvll Ctr 11571 **Fx:**678-4962
(212) 259-8000 .. **Horgan,** John B '10 %Dewey & L LLP -1301 Av of Amer -NY 10019
(914) 961-4441 .. **Horgan,** Michl F Jr. '90 (Begos H&B LLP) -7 Pondfld Rd Bx369 -Bronxvll 10708
(718) 286-6000 .. **Horgan,** Sheila '07 %DA -125-01 Qns Blvd -Kew Gdns 11415
(212) 605-0435 .. **Horgan,** Timothy J '75 -575 Mad Av -NY 10022
(518) 843-0043 .. **Horigan Horigan & Lombardo, PC** -49 E Main Bx520 -Amsterdam 12010 **Fx:**843-0339
(518) 843-0043 .. **Horigan,** Richd T '51 OfCnsl Horigan H&L,PC -49 E Main Bx520 -Amsterdam 12010
(518) 843-0043 .. **Horigan,** Timothy J '77 (Horigan H&L,PC) -49 E Main Bx520 -Amsterdam 12010
(212) 878-4000 .. **Horikoshi,** Aya '00 %Mitsui & Co -200 Park Av -NY 10166 **Fx:**878-4800
(516) 535-1700 .. **Horing Welikson & Rosen,PC** -11 Hillside Av -Williston Pk 11596 **Fx:**535-1701
(212) 278-1322 .. **Horkovich,** Robt M '80 (Anderson K&O,PC) -1251 Av of Amer -NY 10020
(212) 416-8000 .. **Hormozi,** Mitra '96 %Dept of Law -120 Bway -NY 10271
(212) 223-0400 .. **Horn,** Alan B '77 OfCnsl Zeichner E&K LLP -575 Lex Av -NY 10022
(212) 725-5113 .. **Horn,** C Steven '66 -18 E 16th -NY 10003
(516) 355-9600 .. **Horn,** Chas H '97 %Friedman HK&P -3000 Marcus Av -Lk Success 11042
(212) 506-2500 .. **Horn,** Christopher B '06 (Mayer B LLP) -1675 Bway -NY 10019
(518) 487-5460 .. **Horn,** Christopher D '94 %DA -6 Lodge -Albany 12207 **Fx:**487-5093
(212) 704-6000 .. **Horn,** David B '88 (Troutman S LLP) -405 Lex Av -NY 10174
(631) 435-7900 .. **Horn,** Eric A '96 -1010 Suffolk Av -Brentwd 11717 **Fx:**435-7901
(212) 445-7000 .. **Horn,** Eric L '99 Jacoby & M,LLP -39 Bway -NY 10006
(212) 879-1738 .. **Horn,** Fredk M '65 -10 East End Av -NY 10075
(516) 348-0002 .. **Horn,** Gary A '92 -100 Merrick Rd -Rockvll Ctr 11570 **Fx:**348-0004
(914) 997-0500 .. **Horn,** Geoffrey M '94 (Lowey DC&H,PC) -1 N Bway -White Plns 10601
(212) 883-1300 .. **Horn,** Gerald B '75 (Sandler T&R,PA) -551 5th Av -NY 10176
(516) 222-0261 .. **Horn,** Howard I '85 -585 Stewart Av -Gdn Cty 11530 **Fx:**222-2347
(212) 696-4848 .. **Horn,** Jack A '75 Mintz & G LLP -470 Park Av S -NY 10016
(212) 308-6560 .. **Horn,** Janet L '99 %David Carrie LLC -155 E 55th -NY 10022 **Fx:**308-6569
(212) 688-8555 .. **Horn,** Janet S '85 %Fragomen DB&L LLP -7 Hanover Sq -NY 10004
(718) 537-5555 .. **Horn,** Jeffrey A '81 -910 Grnd Cncrs -Bronx 10451
(631) 271-5200 .. **Horn,** Jeffrey S '81 (Horn & H) -780 NY Av -Huntngtn 11743 **Fx:**271-5216
(716) 853-1616 .. **Horn,** John G '99 (Harter S&E LLP) -12 Fountain Plz -Buffalo 14202
(212) 760-0111 .. **Horn,** Jonathan S '00 -350 5th Av -NY 10118
(212) 687-3000 .. **Horn,** Jos A '76 Jaffe & A,LLP -600 3rd Av -NY 10016
(212) 506-1700 .. **Horn,** Kimberly A '04 %Kasowitz BT&F LLP -1633 Bway -NY 10019
(347) 296-1669 .. **Horn,** Linda J '87 %Supreme Ct Law Dept -360 Adams -Brklyn 11201 **Fx:**643-6114
(718) 261-3047 .. **Horn,** Michl D '92 %Queens Law Assoc -118-21 Qns Blvd -Frst Hlls 11375 **Fx:**261-0798
(212) 584-0700 .. **Horn,** Moshe H '94 (Seeger W LLP) -1 William -NY 10004
(917) 320-2812 .. **Horn,** Richd B '04 FDIC -350 5th Av -NY 10118 **Fx:**320-2917
(212) 371-1511 .. **Horn,** Robt A '64 -110 E 59th -NY 10022 **Fx:**223-4911
(212) 505-9080 .. **Horn,** Romy L '92 %Loscalzo & L,PC -14 E 4th -NY 10012
(212) 425-5191 .. **Horn,** Scott T '92 (Mischel & H,PC) -1 Whitehall -NY 10004
(212) 840-3080 .. **Horn,** Shimmie '00 Iroquois Hotel -49 W 44th -NY 10036
(516) 364-1095 .. **Horn,** Spencer R '06 %McBreen & K -500 N Bway -Jericho 11753
(315) 422-8191 .. **Horn,** Susan R '75 %Leg Aid -351 S Warren -Syracuse 13202 **Fx:**472-2819
(631) 831-1561 .. **Horn,** Thos W '06 %Town of E Hampton -159 Pantigo Rd -E Hampton 11937
(212) 351-4000 .. **Hornbaker,** Thos S '99 OfCnsl Gibson D&C LLP -200 Park Av -NY 10166
(631) 207-5654 .. **Hornberger,** Robt E '06 (Wurman & H,PC) -57 E Main -Patchogue 11772
(212) 770-5852 .. **Hornbostel,** John P '88 %AIG -70 Pine -NY 10270
(212) 973-0572 .. **Hornby,** Robt L '01 (Wolff & S PC) -140 Bway -NY 10005
(212) 446-4800 .. **Horne,** Andrew G '02 (Kirkland & E LLP) -153 E 53rd -NY 10022
(212) 836-8000 .. **Horne,** Jonathan R '10 %Kaye S LLP -425 Park Av -NY 10022
(212) 756-2000 .. **Horne,** Neil P '96 SpclCnsl Schulte R&Z LLP -919 3rd Av -NY 10022
(646) 414-6854 .. **Horne,** Richd J '94 Cnsl Lowenstein S PC -1251 Av of Amer -NY 10020 **Fx:**(973) 422-6853

(914) 471-5402 .. **Horne,** Robt A '93 -405 Tarrytown Rd -White Plns 10607 **Fx:**437-5057
(718) 343-1760 .. **Horne,** Roberta '89 -24852 88th Dr -Bellerose 11426
(516) 463-5387 .. **Horne,** Vernadette L '89 Hofstra Law Schl -108 Hofstra Univ -Hempstd 11549
(212) 832-0400 .. **Horne,** Veronique '02 Berdon LLP -360 Mad Av -NY 10017
(212) 558-5500 .. **Horner,** Danl T '09 Weitz & L,PC -700 Bway -NY 10003
(212) 610-6300 .. **Horner,** David B '09 SrCnsl Allen & O -1221 Av of Amer -NY 10020
(212) 418-2618 .. **Horner,** Martin '85 Jones Lang LaSalle Inc -601 Lex Av -NY 10022
(212) 839-5300 .. **Horner,** Neil E '07 %Sidley A LLP -787 7th Av -NY 10019
(845) 471-0044 .. **Horner,** Terry D '82 -329 Main -Poughkeepsie 12601 **Fx:**471-0041
(607) 648-7165 .. **Horner,** Timothy M '82 -309 E Hill Rd -Bnghmtn 13901
(212) 252-1165 .. **Horner,** Wm R '74 -551 5th Av -NY 10176 **Fx:**252-1632
(631) 853-4161 .. **Horney,** Deirdre N '01 %DA -N Cnty Cmplx Bldg 77 -Hauppauge 11788 **Fx:**853-4192
(212) 218-5500 .. **Hornick,** Blake '81 (Seyfarth S LLP) -620 8th Av -NY 10018
(516) 870-1124 .. **Hornig,** Audra L '94 Cnsl Premium Capital Funding -125 Jericho Tpk -Jericho 11753 **Fx:**870-7124
(212) 220-3830 .. **Hornig,** David R '74 (Nicoletti H&S) -88 Pine -NY 10005
(212) 530-4823 .. **Hornik,** Jonathan L '96 (LaRocca HRG&B LLP) -40 Wall -NY 10005
(212) 770-3422 .. **Hornik,** Jos J '96 %AIG -70 Pine -NY 10270
(212) 878-8000 .. **Horning,** Nils E '09 %Clifford C LLP -31 W 52nd -NY 10019
(212) 504-6000 .. **Hornsby,** Zachary D '03 %Cadwalader W&T LLP -1 World Fncl Ctr -NY 10281
(212) 455-2000 .. **Hornstein,** Alison B '08 %Simpson T&B LLP -425 Lex Av -NY 10017
(917) 388-2629 .. **Hornstein,** Edw S '03 Hornstein Capital Prtnrs LP -53 E 34th -NY 10016
(212) 883-4900 .. **Hornstein,** Howard B '63 (Cozen O) -277 Park Av -NY 10172
(646) 252-2928 .. **Hornstein,** Joel M '83 %Transit Auth -2 Bway -NY 10004 **Fx:**252-5559
(212) 416-6180 .. **Hornstein,** Nancy D '81 %Dept of Law -120 Bway -NY 10271
(212) 941-7100 .. **Hornstein Palumbo & Keith** -350 Bway -NY 10013 **Fx:**941-7217
(212) 761-0157 .. **Hornstein,** Rebecca N '02 Morgan Stanley -1585 Bway -NY 10036
(212) 941-7100 .. **Hornstein,** Steven J '83 (Hornstein P&K) -350 Bway -NY 10013
(631) 845-2600 .. **Hornung,** Mary Stanton '92 %Morenus CG&B -58 S Srvc Rd -Melvll 11747
(212) 768-6700 .. **Hornung,** Meir S '07 %Sonnenschein N&R LLP -2 World Fncl Ctr -NY 10281
(212) 837-6000 .. **Hornung,** Stephan E '08 %Hughes H&R LLP -1 Bttry Pk Plz -NY 10004
(716) 885-3500 .. **Horohoe,** Kathleen E '93 %Flaherty & S -329 Elmwood Av -Buffalo 14222 **Fx:**885-3505
(718) 375-2755 .. **Horowitz,** Aimee F '86 -1782 E 2nd -Brklyn 11223
(212) 701-3000 .. **Horowitz,** Craig M '90 (Cahill G&R LLP) -80 Pine -NY 10005 **Fx:**269-5420
(212) 351-4000 .. **Horowitz,** Dan '10 Gibson D&C LLP -200 Park Av -NY 10166
(212) 684-3630 .. **Horowitz,** David '57 (D Horowitz,PC) -276 5th Av -NY 10001 **Fx:**685-8617
(212) 966-6668 .. **Horowitz,** David B '77 Fong & W,PC -254 Canal -NY 10013
(212) 695-6446 .. **Horowitz,** David Paul '88 OfCnsl Ressler & R -48 Wall -NY 10005 **Fx:**268-0287
(212) 337-8550 .. **Horowitz,** Davim L '06 Sylvia Rivera Law Proj -322 8th Av -NY 10001
(212) 701-3000 .. **Horowitz,** Douglas S '02 (Cahill G&R LLP) -80 Pine -NY 10005 **Fx:**269-5420
(212) 728-8000 .. **Horowitz,** Elizabeth K '07 %Willkie F&G LLP -787 7th Av -NY 10019
(516) 569-8399 .. **Horowitz,** Elliot S '79 -47 White Dr N -Cedarhrst 11516
(718) 250-2000 .. **Horowitz,** Emma '07 %DA -350 Jay -Brklyn 11201 **Fx:**250-2314
(212) 245-2222 .. **Horowitz,** Eric S '85 (Zane and R) -601 W 26th -NY 10001
(914) 472-7034 .. **Horowitz,** Fredric R '80 -6 Fountain Ter -Scarsdale 10583
(212) 455-2000 .. **Horowitz,** Gary I '82 (Simpson T&B LLP) -425 Lex Av -NY 10017
(212) 983-4141 .. **Horowitz,** Gary N '78 -400 Mad Av -NY 10017
(212) 715-9100 .. **Horowitz,** Gregory A '91 (Kramer LN&F,LLP) -1177 Av of Amer -NY 10036
(718) 339-1471 .. **Horowitz,** Harold A '77 -1424 E 19th -Brklyn 11230 **Fx:**339-1844
(212) 696-4848 .. **Horowitz,** Harvey J '67 OfCnsl Mintz & G LLP -470 Park Av S -NY 10016
(212) 816-5930 .. **Horowitz,** Hayden M '02 Salomon Smith Barney -388 Greenwich -NY 10013
(516) 921-2077 .. **Horowitz,** Hedy R '87 OfCnsl M Angiulo & Assoc LLC -6800 Jericho Tpk -Syosset 11791 **Fx:**921-1223
(212) 737-9590 .. **Horowitz,** Howard '93 -59 E 78th -NY 10075
(212) 371-2939 .. **Horowitz,** Ian G '98 Galleon Grp -590 Mad Av -NY 10022 **Fx:**371-0092
(516) 227-2140 .. **Horowitz,** Iris '92 -600 Old Cntry Rd -Gdn Cty 11530
(212) 756-2000 .. **Horowitz,** Jamie M '09 %Schulte R&Z LLP -919 3rd Av -NY 10022
(212) 272-2000 .. **Horowitz,** Jared T '05 JP Morgan Chase -383 Mad Av -NY 10179
(516) 228-1300 .. **Horowitz,** Jason B '08 %Sahn WC&B,PLLC -333 Earle Ovngton Blvd -Uniondale 11553
(212) 836-8000 .. **Horowitz,** Jeffrey H '01 (Kaye S LLP) -425 Park Av -NY 10022
(212) 351-4500 .. **Horowitz,** Jennifer M '99 %Epstein B&G,PC -250 Park Av -NY 10177
(212) 442-0589 .. **Horowitz,** Jerald '88 %Law Dept -100 Church -NY 10007 **Fx:**788-0367
(845) 634-3775 .. **Horowitz,** Joanne R '83 %Fellows H&E,PC -254 S Main -New Cty 10956
(212) 393-1000 .. **Horowitz,** Joel A '84 %Burns & H -233 Bway -NY 10279
(212) 878-7900 .. **Horowitz,** John D '01 (Fox R LLP) -100 Park Av -NY 10017
(212) 626-9399 .. **Horowitz,** Jonathan D '88 %Masterworks Dvlpmnt Corp -40 W 45th -NY 10036 **Fx:**391-5453
(212) 960-0051 .. **Horowitz,** Jos L '77 %Yeshiva Univ -500 W 185th -NY 10033 **Fx:**960-5346
(718) 237-0303 .. **Horowitz,** Joshua E '79 -356 Fulton -Brklyn 11201
(212) 661-2900 .. **Horowitz,** Kenneth P '88 (Kriss & F LLP) -360 Lex Av -NY 10017
(212) 696-6000 .. **Horowitz,** Kenneth S '93 %Curtis M-PC&M LLP -101 Park Av -NY 10178
(212) 836-8000 .. **Horowitz,** Larry E '96 %Kaye S LLP -425 Park Av -NY 10022
(914) 949-9663 .. **Horowitz,** Lawr S '87 -150 Grand -White Plns 10601 **Fx:**949-9447
(718) 838-7878 .. **Horowitz,** Leah A '07 Bronx Defenders -860 Crtlandt Av -Bronx 10451 **Fx:**665-0100
(646) 386-5700 .. **Horowitz,** Ledra H '05 %Civil Ct -111 Centre -NY 10013
(516) 695-0008 .. **Horowitz,** Lori E '86 -2921 Judith Dr -Bellmore 11710
(212) 599-3410 .. **Horowitz,** Louise S '82 -260 Mad Av -NY 10016 **Fx:**599-0405
(516) 773-3250 .. **Horowitz,** Mark M '77 -11 Grace Av -Gt Neck 11021
(212) 504-6407 .. **Horowitz,** Michl E '88 (Cadwalader W&T LLP) -1 World Fncl Ctr -NY 10281
(212) 248-4900 .. **Horowitz,** Michl M '83 (Dillon H&G LLP) -11 Hanover Sq -NY 10005
(212) 264-5916 .. **Horowitz,** Michl R '96 US DHS -26 Fed Plz -NY 10278
(914) 684-0551 .. **Horowitz,** Nathan '80 -1 Water -White Plns 10601
(718) 428-6868 .. **Horowitz,** Norman L '79 -38-50 Bell Blvd -Bayside 11361 **Fx:**423-5373
(914) 699-5637 .. **Horowitz,** Paul I '77 -22 W 1st -Mt Vernon 10550 **Fx:**667-5960
(212) 829-8196 .. **Horowitz,** Richd '97 -450 7th Av -NY 10123
(212) 698-3500 .. **Horowitz,** Richd I '86 (Dechert LLP) -1095 Av of Amer -NY 10036
(917) 438-1500 .. **Horowitz,** Richd M '83 Amer Arbitration Assn -20 W 20th -NY 10011
(516) 354-0200 .. **Horowitz,** Robt '56 (Horowitz T&S,PC) -2001 Marcus Av -Lk Success 11042
(212) 801-2194 .. **Horowitz,** Robt A '80 (Greenberg T,LLP) -200 Park Av -NY 10166
(212) 986-8400 .. **Horowitz,** Robt B '85 %Cooper Horowitz -51 E 42nd -NY 10017
(212) 589-4200 .. **Horowitz,** Robt B G '78 (Baker & H LLP) -45 Rckfllr Plz -NY 10111
(631) 390-7700 .. **Horowitz,** Ron J '86 -135 Pinelawn Rd -Melvll 11747
(718) 250-2000 .. **Horowitz,** Sarena Tamar '07 %DA -350 Jay -Brklyn 11201 **Fx:**250-2314
(845) 354-5460 .. **Horowitz,** Saul '94 -21 Rochelle Ln -Spg Vly 10977
(631) 777-5188 .. **Horowitz,** Seth R '90 Falconstor Software -2 Huntngtn Quadrangle -Melvll 11747 **Fx:**501-7633
(212) 269-7444 .. **Horowitz,** Stan G '99 %Cilmi & Assoc PLLC -39 Bway -NY 10006 **Fx:**269-3958
(212) 806-5400 .. **Horowitz,** Steven '84 (Stroock &S&L LLP) -180 Maiden Ln -NY 10038
(212) 867-6800 .. **Horowitz,** Steven '85 -295 Mad Av -NY 10017
(516) 873-2000 .. **Horowitz,** Steven A '85 SrCnsl Moritt HH&H LLP -400 Grdn City Plz -Gdn Cty 11530
(212) 792-7600 .. **Horowitz,** Steven A '98 Peak Cnsl Inc -25 W 31st -NY 10001
(212) 681-9600 .. **Horowitz,** Steven B '99 %Altman Grp -60 E 42nd -NY 10165
(212) 225-2000 .. **Horowitz,** Steven G '88 (Cleary GS&H) -1 Lbrty Plz -NY 10006
(212) 684-3630 .. **Horowitz,** Steven J '02 (D Horowitz,PC) -276 5th Av -NY 10001 **Fx:**685-8617
(516) 877-2900 .. **Horowitz,** Steven S '92 %Bartlett MB&M,LLP -300 Old Cntry Rd -Mineola 11501
(212) 527-8400 .. **Horowitz,** Suzanne L '99 %Oak Hill Cptl Ptnrs -65 E 55th -NY 10022 **Fx:**527-8450
(516) 354-0200 .. **Horowitz Tannenbaum & Silver, PC** -2001 Marcus Av -Lk Success 11042 **Fx:**354-1733
(212) 227-1500 .. **Horowitz,** Victor J '81 -305 Bway -NY 10007 **Fx:**(732) 572-7725
(718) 250-1100 .. **Horowitz,** Yosef E '04 %E Garfinkel -12 Metrotech Ctr -Brklyn 11201 **Fx:**250-1168
(212) 554-7800 .. **Horrocks,** Kerrie C '04 %Moses & S LLP -405 Lex Av -NY 10174
(212) 819-8200 .. **Horsch,** Richd A '81 (White & C LLP) -1155 Av of Amer -NY 10036
(212) 244-9500 .. **Horsfield,** Emily McNally '08 %White and W LLP -1 Penn Plz -NY 10119
(631) 286-7532 .. **Horsley,** Scott A '80 -42 Colonial Ln -Bellprt 11713
(212) 225-2000 .. **Horst,** Nathan T '10 %Cleary GS&H -1 Lbrty Plz -NY 10006
(518) 436-6000 .. **Horstmyer,** Ryan V '09 %Marsh Wassmermann & McHugh,LLC -677 Bway -Albany 12207 **Fx:**436-6009
(212) 431-0513 .. **Hort,** Peter L '98 -153 Hudson -NY 10013 **Fx:**966-8453
(914) 667-8863 .. **Horton,** Barbara Ann '83 -240 N Fulton Av -Mt Vernon 10552
(212) 574-1200 .. **Horton,** Edw S '01 (Seward & K LLP) -1 Bttry Pk Plz -NY 10004
(212) 617-6136 .. **Horton,** Erica B '08 Bloomberg LLP -731 Lex Av -NY 10022
(585) 343-4828 .. **Horton,** Gary A '76 -32 Mntclr Av -Batavia 14020 **Fx:**344-3929
(718) 250-4248 .. **Horton,** Gwyneth S '09 Leg Aid -111 Lvngstn -Brklyn 11201 **Fx:**250-4243
(212) 352-3220 .. **Horton,** Kenneth S '02 Amer Conference Inst -41 W 25th -NY 10010
(212) 373-3000 .. **Horton,** Lesley C '09 %Paul WRW&G LLP -1285 Av of Amer -NY 10019
(212) 264-6524 .. **Horton,** Meagen Sleeper '00 US Dept Homeland Security-Dist Cnsl Ofc -26 Fed Plz -NY 10278
(585) 338-3770 .. **Horton,** Ralph A '65 -1171 Titus Av -Rchstr 14617
(212) 918-3000 .. **Horton,** Scott G '03 %Hogan L LLP -875 3rd Av -NY 10022
(716) 856-0600 .. **Horton,** Scott P '06 %Jaeckle F&M,LLP -12 Fountain Plz -Buffalo 14202
(212) 894-7200 .. **Horton,** Wm B II '85 OfCnsl Entwistle & C LLP -280 Park Av -NY 10017
(212) 310-8000 .. **Horton,** Wm H Jr. '77 (Weil G&M LLP) -767 5th Av -NY 10153
(631) 369-2270 .. **Horvat,** Robt F '83 %J Ryan & Assoc -633 Main Rd -Rvrhead 11901
(212) 808-7800 .. **Horvath,** August T '97 SpclCnsl Kelley D&W LLP -101 Park Av -NY 10178
(646) 429-7500 .. **Horvath,** Fawn M '98 %Macys,Inc -11 Penn Plz -NY 10001 **Fx:**429-7521
(212) 389-8058 .. **Horvath,** James S '95 Collins Stewart LLC -350 Mad Av -NY 10017
(212) 250-2734 .. **Horvath,** Jeffrey T '96 Deutsche Bk Sec -60 Wall -NY 10005
(212) 446-5868 .. **Horvath,** Jordan A '87 Dvlpmnt Corp Israel -575 Lex Av -NY 10022 **Fx:**644-7102
(212) 315-7563 .. **Horvath,** Linda A '03 Wells Fargo Bank -40 W 57th -NY 10019
(716) 853-9555 .. **Horvatits,** Melissa J '07 Leg Aid -237 Main -Buffalo 14203 **Fx:**853-3219
(212) 682-2280 .. **Horwitz,** Abbey M '07 %Holm & O LLP -3 W 35th -NY 10001
(347) 296-1600 .. **Horwitz,** Carol H '90 %Hon R Velasquez -260 Adams -Brklyn 11201
(212) 812-8910 .. **Horwitz,** Danl J '91 (Lankler & C,LLP) -845 3rd Av -NY 10022
(212) 693-0085 .. **Horwitz,** Erica '78 %Appellate Advocates -2 Rector -NY 10006 **Fx:**693-0878
(212) 556-2100 .. **Horwitz,** Ethan '77 (King & S) -1185 Av of Amer -NY 10036
(212) 319-8500 .. **Horwitz,** Harry A '89 (Stevens & L PC) -485 Mad Av -NY 10022
(212) 986-4500 .. **Horwitz Horwitz & Paradis** -405 Lex Av -NY 10174 **Fx:**986-4501

(518) 826-1981 .. **Horwitz**, James D '82 Glens Falls Hsptl -100 Park -Glens Fls 12801 **Fx:**926-1988
(212) 969-3000 .. **Horwitz**, Jeffrey A '85 (Proskauer R LLP) -1585 Bway -NY 10036
(212) 463-2493 .. **Horwitz**, Lisa G '01 Saatchi & Saatchi -375 Hudson -NY 10014
(212) 479-6000 .. **Horwitz**, Lynn D '95 SpclCnsl Cooley LLP -1114 Av of Amer -NY 10036
(212) 310-8000 .. **Horwitz**, Maurice '08 %Weil G&M LLP -767 5th Av -NY 10153
(212) 558-4000 .. **Horwitz**, Michl D '05 %Sullivan & C LLP -125 Broad -NY 10004
(212) 644-1857 .. **Horwitz**, Michl S '83 (Horwitz & Z,PC) -250 W 57th -NY 10107 **Fx:**644-6553
(716) 838-4300 .. **Horwitz**, Morris L '75 (Bulan CH&I) -1320 Millersport Hwy -Williamsvll 14221 **Fx:**204-9728
(212) 962-5352 .. **Horwitz**, Neil M '81 (Schneider & H) -111 John -NY 10038 **Fx:**(646) 378-4410
(212) 691-0950 .. **Horwitz**, Rebecca A '09 %Ctr for Family Representation -116 John -NY 10038
(585) 264-0590 .. **Horwitz**, Richd J '70 -625 Panorama Trl Bldg 1 -Rchstr 14625 **Fx:**264-0277
(212) 373-3000 .. **Horwitz**, Seth J '10 %Paul WRW&G LLP -1285 Av of Amer -NY 10019
(212) 440-4300 .. **Horwitz**, Susan J '91 %Leg Aid -199 Water -NY 10038
(914) 479-0990 .. **Horwitz**, Wm E '98 -923 Saw Mill Rvr Rd -Ardsley 10502
(212) 265-6888 .. **Horwitz**, Wm R '94 Cnsl Porzio B&N,PC -156 W 56th -NY 10019
(212) 310-8000 .. **Horwitz**, Yosef Y '05 %Weil G&M LLP -767 5th Av -NY 10153
(212) 227-0347 .. **Horwitz-Bard**, Ronna L '94 %Weiss W&W,PC -25 Park Pl -NY 10007
(212) 522-5808 .. **Horwood**, Fredk C '95 %Time Inc -1271 Av of Amer -NY 10020 **Fx:**522-0437
(212) 553-0300 .. **Hosaka**, Miwako '06 Moodys -250 Greenwich -NY 10007
(212) 690-9787 .. **Ho-Sang**, Gwinett E '00 HRA -530 W 135th -NY 10031
(212) 593-6700 .. **Hosang**, Phillip W '98 %Aaronson RF&D,LLP -757 3rd Av -NY 10017
(212) 773-3000 .. **Hosbach**, Marguerette N '82 %Ernst & Young,LLP -5 Times Sq -NY 10036
(718) 384-9111 .. **Hoschander**, Abraham '93 -236 Bway -Brklyn 11211 **Fx:**384-5999
(212) 403-1000 .. **Hoschander**, Jeffrey D '07 %Wachtell LR&K -51 W 52nd -NY 10019
(518) 449-8893 .. **Hosford**, Matthew L '97 OfCnsl Wilson EME&D LLP -677 Bway -Albany 12207
(646) 619-1123 .. **Hoshovskyy**, Serhiy '02 -33 W 19th -NY 10011
(631) 509-1500 .. **Hosie-Kingham**, Nicola J '03 -4250 Vets Mem'l Hwy -Holbrook 11741
(914) 323-7000 .. **Ho Sing**, Elizabeth D '08 %Wilson EME&D LLP -3 Gannett Dr -White Plns 10604
(212) 888-3033 .. **Hosinski**, Peter Mitten '92 (Becker GM&M LLP) -299 Park Av -NY 10171
(585) 263-6201 .. **Hosken**, Mark D '82 %Fed Pub Def -28 E Main -Rchstr 14614 **Fx:**263-5871
(212) 257-6960 .. **Hosking**, James M '01 (Chaffetz L LLP) -1350 Av of Amer -NY 10019
(718) 468-2277 .. **Hoskins**, Debra A '80 -108-30 217th Pl -Jamaica 11429 **Fx:**479-3846
(212) 953-6000 .. **Hoskins**, Sharon T '00 %Katsky K LLP -605 3rd Av -NY 10158
(212) 728-8000 .. **Hosmane**, Ameesha N '06 %Willkie F&G LLP -787 7th Av -NY 10019
(212) 325-1283 .. **Hosmane**, Sunil R '03 Credit Suisse -11 Mad Av -NY 10010
(212) 735-3000 .. **Hosmer-Henner**, Adam D '09 %Skadden ASM&F LLP -4 Times Sq -NY 10036
(212) 242-2908 .. **Hossrich**, John '77 -67 8th Av -NY 10014
(212) 691-0950 .. **Host**, Michele E '01 Ctr for Family Representation -116 John -NY 10038 **Fx:**691-0951
(212) 833-3304 .. **Hostin**, Asuncion Cummings '03 Kroll -1166 Av of Amer -NY 10036
(212) 350-2646 .. **Hotai**, Jill Marie '98 Manufacturers & Trade -350 Park Av -NY 10022
(718) 596-9000 .. **Hotaling**, Marybeth '84 %Cohen HEP&T -25 Chapel -Brklyn 11201
(212) 577-2523 .. **Hoth**, Jan '88 %Ctr for Appllt Litigation -74 Trinity Pl -NY 10006 **Fx:**577-2535
(212) 757-0007 .. **Hotis**, Constantinos '07 %Scarola E LLP -888 7th Av -NY 10106
(631) 665-3400 .. **Hotis**, Peter D '90 %Siben & S,LLP -90 E Main Bx149P -Bay Shr 11706
(212) 274-6724 .. **Hotnit**, Carl E '84 %Admin Children's Srvcs -220 Church -NY 10013
(646) 394-6768 .. **Hott**, Douglas R '94 PricewaterhouseCoopers LLP -11 Mad Av -NY 10010
(516) 214-0196 .. **Hott**, Timothy R '80 -11 Summer Av -Gt Neck 11020 **Fx:**(631) 980-3650
(718) 428-9180 .. **Hotter**, Kevin J '06 %Rossi & C,LLP -42-24 235th -Douglastn 11363
(914) 665-2366 .. **Hottinger**, Loretta J '81 Law Dept -City Hall One Roosevelt Sq -Mt Vernon 10550 **Fx:**665-9142
(518) 474-8352 .. **Hotvet**, Martin A '71 %Dept of Law -The Cptl -Albany 12224
(212) 872-1000 .. **Hotz**, Robt H Jr. '93 -One Bryant Park -NY 10036 **Fx:**872-1002
(585) 232-5300 .. **Hou**, David K '00 %Boylan BCV&W,LLP -2400 Chase Sq -Rchstr 14604
(212) 225-2000 .. **Hou**, Victor L '98 (Cleary GS&H) -1 Lbrty Plz -NY 10006
(212) 552-0153 .. **Hou**, Xiaoyang '09 JP Morgan Chase -1 Chase Manh Plz -NY 10005
(212) 918-3000 .. **Houbouyan**, Johanne M '06 %Hogan L LLP -875 3rd Av -NY 10022
(212) 355-1600 .. **Houck**, Michelle Cappucine '98 Pzena Investment Mgmt -120 W 45th -NY 10036
(212) 878-3224 .. **Houck**, Robt G '97 %Clifford C LLP -31 W 52nd -NY 10019
(212) 779-9910 .. **Houck**, Rudolph S '72 (Eaton & V LLP) -3 Park Av -NY 10016
(212) 545-1900 .. **Houck**, Stephen D '73 Cnsl Menaker & H LLP -10 E 40th -NY 10016
(212) 548-7408 .. **Houck**, Thos R '04 Thomson West -530 5th Av -NY 10036
(585) 295-5776 .. **Houde**, Ardeth L '59 %Leg Aid -1 W Main -Rchstr 14614 **Fx:**232-2352
(212) 822-1470 .. **Houdek**, Dennis W '88 -305 Bway -NY 10007 **Fx:**822-1401
(516) 571-3056 .. **Houdek**, Jane M '89 %Cnty Atty -1 West -Mineola 11501 **Fx:**571-6604
(212) 261-8000 .. **Houdlett**, Ronald R '72 (Mendes & M,LLP) -750 7th Av -NY 10019
(212) 548-2100 .. **Hough**, Andrew R '03 (McGuire W LLP) -1345 Av of Amer -NY 10105
(212) 400-7177 .. **Hough**, Christopher K '80 %Garrity GMG&F -40 Wall -NY 10005
(212) 506-2500 .. **Hough**, Duane-David '86 (Mayer B LLP) -1675 Bway -NY 10019
(518) 785-1900 .. **Hough**, Elizabeth S '88 %PEF -1168-70 Troy-Schnctdy Rd Bx12414 -Albany 12212 **Fx:**785-1323
(212) 468-8000 .. **Hough**, James E '87 (Morrison & F LLP) -1290 Av of Amer -NY 10104
(716) 856-8200 .. **Houghtaling**, Julie Ann '97 %Williams & W -43 Court -Buffalo 14202 **Fx:**856-0559
(212) 397-3370 .. **Houghteling**, Charlotte Waisbren '08 (Harris CC&H LLP) -111 Bway -NY 10006 **Fx:**202-6206
(212) 526-1012 .. **Houghtlin**, James G '04 Barclays Capital -745 7th Av -NY 10019 **Fx:**(646) 758-1348
(212) 422-0202 .. **Houghton**, Andrew T '89 (Sedgwick DM&A LLP) -125 Broad -NY 10004
(212) 422-4000 .. **Houghton**, Jonathan M '99 (Goldstein R&R) -80 Pine -NY 10005
(914) 640-1861 .. **Houghton**, Kerry J '94 Starwood Hotels & Resorts -1111 Wnchstr Av -West Harrison 10604
(212) 763-5000 .. **Houk**, Diane L '05 OfCnsl Emery CB&A LLP -75 Rckfllr Plz -NY 10019
(212) 682-0020 .. **Houlihan**, Christopher M '76 (Putney TH&H LLP) -521 5th Av -NY 10175
(212) 506-2500 .. **Houpt**, Christopher J '07 %Mayer B LLP -1675 Bway -NY 10019
(212) 983-8500 .. **Hourican**, Timothy G '93 (Brown G&F LLP) -355 Lex Av -NY 10017
(585) 362-4700 .. **Hourihan**, Edw P Jr. '91 (Bond S&K,PLLC) -350 Linden Oaks -Rchstr 14625
(716) 515-8164 .. **Hourihan**, Kevin W '00 -20 Curley Dr -Orchard Pk 14127 **Fx:**662-0192
(212) 572-6222 .. **Hourihan**, Michl T '81 %Greenfield Manh Prop -300 Park Av -NY 10022
(718) 875-1300 .. **House**, David A '05 %Appllt Div 2nd Dept -45 Monroe Pl -Brklyn 11201 **Fx:**858-2446
(212) 521-5400 .. **House**, Jeffrey C '93 %Reed S LLP -599 Lex Av -NY 10022
(718) 875-1300 .. **House**, Lorien L '06 Appllt Div 2nd Dept -45 Monroe Pl -Brklyn 11201 **Fx:**858-2446
(518) 474-7131 .. **House**, Mary E '85 %Dept of Law -The Cptl -Albany 12224
(212) 918-3000 .. **House**, Theresa M '08 %Hogan L LLP -875 3rd Av -NY 10022
(212) 696-9898 .. **House**, Wm C '86 -170 Bway -NY 10038 **Fx:**696-9150
(585) 428-1893 .. **Housel**, Jessica Birkahn '03 %Hon J Winslow -545 Hall of Justice -Rchstr 14614
(212) 354-5048 .. **Housenbold**, Allison B '98 (Housenbold & H PLLC) -733 3rd Av -NY 10017 **Fx:**354-5055
(212) 354-5048 .. **Housenbold**, Scott R '99 (Housenbold & H PLLC) -733 3rd Av -NY 10017 **Fx:**354-5055
(631) 712-6344 .. **Houser**, Jeffrey D '00 %US Dept of Probation -Bx9012 -Central Islip 11722
(212) 768-6700 .. **Housey**, Paul J '94 (Sonnenschein N&R LLP) -2 World Fncl Ctr -NY 10281
(716) 881-3010 .. **Housh**, Frank T '94 %Cohen & L,PC -343 Elmwood Av Bx5204 -Buffalo 14213
(631) 427-1140 .. **Houslanger**, Todd E '89 (Houslanger & Assoc,PLLC) -372 NY Av -Huntngtn 11743 **Fx:**427-1143 ***[Collection Law]***
(631) 427-1140 .. **Houslanger**, Wm '48 SrCnsl Houslanger & Assoc,PLLC -372 NY Av -Huntngtn 11743 **Fx:**427-1143
(212) 846-3945 .. **Housley**, Michl L '07 Viacom -1515 Bway -NY 10036
(718) 720-6812 .. **Housman**, Anayancy Riley '97 -10 Bayview Pl -Staten Isl 10304
(914) 524-8500 .. **Housman**, Mark E '84 (Housman & Assoc,PC) -150 Wht Plns Rd -Tarrytwn 10591
(212) 403-1000 .. **Houston**, Andrew C '85 (Wachtell LR&K) -51 W 52nd -NY 10019
(212) 668-5663 .. **Houston**, Brent M '03 Hon B Lifland -1 Bowling Grn -NY 10004
(212) 728-8000 .. **Houston**, Carolyn S '09 %Willkie F&G LLP -787 7th Av -NY 10019
(631) 853-5212 .. **Houston**, Lani E '05 %Leg Aid -400 Carleton Av Bx9082 -Central Islip 11722 **Fx:**853-7798
(845) 326-5662 .. **Houston**, Matthew D '90 Balchem Corp -52 Sunrise Park Rd -New Hampton 10958
(212) 935-7400 .. **Houston**, Matthew M '92 (Harwood F LLP) -488 Mad Av -NY 10022
(518) 861-7246 .. **Hout**, Rebecca Morse '78 -161 Maple Av Bx528 -Altamont 12009 **Fx:**861-7246
(212) 436-1096 .. **Houtchens**, Kathryn '90 %IRS -290 Bway -NY 10007 **Fx:**436-1063
(518) 487-7600 .. **Hovancik**, Damian M '88 (Whiteman O&H LLP) -1 Commerce Plz -Albany 12260
(631) 852-2500 .. **Hovani**, Steven A '74 %DA -200 Center Dr -Rvrhead 11901 **Fx:**852-1769
(212) 248-3140 .. **Hovanyetz**, Scott A '09 %Drinker B&R LLP -140 Bway -NY 10005
(212) 940-8800 .. **Hovden**, Jeffrey A '94 (Katten MR LLP) -575 Mad Av -NY 10022
(631) 234-5678 .. **Hove**, David J '94 %Wallace WF&V,PC -600 Suffolk Av -Brentwd 11717
(518) 474-7330 .. **Hove**, Yvonne M '97 %Dept of Law -The Cptl -Albany 12224
(315) 422-1391 .. **Hoveman**, Virginia A '86 (Green & S,PLLC) -One Lincoln Ctr #900 -Syracuse 13202
(518) 935-0935 .. **Hover**, Jason S '07 -420 Warren -Hudson 12534 **Fx:**828-0944
(212) 592-1400 .. **Hoverkamp**, Toni J '06 %Herrick,F LLP -2 Park Av -NY 10016
(212) 821-6980 .. **Hoverman**, Danl S '04 UBS Investment Bk -299 Park Av -NY 10171
(732) 855-6196 .. **Hovey**, Keith L '05 %Wilentz G&S -110 William -NY 10038 **Fx:**726-6576
(716) 285-9338 .. **Hovey & Massaro** -631 Main -Niagara Fls 14301 **Fx:**285-0908
(914) 686-4800 .. **Howansky**, I Paul '98 (Harrington O&M,LLP) -81 Main -White Plns 10601
(212) 259-8000 .. **Howard**, Alan B '88 (Dewey & L LLP) -1301 Av of Amer -NY 10019
(518) 828-2021 .. **Howard**, Andrew B '95 (Freeman H,PC) -441 E Allen Bx1328 -Hudson 12534 **Fx:**828-2420
(716) 824-1021 .. **Howard**, Anita L '04 -2100 Seneca -Buffalo 14210 **Fx:**852-5441
(716) 852-5430 .. **Howard**, Anita L '04 -110 Pearl -Buffalo 14202 **Fx:**852-5441
(718) 746-0087 .. **Howard**, Brian J '00 Cnsl Glaceau -1720 Whitestone Expy -Whitestone 11357
(212) 637-3216 .. **Howard**, Carl R '87 %EPA -290 Bway -NY 10007 **Fx:**637-3096
(212) 559-2938 .. **Howard**, Carl V '88 Citibank NA -425 Park Av -NY 10043 **Fx:**793-4400
(212) 415-8600 .. **Howard**, Casey B '05 %Locke LB&L LLP -3 World Fncl Ctr -NY 10281
(212) 415-9200 .. **Howard**, Cecilie '07 %Dorsey & W LLP -250 Park Av -NY 10177

(212) 504-6000 .. **Howard,** Cheryl L '07 %Cadwalader W&T LLP -1 World Fncl Ctr -NY 10281
(917) 446-9830 .. **Howard,** Cheryl R '83 -539 W 217th -NY 10034 **Fx:**(212) 569-1163
(516) 987-9188 .. **Howard,** Clark E '80 -199 Water -NY 10038
(212) 450-4000 .. **Howard,** Courtney A '07 %Davis P&W LLP -450 Lex Av -NY 10017
(212) 619-5400 .. **Howard,** Damon P '07 %Newman F LLP -1250 Bway -NY 10001
(212) 307-5100 .. **Howard,** Danl A '07 %McElfish & Assoc,LLC -350 5th Av -NY 10118 **Fx:**307-5200
(516) 747-4343 .. **Howard,** Danl R '10 %JP DiMascio & Assoc,LLP -300 Grdn City Plz -Gdn Cty 11530 **Fx:**747-0204
(718) 565-4309 .. **Howard,** David C '86 %NY Mets -Shea Stadium -Flushng 11368 **Fx:**565-4382
(718) 286-6000 .. **Howard,** Denise G '74 %DA -125-01 Qns Blvd -Kew Gdns 11415
(212) 633-1777 .. **Howard,** Douglas A '85 (D Howard,PC) -511 Av of Amer -NY 10011 **Fx:**633-1773
(585) 271-8190 .. **Howard,** Frank J '98 -1441 East Av -Rchstr 14610
(212) 475-2763 .. **Howard,** Frederic K '71 -420 E 23rd -NY 10010 **Fx:**(646) 414-7973
(516) 364-6444 .. **Howard,** Gina '98 (Navaretta & H,LLP) -567 Jericho Tpk -Syosset 11791 **Fx:**364-5005
(914) 765-6366 .. **Howard,** Gloria D '95 IBM -N Castle Dr -Armonk 10504
(914) 328-0366 .. **Howard,** Ingrid A '08 %Sapir & F LLP -399 Knollwood Rd -White Plns 10603
(212) 806-5400 .. **Howard,** Janine '02 %Stroock &S&L LLP -180 Maiden Ln -NY 10038
(914) 681-4437 .. **Howard,** Jay M '70 %AC Israel Entrprs -707 Wstchstr Av -White Plns 10604 **Fx:**681-0856
(516) 829-0363 .. **Howard,** Jennifer Greenhalgh '99 %Israel I&P,LLP -11 Grace Av -Gt Neck 11021 **Fx:**829-0366
(518) 426-4600 .. **Howard,** Joel M III '72 (Couch W,LLP) -540 Bway Bx22222 -Albany 12201
(212) 608-8840 .. **Howard,** John A '00 %Bamundo Z&S,LLP -111 John -NY 10038
(212) 358-1500 .. **Howard,** John R '08 %Kennedy J&M,PC -113 Univ Pl -NY 10003
(646) 386-5700 .. **Howard,** Juliet Pearl '93 %Civil Ct -111 Centre -NY 10013
(212) 879-5500 .. **Howard,** Kirstie M '04 %Metropolitan Museum -1000 5th Av -NY 10028 **Fx:**570-3850
(212) 450-4000 .. **Howard,** Lauren M '10 %Davis P&W LLP -450 Lex Av -NY 10017
(518) 674-3766 .. **Howard,** Lawr E '96 -17 Old Route 66 Bx1000 -Averill Pk 12018 **Fx:**674-3964
(585) 786-0220 .. **Howard,** Lawr M '83 -Bx386 -Warsaw 14569
(917) 650-9262 .. **Howard,** Linda G '81 -340 E 93rd -NY 10128 **Fx:**(212) 722-3692
(631) 361-9494 .. **Howard,** M Angela '79 -732 Smithtwn Bypass -Smithtwn 11787 **Fx:**361-8752
(212) 225-2000 .. **Howard,** Matthew W '05 %Cleary GS&H -1 Lbrty Plz -NY 10006
(516) 877-6146 .. **Howard,** Maura A '03 -114 Old Cntry Rd -Mineola 11501 **Fx:**877-6162
(914) 693-3798 .. **Howard,** Maxine D '85 -11 Rockrdg Rd -Ardsley 10502 **Fx:**693-5580
(585) 232-5300 .. **Howard,** Michl A '80 (Boylan BCV&W,LLP) -2400 Chase Sq -Rchstr 14604
(518) 828-6110 .. **Howard,** Michl C '92 (M Howard,PC) -118 Green Bx642 -Hudson 12534 **Fx:**828-6113
(516) 496-3156 .. **Howard,** Michl H '77 -2 Aron Dr -Woodbury 11797 **Fx:**921-4853
(516) 227-0700 .. **Howard,** Nicole S '08 %Farrell F,PC -1320 RXR Plz -Uniondale 11556
(212) 841-1000 .. **Howard,** Nigel L '93 (Covington & B LLP) -620 8th Av -NY 10018
(914) 683-1333 .. **Howard,** Pamela '88 -1 Water -White Plns 10601
(212) 841-1000 .. **Howard,** Philip K '75 (Covington & B LLP) -620 8th Av -NY 10018
(718) 951-6880 .. **Howard,** Randolph M '84 -1176 E 51st -Brklyn 11234
(516) 747-0300 .. **Howard,** Richd M '80 (Meltzer LG&B,LLP) -190 Willis Av -Mineola 11501
(212) 944-0500 .. **Howard,** Robt D '65 (Hofheimer G&G,LLP) -530 5th Av -NY 10036 **Fx:**897-4984
(516) 747-7400 .. **Howard,** Robt J '99 %Rosenberg C&B LLP -100 Grdn City Plz -Gdn Cty 11530
(631) 723-1100 .. **Howard,** Robt Kendall '90 -103 W Montauk Hwy -Hampton Bays 11946 **Fx:**723-1102
(212) 333-4243 .. **Howard,** Robt L '72 -119 W 57th -NY 10019
(212) 336-2000 .. **Howard,** Scott B '94 (Patterson BW&T LLP) -1133 Av of Amer -NY 10036
(718) 477-2479 .. **Howard,** Steven P '73 -23 Morse Av -Staten Isl 10314
(917) 777-4200 .. **Howard,** Steven R '83 (Bingham M LLP) -1 Bttry Pk Plz -NY 10004
(212) 373-3000 .. **Howard,** Susannah K '09 %Paul WRW&G LLP -1285 Av of Amer -NY 10019
(212) 787-2380 .. **Howard,** Theo P '98 -313 W 71st -NY 10023
(585) 768-8181 .. **Howard,** Theron E '79 -15 Clay Bx250 -Le Roy 14482 **Fx:**768-8248
(212) 248-2936 .. **Howard,** Thos S '78 (Kirsch GH LLP) -11 Penn Plz -NY 10001
(212) 259-8000 .. **Howard-Potter,** Erica B '08 %Dewey & L LLP -1301 Av of Amer -NY 10019
(212) 400-2424 .. **Howarth,** Glenn S '77 J&W Mgmt Corp -505 Park Av -NY 10022 **Fx:**400-2425
(631) 499-5400 .. **Howarth,** Janeen M '01 %Smith CL PC -5036 Jericho Tpk Bx49 -Commack 11725
(212) 858-7575 .. **Howarth,** John S '00 (Wilbraham L&B PC) -140 Bway -NY 10005
(212) 310-8000 .. **Howatt,** Matthew E K '09 %Weil G&M LLP -767 5th Av -NY 10153
(716) 373-2260 .. **Howden,** M Mark '92 -615-616 Community Bk Bldg -Olean 14760
(212) 250-0415 .. **Howe,** Anne B '91 %Deutsche Bank -60 Wall -NY 10005
(845) 624-7474 .. **Howe,** David '85 D Howe PC -250 W Nyack Rd -W Nyack 10994 **Fx:**624-1946
(212) 986-7888 .. **Howe,** David D '83 -747 3rd Av -NY 10017
(315) 477-9900 .. **Howe,** David S '72 (Porter NH LLP) -316 S Clinton -Syracuse 13202 **Fx:**477-9923
(718) 760-6746 .. **Howe,** Deborah '02 %Dept of Parks & Rec -Olmsted Ctr -Flushng 11368 **Fx:**760-6730
(212) 891-8420 .. **Howe,** Gabrielle S '01 %Mitsubishi UFJ -520 Mad Av -NY 10022 **Fx:**593-4691
(585) 325-7515 .. **Howe,** Gordon A II '66 (Forsyth HOK&M,PC) -1 Chase Sq -Rchstr 14604
(212) 715-1348 .. **Howe,** J Cullen '00 -399 Park Av -NY 10022
(607) 753-5008 .. **Howe,** Karen L '90 %DA -46 Greenbush -Cortlnd 13045 **Fx:**756-3477
(315) 655-3505 .. **Howe,** Larry M '75 -3893 Pompey Hllw Rd -Cazenovia 13035
(212) 504-6000 .. **Howe,** Mark P '87 (Cadwalader W&T LLP) -1 World Fncl Ctr -NY 10281
(212) 589-4200 .. **Howe,** Mary E '09 %Baker & H LLP -45 Rckfllr Plz -NY 10111
(212) 558-4000 .. **Howe,** Richd R '68 (Sullivan & C LLP) -125 Broad -NY 10004
(718) 748-9700 .. **Howe,** Robt L '81 -251 86th -Brklyn 11209 **Fx:**630-5279
(718) 909-9415 .. **Howell,** Annamatesha N '00 -185 Merrick Rd -Lynbrk 11563
(631) 844-7027 .. **Howell,** Diane S '97 Adecco Inc -175 Broadhllw Rd -Melvll 11747
(212) 309-1000 .. **Howell,** George C III '08 (Hunton & W) -200 Park Av -NY 10166
(877) 499-5111 .. **Howell,** Jacqueline N '04 AllHipHop.com -244 5th Av -NY 10001
(212) 770-7970 .. **Howell,** Joanne Moore '89 %AIG -70 Pine -NY 10270
(212) 998-6550 .. **Howell,** Katharine M '94 %NYU Law Schl -245 Sullivan -NY 10012
(718) 643-4546 .. **Howell,** Marilyn H '84 %Hon B Staton -283 Adams -Brklyn 11201
(212) 809-7800 .. **Howell,** Melnia '04 %Jaffe & K,LLP -40 Wall -NY 10005
(212) 848-4000 .. **Howell,** Paula M '02 %Shearman & S LLP -599 Lex Av -NY 10022
(718) 579-3000 .. **Howell,** Saml A '94 %Leg Aid -1020 Grnd Cncrs -Bronx 10451 **Fx:**588-2611
(212) 701-3000 .. **Howell,** Timothy '04 %Cahill G&R LLP -80 Pine -NY 10005 **Fx:**269-5420
(212) 351-4000 .. **Howell,** Wesley G '84 (Gibson D&C LLP) -200 Park Av -NY 10166
(212) 956-2600 .. **Howell,** Wm R '86 %Greystone & Co -152 W 57th -NY 10019 **Fx:**956-2244
(516) 747-6300 .. **Hower,** Jennifer '06 %Koeppel M&L,LLP -155 First Bx863 -Mineola 11501
(212) 547-5400 .. **Howes,** B Ted '92 (McDermott W&E LLP) -340 Mad Av -NY 10173
(212) 268-2665 .. **Howfield,** Martin M '04 %Sinel & Assoc,PLLC -7 Penn Plz -NY 10001 **Fx:**268-6250
(212) 474-1000 .. **Howick,** Marie Davies '10 %Cravath S&M LLP -825 8th Av -NY 10019
(631) 654-5942 .. **Howie,** Barbara K '95 (Howie & H) -61 Rose Av Bx271 -Patchogue 11772
(631) 654-5942 .. **Howie,** Donald L W '87 (Howie & H) -61 Rose Av Bx271 -Patchogue 11772
(212) 355-7332 .. **Howitt,** Idelle A '83 Howitt & Assoc -2 Sutton Pl S -NY 10022 **Fx:**355-5255
(212) 878-8000 .. **Howitt,** John P '88 (Clifford C LLP) -31 W 52nd -NY 10019
(212) 220-3000 .. **Howland-Kruse,** Kerri '91 %Broadcast Music Inc -250 Greenwich -NY 10007
(631) 661-4305 .. **Howlett,** Patricia '91 -22 Evelyn Rd -W Islip 11795
(212) 438-2000 .. **Howley,** Christopher P '94 Standard & Poor's -55 Water -NY 10041
(845) 486-2300 .. **Howley,** Francis X '97 %DA -236 Main -Poughkeepsie 12601 **Fx:**486-2324
(718) 945-2700 .. **Howley,** John J '57 -204 Beach 116th Bx940008 -Rckwy Pk 11694
(212) 909-6000 .. **Howley,** Lisa '04 %Debevoise & P LLP -919 3rd Av -NY 10022
(518) 565-4715 .. **Howley,** Michl J '80 %Supreme Ct -36 Clinton -Plattsbrgh 12901 **Fx:**565-4708
(212) 896-6500 .. **Howrey LLP** -601 Lex Av -NY 10022 **Fx:**896-6501
(518) 828-3410 .. **Howser,** Jessica D '02 %Pub Def -610 State -Hudson 12534 **Fx:**828-4076
(914) 238-5465 .. **Howson,** John A '61 -3 Sunset Dr -Chappaqua 10514 **Fx:**238-5465
(212) 675-0849 .. **Hoy,** Justin E Jr. '72 -433 W 21st -NY 10011
(585) 232-6500 .. **Hoy,** Wm A '04 (Harter S&E LLP) -1600 Bausch & Lomb Pl -Rchstr 14604
(718) 330-1200 .. **Hoyes,** Lisa E '00 %Fed Def of NY Inc -1 Pierrepont Plz -Brklyn 11201 **Fx:**855-0760
(212) 493-7484 .. **Hoylman,** Brad M '97 %NYC Partnership -1 Bttry Pk Plz -NY 10004
(212) 837-6000 .. **Hoyns,** John K '80 (Hughes H&R LLP) -1 Bttry Pk Plz -NY 10004
(212) 643-0550 .. **Hoyt,** Christopher W '01 (Hoyt Law Grp,LLC) -350 5th Av -NY 10118 **Fx:**643-0551
(212) 850-2800 .. **Hoyt,** David J '94 %Andrews K LLP -450 Lex Av -NY 10017
(845) 339-4000 .. **Hoyt,** Jonathan C '94 -326 Wall -Kingston 12401
(518) 883-4816 .. **Hoyt,** Kelly D '97 (Hoyt & P) -3734 State Hwy 30 Bx1119 -Broadalbin 12025
(585) 454-7145 .. **Hoyt,** Kevin C '03 %Gallo & I,LLP -39 State -Rchstr 14614
(518) 883-4816 .. **Hoyt & Preston** -3734 State Hwy 30 Bx1119 -Broadalbin 12025 **Fx:**883-3096
(845) 778-1800 .. **Hoyt,** Richd W '85 -43 Orchrd Bx402 -Walden 12586 **Fx:**778-1859
(212) 613-5075 .. **Hozer,** Amy R '04 Leg Assistance Grp -450 W 33rd -NY 10001
(315) 471-8111 .. **Hrab,** Michl J '85 (Scolaro SCF&B,PC) -507 Plum -Syracuse 13204
(315) 788-5900 .. **Hrabchak Gebo & Langone,PC** -216 Wshngtn -Watertwn 13601 **Fx:**788-6085
(973) 596-4995 .. **Hradil,** Jennifer A '98 (Gibbons PC) -1 Penn Plz -NY 10119 **Fx:**639-6487
(212) 698-3500 .. **Hranitzky,** Dennis H '96 Cnsl Dechert LLP -1095 Av of Amer -NY 10036
(718) 855-9000 .. **Hrankiwskyj,** Michl G '07 %Cullen and D LLP -177 Montague -Brklyn 11201
(212) 480-2400 .. **Hrbek,** Deborah L '93 (Hrbek Law LLC) -225 Bway -NY 10007 **Fx:**(646) 478-9490
(845) 246-9596 .. **Hrdlicka,** Albert F '71 (Schirmer H&S) -110 Market Bx240 -Saugerties 12477
(212) 688-5055 .. **Hrdy,** Veronica L '79 Chanel Inc -9 W 57th -NY 10019 **Fx:**303-5979
(718) 932-7070 .. **Hrisikopoulos,** George M '04 -3089 42nd -Astoria 11103
(718) 250-2000 .. **Hristova,** Linda S '10 %DA -350 Jay -Brklyn 11201 **Fx:**250-2314
(212) 918-3000 .. **Hritz,** George F '74 (Hogan L LLP) -875 3rd Av -NY 10022
(212) 275-4995 .. **Hrivnak,** Tamara '02 %Warner Music Grp -75 Rckfllr Plz -NY 10019 **Fx:**489-3342
(212) 682-1818 .. **Hromadkova,** Eva '05 %Murray F&S LLP -275 Mad Av -NY 10016
(212) 416-8658 .. **Hronsky,** Rosalie J '83 %Dept of Law -120 Bway -NY 10271
(212) 474-1000 .. **Hruska,** Alan J '59 SrCnsl Cravath S&M LLP -825 8th Av -NY 10019
(212) 556-2100 .. **Hruska,** Andrew C '95 (King & S) -1185 Av of Amer -NY 10036
(212) 318-6000 .. **Hryb,** Deborah E '08 %Paul HJ&W LLP -75 E 55th -NY 10022
(212) 335-4500 .. **Hryck,** David M '02 (DLA Piper LLP) -1251 Av of Amer -NY 10020
(516) 393-2200 .. **Hsi,** Jason Y '06 %Garfunkel W,PC -111 Grt Nck Rd -Gt Neck 11021
(212) 450-4000 .. **Hsi,** Tabea Y '08 %Davis P&W LLP -450 Lex Av -NY 10017
(516) 542-5900 .. **Hsia,** Richd C '75 (Congdon FORDT&F) -333 Earle Ovngton Blvd -Uniondale 11553
(516) 750-9464 .. **Hsia,** Richd C '75 Wright Risk Mgmt -333 Earle Ovngton Blvd -Uniondale 11553
(212) 530-1800 .. **Hsieh,** Jenny '01 %Richards K&O LLP -1 World Fncl Ctr -NY 10281
(212) 736-1940 .. **Hsieh,** Stephanie '93 Cnsl Davidson D&K LLC -485 7th Av -NY 10018

(212) 836-8000 .. **Hsing,** Benjamin C '92 (Kaye S LLP) -425 Park Av -NY 10022
(212) 227-0066 .. **Hsiung,** Ann '84 -7 Chatham Sq -NY 10038 **Fx:**267-3028
(718) 250-2000 .. **Hsiung,** Mara '09 %DA -350 Jay -Brklyn 11201 **Fx:**250-2314
(212) 872-1000 .. **Hsu,** Alice '05 -One Bryant Park -NY 10036 **Fx:**872-1002
(585) 461-3518 .. **Hsu,** Alice H '00 Deluxe Intl Lawyers -877 Harvard -Rchstr 14610
(212) 735-3000 .. **Hsu,** Angie Yen-Chi '00 %Skadden ASM&F LLP -4 Times Sq -NY 10036
(212) 841-3979 .. **Hsu,** Annie '08 BNP Paribas -787 7th Av -NY 10019
(718) 330-7731 .. **Hsu,** Annie L '07 NLRB -2 Metrotech Ctr -Brklyn 11201 **Fx:**330-7579
(212) 788-1312 .. **Hsu,** Carol J '01 %Law Dept -100 Church -NY 10007 **Fx:**788-0367
(212) 755-3333 .. **Hsu,** Doris S '96 SC Ruchelman -150 E 58th -NY 10155 **Fx:**755-5898
(212) 909-6000 .. **Hsu,** Emilie Tien-Jung '99 Cnsl Debevoise & P LLP -919 3rd Av -NY 10022
(914) 323-7000 .. **Hsu,** John A '04 %Wilson EME&D LLP -3 Gannett Dr -White Plns 10604
(212) 373-3000 .. **Hsu,** Josh M '06 %Paul WRW&G LLP -1285 Av of Amer -NY 10019
(212) 490-3285 .. **Hsu,** Lynn Y '07 %Tiajoloff & K -405 Lex Av -NY 10174 **Fx:**490-3295
(212) 506-1700 .. **Hsu,** Mark K '97 SpclCnsl Kasowitz BT&F LLP -1633 Bway -NY 10019
(212) 925-7700 .. **Hsu,** Yung H '92 -168 Canal -NY 10013
(914) 251-0001 .. **Hsuan,** Abraham B '92 OfCnsl Lane S&L LLP -106 Corp Park Dr -White Plns 10604
(917) 573-2140 .. **Hsueh,** Francis K '03 -48 Allen -NY 10002
(212) 815-1450 .. **Hsueh,** Kim '98 %DC 37 Gen Cnsl -125 Barclay -NY 10007 **Fx:**815-1440
(845) 452-2366 .. **Htoo,** Susan S '81 -290 Hooker Av -Poughkeepsie 12603 **Fx:**485-2771
(212) 277-6500 .. **Hu,** Christopher K '75 (Dickstein S LLP) -1633 Bway -NY 10019
(212) 373-3000 .. **Hu,** Da-Wai '03 Cnsl Paul WRW&G LLP -1285 Av of Amer -NY 10019
(212) 558-4000 .. **Hu,** Ellen C '08 %Sullivan & C LLP -125 Broad -NY 10004
(212) 715-9100 .. **Hu,** Geoffrey G '07 %Kramer LN&F,LLP -1177 Av of Amer -NY 10036
(212) 898-1103 .. **Hu,** Huping '99 -25 Lubber -Stony Brk 11790 **Fx:**898-1103
(718) 539-6216 .. **Hu,** Jee-Min '84 -142-05 Roosevelt Av -Flushng 11354
(212) 318-3000 .. **Hu,** Jianjie '09 %Fulbright & J LLP -666 5th Av -NY 10103
(718) 436-6140 .. **Hu,** Jin '01 J Hu & Assoc,PLLC -305 Bway -NY 10007 **Fx:**436-6137
(212) 448-1100 .. **Hu,** Qian '08 %McLaughlin & S,LLP -260 Mad Av -NY 10016
(212) 916-7863 .. **Hu,** Wen-Chi '94 Rabobank Intl -245 Park Av -NY 10167
(212) 935-3101 .. **Hu,** Xiaoying '07 Bk of China -410 Mad Av -NY 10017
(212) 334-2393 .. **Hua,** Chungmi '06 (Hua & M,LLP) -350 Bway -NY 10013
(212) 878-8000 .. **Hua,** Jennifer N '09 %Clifford C LLP -31 W 52nd -NY 10019
(212) 816-1756 .. **Hua,** Lun '03 Citigroup -388 Greenwich -NY 10013
(212) 358-9516 .. **Hua,** Sanny Boi '01 Company Agenda -648 Bway -NY 10012
(212) 225-2000 .. **Huang,** Angela C '09 %Cleary GS&H -1 Lbrty Plz -NY 10006
(212) 218-2100 .. **Huang,** Anna Y '08 %Fitzpatrick CH&S -1290 Av of Amer -NY 10104
(212) 358-9690 .. **Huang,** Betty '07 %N Datta -237 1st Av -NY 10003 **Fx:**358-1916
(718) 546-0950 .. **Huang,** Bin-Bin K '95 Dept of Correction -75-20 Astoria Blvd -E Elmhrst 11370
(212) 218-2100 .. **Huang,** Cheney H '10 %Fitzpatrick CH&S -1290 Av of Amer -NY 10104
(212) 969-3000 .. **Huang,** Chieh Erh '09 %Proskauer R LLP -1585 Bway -NY 10036
(212) 608-1800 .. **Huang,** Chiung-Hui '00 %Kuzmin & Assoc -225 Bway -NY 10007
(516) 466-1401 .. **Huang,** Elisha '08 %Bai & S -505 Nrthrn Blvd -Gt Neck 11021
(212) 849-7000 .. **Huang,** Eric '98 %Quinn EU&S,LLP -51 Mad Av -NY 10010
(212) 446-4800 .. **Huang,** Helena Chunghuang '01 (Kirkland & E LLP) -153 E 53rd -NY 10022
(212) 728-8000 .. **Huang,** Huang '03 %Willkie F&G LLP -787 7th Av -NY 10019
(212) 578-2211 .. **Huang,** James Pei-Yuen '00 %MetLife -27-01 Qns Plz N -LIC 11101
(212) 922-0450 .. **Huang,** Jennifer '04 %Kaplan M&A,LLC -70 E 55th -NY 10022
(212) 440-7717 .. **Huang,** Jerome C '01 CNA Global Specialty Lines -40 Wall -NY 10005
(718) 321-2911 .. **Huang,** Jin '05 -3609 Main -Flushng 11354
(212) 373-3000 .. **Huang,** Joyce Szuyun '95 (Paul WRW&G LLP) -1285 Av of Amer -NY 10019
(718) 250-2000 .. **Huang,** Melody C '00 %DA -350 Jay -Brklyn 11201 **Fx:**250-2314
(212) 446-2300 .. **Huang,** Mike F '03 %Boies S&F LLP -575 Lex Av -NY 10022
(718) 590-2000 .. **Huang,** Monica C '09 %DA -198 E 161st -Bronx 10451 **Fx:**590-6477
(718) 590-2000 .. **Huang,** Samson '08 %DA -198 E 161st -Bronx 10451 **Fx:**590-6477
(212) 636-5854 .. **Huang,** Sharon Ting '99 %Child Fndtn -1325 6th Av -NY 10019
(646) 473-6040 .. **Huang,** Sonja N '06 %1199SEIU Funds -330 W 42nd -NY 10036
(212) 761-7872 .. **Huang,** Susan Siu-Chin '91 Morgan Stanley -1585 Bway -NY 10036
(212) 679-3124 .. **Huang,** Ying Hua '05 %T McCauley LLC -274 Mad Av -NY 10016 **Fx:**679-3105
(212) 735-3000 .. **Huang,** Yiyang '10 %Skadden ASM&F LLP -4 Times Sq -NY 10036
(212) 343-8584 .. **Huang,** Zhe-Ying '95 -401 Bway -NY 10013 **Fx:**941-1608
(518) 266-1175 .. **Huban,** Yorden C '99 -208 19th -Watervliet 12189 **Fx:**266-9815
(212) 310-8000 .. **Hubana,** Lidija '01 Weil G&M LLP -767 5th Av -NY 10153
(212) 223-9700 .. **Hubbard,** Bruce A '76 B Hubbard,PC -730 3rd Av -NY 10017 **Fx:**752-8881
(212) 599-1892 .. **Hubbard,** David J '98 (Decker H LLC) -315 Mad Av -NY 10017
(718) 243-6267 .. **Hubbard,** Dorothy J '96 Leg Aid -111 Lvngstn -Brklyn 11201 **Fx:**237-8737
(212) 596-9000 .. **Hubbard,** Eric R '88 (Ropes & G LLP) -1211 Av of Amer -NY 10036
(212) 687-8500 .. **Hubbard,** James R '04 (Liddle & R,LLP) -800 3rd Av -NY 10022
(212) 761-6176 .. **Hubbard,** James R Jr. '07 Morgan Stanley -1585 Bway -NY 10036
(607) 652-7343 .. **Hubbard,** John L '91 -72 Main Bx130 -Stamfrd 12167 **Fx:**652-2812
(631) 661-6326 .. **Hubbard,** Jos C '69 -619 Deer Prk Av -Babylon 11702
(914) 395-2410 .. **Hubbard,** K Dean Jr. '88 Sarah Lawrence College -1 Mead Way -Bronxvll 10708
(315) 474-7541 .. **Hubbard,** Peter L '72 (Menter R&T,PC) -308 Maltbie -Syracuse 13204
(212) 416-8267 .. **Hubbard,** Robt L '82 %Dept of Law -120 Bway -NY 10271
(212) 599-1892 .. **Hubbard,** Thos J '56 (Decker H LLC) -315 Mad Av -NY 10017
(212) 618-0630 .. **Hubbert,** James M '82 Bear Wagner Specialists -40 Wall -NY 10005
(212) 682-7195 .. **Hubell,** Richd A '92 (Hubell & Assoc) -100 Park Av -NY 10017
(212) 450-4000 .. **Huber,** Betty Moy '97 Cnsl Davis P&W LLP -450 Lex Av -NY 10017
(516) 739-0300 .. **Huber,** Ezra '83 -200 Old Cntry Rd -Mineola 11501 **Fx:**739-7309
(716) 632-8712 .. **Huber,** James A '70 -Bx1158 -Williamsvll 14231
(631) 425-4100 .. **Huber,** John P '97 (Ré NH&C,LLP) -36 N NY Av -Huntngtn 11743
(212) 298-5043 .. **Huber,** Kate R '01 Leg Aid -49 Thomas -NY 10013 **Fx:**298-5252
(212) 357-2791 .. **Huber,** Michl P '01 Goldman Sachs -1 NY Plz -NY 10004
(212) 381-7000 .. **Huber,** Ralph P '78 (Sabin B&G LLP) -4 Times Sq -NY 10036
(315) 471-4107 .. **Hubert,** Herbert W '61 (Hoffmann H&H,LLP) -4629 Onondaga Blvd -Syracuse 13219
(718) 522-4646 .. **Hubert,** Steven L '91 -32 Court -Brklyn 11201 **Fx:**522-0487
(212) 837-6000 .. **Huberty,** Chas H '09 %Hughes H&R LLP -1 Bttry Pk Plz -NY 10004
(585) 248-9119 .. **Huberty,** Jos P '55 -38 Stonington Dr -Pittsfrd 14534
(212) 532-3850 .. **Hubicki,** Jos '93 %Menagh & F,PC -386 Park Av S -NY 10016
(518) 640-5033 .. **Hubicki,** Kristina M '05 AYCO -25 British Amer Blvd -Latham 12110
(845) 485-6974 .. **Hubner,** Shari S L '86 -80 Wshngtn -Poughkeepsie 12601 **Fx:**485-6995
(212) 340-4821 .. **Hubscher,** Sofia C '93 %Metro-North -347 Mad Av -NY 10017 **Fx:**697-9079
(914) 923-9041 .. **Huchro,** Kimberly J '91 -100 Twr Hill Rd -Scarboro 10510
(212) 455-2000 .. **Huck,** L Francis '73 (Simpson T&B LLP) -425 Lex Av -NY 10017
(212) 578-8872 .. **Huck,** Paul G '90 %MetLife -1 Mad Av -NY 10010
(716) 684-8060 .. **Huckle,** Courtney R '09 %Ecology & Envrmnt Inc -368 Plsnt Vw Dr -Lancaster 14086 **Fx:**684-0844
(845) 225-5827 .. **Hudak,** Elizabeth D '80 (Berkman & H,PC) -38 Gleneida Av -Carmel 10512
(516) 746-0707 .. **Hudak,** Mark W '99 %Hammill OCDP&K,PC -6851 Jericho Tpk -Syosset 11791
(212) 808-7800 .. **Hudak,** Nicole M '09 %Kelley D&W LLP -101 Park Av -NY 10178
(212) 506-2500 .. **Hudanish,** David M '92 (Mayer B LLP) -1675 Bway -NY 10019
(212) 907-7300 .. **Hudders,** Andrew D '80 (Golenbock EAB&P) -437 Mad Av -NY 10022
(212) 765-5070 .. **Hudnell,** Lewis E III '99 (Fish & R,PC) -153 E 53rd -NY 10022
(212) 445-7000 .. **Hudoba,** Mark B '99 Jacoby & M,LLP -39 Bway -NY 10006
(518) 383-9440 .. **Hudson Cook LLP** -636 Plnk Rd -Clifton Pk 12065 **Fx:**383-9401
(212) 691-6398 .. **Hudson,** Eileen E '84 -94 Christopher -NY 10014
(212) 735-3000 .. **Hudson,** Evan W '08 %Skadden ASM&F LLP -4 Times Sq -NY 10036
(212) 765-5070 .. **Hudson,** Irene E '03 (Fish & R,PC) -153 E 53rd -NY 10022
(212) 402-4100 .. **Hudson,** Jalina J '10 %Ofc Applt Def -11 Park Pl -NY 10007 **Fx:**402-4199
(212) 924-1220 .. **Hudson,** Jennifer E '08 Leg Srvc Plan Lcl 237 -216 W 14th -NY 10011 **Fx:**647-9421
(212) 262-2390 .. **Hudson,** Jodi A '97 Cnsl Connell F LLP -888 7th Av -NY 10106
(914) 388-5016 .. **Hudson,** Katherine K '78 KK Hudson Cnsltng -119 Dusinberre Rd -Gardiner 12525 **Fx:**(845) 255-5416
(212) 788-8684 .. **Hudson,** Maurice L '08 %Law Dept -100 Church -NY 10007 **Fx:**788-0367
(212) 653-8700 .. **Hudson,** Scott N '98 (Sheppard MR&H LLP) -30 Rckfllr Plz -NY 10112
(718) 923-8250 .. **Hudson,** Sharen D '97 Hook Community Justice Ctr -88 Visitation Pl -Brklyn 11231
(212) 450-4000 .. **Hudson,** Sophia E '07 %Davis P&W LLP -450 Lex Av -NY 10017
(212) 307-0800 .. **Hudson,** Timothy M '98 %A Wasser Assoc -The Miss Saigon Co LP -NY 10019
(716) 852-1000 .. **Hudson,** Timothy M '07 %PW Beltz,PC -36 Church -Buffalo 14202 **Fx:**852-5887
(718) 263-0550 .. **Hudson-Phillips,** Jennifer A '02 -150-40 71st Av -Flushng 11367
(212) 563-4100 .. **Hudson-Plush,** Evan R '08 %Cohen W&S LLP -330 W 42nd -NY 10036
(212) 490-9000 .. **Huebner,** Christine A '94 %TIAA-CREF -730 3rd Av -NY 10017
(212) 354-5555 .. **Huebner,** Levi '06 (L Huebner & Assoc,PC) -478 Malbone -Brklyn 11225
(212) 450-4000 .. **Huebner,** Marshall S '94 (Davis P&W LLP) -450 Lex Av -NY 10017
(716) 862-0198 .. **Huebsch,** Ronald A '76 -438 Ruskin Rd -Snyder 14226
(315) 638-8283 .. **Huegel,** Teresa C '94 %J Ledden -60 Oswego -Baldwinsvll 13027 **Fx:**638-8843
(212) 770-6769 .. **Huelbig,** Paul S '92 %AIG -70 Pine -NY 10270 **Fx:**514-8949
(212) 336-3500 .. **Huene,** Claire L '03 (Miller & W,PC) -570 Lex Av -NY 10022
(631) 756-2024 .. **Huenke & Rodriguez** -1 Huntngtn Quad -Melvll 11747 **Fx:**756-2033
(631) 756-2024 .. **Huenke,** Theo E '79 (Huenke & R) -1 Huntngtn Quad -Melvll 11747
(212) 519-7878 .. **Huergo,** Pamela A '07 ACLU -125 Broad -NY 10004 **Fx:**549-2651
(646) 602-5600 .. **Huertas,** Carmen V '03 %Urban Justice Ctr -123 William -NY 10038 **Fx:**(212) 533-4598
(718) 624-9391 .. **Hueston,** Michl O '95 (Cardinale H&M) -26 Court -Brklyn 11242
(585) 530-3180 .. **Huether,** Gregory H '81 %Atty Grievance Comm -50 East Av -Rchstr 14604 **Fx:**530-3191
(845) 291-2050 .. **Huey,** David R '79 %DA -255-275 Main -Goshen 10924 **Fx:**291-2085
(914) 631-1500 .. **Huff,** Jean Smiertka '81 (Huff W LLP) -200 Wht Plns Rd -Tarrytwn 10591 **Fx:**631-1501
(212) 805-0202 .. **Huff,** Kevin B '97 %Hon D Cote -500 Pearl -NY 10007
(518) 377-6489 .. **Huff,** Margaret D '87 (McCary & H,LLP) -107 N Ballston Av -Scotia 12302
(212) 421-4100 .. **Huff,** Stephen F '64 (Pryor C LLP) -7 Times Sq -NY 10036
(212) 728-8000 .. **Huffman,** Diana N H '10 %Willkie F&G LLP -787 7th Av -NY 10019
(212) 325-2000 .. **Huffman,** Jennifer I '95 Credit Suisse -1 Mad Av -NY 10010
(315) 781-5131 .. **Huffman,** Laura Crume '93 -1 Franklin Sq -Geneva 14456
(212) 310-2906 .. **Huffman,** Nina R '94 %Colgate-Palmolive -300 Park Av -NY 10022 **Fx:**310-3230
(212) 902-9957 .. **Huffman,** Robyn A '89 %Goldman Sachs -1 NY Plz -NY 10004
(212) 661-1100 .. **Hufford,** D Brian '89 (Pomerantz HG&G LLP) -100 Park Av -NY 10017
(212) 584-5710 .. **Hufft,** Ashley Evans '05 Millennium Promise -432 Park Av S -NY 10016
(914) 664-8400 .. **Hufjay,** Robt A '65 (Alperin & H) -22 W 1st -Mt Vernon 10550
(516) 248-1700 .. **Hufnagel,** Brian J '03 %Forchelli CDSM&T,LLP -333 Earle Ovngton Blvd -Uniondale 11553

(914) 472-7700 .. **Hufnagel,** John E '71 OfCnsl Bertine HHZD&D,LLP -700 Wht Plns Rd -Scarsdale 10583
(518) 283-3288 .. **Hug,** Matthew C '05 -105 Jordan Rd -Troy 12180 **Fx:**833-0589
(518) 270-4040 .. **Hug,** Shane B '09 %DA -80 2nd -Troy 12180 **Fx:**270-4025
(518) 792-2117 .. **Hugabone Vinson,** Jessica '08 %Bartlett PS&R,PC -1 Wshngtn Bx2168 -Glens Fls 12801
(914) 323-1036 .. **Hugel,** Jessica '94 -100 S Bedford -Mt Kisco 10549
(212) 922-1080 .. **Hugel,** Paul S '93 (Clayman & R,LLP) -305 Mad Av -NY 10165
(212) 408-2500 .. **Hugenberger,** Joel A '08 %Baker B,LLP -30 Rckfllr Plz -NY 10112
(516) 571-3800 .. **Huggard,** Anne M '93 %DA -262 Old Cntry Rd -Mineola 11501 **Fx:**248-9479
(212) 395-2258 .. **Huggard,** Eileen E '89 Verizon -140 West -NY 10007
(518) 583-0582 .. **Huggard,** Victor A Jr. '69 -17 Knollwood Dr -Saratoga Spgs 12866
(212) 558-4000 .. **Huggin,** David M '65 SrCnsl Sullivan & C LLP -125 Broad -NY 10004
(631) 957-3029 .. **Huggins,** Allen E '79 %Babylon Town Atty -200 E Sunrise Hwy -Lindenhrst 11757 **Fx:**957-3146
(212) 819-8200 .. **Huggins,** Heather E '08 %White & C LLP -1155 Av of Amer -NY 10036
(646) 264-3650 .. **Huggins,** Jennifer L '02 %US Dept of Labor -201 Varick -NY 10014 **Fx:**264-3660
(212) 578-2211 .. **Huggins,** Kito K '00 %MetLife -27-01 Qns Plz N -LIC 11101
(212) 969-3000 .. **Huggins,** Kristine K '09 %Proskauer R LLP -1585 Bway -NY 10036
(516) 334-3500 .. **Hughes,** Adam M '10 %Malen & Assoc,PC -123 Frost -Westbury 11590
(914) 273-4545 .. **Hughes,** Andrew P '05 MBIA Inc -113 King -Armonk 10504
(315) 798-6420 .. **Hughes,** Barbara E '78 Cnsl Family Ct -200 Elizabeth -Utica 13501
(718) 286-6000 .. **Hughes,** Brian C '08 %DA -125-01 Qns Blvd -Kew Gdns 11415
(631) 765-6911 .. **Hughes,** Brian J '86 -210 Brook Ln -Southold 11971 **Fx:**765-6911
(518) 483-4330 .. **Hughes,** Bryan J '69 (Hughes S&R,PC) -31 Elm Bx788 -Malone 12953
(212) 702-0950 .. **Hughes,** Chas B III '76 Easton Capital -767 3rd Av -NY 10017
(212) 504-6000 .. **Hughes,** Christopher A '74 (Cadwalader W&T LLP) -1 World Fncl Ctr -NY 10281
(718) 243-6306 .. **Hughes,** Clinton '98 %Leg Aid -111 Lvngstn -Brklyn 11201 **Fx:**237-8737
(518) 734-5393 .. **Hughes,** Craig S '84 -Meadow Ln Bx59 -Jewett 12444
(212) 434-0100 .. **Hughes,** Danl T '82 (Litchfield C LLP) -420 Lex Av -NY 10170
(631) 277-5232 .. **Hughes,** Dawn M '02 D Hughes,PC -130 W Main -E Islip 11730 **Fx:**277-5237
(716) 842-6514 .. **Hughes,** Desmond '90 -43 Court -Buffalo 14202
(607) 734-1519 .. **Hughes,** Diana L '92 (Learned RL&H,LLP) -449 E Water -Elmira 14901
(718) 261-3047 .. **Hughes,** Dorothy Ann Riordan '91 %Queens Law Assoc -118-21 Qns Blvd -Frst Hlls 11375 **Fx:**261-0798
(212) 724-4437 .. **Hughes,** Dorothy E '77 -7 W 87th -NY 10024
(718) 254-0700 .. **Hughes,** Dorothy E '90 %Bklyn Defender Srvcs -177 Lvngstn -Brklyn 11201 **Fx:**254-0897
(212) 762-5032 .. **Hughes,** Duane L '92 Morgan Stanley -1221 Av of Amer -NY 10020
(212) 599-8200 .. **Hughes,** Edw J Jr. '91 %Shaub AC&S,LLP -655 3rd Av -NY 10017
(917) 343-1876 .. **Hughes,** Elena Sapozhnicov '06 Goldman Sachs Co -85 Broad -NY 10004
(315) 841-4356 .. **Hughes,** Elizabeth Buenger '80 -2791 State Route 12B -Deansboro 13328 **Fx:**841-4753
(212) 442-5980 .. **Hughes,** Everett N '80 Dept Youth & Commnty Devlpmnt -156 William -NY 10038
(585) 546-5530 .. **Hughes,** Gary A '79 %Thomson West -50 E Broad -Rchstr 14694
(212) 768-6700 .. **Hughes,** Gregory D '08 %Sonnenschein N&R LLP -2 World Fncl Ctr -NY 10281
(212) 248-3140 .. **Hughes,** Heather M '02 %Drinker B&R LLP -140 Bway -NY 10005
(212) 679-3124 .. **Hughes,** Hilary K '96 %T McCauley LLC -274 Mad Av -NY 10016 **Fx:**679-3105
(212) 965-4527 .. **Hughes,** Hillary H '98 (Garvey SB) -100 Wall -NY 10005
(212) 837-6000 .. **Hughes Hubbard & Reed LLP** -1 Bttry Pk Plz -NY 10004 **Fx:**422-4726
(212) 559-9416 .. **Hughes,** James C IV '88 %Citibank NA -153 E 53rd -NY 10043
(315) 471-3151 .. **Hughes,** James E '80 (Hancock & E,LLP) -1500 AXA Twr I Bx4976 -Syracuse 13221
(518) 371-1299 .. **Hughes,** James F '88 -233 Tallow Wood Dr Bx1197 -Clifton Pk 12065 **Fx:**952-7314
(212) 698-3500 .. **Hughes,** Jenny A '07 %Dechert LLP -1095 Av of Amer -NY 10036
(845) 634-5050 .. **Hughes,** John H '02 -20 S Main -New Cty 10956 **Fx:**709-6231
(914) 631-8855 .. **Hughes,** John J Jr. '80 -181 S Bway -Tarrytwn 10591 **Fx:**631-8895
(914) 472-7700 .. **Hughes,** John J '98 (Bertine HHZD&D,LLP) -700 Wht Plns Rd -Scarsdale 10583
(212) 714-0500 .. **Hughes,** John W '75 -421 7th Av -NY 10001 **Fx:**714-0518
(212) 790-0200 .. **Hughes,** Justin J '87 Benj N Cardozo Schl of Law -55 5th Av -NY 10003 **Fx:**790-0345
(212) 373-3000 .. **Hughes,** Karen J '97 %Paul WRW&G LLP -1285 Av of Amer -NY 10019
(212) 312-8770 .. **Hughes,** Katherine C '09 %Fordham Univ Sch of Law -140 W 62nd -NY 10023 **Fx:**636-6899
(518) 474-8211 .. **Hughes,** Kathleen B '00 %Law Reporting Bur -1 Commerce Plz -Albany 12210 **Fx:**463-6869
(516) 897-0988 .. **Hughes,** Kevin T '77 -Bx127 -Point Lookout 11569
(212) 692-1000 .. **Hughes,** Laurence S '82 (Duane M LLP) -1540 Bway -NY 10036
(718) 526-0800 .. **Hughes,** Lawr F '98 %Varsity Transit -114-15 Guy R Brewer Blvd -Jamaica 11434
(212) 451-2900 .. **Hughes,** Leigh Kiersten '05 %Robinson & C LLP -885 3rd Av -NY 10022
(315) 356-0600 .. **Hughes,** Linda A '94 NYS Unified Ct Syst -302 N James -Rome 13440 **Fx:**356-0603
(212) 664-4444 .. **Hughes,** Lisa Stewart '95 %NBC -30 Rckfllr Plz -NY 10112
(212) 318-6000 .. **Hughes,** M Danl '09 %Paul HJ&W LLP -75 E 55th -NY 10022
(212) 416-8000 .. **Hughes,** Mary Ann '87 %Dept of Law -120 Bway -NY 10271
(212) 416-8711 .. **Hughes,** Mary B '98 %Dept of Law -120 Bway -NY 10271 **Fx:**416-6147
(718) 250-2000 .. **Hughes,** Mary D '92 %DA -350 Jay -Brklyn 11201 **Fx:**250-2314
(631) 482-1264 .. **Hughes,** Mary L '02 (M Hughes & Assoc,PLLC) -1 Sawmill Rd -Commack 11725 **Fx:**482-1266
(631) 853-3242 .. **Hughes,** Matthew G '97 %Hon J Pastoressa -400 Carleton Av -Central Islip 11722 **Fx:**853-7727
(516) 571-6066 .. **Hughes,** Meredith A '08 Nassau Cnty Legislature -1550 Franklin Av -Mineola 11501
(718) 261-3047 .. **Hughes,** Michl G '94 %Queens Law Assoc -118-21 Qns Blvd -Frst Hlls 11375 **Fx:**261-0798
(716) 856-0400 .. **Hughes,** Michl J '84 (Hughes & W LLP) -63 Kenmore Av -Buffalo 14226 **Fx:**856-9255
(914) 606-9790 .. **Hughes,** Patricia A '91 Cartafalsa ST&L -560 Wht Plns Rd -Tarrytwn 10591
(516) 932-0255 .. **Hughes,** Patrick J '89 -21 Edward -Bethpage 11714
(212) 262-2390 .. **Hughes,** Patrick J '05 (Connell F LLP) -888 7th Av -NY 10106
(212) 884-6228 .. **Hughes,** Patrick T '94 Guggenheim Advisors -135 E 57th -NY 10022
(212) 217-6300 .. **Hughes,** Paul C '98 CapLease,Inc -1065 Av of Amer -NY 10018 **Fx:**217-6301
(212) 450-4000 .. **Hughes,** Paul P '09 %Davis P&W LLP -450 Lex Av -NY 10017
(212) 884-8200 .. **Hughes,** Priscilla C '86 Thomson Fncl Inc -195 Bway -NY 10007
(212) 558-4000 .. **Hughes,** Rachel A '09 %Sullivan & C LLP -125 Broad -NY 10004
(315) 425-2700 .. **Hughes,** Richd K '73 OfCnsl Hiscock & B,LLP -One Park Pl -Syracuse 13202
(212) 447-5500 .. **Hughes,** Richd O '99 %Quinn M LLP -274 Mad Av -NY 10016 **Fx:**889-2981
(212) 318-4353 .. **Hughes,** Robt K '89 %Goldwater Memorial Hsptl -1 Main -NY 10044 **Fx:**318-4370
(212) 645-5110 .. **Hughes,** Robt L '93 New Visions for Pub Schls -320 W 13th -NY 10014 **Fx:**645-7409
(631) 477-2700 .. **Hughes,** Robt S '94 -316 Front Bx128 -Greenprt 11944
(914) 245-8362 .. **Hughes,** Sherri L '82 -1387 Carters Grove -Yorktwn Hts 10598 **Fx:**245-8527
(212) 221-5499 .. **Hughes,** Stephen C '98 %Verizon -140 West -NY 10007
(716) 381-8960 .. **Hughes,** Stephen M '80 -295 Main -Buffalo 14203
(518) 483-4330 .. **Hughes Stewart & Race, PC** -31 Elm Bx788 -Malone 12953 **Fx:**483-4005
(718) 261-3290 .. **Hughes,** Theresa '96 (Fanning & H,PLLC) -108-18 Qns Blvd -Frst Hlls 11375
(212) 683-9700 .. **Hughes,** Thos D '86 GNY Mutual Ins -200 Mad Av -NY 10016 **Fx:**843-1962
(914) 337-2626 .. **Hughes,** Thos J Jr. '61 -141 Pkwy Rd -Bronxvll 10708 **Fx:**337-3392
(212) 735-3000 .. **Hughes,** Thos J '05 %Skadden ASM&F LLP -4 Times Sq -NY 10036
(315) 223-3043 .. **Hughes,** Thos P '78 -23 Oxford Rd -New Hartfrd 13413 **Fx:**735-7924
(718) 250-1400 .. **Hughes,** Timothy M '87 %BZ Green -12 MetroTech Ctr -Brklyn 11201 **Fx:**250-1401
(212) 558-4000 .. **Hughes,** Wm C '09 %Sullivan & C LLP -125 Broad -NY 10004
(518) 395-6414 .. **Hughes Robillard,** Samantha M '94 %US Dept of Energy -Bx1069 -Schnctdy 12301 **Fx:**395-6390
(212) 839-5300 .. **Hughey,** Matthew M '04 %Sidley A LLP -787 7th Av -NY 10019
(315) 785-3088 .. **Hughson,** Jos P '08 Cnty Atty -175 Arsenal -Watertwn 13601 **Fx:**785-5178
(607) 733-8866 .. **Hughson,** Matthew P '05 (Ziff Law Firm,LLP) -303 William -Elmira 14901 **Fx:**732-6062
(212) 594-8292 .. **Hugo,** Christopher C '04 Vinluan & T -224 W 35th -NY 10001 **Fx:**594-8296
(718) 654-3330 .. **Huguenot,** Michl Z '82 (Vozza & H) -2435 E Chester Rd -Bronx 10469 **Fx:**654-1374
(516) 835-6534 .. **Hugues,** Stephen M J '99 -521 East Dr -Lindenhrst 11757
(212) 728-8000 .. **Huh,** Joon-Yeung '96 OfCnsl Willkie F&G LLP -787 7th Av -NY 10019
(212) 788-0817 .. **Hui,** Jacqueline '06 %Law Dept -100 Church -NY 10007 **Fx:**788-0367
(212) 838-1177 .. **Hui,** John C '96 %Morse ZR&L LLP -405 Park Av -NY 10022
(212) 854-5181 .. **Hui,** Karen Y '05 %Columbia Univ -535 W 116th 412 Low Mem'l Library -NY 10027
(718) 802-2715 .. **Hui,** Kevin J '89 %ACS -330 Jay -Brklyn 11201 **Fx:**802-2798
(212) 986-6000 .. **Hui,** Lawr D '88 (Kleinberg KW&C,PC) -551 5th Av -NY 10176
(718) 533-1111 .. **Hui,** Sally '01 %Yoon & H -75-21 Bway -Elmhrst 11373 **Fx:**429-6786
(212) 735-3000 .. **Hui,** Stephanie D '09 %Skadden ASM&F LLP -4 Times Sq -NY 10036
(716) 667-9700 .. **Hujer,** Tristan D '10 %F Muggia & Assoc,PLLC -6438 W Quaker -Orchard Pk 14127 **Fx:**667-9711
(585) 247-9000 .. **Hulbert,** Anne Miller '84 %Shapiro D&B,LLP -250 Mile Xing Blvd -Rchstr 14624
(212) 652-3890 .. **Hulbert,** Deborah A '83 (Pitta & G LLP) -120 Bway -NY 10271
(607) 432-6720 .. **Hulbert,** Henry L '54 -6 Ford Av -Oneonta 13820 **Fx:**433-1507
(212) 225-2000 .. **Hulbert,** Richd W '56 SrCnsl Cleary GS&H -1 Lbrty Plz -NY 10006
(212) 504-6000 .. **Hulbig,** Ngoc Pham '02 %Cadwalader W&T LLP -1 World Fncl Ctr -NY 10281
(845) 658-7777 .. **Huleatt,** John W '03 Church Communities -2032 Route 213 Bx903 -Rifton 12471 **Fx:**658-7776
(212) 326-3939 .. **Hulet,** Briana R '10 %Jones D -222 E 41st -NY 10017
(518) 452-5600 .. **Hulihan,** Matthew M '09 %Heslin RF&M PC -5 Columbia Cir -Albany 12203
(315) 638-7377 .. **Huling,** Elijah Jr. '77 -7 E Oneida -Baldwinsvll 13027
(315) 475-3425 .. **Huling,** Laura S '98 %S Cominsky,LLC -1500 State Twr Bldg -Syracuse 13202 **Fx:**475-2932
(718) 579-7932 .. **Hulkower,** Adira J '01 %Leg Aid -900 Sheridan Av -Bronx 10451 **Fx:**293-8744
(516) 883-4654 .. **Hulkower,** Bernard '55 -25 Morewood Oaks -Pt Wash 11050
(212) 521-5400 .. **Hull,** Adam C '08 %Reed S LLP -599 Lex Av -NY 10022
(718) 262-3422 .. **Hull,** Angella S '00 ACS -92-31 Union Hall -Jamaica 11433
(212) 356-8100 .. **Hull,** Christopher S '94 %CIR -520 8th Av -NY 10018 **Fx:**356-8111
(585) 453-6437 .. **Hull,** Denise M '91 Excellus BC/BS -165 Court -Rchstr 14647 **Fx:**238-3679
(631) 567-8793 .. **Hull,** Oliver '85 -320 W Main -Sayvll 11782 **Fx:**567-3760
(716) 856-2626 .. **Hull,** Richd A '95 %Tronolone & S,PC -298 Main -Buffalo 14202
(315) 536-9820 .. **Hull,** Robt Kingsley '76 -224 Clinton -Penn Yan 14527 **Fx:**536-9820
(585) 258-2800 .. **Hull,** Ronald G '80 SrCnsl Underberg & K LLP -300 Bausch & Lomb Pl -Rchstr 14604
(607) 772-7006 .. **Hull,** Thos J '67 City Ct -38 Hawley -Bnghmtn 13901 **Fx:**772-7041
(607) 974-9714 .. **Hulme,** Danl S '96 Corning Inc -1 Rvrfrnt Plz SPTI0301 -Corning 14831

(631) 288-2876 .. **Hulme,** James N '86 (Kelly & H) -323 Mill Rd -Westhmptn Bch 11978 **Fx:**288-1328
(518) 486-5258 .. **Hulme,** James W '91 %Insurance Dept -99 Wshngtn Av -Albany 12257 **Fx:**486-2218
(914) 631-7768 .. **Hulnick & Coe** -54 Main -Tarrytwn 10591 **Fx:**631-7583
(716) 855-3272 .. **Hulnick,** Mark A '71 -42 Delaware Av -Buffalo 14202
(631) 821-3667 .. **Hulse,** Jeffrey B '81 -295 N Cntry Rd -Sound Bch 11789
(516) 688-1700 .. **Hulse,** Mark L '84 %IRS -1600 Stewart Av -Westbury 11590 **Fx:**688-1750
(212) 408-2500 .. **Hulseberg,** Danl J '03 (Baker B,LLP) -30 Rckfllr Plz -NY 10112
(212) 872-1000 .. **Hulsh,** Andrew '86 -One Bryant Park -NY 10036 **Fx:**872-1002
(315) 474-2911 .. **Hulslander,** Kevin E '87 (Smith SK&S,PC) -250 S Clinton -Syracuse 13202
(212) 644-4420 .. **Hult,** Ann-Gail B '97 OfCnsl Fabiani C&H,LLP -570 Lex Av -NY 10022
(212) 527-1000 .. **Hulten,** R Alexander '74 OfCnsl Jones HC&B PC -1 Bttry Pk Plz -NY 10004
(212) 455-2000 .. **Hultman,** Christopher O J '10 %Simpson T&B LLP -425 Lex Av -NY 10017
(212) 925-8818 .. **Hum,** Chi Kong '78 (Sung & H) -350 Bway -NY 10013 **Fx:**925-8897
(716) 854-4300 .. **Human,** Jeffrey A '79 (Gross SB&G,PC) -465 Main -Buffalo 14203
(212) 446-4800 .. **Humann,** Adam T '07 %Kirkland & E LLP -153 E 53rd -NY 10022
(716) 551-3341 .. **Humann,** John F '76 %Fed Pub Def -300 Pearl -Buffalo 14202 **Fx:**551-3346
(716) 633-3535 .. **Humann,** Max B '06 %W Mattar,PC -6720 Main -Williamsvll 14221 **Fx:**631-9804
(914) 422-4239 .. **Humbach,** John A '67 %Pace Law Schl -78 N Bway -White Plns 10603 **Fx:**422-4039
(845) 627-1672 .. **Humbach,** Thos E '94 -161 N Mddltwn Rd -Pearl Rvr 10965
(716) 664-2889 .. **Humble,** Scott F '90 -7 Jackson Av -Jamestwn 14701 **Fx:**664-2329
(212) 222-0110 .. **Humburg,** Reinhard '96 -200 Claremont Av -NY 10027 **Fx:**865-3550
(212) 371-6600 .. **Hume,** Danl '92 (Kirby M LLP) -825 3rd Av -NY 10022
(212) 205-7000 .. **Hume,** David G '73 Cnsl Ashurst LLP -7 Times Sq -NY 10036
(914) 286-3400 .. **Hume,** Elizabeth A '09 %Leg Aid -1 N Bway -White Plns 10601 **Fx:**682-4112
(914) 939-7095 .. **Hume,** Wm F '79 -26 Brcknrdg Av -Pt Chester 10573
(860) 275-6761 .. **Humes,** Stephen J '95 (McCarter & E,LLP) -245 Park Av -NY 10167 **Fx:**724-3397
(516) 676-4600 .. **Humes & Wagner** -147 Forest Av Bx546 -Locust Vly 11560 **Fx:**676-4606
(585) 235-6611 .. **Hummel,** Chad M '03 %Panzarella & C -1411 Chili Av -Rchstr 14624 **Fx:**436-9706
(516) 677-5400 .. **Hummel,** Evan S '86 -180 Froehlich Farm Blvd -Woodbury 11797
(212) 408-2500 .. **Hummel,** Ian H '03 %Baker B,LLP -30 Rckfllr Plz -NY 10112
(631) 242-1600 .. **Hummel,** Jeffrey D '97 %Kujawski & D -1637 Deer Prk Av -Deer Pk 11729
(212) 474-1000 .. **Hummel,** Keith R '91 (Cravath S&M LLP) -825 8th Av -NY 10019
(516) 367-4510 .. **Hummel,** Ralph A '83 -137 Woodbury Rd -Woodbury 11797 **Fx:**692-2746
(212) 541-2000 .. **Hummel,** Zachary A '06 (Bryan C LLP) -1290 Av of Amer -NY 10104
(212) 869-5030 .. **Hummell,** Wm D '84 (Kucker & B,LLP) -747 3rd Av -NY 10017
(212) 278-1000 .. **Hummers,** Herbert J '61 (Anderson K&O,PC) -1251 Av of Amer -NY 10020
(718) 802-6644 .. **Humowiecki,** Mark R '02 Workers Comp Bd -111 Lvngstn -Brklyn 11201
(212) 596-9000 .. **Humphreville,** Chas P '08 %Ropes & G LLP -1211 Av of Amer -NY 10036
(212) 559-5617 .. **Humphrey,** Barbara C '84 CitiGroup Private Bk -666 5th Av -NY 10103
(347) 296-1554 .. **Humphrey,** Debbie Irene '81 Hon L Jacobson -360 Adams -Brklyn 11201
(914) 476-0600 .. **Humphrey,** Devyn C '07 %Smith B&J,LLP -733 Ynkrs Av -Ynkrs 10704
(718) 466-3000 .. **Humphrey,** Donna A '84 %Civil Ct -1118 Grnd Cncrs -Bronx 10456 **Fx:**466-3006
(212) 684-0199 .. **Humphrey,** James M '09 (Polsinelli S PC) -7 Penn Plz -NY 10001
(315) 732-4055 .. **Humphrey,** Mary R '99 -4063 Oneida -New Hartfrd 13413 **Fx:**793-1061
(585) 768-6259 .. **Humphrey,** Robt F '72 -3 Main -Le Roy 14482 **Fx:**768-6809
(845) 562-9100 .. **Humphrey,** Shay A '02 %Rider W&F,PC -655 Little Britain Rd -New Windsor 12553
(914) 995-4188 .. **Humphrey,** Wayne A '95 %Cnty Atty -148 Martine Av -White Plns 10601 **Fx:**995-5858
(845) 228-4200 .. **Humphreys,** Andrew W '91 %W Sayegh,PC -65 Gleneida Av -Carmel 10512 **Fx:**228-4832
(631) 501-3100 .. **Humphreys,** John P '87 -3 Huntngtn Quad Bx9028 -Melvll 11747 **Fx:**501-3085
(212) 262-2390 .. **Humphreys,** Noel D '80 OfCnsl Connell F LLP -888 7th Av -NY 10106
(212) 547-5400 .. **Humphreys,** Peter S '84 (McDermott W&E LLP) -340 Mad Av -NY 10173
(212) 468-8000 .. **Humphreys,** Thos A '80 (Morrison & F LLP) -1290 Av of Amer -NY 10104
(212) 909-6000 .. **Humphrey-Skomer,** Jael '09 %Debevoise & P LLP -919 3rd Av -NY 10022
(718) 370-7030 .. **Humphries,** Edw F '85 (Amabile & E,PC) -1000 South Av -Staten Isl 10314
(315) 446-4600 .. **Humpleby,** Craig C '02 -4306 E Genesee -Syracuse 13214 **Fx:**449-9330
(212) 554-1400 .. **Hunciker,** Kurt M '79 Cnsl Bernstein LB&G LLP -1285 Av of Amer -NY 10019
(516) 747-4855 .. **Hundertmark,** J Randolph '82 Hahn F&H -105 Hillside Av -Williston Pk 11596
(212) 547-5400 .. **Hundley,** Rachel E '09 %McDermott W&E LLP -340 Mad Av -NY 10173
(212) 318-5666 .. **Hung,** Michelle Minshang '97 AGI/Klearfold -299 Park Av -NY 10171 **Fx:**318-5697
(212) 607-3300 .. **Hung,** Palyn P '99 %NYCLU -125 Broad -NY 10004
(212) 848-4000 .. **Hung,** Shiu-Kay '09 %Shearman & S LLP -599 Lex Av -NY 10022
(516) 465-8129 .. **Hung,** Trestney '06 NSLIJ Med Ctr -145 Community Dr -Gt Neck 11021
(212) 728-8000 .. **Hungate,** Meghan McKee '10 %Willkie F&G LLP -787 7th Av -NY 10019
(315) 473-9495 .. **Hungerford,** Michl J '80 %MHLS -224 Harrison -Syracuse 13202 **Fx:**473-9646
(646) 386-5700 .. **Hunka,** John K '06 %Civil Ct -111 Centre -NY 10013
(212) 660-3000 .. **Hunkele,** Bryan '07 %Sullivan & W LLP -1290 Av of Amer -NY 10104
(212) 207-7000 .. **Hunn,** Trina R '95 %HarperCollins Pub -10 E 53rd -NY 10022 **Fx:**207-7552
(516) 797-7195 .. **Hunsberger,** Jos L '99 -1000 Park Blvd -Massapequa Pk 11762 **Fx:**797-7193
(212) 416-8005 .. **Hunt,** Carol J '03 %Dept of Law -120 Bway -NY 10271
(212) 530-5000 .. **Hunt,** Danielle J '08 %Milbank TH&M LLP -1 Chase Manh Plz -NY 10005
(845) 687-9496 .. **Hunt,** Douglas Jesse '72 -Bx6 -High Fls 12440 **Fx:**687-4510
(212) 906-1200 .. **Hunt,** Eli G '03 %Latham & W -885 3rd Av -NY 10022
(315) 471-4629 .. **Hunt,** Francis E Jr. '81 (Hunt & O) -250 Harrison -Syracuse 13202 **Fx:**471-5098
(718) 391-1720 .. **Hunt,** Gregory K '93 %Dept Design & Cnstrctn -30-30 Thomson Av -LIC 11101 **Fx:**391-1894
(716) 284-0666 .. **Hunt,** James E '48 -1110 Main -Niagara Fls 14301
(212) 578-2211 .. **Hunt,** James G '90 %MetLife -27-01 Qns Plz N -LIC 11101
(212) 696-0133 .. **Hunt,** John C '93 %M Polovy -192 Lex Av -NY 10016
(718) 923-8400 .. **Hunt,** John L '96 Forest City Ratner -1 Metrotech Ctr N -Brklyn 11201 **Fx:**923-8722
(315) 474-2943 .. **Hunt,** Kevin T '92 (Sugarman Law Firm,LLP) -211 W Jffrsn -Syracuse 13202
(518) 465-3553 .. **Hunt,** Lauren L '10 %Maynard OS&C,LLP -6 Twr Pl -Albany 12203
(518) 474-9502 .. **Hunt,** Linda S '82 %OTDA -40 N Pearl -Albany 12243 **Fx:**474-9389
(315) 474-8411 .. **Hunt,** Marsha A '88 -711 E Genesee -Syracuse 13210 **Fx:**426-0822
(212) 508-6100 .. **Hunt,** Martin J '92 (Bracewell & G,LLP) -1251 Av of Amer -NY 10020
(212) 373-3000 .. **Hunt,** Mary Reece '09 %Paul WRW&G LLP -1285 Av of Amer -NY 10019
(212) 617-8779 .. **Hunt,** Mary V '06 Bloomberg LP -731 Lex Av -NY 10022
(212) 558-4000 .. **Hunt,** Melissa A '09 %Sullivan & C LLP -125 Broad -NY 10004
(212) 858-1000 .. **Hunt,** Peter J '85 (Pillsbury WSP LLP) -1540 Bway -NY 10036
(585) 428-1854 .. **Hunt,** Timothy C '94 NYS Unified Ct Sys -525 Hall of Justice -Rchstr 14614 **Fx:**428-3182
(212) 436-1145 .. **Hunt,** Virginia M '88 IRS -290 Bway -NY 10007
(212) 558-4000 .. **Hunt,** Wm Adam '09 %Sullivan & C LLP -125 Broad -NY 10004
(315) 474-7571 .. **Hunt,** Wm B '04 %Mackenzie H LLP -101 S Salina Bx4967 -Syracuse 13221
(914) 526-1000 .. **Hunte,** Adrian C '81 Hunte Law Grp,PC -3031 Main Bx97 -Mohegan Lk 10547 **Fx:**526-3106
(212) 770-1634 .. **Hunte,** Dale Angela '88 AIGTS -80 Pine -NY 10005
(212) 896-6500 .. **Hunter,** Alexis A '01 %Howrey LLP -601 Lex Av -NY 10022
(845) 291-2454 .. **Hunter,** Anne E '77 %Leg Aid -2 Court Ln Bx328 -Goshen 10924 **Fx:**294-2638
(212) 576-6043 .. **Hunter,** Christine M '95 NY Life Ins Co -51 Mad Av -NY 10010
(212) 401-3452 .. **Hunter,** Christopher P '88 SrCnsl Royal Bk of Scotland -101 Park Av -NY 10178 **Fx:**401-3627
(212) 756-2000 .. **Hunter,** Danl F '96 (Schulte R&Z LLP) -919 3rd Av -NY 10022
(716) 854-4300 .. **Hunter,** Danl T '10 %Gross SB&G,PC -465 Main -Buffalo 14203
(716) 856-9443 .. **Hunter,** Edwin P '77 %Hagerty & B -69 Delaware Av -Buffalo 14202
(914) 328-0366 .. **Hunter,** Elizabeth E '07 %Sapir & F LLP -399 Knollwood Rd -White Plns 10603
(212) 230-8882 .. **Hunter,** Fraser L Jr. '93 (WilmerHale) -399 Park Av -NY 10022
(212) 250-2500 .. **Hunter,** Ian C '01 Deutsche Bk AG -60 Wall -NY 10005
(607) 734-2271 .. **Hunter,** J Philip '67 OfCnsl Sayles & E -1 W Church -Elmira 14901
(718) 380-7272 .. **Hunter,** Jack '64 (J Hunter,PC) -12 Lundy Ln -Larchmnt 10538
(212) 473-6181 .. **Hunter,** Jeffrey '77 -115 E 9th -NY 10003
(212) 416-8000 .. **Hunter,** John M '86 %Dept of Law -120 Bway -NY 10271
(212) 245-7300 .. **Hunter,** John Reid '05 Serling R&F,LLP -119 5th Av -NY 10003
(646) 386-3645 .. **Hunter,** Linell P '86 %Supreme Ct-Law Dept -60 Centre -NY 10007
(516) 296-7000 .. **Hunter,** Lisa S '80 (Certilman BA&H,LLP) -90 Merrick Av -E Meadow 11554
(718) 260-5124 .. **Hunter,** Lise G '85 NYC College of Tech -300 Jay -Brklyn 11201 **Fx:**260-5387
(212) 735-3000 .. **Hunter,** Mary I '07 %Skadden ASM&F LLP -4 Times Sq -NY 10036
(718) 268-8835 .. **Hunter,** Matthew D Jr. '83 -108-18 Qns Blvd -Frst Hlls 11375 **Fx:**268-3239
(518) 481-5000 .. **Hunter,** Richd F '92 %Fischer B&M -Cntry Clb Rd Bx420 -Malone 12953
(212) 779-9800 .. **Hunter,** Richd M '86 (Luboja & T,LLP) -10 E 40th -NY 10016
(845) 794-3660 .. **Hunter,** Robt B '82 %ML Zager,PC -543 Bway Bx948 -Monticello 12701 **Fx:**794-3919
(631) 852-2500 .. **Hunter,** Ryan P '05 %DA -200 Center Dr -Rvrhead 11901 **Fx:**852-1769
(845) 294-0776 .. **Hunter,** Stephen R '73 -140 Main Bx808 -Goshen 10924 **Fx:**294-3689
(212) 742-9280 .. **Hunter,** Travis W '04 Waterfront Commission -39 Bway -NY 10006
(212) 805-0202 .. **Huntington,** Clare '97 %Hon D Cote -500 Pearl -NY 10007
(212) 373-3000 .. **Huntington,** David S '97 (Paul WRW&G LLP) -1285 Av of Amer -NY 10019
(212) 309-1000 .. **Hunton & Williams** -200 Park Av -NY 10166 **Fx:**309-1100
(212) 788-0862 .. **Huntone,** Jeremy I '07 %Law Dept -100 Church -NY 10007 **Fx:**788-0367
(315) 361-7711 .. **Huntzinger,** Steven J '05 Oneida Indian Nation Enterprises -5218 Patrick Rd -Verona 13478 **Fx:**361-8009
(212) 715-9100 .. **Huo,** Zengguang '05 %Kramer LN&F,LLP -1177 Av of Amer -NY 10036
(877) 372-5712 .. **Huonker,** Lynn M '98 Sun Microsystems,Inc -101 Park Av -NY 10178
(212) 558-4000 .. **Huoth,** Derek S '09 %Sullivan & C LLP -125 Broad -NY 10004
(718) 432-0500 .. **Hupart,** Brett R '94 (Krieger W&H) -5602 Bway -Bronx 10463
(212) 431-0962 .. **Hupert,** Danl '81 (Orzick & H) -350 Bway -NY 10013
(212) 345-2483 .. **Hupp,** Jason H '99 Marsh Inc -1166 Av of Amer -NY 10036
(212) 788-0990 .. **Hupper,** John R Jr. '83 %Law Dept -100 Church -NY 10007 **Fx:**788-0367
(212) 770-1816 .. **Huppert,** Alla E '95 %AIG -80 Pine -NY 10005 **Fx:**344-2286

(646) 442-3100 .. **Huq,** Chaumtoli '98 %Legal Srvcs -90 John -NY 10038 **Fx:**(212) 227-9798
(212) 421-4100 .. **Huq,** Muzamil A '06 %Pryor C LLP -7 Times Sq -NY 10036
(212) 471-8500 .. **Hur,** Scott K '09 %Herzfeld & R,PC -125 Broad -NY 10004
(212) 856-9600 .. **Hurand,** Gates S '07 %Morvillo AGIA&B,PC -565 5th Av -NY 10017
(212) 318-6000 .. **Hurd,** Christopher N '06 %Paul HJ&W LLP -75 E 55th -NY 10022
(518) 862-1386 .. **Hurd,** Jeffrey E '94 (Burke SM&H,LLP) -302 Wshngtn Av Ext Bx15085 -Albany 12212
(212) 770-7292 .. **Hurd,** Jeffrey J '94 %AIG -70 Pine -NY 10270
(212) 558-4000 .. **Hurd,** Matthew G '92 (Sullivan & C LLP) -125 Broad -NY 10004
(212) 969-3000 .. **Hurd,** Steven D '95 (Proskauer R LLP) -1585 Bway -NY 10036
(212) 790-4500 .. **Hurdle,** Angela C '04 %Manatt P&P,LLP -7 Times Sq -NY 10036
(212) 335-4500 .. **Hurel,** Marc '87 (DLA Piper LLP) -1251 Av of Amer -NY 10020
(212) 225-2000 .. **Hurford,** Patrick J '07 %Cleary GS&H -1 Lbrty Plz -NY 10006
(212) 751-2700 .. **Hurkin-Torres,** Allen Z '91 JAMS -620 8th Av -NY 10018 **Fx:**751-4099
(518) 465-0400 .. **Hurley,** Anne M '89 O'Connor OB&F,PC -20 Corp Wds Blvd -Albany 12211
(718) 250-2000 .. **Hurley,** Beth Ann '05 %DA -350 Jay -Brklyn 11201 **Fx:**250-2314
(212) 549-8408 .. **Hurley,** Brian F '03 Brookfield Investment Mgmt Inc -200 Vesey -NY 10281
(212) 425-0700 .. **Hurley,** Brian P '87 %Kelner & K -140 Bway -NY 10005
(518) 533-1050 .. **Hurley,** Denis R Jr. '89 OfCnsl Conway & K LLP -9 Cornell Rd -Latham 12110
(212) 285-3300 .. **Hurley,** Erin K '95 %Lipsig SM&M,PC -40 Fulton -NY 10038
(212) 335-9000 .. **Hurley,** Eugene R III '83 %DA -1 Hogan Pl -NY 10013
(917) 297-9429 .. **Hurley,** F Richd Jr. '90 -225 Bway -NY 10007
(212) 698-3500 .. **Hurley,** Geoffrey K '74 (Dechert LLP) -1095 Av of Amer -NY 10036
(516) 229-4300 .. **Hurley,** James '01 %J Bilello & Assoc -875 Merrick Av -Westbury 11590
(212) 402-6822 .. **Hurley,** James E Jr. '85 -75 Maiden Ln -NY 10038
(716) 926-8110 .. **Hurley,** Jennifer A '02 -56 Main -Hambrg 14075
(315) 266-6100 .. **Hurley,** Jennifer D '91 Pub Def -235 Elizabeth -Utica 13501 **Fx:**266-6105
(716) 888-3104 .. **Hurley,** John J '85 Cnsl Canisius College -2001 Main-Bagen 202 -Buffalo 14208
(716) 875-1300 .. **Hurley,** John L '51 -1920 Elmwood Av -Buffalo 14207
(212) 598-8000 .. **Hurley,** John R '76 %Guardian Life Ins -7 Hanover Sq -NY 10004 **Fx:**919-2693
(716) 878-8000 .. **Hurley,** Maureen O'Connell '85 %Rich Products -1 Robert Rich Way -Buffalo 14213 **Fx:**878-8767
(212) 574-1200 .. **Hurley,** Maureen R '98 (Seward & K LLP) -1 Bttry Pk Plz -NY 10004
(914) 253-2000 .. **Hurley,** Megan M '96 %Pepsico -700 Andrsn Hill Rd -Purchase 10577
(212) 382-0700 .. **Hurley,** Michl F '87 OfCnsl Ostrolenk FG&S,LLP -1180 Av of Amer -NY 10036
(212) 972-6161 .. **Hurley,** Michl J '98 (Cassin & C LLP) -711 3rd Av -NY 10017
(212) 872-1000 .. **Hurley,** Mitchell P '97 -One Bryant Park -NY 10036 **Fx:**872-1002
(585) 473-3100 .. **Hurley,** Nell M '85 %Ernstrom & D,LLP -180 Canal Vw Blvd -Rchstr 14623
(518) 465-1100 .. **Hurley,** Paul A '91 (Boeggeman G&C,PC) -46 Columbia -Albany 12207
(518) 399-6609 .. **Hurley,** Richd E '75 -18 Evergreen Blvd -Glenvll 12302 **Fx:**372-4789
(518) 303-4816 .. **Hurley,** Sheila M '00 -61 Thompson -Catskill 12414
(716) 853-1616 .. **Hurley,** Thos J '89 (Harter S&E LLP) -12 Fountain Plz -Buffalo 14202
(716) 626-0404 .. **Hurley,** Thos P '02 %Kantor & G,PLLC -5800 Main -Williamsvll 14221 **Fx:**626-0412
(212) 819-8200 .. **Hurlock,** James B '60 OfCnsl White & C LLP -1155 Av of Amer -NY 10036
(212) 653-8865 .. **Hurlock,** Wm L '04 (Seiger GF,LLP) -330 Mad Av -NY 10017 **Fx:**(646) 495-5009
(212) 277-0781 .. **Hurm,** Corrie A '06 The Hartford -2 Park Av -NY 10016
(212) 407-9129 .. **Hurowitz,** Brian M '97 CKX Inc -650 Mad Av -NY 10022
(212) 285-3800 .. **Hurowitz,** Chas J '91 %Subin Assoc LLP -150 Bway -NY 10007
(516) 571-2631 .. **Hurrell,** David '88 Hon F Gulotta Jr -262 Old Cntry Rd -Mineola 11501
(718) 579-3000 .. **Hurson,** Michl P '88 %Leg Aid -1020 Grnd Cncrs -Bronx 10451 **Fx:**588-2611
(718) 590-2000 .. **Hurst,** Erica R '09 %DA -198 E 161st -Bronx 10451 **Fx:**590-6477
(518) 689-1407 .. **Hurst,** Wm A '98 OfCnsl Greenberg T,LLP -54 State -Albany 12207
(212) 689-8600 .. **Hurt,** Adam '05 %Meissner K&F,LLP -275 Mad Av -NY 10016
(212) 609-6800 .. **Hurtado,** Irene M '01 %McCarter & E,LLP -245 Park Av -NY 10167
(914) 376-3757 .. **Hurtado,** Patty '04 %Leg Srvcs -30 S Bway -Ynkrs 10701 **Fx:**376-8739
(518) 427-2650 .. **Hurteau,** Danl J '89 (Nixon P LLP) -677 Bway -Albany 12207
(518) 457-2070 .. **Hurteau,** Mary Rinaldi '90 %Dept of Tax & Fin -Bldg 9 State Campus -Albany 12227 **Fx:**457-6131
(212) 269-5500 .. **Hurwit,** Joshua S '09 %Gordon & R LLP -90 Broad -NY 10004
(212) 977-7033 .. **Hurwitz,** Adam M '86 %Perecman Firm PLLC -250 W 57th -NY 10107
(212) 832-1977 .. **Hurwitz,** Andrew P '88 (Schreck RDA&H) -1790 Bway -NY 10019 **Fx:**832-2969
(585) 546-5530 .. **Hurwitz,** Bernard R '99 -50 E Broad -Rchstr 14694
(716) 856-1600 .. **Hurwitz & DiMatteo** -424 Main -Buffalo 14202 **Fx:**856-5013
(212) 880-1200 .. **Hurwitz,** Elliot L '85 %Chicago Title/Ticor -711 3rd Av -NY 10017 **Fx:**880-1400
(716) 849-8900 .. **Hurwitz & Fine,PC** -1300 Lbrty Bldg -Buffalo 14202 **Fx:**855-0874
(212) 416-8000 .. **Hurwitz,** Gerald J '61 %Dept of Law -120 Bway -NY 10271
(646) 706-8289 .. **Hurwitz,** Isaac D '88 -638 Mntgmry -Brklyn 11225
(212) 720-5885 .. **Hurwitz,** Ivan J '94 %Fed Reserve Bk -33 Lbrty -NY 10045 **Fx:**785-5748
(585) 750-9888 .. **Hurwitz,** Jayme A '05 -28 E Main -Rchstr 14614 **Fx:**219-5299
(212) 884-7190 .. **Hurwitz,** Jerald P '78 GMAC Commerical Credit -1290 Av of Amer -NY 10104
(212) 534-4924 .. **Hurwitz,** Jill P '82 -305 E 86th -NY 10028 **Fx:**534-3905
(212) 373-3254 .. **Hurwitz,** Jonathan H '87 Cnsl Paul WRW&G LLP -1285 Av of Amer -NY 10019
(212) 548-0600 .. **Hurwitz,** Kenneth D '86 Open Soc Jstc Initiative -400 W 59th -NY 10019 **Fx:**548-4679
(718) 751-3821 .. **Hurwitz,** Lawr T '88 JFK Intl Air Term LLC -Term 4 Rm 161.022 -Jamaica 11430
(212) 436-4256 .. **Hurwitz,** Lisa B '07 Deloitte Tax LLP -2 World Fncl Ctr -NY 10281
(212) 361-0550 .. **Hurwitz,** Mark A '93 %Dept Homeless Srvcs -33 Beaver -NY 10004
(716) 856-1600 .. **Hurwitz,** Melvyn L '62 Hurwitz & D -424 Main -Buffalo 14202
(212) 619-4240 .. **Hurwitz,** Michl '70 (Hurwitz S&R) -299 Bway -NY 10007
(212) 684-3630 .. **Hurwitz,** Michl J '99 %D Horowitz,PC -276 5th Av -NY 10001 **Fx:**685-8617
(212) 687-3000 .. **Hurwitz,** Michl L '06 %Jaffe & A,LLP -600 3rd Av -NY 10016
(212) 757-6767 .. **Hurwitz,** Neal J '61 -111 W 57th -NY 10019
(212) 397-5553 .. **Hurwitz,** Peter A '87 %The Chatterjee Grp -888 7th Av -NY 10106 **Fx:**262-9637
(845) 634-4966 .. **Hurwitz,** Peter A '91 -151 N Main Bx624 -New Cty 10956 **Fx:**634-0872
(585) 527-0300 .. **Hurwitz,** Phillip R '91 -170 Mt Read Blvd -Rchstr 14611
(212) 398-1940 .. **Hurwitz,** Seymour I '55 -19 W 44th -NY 10036 **Fx:**764-5982
(212) 619-4240 .. **Hurwitz Stampur & Roth** -299 Bway -NY 10007 **Fx:**619-6743
(212) 232-1300 .. **Hurzeler,** Nicholas P K '07 %Lewis BB&S LLP -77 Water -NY 10005
(212) 267-5000 .. **Hus,** Mark '75 -225 Bway -NY 10007 **Fx:**267-5008
(212) 556-2100 .. **Husain,** Amene Mamoun '07 %King & S -1185 Av of Amer -NY 10036
(212) 967-3000 .. **Husain,** Parveen '07 %Levine & B,PLLC -350 5th Av -NY 10118
(718) 222-1640 .. **Husbands,** Carl A '96 -26 Court -Brklyn 11242 **Fx:**222-1639
(914) 995-3420 .. **Huseby,** Berit Hayes '04 %DA -111 Martin Luther King Blvd -White Plns 10601 **Fx:**995-3363
(212) 594-5300 .. **Husgen,** Jason M '07 %Milberg LLP -1 Penn Plz -NY 10119
(212) 388-3600 .. **Huss,** Isadore B '81 %32B-J Leg Srvcs -101 Av of Amer -NY 10013 **Fx:**388-3061
(212) 480-6781 .. **Huss,** Patrice Koza '81 %DHCR -25 Beaver -NY 10004 **Fx:**480-7416
(212) 849-7000 .. **Hussain,** Safia Gray '08 %Quinn EU&S,LLP -51 Mad Av -NY 10010
(518) 271-5002 .. **Hussar,** Robt A '97 %NE Health -2212 Burdett Av -Troy 12180
(212) 373-3000 .. **Hussein,** Amran '01 Cnsl Paul WRW&G LLP -1285 Av of Amer -NY 10019
(212) 250-6161 .. **Hussein,** Samir H '95 Deutsche Bk -60 Wall -NY 10005
(212) 735-3000 .. **Hussein,** Shermarkeh '07 %Skadden ASM&F LLP -4 Times Sq -NY 10036
(516) 342-1696 .. **Hussein,** Waiel S '99 W Hussein,PLLC -1233 Walt Whitman Rd -Melvll 11747 **Fx:**777-2776
(212) 986-4343 .. **Husserl,** Kenneth W '77 Berkeley College -3 E 43rd -NY 10017
(212) 416-8455 .. **Hussey,** Jeanna E '89 %Dept of Law -120 Bway -NY 10271
(315) 255-4307 .. **Hussey,** Nancy F '99 Hon T Leone -157 Genesee -Auburn 13021 **Fx:**255-4312
(212) 598-8000 .. **Husslein,** Scott F '92 Guardian Life Ins -7 Hanover Sq -NY 10004 **Fx:**919-2693
(212) 223-6700 .. **Husson DeSampigny,** Guillaume '00 Zukerman GB&C,LLP -875 3rd Av -NY 10022
(212) 977-7033 .. **Huston,** Barry S '73 OfCnsl Perecman Firm PLLC -250 W 57th -NY 10107
(716) 488-0758 .. **Huston,** Lana M '05 %Bly SBP&M -3 Lakevw Av Bx3327 -Jamestwn 14702
(212) 720-5326 .. **Huszar,** Andrew C '02 %Fed Reserve Bk -33 Lbrty -NY 10045 **Fx:**785-5748
(212) 216-8000 .. **Huszar,** Thos G '98 Cnsl Tarter K&D LLP -1350 Bway -NY 10018
(212) 873-1965 .. **Hutar,** Jean R '94 %Gracious Thyme -2191 3rd Av -NY 10035 **Fx:**724-1557
(212) 221-5700 .. **Hutchens,** Jon T '08 %Goldberg WFG LLP -1501 Bway -NY 10036
(212) 848-4000 .. **Hutchens,** Kristen A '10 Shearman & S LLP -599 Lex Av -NY 10022
(212) 325-7417 .. **Hutcher,** Andrew M '89 Credit Suisse -11 Mad Av -NY 10010
(212) 557-7200 .. **Hutcher,** Larry K '76 (Davidoff M&H,LLP) -605 3rd Av -NY 10158
(716) 852-0400 .. **Hutcheson,** Kevin V '03 %Roach BM&G,PC -424 Main -Buffalo 14202
(607) 273-2283 .. **Hutchings,** Betsy Ann '86 Prisoners' Leg Srvcs -114 Prospect -Ithaca 14850 **Fx:**272-9122
(212) 430-3150 .. **Hutchings,** Brian C '01 %Gunderson DSVF&H,LLP -220 W 42nd -NY 10036
(212) 450-4000 .. **Hutchins,** David M '08 %Davis P&W LLP -450 Lex Av -NY 10017
(315) 785-3152 .. **Hutchins,** Julie M '93 (Pub Def) -175 Arsenal -Watertwn 13601 **Fx:**785-5060
(212) 295-6414 .. **Hutchins,** Kathryn A '01 Cnsl WilmerHale -399 Park Av -NY 10022
(212) 790-0000 .. **Hutchinson,** Andrew B '06 OZ Captl Mgt -9 W 57th -NY 10019
(718) 671-0900 .. **Hutchinson,** Bryan J '99 (BJ Hutchinson,PLLC) -1443 E Gun Hill Rd -Bronx 10469 **Fx:**671-1543
(607) 734-2271 .. **Hutchinson,** Cynthia S '79 OfCnsl Sayles & E -1 W Church -Elmira 14901
(212) 210-9552 .. **Hutchinson,** James S '07 (Alston & B LLP) -90 Park Av -NY 10016
(212) 839-5300 .. **Hutchinson,** John G '86 (Sidley A LLP) -787 7th Av -NY 10019
(212) 693-0085 .. **Hutchinson,** Kendra L '06 Appellate Advocates -2 Rector -NY 10006 **Fx:**693-0878
(212) 310-2000 .. **Hutchinson,** Kristine H '05 %Colgate-Palmolive -300 Park Av -NY 10022 **Fx:**310-3406
(516) 694-3000 .. **Hutchinson,** Lisa L '96 %Guercio & G,LLP -77 Conklin -Farmngdl 11735 **Fx:**694-4738
(585) 454-5050 .. **Hutchinson,** Michelle A '93 (Brown & H) -2 State -Rchstr 14614
(212) 837-6826 .. **Hutchinson,** Parker N '10 %Hughes H&R LLP -1 Bttry Pk Plz -NY 10004 **Fx:**299-6826
(516) 922-3000 .. **Hutchinson,** Richd L '90 Hutchinson & H,PC -127 South -Oyster Bay 11771 **Fx:**922-3156
(518) 458-8922 .. **Hutchison,** Fred J '85 (Donohue SV&H,LLP) -24 Aviation Rd -Albany 12205
(607) 734-3380 .. **Hutchison,** Mark P '82 (Hutchison & M) -315 Lk -Elmira 14901 **Fx:**734-3398
(607) 937-8383 .. **Hutchison,** Mark P '82 (Hutchison & M) -9 W 1st -Corning 14830 **Fx:**936-2410
(607) 426-6982 .. **Hutchison,** Robin M '88 (Hutchison Law Ofcs) -Bx701 -Waverly 14892
(212) 468-8000 .. **Huters,** Emily E '08 %Morrison & F LLP -1290 Av of Amer -NY 10104
(212) 474-1000 .. **Huth,** Karl C '05 %Cravath S&M LLP -825 8th Av -NY 10019

(212) 981-9121 .. **Hutner**, Eric S '83 (Hutner K LLP) -1359 Bway -NY 10018 **Fx**:981-9122
(718) 546-0950 .. **Hutner**, Florence A '87 %Dept of Correction -75-20 Astoria Blvd -E Elmhrst 11370
(212) 351-4500 .. **Hutner**, Jos L '59 OfCnsl Epstein B&G,PC -250 Park Av -NY 10177
(212) 888-0658 .. **Hutson**, George J '84 %M Edelman -400 E 56th -NY 10022 **Fx**:888-0695
(716) 332-0990 .. **Hutson**, Horace A '89 Childrens Lgl Ctr -438 Main -Buffalo 14202
(212) 455-2000 .. **Hutson**, Melissa J '03 %Simpson T&B LLP -425 Lex Av -NY 10017
(212) 224-4000 .. **Hutta**, Jane '96 %Sumitomo Mitsui -277 Park Av -NY 10172 **Fx**:593-9522
(212) 547-5400 .. **Huttenlocher**, Michl R '06 %McDermott W&E LLP -340 Mad Av -NY 10173
(212) 335-9000 .. **Hutter**, Barbara J '99 %DA -1 Hogan Pl -NY 10013
(914) 225-6460 .. **Hutter**, Lisa Bianculli '98 Morgan Stanley -2000 Wstchstr Av -Purchase 10577
(518) 432-8000 .. **Hutter**, Lynne Ann '05 %Crane & P -48 Howard -Albany 12207
(518) 465-5995 .. **Hutter**, Michl J Jr. '71 SpclCnsl Powers & S,LLP -39 N Pearl -Albany 12207
(518) 445-2311 .. **Hutter**, Michl J Jr. '71 %Albany Law Schl -80 New Scotland Av -Albany 12208 **Fx**:445-2315
(585) 593-3341 .. **Hutter**, Robt G '80 (Hutter & F) -22 W State Bx1137 -Wellsvll 14895 **Fx**:593-3782
(718) 250-2000 .. **Huttler**, Jos S '92 %DA -350 Jay -Brklyn 11201 **Fx**:250-2314
(212) 947-3793 .. **Huttler**, Steven '91 (Sadis & G LLP) -551 5th Av -NY 10176
(518) 458-8922 .. **Huttner**, Bruce S '86 (Donohue SV&H,LLP) -24 Aviation Rd -Albany 12205
(212) 237-0000 .. **Huttner**, Constance S '81 (Vinson & E LLP) -666 5th Av -NY 10103
(646) 467-9700 .. **Huttner**, Lee Michl '91 -233 Bway -NY 10279
(518) 452-5600 .. **Hutton**, Brett M '99 (Heslin RF&M PC) -5 Columbia Cir -Albany 12203
(212) 404-6988 .. **Hutton**, Frank J '01 %R Yellen & Assoc LLP -111 Bway -NY 10006 **Fx**:404-7857
(212) 396-1200 .. **Hutton**, G Thompson '72 -13 E 69th -NY 10021 **Fx**:472-7711
(212) 682-5702 .. **Hutton & Solomon** -475 5th Av -NY 10017 **Fx**:682-6523
(212) 262-0660 .. **Hutton**, Thos C '77 %Chemed Corp -1270 Av of Amer -NY 10020
(212) 416-6146 .. **Huvane**, Breda A '02 %Dept of Law -120 Bway -NY 10271
(516) 354-8500 .. **Huwel**, George A '82 (Huwel & M) -11 New Hyde Pk Rd -Franklin Sq 11010
(212) 592-1400 .. **Huynh**, Hanh V '05 %Herrick,F LLP -2 Park Av -NY 10016
(212) 373-3000 .. **Huynh**, Philander '08 %Paul WRW&G LLP -1285 Av of Amer -NY 10019
(212) 294-6700 .. **HuYoung**, James D '07 %Winston & S -200 Park Av -NY 10166
(315) 461-4277 .. **Hvozda**, John I '89 %Falge & M,PC -3300 Vickery Rd -N Syracuse 13212
(212) 704-6000 .. **Hwang**, Albert C '08 (Troutman S LLP) -405 Lex Av -NY 10174
(212) 572-4200 .. **Hwang**, Andrew '04 Estee Lauder -767 5th Av -NY 10153 **Fx**:572-3989
(212) 455-2000 .. **Hwang**, Celine C '04 %Simpson T&B LLP -425 Lex Av -NY 10017
(718) 353-7773 .. **Hwang**, Chia-Yin Lois '89 -136-21 Roosevelt Av -Flushng 11354 **Fx**:353-6202
(800) 293-6292 .. **Hwang**, Danl '72 -55 Bway -NY 10006
(212) 925-1208 .. **Hwang**, Henry S-L '08 T Cox -401 Bway -NY 10013
(212) 848-4000 .. **Hwang**, In Young '09 %Shearman & S LLP -599 Lex Av -NY 10022
(212) 837-6599 .. **Hwang**, Jennifer E '03 %Hughes H&R LLP -1 Bttry Pk Plz -NY 10004 **Fx**:299-6599
(917) 777-4200 .. **Hwang**, John Y '02 Cnsl Bingham M LLP -1 Bttry Pk Plz -NY 10004
(212) 558-4000 .. **Hwang**, Jonathan '10 %Sullivan & C LLP -125 Broad -NY 10004
(212) 907-0700 .. **Hwang**, Julie '08 %Labaton S LLP -140 Bway -NY 10005
(212) 335-4500 .. **Hwang**, Jungyoon '10 %DLA Piper LLP -1251 Av of Amer -NY 10020
(212) 683-7763 .. **Hwang**, Kelley K '87 -401 E 34th -NY 10016 **Fx**:725-7123
(212) 773-6325 .. **Hwang**, Michelle H '07 Ernst & Young LP -5 Times Sq -NY 10036
(212) 833-0589 .. **Hwang**, Mirry M '94 %Pru -466 Lex Av -NY 10017
(212) 856-9600 .. **Hwang**, Nahye '10 %Morvillo AGIA&B,PC -565 5th Av -NY 10017
(212) 380-8207 .. **Hwang**, Sang Kyu '07 Sheppard MR&H LLP -30 Rckfllr Plz -NY 10112 **Fx**:653-8701
(212) 418-4821 .. **Hwang**, Soo Won '88 %Sunitomo Trust & Banking Co -527 Mad Av -NY 10022
(914) 639-6200 .. **Hyacinthe**, Maurice K '97 HMH Mgmt Co LLC -Bx625 -Ardsley 10502
(914) 323-7000 .. **Hyacinthe**, Sylvere M '86 (Wilson EME&D LLP) -3 Gannett Dr -White Plns 10604
(914) 669-6710 .. **Hyams**, Ira L '55 -813 Heritage Hills -Somers 10589
(212) 349-2030 .. **Hyams**, Jerrold E '71 -300 E 51st -NY 10022
(914) 461-3153 .. **Hyams**, Paul J '84 (P Hyams,PLLC) -108 Corp Park Dr -White Plns 10604 **Fx**:992-8763
(212) 867-7947 .. **Hyams**, Robt A '90 -295 Mad Av -NY 10017 **Fx**:682-8785
(212) 468-8050 .. **Hyans**, Hollis Lee '81 (Morrison & F LLP) -1290 Av of Amer -NY 10104
(212) 326-2000 .. **Hyatt**, Adam G '08 %O'Melveny & M LLP -7 Times Sq -NY 10036
(585) 424-3270 .. **Hyatt**, Dennis M '75 %Dollinger & Assoc,PC -777 Canal Vw Blvd -Rchstr 14623
(585) 753-4500 .. **Hyatt**, Jennifer L '08 DA -832 Watts Bldg -Rchstr 14614 **Fx**:753-4576
(212) 682-0020 .. **Hyde**, Andrea '71 (Putney TH&H LLP) -521 5th Av -NY 10175
(518) 462-3000 .. **Hyde**, Carol A '85 (Iseman CR&H,LLP) -9 Thurlow Ter -Albany 12203
(716) 753-4478 .. **Hyde**, Jerry D '79 %Dept Soc Srvcs -HR Clothier Bldg -Mayvll 14757
(518) 465-3484 .. **Hyde**, Panagiota K '09 %Carter CCBM&L,PC -20 Corp Wds Blvd -Albany 12211
(716) 934-4588 .. **Hyde**, Sheila Meck '82 -12 Pkwy -Silver Crk 14136
(716) 856-4000 .. **Hyde**, Thos R '93 (Hodgson R LLP) -140 Pearl -Buffalo 14202
(718) 666-8648 .. **Hyder**, Iqbal '01 (I Hyder,LLC) -8801 35th Av -Jcksn Hts 11372 **Fx**:732-2465
(212) 906-1200 .. **Hyder**, Stefanie C '08 %Latham & W -885 3rd Av -NY 10022
(212) 267-3320 .. **Hyer**, Suzanne E '81 (Savona D&H LLC) -111 Bway -NY 10006
(212) 728-8000 .. **Hykal**, Deirdre N '02 %Willkie F&G LLP -787 7th Av -NY 10019
(631) 390-5000 .. **Hyl**, Paul S '00 %Genser DG&C,LLP -445 Broad Hollow Rd -Melvll 11747
(212) 972-6161 .. **Hyland**, Anita M '98 (Cassin & C LLP) -711 3rd Av -NY 10017
(646) 252-2746 .. **Hyland**, Edw D '94 %Transit Auth -2 Bway -NY 10004 **Fx**:252-5559
(212) 697-3050 .. **Hyland**, John A '86 (Sherry & O) -305 Mad Av -NY 10165
(212) 326-3939 .. **Hyland**, John J '77 (Jones D) -222 E 41st -NY 10017
(347) 418-3830 .. **Hyland**, John T '03 %L Miles -36-01 43rd Av -LIC 11101 **Fx**:418-3838
(516) 538-1111 .. **Hyland**, Jos A '00 %Mahon MK&O,LLC -254 Nassau Blvd -Garden City South 11530
(212) 506-1700 .. **Hyland**, Jos P '06 Kasowitz BT&F LLP -1633 Bway -NY 10019
(212) 687-0100 .. **Hyland**, Kevin T '95 (Harris B PLLC) -100 Wall -NY 10005
(212) 574-1200 .. **Hyland**, Mark Jos '81 (Seward & K LLP) -1 Bttry Pk Plz -NY 10004
(212) 460-4584 .. **Hyland**, Michelle M '02 Con Ed -4 Irving Pl -NY 10003
(212) 697-1900 .. **Hyland**, Niamh J '08 Katzenbach Ptnrs LLC -101 Park Av -NY 10178
(212) 980-0120 .. **Hyland**, Nicole I '03 %Frankfurt KK&S,PC -488 Mad Av -NY 10022
(212) 490-3000 .. **Hyland**, Thos W '71 (Wilson EME&D LLP) -150 E 42nd -NY 10017
(212) 788-7302 .. **Hylton**, Christian Brent '99 City Cncl Land Use -250 Bway -NY 10007 **Fx**:788-7337
(212) 841-1000 .. **Hyman**, Andrew C '05 %Covington & B LLP -620 8th Av -NY 10018
(516) 869-7695 .. **Hyman**, Andrew M '81 %Town Atty -220 Plandome Rd -Manhsst 11030 **Fx**:869-7605
(516) 296-7000 .. **Hyman**, Bernard '70 (Certilman BA&H,LLP) -90 Merrick Av -E Meadow 11554
(315) 798-5766 .. **Hyman**, Bernard L Jr. '98 %DA -800 Park Av -Utica 13501 **Fx**:798-5582
(914) 750-5933 .. **Hyman**, Chas '85 (Kissel H&W LLP) -580 Wht Plns Rd -Tarrytwn 10591
(212) 719-3800 .. **Hyman**, Chris Stern '79 (Medical Mediation Grp LLC) -1040 Av of Amer -NY 10018 **Fx**:997-7686
(212) 973-0572 .. **Hyman**, David M '81 (Wolff & S PC) -140 Bway -NY 10005
(212) 286-8585 .. **Hyman**, E Marc '85 (Heidell PM&B,LLP) -99 Park Av -NY 10016
(212) 732-5800 .. **Hyman**, Elisa F '92 OfCnsl Friedman & M LLP -233 Bway -NY 10279
(516) 745-0700 .. **Hyman**, Franklin C '63 (FC Hyman,PC) -595 Stewart Av -Gdn Cty 11530 **Fx**:745-0769
(212) 506-2500 .. **Hyman**, Fredk D '93 (Mayer B LLP) -1675 Bway -NY 10019
(914) 833-5297 .. **Hyman & Gilbert** -1843 Palmer Av -Larchmnt 10538 **Fx**:833-5294
(212) 225-2000 .. **Hyman**, Jerome E '49 SrCnsl Cleary GS&H -1 Lbrty Plz -NY 10006
(212) 523-7191 .. **Hyman**, Jonathan A '99 Continuum Srvcs -555 W 57th -NY 10019
(516) 823-9301 .. **Hyman**, Jordan M '89 -119 N Park Av -Rockvll Ctr 11570 **Fx**:825-6568
(516) 773-3017 .. **Hyman**, Jos D '81 -97 Old Mill Rd -Gt Neck 11023
(347) 449-6398 .. **Hyman**, Julie '98 J Hyman,PC -640 W 237th -Bronx 10463 **Fx**:449-6398
(718) 792-0444 .. **Hyman**, Lauren B '09 Cnsl MHLS -1500 Waters Pl -Bronx 10461 **Fx**:597-7385
(718) 520-9095 .. **Hyman**, Lawr S '86 -125-10 Qns Blvd -Kew Gdns 11415
(914) 428-8290 .. **Hyman**, Lisa J '88 -805 C Maple Ln -Somers 10589
(718) 262-7100 .. **Hyman**, Lori E '90 %Civil Ct -89-17 Sutphin Blvd -Jamaica 11435 **Fx**:262-7107
(516) 296-7000 .. **Hyman**, M Allan '65 (Certilman BA&H,LLP) -90 Merrick Av -E Meadow 11554
(516) 621-0600 .. **Hyman**, Marc H '90 (Sontag & H) -69 Roslyn Rd -Roslyn Hts 11577
(212) 608-8959 .. **Hyman**, Marc S '96 %M Palillo,PC -277 Bway -NY 10007 **Fx**:608-0304
(212) 907-7300 .. **Hyman**, Martin S '80 (Golenbock EAB&P) -437 Mad Av -NY 10022
(212) 869-2300 .. **Hyman**, Marvin J '71 (Toback B&R,LLP) -15 W 44th -NY 10036
(212) 790-9200 .. **Hyman**, Midge M '87 (Cowan L&L,PC) -1133 Av of Amer -NY 10036
(212) 692-1000 .. **Hyman**, Miriam O '78 (Duane M LLP) -1540 Bway -NY 10036
(212) 585-0111 .. **Hyman**, Morton P '59 MPH Enterprises LLC -998 5th Av -NY 10028
(212) 535-3600 .. **Hyman**, Myron A '80 -240 E 82nd -NY 10028
(212) 770-1957 .. **Hyman**, Paul B '93 AIG Tech Srvcs -80 Pine -NY 10005
(718) 590-8545 .. **Hyman**, Shari C '92 %Hon M Clancy -851 Grnd Cncrs -Bronx 10451
(914) 522-0105 .. **Hyman**, Sharon '85 -43 Harvard Rd -Scarsdale 10583 **Fx**:654-0890
(212) 248-3140 .. **Hyman**, Stacey A '09 %Drinker B&R LLP -140 Bway -NY 10005
(631) 324-3262 .. **Hyman**, Stanley '74 -10 Pantigo Rd -E Hampton 11937
(718) 294-1010 .. **Hyman**, Stanley M '71 -432 Claremont Pkwy -Bronx 10457 **Fx**:294-4268
(212) 448-1100 .. **Hyman**, Steven J '66 (McLaughlin & S,LLP) -260 Mad Av -NY 10016
(516) 746-3500 .. **Hyman**, Todd '99 %Brand G&B,PC -600 Old Cntry Rd -Gdn Cty 11530
(585) 258-4538 .. **Hymes**, Allan D '92 %UIA Bd -109 S Union -Rchstr 14607 **Fx**:258-4539
(914) 949-0600 .. **Hymes**, Kevin C '99 (Hymes & Assoc) -445 Hmltn Av -White Plns 10601 **Fx**:946-7950
(718) 624-9200 .. **Hymowitz**, Chas M '98 -26 Court -Brklyn 11242 **Fx**:865-9248
(212) 889-3900 .. **Hymowitz & Freeman** -404 Park Av S -NY 10016 **Fx**:689-3315
(212) 889-3900 .. **Hymowitz**, Lee D '76 (Hymowitz & F) -404 Park Av S -NY 10016
(212) 233-4651 .. **Hymowitz**, Phillip M '86 %Weinstein & Holtzman -29 Park Row -NY 10038
(845) 634-3775 .. **Hymowitz**, Steven R '87 (Fellows H&E,PC) -254 S Main -New Cty 10956
(718) 250-2000 .. **Hynes**, Chas J '63 (DA) -350 Jay -Brklyn 11201 **Fx**:250-2314
(212) 373-3000 .. **Hynes**, John L '06 %Paul WRW&G LLP -1285 Av of Amer -NY 10019
(914) 750-5933 .. **Hynes**, Jos G '87 (Kissel H&W LLP) -580 Wht Plns Rd -Tarrytwn 10591
(212) 776-5081 .. **Hynes**, Lisa '97 %Housing Auth -250 Bway -NY 10007
(518) 371-2684 .. **Hynes**, Mary Beth '91 Precision Valve & Automation -15 Solar Dr -Clifton Pk 12065
(212) 335-4500 .. **Hynes**, Michl D '00 (DLA Piper LLP) -1251 Av of Amer -NY 10020
(212) 610-6300 .. **Hynes**, Patricia M '66 SrCnsl Allen & O -1221 Av of Amer -NY 10020
(212) 335-9000 .. **Hynes**, Patrick J '85 %DA -1 Hogan Pl -NY 10013
(914) 366-7200 .. **Hynes**, Sean P '91 %Stinnes Corp -120 Wht Plns Rd -Tarrytwn 10591 **Fx**:366-8226
(212) 225-2000 .. **Hynes**, Shawn T '07 %Cleary GS&H -1 Lbrty Plz -NY 10006
(516) 739-3525 .. **Hynes**, Thos A '89 (Hynes & C,LLP) -114 Old Cntry Rd -Mineola 11501 **Fx**:739-8742
(212) 506-5000 .. **Hyon**, Elizabeth S '09 %Orrick H&S LLP -51 W 52nd -NY 10019

(212) 239-4788 .. **Hyon,** Yong Hee '80 -450 7th Av -NY 10123 **Fx:**629-5659
(718) 625-6777 .. **Hyppolite,** Cassandra '00 -32 Court -Brklyn 11201
(212) 268-3607 .. **Hyun,** Boyoung '03 %Pak & C,PC -230 Park Av -NY 10169 **Fx:**(201) 886-0111
(212) 691-1038 .. **Hyun,** Christopher C '89 GLC Productions,Inc -302A W 12th -NY 10014
(212) 474-1000 .. **Hyun,** Michl K '10 %Cravath S&M LLP -825 8th Av -NY 10019
(212) 554-1400 .. **Hyun,** Paul J '08 %Bernstein LB&G LLP -1285 Av of Amer -NY 10019
(212) 416-6556 .. **Hyun,** Peter S '06 %Dept of Law -120 Bway -NY 10271
(516) 483-2990 .. **Iaccarino,** Riccardo '90 (Barnes I&S,LLP) -3 Surrey Ln -Hempstd 11550
(646) 557-5100 .. **Iachan,** Melissa '08 %Patton B LLP -1185 Av of Amer -NY 10036
(914) 967-7763 .. **Iacobellis,** Jane Grantmyre '85 -19 Highland Pk Pl -Rye 10580 **Fx:**967-7763
(585) 530-3100 .. **Iacobucci,** Jennifer Powers '96 %Applt Div 4th Dept -50 East Av Ste 200 -Rchstr 14604 **Fx:**530-3247
(212) 267-4876 .. **Iacocca,** Anthony C '00 (Hoagland LMD&D,LLP) -1501 Bway -NY 10036
(516) 292-8100 .. **Iacona,** Lynn Ann '84 Nassau/Sfflk Law Srv -1 Helen Keller Way -Hempstd 11550 **Fx:**292-6529
(914) 684-0090 .. **Iaconis,** Anthony J '91 (Diserio MO&C LLP) -50 Main -White Plns 10606
(315) 687-6093 .. **Iaconis,** Paul F '74 Iaconis Law Ofc,PLLC -282 Genesee -Chittenango 13037 **Fx:**687-5232
(516) 294-8844 .. **Iaconis,** Rosemarie '07 %L'Abbate BC&C,LLP -1001 Franklin Av -Gdn Cty 11530
(917) 685-0537 .. **Iacono,** Frank A '97 -6 Donald Ct W -Blue Pnt 11715
(212) 504-6000 .. **Iacono,** Jennifer A '09 %Cadwalader W&T LLP -1 World Fncl Ctr -NY 10281
(914) 961-0565 .. **Iacono,** Joan '83 -81 Pondfld Rd -Bronxvll 10708 **Fx:**961-3333
(516) 365-3629 .. **Iacono,** John P '77 Alliant Resrcs Grp Inc -64 Blenheim Dr -Manhsst 11030 **Fx:**365-3629
(716) 881-5800 .. **Iacono,** Michl A '88 Siegel K&K -426 Franklin -Buffalo 14202
(585) 454-7145 .. **Iacovangelo,** Anthony B '96 (Gallo & I,LLP) -39 State -Rchstr 14614
(585) 889-4840 .. **Iacovangelo,** Bernard J '74 Faber Homes -3240 Chili Av -Rchstr 14624
(585) 454-7145 .. **Iacovangelo,** Frank B '67 (Gallo & I,LLP) -39 State -Rchstr 14614
(212) 745-5860 .. **Iacovetta,** Ana C '93 IBM -590 Mad Av -NY 10022 **Fx:**745-5868
(212) 695-5454 .. **Iacoviello,** Rocco '95 (Mango & I,LLP) -14 Penn Plz -NY 10122
(212) 818-9494 .. **Iacovino,** Louis T '68 -60 E 42nd -NY 10165 **Fx:**689-9403
(212) 225-2000 .. **Iacovitti,** Danl R '09 %Cleary GS&H -1 Lbrty Plz -NY 10006
(631) 474-1017 .. **Iacueo,** Laurence J '71 Data Strat,Inc -10 Roosevelt Av -Pt Jffrsn Sta 11776 **Fx:**928-1025
(212) 996-8700 .. **Iadevaia,** Anthony '92 -1932 2nd Av -NY 10029 **Fx:**996-4235
(212) 238-2420 .. **Iafrate,** Susanna '93 UIA Bd -59 Maiden Ln -NY 10038 **Fx:**238-2451
(516) 248-2400 .. **Ialenti & Macari** -170 Old Cntry Rd -Mineola 11501 **Fx:**248-2084
(516) 248-2400 .. **Ialenti,** Marc J '87 (Ialenti & M) -170 Old Cntry Rd -Mineola 11501
(516) 333-3665 .. **Iammarino,** Deborah '98 (Iammarino & V PLLC) -2126 Stratford Dr -Westbury 11590 **Fx:**333-3275
(585) 232-7070 .. **Ianacone,** Saml J Jr. '75 (S Ianacone Jr, PC) -311 Alxndr -Rchstr 14604 **Fx:**232-7295
(212) 770-1740 .. **Iandoli,** Anthony J '93 %AIG -80 Pine -NY 10005
(212) 922-2200 .. **Iandoli,** Patricia Ann '96 (Watson F&W LLP) -1133 Av of Amer -NY 10036
(845) 896-7900 .. **Ianelli,** John R '75 JR Ianelli PC -804 Route 9 -Fishkill 12524 **Fx:**896-2100
(845) 896-4711 .. **Ianelli,** Robt P '78 R Ianelli -1436 Route 52 -Fishkill 12524 **Fx:**896-4755
(212) 460-4682 .. **Ianello,** Stephen '85 Con Ed -4 Irving Pl -NY 10003 **Fx:**777-0963
(716) 551-4128 .. **Iannaccone,** Adolph C '79 %Bankruptcy Ct -300 Pearl -Buffalo 14202
(212) 308-4440 .. **Iannaccone,** Giuliano '00 SpclCnsl Ferrante,PLLC -5 W 19th -NY 10011 **Fx:**888-3839
(914) 995-3637 .. **Iannace,** John-Paul A '00 Cnty Atty -148 Martine Av -White Plns 10601 **Fx:**995-2495
(212) 971-0111 .. **Iannace,** Peter A '00 Sapir Organization -384 5th Av -NY 10018
(718) 894-2900 .. **Iannacone,** Randolph Frank '90 (R Frank Iannacone Metro Law Assoc) -290 Larkin Dr -Monroe 10950 **Fx:**894-2929
(212) 770-1731 .. **Iannantuoni,** Jennifer D '98 AIG Toxic Torts -80 Pine -NY 10005
(212) 431-1031 .. **Iannarelli,** Anthony N Jr. '88 -130 Church -NY 10007 **Fx:**(201) 962-8190
(631) 361-7050 .. **Iannarone,** Liberatore J '69 (Mullen & I,PC) -300 E Main -Smithtwn 11787
(212) 503-2191 .. **Iannarone,** Thos L '04 GSO Cptl Prtnrs LLP -280 Park Av -NY 10017
(718) 961-5550 .. **Iannece,** Jerry M '85 -160-05 Horace Hrdng Expy -Flushng 11365 **Fx:**961-5755
(718) 855-2844 .. **Iannelli,** Susan '93 -26 Court -Brklyn 11242 **Fx:**855-5937
(518) 371-8888 .. **Ianniello Anderson & Reilly,PC** -805 Route 146 -Clifton Pk 12065 **Fx:**371-3369
(518) 218-1053 .. **Ianniello Anderson & Reilly,PC** -8 Airline Dr -Albany 12205
(518) 371-8888 .. **Ianniello,** Anthony R '71 (Ianniello A&R,PC) -805 Route 146 -Clifton Pk 12065
(212) 558-5500 .. **Ianniello,** Marie-Louise '87 OfCnsl Weitz & L,PC -700 Bway -NY 10003
(716) 852-0737 .. **Iannini,** Peter L '76 Monroe Title -130 Pearl -Buffalo 14202 **Fx:**852-9847
(516) 739-0400 .. **Ianno,** Kathleen A '92 %Kelly R&K,LLP -330 Old Cntry Rd -Mineola 11501
(516) 333-5000 .. **Iannone,** James L '99 (Gordon S&I PC) -400 Grdn City Plz -Gdn Cty 11530 **Fx:**333-3260
(212) 553-3200 .. **Iannone,** Lisa M '91 (Marulli LE&T,LLP) -5 Hanover Sq -NY 10004
(212) 761-4000 .. **Iannucci,** Laura '03 Morgan Stanley -1221 Av of Amer -NY 10020
(718) 596-0504 .. **Iannucci,** Robt T '76 -139 Henry -Brklyn 11201
(914) 948-9500 .. **Iannuccilli,** Thos '94 %J Killerlane -175 Main -White Plns 10601 **Fx:**948-3004
(585) 546-6688 .. **Iannuzo,** Bruce C '88 -183 E Main -Rchstr 14604
(212) 227-9595 .. **Iannuzzi,** John Nicholas '62 Iannuzzi & I -74 Trinity Pl -NY 10006 **Fx:**227-2099
(212) 732-2000 .. **Iannuzzi,** Michl M '10 %Cullen and D LLP -44 Wall -NY 10005
(631) 567-7600 .. **Iantuono,** Jos G '74 %ASG Consulting Corp -926 Lincoln Av -Holbrook 11741 **Fx:**589-7166
(845) 334-8150 .. **Iapoce,** Michl A '93 -1 N Front Bx3741 -Kingston 12402 **Fx:**338-0868
(914) 962-5513 .. **Iasiello,** Theresa Catanese '01 (Kibbe & I) -1961 Commerce -Yorktwn Hts 10598
(914) 698-0649 .. **Iason,** Cara Nash '79 -606 Walton Av -Mamaroneck 10543
(212) 880-1420 .. **Iason,** Lawr II '71 (Morvillo AGIA&B,PC) -565 5th Av -NY 10017
(212) 735-3000 .. **Iason,** Sara '09 %Skadden ASM&F LLP -4 Times Sq -NY 10036
(585) 454-6850 .. **Iati,** Janice '82 -1 Chase Sq -Rchstr 14604 **Fx:**325-6407
(585) 325-7515 .. **Iati,** Janice '82 OfCnsl Forsyth HOK&M,PC -1 Chase Sq -Rchstr 14604
(212) 557-0990 .. **Iaulus,** Hilah R '82 (Krasner & I) -10 E 40th -NY 10016
(212) 701-3000 .. **Ibarguen,** Diego A '07 %Cahill G&R LLP -80 Pine -NY 10005 **Fx:**269-5420
(631) 951-3700 .. **Ibraham,** Robt M '01 (Ibraham & Assoc) -2025 Brentwd Rd -Brentwd 11717
(718) 237-2000 .. **Ibrahim,** Andrea S '08 Leg Aid -111 Lvngstn -Brklyn 11201 **Fx:**237-8737
(212) 450-4000 .. **Ibrahim,** Ashraf '98 (Davis P&W LLP) -450 Lex Av -NY 10017
(631) 577-7742 .. **Ibuzor,** Aloy O '00 K Dodson -100 Baylis Rd -Melvll 11747 **Fx:**577-7199
(212) 704-6000 .. **Ice,** Robyn E '03 (Troutman S LLP) -405 Lex Av -NY 10174
(212) 455-2000 .. **Ichel,** David W '79 (Simpson T&B LLP) -425 Lex Av -NY 10017
(212) 474-1000 .. **Ichino,** Mayumi '08 %Cravath S&M LLP -825 8th Av -NY 10019
(212) 599-1300 .. **Icklan,** Susan S '95 Lex Terrae Ltd -331 Mad Av -NY 10017 **Fx:**983-2791
(845) 365-0293 .. **Icobelli,** Raymond G '59 -10 Glenwood Dr -Blauvelt 10913 **Fx:**359-3434
(212) 837-6662 .. **Idachaba,** Unekuojo '07 %Hughes H&R LLP -1 Bttry Pk Plz -NY 10004 **Fx:**299-6662
(212) 867-4100 .. **Idahosa-Howard,** R Evon '00 %Furman K&B LLP -61 Bway -NY 10006
(718) 558-4191 .. **Idehen,** Austin I '96 (Idehen & Assoc,PLLC) -89-31 161st -Jamaica 11432 **Fx:**504-4430
(212) 687-1736 .. **Idehen,** Stan N '98 %R Schwartzberg & Assoc,PLLC -60 E 42nd -NY 10165
(212) 944-9112 .. **Idelchik,** Inna '97 Strategic Legal Solutions -110 E 42nd -NY 10017
(212) 302-2900 .. **Iden,** Mitchell S '83 (Tannenbaum D&R) -1140 Av of Amer -NY 10036
(646) 701-4680 .. **Idiatoulina-Duffy,** Ekaterina R '08 %Puygrenier & L LLP -1699 Lex Av -NY 10029 **Fx:**(800) 616-0253
(212) 521-5400 .. **Idilby,** Omar Z '04 %Reed S LLP -599 Lex Av -NY 10022
(718) 961-5533 .. **Idouchi,** John K '88 -136-40 39th Av -Flushng 11354 **Fx:**961-7766
(212) 859-8000 .. **Idrizovic,** Andrew J '09 %Fried FHS&J LLP -1 NY Plz -NY 10004
(212) 697-1900 .. **Idzik,** Danl R '64 %Booz Allen Hamilton -101 Park Av -NY 10178
(716) 664-3906 .. **Idzik,** Martin F '66 (Phillips L LLP) -8 E 3rd Bx1279 -Jamestwn 14702
(716) 832-7777 .. **Ieraci,** Frank S '86 -2140 Eggert Rd -Amherst 14226 **Fx:**832-8915
(516) 741-3900 .. **Ieraci,** Vincenzo '97 Cnsl M Angel,PLLC -170 Old Cntry Rd -Mineola 11501 **Fx:**741-3383
(718) 250-2000 .. **Ierardi,** Joan P Barton '89 %DA -350 Jay -Brklyn 11201 **Fx:**250-2314
(716) 816-8679 .. **Ifandis,** Anastasia '04 -97 Lake -Hambrg 14075 **Fx:**649-9797
(718) 923-4206 .. **Ifaturoti,** Titilola O '01 %OTDA Fair Hearings -14 Boerum Pl -Brklyn 11201
(516) 739-6100 .. **Ife,** Wm B '93 -1140 Franklin Av -Gdn Cty 11530 **Fx:**739-6101
(212) 356-7549 .. **Ifill,** Michele Y '01 Dept of Ed -333 7th Av -NY 10001
(914) 251-2866 .. **Ifill,** Michelle C '86 %MCI -2 Intl Dr -Rye Brook 10573
(212) 735-3000 .. **Ifill,** Vicente A '08 %Skadden ASM&F LLP -4 Times Sq -NY 10036
(718) 205-1010 .. **Ifraimoff,** Elliot '01 (E Ifraimoff & Assoc,PC) -116-16 Qns Blvd -Frst Hlls 11375 **Fx:**205-2066
(347) 556-9583 .. **Igbo,** Nkechi A '09 -146-08 Hillside Av -Jamaica 11435
(914) 238-1000 .. **Iger,** Linda B '89 Reader's Digest -Readers Digest Rd -Plsntvll 10570 **Fx:**241-5644
(212) 361-1400 .. **Iglauer,** Evi F '85 %Envrnmntl Cntrl Brd -66 John -NY 10038 **Fx:**361-1900
(212) 402-9400 .. **Iglesia,** Virginia '08 McKool S,PC -1 Bryant Park -NY 10036
(212) 753-5000 .. **Ignacio,** Mary Eleonor D '09 %Schiff H LLP -900 3rd Av -NY 10022
(212) 232-1300 .. **Ignat,** Florentina '09 %Lewis BB&S LLP -77 Water -NY 10005
(212) 661-9100 .. **Igoe,** John P G '08 %Otterbourg SH&R,PC -230 Park Av -NY 10169
(518) 436-2840 .. **Igoe,** Jos P '09 %Thruway Auth -200 Southrn Blvd Bx189 -Albany 12201 **Fx:**471-4340
(716) 849-2215 .. **Igoe,** Michl J '02 WGRZ TV -259 Delaware Av -Buffalo 14202
(212) 521-5400 .. **Igoe,** Thos J Jr. '73 (Reed S LLP) -599 Lex Av -NY 10022
(845) 296-1001 .. **Igunbor,** Osaruwense '03 -695 Dutchess Tpk -Poughkeepsie 12603
(716) 845-9379 .. **Ihde,** Regan P '82 %Supreme Ct -25 Delaware Av -Buffalo 14202 **Fx:**851-3224
(212) 403-1000 .. **Ihekweazu,** Obinna C '09 %Wachtell LR&K -51 W 52nd -NY 10019
(212) 637-3250 .. **Ihlenburg,** Erick R '07 US EPA -290 Bway -NY 10007
(518) 434-0127 .. **Ihnatolya,** Nicholas M '06 %Sneeringer MPR -50 Chapel -Albany 12207
(516) 741-5252 .. **Ihrig,** Michl L II '09 %Sanders SBWV&G,PC -100 Hrrcks Rd -Mineola 11501
(212) 837-6921 .. **Ike,** U Arinze '07 %Hughes H&R LLP -1 Bttry Pk Plz -NY 10004 **Fx:**299-6921
(716) 636-7600 .. **Ikefugi,** Bruce A '89 %HoganWillig -2410 N Forest Rd -Amherst 14068
(718) 339-4999 .. **Ikhilov,** Z Erik '93 (ZE Ikhilov,PC) -2357 Coney Isl Av -Brklyn 11223
(718) 286-6000 .. **Ikhlas,** Muhammad '05 %DA -125-01 Qns Blvd -Kew Gdns 11415
(646) 386-4051 .. **Ikwild,** Jeannette M '86 %Hon M Obus -100 Centre -NY 10013
(212) 859-8000 .. **Ilacqua,** Danielle K '03 Fried FHS&J LLP -1 NY Plz -NY 10004
(212) 225-2000 .. **Ilan,** Danl '09 Cnsl Cleary GS&H -1 Lbrty Plz -NY 10006
(718) 286-6000 .. **Ilardi,** Charissa '04 %DA -125-01 Qns Blvd -Kew Gdns 11415
(212) 653-8700 .. **Ilardi,** Gina Reif '06 %Sheppard MR&H LLP -30 Rckfllr Plz -NY 10112
(212) 268-5136 .. **Ilardi,** Gregg A '01 (Harwood L) -350 5th Av -NY 10118
(212) 867-6000 .. **Ilardi,** Jolie M '07 %Rosenberg & E,PC -733 3rd Av -NY 10017
(914) 766-1900 .. **Ilardi,** Terry J '78 IBM -294 Route 100 -Somers 10589

(716) 646-1190 .. **Ilardo,** Edwin '59 -5899 S Park Av Bx887 -Hambrg 14075 **Fx:**646-1192
(716) 646-1190 .. **Ilardo,** Mary B '00 -5899 S Park Av Bx887 -Hambrg 14075 **Fx:**646-1192
(212) 480-2222 .. **Ilasz,** Livius M '95 (Ilasz & Assoc) -1 Maiden Ln -NY 10038 **Fx:**480-2958
(212) 685-7411 .. **Ilchert,** George W '89 (Lurie IM&R,LLP) -475 Park Av S -NY 10016 **Fx:**685-9827
(716) 838-4300 .. **Ilecki,** Wm '90 (Bulan CH&I) -1320 Millersport Hwy -Williamsvll 14221 **Fx:**204-9728
(914) 374-5802 .. **Iler,** Iris J '94 -839 Plsntvll Rd -Briarclff Mnr 10510 **Fx:**944-0585
(212) 225-2000 .. **Ilgenfritz,** Heide H '97 Cnsl Cleary GS&H -1 Lbrty Plz -NY 10006
(718) 343-1336 .. **Ilibassi,** John A '86 -253-11 80th Av -Glen Oaks 11004
(516) 781-5105 .. **Ilich,** Rhoda L '88 -2454 Legion -Bellmore 11710
(212) 819-8200 .. **Ilkhani,** Ashkan '05 %White & C LLP -1155 Av of Amer -NY 10036
(315) 234-8590 .. **Illingworth,** Linda L '02 %Hon N McCurn USDC -100 S Clinton Bx7367 -Syracuse 13261
(516) 742-2777 .. **Illmensee,** Thos A '70 -1305 Franklin Av -Gdn Cty 11530
(212) 450-4000 .. **Illouz,** Aharon '10 %Davis P&W LLP -450 Lex Av -NY 10017
(212) 261-8000 .. **Illuzzi,** Lauren '07 %Mendes & M,LLP -750 7th Av -NY 10019
(212) 335-9000 .. **Illuzzi-Orbon,** Joan K '89 %DA -1 Hogan Pl -NY 10013
(718) 528-5270 .. **Ilyaich,** Mikhail '08 -1 Cross Isl Plz -Rosedale 11422 **Fx:**528-3370
(212) 318-3000 .. **Im,** C Andrew '96 SrCnsl Fulbright & J LLP -666 5th Av -NY 10103
(212) 312-2260 .. **Im,** Carolyn Y '07 Leg Aid -60 Lafayette -NY 10013 **Fx:**349-0874
(212) 592-1400 .. **Im,** Richd Y '99 %Herrick,F LLP -2 Park Av -NY 10016
(212) 446-4800 .. **Im,** Yongjin '99 (Kirkland & E LLP) -153 E 53rd -NY 10022
(212) 224-4031 .. **Imai,** Yasuhiko '97 Sumitomo Mitsui -277 Park Av -NY 10172 **Fx:**593-9522
(973) 315-4517 .. **Imbacuan,** Michl H '98 Cnsl Budd L -140 Bway -NY 10005
(212) 279-9090 .. **Imbalzano,** Maria P '84 (Stark & S) -One Penn Plz -NY 10119 **Fx:**279-9113
(800) 724-3828 .. **Imbasciani,** Jos '85 -200 Broadhllw Rd -Melvll 11747
(212) 232-1300 .. **Imbasciani,** Michelle M '05 %Lewis BB&S LLP -77 Water -NY 10005
(516) 745-0707 .. **Imber,** Mark D '77 -100 Q Roosevelt Blvd -Gdn Cty 11530 **Fx:**222-1654
(718) 727-4555 .. **Imber-Gluck,** Ilana B '05 %H Bernstein -1444 Clove Rd -Staten Isl 10301 **Fx:**981-4666
(212) 736-5599 .. **Imbesi,** Vincent J '03 (Weiss I PLLC) -462 7th Av -NY 10018
(718) 590-2000 .. **Imbo,** Susanna L '01 %DA -198 E 161st -Bronx 10451 **Fx:**590-6477
(212) 742-3390 .. **Imbriaco,** Jos E '58 (Lindabury ME&C,PC) -26 Bway -NY 10004
(518) 641-5571 .. **Imbriaco,** Randi B '03 %Cptl Dist Physicians Hlth Plan,Inc -500 Patroon Crk Blvd -Albany 12206 **Fx:**641-5505
(518) 370-4793 .. **Imbriaco,** Steven E '03 MVP Healthcare -Bx2207 -Schnctdy 12301
(212) 527-1000 .. **Imbrogno,** Richd C '80 (Jones HC&B PC) -1 Bttry Pk Plz -NY 10004
(212) 348-7449 .. **Imeh,** Ime Nse '02 %Legal Srvcs -1 W 125th -NY 10027 **Fx:**348-4093
(212) 878-1700 .. **Imeri,** Jeff '90 (Marshall DWC&G) -140 Bway -NY 10005
(212) 213-6996 .. **Imes,** Linda C '84 (Spears & I LLP) -51 Mad Av -NY 10010
(212) 922-2200 .. **Imhof,** John F Jr. '91 (Watson F&W LLP) -1133 Av of Amer -NY 10036
(518) 677-3130 .. **Imhof,** John V '92 -49 W Main -Cambrdg 12816 **Fx:**677-5494
(212) 530-5000 .. **Immergut,** Mel M '72 (Milbank TH&M LLP) -1 Chase Manh Plz -NY 10005
(212) 916-5877 .. **Immerman,** Elaine A '84 %TIAA-CREF -730 3rd Av -NY 10017
(212) 809-1111 .. **Imossi,** Richd T '92 %Morgan MA -39 Bway -NY 10006
(212) 258-3333 .. **Imoto,** Yoshitoshi '09 %Masuda Intl -152 W 57th -NY 10019 **Fx:**957-3939
(718) 286-6000 .. **Impellizzeri,** Frances M '02 %DA -125-01 Qns Blvd -Kew Gdns 11415
(212) 834-0600 .. **Imperato,** Alison M '04 %Gordon & S,PC -355 Lex Av -NY 10017
(845) 639-1415 .. **Imperato,** Donna Garigali '87 Natl Granite Title Ins Co -155 N Main -New Cty 10956 **Fx:**639-1239
(718) 380-2394 .. **Imperato,** Francis P '74 -138-31 78th Av -Flushng 11367
(718) 891-8814 .. **Imperato,** Gerard A '69 -2305 Av Z -Brklyn 11235 **Fx:**769-6433
(212) 705-7000 .. **Imperato,** Justin G '05 %Bingham M LLP -399 Park Av -NY 10022
(212) 805-0216 .. **Imperatore,** Edw A '09 Hon L Kaplan USDC -500 Pearl -NY 10007
(212) 977-9700 .. **Imperatore,** Edw G '77 (Phillips N LLP) -666 5th Av -NY 10103
(212) 326-3939 .. **Imperatore,** Preston J '10 %Jones D -222 E 41st -NY 10017
(914) 949-6227 .. **Imperial,** Maria L '87 YWCA -515 North -White Plns 10605
(212) 837-2250 .. **Inaba,** Gail M '82 %JP Morgan Chase -345 Park Av -NY 10154
(212) 373-3000 .. **Inamasu,** Leslie Kikuno '07 %Paul WRW&G LLP -1285 Av of Amer -NY 10019
(212) 526-3916 .. **Inamdar,** Sonia '05 Barclays Capital Inc -745 7th Av -NY 10019
(212) 336-2000 .. **Inbar,** Tomer J '97 (Patterson BW&T LLP) -1133 Av of Amer -NY 10036
(516) 248-2222 .. **Inbody,** Diane E '89 %LI Advocacy Ctr -999 Hrrcks Rd -New Hyde Pk 11040 **Fx:**248-2290
(631) 853-4530 .. **Incantalupo,** Frank J '83 Dist Ct -400 Carleton Av -Central Islip 11722
(718) 997-1000 .. **Incantalupo,** Thos V '78 (Mitchell & I) -98-20 Metro Av -Frst Hlls 11375
(212) 297-5800 .. **Incardone,** Justin B '08 %Day P LLP -7 Times Sq -NY 10036
(212) 450-4000 .. **Ince,** George R Jr. '69 Cnsl Davis P&W LLP -450 Lex Av -NY 10017
(212) 906-1200 .. **Ince,** Irmak '08 %Latham & W -885 3rd Av -NY 10022
(914) 949-2700 .. **Incorvaia,** Jos M '74 OfCnsl Bleakley P&S,LLP -1 N Lex Av -White Plns 10601
(212) 546-9255 .. **Indeck,** Andrew L '02 (Scarinci H) -107 Grand -NY 10013
(212) 309-6000 .. **Indek,** Ben A '93 (Morgan L&B LLP) -101 Park Av -NY 10178
(914) 995-2660 .. **Indelicato,** Charlene M '80 (Cnty Atty) -148 Martine Av -White Plns 10601 **Fx:**995-5858
(212) 809-7600 .. **Indelicato,** Elizabeth '87 %Cheven K&H -40 Wall -NY 10005
(518) 447-2666 .. **Indelicato,** Jos J Jr. '89 %Tchrs Rtrmnt Sys -10 Corp Woods Dr -Albany 12211 **Fx:**447-2679
(212) 325-6424 .. **Indelicato,** Mario A '99 Credit Suisse -11 Mad Av -NY 10010
(212) 478-7200 .. **Indelicato,** Mark S '86 (Hahn & H LLP) -488 Mad Av -NY 10022
(212) 259-8000 .. **Indelicato,** Vincent '09 %Dewey & L LLP -1301 Av of Amer -NY 10019
(212) 777-8887 .. **Inderwies,** Robyn M '07 %J Kasdon -112 E 19th -NY 10003 **Fx:**777-1850
(914) 478-4850 .. **Indig-Smith,** Jessica '85 -11 Goodwin -Hastings-On-Hud 10706
(914) 788-5775 .. **Indik,** Gloria H '91 %Workers Comp Bd -41 N Division -Peekskill 10566
(315) 234-8600 .. **Indingaro,** Jessica L '06 %Hon G DiBianco -100 S Clinton Bx7396 -Syracuse 13261
(516) 794-3875 .. **Indiviglio,** Frank J '82 -1984 Marion Dr -E Meadow 11554
(585) 352-8900 .. **Indivino,** Deborah A '80 -24 West Av -Spencerprt 14559 **Fx:**352-8709
(212) 558-4000 .. **Indoe,** Wm F '69 (Sullivan & C LLP) -125 Broad -NY 10004
(914) 285-9797 .. **Indriolo,** Joanne S '04 %Kitson LLP -50 Main -White Plns 10606
(212) 554-0400 .. **Indursky,** Arthur I '68 (Grubman I&S,PC) -152 W 57th -NY 10019
(212) 248-3162 .. **Indych,** Marsha J '07 %Drinker B&R LLP -140 Bway -NY 10005
(212) 517-2052 .. **Indyke,** Darren K '92 -301 E 66th -NY 10065
(212) 479-6000 .. **Indyke,** Jay R '82 (Cooley LLP) -1114 Av of Amer -NY 10036
(845) 291-2454 .. **Indzonka,** Erik F '89 %Leg Aid -2 Court Ln Bx328 -Goshen 10924 **Fx:**294-2638
(212) 841-1000 .. **Infante,** Stephen A '91 (Covington & B LLP) -620 8th Av -NY 10018
(718) 590-2000 .. **Infantes,** Delia R '08 %DA -198 E 161st -Bronx 10451 **Fx:**590-6477
(315) 834-6621 .. **Infanti,** Kathleen Walsh '03 -8941 N Seneca Bx458 -Weedsport 13166 **Fx:**834-6029
(585) 428-2488 .. **Infantino,** Fred J '74 %Hon J Ark -229 Hall of Justice -Rchstr 14614
(585) 232-4724 .. **Infantino,** Marc S '97 %Elliott S&C,LLP -1 E Main -Rchstr 14614
(518) 457-2070 .. **Infantino,** Michl B '83 %Dept of Tax & Fin -Bldg 9 State Campus -Albany 12227 **Fx:**457-6131
(516) 933-1515 .. **Infeld,** Wm S '60 -366 N Bway -Jericho 11753 **Fx:**933-1666
(914) 995-3638 .. **Infield,** Daniela '91 %Cnty Atty -148 Martine Av -White Plns 10601 **Fx:**995-2495
(212) 556-2100 .. **Infield-Harm,** Lisa J '06 %King & S -1185 Av of Amer -NY 10036
(631) 543-3663 .. **Infranco,** Jos P '78 (Migliore & I,PC) -353 Vets Mem'l Hwy -Commack 11725
(914) 286-2911 .. **Infurna,** Thos J '87 (Greenberg T,LLP) -445 Hmltn Av -White Plns 10601
(845) 331-0062 .. **Ingalsbe,** Ward W Jr. '59 -41 Pearl Bx3040 -Kingston 12402 **Fx:**331-2754
(845) 331-2525 .. **Ingalsbe,** Ward W III '87 (Ryan R&R,LLP) -115 Green Bx3153 -Kingston 12402
(845) 331-7377 .. **Ingarra,** Jos M '74 J Ingarra,PC -145 Wall Bx3190 -Kingston 12402 **Fx:**331-7817
(212) 641-3913 .. **Ingber,** Abby Lynn '88 Schroeder Investment Mgmt NA,Inc -875 3rd Av -NY 10022
(212) 572-8600 .. **Ingber,** Adam F '95 MacAndrews & Forbes -35 E 62nd -NY 10065
(718) 446-0312 .. **Ingber,** Chas S '82 -40-06 Warren -Elmhrst 11373 **Fx:**779-6984
(212) 867-4466 .. **Ingber,** Craig G '87 (Belkin BW&G,LLP) -270 Mad Av -NY 10016
(845) 794-4400 .. **Ingber,** Jack S '52 (Ingber & I) -230 Bway Bx977 -Monticello 12701 **Fx:**794-1240
(212) 855-3200 .. **Ingber,** Jeffrey F '80 Depository Trust -55 Water -NY 10041 **Fx:**855-3279
(212) 353-1800 .. **Ingber,** Jos S '77 -14 Penn Plz -NY 10122 **Fx:**563-6211
(845) 794-4400 .. **Ingber,** Keith G '78 (Ingber & I) -230 Bway Bx977 -Monticello 12701 **Fx:**794-1240
(212) 695-5670 .. **Ingber,** Larry H '84 (Goldfinger & L LLP) -750 3rd Av -NY 10017
(212) 506-2500 .. **Ingber,** Matthew '99 (Mayer B LLP) -1675 Bway -NY 10019
(212) 683-2210 .. **Ingber,** Miriam F '06 %Childrens Rts Inc -330 7th Av -NY 10001 **Fx:**683-4015
(845) 733-2720 .. **Ingber,** Norman '69 -53 Roe Rd -Bloomngbrg 12721 **Fx:**733-2722
(516) 294-2666 .. **Ingber,** Ronald D '98 (Siler & I,LLP) -301 Mineola Blvd -Mineola 11501
(212) 750-5055 .. **Ingber,** Sidney '61 (Ingber & K) -575 Lex Av -NY 10022
(212) 439-8516 .. **Ingber,** Warren J '84 -435 E 77th -NY 10075
(516) 364-3312 .. **Ingbretsen,** Bruce E '84 -2 Roosevelt Av -Syosset 11791
(631) 300-4960 .. **Ingebretsen,** Erica L '01 %Bello & L -150 Motor Pkwy -Hauppauge 11788
(845) 368-1515 .. **Inger,** Rochelle '01 -1 Dalewood Dr -Suffern 10901 **Fx:**368-1590
(212) 596-9000 .. **Ingerman,** Jeffrey H '83 (Ropes & G LLP) -1211 Av of Amer -NY 10036
(212) 302-3600 .. **Ingerman,** Joanne Sherman '95 %Sherman & G,PC -494 8th Av -NY 10001
(212) 408-5100 .. **Ingerman,** Peter K '82 (Chadbourne & P LLP) -30 Rckfllr Plz -NY 10112
(631) 261-8834 .. **Ingerman Smith LLP** -150 Motor Pkwy -Hauppauge 11788 **Fx:**261-0523
(914) 777-1134 .. **Ingerman Smith LLP** -550 Mamaroneck Av -Harrison 10528
(212) 818-8800 .. **Ingerman,** Steven L '82 (Graubard M) -405 Lex Av -NY 10174
(585) 325-4600 .. **Ingersoll,** Timothy E '90 (Fero & I) -183 E Main -Rchstr 14604 **Fx:**325-1525
(607) 547-8500 .. **Ingham,** Colin E '74 OfCnsl Trosset Grp -31 Pioneer Bx28 -Cooperstwn 13326
(516) 249-3450 .. **Ingham,** Michl F '79 (Carman C&I,LLP) -266 Main -Farmngdl 11735
(716) 531-1639 .. **Ingham,** Michl J '91 -150 Payne Av -N Tonawanda 14120
(718) 250-2000 .. **Ingle,** David L '00 %DA -350 Jay -Brklyn 11201 **Fx:**250-2314
(212) 735-3000 .. **Ingles,** David C '95 (Skadden ASM&F LLP) -4 Times Sq -NY 10036
(212) 373-3000 .. **Inglis,** John D '06 %Paul WRW&G LLP -1285 Av of Amer -NY 10019
(212) 982-9493 .. **Inglis,** Shelley Case '00 UNIFEM -304 E 45th -NY 10017
(212) 836-8000 .. **Ingman,** Tatiana '07 %Kaye S LLP -425 Park Av -NY 10022
(212) 637-1113 .. **Ingoglia,** Eugene E '97 %US Atty -1 St Andrews Plz -NY 10007
(516) 432-0500 .. **Ingoglia,** Glenn J '98 -104 Lng Bch Rd -Isl Pk 11558
(212) 786-6047 .. **Ingoglia,** James M '00 %Morandi Taub & Sarnoff,LLC -1325 Av of Amer -NY 10019 **Fx:**786-6045
(646) 610-5400 .. **Ingoldsby,** John K '95 %NYPD -1 Police Plz -NY 10038
(607) 722-3495 .. **Ingraham,** Chas O '68 (Aswad & I) -46 Front -Bnghmtn 13905
(518) 387-5073 .. **Ingraham,** Donald S '91 GE -1 Rsrch Cir -Schnctdy 12309 **Fx:**387-6110
(585) 419-8800 .. **Ingraham,** Stevens L '77 (Harris B PLLC) -99 Garnsey Rd -Pittsfrd 14534
(212) 918-3000 .. **Ingram,** Jennie E '06 %Hogan L LLP -875 3rd Av -NY 10022
(212) 947-4855 .. **Ingram,** John R '05 %Baldonado & Assoc,PC -481 8th Av -NY 10001

(718) 701-5915 .. **Ingram,** Michele '92 %Bailey & B,LLC -123-20 82nd Av -Kew Gdns 11415 **Fx:**(877) 225-2932
(718) 991-4600 .. **Ingram,** Natasha Y '96 %Leg Aid -953 Southrn Blvd -Bronx 10459 **Fx:**842-2867
(845) 353-2000 .. **Ingram,** Phyllis A '90 %Feerick LM PLLC -96 S Bway -Nyack 10960
(212) 724-7780 .. **Ingram,** Susan '75 (S Ingram,PC) -320 Cntrl Pk W -NY 10025 **Fx:**496-0172
(315) 265-8680 .. **Ingram,** Verner M Jr. '70 (Ingram & P) -63 Market -Potsdam 13676 **Fx:**265-8390
(845) 348-1005 .. **Ingram,** Wm R '92 Eklecco LLC -1000 Palisades Ctr Dr -W Nyack 10994 **Fx:**348-1774
(212) 907-9600 .. **Ingram Yuzek Gainen Carroll & Bertolotti,LLP** -250 Park Av -NY 10177 **Fx:**907-9681
(516) 248-6777 .. **Ingrao,** Jos A '54 (Purcell & I,PC) -204 Willis Av -Mineola 11501
(516) 248-6777 .. **Ingrao,** Lynn A '85 (Purcell & I,PC) -204 Willis Av -Mineola 11501
(516) 248-6777 .. **Ingrao,** Terrance J '78 (Purcell & I,PC) -204 Willis Av -Mineola 11501
(212) 259-8000 .. **Ingrasin,** Tracie E '08 %Dewey & L LLP -1301 Av of Amer -NY 10019
(845) 342-3366 .. **Ingrassia,** Angelo J '50 OfCnsl Larkin AI&T,LLP -626 E Main -Middletwn 10940
(914) 285-8500 .. **Ingrassia,** Christopher '83 %TK Moore -701 Wstchstr Av -White Plns 10604 **Fx:**285-8510
(845) 566-5345 .. **Ingrassia,** John '89 (Larkin AI&T,LLP) -356 Meadow Av -Newburgh 12550
(212) 833-8688 .. **Ingrassia,** John A '86 Sony BMG Music Entrtnmnt -550 Mad Av -NY 10022 **Fx:**833-8406
(516) 741-5252 .. **Ingrassia,** Melissa C '03 %Sanders SBWV&G,PC -100 Hrrcks Rd -Mineola 11501
(212) 906-1200 .. **Ingrassia,** Michl R '07 %Latham & W -885 3rd Av -NY 10022
(212) 816-9915 .. **Ingrassia,** Paul J '85 Citigroup -388 Greenwich -NY 10013
(516) 877-5600 .. **Inguanti,** Marie-Ann '95 %R Tusa -1225 Franklin Av -Gdn Cty 11530 **Fx:**877-5695
(516) 694-1242 .. **Ingvoldstad,** David R '81 -176 Woodbury Rd -Hicksvll 11801
(212) 294-6700 .. **Ingwer,** Rachel M '09 %Winston & S -200 Park Av -NY 10166
(212) 406-4991 .. **Iñiguez,** James E '96 -61 Bway -NY 10006 **Fx:**406-4991
(212) 442-1400 .. **Injeski,** Breanne E '07 Conflicts of Int Bd -2 Lafayette -NY 10007 **Fx:**442-1407
(646) 424-6000 .. **Inkeles,** Chas H A '01 %ING Capital LLC -1325 Av of Amer -NY 10019
(646) 328-0850 .. **Inker,** Jonathan S '94 %Outside Cnsl Solutns LLP -1430 Bway -NY 10018 **Fx:**360-5000
(914) 963-5500 .. **Inlaw,** Evan '92 -20 S Bway -Ynkrs 10701
(212) 536-0617 .. **Innamorati,** Jos E '88 -1251 Av of Amer -NY 10020
(607) 723-9511 .. **Inneo,** Susan A '94 (Coughlin & G,LLP) -19 Chenango Bx2039 -Bnghmtn 13902
(212) 506-1700 .. **Innes,** Jennifer '02 Kasowitz BT&F LLP -1633 Bway -NY 10019
(516) 663-8244 .. **Innes,** Michele K '92 %Winthrop Univ Hsptl -259 1st -Mineola 11501 **Fx:**663-8288
(516) 229-4200 .. **Inniss,** Larry '01 Mendolia & S -875 Merrick Av -Westbury 11590
(212) 913-2373 .. **Innis-Thompson,** Janice L '01 TIAA-CREF -730 3rd Av -NY 10017
(212) 449-1000 .. **Innocentin,** Robt D '01 -4 World Fncl Ctr -NY 10281
(212) 972-4260 .. **Inouye,** Ronald N '72 Inouye & O -90 Park Av -NY 10016 **Fx:**972-4264
(212) 756-2000 .. **Insalaco,** Michl G '03 %Schulte R&Z LLP -919 3rd Av -NY 10022
(585) 275-4838 .. **Insalaco,** Richd C '97 Univ of Rochester -110 Ofc Park Way -Pittsfrd 14534
(718) 738-7700 .. **Insanally,** David I '87 -113-03 Lbrty Av -S Richmond Hll 11419
(914) 777-7737 .. **Insardi,** Janet M '90 Vllg Atty -123 Mamaroneck Av Bx369 -Mamaroneck 10543 **Fx:**777-7769
(212) 430-6526 .. **Insdorf,** Debbie K '81 -65 Bway -NY 10006
(212) 808-7933 .. **Insel,** Michl S '74 (Kelley D&W LLP) -101 Park Av -NY 10178
(212) 319-7125 .. **Inselbuch,** Elihu '62 (Caplin & D) -375 Park Av -NY 10152
(315) 786-3498 .. **Inserra,** Anthony '91 -531 Wshngtn -Watertwn 13601 **Fx:**786-0798
(607) 723-9511 .. **Insinga,** Cheryl '99 %Coughlin & G,LLP -19 Chenango Bx2039 -Bnghmtn 13902
(718) 522-1786 .. **Insler,** Amy Lee '97 %Bonina & B,PC -16 Court -Brklyn 11241 **Fx:**243-0414
(914) 286-3030 .. **Insler,** Lewis B '80 (Insler & H LLP) -80 Grasslands Rd -Elmsfrd 10523 **Fx:**372-1392
(518) 566-0833 .. **Insley,** Kathleen R '00 -187 Margaret -Plattsbrgh 12901
(212) 813-8800 .. **Insolia,** Robt S '85 (Goodwin P LLP) -620 8th Av -NY 10018
(212) 433-1480 .. **Intelisano,** Ross B '95 (Rich & I LLP) -111 Bway -NY 10006 **Fx:**433-1481
(518) 548-7945 .. **Intemann,** Wm H Jr. '62 -177 Golf Course Rd Bx26 -Lk Plsnt 12108 **Fx:**548-9745
(212) 790-0476 .. **Interdonato,** Julie A '84 %Benj N Cardozo Schl of Law -55 5th Av -NY 10003 **Fx:**790-0345
(718) 250-2000 .. **Interiano,** Jose A '09 %DA -350 Jay -Brklyn 11201 **Fx:**250-2314
(585) 454-2181 .. **Interlichia,** Jos G '84 (Trevett CS&A,PC) -2 State -Rchstr 14614
(607) 778-2423 .. **Intermill,** Karin L '03 DA -45 Hawley Bx1766 -Bnghmtn 13902 **Fx:**778-8870
(718) 979-4300 .. **Internicola,** Chas N '96 (Decker DD&I,LLP) -1610 Richmond Rd -Staten Isl 10304
(212) 883-4900 .. **Intriligator,** Marc S '78 (Cozen O) -277 Park Av -NY 10172
(315) 785-3053 .. **Intschert,** Cindy Foote '85 (DA) -175 Arsenal -Watertwn 13601 **Fx:**785-3371
(212) 519-7856 .. **Intzeyiannis,** Constantine '99 ACLU Fndtn -125 Broad -NY 10004 **Fx:**(516) 437-4395
(212) 450-0100 .. **Inuyama,** Hiroaki '04 Marubeni America -375 Lex Av -NY 10017 **Fx:**450-0706
(516) 873-0011 .. **Invidiata,** Christopher R '00 %S Goldstein,LLP -1 Old Cntry Rd -Carle Pl 11514 **Fx:**873-0120
(718) 520-3726 .. **Invidiata,** Robt S '70 %Hon JM Durante -88-11 Sutphin Blvd -Jamaica 11435
(646) 442-3634 .. **Inwald,** Jacob '85 Legal Srvcs NYC -350 Bway -NY 10013 **Fx:**(212) 966-9571
(718) 230-5970 .. **Inwald,** Scott '85 -315 Park Pl -Brklyn 11238 **Fx:**230-0572
(212) 689-4343 .. **Inwood,** Alan R '83 (Hochheiser H&I LLP) -15 Maiden Ln -NY 10038 **Fx:**481-3424
(212) 532-5640 .. **Inzelbuch,** Michl I '95 -276 5th Av -NY 10001 **Fx:**481-9569
(212) 412-4000 .. **Inzerillo,** Jos A '02 Barclays Capital -200 Park Av -NY 10166
(914) 761-4459 .. **Inzero,** Christopher J '95 -399 Knollwood Rd -White Plns 10603 **Fx:**421-9028
(212) 416-8268 .. **Ioannou,** John A '95 %Dept of Law -120 Bway -NY 10271
(212) 593-2800 .. **Ioannou,** John M '83 (Ioannou & Assoc) -414 E 59th -NY 10022 **Fx:**593-2933
(212) 237-1000 .. **Iocco,** Denise L '92 SpclCnsl Windels ML&M,LLP -156 W 56th -NY 10019
(315) 258-9336 .. **Iocolano,** David M '91 -144 Genesee Bx1015 -Auburn 13021
(315) 253-5349 .. **Iocolano,** George R '50 -206 Metcalf Plz -Auburn 13021
(315) 866-6520 .. **Iocovozzi,** Mary M '83 -426 N Main Bx85 -Herkimer 13350 **Fx:**866-6618
(914) 697-5000 .. **Iori,** Massimo '98 %Westminster USA -4 W Red Oak Ln -White Plns 10604 **Fx:**697-5050
(646) 356-8600 .. **Iorillo,** John P '95 Ambrose Employer Grp -199 Water -NY 10038
(631) 581-2310 .. **Iorio,** Gary '85 -1 Sutton Pl -Islip 11751
(631) 761-0552 .. **Iorio,** Neal T '85 -110 Walt Whitman Rd -South Huntington 11746
(212) 736-1940 .. **Ioselevich,** Oleg '06 %Davidson D&K LLC -485 7th Av -NY 10018
(212) 766-9696 .. **Iosepovici,** Zamir '93 (Popescu I LLP) -225 Bway -NY 10007
(518) 434-0600 .. **Iovieno,** Philip J '93 (Boies S&F LLP) -10 N Pearl -Albany 12207
(718) 522-4604 .. **Iovine,** Louis F '66 -188 Montague -Brklyn 11201 **Fx:**596-1766
(212) 318-6000 .. **Iovine,** Luke P III '91 (Paul HJ&W LLP) -75 E 55th -NY 10022
(516) 741-8585 .. **Iovino,** Anthony F '83 (Bondi & I) -1055 Franklin Av -Gdn Cty 11530
(718) 846-6119 .. **Iovino,** Neil '95 -105-02 Metro Av -Frst Hlls 11375
(212) 732-9777 .. **Ip,** K Thos '85 -22 Chatham Sq -NY 10038 **Fx:**349-1735
(716) 856-8200 .. **Ipolito,** Jennifer Ann '05 Williams & W -43 Court -Buffalo 14202 **Fx:**856-0559
(212) 578-2211 .. **Ippen,** Katrina A '03 %MetLife -27-01 Qns Plz N -LIC 11101
(718) 579-3000 .. **Ippolito,** Chas J '82 %Leg Aid -1020 Grnd Cncrs -Bronx 10451 **Fx:**588-2611
(716) 332-7810 .. **Ippolito,** Giuseppe A '06 Hon R Arcara - USDC -68 Court -Buffalo 14202
(914) 385-4100 .. **Ippolito,** Gregory V '03 %Hoffman W&R,LLP -399 Knollwood Rd -White Plns 10603
(585) 232-3730 .. **Ippolito,** Henry R '67 (Chamberlain D LLP) -1600 Crssrds Bldg -Rchstr 14614
(212) 335-9000 .. **Ippolito,** Jos T '77 %DA -1 Hogan Pl -NY 10013
(212) 728-8000 .. **Ippolito,** Loretta A '90 (Willkie F&G LLP) -787 7th Av -NY 10019
(212) 318-6000 .. **Ippolito,** Mario J '85 (Paul HJ&W LLP) -75 E 55th -NY 10022
(716) 858-6599 .. **Ippolito,** Richd N '74 %Dept Soc Srvcs -95 Franklin -Buffalo 14202 **Fx:**858-8072
(914) 631-9090 .. **Ippolito,** Russell J '92 -150 Wht Plns Rd -Tarrytwn 10591 **Fx:**631-0363
(716) 852-6276 .. **Ippolito,** Russell T Jr. '90 %Dept of Law -350 Main Pl Twr -Buffalo 14202 **Fx:**853-8571
(718) 590-2000 .. **Irace,** Paul G '09 %DA -198 E 161st -Bronx 10451 **Fx:**590-6477
(516) 294-9420 .. **Irace,** Steven A '70 -63 Cmmrcial Av -Gdn Cty 11530 **Fx:**742-6221
(212) 683-7700 .. **Irani,** James S '97 -347 5th Av -NY 10016 **Fx:**725-1772
(212) 816-7272 .. **Irazu,** Fernando G '00 %Salomon Smith Barney -388 Greenwich -NY 10013
(212) 991-5468 .. **Ireland,** Gary E '92 -530 5th Av -NY 10036
(518) 429-4200 .. **Ireland,** Meredith A '10 %Hiscock & B,LLP -50 Beaver -Albany 12207
(716) 854-4435 .. **Irene,** Juan E '84 J Irene PLLC -37 Franklin -Buffalo 14202 **Fx:**842-0838
(716) 847-8400 .. **Irey,** Annabelle '85 (Phillips L LLP) -3400 HSBC Ctr -Buffalo 14203
(646) 345-0752 .. **Irgang,** Jay R '55 -60 E 42nd -NY 10165 **Fx:**(212) 370-4276
(212) 335-9000 .. **Irick,** Shirley C '01 %DA -1 Hogan Pl -NY 10013
(212) 260-0940 .. **Irie,** Haruko Jeanette '09 Sunyo,Inc -797 Bway -NY 10003
(516) 767-1915 .. **Irie,** Hisae Helen '96 -34 3rd Av -Pt Wash 11050 **Fx:**944-6577
(212) 834-8348 .. **Irie,** Masako '05 JP Morgan Chase -270 Park Av -NY 10017
(212) 872-9800 .. **Irish,** Corrine Anetra '05 %Squire S&D LLP -30 Rckfllr Plz -NY 10112
(716) 759-2093 .. **Irish-Jones,** Laurie J '88 -5220 Brookhvn Dr -Clarence 14031
(212) 969-3000 .. **Irizarry,** Dawn M '03 %Proskauer R LLP -1585 Bway -NY 10036
(212) 213-6955 .. **Irizarry,** Edw '91 -200 Mad Av -NY 10016 **Fx:**213-6956
(212) 349-1500 .. **Irizarry,** Miguel A '88 -440 45th -Brklyn 11220 **Fx:**(718) 851-3187
(716) 773-6800 .. **Irizarry,** Racheal Christine '02 Cannon Design -2170 Whitehaven Rd -Grand Isl 14072
(212) 722-2000 .. **Irizarry,** Yolanda '87 %Leg Aid -230 E 106th -NY 10029 **Fx:**876-5365
(718) 665-0220 .. **Irom,** Jos M '53 (Irom WFB&S,PC) -349 E 149th -Bronx 10451
(212) 816-6000 .. **Irom,** Larry H '73 Citigroup -388 Greenwich -NY 10013
(718) 665-0220 .. **Irom Wittels Freund Berne & Serra, PC** -349 E 149th -Bronx 10451 **Fx:**665-8004
(718) 273-5444 .. **Ironman,** David G '86 -176 Hart Blvd -Staten Isl 10301
(718) 233-6422 .. **Irons,** Jonathan '81 -1360 Fulton -Brklyn 11216
(646) 240-4872 .. **Irvine,** Sol L '99 (Bortstein & I LLC) -275 Mad Av -NY 10016 **Fx:**(866) 955-9403
(516) 883-5432 .. **Irving,** Christopher L '86 %Publishers Clearing House -382 Channel Dr -Pt Wash 11050
(585) 295-5768 .. **Irving,** David O '07 Leg Aid -1 W Main -Rchstr 14614
(212) 326-3939 .. **Irving,** Euclid A '77 OfCnsl Jones D -222 E 41st -NY 10017
(212) 732-3200 .. **Irving,** Macculloch M '85 (Carter L&M LLP) -2 Wall -NY 10005
(212) 880-6000 .. **Irving,** Mark W '05 %Torys LLP -237 Park Av -NY 10017
(585) 753-4500 .. **Irving,** Paul D '91 %DA -832 Watts Bldg -Rchstr 14614 **Fx:**753-4576
(716) 645-3312 .. **Irving,** Wendy M '92 %University Development -112(A) Ctr for Tomorrow Bx534 -Buffalo 14260
(212) 335-9191 .. **Irvis,** Dana A '07 DA -1 Hogan Pl -NY 10013
(212) 418-8600 .. **Irwin,** Catherine C '00 %Kornstein VW&P,LLP -757 3rd Av -NY 10017
(716) 837-5631 .. **Irwin,** Daire B '93 -210 Voorhees Av -Buffalo 14214
(518) 438-2122 .. **Irwin,** Dennis F '74 -428 Sand Crk Rd -Albany 12205 **Fx:**438-2304
(212) 759-2600 .. **Irwin,** E David '69 (Irwin LC&L,PC) -845 3rd Av -NY 10022
(631) 390-0010 .. **Irwin,** Ethan D '04 %Bruno G&S,LLP -445 Broad Hollow Rd -Melvll 11747
(212) 268-5136 .. **Irwin,** Gregory J '81 (Harwood L) -350 5th Av -NY 10118
(212) 335-9000 .. **Irwin,** John F '87 %DA -1 Hogan Pl -NY 10013
(212) 406-2000 .. **Irwin,** Joshua B '00 (Irwin & P,LLP) -233 Bway -NY 10279
(845) 486-2300 .. **Irwin,** Kevin P '97 %DA -236 Main -Poughkeepsie 12601 **Fx:**486-2324

(212) 759-2600 ..**Irwin Lewin Cohn & Lewin,PC** -845 3rd Av -NY 10022 **Fx**:593-1318
(212) 460-4757 ..**Irwin**, Peter A '72 Con Ed -4 Irving Pl -NY 10003
(212) 909-6000 ..**Irwin**, Peter J '97 (Debevoise & P LLP) -919 3rd Av -NY 10022
(212) 841-1000 ..**Irwin**, Philip A '00 (Covington & B LLP) -620 8th Av -NY 10018
(212) 713-8895 ..**Irwin**, Rebecca S '97 UBS -1285 Av of Amer -NY 10019
(718) 874-8423 ..**Irwin**, Stephen B '88 -59-14 146th -Flushng 11355 **Fx**:874-6843
(516) 801-4990 ..**Irwin**, Veronica '00 (Irwin & S LLC) -1180 Nrthrn Blvd -Manhsst 11030
(212) 344-1048 ..**Iryami**, Dara A '94 %JA Goldberg -42 Bway -NY 10004
(212) 599-1081 ..**Iryami**, Raymond '00 -305 Madison A -NY 10165
(646) 610-5400 ..**Isaac**, Albert '94 NYPD -1 Police Plz -NY 10038
(516) 791-6555 ..**Isaac**, Allen H '58 -854 Oak Ln -Vly Stream 11581
(212) 233-8100 ..**Isaac**, Brian J '85 (Pollack PI&D) -225 Bway -NY 10007
(718) 875-1300 ..**Isaac**, Carol F '85 %Hon V Pizzuto -45 Monroe Pl -Brklyn 11201
(631) 470-5000 ..**Isaac**, David A '90 Garden City Grp Inc -105 Maxess Rd -Melvll 11747 **Fx**:470-5100
(646) 386-5700 ..**Isaac**, Isiris Isela '97 %Civil Ct -111 Centre -NY 10013
(917) 838-5720 ..**Isaac**, Marc M '01 (MM Isaac PLLC) -210 Moore Av -Freeprt 11520 **Fx**:(866) 342-2903
(518) 474-6530 ..**Isaac**, Meredyth L '08 %Dept Pub Srvc -3 ESP -Albany 12223
(212) 268-1000 ..**Isaac**, Michl H '08 %Broach & S,LLP -1 Penn Plz -NY 10119
(716) 674-0380 ..**Isaac**, Paul K '87 -3686 Seneca -W Seneca 14224
(212) 440-4400 ..**Isaacoff**, Lauren '09 Buchanan I&R PC -620 8th Av -NY 10018
(212) 965-6089 ..**Isaacs**, Alison E '03 Prudential Douglas Elliman -90 Hudson -NY 10013
(212) 864-3325 ..**Isaacs**, Audrey J '76 -400 Cntrl Pk W -NY 10025
(212) 373-4875 ..**Isaacs**, Craig A '93 %Miss Universe LP -1370 Av of Amer -NY 10019
(212) 925-3000 ..**Isaacs**, Danl W '92 -305 Bway -NY 10007 **Fx**:925-3666
(212) 292-4412 ..**Isaacs**, Leigh R '73 (Isaacs & E,LLP) -521 5th Av -NY 10175
(516) 561-8000 ..**Isaacs**, Leonard B '77 -108 S Franklin Av -Vly Stream 11580
(347) 592-2200 ..**Isaacs**, Lisa '97 %Leg Srvcs -89-00 Sutphin Blvd -Jamaica 11435 **Fx**:(718) 937-5350
(212) 751-5444 ..**Isaacs**, Marc J '81 (Isaacs & Assoc,PLLC) -260 Mad Av -NY 10016 **Fx**:532-6400
(516) 561-8005 ..**Isaacs**, Mark P '79 -108 S Franklin -Vly Stream 11580
(212) 732-1909 ..**Isaacs**, Marshall R '94 -20 Vesey -NY 10007 **Fx**:766-5899
(631) 283-2163 ..**Isaacs**, Nadine '90 -206 Corrigan -Southampton 11968
(212) 725-7111 ..**Isaacs**, Randi S '93 (Bender RI&R LLP) -451 Park Av S -NY 10016
(917) 551-1300 ..**Isaacs**, Steven A '88 (Koehler & I LLP) -61 Bway -NY 10006
(212) 859-8000 ..**Isaacson**, Allen I '66 OfCnsl Fried FHS&J LLP -1 NY Plz -NY 10004
(631) 439-1720 ..**Isaacson**, Beth '89 MHLS -320 Carleton Av -Central Islip 11722 **Fx**:951-2562
(212) 259-8000 ..**Isaacson**, Brian T '03 %Dewey & L LLP -1301 Av of Amer -NY 10019
(845) 638-3333 ..**Isaacson**, David '53 -130 N Main -New Cty 10956 **Fx**:634-2807
(212) 425-0555 ..**Isaacson**, David A '05 %C Mehta & Assoc,PLLC -2 Wall -NY 10005 **Fx**:425-3282
(516) 747-9700 ..**Isaacson**, Jason A '09 Ryan & H,PC -1 Old Cntry Rd -Carle Pl 11514
(516) 741-7676 ..**Isaacson**, Jonathan B '08 %Miranda SSSV LLP -240 Mineola Blvd -Mineola 11501
(917) 777-4200 ..**Isaacson**, Laurence B '88 OfCnsl Bingham M LLP -1 Bttry Pk Plz -NY 10004
(212) 888-8200 ..**Isaacson**, Leonard A '52 (Feder K LLP) -845 3rd Av -NY 10022
(212) 221-8004 ..**Isaacson**, Marcia '08 SUNY Univ Cnsl -S333 SUNY Plz -Albany 12246 **Fx**:(518) 443-5409
(212) 312-7877 ..**Isaacson**, Paul '80 %State Ins Fund -199 Church -NY 10007 **Fx**:385-9199
(212) 765-7770 ..**Isaacson**, Richd I '90 RI Entertainment -1790 Bway -NY 10019
(212) 267-6557 ..**Isaacson Schiowitz & Korson** -150 Bway -NY 10038 **Fx**:240-0365
(518) 829-5067 ..**Isabel**, Alexander B '82 -155 2nd Av Ext -Fonda 12068 **Fx**:829-5067
(212) 506-5000 ..**Isackson**, Robt M '83 (Orrick H&S LLP) -51 W 52nd -NY 10019
(212) 557-4000 ..**Isacoff**, Harry '93 OfCnsl Grunfeld DLS&K LLP -399 Park Av -NY 10022
(212) 504-6000 ..**Isajiw**, Peter J '03 %Cadwalader W&T LLP -1 World Fncl Ctr -NY 10281
(212) 455-2000 ..**Isak**, Eli '09 %Simpson T&B LLP -425 Lex Av -NY 10017
(718) 590-2000 ..**Isales**, Cynthia '06 DA -198 E 161st -Bronx 10451 **Fx**:590-6477
Isaza, Stella '94 -Bx231 -Poughkeepsie 12602
(917) 626-7336 ..**Isbell**, Alexa D '02 A Isbell PLLC -51 Greene -NY 10013 **Fx**:591-9615
(212) 455-2000 ..**Isby**, Michl R '87 SrCnsl Simpson T&B LLP -425 Lex Av -NY 10017
(212) 326-3939 ..**Iscaro**, Robt '82 Cnsl Jones D -222 E 41st -NY 10017
(718) 250-2000 ..**Isdith**, Robt T '97 %DA -350 Jay -Brklyn 11201 **Fx**:250-2314
(212) 548-2100 ..**Iselin**, Benjamin B '88 (McGuire W LLP) -1345 Av of Amer -NY 10105
(518) 689-1415 ..**Iselin**, Harold N '82 (Greenberg T,LLP) -54 State -Albany 12207
(212) 418-0500 ..**Iselin**, Josephine L '72 Cnsl Morris & M LLP -767 3rd Av -NY 10017
(518) 462-3000 ..**Iseman Cunningham Riester & Hyde,LLP** -9 Thurlow Ter -Albany 12203 **Fx**:462-4199
(845) 473-8100 ..**Iseman Cunningham Riester & Hyde,LLP** -2649 South Rd -Poughkeepsie 12601 **Fx**:473-8777
(518) 895-2715 ..**Iseman**, John C '90 -Route 7 -Quaker Street 12141
(518) 462-3000 ..**Iseman**, Robt H '74 (Iseman CR&H,LLP) -9 Thurlow Ter -Albany 12203
(716) 845-2506 ..**Isenberg**, Andrew B '93 %Hon S Townsend -92 Franklin -Buffalo 14202
(212) 318-6000 ..**Isenberg**, Laura K '05 %Paul HJ&W LLP -75 E 55th -NY 10022
(212) 236-1000 ..**Isenberg**, Michl H '03 Merrill Lynch -225 Lbrty -NY 10080
(212) 902-5396 ..**Isenstein**, Tania B '92 %Goldman Sachs -1 NY Plz -NY 10004
(631) 692-5000 ..**Iserman**, Jordan M '51 Iserman & I -37 Main Bx477 -Cold Spg Hbr 11724 **Fx**:692-5004
(212) 848-4000 ..**Isernhagen**, Mary L '09 %Shearman & S LLP -599 Lex Av -NY 10022
(845) 343-1113 ..**Isgur**, Michl S '96 -125 Wickham Av -Middletwn 10940 **Fx**:343-2010
(212) 629-9400 ..**Ishar**, Iqbal Singh '90 (Yaskhi IC&R LLP) -315 5th Av -NY 10016
(646) 386-5891 ..**Ishee**, Sadie Z '04 %MHLS -41 Mad Av -NY 10010
(845) 473-1137 ..**Ishizuka**, Yumiko '98 Indotronix Intl Corp -331 Main Mall -Poughkeepsie 12601
(212) 848-4000 ..**Ishmael**, Darren K '10 Shearman & S LLP -599 Lex Av -NY 10022
(516) 313-4840 ..**Ishofsky**, Harvey J '71 -15 Parkside Dr -Gt Neck 11021 **Fx**:482-4701
(212) 458-1305 ..**Isidro**, Hermenegildo A '98 Natl Union Fire Ins Co -175 Water -NY 10038
(212) 661-7839 ..**Iskanian-Hashasian**, Talar '94 -275 Mad Av -NY 10016 **Fx**:661-7846
(212) 558-4000 ..**Iskelov**, Diana G '10 %Sullivan & C LLP -125 Broad -NY 10004
(212) 940-8800 ..**Iskowitz**, Jos M '02 (Katten MR LLP) -575 Mad Av -NY 10022
(718) 658-0500 ..**Iskowitz**, Lori B '95 %Law Dept -151-20 Jamaica Av -Jamaica 11432 **Fx**:658-4025
(516) 433-0404 ..**Isler**, Debra V '90 (Isler & I) -25 Cambria Rd -Syosset 11791 **Fx**:433-8524
(631) 727-4100 ..**Isler**, Frank A '77 (Smith FLI&Y) -456 Griffing Av Bx389 -Rvrhead 11901
(516) 433-0404 ..**Isler**, Robt A '91 (Isler & I) -25 Cambria Rd -Syosset 11791 **Fx**:433-8524
(212) 250-8165 ..**Ismael**, Bruce K '74 %Deutsche Bank -60 Wall -NY 10005
(212) 701-3000 ..**Ismail**, Errol '06 %Cahill G&R LLP -80 Pine -NY 10005 **Fx**:269-5420
(212) 608-1800 ..**Ismail**, Khaleel N '05 %Kuzmin & Assoc -225 Bway -NY 10007
(212) 250-2960 ..**Ismailov**, Metin Ilias '95 Deutsche Bk -60 Wall -NY 10005
(212) 661-1010 ..**Isoai**, Toshinori '07 %Ogihara & Assoc,PLLC -122 E 42nd -NY 10168 **Fx**:661-6116
(718) 694-3853 ..**Isola**, Anita T '80 %Transit Auth -130 Lvngstn -Brklyn 11201 **Fx**:694-5726
(516) 806-4967 ..**Isolde**, Richd J '06 OfCnsl Kepanis Law Firm,PC -626 RXR Plz -Uniondale 11556 **Fx**:(866) 314-1386
(212) 326-2000 ..**Isom**, Phillip IV '92 (O'Melveny & M LLP) -7 Times Sq -NY 10036
(212) 549-2594 ..**Ispahani**, Laleh '95 ACLU -125 Broad -NY 10004 **Fx**:549-2651
(718) 377-7722 ..**Ispass**, Kenneth S '75 -3838 Flatlands Av -Brklyn 11234 **Fx**:377-7733
(212) 728-8000 ..**Ispass**, Michl T '10 %Willkie F&G LLP -787 7th Av -NY 10019
(212) 545-4690 ..**Isquith**, Fred T '72 (Wolf HAF&H LLP) -270 Mad Av -NY 10016
(212) 697-3750 ..**Israel**, Alan '75 (Kirschstein IS&P,PC) -425 5th Av -NY 10016
(212) 355-5353 ..**Israel**, Arthur J '74 -260 Mad Av -NY 10016 **Fx**:448-0066
(516) 365-5033 ..**Israel**, Chas J '80 -129 Firestone Cir -Roslyn 11576
(212) 514-5000 ..**Israel**, David M '77 -111 John -NY 10038 **Fx**:514-5004
(845) 371-7400 ..**Israel**, Eric A '93 -1 Exec Blvd -Suffern 10901 **Fx**:371-7450
(212) 558-4000 ..**Israel**, Gary '87 (Sullivan & C LLP) -125 Broad -NY 10004
(212) 416-8321 ..**Israel**, Herbert '73 %Dept of Law -120 Bway -NY 10271
(516) 221-6600 ..**Israel**, Jay M '92 -1200 Route 109 -Lindenhrst 11757 **Fx**:221-4290
(212) 801-9354 ..**Israel**, Jonathan L '94 (Greenberg T,LLP) -200 Park Av -NY 10166
(646) 695-9459 ..**Israel**, Marc '88 KV Natl Land -39 W 37th -NY 10018 **Fx**:417-5035
(516) 829-0363 ..**Israel**, Mardon R '59 (Israel I&P,LLP) -11 Grace Av -Gt Neck 11021 **Fx**:829-0366
(518) 489-8633 ..**Israel**, Mark A '96 -190 Davis Av -Albany 12208
(716) 551-4931 ..**Israel**, Michl J '83 NLRB -130 S Elmwood Av -Buffalo 14202 **Fx**:551-4972
(212) 973-0572 ..**Israel**, Ronald L '97 (Wolff & S PC) -140 Bway -NY 10005
(718) 292-2952 ..**Israel**, Roy S '64 (Yalkut & I) -865B Walton Av -Bronx 10451
(212) 201-5345 ..**Israel**, Sam P '88 (SP Israel,PC) -1 Lbrty Plz -NY 10006 **Fx**:201-5343
(212) 481-9777 ..**Israel**, Sol M '81 -185 Mad Av -NY 10016 **Fx**:447-6204
(718) 392-1000 ..**Israel**, Stanley '58 Pepsi-Cola Bottling -50-35 56th Rd -Maspeth 11378 **Fx**:392-2118
(718) 338-0400 ..**Israel**, Stanley M '60 -1978 Flatbush Av -Brklyn 11234
(516) 829-0363 ..**Israel**, Stuart M '91 (Israel I&P,LLP) -11 Grace Av -Gt Neck 11021 **Fx**:829-0366
(914) 684-2100 ..**Israel**, Susan F '08 %Littman K LLP -399 Knollwood Rd -White Plns 10603
(212) 506-1700 ..**Israeli**, Avi B '05 %Kasowitz BT&F LLP -1633 Bway -NY 10019
(718) 390-5383 ..**Israeli**, Judith D '87 %Supreme Ct Law Dept -18 Richmond Ter -Staten Isl 10301
(212) 645-2383 ..**Israeli**, Millet '96 TPM Media LLC -37 W 20th -NY 10011
(212) 316-5016 ..**Israeloff**, Lawr A '92 -10 Rckfllr Plz -NY 10020
(212) 362-4311 ..**Israels**, Michl J '76 -160 W 66th -NY 10023 **Fx**:595-3123
(516) 576-0101 ..**Israelson**, Paul J '82 -54 Sunnyside Blvd -Plainvw 11803 **Fx**:576-0565
(212) 262-6400 ..**Israelton**, Harvey S '73 Cnsl Schickler & S,LLP -1700 Bway -NY 10019 **Fx**:262-6298
(646) 459-7556 ..**Israelyan**, Souren A '03 -39 Bway -NY 10006 **Fx**:(888) 217-1948
(212) 918-3000 ..**Isralowitz**, Jason P '94 (Hogan L LLP) -875 3rd Av -NY 10022
(718) 694-3829 ..**Issacs-Fisher**, Karen A '86 %Transit Auth -130 Lvngstn -Brklyn 11201 **Fx**:694-5726
(845) 344-4322 ..**Isseks**, Robt N '79 -6 North -Middletwn 10940 **Fx**:341-1760
(212) 788-1222 ..**Isselbacher**, Tina H '84 Law Dept -100 Church -NY 10007 **Fx**:788-0367
(212) 812-5096 ..**Isser**, Steven D '94 -1359 Bway -NY 10018
(212) 479-6724 ..**Isserles**, Marc E '07 (Macht SA&I LLP) -1114 Av of Amer -NY 10036 **Fx**:202-6417
(718) 361-1514 ..**Isserlis**, Nancy L '80 -36-01 43rd Av -LIC 11101 **Fx**:(347) 418-3839
(212) 371-0200 ..**Issler**, Harry '58 H Issler,PLLC -50 Sutton Pl S -NY 10022 **Fx**:371-8853
(212) 309-1000 ..**Itkin**, Judith H '94 (Hunton & W) -200 Park Av -NY 10166
(718) 250-2000 ..**Itkin**, Nicole T '98 %DA -350 Jay -Brklyn 11201 **Fx**:250-2314
(212) 506-1700 ..**Itkin**, Uri A '09 %Kasowitz BT&F LLP -1633 Bway -NY 10019
(646) 822-1801 ..**Itkowitz & Harwood** -305 Bway -NY 10007 **Fx**:(212) 822-1401
(646) 822-1801 ..**Itkowitz**, Jay B '79 (Itkowitz & H) -305 Bway -NY 10007 **Fx**:(212) 822-1402
(212) 323-8194 ..**Iton**, Brian D '91 -67 Wall -NY 10005
(212) 219-3360 ..**Iturralde**, Christina '09 %Latino Justice PRLDEF -99 Hudson -NY 10013 **Fx**:431-4276
(718) 720-2877 ..**Itzkowitz**, Brian B '08 %Votto & C,LLP -60 Bay -Staten Isl 10310
(212) 969-3000 ..**Itzkowitz**, Elizabeth R '07 %Proskauer R LLP -1585 Bway -NY 10036
(212) 503-8862 ..**Itzkowitz**, Eric A '98 Marks Paneth & Shron LLP -622 3rd Av -NY 10017

(718) 625-8940 ..**Itzkowitz,** Roy '88 %B Lawrence -15 Metrotech Ctr N -Brklyn 11201 **Fx:**624-5756
(516) 221-3542 ..**Itzkowitz Schifman,** Lois B '86 -3368 S Mplwd Dr -Wantagh 11793
(914) 941-4885 ..**Itzla,** Amy Lynne '95 -11 Pea Pond Ln -Briarclff Mnr 10510
(914) 946-7770 ..**Iuanow,** Maria '02 OfCnsl Westermann SKS&A,LLP -222 Bloomingdale Rd -White Plns 10605
(845) 291-2050 ..**Iuele,** Albert J '07 %DA -255-275 Main -Goshen 10924 **Fx:**291-2085
(212) 262-2390 ..**Iuso,** Angela A '98 (Connell F LLP) -888 7th Av -NY 10106
(212) 506-1700 ..**Ivan,** Shelley '05 Kasowitz BT&F LLP -1633 Bway -NY 10019
(212) 685-1001 ..**Ivanac,** John '96 Canaui Grp Inc -107 E 34th -NY 10016
(716) 853-5100 ..**Ivancic,** Gregory T '83 (Lippes MWF LLP) -665 Main -Buffalo 14203
(212) 801-9333 ..**Ivanhoe,** Robt J '79 (Greenberg T,LLP) -200 Park Av -NY 10166
(212) 259-8000 ..**Ivanick,** Carol T '63 OfCnsl Dewey & L LLP -1301 Av of Amer -NY 10019
(212) 259-8000 ..**Ivanick,** Peter A '84 (Dewey & L LLP) -1301 Av of Amer -NY 10019
(212) 801-2210 ..**Ivanov,** Dmitry G '04 %Greenberg T,LLP -200 Park Av -NY 10166
(212) 556-3798 ..**Ivanova,** Elena '91 %The NY Times Co -620 8th Av -NY 10018 **Fx:**556-4634
(212) 969-3000 ..**Ivanova,** Suzette '05 %Proskauer R LLP -1585 Bway -NY 10036
(212) 753-5446 ..**Ivanyi,** Thos P '69 Hampton Prtnrs -444 Mad Av -NY 10022
(212) 335-9593 ..**Iverson,** Eric L '09 DA -1 Hogan Pl -NY 10013
(212) 988-5046 ..**Ives,** Garrison '66 -45 E 85th -NY 10028
(212) 486-8484 ..**Ives,** Howard '75 H Ives, PC -110 E 59th -NY 10022 **Fx:**486-3404
(914) 834-9595 ..**Ives,** Howard '75 -84 Briarcliff Rd -Larchmnt 10538 **Fx:**(212) 486-3404
(212) 298-5161 ..**Ives,** Kenneth B '89 %Leg Aid -49 Thomas -NY 10013 **Fx:**298-5252
(212) 704-6000 ..**Ivey,** Edw H '10 %Troutman S LLP -405 Lex Av -NY 10174
(718) 923-4206 ..**Ivey,** Gila '93 %OTDA Fair Hearings -14 Boerum Pl -Brklyn 11201
(631) 656-0996 ..**Ivezaj,** Jonathan D '04 -191 Terry Rd -Smithtwn 11787 **Fx:**265-6273
(212) 547-5400 ..**Ivill,** David S '00 (McDermott W&E LLP) -340 Mad Av -NY 10173
(516) 326-2400 ..**Ivone Devine & Jensen, LLP** -2001 Marcus Av -Lk Success 11042 **Fx:**352-4952
(516) 326-2400 ..**Ivone,** Michl T '61 (Ivone D&J,LLP) -2001 Marcus Av -Lk Success 11042
(212) 619-8387 ..**Ivory,** Paula J '02 %J O'Malley,PC -299 Bway -NY 10007 **Fx:**406-2967
(718) 579-8067 ..**Ivry,** Rebecca A '01 %Leg Aid -900 Sheridan Av -Bronx 10451 **Fx:**293-8744
(585) 238-2000 ..**Ivy,** Brian C '09 %Phillips L LLP -1400 First Fed Plz -Rchstr 14614
(585) 419-8800 ..**Ivy,** Svetlana K '08 %Harris B PLLC -99 Garnsey Rd -Pittsfrd 14534
(212) 868-3341 ..**Iwai,** Emiko '95 WTR,Inc -212 W 35th -NY 10001 **Fx:**(646) 351-8450
(212) 935-3000 ..**Iwamoto,** Michelle A '10 %Mintz LCFG&P,PC -666 3rd Av -NY 10017
(585) 343-4577 ..**Iwanicki,** Don B '64 -43 Jackson -Batavia 14020
(212) 855-0748 ..**Iwaschuk,** Wm J '03 Goldman Sachs -1 NY Plz -NY 10004
(917) 367-9042 ..**Iwata,** Tomoko '07 UN -1 UN Plz -NY 10017
(212) 854-2675 ..**Iwerebon,** E Nkonye '01 Columbia Law Schl -435 W 116th -NY 10027 **Fx:**854-7946
(212) 656-5791 ..**Iyeki,** Marc Hideo '85 NYSE EuroNext -20 Broad -NY 10005
(212) 255-8153 ..**Iyer,** Seema '98 -350 Bway -NY 10013
(212) 558-4000 ..**Iyer,** Vijay '08 %Sullivan & C LLP -125 Broad -NY 10004
(212) 727-2700 ..**Izeman,** Mark A '93 %NRDC -40 W 20th -NY 10011 **Fx:**727-1773
(631) 543-3167 ..**Izen,** Irwin S '86 -357 Vets Mem'l Hwy -Commack 11725 **Fx:**543-3187
(201) 406-9320 ..**Izen,** Jennifer B '08 -520 2nd Av -NY 10016
(212) 848-4000 ..**Izfar,** Sarah '08 %Shearman & S LLP -599 Lex Av -NY 10022
(212) 521-5400 ..**Izower,** Aron S '98 (Reed S LLP) -599 Lex Av -NY 10022
(212) 801-6992 ..**Izower,** Rachel L '01 OfCnsl Greenberg T,LLP -200 Park Av -NY 10166
(212) 335-9000 ..**Izquierdo,** Herculano A '77 %DA -1 Hogan Pl -NY 10013
(212) 857-8863 ..**Izutsu-Keener,** Laurie T '06 US Ct of Appls -40 Foley Sq -NY 10007
(315) 343-9093 ..**Izyk,** Edw J '90 -250 W 5th -Oswego 13126 **Fx:**342-2985
(518) 584-5500 ..**Izzo,** Anthony J '85 -158 W Circular -Saratoga Spgs 12866
(845) 473-8100 ..**Izzo,** Frank P '09 %Iseman CR&H,LLP -2649 South Rd -Poughkeepsie 12601
(315) 472-3434 ..**Izzo,** Janet M '00 R Lahm,PLLC -711 E Genesee -Syracuse 13210 **Fx:**472-8214
(914) 288-8706 ..**Izzo,** Luigi '08 D Klausner,PLLC -150 Grand -White Plns 10601
(718) 522-6767 ..**Izzo,** Richd A '82 -26 Court -Brklyn 11242
(212) 701-3000 ..**Izzo,** Thos J '10 %Cahill G&R LLP -80 Pine -NY 10005 **Fx:**269-5420
(914) 592-4275 ..**Izzo Mignardi,** Loraine J '00 %MHLS -100 Clearbrook Rd -Elmsfrd 10523 **Fx:**592-9404
(212) 335-4500 ..**Jaafar,** Randa A '95 OfCnsl DLA Piper LLP -1251 Av of Amer -NY 10020
(212) 558-4000 ..**Jaang,** Jane J '01 %Sullivan & C LLP -125 Broad -NY 10004
(212) 598-0646 ..**Jabara,** Abdeen '97 -113 Univ Pl -NY 10003
(212) 701-3000 ..**Jabbawy,** Michl R '08 %Cahill G&R LLP -80 Pine -NY 10005 **Fx:**269-5420
(212) 574-1200 ..**Jaber,** Amanda H '10 %Seward & K LLP -1 Bttry Pk Plz -NY 10004
(212) 657-0191 ..**Jaber,** Valerie-Leila '91 Citigroup Global Mrkts -77 Water -NY 10005
(212) 596-9000 ..**Jabido,** Janice V '07 %Ropes & G LLP -1211 Av of Amer -NY 10036
(212) 545-4000 ..**Jabinsky,** Carrie L '03 %Jackson L LLP -666 3rd Av -NY 10017
(516) 229-4427 ..**Jable,** David M '98 Cnsl Kay & G -875 Merrick Av -Westbury 11590
(516) 229-4200 ..**Jable,** Effy Belessis '99 %Mendolia & S -875 Merrick Av -Westbury 11590
(212) 906-1200 ..**Jablon,** Adam D '10 %Latham & W -885 3rd Av -NY 10022
(212) 732-9000 ..**Jablon,** Beth N '02 %Sullivan PBM&C PC -120 Bway -NY 10271
(516) 569-1435 ..**Jablon,** Deborah R '92 -1613 Hewlett Heath Rd -Hewlett 11557 **Fx:**295-5975
(212) 759-3300 ..**Jablon,** Jessica A '07 %Dornbush SS&V,LLP -747 3rd Av -NY 10017
(212) 808-7800 ..**Jablons,** Jane E '79 (Kelley D&W LLP) -101 Park Av -NY 10178
(518) 388-2667 ..**Jablonski,** Dawn K '90 MVP Health Care -625 State -Schnctdy 12305
(315) 594-1066 ..**Jablonski,** Douglas M '93 -12061 E Main -Wolcott 14590 **Fx:**594-1969
(631) 853-4104 ..**Jablonski,** Edw C '74 %DA -400 Carleton Av Bx9082 -Central Islip 11722 **Fx:**853-7838
(716) 566-5400 ..**Jablonski,** John J '94 (Goldberg S LLP) -665 Main -Buffalo 14203
(516) 676-4114 ..**Jablonski,** Mary J '90 (Jablonski & J) -50 Glen -Glen Cove 11542 **Fx:**674-9270
(516) 676-4114 ..**Jablonski,** Stuart R '90 (Jablonski & J) -50 Glen -Glen Cove 11542 **Fx:**674-9270
(631) 234-3030 ..**Jablonsky,** Michelle L Black '98 (Davidow DS&S,LLP) -1601 Vets Mem'l Hwy -Islandia 11749
(212) 776-5000 ..**Jabouin,** Marjorie G '06 NYC Housing Auth -250 Bway -NY 10007 **Fx:**776-5039
(212) 999-5800 ..**Jabri,** Omar '07 %Wilson SG&R -1301 Av of Americas -NY 10019
(718) 250-2000 ..**Jaccarino,** Michl T '08 %DA -350 Jay -Brklyn 11201 **Fx:**250-2314
(718) 852-3000 ..**Jaccoma,** Barbara '80 %CSA -16 Court -Brklyn 11241
(585) 368-9020 ..**Jacek,** Jos W Jr. '84 -31 Erie Canal Dr -Rchstr 14626
(212) 841-1000 ..**Jachimowicz,** David '09 %Covington & B LLP -620 8th Av -NY 10018
(212) 344-5680 ..**Jachimowski,** Adam F '02 %Thompson H LLP -335 Mad Av -NY 10017
(718) 250-2000 ..**Jack,** Aisha J P '06 %DA -350 Jay -Brklyn 11201 **Fx:**250-2314
(518) 767-9051 ..**Jack,** Howard A '73 Audubon Intl -46 Rarick Rd -Selkirk 12158 **Fx:**767-0069
(212) 450-4000 ..**Jack,** Julie N '01 %Davis P&W LLP -450 Lex Av -NY 10017
(212) 255-9252 ..**Jack,** Kathrine D '09 NAFPW -15 W 36th -NY 10018
(347) 404-9433 ..**Jack-Browne,** Sheridan N '07 Criminal Ct -120 Schermerhorn -Brklyn 11201
(212) 223-0200 ..**Jackel,** Sarah K '07 %Stillman F&S,PC -425 Park Av -NY 10022
(212) 393-1300 ..**Jackel,** Stephen M '80 -277 Bway -NY 10007 **Fx:**393-1345
(585) 546-5530 ..**Jacklin,** Beverly L '78 %Thomson West -50 E Broad -Rchstr 14694
(914) 681-0200 ..**Jackman,** Jennifer M '00 %DelBello DWW&W,LLP -1 N Lex Av -White Plns 10601
(212) 474-1000 ..**Jackman,** Phillip E '09 %Cravath S&M LLP -825 8th Av -NY 10019
(212) 284-8194 ..**Jackman,** Robt J '98 Jeffries & Co -520 Mad Av -NY 10022
(212) 267-3170 ..**Jacknowitz,** Melvyn S '75 -19 Fulton -NY 10038 **Fx:**267-2019
(212) 545-1900 ..**Jackowski,** Wojciech '04 %Menaker & H LLP -10 E 40th -NY 10016
(716) 434-8891 ..**Jackson,** Arthur '72 (Jackson & B) -365 Market Bx468 -Lockprt 14095
(716) 434-8891 ..**Jackson & Balkin** -365 Market Bx468 -Lockprt 14095 **Fx:**434-9105
(212) 259-8000 ..**Jackson,** Bernard H III '90 Cnsl Dewey & L LLP -1301 Av of Amer -NY 10019
(212) 336-2000 ..**Jackson,** Christopher M P '01 %Patterson BW&T LLP -1133 Av of Amer -NY 10036
(716) 488-3090 ..**Jackson,** Craig E '02 %Burgett & R -15 E 5th Bx3090 -Jamestwn 14702
(212) 626-4100 ..**Jackson,** D David '97 OfCnsl Baker & M LLP -1114 Av of Amer -NY 10036
(845) 566-5345 ..**Jackson,** Danl C III '05 %Larkin AI&T,LLP -356 Meadow Av -Newburgh 12550
(718) 875-1300 ..**Jackson,** Deidre '02 %Appllt Div 2nd Dept -45 Monroe Pl -Brklyn 11201 **Fx:**858-2446
(518) 473-8418 ..**Jackson,** Derek J '90 %OCFS -52 Wshngtn -Rensselaer 12144 **Fx:**486-6361
(212) 461-2338 ..**Jackson,** Eunice A '78 %Goldstein H -44 Wall -NY 10005 **Fx:**(646) 219-2450
(518) 436-0344 ..**Jackson,** F Matthew '96 (Deily M&G,LLP) -8 Thurlow Ter -Albany 12203
(212) 335-4500 ..**Jackson,** Frank J '98 %DLA Piper LLP -1251 Av of Amer -NY 10020
(212) 709-0839 ..**Jackson,** Garrett D '02 %Cushman & Wakefield -88 Pine -NY 10005
(212) 767-8600 ..**Jackson,** Genise '94 Comedy Central -345 Hudson -NY 10014 **Fx:**767-4284
(718) 250-2000 ..**Jackson,** Howard L '02 %DA -350 Jay -Brklyn 11201 **Fx:**250-2314
(212) 918-3000 ..**Jackson,** Inna Nazarova '04 %Hogan L LLP -875 3rd Av -NY 10022
(516) 486-3279 ..**Jackson,** J Barrington '82 -734 Franklin Av #321 -Gdn Cty 11530
(212) 735-3000 ..**Jackson,** J Russell '91 (Skadden ASM&F LLP) -4 Times Sq -NY 10036
(212) 592-1400 ..**Jackson,** Jack P '84 (Herrick,F LLP) -2 Park Av -NY 10016
(212) 416-8000 ..**Jackson,** Jeffrey '97 %Dept of Law -120 Bway -NY 10271
(718) 546-8314 ..**Jackson,** Jeffrey G '79 NY Dept of Corrections-ACS -120 Mancini Rd -E Elmhrst 11370
(716) 853-9555 ..**Jackson,** Jessamine Ingrid '90 %Leg Aid -237 Main -Buffalo 14203 **Fx:**853-3219
(845) 486-4200 ..**Jackson,** Jillian E '01 %Shaw PM&L,LLP -21 Van Wagner Rd -Poughkeepsie 12603
(917) 551-1300 ..**Jackson,** Joey '96 %Koehler & I LLP -61 Bway -NY 10006
(716) 565-9700 ..**Jackson,** Kathryn Ann '84 -5784 Main -Williamsvll 14221 **Fx:**565-0668
(718) 286-6000 ..**Jackson,** Katrina D '08 %DA -125-01 Qns Blvd -Kew Gdns 11415
(585) 899-1414 ..**Jackson,** LaMarr J '99 (Harris COJW&L) -300 Linden Oaks -Rchstr 14625
(718) 370-1021 ..**Jackson,** LaWanda A '95 -951 Goethals Rd N -Staten Isl 10303
(212) 545-4000 ..**Jackson Lewis LLP** -666 3rd Av -NY 10017 **Fx:**972-3213
(914) 328-0404 ..**Jackson Lewis LLP** -1 N Bway -White Plns 10601 **Fx:**328-1882
(631) 247-0404 ..**Jackson Lewis LLP** -58 S Srvc Rd -Melvll 11747 **Fx:**247-0147
(518) 434-1300 ..**Jackson Lewis LLP** -18 Corp Wds Blvd -Albany 12211
(718) 741-8258 ..**Jackson,** Margaret A '87 Div of Human Rights -1 Fordham Plz -Bronx 10458
(212) 416-2000 ..**Jackson,** Mark H '86 Dow Jones & Co Inc -1155 Av of Amer -NY 10036
(212) 839-5300 ..**Jackson,** Martin B '03 %Sidley A LLP -787 7th Av -NY 10019
(716) 362-0237 ..**Jackson,** Michl L '90 (Jackson & J LLP) -70 W Chippewa -Buffalo 14202
(212) 906-1200 ..**Jackson,** Nicole D '10 %Latham & W -885 3rd Av -NY 10022
(212) 578-2211 ..**Jackson,** Patricia Anne '90 %MetLife -27-01 Qns Plz N -LIC 11101

(914) 995-3121 ..**Jackson,** Peter D '89 %Cnty Atty -148 Martine Av -White Plns 10601 **Fx:**995-5858
(716) 362-0237 ..**Jackson,** Rachel E '00 (Jackson & J LLP) -70 W Chippewa -Buffalo 14202
(585) 262-8100 ..**Jackson,** Rashondra M '03 Rochester City Schl Dist -131 W Broad -Rchstr 14614
(212) 416-6511 ..**Jackson,** Richd O '02 %Dept of Law -120 Bway -NY 10271
(212) 750-1200 ..**Jackson,** Robt B '76 %Trolman G&L,PC -777 3rd Av -NY 10017
(718) 447-2950 ..**Jackson,** Robt E '67 -350 St Marks Pl -Staten Isl 10301
(212) 596-9000 ..**Jackson,** Robt R '71 (Ropes & G LLP) -1211 Av of Amer -NY 10036
(212) 530-1800 ..**Jackson,** Ryan C '01 %Richards K&O LLP -1 World Fncl Ctr -NY 10281
(718) 595-3520 ..**Jackson,** Sandra Salter '76 %DEP -59-17 Junction Blvd -Flushng 11373 **Fx:**595-6543
(212) 223-4000 ..**Jackson,** Sean E '06 %Crowell & M LLP -590 Mad Av -NY 10022
(716) 886-0211 ..**Jackson,** Shaun Bryan '86 %Benderson Dvlpmnt -570 Delaware Av -Buffalo 14202 **Fx:**886-2269
(212) 643-2394 ..**Jackson,** Stephen C '87 -350 5th Av -NY 10118 **Fx:**239-6900
(718) 298-7050 ..**Jackson,** Steven F '76 Envrnmntl Cntrl Bd -144-06 94th Av -Jamaica 11435
(212) 755-0500 ..**Jackson,** Stuart A '58 (Maidman and M,LLP) -70 E 55th -NY 10022
(516) 712-4000 ..**Jackson,** Susan M '99 (Milber MP&S LLP) -1000 Woodbury Rd -Woodbury 11797
(212) 788-0446 ..**Jackson,** Tamara '06 %Law Dept -100 Church -NY 10007 **Fx:**788-0367
(607) 778-2423 ..**Jackson,** Thos D Jr. '02 %DA -45 Hawley Bx1766 -Bnghmtn 13902 **Fx:**778-8870
(212) 977-9700 ..**Jackson,** Thos G '75 (Phillips N LLP) -666 5th Av -NY 10103
(585) 275-8356 ..**Jackson,** Thos H '76 %Univ of Rochester -240 Admin Bldg -Rchstr 14627 **Fx:**256-2473
(212) 504-6000 ..**Jackson,** Tianna E '10 %Cadwalader W&T LLP -1 World Fncl Ctr -NY 10281
(212) 788-7081 ..**Jackson,** Tisha M '02 %City Cncl Leg Div -250 Bway -NY 10007 **Fx:**788-7034
(212) 331-5946 ..**Jackson,** Valarie Y '09 HR Admin-Legal Affairs -180 Water -NY 10038
(212) 820-9620 ..**Jackson,** Wm J '05 %Hawkins D&W LLP -One Chase Manh Plz -NY 10005
(212) 818-9200 ..**Jackson,** Wm M '75 (Satterlee SB&B LLP) -230 Park Av -NY 10169
(646) 264-1302 ..**Jackson-Chase,** Courtenaye Y '93 Midtown Comm Ct -314 W 54th -NY 10019
(516) 463-5887 ..**Jacob,** Bernard E '69 %Hofstra Law Schl -121 Hofstra Univ -Hempstd 11549
(212) 753-5000 ..**Jacob,** Beth D '78 (Schiff H LLP) -900 3rd Av -NY 10022
(212) 336-3500 ..**Jacob,** Chas R III '79 (Miller & W,PC) -570 Lex Av -NY 10022
(212) 524-5000 ..**Jacob,** Edwin J '51 (Jacob M&F) -1270 Av of Amer -NY 10020
(516) 625-8048 ..**Jacob,** Howard D '76 -1500 Old Nrthrn Blvd -Roslyn 11576
(212) 310-8000 ..**Jacob,** Marvin E '64 (Weil G&M LLP) -767 5th Av -NY 10153
(212) 735-3000 ..**Jacob,** Mary '07 %Skadden ASM&F LLP -4 Times Sq -NY 10036
(212) 524-5000 ..**Jacob Medinger & Finnegan** -1270 Av of Amer -NY 10020 **Fx:**524-5050
(212) 415-8600 ..**Jacob,** Shalom '87 (Locke LB&L LLP) -3 World Fncl Ctr -NY 10281
(212) 766-1200 ..**Jacob,** Shibu J '04 %Shestack & Y,LLP -233 Bway -NY 10279
(212) 295-6406 ..**Jacob,** Thos A '03 WilmerHale -399 Park Av -NY 10022
(212) 859-8000 ..**Jacob,** Valerie Ford '79 (Fried FHS&J LLP) -1 NY Plz -NY 10004
(845) 225-3641 ..**Jacobellis,** Thos J '98 %DA -40 Gleneida Av -Carmel 10512
(212) 326-3939 ..**Jacobi,** Eric S '10 %Jones D -222 E 41st -NY 10017
(718) 670-1995 ..**Jacobi,** Kyle J '05 NY Hosptl Queens -56-45 Main -Flushng 11355
(718) 442-4600 ..**Jacobi,** Mordecai J '70 (Jacobi SBP&F,PC) -235 Forest Av -Staten Isl 10301
(718) 442-4600 ..**Jacobi Sieghardt Bousanti Piazza & Fitzpatrick,PC** -235 Forest Av -Staten Isl 10301 **Fx:**442-3148
(212) 685-7474 ..**Jacobi,** Sophie M S '04 %Mayerson SA LLP -292 Mad Av -NY 10017
(212) 852-1000 ..**Jacobi,** Susan M '85 %US Trust Co,NA -114 W 47th -NY 10036 **Fx:**852-1310
(518) 435-1770 ..**Jacobi,** Tara L '98 Legal Project Inc -6 Exec Park Dr -Albany 12203 **Fx:**435-1773
(516) 295-5400 ..**Jacobowitz & Arrick** -650 Central Av Bx209 -Cedarhrst 11516 **Fx:**295-5413
(845) 778-2121 ..**Jacobowitz,** Gerald N '59 (Jacobowitz & G,LLP) -158 Orange Av Bx367 -Walden 12586
(631) 264-0600 ..**Jacobowitz & Graziano, LLP** -43 Ireland Pl Bx668 -Amityvll 11701 **Fx:**264-0003
(845) 778-2121 ..**Jacobowitz & Gubits,LLP** -158 Orange Av Bx367 -Walden 12586 **Fx:**778-5173
(845) 454-6000 ..**Jacobowitz & Gubits,LLP** -1 Civic Ctr Plz -Poughkeepsie 12601
(845) 791-1765 ..**Jacobowitz & Gubits,LLP** -540 Bway -Monticello 12701 **Fx:**794-9781
(212) 770-6327 ..**Jacobowitz,** Harold S '77 %AIG -70 Pine -NY 10270
(914) 632-4700 ..**Jacobowitz,** Howard S '79 (McDonough Law Firm, LLP) -145 Huguenot -New Rchll 10801
(631) 264-0600 ..**Jacobowitz,** Lee S '93 (Jacobowitz & G,LLP) -43 Ireland Pl Bx668 -Amityvll 11701
(212) 484-3900 ..**Jacobowitz,** Lester '87 (Arent F LLP) -1675 Bway -NY 10019
(845) 778-2581 ..**Jacobowitz,** Marcia A '86 (Jacobowitz & P) -156 Orange Av Bx366 -Walden 12586 **Fx:**778-5074
(516) 869-4451 ..**Jacobowitz,** Moshe '02 -445 Central Av -Cedarhrst 11516
(212) 245-6445 ..**Jacobs,** Adele R '84 -80 Broad -NY 10004 **Fx:**(203) 332-7709
(212) 848-9800 ..**Jacobs,** Alan S '72 (Withers B LLP) -430 Park Av -NY 10022
(212) 704-6000 ..**Jacobs,** Albert L Jr. '64 OfCnsl Troutman S LLP -405 Lex Av -NY 10174
(718) 757-2474 ..**Jacobs,** Allan J '09 (O'Brien & J,PLLC) -110 Wall -NY 10005
(212) 458-2880 ..**Jacobs,** Allan R '89 AIG,Inc -175 Water -NY 10038
(212) 701-3000 ..**Jacobs,** Andrew B '10 %Cahill G&R LLP -80 Pine -NY 10005 **Fx:**269-5420
(212) 286-8899 ..**Jacobs,** Andrew M '95 (Balsam J,LLP) -315 Mad Av -NY 10017 **Fx:**(888) 873-6587
(212) 309-1000 ..**Jacobs,** Andrew M '08 %Hunton & W -200 Park Av -NY 10166
(212) 208-1436 ..**Jacobs,** Andrew R '80 (Berman SR&J,PC) -140 Bway -NY 10005
(518) 477-5408 ..**Jacobs,** Andrew S '00 A Jacobs -573 Columbia Tpk -E Greenbush 12061 **Fx:**477-4255
(212) 841-4230 ..**Jacobs,** Andrew S '04 Millennium Prtnrs,LP -666 5th Av -NY 10103
(212) 969-3000 ..**Jacobs,** Arnold S '64 (Proskauer R LLP) -1585 Bway -NY 10036
(212) 207-8787 ..**Jacobs,** Arthur J '68 (Jacobs & B LLP) -445 Park Av -NY 10022
(212) 331-6729 ..**Jacobs,** Barbara J '96 1st NY Securities -90 Park Av -NY 10016
(212) 422-1200 ..**Jacobs,** Barry '81 (Abrams GF&J,PC) -1 Bttry Pk Plz -NY 10004
(914) 725-5568 ..**Jacobs,** Bernadine Rosen '95 -46 Walworth Av -Scarsdale 10583 **Fx:**725-5877
(212) 213-5577 ..**Jacobs,** Betty Jane '74 (Litman & J) -1133 Bway -NY 10010
(212) 448-1100 ..**Jacobs,** Brad M '00 (McLaughlin & S,LLP) -260 Mad Av -NY 10016
(212) 637-2512 ..**Jacobs,** Brian A '05 %US Atty -1 St Andrews Plz -NY 10007
(212) 207-8787 ..**Jacobs & Burleigh LLP** -445 Park Av -NY 10022 **Fx:**207-8727
(212) 940-3170 ..**Jacobs,** Chas P '76 (Nixon P LLP) -437 Mad Av -NY 10022
(716) 853-8100 ..**Jacobs,** Chas P '76 (Nixon P LLP) -40 Fountain Plz -Buffalo 14202
(716) 852-0733 ..**Jacobs,** Christopher L '99 %Avalon Dvlpmnt LLC -700 Seneca -Buffalo 14210
(718) 237-1200 ..**Jacobs & Cohen** -26 Court -Brklyn 11242 **Fx:**237-1393
(518) 432-7511 ..**Jacobs,** Danl A '08 %Gleason DW&O -40 Beaver -Albany 12207
(212) 545-4000 ..**Jacobs,** Danl J '07 %Jackson L LLP -666 3rd Av -NY 10017
(718) 372-7333 ..**Jacobs,** David '82 -40 Brighton 1st Rd -Brklyn 11235
(718) 237-1200 ..**Jacobs,** David S '70 (Jacobs & C) -26 Court -Brklyn 11242
(973) 315-4413 ..**Jacobs,** Donald P '88 (Budd L) -140 Bway -NY 10005
(212) 210-1400 ..**Jacobs,** Douglas P '72 A&E Television Networks -235 E 45th -NY 10017
(212) 859-8000 ..**Jacobs,** Edw J '03 %Fried FHS&J LLP -1 NY Plz -NY 10004
(212) 756-2000 ..**Jacobs,** Eliza G '10 %Schulte R&Z LLP -919 3rd Av -NY 10022
(212) 558-5500 ..**Jacobs,** Erik '93 %Weitz & L,PC -700 Bway -NY 10003
(212) 841-1000 ..**Jacobs,** Ethan I '06 %Covington & B LLP -620 8th Av -NY 10018
(212) 735-3000 ..**Jacobs,** Evan S '07 %Skadden ASM&F LLP -4 Times Sq -NY 10036
(212) 692-1000 ..**Jacobs,** Fran M '80 (Duane M LLP) -1540 Bway -NY 10036
(718) 238-2021 ..**Jacobs,** Freddy '88 OfCnsl M King -256 93rd -Brklyn 11209 **Fx:**238-2099
(516) 773-3107 ..**Jacobs,** Gail '79 -10 St George Rd -Gt Neck 11021 **Fx:**482-8127
(212) 635-2244 ..**Jacobs,** Gerald M '90 %Rosner N&R LLP -110 Wall -NY 10005
(914) 761-6066 ..**Jacobs,** Gloria S '75 -175 Main -White Plns 10601
(718) 237-9795 ..**Jacobs,** Harvey S '67 -26 Court -Brklyn 11242 **Fx:**855-2057
(914) 697-5289 ..**Jacobs,** Howard E '99 Krasdale Foods Inc -65 W Red Oak Ln -West Harrison 10604
(212) 431-3710 ..**Jacobs,** Howard L '60 -401 Bway -NY 10013
(212) 940-8800 ..**Jacobs,** Howard S '68 (Katten MR LLP) -575 Mad Av -NY 10022
(718) 523-3462 ..**Jacobs,** Hyman '77 -148-05 Archer Av Bx344 -Jamaica 11435 **Fx:**523-3581
(212) 460-1916 ..**Jacobs,** J Zalman '91 Leucadia Intl Corp -315 Park Av S -NY 10010
(212) 626-4100 ..**Jacobs,** James D '70 (Baker & M LLP) -1114 Av of Amer -NY 10036
(212) 935-6020 ..**Jacobs,** Jane B '83 (Klein ZR LLP) -485 Mad Av -NY 10022
(607) 723-9511 ..**Jacobs,** Jeffrey M '02 (Coughlin & G,LLP) -19 Chenango Bx2039 -Bnghmtn 13902
(212) 460-4434 ..**Jacobs,** Joan S '00 Con Ed -4 Irving Pl -NY 10003
(212) 258-6000 ..**Jacobs,** John R '86 %Viacom -1515 Bway -NY 10036
(718) 590-3578 ..**Jacobs,** Jonathan A '78 %Hon H Silverman -851 Grnd Cncrs -Bronx 10451
(212) 422-1200 ..**Jacobs,** Jonathan A '09 %Abrams GF&J,PC -1 Bttry Pk Plz -NY 10004
(212) 839-5300 ..**Jacobs,** Jonathan B '03 %Sidley A LLP -787 7th Av -NY 10019
(212) 756-2000 ..**Jacobs,** Jonathan D '06 %Schulte R&Z LLP -919 3rd Av -NY 10022
(212) 841-1000 ..**Jacobs,** Jonathan F '05 %Covington & B LLP -620 8th Av -NY 10018
(914) 476-0600 ..**Jacobs,** Kenneth R '79 (Smith B&J,LLP) -733 Ynkrs Av -Ynkrs 10704
(516) 487-0175 ..**Jacobs,** Kimberly Middle '07 E Schwartz -343 Grt Nck Rd -Gt Neck 11021 **Fx:**773-7706
(646) 386-3600 ..**Jacobs,** Laura J '95 Hon M Schoenfeld Supreme Ct -60 Centre -NY 10007
(607) 652-7511 ..**Jacobs,** Lauren B '09 %Jacobs & J -31 Lake Bx159 -Stamfrd 12167 **Fx:**652-7262
(212) 852-7720 ..**Jacobs,** Lawr A '82 %News Corp -1211 Av of Amer -NY 10036 **Fx:**852-7147
(212) 450-4000 ..**Jacobs,** Lawr E '86 Cnsl Davis P&W LLP -450 Lex Av -NY 10017
(212) 279-9200 ..**Jacobs,** Lee N '08 %Abrams FFEGF&E,LLP -630 3rd Av -NY 10017
(212) 309-7845 ..**Jacobs,** Linda '95 %Lexis/Nexis -125 Park Av -NY 10017 **Fx:**309-8187
(212) 848-4000 ..**Jacobs,** Lisa L '83 (Shearman & S LLP) -599 Lex Av -NY 10022
(212) 578-4009 ..**Jacobs,** Lowell L '77 %MetLife -27-01 Qns Plz N -LIC 11101
(716) 853-8671 ..**Jacobs,** Luke T '96 Barrantys -120 W Tupper -Buffalo 14201 **Fx:**854-0715
(631) 342-5224 ..**Jacobs,** Lynn B '87 %CA,Inc -1 CA Plz -Islandia 11749 **Fx:**342-4866
(212) 632-4967 ..**Jacobs,** M Joy '98 %Scribner -1230 Av of Amer -NY 10020
(212) 922-6000 ..**Jacobs,** Mark Neil '72 Dreyfus -200 Park Av -NY 10166
(212) 421-4100 ..**Jacobs,** Mark R '83 (Pryor C LLP) -7 Times Sq -NY 10036
(212) 730-7750 ..**Jacobs,** Melissa A '99 %Nicoletti GS&O,LLP -555 5th Av -NY 10017
(607) 652-7511 ..**Jacobs,** Michl A '72 (Jacobs & J) -31 Lake Bx159 -Stamfrd 12167 **Fx:**652-7262
(718) 579-7938 ..**Jacobs,** Michelle L '94 %Leg Aid -900 Sheridan Av -Bronx 10451 **Fx:**293-8744
(845) 938-3510 ..**Jacobs,** Nathan P '09 US Military Academy Law Dept -646 Swift Rd -West Pnt 10996
(914) 669-5559 ..**Jacobs,** Neil I '84 -679 Titicus Rd -N Salem 10560 **Fx:**669-9408
(212) 318-3000 ..**Jacobs,** Paul '71 (Fulbright & J LLP) -666 5th Av -NY 10103
(212) 856-9595 ..**Jacobs,** Peter L '60 (P Jacobs & Assoc,PC) -49 W 37th -NY 10018 **Fx:**856-9898
(212) 709-8116 ..**Jacobs,** Randall S D '77 -110 Wall -NY 10005 **Fx:**(973) 226-8897
(845) 220-2667 ..**Jacobs,** Randy '04 %McGillicuddy & S,PC -233 Bway -Newburgh 12550
(718) 253-8800 ..**Jacobs,** Reuven '86 -1907 Av I -Brklyn 11230 **Fx:**253-4033
(212) 267-2600 ..**Jacobs,** Robt A '61 -61 Bway -NY 10006 **Fx:**267-3024

(212) 867-4466 .. **Jacobs,** Robt A '80 (Belkin BW&G,LLP) -270 Mad Av -NY 10016
(310) 312-4360 .. **Jacobs,** Robt A '93 %Manatt P&P,LLP -7 Times Sq -NY 10036 **Fx:**312-4224
(212) 687-4900 .. **Jacobs,** Robt F '68 (Wormser KG&J LLP) -825 3rd Av -NY 10022
(212) 644-0500 .. **Jacobs,** Roger B '80 (Jacobs R,LLC) -777 3rd Av -NY 10017
(212) 376-8900 .. **Jacobs,** Ron '82 (Jacobs & S) -757 3rd Av -NY 10017 **Fx:**376-8989
(212) 644-0500 .. **Jacobs Rosenberg,LLC** -777 3rd Av -NY 10017
(212) 603-6300 .. **Jacobs,** Roy A '73 (Robinson BLGG&G PC) -875 3rd Av -NY 10022
(212) 867-1156 .. **Jacobs,** Roy L '76 (R Jacobs & Assoc) -60 E 42nd -NY 10165 **Fx:**504-8343
(914) 385-6000 .. **Jacobs,** Sanford G '99 %Hodges W&S LLP -55 Church -White Plns 10601 **Fx:**385-6060
(212) 661-5500 .. **Jacobs,** Scott H '98 SH Jacobs & Assoc,LLC -708 3rd Av -NY 10017
(212) 733-3678 .. **Jacobs,** Seth H '86 Cnsl Pfizer Inc -235 E 42nd -NY 10017 **Fx:**573-1445
(212) 351-4000 .. **Jacobs,** Sheera L '09 Gibson D&C LLP -200 Park Av -NY 10166
(212) 335-9000 .. **Jacobs,** Sophi K '07 DA -1 Hogan Pl -NY 10013
(845) 565-9261 .. **Jacobs,** Stacy L '99 B Kulak -484 Temple Hill Rd -New Windsor 12553
(212) 238-4800 .. **Jacobs,** Stephen '79 (Landman CB&F,PC) -120 Bway -NY 10271
(212) 687-9555 .. **Jacobs,** Stephen C '88 Spectrum Grp Mgmt LLC -1250 Bway -NY 10001 **Fx:**983-2322
(212) 310-8000 .. **Jacobs,** Stephen E '62 (Weil G&M LLP) -767 5th Av -NY 10153
(631) 756-4036 .. **Jacobs,** Steven I '83 %State Ins Fund -8 Corp Ctr Dr -Melvll 11747 **Fx:**756-4060
(212) 788-0899 .. **Jacobs,** Stuart E '04 %Law Dept -100 Church -NY 10007 **Fx:**788-0367
(718) 436-3396 .. **Jacobs,** Stuart I '88 -1779 51st -Brklyn 11204 **Fx:**436-4138
(212) 385-1191 .. **Jacobs,** Sue C '80 (Goodman & J LLP) -75 Broad -NY 10004
(646) 264-3650 .. **Jacobs,** Susan B '95 %US Dept of Labor -201 Varick -NY 10014 **Fx:**264-3660
(212) 691-0950 .. **Jacobs,** Susan L '83 %Ctr for Family Representation -116 John -NY 10038 **Fx:**691-0951
(516) 489-5000 .. **Jacobs,** Susan P '94 %Town Atty -Town Hall -Hempstd 11550 **Fx:**489-5150
(212) 558-4000 .. **Jacobs,** Zachary J P '08 %Sullivan & C LLP -125 Broad -NY 10004
(914) 234-9241 .. **Jacobsen,** Alfred III '59 (A Jacobsen & Assoc LLP) -15 Court Bx471 -Bedfrd 10506 **Fx:**234-3940
(212) 218-2100 .. **Jacobsen,** Charlotte C '09 %Fitzpatrick CH&S -1290 Av of Amer -NY 10104
(914) 234-9241 .. **Jacobsen,** Erik P '94 (A Jacobsen & Assoc LLP) -15 Court Bx471 -Bedfrd 10506 **Fx:**234-3940
(212) 902-1445 .. **Jacobsen,** Glade A '90 %Goldman Sachs -1 NY Plz -NY 10004
(212) 450-4000 .. **Jacobsen,** Lin '08 %Davis P&W LLP -450 Lex Av -NY 10017
(212) 506-5000 .. **Jacobsen,** Richd A Jr. '04 %Orrick H&S LLP -51 W 52nd -NY 10019
(845) 338-6322 .. **Jacobsen,** Robt R '05 Ulster Savings Bank -180 Schwenk Dr -Kingston 12401 **Fx:**339-9744
(718) 222-2313 .. **Jacobson,** Amy L '08 %Law Dept -350 Jay -Brklyn 11201 **Fx:**222-2373
(716) 373-4701 .. **Jacobson,** Amy Sigrid '98 %Leg Srvcs -103 S Barry -Olean 14760 **Fx:**373-7771
(212) 836-8000 .. **Jacobson,** Andrea B '89 %Kaye S LLP -425 Park Av -NY 10022
(212) 805-3900 .. **Jacobson,** Andrew C '77 (Clausen M PC) -1 Chase Manh Plz -NY 10005
(212) 790-0218 .. **Jacobson,** Arthur J '75 %Benj N Cardozo Schl of Law -55 5th Av -NY 10003 **Fx:**790-0345
(914) 428-3313 .. **Jacobson,** Austin H '90 %Curan AF&N,LLP -14 Mamaroneck Av -White Plns 10601 **Fx:**949-5800
(718) 923-1000 .. **Jacobson,** Barry S '81 -26 Court -Brklyn 11242 **Fx:**(516) 939-6694
(516) 496-3000 .. **Jacobson,** Chas '74 -7600 Jericho Tpk -Woodbury 11797 **Fx:**496-8667
(212) 270-0329 .. **Jacobson,** Darryl M '00 JP Morgan Chase & Co -270 Park Av -NY 10017
(212) 317-0700 .. **Jacobson,** David H '95 %Fuller & F -845 3rd Av -NY 10022 **Fx:**317-8833
(212) 558-4000 .. **Jacobson,** Eliyahu D '81 (Sullivan & C LLP) -125 Broad -NY 10004
(914) 993-1940 .. **Jacobson,** Elliott B '81 %US Atty -300 Quarropas -White Plns 10601 **Fx:**993-9036
(716) 824-7200 .. **Jacobson,** Frank J '99 %R Lorigo -101 Slade Av -W Seneca 14224 **Fx:**824-8728
(212) 608-1900 .. **Jacobson,** Gary S '77 OfCnsl Lovell SH LLP -61 Bway -NY 10006
(212) 422-1200 .. **Jacobson,** Glenn A '80 (Abrams GF&J,PC) -1 Bttry Pk Plz -NY 10004
(516) 222-2330 .. **Jacobson Goldberg & Kulb,LLP** -585 Stewart Av -Gdn Cty 11530 **Fx:**222-2339
(631) 473-0286 .. **Jacobson,** Harold E '94 -102 W Bway -Pt Jffrsn 11777
(845) 454-1171 .. **Jacobson,** Herbert '60 (Feldman & J) -94 Market -Poughkeepsie 12601
(212) 728-8000 .. **Jacobson,** Hillel Noah '00 (Willkie F&G LLP) -787 7th Av -NY 10019
(914) 699-0600 .. **Jacobson,** Howard '82 (Scancarelli J&U,LLP) -22 W 1st -Mt Vernon 10550
(212) 854-5583 .. **Jacobson,** Howard A '67 Columbia Univ -535 W 116th 412 Low Mem'l Library -NY 10027 **Fx:**854-5828
(212) 344-1500 .. **Jacobson,** Ivy L '00 %Smith C,LLP -110 Wall -NY 10005
(212) 759-9001 .. **Jacobson,** J Jos '97 Madison Capital -55 E 59th -NY 10022
(212) 977-9001 .. **Jacobson,** Janet Carol '82 %RHI Entrtnmnt -1325 Av of Amer -NY 10019 **Fx:**977-9049
(516) 741-1110 .. **Jacobson,** Jay D '94 (Foley GJ&F,LLP) -666 Old Cntry Rd -Gdn Cty 11530
(212) 683-2001 .. **Jacobson,** Jeffrey E '82 Jacobson Firm,PC -60 Mad Av -NY 10010 **Fx:**(516) 374-4127
(212) 909-6000 .. **Jacobson,** Jeffrey S '98 (Debevoise & P LLP) -919 3rd Av -NY 10022
(212) 277-0426 .. **Jacobson,** Jennifer B '05 Hartford Fncl Products -2 Park Av -NY 10016
(212) 969-3000 .. **Jacobson,** Jerold D '66 (Proskauer R LLP) -1585 Bway -NY 10036
(718) 409-9600 .. **Jacobson,** Jerry A '00 -4215 Katonah Av -Bronx 10470
(212) 209-3053 .. **Jacobson,** Jocelyn L '90 (Reitler K&R LLC) -885 3rd Av -NY 10022
(516) 487-4223 .. **Jacobson,** Joel L '63 -Bx397 -Gt Neck 11022
(845) 634-3663 .. **Jacobson,** Jonah '66 (Jacobson & J) -151 S Main -New Cty 10956
(845) 567-6778 .. **Jacobson,** Jonathan G '78 -843 Union Av -New Windsor 12553
(212) 999-5800 .. **Jacobson,** Jonathan M '77 (Wilson SG&R) -1301 Av of Americas -NY 10019
(212) 310-2184 .. **Jacobson,** Judith Ann '76 %Colgate-Palmolive -300 Park Av -NY 10022
(212) 242-0806 .. **Jacobson,** June '80 -156 5th Av -NY 10010 **Fx:**242-0944
(718) 590-2000 .. **Jacobson,** Lauren B '08 %DA -198 E 161st -Bronx 10451 **Fx:**590-6477
(212) 966-1435 .. **Jacobson,** Laurence E '54 -401 Bway -NY 10013
(212) 697-1420 .. **Jacobson,** Leon I '68 (Jacobson M&S,LLP) -52 Vndrblt Av -NY 10017 **Fx:**697-1427
(212) 857-2100 .. **Jacobson,** Loren '03 Hon W Feinberg -40 Centre -NY 10007
(212) 504-6000 .. **Jacobson,** Lowell D '08 %Cadwalader W&T LLP -1 World Fncl Ctr -NY 10281
(212) 563-9884 .. **Jacobson,** M Ari '03 %Samuel & S -38 W 32nd -NY 10001 **Fx:**563-9870
(212) 705-4899 .. **Jacobson,** Marc '78 -488 Mad Av -NY 10022 **Fx:**(646) 807-4599
(212) 794-9445 .. **Jacobson,** Mark H '96 -510 E 85th -NY 10028
(212) 455-2000 .. **Jacobson,** Martin D '77 (Simpson T&B LLP) -425 Lex Av -NY 10017
(212) 589-4200 .. **Jacobson,** Michl B '09 %Baker & H LLP -45 Rckfllr Plz -NY 10111
(212) 697-3122 .. **Jacobson,** Michl C '06 %Martin C&B LLP -220 E 42nd -NY 10017
(212) 806-5400 .. **Jacobson,** Michele L '88 (Stroock &S&L LLP) -180 Maiden Ln -NY 10038
(516) 222-2330 .. **Jacobson,** Miles R '59 (Jacobson G&K,LLP) -585 Stewart Av -Gdn Cty 11530
(212) 227-1219 .. **Jacobson,** Monica R '79 -225 Bway -NY 10007 **Fx:**766-2298
(845) 634-3663 .. **Jacobson,** Murray N '57 (Jacobson & J) -151 S Main -New Cty 10956
(516) 599-0888 .. **Jacobson,** Myron G '69 -197 Merrick Rd -Lynbrk 11563 **Fx:**599-0889
(212) 813-5900 .. **Jacobson,** Nadine H '93 (Fross ZL&Z,PC) -866 UN Plz -NY 10017
(212) 571-2000 .. **Jacobson,** Nancy Alyse '91 OfCnsl Ottinger Firm,PC -19 Fulton -NY 10038 **Fx:**571-0505
(212) 446-7000 .. **Jacobson,** Nancy L '04 %McKinsey & Co -55 E 52nd -NY 10055 **Fx:**688-9521
(212) 336-0095 .. **Jacobson,** Neal R '90 %SEC -3 World Fncl Ctr -NY 10281 **Fx:**336-1323
(585) 428-2064 .. **Jacobson,** Peter A '71 SpclCnsl Hon T Van Strydonck -545 Hall of Justice -Rchstr 14614 **Fx:**428-2105
(212) 308-4411 .. **Jacobson,** Rachel B '08 %Edwards AP&D LLP -750 Lex Av -NY 10022
(518) 456-5188 .. **Jacobson,** Richd P '93 -Bx12994 -Albany 12212 **Fx:**514-1152
(212) 935-5700 .. **Jacobson,** Richd P '96 (Colucci & U) -218 E 50th -NY 10022
(585) 218-6290 .. **Jacobson,** Robt L '81 -1080 Pttsfrd Victor Rd -Pittsfrd 14534
(914) 997-0825 .. **Jacobson,** Roni L '03 (Wilson J,PC) -99 Court -White Plns 10601 **Fx:**997-0830
(845) 634-7679 .. **Jacobson,** Rosalind D '80 -62 Laurel Rd Bx89 -New Cty 10956 **Fx:**634-1150
(212) 796-1460 .. **Jacobson,** Russel N '05 Mark Bruce Intl -55 E 59th -NY 10022 **Fx:**755-1327
(718) 590-2000 .. **Jacobson,** Sara I '97 %DA -198 E 161st -Bronx 10451 **Fx:**590-6477
(212) 659-7300 .. **Jacobson,** Sarah M '09 %Haynes & B,LLP -1221 Av of Amer -NY 10020
(516) 536-0900 .. **Jacobson & Schwartz** -510 Merrick Rd Bx46 -Rockvll Ctr 11571 **Fx:**536-2371
(914) 948-2700 .. **Jacobson,** Simon '60 -7 Alex Dr -White Plns 10605 **Fx:**421-1160
(631) 393-6220 .. **Jacobson,** Stacy E '99 %Harras B&A LLP -445 Broad Hollow Rd -Melvll 11747
(212) 490-5700 .. **Jacobson,** Stephen H '96 %Hecht KP&D -19 W 44th -NY 10036
(212) 935-5700 .. **Jacobson,** Susan B '86 (Colucci & U) -218 E 50th -NY 10022
(607) 255-3626 .. **Jacobson,** Wm A '85 %Cornell Law Schl -Myron Taylor Hall -Ithaca 14853 **Fx:**255-7193
(585) 325-7440 .. **Jacobstein,** Stephen M '67 (Kaman BMJ&G LLP) -135 Corp Woods -Rchstr 14623
(914) 328-0404 .. **Jacobster,** Michl D '77 (Jackson L LLP) -1 N Bway -White Plns 10601
(973) 228-5700 .. **Jacobus,** Belinda S '08 %Brach E LLC -100 Park Av -NY 10017 **Fx:**228-7852
(212) 922-9250 .. **Jacobus,** Sandra L '74 (Ganfer & S LLP) -360 Lex Av -NY 10017
(718) 643-7416 .. **Jacoby,** Aaron '81 %Hon M Cammer -120 Schermerhorn -Brklyn 11201
(212) 753-5000 .. **Jacoby,** David E '79 (Schiff H LLP) -900 3rd Av -NY 10022
(212) 833-8000 .. **Jacoby,** David G '93 Sony BMG Music Entrtnmnt -550 Mad Av -NY 10022 **Fx:**833-8406
(212) 509-9400 .. **Jacoby,** F Warren '05 (Cozen O) -45 Bway Atrium -NY 10006
(212) 872-1500 .. **Jacoby,** Herbert P '37 %Lacher & L-T -460 Park Av -NY 10022
(212) 225-2000 .. **Jacoby,** Leonard C '95 (Cleary GS&H) -1 Lbrty Plz -NY 10006
(212) 310-8000 .. **Jacoby,** Mark A '66 (Weil G&M LLP) -767 5th Av -NY 10153
(212) 756-2000 .. **Jacoby,** Melissa A '09 %Schulte R&Z LLP -919 3rd Av -NY 10022
(631) 289-4600 .. **Jacoby,** Melvyn L '62 (Jacoby & J) -1737 N Ocean Av -Medfrd 11763 **Fx:**654-5095
(212) 909-6000 .. **Jacoby,** Nicole E '05 %Debevoise & P LLP -919 3rd Av -NY 10022
(212) 698-3500 .. **Jacoby,** Nicolle Lipper '93 (Dechert LLP) -1095 Av of Amer -NY 10036
(631) 289-4600 .. **Jacoby,** Richd A '94 (Jacoby & J) -1737 N Ocean Av -Medfrd 11763 **Fx:**654-5095
(212) 634-6385 .. **Jacoby,** Sharon H '92 (McDonald Law Grp,LLC) -641 Lex Av -NY 10022 **Fx:**634-6389
(212) 715-9100 .. **Jacoby,** Tobias B '04 %Kramer LN&F,LLP -1177 Av of Amer -NY 10036
(518) 851-3548 .. **Jacoby,** Wm S '84 -22 State Rt 23 -Claverack 12513
(631) 751-1332 .. **Jacoppi,** Kenneth A '67 -194 Main -E Setauket 11733 **Fx:**751-1205
(646) 595-7005 .. **Jacque,** Laura M '09 %Stavitsky & Assoc LLC -5 Penn Plz -NY 10001
(212) 715-9100 .. **Jacquemot,** Susan '92 SpclCnsl Kramer LN&F,LLP -1177 Av of Amer -NY 10036
(212) 465-6000 .. **Jacqueney,** Stephanie A '83 %Madison Sq Grdn,LP -2 Penn Plz -NY 10121 **Fx:**465-6011

(212) 809-4800 .. **Jacques,** Debora L '85 %N Kanzer -30 Broad -NY 10004 **Fx:**363-3097
(718) 252-3770 .. **Jacques,** Diane '00 -1354 E 49th -Brklyn 11234
(718) 590-2000 .. **Jacques,** Jennifer '09 %DA -198 E 161st -Bronx 10451 **Fx:**590-6477
(518) 462-0110 .. **Jacques,** Keith R '99 (Sheehan GCG&J LLP) -54 State -Albany 12207
(212) 556-2100 .. **Jacques,** Kristi E '06 %King & S -1185 Av of Amer -NY 10036
(518) 473-8418 .. **Jacquinot,** M Mark '88 %OCFS -52 Wshngtn -Rensselaer 12144 **Fx:**486-6361
(716) 852-1300 .. **Jadd,** Robt I '75 (Amigone S&M,LLP) -350 Main -Buffalo 14202
(315) 425-2700 .. **Jadhon,** John A '95 OfCnsl Hiscock & B,LLP -One Park Pl -Syracuse 13202
(718) 706-6105 .. **Jadidian,** David L '94 (Jadidian & J) -26-04 Jackson Av -LIC 11101 **Fx:**706-1720
(718) 706-6105 .. **Jadidian,** Lisa '92 (Jadidian & J) -26-04 Jackson Av -LIC 11101 **Fx:**706-1720
(716) 689-9225 .. **Jadoch,** Christopher J '92 -179 Radcliffe Dr -Getzvll 14068
(212) 497-8065 .. **Jadow,** Anna J '05 %Rayner R,LLP -305 Bway -NY 10007 **Fx:**937-4680
(646) 415-7717 .. **Jadusingh,** Carlene '09 -85 South -NY 10038
(212) 549-2620 .. **Jadwat,** Omar C '03 ACLU -125 Broad -NY 10004 **Fx:**549-2651
(212) 975-4099 .. **Jaeckel,** Howard F '73 %CBS Inc -51 W 52nd -NY 10019 **Fx:**975-3930
(716) 856-0600 .. **Jaeckle Fleischmann & Mugel,LLP** -12 Fountain Plz -Buffalo 14202 **Fx:**856-0432
(716) 250-1800 .. **Jaeckle Fleischmann & Mugel,LLP** -400 Essjay Rd -Amherst 14221 **Fx:**250-1806
(631) 209-1200 .. **Jaedicke Hauser,** Susan E '92 -997 Route 25A Bx465 -Shoreham 11786
(212) 922-9700 .. **Jaeger,** Andrew D '94 1st Amer Title -633 3rd Av -NY 10017 **Fx:**922-0881
(212) 513-6024 .. **Jaeger,** Brad '09 National Futures Assn -120 Bway -NY 10271
(631) 852-2325 .. **Jaeger,** Norman P '77 %MHLS -One Court -Rvrhead 11901 **Fx:**852-3132
(718) 615-0393 .. **Jaeger,** Oscar A '86 -729 Kathleen Pl -Brklyn 11235 **Fx:**615-0393
(212) 733-7279 .. **Jaeger,** Tanya M '99 %Pfizer Inc -235 E 42nd -NY 10017
(516) 482-0992 .. **Jaegers,** Richd J '75 -8 W Mill Dr Bx222038 -Gt Neck 11022 **Fx:**487-8174
(212) 841-5200 .. **Jaensch,** Peter M '04 Columbia Univ-Ctr Addctn & Sbstnc Abuse -633 3rd Av -NY 10017 **Fx:**956-8020
(516) 546-5900 .. **Jafar,** Imtiaz U U '04 -1510 Grand Av -Baldwin 11510
(718) 768-1225 .. **Jaffa,** Helene Rosenthal '89 -475 10th -Brklyn 11215
(516) 536-2645 .. **Jaffa,** Thos P '83 -19 Tarence -Rockvll Ctr 11570
(516) 466-7900 .. **Jaffa,** Thos P '07 %Kiley K&K,PLLC -107 Nrthrn Blvd -Gt Neck 11021
(718) 892-8588 .. **Jaffe,** Adam M '98 -2027 Wllmsbrdg Rd -Bronx 10461 **Fx:**518-0674
(212) 969-3000 .. **Jaffe,** Alan S '64 (Proskauer R LLP) -1585 Bway -NY 10036
(212) 587-2400 .. **Jaffe,** Anne '73 OfCnsl Collins D&M,LLP -277 Bway -NY 10007
(212) 687-3000 .. **Jaffe & Asher,LLP** -600 3rd Av -NY 10016 **Fx:**687-9639
(212) 689-4553 .. **Jaffe,** Bernard '37 (B Jaffe,PC) -10 Waterside Plz -NY 10010 **Fx:**689-4553
(212) 867-4004 .. **Jaffe,** Bernard J '74 (Jaffe & M) -100 Park Av -NY 10017
(212) 957-7600 .. **Jaffe,** Brett D '98 Cnsl Cohen & G LLP -800 3rd Av -NY 10022
(212) 421-2233 .. **Jaffe,** Brian H '83 (Wilk A LLP) -675 3rd Av -NY 10017
(212) 460-2178 .. **Jaffe,** Carolyn W '84 Con Ed Co of NY,Inc -4 Irving Pl -NY 10003
(315) 471-8111 .. **Jaffe,** Chaim J '94 (Scolaro SCF&B,PC) -507 Plum -Syracuse 13204
(212) 858-4762 .. **Jaffe,** David M '87 FINRA -1 Lbrty Plz -NY 10006 **Fx:**858-4389
(212) 751-1700 .. **Jaffe,** Edw '64 (Jaffe R&L LLP) -880 3rd Av -NY 10022
(212) 484-3900 .. **Jaffe,** Elizabeth '05 %Arent F LLP -1675 Bway -NY 10019
(212) 907-7300 .. **Jaffe,** Elizabeth A '83 Cnsl Golenbock EAB&P -437 Mad Av -NY 10022
(631) 232-1111 .. **Jaffe,** Eric M '96 %Conforti & W -140 Fell Ct -Hauppauge 11788 **Fx:**232-2380
(212) 859-8000 .. **Jaffe,** Erica L '10 %Fried FHS&J LLP -1 NY Plz -NY 10004
(212) 310-8000 .. **Jaffe,** Helene D '77 (Weil G&M LLP) -767 5th Av -NY 10153
(607) 432-5201 .. **Jaffe,** Hollie '84 OfCnsl Bookhout Law Ofc -353 Main -Oneonta 13820 **Fx:**432-5202
(212) 317-0020 .. **Jaffe,** Howard A '66 1st Capital Advisors -445 Park Av -NY 10022
(212) 966-5897 .. **Jaffe,** Howard S '70 (Gotlin & J) -100 Lafayette -NY 10013 **Fx:**941-9183
(212) 341-2722 .. **Jaffe,** Jane N '90 SrCnsl Admin Children's Srvcs -150 William -NY 10038 **Fx:**341-2700
(212) 261-2449 .. **Jaffe,** Jay '02 Local 1199 SEIU -310 W 43rd -NY 10036
(212) 986-7714 .. **Jaffe,** Jeffrey R '95 (Propp L&J,LLP) -1500 Bway -NY 10036
(646) 746-1300 .. **Jaffe,** Jos '69 UHY Advisors FLVS -555 5th Av -NY 10017 **Fx:**746-1125
(212) 277-6500 .. **Jaffe,** Joshua '08 %Dickstein S LLP -1633 Bway -NY 10019
(212) 941-0183 .. **Jaffe,** Karen '82 -401 Bway -NY 10013
(718) 875-7900 .. **Jaffe,** Kenneth '90 -189 Montague -Brklyn 11201 **Fx:**875-6797
(212) 809-7800 .. **Jaffe & Koumourdas, LLP** -40 Wall -NY 10005 **Fx:**480-2080
(212) 264-0300 .. **Jaffe,** Leah Z '84 %NLRB -26 Fed Plz -NY 10278 **Fx:**264-8427
(212) 906-1200 .. **Jaffe,** Marc D '94 (Latham & W) -885 3rd Av -NY 10022
(646) 386-3816 .. **Jaffe,** Mark H '07 %Hon H Beeler -71 Thomas -NY 10013
(212) 839-7000 .. **Jaffe,** Mark M '69 (Hill B&N LLP) -200 Lbrty -NY 10281
(212) 245-4680 .. **Jaffe,** Martin B '71 -124 E 55th -NY 10022
(212) 604-4727 .. **Jaffe,** Martin H '70 (Jacoby & M) -350 5th Av -NY 10118
(212) 867-4004 .. **Jaffe & McKenna** -100 Park Av -NY 10017 **Fx:**867-4774
(212) 545-4606 .. **Jaffe,** Michl '89 (Wolf HAF&H LLP) -270 Mad Av -NY 10016
(212) 809-7800 .. **Jaffe,** Michl D '81 (Jaffe & K,LLP) -40 Wall -NY 10005
(212) 227-1212 .. **Jaffe,** Michl E '95 (Pazer E&J,PC) -20 Vesey -NY 10007
(914) 428-5837 .. **Jaffe,** Paul D '64 -202 Mamaroneck Av -White Plns 10601 **Fx:**948-4936
(212) 734-3535 .. **Jaffe,** Phillip '93 -370 E 76th -NY 10021 **Fx:**717-2584
(212) 541-5996 .. **Jaffe,** Rachel D '07 HCC,Inc -777 10th Av -NY 10019
(516) 358-6900 .. **Jaffe,** Richd S '95 (Cohen & J LLP) -2001 Marcus Av -Lk Success 11042
(212) 575-7900 .. **Jaffe,** Robt M '65 (Ballon SB&N,PC) -729 7th Av -NY 10019
(212) 223-0400 .. **Jaffe,** Rosh H '05 %Zeichner E&K LLP -575 Lex Av -NY 10022
(212) 751-1700 .. **Jaffe Ross & Light LLP** -880 3rd Av -NY 10022 **Fx:**751-2235
(212) 967-1800 .. **Jaffe,** Scott R '92 (Bryant BJ&R LLP) -140 Bway -NY 10005
(212) 867-3636 .. **Jaffe,** Sharon E '85 OfCnsl Levin & G,PC -420 Lex Av -NY 10170
(212) 732-9000 .. **Jaffe,** Susan M '89 %Sullivan PBM&C PC -120 Bway -NY 10271
(212) 960-8908 .. **Jaffe,** Wm M '81 -112 Mad Av -NY 10016 **Fx:**689-9680
(212) 417-2000 .. **Jaffee,** Carl D '69 %Battery Pk City Auth -1 Wrld Fncl Ctr -NY 10281 **Fx:**417-2001
(212) 440-7293 .. **Jaffee,** Lisa K '99 CNA Pro Open Brokerage -40 Wall -NY 10005
(212) 512-1912 .. **Jaffee,** Scott D '00 %HBO -1100 Av of Amer -NY 10036 **Fx:**512-1986
(646) 386-3734 .. **Jaffee,** Susan E '81 %Hon D Ling-Cohan -80 Centre -NY 10013
(212) 519-7814 .. **Jaffer,** Jameel '00 %ACLU -125 Broad -NY 10004 **Fx:**549-2651
(518) 587-4419 .. **Jaffe Tastensen,** Elena '99 -358 Bway -Saratoga Spgs 12866 **Fx:**587-1262
(585) 385-1150 .. **Jaffey,** Stephen E '74 -37 S Main Bx120 -Pittsfrd 14534 **Fx:**385-4550
(212) 643-0895 .. **Jaffrey,** Sajid '77 -45 W 34th -NY 10001
(212) 728-8000 .. **Jafri,** Amina '06 %Willkie F&G LLP -787 7th Av -NY 10019
(516) 333-3322 .. **Jafri,** Mohammed H '89 (Jafri & J) -143 Post Av -Westbury 11590 **Fx:**333-3342
(516) 333-3322 .. **Jafri,** Reaz H '92 (Jafri & J) -143 Post Av -Westbury 11590 **Fx:**333-3342
(212) 878-7900 .. **Jagde,** Christine '95 SpclCnsl Fox R LLP -100 Park Av -NY 10017
(585) 419-8800 .. **Jagel,** Christopher D '89 (Harris B PLLC) -99 Garnsey Rd -Pittsfrd 14534
(212) 683-3520 .. **Jager Smith, PC** -485 Mad Av -NY 10022 **Fx:**(617) 951-2414
(516) 747-8830 .. **Jaghab,** Elias '68 (Jaghab & J) -176 Mineola Blvd -Mineola 11501 **Fx:**747-8770
(516) 747-8830 .. **Jaghab,** Elias A '99 %Jaghab & J -176 Mineola Blvd -Mineola 11501 **Fx:**747-8770
(516) 747-8830 .. **Jaghab,** Roy R '95 %Jaghab & J -176 Mineola Blvd -Mineola 11501 **Fx:**747-8770
(212) 644-4420 .. **Jagiani,** Michl N '01 %Fabiani C&H,LLP -570 Lex Av -NY 10022
(212) 508-6700 .. **Jaglom,** Andre R '78 (Tannenbaum HS&H LLP) -900 3rd Av -NY 10022
(212) 940-8800 .. **Jagoda,** Andrew L '85 (Katten MR LLP) -575 Mad Av -NY 10022
(212) 294-6700 .. **Jagoda,** Deborah S K '85 %Winston & S -200 Park Av -NY 10166
(212) 765-4757 .. **Jagoda,** Heidi Jon '93 Sound One Corp -1619 Bway -NY 10019 **Fx:**603-0510
(212) 836-8000 .. **Jagoe,** Christopher T '01 (Kaye S LLP) -425 Park Av -NY 10022
(212) 940-8800 .. **Jahagirdar,** Om M '09 %Katten MR LLP -575 Mad Av -NY 10022
(212) 896-6500 .. **Jahnke,** Michl W '89 (Howrey LLP) -601 Lex Av -NY 10022
(212) 732-8700 .. **Jahre,** Jayne '86 (McAloon & F,PC) -123 William -NY 10038
(212) 247-0800 .. **Jahrmarkt,** Michl H '65 Northlight Fncl LLC -24 W 40th -NY 10018
(212) 425-0555 .. **Jaidi,** Myriam '03 %C Mehta & Assoc,PLLC -2 Wall -NY 10005 **Fx:**425-3282
(212) 725-6422 .. **Jain,** Benita '06 %Immigrant Defense Proj -3 W 29th -NY 10001 **Fx:**(800) 391-5713
(212) 763-5000 .. **Jain,** Eisha '09 %Emery CB&A LLP -75 Rckfllr Plz -NY 10019
(212) 758-9300 .. **Jain,** Jaipat Singh '00 (Lazare P&G LLP) -950 3rd Av -NY 10022
(718) 476-9757 .. **Jain,** Lalit K '78 -61-22 Booth -Rego Pk 11374
(212) 986-6000 .. **Jain,** Monika '03 %Kleinberg KW&C,PC -551 5th Av -NY 10176
(914) 333-0610 .. **Jain,** Nada '97 (N Jain,PC) -560 Wht Plns Rd -Tarrytwn 10591
(212) 848-7126 .. **Jain,** Sheila '10 %Shearman & S LLP -599 Lex Av -NY 10022 **Fx:**(646) 848-7126
(212) 848-4000 .. **Jain,** Sumeet '10 Shearman & S LLP -599 Lex Av -NY 10022
(212) 584-5710 .. **Jain,** Vibhuti '08 Cnsl Millennium Promise -432 Park Av S -NY 10016
(718) 740-8019 .. **Jairam,** Khelanand V '91 (KV Jairam,PC) -189-15 Jamaica Av -Hollis 11423 **Fx:**740-8029
(212) 558-4000 .. **Jaisingh,** Shevani '09 %Sullivan & C LLP -125 Broad -NY 10004
(212) 244-9331 .. **Jaiswal,** Gopaljee '77 -45 W 34th -NY 10001 **Fx:**244-9332
(845) 331-8900 .. **Jaiven,** Mitchell L '86 (Kellar K&J) -14 Pearl Bx3536 -Kingston 12402
(212) 352-8616 .. **Jajan,** Martin I '00 -175 W 12th -NY 10011
(212) 732-9290 .. **Jakab,** Peter A '96 (Fein & J) -233 Bway -NY 10279 **Fx:**227-6479
Jakabovics, Sylvain R '68 -2630 Ocean Av -Brklyn 11229
(518) 385-4791 .. **Jakaitis,** Gary J '81 %GE -2690 Balltown Rd -Schnctdy 12345 **Fx:**385-3345
(212) 728-8000 .. **Jakes,** Peter H '72 (Willkie F&G LLP) -787 7th Av -NY 10019
(212) 839-5300 .. **Jakimo,** Alan L '81 (Sidley A LLP) -787 7th Av -NY 10019
(845) 634-7909 .. **Jaklitsch,** Frank P '01 %Esbin & A,LLP -497 S Main -New Cty 10956 **Fx:**634-4160
(212) 572-4200 .. **Jakobsson,** Anna M '02 %Estee Lauder -767 5th Av -NY 10153 **Fx:**572-3989
(212) 592-1400 .. **Jakoby,** Arthur G '84 (Herrick,F LLP) -2 Park Av -NY 10016
(518) 465-6537 .. **Jakovic,** Jay Harold '77 -662 Mad Av -Albany 12208 **Fx:**465-6566
(914) 328-0404 .. **Jakowsky,** Michl A '07 %Jackson L LLP -1 N Bway -White Plns 10601
(212) 742-8700 .. **Jakub,** Louis E Jr. '95 (Garson D&C LLP) -110 Wall -NY 10005
(585) 271-1500 .. **Jakubek,** John J '05 %Dibble & M,PC -55 Canterbury Rd -Rchstr 14607
(516) 328-3500 .. **Jakubowitz,** David '05 %McDonnell & A,PC -401 Franklin Av -Gdn Cty 11530
(718) 445-1436 .. **Jakubowitz,** Hersh '86 (H Jakubowitz,PC) -42-34 162nd -Flushng 11358 **Fx:**445-1352
(347) 370-9585 .. **Jakubowitz,** Tovia '07 (Jakubowitz & C LLP) -401 Bway -NY 10013 **Fx:**532-1344
(631) 360-0400 .. **Jakubowski,** Edw W '68 OfCnsl Jakubowski RMG&T -969 Jericho Tpk -St James 11780 **Fx:**360-0408
(631) 360-7570 .. **Jakubowski,** Matthew V '01 %Town Atty -99 W Main -Smithtwn 11787 **Fx:**360-7719
(212) 541-2000 .. **Jalalipour,** Shima '09 %Bryan C LLP -1290 Av of Amer -NY 10104
(631) 853-4161 .. **Jalayer,** Saam '03 %DA -N Cnty Cmplx Bldg 77 -Hauppauge 11788 **Fx:**853-4192
(212) 344-5680 .. **Jalil,** James P '74 (Thompson H LLP) -335 Mad Av -NY 10017
(212) 259-8000 .. **Jallad,** Tala '08 %Dewey & L LLP -1301 Av of Amer -NY 10019
(212) 227-8696 .. **Jalosky,** David '60 -11 Park Pl -NY 10007
(212) 374-6700 .. **Jalowski,** Susan K '92 %NYC Dept Educ-OLS -52 Chmbrs -NY 10007 **Fx:**374-5596
(718) 360-9210 .. **Jaloza,** Andrew L '88 -71-27A Myrtle Av -Glendale 11385 **Fx:**907-7925
(646) 452-9642 .. **Jaluria,** Aseem '07 Man Investments -1 Rckfllr Plz -NY 10020

(516) 249-3450 ..**Jamaluddin,** Adeel '06 %Carman C&I,LLP -266 Main -Farmngdl 11735
(212) 940-3152 ..**Jamberdino,** Kristin M '06 %Nixon P LLP -437 Mad Av -NY 10022
(585) 419-8800 ..**James,** Barbara R Heck '80 (Harris B PLLC) -99 Garnsey Rd -Pittsfrd 14534
(718) 670-5991 ..**James,** Carmen R '87 Flushing Hospital -45th Av & Parsons Blvd -Flushng 11355
(212) 310-8000 ..**James,** Cheryl A '09 %Weil G&M LLP -767 5th Av -NY 10153
(212) 583-5811 ..**James,** Christopher J '03 Blackstone Grp -345 Park Av -NY 10154
(212) 532-6333 ..**James,** Clifford '79 -260 Mad Av -NY 10016 **Fx:**(646) 385-7241
(212) 715-9100 ..**James,** Dani R '96 (Kramer LN&F,LLP) -1177 Av of Amer -NY 10036
(718) 254-7000 ..**James,** David C '84 %US Atty -271 Cadman Plz E -Brklyn 11201 **Fx:**254-6479
(845) 201-8373 ..**James,** Diedre M '92 (Murphy & J,LLC) -275 N Mddltwn Rd -Pearl Rvr 10965
(212) 361-7910 ..**James,** Douglas C '05 %Dept Homeless Srvcs -33 Beaver -NY 10004 **Fx:**361-8002
(212) 728-8000 ..**James,** Emma J '08 %Willkie F&G LLP -787 7th Av -NY 10019
(212) 450-4000 ..**James,** Ethan T '95 (Davis P&W LLP) -450 Lex Av -NY 10017
(518) 474-8390 ..**James,** Francine '89 NYS Governor Ofc -Exec Chmbr State Cptl -Albany 12224
(718) 590-2000 ..**James,** Ginger S '00 %DA -198 E 161st -Bronx 10451 **Fx:**590-6477
(212) 292-5390 ..**James,** Harold '58 OfCnsl Epstein DB&J,LLP -60 E 42nd -NY 10165
(631) 853-4289 ..**James,** Heather P S '89 Law Dept -400 Carleton Av -Central Islip 11722
(914) 921-1200 ..**James,** Jacqueline M '91 OfCnsl Maloof B&E LLC -411 Theo Fremd Av -Rye 10580 **Fx:**921-1023
(212) 596-9000 ..**James,** Jacqueline M '09 %Ropes & G LLP -1211 Av of Amer -NY 10036
(718) 906-1128 ..**James,** Joan N G '87 -26 Court -Brklyn 11242
(212) 233-9385 ..**James,** John P '80 (Friedman J&B LLP) -132 Nassau -NY 10038
(212) 227-3067 ..**James,** John S '98 -20 Vesey -NY 10007
(212) 735-3000 ..**James,** Katrina E '08 %Skadden ASM&F LLP -4 Times Sq -NY 10036
(718) 250-2000 ..**James,** Kevin M '05 %DA -350 Jay -Brklyn 11201 **Fx:**250-2314
(212) 867-1940 ..**James,** Kiva V '05 %Macey & A,PC -420 Lex Av -NY 10170
(718) 222-2018 ..**James,** Lindsey M '08 %Law Dept -350 Jay -Brklyn 11201 **Fx:**222-2088
(212) 450-4000 ..**James,** Melissa A '03 Davis P&W LLP -450 Lex Av -NY 10017
(212) 696-6000 ..**James,** Nicholas P '08 %Curtis M-PC&M LLP -101 Park Av -NY 10178
(212) 450-4000 ..**James,** Rajesh S '04 %Davis P&W LLP -450 Lex Av -NY 10017
(315) 474-7571 ..**James,** Richd P '90 (Mackenzie H LLP) -101 S Salina Bx4967 -Syracuse 13221
(212) 577-3646 ..**James,** Seymour W Jr. '75 %Leg Aid -199 Water -NY 10038 **Fx:**509-8431
(212) 250-0757 ..**James,** Shaun H '06 Deutsche Bk -60 Wall -NY 10005
(646) 473-3944 ..**James,** Stuart '90 %USPS- NY Metro Law Ofc -380 W 33rd -NY 10199
(212) 836-8000 ..**James,** Ta-Tanisha D '99 Kaye S LLP -425 Park Av -NY 10022
(212) 575-0007 ..**James,** Timothy W '88 %Cohen HB&R,PC -11 W 42nd -NY 10036
(914) 249-2000 ..**James,** Xavier D '94 MasterCard Intl -2000 Purchase -Purchase 10577
(212) 855-3200 ..**Jameson,** Carol A '86 %Depository Trust -55 Water -NY 10041 **Fx:**855-3279
(212) 572-6200 ..**Jameson,** Constance Hamilton '89 %Derivative Srch Inc -300 Park Av -NY 10022 **Fx:**572-6499
(845) 708-9100 ..**Jameson,** Peter L '04 %J Sexton,PC -130 N Main -New Cty 10956 **Fx:**708-0027
(845) 356-2570 ..**Jameson,** Risa K '04 %Kantrowitz G&G,PC -747 Chestnut Rdg Rd -Chestnut Rdg 10977
(718) 590-2926 ..**Jamet,** Joan '87 %Criminal Ct -265 E 161st -Bronx 10451
(212) 859-8000 ..**Jamgochian,** Richd J '09 %Fried FHS&J LLP -1 NY Plz -NY 10004
(718) 250-2000 ..**Jamieson,** Stacey Mara '93 %DA -350 Jay -Brklyn 11201 **Fx:**250-2314
(518) 434-5050 ..**Jamison,** Jeffrey V '05 Law Dept -106 City Hall -Albany 12207 **Fx:**434-5070
(212) 922-6825 ..**Jamison,** Ronald M '86 Dreyfus Corp -200 Park Av -NY 10166
(212) 661-1151 ..**Jamison,** Russell S '99 %Marin G LLP -40 Wall -NY 10005
(212) 460-6149 ..**Janairo,** Monica Petrovic '06 %Con Ed -4 Irving Pl -NY 10003
(212) 399-0312 ..**Janairo,** Reynald R '07 Abkco Music & Records Inc -1700 Bway -NY 10019
(845) 634-0334 ..**Janata,** Jerrold F '62 -155 N Main -New Cty 10956
(646) 652-6206 ..**Janay,** Barry E '04 BE Janay,PC -101 E 15th -NY 10003 **Fx:**478-9204
(914) 997-9070 ..**Jancko-Baken,** Ellen '90 (Fredman B&K LLP) -333 Wstchstr Av -White Plns 10604
(518) 402-6757 ..**Janco,** Kimmey L '90 %Workers Comp Bd -20 Park -Albany 12207
(718) 263-2010 ..**Jancu,** Robt B '02 -101 Groton -Frst Hlls 11375
(212) 878-8001 ..**Jander,** Klaus H '64 (Clifford C LLP) -31 W 52nd -NY 10019
(212) 326-3939 ..**Jandovitz,** Jessie L '10 %Jones D -222 E 41st -NY 10017
(212) 924-6701 ..**Janego,** Jason W '00 Magnolia Pictures -49 W 27th -NY 10001
(212) 980-9600 ..**Janes,** Michl R '00 %Kaufman B&R -120 Bway -NY 10271
(716) 286-4420 ..**Janese,** Douglas A Jr. '04 Law Dept -745 Main Bx69 -Niagara Fls 14302 **Fx:**286-4424
(585) 232-1928 ..**Janetos,** Spiro P '70 -301 Exchange Blvd -Rchstr 14608
(212) 403-1000 ..**Jang,** David P '09 %Wachtell LR&K -51 W 52nd -NY 10019
(212) 878-8000 ..**Jang,** Euna '08 %Clifford C LLP -31 W 52nd -NY 10019
(212) 225-2000 ..**Jang,** Meejung '10 %Cleary GS&H -1 Lbrty Plz -NY 10006
(212) 336-0177 ..**Janghorbani,** Alexander J '04 %SEC -3 World Fncl Ctr -NY 10281 **Fx:**336-1323
(212) 373-3000 ..**Janghorbani,** Jaren '05 %Paul WRW&G LLP -1285 Av of Amer -NY 10019
(845) 735-0247 ..**Jani,** Bijal M '99 -1 Blue Hill Plz Bx1669 -Pearl Rvr 10965 **Fx:**735-0280
(212) 878-8000 ..**Jani,** Salil P '08 %Clifford C LLP -31 W 52nd -NY 10019
(212) 373-3000 ..**Janian,** Lauren Cutson '08 %Paul WRW&G LLP -1285 Av of Amer -NY 10019
(718) 205-8420 ..**Janicki-Crespo,** Miriam E '91 -83-15 Nrthrn Blvd -Jcksn Hts 11372 **Fx:**205-8425
(212) 629-0027 ..**Janiec,** John J '74 -350 5th Av -NY 10118 **Fx:**629-0075
(212) 431-2373 ..**Janin,** Sandra D '76 NY Law Schl -185 W Bway -NY 10013 **Fx:**343-1860
(212) 883-8200 ..**Janis,** Andrew Y '07 Institute of Intrnl Educ -809 UN Plz -NY 10017 **Fx:**984-5452
(518) 581-2704 ..**Janis,** George G '66 -26F Congress -Saratoga Spgs 12866 **Fx:**583-0917
(212) 533-6300 ..**Janis,** Paul H '67 %NYSUT -52 Bway -NY 10004 **Fx:**995-2347
(212) 566-7500 ..**Janis,** Randolph D '00 Douglas & L -111 John -NY 10038
(212) 297-5800 ..**Janis,** Ronald H '76 (Day P LLP) -7 Times Sq -NY 10036
(212) 455-2000 ..**Janiszewski,** Aleksander '07 %Simpson T&B LLP -425 Lex Av -NY 10017
(845) 434-4550 ..**Jankiewicz,** Sharon L '99 -442 Wolf Lk Rd -Rck Hll 12775 **Fx:**434-0142
(212) 355-1724 ..**Janklow & Ashley** -445 Park Av -NY 10022 **Fx:**355-1719
(212) 355-1724 ..**Janklow,** Morton L '53 OfCnsl Janklow & A -445 Park Av -NY 10022
(212) 371-5700 ..**Jankoff & Gabe,PC** -575 Lex Av -NY 10022 **Fx:**826-5888
(212) 371-5700 ..**Jankoff,** John H '68 (Jankoff & G,PC) -575 Lex Av -NY 10022
(212) 233-9087 ..**Jankowitz,** Mark '87 (Sanpedro & J) -305 Bway -NY 10007
(516) 775-2236 ..**Jankowski,** James W '93 %Santangelo B&S -1800 Nrthrn Blvd -Roslyn 11576
(845) 331-7966 ..**Jankowski,** Matthew M '08 %D Clegg & Assoc -48 Main Bx3448 -Kingston 12402 **Fx:**331-6994
(718) 921-6453 ..**Jankowski,** Z Robt '81 -425 73rd -Brklyn 11209
(212) 349-6009 ..**Jankunas,** Joy '04 %Sanctuary for Families -110 Wall -NY 10005 **Fx:**566-0344
(410) 341-3939 ..**Jannace,** Chas J III '84 -32 Union Sq E -NY 10003 **Fx:**341-3944
(516) 802-0630 ..**Jannace,** Steven D '87 (Simmons J,LLP) -115 Eileen Way -Syosset 11791
(516) 802-0630 ..**Jannace,** Susan Henion '93 OfCnsl Simmons J,LLP -115 Eileen Way -Syosset 11791
(212) 264-0660 ..**Jannaco,** Patricia '86 %US DOJ Antitrust Div -26 Fed Plz Ste 3630 -NY 10278
(516) 227-7447 ..**Jannone,** Justin J A '94 Dept of Social Svcs -60 Chas Lindbergh Blvd -Uniondale 11553 **Fx:**227-8433
(631) 298-8065 ..**Jannuzzi,** David Jude '99 -Bx1672 -Mattituck 11952 **Fx:**298-4214
(631) 385-8182 ..**Jannuzzi,** Dolores A '87 %M Jannuzzi -775 Park Av -Huntngtn 11743 **Fx:**385-7664
(631) 385-8182 ..**Jannuzzi,** Michl J '87 -775 Park Av -Huntngtn 11743 **Fx:**385-7664
(212) 932-8524 ..**Jannuzzo,** Jeffrey A '77 (Jannuzzo Law Ofcs) -375 Riverside Dr -NY 10025 **Fx:**932-1165
(212) 648-0417 ..**Janoff,** Chas J '78 JP Morgan Chase -245 Park Av -NY 10167
(212) 829-9200 ..**Janoff & Gurevich,LLP** -216 E 49th -NY 10017 **Fx:**829-9838
(212) 829-9200 ..**Janoff,** Peter L '82 (Janoff & G,LLP) -216 E 49th -NY 10017
(516) 542-1000 ..**Janofsky,** Jonathan R '04 %Geisler & G,LLP -100 Q Roosevelt Blvd -Gdn Cty 11530
(212) 449-7553 ..**Janover,** James T '90 Merrill Lynch -4 World Fncl Ctr -NY 10080
(212) 715-9100 ..**Janover,** Thos T '87 (Kramer LN&F,LLP) -1177 Av of Amer -NY 10036
(212) 676-7824 ..**Janovitz,** Olivia '89 ACS/OLA Div Foster Care -220 Church -NY 10013
(212) 223-0400 ..**Janovsky,** Peter '88 (Zeichner E&K LLP) -575 Lex Av -NY 10022
(914) 725-2165 ..**Janow,** Adele Lerman '94 %Assoc in Law & Mediation -105 Saxon Woods Rd -Scarsdale 10583 **Fx:**725-9219
(914) 725-2449 ..**Janow,** David J '98 Citadel Intl Corp -105 Saxon Woods Rd -Scarsdale 10583
(845) 735-8385 ..**Janow,** Hugh '66 -1 Blue Hill Plz Bx1586 -Pearl Rvr 10965 **Fx:**735-1054
(212) 854-1724 ..**Janow,** Merit E '89 Columbia Univ-East Asian Ins -420 W 118th -NY 10027
(718) 260-2550 ..**Janowitz,** Brenda M '99 %Hon M Go -225 Cadman Plz E -Brklyn 11201
(212) 421-4100 ..**Janowitz,** James A '72 (Pryor C LLP) -7 Times Sq -NY 10036
Janowitz, Richd '75 -229 7th -Gdn Cty 11530
(516) 378-1700 ..**Janowski,** John F '84 (Chesney & M) -2305 Grand Av -Baldwin 11510
(315) 263-6585 ..**Janowski,** Susan Basile '99 -181 Blackberry Rd -Liverpool 13090 **Fx:**638-4739
(212) 345-5628 ..**Janowski,** Ziporah '83 %Marsh USA -1166 Av of Amer -NY 10036 **Fx:**345-4808
(315) 218-8000 ..**Janowsky,** Brian K '07 %Bond S&K,PLLC -1 Lincoln Ctr -Syracuse 13202
(914) 761-9400 ..**Jansen,** Karen M '00 %Farber P&C -200 E Post Rd -White Plns 10601
(212) 600-9637 ..**Jansen,** Richd C Jr. '98 CCMP Capital Advisors LLC -245 Park Av -NY 10167
(212) 600-9637 ..**Jansen,** Richd G '84 CCMP Capital Advisors,LLC -245 Park Av -NY 10167
(212) 412-9500 ..**Jansenson,** Dina R '85 OfCnsl Flemming ZWZ LLP -1 Lbrty Plz -NY 10006
(585) 786-3070 ..**Janson,** Bradley A '01 -52 N Main -Warsaw 14569 **Fx:**786-3065
(212) 373-3000 ..**Janson,** Brian M '07 %Paul WRW&G LLP -1285 Av of Amer -NY 10019
(212) 513-3200 ..**Janson,** Francois '98 SrCnsl Holland & K LLP -31 W 52nd -NY 10019
(212) 474-1000 ..**Janson,** Katherine Deringer '06 %Cravath S&M LLP -825 8th Av -NY 10019
(212) 530-5000 ..**Janson,** Thos C Jr. '82 (Milbank TH&M LLP) -1 Chase Manh Plz -NY 10005
(212) 371-6873 ..**Janssen-Spinosa,** Tina P '00 Leg Assist Grp -450 W 33rd -NY 10001 **Fx:**750-0820
(718) 928-3700 ..**Jantarasami,** James J '05 %LSNYC-Bronx -579 Courtlandt Av -Bronx 10451 **Fx:**402-7586
(914) 428-4034 ..**January,** Derick C '67 (Brinton & J) -50 Main -White Plns 10606
(212) 849-7000 ..**Janus,** Kevin A '02 %Quinn EU&S,LLP -51 Mad Av -NY 10010
(516) 683-1200 ..**Janus,** Michl E '92 (Janus & T PC) -825 E Gate Blvd -Gdn Cty 11530 **Fx:**222-5510
(718) 624-5760 ..**Janusas,** John V '00 -26 Court -Brklyn 11242 **Fx:**569-0982
(212) 421-2800 ..**Janush,** Evan M '00 %Lanier Law Firm,PLLC -126 E 56th -NY 10022 **Fx:**421-2878
(212) 701-3000 ..**Januszewski,** David G '91 (Cahill G&R LLP) -80 Pine -NY 10005 **Fx:**269-5420

(212) 415-3313 .. **Januzzi**, Louis F '02 Diversified Agncy Srvcs -437 Mad Av -NY 10022
(212) 430-5400 .. **Janvey**, Richd I '71 (Diamond M LLP) -620 8th Av -NY 10018
(516) 574-6142 .. **Janvier**, Melissa N '08 %JP Morgan Chase -1985 Marcus Av -New Hyde Pk 11040
(718) 548-3674 .. **Janvier**, Pierre M '95 -314 W 231st -Bronx 10463
(212) 848-4000 .. **Janzen**, Lesley A '06 %Shearman & S LLP -599 Lex Av -NY 10022
(718) 590-6164 .. **Janzen**, Ralph '97 %Law Dept -198 E 161st -Bronx 10451 **Fx:**590-2686
(914) 789-8698 .. **Japal**, Vincere N '01 SrCnsl FUJIFILM Holdings Amer Corp -200 Summit Lk Dr -Valhalla 10595 **Fx:**789-8514
(518) 431-0247 .. **Jaquith**, Grant C '88 %US Atty -445 Bway -Albany 12207 **Fx:**431-0249
(718) 460-6333 .. **Jaramillo**, Carol '96 -43-64 Smart -Flushng 11355 **Fx:**460-3032
(212) 868-6300 .. **Jaramillo**, Noelia E '09 %Cary K LLP -1350 Bway -NY 10018
(212) 833-1182 .. **Jarashow**, Kizzy L '08 %Friedman KS&A LLP -1633 Bway -NY 10019 **Fx:**373-7982
(212) 806-5400 .. **Jarashow**, Mark S '08 %Stroock &S&L LLP -180 Maiden Ln -NY 10038
(212) 548-2100 .. **Jarashow**, Richd L '72 (McGuire W LLP) -1345 Av of Amer -NY 10105
(212) 208-1436 .. **Jardim**, Thos C '96 (Berman SR&J,PC) -140 Bway -NY 10005
(845) 732-7500 .. **Jardine**, Anne Schaible '87 %Medicaid Fraud Cntrl -1 Blue Hill Plz Bx1557 -Pearl Rvr 10965 **Fx:**732-7555
(212) 592-1400 .. **Jardine**, Kerry K '07 %Herrick,F LLP -2 Park Av -NY 10016
(212) 839-5300 .. **Jardine**, Richd J '95 Cnsl Sidley A LLP -787 7th Av -NY 10019
(212) 576-7986 .. **Jaret**, Debra A '80 %NYLIM -51 Mad Av -NY 10010
(212) 351-4000 .. **Jarit**, Lee A '07 %Gibson D&C LLP -200 Park Av -NY 10166
(212) 725-0200 .. **Jarman**, Rufus E Jr. '65 (Barnes R&C) -475 Park Av S -NY 10016
(212) 788-3826 .. **Jarman**, Wm B '07 ACS -220 Church -NY 10013
(212) 310-8000 .. **Jarmer**, Christine T '05 %Weil G&M LLP -767 5th Av -NY 10153
(516) 594-0909 .. **Jarmol**, Les D '92 %Polsky S&R,PC -500 Merrick Rd -Rockvll Ctr 11570
(212) 522-5650 .. **Jaroff**, Jill Ann '89 Sports Illustrated -1271 Av of Amer -NY 10020
(516) 352-1922 .. **Jaronczyk**, Donna M '98 %Sweetbaum & S -3000 Marcus Av -Lk Success 11042 **Fx:**354-6923
(212) 227-2780 .. **Jaros**, Abraham '73 %Jaroslawicz & J -225 Bway -NY 10007
(212) 998-6550 .. **Jaros**, David M '02 %NYU Law Schl -245 Sullivan -NY 10012
(716) 677-6666 .. **Jaros**, Jason P '99 -8205 Main -Buffalo 14221
(716) 634-7132 .. **Jaros**, Ronald L Jr. '98 %NYSUT -270 Essjay Rd -Buffalo 14221
(212) 564-6633 .. **Jarosak**, Sarah A '84 OfCnsl White & M,PC -875 Av of Amer -NY 10001
(212) 788-1857 .. **Jarosch**, Richd '07 NYPD Legal Bureau -1 Police Plz -NY 10038
(212) 524-5000 .. **Jaroslaw**, David W '89 (Jacob M&F) -1270 Av of Amer -NY 10020
(718) 254-7000 .. **Jaroslaw**, Ilene Weininger '89 %US Atty -271 Cadman Plz E -Brklyn 11201 **Fx:**254-6479
(212) 227-2780 .. **Jaroslawicz**, David '72 (Jaroslawicz & J) -225 Bway -NY 10007
(718) 250-2000 .. **Jaroslawicz**, Debra E '08 %DA -350 Jay -Brklyn 11201 **Fx:**250-2314
(212) 227-2780 .. **Jaroslawicz & Jaros** -225 Bway -NY 10007
(716) 483-2116 .. **Jaroszynski**, Sally Ann '93 -111 W 2nd -Jamestwn 14701
(516) 798-0583 .. **Jarowski**, Stephen A '81 -67 Hrbr Ln -Massapequa Pk 11762
(212) 416-8000 .. **Jarrett**, Karlton S '09 %Dept of Law -120 Bway -NY 10271
(518) 464-6000 .. **Jarrett**, Karonne P '09 %Arroyo Copland & Assoc,PLLC -300 Great Oaks Blvd -Albany 12203 **Fx:**464-6014
(212) 765-9000 .. **Jarushewsky**, Jayson '92 OfCnsl Gazes,LLC -32 Av of Amer -NY 10013 **Fx:**765-9675
(212) 416-8876 .. **Jarusinsky**, Renee L '01 %Dept of Law -120 Bway -NY 10271
(212) 478-7200 .. **Jarvinen**, Christopher A '00 (Hahn & H LLP) -488 Mad Av -NY 10022
(646) 722-8500 .. **Jarvis**, Geoffrey C '06 (Grant & E,PA) -485 Lex Av -NY 10017
(716) 645-5000 .. **Jarvis**, James L Jr. '89 Univ of Buffalo -120 Crofts Hall -Buffalo 14260
(212) 407-1200 .. **Jarvis**, Pamela '79 -485 Lex Av -NY 10017 **Fx:**407-1299
(315) 426-1525 .. **Jarvis**, Richd H '85 -1 Lincoln Ctr -Syracuse 13202 **Fx:**426-8585
(518) 482-7368 .. **Jarvis**, Robt J '83 -12 Wdrdg Dr -Loudonvll 12211
(716) 858-6092 .. **Jarzembek**, Jos T '87 Dept Soc Srvcs -478 Main -Buffalo 14202
(212) 564-6633 .. **Jarzombek**, Tracey L '96 %White & M,PC -875 Av of Amer -NY 10001
(973) 912-7175 .. **Jasaitis**, James E '97 (Sonnenschein N&R LLP) -1221 Av of Amer -NY 10020
(212) 848-9800 .. **Jasani**, Azmina N '09 %Withers B LLP -430 Park Av -NY 10022
(716) 848-9500 .. **Jasen & Jasen,PC** -69 Delaware Av -Buffalo 14202 **Fx:**849-7434
(716) 848-9500 .. **Jasen**, Peter M '75 (Jasen & J,PC) -69 Delaware Av -Buffalo 14202
(347) 648-2017 .. **Jasen**, Raymond D '92 Citigroup -2 Court Sq -LIC 11120
(212) 826-0100 .. **Jasiak**, Dawn L '95 FSA -31 W 52nd -NY 10019 **Fx:**893-2710
(212) 479-4300 .. **Jasie**, Elisheva '03 %Coty Inc -2 Park Av -NY 10016
(212) 486-7304 .. **Jasilli**, John A '79 -708 3rd Av -NY 10017 **Fx:**202-4376
(212) 861-8134 .. **Jasinska**, Maria B '85 -430 E 72nd -NY 10021
(607) 762-4315 .. **Jasinski**, Kenneth M '75 %Electric & Gas Corp -4500 Vestal Pkwy E -Bnghmtn 13902 **Fx:**762-4345
(718) 499-9431 .. **Jasinski**, M Diane '80 -204 8th Av -Brklyn 11215
(347) 418-4250 .. **Jasinski**, Paul C '81 %British Airways -75-20 Astoria Blvd -Jcksn Hts 11370 **Fx:**418-4204
(212) 661-9400 .. **Jaskiel**, Solomon J '85 OfCnsl Klein & S LLP -275 Mad Av -NY 10016
(212) 599-0520 .. **Jaskiewicz**, Christopher M '97 Gotham Org -1010 Av of Amer -NY 10018
(212) 922-9250 .. **Jaskola**, Wm A '97 %Ganfer & S LLP -360 Lex Av -NY 10017
(315) 798-5742 .. **Jaskolka**, Chester W '98 %Dept Soc Srvcs -800 Park Av -Utica 13501 **Fx:**798-6425
(315) 734-2063 .. **Jaskolka**, Jason W '98 Utica Natl Insurance Grp -180 Genesse -New Hartfrd 13413
(212) 935-7900 .. **Jaskot**, Anita M '01 %R Brill LLC -880 3rd Av -NY 10022 **Fx:**935-6524
(212) 809-7800 .. **Jaskot**, Katherine M '01 Jaffe & K,LLP -40 Wall -NY 10005
(212) 682-8811 .. **Jaskowiak**, Adam M '08 %Dunnington B&M LLP -1359 Bway -NY 10018
(212) 593-3000 .. **Jaslow**, Howard M '88 (Platzer SKLG&J,LLP) -1065 Av of Amer -NY 10018
(914) 997-1212 .. **Jasne & Florio,LLP** -30 Glenn -White Plns 10603 **Fx:**682-8692
(914) 997-1212 .. **Jasne**, Hugh G '89 (Jasne & F,LLP) -30 Glenn -White Plns 10603
(845) 565-1100 .. **Jason**, Jay F '80 SpclCnsl Tarshis CLM&M,PLLC -One Corwin Ct -Newburgh 12550
(212) 336-8000 .. **Jason**, Marc J '91 SrCnsl Amster R&E -90 Park Av -NY 10016
(212) 816-8969 .. **Jason**, Marilyn S '79 Citigroup -388 Greenwich -NY 10013
(914) 723-6515 .. **Jason**, Paul S '72 Cohen & J -14 Harwood Ct -Scarsdale 10583 **Fx:**723-9137
(516) 746-8000 .. **Jaspan**, Arthur W '65 (Jaspan S LLP) -300 Grdn City Plz -Gdn Cty 11530
(516) 931-4088 .. **Jaspan**, Michele K '87 OfCnsl Weltman & M,LLP -575 Underhill Blvd -Syosset 11791
(212) 684-7800 .. **Jaspan**, Michele K '87 OfCnsl Weltman & M,LLP -270 Mad Av -NY 10016
(516) 746-8000 .. **Jaspan Schlesinger LLP** -300 Grdn City Plz -Gdn Cty 11530 **Fx:**393-8282
(917) 751-3912 .. **Jaspan**, Steven A '07 Egatniv,LLC -150 W 46th -NY 10036
(212) 732-2292 .. **Jasper**, Harvey M '58 (Jasper & J) -299 Bway -NY 10007 **Fx:**349-1724
(914) 533-5096 .. **Jasper**, Margaret C '91 Jasperlaw.com -10 Deepwell Farms Rd -S Salem 10590 **Fx:**533-5097
(212) 732-2292 .. **Jasper**, Merrill Gayle '95 %Jasper & J -299 Bway -NY 10007 **Fx:**349-1724
(212) 689-3858 .. **Jasper**, Richd M Jr. '85 -276 5th Av -NY 10001 **Fx:**779-7544
(212) 818-9200 .. **Jasper**, Zoe E '04 %Satterlee SB&B LLP -230 Park Av -NY 10169
(516) 877-5600 .. **Jassem**, Julie L '93 %R Tusa -1225 Franklin Av -Gdn Cty 11530 **Fx:**877-5695
(212) 734-4884 .. **Jassen**, Sheryl D '93 -785 Park Av -NY 10021
(516) 683-1000 .. **Jassey**, Adam P '03 Abstracts, Inc -585 Stewart Av -Gdn Cty 11530
(212) 465-5000 .. **Jassey**, Hillary F '99 %Parsons Brinckerhoff -1 Penn Plz -NY 10119
(212) 354-4442 .. **Jassin**, Lloyd J '91 -1560 Bway -NY 10036 **Fx:**840-1124
(212) 259-8000 .. **Jassy**, Everett L '60 OfCnsl Dewey & L LLP -1301 Av of Amer -NY 10019
(516) 426-2767 .. **Jauck**, Shannon M '06 -3350 Woodward Av -Wantagh 11793
(914) 323-7000 .. **Jauert**, Katherine L '09 %Wilson EME&D LLP -3 Gannett Dr -White Plns 10604
(212) 906-1200 .. **Jauregui**, Eddie A '08 %Latham & W -885 3rd Av -NY 10022
(212) 645-8111 .. **Jaureguilorda**, Ignacio '03 Housing Works Inc -320 W 13th -NY 10014
(718) 250-2000 .. **Jaus**, Rhonnie Broder '82 %DA -350 Jay -Brklyn 11201 **Fx:**250-2314
(212) 249-6493 .. **Jauvtis**, Robt L '74 -230 E 79th -NY 10075 **Fx:**223-4134
(716) 852-0400 .. **Java**, Joel J Jr. '99 %Roach BM&G,PC -424 Main -Buffalo 14202
(212) 230-8839 .. **Javaid**, Imran S '08 %WilmerHale -399 Park Av -NY 10022
(631) 234-3030 .. **Javaras**, Hariklea D '07 %Davidow DS&S,LLP -1601 Vets Mem'l Hwy -Islandia 11749
(914) 761-2252 .. **Javer**, David M '01 %Boeggeman G&C,PC -1 Water -White Plns 10601
(585) 258-5565 .. **Javery**, Mary J '97 %JP Morgan Chase -1 Chase Sq -Rchstr 14643 **Fx:**258-6458
(212) 903-9000 .. **Javian**, Aaron G M '06 %Linklaters -1345 Av of Amer -NY 10105
(212) 698-7000 .. **Javit**, Felice E '90 %Simon & Schuster -1230 Av of Amer -NY 10020 **Fx:**698-7171
(212) 953-8890 .. **Javitch**, Rikki A '03 %Drechsler & D LLP -60 E 42nd -NY 10165 **Fx:**953-8899
(631) 666-6200 .. **Javits**, Darlene C '97 (PF Adams,PC) -49 5th Av Bx1089M -Bay Shr 11706 **Fx:**665-6739
(212) 213-3676 .. **Jaw**, Evelyn '97 (Popick R&J,LLP) -41 Elizabeth -NY 10013
(212) 450-4000 .. **Jawanda**, Bhawandeep S '09 %Davis P&W LLP -450 Lex Av -NY 10017
(212) 605-0308 .. **Jawin**, Michele Rodin '01 Mestel & Co -575 Mad Av -NY 10022
(516) 735-3650 .. **Jawitz**, Lynn M '83 -797 Helene -Wantagh 11793
(716) 895-4210 .. **Jaworski**, David V '89 -2988 William -Cheektowaga 14227 **Fx:**895-2516
(212) 278-0400 .. **Jaworski**, Richd F '92 (Cooper & D LLP) -30 Rckfllr Plz -NY 10112
(631) 421-3500 .. **Jay**, Christopher S '99 -9 Bellprt Ln -Bellprt 11713 **Fx:**423-1346
(716) 856-6300 .. **Jay**, David G '67 -69 Delaware Av -Buffalo 14202 **Fx:**856-6100
(212) 618-0641 .. **Jay**, Evan D '92 Bear Wagner Specialists LLC -40 Wall -NY 10005
(716) 858-2424 .. **Jay**, Hope R '05 %DA -25 Delaware Av -Buffalo 14202 **Fx:**858-7425
(718) 261-4000 .. **Jay**, Michl A '69 -125-10 Qns Blvd -Kew Gdns 11415
(212) 343-1771 .. **Jayaraman**, Sarumathi '01 ROC NY -275 7th Av -NY 10001
(212) 750-8700 .. **Jayaratnam**, Ashwini '09 %Friedman & W,PC -600 Lex Av -NY 10022
(212) 461-1467 .. **Jayashankar**, Srinivas M '93 (Shankar & Assoc,PC) -40 Exch Pl -NY 10005 **Fx:**461-1468
(212) 484-3299 .. **Jayasinghe**, Marapullige G '09 American Arbitration Assn -1633 Bway -NY 10019
(212) 817-5424 .. **Jaycox**, Thos D '90 %King World Prdctns -555 W 57th -NY 10019
(516) 742-9200 .. **Jaye**, Wm T '80 (Edelman K&J PLLC) -1 Old Cntry Rd -Carle Pl 11514
(212) 268-7535 .. **Jayne**, Mindy L '02 %Bonner KT&C,LLP -350 5th Av -NY 10118
(716) 636-0273 .. **Jayson**, Jeffrey M '91 (J Jayson & Assoc) -2350 N Forest Rd -Getzvll 14068 **Fx:**636-0466
(212) 448-9933 .. **Jayson**, Sherri A '02 %Finder & C LLP -9 E 38th -NY 10016
(212) 805-6165 .. **Jazayerli**, Rana '97 %Hon W Knapp -40 Foley Sq -NY 10007
(212) 818-8000 .. **Jazbik Filho**, Marun '88 ITOCHU Intl Inc -335 Mad Av -NY 10017 **Fx:**818-8543
(212) 506-2500 .. **Jealous**, Bradford '04 %Mayer B LLP -1675 Bway -NY 10019
(718) 590-2000 .. **Jean**, Alexander '09 %DA -198 E 161st -Bronx 10451 **Fx:**590-6477
(212) 859-8000 .. **Jean**, Courtney A '08 %Fried FHS&J LLP -1 NY Plz -NY 10004
(516) 837-3892 .. **Jean**, Denis J '90 -1018 Jerome Rd -Franklin Sq 11010
(212) 809-7074 .. **Jean**, Fania '01 %Armienti DG&R,LLP -39 Bway -NY 10006
(718) 783-4468 .. **Jean**, Fritz G '92 -890 Atl Av -Brklyn 11238
(718) 250-2000 .. **Jean**, Grace S '04 %DA -350 Jay -Brklyn 11201 **Fx:**250-2314
(212) 506-1700 .. **Jean**, Jos D '98 Cnsl Kasowitz BT&F LLP -1633 Bway -NY 10019
(212) 425-7200 .. **Jean**, Patrice Polyxene '03 %Kenyon & K,LLP -1 Bway -NY 10004
(212) 770-1961 .. **Jean**, Sidney R '97 AIGTS -80 Pine -NY 10005
(212) 331-5911 .. **Jean**, Stephanie I '08 NYC Human Resources Admin Ofc -180 Water -NY 10038
(212) 895-1066 .. **Jean-Baptiste**, Marie-Claude '09 %ISLP -31 W 52nd -NY 10019 **Fx:**878-8375
(212) 298-5000 .. **Jean-Baptiste**, Natasha R '05 Leg Aid -199 Water -NY 10038

(212) 480-5284 .. **Jean-Baptiste,** Pascale '00 %Insurance Dept -25 Beaver -NY 10004 **Fx:**480-5272
(646) 251-3293 .. **Jean-Charles,** Lewis Y '95 -1184 E 56th -Brklyn 11234 **Fx:**(877) 280-3487
(631) 847-5450 .. **Jean-Claude,** Carine L '93 %Arrow Electronics -50 Marcus Dr -Melvll 11747
(212) 552-7416 .. **Jean-Claude,** Enid D '98 JP Morgan Chase & Co -1 Chase Manh Plz -NY 10005
(212) 841-1000 .. **Jeanfreau,** Chas H '99 SpclCnsl Covington & B LLP -620 8th Av -NY 10018
(917) 204-1007 .. **Jean-Gilles,** Fabiola '92 -177 Thompson -NY 10012
(212) 244-9500 .. **Jeanite,** Sedgwick M '01 %White and W LLP -1 Penn Plz -NY 10119
(347) 404-9929 .. **Jean-Jacques,** Betsey '07 %MHLS -120 Schermerhorn -Brklyn 11201 **Fx:**(718) 243-2408
(212) 732-3665 .. **Jean-Jacques,** Michelle '99 %Harmon L&R -42 Bway -NY 10004
(718) 462-2600 .. **Jean-Jerome,** Menez '89 -4512 Church Av -Brklyn 11203 **Fx:**287-3958
(212) 964-3434 .. **Jean-Louis,** Macx I '01 (M Jean-Louis,PC) -305 Bway -NY 10007
(212) 343-5721 .. **Jean-Louis,** Ramcess '98 %Phenom Rand Communications -130 Prince -NY 10012
(516) 326-7761 .. **Jeanne-Porter,** Tierre '88 IPRO -1979 Marcus Av -New Hyde Pk 11042
(212) 343-2200 .. **Jeanneret,** Christine '03 Ultra Records Inc -235 W 23rd -NY 10011
(212) 264-8562 .. **Jeannopoulos,** Amanda R '06 Cnsl DHS -26 Fed Plz -NY 10278
(212) 857-8200 .. **Jean-Pierre,** Andy D '01 Amer Transit Ins Co -330 W 34th -NY 10001
(212) 250-8154 .. **Jean-Pierre,** Leslie A '96 -60 Wall -NY 10005
(914) 995-2660 .. **Jeanty,** Wienia '03 %Cnty Atty -148 Martine Av -White Plns 10601 **Fx:**995-5858
(212) 558-4000 .. **Jebb,** Brian D '06 %Sullivan & C LLP -125 Broad -NY 10004
(212) 474-1000 .. **Jebejian,** Sarkis '95 (Cravath S&M LLP) -825 8th Av -NY 10019
(212) 261-8000 .. **Jeberg,** Wm H '02 (Mendes & M,LLP) -750 7th Av -NY 10019
(212) 835-2765 .. **Jedlicka,** Amy '90 Alliance for Dwntwn NY,Inc -120 Bway -NY 10271
(718) 654-8988 .. **Jednak,** Jos T '88 (Koors & J) -4234 Viero Av -Bronx 10470
(212) 506-1700 .. **Jedreski,** Matthew R '09 %Kasowitz BT&F LLP -1633 Bway -NY 10019
(212) 225-2000 .. **Jedrey,** Nathaniel E '09 %Cleary GS&H -1 Lbrty Plz -NY 10006
(212) 513-1551 .. **Jedrlinic,** Judith A '91 Deloitte & Touche LLP -2 World Fncl Ctr -NY 10281
(516) 295-5922 .. **Jedwab,** Brian D '96 Hymax Grp,Inc -Bx357 -Cedarhrst 11516 **Fx:**295-4598
(914) 251-5811 .. **Jedwab,** Joshua '85 Knight Capital Markets,LLC -100 Manhattanvll Rd -Purchase 10577
(212) 732-4800 .. **Jeffer,** Herman '90 (Jeffer H&V) -150 Bway -NY 10038
(212) 732-4800 .. **Jeffer Hopkinson & Vogel** -150 Bway -NY 10038
(518) 438-2000 .. **Jeffers,** Dale F '73 OfCnsl Lombardi WWHA&D PC -III Winners Cir -Albany 12205
(518) 449-8893 .. **Jeffers,** Darrell E '97 (Wilson EME&D LLP) -677 Bway -Albany 12207
(518) 464-9874 .. **Jeffers,** F Patrick '79 -435 New Karner Rd -Albany 12205 **Fx:**464-1809
(212) 222-3245 .. **Jeffers,** Jack '83 -119 Manh Av -NY 10025
(718) 658-0500 .. **Jeffers,** Latoya S '07 %Law Dept -151-20 Jamaica Av -Jamaica 11432 **Fx:**658-4025
(518) 674-0000 .. **Jeffers,** Valarie M '89 -10 Chaundry Ln -Averill Pk 12018
(347) 404-9400 .. **Jefferson,** Cyril A '87 %Criminal Ct -120 Schermerhorn -Brklyn 11201 **Fx:**(718) 643-3538
(845) 357-2660 .. **Jefferson,** Jerome S '92 (Kornfeld RN&S) -46 Wshngtn Av Bx177 -Suffern 10901
(212) 975-7266 .. **Jefferson,** Richd N '92 %CBS News -524 W 57th -NY 10019
(212) 388-3617 .. **Jefferson,** Theresa '00 SEIU Local 32BJ -101 Av of Amer -NY 10013
(212) 218-5500 .. **Jeffrey,** Alexander M Jr. '98 %Seyfarth S LLP -620 8th Av -NY 10018
(212) 627-8100 .. **Jeffrey,** Pamela C '92 (Levy R,PC) -80 8th Av -NY 10011
(212) 613-5000 .. **Jeffrey,** Randal S '95 %Leg Assist Grp -450 W 33rd -NY 10001 **Fx:**750-0820
(631) 853-4049 .. **Jeffreys,** Christopher A '88 %Cnty Atty -Dennison Bldg Bx6100 -Hauppauge 11788 **Fx:**853-5169
(718) 286-6000 .. **Jeffries,** David J '03 %DA -125-01 Qns Blvd -Kew Gdns 11415
(718) 286-6000 .. **Jeffries,** Frederica Brown '91 %DA -125-01 Qns Blvd -Kew Gdns 11415
(212) 742-9700 .. **Jeffries,** Hakeem Sekou '98 OfCnsl Godosky & G,PC -61 Bway -NY 10006
(212) 764-4222 .. **Jeffries,** Stephen D '80 (S Jeffries & Assoc) -1560 Bway -NY 10036 **Fx:**764-4229
(212) 259-8000 .. **Jeffries,** Tevia R M '09 %Dewey & L LLP -1301 Av of Amer -NY 10019
(917) 653-0926 .. **Jeger,** Meyer '80 -135-20 78th Rd -Flushng 11367 **Fx:**(718) 591-9189
(212) 732-3320 .. **Jehle,** Amanda A '06 %Short & B,PC -217 Bway -NY 10007
(716) 848-2745 .. **Jehrio,** Julie E '05 M & T Bank -One Fountain Plz -Buffalo 14203
(212) 966-1303 .. **Jeidel,** Gavriel '84 -16 E 34th -NY 10016
(212) 686-7008 .. **Jekielek,** Jon D '07 (Meyerowitz J,PLLC) -295 Mad Av -NY 10017 **Fx:**542-8883
(718) 755-8074 .. **Jelen,** Marc S '03 -2681 Martin Av -Bellmore 11710
(212) 572-6797 .. **Jelinek,** Wm '94 %Estee Lauder -767 5th Av -NY 10153 **Fx:**572-3989
(914) 793-7534 .. **Jellen,** Patricia A '92 -245 Park Dr -Eastchstr 10709 **Fx:**793-7534
(631) 265-8500 .. **Jellenik,** Stephen R '61 (Scheyer & J) -110 Lk Av S -Nesconset 11767
(914) 644-8300 .. **Jellinek,** Russ F '92 %Schuman S&G -1 N Lex Av -White Plns 10601
(631) 231-1832 .. **Jelnicky,** Sandra Anne '94 -Bx2041 -Brentwd 11717 **Fx:**231-2340
(516) 746-5599 .. **Jemal,** Joshua M '99 (Bee RFH&D,LLP) -170 Old Cntry Rd -Mineola 11501
(718) 461-6633 .. **Jen,** Ann '03 Mallilo & G -163-09 Nrthrn Blvd -Flushng 11358
(212) 259-8000 .. **Jenab,** Michelle M '01 %Dewey & L LLP -1301 Av of Amer -NY 10019
(212) 788-0993 .. **Jenerette,** Tonya '95 %Law Dept -100 Church -NY 10007 **Fx:**788-0367
(212) 259-8000 .. **Jeng,** Saml S '09 %Dewey & L LLP -1301 Av of Amer -NY 10019
(516) 935-0709 .. **Jenis,** Lori Haber '87 (Haber & H) -302 Vista Dr -Jericho 11753
(212) 563-3006 .. **Jenis,** Richd E '97 Wolters Kluwer Health -333 7th Av -NY 10001
(516) 328-3500 .. **Jenkelowitz,** Jacob M '07 %McDonnell & A,PC -401 Franklin Av -Gdn Cty 11530
(518) 266-3036 .. **Jenkins,** Carroll R '76 %Tax Appls Tribunal -500 Fed -Troy 12180 **Fx:**271-0886
(718) 802-6645 .. **Jenkins,** Ernestine L '98 %Workers Comp Bd -111 Lvngstn -Brklyn 11201
(914) 345-0846 .. **Jenkins,** Gary A '91 Divine Records -76 Palisade Av -White Plns 10607
(212) 820-9567 .. **Jenkins,** J Spencer '07 %Hawkins D&W LLP -One Chase Manh Plz -NY 10005
(585) 232-6500 .. **Jenkins,** James M '90 (Harter S&E LLP) -1600 Bausch & Lomb Pl -Rchstr 14604
(212) 903-9000 .. **Jenkins,** Jared R '08 %Linklaters -1345 Av of Amer -NY 10105
(518) 463-6649 .. **Jenkins,** Joanne E '85 %Life Ins Cncl of NY -111 Wshngtn Av -Albany 12210
(212) 225-2000 .. **Jenkins,** Johnathan A '10 %Cleary GS&H -1 Lbrty Plz -NY 10006
(212) 660-3000 .. **Jenkins,** Jon M '82 (Sullivan & W LLP) -1290 Av of Amer -NY 10104
(212) 533-6300 .. **Jenkins,** Kevin G '83 %NYSUT -52 Bway -NY 10004 **Fx:**995-2347
(212) 878-1033 .. **Jenkins,** Lawr '75 %MTA -347 Mad Av -NY 10017
(518) 435-1770 .. **Jenkins,** Lorraine R '06 Legal Project,Inc -6 Exec Park Dr -Albany 12203
(212) 484-3900 .. **Jenkins,** Marylee '92 (Arent F LLP) -1675 Bway -NY 10019
(212) 783-3996 .. **Jenkins,** Melanie A '92 Morgan Stanley Smith Barney -485 Lex Av -NY 10017
(212) 704-6000 .. **Jenkins,** Norman A '78 (Troutman S LLP) -405 Lex Av -NY 10174
(315) 428-3248 .. **Jenkins,** Robt J '78 Supreme Ct-Matrimonial Referee -Cnty Cthse -Syracuse 13202
(212) 735-3000 .. **Jenkins,** Rose E '09 %Skadden ASM&F LLP -4 Times Sq -NY 10036
(212) 406-1700 .. **Jenkins,** Stephen '75 %Queller FWF&K LLP -233 Bway -NY 10279
(518) 434-0155 .. **Jenkins,** Wm Raymond '89 Albany Tile Supply -452 N Pearl -Albany 12204
(212) 657-1085 .. **Jenkins Hines,** Illonka Javette '01 -111 Wall -NY 10005
(212) 373-3000 .. **Jenkinson,** Michéle R '82 Cnsl Paul WRW&G LLP -1285 Av of Amer -NY 10019
(212) 474-1000 .. **Jenks,** Brian M '10 %Cravath S&M LLP -825 8th Av -NY 10019
(516) 741-2920 .. **Jenks,** Edw P '83 -332 Willis Av -Mineola 11501 **Fx:**747-3136
(585) 586-4192 .. **Jenks,** Laura A '03 -86 Langston Pt -Pittsfrd 14534 **Fx:**586-4192
(516) 378-1700 .. **Jenks,** Michl J '96 %Chesney & M -2305 Grand Av -Baldwin 11510
(212) 273-7305 .. **Jenkyn,** Alexander M '02 Gleacher & Co Securities,Inc -677 Bway -Albany 12207 **Fx:**(800) 887-4129
(212) 816-4626 .. **Jenman,** Camille C '02 Citigroup -388 Greenwich -NY 10013
(315) 785-3224 .. **Jenne,** Susan Drake '94 %Jefferson Cnty Ct -163 Arsenal -Watertwn 13601
(212) 891-1600 .. **Jenner & Block LLP** -919 3rd Av -NY 10022 **Fx:**891-1699
(212) 596-9000 .. **Jenner,** Jesse J '73 (Ropes & G LLP) -1211 Av of Amer -NY 10036
(585) 454-0700 .. **Jennette,** Scott R '90 (Ward GH&R LLP) -300 State -Rchstr 14614
(212) 358-1500 .. **Jennik,** Susan M '82 (Kennedy J&M,PC) -113 Univ Pl -NY 10003
(607) 582-6844 .. **Jennings,** Chas H '51 -2153 E Seneca Bx407 -Lodi 14860
(518) 449-8893 .. **Jennings,** Gerald J '99 (Wilson EME&D LLP) -677 Bway -Albany 12207
(585) 232-6500 .. **Jennings,** John M '04 %Harter S&E LLP -1600 Bausch & Lomb Pl -Rchstr 14604
(518) 285-8435 .. **Jennings,** Kathleen J '83 %Family Ct -620 State -Schnctdy 12305
(212) 277-2361 .. **Jennings,** Kathleen L '97 Estee Lauder Co Inc -767 5th Av -NY 10153
(212) 370-5050 .. **Jennings,** Leslie A '94 -207-01 Hillside Av -Qns Vllg 11427 **Fx:**370-5066
(516) 294-5200 .. **Jennings,** Michl '72 %Picciano & S -900 Merchants Cncrs -Westbury 11590
(212) 558-4000 .. **Jennings,** Nelle P '95 SpclCnsl Sullivan & C LLP -125 Broad -NY 10004
(347) 404-9133 .. **Jennings,** Norma J '91 %Civil Ct -141 Lvngstn -Brklyn 11201 **Fx:**(718) 643-3733
(518) 226-0425 .. **Jennings,** Patrick J '96 -42 Glenham Rd -Saratoga Spgs 12866 **Fx:**(201) 342-5848
(973) 228-5700 .. **Jennings,** Rita M '02 %Brach E LLC -100 Park Av -NY 10017 **Fx:**228-7852
(212) 756-2000 .. **Jennings,** Taleah '04 %Schulte R&Z LLP -919 3rd Av -NY 10022
(212) 732-0091 .. **Jennings,** Walter S '71 (W Jennings,PC) -708 3rd Av -NY 10017 **Fx:**732-0579
(212) 794-5382 .. **Jennis,** Abby L '84 %CUNY -535 E 80th -NY 10075 **Fx:**794-5426
(716) 825-0850 .. **Jenny,** John '68 -609 Ridge Rd -Buffalo 14218
(212) 272-2000 .. **Jens,** Linda Kolodny '00 JP Morgan Chase -1 Chase Manh Plz -NY 10005
(212) 262-2390 .. **Jensen,** Christian J '07 %Connell F LLP -888 7th Av -NY 10106
(212) 309-6000 .. **Jensen,** Christopher T '81 (Morgan L&B LLP) -101 Park Av -NY 10178
(646) 200-6300 .. **Jensen,** Douglas R '83 (Park & J LLP) -630 3rd Av -NY 10017 **Fx:**200-6301
(212) 513-3200 .. **Jensen,** Frode I '77 (Holland & K LLP) -31 W 52nd -NY 10019
(516) 486-2268 .. **Jensen,** Gail S '74 -358 Spruce Ln -E Meadow 11554
(212) 790-9204 .. **Jensen,** J Christopher '74 (Cowan L&L,PC) -1133 Av of Amer -NY 10036
(518) 792-5693 .. **Jensen,** Jennifer A '84 -130 Dix Av Bx447 -Glens Fls 12801 **Fx:**792-5987
(212) 837-6828 .. **Jensen,** Jesse L '10 %Hughes H&R LLP -1 Bttry Pk Plz -NY 10004 **Fx:**299-6828
(212) 944-1377 .. **Jensen,** Marianne M N '91 %M Kassimir & Assoc,PC -1065 Av of Amer -NY 10018 **Fx:**790-5868
(212) 225-2000 .. **Jensen,** Meredith J '04 %Cleary GS&H -1 Lbrty Plz -NY 10006
(212) 836-8000 .. **Jensen,** Penelope J '08 %Kaye S LLP -425 Park Av -NY 10022
(212) 737-5800 .. **Jensen,** Peter T '90 (Jensen & J) -1212 Av Of The Americas -NY 10036 **Fx:**737-5900
(212) 237-1000 .. **Jensen,** Preben '59 SpclCnsl Windels ML&M,LLP -156 W 56th -NY 10019
(516) 326-2400 .. **Jensen,** Richd C '66 (Ivone D&J,LLP) -2001 Marcus Av -Lk Success 11042

(914) 422-4294 ..**Jensen**, Ronald H '64 %Pace Law Schl -78 N Bway -White Plns 10603 **Fx:**422-4039
(518) 473-3303 ..**Jensen**, Sandra '98 %Dept of Health -Corning Twr 24th Fl -Albany 12237 **Fx:**473-2019
(212) 880-6000 ..**Jensen**, Sarah L '04 %Torys LLP -237 Park Av -NY 10017
(585) 987-2800 ..**Jensen**, Sean D '02 %Woods OG LLP -2 State -Rchstr 14614
(607) 778-2423 ..**Jensen**, Sophie A '08 DA -45 Hawley Bx1766 -Bnghmtn 13902 **Fx:**778-8870
(212) 403-7300 ..**Jensen**, Tara '07 Vladeck WE&E,PC -1501 Bway -NY 10036
(914) 997-2500 ..**Jenson**, Pamela J '85 %Bodnar & M LLP -140 Grand -White Plns 10601 **Fx:**997-8155
(212) 729-9987 ..**Jentis**, Wayne F '01 Jentis-USA -130 Malcolm X Blvd -NY 10026 **Fx:**(888) 471-5693
(212) 417-3700 ..**Jentsch**, Bernadette Dino '04 %MFY Legal Srvcs -299 Bway -NY 10007 **Fx:**417-3890
(212) 625-1001 ..**Jeon**, Matthew J '90 (M Jeon,PC) -401 Bway -NY 10013 **Fx:**625-1202
(718) 460-2783 ..**Jeon**, Peter Seokmok '02 -147-48 Roosevelt Av -Flushng 11354
(212) 967-3966 ..**Jeong**, Seong Ho '90 -120 W 31st -NY 10001 **Fx:**967-0596
(516) 294-1333 ..**Jeong**, Yongil '07 (DeMartini & Y LLP) -264 Hillside Av -Williston Pk 11596
(518) 463-2251 ..**Jeram**, Thos W '61 (D'Agostino HF&J,PC) -187 Wolf Rd -Albany 12205
(315) 785-3053 ..**Jeram**, Walter M Jr. '88 %DA -175 Arsenal -Watertwn 13601 **Fx:**785-3371
(212) 407-1200 ..**Jerdee**, Peter R '97 -485 Lex Av -NY 10017 **Fx:**407-1299
(518) 462-5601 ..**Jerian**, Kathryn E '08 %O'Connell & A -54 State -Albany 12207
(718) 694-3672 ..**Jerman**, John E '94 Transit Auth -130 Lvngstn -Brklyn 11201 **Fx:**694-5726
(212) 574-1200 ..**Jernigan**, Lindsay M '06 %Seward & K LLP -1 Bttry Pk Plz -NY 10004
(518) 884-0200 ..**Jerome**, Chad A '07 %Donnellan & K,PLLC -20 Prospect -Ballston Spa 12020 **Fx:**884-0343
(212) 541-2000 ..**Jerome**, Eva Linnell '95 (Bryan C LLP) -1290 Av of Amer -NY 10104
(914) 632-5400 ..**Jerome**, Marc M '93 %Monroe College -434 Main -New Rchll 10801
(212) 818-8800 ..**Jerome**, Marisa A '09 %Graubard M -405 Lex Av -NY 10174
(212) 756-2000 ..**Jerow**, John G '01 %Schulte R&Z LLP -919 3rd Av -NY 10022
(631) 864-4460 ..**Jerozal**, Jason T '03 Primary Land Srvcs LLC -353 Vets Mem'l Hwy -Commack 11725
(718) 262-3671 ..**Jerozal**, Lauren '02 ACS-DLS -92-31 Union Hall -Jamaica 11433
(518) 862-1090 ..**Jerry**, Jacquelyn Ladd '77 %NYSERDA -17 Columbia Cir -Albany 12203 **Fx:**862-1091
(800) 424-2233 ..**Jerushalmy**, Lee '93 %M Weiss & Assoc,PC -875 Av of Amer -NY 10001 **Fx:**(732) 418-9115
(607) 432-3611 ..**Jervis**, Eric V '06 (Harlem & J) -493 Chestnut -Oneonta 13820 **Fx:**432-9761
(212) 538-6181 ..**Jesberger**, Jacklyn A '02 Credit Suisse 1st Boston -11 Mad Av -NY 10010
(315) 472-5827 ..**Jeschke**, Eric B '91 -250 Harrison -Syracuse 13202 **Fx:**476-5350
(716) 754-4300 ..**Jesella**, Edw P Jr. '72 -900 Center -Lewiston 14092 **Fx:**754-0747
(212) 477-2400 ..**Jeselsohn**, Paul '77 -799 Bway -NY 10003
(518) 292-5700 ..**Jesep**, Paul P '93 NYSTAR -30 S Pearl -Albany 12207
(212) 765-5070 ..**Jesien**, Karolina '08 %Fish & R,PC -153 E 53rd -NY 10022
(212) 326-3939 ..**Jesner**, Lisa Rothman '01 %Jones D -222 E 41st -NY 10017
(212) 230-8800 ..**Jessee**, Seth M '10 %WilmerHale -399 Park Av -NY 10022
(585) 428-3542 ..**Jesserer**, Henry L III '74 State of NY -99 Exchange Blvd -Rchstr 14614 **Fx:**428-2190
(716) 853-9555 ..**Jessey**, Deborah K '04 %Leg Aid -237 Main -Buffalo 14203 **Fx:**853-3219
(212) 891-1600 ..**Jestin**, Katya T P '97 (Jenner & B LLP) -919 3rd Av -NY 10022
(212) 695-5506 ..**Jethmalani**, Anil '87 -875 Av of Amer -NY 10001 **Fx:**695-0399
(518) 473-1416 ..**Jetkiewicz**, Valerie A '98 Gov Ofc of Employee Relations -2 ESP -Albany 12223
(347) 296-1628 ..**Jette**, Myra N '90 %Supreme Ct Law Dept -360 Adams -Brklyn 11201 **Fx:**643-6114
(212) 425-0055 ..**Jetter**, Sherry L '87 OfCnsl Sharretts PC&B -75 Broad -NY 10004
(716) 856-8200 ..**Jetty**, Kimberly A '06 %Williams & W -43 Court -Buffalo 14202 **Fx:**856-0559
(212) 710-0000 ..**Jeun**, Paul B '96 (Drohan L,LLP) -489 5th Av -NY 10017
(212) 309-6000 ..**Jeung**, Audrey A '07 %Morgan L&B LLP -101 Park Av -NY 10178
(212) 270-6000 ..**Jew**, Anthony J '03 JP Morgan Chase & Co -270 Park Av -NY 10017
(516) 248-5757 ..**Jew**, Michl D '97 %Colleran O&M,LLP -1225 Franklin Av -Gdn Cty 11530
(212) 788-1195 ..**Jewell**, Eric P '90 %Law Dept -100 Church -NY 10007 **Fx:**788-0367
(212) 408-2500 ..**Jewell**, Katherine Campbell '10 %Baker B,LLP -30 Rckfllr Plz -NY 10112
(516) 280-2211 ..**Jewell**, Keith C '98 KC Jewell,PC -393 Old Cntry Rd -Carle Pl 11514 **Fx:**280-6916
(516) 742-2700 ..**Jewell**, Robt H '58 -100 Q Roosevelt Blvd Bx8009 -Gdn Cty 11530 **Fx:**742-2700
(212) 807-5528 ..**Jewell**, Robt Kenneth '99 -315 Mad Av -NY 10017 **Fx:**721-9146
(212) 698-3500 ..**Jewell**, Ronald R '75 (Dechert LLP) -1095 Av of Amer -NY 10036
(212) 953-2381 ..**Jewels**, Mary A '99 %Rubin F&F,LLP -292 Mad Av -NY 10017
(212) 264-3650 ..**Jewett**, Peter W '09 %SSA Ofc Genl Cnsl -26 Fed Plz -NY 10278 **Fx:**264-6372
(212) 885-6420 ..**Jezic**, Nina L '04 Constellation Energy -810 7th Av -NY 10019
(718) 225-4026 ..**Jha**, Asha '93 -64-33 211th -Oakland Gdns 11364
(212) 455-2000 ..**Jhaveri**, Ketan Priyavadan '00 %Simpson T&B LLP -425 Lex Av -NY 10017
(718) 897-9300 ..**Jhaveri**, Rashmi R '00 Jhaveri & Assoc,PLLC -205 Woodbury Rd -Woodbury 11797
(212) 859-8000 ..**Jhaveri**, Sujata M '10 %Fried FHS&J LLP -1 NY Plz -NY 10004
(212) 696-2776 ..**Jho**, Harry '00 -10 E 38th -NY 10016
(212) 318-6000 ..**Ji**, Gongjun Gary '03 %Paul HJ&W LLP -75 E 55th -NY 10022
(212) 819-8200 ..**Ji**, Sang I '97 (White & C LLP) -1155 Av of Amer -NY 10036
(646) 896-1536 ..**Ji**, Wei '08 Alliance Law PLLC -800 2nd Av -NY 10017
(212) 704-6000 ..**Jiang**, Howard H '93 (Troutman S LLP) -405 Lex Av -NY 10174
(212) 319-4755 ..**Jiang**, James Y '93 King & W -444 Mad Av -NY 10022
(212) 986-5303 ..**Jiang**, Kenneth W '96 -18 E 41st -NY 10017 **Fx:**696-2383
(212) 773-8872 ..**Jiang**, Zheng Anwen '01 Ernst & Young LLP -5 Times Sq -NY 10036
(212) 735-3000 ..**Jiang**, Zhenyu '09 %Skadden ASM&F LLP -4 Times Sq -NY 10036
(212) 416-8206 ..**Jiao**, Chenxi '08 %Dept of Law -120 Bway -NY 10271
(212) 416-8000 ..**Jiggetts**, Sabrina '01 %Dept of Law -120 Bway -NY 10271
(631) 329-4660 ..**Jilnicki**, John C '85 -10 Pantigo Rd Bx2184 -E Hampton 11937
(516) 357-3000 ..**Jim**, Sui Y '08 %Rivkin R LLP -926 RXR Plz -Uniondale 11556
(212) 239-6000 ..**Jimenez**, Angela B '05 %Div Of Parole -314 W 40th -NY 10018 **Fx:**239-6160
(212) 455-2000 ..**Jimenez**, Dora '07 %Simpson T&B LLP -425 Lex Av -NY 10017
(212) 270-3634 ..**Jimenez**, Emilio '93 JP Morgan Chase & Co -270 Park Av -NY 10017
(212) 217-3168 ..**Jimenez**, Guillermo C '04 FIT -227 W 27th -NY 10001
(212) 687-6262 ..**Jimenez**, Jessica M '05 %Barton B&P,LLP -420 Lex Av -NY 10170
(212) 446-2300 ..**Jimenez**, Magda M '96 (Boies S&F LLP) -575 Lex Av -NY 10022
(212) 592-1400 ..**Jimenez**, Mari-Claudia '05 %Herrick,F LLP -2 Park Av -NY 10016
(212) 279-1069 ..**Jimenez**, Michl A '04 %Feinsilver Law Grp,PC -26 Court -Brklyn 11242 **Fx:**(973) 376-4405
(212) 566-4670 ..**Jimenez**, Miriam '95 -160 Bway -NY 10038
(607) 776-9631 ..**Jimenez**, Patricio '95 %DA -3 E Pulteney Sq -Bath 14810 **Fx:**776-7052
(212) 326-3939 ..**Jimenez**, Pedro A '06 (Jones D) -222 E 41st -NY 10017
(718) 993-0909 ..**Jimenez**, Ramon J '75 -145 E 149th -Bronx 10451 **Fx:**993-2156
(718) 366-3800 ..**Jimenez**, Sergio '08 Bushwick Housing & Legal Assistance -217 Wyckoff Av -Brklyn 11237
(212) 492-3857 ..**Jin**, Annica H '98 %Deloitte LLP -1633 Bway -NY 10019 **Fx:**653-2502
(212) 455-2000 ..**Jin**, Hyunsoo '07 %Simpson T&B LLP -425 Lex Av -NY 10017
(212) 326-3939 ..**Jin**, Soyon Angela '09 %Jones D -222 E 41st -NY 10017
(212) 949-4700 ..**Jing**, Wei '08 %Bushell SO&G LLP -60 E 42nd -NY 10165 **Fx:**286-0513
(212) 871-3767 ..**Jing**, Xiao-Hong '96 Asset Alliance Corp -800 3rd Av -NY 10022
(718) 590-2000 ..**Jittraracht**, Ellen Magid '06 DA -198 E 161st -Bronx 10451 **Fx:**590-6477
(845) 256-3036 ..**Jiudice**, Joyce Ellen '82 %DEC -21 S Putt Crnrs Rd -New Paltz 12561 **Fx:**255-4659
(212) 735-3000 ..**Jjingo**, Mary J '06 %Skadden ASM&F LLP -4 Times Sq -NY 10036
(212) 732-3320 ..**Jnane**, Helene '91 %Short & B,PC -217 Bway -NY 10007
(516) 437-4385 ..**Jo**, Eun Chong '09 %Vishnick MM LLP -3000 Marcus Av -Lk Success 11042
(646) 253-8804 ..**Jo**, Michl H '01 CW Capital LLC -1540 Bway -NY 10036
(212) 298-5212 ..**Jo**, Sunny '06 %Leg Aid -49 Thomas -NY 10013 **Fx:**298-5252
(212) 692-1000 ..**Jo**, Suzan '07 %Duane M LLP -1540 Bway -NY 10036
(516) 354-1570 ..**Joachim**, Edw B '53 (E Joachim & Assoc,PC) -1040 Hempstd Tpk -Franklin Sq 11010
(718) 703-1769 ..**Joachim**, Jan P '99 (J Joachim,PC) -1655 Bedford Av -Brklyn 11225 **Fx:**233-3152
(212) 508-6100 ..**Joachim**, Mark B '93 (Bracewell & G,LLP) -1251 Av of Amer -NY 10020
(212) 578-2211 ..**Joachim**, Nancy '02 %MetLife -27-01 Qns Plz N -LIC 11101
(212) 799-6416 ..**Joachim**, W Lawr '75 -160 W 77th -NY 10024 **Fx:**799-6416
(845) 373-8521 ..**Joannides**, Richd A '70 -528 Smithfld Rd -Millerton 12546 **Fx:**373-8082
(212) 232-0468 ..**Job**, Bronwen '89 Dept Probation -33 Beaver -NY 10004
(518) 474-2518 ..**Jobin-Davis**, Camille S '96 %Dept of State -41 State -Albany 12231 **Fx:**474-1927
(718) 250-2000 ..**Joblove**, Leonard S '83 %DA -350 Jay -Brklyn 11201 **Fx:**250-2314
(212) 474-1000 ..**Jobson**, Kevin A '09 %Cravath S&M LLP -825 8th Av -NY 10019
(212) 547-5400 ..**Jocelyn**, Danl N '98 (McDermott W&E LLP) -340 Mad Av -NY 10173
(607) 272-7279 ..**Joch**, Jos '70 (Joch & K) -319 N Aurora Bx396 -Ithaca 14851 **Fx:**272-9976
(518) 591-8774 ..**Jochnowitz**, Leona D '82 SUNY-Schl of Criminal Justice -135 Wstrn Av -Albany 12203
(212) 891-1600 ..**Jock**, Paul F II '90 (Jenner & B LLP) -919 3rd Av -NY 10022
(212) 998-6430 ..**Jockers**, Kenneth A '97 NYU Law Schl -245 Sullivan -NY 10012 **Fx:**995-4031
(914) 761-2252 ..**Jockimo**, Karen A D '94 (Boeggeman G&C,PC) -1 Water -White Plns 10601
(212) 788-0523 ..**Jody**, Nina '84 %Law Dept -100 Church -NY 10007 **Fx:**788-0367
(718) 262-4676 ..**Joe**, Chan '92 %DHCR -92-31 Union Hall -Jamaica 11433 **Fx:**262-7938
(212) 858-1000 ..**Joe**, K Brian '10 %Pillsbury WSP LLP -1540 Bway -NY 10036
(212) 566-5000 ..**Joe**, Valerie '04 NYC Bldgs Dept -280 Bway -NY 10007
(212) 697-3122 ..**Joelson**, Benjamin R '10 %Martin C&B LLP -220 E 42nd -NY 10017
(212) 873-7063 ..**Joelson**, Kenneth '76 (Joelson & R) -149 W 72nd -NY 10023
(212) 962-1190 ..**Joelson**, Marissa B '06 %Sanocki N&T,LLP -225 Bway -NY 10007
(212) 873-7063 ..**Joelson & Rochkind** -149 W 72nd -NY 10023 **Fx:**496-9598
(716) 433-1909 ..**Joerg**, Claude A '80 -260 East Av -Lockprt 14094 **Fx:**433-4065
(212) 541-2000 ..**Joerger**, Martha E '05 %Bryan C LLP -1290 Av of Amer -NY 10104
(518) 427-1240 ..**Joern**, Pamela J '89 -750 Bway -Albany 12207
(212) 450-4000 ..**Joffe**, David A '09 %Davis P&W LLP -450 Lex Av -NY 10017
(212) 506-1700 ..**Joffe**, Dimitry '99 SpclCnsl Kasowitz BT&F LLP -1633 Bway -NY 10019
(212) 577-7185 ..**Joffe**, Michl '94 -277 Bway -NY 10007
(212) 907-0855 ..**Joffe**, Richd T '94 OfCnsl Labaton S LLP -140 Bway -NY 10005
(212) 499-3650 ..**Joffe**, Steven '77 FTI Consulting -3 Times Sq -NY 10036
(607) 763-9200 ..**Joggerst**, Elizabeth K '82 (Levene G&T,LLP) -BxF-1706 -Bnghmtn 13902
(212) 373-3000 ..**Jogi**, Piibe '09 %Paul WRW&G LLP -1285 Av of Amer -NY 10019
(845) 855-8900 ..**Johannesen**, Amy J '93 (Cerny Assoc,PC) -24 Smith -Pawling 12564 **Fx:**855-8904
(631) 821-6234 ..**Johannesen**, Annmarie R '91 (Johannesen & J, PLLC) -544 Business Route 25A -Rocky Pnt 11778 **Fx:**821-6171
(718) 590-2000 ..**Johannesen**, Rebecca L '06 DA -198 E 161st -Bronx 10451 **Fx:**590-6477
(631) 821-6234 ..**Johannesen**, Richd '89 (Johannesen & J, PLLC) -544 Business Route 25A -Rocky Pnt 11778 **Fx:**821-6171
(212) 596-9000 ..**Johannessen**, Pristine S '03 %Ropes & G LLP -1211 Av of Amer -NY 10036

(212) 364-8475 .. **Johanns,** Gretchen A '99 Time Warner Cable -60 Columbus Av -NY 10023 **Fx:**364-8460
(212) 468-8000 .. **Johanns,** Heidi J '07 %Morrison & F LLP -1290 Av of Amer -NY 10104
(212) 819-8200 .. **Johansen,** David M '98 (White & C LLP) -1155 Av of Amer -NY 10036
(914) 422-4069 .. **Johansen,** Karen L '05 Pace Women's Jstc Ctr -78 N Bway -White Plns 10603
(212) 517-2750 .. **Johansson,** Jan G '90 -360 E 72nd -NY 10021 **Fx:**988-3285
(212) 785-2929 .. **John,** Darrell '00 %Conway FC&K,PC -48 Wall -NY 10005
(914) 345-3020 .. **John,** Fincey '09 %Knuckles K&E,LLP -565 Taxter Rd -Elmsfrd 10523
(212) 735-3000 .. **John,** Ian Grant '96 (Skadden ASM&F LLP) -4 Times Sq -NY 10036
(516) 364-6006 .. **John,** Leandre M '02 Cohen & S,LLP -199 Crsswys Park Dr Bx9004 -Woodbury 11797
(516) 357-3000 .. **John,** Maria C '02 %Rivkin R LLP -926 RXR Plz -Uniondale 11556
(315) 422-8191 .. **John,** Mary C '97 %Leg Aid -351 S Warren -Syracuse 13202 **Fx:**472-2819
(607) 758-6244 .. **John,** Richd T '87 Intertek Testing Svcs -3933 Route 11 -Cortlnd 13045
(718) 250-2000 .. **John-Drigo,** Marie E '93 %DA -350 Jay -Brklyn 11201 **Fx:**250-2314
(212) 269-0927 .. **Johnmar,** Sotheary '04 %D'Amato & L,LLP -2 World Fncl Ctr -NY 10281
(845) 624-8661 .. **Johns,** Craig E '80 -154 S Mddltwn Rd -Nanuet 10954 **Fx:**624-3586
(585) 394-2665 .. **Johns,** David A '71 (Croucher J&J) -70 S Main -Canandaigua 14424
(917) 343-8131 .. **Johns,** Kimberly A '98 Goldman Sachs -1 NY Plz -NY 10004
(315) 437-7600 .. **Johns,** Susan T '85 (Ferrara FLB&R,PC) -5010 Campuswood Dr -E Syracuse 13057
(212) 393-9697 .. **Johns,** Thos L '87 -200 W 57th -NY 10019 **Fx:**385-0849
(212) 294-6700 .. **Johnsen,** Edw J '87 (Winston & S) -200 Park Av -NY 10166
(716) 854-0007 .. **Johnsen,** Jonathan G '92 (Creighton PJ&G) -295 Main -Buffalo 14203 **Fx:**854-0004
(212) 425-7200 .. **Johnson,** Aaron D '09 %Kenyon & K,LLP -1 Bway -NY 10004
(212) 969-1000 .. **Johnson,** Adam H '02 Alliance Capital Mgmt Corp -1345 Av of Amer -NY 10105
(718) 907-6220 .. **Johnson,** Aisha L '02 (Johnson L Law Grp LLC) -45 Main -Brklyn 11201 **Fx:**228-8425
(212) 832-0400 .. **Johnson,** Alan R '69 Berdon LLP -360 Mad Av -NY 10017
(607) 273-2283 .. **Johnson,** Alba S '95 %Prisoners' Leg Srvcs -114 Prospect -Ithaca 14850 **Fx:**272-9122
(212) 918-3000 .. **Johnson,** Alexander B '97 (Hogan L LLP) -875 3rd Av -NY 10022
(212) 732-8700 .. **Johnson,** Alexander S '90 (McAloon & F,PC) -123 William -NY 10038
(718) 553-3285 .. **Johnson,** Alfred R Jr. '80 %FAA -1 Aviation Plz -Jamaica 11434 **Fx:**995-5699
(212) 487-7219 .. **Johnson,** Allison R '07 Dept Consumer Affrs -42 Bway -NY 10004
(518) 348-1190 .. **Johnson,** Andrew M '95 TRC Envrnmtl Corp -10 Maxwell Dr -Clifton Pk 12065 **Fx:**348-1194
(718) 875-2145 .. **Johnson,** Angelyn D '87 -26 Court -Brklyn 11242 **Fx:**722-7887
(845) 562-0203 .. **Johnson,** Ann R '95 (Finkelstein & Prtnrs,LLP) -1279 Route 300 Bx1111 -Newburgh 12550
(212) 263-7921 .. **Johnson,** Annette B '81 %NYU Ofc Leg Cnsl -70 Wshngtn Sq S -NY 10012 **Fx:**995-3048
(718) 262-7100 .. **Johnson,** Autrey G '03 %Civil Ct -89-17 Sutphin Blvd -Jamaica 11435 **Fx:**262-7107
(212) 557-7700 .. **Johnson,** Berkeley D Jr. '61 OfCnsl Davidson D&C LLP -60 E 42nd -NY 10165
(212) 637-2276 .. **Johnson,** Boyd M III '93 %US Atty -1 St Andrews Plz -NY 10007
(212) 858-1000 .. **Johnson,** Brandon R '07 %Pillsbury WSP LLP -1540 Bway -NY 10036
(212) 937-7206 .. **Johnson,** Brian A '00 (WilmerHale) -399 Park Av -NY 10022
(212) 421-2233 .. **Johnson,** Bruce C '78 OfCnsl Wilk A LLP -675 3rd Av -NY 10017
(631) 271-4684 .. **Johnson,** Bryan R '07 %RJ Delcol -1038 W Jericho Tpk -Smithtwn 11787 **Fx:**629-4583
(212) 554-1400 .. **Johnson,** C Chad '98 (Bernstein LB&G LLP) -1285 Av of Amer -NY 10019
(607) 739-3581 .. **Johnson,** C Douglas '97 GST BOCES -459 Philo Rd -Elmira 14903
(212) 264-5916 .. **Johnson,** Carrie Carnduff '04 DHS -26 Fed Plz -NY 10278
(315) 234-8600 .. **Johnson,** Casey A '07 US Dist Ct-NDNY -100 S Clinton -Syracuse 13261 **Fx:**234-8601
(315) 663-2100 .. **Johnson,** Catherine K '88 Cor Devlpmnt Corp -540 Towne Dr -Fayettevll 13066
(585) 262-8412 .. **Johnson,** Chas G '89 Rochester Schl Dist -131 W Broad -Rchstr 14614
(212) 446-8147 .. **Johnson,** Christian P '95 McKinsey & Co -55 E 52nd -NY 10055
(716) 853-3801 .. **Johnson,** Christopher A '05 %Kenney SL&N,LLP -14 Lafayette Sq -Buffalo 14203
(585) 415-3803 .. **Johnson,** Christopher G '89 -1800 Hudson Av -Rchstr 14617 **Fx:**342-4514
(646) 252-2745 .. **Johnson,** Christopher J '83 %Transit Auth -2 Bway -NY 10004 **Fx:**252-5559
(212) 496-7278 .. **Johnson,** Christopher J '84 -459 Columbus Av -NY 10024
(212) 872-3670 .. **Johnson,** Christopher K '01 KPMG LLP -345 Park Av -NY 10154
(212) 506-1700 .. **Johnson,** Christopher P '87 (Kasowitz BT&F LLP) -1633 Bway -NY 10019
(212) 230-8800 .. **Johnson,** Clarion E '08 %WilmerHale -399 Park Av -NY 10022
(845) 735-7000 .. **Johnson & Cohen,LLP** -1 Blue Hill Plz -Pearl Rvr 10965 **Fx:**735-7585
(914) 995-3000 .. **Johnson,** Courtney L '07 %DA -111 Martin Luther King Blvd -White Plns 10601 **Fx:**995-3363
(516) 612-7146 .. **Johnson,** Craig B '97 (C Johnson,LLC) -85 W Hawthorne Av -Vly Stream 11580 **Fx:**612-7147
(716) 286-4420 .. **Johnson,** Craig H '79 Law Dept -745 Main Bx69 -Niagara Fls 14302 **Fx:**286-4424
(516) 746-8000 .. **Johnson,** Craig M '97 OfCnsl Jaspan S LLP -300 Grdn City Plz -Gdn Cty 11530
(914) 302-2210 .. **Johnson,** Cris E '81 -975 Hanover -Yorktwn Hts 10598 **Fx:**(661) 749-8509
(212) 609-6800 .. **Johnson,** Curtis A '84 (McCarter & E,LLP) -245 Park Av -NY 10167
(212) 530-5000 .. **Johnson,** Curtis A '08 %Milbank TH&M LLP -1 Chase Manh Plz -NY 10005
(315) 634-1100 .. **Johnson,** Dale B '81 -990 7th N -Liverpool 13088
(607) 274-5461 .. **Johnson,** Danl W '05 DA -320 N Tioga -Ithaca 14850 **Fx:**274-5429
(718) 855-7874 .. **Johnson,** Darius X '07 D Johnson,PC -188 Montague -Brklyn 11201
(212) 373-3000 .. **Johnson,** Darren W '02 Cnsl Paul WRW&G LLP -1285 Av of Amer -NY 10019
(518) 465-9313 .. **Johnson,** David B '95 (Read and L,LLP) -25 Eagle -Albany 12207
(212) 484-8000 .. **Johnson,** David H '74 %Warner Music Grp -75 Rckfllr Plz -NY 10019 **Fx:**489-3342
(212) 574-1200 .. **Johnson,** David R '08 %Seward & K LLP -1 Bttry Pk Plz -NY 10004
(518) 359-3394 .. **Johnson,** David W '61 DW Johnson,LLC -51 Lake -Tupper Lk 12986 **Fx:**359-7875
(718) 261-3116 .. **Johnson,** Denise N '98 -88-11 Sutphin Blvd -Jamaica 11435
(845) 373-7406 .. **Johnson,** Dennis D '07 -149 Haight Rd -Amenia 12501
(212) 788-7000 .. **Johnson,** Denora M '06 %City Cncl Leg Div -250 Bway -NY 10007 **Fx:**788-7034
(631) 475-0200 .. **Johnson,** Edw M '85 (Dranitzke LT&J) -73 N Ocean Av Bx510 -Patchogue 11772
(718) 588-6800 .. **Johnson,** Edw T '96 -903 Sheridan Av -Bronx 10451
(212) 449-1778 .. **Johnson,** Elissa Shendalman '97 %Merrill Lynch -4 Wrld Fncl Ctr -NY 10080
(212) 997-7499 .. **Johnson,** Elizabeth Martin '90 -500 5th Av -NY 10110 **Fx:**997-7707
(212) 973-1171 .. **Johnson,** Emily F '75 OfCnsl G & L Blumberg,LLP -521 5th Av -NY 10175 **Fx:**697-9570
(315) 474-2911 .. **Johnson,** Eric G '87 (Smith SK&S,PC) -250 S Clinton -Syracuse 13202
(212) 754-6120 .. **Johnson,** Eric R '96 %Stout & T -477 Mad Av -NY 10022 **Fx:**754-6809
(845) 838-6900 .. **Johnson,** Erin A '07 Beacon City Schl District -10 Educ Dr -Beacon 12508
(212) 474-1000 .. **Johnson,** G Douglas '85 Cravath S&M LLP -825 8th Av -NY 10019
(631) 369-2270 .. **Johnson,** G Randi '89 %J Ryan & Assoc -633 Main Rd -Rvrhead 11901
(914) 663-9122 .. **Johnson,** Garrett M '88 -6 Gramatan Av -Mt Vernon 10550
(518) 474-6988 .. **Johnson,** Gary '86 Ofc Emp Rltns -Agncy Bldg 2 ESP -Albany 12223 **Fx:**473-6795
(718) 442-7004 .. **Johnson,** Gary W '83 (Johnson & L,PC) -1688 Victory Blvd -Staten Isl 10314 **Fx:**442-9086
(718) 248-6541 .. **Johnson,** Geneva M '00 Citicorp Credit Srvcs -1 Court Sq -LIC 11120
(201) 447-5600 .. **Johnson,** Geoffrey M '78 (Johnson & C,LLP) -307 7th Av -NY 10001 **Fx:**447-2080
(347) 404-9133 .. **Johnson,** Gerry T '08 Civil Ct -141 Lvngstn -Brklyn 11201 **Fx:**(718) 643-3733
(718) 999-2040 .. **Johnson,** Gloria '84 %Fire Dept Bureau Leg Afrs -9 Metrotech Ctr -Brklyn 11201
(212) 878-4633 .. **Johnson,** Gordon J '75 %MTA -347 Mad Av -NY 10017
(315) 732-5121 .. **Johnson,** Grant E '59 OfCnsl Helmer JM&K -405 Court -Utica 13502
(518) 899-5700 .. **Johnson,** Gregg T '93 (Lemire J,LLC) -2534 Route 9 Bx2485 -Malta 12020 **Fx:**899-5487
(212) 940-8800 .. **Johnson,** Gregory C '09 %Katten MR LLP -575 Mad Av -NY 10022
(212) 834-4616 .. **Johnson,** Gregory J '91 JP Morgan Chase & Co -270 Park Av -NY 10017
(914) 997-9488 .. **Johnson,** Harold J '76 -175 Main -White Plns 10601 **Fx:**949-6810
(716) 204-2400 .. **Johnson,** Heather A '01 %SJ Baum,PC -220 Nrthpnte Pkwy Bx1291 -Buffalo 14240 **Fx:**204-4600
(212) 223-2100 .. **Johnson,** Heather M '98 %Menz B&K LLP -444 Mad Av -NY 10022
(212) 756-2000 .. **Johnson,** Heather N '09 %Schulte R&Z LLP -919 3rd Av -NY 10022
(914) 747-2263 .. **Johnson,** Helen A '67 -194 Deerfld Ln N -Plsntvll 10570 **Fx:**741-0399
(631) 421-5087 .. **Johnson,** J Wm '65 -6 Van Wyck Ln -Huntngtn 11743
(212) 526-0480 .. **Johnson,** Jack L '00 %Barclays Capital Inc -745 7th Av -NY 10019
(718) 579-3025 .. **Johnson,** Jamal L '01 Leg Aid -1020 Grnd Cncrs -Bronx 10451
(212) 839-5300 .. **Johnson,** James D '94 SrCnsl Sidley A LLP -787 7th Av -NY 10019
(212) 909-6000 .. **Johnson,** James E '87 (Debevoise & P LLP) -919 3rd Av -NY 10022
(212) 907-0859 .. **Johnson,** James W '87 (Labaton S LLP) -140 Bway -NY 10005
(212) 450-4000 .. **Johnson,** Jami S '10 %Davis P&W LLP -450 Lex Av -NY 10017
(516) 571-3800 .. **Johnson,** Jamie B '05 %DA -262 Old Cntry Rd -Mineola 11501 **Fx:**248-9479
(914) 422-4265 .. **Johnson,** Janet A '94 %Pace Law Schl -78 N Bway -White Plns 10603 **Fx:**422-4039
(212) 218-2100 .. **Johnson,** Jason E '06 %Fitzpatrick CH&S -1290 Av of Amer -NY 10104
(518) 455-4166 .. **Johnson,** Jeanine R '04 %NYS Assembly -452 Lgsltv Ofc Bldg -Albany 12248
(212) 421-4100 .. **Johnson,** Jeffrey C '85 (Pryor C LLP) -7 Times Sq -NY 10036
(646) 552-3330 .. **Johnson,** Jeffrey D '98 -225 Bway -NY 10007 **Fx:**(212) 406-6043
(718) 981-6650 .. **Johnson,** Jeffrey W '92 -136 Bay -Staten Isl 10301
(212) 407-7700 .. **Johnson,** Jennifer A '04 %Vedder P,PC -1633 Bway -NY 10019
(212) 416-8600 .. **Johnson,** Jennifer L '98 Dept of Law -120 Bway -NY 10271
(212) 335-4500 .. **Johnson,** Jeremy R '05 (DLA Piper LLP) -1251 Av of Amer -NY 10020
(718) 590-2000 .. **Johnson,** Jevet T '02 %DA -198 E 161st -Bronx 10451 **Fx:**590-6477
(845) 331-2525 .. **Johnson,** Jill M '95 %Ryan R&R,LLP -115 Green Bx3153 -Kingston 12402
(212) 483-2323 .. **Johnson,** Joanne E '86 %JP Morgan Chase -345 Park Av -NY 10154
(212) 758-9300 .. **Johnson,** Jodi '96 %Lazare P&G LLP -950 3rd Av -NY 10022
(212) 566-3019 .. **Johnson,** John '93 -225 Bway -NY 10007 **Fx:**732-7091
(212) 765-5070 .. **Johnson,** John T '94 (Fish & R,PC) -153 E 53rd -NY 10022
(516) 741-2585 .. **Johnson,** Jos H '09 %Rosicki R & Assoc,PC -51 E Bethpage Rd -Plainvw 11803 **Fx:**741-4748
(212) 779-9910 .. **Johnson,** Jos T III '95 (Eaton & V LLP) -3 Park Av -NY 10016
(716) 332-7192 .. **Johnson,** Julian C '86 (Johnson & K LLC) -534 Delaware Av -Buffalo 14202 **Fx:**332-7170

(212) 310-8000 .. **Johnson,** Junine K '05 %Weil G&M LLP -767 5th Av -NY 10153
(212) 816-4415 .. **Johnson,** K Bridget '91 Citigroup -388 Greenwich -NY 10013
(212) 992-8904 .. **Johnson,** Karen K '02 %NYU Law Schl -245 Sullivan -NY 10012 **Fx:**995-4600
(212) 201-5815 .. **Johnson,** Karl E '03 Cedar Hill Capital -445 Park Av -NY 10022
(718) 243-6881 .. **Johnson,** Kathleen '03 %Leg Aid -111 Lvngstn -Brklyn 11201 **Fx:**237-8737
(212) 790-4500 .. **Johnson,** Kathleen R '07 %Manatt P&P,LLP -7 Times Sq -NY 10036
(212) 577-3001 .. **Johnson,** Kendall A '91 %HIV Law Proj -15 Maiden Ln -NY 10038 **Fx:**577-3192
(845) 457-5332 .. **Johnson,** Kenneth D '68 -15 Scotts Crnrs Dr Bx664 -Montgmry 12549 **Fx:**457-5931
(212) 749-5272 .. **Johnson,** Kenneth L '90 -340 Riverside Dr -NY 10025
(212) 408-5100 .. **Johnson,** Kenneth L '00 Cnsl Chadbourne & P LLP -30 Rckfllr Plz -NY 10112
(585) 637-3911 .. **Johnson,** Kevin G '09 %Klafehn & H -13 Water -Brockprt 14420
(212) 815-1818 .. **Johnson,** Kimberly F '05 DC 37 MELS -125 Barclay -NY 10007 **Fx:**815-1343
(845) 634-7010 .. **Johnson,** Kurt E '67 %Montalbano C&F,PC -67 N Main Bx1070 -New Cty 10956
(212) 770-1884 .. **Johnson,** Lance J '97 %AIG -80 Pine -NY 10005
(212) 992-8374 .. **Johnson,** Larry D '71 NYU Ctr for Global Affrs -15 Barclay -NY 10279
(212) 416-6184 .. **Johnson,** Laura R '86 %Dept of Law -120 Bway -NY 10271
(716) 885-6883 .. **Johnson,** LeRoi C '89 -181 Franklin -Buffalo 14202 **Fx:**365-1520
(607) 723-5341 .. **Johnson,** Linda Blom '02 %Hinman H&K,LLP -80 Exchange Bx5250 -Bnghmtn 13902
(518) 474-4098 .. **Johnson,** Lisette M '91 %Insurance Dept -99 Wshngtn Av -Albany 12257 **Fx:**474-3397
(212) 859-8000 .. **Johnson,** Lynne '81 SpclCnsl Fried FHS&J LLP -1 NY Plz -NY 10004
(212) 867-9500 .. **Johnson,** M Davis '75 (Kurzman K&F,LLP) -230 Park Av -NY 10169
(315) 423-1026 .. **Johnson,** Marc J '81 %Workers Comp Bd -935 James -Syracuse 13203 **Fx:**423-2938
(718) 240-6163 .. **Johnson,** Margaret M '90 %Brookdale Hsptl Med Ctr -One Brookdale Plz -Brklyn 11212 **Fx:**240-6169
(212) 248-3140 .. **Johnson,** Marion B '03 %Drinker B&R LLP -140 Bway -NY 10005
(212) 264-8335 .. **Johnson,** Mark S '79 %US GSA -26 Fed Plz -NY 10278 **Fx:**264-1987
(212) 909-6000 .. **Johnson,** Marques S '09 %Debevoise & P LLP -919 3rd Av -NY 10022
(212) 735-3000 .. **Johnson,** Marti A '03 %Skadden ASM&F LLP -4 Times Sq -NY 10036
(845) 735-7000 .. **Johnson,** Martin T '81 (Johnson & C,LLP) -1 Blue Hill Plz -Pearl Rvr 10965
(315) 734-2688 .. **Johnson,** Mary E '99 %Utica Natl Ins -180 Genesee Bx530 -Utica 13502 **Fx:**734-2662
(212) 653-8700 .. **Johnson,** Mary L '92 SpclCnsl Sheppard MR&H LLP -30 Rckfllr Plz -NY 10112
(212) 335-9000 .. **Johnson,** Maurice A '04 %DA -1 Hogan Pl -NY 10013
(212) 798-6100 .. **Johnson,** Megan E '01 Fortress Invstmt Grp -1345 Av of Amer -NY 10105
(917) 343-5694 .. **Johnson,** Megan M '07 Goldman Sachs Trust Co,NA -1 NY Plz -NY 10004
(518) 842-9466 .. **Johnson,** Melissa Kahn '03 %Leg Aid -1 Kimball -Amsterdam 12010 **Fx:**843-1792
(212) 474-1000 .. **Johnson,** Merritt S '07 %Cravath S&M LLP -825 8th Av -NY 10019
(212) 210-9584 .. **Johnson,** Michl E '95 (Alston & B LLP) -90 Park Av -NY 10016
(518) 474-2063 .. **Johnson,** Michl L '97 Bd of Elections -40 Steuben -Albany 12207 **Fx:**486-6627
(212) 728-8000 .. **Johnson,** Michl W '02 %Willkie F&G LLP -787 7th Av -NY 10019
(516) 767-7664 .. **Johnson,** Michele P '87 -118 Huntngtn Rd -Pt Wash 11050 **Fx:**767-7813
(718) 590-2000 .. **Johnson,** Michelle M '07 %DA -198 E 161st -Bronx 10451 **Fx:**590-6477
(585) 442-2551 .. **Johnson Mullan & Brundage,PC** -1399 Monroe Av -Rchstr 14618 **Fx:**442-2556
(347) 404-9133 .. **Johnson,** Nadine C '99 %Civil Ct -141 Lvngstn -Brklyn 11201 **Fx:**(718) 643-3733
(585) 428-5210 .. **Johnson,** Nathan L '05 Pub Def -10 N Fitzhugh -Rchstr 14614 **Fx:**428-2234
(716) 885-2984 .. **Johnson,** Nels M '87 -3 Rabin Ter -Buffalo 14201
(212) 715-1000 .. **Johnson,** Nelson D '93 Cnsl Arnold & P LLP -399 Park Av -NY 10022
(914) 665-2366 .. **Johnson,** Nichelle Aniece '95 %Law Dept -City Hall One Roosevelt Sq -Mt Vernon 10550 **Fx:**665-9142
(212) 552-8296 .. **Johnson,** Nicole C '97 JP Morgan Chase -1 Chase Manh Plz -NY 10081
(518) 388-1270 .. **Johnson,** Patricia W '82 %CQC -401 State -Schnctdy 12305 **Fx:**388-1275
(718) 745-5530 .. **Johnson,** Patrick W '89 %W Johnson -9118 3rd Av -Brklyn 11209
(212) 663-0918 .. **Johnson,** Peter C '96 -134 W 93rd -NY 10025 **Fx:**663-6968
(631) 265-4500 .. **Johnson,** Peter D '86 OfCnsl Meyer M&K -28 Manor Rd -Smithtwn 11787
(212) 269-7308 .. **Johnson,** Peter J '49 (Leahey & J PC) -120 Wall -NY 10005
(212) 269-7336 .. **Johnson,** Peter James Jr. '87 (Leahey & J PC) -120 Wall -NY 10005 **Fx:**968-7358
(716) 484-7196 .. **Johnson,** Peter R '02 %Fessenden L&D -81 Forest Av Bx590 -Jamestwn 14702
(607) 763-9200 .. **Johnson,** Philip C '73 (Levene G&T,LLP) -BxF-1706 -Bnghmtn 13902
(718) 222-2267 .. **Johnson,** Porsha R '09 %Law Dept -350 Jay -Brklyn 11201 **Fx:**222-2088
(212) 416-8207 .. **Johnson,** R Verle Jr. '90 %Dept of Law -120 Bway -NY 10271 **Fx:**416-8816
(845) 338-7800 .. **Johnson,** R Wayne '88 (Johnson Auto Grp Inc) -128 Route 28 -Kingston 12401 **Fx:**340-1926
(518) 654-9400 .. **Johnson,** Raeann C '99 -261 Main -Corinth 12822 **Fx:**654-9402
(607) 647-5278 .. **Johnson,** Rand D '80 -447 Balsam Tyler Rd -McDonough 13801
(914) 995-2243 .. **Johnson,** Reginald J '94 %Cnty Atty -148 Martine Av -White Plns 10601 **Fx:**995-5858
(718) 520-4662 .. **Johnson,** Richd C Jr. '88 Hon D Lewis -125-01 Qns Blvd -Kew Gdns 11415
(347) 404-9133 .. **Johnson,** Richd E '02 %Civil Ct -141 Lvngstn -Brklyn 11201 **Fx:**(718) 643-3733
(718) 835-2677 .. **Johnson,** Richd G '89 -110-22 Lbrty Av -S Richmond Hll 11419 **Fx:**835-2672
(631) 615-2171 .. **Johnson,** Richd J '05 -77 W 5th -Ronkonkoma 11779
(212) 872-1000 .. **Johnson,** Robt A '88 -One Bryant Park -NY 10036 **Fx:**872-1002
(585) 238-2000 .. **Johnson,** Robt C '74 (Phillips L LLP) -1400 First Fed Plz -Rchstr 14614
(212) 619-6744 .. **Johnson,** Robt E '83 (Johnson L,LLP) -305 Bway -NY 10007 **Fx:**619-1358
(716) 842-1010 .. **Johnson,** Robt P '75 -69 Delaware Av -Buffalo 14202
(516) 746-2300 .. **Johnson,** Robt P '78 %A Capetola -2C Hillside Av -Williston Pk 11596 **Fx:**746-2318
(718) 590-2000 .. **Johnson,** Robt T '76 (DA) -198 E 161st -Bronx 10451 **Fx:**590-6477
(518) 272-6565 .. **Johnson,** Robt W III '74 (Martin SWD&J) -279 River Bx1530 -Troy 12181
(718) 745-5530 .. **Johnson,** Robt W '97 -9118 3rd Av -Brklyn 11209
(845) 357-5828 .. **Johnson,** Ronald E '69 %Johnson J&T -10 Burlngtn Av -Suffern 10901
(716) 858-2424 .. **Johnson,** Rosanne Eimer '88 %DA -25 Delaware Av -Buffalo 14202 **Fx:**858-7425
(315) 334-4670 .. **Johnson,** Russell D Jr. '95 -6707 Golf Course Rd -Rome 13440
(212) 819-8200 .. **Johnson,** Ryan P '08 %White & C LLP -1155 Av of Amer -NY 10036
(212) 478-0833 .. **Johnson,** Sarah S '04 DE Shaw & Co -120 W 45th -NY 10036
(212) 484-3900 .. **Johnson,** Shawanna '09 %Arent F LLP -1675 Bway -NY 10019
(607) 256-6478 .. **Johnson,** Sheri L '80 %Cornell Law Schl -Myron Taylor Hall -Ithaca 14853 **Fx:**255-7193
(212) 484-3900 .. **Johnson,** Sonya D '94 %Arent F LLP -1675 Bway -NY 10019
(212) 407-4000 .. **Johnson,** Stanley M '82 (Loeb & L,LLP) -345 Park Av -NY 10154
(212) 450-4000 .. **Johnson,** Stefani L '10 %Davis P&W LLP -450 Lex Av -NY 10017
(212) 440-2350 .. **Johnson,** Stephanie Ann '93 C Siegel -40 Wall -NY 10005 **Fx:**440-2385
(315) 218-8000 .. **Johnson,** Stephen L '69 (Bond S&K,PLLC) -1 Lincoln Ctr -Syracuse 13202
(212) 504-6000 .. **Johnson,** Stephen M '10 %Cadwalader W&T LLP -1 World Fncl Ctr -NY 10281
(212) 248-2220 .. **Johnson,** Steven D '87 (Kennedy JG LLC) -99 Wall -NY 10005 **Fx:**248-0170
(718) 237-5500 .. **Johnson,** Susan C '09 %Leg Srvcs -105 Court -Brklyn 11201 **Fx:**855-0733
(212) 816-1997 .. **Johnson,** Susan O'Connell '86 %Citi Markets & Banking -388 Greenwich -NY 10013
(518) 762-3505 .. **Johnson,** Susan Palmer '91 -17 W Main -Johnstwn 12095 **Fx:**762-3011
(716) 845-1088 .. **Johnson,** Susan S '04 Roswell Park Cancer Inst -Elm & Carlton -Buffalo 14263
(718) 579-7900 .. **Johnson,** Tajuana B '08 Leg Aid -900 Sheridan Av -Bronx 10451 **Fx:**293-8744
(585) 238-4207 .. **Johnson,** Tara R '03 Excellus Health Plan Inc -165 Court -Rchstr 14647
(212) 332-8900 .. **Johnson,** Terrence J '03 %Simon & Prtnrs LLP -551 5th Av -NY 10176 **Fx:**332-8909
(518) 456-0082 .. **Johnson,** Thos J '78 (Bailey K&J,PC) -5 Pine West Plz -Albany 12205 **Fx:**456-4767
(718) 286-2000 .. **Johnson,** Thos P '88 %Leg Aid -120-46 Qns Blvd -Kew Gdns 11415 **Fx:**286-2286
(518) 465-3484 .. **Johnson,** Tichina L '10 %Carter CCBM&L,PC -20 Corp Wds Blvd -Albany 12211
(718) 613-2440 .. **Johnson,** Timothy N '07 Hon IL Glasser -225 Cadman Plz E -Brklyn 11201
(716) 849-8900 .. **Johnson,** Timothy P '81 (Hurwitz & F,PC) -1300 Lbrty Bldg -Buffalo 14202
(607) 263-5741 .. **Johnson,** Timothy R '86 -144 Main Bx238 -Morris 13808
(607) 965-8343 .. **Johnson,** Timothy R '86 -7 West Bx306 -Edmeston 13335 **Fx:**965-8331
(607) 547-4413 .. **Johnson,** Timothy R '86 -203 Main -Cooperstwn 13326
(646) 502-7001 .. **Johnson,** Tobe '01 (JSBarkats PLLC) -100 Church -NY 10007 **Fx:**607-5544
(212) 941-9090 .. **Johnson,** Travis M '04 The Door -121 Av of Amer -NY 10013 **Fx:**941-0714
(212) 230-8800 .. **Johnson,** Trisha L '09 (WilmerHale) -399 Park Av -NY 10022
(585) 238-8143 .. **Johnson,** Valerie R '96 Ofc of Chldrn & Families -259 Monroe Av -Rchstr 14607 **Fx:**238-8169
(716) 847-3004 .. **Johnson,** Vera R '91 %OTDA -295 Main -Buffalo 14203 **Fx:**847-3699
(212) 557-7700 .. **Johnson,** W Macy '78 (Davidson D&C LLP) -60 E 42nd -NY 10165
(212) 523-2891 .. **Johnson,** Wade E '96 -1123 Bway -NY 10010
(718) 558-8352 .. **Johnson,** Walter III '95 %LIRR -Jamaica Station -Jamaica 11435 **Fx:**558-8211
(212) 859-8000 .. **Johnson,** Wm F '97 (Fried FHS&J LLP) -1 NY Plz -NY 10004
(212) 715-9100 .. **Johnson,** Wm J '08 %Kramer LN&F,LLP -1177 Av of Amer -NY 10036
(716) 688-3800 .. **Johnson,** Wm P '87 (Nesper F&D,LLP) -501 JJ Audobon Pkwy -Amherst 14228
(585) 475-2140 .. **Johnson,** Wm P '09 %Rochester Inst of Tech -78 Lomb Mem'l Dr -Rchstr 14623 **Fx:**475-2178
(718) 745-5530 .. **Johnson,** Wm R '59 -9118 3rd Av -Brklyn 11209
(212) 918-4661 .. **Johnson,** Zachary H '03 (Galluzzo & J LLP) -48 Wall -NY 10005
(716) 278-1890 .. **Johnson-Granat,** Judy L '87 Family Ct -775 3rd -Niagara Fls 14301
(716) 853-9555 .. **Johnson-Lee,** Barbara R '91 %Leg Aid -237 Main -Buffalo 14203 **Fx:**853-3219
(914) 378-1010 .. **Johnson-Pertet,** Margaret E '84 %Fitzgerald & F -538 Riverdale Av -Ynkrs 10705
(212) 880-6000 .. **Johnson-Spina,** Amy C '01 (Torys LLP) -237 Park Av -NY 10017
(631) 370-1178 .. **Johnston,** Brian M '09 %Puleo D,LLC -444 Route 111 -Smithtwn 11787 **Fx:**370-1278
(212) 644-2300 .. **Johnston,** Claude E '79 Pearl Meyer & Prtnrs -445 Park Av -NY 10022 **Fx:**644-2320
(646) 375-2035 .. **Johnston,** Dan L '73 -116 W 23rd -NY 10011

(716) 845-7440 .. **Johnston,** Danl S '80 %Family Ct -1 Niagara Plz -Buffalo 14202 **Fx:**858-8432
(631) 734-5890 .. **Johnston,** E Brownell Jr. '70 -4001 Wells Rd -Peconic 11958 **Fx:**734-5891
(212) 701-3000 .. **Johnston,** Gail E '95 %Cahill G&R LLP -80 Pine -NY 10005 **Fx:**269-5420
(212) 935-3000 .. **Johnston,** Garrett T '10 %Mintz LCFG&P,PC -666 3rd Av -NY 10017
(212) 264-2835 .. **Johnston,** Glenn M '07 US Ct of Intl Trade -1 Fed Plz -NY 10278
(718) 237-2000 .. **Johnston,** Gregory J '04 %Leg Aid -111 Lvngstn -Brklyn 11201 **Fx:**237-8737
(212) 468-4800 .. **Johnston,** James L '99 (Davis & G LLP) -1740 Bway -NY 10019
(212) 456-1000 .. **Johnston,** Janice S '96 ABC -147 W 66th -NY 10023
(914) 277-3460 .. **Johnston,** John J Jr. '64 -27 Sunset Dr -N Salem 10560 **Fx:**277-3460
(212) 237-0000 .. **Johnston,** John P '07 %Vinson & E LLP -666 5th Av -NY 10103
(212) 699-8581 .. **Johnston,** Julius IV '02 VanWagner Communications LLC -800 3rd Av -NY 10022 **Fx:**986-0927
(607) 652-7343 .. **Johnston,** June F '88 Johnston Law Firm -72 Main Bx130 -Stamfrd 12167 **Fx:**652-2812
(516) 330-3412 .. **Johnston,** Karen E '91 -734 Franklin Av -Gdn Cty 11530
(631) 666-5766 .. **Johnston,** Kevin R '88 (Long TBSWJ&S) -120 4th Av Bx5591 -Bay Shr 11706
(607) 273-4200 .. **Johnston,** Laurie M '92 (Miller M,LLP) -202 E State -Ithaca 14850
(914) 237-6635 .. **Johnston,** Lisa L '92 (L Johnston & Assoc) -1032 McLean Av -Ynkrs 10704 **Fx:**237-6473
(212) 517-7880 .. **Johnston,** Lowell D '90 (Johnston & O) -36 E 72nd -NY 10021 **Fx:**517-7889
(212) 526-0619 .. **Johnston,** Lynne E '87 %Barclays Capital Inc -1271 Av of Amer -NY 10020
(212) 610-6300 .. **Johnston,** M Elaine '88 (Allen & O) -1221 Av of Amer -NY 10020
(516) 623-1111 .. **Johnston,** Melissa L '03 %Curtis V PC -2174 Hewlett Av Bx801 -Merrick 11566 **Fx:**623-0758
(212) 480-4800 .. **Johnston,** Michl F '67 (Fox H&C LLP) -825 3rd Av -NY 10022
(718) 992-5209 .. **Johnston,** R Hamilton '67 -2222 Haviland Av -Bronx 10462
(212) 513-3200 .. **Johnston,** R Scott '85 (Holland & K LLP) -31 W 52nd -NY 10019
(212) 788-0846 .. **Johnston,** Raegan M '06 %ACS -220 Church -NY 10013
(212) 335-4500 .. **Johnston,** Robt A '09 %DLA Piper LLP -1251 Av of Amer -NY 10020
(212) 918-3000 .. **Johnston,** Russell W '06 %Hogan L LLP -875 3rd Av -NY 10022
(212) 943-0110 .. **Johnston,** Scott R '84 %Poles TS&G, LLP -46 Trinity Pl -NY 10006
(518) 561-9550 .. **Johnston,** Stephen A '80 -11 Oak -Plattsbrgh 12901 **Fx:**561-9584
(212) 841-1000 .. **Johnston,** Susan Power '80 OfCnsl Covington & B LLP -620 8th Av -NY 10018
(212) 265-6888 .. **Johnston,** Thos O '99 (Porzio B&N,PC) -156 W 56th -NY 10019
(631) 854-6550 .. **Johnston,** Wm A '93 %Cnty Probation Ofc -250-Z Exec Dr -Edgewood 11717
(518) 686-7324 .. **Johnston,** Wm C '68 (Holbrook J&T) -12 Main Bx146 -Hoosick Fls 12090
(908) 233-9000 .. **Johnstone,** I Blakeley III '81 (Johnstone SL&L) -225 Bway -NY 10007
(585) 899-1414 .. **Johnstone,** Jeffrey M '75 (Harris COJW&L) -300 Linden Oaks -Rchstr 14625
(908) 233-9000 .. **Johnstone Skok Loughlin & Lane** -225 Bway -NY 10007 **Fx:**233-5612
(212) 374-6888 .. **John-Stull,** Minerva A '99 %NYC Dept Educ-OLS -52 Chmbrs -NY 10007 **Fx:**374-5596
(631) 755-0101 .. **Johs,** Fredk C '81 (Lewis JAA,LLP) -425 Broad Hollow Rd -Melvll 11747
(212) 551-0768 .. **Joiner,** Devina S '95 %Mutual Marine -919 3rd Av -NY 10022
(607) 776-0695 .. **Joint,** Wm B '86 -12 W Pulteney Sq Bx346 -Bath 14810 **Fx:**776-0696
(212) 474-1000 .. **Jois,** Goutam U '08 %Cravath S&M LLP -825 8th Av -NY 10019
(212) 374-1511 .. **Joishy,** Mahima '02 %Bonnaig & Assoc -25 Murray -NY 10007 **Fx:**374-1703
(212) 768-6700 .. **Jokinen,** Deborah L '08 %Sonnenschein N&R LLP -1221 Av of Amer -NY 10020
(315) 478-3138 .. **Jokl,** Robt L Jr. '90 -2 Clinton Sq -Syracuse 13202 **Fx:**478-3148
(212) 878-8000 .. **Joksimovic,** Tomislav '07 %Clifford C LLP -31 W 52nd -NY 10019
(585) 256-5278 .. **Joles,** Amber M '99 Danisco US,Inc-Genecor -3490 Winton Pl -Rchstr 14623 **Fx:**244-2806
(212) 443-4872 .. **Jolley,** Craig A '06 NYU -75 3rd Av -NY 10003
(607) 974-7430 .. **Jolly,** Linda E '99 Corning Inc -1 Rvrfrnt Plz -Corning 14831
(212) 522-3083 .. **Jollymore,** Nicholas J '79 %Time Inc -1271 Av of Amer -NY 10020 **Fx:**522-0437
(212) 808-2700 .. **Jonaitis,** Stephanie L '03 %Pepper H LLP -620 8th Av -NY 10018
(212) 431-2198 .. **Jonakait,** Randolph N '71 %NY Law Schl -185 W Bway -NY 10013 **Fx:**431-9205
(212) 637-2472 .. **Jonas,** Bonnie Brooks '96 %US Atty -1 St Andrews Plz -NY 10007
(718) 260-8001 .. **Jonas,** Brian S '06 Blackbird Artists Agncy LLC -45 Main -Brklyn 11201
(315) 624-3208 .. **Jonas,** Danl S '90 Conmed Corp -525 French Rd -Utica 13502 **Fx:**793-8929
(315) 724-5545 .. **Jonas,** Marc '76 -502 Court -Utica 13502 **Fx:**724-5807
(212) 935-2600 .. **Jonas,** Marla '92 OfCnsl Halperin & H,PC -18 E 48th -NY 10017 **Fx:**753-9173
(585) 593-0715 .. **Jonas,** Nicholas G '81 -1584 Alma Hill Rd -Wellsvll 14895
(718) 488-2198 .. **Jonas,** Robt L '98 IRS -625 Fulton -Brklyn 11201
(585) 454-0700 .. **Jonascu,** Michl E '10 %Ward GH&R LLP -300 State -Rchstr 14614
(212) 637-3843 .. **Jonathan,** Grant W '05 EPA -290 Bway -NY 10007 **Fx:**637-3096
(212) 653-8700 .. **Joneja,** Bhavana '04 SpclCnsl Sheppard MR&H LLP -30 Rckfllr Plz -NY 10112
(212) 438-1113 .. **Jones,** Aaron D '01 Standard & Poor's -55 Water -NY 10041
(212) 508-6100 .. **Jones,** Alexander W '05 %Bracewell & G,LLP -1251 Av of Amer -NY 10020
(212) 681-3825 .. **Jones,** Alfred C III '70 %Den Norske Bk -200 Park Av -NY 10166 **Fx:**681-3900
(212) 867-4100 .. **Jones,** Andrew R '03 %Furman K&B LLP -61 Bway -NY 10006
(212) 572-6446 .. **Jones,** Anthony J M '06 -300 Park Av -NY 10022
(718) 792-0444 .. **Jones,** Barbara E '83 %MHLS -1500 Waters Pl -Bronx 10461 **Fx:**597-7385
(518) 745-1500 .. **Jones,** Barry J '81 -Bx108 -Hudson Fls 12839
(212) 592-1800 .. **Jones,** Barton T '72 The Church Pension Fund -445 5th Av -NY 10016 **Fx:**592-9428
(718) 780-7957 .. **Jones,** Beryl R '84 %Bklyn Law Schl -250 Joralemon -Brklyn 11201 **Fx:**780-0393
(212) 876-7700 .. **Jones,** Beverly J '03 ASPCA -424 E 92nd -NY 10128 **Fx:**860-3560
(212) 788-5010 .. **Jones,** Beverly Jo Vonne '99 Dept Hlth & Mental Hygiene -125 Worth CN-30 -NY 10013 **Fx:**442-8965
(518) 373-0333 .. **Jones,** Bonnie McGuire '82 (Jones W&P PLLC) -5 Emma Ln -Clifton Pk 12065
(917) 637-3600 .. **Jones,** Bonnie S '03 Ctr for Reproductive Rts -120 Wall -NY 10005
(845) 452-5900 .. **Jones,** Brett E '00 %Van DeWater & V,LLP -85 Civic Ctr Plz Bx112 -Poughkeepsie 12602
(718) 624-7237 .. **Jones,** Brian A '71 -10 Clinton -Brklyn 11201 **Fx:**624-7237
(718) 205-4445 .. **Jones,** Brian S '64 -8456 Grand Av -Elmhrst 11373
(212) 751-3001 .. **Jones,** Carie M '06 %Thompson & K LLP -919 3rd Av -NY 10022
(212) 373-3000 .. **Jones,** Charlene A '10 Paul WRW&G LLP -1285 Av of Amer -NY 10019
(315) 474-7571 .. **Jones,** Christian P '96 %Mackenzie H LLP -101 S Salina Bx4967 -Syracuse 13221
(212) 452-3800 .. **Jones,** Christopher '67 %Fox News -205 E 67th -NY 10065 **Fx:**249-1182
(914) 467-5260 .. **Jones,** Christopher W '82 IGT -520 Wht Plns Rd -Tarrytwn 10591
(212) 226-5054 .. **Jones,** David A '10 %Powley & G,PC -304 Hudson -NY 10013 **Fx:**266-5085
(315) 422-1311 .. **Jones,** David B '04 (Melvin & M,PLLC) -217 S Salina -Syracuse 13202
(212) 791-0285 .. **Jones,** David H '98 Malaby & B,LLC -150 Bway -NY 10038 **Fx:**791-0286
(716) 875-5750 .. **Jones,** David L '70 -22 Victoria Blvd -Kenmore 14217
(212) 614-5426 .. **Jones,** David R '75 %Community Srvc Soc -105 E 22nd -NY 10010 **Fx:**260-6218
(212) 637-2739 .. **Jones,** David S '91 %US Atty -86 Chmbrs -NY 10007
(212) 326-3939 .. **Jones Day** -222 E 41st -NY 10017 **Fx:**755-7306
(631) 715-7900 .. **Jones,** Demetri M '85 %US Atty -610 Fed Plz -Central Islip 11722
(716) 769-7426 .. **Jones,** Dennis W '78 -Bx590 -Findley Lk 14736
(718) 477-9356 .. **Jones,** Donna G '92 -339A Grand Av -Brklyn 11238
(212) 848-4000 .. **Jones,** Douglas E '08 %Shearman & S LLP -599 Lex Av -NY 10022
(845) 926-3449 .. **Jones,** Douglas M '91 -260 Main -Goshen 10924 **Fx:**651-5111
(212) 916-6018 .. **Jones,** E Laverne '84 %TIAA-CREF -730 3rd Av -NY 10017
(518) 274-5820 .. **Jones,** E Stewart Jr. '66 -28 2nd -Troy 12181 **Fx:**274-5875
(716) 831-9947 .. **Jones,** E Thos '82 -17 Beresford Ct -Buffalo 14221
(212) 258-8000 .. **Jones,** Elizabeth Osborne '09 %MTV Networks -1515 Bway -NY 10036 **Fx:**258-8358
(516) 505-0400 .. **Jones,** Ernest R '95 (Jones & Assoc) -24 Main -Hempstd 11550
(914) 995-2672 .. **Jones,** Fay A '88 %Cnty Atty -148 Martine Av -White Plns 10601 **Fx:**995-5858
(518) 587-0080 .. **Jones Ferradino** -68 West Av Bx4400 -Saratoga Spgs 12866 **Fx:**580-0857
(914) 472-2300 .. **Jones Garneau,LLP** -670 Wht Plns Rd -Scarsdale 10583 **Fx:**472-2312
(212) 759-2500 .. **Jones Garneau,LLP** -60 E 42nd -NY 10165 **Fx:**661-4174
(516) 931-2600 .. **Jones,** George '86 (Churbuck CJ&M PC) -43A E Barclay -Hicksvll 11801
(212) 506-5000 .. **Jones,** Glenn K '99 %Orrick H&S LLP -51 W 52nd -NY 10019
(845) 473-9118 .. **Jones,** Graham S II '61 -42 Barnard Av -Poughkeepsie 12601
(518) 388-0690 .. **Jones,** Gregory K '75 %CQC -401 State -Schnctdy 12305
(516) 873-8700 .. **Jones,** Harold D '79 (Jones & S,PC) -1 Old Cntry Rd -Carle Pl 11514 **Fx:**873-8711
(212) 277-4000 .. **Jones,** Helen S '08 %Freshfields BD LLP -520 Mad Av -NY 10022
(516) 564-8390 .. **Jones,** Henry F '90 -366 N Bway -Jericho 11753 **Fx:**564-9075
(585) 428-4154 .. **Jones,** Henry Ware IV '87 %Hon JS Kohout -316 Hall of Justice -Rchstr 14614
(212) 527-1000 .. **Jones Hirsch Connors & Bull PC** -1 Bttry Pk Plz -NY 10004 **Fx:**527-1680
(516) 248-8842 .. **Jones Hirsch Connors & Bull PC** -200 Old Cntry Rd -Mineola 11501 **Fx:**535-5563
(646) 964-5749 .. **Jones,** Ingrid Green '99 (Walker GW&B,LLC) -1825 Park Av -NY 10035 **Fx:**(866) 422-4858
(212) 609-6800 .. **Jones,** J Forrest '85 (McCarter & E,LLP) -245 Park Av -NY 10167
(585) 243-0313 .. **Jones,** J Michl '65 OfCnsl Jones & S -31 Main -Geneseo 14454 **Fx:**243-3625
(315) 474-7571 .. **Jones,** Jacqueline B '95 (Mackenzie H LLP) -101 S Salina Bx4967 -Syracuse 13221
(212) 998-6550 .. **Jones,** Jacqueline D '96 %NYU Law Schl -245 Sullivan -NY 10012
(212) 309-1000 .. **Jones,** James A III '84 (Hunton & W) -200 Park Av -NY 10166
(212) 506-5000 .. **Jones,** James B '09 %Orrick H&S LLP -51 W 52nd -NY 10019
(212) 813-5900 .. **Jones,** Jason D '05 %Fross ZL&Z,PC -866 UN Plz -NY 10017
(516) 228-3908 .. **Jones,** Jean Bell '84 %UIA Bd -400 Oak -Gdn Cty 11530 **Fx:**794-1061
(212) 326-3939 .. **Jones,** Jeffrey D '10 %Jones D -222 E 41st -NY 10017
(914) 923-3722 .. **Jones,** Jeffrey E '83 -38 Walnut Pl -Briarclff Mnr 10510
(212) 969-3000 .. **Jones,** Jennifer L '05 %Proskauer R LLP -1585 Bway -NY 10036
(585) 258-5403 .. **Jones,** Jennifer Lynn '88 %JP Morgan Chase -1 Chase Sq -Rchstr 14643 **Fx:**258-6458
(631) 852-2325 .. **Jones,** Jessie A '78 %MHLS -One Court -Rvrhead 11901
(607) 723-5341 .. **Jones,** John E '89 (Hinman H&K,LLP) -80 Exchange Bx5250 -Bnghmtn 13902
(631) 231-1199 .. **Jones,** John J J '50 OfCnsl Reynolds CGHL&Q,LLP -35 Arkay Dr -Hauppauge 11788
(718) 222-8880 .. **Jones Jones O'Connell** -45 Main -Brklyn 11201 **Fx:**222-0208
(212) 709-8301 .. **Jones,** Jos K '06 JK Jones,LLC -67 Wall -NY 10005
(518) 229-1841 .. **Jones,** Josiah B '03 Police Dept -526 Central Av -Albany 12206
(315) 637-5151 .. **Jones,** Julie Anne '97 %F Josef,PC -519 E Genesee -Fayettevll 13066 **Fx:**637-3436
(212) 589-2700 .. **Jones,** Julie Cassidy '05 %Weight Watchers -11 Mad Av -NY 10010
(212) 687-0100 .. **Jones,** Kelly E '06 %Harris B PLLC -100 Wall -NY 10005
(212) 720-1574 .. **Jones,** Kenneth H '97 %Fed Reserve Bk of NY -33 Lbrty -NY 10045
(607) 753-5008 .. **Jones,** Kevin A '92 %DA -46 Greenbush -Cortlnd 13045 **Fx:**756-3477
(212) 225-2000 .. **Jones,** Kevin C '08 %Cleary GS&H -1 Lbrty Plz -NY 10006

(518) 457-4380 .. **Jones,** Kevin E '96 %Dept of Labor -State Campus Bldg 12 -Albany 12240 **Fx:**485-1819
(212) 334-4577 .. **Jones,** Kevin W '96 (Jones C LLP) -225 Bway -NY 10007 **Fx:**406-6890
(212) 309-1000 .. **Jones,** Kevin W '08 (Hunton & W) -200 Park Av -NY 10166
(212) 553-3200 .. **Jones,** Kimberly A '08 %Marulli LE&T,LLP -5 Hanover Sq -NY 10004
(212) 686-4655 .. **Jones,** Lauren A '09 %Abraham L&A LLP -292 Mad Av -NY 10017
(914) 935-5476 .. **Jones,** Laurence B '76 Compass Grp USA,Inc -3 Intl Dr -Rye Brook 10573
(516) 747-1141 .. **Jones,** Lawr T '76 Jones & J -1000 Franklin Av -Gdn Cty 11530 **Fx:**741-5842
(347) 401-9580 .. **Jones,** Leila M '89 %Appllt Term -141 Lvngstn -Brklyn 11201 **Fx:**(718) 643-7889
(607) 277-2121 .. **Jones,** Leslie F '01 -119 E Buffalo -Ithaca 14850 **Fx:**277-2120
(914) 725-4800 .. **Jones,** Leslie H '93 -455 Cntrl Pk Av -Scarsdale 10583
(585) 343-1366 .. **Jones,** Linda M '93 -22 Wshngtn Av -Batavia 14020
(212) 219-1800 .. **Jones,** Lindsey B '06 %Lawyers Alliance NY -171 Mad Av -NY 10016 **Fx:**941-7458
(212) 790-9200 .. **Jones,** Lindsey F '96 %Cowan L&L,PC -1133 Av of Amer -NY 10036
(516) 466-4110 .. **Jones,** Lori Lapin '85 (LL Jones,PLLC) -98 Cuttermill Rd -Gt Neck 11021 **Fx:**466-4009
(718) 991-4600 .. **Jones,** Margarita R '09 %Leg Aid -953 Southrn Blvd -Bronx 10459 **Fx:**842-2867
(212) 715-9100 .. **Jones,** Maria T '76 (Kramer LN&F,LLP) -1177 Av of Amer -NY 10036
(212) 858-1000 .. **Jones,** Mark C '00 %Pillsbury WSP LLP -1540 Bway -NY 10036
(212) 421-4100 .. **Jones,** Martin J '97 OfCnsl Pryor C LLP -7 Times Sq -NY 10036
(518) 587-0080 .. **Jones,** Matthew J '80 (Jones F) -68 West Av Bx4400 -Saratoga Spgs 12866
(516) 742-0707 .. **Jones,** Matthew J '82 %Sullivan PBM&C PC -55 Mineola Blvd -Mineola 11501
(212) 554-0400 .. **Jones,** Megan A '08 %Grubman I&S,PC -152 W 57th -NY 10019
(212) 281-5879 .. **Jones,** Melanie Adrienne '07 -684 Riverside Dr -NY 10031
(212) 619-5000 .. **Jones,** Meredith J '75 %EDC -110 William -NY 10038 **Fx:**312-3912
(718) 643-3913 .. **Jones,** Meredith R '97 Surrogates Ct -2 Johnson -Brklyn 11201
(585) 924-9151 .. **Jones,** Michl A Jr. '99 (Jones & M) -98 W Main -Victor 14564 **Fx:**924-1744
(716) 824-5353 .. **Jones,** Michl B '88 %M Stachowski -2025 Clinton -Buffalo 14206 **Fx:**824-6674
(212) 858-4000 .. **Jones,** Michl E '89 %FINRA -1 Lbrty Plz -NY 10006
(518) 435-1919 .. **Jones,** Michl G '06 %Stockton B&M,LLP -2 Twr Pl -Albany 12203
(631) 421-1211 .. **Jones,** Michl P '02 %Martin F&M -100 E Carver -Huntngtn 11743
(212) 336-2000 .. **Jones,** Michl R '07 %Patterson BW&T LLP -1133 Av of Amer -NY 10036
(716) 433-5907 .. **Jones,** Morgan L Jr. '75 (Seaman JH&B,LLP) -76 West Av -Lockprt 14094
(212) 468-8000 .. **Jones,** Nadia R '05 Morrison & F LLP -1290 Av of Amer -NY 10104
(518) 457-2411 .. **Jones,** Nancy E '79 %DOT -50 Wolf Rd -Albany 12232 **Fx:**457-4021
(646) 228-5710 .. **Jones,** Nathaniel '92 -244 5th Av -NY 10001
Jones, Pamela Y '89 -Bx497 -White Plns 10602
(212) 351-4500 .. **Jones,** Patrick W '98 OfCnsl Epstein B&G,PC -250 Park Av -NY 10177
(716) 847-8400 .. **Jones,** Paul F '74 (Phillips L LLP) -3400 HSBC Ctr -Buffalo 14203
(518) 584-5212 .. **Jones,** Paul L '51 -2 Elizabeth Ln -Saratoga Spgs 12866
(212) 460-4132 .. **Jones,** Paula F '91 Con Ed -4 Irving Pl -NY 10003
(585) 362-4700 .. **Jones,** Peter A '93 (Bond S&K,PLLC) -350 Linden Oaks -Rchstr 14625
(315) 218-8000 .. **Jones,** Peter A '93 (Bond S&K,PLLC) -1 Lincoln Ctr -Syracuse 13202
(518) 274-3510 .. **Jones,** Peter B '84 (Bartle MD&J,LLP) -251 River Bx448 -Troy 12181
(718) 579-3000 .. **Jones,** Peter H '90 %Leg Aid -1020 Grnd Cncrs -Bronx 10451 **Fx:**588-2611
(914) 214-5579 .. **Jones,** R Scott '97 (Goldstein J LLP) -Bx507 -Yorktwn Hts 10598 **Fx:**462-4040
(718) 243-6801 .. **Jones,** Rachel I '03 Leg Aid -111 Lvngstn -Brklyn 11201 **Fx:**237-8737
(718) 221-0800 .. **Jones,** Ray Alfred Jr. '84 -1142 Dean -Brklyn 11216 **Fx:**771-4470
(212) 839-5300 .. **Jones,** Raynard O '09 %Sidley A LLP -787 7th Av -NY 10019
(585) 454-5255 .. **Jones,** Rhian D '02 -16 W Main -Rchstr 14614
(518) 435-9426 .. **Jones,** Robt A '84 (Chamberlain K&J) -35 Fuller Rd -Albany 12205 **Fx:**435-9102
(212) 818-1110 .. **Jones,** Robt I '84 (Butzel L,PC) -380 Mad Av -NY 10017
(607) 723-9511 .. **Jones,** Robt R '91 (Coughlin & G,LLP) -19 Chenango Bx2039 -Bnghmtn 13902
(718) 520-7956 .. **Jones,** Robt W '91 -80-02 Kew Grdns Rd -Kew Gdns 11415
(518) 479-1008 .. **Jones,** Robt W '09 -75 Troy Rd -E Greenbush 12061
(716) 603-9867 .. **Jones,** Rochelle M '00 JP&J Legal -69 Deerfld Av -Buffalo 14215
(212) 315-0170 .. **Jones,** Roland G '91 (Jones & Assoc) -1285 Av of Amer -NY 10019
(718) 625-6777 .. **Jones,** S Kenneth F '95 (Jones R PC) -32 Court -Brklyn 11201 **Fx:**625-6977
(212) 384-1000 .. **Jones,** Sara J '02 %FBI -26 Fed Plz -NY 10278
(212) 538-5922 .. **Jones,** Sarah S '03 Credit Suisse Securities -1 Mad Av -NY 10010
(518) 464-9003 .. **Jones,** Scott R '01 -4 Pine West Plz -Albany 12205
(718) 254-7000 .. **Jones,** Shannon C '99 US Atty -271 Cadman Plz E -Brklyn 11201 **Fx:**254-6479
(212) 728-8000 .. **Jones,** Shaunna D '04 %Willkie F&G LLP -787 7th Av -NY 10019
(212) 474-1000 .. **Jones,** Shawndra G '09 %Cravath S&M LLP -825 8th Av -NY 10019
(585) 263-1000 .. **Jones,** Shelley A '05 %Nixon P LLP -1100 Clinton Sq -Rchstr 14604
(518) 591-5232 .. **Jones,** Stanley J Jr. '80 %NYS ORPTS -WA Harriman State Campus -Albany 12227 **Fx:**474-3657
(212) 889-8790 .. **Jones,** Stephanie '94 WEA Enterprises,Inc -902 Bway -NY 10010
(914) 472-2300 .. **Jones,** Stephen J '94 (Jones G,LLP) -670 Wht Plns Rd -Scarsdale 10583
(585) 263-1000 .. **Jones,** Stephen J '01 (Nixon P LLP) -1100 Clinton Sq -Rchstr 14604
(315) 684-3400 .. **Jones,** Steven R '79 -15 Eaton Bx130 -Morrisvll 13408 **Fx:**684-7066
(914) 592-4411 .. **Jones,** Susan Bloom '75 %NYSUT -520 Wht Plns Rd -Tarrytwn 10591
(585) 394-7860 .. **Jones,** Susan G '85 -21 Sly -Canandaigua 14424
(585) 786-8450 .. **Jones,** Susan K '82 %Leg Aid -18 Linwood Av -Warsaw 14569 **Fx:**786-8478
(212) 530-5000 .. **Jones,** Tarnetta V '08 %Milbank TH&M LLP -1 Chase Manh Plz -NY 10005
(631) 784-7820 .. **Jones,** Timothy E '00 (Jones & B,PC) -23 Green -Huntngtn 11743 **Fx:**784-7821
(212) 980-0404 .. **Jones,** Timothy F X '90 J Dearie & Assoc -515 Mad Av -NY 10022 **Fx:**980-0555
(646) 855-5378 .. **Jones,** Trent M '02 Bk of Amer Client Integration Grp -1 Bryant Park -NY 10036
(518) 274-5820 .. **Jones,** W Farley '83 -28 2nd -Troy 12181 **Fx:**274-5875
(212) 876-5500 .. **Jones,** Walter Patrick '88 %Neighborhood Def Srv -317 Lenox Av -NY 10027 **Fx:**876-5586
(585) 394-2665 .. **Jones,** Walter W Jr. '73 (Croucher J&J) -70 S Main -Canandaigua 14424
(518) 373-0333 .. **Jones Wilcenski & Pleat PLLC** -5 Emma Ln -Clifton Pk 12065 **Fx:**383-6773
(718) 222-8880 .. **Jones,** Wm S '87 (Jones JO) -45 Main -Brklyn 11201
(212) 312-2356 .. **Jones,** Willie E '81 %Leg Aid -60 Lafayette -NY 10013 **Fx:**349-0874
(212) 527-1000 .. **Jones,** Winfield P '67 (Jones HC&B PC) -1 Bttry Pk Plz -NY 10004
(718) 780-0626 .. **Jones Sculli,** Julie '03 %Bklyn Law Schl -250 Joralemon -Brklyn 11201 **Fx:**780-7548
(212) 474-1000 .. **Jong,** Susan K '05 %Cravath S&M LLP -825 8th Av -NY 10019
(585) 247-9170 .. **Jong,** Tracy P '94 -2775 Buffalo Rd -Rchstr 14624 **Fx:**247-9171
(212) 474-1000 .. **Jonnalagadda,** Megha '09 %Cravath S&M LLP -825 8th Av -NY 10019
(212) 545-0322 .. **Jonnalagadda,** Srinivasa R '97 -1270 Bway -NY 10001 **Fx:**545-0323
(585) 987-2800 .. **Jonsson,** Kristin S '07 %Woods OG LLP -2 State -Rchstr 14614
(212) 297-0503 .. **Jonusas,** Natalia M '09 %Segal & G LLP -179 Franklin -NY 10013 **Fx:**297-0572
(212) 447-1600 .. **Joo,** Chan-Yun '99 -303 5th Av -NY 10016 **Fx:**447-0324
(212) 903-9000 .. **Joo,** David S '10 %Linklaters -1345 Av of Amer -NY 10105
(212) 626-4100 .. **Joo,** Seunghee Lucy '07 %Baker & M LLP -1114 Av of Amer -NY 10036
(212) 837-6000 .. **Joosten,** Jan J H '94 (Hughes H&R LLP) -1 Bttry Pk Plz -NY 10004
(718) 482-4900 .. **Joplin,** Megan J '05 %DEC -1 Hunters Pnt Plz -LIC 11101 **Fx:**482-4962
(212) 351-4000 .. **Joralemon,** Christopher M '98 (Gibson D&C LLP) -200 Park Av -NY 10166
(845) 602-4669 .. **Joran,** A David '97 Pfizer,Inc -401 N Mddltwn Rd -Pearl Rvr 10965
(718) 237-2000 .. **Jordan,** Allison P '06 %Leg Aid -111 Lvngstn -Brklyn 11201 **Fx:**237-8737
(716) 564-3288 .. **Jordan,** Amanda R '06 %K Hiller -2001 Niagara Flls Blvd -Amherst 14228 **Fx:**564-3291
(315) 379-2115 .. **Jordan,** Anthony '06 Pub Def -Cnty Cthse -Canton 13617 **Fx:**386-8241
(212) 553-5662 .. **Jordan,** Bryan T '97 Zurich Ins Co -1 Lbrty Plz -NY 10006
(914) 813-5648 .. **Jordan,** Carol A '89 %Family Ct -420 North Av -New Rchll 10801
(315) 474-2644 .. **Jordan,** Casey E '88 (Rose & J) -300 S State -Syracuse 13202
(212) 635-1517 .. **Jordan,** Catherine A '81 Bk of NY Mellon -1 Wall -NY 10286
(212) 599-1300 .. **Jordan,** Chas V '78 %Lex Terrae Ltd -331 Mad Av -NY 10017 **Fx:**983-2791
(212) 661-8000 .. **Jordan,** Christina M '08 %Lucas & M,LLP -475 Park Av S -NY 10016
(212) 488-1598 .. **Jordan,** Deborah Peters '05 %Havkins RR&V,LLP -11 Penn Plz -NY 10001
(212) 417-4145 .. **Jordan,** Emily B '04 Medicaid Insp Gen -217 Bway -NY 10007
(212) 566-2294 .. **Jordan,** Eunice C '90 -225 Bway -NY 10007
(212) 986-2340 .. **Jordan,** Frank J '61 (Jordan & H) -122 E 42nd -NY 10168
(212) 986-2340 .. **Jordan & Hamburg** -122 E 42nd -NY 10168 **Fx:**953-7733
(212) 230-8800 .. **Jordan,** Heather C P '04 %WilmerHale -399 Park Av -NY 10022
(518) 692-9441 .. **Jordan,** J Anthony '97 (Jordan & K LLC) -4 Fisher -Greenwich 12834 **Fx:**692-1222
(212) 938-1080 .. **Jordan,** Jennifer M '03 %Conway & C -1700 Bway -NY 10019 **Fx:**938-1207
(716) 842-2558 .. **Jordan,** John K '91 -227 Niagara -Buffalo 14201 **Fx:**842-2580
(585) 325-5150 .. **Jordan,** Julie S '05 %Faraci L,LLP -28 E Main -Rchstr 14614
(212) 425-7200 .. **Jordan,** Kevin B '09 %Kenyon & K,LLP -1 Bway -NY 10004
(914) 945-3255 .. **Jordan,** Kevin M '95 IBM Intellectual Prop -Bx218 -Yorktwn Hts 10598 **Fx:**241-4038
(212) 492-5909 .. **Jordan,** Kristin L '98 Kaplan Inc -888 7th Av -NY 10106
(914) 323-7000 .. **Jordan,** Laura B '94 (Wilson EME&D LLP) -3 Gannett Dr -White Plns 10604
(518) 465-5995 .. **Jordan,** Laura M '04 %Powers & S,LLP -39 N Pearl -Albany 12207
(212) 351-4500 .. **Jordan,** Lori A '03 %Epstein B&G,PC -250 Park Av -NY 10177
(212) 833-7795 .. **Jordan,** Marc A '96 Rebel-One -142 W 5th -NY 10019
(518) 943-7775 .. **Jordan,** Mark S '93 (Jordan & D) -277 Main -Catskill 12414 **Fx:**943-7177
(212) 857-2152 .. **Jordan,** Michl D '03 %Hon D Jacobs-US Ct Appls -500 Pearl -NY 10007
(845) 339-6860 .. **Jordan,** Michl F '82 (Findholt & J) -204 Fair Bx4120 -Kingston 12402 **Fx:**339-7063
(212) 450-4000 .. **Jordan,** Nora M '84 (Davis P&W LLP) -450 Lex Av -NY 10017
(212) 732-1933 .. **Jordan,** P Conrad '87 -233 Bway -NY 10279
(718) 261-3047 .. **Jordan,** Pamela '81 %Queens Law Assoc -118-21 Qns Blvd -Frst Hlls 11375 **Fx:**261-0798
(631) 853-4049 .. **Jordan,** Patricia '91 %Cnty Atty -Dennison Bldg Bx6100 -Hauppauge 11788 **Fx:**853-5169
(518) 434-5050 .. **Jordan,** Patrick K '03 Law Dept -106 City Hall -Albany 12207 **Fx:**434-5070
(212) 916-4241 .. **Jordan,** Peter M '66 %TIAA-CREF -730 3rd Av -NY 10017
(516) 739-0000 .. **Jordan,** Phillip A Jr. '78 %Martyn T&M -330 Old Cntry Rd -Mineola 11501
(212) 559-4771 .. **Jordan,** R Duff '88 -425 Park Av -NY 10022
(212) 888-5222 .. **Jordan,** Robt F '05 %Third Av Mgmt LLC -622 3rd Av -NY 10017
(212) 836-8000 .. **Jordan,** Silvia '07 %Kaye S LLP -425 Park Av -NY 10022

(516) 294-5200 .. **Jordan,** Stephen D '88 %Picciano & S -900 Merchants Cncrs -Westbury 11590
(212) 872-1000 .. **Jordan,** Stephen M '01 -One Bryant Park -NY 10036 **Fx:**872-1002
(518) 464-9003 .. **Jordan,** Thos J '85 -4 Pine West Plz -Albany 12205 **Fx:**464-9340
(212) 972-6161 .. **Jordan,** Toni S '98 (Cassin & C LLP) -711 3rd Av -NY 10017
(212) 698-7000 .. **Jordan,** Veronica '93 %Simon & Schuster -1230 Av of Amer -NY 10020 **Fx:**698-7171
(914) 961-8411 .. **Jordan,** Wayne P '78 -9 Tanglewylde Av -Bronxvll 10708 **Fx:**961-0044
(212) 455-2000 .. **Jordan,** Whitney J '09 %Simpson T&B LLP -425 Lex Av -NY 10017
(516) 783-8508 .. **Jordan,** Wm '76 -55 Grdn Blvd -Hicksvll 11801
(212) 227-3365 .. **Jorgensen,** Jeremy L '09 %Law Dept -100 Church -NY 10007 **Fx:**788-0367
(631) 376-1000 .. **Jorgensen,** Joy E '88 -500 W Main -Babylon 11702 **Fx:**893-7008
(516) 571-3800 .. **Jorgenson,** Wm H '91 %DA -262 Old Cntry Rd -Mineola 11501 **Fx:**248-9479
(212) 876-5500 .. **Jorif-Mangane,** Darlene M '94 Neighborhood Def Srv -317 Lenox Av -NY 10027 **Fx:**876-5586
(516) 466-1986 .. **Jorisch,** Bertram M '91 -366 N Bway -Jericho 11753
(212) 506-2500 .. **Jorissen,** Paul A '03 (Mayer B LLP) -1675 Bway -NY 10019
(212) 715-1000 .. **Jorns,** Amalia Wylder '06 %Arnold & P LLP -399 Park Av -NY 10022
(914) 234-4720 .. **Jorquera,** Sarah V '90 (Kulowiec & J,LLP) -460 Old Post Rd -Bedfrd 10506 **Fx:**234-7210
(716) 204-9480 .. **Jose,** Dennis '05 %SJ Baum,PC -900 Merchants Cncrs -Westbury 11590 **Fx:**204-9680
(212) 577-7700 .. **Jose,** Mary '03 %Safe Horizon -2 Lafayette -NY 10007 **Fx:**385-0331
(845) 791-7800 .. **Jose-Decker,** E Danielle '00 (Ricciani & J,LLP) -17 St John -Monticello 12701 **Fx:**791-5923
(315) 637-5151 .. **Josef,** Franklin A '66 (F Josef,PC) -519 E Genesee -Fayettevll 13066 **Fx:**637-3436
(716) 856-4000 .. **Joseffer,** Alice A '84 (Hodgson R LLP) -140 Pearl -Buffalo 14202
(212) 542-9615 .. **Josefowicz,** Barbara G '72 %Grant Thornton LLP -666 3rd Av -NY 10017 **Fx:**370-4520
(212) 554-1400 .. **Josefson,** Avi '03 SrCnsl Bernstein LB&G LLP -1285 Av of Amer -NY 10019
(212) 837-6448 .. **Josel,** Wayne M '93 Cnsl Hughes H&R LLP -1 Bttry Pk Plz -NY 10004 **Fx:**299-6448
(212) 474-1000 .. **Joseloff,** Benjamin G '09 %Cravath S&M LLP -825 8th Av -NY 10019
(914) 381-6250 .. **Joselson,** Henry C '86 OfCnsl Warner & S -5 Leatherstocking Ln -Mamaroneck 10543 **Fx:**381-6253
(212) 577-3688 .. **Joselson,** Richd '86 %Leg Aid -199 Water -NY 10038 **Fx:**509-8431
(212) 632-4630 .. **Josem,** Ellen D '81 JBFCS -120 W 57th -NY 10019 **Fx:**956-5676
(516) 496-5822 .. **Josen,** Mohina Kaur '93 %T Spina -170 Froehlich Farm Blvd -Woodbury 11797 **Fx:**496-5420
(914) 681-8700 .. **Joseph,** Aisha L '02 %Milber MP&S LLP -3 Barker Av -White Plns 10601
(718) 366-6418 .. **Joseph,** Alan H '66 -69-38 Myrtle Av -Glendale 11385
(845) 294-1100 .. **Joseph,** Alan L '80 -261 Greenwich Av -Goshen 10924 **Fx:**294-1447
(212) 248-3140 .. **Joseph,** Andrew B '93 (Drinker B&R LLP) -140 Bway -NY 10005
(212) 885-5000 .. **Joseph,** Carol M '85 (Blank R LLP) -405 Lex Av -NY 10174
(212) 897-1687 .. **Joseph,** Cassondra E '76 Integrated Mgmt Solutions -39 Bway -NY 10006 **Fx:**796-1531
(212) 688-5640 .. **Joseph,** Chas E '91 (Joseph & H LLP) -757 3rd Av -NY 10017
(212) 360-1417 .. **Joseph,** Cheryl C '04 Dept Parks & Rec -1234 5th Av -NY 10029
(718) 875-1300 .. **Joseph,** Darrell M '87 %Applt Div 2nd Dept -45 Monroe Pl -Brklyn 11201 **Fx:**858-2446
(212) 610-2822 .. **Joseph,** Elliott '81 Property Marketing Grp -5 E 17th -NY 10003
(201) 567-6288 .. **Joseph & Feldman** -711 3rd Av -NY 10017 **Fx:**567-0709
(718) 403-3600 .. **Joseph,** Frances R '00 Dept of Finance -345 Adams -Brklyn 11201 **Fx:**403-3650
(716) 626-5200 .. **Joseph,** Gary A '83 (Sarles F&J) -5800 Main -Williamsvll 14221
(212) 407-1200 .. **Joseph,** Gregory P '75 -485 Lex Av -NY 10017 **Fx:**407-1299
(347) 404-9133 .. **Joseph,** Henry J '96 %Civil Ct -141 Lvngstn -Brklyn 11201 **Fx:**(718) 643-3733
(212) 688-5640 .. **Joseph & Herzfeld LLP** -757 3rd Av -NY 10017 **Fx:**688-2548
(516) 496-0202 .. **Joseph,** James N '93 (Joseph & T,LLP) -2 Roosevelt Av -Syosset 11791 **Fx:**921-7785
(516) 542-2000 .. **Joseph,** James P '94 (JP Joseph & Assoc) -666 Old Cntry Rd -Gdn Cty 11530 **Fx:**542-2001
(718) 694-3831 .. **Joseph,** Jamila E '03 %Transit Auth -130 Lvngstn -Brklyn 11201 **Fx:**694-5726
(914) 948-1300 .. **Joseph,** Jeffrey F '67 -180 S Bway -White Plns 10605
(212) 735-3000 .. **Joseph,** Jillian E '06 %Skadden ASM&F LLP -4 Times Sq -NY 10036
(914) 686-0140 .. **Joseph,** Joy S '86 -399 Knollwood Rd -White Plns 10603
(201) 567-6288 .. **Joseph,** Judith '79 (Joseph & F) -711 3rd Av -NY 10017
(212) 336-0097 .. **Joseph,** Ken C '01 %SEC -3 World Fncl Ctr -NY 10281 **Fx:**336-1323
(518) 432-1200 .. **Joseph,** Kevin C '05 %McGlinchey S PLLC -194 Wshngtn Av -Albany 12210
(718) 261-3047 .. **Joseph,** Kirlyn H '91 Queens Law Assoc -118-21 Qns Blvd -Frst Hlls 11375 **Fx:**261-0798
(718) 990-6014 .. **Joseph,** Lawr '82 %St John's Law Schl -8000 Utopia Pkwy -Jamaica 11439 **Fx:**591-1855
(212) 259-8000 .. **Joseph,** Leonard '49 OfCnsl Dewey & L LLP -1301 Av of Amer -NY 10019
(212) 416-6142 .. **Joseph,** Linda D '91 %Dept of Law -120 Bway -NY 10271 **Fx:**416-6147
(716) 881-4900 .. **Joseph,** Linda H '76 (Schröder J & Assoc) -766 Ellicott -Buffalo 14203
(201) 567-6288 .. **Joseph,** Marc '50 (Joseph & F) -711 3rd Av -NY 10017
(212) 625-9949 .. **Joseph,** Mario Alex '97 (Joseph & S,LLC) -2 Rector -NY 10006
(347) 404-9929 .. **Joseph,** Martine N '08 %MHLS -120 Schermerhorn -Brklyn 11201 **Fx:**(718) 243-2408
(212) 644-4420 .. **Joseph,** Mary J '98 %Fabiani C&H,LLP -570 Lex Av -NY 10022
(917) 777-4200 .. **Joseph,** Matthew P '95 (Bingham M LLP) -1 Bttry Pk Plz -NY 10004
(914) 761-3168 .. **Joseph,** Michl H '00 M Joseph, PLLC -184 Martine Av -White Plns 10601 **Fx:**761-8076
(212) 964-2500 .. **Joseph,** Michl P '72 (Kliegerman & J LLP) -2 Rector -NY 10006 **Fx:**587-0075
(212) 233-3060 .. **Joseph,** Narissa A '03 -277 Bway -NY 10007 **Fx:**608-0304
(212) 849-7000 .. **Joseph,** Nicholas F '04 %Quinn EU&S,LLP -51 Mad Av -NY 10010
(212) 261-7000 .. **Joseph,** Nicole E '02 %Calyon -1301 Av of Amer -NY 10019
(845) 638-3333 .. **Joseph,** Peter A '74 OfCnsl Isaacson & J -130 N Main -New Cty 10956 **Fx:**634-2807
(212) 705-7000 .. **Joseph,** Roger P '77 (Bingham M LLP) -399 Park Av -NY 10022
(212) 238-4800 .. **Joseph,** Ronald E '84 (Landman CB&F,PC) -120 Bway -NY 10271
(212) 863-7173 .. **Joseph,** Ronit Benezry '99 %HPD -100 Gold -NY 10038
(212) 480-7441 .. **Joseph,** Sandra A '05 DHCR -25 Beaver -NY 10004 **Fx:**480-7416
(212) 349-3000 .. **Joseph,** Serge '92 (Himmelstein MGD&J) -15 Maiden Ln -NY 10038
(212) 625-9949 .. **Joseph & Smargiassi,LLC** -2 Rector -NY 10006 **Fx:**625-9193
(212) 754-3086 .. **Joseph,** Stephanie R '71 %The Director's Network -241 Cntrl Pk W -NY 10024 **Fx:**754-3087
(716) 856-4000 .. **Joseph,** Todd M '75 (Hodgson R LLP) -140 Pearl -Buffalo 14202
(718) 977-4132 .. **Joseph,** Vivia L '99 -229-22 Linden Blvd -Cambria Hts 11411 **Fx:**977-4587
(212) 233-2100 .. **Josepher,** Myron J '60 (Oshman & M,LLP) -42 Bway -NY 10004
(212) 644-5712 .. **Josephs,** Bonnie P '66 -1776 Bway -NY 10019 **Fx:**838-9534
(212) 436-1000 .. **Josephs,** Cheryl A '07 IRS -290 Bway -NY 10007
(631) 751-5456 .. **Josephs,** Gary S '74 -60 Route 25A -Setauket 11733 **Fx:**751-5677
(315) 443-9573 .. **Josephs,** Hilary K '80 %Syracuse Univ Cllg of Law -Wht Hall -Syracuse 13244 **Fx:**443-4213
(914) 749-8200 .. **Josephs,** Laurie R '82 Cnsl Boies S&F LLP -333 Main -Armonk 10504
(212) 880-3809 .. **Josephs,** Lori S '83 Philip Morris Mgt Corp -120 Park Av -NY 10017
(646) 471-1583 .. **Josephs,** Michl H '91 %PricewaterhouseCoopers LLP -300 Mad Av -NY 10017 **Fx:**(212) 259-1334
(718) 490-9970 .. **Josephs,** Michl I '78 -68-37 Yllwstn Blvd -Frst Hlls 11375 **Fx:**255-6274
(212) 661-1151 .. **Josephs,** Paul B '98 %Marin G LLP -40 Wall -NY 10005
(212) 596-9000 .. **Josephsen,** Jared R '10 %Ropes & G LLP -1211 Av of Amer -NY 10036
(631) 324-3288 .. **Josephson,** Celia M '88 -2 Dune Alpin Dr N -E Hampton 11937 **Fx:**324-3288
(718) 237-5500 .. **Josephson,** Edw J '89 %Leg Srvcs -105 Court -Brklyn 11201 **Fx:**855-0733
(212) 906-1713 .. **Josephson,** Gregg D '99 -885 3rd Av -NY 10022
(212) 496-0533 .. **Josephson,** Jessica J '84 -365 West End Av -NY 10024
(212) 644-2100 .. **Josephson,** Mark A '99 -425 Mad Av -NY 10017 **Fx:**644-9802
(516) 343-0090 .. **Josephson,** Maury B '86 -626 Reckson Plz -Uniondale 11556
(516) 521-7433 .. **Josephson,** Roy H '58 -43 Morris Av W -Malverne 11565
(212) 859-8220 .. **Josephson,** Wm H '56 OfCnsl Fried FHS&J LLP -1 NY Plz -NY 10004 **Fx:**859-8582
(718) 618-3662 .. **Joseph Varlack,** Camille M '04 Supreme Ct -265 E 161st -Bronx 10451
(212) 756-2000 .. **Joshi,** Atul '99 %Schulte R&Z LLP -919 3rd Av -NY 10022
(212) 735-3000 .. **Joshi,** Mahesh M '04 %Skadden ASM&F LLP -4 Times Sq -NY 10036
(212) 442-8750 .. **Joshi,** Meera '96 %CCRB -40 Rector -NY 10006 **Fx:**442-8800
(212) 684-3630 .. **Joslin,** Christopher S '94 OfCnsl D Horowitz,PC -276 5th Av -NY 10001 **Fx:**685-8617
(631) 465-2071 .. **Joslin,** Lana E '94 -68 S Srvc Rd -Melvll 11747 **Fx:**465-2072
(518) 432-7511 .. **Joslin,** Lisa Ferro '98 (Gleason DW&O) -40 Beaver -Albany 12207
(518) 465-0400 .. **Joslin,** Peter B Jr. '98 (O'Connor OB&F,PC) -20 Corp Wds Blvd -Albany 12211
(917) 778-6079 .. **Joslyn,** Jason D '02 St Paul Travelers -485 Lex Av -NY 10017
(646) 562-3405 .. **Josma Nazaire,** Erlyne '00 %PLC -747 3rd Av -NY 10017
(914) 767-6000 .. **Joss,** Marisa '92 Pepsi Bottling Grp -1 Pepsi Way -Somers 10589
(212) 635-1126 .. **Josselsohn,** Bennett E '85 Bk of NY Mellon -1 Wall -NY 10286 **Fx:**635-1999
(212) 574-1200 .. **Josselson,** Benay L '06 %Seward & K LLP -1 Bttry Pk Plz -NY 10004
(212) 902-3761 .. **Josselyn,** Kenneth L '81 %Goldman Sachs -1 NY Plz -NY 10004
(212) 698-3500 .. **Jossen,** Robt J '73 (Dechert LLP) -1095 Av of Amer -NY 10036
(212) 859-8000 .. **Jost,** Zachary P '06 %Fried FHS&J LLP -1 NY Plz -NY 10004
(845) 425-8871 .. **Jotkowitz,** Tirtza R '95 %SSA -19 Nelson Rd -Monsey 10952 **Fx:**426-5088
(212) 943-9000 .. **Jou,** Chi-Ru '06 %Dewey P&K LLP -220 E 42nd -NY 10017
(212) 530-5000 .. **Jou,** Jacob K '10 %Milbank TH&M LLP -1 Chase Manh Plz -NY 10005
(212) 876-5500 .. **Joubin,** Cyrus '07 Neighborhood Def Srv -317 Lenox Av -NY 10027 **Fx:**876-5586
(518) 399-2141 .. **Jourdanais,** Tatha R '04 Jourdanais Law Firm,PC -763 Saratoga Rd -Burnt Hlls 12027 **Fx:**384-1781
(212) 506-1700 .. **Jouvin,** Zoe Synthia '07 Kasowitz BT&F LLP -1633 Bway -NY 10019
(315) 445-7963 .. **Joy,** Kathleen '87 Bankers Title & Abstract LLC -5010 Campuswood Dr -E Syracuse 13057
(212) 373-3000 .. **Joy,** Kripa M '10 Paul WRW&G LLP -1285 Av of Amer -NY 10019
(212) 417-8700 .. **Joy,** Leonard F '56 %Fed Def of NY Inc -52 Duane -NY 10007 **Fx:**571-0392
(212) 431-5757 .. **Joy,** Mark '91 (Lutwin & J) -401 Bway -NY 10013 **Fx:**431-5759
(212) 335-9000 .. **Joy,** Megan E '04 %DA -1 Hogan Pl -NY 10013
(716) 633-3200 .. **Joy,** Michl P '03 (Lipman B&J,LLP) -333 Intl Dr -Williamsvll 14221
(212) 450-4000 .. **Joy,** Sarah '10 %Davis P&W LLP -450 Lex Av -NY 10017
(315) 475-2559 .. **Joyal,** Thane '01 -716 E Wshngtn -Syracuse 13210
(212) 536-3900 .. **Joyce,** Allison C '08 %K&L Gates LLP -599 Lex Av -NY 10022
(516) 832-9100 .. **Joyce,** Amy '98 %Schaeffer & Sam PC -1232 RXR Plz -Uniondale 11556
(518) 447-2510 .. **Joyce,** Amy E '98 %Hon M Lynch -112 State -Albany 12207 **Fx:**447-7181
(716) 856-0600 .. **Joyce,** Brenda J '87 (Jaeckle F&M,LLP) -12 Fountain Plz -Buffalo 14202
(518) 564-4038 .. **Joyce,** Catherine M '95 %Ctr for Earth & Env Sci SUNY -101 Broad -Plattsbrgh 12901 **Fx:**564-5267
(716) 856-0600 .. **Joyce,** Danl P '87 (Jaeckle F&M,LLP) -12 Fountain Plz -Buffalo 14202
(212) 819-8200 .. **Joyce,** David E '82 (White & C LLP) -1155 Av of Amer -NY 10036

(212) 839-5300 ..**Joyce,** Eamon P '03 %Sidley A LLP -787 7th Av -NY 10019
(212) 326-3939 ..**Joyce,** Edw M '87 (Jones D) -222 E 41st -NY 10017
(212) 525-2400 ..**Joyce,** Gerard F Jr. '83 %HSBC Bank -452 5th Av -NY 10018
(212) 581-3320 ..**Joyce,** James L '89 %Wasserman G&R,LLP -1700 Bway -NY 10019
(212) 541-2000 ..**Joyce,** Janet M '85 %Bryan C LLP -1290 Av of Amer -NY 10104
(646) 386-4800 ..**Joyce,** Jean M '97 %Comm Judicial Cndct -61 Bway -NY 10006 **Fx:**458-0037
(212) 669-5100 ..**Joyce,** John A '99 %Standard Credit -75 Park Pl -NY 10007
(212) 696-6000 ..**Joyce,** Josh M '10 %Curtis M-PC&M LLP -101 Park Av -NY 10178
(716) 645-3041 ..**Joyce,** Kenneth F '75 %SUNY Buffalo Lw Schl -O'Brian Hall -Buffalo 14260 **Fx:**645-5968
(631) 859-1900 ..**Joyce,** Kim Brennan '90 -130 W Main -E Islip 11730 **Fx:**859-9233
(212) 312-3000 ..**Joyce,** Martin R '85 %FGIC -125 Park Av -NY 10017 **Fx:**312-3221
(718) 928-3700 ..**Joyce,** Maryanne J '00 %LSNYC-Bronx -579 Courtlandt Av -Bronx 10451 **Fx:**402-7586
(212) 707-3054 ..**Joyce,** Megan K '05 Atlantic Recording Corp -1290 Av of Amer -NY 10104
(212) 285-2299 ..**Joyce,** Patrick J '84 -70 Lafayette -NY 10013 **Fx:**513-1989
(716) 853-4080 ..**Joyce,** Paul G '01 %Colucci & G,PC -424 Main -Buffalo 14202
(914) 417-3400 ..**Joyce,** Robt L '86 (Littleton JUP&K LLP) -1 Manhattanvll Rd -Purchase 10577
(212) 455-9255 ..**Joyce,** Rosemary P '04 %Rao & T LLP -90 Park Av -NY 10016 **Fx:**297-0005
(607) 674-4770 ..**Joyce,** Stephen P '81 (Joyce & H) -26 N Main Bx705 -Sherburne 13460 **Fx:**674-5415
(607) 432-0525 ..**Joyce,** Stephen P '81 -129 Oneida -Oneonta 13820
(315) 738-0879 ..**Joyce,** Stephen P '81 -107 Genesee -New Hartfrd 13413
(631) 283-8456 ..**Joyce,** Thos W E Jr. '63 -668 Hill Bx1414 -Southampton 11969
(914) 949-2700 ..**Joyce,** Timothy J '75 OfCnsl Bleakley P&S,LLP -1 N Lex Av -White Plns 10601
(212) 313-3600 ..**Joyce,** Wm D III '96 (Barry M&M) -2 Rector -NY 10006
(212) 374-6888 ..**Joyce,** Wm R '85 NYC Dept Educ-OLS -52 Chmbrs -NY 10007 **Fx:**374-5596
(212) 530-5000 ..**Joyce-Schleimer,** Jared E '09 %Milbank TH&M LLP -1 Chase Manh Plz -NY 10005
(212) 640-3172 ..**Joyner,** Lauren C '93 %Amer Exp -200 Vesey -NY 10285
(914) 730-9223 ..**Joyner,** Lovetts '96 -244 5th Av -NY 10001
(716) 849-0701 ..**Joynt,** Anne E '06 %Lipsitz & P LLC -135 Delaware Av -Buffalo 14202
(585) 381-3290 ..**Joynt,** Margaret M '76 -32 Sandpiper Ln -Pittsfrd 14534
(631) 421-0993 ..**Jozwicki,** Edw M '65 -44 Old Town Ln -Huntngtn 11743
(212) 225-2000 ..**Ju,** Jung Whan '08 %Cleary GS&H -1 Lbrty Plz -NY 10006
(212) 756-2000 ..**Ju,** Lisa N '07 %Schulte R&Z LLP -919 3rd Av -NY 10022
(212) 225-2000 ..**Juantorena,** Jorge U '94 (Cleary GS&H) -1 Lbrty Plz -NY 10006
(212) 937-7205 ..**Juarez,** Orlando F '07 %WilmerHale -399 Park Av -NY 10022
(716) 858-2424 ..**Juarez,** René '10 %DA -25 Delaware Av -Buffalo 14202 **Fx:**858-7425
(212) 733-1092 ..**Juarez,** Zaira E '01 Pfizer Inc -150 E 42nd -NY 10017
(212) 504-6000 ..**Jubin,** Gregg S '93 (Cadwalader W&T LLP) -1 World Fncl Ctr -NY 10281
(212) 859-8000 ..**Juceam,** Robt E '65 OfCnsl Fried FHS&J LLP -1 NY Plz -NY 10004
(518) 377-3077 ..**Juda,** Mark A '93 -115 Clinton -Schnctdy 12305 **Fx:**377-7928
(716) 842-6230 ..**Juda,** Richd S Jr. '84 -37 Franklin -Buffalo 14202 **Fx:**842-6205
(212) 267-9020 ..**Judd,** Jeffrey M '90 (Shapiro B&A LLP) -225 Bway -NY 10007
(212) 488-1598 ..**Judd,** Jonathan A '90 (Havkins RR&V,LLP) -11 Penn Plz -NY 10001
(518) 761-6350 ..**Judd,** Karen L '96 Cnsl Dept of Social Srvcs -1340 State Route 9 -Lk George 12845 **Fx:**761-6314
(631) 283-9696 ..**Judd,** Kimberly A '97 %Bennett & R -212 Windmill Ln -Southampton 11968
(516) 294-7301 ..**Judd,** Meaghan '97 %D Smith -500 Old Cntry Rd -Gdn Cty 11530 **Fx:**393-7594
(631) 981-9110 ..**Judd,** Stephanie '87 (Judd & M,PC) -3505 Vets Mem'l Hwy -Ronkonkoma 11779 **Fx:**981-9004
(607) 547-7585 ..**Judd,** Stephen H '81 OCA-6th Jud Dist -197 Main -Cooperstwn 13326 **Fx:**547-7582
(212) 850-2800 ..**Judell,** Lynn E '89 (Andrews K LLP) -450 Lex Av -NY 10017
(845) 695-2002 ..**Judelson,** Chas A '68 (Bull MJ&D,PC) -90 Crystal Run Rd -Middletwn 10941
(718) 255-5610 ..**Judelson,** Steven M '86 Judelson Dvlpmnt Grp Ltd -79 Alxndr Av -Bronx 10454 **Fx:**585-5211
(518) 886-4118 ..**Judge,** Chas W '99 AYCO -321 Bway Bx860 -Saratoga Spgs 12866
(518) 745-5030 ..**Judge & Duffy** -1 Broad Street Plz Bx2850 -Glens Fls 12801 **Fx:**745-5029
(518) 745-5030 ..**Judge,** H Wayne '64 (Judge & D) -1 Broad Street Plz Bx2850 -Glens Fls 12801
(212) 921-2200 ..**Judge,** Kiran B '04 Update Legal -1140 Av of Amer -NY 10036
(718) 875-5802 ..**Judge,** Robt E '92 -44 Court -Brklyn 11201
(315) 451-3810 ..**Judge,** Steven C '07 %O'Hara O&C,PC -7207 E Genesee -Fayettevll 13066
(516) 944-3637 ..**Judge,** Thos E Jr. '71 (Judge & Assoc) -74 Juniper Rd -Pt Wash 11050 **Fx:**570-2417
(212) 880-6000 ..**Judovits,** Mayah Y '03 %Torys LLP -237 Park Av -NY 10017
(914) 725-0300 ..**Judy Miller & O'Connor,PC** -700 Wht Plns Rd -Scarsdale 10583 **Fx:**725-8215
(917) 637-3600 ..**Jueds,** Victoria Howard '02 %Ctr for Reproductive Rts -120 Wall -NY 10005 **Fx:**637-3666
(631) 738-0505 ..**Juengst,** Jennifer A '91 (Gordon & J,PC) -1785 Express Dr N -Hauppauge 11788
(212) 762-4649 ..**Juergens,** Benjamin J '09 Morgan Stanley -1221 Av of Amer -NY 10020
(585) 392-2161 ..**Juergens,** David R '84 -32 South Av -Hilton 14468
(585) 392-2161 ..**Juergens,** Risa R '85 -32 South Av -Hilton 14468
(212) 438-5638 ..**Juette,** Nancy A '01 Standard & Poor's -55 Water -NY 10041
(914) 693-0941 ..**Juettner,** Diana D '84 -598 Ashford Av -Ardsley 10502 **Fx:**693-5986
(914) 693-0941 ..**Juettner,** Paul J '79 -598 Ashford Av -Ardsley 10502 **Fx:**693-5986
(212) 980-9600 ..**Juffa,** Laura Baldwin '07 %Kaufman B&R -120 Bway -NY 10271
(212) 761-7874 ..**Juhas,** Peter L '98 Morgan Stanley -1585 Bway -NY 10036
(212) 270-5907 ..**Juhase,** Kathleen A '82 JP Morgan Chase & Co -270 Park Av -NY 10017
(516) 569-3030 ..**Juhase,** Kim Steven '78 (Novak J&S) -483 Chestnut -Cedarhrst 11516
(212) 233-0130 ..**Juidiciani,** Jos A '06 %Nelson Ld&H -120 Bway -NY 10271
(212) 335-9000 ..**Jujjavarapu,** Nagasilpa '07 DA -1 Hogan Pl -NY 10013
(516) 489-3340 ..**Julian,** Kathleen F '98 -954 Madison Pl -Merrick 11566 **Fx:**505-2666
(212) 735-3000 ..**Julian,** Peter S '83 Cnsl Skadden ASM&F LLP -4 Times Sq -NY 10036
(315) 733-2396 ..**Julian,** Robt F '76 (Brindisi MBPJ&P,LLP) -2713 Genesee -Utica 13501
(212) 973-2900 ..**Juliana,** Chas N '07 AECOM Tech Corp -605 3rd Av -NY 10158
(212) 218-7418 ..**Juliano,** Anthony '92 Dubai Investment Grp -45 Rckfllr Plz -NY 10111
(973) 228-5700 ..**Juliano,** Anthony M '00 %Brach E LLC -100 Park Av -NY 10017 **Fx:**228-7852
(631) 499-9300 ..**Juliano,** John L '70 SrCnsl J Juliano,PC -39 Doyle Ct -E Northprt 11731 **Fx:**462-2532
(631) 499-9300 ..**Juliano,** Jonathan C '98 -39 Doyle Ct -E Northprt 11731 **Fx:**462-2532
(516) 248-1047 ..**Juliano,** Jos '95 -1527 Franklin Av -Mineola 11501 **Fx:**248-1048
(212) 446-4247 ..**Juliano,** Michl J '08 %Gruss Asset Mgt LP -667 Mad Av -NY 10065
(716) 885-2889 ..**Juliano,** Peter T '04 %Eoannou L&D -484 Delaware Av -Buffalo 14202
(212) 808-7800 ..**Julie,** Douglas E '05 %Kelley D&W LLP -101 Park Av -NY 10178
(212) 687-1466 ..**Julie,** Franklin H '88 (Koppel KJ LLP) -551 5th Av -NY 10176
(212) 331-5987 ..**Julien,** Christine '09 NYC HR Admin -180 Water -NY 10038
(212) 221-7575 ..**Julien,** Jay '46 -1501 Bway -NY 10036 **Fx:**221-7386
(718) 595-6516 ..**Julien,** Roseann C '05 DEP -59-17 Junction Blvd -Flushng 11373 **Fx:**595-6543
(212) 962-8020 ..**Julien & Schlesinger,PC** -1 Whitehall -NY 10004
(609) 475-5745 ..**Julio,** Jeffrey R '09 -1087 Flushing Av -Brklyn 11237
(516) 741-8200 ..**Julius,** Martin C '70 -200 Willis Av -Mineola 11501 **Fx:**741-9415
(212) 849-7000 ..**Juman,** Robt C '96 (Quinn EU&S,LLP) -51 Mad Av -NY 10010
(212) 344-1500 ..**Jump,** Alice Keeney '83 %Smith C,LLP -110 Wall -NY 10005
(914) 741-6100 ..**Jumper,** Aisling A '09 %Kaufman B&R -200 Summit Lk Dr -Valhalla 10595
(212) 859-8000 ..**Jun,** Eun Seo '10 %Fried FHS&J LLP -1 NY Plz -NY 10004
(212) 841-3020 ..**Jun,** Jason J '03 BNP Paaribas -787 7th Av -NY 10019
(212) 279-5442 ..**Jun,** Soohyun '03 -45 W 34th -NY 10001
(716) 836-1500 ..**Juncewicz,** Nina F '97 (N Juncewicz,PC) -1645 Hertel Av -Buffalo 14216 **Fx:**836-1516
(212) 735-3000 ..**Junck,** Ryan D '04 %Skadden ASM&F LLP -4 Times Sq -NY 10036
(212) 566-8487 ..**Juneau,** Ana M '90 -160 Bway -NY 10038 **Fx:**566-4749
(518) 447-3200 ..**Juneau,** David R '91 (McNamee LT&W,PC) -677 Bway -Albany 12207
(212) 244-6600 ..**Juneau,** Thos V Jr. '92 %Schechter & B,PC -350 5th Av -NY 10118
(212) 596-9000 ..**Jung,** Christine Y '09 %Ropes & G LLP -1211 Av of Amer -NY 10036
(212) 558-4000 ..**Jung,** Gina Jimi '03 %Sullivan & C LLP -125 Broad -NY 10004
(212) 848-4000 ..**Jung,** Gloria H '06 %Shearman & S LLP -599 Lex Av -NY 10022
(212) 481-0800 ..**Jung,** Hong Keun '97 Jung & Assoc,PC -470 Park Av S -NY 10016 **Fx:**481-0820
(646) 471-2853 ..**Jung,** Jennifer S '06 PricewaterhouseCoopers -300 Mad Av -NY 10017
(718) 349-5413 ..**Jung,** Michelle S '98 NYC Dept of Ed-DSF -44-36 Vernon Blvd -LIC 11101 **Fx:**610-0105
(212) 336-0479 ..**Jung,** Rhonda L '96 %SEC -3 World Fncl Ctr -NY 10281 **Fx:**336-1323
(718) 590-2000 ..**Jung,** Stephen H '08 %DA -198 E 161st -Bronx 10451 **Fx:**590-6477
(212) 633-2000 ..**Jung,** Veronica S '03 Korean Amer League -149 W 24th -NY 10011 **Fx:**633-0707
(212) 541-2000 ..**Jungblut,** Erika M '08 %Bryan C LLP -1290 Av of Amer -NY 10104
(718) 220-5430 ..**Junge,** Evelyn J '69 Wildlife Conservation Soc -2300 Southrn Blvd -Bronx 10460
(212) 269-0061 ..**Junge,** Peter A '74 (Junge & M,LLP) -250 W 57th -NY 10107 **Fx:**269-0515
(212) 813-8800 ..**Jungreis,** Rivka '09 %Goodwin P LLP -620 8th Av -NY 10018
(718) 250-2000 ..**Junior,** Nicole S '08 %DA -350 Jay -Brklyn 11201 **Fx:**250-2314
(646) 200-6300 ..**Junker,** Barry H '07 %Park & J LLP -630 3rd Av -NY 10017 **Fx:**200-6301
(212) 315-3755 ..**Juntikka,** Chas W '83 (C Juntikka & Assoc,LLP) -350 5th Av -NY 10118 **Fx:**315-9032
(212) 506-1700 ..**Juntunen,** Kristina R '04 %Kasowitz BT&F LLP -1633 Bway -NY 10019
(212) 455-2000 ..**Jupiter,** Dana A '10 %Simpson T&B LLP -425 Lex Av -NY 10017
(518) 457-1260 ..**Juracka-Maher,** Wendy A '91 %DCJS -4 Twr Pl -Albany 12203 **Fx:**457-3089
(718) 590-8555 ..**Jurado,** Enis L '98 %Borough Pres -851 Grnd Cncrs -Bronx 10451 **Fx:**590-2668
(212) 791-7646 ..**Jurakhan,** Nirmala '93 -299 Bway -NY 10007
(845) 339-4313 ..**Juran,** Brian '97 -654 Aaron Ct -Kingston 12401 **Fx:**340-9672
(212) 758-9700 ..**Juran,** Kevin A '84 %KPMG LLP -345 Park Av -NY 10154
(212) 972-3000 ..**Jureller,** John E Jr. '94 (Klestadt & W,LLP) -292 Mad Av -NY 10017
(518) 464-6770 ..**Jureller,** Paul D '93 (Thorn GT&B,LLP) -5 Wembley Ct Bx15054 -Albany 12212
(518) 463-2280 ..**Jurena,** Michl D '93 -817 Mad Av -Albany 12208 **Fx:**427-6720
(212) 504-6000 ..**Jurgens,** Jason '00 SpclCnsl Cadwalader W&T LLP -1 World Fncl Ctr -NY 10281
(212) 533-6300 ..**Jurgens,** John H '81 %NYSUT -52 Bway -NY 10004 **Fx:**995-2347
(631) 547-9646 ..**Jurgens,** Jos L III '01 %Ferrari & W,LLP -290 Broadhllw Rd -Melvll 11747
(212) 506-1700 ..**Jurgens,** Melonie S '01 %Kasowitz BT&F LLP -1633 Bway -NY 10019
(845) 223-5514 ..**Jurina,** Raymond P Jr. '73 -296 Waterbury Hill Rd -LaGrangevll 12540 **Fx:**223-3179
(212) 880-9475 ..**Juris,** Stephen M '99 (Morvillo AGIA&B,PC) -565 5th Av -NY 10017
(516) 781-4495 ..**Jurist,** Eric '73 MBR Asset Srvc,LLC -2864 Mandalay Beach Rd -Wantagh 11793
(516) 222-0500 ..**Jurist,** Howard C '77 (Goodman J&P,LLP) -1103 Stewart Av -Gdn Cty 11530
(914) 761-1300 ..**Jurist,** Kenneth F '78 (Cuddy & F LLP) -445 Hmltn Av -White Plns 10601

(212) 566-7188 .. **Jurista,** Michl J '09 %Genova B&G -115 Bway -NY 10006
(212) 272-3358 .. **Jurkowski,** Jos T Jr. '88 %JP Morgan Chase -383 Mad Av -NY 10179
(718) 454-1341 .. **Juron,** Albert A '51 -67-62 198th -Fresh Mdws 11365 **Fx:**454-1341
(716) 542-5413 .. **Juron,** Jason R '05 Nicholas PSB&Z -12364 Main Rd Bx176 -Akron 14001
(718) 595-2990 .. **Juron,** Marc B '85 -67-62 198th -Fresh Mdws 11365 **Fx:**454-1341
(631) 619-5251 .. **Jurow,** Bill Ian '79 -349 Cypress Dr -Mastic Bch 11951
(716) 858-2424 .. **Jurusik,** Christopher P '99 %DA -25 Delaware Av -Buffalo 14202 **Fx:**858-7425
(212) 421-2233 .. **Jury,** Hillary A '04 %Wilk A LLP -675 3rd Av -NY 10017
(631) 588-3155 .. **Jusino,** Phillip J '90 -2780 Middle Cntry Rd -Lk Grove 11755 **Fx:**588-0603
(212) 425-1900 .. **Juska,** Wm L Jr. '70 (Freehill H&M LLP) -80 Pine -NY 10005
(212) 953-1600 .. **Juste,** Isaiah '06 %S Rosenfeld,PC -777 3rd -NY 10017 **Fx:**953-1801
(212) 373-0627 .. **Juste,** Jerry A '95 %Universal Music Grp -1755 Bway -NY 10019
(212) 465-8840 .. **Juste,** Jessica '07 %Hofmann & S -360 W 31st -NY 10001 **Fx:**465-8849
(212) 371-2241 .. **Juster,** Chas P '82 World Wise -5 E 57th -NY 10022
(516) 746-8000 .. **Juster,** Holly '83 %Jaspan S LLP -300 Grdn City Plz -Gdn Cty 11530
(631) 853-4336 .. **Justesen,** Elizabeth A '07 Leg Aid -400 Carleton Av -Central Islip 11722
(718) 590-2000 .. **Justice,** Caroline M '10 %DA -198 E 161st -Bronx 10451 **Fx:**590-6477
(585) 467-6068 .. **Justice,** Douglas W '73 -3142 Cullver Rd -Rchstr 14622
(518) 462-7770 .. **Justice,** Heather N '04 %Daniels & P,LLP -119 Wshngtn Av -Albany 12210
(212) 759-2300 .. **Justice,** Jennifer L '97 Carroll G&G,LLP -1790 Bway -NY 10019
(518) 886-4221 .. **Justice,** John R '95 %AYCO -Bx860 -Saratoga Spgs 12866
(518) 434-8435 .. **Justice,** Lawr P '69 (Rice & J) -111 Wshngtn Av -Albany 12210
(212) 697-8500 .. **Justice,** Roy C '82 (Konner T&G) -462 7th Av -NY 10018
(516) 678-3885 .. **Justiz,** Jos E '72 (Land & J) -4029 Lng Bch Rd -Isl Pk 11558
(212) 415-1462 .. **Justvig,** Gerard '91 McKinsey & Co -55 E 52nd -NY 10055 **Fx:**688-9521
(212) 697-2310 .. **Justvig,** Howard '77 (Becker R LLP) -317 Mad Av -NY 10017
(212) 880-9580 .. **Juteau,** Jasmine M '04 %Morvillo AGIA&B,PC -565 5th Av -NY 10017
(212) 464-1654 .. **Juterbock,** Richd E '72 %JP Morgan Chase -345 Park Av -NY 10154
(212) 415-9200 .. **Jutsen,** Mark '99 (Dorsey & W LLP) -250 Park Av -NY 10177
(646) 282-1670 .. **Juvelier,** Martin D '66 (M Juvelier,PLLC) -470 Park Av S -NY 10016 **Fx:**282-1674
(212) 272-3008 .. **Ka,** Mimi M '95 %JP Morgan Chase -383 Mad Av -NY 10179
(212) 558-4000 .. **Kaal,** Amina M '06 %Sullivan & C LLP -125 Broad -NY 10004
(212) 667-4395 .. **Kaback,** Deborah '76 Oppenheimer Asset Mgt -200 Park Av -NY 10166
(212) 249-2404 .. **Kaback,** Hoffer '73 (H Kaback,PC) -233 E 69th -NY 10021 **Fx:**517-7433
(212) 586-5100 .. **Kabak,** Wayne S '78 %Wm Morris Agency -1325 Av of Amer -NY 10019 **Fx:**903-1473
(212) 450-4000 .. **Kabakov,** Loren Paige '98 Davis P&W LLP -450 Lex Av -NY 10017
(212) 735-3000 .. **Kabealo,** John P '08 %Skadden ASM&F LLP -4 Times Sq -NY 10036
(212) 788-3300 .. **Kabel,** Janice '85 %Hlth & Hsptl Corp -125 Worth -NY 10013 **Fx:**267-6905
(212) 284-7332 .. **Kabir,** Naveen '09 ACLU -125 Broad -NY 10004
(212) 799-0509 .. **Kable,** Edw E '65 Polo Ralph Lauren Corp -650 Mad Av -NY 10022
(212) 889-3700 .. **Kaboolian,** Nancy '90 (Abbey SR&A LLP) -212 E 39th -NY 10016
(914) 323-7000 .. **Kachadoorian,** James W '87 (Wilson EME&D LLP) -3 Gannett Dr -White Plns 10604
(607) 722-2270 .. **Kachadourian,** Mark '85 -209 Court -Bnghmtn 13901 **Fx:**722-0414
(914) 220-5324 .. **Kachalsky,** Alan N '81 -800 Wstchstr Av -Rye Brook 10573 **Fx:**696-0450
(212) 812-8910 .. **Kachmar,** Laryssa C '03 %Lankler & C,LLP -845 3rd Av -NY 10022
(212) 752-9700 .. **Kachnykewych,** Vera O '95 (Gersten S LLP) -600 Lex Av -NY 10022
(212) 262-2390 .. **Kachonick,** Laurie B '06 %Connell F LLP -888 7th Av -NY 10106
(716) 626-3429 .. **Kachur,** Tracy A '00 -300 Intl Dr -Williamsvll 14221 **Fx:**626-3001
(516) 571-3800 .. **Kaczmarek-Corrigan,** Teresa D '90 DA -262 Old Cntry Rd -Mineola 11501 **Fx:**248-9479
(716) 645-6429 .. **Kaczmarski,** Karen R '90 SUNY Buffalo Lw Schl -O'Brian Hall -Buffalo 14260 **Fx:**645-5968
(212) 458-3297 .. **Kaczor,** Phillip M '05 Amer Intl Underwriters -175 Water -NY 10038
(212) 636-6000 .. **Kaczorowski,** Robt J '83 %Fordham Univ Sch of Law -140 W 62nd -NY 10023 **Fx:**636-6899
(718) 875-6706 .. **Kadanoff,** Jacqueline F '94 (Kadanoff & K PC) -26 Court -Brklyn 11242 **Fx:**797-4600
(914) 422-8700 .. **Kadanoff,** Peri A '95 %OCTF -101 E Post Rd -White Plns 10601 **Fx:**422-8795
(718) 875-6706 .. **Kadanoff,** Philip G '62 (Kadanoff & K PC) -26 Court -Brklyn 11242 **Fx:**797-4600
(212) 661-1400 .. **Kadden,** Ronald S '71 (Von Maltitz DKJ&G) -60 E 42nd -NY 10017
(212) 752-6700 .. **Kaddour,** Nadia '01 %K MacCarthy Assoc -150 E 55th -NY 10022 **Fx:**319-7584
(212) 335-9000 .. **Kade,** Larken S '07 DA -1 Hogan Pl -NY 10013
(212) 578-2211 .. **Kaden,** Heather '02 %MetLife -27-01 Qns Plz N -LIC 11101
(212) 684-3900 .. **Kaden,** Jeffrey M '86 (Gottlieb R&R,PC) -270 Mad Av -NY 10016
(212) 793-8045 .. **Kaden,** Lewis B '70 %Citigroup -399 Park Av -NY 10022
(212) 425-9300 .. **Kadian,** Dennis E '04 %Bressler A&R,PC -17 State -NY 10004
(212) 435-3571 .. **Kadin,** Howard Jr. '80 %Port Auth of NY/NJ -225 Park Av S -NY 10003 **Fx:**435-3555
(212) 682-6688 .. **Kadish,** Abbe L '80 DRJAYS.COM -853 Bway -NY 10003 **Fx:**334-7997
(212) 801-6846 .. **Kadish,** Allen G '88 (Greenberg T,LLP) -200 Park Av -NY 10166
(212) 867-3686 .. **Kadish,** Gerald '62 -261 Mad Av -NY 10016 **Fx:**490-0606
(716) 831-0188 .. **Kadish,** Keith I '86 (Kadish & F) -3517 Genesee -Buffalo 14225 **Fx:**831-0177
(315) 449-3239 .. **Kadish,** Kenneth F '72 -6100 Bay Hill Cir -Jamesvll 13078
(212) 250-5081 .. **Kadish,** Michl L '03 %Deutsche Bank -60 Wall -NY 10005
(212) 930-8071 .. **Kadison,** Danl S '00 NY Post -1211 Av of Amer -NY 10036
(716) 856-4000 .. **Kadle,** Ranjana D '97 (Hodgson R LLP) -140 Pearl -Buffalo 14202
(212) 735-3000 .. **Kadlick,** Richd F '85 (Skadden ASM&F LLP) -4 Times Sq -NY 10036
(212) 416-6697 .. **Kadosh,** Shmuel '09 %Dept of Law -120 Bway -NY 10271
(516) 997-6000 .. **Kadushin,** Jeffrey D '86 %Marshall & M -30 Jericho Exec Plz -Jericho 11753 **Fx:**997-0860
(718) 838-7878 .. **Kadushin,** Matthew D '06 %Bronx Defenders -860 Crtlandt Av -Bronx 10451 **Fx:**665-0100
(518) 885-2263 .. **Kaelin,** Debra A '84 %DA -25 W High -Ballston Spa 12020 **Fx:**884-8627
(212) 446-4800 .. **Kaeser,** Cheryl L '88 OfCnsl Kirkland & E LLP -153 E 53rd -NY 10022
(212) 753-5000 .. **Kaeser,** Hans F '83 (Schiff H LLP) -900 3rd Av -NY 10022
(845) 290-5298 .. **Kaess,** Laura '86 -5 Antoinette Ct -Suffern 10901
(585) 753-4500 .. **Kaeuper,** Geoffrey A '07 %DA -832 Watts Bldg -Rchstr 14614 **Fx:**753-4576
(212) 505-9080 .. **Kafer,** Michl S '81 %Loscalzo & L,PC -14 E 4th -NY 10012
(212) 643-9140 .. **Kafer,** Susan M '76 (Schwaber & K) -350 7th Av -NY 10001 **Fx:**643-9151
(607) 936-3785 .. **Kaffenbarger,** James A Jr. '02 JG Ullman & Assoc Inc -51 E Market -Corning 14830 **Fx:**936-8361
(212) 969-3000 .. **Kafin,** Robt J '67 (Proskauer R LLP) -1585 Bway -NY 10036
(516) 222-1010 .. **Kafka,** Steven M '82 (Kafka & B) -585 Stewart Av -Gdn Cty 11530
(718) 319-8902 .. **Kafko,** Neil R '78 (Kafko S) -7 Hugh Grant Cir -Bronx 10462 **Fx:**319-8915
(718) 250-2000 .. **Kaftal,** Robt '06 %DA -350 Jay -Brklyn 11201 **Fx:**250-2314
(646) 502-7001 .. **Kagan,** David H '82 OfCnsl JSBarkats PLLC -100 Church -NY 10007 **Fx:**607-5544
(516) 334-0870 .. **Kagan,** Erran '95 Electro Indstrs -180 Shams Dr -Westbury 11590
(718) 258-8080 .. **Kagan & Gertel** -1575 E 19th -Brklyn 11230 **Fx:**253-3278
(718) 258-8080 .. **Kagan,** Howard '89 (Kagan & G) -1575 E 19th -Brklyn 11230
(212) 447-7400 .. **Kagan,** Irving '58 Kagan Consultants -245 Park Av -NY 10167
(718) 250-2000 .. **Kagan,** Jacqueline R '95 %DA -350 Jay -Brklyn 11201 **Fx:**250-2314
(718) 588-8584 .. **Kagan,** Linda A '90 -26 N Clover Dr -Gt Neck 11021
(212) 848-9417 .. **Kagan,** Linda S '93 KaganLaw -575 Lex Av -NY 10022 **Fx:**937-5222
(212) 252-0300 .. **Kagan Lubic Lepper Lewis Gold & Colbert,LLP** -200 Mad Av -NY 10016 **Fx:**779-7295
(718) 951-1070 .. **Kagan,** Mark M '97 -858 E 23rd -Brklyn 11210
(212) 225-2000 .. **Kagan,** Michl A '09 %Cleary GS&H -1 Lbrty Plz -NY 10006
(212) 401-4465 .. **Kagan,** Nancy A '81 AFCO Credit Corp -14 Wall -NY 10005
(518) 561-2771 .. **Kagan,** Robt A '77 -59 Court -Plattsbrgh 12901 **Fx:**561-8649
(718) 981-0219 .. **Kagan,** Siri L '95 Leg Aid -60 Bay -Staten Isl 10301 **Fx:**981-6623
(212) 504-6000 .. **Kagan,** Stewart A '90 (Cadwalader W&T LLP) -1 World Fncl Ctr -NY 10281
(212) 839-5300 .. **Kagan,** Stuart P '07 %Sidley A LLP -787 7th Av -NY 10019
(212) 625-8910 .. **Kaganovich,** Marina '10 %B Kogan & Assoc,PC -277 Bway -NY 10007 **Fx:**219-2728
(212) 688-5900 .. **Kagen,** Stuart '96 (Shustak F & Prtnrs) -400 Park Av -NY 10022 **Fx:**688-6151
(212) 790-4500 .. **Kagle,** Abigail M '06 %Manatt P&P,LLP -7 Times Sq -NY 10036
(212) 696-6000 .. **Kahale,** George III '75 (Curtis M-PC&M LLP) -101 Park Av -NY 10178
(718) 677-0700 .. **Kahan,** Abraham J '00 Odyssey Funding LLC -1206 Av J -Brklyn 11230
(212) 343-1645 .. **Kahan,** Adam M '96 %Empire Entertainment -560 Bway -NY 10012
(212) 403-1000 .. **Kahan,** David E '01 (Wachtell LR&K) -51 W 52nd -NY 10019
(212) 566-2566 .. **Kahan,** Douglas E '87 (Kahan & K) -225 Bway -NY 10007 **Fx:**566-8165
(917) 351-1335 .. **Kahan,** Eric H '94 (Sperber D&K,PC) -48 W 37th -NY 10018
(212) 998-6268 .. **Kahan,** Marcel '89 %NYU Law Schl -40 Wshngtn Sq S -NY 10012 **Fx:**995-4692
(212) 578-5170 .. **Kahan,** Martin J '92 %MetLife -27-01 Qns Plz N -LIC 11101 **Fx:**578-8435
(845) 425-8999 .. **Kahan,** Nathan '79 -127 Route 59 -Monsey 10952 **Fx:**425-8396
(212) 506-2500 .. **Kahan,** Rebecca S '07 %Mayer B LLP -1675 Bway -NY 10019
(516) 333-5762 .. **Kahan,** Robt '65 (Kahan & K) -242 Maple Av -Westbury 11590 **Fx:**333-5762
(845) 473-1410 .. **Kahan,** Sheldon '63 -35 Market -Poughkeepsie 12601 **Fx:**473-8122
(914) 422-3900 .. **Kahan,** Stuart E '82 %Oxman TKW&G LLP -120 Bloomingdale Rd -White Plns 10605
(845) 569-3151 .. **Kahana,** Jeffrey S '07 Mount St Mary College -330 Powell Av -Newburgh 12550
(212) 808-4000 .. **Kahane,** Jason A '07 The Moinian Grp -530 5th Av -NY 10036 **Fx:**808-4118
(914) 712-0272 .. **Kahaner,** Steven M '90 %Juriscribe -115 6th Av -Pelham 10803
(212) 788-3300 .. **Kahaner,** Vicki R '95 %Hlth & Hsptl Corp -125 Worth -NY 10013 **Fx:**267-6905
(718) 479-1500 .. **Kahen,** Behnam '96 -75-81 183rd -Fresh Mdws 11366
(212) 903-8700 .. **Kahen,** David E '84 (Roberts & H,LLP) -825 8th Av -NY 10019
(212) 759-5400 .. **Kahl,** Manfred Dieter '02 -575 Mad Av -NY 10022
(718) 298-8900 .. **Kahle,** Shannon T '07 Leg Aid -153-01 Jamaica Av -Jamaica 11432 **Fx:**657-0537
(518) 445-2311 .. **Kahler,** Annette M '06 Albany Law Schl -80 New Scotland Av -Albany 12208 **Fx:**445-2315
(315) 733-0419 .. **Kahler,** Camille T '84 (Saunders K,LLP) -185 Genesee -Utica 13501
(914) 834-6214 .. **Kahler,** Judith Fine '84 -27 Oak Av -Larchmnt 10538
(212) 704-6000 .. **Kahler,** Timothy I '86 (Troutman S LLP) -405 Lex Av -NY 10174
(212) 657-2996 .. **Kahl-Parham,** Michelle L '01 Citigroup,Inc -111 Wall -NY 10043
(646) 688-6095 .. **Kahman,** Jacqueline S '08 %Calabro & Assoc,PC -450 7th Av -NY 10123 **Fx:**688-6096
(212) 612-3270 .. **Kahn,** Aimee R '08 %Mishcon de R NY LLP -200 Park Av -NY 10166
(212) 271-4345 .. **Kahn,** Alan E '56 -61 Bway -NY 10006 **Fx:**363-8202
(212) 336-0102 .. **Kahn,** Allan I '01 SEC -3 World Fncl Ctr -NY 10281 **Fx:**336-1323
(718) 923-4215 .. **Kahn,** Alyssa '06 %OTDA Fair Hearings -14 Boerum Pl -Brklyn 11201
(212) 808-7800 .. **Kahn,** Andrea G '07 %Kelley D&W LLP -101 Park Av -NY 10178
(212) 819-8200 .. **Kahn,** Anthony F '81 (White & C LLP) -1155 Av of Amer -NY 10036

(212) 872-1000 .. **Kahn,** Brad M '08 -One Bryant Park -NY 10036 **Fx:**872-1002
(212) 874-1063 .. **Kahn,** Chavie N '90 -165 West End Av -NY 10023 **Fx:**362-1088
(212) 369-5656 .. **Kahn,** David S '95 -201 E 86th -NY 10028
(518) 474-7668 .. **Kahn,** Deborah A '84 %Insurance Dept -99 Wshngtn Av -Albany 12257 **Fx:**486-2218
(212) 308-7697 .. **Kahn,** Deborah Beth '85 (Butterman & K,LLP) -425 Park Av -NY 10022
(716) 881-5800 .. **Kahn,** Dennis A '77 Siegel K&K -426 Franklin -Buffalo 14202
(212) 545-4000 .. **Kahn,** Dona Seeman '93 OfCnsl Jackson L LLP -666 3rd Av -NY 10017
(212) 583-9600 .. **Kahn,** Elias J '04 %Littler M,PC -900 3rd Av -NY 10022
(212) 541-2000 .. **Kahn,** Erik Wolff '93 (Bryan C LLP) -1290 Av of Amer -NY 10104
(212) 969-3000 .. **Kahn,** Evan L '93 (Proskauer R LLP) -1585 Bway -NY 10036
(716) 282-6000 .. **Kahn,** F Warren '60 -763 Cayuga -Lewiston 14092
(718) 520-2580 .. **Kahn,** Francis A '96 Supreme Ct -88-11 Sutphin Blvd -Jamaica 11435
(212) 688-2400 .. **Kahn,** Gerald '57 OfCnsl Smith B&J,LLP -500 5th Av -NY 10110
(212) 233-2040 .. **Kahn Gordon Timko & Rodriques,PC** -20 Vesey -NY 10007 **Fx:**732-4666
(212) 878-8000 .. **Kahn,** Greg '04 %Clifford C LLP -31 W 52nd -NY 10019
(631) 424-6850 .. **Kahn,** Ira M '86 (Silverstein & K) -1160 E Jericho Tpk -Huntngtn 11743 **Fx:**424-0636
(212) 227-8075 .. **Kahn,** Irwin '58 (Kahn & H,PC) -160 Bway -NY 10038 **Fx:**(516) 826-4341
(914) 761-1800 .. **Kahn,** James C '86 Kahn & K -175 Main -White Plns 10601 **Fx:**761-1871
(212) 746-0463 .. **Kahn,** James R '81 Weill Medical Cllg -445 E 69th -NY 10021 **Fx:**746-0495
(212) 947-3793 .. **Kahn,** Jarret A '00 %Sadis & G LLP -551 5th Av -NY 10176
(212) 574-1200 .. **Kahn,** Jason P '10 %Seward & K LLP -1 Bttry Pk Plz -NY 10004
(212) 598-5900 .. **Kahn,** Jaymee H '95 (Alonso A&K PC) -920 Bway -NY 10010
(212) 318-3000 .. **Kahn,** Joann R '06 %Fulbright & J LLP -666 5th Av -NY 10103
(516) 571-3800 .. **Kahn,** Joshua R '06 %DA -262 Old Cntry Rd -Mineola 11501 **Fx:**248-9479
(212) 842-3004 .. **Kahn,** L Todd '90 Accessory Ntwrk Grp -350 5th Av -NY 10118
(845) 623-4559 .. **Kahn,** Lawr B '58 -5 Lilac Ct -Nanuet 10954 **Fx:**623-9362
(212) 425-1900 .. **Kahn,** Lawr J '98 %Freehill H&M LLP -80 Pine -NY 10005
(212) 788-0600 .. **Kahn,** Lawr S '73 %Law Dept -100 Church -NY 10007 **Fx:**788-0367
(212) 685-7474 .. **Kahn,** Leigh Baseheart '97 %Mayerson SA LLP -292 Mad Av -NY 10017
(718) 250-2000 .. **Kahn,** Leslie D '92 %DA -350 Jay -Brklyn 11201 **Fx:**250-2314
(845) 638-0800 .. **Kahn,** Lisa J '85 (Kahn & L) -369 S Main -New Cty 10956 **Fx:**638-0707
(212) 318-6000 .. **Kahn,** Marguerite R '79 (Paul HJ&W LLP) -75 E 55th -NY 10022
(212) 596-9000 .. **Kahn,** Michl P '02 %Ropes & G LLP -1211 Av of Amer -NY 10036
(212) 687-5066 .. **Kahn,** Michele '88 (Kahn & G,LLP) -708 3rd Av -NY 10017 **Fx:**983-8415
(212) 742-2400 .. **Kahn,** Mitchell R '92 -192 Lex Av -NY 10016
(212) 233-2040 .. **Kahn,** Myron '56 (Kahn GT&R,PC) -20 Vesey -NY 10007
(518) 457-2070 .. **Kahn,** Patricia Oveis '86 %Dept of Tax & Fin -Bldg 9 State Campus -Albany 12227 **Fx:**457-6131
(845) 638-0800 .. **Kahn,** Paul B '98 (Kahn & L) -369 S Main -New Cty 10956 **Fx:**638-0707
(845) 371-4700 .. **Kahn,** Philip A '73 (Fein SK&S,PC) -747 Chestnut Rdg Rd -Spg Vly 10977
(212) 688-5900 .. **Kahn,** Philip J '94 -400 Park Av -NY 10022
(212) 558-4000 .. **Kahn,** Richd A '86 SpclCnsl Sullivan & C LLP -125 Broad -NY 10004
(718) 295-5605 .. **Kahn,** Richd N '96 %Bronx AIDS Srvcs -540 E Fordham Rd -Bronx 10458 **Fx:**733-3429
(212) 293-5556 .. **Kahn,** Robt L '92 (Kaufman & K,LLP) -747 3rd Av -NY 10017 **Fx:**355-5009
(518) 465-3444 .. **Kahn,** Robt W '52 (Kahn & R) -90 State Bx22006 -Albany 12201 **Fx:**465-3447
(718) 435-0363 .. **Kahn,** Roberta '83 -1450 48th -Brklyn 11219 **Fx:**435-0363
(718) 797-0700 .. **Kahn,** Robin J '88 -16 Court -Brklyn 11241 **Fx:**855-2427
(212) 541-6222 .. **Kahn,** S Reid '76 (Kane K,PC) -1350 Av of Amer -NY 10019
(212) 577-6877 .. **Kahn,** Sami '98 -305 Bway -NY 10007
(212) 474-1000 .. **Kahn,** Sarah R '10 %Cravath S&M LLP -825 8th Av -NY 10019
(212) 468-8000 .. **Kahn,** Sherman W '04 OfCnsl Morrison & F LLP -1290 Av of Amer -NY 10104
(914) 962-0087 .. **Kahn,** Stephen B '84 -53 Acorn Ln -Yorktwn Hts 10598
(212) 310-8000 .. **Kahn,** Stephen D '69 (Weil G&M LLP) -767 5th Av -NY 10153
(212) 966-8686 .. **Kahn,** Stephen H '77 Kahn O,LLP -228 E 45th -NY 10017
(718) 585-6551 .. **Kahn,** Steven L '94 (Pena & K,PLLC) -1200 Waters Pl -Bronx 10461 **Fx:**585-6618
(516) 694-3000 .. **Kahn,** Tara E '06 %Guercio & G,LLP -77 Conklin -Farmngdl 11735 **Fx:**694-4738
(888) 812-5100 .. **Kahne,** Bruce J '93 EnTrust Capital Inc -717 5th Av -NY 10022
(718) 613-2230 .. **Kahne,** David J '08 Hon B Cogan -225 Cadman Plz E -Brklyn 11201
(212) 455-2000 .. **Kahng,** Joohee '08 %Simpson T&B LLP -425 Lex Av -NY 10017
(212) 506-1700 .. **Kahnowitz,** Marcia A '09 %Kasowitz BT&F LLP -1633 Bway -NY 10019
(917) 596-0158 .. **Kaiafas,** George P '04 -419 Clinton -Brklyn 11231 **Fx:**(718) 852-4287
(212) 626-6879 .. **Kaidanow,** Jos '81 %Headquarters Co -1120 6th Av -NY 10036 **Fx:**626-6932
(917) 521-3473 .. **Kaigh,** Edw J '06 %Dept Homeless Svcs -346 Powers Av -Bronx 10454
(212) 896-6500 .. **Kaigh,** Laya R '06 %Howrey LLP -601 Lex Av -NY 10022
(212) 309-6000 .. **Kail,** Kenneth S '81 (Morgan L&B LLP) -101 Park Av -NY 10178
(212) 209-3012 .. **Kailas,** Leo G '74 (Reitler K&R LLC) -885 3rd Av -NY 10022
(212) 609-6800 .. **Kailes,** Howard '78 (McCarter & E,LLP) -245 Park Av -NY 10167
(518) 456-0082 .. **Kaim,** Marc J '08 %Bailey K&J,PC -5 Pine West Plz -Albany 12205 **Fx:**456-4767
(212) 610-2855 .. **Kaiman,** Franklin R '78 Property Mrkts Grp -5 E 17th -NY 10003 **Fx:**610-2856
(516) 627-0590 .. **Kaiman,** Jonathan S '89 Town of N Hempstead -220 Plandome Rd -Manhsst 11030 **Fx:**627-4204
(212) 726-0773 .. **Kaiman,** Mark S '97 Midtown Equities LLC -417 5th Av -NY 10016
(212) 940-8750 .. **Kain,** Milton J '61 Cnsl Katten MR LLP -575 Mad Av -NY 10022
(212) 636-6000 .. **Kainen,** James L '79 %Fordham Univ Sch of Law -140 W 62nd -NY 10023 **Fx:**636-6899
(212) 259-8000 .. **Kaiser,** Adam J '93 (Dewey & L LLP) -1301 Av of Amer -NY 10019
(845) 634-0888 .. **Kaiser,** Albert J '85 OfCnsl Freeman & L RLLP -4 Laurel Rd -New Cty 10956
(914) 472-2900 .. **Kaiser,** Barry S '77 (Gralicer & K) -455 Cntrl Pk Av -Scarsdale 10583
(212) 338-9100 .. **Kaiser,** Danl J '90 (Kaiser S&M,PC) -111 Bway -NY 10006
(585) 232-1840 .. **Kaiser,** David D '79 Cnsl Catholic Family Cntr -30 Clinton Av N -Rchstr 14604 **Fx:**454-6286
(212) 715-9100 .. **Kaiser,** Eliza A '04 %Kramer LN&F,LLP -1177 Av of Amer -NY 10036
(631) 715-7900 .. **Kaiser,** Geoffrey R '88 %US Atty -610 Fed Plz -Central Islip 11722
(212) 210-2583 .. **Kaiser,** Karen I '00 Tribune Co -220 E 42nd -NY 10017
(516) 802-7007 .. **Kaiser,** Marcy Udasin '90 SrCnsl Levy S&C,LLP -1425 RXR Plz -Uniondale 11556
(212) 517-3823 .. **Kaiser,** Monica L '91 -450 7th Av -NY 10123 **Fx:**517-6741
(212) 218-5500 .. **Kaiser,** Nicholas J '83 (Seyfarth S LLP) -620 8th Av -NY 10018
(212) 732-8700 .. **Kaiser,** Patricia H '02 McAloon & F,PC -123 William -NY 10038
(716) 856-4000 .. **Kaiser,** Richd W '82 (Hodgson R LLP) -140 Pearl -Buffalo 14202
(716) 882-5049 .. **Kaiser,** Robt B '64 -200 Linwood Av -Buffalo 14209
(212) 338-9100 .. **Kaiser Saurborn & Mair,PC** -111 Bway -NY 10006 **Fx:**338-9088
(212) 541-2000 .. **Kaiser,** Scott H '05 %Bryan C LLP -1290 Av of Amer -NY 10104
(212) 209-4800 .. **Kaiser,** Shoshana B '09 %Brown R LLP -7 Times Sq -NY 10036
(212) 225-2000 .. **Kaiser,** Stephen T '04 %Cleary GS&H -1 Lbrty Plz -NY 10006
(718) 537-0909 .. **Kaiser,** Steven J '76 -840 Grnd Cncrs -Bronx 10451 **Fx:**537-2355
(516) 222-2111 .. **Kaiser,** Steven S '79 (Baram & K) -600 Old Cntry Rd -Gdn Cty 11530 **Fx:**745-0456
(212) 239-9669 .. **Kaiser,** Steven W '99 %Catafago Law Firm -350 5th Av -NY 10118 **Fx:**239-9688
(212) 245-6600 .. **Kaiser,** Suzanne E '95 Project Renewal-Holland House -351 W 42nd -NY 10036
(212) 338-9100 .. **Kaiser,** Wm H '97 (Kaiser S&M,PC) -111 Bway -NY 10006
(212) 538-1962 .. **Kaiserman,** Bruce S '99 Credit Suisse -11 Mad Av -NY 10010
(516) 873-1711 .. **Kaiteris,** Peter C '97 %Solferino & S,LLP -15 Roslyn Rd -Mineola 11501 **Fx:**873-1721
(212) 484-3900 .. **Kaizer,** Andrew D '87 (Arent F LLP) -1675 Bway -NY 10019
(212) 480-4000 .. **Kaizer,** Nicholas G '88 (Levitt & K) -40 Fulton -NY 10038 **Fx:**480-4444
(212) 537-0403 .. **Kajon,** Nicholas F '86 (Stevens & L PC) -485 Mad Av -NY 10022 **Fx:**(610) 371-1223
(212) 416-8685 .. **Kakalec,** Patricia Coyle '94 %Dept of Law -120 Bway -NY 10271
(212) 935-3000 .. **Kakalia,** Narges M '04 %Mintz LCFG&P,PC -666 3rd Av -NY 10017
(718) 876-6300 .. **Kakani,** Om M '05 DA -130 Styvsnt Pl -Staten Isl 10301
(212) 878-8000 .. **Kakar,** Sandip '01 %Clifford C LLP -31 W 52nd -NY 10019
(212) 867-2969 .. **Kakkar,** Balram '92 -261 Mad Av -NY 10016 **Fx:**867-3065
(212) 270-2074 .. **Kako,** Cris T '80 JP Morgan Chase -245 Park Av -NY 10167
(212) 269-0927 .. **Kakoullis,** Bill V '82 (D'Amato & L,LLP) -2 World Fncl Ctr -NY 10281
(212) 878-1851 .. **Kakouros,** Georgia '09 %Minerals Tech -622 3rd Av -NY 10017
(212) 848-4000 .. **Kakoyiannis,** Jason P '08 %Shearman & S LLP -599 Lex Av -NY 10022
(212) 752-1000 .. **Kakoyiannis,** Peter '75 (Eiseman LL&K,PC) -805 3rd Av -NY 10022
(212) 752-1000 .. **Kakoyiannis,** Theo M '94 OfCnsl Eiseman LL&K,PC -805 3rd Av -NY 10022
(212) 643-7000 .. **Kakstys,** Clint B '06 %Sills C&G PC -One Rckfllr Plz -NY 10020
(315) 253-3293 .. **Kalabanka,** David A '85 (Michaels & S,PC) -71 South -Auburn 13021
(631) 262-0780 .. **Kalachman,** Rose Angela '99 -42 Yeoman Dr -E Northprt 11731 **Fx:**262-0780
(212) 403-1000 .. **Kalafat,** Vincent G '07 %Wachtell LR&K -51 W 52nd -NY 10019
(212) 412-7544 .. **Kalaher,** Kathleen M '99 Barclays Capital Inc -745 7th Av -NY 10019
(212) 310-8000 .. **Kalamakis,** Irini '08 %Weil G&M LLP -767 5th Av -NY 10153
(718) 491-0758 .. **Kalamaras,** Demetrius G '88 -484 81st -Brklyn 11209
(212) 302-6600 .. **Kalamaras,** James '97 -2016 Grand Av -Baldwin 11510 **Fx:**208-4465
(212) 564-1250 .. **Kalamotousakis,** Thos J '95 (Karp & K) -370 7th Av -NY 10001
(212) 858-5156 .. **Kalan,** Stephanie E '09 FINRA -1 Lbrty Plz -NY 10006
(415) 875-6600 .. **Kalanithi,** Emily Costello '04 %Quinn EU&S,LLP -51 Mad Av -NY 10010 **Fx:**875-6700
(212) 468-8000 .. **Kalansky,** Shai '09 %Morrison & F LLP -1290 Av of Amer -NY 10104
(607) 255-3736 .. **Kalantry,** Sital '99 Cornell Law Schl -G49 Myron Taylor Hall -Ithaca 14853 **Fx:**255-7193
(212) 227-0347 .. **Kalantzopoulos,** Calliopi '95 %Weiss W&W,PC -25 Park Pl -NY 10007
(212) 644-9691 .. **Kalapoutis,** Taso P '94 -800 Wstchstr Av -Pt Chester 10573
(212) 454-6843 .. **Kalaria,** Niral P '97 %Deutsche Bank -60 Wall -NY 10005
(516) 495-7037 .. **Kalas,** John J '99 Amer Home Mortgage -538 Broadhllw Rd -Melvll 11747
(631) 909-3506 .. **Kalata,** Jean '06 -Bx402 -S Jamesport 11970 **Fx:**909-3506
(718) 424-2220 .. **Kalathara,** Stanley J '98 S Kalathara PC -7048 Bway -Jcksn Hts 11372
(718) 748-5828 .. **Kalavesios,** Theo '92 -49 Bay 8th -Brklyn 11228 **Fx:**748-6049
(516) 222-6200 .. **Kalb,** Adam S '93 %Berkman HPP&F,PC -100 Grdn City Plz -Gdn Cty 11530
(718) 857-3813 .. **Kalb,** James B '79 -110 St Marks Av -Brklyn 11217
(212) 578-8716 .. **Kalb,** Jennifer J '78 %MetLife -27-01 Qns Plz N -LIC 11101
(585) 325-7515 .. **Kalb,** Robt J '77 (Forsyth HOK&M,PC) -1 Chase Sq -Rchstr 14604
(631) 499-3800 .. **Kalb & Rosenfeld,PC** -283 Commack Rd -Commack 11725 **Fx:**499-0534
(347) 533-4826 .. **Kalba,** Stephen E '09 Kalba Law Firm,PC -590 E 94th -Brklyn 11236 **Fx:**533-4829
(212) 682-0020 .. **Kalban,** Philip H '71 (Putney TH&H LLP) -521 5th Av -NY 10175
(212) 852-6187 .. **Kalbaugh,** Gary E '00 Cnsl WestLB AG -1211 Av of Amer -NY 10036
(212) 788-3300 .. **Kalbitzer,** Ruth '99 %Hlth & Hsptl Corp -125 Worth -NY 10013 **Fx:**267-6905
(212) 306-7714 .. **Kale,** Sheetal J '06 Comm on Human Rights -40 Rector -NY 10006 **Fx:**306-7414

(917) 714-5821 .. **Kaleda**, Meryle A '88 -51-02 Redfld -Douglastn 11362 **Fx:**(718) 229-4566
(212) 504-6000 .. **Kalembka**, Lech R '89 SpclCnsl Cadwalader W&T LLP -1 World Fncl Ctr -NY 10281
(516) 877-5600 .. **Kalenka**, Jeffrey M '91 %R Tusa -1225 Franklin Av -Gdn Cty 11530 **Fx:**877-5695
(516) 621-9018 .. **Kalenscher**, Evelyn '89 -39 Center Ct -Roslyn Hts 11577 **Fx:**621-0460
(212) 619-3730 .. **Kaley**, John F '76 (Doar RK&M) -217 Bway -NY 10007
(212) 490-3000 .. **Kalfayan**, Armand S '07 %Wilson EME&D LLP -150 E 42nd -NY 10017
(212) 636-7699 .. **Kalhan**, Anil '00 %Fordham Univ Sch of Law -140 W 62nd -NY 10023 **Fx:**636-6899
(212) 736-9721 .. **Kalhous**, Clara S '09 R Blanch,PC -350 5th Av -NY 10118
(212) 732-3200 .. **Kalib**, Susan B '99 Cnsl Carter L&M LLP -2 Wall -NY 10005
(646) 386-3807 .. **Kalicharan**, Susan '00 Hon R Acosta -71 Thomas -NY 10013
(212) 737-6477 .. **Kalichstein**, Rowain '91 -60 E 42nd -NY 10165 **Fx:**(201) 624-7517
(914) 323-7000 .. **Kalick**, Lindsay J '07 %Wilson EME&D LLP -3 Gannett Dr -White Plns 10604
(212) 903-8700 .. **Kalickstein**, Lana A '02 %Roberts & H,LLP -825 8th Av -NY 10019
(212) 471-8545 .. **Kalik**, Lawr '48 OfCnsl Herzfeld & R,PC -125 Broad -NY 10004
(212) 245-0798 .. **Kalik**, Mark J '69 Kalik & K -250 W 57th -NY 10107
(212) 455-2000 .. **Kalik**, Mildred '73 (Simpson T&B LLP) -425 Lex Av -NY 10017
(914) 422-4159 .. **Kalika**, Yelena '05 Pace Inst of Intl Commrcl Law -78 N Bway -White Plns 10603
(718) 491-5502 .. **Kalikhman**, David '97 -1860 E 23rd -Brklyn 11229
(516) 876-4800 .. **Kalikow**, Edw M '79 Kalikow Grp -7001 Brush Hllw Rd -Westbury 11590 **Fx:**876-6811
(212) 848-4000 .. **Kalikow**, Jeffrey L '10 Shearman & S LLP -599 Lex Av -NY 10022
(212) 284-4326 .. **Kalikow**, Jonathan G '96 Solus LP -430 Park Av -NY 10022
(212) 577-3688 .. **Kalikow**, Karen M '85 %Leg Aid -199 Water -NY 10038 **Fx:**509-8431
(212) 430-5418 .. **Kalikow**, Richd R '75 (Diamond M LLP) -620 8th Av -NY 10018
(212) 848-4000 .. **Kalil**, Amelia K '08 %Shearman & S LLP -599 Lex Av -NY 10022
(315) 797-1150 .. **Kalil**, Christopher J '92 %Kalil & K PC -1602 Sunset Av -Utica 13502 **Fx:**797-1519
(315) 797-7959 .. **Kalil**, John N '75 -289 Genesee -Utica 13501 **Fx:**797-9040
(315) 797-1150 .. **Kalil**, Michl N '87 (Kalil & K PC) -1602 Sunset Av -Utica 13502 **Fx:**797-1519
(315) 797-1150 .. **Kalil**, Waddie N '58 (Kalil & K PC) -1602 Sunset Av -Utica 13502 **Fx:**797-1519
(212) 770-2617 .. **Kaliman**, Tracey L '88 %AIG -80 Pine -NY 10005 **Fx:**742-1164
(516) 488-3000 .. **Kalimian**, Eric J '05 Lalezarian Developers -1999 Marcus Av -New Hyde Pk 11042
(845) 352-4751 .. **Kalin**, Beatrice C '83 -Bx407 -Monsey 10952
(212) 661-7300 .. **Kalin**, John T '95 %Malapero & P LLP -295 Mad Av -NY 10017
(516) 822-4400 .. **Kalina**, Jeremy R '96 (Tunstead & S) -500 N Bway -Jericho 11753
(718) 263-9700 .. **Kalina**, Paul J '57 -117-01 Park Ln S -Richmnd Hll 11418 **Fx:**441-4483
(212) 448-1222 .. **Kalina**, Robt I '67 -260 Mad Av -NY 10016 **Fx:**448-0066
(646) 414-6840 .. **Kalina**, Stefan B '97 Cnsl Lowenstein S PC -1251 Av of Amer -NY 10020 **Fx:**(973) 422-6869
(212) 804-4200 .. **Kaliner**, Bruce R '87 (Mound CW&G) -One Bttry Pk Plz -NY 10004
(212) 309-6000 .. **Kalinowski**, Matthew R '07 %Morgan L&B LLP -101 Park Av -NY 10178
(212) 506-1700 .. **Kalirao**, Manjit Kaur '05 Kasowitz BT&F LLP -1633 Bway -NY 10019
(212) 373-3000 .. **Kalish**, Arthur '56 OfCnsl Paul WRW&G LLP -1285 Av of Amer -NY 10019
(914) 761-6177 .. **Kalish**, Danl A '86 -199 Main -White Plns 10601
(212) 848-4000 .. **Kalish**, Danielle B '06 %Shearman & S LLP -599 Lex Av -NY 10022
(718) 258-7797 .. **Kalish**, Hannah '92 -855 E 24th -Brklyn 11210
(212) 353-7480 .. **Kalish**, Jason D '03 Uptown Tech -115 5th Av -NY 10003 **Fx:**353-7441
(212) 225-2000 .. **Kalish**, Joshua M '09 %Cleary GS&H -1 Lbrty Plz -NY 10006
(212) 869-6565 .. **Kalish**, Mark C '85 -130 W 42nd -NY 10036 **Fx:**869-6953
(212) 867-4488 .. **Kalish**, Mark L '76 (Moss & K) -122 E 42nd -NY 10168
(516) 746-3000 .. **Kalish**, Melvin J '74 -114 Old Cntry Rd -Mineola 11501 **Fx:**746-3079
(212) 351-4500 .. **Kalish**, Michl A '86 (Epstein B&G,PC) -250 Park Av -NY 10177
(212) 737-8142 .. **Kalish**, Myron '44 -50 E 79th -NY 10075 **Fx:**288-6102
(212) 455-2000 .. **Kalish**, Sharon Jill '05 %Simpson T&B LLP -425 Lex Av -NY 10017
(631) 225-7183 .. **Kalish**, Thos J '91 -211 S Wellwood Av -Lindenhrst 11757 **Fx:**225-7198
(718) 784-0493 .. **Kalisz**, Lucy W '84 -39-24 47th -Sunnyside 11104
(212) 715-1000 .. **Kalivas**, Tanya E '09 %Arnold & P LLP -399 Park Av -NY 10022
(516) 741-1424 .. **Kalka**, Howard A '66 -2 Knolls Dr -Old Westbury 11568 **Fx:**414-0931
(212) 841-1000 .. **Kalka**, Michelle B '06 %Covington & B LLP -620 8th Av -NY 10018
(718) 275-0780 .. **Kalker**, Terri B '92 -139-12 73rd Ter -Flushng 11367 **Fx:**544-8435
(212) 790-4500 .. **Kalkines**, George '65 (Manatt P&P,LLP) -7 Times Sq -NY 10036
(212) 788-1030 .. **Kalkstein**, Julian L '73 %Law Dept -100 Church -NY 10007 **Fx:**788-0367
(631) 738-2400 .. **Kall**, Patricia A '90 %Symbol Tech -1 Symbol Plz -Holtsvll 11742
(315) 437-3321 .. **Kall**, Sheldon G '60 (Kall & R) -3522 James -Syracuse 13206 **Fx:**437-0091
(315) 754-6214 .. **Kall**, Sheldon G '60 (Kall & R) -6819 Main Bx189 -Red Crk 13143 **Fx:**754-6237
(212) 804-4200 .. **Kallal**, Amy Justine '98 (Mound CW&G) -One Bttry Pk Plz -NY 10004
(212) 973-0929 .. **Kallan**, Lisa J '87 -122 E 42nd -NY 10168 **Fx:**983-5276
(212) 569-5779 .. **Kallas**, Christina '77 -5009 Bway -NY 10034
(212) 447-7070 .. **Kallas**, Edith M '88 (Whatley D&K LLC) -1540 Bway -NY 10036
(212) 218-2100 .. **Kallas**, Nicholas N '83 (Fitzpatrick CH&S) -1290 Av of Amer -NY 10104
(212) 569-5779 .. **Kallas**, Stephan J '80 -5009 Bway -NY 10034 **Fx:**569-7294
(212) 816-3420 .. **Kallash**, H Leena '05 Citigroup -388 Greenwich -NY 10013
(585) 232-5300 .. **Kallaur**, Lawr A '01 %Boylan BCV&W,LLP -2400 Chase Sq -Rchstr 14604
(845) 638-5358 .. **Kallen**, Edw P '72 Hon A Weiner -1 S Main -New Cty 10956
(646) 216-9914 .. **Kallen**, Laurel L '02 -4601 H Hdsn Pkwy W -Bronx 10471 **Fx:**216-9401
(212) 713-9250 .. **Kallenekos**, Constantine '87 UBS Fncl Srvcs Inc -1285 Av of Amer -NY 10019
(212) 720-5026 .. **Kaller**, Danl '09 %Fed Reserve Bk -33 Lbrty -NY 10045 **Fx:**785-5748
(212) 272-3352 .. **Kallet-Neuman**, Beth R '98 %JP Morgan Chase -383 Mad Av -NY 10179
(914) 468-7300 .. **Kallman**, Irwin '56 Win Properties -10 Rye Ridge Plz -Rye Brook 10573
(516) 222-2006 .. **Kallman**, Marc S '88 MS Kallman PC -1101 Stewart Av -Gdn Cty 11530 **Fx:**222-1080
(212) 759-7667 .. **Kallman**, Stanley W '56 SW Kallman,PC -245 E 58th -NY 10022
(212) 406-1919 .. **Kallmann**, Stanley W '84 (Gennet KA&R,PC) -140 Bway -NY 10005
(518) 447-7117 .. **Kallner**, Jamie J '91 %Legislative Cnsl -112 State -Albany 12207
(212) 600-4960 .. **Kallos**, Benjamin J '06 -215 E 95th -NY 10128 **Fx:**600-4965
(845) 567-0020 .. **Kallus**, Harvey C '87 -1161 Little Britain Rd -New Windsor 12553
(315) 446-0300 .. **Kallusch**, H A Jr. '73 (Kallusch & K) -4455 E Genesee -DeWitt 13214 **Fx:**445-9127
(212) 925-0017 .. **Kalm**, David P '96 RMTS Assoc,LLC -6 Harrison -NY 10013 **Fx:**925-8760
(516) 267-7360 .. **Kalmaer**, Brian P '99 Steve & Barrys Univ Sportswear -12 Hrbr Park Dr -Pt Wash 11050
(212) 972-1000 .. **Kalman**, Brian A '94 (London F LLP) -59 Maiden Ln -NY 10038
(718) 522-0366 .. **Kalman**, Elliot R '56 -105 Court -Brklyn 11201
(718) 522-0366 .. **Kalman**, Neil K '79 -105 Court -Brklyn 11201
(212) 506-1700 .. **Kalman**, Suzanne B '80 Kasowitz BT&F LLP -1633 Bway -NY 10019
(718) 590-2000 .. **Kalman-Blustein**, Rachel '08 %DA -198 E 161st -Bronx 10451 **Fx:**590-6477
(212) 768-6700 .. **Kalmanson**, Kimberly '09 %Sonnenschein N&R LLP -1221 Av of Amer -NY 10020
(631) 261-6666 .. **Kalmar**, Gregory W '04 -215 E Main -Huntngtn 11743
(516) 741-2585 .. **Kalmar**, Jason A '09 %Rosicki R & Assoc,PC -51 E Bethpage Rd -Plainvw 11803 **Fx:**741-4748
(212) 267-2300 .. **Kalmus**, Michl '81 M Kalmus,PC -100 Wall -NY 10005 **Fx:**943-7454
(212) 267-9090 .. **Kalmus**, Michl L '81 %S Salles -225 Bway -NY 10007 **Fx:**267-9175
(212) 751-2400 .. **Kalnick Klee & Green,LLP** -767 3rd Av -NY 10017 **Fx:**751-3175
(212) 751-2400 .. **Kalnick**, Michl C '66 (Kalnick K&G,LLP) -767 3rd Av -NY 10017
(212) 479-6000 .. **Kalnit**, Richelle P '06 %Cooley LLP -1114 Av of Amer -NY 10036
(973) 491-3373 .. **Kalocsay**, Robyn Gnudi '89 (LeClairRyan,PC) -830 3rd Av -NY 10022 **Fx:**491-3555
(212) 310-8000 .. **Kalogeras**, Steven M '07 %Weil G&M LLP -767 5th Av -NY 10153
(212) 732-3320 .. **Kalogiannis**, Mary J '06 %Short & B,PC -217 Bway -NY 10007
(212) 670-0175 .. **Kalola**, Bina '99 Merrill Lynch -222 Bway -NY 10038
(718) 543-2302 .. **Kalomiris**, Errika '95 -3265 Johnson Av -Bronx 10463 **Fx:**543-2304
(212) 610-6300 .. **Kalorides**, Maria L '99 SrCnsl Allen & O -1221 Av of Amer -NY 10020
(718) 624-3894 .. **Kalos**, Bradley G '86 Brooklyn Bar Assn -123 Remsen -Brklyn 11201
(212) 312-2314 .. **Kalos**, Carolyn J '94 %Leg Aid -60 Lafayette -NY 10013 **Fx:**349-0874
(516) 627-8487 .. **Kalos**, Matthew D '79 -Bx1247 -Manhsst 11030 **Fx:**627-6533
(212) 872-1000 .. **Kaloudis**, Dionisia '05 -One Bryant Park -NY 10036 **Fx:**872-1002
(212) 813-1600 .. **Kalow**, David A '77 (Kalow & S) -488 Mad Av -NY 10022
(212) 551-5731 .. **Kalow**, Gwenn M '99 %Royal Alliance Assoc -1 World Fncl Ctr -NY 10281 **Fx:**551-5620
(212) 355-8282 .. **Kalow**, Henry Norr '59 -488 Mad Av -NY 10022 **Fx:**813-9600
(212) 813-1600 .. **Kalow & Springut** -488 Mad Av -NY 10022
(212) 776-5000 .. **Kaloyanides**, Sonya M '88 %NYC Housing Auth -250 Bway -NY 10007 **Fx:**776-5039
(718) 897-2211 .. **Kalra**, Neil '99 -100-15 Qns Blvd -Frst Hlls 11375
(212) 415-9200 .. **Kals**, Stephen A '73 (Dorsey & W LLP) -250 Park Av -NY 10177
(212) 349-3000 .. **Kalson**, Janet R '85 %Himmelstein MGD&J -15 Maiden Ln -NY 10038
(718) 423-5333 .. **Kalstein**, Kenneth R '01 -3850 Bell Blvd -Bayside 11361
(212) 720-5026 .. **Kalstein**, Michele H '94 %Fed Reserve Bk -33 Lbrty -NY 10045 **Fx:**785-5748
(914) 745-4284 .. **Kalten**, Wm A '96 Towers Watson -100 Summit Lk Dr -Valhalla 10595
(212) 527-1000 .. **Kaltenbach**, Kerry J '95 (Jones HC&B PC) -1 Bttry Pk Plz -NY 10004
(518) 457-1153 .. **Kaltenborn**, Marilyn '75 Dept of Tax & Fin -Bldg 9 State Campus -Albany 12227
(212) 964-5485 .. **Kalter**, Albert '61 -225 Bway -NY 10007
(212) 964-5485 .. **Kalter**, Dahlia '97 -225 Bway -NY 10007 **Fx:**964-8696
(212) 335-9000 .. **Kalter**, Ilene M '09 %DA -1 Hogan Pl -NY 10013
(845) 647-4110 .. **Kalter**, Ivan '64 (Kalter KZ&F) -47 N Main Bx186 -Ellenvll 12428
(845) 434-4777 .. **Kalter**, Ivan '64 (Kalter KZ&F) -6166 State Rte 42 Bx30 -Woodbourne 12788
(845) 434-4777 .. **Kalter Kaplan Zeiger & Forman** -6166 State Rte 42 Bx30 -Woodbourne 12788 **Fx:**436-8156
(845) 647-4110 .. **Kalter Kaplan Zeiger & Forman** -47 N Main Bx186 -Ellenvll 12428 **Fx:**647-6232
(516) 746-8000 .. **Kalva**, Jessica K '09 %Jaspan S LLP -300 Grdn City Plz -Gdn Cty 11530
(732) 855-6124 .. **Kalver**, Brian '90 Cnsl Wilentz G&S -110 William -NY 10038 **Fx:**726-6663
(518) 885-2613 .. **Kalwa**, Kathleen D '86 -17 Milton Av -Ballston Spa 12020 **Fx:**885-2616
(212) 294-4757 .. **Kalyvas**, John G '98 (Winston & S) -200 Park Av -NY 10166
(212) 542-8882 .. **Kam**, Jordan M '04 (Roth Law Firm,PLLC) -295 Mad Av -NY 10017 **Fx:**542-8883
(212) 310-8000 .. **Kam**, Michl K '87 (Weil G&M LLP) -767 5th Av -NY 10153
(212) 640-7146 .. **Kam**, Mireya E '99 AMEX -200 Vesey -NY 10285
(212) 808-7800 .. **Kam**, Sarah K '07 %Kelley D&W LLP -101 Park Av -NY 10178
(212) 308-4411 .. **Kamaiko**, Laurie A '81 (Edwards AP&D LLP) -750 Lex Av -NY 10022
(212) 963-1670 .. **Kamali-Miyamoto**, Maryam D '00 UN Ofc of Leg Affrs -318 Mad Av -NY 10017 **Fx:**963-6430

(585) 325-7440 .. **Kaman Berlove Marafioti Jacobstein & Goldman LLP** -135 Corp Woods -Rchstr 14623 **Fx:**454-3559
(585) 248-9426 .. **Kaman,** John B '85 %Pyramid Brokerage Co Inc -255 Woodcliff Dr -Fairprt 14450 **Fx:**248-3981
(212) 336-0090 .. **Kamar,** Barry A '07 SEC -3 World Fncl Ctr -NY 10281 **Fx:**336-1323
(718) 694-3897 .. **Kamara,** Baimusa '98 Transit Auth -130 Lvngstn -Brklyn 11201 **Fx:**694-5726
(212) 629-9690 .. **Kamara,** Saml A '99 %P Merani -298 5th Av -NY 10001 **Fx:**629-9664
(212) 762-4597 .. **Kamara,** Tamiko '95 Morgan Stanley -1221 Av of Amer -NY 10020
(212) 856-9600 .. **Kamaraju,** Sidhardha '08 %Morvillo AGIA&B,PC -565 5th Av -NY 10017
(718) 625-9600 .. **Kamaras,** Philip L '84 -26 Court -Brklyn 11242
(212) 557-1818 .. **Kamback,** Craig J '04 %Silverson P&L -192 Lex Av -NY 10016
(212) 920-3072 .. **Kamber,** Scott A '92 (KamberEdelson,LLC) -11 Bway -NY 10004 **Fx:**202-6364
(212) 438-1168 .. **Kambeseles,** Panayotis '99 %Standard & Poor's -55 Water -NY 10041
(631) 715-7852 .. **Kambic,** Robt B '90 %US Atty -610 Fed Plz -Central Islip 11722
(716) 836-1500 .. **Kamble,** Tara N '01 (N Juncewicz,PC) -1645 Hertel Av -Buffalo 14216 **Fx:**836-1516
(646) 447-7828 .. **Kambolis,** Nicholas P '94 Cnsl Emblem Health -55 Water -NY 10041 **Fx:**(877) 620-8096
(212) 776-5000 .. **Kambos,** Irene '05 NYC Housing Auth -250 Bway -NY 10007 **Fx:**776-5039
(212) 484-8000 .. **Kambour,** Annaliese S '87 %Time Warner -1 Time Warner Ctr -NY 10019
(718) 330-1200 .. **Kamdang,** Len H '05 %Fed Def of NY Inc -1 Pierrepont Plz -Brklyn 11201 **Fx:**855-0760
(212) 320-3000 .. **Kamdar,** Kevin P '01 Shields & Co -140 Bway -NY 10005
(845) 359-8258 .. **Kamel,** Alan M '83 (Glazer & K) -21 Valenza Ln -Blauvelt 10913
(212) 254-4623 .. **Kamelhar,** Leslie C '81 -276 1st Av -NY 10009 **Fx:**788-3518
(631) 444-5200 .. **Kamen,** Barry A '75 -26 Hallock Meadow Dr -Stony Brk 11790 **Fx:**444-5534
(212) 408-5100 .. **Kamen,** Garrett S '09 %Chadbourne & P LLP -30 Rckfllr Plz -NY 10112
(212) 953-1217 .. **Kamen,** Harry P '58 %MetLife -200 Park Av -NY 10166
(212) 506-2500 .. **Kamen,** Joshua A '06 %Mayer B LLP -1675 Bway -NY 10019
(212) 442-2861 .. **Kamen,** Kelly A '04 Dept of Bldgs -280 Bway -NY 10007
(212) 249-7182 .. **Kamen,** Peggy A '75 -360 E 72nd -NY 10021
(212) 442-5924 .. **Kamen,** Wm M '84 Cnsl Dept Youth & Cmmnty Dvlpmnt -156 William -NY 10038
(212) 984-8134 .. **Kamenetsky,** Gary '96 CB Richard Ellis -200 Park Av -NY 10166 **Fx:**984-8040
(212) 302-1020 .. **Kamens,** Joshua A '00 Anndorll Corp -305 Mad Av -NY 10165
(212) 532-8100 .. **Kamensky,** Allison J '03 %Stern & M,LLP -115 Bway -NY 10006
(914) 939-3300 .. **Kamensky,** Mark J '85 (Pierro & K) -327 Irving Av Bx471 -Pt Chester 10573
(212) 400-4930 .. **Kamerman,** Jerome '52 OfCnsl Kamerman & S PC -708 3rd Av -NY 10017
(212) 400-4930 .. **Kamerman,** Joshua '81 %Kamerman & S PC -708 3rd Av -NY 10017
(212) 859-8000 .. **Kamerman,** Russell L '09 %Fried FHS&J LLP -1 NY Plz -NY 10004
(212) 400-4930 .. **Kamerman & Soniker PC** -708 3rd Av -NY 10017 **Fx:**400-4935
(212) 355-1777 .. **Kamerman,** Steven '77 (S Kamerman,PC) -110 E 57th -NY 10022 **Fx:**355-1666
(212) 940-3000 .. **Kameros,** Ilana F '05 %Nixon P LLP -437 Mad Av -NY 10022
(212) 688-1900 .. **Kamlen,** Kalvin '77 (Greenberg T&H,LLP) -767 3rd Av -NY 10017
(212) 417-7000 .. **Kamijyo,** Miki Okabe '07 %Brookfield Asset Mgmt -3 World Fncl Ctr -NY 10281
(212) 867-6000 .. **Kamillatos,** Nicholas '83 (Rosenberg & E,PC) -733 3rd Av -NY 10017
(718) 225-9223 .. **Kamin,** Lewis P '84 -42-40 Bell Blvd -Bayside 11361 **Fx:**225-9093
(212) 969-3000 .. **Kamine,** Elida '07 %Proskauer R LLP -1585 Bway -NY 10036
(646) 312-3584 .. **Kaminer,** Deborah N '92 %Baruch College -17 Lex Av Bx 316 -NY 10010
(212) 921-5525 .. **Kaminer,** Maggie I '05 (Kaminer K&B LLP) -369 Lex Av -NY 10017 **Fx:**(646) 269-7669
(212) 317-8500 .. **Kaminetsky,** Danl I '03 %Snitow KH&M,LLP -575 Lex Av -NY 10022
(212) 450-4000 .. **Kaminetzky,** Benjamin S '96 (Davis P&W LLP) -450 Lex Av -NY 10017
(516) 374-0074 .. **Kaminetzky,** Deborah E '91 -132 Spruce -Cedarhrst 11516
(212) 535-0245 .. **Kaming,** Elizabeth C '73 (Kaming & K) -156 E 65th -NY 10065
(212) 535-0245 .. **Kaming,** Jos S '59 (Kaming & K) -156 E 65th -NY 10065
(212) 559-1437 .. **Kamins,** Bruce L '80 %Citibank NA -909 3rd Av -NY 10022 **Fx:**793-8859
(212) 969-3000 .. **Kaminska,** Anna G '04 %Proskauer R LLP -1585 Bway -NY 10036
(516) 294-5433 .. **Kaminska,** Glenn A '98 (Ahmuty D&M) -200 IU Willets Rd -Albertson 11507
(718) 389-0450 .. **Kaminski,** Andrew '02 (A Kaminski,PC) -79 Greenpoint Av -Brklyn 11222 **Fx:**389-0462
(212) 968-2300 .. **Kaminski,** Danielle Sullivan '99 -39 Bway -NY 10006 **Fx:**968-2400
(315) 724-8048 .. **Kaminski,** Edw G '83 -1522 Genesee -Utica 13502 **Fx:**735-4647
(585) 546-5530 .. **Kaminski,** Michele C '97 %Thomson West -50 E Broad -Rchstr 14694
(212) 355-5886 .. **Kaminski,** Robt V '97 -350 5th Av -NY 10118
(212) 403-1000 .. **Kaminsky,** Adam J '06 %Wachtell LR&K -51 W 52nd -NY 10019
(212) 232-1300 .. **Kaminsky,** Alan '84 (Lewis BB&S LLP) -77 Water -NY 10005
(716) 854-4400 .. **Kaminsky,** Allan H '55 R Slisz -14 Lafayette Sq -Buffalo 14203 **Fx:**856-5801
(516) 365-8028 .. **Kaminsky,** Arthur C '74 (Athletes and Artists,Inc) -25 Middle Dr -Plandome 11030 **Fx:**365-1065
(212) 403-1000 .. **Kaminsky,** Blair E '09 %Wachtell LR&K -51 W 52nd -NY 10019
(718) 854-1505 .. **Kaminsky,** Carl I '55 -135 Ocean Pkwy -Brklyn 11218
(718) 613-2380 .. **Kaminsky,** Clay H '10 Hon A Ross USDC -225 Cadman Plz E -Brklyn 11201 **Fx:**613-2386
(212) 571-1227 .. **Kaminsky,** David A '84 (D Kaminsky & Assoc,PC) -325 Bway -NY 10007 **Fx:**571-7004
(212) 750-3636 .. **Kaminsky,** Edw A '84 (Handsman & K LLP) -900 3rd Av -NY 10022 **Fx:**750-4699
(212) 253-7126 .. **Kaminsky,** Howard S '93 -32 Union Sq E -NY 10003
(212) 801-6892 .. **Kaminsky,** Martin I '65 Cnsl Greenberg T,LLP -200 Park Av -NY 10166
(212) 279-7900 .. **Kaminsky,** Martin L '77 -7 Penn Plz -NY 10001 **Fx:**279-7901
(718) 250-2000 .. **Kaminsky,** Michelle Lee '93 %DA -350 Jay -Brklyn 11201 **Fx:**250-2314
(914) 682-8180 .. **Kaminsky & Rich** -399 Knollwood Rd -White Plns 10603 **Fx:**682-2966
(718) 254-7000 .. **Kaminsky,** Todd D '04 %US Atty -271 Cadman Plz E -Brklyn 11201 **Fx:**254-6479
(212) 355-7188 .. **Kaminsky-Meyers,** Judith '94 Meyers & H LLP -444 Mad Av -NY 10022 **Fx:**355-7190
(718) 590-2000 .. **Kamlet,** Bari L '08 %DA -198 E 161st -Bronx 10451 **Fx:**590-6477
(607) 770-0155 .. **Kamlet,** Kenneth S '99 Newman Dvlpmnt Grp LLC -3101 Shippers Rd Bx678 -Vestal 13851 **Fx:**770-3482
(212) 422-1200 .. **Kamlet,** Leonard G '77 (Abrams GF&J,PC) -1 Bttry Pk Plz -NY 10004
(212) 745-4195 .. **Kamm,** Lisa '96 IBM -11 Mad Av -NY 10010 **Fx:**745-5868
(646) 386-3025 .. **Kamman,** Barbara Weingrad '92 Supreme Ct Pro Se Ofc -60 Centre -NY 10007
(212) 326-3939 .. **Kamman,** Edw G '94 (Jones D) -222 E 41st -NY 10017
(716) 858-2200 .. **Kammer,** Gregory P '02 %Cnty Atty -95 Franklin -Buffalo 14202 **Fx:**858-2281
(518) 402-2225 .. **Kammerer,** Keith E '79 %Dept of Law -The Cptl -Albany 12224
(212) 594-4400 .. **Kammerman,** Joshua L '97 (Kammerman Assoc) -146 W 29th -NY 10001 **Fx:**594-4808
(212) 594-5300 .. **Kammerman,** Todd L '03 %Milberg LLP -1 Penn Plz -NY 10119
(212) 259-8000 .. **Kammoun,** Martha N '06 %Dewey & L LLP -1301 Av of Amer -NY 10019
(212) 323-1200 .. **Kamnik,** Christopher M '07 OCME -421 E 26th -NY 10016
(212) 425-0055 .. **Kamnitz,** Allan H '59 %Sharretts PC&B -75 Broad -NY 10004
(646) 315-7300 .. **Kampel,** Andrew D '91 FINRA -14 Wall -NY 10005 **Fx:**315-7440
(718) 238-6800 .. **Kampessis,** Basil J '07 %DiConza LD&K -478 Bay Ridge Pkwy -Brklyn 11209
(212) 373-3000 .. **Kampfer,** Cory R '08 %Paul WRW&G LLP -1285 Av of Amer -NY 10019
(631) 582-1200 .. **Kampfer,** Paul M '06 %DeHaan B LLP -300 Rabro Dr -Hauppauge 11788
(212) 326-3939 .. **Kamphaus,** Nicholas C '09 %Jones D -222 E 41st -NY 10017
(212) 312-2363 .. **Kampil,** James '02 Leg Aid -60 Lafayette -NY 10013 **Fx:**349-0874
(212) 326-3939 .. **Kampmeier,** Stephen F '03 %Jones D -222 E 41st -NY 10017
(212) 398-3073 .. **Kampner-Rudin,** Alissa C '86 Lantern Org -49 W 37th -NY 10018
(718) 796-3703 .. **Kampton,** Harvey D '82 -5900 Arlngtn Av -Bronx 10471 **Fx:**796-8349
(516) 663-6280 .. **Kamran,** Peter K '05 Private Capital Grp,LLC -2 Jericho Plz -Jericho 11753 **Fx:**663-6299
(516) 741-7800 .. **Kamskaya,** Bella '05 %Krupnick Firm,PC -23 Vllg Sq -Glen Cove 11542 **Fx:**385-1817
(212) 225-2000 .. **Kamuf,** Joann D '07 %Cleary GS&H -1 Lbrty Plz -NY 10006
(212) 571-3896 .. **Kamysek,** Phyllis M '85 -305 Bway -NY 10007 **Fx:**571-0176
(212) 401-4040 .. **Kan,** Christina '08 %Teplen & Assoc,PLLC -350 5th Av -NY 10118 **Fx:**401-4041
(718) 209-0682 .. **Kanabrocki,** Michl L '98 SrCnsl US Army-JAG Corps -10415 Av L -Brklyn 11236
(212) 326-3939 .. **Kanaga,** Mark A '07 %Jones D -222 E 41st -NY 10017
(212) 554-7800 .. **Kanaga,** Vanessa L '07 %Moses & S LLP -405 Lex Av -NY 10174
(716) 855-1111 .. **Kanaley,** Gary M '80 (Duke HP&G LLP) -350 Main -Buffalo 14202
(716) 855-5714 .. **Kanaley,** Michl J Jr. '84 L Ogden -60 Lakefront Blvd -Buffalo 14202
(212) 859-8000 .. **Kanarek,** David A '05 %Fried FHS&J LLP -1 NY Plz -NY 10004
(718) 237-2000 .. **Kanas,** Melissa '02 %Leg Aid -111 Lvngstn -Brklyn 11201 **Fx:**237-8737
(516) 333-2553 .. **Kanas,** Wm S '95 %S Pirotin,PC -323 Madison -Westbury 11590
(212) 373-5975 .. **Kanazawa,** Sumiko '00 Mizuho Trust & Bnking Co -135 W 50th -NY 10020
(914) 632-4700 .. **Kanca,** Diane K '83 (McDonough Law Firm,LLP) -44 W Wall -NY 10005 **Fx:**632-3329
(212) 298-5176 .. **Kandathil,** Rosy '06 %Leg Aid -49 Thomas -NY 10013 **Fx:**298-5252
(914) 946-4777 .. **Kandel,** Amanda E '03 %Keane & B,PC -445 Hmltn Av -White Plns 10601
(212) 670-0302 .. **Kandel,** Andrew '87 %Merrill Lynch -222 Bway -NY 10038
(631) 853-4049 .. **Kandel,** Ann K '82 %Cnty Atty -Dennison Bldg Bx6100 -Hauppauge 11788 **Fx:**853-5169
(212) 980-9600 .. **Kandel,** Elan R '01 (Kaufman B&R) -120 Bway -NY 10271
(212) 277-0447 .. **Kandel,** Lisa J '86 Hartford Fncl Prdcts -2 Park Av -NY 10016
(212) 744-5022 .. **Kandel,** Mia R '07 Lenox Hill Neighbrhd House -331 E 70th -NY 10021
(212) 836-8000 .. **Kandel,** Robt A '73 OfCnsl Kaye S LLP -425 Park Av -NY 10022
(212) 373-3000 .. **Kandel,** Susanne M '05 %Paul WRW&G LLP -1285 Av of Amer -NY 10019
(212) 238-3000 .. **Kandel,** Tyler J '96 OfCnsl Emmet M&M,LLP -120 Bway -NY 10271
(212) 570-9064 .. **Kandel,** Wm L '65 -880 5th Av -NY 10021
(718) 819-0200 .. **Kandel,** Zhanna Shpaykher '97 (Orenstein & K PC) -217-04 Nrthrn Blvd -Bayside 11361 **Fx:**819-0201
(212) 474-1000 .. **Kandel-Burg,** Ellen '02 %Cravath S&M LLP -825 8th Av -NY 10019
(718) 351-2656 .. **Kandell,** Adam C '88 Kandell & Assoc -2141 Richmond Rd -Staten Isl 10306 **Fx:**351-2809
(718) 237-3100 .. **Kandhari,** Sandeep S '07 Leg Aid -111 Lvngstn -Brklyn 11201 **Fx:**250-4243
(212) 248-8800 .. **Kandler,** Michl P '89 (Callan KB&B LLP) -1 Whitehall -NY 10004
(212) 248-3140 .. **Kandravy,** John '82 (Drinker B&R LLP) -140 Bway -NY 10005
(212) 244-9500 .. **Kane,** Alexandria E '00 %White and W LLP -1 Penn Plz -NY 10119
(917) 534-4832 .. **Kane,** Alice T '72 -105 E 17th -NY 10003
(718) 618-2500 .. **Kane,** Alison M '09 %Civil Ct -851 Grnd Cncrs -Bronx 10451 **Fx:**590-7294
(212) 259-8000 .. **Kane,** Arielle D '03 %Dewey & L LLP -1301 Av of Amer -NY 10019
(866) 331-3271 .. **Kane,** Brian '84 %SSA-ODAR -100 State -Rchstr 14614 **Fx:**(585) 263-5792
(718) 286-6000 .. **Kane,** Catherine C '96 %DA -125-01 Qns Blvd -Kew Gdns 11415
(212) 775-0055 .. **Kane,** Christopher M '83 (Simon G&K LLP) -1700 Bway -NY 10019
(631) 715-7825 .. **Kane,** Colleen M '90 US Atty Ofc -610 Fed Plz -Central Islip 11722

(716) 362-1158 .. **Kane,** Danl B '87 (Higgins K,PC) -70 Niagara -Buffalo 14202 **Fx:**362-1162
(914) 965-5536 .. **Kane,** Dara M '71 -479 Park Av -Ynkrs 10703
(212) 415-8600 .. **Kane,** David H T '63 OfCnsl Locke LB&L LLP -3 World Fncl Ctr -NY 10281
(315) 366-2393 .. **Kane,** Edw M '72 %Cnty Cts -Cnty Cthse Bx607 -Wampsville 13163 **Fx:**366-2539
(607) 778-2158 .. **Kane,** Eileen M '81 %Family Ct -George Harvey Justice Bldg -Bnghmtn 13901
(212) 799-9638 .. **Kane,** Elizabeth '87 %West Side SRO Lw Prj -647 Columbus Av -NY 10025 **Fx:**721-1514
(718) 237-2000 .. **Kane,** Emily S '06 %Leg Aid -111 Lvngstn -Brklyn 11201 **Fx:**237-8737
(212) 735-3000 .. **Kane,** H Lacey '08 %Skadden ASM&F LLP -4 Times Sq -NY 10036
(845) 735-0088 .. **Kane,** James P '91 (Brown B&K,LLP) -275 N Mddltwn Rd -Pearl Rvr 10965 **Fx:**735-7660
(585) 381-3820 .. **Kane,** Jason J '08 %Pearl Law Firm,PA -1159 Pttsfrd Victor Rd -Pittsfrd 14534 **Fx:**381-3886
(212) 709-1640 .. **Kane,** Jeffrey "Jay" '86 %Banking Dept -1 State -NY 10004 **Fx:**709-1655
(914) 232-8416 .. **Kane,** Jeffrey J '81 -200 Katonah Av Bx554 -Katonah 10536 **Fx:**232-2770
(212) 492-4361 .. **Kane,** Joanna D '06 %Deloitte Tax LLP -1633 Bway -NY 10019
(212) 335-9000 .. **Kane,** Jodie Eden '96 %DA -1 Hogan Pl -NY 10013
(212) 326-3939 .. **Kane,** John K '00 (Jones D) -222 E 41st -NY 10017
(585) 454-1920 .. **Kane,** Jonathan A '93 -301 Exchange Blvd -Rchstr 14608 **Fx:**325-4568
(212) 417-7000 .. **Kane,** Kathleen G '89 %Brookfield Fncl Prop -3 World Fncl Ctr -NY 10281 **Fx:**417-7214
(631) 853-4343 .. **Kane,** Kathleen McKinley '04 %Leg Aid -400 Carleton Av Bx9082 -Central Islip 11722 **Fx:**853-7798
(917) 536-6751 .. **Kane,** Kenneth P '80 -240 W 35th -NY 10001 **Fx:**(212) 689-5398
(212) 541-6222 .. **Kane Kessler,PC** -1350 Av of Amer -NY 10019 **Fx:**245-3009
(716) 853-8530 .. **Kane,** Kevin J '85 OCTF -350 Main Pl Twr -Buffalo 14202 **Fx:**853-8550
(718) 286-6000 .. **Kane,** Kristen A '90 %DA -125-01 Qns Blvd -Kew Gdns 11415
(212) 596-9000 .. **Kane,** Madeleine P '08 %Ropes & G LLP -1211 Av of Amer -NY 10036
(212) 662-4007 .. **Kane,** Margaret A '89 -90 LaSalle -NY 10027 **Fx:**665-5015
(718) 793-5700 .. **Kane,** Martin D '63 -125-10 Qns Blvd -Kew Gdns 11415 **Fx:**793-4719
(607) 723-5341 .. **Kane,** Martin J '79 SpclCnsl Hinman H&K,LLP -80 Exchange Bx5250 -Bnghmtn 13902
(716) 843-5700 .. **Kane,** Mary C '91 %US Atty -138 Delaware Av -Buffalo 14202 **Fx:**551-3052
(631) 852-1715 .. **Kane,** Mary K '81 Surrogates Ct -320 Center Dr -Rvrhead 11901
(212) 490-4100 .. **Kane,** Matthew D '04 %Storch A&M,PC -140 E 45th -NY 10017
(212) 752-5258 .. **Kane,** Matthew I '92 (Schwartz SE&C LLC) -845 3rd Av -NY 10022
(212) 373-3000 .. **Kane,** Meredith J '83 (Paul WRW&G LLP) -1285 Av of Amer -NY 10019
(212) 526-3783 .. **Kane,** Michl D '04 Barclays Capital Inc -745 7th Av -NY 10019
(212) 685-5263 .. **Kane,** Michl H '78 -240 W 35th -NY 10001 **Fx:**689-5398
(212) 457-9543 .. **Kane,** Patricia D '97 IncisiveMedia /NYLJ -120 Bway -NY 10271
(212) 776-5000 .. **Kane,** Patrick J '81 %NYC Housing Auth -250 Bway -NY 10007 **Fx:**776-5039
(212) 479-6000 .. **Kane,** Rachel B '03 %Cooley LLP -1114 Av of Amer -NY 10036
(212) 857-8230 .. **Kane,** Richd M '97 %Baker MM&M,PC -330 W 34th -NY 10001
(212) 272-9867 .. **Kane,** Robt K '94 JP Morgan Chase -320 Park Av -NY 10022
(212) 455-2000 .. **Kane,** Ryan A '03 %Simpson T&B LLP -425 Lex Av -NY 10017
(516) 203-7180 .. **Kane,** Sara W '99 (Valli K&V,LLP) -600 Old Cntry Rd -Gdn Cty 11530 **Fx:**706-0248
(212) 770-0630 .. **Kane,** Sean M '00 AIU Holdings,Inc -80 Pine -NY 10005
(212) 858-1453 .. **Kane,** Sean-Francis '99 Cnsl Pillsbury WSP LLP -1540 Bway -NY 10036
(212) 225-2000 .. **Kane,** Sheilah M '01 Cleary GS&H -1 Lbrty Plz -NY 10006
(212) 415-8600 .. **Kane,** Siegrun D '63 OfCnsl Locke LB&L LLP -3 World Fncl Ctr -NY 10281
(212) 264-2840 .. **Kane,** Susan H '05 %Hon R Eaton -1 Fed Plz -NY 10278
(718) 286-6000 .. **Kane,** Susan M '78 %DA -125-01 Qns Blvd -Kew Gdns 11415
(716) 845-9484 .. **Kane,** Timothy J '73 %Supreme Ct -50 Delaware Av -Buffalo 14202
(716) 635-4360 .. **Kane,** Timothy L '90 Merrill Lynch -6245 Sheridan Dr -Williamsvll 14221 **Fx:**635-4348
(212) 868-6300 .. **Kane,** Walter M '99 (Cary K LLP) -1350 Bway -NY 10018
(718) 520-3363 .. **Kane,** Wm C Jr. '83 %Criminal Ct -125-01 Qns Blvd -Kew Gdns 11415
(212) 553-0300 .. **Kanef,** Michl B '93 %Moody's Invstr Srvc -250 Greenwich -NY 10007
(212) 922-6424 .. **Kanefsky,** David H '91 Dreyfus Corp -200 Park Av -NY 10166 **Fx:**922-6880
(212) 308-4411 .. **Kanefsky,** E Paul '80 (Edwards AP&D LLP) -750 Lex Av -NY 10022
(585) 247-9000 .. **Kanellis,** Gary M '99 %Shapiro D&B,LLP -250 Mile Xing Blvd -Rchstr 14624
(718) 286-6000 .. **Kanellopoulos,** George '07 %DA -125-01 Qns Blvd -Kew Gdns 11415
(212) 395-0017 .. **Kanengiser,** Amy D '83 Verizon -560 Lex Av -NY 10022
(718) 739-6400 .. **Kaner,** Debra M '85 %DHCR -92-31 Union Hall -Jamaica 11433 **Fx:**262-7938
(914) 636-7100 .. **Kaner,** Morton Elliott '55 (Novick & K) -56 Harrison -New Rchll 10801
(212) 508-6700 .. **Kanes,** Yolanda '85 (Tannenbaum HS&H LLP) -900 3rd Av -NY 10022
(212) 336-0103 .. **Kanevski Suh,** Simona '02 %SEC -3 World Fncl Ctr -NY 10281 **Fx:**336-1323
(212) 508-6700 .. **Kanfer,** David J '02 %Tannenbaum HS&H LLP -900 3rd Av -NY 10022
(212) 317-8500 .. **Kanfer,** Kenneth A '88 (Snitow KH&M,LLP) -575 Lex Av -NY 10022
(516) 482-6293 .. **Kanfer,** Martin R '88 -3 Nrthrn Blvd -Gt Neck 11021 **Fx:**(208) 728-6963
(212) 756-2000 .. **Kang,** Ana P '03 %Schulte R&Z LLP -919 3rd Av -NY 10022
(212) 527-1000 .. **Kang,** Bella Soohee '00 %Jones HC&B PC -1 Bttry Pk Plz -NY 10004
(212) 858-4009 .. **Kang,** Christina J '02 FINRA -1 Lbrty Plz -NY 10006 **Fx:**858-4389
(212) 478-7200 .. **Kang,** Christina J '02 %Hahn & H LLP -488 Mad Av -NY 10022
(212) 715-1000 .. **Kang,** Eunice Y '04 %Arnold & P LLP -399 Park Av -NY 10022
(212) 858-1000 .. **Kang,** H Marty '09 %Pillsbury WSP LLP -1540 Bway -NY 10036
(212) 455-2000 .. **Kang,** Heesun '07 %Simpson T&B LLP -425 Lex Av -NY 10017
(212) 318-6000 .. **Kang,** Hyun Ah '10 %Paul HJ&W LLP -75 E 55th -NY 10022
(212) 318-6000 .. **Kang,** Hyungsuk '09 %Paul HJ&W LLP -75 E 55th -NY 10022
(212) 809-7800 .. **Kang,** Jean Hee '00 %Jaffe & K,LLP -40 Wall -NY 10005
(212) 902-1590 .. **Kang,** Jeannie S '95 %Goldman Sachs -1 NY Plz -NY 10004
(516) 777-7770 .. **Kang,** John M '92 %Earth Therapeutics -163 E Bethpage Rd -Plainvw 11803
(212) 701-3000 .. **Kang,** Jun '03 %Cahill G&R LLP -80 Pine -NY 10005 **Fx:**269-5420
(212) 902-9636 .. **Kang,** Linda Tae-Ryung '01 Goldman Sachs & Co -85 Broad -NY 10004
(212) 450-4000 .. **Kang,** Mi-Hyang Charlotte '09 %Davis P&W LLP -450 Lex Av -NY 10017
(212) 826-0900 .. **Kang,** Shin-Taeg '01 Korea Trade -460 Park Av -NY 10022
(212) 564-5550 .. **Kang,** Sook J '92 -39 W 32nd -NY 10001
(646) 497-4067 .. **Kang,** Suesie '05 Neuberger Berman,LLC -605 3rd Av -NY 10158
(212) 261-8000 .. **Kang,** Tae (Thomas) Y '06 %Mendes & M,LLP -750 7th Av -NY 10019
(914) 946-4777 .. **Kang,** Wm S '08 %Keane & B,PC -445 Hmltn Av -White Plns 10601
(212) 252-9550 .. **Kang,** Yilo J '02 %Freiberg & P -49 W 37th -NY 10018
(212) 875-6303 .. **Kang-Huneke,** Myung H '90 Sesame Workshop -1 Lincoln Plz -NY 10023 **Fx:**875-6124
(516) 832-3200 .. **Kania,** John T '86 %1st Amer Title -333 Earle Ovngton Blvd -Uniondale 11553 **Fx:**832-3299
(716) 856-3646 .. **Kania,** Nancy Sorrentino '94 %Cole SHH&G,PC -37 Franklin -Buffalo 14202
(212) 687-3860 .. **Kanian,** Mark A '83 Snow BK,PC -605 3rd Av -NY 10158
(212) 878-8000 .. **Kaniaru,** Wangui W '09 %Clifford C LLP -31 W 52nd -NY 10019
(212) 878-8000 .. **Kanji,** Farzana Salim '00 %Clifford C LLP -31 W 52nd -NY 10019
(914) 948-4700 .. **Kanlong,** Christina S '02 %Kent HWCV&F,LLP -111 Church -White Plns 10601
(212) 836-8000 .. **Kann,** Elisabeth C '01 %Kaye S LLP -425 Park Av -NY 10022
(716) 645-2406 .. **Kannar,** George '79 %SUNY Buffalo Lw Schl -O'Brian Hall -Buffalo 14260 **Fx:**645-5968
(877) 222-1814 .. **Kannengieser,** John V '79 %B Rothenberg -100 Duffy Av -Hicksvll 11801 **Fx:**(866) 894-2182
(212) 735-3000 .. **Kanner,** Ellen H '08 %Skadden ASM&F LLP -4 Times Sq -NY 10036
(212) 259-8000 .. **Kanner,** Fredk W '69 (Dewey & L LLP) -1301 Av of Amer -NY 10019
(212) 812-2615 .. **Kanner,** Hillel '03 Nationwide Settlements LLC -1333 60th Rd -Brklyn 11219
(212) 286-1666 .. **Kanner,** Jacob '83 %S Bing -276 5th Av -NY 10001 **Fx:**286-1616
(212) 446-4800 .. **Kanner,** Jason S '98 (Kirkland & E LLP) -153 E 53rd -NY 10022
(212) 303-8050 .. **Kanner,** Lisa B '02 %Hadassah -50 W 58th -NY 10019 **Fx:**303-7436
(212) 984-7720 .. **Kannry,** Jack S '68 (Warshaw BCS&K,LLP) -555 5th Av -NY 10017
(212) 832-0400 .. **Kanousis,** Sean P '06 Berdon LLP -360 Mad Av -NY 10017
(212) 287-2800 .. **Kanover,** Jared A '03 SrCnsl Sterling Stamos Capital Mgmt,LP -450 Park Av -NY 10022 **Fx:**287-2900
(718) 435-2847 .. **Kanovsky,** Yaakov '90 -1138 52nd -Brklyn 11219 **Fx:**435-3077
(212) 479-6000 .. **Kanowitz,** Richd S '93 (Cooley LLP) -1114 Av of Amer -NY 10036
(917) 421-4665 .. **Kanrek,** Victoria J '91 IRS Chief Cnsl LMSB -33 Maiden Ln -NY 10038 **Fx:**421-3937
(212) 732-6282 .. **Kansas,** Tina E '98 -305 Bway -NY 10007 **Fx:**385-1436
(212) 973-0572 .. **Kantar,** Brian '07 %Wolff & S PC -140 Bway -NY 10005 **Fx:**(973) 530-2312
(646) 471-5608 .. **Kantemeridis,** Catherine '02 PricewaterhouseCoopers LLP -1177 Av of Amer -NY 10036
(315) 443-2524 .. **Kanter,** Arlene S '82 %Syracuse Univ Cllg of Law -Wht Hall -Syracuse 13244 **Fx:**443-4213
(212) 412-9500 .. **Kanter,** Gregg H '92 OfCnsl Flemming ZWZ LLP -1 Lbrty Plz -NY 10006
(212) 504-6000 .. **Kanter,** Jonathan S '99 (Cadwalader W&T LLP) -1 World Fncl Ctr -NY 10281
(212) 918-3000 .. **Kanter,** Lauren B '08 %Hogan L LLP -875 3rd Av -NY 10022
(631) 738-9100 .. **Kanter,** Lauren D '09 %Campolo M&M,LLP -3340 Vets Mem'l Hwy -Bohemia 11716 **Fx:**738-0659
(212) 468-4800 .. **Kanter,** Leslie G '89 Davis & G LLP -1740 Bway -NY 10019
(631) 845-7100 .. **Kanter,** Marc J '94 -151 W Carver -Huntngtn 11743
(212) 530-5000 .. **Kanter,** Matthew L '10 %Milbank TH&M LLP -1 Chase Manh Plz -NY 10005
(516) 728-3014 .. **Kanter,** Michelle B '96 -Bellmore 11710
(631) 845-1400 .. **Kanter,** Richd V '95 -510 Broadhllw Rd -Melvll 11747 **Fx:**752-4603
(646) 386-3040 .. **Kanter,** Robt M '74 %Supreme Ct Appllt Term -60 Centre -NY 10007
(212) 735-3497 .. **Kanter,** Stacy J '85 (Skadden ASM&F LLP) -4 Times Sq -NY 10036
(212) 915-8401 .. **Kanterman,** Emily M '07 Willis of NY Inc -200 Lbrty -NY 10281
(914) 457-2300 .. **Kanterman,** Erin H '04 %Kanterman & S,LLP -50 Main -White Plns 10606
(914) 457-2300 .. **Kanterman,** Lawr R '75 (Kanterman & S,LLP) -50 Main -White Plns 10606
(914) 457-2300 .. **Kanterman & Soscia, LLP** -50 Main -White Plns 10606 **Fx:**457-2301
(718) 286-6000 .. **Kanth,** Antara D '07 %DA -125-01 Qns Blvd -Kew Gdns 11415
(516) 237-7863 .. **Kantor,** Andrea D '83 800-Flowers.com -1 Old Cntry Rd -Carle Pl 11514
(212) 682-8383 .. **Kantor Davidoff Wolfe Mandelker Twomey & Gallanty,PC** -51 E 42nd -NY 10017 **Fx:**949-5206
(212) 206-6191 .. **Kantor & DeMarco** -55 5th Av -NY 10003 **Fx:**727-0563
(631) 231-1450 .. **Kantor,** Glenn L '84 Feldman K&M,PC -330 Vndrblt Motor Pkwy -Hauppauge 11788
(516) 352-4100 .. **Kantor,** Harris D '84 -3000 Marcus Av -Lk Success 11042 **Fx:**326-1576
(212) 682-8383 .. **Kantor,** Herbert C '55 (Kantor DWMT&G,PC) -51 E 42nd -NY 10017
(516) 938-9309 .. **Kantor,** Isa Doppelt '81 (Kantor & K) -183 Bway -Hicksvll 11801
(212) 825-3336 .. **Kantor,** John B '93 %Dept of Invstgtn -80 Maiden Ln -NY 10038 **Fx:**825-2860

(516) 938-9309 ..**Kantor & Kopman** -183 Bway -Hicksvll 11801 **Fx:**938-9401
(716) 439-7172 ..**Kantor,** Kristie Ann '93 Family Ct -Cthse -Lockprt 14094 **Fx:**439-7170
(212) 308-4411 ..**Kantor,** Patricia L '84 (Edwards AP&D LLP) -750 Lex Av -NY 10022
(212) 206-6179 ..**Kantor,** Robt A '85 (Kantor & D) -55 5th Av -NY 10003
(716) 626-0404 ..**Kantor,** Steven L '90 (Kantor & G,PLLC) -5800 Main -Williamsvll 14221 **Fx:**626-0412
(914) 328-0404 ..**Kantor,** Susanne '97 OfCnsl Jackson L LLP -1 N Bway -White Plns 10601
(585) 262-4700 ..**Kantor,** Theo S '70 (Bilgore RLK&K) -950 Rynlds Arcd Bldg -Rchstr 14614
(212) 867-9655 ..**Kantorowitz,** Steven R '91 -12 W 37th -NY 10018
(973) 966-8108 ..**Kantowitz,** Jeffrey L '83 Cnsl Day P LLP -7 Times Sq -NY 10036 **Fx:**966-1065
(631) 423-8527 ..**Kantrow,** Fred S '04 %A Rosen -38 New -Huntngtn 11743 **Fx:**423-4536
(845) 356-2570 ..**Kantrowitz,** Barry S '86 (Kantrowitz G&G,PC) -747 Chestnut Rdg Rd -Chestnut Rdg 10977
(845) 356-2570 ..**Kantrowitz Goldhamer & Graifman,PC** -747 Chestnut Rdg Rd -Chestnut Rdg 10977 **Fx:**356-4335
(212) 335-4500 ..**Kantrowitz,** Jack I '91 (DLA Piper LLP) -1251 Av of Amer -NY 10020
(212) 617-6068 ..**Kantrowitz,** Naomi L '06 %Bloomberg -731 Lex Av -NY 10022
(212) 940-8800 ..**Kantrowitz,** Sharon '93 SpclCnsl Katten MR LLP -575 Mad Av -NY 10022
(845) 356-2570 ..**Kantrowitz,** Walter L '55 SpclCnsl Kantrowitz G&G,PC -747 Chestnut Rdg Rd -Chestnut Rdg 10977
(212) 488-1598 ..**Kanuck,** Jonathan M '06 %Havkins RR&V,LLP -11 Penn Plz -NY 10001
(212) 833-5730 ..**Kanusher,** Lawr A '89 Sony BMG Music Entrtnmnt -550 Mad Av -NY 10022 **Fx:**833-8406
(718) 780-0696 ..**Kanwar,** Joy '00 %Bklyn Law Schl -250 Joralemon -Brklyn 11201 **Fx:**780-0393
(585) 546-8430 ..**Kanyuck,** Dwight E '09 %Knauf S LLP -2 State -Rchstr 14614
(212) 352-9200 ..**Kanzer,** Adam M '93 %Domini Social Investments -536 Bway -NY 10012
(212) 210-9480 ..**Kanzer,** Alan '69 SrCnsl Alston & B LLP -90 Park Av -NY 10016
(718) 769-7200 ..**Kanzer,** Michl F '88 (M Kanzer & Assoc) -2110 Av U -Brklyn 11229 **Fx:**(347) 702-8208
(516) 741-2121 ..**Kanzer,** Neil L '74 -1325 Franklin Av -Gdn Cty 11530 **Fx:**741-3930
(212) 809-4800 ..**Kanzer,** Neil L '74 -30 Broad -NY 10004 **Fx:**363-3097
(516) 433-3000 ..**Kanzler,** John S '89 %Finz & F,PC -410 E Jericho Tpk -Mineola 11501 **Fx:**433-3001
(212) 755-8880 ..**Kao,** Annie '85 (Wu & K,PLLC) -747 3rd Av -NY 10017 **Fx:**755-8890
(212) 596-9000 ..**Kao,** Brian '08 %Ropes & G LLP -1211 Av of Amer -NY 10036
(718) 460-8999 ..**Kao,** Chenmao Jeff '89 -39-07 Prince -Flushng 11354 **Fx:**461-9124
(212) 788-3160 ..**Kao,** Cynthia '01 %Law Dept -60 Lafayette -NY 10013 **Fx:**442-6865
(212) 583-5047 ..**Kao,** Ja Lee '02 Blackstone Grp -345 Park Av -NY 10154
(212) 906-1200 ..**Kao,** Robt '07 %Latham & W -885 3rd Av -NY 10022
(212) 601-6151 ..**Kao,** Yvonne R '07 Western Asset Mgmt Co -620 8th Av -NY 10018
(212) 834-0600 ..**Kaouris,** Christina '93 (Gordon & S,PC) -355 Lex Av -NY 10017
(212) 332-4225 ..**Kapadia,** Aman F '05 %Fir Tree Prtnrs -505 5th Av -NY 10017
(212) 577-7700 ..**Kapadia,** Sneha Subhash '03 %Safe Horizon -2 Lafayette -NY 10007 **Fx:**385-0331
(212) 895-5100 ..**Kapassakis,** Paul '96 Dresdner Kleinwort & Srvcs LLC -2 World Fncl Ctr -NY 10281
(212) 692-9708 ..**Kapchan,** Jordan W '84 J Kapchan,PC -99 Park Av -NY 10016 **Fx:**681-0810
(212) 683-2210 ..**Kapell,** Wm A '86 %Childrens Rts Inc -330 7th Av -NY 10001 **Fx:**683-4015
(212) 563-2010 ..**Kapelman,** David A '77 (D Kapelman,PC) -3 W 35th -NY 10001 **Fx:**594-0019
(212) 244-2600 ..**Kapelman,** Jeffrey D '77 %Hilldun Corp -225 W 35th -NY 10001
(516) 227-0700 ..**Kapen,** Alon Y '88 (Farrell F,PC) -1320 RXR Plz -Uniondale 11556
(212) 449-2853 ..**Kaperst,** Stuart C '85 Merrill Lynch -250 Vesey -NY 10080
(718) 777-3800 ..**Kapetanos & Belibasakis,LLP** -23-56 Steinway -Astoria 11105 **Fx:**777-3801
(718) 777-3800 ..**Kapetanos,** Constantine S '94 (Kapetanos & B,LLP) -23-56 Steinway -Astoria 11105
(516) 745-8000 ..**Kapetanos,** Steven J '04 %Wolfson & G LLP -1600 Stewart Av -Westbury 11590
(212) 576-6127 ..**Kapili,** Bernee V '04 NY Life Ins -51 Mad Av -NY 10010
(212) 808-8100 ..**Kapiloff,** Arnold Y '62 Cnsl Kostelanetz & F,LLP -7 Wrld Trd Ctr -NY 10007
(631) 844-7408 ..**Kapitansky,** Sharon Haut '97 %Adecco -175 Broadhllw Rd -Melvll 11747 **Fx:**844-7266
(516) 535-1700 ..**Kaplain,** Leonard R '87 (Horing W&R,PC) -11 Hillside Av -Williston Pk 11596
(718) 590-2000 ..**Kaplan,** Aaron B '98 %DA -198 E 161st -Bronx 10451 **Fx:**590-6477
(716) 856-4829 ..**Kaplan,** Aaron E '05 %Sammarco M&S,LLP -250 Delaware Av -Buffalo 14202
(212) 695-2800 ..**Kaplan,** Adam J '02 %Pinnacle Grp -1 Penn Plz -NY 10119
(212) 861-0469 ..**Kaplan,** Adam L '97 -370 E 76th -NY 10021
(516) 365-9802 ..**Kaplan,** Aimee L '07 %Collard & R,PC -1077 Nrthrn Blvd -Roslyn 11576
(212) 412-6910 ..**Kaplan,** Alan B '84 Barclays Capital Inc -745 7th Av -NY 10019
(212) 592-1400 ..**Kaplan,** Alan D '81 (Herrick,F LLP) -2 Park Av -NY 10016
(212) 839-5300 ..**Kaplan,** Alex J '03 %Sidley A LLP -787 7th Av -NY 10019
(212) 969-3000 ..**Kaplan,** Alexander '01 %Proskauer R LLP -1585 Bway -NY 10036
(516) 877-2525 ..**Kaplan,** Alexander M '76 (Weinstein K&C,PC) -1325 Franklin Av -Gdn Cty 11530
(212) 455-2000 ..**Kaplan,** Alexandra '03 %Simpson T&B LLP -425 Lex Av -NY 10017
(212) 824-0367 ..**Kaplan,** Alison G '92 Muze Inc -304 Hudson -NY 10013
(212) 231-7100 ..**Kaplan,** Alissa G '02 24/7 Real Media Inc -132 W 31st -NY 10001
(914) 282-0575 ..**Kaplan,** Alvin '61 -33 Lady Godiva Way -New Cty 10956 **Fx:**(561) 997-0950
(212) 593-6700 ..**Kaplan,** Andrew I '94 (Aaronson RF&D,LLP) -757 3rd Av -NY 10017
(212) 801-9250 ..**Kaplan,** Barbara T '76 (Greenberg T,LLP) -200 Park Av -NY 10166
(212) 779-3535 ..**Kaplan,** Barry M '75 -10 E 40th -NY 10016 **Fx:**689-2079
(914) 946-2869 ..**Kaplan,** Barry N '72 -25 Hillside Av -White Plns 10601
(516) 801-6363 ..**Kaplan,** Bart D '76 (Kaplan & K LLP) -1 Schl -Glen Cove 11542 **Fx:**801-6364
(516) 745-1100 ..**Kaplan Belsky Ross Bartell, LLP** -666 Old Cntry Rd -Gdn Cty 11530 **Fx:**745-6912
(212) 468-8000 ..**Kaplan,** Ben '01 %Morrison & F LLP -1290 Av of Amer -NY 10104
(212) 777-0320 ..**Kaplan,** Benjamin R '51 -30 Av B -NY 10009 **Fx:**674-1729
(516) 829-6900 ..**Kaplan,** Benjamin S '07 %Ackerman LCB&L,LLP -1010 Nrthrn Blvd -Gt Neck 11021
(212) 752-5258 ..**Kaplan,** Brad M '98 (Schwartz SE&C LLC) -845 3rd Av -NY 10022
(212) 269-2363 ..**Kaplan,** Brian I '91 (Goldberg & K) -11 Park Pl -NY 10007
(212) 506-1700 ..**Kaplan,** Brian S '95 (Kasowitz BT&F LLP) -1633 Bway -NY 10019
(212) 639-9000 ..**Kaplan,** Bruce H '86 -44 Wall -NY 10005
(212) 833-1101 ..**Kaplan,** Bruce S '67 (Friedman KS&A LLP) -1633 Bway -NY 10019 **Fx:**373-7901
(845) 344-2524 ..**Kaplan,** Bryan R '98 %C Curcio -1 Edgewtr Dr -Middletwn 10940 **Fx:**344-2528
(212) 318-6000 ..**Kaplan,** Bryan R '02 %Paul HJ&W LLP -75 E 55th -NY 10022
(212) 577-2523 ..**Kaplan,** Carl S '96 %Ctr for Appllt Litigation -74 Trinity Pl -NY 10006 **Fx:**577-2535
(212) 373-3000 ..**Kaplan,** Carol M '01 Cnsl Paul WRW&G LLP -1285 Av of Amer -NY 10019
(718) 596-8800 ..**Kaplan,** Cary H '03 (Kaplan & K) -16 Court -Brklyn 11241 **Fx:**596-9657
(212) 839-5300 ..**Kaplan,** Cathy M '78 (Sidley A LLP) -787 7th Av -NY 10019
(212) 422-0202 ..**Kaplan,** Chas H '80 (Sedgwick DM&A LLP) -125 Broad -NY 10004
(631) 923-1444 ..**Kaplan,** Cindy R '94 (Kaplan & K,PC) -707 Walt Whitman Rd -Melvll 11747
(631) 271-8505 ..**Kaplan,** Cori L '92 -275 Nassau Rd -Huntngtn 11743 **Fx:**547-8201
(212) 254-1111 ..**Kaplan,** Craig B '75 OfCnsl Rabinowitz BSK&L,PC -111 Bway -NY 10006
(212) 425-7200 ..**Kaplan,** Dana R '93 (Kenyon & K,LLP) -1 Bway -NY 10004
(212) 455-2000 ..**Kaplan,** Danl L '10 %Simpson T&B LLP -425 Lex Av -NY 10017
(212) 541-2000 ..**Kaplan,** Danl R '56 OfCnsl Bryan C LLP -1290 Av of Amer -NY 10104
(516) 773-6090 ..**Kaplan,** Darren T '92 (Chitwood HH LLP) -185 Grt Nck Rd -Gt Neck 11021
(212) 445-4479 ..**Kaplan,** David A '82 %Newsweek -395 Hudson -NY 10014
(212) 645-1253 ..**Kaplan,** David A '87 -225 W 25th -NY 10001 **Fx:**242-9018
(516) 222-9260 ..**Kaplan,** David H '78 Kaplan & K -666 Old Cntry Rd -Gdn Cty 11530
(516) 921-0800 ..**Kaplan,** David J '90 Blumenfeld Dvlmnt Grp, Ltd -300 Robbins Ln -Syosset 11791 **Fx:**921-0053
(212) 826-6658 ..**Kaplan,** David J '92 -551 Mad Av -NY 10022 **Fx:**826-6669
(212) 371-8008 ..**Kaplan,** David J '96 %Guzov O,LLC -600 Mad Av -NY 10022
(212) 425-7200 ..**Kaplan,** David J '07 %Kenyon & K,LLP -1 Bway -NY 10004
(718) 454-9411 ..**Kaplan,** David M '56 -67-23 198th -Flushng 11365 **Fx:**454-9606
(212) 589-4200 ..**Kaplan,** Deborah A '08 %Baker & H LLP -45 Rckfllr Plz -NY 10111
(212) 661-9100 ..**Kaplan,** Diane B '81 OfCnsl Otterbourg SH&R,PC -230 Park Av -NY 10169
(914) 773-2148 ..**Kaplan,** Dina S '96 -226 Central Av -Plsntvll 10570 **Fx:**773-2149
(212) 584-5100 ..**Kaplan,** Douglas A '94 %CD Radio Inc -1221 Av of Amer -NY 10020 **Fx:**584-5200
(516) 868-8700 ..**Kaplan,** Douglas J '83 -124 N Merrick Av -Merrick 11566
(518) 263-5077 ..**Kaplan,** Edw I '02 -7759 Main Bx155 -Hunter 12442 **Fx:**263-5078
(718) 855-3627 ..**Kaplan,** Eileen Schmerler '94 %C Berkman,LLC -111 Lvngstn -Brklyn 11201 **Fx:**855-4696
(516) 484-8479 ..**Kaplan,** Elayna C '88 -25 Woodgreen Ln -Roslyn Hts 11577 **Fx:**484-7835
(914) 682-0371 ..**Kaplan,** Eliot L '69 -175 Main -White Plns 10601 **Fx:**948-6051
(718) 739-6400 ..**Kaplan,** Ellen '76 %DHCR -92-31 Union Hall -Jamaica 11433 **Fx:**262-7938
(212) 345-6650 ..**Kaplan,** Ellyn B '93 Marsh & McLennan Cos -1166 Av of Amer -NY 10036 **Fx:**345-5627
(718) 298-8977 ..**Kaplan,** Emily '02 %Leg Aid -153-01 Jamaica Av -Jamaica 11432 **Fx:**657-0537
(212) 708-0280 ..**Kaplan,** Eric S '02 Bristol Consultantes LLC -335 Mad Av -NY 10017
(212) 782-3676 ..**Kaplan,** Eric T '04 Mizuho Corp Bk -1251 Av of Amer -NY 10020
(212) 593-1700 ..**Kaplan,** Eugene N '74 (Kaplan L LLP) -1065 Av of Amer -NY 10018
(212) 687-1980 ..**Kaplan Fox & Kilsheimer LLP** -850 3rd Av -NY 10022 **Fx:**687-7714
(845) 786-4855 ..**Kaplan,** Francine Spilke '80 %Dept of Law -Route 9 W-Helen Hayes Hsptl -W Haverstraw 10993 **Fx:**942-1452
(212) 859-8000 ..**Kaplan,** Gary L '99 (Fried FHS&J LLP) -1 NY Plz -NY 10004
(516) 224-1622 ..**Kaplan,** George M '77 %Dilworth & B,LLP -1000 Woodbury Rd -Woodbury 11797
(718) 739-1171 ..**Kaplan,** Glenn E '90 -9050 Parsons Blvd -Jamaica 11432
(312) 832-4393 ..**Kaplan,** Harold L '76 (Foley & L LLP) -90 Park Av -NY 10016
(212) 735-3000 ..**Kaplan,** Helene L '67 OfCnsl Skadden ASM&F LLP -4 Times Sq -NY 10036
(914) 378-3900 ..**Kaplan,** Howard J '82 (Kaplan & M) -1 Exec Blvd -Ynkrs 10701
(212) 333-0200 ..**Kaplan,** Howard J '89 (Arkin KR LLP) -590 Mad Av -NY 10022
(212) 909-4135 ..**Kaplan,** Hyla R '02 %Fragomen DB&L LLP -7 Hanover Sq -NY 10004 **Fx:**935-9838
(516) 293-1788 ..**Kaplan,** Ira S '96 -20 Melbourne Ln -Old Bethpage 11804
(718) 596-8800 ..**Kaplan,** Irwin R '63 (Kaplan & K) -16 Court -Brklyn 11241 **Fx:**596-9657
(212) 732-3200 ..**Kaplan,** Jack '63 Cnsl Carter L&M LLP -2 Wall -NY 10005
(212) 626-4100 ..**Kaplan,** Jacob M '03 %Baker & M LLP -1114 Av of Amer -NY 10036
(212) 310-8000 ..**Kaplan,** Jaime Singer '06 %Weil G&M LLP -767 5th Av -NY 10153
(212) 493-8353 ..**Kaplan,** James I '05 Brown Bros Harriman -140 Bway -NY 10005 **Fx:**493-8206
(212) 704-6000 ..**Kaplan,** James M '71 (Troutman S LLP) -405 Lex Av -NY 10174
(212) 878-8000 ..**Kaplan,** James M '07 %Clifford C LLP -31 W 52nd -NY 10019
(212) 471-8546 ..**Kaplan,** James S '76 (Herzfeld & R,PC) -125 Broad -NY 10004
(315) 428-4634 ..**Kaplan,** Jami E '04 NYS Div Human Rights -333 E Wshngtn -Syracuse 13202
(518) 482-8986 ..**Kaplan,** Janet S '83 Swyer Cos -10 Exec Park Dr -Albany 12203 **Fx:**482-5190

(516) 801-6363 .. **Kaplan**, Jared S '03 (Kaplan & K LLP) -1 Schl -Glen Cove 11542 **Fx:**801-6364

(212) 530-5000 .. **Kaplan**, Jason I '08 %Milbank TH&M LLP -1 Chase Manh Plz -NY 10005

(516) 228-1300 .. **Kaplan**, Jason L '10 %Sahn WC&B,PLLC -333 Earle Ovngton Blvd -Uniondale 11553

(212) 756-2000 .. **Kaplan**, Jason S '02 (Schulte R&Z LLP) -919 3rd Av -NY 10022

(212) 918-3000 .. **Kaplan**, Jason W '93 (Hogan L LLP) -875 3rd Av -NY 10022

(845) 331-3258 .. **Kaplan**, Jay A '73 JA Kaplan,PC -24 John -Kingston 12401 **Fx:**331-7648

(845) 647-4110 .. **Kaplan**, Jeffrey '78 (Kalter KZ&F) -47 N Main Bx186 -Ellenvll 12428

(845) 434-4777 .. **Kaplan**, Jeffrey '78 (Kalter KZ&F) -6166 State Rte 42 Bx30 -Woodbourne 12788

(212) 485-9804 .. **Kaplan**, Jeffrey A '95 (Schwartz L&K,PLLC) -60 E 42nd -NY 10165

(212) 541-2000 .. **Kaplan**, Jeffrey H '83 Cnsl Bryan C LLP -1290 Av of Amer -NY 10104

(212) 532-8100 .. **Kaplan**, Jennifer L '04 %Stern & M,LLP -115 Bway -NY 10006

(212) 247-0848 .. **Kaplan**, Jeremy B '06 %Bienstock & M,PC -250 W 57th -NY 10107

(516) 868-3963 .. **Kaplan**, Jerrold M '92 -2163 Vine Dr -Merrick 11566

(212) 213-8844 .. **Kaplan**, Jesse A '03 %Allyn & F LLP -200 Mad Av -NY 10016

(646) 865-1541 .. **Kaplan**, Joel '81 NYS IOLA -11 E 44th -NY 10017

(516) 745-1100 .. **Kaplan**, Joel S '62 (Kaplan BRB,LLP) -666 Old Cntry Rd -Gdn Cty 11530

(212) 262-6699 .. **Kaplan**, Jos C '72 Cnsl Tenzer & L LLP -1775 Bway -NY 10019

(212) 380-5885 .. **Kaplan**, Jos M '05 %Cyrus Cptl Ptnrs -399 Park Av -NY 10022

(212) 839-5300 .. **Kaplan**, Joshua A '08 %Sidley A LLP -787 7th Av -NY 10019

(212) 250-7523 .. **Kaplan**, Joshua H '03 %Deutsche Bank -60 Wall -NY 10005

(212) 805-0431 .. **Kaplan**, Joshua I '05 %Hon G Lynch -500 Pearl -NY 10007

(212) 450-4000 .. **Kaplan**, Joshua M '08 Davis P&W LLP -450 Lex Av -NY 10017

(516) 571-3800 .. **Kaplan**, Kara R '02 %DA -262 Old Cntry Rd -Mineola 11501 **Fx:**248-9479

(516) 248-6000 .. **Kaplan**, Keith L '97 (Kaufman B&R) -1205 Franklin Av -Gdn Cty 11530

(212) 750-3100 .. **Kaplan**, Kenneth J '72 (Kaplan & K) -767 3rd Av -NY 10017

(212) 593-1700 .. **Kaplan Landau LLP** -1065 Av of Amer -NY 10018 **Fx:**593-1707

(212) 815-1818 .. **Kaplan**, Lee S S '04 DC 37 MELS -125 Barclay -NY 10007 **Fx:**815-1343

(212) 244-9500 .. **Kaplan**, Leor J '05 %White and W LLP -1 Penn Plz -NY 10119

(212) 983-6900 .. **Kaplan & Levenson PC** -630 3rd Av -NY 10017 **Fx:**983-9210

(212) 878-8000 .. **Kaplan**, Lindsay R '04 %Clifford C LLP -31 W 52nd -NY 10019

(212) 554-7800 .. **Kaplan**, Lindsay R '10 %Moses & S LLP -405 Lex Av -NY 10174

(212) 354-1166 .. **Kaplan**, Marc A '05 %Triumph Srch Cnsltnts -130 W 42nd -NY 10036 **Fx:**354-1141

(212) 417-4357 .. **Kaplan**, Marcia E '83 %Dept of Health -90 Church -NY 10007 **Fx:**417-4392

(212) 878-0000 .. **Kaplan**, Marcie B '83 %MTA -2 Penn Plz -NY 10121

(212) 549-2500 .. **Kaplan**, Margo '05 %ACLU -125 Broad -NY 10004 **Fx:**549-2651

(212) 373-2646 .. **Kaplan**, Marjorie S '89 Paul WRW&G LLP -1285 Av of Amer -NY 10019

(212) 735-3000 .. **Kaplan**, Mark N '53 OfCnsl Skadden ASM&F LLP -4 Times Sq -NY 10036

(718) 855-7728 .. **Kaplan**, Marshall G '49 -40 Clinton -Brklyn 11201 **Fx:**802-1248

(718) 258-9100 .. **Kaplan**, Martin '57 -2917 Av P -Brklyn 11229 **Fx:**258-9106

(212) 269-1400 .. **Kaplan**, Martin H '75 (Gusrae KB&N PLLC) -120 Wall -NY 10005

(212) 937-7272 .. **Kaplan**, Martin S '02 WilmerHale -399 Park Av -NY 10022

(212) 922-0450 .. **Kaplan Massamillo & Andrews,LLC** -70 E 55th -NY 10022 **Fx:**922-0530

(212) 974-7474 .. **Kaplan**, Matthew A '01 %Cowan DA&S LLP -41 Mad Av -NY 10010

(212) 909-6000 .. **Kaplan**, Matthew E '97 (Debevoise & P LLP) -919 3rd Av -NY 10022

(212) 728-8000 .. **Kaplan**, Matthew I '06 %Willkie F&G LLP -787 7th Av -NY 10019

(212) 298-5297 .. **Kaplan**, Melissa '06 %Leg Aid -49 Thomas -NY 10013 **Fx:**298-5252

(212) 373-3000 .. **Kaplan**, Menachem '06 %Paul WRW&G LLP -1285 Av of Amer -NY 10019

(718) 833-4400 .. **Kaplan**, Michl A '92 M Kaplan,PC -53 Harmon -Long Bch 11561 **Fx:**833-4472

(212) 582-6700 .. **Kaplan**, Michl B '99 %Ripplewood Holdings -1 Rckfllr Plz -NY 10020

(718) 377-0600 .. **Kaplan**, Michl L '83 -2911 Kings Hwy -Brklyn 11229 **Fx:**377-7420

(212) 450-4000 .. **Kaplan**, Michl P '96 (Davis P&W LLP) -450 Lex Av -NY 10017

(212) 362-9800 .. **Kaplan**, Mitchell D '90 -170 W 74th -NY 10023

(212) 218-5500 .. **Kaplan**, Mitchell S '85 (Seyfarth S LLP) -620 8th Av -NY 10018

(212) 986-6000 .. **Kaplan**, Myron L '70 (Kleinberg KW&C,PC) -551 5th Av -NY 10176

(212) 350-9990 .. **Kaplan**, Natalie J '74 -100 Park Av -NY 10017 **Fx:**350-1597

(718) 803-4089 .. **Kaplan**, Neal H '02 Sterling Mets LP -Citi Field -Flushng 11368 **Fx:**205-8123

(516) 364-6400 .. **Kaplan**, Neal S '78 %Kabro Assoc -113 Crsswys Park Dr -Woodbury 11797 **Fx:**364-7646

(212) 839-5300 .. **Kaplan**, Neil J '84 (Sidley A LLP) -787 7th Av -NY 10019

(212) 421-4100 .. **Kaplan**, Nicole E '98 OfCnsl Pryor C LLP -7 Times Sq -NY 10036

(212) 801-3150 .. **Kaplan**, Nicole H '08 %Greenberg T,LLP -200 Park Av -NY 10166

(516) 487-4300 .. **Kaplan**, Norman A '73 -111 Grt Nck Rd -Gt Neck 11021 **Fx:**773-4516

(212) 808-7800 .. **Kaplan**, Pamela D '84 SpclCnsl Kelley D&W LLP -101 Park Av -NY 10178

(315) 472-8472 .. **Kaplan**, Pamela R '77 -222 Hawley Av Bx6062 -Syracuse 13217 **Fx:**472-8419

(212) 484-3900 .. **Kaplan**, Paul M '91 (Arent F LLP) -1675 Bway -NY 10019

(914) 234-9462 .. **Kaplan**, Peter D '83 -127 Indn Hill Rd -Bedfrd 10506 **Fx:**234-3843

(585) 262-6390 .. **Kaplan**, Peter M '83 (Hamberger & W) -1 S Wshngtn -Rchstr 14614

(718) 442-6262 .. **Kaplan**, Philip J '63 -350 St Marks Pl -Staten Isl 10301 **Fx:**442-0708

(914) 766-3470 .. **Kaplan**, Richd J '85 IBM -294 Route 100 -Somers 10589

(212) 907-7300 .. **Kaplan**, Richd S '94 (Golenbock EAB&P) -437 Mad Av -NY 10022

(718) 268-4200 .. **Kaplan**, Robt A '86 R Kaplan,PC -70-20 Austin -Frst Hlls 11375 **Fx:**268-0823

(212) 833-1104 .. **Kaplan**, Robt D '84 (Friedman KS&A LLP) -1633 Bway -NY 10019 **Fx:**373-7904

(212) 964-0600 .. **Kaplan**, Robt J '76 -15 Maiden Ln -NY 10038

(212) 944-2200 .. **Kaplan**, Robt M '81 (Ferber CE&C,LLP) -530 5th Av -NY 10036

(212) 687-1980 .. **Kaplan**, Robt N '64 (Kaplan F&K LLP) -850 3rd Av -NY 10022

(212) 373-3000 .. **Kaplan**, Roberta A '92 (Paul WRW&G LLP) -1285 Av of Amer -NY 10019

(631) 247-0404 .. **Kaplan**, Roger S '67 (Jackson L LLP) -58 S Srvc Rd -Melvll 11747

(212) 766-1423 .. **Kaplan**, Ron '85 -325 Bway -NY 10007 **Fx:**571-7004

(212) 925-3179 .. **Kaplan**, Rosanne L '75 -177 Duane -NY 10013 **Fx:**989-8873

(212) 878-7900 .. **Kaplan**, Seth M '98 SpclCnsl Fox R LLP -100 Park Av -NY 10017

(516) 938-9500 .. **Kaplan**, Sherri L '88 -575 Jericho Tpk -Jericho 11753 **Fx:**938-9508

(212) 269-1400 .. **Kaplan**, Shirley '85 Gusrae KB&N PLLC -120 Wall -NY 10005

(718) 824-9650 .. **Kaplan**, Solomon H '54 -2311 Wht Plns Rd -Bronx 10467 **Fx:**231-2330

(212) 468-8000 .. **Kaplan**, Stacy L '05 %Morrison & F LLP -1290 Av of Amer -NY 10104

(516) 677-0870 .. **Kaplan**, Stacy Lee '95 -60 Calvin Av -Syosset 11791

(516) 877-9200 .. **Kaplan**, Stanford '69 -200 Willis Av -Mineola 11501 **Fx:**877-2554

(718) 590-2000 .. **Kaplan**, Stanley R '86 %DA -198 E 161st -Bronx 10451 **Fx:**590-6477

(212) 687-4900 .. **Kaplan**, Stefi N '07 %Wormser KG&J LLP -825 3rd Av -NY 10022

(212) 298-5220 .. **Kaplan**, Stephanie I '86 %Leg Aid -49 Thomas -NY 10013 **Fx:**298-5252

(212) 448-1100 .. **Kaplan**, Steven H '78 (McLaughlin & S,LLP) -260 Mad Av -NY 10016

(212) 527-1000 .. **Kaplan**, Steven H '82 (Jones HC&B PC) -1 Bttry Pk Plz -NY 10004

(631) 923-1444 .. **Kaplan**, Steven L '92 (Kaplan & K,PC) -707 Walt Whitman Rd -Melvll 11747

(212) 682-1400 .. **Kaplan**, Steven M '79 (Rosenfeld & K) -535 5th Av -NY 10017

(212) 983-6900 .. **Kaplan**, Steven M '93 (Kaplan & L PC) -630 3rd Av -NY 10017

(212) 885-5000 .. **Kaplan**, Stuart D '86 (Blank R LLP) -405 Lex Av -NY 10174

(212) 877-5998 .. **Kaplan**, Susan '75 -165 W End Av -NY 10023

(212) 319-3737 .. **Kaplan**, Tara L '02 %J Silberman Assoc,PC -145 E 57th -NY 10022 **Fx:**319-8188

(516) 791-5305 .. **Kaplan**, Theo '54 -140 Hungry Hrbr Rd -Vly Stream 11581 **Fx:**791-1108

(212) 687-1980 .. **Kaplan**, Theo N '69 (Kaplan F&K LLP) -850 3rd Av -NY 10022

(212) 953-0000 .. **Kaplan**, Theo P '98 -260 Mad Av -NY 10016 **Fx:**(646) 964-6646

(212) 986-6000 .. **Kaplan**, Todd B '08 %Kleinberg KW&C,PC -551 5th Av -NY 10176

(516) 678-4055 .. **Kaplan**, Victoria Saunders '95 (V Kaplan,PC) -2787 Lng Bch Rd -Oceanside 11572 **Fx:**678-2903

(516) 663-6600 .. **Kaplan**, Wayne L '82 (Ruskin MF,PC) -1425 RXR Plz -Uniondale 11556

(212) 480-4800 .. **Kaplan**, Wm I '83 (Fox H&C LLP) -825 3rd Av -NY 10022

(914) 747-4410 .. **Kaplen**, Michl V '80 (DeCaro & K,LLP) -427 Bedford Rd -Plsntvll 10570

(212) 640-9990 .. **Kaplicer**, Brett I '01 Amer Exp -200 Vesey -NY 10285

(718) 238-6800 .. **Kaplin**, Richd A '84 (DiConza LD&K) -478 Bay Ridge Pkwy -Brklyn 11209

(212) 425-9300 .. **Kaplon**, Jon D '87 Cnsl Bressler A&R,PC -17 State -NY 10004

(212) 233-6363 .. **Kaplow**, Alicia '78 -30 Vesey -NY 10007 **Fx:**962-9696

(518) 436-0751 .. **Kaplowitz**, Bernard '62 (Hinman S PC) -121 State -Albany 12207

(212) 839-5300 .. **Kaplowitz**, Brian M '82 (Sidley A LLP) -787 7th Av -NY 10019

(914) 633-3800 .. **Kaplowitz**, Isaac '52 (Kaplowitz & K) -145 Huguenot -New Rchll 10801 **Fx:**637-6299

(518) 459-3984 .. **Kaplowitz**, Jack A '76 -44 Oakwood -Albany 12208 **Fx:**459-3984

(212) 752-9700 .. **Kaplowitz**, Jay M '72 (Gersten S LLP) -600 Lex Av -NY 10022

(212) 687-3000 .. **Kaplowitz**, Mark '06 %Jaffe & A,LLP -600 3rd Av -NY 10016

(718) 298-1202 .. **Kaplowitz**, Mark D '07 %Supreme Ct -88-11 Sutphin Blvd -Jamaica 11435

(914) 232-6086 .. **Kaplowitz**, Michl B '85 -26 Lalli Dr -Katonah 10536

(914) 633-3800 .. **Kaplowitz**, Richd H '01 (Kaplowitz & K) -145 Huguenot -New Rchll 10801 **Fx:**637-6299

(212) 907-7300 .. **Kaplun**, Alexander '00 OfCnsl Golenbock EAB&P -437 Mad Av -NY 10022

(212) 907-6413 .. **Kaplun**, Allen '05 -405 Lex Av -NY 10174

(212) 619-6000 .. **Kaplun**, Oleg Feygin '98 (Fay K&M,LLP) -150 Bway -NY 10038 **Fx:**208-6879

(212) 687-5464 .. **Kapner**, Alyssa L '10 %JD Davis,PC -99 Park Av -NY 10016 **Fx:**557-0565

(212) 298-5124 .. **Kapner**, David M '89 %Leg Aid -49 Thomas -NY 10013 **Fx:**298-5252

(212) 697-3122 .. **Kapner**, Erik '76 (Martin C&B LLP) -220 E 42nd -NY 10017

(212) 836-8397 .. **Kapner**, Jeffrey H '98 (Kaye S LLP) -425 Park Av -NY 10022

(212) 596-9000 .. **Kapner**, Sara L '09 %Ropes & G LLP -1211 Av of Amer -NY 10036

(845) 371-4700 .. **Kapnick**, Eric S '82 (Fein SK&S,PC) -747 Chestnut Rdg Rd -Spg Vly 10977

(212) 808-7800 .. **Kapoor**, Anjna R '03 %Kelley D&W LLP -101 Park Av -NY 10178

(212) 350-2700 .. **Kapoor**, Ankur '02 (Constantine C,PC) -450 Lex Av -NY 10017

(212) 808-7800 .. **Kapoor**, Ila '08 %Kelley D&W LLP -101 Park Av -NY 10178

(212) 450-4000 .. **Kapoor**, Kirtee '00 (Davis P&W LLP) -450 Lex Av -NY 10017

(631) 843-5500 .. **Kapoor**, Kristen M '01 Henry Schein Inc -135 Duryea Rd -Melvll 11747

(212) 307-5500 .. **Kapoor**, Rishi '09 %Venable LLP -1270 Av of Amer -NY 10020

(718) 260-8547 .. **Kapoor**, Sapna '04 %ACS -345 Adams -Brklyn 11201

(516) 571-2777 .. **Kapoor**, Sarika '05 Supreme Ct -100 Supreme Ct Dr -Mineola 11501

(631) 348-0195 .. **Kapp**, David S '92 -1 Suffolk Sq -Islandia 11749 **Fx:**234-8876

(212) 788-8907 .. **Kapp**, Norman '50 %Law Dept -100 Church -NY 10007 **Fx:**788-0367

(718) 590-2059 .. **Kapp**, Thos D '89 %DA -198 E 161st -Bronx 10451 **Fx:**590-6477

(212) 736-1940 .. **Kappel**, Cary S '93 (Davidson D&K LLC) -485 7th Av -NY 10018

(212) 594-2020 .. **Kappel**, Michl J '95 Resnick Druckman Grp LLC -469 7th Av -NY 10018 **Fx:**629-0293

(516) 357-3000 .. **Kappus**, George D '74 (Rivkin R LLP) -926 RXR Plz -Uniondale 11556

(212) 688-8555 .. **Kappy**, Pia K '05 %Fragomen DB&L LLP -7 Hanover Sq -NY 10004

(212) 566-7188 .. **Kapralos**, Harry G '89 Cnsl Genova B&G -115 Bway -NY 10006

(516) 466-6500 .. **Kapralos**, James G '94 %Parker WA LLP -6 Hrbr Park Dr S -Pt Wash 11050

(718) 767-5300 .. **Kapsalis**, John P '00 (Kapsalis Assoc,PC) -12-52 Clintonvll -Whitestone 11357 **Fx:**767-5304

(631) 853-4049 .. **Kapsalis**, Leonard G '80 %Cnty Atty -Dennison Bldg Bx6100 -Hauppauge 11788 **Fx:**853-5169

(718) 391-1720 .. **Kaptzis**, Irene S '05 %Dept Design & Cnstrctn -30-30 Thomson Av -LIC 11101 **Fx:**391-1894
(607) 785-3389 .. **Kapur**, David E '79 Petrick & K,PC -2200 E Main -Endicott 13760 **Fx:**785-4830
(212) 878-0000 .. **Kapur**, Nicholas P '88 %MTA -2 Penn Plz -NY 10121
(212) 436-3648 .. **Kapusta**, Scott M '96 Deloitte & Touche LLP -2 World Fncl Ctr -NY 10281
(212) 903-9000 .. **Kapych**, Yekaterina '09 %Linklaters -1345 Av of Amer -NY 10105
(212) 681-8313 .. **Karaahmet**, Barbaros M '99 (Karaahmet L&G LLP) -370 Lex Av -NY 10017 **Fx:**208-2917
(212) 688-8555 .. **Karaahmet**, Parisa Kazemian '00 (Fragomen DB&L LLP) -7 Hanover Sq -NY 10004
(516) 877-1800 .. **Karabatos**, Elena '87 (Schlissel OK,PLLC) -200 Grdn City Plz -Gdn Cty 11530
(845) 592-7000 .. **Karabel**, Aron Z '06 %Donoghue TA&D LLP -2517 Route 52 -Hopewell Junct 12533
(631) 844-7800 .. **Karabelas**, Diana R '93 %Olsten Corp -175 Broadhllw Rd -Melvll 11747 **Fx:**844-7414
(718) 274-1600 .. **Karabelas**, Kyriakos T '95 (Karabelas & P LLP) -31-10 37th Av -LIC 11101 **Fx:**204-7100
(212) 732-3200 .. **Karabell**, David I '67 (Carter L&M LLP) -2 Wall -NY 10005
(607) 432-1499 .. **Karabinis**, Anastasios P '03 B&K Coffee -127 Commerce Rd -Oneonta 13820
(646) 746-8189 .. **Karacostas**, Nicholas A '91 Arch Ins Grp -1 Lbrty Plz -NY 10006 **Fx:**746-8248
(212) 335-4500 .. **Karaffa**, Jason M '07 %DLA Piper LLP -1251 Av of Amer -NY 10020
(212) 415-9200 .. **Karagheuzoff**, Christopher G '96 (Dorsey & W LLP) -250 Park Av -NY 10177
(212) 759-2300 .. **Karalian**, Renee L '04 %Carroll G&G,LLP -1790 Bway -NY 10019
(212) 883-1700 .. **Karalis**, Themes '04 %Duval & S LLP -101 Park Av -NY 10178
(718) 613-2424 .. **Karam**, Alexander R '05 %Hon F Block USDC -225 Cadman Plz E -Brklyn 11201
(212) 558-4000 .. **Karam**, Bachir P '09 %Sullivan & C LLP -125 Broad -NY 10004
(646) 722-8500 .. **Karam**, Francis P '82 (Grant & E,PA) -485 Lex Av -NY 10017
(212) 454-3467 .. **Karam**, Jennifer C '96 %Deutsche Bank -60 Wall -NY 10005
(212) 712-0008 .. **Karam**, Lawr M '80 (L Karam,PC) -41 W 72nd -NY 10023 **Fx:**712-0003
(518) 474-6750 .. **Karamanol**, Paul S '03 Liquor Auth -80 S Swan -Albany 12210 **Fx:**402-2304
(914) 686-9010 .. **Karamitsos**, Alexandra Cleveland '93 %Wilson BCC&C,PC -2 William -White Plns 10601
(212) 436-2000 .. **Karamon**, Martin C '05 Deloitte & Touche,LLP -2 World Fncl Ctr -NY 10281
(516) 678-6660 .. **Karamouzis**, Andrew P '89 (Moran K LLP) -265 Sunrise Hwy -Rockvll Ctr 11570
(212) 425-2125 .. **Karamouzis**, Andrew P '89 (Moran K LLP) -475 Park Av -NY 10016
(212) 272-8806 .. **Karamsingh**, Ravind '97 %JP Morgan Chase -383 Mad Av -NY 10179
(212) 766-1888 .. **Karan**, Gail S '96 %Morris DA&F -2 Rector -NY 10006
(718) 260-9150 .. **Karan**, Jeffrey D '84 -32 Court -Brklyn 11201
(212) 754-9400 .. **Karan**, Paul R '61 (Todtman NS&J,PC) -425 Park Av -NY 10022
(212) 323-2250 .. **Karanas**, Catherine L '88 %HHC-OLA-Medical Litigation -346 Bway -NY 10013 **Fx:**323-2251
(212) 416-8000 .. **Karanjia**, Peter '00 Dept of Law -120 Bway -NY 10271
(212) 373-3000 .. **Karansky**, Joel P '03 %Paul WRW&G LLP -1285 Av of Amer -NY 10019
(212) 848-4000 .. **Karapetyan**, Irene Kelly '02 %Shearman & S LLP -599 Lex Av -NY 10022
(212) 973-2800 .. **Karas**, Elizabeth J '87 Court TV -600 3rd Av -NY 10016 **Fx:**973-3355
(212) 683-0220 .. **Karas**, Helene L '86 (Hecht-Law,LLC) -60 Mad Av -NY 10010 **Fx:**683-2325
(212) 302-6574 .. **Karas**, James N Jr. '74 (Riker DSH&P LLP) -500 5th Av -NY 10110
(212) 504-6000 .. **Karas**, Jonathan M '08 %Cadwalader W&T LLP -1 World Fncl Ctr -NY 10281
(212) 715-9100 .. **Karasik**, Adam S '02 %Kramer LN&F,LLP -1177 Av of Amer -NY 10036
(212) 455-0450 .. **Karasik**, Howard '61 (Sherman C&K,PC) -605 3rd Av -NY 10158
(212) 233-3800 .. **Karasyk & Moschella,LLP** -225 Bway -NY 10007 **Fx:**233-3801
(212) 233-3800 .. **Karasyk**, Philip E '79 (Karasyk & M,LLP) -225 Bway -NY 10007
(718) 250-4236 .. **Karasyk**, Robin H '85 %Leg Aid -111 Lvngstn -Brklyn 11201 **Fx:**250-4243
(212) 889-4220 .. **Karasz**, Valerie '02 %Buchman Law Firm,LLP -10 E 40th -NY 10016 **Fx:**889-4221
(716) 204-2400 .. **Karaszewski**, Darleen V '00 %SJ Baum,PC -220 Nrthpnte Pkwy Bx1291 -Buffalo 14240 **Fx:**204-4600
(716) 843-5700 .. **Karaszewski**, Jos J '89 %US Atty -138 Delaware Av -Buffalo 14202 **Fx:**551-3052
(585) 723-8250 .. **Karatas**, Nigos '83 -1109 English Rd -Rchstr 14616 **Fx:**723-3852
(212) 858-1000 .. **Karatz**, Wm W '53 SrCnsl Pillsbury WSP LLP -1540 Bway -NY 10036
(646) 328-2626 .. **Karavias**, George L '95 -1001 Av of Amer -NY 10018
(718) 729-5959 .. **Karavias**, Jason L '01 -31-87 Steinway -Astoria 11103 **Fx:**729-3003
(212) 858-1000 .. **Karavolas**, Nickolas J '09 %Pillsbury WSP LLP -1540 Bway -NY 10036
(516) 496-5822 .. **Karayiannis**, Peter G '05 %T Spina -170 Froehlich Farm Blvd -Woodbury 11797 **Fx:**496-5420
(212) 836-8000 .. **Karbalai**, Hasneen '05 %Kaye S LLP -425 Park Av -NY 10022
(718) 277-5324 .. **Karben**, Ronald L '76 MHLS -888 Fountain Av -Brklyn 11208 **Fx:**235-3671
(914) 536-4402 .. **Karben**, Ryan Scott '00 -1 Melaney Dr -Monsey 10952 **Fx:**(845) 503-2193
(212) 956-0899 .. **Karch**, Chas P '79 -106 Cntrl Pk S -NY 10019 **Fx:**(973) 283-2608
(212) 259-8000 .. **Karcher**, Timothy Q '00 (Dewey & L LLP) -1301 Av of Amer -NY 10019
(212) 207-8787 .. **Karcioglu**, Zeynel Memed '02 Jacobs & B LLP -445 Park Av -NY 10022
(212) 640-2000 .. **Karczmer**, Aaron S '00 %Amer Exp -200 Vesey -NY 10285
(212) 450-4000 .. **Karczmer**, Ada Dekhtyar '00 Cnsl Davis P&W LLP -450 Lex Av -NY 10017
(212) 785-5050 .. **Kardaras & Kelleher LLP** -44 Wall -NY 10005 **Fx:**785-5055
(212) 785-5050 .. **Kardaras**, Peter W '98 OfCnsl Kardaras & K LLP -44 Wall -NY 10005
(212) 785-5050 .. **Kardaras**, Wm P '61 (Kardaras & K LLP) -44 Wall -NY 10005
(516) 255-4160 .. **Kardisch**, Josh H '86 (Kardisch L & Assoc PC) -80 E Old Cntry Rd -Mineola 11501 **Fx:**255-4163
(212) 478-7200 .. **Kardon**, James C '79 (Hahn & H LLP) -488 Mad Av -NY 10022
(212) 735-3000 .. **Kardon**, Saml M '08 %Skadden ASM&F LLP -4 Times Sq -NY 10036
(973) 618-5172 .. **Kardos**, Elizabeth S '98 Zolfo C,LLC -1114 Av of Amer -NY 10036 **Fx:**618-9430
(212) 756-2000 .. **Kareff**, Scott M '95 SpclCnsl Schulte R&Z LLP -919 3rd Av -NY 10022
(585) 295-4400 .. **Kareken**, Ronald S '65 OfCnsl Hiscock & B,LLP -2000 HSBC Plz -Rchstr 14604
(212) 285-0510 .. **Karel**, David B '81 (Wilkofsky FK&C) -299 Bway -NY 10007
(212) 371-9400 .. **Karelas**, Maria Demetriades '95 %Newman & N,PC -460 Park Av -NY 10022 **Fx:**371-8022
(718) 590-2000 .. **Karen**, Allen P W '73 %DA -198 E 161st -Bronx 10451 **Fx:**590-6477
(212) 455-2000 .. **Karen**, Jonathan A '02 %Simpson T&B LLP -425 Lex Av -NY 10017
(212) 407-7700 .. **Karesh**, John I '71 (Vedder P,PC) -1633 Bway -NY 10019
(212) 885-8156 .. **Karges**, Martin H '05 BDO Seidman LLP -330 Mad Av -NY 10017
(212) 286-1500 .. **Kargman**, Steven T '88 (Kargman Assoc) -500 E 77th -NY 10162 **Fx:**286-1588
(212) 521-5400 .. **Karides**, Constantine '95 (Reed S LLP) -599 Lex Av -NY 10022
(212) 909-6787 .. **Karig**, Adele M '81 (Debevoise & P LLP) -919 3rd Av -NY 10022
(212) 227-6333 .. **Karikari**, Gerald '02 -305 Bway -NY 10007 **Fx:**227-6336
(845) 638-5001 .. **Karim**, Ameenah '02 %DA -1 S Main -New Cty 10956 **Fx:**638-5070
(212) 648-4071 .. **Karim**, Irshad S '87 %JP Morgan Chase & Co -60 Wall -NY 10260
(347) 592-2200 .. **Karim**, Sheba '03 Leg Srvcs -89-00 Sutphin Blvd -Jamaica 11435 **Fx:**(718) 937-5350
(718) 843-8390 .. **Karin**, Michele J '98 %PS 100 -111-11 118th -S Ozone Pk 11420
(212) 468-4800 .. **Karin**, Robt A '79 (Davis & G LLP) -1740 Bway -NY 10019
(518) 391-5665 .. **Karis-Nix**, Olivia T '08 -34 Griffin Rd -Stephentwn 12169
(212) 210-9452 .. **Kariss**, Richd C '03 (Alston & B LLP) -90 Park Av -NY 10016
(212) 909-6000 .. **Kariyev**, Rafael '00 Cnsl Debevoise & P LLP -919 3rd Av -NY 10022
(212) 310-8000 .. **Karkar**, Nadia M '09 %Weil G&M LLP -767 5th Av -NY 10153
(212) 449-1000 .. **Karkhanechi**, Soheil M '02 Merrill Lynch -4 World Fncl Ctr -NY 10080
(212) 687-3000 .. **Karki**, Roshana '00 %Jaffe & A,LLP -600 3rd Av -NY 10016
(212) 458-2361 .. **Karkowsky**, Adam Zev '02 AIG -175 Water -NY 10038
(516) 569-4795 .. **Karkowsky**, Mayeer '78 -357 Edward Av -Woodmere 11598
(212) 373-3000 .. **Karkowsky**, Michelle '10 %Paul WRW&G LLP -1285 Av of Amer -NY 10019
(212) 909-6000 .. **Karkus**, Erzsebet '03 %Debevoise & P LLP -919 3rd Av -NY 10022
(646) 425-4444 .. **Karl**, Ellery Frederic '97 -Canal St Sta Bx253 -NY 10013
(585) 232-6500 .. **Karl**, Gary L '85 (Harter S&E LLP) -1600 Bausch & Lomb Pl -Rchstr 14604
(585) 258-2800 .. **Karl**, Katherine H '88 (Underberg & K LLP) -300 Bausch & Lomb Pl -Rchstr 14604
(212) 318-6000 .. **Karl**, Lindsey M '10 %Paul HJ&W LLP -75 E 55th -NY 10022
(315) 735-6481 .. **Karl**, Peter A III '79 (Paravati KG&D) -12 Steuben Pk -Utica 13501
(631) 265-7200 .. **Karl**, Terry J '83 (Russo KW&C) -400 Townline Rd -Hauppauge 11788
(718) 222-2395 .. **Karla**, Shannon '09 %Law Dept -350 Jay -Brklyn 11201 **Fx:**222-2088
(718) 681-5600 .. **Karlan**, Diane V '83 -881 Gerard Av -Bronx 10452
(212) 351-4000 .. **Karlan**, Mitchell A '80 (Gibson D&C LLP) -200 Park Av -NY 10166
(212) 259-8000 .. **Karlberg**, Magnus K '07 %Dewey & L LLP -1301 Av of Amer -NY 10019
(585) 753-4500 .. **Karle**, Kristina Anna '98 %DA -832 Watts Bldg -Rchstr 14614 **Fx:**753-4576
(212) 456-7777 .. **Karle**, Theresa W '91 %ABC -77 W 66th -NY 10023 **Fx:**456-6202
(914) 949-4600 .. **Karlen**, Andrew N '74 (Karlen S&R,LLP) -1 N Bway -White Plns 10601
(212) 867-0303 .. **Karlen**, Gerard M '83 -60 E 42nd -NY 10165
(914) 949-4600 .. **Karlen Stolzar & Reimann, LLP** -1 N Bway -White Plns 10601 **Fx:**682-0387
(800) 476-2970 .. **Karlick**, Gideon J '78 -Bx7227 -NY 10150
(718) 655-2900 .. **Karlin**, David A '89 %Belovin & F -2311 Wht Plns Rd -Bronx 10467
(212) 306-7450 .. **Karlin**, Raymond W '82 %Comm on Human Rights -40 Rector -NY 10006 **Fx:**306-7414
(212) 267-9020 .. **Karlin**, Roy J '76 (Shapiro B&A LLP) -225 Bway -NY 10007
(212) 593-3000 .. **Karlin**, Steven D '81 (Platzer SKLG&J,LLP) -1065 Av of Amer -NY 10018
(212) 732-9450 .. **Karlin**, Stewart L '82 -9 Murray -NY 10007 **Fx:**571-9893
(718) 260-9100 .. **Karliner**, Saml J '90 (Adler & K) -26 Court -Brklyn 11242 **Fx:**246-1423
(212) 325-2266 .. **Karlinsky**, Jason S '01 Credit Suisse -11 Mad Av -NY 10010
(212) 818-1110 .. **Karlinsky**, Martin E '77 (Butzel L,PC) -380 Mad Av -NY 10017
(646) 289-8900 .. **Karlitz**, Herbert S '82 Karlitz & Co,Inc -95 Mad Av -NY 10016
(315) 422-7725 .. **Karlovitz**, Kathleen A '85 %J McGraw -333 E Onondaga -Syracuse 13202 **Fx:**422-7741
(518) 756-3764 .. **Karlson**, Karleen I '92 -RR 1 Bx 39A -Hannacroix 12087
(212) 348-1276 .. **Karlson**, Michl K '91 -315 E 86th -NY 10028
(212) 608-3284 .. **Karlsson**, Gail V '82 -258 Bway -NY 10007
(212) 406-3070 .. **Karlsson**, Kent '69 (Karlsson & N,PC) -305 Bway -NY 10007
(914) 764-0105 .. **Karlsson**, Kent '69 -254 Trinity Pass -Pound Rdg 10576 **Fx:**764-9616
(914) 835-1818 .. **Karlsson**, Michl B II '08 %E Vecchio & Assoc -550 Mamaroneck Av -Harrison 10528 **Fx:**835-1858
(212) 406-3070 .. **Karlsson & Ng,PC** -305 Bway -NY 10007 **Fx:**964-9636
(212) 213-6996 .. **Karlstein**, Debra A '93 Cnsl Spears & I LLP -51 Mad Av -NY 10010
(888) 472-4878 .. **Karlstein**, Ira S '65 -11 Hanover Sq -NY 10005
(212) 714-3599 .. **Karmaker**, Ashok K '04 (A Karmaker,PC) -350 5th Av -NY 10118 **Fx:**714-6872
(212) 651-9653 .. **Karmali**, Rashida A '94 Technology Law Practice -99 Wall -NY 10005 **Fx:**651-9654

(631) 220-4416 .. **Karman,** Dina M '07 Cnsl NBTY Inc -2100 Smithtown Av -Ronkonkoma 11779
(718) 816-0005 .. **Karmazin,** Alan G '92 %Angiuli K&G,LLP -60 Bay -Staten Isl 10301
(212) 859-8000 .. **Karmazin,** Sarah E '10 %Fried FHS&J LLP -1 NY Plz -NY 10004
(518) 473-3303 .. **Karmel,** Jonathan B '99 %Dept of Health -Corning Twr 24th Fl -Albany 12237 **Fx:**473-2019
(516) 482-9050 .. **Karmel,** Lloyd G '91 %Advance Media Corp -560 Nrthrn Blvd -Gt Neck 11021 **Fx:**482-9348
(212) 541-2000 .. **Karmel,** Philip E '89 (Bryan C LLP) -1290 Av of Amer -NY 10104
(212) 755-0224 .. **Karmel,** Randi L '92 R Karmel,PLLC -425 Park Av -NY 10022 **Fx:**755-0334
(718) 780-7946 .. **Karmel,** Roberta S '62 %Bklyn Law Schl -250 Joralemon -Brklyn 11201 **Fx:**780-0393
(914) 846-7000 .. **Karmen,** Robt '84 %NY Life Ins -1 Rockwood Rd -Sleepy Hollow 10591 **Fx:**846-4755
(315) 435-2585 .. **Karmen,** Zachary L '85 %Dept Social Srvcs -421 Mntgmry -Syracuse 13202
(516) 741-7994 .. **Karmiol,** Harold '46 -179 Oxford Blvd -Gdn Cty 11530
(212) 667-9300 .. **Karna,** Angie '00 %Nomura Securities Intl -2 World Fncl Ctr -NY 10281
(716) 842-2244 .. **Karnath,** Stephen B '80 -516 Lafayette Av -Buffalo 14222
(212) 859-8000 .. **Karneeb,** Kelly Jo '10 %Fried FHS&J LLP -1 NY Plz -NY 10004
(718) 585-3512 .. **Karnes,** Michl D '87 %Gallin & N -860 Grnd Cncrs -Bronx 10451 **Fx:**993-3712
(212) 672-5393 .. **Karnofsky,** Jon D '79 %Bayerische Hypo & Vereinsbank Inc -150 E 42nd -NY 10017
(212) 720-3400 .. **Karnovsky,** David M '88 Dept City Planning -22 Reade -NY 10007 **Fx:**720-3219
(585) 325-6202 .. **Karns,** Adam J '08 Relin G&C LLP -28 E Main -Rchstr 14614
(716) 945-1790 .. **Karns,** Christopher A '95 Seneca Nation of Indians -Bx231 -Salamanca 14779
(718) 579-3000 .. **Karny,** Thalia '97 %Leg Aid -1020 Grnd Cncrs -Bronx 10451 **Fx:**588-2611
(585) 428-5210 .. **Karnyski,** Kevin J '99 %Pub Def -10 N Fitzhugh -Rchstr 14614 **Fx:**428-2234
(212) 610-6300 .. **Karol,** E Michl '98 SrCnsl Allen & O -1221 Av of Amer -NY 10020
(516) 745-0066 .. **Karol Hausman & Sosnik, PC** -600 Old Cntry Rd -Gdn Cty 11530 **Fx:**222-1499
(212) 644-6644 .. **Karol,** John A '04 %R Rosen,PLLC -110 E 59th -NY 10022 **Fx:**644-3344
(516) 745-0066 .. **Karol,** Louis P '85 (Karol H&S,PC) -600 Old Cntry Rd -Gdn Cty 11530
(212) 337-2083 .. **Karonis,** Andrew '97 US Dept of Labor -201 Varick -NY 10014
(718) 286-6040 .. **Karonis,** Mario T '92 %DA -125-01 Qns Blvd -Kew Gdns 11415
(646) 610-5424 .. **Karopkin,** Martin G '72 NYPD -1 Police Plz -NY 10038
(212) 310-8000 .. **Karotkin,** Stephen '77 (Weil G&M LLP) -767 5th Av -NY 10153
(518) 377-0231 .. **Karowe,** Marjorie E '75 -813 Londonderry Rd -Schnctdy 12309 **Fx:**393-6049
(212) 416-8401 .. **Karp,** Amy C '92 %Dept of Law -120 Bway -NY 10271
(212) 635-7399 .. **Karp,** Andrew T '90 Bk of NY Mellon -1 Wall -NY 10286
(518) 828-4273 .. **Karp,** Bernhardt '64 -One Hudson City Ctr -Hudson 12534 **Fx:**828-4065
(212) 373-3000 .. **Karp,** Brad S '86 (Paul WRW&G LLP) -1285 Av of Amer -NY 10019
(212) 589-4200 .. **Karp,** Brian S '07 %Baker & H LLP -45 Rckfllr Plz -NY 10111
(212) 645-2200 .. **Karp,** Bruce O '82 -420 W 23rd -NY 10011
(212) 564-1250 .. **Karp,** Chad L '95 (Karp & K) -370 7th Av -NY 10001
(212) 714-0421 .. **Karp,** David '95 %M Fuld,PC -38 W 32nd -NY 10001 **Fx:**714-0436
(516) 766-4869 .. **Karp,** David A '83 (Karp & K) -Bx878 -Rockvll Ctr 11571
(212) 403-1000 .. **Karp,** David C '94 (Wachtell LR&K) -51 W 52nd -NY 10019
(212) 756-2000 .. **Karp,** David J '02 SpclCnsl Schulte R&Z LLP -919 3rd Av -NY 10022
(212) 732-4845 .. **Karp,** George '62 -305 Bway -NY 10007 **Fx:**406-7265
(212) 310-8000 .. **Karp,** Hope L '01 %Weil G&M LLP -767 5th Av -NY 10153
(585) 428-5004 .. **Karp,** Jason '71 %Family Ct -332 Hall of Justice -Rchstr 14614 **Fx:**428-2597
(718) 780-1969 .. **Karp,** Jeffrey S '74 LI College Hospital -339 Hicks -Brklyn 11201 **Fx:**780-2840
(718) 852-4454 .. **Karp,** Jerome '51 (J Karp,PC) -26 Court -Brklyn 11242 **Fx:**875-5075
(914) 253-3785 .. **Karp,** Jonas '03 Pepsi Co -700 Andrsn Hill Rd -Purchase 10577
(315) 458-5040 .. **Karp,** Jonathan R '06 %Karp -428 S Main -N Syracuse 13212 **Fx:**458-4321
(631) 232-0200 .. **Karp,** Jordan B '02 %Fumuso KDSS&F,LLP -110 Marcus Blvd -Hauppauge 11788
(212) 564-1250 .. **Karp & Kalamotousakis** -370 7th Av -NY 10001 **Fx:**564-1801
(212) 756-2000 .. **Karp,** Melissa B '10 %Schulte R&Z LLP -919 3rd Av -NY 10022
(212) 292-5066 .. **Karp,** Michl N '85 -2 Penn Plz -NY 10121
(718) 979-5200 .. **Karp,** Miriam '79 %W Leininger,PC -34 Dumont Av -Staten Isl 10305 **Fx:**667-7128
(212) 629-9158 .. **Karp,** Mitchell '82 Karp Consulting -225 W 34th -NY 10122 **Fx:**787-4646
(212) 490-3000 .. **Karp,** Paul J '88 (Wilson EME&D LLP) -150 E 42nd -NY 10017
(914) 428-8922 .. **Karp,** Sandra Y '95 (S Karp,PC) -399 Knollwood Rd -White Plns 10603 **Fx:**428-6486
(212) 722-2000 .. **Karp,** Sheryl R '81 %Leg Aid -230 E 106th -NY 10029 **Fx:**876-5365
(315) 458-5040 .. **Karp,** Stephen S '68 Karp -428 S Main -N Syracuse 13212 **Fx:**458-4321
(212) 801-6824 .. **Karp,** Warren J '74 (Greenberg T,LLP) -200 Park Av -NY 10166
(212) 254-9290 .. **Karpas,** Seymour '51 -40 E 9th -NY 10003 **Fx:**460-9166
(212) 336-0104 .. **Karpati,** Bruce '97 %SEC -3 World Fncl Ctr -NY 10281 **Fx:**336-1323
(646) 865-9930 .. **Karpatkin,** Deborah H '82 -99 Park Av -NY 10016 **Fx:**(212) 557-0565
(212) 244-9500 .. **Karpe,** Karel S '89 Cnsl White and W LLP -1 Penn Plz -NY 10119
(212) 456-7086 .. **Karpeh,** Enid J H '84 ABC,Inc -77 W 66th -NY 10023
(212) 986-6000 .. **Karpel,** Max '00 (Kleinberg KW&C,PC) -551 5th Av -NY 10176
(917) 778-6600 .. **Karpel,** Scott M '86 %J Toomey -485 Lex Av -NY 10017 **Fx:**778-7048
(518) 486-7432 .. **Karpen,** Judith S '86 %Dept of Law -The Cptl -Albany 12224
(212) 704-6000 .. **Karpen,** Michl A '82 (Troutman S LLP) -405 Lex Av -NY 10174
(631) 851-0400 .. **Karpf,** Andrew C '89 (Bark & K) -842 Route 25A -Northprt 11768
(212) 225-2864 .. **Karpf,** Jeffrey D '95 (Cleary GS&H) -1 Lbrty Plz -NY 10006
(917) 262-1822 .. **Karpf,** Robt A '02 Marc Ecko Entrprs -40 W 23rd -NY 10010
(646) 471-4000 .. **Karpiak,** Carl P '96 %PricewaterhouseCoopers LLP -300 Mad Av -NY 10017
(315) 253-6219 .. **Karpinski,** John A '71 (Karpinski SG&T) -110 Genesee -Auburn 13021
(315) 253-6219 .. **Karpinski Stapleton Galbato & Tehan** -110 Genesee -Auburn 13021 **Fx:**253-6368
(646) 307-4383 .. **Karpman,** Anna L '00 Capital Market Srvcs LLC -350 5th Av -NY 10118
(347) 245-4929 .. **Karpman,** Randy '88 -58-09 28th Av -Woodside 11377
(914) 749-8200 .. **Karpoff,** Timothy '07 %Boies S&F LLP -333 Main -Armonk 10504
(212) 425-1900 .. **Karpousis,** John F '94 (Freehill H&M LLP) -80 Pine -NY 10005
(914) 967-9115 .. **Karpovich,** Sherri L '96 -65 Orchrd Av -Rye 10580
(631) 852-1688 .. **Karpp,** Russell J '86 %Supreme Ct -Center Dr S -Rvrhead 11901 **Fx:**852-2020
(315) 386-4586 .. **Karr,** Jennifer K '09 %Leg Aid -17 Hodskin Bx648 -Canton 13617 **Fx:**386-2868
(212) 325-1021 .. **Karrandjas,** Nanci R '05 Credit Suisse -11 Mad Av -NY 10010
(585) 482-4370 .. **Karron,** Elaine Tanner '84 -430 Corwin Rd -Rchstr 14610 **Fx:**482-4370
(212) 752-9700 .. **Kars,** Larry '69 (L Kars,PC) -101 E 52nd -NY 10022 **Fx:**980-5192
(212) 952-1111 .. **Karsch,** Dennis M '73 (H Gladstein & Prtnrs LLC) -110 Wall -NY 10005 **Fx:**943-7427
(212) 468-4800 .. **Karsch,** Mitchell W '92 (Davis & G LLP) -1740 Bway -NY 10019
(212) 619-2700 .. **Karsch,** Stephen E '68 P Gentile,PC -261 Mad Av -NY 10016 **Fx:**619-3626
(631) 298-4200 .. **Karsch,** Tracy L '02 OfCnsl Goggins & P -13105 Main Rd Bx65 -Mattituck 11952 **Fx:**298-4214
(212) 504-6000 .. **Karsh,** Rielly A '07 %Cadwalader W&T LLP -1 World Fncl Ctr -NY 10281
(212) 248-7200 .. **Karshan,** Ali Levine '01 %McCabe & F,LLP -1 Whitehall -NY 10004
(212) 373-3000 .. **Karsnitz,** Patrick N '06 %Paul WRW&G LLP -1285 Av of Amer -NY 10019
(212) 490-8026 .. **Karson,** Barry M '67 (Karson & L LLP) -600 3rd Av -NY 10016 **Fx:**490-8413
(212) 593-1000 .. **Karson,** Danl E '74 %Kroll Assoc -1166 Av of Amer -NY 10036 **Fx:**593-2631
(212) 554-0400 .. **Karson,** Gil A '86 (Grubman I&S,PC) -152 W 57th -NY 10019
(212) 609-6800 .. **Karson,** Jamieson A '84 SpclCnsl McCarter & E,LLP -245 Park Av -NY 10167
(646) 386-5206 .. **Karson,** Lisa Ann '86 %Family Ct -60 Lafayette -NY 10013
(516) 228-6600 .. **Karson,** Lori S '90 -595 Stewart Av -Gdn Cty 11530
(631) 694-2300 .. **Karson,** Scott M '76 (Lamb & B,LLP) -534 Broadhllw Rd Bx9034 -Melvll 11747
(212) 372-1000 .. **Karst,** Laurence J '80 (RSM McGladrey Inc) -1185 Av of Amer -NY 10036 **Fx:**372-1483
(585) 454-4060 .. **Karsten,** Alexander Y '09 %Empire Justice Ctr -1 W Main -Rchstr 14614 **Fx:**454-4019
(212) 732-9600 .. **Kartagener,** Steven R '74 -225 Bway -NY 10007 **Fx:**732-6966
(212) 826-3800 .. **Karten,** Susan M '84 (S Karten & Assoc,LLP) -355 Lex Av -NY 10017 **Fx:**486-6583
(212) 965-2200 .. **Karteron,** Alexis B '06 %NAACP/LDF -99 Hudson -NY 10013 **Fx:**226-7592
(212) 610-6300 .. **Kartheiser,** Robt D '88 (Allen & O) -1221 Av of Amer -NY 10020
(516) 496-1919 .. **Kartzinel,** Steven R '00 %Keller O&W,PC -242 Crsswys Park Dr W -Woodbury 11797
(516) 222-6200 .. **Karvay,** Rudolf J '93 %Berkman HPP&F,PC -100 Grdn City Plz -Gdn Cty 11530
(212) 318-6000 .. **Karvosky,** Laura B '08 %Paul HJ&W LLP -75 E 55th -NY 10022
(212) 447-5599 .. **Karyo,** Jessica I '01 %Agins SR&B,LLP -386 Park Av S -NY 10016
(585) 394-5755 .. **Karz,** Laurence M '77 (Hall & K) -6 Gorham -Canandaigua 14424
(212) 922-1920 .. **Kasai,** Sara Y '06 %West Group -530 5th Av -NY 10036 **Fx:**867-2404
(212) 541-2000 .. **Kasakove,** David P '96 (Bryan C LLP) -1290 Av of Amer -NY 10104
(646) 610-8666 .. **Kasanof,** Adam P '89 NYPD -1 Police Plz -NY 10038
(718) 932-5040 .. **Kasapis,** Theo '91 -30-33 32nd -Astoria 11102
(212) 225-2000 .. **Kasara,** Mbabazi '10 %Cleary GS&H -1 Lbrty Plz -NY 10006
(914) 358-4302 .. **Kasarda,** Steven C '03 (S Kasarda,PC) -445 Hmltn Av -White Plns 10601 **Fx:**829-9010
(212) 506-1700 .. **Kaschel,** Nancy E '97 SpclCnsl Kasowitz BT&F LLP -1633 Bway -NY 10019
(212) 336-8000 .. **Kasdan,** Abraham '86 (Amster R&E) -90 Park Av -NY 10016
(212) 612-4200 .. **Kasdan,** David S '86 (Hoey KT&E) -55 Water -NY 10041
(212) 549-2500 .. **Kasdan,** Diana '02 %ACLU -125 Broad -NY 10004 **Fx:**549-2651
(212) 336-8000 .. **Kasdan,** Michl J '02 %Amster R&E -90 Park Av -NY 10016
(212) 777-8887 .. **Kasdon,** James E '92 -112 E 19th -NY 10003 **Fx:**777-1850
(212) 755-5510 .. **Kase,** David A '03 %Loeb B & Prtnrs -505 Park Av -NY 10022
(516) 746-4300 .. **Kase & Druker** -1325 Franklin Av -Gdn Cty 11530 **Fx:**742-9415
(516) 746-4300 .. **Kase,** Elizabeth S '00 (Kase & D) -1325 Franklin Av -Gdn Cty 11530
(212) 605-1000 .. **Kasell,** Danl M '05 Square Mile Capital Mgmt LLC -450 Park Av -NY 10022
(212) 947-3793 .. **Kasell,** David M '96 %Sadis & G LLP -551 5th Av -NY 10176
(212) 790-9200 .. **Kasell,** Elise C '07 %Cowan L&L,PC -1133 Av of Amer -NY 10036
(212) 447-0418 .. **Kasen,** Anita S '84 -350 E 30th -NY 10016 **Fx:**447-0418
(212) 310-8000 .. **Kasenetz,** Eric D '10 %Weil G&M LLP -767 5th Av -NY 10153
(718) 923-0690 .. **Kaser,** Chas W '07 %R Santoriella PC -335 Adams -Brklyn 11201 **Fx:**923-0683
(631) 853-5155 .. **Kash,** Catherine S '84 Hon J Bivona -400 Carleton Av -Central Islip 11722
(585) 262-8412 .. **Kash,** Louis N '69 %Rochester School District -131 W Broad -Rchstr 14614
(212) 416-8000 .. **Kasha,** Jeremy R '99 Dept of Law -120 Bway -NY 10271
(516) 365-1563 .. **Kashanian,** Shahriar '85 -69 Stonehenge Rd -Manhsst 11030
(212) 819-8200 .. **Kashar,** Gary A '05 (White & C LLP) -1155 Av of Amer -NY 10036
(212) 403-3408 .. **Kashima,** Shinichiro '02 Nippon Life Ins -1251 Av of Amer -NY 10020
(516) 227-0700 .. **Kashimer,** Jonathan M '04 %Farrell F,PC -1320 RXR Plz -Uniondale 11556
(212) 941-9090 .. **Kashkin,** Stephanie L '97 %The Door -121 Av of Amer -NY 10013 **Fx:**941-9579
(212) 684-3900 .. **Kashman,** David S '76 (Gottlieb R&R,PC) -270 Mad Av -NY 10016

(212) 940-8800 .. **Kashner,** Howard J '65 Cnsl Katten MR LLP -575 Mad Av -NY 10022
(718) 248-6544 .. **Kashtan,** Robt J '88 Citicorp Credit Srvcs -1 Court Sq -LIC 11101
(212) 621-7993 .. **Kasi,** Srinandan R '97 Associated Press -50 Rckfllr Plz -NY 10020
(212) 655-3500 .. **Kasindorf,** Matthew E '84 (Meister S&F LLP) -140 E 45th -NY 10017
(845) 565-3098 .. **Kasinki,** John A '94 -Bx2555 -Newburgh 12550 **Fx:**565-3136
(718) 232-1111 .. **Kasirer,** Ben '95 Saul Friedman & Co -6201 15th Av -Brklyn 11219
(516) 564-4975 .. **Kaslow,** Judith '01 %OTDA -50 Clinton -Hempstd 11550
(516) 224-5651 .. **Kasman,** Andrew T '85 CLK Mgmt Corp -135 Crsswys Park Dr -Woodbury 11797 **Fx:**224-6751
(315) 435-2470 .. **Kasmarek,** Michl A '05 %DA -505 S State -Syracuse 13202 **Fx:**435-3969
(315) 443-1941 .. **Kasmarek,** Samantha D '05 %Syracuse Univ Cllg of Law -Wht Hall -Syracuse 13244 **Fx:**443-4213
(212) 593-6700 .. **Kasmir,** Justin M '03 %Aaronson RF&D,LLP -757 3rd Av -NY 10017
(212) 226-5054 .. **Kasner,** Jason H '06 %Powley & G,PC -304 Hudson -NY 10013 **Fx:**266-5085
(212) 735-3000 .. **Kasner,** Jay B '81 (Skadden ASM&F LLP) -4 Times Sq -NY 10036
(845) 485-7058 .. **Kasnia,** Cynthia G '98 (Kasnia & K,PLLC) -19 Dutchess Av -Poughkeepsie 12601 **Fx:**485-1026
(516) 572-2000 .. **Kasnicki,** Kristofer J '09 %DA -99 Main -Hempstd 11550 **Fx:**572-2606
(718) 295-5605 .. **Kaso,** Joana '08 %Bronx AIDS Srvcs -540 E Fordham Rd -Bronx 10458 **Fx:**733-3429
(212) 506-1700 .. **Kasowitz Benson Torres & Friedman LLP** -1633 Bway -NY 10019 **Fx:**506-1800
(212) 788-4733 .. **Kasowitz,** Jesse E '91 ACS-Div Leg Srvcs -220 Church -NY 10013 **Fx:**788-3943
(212) 506-1700 .. **Kasowitz,** Marc E '78 (Kasowitz BT&F LLP) -1633 Bway -NY 10019
(646) 386-3722 .. **Kaspar,** Eileen '93 Hon J Gische -60 Centre -NY 10007 **Fx:**(212) 401-9288
(203) 330-2119 .. **Kasper,** George J '87 (Pullman & C,LLC) -50 Main -White Plns 10606
(718) 935-2248 .. **Kasper,** Mitchell L '84 %NYC Bd of Ed -65 Court -Brklyn 11201
(212) 681-8680 .. **Kasper,** Stephen M '90 -230 Park Av -NY 10169 **Fx:**661-2153
(845) 569-9110 .. **Kasper-Buckareff,** Lara E '08 Leg Srvcs -123 Grand -Newburgh 12550 **Fx:**569-9120
(585) 423-8290 .. **Kasperek,** Lawr L '85 (Easton TKS,LLP) -16 W Main -Rchstr 14614 **Fx:**423-0890
(212) 696-6000 .. **Kaspersen,** Andrew N '10 %Curtis M-PC&M LLP -101 Park Av -NY 10178
(212) 656-5226 .. **Kasprzak,** Stephen A '97 FINRA -20 Broad -NY 10005
(212) 629-9690 .. **Kass,** Adam J '04 %P Merani -298 5th Av -NY 10001 **Fx:**629-9664
(845) 291-2050 .. **Kass,** Andrew R '93 %DA -255-275 Main -Goshen 10924 **Fx:**291-2085
(212) 859-8000 .. **Kass,** Barri S '07 %Fried FHS&J LLP -1 NY Plz -NY 10004
(516) 627-3136 .. **Kass,** David N '82 -14 Woodlnd Rd -Roslyn 11576 **Fx:**627-0920
(516) 742-6500 .. **Kass,** Howard S '63 (H Kass,PC) -1 Old Cntry Rd -Carle Pl 11514 **Fx:**742-6596
(212) 442-6818 .. **Kass,** Ilene '80 %Law Dept -52 Duane -NY 10007 **Fx:**442-6868
(516) 221-7610 .. **Kass,** Ira '56 -2544 Towne Hse Cir -N Bellmore 11710 **Fx:**221-7610
(212) 819-8200 .. **Kass,** Jonathan M '05 %White & C LLP -1155 Av of Amer -NY 10036
(646) 386-3655 .. **Kass,** Kathy M '82 %Supreme Ct-Law Dept -60 Centre -NY 10007
(212) 530-5000 .. **Kass,** Lawr T '96 %Milbank TH&M LLP -1 Chase Manh Plz -NY 10005
(212) 578-3317 .. **Kass,** Lowell D '96 %MetLife -27-01 Qns Plz N -LIC 11101 **Fx:**578-3916
(212) 218-5500 .. **Kass,** Melissa K '01 %Seyfarth S LLP -620 8th Av -NY 10018
(646) 253-2300 .. **Kass,** Richd G '86 (Bond S&K,PLLC) -330 Mad Av -NY 10017
(212) 374-1144 .. **Kass,** Richd M '81 -299 Bway -NY 10007 **Fx:**285-0531
(212) 974-7474 .. **Kass,** Roger E '90 OfCnsl Cowan DA&S LLP -41 Mad Av -NY 10010
(212) 909-6000 .. **Kass,** Sean N '09 %Debevoise & P LLP -919 3rd Av -NY 10022
(212) 556-2100 .. **Kass,** Sheryl A '07 %King & S -1185 Av of Amer -NY 10036
(718) 270-3018 .. **Kass,** Stephan '84 %SUNY Hlth Sci Ctr -450 Clarkson Av -Brklyn 11203
(212) 843-0050 .. **Kass,** Stephen B '93 -225 Bway -NY 10007 **Fx:**571-0640
(212) 732-3200 .. **Kass,** Stephen L '64 (Carter L&M LLP) -2 Wall -NY 10005
(631) 574-4554 .. **Kass,** Steven A '93 (S Kass,PC) -105 Maxess Rd -Melvll 11747 **Fx:**574-4553
(212) 599-1717 .. **Kass,** Susan B '86 (Barnett EGK&L,PC) -122 E 42nd -NY 10168
(212) 682-8383 .. **Kass,** Thos E '84 (Kantor DWMT&G,PC) -51 E 42nd -NY 10017
(212) 788-1186 .. **Kass,** Zachary B '79 %Law Dept -100 Church -NY 10007 **Fx:**788-0367
(212) 454-8660 .. **Kassa,** Jote W '91 %Deutsche Bank -60 Wall -NY 10005
(212) 735-3000 .. **Kassal,** Bentley '40 Cnsl Skadden ASM&F LLP -4 Times Sq -NY 10036
(212) 922-9499 .. **Kassam,** Aminmohamed S '05 %DeVore & D LLP -99 Park Av -NY 10016 **Fx:**922-1799
(917) 699-4408 .. **Kassamali,** Reyaz A '99 Brand Matter -1350 Bway -NY 10018
(516) 741-5252 .. **Kassan,** Randi A '06 %Sanders SBWV&G,PC -100 Hrrcks Rd -Mineola 11501
(212) 487-4444 .. **Kassapian,** Susan M '80 %Dept Cnsmr Affrs -42 Bway -NY 10004 **Fx:**487-4390
(212) 233-3079 .. **Kassar,** Camille Jos '92 %Maloof LC&O,PA -299 Bway -NY 10007
(516) 746-8000 .. **Kasschau,** Jared A '06 %Jaspan S LLP -300 Grdn City Plz -Gdn Cty 11530
(212) 225-2000 .. **Kassel,** Judith R '86 SpclCnsl Cleary GS&H -1 Lbrty Plz -NY 10006
(516) 294-8300 .. **Kassel,** Penny B '84 (P Kassel & Assoc,PC) -100 Ring Rd -Gdn Cty 11530 **Fx:**294-9291
(212) 986-0656 .. **Kassel,** Philip J '45 -340 W 86th -NY 10024 **Fx:**986-0658
(212) 727-2700 .. **Kassel,** Richd A '89 %NRDC -40 W 20th -NY 10011 **Fx:**727-1773
(212) 594-0144 .. **Kassel,** Richd A '93 (R Kassel,LLC) -350 5th Av -NY 10118 **Fx:**594-0155
(212) 449-9509 .. **Kassel,** Terry '75 %Merrill Lynch -220 Bway -NY 10038
(516) 621-5171 .. **Kasselman,** Diane J '97 -1044 Nrthrn Blvd -Roslyn 11576 **Fx:**621-4271
(516) 621-5171 .. **Kasselman,** Stevens J '81 -1044 Nrthrn Blvd -Roslyn 11576 **Fx:**621-4271
(212) 965-9081 .. **Kassem,** Ramzi '05 %Neufeld S&B -99 Hudson -NY 10013
(212) 801-2157 .. **Kassenoff,** Allan A '99 (Greenberg T,LLP) -200 Park Av -NY 10166
(212) 619-5400 .. **Kassenoff,** Jarred I '99 (Newman F LLP) -1250 Bway -NY 10001
(212) 613-2000 .. **Kassim,** Ahmed J '09 %Gibbons PC -1 Penn Plz -NY 10119
(212) 944-1377 .. **Kassimir,** Maurice R '81 (M Kassimir & Assoc,PC) -1065 Av of Amer -NY 10018 **Fx:**790-5868
(212) 227-7147 .. **Kassin,** Morris J '65 -150 Bway -NY 10038
(212) 341-4355 .. **Kassirer,** Paul L '77 (Lester SK&D) -120 Bway -NY 10271
(212) 954-7400 .. **Kassman,** Donna J '92 %KPMG LLP -345 Park Av -NY 10154
(631) 232-9479 .. **Kassman,** Shawn R '00 -110 Carleton Av -Central Islip 11722
(716) 845-7449 .. **Kassman,** Tracey A '86 %Family Ct -1 Niagara Plz -Buffalo 14202 **Fx:**858-4739
(518) 388-4305 .. **Kassner,** Eileen B '92 %Family Ct -620 State -Schnctdy 12305 **Fx:**388-4496
(518) 377-3423 .. **Kassner,** Mark A '94 -1334 Union -Schnctdy 12308 **Fx:**374-3466
(212) 261-1107 .. **Kassof,** Lindsay '07 Elizabeth Arden Inc -200 Park Av S -NY 10003
(516) 766-7700 .. **Kassoff,** Edwin '54 (Kassoff R&L) -100 Merrick Rd -Rockvll Ctr 11570
(212) 406-1776 .. **Kassoff,** Mitchell J '79 -217 Bway -NY 10007
(516) 766-7700 .. **Kassoff Robert & Lerner** -100 Merrick Rd -Rockvll Ctr 11570 **Fx:**766-0738
(212) 267-9020 .. **Kasson,** Manuel '64 OfCnsl Shapiro B&A LLP -225 Bway -NY 10007
(212) 302-1221 .. **Kassouf,** Nadine M '99 %Max Mara USA Inc -530 7th Av -NY 10018
(212) 716-3810 .. **Kassover,** Peter J '96 Williams Real Estate Co -380 Mad Av -NY 10017
(212) 236-2989 .. **Kassover,** Randi F '97 Merrill Lynch -2 Wrld Fncl Ctr -NY 10281
(516) 541-5820 .. **Kast,** Paul E '53 -5400 Merrick Rd -Massapequa 11758 **Fx:**541-5898
(718) 923-0007 .. **Kastell,** Paul H '98 -760 Bway -Brklyn 11206 **Fx:**963-8529
(212) 826-0100 .. **Kastellec,** Philip R '78 %FSA -31 W 52nd -NY 10019 **Fx:**893-2710
(800) 890-3090 .. **Kasten,** Wm R '92 Jacoby & M,LLP -39 Bway -NY 10002 **Fx:**(212) 344-9400
(212) 541-2000 .. **Kaster,** Lewis R '54 OfCnsl Bryan C LLP -1290 Av of Amer -NY 10104
(212) 596-9000 .. **Kasthuri,** Ramya '09 %Ropes & G LLP -1211 Av of Amer -NY 10036
(212) 373-3000 .. **Kastiel,** Jacobe '09 %Paul WRW&G LLP -1285 Av of Amer -NY 10019
(212) 326-3939 .. **Kastin,** Jessica '02 %Jones D -222 E 41st -NY 10017
(516) 742-2187 .. **Kastin,** Robt '72 -114 Old Cntry Rd -Mineola 11501 **Fx:**(253) 461-4357
(212) 693-0085 .. **Kastin,** Wm G '94 %Appellate Advocates -2 Rector -NY 10006 **Fx:**693-0878
(212) 416-8888 .. **Kastleman,** Hilary R '01 %Dept of Law -120 Bway -NY 10271
(718) 875-1552 .. **Kastner,** Chas D '95 %United Management -166 Montague -Brklyn 11201
(516) 742-3470 .. **Kastner,** Elizabeth Gelfand '92 OfCnsl Kral CRRP&G,LLP -538 Broadhllw Rd -Melvll 11747
(212) 969-3000 .. **Kastner,** Jessica J '08 %Proskauer R LLP -1585 Bway -NY 10036
(917) 454-1155 .. **Kastner,** Marie '07 NYPD -2 Lafayette -NY 10007
(212) 509-9400 .. **Kastner,** Menachem J '77 (Cozen O) -45 Bway Atrium -NY 10006
(516) 873-3040 .. **Kaston,** David '91 (Kaston & A) -259 Mineola Blvd -Mineola 11501 **Fx:**873-5166
(917) 534-4949 .. **Kaston,** David M '89 ZNA Srvcs LLC -105 E 17th -NY 10003
(518) 457-2070 .. **Kastor,** Bruce B '82 %Dept of Tax & Fin -Bldg 9 State Campus -Albany 12227 **Fx:**457-6131
(212) 335-4500 .. **Kastrinakis,** Anastasios G '06 %DLA Piper LLP -1251 Av of Amer -NY 10020
(212) 297-5800 .. **Kastrinsky,** Stefanie H '05 %Day P LLP -7 Times Sq -NY 10036
(212) 637-2411 .. **Kasulis,** Telemachus P '03 %US Atty -1 St Andrews Plz -NY 10007
(718) 458-4121 .. **Kasuri,** Kuldip S '87 -37-05 74th -Jcksn Hts 11372 **Fx:**458-9808
(212) 223-6444 .. **Kaswan,** Beth '84 Scott +S,LLP -500 5th Av -NY 10110 **Fx:**223-6334
(212) 888-8200 .. **Kaszovitz,** Gabriel '55 (Feder K LLP) -845 3rd Av -NY 10022
(315) 461-4277 .. **Kaszycki,** Rebecca L '09 %Falge & M,PC -3300 Vickery Rd -N Syracuse 13212
(212) 806-5400 .. **Kata,** Lori E '03 %Stroock &S&L LLP -180 Maiden Ln -NY 10038
(212) 317-8100 .. **Kataoka,** Tomoko '01 %E Grosz -757 3rd Av -NY 10017 **Fx:**679-7426
(212) 909-6000 .. **Kataria,** Amit '08 %Debevoise & P LLP -919 3rd Av -NY 10022
(212) 966-6420 .. **Kataria,** Priti P '05 Lwyrs For Children -110 Lafayette -NY 10013 **Fx:**966-0531
(212) 506-5000 .. **Katayama,** Yoichi '93 (Orrick H&S LLP) -51 W 52nd -NY 10019
(718) 876-6300 .. **Katchen,** Anthony L '06 DA -130 Styvsnt Pl -Staten Isl 10301
(212) 355-4449 .. **Katcher,** Danl E '93 (Joele Frank Wilkinson Brimmer Katcher) -140 E 45th -NY 10017 **Fx:**355-4554
(212) 687-1980 .. **Katcher,** Elana '04 %Kaplan F&K LLP -850 3rd Av -NY 10022
(212) 504-6000 .. **Katcher,** Joshua D '10 %Cadwalader W&T LLP -1 World Fncl Ctr -NY 10281
(516) 791-7633 .. **Katcher,** Karl S '63 -83 Rosedale Rd -N Woodmere 11581
(516) 932-8122 .. **Katcher,** Kimberly T '00 (Katcher & K) -15 E Carl -Hicksvll 11801 **Fx:**932-8129
(212) 737-6053 .. **Katcher,** Paul '56 -715 Park Av -NY 10021
(212) 403-1000 .. **Katcher,** Richd D '66 (Wachtell LR&K) -51 W 52nd -NY 10019
(516) 932-8122 .. **Katcher,** Robt J '73 (Katcher & K) -15 E Carl -Hicksvll 11801 **Fx:**932-8129
(914) 771-4200 .. **Katcher,** Scott G '94 Pop Displays -555 Tuckahoe Rd -Ynkrs 10710
(212) 751-4300 .. **Katcherian,** Amy L '05 %Hodgson R LLP -1540 Bway -NY 10036
(212) 836-8000 .. **Katcoff,** Joel '81 (Kaye S LLP) -425 Park Av -NY 10022
(516) 229-4400 .. **Katechis,** Chris '01 %Kay & G -875 Merrick Av -Westbury 11590
(718) 875-1300 .. **Katehos,** Jennifer M '06 Appllt Div 2nd Dept -45 Monroe Pl -Brklyn 11201 **Fx:**858-2446
(212) 455-2000 .. **Katerberg,** Craig A '10 %Simpson T&B LLP -425 Lex Av -NY 10017
(585) 820-3818 .. **Kates,** Cheryl L '03 -Bx711 -Honeoye 14471
(212) 589-4200 .. **Kates,** Elyssa S '01 %Baker & H LLP -45 Rckfllr Plz -NY 10111
(212) 279-5979 .. **Kates Nussman Rapone Ellis & Farhi, LLP** -845 3rd Av -NY 10022 **Fx:**(201) 488-1210

(212) 788-1587 .. **Kath,** Susan M '86 %Law Dept -100 Church -NY 10007 **Fx:**788-0367
(212) 506-5000 .. **Kathawala,** Rene A '97 Orrick H&S LLP -51 W 52nd -NY 10019
(631) 751-8600 .. **Katims,** Joel D '67 (J Katims,PC) -3771 Nesconset Hwy -South Setauket 11720 **Fx:**751-8665
(212) 553-8300 .. **Katirachi,** Shahab '87 %Cohen K & Assoc -2 Park Av -NY 10016 **Fx:**553-8721
(718) 507-4646 .. **Katiraei,** Ron '95 (Katiraei & Assoc) -8219 Roosevelt Av -Jcksn Hts 11372
(718) 816-0005 .. **Katkin,** Alan S '83 (Angiuli K&G,LLP) -60 Bay -Staten Isl 10301
(315) 448-0672 .. **Katko,** John M '89 %US Atty -100 S Clinton Bx7198 -Syracuse 13261 **Fx:**448-0689
(212) 271-7600 .. **Katlowitz,** Moshe Y '80 (Katlowitz & Assoc) -270 Mad Av -NY 10016 **Fx:**271-7601
(212) 459-7894 .. **Kato,** Bruce K '81 %Dept of Tax & Fin -1740 Bway -NY 10019 **Fx:**459-7897
(212) 541-3720 .. **Kato,** Keiko '99 -590 Mad Av -NY 10022
(212) 848-4000 .. **Kato,** Satoko '01 %Shearman & S LLP -599 Lex Av -NY 10022
(212) 878-8000 .. **Kato,** Tomoya '01 %Clifford C LLP -31 W 52nd -NY 10019
(212) 944-1529 .. **Katona,** David G '01 (Katona & M) -49 W 37th -NY 10018 **Fx:**553-7370
(212) 872-6441 .. **Katovitz,** Michl '83 %KPMG LLP -345 Park Av -NY 10154
(212) 233-1477 .. **Katowitz,** Philip R '71 -320 7th Av PMB 255 -Brklyn 11215
(212) 574-1200 .. **Katragadda,** Srikanth '07 %Seward & K LLP -1 Bttry Pk Plz -NY 10004
(212) 839-5300 .. **Katris,** Darcy M '86 Cnsl Sidley A LLP -787 7th Av -NY 10019
(631) 853-5212 .. **Katrivanos,** Alison J '00 %Leg Aid -400 Carleton Av Bx9082 -Central Islip 11722 **Fx:**853-7798
(347) 451-7318 .. **Kats,** James '83 -407 Woodstock Av -Staten Isl 10301 **Fx:**(718) 524-6991
(518) 487-7600 .. **Kats,** Lucy '03 %Whiteman O&H LLP -1 Commerce Plz -Albany 12260
(800) 529-1917 .. **Kats,** Marina '96 %Kats & Assoc -4121 18th Av -Brklyn 11218 **Fx:**(718) 854-6550
(646) 471-4000 .. **Katsanos,** John C V '98 %PricewaterhouseCoopers LLP -300 Mad Av -NY 10017
(212) 574-1200 .. **Katsanos,** Nick V '00 %Seward & K LLP -1 Bttry Pk Plz -NY 10004
(212) 233-0130 .. **Katsaros,** Konstantinos '05 %Nelson Ld&H -120 Bway -NY 10271
(212) 973-8000 .. **Katsh,** Salem M '73 (Schnader HS&L LLP) -140 Bway -NY 10005
(212) 896-6500 .. **Katsiris,** Konstantinos D '00 OfCnsl Howrey LLP -601 Lex Av -NY 10022
(212) 953-6000 .. **Katsky,** David L '67 (Katsky K LLP) -605 3rd Av -NY 10158
(212) 953-6000 .. **Katsky Korins LLP** -605 3rd Av -NY 10158 **Fx:**953-6899
(516) 295-9680 .. **Katsman,** Aaron I '98 (A Katsman,PC) -65 Roosevelt Av -Vly Stream 11581 **Fx:**295-9685
(212) 697-3122 .. **Katsnelson,** Elena '09 %Martin C&B LLP -220 E 42nd -NY 10017
(718) 306-1570 .. **Katsnelson,** Elliott '98 -1711 Kings Hwy -Brklyn 11229 **Fx:**306-1571
(212) 905-2340 .. **Katsoolis,** Krysanne '93 Cactus Three -440 Lafayette -NY 10003
(718) 591-6900 .. **Katsorhis,** Kerry J '71 (Ginsberg & K) -77-53 Main -Flushng 11367
(718) 591-6900 .. **Katsorhis,** Nicole Demetra '02 %Ginsberg & K -77-53 Main -Flushng 11367
(516) 496-5822 .. **Katsorhis,** Valerie '09 T Spina -170 Froehlich Farm Blvd -Woodbury 11797 **Fx:**496-5420
(212) 636-6000 .. **Katsoris,** Constantine N '57 %Fordham Univ Sch of Law -140 W 62nd -NY 10023 **Fx:**636-6899
(914) 921-9250 .. **Katsoris,** Louis '95 Sotheby's Intl Realty -49 Purchase -Rye 10580
(212) 956-5803 .. **Katsoris,** Nicholas C '92 Red Apple Grp -823 11th Av -NY 10019
(914) 476-0600 .. **Katsoris,** Voula T '97 %Smith B&J,LLP -733 Ynkrs Av -Ynkrs 10704
(212) 421-0307 .. **Katsos,** Barbara H '97 (B Katsos,PC) -777 3rd Av -NY 10017 **Fx:**838-5026
(631) 501-5700 .. **Katsougrakis,** John '07 %Carter DF&S LLP -445 Broadhallow Rd -Melvll 11747
(212) 816-8389 .. **Katsoulis,** Timothy E '96 Citigroup Global Mrkts -388 Greenwich -NY 10013
(914) 355-2955 .. **Kattan,** Julie S '99 -271 North Av -New Rchll 10801 **Fx:**355-2954
(212) 768-6700 .. **Kattan,** Justin N '01 (Sonnenschein N&R LLP) -1221 Av of Amer -NY 10020
(212) 490-0988 .. **Kattas,** Paul L '98 %Reppert K,LLC -570 Lex Av -NY 10022
(212) 940-8800 .. **Katten Muchin Rosenman LLP** -575 Mad Av -NY 10022 **Fx:**940-8776
(212) 809-4293 .. **Katter,** Ronald J '86 -61 Bway -NY 10006 **Fx:**968-0949
(212) 538-1026 .. **Katz,** Aaron M '91 Credit Suisse -11 Mad Av -NY 10010
(718) 747-0100 .. **Katz,** Abraham J '79 -1979 Marcus Av -New Hyde Pk 11042 **Fx:**747-7710
(516) 466-6680 .. **Katz,** Adam '89 %Roxann Mgmt Corp -29 Barstow Rd -Gt Neck 11021 **Fx:**466-6684
(516) 617-3416 .. **Katz,** Adam F '07 -1042 Reads Ln -Far Rckwy 11691
(212) 756-2000 .. **Katz,** Adam J '96 (Schulte R&Z LLP) -919 3rd Av -NY 10022
(212) 857-8832 .. **Katz,** Adam J '05 US Ct of Appls -40 Foley Sq -NY 10007
(631) 756-7020 .. **Katz,** Alan B '74 -14 Dubon Ct -Farmngdl 11735 **Fx:**756-7023
(212) 818-9600 .. **Katz,** Alan E '69 (Greenfield S&S,LLP) -600 3rd Av -NY 10016
(516) 741-5747 .. **Katz,** Alan F '85 -734 Franklin Av -Gdn Cty 11530
(212) 973-9797 .. **Katz,** Alan G '83 (Saretsky KD&G,LLP) -475 Park Av S -NY 10016
(516) 663-2501 .. **Katz,** Alan J '94 %Winthrop Univ Hsptl -259 1st Av -Mineola 11501 **Fx:**663-8558
(914) 997-2323 .. **Katz,** Alan R '68 (Katz & K,PC) -30 Glenn -White Plns 10603 **Fx:**644-8290
(212) 696-4848 .. **Katz,** Alan S '85 (Mintz & G LLP) -470 Park Av S -NY 10016
(914) 591-3278 .. **Katz,** Alayne P '87 (A Katz,PC) -76 Greenway Dr -Irvngtn 10533 **Fx:**591-8514
(212) 325-5889 .. **Katz,** Alexander S '01 %Credit Suisse -11 Mad Av -NY 10010
(212) 894-8940 .. **Katz,** Alyssa R '07 CT Corp -111 8th Av -NY 10011
(718) 590-7807 .. **Katz,** Amanda G '04 ACS -900 Sheridan Av -Bronx 10451
(518) 506-3774 .. **Katz,** Amy L '94 -71 Hicks Ln -Gt Neck 11024
(212) 298-5017 .. **Katz,** Andrew L '87 %Leg Aid -49 Thomas -NY 10013 **Fx:**298-5252
(212) 715-9100 .. **Katz,** Arielle Warshall '06 %Kramer LN&F,LLP -1177 Av of Amer -NY 10036
(212) 826-8800 .. **Katz,** Arnold I '73 (Calinoff & K,LLP) -245 5th Av -NY 10016
(212) 267-4033 .. **Katz,** Arthur '63 -225 Bway -NY 10007 **Fx:**385-2689
(212) 661-9100 .. **Katz,** Arthur A '67 (Otterbourg SH&R,PC) -230 Park Av -NY 10169
(646) 688-2353 .. **Katz,** Arthur Shaye '84 -1230 Av of Amer -NY 10020
(914) 358-1280 .. **Katz,** Ascher '52 OfCnsl Katz & K -202 Mamaroneck Av -White Plns 10601
(212) 687-3747 .. **Katz,** Audrey S '83 OfCnsl Tuchman KWL&G,LLP -6 E 45th -NY 10017
(212) 259-8000 .. **Katz,** Autumn C '06 %Dewey & L LLP -1301 Av of Amer -NY 10019
(212) 338-5340 .. **Katz,** Avi '87 %Loral Space & Comm Inc -600 3rd Av -NY 10016 **Fx:**338-5320
(212) 242-1719 .. **Katz,** Barry M '88 BM Katz,PC -731 Greenwich -NY 10014 **Fx:**402-1736
(212) 575-2536 .. **Katz,** Benjamin S '97 Sterling Natl Bk -500 7th Av -NY 10018 **Fx:**764-0552
(212) 766-4700 .. **Katz,** Bennett R '90 (Katz & R) -116 John -NY 10038 **Fx:**766-4705
(212) 243-4679 .. **Katz,** Beverly I '75 -64 W 15th -NY 10011 **Fx:**414-8263
(212) 250-0782 .. **Katz,** Beverly R '98 Deutsche Bk -60 Wall -NY 10005
(212) 705-7000 .. **Katz,** Brian A '07 %Bingham M LLP -399 Park Av -NY 10022
(212) 233-3434 .. **Katz,** Bruce D '85 -225 Bway -NY 10007
(212) 244-4630 .. **Katz,** Bruce D '94 (Katz & M,PC) -1350 Av of Amer -NY 10019 **Fx:**(646) 219-5717
(212) 753-7994 .. **Katz,** Caroline '79 -136 E 55th -NY 10022
(212) 883-1700 .. **Katz,** Caroline B '06 %Duval & S LLP -101 Park Av -NY 10178
(716) 853-9555 .. **Katz,** Chas R '85 %Leg Aid -237 Main -Buffalo 14203 **Fx:**853-3219
(347) 592-2200 .. **Katz,** Cindy R '86 %Leg Srvcs -42-15 Crescent -LIC 11101 **Fx:**(718) 937-5350
(212) 593-3000 .. **Katz,** Clifford A '89 (Platzer SKLG&J,LLP) -1065 Av of Amer -NY 10018
(212) 213-2981 .. **Katz,** Clifford E '87 Mobius Realty Holdings LLC -304 Park Av S -NY 10010 **Fx:**208-4370
(212) 808-7800 .. **Katz,** Clifford E '03 %Kelley D&W LLP -101 Park Av -NY 10178
(516) 466-6680 .. **Katz,** Curtis '53 -29 Barstow Rd -Gt Neck 11021
(212) 878-7900 .. **Katz,** Dana Sichel '10 %Fox R LLP -100 Park Av -NY 10017
(212) 684-0300 .. **Katz,** Danl E '82 (Bauman K&G LLP) -28 W 44th -NY 10036
(212) 228-2528 .. **Katz,** David '82 (D Katz & Assoc,LLP) -116 E 16th -NY 10003 **Fx:**228-4744
(212) 403-1000 .. **Katz,** David A '88 (Wachtell LR&K) -51 W 52nd -NY 10019
(718) 228-1900 .. **Katz,** David B '84 -45-17 Marathon Pkwy -Little Neck 11362 **Fx:**228-9910
(212) 682-3025 .. **Katz,** David C '89 %Weiss & L -551 5th Av -NY 10176
(212) 735-3000 .. **Katz,** David F '08 %Skadden ASM&F LLP -4 Times Sq -NY 10036
(212) 344-5400 .. **Katz,** David J '93 OfCnsl Schlam S&D LLP -26 Bway -NY 10004
(212) 476-9000 .. **Katz,** David L '95 %Neuberger Berman Mgmt Inc -605 3rd Av -NY 10158 **Fx:**476-5781
(212) 839-5300 .. **Katz,** David M '84 (Sidley A LLP) -787 7th Av -NY 10019
(212) 935-3000 .. **Katz,** David M '04 %Mintz LCFG&P,PC -666 3rd Av -NY 10017
(212) 362-4772 .. **Katz,** David S '86 MacArthur Holdings,LLC -2130 Bway -NY 10023 **Fx:**769-4282
(914) 761-7190 .. **Katz,** Dennis G '73 ODAR-SSA -75 S Bway -White Plns 10601
(212) 758-1433 .. **Katz,** Dennis R '66 -845 3rd Av -NY 10022
(585) 641-8001 .. **Katz,** Diane S '81 (Allen & O) -625 Panorama Trl -Rchstr 14625
(516) 561-0210 .. **Katz,** Edw C '76 -108 S Franklin Av -Vly Stream 11580 **Fx:**561-0218
(716) 847-0650 .. **Katz,** Eileen '77 %Leg Srvcs -237 Main -Buffalo 14203 **Fx:**847-0227
(212) 701-3000 .. **Katz,** Elai E '97 (Cahill G&R LLP) -80 Pine -NY 10005 **Fx:**269-5420
(585) 546-5530 .. **Katz,** Eliot J '90 %Thomson West -50 E Broad -Rchstr 14694
(212) 408-5100 .. **Katz,** Eliyohu M '00 (Chadbourne & P LLP) -30 Rckfllr Plz -NY 10112
(212) 773-3000 .. **Katz,** Elliot '09 %Ernst & Young,LLP -5 Times Sq -NY 10036
(212) 310-8000 .. **Katz,** Emily L '08 %Weil G&M LLP -767 5th Av -NY 10153
(914) 238-1000 .. **Katz,** Erica S '97 Reader's Digest -Readers Digest Rd -Plsntvll 10570 **Fx:**241-5644
(212) 684-6272 .. **Katz,** Gary Jay '79 %Lisette Handbags Ltd -1 E 33rd -NY 10016 **Fx:**213-1868
(212) 973-0642 .. **Katz,** Gary M '67 -230 Park Av -NY 10169 **Fx:**973-0645
(914) 997-2323 .. **Katz,** Gary R '06 %Katz & K,PC -30 Glenn -White Plns 10603 **Fx:**644-8290
(914) 683-9613 .. **Katz,** Gary W '98 Downtown Capital Prtnrs -1 Barker Av -White Plns 10601
(212) 425-8666 .. **Katz,** Gilbert '53 -29 Bway -NY 10006 **Fx:**785-1618
(212) 641-3200 .. **Katz,** Gregory '74 NCH Capital -712 5th Av -NY 10019
(212) 232-1300 .. **Katz,** Gregory S '91 (Lewis BB&S LLP) -77 Water -NY 10005
(212) 925-2455 .. **Katz,** H Hershel '73 -100 Lafayette -NY 10013 **Fx:**941-9183
(212) 918-3000 .. **Katz,** Hali R '05 %Hogan L LLP -875 3rd Av -NY 10022
(212) 221-6900 .. **Katz,** Harris B '06 %Winget S&S,LLP -45 Bway -NY 10006
(718) 463-3700 .. **Katz,** Harry I '73 (H Katz,PC) -61-25 Utopia Pkwy -Fresh Mdws 11365
(516) 536-2900 .. **Katz,** Harry S '57 OfCnsl Gross & G LLP -371 Merrick Rd -Rockvll Ctr 11570 **Fx:**536-2870
(212) 878-7900 .. **Katz,** Harvey M '82 (Fox R LLP) -100 Park Av -NY 10017
(212) 693-1330 .. **Katz,** Herbert W '59 (Katz & K LLP) -61 Bway -NY 10006
(212) 627-3000 .. **Katz,** Howard J '92 %Bellmarc Realty -16 E 12th -NY 10003
(212) 732-3435 .. **Katz,** Howard M '83 -225 Bway -NY 10007
(212) 506-1700 .. **Katz,** Ian D '96 (Kasowitz BT&F LLP) -1633 Bway -NY 10019
(212) 530-1800 .. **Katz,** Igal L '02 %Richards K&O LLP -1 World Fncl Ctr -NY 10281
(212) 859-8000 .. **Katz,** Ilan '07 %Fried FHS&J LLP -1 NY Plz -NY 10004
(212) 265-7000 .. **Katz,** Ira Jay '90 %UNITE HERE -275 7th Av -NY 10001 **Fx:**307-6904
(516) 466-6680 .. **Katz,** Jason '89 %Roxann Mgmt Corp -29 Barstow Rd -Gt Neck 11021 **Fx:**466-6684
(212) 451-2300 .. **Katz,** Jason P '10 %Olshan GFR&W LLP -65 E 55th -NY 10022
(631) 755-0101 .. **Katz,** Jason T '92 (Lewis JAA,LLP) -425 Broad Hollow Rd -Melvll 11747
(212) 483-9490 .. **Katz,** Jay A '69 OfCnsl McElroy DM&C,LLP -88 Pine -NY 10005
(212) 868-8333 .. **Katz,** Jay H '88 -450 7th Av -NY 10123 **Fx:**947-2946
(212) 808-7800 .. **Katz,** Jeffrey A '90 (Kelley D&W LLP) -101 Park Av -NY 10178
(212) 468-4800 .. **Katz,** Jeffrey C '80 (Davis & G LLP) -1740 Bway -NY 10019
(212) 450-4000 .. **Katz,** Jeffrey D '07 %Davis P&W LLP -450 Lex Av -NY 10017
(716) 633-3363 .. **Katz,** Jeffrey H '88 (Katz & B) -8604 Main -Williamsvll 14221
(212) 698-3500 .. **Katz,** Jeffrey M '86 (Dechert LLP) -1095 Av of Amer -NY 10036
(212) 521-5400 .. **Katz,** Jennifer D '05 %Reed S LLP -599 Lex Av -NY 10022
(518) 640-5116 .. **Katz,** Jennifer L '96 AYCO -25 British Amer Blvd -Latham 12110
(212) 596-9000 .. **Katz,** Jerome C '76 (Ropes & G LLP) -1211 Av of Amer -NY 10036

(212) 943-1090 .. **Katz,** Jerome I '72 (Gair GCSMB&R) -80 Pine -NY 10005
(212) 909-6000 .. **Katz,** Jessica R '09 %Debevoise & P LLP -919 3rd Av -NY 10022
(212) 838-1000 .. **Katz,** Jill B '02 Trump Grp -404 Park Av S -NY 10016
(518) 272-2300 .. **Katz,** Jo M '84 -68 2nd -Troy 12180 **Fx:**272-0540
(631) 342-5224 .. **Katz,** Joel H '95 %CA,Inc -1 CA Plz -Islandia 11749 **Fx:**342-4866
(212) 760-2222 .. **Katz,** John D '97 %Kolenovsky & S,LLP -135 W 29th -NY 10001
(212) 261-3009 .. **Katz,** Jonas C '02 Indus Capital Prtnrs,LLC -152 W 57th -NY 10019
(845) 255-7635 .. **Katz,** Jonathan D '83 -126 Main -New Paltz 12561 **Fx:**255-7515
(212) 270-4565 .. **Katz,** Jonathan E '97 %Chase Securities Inc -270 Park Av -NY 10017
(212) 474-1000 .. **Katz,** Jonathan J '08 %Cravath S&M LLP -825 8th Av -NY 10019
(212) 489-3333 .. **Katz,** Jonathan S '99 Pressman Film Corp -47 Murray -NY 10007
(631) 454-8059 .. **Katz,** Jordan S '92 JS Katz,PC -395 N Srvc Rd -Melvll 11747 **Fx:**454-8169
(516) 747-0300 .. **Katz,** Jos '68 (Meltzer LG&B,LLP) -190 Willis Av -Mineola 11501
(718) 743-3700 .. **Katz,** Jos '99 -2626 E 14th -Brklyn 11235
(212) 421-4300 .. **Katz,** Joshua '08 Kent B&G,LLP -425 Park Av -NY 10022
(718) 268-8111 .. **Katz,** Joshua R '94 %D Mastrodomenico -107-19 71st Av -Frst Hlls 11375 **Fx:**268-7382
(845) 639-7800 .. **Katz,** Kara Scheinmann '93 (Mandel K&B,LLP) -210 Route 303 -Vly Cottage 10989
(518) 445-2311 .. **Katz,** Katheryn D '71 Albany Law Schl -80 New Scotland Av -Albany 12208 **Fx:**445-2315
(914) 779-7555 .. **Katz,** Kenneth A '94 (B Katz & Co,PC) -1 Mayfair Rd -Eastchstr 10709 **Fx:**779-0024
(212) 460-5757 .. **Katz,** Kenneth J '04 Gellis & M,LLP -137 5th Av -NY 10010
(212) 837-6000 .. **Katz,** Kenneth M '03 %Hughes H&R LLP -1 Bttry Pk Plz -NY 10004
(914) 271-6601 .. **Katz & Klein** -1 Croton Pnt Av Bx626 -Croton-On-Hud 10520 **Fx:**271-6602
(914) 358-1280 .. **Katz & Klein** -202 Mamaroneck Av -White Plns 10601
(516) 741-1710 .. **Katz & Kreinces,LLP** -170 Old Cntry Rd -Mineola 11501 **Fx:**741-0546
(516) 374-2118 .. **Katz,** Lawr '86 -445 Central Av -Cedarhrst 11516
(718) 966-1186 .. **Katz,** Lawr H '00 -101 Dent Rd -Staten Isl 10308 **Fx:**966-7070
(516) 741-1710 .. **Katz,** Lawr K '65 (Katz & K,LLP) -170 Old Cntry Rd -Mineola 11501
(212) 436-2133 .. **Katz,** Lawr R '91 Deloitte & Touche LLP -2 World Fncl Ctr -NY 10281
(212) 962-3362 .. **Katz Leidman Grossman Wolfe & Freund** -277 Bway -NY 10007 **Fx:**233-3065
(718) 624-0154 .. **Katz,** Leigh J '90 Katz & Assoc -26 Court -Brklyn 11242 **Fx:**624-4212
(718) 261-4800 .. **Katz,** Linda F '82 -108-18 Qns Blvd -Frst Hlls 11375 **Fx:**261-7645
(212) 379-8313 .. **Katz,** Lloyd A '83 -352 7th Av -NY 10001 **Fx:**379-8311
(914) 997-2323 .. **Katz,** Louise '70 (Katz & K,PC) -30 Glenn -White Plns 10603 **Fx:**644-8290
(212) 558-4000 .. **Katz,** Malcolm G '08 %Sullivan & C LLP -125 Broad -NY 10004
(212) 878-7900 .. **Katz,** Marcy H '06 %Fox R LLP -100 Park Av -NY 10017
(718) 286-6000 .. **Katz,** Mark L '92 %DA -125-01 Qns Blvd -Kew Gdns 11415
(212) 804-4200 .. **Katz,** Mark S '94 (Mound CW&G) -One Bttry Pk Plz -NY 10004
(212) 309-6000 .. **Katz,** Marsha Stern '98 %Morgan L&B LLP -101 Park Av -NY 10178
(718) 237-2000 .. **Katz,** Martin V '71 %Leg Aid -111 Lvngstn -Brklyn 11201 **Fx:**237-8737
(212) 486-6001 .. **Katz,** Marvin '69 -45 Sutton Pl S -NY 10022
(212) 277-6300 .. **Katz,** Matthew A '05 %Schindler C&H LLP -100 Wall -NY 10005
(212) 727-0777 .. **Katz,** Max Markus '71 MM Katz,PC -88 Univ Pl -NY 10003 **Fx:**727-7691
(212) 909-6000 .. **Katz,** Meir D '05 %Debevoise & P LLP -919 3rd Av -NY 10022
(212) 801-6883 .. **Katz,** Melinda R '91 (Greenberg T,LLP) -200 Park Av -NY 10166
(212) 687-7721 .. **Katz,** Melissa S '06 %AABGU -1430 Bway -NY 10018 **Fx:**302-6443
(212) 554-7800 .. **Katz,** Melvin '56 (Moses & S LLP) -405 Lex Av -NY 10174
(212) 964-6611 .. **Katz,** Melvin '60 OfCnsl Lester SK&D -120 Bway -NY 10271
(516) 746-4690 .. **Katz,** Meryl Z '88 -114 Old Cntry Rd -Mineola 11501
(212) 821-3000 .. **Katz,** Michl '01 UBS Securities LLC -299 Park Av -NY 10171
(212) 682-6260 .. **Katz,** Michl A '83 -630 3rd Av -NY 10017 **Fx:**(914) 232-8673
(212) 558-4000 .. **Katz,** Michl A '95 SpclCnsl Sullivan & C LLP -125 Broad -NY 10004
(212) 294-6700 .. **Katz,** Michl D '09 %Winston & S -200 Park Av -NY 10166
(212) 269-4310 .. **Katz,** Michl I '82 (Frankenthaler KS&K) -420 Lex Av -NY 10170
(646) 386-3226 .. **Katz,** Michl L '93 Supreme Ct Civil -60 Centre -NY 10007
(914) 761-1300 .. **Katz,** Michl L '94 (Cuddy & F LLP) -445 Hmltn Av -White Plns 10601
(212) 526-1767 .. **Katz,** Michal '92 %Barclays Capital Inc -745 7th Av -NY 10019
(212) 980-4500 .. **Katz,** Michele A '82 (Cohen L LLP) -885 3rd Av -NY 10022
(212) 425-7775 .. **Katz,** Michelle R '86 OfCnsl SL Salzman,PC -1350 Bway -NY 10018 **Fx:**643-1882
(315) 474-7541 .. **Katz,** Mitchell J '87 (Menter R&T,PC) -308 Maltbie -Syracuse 13204
(718) 250-4526 .. **Katz,** Mitchell Lewis '99 %Leg Aid -111 Lvngstn -Brklyn 11201 **Fx:**250-4243
(201) 569-4040 .. **Katz,** Mordecai D '78 -110 Wall -NY 10005
(212) 267-6021 .. **Katz,** Morton '66 -132 Nassau -NY 10038 **Fx:**619-2340
(845) 225-7100 .. **Katz,** Naomi '86 -Bx611 -Mahopac 10541
(212) 290-7800 .. **Katz,** Neal B '78 -295 Mad Av -NY 10017 **Fx:**290-2422
(516) 364-5100 .. **Katz,** Neil D '91 (Katz B&K) -6900 Jericho Tpk -Syosset 11791 **Fx:**364-5166
(716) 688-0849 .. **Katz,** Neil J '72 -27 Ranch Trl -Williamsvll 14221 **Fx:**688-0849
(212) 964-6611 .. **Katz,** Noah R '01 Cnsl Lester SK&D -120 Bway -NY 10271
(212) 973-9797 .. **Katz,** Norman '49 Cnsl Saretsky KD&G,LLP -475 Park Av S -NY 10016
(518) 292-1736 .. **Katz,** Pamela Sue '87 Sage Colleges -140 New Scotland Av -Albany 12208
(212) 393-1006 .. **Katz,** Paula F '84 (Gluck & K) -156 William -NY 10038 **Fx:**267-7695
(212) 621-6000 .. **Katz,** Paula G '88 %ASCAP -1 Lincoln Plz -NY 10023 **Fx:**787-1381
(212) 385-1373 .. **Katz,** Philip '97 (Fink & K,PLLC) -40 Exch Pl -NY 10005
(212) 349-2875 .. **Katz,** Philippe D '90 %United Equities -160 Bway -NY 10038 **Fx:**227-3208
(212) 577-2490 .. **Katz,** Phillip '86 -305 Bway -NY 10007 **Fx:**227-9695
(212) 697-2800 .. **Katz,** Randi J '03 %Sofer & H,LLP -317 Mad Av -NY 10017
(212) 430-5400 .. **Katz,** Raphael '06 Diamond M LLP -620 8th Av -NY 10018
(212) 779-1414 .. **Katz,** Rebecca M '91 (Bernstein L LLP) -10 E 40th -NY 10016
(212) 553-3200 .. **Katz,** Rhonda P '91 %Marulli LE&T,LLP -5 Hanover Sq -NY 10004
(212) 935-8880 .. **Katz,** Richd A '67 RA Katz PC -301 N Main -New Cty 10956 **Fx:**(845) 638-6725
(212) 754-4001 .. **Katz,** Richd A '03 -8 E 48th -NY 10017
(646) 840-6666 .. **Katz,** Richd C '73 OfCnsl Cameron & H -230 Park Av -NY 10169
(718) 980-3882 .. **Katz,** Richd D '94 -43 New Dorp Plz -Staten Isl 10306 **Fx:**987-3929
(212) 233-1515 .. **Katz,** Richd J '85 -80 Broad -NY 10004 **Fx:**571-3415
(212) 833-8972 .. **Katz,** Richd S '90 %Sony Classical Business Affairs -550 Mad Av -NY 10022
(212) 635-1143 .. **Katz,** Richd W '80 Bk of NY Mellon -1 Wall -NY 10286
(516) 364-5100 .. **Katz,** Robt '65 (Katz B&K) -6900 Jericho Tpk -Syosset 11791 **Fx:**364-5166
(212) 587-2400 .. **Katz,** Robt A '63 -277 Bway -NY 10007 **Fx:**587-2410
(212) 278-0400 .. **Katz,** Robt D '84 (Cooper & D LLP) -30 Rckfllr Plz -NY 10112
(212) 902-1000 .. **Katz,** Robt J '73 %Goldman Sachs -1 NY Plz -NY 10004
(212) 788-0962 .. **Katz,** Robt M '74 %Law Dept -100 Church -NY 10007 **Fx:**788-0367
(212) 848-4000 .. **Katz,** Robt M '02 (Shearman & S LLP) -599 Lex Av -NY 10022
(516) 741-1130 .. **Katz,** Robt S '75 (Herman KC&C,LLP) -400 Grdn City Plz -Gdn Cty 11530 **Fx:**(212) 627-0432
(212) 953-5000 .. **Katz,** Robt S '75 (Herman KC&C,LLP) -630 3rd Av -NY 10017
(845) 357-3769 .. **Katz,** Roberta M '89 -6 Kings Gate Rd -Suffern 10901 **Fx:**(978) 336-0575
(646) 386-3329 .. **Katz,** Rochelle '88 %Supreme Ct-Law Dept -60 Centre -NY 10007
(212) 885-5000 .. **Katz,** Ronald S '72 (Blank R LLP) -405 Lex Av -NY 10174
(212) 986-8444 .. **Katz & Ross** -60 E 42nd -NY 10165
(212) 652-3800 .. **Katz,** Ross S '97 Cnsl Schlesinger G&L LLP -535 Mad Av -NY 10022
(212) 872-9600 .. **Katz,** Russell S '97 Family Mgmt Corp -485 Mad Av -NY 10022 **Fx:**758-4020
(212) 872-1000 .. **Katz,** Ryan M '02 -One Bryant Park -NY 10036 **Fx:**872-1002
(212) 683-6949 .. **Katz,** Saml '88 -315 Mad Av -NY 10017 **Fx:**779-4732
(212) 583-0500 .. **Katz,** Sandra C '69 -425 Park Av -NY 10022 **Fx:**583-0419
(212) 506-1700 .. **Katz,** Sarah G '09 %Kasowitz BT&F LLP -1633 Bway -NY 10019
(516) 466-6436 .. **Katz,** Saul S '55 -71 Hicks Ln -Gt Neck 11024 **Fx:**504-0711
(718) 876-8105 .. **Katz,** Seth Ian '99 (Katz Law Ofcs) -36 Richmond Ter -Staten Isl 10301 **Fx:**876-8964
(212) 545-7373 .. **Katz,** Seth M '92 K Wilhelm -445 Park Av -NY 10022 **Fx:**545-9093
(212) 869-5030 .. **Katz,** Shari J '02 %Kucker & B,LLP -747 3rd Av -NY 10017
(212) 450-4000 .. **Katz,** Sharon '82 (Davis P&W LLP) -450 Lex Av -NY 10017
(212) 872-6084 .. **Katz,** Sharon D '85 KPMG LLP -345 Park Av -NY 10154
(631) 928-1800 .. **Katz,** Sheldon D '58 -18 Cliffside Dr -Pt Jffrsn 11777
(718) 222-2041 .. **Katz,** Stacey L '06 %Law Dept -350 Jay -Brklyn 11201 **Fx:**222-2088
(845) 480-5338 .. **Katz,** Stanley '59 -1 Salisbury Pt -South Nyack 10960 **Fx:**480-5338
(212) 966-7722 .. **Katz,** Stanley B '76 -1397 2nd Av -NY 10021
(212) 859-8000 .. **Katz,** Stanley I '80 OfCnsl Fried FHS&J LLP -1 NY Plz -NY 10004
(914) 681-7148 .. **Katz,** Stanley M '55 -4 New King -White Plns 10604 **Fx:**681-1383
(212) 349-6400 .. **Katz,** Stephen A '83 (S Katz,PC) -111 John -NY 10038 **Fx:**349-6407
(212) 382-0909 .. **Katz,** Stephen P '93 (Peckar & A,PC) -41 Mad Av -NY 10154
(212) 940-8800 .. **Katz,** Steven J '03 %Katten MR LLP -575 Mad Av -NY 10022
(212) 313-9869 .. **Katz,** Steven R '95 BBR Partners LLC -140 E 45th -NY 10017
(212) 973-0572 .. **Katz,** Steven S '88 Cnsl Wolff & S PC -140 Bway -NY 10005
(914) 828-8998 .. **Katz,** Stuart B '89 Swiss Re -175 King -Armonk 10504
(212) 859-8000 .. **Katz,** Stuart Z '68 OfCnsl Fried FHS&J LLP -1 NY Plz -NY 10004
(212) 906-1200 .. **Katz,** Tamara C '07 %Latham & W -885 3rd Av -NY 10022
(516) 997-0997 .. **Katz,** Terry Israel '92 (T Katz & Assoc,PC) -300 Jericho Quad -Jericho 11753 **Fx:**997-0001
(212) 697-3122 .. **Katz,** Tracy S '03 %Martin C&B LLP -220 E 42nd -NY 10017
(212) 969-3000 .. **Katz,** Wayne D '92 (Proskauer R LLP) -1585 Bway -NY 10036
(212) 751-3001 .. **Katz,** Wm M Jr. '03 (Thompson & K LLP) -919 3rd Av -NY 10022
(914) 478-0177 .. **Katz Wittenberg Levine & Silverman** -10 Old Jackson Av -Hastings-On-Hud 10706 **Fx:**478-7653
(212) 318-6000 .. **Katz,** Yariv C '02 %Paul HJ&W LLP -75 E 55th -NY 10022
(516) 803-3000 .. **Katzav,** Barbara L '93 Rainbow Prog -1111 Stewart Av -Bethpage 11714
(212) 400-7177 .. **Katzban,** Jo Ann '95 (Garrity GMG&F) -40 Wall -NY 10005
(212) 750-3100 .. **Katzberg,** Robt F '72 (Kaplan & K) -767 3rd Av -NY 10017
(212) 536-3900 .. **Katze,** Samantha J '08 %K&L Gates LLP -599 Lex Av -NY 10022
(212) 770-5080 .. **Katzel,** Aaron J '98 %AIG -70 Pine -NY 10270
(585) 454-5650 .. **Katzen,** Leon '42 SrCnsl Lacy K LLP -130 E Main -Rchstr 14604
(516) 466-3200 .. **Katzen,** Michl S '08 %J Halpern -525 Nrthrn Blvd -Gt Neck 11021
(212) 836-8000 .. **Katzenberg,** Jordan T '02 %Kaye S LLP -425 Park Av -NY 10022
(866) 348-5819 .. **Katzenelson,** Judith D '75 %SSA-ODAR -50 Fountain Plz -Buffalo 14202 **Fx:**(716) 551-4078
(212) 984-1703 .. **Katzenstein,** Chas B '80 %Rockrose Dvlpmnt Corp -290 Park Av S -NY 10010 **Fx:**949-6054
(212) 509-3456 .. **Katzenstein,** David M '89 (McGivney & K,PC) -80 Broad -NY 10004
(212) 735-2245 .. **Katzenstein,** Steven R '82 -4 Times Sq -NY 10036 **Fx:**(917) 777-2245
(518) 478-0006 .. **Katzer,** Michl '78 -Bx1001 -Slingerlnds 12159 **Fx:**475-0908
(212) 735-3000 .. **KatzGraham,** Shari A '07 %Skadden ASM&F LLP -4 Times Sq -NY 10036
(917) 637-3600 .. **Katzive,** Laura E '98 %Ctr for Reproductive Rts -120 Wall -NY 10005 **Fx:**637-3666
(212) 500-5030 .. **Katzive,** Marion C '65 (Kehl K&S,LLP) -317 Mad Av -NY 10017
(212) 319-3900 .. **Katzke,** Michl S '85 OfCnsl JE Bachelder LLP -437 Mad Av -NY 10022 **Fx:**319-3070
(718) 578-5097 .. **Katzman,** Eyal '00 -84-15 Cuthbert Rd -Kew Gdns 11415 **Fx:**805-1355
(518) 445-7200 .. **Katzman,** Gerald H '75 Albany Cllg Pharmacy-Union Univ -106 New Scotland Av -Albany 12208
(212) 455-2000 .. **Katzman,** Harlene G '96 Cnsl Simpson T&B LLP -425 Lex Av -NY 10017
(212) 506-3900 .. **Katzman,** Jennifer S '06 %Steptoe & J LLP -750 7th Av -NY 10019
(212) 698-3500 .. **Katzman,** Joshua S '04 Dechert LLP -1095 Av of Amer -NY 10036
(718) 237-3100 .. **Katzman,** Lauren R '09 %Leg Aid -111 Lvngstn -Brklyn 11201 **Fx:**250-4243
(516) 832-8070 .. **Katzman,** Martin '70 -1103 Stewart Av -Gdn Cty 11530 **Fx:**832-8071
(212) 599-0700 .. **Katzman,** Peter B '04 %Mazzeo S&B LLP -708 3rd Av -NY 10017 **Fx:**599-8400
(518) 587-5500 .. **Katzman,** Robt L '66 Katzman Law Firm,PLLC -376 Bway -Saratoga Spgs 12866 **Fx:**587-6054
(718) 589-3999 .. **Katzner,** Danl M '05 -1025 Longwood Av -Bronx 10459

(315) 425-2700 .. **Katzoff,** Susan R '91 (Hiscock & B,LLP) -One Park Pl -Syracuse 13202

(212) 883-6406 .. **Katzovicz,** Roy J '00 SrCnsl Pershing Square Capital Mgmt,LP -888 7th Av -NY 10106 **Fx:**286-1133

(212) 880-6000 .. **Kau,** Alexandra A '04 (Torys LLP) -237 Park Av -NY 10017

(212) 310-8000 .. **Kau,** Gregory L '10 %Weil G&M LLP -767 5th Av -NY 10153

(914) 271-6106 .. **Kauderer,** Bruce M '73 -6 Georgia Ln -Croton-On-Hud 10520 **Fx:**271-8993

(516) 832-7777 .. **Kaufer,** Jason M '95 Cnsl Silberstein A&M,PC -600 Old Cntry Rd -Gdn Cty 11530

(212) 644-1010 .. **Kauff,** Jerome B '62 (Kauff M&M LLP) -950 3rd Av -NY 10022

(212) 644-1010 .. **Kauff McGuire & Margolis LLP** -950 3rd Av -NY 10022 **Fx:**644-1936

(212) 547-2600 .. **Kauff,** Steven B '99 %North Star Realty Finance Corp -399 Park Av -NY 10022 **Fx:**547-2700

(212) 321-7080 .. **Kauffman,** Brad A '96 -40 Exch Pl -NY 10005 **Fx:**321-7079

(518) 449-3300 .. **Kauffman,** Madeline H Kibrick '87 (Nolan & H,LLP) -39 N Pearl -Albany 12207

(212) 632-5500 .. **Kauffman,** Michl R '07 %Salans LLP -620 5th Av -NY 10020

(212) 846-3543 .. **Kauffman,** Stuart '00 %MTV Networks -1515 Bway -NY 10036 **Fx:**258-8358

(212) 849-7000 .. **Kaufman,** Aaron S '08 %Quinn EU&S,LLP -51 Mad Av -NY 10010

(516) 228-8823 .. **Kaufman,** Adam B '95 A Kaufman & Assoc,PLLC -585 Stewart Av -Gdn Cty 11530 **Fx:**228-8824

(212) 751-8000 .. **Kaufman,** Adam B '02 %Dankner & M,PC -41 E 57th -NY 10022

(212) 403-1000 .. **Kaufman,** Adam K '08 %Wachtell LR&K -51 W 52nd -NY 10019

(212) 922-1800 .. **Kaufman,** Alan F '00 OfCnsl McKenna L&A -230 Park Av -NY 10169

(212) 833-6752 .. **Kaufman,** Alan H '77 %Sony Corp of America -555 Mad Av -NY 10022 **Fx:**833-6797

(212) 826-5579 .. **Kaufman,** Alan J '71 -1212 Av of Amer -NY 10036

(718) 459-5400 .. **Kaufman,** Alan L '88 (Farber R&K PC) -97-77 Qns Blvd -Rego Pk 11374

(212) 808-7800 .. **Kaufman,** Alan R '71 (Kelley D&W LLP) -101 Park Av -NY 10178

(518) 435-9426 .. **Kaufman,** Alan S '78 (Chamberlain K&J) -35 Fuller Rd -Albany 12205 **Fx:**435-9102

(718) 454-2230 .. **Kaufman,** Albert M '58 -186-46 Avon Rd -Jamaica 11432

(212) 715-9100 .. **Kaufman,** Alexander S '08 %Kramer LN&F,LLP -1177 Av of Amer -NY 10036

(212) 834-0600 .. **Kaufman,** Andrew B '91 (Gordon & S,PC) -355 Lex Av -NY 10017

(718) 286-6000 .. **Kaufman,** Andrew H '91 %DA -125-01 Qns Blvd -Kew Gdns 11415

(212) 826-0820 .. **Kaufman,** Andrew H '01 -277 Park Av -NY 10172

(212) 980-9600 .. **Kaufman,** Andrew S '79 (Kaufman B&R) -120 Bway -NY 10271

(516) 681-1100 .. **Kaufman,** Arthur R '67 (Kaufman DV&G,LLP) -135 Crsswys Park Dr -Woodbury 11797

(212) 859-8000 .. **Kaufman,** Arthur S '72 (Fried FHS&J LLP) -1 NY Plz -NY 10004

(212) 450-4000 .. **Kaufman,** Aryeh L '09 %Davis P&W LLP -450 Lex Av -NY 10017

(914) 668-6167 .. **Kaufman,** Barbara '83 -311 E Devonia Av -Mt Vernon 10552

(845) 485-3900 .. **Kaufman,** Barry '76 %Dept of Law -235 Main -Poughkeepsie 12601 **Fx:**452-3303

(212) 594-5300 .. **Kaufman,** Benjamin Y '90 (Milberg LLP) -1 Penn Plz -NY 10119

(212) 987-4000 .. **Kaufman Bern Deutsch & Leibman,LLP** -888 7th Av -NY 10106

(212) 661-5030 .. **Kaufman,** Beth L '78 (Schoeman U&K,LLP) -60 E 42nd -NY 10165

(212) 980-9600 .. **Kaufman Borgeest & Ryan** -120 Bway -NY 10271 **Fx:**980-9291

(914) 741-6100 .. **Kaufman Borgeest & Ryan** -200 Summit Lk Dr -Valhalla 10595 **Fx:**741-0025

(516) 248-6000 .. **Kaufman Borgeest & Ryan** -1205 Franklin Av -Gdn Cty 11530 **Fx:**248-0677

(212) 421-4100 .. **Kaufman,** Bradley A '83 (Pryor C LLP) -7 Times Sq -NY 10036

(631) 390-0010 .. **Kaufman,** Brian E '09 %Bruno G&S,LLP -445 Broad Hollow Rd -Melvll 11747

(516) 481-5025 .. **Kaufman,** Celeste P '83 -955 Front -Uniondale 11553

(212) 504-6000 .. **Kaufman,** Chas '08 %Cadwalader W&T LLP -1 World Fncl Ctr -NY 10281

(212) 825-0365 .. **Kaufman,** Colin E '79 (AL Bailey,PC) -120 Bway -NY 10271 **Fx:**825-0999

(212) 698-3500 .. **Kaufman,** Danl S '03 %Dechert LLP -1095 Av of Amer -NY 10036

(212) 506-1700 .. **Kaufman,** Dara J '04 Kasowitz BT&F LLP -1633 Bway -NY 10019

(212) 468-8000 .. **Kaufman,** David H '84 (Morrison & F LLP) -1290 Av of Amer -NY 10104

(631) 342-8070 .. **Kaufman,** David M '89 (Tinari OO&K,LLP) -320 Carleton Av -Central Islip 11722

(212) 558-5500 .. **Kaufman,** David M '09 Weitz & L,PC -700 Bway -NY 10003

(212) 918-3000 .. **Kaufman,** Dena Copulsky '03 %Hogan L LLP -875 3rd Av -NY 10022

(315) 475-3127 .. **Kaufman,** Dennis A '74 %Leg Srvcs -472 S Salina -Syracuse 13202 **Fx:**475-2706

(212) 506-2500 .. **Kaufman,** Diane K '07 %Mayer B LLP -1675 Bway -NY 10019

(212) 705-7000 .. **Kaufman,** Dina R '09 %Bingham M LLP -399 Park Av -NY 10022

(516) 681-1100 .. **Kaufman Dolowich Voluck & Gonzo,LLP** -135 Crsswys Park Dr -Woodbury 11797 **Fx:**681-1101

(212) 485-9600 .. **Kaufman Dolowich Voluck & Gonzo,LLP** -100 William -NY 10038 **Fx:**485-9700

(212) 335-9000 .. **Kaufman,** Douglas P '01 %DA -1 Hogan Pl -NY 10013

(631) 761-7000 .. **Kaufman,** Eileen R '76 %Touro Cllg Law Ctr -225 Eastvw Dr -Central Islip 11722

(212) 332-3373 .. **Kaufman,** Eric R '67 Kaufman & K -620 5th Av -NY 10020 **Fx:**332-3374

(212) 688-8555 .. **Kaufman,** Ethan E '88 (Fragomen DB&L LLP) -7 Hanover Sq -NY 10004

(914) 633-6608 .. **Kaufman,** Eugene M '60 -30 Church -New Rchll 10801 **Fx:**633-6608

(631) 367-7100 .. **Kaufman,** Evan J '96 (Coughlin SGR&R LLP) -58 S Srvc Rd -Melvll 11747

(212) 512-2543 .. **Kaufman,** Frank J '73 %McGraw-Hill Co,Inc -1221 Av of Amer -NY 10020

(212) 687-1700 .. **Kaufman Friedman Plotnicki & Grun,LLP** -300 E 42nd -NY 10017 **Fx:**687-3179

(212) 975-6792 .. **Kaufman,** Gary '76 %CBS Inc -51 W 52nd -NY 10019

(212) 682-7250 .. **Kaufman,** Gerald S '60 (Kaufman & G) -370 Lex Av -NY 10017

(212) 476-8029 .. **Kaufman,** Glenn B '94 American Securities -666 3rd Av -NY 10017 **Fx:**697-5524

(212) 682-7250 .. **Kaufman & Gluck** -370 Lex Av -NY 10017 **Fx:**953-7257

(212) 682-7250 .. **Kaufman,** H Sheldon '53 (Kaufman & G) -370 Lex Av -NY 10017

(212) 260-0228 .. **Kaufman,** Harley D '90 -441 E 20th -NY 10010

(914) 242-3222 .. **Kaufman,** Harry C '78 (Kaufman & K) -37 W Main -Mt Kisco 10549 **Fx:**242-6082

(212) 880-0842 .. **Kaufman,** Henry R '73 H Kaufman,PC -60 E 42nd -NY 10165 **Fx:**682-1965

(877) 964-1115 .. **Kaufman,** Herman '69 -Bx242 -Pt Chester 10573 **Fx:**(772) 325-7670

(845) 351-2900 .. **Kaufman,** Howard '80 Leyland Devlpmnt LLC -16 Sterling Lk Rd -Tuxedo Pk 10987

(212) 363-3100 .. **Kaufman,** Ian H '03 %Bivona & C,PC -88 Pine -NY 10005

(212) 336-0106 .. **Kaufman,** Jack '90 %SEC -3 World Fncl Ctr -NY 10281 **Fx:**336-1323

(212) 580-6378 .. **Kaufman,** Jack S '99 Kosher Mrkt Pl -2442 Bway -NY 10024

(212) 381-7323 .. **Kaufman,** James '69 -420 Lex Av -NY 10170 **Fx:**682-3373

(212) 302-2400 .. **Kaufman,** Jason '09 %Lynch DE LLP -264 W 40th -NY 10018

(212) 592-1400 .. **Kaufman,** Jeffrey H '75 (Herrick,F LLP) -2 Park Av -NY 10016

(212) 909-6000 .. **Kaufman,** Jennifer Correll '04 %Debevoise & P LLP -919 3rd Av -NY 10022

(845) 794-3344 .. **Kaufman,** Jeremy B '09 %DA -414 Bway -Monticello 12701 **Fx:**794-3646

(212) 468-8000 .. **Kaufman,** Jessica '07 %Morrison & F LLP -1290 Av of Amer -NY 10104

(202) 607-3376 .. **Kaufman,** Jocelyn D '08 -345 Union -Brklyn 11231

(914) 993-0700 .. **Kaufman,** John L '77 (Canavan & K) -1 Barker Av -White Plns 10601 **Fx:**993-9298

(212) 691-8871 .. **Kaufman,** Jon M '53 -37 W 12th -NY 10011 **Fx:**924-9413

(631) 421-4488 .. **Kaufman,** Jonathan H '88 (Serpe A&K) -149 Main Bx165 -Huntngtn 11743

(212) 816-1481 .. **Kaufman,** Jonathan J '90 %Citigroup -388 Greenwich -NY 10013

(212) 455-2000 .. **Kaufman,** Jos H '95 (Simpson T&B LLP) -425 Lex Av -NY 10017

(212) 735-3000 .. **Kaufman,** Joshua A '03 %Skadden ASM&F LLP -4 Times Sq -NY 10036

(212) 445-8158 .. **Kaufman,** Joshua P '97 CMG -919 3rd Av -NY 10022

(914) 725-6826 .. **Kaufman,** Judith A '74 -Bx1641 -White Plns 10602

(212) 416-8959 .. **Kaufman,** Judith E '79 %Dept of Law -120 Bway -NY 10271

(212) 479-4338 .. **Kaufman,** Jules P '84 Coty Inc -2 Park Av -NY 10016

(718) 585-7000 .. **Kaufman,** Julian '82 (Rogers WKC&Z) -800 Grnd Cncrs -Bronx 10451 **Fx:**585-8969

(516) 228-0348 .. **Kaufman,** Lewis '70 %Goldman H&C,LLP -47 Post Av -Westbury 11590

(631) 348-3535 .. **Kaufman,** Lita C '97 Dasnet Corp -20 Orvll Dr -Bohemia 11716

(212) 599-1900 .. **Kaufman,** Marc '08 -60 E 42nd -NY 10165

(212) 310-8000 .. **Kaufman,** Marcie R '07 %Weil G&M LLP -767 5th Av -NY 10153

(212) 293-5556 .. **Kaufman,** Mark S '90 (Kaufman & K,LLP) -747 3rd Av -NY 10017 **Fx:**355-5009

(914) 472-2356 .. **Kaufman,** Martin S '66 -322 Heathcote Rd -Scarsdale 10583 **Fx:**472-5544

(914) 834-3322 .. **Kaufman,** Martin S '66 Cnsl Atlantic Lgl Fndtn -2039 Palmer Av -Larchmnt 10538 **Fx:**833-1022

(212) 374-0680 .. **Kaufman,** Matthew A '80 Rimland & Assoc -225 Bway -NY 10007 **Fx:**374-0681

(646) 485-5524 .. **Kaufman,** Matthew J '06 Goldman Sachs -32 Old Slip -NY 10005

(212) 682-9200 .. **Kaufman,** Matthew L '01 (Ostrow K&F LLP) -405 Lex Av -NY 10174

(516) 681-1100 .. **Kaufman,** Michl A '93 (Kaufman DV&G,LLP) -135 Crsswys Park Dr -Woodbury 11797

(212) 583-8989 .. **Kaufman,** Michl B '92 Geller & Co -800 3rd Av -NY 10022

(212) 701-3000 .. **Kaufman,** Michl W '03 %Cahill G&R LLP -80 Pine -NY 10005 **Fx:**269-5420

(718) 934-0900 .. **Kaufman,** Mitchell A '78 -3558 Nostrand Av -Brklyn 11229 **Fx:**934-0988

(718) 298-1125 .. **Kaufman,** Mitchell L '80 %Hon J Golia -88-11 Sutphin Blvd -Jamaica 11435

(516) 248-6400 .. **Kaufman,** Neil M '85 (Davidoff M&H,LLP) -200 Grdn City Plz -Gdn Cty 11530

(212) 902-1000 .. **Kaufman,** Neil S '00 Goldman Sachs & Co -85 Broad -NY 10004

(212) 808-7210 .. **Kaufman,** Nina L '92 -230 Park Av -NY 10169 **Fx:**481-4039

(718) 254-7000 .. **Kaufman,** Paul '92 %US Atty -271 Cadman Plz E -Brklyn 11201 **Fx:**254-6479

(212) 987-4000 .. **Kaufman,** Paul C '74 (Kaufman BD&L,LLP) -888 7th Av -NY 10106

(212) 486-3600 .. **Kaufman,** Peter S '79 %Gordian Grp -500 Park Av -NY 10022 **Fx:**486-3616

(212) 715-9100 .. **Kaufman,** Philip S '77 (Kramer LN&F,LLP) -1177 Av of Amer -NY 10036

(212) 294-6700 .. **Kaufman,** Rachel H '10 %Winston & S -200 Park Av -NY 10166

(845) 638-5300 .. **Kaufman,** Rachelle Congemi '92 %Rockland Cnty Family Ct -1 S Main -New Cty 10956 **Fx:**638-5319

(914) 694-4444 .. **Kaufman,** Richd A '80 %Natl Rlty & Dvlpmnt -3 Manhattanvll Rd -Purchase 10577 **Fx:**694-5448

(716) 843-5700 .. **Kaufman,** Richd D '81 %US Atty -138 Delaware Av -Buffalo 14202 **Fx:**551-3052

(516) 747-2433 .. **Kaufman,** Richd G '85 (Seiden & K) -1 Old Cntry Rd -Carle Pl 11514

(631) 331-0950 .. **Kaufman,** Richd J '78 -646 Main -Pt Jffrsn 11777 **Fx:**474-4282

(212) 998-6295 .. **Kaufman,** Risa E '98 NYU Schl of Law -245 Sullivan -NY 10012

(212) 969-3000 .. **Kaufman,** Robt M '57 (Proskauer R LLP) -1585 Bway -NY 10036

(516) 938-6299 .. **Kaufman,** Roberta N '94 -183 Bway -Hicksvll 11801 **Fx:**938-9401

(212) 869-3500 .. **Kaufman,** Rosalind Fuchsberg '78 SrCnsl J Fuchsberg Law Firm,LLP -500 5th Av -NY 10110 **Fx:**398-1532

(212) 801-9380 .. **Kaufman,** Ross '81 (Greenberg T,LLP) -200 Park Av -NY 10166

(516) 365-6690 .. **Kaufman,** Roy F '85 PRI -1800 Nrthrn Blvd -Roslyn 11576

(718) 651-1948 .. **Kaufman,** Scott G '94 (Crowley C&K) -84-56 Grand Av -Elmhrst 11373

(212) 490-1700 .. **Kaufman,** Scott L '91 (Wiggin & D) -450 Lex Av -NY 10017

(212) 732-6366 .. **Kaufman & Serota,PC** -225 Bway -NY 10007 **Fx:**385-3425

(516) 791-8888 .. **Kaufman & Serota,PC** -896 Longvw Av -N Woodmere 11581 **Fx:**791-6048

(212) 255-4414 .. **Kaufman,** Seth M '02 Kaufman,PLLC -61 Bway -NY 10006

(516) 239-4015 .. **Kaufman,** Stanley J '55 -1327 Park -Atlantic Bch 11509 **Fx:**(718) 522-2146

(212) 687-1700 .. **Kaufman,** Stanley M '78 (Kaufman FP&G,LLP) -300 E 42nd -NY 10017

(516) 833-5630 .. **Kaufman,** Stephanie J '00 (Beekman SK&L,LLP) -1050 Franklin Av -Gdn Cty 11530
(718) 822-0500 .. **Kaufman,** Stephen B '68 (Alpert & K, LLP) -2916 Bruckner Blvd -Bronx 10465
(212) 349-2000 .. **Kaufman,** Stephen B '68 (Alpert & K, LLP) -233 Bway -NY 10279
(914) 945-3197 .. **Kaufman,** Stephen C '78 IBM -Bx218 -Yorktwn Hts 10598
(212) 826-0820 .. **Kaufman,** Stephen E '58 -277 Park Av -NY 10172 **Fx:**832-8532
(718) 807-9492 .. **Kaufman,** Stephen H '83 -72-61 113th -Frst Hlls 11375
(212) 564-9633 .. **Kaufman,** Steven B '85 -225 Bway -NY 10007 **Fx:**564-9639
(212) 883-4021 .. **Kaufman,** Steven J '74 Cluett American Corp -48 W 38th -NY 10018
(518) 587-5188 .. **Kaufman,** Stuart A '06 Leg Aid -112 Spring -Saratoga Spgs 12866 **Fx:**587-0959
(212) 455-2000 .. **Kaufman,** Susan B '79 Cnsl Simpson T&B LLP -425 Lex Av -NY 10017
(516) 239-4015 .. **Kaufman,** Susan L '91 %S Kaufman -1327 Park -Atlantic Bch 11509 **Fx:**(718) 522-2146
(914) 723-7592 .. **Kaufman,** Susan W '72 -17 Withington Rd -Scarsdale 10583
(917) 453-3384 .. **Kaufman,** Uri '90 -220-46 73rd Av -Oakland Gdns 11364
(212) 458-7455 .. **Kaufman,** Wayne R '98 AIG -175 Water -NY 10038 **Fx:**458-7080
(212) 335-9000 .. **Kaufmann,** Adam S '95 %DA -1 Hogan Pl -NY 10013
(212) 755-3100 .. **Kaufmann,** David J '77 (Kaufmann GR&O LLP) -777 3rd Av -NY 10017
(212) 825-1044 .. **Kaufmann,** Ernest W Jr. '59 -26 Bway -NY 10004
(212) 755-3100 .. **Kaufmann Gildin Robbins & Oppenheim LLP** -777 3rd Av -NY 10017 **Fx:**755-3174
(914) 834-9500 .. **Kaufmann,** Henry M '57 (H Kaufmann Assoc) -2 East Av -Larchmnt 10538 **Fx:**834-9515
(646) 471-4000 .. **Kaufmann,** John '97 %PricewaterhouseCoopers LLP -300 Mad Av -NY 10017
(212) 536-3900 .. **Kaufmann,** John W '82 (K&L Gates LLP) -599 Lex Av -NY 10022
(518) 486-2921 .. **Kaufmann,** Karen '79 Cnsl OPRHP -Agncy Bldg 1 ESP -Albany 12238 **Fx:**474-5106
(607) 272-5590 .. **Kaufmann,** Karen E '79 Friedlander & F,PC -103 W Seneca Bx6577 -Ithaca 14851 **Fx:**272-5594
(914) 969-5319 .. **Kaufmann,** Kenneth J '81 -Bx481 -Bronxvll 10708
(212) 735-3000 .. **Kaufmann,** Laura A '03 %Skadden ASM&F LLP -4 Times Sq -NY 10036
(212) 556-2100 .. **Kaufmann,** Sebastian F C '00 (King & S) -1185 Av of Amer -NY 10036
(212) 517-8634 .. **Kaufthal,** Abby L '04 David Berg Fndtn -16 E 73rd -NY 10021
(718) 361-0555 .. **Kauftheil,** Leonard K '92 %GHP -25-07 36th Av -LIC 11106
(718) 833-2496 .. **Kauget,** Gary P '83 -9201 4th Av -Brklyn 11209 **Fx:**921-4526
(212) 525-8042 .. **Kauh,** Jane H '01 %HSBC Bank -452 5th Av -NY 10018
(585) 419-9100 .. **Kaul,** Richd A '74 -290 Linden Oaks -Rchstr 14625 **Fx:**419-8061
(845) 758-9786 .. **Kaumeyer,** Linda Louise '82 -14 Cntry Clb Dr -Red Hook 12571
(212) 728-8000 .. **Kaunfer,** Rachel Pressman '05 %Willkie F&G LLP -787 7th Av -NY 10019
(718) 792-0444 .. **Kaur,** Anup '00 %MHLS -1500 Waters Pl -Bronx 10461 **Fx:**597-7385
(516) 496-5822 .. **Kaur,** Jasleen '08 T Spina -170 Froehlich Farm Blvd -Woodbury 11797 **Fx:**496-5420
(212) 446-4800 .. **Kaushik,** Srinivas S '01 (Kirkland & E LLP) -153 E 53rd -NY 10022
(212) 819-8200 .. **Kautz,** Matthew J '99 (White & C LLP) -1155 Av of Amer -NY 10036
(732) 855-6451 .. **Kautz,** Robt C '85 (Wilentz G&S) -110 William -NY 10038 **Fx:**726-6685
(518) 587-5188 .. **Kautzman,** Carol '93 %Leg Aid -112 Spring -Saratoga Spgs 12866 **Fx:**587-0959
(212) 610-6300 .. **Kauvar,** Eloise M '08 %Allen & O -1221 Av of Amer -NY 10020
(212) 902-1000 .. **Kava,** Alan S '91 %Goldman Sachs -1 NY Plz -NY 10004
(914) 328-7272 .. **Kava,** Jody L '85 %J Sapir -399 Knollwood Rd -White Plns 10603 **Fx:**328-8608
(212) 701-3000 .. **Kavaler,** Thos J '73 (Cahill G&R LLP) -80 Pine -NY 10005 **Fx:**269-5420
(212) 593-6700 .. **Kavallieratos,** Jennifer P '08 %Aaronson RF&D,LLP -757 3rd Av -NY 10017
(914) 729-6319 .. **Kavalos,** Kaliopi '03 (Fazio & K,PLLC) -10 Bank -White Plns 10606
(212) 425-9300 .. **Kavanagh,** Caoilfhionn P '10 %Bressler A&R,PC -17 State -NY 10004
(212) 852-3558 .. **Kavanagh,** Christopher M '97 %US Trust Co,NA -114 W 47th -NY 10036 **Fx:**852-1310
(516) 484-0254 .. **Kavanagh,** Donald J Jr. '77 OfCnsl B Somerstein & Assoc,PC -203 Glen Cove Av -Sea Cliff 11579
(516) 674-0707 .. **Kavanagh,** Edw L '86 (E Kavanagh,PC) -3 Schl -Glen Cove 11542 **Fx:**674-8353
(212) 837-6000 .. **Kavanagh,** Frances C '08 Hughes H&R LLP -1 Bttry Pk Plz -NY 10004
(212) 207-8400 .. **Kavanagh,** J Hayes '74 (Kavanagh M&O LLP) -415 Mad Av -NY 10017
(516) 796-8590 .. **Kavanagh,** John G '84 -37 Sandpiper Ln -Levittwn 11756
(212) 524-5000 .. **Kavanagh,** Keelin '88 (Jacob M&F) -1270 Av of Amer -NY 10020
(212) 207-8400 .. **Kavanagh Maloney & Osnato LLP** -415 Mad Av -NY 10017 **Fx:**888-7324
(845) 331-9434 .. **Kavanagh,** Michl J '99 %Mainetti M&O,PC -303 Clinton Av Bx3058 -Kingston 12402
(718) 286-6000 .. **Kavanagh,** Michl P '82 %DA -125-01 Qns Blvd -Kew Gdns 11415
(631) 286-3500 .. **Kavanagh,** Tara A '94 (Gunkel & K,PC) -9 Station Ct -Bellprt 11713 **Fx:**286-6188
(518) 283-3000 .. **Kavanaugh,** David J '92 (Frost & K,PC) -287 N Greenbush Rd -Troy 12180 **Fx:**283-8060
(518) 485-8495 .. **Kavaney,** Mary B '92 %DCJS -4 Twr Pl -Albany 12203 **Fx:**457-3089
(212) 592-3947 .. **Kavanna,** W Ashwood '84 -1487 York Av Bx20322 -NY 10021
(845) 562-1234 .. **Kave,** Howard A '73 -815 Blooming Grove Tpk -New Windsor 12553 **Fx:**562-5271
(212) 385-1191 .. **Kavesh,** Jos S '98 %Goodman & J LLP -75 Broad -NY 10004
(718) 965-6146 .. **Kaviar,** Eric B '79 -712 3rd Av -Brklyn 11232 **Fx:**768-5077
(716) 845-6000 .. **Kavinoky Cook LLP** -726 Exchange -Buffalo 14210 **Fx:**845-6474
(212) 819-8200 .. **Kavoukjian,** Michl E '86 (White & C LLP) -1155 Av of Amer -NY 10036
(914) 287-8850 .. **Kavounas,** Edmond A '65 (Rockwood Capital,LLC) -10 Bank -White Plns 10606 **Fx:**761-3100
(212) 297-1026 .. **Kavourias,** Michl G '90 Gramercy Capital Corp -420 Lex Av -NY 10170 **Fx:**297-1090
(516) 773-3516 .. **Kavoussi,** Mandana '03 (Zervos & K) -505 Nrthrn Blvd -Gt Neck 11021 **Fx:**759-6120
(718) 875-7686 .. **Kavowras,** Mona '91 -1421 Oriental Blvd -Brklyn 11235
(212) 278-0400 .. **Kavrukov,** Ivan S '68 (Cooper & D LLP) -30 Rckfllr Plz -NY 10112
(516) 616-0734 .. **Kavulich,** Gary M '96 %Century Credit & Collection -813 Jericho Tpk -New Hyde Pk 11040
(914) 762-6625 .. **Kavy,** Irwin J '82 -573 N State Rd -Briarclff Mnr 10510 **Fx:**762-6877
(315) 422-4742 .. **Kawa,** Michl J '73 -304 S Franklin -Syracuse 13202 **Fx:**478-6503
(716) 852-3600 .. **Kawalec,** Thos P '98 (Chelus HS&M,PC) -438 Main -Buffalo 14202
(212) 962-2232 .. **Kawano,** Arnold H '78 Harold Lee & Sons Ins Co -31 Pell -NY 10013
(914) 833-0792 .. **Kawas,** Paul T '91 -131 Larchmnt Av -Larchmnt 10538
(212) 450-4000 .. **Kawata,** Yukako '83 (Davis P&W LLP) -450 Lex Av -NY 10017
(212) 331-2803 .. **Kawejsza,** Jason B '04 Universal Music Grp -1755 Bway -NY 10019
(718) 262-2983 .. **Kawinski,** Magdalen C '07 %CUNY Citizenshp & Immig Prjct -94-20 Guy R Brewer Blvd -Jamaica 11450
(212) 506-2500 .. **Kay,** Alicia R '09 %Mayer B LLP -1675 Bway -NY 10019
(212) 732-2000 .. **Kay,** Crystal '10 %Cullen and D LLP -44 Wall -NY 10005
(212) 455-2000 .. **Kay,** Danl R '08 %Simpson T&B LLP -425 Lex Av -NY 10017
(516) 222-6200 .. **Kay,** David R '67 OfCnsl Berkman HPP&F,PC -100 Grdn City Plz -Gdn Cty 11530
(212) 270-2804 .. **Kay,** Deborah J '03 JP Morgan Chase & Co -270 Park Av -NY 10017
(212) 939-7251 .. **Kay,** Elliot S '03 -115 E 57th -NY 10022
(973) 596-4681 .. **Kay,** Elyssa '08 %Gibbons PC -1 Penn Plz -NY 10119 **Fx:**639-6331
(516) 229-4400 .. **Kay,** Emanuel M '74 (Kay & G) -875 Merrick Av -Westbury 11590
(212) 849-7000 .. **Kay,** Eric M '96 OfCnsl Quinn EU&S,LLP -51 Mad Av -NY 10010
(516) 229-4400 .. **Kay & Gray** -875 Merrick Av -Westbury 11590 **Fx:**229-4403
(631) 666-6200 .. **Kay,** James P '98 %PF Adams,PC -49 5th Av Bx1089M -Bay Shr 11706 **Fx:**665-6739
(631) 271-2350 .. **Kay,** John Andrew '05 -1445 NY Av -Huntngtn Sta 11746 **Fx:**271-2356
(212) 337-2228 .. **Kay,** Jonathan M '79 %US Dept Labor -201 Varick -NY 10014
(518) 477-4800 .. **Kay,** Jos L '77 -Bx444 -E Greenbush 12061 **Fx:**477-5666
(718) 935-3620 .. **Kay,** Judith K '75 Bd of Ed -131 Lvngstn -Brklyn 11201
(718) 250-0400 .. **Kay,** Michl John '95 %R Tusa -1 MetroTech Ctr -Brklyn 11201 **Fx:**250-0591
(212) 594-1991 .. **Kay,** Mitchell N '62 -7 Penn Plz -NY 10001 **Fx:**847-8220
(716) 822-8784 .. **Kay,** Randall J '83 -6 Mokinley Pkwy -Buffalo 14220
(212) 943-1090 .. **Kay,** Rhonda E '91 (Gair GCSMB&R) -80 Pine -NY 10005
(212) 421-4100 .. **Kay,** Richd L '62 (Pryor C LLP) -7 Times Sq -NY 10036
(718) 392-0200 .. **Kay,** Sanford '78 -37-18 Nrthrn Blvd -LIC 11101
(212) 669-3749 .. **Kay,** Sara C '92 %Comptroller -1 Centre -NY 10007 **Fx:**669-2884
(212) 351-4500 .. **Kay,** Stanley L '68 (Epstein B&G,PC) -250 Park Av -NY 10177
(646) 315-7351 .. **Kay,** Thos G '00 FINRA -14 Wall -NY 10005
(212) 586-8078 .. **Kayatt,** Arlene S '87 -250 W 57th -NY 10107 **Fx:**977-7035
(212) 530-5000 .. **Kaye,** Alexander M '92 (Milbank TH&M LLP) -1 Chase Manh Plz -NY 10005
(212) 964-5858 .. **Kaye,** Allen E '65 -111 Bway -NY 10006
(212) 834-0600 .. **Kaye,** Andrew C '04 %Gordon & S,PC -355 Lex Av -NY 10017
(212) 385-8000 .. **Kaye,** Bruce K '88 OfCnsl Barasch MS&P -11 Park Pl -NY 10007
(516) 747-5900 .. **Kaye,** Corey B '85 (Kaye & L) -220 Mineola Blvd -Mineola 11501
(716) 565-0080 .. **Kaye,** Danl L '58 -Bx683 -Williamsvll 14231 **Fx:**565-9880
(212) 530-5000 .. **Kaye,** David B '09 %Milbank TH&M LLP -1 Chase Manh Plz -NY 10005
(212) 878-8000 .. **Kaye,** David E '08 %Clifford C LLP -31 W 52nd -NY 10019
(212) 674-5151 .. **Kaye,** David N '75 -175 5th Av -NY 10010 **Fx:**529-0594
(212) 635-6612 .. **Kaye,** Deborah H '81 Bk of NY Mellon -1 Wall -NY 10286
(914) 944-0760 .. **Kaye,** Edw P '95 -24 Whitson Rd -Briarclff Mnr 10510
(718) 260-2460 .. **Kaye,** Elliot F '05 Hon S Johnson -225 Cadman Plz E -Brklyn 11201
(212) 791-2498 .. **Kaye,** Emily C '96 %SSA -26 Fed Plz -NY 10278 **Fx:**791-2973
(212) 782-7102 .. **Kaye,** James E '90 Moore Cap Mgt -1251 6th Av -NY 10020
(718) 746-5017 .. **Kaye,** Jonathan '85 -3516 Bell Blvd -Bayside 11361 **Fx:**281-4746
(718) 250-2000 .. **Kaye,** Jonathan S '98 %DA -350 Jay -Brklyn 11201 **Fx:**250-2314
(212) 715-9100 .. **Kaye,** Jordan D '04 %Kramer LN&F,LLP -1177 Av of Amer -NY 10036
(212) 805-6387 .. **Kaye,** Joshua D '08 %Hon WH Pauley III -500 Pearl -NY 10007
(212) 735-3000 .. **Kaye,** Judith S '63 OfCnsl Skadden ASM&F LLP -4 Times Sq -NY 10036
(212) 669-2138 .. **Kaye,** Laurie Kammler '79 %DCAS-DLS -1 Centre -NY 10007 **Fx:**669-2139
(718) 243-2262 .. **Kaye,** Lawr L '80 (LL Kaye,PC) -44 Court -Brklyn 11201 **Fx:**(866) 299-5193
(212) 592-1400 .. **Kaye,** Lawr M '71 (Herrick,F LLP) -2 Park Av -NY 10016
(516) 747-5900 .. **Kaye & Lenchner** -220 Mineola Blvd -Mineola 11501 **Fx:**747-7633
(212) 576-5965 .. **Kaye,** Leonard B '80 NY Life Ins -51 Mad Av -NY 10010
(212) 545-4000 .. **Kaye,** Marjorie N Jr. '91 (Jackson L LLP) -666 3rd Av -NY 10017
(718) 229-6146 .. **Kaye,** Michl A '77 (M Kaye,PC) -838 Union -Brklyn 11215
(212) 370-1300 .. **Kaye,** Richd P '79 (Ellenoff G&S LLP) -150 E 42nd -NY 10017
(914) 712-1100 .. **Kaye,** Richd S '79 %Murphy & H,LLP -1 Radisson Plz -New Rchll 10801
(212) 836-8000 .. **Kaye Scholer LLP** -425 Park Av -NY 10022 **Fx:**836-8760
(212) 248-8800 .. **Kaye,** Steven M Jr. '10 %Callan KB&B LLP -1 Whitehall -NY 10004
(415) 773-5463 .. **Kaye,** Tchienyonnoh '07 %Orrick H&S LLP -51 W 52nd -NY 10019 **Fx:**773-5759
(212) 310-8000 .. **Kaye Watson,** Vanessa A '03 %Weil G&M LLP -767 5th Av -NY 10153
(212) 530-5000 .. **Kayle,** Bruce E '83 (Milbank TH&M LLP) -1 Chase Manh Plz -NY 10005
(718) 998-1010 .. **Kaylie,** Rachel L '95 %W Pager -203-205 Kings Hwy -Brklyn 11223 **Fx:**998-8046
(212) 227-8283 .. **Kayman,** Ann Gardner '88 NY Grant Co -29 Bway -NY 10006 **Fx:**214-0814
(718) 438-2525 .. **Kayman,** Gershon S '02 NC Caller,PC -4309 13th Av -Brklyn 11219 **Fx:**972-4154
(212) 969-3000 .. **Kayman,** Steven M '82 (Proskauer R LLP) -1585 Bway -NY 10036
(212) 259-8000 .. **Kayne,** Alexander M '98 (Dewey & L LLP) -1301 Av of Amer -NY 10019

(212) 578-6234 .. **Kayne,** Michele S '98 %MetLife -27-01 Qns Plz N -LIC 11101
(212) 906-1200 .. **Kay-Oliphant,** Eli J '06 %Latham & W -885 3rd Av -NY 10022
(212) 935-5057 .. **Kayser,** Leo III '70 (Kayser & R,LLP) -515 Mad Av -NY 10022
(212) 935-5057 .. **Kayser & Redfern, LLP** -515 Mad Av -NY 10022 **Fx:**935-6424
(212) 692-1000 .. **Kayser,** Susan V '83 (Duane M LLP) -1540 Bway -NY 10036
(212) 701-3000 .. **Kazakevich,** Michl '05 %Cahill G&R LLP -80 Pine -NY 10005 **Fx:**269-5420
(212) 613-5000 .. **Kazakina,** Alla '02 Leg Assist Grp -450 W 33rd -NY 10001 **Fx:**750-0820
(212) 848-9800 .. **Kazakova,** Anna '07 %Withers B LLP -430 Park Av -NY 10022
(212) 859-8000 .. **Kazakova,** Joanna M '07 %Fried FHS&J LLP -1 NY Plz -NY 10004
(212) 344-5680 .. **Kazan,** Barry Mark '95 (Thompson H LLP) -335 Mad Av -NY 10017
(518) 474-3219 .. **Kazanjian,** George M '97 NYSHESC -99 Wshngtn Av -Albany 12255 **Fx:**486-6515
(212) 702-5400 .. **Kazanjian,** John H '76 (Beveridge & D,PC) -477 Mad Av -NY 10022
(212) 455-2000 .. **Kazanoff,** Peter E '98 (Simpson T&B LLP) -425 Lex Av -NY 10017
(212) 490-3000 .. **Kazansky,** Adam M '07 %Wilson EME&D LLP -150 E 42nd -NY 10017
(917) 778-6600 .. **Kazansky,** Evy '97 %J Toomey -485 Lex Av -NY 10017 **Fx:**778-7048
(718) 222-5300 .. **Kazansky,** Matthew J '99 (Nangia & K LLP) -26 Court -Brklyn 11242
(718) 849-4811 .. **Kazas,** Paul M '85 -87-28 97th -Woodhvn 11421
(212) 490-1700 .. **Kazazian,** Arsineh '03 %Wiggin & D -450 Lex Av -NY 10017
(646) 349-3462 .. **Kazazian,** Nina H '99 (Kazazian & Assoc LLC) -545 5th Av -NY 10017 **Fx:**349-3462
(718) 361-0075 .. **Kazazis,** George '66 (Kazazis & A,LLP) -36-12 34th Av -LIC 11106 **Fx:**361-5516
(718) 254-7000 .. **Kazemi,** Ali '08 %US Atty -271 Cadman Plz E -Brklyn 11201 **Fx:**254-6479
(516) 466-6500 .. **Kazepis,** Christina J '96 %Parker WA LLP -6 Hrbr Park Dr S -Pt Wash 11050
(718) 365-2288 .. **Kazimiroff,** Emelia P '54 -293 E 201st -Bronx 10458
(516) 812-4500 .. **Kazin,** Andrew S '00 (Stagg TC&W LLP) -401 Franklin Av -Gdn Cty 11530
(631) 293-0030 .. **Kazin,** Philip M '70 Cnsl Natural Organics,Inc -548 Broadhllw Rd -Melvll 11747
(212) 218-5500 .. **Kazlow,** Alan L '62 OfCnsl Seyfarth S LLP -620 8th Av -NY 10018
(212) 872-1000 .. **Kazlow,** David A '08 -One Bryant Park -NY 10036 **Fx:**872-1002
(212) 947-2900 .. **Kazlow,** Gene R '61 (Kazlow & K) -237 W 35th -NY 10001
(718) 268-9223 .. **Kazlow,** Ira '80 -118-21 Qns Blvd -Frst Hlls 11375 **Fx:**544-4803
(212) 947-2900 .. **Kazlow & Kazlow** -237 W 35th -NY 10001 **Fx:**563-0629
(718) 446-7474 .. **Kazmi,** Shakeel H '97 -72-28 Bway -Jcksn Hts 11372
(718) 441-5460 .. **Kazmierczuk,** Jos J '96 (Kazmierczuk & M) -103-16 Metro Av -Frst Hlls 11375 **Fx:**441-5537
(212) 336-0107 .. **Kazon,** Leslie '83 %SEC -3 World Fncl Ctr -NY 10281 **Fx:**336-1323
(518) 561-5381 .. **Keable,** James E '59 -68 Court -Plattsbrgh 12901 **Fx:**561-2085
(716) 854-4300 .. **Keable,** Thos J '82 (Gross SB&G,PC) -465 Main -Buffalo 14203
(518) 434-1718 .. **Keach,** Elmer R III '97 -1040 Rvrfrnt Ctr Bx70 -Amsterdam 12010 **Fx:**770-1558
(631) 361-5360 .. **Keahon,** Wm J '72 (Keahon FD&F) -1393 Vets Mem'l Hwy -Hauppauge 11788 **Fx:**361-5365
(518) 929-6506 .. **Kealy,** Janet '06 -330 Allen -Hudson 12534
(518) 452-1800 .. **Kean,** Elena DeFio '94 (Towne R & Prtnrs,PC) -450 New Karner Rd Bx15072 -Albany 12212
(212) 839-5300 .. **Kean,** Jesse C '09 %Sidley A LLP -787 7th Av -NY 10019
(914) 834-4203 .. **Kean,** Paul H '75 -45 Knollwood Rd -Elmsfrd 10523 **Fx:**834-4070
(845) 744-3048 .. **Kean,** Robt J '92 -Boniface Dr Bx179 -Pine Bush 12566
(212) 848-4000 .. **Kean,** Seth M '00 %Shearman & S LLP -599 Lex Av -NY 10022
(914) 946-4777 .. **Keane & Beane,PC** -445 Hmltn Av -White Plns 10601 **Fx:**946-6868
(212) 325-6459 .. **Keane,** Brendan J '89 Credit Suisse -11 Mad Av -NY 10010
(212) 572-6210 .. **Keane,** Christopher '76 (Keane & M) -300 Park Av -NY 10022
(212) 482-0001 .. **Keane,** Christopher G '98 %Russo K&T LLP -33 Whitehall -NY 10004
(212) 721-7281 .. **Keane,** Cynthia '91 -2350 Bway -NY 10024 **Fx:**579-0205
(631) 665-1100 .. **Keane,** Danl J '01 -109 Cncrs W -Brightwtrs 11718
(914) 509-5823 .. **Keane,** Donna M '03 -29 Sparrow Cir -White Plns 10605 **Fx:**509-6550
(212) 385-1422 .. **Keane,** Edw A '77 (Mahoney & K,LLP) -76 Beaver -NY 10005
(212) 558-4000 .. **Keane,** Edw W '60 SrCnsl Sullivan & C LLP -125 Broad -NY 10004
(716) 845-7488 .. **Keane,** Lynn M '94 Family Ct -1 Niagara Plz -Buffalo 14202 **Fx:**858-7756
(212) 373-3202 .. **Keane,** Maria H '87 Cnsl Paul WRW&G LLP -1285 Av of Amer -NY 10019
(212) 572-6210 .. **Keane & Marlowe** -300 Park Av -NY 10022 **Fx:**572-6499
(718) 898-8100 .. **Keane,** Martin F '84 -63-48 Alderton -Rego Pk 11374 **Fx:**458-5281
(516) 393-2200 .. **Keane,** Michl J '88 (Garfunkel W,PC) -111 Grt Nck Rd -Gt Neck 11021
(212) 416-8550 .. **Keane,** Michl J '89 %Dept of Law -120 Bway -NY 10271
(716) 853-4080 .. **Keane,** Michl J '93 Colucci & G,PC -424 Main -Buffalo 14202
(212) 344-7042 .. **Keane,** Paul M '74 (Cichanowicz CKV&T,LLP) -61 Bway -NY 10006
(518) 862-1090 .. **Keane,** Peter R '98 %NYSERDA -17 Columbia Cir -Albany 12203 **Fx:**862-1091
(914) 238-2805 .. **Keane,** Susan '92 (Keane & K) -26 Glenside Pl -Chappaqua 10514
(212) 482-0001 .. **Keane,** Thos F '86 (Russo K&T LLP) -33 Whitehall -NY 10004
(914) 238-2805 .. **Keane,** Thos F '86 (Keane & K) -26 Glenside Pl -Chappaqua 10514
(914) 345-0005 .. **Keane,** Thos J '81 (Nesci K,PLLC) -40 Saw Mill Rvr Rd -Hawthorne 10532
(212) 880-9482 .. **Keane,** Thos M '98 Morvillo AGIA&B,PC -565 5th Av -NY 10017
(212) 319-1000 .. **Keane,** Timothy J '91 (Quirk & B,PC) -845 3rd Av -NY 10022
(212) 706-0248 .. **Keaney,** James B '75 (Hollyer B LLP) -60 E 42nd -NY 10165 **Fx:**(646) 652-5336
(212) 768-6700 .. **Keaney,** Lydia A '08 %Sonnenschein N&R LLP -1221 Av of Amer -NY 10020
(212) 319-1900 .. **Keany,** Sutton '71 OfCnsl Berger & W,LLP -1633 Bway -NY 10019
(516) 326-3350 .. **Kearke,** Vinod '97 -266 Jericho Tpk -Floral Pk 11001 **Fx:**326-3353
(212) 309-6000 .. **Kearney,** Amy M '09 %Morgan L&B LLP -101 Park Av -NY 10178
(212) 373-3000 .. **Kearney,** Benet J '10 %Paul WRW&G LLP -1285 Av of Amer -NY 10019
(845) 876-5260 .. **Kearney,** Brian J '87 -60 Chestnut -Rhinebeck 12572
(646) 442-3582 .. **Kearney,** Caroline '76 Legal Srvcs NYC -350 Bway -NY 10013 **Fx:**442-3583
(212) 836-8000 .. **Kearney,** Christine M '08 %Kaye S LLP -425 Park Av -NY 10022
(516) 237-7863 .. **Kearney,** Colleen M '02 %800-Flowers.com -1 Old Cntry Rd -Carle Pl 11514
(212) 906-1200 .. **Kearney,** James V '73 (Latham & W) -885 3rd Av -NY 10022
(516) 877-5600 .. **Kearney,** Janet E '91 %R Tusa -1225 Franklin Av -Gdn Cty 11530 **Fx:**877-5695
(516) 355-7901 .. **Kearney,** John J '95 %Paganini GCC&F -1979 Marcus Av -Lk Success 11042
(212) 450-4000 .. **Kearney,** Keith L '78 (Davis P&W LLP) -450 Lex Av -NY 10017
(718) 852-5900 .. **Kearney,** Kevin M '78 (Wingate K&C) -45 Main -Brklyn 11201
(716) 856-4000 .. **Kearney,** Kevin M '92 (Hodgson R LLP) -140 Pearl -Buffalo 14202
(212) 735-8600 .. **Kearney,** Michl J '03 %Morrison C LLP -909 3rd Av -NY 10022
(718) 590-2000 .. **Kearney,** Richd P '00 %DA -198 E 161st -Bronx 10451 **Fx:**590-6477
(212) 354-0600 .. **Kearney-Wood,** Annmarie '92 (Stark A&L,LLP) -7 Penn Plz -NY 10001
(631) 427-7790 .. **Kearns,** Brendan J '04 Lewin GB,LLP -900 Walt Whitman Rd -Melvll 11747
(518) 455-4191 .. **Kearns,** Carolyn S '90 %Ofc Cnsl to Majority -448M State Cptl -Albany 12248 **Fx:**455-4103
(212) 250-7546 .. **Kearns,** Christopher D '85 %Deutsche Bank -60 Wall -NY 10005
(212) 827-4422 .. **Kearns,** Christopher J '09 Ace Grp -1133 Av of Amer -NY 10036 **Fx:**827-4449
(518) 445-2328 .. **Kearns,** Deborah S '01 Albany Law Schl -80 New Scotland Av -Albany 12208 **Fx:**445-2315
(718) 330-7713 .. **Kearns,** James P '89 %NLRB -2 Metrotech Ctr -Brklyn 11201 **Fx:**330-7579
(646) 610-5483 .. **Kearns,** Kathleen M '93 %NYPD -1 Police Plz -NY 10038
(212) 382-0909 .. **Kearns,** Scott G '96 %Peckar & A,PC -41 Mad Av -NY 10154
(212) 480-6791 .. **Kearns,** Susan E '96 DHCR -25 Beaver -NY 10004 **Fx:**480-7416
(212) 451-2300 .. **Kearns,** Thos D '85 (Olshan GFR&W LLP) -65 E 55th -NY 10022
(631) 852-2500 .. **Kearon,** Kathleen A '07 %DA -200 Center Dr -Rvrhead 11901 **Fx:**852-1769
(631) 963-4880 .. **Kearon,** Kevin T '86 -121 W Oak -Amityvll 11701 **Fx:**963-4877
(631) 853-4161 .. **Kearon,** Robt V '75 %DA -N Cnty Cmplx Bldg 77 -Hauppauge 11788 **Fx:**853-4192
(212) 422-1200 .. **Kearse,** Alexandra R '08 %Abrams GF&J,PC -1 Bttry Pk Plz -NY 10004
(212) 425-6244 .. **Kearse,** Brendan P '97 -67 Wall -NY 10005
(718) 923-6300 .. **Kearse,** Diana Maxfield '80 %Atty Grievance Comm -335 Adams -Brklyn 11201 **Fx:**624-2978
(631) 231-3775 .. **Kearse,** Michl J '79 %Atty Grievance Comm -150 Motor Pkwy -Hauppauge 11788
(212) 848-4000 .. **Kearse,** Nicole E '05 %Shearman & S LLP -599 Lex Av -NY 10022
(518) 457-8413 .. **Keating,** Deirdre Ann '93 %DCJS -4 Twr Pl -Albany 12203
(845) 639-8160 .. **Keating,** Elizabeth Bernstein '87 Sterling Abstract Corp -60 S Main -New Cty 10956 **Fx:**639-8163
(917) 604-6600 .. **Keating,** John F Jr. '83 (Keating & M) -204-54 8th Av -Breezy Point 11697 **Fx:**(866) 408-1843
(212) 608-5657 .. **Keating,** John F Jr. '83 (Keating & M) -132 Nassau -NY 10038 **Fx:**(866) 408-1843
(845) 932-8781 .. **Keating,** John J '76 -Bx77 -Cochecton 12726
(212) 609-6800 .. **Keating,** Kathleen O'Connell '86 %McCarter & E,LLP -245 Park Av -NY 10167
(516) 222-1099 .. **Keating,** Kevin J '88 -666 Old Cntry Rd -Gdn Cty 11530 **Fx:**683-8410
(716) 691-4870 .. **Keating,** Lisa Massaro '90 -573 Kaymar Dr -Amherst 14228
(212) 344-4700 .. **Keating,** Marshall P '56 OfCnsl DeOrchis & Prtnrs LLP -61 Bway -NY 10006
(914) 961-1515 .. **Keating,** Matthew J '81 (Maffei M&K) -35 E Grassy Sprain Rd -Ynkrs 10710 **Fx:**961-2976
(212) 691-0950 .. **Keating,** Maura A '02 Ctr for Family Representation -116 John -NY 10038 **Fx:**691-0951
(212) 554-1234 .. **Keating,** Maurya Crawford '88 %AXA Financial Inc -1290 Av of Amer -NY 10104 **Fx:**707-3963
(914) 949-2232 .. **Keating,** Michl '65 -2 William -White Plns 10601
(212) 483-9490 .. **Keating,** Michl G '86 (McElroy DM&C,LLP) -88 Pine -NY 10005
(212) 346-1855 .. **Keating,** Robt G M '68 Pace University -1 Pace Plz -NY 10038
(716) 855-7398 .. **Keating,** Ruth '84 %NFTA -181 Ellicott -Buffalo 14203 **Fx:**855-7657
(914) 793-2614 .. **Keating,** Sara L '94 -115 Grandvw Blvd -Ynkrs 10710 **Fx:**793-2614
(516) 620-8585 .. **Keating,** Stephanie M '03 %Schwartz & F,PC -3000 Marcus Av -Lk Success 11042 **Fx:**488-1238
(646) 346-7317 .. **Keating,** Stephen J '81 Cantor Fitzgerald -1 Seaport Plz -NY 10038
(914) 437-7023 .. **Keating,** Thos T '89 -8 Chester Av -White Plns 10601
(212) 857-8230 .. **Keats,** Andrew A '00 %Baker MM&M,PC -330 W 34th -NY 10001
(212) 902-4315 .. **Keats,** Michl C '96 Goldman Sachs -1 NY Plz -NY 10004
(516) 248-0100 .. **Keats,** Steven L '62 -131 Mineola Blvd Bx542 -Mineola 11501 **Fx:**248-4256
(212) 483-9490 .. **Keatts,** Brian W '01 %McElroy DM&C,LLP -88 Pine -NY 10005
(212) 238-4800 .. **Keaveney,** Andrew P '99 (Landman CB&F,PC) -120 Bway -NY 10271
(212) 701-3000 .. **Keaveny,** John K '08 %Cahill G&R LLP -80 Pine -NY 10005 **Fx:**269-5420
(716) 834-4685 .. **Keavey,** John M '97 -282 Norwalk Av -Buffalo 14216
(914) 733-7745 .. **Kebbe,** Timothy P A '88 -1 N Bway -White Plns 10601
(914) 683-5532 .. **Kebrdle,** Jerry F II '93 -175 Main -White Plns 10601 **Fx:**683-6953
(917) 637-3600 .. **Kebriaei,** Pardiss '05 Ctr for Reproductive Rts -120 Wall -NY 10005 **Fx:**637-3666
(212) 359-9599 .. **Keck,** Richd P '08 (Macmillan K) -469 7th Av -NY 10018 **Fx:**(646) 349-4989
(212) 596-9000 .. **Kedem,** Tal '09 %Ropes & G LLP -1211 Av of Amer -NY 10036
(718) 254-7000 .. **Kedeshian,** Claire Siran '91 %US Atty -271 Cadman Plz E -Brklyn 11201 **Fx:**254-6479
(212) 681-0202 .. **Kedia,** Sarita '95 -5 E 22nd -NY 10010 **Fx:**614-0202
(716) 852-1380 .. **Kedzielawa,** Frank S '76 (Abbarno M&K) -314 Brisbane Bldg -Buffalo 14203
(212) 625-0300 .. **Kee & Lau-Kee, PLLC** -354 Broome -NY 10013 **Fx:**625-1812
(212) 625-0300 .. **Kee,** Norman Lau '56 (Kee & L-K,PLLC) -354 Broome -NY 10013

(212) 336-2000 .. **Kee,** Norman W '05 %Patterson BW&T LLP -1133 Av of Amer -NY 10036
(212) 310-8000 .. **Kee,** Peter J '10 %Weil G&M LLP -767 5th Av -NY 10153
(518) 622-3235 .. **Keefe,** James F '68 -527 Main Bx1136 -Cairo 12413
(516) 741-2650 .. **Keefe,** James J Jr. '71 JJ Keefe,PC -301 Mineola Blvd -Mineola 11501 **Fx:**908-7961
(212) 239-5712 .. **Keefe,** Jeanne M '85 %Div Of Parole -314 W 40th -NY 10018 **Fx:**239-6160
(716) 856-4222 .. **Keefe,** Jos W '72 -1717 Lbrty Bldg -Buffalo 14202 **Fx:**842-0619
(518) 488-7079 .. **Keefe,** Mark S '97 -181 Green Hllw Rd -Petersburg 12138
(585) 538-4727 .. **Keefe,** Patrick M '59 -3152 State Bx80 -Caledonia 14423 **Fx:**538-2139
(212) 254-8900 .. **Keefe,** Paul F '08 %Community Srvc Soc -105 E 22nd -NY 10010 **Fx:**260-6218
(716) 565-0001 .. **Keefe,** Thos F '93 -4455 Transit Rd -Williamsvll 14221 **Fx:**565-2738
(212) 759-4888 .. **Keefer,** Wm P '92 (Phillips L LLP) -437 Mad Av -NY 10022
(716) 847-8400 .. **Keefer,** Wm P '92 (Phillips L LLP) -3400 HSBC Ctr -Buffalo 14203
(914) 277-7415 .. **Keeffe,** John A '56 -315A Heritage Hills -Somers 10589 **Fx:**277-7416
(212) 898-5000 .. **Keegan,** Christopher J '85 Marsh USA -1166 Av of Amer -NY 10036
(212) 489-8230 .. **Keegan,** Colleen M '00 OfCnsl Davis WT LLP -1633 Bway -NY 10019
(516) 222-2224 .. **Keegan,** David V '68 -666 Old Cntry Rd -Gdn Cty 11530 **Fx:**222-6075
(516) 741-0099 .. **Keegan,** Diane L '88 -127 2nd -Gdn Cty 11530
(212) 210-9558 .. **Keegan,** Gerard C '99 (Alston & B LLP) -90 Park Av -NY 10016
(914) 964-9638 .. **Keegan,** Glenn F '77 -1 David Ln -Ynkrs 10701
(914) 683-1100 .. **Keegan,** Jeffrey J '97 %Keegan KK&S,LLP -81 Main -White Plns 10601
(914) 683-1100 .. **Keegan,** John W Jr. '80 (Keegan KK&S,LLP) -81 Main -White Plns 10601
(212) 980-9600 .. **Keegan,** Julie A '98 %Kaufman B&R -120 Bway -NY 10271
(518) 457-5835 .. **Keegan,** Julie M '99 Ofc for the Prevention of Dom Violence -80 Wolf Rd -Albany 12205 **Fx:**457-5810
(914) 683-1100 .. **Keegan Keegan Keegan & Strutt,LLP** -81 Main -White Plns 10601 **Fx:**683-7363
(631) 475-9400 .. **Keegan & Keegan, Ross & Rosner,LLP** -147 N Ocean Av Bx918 -Patchogue 11772 **Fx:**475-0601
(718) 675-8510 .. **Keegan,** Laura Lopez '08 %Surrogates Ct -18 Richmond Ter -Staten Isl 10301
(914) 967-9421 .. **Keegan,** Mark '96 Keegan & Co,LLC -350 Theo Fremd Av -Rye 10580
(845) 338-8884 .. **Keegan,** Maureen A '86 (Basch & K,LLP) -307 Clinton Av Bx4235 -Kingston 12402
(914) 683-1100 .. **Keegan,** Raymond J '64 (Keegan KK&S,LLP) -81 Main -White Plns 10601
(631) 475-9400 .. **Keegan,** Thos J Jr. '78 (Keegan &KR&R,LLP) -147 N Ocean Av Bx918 -Patchogue 11772
(212) 490-3000 .. **Keegan-Natola,** Vanessa L '10 %Wilson EME&D LLP -150 E 42nd -NY 10017
(518) 402-9521 .. **Keehn,** David H '90 %DEC -625 Bway -Albany 12233 **Fx:**402-9018
(212) 225-2000 .. **Keele,** Jeremy J '07 %Cleary GS&H -1 Lbrty Plz -NY 10006
(518) 828-4081 .. **Keeler,** Eugene '79 -75 Spook Rock Rd -Hudson 12534
(917) 603-1946 .. **Keeler,** John C '99 DDG Industries -40 LeRoy -NY 10014
(607) 723-5341 .. **Keeler,** John M '61 OfCnsl Hinman H&K,LLP -80 Exchange Bx5250 -Bnghmtn 13902
(212) 225-2000 .. **Keeley,** Chas J III '08 %Cleary GS&H -1 Lbrty Plz -NY 10006
(212) 473-4305 .. **Keeley,** Doris B '60 -39 Gramercy Park N -NY 10010
(212) 209-3119 .. **Keeley,** Elizabeth A '96 Taconic Captl Advsrs -450 Park Av -NY 10022
(212) 268-2665 .. **Keeley,** Jessica A '09 %Sinel & Assoc,PLLC -7 Penn Plz -NY 10001 **Fx:**268-6250
(212) 728-2200 .. **Keeley,** Michl L '97 (Axinn V&H LLP) -114 W 47th -NY 10036
(212) 402-4100 .. **Keeling,** Alexandra H '04 %Ofc Applt Def -11 Park Pl -NY 10007 **Fx:**402-4199
(212) 809-7600 .. **Keely,** Harry A '77 (Cheven K&H) -40 Wall -NY 10005
(212) 918-3000 .. **Keely,** Sean T '98 (Hogan L LLP) -875 3rd Av -NY 10022
(315) 474-1285 .. **Keem,** Bradley E '08 %DJ & JA Cirando -101 S Salina -Syracuse 13202
(212) 552-0921 .. **Keen,** Andrew N '82 JP Morgan Chase -1 Chase Manh Plz -NY 10081
(212) 259-8000 .. **Keen,** Kathryn A '09 %Dewey & L LLP -1301 Av of Amer -NY 10019
(212) 468-4800 .. **Keen,** Shirin '05 %Davis & G LLP -1740 Bway -NY 10019
(212) 455-2000 .. **Keenaghan,** Danl J '74 %Simpson T&B LLP -425 Lex Av -NY 10017
(212) 393-1000 .. **Keenan,** Alison R '06 %Burns & H -233 Bway -NY 10279
(212) 536-3900 .. **Keenan,** Catherine R '00 %K&L Gates LLP -599 Lex Av -NY 10022
(914) 946-7770 .. **Keenan,** Christopher P '91 (Westermann SKS&A,LLP) -222 Bloomingdale Rd -White Plns 10605
(212) 310-8000 .. **Keenan,** Eoghan P '08 %Weil G&M LLP -767 5th Av -NY 10153
(212) 947-1999 .. **Keenan,** Frank J '86 %Methfessel & W,PC -450 7th Av -NY 10123
(212) 326-3939 .. **Keenan,** Jeremy S '07 %Jones D -222 E 41st -NY 10017
(212) 571-4067 .. **Keenan,** Joan W '79 OfCnsl Dwyer & B -7 Dey -NY 10007
(518) 432-5100 .. **Keenan,** John T III '99 -600 Bway -Albany 12207 **Fx:**432-0981
(212) 943-0280 .. **Keenan,** Jos F '81 (McCanliss & E LLP) -88 Pine -NY 10005
(212) 336-3705 .. **Keenan,** Judy A '92 EEOC -33 Whitehall -NY 10004 **Fx:**336-3623
(212) 836-8000 .. **Keenan,** Kelli M '06 %Kaye S LLP -425 Park Av -NY 10022
(212) 259-8000 .. **Keenan,** Lisa A '03 %Dewey & L LLP -1301 Av of Amer -NY 10019
(212) 836-8000 .. **Keenan,** Michl D '05 %Kaye S LLP -425 Park Av -NY 10022
(518) 434-1022 .. **Keenan,** Michl J '86 (Sullivan KO&V, LLP) -152 Central Av -Albany 12206
(212) 728-8000 .. **Keenan,** Neil R '10 %Willkie F&G LLP -787 7th Av -NY 10019
(212) 385-0777 .. **Keenan,** Paul '86 -335 Bway -NY 10013
(212) 808-7800 .. **Keenan,** Paul A '95 (Kelley D&W LLP) -101 Park Av -NY 10178
(212) 880-6000 .. **Keenan,** Peter J '91 (Torys LLP) -237 Park Av -NY 10017
(631) 787-6161 .. **Keenan Powers & Andrews,PC** -2150 Joshuas Path -Hauppauge 11788 **Fx:**231-6121
(631) 231-0840 .. **Keenan Powers & Andrews,PC** -95 Oser Av -Hauppauge 11788 **Fx:**231-0733
(212) 278-1888 .. **Keenan,** R Mark '75 (Anderson K&O,PC) -1251 Av of Amer -NY 10020
(516) 694-3000 .. **Keenan,** Raymond G '99 (Guercio & G,LLP) -77 Conklin -Farmngdl 11735 **Fx:**694-4738
(516) 227-6363 .. **Keenan,** Richd S '96 %Amato & Assoc,PC -666 Old Cntry Rd -Gdn Cty 11530 **Fx:**227-6367
(631) 753-4400 .. **Keenan,** Sarah M '85 (Sferrazza & K,PLLC) -532 Broad Hollow Rd -Melvll 11747
(212) 504-6000 .. **Keenan,** Sonja '07 %Cadwalader W&T LLP -1 World Fncl Ctr -NY 10281
(716) 854-5063 .. **Keenan,** Wm F '57 -268 Main -Buffalo 14202 **Fx:**854-1069
(607) 565-8283 .. **Keene,** Betty Josephson '84 Keene & K -443 Fulton -Waverly 14892 **Fx:**565-2327
(607) 687-4344 .. **Keene,** Gerald A '81 DA -20 Court Bx300 -Owego 13827
(516) 466-6050 .. **Keene,** Glen E '82 %N Shore Abstrct -1010 Nrthrn Blvd -Gt Neck 11021 **Fx:**466-6011
(212) 354-5650 .. **Keene,** John M '70 %Graham C PC -36 W 44th -NY 10036
(212) 357-4876 .. **Keene,** Lonnie S '99 Goldman Sachs -85 Broad -NY 10004
(845) 368-0104 .. **Keene,** Susan '91 (Schulman K&K,PC) -1 Exec Blvd #202 -Suffern 10901
(718) 430-1127 .. **Keeney,** Brian D '89 -3221 Tierney Pl -Bronx 10465 **Fx:**430-1127
(516) 364-3436 .. **Keeney,** Brian J '80 First Natl Bank Of Long Island -800 Woodbury Rd -Woodbury 11797
(518) 274-5820 .. **Keenholts,** Meghan R '06 %ES Jones -28 2nd -Troy 12181 **Fx:**274-5875
(212) 825-1212 .. **Keenoy,** Christopher P '09 %Morrison M LLP -17 State -NY 10004
(914) 937-3880 .. **Keesee,** Michl F '74 -327 Irving Av -Pt Chester 10573 **Fx:**937-3950
(212) 312-3000 .. **Kegg,** Laura Lee '98 %FGIC -125 Park Av -NY 10017 **Fx:**312-3221
(718) 852-8100 .. **Keghida,** Sihame '01 Schneider & K,PC -241 Carroll -Brklyn 11231 **Fx:**875-2728
(877) 222-1814 .. **Kehagias,** Argyria A N '00 %B Rothenberg -100 Duffy Av -Hicksvll 11801 **Fx:**(866) 894-2182
(212) 500-5030 .. **Kehl,** Jeffrey A '74 (Kehl K&S,LLP) -317 Mad Av -NY 10017
(212) 500-5030 .. **Kehl Katzive & Simon, LLP** -317 Mad Av -NY 10017 **Fx:**500-5031
(212) 500-5030 .. **Kehl,** Shelley Sanders '81 (Kehl K&S,LLP) -317 Mad Av -NY 10017
(516) 795-3434 .. **Kehm,** George F '66 -Bx302 -Massapequa 11758
(631) 852-2832 .. **Kehoe,** Athena D '93 %Hon R Costello -1 Court -Rvrhead 11901
(212) 446-4800 .. **Kehoe,** Brendan T '07 %Kirkland & E LLP -153 E 53rd -NY 10022
(212) 556-2100 .. **Kehoe,** Edw G '91 (King & S) -1185 Av of Amer -NY 10036
(631) 269-1515 .. **Kehoe,** Francis P '95 (Sullivan & K,LLP) -44 Main -Kings Pk 11754
(585) 263-6237 .. **Kehoe,** J Michl '94 %Hon C Siragusa -100 State -Rchstr 14614
(315) 798-5870 .. **Kehoe,** James F '76 %Pub Def -321 Main -Utica 13501 **Fx:**798-6419
(631) 577-2400 .. **Kehoe,** James S '78 (Tromello M&K) -25 Melvll Park Rd Bx9038 -Melvll 11747
(607) 432-4242 .. **Kehoe,** Jos F '75 Kehoe & M,PC -8-12 Dietz -Oneonta 13820
(585) 899-1414 .. **Kehoe,** L Paul '62 SrCnsl Harris COJW&L -300 Linden Oaks -Rchstr 14625
(518) 452-8000 .. **Kehoe,** Martin J III '88 (M Kehoe & Assoc,PC) -2009 Wstrn Av -Albany 12203 **Fx:**452-1116
(607) 432-4242 .. **Kehoe & Merzig,PC** -8-12 Dietz -Oneonta 13820
(718) 641-4700 .. **Kehoe,** Patrick L '96 NY Racing Assn -Bx90 -Ozone Pk 11417 **Fx:**835-2432
(518) 432-4318 .. **Kehoe,** Peter R '71 -18 Hawthorne Av -Troy 12180 **Fx:**434-9093
(518) 465-2211 .. **Kehoe,** Randall E '90 -127 Mad Av -Albany 12202 **Fx:**462-9528
(585) 637-5900 .. **Kehoe,** Sharon M '80 -320 Main -Brockprt 14420 **Fx:**637-2319
(716) 951-8095 .. **Kehrer,** Andrew D '94 -71 Main -Silver Crk 14136
(718) 661-3838 .. **Kei,** Howard F '07 Franklin Land Srvcs Inc -13620 38th Av -Flushng 11354
(315) 492-3000 .. **Keib Smith,** Mary '93 Cramer S&M,PC -3175 E Genesee -Syracuse 13224
(914) 948-7000 .. **Keidel,** James C '89 (Keidel W&C LLP) -925 Wstchstr Av -White Plns 10604
(914) 948-7000 .. **Keidel Weldon & Cunningham LLP** -925 Wstchstr Av -White Plns 10604 **Fx:**948-7010
(315) 425-1100 .. **Keidel Weldon & Cunningham LLP** -4625 Onondaga Blvd -Syracuse 13219 **Fx:**399-4912
(917) 757-5574 .. **Keil,** Alison C '01 (Keil & S,LLP) -1983 Marcus Av -Lk Success 11042
(212) 758-7600 .. **Keil,** John P '00 %Collazo C&M -747 3rd Av -NY 10017
(212) 205-7000 .. **Keil,** Tamar L '06 %Ashurst LLP -7 Times Sq -NY 10036
(516) 775-7007 .. **Keilbach,** Eric J '99 %Gutman MB&S,PC -813 Jericho Tpk -New Hyde Pk 11040
(212) 302-7760 .. **Keilin,** Nina H '96 -130 W 42nd -NY 10036
(516) 295-7718 .. **Keilson,** Avram '95 (Keilson & K) -337R Central Av -Lawrence 11559 **Fx:**295-0722
(516) 295-7718 .. **Keilson,** Lloyd F '74 (Keilson & K) -337R Central Av -Lawrence 11559 **Fx:**295-0722
(516) 248-0251 .. **Keilson,** Robt C '82 -1000 Franklin Av -Gdn Cty 11530 **Fx:**478-4193
(212) 773-9447 .. **Keim,** James M '01 Ernst & Young LLP -5 Times Sq -NY 10036 **Fx:**773-2794
(212) 259-8000 .. **Keim,** Steffanie '08 %Dewey & L LLP -1301 Av of Amer -NY 10019
(212) 756-2000 .. **Keinan,** David '07 %Schulte R&Z LLP -919 3rd Av -NY 10022
(212) 801-6826 .. **Keinan,** Yoram '08 (Greenberg T,LLP) -200 Park Av -NY 10166
(315) 735-6185 .. **Keinz,** Donald E '52 -2045 Genesee -Utica 13501 **Fx:**797-5521
(914) 428-8800 .. **Keiser,** Laurence '76 (Stern KP&W,LLP) -1025 Wstchstr Av -White Plns 10604
(845) 439-5550 .. **Keiser,** Michl S '66 (Keiser & K) -75 Main Bx350 -Lvngstn Mnr 12758 **Fx:**(914) 674-4040
(914) 674-4440 .. **Keiser,** Michl S '66 (Keiser & K) -3 Farm Rd -Ardsley 10502
(212) 259-8000 .. **Keiserman,** John P '99 (Dewey & L LLP) -1301 Av of Amer -NY 10019
(212) 578-2211 .. **Keisman,** Howard I '65 %MetLife -27-01 Qns Plz N -LIC 11101
(212) 468-4800 .. **Keisner,** C Andrew '09 %Davis & G LLP -1740 Bway -NY 10019
(631) 843-5500 .. **Keitel,** Martin A '98 Henry Schein,Inc -135 Duryea Rd -Melvll 11747
(212) 941-7100 .. **Keith,** Arnold P Jr. '83 (Hornstein P&K) -350 Bway -NY 10013
(516) 222-0200 .. **Keith,** Kenneth M '78 (Keith S&F) -666 Old Cntry Rd -Gdn Cty 11530
(212) 351-4000 .. **Keith,** Lisa Debin '10 Gibson D&C LLP -200 Park Av -NY 10166

(516) 222-0200 .. **Keith Shapiro & Ford** -666 Old Cntry Rd -Gdn Cty 11530 **Fx:**745-0573
(212) 659-1959 .. **Keith,** Sonja '91 Classic Media,Inc -860 Bway -NY 10003
(212) 336-2000 .. **Keithley,** Todd S '07 %Patterson BW&T LLP -1133 Av of Amer -NY 10036
(212) 621-1500 .. **Keitt,** John K Jr. '85 Associated Press -50 Rckfllr Plz -NY 10020
(212) 584-0700 .. **Kekatos,** Diogenes P '84 (Seeger W LLP) -1 William -NY 10004
(212) 906-1200 .. **Kelban,** Michelle V '01 (Latham & W) -885 3rd Av -NY 10022
(212) 687-6975 .. **Kelban,** Steven A '72 Andrus Family Fund -330 Mad Av -NY 10017 **Fx:**687-6978
(212) 530-5000 .. **Kelberg,** Howard S '70 (Milbank TH&M LLP) -1 Chase Manh Plz -NY 10005
(718) 855-9000 .. **Kelch,** Hayley M '07 %Cullen and D LLP -177 Montague -Brklyn 11201
(315) 443-2524 .. **Kelder,** Gary T '96 %Syracuse Univ Cllg of Law -Wht Hall -Syracuse 13244 **Fx:**443-4213
(518) 429-4200 .. **Keleher,** Ryan P '09 Hiscock & B,LLP -50 Beaver -Albany 12207
(315) 218-8000 .. **Keleher,** Thos D '80 (Bond S&K,PLLC) -1 Lincoln Ctr -Syracuse 13202
(716) 855-0203 .. **Kelemen,** Jos '81 %Western NY Law Ctr -237 Main -Buffalo 14203 **Fx:**270-4005
(315) 425-2700 .. **Kelepurovski,** John Jr. '00 %Hiscock & B,LLP -One Park Pl -Syracuse 13202
(212) 964-7400 .. **Kelhoffer,** Alan C '96 %Smith MDWY&Y,PC -111 John -NY 10038
(716) 856-4000 .. **Kelkenberg,** Stephen W '03 (Hodgson R LLP) -140 Pearl -Buffalo 14202
(212) 335-9000 .. **Kellachan,** Lisa M '00 %DA -1 Hogan Pl -NY 10013
(917) 953-3304 .. **Kellaghan,** P Colm '96 -531 E 72nd -NY 10021
(212) 742-3390 .. **Kellar,** James A '08 %Lindabury ME&C,PC -26 Bway -NY 10004
(845) 331-8900 .. **Kellar Kellar & Jaiven** -14 Pearl Bx3536 -Kingston 12402 **Fx:**331-0632
(845) 331-8900 .. **Kellar,** Norman '40 (Kellar K&J) -14 Pearl Bx3536 -Kingston 12402
(845) 331-8900 .. **Kellar,** Paul T '78 (Kellar K&J) -14 Pearl Bx3536 -Kingston 12402
(212) 906-1200 .. **Kelleher,** Brendan K '08 %Latham & W -885 3rd Av -NY 10022
(716) 856-4000 .. **Kelleher,** Brendan P '02 %Hodgson R LLP -140 Pearl -Buffalo 14202
(212) 701-3000 .. **Kelleher,** Brian S '03 %Cahill G&R LLP -80 Pine -NY 10005 **Fx:**269-5420
(212) 756-2000 .. **Kelleher,** Bryanne E '08 %Schulte R&Z LLP -919 3rd Av -NY 10022
(718) 802-2736 .. **Kelleher,** Cassandra M '05 ACS -330 Jay -Brklyn 11201
(212) 422-0202 .. **Kelleher,** Catherine B '04 %Sedgwick DM&A LLP -125 Broad -NY 10004
(718) 748-9600 .. **Kelleher,** Denis P '69 (Twohy & K) -477 86th -Brklyn 11209
(212) 825-1700 .. **Kelleher,** Denis P '94 OfCnsl D Kelleher,PLLC -17 Battery Pl -NY 10004 **Fx:**825-1108
(212) 455-2000 .. **Kelleher,** Gabrielle '04 %Simpson T&B LLP -425 Lex Av -NY 10017
(845) 352-9240 .. **Kelleher,** Glenn W '80 %Finkelstein & Prtnrs,LLP -296 Main -Spg Vly 10977
(716) 881-5800 .. **Kelleher,** J Michl '71 Siegel K&K -426 Franklin -Buffalo 14202
(518) 561-4400 .. **Kelleher,** Jacqueline M '00 (Stafford OC&T,PLLC) -1 Cumberland Av Bx2947 -Plattsbrgh 12901
(212) 349-2025 .. **Kelleher,** James P '75 -20 Vesey -NY 10007
(716) 849-8900 .. **Kelleher,** Jennifer A '08 %Hurwitz & F,PC -1300 Lbrty Bldg -Buffalo 14202
(607) 753-5353 .. **Kelleher,** John J '69 %Family Ct -46 Greenbush -Cortlnd 13045 **Fx:**753-3409
(518) 464-4400 .. **Kelleher,** John J '99 (Kelleher & M,LLP) -113 Great Oaks Blvd -Albany 12203 **Fx:**464-2620
(212) 816-0279 .. **Kelleher,** Jos J '92 Citibank NA -388 Greenwich -NY 10013
(212) 440-4300 .. **Kelleher,** Kathleen M '94 %Leg Aid -199 Water -NY 10038
(518) 943-1111 .. **Kelleher,** Kevin M '77 (Brown K&Z,LLP) -370 Main -Catskill 12414
(212) 785-5050 .. **Kelleher,** Louise A '87 (Kardaras & K LLP) -44 Wall -NY 10005
(845) 398-4121 .. **Kelleher,** Mary P '85 St Thomas Aquinas Cllg -125 Route 340 -Sparkill 10976
(518) 456-0082 .. **Kelleher,** Nannette R '98 (Bailey K&J,PC) -5 Pine West Plz -Albany 12205 **Fx:**456-4767
(716) 887-7178 .. **Kelleher,** Patricia A '02 Cnsl HealthNow NY Inc -257 W Genesee -Buffalo 14202 **Fx:**887-8614
(212) 839-5300 .. **Kelleher,** Rory '73 (Sidley A LLP) -787 7th Av -NY 10019
(212) 906-1170 .. **Kelleher,** Sarah S '04 3rd Av Mgmt LLC -622 3rd Av -NY 10017 **Fx:**735-0003
(914) 214-5514 .. **Kelleher,** Sean L '06 (Kelleher IP PLLC) -4 Manorshire Dr -Fairprt 14450 **Fx:**358-0510
(631) 390-0010 .. **Kelleher,** Shawn P '08 %Bruno G&S,LLP -445 Broad Hollow Rd -Melvll 11747
(518) 786-3900 .. **Kelleher,** Timothy P '78 (Kelleher & Assoc) -17 British Amer Blvd -Latham 12110 **Fx:**786-6446
(516) 766-3131 .. **Kelleher,** Wm J Jr. '75 -100 Merrick Rd -Rockvll Ctr 11570
(212) 821-0512 .. **Keller,** Andrea Dubin '87 %Cornell Med Ctr -525 E 68th Bx123 -NY 10021
(212) 455-2000 .. **Keller,** Andrew R '85 (Simpson T&B LLP) -425 Lex Av -NY 10017
(212) 984-7790 .. **Keller,** Arthur '66 (Warshaw BCS&K,LLP) -555 5th Av -NY 10017
(212) 272-1733 .. **Keller,** Barbara A '99 %JP Morgan Chase -383 Mad Av -NY 10179
(212) 788-3300 .. **Keller,** Barbara R '86 %Hlth & Hsptl Corp -125 Worth -NY 10013 **Fx:**267-6905
(212) 813-8800 .. **Keller,** Benjamin A '10 %Goodwin P LLP -620 8th Av -NY 10018
(212) 530-5000 .. **Keller,** Benjamin M '09 %Milbank TH&M LLP -1 Chase Manh Plz -NY 10005
(212) 983-9330 .. **Keller,** Beth A '03 Faruqi & F,LLP -369 Lex Av -NY 10017 **Fx:**983-9331
(212) 909-6000 .. **Keller,** Bruce P '80 (Debevoise & P LLP) -919 3rd Av -NY 10022
(716) 858-5000 .. **Keller,** Bryan J '79 Delaware North -40 Fountain Plz -Buffalo 14202 **Fx:**858-5056
(315) 473-0899 .. **Keller,** Chas A III '99 %Anelli X,PC -441 S Salina -Syracuse 13202 **Fx:**473-0530
(212) 907-0853 .. **Keller,** Christopher J '98 (Labaton S LLP) -140 Bway -NY 10005
(516) 496-1919 .. **Keller,** Clifford B '77 (Keller O&W,PC) -242 Crsswys Park Dr W -Woodbury 11797
(646) 536-2719 .. **Keller,** Danl L '02 (Keller F&J LLP) -62 William -NY 10005 **Fx:**349-3329
(212) 310-8000 .. **Keller,** David B '10 %Weil G&M LLP -767 5th Av -NY 10153
(516) 572-2385 .. **Keller,** Debra S '94 %Dist Ct -99 Main -Hempstd 11550 **Fx:**572-2600
(212) 431-1300 .. **Keller,** Dorothy M '83 (Borah GAN&G PC) -377 Bway -NY 10013
(212) 770-7417 .. **Keller,** Elan P '99 AIG -70 Pine -NY 10270
(516) 773-6090 .. **Keller,** Gregory E '95 (Chitwood HH LLP) -185 Grt Nck Rd -Gt Neck 11021
(212) 762-7726 .. **Keller,** Jacqueline '97 Morgan Stanley -1221 Av of Amer -NY 10020
(212) 208-4161 .. **Keller,** Jane E '84 Liberty Intl Underwriters -55 Water -NY 10041
(718) 206-4734 .. **Keller,** Janet E '95 %Law Dept -89-17 Sutphin Blvd -Jamaica 11435 **Fx:**206-4702
(212) 889-2498 .. **Keller,** Jay '86 %Fager & A,LLP -2 Park Av -NY 10016
(212) 872-3052 .. **Keller,** Jonathan C '99 KPMG LLP -345 Park Av -NY 10154
(212) 594-5300 .. **Keller,** Joshua E '05 %Milberg LLP -1 Penn Plz -NY 10119
(212) 726-6500 .. **Keller,** Kristen J '94 Atari Inc -417 5th Av -NY 10016
(585) 258-2800 .. **Keller,** Lawr P '71 (Underberg & K LLP) -300 Bausch & Lomb Pl -Rchstr 14604
(212) 815-1818 .. **Keller,** Linda M '90 %DC 37 MELS -125 Barclay -NY 10007 **Fx:**815-1343
(516) 746-7371 .. **Keller,** Linda N '09 %Burns RT&R,LLP -390 Old Cntry Rd -Gdn Cty 11530
(914) 238-5764 .. **Keller,** Margaret M '68 -375 Whippoorwill Rd -Chappaqua 10514
(718) 478-5222 .. **Keller,** Mark J '93 (Abramson & K) -6008 Woodside Av -Woodside 11377 **Fx:**478-5352
(914) 467-5256 .. **Keller,** Martha J '99 -520 Wht Plns Rd -Tarrytwn 10591 **Fx:**(203) 661-7286
(718) 590-5944 .. **Keller,** Melissa S '96 ACS -900 Sheridan Av -Bronx 10451
(646) 386-4039 .. **Keller,** Nina '88 Hon L Stone -111 Centre -NY 10013
(516) 496-1919 .. **Keller O'Reilly & Watson,PC** -242 Crsswys Park Dr W -Woodbury 11797 **Fx:**496-9791
(212) 937-7273 .. **Keller,** Paul B '98 (WilmerHale) -399 Park Av -NY 10022
(716) 855-3611 .. **Keller,** Robt E '71 OfCnsl Smith MO&S,LLP -69 Delaware Av -Buffalo 14202
(212) 918-3000 .. **Keller,** Robin E '79 (Hogan L LLP) -875 3rd Av -NY 10022
(212) 787-1882 .. **Keller,** Ronald I '84 -103 W 86th -NY 10024
(212) 559-5093 .. **Keller,** Stacey Berg '94 %Citigroup Inc -909 3rd Av -NY 10022
(212) 326-2000 .. **Kellerman,** Elizabeth A '08 Cnsl O'Melveny & M LLP -7 Times Sq -NY 10036
(518) 474-2705 .. **Kellett,** Christine Marbach '78 NYS Div Human Rights -ESP Corning Twr Bx2049 -Albany 12220
(212) 223-4000 .. **Kellett,** James E '89 (Crowell & M LLP) -590 Mad Av -NY 10022
(716) 332-0151 .. **Kellett,** Leo C '93 %Galbo & Assoc -420 Main -Buffalo 14202 **Fx:**332-0153
(212) 435-3571 .. **Kellett,** Philip J '90 Port Auth of NY/NJ -225 Park Av S -NY 10003 **Fx:**435-3555
(631) 727-2180 .. **Kelley,** Christopher D '82 (Twomey LSKD&Q,LLP) -33 W 2nd Bx9398 -Rvrhead 11901
(212) 701-3000 .. **Kelley,** David N '87 (Cahill G&R LLP) -80 Pine -NY 10005 **Fx:**269-5420
(631) 853-3158 .. **Kelley,** Dennis R '89 Dept of Hlth Srvcs -225 Rabro Dr E -Hauppauge 11788
(212) 407-4000 .. **Kelley,** Dobromira M '06 %Loeb & L,LLP -345 Park Av -NY 10154
(212) 866-4289 .. **Kelley,** Donald P '78 -900 West End Av -NY 10025
(212) 808-7800 .. **Kelley Drye & Warren LLP** -101 Park Av -NY 10178 **Fx:**808-7897
(315) 218-8000 .. **Kelley,** Edwin J Jr. '82 (Bond S&K,PLLC) -1 Lincoln Ctr -Syracuse 13202
(212) 335-4500 .. **Kelley,** Eric O'Brien '95 %DLA Piper LLP -1251 Av of Amer -NY 10020
(212) 286-8585 .. **Kelley,** Erin K '05 %Heidell PM&B,LLP -99 Park Av -NY 10016
(212) 370-4900 .. **Kelley,** Eurydice A '04 %Rosenthal & H,PC -420 Lex Av -NY 10170
(212) 277-4000 .. **Kelley,** Glen N '03 Cnsl Freshfields BD LLP -520 Mad Av -NY 10022
(646) 594-4198 .. **Kelley,** Ian L '97 -245 Carlton Av -Brklyn 11205
(718) 447-8841 .. **Kelley,** James L '67 (Lahr DMK&P) -33 Decker Av -Staten Isl 10302
(845) 452-6100 .. **Kelley,** James P '83 (Rizzo & K) -272 Mill -Poughkeepsie 12601 **Fx:**452-8459
(212) 341-6700 .. **Kelley,** John J '88 Liquidation Bur -123 William -NY 10038 **Fx:**608-3398
(212) 455-2000 .. **Kelley,** Karen Hsu '03 %Simpson T&B LLP -425 Lex Av -NY 10017
(212) 648-0427 .. **Kelley,** Kevin C '77 JP Morgan Chase -245 Park Av -NY 10167
(518) 785-9000 .. **Kelley,** Kevin J '81 Coldwell Banker -621 Columbia -Cohoes 12047
(212) 351-4000 .. **Kelley,** Kevin W '88 (Gibson D&C LLP) -200 Park Av -NY 10166
(716) 849-1333 .. **Kelley,** Laraine '80 (Lipsitz GSC LLP) -42 Delaware Av -Buffalo 14202
(518) 459-6422 .. **Kelley,** Laurel Lei '95 %Capitol Dist Ctr for Independence -875 Central Av -Albany 12206
(866) 348-5819 .. **Kelley,** Mary M '89 %SSA-ODAR -50 Fountain Plz -Buffalo 14202 **Fx:**(716) 551-4078
(212) 547-5400 .. **Kelley,** Nathanael '07 %McDermott W&E LLP -340 Mad Av -NY 10173
(212) 833-8000 .. **Kelley,** Palisa R '96 Sony BMG Music Entrtnmnt -550 Mad Av -NY 10022 **Fx:**833-8406
(212) 387-7787 .. **Kelley,** Peter J '80 (P Kelley & Assoc) -36 E 20th -NY 10003 **Fx:**387-0382
(212) 768-6700 .. **Kelley,** Ralph B '64 OfCnsl Sonnenschein N&R LLP -1221 Av of Amer -NY 10020
(516) 240-8900 .. **Kelley,** Sean P '96 %Torre LGG&R,LLP -100 Jericho Quad -Jericho 11753
(716) 883-3300 .. **Kelley,** Sean P '06 %R Cercone -484 Delaware Av -Buffalo 14202 **Fx:**883-2163
(585) 546-9557 .. **Kelley,** Stephen M '99 Fleet Bank -1 East Av -Rchstr 14638
(585) 382-3557 .. **Kelley,** Wm J '89 -4984 Chestnut -Leicester 14481
(212) 351-3400 .. **Kellman,** Alan S '00 (Desmarais LLP) -230 Park Av -NY 10169 **Fx:**351-3401
(212) 753-7500 .. **Kellman,** David A '75 (Hartman & C LLP) -488 Mad Av -NY 10022
(212) 809-4800 .. **Kellman,** Debra A '97 %N Kanzer -30 Broad -NY 10004 **Fx:**363-3097
(212) 663-9220 .. **Kellman,** Ira S '65 %Irana Realty Corp -840 W End Av -NY 10025 **Fx:**663-9230
(914) 328-0900 .. **Kellman,** Nancy D '86 -123 Main -White Plns 10601 **Fx:**328-0916
(718) 783-8200 .. **Kellman,** Susan G '79 -25 8th Av -Brklyn 11217

(212) 889-2121 .. **Kellner,** Douglas A '78 (Kellner HG&F) -470 Park Av S -NY 10016
(212) 345-5530 .. **Kellner,** Elizabeth Krob '87 %Marsh USA -1166 Av of Amer -NY 10036 **Fx:**345-4808
(631) 360-2175 .. **Kellner,** Herbert S '87 (Guttmann & K PC) -25 W Main -Smithtwn 11787 **Fx:**360-3393
(212) 889-2121 .. **Kellner Herlihy Getty & Friedman** -470 Park Av S -NY 10016 **Fx:**684-6224
(212) 319-6898 .. **Kellner,** Leland I '02 (Lavin ORC&D) -420 Lex Av -NY 10170
(518) 434-4377 .. **Kellogg,** Amy J '03 %Harter S&E LLP -111 Wshngtn Av -Albany 12210
(518) 474-9502 .. **Kellogg,** David S '73 %OTDA -40 N Pearl -Albany 12243 **Fx:**474-9389
(716) 856-4000 .. **Kellogg,** Leslie R '96 (Hodgson R LLP) -140 Pearl -Buffalo 14202
(212) 763-0600 .. **Kellogg,** Michl T '82 %Century Direct -30-00 47th Av -LIC 11101
(716) 881-3519 .. **Kellogg,** Stephen '67 -55 Windsor Av -Buffalo 14209 **Fx:**881-3519
(212) 259-8000 .. **Kellogg,** Wm E '09 %Dewey & L LLP -1301 Av of Amer -NY 10019
(212) 741-8282 .. **Kelly,** Adam '00 Cnsl Ofc & Prof Employee Intl Union -265 W 14th -NY 10011 **Fx:**463-9479
(212) 237-0000 .. **Kelly,** Alexandra Shaw '06 %Vinson & E LLP -666 5th Av -NY 10103
(212) 455-2000 .. **Kelly,** Alison M '08 %Simpson T&B LLP -425 Lex Av -NY 10017
(716) 636-7600 .. **Kelly,** Amanda J '09 %HoganWillig -2410 N Forest Rd -Amherst 14068
(516) 867-5100 .. **Kelly,** Amelia Jean '79 Seaport Title Agncy -106 Woodcleft Av -Freeprt 11520
(518) 692-1200 .. **Kelly,** Andrew C '96 (Jordan & K LLC) -4 Fisher -Greenwich 12834 **Fx:**692-1222
(516) 294-5433 .. **Kelly,** Andria Simone '93 %Ahmuty D&M -200 IU Willets Rd -Albertson 11507
(212) 208-3355 .. **Kelly,** Anne G '89 %Ambac Assurance -1 State Street Plz -NY 10004 **Fx:**785-1178
(212) 209-4800 .. **Kelly,** Barbara J '82 Brown R LLP -7 Times Sq -NY 10036
(631) 473-4660 .. **Kelly,** Barbara Jane '94 -218 Main #213 -E Setauket 11733
(212) 735-3000 .. **Kelly,** Barbara Krasa '80 Cnsl Skadden ASM&F LLP -4 Times Sq -NY 10036
(718) 553-3285 .. **Kelly,** Brendan A '91 %FAA -1 Aviation Plz -Jamaica 11434 **Fx:**995-5699
(518) 474-7700 .. **Kelly,** Brian A '80 %NYS OPWDD -44 Holland Av -Albany 12229 **Fx:**474-7382
(845) 634-2105 .. **Kelly,** Brian A '98 -118 Maple Av -New Cty 10956 **Fx:**634-2156
(718) 579-3000 .. **Kelly,** Brian E '81 %Leg Aid -1020 Grnd Cncrs -Bronx 10451 **Fx:**588-2611
(212) 530-5000 .. **Kelly,** Brian P '01 %Milbank TH&M LLP -1 Chase Manh Plz -NY 10005
(212) 715-1000 .. **Kelly,** Bruce R '78 (Arnold & P LLP) -399 Park Av -NY 10022
(516) 571-3800 .. **Kelly,** Carolyn E '93 %DA -262 Old Cntry Rd -Mineola 11501 **Fx:**248-9479
(631) 715-7900 .. **Kelly,** Chas '78 %US Atty -610 Fed Plz -Central Islip 11722
(716) 649-5533 .. **Kelly,** Chas E '75 -110 Woodvw Av -Hambrg 14075
(212) 513-3200 .. **Kelly,** Christopher G '87 (Holland & K LLP) -31 W 52nd -NY 10019
(518) 457-2070 .. **Kelly,** Christopher J '95 %Dept of Tax & Fin -Bldg 9 State Campus -Albany 12227 **Fx:**457-6131
(212) 474-1000 .. **Kelly,** Christopher J '00 Cravath S&M LLP -825 8th Av -NY 10019
(212) 326-3939 .. **Kelly,** Christopher M '88 (Jones D) -222 E 41st -NY 10017
(212) 607-8661 .. **Kelly,** Christopher M '02 Dept of Labor -33 Whitehall -NY 10004
(845) 568-5142 .. **Kelly,** Christopher M '07 %DA -255-275 Main -Goshen 10924 **Fx:**291-2085
(212) 490-0988 .. **Kelly,** Christopher P '00 (Reppert K,LLC) -570 Lex Av -NY 10022
(212) 506-1700 .. **Kelly,** Cindy Caranella '93 (Kasowitz BT&F LLP) -1633 Bway -NY 10019
(718) 780-0398 .. **Kelly,** Claire R '94 %Bklyn Law Schl -250 Joralemon -Brklyn 11201 **Fx:**780-0393
(212) 373-3000 .. **Kelly,** Colin S '09 %Paul WRW&G LLP -1285 Av of Amer -NY 10019
(716) 853-8470 .. **Kelly,** Cydney A '95 %Dept of Law -350 Main Pl Twr -Buffalo 14202 **Fx:**853-8571
(718) 250-2000 .. **Kelly,** David C '88 %DA -350 Jay -Brklyn 11201 **Fx:**250-2314
(212) 218-2100 .. **Kelly,** David M '08 %Fitzpatrick CH&S -1290 Av of Amer -NY 10104
(716) 362-0470 .. **Kelly,** David S '99 (Riordan & K,LLC) -2982 Delaware Av -Kenmore 14217 **Fx:**362-0480
(917) 551-1300 .. **Kelly,** Dawn K '92 %Koehler & I LLP -61 Bway -NY 10006
(516) 739-3737 .. **Kelly,** Deborah A '96 %Alexander P,LLC -666 Old Cntry Rd -Gdn Cty 11530
(212) 483-0105 .. **Kelly,** Deborah A '06 %Coughlin D LLP -88 Pine-Wall St Plz -NY 10005
(718) 320-3420 .. **Kelly,** Debra A '00 %Riverbay Corp -2049 Bartow Av -Bronx 10475
(516) 897-0800 .. **Kelly,** Denis G '93 (D Kelly & Assoc PC) -100 W Park Av -Long Bch 11561
(631) 864-5575 .. **Kelly,** Dennis J '88 (Kelly G&F,LLP) -901A Motor Pkwy -Hauppauge 11788
(212) 819-8200 .. **Kelly,** Derek R '10 %White & C LLP -1155 Av of Amer -NY 10036
(585) 237-2111 .. **Kelly,** Devon M '10 M Kelly -24 Lake Bx 92 -Perry 14530 **Fx:**237-6901
(718) 428-2573 .. **Kelly,** Diana H '91 -153-01 Jamaica Av -Jamaica 11432 **Fx:**725-4206
(315) 472-0972 .. **Kelly,** Donald E '96 -2105 W Genesee -Syracuse 13219 **Fx:**472-9818
(914) 948-1024 .. **Kelly,** Donna M '84 -202 Mamaroneck Av -White Plns 10601 **Fx:**948-1320
(212) 593-1400 .. **Kelly,** Edw P '82 (Fisher F PC) -30 Vesey -NY 10007
(212) 490-3285 .. **Kelly,** Edw P '84 (Tiajoloff & K) -405 Lex Av -NY 10174 **Fx:**490-3295
(518) 438-5237 .. **Kelly,** Eileen M '93 -95 Pinewood Av -Albany 12208 **Fx:**435-9809
(212) 848-4000 .. **Kelly,** Erin P '06 %Shearman & S LLP -599 Lex Av -NY 10022
(518) 357-2068 .. **Kelly,** Eugene J Jr. '88 %DEC -1150 N Westcott Rd -Schnctdy 12306 **Fx:**357-2087
(718) 279-4500 .. **Kelly,** Frank T '84 -42-40 Bell Blvd -Bayside 11361 **Fx:**281-0850
(718) 892-0400 .. **Kelly,** Frank V '89 %W Gallina -1180 Morris Park Av -Bronx 10461 **Fx:**892-0033
(212) 785-2929 .. **Kelly,** Gail M '89 (Conway FC&K,PC) -48 Wall -NY 10005
(212) 956-3355 .. **Kelly,** Gary M '83 %Elegant Logic -305 Mad Av -NY 10165
(607) 974-4152 .. **Kelly,** Grace Park '02 %Corning -1 Rvrfrnt Plz -Corning 14831 **Fx:**974-6135
(631) 864-5575 .. **Kelly Grossman & Flanagan, LLP** -901A Motor Pkwy -Hauppauge 11788 **Fx:**594-3114
(212) 713-8663 .. **Kelly,** James B III '98 UBS Securities LLC -1285 Av of Amer -NY 10019
(212) 759-4600 .. **Kelly,** James C '05 %Wolf P LLP -845 3rd Av -NY 10022
(716) 626-0700 .. **Kelly,** James E '73 -5820 Main -Williamsvll 14221
(212) 557-7700 .. **Kelly,** James F '89 (Davidson D&C LLP) -60 E 42nd -NY 10165
(516) 355-7901 .. **Kelly,** James G '81 %Paganini GCC&F -1979 Marcus Av -Lk Success 11042
(631) 667-1510 .. **Kelly,** James J '51 (Kelly L&A) -2023 Deer Prk Av -Deer Pk 11729
(718) 821-1690 .. **Kelly,** James J '81 -409 Linden -Brklyn 11237
(212) 858-1000 .. **Kelly,** James L '00 (Pillsbury WSP LLP) -1540 Bway -NY 10036
(212) 480-7421 .. **Kelly,** Jeffrey G '94 %DHCR -25 Beaver -NY 10004 **Fx:**480-7416
(212) 770-5065 .. **Kelly,** Jennifer A '02 AIGTS -70 Pine -NY 10270
(718) 248-2855 .. **Kelly,** Jo-Anne M '89 %Citigroup -1 Court Sq -LIC 11101
(914) 694-2822 .. **Kelly,** John B F '80 Senerchia & K,PC -4 W Red Oak Ln -White Plns 10604 **Fx:**696-0672
(212) 609-6800 .. **Kelly,** John C '95 (McCarter & E,LLP) -245 Park Av -NY 10167
(646) 392-9250 .. **Kelly,** John F '85 %M Klein & Assoc -200 Mad Av -NY 10016 **Fx:**(212) 779-1499
(212) 940-3790 .. **Kelly,** John L '75 (Nixon P LLP) -437 Mad Av -NY 10022
(212) 264-3650 .. **Kelly,** John M '95 Soc Sec-Ofc of Gen Cnsl -26 Fed Plz -NY 10278
(212) 341-6400 .. **Kelly,** John Pearson '85 Liquidation Bur -123 William -NY 10038 **Fx:**608-3398
(212) 704-0500 .. **Kelly,** John Q '81 -9 E 40th -NY 10016 **Fx:**764-0900
(718) 293-1101 .. **Kelly,** John R '03 -901 Sheridan Av -Bronx 10451 **Fx:**293-5395
(732) 855-6139 .. **Kelly,** John T '83 (Wilentz G&S) -110 William -NY 10038 **Fx:**726-6582
(914) 769-6876 .. **Kelly,** John W '67 -104 Bway -Plsntvll 10570 **Fx:**769-6876
(212) 687-6262 .. **Kelly,** Jonathan '10 %Barton B&P,LLP -420 Lex Av -NY 10170
(212) 839-5300 .. **Kelly,** Jonathan J '97 (Sidley A LLP) -787 7th Av -NY 10019
(914) 682-2049 .. **Kelly,** Jos A '96 -50 Main -White Plns 10606 **Fx:**819-0802
(212) 839-5300 .. **Kelly,** Jos C T '01 (Sidley A LLP) -787 7th Av -NY 10019
(212) 363-3100 .. **Kelly,** Jos E Jr. '86 (Bivona & C,PC) -88 Pine -NY 10005
(315) 435-5250 .. **Kelly,** Jos M '74 Dept of Social Srvcs -421 Mntgmry -Syracuse 13202 **Fx:**435-2159
(212) 742-9280 .. **Kelly,** Joy M '89 %Waterfront Comm -39 Bway -NY 10006 **Fx:**480-0587
(212) 546-4852 .. **Kelly,** Katherine R '02 %Bristol-Myers Squibb -345 Park Av -NY 10154 **Fx:**546-9562
(845) 353-2000 .. **Kelly Kelly Marotta & Lafferty LLC** -96 S Bway -South Nyack 10960
(212) 351-4606 .. **Kelly,** Kenneth J '72 (Epstein B&G,PC) -250 Park Av -NY 10177
(631) 852-2500 .. **Kelly,** Kerriann '87 %DA -200 Center Dr -Rvrhead 11901 **Fx:**852-1769
(212) 785-2929 .. **Kelly,** Kevin J '75 (Conway FC&K,PC) -48 Wall -NY 10005
(212) 968-8300 .. **Kelly,** Kevin L '84 (Mintzer SZL&M LLP) -39 Bway -NY 10006
(845) 353-2000 .. **Kelly,** Kevin P '92 (Kelly KM&L LLC) -96 S Bway -South Nyack 10960
(917) 592-4779 .. **Kelly,** Kevin P '01 (McMahon & K,LLP) -545 W 45TH -NY 10036
(607) 776-9631 .. **Kelly,** Kevin T '05 Pub Def -3 E Pulteney Sq -Bath 14810 **Fx:**664-2496
(646) 733-3200 .. **Kelly,** Kimberly T '99 US Customs -1 Penn Plz -NY 10119
(212) 609-6800 .. **Kelly,** Laura A '03 (McCarter & E,LLP) -245 Park Av -NY 10167
(212) 408-5100 .. **Kelly,** Lauren D '85 (Chadbourne & P LLP) -30 Rckfllr Plz -NY 10112
(631) 751-5757 .. **Kelly,** Lawr E '83 (Glynn M&P,LLP) -57 North Cntry Rd Bx712 -Stony Brk 11790
(518) 792-1582 .. **Kelly,** Leah M A '09 %Caffry & F -100 Bay -Glens Fls 12801
(716) 849-8432 .. **Kelly,** Lois Varisco '93 %Erie Cnty Water Authority -295 Main -Buffalo 14203
(516) 676-6262 .. **Kelly Lucas & Pacifico** -23 Birch Hill Rd -Locust Vly 11560 **Fx:**676-6382
(631) 667-1510 .. **Kelly Luglio & Arcuri** -2023 Deer Prk Av -Deer Pk 11729 **Fx:**667-1514
(212) 382-6600 .. **Kelly,** Lynn M '83 %NYC Bar -42 W 44th -NY 10036 **Fx:**398-6634
(212) 813-5900 .. **Kelly,** Marilyn F '03 %Fross ZL&Z,PC -866 UN Plz -NY 10017
(212) 953-2626 .. **Kelly,** Mark C '78 (Kelly & H) -380 Lex Av -NY 10168 **Fx:**983-5271
(914) 631-2657 .. **Kelly,** Mary F '72 (Kelly & K) -399 Knollwood Rd -White Plns 10603 **Fx:**631-7795
(212) 450-4000 .. **Kelly,** Matthew A '10 %Davis P&W LLP -450 Lex Av -NY 10017
(212) 349-5150 .. **Kelly,** Matthew D '99 %Galvano & X,PC -150 Bway -NY 10038
(914) 948-4500 .. **Kelly,** Matthew E '08 %O'Connor MCD&O -1 Barker Av -White Plns 10601
(518) 464-1300 .. **Kelly,** Matthew J '80 (Roemer WG&M LLP) -13 Columbia Cir -Albany 12203
(212) 973-8000 .. **Kelly,** Matthew J Jr. '06 %Schnader HS&L LLP -140 Bway -NY 10005
(212) 670-0278 .. **Kelly,** Maura T '95 %Merrill Lynch -222 Bway -NY 10038
(845) 359-5178 .. **Kelly,** Maureen D '97 -Bx183 -Tappan 10983 **Fx:**359-0974
(845) 454-4244 .. **Kelly & Meenagh, LLP** -135 N Water -Poughkeepsie 12601 **Fx:**454-5272
(212) 301-5494 .. **Kelly,** Megyn M '97 %FOX News -1211 Av of Amer -NY 10036
(212) 309-6000 .. **Kelly,** Melissa R '08 %Morgan L&B LLP -101 Park Av -NY 10178
(718) 646-4156 .. **Kelly,** Michl F '86 -2305 Av Z -Brklyn 11235
(631) 363-3014 .. **Kelly,** Michl F '02 Pulte Homes of NY -570 Expwy Dr S -Medfrd 11763
(516) 741-4104 .. **Kelly,** Michl J '79 Fidelity Natl Title -330 Old Cntry Rd -Mineola 11501
(631) 549-4677 .. **Kelly,** Michl J '80 (Sobel K&S,PC) -464 NY Av -Huntngtn 11743
(212) 425-7200 .. **Kelly,** Michl J '04 %Kenyon & K,LLP -1 Bway -NY 10004
(516) 708-1767 .. **Kelly,** Michl J '07 -21 Schenck Av -Gt Neck 11021 **Fx:**708-1767
(585) 237-2111 .. **Kelly,** Michl J T '73 -24 Lake Bx 92 -Perry 14530 **Fx:**237-6901
(212) 554-1700 .. **Kelly,** Michl John '89 Monarch Alternative Capital -535 Mad Av -NY 10022 **Fx:**554-1701
(585) 225-3446 .. **Kelly,** Michl Jos '89 (Darweesh LK&V,LLP) -1081 Long Pond Rd -Rchstr 14626
(631) 232-0200 .. **Kelly,** Michl K '77 (Fumuso KDSS&F,LLP) -110 Marcus Blvd -Hauppauge 11788
(516) 248-8842 .. **Kelly,** Michl P '95 %Jones HC&B PC -200 Old Cntry Rd -Mineola 11501
(212) 408-5100 .. **Kelly,** Michl R '06 %Chadbourne & P LLP -30 Rckfllr Plz -NY 10112

(716) 886-1922 .. **Kelly,** Michl T '74 -207 Admirals Walk -Buffalo 14202
(212) 251-8200 .. **Kelly,** Michl T '79 %Moet Hennessy -85 Tenth Av -NY 10011 **Fx:**251-8390
(212) 788-0482 .. **Kelly,** Monica '00 %Law Dept -100 Church -NY 10007 **Fx:**788-0367
(516) 221-4736 .. **Kelly,** Pamela Bannon '89 -1555 Earl Rd -Wantagh 11793
(212) 552-4131 .. **Kelly,** Patricia M '89 JP Morgan Chase -1 Chase Manh Plz -NY 10081
(716) 634-2497 .. **Kelly,** Patrick M '82 (Kelly & S) -5678 Main -Williamsvll 14221
(585) 546-6448 .. **Kelly,** Paul D '81 (Davidson F LLP) -28 E Main -Rchstr 14614
(518) 485-9373 .. **Kelly,** Paul F '84 Ofc of State Review -80 Wolf Rd -Albany 12205
(212) 440-2222 .. **Kelly,** Paul G '88 NYC EDC -110 William -NY 10038 **Fx:**480-4320
(914) 632-8382 .. **Kelly,** Paula Johnson '94 %Goodstein & Assoc -270 North Av -New Rchll 10801 **Fx:**632-1833
(516) 663-6600 .. **Kelly,** Peter K '76 Cnsl Ruskin MF,PC -1425 RXR Plz -Uniondale 11556
(212) 344-4700 .. **Kelly,** R Brett '93 DeOrchis & Prtnrs LLP -61 Bway -NY 10006
(347) 446-2407 .. **Kelly,** Rachel G '02 Citi Habitats -32 E 22nd -NY 10010
(518) 463-4569 .. **Kelly,** Raymond A Jr. '74 -112 State -Albany 12207
(914) 948-1957 .. **Kelly,** Regina F '83 -99 Court -White Plns 10601 **Fx:**948-7848
(516) 676-6262 .. **Kelly,** Richd B '68 (Kelly L&P) -23 Birch Hill Rd -Locust Vly 11560
(518) 876-3086 .. **Kelly,** Robt '74 Cnsl First Niagara Bank -161 Church -Amsterdam 12010 **Fx:**842-5843
(631) 288-2876 .. **Kelly,** Robt A Jr. '90 (Kelly & H) -323 Mill Rd -Westhmptn Bch 11978 **Fx:**288-1328
(518) 761-0213 .. **Kelly,** Robt E '76 -37 Lincoln Av -Glens Fls 12801 **Fx:**761-6160
(212) 483-0105 .. **Kelly,** Robt J '90 (Coughlin D LLP) -88 Pine-Wall St Plz -NY 10005
(212) 819-8200 .. **Kelly,** Robt M '72 Cnsl White & C LLP -1155 Av of Amer -NY 10036
(518) 587-7878 .. **Kelly,** Robt M '94 -376 Bway -Saratoga Spgs 12866 **Fx:**587-0269
(914) 777-1577 .. **Kelly,** Robt P '86 -480 Mamaroneck Av -Harrison 10528
(212) 691-9393 .. **Kelly,** Robt P '87 (Kelly & R,LLP) -275 7th Av -NY 10001
(516) 739-0400 .. **Kelly Rode & Kelly,LLP** -330 Old Cntry Rd -Mineola 11501 **Fx:**739-0434
(631) 727-0110 .. **Kelly Rode & Kelly,LLP** -218 Griffing -Rvrhead 11901
(212) 284-2316 .. **Kelly,** Roland T '05 Jefferies & Co Inc -520 Mad Av -NY 10022
(914) 333-0900 .. **Kelly,** Ronald F '80 (Rubin & K) -660 Wht Plns Rd -Tarrytwn 10591 **Fx:**333-0495
(718) 590-6366 .. **Kelly,** Rori '94 Supreme Ct -851 Grnd Cncrs -Bronx 10451
(212) 691-9393 .. **Kelly & Rubin, LLP** -275 7th Av -NY 10001 **Fx:**691-1485
(518) 438-8395 .. **Kelly,** Ruth M '74 -187 Euclid Av -Albany 12208
(516) 357-3700 .. **Kelly,** Ryan P '04 %Cullen and D LLP -100 Q Roosevelt Blvd -Gdn Cty 11530
(212) 499-6644 .. **Kelly,** Sakima V '08 %M Cohen & Assoc,PC -7 Penn Plz -NY 10001 **Fx:**818-0625
(212) 735-3000 .. **Kelly,** Sarah N '07 %Skadden ASM&F LLP -4 Times Sq -NY 10036
(631) 737-4110 .. **Kelly,** Sean P '97 (Gruenberg & K,PC) -3275 Vets Mem'l Hwy -Ronkonkoma 11779 **Fx:**737-4155
(212) 461-2323 .. **Kelly,** Sean R '90 (Saiber LLC) -44 Wall -NY 10005
(718) 354-3200 .. **Kelly,** Shane M '05 %Battiste A&S,Inc -60 Bay -Staten Isl 10301
(716) 856-4000 .. **Kelly,** Sharon M '90 (Hodgson R LLP) -140 Pearl -Buffalo 14202
(631) 727-0110 .. **Kelly,** Shawn P '78 (Kelly R&K,LLP) -218 Griffing -Rvrhead 11901
(516) 739-0400 .. **Kelly,** Shawn P '78 (Kelly R&K,LLP) -330 Old Cntry Rd -Mineola 11501
(716) 689-2403 .. **Kelly,** Sienie '89 -209 Northington Dr -E Amherst 14051
(212) 964-7400 .. **Kelly,** Stacey Schwartz '96 Smith MDWY&Y,PC -111 John -NY 10038
(212) 545-4728 .. **Kelly,** Stacey T '01 %Wolf HAF&H LLP -270 Mad Av -NY 10016
(212) 756-2781 .. **Kelly,** Steven T '10 %Schulte R&Z LLP -919 3rd Av -NY 10022
(518) 431-0247 .. **Kelly,** Terrence '74 %US Atty -445 Bway -Albany 12207 **Fx:**431-0249
(631) 547-5900 .. **Kelly,** Theresa A '01 (Kelly & S,LLP) -150 Broadhllw Rd -Melvll 11747 **Fx:**547-9125
(212) 506-1700 .. **Kelly,** Thos B '09 %Kasowitz BT&F LLP -1633 Bway -NY 10019
(518) 884-0080 .. **Kelly,** Thos E '89 (Kelly & L,LLP) -199 Milton Av -Ballston Spa 12020 **Fx:**884-0083
(607) 337-1828 .. **Kelly,** Thos E '93 Cnty Multi-Court -5 Court -Norwich 13815 **Fx:**337-1834
(845) 454-4244 .. **Kelly,** Thos F III '81 (Kelly & M,LLP) -135 N Water -Poughkeepsie 12601
(716) 854-2620 .. **Kelly,** Thos J '52 (Brown & K,LLP) -1500 Lbrty Bldg -Buffalo 14202
(212) 588-8868 .. **Kelly,** Thos J '90 Gilberti SH&S,PC -885 3rd Av -NY 10022
(914) 694-5900 .. **Kelly,** Thos L '94 %West World Mgt Inc -4 Manhattanvll Rd -Purchase 10577
(212) 909-6907 .. **Kelly,** Thos M '85 (Debevoise & P LLP) -919 3rd Av -NY 10022
(212) 363-6900 .. **Kelly,** Thos M '97 Faust GS&B LLP -2 Rector -NY 10006
(212) 733-6382 .. **Kelly,** Thos R '86 Pfizer -235 E 42nd -NY 10017
(212) 218-2100 .. **Kelly,** Timothy J '92 (Fitzpatrick CH&S) -1290 Av of Amer -NY 10104
(212) 458-2182 .. **Kelly,** Tracey L '90 %AIG -175 Water -NY 10038
(212) 855-0211 .. **Kelly,** Vanessa '00 Goldman Sachs -1 NY Plz -NY 10004 **Fx:**(917) 977-4356
(212) 801-6864 .. **Kelly,** W Michl '75 (Greenberg T,LLP) -200 Park Av -NY 10166
(212) 776-5000 .. **Kelly,** Walter P '75 %NYC Housing Auth -250 Bway -NY 10007 **Fx:**776-5039
(315) 724-3158 .. **Kelly & Walthall** -239 Genesee -Utica 13501 **Fx:**724-3150
(585) 247-2925 .. **Kelly,** Wm C '54 -17 Brwstr Ln -Rchstr 14624 **Fx:**247-2925
(212) 714-1720 .. **Kelly,** Wm C '91 (Tompkins MW&B LLP) -140 Bway -NY 10005
(914) 798-5400 .. **Kelly,** Wm G '78 (Goldberg S LLP) -11 Martine Av -White Plns 10606
(518) 434-5050 .. **Kelly,** Wm G '04 %Law Dept -106 City Hall -Albany 12207 **Fx:**434-5070
(914) 323-7000 .. **Kelly,** Wm J '01 OfCnsl Wilson EME&D LLP -3 Gannett Dr -White Plns 10604
(212) 732-6000 .. **Kelly,** Wm P '92 (McCarthy & K LLP) -52 Duane -NY 10007
(212) 944-7333 .. **Kelly-Kobayashi,** Eleanore '80 %Rode & Q -55 W 39th -NY 10018
(518) 762-3840 .. **Kelly-May,** Beth V '94 %Family Ct -11 N William -Johnstwn 12095
(212) 906-1200 .. **Kelly-Najah,** Noreen A '99 (Latham & W) -885 3rd Av -NY 10022
(516) 432-9400 .. **Kelly Peknic,** Loreen M '95 %Peknic P&S LLC -1005 W Beech -Long Bch 11561 **Fx:**432-5396
(516) 571-3800 .. **Kelly-Pincus,** Pamela '87 %DA -262 Old Cntry Rd -Mineola 11501 **Fx:**248-9479
(212) 869-3500 .. **Kelmachter,** Leslie D '78 (J Fuchsberg Law Firm,LLP) -500 5th Av -NY 10110 **Fx:**398-1532
(212) 552-0917 .. **Kelman,** Alyssa '87 JP Morgan Chase -1 Chase Manh Plz -NY 10081
(212) 371-9490 .. **Kelman,** Edw M '69 -100 Park Av -NY 10017
(516) 887-0730 .. **Kelman,** Lorne J '95 (L Kelman,PC) -20 E Sunrise Hwy -Vly Stream 11581 **Fx:**887-0751
(212) 485-3465 .. **Kelman,** Matthew S '98 MLB Advanced Media LP -75 9th Av -NY 10011
(212) 966-3730 .. **Kelman,** Richd '76 (Kelman W&V) -2 Rector -NY 10006
(212) 966-3730 .. **Kelman Winston & Vallone** -2 Rector -NY 10006 **Fx:**925-0290
(212) 779-3510 .. **Kelmenson,** Lee D '82 %AB Stollow,PC -475 Park Av S -NY 10016 **Fx:**679-9064
(516) 873-1200 .. **Kelner,** Gail Stein '74 %Kelner & K -1 Old Cntry Rd -Carle Pl 11514
(212) 425-0700 .. **Kelner,** Gail Stein '74 %Kelner & K -140 Bway -NY 10005
(212) 425-0700 .. **Kelner,** Joshua D '05 %Kelner & K -140 Bway -NY 10005
(212) 425-0700 .. **Kelner & Kelner** -140 Bway -NY 10005 **Fx:**425-0007
(516) 873-1200 .. **Kelner & Kelner** -1 Old Cntry Rd -Carle Pl 11514 **Fx:**873-1230
(212) 425-0700 .. **Kelner,** Robt S '72 (Kelner & K) -140 Bway -NY 10005
(516) 873-1200 .. **Kelner,** Robt S '72 (Kelner & K) -1 Old Cntry Rd -Carle Pl 11514
(516) 374-0371 .. **Kelner,** Saml H '53 -670 Arbuckle Av -Woodmere 11598
(718) 590-2000 .. **Kelsch,** Meridith L '07 %DA -198 E 161st -Bronx 10451 **Fx:**590-6477
(607) 753-5008 .. **Kelsen,** Mardis '98 %DA -46 Greenbush -Cortlnd 13045 **Fx:**756-3477
(607) 756-4585 .. **Kelsen,** Mardis '98 Law Ofc-the Higgins Hse -20 Court -Cortlnd 13045 **Fx:**756-5329
(914) 967-5965 .. **Kelsey,** Alan R '77 -179 Grace Church -Rye 10580
(518) 456-6767 .. **Kelsey,** Andrea L '84 (Young FK&B,PC) -1881 Wstrn Av -Albany 12203
(718) 723-5954 .. **Kelsey,** Fredk T '93 %DOJ INS -1 Cross Isl Plz -Rosedale 11422 **Fx:**723-1121
(212) 351-4000 .. **Kelsey,** Matthew K '04 %Gibson D&C LLP -200 Park Av -NY 10166
(212) 455-2000 .. **Kelsey,** Parker B '08 %Simpson T&B LLP -425 Lex Av -NY 10017
(212) 230-8800 .. **Kelsey,** Sara A '77 Cnsl WilmerHale -399 Park Av -NY 10022
(212) 547-5400 .. **Kelson,** Evan B '04 %McDermott W&E LLP -340 Mad Av -NY 10173
(845) 569-7335 .. **Kelson,** Michelle J '92 %Law Dept -83 Bway -Newburgh 12550 **Fx:**569-7338
(845) 567-3010 .. **Kelson,** Todd A '86 T Kelson,PC -542 Union Av -New Windsor 12553 **Fx:**561-2128
(845) 794-1000 .. **Kelson,** Zachary D '83 -10 St John Bx1210 -Monticello 12701 **Fx:**794-1422
(212) 687-8700 .. **Keltner,** Thos N Jr. '75 (Malkin Hldngs,LLC) -60 E 42nd -NY 10165 **Fx:**986-7679
(212) 357-9762 .. **Kelton,** C Annette '01 Goldman Sachs -1 NY Plz -NY 10004
(516) 393-5840 .. **Kelton,** Chas S '79 (Kelton & T) -6800 Jericho Tpk -Syosset 11791 **Fx:**393-5839
(212) 489-1400 .. **Kelton,** Justin T '09 %Bickel & B -767 5th Av -NY 10153
(212) 279-9200 .. **Kelton,** Michl S '78 (Abrams FFEGF&E,LLP) -630 3rd Av -NY 10017
(914) 798-4251 .. **Kelty,** John C '93 %Mariner Invstmt Grp -500 Mamaroneck Av -Harrison 10528
(212) 687-3000 .. **Kelty,** Thos M Jr. '02 %Jaffe & A,LLP -600 3rd Av -NY 10016
(718) 937-2123 .. **Keltz,** Eric L '96 Major Automotive Co,INC -4340 Nrthrn Blvd -LIC 11101
(914) 824-5643 .. **Keltz,** Jody B '86 %Surrogates Ct -111 Dr MLK Jr Blvd -White Plns 10601 **Fx:**995-3728
(212) 816-2211 .. **Keltz,** Steven '78 Citigroup Global Mrkts -250 West -NY 10013
(845) 342-2314 .. **Kelvasa,** Anthony Jr. '54 -44 W Main Bx2162 -Middletwn 10940 **Fx:**342-3006
(212) 848-4000 .. **Kemnitz,** Catherine M '00 %Shearman & S LLP -599 Lex Av -NY 10022
(917) 557-7420 .. **Kemp,** Antoinette L '09 -70 W 95th -NY 10025
(914) 941-5668 .. **Kemp,** Audra A '98 %Collen IP -80 S Highland Av -Ossining 10562 **Fx:**941-6091
(585) 238-2000 .. **Kemp,** Chandy Z '95 %Phillips L LLP -1400 First Fed Plz -Rchstr 14614
(518) 449-8893 .. **Kemp,** Douglas R '01 %Wilson EME&D LLP -677 Bway -Albany 12207
(212) 848-4000 .. **Kemp,** Felicia M '09 %Shearman & S LLP -599 Lex Av -NY 10022
(718) 464-1125 .. **Kemp,** Laurette A '95 -100-01 Bellaire Pl -Qns Vllg 11429
(516) 569-3700 .. **Kemp,** Marc D '88 %Basser Kaufman -151 Irving Pl -Woodmere 11598 **Fx:**569-7528
(716) 853-9555 .. **Kemp,** Robt L '00 %Leg Aid -237 Main -Buffalo 14203 **Fx:**853-3219
(845) 486-6800 .. **Kemp,** Sean M '05 %McCabe & M LLP -63 Wshngtn Bx509 -Poughkeepsie 12602
(212) 761-7321 .. **Kempf,** Donald G Jr. '86 Morgan Stanley -1585 Bway -NY 10036 **Fx:**761-0331
(212) 424-8604 .. **Kempler,** Cecelia '80 -125 W 55th -NY 10019 **Fx:**424-8500
(212) 792-2200 .. **Kempner,** Brian G '89 Firstmark Capital,LLC -1221 Av of Amer -NY 10020 **Fx:**391-5700
(718) 875-2034 .. **Kempner,** Maria '89 -65-35 108th -Frst Hlls 11375
(718) 237-5574 .. **Kempner,** Peter A '02 Leg Srvcs -105 Court -Brklyn 11201 **Fx:**855-0733
(585) 295-4400 .. **Kendall,** Amy K '99 Cnsl Hiscock & B,LLP -2000 HSBC Plz -Rchstr 14604
(212) 431-2119 .. **Kendall,** Chris A '02 NY Law Schl -185 W Bway -NY 10013 **Fx:**343-1537
(315) 824-2179 .. **Kendall,** Christopher '90 -9 Payne Bx248 -Hamilton 13346 **Fx:**824-2187
(212) 310-8000 .. **Kendall,** Consuelo A '09 %Weil G&M LLP -767 5th Av -NY 10153
(212) 935-3960 .. **Kendall,** Katie Jo '05 Municipal Art Society -457 Mad Av -NY 10022 **Fx:**753-1816
(212) 509-9400 .. **Kende,** Christopher B '74 (Cozen O) -45 Bway Atrium -NY 10006
(516) 281-9800 .. **Kendric,** Christopher '89 SpclCnsl Goldberg S LLP -200 Old Cntry Rd -Mineola 11501
(212) 578-2506 .. **Kendrick,** Carol Y '78 SrCnsl MetLife -1095 Av of Amer -NY 10036
(212) 461-6950 .. **Kendrick,** James M '84 -254 W 31st -NY 10001
(716) 855-2251 .. **Kendrick,** Joy A '82 -Bx735 -Buffalo 14205 **Fx:**855-2253
(718) 254-0700 .. **Kendrick,** Joyce D '96 %Bklyn Defender Srvcs -177 Lvngstn -Brklyn 11201 **Fx:**254-0897

(315) 671-2030 .. **Kendrick-Gaffney,** Mary E '87 Hon M Pirro Bailey -401 Mntgmry -Syracuse 13202
(212) 808-7800 .. **Keneally,** James M '83 (Kelley D&W LLP) -101 Park Av -NY 10178
(631) 265-4500 .. **Keneally,** Jos P '92 (Meyer M&K) -28 Manor Rd -Smithtwn 11787
(212) 318-3000 .. **Keneally,** Kathryn '83 (Fulbright & J LLP) -666 5th Av -NY 10103
(585) 258-2800 .. **Keneally,** Paul F '94 (Underberg & K LLP) -300 Bausch & Lomb Pl -Rchstr 14604
(516) 795-6000 .. **Kenealy,** J Bradford '80 (Kenealy & L) -553 Bway -Massapequa 11758 **Fx:**795-6148
(315) 732-5121 .. **Kenealy,** John F '99 (Helmer JM&K) -405 Court -Utica 13502
(518) 862-9292 .. **Kenealy,** Kimberly E '97 (Napierski V&N,LLP) -296 Wshngtn Av Ext -Albany 12203
(518) 270-3795 .. **Kenefick,** Christine L '94 %Hon A Carpinello -2nd & Congress -Troy 12180 **Fx:**270-3799
(212) 986-5993 .. **Kenepaske,** Linda '83 L Kenepaska PLLC -261 5th Av -NY 10016 **Fx:**889-5697
(212) 840-0080 .. **Kenerson,** Martha L '80 (Bierce & K,PC) -420 Lex Av -NY 10170
(516) 357-3000 .. **Kenigsberg,** Jay D '88 (Rivkin R LLP) -926 RXR Plz -Uniondale 11556
(212) 521-5400 .. **Kenin,** Christa A '06 %Reed S LLP -599 Lex Av -NY 10022
(518) 464-0640 .. **Keniry,** Laurie S '98 OfCnsl Devine M&S LLP -52 Corp Cir -Albany 12203
(518) 465-9500 .. **Keniry,** Wm H '55 OfCnsl Tabner R&K,LLP -18 Corp Wds Blvd -Albany 12211
(518) 465-9500 .. **Keniry,** Wm J '90 (Tabner R&K,LLP) -18 Corp Wds Blvd -Albany 12211
(212) 513-3200 .. **Kenlon,** Jennivere L '07 %Holland & K LLP -31 W 52nd -NY 10019
(315) 443-4582 .. **Kenn,** Deborah S '81 %Syracuse Univ Cllg of Law -Wht Hall -Syracuse 13244 **Fx:**443-4213
(212) 804-4200 .. **Kenna,** David W '97 (Mound CW&G) -One Bttry Pk Plz -NY 10004
(646) 386-3500 .. **Kenna,** Francis K '91 OCA -25 Beaver -NY 10004
(518) 783-2600 .. **Kenna,** Timothy M '00 Zappone & Per -6 Century Hill Dr -Latham 12110 **Fx:**783-2607
(212) 768-6700 .. **Kenneally,** Brian P '07 Sonnenschein N&R LLP -1221 Av of Amer -NY 10020
(518) 813-9775 .. **Kenneally,** Colin J '78 -16 Miracle Ln -Albany 12211
(212) 613-5000 .. **Kenneally,** Kevin Martin '01 Leg Assist Grp -450 W 33rd -NY 10001 **Fx:**750-0820
(518) 465-7933 .. **Kenneally,** Michl E '04 Assn of Towns of NYS -150 State -Albany 12207
(518) 792-6516 .. **Kenneally & Tarantino** -470 Glen Bx379 -Glens Fls 12801 **Fx:**798-8358
(518) 379-1282 .. **Kenneally,** Wm J '77 %Golub Corp -501 Duanesburg Rd Bx1074 -Schnctdy 12306 **Fx:**379-3536
(212) 770-5618 .. **Kennedy,** Andrew J '84 %AIG -70 Pine -NY 10270 **Fx:**571-6432
(212) 407-4000 .. **Kennedy,** Anne E '07 %Loeb & L,LLP -345 Park Av -NY 10154
(716) 856-9090 .. **Kennedy,** Beatrice D '42 (Kennedy S&M) -1100 Lbrty Bldg -Buffalo 14202
(516) 794-6500 .. **Kennedy,** Bernard P '83 (Kennedy & G) -1050 Franklin Av -Gdn Cty 11530 **Fx:**794-5171
(718) 722-6399 .. **Kennedy,** Brian E '94 %Applt Div 2nd Dept -45 Monroe Pl -Brklyn 11201 **Fx:**858-2446
(212) 687-0099 .. **Kennedy,** Brian O '93 -909 3rd Av -NY 10022
(516) 221-4502 .. **Kennedy,** Brian R '95 -3644 Demott Av -Wantagh 11793
(631) 691-0100 .. **Kennedy,** Bruce '73 (B Kennedy,PC) -31 Greene Av -Amityvll 11701 **Fx:**691-1029
(212) 509-3456 .. **Kennedy,** Christine P '09 %McGivney & K,PC -80 Broad -NY 10004
(212) 859-8000 .. **Kennedy,** Coleman W '08 %Fried FHS&J LLP -1 NY Plz -NY 10004
(631) 271-6363 .. **Kennedy,** Colleen M '89 %Cannon & A,LLP -1923 NY Av -Huntngtn Sta 11746 **Fx:**271-7128
(212) 637-2733 .. **Kennedy,** David J '98 %US Atty -86 Chmbrs -NY 10007
(516) 741-2121 .. **Kennedy,** Denis J '92 %N Kanzer -1325 Franklin Av -Gdn Cty 11530 **Fx:**741-3930
(212) 732-3200 .. **Kennedy,** Donald J '73 (Carter L&M LLP) -2 Wall -NY 10005
(212) 430-0800 .. **Kennedy,** Donald M '60 SpclCnsl Kennedy LS&E -75 Maiden Ln -NY 10038
(516) 248-1188 .. **Kennedy,** Dwight A '03 %Carrieri & C,PC -200 Old Cntry Rd -Mineola 11501 **Fx:**248-1794
(212) 326-3939 .. **Kennedy,** Edw T '94 (Jones D) -222 E 41st -NY 10017
(212) 291-3134 .. **Kennedy,** Eileen E '88 %Citigroup -125 Broad -NY 10004
(212) 479-6724 .. **Kennedy,** Elizabeth F '04 Macht SA&I LLP -1114 Av of Amer -NY 10036 **Fx:**202-6417
(212) 506-1700 .. **Kennedy,** Garret D '10 Kasowitz BT&F LLP -1633 Bway -NY 10019
(718) 487-1300 .. **Kennedy,** Geraldine A '85 %Leg Srvcs Corp A -80 Jamaica Av -Brklyn 11207 **Fx:**342-1780
(212) 251-9443 .. **Kennedy,** Glen P '95 Structure Tone Inc -770 Bway -NY 10003
(212) 728-8000 .. **Kennedy,** Henry J '87 Willkie F&G LLP -787 7th Av -NY 10019
(212) 421-2233 .. **Kennedy,** James C '86 (Wilk A LLP) -675 3rd Av -NY 10017
(518) 457-4951 .. **Kennedy,** James L '73 Dept Correctional Srvcs -1220 Wshngtn Av -Albany 12226 **Fx:**457-7555
(716) 843-5700 .. **Kennedy,** James P Jr. '89 %US Atty -138 Delaware Av -Buffalo 14202 **Fx:**551-3052
(212) 248-2220 .. **Kennedy,** James W '85 (Kennedy JG LLC) -99 Wall -NY 10005 **Fx:**248-0170
(631) 853-4104 .. **Kennedy,** Jennifer R '10 %DA -400 Carleton Av Bx9082 -Central Islip 11722 **Fx:**853-7838
(212) 358-1500 .. **Kennedy Jennik & Murray, PC** -113 Univ Pl -NY 10003 **Fx:**358-0207
(212) 259-8000 .. **Kennedy,** John B '86 (Dewey & L LLP) -1301 Av of Amer -NY 10019
(212) 373-3000 .. **Kennedy,** John C Jr. '89 (Paul WRW&G LLP) -1285 Av of Amer -NY 10019
(914) 734-7056 .. **Kennedy,** John E '92 -400 Nelson Av -Peekskill 10566 **Fx:**470-2350
(516) 573-7215 .. **Kennedy,** John G '94 %Cnty Police -1490 Franklin Av -Mineola 11501 **Fx:**573-7926
(607) 256-1000 .. **Kennedy,** John I '54 (Kennedy & K) -28 Dove Dr -Ithaca 14850
(845) 702-3819 .. **Kennedy,** John M '65 -2 Mansion Dr -Hyde Pk 12538
(631) 724-2689 .. **Kennedy,** John M Jr. '95 -15 Addie Ln -Nesconset 11767
(212) 715-9100 .. **Kennedy,** Karen Steinberg '91 %Kramer LN&F,LLP -1177 Av of Amer -NY 10036
(518) 537-3054 .. **Kennedy,** Kathleen A '92 -2709 Route 9 -Hudson 12534
(914) 995-3419 .. **Kennedy,** Kevin '84 %DA -111 Martin Luther King Blvd -White Plns 10601 **Fx:**995-3363
(845) 294-9771 .. **Kennedy,** Lawr X '69 -26 Scotchtown Av Bx857 -Goshen 10924
(631) 265-9191 .. **Kennedy,** Lillian M '88 Epstein & G -1393 Vets Mem'l Hwy -Hauppauge 11788
(212) 430-0800 .. **Kennedy Lillis Schmidt & English** -75 Maiden Ln -NY 10038 **Fx:**430-0810
(516) 326-2976 .. **Kennedy,** Louis L '84 -1542 Rosser Av -Elmont 11003
(914) 642-4705 .. **Kennedy,** Louise Leduc '01 IBM -1133 Wstchstr Av -White Plns 10604
(518) 463-1311 .. **Kennedy,** Madeleine M '85 (Scheiberling R&M) -100 State -Albany 12207
(914) 843-4552 .. **Kennedy & Madonna LLP** -78 N Bway -White Plns 10603 **Fx:**422-4437
(914) 224-3409 .. **Kennedy,** Margaret A '03 Supreme Ct -111 Dr MLK Jr Blvd -White Plns 10601
(845) 561-0550 .. **Kennedy,** Marianna R '92 (Drake LHKGG&R PLLC) -555 Hudson Valley Av -New Windsor 12553
(718) 625-8940 .. **Kennedy,** Marilyn Pringle '88 %B Lawrence -15 Metrotech Ctr N -Brklyn 11201 **Fx:**624-5756
(914) 946-0600 .. **Kennedy,** Matthew D '03 OfCnsl Pino & Assoc -50 Main -White Plns 10606 **Fx:**946-0650
(212) 935-4500 .. **Kennedy,** Michl '76 -419 Park Av S -NY 10016 **Fx:**980-6881
(631) 435-0781 .. **Kennedy,** Michl C '82 (Borda KA&G,LLP) -1805 5th Av -Bay Shr 11706
(516) 538-2400 .. **Kennedy,** Michl F '90 (Lawrence and W,PC) -215 Hilton Av Bx1200 -Hempstd 11551
(212) 397-8199 .. **Kennedy,** Michl W '89 -315 Bway -NY 10007 **Fx:**267-9589
(212) 732-0002 .. **Kennedy,** Mina '03 %Cohen F&R,LLP -20 Vesey -NY 10007
(212) 504-6000 .. **Kennedy,** Nicholas W '10 %Cadwalader W&T LLP -1 World Fncl Ctr -NY 10281
(914) 694-3999 .. **Kennedy,** Paul L '74 %1870 Corp -2 Manhattanvll Rd -Purchase 10577
(718) 590-2000 .. **Kennedy,** Peter O '07 DA -198 E 161st -Bronx 10451 **Fx:**590-6477
(518) 783-2704 .. **Kennedy,** Rebekah R '08 Colonie Town Atty -Mem'l Town Hall Bx508 -Newtonville 12128 **Fx:**786-7324
(716) 856-4000 .. **Kennedy,** Rick W '83 (Hodgson R LLP) -140 Pearl -Buffalo 14202
(914) 843-4552 .. **Kennedy,** Robt F Jr. '85 (Kennedy & M LLP) -78 N Bway -White Plns 10603
(212) 326-3939 .. **Kennedy,** Robt F '94 (Jones D) -222 E 41st -NY 10017
(518) 463-3200 .. **Kennedy,** Ronald F '85 %NYS Bar Assn -1 Elk -Albany 12207 **Fx:**487-5544
(607) 256-1000 .. **Kennedy,** Sean A '97 (Kennedy & K) -28 Dove Dr -Ithaca 14850
(718) 858-3791 .. **Kennedy,** Sharon Callahan '80 -66 S Elliot Pl -Brklyn 11217
(917) 442-4181 .. **Kennedy,** Stephen G '87 -305 Bway -NY 10007
(212) 710-3900 .. **Kennedy,** Stephen M '96 (Clyde & Co US LLP) -405 Lex Av -NY 10174 **Fx:**710-3950
(716) 856-9090 .. **Kennedy Stoeckl & Martin** -1100 Lbrty Bldg -Buffalo 14202
(212) 450-4000 .. **Kennedy,** Susan D '84 Cnsl Davis P&W LLP -450 Lex Av -NY 10017
(212) 820-9428 .. **Kennedy,** Susan V '05 %Hawkins D&W LLP -One Chase Manh Plz -NY 10005
(212) 657-2885 .. **Kennedy,** Thos G '00 Citigroup Global -111 Wall -NY 10005
(212) 735-3000 .. **Kennedy,** Thos H Jr. '82 (Skadden ASM&F LLP) -4 Times Sq -NY 10036
(212) 682-1818 .. **Kennedy,** Thos J '96 %Murray F&S LLP -275 Mad Av -NY 10016
(315) 218-8000 .. **Kennedy,** Thos L '06 %Bond S&K,PLLC -1 Lincoln Ctr -Syracuse 13202
(212) 358-1500 .. **Kennedy,** Thos M '75 (Kennedy J&M,PC) -113 Univ Pl -NY 10003
(914) 997-7208 .. **Kennedy,** Thos V '82 -30 Hawthorne -White Plns 10603
(212) 653-8700 .. **Kennedy,** Tracey A '06 (Sheppard MR&H LLP) -30 Rckfllr Plz -NY 10112
(646) 708-8088 .. **Kennedy,** Victoria '02 Fidelity Natl Law Grp -350 5th Av -NY 10118 **Fx:**(212) 594-8378
(716) 852-4100 .. **Kennedy,** Wm K '94 %D Coppola -37 Franklin -Buffalo 14202 **Fx:**852-0002
(212) 940-3744 .. **Kennedy,** Wm P '81 Cnsl Nixon P LLP -437 Mad Av -NY 10022
(212) 225-2000 .. **Kennedy Park,** Jennifer '04 %Cleary GS&H -1 Lbrty Plz -NY 10006
(716) 773-5461 .. **Kennedy-Rogoza,** Deborah '88 Pritchard & K -1990 Whitehaven Rd Bx40 -Grand Isl 14072 **Fx:**773-9373
(607) 273-4044 .. **Kennedy-Smith,** Maura A '99 (Shapiro & K-S) -120 W State -Ithaca 14850 **Fx:**697-0113
(212) 839-5300 .. **Kennell,** Patrick E III '08 %Sidley A LLP -787 7th Av -NY 10019
(212) 485-9600 .. **Kennell,** Patrick M '03 (Kaufman DV&G,LLP) -100 William -NY 10038
(212) 530-3900 .. **Kennelly,** Beth A '93 %Hannum FP&M, LLC -55 Bway -NY 10006
(212) 269-1696 .. **Kennelly,** Donald P '79 Kennelly Dvlpmnt -304 E 52nd -NY 10022
(212) 770-1862 .. **Kennelly,** Edw J '87 %AIG -70 Pine -NY 10270
(212) 932-1172 .. **Kennelty,** Timothy J '84 -40 W 88th -NY 10024
(212) 338-9699 .. **Kenner,** Lynn E '68 -420 Lex Av -NY 10170
(212) 403-1000 .. **Kenner,** Morgan U '09 %Wachtell LR&K -51 W 52nd -NY 10019
(516) 248-2002 .. **Kenney,** Brian R '10 %Gallagher WB&P -98 Willis Av -Mineola 11501
(516) 741-3900 .. **Kenney,** Gemma '01 %M Angel,PLLC -170 Old Cntry Rd -Mineola 11501 **Fx:**741-3383
(631) 265-1700 .. **Kenney Goidel Wrenn & Schmid,LLP** -50 Route 111 -Smithtwn 11787 **Fx:**863-3018
(212) 689-8808 .. **Kenney,** John J '70 (Hoguet NR&K,LLP) -10 E 40th -NY 10016
(631) 265-1700 .. **Kenney,** Lawr M '67 (Kenney GW&S,LLP) -50 Route 111 -Smithtwn 11787
(212) 688-8555 .. **Kenney,** Mary M '08 %Fragomen DB&L LLP -7 Hanover Sq -NY 10004
(716) 853-3801 .. **Kenney,** Patrick S '85 (Kenney SL&N,LLP) -14 Lafayette Sq -Buffalo 14203
(212) 877-4039 .. **Kenney,** Paul R '00 -155 W 72nd -NY 10023 **Fx:**877-3779
(212) 944-0500 .. **Kenney,** Robt J Jr. '91 OfCnsl Hofheimer G&G,LLP -530 5th Av -NY 10036
(518) 402-3490 .. **Kenney,** Sara O'Connor '07 %State Comptroller -110 State -Albany 12236 **Fx:**473-9104
(212) 536-3900 .. **Kenney,** Sarah Peck '06 %K&L Gates LLP -599 Lex Av -NY 10022

(716) 853-3801 .. **Kenney Shelton Liptak & Nowak,LLP** -14 Lafayette Sq -Buffalo 14203 **Fx:**853-0265
(518) 274-5221 .. **Kenney,** Thos V Jr. '72 -65 2nd -Troy 12180 **Fx:**274-5222
(212) 310-4431 .. **Kenniff,** Alice M '00 Instinet -3 Times Sq -NY 10036
(718) 838-7878 .. **Kenniff,** James F '96 Bronx Defenders -860 Crtlandt Av -Bronx 10451 **Fx:**665-0100
(516) 742-7600 .. **Kenniff,** Thos A '01 (Raiser & K,PC) -1517 Franklin Av -Mineola 11501
(212) 809-2700 .. **Kenny,** Alfreida B '76 -11 Park Pl -NY 10007
(212) 752-5258 .. **Kenny,** Alison L '09 %Schwartz SE&C LLC -845 3rd Av -NY 10022
(631) 852-2370 .. **Kenny,** Barbara J '75 %Hon L Gerard -235 Griffing Av -Rvrhead 11901
(914) 631-2979 .. **Kenny,** Bernadette '84 -48 Wilson Park Dr -Tarrytwn 10591 **Fx:**332-4735
(212) 947-6147 .. **Kenny,** Cathy A '82 %NYS Petroleum Cncl -1250 Bway -NY 10001 **Fx:**947-6192
(315) 474-7541 .. **Kenny,** Celia E '07 %Menter R&T,PC -308 Maltbie -Syracuse 13204
(212) 382-0909 .. **Kenny,** Chas F '80 (Peckar & A,PC) -41 Mad Av -NY 10154
(845) 566-4400 .. **Kenny,** Dennis '91 (D Kenny,PC) -288 N Plnk Rd -Newburgh 12550
(914) 949-8883 .. **Kenny,** Dennis J '62 -39 Club Pnte Dr -White Plns 10605 **Fx:**949-8883
(212) 264-0480 .. **Kenny,** Edw F III '91 US DOJ -26 Fed Plz -NY 10278 **Fx:**264-1916
(914) 828-8079 .. **Kenny,** Elissa B '88 %Swiss Re Life & Hlth Amer Inc -175 King -Armonk 10504
(607) 674-7065 .. **Kenny,** Elizabeth A '04 NY Cntrl Mutual Fire Ins -16 Chapel -Sherburne 13460
(212) 262-2390 .. **Kenny,** George J '83 (Connell F LLP) -888 7th Av -NY 10106
(212) 762-5137 .. **Kenny,** Heather W '97 Morgan Stanley -1221 Av of Amer -NY 10020
(212) 309-6000 .. **Kenny,** Howard A '85 (Morgan L&B LLP) -101 Park Av -NY 10178
(212) 422-6111 .. **Kenny,** James M '66 (Kenny S&Z) -26 Bway -NY 10004
(518) 474-6740 .. **Kenny,** John E '96 %Dept of State -41 State -Albany 12231 **Fx:**473-9211
(212) 425-7200 .. **Kenny,** John R '92 (Kenyon & K,LLP) -1 Bway -NY 10004
(315) 471-0524 .. **Kenny,** John S '56 %Kenny & K PLLC -W 315 Fayette -Syracuse 13202 **Fx:**471-4238
(718) 855-6062 .. **Kenny,** Jos G '81 -142 Joralemon -Brklyn 11201 **Fx:**855-6065
(212) 701-3000 .. **Kenny,** Kendra M '96 %Cahill G&R LLP -80 Pine -NY 10005 **Fx:**269-5420
(212) 449-1000 .. **Kenny,** Keric J '03 Merril Lynch -250 Vesey -NY 10080
(866) 348-5819 .. **Kenny,** Mary J '93 %SSA-ODAR -50 Fountain Plz -Buffalo 14202 **Fx:**(716) 551-4078
(718) 248-9093 .. **Kenny,** Michl A '78 %Citibank -1 Court Sq -LIC 11101
(315) 471-0524 .. **Kenny,** Michl P '88 (Kenny & K PLLC) -W 315 Fayette -Syracuse 13202 **Fx:**471-4238
(518) 965-7990 .. **Kenny,** Monica M '06 -Bx358 -Cairo 12413 **Fx:**943-5611
(516) 328-5124 .. **Kenny,** Pamela M '89 Canon USA -1 Canon Plz -Lk Success 11042
(212) 513-7788 .. **Kenny,** Patrick J '77 (Ahmuty D&M) -123 William -NY 10038
(347) 401-9593 .. **Kenny,** Paul J '87 Appellate Term-2nd Dept -141 Lvngstn -Brklyn 11201
(212) 421-0300 .. **Kenny,** Richd M '91 -777 3rd Av -NY 10017
(212) 422-6111 .. **Kenny Stearns & Zonghetti** -26 Bway -NY 10004 **Fx:**422-6544
(845) 627-0884 .. **Kenny,** Teresa M '91 -334 S Mddltwn Rd -Nanuet 10954 **Fx:**623-6977
(516) 629-3636 .. **Kenowitz,** Gail '81 -600 Old Cntry Rd -Gdn Cty 11530 **Fx:**222-0088
(914) 666-7393 .. **Kensing,** Henry V '60 -15 Moore Av -Mt Kisco 10549 **Fx:**241-0181
(212) 278-1814 .. **Kensington,** Costa N '73 (Anderson K&O,PC) -1251 Av of Amer -NY 10020
(212) 973-0572 .. **Kent,** Andrew S '93 Cnsl Wolff & S PC -140 Bway -NY 10005
(212) 709-3503 .. **Kent,** Barbara '75 %Banking Dept -1 State -NY 10004 **Fx:**709-1655
(212) 421-4300 .. **Kent Beatty & Gordon, LLP** -425 Park Av -NY 10022 **Fx:**421-4303
(518) 432-3612 .. **Kent,** Carolyn V '86 -3 Loudon Heights S -Loudonvll 12211 **Fx:**432-3612
(631) 727-3417 .. **Kent,** Christopher E '88 -130 Ostrander Av -Rvrhead 11901 **Fx:**727-7005
(212) 554-1234 .. **Kent,** Doris Cirignano '91 %AXA Financial Inc -1290 Av of Amer -NY 10104 **Fx:**707-3963
(212) 790-4500 .. **Kent,** Felix H '50 Cnsl Manatt P&P,LLP -7 Times Sq -NY 10036
(914) 948-4700 .. **Kent Hazzard Wilson Conroy Verni & Freeman, LLP** -111 Church -White Plns 10601 **Fx:**948-4721
(212) 636-6000 .. **Kent,** J Andrew '00 %Fordham Univ Sch of Law -140 W 62nd -NY 10023 **Fx:**636-6899
(716) 849-3500 .. **Kent,** Kristin H '76 (Hagelin & K LLC) -135 Delaware Av -Buffalo 14202 **Fx:**849-3501
(212) 421-4300 .. **Kent,** Michl B '77 (Kent B&G,LLP) -425 Park Av -NY 10022
(212) 836-8000 .. **Kent,** Regina O '04 %Kaye S LLP -425 Park Av -NY 10022
(518) 485-2312 .. **Kent,** Robt A '88 OASAS -1450 Wstrn Av -Albany 12203 **Fx:**485-2335
(212) 490-3000 .. **Kent,** Steven '79 (Wilson EME&D LLP) -150 E 42nd -NY 10017
(212) 318-6000 .. **Kent,** Thos L '93 (Paul HJ&W LLP) -75 E 55th -NY 10022
(212) 310-8000 .. **Kenter,** Doron P '10 %Weil G&M LLP -767 5th Av -NY 10153
(212) 704-6000 .. **Kenter,** Jonathan A '87 (Troutman S LLP) -405 Lex Av -NY 10174
(212) 312-9689 .. **Kent-Friedman,** Alison '89 %State Ins Fund -199 Church -NY 10007 **Fx:**385-9199
(914) 766-2090 .. **Kentros,** Arthur G '82 IBM -294 Route 100 -Somers 10589
(212) 575-8333 .. **Kenworthey,** Tamara '06 %Wincig & W -137 5th Av -NY 10010 **Fx:**575-8525
(212) 436-3750 .. **Kenworthy,** James H '80 Deloitte & Touche,LLP -2 World Fncl Ctr -NY 10281
(518) 587-0316 .. **Kenyon,** Briana Vaughn '07 Herkenham & D,PC -18 Division -Saratoga Spgs 12866 **Fx:**583-2936
(914) 833-3090 .. **Kenyon,** Debra M '83 -1865 Palmer Av -Larchmnt 10538 **Fx:**833-3092
(585) 394-2068 .. **Kenyon,** Edw C '94 %Kenyon & K -11 North -Canandaigua 14424 **Fx:**394-5227
(212) 425-7200 .. **Kenyon & Kenyon, LLP** -1 Bway -NY 10004 **Fx:**425-5288
(607) 741-3929 .. **Kenyon,** Mark A '89 %State Ins Fund -2001 Perimeter Rd E -Endicott 13760 **Fx:**741-5029
(212) 297-0050 .. **Kenyon,** Todd P '84 (Betancourt VHG&K LLC) -46 Trinity Pl -NY 10006
(585) 394-2068 .. **Kenyon,** Wm R '67 (Kenyon & K) -11 North -Canandaigua 14424 **Fx:**394-5227
(914) 993-0600 .. **Keogh,** Anthony J '84 (Keogh T&M) -1 N Bway -White Plns 10601 **Fx:**993-0251
(212) 818-0600 .. **Keogh,** Dorothy M '87 (Keogh C,PC) -521 5th Av -NY 10175 **Fx:**818-0180
(212) 389-7700 .. **Keogh,** Eugene L '74 %Coty Inc -1 Park Av -NY 10016
(212) 967-2224 .. **Keogh,** Gerard L '83 -350 5th Av -NY 10118
(212) 819-8200 .. **Keogh,** Kevin '69 (White & C LLP) -1155 Av of Amer -NY 10036
(212) 815-1550 .. **Keogh,** Michl P '90 %DC 37 - Political Action -125 Barclay -NY 10007
(516) 656-3100 .. **Keogh,** Terri Austin '93 %Austin Intl Realty -95 Forest Av -Locust Vly 11560
(212) 506-5000 .. **Keohane,** John J '75 (Orrick H&S LLP) -51 W 52nd -NY 10019
(212) 227-3550 .. **Keough,** John R III '81 (Waesche S&O,PC) -111 Bway -NY 10006
(212) 318-6000 .. **Keough,** Owen M '10 %Paul HJ&W LLP -75 E 55th -NY 10022
(516) 806-4967 .. **Kepanis,** Douglas S '03 (Kepanis Law Firm,PC) -626 RXR Plz -Uniondale 11556 **Fx:**(866) 314-1386
(516) 742-9090 .. **Kephart,** Wm J '96 (Terino K&F) -Bx1185 -Syosset 11791
(212) 245-2700 .. **Kepke,** Matthew A '02 Argyle Scrty,Inc -40 W 37th -NY 10018
(585) 454-0700 .. **Kepner,** Adrienne L '09 %Ward GH&R LLP -300 State -Rchstr 14614
(585) 423-9215 .. **Kepner,** Kevin R '87 %Xerox -100 Clinton Av S -Rchstr 14644
(212) 538-4500 .. **Kepple,** Douglas J '91 CSFB -11 Mad Av -NY 10010
(212) 806-5400 .. **Keppler,** Abbey L '90 SpclCnsl Stroock &S&L LLP -180 Maiden Ln -NY 10038
(212) 681-1600 .. **Kera,** Martin S '72 (Kera & G) -240 Mad Av -NY 10016 **Fx:**681-1601
(212) 558-4000 .. **Keranen,** Kristin L '08 %Sullivan & C LLP -125 Broad -NY 10004
(718) 575-8282 .. **Kerben,** Lawr S '79 -12526 Qns Blvd -Kew Gdns 11415
(631) 912-9542 .. **Kerber,** Kim E '98 -248 Larkfld Rd -E Northprt 11731
(212) 428-2150 .. **Kerby,** Shawn '93 %OCA -25 Beaver -NY 10004 **Fx:**428-2155
(212) 849-7000 .. **Kercher,** Christopher D '05 %Quinn EU&S,LLP -51 Mad Av -NY 10010
(845) 565-0070 .. **Kerchman,** Marc C '82 -1200 Stony Brook Ct -Newburgh 12550 **Fx:**565-0097
(212) 504-6000 .. **Kerdman,** Alexander '08 %Cadwalader W&T LLP -1 World Fncl Ctr -NY 10281
(212) 872-1000 .. **Kerdock,** Anastasia M '10 -One Bryant Park -NY 10036 **Fx:**872-1002
(212) 698-3500 .. **Kerfoot,** Matthew K '00 Cnsl Dechert LLP -1095 Av of Amer -NY 10036
(212) 803-5100 .. **Kerins,** John E '88 %NY Cnty Defender Srvcs -225 Bway -NY 10007 **Fx:**571-6035
(516) 538-1111 .. **Kerins,** Richd T '87 (Mahon MK&O,LLC) -254 Nassau Blvd -Garden City South 11530
(516) 304-5725 .. **Kerker,** Howard J '75 (H Kerker,PC) -25 Kensngtn Cir -Manhsst 11030 **Fx:**304-5726
(845) 634-6014 .. **Kerker,** Lawr L '54 -4 Lisa Ct -New Cty 10956 **Fx:**634-6014
(212) 613-1427 .. **Kerker,** Mindy S '92 %HIAS -333 7th Av -NY 10001 **Fx:**967-4356
(917) 439-9920 .. **Kerker,** Susan J '87 -350 5th Av -NY 10118 **Fx:**(212) 594-2944
(212) 895-7943 .. **Kerker,** Susan Wynne '91 Weizmann Inst of Science -633 3rd Av -NY 10017 **Fx:**895-7978
(518) 456-4300 .. **Kerker,** Valerie '84 (Kerker & G PC) -286 Wshngtn Av Ext -Albany 12203 **Fx:**456-5700
(516) 409-6200 .. **Kerley,** Brian P '83 (Furey KWM&C,PC) -2174 Jackson Av -Seafrd 11783
(315) 473-9648 .. **Kerling,** Bridget P '09 %McGivney & K,PC -110 W Fayette -Syracuse 13202
(212) 689-6700 .. **Kerman,** Jeffrey A '06 SrCnsl Wealth Ptrnrs,LLC -286 Mad Av -NY 10017 **Fx:**689-7010
(716) 834-9181 .. **Kerman,** Larry '81 (Blair & R,LLP) -2645 Sheridan Dr -Tonawanda 14150
(212) 230-1300 .. **Kerman,** Thea J '75 %Beigelman F&F,PC -100 Wall -NY 10005 **Fx:**230-1090
(212) 335-9000 .. **Kermani,** Leila M '98 %DA -1 Hogan Pl -NY 10013
(646) 315-7353 .. **Kerman-Mastour,** Tahra N '01 %FINRA -14 Wall -NY 10005 **Fx:**315-7440
(631) 844-7276 .. **Kern,** Amy L '01 Adecco -175 Broadhllw Rd -Melvll 11747
(516) 294-5432 .. **Kern Augustine Conroy & Schoppmann,PC** -1325 Franklin Av -Gdn Cty 11530 **Fx:**294-5414
(212) 697-3122 .. **Kern,** Brace E '06 %Martin C&B LLP -220 E 42nd -NY 10017
(212) 693-1330 .. **Kern,** Chet W '81 (Katz & K LLP) -61 Bway -NY 10006
(212) 710-9468 .. **Kern,** Cynthia R '00 SrCnsl TitleVest Agency,Inc -44 Wall -NY 10005 **Fx:**757-0466
(716) 845-8682 .. **Kern,** Emily A '86 %Dept of Law -Roswell Pk Cancer Inst -Buffalo 14263 **Fx:**845-8792
(212) 558-4000 .. **Kern,** George C Jr. '53 SrCnsl Sullivan & C LLP -125 Broad -NY 10004
(212) 858-4000 .. **Kern,** Jeffrey T '88 FINRA -1 Lbrty Plz -NY 10006 **Fx:**858-4389
(516) 578-5581 .. **Kern,** Jos F Jr. '07 Carroll St Capital LLC -142 Wellngtn Rd -Mineola 11501
(212) 909-6000 .. **Kern,** Katherine Webber '10 %Debevoise & P LLP -919 3rd Av -NY 10022
(212) 335-9000 .. **Kern,** Kenn '05 %DA -1 Hogan Pl -NY 10013
(631) 390-5000 .. **Kern,** Kenneth M '06 %Genser DG&C,LLP -445 Broad Hollow Rd -Melvll 11747
(973) 228-5700 .. **Kern,** Lindsay P '05 %Brach E LLC -100 Park Av -NY 10017 **Fx:**228-7852
(212) 576-9842 .. **Kern,** Martin L '80 %AHPIA -1250 Bway -NY 10001
(516) 802-0630 .. **Kern,** Michl D '99 %Simmons J,LLP -115 Eileen Way -Syosset 11791
(212) 228-6398 .. **Kern,** Richd A '94 -50 E 8th -NY 10003
(212) 554-7800 .. **Kern,** Robt C '94 (Moses & S LLP) -405 Lex Av -NY 10174
(212) 674-1222 .. **Kern,** Robt P '63 -36 E 20th -NY 10003 **Fx:**387-0382
(914) 592-5740 .. **Kern,** Steven H '88 %Barnes I&S,LLP -258 Saw Mill Rvr Rd -Elmsfrd 10523
(212) 270-8474 .. **Kern,** Steven T '96 JP Morgan Chase -270 Park Av -NY 10017
(716) 847-8400 .. **Kernan,** David H '78 (Phillips L LLP) -3400 HSBC Ctr -Buffalo 14203

(212) 966-6420 .. **Kernan,** Emily R '08 Lwyrs For Children -110 Lafayette -NY 10013 **Fx:**966-0531
(315) 797-8300 .. **Kernan,** James S Jr. '40 OfCnsl Kernan and K,PC -258 Genesee -Utica 13502 **Fx:**797-6467
(315) 946-7472 .. **Kernan,** James S III '81 %Pub Def -26 Church -Lyons 14489 **Fx:**946-7478
(585) 546-6448 .. **Kernan,** Leslie W Jr. '81 (Davidson F LLP) -28 E Main -Rchstr 14614 **Fx:**760-7261
(315) 736-0816 .. **Kernan,** Martin J '03 (Kernan Prof Grp,LLP) -1310 Utica Bx750 -Oriskany 13424 **Fx:**736-8731
(518) 432-8000 .. **Kernan,** Thos M '04 %Crane & P -48 Howard -Albany 12207
(212) 675-4030 .. **Kerner,** Chas A '79 -322 8th Av -NY 10001
(212) 830-6655 .. **Kerner,** Gerald '76 %Duquesne Capital Mgmt,LLC -40 W 57th -NY 10019
(212) 813-8800 .. **Kerner,** Glenn S '88 (Goodwin P LLP) -620 8th Av -NY 10018
(212) 389-5000 .. **Kerner,** Jessica L '09 %Sutherland A&B LLP -1114 Av of Amer -NY 10036
(212) 964-1098 .. **Kerner,** Kenneth T '89 Cnsl Kerner & K -74 Trinity Pl -NY 10006 **Fx:**385-9072
(914) 754-5956 .. **Kerner,** Marty-Ann '78 -207 Uppr Shad Rd -Pound Rdg 10576
(212) 964-1098 .. **Kerner,** Richd A '58 (Kerner & K) -74 Trinity Pl -NY 10006 **Fx:**385-9072
(516) 249-1342 .. **Kerner,** Sherman B '81 %Grey & G,LLP -360 Main -Farmngdl 11735
(718) 796-6454 .. **Kerner,** Stuart M '91 (S Kerner,PC) -269 W 231st -Bronx 10463 **Fx:**796-4412
(518) 457-2153 .. **Kerner,** Todd M '89 %Dept of Tax & Fin -Bldg 9 State Campus -Albany 12227 **Fx:**457-6131
(212) 701-3000 .. **Kerner,** Zachary A '10 %Cahill G&R LLP -80 Pine -NY 10005 **Fx:**269-5420
(212) 908-0500 .. **Kernis,** Lainie L '99 Fitch,Inc -1 State Street Plz -NY 10004 **Fx:**968-8839
(212) 576-5904 .. **Kernkamp,** Anke N '04 NY Life Ins Co -51 Mad Av -NY 10010
(516) 873-5300 .. **Kerno,** Raymond E '73 R Kerno -1527 Franklin Av -Mineola 11501 **Fx:**873-6008
(646) 386-3623 .. **Kern-Rappy,** Michele E '89 %Supreme Ct-Law Dept -60 Centre -NY 10007
(212) 354-4901 .. **Kerr,** Brian C '97 (Browne WG LLP) -49 W 37th -NY 10018 **Fx:**354-4904
(212) 837-6000 .. **Kerr,** Carla A '87 (Hughes H&R LLP) -1 Bttry Pk Plz -NY 10004
(518) 591-4634 .. **Kerr,** Carolyn Betz '04 United Hlth Grp -90 State -Albany 12207
(212) 468-8043 .. **Kerr,** Chas L '84 (Morrison & F LLP) -1290 Av of Amer -NY 10104
(716) 856-7091 .. **Kerr,** Christopher C '84 (J Freedman) -424 Main -Buffalo 14202 **Fx:**856-7097
(212) 450-4000 .. **Kerr,** Diane G '82 (Davis P&W LLP) -450 Lex Av -NY 10017
(212) 237-1000 .. **Kerr,** Gregory J '96 %Windels ML&M,LLP -156 W 56th -NY 10019
(315) 474-6055 .. **Kerr,** J Craig '72 (Nottingham Law Ofc) -One Lincoln Ctr -Syracuse 13202 **Fx:**474-6049
(518) 782-9500 .. **Kerr,** James D '95 (Kerr S PC) -12 Cornell Rd -Latham 12110 **Fx:**782-9700
(212) 450-4000 .. **Kerr,** James L '73 Cnsl Davis P&W LLP -450 Lex Av -NY 10017
(212) 345-8621 .. **Kerr,** Jason S '05 Cnsl Mercer HR Cnsltng -1166 Av of Amer -NY 10036
(212) 455-2000 .. **Kerr,** John J Jr. '77 (Simpson T&B LLP) -425 Lex Av -NY 10017
(315) 266-1159 .. **Kerr,** Kathleen Greey '07 US 2nd Dist Ct of Appeals -10 Broad -Utica 13501
(718) 590-6174 .. **Kerr,** Margaret A '89 %Law Dept -198 E 161st -Bronx 10451 **Fx:**590-2686
(631) 736-0500 .. **Kerr,** Patrick M '94 %Sallah Law Firm PC -110 Wshngtn Av -Holtsvll 11742 **Fx:**736-0179
(631) 852-2500 .. **Kerr,** Robt V '02 %DA -200 Center Dr -Rvrhead 11901 **Fx:**852-1769
(212) 577-3530 .. **Kerr,** Sarah '94 %Leg Aid -199 Water -NY 10038 **Fx:**425-2465
(631) 852-2500 .. **Kerr,** Shauna L '04 %DA -200 Center Dr -Rvrhead 11901 **Fx:**852-1769
(212) 815-0856 .. **Kerr,** Susan M '98 NYS Supreme Ct -71 Thomas -NY 10013 **Fx:**815-0892
(631) 226-8071 .. **Kerr,** Timothy P '95 -495 N Broome Av -Lindenhrst 11757
(607) 272-1400 .. **Kerrigan,** James M '69 -1021 W Seneca -Ithaca 14850 **Fx:**273-1200
(914) 202-9905 .. **Kerrigan,** Robt M '75 -65 Pondfld Rd -Bronxvll 10708
(516) 688-1700 .. **Kerrigan,** Thos J '95 %IRS -1600 Stewart Av -Westbury 11590 **Fx:**688-1750
(212) 989-9100 .. **Kerrigan,** Thos P '78 (Finder NK LLP) -276 Park Av S -NY 10010
(845) 358-0074 .. **Kerrigan,** Wm K '75 (MacCartney MK&M) -13 N Bway Bx350 -Nyack 10960
(518) 462-5461 .. **Kerry,** Natasha '03 NYC Council -111 Wshngtn Av -Albany 12210
(516) 294-6666 .. **Kersch,** Carolyn D '05 %Samuelson H&S -300 Grdn City Plz -Gdn Cty 11530
(212) 345-3298 .. **Kerschner,** Barry J '80 Marsh USA -1166 Av of Amer -NY 10036 **Fx:**345-4808
(212) 848-4000 .. **Kerschner,** Seth '07 %Shearman & S LLP -599 Lex Av -NY 10022
(212) 318-6000 .. **Kersey,** Leslie E '10 %Paul HJ&W LLP -75 E 55th -NY 10022
(518) 285-8592 .. **Kersey,** Tara A '02 Hon G Connolly -112 State -Albany 12207
(212) 207-8181 .. **Kersh,** Alan L '86 Savoy Capital Advisors -445 Park Av -NY 10022
(212) 980-0120 .. **Kersh,** Candice Stein '90 (Frankfurt KK&S,PC) -488 Mad Av -NY 10022
(914) 332-0438 .. **Kershaw,** Anne E '87 (A Kershaw,PC) -303 S Bway -Tarrytwn 10591 **Fx:**(888) 231-3577
(212) 848-4000 .. **Kershaw,** Derek P '09 %Shearman & S LLP -599 Lex Av -NY 10022
(212) 449-4974 .. **Kershaw,** Michele Ann '93 %Merrill Lynch -220 Bway -NY 10038
(516) 798-2688 .. **Kershen,** Harry '91 -25 E Shore Dr -Massapequa 11758 **Fx:**797-7146
(518) 785-1900 .. **Kershko,** John F '89 %PEF -1168-70 Troy-Schnctdy Rd Bx12414 -Albany 12212 **Fx:**785-1323
(518) 388-4305 .. **Kershko,** Paulette M '92 Family Ct -620 State -Schnctdy 12305
(212) 733-0538 .. **Kershner,** David L '06 Pfizer Inc -150 E 42nd -NY 10017
(212) 808-7800 .. **Kersis,** Danielle C '08 %Kelley D&W LLP -101 Park Av -NY 10178
(212) 763-6800 .. **Kerson,** Edw W '77 Cnsl Vandenberg & F,LLP -60 E 42nd -NY 10165
(212) 973-9339 .. **Kerson,** Paul E '76 (Leavitt K&D) -228 E 45th -NY 10017
(718) 793-8822 .. **Kerson,** Paul E '76 (Leavitt K&D) -118-35 Qns Blvd -Frst Hlls 11375
(212) 351-4000 .. **Kerstein,** David J '00 %Gibson D&C LLP -200 Park Av -NY 10166
(212) 326-2000 .. **Kerstein,** Erica '02 Cnsl O'Melveny & M LLP -7 Times Sq -NY 10036
(212) 819-8200 .. **Kerstetter,** Michl '07 %White & C LLP -1155 Av of Amer -NY 10036
(516) 222-1860 .. **Kert,** Arnold L '73 A Kert PLLC -666 Old Cntry Rd -Gdn Cty 11530 **Fx:**222-1713
(917) 286-3300 .. **Kert,** Jeffrey W '99 Hudson Advisors LLC -888 7th Av -NY 10106
(212) 530-5000 .. **Kertesz,** Kevin M '07 %Milbank TH&M LLP -1 Chase Manh Plz -NY 10005
(212) 801-6771 .. **Kertzer,** Seth E '09 %Greenberg T,LLP -200 Park Av -NY 10166
(212) 766-9651 .. **Kertzner,** Michl J '05 Joy Construction Corp -40 Fulton -NY 10038 **Fx:**766-9654
(718) 742-6572 .. **Kerulo,** Keith D '01 NYC Dept of Ed -501 Courtlandt Av -Bronx 10451
(518) 474-3340 .. **Kerwin,** Adrienne J '99 %Dept of Law -The Cptl -Albany 12224
(518) 486-1295 .. **Kerwin,** Donna M '05 State Comptroller -110 State -Albany 12236 **Fx:**473-9104
(212) 336-2000 .. **Kerwin,** James L '07 %Patterson BW&T LLP -1133 Av of Amer -NY 10036
(518) 463-3200 .. **Kerwin,** Kevin M '04 %NYS Bar Assn -1 Elk -Albany 12207 **Fx:**487-5544
(315) 425-2700 .. **Kerwin,** Matthew T '01 %Hiscock & B,LLP -One Park Pl -Syracuse 13202
(315) 487-1728 .. **Kerwin,** Michl J '95 -4679 Watch Hill Rd -Manlius 13104
(518) 486-4645 .. **Kerwin,** Stephen M '83 %Dept of Law -The Cptl -Albany 12224 **Fx:**473-1572
(212) 574-1200 .. **Kerzhner,** Irina E '06 %Seward & K LLP -1 Bttry Pk Plz -NY 10004
(212) 859-3506 .. **Kerzner,** David S '93 -110 Wall -NY 10005 **Fx:**943-2300
(718) 366-0940 .. **Kerzner,** Paul '76 (Kerzner & H,LLC) -74-09 Myrtle Av -Glendale 11385 **Fx:**366-0922
(212) 412-9500 .. **Kesch,** Craig S '02 %Flemming ZWZ LLP -1 Lbrty Plz -NY 10006
(212) 574-1200 .. **Keshavarz,** Kamand '08 %Seward & K LLP -1 Bttry Pk Plz -NY 10004
(800) 496-0187 .. **Keshner,** Robt '72 -2027 Wllmsbrdg Rd -Bronx 10461 **Fx:**(718) 379-0106
(212) 450-4000 .. **Keshvargar,** Yasin '09 %Davis P&W LLP -450 Lex Av -NY 10017
(212) 635-6851 .. **Keskinyan,** Julian R '99 Bank of NY -1 Wall -NY 10005
(212) 930-9700 .. **Kesner,** Harvey J '90 (Sichenzia RFF LLP) -61 Bway -NY 10006
(631) 853-5212 .. **Kesner,** Stephen D '86 %Leg Aid -400 Carleton Av Bx9082 -Central Islip 11722 **Fx:**853-7798
(631) 878-4171 .. **Kesnig,** Richd C '86 -32 Gtwy Ln -Manorvll 11949 **Fx:**874-5058
(212) 609-6800 .. **Kesoglou,** Thos '99 (McCarter & E,LLP) -245 Park Av -NY 10167
(212) 455-2000 .. **Kess,** Avrohom J '95 (Simpson T&B LLP) -425 Lex Av -NY 10017
(212) 450-4000 .. **Kess,** Lydia E '63 SrCnsl Davis P&W LLP -450 Lex Av -NY 10017
(973) 848-4700 .. **Kessel,** I Michl '91 SpclCnsl Littler M,PC -900 3rd Av -NY 10022 **Fx:**643-5626
(212) 684-3900 .. **Kessel,** Maris R '09 %Gottlieb R&R,PC -270 Mad Av -NY 10016
(212) 632-5408 .. **Kessel,** Mark '66 Symphony Capital LLC -875 3rd Av -NY 10022
(212) 592-1400 .. **Kessel,** Michl H '96 (Herrick,F LLP) -2 Park Av -NY 10016
(212) 382-6600 .. **Kesselman,** Deborah '84 %NYC Bar -42 W 44th -NY 10036 **Fx:**768-0768
(718) 237-3100 .. **Kesselman,** Dena '07 Leg Aid -111 Lvngstn -Brklyn 11201 **Fx:**250-4243
(212) 218-5500 .. **Kesselman,** Dov '97 (Seyfarth S LLP) -620 8th Av -NY 10018
(212) 937-9572 .. **Kesselman,** Edw C '85 -60 E 42nd -NY 10165 **Fx:**564-6961
(212) 799-8723 .. **Kesselman,** Elayne B '81 -165 W 91st -NY 10024 **Fx:**799-6491
(212) 786-6094 .. **Kesselman,** Todd '92 Precision Capital Advsrs -787 7th Av -NY 10019
(585) 234-0425 .. **Kesselring,** Leo J '58 -43 Chasewood Cir -Rchstr 14618
(212) 506-1928 .. **Kessing,** Shaddy W F '99 Kasowitz BT&F LLP -1633 Bway -NY 10019
(212) 474-1000 .. **Kessing,** Stephen M '06 %Cravath S&M LLP -825 8th Av -NY 10019
(914) 703-6904 .. **Kesslen,** Jay H '00 SrCnsl Kinetics Asset Mgmt,Inc -555 Taxter Rd -Elmsfrd 10523 **Fx:**703-6899
(845) 259-8400 .. **Kessler,** Amy McCrae '00 Turning Earth LLC -97 Maple Wood Dr -Brewstr 10509 **Fx:**622-3649
(212) 773-3616 .. **Kessler,** Andrew S '97 Ernst & Young LLP -5 Times Sq -NY 10036
(212) 260-0415 .. **Kessler,** Barbara R '93 -163 3rd Av -NY 10003
(212) 687-1466 .. **Kessler,** Barry '68 (Koppel KJ LLP) -551 5th Av -NY 10176
(212) 909-6000 .. **Kessler,** Bryan P '07 %Debevoise & P LLP -919 3rd Av -NY 10022
(516) 433-4220 .. **Kessler,** Cary D '88 (Farley & K,PC) -55 Jericho Tpk -Jericho 11753
(212) 262-2390 .. **Kessler,** Danl B '06 %Connell F LLP -888 7th Av -NY 10106
(212) 819-8200 .. **Kessler,** Danl J '97 Cnsl White & C LLP -1155 Av of Amer -NY 10036
(212) 381-7000 .. **Kessler,** Daryl I '96 (Sabin B&G LLP) -4 Times Sq -NY 10036
(212) 869-9911 .. **Kessler,** David '61 -570 7th Av -NY 10018 **Fx:**819-9465
(516) 569-5001 .. **Kessler,** Deena '91 %Schonfeld & G,LLP -112 Spruce -Cedarhrst 11516
(212) 916-4387 .. **Kessler,** Deirdre G '81 %TIAA-CREF -730 3rd Av -NY 10017
(212) 935-1400 .. **Kessler,** Elise J '84 SrCnsl Seiden & S,PC -570 Lex Av -NY 10022
(516) 663-6600 .. **Kessler,** Ellen F '87 (Ruskin MF,PC) -1425 RXR Plz -Uniondale 11556
(212) 427-0373 .. **Kessler,** Ellyn D '76 -45 E 89th -NY 10128
(212) 986-0960 .. **Kessler,** Emanuel '48 (Kessler & K) -122 E 42nd -NY 10168
(212) 577-3688 .. **Kessler,** Eve S '86 %Leg Aid -199 Water -NY 10038 **Fx:**509-8431
(212) 382-3300 .. **Kessler,** Fredk R '89 (Wollmuth M&D LLP) -500 5th Av -NY 10110
(718) 858-7484 .. **Kessler,** George H '65 -75 Henry -Brklyn 11201
(718) 488-9100 .. **Kessler,** Glenn S '89 -32 Court -Brklyn 11201
(845) 425-2000 .. **Kessler,** Gordon M '94 LeCroy Corp -700 Chestnut Rdg Rd -Chestnut Rdg 10977
(914) 693-1008 .. **Kessler,** Howard S '75 -33 Capt Honeywells Rd -Ardsley 10502
(585) 258-2800 .. **Kessler,** Irving L '53 (Underberg & K LLP) -300 Bausch & Lomb Pl -Rchstr 14604
(212) 455-2000 .. **Kessler,** Jaclyn H '08 %Simpson T&B LLP -425 Lex Av -NY 10017
(212) 980-0120 .. **Kessler,** Jason '07 %Frankfurt KK&S,PC -488 Mad Av -NY 10022
(914) 220-1088 .. **Kessler,** Jason B '03 -111 Church -White Plns 10601 **Fx:**931-1722

(212) 259-8000 .. **Kessler**, Jeffrey L '78 (Dewey & L LLP) -1301 Av of Amer -NY 10019
(212) 421-8495 .. **Kessler**, Joan B '77 (Pines & K) -110 E 59th -NY 10022 **Fx:**421-8492
(212) 657-8855 .. **Kessler**, Katherine Allen '94 Citigroup Global Mrkts -77 Water -NY 10005
(212) 986-0960 .. **Kessler & Kessler** -122 E 42nd -NY 10168 **Fx:**297-0777
(212) 509-9400 .. **Kessler**, Kevin C '10 %Cozen O -45 Bway Atrium -NY 10006
(212) 779-1414 .. **Kessler**, Khara J '06 %Bernstein L LLP -10 E 40th -NY 10016
(212) 909-6000 .. **Kessler**, Kimberly A '04 %Debevoise & P LLP -919 3rd Av -NY 10022
(516) 463-5894 .. **Kessler**, Lawr W '67 %Hofstra Law Schl -121 Hofstra Univ -Hempstd 11549
(845) 355-2020 .. **Kessler**, Leonard '79 -2022 Route 284 Bx50 -Slate Hll 10973 **Fx:**355-2022
(212) 538-1293 .. **Kessler**, Marcia Lucas '81 Credit Suisse -1 Mad Av -NY 10010
(212) 553-7884 .. **Kessler**, Margaret Lyons '83 %Moody's Invstr Srvc -250 Greenwich -NY 10007
(212) 389-2030 .. **Kessler**, Maria M '92 Jupiter Images Corp -475 Park Av S -NY 10016
(212) 878-8000 .. **Kessler**, Michl J '05 %Clifford C LLP -31 W 52nd -NY 10019
(212) 259-8000 .. **Kessler**, Michl P '02 (Dewey & L LLP) -1301 Av of Amer -NY 10019
(518) 464-0444 .. **Kessler**, Michl W '73 (Rosenblum RK&S,LLP) -110 Great Oaks Blvd -Albany 12203
(212) 268-2677 .. **Kessler**, Mitchell D '84 -7 Penn Plz -NY 10001
(518) 235-6312 .. **Kessler**, Mitchell S '90 -63 Pike Crk Dr -Cohoes 12047 **Fx:**235-6316
(212) 986-0960 .. **Kessler**, Muriel S '48 (Kessler & K) -122 E 42nd -NY 10168
(914) 323-7000 .. **Kessler**, Peter S '09 %Wilson EME&D LLP -3 Gannett Dr -White Plns 10604
(212) 676-4753 .. **Kessler**, Philip J '09 (Butzel L,PC) -380 Mad Av -NY 10017
(212) 935-8880 .. **Kessler**, Phyllis J '75 Cnsl Foreht LL&K,LLP -228 E 45th -NY 10017
(914) 694-4102 .. **Kessler**, Ralph K '68 SpclCnsl Hinman H&K,LLP -106 Corp Park Dr -White Plns 10604
(212) 867-6000 .. **Kessler**, Robt M '86 (Rosenberg & E,PC) -733 3rd Av -NY 10017
(585) 987-2800 .. **Kessler**, Robt W '69 (Woods OG LLP) -2 State -Rchstr 14614
(212) 474-1000 .. **Kessler**, Sarah S '10 %Cravath S&M LLP -825 8th Av -NY 10019
(718) 286-6000 .. **Kessler**, Scott E '89 %DA -125-01 Qns Blvd -Kew Gdns 11415
(212) 438-9528 .. **Kessler**, Scott H '96 %Standard & Poor's -55 Water -NY 10041
(212) 880-3800 .. **Kessler**, Scott M '04 %Akerman S -335 Mad Av -NY 10017
(212) 768-8120 .. **Kessler**, Stephen D '78 -105 5th Av -NY 10003 **Fx:**768-7679
(212) 250-8202 .. **Kessler**, Steven '86 %Deutsche Bank -60 Wall -NY 10005
(212) 709-8024 .. **Kessler**, Steven A '84 -100 Wall -NY 10005
(212) 661-1500 .. **Kessler**, Steven L '83 -122 E 42nd -NY 10168 **Fx:**297-0777
(914) 693-3656 .. **Kessler**, Stuart '57 -15 Agnes Cir -Ardsley 10502 **Fx:**693-1459
(212) 477-3200 .. **Kessler**, Tedd E '83 T Kessler,PC -302 5th Av -NY 10001 **Fx:**388-1714
(631) 499-9100 .. **Kessler**, Troy L '97 (Shulman K,LLP) -510 Broadhllw Rd -Melvll 11747
(212) 216-1721 .. **Kessner**, Neil H '83 SL Green Realty Corp -420 Lex Av -NY 10170
(212) 685-9800 .. **Kestan**, Michl D '90 Counsel Press,LLC -520 8th Av -NY 10018
(516) 561-8447 .. **Kestel**, Jean M '85 -44 S Central Av -Vly Stream 11580 **Fx:**561-7235
(212) 468-4800 .. **Kesten**, Danl L '03 (Davis & G LLP) -1740 Bway -NY 10019
(212) 682-8383 .. **Kesten**, Matthew C '85 (Kantor DWMT&G,PC) -51 E 42nd -NY 10017
(718) 281-0100 .. **Kestenbaum**, Alan C '81 Weil & K -42-40 Bell Blvd -Bayside 11361 **Fx:**281-0850
(516) 747-0300 .. **Kestenbaum**, Avi Z '99 (Meltzer LG&B,LLP) -190 Willis Av -Mineola 11501
(212) 486-3370 .. **Kestenbaum Dannenberg & Klein,LLP** -104 W 40th -NY 10018 **Fx:**486-3371
(516) 742-7777 .. **Kestenbaum**, Elise B '82 %Frazer & F,LLP -1415 Kellum Pl -Gdn Cty 11530
(516) 663-6600 .. **Kestenbaum**, Harold L '76 OfCnsl Ruskin MF,PC -1425 RXR Plz -Uniondale 11556
(718) 237-5586 .. **Kestenbaum**, Jeffrey K '96 -26 Court -Brklyn 11242
(516) 466-0410 .. **Kestenbaum & Mark** -40 Cuttermill Rd -Gt Neck 11021 **Fx:**829-3729
(914) 428-1438 .. **Kestenbaum**, Michl '87 %T Bona,PC -123 Main -White Plns 10601 **Fx:**428-1413
(212) 841-1000 .. **Kestenbaum**, Nancy L '93 (Covington & B LLP) -620 8th Av -NY 10018
(212) 486-3370 .. **Kestenbaum**, Richd A '85 (Kestenbaum D&K,LLP) -104 W 40th -NY 10018
(516) 466-0410 .. **Kestenbaum**, Richd S '75 (Kestenbaum & M) -40 Cuttermill Rd -Gt Neck 11021
(212) 530-5000 .. **Kestenbaum**, Russell J '99 %Milbank TH&M LLP -1 Chase Manh Plz -NY 10005
(212) 582-2500 .. **Kestin**, Lawr A '79 Glenmont Capital Mgmt LLC -40 W 57th -NY 10019
(212) 854-0780 .. **Kestler**, Jeffrey '72 %Columbia Univ -535 W 116th 412 Low Mem'l Library -NY 10027 **Fx:**854-5839
(631) 423-4390 .. **Ketcham**, Malik A '02 Mincone & M,PC -110 Walt Whitman Rd -South Huntington 11746 **Fx:**423-4408
(212) 688-8555 .. **Ketcher**, Adam J '07 %Fragomen DB&L LLP -7 Hanover Sq -NY 10004
(718) 928-3700 .. **Ketcher**, Maxine A '87 %LSNYC-Bronx -579 Courtlandt Av -Bronx 10451 **Fx:**402-7586
(914) 967-1450 .. **Ketchum**, Wm C Jr. '53 -241 Grace Church -Rye 10580
(516) 877-2000 .. **Ketover**, Joshua S '97 (Ketover & Assoc,LLC) -1225 Franklin Av -Gdn Cty 11530 **Fx:**877-2586
(718) 838-7878 .. **Ketteringham**, Emma S '00 %Bronx Defenders -860 Crtlandt Av -Bronx 10451 **Fx:**665-0100
(212) 837-6306 .. **Kettle**, Kamanta C '08 %Hughes H&R LLP -1 Bttry Pk Plz -NY 10004 **Fx:**299-6306
(914) 632-7700 .. **Kettner**, Susan I '90 Kettner & K -270 North Av -New Rchll 10801 **Fx:**632-7706
(212) 336-2000 .. **Ketty**, Nivritha '08 %Patterson BW&T LLP -1133 Av of Amer -NY 10036
(212) 334-2025 .. **Ketyer**, Orin J '90 Buro Happold Cnsltng Engineers -100 Bway -NY 10005
(212) 661-2900 .. **Keusch**, David I '04 %Kriss & F LLP -360 Lex Av -NY 10017
(516) 496-3868 .. **Keusey**, Edwin H '91 (Keusey T&B,PC) -20 Crsswys Park Dr N -Woodbury 11797
(516) 496-3868 .. **Keusey Tutunjian & Bitetto,PC** -20 Crsswys Park Dr N -Woodbury 11797 **Fx:**496-3869
(845) 485-4901 .. **Keutmann**, Kenneth F '82 -2 Cannon -Poughkeepsie 12601 **Fx:**485-4914
(212) 422-0202 .. **Kevane**, Timothy D '01 %Sedgwick DM&A LLP -125 Broad -NY 10004
(212) 503-8980 .. **Kevelson**, Ira Z '75 Marks Paneth & Shron LLP -622 3rd Av -NY 10017 **Fx:**503-8981
(212) 355-2894 .. **Kevin**, Gary M '80 -335 E 51st -NY 10022
(212) 790-9200 .. **Kevlin**, Mary L '84 (Cowan L&L,PC) -1133 Av of Amer -NY 10036
(212) 213-7753 .. **Kevorkian**, Corinne P '84 F Schumacher & Co -79 Mad Av -NY 10016 **Fx:**213-7664
(212) 554-7800 .. **Kewalramani**, Devika '96 (Moses & S LLP) -405 Lex Av -NY 10174
(212) 455-2000 .. **Key**, A Timothy '06 %Simpson T&B LLP -425 Lex Av -NY 10017
(716) 332-7192 .. **Key**, Edw E '03 (Johnson & K LLC) -534 Delaware Av -Buffalo 14202 **Fx:**332-7170
(212) 732-3200 .. **Keyes**, Austin D '98 (Carter L&M LLP) -2 Wall -NY 10005
(518) 464-2338 .. **Keyes**, Margaret M '89 AYCO -1 Wall Bx15073 -Albany 12212
(800) 320-6757 .. **Keyes**, Robt H '87 (Haymond Law,PLLC) -399 Knollwood Rd -White Plns 10603 **Fx:**(203) 330-6762
(212) 336-0109 .. **Keyes**, Robt J '03 %SEC -3 World Fncl Ctr -NY 10281 **Fx:**336-1323
(212) 756-2000 .. **Keyes**, Theo A '92 SpclCnsl Schulte R&Z LLP -919 3rd Av -NY 10022
(212) 951-6400 .. **Keyes**, Wayne L '82 %Dept of Education -475 Park Av S -NY 10016 **Fx:**951-6465
(212) 858-1000 .. **Keyko**, David G '78 (Pillsbury WSP LLP) -1540 Bway -NY 10036
(212) 208-3600 .. **Keyles**, Claire G '86 Zurich Capital Mrkts -105 E 17th -NY 10003
(212) 765-9100 .. **Keynes**, Jocelyn '99 %Halperin BR,LLP -555 Mad Av -NY 10022
(716) 861-1226 .. **Keysa**, Stanley Jay '67 -5455 Bway -Lancaster 14086 **Fx:**685-3029
(716) 854-2907 .. **Keyse**, Mary Jane '87 %Chicago Title Ins -424 Main -Buffalo 14202 **Fx:**852-7346
(607) 734-0990 .. **Keyser Maloney & Winner LLP** -150 Lk -Elmira 14901 **Fx:**378-6204
(607) 734-0990 .. **Keyser**, Richd D '81 (Keyser M&W LLP) -150 Lk -Elmira 14901
(212) 735-3000 .. **Keyte**, James A '87 (Skadden ASM&F LLP) -4 Times Sq -NY 10036
(212) 859-8000 .. **Kezsbom**, Allen '66 OfCnsl Fried FHS&J LLP -1 NY Plz -NY 10004
(212) 310-8000 .. **Khachaturian**, Serj Alex '09 %Weil G&M LLP -767 5th Av -NY 10153
(212) 415-9200 .. **Khadavi**, Steven '97 (Dorsey & W LLP) -250 Park Av -NY 10177
(631) 981-6808 .. **Khadem**, Ali '86 -17 Gatelot Av -Ronkonkoma 11779
(914) 963-5529 .. **Khader**, Michl J '02 (MJ Khader,PC) -733 Ynkrs Av -Ynkrs 10704
(212) 474-1000 .. **Khadpe**, Marc J '07 %Cravath S&M LLP -825 8th Av -NY 10019
(718) 797-2488 .. **Khafif**, Albert R '93 (Friedman K&S,LLP) -16 Court -Brklyn 11241 **Fx:**797-4304
(718) 694-3991 .. **Khahaifa**, Weslii V '01 %Transit Auth -130 Lvngstn -Brklyn 11201 **Fx:**694-5726
(212) 725-3846 .. **Khalaf**, Aman '02 %O Mohammedi,LLC -233 Bway -NY 10279 **Fx:**202-7621
(212) 661-7300 .. **Khalatbari**, Odessa '97 %Malapero & P LLP -295 Mad Av -NY 10017
(914) 242-3222 .. **Khaldarov**, Julia '01 (Kaufman & K) -37 W Main -Mt Kisco 10549 **Fx:**242-6082
(212) 225-2000 .. **Khalid**, Humayun '08 %Cleary GS&H -1 Lbrty Plz -NY 10006
(212) 608-3015 .. **Khalife**, Elias M '07 %R Roth -233 Bway -NY 10279 **Fx:**608-2177
(914) 997-0500 .. **Khalil**, John I '10 %Lowey DC&H,PC -1 N Bway -White Plns 10601
(212) 446-4800 .. **Khalil**, Junaid '03 %Kirkland & E LLP -153 E 53rd -NY 10022
(212) 506-1700 .. **Khalil**, Ranya '07 Kasowitz BT&F LLP -1633 Bway -NY 10019
(212) 589-4200 .. **Khalil**, Rebecca S T '08 %Baker & H LLP -45 Rckfllr Plz -NY 10111
(212) 530-5000 .. **Khalil**, Saml A '04 %Milbank TH&M LLP -1 Chase Manh Plz -NY 10005
(718) 590-2000 .. **Khalil**, Vivian '02 %DA -198 E 161st -Bronx 10451 **Fx:**590-6477
(212) 230-8800 .. **Khamis**, Samia '06 WilmerHale -399 Park Av -NY 10022
(212) 614-9124 .. **Khan**, Amiena A '88 -150 Bway -NY 10038 **Fx:**217-2427
(516) 560-7745 .. **Khan**, Arif A '05 Workers Comp Bd -175 Fulton Av -Hempstd 11550
(845) 566-5345 .. **Khan**, Azra Jabeen '96 %Larkin AI&T,LLP -356 Meadow Av -Newburgh 12550
(212) 825-5900 .. **Khan**, Faisal '02 %Dept of Invstgtn -80 Maiden Ln -NY 10038 **Fx:**825-2860
(914) 323-7000 .. **Khan**, Faisal A '06 %Wilson EME&D LLP -3 Gannett Dr -White Plns 10604
(212) 983-7713 .. **Khan**, Fizza A '06 Counsel Works LLC -420 Lex Av -NY 10170
(212) 419-0616 .. **Khan**, Freda Mushtaq '01 Khan Law Grp,PC -22 Crtlandt -NY 10007 **Fx:**419-0617
(212) 207-8900 .. **Khan**, Hamid H '04 (H Khan,PC) -59 E 54th -NY 10022 **Fx:**664-8754
(212) 373-3000 .. **Khan**, Iqbal I '09 Paul WRW&G LLP -1285 Av of Amer -NY 10019
(212) 588-5500 .. **Khan**, Jamshaid Nisar '05 %Davies WP&V LLP -625 Mad Av -NY 10022
(212) 310-8000 .. **Khan**, Kamran A '04 Weil G&M LLP -767 5th Av -NY 10153
(845) 454-5185 .. **Khan**, Karen '05 -Bx1782 -Poughkeepsie 12601 **Fx:**454-5185
(212) 632-8421 .. **Khan**, M Fyzul '98 %Silver Leaf Ptrns LLC -420 Lex Av -NY 10170
(516) 496-5822 .. **Khan**, Mehreen '09 T Spina -170 Froehlich Farm Blvd -Woodbury 11797 **Fx:**496-5420
(212) 742-8700 .. **Khan**, Naureen Salmah '05 %Garson D&C LLP -110 Wall -NY 10005
(212) 728-8000 .. **Khan**, Naz '09 %Willkie F&G LLP -787 7th Av -NY 10019
(718) 577-9302 .. **Khan**, Nazar M '05 -16 Court -Brklyn 11241
(212) 230-8800 .. **Khan**, Omar A '07 %WilmerHale -399 Park Av -NY 10022
(718) 262-3410 .. **Khan**, Rayaaz N '02 ACS -92-31 Union Hall -Jamaica 11433
(212) 770-8943 .. **Khan**, Saira '00 AIG Invstmnts -70 Pine -NY 10270
(212) 558-4000 .. **Khan**, Samiul E '10 %Sullivan & C LLP -125 Broad -NY 10004
(646) 467-7392 .. **Khan**, Shahla '03 -1375 Bway -NY 10018 **Fx:**253-1258
(212) 351-4000 .. **Khan**, Sophia N '10 Gibson D&C LLP -200 Park Av -NY 10166
(212) 808-7800 .. **Khan**, Tania '07 %Kelley D&W LLP -101 Park Av -NY 10178

(212) 442-0144 .. **Khandakar**, Shakera '10 %Law Dept -100 Church -NY 10007 **Fx**:788-0367
(212) 808-7800 .. **Khandhar**, Lisa R '06 %Kelley D&W LLP -101 Park Av -NY 10178
(212) 455-2000 .. **Khanduja**, Nisha '07 %Simpson T&B LLP -425 Lex Av -NY 10017
(212) 371-0330 .. **Khani**, James J '78 (Cohen & K) -444 Mad Av -NY 10022
(212) 474-1000 .. **Khanna**, Aditya '09 %Cravath S&M LLP -825 8th Av -NY 10019
(212) 373-3000 .. **Khanna**, Amit '08 %Paul WRW&G LLP -1285 Av of Amer -NY 10019
(718) 641-2900 .. **Khanna**, Anil K '04 -131-09 Rockaway Blvd -S Ozone Pk 11420
(212) 536-3900 .. **Khanna**, Rajiv '85 (K&L Gates LLP) -599 Lex Av -NY 10022
(212) 940-8800 .. **Khanna**, Vikas '08 %Katten MR LLP -575 Mad Av -NY 10022
(315) 762-2992 .. **Khanzadian**, Karen '90 %DePerno & K -Bx83 -Sylvan Bch 13157
(212) 839-5300 .. **Khara**, Rahul B '09 %Sidley A LLP -787 7th Av -NY 10019
(212) 344-3800 .. **Kharash**, Alexander '05 Christophe & Assoc,PC -2 Wall -NY 10005 **Fx**:344-3212
(212) 224-4000 .. **Khareyn**, Paul '05 SMBC Capital Mrkts Inc -277 Park Av -NY 10172
(718) 590-2000 .. **Kharkover**, Ilya '09 %DA -198 E 161st -Bronx 10451 **Fx**:590-6477
(212) 632-8421 .. **Kharnak**, Elina '95 Standard & Poor's -55 Water -NY 10041
(212) 964-5570 .. **Khashmati**, Lyaman F '05 %Sacks & S -150 Bway -NY 10038 **Fx**:349-2141
(212) 376-3083 .. **Khashu**, Anita '95 Vera Inst of Justice -233 Bway -NY 10279 **Fx**:941-9407
(212) 421-1011 .. **Khatamee**, Neda N '95 Major Lindsey & Africa -551 Fifth Av -NY 10176
(212) 762-7695 .. **Khatcherian**, Sylvia '80 Morgan Stanley -1221 Av of Amer -NY 10020
(212) 271-3719 .. **Khatib**, Sinan '04 Thomas Weisel Prtnrs -390 Park Av -NY 10022
(646) 562-3405 .. **Khattak**, Nadia '07 %PLC -747 3rd Av -NY 10017
(212) 659-1959 .. **Khavin**, Natalya '05 Classic Media,Inc -860 Bway -NY 10003
(718) 421-3815 .. **Khavinson**, Eugene A '01 (Khavinson & Assoc,PC) -1122 Coney Isl Av -Brklyn 11230
(516) 746-0232 .. **Khavkin**, Mark '98 %Farley G&H,LLP -200 Old Cntry Rd -Mineola 11501
(212) 964-7990 .. **Khavulya**, Mirra '97 OfCnsl Mallow K&N,PC -321 Bway -NY 10007
(212) 446-4800 .. **Khawaja**, Atif N '03 (Kirkland & E LLP) -153 E 53rd -NY 10022
(212) 446-7000 .. **Khedouri**, Robt K '96 %McKinsey & Co -55 E 52nd -NY 10055 **Fx**:688-9521
(212) 770-5925 .. **Kheel**, Danl J '98 %AIG -70 Pine -NY 10270
(212) 408-5100 .. **Kheit**, John '03 (Chadbourne & P LLP) -30 Rckfllr Plz -NY 10112
(212) 837-6851 .. **Khemani**, Sharad J '06 %Hughes H&R LLP -1 Bttry Pk Plz -NY 10004
(718) 787-9500 .. **Khenkin**, Alexander '02 (Khenkin & S,PC) -9712 3rd Av -Brklyn 11209 **Fx**:787-9502
(212) 225-2000 .. **Khentov**, Boris '10 %Cleary GS&H -1 Lbrty Plz -NY 10006
(212) 839-5300 .. **Khera**, Sheetal '08 %Sidley A LLP -787 7th Av -NY 10019
(212) 326-3939 .. **Kheyfits**, Dmitriy A '09 %Jones D -222 E 41st -NY 10017
(212) 906-1200 .. **Khiani**, Shashi N '09 %Latham & W -885 3rd Av -NY 10022
(212) 786-1500 .. **Khine**, Sandy '93 -299 Bway -NY 10007 **Fx**:786-1503
(718) 222-2108 .. **Khishchenko**, Agatha '07 %Law Dept -350 Jay -Brklyn 11201 **Fx**:222-2393
(917) 204-8301 .. **Khiterer**, Inna '04 %I & S Properties -Bx320160 -Brklyn 11232
(914) 749-8200 .. **Kho**, Melissa Sia '05 %Boies S&F LLP -333 Main -Armonk 10504
(212) 510-0500 .. **Khodorovsky**, Nazar '07 %US Trustees Ofc -33 Whitehall -NY 10004 **Fx**:668-2255
(212) 506-1700 .. **Khojasteh**, Sarmad M '07 %Kasowitz BT&F LLP -1633 Bway -NY 10019
(212) 819-8200 .. **Khokhar**, Someera F '05 (White & C LLP) -1155 Av of Amer -NY 10036
(212) 935-3000 .. **Khondker**, Omar A '08 %Mintz LCFG&P,PC -666 3rd Av -NY 10017
(212) 878-8000 .. **Khoo**, Shireen L H '08 %Clifford C LLP -31 W 52nd -NY 10019
(212) 557-4000 .. **Khorsandi**, Michl J '07 %Grunfeld DLS&K LLP -399 Park Av -NY 10022
(212) 530-5000 .. **Khosla**, Mohineet K '02 %Milbank TH&M LLP -1 Chase Manh Plz -NY 10005
(212) 357-6979 .. **Khosla**, Sandip S '01 Goldman Sachs -1 NY Plz -NY 10004
(212) 237-0000 .. **Khosla**, Vikas '07 %Vinson & E LLP -666 5th Av -NY 10103
(518) 653-2662 .. **Khosrova**, Mitchell '86 -130 Raup Rd -Chatham 12037
(212) 298-5381 .. **Khot**, Afsi '05 %Leg Aid -49 Thomas -NY 10013 **Fx**:298-5252
(212) 688-4021 .. **Khouri**, George J '73 -126 E 56th -NY 10022 **Fx**:888-0669
(212) 373-5640 .. **Khoury**, Ivan F '95 %NYC Transit Auth -2 Bway -NY 10004
(516) 746-3500 .. **Khrinenko**, Peter M '03 Brand G&B,PC -600 Old Cntry Rd -Gdn Cty 11530
(212) 594-5300 .. **Khurana**, Arvind '00 (Milberg LLP) -1 Penn Plz -NY 10119
(212) 969-3000 .. **Khurana**, Kevin K '10 %Proskauer R LLP -1585 Bway -NY 10036
(212) 269-1400 .. **Khurana**, Sarah Yeang '08 %Gusrae KB&N PLLC -120 Wall -NY 10005
(914) 761-2270 .. **Khurana**, Sunil '96 -2 William -White Plns 10601
(212) 920-2940 .. **Khutorsky**, Alexander '97 Dahlman Rose & Co -142 W 57th -NY 10019 **Fx**:920-2995
(202) 551-4894 .. **Khuzami**, Robt S '84 SEC -3 World Fncl Ctr -NY 10281 **Fx**:(212) 336-1323
(212) 309-1000 .. **Khvatskaya**, Olga '01 Cnsl Hunton & W -200 Park Av -NY 10166
(718) 591-4696 .. **Khwaja**, Samrin '97 -82-16 164th Pl -Jamaica 11432
(718) 445-1300 .. **Khym**, Chas Chulwon '94 -39-01 Main -Flushng 11354 **Fx**:445-8616
(212) 679-4200 .. **Kia**, Atossa '03 (Kia Law Firm,LLC) -234 5th Av -NY 10001 **Fx**:679-4155
(585) 258-2183 .. **Kiba**, John M '94 State Ins Fund -100 Chestnut -Rchstr 14604 **Fx**:258-8143
(914) 962-5513 .. **Kibbe & Iasiello** -1961 Commerce -Yorktwn Hts 10598 **Fx**:962-5515
(914) 962-5513 .. **Kibbe**, John R '50 (Kibbe & I) -1961 Commerce -Yorktwn Hts 10598
(212) 530-1800 .. **Kibbe**, Jonathan '81 (Richards K&O LLP) -1 World Fncl Ctr -NY 10281
(585) 591-1800 .. **Kibbe King & Moran** -2 Main Bx268 -Attica 14011 **Fx**:591-0987
(212) 907-9700 .. **Kibel**, Beth N '93 Cnsl Smith G&R,LLP -250 Park Av -NY 10177
(212) 468-4800 .. **Kibel**, Gary A '00 (Davis & G LLP) -1740 Bway -NY 10019
(914) 739-2195 .. **Kibel**, Shari B '96 -248 Treetop Ln -Rye Brook 10573 **Fx**:973-2196
(212) 610-6300 .. **Kibler**, John W '94 SrCnsl Allen & O -1221 Av of Amer -NY 10020
(585) 786-3148 .. **Kibler**, Keith D '95 %Cnty Ct -147 N Main -Warsaw 14569 **Fx**:786-3800
(716) 852-5875 .. **Kibler**, Matthew J '10 %Feldman K LLP -110 Pearl -Buffalo 14202
(212) 237-1000 .. **Kicenuik**, Maryann P '88 (Windels ML&M,LLP) -156 W 56th -NY 10019
(212) 374-2988 .. **Kicinski**, Christine J '86 %NYC Dept Educ-OLS -52 Chmbrs -NY 10007 **Fx**:374-5939
(212) 474-1000 .. **Kicken**, Johannes L A '08 %Cravath S&M LLP -825 8th Av -NY 10019
(212) 455-2000 .. **Kidd**, Catherine M '05 %Simpson T&B LLP -425 Lex Av -NY 10017
(845) 485-7058 .. **Kidd**, Diana L '99 (Kasnia & K,PLLC) -19 Dutchess Av -Poughkeepsie 12601 **Fx**:485-1026
(212) 351-4000 .. **Kidd**, Matthew A '02 %Gibson D&C LLP -200 Park Av -NY 10166
(212) 268-2128 .. **Kidd**, Novlette R '01 %Fagenson & P -450 7th Av -NY 10123
(212) 735-3000 .. **Kidd**, Richd W '99 Cnsl Skadden ASM&F LLP -4 Times Sq -NY 10036
(716) 483-6646 .. **Kidder**, Rolland E '75 RH Jackson Ctr -305 E 4th -Jamestwn 14701
(212) 490-3000 .. **Kideckel**, Arnold '64 OfCnsl Wilson EME&D LLP -150 E 42nd -NY 10017
(585) 546-7430 .. **Kidera**, Thos J '80 %Dept of Law -144 Exchange Blvd -Rchstr 14614 **Fx**:546-7514
(212) 541-2000 .. **Kiderman**, Jamie E '04 %Bryan C LLP -1290 Av of Amer -NY 10104
(212) 756-2000 .. **Kidouchim**, Rami '97 %Schulte R&Z LLP -919 3rd Av -NY 10022
(212) 450-4000 .. **Kiechel**, Julia Graham '10 %Davis P&W LLP -450 Lex Av -NY 10017
(845) 477-9226 .. **Kiedaisch**, Robt F '83 -10 Hemlock Hill Bx1268 -Greenwd Lk 10925
(516) 803-2300 .. **Kiefer**, Alfred G Jr. '87 %Cablevision Sys -1111 Stewart Av -Bethpage 11714
(585) 454-3030 .. **Kiefer**, Jason M '04 Merzbach,PC -73 State -Rchstr 14614 **Fx**:454-3044
(212) 490-4949 .. **Kieffer & Hahn LLP** -230 Park Av -NY 10169 **Fx**:(646) 478-9191
(585) 586-5556 .. **Kieffer**, James M '49 -422 Stoutenburgh Ln -Pittsfrd 14534 **Fx**:586-7404
(716) 886-0211 .. **Kieffer**, Jos P '92 %Benderson Dvlpmnt -570 Delaware Av -Buffalo 14202 **Fx**:886-2269
(315) 703-6600 .. **Kieffer**, Maureen P '91 %Leg Aid -472 S Salina -Syracuse 13202 **Fx**:671-0062
(585) 232-5151 .. **Kieffer**, Michl J '79 -134 S Fitzhugh -Rchstr 14608 **Fx**:262-6015
(212) 909-6000 .. **Kiehn**, Kristin D '01 %Debevoise & P LLP -919 3rd Av -NY 10022
(212) 486-6995 .. **Kiel**, Gerald H '69 -400 E 56th -NY 10022
(718) 231-5044 .. **Kiely**, Denis J '00 -4288 Katonah Av -Bronx 10470
(212) 918-3000 .. **Kiely**, Dennis D '97 Cnsl Hogan L LLP -875 3rd Av -NY 10022
(914) 286-3400 .. **Kiely**, Jerome '72 Leg Aid -1 N Bway -White Plns 10601 **Fx**:682-4112
(518) 459-2700 .. **Kiely**, Jessica L '07 Ettinger,PC -125 Wolf Rd -Albany 12205 **Fx**:459-2714
(212) 450-4000 .. **Kiely**, Lena V '02 %Davis P&W LLP -450 Lex Av -NY 10017
(631) 298-2128 .. **Kiely**, Stephen F '05 OfCnsl E Burke Jr & Assoc,LLC -Bx567 -Mattituck 11952
(212) 351-4000 .. **Kiem**, Theo A '05 %Gibson D&C LLP -200 Park Av -NY 10166
(607) 723-9511 .. **Kieper**, Carl A '85 (Coughlin & G,LLP) -19 Chenango Bx2039 -Bnghmtn 13902
(518) 459-8299 .. **Kiepura**, Frank '69 (F Kiepura & Assoc,PC) -116 Everett Rd -Albany 12205 **Fx**:459-8311
(347) 296-1076 .. **Kieran**, Brian '99 Supreme Ct -320 Jay -Brklyn 11201
(718) 478-6744 .. **Kiernan**, James A '73 (Strauch & K) -34-21 87th -Jcksn Hts 11372 **Fx**:478-2381
(516) 248-6400 .. **Kiernan**, John B '73 Davidoff M&H,LLP -200 Grdn City Plz -Gdn Cty 11530
(914) 428-7200 .. **Kiernan**, John E '96 Misys PLC -123 Main -White Plns 10601
(212) 323-5020 .. **Kiernan**, John G '89 Oppenheimer Funds Inc -225 Lbrty -NY 10281
(212) 909-6692 .. **Kiernan**, John S '82 (Debevoise & P LLP) -919 3rd Av -NY 10022
(718) 875-1300 .. **Kiernan**, Matthew G '88 %Appllt Div 2nd Dept -45 Monroe Pl -Brklyn 11201 **Fx**:858-2446
(518) 474-8343 .. **Kiernan**, Peter J '68 Cnsl Gov's Cnsls Ofc -242 State Cptl -Albany 12224 **Fx**:474-8099
(914) 391-4016 .. **Kierszenbaum**, Adriana E '92 Town Atty Ofc -363 Underhill Av -Yorktwn Hts 10598
(212) 558-4000 .. **Kies**, David M '68 OfCnsl Sullivan & C LLP -125 Broad -NY 10004
(212) 302-3300 .. **Kiesel**, Michl T '73 Graf Repetti & Co -1114 Av of Amer -NY 10036 **Fx**:302-9661
(212) 756-2000 .. **Kiesel**, Robt R '92 (Schulte R&Z LLP) -919 3rd Av -NY 10022
(518) 785-7800 .. **Kieselstein**, Steve '84 (Kieselstein PLLC) -1187 Troy Schenectady Rd -Latham 12110
(212) 474-1000 .. **Kiessling**, B Robbins '77 (Cravath S&M LLP) -825 8th Av -NY 10019
(212) 225-2000 .. **Kietlinski**, Piotr J '09 %Cleary GS&H -1 Lbrty Plz -NY 10006
(518) 439-8311 .. **Kietzman**, Paul R '73 Cnsl NYSARC,Inc -393 Delaware Av -Delmar 12054
(212) 450-4000 .. **Kiew**, Chiawen O '06 %Davis P&W LLP -450 Lex Av -NY 10017
(914) 946-3700 .. **Kiggins**, Robt J '75 OfCnsl McCarthy F LLP -11 Martine Av -White Plns 10606
(212) 664-7728 .. **Kiick**, James A '02 %NBC -30 Rckfllr Plz -NY 10112 **Fx**:664-3667
(212) 764-4222 .. **Kikel**, Danl J '03 %S Jeffries & Assoc -1560 Bway -NY 10036 **Fx**:764-4229
(516) 222-0454 .. **Kilada**, Jos F '01 (J Kilada,PC) -666 Old Cntry Rd -Gdn Cty 11530
(212) 808-7800 .. **Kilar**, Stephen W '08 %Kelley D&W LLP -101 Park Av -NY 10178
(212) 318-2371 .. **Kilb**, Karl P '95 %Bloomberg LP -499 Park Av -NY 10022 **Fx**:940-1944
(914) 481-6249 .. **Kilbourn**, Jos A '53 (Cone & K) -83 S Bedford Rd -Mt Kisco 10549
(716) 881-1192 .. **Kilbridge**, Barbara A '89 -155 Summer -Buffalo 14222
(212) 841-7500 .. **Kilbridge**, Valerie Fabregas '05 %Cushman & Wakefield -1290 Av of Amer -NY 10104
(718) 488-1900 .. **Kilduff**, James A '97 %Lazzaro & G,PC -360 Court -Brklyn 11231
(212) 557-7200 .. **Kilduff**, Patrick J '96 (Davidoff M&H,LLP) -605 3rd Av -NY 10158
(914) 741-6100 .. **Kilduff**, Rebecca C '96 %Kaufman B&R -200 Summit Lk Dr -Valhalla 10595
(516) 466-7900 .. **Kiley**, Donald T '56 OfCnsl Kiley K&K,PLLC -107 Nrthrn Blvd -Gt Neck 11021
(516) 466-7900 .. **Kiley**, Donald T Jr. '84 (Kiley K&K,PLLC) -107 Nrthrn Blvd -Gt Neck 11021

(516) 466-7900 .. **Kiley,** James D '98 (Kiley K&K,PLLC) -107 Nrthrn Blvd -Gt Neck 11021
(585) 987-2800 .. **Kiley,** James W '73 (Woods OG LLP) -2 State -Rchstr 14614
(212) 808-7800 .. **Kiley,** John E '90 (Kelley D&W LLP) -101 Park Av -NY 10178
(518) 473-5671 .. **Kiley,** Kathleen M '00 %Dept of Parole -97 Central Av -Albany 12206
(516) 466-7900 .. **Kiley,** Kevin J '86 (Kiley K&K,PLLC) -107 Nrthrn Blvd -Gt Neck 11021
(516) 466-7900 .. **Kiley Kiley & Kiley, PLLC** -107 Nrthrn Blvd -Gt Neck 11021 **Fx:**466-7903
(607) 763-9200 .. **Kiley,** Lauren A '08 %Levene G&T,LLP -BxF-1706 -Bnghmtn 13902
(212) 705-7000 .. **Kilfoyle,** Colleen M '08 %Bingham M LLP -399 Park Av -NY 10022
(718) 643-6130 .. **Kilfoyle,** Thos R '85 %Supreme Ct -360 Adams -Brklyn 11201 **Fx:**643-4221
(718) 499-9061 .. **Kilgallen,** Michl A '84 -547 4th -Brklyn 11215
(631) 853-4310 .. **Kilgallon,** John M '78 %Family Ct -400 Carleton Av Bx9076 -Central Islip 11722 **Fx:**853-4288
(516) 746-5530 .. **Kilgannon,** Frank X '65 (FX Kilgannon PC) -1551 Kellum Pl -Mineola 11501 **Fx:**746-5538
(914) 277-3637 .. **Kilgannon,** Mary Beth '84 Town of Somers -335 Route 202 -Somers 10589
(212) 419-1492 .. **Kilhenny,** Regina T '87 (Kilhenny & F) -350 7th Av -NY 10001 **Fx:**419-1499
(212) 596-9000 .. **Kilian,** Mary E '10 %Ropes & G LLP -1211 Av of Amer -NY 10036
(212) 841-7500 .. **Kilkeary,** Martin J '73 %Cushman & Wakefield -1290 Av of Amer -NY 10104
(718) 225-7871 .. **Kilkelly,** Francis J '61 -46-04 192nd -Flushng 11358 **Fx:**225-7871
(718) 618-2500 .. **Kilkenny,** David J P '89 %Civil Ct -851 Grnd Cncrs -Bronx 10451 **Fx:**590-7294
(646) 610-5400 .. **Kilker,** Mary C '85 %NYPD -1 Police Plz -NY 10038
(607) 748-9907 .. **Kilker,** Patrick J '94 -231-241 Main -Vestal 13850
(212) 278-1000 .. **Kill,** Lawr '61 (Anderson K&O,PC) -1251 Av of Amer -NY 10020
(518) 402-9184 .. **Killcommons-Konz,** Jeanne '93 DEC -625 Bway -Albany 12233 **Fx:**402-9018
(716) 662-0332 .. **Killeen,** Allithea E '84 (Killeen & K) -9080 Cole Rd -Boston 14025
(518) 370-1233 .. **Killeen & Bradt** -179½ Jay -Schnctdy 12305 **Fx:**370-1818
(212) 309-6000 .. **Killeen,** Brendan T '08 %Morgan L&B LLP -101 Park Av -NY 10178
(518) 370-1233 .. **Killeen,** Fredk W '77 (Killeen & B) -179½ Jay -Schnctdy 12305
(716) 662-0332 .. **Killeen,** Henry W III '76 (Killeen & K) -9080 Cole Rd -Boston 14025
(201) 533-3164 .. **Killeen,** Kevin T '90 %HSBC Bank -452 5th Av -NY 10018
(516) 227-0700 .. **Killeen,** Thos J '73 (Farrell F,PC) -1320 RXR Plz -Uniondale 11556
(716) 849-1333 .. **Killelea,** Danl M '98 %Lipsitz GSC LLP -42 Delaware Av -Buffalo 14202
(212) 308-4411 .. **Killelea,** James T '06 %Edwards AP&D LLP -750 Lex Av -NY 10022
(914) 948-9500 .. **Killerlane,** Christina M '97 %J Killerlane -175 Main -White Plns 10601 **Fx:**948-3004
(914) 948-9500 .. **Killerlane,** James J '81 -175 Main -White Plns 10601 **Fx:**948-3004
(212) 762-4715 .. **Killerlane,** James J III '97 %Morgan Stanley -1221 Av of Amer -NY 10020
(845) 292-4369 .. **Killian,** Elissa Y '88 -59 Benton Hllw Rd Bx126 -Liberty 12754 **Fx:**363-4469
(718) 590-6759 .. **Killian,** Nancy D '88 %DA -198 E 161st -Bronx 10451 **Fx:**590-6477
(631) 751-1984 .. **Killian,** Patrick O '82 -Bx567 -Stony Brk 11790
(631) 642-2588 .. **Killian,** Paul M '91 -250 Montauk Hwy -E Moriches 11940
(845) 339-2572 .. **Killigan,** Kenneth D '77 -111 Green Bx3605 -Kingston 12402 **Fx:**339-6144
(917) 368-2416 .. **Killion,** Kim '99 Abp Invstmnts US Inc -666 3rd Av -NY 10017
(212) 872-1000 .. **Killip,** Douglas W '88 -One Bryant Park -NY 10036 **Fx:**872-1002
(315) 476-2812 .. **Kilmartin,** Patrick M '95 P Kilmartin,PLLC -221 Walton -Syracuse 13202 **Fx:**476-3408
(914) 237-6000 .. **Kilmartin,** Paul G '93 (Kilmartin & K) -876 McLean Av -Ynkrs 10704 **Fx:**237-3325
(914) 237-6000 .. **Kilmartin,** Ronald F '55 (Kilmartin & K) -876 McLean Av -Ynkrs 10704 **Fx:**237-3325
(914) 237-6000 .. **Kilmartin,** Ronald F Jr. '86 (Kilmartin & K) -876 McLean Av -Ynkrs 10704 **Fx:**237-3325
(607) 772-1663 .. **Kilmer,** Robt C '93 -Bx2546 -Bnghmtn 13902
(607) 363-7648 .. **Kilpatrick,** Alan R '86 -24461 State Hwy 206 -Downsvll 13755
(845) 486-2280 .. **Kilpatrick,** Brittany '93 %Pub Def -22 Market -Poughkeepsie 12601 **Fx:**486-2266
(212) 858-1000 .. **Kilpatrick,** Donald G '82 (Pillsbury WSP LLP) -1540 Bway -NY 10036
(212) 364-1386 .. **Kilpatrick,** Heather '73 %Hachette Book Grp -1271 Av of Amer -NY 10020
(315) 474-6448 .. **Kilpatrick,** Loretta R '91 %Byrne C&P PC -100 Madison -Syracuse 13202
(212) 775-8700 .. **Kilpatrick Stockton,LLP** -31 W 52nd -NY 10019 **Fx:**775-8800
(212) 878-8000 .. **Kilroy,** Stephen Winthrop '04 %Clifford C LLP -31 W 52nd -NY 10019
(914) 965-8473 .. **Kilsch,** Gunther H '64 G Kilsch,PC -46 Sunnyside Dr -Ynkrs 10705
(212) 687-1980 .. **Kilsheimer,** Richd J '76 (Kaplan F&K LLP) -850 3rd Av -NY 10022
(212) 998-2240 .. **Kilson,** Nancy A '79 (NYU Ofc Leg Cnsl) -70 Wshngtn Sq S -NY 10012 **Fx:**995-3048
(201) 791-7797 .. **Kilstein,** Neil I '62 (Kilstein & K) -160 E 65th -NY 10065 **Fx:**791-7091
(212) 840-8181 .. **Kim,** Albert T '98 Jujamayn Theathers LLC -246 W 44th -NY 10036
(212) 859-8000 .. **Kim,** Alexander M '98 SpclCnsl Fried FHS&J LLP -1 NY Plz -NY 10004
(212) 258-8000 .. **Kim,** Alice J '96 %MTV Networks -1515 Bway -NY 10036 **Fx:**258-8358
(212) 404-5777 .. **Kim,** Amanda Y '08 %Littleton JUP&K LLP -39 Bway -NY 10006
(212) 762-5079 .. **Kim,** Amy Yongmi '93 Morgan Stanley -1221 Av of Amer -NY 10020
(347) 592-2200 .. **Kim,** Andrea Y '02 %Leg Srvcs -89-00 Sutphin Blvd -Jamaica 11435 **Fx:**(718) 937-5350
(212) 340-0400 .. **Kim,** Angela Koh '93 %Appllt Div 1st Dept -27 Mad Av -NY 10010 **Fx:**889-4412
(212) 342-8028 .. **Kim,** Anna L '99 Tykhe Capital LLC -330 Mad Av -NY 10017
(212) 432-4600 .. **Kim,** Anne-Marie C '99 Ancharge Advisors LLC -610 Bway -NY 10012
(212) 474-1000 .. **Kim,** Annie '04 %Cravath S&M LLP -825 8th Av -NY 10019
(212) 205-7000 .. **Kim,** Anthony S '09 %Ashurst LLP -7 Times Sq -NY 10036
(212) 319-6888 .. **Kim & Bae PC** -110 E 59th -NY 10022 **Fx:**319-7539
(718) 391-1720 .. **Kim,** Beatriz C '06 %Dept Design & Cnstrctn -30-30 Thomson Av -LIC 11101 **Fx:**391-1894
(212) 319-6888 .. **Kim,** Bong June '93 (Kim & B PC) -110 E 59th -NY 10022
(212) 779-9910 .. **Kim,** Bonnie Rhenhwa '06 %Eaton & V LLP -3 Park Av -NY 10016
(212) 872-1000 .. **Kim,** Brian '01 -One Bryant Park -NY 10036 **Fx:**872-1002
(212) 351-4000 .. **Kim,** Brian J '10 Gibson D&C LLP -200 Park Av -NY 10166
(212) 653-8700 .. **Kim,** Byoung Soo '02 (Sheppard MR&H LLP) -30 Rckfllr Plz -NY 10112
(212) 878-8000 .. **Kim,** Caroline '07 %Clifford C LLP -31 W 52nd -NY 10019
(212) 839-5300 .. **Kim,** Caroline Yelee '01 %Sidley A LLP -787 7th Av -NY 10019
(212) 549-2500 .. **Kim,** Catherine Yonsoo '03 %ACLU -125 Broad -NY 10004 **Fx:**549-2651
(718) 888-9500 .. **Kim & Cha,LLP** -158-14 Nrthrn Blvd -Flushng 11358 **Fx:**661-3678
(212) 248-7200 .. **Kim,** Chan '00 %McCabe & F,LLP -1 Whitehall -NY 10004
(212) 801-6995 .. **Kim,** Chang Joo '96 (Greenberg T,LLP) -200 Park Av -NY 10166
(212) 408-2500 .. **Kim,** Chang Sik '04 %Baker B,LLP -30 Rckfllr Plz -NY 10112
(212) 601-9700 .. **Kim,** Charen '10 %Ginarte OGG&W,LLP -225 Bway -NY 10007
(212) 732-9000 .. **Kim,** Cheol I '97 %Sullivan PBM&C PC -120 Bway -NY 10271
(212) 839-5300 .. **Kim,** Chisoo '05 %Sidley A LLP -787 7th Av -NY 10019
(212) 878-8000 .. **Kim,** Chong Woo '08 %Clifford C LLP -31 W 52nd -NY 10019
(646) 240-4872 .. **Kim,** Chongjin C J '03 %Bortstein & I LLC -275 Mad Av -NY 10016 **Fx:**(866) 955-9403
(212) 735-3000 .. **Kim,** Chris Jason '09 %Skadden ASM&F LLP -4 Times Sq -NY 10036
(212) 986-1544 .. **Kim,** Chris S '06 %Gleason & K,LLP -122 E 42nd -NY 10169 **Fx:**986-1379
(212) 848-4000 .. **Kim,** Christine B '07 %Shearman & S LLP -599 Lex Av -NY 10022
(718) 222-2358 .. **Kim,** Christine C '08 %Law Dept -350 Jay -Brklyn 11201 **Fx:**222-2373
(212) 896-3310 .. **Kim,** Cindi '06 %PS Schram,PC -350 Bway -NY 10013 **Fx:**896-3316
(212) 258-8000 .. **Kim,** Clara K '89 %MTV Networks -1515 Bway -NY 10036 **Fx:**258-8358
(212) 318-6000 .. **Kim,** Claudia J '08 %Paul HJ&W LLP -75 E 55th -NY 10022
(917) 673-1522 .. **Kim,** Dae H '07 -170 Thompson -NY 10012
(718) 250-2000 .. **Kim,** Dana C '04 %DA -350 Jay -Brklyn 11201 **Fx:**250-2314
(212) 643-0090 .. **Kim,** Danbee '05 %D Kim -170 Bway -NY 10038 **Fx:**(646) 349-1732
(212) 643-0090 .. **Kim,** Danl D '92 -170 Bway -NY 10038 **Fx:**(646) 349-1732
(718) 358-9500 .. **Kim,** Danl D '04 -164-10 Nrthrn Blvd -Flushng 11358
(212) 549-8465 .. **Kim,** Danl S '01 Hyperion Capital Mgmt -1 Lbrty Plz -NY 10006
(212) 225-2000 .. **Kim,** Daseul '09 %Cleary GS&H -1 Lbrty Plz -NY 10006
(718) 250-2000 .. **Kim,** David D '07 %DA -350 Jay -Brklyn 11201 **Fx:**250-2314
(518) 402-0205 .. **Kim,** David H '90 %UIA Bd -Troy Atrium Bx15126 -Albany 12212 **Fx:**402-6208
(212) 267-2555 .. **Kim,** David K '02 %Bretz & C,LLP -305 Bway -NY 10007
(212) 609-6800 .. **Kim,** David S '07 %McCarter & E,LLP -245 Park Av -NY 10167
(212) 490-9100 .. **Kim,** Diana K '06 %Condon & F LLP -7 Times Sq -NY 10036
(516) 775-2236 .. **Kim,** Diane C '94 %Santangelo B&S -1800 Nrthrn Blvd -Roslyn 11576
(212) 918-3000 .. **Kim,** Dillon '03 %Hogan L LLP -875 3rd Av -NY 10022
(212) 213-1918 .. **Kim,** Donald S '90 -15 E 32nd -NY 10016 **Fx:**447-0968
(212) 850-2800 .. **Kim,** Donna D '07 (Andrews K LLP) -450 Lex Av -NY 10017
(212) 223-3562 .. **Kim,** Donna E '09 %Turek RM LLP -377 5th Av -NY 10016
(212) 715-0300 .. **Kim,** Dorhee '07 Tishman Speyer Prop -45 Rckfllr Plz -NY 10111 **Fx:**332-6603
(212) 530-5000 .. **Kim,** Douglas Y '08 %Milbank TH&M LLP -1 Chase Manh Plz -NY 10005
(718) 321-9797 .. **Kim,** Dujeong Jenny '02 (Rha & K,LLP) -40-45 Utopia Pkwy -Flushng 11363
(516) 538-2500 .. **Kim,** Edw '03 %Furey FLMW&D,PC -600 Front -Hempstd 11550
(212) 637-2401 .. **Kim,** Edw Y '05 %US Atty -1 St Andrews Plz -NY 10007
(212) 468-8000 .. **Kim,** Elise '05 %Morrison & F LLP -1290 Av of Amer -NY 10104
(718) 423-3200 .. **Kim,** Elizabeth H '01 EH Kim & Assoc,PLLC -215-10 Nrthrn Blvd -Bayside 11361 **Fx:**423-2612
(212) 265-6888 .. **Kim,** Elizabeth H '10 %Porzio B&N,PC -156 W 56th -NY 10019
(212) 619-5000 .. **Kim,** Elizabeth J '05 EDC -110 William -NY 10038 **Fx:**312-3909
(212) 486-1455 .. **Kim,** Ellen C '00 OfCnsl Post PGM&S,PA -575 Mad Av -NY 10022
(212) 715-1000 .. **Kim,** Emily A '06 %Arnold & P LLP -399 Park Av -NY 10022
(646) 428-3900 .. **Kim,** Emma Yoonhee '01 Dept of Educ -32 Old Slip -NY 10005 **Fx:**428-3890
(212) 319-5240 .. **Kim,** Eric H '08 %Flicker G & Assoc,LLP -45 Bway -NY 10006
(212) 790-4500 .. **Kim,** Esther '04 %Manatt P&P,LLP -7 Times Sq -NY 10036
(212) 309-6000 .. **Kim,** Esther K '05 %Morgan L&B LLP -101 Park Av -NY 10178
(212) 530-1800 .. **Kim,** Eugene '02 %Richards K&O LLP -1 World Fncl Ctr -NY 10281
(212) 558-4000 .. **Kim,** Eugene K '09 %Sullivan & C LLP -125 Broad -NY 10004
(212) 225-2000 .. **Kim,** Eugene S '09 %Cleary GS&H -1 Lbrty Plz -NY 10006
(212) 554-0400 .. **Kim,** Grace Y '07 %Grubman I&S,PC -152 W 57th -NY 10019
(914) 423-8880 .. **Kim,** Gretchen Mullins '93 -1250 Cntrl Pk Av -Ynkrs 10704 **Fx:**423-8964
(212) 980-0120 .. **Kim,** H Sujin '99 Cnsl Frankfurt KK&S,PC -488 Mad Av -NY 10022
(718) 279-7928 .. **Kim,** Haenoon '07 -43-19 207th -Bayside 11361
(212) 720-5026 .. **Kim,** Haeran '90 %Fed Reserve Bk -33 Lbrty -NY 10045 **Fx:**785-5748
(718) 445-0123 .. **Kim,** Hakyong '03 -159-15 Nrthrn Blvd -Flushng 11358
(212) 439-4094 .. **Kim,** Hana '10 Rep of Korea Mission to UN -335 E 45th -NY 10017
(646) 416-6394 .. **Kim,** Hana '10 -7 Penn Plz -NY 10001
(718) 286-6000 .. **Kim,** Hana C '06 %DA -125-01 Qns Blvd -Kew Gdns 11415
(212) 310-8000 .. **Kim,** Hansem Dawn '05 %Weil G&M LLP -767 5th Av -NY 10153
(212) 521-5400 .. **Kim,** Hayoung '07 %Reed S LLP -599 Lex Av -NY 10022
(212) 335-4500 .. **Kim,** Hee-Jean '09 %DLA Piper LLP -1251 Av of Amer -NY 10020
(212) 610-6300 .. **Kim,** Helen S '08 %Allen & O -1221 Av of Amer -NY 10020
(718) 539-7400 .. **Kim,** Henry L '01 (Kim C&L,LLC) -136-40 39th Av -Flushng 11354
(212) 225-2000 .. **Kim,** Hoon-Jung '05 %Cleary GS&H -1 Lbrty Plz -NY 10006
(212) 903-9000 .. **Kim,** Hyejin Jennifer '10 %Linklaters -1345 Av of Amer -NY 10105
(845) 291-3150 .. **Kim,** Hyun Chin '96 Cnty Atty -255 Main -Goshen 10924 **Fx:**291-3167
(212) 438-1211 .. **Kim,** Hyun Jung '05 Standard & Poors -55 Water -NY 10041
(212) 310-8000 .. **Kim,** Hyun Kang '10 %Weil G&M LLP -767 5th Av -NY 10153
(212) 310-8000 .. **Kim,** Hyun Kyung '05 %Weil G&M LLP -767 5th Av -NY 10153

(212) 848-4000 .. **Kim,** Hyun-Jeong '08 %Shearman & S LLP -599 Lex Av -NY 10022
(718) 539-7400 .. **Kim,** Hyung Seok '06 %Kim C&L,LLC -136-40 39th Av -Flushng 11354
(212) 952-0602 .. **Kim,** Hyunjung '05 %Brualdi Law -29 Bway -NY 10006 **Fx:**952-0608
(212) 455-2000 .. **Kim,** Iksoo '09 %Simpson T&B LLP -425 Lex Av -NY 10017
(212) 820-9467 .. **Kim,** J Sarah '95 Cnsl Hawkins D&W LLP -One Chase Manh Plz -NY 10005
(718) 322-5580 .. **Kim,** Jack B '98 (J Kim,PC) -117-01 Lbrty Av -S Richmond Hll 11419
(212) 245-6221 .. **Kim,** Jackie Jaewun '97 %P Thall -10 W End Av -NY 10023
(212) 852-3242 .. **Kim,** Jaclyn S '02 US Trust, Bk of America -114 W 47th -NY 10036
(212) 925-3333 .. **Kim,** Jae Kuan '07 Cantor Pecorella,Inc -54 Greene -NY 10013
(212) 450-4000 .. **Kim,** Jae Myung '06 %Davis P&W LLP -450 Lex Av -NY 10017
(646) 602-5600 .. **Kim,** Jae Y '04 %Urban Justice Ctr -123 William -NY 10038 **Fx:**(212) 533-4598
(212) 310-8000 .. **Kim,** Jae Yeon '06 %Weil G&M LLP -767 5th Av -NY 10153
(212) 506-1700 .. **Kim,** Jae Youn J '05 %Kasowitz BT&F LLP -1633 Bway -NY 10019
(718) 286-1500 .. **Kim,** Jaemin '97 %Leg Srvcs -97-77 Qns Blvd -Rego Pk 11374 **Fx:**275-5352
(212) 812-8913 .. **Kim,** James '01 %Lankler & C,LLP -845 3rd Av -NY 10022
(212) 225-2000 .. **Kim,** Jane '03 %Cleary GS&H -1 Lbrty Plz -NY 10006
(718) 250-2000 .. **Kim,** Jane Choi '99 %DA -350 Jay -Brklyn 11201 **Fx:**250-2314
(212) 551-0974 .. **Kim,** Jane Soon '98 %International Rescue Committee -122 E 42nd -NY 10168
(212) 584-0058 .. **Kim,** Jay H '01 (Yoon & K LLP) -11 E 44th -NY 10017
(212) 596-9000 .. **Kim,** Jay J '90 (Ropes & G LLP) -1211 Av of Amer -NY 10036
(718) 222-2015 .. **Kim,** Jay Young '09 %Law Dept -350 Jay -Brklyn 11201 **Fx:**222-2088
(212) 208-3530 .. **Kim,** Jean '94 %Ambac Assurance -1 State Street Plz -NY 10004 **Fx:**785-1178
(212) 350-2700 .. **Kim,** Jean '00 %Constantine C,PC -450 Lex Av -NY 10017
(212) 506-1700 .. **Kim,** Jean J '04 Kasowitz BT&F LLP -1633 Bway -NY 10019
(212) 325-2000 .. **Kim,** Jeen '02 Credit Suisse -1 Mad Av -NY 10010
(917) 599-8161 .. **Kim,** Jeeyoung '03 -Bx527578 -Flushng 11352
(718) 428-4949 .. **Kim,** Jeffrey K S '97 (Kim P&S,PC) -42-40 Bell Blvd -Bayside 11361 **Fx:**428-1316
(914) 949-1305 .. **Kim,** Jennie G '07 Leg Srvcs -90 Maple Av -White Plns 10601 **Fx:**949-6213
(718) 590-2000 .. **Kim,** Jennifer H '08 %DA -198 E 161st -Bronx 10451 **Fx:**590-6477
(212) 382-6600 .. **Kim,** Jennifer Hee-Jin '01 %NYC Bar -42 W 44th -NY 10036 **Fx:**398-6634
(212) 225-2000 .. **Kim,** Jennifer J '04 Cleary GS&H -1 Lbrty Plz -NY 10006
(212) 859-8000 .. **Kim,** Jennifer K '08 %Fried FHS&J LLP -1 NY Plz -NY 10004
(212) 891-9100 .. **Kim,** Jenny '05 %Goldfarb & F LLP -345 Park Av -NY 10154
(212) 506-1700 .. **Kim,** Jenny H '05 %Kasowitz BT&F LLP -1633 Bway -NY 10019
(212) 766-1888 .. **Kim,** Jeoungson '95 (Morris DA&F) -2 Rector -NY 10006
(212) 687-3000 .. **Kim,** Jeremy '03 %Jaffe & A,LLP -600 3rd Av -NY 10016
(212) 736-3116 .. **Kim,** Jerry Jinyoung '89 -1270 Bway -NY 10001 **Fx:**564-1649
(212) 407-7700 .. **Kim,** Ji Woon '05 %Vedder P,PC -1633 Bway -NY 10019
(914) 642-3102 .. **Kim,** Jihwan '01 IBM -1133 Wstchstr Av -White Plns 10604
(718) 353-3260 .. **Kim,** Jin H '00 -16332 Nrthrn Blvd -Flushng 11358 **Fx:**353-5285
(212) 474-1000 .. **Kim,** Jin Hee '05 %Cravath S&M LLP -825 8th Av -NY 10019
(212) 819-8200 .. **Kim,** Jin Koo '95 (White & C LLP) -1155 Av of Amer -NY 10036
(212) 450-4000 .. **Kim,** Jinsoo H '96 (Davis P&W LLP) -450 Lex Av -NY 10017
(212) 239-2378 .. **Kim,** Jiwon '04 %Pak & W LLC -16 W 32nd -NY 10001 **Fx:**239-8732
(718) 210-4794 .. **Kim,** John C '00 -50 Court -Brklyn 11201
(212) 679-3482 .. **Kim,** John H '85 -445 5th Av -NY 10016 **Fx:**679-4133
(212) 454-6849 .. **Kim,** John H '96 %Deutsche Bank -60 Wall -NY 10005
(212) 768-6700 .. **Kim,** John J '93 (Sonnenschein N&R LLP) -2 World Fncl Ctr -NY 10281
(917) 639-4034 .. **Kim,** John J B '95 -1230 6th Av -NY 10020 **Fx:**639-4005
(212) 698-3500 .. **Kim,** Jonathan '03 %Dechert LLP -1095 Av of Amer -NY 10036
(212) 357-1999 .. **Kim,** Jonathan J '97 Goldman Sachs -1 NY Plz -NY 10004
(212) 504-6000 .. **Kim,** Joo H '06 %Cadwalader W&T LLP -1 World Fncl Ctr -NY 10281
(212) 806-5400 .. **Kim,** Joon H '08 %Stroock &S&L LLP -180 Maiden Ln -NY 10038
(212) 225-2000 .. **Kim,** Joon Hyun '97 (Cleary GS&H) -1 Lbrty Plz -NY 10006
(212) 599-2200 .. **Kim,** Joon S '94 Lucas Group -52 Vndrblt Av -NY 10017
(212) 480-4800 .. **Kim,** JooYun '02 %Fox H&C LLP -825 3rd Av -NY 10022
(914) 253-3520 .. **Kim,** Jos O '97 %Pepsico -700 Andrsn Hill Rd -Purchase 10577
(718) 461-3654 .. **Kim,** Joung H '92 -36-09 Main -Flushng 11354 **Fx:**461-2425
(212) 225-2000 .. **Kim,** Joyce S '10 %Cleary GS&H -1 Lbrty Plz -NY 10006
(212) 859-8000 .. **Kim,** Judy E '99 %Fried FHS&J LLP -1 NY Plz -NY 10004
(212) 341-6400 .. **Kim,** Judy Hee-Jung '99 Liquidation Bur -123 William -NY 10038 **Fx:**608-3398
(212) 687-2770 .. **Kim,** Julia S '92 (Cohen PL&P) -551 5th Av -NY 10176
(212) 506-1700 .. **Kim,** Julia Young '03 Kasowitz BT&F LLP -1633 Bway -NY 10019
(212) 847-3907 .. **Kim,** Julie A '05 Meadowlands Dvlpmnt -601 W 26th -NY 10001
(212) 484-8000 .. **Kim,** Julie Y '00 %Time Warner -1 Time Warner Ctr -NY 10019
(212) 422-0202 .. **Kim,** Julie Y '08 %Sedgwick DM&A LLP -125 Broad -NY 10004
(212) 878-8000 .. **Kim,** JungAh '08 %Clifford C LLP -31 W 52nd -NY 10019
(718) 956-8144 .. **Kim,** Juston K '92 -36-19 Bway -Astoria 11106
(212) 545-1900 .. **Kim,** Karen '08 %Menaker & H LLP -10 E 40th -NY 10016
(212) 474-1000 .. **Kim,** Karen '10 %Cravath S&M LLP -825 8th Av -NY 10019
(201) 615-5709 .. **Kim,** Kathy K '10 -48 East End Av -NY 10028
(212) 697-3122 .. **Kim,** Kenneth '08 %Martin C&B LLP -220 E 42nd -NY 10017
(212) 566-8080 .. **Kim,** Kenneth '08 %Wong W & Assoc,PC -150 Bway -NY 10038 **Fx:**566-8960
(718) 321-1616 .. **Kim,** Kenneth Sungkon '90 -150-52 Nrthrn Blvd -Flushng 11354 **Fx:**321-9350
(212) 940-8800 .. **Kim,** Keun Dong '09 %Katten MR LLP -575 Mad Av -NY 10022
(212) 596-9000 .. **Kim,** Kristen C '08 %Ropes & G LLP -1211 Av of Amer -NY 10036
(212) 279-6200 .. **Kim,** Kyu O '98 %McGovern & Assoc -16 W 32nd -NY 10001
(212) 806-5400 .. **Kim,** Linda Y '08 %Stroock &S&L LLP -180 Maiden Ln -NY 10038
(212) 302-2400 .. **Kim,** Lois '08 %Lynch DE LLP -264 W 40th -NY 10018
(212) 205-7000 .. **Kim,** M Sharon '08 %Ashurst LLP -7 Times Sq -NY 10036
(212) 902-2049 .. **Kim,** Marianne M '06 Goldman Sachs & Co -1 NY Plz -NY 10004
(646) 591-3272 .. **Kim,** Martha V '03 -350 5th Av -NY 10118
(718) 722-3100 .. **Kim,** Mary Hye Kyung '99 %Leg Aid -111 Lvngstn -Brklyn 11201 **Fx:**722-3093
(212) 825-1565 .. **Kim,** Mary Y J '96 %Ptashnik & Assoc -45 Bway -NY 10006 **Fx:**825-1559
(212) 878-8000 .. **Kim,** Maxwell S '04 %Clifford C LLP -31 W 52nd -NY 10019
(212) 468-8000 .. **Kim,** Mee Jung '92 OfCnsl Morrison & F LLP -1290 Av of Amer -NY 10104
(212) 820-9300 .. **Kim,** Meenah Yoon '07 %Hawkins D&W LLP -One Chase Manh Plz -NY 10005
(212) 768-6700 .. **Kim,** Michl '98 %Sonnenschein N&R LLP -2 World Fncl Ctr -NY 10281
(212) 762-5080 .. **Kim,** Michl '02 Morgan Stanley -1585 Bway -NY 10036
(212) 446-4800 .. **Kim,** Michl '03 (Kirkland & E LLP) -153 E 53rd -NY 10022
(212) 488-1200 .. **Kim,** Michl S '96 (Kobre & K,LLP) -800 3rd Av -NY 10022
(212) 545-0818 .. **Kim,** Michele '98 ILW.COM -Bx1830 -NY 10156 **Fx:**545-0869
(212) 364-8480 .. **Kim,** Michelle N '97 Time Warner Cable -60 Columbus Av -NY 10023 **Fx:**364-8460
(718) 286-2000 .. **Kim,** Mihea '90 %Leg Aid -120-46 Qns Blvd -Kew Gdns 11415 **Fx:**286-2286
(212) 559-8580 .. **Kim,** Millie '86 -399 Park Av -NY 10022
(212) 652-6392 .. **Kim,** Mimi Okkyung '97 AOL -1325 Av of Amer -NY 10019
(212) 878-8000 .. **Kim,** Mina '03 %Clifford C LLP -31 W 52nd -NY 10019
(212) 416-8000 .. **Kim,** Mina A '06 %Dept of Law -120 Bway -NY 10271
(212) 609-6800 .. **Kim,** Minji '10 %McCarter & E,LLP -245 Park Av -NY 10167
(716) 847-8400 .. **Kim,** Minryu Sarah '07 %Phillips L LLP -3400 HSBC Ctr -Buffalo 14203
(212) 755-5510 .. **Kim,** Miree '04 %Loeb B & Prtnrs -505 Park Av -NY 10022
(212) 452-5300 .. **Kim,** Morae '07 %Darger & E,LLP -116 E 27th -NY 10016
(212) 632-6000 .. **Kim,** Namsun '08 Lazard Freres -30 Rckfllr Plz -NY 10112 **Fx:**632-6060
(212) 699-8865 .. **Kim,** Nayoung '05 Berdon LLP -360 Mad Av -NY 10017
(212) 422-0202 .. **Kim,** P Stephen '99 %Sedgwick DM&A LLP -125 Broad -NY 10004
(212) 547-5400 .. **Kim,** Paul June-IL '94 McDermott W&E LLP -340 Mad Av -NY 10173
(914) 323-7000 .. **Kim,** Paul Myung Han '09 %Wilson EME&D LLP -3 Gannett Dr -White Plns 10604
(212) 969-3000 .. **Kim,** Pauline S '08 %Proskauer R LLP -1585 Bway -NY 10036
(212) 833-8676 .. **Kim,** Peter J '96 Sony Corp of America -550 Mad Av -NY 10022
(212) 909-6000 .. **Kim,** Peter J '10 %Debevoise & P LLP -919 3rd Av -NY 10022
(212) 259-8000 .. **Kim,** Peter S '08 %Dewey & L LLP -1301 Av of Amer -NY 10019
(212) 450-4000 .. **Kim,** Peter S '10 %Davis P&W LLP -450 Lex Av -NY 10017
(212) 299-2245 .. **Kim,** Philip D '04 NYMEX -1 North End Av -NY 10282 **Fx:**301-4700
(212) 686-1060 .. **Kim,** Phillip '03 %Rosen Law Firm -350 5th Av -NY 10118
(212) 261-8000 .. **Kim,** Rachel H '06 %Mendes & M,LLP -750 7th Av -NY 10019
(646) 541-7327 .. **Kim,** Richd '08 JP Morgan Chase -245 Park Av -NY 10167
(212) 455-2000 .. **Kim,** Richd C '07 %Simpson T&B LLP -425 Lex Av -NY 10017
(212) 403-1000 .. **Kim,** Richd K '02 (Wachtell LR&K) -51 W 52nd -NY 10019
(516) 625-9292 .. **Kim,** Richd Kwang-Ho '84 Kiss Products Inc -57 Seaview Blvd -Pt Wash 11050 **Fx:**299-5282
(212) 732-3200 .. **Kim,** Richd N '02 %Carter L&M LLP -2 Wall -NY 10005
(718) 445-0095 .. **Kim,** Rick Chan Yong '97 -159-15 Nrthrn Blvd -Flushng 11358
(212) 385-4575 .. **Kim,** Robt D '03 OfCnsl YL Poon.PLLC -11 E Bway -NY 10038 **Fx:**385-4792
(212) 599-3940 .. **Kim,** Robt M '02 Citigroup -909 3rd Av -NY 10022
(212) 504-6000 .. **Kim,** Robt S '96 SpclCnsl Cadwalader W&T LLP -1 World Fncl Ctr -NY 10281
(212) 745-5826 .. **Kim,** Roger C '02 IBM -590 Mad Av -NY 10022
(518) 581-8416 .. **Kim,** Ronald J '90 -36 Long Alley Bx318 -Saratoga Spgs 12866 **Fx:**583-9059
(212) 849-7000 .. **Kim,** Rosa W '07 %Quinn EU&S,LLP -51 Mad Av -NY 10010
(212) 317-5032 .. **Kim,** Samantha J '93 Swiss Re -55 E 52nd -NY 10055
(212) 733-8174 .. **Kim,** Sandra '06 %Pfizer -150 E 42nd -NY 10017
(212) 941-9213 .. **Kim,** Sandra M '93 -1775 York Av -NY 10128
(212) 902-8680 .. **Kim,** Sang Yong '98 %Goldman Sachs -1 NY Plz -NY 10004
(212) 823-1996 .. **Kim,** Sarah '06 %Metalmark Cptl -1177 Av of Amer -NY 10036
(212) 239-9266 .. **Kim,** Seo Mahn Bryan '96 -16 W 32nd -NY 10001 **Fx:**239-9296
(212) 836-8000 .. **Kim,** Seong '07 %Kaye S LLP -425 Park Av -NY 10022
(212) 684-7407 .. **Kim,** Seoun K '93 -15 E 32nd -NY 10016
(212) 808-7800 .. **Kim,** Seunghwan '02 Kelley D&W LLP -101 Park Av -NY 10178
(212) 282-5000 .. **Kim,** Si-Yeon '00 Avon Products -1345 Av of Amer -NY 10105
(646) 356-0550 .. **Kim,** Simone Sun Min '02 Hire Cnsl -575 Mad Av -NY 10022 **Fx:**356-0565
(212) 479-6000 .. **Kim,** Soo Y '08 %Cooley LLP -1114 Av of Amer -NY 10036
(212) 422-0202 .. **Kim,** Soo Yeon '02 %Sedgwick DM&A LLP -125 Broad -NY 10004
(212) 878-8000 .. **Kim,** Soo Young '05 %Clifford C LLP -31 W 52nd -NY 10019
(718) 888-9500 .. **Kim,** Soo-Hyun '97 (Kim & C,LLP) -158-14 Nrthrn Blvd -Flushng 11358
(212) 389-2560 .. **Kim,** Sophie Sokhun '05 Ore Hill Prtnrs LLC -650 5th Av -NY 10019
(212) 756-2000 .. **Kim,** Stephanie '07 %Schulte R&Z LLP -919 3rd Av -NY 10022
(718) 206-4728 .. **Kim,** Stephen Sanghyun '08 %Law Dept -89-17 Sutphin Blvd -Jamaica 11435 **Fx:**206-4702
(212) 373-3000 .. **Kim,** Steve D '04 %Paul WRW&G LLP -1285 Av of Amer -NY 10019
(718) 254-7000 .. **Kim,** Steven J '06 %US Atty -271 Cadman Plz E -Brklyn 11201 **Fx:**254-6479
(212) 218-2100 .. **Kim,** Steven S Y '06 %Fitzpatrick CH&S -1290 Av of Amer -NY 10104
(212) 279-8740 .. **Kim,** Stuart S '94 -Bx20084 -NY 10001 **Fx:**279-8742
(646) 386-4200 .. **Kim,** Sun E '07 %OCA -25 Beaver -NY 10004
(212) 848-4000 .. **Kim,** Sung Eun '09 %Shearman & S LLP -599 Lex Av -NY 10022
(212) 596-9000 .. **Kim,** Sung Hoon '10 %Ropes & G LLP -1211 Av of Amer -NY 10036
(212) 442-1400 .. **Kim,** Sung Mo '02 %Conflicts of Int Bd -2 Lafayette -NY 10007 **Fx:**442-1407
(212) 808-7800 .. **Kim,** Sung Wan '05 %Kelley D&W LLP -101 Park Av -NY 10178
(212) 479-6000 .. **Kim,** Sung Yoon '04 %Cooley LLP -1114 Av of Amer -NY 10036
(914) 428-2100 .. **Kim,** Sung-Teak Dean '95 %Welby B&G,LLP -11 Martine Av -White Plns 10606
(212) 558-4000 .. **Kim,** Sunjung Melissa '10 %Sullivan & C LLP -125 Broad -NY 10004
(212) 344-5680 .. **Kim,** Sunny '01 %Thompson H LLP -335 Mad Av -NY 10017
(212) 575-7900 .. **Kim,** Sunny '03 %Ballon SB&N,PC -729 7th Av -NY 10019
(212) 556-2100 .. **Kim,** Susan A '04 %King & S -1185 Av of Amer -NY 10036

(212) 605-3053 .. **Kim,** Susan Soyon '96 Bloomberg LP -499 Park Av -NY 10022
(212) 407-4000 .. **Kim,** Susie L '04 %Loeb & L,LLP -345 Park Av -NY 10154
(212) 506-5000 .. **Kim,** Suzy '02 %Orrick H&S LLP -51 W 52nd -NY 10019
(212) 553-1684 .. **Kim,** Taehun '96 Moody's Invstr Srvc -250 Greenwich -NY 10007
(212) 756-2000 .. **Kim,** Taejin '10 %Schulte R&Z LLP -919 3rd Av -NY 10022
(212) 374-6759 .. **Kim,** Taejong '00 NYC Dept Educ -51 Chmbrs -NY 10007
(631) 698-3900 .. **Kim,** Tai Hee '00 -1305 Middle Cntry Rd -Selden 11784 **Fx:**698-3968
(212) 790-4500 .. **Kim,** Terry N '07 %Manatt P&P,LLP -7 Times Sq -NY 10036
(646) 223-4200 .. **Kim,** Thos Sang '02 %Reuters -3 Times Sq -NY 10036 **Fx:**223-4250
(212) 848-4000 .. **Kim,** Tracey J '08 %Shearman & S LLP -599 Lex Av -NY 10022
(212) 596-9000 .. **Kim,** Wm Y '89 (Ropes & G LLP) -1211 Av of Amer -NY 10036
(212) 808-7800 .. **Kim,** Wook '06 %Kelley D&W LLP -101 Park Av -NY 10178
(212) 869-7000 .. **Kim,** Yong Hak '87 (Feldman W&S LLP) -420 Lex Av -NY 10170
(646) 295-0287 .. **Kim,** Yong Ig '02 -1261 Bway -NY 10001
(212) 584-0058 .. **Kim,** Young Danl '09 %Yoon & K LLP -11 E 44th -NY 10017
(212) 371-1000 .. **Kim,** Young J '93 NY Catholic Ctr -1011 1st Av -NY 10022
(716) 631-2300 .. **Kim,** Yung Mo '91 -6470 Main -Williamsvll 14221 **Fx:**631-2316
(212) 704-6000 .. **Kim,** Yunhee '09 %Troutman S LLP -405 Lex Av -NY 10174
(212) 455-2000 .. **Kiman,** Joshua D '08 %Simpson T&B LLP -425 Lex Av -NY 10017
(315) 445-0600 .. **Kimball,** Emily D '01 (McDonald & K PC) -120 E Wshngtn -Syracuse 13202
(845) 424-3487 .. **Kimball,** Harris L '73 -559 Route 9D Bx54 -Garrison 10524 **Fx:**424-4560
(212) 238-3000 .. **Kimball,** J Dudley B '75 (Emmet M&M,LLP) -120 Bway -NY 10271
(212) 885-5000 .. **Kimball,** John D '76 (Blank R LLP) -405 Lex Av -NY 10174
(518) 283-1650 .. **Kimball,** Karen L '91 -26 Sand Lk Rd -Wynantskill 12198
(914) 328-0674 .. **Kimball,** Leslie Y '01 Pro Bono Prtnrshp,Inc -237 Mamaroneck Av -White Plns 10605 **Fx:**328-0538
(212) 417-2000 .. **Kimball,** Wilson '01 %Battery Pk City Auth -1 Wrld Fncl Ctr -NY 10281 **Fx:**417-2001
(607) 255-5124 .. **Kimberly,** Michl G '68 %Cornell Univ -300 CCC Bldg-Grdn Av -Ithaca 14853 **Fx:**255-2794
(212) 230-3983 .. **Kimble,** Michl J '93 MacKay Shields LLC -9 W 57th -NY 10019
(212) 264-2908 .. **Kimble,** Tina Potuto '08 US Ct of Intl Trade -1 Fed Plz -NY 10278
(212) 944-6225 .. **Kim-Bookstein,** Desirée '91 %Law Dept -100 Church -NY 10007 **Fx:**788-0367
(914) 524-6819 .. **Kimbro,** Lawanna R '09 Prestige Brands -90 N Bway -Irvngtn 10533
(212) 449-9892 .. **Kimbrough,** Colette D '87 %Merrill Lynch -220 Bway -NY 10038
(212) 227-8140 .. **Kimelman,** Glenn A '89 (Taubman K&S LLP) -30 Vesey -NY 10007
(718) 590-2000 .. **Kimelman,** Jeffrey M '09 %DA -198 E 161st -Bronx 10451 **Fx:**590-6477
(212) 848-0219 .. **Kimelman,** Martin '62 ADCO Grp -645 5th Av -NY 10022 **Fx:**355-5057
(917) 496-7192 .. **Kimelman,** Michl A '98 Incremental Capital -110 E 55th -NY 10022
(212) 484-3900 .. **Kimelman,** Steven '73 (Arent F LLP) -1675 Bway -NY 10019
(914) 428-8300 .. **Kimenker,** Nina L '85 %Sacks,PC -707 Wstchstr Av -White Plns 10604 **Fx:**682-1707
(914) 761-1300 .. **Kimerling,** Joshua E '95 (Cuddy & F LLP) -445 Hmltn Av -White Plns 10601
(212) 966-5932 .. **Kimerling,** Kenneth '69 %AALDEF -99 Hudson -NY 10013 **Fx:**966-4303
(516) 437-4385 .. **Kimler,** Andrew A '79 (Vishnick MM LLP) -3000 Marcus Av -Lk Success 11042
(212) 704-6000 .. **Kim-Levy,** Susie '94 (Troutman S LLP) -405 Lex Av -NY 10174
(212) 968-8600 .. **Kimm,** April S '05 %Manchanda Law Ofc,PLLC -80 Wall -NY 10005 **Fx:**968-8601
(212) 867-3141 .. **Kimmel,** Brett H '93 (B Kimmel,PC) -275 Mad Av -NY 10016
(212) 404-7069 .. **Kimmel,** Brian S '07 %De Lotto & F LLP -44 Wall -NY 10005
(212) 438-1575 .. **Kimmel,** George L '86 Standard & Poor's -55 Water -NY 10041 **Fx:**438-2652
(212) 422-1200 .. **Kimmel,** James E '03 %Abrams GF&J,PC -1 Bttry Pk Plz -NY 10004
(212) 661-8838 .. **Kimmel,** Jay '80 (Kimmel & K) -270 Mad Av -NY 10016 **Fx:**490-3736
(212) 655-3500 .. **Kimmel,** Jeffrey A '96 (Meister S&F LLP) -140 E 45th -NY 10017
(212) 267-1950 .. **Kimmel,** Jeffrey M '92 (Salenger SSK&B,LLP) -233 Bway -NY 10279
(212) 684-5454 .. **Kimmel,** Jeffrey S '99 -160 Bway -NY 10038 **Fx:**202-7941
(212) 867-3141 .. **Kimmel,** Jodi J '02 (B Kimmel,PC) -275 Mad Av -NY 10016
(212) 787-2306 .. **Kimmel,** Jonathan L '84 -160 West End Av -NY 10023
(212) 966-6420 .. **Kimmel,** Kristin S '97 %Lwyrs For Children -110 Lafayette -NY 10013 **Fx:**966-0531
(718) 643-9558 .. **Kimmel,** Leo J '66 -26 Court -Brklyn 11242 **Fx:**643-0025
(305) 532-8578 .. **Kimmel,** Melvin '58 -2247 Coney Isl Av -Brklyn 11223
(212) 403-3500 .. **Kimmel,** Roger H '72 Rothschild Inc -1251 Av of Amer -NY 10020 **Fx:**403-5515
(212) 526-2439 .. **Kimmel,** Scott L '89 Barclays Capital Inc -745 7th Av -NY 10019
(845) 496-8717 .. **Kimmel,** Steven A '81 -Bx258 -Washingtnvll 10992 **Fx:**(877) 594-1293
(212) 556-2100 .. **Kimmel,** Tracy '93 (King & S) -1185 Av of Amer -NY 10036
(212) 661-8838 .. **Kimmel,** Tuvia L '07 %Kimmel & K -270 Mad Av -NY 10016 **Fx:**490-3736
(212) 310-8000 .. **Kimmelman,** Cassie L '09 %Weil G&M LLP -767 5th Av -NY 10153
(718) 248-9102 .. **Kimmelman,** Gary A '82 %Citibank -1 Court Sq -LIC 11101
(212) 610-6300 .. **Kimmelman,** Louis B '77 (Allen & O) -1221 Av of Amer -NY 10020
(212) 962-3630 .. **Kimmelman,** Michl L '84 -170 Bway -NY 10038 **Fx:**571-6083
(212) 341-3127 .. **Kimmelman,** Raymond L '84 Admin Childrens Srvcs -150 William -NY 10038 **Fx:**341-2679
(212) 506-5000 .. **Kimmet,** George T '10 %Orrick H&S LLP -51 W 52nd -NY 10019
(212) 761-4000 .. **Kimmett,** Krysten M '02 Morgan Stanley -1221 Av of Amer -NY 10020
(516) 876-3270 .. **Kimmins,** Wm P '68 SUNY -Bx210 -Old Westbury 11568
(315) 472-4481 .. **Kimpel,** David S '83 (Ali P&C) -614 James -Syracuse 13203
(845) 928-9444 .. **Kimple,** Justin E '07 %Levinson R&O,PC -Bx244 -Centrl Vly 10917
(212) 373-3000 .. **Kimpler,** Kyle J '09 %Paul WRW&G LLP -1285 Av of Amer -NY 10019
(212) 756-2000 .. **Kim-Reuter,** Sena H '01 %Schulte R&Z LLP -919 3rd Av -NY 10022
(212) 373-3000 .. **Kinburn,** Rebecca '09 Paul WRW&G LLP -1285 Av of Amer -NY 10019
(914) 945-3766 .. **Kincaid,** Sandra K '72 IBM -Bx218 -Yorktwn Hts 10598
(718) 305-1543 .. **Kinch,** Cheryl J '04 -26 Court -Brklyn 11242 **Fx:**802-9369
(914) 286-4737 .. **Kinch,** Julie M '88 Heineken USA -360 Hmltn Av -White Plns 10601
(516) 487-3919 .. **Kind,** Esther Drapacz '84 -92 Merrivale Rd -Gt Neck 11020
(212) 421-2233 .. **Kinderlehrer,** Aaron C '74 (Wilk A LLP) -675 3rd Av -NY 10017
(212) 451-2300 .. **Kindler,** Hyman '89 Cnsl Olshan GFR&W LLP -65 E 55th -NY 10022
(631) 232-2400 .. **Kindler,** Marissa Luchs '91 %Nassau/Sfflk Law Srv -1757 Vets Hwy -Islandia 11749 **Fx:**232-2489
(212) 761-7895 .. **Kindler,** Robt A '81 Morgan Stanley -1585 Bway -NY 10036
(518) 434-1493 .. **Kindlon,** Lee C '02 %Kindlon & S,PC -74 Chapel -Albany 12207
(518) 434-1493 .. **Kindlon & Shanks,PC** -74 Chapel -Albany 12207 **Fx:**432-7806
(518) 434-1493 .. **Kindlon,** Terence L '74 (Kindlon & S,PC) -74 Chapel -Albany 12207
(585) 232-6500 .. **Kinel,** Danl R '96 (Harter S&E LLP) -1600 Bausch & Lomb Pl -Rchstr 14604
(212) 262-6700 .. **Kinel,** Norman N '84 (Lowenstein S PC) -1251 Av of Amer -NY 10020
(212) 272-1731 .. **Kinet,** Sandra J '77 %JP Morgan Chase -383 Mad Av -NY 10179
(518) 584-2200 .. **King Adang & Arpey** -2911 Route 9 Bx4580 -Saratoga Spgs 12866 **Fx:**584-4075
(212) 836-8000 .. **King,** Alison M '97 Cnsl Kaye S LLP -425 Park Av -NY 10022
(631) 232-2400 .. **King,** Amy E '02 %Nassau/Sfflk Law Srv -1757 Vets Hwy -Islandia 11749 **Fx:**232-2489
(315) 677-9363 .. **King,** Andrea '86 -5968 Route 20 -LaFayette 13084 **Fx:**677-9514
(212) 455-2000 .. **King,** Anthony D '04 %Simpson T&B LLP -425 Lex Av -NY 10017
(518) 218-7100 .. **King,** Barbara J '88 OfCnsl Tully R,PLLC -441 New Karner Rd -Albany 12205
(718) 858-2994 .. **King,** Bernard R '85 -32 Court -Brklyn 11201
(315) 422-7111 .. **King,** Bernard T '59 (Blitman & K LLP) -443 N Franklin -Syracuse 13204
(516) 741-3441 .. **King,** Bradley D '78 (Bergman & K,PC) -500 Old Cntry Rd -Gdn Cty 11530
(212) 661-7762 .. **King,** Bradley T '06 Hon C Ciparick -122 E 42nd -NY 10168
(315) 474-2911 .. **King,** Brandon R '96 (Smith SK&S,PC) -250 S Clinton -Syracuse 13202
(917) 783-7024 .. **King,** Brian A '99 -110 Wall -NY 10005
(212) 883-8833 .. **King,** Brian E '06 %Tacopina & A -275 Mad Av -NY 10016
(212) 513-7800 .. **King,** Brian M '88 -111 John -NY 10038
(315) 218-8000 .. **King,** Catherine Ann '91 (Bond S&K,PLLC) -1 Lincoln Ctr -Syracuse 13202
(212) 335-9000 .. **King,** Chas E III '83 %DA -1 Hogan Pl -NY 10013
(718) 739-6400 .. **King,** Cheryl '90 %DHCR -92-31 Union Hall -Jamaica 11433 **Fx:**262-7938
(716) 854-3455 .. **King,** Christine M '08 Gielowski F&C,LLP -135 Delaware Av -Buffalo 14202 **Fx:**854-2797
(212) 788-1235 .. **King,** Christopher G '93 %Law Dept -100 Church -NY 10007 **Fx:**788-0367
(212) 325-9880 .. **King,** Christopher J '94 %Credit Suisse First Boston -11 Mad Av -NY 10010
(212) 848-4000 .. **King,** Dana M '07 %Shearman & S LLP -599 Lex Av -NY 10022
(315) 376-6565 .. **King,** Danl R '93 (Dunckel & K LLP) -5423 Shady Av Bx473 -Lowvll 13367 **Fx:**376-8418
(585) 442-2551 .. **King,** David C '76 OfCnsl Johnson M&B,PC -1399 Monroe Av -Rchstr 14618
(212) 592-1400 .. **King,** David R '99 (Herrick,F LLP) -2 Park Av -NY 10016
(212) 374-2985 .. **King,** Deborah A L '85 %NYC Dept Educ-OLS -52 Chmbrs -NY 10007 **Fx:**374-5939
(631) 269-3998 .. **King,** Donald J '66 -75 E Main Bx304 -Kings Pk 11754
(718) 919-1706 .. **King,** Edw H '84 -457 Putnam Av -Brklyn 11221
(516) 431-3333 .. **King,** Edw L '88 -522 W Beech -Long Bch 11561 **Fx:**431-3333
(212) 812-5080 .. **King,** Eileen S '84 -110 E 59th -NY 10022 **Fx:**812-5078
(518) 843-5029 .. **King,** Eliot '81 -22 Vanderveer -Amsterdam 12010 **Fx:**842-1812
(718) 590-2000 .. **King,** Gabriela '00 %DA -198 E 161st -Bronx 10451 **Fx:**590-6477
(518) 408-4906 .. **King,** George S '75 %State Comptroller -110 State -Albany 12236 **Fx:**473-9104
(518) 474-5259 .. **King,** Glenn C '99 %Dept of Law -The Cptl -Albany 12224
(212) 612-4200 .. **King,** Harold Kenneth Jr. '79 (Hoey KT&E) -55 Water -NY 10041
(212) 450-4000 .. **King,** Henry L '52 SrCnsl Davis P&W LLP -450 Lex Av -NY 10017
(212) 506-1700 .. **King,** J Anthony '04 %Kasowitz BT&F LLP -1633 Bway -NY 10019
(518) 426-4600 .. **King,** James S '98 (Couch W,LLP) -540 Bway Bx22222 -Albany 12201
(315) 772-6371 .. **King,** James T Jr. '79 OSJA -141 Lewis Av -Fort Drum 13602
(212) 248-3140 .. **King,** Jason F '04 %Drinker B&R LLP -140 Bway -NY 10005
(718) 595-5062 .. **King,** Jennifer M '99 %DEP-BWT -96-05 Horace Hrdng Expy -Corona 11368 **Fx:**595-6950
(212) 277-6500 .. **King,** Jeremy M '02 %Dickstein S LLP -1633 Bway -NY 10019
(516) 229-6000 .. **King,** Jill R '83 %R Lau & Assoc -300 Jericho Quad Bx9040 -Jericho 11753 **Fx:**229-6167
(315) 471-8111 .. **King,** John S '97 (Scolaro SCF&B,PC) -507 Plum -Syracuse 13204
(631) 261-5492 .. **King,** John W Jr. '73 -Bx523 -Centerprt 11721
(212) 566-7188 .. **King,** Jonathan B '09 %Genova B&G -115 Bway -NY 10006
(212) 790-9200 .. **King,** Jonathan Z '92 %Cowan L&L,PC -1133 Av of Amer -NY 10036
(631) 853-5212 .. **King,** Jos H '94 %Leg Aid -400 Carleton Av Bx9082 -Central Islip 11722 **Fx:**853-7798
(914) 422-4220 .. **King,** Josephine Y '65 %Pace Law Schl -78 N Bway -White Plns 10603 **Fx:**422-4039
(212) 373-3000 .. **King,** Karen R '01 %Paul WRW&G LLP -1285 Av of Amer -NY 10019
(212) 335-9000 .. **King,** Kassandra A '06 %DA -1 Hogan Pl -NY 10013
(212) 969-3000 .. **King,** Kawana T '09 %Proskauer R LLP -1585 Bway -NY 10036
(212) 808-2700 .. **King,** Kenneth J '83 (Pepper H LLP) -620 8th Av -NY 10018
(516) 572-2000 .. **King,** Kevin C '09 %DA -99 Main -Hempstd 11550 **Fx:**572-2606
(518) 474-3997 .. **King,** Kevin J '94 %State Comptroller -110 State -Albany 12236 **Fx:**473-9104
(718) 896-6554 .. **King & King LLP** -27-12 37th Av -LIC 11101 **Fx:**275-5081
(718) 803-3782 .. **King,** Kleo J '88 %United Spinal Assn -75-20 Astoria Blvd -E Elmhrst 11370 **Fx:**803-0414

(518) 456-3579 .. **King**, Kristen '90 -292 Wshngtn Av Ext -Albany 12203 **Fx**:456-8258
(212) 582-8000 .. **King**, Kristin J '97 (Feingold & A,LLP) -1330 Av of Amer -NY 10019
(212) 259-8000 .. **King**, Lauren '06 %Dewey & L LLP -1301 Av of Amer -NY 10019
(212) 687-1980 .. **King**, Laurence D '89 (Kaplan F&K LLP) -850 3rd Av -NY 10022
(631) 293-6060 .. **King**, Lisa Faro '08 (Cellino & B,PC) -445 Broad Hollow Rd -Melvll 11747
(631) 269-3998 .. **King**, Lisa M '92 -75 E Main Bx304 -Kings Pk 11754
(518) 785-1900 .. **King**, Lisa Marie '88 %PEF -1168-70 Troy-Schnctdy Rd Bx12414 -Albany 12212 **Fx**:785-1323
(212) 788-0472 .. **King**, Margaret G '77 %Law Dept -100 Church -NY 10007 **Fx**:788-0367
(212) 351-4000 .. **King**, Marshall R '92 %Gibson D&C LLP -200 Park Av -NY 10166
(914) 241-4545 .. **King**, Martin J '69 M King,PC -6 Oxford Rd -White Plns 10605 **Fx**:560-2234
(315) 471-3151 .. **King**, Mary C '05 %Hancock & E,LLP -1500 AXA Twr I Bx4976 -Syracuse 13221
(516) 741-3441 .. **King**, Matthew B '87 (Bergman & K,PC) -500 Old Cntry Rd -Gdn Cty 11530
(212) 468-8000 .. **King**, Matthew R '08 %Morrison & F LLP -1290 Av of Amer -NY 10104
(212) 336-0111 .. **King**, Maureen P '03 SEC -3 World Fncl Ctr -NY 10281 **Fx**:336-1323
(212) 450-4000 .. **King**, Melissa C '10 %Davis P&W LLP -450 Lex Av -NY 10017
(845) 452-6400 .. **King**, Michl '02 OfCnsl O'Neil & B -301 Mnchstr Rd -Poughkeepsie 12603
(718) 240-0135 .. **King**, Michl A '97 -41 Schermerhorn -Brklyn 11201
(518) 734-6713 .. **King**, Michl F '79 -19 Brook Hllw Ln Bx962 -Windham 12496 **Fx**:734-6885
(718) 238-2021 .. **King**, Michl F '79 -256 93rd -Brklyn 11209 **Fx**:238-2099
(212) 918-3000 .. **King**, Michl H '64 (Hogan L LLP) -875 3rd Av -NY 10022
(212) 701-3000 .. **King**, Michl P '00 %Cahill G&R LLP -80 Pine -NY 10005 **Fx**:269-5420
(518) 465-9313 .. **King**, Richd C '73 OfCnsl Read and L,LLP -25 Eagle -Albany 12207
(914) 993-9393 .. **King**, Richd J '94 %Stewart Title Ins -707 Wstchstr Av -White Plns 10604 **Fx**:997-1698
(212) 878-8209 .. **King**, Robt E Jr. '85 (Clifford C LLP) -31 W 52nd -NY 10019
(212) 909-6000 .. **King**, Robt L '61 SrCnsl Debevoise & P LLP -919 3rd Av -NY 10022
(585) 753-4500 .. **King**, Robt S '08 %DA -832 Watts Bldg -Rchstr 14614 **Fx**:753-4576
(516) 741-3441 .. **King**, Rochelle Bergman '78 (Bergman & K,PC) -500 Old Cntry Rd -Gdn Cty 11530
(212) 267-7767 .. **King**, Sean P '93 %Gess G&S,PC -30 Vesey -NY 10007
(212) 556-2100 .. **King & Spalding** -1185 Av of Amer -NY 10036 **Fx**:556-2222
(212) 845-2517 .. **King**, Stephen P '97 KBC Fncl Prdcts -140 E 45th -NY 10017
(315) 378-4464 .. **King**, Susan L M '00 Sanza Capital Advisors LLC -5792 Widewaters Pkwy -Syracuse 13214
(212) 487-9701 .. **King**, Thos J '81 (Robin HK&F) -1 Bttry Pk Plz -NY 10014
(585) 412-6036 .. **King**, Victoria L '05 -21 Sly -Canandaigua 14424
(585) 242-9900 .. **King**, Wm H Jr. '98 -774 Monroe Av -Rchstr 14607 **Fx**:242-9105
(212) 966-7400 .. **King**, Wm Ng '77 -5 Division -NY 10002 **Fx**:941-7543
(212) 319-4755 .. **King & Wood** -444 Mad Av -NY 10022 **Fx**:421-1101
(212) 456-2164 .. **King**, Yvenne M '00 ESPN Inc -730 Columbus Av -NY 10025
(212) 267-4177 .. **King**, Yvette M '01 %Kramer DL&M -217 Bway -NY 10007
(212) 683-7050 .. **King**, Zaida E '08 %JM Abramson -375 5th Av -NY 10016 **Fx**:683-7076
(212) 801-3067 .. **King-Brown**, Kristie G '07 %Greenberg T,LLP -200 Park Av -NY 10166
(212) 624-3300 .. **Kingfield**, Michl T '07 UGO Networks Inc -670 Bway -NY 10012
(212) 696-6000 .. **Kingham**, T Barry '69 (Curtis M-PC&M LLP) -101 Park Av -NY 10178
(631) 462-3434 .. **King Richards**, Sheryl D '05 %Wand P&G -1776 E Jericho Tpk -Huntngtn 11743 **Fx**:462-3939
(212) 964-3344 .. **King-Robinson**, Arlene '82 -321 Bway -NY 10007 **Fx**:571-4309
(212) 355-6800 .. **Kingsley**, Alfred D '67 %Greenway Partners -150 E 57th -NY 10022 **Fx**:207-3901
(212) 682-8300 .. **Kingsley**, Bonni L '91 Medialink Worldwide Inc -708 3rd Av -NY 10017
(212) 755-8555 .. **Kingsley**, Carrie B '04 M Safra & Co -499 Park Av -NY 10022
(518) 499-0270 .. **Kingsley**, Frank H Jr. '57 -167 Bway Bx300 -Whitehall 12887 **Fx**:499-2615
(212) 599-2789 .. **Kingsley**, Gordon F Jr. '88 Forum Asset Mgmt,LLC -140 E 45th -NY 10017 **Fx**:599-2730
(516) 931-0064 .. **Kingsley**, Harold M '69 (Kingsley K&C) -91 W Cherry -Hicksvll 11801 **Fx**:931-4313
(212) 867-6000 .. **Kingsley**, Howard W '89 (Rosenberg & E,PC) -733 3rd Av -NY 10017
(212) 947-1999 .. **Kingsley**, Jared P '94 Cnsl Methfessel & W,PC -450 7th Av -NY 10123
(716) 566-5400 .. **Kingsley**, Jeffrey L '03 (Goldberg S LLP) -665 Main -Buffalo 14203
(516) 931-0064 .. **Kingsley**, Joan S '81 (Kingsley K&C) -91 W Cherry -Hicksvll 11801 **Fx**:931-4313
(518) 943-3399 .. **Kingsley**, John P '66 JP Kingsley,PC -329 Main -Catskill 12414 **Fx**:943-3049
(212) 836-8000 .. **Kingsley**, Mark S '92 (Kaye S LLP) -425 Park Av -NY 10022
(212) 450-4000 .. **Kingsley**, Paul R '84 (Davis P&W LLP) -450 Lex Av -NY 10017
(212) 807-5787 .. **Kingston**, Jonathan S '98 (J Kingston & Assoc,PC) -31 Smith -Brklyn 11201
(631) 878-2044 .. **Kingston**, Wm W '88 -15 Dundalk Rd -Manorvll 11949
(212) 285-9300 .. **Kinigstein**, Noah A '81 -315 Bway -NY 10007 **Fx**:385-2608
(631) 727-2180 .. **Kinirons**, Kelly E '05 %Twomey LSKD&Q,LLP -33 W 2nd Bx9398 -Rvrhead 11901
(631) 231-2424 .. **Kinirons**, Kimberly Ann '97 %Dept of Law -300 Motor Pkwy -Hauppauge 11788 **Fx**:435-4757
(212) 416-8000 .. **Kini-Tandon**, Sunita '06 %Dept of Law -120 Bway -NY 10271
(518) 455-2701 .. **Kink**, Michl J '89 Senate Minority Cnsl -907 Legislatvie Ofc Bldg -Albany 12247 **Fx**:455-2816
(212) 984-4711 .. **Kinnally**, Robt G '97 %L'Oreal USA -575 5th Av -NY 10017
(212) 688-5151 .. **Kinnally**, Wm L Jr. '73 (Gibney A&F,LLP) -665 5th Av -NY 10022
(845) 433-1175 .. **Kinnaman**, Wm A Jr. '75 %IBM -522 South Rd Bldg 708/P386 -Poughkeepsie 12601
(212) 335-4500 .. **Kinney**, Amanda R '09 %DLA Piper LLP -1251 Av of Amer -NY 10020
(212) 530-5000 .. **Kinney**, Brian '04 %Milbank TH&M LLP -1 Chase Manh Plz -NY 10005
(212) 483-0105 .. **Kinney**, Justin N '94 (Coughlin D LLP) -88 Pine-Wall St Plz -NY 10005
(212) 407-4000 .. **Kinney**, Michl B '84 (Loeb & L,LLP) -345 Park Av -NY 10154
(212) 309-6000 .. **Kinney**, Stephen H Jr. '74 SrCnsl Morgan L&B LLP -101 Park Av -NY 10178
(212) 221-5999 .. **Kinney**, Thos P '96 %Antin E&E,LLP -49 W 37th -NY 10018
(917) 750-2810 .. **Kinosian**, Craig K '92 -40 Cntrl Pk S -NY 10019
(518) 626-9000 .. **Kinsch**, Noelle M '97 (Dewey & L LLP) -99 Wshngtn Av -Albany 12210
(212) 735-3000 .. **Kinschots**, Cedric R L '07 %Skadden ASM&F LLP -4 Times Sq -NY 10036
(518) 449-3125 .. **Kinsella**, Donald T '74 OfCnsl Stockli GS&P,LLP -90 State -Albany 12207
(315) 451-7955 .. **Kinsella**, John D '71 -6834 Buckley Rd -N Syracuse 13212 **Fx**:451-7958
(518) 213-6000 .. **Kinsella**, Pauline Rogers '76 %NYSUT -800 Troy-Schnctdy Rd -Latham 12110 **Fx**:213-6488
(315) 423-7100 .. **Kinsella**, Wendy Ann '96 (Harris B PLLC) -300 S State -Syracuse 13202
(212) 818-9200 .. **Kinsey**, Dwight A '81 (Satterlee SB&B LLP) -230 Park Av -NY 10169
(518) 473-6288 .. **Kinsey**, Roger W '96 %Dept of Law -The Cptl -Albany 12224
(585) 641-8000 .. **Kinsler**, Townsend B '08 %Fix SB&G,PC -295 Woodcliff Dr -Fairprt 14450
(631) 722-2100 .. **Kinslow**, Diane B '80 -Bx980 -Aquebogue 11931
(212) 297-5800 .. **Kintiroglou**, Achilles B '06 %Day P LLP -7 Times Sq -NY 10036
(518) 447-3200 .. **Kinum**, John B '58 OfCnsl McNamee LT&W,PC -677 Bway -Albany 12207
(518) 533-3000 .. **Kinum**, Michl L '98 SrCnsl Bond S&K,PLLC -111 Wshngtn Av -Albany 12210
(212) 363-6900 .. **Kinzel**, Christopher B '03 %Faust GS&B LLP -2 Rector -NY 10006
(631) 321-6694 .. **Kinzer**, Michl A '91 -384 W Main -Babylon 11702 **Fx**:321-1440
(212) 613-2095 .. **Kinzey**, John S '75 Cnsl Gibbons PC -1 Penn Plz -NY 10119 **Fx**:554-9690
(212) 758-6313 .. **Kinzler**, Alexander C '86 %Barnwell Ind -425 E 58th -NY 10022 **Fx**:751-2949
(516) 333-7730 .. **Kinzler**, Jeffrey L '85 J Kinzler & Assoc -393 Old Cntry Rd -Carle Pl 11514
(212) 808-7800 .. **Kinzler**, Thos B '76 (Kelley D&W LLP) -101 Park Av -NY 10178
(212) 253-5495 .. **Kiok**, Joan Stern '55 -442 E 20th -NY 10009 **Fx**:253-2229
(518) 464-4095 .. **Kiosse**, Leyla A '06 %M Tabak -100 Great Oaks Blvd -Albany 12203 **Fx**:464-4096
(315) 768-7246 .. **Kipers**, Kristine A '04 -Bx823 -New Hartfrd 13413 **Fx**:736-2510
(718) 624-2058 .. **Kipiniak**, Monica '92 -26 Court -Brklyn 11242
(212) 837-6000 .. **Kiplok**, Christopher K '01 (Hughes H&R LLP) -1 Bttry Pk Plz -NY 10004
(212) 808-0800 .. **Kipnees**, Glenn E '86 %D Skrilow -551 5th Av -NY 10176 **Fx**:808-0807
(917) 648-7837 .. **Kipnes**, Todd A '00 The Pension Co -207 E 74th -NY 10021
(914) 461-3222 .. **Kipness**, Robt S '99 Kipness & Assoc -460 Old Post Rd -Bedfrd 10506 **Fx**:(800) 414-2044
(212) 682-6800 .. **Kipnis**, Alexander M '08 %Zetlin & D LLP -801 2nd Av -NY 10017
(516) 328-3500 .. **Kipnis**, Pamela Gould '87 %McDonnell & A,PC -401 Franklin Av -Gdn Cty 11530
(212) 944-0500 .. **Kipnis**, Scott R '92 (Hofheimer G&G,LLP) -530 5th Av -NY 10036 **Fx**:897-4999
(212) 258-8000 .. **Kippen**, Erin '98 %MTV Networks -1515 Bway -NY 10036 **Fx**:258-8358
(212) 836-8000 .. **Kipperman**, Evan S '06 %Kaye S LLP -425 Park Av -NY 10022
(212) 893-7759 .. **Kipperman**, Steffi '88 %The Estee Lauder Co Inc -767 5th Av -NY 10153
(718) 222-3610 .. **Kirberger**, Elizabeth A '91 -81 Wshngtn -Brklyn 11201
(212) 698-3500 .. **Kirberger**, Steven P '02 %Dechert LLP -1095 Av of Amer -NY 10036
(518) 533-1050 .. **Kirby**, Andrew W '93 (Conway & K LLP) -9 Cornell Rd -Latham 12110
(516) 746-5040 .. **Kirby**, Christopher G '97 Scher Law Firm,LLP -1 Old Cntry Rd -Carle Pl 11514 **Fx**:747-9100
(212) 513-3200 .. **Kirby**, Danielle J '10 %Holland & K LLP -31 W 52nd -NY 10019
(212) 661-0009 .. **Kirby**, David V '83 OfCnsl Krantz & B LLP -747 3rd Av -NY 10017 **Fx**:355-5009
(516) 334-2500 .. **Kirby**, Gerald F '82 (Feldman RK&F,PC) -410 Jericho Tpk -Jericho 11753
(518) 436-8495 .. **Kirby**, Jeffery H '84 %NY Farm Bureau -159 Wolf Rd Bx5330 -Albany 12205 **Fx**:431-5656
(914) 255-5616 .. **Kirby**, Justine E '00 %Morgan Stanley -2000 Wstchstr Av -Purchase 10577
(716) 853-5100 .. **Kirby**, Kenneth R '83 Cnsl Lippes MWF LLP -665 Main -Buffalo 14203
(202) 624-5907 .. **Kirby**, Maria L '05 %Law Dept -100 Church -NY 10007 **Fx**:(212) 788-0367
(212) 371-6600 .. **Kirby McInerney LLP** -825 3rd Av -NY 10022 **Fx**:751-2540
(516) 741-1818 .. **Kirby**, Richd P '87 (O'Reilly M&C,PC) -222 Old Cntry Rd -Mineola 11501
(212) 408-5100 .. **Kirby**, Robt M '08 %Chadbourne & P LLP -30 Rckfllr Plz -NY 10112
(212) 371-6600 .. **Kirby**, Roger W '73 (Kirby M LLP) -825 3rd Av -NY 10022
(212) 653-8700 .. **Kirby**, Sean J '07 %Sheppard MR&H LLP -30 Rckfllr Plz -NY 10112
(607) 272-7279 .. **Kirby**, Susan Craigie '92 (Joch & K) -319 N Aurora Bx396 -Ithaca 14851 **Fx**:272-9976
(212) 559-2108 .. **Kirchen**, Karen J '78 Citigroup -425 Park Av -NY 10022
(212) 541-2000 .. **Kircher**, John D '04 %Bryan C LLP -1290 Av of Amer -NY 10104
(585) 724-5408 .. **Kircher**, Susan M '97 Eastman Kodak Co -343 State -Rchstr 14650
(718) 330-1200 .. **Kirchheimer**, R Peter '75 %Fed Def of NY Inc -1 Pierrepont Plz -Brklyn 11201 **Fx**:855-0760
(518) 473-6084 .. **Kirchheimer**, Susan S '90 %Dept of Law -The Cptl -Albany 12224 **Fx**:402-2163
(631) 784-7779 .. **Kirchhoff**, Diane E '98 -775 Park Av -Huntngtn 11743
(212) 455-2000 .. **Kirchner**, Max P '06 %Simpson T&B LLP -425 Lex Av -NY 10017
(585) 362-4700 .. **Kirchner**, Robt H '87 (Bond S&K,PLLC) -350 Linden Oaks -Rchstr 14625

(315) 218-8000 .. **Kirchner,** Robt H '87 (Bond S&K,PLLC) -1 Lincoln Ctr -Syracuse 13202
(212) 896-3310 .. **Kirchner,** Shawna A '09 %PS Schram,PC -350 Bway -NY 10013 **Fx:**896-3316
(212) 208-3344 .. **Kirchoff,** Eileen L '84 %Ambac Assurance -1 State Street Plz -NY 10004 **Fx:**785-1178
(212) 367-1000 .. **Kirdahy,** Thos J '90 %GMHC,Inc -119 W 24th -NY 10011 **Fx:**367-1305
(212) 558-4000 .. **Kirgis,** Adam T '10 %Sullivan & C LLP -125 Broad -NY 10004
(718) 990-6600 .. **Kirgis,** Paul F '04 %St John's Law Schl -8000 Utopia Pkwy -Jamaica 11439 **Fx:**591-1855
(716) 852-1102 .. **Kirisits,** James J '66 -80 W Huron -Buffalo 14202 **Fx:**852-8013
(315) 422-1391 .. **Kiritsis-Cappers,** Dafni S '01 %Green & S,PLLC -One Lincoln Ctr #900 -Syracuse 13202
(845) 471-1818 .. **Kirk,** Adam G '89 -4 Lbrty -Poughkeepsie 12601
(212) 422-0202 .. **Kirk,** Edw J '98 (Sedgwick DM&A LLP) -125 Broad -NY 10004
(212) 609-6800 .. **Kirk,** Francis A '93 (McCarter & E,LLP) -245 Park Av -NY 10167
(212) 326-3939 .. **Kirk,** James A A '08 %Jones D -222 E 41st -NY 10017
(212) 808-7800 .. **Kirk,** James J '81 (Kelley D&W LLP) -101 Park Av -NY 10178
(716) 616-6713 .. **Kirk,** Janice B '92 %Ingram Micro Inc -1759 Wehrle Dr -Williamsvll 14221
(212) 859-8000 .. **Kirk,** Kim J '84 SpclCnsl Fried FHS&J LLP -1 NY Plz -NY 10004
(212) 486-5555 .. **Kirk,** Patrick J '94 %Wall St By Fax Inc -650 Mad Av -NY 10022 **Fx:**486-5556
(845) 338-4477 .. **Kirk,** Ralph M '78 -9 Main Bldg Bx4466 -Kingston 12402 **Fx:**338-2892
(516) 249-5600 .. **Kirk,** Robt P Jr. '85 R Kirk Jr,PC -1 West -Farmngdl 11735 **Fx:**249-5601
(607) 778-2418 .. **Kirkaldy,** Marjorie M '82 %Hon ME Smith -George Harvey Justice Bldg Bx1766 -Bnghmtn 13902
(212) 687-3860 .. **Kirkham,** Ashley S '06 %Snow BK,PC -605 3rd Av -NY 10158
(212) 455-2000 .. **Kirkland,** Christine S '04 %Simpson T&B LLP -425 Lex Av -NY 10017
(212) 446-4800 .. **Kirkland & Ellis LLP** -153 E 53rd -NY 10022 **Fx:**446-4900
(718) 741-8326 .. **Kirkland,** Galen D '78 %Div of Human Rights -1 Fordham Plz -Bronx 10458 **Fx:**741-8102
(212) 218-2100 .. **Kirkland,** John W '05 %Fitzpatrick CH&S -1290 Av of Amer -NY 10104
(914) 422-3900 .. **Kirkpatrick,** Andrew R '10 Oxman TKW&G LLP -120 Bloomingdale Rd -White Plns 10605
(212) 450-4000 .. **Kirkpatrick,** Deanna L '90 (Davis P&W LLP) -450 Lex Av -NY 10017
(716) 849-1333 .. **Kirkpatrick,** James W '59 SpclCnsl Lipsitz GSC LLP -42 Delaware Av -Buffalo 14202
(914) 422-3900 .. **Kirkpatrick,** John B '80 (Oxman TKW&G LLP) -120 Bloomingdale Rd -White Plns 10605
(518) 993-4391 .. **Kirkpatrick,** John L '77 Kirkpatrick & K,PC -83 Canal Bx350 -Ft Plain 13339 **Fx:**993-4396
(212) 867-4466 .. **Kirkpatrick,** Steven N '94 (Belkin BW&G,LLP) -270 Mad Av -NY 10016
(716) 858-2200 .. **Kirkpatrick,** Thos F '97 %Cnty Atty -95 Franklin -Buffalo 14202 **Fx:**858-2281
(212) 954-2515 .. **Kirkwood,** Elizabeth A '09 KPMG LLP -757 3rd Av -NY 10017
(716) 376-8237 .. **Kirkwood,** Pamela J '05 %Cattaraugus-Allegany BOCES -1825 Windfall Rd -Olean 14760
(607) 746-2325 .. **Kirkwood,** Porter L '94 Delaware Cnty DSS -111 Main -Delhi 13753 **Fx:**746-6242
(914) 769-9070 .. **Kirkwood,** Robt C '81 -91 Wshngtn Av -Plsntvll 10570 **Fx:**769-4706
(212) 762-3165 .. **Kirkwood,** Wm T '99 %Morgan Stanley -750 7th Av -NY 10019
(914) 428-4709 .. **Kirley,** Jos P '62 -149 Grand -White Plns 10601 **Fx:**761-5444
(212) 403-1000 .. **Kirman,** Igor '97 (Wachtell LR&K) -51 W 52nd -NY 10019
(212) 839-5300 .. **Kirmayer,** Asi '01 %Sidley A LLP -787 7th Av -NY 10019
(212) 596-9000 .. **Kirova,** Iliana V '09 %Ropes & G LLP -1211 Av of Amer -NY 10036
(212) 849-7000 .. **Kirpalani,** Susheel '95 (Quinn EU&S,LLP) -51 Mad Av -NY 10010
(212) 267-1900 .. **Kirrane,** Wm K '02 %Wade CM -111 Bway -NY 10006
(212) 389-5000 .. **Kirsch,** Clifford E '86 (Sutherland A&B LLP) -1114 Av of Amer -NY 10036
(718) 590-2000 .. **Kirsch,** David '07 %DA -198 E 161st -Bronx 10451 **Fx:**681-1129
(212) 683-1836 .. **Kirsch,** David A '87 -210 5th Av -NY 10010
(212) 521-5400 .. **Kirsch,** Emily Bab '96 Cnsl Reed S LLP -599 Lex Av -NY 10022
(212) 278-0400 .. **Kirsch,** Eric '96 (Cooper & D LLP) -30 Rckfllr Plz -NY 10112
(212) 698-3500 .. **Kirsch,** Eric C '06 %Dechert LLP -1095 Av of Amer -NY 10036
(212) 248-2936 .. **Kirsch Gartenberg Howard LLP** -11 Penn Plz -NY 10001 **Fx:**(201) 488-6842
(718) 237-0712 .. **Kirsch,** Howard '71 -50 Court -Brklyn 11201 **Fx:**852-6086
(718) 651-0500 .. **Kirsch,** Jed N '81 %B Lassin -39-18 63rd -Woodside 11377 **Fx:**651-0262
(212) 697-7383 .. **Kirsch,** Jeffrey C '85 %Mandel Law Firm -370 Lex Av -NY 10017 **Fx:**681-6157
(845) 292-4412 .. **Kirsch,** Jeffrey L '81 (Eisenberg & K) -25 Darbee Ln Bx715 -Liberty 12754
(212) 258-4000 .. **Kirsch,** Joel A '94 %Siemens Corp -153 E 53rd -NY 10022 **Fx:**767-0580
(212) 278-0520 .. **Kirsch,** Jules P '68 -1185 Av of Amer -NY 10036 **Fx:**391-0525
(716) 852-1380 .. **Kirsch,** Kathryn M '97 %Abbarno M&K -314 Brisbane Bldg -Buffalo 14203
(518) 463-2051 .. **Kirsch,** Lawr A '83 G Weinberg,PC -90 State -Albany 12207 **Fx:**463-0079
(516) 364-1095 .. **Kirsch,** Leonard D '81 (McBreen & K) -500 N Bway -Jericho 11753
(212) 351-4000 .. **Kirsch,** Mark A '88 (Gibson D&C LLP) -200 Park Av -NY 10166
(212) 406-2181 .. **Kirsch,** Melinda '95 %G Caplan PC -160 Bway -NY 10038 **Fx:**732-1425
(315) 474-7541 .. **Kirsch,** Trisha L '08 %Menter R&T,PC -308 Maltbie -Syracuse 13204
(212) 836-8000 .. **Kirschbaum,** Myron '75 (Kaye S LLP) -425 Park Av -NY 10022
(631) 232-0200 .. **Kirschbaum,** Seth E '99 %Fumuso KDSS&F,LLP -110 Marcus Blvd -Hauppauge 11788
(585) 325-4500 .. **Kirschen,** Michl B '74 %Ct of Claims -144 Exchange Blvd -Rchstr 14614 **Fx:**262-5715
(212) 692-8423 .. **Kirschenbaum,** Benjamin C '80 %Insignia Residntl Grp -675 3rd Av -NY 10017 **Fx:**692-8449
(212) 688-5640 .. **Kirschenbaum,** Danl M '06 %Joseph & H LLP -757 3rd Av -NY 10017
(212) 868-6300 .. **Kirschenbaum,** George A '74 (Cary K LLP) -1350 Bway -NY 10018
(516) 746-1144 .. **Kirschenbaum,** Irwin S '72 (Kirschenbaum & P,PC) -3000 Hempstd Tpk -Levittwn 11756
(516) 747-6700 .. **Kirschenbaum,** Jennifer A '07 %Kirschenbaum & K -200 Grdn City Plz -Gdn Cty 11530 **Fx:**747-6781
(516) 747-6700 .. **Kirschenbaum,** Kenneth '75 (Kirschenbaum & K) -200 Grdn City Plz -Gdn Cty 11530 **Fx:**747-6781
(212) 552-7128 .. **Kirschenbaum,** Peter C '81 JP Morgan Chase -1 Chase Manh Plz -NY 10081
(516) 746-1144 .. **Kirschenbaum & Philips,PC** -3000 Hempstd Tpk -Levittwn 11756 **Fx:**742-2735
(516) 747-6700 .. **Kirschenbaum,** Saml '42 (Kirschenbaum & K) -200 Grdn City Plz -Gdn Cty 11530 **Fx:**747-6781
(212) 731-2144 .. **Kirschner,** Adam L '00 -670 W End Av -NY 10025
(718) 520-3745 .. **Kirschner,** Agnes K '87 %Hon J O'Donoghue -88-11 Sutphin Blvd -Jamaica 11435 **Fx:**520-6435
(845) 758-6991 .. **Kirschner,** Anna W '89 -254 Middle Rd -Rhinebeck 12572 **Fx:**758-6992
(212) 370-3000 .. **Kirschner,** Chas '74 -2 Rector -NY 10006 **Fx:**779-8208
(516) 466-8331 .. **Kirschner & Cohen** -305 Nrthrn Blvd -Gt Neck 11021 **Fx:**466-1386
(718) 590-3765 .. **Kirschner,** David J '90 Hon L Bernstein -851 Grnd Cncrs -Bronx 10451
(212) 310-8000 .. **Kirschner,** Elyse G '94 (Weil G&M LLP) -767 5th Av -NY 10153
(212) 525-8119 .. **Kirschner,** Ian M '80 HSBC Securities -452 5th Av -NY 10018
(212) 506-2500 .. **Kirschner,** Jason I '06 %Mayer B LLP -1675 Bway -NY 10019
(212) 643-2008 .. **Kirschner,** Kenneth '62 -330 7th Av -NY 10001
(212) 918-3000 .. **Kirschner,** Kenneth H '79 (Hogan L LLP) -875 3rd Av -NY 10022
(917) 459-6964 .. **Kirschner,** Marc S '68 -18 E 94th -NY 10128
(845) 339-0892 .. **Kirschner,** Philip W '88 -1 N Front Bx4151 -Kingston 12402 **Fx:**338-0868
(212) 438-1170 .. **Kirschner,** Rhonda G '85 Standard & Poor's -55 Water -NY 10041 **Fx:**438-6290
(212) 883-6850 .. **Kirschner,** Richd D '74 %Marley Grp -400 E 59th -NY 10022
(212) 598-1239 .. **Kirschner,** Robt D '84 Guardian Life -7 Hanover Sq -NY 10004
(646) 369-4546 .. **Kirschner,** Saml '95 Park Shore Capital Mgmt LLC -1114 Av of Amer -NY 10036
(516) 466-8331 .. **Kirschner,** Steven B '74 (Kirschner & C) -305 Nrthrn Blvd -Gt Neck 11021
(212) 953-9595 .. **Kirschner,** Uri A '97 (Silberberg & K LLP) -360 Lex Av -NY 10017 **Fx:**953-7755
(212) 697-3750 .. **Kirschstein,** David B '52 (Kirschstein IS&P,PC) -425 5th Av -NY 10016
(212) 697-3750 .. **Kirschstein Israel Schiffmiller & Pieroni, PC** -425 5th Av -NY 10016 **Fx:**949-1690
(212) 527-5644 .. **Kirsh,** Jeffrey H '92 %Revlon -237 Park Av -NY 10017 **Fx:**527-5299
(212) 541-8100 .. **Kirsh,** Rachel L '99 Oliver Wyman -1166 Av of Amer -NY 10036
(212) 577-2523 .. **Kirshbaum,** Jonathan M '97 %Ctr for Appllt Litigation -74 Trinity Pl -NY 10006 **Fx:**577-2535
(718) 298-0186 .. **Kirshblum,** David A '91 Family Ct -151-20 Jamaica Av -Jamaica 11432
(212) 682-4001 .. **Kirshenbaum,** Karen L '95 (Lynch R LLP) -630 3rd Av -NY 10017
(212) 836-8000 .. **Kirshenbaum,** Lester M '77 (Kaye S LLP) -425 Park Av -NY 10022
(212) 777-4400 .. **Kirshenbaum,** Melissa P '02 STV Grp Inc -225 Park Av S -NY 10003
(212) 969-3000 .. **Kirshenbaum,** Steven L '77 (Proskauer R LLP) -1585 Bway -NY 10036
(212) 801-2186 .. **Kirshenberg,** Robt J '90 (Greenberg T,LLP) -200 Park Av -NY 10166
(212) 384-1000 .. **Kirshner,** Allison A '04 %FBI -26 Fed Plz -NY 10278
(212) 922-1080 .. **Kirshner,** Isabelle A '82 (Clayman & R,LLP) -305 Mad Av -NY 10165
(718) 488-1900 .. **Kirshner,** James W '03 %Lazzaro & G,PC -360 Court -Brklyn 11231
(212) 521-6986 .. **Kirshner,** Jeffrey T '97 Harbinger Capital Partners -555 Mad Av -NY 10022
(212) 450-4000 .. **Kirshner,** Jodie A '07 %Davis P&W LLP -450 Lex Av -NY 10017
(631) 581-6054 .. **Kirshner,** Mark G '80 -265 E Main -E Islip 11730 **Fx:**581-5894
(212) 335-4500 .. **Kirshnitz,** Eliot J '02 %DLA Piper LLP -1251 Av of Amer -NY 10020
(315) 797-1970 .. **Kirshtein,** Murray J S '59 -811 Court -Utica 13502 **Fx:**797-1976
(631) 287-1251 .. **Kirst,** David M '06 -376 CR 39 -Southampton 11968
(212) 810-4099 .. **Kirstein,** Allan E '73 -708 3rd Av -NY 10017 **Fx:**810-4098
(212) 969-2108 .. **Kirstein,** Philip L '74 Alliance Bernstein LP -1345 Av of Amer -NY 10105 **Fx:**554-4639
(516) 767-6600 .. **Kirtland,** Robt A '50 -45 N Bayles Av -Pt Wash 11050 **Fx:**767-9308
(347) 404-9400 .. **Kirton,** Darren L '96 %Criminal Ct -120 Schermerhorn -Brklyn 11201 **Fx:**(718) 643-3538
(914) 995-4526 .. **Kirton,** Lila E '86 Cnty Legislature -148 Martine Av -White Plns 10601
(646) 435-5519 .. **Kirton,** Marlon G '91 -230 Park Av -NY 10169 **Fx:**(212) 808-3020
(914) 377-6150 .. **Kirven,** Louis C III '96 Dept of Planning -40 S Bway -Ynkrs 10701
(516) 248-2727 .. **Kirwan,** Barbara M '89 %K Brodzansky -300 Grdn City Plz -Gdn Cty 11530 **Fx:**248-6929
(718) 579-7921 .. **Kirwan,** D Antoinette '05 %Leg Aid -900 Sheridan Av -Bronx 10451 **Fx:**293-8744
(212) 223-3900 .. **Kirwan,** Stephanie E '05 %Zwerling S&Z,LLP -41 Mad Av -NY 10010
(315) 452-2443 .. **Kirwan,** Terry J Jr. '91 (Primo P&K,LLP) -7075 Manlius Ctr Rd -E Syracuse 13057
(315) 342-7214 .. **Kirwan,** Timothy J '97 (Rodak & K) -55 W 2nd -Oswego 13126
(212) 869-8220 .. **Kirwin,** Andrew C '93 %S&E Azriliant,PC -36 W 44th -NY 10036 **Fx:**840-2540
(212) 840-6543 .. **Kirwin,** Andrew C '93 (Weinstein S&K) -36 W 44th -NY 10036
(212) 804-4200 .. **Kirwin,** Bernadette K '01 (Mound CW&G) -One Bttry Pk Plz -NY 10004
(518) 274-1500 .. **Kirwin,** Fredk W '82 -1 State -Troy 12180 **Fx:**274-7730
(212) 608-5000 .. **Kirwin,** Peter M '94 %F Seeman -170 Bway -NY 10038 **Fx:**385-8161

(516) 877-2900 .. **Kirzner,** Kim B '02 %Bartlett MB&M,LLP -300 Old Cntry Rd -Mineola 11501
(212) 846-3625 .. **Kisch,** Alexander D '00 %MTV Networks -1515 Bway -NY 10036 **Fx:**258-8358
(212) 478-7200 .. **Kisch,** Rhona J '96 (Hahn & H LLP) -488 Mad Av -NY 10022
(518) 842-0704 .. **Kiselis,** Anthony J M '78 -32 Romeyn Av -Amsterdam 12010 **Fx:**842-0704
(212) 446-4800 .. **Kiser,** Jessica M '08 %Kirkland & E LLP -153 E 53rd -NY 10022
(914) 323-7000 .. **Kiser,** Miriam '09 %Wilson EME&D LLP -3 Gannett Dr -White Plns 10604
(718) 590-6218 .. **Kish,** Rachel A '07 %Law Dept -198 E 161st -Bronx 10451 **Fx:**590-2686
(212) 801-9238 .. **Kishel,** Jos F '86 (Greenberg T,LLP) -200 Park Av -NY 10166
(212) 808-7800 .. **Kishinevsky,** Lily '02 %Kelley D&W LLP -101 Park Av -NY 10178
(212) 585-3425 .. **Kishner,** Bryan W '91 (B Kishner & Assoc) -420 Lex Av -NY 10170 **Fx:**752-1810
(212) 592-1400 .. **Kishner,** Irwin '88 (Herrick,F LLP) -2 Park Av -NY 10016
(585) 987-2800 .. **Kisicki,** Ronald J '87 (Woods OG LLP) -2 State -Rchstr 14614
(212) 867-6000 .. **Kisish,** Elvira A '00 (Rosenberg & E,PC) -733 3rd Av -NY 10017
(212) 869-8530 .. **Kiskaddon,** Walter D '95 %Actors Equity Assn -165 W 46th -NY 10036
(212) 973-0572 .. **Kisker,** Stephen A '95 OfCnsl Wolff & S PC -140 Bway -NY 10005
(212) 929-7099 .. **Kislak,** Barbara Maier '95 -135 W 17th -NY 10011
(212) 256-8000 .. **Kislin,** Scott A '93 Atticus Capital LP -767 5th Av -NY 10153
(212) 776-5000 .. **Kiss,** Danl '02 NYC Housing Auth -250 Bway -NY 10007 **Fx:**776-5039
(718) 822-0707 .. **Kiss,** Edw N '04 -984 Morris Park Av -Bronx 10462 **Fx:**904-1030
(212) 656-2039 .. **Kissane,** Janet M '97 NYSE -20 Broad -NY 10005
(212) 922-2200 .. **Kissane,** John G '94 %Watson F&W LLP -1133 Av of Amer -NY 10036
(212) 674-7016 .. **Kissane,** Mary Elizabeth '97 %Abernathy MacGregor Grp -501 Mad Av -NY 10022
(315) 473-9495 .. **Kissane,** Maureen T '03 %MHLS -224 Harrison -Syracuse 13202 **Fx:**473-9646
(212) 344-5400 .. **Kissane,** Thos A '88 (Schlam S&D LLP) -26 Bway -NY 10004
(914) 750-5933 .. **Kissel Hirsch & Wilmer LLP** -580 Wht Plns Rd -Tarrytwn 10591 **Fx:**750-5922
(716) 691-3133 .. **Kissel,** James E '86 -119 Sundrdg Dr -Amherst 14228
(845) 368-0104 .. **Kissel,** Marc I '91 (Schulman K&K,PC) -1 Exec Blvd #202 -Suffern 10901
(914) 750-5933 .. **Kissel,** Richd A '80 (Kissel H&W LLP) -580 Wht Plns Rd -Tarrytwn 10591
(518) 523-1980 .. **Kissel,** Wm H '68 -2465 Main Bx1598 -Lk Placid 12946
(718) 421-3815 .. **Kissen,** Anatoly '04 Khavinson & Assoc,PC -1122 Coney Isl Av -Brklyn 11230
(212) 973-9100 .. **Kissin,** Gary '81 (Rose & K LLP) -757 3rd Av -NY 10017 **Fx:**973-9101
(212) 290-8200 .. **Kissinger,** Laura E '06 %Open Space Inst -1350 Bway -NY 10018 **Fx:**244-3441
(212) 883-4900 .. **Kissoon,** Dave '01 (Cozen O) -277 Park Av -NY 10172
(212) 885-5000 .. **Kistler,** David C '04 %Blank R LLP -405 Lex Av -NY 10174
(516) 294-9200 .. **Kistler,** Graham W '02 -114 Old Cntry Rd -Mineola 11501 **Fx:**746-1071
(212) 407-4000 .. **Kistler,** Michl J '03 %Loeb & L,LLP -345 Park Av -NY 10154
(845) 473-4646 .. **Kistner,** Michl J '83 -4 Lbrty -Poughkeepsie 12601
(212) 756-2000 .. **Kit,** Wu-Kwan '08 %Schulte R&Z LLP -919 3rd Av -NY 10022
(716) 854-1744 .. **Kita,** Wm John '79 (Burgio K&C) -2150 Main Place Twr -Buffalo 14202
(212) 782-4375 .. **Kitagawa,** Rie '98 %Bk of Tokyo-Mitsubishi -1251 Av of Amer -NY 10020 **Fx:**782-6420
(646) 315-7355 .. **Kitay,** Cynthia '92 %FINRA -14 Wall -NY 10005 **Fx:**315-7440
(718) 250-4283 .. **Kitay,** Emily L '78 %Leg Aid -111 Lvngstn -Brklyn 11201 **Fx:**250-4243
(212) 719-2900 .. **Kitay,** Harvey R '57 (Kolleeny K&H) -500 5th Av -NY 10110
(212) 813-8800 .. **Kitay,** Valerie H '04 %Goodwin P LLP -620 8th Av -NY 10018
(212) 617-3525 .. **Kitchen,** Adrienne N '04 Bloomberg -731 Lex Av -NY 10022
(212) 446-4800 .. **Kitchen,** Christopher A '05 %Kirkland & E LLP -153 E 53rd -NY 10022
(716) 631-5661 .. **Kitchen,** Denis A Jr. '76 DA Kitchen,PC -8899 Main -Williamsvll 14221 **Fx:**631-0613
(518) 402-0205 .. **Kitchen,** E Yvette '82 %UIA Bd -Troy Atrium Bx15126 -Albany 12212 **Fx:**402-6208
(845) 454-8800 .. **Kitchen,** Heather L '89 -2 Cannon -Poughkeepsie 12601 **Fx:**473-6056
(212) 259-8000 .. **Kitchens,** Justin K '08 %Dewey & L LLP -1301 Av of Amer -NY 10019
(516) 742-9200 .. **Kitchner,** Stuart L '95 %Edelman K&J PLLC -1 Old Cntry Rd -Carle Pl 11514
(845) 358-7270 .. **Kitman,** Jamie Lincoln '85 Hornblow Grp USA,Inc -Bx176 -Palisades 10964 **Fx:**358-8041
(631) 952-6528 .. **Kitograd,** Sheldon M '65 NYS Traffic Violtn Bur -State Ofc Bldg Vets Hwy -Hauppauge 11788
(212) 335-9000 .. **Kitsis,** Michl D '84 %DA -1 Hogan Pl -NY 10013
(914) 285-9797 .. **Kitson,** Kevin J '74 (Kitson LLP) -50 Main -White Plns 10606
(914) 285-9797 .. **Kitson Law Firm, LLP** -50 Main -White Plns 10606 **Fx:**285-9817
(914) 285-9797 .. **Kitson,** Patricia G '80 (Kitson LLP) -50 Main -White Plns 10606
(718) 423-6800 .. **Kitt,** Edw K '81 %MacKay W&B LLP -40-26 235th -Douglastn 11363
(518) 474-3494 .. **Kitt,** Stacy '88 %State Comptroller -110 State -Albany 12236 **Fx:**473-9104
(212) 702-5200 .. **Kittay,** David M '89 Promethean Capital Grp,LLC -55 5th Av -NY 10003
(914) 332-8000 .. **Kittay,** David R '78 (Kittay & G,PC) -100 Wht Plns Rd -Tarrytwn 10591
(212) 768-9500 .. **Kittay,** David R '78 (Kittay & G,PC) -1 Exch Plz 55 Bway -NY 10016
(914) 332-8000 .. **Kittay & Gershfeld,PC** -100 Wht Plns Rd -Tarrytwn 10591 **Fx:**332-8001
(212) 768-9500 .. **Kittay & Gershfeld,PC** -1 Exch Plz 55 Bway -NY 10016 **Fx:**685-1573
(212) 841-1000 .. **Kittay,** Leo B '09 %Covington & B LLP -620 8th Av -NY 10018
(631) 629-4287 .. **Kittenplan,** Joshua A '04 J Kittenplan,PC -20 Broadhllw Rd -Melvll 11747
(212) 416-8000 .. **Kittilsen,** Loren E '08 %Dept of Law -120 Bway -NY 10271
(212) 506-2500 .. **Kittle,** Brian W '04 %Mayer B LLP -1675 Bway -NY 10019
(315) 479-3380 .. **Kittleman,** Steven C '90 %UIA Bd -450 S Salina -Syracuse 13202 **Fx:**479-3418
(516) 826-1100 .. **Kitton,** Cheryl H '85 C Kitton,PC -103 Bedford Av -Bellmore 11710 **Fx:**826-0670
(212) 220-3830 .. **Kitton,** Fara N '09 %Nicoletti H&S -88 Pine -NY 10005
(212) 530-4833 .. **Kittredge,** David N '92 LaRocca HRG&B LLP -40 Wall -NY 10005
(718) 277-5324 .. **Kittrell,** Rebecca S '03 %MHLS -888 Fountain Av -Brklyn 11208 **Fx:**235-3671
(212) 745-1316 .. **Kittsley,** James F '68 %Chase Manhattan Bk -726 Mad Av -NY 10065 **Fx:**223-2138
(718) 701-6500 .. **Kitzen,** Adam I '03 Titledge -654 Sharrotts Rd -Staten Isl 10309
(212) 788-0849 .. **Kitzinger,** Stephen E '96 %Law Dept -100 Church -NY 10007 **Fx:**788-0367
(212) 680-5150 .. **Kitzman,** Tracey L '95 Friedman Law Grp LLP -270 Lafayette -NY 10012
(631) 231-5195 .. **Kivett,** Chas H '81 -330 Motor Pkwy -Hauppauge 11788
(212) 735-3000 .. **Kivitz,** Hilary C '02 %Skadden ASM&F LLP -4 Times Sq -NY 10036
(518) 477-1018 .. **Kivitz,** Larry P '84 -738 Columbia Tpk -E Greenbush 12061 **Fx:**477-1021
(212) 819-1130 .. **Kivler,** Russell A '03 (Hirschen S&E) -902 Bway -NY 10010
(212) 490-4021 .. **Kivowitz,** Michl S '05 UBS Fncl Srvcs Inc -200 Park Av -NY 10166
(212) 637-3183 .. **Kivowitz,** Sharon E '86 %EPA -290 Bway -NY 10007 **Fx:**637-3096
(212) 264-3940 .. **Kiwak,** Danielle J '04 %Hon T Stanceu -1 Fed Plz -NY 10278
(212) 824-5700 .. **Kiwi,** Tamara Chesna '96 %Practising Law Inst -810 7th Av -NY 10019
(212) 330-9808 .. **Kizner,** Gail Ann '90 -24 5th Av -NY 10011
(212) 790-9200 .. **Kjellberg,** Thos G '99 %Cowan L&L,PC -1133 Av of Amer -NY 10036
(212) 536-3900 .. **K&L Gates LLP** -599 Lex Av -NY 10022 **Fx:**536-3901
(716) 854-2620 .. **Klaasesz,** Peter E '61 Cnsl Brown & K,LLP -1500 Lbrty Bldg -Buffalo 14202
(585) 637-3911 .. **Klafehn & Heise** -13 Water -Brockprt 14420 **Fx:**637-7546
(585) 637-3911 .. **Klafehn,** Mark H '58 OfCnsl Klafehn & H -13 Water -Brockprt 14420
(607) 432-4100 .. **Klafehn,** Rodney L '76 -172 Gilbert Lk Rd Bx305 -Laurens 13796 **Fx:**432-4806
(631) 385-4020 .. **Klaffky,** Kenneth R '72 -47 Dumbarton Dr -Huntngtn 11743
(212) 286-0300 .. **Klafter,** David S '81 %Gotham Partners -888 7th Av -NY 10106
(914) 934-9200 .. **Klafter,** Jeffrey A '80 (Klafter O&L LLP) -2 Intl Dr -Rye Brook 10573 **Fx:**934-9220
(718) 721-5740 .. **Klafter,** Mitchell K '89 (M Klafter,PC) -2215 31st -Astoria 11105 **Fx:**721-9645
(718) 250-1400 .. **Klag,** Michl F '88 %BZ Green -12 MetroTech Ctr -Brklyn 11201 **Fx:**250-1401
(212) 448-1100 .. **Klagsbrun,** Edw '61 OfCnsl McLaughlin & S,LLP -260 Mad Av -NY 10016
(212) 742-3390 .. **Klahr,** Deborah E '93 Cnsl Lindabury ME&C,PC -26 Bway -NY 10004
(212) 813-8800 .. **Klahr,** Shmuel M '05 %Goodwin P LLP -620 8th Av -NY 10018
(212) 530-5000 .. **Klaiber,** James R '97 %Milbank TH&M LLP -1 Chase Manh Plz -NY 10005
(718) 656-6066 .. **Klainberg,** Dennis S '91 %Berklay Air Srvcs -Bldg 80 JFK Airport Bx665 -Jamaica 11430
(718) 250-2000 .. **Klam,** Tania L '10 %DA -350 Jay -Brklyn 11201 **Fx:**250-2314
(212) 788-0516 .. **Klann,** Rita M '93 %Law Dept -100 Church -NY 10007 **Fx:**788-0367
(212) 345-7000 .. **Klapak,** Timothy J '92 %Mercer HR Cnsltng -1166 Av of Amer -NY 10036
(516) 239-2288 .. **Klaperman,** Gilbert '78 -64 Muriel Av -Lawrence 11559
(212) 848-8021 .. **Klaperman,** Joel S '74 (Shearman & S LLP) -599 Lex Av -NY 10022
(212) 696-2666 .. **Klaplsch,** Steven M '75 (Weisberg F&K) -261 5th Av -NY 10016
(212) 474-1000 .. **Klapp,** Robt D '92 Cravath S&M LLP -825 8th Av -NY 10019
(212) 446-4800 .. **Klapper,** Alyssa D '08 %Kirkland & E LLP -153 E 53rd -NY 10022
(718) 447-2536 .. **Klapper,** Andrew D '90 Klapper & K -888 Forest Av -Staten Isl 10310 **Fx:**442-5088
(212) 750-5055 .. **Klapper,** Benjamin S '65 (Ingber & K) -575 Lex Av -NY 10022
(631) 715-7900 .. **Klapper,** Bonnie S '83 %US Atty -610 Fed Plz -Central Islip 11722
(212) 264-6913 .. **Klapper,** Hanna '86 %IRS -290 Bway -NY 10007 **Fx:**264-4089
(914) 287-6466 .. **Klapper,** Joshua H '78 (Klapper & F) -170 Hmltn Av -White Plns 10601 **Fx:**287-6422
(212) 431-6888 .. **Klapper,** Judith N '95 -100 Lafayette -NY 10013 **Fx:**431-6773
(212) 795-5541 .. **Klapper,** Molly '89 Mediator/Arbitrator -720 Ft Wshngtn Av -NY 10040 **Fx:**795-5542
(212) 558-4000 .. **Klapper,** Richd H '81 (Sullivan & C LLP) -125 Broad -NY 10004
(718) 654-2000 .. **Klapper,** Robt J '55 Eastern Abstract -2500 Wllmsbrdg Rd -Bronx 10469 **Fx:**654-2221
(212) 756-2000 .. **Klaproth,** Elizabeth S '08 %Schulte R&Z LLP -919 3rd Av -NY 10022
(212) 606-0850 .. **Klar,** Edw I '77 -909 5th Av -NY 10021
(212) 683-7100 .. **Klar,** Howard P '90 (Gallo V&K,LLP) -90 Broad -NY 10004
(516) 746-6565 .. **Klar,** Michl N '69 -One Old Cntry Rd -Carle Pl 11514 **Fx:**746-6633
(516) 248-8800 .. **Klar,** Richd B '83 -145 Willis Av -Mineola 11501
(718) 515-6000 .. **Klar,** Ronald M '68 (Corpina PK&P,LLP) -2344 Eastchstr Rd -Bronx 10469
(516) 735-1717 .. **Klar,** Steven A '73 -2580 Hempstd Tpk -E Meadow 11554
(212) 450-4000 .. **Klar,** Steven R '09 %Davis P&W LLP -450 Lex Av -NY 10017
(914) 698-0712 .. **Klarberg,** Richd B '71 -825 Taylors Ln -Mamaroneck 10543
(518) 445-3345 .. **Klare,** Kathe A '03 %Albany Law Schl -80 New Scotland Av -Albany 12208 **Fx:**445-2315
(212) 286-5857 .. **Klaris,** Edw J '93 The New Yorker -4 Times Sq -NY 10036 **Fx:**286-5025
(212) 868-3777 .. **Klarish,** Noah '84 (Hutner K LLP) -1359 Bway -NY 10018 **Fx:**868-3778
(914) 736-0144 .. **Klarl,** John J '80 (Wood & K) -2131 Albany Post Rd -Montrose 10548
(212) 768-6700 .. **Klarquist,** Scott R '02 %Sonnenschein N&R LLP -2 World Fncl Ctr -NY 10281
(212) 508-6700 .. **Klarreich,** Joel A '68 (Tannenbaum HS&H LLP) -900 3rd Av -NY 10022
(212) 889-0707 .. **Klarsfeld,** Jeffrey H '92 (Platte KL&L,LLP) -10 E 40th -NY 10016
(212) 398-3550 .. **Klarsfeld,** S Herman '55 -25 W 43rd -NY 10036

(212) 688-0004 .. **Klasfeld,** Norman '72 -845 3rd Av -NY 10022 **Fx:**688-7250
(585) 258-8141 .. **Klash,** Rudolph M '89 %State Ins Fund -100 Chestnut -Rchstr 14604 **Fx:**258-8143
(212) 448-9570 .. **Klasna,** Chad L '06 %Callahan & F,LLC -40 Exch Pl -NY 10005
(212) 309-6000 .. **Klass,** Jennifer Lynd '05 (Morgan L&B LLP) -101 Park Av -NY 10178
(718) 643-6063 .. **Klass,** Richd A '92 (R Klass) -16 Court -Brklyn 11241 **Fx:**643-9788
(212) 541-7800 .. **Klassel,** Dara '79 %Planned Parenthood -434 W 33rd -NY 10001 **Fx:**868-4677
(212) 691-4560 .. **Klasson,** Walter B '77 -236 W 26th -NY 10001
(212) 254-1111 .. **Klatell,** Christopher J '00 (Rabinowitz BSK&L,PC) -111 Bway -NY 10006
(212) 909-6000 .. **Klatell,** Jeremy N '05 %Debevoise & P LLP -919 3rd Av -NY 10022
(212) 725-4423 .. **Klatsky,** James '85 OfCnsl Paykin K&A LLP -185 Mad Av -NY 10016
(212) 759-1200 .. **Klauber,** Amy B '91 (Klauber & K,LLP) -444 Mad Av -NY 10022 **Fx:**317-8717
(212) 661-7300 .. **Klauber,** Andrew L '83 (Malapero & P LLP) -295 Mad Av -NY 10017
(212) 759-1200 .. **Klauber,** Richd H '88 (Klauber & K,LLP) -444 Mad Av -NY 10022 **Fx:**317-8717
(212) 259-8000 .. **Klauberg,** John G '82 (Dewey & L LLP) -1301 Av of Amer -NY 10019
(212) 785-2929 .. **Klaum,** Teresa A '92 (Conway FC&K,PC) -48 Wall -NY 10005
(212) 750-2500 .. **Klaus,** Mortimer '60 %Burma Bibas Inc -597 5th Av -NY 10017 **Fx:**750-2834
(718) 442-1700 .. **Klaus,** Wm A '95 %Connors & C,PC -766 Castleton Av -Staten Isl 10310 **Fx:**442-1717
(607) 272-0800 .. **Klausner,** Adam A '99 -409 Taughannock Blvd -Ithaca 14850
(914) 288-8706 .. **Klausner,** David S '94 D Klausner,PLLC -150 Grand -White Plns 10601
(212) 468-4800 .. **Klausner,** Jennifer Tafet '93 (Davis & G LLP) -1740 Bway -NY 10019
(718) 389-2427 .. **Klausner,** Jeremy M '95 %Agostino & Assoc,PC -500 Kngslnd Av -Brklyn 11222
(212) 468-4800 .. **Klausner,** Neal H '87 (Davis & G LLP) -1740 Bway -NY 10019
(212) 490-1002 .. **Klausner,** Paul J '82 Sierra Rlty -12 E 46th -NY 10017
(212) 980-3500 .. **Klausner,** Peter L '66 Cnsl Pavia & H LLP -600 Mad Av -NY 10022
(212) 297-5800 .. **Klausner,** Robt A '87 (Day P LLP) -7 Times Sq -NY 10036
(212) 926-7000 .. **Klausner,** Ronald B '79 -222 W 145th -NY 10039
(212) 999-5800 .. **Klausner,** Tonia Ouellette '94 (Wilson SG&R) -1301 Av of Americas -NY 10019
(212) 461-7152 .. **Klauss,** Patrick M '05 (Berd & K PLLC) -44 Wall -NY 10005 **Fx:**461-7153
(516) 759-2110 .. **Kle,** John P '50 -24 Prospect Av -Sea Cliff 11579
(516) 906-2102 .. **Klear,** Jay C '04 %Futurtec Cptl Corp -111 Grt Nck Rd -Gt Neck 11021
(212) 579-5943 .. **Klear,** Jennifer A '03 -445 Park Av -NY 10022
(516) 681-7176 .. **Klebanoff,** Richd E '86 -2 Prsdntl Dr E -Plainvw 11803 **Fx:**681-1365
(212) 737-9719 .. **Kleckner,** Robt G Jr. '64 -80 East End Av -NY 10028
(631) 261-7777 .. **Kleczka,** Mark D '84 (Bushell K&M) -7 Bayview Av -Northprt 11768
(914) 524-6878 .. **Klee,** Eric S '98 Prestige Brands Hldngs -90 N Bway -Irvngtn 10533
(516) 294-5775 .. **Klee,** Jonathan R '93 (Klee & W,LLP) -350 Willis Av -Mineola 11501
(718) 935-0582 .. **Klee,** Lewis M '78 -41 Schermerhorn -Brklyn 11201 **Fx:**228-4158
(212) 751-2400 .. **Klee,** Richd '69 (Kalnick K&G,LLP) -767 3rd Av -NY 10017
(516) 294-5775 .. **Klee & Woolf,LLP** -350 Willis Av -Mineola 11501 **Fx:**228-0044
(212) 490-5700 .. **Kleeger,** Judd Franklin '96 (Hecht KP&D) -19 W 44th -NY 10036
(212) 763-4100 .. **Kleeman,** Jan '87 Cnsl Reavis PL LLP -41 Mad Av -NY 10010
(212) 682-4001 .. **Kleeman,** Julie A '06 %Lynch R LLP -630 3rd Av -NY 10017
(917) 778-6500 .. **Kleen,** Wm P '80 %K Dodson -485 Lex Av -NY 10017
(516) 938-6076 .. **Kleger,** Lawr A '77 -38 Club Dr N -Jericho 11753 **Fx:**827-0981
(212) 326-3939 .. **Klehm,** Henry III '91 (Jones D) -222 E 41st -NY 10017
(212) 974-5700 .. **Kleidman,** Carl G '83 %Barington Cptl Grp -888 7th Av -NY 10106
(212) 223-3900 .. **Kleidman,** Paul '02 %Zwerling S&Z,LLP -41 Mad Av -NY 10010
(516) 482-6166 .. **Kleiger,** Howard L '56 (Kleiger & K) -80 Cuttermill Rd -Gt Neck 11021 **Fx:**482-6240
(212) 351-4500 .. **Kleiman,** Alan S '75 OfCnsl Epstein B&G,PC -250 Park Av -NY 10177
(212) 969-3000 .. **Kleiman,** Andrew H '06 %Proskauer R LLP -1585 Bway -NY 10036
(212) 945-4077 .. **Kleiman,** Diane L '87 -380 Rector Pl -NY 10280
(716) 856-1289 .. **Kleiman,** Howard '81 (Lavin & K) -528 Brisbane Bldg -Buffalo 14203 **Fx:**856-8808
(212) 758-6160 .. **Kleiman,** Ira '83 (Brief C&K,LLP) -805 3rd Av -NY 10022
(212) 355-6161 .. **Kleiman,** Jeremy P '95 Coastal Dvlpmnt LLC -745 5th Av -NY 10151 **Fx:**355-4461
(212) 839-5300 .. **Kleiman,** Laurin Blumenthal '85 (Sidley A LLP) -787 7th Av -NY 10019
(718) 523-6868 .. **Kleiman,** Mark '72 %Comm Mediation Svcs -89-64 163rd -Jamaica 11432 **Fx:**523-8204
(212) 682-2900 .. **Kleiman,** Rachel M '87 (Braverman & Assoc,PC) -331 Mad Av -NY 10017 **Fx:**682-7718
(212) 318-6000 .. **Klein,** Aaron M '06 %Paul HJ&W LLP -75 E 55th -NY 10022
(212) 245-1000 .. **Klein,** Adam T '91 (Outten & G LLP) -3 Park Av -NY 10016
(845) 348-3168 .. **Klein,** Adrienne R '80 -15 N Mill -Nyack 10960 **Fx:**348-3167
(212) 455-2000 .. **Klein,** Alan M '86 (Simpson T&B LLP) -425 Lex Av -NY 10017
(212) 317-8500 .. **Klein,** Alan V '09 %Snitow KH&M,LLP -575 Lex Av -NY 10022 **Fx:**317-1308
(212) 506-1700 .. **Klein,** Alana Sher '08 %Kasowitz BT&F LLP -1633 Bway -NY 10019
(518) 533-3000 .. **Klein,** Amelia M '91 (Bond S&K,PLLC) -111 Wshngtn Av -Albany 12210
(518) 455-7700 .. **Klein,** Andrew '78 %Ct of Appls -20 Eagle -Albany 12207
(212) 373-3000 .. **Klein,** Andrew J '05 %Paul WRW&G LLP -1285 Av of Amer -NY 10019
(212) 822-9521 .. **Klein,** Anne C '93 Advocates for Children -151 W 30th -NY 10001
(212) 526-1693 .. **Klein,** Arlene '90 Barclays Capital Inc -745 7th Av -NY 10019
(516) 354-0800 .. **Klein,** Arnold S '78 (Koopersmith K LLC) -200 Grdn City Plz -Gdn Cty 11530 **Fx:**488-4387
(212) 232-1300 .. **Klein,** Bari R '02 %Lewis BB&S LLP -77 Water -NY 10005
(516) 487-0143 .. **Klein,** Bart J '79 -343 Grt Nck Rd -Gt Neck 11021
(718) 722-4100 .. **Klein,** Brett H '98 (Leventhal & K,LLP) -45 Main -Brklyn 11201
(718) 401-2600 .. **Klein,** Bruce D '81 -888 Grnd Cncrs -Bronx 10451
(718) 319-1400 .. **Klein Calderoni & Santucci LLP** -1614 Wllmsbrdg Rd -Bronx 10461 **Fx:**239-0716
(516) 221-3613 .. **Klein,** Carl S '50 -955 Sienns Ct -N Bellmore 11710
(718) 237-3100 .. **Klein,** Catherine M '05 Leg Aid -111 Lvngstn -Brklyn 11201 **Fx:**250-4243
(212) 476-8062 .. **Klein,** Chas D '64 American Securities -666 3rd Av -NY 10017
(212) 557-7200 .. **Klein,** Chas H '78 (Davidoff M&H,LLP) -605 3rd Av -NY 10158
(516) 431-1000 .. **Klein,** Corey E '95 %Corp Cnsl -1 W Chester -Long Bch 11561 **Fx:**431-1016
(718) 590-2000 .. **Klein,** Danl L '02 %DA -198 E 161st -Bronx 10451 **Fx:**590-6477
(212) 632-6503 .. **Klein,** Danl P '97 %Lazard Freres -30 Rckfllr Plz -NY 10112 **Fx:**632-6060
(212) 450-4000 .. **Klein,** Darren S '08 %Davis P&W LLP -450 Lex Av -NY 10017
(212) 344-9022 .. **Klein,** David '05 Klein Law Grp,PC -11 Bway -NY 10004 **Fx:**344-0301
(212) 446-8415 .. **Klein,** David B '89 %McKinsey & Co -55 E 52nd -NY 10055 **Fx:**688-9521
(973) 228-5700 .. **Klein,** David J '87 Cnsl Brach E LLC -100 Park Av -NY 10017 **Fx:**228-7852
(212) 553-3200 .. **Klein,** David L '74 (Marulli LE&T,LLP) -5 Hanover Sq -NY 10004
(845) 357-7900 .. **Klein,** David M '73 (Klein & K) -2 Exec Blvd -Suffern 10901 **Fx:**357-7127
(212) 318-6000 .. **Klein,** David M '93 (Paul HJ&W LLP) -75 E 55th -NY 10022
(212) 756-2000 .. **Klein,** David M '08 %Schulte R&Z LLP -919 3rd Av -NY 10022
(212) 935-6020 .. **Klein,** David O '93 (Klein ZR LLP) -485 Mad Av -NY 10022
(212) 815-1450 .. **Klein,** Dena '07 %DC 37 Gen Cnsl -125 Barclay -NY 10007 **Fx:**815-1440
(212) 753-5000 .. **Klein,** Donald A '03 OfCnsl Schiff H LLP -900 3rd Av -NY 10022
(212) 603-6300 .. **Klein,** Donald M '73 Cnsl Robinson BLGG&G PC -875 3rd Av -NY 10022
(212) 297-5800 .. **Klein,** Doreen '83 SrCnsl Day P LLP -7 Times Sq -NY 10036
(631) 486-4900 .. **Klein,** Edw C '84 %E Berman,PC -100 Grdn City Plz -Gdn Cty 11530 **Fx:**486-4997
(212) 661-9400 .. **Klein,** Edw E '82 (Klein & S LLP) -275 Mad Av -NY 10016
(718) 380-5362 .. **Klein,** Edw J '64 -179-54 80th Rd -Jamaica 11432 **Fx:**380-5362
(315) 424-3854 .. **Klein,** Edw W '90 -217 Mntgmry -Syracuse 13202 **Fx:**424-6826
(212) 756-2000 .. **Klein,** Eleazer '92 (Schulte R&Z LLP) -919 3rd Av -NY 10022
(212) 782-6019 .. **Klein,** Eric T '91 Moore Capital Mgmt,Inc -1251 Av of Amer -NY 10020
(212) 715-9100 .. **Klein,** Erica D '99 (Kramer LN&F,LLP) -1177 Av of Amer -NY 10036
(212) 403-1000 .. **Klein,** Erica Mitnick '09 %Wachtell LR&K -51 W 52nd -NY 10019
(212) 692-1000 .. **Klein,** Eve I '86 (Duane M LLP) -1540 Bway -NY 10036
(212) 298-9416 .. **Klein,** Faige P '01 Skidmore O&M LLP -14 Wall -NY 10005
(646) 723-1032 .. **Klein,** Frank H '62 -60 E 42nd -NY 10165
(212) 867-1080 .. **Klein,** Frank J '66 -511 5th Av -NY 10017
(631) 952-6400 .. **Klein,** Fred B '80 %Medicaid Fraud Cntrl -300 Motor Pkwy -Hauppauge 11788 **Fx:**952-6382
(212) 935-6020 .. **Klein,** Fred C '68 (Klein ZR LLP) -485 Mad Av -NY 10022
(212) 695-0910 .. **Klein,** Fredk M '95 %Sullivan Law Grp,LLP -1350 Bway -NY 10018 **Fx:**695-0915
(212) 558-5500 .. **Klein,** Gary R '92 %Weitz & L,PC -700 Bway -NY 10003
(212) 402-9400 .. **Klein,** Gayle '04 (McKool S,PC) -1 Bryant Park -NY 10036
(718) 575-3373 .. **Klein,** George '84 -70-09 Austin -Frst Hlls 11375 **Fx:**575-2656
(914) 271-6601 .. **Klein,** Gerald M '70 (Katz & K) -1 Croton Pnt Av Bx626 -Croton-On-Hud 10520
(718) 852-5266 .. **Klein,** Harry L '63 -26 Court -Brklyn 11242 **Fx:**852-5838
(212) 446-4800 .. **Klein,** Howard M '02 (Kirkland & E LLP) -153 E 53rd -NY 10022
(516) 374-6600 .. **Klein,** Irwin G '77 (Hein W&K) -825 E Gate Blvd -Gdn Cty 11530
(212) 586-4567 .. **Klein,** Jack '57 -1650 Bway -NY 10019 **Fx:**397-3794
(212) 436-3421 .. **Klein,** James P '74 Deloitte & Touche LLP -2 World Fncl Ctr -NY 10281
(516) 488-3452 .. **Klein,** James R '73 -276 Jericho Tpk Bx215 -Floral Pk 11002 **Fx:**437-9535
(212) 408-6324 .. **Klein,** Jason M '00 Cnsl MOMA -11 W 53rd -NY 10019
(212) 761-4000 .. **Klein,** Jay J '06 Morgan Stanley -1633 Bway -NY 10019
(212) 578-2211 .. **Klein,** Jay W '83 %MetLife -27-01 Qns Plz N -LIC 11101
(516) 783-0380 .. **Klein,** Jeffrey '78 (Mulhern & K) -3330 Park Av -Wantagh 11793
(718) 319-1400 .. **Klein,** Jeffrey D '94 (Klein C&S LLP) -1614 Wllmsbrdg Rd -Bronx 10461
(212) 620-7310 .. **Klein,** Jeffrey H '05 LGBT Community Ctr -208 W 13th -NY 10011
(914) 946-2822 .. **Klein,** Jeffrey I '71 OfCnsl O'Kelley & F,PC -445 Hmltn Av -White Plns 10601
(212) 813-8800 .. **Klein,** Jeffrey I '03 (Goodwin P LLP) -620 8th Av -NY 10018
(212) 310-8000 .. **Klein,** Jeffrey S '82 (Weil G&M LLP) -767 5th Av -NY 10153
(212) 819-0089 .. **Klein,** Jenean M '01 %Edmonds & Co,PC -112 Mad Av -NY 10016 **Fx:**819-0189
(212) 455-2000 .. **Klein,** Jennifer P '08 %Simpson T&B LLP -425 Lex Av -NY 10017
(212) 558-4000 .. **Klein,** Jessica '04 %Sullivan & C LLP -125 Broad -NY 10004
(631) 249-6565 .. **Klein,** John V N '56 (Meyer SE&K,PC) -425 Broadhllw Rd Bx9064 -Melvll 11747
(212) 335-4500 .. **Klein,** Jonathan '88 (DLA Piper LLP) -1251 Av of Amer -NY 10020
(718) 222-2021 .. **Klein,** Jonathan D '01 %Law Dept -350 Jay -Brklyn 11201 **Fx:**222-2088
(914) 633-7400 .. **Klein,** Jonathan Saml '94 %Marcus O&K LLP -145 Huguenot -New Rchll 10801
(212) 637-2397 .. **Klein,** Josh '94 %US Atty -1 St Andrews Plz -NY 10007
(212) 883-1700 .. **Klein,** Joshua C '02 (Duval & S LLP) -101 Park Av -NY 10178
(914) 237-1922 .. **Klein,** Judith A '87 %Dr P Klein -928 McLean Av -Ynkrs 10704
(212) 818-9200 .. **Klein,** Justin E '04 %Satterlee SB&B LLP -230 Park Av -NY 10169
(845) 482-5000 .. **Klein,** Kenneth C '86 -4880 State Route 52 Bx600 -Jffrsnvll 12748 **Fx:**482-5002
(845) 295-0100 .. **Klein,** Kenneth C '86 -2 Schl Bx670 -Liberty 12754 **Fx:**295-0120
(212) 804-4200 .. **Klein,** Kenneth W '09 %Mound CW&G -One Bttry Pk Plz -NY 10004
(212) 225-2000 .. **Klein,** Kerrin T '10 %Cleary GS&H -1 Lbrty Plz -NY 10006
(212) 968-9607 .. **Klein,** Kerry '77 %M Weisman -45 Bway -NY 10006 **Fx:**968-0296
(212) 554-7800 .. **Klein,** Kimberly '98 (Moses & S LLP) -405 Lex Av -NY 10174
(914) 946-4777 .. **Klein,** Lance H '91 (Keane & B,PC) -445 Hmltn Av -White Plns 10601

(212) 522-6809 .. **Klein,** Lauren Ezrol '92 %Time Inc -1271 Av of Amer -NY 10020 **Fx:**522-0437
(212) 422-0202 .. **Klein,** Lawr J '85 (Sedgwick DM&A LLP) -125 Broad -NY 10004
(845) 565-2100 .. **Klein,** Lawr M '60 -17 N Plnk Rd -Newburgh 12550 **Fx:**565-2111
(516) 746-3500 .. **Klein,** Lawr W '03 %Brand G&B,PC -600 Old Cntry Rd -Gdn Cty 11530
(845) 454-9200 .. **Klein,** Lee David '83 -11 Market -Poughkeepsie 12601 **Fx:**454-6612
(212) 730-5405 .. **Klein,** Leo N '83 -15 W 44th -NY 10036 **Fx:**869-2303
(845) 454-3250 .. **Klein,** Leonard '66 (Gellert & K,PC) -75 Wshngtn -Poughkeepsie 12601
(212) 816-0330 .. **Klein,** Leslie A '76 Citigroup -388 Greenwich -NY 10013 **Fx:**816-4447
(212) 683-7300 .. **Klein & Liss** -470 Park Av S -NY 10016 **Fx:**683-7737
(845) 331-0396 .. **Klein,** Louis M '67 (Klein & K,PC) -70 Maiden Ln Bx3158 -Kingston 12402 **Fx:**331-1482
(516) 365-8675 .. **Klein,** Luise M '90 -58 Monterey Dr Bx3951 -Manhsst Hlls 11040 **Fx:**365-8682
(516) 877-2900 .. **Klein,** M David '94 (Bartlett MB&M,LLP) -300 Old Cntry Rd -Mineola 11501
(646) 392-9250 .. **Klein,** Margaret G '84 (M Klein & Assoc) -200 Mad Av -NY 10016 **Fx:**(212) 779-1499
(212) 907-9600 .. **Klein,** Mark E '79 (Ingram YGC&B,LLP) -250 Park Av -NY 10177
(212) 821-6543 .. **Klein,** Mark N '92 UBS Global Asset Mgmt -299 Park Av -NY 10171
(716) 856-4000 .. **Klein,** Mark S '83 (Hodgson R LLP) -140 Pearl -Buffalo 14202
(212) 753-9200 .. **Klein,** Martin I '73 (M Klein,PC) -350 E 79th -NY 10075 **Fx:**753-9229
(212) 400-4930 .. **Klein,** Martin S '83 %Kamerman & S PC -708 3rd Av -NY 10017
(212) 923-1400 .. **Klein,** Matthew '99 %Blue Ridge Fndtn NY -660 Mad Av -NY 10065
(212) 791-1881 .. **Klein,** Megan J '07 EarthJustice -156 William -NY 10038
(212) 506-1700 .. **Klein,** Menachem C '07 Kasowitz BT&F LLP -1633 Bway -NY 10019
(315) 671-1100 .. **Klein,** Michl A '77 %Hon J Tormey III -400 Cnty Cthse -Syracuse 13202
(212) 479-6000 .. **Klein,** Michl A '05 %Cooley LLP -1114 Av of Amer -NY 10036
(212) 201-2500 .. **Klein,** Michl F '89 Aetos Captl -875 3rd Av -NY 10022 **Fx:**201-2525
(212) 486-3370 .. **Klein,** Michl H '75 (Kestenbaum D&K,LLP) -104 W 40th -NY 10018
(212) 687-7230 .. **Klein,** Michl J '05 Stull S&B -6 E 45th -NY 10017
(845) 357-7900 .. **Klein,** Michl L '79 (Klein & K) -2 Exec Blvd -Suffern 10901 **Fx:**357-7127
(914) 934-8792 .. **Klein,** Michele '87 (Klein & F) -219 Wstchstr Av -Pt Chester 10573 **Fx:**934-8793
(914) 683-8792 .. **Klein,** Michele '87 (Klein & F) -1849 Route 6 -Carmel 10512 **Fx:**683-8790
(212) 553-5513 .. **Klein,** Michelle R '91 %Zurich NA -1 Lbrty Plz -NY 10006
(212) 949-5800 .. **Klein,** Mitchell '78 (Brady K&W,LLP) -501 5th Av -NY 10017
(516) 222-6855 .. **Klein,** Mitchell P '91 -114 Old Cntry Rd -Mineola 11501
(518) 457-5973 .. **Klein,** Monte A '79 %PERB -80 Wolf Rd -Albany 12205 **Fx:**457-2664
(516) 466-0033 .. **Klein,** Murray R '55 -475 Nrthrn Blvd -Gt Neck 11021 **Fx:**466-3867
(212) 869-2147 .. **Klein,** Norman I '62 (Carlet GK&Z) -645 5th Av -NY 10022
(718) 376-5079 .. **Klein,** Pace C '94 -2136 E 5th -Brklyn 11223
(315) 458-1450 .. **Klein,** Pamela J '91 -801 Church -N Syracuse 13212
(212) 924-3738 .. **Klein,** Paul L '58 -241 Av of Amer -NY 10014 **Fx:**924-4927
(914) 993-9393 .. **Klein,** Paula L '79 Stewart Title Ins -707 Wstchstr Av -White Plns 10604 **Fx:**997-1698
(716) 856-0600 .. **Klein,** Peter G '80 (Jaeckle F&M,LLP) -12 Fountain Plz -Buffalo 14202
(212) 230-8800 .. **Klein,** Peter R '05 %WilmerHale -399 Park Av -NY 10022
(212) 683-7300 .. **Klein,** Philip E '79 (Klein & L) -470 Park Av S -NY 10016
(212) 774-2194 .. **Klein,** Phyllis A '93 Hospital for Special Surgery -535 E 70th -NY 10021 **Fx:**517-8781
(516) 240-1716 .. **Klein,** Randy M '97 Ivy Asset Mgmt Corp -1 Jericho Plz -Jericho 11753
(212) 697-4455 .. **Klein,** Reuven '82 (Klein & H) -521 5th Av -NY 10175 **Fx:**697-1958
(914) 671-6162 .. **Klein,** Richd '90 -15 Bank -White Plns 10606
(646) 471-4000 .. **Klein,** Richd A '84 %PricewaterhouseCoopers LLP -300 Mad Av -NY 10017
(631) 761-7000 .. **Klein,** Richd D '73 %Touro Cllg Law Ctr -225 Eastvw Dr -Central Islip 11722
(516) 663-5151 .. **Klein,** Richd D '07 Diamond Law Grp -244 Mineola Blvd -Mineola 11501 **Fx:**663-5152
(212) 944-0500 .. **Klein,** Richd G '73 (Hofheimer G&G,LLP) -530 5th Av -NY 10036 **Fx:**897-4982
(212) 490-3000 .. **Klein,** Richd S '74 (Wilson EME&D LLP) -150 E 42nd -NY 10017
(845) 356-3840 .. **Klein,** Robt '80 -2 Sands Pnt Rd -Monsey 10952
(914) 584-8477 .. **Klein,** Robt C '83 -179 Madison Rd -Scarsdale 10583
(212) 768-6700 .. **Klein,** Ronald L '08 %Sonnenschein N&R LLP -2 World Fncl Ctr -NY 10281
(212) 916-4220 .. **Klein,** Roseanne M '75 %TIAA-CREF -730 3rd Av -NY 10017
(631) 777-1313 .. **Klein,** Roy A '78 -532 Broadhllw Rd -Melvll 11747
(212) 696-4848 .. **Klein,** Scott A '96 %Mintz & G LLP -470 Park Av S -NY 10016
(718) 522-3311 .. **Klein,** Scott H '77 -26 Court -Brklyn 11242
(718) 382-7000 .. **Klein,** Simon '74 (Suslovich & K) -1507 Av M -Brklyn 11230 **Fx:**382-5797
(212) 661-9400 .. **Klein & Solomon LLP** -275 Mad Av -NY 10016 **Fx:**661-6606
(212) 575-0202 .. **Klein,** Solomon N '01 -1410 Bway -NY 10018
(212) 468-8000 .. **Klein,** Spencer D '91 (Morrison & F LLP) -1290 Av of Amer -NY 10104
(631) 584-8000 .. **Klein,** Stacey J '96 (Valente & K,PC) -112 Terry Rd -Smithtwn 11787 **Fx:**584-8808
(212) 969-3000 .. **Klein,** Stacey P '08 %Proskauer R LLP -1585 Bway -NY 10036
(212) 581-1340 .. **Klein,** Stanley M '59 -250 W 57th -NY 10107
(914) 345-8750 .. **Klein,** Stephanie A '93 -500 Exec Blvd -Elmsfrd 10523 **Fx:**345-5792
(212) 728-8000 .. **Klein,** Steven D '87 (Willkie F&G LLP) -787 7th Av -NY 10019
(212) 458-2224 .. **Klein,** Steven E '02 Chartis Inc -175 Water -NY 10038
(518) 785-1900 .. **Klein,** Steven M '89 %PEF -1168-70 Troy-Schnctdy Rd Bx12414 -Albany 12212 **Fx:**785-1323
(718) 338-6160 .. **Klein,** Stewart '89 -1089 E 18th -Brklyn 11230
(212) 564-7560 .. **Klein,** Stuart A '73 -99 Mad Av -NY 10016 **Fx:**564-7845
(518) 533-3000 .. **Klein,** Stuart F '00 (Bond S&K,PLLC) -111 Wshngtn Av -Albany 12210
(212) 344-9022 .. **Klein,** Susan '86 (Klein Law Grp,PC) -11 Bway -NY 10004 **Fx:**344-0301
(212) 294-6700 .. **Klein,** Susan F '71 (Winston & S) -200 Park Av -NY 10166
(212) 298-5127 .. **Klein,** Thos M '82 %Leg Aid -49 Thomas -NY 10013 **Fx:**298-5252
(212) 351-4500 .. **Klein,** Traycee Ellen '94 (Epstein B&G,PC) -250 Park Av -NY 10177
(631) 587-2300 .. **Klein & Vizzi,LLP** -370 B Sunrise Hwy -W Babylon 11704 **Fx:**587-2010
(212) 227-7200 .. **Klein Wagner & Morris** -277 Bway -NY 10007 **Fx:**385-0792
(631) 587-2300 .. **Klein,** Warren J '87 (Klein & V,LLP) -370 B Sunrise Hwy -W Babylon 11704
(212) 935-6020 .. **Klein Zelman Rothermel LLP** -485 Mad Av -NY 10022 **Fx:**753-8101
(718) 876-6300 .. **Kleinbart,** Morrie I '87 %DA -130 Styvsnt Pl -Staten Isl 10301
(518) 794-8703 .. **Kleinbaum,** Chas '65 -763 Cnty Route 13 -Old Chatham 12136 **Fx:**794-8704
(914) 644-2000 .. **Kleinbaum,** Clifford G '64 -11 Martine Av -White Plns 10606 **Fx:**946-0134
(212) 599-2500 .. **Kleinbaum,** Gerald M '59 -260 Mad Av -NY 10016 **Fx:**599-2579
(212) 801-6899 .. **Kleinbaum,** Glenn A '92 (Greenberg T,LLP) -200 Park Av -NY 10166
(518) 794-8708 .. **Kleinbaum,** James E '95 (J Kleinbaum) -18 Park Row -Chatham 12037 **Fx:**794-8709
(718) 248-9103 .. **Kleinbaum,** Wendy Slote '72 %Citibank -1 Court Sq -LIC 11101
(516) 334-4500 .. **Kleinberg,** Adam I '00 Sokoloff S LLP -355 Post Av -Westbury 11590 **Fx:**334-4501
(718) 254-7000 .. **Kleinberg,** Chas S '77 %US Atty -271 Cadman Plz E -Brklyn 11201 **Fx:**254-6479
(212) 372-2156 .. **Kleinberg,** Elaine '91 Cnsl Newmark Knight Frank -125 Park Av -NY 10017 **Fx:**372-2386
(212) 986-6000 .. **Kleinberg,** Fredric A '68 (Kleinberg KW&C,PC) -551 5th Av -NY 10176
(516) 741-6565 .. **Kleinberg,** Howard B '90 (Meyer SE&K,PC) -990 Stewart Av Bx9194 -Gdn Cty 11530
(212) 986-6000 .. **Kleinberg Kaplan Wolff & Cohen,PC** -551 5th Av -NY 10176 **Fx:**986-8866
(212) 837-6000 .. **Kleinberg,** Norman C '73 (Hughes H&R LLP) -1 Bttry Pk Plz -NY 10004
(212) 421-2233 .. **Kleinberg,** Pamela L '88 %Wilk A LLP -675 3rd Av -NY 10017
(212) 301-4000 .. **Kleinberg,** Robt I '62 %National Fncl Partners -787 7th Av -NY 10019
(212) 689-8600 .. **Kleinberg,** Ronald M '69 (Meissner K&F,LLP) -275 Mad Av -NY 10016
(212) 770-2217 .. **Kleinberger,** Alan E '92 AIG Tech Srvcs -80 Pine -NY 10005
(518) 765-4721 .. **Kleinberger,** George H '60 -193 New Salem South Rd -Voorheesvll 12186
(917) 326-5523 .. **Kleinberger,** Thos R '93 (TR Kleinberger,PLLC) -411 5th Av -NY 10016 **Fx:**326-5525
(212) 237-0000 .. **Kleiner,** Barry R '95 (Vinson & E LLP) -666 5th Av -NY 10103
(347) 739-9739 .. **Kleiner,** Chas J '86 -450 7th Av -NY 10123 **Fx:**(212) 629-5825
(212) 880-3800 .. **Kleiner,** H Frances '86 (Akerman S) -335 Mad Av -NY 10017
(212) 839-7000 .. **Kleiner,** James D '79 (Hill B&N LLP) -200 Lbrty -NY 10281
(212) 935-4400 .. **Kleiner,** Jeffrey W '03 %LePatner & Assoc LLP -600 Lex Av -NY 10022 **Fx:**935-4404
(212) 356-1400 .. **Kleiner,** Kenneth R '92 %Rosenthal & Rosenthal, Inc -1370 Bway -NY 10018
(212) 686-3838 .. **Kleiner,** Philip J '74 (Barst M&K LLP) -2 Park Av -NY 10016
(845) 359-5100 .. **Kleiner,** Thom '85 -26 Orangebrg Rd -Orangebrg 10962 **Fx:**359-2623
(212) 918-3000 .. **Kleinerman,** Michl R '65 (Hogan L LLP) -875 3rd Av -NY 10022
(845) 679-8986 .. **Kleinfeld,** Harold A '52 -68 Tanglewood Rd -W Hurley 12491 **Fx:**679-3739
(716) 551-4931 .. **Kleingardner,** Lillian '00 %NLRB -130 S Elmwood Av -Buffalo 14202 **Fx:**551-4972
(212) 977-9700 .. **Kleinhandler,** Neil C '67 (Phillips N LLP) -666 5th Av -NY 10103
(212) 581-3791 .. **Kleinhans,** Elysabeth '89 Omnispective Mgt Co -240 Cntrl Pk S -NY 10019
(516) 223-7714 .. **Kleinhardt,** Chas R '57 (Kleinhardt & K) -2300 Grand Av -Baldwin 11510 **Fx:**223-0634
(516) 223-7714 .. **Kleinhardt,** Lee D '89 %Kleinhardt & K -2300 Grand Av -Baldwin 11510 **Fx:**223-0634
(212) 504-6000 .. **Kleinhaus,** Brian W '07 %Cadwalader W&T LLP -1 World Fncl Ctr -NY 10281
(212) 403-1000 .. **Kleinhaus,** Emil A '03 %Wachtell LR&K -51 W 52nd -NY 10019
(212) 455-2000 .. **Kleinhaus,** Joanna L '05 %Simpson T&B LLP -425 Lex Av -NY 10017
(212) 909-9500 .. **Kleinhendler,** Howard '95 (Wachtel & M,LLP) -885 2nd Av -NY 10017
(212) 553-9200 .. **Kleinick,** Arnold L '54 (K Kleinick PLLC) -233 Bway -NY 10279 **Fx:**233-5070
(212) 318-6000 .. **Kleinick,** Jodi A '95 (Paul HJ&W LLP) -75 E 55th -NY 10022
(212) 233-5433 .. **Kleinick,** Keith A '90 (K Kleinick PLLC) -233 Bway -NY 10279 **Fx:**233-5070
(212) 859-8000 .. **Kleinman,** Aaron J '10 %Fried FHS&J LLP -1 NY Plz -NY 10004
(516) 522-2621 .. **Kleinman,** Abraham '99 -626 RXR Plz -Uniondale 11556
(845) 624-6240 .. **Kleinman,** Abraham N '72 -Bx211 -W Nyack 10994 **Fx:**623-0408
(212) 788-1012 .. **Kleinman,** Alan H '79 %Law Dept -100 Church -NY 10007 **Fx:**788-0367
(516) 294-8844 .. **Kleinman,** Andrea S '07 %L'Abbate BC&C,LLP -1001 Franklin Av -Gdn Cty 11530
(914) 644-6660 .. **Kleinman,** Bernard V '75 -2 Gannett Dr -White Plns 10604
(732) 855-6123 .. **Kleinman,** Bruce M '79 (Wilentz G&S) -110 William -NY 10038 **Fx:**726-4720
(212) 285-3800 .. **Kleinman,** David '05 Subin Assoc LLP -150 Bway -NY 10007
(212) 819-8200 .. **Kleinman,** David L '06 %White & C LLP -1155 Av of Amer -NY 10036
(516) 496-2322 .. **Kleinman,** David M '07 AFA Protective Systems,Inc -155 Michl Dr -Syosset 11791
(212) 801-6486 .. **Kleinman,** Gary S '83 (Greenberg T,LLP) -200 Park Av -NY 10166
(212) 698-3500 .. **Kleinman,** Howard M '89 (Dechert LLP) -1095 Av of Amer -NY 10036

(718) 739-6916 .. **Kleinman,** Ira E '92 %Admin Children's Srvcs -151-20 Jamaica Av -Jamaica 11432 **Fx:**739-4493
(212) 878-8000 .. **Kleinman,** Jason M '07 %Clifford C LLP -31 W 52nd -NY 10019
(212) 373-3000 .. **Kleinman,** Jeffrey '07 %Paul WRW&G LLP -1285 Av of Amer -NY 10019
(212) 801-6454 .. **Kleinman,** Justin B '04 %Greenberg T,LLP -200 Park Av -NY 10166
(212) 449-1777 .. **Kleinman,** Larry M '95 %Merrill Lynch -4 World Fncl Ctr -NY 10080 **Fx:**738-2107
(845) 639-6666 .. **Kleinman,** Laurence D '62 (Kleinman S&B,PC) -151 N Main Bx947 -New Cty 10956
(516) 377-1758 .. **Kleinman,** Max L '55 -2142 Holland Way -Merrick 11566 **Fx:**377-1764
(718) 544-8881 .. **Kleinman,** Michelle F '01 (Kleinman & S) -14415 Melbourne Av -Flushng 11367 **Fx:**544-7281
(212) 323-8404 .. **Kleinman,** Mitchell B '79 %Keefe Bruyette & Woods Inc -787 7th Av -NY 10019
(212) 532-8100 .. **Kleinman,** Mitchell S '00 %Stern & M,LLP -115 Bway -NY 10006
(212) 277-5853 .. **Kleinman,** Rachel M '06 %Beldock L&H LLP -99 Park Av -NY 10016
(516) 364-1152 .. **Kleinman,** Robt D '79 AFA Protective -155 Michl Dr -Syosset 11791
(845) 639-6666 .. **Kleinman Saltzman & Bolnick,PC** -151 N Main Bx947 -New Cty 10956 **Fx:**639-0752
(212) 809-7800 .. **Kleinman,** Shana A '03 %Jaffe & K,LLP -40 Wall -NY 10005
(718) 592-6400 .. **Kleinman,** Simon A '98 Rego Park Nursing Home -111-26 Corona Av -Flushng 11368
(516) 932-8810 .. **Kleinman,** Steven C '77 -500 N Bway -Jericho 11753 **Fx:**932-8731
(212) 216-8000 .. **Kleinmann,** David N '05 %Tarter K&D LLP -1350 Bway -NY 10018
(518) 455-4928 .. **Kleinmann,** Teri '89 NYS Assembly -520 The Cptl -Albany 12248
(212) 360-1313 .. **Kleitman,** Amy F '01 %Dept of Parks & Rec -The Arsenal Cntrl Pk -NY 10065 **Fx:**360-1373
(646) 610-5400 .. **Klejman,** Nathan G '90 %NYPD -1 Police Plz -NY 10038
(212) 416-8592 .. **Klekman,** Michl R '75 %Dept of Law -120 Bway -NY 10271 **Fx:**416-6009
(212) 577-2523 .. **Klem,** David J '95 %Ctr for Applit Litigation -74 Trinity Pl -NY 10006 **Fx:**577-2535
(212) 832-9021 .. **Kleman,** Debbie I '92 -310 E 55th -NY 10022
(212) 282-5000 .. **Klemann,** Gilbert L II '75 %Avon Products -1345 Av of Amer -NY 10105
(516) 746-7660 .. **Klemanowicz,** Benjamin J Jr. '63 (Klemanowicz H&VS,LLP) -300 Old Cntry Rd -Mineola 11501 **Fx:**747-7292
(518) 880-1500 .. **Klembczyk,** Jeffrey R '94 SrCnsl X-Ray Optical Systems -Bx822 -Guilderlnd 12084 **Fx:**880-1510
(718) 643-2677 .. **Klemes,** Jane E '85 %Hon H Kramer -360 Adams -Brklyn 11201
(914) 377-6240 .. **Klemperer,** Michelle H '88 %Law Dept -300 City Hall -Ynkrs 10701 **Fx:**964-0563
(212) 261-7000 .. **Klemperer,** Sally '94 %Calyon -1301 Av of Amer -NY 10019
(646) 386-5700 .. **Klempner,** Rochelle K '87 %Civil Ct -111 Centre -NY 10013
(212) 655-0880 .. **Klempner,** Ronald E '88 %NBPA -310 Lennox Av -NY 10027 **Fx:**655-0881
(718) 250-2000 .. **Klengler,** Roland '87 %DA -350 Jay -Brklyn 11201 **Fx:**250-2314
(212) 788-0897 .. **Klepfish,** Isaac '75 %Law Dept -100 Church -NY 10007 **Fx:**788-0367
(516) 829-8585 .. **Klepner,** Philip S '87 -1 Linford Rd -Gt Neck 11021
(212) 728-8000 .. **Klesh,** Kevin J '02 %Willkie F&G LLP -787 7th Av -NY 10019
(212) 836-8000 .. **Kless,** Rachel S '02 Cnsl Kaye S LLP -425 Park Av -NY 10022
(845) 278-1670 .. **Klessen,** Helga '82 -341 Gage Rd -Brewstr 10509 **Fx:**278-2622
(212) 557-4000 .. **Klestadt,** Alan R '84 (Grunfeld DLS&K LLP) -399 Park Av -NY 10022
(212) 557-4000 .. **Klestadt,** Peter W '84 (Grunfeld DLS&K LLP) -399 Park Av -NY 10022 ***[Customs Law]***
(212) 972-3000 .. **Klestadt,** Tracy L '86 (Klestadt & W,LLP) -292 Mad Av -NY 10017
(212) 972-3000 .. **Klestadt & Winters,LLP** -292 Mad Av -NY 10017 **Fx:**972-2245
(718) 250-2000 .. **Klestzick,** David Z '97 %DA -350 Jay -Brklyn 11201 **Fx:**250-2314
(516) 328-3500 .. **Klestzick,** Evan W '91 (McDonnell & A,PC) -401 Franklin Av -Gdn Cty 11530
(212) 867-3636 .. **Kletnick,** Amy B '07 %Levin & G,PC -420 Lex Av -NY 10170
(212) 831-9700 .. **Klett,** John C Jr. '49 -118 E 91st -NY 10128 **Fx:**831-2255
(718) 761-9300 .. **Klette,** M Maureen '93 %Vaslas LH&D LLP -201 Edward Curry Av -Staten Isl 10314
(212) 239-4999 .. **Kletter,** Joni Haviva '05 %Meyer SE&K,PC -1350 Bway Bx822 -NY 10018
(646) 855-1186 .. **Kletter,** Justin M '02 Bk of Amer -1 Bryant Pk -NY 10036
(914) 332-1008 .. **Kletter,** Matthew L '85 -31 Mamaroneck Av -White Plns 10601
(212) 224-1560 .. **Kleva,** Gregory A Jr. '75 Mutual of America -320 Park Av -NY 10022
(212) 224-1560 .. **Kleva,** Gregory A III '01 Mutual of Amer -320 Park Av -NY 10022
(718) 234-5353 .. **Kleyman,** Val '04 (Kleyman & Assoc,PC) -2227 86th -Brklyn 11214
(212) 735-3000 .. **Kleyman,** Vladimir A '07 %Skadden ASM&F LLP -4 Times Sq -NY 10036
(212) 715-1000 .. **Kleyna,** Mark A '06 %Arnold & P LLP -399 Park Av -NY 10022
(718) 759-1909 .. **Kleynerman,** Ilya '00 -6902 11th Av -Brklyn 11228 **Fx:**759-1907
(516) 569-6347 .. **Klibanoff,** Herbert A '77 -78 Burton Av -Woodmere 11598
(845) 371-4700 .. **Klics,** Kristen A '07 %Fein SK&S,PC -747 Chestnut Rdg Rd -Spg Vly 10977
(718) 459-9000 .. **Klie,** Rosemarie A '91 %Sweeney GR&B,LLP -95-25 Qns Blvd -Rego Pk 11374
(212) 766-8700 .. **Klieger,** Louis '83 -11 Park Pl -NY 10007 **Fx:**227-2087
(212) 964-2500 .. **Kliegerman,** Ronald E '72 (Kliegerman & J LLP) -2 Rector -NY 10006 **Fx:**587-0075
(718) 263-0700 .. **Kliegman,** David R '68 -125-10 Qns Blvd -Kew Gdns 11415 **Fx:**793-4719
(516) 393-5899 .. **Kliegman,** Jos H '84 J Kliegman,PC -6800 Jericho Tpk -Syosset 11791 **Fx:**393-5837
(212) 705-7000 .. **Kliegman,** Matthew I '96 OfCnsl Bingham M LLP -399 Park Av -NY 10022
(516) 681-1100 .. **Kligman,** Gregg M '07 %Kaufman DV&G,LLP -135 Crsswys Park Dr -Woodbury 11797
(315) 446-4266 .. **Klim,** Barbara Kurr '79 -605 Bradford Pkwy -Syracuse 13224 **Fx:**472-7225
(718) 237-2000 .. **Kliman,** Steven E '92 %Leg Aid -111 Lvngstn -Brklyn 11201 **Fx:**237-8737
(212) 816-4784 .. **Klimashousky,** Wm J '79 Citibank -388 Greenwich -NY 10013
(212) 768-6700 .. **Klimerman,** Edw '68 (Sonnenschein N&R LLP) -1221 Av of Amer -NY 10020
(212) 558-4000 .. **Klimoski,** Donald II '08 %Sullivan & C LLP -125 Broad -NY 10004
(212) 225-2000 .. **Klimpel,** Laura C '08 %Cleary GS&H -1 Lbrty Plz -NY 10006
(212) 508-6700 .. **Klimpl,** Jason B '08 %Tannenbaum HS&H LLP -900 3rd Av -NY 10022
(212) 704-6000 .. **Kline,** Craig M '96 (Troutman S LLP) -405 Lex Av -NY 10174
(315) 637-0160 .. **Kline,** David A '78 -7136 E Genesee -Fayettevll 13066 **Fx:**(309) 418-1151
(212) 977-9700 .. **Kline,** Eugene M '35 Cnsl Phillips N LLP -666 5th Av -NY 10103
(607) 723-9511 .. **Kline,** Gary B '87 (Coughlin & G,LLP) -19 Chenango Bx2039 -Bnghmtn 13902
(212) 627-9810 .. **Kline,** Gary R '96 (Kline & S LLP) -440 W 15th -NY 10011 **Fx:**727-2144
(607) 723-9511 .. **Kline,** Herbert A '54 OfCnsl Coughlin & G,LLP -19 Chenango Bx2039 -Bnghmtn 13902
(212) 750-8700 .. **Kline,** Ivan O '84 (Friedman & W,PC) -600 Lex Av -NY 10022
(212) 907-9700 .. **Kline,** Jonathan '95 Cnsl Smith G&R,LLP -250 Park Av -NY 10177
(607) 723-9511 .. **Kline,** Nancy E '90 OfCnsl Coughlin & G,LLP -19 Chenango Bx2039 -Bnghmtn 13902
(917) 723-5044 .. **Kline,** Stephen Lee '97 Privo.com -7618 6th Av -Brklyn 11209
(212) 218-2100 .. **Kline,** Steven C '90 (Fitzpatrick CH&S) -1290 Av of Amer -NY 10104
(516) 873-2000 .. **Klineberg,** Brandi P '04 %Moritt HH&H LLP -400 Grdn City Plz -Gdn Cty 11530
(212) 715-7300 .. **Kling,** Arnold P '84 %GH Venture Prtnrs,Inc -1370 Av of Amer -NY 10019 **Fx:**715-7313
(212) 735-3000 .. **Kling,** Lou R '78 (Skadden ASM&F LLP) -4 Times Sq -NY 10036
(212) 446-4800 .. **Klingbaum,** Leonard '00 (Kirkland & E LLP) -153 E 53rd -NY 10022
(518) 798-1758 .. **Klingebiel,** David C '06 %R Newell -1 South Wstrn Plz Bx2152 -Glens Fls 12801 **Fx:**798-0740
(212) 768-6700 .. **Klingenberg,** Erik D '94 (Sonnenschein N&R LLP) -2 World Fncl Ctr -NY 10281
(716) 884-1115 .. **Klingensmith,** Robt W '76 %NYSUT -271 Porter Av -Buffalo 14201 **Fx:**881-6678
(212) 806-5400 .. **Klinger,** Alan M '82 (Stroock &S&L LLP) -180 Maiden Ln -NY 10038
(212) 682-1800 .. **Klinger,** Andrew M '68 (Grant HS&K LLP) -675 3rd Av -NY 10017
(212) 715-9100 .. **Klinger,** Carole E '90 %Kramer LN&F,LLP -1177 Av of Amer -NY 10036
(516) 442-2971 .. **Klinger,** Edw J '65 -485 Park Av -Merrick 11566 **Fx:**442-2975
(212) 735-3000 .. **Klinger,** Jane M '09 %Skadden ASM&F LLP -4 Times Sq -NY 10036
(212) 984-7727 .. **Klingman,** Barry '69 (Warshaw BCS&K,LLP) -555 5th Av -NY 10017
(212) 775-0055 .. **Klingon,** Robt M '90 Simon G&K LLP -1700 Bway -NY 10019
(212) 836-8000 .. **Klingsberg,** David '58 SpclCnsl Kaye S LLP -425 Park Av -NY 10022
(212) 225-2000 .. **Klingsberg,** Ethan A '91 (Cleary GS&H) -1 Lbrty Plz -NY 10006
(212) 783-2013 .. **Klinker,** David J '05 Morgan Stanley Smith Barney LLC -787 7th Av -NY 10019 **Fx:**783-2136
(914) 969-4848 .. **Kliot,** Nancy M '93 %Fred Straus Inc -104 St Andrews Pl -Ynkrs 10705
(917) 777-4200 .. **Klippert,** Barbara D '76 (Bingham M LLP) -1 Bttry Pk Plz -NY 10004
(212) 575-7900 .. **Klipstein,** Robt A '60 (Ballon SB&N,PC) -729 7th Av -NY 10019
(973) 596-4757 .. **Klock,** John H '77 (Gibbons PC) -1 Penn Plz -NY 10119 **Fx:**639-6270
(516) 823-0460 .. **Kloeckener,** Theresa F '89 -26 W Merrick Rd -Vly Stream 11580
(516) 686-7792 .. **Kloepfer,** Stephen J '87 NY Inst of Tech -Nrthrn Blvd Bx8000 -Old Westbury 11568 **Fx:**686-7442
(212) 464-1671 .. **Kloin,** Scott E '02 JP Morgan Sec -345 Park Av -NY 10154
(585) 328-0700 .. **Kloner,** Cyrus '75 -20 Paige -Rchstr 14619 **Fx:**436-8216
(212) 839-5300 .. **Kloner,** Dean '88 Cnsl Sidley A LLP -787 7th Av -NY 10019
(212) 821-4789 .. **Kloner,** Kenneth J '99 UBS -299 Park Av -NY 10171
(585) 425-3310 .. **Klonick,** Thos A '80 -7700 Pttsfrd-Palmyra Rd -Fairprt 14450 **Fx:**425-7176
(212) 308-0888 .. **Klonsky,** Aryeh S '06 %Widowski & S LLP -425 Mad Av -NY 10017
(212) 542-5591 .. **Klonsky,** Edw L '83 SrCnsl Excalibur Title Agency,LLC -44 Wall -NY 10005 **Fx:**542-5592
(718) 579-7918 .. **Kloogman,** Helen J '85 %Leg Aid -900 Sheridan Av -Bronx 10451 **Fx:**293-8744
(212) 756-2000 .. **Kloos,** Wm E '09 %Schulte R&Z LLP -919 3rd Av -NY 10022
(212) 578-1930 .. **Klopfer,** Jason P '04 OSG Ship Mgmt,Inc -666 3rd Av -NY 10017
(718) 546-0950 .. **Klopman,** David K '85 Dept of Correction -75-20 Astoria Blvd -E Elmhrst 11370
(716) 856-0600 .. **Klos,** Kayla E '93 %Jaeckle F&M,LLP -12 Fountain Plz -Buffalo 14202
(845) 727-7727 .. **Klose,** Peter '94 -99 Main -Nyack 10960 **Fx:**727-7725
(212) 813-8800 .. **Klosek,** Jacqueline '98 SrCnsl Goodwin P LLP -620 8th Av -NY 10018
(212) 838-2100 .. **Klosk,** Craig B '85 %The Wicks Grp -405 Park Av -NY 10022
(914) 666-7806 .. **Klosner,** Lise H '95 -161 McLain -Bedford Corners 10549
(315) 867-1155 .. **Klosner,** Prescott E '98 %DA -301 N Wshngtn -Herkimer 13350 **Fx:**867-1348
(516) 873-2000 .. **Klosowski,** Henry E Jr. '88 (Moritt HH&H LLP) -400 Grdn City Plz -Gdn Cty 11530
(716) 853-1111 .. **Kloss,** David W '86 (Kloss S&L) -69 Delaware Av -Buffalo 14202 **Fx:**847-2924
(315) 453-6530 .. **Klotz,** David R '93 State Ins Fund -1045 7th N -Liverpool 13088 **Fx:**453-6540
(212) 661-5858 .. **Klotz,** Emily Ann '82 -30 W 26th -NY 10010 **Fx:**255-4285
(631) 755-0101 .. **Klotz,** Jessica D '94 %Lewis JAA,LLP -425 Broad Hollow Rd -Melvll 11747
(212) 630-2600 .. **Klotz,** John C '60 -350 5th Av -NY 10118
(212) 728-8000 .. **Klotz,** Martin B '82 (Willkie F&G LLP) -787 7th Av -NY 10019
(518) 363-2754 .. **Kluckowski,** Stephen A '05 State Farm Ins -101 State Farm Plz -Ballston Spa 12020
(315) 474-2943 .. **Klucsik,** Jenna W '07 %Sugarman Law Firm,LLP -211 W Jffrsn -Syracuse 13202

(315) 442-0100 .. **Klucsik,** John F '89 %Gilberti SH&S,PC -555 E Genesee -Syracuse 13202
(516) 747-1990 .. **Kluepfel,** David F '96 (Cascone & K,LLP) -1399 Franklin Av -Gdn Cty 11530
(212) 506-1700 .. **Kluewer,** Joshua T '07 %Kasowitz BT&F LLP -1633 Bway -NY 10019
(845) 758-8893 .. **Klug,** Alessandra D '09 %Walsh W&S -7405 S Bway -Red Hook 12571
(212) 609-6800 .. **Klug,** Amy Todd '06 %McCarter & E,LLP -245 Park Av -NY 10167
(518) 459-2100 .. **Klug,** Christopher M '09 %Pierro Law Grp,LLC -20 Corp Wds Blvd -Albany 12211 **Fx:**459-2200
(212) 336-0112 .. **Klug,** Yitzchok '03 %SEC -3 World Fncl Ctr -NY 10281 **Fx:**336-1323
(212) 480-5284 .. **Kluger,** Barbara A '80 %Insurance Dept -25 Beaver -NY 10004 **Fx:**480-5272
(212) 878-0000 .. **Kluger,** Barry L '75 %MTA -2 Penn Plz -NY 10121
(212) 837-6048 .. **Kluger,** Eric J '09 %Hughes H&R LLP -1 Bttry Pk Plz -NY 10004
(212) 209-3057 .. **Kluger,** Lauren K '95 SrCnsl Reitler K&R LLC -885 3rd Av -NY 10022
(718) 293-4900 .. **Kluger,** Matthew J '96 -859 Cncrs Vlg W -Bronx 10451
(212) 888-3033 .. **Klugman,** Bonnie Rattner '90 (Becker GM&M LLP) -299 Park Av -NY 10171
(212) 356-0327 .. **Klugman,** Debra E '79 SBLI USA Mutual Life Ins -460 W 34th -NY 10001
(212) 446-4800 .. **Klugman,** Maura M '09 %Kirkland & E LLP -153 E 53rd -NY 10022
(516) 222-2655 .. **Klugman,** Robt A '94 -1305 Franklin Av -Gdn Cty 11530 **Fx:**228-6569
(718) 254-7000 .. **Klugman,** Scott B '98 %US Atty -271 Cadman Plz E -Brklyn 11201 **Fx:**254-6479
(212) 909-6000 .. **Klugman,** Steven '79 (Debevoise & P LLP) -919 3rd Av -NY 10022
(716) 888-2695 .. **Klump,** Robt A '84 Canisius College -2001 Main -Buffalo 14208
(212) 373-3000 .. **Klunder,** Michl '09 %Paul WRW&G LLP -1285 Av of Amer -NY 10019
(212) 558-4000 .. **Klurfeld,** Jason '05 %Sullivan & C LLP -125 Broad -NY 10004
(212) 259-8000 .. **Klutkowski,** Steven W '06 %Dewey & L LLP -1301 Av of Amer -NY 10019
(718) 261-4128 .. **Klyde,** Andrew J '89 -141-15 72nd Av -Flushng 11367
(914) 422-3101 .. **Kmetz,** Steven P '84 Kelly & K -175 Main -White Plns 10601 **Fx:**422-3105
(716) 848-9000 .. **Knab,** Thos F '89 (Underberg & K LLP) -1900 Main Pl Twr -Buffalo 14202
(585) 243-7924 .. **Knaier,** Robt G '04 Hon RC Wesley -6 Court -Geneseo 14454
(607) 722-6427 .. **Knaphle,** Thos L '73 Law Clinic -160 Court -Bnghmtn 13901 **Fx:**722-6428
(212) 906-4400 .. **Knapp,** Chas E '81 Allcapital (US),LLC -153 E 53rd -NY 10022
(212) 991-9590 .. **Knapp,** Danl R '03 OfCnsl Lustrin T,LLP -28 W 44th -NY 10036 **Fx:**991-9595
(212) 859-8000 .. **Knapp,** David M '08 %Fried FHS&J LLP -1 NY Plz -NY 10004
(212) 490-3000 .. **Knapp,** Elizabeth L '08 %Wilson EME&D LLP -150 E 42nd -NY 10017
(718) 254-7000 .. **Knapp,** James H '99 %US Atty -271 Cadman Plz E -Brklyn 11201 **Fx:**254-6479
(212) 336-2000 .. **Knapp,** John C '05 %Patterson BW&T LLP -1133 Av of Amer -NY 10036
(914) 962-5525 .. **Knapp,** Jos A '85 -3360 Deerfld Av -Yorktwn Hts 10598
(716) 649-6700 .. **Knapp,** Kenneth W '60 (Abbott T&K,LLP) -44 Union -Hambrg 14075
(212) 450-4000 .. **Knapp,** Lindsey Taylor '08 %Davis P&W LLP -450 Lex Av -NY 10017
(845) 486-2300 .. **Knapp,** Melissa A '08 %DA -236 Main -Poughkeepsie 12601 **Fx:**486-2324
(518) 786-9069 .. **Knapp,** Paul B '86 (Schiller & K LLP) -950 New Loudon Rd -Latham 12110
(845) 486-2300 .. **Knapp,** Robt J '95 %DA -236 Main -Poughkeepsie 12601 **Fx:**486-2324
(212) 702-9027 .. **Knapp,** Robt P III '78 (Mulholland & K,LLP) -641 Lex Av -NY 10022 **Fx:**702-9092
(518) 474-6402 .. **Knapp,** Sharon A '86 %Dept of Law -The Cptl -Albany 12224
(212) 891-1600 .. **Knapp,** Tobias L '00 (Jenner & B LLP) -919 3rd Av -NY 10022
(718) 263-9000 .. **Knapp,** Victor '81 -125-10 Qns Blvd -Kew Gdns 11415 **Fx:**793-6975
(212) 489-7100 .. **Knapp,** Whitman G S '94 James Mintz Grp,Inc -32 Av of Amer -NY 10013 **Fx:**489-7037
(716) 843-5700 .. **Knapp,** Wm J '75 %US Atty -138 Delaware Av -Buffalo 14202 **Fx:**551-3052
(914) 251-1618 .. **Knarich,** Jennifer M '05 %Price MS&D,PC -106 Corp Park Dr -White Plns 10604
(212) 297-5800 .. **Knarr,** Ellen S '08 %Day P LLP -7 Times Sq -NY 10036
(212) 702-5400 .. **Knaub,** Zackary D '04 %Beveridge & D,PC -477 Mad Av -NY 10022
(212) 266-0400 .. **Knauer,** Edwin H '71 %Krez & F,LLP -225 Bway -NY 10007
(212) 421-2150 .. **Knauer,** Elizabeth R '00 %Sive P&R,PC -460 Park Av -NY 10022
(631) 694-2400 .. **Knauer,** Todd A '74 (Hamburger MYK&M,LLP) -225 Broadhllw Rd -Melvll 11747
(585) 546-8430 .. **Knauf,** Alan J '81 (Knauf S LLP) -2 State -Rchstr 14614
(716) 515-4810 .. **Knauf,** Mary K '82 %Ct of Claims -125 Main -Buffalo 14203 **Fx:**515-4813
(585) 546-8430 .. **Knauf Shaw LLP** -2 State -Rchstr 14614 **Fx:**546-4324
(585) 544-1340 .. **Knauf,** Thos S '81 Knauf & K -367 Titus Av -Rchstr 14617 **Fx:**544-8831
(716) 856-7091 .. **Knauth,** Brian D '91 %J Freedman -424 Main -Buffalo 14202 **Fx:**856-7097
(718) 741-8416 .. **Knauth,** Christopher R '57 %Div of Human Rights -1 Fordham Plz -Bronx 10458 **Fx:**741-8102
(917) 701-3750 .. **Knauth,** Danl C '99 -3318 21st Av -Astoria 11105
(212) 841-1000 .. **Knecht,** Fredk J '88 (Covington & B LLP) -620 8th Av -NY 10018
(212) 876-5500 .. **Knecht,** Matthew W '00 Neighborhood Def Srv -317 Lenox Av -NY 10027 **Fx:**876-5586
(212) 715-9100 .. **Knecht,** Steven M '92 SpclCnsl Kramer LN&F,LLP -1177 Av of Amer -NY 10036
(212) 832-0400 .. **Knee,** Lisa Bari '00 Berdon LLP -360 Mad Av -NY 10017
(212) 536-3990 .. **Kneis,** Kirsten Alford '00 %K&L Gates LLP -599 Lex Av -NY 10022
(212) 857-8230 .. **Knel,** David H '95 %Baker MM&M,PC -330 W 34th -NY 10001
(646) 315-7300 .. **Kneller,** Howard L '89 %FINRA -14 Wall -NY 10005 **Fx:**315-7440
(212) 483-9490 .. **Knepper,** Randi F '95 (McElroy DM&C,LLP) -88 Pine -NY 10005
(212) 242-7480 .. **Knets,** Talis B '05 %M Lubelsky & Assoc -123 W 18th -NY 10011
(718) 403-0934 .. **Knickerbocker,** Helaine Joyce '52 -50 Cheever Pl -Brklyn 11231 **Fx:**855-4680
(607) 753-8023 .. **Knickerbocker,** Lawr J '83 -Bx5561 -Cortlnd 13045 **Fx:**753-6540
(212) 870-3222 .. **Knickerbocker,** Peter '89 Morality in Media -475 Riverside Dr -NY 10115
(212) 859-8000 .. **Kniesly,** Brian W '01 (Fried FHS&J LLP) -1 NY Plz -NY 10004
(516) 921-2805 .. **Kniffin,** Lesley Ann '99 %The Princeton Review -6900 Jericho Tpk -Syosset 11791
(718) 990-6634 .. **Kniffin,** Margaret N '73 %St John's Law Schl -8000 Utopia Pkwy -Jamaica 11439 **Fx:**591-1855
(212) 688-5000 .. **Knight,** Alfred C '72 %Westvaco -299 Park Av -NY 10171
(212) 698-3500 .. **Knight,** Alvin C '98 Dechert LLP -1095 Av of Amer -NY 10036
(212) 455-2000 .. **Knight,** Anne L '06 %Simpson T&B LLP -425 Lex Av -NY 10017
(212) 996-2009 .. **Knight,** Carolynne M '77 -114 E 90th -NY 10128
(212) 930-4241 .. **Knight,** Clifton B Jr. '74 BMG/Columbia House -250 W 34th -NY 10119 **Fx:**930-4755
(973) 642-1440 .. **Knight,** Dexter L '92 -1234 Park Av -NY 10128
(845) 268-3497 .. **Knight,** Donald B '52 -30 Old Lk Rd Bx84 -Congers 10920
(212) 455-2000 .. **Knight,** James T '80 (Simpson T&B LLP) -425 Lex Av -NY 10017
(212) 525-8134 .. **Knight,** Jane M '85 %HSBC Bank -452 5th Av -NY 10018
(212) 450-4000 .. **Knight,** John K Jr. '90 (Davis P&W LLP) -450 Lex Av -NY 10017
(212) 207-8400 .. **Knight,** Kirstin Torgerson '96 (Kavanagh M&O LLP) -415 Mad Av -NY 10017
(212) 858-7787 .. **Knight,** Lisa M '98 -140 Bway -NY 10005
(212) 402-4100 .. **Knight,** Margaret E '03 Ofc Applt Def -11 Park Pl -NY 10007 **Fx:**402-4199
(518) 434-1935 .. **Knight,** Michl J '91 %NY Lawyers Fund -119 Wshngtn Av -Albany 12210 **Fx:**434-5641
(315) 366-2592 .. **Knight,** Suzanne '02 Dept of Social Srvcs -Bx637 -Wampsville 13163
(212) 696-6000 .. **Knight,** Townsend J '52 Cnsl Curtis M-PC&M LLP -101 Park Av -NY 10178
(212) 421-4100 .. **Knight,** W Wilder II '86 OfCnsl Pryor C LLP -7 Times Sq -NY 10036
(516) 496-5822 .. **Knight-Mingo,** Joan P '00 %T Spina -170 Froehlich Farm Blvd -Woodbury 11797 **Fx:**496-5420
(718) 421-6521 .. **Knights,** Stephen N '93 -2009 Nostrand Av -Brklyn 11210 **Fx:**421-6883
(212) 940-6830 .. **Knipe,** Jonathan W '98 Fisher Bros -299 Park Av -NY 10171
(347) 462-9900 .. **Knipel,** Lori E '99 OfCnsl Shapiro & S,LLP -3145 Coney Isl Av -Brklyn 11235
(212) 544-8892 .. **Knipping,** Francisco A '99 (Rosenblatt F&K-D,LLC) -4791 Bway -NY 10034
(718) 459-2808 .. **Knisley,** Wm P '78 -97-12 63rd Dr -Rego Pk 11374
(631) 864-7589 .. **Knispel,** Howard E '89 -354 Vets Hwy -Commack 11725 **Fx:**864-0968
(212) 564-2800 .. **Knispel,** Jay S '92 -450 7th Av -NY 10123 **Fx:**564-2818
(212) 229-6000 .. **Knob,** Damien M '06 %Turner Construction Co -375 Hudson -NY 10014
(212) 609-6800 .. **Knob,** Peter M '09 %McCarter & E,LLP -245 Park Av -NY 10167
(845) 353-3500 .. **Knoebel,** Robt S Jr. '91 (Dorfman K&C LLP) -51 N Bway -Nyack 10960
(212) 710-3900 .. **Knoerzer,** Michl A '88 (Clyde & Co US LLP) -405 Lex Av -NY 10174 **Fx:**710-3950
(212) 506-5000 .. **Knoll,** Alan M '89 (Orrick H&S LLP) -51 W 52nd -NY 10019
(315) 471-8111 .. **Knoll,** Andrew M '04 %Scolaro SCF&B,PC -507 Plum -Syracuse 13204
(518) 528-2514 .. **Knoll,** Bruce Evans '93 -ESP Bx2072 -Albany 12220
(212) 521-4410 .. **Knoll,** Lawr I '89 -590 Mad Av -NY 10022
(212) 425-9300 .. **Knoll,** Mark D '01 Cnsl Bressler A&R,PC -17 State -NY 10004
(212) 490-3000 .. **Knopf,** Fred N '91 (Wilson EME&D LLP) -150 E 42nd -NY 10017
(914) 323-7000 .. **Knopf,** Fred N '91 (Wilson EME&D LLP) -3 Gannett Dr -White Plns 10604
(646) 556-6395 .. **Knopf,** Judith Margulies '07 JM Knopf,PC -845 3rd Av -NY 10022 **Fx:**556-6396
(914) 765-3537 .. **Knopf,** Michl S '93 MBIA Ins Corp -113 King -Armonk 10504
(212) 839-5300 .. **Knopf,** Siegfried P '83 SrCnsl Sidley A LLP -787 7th Av -NY 10019
(646) 674-2000 .. **Knopp,** Cheryl J '96 Liquidnet Holdings,Inc -498 Fashion Av -NY 10018 **Fx:**674-2003
(516) 393-2200 .. **Knothe,** Barbara D '85 SrCnsl Garfunkel W,PC -111 Grt Nck Rd -Gt Neck 11021
(212) 872-5908 .. **Knott,** Alvin D '84 KPMG LLP -345 Park Av -NY 10154
(518) 585-2749 .. **Knott,** Heather L '91 -801 New Hague Rd -Hague 12836 **Fx:**585-2749
(518) 487-5460 .. **Knowles,** Brett M '06 %DA -6 Lodge -Albany 12207 **Fx:**487-5093
(212) 348-4287 .. **Knowles,** Clayton P Jr. '72 -315 E 86th -NY 10028 **Fx:**348-0567
(718) 260-8701 .. **Knowles,** Norris W '04 ACS -345 Adams -Brklyn 11201
(212) 998-6562 .. **Knowles,** Robt H '05 %NYU Law Schl -245 Sullivan -NY 10012
(212) 838-3333 .. **Knowlton,** Steven P '92 (Locks Law Firm,PLLC) -747 3rd Av -NY 10017 **Fx:**838-3735
(212) 474-1000 .. **Knowsley,** Fleur J '09 %Cravath S&M LLP -825 8th Av -NY 10019
(516) 676-4600 .. **Knox,** Christine K '07 %Humes & W -147 Forest Av Bx546 -Locust Vly 11560
(212) 577-3001 .. **Knox,** Cynthia B '90 %HIV Law Proj -15 Maiden Ln -NY 10038 **Fx:**577-3192
(212) 605-2126 .. **Knox,** Diane G '97 %Mitsubishi Intl -655 3rd Av -NY 10017
(914) 763-0611 .. **Knox,** Donna M '86 -3 Gideon Reynolds Rd -Cross Rvr 10518 **Fx:**763-0611
(212) 335-4500 .. **Knox,** Jamie C '06 (DLA Piper LLP) -1251 Av of Amer -NY 10020
(718) 455-2251 .. **Knox,** Jeffrey H '00 %US Atty -271 Cadman Plz E -Brklyn 11201 **Fx:**254-6479
(212) 351-4000 .. **Knox,** Matthew W '10 Gibson D&C LLP -200 Park Av -NY 10166
(212) 425-9300 .. **Knox,** Stephen R '85 (Bressler A&R,PC) -17 State -NY 10004
(212) 785-9100 .. **Knox,** Willard R '01 %Paduano & W LLP -1251 Av of Amer -NY 10020
(516) 741-2585 .. **Knox,** Wm J '08 %Rosicki R & Assoc,PC -51 E Bethpage Rd -Plainvw 11803 **Fx:**741-4748
(718) 389-2427 .. **Knuckles,** Dolores Clarizio '93 %Agostino & Assoc,PC -500 Kngslnd Av -Brklyn 11222
(718) 325-8844 .. **Knuckles,** Kenneth J '82 -4624 Carpenter Av -Bronx 10470

(914) 345-3020 .. **Knuckles, Komosinski & Elliott, LLP** -565 Taxter Rd -Elmsfrd 10523 **Fx:**366-0080
(914) 345-3020 .. **Knuckles,** Mark R '93 (Knuckles K&E,LLP) -565 Taxter Rd -Elmsfrd 10523
(212) 735-3000 .. **Knudsen,** Jens S '08 %Skadden ASM&F LLP -4 Times Sq -NY 10036
(212) 416-8625 .. **Knudsen,** John E '96 %Dept of Law -120 Bway -NY 10271
(212) 921-1122 .. **Knudsen,** Katherine J '96 Reis, Inc -530 5th Av -NY 10036
(315) 431-4000 .. **Knudsen,** Kurt D L '90 (Knudsen Leg Srvcs) -2711 James -Syracuse 13206 **Fx:**431-4363
(212) 349-8173 .. **Knudsen,** Stephen M '87 %Durkin & D -111 Bway -NY 10006 **Fx:**285-1968
(212) 571-0068 .. **Knull,** Chas H '83 Cnsl Ullman S&U,LLP -299 Bway -NY 10007
(212) 640-2000 .. **Knurr,** Joshua J '07 %Amer Exp -200 Vesey -NY 10285
(518) 884-0200 .. **Knussman,** Amy J '03 (Donnellan & K,PLLC) -20 Prospect -Ballston Spa 12020 **Fx:**884-0343
(646) 200-6300 .. **Knuts,** Robt N '82 (Park & J LLP) -630 3rd Av -NY 10017 **Fx:**200-6301
(212) 848-4000 .. **Knutson,** Ryan C '09 %Shearman & S LLP -599 Lex Av -NY 10022
(315) 449-0106 .. **Knych,** Lisa Quinn '86 -6104 Wolfeboro Rd -Jamesvll 13078 **Fx:**449-1012
(315) 472-1175 .. **Knych,** Peter W '86 (Knych & W,LLC) -300 S State -Syracuse 13202
(315) 472-1175 .. **Knych & Whritenour,LLC** -300 S State -Syracuse 13202 **Fx:**234-4119
(212) 446-4800 .. **Ko,** Henry '09 %Kirkland & E LLP -153 E 53rd -NY 10022
(516) 364-0400 .. **Ko,** Johnny C '98 Polar Electro -1111 Marcus Av -Lk Success 11042
(212) 782-4000 .. **Ko,** Kwanghyon Thos '02 Bank of Tokyo-Mitsubishi UFJ Ltd -1251 Av of Amer -NY 10020
(518) 285-7210 .. **Ko,** Pamela R '04 Pitney Bowes Sftwr -1 Global VW -Troy 12180
(212) 657-0838 .. **Ko,** Patty S '92 Citigroup Global Mrkts -77 Water -NY 10005
(212) 454-7722 .. **Ko,** Roger W '07 Deutsche Bk -280 Park Av -NY 10017
(212) 657-8774 .. **Ko,** Un Suk '90 %Citibank NA -111 Wall -NY 10005
(212) 986-1544 .. **Koatz,** Fernando O '86 (Gleason & K,LLP) -122 E 42nd -NY 10169 **Fx:**986-1379
(212) 577-7700 .. **Kob,** Jennifer Liebre '06 %Safe Horizon -2 Lafayette -NY 10007 **Fx:**385-0331
(914) 323-7000 .. **Koba,** Nancy Quinn '86 OfCnsl Wilson EME&D LLP -3 Gannett Dr -White Plns 10604
(212) 837-6000 .. **Kobak,** James B Jr. '72 (Hughes H&R LLP) -1 Bttry Pk Plz -NY 10004
(516) 328-2300 .. **Kobak,** Lawr F '02 (Abrams FFEGF&E,LLP) -1111 Marcus Av -Lk Success 11042
(212) 455-2000 .. **Kobak,** Scott M '93 (Simpson T&B LLP) -425 Lex Av -NY 10017
(212) 310-6839 .. **Kobak,** Vickie G '82 -767 5th Av -NY 10153 **Fx:**310-8007
(516) 997-0293 .. **Kobayashi,** Beatrice '97 -480 Maple Av -Westbury 11590
(718) 459-0427 .. **Kobayashi,** David Y '00 -7050 Austin -Frst Hlls 11375
(845) 623-0883 .. **Kobb,** James S '85 (Scheinert & K) -404 E Route 59 Bx220 -Nanuet 10954
(212) 609-6800 .. **Kobelt,** Werner H '87 (McCarter & E,LLP) -245 Park Av -NY 10167
(212) 407-1200 .. **Kober,** Honey L '88 OfCnsl Joseph Law Ofcs LLC -485 Lex Av -NY 10017 **Fx:**407-1299
(212) 530-4001 .. **Kober,** Thos W '79 %Home Ins -59 Maiden Ln -NY 10038
(212) 858-1000 .. **Kober,** Timothy P '06 %Pillsbury WSP LLP -1540 Bway -NY 10036
(516) 714-7378 .. **Kobets,** Anthony N '02 Cnsl T Spina -170 Froehlich Farm Blvd -Woodbury 11797 **Fx:**496-5420
(212) 526-6259 .. **Kobi,** Danl Casey '02 Barclays Capital Inc -745 7th Av -NY 10019
(716) 362-9776 .. **Kobialka,** Anna M '01 -17 Beresford Ct -Williamsvll 14221
(212) 750-4949 .. **Kobin,** Jason M '01 %Shearer & E,LLP -50 Bway -NY 10004
(212) 630-5620 .. **Kobin,** Tamara I '99 Advance Magazine Grp -750 3rd Av -NY 10017
(516) 357-3000 .. **Koblenz,** Adam H '07 %Rivkin R LLP -926 RXR Plz -Uniondale 11556
(518) 462-4242 .. **Koblenz,** Mark L '79 OfCnsl Colwell C&P,LLP -20 Corp Wds Blvd -Albany 12211 **Fx:**724-3299
(212) 804-4200 .. **Koblenz,** Michl R '80 (Mound CW&G) -One Bttry Pk Plz -NY 10004
(212) 776-5069 .. **Kobocow,** Sara B '88 %Housing Auth -250 Bway -NY 10007 **Fx:**776-5430
(212) 819-8200 .. **Kobori,** Aya '03 %White & C LLP -1155 Av of Amer -NY 10036
(516) 571-0710 .. **Kobos,** Dana L '04 Cnty Atty -1 West -Mineola 11501 **Fx:**571-6604
(516) 295-7364 .. **Kobre,** Eytan A '91 -337R Central Av -Lawrence 11559 **Fx:**295-0722
(212) 488-1200 .. **Kobre & Kim,LLP** -800 3rd Av -NY 10022 **Fx:**488-1220
(212) 488-1200 .. **Kobre,** Steven G '94 (Kobre & K,LLP) -800 3rd Av -NY 10022
(212) 770-7725 .. **Kobrick,** Eric S '89 %AIG -70 Pine -NY 10270
(516) 248-9500 .. **Kobrick,** Saul '67 -1305 Franklin Av -Gdn Cty 11530 **Fx:**248-7606
(212) 373-3000 .. **Kobrin,** Joshua A '07 %Paul WRW&G LLP -1285 Av of Amer -NY 10019
(212) 701-3000 .. **Kobrin,** Lawr A '57 SrCnsl Cahill G&R LLP -80 Pine -NY 10005 **Fx:**269-5420
(212) 763-6800 .. **Kobrin Levy,** Debra '06 %Vandenberg & F,LLP -60 E 42nd -NY 10165
(212) 695-8100 .. **Kobroff,** Bernard '69 %Goetz F,LLP -1 Penn Plz -NY 10119
(212) 735-3000 .. **Kobulnik,** Reuben '05 %Skadden ASM&F LLP -4 Times Sq -NY 10036
(718) 291-3400 .. **Kobus,** Raymond '78 -148-55 Hillside Av -Jamaica 11435
(212) 753-7500 .. **Koby,** Richd H '76 (Hartman & C LLP) -488 Mad Av -NY 10022
(212) 953-6000 .. **Koch,** Adrienne B '91 (Katsky K LLP) -605 3rd Av -NY 10158
(516) 410-1230 .. **Koch,** Andrea P '03 -143 Willis Av -Mineola 11501
(212) 640-1230 .. **Koch,** Barry M '81 Amer Exp -200 Vesey -NY 10285
(718) 248-3638 .. **Koch,** Carol B '83 %Citigroup -1 Court Sq -LIC 11101
(516) 294-9710 .. **Koch,** David G '65 -170 Old Cntry Rd -Mineola 11501 **Fx:**248-0512
(212) 785-5454 .. **Koch,** Donald G '72 -26 Bway -NY 10004 **Fx:**843-6919
(631) 224-4592 .. **Koch,** Donald K '84 (DK Koch,PC) -42 Laurel Av -E Islip 11730
(212) 541-2000 .. **Koch,** Edw I '49 (Bryan C LLP) -1290 Av of Amer -NY 10104
(718) 283-7441 .. **Koch,** Irene M '90 %Maimonides Med Ctr -4802 10th Av -Brklyn 11219 **Fx:**283-7180
(212) 788-6568 .. **Koch,** Joey K '03 Dept Info Tech -75 Park Pl -NY 10007
(212) 935-3000 .. **Koch,** Kenneth R '81 (Mintz LCFG&P,PC) -666 3rd Av -NY 10017
(212) 947-1999 .. **Koch,** Leslie A '06 %Methfessel & W,PC -450 7th Av -NY 10123
(212) 715-9100 .. **Koch,** Matan A '09 %Kramer LN&F,LLP -1177 Av of Amer -NY 10036
(212) 656-3000 .. **Koch,** Michelle '06 NYSE Euronext -20 Broad -NY 10005
(516) 688-1700 .. **Koch,** Monica E '87 %IRS -1600 Stewart Av -Westbury 11590 **Fx:**688-1750
(845) 463-2330 .. **Koch,** Nancy Brodey '91 -31 Pasture Ln -Poughkeepsie 12603
(212) 841-7799 .. **Koch,** Rebecca L '94 %Cushman & Wakefield -51 W 52nd -NY 10019
(212) 659-7300 .. **Koch,** Steven '85 (Haynes & B,LLP) -1221 Av of Amer -NY 10020
(718) 590-2000 .. **Kocheulov,** Vladimir '09 %DA -198 E 161st -Bronx 10451 **Fx:**590-6477
(212) 872-1000 .. **Kochian,** Jeffrey L '00 -One Bryant Park -NY 10036 **Fx:**872-1002
(212) 233-0130 .. **Kochis,** Kymberly '02 (Nelson Ld&H) -120 Bway -NY 10271
(212) 643-2828 .. **Kochman,** Allison B '05 %GNYHCFA -360 W 31st -NY 10001 **Fx:**643-2956
(212) 521-5400 .. **Kochman,** David A '05 %Reed S LLP -599 Lex Av -NY 10022
(212) 687-0100 .. **Kochman,** David H '86 (Harris B PLLC) -100 Wall -NY 10005
(718) 252-1113 .. **Kochman,** Rosalind A '75 %Kochman Eye SurgFclt -1301 Av J -Brklyn 11230 **Fx:**692-4456
(973) 848-4700 .. **Kochman,** Tedd J '96 (Littler M,PC) -900 3rd Av -NY 10022 **Fx:**643-5626
(718) 262-3916 .. **Koch-Nir,** Randi B '88 %DA -125-01 Qns Blvd -Kew Gdns 11415
(917) 604-6928 .. **Kocian,** Thos A '00 (T Kocian,PC) -72 Toddy Av -Staten Isl 10314 **Fx:**(718) 761-4544
(631) 231-1199 .. **Kocienda,** Katherine '10 %Reynolds CGHL&Q,LLP -35 Arkay Dr -Hauppauge 11788
(212) 319-2787 .. **Kocinski,** Kelly L '08 VLA -1 E 53rd -NY 10022 **Fx:**752-6575
(212) 626-4100 .. **Kocis,** Jamie D '01 %Baker & M LLP -1114 Av of Amer -NY 10036
(516) 247-7010 .. **Kocoris,** James '98 %Moberg & Assoc -333 Earle Ovngton Blvd -Uniondale 11553 **Fx:**247-7031
(914) 476-4079 .. **Kocur,** Michl '89 -38 Morsemere Pl -Ynkrs 10701 **Fx:**476-4079
(518) 473-6486 .. **Koczaja,** Jos '84 %Dept of Law -The Cptl -Albany 12224
(212) 344-5680 .. **Koczko,** Jos B '99 (Thompson H LLP) -335 Mad Av -NY 10017
(718) 590-2000 .. **Kodjo,** Denise R '01 %DA -198 E 161st -Bronx 10451 **Fx:**590-6477
(212) 363-3100 .. **Koeberle,** Christopher D '08 %Bivona & C,PC -88 Pine -NY 10005
(212) 255-7744 .. **Koegel,** John B '73 Koegel Grp LLP -161 Av of Amer -NY 10013 **Fx:**337-1103
(585) 232-5225 .. **Koegel,** Robt B '77 OfCnsl Remington GW&C,LLP -183 E Main -Rchstr 14604
(212) 351-4000 .. **Koehl,** Richd M '04 %Gibson D&C LLP -200 Park Av -NY 10166
(718) 896-9600 .. **Koehler,** Danielle '07 Algin Mgmt Co,LLC -64-35 Yllwstn Blvd -Frst Hlls 11375 **Fx:**997-8084
(917) 551-1300 .. **Koehler & Isaacs LLP** -61 Bway -NY 10006 **Fx:**551-0030
(516) 227-0700 .. **Koehler,** Jennifer C '09 %Farrell F,PC -1320 RXR Plz -Uniondale 11556
(516) 746-0707 .. **Koehler,** Richd C '91 (Hammill OCDP&K,PC) -6851 Jericho Tpk -Syosset 11791
(917) 551-1300 .. **Koehler,** Richd J '78 (Koehler & I LLP) -61 Bway -NY 10006
(914) 238-5530 .. **Koehn,** Susan B '81 -335 Whippoorwill Rd -Chappaqua 10514 **Fx:**238-5917
(716) 856-4000 .. **Koelbl,** Christian G III '72 (Hodgson R LLP) -140 Pearl -Buffalo 14202
(212) 788-0500 .. **Koeleveld,** Celeste L '90 %Law Dept -100 Church -NY 10007 **Fx:**788-0367
(718) 250-2000 .. **Koelsch,** Adam M '08 %DA -350 Jay -Brklyn 11201 **Fx:**250-2314
(845) 228-1400 .. **Koelsch,** Fredk J '89 Camarda Rlty Invstmnts -1699 Route 6 -Carmel 10512 **Fx:**228-5400
(212) 846-6782 .. **Koen,** Kenneth F '88 %Viacom -1515 Bway -NY 10036 **Fx:**846-1712
(212) 335-4500 .. **Koen,** Robt G '73 (DLA Piper LLP) -1251 Av of Amer -NY 10020
(518) 886-4000 .. **Koenen,** Erin K '98 %AYCO -321 Bway Bx860 -Saratoga Spgs 12866
(516) 693-0038 .. **Koenig,** Arnold '63 (Koenig & S) -300 Old Cntry Rd -Mineola 11501 **Fx:**693-0042
(516) 357-3000 .. **Koenig,** David V '03 %Rivkin R LLP -926 RXR Plz -Uniondale 11556
(212) 822-1439 .. **Koenig,** James L '88 (Pollard & K) -305 Bway -NY 10007 **Fx:**822-1441
(212) 761-4057 .. **Koenig,** Jason S '01 Morgan Stanley -1585 Bway -NY 10036
(212) 227-3636 .. **Koenig,** Jeffrey L '03 %Spar & B,PC -225 Bway -NY 10007
(212) 841-8656 .. **Koenig,** Jeffrey S '06 Universal Motown Records Corp -1755 Bway -NY 10019 **Fx:**373-0676
(212) 989-2369 .. **Koenig,** Kenneth W '66 -440 W 24th -NY 10011
(212) 891-7529 .. **Koenig,** Lisa M '93 %Fragomen DB&L LLP -7 Hanover Sq -NY 10004 **Fx:**480-9930
(716) 636-7600 .. **Koenig,** Marianne E '05 %HoganWillig -2410 N Forest Rd -Amherst 14068
(212) 403-1000 .. **Koenig,** Mark A '01 %Wachtell LR&K -51 W 52nd -NY 10019
(518) 689-1414 .. **Koenig,** Michl L '94 (Greenberg T,LLP) -54 State -Albany 12207
(914) 235-3200 .. **Koenig,** Michl R '94 -524 North Av -New Rchll 10801 **Fx:**235-8760
(212) 964-3991 .. **Koenig,** Peter S '76 -299 Bway -NY 10007
(516) 949-2363 .. **Koenig,** Rosalie A '86 Travelers -2 Jericho Plz -Jericho 11753
(212) 407-8345 .. **Koenig,** Wm S '88 NBA Properties -645 5th Av -NY 10022
(212) 788-8719 .. **Koenig-Berman,** Mindy R '90 %Law Dept -100 Church -NY 10007 **Fx:**788-0367
(212) 408-5100 .. **Koenigsberg,** Benjamin Y '02 %Chadbourne & P LLP -30 Rckfllr Plz -NY 10112
(212) 678-0563 .. **Koenigsberg,** Bernard '58 -250 W 94th -NY 10025 **Fx:**932-2083
(212) 223-2100 .. **Koenigsberg,** David A '83 (Menz B&K LLP) -444 Mad Av -NY 10022 **Fx:**223-2185
Koenigsberg, Herman M '51 -112 Audley -Kew Gdns 11415
(212) 819-8200 .. **Koenigsberg,** I Fred '73 (White & C LLP) -1155 Av of Amer -NY 10036
(718) 336-2000 .. **Koenigsberg,** Paul D '83 (Koenigsberg & Assoc,PC) -1213 Av U -Brklyn 11229 **Fx:**998-5527
(212) 964-9292 .. **Koenigsberg,** Robt '92 -305 Bway #800 -NY 10007 **Fx:**267-5183
(212) 273-6290 .. **Koenigsberg,** Roberta G '83 %YAI/Natl Inst for People with Disablities -460 W 34th -NY 10001 **Fx:**273-6531
(518) 785-7800 .. **Koenitzer,** Erik A '05 %Kieselstein PLLC -1187 Troy Schenectady Rd -Latham 12110
(212) 326-2000 .. **Koepff,** Paul R '74 (O'Melveny & M LLP) -7 Times Sq -NY 10036
(212) 344-2150 .. **Koeppel,** Bevin D '49 OfCnsl Adler C&K -575 Lex Av -NY 10022

(212) 344-2150 .. **Koeppel**, Caleb D '84 (Adler C&K) -575 Lex Av -NY 10022
(212) 344-2150 .. **Koeppel**, David J '84 (Adler C&K) -575 Lex Av -NY 10022
(716) 853-8100 .. **Koeppel**, John J '99 (Nixon P LLP) -40 Fountain Plz -Buffalo 14202
(516) 747-6300 .. **Koeppel Martone & Leistman,LLP** -155 First Bx863 -Mineola 11501 **Fx:**747-8227
(718) 858-5727 .. **Koeppel**, Robt R '60 -44 Court -Brklyn 11201
(212) 751-8334 .. **Koeppel**, Roberta Levy '81 Koeppel Mgmt -Bx287146 -NY 10128
(631) 789-4700 .. **Koeppel**, Ronald H '92 Contential Accessory Corp -150 New Hwy -Amityvll 11701
(716) 913-2422 .. **Koepsell**, David R '96 -Bx410 -Penfld 14526
(212) 848-9800 .. **Koerner**, Alyssa N '05 %Withers B LLP -430 Park Av -NY 10022
(212) 244-9500 .. **Koerner**, Carl Seldin '76 Cnsl White and W LLP -1 Penn Plz -NY 10119
(212) 461-4377 .. **Koerner**, Gregory O '96 (Koerner & Assoc,LLC) -10 E 40th -NY 10016 **Fx:**453-0658
(212) 788-1010 .. **Koerner**, Leonard '68 %Law Dept -100 Church -NY 10007 **Fx:**788-0367
(718) 855-8777 .. **Koerner**, Ronald J '59 Rose & K -26 Court -Brklyn 11242 **Fx:**855-0156
(718) 671-8700 .. **Koester**, Edw L '86 -1457 Knapp -Bronx 10469 **Fx:**320-2229
(516) 803-4813 .. **Koester**, Jennifer V '98 Cablevision Sys Corp -1111 Stewart Av -Bethpage 11714
(516) 877-2900 .. **Koester**, John P '88 (Bartlett MB&M,LLP) -300 Old Cntry Rd -Mineola 11501
(212) 715-9100 .. **Koestler**, Mark D '92 (Kramer LN&F,LLP) -1177 Av of Amer -NY 10036
(212) 506-1700 .. **Koevary**, Danl J '06 %Kasowitz BT&F LLP -1633 Bway -NY 10019
(212) 373-3000 .. **Koevary**, Jonathan T '05 %Paul WRW&G LLP -1285 Av of Amer -NY 10019
(212) 318-6000 .. **Koff**, Douglas I '95 (Paul HJ&W LLP) -75 E 55th -NY 10022
(518) 463-5530 .. **Koff**, Howard M '65 (H Koff,PC) -54 State -Albany 12207 **Fx:**514-2700
(212) 841-1000 .. **Koff**, Lisa L '85 OfCnsl Covington & B LLP -620 8th Av -NY 10018
(212) 295-6303 .. **Koffer**, Thos J '04 Cnsl WilmerHale -399 Park Av -NY 10022
(516) 681-3636 .. **Koffler**, David S '89 (Post H&K LLP) -2 Jericho Plz -Jericho 11753
(212) 418-6000 .. **Koffler**, Peter D '83 %21st Sec Corp -780 3rd Av -NY 10017 **Fx:**418-6038
(212) 806-5400 .. **Koffler**, Peter G '89 (Stroock &S&L LLP) -180 Maiden Ln -NY 10038
(212) 837-6000 .. **Koffman**, Heather N '09 %Hughes H&R LLP -1 Bttry Pk Plz -NY 10004
(212) 596-9000 .. **Koffman**, Natalie '08 %Ropes & G LLP -1211 Av of Amer -NY 10036
(212) 691-9353 .. **Koffman**, Phyllis S '79 -175 W 13th -NY 10011 **Fx:**691-9353
(212) 813-8800 .. **Koffman**, Valerie A '09 %Goodwin P LLP -620 8th Av -NY 10018
(315) 232-4551 .. **Koffs**, Melissa L '05 %McClusky Law Firm,LLC -8 Main Bx97 -Adams 13605 **Fx:**232-2562
(631) 435-6000 .. **Koffsky**, Mark I '96 SMSC -80 Arkay Dr -Hauppauge 11788
(212) 403-1000 .. **Kofke**, Lauren M '07 %Wachtell LR&K -51 W 52nd -NY 10019
(718) 758-2200 .. **Kofman**, Martin E '87 (Lowenthal & K,PC) -2001 Flatbush Av -Brklyn 11234
(212) 833-4920 .. **Kofman**, Stephanie Wank '97 Sony Corp of Amer -550 Mad Av -NY 10022
(212) 575-1292 .. **Kofsky**, Jeffrey S '90 %Uncyk B&N,LLP -555 5th Av -NY 10017
(212) 728-8000 .. **Kofsky**, Robt G '09 %Willkie F&G LLP -787 7th Av -NY 10019
(718) 275-3376 .. **Kogan**, Boris '89 -98-26 64th Av -Rego Pk 11374
(212) 625-8910 .. **Kogan**, Boris '95 (B Kogan & Assoc,PC) -277 Bway -NY 10007 **Fx:**219-2728
(718) 621-5970 .. **Kogan**, Irina '97 -2612 Av Y -Brklyn 11235 **Fx:**621-5970
(212) 553-0300 .. **Kogan**, Jamie L '92 %Moody's Invstr Srvc -250 Greenwich -NY 10007
(212) 636-5400 .. **Kogan**, Jay S '87 %DC Comics -1700 Bway -NY 10019 **Fx:**636-5595
(212) 446-4800 .. **Kogan**, Joshua Michl '04 %Kirkland & E LLP -153 E 53rd -NY 10022
(917) 777-4200 .. **Kogan**, Leo '09 %Bingham M LLP -1 Bttry Pk Plz -NY 10004
(516) 739-5100 .. **Kogan**, Matthew B '02 %Farber B&Z LLP -51 Charles -Mineola 11501
(212) 558-4000 .. **Kogan**, Maxim A '09 %Sullivan & C LLP -125 Broad -NY 10004
(212) 574-1200 .. **Kogan**, Samara L '05 %Seward & K LLP -1 Bttry Pk Plz -NY 10004
(718) 984-3789 .. **Kogan**, Simon S '84 -27 Weaver -Staten Isl 10312
(212) 308-9000 .. **Kogan**, Wm S '94 Andalex Grp -430 Park Av -NY 10022 **Fx:**308-9265
(212) 385-0777 .. **Kogelman**, David '79 -335 Bway -NY 10013
(212) 788-0905 .. **Kogel-Smucker**, Sarah A '09 %Law Dept -100 Church -NY 10007 **Fx:**788-0367
(212) 964-6079 .. **Kogler**, Matthew J '92 -7 Dey -NY 10007 **Fx:**964-5078
(315) 218-8000 .. **Kogut**, Barry R '78 (Bond S&K,PLLC) -1 Lincoln Ctr -Syracuse 13202
(315) 474-6181 .. **Kogut**, Walter D '79 (W Kogut,PC) -500 S Salina -Syracuse 13202 **Fx:**474-5140
(212) 626-4100 .. **Koh**, Catherine Y '03 %Baker & M LLP -1114 Av of Amer -NY 10036
(212) 264-2918 .. **Koh**, Hea Jin '05 Hon N Tsoucala -1 Fed Plz -NY 10278
(212) 655-3500 .. **Koh**, Howard S '90 %Meister S&F LLP -140 E 45th -NY 10017
(212) 553-8300 .. **Koh**, Sung Hee K '91 %Cohen K & Assoc -2 Park Av -NY 10016 **Fx:**553-8721
(212) 213-3319 .. **Koh**, Sungchurl '99 -303 5th Av -NY 10016
(516) 625-4400 .. **Kohan**, Michl '09 %Sanders Litgtn Assoc,PC -69 Roslyn Rd -Roslyn Hts 11577 **Fx:**625-4410
(518) 589-5450 .. **Kohan**, Susan J '79 -6055 Main Bx548 -Tannersvll 12485
(716) 849-8900 .. **Kohane**, Dan D '80 (Hurwitz & F,PC) -1300 Lbrty Bldg -Buffalo 14202
(212) 315-3333 .. **Kohane**, Tobin '75 -450 Fashion Av -NY 10123
(212) 716-0062 .. **Kohane**, Wm I '89 Apple Core Hotels,Inc -1450 Bway -NY 10018
(516) 745-1242 .. **Kohanim**, Mehrdad '95 -595 Stewart Av -Gdn Cty 11530 **Fx:**745-1244
(718) 510-3195 .. **Kohanowski**, K Scott '02 -61 Wycoff -Brklyn 11201
(212) 509-9400 .. **Kohel**, Matthew D '03 %Cozen O -45 Bway Atrium -NY 10006
(212) 309-6000 .. **Kohen**, Jamie M '09 %Morgan L&B LLP -101 Park Av -NY 10178
(212) 455-2000 .. **Kohen**, Julia I '08 %Simpson T&B LLP -425 Lex Av -NY 10017
(845) 562-0203 .. **Kohl**, George A II '82 (Finkelstein & Prtnrs,LLP) -1279 Route 300 Bx1111 -Newburgh 12550
(631) 962-9600 .. **Kohl**, Jonathan M '99 Vernit Systems Inc -330 S Srvc Rd -Melvll 11747
(516) 746-1144 .. **Kohl**, Michl L '78 Cnsl Kirschenbaum & P,PC -3000 Hempstd Tpk -Levittwn 11756
(212) 940-8800 .. **Kohl**, Robt L '68 (Katten MR LLP) -575 Mad Av -NY 10022
(585) 428-4555 .. **Kohl**, Walter A Jr. '78 %Hon F Affronti -Hall of Justice -Rchstr 14614
(212) 735-3000 .. **Kohlberger**, Richd '04 %Skadden ASM&F LLP -4 Times Sq -NY 10036
(212) 670-7595 .. **Kohler**, Andrew J '96 Merrill Lynch -222 Bway -NY 10038
(585) 266-2843 .. **Kohler**, Donald A '78 -95 Parkside Ln -Rchstr 14612
(212) 308-4411 .. **Kohler**, Jeanne M '96 (Edwards AP&D LLP) -750 Lex Av -NY 10022
(212) 839-5300 .. **Kohler**, Michl T '89 (Sidley A LLP) -787 7th Av -NY 10019
(845) 897-7770 .. **Kohler**, Wm R '66 (Kohler & B,PC) -300 Westage Business Ctr -Fishkill 12524 **Fx:**897-7711
(212) 336-2000 .. **Kohley**, Matthew J '09 %Patterson BW&T LLP -1133 Av of Amer -NY 10036
(212) 310-8000 .. **Kohli**, Sachin '07 %Weil G&M LLP -767 5th Av -NY 10153
(718) 590-2000 .. **Kohlmann**, Allyson A '07 %DA -198 E 161st -Bronx 10451 **Fx:**590-6477
(212) 891-1600 .. **Kohlmann**, Susan J '83 (Jenner & B LLP) -919 3rd Av -NY 10022
(631) 929-7203 .. **Kohlus**, Lois A '88 (Kohlus & K) -4 Elms Ln -Wading Rvr 11792 **Fx:**929-7204
(631) 929-7203 .. **Kohlus**, Robt W '80 (Kohlus & K) -4 Elms Ln -Wading Rvr 11792 **Fx:**929-7204
(718) 286-6000 .. **Kohm**, Brian E '98 %DA -125-01 Qns Blvd -Kew Gdns 11415
(845) 679-6919 .. **Kohn**, Aaron '49 -629 Izena Highwood Rd -Kingston 12401
(212) 225-2000 .. **Kohn**, Arthur H '87 (Cleary GS&H) -1 Lbrty Plz -NY 10006
(212) 756-2000 .. **Kohn**, Brian '04 %Schulte R&Z LLP -919 3rd Av -NY 10022
(212) 373-3000 .. **Kohn**, Brian '08 %Paul WRW&G LLP -1285 Av of Amer -NY 10019
(212) 594-8515 .. **Kohn**, Christopher P '95 %Fidelity Natl Title Grp -350 5th Av -NY 10118 **Fx:**594-8378
(212) 872-6622 .. **Kohn**, David L '94 KPMG LLP -345 Park Av -NY 10154
(718) 591-2212 .. **Kohn**, David S '93 (Kohn & K) -69-27 164th -Flushng 11365
(718) 409-5500 .. **Kohn**, Evan W '87 -2000 Wht Plns Rd -Bronx 10462
(716) 856-2700 .. **Kohn**, Gerald L '65 (Rolls K,LLP) -438 Main -Buffalo 14202 **Fx:**856-2777
(718) 972-7000 .. **Kohn**, Henry '86 -4912 13th Av -Brklyn 11219
(212) 326-2000 .. **Kohn**, Jeffrey I '85 (O'Melveny & M LLP) -7 Times Sq -NY 10036
(631) 853-4049 .. **Kohn**, Jennifer B '85 %Cnty Atty -Dennison Bldg Bx6100 -Hauppauge 11788 **Fx:**853-5169
(718) 409-1200 .. **Kohn**, Kevin J '91 Kohn Law Firm -1200 Morris Park Av -Bronx 10461 **Fx:**823-3533
(718) 591-2212 .. **Kohn**, Michl J '80 (Kohn & K) -69-27 164th -Flushng 11365
(315) 831-3581 .. **Kohn & Moseman** -9580 Main Bx248 -Remsen 13438
(315) 443-6565 .. **Kohn**, Nina A '03 %Syracuse Univ Cllg of Law -Wht Hall -Syracuse 13244 **Fx:**443-4213
(518) 458-8080 .. **Kohn**, Richd A '63 -74 Chapel -Albany 12207
(212) 294-6700 .. **Kohn**, Saml S '00 (Winston & S) -200 Park Av -NY 10166
(718) 268-8111 .. **Kohn**, Susan J '01 %D Mastrodomenico -107-19 71st Av -Frst Hlls 11375 **Fx:**268-7382
(212) 756-2000 .. **Kohut**, Kristyn E '09 %Schulte R&Z LLP -919 3rd Av -NY 10022
(212) 735-3000 .. **Kohut**, Ronald D '04 %Skadden ASM&F LLP -4 Times Sq -NY 10036
(212) 446-4800 .. **Koiffman**, Karyn K '05 %Kirkland & E LLP -153 E 53rd -NY 10022
(212) 264-0300 .. **Koike**, Simon-Jon H '01 %NLRB -26 Fed Plz -NY 10278 **Fx:**264-8427
(718) 466-3000 .. **Kojalowicz-Kreig**, Alisa M '05 %Civil Ct -1118 Grnd Cncrs -Bronx 10456 **Fx:**466-3006
(212) 855-0478 .. **Kojima**, Jay Christopher '96 Goldman Sachs & Co -32 Old Slip -NY 10005
(212) 508-6100 .. **Kokalas**, Thos '01 %Bracewell & G,LLP -1251 Av of Amer -NY 10020
(914) 701-8000 .. **Kokas**, Adam R '00 Atlas Air,Inc -2000 Wstchstr Av -Purchase 10577 **Fx:**701-8333
(914) 681-0444 .. **Koke**, Roland T '95 (Rende R&D,LLP) -202 Mamaroneck Av -White Plns 10601
(212) 505-1121 .. **Kokel**, Richd W '82 -Bx527 -NY 10274
(212) 682-8383 .. **Kokhba**, Danl S '04 %Kantor DWMT&G,PC -51 E 42nd -NY 10017
(914) 682-6884 .. **Kokkalenios**, George '00 -50 Main -White Plns 10606
(212) 669-7778 .. **Kokkoris**, Constantine P '95 Comptroller -1 Centre -NY 10007 **Fx:**669-2884
(212) 254-1444 .. **Kokkosis**, Katherine A '04 %Gold SM PLLC -134 Spring -NY 10012 **Fx:**966-2322
(718) 545-1111 .. **Kokolakis**, John A '99 (Kokolakis & Assoc,PC) -31-16 30th Av -Astoria 11102
(212) 695-1735 .. **Kokot**, Arthur '74 -240 W 35th -NY 10001 **Fx:**689-5398
(212) 953-6000 .. **Kokot**, Eugene V '75 (Katsky K LLP) -605 3rd Av -NY 10158
(716) 856-5500 .. **Kolaga**, John T '86 SpclCnsl Damon M LLP -200 Delaware Av -Buffalo 14202
(518) 283-3546 .. **Kolakowski**, Albert P '93 -298 N Greenbush Rd -Troy 12180 **Fx:**283-4709
(212) 310-8000 .. **Kolar**, Jordan K '04 %Weil G&M LLP -767 5th Av -NY 10153
(212) 401-0800 .. **Kolar**, Roberta N '91 %Disciplinary Comm -61 Bway -NY 10006 **Fx:**287-1045
(212) 458-1175 .. **Kolari**, Vullnet '02 AIG -175 Water -NY 10038
(518) 436-0751 .. **Kolarsey**, E Raymond '94 (Hinman S PC) -121 State -Albany 12207
(212) 556-2100 .. **Kolassa**, Scott E '05 %King & S -1185 Av of Amer -NY 10036
(212) 586-5800 .. **Kolatch**, Sari E '86 (Cohen TS&W PC) -420 Lex Av -NY 10170
(718) 250-1100 .. **Kolb**, Christopher M '99 %E Garfinkel -12 Metrotech Ctr -Brklyn 11201 **Fx:**250-1168
(212) 596-9000 .. **Kolb**, Danl C '93 (Ropes & G LLP) -1211 Av of Amer -NY 10036
(212) 450-4000 .. **Kolb**, Danl F '66 (Davis P&W LLP) -450 Lex Av -NY 10017
(845) 562-3366 .. **Kolb**, Michl '76 %Larkin AI&T,LLP -34 Route 17K -Newburgh 12550
(718) 351-1400 .. **Kolb**, Robt '71 -226 Cannon Blvd -Staten Isl 10306
(212) 883-1700 .. **Kolb**, Sara B '09 %Duval & S LLP -101 Park Av -NY 10178
(212) 804-4200 .. **Kolb**, Wm C '95 (Mound CW&G) -One Bttry Pk Plz -NY 10004
(212) 759-7466 .. **Kolbe**, George S '95 (Raven & K,LLP) -126 E 56th -NY 10022
(212) 222-7893 .. **Kolben**, Alexander A '66 -425 Riverside Dr -NY 10025 **Fx:**901-1941

(845) 918-1277 .. **Kolber,** Allen A '89 -134 Route 59 -Suffern 10901 **Fx:**369-0673
(212) 558-6668 .. **Kolber,** Mark L '78 (Foley SO&W) -100 William -NY 10038
(201) 227-1114 .. **Kolber,** Richd J '02 %Profita & Assoc,LLC -11 Bway -NY 10004 **Fx:**227-1115
(631) 543-3936 .. **Kolber,** Ronald H '90 -90 Fla Av -Commack 11725
(212) 554-7800 .. **Kolbig,** Kent C '04 %Moses & S LLP -405 Lex Av -NY 10174
(212) 682-2900 .. **Kolbrener,** Jonathan '83 (Braverman & Assoc,PC) -331 Mad Av -NY 10017 **Fx:**682-7718
(516) 248-7575 .. **Kolbrener,** Peter D '60 Cnsl Levine & G -114 Old Cntry Rd -Mineola 11501
(315) 798-5742 .. **Kolch,** Kimberly A '94 %Dept Soc Srvcs -800 Park Av -Utica 13501
(585) 987-2800 .. **Kolcon,** Greta K '95 (Woods OG LLP) -2 State -Rchstr 14614
(212) 562-4961 .. **Kolcun,** Susan L '00 %MHLS -Bellevue Hsptl 27th & 1st Av -NY 10016
(315) 463-4032 .. **Koldin,** Leonard C '62 (Koldin Law Ctr) -6661 Kirkvll Rd Bx279 -E Syracuse 13057 **Fx:**463-6512
(315) 463-4032 .. **Koldin,** Scott E '95 (Koldin Law Ctr) -6661 Kirkvll Rd Bx279 -E Syracuse 13057 **Fx:**463-6512
(315) 463-4032 .. **Koldin,** Stephen K '89 %Koldin Law Ctr -6661 Kirkvll Rd Bx279 -E Syracuse 13057 **Fx:**463-6512
(212) 248-3140 .. **Kole,** Deirdre Russo '06 %Drinker B&R LLP -140 Bway -NY 10005
(212) 688-6400 .. **Kole,** James A '69 Kole & K -270 Mad Av -NY 10016 **Fx:**671-1462
(212) 408-2500 .. **Kole,** Lisa B '95 (Baker B,LLP) -30 Rckfllr Plz -NY 10112
(212) 637-3167 .. **Kolenberg,** Beverly '85 %EPA -290 Bway -NY 10007 **Fx:**637-3096
(212) 489-7700 .. **Kolenda,** Helena K '90 The Henry Luce Fndtn,Inc -51 Mad Av -NY 10010
(212) 465-9200 .. **Kolenda,** John D '86 (Kolenda & L,LLP) -450 7th Av -NY 10001
(212) 760-2222 .. **Kolenovsky,** Maryanne '92 (Kolenovsky & S,LLP) -135 W 29th -NY 10001
(212) 760-2222 .. **Kolenovsky & Spiegel, LLP** -135 W 29th -NY 10001 **Fx:**760-2530
(212) 524-6833 .. **Koles,** Jonathan '81 -233 Bway -NY 10279
(914) 666-5600 .. **Kolev,** Diana Bunin '06 %Shamberg MD&H,PC -55 Smith Av -Mt Kisco 10549
(917) 421-4651 .. **Koleva,** Sashka Todorova '06 IRS -33 Maiden Ln -NY 10038
(212) 715-9100 .. **Kolevzon,** Peter S '66 (Kramer LN&F,LLP) -1177 Av of Amer -NY 10036
(212) 816-0645 .. **Koleyni,** Kenneth C '02 Citigroup Global Mrkt -388 Greenwich -NY 10013
(212) 435-3571 .. **Kolikoff,** Arnold D '79 %Port Auth of NY/NJ -225 Park Av S -NY 10003 **Fx:**435-3555
(212) 788-0716 .. **Kolikoff,** Fred '79 %Law Dept -100 Church -NY 10007 **Fx:**788-0367
(212) 803-5100 .. **Kolins,** Allison L '97 NY Cnty Defender Srvcs -225 Bway -NY 10007 **Fx:**571-6035
(716) 854-1541 .. **Kolken,** Matthew L '97 (Kolken & K) -135 Delaware Av -Buffalo 14202 **Fx:**854-6223
(716) 854-1541 .. **Kolken,** Robt D '65 (Kolken & K) -135 Delaware Av -Buffalo 14202 **Fx:**854-6223
(212) 806-5400 .. **Kolker,** Dina K '04 %Stroock &S&L LLP -180 Maiden Ln -NY 10038
(212) 545-4672 .. **Kolker,** Lawr P '84 (Wolf HAF&H LLP) -270 Mad Av -NY 10016
(212) 225-2000 .. **Kolkin,** Zachary '09 %Cleary GS&H -1 Lbrty Plz -NY 10006
(914) 948-4800 .. **Kolko,** Danl M '78 SrCnsl A Greene & Assoc,PC -202 Mamaroneck Av -White Plns 10601 **Fx:**948-4936
(212) 239-4999 .. **Kolko,** Hanan B '91 (Meyer SE&K,PC) -1350 Bway Bx822 -NY 10018
(212) 474-1000 .. **Kollander,** Jason S '09 %Cravath S&M LLP -825 8th Av -NY 10019
(212) 878-8000 .. **Kollar,** Thos '03 %Clifford C LLP -31 W 52nd -NY 10019
(212) 719-2900 .. **Kolleeny Kitay & Hort** -500 5th Av -NY 10110 **Fx:**575-3093
(917) 690-3836 .. **Kolleeny,** Leonard '52 -10 Park Av -NY 10016 **Fx:**(305) 932-3033
(212) 735-3000 .. **Kolleeny,** Steven J '80 SpclCnsl Skadden ASM&F LLP -4 Times Sq -NY 10036
(631) 236-4105 .. **Kollen-Rice,** Melissa S '05 %Goldson NC,PC -145 Marcus Blvd -Hauppauge 11788 **Fx:**236-4110
(718) 556-7090 .. **Koller,** Timothy J '81 %DA -130 Styvsnt Pl -Staten Isl 10301
(212) 589-4200 .. **Kolm,** Julie A '05 %Baker & H LLP -45 Rckfllr Plz -NY 10111
(212) 267-4700 .. **Kolman,** Annette Z '78 -30 Vesey -NY 10007 **Fx:**385-0662
(212) 427-0671 .. **Kolmes,** Matthew L '99 -501 5th Av -NY 10017 **Fx:**(646) 367-4979
(212) 415-8600 .. **Kolmykov,** Sergey '04 Cnsl Locke LB&L LLP -3 World Fncl Ctr -NY 10281
(914) 965-7533 .. **Kolnik,** Stephen '81 -20 Colin -Ynkrs 10701
(212) 554-7800 .. **Kolod,** Alan '74 (Moses & S LLP) -405 Lex Av -NY 10174
(212) 826-0100 .. **Kolodner,** Eric A '96 %FSA -31 W 52nd -NY 10019 **Fx:**893-2710
(212) 637-2561 .. **Kolodner,** Jonathan S '01 %US Atty -1 St Andrews Plz -NY 10007
(212) 541-6222 .. **Kolodney,** Robt '70 OfCnsl Kane K,PC -1350 Av of Amer -NY 10019
(212) 508-6700 .. **Kolodny,** David S '88 (Tannenbaum HS&H LLP) -900 3rd Av -NY 10022
(212) 977-9700 .. **Kolodny,** Jeffrey B '96 (Phillips N LLP) -666 5th Av -NY 10103
(914) 366-5700 .. **Kolodny,** Michelle Rivlin '04 %MA Bjork -660 Wht Plns Rd -Tarrytwn 10591 **Fx:**366-5759
(212) 223-0200 .. **Kolodny,** Nathaniel I '05 %Stillman F&S,PC -425 Park Av -NY 10022
(212) 349-7771 .. **Kolodny,** Peter A '77 (Kolodny PC) -338 Greenwich -NY 10013
(518) 725-8922 .. **Kolodziej,** J Paul '82 -350 N Main -Gloversvll 12078 **Fx:**725-1727
(212) 735-3000 .. **Kolontyrsky,** Anna '09 %Skadden ASM&F LLP -4 Times Sq -NY 10036
(212) 416-6681 .. **Kolp,** Peter W '02 %Dept of Law -120 Bway -NY 10271
(212) 739-6577 .. **Kolsun,** Barbara '83 Kate Spade LLC -48 W 25th -NY 10010 **Fx:**206-8015
(631) 853-7577 .. **Kolterman,** Robt '86 %Hon M Floyd -400 Carleton Av Bx9070 -Central Islip 11722 **Fx:**853-4543
(212) 866-1565 .. **Koltun,** Elizabeth S '80 -515 Cathedral Pkwy -NY 10025
(631) 242-7815 .. **Koltun,** Scott A '85 (Frankfort & K) -2061 Deer Prk Av -Deer Pk 11729 **Fx:**586-6029
(212) 408-5100 .. **Kolyer,** Peter R '76 (Chadbourne & P LLP) -30 Rckfllr Plz -NY 10112
(212) 878-8473 .. **Kolyer,** Steven T '82 (Clifford C LLP) -31 W 52nd -NY 10019
(585) 232-5300 .. **Komanecky,** Bradley W '89 OfCnsl Boylan BCV&W,LLP -2400 Chase Sq -Rchstr 14604
(631) 549-5600 .. **Komansky,** Danl S '83 -105 Maxess Rd -Melvll 11747 **Fx:**549-5690
(212) 789-1500 .. **Komansky,** Susan Jane '88 %Donna Karan Co -550 7th Av -NY 10018 **Fx:**789-1688
(212) 482-0001 .. **Komar,** John J '88 %Russo K&T LLP -33 Whitehall -NY 10004
(212) 223-2100 .. **Komar,** Michl S '93 (Menz B&K LLP) -444 Mad Av -NY 10022
(212) 776-5026 .. **Komar,** Wm P '73 NYCHA -250 Bway -NY 10007
(212) 969-3000 .. **Komaroff,** Stanley '59 (Proskauer R LLP) -1585 Bway -NY 10036
(212) 969-3000 .. **Komaroff,** Wm C '95 SrCnsl Proskauer R LLP -1585 Bway -NY 10036
(212) 687-0100 .. **Komaromi,** Andras '99 (Harris B PLLC) -100 Wall -NY 10005
(516) 880-8484 .. **Komaromi,** Andras '99 (Harris B PLLC) -333 Earle Ovngton Blvd -Uniondale 11553
(845) 298-8155 .. **Komarow,** Michl S '96 -169 Myers Crnrs Rd -Wappingers Fls 12590
(212) 404-6988 .. **Kombol,** Brendan C '08 R Yellen & Assoc LLP -111 Bway -NY 10006 **Fx:**404-7857
(631) 727-2180 .. **Kombrink,** Lisa Clare '84 (Twomey LSKD&Q,LLP) -33 W 2nd Bx9398 -Rvrhead 11901
(718) 298-8900 .. **Kominos,** Teresa M '08 Leg Aid -153-01 Jamaica Av -Jamaica 11432 **Fx:**657-0537
(212) 779-8600 .. **Kominsky,** Adam G '92 (Silverman SS&B PLLC) -381 Park Av S -NY 10016
(347) 404-9133 .. **Komissaroff,** Carol L '82 %Civil Ct -141 Lvngstn -Brklyn 11201 **Fx:**(718) 643-3733
(212) 672-7000 .. **Komitee,** Eric R '96 Viking Global Investors -280 Park Av -NY 10017
(516) 536-7156 .. **Komitee,** Ira '68 -307 5th Av -NY 10016
(212) 605-6200 .. **Komitor,** Robt I '81 (Levy P&K,LLP) -800 3rd Av -NY 10022
(212) 983-9330 .. **Komlossy,** Emily C '90 Faruqi & F,LLP -369 Lex Av -NY 10017 **Fx:**983-9331
(914) 633-7400 .. **Kommer,** John S '77 (Marcus O&K LLP) -145 Huguenot -New Rchll 10801
(516) 228-9181 .. **Kommor,** Steven D '92 OfCnsl Gassman BB&T,PC -666 Old Cntry Rd -Gdn Cty 11530
(212) 683-4141 .. **Komor,** Mikelle V '00 %Lynch & Assoc -462 7th Av -NY 10018 **Fx:**208-0948
(914) 345-3020 .. **Komosinski,** Richd F '96 (Knuckles K&E,LLP) -565 Taxter Rd -Elmsfrd 10523
(212) 669-0600 .. **Komsa,** Lauren E '09 %Hill R LLP -45 Bway -NY 10006
(516) 458-5051 .. **Komsky,** Lawr J '85 -575 Chustnut -Cedarhrst 11516
(212) 425-9300 .. **Komyati,** Nikolas S '05 %Bressler A&R,PC -17 State -NY 10004
(212) 549-2690 .. **Konanova,** Yelena '09 ACLU -125 Broad -NY 10004
(585) 334-4110 .. **Konar,** Howard E '82 -75 Thruway Park Dr -W Henrietta 14586
(631) 324-9800 .. **Koncelik,** Lawr J Jr. '80 -37 Mill Hill Rd -E Hampton 11937 **Fx:**324-8948
(212) 848-4000 .. **Kondo,** Sayo '07 %Shearman & S LLP -599 Lex Av -NY 10022
(516) 229-4300 .. **Kondulis,** John W '77 %J Bilello & Assoc -875 Merrick Av -Westbury 11590
(718) 928-4472 .. **Kone,** Allen J '77 -376 Pacific -Brklyn 11217 **Fx:**(646) 365-3024
(914) 285-9800 .. **Konefal,** Christine Cuccia '97 OfCnsl Kurzman EC&L,LLP -1 N Bway -White Plns 10601
(212) 964-9414 .. **Koney,** Ebenezer E O '85 -277 Bway -NY 10007
(212) 248-3152 .. **Kong,** Christine M '04 Cnsl Drinker B&R LLP -140 Bway -NY 10005
(212) 661-7300 .. **Kong,** David W '07 %Malapero & P LLP -295 Mad Av -NY 10017
(212) 925-0101 .. **Kong,** Dominic Kang-Ching '97 %C Slovinsky -401 Bway -NY 10013 **Fx:**219-9412
(212) 446-4800 .. **Kong,** Hee Kyung Hannah '03 (Kirkland & E LLP) -153 E 53rd -NY 10022
(212) 723-2186 .. **Kong,** Myongsu '96 Citigroup Global Mrkts -250 West -NY 10013
(212) 480-7419 .. **Konig,** Danl E '85 %DHCR -25 Beaver -NY 10004 **Fx:**480-7416
(212) 310-8000 .. **Konig,** Robt Y '04 %Weil G&M LLP -767 5th Av -NY 10153
(212) 605-6200 .. **Konigsberg,** Alan J '67 (Levy P&K,LLP) -800 3rd Av -NY 10022
(516) 741-4700 .. **Konigsberg,** Frederic Z '73 (F Konigsberg,PC) -1 Hrrcks Rd -New Hyde Pk 11040 **Fx:**873-1987
(845) 634-0971 .. **Konigsberg,** Jay M '75 -155 N Main -New Cty 10956
(212) 788-9895 .. **Konigsberg,** Matthew F '08 Cnsl Law Dept -100 Church -NY 10007 **Fx:**788-8896
(212) 685-7215 .. **Konigsberg,** Paul J '62 -440 Park Av S -NY 10016
(718) 590-2000 .. **Konigsberg,** Sheryl A '09 %DA -198 E 161st -Bronx 10451 **Fx:**590-6477
(718) 590-3653 .. **Konigsberg,** Steven I '83 %Hon A Saks -851 Grnd Cncrs -Bronx 10451
(212) 224-4846 .. **Konishi,** Takaya '09 Sumitomo Mitsui Banking Corp -277 Park Av -NY 10172
(516) 524-0453 .. **Konits,** Sharon Cerelle '92 -998 Old Cntry Rd -Plainvw 11803
(718) 979-1646 .. **Konka,** Veera V '84 -12 Grdn Ct -Staten Isl 10304
(212) 453-5900 .. **Konkel,** Mark A '01 SrCnsl Ford & H LLP -100 Park Av -NY 10017
(845) 306-1000 .. **Konken,** Beth L '08 Watchtower -100 Watchtower Dr -Patterson 12563 **Fx:**306-0709
(845) 398-1647 .. **Konkol,** Shimona '02 Radiancy Inc -40 Ramland Rd -Orangebrg 10962
(212) 692-1000 .. **Konner,** Dennis A '67 (Duane M LLP) -1540 Bway -NY 10036
(212) 697-8500 .. **Konner,** Scott C '86 (Konner T&G) -462 7th Av -NY 10018
(212) 697-8500 .. **Konner Teitelbaum & Gallagher** -462 7th Av -NY 10018 **Fx:**697-4512
(212) 728-8000 .. **Konoff,** Jonathan J '92 SpclCnsl Willkie F&G LLP -787 7th Av -NY 10019
(914) 997-9488 .. **Konon,** Natasha V '95 %H Johnson -175 Main -White Plns 10601 **Fx:**949-6810
(914) 793-1431 .. **Konop,** Thos F '70 -5 Bacon Ct -Bronxvll 10708
(212) 385-4800 .. **Konopka,** Michl '83 -277 Bway -NY 10007
(212) 309-1000 .. **Konor,** Estee M '07 %Hunton & W -200 Park Av -NY 10166
(212) 897-5832 .. **Konoski,** Bryan M '03 (Treyvus & K,PC) -305 Bway -NY 10007
(914) 761-6388 .. **Konove,** Ronald L '74 Konove & K,PC -301 Old Tarrytown Rd -White Plns 10603 **Fx:**681-8730
(212) 221-7999 .. **Konovitch,** Jonathan S '99 %Moskowitz B&W,LLP -345 7th Av -NY 10001
(212) 416-8549 .. **Konowitz,** Marc A '96 %Dept of Law -120 Bway -NY 10271 **Fx:**416-6075
(607) 751-3276 .. **Konrad,** Christopher J '99 %Lockheed Martin Fed Syst -1801 Route 17C -Owego 13827
(212) 455-2000 .. **Konrad,** Kerry L '83 (Simpson T&B LLP) -425 Lex Av -NY 10017
(212) 696-6000 .. **Konschnik,** Kristin E '03 %Curtis M-PC&M LLP -101 Park Av -NY 10178
(716) 601-1000 .. **Konst,** Harry N '01 -5511 Bway -Lancaster 14086
(716) 822-9929 .. **Konst,** Nicholas '49 -615 Ridge Rd -Lackawanna 14218

(212) 964-5570 .. **Konstadt,** Sanford '55 %Sacks & S -150 Bway -NY 10038 **Fx:**349-2141
(212) 964-7990 .. **Konstam,** Abe H '75 (Mallow K&N,PC) -321 Bway -NY 10007
(212) 512-1000 .. **Konstan,** Eve A '93 %HBO -1100 Av of Amer -NY 10036 **Fx:**512-1986
(212) 230-8800 .. **Konstandt,** Brad E '05 %WilmerHale -399 Park Av -NY 10022
(212) 705-0127 .. **Konstant,** Elana V '04 Childrens Advertsng Review Unit -70 W 36th -NY 10018
(212) 225-2000 .. **Konstant,** John W '05 %Cleary GS&H -1 Lbrty Plz -NY 10006
(716) 822-9929 .. **Konstantakis,** George N '85 -615 Ridge Rd -Lackawanna 14218
(718) 361-5555 .. **Konstantinides,** Daphne '07 Omega EMS Brokerage -3420 31st -Astoria 11106
(607) 432-2245 .. **Konstanty,** James E '67 -252 Main -Oneonta 13820 **Fx:**432-4337
(212) 733-6380 .. **Konstas,** Kristina L '94 %Pfizer Inc -235 E 42nd -NY 10017
(212) 732-0002 .. **Konta,** Adam B '08 %Cohen F&R,LLP -20 Vesey -NY 10007
(212) 626-4100 .. **Konta,** Fredk P '69 (Baker & M LLP) -1114 Av of Amer -NY 10036
(516) 767-3600 .. **Kontakis,** George K '08 %Chalos O&D -366 Main -Pt Wash 11050
(212) 309-1000 .. **Konther,** John T '71 (Hunton & W) -200 Park Av -NY 10166
(914) 368-4525 .. **Kontogiannis,** George '01 OfCnsl Marino & Assoc,PC -30 Glenn -White Plns 10603 **Fx:**368-4527
(518) 436-0751 .. **Kontogiannis,** Leanne R '97 (Hinman S PC) -121 State -Albany 12207
(212) 486-1455 .. **Kontos,** Michl J '06 %Post PGM&S,PA -575 Mad Av -NY 10022
(212) 858-1000 .. **Konvisser,** Joshua B '98 (Pillsbury WSP LLP) -1540 Bway -NY 10036
(215) 864-6334 .. **Konzelmann,** Christopher '01 (White and W LLP) -1 Penn Plz -NY 10119 **Fx:**789-7636
(212) 872-1000 .. **Koo,** Angeline L '05 -One Bryant Park -NY 10036 **Fx:**872-1002
(212) 294-6700 .. **Koo,** Calvin K '08 %Winston & S -200 Park Av -NY 10166
(212) 486-2400 .. **Koo,** Gloria E '97 %Leader & B LLP -630 3rd Av -NY 10017
(716) 858-5000 .. **Koo,** In Suk C '99 Delaware North -40 Fountain Plz -Buffalo 14202 **Fx:**858-5056
(914) 205-4370 .. **Koo,** Richd '82 -7 Oregon Rd -Armonk 10504 **Fx:**239-4800
(212) 373-3000 .. **Koo,** Stephen K '88 Cnsl Paul WRW&G LLP -1285 Av of Amer -NY 10019
(914) 964-8888 .. **Koob,** Elizabeth L '77 (Koob & M) -221 Devoe Av -Ynkrs 10705
(914) 964-8888 .. **Koob & Magoolaghan** -221 Devoe Av -Ynkrs 10705
(212) 556-5600 .. **Kooij,** Maarten B '88 %ICM -825 8th Av -NY 10019 **Fx:**556-5665
(347) 592-2200 .. **Kook,** Heejung '08 Leg Srvcs -89-00 Sutphin Blvd -Jamaica 11435 **Fx:**(718) 937-5350
(212) 763-6800 .. **Kook,** Mark R '79 (Vandenberg & F,LLP) -60 E 42nd -NY 10165
(212) 406-1700 .. **Kool,** Jonny '89 (Queller FWF&K LLP) -233 Bway -NY 10279
(212) 715-1000 .. **Koolyk,** Reuben S '77 SpclCnsl Arnold & P LLP -399 Park Av -NY 10022
(212) 489-8230 .. **Koonce,** Lance H III '98 (Davis WT LLP) -1633 Bway -NY 10019
(212) 839-5300 .. **Koonce,** Stuart S '03 (Sidley A LLP) -787 7th Av -NY 10019
(516) 482-0811 .. **Koondel,** Ira S '66 -10 Cypress Av -Gt Neck 11024
(212) 839-5300 .. **Koontz,** Mark R '04 %Sidley A LLP -787 7th Av -NY 10019
(718) 921-6601 .. **Koop,** Scott E '10 %T Beinert -155 Bay Ridge Av -Brklyn 11220 **Fx:**921-6609
(845) 647-4110 .. **Kooperman Kooperman & Tso** -47 N Main Bx511 -Ellenvll 12428 **Fx:**647-6232
(516) 393-2200 .. **Koopersmith,** Eve Green '83 SrCnsl Garfunkel W,PC -111 Grt Nck Rd -Gt Neck 11021
(516) 873-1000 .. **Koopersmith,** Glenn S '82 -1103 Stewart Av -Gdn Cty 11530 **Fx:**222-2462
(516) 354-0800 .. **Koopersmith,** Kenneth '56 (Koopersmith K LLC) -200 Grdn City Plz -Gdn Cty 11530 **Fx:**488-4387
(212) 872-1000 .. **Koopersmith,** Kim '85 -One Bryant Park -NY 10036 **Fx:**872-1002
(631) 537-4601 .. **Kooperstein,** Deborah '85 D Kooperstein & Assoc -106 Lumber Ln Bx3028 -Brdghmptn 11932
(212) 770-1892 .. **Koopmann,** Ann Spinning '89 %AIG Tech Srvcs -80 Pine -NY 10005 **Fx:**344-2286
(718) 654-8988 .. **Koors,** Paul W '76 (Koors & J) -4234 Viero Av -Bronx 10470
(516) 294-1333 .. **Koos,** Dana M '03 %DeMartini & Y LLP -264 Hillside Av -Williston Pk 11596
(212) 536-3900 .. **Koosed,** Brian D '06 %K&L Gates LLP -599 Lex Av -NY 10022
(716) 858-2424 .. **Kooshoian,** Michl H '08 %DA -25 Delaware Av -Buffalo 14202 **Fx:**858-7425
(716) 852-1102 .. **Kooshoian,** Peter M '66 -80 W Huron -Buffalo 14202 **Fx:**852-8013
(716) 854-1300 .. **Kooshoian,** Peter M '02 %Rosenthal S&M,LLP -300 Main -Buffalo 14202
(518) 885-2263 .. **Kopach,** Danl J '99 %DA -25 W High -Ballston Spa 12020 **Fx:**884-8627
(212) 547-5400 .. **Kopacz,** Gregory A '10 %McDermott W&E LLP -340 Mad Av -NY 10173
(716) 648-3030 .. **Kopacz,** Tiffany M '99 %Chiacchia & F,LLP -5113 S Park Av -Hambrg 14075
(212) 735-3000 .. **Kopald,** Adam E '09 %Skadden ASM&F LLP -4 Times Sq -NY 10036
(845) 446-4764 .. **Kopald,** Ned '65 (Kopald & K,PC) -189 Main Bx274 -Highlnd Fls 10928 **Fx:**446-4788
(212) 358-6400 .. **Kopans,** Nancy A '94 JSTOR -149 5th Av -NY 10010
(212) 269-5500 .. **Kopco,** Jeffrey A '06 %Gordon & R LLP -90 Broad -NY 10004
(212) 756-2000 .. **Kopco,** Leah M '08 %Schulte R&Z LLP -919 3rd Av -NY 10022
(212) 682-8811 .. **Kopcsak,** Michl J '75 (Dunnington B&M LLP) -1359 Bway -NY 10018
(212) 326-2000 .. **Kopczynski,** Jeffrey A N '08 %O'Melveny & M LLP -7 Times Sq -NY 10036
(212) 373-3000 .. **Kopczynski,** Philip A '08 %Paul WRW&G LLP -1285 Av of Amer -NY 10019
(212) 878-8000 .. **Kopec,** Aleksandra '08 %Clifford C LLP -31 W 52nd -NY 10019
(518) 677-8819 .. **Kopec,** Christine C '77 (Wrigley & K) -27 W Main Bx255 -Cambrdg 12816
(212) 250-2500 .. **Kopec,** Jos C '90 %Deutsche Bank -60 Wall -NY 10005
(212) 261-7000 .. **Kopech,** Susan D '81 %Calyon -1301 Av of Amer -NY 10019
(516) 837-6103 .. **Kopel,** Howard J '76 Sutton Alliance -515 Rockaway Av -Vly Stream 11581 **Fx:**837-6403
(212) 697-6484 .. **Kopel,** Noson A '00 OfCnsl Bronstein G&G,LLC -60 E 42nd -NY 10165 **Fx:**697-0877
(212) 408-2500 .. **Kopel,** Reuben '02 SpclCnsl Baker B,LLP -30 Rckfllr Plz -NY 10112
(212) 891-1600 .. **Kopelman,** Andrew J '07 %Jenner & B LLP -919 3rd Av -NY 10022
(212) 629-0733 .. **Kopelman,** Carol Weinflash '95 (Kopelman & K) -1 Penn Plz -NY 10119 **Fx:**(201) 489-7755
(212) 705-7000 .. **Kopelman,** Kenneth A '85 (Bingham M LLP) -399 Park Av -NY 10022
(212) 715-9100 .. **Kopelman,** Kenneth P '77 (Kramer LN&F,LLP) -1177 Av of Amer -NY 10036
(212) 629-0733 .. **Kopelman,** Michl S '82 (Kopelman & K) -1 Penn Plz -NY 10119 **Fx:**(201) 489-7755
(212) 867-6000 .. **Kopelowitz,** Joshua R '04 %Rosenberg & E,PC -733 3rd Av -NY 10017
(845) 339-4230 .. **Kopf,** Bruce I '96 Adirondack Trailways -499 Hurley Av -Hurley 12443
(212) 244-2999 .. **Kopff Nardelli & Dopf LLP** -440 9th Av -NY 10001 **Fx:**643-0862
(212) 244-2999 .. **Kopff,** Peter C '76 (Kopff N&D LLP) -440 9th Av -NY 10001
(516) 747-4770 .. **Kopilow,** Stanley R '73 (Hopkins & K) -100 Q Roosevelt Blvd -Gdn Cty 11530
(718) 472-1200 .. **Kopit,** Sarah E '03 Dial-A-Mattress -3110 48th Av -LIC 11101
(212) 362-4501 .. **Kopitko,** Stephen L '72 -1995 Bway -NY 10023 **Fx:**362-4510
(718) 834-9200 .. **Kopito,** Ira M '93 -32 Court -Brklyn 11201 **Fx:**875-0821
(646) 223-4200 .. **Kopits,** Laszlo Imre '93 %Reuters -3 Times Sq -NY 10036 **Fx:**223-4250
(607) 272-0479 .. **Kopko,** Edw E '01 (Wiggins & K,LLP) -308 N Tioga -Ithaca 14850
(845) 623-7070 .. **Koplen,** Michl A '82 -14 S Main -New Cty 10956 **Fx:**708-5597
(212) 953-1010 .. **Koplik,** Marc S '73 (Henderson & K) -420 Lex Av -NY 10170 **Fx:**953-1025
(212) 788-1336 .. **Koplik,** Pamela Ann '96 %Law Dept -100 Church -NY 10007 **Fx:**788-0367
(215) 772-1700 .. **Koplin,** Bernice J '93 -92 Prospect Pl -Brklyn 11217 **Fx:**772-0312
(212) 687-6262 .. **Koplin,** Kevin S '95 (Barton B&P,LLP) -420 Lex Av -NY 10170
(212) 687-7770 .. **Koplovitz,** Deborah B '06 %Rosen L&C LLP -275 Mad Av -NY 10016
(845) 679-7207 .. **Koplovitz,** Joshua N '61 (Wapner K&F,PLLC) -45 Mill Hill Rd Bx572 -Woodstock 12498
(845) 331-0100 .. **Koplovitz,** Joshua N '61 (Wapner K&F,PLLC) -239 Wall Bx3268 -Kingston 12402
(212) 403-1000 .. **Koplow,** Meyer G '77 (Wachtell LR&K) -51 W 52nd -NY 10019
(718) 568-3678 .. **Koplow,** Sean I '94 (S Koplow,PC) -900 South Av -Staten Isl 10314 **Fx:**568-3612
(718) 923-3379 .. **Koplowitz,** Aaron '82 OTDA Fair Hearings -14 Boerum Pl -Brklyn 11201
(516) 938-9309 .. **Kopman,** Barbara H '81 (Kantor & K) -183 Bway -Hicksvll 11801
(516) 560-6400 .. **Kopmar,** Ilana '92 %Leg Aid -1 Helen Keller Way -Hempstd 11550 **Fx:**565-3694
(315) 474-7541 .. **Kopnitsky,** Vic J Jr. '84 (Menter R&T,PC) -308 Maltbie -Syracuse 13204
(212) 637-2210 .. **Kopp,** Glen A '03 US Atty -1 St Andrews Plz -NY 10007
(585) 263-1000 .. **Kopp,** J Brian '92 (Nixon P LLP) -1100 Clinton Sq -Rchstr 14604
(212) 274-9500 .. **Kopp,** Jonathan H '94 %Shepardson Stern & Kaminsky -88 Pine -NY 10005
(212) 205-7000 .. **Kopp,** Steven L '93 (Ashurst LLP) -7 Times Sq -NY 10036
(212) 687-1466 .. **Koppel Kessler Julie LLP** -551 5th Av -NY 10176
(212) 373-3000 .. **Koppel,** Paul R '01 %Paul WRW&G LLP -1285 Av of Amer -NY 10019
(212) 326-3939 .. **Koppel,** Steven C '86 (Jones D) -222 E 41st -NY 10017
(212) 768-6700 .. **Koppele,** Jeffrey H '91 (Sonnenschein N&R LLP) -2 World Fncl Ctr -NY 10281
(212) 867-3838 .. **Koppell,** G Oliver '66 -99 Park Av -NY 10016 **Fx:**681-0810
(212) 577-6580 .. **Koppelman,** Robt '67 -585 West End Av -NY 10024 **Fx:**619-2767
(845) 708-8700 .. **Koppelman,** Ronald S '72 (Blatt & K,PC) -151 N Main -New Cty 10956
(212) 735-3423 .. **Koppman,** Katherine L '01 Skadden ASM&F LLP -4 Times Sq -NY 10036
(212) 501-1901 .. **Kopsick,** Steven C '90 -1053 Admont Av -Franklin Sq 11010 **Fx:**501-1912
(212) 816-1765 .. **Korab,** Marc J '06 Citigroup Global Mrkts Inc -388 Greenwich -NY 10013
(212) 688-2550 .. **Korach,** Jane E '05 Owl Creek Asset Mgmt,LP -640 5th Av -NY 10019
(212) 567-2211 .. **Korahais,** Wm A '07 M&N Mgmt -5047 Bway -NY 10034
(212) 407-7700 .. **Koral,** Alan M '77 (Vedder P,PC) -1633 Bway -NY 10019
(212) 479-6000 .. **Koral,** Jason M '98 (Cooley LLP) -1114 Av of Amer -NY 10036
(914) 763-5328 .. **Koral,** Richd L '79 -180 Rdgfld Av -S Salem 10590
(718) 377-1156 .. **Koral,** Robt H '79 -2425 Kings Hwy -Brklyn 11229
(212) 632-1390 .. **Korb,** Lawr J Jr. '04 Lazard Alternative Invstmnts LLC -30 Rckfllr Plz -NY 10112
(212) 592-1400 .. **Korbey,** Mitchell A '04 (Herrick,F LLP) -2 Park Av -NY 10016
(631) 298-0106 .. **Korbin,** Helene '91 (Hilgendorff & K) -2160 Reeve Rd -Mattituck 11952
(607) 722-5000 .. **Korchak,** Michl A '90 C Garufi -68 Oak -Bnghmtn 13905 **Fx:**722-5626
(212) 455-2000 .. **Korchin,** Brian E '09 %Simpson T&B LLP -425 Lex Av -NY 10017
(631) 580-3400 .. **Korcz,** Amy B '92 (Schondebare & K) -3555 Vets Mem'l Hwy -Ronkonkoma 11779 **Fx:**581-3030
(212) 218-5500 .. **Korda,** Peter J '80 (Seyfarth S LLP) -620 8th Av -NY 10018
(718) 392-8000 .. **Kordas & Marinis** -5-47 47th Rd -LIC 11101 **Fx:**482-9000
(718) 392-8000 .. **Kordas,** Nicholas '77 (Kordas & M) -5-47 47th Rd -LIC 11101
(914) 833-0500 .. **Korder,** Mitchell L '76 (Eppinger R&K) -131 Larchmnt Av Bx868 -Larchmnt 10538
(212) 829-0535 .. **Kordes,** Linda L '85 -485 Mad Av -NY 10022 **Fx:**588-0471
(518) 464-6770 .. **Kordich,** Kyle N '99 (Thorn GT&B,LLP) -5 Wembley Ct Bx15054 -Albany 12212
(718) 821-1884 .. **Kordisch,** Steven E '87 S Kordisch,PC -72-41 Cooper Av -Glendale 11385
(212) 225-2000 .. **Kordula,** Chantal E '98 (Cleary GS&H) -1 Lbrty Plz -NY 10006
(516) 229-4501 .. **Koreen,** Amy J '94 %Russo A&T -875 Merrick Av -Westbury 11590
(212) 326-2000 .. **Korehbandi,** Carmen R '08 %O'Melveny & M LLP -7 Times Sq -NY 10036
(212) 385-4410 .. **Korek,** Jeff S '87 (Gersowitz L&K,PC) -111 Bway -NY 10006
(212) 782-2000 .. **Koren,** Ayelet A '03 %Bk Hapoalim -1177 Av of Amer -NY 10036 **Fx:**782-2141
(716) 838-4600 .. **Koren,** Bruce Kevin '77 -2655 Sheridan Dr -Tonawanda 14150 **Fx:**838-4646
(917) 587-6742 .. **Koren,** Jonathan '03 -2241 E 1st -Brklyn 11223 **Fx:**(212) 799-5287

(212) 735-3000 .. **Koren,** Kristine M '05 %Skadden ASM&F LLP -4 Times Sq -NY 10036
(917) 551-1300 .. **Koren,** Mark L '85 %Koehler & I LLP -61 Bway -NY 10006
(212) 637-2266 .. **Korenbaum,** Laurie A '97 %US Atty -1 St Andrews Plz -NY 10007
(212) 587-0018 .. **Korenbaum,** Scott A '89 -111 Bway -NY 10006 **Fx:**346-4665
(718) 923-6300 .. **Korenberg,** Susan '94 %Atty Grievance Comm -335 Adams -Brklyn 11201 **Fx:**624-2978
(212) 783-2268 .. **Korenman,** Stephanie '99 Citigroup Inc -787 7th Av -NY 10019
(212) 335-9000 .. **Korenstein,** Hope '00 %DA -1 Hogan Pl -NY 10013
(212) 556-2100 .. **Koretz,** Alexander E '08 %King & S -1185 Av of Amer -NY 10036
(845) 294-1611 .. **Koretzky,** Marsha E '84 -210 Main Bx943 -Goshen 10924 **Fx:**294-9667
(212) 610-6300 .. **Koretzky,** Todd A '07 %Allen & O -1221 Av of Amer -NY 10020
(917) 777-4200 .. **Korff,** Jennifer Z '97 Cnsl Bingham M LLP -1 Bttry Pk Plz -NY 10004
(212) 702-5851 .. **Korff,** Jos '69 ARC Devlpmnt -250 Park Av -NY 10177
(212) 446-4800 .. **Korff,** Joshua N '94 (Kirkland & E LLP) -153 E 53rd -NY 10022
(212) 735-3000 .. **Korff,** Phyllis G '82 (Skadden ASM&F LLP) -4 Times Sq -NY 10036
(212) 708-9289 .. **Korfmann,** Laura E '96 Bessemer Trst Co -630 5th Av -NY 10111 **Fx:**265-5826
(212) 841-1000 .. **Korgaonkar,** Natasha M '09 %Covington & B LLP -620 8th Av -NY 10018
(212) 541-6980 .. **Korik,** Michl '05 %Monaghan ML&M -401 E 65th -NY 10019
(516) 357-9191 .. **Korinman,** Gabriel R '05 %Lester & W,PC -600 Old Cntry Rd -Gdn Cty 11530 **Fx:**357-9281
(646) 752-4656 .. **Korins,** Jeffrey M '99 Kelly Law Registry -237 Park Av -NY 10017
(212) 953-6000 .. **Korins,** Roy M '66 (Katsky K LLP) -605 3rd Av -NY 10158
(212) 935-7400 .. **Korkhov,** Tanya '06 %Harwood F LLP -488 Mad Av -NY 10022
(518) 489-1117 .. **Korkosz,** Fredk P '89 %A Berke -930 Mad Av -Albany 12208 **Fx:**446-1798
(716) 858-2424 .. **Korkuc,** Karen A '86 DA -25 Delaware Av -Buffalo 14202 **Fx:**858-7425
(716) 691-0010 .. **Korman,** Alan S '94 Ivoclar Vivadent,Inc -175 Pinevw Dr -Amherst 14228 **Fx:**691-2280
(212) 785-4823 .. **Korman,** Brian '05 %Carcagno & Assoc -80 Broad -NY 10004 **Fx:**785-0437
(516) 357-3000 .. **Korman,** Cheryl F '91 (Rivkin R LLP) -926 RXR Plz -Uniondale 11556
(212) 571-4900 .. **Korman,** Hilary F '09 %M Harris & Assoc LLC -5 Hanover Sq -NY 10004 **Fx:**571-0965
(212) 306-8848 .. **Korman,** Howard M '83 Housing Auth -250 Bway -NY 10007
(212) 480-6235 .. **Korman,** Iris J '79 %DHCR -25 Beaver -NY 10004 **Fx:**480-7416
(212) 732-4992 .. **Korman,** John G '98 OfCnsl Arye L&S,PC -20 Vesey -NY 10007
(716) 633-5432 .. **Korman,** Joshua '06 -5547 Main -Williamsvll 14221
(718) 701-6454 .. **Korman,** Lawr A '81 Integrity Title Agency -654 Sharrotts Rd -Staten Isl 10309
(212) 336-2000 .. **Korman,** Rochelle '74 OfCnsl Patterson BW&T LLP -1133 Av of Amer -NY 10036
(516) 294-4411 .. **Korman,** Steven S '89 -50 Chas Lindbergh Blvd -Uniondale 11553 **Fx:**294-4436
(516) 571-0648 .. **Korn,** Alan I '75 %Cnty Atty -1 West -Mineola 11501 **Fx:**571-6604
(212) 859-8000 .. **Korn,** Alexander T '06 %Fried FHS&J LLP -1 NY Plz -NY 10004
(718) 838-7878 .. **Korn,** Allison E '09 Bronx Defenders -860 Crtlandt Av -Bronx 10451 **Fx:**665-0100
(516) 877-5600 .. **Korn,** Gary L '91 %R Tusa -1225 Franklin Av -Gdn Cty 11530 **Fx:**877-5695
(212) 935-4400 .. **Korn,** Henry H '74 (LePatner & Assoc LLP) -600 Lex Av -NY 10022 **Fx:**935-4404
(212) 728-8000 .. **Korn,** Jeffrey B '01 %Willkie F&G LLP -787 7th Av -NY 10019
(718) 237-2000 .. **Korn,** Joyce B '87 %Leg Aid -111 Lvngstn -Brklyn 11201 **Fx:**237-8737
(716) 845-5500 .. **Korn,** Lindy '79 -424 Main -Buffalo 14202
(212) 968-1000 .. **Korn,** Mark E '00 -64 Beaver -NY 10004
(212) 603-6300 .. **Korn,** Michl A '06 %Robinson BLGG&G PC -875 3rd Av -NY 10022
(212) 768-6700 .. **Korn,** Peter L Jr. '97 (Sonnenschein N&R LLP) -2 World Fncl Ctr -NY 10281
(718) 858-2898 .. **Korn,** Richd J '80 -31 Smith -Brklyn 11201
(212) 290-4000 .. **Korn,** Tyler B '01 OfCnsl Ebert & Assoc,LLC -110 E 30th -NY 10016 **Fx:**290-1717
(716) 285-0640 .. **Kornaker,** Dawn M '04 %Clayton & B -650 4th -Niagara Fls 14301 **Fx:**285-0663
(212) 373-3000 .. **Kornberg,** Alan W '78 (Paul WRW&G LLP) -1285 Av of Amer -NY 10019
(212) 279-3200 .. **Kornblatt,** Danl H '83 -2 Wall -NY 10005
(212) 288-5204 .. **Kornblau,** Allan I '73 -1520 York Av -NY 10028 **Fx:**288-5069
(516) 571-3800 .. **Kornblau,** Barbara '85 %DA -262 Old Cntry Rd -Mineola 11501 **Fx:**248-9479
(516) 627-4390 .. **Kornblau,** David L '81 -36 Drake Ln -Manhsst 11030
(212) 841-1000 .. **Kornblau,** David L '87 (Covington & B LLP) -620 8th Av -NY 10018
(718) 624-2302 .. **Kornblau,** Eric M '85 (Kornblau & K,PC) -16 Court -Brklyn 11241 **Fx:**624-2763
(718) 624-2323 .. **Kornblau,** Jules H '58 (Kornblau & K,PC) -16 Court -Brklyn 11241 **Fx:**624-2763
(212) 541-2000 .. **Kornblau,** Steven M '88 (Bryan C LLP) -1290 Av of Amer -NY 10104
(212) 879-9300 .. **Kornblit,** Sandra C '75 %Natl Jewish Fund -42 E 69th -NY 10021
(718) 654-4931 .. **Kornbluh,** James A '94 %EARS -3319 Rochambeau Av -Bronx 10467
(212) 521-5400 .. **Kornbluh,** Sara K '09 %Reed S LLP -599 Lex Av -NY 10022
(212) 816-8988 .. **Kornblum,** Amir I '92 Citigroup -388 Greenwich -NY 10013
(914) 948-3666 .. **Kornblum,** Leslie M '89 Mercy Cllg -277 Martine Av -White Plns 10601
(516) 357-3000 .. **Kornblum,** Yaron J '93 %Rivkin R LLP -926 RXR Plz -Uniondale 11556
(631) 324-3666 .. **Kornbluth,** Ira '82 -11 Muchmore Ln -E Hampton 11937 **Fx:**287-7337
(212) 592-1400 .. **Kornbluth,** Seth F '00 %Herrick,F LLP -2 Park Av -NY 10016
(212) 208-9516 .. **Kornell,** Darah R '05 Liberty Intl Underwriters -55 Water -NY 10041
(212) 577-3688 .. **Kornfeind,** Svetlana Milloy '93 %Leg Aid -199 Water -NY 10038 **Fx:**509-8431
(212) 561-7700 .. **Kornfeld,** Alan J '04 (Pachulski SZ&J) -780 3rd Av -NY 10017
(914) 949-6400 .. **Kornfeld,** Alice D '93 %McCullough G&S,LLP -1311 Mamaroneck Av -White Plns 10605
(315) 422-7111 .. **Kornfeld,** Danl E '04 (Blitman & K LLP) -443 N Franklin -Syracuse 13204
(718) 382-9300 .. **Kornfeld,** H Jos '79 -1867 E 13th -Brklyn 11229
(212) 227-4492 .. **Kornfeld,** Howard A '85 -20 Vesey -NY 10007
(914) 733-3914 .. **Kornfeld,** Janet Phillips '91 -660 Wht Plns Rd -Tarrytwn 10591 **Fx:**468-0301
(718) 382-9300 .. **Kornfeld,** Jason R '09 %HJ Kornfeld -1867 E 13th -Brklyn 11229
(212) 521-3500 .. **Kornfeld,** John A '88 (Aronson M&S, LLP) -485 Lex Av -NY 10017
(914) 472-4914 .. **Kornfeld,** Julie E '96 -206 Brwstr Rd -Scarsdale 10583
(212) 488-1200 .. **Kornfeld,** Karyn R '98 %Kobre & K,LLP -800 3rd Av -NY 10022
(914) 737-4585 .. **Kornfeld,** Leon '63 -1011 Park -Peekskill 10566 **Fx:**737-4587
(212) 589-4200 .. **Kornfeld,** Mark A '93 (Baker & H LLP) -45 Rckfllr Plz -NY 10111
(212) 867-4100 .. **Kornfeld,** Neil S '89 (Furman K&B LLP) -61 Bway -NY 10006
(212) 759-6767 .. **Kornfeld,** Randy M '80 -570 Lex Av -NY 10022 **Fx:**759-6766
(845) 357-2660 .. **Kornfeld Rew Newman & Simeone** -46 Wshngtn Av Bx177 -Suffern 10901 **Fx:**357-6977
(212) 859-8000 .. **Kornfeld,** Todd R '97 SpclCnsl Fried FHS&J LLP -1 NY Plz -NY 10004
(585) 546-2434 .. **Kornfield,** Bryan S '02 %Hirsch & T PC -1000 Rynlds Arcd Bldg -Rchstr 14614
(212) 431-2154 .. **Korngold,** Gerald '09 NY Law Schl -185 W Bway -NY 10013 **Fx:**431-1864
(914) 576-1904 .. **Korngold,** Laurie J '80 -155 Oxford Rd -New Rchll 10804
(914) 834-3899 .. **Korngold,** Leslie A '73 %Healthcare Acquisitions Inc -681 Forest Av -Larchmnt 10538
(212) 687-3747 .. **Korngold,** Paul J '77 (Tuchman KWL&G,LLP) -6 E 45th -NY 10017
(718) 250-2000 .. **Korngold,** Pinhas David '07 %DA -350 Jay -Brklyn 11201 **Fx:**250-2314
(212) 504-6000 .. **Korngut,** Benjamin A '08 %Cadwalader W&T LLP -1 World Fncl Ctr -NY 10281
(212) 566-5021 .. **Korngut,** David I '75 -225 Bway -NY 10007 **Fx:**766-2628
(718) 875-0605 .. **Kornhaber,** Ari P '98 %LawCash -26 Court -Brklyn 11242
(212) 969-3000 .. **Kornreich,** Edw S '78 (Proskauer R LLP) -1585 Bway -NY 10036
(212) 916-6973 .. **Kornreich,** Meredith '83 %TIAA-CREF -730 3rd Av -NY 10017
(212) 759-4600 .. **Kornreich,** Robt M '69 (Wolf P LLP) -845 3rd Av -NY 10022
(212) 969-3000 .. **Kornreich,** Ronald S '97 (Proskauer R LLP) -1585 Bway -NY 10036
(212) 772-3548 .. **Kornreich,** Stephen J '63 -400 E 71st -NY 10021 **Fx:**535-1594
(646) 471-6790 .. **Kornreich,** Wendy L '90 %PricewaterhouseCoopers LLP -300 Mad Av -NY 10017 **Fx:**(212) 707-6717
(212) 351-7000 .. **Kornrich,** Evan K '91 %Monster Worldwide -622 3rd Av -NY 10017 **Fx:**351-7097
(212) 418-8600 .. **Kornstein,** Danl J '74 (Kornstein VW&P,LLP) -757 3rd Av -NY 10017
(212) 536-3900 .. **Kornstein,** Israel E '80 (K&L Gates LLP) -599 Lex Av -NY 10022
(518) 449-3900 .. **Kornstein,** Michl A '78 (Cooper E&S,LLP) -39 N Pearl -Albany 12207
(212) 445-8213 .. **Kornstein,** Steven '86 %Cerberus Cptl Mgmt LP -299 Park Av -NY 10171 **Fx:**445-8276
(212) 418-8600 .. **Kornstein Veisz Wexler & Pollard,LLP** -757 3rd Av -NY 10017 **Fx:**826-3640
(718) 876-6300 .. **Korode,** Joshua O '06 %DA -130 Styvsnt Pl -Staten Isl 10301
(518) 347-3318 .. **Koroghlian,** Anoush M '92 Bellevue Womens Hosptl -2210 Troy Rd -Schnctdy 12309
(718) 445-5330 .. **Koroghlian,** Haig E '97 -3901 Main -Flushng 11354 **Fx:**445-5790
(917) 442-1928 .. **Koroleva,** Anastasia Y '01 Intermedia.net,INC -156 W 56th -NY 10019
(516) 873-2000 .. **Koroleva,** Lana '09 %Moritt HH&H LLP -400 Grdn City Plz -Gdn Cty 11530
(212) 637-2406 .. **Korologos,** Lisa P '94 %US Atty -1 St Andrews Plz -NY 10007
(212) 446-2300 .. **Korologos,** Philip C '92 (Boies S&F LLP) -575 Lex Av -NY 10022
(585) 327-4100 .. **Korona,** Mary Jo '88 (Leclair KGC,LLP) -150 State -Rchstr 14614 **Fx:**327-4200
(585) 387-0500 .. **Korona,** Matthew M '86 (Olver K LLP) -100 Ofc Park Way -Pittsfrd 14534
(212) 425-7200 .. **Korostash,** Yekaterina T '06 %Kenyon & K,LLP -1 Bway -NY 10004
(646) 315-7357 .. **Korostoff,** Steven F '91 %FINRA -14 Wall -NY 10005 **Fx:**315-7440
(212) 553-0300 .. **Korot,** Emily C '06 %Moody's Invstr Srvc -250 Greenwich -NY 10007
(212) 530-5000 .. **Korot,** Mia C '04 %Milbank TH&M LLP -1 Chase Manh Plz -NY 10005
(212) 526-4842 .. **Korot,** Philip '75 %Lehman Bros Inc -399 Park Av -NY 10022
(585) 419-5714 .. **Korotkin,** Alexander '95 -70 Linden Oaks -Rchstr 14625
(212) 715-9100 .. **Korotkin,** Michl P '63 (Kramer LN&F,LLP) -1177 Av of Amer -NY 10036
(718) 237-2000 .. **Korotzer,** Daniella '95 %Leg Aid -111 Lvngstn -Brklyn 11201 **Fx:**237-8737
(718) 260-8700 .. **Korovin,** Arthur J '86 %Admin Children's Srvcs -345 Adams -Brklyn 11201
(212) 506-1700 .. **Korpus,** Sheron '97 (Kasowitz BT&F LLP) -1633 Bway -NY 10019
(212) 259-8000 .. **Korrapati,** Smita G '07 %Dewey & L LLP -1301 Av of Amer -NY 10019
(914) 948-1188 .. **Korren,** Robt A '84 (R Korren,PLLC) -1 Barker Av -White Plns 10601 **Fx:**997-1096
(212) 558-4000 .. **Korry,** Alexandra D '88 (Sullivan & C LLP) -125 Broad -NY 10004
(212) 858-7706 .. **Korsh,** Barry L '95 %Slowinski A,LLP -140 Bway PMB 46039 -NY 10005
(718) 799-1000 .. **Korshalla,** Lauren E '08 %AW Chan,PLLC -141-07 20th Av -Whitestone 11357 **Fx:**357-8615
(516) 496-5822 .. **Korshin,** Michl A '02 %T Spina -170 Froehlich Farm Blvd -Woodbury 11797 **Fx:**496-5420
(212) 277-0458 .. **Korshukin,** Marianna '09 Hartford Ins Co -2 Park Av -NY 10016
(212) 363-7500 .. **Korsinsky,** Eduard '96 (Levi & K LLP) -30 Broad -NY 10004
(212) 363-7500 .. **Korsinsky,** Michl '01 Cnsl Levi & K LLP -30 Broad -NY 10004
(212) 596-9000 .. **Korson,** Margaret W '08 %Ropes & G LLP -1211 Av of Amer -NY 10036
(212) 267-6557 .. **Korson,** Michl S '70 (Isaacson S&K) -150 Bway -NY 10038
(516) 296-7000 .. **Korth,** Donna-Marie '87 (Certilman BA&H,LLP) -90 Merrick Av -E Meadow 11554
(516) 599-4077 .. **Korth,** Jay F '48 (Korth & K) -129 Charles -Lynbrk 11563 **Fx:**599-4077

(516) 599-4077 .. **Korth**, Jay T '88 %Korth & K -129 Charles -Lynbrk 11563 **Fx**:599-4077
(516) 741-2121 .. **Korth**, Lorraine M '81 %N Kanzer -1325 Franklin Av -Gdn Cty 11530 **Fx**:741-3930
(212) 207-6415 .. **Korth**, Timothy W '93 MFA Mortgage Invstmnts -350 Park Av -NY 10022 **Fx**:207-6420
(212) 662-5761 .. **Kortis**, Bryan L '98 Neighborhood Cats,Inc -2565 Bway -NY 10025
(212) 660-3000 .. **Kortmansky**, Jonathan G '95 (Sullivan & W LLP) -1290 Av of Amer -NY 10104
(518) 746-2525 .. **Kortright**, Kevin C '88 (DA) -383 Bway -Ft Edward 12828 **Fx**:746-2568
(212) 450-4000 .. **Kortright**, Richd T '73 Cnsl Davis P&W LLP -450 Lex Av -NY 10017
(914) 269-8120 .. **Korus**, Roberta '84 -3 Emmalon Av -N White Plns 10603 **Fx**:831-2174
(212) 407-7700 .. **Korval**, Neal I '82 (Vedder P,PC) -1633 Bway -NY 10019
(212) 697-5550 .. **Koryakin**, Paulina '08 %G & L Blumberg,LLP -521 5th Av -NY 10175 **Fx**:697-9570
(518) 402-1971 .. **Korycinski**, Kathleen Ann '89 %Medicaid Fraud Cntrl -The Cptl -Albany 12223 **Fx**:474-4519
(716) 282-4488 .. **Koryl**, Robt T '80 -701 Pine Av -Niagara Fls 14301 **Fx**:282-6945
(212) 552-0919 .. **Korzec**, Arthur '89 JP Morgan Chase -1 Chase Manh Plz -NY 10081
(212) 268-7535 .. **Korzen**, Alan L '91 OfCnsl Bonner KT&C,LLP -350 5th Av -NY 10118
(716) 853-9555 .. **Korzeniewski**, Lawr F '80 %Leg Aid -237 Main -Buffalo 14203 **Fx**:853-3219
(212) 752-9200 .. **Korzenik**, David S '80 (Miller KS LLP) -488 Mad Av -NY 10022 **Fx**:688-3996
(212) 523-2162 .. **Korzenik**, Deborah B '85 %Beth Israel Med Ctr -555 W 57th -NY 10019
(973) 503-5909 .. **Korzha**, Ilona I '06 %Kelley D&W LLP -101 Park Av -NY 10178 **Fx**:503-5950
(212) 589-4200 .. **Kosack**, Melissa L '06 %Baker & H LLP -45 Rckfllr Plz -NY 10111
(631) 650-1200 .. **Kosakoff**, David B '87 (Sinnreich K&M LLP) -267 Carleton Av -Central Islip 11722
(212) 903-8700 .. **Kosakoff**, Debra G '81 OfCnsl Roberts & H,LLP -825 8th Av -NY 10019
(212) 448-1100 .. **Kosakow**, James M '85 (McLaughlin & S,LLP) -260 Mad Av -NY 10016
(212) 630-6341 .. **Kosakowski**, John R Jr. '02 Amtrak Police Dept -234 W 33rd -NY 10001
(914) 997-9070 .. **Kosan**, E Michl '78 (Fredman B&K LLP) -333 Wstchstr Av -White Plns 10604
(212) 867-6000 .. **Kosar**, Devin P '09 %Rosenberg & E,PC -733 3rd Av -NY 10017
(212) 947-9779 .. **Kosberg**, Jana B '02 AFC -151 W 30th -NY 10001
(845) 895-3030 .. **Koschei**, Jonathan E '81 -81 Bona Ventura Av BxR -Wallkill 12589 **Fx**:895-8440
(718) 377-7798 .. **Kosches**, Jon B '99 M Reinhardt & Assoc -2990 Av U -Brklyn 11229 **Fx**:692-1012
(212) 819-8200 .. **Koschik**, David N '85 (White & C LLP) -1155 Av of Amer -NY 10036
(212) 508-6100 .. **Koscuiszka**, Kelly A '07 %Bracewell & G,LLP -1251 Av of Amer -NY 10020
(212) 331-5067 .. **Kosefas**, Theoni '98 HRA -180 Water -NY 10038
(212) 458-1693 .. **Kosh**, Richd J '85 %AIG -175 Water -NY 10038
(212) 455-2000 .. **Koshal**, Arjun '02 %Simpson T&B LLP -425 Lex Av -NY 10017
(212) 530-5000 .. **Kosharovsky**, Marianna '09 %Milbank TH&M LLP -1 Chase Manh Plz -NY 10005
(212) 371-6600 .. **Kosharskyy**, Karina '08 %Kirby M LLP -825 3rd Av -NY 10022
(212) 878-8000 .. **Koshelev**, Alexey '08 %Clifford C LLP -31 W 52nd -NY 10019
(212) 201-1170 .. **Koshers**, David R '07 %Abrams GMB,LLP -237 W 35th -NY 10001
(212) 644-0303 .. **Koshetz**, Rae Downes '78 RD Koshetz,PC -515 Mad Av -NY 10022 **Fx**:644-4818
(518) 452-0941 .. **Koshgarian**, Robt J '87 %Segel GM&S,PC -9 Wshngtn Sq -Albany 12205
(212) 468-8000 .. **Koshgerian**, Stephen P '10 %Morrison & F LLP -1290 Av of Amer -NY 10104
(212) 723-2889 .. **Koshy**, Sunita E '02 Citigrp Glbl Mkts -250 West -NY 10013
(518) 449-3300 .. **Koshykar**, Marco B '05 %Nolan & H,LLP -39 N Pearl -Albany 12207
(212) 599-2200 .. **Kosiba**, Lauren N '06 Lucas Grp -52 Vndrblt Av -NY 10017 **Fx**:599-2014
(518) 966-4412 .. **Kosich**, Jon A '94 -4840 State Route 81 -Greenvll 12083 **Fx**:966-8258
(518) 943-5050 .. **Kosich**, Veronica M '99 -24 Hambrg Rd Bx591 -Catskill 12414 **Fx**:943-2213
(718) 286-6000 .. **Kosinski**, John W Jr. '92 %DA -125-01 Qns Blvd -Kew Gdns 11415
(518) 474-6236 .. **Kosinski**, Peter S '88 %Bd of Elections -40 Steuben -Albany 12207
(718) 388-3330 .. **Kosiorek**, Wioletta '99 %Zawisny & Z,PC -578 Driggs Av -Brklyn 11211 **Fx**:338-3877
(585) 530-3112 .. **Koski-Taylor**, Kim '03 Appllt Div 4th Dept -50 East Av Ste 200 -Rchstr 14604 **Fx**:530-3247
(516) 496-5822 .. **Koski-Troxler**, Ann K '05 %T Spina -170 Froehlich Farm Blvd -Woodbury 11797 **Fx**:496-5420
(212) 552-4672 .. **Kosloff**, Andrew '74 JP Morgan Chase -1 Chase Manh Plz -NY 10081
(315) 724-5477 .. **Koslosky**, John G '86 (Koslosky & K) -2635 Genesee -Utica 13501
(315) 724-5477 .. **Koslosky**, Wm L '88 (Koslosky & K) -2635 Genesee -Utica 13501
(212) 787-7136 .. **Koslow**, Esther S '80 -588 West End Av -NY 10024
(212) 735-3000 .. **Koslow**, Jonathan L '78 (Skadden ASM&F LLP) -4 Times Sq -NY 10036
(212) 455-2000 .. **Koslowe**, Jamin R '97 Cnsl Simpson T&B LLP -425 Lex Av -NY 10017
(212) 889-4220 .. **Koslowe**, Jonathan M '10 %Buchman Law Firm,LLP -10 E 40th -NY 10016 **Fx**:889-4221
(212) 889-4220 .. **Koslowe**, Mark A '77 (Buchman Law Firm,LLP) -10 E 40th -NY 10016 **Fx**:889-4221
(212) 687-7770 .. **Kosmark**, Mary L '85 (Rosen L&C LLP) -275 Mad Av -NY 10016
(585) 492-5191 .. **Kosmerl**, John K '88 -7817 Cntyline Rd -Arcade 14009
(716) 845-2660 .. **Kosmerl**, Mary T '80 %Supreme Ct -50 Delaware Av -Buffalo 14202
(212) 294-6700 .. **Kosmidis**, John '07 %Winston & S -200 Park Av -NY 10166
(718) 746-9777 .. **Kosnik**, George A '94 -12-55 150th -Whitestone 11357 **Fx**:746-9778
(212) 326-3939 .. **Kosnik**, Richd M '83 (Jones D) -222 E 41st -NY 10017
(585) 223-5730 .. **Kosoff-Roth**, Karen L '85 -Bx455 -Fairprt 14450 **Fx**:223-5962
(845) 359-5803 .. **Kosofsky**, Jos '51 -22 Lbrty Rd -Tappan 10983 **Fx**:359-2847
(800) 323-3266 .. **Kosofsky**, Mark '89 -1600 Harrison Av -Mamaroneck 10543
(212) 848-4000 .. **Kosonen**, Amanda R '05 %Shearman & S LLP -599 Lex Av -NY 10022
(718) 855-0660 .. **Kosover**, Irwin S '58 -32 Court -Brklyn 11201
(212) 682-0020 .. **Kosovych**, Adriana S '09 %Putney TH&H LLP -521 5th Av -NY 10175
(212) 751-3001 .. **Kosovych**, Bohdan S '82 SrCnsl Thompson & K LLP -919 3rd Av -NY 10022
(212) 331-5052 .. **Kosowitz**, Susan M '92 %HRA -180 Water -NY 10038
(212) 504-6000 .. **Kosowsky**, Amanda L '00 SpclCnsl Cadwalader W&T LLP -1 World Fncl Ctr -NY 10281
(914) 225-5552 .. **Kosowsky**, Danl E '97 Morgan Stanley -2000 Wstchstr Av -Purchase 10577
(212) 796-8914 .. **Koss**, Allen V '00 (Koss & S,LLP) -500 5th Av -NY 10110 **Fx**:(801) 650-8733
(212) 578-5912 .. **Koss**, Barri N '02 %MetLife -27-01 Qns Plz N -LIC 11101
(585) 637-3961 .. **Koss**, Larry R '74 -58 Market -Brockprt 14420 **Fx**:637-4298
(718) 250-2000 .. **Koss**, Taylor A '01 %DA -350 Jay -Brklyn 11201 **Fx**:250-2314
(845) 343-5111 .. **Kossar**, Ronald S '74 -402 E Main Bx548 -Middletwn 10940 **Fx**:343-5222
(845) 561-0550 .. **Kossar**, Stuart L '08 %Drake LHKGG&R PLLC -555 Hudson Valley Av -New Windsor 12553
(718) 956-4211 .. **Kossaris**, Emmanuel '97 -28-03 43rd -Astoria 11103 **Fx**:626-6553
(718) 206-4684 .. **Kossegi**, Terrence T '99 %Law Dept -89-17 Sutphin Blvd -Jamaica 11435 **Fx**:206-4702
(631) 439-1723 .. **Kossin**, Nan Shapiro '86 %MHLS -320 Carleton Av -Central Islip 11722 **Fx**:273-9365
(845) 426-6503 .. **Kossin**, Warren P '69 -300 Airport Exec Pk -Nanuet 10954 **Fx**:426-6584
(212) 267-6364 .. **Kossoff**, Mitchell H '79 (Kossoff & U) -217 Bway -NY 10007
(212) 267-6364 .. **Kossoff & Unger** -217 Bway -NY 10007 **Fx**:385-2558
(516) 294-8844 .. **Kossove**, Scott E '98 (L'Abbate BC&C,LLP) -1001 Franklin Av -Gdn Cty 11530
(845) 255-4655 .. **Kossover**, Andrew '79 -40 Main Bx399 -New Paltz 12561 **Fx**:255-4657
(845) 255-4655 .. **Kossover**, Victoria '80 -40 Main Bx399 -New Paltz 12561 **Fx**:255-4657
(585) 232-5300 .. **Kossow**, Mark R '97 (Boylan BCV&W,LLP) -2400 Chase Sq -Rchstr 14604
(212) 972-1000 .. **Kost**, Gillian H '06 %London F LLP -59 Maiden Ln -NY 10038
(212) 763-6800 .. **Kost**, John G '87 Cnsl Vandenberg & F,LLP -60 E 42nd -NY 10165
(212) 431-2157 .. **Kostant**, Peter C '79 %NY Law Schl -185 W Bway -NY 10013 **Fx**:431-1804
(212) 808-8100 .. **Kostelanetz & Fink, LLP** -7 Wrld Trd Ctr -NY 10007 **Fx**:808-8108
(718) 248-7801 .. **Koster**, Anelys Garcia '03 Citigroup -1 Court Sq -LIC 11120
(212) 938-5000 .. **Koster**, Caroline Aiken '93 Cantor Fitzgerald -110 E 59th -NY 10022
(212) 788-7295 .. **Koster**, Craig R '01 %Law Dept -100 Church -NY 10007 **Fx**:788-0367
(914) 285-9800 .. **Koster**, Eric D '75 (Kurzman EC&L,LLP) -1 N Bway -White Plns 10601
(212) 259-8000 .. **Koster**, Evan M '08 (Dewey & L LLP) -1301 Av of Amer -NY 10019
(212) 651-2013 .. **Koster**, Katherine E '93 %Oxygen Media LLC -75 9th Av -NY 10011
(212) 269-5500 .. **Koster**, Matthew J '06 %Gordon & R LLP -90 Broad -NY 10004
(516) 227-2260 .. **Koster**, Warren S '76 (Callan KB&B LLP) -333 Earle Ovngton Blvd -Uniondale 11553
(212) 248-8800 .. **Koster**, Warren S '76 (Callan KB&B LLP) -1 Whitehall -NY 10004
(914) 395-0055 .. **Kosterich**, Jeffrey '83 (Kosterich & Assoc) -68 Main -Tuckahoe 10707 **Fx**:395-0230
(212) 541-2000 .. **Kostman**, David B '93 Cnsl Bryan C LLP -1290 Av of Amer -NY 10104
(212) 554-7800 .. **Kostopoulos**, Mary '08 %Moses & S LLP -405 Lex Av -NY 10174
(516) 829-4488 .. **Kostrinsky**, Albert '65 -150 Grt Nck Rd -Gt Neck 11021 **Fx**:829-3914
(212) 373-3000 .. **Kostrzewa**, Benjamin O '08 %Paul WRW&G LLP -1285 Av of Amer -NY 10019
(212) 909-6000 .. **Kostrzewa**, Elizabeth A '10 %Debevoise & P LLP -919 3rd Av -NY 10022
(212) 254-2677 .. **Kostyn**, Kevin F '85 -647 E 9th -NY 10009 **Fx**:677-7928
(516) 599-1840 .. **Kostyrka**, Jeanette P '57 -57 Earle Av -Lynbrk 11563
(914) 835-1882 .. **Koszkul**, Christine L '93 -240 Halstead Av -Harrison 10528 **Fx**:835-6028
(212) 609-6800 .. **Kot**, Julie A '08 %McCarter & E,LLP -245 Park Av -NY 10167
(585) 232-1760 .. **Kotary**, Christopher '73 %Mark IV Construction -301 Exchange Blvd -Rchstr 14608
(914) 499-4876 .. **Kotary**, Jessica L '00 IBM -1 New Orchrd Rd -Armonk 10504
(716) 847-8400 .. **Kotaska**, Gary F '75 (Phillips L LLP) -3400 HSBC Ctr -Buffalo 14203
(607) 772-8440 .. **Kotchick**, John L III '87 %R Perot -20-24 Wall -Bnghmtn 13901 **Fx**:772-8339
(212) 964-6611 .. **Kotec**, Victor '03 %Lester SK&D -120 Bway -NY 10271
(914) 684-0090 .. **Koteen**, Barbara S '96 %Diserio MO&C LLP -50 Main -White Plns 10606
(212) 768-6700 .. **Kotel**, Ira L '90 (Sonnenschein N&R LLP) -2 World Fncl Ctr -NY 10281
(914) 965-1997 .. **Kotelez**, Richd M '67 -12 Lake Av -Ynkrs 10703 **Fx**:963-8489
(212) 980-4500 .. **Kothari**, Raunak Paresh '05 -885 3rd Av -NY 10022 **Fx**:980-3448
(212) 308-4440 .. **Kothari**, Rupal H '03 %Ferrante,PLLC -5 W 19th -NY 10011 **Fx**:888-3839
(212) 836-8000 .. **Kothari**, Shefali M '04 %Kaye S LLP -425 Park Av -NY 10022
(212) 698-3500 .. **Kothari**, Sonia K '08 %Dechert LLP -1095 Av of Amer -NY 10036
(212) 535-6403 .. **Kotick**, Joel M '83 -501 E 79th -NY 10075
(212) 949-5800 .. **Kotik**, Lawr H '85 (Brady K&W,LLP) -501 5th Av -NY 10017
(845) 791-6141 .. **Kotin**, Sandra M '87 -541 Bway Bx550 -Monticello 12701 **Fx**:791-6141
(212) 696-6000 .. **Kotite**, Edw A '79 (Curtis M-PC&M LLP) -101 Park Av -NY 10178

(718) 780-7994 .. **Kotkin,** Minna J '76 %Bklyn Law Schl -250 Joralemon -Brklyn 11201 **Fx:**780-0393
(631) 425-0451 .. **Kotler,** Herbert '61 -7 E Carver -Huntngtn 11743
(212) 792-8484 .. **Kotler,** Jonathan A '09 %Stern T&B LLP -380 Lex Av -NY 10168
(212) 225-2000 .. **Kotler,** Meredith E '97 (Cleary GS&H) -1 Lbrty Plz -NY 10006
(212) 832-0400 .. **Kotler,** Stuart B '83 Berdon LLP -360 Mad Av -NY 10017
(212) 655-4000 .. **Kotlyarsky,** Jennifer '02 %M Gershweir -120 Bway -NY 10271 **Fx:**655-5039
(212) 972-5430 .. **Kotner,** Jill R '00 %Rosin SM -801 2nd Av -NY 10017
(212) 546-9302 .. **Kotokawa,** Rie '00 -445 Park Av -NY 10022
(212) 416-6141 .. **Koton,** Steven Z '81 %Dept of Law -120 Bway -NY 10271 **Fx:**416-6147
(212) 558-4000 .. **Kotran,** Stephen M '93 (Sullivan & C LLP) -125 Broad -NY 10004
(212) 973-8000 .. **Kotsinis,** Carol Notias '03 %Schnader HS&L LLP -140 Bway -NY 10005
(212) 355-6527 .. **Kotsopoulos,** Alexia '03 -900 3rd Av -NY 10022
(212) 609-6800 .. **Kott,** David R '84 (McCarter & E,LLP) -245 Park Av -NY 10167
(212) 761-3140 .. **Kott,** Geoffrey D '03 Morgan Stanley -1585 Bway -NY 10036
(516) 683-5633 .. **Kottler,** Ellen D '90 IRS -107 Charles Lindergh Blvd -Gdn Cty 11530 **Fx:**683-5653
(607) 746-8730 .. **Kottmeier,** Gregory L '97 -145 Main Bx125 -Delhi 13753 **Fx:**746-6767
(516) 357-3000 .. **Kotula,** Michl A '95 (Rivkin R LLP) -926 RXR Plz -Uniondale 11556
(212) 894-8519 .. **Kotulski,** Absalom S '06 Wolters Kluwer -111 8th Av -NY 10011
(212) 880-6000 .. **Kotwal,** Dean '07 %Torys LLP -237 Park Av -NY 10017
(585) 238-8300 .. **Kotwas,** Paul T '94 Workers Comp Bd -130 W Main -Rchstr 14614
(212) 574-1200 .. **Kotwick,** Mark D '90 (Seward & K LLP) -1 Bttry Pk Plz -NY 10004
(718) 291-3400 .. **Kotzamanis,** Dimitri '90 %Shaevitz & S -148-55 Hillside Av -Jamaica 11435 **Fx:**739-5654
(212) 648-1451 .. **Kotzen,** Jennifer Wallis '95 JP Morgan Chase -383 Mad Av -NY 10179
(516) 921-8600 .. **Koubek,** Robt A '02 %McAndrew C&P -95 Froehlich Farm Blvd -Woodbury 11797
(718) 590-2000 .. **Koubek-Fonseca,** Donna J '00 %DA -198 E 161st -Bronx 10451 **Fx:**590-6477
(212) 490-9100 .. **Koueiter,** Michl G '06 %Condon & F LLP -7 Times Sq -NY 10036
(631) 324-1818 .. **Kouffman,** Robt H '83 -300 Pantigo Pl -E Hampton 11937 **Fx:**324-7923
(212) 335-9000 .. **Kougasian,** Peter M '80 %DA -1 Hogan Pl -NY 10013
(347) 267-5367 .. **Kougentakis,** Anna G '02 Beys Genl Construction Corp -2520 Coney Isl Av -Brklyn 11223
(212) 608-3015 .. **Koukoulas,** Demetra '95 %R Roth -233 Bway -NY 10279 **Fx:**608-2177
(718) 299-7555 .. **Koulikourdis,** Peter J '92 (Koulikourdis & Assoc) -217 E Tremont Av -Bronx 10457 **Fx:**(201) 489-3575
(718) 590-3927 .. **Koulish,** Steven M '74 %Law Dept -198 E 161st -Bronx 10451 **Fx:**590-2686
(212) 880-6000 .. **Koumanakos,** James S '09 %Torys LLP -237 Park Av -NY 10017
(212) 809-7800 .. **Koumourdas,** Paul '92 (Jaffe & K,LLP) -40 Wall -NY 10005
(631) 501-5700 .. **Kountotsis,** Theodosios '09 %Carter DF&S LLP -445 Broadhallow Rd -Melvll 11747
(212) 310-8000 .. **Kourabas,** Michl N '09 %Weil G&M LLP -767 5th Av -NY 10153
(914) 395-0871 .. **Kourakos,** Hippocrates P '63 (Kourakos & K) -271 Main -Eastchstr 10709 **Fx:**395-0415
(914) 395-0871 .. **Kourakos,** John G '93 (Kourakos & K) -271 Main -Eastchstr 10709 **Fx:**395-0415
(518) 374-1200 .. **Kouray,** Steven X '76 (Kouray & K) -525 State -Schnctdy 12305 **Fx:**374-7414
(631) 427-5455 .. **Kourbage,** Allison M '02 -1 Schwab Rd -Melvll 11747
(212) 770-6490 .. **Kourides,** P Nicholas '73 AIG -70 Pine -NY 10270
(631) 845-1900 .. **Kouril,** Cynthia A '87 (RL Folks & Assoc,LLP) -510 Broadhllw Rd -Melvll 11747 **Fx:**845-8779
(212) 223-1100 .. **Kourland,** Nancy L '89 %Rosen & Assoc,PC -747 3rd Av -NY 10017 **Fx:**223-1102
(585) 232-8314 .. **Kourofsky,** Kevin P '86 (Buckner & K) -1 S Wshngtn -Rchstr 14614
(718) 281-4000 .. **Kouroupas,** John K '04 %Papa D&B -42-40 Bell Blvd -Bayside 11361 **Fx:**281-4030
(212) 350-2700 .. **Koury,** Marlene '06 %Constantine C,PC -450 Lex Av -NY 10017
(212) 895-6725 .. **Koury,** Paul J '95 Commerz Bnk AG -2 World Fncl Ctr -NY 10281
(212) 474-1000 .. **Kousoula,** Aikaterini '09 %Cravath S&M LLP -825 8th Av -NY 10019
(212) 509-2566 .. **Kousoulas,** Antonia C '90 (Kousoulas & Assoc) -48 Wall -NY 10005
(718) 575-5450 .. **Kousouros,** Debra K '86 -80-02 Kew Grdns Rd -Kew Gdns 11415 **Fx:**793-0165
(212) 532-1934 .. **Kousouros,** James '86 -260 Mad Av -NY 10016 **Fx:**532-1939
(212) 879-2223 .. **Koutsos,** John C '77 -415 E 85th -NY 10028
(917) 551-1300 .. **Koutsoudakis,** Andreas '09 %Koehler & I LLP -61 Bway -NY 10006
(585) 464-9400 .. **Kouwe,** Robt E '82 %Wilmorite -1265 Scottsvll Rd -Rchstr 14624 **Fx:**328-1784
(212) 509-9400 .. **Kouyoumdjian,** Philip Y '97 (Cozen O) -45 Bway Atrium -NY 10006
(212) 921-5525 .. **Kouzi,** Jennifer '02 (Kaminer K&B LLP) -369 Lex Av -NY 10017 **Fx:**(646) 269-7669
(212) 922-1226 .. **Kovac,** Elisabeth M '01 -90 Park Av -NY 10016 **Fx:**(646) 478-9690
(212) 308-4411 .. **Kovacs,** David L '80 (Edwards AP&D LLP) -750 Lex Av -NY 10022
(212) 310-8000 .. **Kovacs,** Eva '09 %Weil G&M LLP -767 5th Av -NY 10153
(845) 638-5001 .. **Kovacs,** Janine M '07 %DA -1 S Main -New Cty 10956 **Fx:**638-5070
(845) 331-4100 .. **Kovacs,** Jason J '04 %Rusk WH&M,LLP -255 Fair Bx3356 -Kingston 12402
(845) 331-1899 .. **Kovacs,** Leanora A '90 Surrogate Ct -240 Fair -Kingston 12401
(212) 556-2100 .. **Kovacs,** Valerie S '03 (King & S) -1185 Av of Amer -NY 10036
(516) 485-3800 .. **Koval,** Mitchell B '92 %Zemsky & S,PC -95 Front -Hempstd 11550 **Fx:**485-3280
(212) 367-2669 .. **Koval,** Nikki '99 Forbes -60 5th Av -NY 10011
(212) 836-8000 .. **Koval,** Stephen C '85 (Kaye S LLP) -425 Park Av -NY 10022
(607) 656-2394 .. **Koval,** Timothy J '84 Raymond Corp -20 S Canal Bx130 -Greene 13778 **Fx:**656-2466
(212) 735-3000 .. **Kovalski,** Ron '07 %Skadden ASM&F LLP -4 Times Sq -NY 10036
(212) 656-2631 .. **Kovar,** Elyse Dranoff '89 NYSE Regulation,Inc-Div of Enforcement -14 Wall -NY 10005 **Fx:**656-2622
(212) 751-9442 .. **Kovarcik,** Thos J '86 -590 Mad Av -NY 10022 **Fx:**751-9443
(212) 618-1225 .. **Kovarik,** Jaromir '04 (KTHL Law Ofcs,PC) -14 Wall -NY 10005 **Fx:**618-1226
(212) 371-6600 .. **Kovel,** David E '03 (Kirby M LLP) -825 3rd Av -NY 10022
(516) 208-7733 .. **Kovel,** Rod E '87 -2116 Merrick Av -Merrick 11566 **Fx:**208-7732
(212) 736-7432 .. **Koven & Krausz** -350 5th Av -NY 10118 **Fx:**967-2755
(212) 736-7432 .. **Koven,** Murray T '38 (Koven & K) -350 5th Av -NY 10118
(212) 977-5597 .. **Koven,** Sophia Coquillette '06 HR&A Advisors,Inc -99 Hudson -NY 10013 **Fx:**977-6202
(212) 407-7700 .. **Kover,** Ezra W '09 %Vedder P,PC -1633 Bway -NY 10019
(516) 489-5000 .. **Kovit,** Chas S '84 %Town Atty -Town Hall -Hempstd 11550 **Fx:**489-5150
(516) 775-3300 .. **Kovit,** Meryl '85 -248-52 Jericho Tpk -Floral Pk 11001 **Fx:**775-3320
(212) 836-8000 .. **Kovner,** Nicholas A '05 %Kaye S LLP -425 Park Av -NY 10022
(212) 953-2381 .. **Kovner,** Paul '78 (Rubin F&F,LLP) -292 Mad Av -NY 10017
(212) 637-2470 .. **Kovner,** Rachel P '09 US Atty -1 St Andrews Plz -NY 10007
(212) 489-8230 .. **Kovner,** Victor A '62 (Davis WT LLP) -1633 Bway -NY 10019
(646) 855-0831 .. **Kowal,** Darryl H '02 Bank of America Securities LLC -1 Bryant Pk -NY 10036
(914) 251-1618 .. **Kowal,** Dorothy A '92 %Price MS&D,PC -106 Corp Park Dr -White Plns 10604
(212) 921-9099 .. **Kowal,** Michl J '05 %Caithness Corp -565 5th Av -NY 10017
(212) 227-3900 .. **Kowalchyn,** Nicholas Wm '84 %F Lewis -7 Dey -NY 10007 **Fx:**406-9571
(212) 559-2459 .. **Kowalcyk,** Edw J '80 %Citibank -399 Park Av -NY 10022
(716) 854-2620 .. **Kowalczuk,** Renata '98 (Brown & K,LLP) -1500 Lbrty Bldg -Buffalo 14202
(315) 724-3164 .. **Kowalczyk,** Andrew S Jr. '62 (Kowalczyk TD&H,LLP) -185 Genesee -Utica 13501
(315) 724-3164 .. **Kowalczyk,** Andrew S III '83 (Kowalczyk TD&H,LLP) -185 Genesee -Utica 13501
(315) 724-3164 .. **Kowalczyk,** Bradley M '89 OfCnsl Kowalczyk TD&H,LLP -185 Genesee -Utica 13501
(718) 590-2000 .. **Kowalczyk,** Gina T '07 %DA -198 E 161st -Bronx 10451 **Fx:**590-6477
(518) 474-7330 .. **Kowalczyk,** Jos M Jr. '89 %Dept of Law -The Cptl -Albany 12224
(212) 506-1700 .. **Kowalczyk,** Noelle M '95 (Kasowitz BT&F LLP) -1633 Bway -NY 10019
(585) 786-8256 .. **Kowalczyk,** Teresa '80 -30 Park -Warsaw 14569 **Fx:**786-8256
(315) 724-3164 .. **Kowalczyk Tolles Deery & Hilton, LLP** -185 Genesee -Utica 13501 **Fx:**724-3212
(518) 443-5400 .. **Kowalczyk,** Wendy L '89 %SUNY Univ Cnsl -S333 SUNY Plz -Albany 12246 **Fx:**443-5409
(631) 736-0500 .. **Kowalenko,** Wm Alan '00 %Sallah Law Firm PC -110 Wshngtn Av -Holtsvll 11742 **Fx:**736-0179
(518) 383-0200 .. **Kowalewski,** Edw Jr. '91 (Fox & K,LLP) -4 Old Route 146 Bx958 -Clifton Pk 12065
(716) 824-6481 .. **Kowalski,** Anthony S '65 -70 Spann -Buffalo 14206
(631) 582-4990 .. **Kowalski,** Edw S '78 (LaCapra S&K,LLP) -320 Carleton Av -Central Islip 11722 **Fx:**582-4690
(212) 859-8000 .. **Kowalski,** Elliot H '09 %Fried FHS&J LLP -1 NY Plz -NY 10004
(212) 455-2000 .. **Kowalski,** Francis X '07 %Simpson T&B LLP -425 Lex Av -NY 10017
(516) 937-1010 .. **Kowalski,** Jan E '96 %F Laine,PC -449 S Oyster Bay Rd -Plainvw 11803
(212) 578-2211 .. **Kowalski,** Juliane '96 %MetLife -27-01 Qns Plz N -LIC 11101
(212) 556-2100 .. **Kowalski,** Karen R '02 %King & S -1185 Av of Amer -NY 10036
(718) 250-1100 .. **Kowalski,** Leon R '98 %E Garfinkel -12 Metrotech Ctr -Brklyn 11201 **Fx:**250-1168
(716) 551-4931 .. **Kowalski,** Linda M '00 %NLRB -130 S Elmwood Av -Buffalo 14202 **Fx:**551-4972
(212) 588-0800 .. **Kowalski,** Thos J '87 (Frommer L&H LLP) -745 5th Av -NY 10151
(518) 828-9985 .. **Koweek Cranna & McEvoy,PC** -445 Warren -Hudson 12534 **Fx:**828-2362
(518) 828-9985 .. **Koweek,** Richd M '79 (Koweek C&M,PC) -445 Warren -Hudson 12534
(518) 474-9778 .. **Koweek,** Toni Greenberg '83 %OCFS -52 Wshngtn -Rensselaer 12144 **Fx:**486-6378
(212) 384-1000 .. **Kowel,** Eugene S '02 %FBI -26 Fed Plz -NY 10278
(212) 867-4100 .. **Kowlowitz,** Andrew S '03 %Furman K&B LLP -61 Bway -NY 10006
(212) 557-4190 .. **Kownacki,** David P '76 (D Kownacki,PC) -420 Lex Av -NY 10170 **Fx:**557-4188
(631) 329-2828 .. **Kowtna,** Erin B '07 %Egan & G,LLP -393 Montauk Hwy Bx338 -Wainscott 11975 **Fx:**324-2472
(718) 830-0595 .. **Koya,** Mansukhlal A '74 -102-58 62nd Dr -Frst Hlls 11375
(212) 343-0222 .. **Koyama,** Kelly R '02 Marc Jacobs Intl LLC -72 Spring -NY 10012
(212) 597-1400 .. **Koyfman,** Isaac '97 WestLB AG -1211 Av of Amer -NY 10036
(718) 236-3000 .. **Koyonda,** Samson O '04 Catholic Migration Ofc -1258 65th -Brklyn 11219
(212) 704-6000 .. **Koza,** Arielle I '09 %Troutman S LLP -405 Lex Av -NY 10174
(646) 386-4800 .. **Kozac,** Karen '79 Comm Judicial Cndct -61 Bway -NY 10006 **Fx:**458-0037
(212) 238-4800 .. **Kozak,** Christopher S '97 (Landman CB&F,PC) -120 Bway -NY 10271
(718) 734-9333 .. **Kozak,** Felix '96 -1209 Av Z -Brklyn 11235
(914) 328-0404 .. **Kozak,** Jonathan M '98 (Jackson L LLP) -1 N Bway -White Plns 10601
(212) 264-6373 .. **Kozak,** Maryalice '91 %HHS -26 Fed Plz -NY 10278 **Fx:**264-6364
(646) 313-6114 .. **Kozak,** Thos '03 IPSOS -1700 Bway -NY 10019
(516) 520-1263 .. **Kozak,** Timothy '00 -64 Divison Av -Levittwn 11756
(212) 684-3933 .. **Kozak,** Zachary A '07 %Hantman & Assoc -1515 Bway -NY 10036 **Fx:**520-4301
(212) 210-9440 .. **Kozar,** Jennifer S '06 %Alston & B LLP -90 Park Av -NY 10016
(914) 683-3512 .. **Kozek,** Neil E '95 (Kramer K,LLP) -445 Hmltn Av -White Plns 10601
(518) 436-0751 .. **Kozemko,** Deborah A '82 (Hinman S PC) -121 State -Albany 12207
(212) 682-2280 .. **Kozhich,** Valeria '07 %Holm & O LLP -3 W 35th -NY 10001
(914) 969-1900 .. **Kozicky & Cichowlas,PLLC** -125 Corp Blvd -Ynkrs 10701 **Fx:**969-2425
(914) 969-1900 .. **Kozicky,** Roman G '84 (Kozicky & C,PLLC) -125 Corp Blvd -Ynkrs 10701
(212) 272-2000 .. **Kozinn,** Benjamin E '02 %JP Morgan Chase -383 Mad Av -NY 10179

(212) 227-8343 .. **Kozinn,** Paul '57 Kozinn & K -225 Bway -NY 10007 **Fx:**962-1662
(315) 735-2271 .. **Koziol,** Leon R '86 -1518 Genesee -Utica 13502 **Fx:**735-0991
(212) 214-5107 .. **Kozlark,** Thos H '82 Wachovia Corp -375 Park Av -NY 10152
(646) 502-7001 .. **Kozlenko,** Yakov '08 SpclCnsl JSBarkats PLLC -100 Church -NY 10007 **Fx:**607-5544
(212) 521-5400 .. **Kozlov,** Herbert F '78 (Reed S LLP) -599 Lex Av -NY 10022
(212) 636-6000 .. **Kozlova,** Yelena '10 Fordham Univ Sch of Law -140 W 62nd -NY 10023 **Fx:**636-6899
(716) 842-5488 .. **Kozlowski,** Andrea Ruta '02 M&T Bank -One M&T Plz -Buffalo 14203
(212) 484-3900 .. **Kozlowski,** David J '07 %Arent F LLP -1675 Bway -NY 10019
(212) 859-8000 .. **Kozlowski,** Elizabeth P '09 %Fried FHS&J LLP -1 NY Plz -NY 10004
(212) 830-4364 .. **Kozlowski,** Gregory J '01 Air France -125 W 55th -NY 10019
(212) 660-3000 .. **Kozlowski,** Karen M '02 (Sullivan & W LLP) -1290 Av of Amer -NY 10104
(716) 332-0990 .. **Kozlowski,** Kristin G '01 Childrens Leg Ctr -438 Main -Buffalo 14202 **Fx:**332-0997
(716) 634-1704 .. **Kozlowski,** Nanette M '89 -51 Sudbury Ln -Williamsvll 14221
(212) 325-2000 .. **Kozlowski,** Peter J '97 Credit Suisse -1 Mad Av -NY 10010
(212) 867-9876 .. **Kozlowski,** Sandra L '04 %Heidrick & Struggles -1114 Av of Amer -NY 10036
(212) 685-2422 .. **Kozminsky,** Ellen C '77 -333 7th Av -NY 10001 **Fx:**863-4141
(607) 723-3551 .. **Kozol,** George B '77 Security Mtl Life -Bx1625 -Bnghmtn 13902 **Fx:**772-2114
(212) 436-1503 .. **Kozoulina,** Anna '01 %IRS-Chief Cnsl Ofc -290 Bway -NY 10007 **Fx:**436-1430
(914) 277-2823 .. **Kozupsky,** Allen J '61 (Kozupsky & K) -672 C Heritage Hills -Somers 10589
(914) 277-2823 .. **Kozupsky,** Deborah L '88 (Kozupsky & K) -672 C Heritage Hills -Somers 10589
(212) 267-9020 .. **Kozupsky,** Harold D '53 OfCnsl Shapiro B&A LLP -225 Bway -NY 10007
(212) 907-9700 .. **Kozupsky,** Roy P '86 (Smith G&R,LLP) -250 Park Av -NY 10177
(212) 728-8000 .. **Kozusko,** Dan C '04 %Willkie F&G LLP -787 7th Av -NY 10019
(212) 574-1200 .. **Kozyra,** Arthur '01 %Seward & K LLP -1 Bttry Pk Plz -NY 10004
(212) 768-2100 .. **Kraditor & Haber,PC** -75 9th Av -NY 10011 **Fx:**768-2450
(212) 687-4185 .. **Kraebel,** Barbara '68 -60 E 42nd -NY 10165
(315) 348-5326 .. **Kraeger,** Susan J '86 -Bx181 -Brantingham 13312 **Fx:**348-5326
(718) 359-1328 .. **Kraemer,** Alan J '77 -14-54 Cllg Pnt Blvd Bx560121 -Cllg Pnt 11356 **Fx:**359-7355
(516) 334-2320 .. **Kraemer,** Dwight D '70 (Kraemer & M) -342 Post Av -Westbury 11590
(516) 465-8090 .. **Kraemer,** Laurence A '82 %North Shore-LIJ Hlth Systm -145 Community Dr -Gt Neck 11021 **Fx:**465-8013
(212) 455-2000 .. **Kraemer,** Lillian E '65 OfCnsl Simpson T&B LLP -425 Lex Av -NY 10017
(516) 334-2320 .. **Kraemer & Mulligan** -342 Post Av -Westbury 11590 **Fx:**338-6745
(716) 855-1111 .. **Kraengel,** Elizabeth A '08 %Duke HP&G LLP -350 Main -Buffalo 14202
(845) 331-5111 .. **Kraft,** Christopher R '89 (Dall Vechia &K LLP) -115 Green -Kingston 12401
(212) 558-5500 .. **Kraft,** Danny R Jr. '03 Weitz & L,PC -700 Bway -NY 10003
(516) 795-6099 .. **Kraft,** John M '77 -567 Bway -Massapequa 11758 **Fx:**795-6083
(212) 556-7491 .. **Kraft,** Marcijane '76 %The NY Times Co -620 8th Av -NY 10018 **Fx:**556-4634
(212) 986-4700 .. **Kraft,** Michl '70 %Kraft & K,Inc -360 Lex Av -NY 10017 **Fx:**986-4730
(845) 735-8651 .. **Kraft,** Paul '91 -6 Imperial Ln -Chestnut Rdg 10977 **Fx:**735-4601
(212) 416-8632 .. **Kraft,** Robt L '85 %Dept of Law -120 Bway -NY 10271
(516) 466-9789 .. **Kraft,** Ruth Bogatyrow '80 -4 Melbourne Rd -Gt Neck 11021 **Fx:**829-2780
(845) 692-8700 .. **Kraham,** Bonnie '96 %Ettinger,PC -75 Crystal Run Rd -Middletwn 10941 **Fx:**692-8708
(203) 570-5754 .. **Krahel,** Wioletta '05 Morgan Stanley -2000 Wstchstr Av -Purchase 10577
(845) 291-2577 .. **Krahulik,** Christine M '91 Family Ct -285 Main -Goshen 10924 **Fx:**291-4520
(845) 986-1156 .. **Krahulik,** Emil R '59 (Bonacic KCM&B,LLP) -2 Bank Bx391 -Warwick 10990
(845) 986-1156 .. **Krahulik,** Robt E '91 (Bonacic KCM&B,LLP) -2 Bank Bx391 -Warwick 10990
(845) 703-3101 .. **Krahulik,** Robt E '91 (Bonacic KCM&B,LLP) -90 Crystal Run Rd -Middletwn 10941
(212) 610-6300 .. **Kraidin,** Lisa J '01 SrCnsl Allen & O -1221 Av of Amer -NY 10020
(212) 841-1000 .. **Kraiem,** Ruben '82 (Covington & B LLP) -620 8th Av -NY 10018
(518) 884-0200 .. **Kraigenow,** John W '03 Donnellan & K,PLLC -20 Prospect -Ballston Spa 12020 **Fx:**884-0343
(212) 318-3000 .. **Kraines,** Merrill M '80 (Fulbright & J LLP) -666 5th Av -NY 10103
(212) 702-5400 .. **Krainin,** Danl M '03 (Beveridge & D,PC) -477 Mad Av -NY 10022
(212) 750-9720 .. **Krainin,** Harold L '53 Krainin & M -880 3rd Av -NY 10022 **Fx:**750-9721
(212) 484-3900 .. **Krainin,** Richd J '87 (Arent F LLP) -1675 Bway -NY 10019
(212) 265-6888 .. **Krais,** Wm A '91 (Porzio B&N,PC) -156 W 56th -NY 10019
(845) 565-4464 .. **Kraiza,** Michl A '86 -67 S Plnk Rd -Newburgh 12550 **Fx:**561-9832
(212) 258-4381 .. **Krajci,** Jos R '76 %Siemens Corp -153 E 53rd -NY 10022 **Fx:**767-0580
(212) 479-6000 .. **Krajeck,** Katie M '08 %Cooley LLP -1114 Av of Amer -NY 10036
(716) 681-3355 .. **Krajewski,** Jeffrey S '89 -2956 Union Rd -Cheektowaga 14227 **Fx:**685-9844
(716) 854-2620 .. **Krajewski,** Kenneth A '92 (Brown & K,LLP) -1500 Lbrty Bldg -Buffalo 14202
(212) 269-5141 .. **Krakauer,** Ronald '76 -29 Bath -Lido Bch 11561 **Fx:**269-2339
(212) 735-3000 .. **Krakaur,** Keith D '86 (Skadden ASM&F LLP) -4 Times Sq -NY 10036
(212) 940-8800 .. **Kraker,** Theresa A '05 %Katten MR LLP -575 Mad Av -NY 10022
(516) 572-2381 .. **Kraker,** Walter J '79 %Dist Ct -99 Main -Hempstd 11550 **Fx:**572-2507
(212) 361-1597 .. **Krakow,** Joshua '87 %Envrnmntl Cntrl Bd -66 John -NY 10038
(516) 354-3300 .. **Krakow,** Robt J '80 -1205 Franklin Av -Gdn Cty 11530 **Fx:**(646) 349-1771
(845) 215-9430 .. **Krakower & Goldman** -55 Old Tpk Rd -Nanuet 10954 **Fx:**624-0288
(212) 268-3222 .. **Krakower,** Jason S '04 %Raphaelson & L,PC -14 Penn Plz -NY 10122 **Fx:**268-3313
(845) 215-9430 .. **Krakower,** Michl J '68 (Krakower & G) -55 Old Tpk Rd -Nanuet 10954
(845) 462-4336 .. **Krakower,** Stephan L '94 -646 South Rd -Poughkeepsie 12601 **Fx:**462-7078
(845) 510-2202 .. **Krakower,** Todd J '94 (Glass K LLP) -169 S Main -New Cty 10956 **Fx:**510-2219
(718) 875-1300 .. **Krakowski,** Melissa J '01 %Appllt Div 2nd Dept -45 Monroe Pl -Brklyn 11201 **Fx:**858-2446
(212) 833-1154 .. **Krakowsky,** Jennifer P '07 Friedman KS&A LLP -1633 Bway -NY 10019 **Fx:**373-7954
(212) 557-7200 .. **Krakowsky,** Joshua S '02 %Davidoff M&H,LLP -605 3rd Av -NY 10158
(516) 742-3470 .. **Kral Clerkin Redmond Ryan Perry & Girvan,LLP** -538 Broadhllw Rd -Melvll 11747 **Fx:**742-6243
(212) 406-9710 .. **Kral Clerkin Redmond Ryan Perry & Girvan,LLP** -170 Bway -NY 10038 **Fx:**571-0874
(516) 393-2200 .. **Kraljic,** John P '88 %Garfunkel W,PC -111 Grt Nck Rd -Gt Neck 11021
(516) 746-5599 .. **Krall,** Michl '03 %Bee RFH&D,LLP -170 Old Cntry Rd -Mineola 11501
(845) 426-3790 .. **Kram,** Marc Palmer '93 CCH -42 Melnick Dr -Monsey 10952 **Fx:**426-6275
(315) 478-9290 .. **Kram,** Richd C '75 -447 E Wshngtn -Syracuse 13202 **Fx:**478-4352
(212) 943-9000 .. **Kramarsky,** Stephen M '94 (Dewey P&K LLP) -220 E 42nd -NY 10017
(914) 948-1957 .. **Kramen-Martell,** Holly K '97 %RF Kelly -99 Court -White Plns 10601 **Fx:**948-7848
(212) 249-9531 .. **Kramer,** Alan M '69 -880 5th Av -NY 10021 **Fx:**249-9531
(917) 488-3268 .. **Kramer,** Alan T '86 AT Kramer,PC -260 W 52nd -NY 10019 **Fx:**(212) 924-8829
(212) 233-0580 .. **Kramer,** Allen '83 -30 Vesey -NY 10007 **Fx:**(516) 569-2782
(212) 637-2478 .. **Kramer,** Amanda K '04 %US Atty -1 St Andrews Plz -NY 10007
(212) 972-1000 .. **Kramer,** Amy M '91 %London F LLP -59 Maiden Ln -NY 10038
(914) 273-4545 .. **Kramer,** Amy Schimmel '83 %MBIA Ins Corp -113 King -Armonk 10504
(212) 451-2900 .. **Kramer,** Andrew L '88 (Robinson & C LLP) -885 3rd Av -NY 10022
(212) 661-9100 .. **Kramer,** Andrew M '83 (Otterbourg SH&R,PC) -230 Park Av -NY 10169
(212) 521-5400 .. **Kramer,** Ann V '85 (Reed S LLP) -599 Lex Av -NY 10022
(212) 799-2548 .. **Kramer,** Barry P '93 Advantage Testing -241 E 86th -NY 10028 **Fx:**439-9602
(212) 344-5400 .. **Kramer,** Bennette D '88 (Schlam S&D LLP) -26 Bway -NY 10004
(212) 536-3900 .. **Kramer,** Beth R '87 (K&L Gates LLP) -599 Lex Av -NY 10022
(212) 966-6420 .. **Kramer,** Betsy '91 %Lwyrs For Children -110 Lafayette -NY 10013 **Fx:**966-0531
(718) 292-8400 .. **Kramer,** Bob A '69 -888 Grnd Cncrs -Bronx 10451 **Fx:**742-2058
(212) 571-4080 .. **Kramer,** Bruce M '73 SrCnsl Sokolski & Z,PC -305 Bway -NY 10007 **Fx:**571-4079
(718) 522-3333 .. **Kramer,** Callie M '04 Children's Law Ctr -44 Court -Brklyn 11201 **Fx:**522-7376
(212) 325-2000 .. **Kramer,** Carolyn Merin '98 Credit Suisse -11 Mad Av -NY 10010
(212) 254-5093 .. **Kramer,** Chas B '83 -200 E 10th -NY 10003 **Fx:**208-4446
(914) 612-4000 .. **Kramer,** Colleen M '06 %Cadbury -900 King -Rye Brook 10573
(212) 373-3000 .. **Kramer,** Danl J '85 (Paul WRW&G LLP) -1285 Av of Amer -NY 10019
(914) 328-0366 .. **Kramer,** David '57 -399 Knollwood Rd -White Plns 10603 **Fx:**682-9128
(516) 482-6300 .. **Kramer,** Debra '85 -98 Cutter Mill Rd -Gt Neck 11021 **Fx:**482-6317
(212) 267-4177 .. **Kramer Dillof Livingston & Moore** -217 Bway -NY 10007 **Fx:**233-8525
(212) 226-6662 .. **Kramer & Dunleavy** -350 Bway -NY 10013 **Fx:**226-8089
(212) 490-1616 .. **Kramer,** Edw C '77 -488 Mad Av -NY 10022
(516) 937-5900 .. **Kramer,** Edw I '59 OfCnsl Moomjian WW&C LLP -100 Jericho Quad -Jericho 11753
(718) 254-6372 .. **Kramer,** Elizabeth J '99 US Atty EDNY -147 Pierrepont -Brklyn 11201
(516) 227-0700 .. **Kramer,** Eric M '89 (Farrell F,PC) -1320 RXR Plz -Uniondale 11556
(212) 859-8000 .. **Kramer,** Etai I '09 %Fried FHS&J LLP -1 NY Plz -NY 10004
(516) 293-4747 .. **Kramer,** Fredk J '85 -640 Fulton -Farmngdl 11735 **Fx:**293-5204
(914) 683-3515 .. **Kramer,** Georgia '67 (Kramer K,LLP) -445 Hmltn Av -White Plns 10601
(212) 563-1710 .. **Kramer,** Glenn R '06 Schindel FLG&R LLP -14 Penn Plz -NY 10122
(212) 986-6000 .. **Kramer,** Gregory D '06 %Kleinberg KW&C,PC -551 5th Av -NY 10176
(516) 775-0300 .. **Kramer,** Gregory P '87 (Kramer & Assoc,PC) -99 Tulip Av -Floral Pk 11001 **Fx:**775-0352
(212) 227-1010 .. **Kramer,** Herbert '53 (Berger & K) -225 Bway -NY 10007
(631) 231-1450 .. **Kramer,** Herbert '78 (Feldman K&M,PC) -330 Vndrblt Motor Pkwy -Hauppauge 11788
(646) 660-8871 .. **Kramer,** Jacob J '03 University Sports Publications Co Inc -519 8th Av -NY 10018
(212) 902-1000 .. **Kramer,** Jared G '06 Goldman Sachs -1 NY Plz -NY 10004
(212) 753-5420 .. **Kramer,** Jay Douglass '68 -115 E 57th -NY 10022
(212) 384-1000 .. **Kramer,** Jay F '94 %FBI -26 Fed Plz -NY 10278
(718) 522-6788 .. **Kramer,** Jeffrey M '88 -26 Court -Brklyn 11242
(212) 848-4000 .. **Kramer,** Jessica A '06 %Shearman & S LLP -599 Lex Av -NY 10022
(516) 248-2002 .. **Kramer,** John J '02 %Gallagher WB&P -98 Willis Av -Mineola 11501
(212) 592-1400 .. **Kramer,** Jonathan A '03 %Herrick,F LLP -2 Park Av -NY 10016
(212) 425-3333 .. **Kramer,** Joyce L '81 %JCCA -120 Wall -NY 10005
(718) 522-3333 .. **Kramer,** Judith T '71 Childrens Law Ctr -44 Court -Brklyn 11201
(212) 869-8100 .. **Kramer,** Judy '89 %Pohl Law Grp,LLC -60 E 42nd -NY 10165 **Fx:**869-8270
(516) 572-2000 .. **Kramer,** Justin M '08 %DA -99 Main -Hempstd 11550 **Fx:**572-2606
(212) 751-2700 .. **Kramer,** Kenneth M '73 JAMS -620 8th Av -NY 10018 **Fx:**751-4099
(212) 310-8000 .. **Kramer,** Kevin W '10 %Weil G&M LLP -767 5th Av -NY 10153
(212) 637-3238 .. **Kramer,** Kim M '98 EPA -290 Bway -NY 10007 **Fx:**637-3096
(914) 683-3500 .. **Kramer Kozek,LLP** -445 Hmltn Av -White Plns 10601 **Fx:**428-1660

(718) 243-2100 .. **Kramer,** Lance C '85 -26 Court -Brklyn 11242
(516) 742-8897 .. **Kramer,** Larry J '90 (Kramer & P,LLP) -143 Willis Av -Mineola 11501
(914) 273-0030 .. **Kramer,** Laurence '75 -80 Business Park Dr -Armonk 10504 **Fx:**273-2337
(516) 773-3237 .. **Kramer,** Lawr M '89 -14 Bond -Gt Neck 11021
(212) 226-6662 .. **Kramer,** Lenore '77 (Kramer & D) -350 Bway -NY 10013
(631) 581-6464 .. **Kramer,** Leonard G '50 -24 E Main -Bay Shr 11706 **Fx:**581-6465
(212) 715-9100 .. **Kramer Levin Naftalis & Frankel,LLP** -1177 Av of Amer -NY 10036 **Fx:**715-8000
(212) 363-6900 .. **Kramer,** Lisa R '02 %Faust GS&B LLP -2 Rector -NY 10006
(631) 761-7127 .. **Kramer,** Lynne Adair '77 Touro Cllg Law Ctr -225 Eastvw Dr -Central Islip 11722
(631) 207-2500 .. **Kramer,** Marc A '02 N Cardiello,PC -66A Medford Av -Patchogue 11772
(212) 556-1234 .. **Kramer,** Marc Z '81 %The NY Times Co -620 8th Av -NY 10018
(718) 643-0530 .. **Kramer,** Martin R '67 -250 93rd -Brklyn 11209 **Fx:**238-2099
(718) 748-5000 .. **Kramer,** Martin R '67 OfCnsl Hindy & Assoc,PC -233 87th -Brklyn 11209 **Fx:**748-9695
(914) 949-5561 .. **Kramer,** Michl A '71 -1311 Mamaroneck Av -White Plns 10605
(212) 319-0304 .. **Kramer,** Michl B '74 M Kramer & Assoc -150 E 58th -NY 10155 **Fx:**319-0545
(212) 735-3000 .. **Kramer,** Morris J '66 (Skadden ASM&F LLP) -4 Times Sq -NY 10036
(212) 903-8700 .. **Kramer,** Morris L '60 (Roberts & H,LLP) -825 8th Av -NY 10019
(212) 349-5890 .. **Kramer,** Nancy '66 NYS Trial Lawyers Assn -132 Nassau -NY 10038 **Fx:**608-2310
(212) 697-3750 .. **Kramer,** Nathaniel D '67 Kirschstein IS&P,PC -425 5th Av -NY 10016
(212) 935-3000 .. **Kramer,** Pamela L '99 %Mintz LCFG&P,PC -666 3rd Av -NY 10017
(516) 742-8897 .. **Kramer & Pollack,LLP** -143 Willis Av -Mineola 11501
(212) 682-7474 .. **Kramer,** Rachel E '06 %Foley & L LLP -90 Park Av -NY 10016
(212) 776-5000 .. **Kramer,** Randi B '06 NYC Housing Auth -250 Bway -NY 10007 **Fx:**776-5039
(212) 442-4900 .. **Kramer,** Raymond E '79 %Ofc Admin Trials -40 Rector -NY 10006 **Fx:**442-4947
(718) 286-6485 .. **Kramer,** Rebecca L '02 %DA -125-01 Qns Blvd -Kew Gdns 11415
(718) 461-7650 .. **Kramer,** Richd P '58 -149-06 Beech Av -Flushng 11355
(212) 402-9400 .. **Kramer,** Robt G '95 SrCnsl McKool S,PC -1 Bryant Park -NY 10036
(212) 715-9100 .. **Kramer,** Robin A '80 %Kramer LN&F,LLP -1177 Av of Amer -NY 10036
(212) 446-2323 .. **Kramer,** Ross M '05 %G Shargel -570 Lex Av -NY 10022 **Fx:**446-2330
(212) 285-2290 .. **Kramer,** Saml E '83 -225 Bway -NY 10007 **Fx:**964-4506
(212) 776-5206 .. **Kramer,** Seth E '02 %NYC Housing Auth -250 Bway -NY 10007 **Fx:**776-5039
(718) 520-1600 .. **Kramer & Shapiro** -80-02 Kew Grdns Rd -Kew Gdns 11415 **Fx:**520-8751
(212) 820-9470 .. **Kramer,** Stanley R '80 (Hawkins D&W LLP) -One Chase Manh Plz -NY 10005
(212) 977-9700 .. **Kramer,** Stephen D '75 (Phillips N LLP) -666 5th Av -NY 10103
(212) 566-3540 .. **Kramer,** Stephen P '73 -280 Bway -NY 10007 **Fx:**566-3865
(718) 250-2000 .. **Kramer,** Steven D '90 %DA -350 Jay -Brklyn 11201 **Fx:**250-2314
(518) 474-6530 .. **Kramer,** Steven J '95 %Dept Pub Srvc -3 ESP -Albany 12223
(631) 231-1450 .. **Kramer,** Steven N '98 Feldman K&M,PC -330 Vndrblt Motor Pkwy -Hauppauge 11788
(914) 949-2909 .. **Kramer,** Steven R '90 (Eckert SC&M,LLC) -10 Bank -White Plns 10606
(845) 452-7400 .. **Kramer,** Timothy W '07 %Spiegel BF&C,LLP -272 Mill -Poughkeepsie 12601
(914) 271-3283 .. **Kraminitz,** Roger S '86 -17 Hillside Av -Croton-On-Hud 10520
(718) 839-1159 .. **Kramnick,** Rebecca K '93 Womens Housing & Economic Dvlpmnt Corp -50 E 168th -Bronx 10452
(212) 989-2674 .. **Krampner,** Robt '42 -152 W 20th -NY 10011 **Fx:**243-1266
(212) 788-1031 .. **Krams,** Alan G '75 %Law Dept -100 Church -NY 10007 **Fx:**788-0367
(718) 356-4909 .. **Kramsky,** Les R '90 -43 New Dorp Plz -Staten Isl 10306 **Fx:**356-5279
(212) 766-5222 .. **Kran,** Alexander III '88 %Leav & S LLP -120 Bway -NY 10271 **Fx:**693-2377
(212) 885-7873 .. **Kranczer,** Lori R '95 %ADL -605 3rd Av -NY 10158 **Fx:**867-0779
(212) 726-4278 .. **Krane,** Jennifer A '93 %GT Interactive Software -417 5th Av -NY 10016 **Fx:**726-4214
(585) 454-6180 .. **Krane,** Joel N '66 -36 W Main -Rchstr 14614
(914) 761-5327 .. **Kraner,** Richd L '56 -2 Carriage Way -White Plns 10605
(516) 466-6500 .. **Krangle,** David B '95 %Parker WA LLP -6 Hrbr Park Dr S -Pt Wash 11050
(212) 267-6700 .. **Krangle,** David B '95 %Parker WA LLP -111 John -NY 10038
(212) 608-8965 .. **Kranich,** Richd D '72 -531 Main -NY 10044 **Fx:**608-0886
(845) 454-1123 .. **Kranis,** Michl D '81 -40 Grdn -Poughkeepsie 12601 **Fx:**454-1322
(646) 216-2400 .. **Kranjac,** Mario M '91 (Kranjac M&V LLP) -40 Wall -NY 10005 **Fx:**216-2373
(212) 381-7000 .. **Kransdorf,** Andrew P '92 (Sabin B&G LLP) -4 Times Sq -NY 10036
(646) 442-3646 .. **Kransdorf,** Wm Z '08 Legal Srvcs NYC -350 Bway -NY 10013 **Fx:**(212) 966-9571
(212) 869-1924 .. **Krantz,** Gloria J '03 (Krantz & K,LLP) -500 Mamaroneck Av -Harrison 10528 **Fx:**(914) 220-8305
(518) 668-2199 .. **Krantz,** Howard I '72 -161 Ottawa -Lk George 12845 **Fx:**668-4653
(212) 580-6500 .. **Krantz,** Jason G '94 (Phillips K & Assoc,LLP) -204 W 84th -NY 10024
(212) 661-0279 .. **Krantz,** Jeremy J '88 (Smith & K,LLP) -122 E 42nd -NY 10168
(212) 661-0009 .. **Krantz,** Larry H '81 (Krantz & B LLP) -747 3rd Av -NY 10017 **Fx:**355-5009
(212) 869-1924 .. **Krantz,** Saml J '02 (Krantz & K,LLP) -500 Mamaroneck Av -Harrison 10528 **Fx:**(914) 220-8305
(518) 474-1310 .. **Krantz,** Steven '83 Executive Chamber -242 State Cptl -Albany 12224
(631) 543-3750 .. **Krantz,** Steven L '85 (Savitt K&S PC) -353 Vets Mem'l Hwy -Commack 11725
(516) 485-5577 .. **Kranz,** Allen M '74 (Rosenthal C&K,LLP) -1600 Front -E Meadow 11554
(212) 697-5520 .. **Kranz,** Denise Mortner '86 -570 Lex Av -NY 10022
(516) 485-5577 .. **Kranz,** Elizabeth Schulman '77 OfCnsl Rosenthal C&K,LLP -1600 Front -E Meadow 11554
(212) 269-0927 .. **Kranz,** Jonathan L '97 %D'Amato & L,LLP -2 World Fncl Ctr -NY 10281
(212) 645-2410 .. **Kranz,** Joshua Elan '95 %GF Dunne -156 5th Av -NY 10010 **Fx:**645-2435
(212) 573-8000 .. **Kranz,** Kenneth H '75 -2 E End Av -NY 10075
(718) 382-5700 .. **Kranz,** Mark M '07 %Suslovich & K -1507 Av M -Brklyn 11230 **Fx:**382-5796
(718) 590-3344 .. **Krapes,** Mitchell G '89 %Family Ct -900 Sheridan Av -Bronx 10451
(212) 223-4000 .. **Krapf,** Jamie C '04 %Crowell & M LLP -590 Mad Av -NY 10022
(212) 400-7161 .. **Kraselnik,** Robt L '98 (Kraselnik & L,PLLC) -40 Wall -NY 10005 **Fx:**400-7162
(212) 400-7161 .. **Kraselnik,** Robt L '98 OfCnsl Zaremba B&B PLLC -40 Wall -NY 10005 **Fx:**(646) 512-5607
(212) 682-8552 .. **Krasilovsky,** M Wm '69 -51 E 42nd -NY 10017 **Fx:**983-3228
(516) 742-9200 .. **Krasin,** Lawr P '95 (Edelman K&J PLLC) -1 Old Cntry Rd -Carle Pl 11514
(212) 309-6000 .. **Krasinski,** Leon G '08 SrCnsl Morgan L&B LLP -101 Park Av -NY 10178
(212) 789-1500 .. **Kraske,** Anna Nabiha '95 %Donna Karan Co -550 7th Av -NY 10018 **Fx:**789-1688
(631) 756-8300 .. **Kraslow,** Richd A '86 -425 Broad Hollow Rd -Melvll 11747 **Fx:**756-3684
(516) 889-9353 .. **Krasner,** Bennett D '87 -1233 Beech -Atlantic Bch 11509 **Fx:**432-7016
(516) 889-9353 .. **Krasner,** Bonnie Ellen '84 -1233 Beech -Atlantic Bch 11509 **Fx:**432-7016
(212) 545-4670 .. **Krasner,** Danl W '66 (Wolf HAF&H LLP) -270 Mad Av -NY 10016
(212) 292-5108 .. **Krasner,** Dennis R '75 -2 Penn Plz -NY 10121 **Fx:**629-4568
(212) 984-7828 .. **Krasner,** Harvey I '74 (Warshaw BCS&K,LLP) -555 5th Av -NY 10017
(212) 557-0990 .. **Krasner & Iaulus** -10 E 40th -NY 10016 **Fx:**557-1917
(212) 557-0990 .. **Krasner,** Jeffrey M '81 (Krasner & I) -10 E 40th -NY 10016
(212) 677-7171 .. **Krasner,** Kenneth A '78 %Trst for Public Land -666 Bway -NY 10012 **Fx:**353-2052
(212) 723-9941 .. **Krasner,** Leslie J M '96 %Salomon Smith Barney -388 Greenwich -NY 10013
(212) 940-3062 .. **Krasney,** Keith L '85 (Nixon P LLP) -437 Mad Av -NY 10022
(212) 759-7477 .. **Krasnogor,** Julie B '96 (Krasnogor & K LLP) -530 5th Av -NY 10036 **Fx:**759-4450
(518) 449-3300 .. **Krasnokutski,** Shannan C '03 %Nolan & H,LLP -39 N Pearl -Albany 12207
(212) 336-2000 .. **Krasnoo,** Ethan M '08 %Patterson BW&T LLP -1133 Av of Amer -NY 10036
(516) 775-6222 .. **Krasnow,** Donald B '60 -90 Elmont Rd Bx125 -Elmont 11003 **Fx:**437-6580
(212) 530-5000 .. **Krasnow,** Joel I '90 (Milbank TH&M LLP) -1 Chase Manh Plz -NY 10005
(212) 880-6000 .. **Krasnow,** Lauren G '96 %Torys LLP -237 Park Av -NY 10017
(212) 310-8000 .. **Krasnow,** Richd P '72 (Weil G&M LLP) -767 5th Av -NY 10153
(212) 661-8033 .. **Krasnow,** Robt L '73 -380 Lex Av -NY 10168 **Fx:**792-8489
(212) 683-3636 .. **Krass Snow & Schmutter,PC** -419 Park Av S -NY 10016 **Fx:**481-7692
(212) 683-3636 .. **Krass,** Stephen J '63 (Krass S&S,PC) -419 Park Av S -NY 10016
(212) 564-1900 .. **Krassner,** Mark '81 (Cohen & K) -450 7th Av -NY 10123
(212) 310-8000 .. **Krassy,** Jos G '77 SpclCnsl Weil G&M LLP -767 5th Av -NY 10153
(212) 551-5100 .. **Krat,** Gary W '74 %Royal Alliance Assoc -1 World Fncl Ctr -NY 10281 **Fx:**551-5620
(212) 547-5400 .. **Kratenstein,** Andrew B '00 (McDermott W&E LLP) -340 Mad Av -NY 10173
(516) 829-0363 .. **Kratenstein,** Brian S '99 %Israel I&P,LLP -11 Grace Av -Gt Neck 11021 **Fx:**829-0366
(212) 697-2310 .. **Kratenstein,** Wm C '68 (Becker R LLP) -317 Mad Av -NY 10017
(212) 695-0060 .. **Kratka,** Danl S '01 %Wilens & B,PC -450 7th Av -NY 10123
(212) 345-9116 .. **Kratochvil,** Thos J '96 %Marsh USA -1166 Av of Amer -NY 10036 **Fx:**345-4808
(212) 941-1277 .. **Kratt,** Edw M '75 -350 Bway -NY 10013 **Fx:**274-1189
(212) 693-0085 .. **Kratter,** Jonathan '76 %Appellate Advocates -2 Rector -NY 10006 **Fx:**693-0878
(845) 368-4355 .. **Kratter,** Stuart '73 -2 Sunderland Pl -Suffern 10901 **Fx:**368-4355
(212) 335-9141 .. **Kratville,** Eryck N '09 DA -1 Hogan Pl -NY 10013
(631) 723-1800 .. **Kratz,** Jane R '86 (JR Katz,PC) -223 W Montauk Hwy Bx742 -Hampton Bays 11946 **Fx:**723-1804
(914) 750-5933 .. **Kratz,** Ryan A '10 %Kissel H&W LLP -580 Wht Plns Rd -Tarrytwn 10591
(212) 223-8409 .. **Kraus,** Amelie R '00 -150 E 58th -NY 10155 **Fx:**317-2946
(212) 848-4000 .. **Kraus,** Barbara K '98 Shearman & S LLP -599 Lex Av -NY 10022
(212) 563-3602 .. **Kraus,** Bernd D '91 -40 W 37th -NY 10018
(212) 357-3618 .. **Kraus,** Caroline L '03 Goldman Sachs -1 NY Plz -NY 10004
(212) 852-1000 .. **Kraus,** Christian D '96 %US Trust Co,NA -114 W 47th -NY 10036 **Fx:**852-1310
(212) 431-1300 .. **Kraus,** Craig A '80 Cnsl Borah GAN&G PC -377 Bway -NY 10013
(212) 915-7000 .. **Kraus,** David C '76 XL Insurance -200 Lbrty -NY 10281 **Fx:**945-0820
(212) 735-3000 .. **Kraus,** Douglas M '74 (Skadden ASM&F LLP) -4 Times Sq -NY 10036
(718) 368-0515 .. **Kraus,** Eliezer B '88 -2405 Av U -Brklyn 11229
(212) 759-4888 .. **Kraus,** Eric M '80 (Phillips L LLP) -437 Mad Av -NY 10022
(315) 414-1000 .. **Kraus,** James S '82 Kraus & Assoc -6701 Manlius Ctr Rd -E Syracuse 13057
(516) 365-1400 .. **Kraus,** Jos E '04 %Cooperman LM LLP -1129 Nrthrn Blvd -Manhsst 11030
(585) 241-5999 .. **Kraus,** Kenneth R '06 %Evans & F LLP -95 Allens Crk Rd -Rchstr 14618
(212) 506-1700 .. **Kraus,** Matthew A '07 %Kasowitz BT&F LLP -1633 Bway -NY 10019
(212) 488-1598 .. **Kraus,** Matthew D '03 %Havkins RR&V,LLP -11 Penn Plz -NY 10001
(718) 241-5000 .. **Kraus,** Mitchell H '99 -33-01 Vernon Blvd -LIC 11106
(212) 869-4646 .. **Kraus,** Robt D '85 (Kraus & Z LLP) -500 5th Av -NY 10110
(914) 332-0222 .. **Kraus,** Robt J '80 %Philips Electronics -345 Scarborough Rd Bx3001 -Briarcliff Mnr 10510 **Fx:**332-0615

(212) 515-4191 .. **Kraus,** Roberta '99 Lumenis Inc -375 Park Av -NY 10152
(212) 770-1783 .. **Kraus,** Sallie B '91 %AIG -80 Pine -NY 10005 **Fx:**344-2286
(212) 471-6204 .. **Kraus,** Schuyler Blake '00 (Hinshaw & C LLP) -780 3rd Av -NY 10017
(585) 262-3360 .. **Kraus,** Sherry S '76 -513 Times Sq Bldg -Rchstr 14614
(914) 949-5300 .. **Kraus,** Steven W '86 (Brown & T,LLC) -1 N Bway -White Plns 10601
(212) 869-4646 .. **Kraus & Zuchlewski LLP** -500 5th Av -NY 10110 **Fx:**869-4648
(212) 889-2121 .. **Krausche,** Chas E II '00 %Kellner HG&F -470 Park Av S -NY 10016
(212) 450-4000 .. **Krause,** Andrew E '06 %Davis P&W LLP -450 Lex Av -NY 10017
(518) 580-5700 .. **Krause,** Barbara L '00 Skidmore Cllg -815 N Bway -Saratoga Spgs 12866
(212) 735-3000 .. **Krause,** Brian D '07 %Skadden ASM&F LLP -4 Times Sq -NY 10036
(212) 439-9751 .. **Krause,** Geni Spells '74 -308 E 72nd -NY 10021 **Fx:**794-8818
(315) 986-8500 .. **Krause,** J Mark '89 (M Krause & Assoc) -19 W Main -Macedon 14502 **Fx:**986-8619
(212) 446-2300 .. **Krause,** Jason K '07 %Boies S&F LLP -575 Lex Av -NY 10022
(212) 218-2100 .. **Krause,** John A '71 (Fitzpatrick CH&S) -1290 Av of Amer -NY 10104
(212) 773-3000 .. **Krause,** Katharine E '08 Ernst & Young,LLP -5 Times Sq -NY 10036
(212) 310-8000 .. **Krause,** Katherine M '07 %Weil G&M LLP -767 5th Av -NY 10153
(212) 267-7868 .. **Krause,** Leslie E '74 -11 Park Pl -NY 10007 **Fx:**267-7579
(212) 389-1500 .. **Krause,** Peter C '75 %Greenhill & Co -300 Park Av -NY 10022
(516) 542-5900 .. **Krause,** Robt T '74 %Congdon FORDT&F -333 Earle Ovngton Blvd -Uniondale 11553
(212) 336-2000 .. **Krause,** Robin '91 (Patterson BW&T LLP) -1133 Av of Amer -NY 10036
(212) 735-3000 .. **Krause,** Serhat T '07 %Skadden ASM&F LLP -4 Times Sq -NY 10036
(212) 986-9700 .. **Krause,** Sheldon '81 (Eilenberg & K LLP) -11 E 44th -NY 10017
(212) 450-4000 .. **Krause,** Steven C '08 %Davis P&W LLP -450 Lex Av -NY 10017
(212) 223-0400 .. **Krause,** Stuart A '77 (Zeichner E&K LLP) -575 Lex Av -NY 10022
(212) 839-5300 .. **Krause,** Todd L '98 (Sidley A LLP) -787 7th Av -NY 10019
(607) 753-5008 .. **Krause,** Veronica M '08 %DA -46 Greenbush -Cortlnd 13045 **Fx:**756-3477
(518) 792-1174 .. **Krause,** W Bradley '99 (McPhillips F&C,LLP) -288 Glen Bx299 -Glens Fls 12801
(212) 558-4000 .. **Krause-Vilmar,** Georg '07 %Sullivan & C LLP -125 Broad -NY 10004
(845) 371-1100 .. **Kraushaar,** Danl N '89 -300 Airport Exec Pk -Nanuet 10954 **Fx:**371-4790
(212) 416-8686 .. **Kraushar,** Estelle C '82 %Dept of Law -120 Bway -NY 10271
(212) 269-7308 .. **Krausman,** Gabriel M '60 SpclCnsl Leahey & J PC -120 Wall -NY 10005
(914) 347-2600 .. **Krauss,** Adam D '90 (Traub LS&S LLP) -7 Skyline Dr -Hawthorne 10532
(845) 225-3641 .. **Krauss,** Chana '91 %DA -40 Gleneida Av -Carmel 10512
(212) 478-7200 .. **Krauss,** Danl J '74 (Hahn & H LLP) -488 Mad Av -NY 10022
(212) 965-1161 .. **Krauss,** David B '92 -111 John -NY 10038
(607) 770-2717 .. **Krauss,** Geoffrey H '75 BAE Systems -600 Main -Johnson Cty 13790
(914) 949-9100 .. **Krauss,** Geri S '77 Krauss PLLC -1 N Bway -White Plns 10601 **Fx:**949-9109
(212) 237-1000 .. **Krauss,** Gregory T '06 %Windels ML&M,LLP -156 W 56th -NY 10019
(212) 687-3860 .. **Krauss,** Harvey '61 (Snow BK,PC) -605 3rd Av -NY 10158
(212) 806-5400 .. **Krauss,** Jill A '08 %Stroock &S&L LLP -180 Maiden Ln -NY 10038
(516) 571-3056 .. **Krauss,** Mindy H '01 %Cnty Atty -1 West -Mineola 11501 **Fx:**571-6604
(212) 764-3377 .. **Krauss,** Sandor D '02 -1040 Av of Amer -NY 10018
(212) 969-3000 .. **Krauss,** Sara B '94 %Proskauer R LLP -1585 Bway -NY 10036
(212) 537-1627 .. **Krauss,** Seth D '96 Morgan Stanley -1633 Bway -NY 10019
(914) 694-4444 .. **Krauss,** Steven V '87 %Natl Rlty & Dvlpmnt -3 Manhattanvll Rd -Purchase 10577 **Fx:**694-5448
(212) 885-5000 .. **Krauss-Browne,** Caroline '92 (Blank R LLP) -405 Lex Av -NY 10174
(212) 244-5292 .. **Krausz,** Diane F '85 D Krausz & Assoc -322 8th Av -NY 10001 **Fx:**244-5750
(212) 736-7432 .. **Krausz,** Mordchai '90 (Koven & K) -350 5th Av -NY 10118
(516) 294-4111 .. **Kraut,** Alan G '71 -1325 Franklin Av -Gdn Cty 11530 **Fx:**742-9416
(212) 902-2000 .. **Kraut,** David T '01 Goldman Sachs -1 NY Plz -NY 10004
(914) 701-0800 .. **Kraut,** Jonathan D '94 (Friedman HK&P) -2975 Wstchstr Av -Purchase 10577
(212) 309-6000 .. **Kraut,** Michl S '00 (Morgan L&B LLP) -101 Park Av -NY 10178
(631) 694-2300 .. **Krauthamer,** Michl B '96 (Lamb & B,LLP) -534 Broadhllw Rd Bx9034 -Melvll 11747
(212) 451-2300 .. **Krauthamer,** Nina '76 (Olshan GFR&W LLP) -65 E 55th -NY 10022
(716) 753-4339 .. **Krauza,** Kathleen Downing '86 %Surrogates Ct -Gerace Ofc Bldg BxC -Mayvll 14757
(516) 877-2225 .. **Krauzlis,** James P '81 %Badiak & W,LLP -106 3rd -Mineola 11501
(212) 599-5455 .. **Kravaris,** Eleftherios (Terry) '05 %Simon Lesser,PC -420 Lex Av -NY 10170 **Fx:**599-5459
(516) 512-6333 .. **Kravatz,** Cheryl Spinner '89 (Gold SKB LLP) -1025 Old Cntry Rd -Westbury 11590
(212) 244-9000 .. **Kraver,** Michl E '03 %Matalon SE -450 7th Av -NY 10123 **Fx:**244-4615
(516) 293-2000 .. **Kravet,** Cary '84 %Kravet Fabrics -225 Central Av S -Bethpage 11714 **Fx:**293-2158
(212) 997-7634 .. **Kravet,** Donald J '84 (Kravet & V,LLP) -1040 Av of Amer -NY 10018 **Fx:**997-7686
(718) 931-3131 .. **Kravet Hoefer & Maher, PC** -1135A Morris Park Av -Bronx 10461 **Fx:**931-3387
(516) 293-2000 .. **Kravet,** Lisa G '84 %Kravet Fabrics -225 Central Av S -Bethpage 11714 **Fx:**293-2158
(212) 376-0900 .. **Kravet,** Martin R '85 %Royal Abstract -500 5th Av -NY 10110 **Fx:**376-0911
(212) 376-0900 .. **Kravet,** Stanley W '59 %Royal Abstract -500 5th Av -NY 10110 **Fx:**376-0911
(212) 213-3930 .. **Kravetz,** David '58 -489 5th Av -NY 10017 **Fx:**644-0544
(212) 715-0300 .. **Kravetz,** Gary M '99 Tishman Speyer Prop -45 Rckfllr Plz -NY 10111 **Fx:**332-6603
(212) 286-9499 .. **Kravetz,** Nina A '05 %M Nolfo -275 Mad Av -NY 10016 **Fx:**286-8881
(212) 252-0550 .. **Kravit,** Craig B '90 (Kravit Prtnrs) -90 John -NY 10038
(212) 506-2500 .. **Kravitt,** Jason H P '02 (Mayer B LLP) -1675 Bway -NY 10019
(718) 834-8078 .. **Kravitz,** David '85 -189 Montague -Brklyn 11201 **Fx:**858-0284
(212) 940-8800 .. **Kravitz,** David S '07 %Katten MR LLP -575 Mad Av -NY 10022
(212) 490-2020 .. **Kravitz,** Ellyn S '93 (Littman K LLP) -655 3rd Av -NY 10017
(914) 738-2222 .. **Kravitz,** Lester J '77 -89 Wolfs Ln -Pelham 10803 **Fx:**738-8007
(212) 859-8000 .. **Kravitz,** Rachel G '09 %Fried FHS&J LLP -1 NY Plz -NY 10004
(212) 373-3000 .. **Kravitz,** Robt N '89 Cnsl Paul WRW&G LLP -1285 Av of Amer -NY 10019
(212) 799-8134 .. **Kravitz,** Robin R '77 -160 West End Av -NY 10023 **Fx:**202-3506
(718) 533-8444 .. **Kravitz,** Wm N '05 %Roman & S,LLP -37-18 73rd -Jcksn Hts 11372
(718) 428-4828 .. **Krawczyk,** Antonina '87 -210-09 41st Av -Bayside 11361
(212) 704-6000 .. **Krawczyk,** Laura E '06 %Troutman S LLP -405 Lex Av -NY 10174
(716) 856-5500 .. **Krawiec,** Marc '07 %Damon M LLP -200 Delaware Av -Buffalo 14202
(212) 735-3000 .. **Krawitz,** Aaron '08 %Skadden ASM&F LLP -4 Times Sq -NY 10036
(212) 682-0707 .. **Krawitz,** Stephen R '78 (S Krawitz,LLC) -271 Mad Av -NY 10016 **Fx:**682-8821
(212) 909-6000 .. **Kraybill,** Jaime Barker '09 %Debevoise & P LLP -919 3rd Av -NY 10022
(212) 460-1340 .. **Krayeske,** Mary L '95 Con Ed -4 Irving Pl -NY 10003
(585) 409-5200 .. **Kraynik,** Michele M '01 -9 St marks -Le Roy 14482
(212) 675-6181 .. **Krebs,** Betsy '88 %Youth Advocacy Ctr -281 Av of Amer -NY 10014
(845) 256-3038 .. **Krebs,** Carol Backman '91 %DEC -21 S Putt Crnrs Rd -New Paltz 12561 **Fx:**255-4659
(914) 681-8700 .. **Krebs,** Debra Miller '94 %Milber MP&S LLP -3 Barker Av -White Plns 10601
(212) 269-5500 .. **Krebs,** Diane '95 (Gordon & R LLP) -90 Broad -NY 10004
(716) 854-1300 .. **Krebs,** Ellen M '80 %Rosenthal S&M,LLP -300 Main -Buffalo 14202
(516) 248-5757 .. **Krebs,** Glenn A '85 OfCnsl Colleran O&M,LLP -1225 Franklin Av -Gdn Cty 11530
(516) 901-5170 .. **Krebs,** Howard S '92 -25 Seaview Ln -Pt Wash 11050 **Fx:**883-6633
(212) 825-9811 .. **Krebsbach & Snyder,PC** -55 Bway -NY 10006 **Fx:**825-9828
(212) 692-1000 .. **Krebsbach,** Spensyr Ann '09 %Duane M LLP -1540 Bway -NY 10036
(212) 825-9811 .. **Krebsbach,** Theo A '79 (Krebsbach & S,PC) -55 Bway -NY 10006
(212) 237-1000 .. **Krechmer,** Leonid D '00 %Windels ML&M,LLP -156 W 56th -NY 10019
(212) 285-0220 .. **Kreeger,** Susan L '86 Medical & Hlth Resrch Assoc -40 Worth -NY 10013
(646) 386-5700 .. **Krefetz,** Claudia L '90 %Civil Ct -111 Centre -NY 10013
(212) 770-7000 .. **Krefft,** Alexander R '02 %AIG -70 Pine -NY 10270
(516) 942-0285 .. **Kreger-Grella,** Cheryl L '80 -420 Jericho Tpke -Jericho 11753
(716) 856-4000 .. **Kreher,** Julia S '95 (Hodgson R LLP) -140 Pearl -Buffalo 14202
(585) 815-0288 .. **Krehl,** Christine L '09 %Rosicki R & Assoc,PC -26 Harvester Av -Batavia 14020 **Fx:**815-0299
(646) 831-8401 .. **Kreidman,** Melvin '63 -4705 H Hdsn Pkwy -Bronx 10471
(212) 972-1000 .. **Kreidman,** Perry I '77 (London F LLP) -59 Maiden Ln -NY 10038
(585) 232-6500 .. **Kreienberg,** Wm L '84 (Harter S&E LLP) -1600 Bausch & Lomb Pl -Rchstr 14604
(212) 935-3000 .. **Kreifels,** Carrie A '08 %Mintz LCFG&P,PC -666 3rd Av -NY 10017
(212) 770-6176 .. **Kreiger,** Sean E '04 AIG Global Invstmnt Grp -70 Pine -NY 10270
(516) 735-6666 .. **Kreinces,** Howard W '58 -119 Spindle Rd -Hicksvll 11801
(516) 227-6500 .. **Kreinces,** Leonard '60 (Kreinces & R,PC) -900 Merchants Cncrs -Westbury 11590 **Fx:**227-6594
(516) 741-1710 .. **Kreinces,** Matthew R '94 (Katz & K,LLP) -170 Old Cntry Rd -Mineola 11501
(212) 977-9700 .. **Kreindler,** Donald L '56 (Phillips N LLP) -666 5th Av -NY 10103
(212) 687-8181 .. **Kreindler,** James P '80 (Kreindler & K) -750 3rd Av -NY 10017
(212) 687-8181 .. **Kreindler & Kreindler** -750 3rd Av -NY 10017 **Fx:**972-9432
(212) 715-9100 .. **Kreiner,** Michl L '09 %Kramer LN&F,LLP -1177 Av of Amer -NY 10036
(212) 619-4350 .. **Kreines,** Chas W '84 (Newman MKGH,PC) -14 Wall -NY 10005
(516) 877-1717 .. **Kreines,** Melvyn '64 M Kreines & Assoc,PC -500 Old Cntry Rd -Gdn Cty 11530 **Fx:**877-1747
(212) 682-7900 .. **Kreinik,** Gary A '81 (Kreinik Assoc,LLC) -275 Mad Av -NY 10016 **Fx:**682-0030
(212) 850-7500 .. **Kreinik,** Steven M '92 %Ave Cptl Grp -535 Mad Av -NY 10022 **Fx:**850-7598
(212) 629-4970 .. **Kreisberg,** Jeffrey L '71 (Kreisberg & M,LLP) -116 John -NY 10038
(212) 629-4970 .. **Kreisberg & Maitland,LLP** -116 John -NY 10038 **Fx:**268-0544
(212) 453-5900 .. **Kreismann,** Ronald '70 (Ford & H LLP) -100 Park Av -NY 10017
(914) 467-1000 .. **Kreiss,** David M '95 %Oxford Health Plans, Inc -44 S Bway -White Plns 10601
(212) 576-7000 .. **Kreis Strutton,** Emily R '00 %NYLIM -51 Mad Av -NY 10010
(212) 559-7044 .. **Kreiswirth,** Brian J '00 Citigroup -850 3rd Av -NY 10022
(212) 318-6000 .. **Kreitman,** Mark A '85 (Paul HJ&W LLP) -75 E 55th -NY 10022
(646) 429-7500 .. **Kreitman,** Michl E '92 %Macys,Inc -11 Penn Plz -NY 10001 **Fx:**429-7521
(212) 839-8637 .. **Kreitman,** Robt M '86 (Sidley A LLP) -787 7th Av -NY 10019
(631) 451-4705 .. **Kreitzer,** Ilene S '95 %Sfflk Cnty Comm Cllg -533 Cllg Rd -Selden 11784 **Fx:**451-4681
(212) 252-9050 .. **Kreitzman,** David I '68 (Kreitzman M&B) -100 Wall -NY 10005
(631) 342-8388 .. **Kreitzman,** Elena M '94 (Spina & K) -300 Rabro Dr -Hauppauge 11788
(212) 252-9050 .. **Kreitzman Mortensen & Borden** -100 Wall -NY 10005 **Fx:**252-9310
(212) 837-6000 .. **Kreitzman,** Ralph J '71 Cnsl Hughes H&R LLP -1 Bttry Pk Plz -NY 10004
(212) 805-3900 .. **Krejci,** Eric T '00 %Clausen M PC -1 Chase Manh Plz -NY 10005
(212) 732-2000 .. **Krejci,** Wm G '90 %Cullen and D LLP -44 Wall -NY 10005
(516) 479-6300 .. **Krell,** Justin S '07 %Silverman A LLP -100 Jericho Quad -Jericho 11753
(212) 336-2000 .. **Krell,** Meridith Bogart '05 %Patterson BW&T LLP -1133 Av of Amer -NY 10036

(516) 747-1010 .. **Krellen**, Joshua N '90 %Dollinger G&G -1 Old Cntry Rd -Carle Pl 11514
(914) 763-6323 .. **Krellenstein**, Jason M '94 -Bx422 -S Salem 10590 **Fx**:763-6331
(212) 808-2700 .. **Krembs**, Susan J '00 (Pepper H LLP) -620 8th Av -NY 10018
(212) 859-8000 .. **Kremen**, Alexis R '05 %Fried FHS&J LLP -1 NY Plz -NY 10004
(212) 481-5858 .. **Kremen**, Andrea S '73 %Fidelity Natl Title Ins -1 Park Av -NY 10016 **Fx**:481-8747
(212) 233-2100 .. **Kremen**, David L '92 %Oshman & M,LLP -42 Bway -NY 10004
(914) 368-0400 .. **Kremenezky**, Tina C '89 Nokia -102 Corp Park Dr -White Plns 10604
(585) 546-6040 .. **Kremer**, Alfred P '66 -135 Dartford Rd -Rchstr 14618 **Fx**:325-3833
(516) 663-6600 .. **Kremer**, Arthur J '59 (Ruskin MF,PC) -1425 RXR Plz -Uniondale 11556
(518) 436-8313 .. **Kremer**, Brian S '92 (Goldberger & K) -39 N Pearl -Albany 12207 **Fx**:436-8316
(516) 741-5300 .. **Kremer**, Fredk D '83 L & E Intl,Ltd -100 Ring Rd W -Gdn Cty 11530 **Fx**:741-6090
(716) 849-0701 .. **Kremer**, Jos T '89 %Lipsitz & P LLC -135 Delaware Av -Buffalo 14202
(516) 681-1100 .. **Kremin**, Todd D '06 %Kaufman DV&G,LLP -135 Crsswys Park Dr -Woodbury 11797
(212) 587-3434 .. **Kremins**, Michl F '81 (Raskin & K LLP) -160 Bway -NY 10038
(212) 672-1906 .. **Kremner**, Jonathan '94 -245 Park Av -NY 10167
(212) 326-0842 .. **Kremnitzer**, Ronald B '78 (Pryor C LLP) -7 Times Sq -NY 10036
(516) 593-0202 .. **Krendel**, Veronica Sympson '93 OfCnsl S Stone PLLC -340 Atl Av -E Rockaway 11518 **Fx**:593-0297
(585) 546-1383 .. **Krenitsky**, Albert G '72 (Lubelle L & K) -19 W Main -Rchstr 14614 **Fx**:546-1385
(716) 842-5401 .. **Krenitsky**, John C '92 %M&T Bk -1 M & T Plz -Buffalo 14203 **Fx**:842-5376
(716) 631-5700 .. **Krenitsky**, Jos G '82 %Sargent & C,LLP -6245 Sheridan Dr -Williamsvll 14221 **Fx**:631-9120
(518) 455-3121 .. **Krenrich**, Michl T '03 Sen Lavalle -LOB 806 -Albany 12247
(212) 227-2900 .. **Krentsel**, Steven '97 (Krentsel & G LLP) -17 Battery Pl -NY 10004 **Fx**:(646) 929-9045
(718) 544-6257 .. **Krentz**, Danl J '69 -67-96 Clyde -Frst Hlls 11375
(585) 328-3180 .. **Krenzer**, Cyril A '67 -7347 E Main -Lima 14485 **Fx**:624-1723
(518) 689-0966 .. **Krenzer**, Cyril A '67 OfCnsl Hite & B,PC -20 Corp Wds Blvd -Albany 12211
(212) 879-5580 .. **Kreoll**, Jos P '04 %R Malagiere,PC -17 Battery Pl -NY 10004 **Fx**:879-5583
(212) 925-1366 .. **Kreplin**, Hannah Selby '92 -67 Vestry -NY 10013
(212) 925-6670 .. **Kreppel**, Jerald D '75 -401 Bway -NY 10013
(914) 633-7900 .. **Kreppel**, Milton M '79 -271 North Av -New Rchll 10801 **Fx**:576-0947
(716) 631-1518 .. **Kreppel**, Robt J '84 US Energy Prntrs LLC -8205 Main -Buffalo 14221
(212) 599-6000 .. **Kresch**, Ari '78 (Kresch Leg Srvcs) -122 E 42nd -NY 10168 **Fx**:(800) 529-9071
(212) 657-1252 .. **Kresch**, Scott E '83 Citigroup -77 Water -NY 10005
(212) 599-6000 .. **Kresch**, Simon P '77 (Kresch Leg Srvcs) -122 E 42nd -NY 10168 **Fx**:(800) 529-9071
(212) 986-3500 .. **Kresge**, Donald M '64 -711 3rd Av -NY 10017 **Fx**:599-7909
(518) 402-9188 .. **Kreshik**, Monica L '95 DEC -625 Bway -Albany 12233 **Fx**:402-9018
(212) 581-1516 .. **Kresky**, Harry '72 -250 W 57th -NY 10107 **Fx**:581-1352
(212) 268-8888 .. **Kresman**, David J '02 (Kresman & W) -7 Penn Plz -NY 10001
(585) 232-6500 .. **Kresock**, David M '95 (Harter S&E LLP) -1600 Bausch & Lomb Pl -Rchstr 14604
(212) 944-6622 .. **Kress**, Alan H '74 -24 W 40th -NY 10018 **Fx**:768-2766
(212) 836-8000 .. **Kress**, Andrew A '80 (Kaye S LLP) -425 Park Av -NY 10022 **Fx**:836-6728
(585) 325-7515 .. **Kress**, Danielle B '96 %Forsyth HOK&M,PC -1 Chase Sq -Rchstr 14604
(718) 354-3200 .. **Kress**, Gillian '06 %Battiste A&S,Inc -60 Bay -Staten Isl 10301
(212) 418-4700 .. **Kress**, Joel S '02 Icon Cptl Corp -100 5th Av -NY 10011
(718) 948-4873 .. **Kress**, Robt J '84 -6735 Amboy Rd -Staten Isl 10309 **Fx**:317-8668
(212) 381-7000 .. **Kress**, Sidney D '82 (Sabin B&G LLP) -4 Times Sq -NY 10036
(716) 843-5700 .. **Kresse**, MaryEllen '92 %US Atty -138 Delaware Av -Buffalo 14202 **Fx**:551-3052
(716) 566-1300 .. **Kresse**, Robt J '54 OfCnsl Hiscock & B,LLP -1100 M&T Ctr -Buffalo 14203
(212) 973-0572 .. **Kressel**, Dorit Fuchs '98 Cnsl Wolff & S PC -140 Bway -NY 10005
(516) 798-5363 .. **Kressel Rothlein Walsh & Roth,LLC** -684 Bway -Massapequa 11758 **Fx**:798-5498
(516) 798-5363 .. **Kressel**, Stephen '64 (Kressel RW&R,LLC) -684 Bway -Massapequa 11758
(914) 739-3394 .. **Kressin**, Marsha D '91 -832 South -Peekskill 10566 **Fx**:739-4601
(212) 310-8000 .. **Kressler**, Noah B '07 %Weil G&M LLP -767 5th Av -NY 10153
(516) 596-8607 .. **Kret**, Jeffrey '02 (J Kret,PLLC) -466 Central Av -Cedarhrst 11516 **Fx**:596-8608
(516) 596-8607 .. **Kret**, Jonathan '09 %J Kret,PLLC -466 Central Av -Cedarhrst 11516 **Fx**:596-8608
(212) 310-8000 .. **Kretchmar**, Thos M '09 %Weil G&M LLP -767 5th Av -NY 10153
(212) 465-8448 .. **Kretchmer**, Jerome '58 %KB Companies -350 5th Av -NY 10118
(716) 548-7627 .. **Kretschman**, Brenda Lee '97 -17 Beresford Ct -Williamsvll 14221
(212) 213-5000 .. **Kretschmann**, Paul H '76 (Matays & K) -271 Mad Av -NY 10016
(212) 788-7210 .. **Kretz**, Caroline R '92 City Cncl Spkrs Ofc -City Hall -NY 10007 **Fx**:788-7207
(631) 957-2000 .. **Kretz**, Stephen W '75 (Donohue K&G) -36 E Montauk Hwy -Lindenhrst 11757
(212) 371-4500 .. **Kretz**, Walter A Jr. '80 (Seiff K&A) -444 Mad Av -NY 10022
(516) 746-8000 .. **Kretzing**, Laurel Row '86 (Jaspan S LLP) -300 Grdn City Plz -Gdn Cty 11530
(212) 527-4000 .. **Kretzman**, Robt K '78 %Revlon -237 Park Av -NY 10017 **Fx**:527-5299
(212) 903-9000 .. **Kretzmann**, Hollin N '09 %Linklaters -1345 Av of Amer -NY 10105
(607) 351-0556 .. **Kretzmann**, Julia A '99 -408 N Tioga -Ithaca 14850
(516) 466-8005 .. **Kreutzer**, Robt H '58 OfCnsl Tashlik KG&C PC -40 Cuttermill Rd -Gt Neck 11021
(212) 902-1000 .. **Krevitt**, Jennifer B '93 %Goldman Sachs -1 NY Plz -NY 10004
(212) 351-4000 .. **Krevitt**, Josh A '93 (Gibson D&C LLP) -200 Park Av -NY 10166
(212) 733-1095 .. **Krex**, Brian R '03 %Pfizer Inc -235 E 42nd -NY 10017
(914) 323-7000 .. **Kreymer**, Peter '00 %Wilson EME&D LLP -3 Gannett Dr -White Plns 10604
(212) 450-4000 .. **Kreynin**, Leonard '90 (Davis P&W LLP) -450 Lex Av -NY 10017
(212) 266-0400 .. **Krez & Flores,LLP** -225 Bway -NY 10007
(212) 980-9600 .. **Krez**, Loretta A '86 (Kaufman B&R) -120 Bway -NY 10271
(212) 266-0400 .. **Krez**, Paul A '78 (Krez & F,LLP) -225 Bway -NY 10007
(212) 504-6000 .. **Krezalek**, Martin S '09 %Cadwalader W&T LLP -1 World Fncl Ctr -NY 10281
(315) 251-3015 .. **Kribs**, Robt J Sr. '84 AutoOne Ins -5788 Widewaters Pkwy -Syracuse 13214
(212) 676-0750 .. **Krichmar**, Todd A '94 %Law Dept -100 Church -NY 10007 **Fx**:788-0367
(212) 924-1625 .. **Kridel**, James A Jr. '81 (Kridel Law Grp) -575 Mad Av -NY 10022
(718) 286-6000 .. **Krider**, LaToya S '07 %DA -125-01 Qns Blvd -Kew Gdns 11415
(212) 725-4423 .. **Krieg**, Chas D '94 (Paykin K&A LLP) -185 Mad Av -NY 10016
(631) 499-8409 .. **Krieg**, Marc S '72 (Krieg Assoc,PC) -5 Heather Ct -Dix Hlls 11746 **Fx**:493-0763
(631) 499-8409 .. **Krieg**, Randi J '94 (Krieg Assoc,PC) -5 Heather Ct -Dix Hlls 11746 **Fx**:493-0763
(212) 371-5999 .. **Kriegel**, Jay L '66 Abernathy MacGregor Grp -501 Mad Av -NY 10022
(212) 553-5400 .. **Kriegel**, Julie A '01 Zurich NA -1 Lbrty Plz -NY 10006
(718) 615-4550 .. **Kriegel**, Tamir '04 %S Hilsenrath -1803 Gravesend Neck Rd -Brklyn 11229 **Fx**:615-4557
(516) 741-6565 .. **Krieger**, Abraham B '76 (Meyer SE&K,PC) -990 Stewart Av Bx9194 -Gdn Cty 11530
(718) 330-2851 .. **Krieger**, Amy Spring '90 %NLRB -2 Metrotech Ctr -Brklyn 11201 **Fx**:330-7579
(845) 562-2333 .. **Krieger**, Andrew S '77 -225 Pkwy Dr -New Windsor 12553
(212) 806-5400 .. **Krieger**, Arlene G '85 SpclCnsl Stroock &S&L LLP -180 Maiden Ln -NY 10038
(212) 756-2000 .. **Krieger**, Beate '03 SpclCnsl Schulte R&Z LLP -919 3rd Av -NY 10022
(212) 953-6000 .. **Krieger**, Dennis C '71 (Katsky K LLP) -605 3rd Av -NY 10158
(718) 793-7400 .. **Krieger**, Douglas '59 -71-21 Austin -Frst Hlls 11375
(212) 258-6000 .. **Krieger**, Elana L '04 %Viacom -1515 Bway -NY 10036
(212) 656-4517 .. **Krieger**, Frederic M '89 NYSE Regulation -20 Broad -NY 10005
(718) 432-0500 .. **Krieger**, Harvey W '81 (Krieger W&H) -5602 Bway -Bronx 10463
(212) 986-6000 .. **Krieger**, Jodi F '88 OfCnsl Kleinberg KW&C,PC -551 5th Av -NY 10176
(212) 798-6100 .. **Krieger**, Kevin P '98 Fortress Invsmt Grp -1345 Av of Amer -NY 10105
(585) 325-2640 .. **Krieger**, Lawr '92 L Krieger -8 Exchange Blvd -Rchstr 14614 **Fx**:325-1946
(914) 684-6000 .. **Krieger**, Michl J '99 (LaPietra & K) -30 Glenn -White Plns 10603 **Fx**:287-6460
(212) 637-1084 .. **Krieger**, Paul M '04 US Atty -1 St Andrews Plz -NY 10007
(212) 415-2000 .. **Krieger**, Philip S '80 DDB Worldwide -437 Mad Av -NY 10022 **Fx**:415-3506
(212) 363-2900 .. **Krieger & Prager LLP** -39 Bway -NY 10006 **Fx**:363-2999
(716) 200-5050 .. **Krieger**, Richd P '91 OfCnsl Harris B PLLC -726 Exchange -Buffalo 14210
(212) 406-3346 .. **Krieger**, Ronald E '85 -376 Bway -NY 10013 **Fx**:406-3578
(212) 363-2900 .. **Krieger**, Saml M '75 (Krieger & P LLP) -39 Bway -NY 10006
(212) 859-8000 .. **Krieger**, Sanford '71 OfCnsl Fried FHS&J LLP -1 NY Plz -NY 10004
(845) 434-6655 .. **Krieger**, Seymour '51 -61 Novogrodsky Rd Bx456 -Woodrdg 12789 **Fx**:434-4814
(516) 463-6078 .. **Krieger**, Stefan H '94 %Hofstra Law Schl -121 Hofstra Univ -Hempstd 11549
(516) 887-9600 .. **Krieger**, Steven '86 %Engel Group -124 Atl Av -Lynbrk 11563 **Fx**:887-9614
(212) 935-1622 .. **Krieger**, Vivien R '07 %Goldman H LLC -475 Park Av S -NY 10016 **Fx**:935-2651
(718) 432-0500 .. **Krieger Wilansky & Hupart** -5602 Bway -Bronx 10463 **Fx**:432-1803
(212) 326-7797 .. **Krieger**, Yulia P '97 %UNICEF -3 UN Plz -NY 10017 **Fx**:326-7165
(212) 232-1300 .. **Kriegstein**, Megan E '07 %Lewis BB&S LLP -77 Water -NY 10005
(212) 986-5300 .. **Kriesberg**, Carol N '75 -225 Bway -NY 10007
(914) 633-6300 .. **Kriesberg**, Carol N '75 -302 Union Av -New Rchll 10801
(718) 677-6500 .. **Kriger**, Morton '63 -1122 Av J -Brklyn 11230 **Fx**:677-3786
(212) 907-0700 .. **Kriger**, Ryan G '05 %Labaton S LLP -140 Bway -NY 10005
(646) 724-0362 .. **Krigsfeld**, Michl '04 (Krigsfeld & Assoc PC) -2350 Ocean Av -Brklyn 11229 **Fx**:(718) 336-2176
(631) 665-0609 .. **Krikorian**, Marina '99 %Sherman FS&L LLP -8 E Main -Bay Shr 11706
(914) 439-4333 .. **Krikorian**, Van Z '94 -5 Fredrck Ct -Harrison 10528
(212) 827-0341 .. **Krim**, Gary M '92 (Krim & K,PC) -114 W 47th -NY 10036 **Fx**:827-0351
(516) 227-0700 .. **Krimitsos**, Chris D '04 %Farrell F,PC -1320 RXR Plz -Uniondale 11556
(718) 522-2700 .. **Krimko**, Melvin R '69 -267 Flatbush Av -Brklyn 11217
(516) 294-4141 .. **Krimmer**, Danl L '80 Class Abstract Srvcs -72 Jericho Tpk -Mineola 11501
(212) 530-5000 .. **Kringen**, Karin M '09 %Milbank TH&M LLP -1 Chase Manh Plz -NY 10005
(516) 357-3000 .. **Krinick**, Evan H '86 (Rivkin R LLP) -926 RXR Plz -Uniondale 11556
(212) 521-3133 .. **Krinitz**, Joel M '89 (Krinitz & K PC) -1775 Bway -NY 10019
(212) 521-3133 .. **Krinitz**, Meyer '58 (Krinitz & K PC) -1775 Bway -NY 10019
(212) 216-8000 .. **Krinsky**, Andrew N '77 (Tarter K&D LLP) -1350 Bway -NY 10018
(718) 643-1878 .. **Krinsky**, Barry H '70 -50 Court -Brklyn 11201
(718) 643-1878 .. **Krinsky**, Melvyn '67 -50 Court -Brklyn 11201
(212) 254-1111 .. **Krinsky**, Michl R '73 (Rabinowitz BSK&L,PC) -111 Bway -NY 10006
(212) 505-4020 .. **Krinsky**, Pery D '02 %M Ross -60 E 42nd -NY 10165 **Fx**:505-4054
(718) 645-3999 .. **Krinsky**, Richd M '94 -2117 Av R -Brklyn 11229
(212) 593-1100 .. **Krinsky**, Scott '86 (Backenroth F&K,LLP) -489 5th Av -NY 10017
(212) 532-1973 .. **Krinsky**, Seymour '54 (Krinsky & M) -274 Mad Av -NY 10016 **Fx**:545-7211
(718) 237-2000 .. **Kripke**, Nanette R '75 %Leg Aid -111 Lvngstn -Brklyn 11201 **Fx**:237-8737
(212) 839-5300 .. **Krisberg**, Brian '85 (Sidley A LLP) -787 7th Av -NY 10019

(212) 446-2300 .. **Krisbergh,** Jonathan P '07 %Boies S&F LLP -575 Lex Av -NY 10022
(212) 815-0491 .. **Krischel,** Susan K '96 %DA -1 Hogan Pl -NY 10013
(718) 222-1720 .. **Krisel,** Andrew M '80 -44 Court -Brklyn 11201
(516) 571-0646 .. **Krisel,** Martha '81 %Cnty Atty -1 West -Mineola 11501 **Fx:**571-4080
(212) 969-3000 .. **Krisel,** Wm E '81 (Proskauer R LLP) -1585 Bway -NY 10036
(718) 304-7590 .. **Krishna,** Akhilesh '03 -12721 Lbrty Av -Richmnd Hll 11419
(646) 602-5600 .. **Krishna,** Gowri J '07 Urban Justice Ctr -123 William -NY 10038 **Fx:**(212) 533-4598
(718) 990-2639 .. **Krishnakumar,** Anita S '01 %St John's Law Schl -8000 Utopia Pkwy -Jamaica 11439 **Fx:**591-1855
(212) 336-0116 .. **Krishnamurthy,** Preethi '03 %SEC -3 World Fncl Ctr -NY 10281 **Fx:**336-1323
(212) 264-1650 .. **Krishnan,** Katherine S '96 %ODAR-SSA -26 Fed Plz -NY 10278
(212) 442-0588 .. **Krishnan,** Sabita L '06 %Law Dept -100 Church -NY 10007 **Fx:**788-0367
(212) 642-7883 .. **Krishnan,** Suresh '93 ACE USA -1133 Av of Amer -NY 10036 **Fx:**642-7889
(631) 239-6817 .. **Krishnaraj,** Hariharan '03 %E Troy -44 Bway -Greenlawn 11740 **Fx:**239-6816
(914) 328-0366 .. **Krishnasamy,** Bindu '08 %Sapir & F LLP -399 Knollwood Rd -White Plns 10603
(718) 237-5500 .. **Krishnaswamy,** Pavita '03 %Leg Srvcs -105 Court -Brklyn 11201 **Fx:**855-0733
(212) 351-7400 .. **Krishtul,** Steve V '04 Hudson Legal -560 Lex Av -NY 10022
(212) 608-1900 .. **Krisiloff,** Jody R '80 %Lovell SH LLP -61 Bway -NY 10006
(845) 334-5290 .. **Krisjanis,** Elisabeth E '91 %Dept of Social Srvcs -1041 Development Ct -Kingston 12401
(212) 577-2000 .. **Kriss,** Arnold N '73 -123 William -NY 10038 **Fx:**577-2138
(212) 610-6300 .. **Kriss,** Bethany E '09 %Allen & O -1221 Av of Amer -NY 10020
(518) 449-2037 .. **Kriss,** Chas T '80 (Kriss K&B,LLP) -350 Nrthrn Blvd -Albany 12204
(212) 661-2900 .. **Kriss,** David S '82 (Kriss & F LLP) -360 Lex Av -NY 10017
(212) 661-2900 .. **Kriss & Feuerstein LLP** -360 Lex Av -NY 10017 **Fx:**661-9397
(518) 449-2037 .. **Kriss Kriss & Brignola, LLP** -350 Nrthrn Blvd -Albany 12204 **Fx:**449-7875
(518) 449-2037 .. **Kriss,** Mark C '79 (Kriss K&B,LLP) -350 Nrthrn Blvd -Albany 12204
(212) 297-0606 .. **Krissoff,** Robt L '61 -250 Park Av -NY 10177 **Fx:**557-4642
(914) 993-1928 .. **Krissoff,** Sarah R '03 US Atty -300 Quarropas -White Plns 10601 **Fx:**993-9036
(212) 825-3650 .. **Krist,** Brian J '09 Dept of Investigation -80 Maiden Ln -NY 10038
(212) 685-2277 .. **Kristal,** Carolyn R '80 -33 E 33rd -NY 10016
(212) 558-5500 .. **Kristal,** Jerry M '91 %Weitz & L,PC -700 Bway -NY 10003
(914) 287-0230 .. **Kristal,** Jocelyne S '89 -19 Court -White Plns 10601 **Fx:**945-9585
(212) 677-3950 .. **Kristal,** Lisa J '83 -57 2nd Av -NY 10003 **Fx:**677-3950
(585) 546-6330 .. **Kristal,** Peter L '80 -30 W Broad -Rchstr 14614 **Fx:**546-3641
(914) 997-2500 .. **Kristensen,** Erik '97 %Bodnar & M LLP -140 Grand -White Plns 10601 **Fx:**997-8155
(716) 856-4000 .. **Kristoff,** Karl W '76 (Hodgson R LLP) -140 Pearl -Buffalo 14202
(718) 254-0700 .. **Kristt,** Dara S '07 Bklyn Defender Srvcs -177 Lvngstn -Brklyn 11201 **Fx:**254-0897
(212) 819-8200 .. **Kritzalis,** Alexander S '70 (White & C LLP) -1155 Av of Amer -NY 10036
(914) 422-4159 .. **Kritzer,** Albert H '52 Pace Law Schl -78 N Bway -White Plns 10603 **Fx:**422-4039
(631) 271-4777 .. **Kritzer,** David S '92 (D Kritzer & Assoc,PC) -187 E Main -Huntngtn 11743 **Fx:**271-2530
(212) 682-5700 .. **Kritzer,** Harry A '81 %Maya M,PC -261 Mad Av -NY 10016 **Fx:**697-4432
(212) 446-4800 .. **Kritzer,** Nathaniel J '09 %Kirkland & E LLP -153 E 53rd -NY 10022
(516) 742-4343 .. **Krivisky,** Barry M '76 Cnsl Scully SM&P PC -400 Grdn City Plz -Gdn Cty 11530
(212) 408-5100 .. **Krivoy,** Clara '94 Cnsl Chadbourne & P LLP -30 Rckfllr Plz -NY 10112
(212) 237-1000 .. **Kriz,** John M '62 Cnsl Windels ML&M,LLP -156 W 56th -NY 10019
(585) 343-7307 .. **Krna,** Steven P '88 %Genesee Patrons Ins -218 E Main -Batavia 14020 **Fx:**343-5036
(212) 401-8756 .. **Kroczynski,** Elizabeth '02 Nasdaq -1 Lbrty -NY 10005
(212) 294-6700 .. **Kroczynski,** Robt J '09 %Winston & S -200 Park Av -NY 10166
(516) 222-8500 .. **Kroczynski,** Thos J '96 (Martin C&B LLP) -90 Merrick Av -E Meadow 11554
(212) 363-3100 .. **Kroeger,** W Richd '05 (Bivona & C,PC) -88 Pine -NY 10005
(585) 343-3700 .. **Kroemer,** Lisa M '90 -121 Wshngtn Av -Batavia 14020 **Fx:**343-3796
(212) 788-0848 .. **Kroening,** Jos J '04 %Law Dept -100 Church -NY 10007 **Fx:**788-0367
(212) 237-0000 .. **Kroetsch,** Jos F '06 %Vinson & E LLP -666 5th Av -NY 10103
(607) 272-2314 .. **Krogh,** Guy K '90 (Thaler & T) -309 N Tioga Bx266 -Ithaca 14851 **Fx:**272-8466
(212) 808-7800 .. **Krohley,** Wm A '71 (Kelley D&W LLP) -101 Park Av -NY 10178
(845) 778-2121 .. **Krohn,** Mark A '86 (Jacobowitz & G,LLP) -158 Orange Av Bx367 -Walden 12586
(718) 875-7431 .. **Krohn,** Paul I '73 -40 Clinton -Brklyn 11201 **Fx:**875-7432
(516) 868-0808 .. **Krohn Rosenblum & Rosenblum** -25 Merrick Av -Merrick 11566 **Fx:**379-5020
(212) 789-2745 .. **Krokoff,** Scott D '99 NHL -1185 Av of Amer -NY 10036
(212) 278-0400 .. **Krol,** Adam C '10 %Cooper & D LLP -30 Rckfllr Plz -NY 10112
(212) 595-8009 .. **Krol,** Igor '81 (Krol & O) -320 W 81st -NY 10024 **Fx:**595-8149
(718) 262-7100 .. **Krol,** Jill R '91 %Civil Ct -89-17 Sutphin Blvd -Jamaica 11435 **Fx:**262-7107
(914) 428-2100 .. **Krol,** John J P '82 OfCnsl Welby B&G,LLP -11 Martine Av -White Plns 10606
(716) 655-4000 .. **Krol,** Thos M '04 Steuben Foods,Inc -1150 Maple Rd -Elma 14059
(718) 624-5521 .. **Krolak,** Steven T '04 %M Tulip -26 Court -Brklyn 11242 **Fx:**875-2811
(914) 632-6990 .. **Kroleski,** Steven L '76 -201 Wolfs Ln -Pelham 10803 **Fx:**632-8560
(212) 808-7800 .. **Krolewski,** Martin A '99 %Kelley D&W LLP -101 Park Av -NY 10178
(212) 891-6147 .. **Krolick,** Ronald S '75 -9 W 57th -NY 10019
(212) 826-2900 .. **Krolik,** Babette '83 %Zeckendorf Realty LP -770 Lex Av -NY 10065 **Fx:**355-0891
(212) 644-3291 .. **Krolik,** Day III '76 %NBC -30 Rckfllr Plz -NY 10112
(212) 608-6800 .. **Krolik,** Maurice M '59 -291 Bway -NY 10007 **Fx:**608-6802
(212) 468-4800 .. **Kroll,** Alan D '71 (Davis & G LLP) -1740 Bway -NY 10019
(212) 484-3900 .. **Kroll,** Elliot M '78 (Arent F LLP) -1675 Bway -NY 10019
(845) 733-1065 .. **Kroll,** Glenn D '97 (G Kroll Assoc) -92 Main Bx10 -Bloomngbrg 12721 **Fx:**733-1055
(718) 222-2316 .. **Kroll,** Jason A '06 %Law Dept -350 Jay -Brklyn 11201 **Fx:**222-2373
(516) 873-8000 .. **Kroll,** Jonathan E '94 (Kroll M&K,LLP) -400 Grdn City Plz -Gdn Cty 11530
(212) 593-1000 .. **Kroll,** Jules B '67 (Kroll Assoc) -1166 Av of Amer -NY 10036 **Fx:**593-2631
(585) 262-4700 .. **Kroll,** Loren H '70 (Bilgore RLK&K) -950 Rynlds Arcd Bldg -Rchstr 14614
(585) 271-4470 .. **Kroll,** Marcus W '08 %R Kroll -2425 Clover -Rchstr 14618 **Fx:**271-0847
(585) 381-4055 .. **Kroll,** Merwyn M '62 -3955 East Av -Rchstr 14618
(516) 367-7777 .. **Kroll,** Michl I '73 -115 Eileen Way -Syosset 11791 **Fx:**692-2787
(516) 873-8000 .. **Kroll Moss & Kroll,LLP** -400 Grdn City Plz -Gdn Cty 11530 **Fx:**873-8009
(585) 271-4470 .. **Kroll,** Richd A '72 -2425 Clover -Rchstr 14618 **Fx:**271-0847
(516) 378-3051 .. **Kroll,** S Robt '58 -1400 Old Cntry Rd -Westbury 11590 **Fx:**623-3340
(716) 847-2923 .. **Kroll,** Scott W '01 -69 Delaware Av -Buffalo 14202
(845) 331-5733 .. **Krom,** Chester G '71 -86 Elmendorf Bx3385 -Kingston 12402 **Fx:**331-5736
(212) 676-7938 .. **Kroman,** Hilit '05 ACS -220 Church -NY 10013
(212) 521-5400 .. **Kromberg,** Jonathan B '03 %Reed S LLP -599 Lex Av -NY 10022
(631) 737-8381 .. **Krome,** Michl S '91 (M Krome,PC) -8 Teak Ct -Lk Grove 11755 **Fx:**737-8382
(212) 223-3900 .. **Kromm,** David R '01 %Zwerling S&Z,LLP -41 Mad Av -NY 10010
(212) 598-5900 .. **Kromo,** Yana '09 %Alonso A&K PC -920 Bway -NY 10010
(212) 696-1888 .. **Kron,** Danl L '07 %M Kron -295 Mad Av -NY 10017 **Fx:**696-4111
(212) 696-1888 .. **Kron,** Lindsay A '07 %M Kron -295 Mad Av -NY 10017 **Fx:**696-4111
(212) 696-1888 .. **Kron,** Martin A '81 -295 Mad Av -NY 10017 **Fx:**696-4111
(914) 948-7000 .. **Kronberg,** Howard S '85 (Keidel W&C LLP) -925 Wstchstr Av -White Plns 10604
(516) 338-0600 .. **Kronbichler,** Eileen M '86 -393 Old Cntry Rd -Carle Pl 11514 **Fx:**338-5310
(718) 543-2252 .. **Kronen,** Sheldon H '60 -2621 Palisade Av -Bronx 10463 **Fx:**543-2264
(212) 504-6000 .. **Kronenberg,** David E '08 %Cadwalader W&T LLP -1 World Fncl Ctr -NY 10281
(212) 387-8400 .. **Kronenberg,** David I '02 (Goldfarb AS&K LLP) -350 5th Av -NY 10118
(646) 328-0850 .. **Kronenberg,** Ely M '03 %Outside Cnsl Solutns LLP -1430 Bway -NY 10018 **Fx:**360-5000
(212) 708-9311 .. **Kronenberg,** James L '95 Bessemer Trst Co -630 5th Av -NY 10111 **Fx:**265-5826
(718) 854-1400 .. **Kronenberg,** Lea Miller '03 Pkwy Realty -1205 47th -Brklyn 11219
(631) 234-4434 .. **Kronenberg,** Robt B '04 -1355 Motor Pkwy -Hauppauge 11749 **Fx:**234-4469
(646) 278-2015 .. **Kronenfeld,** Suzanne J '93 Esperanza NY -636 Bway -NY 10012
(212) 450-4000 .. **Kronfeld,** Nicholas Adams '91 (Davis P&W LLP) -450 Lex Av -NY 10017
(516) 482-2282 .. **Kronfeld,** Penny '81 (Feldman K&B) -45 N Station Plz -Gt Neck 11021
(212) 425-0230 .. **Kronfeld,** Penny '81 (Feldman K&B) -42 Bway -NY 10004
(212) 279-3467 .. **Krongold,** Jeffrey B '73 (Schaeffer & K LLP) -450 7th Av -NY 10123
(914) 946-8484 .. **Kronick,** Arnold S '74 (Lehrman & K) -199 Main -White Plns 10601
(212) 940-8800 .. **Kronick,** Elizabeth K '08 %Katten MR LLP -575 Mad Av -NY 10022
(212) 922-2200 .. **Kroningold,** Randi S '09 %Watson F&W LLP -1133 Av of Amer -NY 10036
(845) 634-3425 .. **Kronish,** Arnold '48 -5 Plains Dr -New Cty 10956
(212) 310-8000 .. **Kronman,** Ariel Z '94 Weil G&M LLP -767 5th Av -NY 10153
(716) 646-5530 .. **Kronman,** Joan M '75 %UAW Ford Leg Srvcs -4819 S Park Av -Hambrg 14075 **Fx:**646-1519
(212) 266-8240 .. **Kronman,** Mark J '59 %FBE Ltd -111 Bway -NY 10006 **Fx:**732-1824
(212) 490-3000 .. **Kronman,** Rachel R '10 %Wilson EME&D LLP -150 E 42nd -NY 10017
(212) 593-6700 .. **Kronovet,** Steven Z '73 (Aaronson RF&D,LLP) -757 3rd Av -NY 10017
(718) 461-6633 .. **Kronrad,** Jessica L '01 %Mallilo & G -163-09 Nrthrn Blvd -Flushng 11358
(212) 408-5100 .. **Kronstadt,** Alison H '09 %Chadbourne & P LLP -30 Rckfllr Plz -NY 10112
(212) 850-2800 .. **Kronthal,** Richd H '84 (Andrews K LLP) -450 Lex Av -NY 10017
(917) 405-1319 .. **Kronzon,** Lori E '03 -1755 York Av -NY 10128
(212) 490-2020 .. **Krooks,** Bernard A '86 (Littman K LLP) -655 3rd Av -NY 10017
(914) 684-2100 .. **Krooks,** Bernard A '86 (Littman K LLP) -399 Knollwood Rd -White Plns 10603
(914) 253-9255 .. **Krooks,** Howard S '90 OfCnsl Amoruso & A,LLP -800 Wstchstr Av -Rye Brook 10573 **Fx:**253-9162
(516) 861-6454 .. **Krosser,** Nancy J '00 -300 Jericho Quad -Jericho 11753
(212) 373-3000 .. **Krotman,** Adam S '10 %Paul WRW&G LLP -1285 Av of Amer -NY 10019
(631) 293-3555 .. **Krotman,** Max T '71 -1 Huntngtn Quad -Melvll 11747
(631) 853-8333 .. **Krotschinsky,** Frank '84 Cnty Ofc of Handicapped Srvcs -Bldg 158 N Cnty Cmplx Bx6100 -Hauppauge 11788 **Fx:**853-8339
(631) 367-7100 .. **Kroub,** Edw Y '05 %Coughlin SGR&R LLP -58 S Srvc Rd -Melvll 11747
(212) 801-2126 .. **Kroub,** Gaston '02 (Greenberg T,LLP) -200 Park Av -NY 10166
(212) 715-9100 .. **Krouner,** Shari K '85 (Kramer LN&F,LLP) -1177 Av of Amer -NY 10036
(914) 238-5800 .. **Krouner,** Todd J '85 -93 N Greeley Av -Chappaqua 10514
(212) 373-3000 .. **Kroup,** George W '09 %Paul WRW&G LLP -1285 Av of Amer -NY 10019
(212) 479-6000 .. **Kroupa,** Lesley A '07 %Cooley LLP -1114 Av of Amer -NY 10036
(212) 455-2000 .. **Krouse,** George R Jr. '71 OfCnsl Simpson T&B LLP -425 Lex Av -NY 10017
(212) 909-6000 .. **Krouzman,** Donna '05 %Debevoise & P LLP -919 3rd Av -NY 10022

(212) 370-9400 .. **Krowitz**, Scott J '88 Lexolution,LLC -295 Mad Av -NY 10017 **Fx**:370-9401
(212) 819-8200 .. **Kroyer**, Kellie M '10 %White & C LLP -1155 Av of Amer -NY 10036
(212) 710-5500 .. **Kruce**, Hilary A '91 FNF Title Intl -711 3rd Av -NY 10017
(212) 972-6161 .. **Krucher**, Jennifer H '94 %Cassin & C LLP -711 3rd Av -NY 10017
(718) 439-6300 .. **Krueger**, David A '88 %Davidson Pipe Supply Co -5002 2nd Av -Brklyn 11232 **Fx**:439-8078
(212) 351-4500 .. **Krueger**, Donald S '81 SrCnsl Epstein B&G,PC -250 Park Av -NY 10177
(585) 232-3730 .. **Krueger**, Mikal J '04 %Chamberlain D LLP -1600 Crssrds Bldg -Rchstr 14614
(518) 270-4040 .. **Kruegler**, Laura M '02 %DA -80 2nd -Troy 12180 **Fx**:270-4025
(212) 317-5546 .. **Kruft**, Stephen R '76 %Swiss Re New Markets -55 E 52nd -NY 10055 **Fx**:317-5230
(716) 856-6086 .. **Krug**, Thos E '65 (Tiernan K&S) -110 Pearl -Buffalo 14202
(631) 273-4445 .. **Kruger**, Frances Petronelli '96 %Innovative Marbile & Tile -130 Motor Pkwy -Hauppauge 11788
(716) 854-1541 .. **Kruger**, Julie E '10 %Kolken & K -135 Delaware Av -Buffalo 14202 **Fx**:854-6223
(212) 806-5400 .. **Kruger**, Lewis '59 (Stroock &S&L LLP) -180 Maiden Ln -NY 10038
(212) 841-1000 .. **Kruger**, Richd D '09 %Covington & B LLP -620 8th Av -NY 10018
(212) 732-5556 .. **Kruger**, Robt '64 -232 Mad Av -NY 10016 **Fx**:986-5994
(518) 853-4250 .. **Kruger**, Robt J '80 (Leonhardt & K,PC) -6 Main Bx442 -Fultonvll 12072 **Fx**:853-4933
(212) 331-7567 .. **Kruger**, Thea K '07 Berdon LLP -360 Mad Av -NY 10017
(212) 318-6000 .. **Kruger**, Thos E '70 (Paul HJ&W LLP) -75 E 55th -NY 10022
(212) 455-2000 .. **Kruglak**, Seth M '04 %Simpson T&B LLP -425 Lex Av -NY 10017
(212) 701-3000 .. **Krugman**, Edw P '80 (Cahill G&R LLP) -80 Pine -NY 10005 **Fx**:269-5420
(212) 558-4000 .. **Krugman**, Maya '10 %Sullivan & C LLP -125 Broad -NY 10004
(212) 918-3000 .. **Kruk**, Carolyn E '08 %Hogan L LLP -875 3rd Av -NY 10022
(585) 624-5030 .. **Kruk**, Stephen M '83 (Kruk & C) -7312 E Main Bx30-A -Lima 14485 **Fx**:624-3972
(585) 546-5530 .. **Kruk**, Theresa Ludwig '83 %Thomson West -50 E Broad -Rchstr 14694
(516) 203-4001 .. **Krukas**, Eugene W '03 -1225 Franklin Av -Gdn Cty 11530 **Fx**:320-8071
(716) 849-1333 .. **Krull**, Gregory P '90 (Lipsitz GSC LLP) -42 Delaware Av -Buffalo 14202
(716) 854-1002 .. **Krull**, John A '52 OfCnsl Miserendino CS&E,PC -295 Main -Buffalo 14203
(516) 599-6420 .. **Kruman**, Henry E '80 (Kruman & K) -353 Hempstd Av -Malverne 11565
(516) 599-6420 .. **Kruman & Kruman** -353 Hempstd Av -Malverne 11565 **Fx**:599-1761
(516) 599-6420 .. **Kruman**, Martin J '63 (Kruman & K) -353 Hempstd Av -Malverne 11565
(877) 222-1814 .. **Krumholz**, George R '75 %B Rothenberg -100 Duffy Av -Hicksvll 11801 **Fx**:(866) 894-2182
(212) 815-1818 .. **Krummel**, Jos C '01 DC 37 MELS -125 Barclay -NY 10007 **Fx**:815-1343
(516) 224-5100 .. **Kruper**, Debra A '07 %J Novick -100 Crsswys Park W -Woodbury 11797 **Fx**:422-6199
(212) 545-4000 .. **Krupman**, Wm A '62 (Jackson L LLP) -666 3rd Av -NY 10017
(516) 741-7800 .. **Krupnick**, Kevin P '08 SrCnsl Krupnick Firm,PC -23 Vllg Sq -Glen Cove 11542 **Fx**:385-1817
(212) 335-9000 .. **Krupnick**, Marc A '98 %DA -1 Hogan Pl -NY 10013
(212) 897-5816 .. **Krupnik**, Alla '01 -305 Bway -NY 10007
(212) 506-1700 .. **Krupp**, Adam J '05 %Kasowitz BT&F LLP -1633 Bway -NY 10019
(716) 854-3400 .. **Kruppa**, Kevin J '03 %Rupp BPC&C LLC -1600 Lbrty Bldg -Buffalo 14202
(518) 486-3298 .. **Kruppenbacher-Meyer**, Sonia '01 %OCFS -52 Wshngtn -Rensselaer 12144 **Fx**:486-6361
(212) 373-1919 .. **Krusch**, Jos G '57 (Krusch & M) -10 Rckfllr Plz -NY 10020
(212) 373-1919 .. **Krusch & Modell** -10 Rckfllr Plz -NY 10020 **Fx**:373-1920
(212) 309-1000 .. **Kruse**, Michl B '08 %Hunton & W -200 Park Av -NY 10166
(518) 266-1000 .. **Kruse**, Rachael E '08 %Pattison SG&G,PC -22 1st Bx208 -Troy 12181
(845) 354-3900 .. **Kruse**, Raymond G '61 R Kruse,PC -865 N Main -Spg Vly 10977 **Fx**:354-0521
(212) 728-8000 .. **Kruse**, Rosalind Fahey '96 (Willkie F&G LLP) -787 7th Av -NY 10019
(212) 547-5400 .. **Kruse**, Toni Ann '09 %McDermott W&E LLP -340 Mad Av -NY 10173
(212) 635-1038 .. **Krusik**, Brent H '00 Bk of NY Mellon -1 Wall -NY 10286
(212) 446-7000 .. **Krusko**, Michelle L '01 %McKinsey & Co -55 E 52nd -NY 10055 **Fx**:688-9521
(631) 549-5900 .. **Krusos**, Denis '69 -900 Walt Whitman Rd -Huntngtn Sta 11747 **Fx**:549-3813
(845) 279-0449 .. **Kruta**, James M '83 -47 Empire Dr -Patterson 12563 **Fx**:279-0449
(585) 428-1803 .. **Krutell**, Christopher T '01 %Surrogates Ct -1 Hall of Justice -Rchstr 14614
(845) 434-3000 .. **Krutman**, Robt '63 (Gaiman & K) -5214 Main Bx366 -S Fallsbrg 12779
(845) 369-0912 .. **Krutoff**, Glenn S '88 -16 Bon Aire Cir -Suffern 10901 **Fx**:369-0444
(212) 335-9000 .. **Krutoy**, Evan S '96 %DA -1 Hogan Pl -NY 10013
(315) 432-8188 .. **Kruttschnitt**, Donald B '72 -255 N Collingwood Av -Syracuse 13206 **Fx**:432-8188
(212) 267-6456 .. **Krutzel**, Martin '77 (Fischer Bros) -217 Bway -NY 10007 **Fx**:267-6468
(212) 269-1400 .. **Kruzhkov**, Marlen '99 Gusrae KB&N PLLC -120 Wall -NY 10005
(631) 369-7600 .. **Kruzynski**, Michl G '96 (Lewis JAA,LLP) -21 E 2nd -Rvrhead 11901
(212) 975-3534 .. **Kryle**, Sanford I '76 %CBS Inc -51 W 52nd -NY 10019 **Fx**:975-3930
(212) 294-6700 .. **Krylov**, Nikolai B '95 (Winston & S) -200 Park Av -NY 10166
(718) 643-9333 .. **Krysinski**, Nicole L '06 %H Schwartz -50 Court -Brklyn 11201 **Fx**:522-5644
(212) 640-0201 .. **Krystal**, Donna Bleiberg '80 %Amer Exp -200 Vesey -NY 10285
(212) 837-8001 .. **Kryston**, Danl J '68 %Dept of Sanitation -44 Beaver -NY 10004 **Fx**:785-3952
(212) 701-3000 .. **Kryszak**, Nathaniel N '03 %Cahill G&R LLP -80 Pine -NY 10005 **Fx**:269-5420
(212) 349-6009 .. **Kryszko**, Barbara C '99 %Sanctuary for Families -110 Wall -NY 10005 **Fx**:566-0344
(585) 546-3770 .. **Krzanowicz**, Ella '92 %S Hall -36 W Main -Rchstr 14614
(212) 483-9490 .. **Krzastek**, Walter R '99 (McElroy DM&C,LLP) -88 Pine -NY 10005
(518) 373-9900 .. **Krzykowski**, Brian P '84 OfCnsl Mills Law Firm,LLP -1520 Crescent Rd -Clifton Pk 12065 **Fx**:383-7162
(518) 842-3795 .. **Krzys**, Robt J '77 -107 Division -Amsterdam 12010 **Fx**:843-4312
(716) 852-6923 .. **Krzywicki**, Cheryl Ann '96 %Taylor & Santacrose -300 Pearl -Buffalo 14202 **Fx**:856-7417
(212) 474-1000 .. **Krzyzowski**, Marek P '05 %Cravath S&M LLP -825 8th Av -NY 10019
(212) 208-3128 .. **Ksenak**, Stephen M '94 %Ambac Assurance -1 State Street Plz -NY 10004 **Fx**:785-1178
(212) 701-3000 .. **Kshirsagar**, Mihir '07 %Cahill G&R LLP -80 Pine -NY 10005 **Fx**:269-5420
(516) 463-4237 .. **Ku**, Julian Gei-Lun '01 %Hofstra Law Schl -121 Hofstra Univ -Hempstd 11549
(212) 715-1000 .. **Ku**, Karen Young '06 %Arnold & P LLP -399 Park Av -NY 10022
(212) 373-3000 .. **Ku**, Sena '09 %Paul WRW&G LLP -1285 Av of Amer -NY 10019
(212) 907-0700 .. **Ku**, Vicky '07 %Labaton S LLP -140 Bway -NY 10005
(212) 274-0777 .. **Kuan**, Julia P '92 (Romano & K,PLLC) -100 Lafayette -NY 10013
(212) 986-6000 .. **Kuan**, Mary C M '00 (Kleinberg KW&C,PC) -551 5th Av -NY 10176
(212) 244-7676 .. **Kuba**, Lance E '88 (Ferro KMS,PC) -424 W 33rd -NY 10001
(212) 732-5050 .. **Kuba**, Ronald J '61 Kuba Law Firm -321 Bway -NY 10007 **Fx**:766-0049
(716) 856-0600 .. **Kubarek**, Jos P '83 (Jaeckle F&M,LLP) -12 Fountain Plz -Buffalo 14202
(212) 909-6000 .. **Kubek**, Gary W '79 (Debevoise & P LLP) -919 3rd Av -NY 10022
(212) 813-2680 .. **Kuber**, Douglas A '00 (Kuber Law Grp,PC) -575 Mad Av -NY 10022
(631) 852-2500 .. **Kubetz**, Jacob T '02 %DA -200 Center Dr -Rvrhead 11901 **Fx**:852-1769
(212) 574-1200 .. **Kubiak**, Deborah P '82 %Seward & K LLP -1 Bttry Pk Plz -NY 10004
(716) 855-1777 .. **Kubiak**, Fonda D '95 -403 Main -Buffalo 14203 **Fx**:855-1317
(718) 463-3993 .. **Kubic**, Carl J '72 -29-03 167th -Flushng 11358
(516) 572-2000 .. **Kubic**, Christian J '09 %DA -99 Main -Hempstd 11550 **Fx**:572-2606
(631) 261-2117 .. **Kubic**, Thos A '80 -8 Pine Hill Ct -Northprt 11768 **Fx**:261-2120
(212) 684-7541 .. **Kubick**, Richd A '95 (Kubick & Assoc,PC) -40 Worth -NY 10013 **Fx**:643-8182
(212) 684-7541 .. **Kubick**, Richd J '87 -40 Worth -NY 10013
(212) 806-5400 .. **Kubikian**, David A '06 %Stroock &S&L LLP -180 Maiden Ln -NY 10038
(212) 735-3000 .. **Kubilus**, Eric M '10 %Skadden ASM&F LLP -4 Times Sq -NY 10036
(716) 873-9161 .. **Kubiniec**, Judith M '88 -402 Amherst -Buffalo 14207
(716) 873-9161 .. **Kubiniec**, Richd J '58 -402 Amherst -Buffalo 14207
(716) 858-2424 .. **Kubiniec**, Thos D '98 %DA -25 Delaware Av -Buffalo 14202 **Fx**:858-7425
(516) 393-2200 .. **Kubit**, Melissa S '07 %Garfunkel W,PC -111 Grt Nck Rd -Gt Neck 11021
(212) 349-0900 .. **Kubitschek**, Carolyn A '74 (Lansner KS&Z) -325 Bway -NY 10007
(212) 785-4100 .. **Kublanovsky**, Eugene D '06 %Fensterstock & Prtnrs LLP -30 Wall -NY 10005
(315) 424-1105 .. **Kublick**, Jan Scott '78 (McMahon K&S,PC) -500 S Salina -Syracuse 13202
(315) 682-4456 .. **Kublin**, Rhonda B '84 (R Kublin,PC) -8261 Iliad Dr -Manlius 13104 **Fx**:682-4177
(718) 222-2395 .. **Kubly**, Gregory A '08 %Law Dept -350 Jay -Brklyn 11201 **Fx**:222-2088
(212) 230-8821 .. **Kubota**, Kohki M '02 Cnsl WilmerHale -399 Park Av -NY 10022
(212) 521-5400 .. **Kubow**, Janice D '04 %Reed S LLP -599 Lex Av -NY 10022
(212) 529-0223 .. **Kuby & Perez,LLP** -119 W 23rd -NY 10011 **Fx**:529-0644
(212) 529-0223 .. **Kuby**, Ronald L '84 (Kuby & P,LLP) -119 W 23rd -NY 10011
(631) 852-2500 .. **Kucera**, Marcia R '90 %DA -200 Center Dr -Rvrhead 11901 **Fx**:852-1769
(212) 578-2605 .. **Kuch**, Stacey A '95 MetLife -27-01 Qns Plz N -LIC 11101
(212) 756-2000 .. **Kuchar**, Kara A '07 %Schulte R&Z LLP -919 3rd Av -NY 10022
(212) 836-8000 .. **Kucharzyk**, Jakub D '09 Kaye S LLP -425 Park Av -NY 10022
(212) 564-5005 .. **Kucherovsky**, Leon '98 -212 W 35th -NY 10001 **Fx**:564-5121
(516) 873-2000 .. **Kucica**, Dennis '99 %Moritt HH&H LLP -400 Grdn City Plz -Gdn Cty 11530
(631) 424-7443 .. **Kucich**, Jacqueline M '95 -5 Blue Grass Ct -Huntngtn 11743 **Fx**:424-7443
(212) 735-3000 .. **Kuck**, Lea Haber '91 (Skadden ASM&F LLP) -4 Times Sq -NY 10036
(646) 452-9644 .. **Kuckelman**, Solomon E '06 Man Invstmnts -1 Rckfllr Plz -NY 10020 **Fx**:452-9701
(212) 869-5030 .. **Kucker**, Alan D '80 (Kucker & B,LLP) -747 3rd Av -NY 10017
(212) 869-5030 .. **Kucker & Bruh, LLP** -747 3rd Av -NY 10017 **Fx**:944-5818
(718) 286-6000 .. **Kucker-Horland**, Alix F '88 %DA -125-01 Qns Blvd -Kew Gdns 11415
(646) 386-3619 .. **Kucsma**, P Michelle '95 Supreme Ct-Law Dept -60 Centre -NY 10007
(914) 245-7200 .. **Kuczinski**, Gregory '95 (G Kuczinski,PC) -2649 Strang Blvd -Yorktwn Hts 10598 **Fx**:245-7208
(315) 423-4400 .. **Kudarauskas**, Michl A '96 (Wolff G&G,LLP) -217 Mntgmry -Syracuse 13202
(212) 768-6700 .. **Kudenholdt**, Stephen S '81 (Sonnenschein N&R LLP) -2 World Fncl Ctr -NY 10281
(212) 481-4870 .. **Kudera**, Loreto S '07 Trustforte Corp -271 Mad Av -NY 10016
(212) 963-7305 .. **Kudiabor**, Cyril F '02 %UN Reproduction Unit -1 UN Plz -NY 10017
(212) 373-3000 .. **Kudiya**, Asad I '09 %Paul WRW&G LLP -1285 Av of Amer -NY 10019
(212) 333-8592 .. **Kudler**, Heath N '97 %Mercury Records -825 8th Av -NY 10019 **Fx**:333-1077
(212) 480-3030 .. **Kudler**, Seth I '92 %M Pressman -125 Maiden Ln -NY 10038 **Fx**:480-2590
(212) 878-7389 .. **Kudler**, Stacy Tick '93 %MTA -347 Mad Av -NY 10017
(212) 868-1010 .. **Kudman**, Stuart R '83 (Kudman TA LLP) -350 5th Av -NY 10118
(212) 868-1010 .. **Kudman**, Tama Beth '96 TB Kudman,PA -350 5th Av -NY 10118 **Fx**:868-0013
(212) 868-1010 .. **Kudman Trachten Aloe LLP** -350 5th Av -NY 10118 **Fx**:868-0013
(212) 506-5000 .. **Kudon**, Jeremy N '01 %Orrick H&S LLP -51 W 52nd -NY 10019

(518) 561-6274 .. **Kudrle,** Larry A '94 Law Guardian Ofc -55 Court -Plattsbrgh 12901 **Fx:**561-6218
(212) 972-1000 .. **Kudrle,** Stephanie I '09 %London F LLP -59 Maiden Ln -NY 10038
(914) 347-2600 .. **Kuebler,** Jamie R '10 %Traub LS&S LLP -7 Skyline Dr -Hawthorne 10532
(212) 449-4715 .. **Kuebler,** Paul A '04 %Merrill Lynch & Co Inc/Bk of America -4 World Fncl Ctr -NY 10080
(212) 986-3114 .. **Kueffner,** Friedrich '85 -317 Mad Av -NY 10017
(631) 852-8800 .. **Kuehhas,** Steven J '88 %DA -116 Hmptn Rd -Southampton 11968 **Fx:**852-8806
(212) 637-2741 .. **Kuehler,** Natalie N '06 %US Atty -86 Chmbrs -NY 10007
(212) 310-8000 .. **Kuehn,** Brant D '07 %Weil G&M LLP -767 5th Av -NY 10153
(631) 734-6308 .. **Kuehn,** Christopher K '85 -2625 W Crk Av -Cutchogue 11935
(212) 695-8100 .. **Kuehn,** David '05 Goetz F,LLP -1 Penn Plz -NY 10119
(212) 446-4800 .. **Kuehn,** John L '98 (Kirkland & E LLP) -153 E 53rd -NY 10022
(212) 308-5858 .. **Kuehn,** Justin A '08 %Bragar WE&S,PC -885 3rd Av -NY 10022
(212) 269-4900 .. **Kuehn,** Michl R '09 %Ford MEW&G,LLP -Wall Street Plz -NY 10005
(212) 770-3410 .. **Kuehn,** Robt P '92 %AIG -80 Pine -NY 10005
(315) 474-8888 .. **Kuehner,** Kevin P '00 -217 Mntgmry -Syracuse 13202
(212) 351-4500 .. **Kuesel,** Jane Lembeck '91 Epstein B&G,PC -250 Park Av -NY 10177
(212) 326-2000 .. **Kuesel,** Wm B '88 (O'Melveny & M LLP) -7 Times Sq -NY 10036
(212) 269-0927 .. **Kuffler,** David J '96 (D'Amato & L,LLP) -2 World Fncl Ctr -NY 10281
(212) 679-3124 .. **Kuflik,** Melina F '94 -274 Mad Av -NY 10016 **Fx:**679-3105
(212) 608-2700 .. **Kuflik,** Sidney H '77 (Lamb & L) -233 Bway -NY 10279
(631) 361-6699 .. **Kugal,** Douglas A '98 %Binder & B,PC -300 Rabro Dr -Hauppauge 11788 **Fx:**361-6475
(212) 372-7218 .. **Kugel,** Rachel L '05 -1838 2nd Av -NY 10128
(718) 520-4727 .. **Kugelman,** Mark J '94 %Hon A Weiss -88-11 Sutphin Blvd -Jamaica 11435
(914) 421-9200 .. **Kugelmas,** Jerry '86 -120 Bloomingdale Rd -White Plns 10605 **Fx:**422-3636
(212) 848-4000 .. **Kugelmass,** Rachel '07 %Shearman & S LLP -599 Lex Av -NY 10022
(212) 867-9595 .. **Kugielska,** Lauren M '10 %Goldberg and W -630 3rd Av -NY 10017
(631) 598-0337 .. **Kugler,** Ellen B '91 (Ansanelli K&S,LLP) -92 Bway -Amityvll 11701 **Fx:**598-0352
(718) 286-6000 .. **Kugler,** Rona I '97 %DA -125-01 Qns Blvd -Kew Gdns 11415
(212) 732-3665 .. **Kugler,** Stacy J '97 %Harmon L&R -42 Bway -NY 10004
(516) 463-5858 .. **Kuh,** Katrina Fischer '04 %Hofstra Law Schl -121 Hofstra Univ -Hempstd 11549
(212) 906-1200 .. **Kuh,** Michl J '04 %Latham & W -885 3rd Av -NY 10022
(212) 984-7830 .. **Kuh,** Richd H '48 (Warshaw BCS&K,LLP) -555 5th Av -NY 10017
(212) 228-1331 .. **Kuharski Levitz & Giovinazzo** -176 Hart Blvd -Staten Isl 10301 **Fx:**406-1331
(212) 228-1331 .. **Kuharski,** Michl J '89 (Kuharski L&G) -176 Hart Blvd -Staten Isl 10301
(914) 684-1200 .. **Kuhfahl,** Ingo '80 -99 Church -White Plns 10601 **Fx:**684-0401
(516) 795-1800 .. **Kuhl,** Charlene M '87 -670 Bway -Massapequa 11758
(607) 776-2877 .. **Kuhl,** John R Jr. '70 -10 Gansevoort -Bath 14810
(347) 404-9920 .. **Kuhlman,** Alison L '05 %MHLS -120 Schermerhorn -Brklyn 11201 **Fx:**(718) 243-2410
(516) 877-5600 .. **Kuhlman,** Jeffrey G '87 %R Tusa -1225 Franklin Av -Gdn Cty 11530 **Fx:**877-5695
(212) 524-5000 .. **Kuhlman,** Jonathan R '92 (Jacob M&F) -1270 Av of Amer -NY 10020
(718) 720-3900 .. **Kuhn,** Danl D '92 (Kuhn & O,LLP) -1 Edgewtr Plz -Staten Isl 10305
(212) 715-1000 .. **Kuhn,** Danl M '02 %Arnold & P LLP -399 Park Av -NY 10022
(585) 262-6390 .. **Kuhn,** Danl P '09 %Hamberger & W -1 S Wshngtn -Rchstr 14614
(212) 803-5100 .. **Kuhn,** David R '94 %NY Cnty Defender Srvcs -225 Bway -NY 10007 **Fx:**571-6035
(212) 480-4800 .. **Kuhn,** Eric D '98 %Fox H&C LLP -825 3rd Av -NY 10022
(518) 626-9000 .. **Kuhn,** Jeffrey D '03 %Dewey & L LLP -99 Wshngtn Av -Albany 12210
(631) 427-2246 .. **Kuhn,** John F '75 -22 Oakwood Rd -Huntngtn 11743 **Fx:**427-3355
(718) 720-3900 .. **Kuhn & O'Toole,LLP** -1 Edgewtr Plz -Staten Isl 10305 **Fx:**720-2116
(212) 848-4000 .. **Kuhn,** Patricia A '90 Cnsl Shearman & S LLP -599 Lex Av -NY 10022
(212) 837-6000 .. **Kuhn,** Perla M '68 (Hughes H&R LLP) -1 Bttry Pk Plz -NY 10004
(718) 720-3900 .. **Kuhn,** Richd D '58 (Kuhn & O,LLP) -1 Edgewtr Plz -Staten Isl 10305
(212) 270-4222 .. **Kuhn,** Robt A '77 %Chem Bk -270 Park Av -NY 10017
(212) 343-1006 .. **Kuhn,** Robt W '86 -100 Park Av -NY 10017 **Fx:**343-1009
(212) 872-1000 .. **Kuhn,** Stephen B '91 -One Bryant Park -NY 10036 **Fx:**872-1002
(631) 928-8000 .. **Kuhn,** Steven P '82 (Winkler KW&K,LLP) -310 Hallock Av -Pt Jffrsn Sta 11776
(212) 553-8300 .. **Kuhn,** Terrence F '88 Cohen K & Assoc -2 Park Av -NY 10016 **Fx:**553-8721
(631) 853-4343 .. **Kuhnla,** Marie '01 %Leg Aid -400 Carleton Av Bx9082 -Central Islip 11722 **Fx:**853-7798
(212) 906-1200 .. **Kui,** Rachel '08 %Latham & W -885 3rd Av -NY 10022
(212) 969-7590 .. **Kujawski,** Audra B '93 King Features -300 W 57th -NY 10019
(631) 242-1600 .. **Kujawski,** Bryan P '72 (Kujawski & D) -1637 Deer Prk Av -Deer Pk 11729
(631) 242-1600 .. **Kujawski & DelliCarpini** -1637 Deer Prk Av -Deer Pk 11729 **Fx:**242-1814
(631) 242-1600 .. **Kujawski,** Mark C '01 %Kujawski & D -1637 Deer Prk Av -Deer Pk 11729
(212) 906-1200 .. **Kukish,** Paul F '05 %Latham & W -885 3rd Av -NY 10022
(315) 637-7253 .. **Kukla,** Karen K '93 -201 W Genesee -Fayettevll 13066 **Fx:**637-7253
(718) 780-7959 .. **Kuklin,** Bailey H '70 %Bklyn Law Schl -250 Joralemon -Brklyn 11201 **Fx:**780-0393
(607) 763-9200 .. **Kukol,** Albert B '91 (Levene G&T,LLP) -BxF-1706 -Bnghmtn 13902
(914) 493-2800 .. **Kukowski,** Barbara Flynn '89 %Cnty Hlthcr Corp -95 Grasslands Rd -Valhalla 10595 **Fx:**493-2321
(914) 681-8700 .. **Kukowski,** Thos H '89 (Milber MP&S LLP) -3 Barker Av -White Plns 10601
(212) 594-0977 .. **Kukreja,** Gopal T '03 -147 W 35th -NY 10001 **Fx:**594-3643
(212) 259-8000 .. **Kukulski,** Jonathan D '04 %Dewey & L LLP -1301 Av of Amer -NY 10019
(315) 597-4641 .. **Kukuvka,** Cynthia M '84 -330 E Main -Palmyra 14522 **Fx:**597-6637
(203) 671-7208 .. **Kul,** Stephanie Lawton '10 -155 E 29th -NY 10016
(212) 977-9700 .. **Kula,** Christopher J '03 %Phillips N LLP -666 5th Av -NY 10103
(631) 852-1613 .. **Kulahcioglu,** Esin '92 %Supreme Ct -Center Dr S -Rvrhead 11901 **Fx:**852-2020
(212) 219-2600 .. **Kulak,** Andrew H '80 (Kulak & Z) -401 Bway -NY 10013
(845) 565-9261 .. **Kulak,** Bryan M '84 B Kulak -484 Temple Hill Rd -New Windsor 12553
(212) 735-8600 .. **Kulak,** Kelly A '00 %Morrison C LLP -909 3rd Av -NY 10022
(212) 644-1010 .. **Kulak,** Marjorie B '03 %Kauff M&M LLP -950 3rd Av -NY 10022
(212) 219-2600 .. **Kulak & Zaslowsky** -401 Bway -NY 10013 **Fx:**941-0143
(718) 726-5400 .. **Kulakis,** Christopher G '84 (Kulakis & C) -21-74 Steinway -Astoria 11105 **Fx:**726-8777
(718) 793-6327 .. **Kulakoff,** David S '82 -67-71 Yllwstn Blvd -Frst Hlls 11375
(212) 250-8412 .. **Kulawas,** Christina H '86 %Deutsche Bank -60 Wall -NY 10005
(212) 310-8000 .. **Kulawik,** Tomasz '08 %Weil G&M LLP -767 5th Av -NY 10153
(516) 222-2330 .. **Kulb,** Amy T '80 (Jacobson G&K,LLP) -585 Stewart Av -Gdn Cty 11530
(212) 906-1200 .. **Kulback,** John A '08 %Latham & W -885 3rd Av -NY 10022
(212) 352-1700 .. **Kulcsar,** Roy R '68 -27 Union Square W -NY 10003
(516) 746-2300 .. **Kule,** Linda '97 %A Capetola -2C Hillside Av -Williston Pk 11596 **Fx:**746-2318
(212) 693-1671 .. **Kulefsky,** Herschel '82 -111 John -NY 10038 **Fx:**385-4846
(718) 261-0181 .. **Kule-Korgood,** Michele G '94 -118-35 Qns Blvd -Frst Hlls 11375 **Fx:**268-2633
(212) 213-6110 .. **Kulen,** Remzi G '01 Acar Law Firm,PLLC -404 Park Av S -NY 10016
(516) 873-2329 .. **Kulewicz,** Mark J '96 %AAA NY -1415 Kellum Pl -Gdn Cty 11530
(212) 920-8172 .. **Kulick,** Mitchell R '94 Iroquois Capital Mgmt,LLC -641 Lex Av -NY 10022
(212) 277-6500 .. **Kulidzhanova,** Ketevan '05 %Dickstein S LLP -1633 Bway -NY 10019
(212) 902-1000 .. **Kulikov,** Maxim S '99 Goldman Sachs & Co -85 Broad -NY 10004
(212) 208-1450 .. **Kulish,** Jonathan A '98 Cormorant Co Inc -140 Bway -NY 10005 **Fx:**208-1451
(212) 656-4878 .. **Kulka,** Holly K '01 NYSE Euronext Inc -11 Wall -NY 10005
(646) 386-5700 .. **Kullas,** Joel R '98 %Civil Ct -111 Centre -NY 10013
(212) 449-4988 .. **Kullerkupp,** Anu '02 %Merrill Lynch -4 World Fncl Ctr -NY 10080
(212) 677-7171 .. **Kulleseid,** L Erik '90 %Trst for Public Land -666 Bway -NY 10012 **Fx:**353-2052
(518) 486-7815 .. **Kullman,** Doris J '99 %Insurance Dept -99 Wshngtn Av -Albany 12257 **Fx:**474-3397
(716) 856-4400 .. **Kullman,** Paul W '88 (Gibbons SG&K,PC) -181 Franklin -Buffalo 14202
(212) 806-5400 .. **Kulman,** Bradley G '88 (Stroock &S&L LLP) -180 Maiden Ln -NY 10038
(914) 234-4720 .. **Kulowiec,** David '88 (Kulowiec & J,LLP) -460 Old Post Rd -Bedfrd 10506 **Fx:**234-7210
(716) 853-9555 .. **Kulpit,** Jessica A '09 Leg Aid -237 Main -Buffalo 14203 **Fx:**853-3219
(212) 735-3000 .. **Kultgen,** Megan E '07 %Skadden ASM&F LLP -4 Times Sq -NY 10036
(212) 474-1000 .. **Kultgen,** Michelle E '05 %Cravath S&M LLP -825 8th Av -NY 10019
(718) 590-2000 .. **Kum,** Jan D '01 %DA -198 E 161st -Bronx 10451 **Fx:**590-6477
(212) 682-9626 .. **Kumada-Lawrence,** Naoko '96 (Kumada-Lawrence & Assoc,PLLC) -100 Park Av -NY 10017
(212) 282-3253 .. **Kumamoto,** Noritaka '03 Mizuho Corp Bk,Ltd -1251 Av of Amer -NY 10020
(718) 544-7688 .. **Kumar,** Chandini Shireen '93 -414 Burns -Frst Hlls 11375
(212) 408-5100 .. **Kumar,** Chlraag '09 %Chadbourne & P LLP -30 Rckfllr Plz -NY 10112
(212) 468-8000 .. **Kumar,** Neeraj '10 %Morrison & F LLP -1290 Av of Amer -NY 10104
(212) 903-9000 .. **Kumar,** Poonam '08 %Linklaters -1345 Av of Amer -NY 10105
(718) 613-2450 .. **Kumar,** Poonam '08 Hon J Gleeson -225 Cadman Plz -Brklyn 11201
(212) 848-4000 .. **Kumar,** Shekhar '10 Shearman & S LLP -599 Lex Av -NY 10022
(212) 373-3000 .. **Kumaraswami,** Nita N '10 %Paul WRW&G LLP -1285 Av of Amer -NY 10019
(212) 306-8096 .. **Kumbatovic,** Robt J '95 Housing Auth -250 Bway -NY 10007
(212) 319-3633 .. **Kumble,** Steven J '60 %Lincolnshire Mgt -780 3rd Av -NY 10017 **Fx:**755-5457
(716) 204-2400 .. **Kumiega,** Brian B '93 SJ Baum,PC -220 Nrthpnte Pkwy Bx1291 -Buffalo 14240 **Fx:**204-4600
(716) 854-3400 .. **Kumm,** Jessica M '07 %Rupp BPC&C LLC -1600 Lbrty Bldg -Buffalo 14202
(212) 664-4444 .. **Kummer,** Danl M '89 %NBC -30 Rckfllr Plz -NY 10112
(212) 277-6500 .. **Kummer,** Victoria A '93 (Dickstein S LLP) -1633 Bway -NY 10019
(212) 869-5300 .. **Kumro,** Richd A '85 Cnsl CPC -28 E 28th -NY 10016 **Fx:**683-2909
(845) 486-2300 .. **Kunca,** David A '04 %DA -236 Main -Poughkeepsie 12601 **Fx:**486-2324
(212) 655-5000 .. **Kundanmal,** Nita '03 %Gannon R&M -120 Bway -NY 10271
(212) 480-4800 .. **Kundar,** Kathleen M '74 (Fox H&C LLP) -825 3rd Av -NY 10022
(212) 571-0111 .. **Kundla,** Mark S '90 (Hardin KM&P,PA) -110 William -NY 10038
(212) 852-3212 .. **Kunego,** Todd M '96 %US Trust Co,NA -114 W 47th -NY 10036 **Fx:**852-1310
(845) 651-4021 .. **Kunert,** Bernard I '62 -62 N Main -Florida 10921 **Fx:**651-4022
(212) 720-8606 .. **Kung,** Catherine '95 Fed Reserve Bk -33 Lbrty -NY 10045 **Fx:**785-5748
(212) 351-4000 .. **Kung,** Teresa R '10 Gibson D&C LLP -200 Park Av -NY 10166
(212) 578-2477 .. **Kunin,** Max B '85 %MetLife -27-01 Qns Plz N -LIC 11101
(516) 571-3800 .. **Kunken,** Kenneth J '83 %DA -262 Old Cntry Rd -Mineola 11501 **Fx:**248-9479
(631) 462-5950 .. **Kunken,** Stephen '72 -6165 Jericho Tpk -Commack 11725
(212) 449-3117 .. **Kunkes,** Eric L '92 %Merrill Lynch -220 Bway -NY 10038
(212) 563-1710 .. **Kunkin,** Marc I '97 %Schindel FLG&R LLP -14 Penn Plz -NY 10122
(212) 564-3555 .. **Kunkis,** Martha H '81 %Bauman & K,PC -14 Penn Plz -NY 10122
(212) 564-3555 .. **Kunkis,** Roger M '69 (Bauman & K,PC) -14 Penn Plz -NY 10122
(212) 806-5400 .. **Kunkle,** Nathaniel I '09 %Stroock &S&L LLP -180 Maiden Ln -NY 10038

(212) 605-2115 .. **Kuno,** Tetsuharu '07 Mitsubishi Intl Corp -655 3rd Av -NY 10017
(914) 428-8800 .. **Kunreuther,** Judith Berry '92 (Stern KP&W,LLP) -1025 Wstchstr Av -White Plns 10604
(646) 602-5600 .. **Kuns,** Mara A '09 %Urban Justice Ctr -123 William -NY 10038 **Fx:**(212) 533-4598
(212) 398-8881 .. **Kunstadt,** Robt M '79 (R Kunstadt,PC) -875 6th Av -NY 10001 **Fx:**398-2922
(212) 924-7025 .. **Kunstler,** Margaret Ratner '70 -14 7th Av -Brklyn 11217
(212) 446-2300 .. **Kunstler,** Marilyn Clapp '92 (Boies S&F LLP) -575 Lex Av -NY 10022
(718) 783-3682 .. **Kunstler,** Sarah '05 %E Fink -36 Plz St E -Brklyn 11238 **Fx:**783-5853
(212) 945-4190 .. **Kunstler,** Susan Y '75 -355 South End Av -NY 10280 **Fx:**432-0852
(845) 689-2400 .. **Kunstlinger,** Jos '94 (Kunstlinger & W PLLC) -235 N Main -Spg Vly 10977 **Fx:**689-2401
(718) 231-2934 .. **Kuntu-Blankson,** George '87 -770 E 233rd -Bronx 10466 **Fx:**231-2937
(212) 818-1669 .. **Kuntz,** Carl M '79 -276 5th Av -NY 10001 **Fx:**477-1731
(212) 848-4000 .. **Kuntz,** Lee A '68 (Shearman & S LLP) -599 Lex Av -NY 10022
(914) 234-6363 .. **Kuntz,** Raymond G '63 (Kuntz S&M,PC) -444 Old Post Rd -Bedfrd 10506 **Fx:**234-6249
(914) 234-6363 .. **Kuntz,** Raymond G III '92 %Kuntz S&M,PC -444 Old Post Rd -Bedfrd 10506 **Fx:**234-6249
(212) 589-4200 .. **Kuntz,** Wm F II '78 (Baker & H LLP) -45 Rckfllr Plz -NY 10111
(212) 735-3000 .. **Kunz,** C Thos '76 OfCnsl Skadden ASM&F LLP -4 Times Sq -NY 10036
(518) 462-5300 .. **Kunz,** David F '68 (DeGraff F&K LLP) -90 State -Albany 12207
(212) 530-5000 .. **Kunz,** Emily J '04 %Milbank TH&M LLP -1 Chase Manh Plz -NY 10005
(212) 788-0422 .. **Kunz,** Morgan David '07 %Law Dept -100 Church -NY 10007 **Fx:**788-0367
(212) 303-9430 .. **Kunz,** Paul E '94 Halcyon Prtnrs -477 Mad Av -NY 10022
(585) 262-2120 .. **Kunze,** Kaaren A '92 (Bressler & K) -16 W Main -Rchstr 14614 **Fx:**262-2625
(585) 262-2120 .. **Kunze,** Karl W '92 (Bressler & K) -16 W Main -Rchstr 14614 **Fx:**262-2625
(845) 371-7680 .. **Kunzier,** Frank J '88 (Zimmerer MC&K) -10 Esquire Rd -New Cty 10956
(914) 847-9122 .. **Kuo,** Jos '98 NY Life -1 Rockwood Rd -Sleepy Hollow 10591
(646) 471-4432 .. **Kuo,** Lisa W '00 PricewaterhouseCoopers LLP -300 Mad Av -NY 10017
(212) 656-6928 .. **Kuo,** Peggy '89 NYSE Regulation -20 Broad -NY 10005
(212) 538-3309 .. **Kuo,** Timothy D '01 Credit Suisse -11 Mad Av -NY 10010
(212) 221-5700 .. **Kuper,** Lewis '79 OfCnsl Goldberg WFG LLP -1501 Bway -NY 10036
(212) 719-0990 .. **Kuperman,** Eric J '98 -10 East 39th -NY 10016
(516) 296-7000 .. **Kuperschmid,** Steven J '86 (Certilman BA&H,LLP) -90 Merrick Av -E Meadow 11554
(212) 244-5588 .. **Kupfer,** Corey S '86 (Kupfer & Assoc,PLLC) -350 5th Av -NY 10125 **Fx:**244-5225
(212) 756-1184 .. **Kupfer,** Judah I '08 %Allen & O -1221 Av of Amer -NY 10020
(718) 435-1001 .. **Kupfer,** Stanley P '02 S Kupfer,PC -5422 16th Av -Brklyn 11204 **Fx:**435-0217
(212) 554-7800 .. **Kupferberg,** Alan '80 %Moses & S LLP -405 Lex Av -NY 10174
(212) 696-5500 .. **Kupferberg,** Alice W '86 (Budin RK&B) -112 Mad Av -NY 10016
(212) 857-8230 .. **Kupferberg,** Jeffrey '85 Baker MM&M,PC -330 W 34th -NY 10001
(212) 223-3905 .. **Kupferberg,** Jill '76 OfCnsl T Fisher,PC -10 E 40th -NY 10016 **Fx:**683-2184
(212) 566-7188 .. **Kupferberg,** Matthew I '99 Cnsl Genova B&G -115 Bway -NY 10006
(212) 416-8856 .. **Kupferberg,** Seth M '80 %Dept of Law -120 Bway -NY 10271
(212) 442-9370 .. **Kupferman,** Jack '82 %Dept Aging SCRIE -2 Lafayette -NY 10007
(917) 414-1983 .. **Kupferman,** Joel R '91 -351 Bway -NY 10013
(518) 474-6191 .. **Kupferman,** Michl E '80 %State Comptroller -110 State -Albany 12236 **Fx:**473-9104
(718) 768-3046 .. **Kupferman,** Neil H '96 -459 6th Av -Brklyn 11215 **Fx:**768-7645
(518) 885-5011 .. **Kupferman,** Richd '88 -30 Remsen -Ballston Spa 12020 **Fx:**885-5298
(917) 873-7592 .. **Kupferman,** Stephanie E '92 (Kupferman & K LLP) -132 Titicus Rd Bx641 -N Salem 10560 **Fx:**(212) 937-3552
(212) 594-5300 .. **Kupillas,** Matthew A '02 (Milberg LLP) -1 Penn Plz -NY 10119
(516) 829-3508 .. **Kupillas & Unger** -11 Grace Av -Gt Neck 11021 **Fx:**482-8334
(212) 883-1700 .. **Kupin,** Michl B '86 (Duval & S LLP) -101 Park Av -NY 10178
(315) 696-8918 .. **Kuppermann,** Jane G '91 (Riehlman S&S) -397 Route 281 Bx430 -Tully 13159
(212) 956-9436 .. **Kupperstein,** Gordon E '96 -100 W 57th -NY 10019
(518) 465-1500 .. **Kuracina,** David C '96 (Cannon H&W,LLP) -54 State -Albany 12207
(212) 957-0500 .. **Kuramoto,** Ken '02 %R Goldstein,PC -145 W 57th -NY 10019 **Fx:**957-2020
(212) 373-3000 .. **Kurasz,** Lindsay B '10 %Paul WRW&G LLP -1285 Av of Amer -NY 10019
(212) 488-1200 .. **Kurcias,** Lisa M '03 %Kobre & K,LLP -800 3rd Av -NY 10022
(516) 829-5890 .. **Kurcias,** Michl G '60 -98 Cuttermill Rd -Gt Neck 11021 **Fx:**829-3605
(516) 482-7777 .. **Kurcias,** Stephen S '64 -111 Grt Nck Rd -Gt Neck 11021
(212) 701-3000 .. **Kurdes,** Julie M '07 %Cahill G&R LLP -80 Pine -NY 10005 **Fx:**269-5420
(212) 609-6800 .. **Kurdian,** Grace S '99 (McCarter & E,LLP) -245 Park Av -NY 10167
(212) 857-8800 .. **Kurella,** Vidya '01 US Ct Appls 2nd Circ -40 Foley Sq -NY 10007
(212) 441-1722 .. **Kurens,** Jonathan H '91 AON Risk Srvcs -199 Water -NY 10038
(212) 688-9200 .. **Kurfist,** Melissa D '05 Empire Search Prtnrs -445 Park Av -NY 10022
(212) 267-9222 .. **Kuriloff,** Roy A '78 %Gorayeb & Assoc,PC -100 William -NY 10038 **Fx:**962-5418
(212) 541-8100 .. **Kuritzkes,** Andrew P '87 %Oliver Wyman & Co -1166 Av of Amer -NY 10036
(212) 354-0020 .. **Kuritzky,** Steven M '92 -1501 Bway -NY 10036 **Fx:**354-1343
(718) 237-1850 .. **Kurkemelis,** John M '83 -32 Court -Brklyn 11201 **Fx:**254-9242
(607) 763-9200 .. **Kurkoski,** Scott R '90 (Levene G&T,LLP) -BxF-1706 -Bnghmtn 13902
(212) 983-0662 .. **Kurkowski,** Elzbieta '92 (E Kurkowski,PC) -501 5th Av -NY 10017 **Fx:**(646) 367-4901
(212) 218-2100 .. **Kurlancheek,** Dara M '09 %Fitzpatrick CH&S -1290 Av of Amer -NY 10104
(845) 638-4700 .. **Kurland,** Adam K '95 (Fenster & K LLP) -337 N Main -New Cty 10956 **Fx:**638-4767
(212) 506-1700 .. **Kurland,** Andrew R '10 Kasowitz BT&F LLP -1633 Bway -NY 10019
(585) 454-0700 .. **Kurland,** Harold A '77 (Ward GH&R LLP) -300 State -Rchstr 14614
(516) 296-7000 .. **Kurland,** Jason M '01 (Certilman BA&H,LLP) -90 Merrick Av -E Meadow 11554
(516) 222-2299 .. **Kurland,** Lauren B '02 %J Schecter & Assoc -595 Stewart Av -Gdn Cty 11530 **Fx:**222-2303
(212) 541-2000 .. **Kurland,** Lawr G '66 (Bryan C LLP) -1290 Av of Amer -NY 10104
(212) 836-8000 .. **Kurland,** Michl J '05 %Kaye S LLP -425 Park Av -NY 10022
(212) 687-3860 .. **Kurland,** Paul C '71 (Snow BK,PC) -605 3rd Av -NY 10158
(212) 788-0821 .. **Kurland,** Sherrill M '79 %Law Dept -100 Church -NY 10007 **Fx:**788-0367
(516) 229-4200 .. **Kurland,** Stuart M '94 Mendolia & S -875 Merrick Av -Westbury 11590
(212) 253-6911 .. **Kurland,** Yetta G '01 (Kurland B& Assoc,PC) -304 Park Av S -NY 10010
(212) 446-4800 .. **Kurlander,** Glenn '85 Smith Barney -388 Greenwich -NY 10013
(212) 431-1300 .. **Kurlander,** Gregg R '00 (Borah GAN&G PC) -377 Bway -NY 10013
(718) 246-9060 .. **Kurlander,** Martin '59 -32 Court -Brklyn 11201
(212) 924-6800 .. **Kurlander,** Neil R '86 Spa Finder -257 Park Av S -NY 10010
(212) 872-1000 .. **Kurlanzik,** Stefanie L '08 -One Bryant Park -NY 10036 **Fx:**872-1002
(212) 762-5095 .. **Kurman,** Lee M '87 Morgan Stanley -1221 Av of Amer -NY 10020
(212) 596-9000 .. **Kurmanova,** Aselle '09 %Ropes & G LLP -1211 Av of Amer -NY 10036
(212) 846-7507 .. **Kurnit,** Melissa N '95 %Nickelodeon -1515 Bway -NY 10036 **Fx:**846-1756
(212) 980-0120 .. **Kurnit,** Richd A '76 (Frankfurt KK&S,PC) -488 Mad Av -NY 10022
(646) 257-3683 .. **Kuroda,** Ai '07 %Ohashi & H LLP -1140 Av of Amer -NY 10036
(212) 964-7990 .. **Kurolapnik,** Alla '01 %Mallow K&N,PC -321 Bway -NY 10007
(212) 487-9701 .. **Kuroly,** Jos B '98 %Robin HK&F -1 Bttry Pk Plz -NY 10014
(914) 761-9450 .. **Kuropatkin,** Jeffrey '81 %Mitsubishi Chem Amer -1 N Lex Av -White Plns 10601 **Fx:**761-0108
(516) 829-7900 .. **Kurre,** Robt J '91 (R Kurre & Assoc,PC) -1010 Nrthrn Blvd -Gt Neck 11021 **Fx:**829-7920
(212) 878-8000 .. **Kurrik,** Ilomai C '05 %Clifford C LLP -31 W 52nd -NY 10019
(860) 424-4331 .. **Kurs,** Michl A '82 (Pullman & C,LLC) -50 Main -White Plns 10606
(212) 471-8547 .. **Kurshan,** Peter J '79 (Herzfeld & R,PC) -125 Broad -NY 10004
(212) 592-1400 .. **Kursman,** Benjamin F '78 (Herrick,F LLP) -2 Park Av -NY 10016
(212) 930-9700 .. **Kurta,** Jonathan A '08 %Sichenzia RFF LLP -61 Bway -NY 10006
(212) 474-1000 .. **Kurta,** Mile T '02 %Cravath S&M LLP -825 8th Av -NY 10019
(212) 785-9100 .. **Kurta,** Paula A '04 %Paduano & W LLP -1251 Av of Amer -NY 10020
(212) 408-5100 .. **Kurth,** Rachel M '09 %Chadbourne & P LLP -30 Rckfllr Plz -NY 10112
(212) 672-1629 .. **Kurtin,** Owen D '86 Vinland Grp LLC -245 Park Av -NY 10167
(914) 686-3171 .. **Kurtis,** Glen A '98 (G Kurtis,PC) -175 Main -White Plns 10601 **Fx:**686-8175
(212) 294-6700 .. **Kurtis,** Jennifer C '96 (Winston & S) -200 Park Av -NY 10166
(212) 836-8791 .. **Kurtyka,** Ruthanne '74 Kaye S LLP -425 Park Av -NY 10022
(212) 974-6000 .. **Kurtz,** Andrew J '93 %Elliott Assoc,LP -712 5th Av -NY 10019
(212) 223-4000 .. **Kurtz,** Birgit '97 Cnsl Crowell & M LLP -590 Mad Av -NY 10022
(516) 267-6300 .. **Kurtz,** Christopher T '04 %Bond S&K,PLLC -1399 Franklin Av -Gdn Cty 11530
(212) 735-3390 .. **Kurtz,** Danl L '68 (Skadden ASM&F LLP) -4 Times Sq -NY 10036
(516) 579-6500 .. **Kurtz,** Deborah '84 %A Clark & Assoc,LLC -650 Wantagh Av -Levittwn 11756 **Fx:**579-6604
(845) 331-0702 .. **Kurtz,** Eric M '86 (Cook NCK&M,PC) -85 Main Bx3939 -Kingston 12402
(212) 819-8200 .. **Kurtz,** Glenn M '90 (White & C LLP) -1155 Av of Amer -NY 10036
(631) 761-0800 .. **Kurtz,** Jennifer M '03 %Lazer AR&Y,PC -225 Old Cntry Rd -Melvll 11747
(212) 218-5500 .. **Kurtz,** Joshua A '05 %Seyfarth S LLP -620 8th Av -NY 10018
(212) 484-7052 .. **Kurtz,** Joy Marcus '87 Time Warner Global Mrkts -1 Time Warner Ctr -NY 10019
(212) 509-3456 .. **Kurtz,** Justin K '08 %McGivney & K,PC -80 Broad -NY 10004
(914) 345-9001 .. **Kurtz,** Michl J '75 %Taro Pharmaceuticals USA Inc -5 Skyline Dr -Hawthorne 10532
(973) 639-7981 .. **Kurtz,** Mitchell S '02 %McCarter & E,LLP -245 Park Av -NY 10167 **Fx:**624-7070
(631) 537-5311 .. **Kurtz,** Nat '56 -61 Jennifer Ln Bx1643 -Brdghmptn 11932
(347) 296-1626 .. **Kurtz,** Nina L '83 Supreme Ct Law Dept -360 Adams -Brklyn 11201 **Fx:**643-6114
(212) 580-4747 .. **Kurtz,** Normand R '63 -228 W 71st -NY 10023
(212) 889-3700 .. **Kurtz,** Orin R '05 %Abbey SR&A LLP -212 E 39th -NY 10016
(516) 741-0010 .. **Kurtz,** Robt I '75 -1205 Franklin Av -Gdn Cty 11530
(212) 698-4570 .. **Kurtz,** Ruth G '76 (Stapper & V) -10 Rckfllr Plz -NY 10020
(631) 928-8000 .. **Kurtz,** Sanders L '76 (Winkler KW&K,LLP) -310 Hallock Av -Pt Jffrsn Sta 11776
(914) 328-9797 .. **Kurtz,** Sandra Koss '80 -81 Main -White Plns 10601 **Fx:**693-4879
(212) 889-0420 .. **Kurtz,** Steven E '88 -240 Mad Av -NY 10016
(315) 752-0325 .. **Kurtz,** Wm J '81 -5793 Crabtree Ln -Cicero 13039
(516) 932-6350 .. **Kurtzberg,** Howard '83 -380 N Bway -Jericho 11753 **Fx:**932-8353
(631) 423-4600 .. **Kurtzberg,** Ira B '64 (Kurtzberg & K,PC) -20 Broadhllw Rd -Melvll 11747 **Fx:**423-4617
(212) 701-3000 .. **Kurtzberg,** Joel L '97 (Cahill G&R LLP) -80 Pine -NY 10005 **Fx:**269-5420
(631) 423-4600 .. **Kurtzberg,** Linda Anna '86 (Kurtzberg & K,PC) -20 Broadhllw Rd -Melvll 11747 **Fx:**423-4617
(718) 250-2000 .. **Kurtzberg,** Sara R '07 %DA -350 Jay -Brklyn 11201 **Fx:**250-2314
(212) 943-1090 .. **Kurtz-Citrin,** Lynne R '98 %Gair GCSMB&R -80 Pine -NY 10005
(716) 652-9560 .. **Kurtzhalts,** Joel R '83 (Bennett D&K,LLP) -681 Main -E Aurora 14052
(716) 297-3850 .. **Kurtzman,** Bryant S '54 -1625 Buffalo Av -Niagara Fls 14303 **Fx:**297-4552
(212) 836-8000 .. **Kurtzman,** Jill E '85 (Kaye S LLP) -425 Park Av -NY 10022
(845) 352-8800 .. **Kurtzman Matera PC** -664 Chestnut Rdg Rd -Spg Vly 10977 **Fx:**352-8865

(631) 852-2500 .. **Kurtzrock**, Glenn R '99 %DA -200 Center Dr -Rvrhead 11901 **Fx:**852-1769
(212) 631-0886 .. **Kuruvila**, Bikku K '99 NY Jobs for Justice -50 Bway -NY 10004 **Fx:**(646) 452-5636
(631) 499-0105 .. **Kury**, Channing R '86 -15 Saratoga -Commack 11725
(845) 548-1142 .. **Kurz**, Aryeh Y '07 -11 Dover Ter -Monsey 10952
(516) 746-7337 .. **Kurz**, Douglas L '86 %M Kurz & Co -128 Lbrty Av -Mineola 11501
(516) 883-8033 .. **Kurz**, Eleanor Halpern '55 -2 Woodlnd Dr -Sands Pnt 11050 **Fx:**883-8033
(518) 218-9000 .. **Kurz**, Michl '88 Kurz & Assoc,LLC -2212 Wstrn Av Bx1502 -Guilderlnd 12084 **Fx:**218-0905
(631) 431-3066 .. **Kurz**, Regina Anzalone '89 -150 Broadhllw Rd -Melvll 11747
(212) 909-6000 .. **Kurz**, Theo A '65 OfCnsl Debevoise & P LLP -919 3rd Av -NY 10022
(212) 858-1000 .. **Kurz**, Wm C F '68 (Pillsbury WSP LLP) -1540 Bway -NY 10036
(516) 328-1100 .. **Kurzatkowski**, Marcin J '10 %Ryan B&D LLP -131 Tulip Av -Floral Pk 11001
(212) 969-3000 .. **Kurzban**, Jessica F '01 %Proskauer R LLP -1585 Bway -NY 10036
(914) 238-3891 .. **Kurzban**, Stanley A '96 -62 Pond Vw Ln -Chappaqua 10514
(212) 530-5000 .. **Kurzer**, Michl D '05 %Milbank TH&M LLP -1 Chase Manh Plz -NY 10005
(914) 285-9800 .. **Kurzman Eisenberg Corbin & Lever,LLP** -1 N Bway -White Plns 10601 **Fx:**285-9855
(212) 661-2150 .. **Kurzman Eisenberg Corbin & Lever,LLP** -360 Lex Av -NY 10017
(212) 557-7700 .. **Kurzman**, Jayne M '72 (Davidson D&C LLP) -60 E 42nd -NY 10165
(212) 867-9500 .. **Kurzman Karelsen & Frank,LLP** -230 Park Av -NY 10169 **Fx:**599-1759
(914) 285-9800 .. **Kurzman**, Robt G '59 (Kurzman EC&L,LLP) -1 N Bway -White Plns 10601
(212) 577-9450 .. **Kurzman**, Ronny L '03 DecisionQuest -2 Rector -NY 10006 **Fx:**577-9460
(718) 999-0375 .. **Kurzman**, Tayo '00 FDNY -9 Metrotech Ctr -Brklyn 11201
(845) 735-6300 .. **Kurzmann**, Hillel M '04 %Kurzmann Law Ofc -275 N Mddltwn Rd -Pearl Rvr 10965 **Fx:**735-7660
(212) 755-5700 .. **Kurzmann**, Mark J '83 OfCnsl Steinberg BG&F,LLP -767 3rd Av -NY 10017 **Fx:**758-6963
(845) 735-6300 .. **Kurzmann**, Mark J '83 -275 N Mddltwn Rd -Pearl Rvr 10965 **Fx:**735-7660
(212) 867-9149 .. **Kurzner**, Wayne D '82 -555 5th Av -NY 10017 **Fx:**986-5316
(212) 571-2000 .. **Kurzon**, Carrie R '03 %Ottinger Firm,PC -19 Fulton -NY 10038 **Fx:**571-0505
(646) 416-0382 .. **Kurzon**, Jeffrey Mead '03 -305 Bway -NY 10007 **Fx:**(212) 822-1437
(212) 588-0800 .. **Kurzrok**, Julie E '09 %Frommer L&H LLP -745 5th Av -NY 10151
(212) 906-1200 .. **Kurzweil**, David A '98 (Latham & W) -885 3rd Av -NY 10022
(212) 259-8000 .. **Kurzweil**, Harvey '70 (Dewey & L LLP) -1301 Av of Amer -NY 10019
(212) 756-2000 .. **Kurzweil**, Judith '90 SpclCnsl Schulte R&Z LLP -919 3rd Av -NY 10022
(212) 609-6800 .. **Kurzweil**, Lanny S '87 (McCarter & E,LLP) -245 Park Av -NY 10167
(212) 554-7800 .. **Kurzweil**, Marc S '06 %Moses & S LLP -405 Lex Av -NY 10174
(212) 857-2310 .. **Kurzweil**, Martin A '08 Hon P Leval -40 Foley Sq -NY 10007
(585) 393-0790 .. **Kusak**, Albert '88 -23 Coach -Canandaigua 14424
(718) 263-2760 .. **Kusakabe**, Dean T '96 (Dezelic & K,LLC) -108-18 Qns Blvd -Frst Hlls 11375 **Fx:**228-5558
(631) 878-0986 .. **Kushel**, Barry J '65 -Bx608 -Manorvll 11949 **Fx:**878-0305
(718) 646-0731 .. **Kushel**, Glenn E '76 -2660 Haring -Brklyn 11235
(347) 825-2369 .. **Kushel**, Irina '09 Kushel & F -299 Bway -NY 10007 **Fx:**(212) 994-9470
(914) 835-0222 .. **Kushel**, Stephen J '62 -4 Kassel Ct -Mamaroneck 10543 **Fx:**835-1115
(917) 747-3285 .. **Kushen**, Robt A '91 Open Society Institute -400 W 59th -NY 10019
(212) 687-8181 .. **Kushlefsky**, Noah H '87 (Kreindler & K) -750 3rd Av -NY 10017
(212) 262-6700 .. **Kushner**, Amiad M '04 Cnsl Lowenstein S PC -1251 Av of Amer -NY 10020
(212) 403-1000 .. **Kushner**, Caith M '06 %Wachtell LR&K -51 W 52nd -NY 10019
(516) 248-1700 .. **Kushner**, Gary M '89 (Forchelli CDSM&T,LLP) -333 Earle Ovngton Blvd -Uniondale 11553
(516) 328-7181 .. **Kushner**, Jay '55 SrCnsl Alvy & T,LLP -1979 Marcus Av -Lk Success 11042
(212) 846-6161 .. **Kushner**, Jay M '82 %Viacom -1515 Bway -NY 10036
(212) 436-4341 .. **Kushner**, Jonathan M '82 Deloitte & Touche,LLP -2 World Fncl Ctr -NY 10281
(718) 250-2000 .. **Kushner**, Kenneth A '06 %DA -350 Jay -Brklyn 11201 **Fx:**250-2314
(212) 218-2100 .. **Kushner**, Leslie J '10 %Fitzpatrick CH&S -1290 Av of Amer -NY 10104
(212) 867-5800 .. **Kushner**, Marc A '89 (Osler H&H LLP) -620 8th Av -NY 10018
(212) 692-1000 .. **Kushner**, Marc A '93 (Duane M LLP) -1540 Bway -NY 10036
(914) 328-0404 .. **Kushner**, Michl G '05 Cnsl Jackson L LLP -1 N Bway -White Plns 10601
(212) 202-2634 .. **Kushner**, Michl P '05 -1133 Bway -NY 10010
(212) 707-2000 .. **Kushner**, Michl S '82 %Atlantic Recording Corp -1290 Av of Amer -NY 10104
(212) 308-2210 .. **Kushner**, Paul D '97 (Eviction Intrvntn Srvcs) -1233 2nd Av -NY 10065 **Fx:**888-7140
(212) 850-7740 .. **Kushner**, Shari L '86 %C-BASS -335 Mad Av -NY 10017 **Fx:**850-7760
(518) 457-2411 .. **Kushner**, Susan M '86 %DOT -50 Wolf Rd -Albany 12232 **Fx:**457-4021
(212) 801-9298 .. **Kushnick**, Heath B '93 (Greenberg T,LLP) -200 Park Av -NY 10166
(631) 752-7100 .. **Kushnick**, Lawr A '89 (Kushnick & Assoc,PC) -445 Broad Hollow Rd -Melvll 11747 **Fx:**777-7732
(631) 427-5700 .. **Kushnick**, Martin J '56 (Gordon K&G) -780 NY Av -Huntngtn 11743
(518) 455-5359 .. **Kushnir**, Andrey August '95 -21 Melrose Av -Albany 12203
(212) 310-8000 .. **Kusinitz**, Alan R '86 %Weil G&M LLP -767 5th Av -NY 10153
(212) 806-5400 .. **Kusko**, Jonathan S '77 (Stroock &S&L LLP) -180 Maiden Ln -NY 10038
(718) 875-6060 .. **Kuslansky & Dorfman** -26 Court -Brklyn 11242 **Fx:**596-8944
(212) 479-6000 .. **Kusmin**, Ben J '07 %Cooley LLP -1114 Av of Amer -NY 10036
(212) 756-2000 .. **Kusnetz**, Dan A '83 (Schulte R&Z LLP) -919 3rd Av -NY 10022
(914) 997-9181 .. **Kusnetz**, Marcia E '82 (Most & K LLC) -222 Bloomingdale Rd -White Plns 10605 **Fx:**997-9180
(631) 424-3597 .. **Kusnetz**, Philip A '00 %B Salamone & Assoc,PC -8 Ford Pl -Dix Hlls 11746 **Fx:**424-5023
(212) 809-7600 .. **Kusnetz**, Stephen F '98 %Cheven K&H -40 Wall -NY 10005
(716) 837-1515 .. **Kustell**, Carl B '65 (Kustell Law Grp,LLP) -1660 Kensngtn Av -Buffalo 14215 **Fx:**837-0090
(716) 837-1515 .. **Kustell**, Carl P '96 %Kustell Law Grp,LLP -1660 Kensngtn Av -Buffalo 14215 **Fx:**837-0090
(212) 839-5300 .. **Kuster**, John J '92 (Sidley A LLP) -787 7th Av -NY 10019
(212) 872-1000 .. **Kustin**, Ira P '00 -One Bryant Park -NY 10036 **Fx:**872-1002
(212) 267-4876 .. **Kuszmerski**, Danl R '06 %Hoagland LMD&D,LLP -1501 Bway -NY 10036
(212) 370-1300 .. **Kutcher**, David E '09 %Ellenoff G&S LLP -150 E 42nd -NY 10017
(718) 896-6554 .. **Kutil**, Peter M '86 (King & K LLP) -27-12 37th Av -LIC 11101
(212) 399-8020 .. **Kutler**, Ileana H '96 %Interpublic Grp -1271 Av of Amer -NY 10020
(212) 308-0210 .. **Kutner**, Chas E '82 -110 E 59th -NY 10022 **Fx:**308-0213
(516) 227-0700 .. **Kutner**, Christopher J '90 (Farrell F,PC) -1320 RXR Plz -Uniondale 11556
(212) 696-4848 .. **Kutner**, Eric M '94 OfCnsl Mintz & G LLP -470 Park Av S -NY 10016
(516) 248-0650 .. **Kutner**, Eric M '94 -200 Old Cntry Rd -Mineola 11501 **Fx:**248-2728
(516) 746-0333 .. **Kutner & Gurlides** -300 Old Cntry Rd -Mineola 11501 **Fx:**746-5109
(516) 741-1400 .. **Kutner**, Harry H Jr. '74 -136 Willis Av -Mineola 11501 **Fx:**741-8712
(212) 683-7100 .. **Kutner**, Kenneth J '92 (Gallo V&K,LLP) -90 Broad -NY 10004
(212) 684-0088 .. **Kutner**, Kenneth L '81 -100 Park Av -NY 10017 **Fx:**684-7390
(212) 308-0210 .. **Kutner**, Marianne Dakin '82 OfCnsl C Kutner,LLP -110 E 59th -NY 10022 **Fx:**308-0213
(516) 746-0333 .. **Kutner**, Stephen D '77 (Kutner & G) -300 Old Cntry Rd -Mineola 11501
(212) 489-1400 .. **Kutscher**, Andrew H '10 %Bickel & B -767 5th Av -NY 10153
(914) 428-7800 .. **Kuttas**, John '56 -576 Kimball Av -Ynkrs 10704 **Fx:**949-0086
(212) 421-2800 .. **Kuttles**, David '02 %Lanier Law Firm,PLLC -126 E 56th -NY 10022 **Fx:**421-2878
(212) 480-7439 .. **Kuttner**, Jack '80 %DHCR -25 Beaver -NY 10004 **Fx:**480-7416
(212) 306-4264 .. **Kutzbach**, Dale C '78 %Housing Auth -250 Bway -NY 10007
(315) 435-2170 .. **Kutzer**, Thos H '85 %Cnty Atty -421 Mntgmry -Syracuse 13202 **Fx:**435-5729
(212) 387-8400 .. **Kutzin**, Michl S '88 (Goldfarb AS&K LLP) -350 5th Av -NY 10118
(585) 492-1460 .. **Kutzuba**, Robt H '74 (Ward & K) -364 W Main Bx321 -Arcade 14009 **Fx:**492-1178
(212) 442-9367 .. **Kuwahara**, Myles H '86 %Law Dept -100 Church -NY 10007 **Fx:**788-0367
(646) 562-3405 .. **Kuyumjian**, Alain '03 %PLC -747 3rd Av -NY 10017
(212) 310-8000 .. **Kuyumjian**, Arman J '02 %Weil G&M LLP -767 5th Av -NY 10153
(716) 366-6966 .. **Kuzdale**, John M '84 -314 Central Av Bx271 -Dunkirk 14048
(212) 480-3400 .. **Kuzecki**, Yerachmial N '04 %Tamir Law Grp -55 Broad -NY 10004
(718) 802-4416 .. **Kuziw**, Gregory R '84 %Dept Probation -210 Joralemon -Brklyn 11201
(212) 268-5136 .. **Kuzma**, Eileen P '98 %Harwood L -350 5th Av -NY 10118
(716) 822-7645 .. **Kuzma**, Michl '98 -1893 Clinton -Buffalo 14206 **Fx:**823-1815
(212) 732-9450 .. **Kuzma**, Nathaniel J '07 %N Rosenberg -9 Murray -NY 10007 **Fx:**571-9893
(631) 345-6600 .. **Kuzma**, Stephen J '91 -220 Middle Cntry Rd -Middl Isl 11953 **Fx:**345-3876
(212) 588-0800 .. **Kuzmich**, Sandra '02 (Frommer L&H LLP) -745 5th Av -NY 10151
(212) 623-6178 .. **Kuzmicz**, Michl J '92 JP Morgan Chase Bnk NA -4 NY Plz -NY 10004
(212) 664-3319 .. **Kuzmik**, Anna M '95 %NBC Universal -30 Rckfllr Plz -NY 10112
(718) 891-4211 .. **Kuzmin**, Roman '07 (R Kuzmin & Assoc,PC) -2747 Coney Isl Av -Brklyn 11235 **Fx:**891-4217
(212) 608-1800 .. **Kuzmin**, Vlad A '98 (Kuzmin & Assoc) -225 Bway -NY 10007
(212) 619-3892 .. **Kuznicki**, Abraham '04 -2 Rector -NY 10006
(212) 242-0500 .. **Kuznicki**, Susan '95 (L Behar,PC) -347 5th Av -NY 10016 **Fx:**242-0518
(516) 794-7500 .. **Kuzow**, Michl F '82 (Westermann SKS&A,LLP) -333 Earle Ovngton Blvd -Uniondale 11553
(646) 471-4777 .. **Kuzyk**, Stephen A '95 PricewaterhouseCoopers -300 Mad Av -NY 10017
(212) 733-8412 .. **Kvachatadze**, Kakhaber '04 %Pfizer Inc -235 E 42nd -NY 10017
(212) 705-7000 .. **Kvurt**, Yelina '08 %Bingham M LLP -399 Park Av -NY 10022
(212) 658-7567 .. **Kwa**, Dwight '00 Ambac Assurance Corp -1 State Street Plz -NY 10004
(212) 872-3503 .. **Kwak**, Jangwoon '00 KPMG LLP -345 Park Av -NY 10154
(212) 859-8000 .. **Kwak**, Jin Young '99 %Fried FHS&J LLP -1 NY Plz -NY 10004
(718) 286-6000 .. **Kwalbrun**, Robin Lee '90 %DA -125-01 Qns Blvd -Kew Gdns 11415
(212) 412-5822 .. **Kwalwasser**, Chas S '02 Barclays Capital Inc -200 Park Av -NY 10166
(212) 969-3000 .. **Kwalwasser**, Edw A '65 SrCnsl Proskauer R LLP -1585 Bway -NY 10036
(646) 610-5400 .. **Kwalwasser**, Robt L '93 %NYPD -1 Police Plz -NY 10038
(212) 839-5300 .. **Kwan**, Angelica '94 (Sidley A LLP) -787 7th Av -NY 10019
(718) 286-6000 .. **Kwan**, Catherine J '08 %DA -125-01 Qns Blvd -Kew Gdns 11415
(212) 728-8000 .. **Kwan-Gett**, Mei Lin '03 (Willkie F&G LLP) -787 7th Av -NY 10019
(212) 490-9100 .. **Kwarta**, Evan M '06 Condon & F LLP -7 Times Sq -NY 10036
(212) 310-8000 .. **Kwartner**, Jason K '09 %Weil G&M LLP -767 5th Av -NY 10153
(518) 785-1900 .. **Kwasniewski**, R Eric '06 %PEF -1168-70 Troy-Schnctdy Rd Bx12414 -Albany 12212 **Fx:**785-1323
(212) 220-3000 .. **Kwasnik**, Fiana R '06 %Broadcast Music Inc -250 Greenwich -NY 10007
(212) 808-5440 .. **Kwasnik**, Richd E '67 -2170 Maple Av -Cortlandt Manor 10567
(212) 776-5000 .. **Kwasnik**, Thaddeus D '84 %NYC Housing Auth -250 Bway -NY 10007 **Fx:**776-5039
(631) 261-8834 .. **Kwee**, David F '99 %Ingerman S LLP -150 Motor Pkwy -Hauppauge 11788
(212) 872-1000 .. **Kweit**, Lewis J '96 -One Bryant Park -NY 10036 **Fx:**872-1002
(212) 301-3002 .. **Kweit**, Mitchell S '90 Fox News -1211 Av of Amer -NY 10036
(718) 380-1122 .. **Kweller**, Leor E '07 %Levi & M,LLP -15916 Union Tpk -Fresh Mdws 11366 **Fx:**380-1124
(212) 335-9000 .. **Kweskin**, Abigail E '05 %DA -1 Hogan Pl -NY 10013

(631) 761-7000 .. **Kwestel,** Sidney '62 %Touro Cllg Law Ctr -225 Eastvw Dr -Central Islip 11722
(800) 499-2610 .. **Kwestel,** Steven J '96 (Zucker & K,LLP) -77 Spruce -Cedarhrst 11516
(516) 354-1900 .. **Kwiatkowski,** John W '98 (Kwiatkowski & K) -131 Tulip Av -Floral Pk 11001 **Fx:**354-0462
(585) 987-2800 .. **Kwiatkowski,** Sarah J '07 %Woods OG LLP -2 State -Rchstr 14614
(718) 388-3330 .. **Kwiatkowski,** Thos '01 -578 Driggs Av -Brklyn 11211 **Fx:**388-3877
(516) 354-1900 .. **Kwiatkowski,** Thos J '67 (Kwiatkowski & K) -131 Tulip Av -Floral Pk 11001 **Fx:**354-0462
(716) 668-0001 .. **Kwieciak,** Richd S '70 (Kwieciak K&K,LLP) -2448 Union Rd -Cheektowaga 14227
(716) 668-0001 .. **Kwieciak,** Stanley III '07 (Kwieciak K&K,LLP) -2448 Union Rd -Cheektowaga 14227
(212) 637-2415 .. **Kwok,** Chi T Steve '05 %US Atty -1 St Andrews Plz -NY 10007
(212) 455-2000 .. **Kwok,** Frank L L '07 %Simpson T&B LLP -425 Lex Av -NY 10017
(212) 687-4900 .. **Kwon,** Barbara J '06 %Wormser KG&J LLP -825 3rd Av -NY 10022
(718) 579-7900 .. **Kwon,** Carolyn '09 Leg Aid -900 Sheridan Av -Bronx 10451 **Fx:**293-8744
(516) 357-9545 .. **Kwon,** Chas '84 -1740 Hempstd Tpk -E Meadow 11554
(212) 816-1197 .. **Kwon,** Eugene '96 Citigroup -388 Greenwich -NY 10013
(212) 412-1473 .. **Kwon,** Julianne S '01 Barclays Capital Inc -200 Park Av -NY 10166
(212) 594-5300 .. **Kwon,** Julie '08 %Milberg LLP -1 Penn Plz -NY 10119
(800) 742-9696 .. **Kwon,** Kristine S '96 %Binder & B,PC -33-00 Nrthrn Blvd -LIC 11101 **Fx:**(718) 512-2424
(212) 756-2000 .. **Kwon,** Michl '08 %Schulte R&Z LLP -919 3rd Av -NY 10022
(212) 259-8000 .. **Kwon,** Minsoo '09 %Dewey & L LLP -1301 Av of Amer -NY 10019
(212) 259-8000 .. **Kwon,** Sohyon '06 %Dewey & L LLP -1301 Av of Amer -NY 10019
(516) 883-1142 .. **Kwon,** Tae Jin '91 -51 W Overlook -Pt Wash 11050
(212) 310-8000 .. **Kwon,** U-Hyeon '09 %Weil G&M LLP -767 5th Av -NY 10153
(212) 259-8000 .. **Kwon,** Yoo-Kyeong '03 %Dewey & L LLP -1301 Av of Amer -NY 10019
(631) 853-4161 .. **Kwon-Cho,** Lucie M '02 %DA -N Cnty Cmplx Bldg 77 -Hauppauge 11788 **Fx:**853-4192
(212) 998-2239 .. **Kwong,** Jennifer W '09 NYU Ofc Leg Cnsl -70 Wshngtn Sq S -NY 10012 **Fx:**995-3048
(212) 854-7580 .. **Kwong,** Joanne Ng '03 Barnard College -3009 Bway -NY 10027 **Fx:**749-6531
(518) 486-5824 .. **Kwong,** Lisa S '93 %Dept of Law -The Cptl -Albany 12224 **Fx:**473-2534
(516) 299-5556 .. **Kye,** Matthew F '97 (Magnozzi & K,LLP) -1 Expwy Plz -Roslyn Hts 11577 **Fx:**299-5598
(212) 584-0058 .. **Kye,** Sammy J '07 %Yoon & K LLP -11 E 44th -NY 10017
(212) 705-7000 .. **Kyle,** Amy L '05 (Bingham M LLP) -399 Park Av -NY 10022
(212) 450-4000 .. **Kyle,** Ashleigh S '03 %Davis P&W LLP -450 Lex Av -NY 10017
(212) 558-4000 .. **Kyle,** Joshua S '09 %Sullivan & C LLP -125 Broad -NY 10004
(315) 785-3053 .. **Kyle,** Nicole L '99 %DA -175 Arsenal -Watertwn 13601 **Fx:**785-3371
(315) 785-3053 .. **Kyle,** Rodney W '03 %DA -175 Arsenal -Watertwn 13601 **Fx:**785-3371
(718) 727-9600 .. **Kyle,** Thos S '78 -803 Castleton Av -Staten Isl 10310 **Fx:**727-6446
(315) 798-5870 .. **Kyles,** Ray A '06 %Pub Def -321 Main -Utica 13501 **Fx:**798-6419
(914) 834-3500 .. **Kyme,** Gary P '98 (McMillan CM&P LLP) -2180 Bstn Post Rd -Larchmnt 10538
(212) 354-3800 .. **Kyne,** Stephen P '74 (Burke & P) -100 Park Av -NY 10017
(718) 254-6431 .. **Kyriakakis,** Anthony G '03 US Atty -271 Cadman Plz E -Brklyn 11201 **Fx:**254-6479
(212) 735-3000 .. **Kyriakides,** Helen '00 %Skadden ASM&F LLP -4 Times Sq -NY 10036
(212) 716-5800 .. **Kyriakides,** Simon P '95 %Amer Arbtrtn Assn -1633 Bway -NY 10019
(212) 489-1600 .. **Kyriakopoulos,** Ageliki V '04 %Deloitte LLP -1633 Bway -NY 10019 **Fx:**492-4201
(315) 379-2225 .. **Kyriakopoulos,** Efstathia G '02 %DA -48 Court -Canton 13617 **Fx:**379-2301
(212) 272-7098 .. **Kyriazos,** Chas S '94 %JP Morgan Chase -383 Mad Av -NY 10179
(212) 404-5777 .. **Kyriss,** Marie Cressy '04 OfCnsl Littleton JUP&K LLP -39 Bway -NY 10006
(212) 450-4000 .. **Kyrwood,** Jason J '02 (Davis P&W LLP) -450 Lex Av -NY 10017
(718) 780-7545 .. **Kysar,** Rebecca M '05 Bklyn Law Schl -250 Joralemon -Brklyn 11201 **Fx:**780-0393
(716) 532-2284 .. **Kysor & Della Posta** -95 W Main Bx 270 -Gowanda 14070 **Fx:**532-0474
(716) 857-7991 .. **Kyzmir,** Anne K '96 %Natl Fuel Gas -6363 Main -Williamsvll 14221 **Fx:**857-7614
(212) 596-9000 .. **La,** Chia-Hao '09 %Ropes & G LLP -1211 Av of Amer -NY 10036
(845) 569-1400 .. **Laager,** Creston F IV '02 -288 N Plnk Rd -Newburgh 12550
(212) 295-8270 .. **Labaj,** Pamela J '91 Integro Ins Brokers -1 State Street Plz -NY 10004 **Fx:**295-8271
(716) 893-4807 .. **Labaki,** Paul F '91 -91 Westland Pkwy -Buffalo 14225 **Fx:**893-4818
(585) 586-2565 .. **Labanowski,** Robt A '80 -29 Kilbourn Rd -Rchstr 14618
(718) 596-9366 .. **LaBarbera,** Jos J '77 (J LaBarbera,PC) -55 Washington -Brklyn 11201 **Fx:**596-9167
(516) 571-2679 .. **LaBarbera,** Moira A '01 Cnsl Cnty Comptroller Ofc -240 Old Cntry Rd -Mineola 11501 **Fx:**571-5900
(845) 291-1900 .. **LaBarbera,** Stephen P '81 OfCnsl Cohen E & Assoc,LLP -40 Matthews -Goshen 10924 **Fx:**291-8601
(212) 237-1000 .. **LaBarbiera,** Leonard A '89 SpclCnsl Windels ML&M,LLP -156 W 56th -NY 10019
(212) 962-2211 .. **LaBarca,** Kenneth A '90 -305 Bway -NY 10007 **Fx:**962-2255
(585) 263-1000 .. **LaBarge,** Jeffrey H '99 %Nixon P LLP -1100 Clinton Sq -Rchstr 14604
(607) 762-7381 .. **LaBarge,** Lisa K '99 %Electric & Gas Corp -Corp Dr Kirkwood Ind Pk Bx5224 -Bnghmtn 13902 **Fx:**762-8564
(212) 907-0850 .. **Labaton,** Edw '57 (Labaton S LLP) -140 Bway -NY 10005
(212) 907-0700 .. **Labaton Sucharow LLP** -140 Bway -NY 10005 **Fx:**818-0477
(212) 805-0232 .. **Labaton,** Vivien M '05 Hon C Baker Motley -500 Pearl -NY 10007
(518) 449-0044 .. **LaBatt,** John W '02 %Hoffman W&D LLC -75 State -Albany 12207 **Fx:**449-0047
(516) 294-8844 .. **L'Abbate Balkan Colavita & Contini,LLP** -1001 Franklin Av -Gdn Cty 11530 **Fx:**294-8202
(516) 294-8844 .. **L'Abbate,** Donald R '70 Cnsl L'Abbate BC&C,LLP -1001 Franklin Av -Gdn Cty 11530
(212) 804-4200 .. **Labbate,** Kenneth M '93 (Mound CW&G) -One Bttry Pk Plz -NY 10004
(212) 607-8622 .. **Labbees,** Cassandra '08 US Dept of Labor -33 Whitehall -NY 10004
(212) 487-9701 .. **Labe,** Mark S '97 Cnsl Robin HK&F -1 Bttry Pk Plz -NY 10014
(212) 687-8700 .. **Labell,** Mark '85 Cnsl Malkin Hldngs,LLC -60 E 42nd -NY 10165 **Fx:**986-7679
(718) 238-6966 .. **LaBella,** Anthony A Jr. '77 -110 Bay Ridge Av -Brklyn 11220
(914) 358-4934 .. **Labella,** Rocco J '89 (Ferro L&Z LLC) -1025 Wstchstr Av -White Plns 10604
(516) 378-1700 .. **LaBella,** Tara A '87 (Chesney & M) -2305 Grand Av -Baldwin 11510
(518) 584-4160 .. **LaBelle,** Lawr J '53 (LaBelle & L) -444 Bway Bx574 -Saratoga Spgs 12866 **Fx:**587-3999
(212) 969-3000 .. **Laben,** Leah E '07 %Proskauer R LLP -1585 Bway -NY 10036
(212) 689-1113 .. **Labendz,** Asher I '98 %Garbarini & S,PC -432 Park Av S -NY 10016
(315) 455-2000 .. **LaBerge,** Ellen T '84 C&S Companies -499 Col Eileen Collins Blvd -Syracuse 13212 **Fx:**455-9467
(315) 218-8000 .. **LaBerge,** Robt A '84 (Bond S&K,PLLC) -1 Lincoln Ctr -Syracuse 13202
(516) 883-5432 .. **Labert,** Jill S '96 %Publishers Clearing House -382 Channel Dr -Pt Wash 11050
(516) 228-4800 .. **Labert,** Louis S '65 -666 Old Cntry Rd -Gdn Cty 11530
(716) 631-9981 .. **Labin & Buffomante** -531 Farber Lks Dr -Williamsvll 14221 **Fx:**633-4421
(716) 631-9981 .. **Labin,** Thos S '67 (Labin & B) -531 Farber Lks Dr -Williamsvll 14221
(845) 279-7432 .. **Labis,** Keith L '82 -2435 Route 6 -Brewstr 10509 **Fx:**279-7461
(518) 587-6210 .. **LaBoda,** John J Jr. '73 -60 Woodlawn Av Bx1044 -Saratoga Spgs 12866 **Fx:**587-5869
(585) 263-1000 .. **Laboda,** John J III '07 %Nixon P LLP -1100 Clinton Sq -Rchstr 14604
(518) 474-8211 .. **LaBoda,** Katherine Dorsey '91 %Law Reporting Bur -1 Commerce Plz -Albany 12210 **Fx:**463-6869
(212) 906-1200 .. **Labonski,** Peter M '94 (Latham & W) -885 3rd Av -NY 10022
(516) 873-3000 .. **LaBonte,** Stevan H '05 %Bellavia G & Assoc,LLP -200 Old Cntry Rd -Mineola 11501 **Fx:**873-9032
(212) 735-3000 .. **LaBorde,** Vivienne C '00 %Skadden ASM&F LLP -4 Times Sq -NY 10036
(212) 878-7020 .. **LaBosco,** Teresa E '86 %MTA -347 Mad Av -NY 10017
(212) 306-7450 .. **Labossiere,** Paul E '02 %Comm on Human Rights -40 Rector -NY 10006 **Fx:**306-7414
(212) 704-6526 .. **Labouriau,** Gabriela Nossar '99 Sojitz Corp of America -1211 Av of Amer -NY 10036
(212) 308-4411 .. **Labov,** Paul J '03 %Edwards AP&D LLP -750 Lex Av -NY 10022
(212) 656-2081 .. **Labovitz,** Danl M '96 NYSE -20 Broad -NY 10005
(212) 446-4800 .. **Labovitz,** M Natasha '97 (Kirkland & E LLP) -153 E 53rd -NY 10022
(212) 308-1681 .. **La Bow,** Ronald '63 WPN Corp -641 5th Av -NY 10022
(212) 431-7500 .. **Laboz,** Albert '86 United Amer Land LLC -430 W Bway -NY 10012
(212) 732-3350 .. **Labozzetta,** Anthony V '76 Wall St Realty Capital -555 5th Av -NY 10017
(212) 688-8555 .. **La Brie,** Christina B '01 %Fragomen DB&L LLP -7 Hanover Sq -NY 10004
(212) 548-0100 .. **LaBrie,** Raquiba '96 %Open Society Inst -400 W 59th -NY 10019
(212) 872-1000 .. **Labritz,** Kelly Jo '09 -One Bryant Park -NY 10036 **Fx:**872-1002
(212) 504-6000 .. **LaBrun,** Henry A '90 (Cadwalader W&T LLP) -1 World Fncl Ctr -NY 10281
(516) 328-8899 .. **Labuda,** Jos M '95 %Milman L Law Grp PLLC -3000 Marcus Av -Lk Success 11042 **Fx:**328-0082
(585) 325-4110 .. **LaBue,** Eugene P '64 (Goldstein & L) -45 Exchange Blvd -Rchstr 14614
(585) 671-5704 .. **LaBue,** Michl J '77 -1050 Gravel Rd -Webster 14580 **Fx:**671-1343
(585) 265-9299 .. **LaBue,** Richd H '90 Temporary & Disability Assistance -259 Monroe Av -Rchstr 14607
(845) 634-0334 .. **LaCap,** Henry '97 -155 N Main -New Cty 10956
(631) 582-4990 .. **LaCapra,** Jos G '97 (LaCapra S&K,LLP) -320 Carleton Av -Central Islip 11722 **Fx:**582-4690
(212) 742-8700 .. **LaCava,** Jos D '98 (Garson D&C LLP) -110 Wall -NY 10005
(212) 547-5400 .. **LaCava,** Lindsay M '06 McDermott W&E LLP -340 Mad Av -NY 10173
(212) 277-6500 .. **LaCava,** Richd '98 (Dickstein S LLP) -1633 Bway -NY 10019
(212) 310-8000 .. **Lacayo,** Isabella C '07 %Weil G&M LLP -767 5th Av -NY 10153
(212) 578-2211 .. **Lacek,** Michl J '81 %MetLife -27-01 Qns Plz N -LIC 11101
(212) 480-7440 .. **Lacerenza,** Mary E '80 %DHCR -25 Beaver -NY 10004 **Fx:**480-7416
(212) 416-6199 .. **Lacewell,** Linda A '91 %Dept of Law -120 Bway -NY 10271
(212) 259-8000 .. **Lacey,** Fredk B '48 SpclCnsl Dewey & L LLP -1301 Av of Amer -NY 10019
(716) 845-3650 .. **Lacey,** Jeffrey T '79 MHLS -438 Main -Buffalo 14202 **Fx:**874-7794
(212) 733-6834 .. **Lacey,** Kevin C '05 Pfizer,Inc -235 E 42nd -NY 10017
(212) 701-3000 .. **Lacey,** Ted B '09 %Cahill G&R LLP -80 Pine -NY 10005 **Fx:**269-5420
(518) 785-4387 .. **LaChapelle,** Ginger B '03 %Blitman & K LLP -800 Troy-Schnctdy Rd -Latham 12110
(212) 403-1000 .. **La Chapelle,** Jonathan R '07 %Wachtell LR&K -51 W 52nd -NY 10019
(518) 438-1600 .. **LaChapelle,** Kinga M '74 United Publishing Co -21A Railroad Av -Albany 12205 **Fx:**459-4576
(212) 633-6967 .. **LaCheen,** Caroline G '89 Natl Ctr Law & Economic Justice -275 7th Av -NY 10001 **Fx:**633-6371
(212) 407-4000 .. **Lachenauer,** Robt B '90 (Loeb & L,LLP) -345 Park Av -NY 10154
(212) 436-1138 .. **Lacher,** Alan E '72 %IRS -290 Bway -NY 10007 **Fx:**436-1063
(914) 729-7700 .. **Lacher,** David '78 -270 North Av -New Rchll 10801 **Fx:**235-8926
(212) 872-1500 .. **Lacher & Lovell-Taylor** -460 Park Av -NY 10022 **Fx:**872-1630
(212) 872-1500 .. **Lacher,** Michl A '65 (Lacher & L-T) -460 Park Av -NY 10022
(516) 747-0440 .. **Lacher,** Stanley J '73 Globe Title -400 S Oyster Bay Rd -Hicksvll 11801 **Fx:**741-3346
(516) 295-3094 .. **Lachman,** Moses '86 -377 Bucknghm Rd -Cedarhrst 11516 **Fx:**295-4497

(212) 553-0300 .. **Lachnicht,** Christine C '90 %Moody's Invstr Srvc -250 Greenwich -NY 10007
(212) 522-8307 .. **Lachow,** Andrew B '87 Time Inc -1271 Av of Amer -NY 10020 **Fx:**522-0437
(212) 918-3000 .. **Lachter,** Katie M '04 %Hogan L LLP -875 3rd Av -NY 10022
(212) 889-0707 .. **Lachtman,** David R '96 %Platte KL&L,LLP -10 E 40th -NY 10016
(212) 408-5453 .. **Lacina,** Chas F '85 Chadbourne & P LLP -30 Rckfllr Plz -NY 10112
(716) 845-2560 .. **LaCivita,** Rebecca Diina '03 Surrogates Ct -92 Franklin -Buffalo 14202 **Fx:**853-3741
(212) 833-1108 .. **Lack,** Robt J '82 (Friedman KS&A LLP) -1633 Bway -NY 10019 **Fx:**373-7908
(845) 471-5140 .. **Lackaye,** Edw J Jr. '75 -90 Market Box 5188 -Poughkeepsie 12601 **Fx:**471-5148
(845) 471-3140 .. **Lackaye,** Robt J '74 -90 Market Bx5188 -Poughkeepsie 12602 **Fx:**471-5148
(718) 576-1248 .. **Lackenbach,** Carol K '82 -29 Cooper Ter -Staten Isl 10314
(914) 723-4300 .. **Lackenbach Siegel LLP** -1 Chase Rd -Scarsdale 10583 **Fx:**723-4301
(212) 277-6500 .. **Lackert,** Clark W '78 (Dickstein S LLP) -1633 Bway -NY 10019
(212) 918-3000 .. **Lackman,** Eleanor M '04 %Hogan L LLP -875 3rd Av -NY 10022
(212) 752-9700 .. **Lackowitz,** David A '00 %Gersten S LLP -600 Lex Av -NY 10022
(212) 225-2000 .. **Lacks,** Jeremy R '09 %Cleary GS&H -1 Lbrty Plz -NY 10006
(315) 422-7111 .. **Laclair,** Brian J '07 %Blitman & K LLP -443 N Franklin -Syracuse 13204
(315) 461-4277 .. **Laclair,** Dean C '02 %Falge & M,PC -3300 Vickery Rd -N Syracuse 13212
(212) 742-0500 .. **LaClair,** Paul L '83 %Gucciardo Law Firm -99 Wall -NY 10005 **Fx:**742-0815
(212) 348-7449 .. **Lacoff,** Judith '76 %Legal Srvcs -1 W 125th -NY 10027 **Fx:**348-4093
(518) 897-1227 .. **Lacombe,** Christopher A '87 %DEC -1115 Route 86 Bx296 -Ray Brk 12977 **Fx:**897-1394
(212) 318-6000 .. **Lacour,** Justin B '10 %Paul HJ&W LLP -75 E 55th -NY 10022
(212) 474-1000 .. **Lacoursiere,** Lynne A '03 %Cravath S&M LLP -825 8th Av -NY 10019
(212) 506-2500 .. **Lacovara,** Philip A '67 SrCnsl Mayer B LLP -1675 Bway -NY 10019
(585) 454-5650 .. **Lacy Katzen LLP** -130 E Main -Rchstr 14604 **Fx:**269-3077
(585) 494-1382 .. **Lacy Katzen LLP** -16 N Lake -Bergen 14416
(585) 225-2470 .. **Lacy Katzen LLP** -20 Main -Hilton 14468 **Fx:**269-3067
(585) 394-5220 .. **Lacy Katzen LLP** -23 North -Canandaigua 14424 **Fx:**394-7973
(585) 225-2470 .. **Lacy Katzen LLP** -1101-C English Rd -Rchstr 14616 **Fx:**225-5620
(585) 663-4543 .. **Lacy Katzen LLP** -4292 Lk Av -Rchstr 14612 **Fx:**663-6785
(585) 454-5650 .. **Lacy Katzen LLP** -319 W Main -Batavia 14020
(585) 454-5650 .. **Lacy Katzen LLP** -1173 Pttsfrd-Vctr Rd -Pittsfrd 14534 **Fx:**269-3077
(315) 524-5000 .. **Lacy Katzen LLP** -1276 Ridge Rd -Ontario 14519 **Fx:**524-5600
(914) 681-0444 .. **Lacy,** Patricia '90 (Rende R&D,LLP) -202 Mamaroneck Av -White Plns 10601
(212) 558-4000 .. **Lacy,** Robinson B '78 (Sullivan & C LLP) -125 Broad -NY 10004
(212) 343-0303 .. **Laczynski,** Christine M '81 -350 Bway -NY 10013
(845) 343-5100 .. **Ladanyi,** Robt A '79 -453 Rt 211E -Middletwn 10940 **Fx:**342-6088
(212) 708-1800 .. **Ladas & Parry** -26 W 61st -NY 10023 **Fx:**246-8959
(212) 524-5000 .. **Ladd,** Ann T '80 OfCnsl Jacob M&F -1270 Av of Amer -NY 10020
(516) 294-7879 .. **Ladd,** David R '03 D Ladd,PC -Bx364 -Farmngdl 11735 **Fx:**877-2586
(212) 728-8000 .. **Ladd,** Delano W '09 %Willkie F&G LLP -787 7th Av -NY 10019
(212) 846-3860 .. **Ladd,** Jonathan E '90 -1515 Bway -NY 10036
(212) 278-1000 .. **Ladd,** Marc T '10 %Anderson K&O,PC -1251 Av of Amer -NY 10020
(518) 461-2842 .. **Ladd,** Pamela A '97 Ladd Law Firm,PC -Bx68 -Fonda 12068
(212) 733-6103 .. **Ladd,** Robt A '00 Pfizer -150 E 42nd -NY 10017
(718) 590-2000 .. **Ladd,** Tara M '09 %DA -198 E 161st -Bronx 10451 **Fx:**590-6477
(585) 786-8135 .. **Ladd,** Vincent O '67 -34 N Main Bx9 -Warsaw 14569 **Fx:**786-8135
(212) 292-4444 .. **Ladds,** Arthur '54 -521 5th Av -NY 10175
(631) 844-7800 .. **Laderoute,** Laurin L Jr. '67 %Olsten Corp -175 Broadhllw Rd -Melvll 11747 **Fx:**844-7414
(315) 471-1664 .. **La Dieu,** Heather R '01 %Meggesto C&V,LLP -313 E Willow -Syracuse 13203
(212) 649-2000 .. **Ladin,** Timothy E '97 %Hearst Corp -300 W 57th -NY 10019 **Fx:**649-2035
(212) 267-7600 .. **Ladislaw,** Robt A '04 %Solomon PBH&S LLP -40 Wall -NY 10005
(212) 551-0600 .. **Ladner,** China '94 Mutual Marine Ofc Inc -919 3rd Av -NY 10022
(212) 468-8035 .. **Ladner,** Mark P '79 (Morrison & F LLP) -1290 Av of Amer -NY 10104
(212) 318-3000 .. **Ladner,** Stanford G '80 (Fulbright & J LLP) -666 5th Av -NY 10103
(212) 728-8000 .. **Ladoff,** Brandon P '09 %Willkie F&G LLP -787 7th Av -NY 10019
(518) 457-2070 .. **Ladouceur,** Mary Ellen '98 Dept of Tax & Fin -Bldg 9 State Campus -Albany 12227 **Fx:**457-6131
(315) 265-2747 .. **Ladouceur,** Michelle H '00 (Cappello L&L) -76 Market Bx5153 -Potsdam 13676
(315) 386-4595 .. **Ladouceur,** Michelle H '00 %Oliver Law Firm -117 Main -Canton 13617 **Fx:**379-1240
(212) 519-7896 .. **Ladov,** Mark H '07 ACLU -125 Broad -NY 10004
(212) 704-6000 .. **Ladow,** Danl A '86 OfCnsl Troutman S LLP -405 Lex Av -NY 10174
(646) 290-6789 .. **Ladson,** Erick V '01 -2298 1st Av -NY 10035
(585) 327-5045 .. **LaDuca,** Anthony J '95 -125 State -Rchstr 14614 **Fx:**454-1254
(585) 327-5045 .. **LaDuca,** Heidi E '95 -125 State -Rchstr 14614 **Fx:**454-1254
(585) 327-5045 .. **LaDuca,** John J '68 -125 State -Rchstr 14614 **Fx:**454-1254
(518) 523-2786 .. **La Duke,** Gregory D '97 -2038 Saranac Av -Lk Placid 12946 **Fx:**523-2143
(212) 326-3939 .. **Laduzinski,** Colleen E '01 (Jones D) -222 E 41st -NY 10017
(212) 773-3000 .. **Laduzinski,** Steven M '01 %Ernst & Young,LLP -5 Times Sq -NY 10036
(212) 325-2000 .. **Laemmle,** Ann K '90 Credit Suisse -1 Mad Av -NY 10010
(516) 877-2800 .. **Laface,** Jos J '77 -229 7th -Gdn Cty 11530 **Fx:**877-2818
(631) 673-9231 .. **LaFace-Sapienza,** Laura C '81 -42 Salem Ridge Dr -Huntngtn 11743 **Fx:**673-6362
(315) 793-8800 .. **LaFache,** Anthony J '72 -286-288 Genesee -Utica 13502 **Fx:**793-0064
(315) 793-8800 .. **Lafache,** Trisha E '03 -288 Genesee -Utica 13502
(212) 236-6301 .. **Lafaire,** Anthony J '87 %Merrill Lynch -225 Lbrty -NY 10080
(716) 636-7600 .. **LaFalce,** John J '64 SpclCnsl HoganWillig -2410 N Forest Rd -Amherst 14068
(212) 571-0111 .. **Lafarga,** David '07 %Hardin KM&P,PA -110 William -NY 10038
(212) 335-9000 .. **Lafarge,** Erin M '08 DA -1 Hogan Pl -NY 10013
(212) 735-3000 .. **Lafata,** Paul A '08 %Skadden ASM&F LLP -4 Times Sq -NY 10036
(631) 724-5370 .. **LaFauci,** Thos J '78 (TJ LaFauci,PC) -23 Swan Ln -Hauppauge 11788
(718) 797-2897 .. **LaFaurie,** Wilson A '95 -44 Court -Brklyn 11201
(518) 782-4900 .. **LaFave,** Cynthia S '82 (LaFave L&S,LLP) -951 Albany Shaker Rd -Latham 12110 **Fx:**785-9705
(585) 338-5093 .. **LaFave,** John F '83 %Bausch & Lomb -One Bausch & Lomb Pl -Rchstr 14604 **Fx:**338-8706
(212) 994-9963 .. **LaFave,** Wm E III '05 Federman S LLP -220 E 42nd -NY 10017 **Fx:**685-5199
(585) 325-4064 .. **LaFay,** Anthony P '67 (LaFay B&L,PC) -36 W Main -Rchstr 14614 **Fx:**325-5362
(585) 325-4064 .. **LaFay,** Jos H '96 (LaFay B&L,PC) -36 W Main -Rchstr 14614 **Fx:**325-5362
(212) 451-2300 .. **Lafayette,** Mark S '85 OfCnsl Olshan GFR&W LLP -65 E 55th -NY 10022
(516) 227-0700 .. **LaFerlita,** Jos T '05 %Farrell F,PC -1320 RXR Plz -Uniondale 11556
(914) 390-4132 .. **La Ferlita,** Lea L '02 Hon Smith -300 Quarropas -White Plns 10601
(518) 465-3484 .. **Laferriere,** Alaina K '10 %Carter CCBM&L,PC -20 Corp Wds Blvd -Albany 12211
(212) 819-8200 .. **Laferriere,** Melissa M '07 %White & C LLP -1155 Av of Amer -NY 10036
(585) 454-6480 .. **Lafever-Koch,** Aimee '96 (Osborn R&B,LLP) -45 Exchange Blvd -Rchstr 14614
(516) 877-0955 .. **Laffan,** Maura V '90 (Laffan & L LLP) -221 Mineola Blvd -Mineola 11501 **Fx:**877-0957
(516) 877-0955 .. **Laffan,** Wm F Jr. '54 (Laffan & L LLP) -221 Mineola Blvd -Mineola 11501 **Fx:**877-0957
(516) 944-3596 .. **Laffer,** Renee F '81 -28A Murray Av -Pt Wash 11050
(646) 562-3405 .. **Lafferty,** Christopher C '07 %PLC -747 3rd Av -NY 10017
(212) 574-1200 .. **Lafferty,** Ellen E '03 %Seward & K LLP -1 Bttry Pk Plz -NY 10004
(718) 590-2000 .. **Lafferty,** Jennifer M Newton '07 DA -198 E 161st -Bronx 10451 **Fx:**590-6477
(516) 745-0160 .. **Lafferty,** Jos A '84 Benjamin Dvlpmnt -377 Oak -Gdn Cty 11530
(212) 789-7601 .. **Lafferty,** Robt M '04 Millennium B'way Hotel -145 W 44th -NY 10036
(212) 521-5400 .. **Laffey,** Casey D '05 %Reed S LLP -599 Lex Av -NY 10022
(212) 969-2179 .. **Laffey,** Stephen J '04 %Alliance Bernstein LP -1345 Av of Amer -NY 10105 **Fx:**554-4639
(516) 327-2700 .. **Laffin,** Kevin R '99 BWD Grp LLC -BWD Plz Bx9050 -Jericho 11753 **Fx:**327-2800
(631) 866-4173 .. **Laffler,** Margaret M '04 Perfumania Holdings,Inc -35 Sawgrss Dr -Bellprt 11713
(518) 449-8893 .. **LaFlam,** Jason M '04 %Wilson EME&D LLP -677 Bway -Albany 12207
(212) 872-1000 .. **Laflamme,** Elaine M '88 -One Bryant Park -NY 10036 **Fx:**872-1002
(212) 259-8000 .. **LaFond,** Carol A '04 %Dewey & L LLP -1301 Av of Amer -NY 10019
(518) 426-4600 .. **LaFond,** Melanie J '03 (Couch W,LLP) -540 Bway Bx22222 -Albany 12201
(718) 254-0700 .. **LaFontaine,** Richd M '88 %Bklyn Defender Srvcs -177 Lvngstn -Brklyn 11201 **Fx:**254-0897
(716) 852-5200 .. **LaForce,** Mary K '99 (Hamberger & W) -700 Main Pl Twr -Buffalo 14202
(212) 813-8800 .. **LaForce,** Ryan H '05 %Goodwin P LLP -620 8th Av -NY 10018
(845) 294-5297 .. **LaForge,** Gladys C '81 -305 Main -Goshen 10924 **Fx:**294-3075
(212) 319-3560 .. **La Forge,** James C '81 -126 E 56th -NY 10022 **Fx:**319-3587
(718) 287-0010 .. **LaForgia,** Madeline '00 CAMBA -885 Flatbush Av -Brklyn 11226 **Fx:**282-5997
(585) 232-6500 .. **La Forte,** Wm N '75 (Harter S&E LLP) -1600 Bausch & Lomb Pl -Rchstr 14604
(718) 254-0700 .. **LaFranchi,** Christie L '05 %Bklyn Defender Srvcs -177 Lvngstn -Brklyn 11201 **Fx:**254-0897
(212) 902-3079 .. **LaFreniere,** Owen C '03 Goldman Sachs & Co -85 Broad -NY 10004
(212) 983-9700 .. **Lagalante,** Louis M '88 (Gallagher H&L LLP) -380 Lex Av -NY 10168
(212) 735-8600 .. **LaGalia,** David P '02 SrCnsl Morrison C LLP -909 3rd Av -NY 10022
(212) 722-2000 .. **LaGamma,** Diane E '87 %Leg Aid -230 E 106th -NY 10029 **Fx:**876-5365
(718) 932-2550 .. **Lagan,** John F '92 -4402 23rd -LIC 11101
(518) 464-2411 .. **Lagan,** Thos K '86 AYCO -1 Wall Bx15073 -Albany 12212
(914) 682-2611 .. **Lagano,** Christopher '94 %Trow & S,PC -50 Main -White Plns 10606
(845) 623-0090 .. **Lagano,** Frank '08 %Weiner & S -119 Rockland Ctr -Nanuet 10954
(212) 733-4644 .. **Lagano,** Roxanne '91 %Pfizer Inc -235 E 42nd -NY 10017
(718) 846-4465 .. **La Garenne,** Robt J '87 -87-16 Woodhvn Blvd -Woodhvn 11421 **Fx:**846-4701
(212) 935-3000 .. **Lagasse,** David R '97 (Mintz LCFG&P,PC) -666 3rd Av -NY 10017
(646) 366-5500 .. **LaGatta,** Michl A '03 1st Solar,Inc -620 8th Av -NY 10018
(212) 785-9800 .. **LaGattuta,** Paul F III '99 (Fixler & L) -61 Bway -NY 10006
(212) 599-0990 .. **Lagemann,** Jonathan K '72 -300 E 42nd -NY 10017 **Fx:**922-0518
(212) 839-5300 .. **Lagemann,** Nicholas K '03 %Sidley A LLP -787 7th Av -NY 10019
(914) 345-3701 .. **Lager,** Karen M '08 %Marks OO&C,PC -530 Saw Mill Rvr Rd -Elmsfrd 10523
(212) 245-7300 .. **Lager,** Stacey L '04 %Serling R&F,LLP -119 5th Av -NY 10003
(718) 250-2000 .. **Laghezza,** Frank Jr. '89 %DA -350 Jay -Brklyn 11201 **Fx:**250-2314
(212) 210-9478 .. **Laginestra,** Jaime '10 %Alston & B LLP -90 Park Av -NY 10016
(518) 462-3000 .. **Lagios,** James P '98 (Iseman CR&H,LLP) -9 Thurlow Ter -Albany 12203
(646) 526-5573 .. **Lagnado,** Michl P '89 -15 Broad -NY 10005 **Fx:**652-5359
(212) 218-5500 .. **Lagno,** Christopher J '79 (Seyfarth S LLP) -620 8th Av -NY 10018
(212) 816-8820 .. **Lago,** Marisa '84 Citigroup -388 Greenwich -NY 10013
(716) 855-6741 .. **Lagona,** James F '87 %BMHA -300 Perry -Buffalo 14204 **Fx:**855-6761
(914) 245-7500 .. **Lagonia,** Salvatore A '92 -1925 Commerce Bx571 -Yorktwn Hts 10598 **Fx:**245-7563

(845) 246-9575 .. **LaGorga,** Anne M '88 -1 W Brdg Bx300 -Saugerties 12477 **Fx:**246-1905
(718) 777-3800 .. **Lagoudes,** Anna M '98 OfCnsl Kapetanos & B,LLP -23-56 Steinway -Astoria 11105
(516) 572-4189 .. **LaGreca,** Linda '89 Sheriff's Ofc -100 Carman Av -E Meadow 11554
(212) 762-5865 .. **LaGreca,** Vincent J '80 Morgan Stanley -1221 Av of Amer -NY 10020
(516) 795-6000 .. **La Grega,** Donald J Jr. '84 (Kenealy & L) -553 Bway -Massapequa 11758 **Fx:**795-6148
(914) 741-2567 .. **LaGrotta,** Thos '79 -Bx136 -Plsntvll 10570
(516) 512-6333 .. **La Grua,** Lauren A '06 %Gold SKB LLP -1025 Old Cntry Rd -Westbury 11590
(212) 848-4000 .. **Laguardia,** Danl H R '00 (Shearman & S LLP) -599 Lex Av -NY 10022
(716) 849-8900 .. **Lagueras,** Margo M '06 %Hurwitz & F,PC -1300 Lbrty Bldg -Buffalo 14202
(718) 999-0338 .. **Laguerre-Brown,** Caroline W '98 NYC Fire Dept-OEEO -9 Metrotech Ctr -Brklyn 11201 **Fx:**999-1289
(212) 336-2000 .. **LaGueux,** Jeffrey E '83 (Patterson BW&T LLP) -1133 Av of Amer -NY 10036
(516) 741-5001 .. **LaGueux,** Linda T '84 -51 Chestnut -Gdn Cty 11530
(914) 253-6554 .. **LaGumina,** John J '87 LaGumina,PLLC -2500 Wstchstr Av -Purchase 10577 **Fx:**253-8641
(212) 908-0212 .. **Laguzza,** Gian-Carlo '04 Fitch Ratings -1 State Street Plz -NY 10004
(212) 238-3000 .. **Lah,** Robt D '98 %Emmet M&M,LLP -120 Bway -NY 10271
(212) 872-1000 .. **Lahaie,** Meredith A '07 -One Bryant Park -NY 10036 **Fx:**872-1002
(212) 310-8000 .. **Lahav,** Etai Y '07 %Weil G&M LLP -767 5th Av -NY 10153
(585) 238-8145 .. **LaHaye,** Michl P '74 %OCFS -259 Monroe Av -Rchstr 14607 **Fx:**238-8169
(518) 473-7051 .. **Lahey,** Mark E '80 %OTDA-Fair Hearings -40 N Pearl -Albany 12243 **Fx:**473-6735
(845) 454-9700 .. **Lahey,** Paul A '96 %Ouimette G&A -88 Market Bx192 -Poughkeepsie 12601
(212) 416-8641 .. **Lahiff,** Jeanne '89 %Dept of Law -120 Bway -NY 10271
(212) 559-2543 .. **Lahiff,** Thos M Jr. '80 Citicorp -425 Park Av -NY 10043 **Fx:**793-4400
(845) 750-6386 .. **Lahiri,** Arun Kumar '99 (Lahiri & N) -254 Fair -Kingston 12401 **Fx:**255-9039
(212) 408-2500 .. **Lahiri,** Yasho '93 (Baker B,LLP) -30 Rckfllr Plz -NY 10112
(212) 878-8000 .. **Lahlou,** Yasmine '03 %Clifford C LLP -31 W 52nd -NY 10019
(315) 472-3434 .. **Lahm,** Robt E '75 R Lahm,PLLC -711 E Genesee -Syracuse 13210 **Fx:**472-8214
(585) 232-6660 .. **Lahman,** Janice Allen '88 -Bx17687 -Rchstr 14617 **Fx:**232-6117
(718) 519-4165 .. **Lahn,** Lori H '90 %Comprehesive Care -612 Allerton Av -Bronx 10467
(212) 963-5363 .. **Lahoud,** Nina J '82 %United Nations-DPKO -42nd & 1st Av -NY 10017
(212) 244-4111 .. **Lahovitsky,** Anat '06 Shiboleth YR&Z,LLP -1 Penn Plz -NY 10119
(718) 447-8841 .. **Lahr Dillon Manzulli Kelley & Penett** -33 Decker Av -Staten Isl 10302 **Fx:**981-6778
(212) 422-0202 .. **Lahr,** J Gregory '99 %Sedgwick DM&A LLP -125 Broad -NY 10004
(646) 602-5600 .. **Lai,** Anne '07 Urban Justice Ctr -123 William -NY 10038 **Fx:**(212) 533-4598
(212) 633-2225 .. **Lai,** Gordon C '96 %M Stumer & Assoc,PC -306 5th Av -NY 10001 **Fx:**691-3642
(212) 274-6002 .. **Lai,** Helen '01 Admin Childrens Srvcs -220 Church -NY 10013
(718) 259-4500 .. **Lai,** Hon K '94 %Vanchieri & F -1724 86th -Brklyn 11214
(212) 683-7100 .. **Lai,** Lesley M '03 %Gallo V&K,LLP -90 Broad -NY 10004
(212) 373-3000 .. **Lai,** Mei Ying '08 %Paul WRW&G LLP -1285 Av of Amer -NY 10019
(212) 839-5300 .. **Lai,** Nicole N '09 %Sidley A LLP -787 7th Av -NY 10019
(212) 728-2200 .. **Lai,** Patrick V '05 %Axinn V&H LLP -114 W 47th -NY 10036
(212) 773-0366 .. **Lai,** Qin '04 Intl Tax Svc -5 Times Sq -NY 10036
(212) 637-1944 .. **Lai,** Sarah Y '99 US Atty -1 St Andrews Plz -NY 10007
(315) 671-2032 .. **Laidlaw,** John F '73 Hon R Rossi -401 Mntgmry -Syracuse 13202 **Fx:**671-1168
(914) 767-0646 .. **Laidlaw,** Moira Schneider '95 Laidlaw Firm,LLC -95 Katonah Av -Katonah 10536
(212) 233-4600 .. **Laidlow,** Earl Ian '99 (E Laidlow,PC) -225 Bway -NY 10007 **Fx:**233-4604
(212) 877-0919 .. **Laifer,** Danl M '94 -100 W 89th -NY 10024
(212) 344-1400 .. **Laifer,** Mark S '77 (Friedland L&R,LLP) -62 William -NY 10005
(516) 937-1010 .. **Laine,** Frank J '92 -449 S Oyster Bay Rd -Plainvw 11803
(212) 364-8482 .. **Laine,** Julie P '97 Time Warner Cable -60 Columbus Av -NY 10023 **Fx:**364-8460
(716) 854-4080 .. **Laing,** Linda Callahan '85 (Notaro L&N,PC) -1 Niagara Sq -Buffalo 14202 **Fx:**854-0059
(212) 730-7750 .. **Lainhart,** Angela A '92 %Nicoletti GS&O,LLP -555 5th Av -NY 10017
(716) 689-4972 .. **Laino,** Jos B '00 Cnsl Mark IV Indstrs,Inc -501 John James Audubon Pkwy Bx810 -Amherst 14226 **Fx:**689-7409
(516) 873-2000 .. **Laino,** Wm P '74 (Moritt HH&H LLP) -400 Grdn City Plz -Gdn Cty 11530
(315) 483-6931 .. **Lair,** Sean D '04 (DeValk P&L,PC) -6 E Main -Sodus 14551
(518) 465-3484 .. **Laird,** Edw D Jr. '78 (Carter CCBM&L,PC) -20 Corp Wds Blvd -Albany 12211
(212) 336-2000 .. **Laird,** Jo Backer '81 OfCnsl Patterson BW&T LLP -1133 Av of Amer -NY 10036
(212) 490-3000 .. **Laird,** Jos '97 (Wilson EME&D LLP) -150 E 42nd -NY 10017
(212) 277-0835 .. **Laird,** Liesel K '05 %Hartford Fncl Grp -2 Park Av -NY 10016
(516) 883-3639 .. **Laird,** Sherry S '87 -231 Manorhaven Blvd -Pt Wash 11050
(518) 745-1400 .. **Lais,** Kara I '04 %FitzGerald MBF -16 Pearl Bx2017 -Glens Fls 12801
(212) 693-0085 .. **Laisure,** Paul Skip '91 %Appellate Advocates -2 Rector -NY 10006 **Fx:**693-0878
(516) 228-6666 .. **Laitman,** Arthur S '00 (Rosenberg F&L,LLP) -666 Old Cntry Rd -Gdn Cty 11530
(212) 581-0680 .. **Laitman,** Danl E '55 (D Laitman,PC) -1500 Bway -NY 10036 **Fx:**581-0686
(212) 838-7797 .. **Laitman,** Joel P '87 Cohen MS&T,PLLC -88 Pine -NY 10005
(212) 687-3000 .. **Lajam,** Michl E '06 %Jaffe & A,LLP -600 3rd Av -NY 10016
(212) 805-0125 .. **Lajoie,** Sara K '07 Hon K Wood -500 Pearl -NY 10007
(518) 452-5832 .. **Lajoy,** Marcel J '91 -1842 Wstrn Av -Albany 12203 **Fx:**456-5716
(212) 846-3954 .. **Lake,** Deborah Principe '99 %MTV Networks -1515 Bway -NY 10036
(631) 543-5400 .. **Lake,** Edw J '93 (Gacovino L & Assoc,PC) -270 W Main -Sayvll 11782 **Fx:**543-5450
(646) 747-3485 .. **Lake,** Kevin J '84 K Lake,PC -335 Mad Av -NY 10017
(212) 530-5000 .. **Lake,** Konata T '09 %Milbank TH&M LLP -1 Chase Manh Plz -NY 10005
(212) 554-7800 .. **Lake,** Mark G '56 OfCnsl Moses & S LLP -405 Lex Av -NY 10174
(845) 778-2121 .. **Lake,** Tobias A '08 %Jacobowitz & G,LLP -158 Orange Av Bx367 -Walden 12586
(212) 735-3000 .. **Lakel,** Zachariah '10 %Skadden ASM&F LLP -4 Times Sq -NY 10036
(212) 310-8000 .. **Laken,** Lacey B '08 %Weil G&M LLP -767 5th Av -NY 10153
(212) 626-4100 .. **Lakes,** Joi M '08 %Baker & M LLP -1114 Av of Amer -NY 10036
(212) 277-4000 .. **Lakin,** Kyle B '09 %Freshfields BD LLP -520 Mad Av -NY 10022
(212) 504-6000 .. **Lakin,** Mark B '09 %Cadwalader W&T LLP -1 World Fncl Ctr -NY 10281
(212) 451-2300 .. **Lakin,** Mark L '03 %Olshan GFR&W LLP -65 E 55th -NY 10022
(212) 237-1000 .. **Lakind,** Howard P '77 (Windels ML&M,LLP) -156 W 56th -NY 10019
(212) 357-6584 .. **Lakis,** Aina '00 %Thomson Reuters -195 Bway -NY 10007
(516) 739-6668 .. **Lakis,** Dean '91 -99 Powerhse Rd -Roslyn Hts 11577 **Fx:**209-4661
(212) 344-4700 .. **Lakis,** Wm E '94 (DeOrchis & Prtnrs LLP) -61 Bway -NY 10006
(518) 429-4200 .. **Laks,** Eugene M '67 OfCnsl Hiscock & B,LLP -50 Beaver -Albany 12207
(914) 478-2801 .. **Laks,** Jason R '98 %R Greenspan,PC -220 Heatherdell Rd -Ardsley 10502 **Fx:**478-2913
(212) 635-4155 .. **Lakshminarasimh,** Iyengar '88 -11 Bway -NY 10004 **Fx:**635-4156
(212) 260-8880 .. **Lal,** Sandy K '01 S Lal & Assoc,LLC -40 E 9th -NY 10003
(212) 836-8000 .. **Lalan,** Christopher P '04 %Kaye S LLP -425 Park Av -NY 10022
(718) 217-7146 .. **La Lande,** Fearonce G '00 -207-01 Hillside Av -Qns Vllg 11427 **Fx:**217-7149
(212) 351-4000 .. **La Lande,** Rashida K '99 (Gibson D&C LLP) -200 Park Av -NY 10166
(212) 538-7648 .. **Lalime,** Crystal M '06 %Credit Suisse -1 Mad Av -NY 10010
(718) 250-2000 .. **Laline,** Christopher J '05 DA -350 Jay -Brklyn 11201 **Fx:**250-2314
(516) 433-4152 .. **Lall,** Arvind '90 -333 Jericho Tpk -Jericho 11753 **Fx:**433-4121
(718) 843-4000 .. **Lall,** Jagat P '00 Lall & Assoc,PC -101-13 101st Av -Ozone Pk 11416 **Fx:**843-8044
(646) 471-7895 .. **Lall,** Keston D '06 %PricewaterhouseCoopers LLP -300 Mad Av -NY 10017
(718) 298-8900 .. **Lall,** Sabrina L '08 Leg Aid -153-01 Jamaica Av -Jamaica 11432 **Fx:**657-0537
(516) 803-4943 .. **Lall,** Sharmalee Bhanumati '98 Rainbow Media Holdings -200 Jericho Quad -Jericho 11753
(914) 848-4800 .. **Lalla,** Thos R Jr. '76 %Pernod Ricard USA -100 Manhattanvll Rd -Purchase 10577
(212) 468-4800 .. **Lalla,** Vejay G '01 %Davis & G LLP -1740 Bway -NY 10019
(607) 770-2717 .. **Lalley,** Robt J '06 Cnsl BAE Systems Controls Inc -600 Main -Johnson Cty 13790
(646) 253-2300 .. **Lalli,** Dennis A '80 OfCnsl Bond S&K,PLLC -330 Mad Av -NY 10017
(914) 287-7711 .. **Lallis,** Danny C '07 %Pisciotti M&B,PC -445 Hmltn Av -White Plns 10601 **Fx:**287-7715
(212) 508-6700 .. **Lallouz,** David R '08 %Tannenbaum HS&H LLP -900 3rd Av -NY 10022
(631) 475-4400 .. **Lally,** Campion '91 OfCnsl Roe TT&P,LLP -One Corp Dr -Bohemia 11716
(516) 741-2666 .. **Lally,** Grant M '87 (Lally M&R LLP) -220 Old Cntry Rd -Mineola 11501
(516) 741-2666 .. **Lally,** Lawr M '61 -220 Old Cntry Rd -Mineola 11501 **Fx:**742-8533
(516) 741-2666 .. **Lally Mahon & Rooney LLP** -220 Old Cntry Rd -Mineola 11501 **Fx:**742-8533
(212) 584-2990 .. **Lally Mahon & Rooney LLP** -36 W 44th -NY 10036 **Fx:**584-2991
(516) 741-2666 .. **Lally,** Regan U '90 -220 Old Cntry Rd -Mineola 11501 **Fx:**742-8533
(518) 758-1485 .. **Lally,** Sean P '93 Lally & L -2 Broad Bx778 -Kinderhook 12106 **Fx:**758-1484
(212) 758-0050 .. **Lally-Ardrey,** Stefanie F '03 Title Assoc -825 3rd Av -NY 10022 **Fx:**758-8223
(518) 402-6757 .. **Lally Clark,** Maria '90 %Workers Comp Bd -20 Park -Albany 12207
(518) 758-6214 .. **Lally Clark,** Maria '90 -Bx654 -Valatie 12184 **Fx:**758-6846
(516) 431-4441 .. **Lally Fitzgerald,** Eileen '96 %J Petrilli -370 W Park Av -Long Bch 11561 **Fx:**889-8904
(315) 361-5500 .. **Lalonde,** Andrew V '83 Madison-Oneida BOCES -4937 Spring Rd -Verona 13478 **Fx:**361-5595
(607) 277-6863 .. **LaLonde,** Robt R '97 -102 E State -Ithaca 14850
(518) 426-4600 .. **Lalone,** Mathew R '10 %Couch W,LLP -540 Bway Bx22222 -Albany 12201
(516) 227-2300 .. **Lalor,** Thos P '91 Wright Risk Mgmt -333 Earle Ovngton Blvd -Uniondale 11553 **Fx:**227-2352
(212) 261-8000 .. **Lalor,** Wm P '00 %Mendes & M,LLP -750 7th Av -NY 10019
(585) 295-4400 .. **Laluk,** Susan Schultz '86 (Hiscock & B,LLP) -2000 HSBC Plz -Rchstr 14604
(718) 229-3555 .. **LaLumia,** Peter A '69 -21528 47th Av -Bayside 11361 **Fx:**229-3555
(646) 557-5100 .. **Lalwani,** Manisha N '04 %Patton B LLP -1185 Av of Amer -NY 10036
(646) 708-8088 .. **Lam,** Alison R '05 Fidelity Natl Law Grp -350 5th Av -NY 10118 **Fx:**(212) 594-8378
(212) 277-4000 .. **Lam,** Alison Tu-Ly '06 %Freshfields BD LLP -520 Mad Av -NY 10022
(212) 403-1000 .. **Lam,** David K '02 (Wachtell LR&K) -51 W 52nd -NY 10019
(917) 778-6083 .. **Lam,** Donna T '04 Travelers -485 Lex Av -NY 10017
(212) 966-7000 .. **Lam,** Frank '78 (Lam & L) -109 Lafayette -NY 10013 **Fx:**226-5110
(718) 286-6000 .. **Lam,** Gloria Tam Dac '08 DA -125-01 Qns Blvd -Kew Gdns 11415
(718) 260-8700 .. **Lam,** Janet Kelly '90 %Admin Children's Srvcs -345 Adams -Brklyn 11201
(212) 530-5000 .. **Lam,** Kristen '09 %Milbank TH&M LLP -1 Chase Manh Plz -NY 10005
(212) 909-6000 .. **Lam,** Le V '05 %Debevoise & P LLP -919 3rd Av -NY 10022

(212) 943-2422 .. **Lam,** Man-Ying '00 CLS Bank Intl -39 Bway -NY 10006
(212) 259-8000 .. **Lam,** Margaret Shui-Kei '02 %Dewey & L LLP -1301 Av of Amer -NY 10019
(212) 261-5538 .. **Lam,** Margaret Y '00 Assured Guaranty -1325 Av of Amer -NY 10019
(212) 966-7000 .. **Lam,** Michl '90 (Lam & L) -109 Lafayette -NY 10013 **Fx:**226-5110
(212) 506-5000 .. **Lam,** Nicholas H '09 %Orrick H&S LLP -51 W 52nd -NY 10019
(212) 820-9580 .. **Lam,** Peter K '00 %Hawkins D&W LLP -One Chase Manh Plz -NY 10005
(212) 440-4300 .. **Lam,** Stacy M '97 %Leg Aid -199 Water -NY 10038
(212) 735-3000 .. **Lam,** Suling '04 Cnsl Skadden ASM&F LLP -4 Times Sq -NY 10036
(212) 966-9893 .. **Lam,** Tung Hak '99 -90 Bowery -NY 10013
(607) 275-3425 .. **Lama,** Diane M '07 Lama Law Firm,LLP -2343 N Triphammer Rd -Ithaca 14850
(607) 275-3425 .. **Lama,** Luciano J '00 Lama Law,LLP -2343 N Triphammer Rd -Ithaca 14850
(607) 275-3425 .. **Lama,** Luciano L '94 Lama Law,LLP -2343 N Triphammer Rd -Ithaca 14850
(516) 775-2236 .. **LaMacchia,** Dana M '00 %Santangelo B&S -1800 Nrthrn Blvd -Roslyn 11576
(212) 431-1211 .. **La Macchia,** Maria A '90 -350 Bway -NY 10013 **Fx:**625-8367
(212) 345-2720 .. **LaMagna,** Donna L '87 %March & McLennan Cos -1166 Av of Amer -NY 10036
(516) 228-3333 .. **LaMagna,** Stephen W '89 (Martello & L,PC) -666 Old Cntry Rd -Gdn Cty 11530
(212) 670-0426 .. **LaMaina,** Michl '00 Merrill Lynch -222 Bway -NY 10038 **Fx:**670-4703
(212) 302-0410 .. **Lamal,** Christopher T '82 OfCnsl Wrobel & S LLP -1040 Av of Amer -NY 10018
(718) 286-7100 .. **LaManna,** Christopher J '96 %FBI -8002 Kew Grdns Rd -Kew Gdns 11415
(315) 478-1122 .. **La Manna,** Judith A '82 (Rivette & R,PC) -224 Harrison -Syracuse 13202 **Fx:**461-1243
(718) 222-3635 .. **Lamanna,** Julia M '98 -67 Butler -Brklyn 11231 **Fx:**799-5513
(718) 497-2006 .. **Lamanna,** Lawr J '57 -65-09 Fresh Pond Rd -Rdgwd 11385 **Fx:**381-3966
(516) 571-0185 .. **Lamanna,** Paul L '92 %Supreme Ct Law Dept -Supreme Ct Bldg -Mineola 11501
(716) 836-2382 .. **Lamantia,** Stephen R '68 -102 Larchmont Rd -Buffalo 14214
(212) 547-5400 .. **Lamar,** Clifford R II '10 %McDermott W&E LLP -340 Mad Av -NY 10173
(212) 480-7137 .. **Lamar,** Kathleen Frances '82 %DHCR -25 Beaver -NY 10004 **Fx:**480-7416
(516) 677-9000 .. **LaMarca,** Anthony J '66 A LaMarca,PC -186 Birch Hill Rd -Locust Vly 11560 **Fx:**677-0190
(212) 980-9600 .. **La Marca,** Cristina M '06 %Kaufman B&R -120 Bway -NY 10271
(516) 797-8686 .. **LaMarca,** Gregory R '93 G LaMarca,PC -898 N Bway -Massapequa 11758 **Fx:**797-8558
(212) 286-8585 .. **LaMarche,** Gabrielle R '00 %Heidell PM&B,LLP -99 Park Av -NY 10016
(518) 274-5820 .. **La Marche,** George E III '01 %ES Jones -28 2nd -Troy 12181 **Fx:**274-5875
(212) 251-3335 .. **Lamari-Burden,** Maria '96 Castlerock Mgmt -101 Park Av -NY 10178
(212) 637-2206 .. **Lamarque,** Natalie '04 US Atty -1 St Andrews Plz -NY 10007
(212) 356-0316 .. **Lamasney,** Kevin M '96 SBLI USA Mutual Life Ins Co Inc -460 W 34th -NY 10001
(212) 308-8505 .. **Lamatina,** Louis J '83 OfCnsl Akabas & S -488 Mad Av -NY 10022
(212) 756-2000 .. **Lamb,** Abigail '10 %Schulte R&Z LLP -919 3rd Av -NY 10022
(631) 694-2300 .. **Lamb & Barnosky,LLP** -534 Broadhllw Rd Bx9034 -Melvll 11747 **Fx:**694-2309
(212) 259-8000 .. **Lamb,** Brian K '03 %Dewey & L LLP -1301 Av of Amer -NY 10019
(212) 312-2358 .. **Lamb,** Brian T '93 %Leg Aid -60 Lafayette -NY 10013 **Fx:**349-0874
(212) 417-3700 .. **Lamb,** Christopher D '87 %MFY Legal Srvcs -299 Bway -NY 10007 **Fx:**417-3890
(845) 246-2888 .. **Lamb,** Danl N Jr. '78 Rosenblum & L -41 Market Bx270 -Saugerties 12477
(631) 331-0020 .. **Lamb,** Eugene G '50 -4089 Nesconset Hwy -Centereach 11720
(718) 250-3230 .. **Lamb,** James E '87 %DA -350 Jay -Brklyn 11201 **Fx:**250-2314
(315) 245-5489 .. **Lamb,** Jason C '02 Cnsl Christmas & Assoc,Inc -Bx200 -Camden 13316 **Fx:**245-5538
(845) 340-3315 .. **Lamb,** Joan '78 %DA -285 Wall -Kingston 12401 **Fx:**340-3185
(212) 979-1012 .. **Lamb,** John B '00 Jewel Bako -239 E 5th -NY 10003
(315) 432-9171 .. **Lamb,** Kathleen E '90 POMCO,Inc -2525 James -Syracuse 13206 **Fx:**437-9466
(585) 454-1730 .. **Lamb,** Kirsten W '05 Closing USA LLC -250 Mile Xing Blvd -Rchstr 14624
(212) 608-2700 .. **Lamb & Lerch** -233 Bway -NY 10279 **Fx:**513-7206
(518) 786-2700 .. **Lamb,** Matthew R '96 Med Liability Mutl Ins Co -8 British Amer Blvd -Latham 12110
(585) 325-6700 .. **Lamb,** Maureen P '76 (Lamb Law Ofc) -1 E Main -Rchstr 14614 **Fx:**325-1372
(914) 232-3100 .. **Lamb,** Nancy R Axelrod '79 -8 Cantitoe -Katonah 10536
(212) 333-4444 .. **Lamb,** Owen H '86 -356 W 58th -NY 10019 **Fx:**581-5511
(718) 526-2222 .. **Lamb,** Owen H '86 -171-08 111th Av -Jamaica 11433 **Fx:**526-2111
(631) 694-2300 .. **Lamb,** P L '70 (Lamb & B,LLP) -534 Broadhllw Rd Bx9034 -Melvll 11747
(718) 250-2000 .. **Lamb,** Robt E '79 %DA -350 Jay -Brklyn 11201 **Fx:**250-2314
(585) 325-6700 .. **Lamb,** Robt G Jr. '72 -1 E Main -Rchstr 14614 **Fx:**325-1372
(518) 273-1662 .. **Lamb,** Thos E '84 (Lamb & L) -516 3rd Av -Watervliet 12189 **Fx:**273-2472
(212) 784-5800 .. **Lamb,** Todd V '95 (Hiscock & B,LLP) -7 Times Sq -NY 10036 **Fx:**784-5768
(518) 273-1662 .. **Lamb,** Vincent A '58 (Lamb & L) -516 3rd Av -Watervliet 12189 **Fx:**273-2472
(212) 259-8000 .. **Lamb,** Wm S '86 (Dewey & L LLP) -1301 Av of Amer -NY 10019
(631) 981-1411 .. **Lambadis,** A Stacey '95 -40 Southvw Cir -Lk Grove 11755 **Fx:**981-1411
(518) 452-0941 .. **Lambek,** Debra J '94 %Segel GM&S,PC -9 Wshngtn Sq -Albany 12205
(212) 735-3000 .. **Lambert,** Amy M '06 %Skadden ASM&F LLP -4 Times Sq -NY 10036
(212) 344-3100 .. **Lambert,** Arthur N '68 (Frenkel LWW&G,LLP) -1 Whitehall -NY 10004
(212) 580-8008 .. **Lambert,** Benjamin F '72 -315 W 70th -NY 10023 **Fx:**(845) 565-4252
(212) 704-0035 .. **Lambert,** Betsy '90 -18 E 48th -NY 10017 **Fx:**704-0198
(212) 313-3600 .. **Lambert,** Edwin F '76 (Barry M&M) -2 Rector -NY 10006
(718) 983-5050 .. **Lambert,** James R '89 -1491 Richmond Rd -Staten Isl 10304 **Fx:**983-5088
(212) 492-4266 .. **Lambert,** Jos J '84 Deloitte & Touche Tohmatsu -1633 Bway -NY 10019
(212) 888-7727 .. **Lambert,** Judith A '85 -245 E 54th -NY 10022 **Fx:**980-4439
(631) 969-7777 .. **Lambert,** Lawr B '93 %Frenkel LWW&G,LLP -20 W Main -Bay Shr 11706 **Fx:**206-0540
(631) 853-4311 .. **Lambert,** Mary Regina '83 Family Ct -400 Carleton Av -Central Islip 11722
(212) 221-5700 .. **Lambert,** Matthew J '07 %Goldberg WFG LLP -1501 Bway -NY 10036
(212) 425-3220 .. **Lambert,** Michl C '75 (Gilmartin P&S LLP) -845 Third Av -NY 10022
(845) 486-4200 .. **Lambert,** Michl K '93 (Shaw PM&L,LLP) -21 Van Wagner Rd -Poughkeepsie 12603
(914) 417-1144 .. **Lambert,** Michl L '08 -2 Gannett Dr -White Plns 10604
(212) 448-1100 .. **Lambert,** Paul C '56 (McLaughlin & S,LLP) -260 Mad Av -NY 10016
(718) 566-6100 .. **Lambert,** Raegan L '01 Bd of Ed -1106 E 95th -Brklyn 11236
(212) 344-3100 .. **Lambert,** Richd A '90 (Frenkel LWW&G,LLP) -1 Whitehall -NY 10004
(212) 688-1900 .. **Lambert,** Richd J '87 %Greenberg T&H,LLP -767 3rd Av -NY 10017
(212) 684-6564 .. **Lambert,** Richd S '74 -166 E 34th -NY 10016
(800) 416-5454 .. **Lambert,** Thos A '91 (Fusco B&R) -180 Froehlich Farm Blvd -Woodbury 11797
(212) 370-4040 .. **Lambert,** Thos C '69 (Lambert & S,PLLC) -274 Mad Av -NY 10016 **Fx:**697-7919
(516) 795-5030 .. **Lamberta,** Jos '46 J Lamberta,PC -551 Bway -Massapequa 11758 **Fx:**795-5082
(212) 453-7553 .. **Lamberth,** Julie '07 Kaplan -1440 Bway -NY 10018
(212) 701-3000 .. **Lamberti,** Amy Desmond '05 %Cahill G&R LLP -80 Pine -NY 10005 **Fx:**269-5420
(718) 238-9826 .. **Lamberti,** Anthony J '91 -435 77th -Brklyn 11209 **Fx:**238-4950
(516) 364-5300 .. **Lamberti,** Michl T '89 -180 Froehlich Farm Blvd -Woodbury 11797 **Fx:**364-5453
(212) 682-0020 .. **Lamberti,** Thos M '57 (Putney TH&H LLP) -521 5th Av -NY 10175
(212) 932-3857 .. **Lambert-Watkins,** Tanya '92 SrCnsl Workers Comp Bd -215 W 125th -NY 10027 **Fx:**932-3800
(845) 291-7100 .. **Lambiase,** Donald J '83 (Murphy & L) -1997 State Route 17M -Goshen 10924
(212) 683-2210 .. **Lambiase,** Susan T '87 %Childrens Rts Inc -330 7th Av -NY 10001 **Fx:**683-4015
(212) 840-0097 .. **Lambiris,** Elias J '88 Novozymes N Amer Inc -500 5th Av -NY 10110
(516) 249-3450 .. **Lamboley,** Wm C '08 Carman C&I,LLP -266 Main -Farmngdl 11735
(917) 671-6217 .. **Lamborn,** Richd D '87 -327 E 149th -Bronx 10451 **Fx:**(646) 349-3819
(212) 381-9700 .. **Lambos,** Carol Notias '95 (Lambos Firm,LLP) -303 S Bway -Tarrytwn 10591 **Fx:**797-9213
(718) 232-1250 .. **Lambrakos,** Elena Evagelia '02 %Polizzotto & P -6911 18th Av -Brklyn 11204 **Fx:**256-0966
(315) 442-0100 .. **Lambrecht,** Timothy J '00 %Gilberti SH&S,PC -555 E Genesee -Syracuse 13202
(212) 277-6500 .. **Lambrianakos,** Peter '98 %Dickstein S LLP -1633 Bway -NY 10019
(315) 422-7111 .. **Lambright,** Nathaniel G '00 (Blitman & K LLP) -443 N Franklin -Syracuse 13204
(585) 325-2520 .. **Lambrix,** Laurie M '91 %Leg Assistance -1 W Main -Rchstr 14614 **Fx:**325-2559
(212) 430-6474 .. **Lambros,** John M '98 -11 Bway -NY 10004 **Fx:**(917) 591-7550
(212) 797-4600 .. **Lambros,** Peter N '88 (Coritsidis & L,PLLC) -46 Trinity Pl -NY 10006
(212) 285-2100 .. **Lambrou,** Lambros Y '98 (McHugh & L LLP) -233 Bway -NY 10279 **Fx:**285-2110
(212) 225-7000 .. **Lambrou,** Sofia '05 %Zurich Amer Ins Co -165 Bway -NY 10006
(718) 830-0124 .. **Lame,** Lawr B '71 -98-30 67th Av -Rego Pk 11374
(212) 361-1400 .. **Lamel,** Bradley S '88 %Envrnmntl Cntrl Brd -66 John -NY 10038 **Fx:**361-1900
(212) 274-7115 .. **Lamelas,** Mel '93 Jobson Pblshng LLC -100 Av of Amer -NY 10013 **Fx:**208-3098
(315) 473-9414 .. **Lamendola,** Jos E '90 SpclCnsl Hinman H&K,LLP -224 Harrison -Syracuse 13202
(518) 462-1800 .. **Lamendola,** Kelly Mercure '96 OfCnsl Plunkett & J/ML&A -111 Wshngtn Av -Albany 12210
(716) 854-6631 .. **LaMendola,** Lee C '77 -70 Niagara -Buffalo 14202 **Fx:**854-6725
(914) 785-5300 .. **Lamer,** Alan I '77 -555 Taxter Rd -Elmsfrd 10523 **Fx:**347-4269
(212) 206-9290 .. **Lamia,** Thos R '90 -54 Charles -NY 10014
(212) 272-9050 .. **La Micela,** Jos M '02 %JP Morgan Chase -383 Mad Av -NY 10179
(315) 701-5780 .. **Lamitie,** Wm J '93 %Olinsky & S -300 S State -Syracuse 13202
(212) 697-3122 .. **Lamkay,** Laura M '09 %Martin C&B LLP -220 E 42nd -NY 10017
(631) 231-1450 .. **Lamkin,** Andrew M '07 %Feldman K&M,PC -330 Vndrblt Motor Pkwy -Hauppauge 11788
(212) 687-7410 .. **Lamm,** Eric S '80 (Clifton B&D,LLP) -420 Lex Av -NY 10170
(718) 858-6555 .. **Lamm,** Michl '79 -26 Court -Brklyn 11242 **Fx:**488-8544
(212) 733-4467 .. **Lamm,** Robt B '72 Pfizer,Inc -235 E 42nd -NY 10017
(631) 852-2500 .. **Lamm,** Ronnie J '04 %DA -200 Center Dr -Rvrhead 11901 **Fx:**852-1769
(518) 447-3200 .. **Lamme,** Jacob F '06 %McNamee LT&W,PC -677 Bway -Albany 12207
(914) 674-4100 .. **Lammers,** Edw G '94 (Stecich M&L,LLP) -828 S Bway -Tarrytwn 10591
(914) 824-5589 .. **Lammers,** Stephanie J '95 %Family Ct -111 Dr Martin Luther King Blvd -White Plns 10601
(718) 391-0225 .. **Lamond,** Michl J '02 M Lamond,PC -34-11 Qns Blvd -LIC 11101
(914) 286-3400 .. **Lamond,** Todd G '89 %Leg Aid -1 N Bway -White Plns 10601 **Fx:**682-4112

(516) 826-6500 .. **LaMonica Herbst & Maniscalco LLP** -3305 Jerusalem Av -Wantagh 11793 **Fx:**826-0222
(212) 421-4100 .. **Lamonica,** Robt C '08 %Pryor C LLP -7 Times Sq -NY 10036
(516) 826-6500 .. **LaMonica,** Salvatore '89 (LaMonica H&M LLP) -3305 Jerusalem Av -Wantagh 11793
(212) 421-2233 .. **LaMons,** Eric B '03 Wilk A LLP -675 3rd Av -NY 10017
(718) 275-3300 .. **Lamonsoff,** Eric J '92 (Bergman BG&L,LLP) -108-18 Qns Blvd -Frst Hlls 11375
(212) 962-1020 .. **Lamonsoff,** Michl S '91 -80 Maiden Ln -NY 10038 **Fx:**962-3078
(212) 906-1200 .. **Lamont,** Dennis D '96 (Latham & W) -885 3rd Av -NY 10022
(212) 248-3140 .. **LaMont,** Jennifer '99 Cnsl Drinker B&R LLP -140 Bway -NY 10005
(315) 447-2025 .. **LaMora,** Christine R '96 -201 W Genesee -Fayettevll 13066
(212) 637-2746 .. **LaMorte,** Tara M '04 US Atty -86 Chmbrs -NY 10007
(631) 852-2325 .. **LaMothe,** Mary Kate '88 %MHLS -One Court -Rvrhead 11901 **Fx:**852-3132
(212) 734-2305 .. **Lamour,** Henry M '71 -1646 1st Av -NY 10028 **Fx:**734-1682
(212) 576-7000 .. **Lamp,** Karen Jean '88 %NY Life Ins -51 Mad Av -NY 10010 **Fx:**447-0569
(212) 969-3000 .. **Lamparello,** Patrick J III '04 %Proskauer R LLP -1585 Bway -NY 10036
(516) 993-3572 .. **Lampasona,** Maureen '91 -197 Toronto Av -Massapequa 11758
(914) 328-2308 .. **Lampasona,** Peter C '99 Mastercard Intl Inc -25 Rockldg Av -White Plns 10601
(631) 756-4254 .. **Lampasona,** Peter J '98 %State Ins Fund -8 Corp Ctr Dr -Melvll 11747 **Fx:**756-4060
(212) 326-3939 .. **Lampe,** Matthew W '08 (Jones D) -222 E 41st -NY 10017
(631) 467-1948 .. **Lampert,** Allison L '02 -650 Portion Rd -Ronkonkoma 11779
(212) 574-1200 .. **Lampert,** Dmitriy '08 %Seward & K LLP -1 Bttry Pk Plz -NY 10004
(516) 481-9500 .. **Lampert,** Jay S '01 Raynor Mrktng Ltd -525 Hempstd Tpk -W Hempstead 11552
(516) 571-3800 .. **Lampert,** Matthew A '04 DA -262 Old Cntry Rd -Mineola 11501 **Fx:**248-9479
(212) 655-3500 .. **Lampert,** Mitchell L '86 (Meister S&F LLP) -140 E 45th -NY 10017
(212) 835-1572 .. **Lampf Lipkind Prupis & Petigrow** -5 Penn Plz 19th Fl -NY 10119
(518) 356-7530 .. **Lampi,** Mary C '78 NY Indpndnt System Operator -3890 Carman Rd -Schnctdy 12303 **Fx:**356-4702
(212) 619-1819 .. **Lampiasi,** Jeffrey M '88 (Lampiasi & Assoc LLP) -434 Bway -NY 10013 **Fx:**619-1869
(212) 698-3500 .. **Lampland,** Bethany A '04 %Dechert LLP -1095 Av of Amer -NY 10036
(212) 455-2000 .. **Lamprecht,** Thos F '07 %Simpson T&B LLP -425 Lex Av -NY 10017
(212) 451-2300 .. **Lamson,** Amanda S '09 %Olshan GFR&W LLP -65 E 55th -NY 10022
(212) 277-6500 .. **Lamson,** Justin W '09 %Dickstein S LLP -1633 Bway -NY 10019
(631) 761-0800 .. **Lamstein,** Matthew C '94 (Lazer AR&Y,PC) -225 Old Cntry Rd -Melvll 11747
(212) 349-5150 .. **Lamster,** Craig A '96 %Galvano & X,PC -150 Bway -NY 10038
(631) 654-4900 .. **La Mura,** John J '82 Cartier BA&D,PC -100 Austin -Patchogue 11772
(212) 474-1000 .. **Lan,** Baolu '10 %Cravath S&M LLP -825 8th Av -NY 10019
(718) 461-9434 .. **Lan,** Dennis B '01 -3901 Main -Flushng 11354
(212) 637-2263 .. **Lan,** Iris '03 %US Atty -1 St Andrews Plz -NY 10007
(212) 921-4141 .. **Lan,** Mario E '99 Horizon Land Srvcs LLC -15 W 44th -NY 10036
(646) 366-4821 .. **Lan,** Shawn '01 Bank of Amer -50 Rckfllr Plz -NY 10020
(212) 421-4100 .. **Lan,** Vanessa G '08 %Pryor C LLP -7 Times Sq -NY 10036
(716) 885-2889 .. **Lana,** Anthony J '93 (Eoannou L&D) -484 Delaware Av -Buffalo 14202
(516) 334-6727 .. **Lanahan,** Judith '92 %Fidelity Natl Title Ins -900 Merchants Cncrs -Westbury 11590 **Fx:**334-7459
(212) 222-5559 .. **Lancaster,** Deborah D '72 -35 Claremont Av -NY 10027
(212) 351-4000 .. **Lance,** Andrew A '84 (Gibson D&C LLP) -200 Park Av -NY 10166
(646) 831-3818 .. **Lance,** Marla S '03 -180 East End Av -NY 10128 **Fx:**(212) 744-8318
(518) 943-5711 .. **Lance,** Philip A '79 %OCA -320 Main -Catskill 12414 **Fx:**943-7763
(718) 686-3320 .. **Lancer,** Adam D '97 %Ohel Childrens Home -4510 16th Av -Brklyn 11204
(716) 855-1660 .. **Lancer,** Michl C '97 (Cascone & K LLP) -110 Pearl -Buffalo 14202
(718) 590-2000 .. **Lancer,** Thos '07 %DA -198 E 161st -Bronx 10451 **Fx:**590-6477
(212) 922-1920 .. **Lancet,** Douglas E '95 %West Group -530 5th Av -NY 10036
(609) 632-0475 .. **Lanchantin,** Denise T '85 -900 W 190th -NY 10040 **Fx:**632-1255
(518) 462-0300 .. **Lanchantin,** Kristine Amodeo '86 (Girvin & F,PC) -20 Corp Wds Blvd -Albany 12211
(917) 885-7949 .. **Lanchner,** Bertrand M '56 -170 E 79th -NY 10075 **Fx:**(212) 744-2032
(212) 964-3157 .. **Lancia,** Thos M '89 (TM Lancia PLLC) -22 Crtlandt -NY 10007
(718) 298-1097 .. **Lancman,** Modjgan '95 Supreme Ct -89-17 Sutphin Blvd -Jamaica 11435
(212) 751-9800 .. **Lancman,** Rory I '96 %Morelli R PC -950 3rd Av -NY 10022
(212) 335-4500 .. **Land,** Christopher C '03 %DLA Piper LLP -1251 Av of Amer -NY 10020
(516) 678-3885 .. **Land,** Dorothy M '88 Land & J -4029 Lng Bch Rd -Isl Pk 11558
(212) 479-7724 .. **Land,** Edw W '91 -245 8th Av Bx 127 -NY 10011
(212) 238-4800 .. **Land,** Elizabeth Gannett '07 %Landman CB&F,PC -120 Bway -NY 10271
(516) 678-3885 .. **Land,** Elyse P '82 %Land & J -40-29 Lng Bch Rd -Isl Pk 11558
(516) 678-3885 .. **Land,** Frank R '65 (Land & J) -4029 Lng Bch Rd -Isl Pk 11558
(212) 309-6000 .. **Land,** Kerry J '08 %Morgan L&B LLP -101 Park Av -NY 10178
(212) 431-2103 .. **Land,** Molly Beutz '02 NY Law Schl -185 W Bway -NY 10013 **Fx:**791-2144
(212) 903-9000 .. **Land,** Stephen B '80 (Linklaters) -1345 Av of Amer -NY 10105
(631) 218-5900 .. **Landa,** Alan '09 Affinity Skilled Living -305 Locust Av -Oakdale 11769
(212) 267-6456 .. **Landa,** Elissa B '96 %Fischer Bros -217 Bway -NY 10007 **Fx:**267-6468
(212) 425-1999 .. **Landa,** Evan M '07 Edelsteins F&B,LLP -61 Bway -NY 10006
(914) 406-7000 .. **Landa,** Howard M '68 OfCnsl Rand RR&G LLP -50 Main -White Plns 10606
(516) 222-1500 .. **Landa,** Jay '55 -595 Stewart Av -Gdn Cty 11530 **Fx:**222-2971
(212) 450-4000 .. **Landa,** Leor S '98 (Davis P&W LLP) -450 Lex Av -NY 10017
(212) 825-5900 .. **Landa,** Marjorie B '84 %Dept of Invstgtn -80 Maiden Ln -NY 10038 **Fx:**825-2860
(516) 229-4300 .. **Landa,** Martin L '88 %J Bilello & Assoc -875 Merrick Av -Westbury 11590
(212) 964-3855 .. **Landa,** Yolanda R '85 %R Cardali & Assoc,LLP -39 Bway -NY 10006 **Fx:**634-4856
(212) 940-8800 .. **Landau,** David H '88 (Katten MR LLP) -575 Mad Av -NY 10022
(212) 558-5500 .. **Landau,** Debbi S '89 %Weitz & L,PC -700 Bway -NY 10003
(212) 318-6000 .. **Landau,** Eric R '87 (Paul HJ&W LLP) -75 E 55th -NY 10022
(631) 225-9117 .. **Landau,** Eric R '91 -799 Pecan -Lindenhrst 11757
(914) 723-4300 .. **Landau,** Geoffrey I '89 %Lackenbach S LLP -1 Chase Rd -Scarsdale 10583
(914) 761-5200 .. **Landau,** Harvey G '70 -222 Bloomingdale Rd -White Plns 10605 **Fx:**761-5999
(212) 751-1926 .. **Landau,** Hortense R '48 -200 E 66th -NY 10065
(212) 964-1661 .. **Landau,** James K '87 (Trokie L LLP) -225 Bway -NY 10007
(914) 694-9500 .. **Landau,** James K '87 (Trokie L LLP) -1133 Wstchstr Av -White Plns 10604
(212) 349-6006 .. **Landau,** Jerome '51 OfCnsl L Reicher -60 E 42nd -NY 10165
(518) 445-6050 .. **Landau,** Joel '91 %Prisoners' Leg Srvcs -41 State -Albany 12207 **Fx:**445-6053
(212) 854-2606 .. **Landau,** Jos B '03 Columbia Law Schl -435 W 116th -Brklyn 11201
(973) 985-9008 .. **Landau,** Julie B '07 -305 W 13th -NY 10014
(516) 747-1100 .. **Landau,** Kenneth J '81 (Shayne DCS&D) -114 Old Cntry Rd -Mineola 11501
(212) 398-0055 .. **Landau,** Kevin S '97 (Garwin G&F,LLP) -1501 Bway -NY 10036
(212) 310-8000 .. **Landau,** Malcolm E '94 (Weil G&M LLP) -767 5th Av -NY 10153
(212) 593-1700 .. **Landau,** Mark '75 (Kaplan L LLP) -1065 Av of Amer -NY 10018
(212) 490-3000 .. **Landau,** Melissa D '08 %Wilson EME&D LLP -150 E 42nd -NY 10017
(212) 935-8880 .. **Landau,** Peter '59 (Foreht LL&K,LLP) -228 E 45th -NY 10017
(212) 972-6161 .. **Landau,** Rebecca L '06 %Cassin & C LLP -711 3rd Av -NY 10017
(718) 248-6009 .. **Landau,** Rhona L '82 Citibank NA -1 Court Sq -LIC 11120
(914) 328-0404 .. **Landau,** Richd D '90 (Jackson L LLP) -1 N Bway -White Plns 10601
(212) 227-4000 .. **Landau,** Ronald J '85 (Mirman M&L,PC) -291 Bway -NY 10007
(631) 766-7878 .. **Landau,** Ronald W '78 -6 Unity Ct -Nesconset 11767 **Fx:**361-8814
(212) 315-4600 .. **Landau,** Saml J '58 -250 W 57th -NY 10107 **Fx:**262-6128
(212) 858-1000 .. **Landau,** Scott E '96 (Pillsbury WSP LLP) -1540 Bway -NY 10036
(718) 254-7035 .. **Landau,** Scott R '03 US Atty -271 Cadman Plz E -Brklyn 11201 **Fx:**254-6479
(212) 643-5727 .. **Landau,** Shawn P '95 Smith Barney -1 Penn Plz -NY 10119
(845) 639-6031 .. **Landau,** Steven M '83 %Bialek & B,LLP -337 N Main -New Cty 10956 **Fx:**639-6034
(212) 924-8893 .. **Landau,** Sybil H '65 -8 W 13th -NY 10011
(646) 471-2564 .. **Landau,** Todd M '83 %PricewaterhouseCoopers LLP -300 Mad Av -NY 10017
(212) 558-4000 .. **Landau,** W Loeber '56 SrCnsl Sullivan & C LLP -125 Broad -NY 10004
(212) 693-0085 .. **Landau,** Warren S '81 %Appellate Advocates -2 Rector -NY 10006 **Fx:**693-0878
(212) 421-4100 .. **Landauer,** Tracy Green '86 (Pryor C LLP) -7 Times Sq -NY 10036
(212) 974-5700 .. **Landaw,** Jared L '91 Barington Capitol Grp -888 7th Av -NY 10106
(212) 586-5600 .. **Landay,** David S '65 -353 W 56th -NY 10019 **Fx:**246-2319
(212) 490-2370 .. **Lande,** David S '69 (Lande PC) -305 Mad Av -NY 10165 **Fx:**490-2372
(212) 815-8119 .. **Lande,** Kimberly Ann '98 Bk of NY Mellon -101 Barclay -NY 10007
(212) 705-5000 .. **Lande,** Mark P '03 Island Cptl Grp -717 5th Av -NY 10022
(212) 725-0200 .. **Lander,** Eric W '02 %Barnes R&C -475 Park Av S -NY 10016
(212) 732-3200 .. **Lander,** Guy P '79 (Carter L&M LLP) -2 Wall -NY 10005
(631) 661-3540 .. **Lander,** John E '76 -484 W Main -Babylon 11702 **Fx:**661-2722
(212) 969-3000 .. **Lander,** Nathan R '04 %Proskauer R LLP -1585 Bway -NY 10036
(845) 888-2259 .. **Lander,** Robt M II '79 -177 Sullivan Bx130 -Wurtsboro 12790
(718) 898-9400 .. **Landers,** Anne '82 -62-87 Woodhvn Blvd -Rego Pk 11374 **Fx:**898-9823
(718) 923-6300 .. **Landers,** Colette M '90 %Atty Grievance Comm -335 Adams -Brklyn 11201 **Fx:**624-2978
(718) 898-9400 .. **Landers,** John T '49 T Mahoney -62-87 Woodhvn Blvd -Rego Pk 11374 **Fx:**898-9823
(212) 594-5300 .. **Landers,** Jonathan M '66 (Milberg LLP) -1 Penn Plz -NY 10119
(646) 325-5247 .. **Landers,** Lance A '84 -168 2nd Av -NY 10003 **Fx:**(212) 505-8297
(516) 742-6000 .. **Landers,** Stanley A '77 (Landers & C,PC) -1 Old Cntry Rd -Carle Pl 11514 **Fx:**742-6066
(212) 373-3000 .. **Landers,** Steven E '74 OfCnsl Paul WRW&G LLP -1285 Av of Amer -NY 10019
(212) 239-5715 .. **Landes,** Danl A '77 Div of Parole -314 W 40th -NY 10018
(212) 867-0700 .. **Landes,** David J '85 %The Provident Grp -122 E 42nd -NY 10168
(518) 486-4568 .. **Landes,** Jane H '02 Supreme Ct -Bx7288 -Albany 12224
(212) 351-4601 .. **Landes,** Jeffrey M '93 (Epstein B&G,PC) -250 Park Av -NY 10177
(212) 242-3330 .. **Landes,** Michl S '66 -180 W 20th -NY 10011 **Fx:**691-2269
(718) 287-2600 .. **Landes,** Robin A '90 CAMBA -1720 Church Av -Brklyn 11226
(914) 428-9766 .. **Landes,** Wendy E '81 -399 Knollwood Rd -White Plns 10603 **Fx:**285-9769
(212) 564-9800 .. **Landesman,** Wayne R '83 (D'Agostino L&L,LLP) -345 7th Av -NY 10001
(718) 767-3333 .. **Landicino,** Carl J '91 (Borchert GL&L,PC) -19-02 Whitestone Expy -Whitestone 11357
(914) 949-6337 .. **Landis,** Donald M '57 -17 Glenbrooke Dr -White Plns 10605
(212) 977-9700 .. **Landis,** Marc A '88 (Phillips N LLP) -666 5th Av -NY 10103
(212) 474-1000 .. **Landis,** Robin C '83 %Cravath S&M LLP -825 8th Av -NY 10019
(212) 308-5035 .. **Landis,** Steven S '93 (S Landis,PC) -485 Mad Av -NY 10022
(212) 532-8100 .. **Landivar,** James '08 %Stern & M,LLP -115 Bway -NY 10006
(212) 238-4800 .. **Landman Corsi Ballaine & Ford,PC** -120 Bway -NY 10271 **Fx:**238-4848
(212) 238-4800 .. **Landman,** Mark S '77 (Landman CB&F,PC) -120 Bway -NY 10271
(212) 504-6000 .. **Landman,** Pamela '95 SpclCnsl Cadwalader W&T LLP -1 World Fncl Ctr -NY 10281
(212) 233-7867 .. **Landman,** Richd M '88 -261 Bway -NY 10007
(212) 875-4900 .. **Landman,** Scott P '90 Millenium Prtnrs -1995 Bway -NY 10023
(914) 251-0010 .. **Lando,** Brett S '08 (Gahagan & L,LLP) -2900 Wstchstr Av -Purchase 10577 **Fx:**251-0020
(212) 867-5800 .. **Lando,** Robt C B '91 (Osler H&H LLP) -620 8th Av -NY 10018
(212) 751-5252 .. **Lando,** S Dov '96 Arden Asset Mgmt LLC -375 Park Av -NY 10152
(518) 843-1300 .. **Landon,** Douglas E '90 -3 Market -Amsterdam 12010 **Fx:**842-5331

(718) 537-4958 .. **Landow,** Mindy E '89 %ODAR-SSA -226 E 161st -Bronx 10451 **Fx:**590-1673
(347) 422-5324 .. **Landowne,** Lori S '88 %Leg Aid -60 Bay -Staten Isl 10301 **Fx:**(718) 981-6623
(212) 859-5048 .. **Landres,** Norman '66 -110 Wall -NY 10005
(716) 843-8495 .. **Landreth,** Matthew C '09 US Customs & Border Protection -726 Exchange -Buffalo 14210
(716) 881-4900 .. **Landreth,** Megan A '09 %Schröder J & Assoc -766 Ellicott -Buffalo 14203
(212) 969-3000 .. **Landrey,** Francis D '76 SrCnsl Proskauer R LLP -1585 Bway -NY 10036
(914) 946-3700 .. **Landrigan,** Phillip C '85 OfCnsl McCarthy F LLP -11 Martine Av -White Plns 10606
(631) 844-1028 .. **Landron,** Michel J '78 North Fork Bk -275 Broad Hollow Rd -Melvll 11747 **Fx:**844-0242
(212) 656-4947 .. **Landron,** Sandra L '05 NYSE Regulation Inc -14 Wall -NY 10005 **Fx:**656-5788
(518) 237-3671 .. **Landry,** Francis W '53 -74 3rd -Cohoes 12047
(518) 449-3333 .. **Landry,** Michl J '88 %NY Capitol Consultants -120 Wshngtn Av -Albany 12210
(212) 918-3000 .. **Landry,** Nicole Savaria '06 %Hogan L LLP -875 3rd Av -NY 10022
(518) 274-7252 .. **Landry,** Philip J III '86 -54 2nd -Troy 12180 **Fx:**274-0348
(914) 779-2400 .. **Landry,** Thos K '90 -Bx159 -Bronxvll 10708
(718) 237-5500 .. **Landry-Reyes,** Jane M '94 %Leg Srvcs -105 Court -Brklyn 11201 **Fx:**855-0733
(212) 812-7000 .. **Landsberg,** Howard S '94 (Weiser LLP) -135 W 50th -NY 10020 **Fx:**375-6888
(212) 527-7575 .. **Landsberg,** Simon B '06 %Grover & F,PC -750 3rd Av -NY 10017
(718) 238-6500 .. **Landskind,** Renata '00 %Connors & S,PC -7408 5th Av -Brklyn 11209
(212) 421-4100 .. **Landsman,** Barry C '97 OfCnsl Pryor C LLP -7 Times Sq -NY 10036
(718) 665-6727 .. **Landsman,** Ira J '95 -184 East 161st -Bronx 10451
(212) 949-6100 .. **Landsman,** Jonathan M '88 -260 Mad Av -NY 10016
(212) 336-2000 .. **Landsman,** Kim J '81 (Patterson BW&T LLP) -1133 Av of Amer -NY 10036
(212) 888-3033 .. **Landsman,** M Zeb '91 (Becker GM&M LLP) -299 Park Av -NY 10171
(516) 741-6565 .. **Landsman,** Marie A '98 %Meyer SE&K,PC -990 Stewart Av Bx9194 -Gdn Cty 11530
(212) 610-6300 .. **Landsman,** Mark E '08 %Allen & O -1221 Av of Amer -NY 10020
(212) 682-2280 .. **Landsman,** Michl L '00 (Holm & O LLP) -3 W 35th -NY 10001
(212) 697-4555 .. **Landsman,** Paul '72 (P Landsman,PC) -18 E 48th -NY 10017 **Fx:**471-2509
(845) 783-6049 .. **Landstrom,** Ruth M '86 -103 Lk Region Blvd -Monroe 10950
(212) 756-2000 .. **Landy,** Alan G '10 %Schulte R&Z LLP -919 3rd Av -NY 10022
(914) 967-2809 .. **Landy,** Brian R '83 -6 Bradford Av -Rye 10580
(212) 382-0909 .. **Landy,** Craig A '77 SpclCnsl Peckar & A,PC -41 Mad Av -NY 10154
(212) 610-6300 .. **Landy,** Douglas J '94 (Allen & O) -1221 Av of Amer -NY 10020
(212) 450-4000 .. **Landy,** Katherine R Steele '07 %Davis P&W LLP -450 Lex Av -NY 10017
(914) 766-4378 .. **Landy,** Lauren D '91 IBM -294 Route 100 -Somers 10589 **Fx:**766-8444
(212) 833-1139 .. **Landy,** Robt S '05 %Friedman KS&A LLP -1633 Bway -NY 10019 **Fx:**373-7969
(212) 682-8510 .. **Landy,** Steven '86 (S Landy & Assoc,PLLC) -270 Mad Av -NY 10016 **Fx:**682-8514
(212) 237-1000 .. **Landzberg,** Alan J '79 (Windels ML&M,LLP) -156 W 56th -NY 10019
(631) 730-2274 .. **Lane,** Andrew B '83 Hain Celestial Grp,Inc -58 S Srvc Rd -Melvll 11747 **Fx:**(720) 622-3728
(631) 694-2300 .. **Lane,** Arthur A '71 (Lamb & B,LLP) -534 Broadhllw Rd Bx9034 -Melvll 11747
(516) 463-5886 .. **Lane,** Eric F '71 %Hofstra Law Schl -121 Hofstra Univ -Hempstd 11549
(212) 599-8200 .. **Lane,** Erika '09 %Shaub AC&S,LLP -655 3rd Av -NY 10017
(315) 445-9405 .. **Lane,** Eugene W '08 Special Funds Conservation Comm -5789 Widewaters Pkwy -Dewitt 13214 **Fx:**445-2831
(646) 386-3642 .. **Lane,** Francis J '91 %Supreme Ct-Law Dept -60 Centre -NY 10007
(845) 452-2022 .. **Lane,** Gary E '75 (Brenner G&L) -219 Church -Poughkeepsie 12601
(585) 899-6030 .. **Lane,** Gregory W '87 (Gilberti SH&S,PC) -1173 Pttsfrd-Vctr Rd -Pittsfrd 14534
(212) 664-2022 .. **Lane,** Hilary '90 NBC Universal Inc -30 Rckfllr Plz -NY 10112
(212) 318-6000 .. **Lane,** Ian T '04 %Paul HJ&W LLP -75 E 55th -NY 10022
(914) 251-0001 .. **Lane,** J Mark '92 (Lane S&L LLP) -106 Corp Park Dr -White Plns 10604
(631) 436-0181 .. **Lane,** Jamie Ann '97 -34 E Main -Smithtwn 11787
(212) 705-7000 .. **Lane,** Jason D '05 %Bingham M LLP -399 Park Av -NY 10022
(914) 232-1419 .. **Lane,** Jeannine J '88 -46 Croton Lk Rd -Katonah 10536
(212) 554-7800 .. **Lane,** Jill R '94 (Moses & S LLP) -405 Lex Av -NY 10174
(212) 363-8048 .. **Lane,** John C '75 -140 Bway PMB 46013 -NY 10005 **Fx:**(201) 848-6808
(212) 588-0800 .. **Lane,** John R '85 (Frommer L&H LLP) -745 5th Av -NY 10151
(212) 593-4202 .. **Lane,** Kathy '98 %Dichter Law,LLC -488 Mad Av -NY 10022 **Fx:**994-5394
(716) 853-2050 .. **Lane,** Kevin A '86 (Sliwa & L) -237 Main -Buffalo 14203
(212) 692-1000 .. **Lane,** Kimball Ann '83 (Duane M LLP) -1540 Bway -NY 10036
(212) 265-5431 .. **Lane,** Lisa S '89 %Promo Cup -599 11th Av -NY 10036 **Fx:**262-7279
(212) 294-6700 .. **Lane,** Maureen E '09 %Winston & S -200 Park Av -NY 10166
(607) 844-8440 .. **Lane,** Michl Edmond '76 -12 South Bx835 -Dryden 13053
(212) 278-1568 .. **Lane,** Michl J '86 (Anderson K&O,PC) -1251 Av of Amer -NY 10020
(718) 248-5431 .. **Lane,** Neil L '91 %Citicorp Invstmt Srvcs -1 Court Sq -LIC 11120
(718) 286-6000 .. **Lane,** Nicole M '10 %DA -125-01 Qns Blvd -Kew Gdns 11415
(585) 546-2500 .. **Lane,** Patrick J '74 OfCnsl McConville CC&M,PC -25 E Main -Rchstr 14614
(718) 298-0500 .. **Lane,** Peter F '92 %Surrogate's Ct -88-11 Sutphin Blvd -Jamaica 11435 **Fx:**520-5048
(212) 878-1700 .. **Lane,** R David Jr. '10 %Marshall DWC&G -140 Bway -NY 10005
(716) 856-4000 .. **Lane,** Robt J Jr. '84 (Hodgson R LLP) -140 Pearl -Buffalo 14202
(315) 452-8091 .. **Lane,** Robt P Jr. '91 Syracuse Research Corp -6225 Running Ridge Rd -N Syracuse 13212
(212) 940-2448 .. **Lane,** Sandra K '99 %Saks Fifth Ave -611 5th Av -NY 10022
(914) 251-0001 .. **Lane Sash & Larrabee LLP** -106 Corp Park Dr -White Plns 10604 **Fx:**251-0969
(516) 825-5577 .. **Lane,** Seymour S '52 -85 W Hawthorne Av -Vly Stream 11580 **Fx:**561-8248
(212) 661-9100 .. **Lane,** Stanley L Jr. '82 (Otterbourg SH&R,PC) -230 Park Av -NY 10169
(516) 741-6800 .. **Lane,** Steven T '94 %K Ready & Assoc -1565 Franklin Av -Mineola 11501
(212) 294-6700 .. **Lane,** Thos P '92 (Winston & S) -200 Park Av -NY 10166
(716) 842-2800 .. **Lane,** Thos S '98 (Webster S LLP) -1400 Lbrty Bldg -Buffalo 14202
(212) 962-0800 .. **Lane,** Veronica M '02 (Estrin B&L) -225 Bway -NY 10007 **Fx:**732-1408
(518) 689-1458 .. **Lane,** Victoria P '03 %Greenberg T,LLP -54 State -Albany 12207
(914) 681-6200 .. **Lane,** Wendy M '79 %NYPA -123 Main -White Plns 10601 **Fx:**390-8038
(212) 417-4213 .. **Laner,** Jeffrey P '03 Battery Pk City Auth -1 Wrld Fncl Ctr -NY 10281 **Fx:**417-2001
(212) 259-8000 .. **Lang,** Aaron C '07 %Dewey & L LLP -1301 Av of Amer -NY 10019
(516) 355-9600 .. **Lang,** Andrew C '89 %Friedman HK&P -3000 Marcus Av -Lk Success 11042
(212) 872-1000 .. **Lang,** Ashley E '07 -One Bryant Park -NY 10036 **Fx:**872-1002
(716) 852-2500 .. **Lang,** Cornelius J '74 -17 Court -Buffalo 14202 **Fx:**852-8263
(212) 813-8800 .. **Lang,** Danl A '07 %Goodwin P LLP -620 8th Av -NY 10018
(212) 487-4444 .. **Lang,** Elizabeth '76 %Dept Cnsmr Affrs -42 Bway -NY 10004 **Fx:**487-4197
(518) 690-0668 .. **Lang,** Frank W '90 Lang Law Firm PLLC -12 Cornell Rd -Latham 12110 **Fx:**782-9101
(716) 681-8000 .. **Lang,** Fred M '80 -6332 Bway -Lancaster 14086
(212) 421-2233 .. **Lang,** Jay A '83 (Wilk A LLP) -675 3rd Av -NY 10017
(212) 479-6000 .. **Lang,** Jeffrey W '04 %Cooley LLP -1114 Av of Amer -NY 10036
(212) 300-0646 .. **Lang,** John F '70 -60 E 42nd -NY 10165 **Fx:**300-0648
(212) 227-8490 .. **Lang,** Judy A '78 -111 John -NY 10038
(212) 484-2703 .. **Lang,** Julius F Jr. '86 %Midtown Community Ct -314 W 54th -NY 10019 **Fx:**586-1144
(518) 426-4600 .. **Lang,** Kevin M '92 (Couch W,LLP) -540 Bway Bx22222 -Albany 12201
(212) 335-9338 .. **Lang,** Lucy J '07 DA -1 Hogan Pl -NY 10013
(212) 698-3500 .. **Lang,** Matthew J '03 %Dechert LLP -1095 Av of Amer -NY 10036
(516) 798-4111 .. **Lang,** Michl J '60 -686 Bway -Massapequa 11758 **Fx:**798-4103
(718) 485-3699 .. **Lang,** Michl S '79 Rainbow Apparel Dist Cntr Corp -1000 Penn Av -Brklyn 11207 **Fx:**485-3807
(212) 669-4058 .. **Lang,** Nancy F '79 DCAS-DLS -1 Centre -NY 10007 **Fx:**669-2139
(212) 361-6401 .. **Lang,** Niles '90 -75 Wall -NY 10005 **Fx:**361-6050
(212) 804-3091 .. **Lang,** Raymond B '86 BNY Capital Mrkts -32 Old Slip -NY 10005
(212) 269-0927 .. **Lang,** Robt D '74 (D'Amato & L,LLP) -2 World Fncl Ctr -NY 10281
(212) 310-8000 .. **Lang,** Robt Todd '47 (Weil G&M LLP) -767 5th Av -NY 10153
(212) 269-0927 .. **Lang,** Robt W '78 (D'Amato & L,LLP) -2 World Fncl Ctr -NY 10281
(212) 259-8000 .. **Lang,** Ryan W '09 %Dewey & L LLP -1301 Av of Amer -NY 10019
(212) 644-3030 .. **Lang,** Stuart R '85 -777 3rd Av -NY 10017 **Fx:**421-1774
(315) 445-1831 .. **Lang,** Vaughn D '74 V Lang -333 Butternut Dr Bx503 -Syracuse 13214 **Fx:**445-1167
(585) 263-7229 .. **Lang,** Vipan S '95 %PricewaterhouseCoopers LLP -1100 Bausch & Lomb Plz -Rchstr 14604
(212) 940-3095 .. **Lang,** Wm X '02 %Nixon P LLP -437 Mad Av -NY 10022
(315) 423-4400 .. **Langan,** Geoffrey J '08 %Wolff G&G,LLP -217 Mntgmry -Syracuse 13202
(315) 425-2700 .. **Langan,** John P '88 (Hiscock & B,LLP) -One Park Pl -Syracuse 13202
(315) 218-8000 .. **Langan,** Kerry W '08 %Bond S&K,PLLC -1 Lincoln Ctr -Syracuse 13202
(315) 234-8610 .. **Langan,** Michl G '99 Hon G Lowe -100 S Clinton Bx7346 -Syracuse 13261 **Fx:**234-8611
(212) 940-3140 .. **Langan,** Richd F Jr. '81 (Nixon P LLP) -437 Mad Av -NY 10022
(212) 673-6753 .. **Langan,** Richd H II '03 -325 E 8th -NY 10009
(315) 435-2170 .. **Langan,** Sara J '02 %Cnty Atty -421 Mntgmry -Syracuse 13202 **Fx:**435-5729
(315) 445-9761 .. **Langan,** Terence A '82 (Langan & L) -333 Butternut Dr -DeWitt 13214 **Fx:**445-9573
(914) 737-0030 .. **Langan,** Thos R '79 Dempsey & L -1200 Brown -Peekskill 10566
(516) 997-0997 .. **Langdale,** Margaret A '04 %T Katz & Assoc,PC -300 Jericho Quad -Jericho 11753 **Fx:**997-0001
(212) 728-8000 .. **Langdon,** Robt T '01 (Willkie F&G LLP) -787 7th Av -NY 10019
(212) 589-4200 .. **Lange,** Christoph '83 (Baker & H LLP) -45 Rckfllr Plz -NY 10111
(518) 724-7788 .. **Lange,** Danielle R '06 HMS -16 Corp Wds Blvd -Albany 12211
(212) 364-8484 .. **Lange,** David M '00 Time Warner Cable -60 Columbus Av -NY 10023 **Fx:**364-8460
(516) 240-8900 .. **Lange,** Jason A '07 %Torre LGG&R,LLP -100 Jericho Quad -Jericho 11753
(914) 666-8033 .. **Lange,** Kenneth H '60 Cnsl Banks SG&W,LLP -118 N Bedford Rd Bx320 -Mt Kisco 10549
(212) 804-4200 .. **Lange,** Kenneth R '01 %Mound CW&G -One Bttry Pk Plz -NY 10004
(212) 508-6100 .. **Lange,** Marvin R '72 (Bracewell & G,LLP) -1251 Av of Amer -NY 10020
(212) 385-1215 .. **Lange,** Paul A '87 -445 Park Av -NY 10022 **Fx:**608-1215
(585) 325-5150 .. **Lange,** Paul K '62 (Faraci L,LLP) -28 E Main -Rchstr 14614
(212) 354-6270 .. **Langeland,** Erik H '95 (E Langeland,PC) -500 5th Av -NY 10110 **Fx:**898-9086
(631) 285-7500 .. **Langella,** Michl S '85 -2459 Ocean Av -Ronkonkoma 11779 **Fx:**285-7510
(716) 858-2424 .. **Langenfeld,** Brian D '06 %DA -25 Delaware Av -Buffalo 14202 **Fx:**858-7425
(212) 973-8000 .. **Langenus,** Peter C '73 Cnsl Schnader HS&L LLP -140 Bway -NY 10005
(212) 944-9112 .. **Langer,** Bobbi A '84 %Strategic Leg Solutions -110 E 42nd -NY 10017 **Fx:**944-8448
(212) 448-1100 .. **Langer,** Bruce A '79 (McLaughlin & S,LLP) -260 Mad Av -NY 10016
(914) 777-8600 .. **Langer,** Craig J '86 -480 Mamaroneck Av -Harrison 10528 **Fx:**777-8605
(212) 906-1200 .. **Langer,** David S '90 OfCnsl Latham & W -885 3rd Av -NY 10022

(212) 998-2252 .. **Langer,** Denise '84 %NYU Ofc Leg Cnsl -70 Wshngtn Sq S -NY 10012 **Fx:**995-3048
(914) 722-0066 .. **Langer,** Florence H '84 -178 Webster Rd -Scarsdale 10583
(914) 997-8200 .. **Langer,** Gary J '67 OfCnsl EH Odesser,LLC -81 Main -White Plns 10601 **Fx:**898-0083
(914) 948-1556 .. **Langer,** Ira '65 (Danziger & M LLP) -123 Main -White Plns 10601
(212) 999-5800 .. **Langer,** Matthew E '99 (Wilson SG&R) -1301 Av of Americas -NY 10019
(845) 620-0999 .. **Langer,** Michl A '89 %Bio Livestock -1 Blue Hill Plz -Pearl Rvr 10965
(516) 742-1400 .. **Langer,** Michl J '02 %K Weinstein -100 Grdn City Plz -Gdn Cty 11530 **Fx:**741-3811
(716) 984-5146 .. **Langer,** Nancy M '92 -115 Wdbrdg Av -Buffalo 14214
(800) 553-9940 .. **Langer,** Oren D '04 %Robins KM&C LLP -499 Park Av -NY 10022
(212) 424-0977 .. **Langer,** Patricia '80 %Lifetime TV -309 W 49th -NY 10019 **Fx:**957-4447
(518) 447-3200 .. **Langer,** Richd A '72 (McNamee LT&W,PC) -677 Bway -Albany 12207
(914) 472-5923 .. **Langer,** Richd P '87 -111 Brook -Scarsdale 10583
(212) 659-7300 .. **Langer,** Robt E '87 (Haynes & B,LLP) -1221 Av of Amer -NY 10020
(718) 601-4993 .. **Langer,** Sidney '94 -560 W 231st -Bronx 10463
(212) 688-6400 .. **Langer,** Stanley M '55 -270 Mad Av -NY 10016 **Fx:**688-6457
(516) 352-2400 .. **Langer,** Steven H '85 -199 Jericho Tpk -Floral Pk 11001 **Fx:**352-2346
(212) 687-2770 .. **Langer,** Thos '75 (Cohen PL&P) -551 5th Av -NY 10176
(315) 422-1152 .. **Langey,** John R '91 (Costello C&F,PLLC) -500 Plum -Syracuse 13204
(518) 873-3335 .. **Langey,** Michl P '99 %DA -Cthse -Elizabethtwn 12932 **Fx:**873-3788
(212) 832-0200 .. **Langfan,** Dayna K '88 %The Langfan Co -135 E 55th -NY 10022
(212) 832-0200 .. **Langfan,** Mark E '87 -135 E 55th -NY 10022
(212) 906-1340 .. **Langham,** Andrew N '01 Icahn Assoc Corp -767 5th Av -NY 10153
(718) 260-4750 .. **Langhenry,** Patrick J '96 Leg Aid -111 Lvngstn -Brklyn 11201 **Fx:**260-4744
(212) 408-5100 .. **Langhoff,** Danielle Pareja '96 Cnsl Chadbourne & P LLP -30 Rckfllr Plz -NY 10112
(212) 809-1111 .. **Langholz,** Douglas '92 (Morgan MA) -39 Bway -NY 10006
(212) 272-3723 .. **Langhorne,** Magali R '06 JP Morgan Chase -320 Park Av -NY 10022
(516) 222-6500 .. **Langione,** James R '82 (Galasso LC&L,LLP) -377 Oak -Gdn Cty 11530
(718) 746-0087 .. **Lang Kaplowitz,** Wendy S '00 Energy Brands,Inc -17-20 Whitestone Expwy -Whitestone 11357
(631) 852-2500 .. **Langlan,** Jeffrey D '03 %DA -200 Center Dr -Rvrhead 11901 **Fx:**852-1769
(631) 853-4161 .. **Langlan,** Kathleen B '99 %DA -N Cnty Cmplx Bldg 77 -Hauppauge 11788 **Fx:**853-4192
(845) 452-0200 .. **Langley,** Jennifer Lee '95 %Basso & Assoc,PC -1171 Route 55 -LaGrangevll 12540 **Fx:**452-0261
(212) 446-4800 .. **Langley,** Matthew J '10 %Kirkland & E LLP -153 E 53rd -NY 10022
(212) 408-2500 .. **Langley,** Robt Scott Jr. '82 OfCnsl Baker B,LLP -30 Rckfllr Plz -NY 10112
(518) 474-3684 .. **Langlie,** Konrad '75 %Dept of Law -The Cptl -Albany 12224
(518) 462-0300 .. **Langlois,** Christopher P '96 (Girvin & F,PC) -20 Corp Wds Blvd -Albany 12211
(212) 389-5000 .. **Langlois,** David P '71 (Sutherland A&B LLP) -1114 Av of Amer -NY 10036
(212) 373-3000 .. **Langman,** Barry '94 Cnsl Paul WRW&G LLP -1285 Av of Amer -NY 10019
(212) 609-2634 .. **Langman,** Ron L '01 %Gibson & B,PC -14 Wall -NY 10005
(914) 923-0125 .. **Langnas,** George '92 -12 Noel Dr -Ossining 10562 **Fx:**923-0125
(212) 258-6471 .. **Langner,** Lola E '85 %Viacom -1515 Bway -NY 10036
(315) 788-5900 .. **Langone,** Eugene J '88 (Hrabchak G&L,PC) -216 Wshngtn -Watertwn 13601
(212) 337-2228 .. **Langone,** Nichelle Alt '98 US Dept Labor -201 Varick -NY 10014
(516) 795-2424 .. **Langone,** Richd M '05 (Langone & Assoc,PLLC) -3601 Hempstd Tpke -Levittwn 11756 **Fx:**795-2400
(914) 995-2684 .. **Langrin,** Taryn '89 %Cnty Atty -148 Martine Av -White Plns 10601 **Fx:**995-5858
(212) 869-7000 .. **Langs,** Lawr J '89 SpclCnsl Feldman W&S LLP -420 Lex Av -NY 10170
(212) 759-4888 .. **Langs,** Sandra E '84 Phillips L LLP -437 Mad Av -NY 10022
(212) 836-8000 .. **Langsam,** Abigail S '05 %Kaye S LLP -425 Park Av -NY 10022
(212) 421-4100 .. **Langsam,** Andrew S '79 (Pryor C LLP) -7 Times Sq -NY 10036
(212) 742-2700 .. **Langsam,** Elise Hagouel '79 -7 Dey -NY 10007
(718) 875-1300 .. **Langsam,** Ira '87 %Applt Div 2nd Dept -45 Monroe Pl -Brklyn 11201 **Fx:**858-2446
(718) 250-2000 .. **Langsam,** Tziyonah M '00 %DA -350 Jay -Brklyn 11201 **Fx:**250-2314
(212) 617-3139 .. **Langsten,** Zoe S '01 Bloomberg -731 Lex Av -NY 10022
(212) 504-6000 .. **Langston,** James E Jr. '06 %Cadwalader W&T LLP -1 World Fncl Ctr -NY 10281
(212) 909-9500 .. **Langston,** Wm H '97 OfCnsl Wachtel & M,LLP -885 2nd Av -NY 10017
(212) 349-3000 .. **Languedoc,** Ronald S '82 %Himmelstein MGD&J -15 Maiden Ln -NY 10038
(914) 684-9890 .. **Langus,** Sandra '80 -175 Main -White Plns 10601
(516) 765-2800 .. **Langweber,** Denise R '82 (D Langweber LLP) -3332 Sunrise Hwy -Wantagh 11793 **Fx:**781-0347
(518) 295-7989 .. **Langwig,** J Russell III '85 -138 Grand Bx118 -Schoharie 12157 **Fx:**295-7975
(718) 442-7004 .. **Langworthy,** Leslie M '80 (Johnson & L,PC) -1688 Victory Blvd -Staten Isl 10314 **Fx:**442-9086
(716) 847-8400 .. **Lanham,** Donna M '89 SpclCnsl Phillips L LLP -3400 HSBC Ctr -Buffalo 14203
(516) 599-8999 .. **Laniado,** David '96 -411 Wstmnstr Rd -Cedarhrst 11516
(518) 465-9313 .. **Laniado,** Sam '77 (Read and L,LLP) -25 Eagle -Albany 12207
(212) 421-2800 .. **Lanier,** Wm Mark '05 (Lanier Law Firm,PLLC) -126 E 56th -NY 10022 **Fx:**421-2878
(631) 360-7333 .. **Lanigan,** Christopher J '95 %De Sena & S -1383 Vets Mem'l Hwy -Hauppauge 11788
(212) 918-3000 .. **Lanigan,** Danl J '10 %Hogan L LLP -875 3rd Av -NY 10022
(518) 402-6969 .. **Lanigan,** Jeffrey M '88 %Envrnmtl Facilities -625 Bway -Albany 12207 **Fx:**402-6972
(212) 331-5890 .. **Lanigan,** Jill C '07 NYC HR Admin -180 Water -NY 10038
(631) 928-9229 .. **Lanigan,** Patrick '73 -52 Sequoia Dr -Coram 11727
(212) 741-8276 .. **Lanigan,** Richd J '92 %Prf Emp Intl Union -265 W 14th -NY 10011 **Fx:**727-3466
(631) 712-5650 .. **Lanin,** Debbie E '95 %Hon D Hurley -934 Fed Plz Bx1094 -Central Islip 11722
(212) 764-7250 .. **Lanin,** Scott L '90 (Lanin Law PC) -1065 Av of Amer -NY 10018 **Fx:**(646) 365-3054
(631) 843-5569 .. **Lanis,** Nancy F '84 %H Schein Inc -135 Duryea Rd -Melvll 11747
(212) 678-0094 .. **Lanius,** P Baxter III '78 -1 St Nicholas Ter -NY 10027 **Fx:**678-1525
(212) 458-2077 .. **Lanka,** Sumani V '06 AIG,Inc -175 Water -NY 10038
(212) 581-5005 .. **Lankenau,** John C '55 (Lankenau & M LLP) -132 Nassau -NY 10038
(212) 581-5005 .. **Lankenau & Miller LLP** -132 Nassau -NY 10038 **Fx:**581-2266
(716) 856-3500 .. **Lankenau,** Susan M '81 SpclCnsl Magavern MG LLP -1100 Rand Bldg -Buffalo 14203
(585) 419-8800 .. **Lankford,** Gavin M '04 %Harris B PLLC -99 Garnsey Rd -Pittsfrd 14534
(716) 856-0600 .. **Lankford,** Jessica E '04 %Jaeckle F&M,LLP -12 Fountain Plz -Buffalo 14202
(212) 812-8912 .. **Lankler,** Andrew M '92 (Lankler & C,LLP) -845 3rd Av -NY 10022
(212) 812-8910 .. **Lankler & Carragher,LLP** -845 3rd Av -NY 10022 **Fx:**812-8920
(212) 733-0752 .. **Lankler,** Douglas M '91 %Pfizer Inc -235 E 42nd -NY 10017
(212) 921-8399 .. **Lankler,** Roderick C '63 (Lankler S&W LLP) -500 5th Av -NY 10110
(212) 921-8399 .. **Lankler Siffert & Wohl LLP** -500 5th Av -NY 10110 **Fx:**764-3701
(212) 972-2929 .. **Lanman,** Henry A '97 Trachtenberg R&F LLP -545 5th Av -NY 10017 **Fx:**972-7581
(914) 946-0534 .. **Lanman,** Jonathan J '04 -7 Mdlnd Av -White Plns 10606
(516) 574-5427 .. **Lannan,** Edw C '05 Allstate Ins Co -1111 Marcus Av -New Hyde Pk 11042
(914) 834-6600 .. **Lanni,** Jos '86 -138 Chatsworth Av -Larchmnt 10538 **Fx:**834-0152
(516) 280-7105 .. **Lanni,** Paul A '97 %Blodnick F & Assoc,PC -1325 Franklin Av -Gdn Cty 11530 **Fx:**280-7102
(212) 318-6000 .. **Lanning,** Ronald N Jr. '96 OfCnsl Paul HJ&W LLP -75 E 55th -NY 10022
(716) 853-6001 .. **Lannon,** J Patrick '09 %Wilder & L,LLP -403 Main at Court -Buffalo 14203
(718) 276-9400 .. **Lanoix,** Lesley J '03 (LJ Lanoix,PC) -8931 161st -Jamaica 11432 **Fx:**276-9408
(518) 437-8100 .. **Lanotte,** Michl A '94 %Credit Union Assn -1021 Watervliet-Shaker Rd Bx15118 -Albany 12212 **Fx:**437-8500
(212) 903-9098 .. **Lanoue,** Marc S '05 %Linklaters -1345 Av of Amer -NY 10105
(607) 723-5341 .. **Lanouette,** Dawn J '02 %Hinman H&K,LLP -80 Exchange Bx5250 -Bnghmtn 13902
(607) 235-3005 .. **Lanouette,** Ronald J Jr. '03 R Lanouette,PLLC -53 Chenango -Bnghmtn 13901
(212) 637-2399 .. **Lanpher,** Mark D '04 US Atty -1 St Andrews Plz -NY 10007
(212) 980-4500 .. **Lans,** Deborah E '75 (Cohen L LLP) -885 3rd Av -NY 10022
(212) 930-0082 .. **Lansburgh,** Matthew S '98 %NY Public Lib -5th Av & 42nd -NY 10018 **Fx:**391-2503
(914) 631-6600 .. **Lansch,** James A '95 Ampacet Corp -660 Wht Plns Rd -Tarrytwn 10591
(212) 697-3122 .. **Lansen,** Thos R '06 %Martin C&B LLP -220 E 42nd -NY 10017
(518) 429-4200 .. **Lansing,** Mark D '85 (Hiscock & B,LLP) -50 Beaver -Albany 12207
(212) 962-0098 .. **Lansky,** Maryna '77 -609 Greenwich -NY 10014 **Fx:**608-1659
(516) 712-4000 .. **Lansky,** Samantha B '03 %Milber MP&S LLP -1000 Woodbury Rd -Woodbury 11797
(212) 349-0900 .. **Lansner,** David J '72 (Lansner KS&Z) -325 Bway -NY 10007
(212) 349-0900 .. **Lansner Kubitschek Schaffer & Zuccardy** -325 Bway -NY 10007 **Fx:**349-0694
(212) 513-3200 .. **Lansner,** Ruth L '75 (Holland & K LLP) -31 W 52nd -NY 10019
(631) 472-5550 .. **Lanteri,** Antoinette '92 -111 Bayport Av -Bayport 11705 **Fx:**472-4999
(212) 732-8700 .. **Lantier,** Brendan J '75 (McAloon & F,PC) -123 William -NY 10038
(315) 474-2911 .. **Lantier,** James D '74 (Smith SK&S,PC) -250 S Clinton -Syracuse 13202
(516) 496-5822 .. **Lantier,** Wm Xavier '98 T Spina -170 Froehlich Farm Blvd -Woodbury 11797 **Fx:**496-5420
(718) 998-5624 .. **Lantner,** Melvin E '57 -1624 E 14th -Brklyn 11229 **Fx:**998-5639
(212) 610-6300 .. **Lantsberg,** Yana '09 %Allen & O -1221 Av of Amer -NY 10020
(516) 624-0466 .. **Lanuti,** Gregory M '95 -1225 Franklin Av -Gdn Cty 11530 **Fx:**624-0483
(212) 735-3000 .. **Lanz,** Julie M '10 %Skadden ASM&F LLP -4 Times Sq -NY 10036
(718) 984-5151 .. **Lanza,** Andrew J '93 NYC Cncl -10 Rustic Pl -Staten Isl 10308
(212) 374-5400 .. **Lanza,** Craig S '04 %Balestriere L PLLC -225 Bway -NY 10007 **Fx:**208-2613
(516) 538-2500 .. **Lanza,** Elena R '90 (Furey FLMW&D,PC) -600 Front -Hempstd 11550
(914) 835-6000 .. **Lanza,** Gene A Jr. '86 -18 Halstead Av -Harrison 10528
(212) 336-2000 .. **Lanza,** Jean-Claude '99 %Patterson BW&T LLP -1133 Av of Amer -NY 10036
(516) 328-3500 .. **Lanza,** Joann Fahey '99 %McDonnell & A,PC -401 Franklin Av -Gdn Cty 11530
(914) 681-8700 .. **Lanza,** Marisa L '01 (Milber MP&S LLP) -3 Barker Av -White Plns 10601
(212) 816-2241 .. **Lanza,** Paul R '94 Citigroup -388 Greenwich -NY 10013
(212) 784-5800 .. **Lanza,** Robt J '86 (Hiscock & B,LLP) -7 Times Sq -NY 10036
(631) 979-4300 .. **Lanza,** Ronald S '00 (Futterman & L,LLP) -222 E Main -Smithtwn 11787 **Fx:**979-9546
(315) 598-1928 .. **Lanza,** Salvatore F '85 -154 S 2nd -Fulton 13069 **Fx:**598-1601
(716) 373-4701 .. **Lanza,** Steven A '07 Leg Srvcs -103 S Barry -Olean 14760 **Fx:**373-7771
(585) 232-6500 .. **Lanzafame,** Ross P '87 (Harter S&E LLP) -1600 Bausch & Lomb Pl -Rchstr 14604
(212) 848-4000 .. **Lanzalotto,** Christopher '09 %Shearman & S LLP -599 Lex Av -NY 10022
(212) 636-6837 .. **Lanzarone,** Michl R '63 %Fordham Univ Sch of Law -140 W 62nd -NY 10023 **Fx:**636-6899
(212) 815-0406 .. **Lanzatella,** Susan N '96 %DA -1 Hogan Pl -NY 10013
(212) 863-6300 .. **Lanzer,** Alyson L '03 HPD -100 Gold -NY 10038 **Fx:**863-8201
(212) 995-8757 .. **Lanzet,** Jeffrey S '00 %Wolk N&M -304 Park Av S -NY 10010
(718) 224-4746 .. **Lanzetta,** Claudia '04 %AM Carrozza -213-38 40th Av -Bayside 11361 **Fx:**224-4794

(631) 653-9100 .. **Lanzetta,** Donna J '88 (Lanzetta & Assoc PC) -472 Montauk Hwy -E Quogue 11942 **Fx:**653-5800
(212) 592-1400 .. **Lanzillotta,** Lawr C '04 %Herrick,F LLP -2 Park Av -NY 10016
(212) 654-8538 .. **Lanzillotta,** Michl '01 MTV Ntwrks -1633 Bway -NY 10019
(718) 725-3200 .. **Lanzilotta,** Lenore L '02 Admin Children's Srvcs -151-20 Jamaica Av -Jamaica 11432
(212) 225-2000 .. **Lanzkron,** Jos '10 %Cleary GS&H -1 Lbrty Plz -NY 10006
(212) 878-0012 .. **Lanzo,** Frank C '81 MTA -2 Penn Plz -NY 10121
(718) 322-3006 .. **Lao,** Mona L F '03 %G Russo & Assoc PC -96-11 101st Av -Ozone Pk 11416
(212) 848-4000 .. **Laorno,** Robt J '06 %Shearman & S LLP -599 Lex Av -NY 10022
(914) 328-0640 .. **LaPaglia,** James W '83 -175 Main -White Plns 10601 **Fx:**948-5695
(315) 435-2470 .. **LaPaglia,** Lauren J '07 %DA -505 S State -Syracuse 13202 **Fx:**435-3969
(212) 619-5000 .. **LaPalme,** Robt S '89 %EDC -110 William -NY 10038 **Fx:**312-3912
(518) 745-5000 .. **LaPann,** James L '83 J LaPann,PC -107 Bay -Glens Fls 12801 **Fx:**745-5080
(315) 452-2440 .. **LaParo,** John B '60 OfCnsl Primo P&K,LLP -7075 Manlius Ctr Rd -E Syracuse 13057
(212) 817-6650 .. **Lapatine,** Jeffrey D '74 Siegel & Gale -437 Mad Av -NY 10022 **Fx:**453-0401
(212) 801-3189 .. **Lapatine,** Kenneth A '69 (Greenberg T,LLP) -200 Park Av -NY 10166
(212) 560-6984 .. **LaPayover,** Shari P '90 %EBC -450 W 33rd -NY 10001 **Fx:**560-3191
(518) 641-5571 .. **Lape Handy,** Valerie R '98 %Cptl Dist Physicians Hlth Plan,Inc -500 Patroon Crk Blvd -Albany 12206 **Fx:**641-5505
(212) 259-8000 .. **Lapenn,** James A '72 OfCnsl Dewey & L LLP -1301 Av of Amer -NY 10019
(516) 747-4082 .. **Lapenna,** Evan M '07 %Montfort HM&S LLP -1140 Franklin Av Bx7677 -Gdn Cty 11530
(845) 942-5500 .. **LaPerch,** Frank J '99 -148 S Lbrty Dr -Stony Pnt 10980
(212) 351-4000 .. **La Perla,** Jos L '09 %Gibson D&C LLP -200 Park Av -NY 10166
(718) 273-8313 .. **LaPerna,** Jos J '87 -2071 Clove Rd -Staten Isl 10304
(518) 257-3000 .. **Lapetina,** Mauro J '75 %Dormitory Auth -515 Bway -Albany 12207 **Fx:**257-3101
(212) 770-8635 .. **Lapham,** Craig L '96 %AIG -70 Pine -NY 10270 **Fx:**341-6950
(518) 270-8254 .. **Lapham,** Jeffrey K '02 -1835 5th Av -Troy 12180 **Fx:**279-9172
(585) 658-2180 .. **LaPiana,** James D '00 -18 Chapel Bx279 -Mt Morris 14510 **Fx:**658-2183
(631) 921-6297 .. **LaPiana,** Peter M '03 -29 S Howell Av -Farmngvll 11738 **Fx:**585-4948
(212) 431-2883 .. **LaPiana,** Wm P '80 %NY Law Schl -185 W Bway -NY 10013 **Fx:**431-1830
(212) 801-9208 .. **Lapides,** Ivy J '00 (Greenberg T,LLP) -200 Park Av -NY 10166
(212) 885-5000 .. **Lapidow,** Seth J '89 (Blank R LLP) -405 Lex Av -NY 10174
(347) 401-9580 .. **Lapidus,** Darryl E '93 Appllt Term -141 Lvngstn -Brklyn 11201 **Fx:**(718) 643-7889
(718) 631-6262 .. **Lapidus,** Howard L '67 %Queensboro Comm Cllg -222-05 56th Av -Bayside 11364 **Fx:**279-8295
(718) 518-2779 .. **Lapidus,** Karen C '85 Loehmanns Inc -2500 Halsey -Bronx 10461
(212) 612-4365 .. **Lapidus,** Laura R '92 Chubb Grp -55 Water -NY 10041
(212) 549-2668 .. **Lapidus,** Lenora M '91 ACLU-Womens Rts Project -125 Broad -NY 10004 **Fx:**549-2580
(212) 986-7714 .. **Lapidus,** Mitchell '87 (Propp L&J,LLP) -1500 Bway -NY 10036
(631) 218-8242 .. **Lapidus,** Myra Paiewonsky '84 OfCnsl R Lapidus,PC -4875 Sunrise Hwy -Bohemia 11716 **Fx:**218-8245
(631) 218-8242 .. **Lapidus,** Rodney S '73 R Lapidus,PC -4875 Sunrise Hwy -Bohemia 11716 **Fx:**218-8245
(212) 576-7000 .. **LaPier,** Theo '80 %NY Life Ins -51 Mad Av -NY 10010 **Fx:**447-0569
(914) 684-6000 .. **LaPietra,** Louis C '98 (LaPietra & K) -30 Glenn -White Plns 10603 **Fx:**287-6460
(518) 783-4762 .. **LaPietra,** Pasquale A '90 -3 Lucia Ln -Latham 12110
(212) 751-7528 .. **Lapin,** Jonathan B '77 -575 Mad Av -NY 10022 **Fx:**755-6385
(585) 641-8000 .. **Lapin,** Paula A '76 OfCnsl Fix SB&G,PC -295 Woodcliff Dr -Fairprt 14450
(585) 454-6690 .. **Lapine,** Felix V '69 -1 E Main -Rchstr 14614
(518) 295-2272 .. **Lapinel,** David '88 %DA -Bx888 -Schoharie 12157 **Fx:**295-2273
(212) 803-5100 .. **Lapiner,** Natasha S '88 %NY Cnty Defender Srvcs -225 Bway -NY 10007 **Fx:**571-6035
(718) 899-3200 .. **Lapinski,** Alexander J '62 -42-57 Layton -Elmhrst 11373 **Fx:**457-4693
(518) 402-9509 .. **Lapinski,** Ann '88 %DEC -625 Bway -Albany 12233 **Fx:**402-9018
(732) 855-6066 .. **Lapinski,** Danl R '02 %Wilentz G&S -110 William -NY 10038 **Fx:**726-4735
(631) 231-1199 .. **La Pinta,** Anthony M '93 (Reynolds CGHL&Q,LLP) -35 Arkay Dr -Hauppauge 11788
(516) 694-3000 .. **LaPlace,** Christine M '98 %Guercio & G,LLP -77 Conklin -Farmngdl 11735 **Fx:**694-4738
(212) 607-3300 .. **Laplace,** Lisa J '91 %NYCLU -125 Broad -NY 10004
(518) 481-5983 .. **LaPlant,** David E '96 -362 W Main -Malone 12953 **Fx:**483-3945
(860) 527-9699 .. **LaPlante,** Suzanne M '97 %Berman & S LLC -58 W 58th -NY 10019 **Fx:**527-9077
(585) 232-6500 .. **Lapoff,** Lucinda Odell '96 %Harter S&E LLP -1600 Bausch & Lomb Pl -Rchstr 14604
(631) 451-6477 .. **Lapointe,** Alison A '09 Bd of Appls -1 Indpndnc Hl -Farmngvll 11738 **Fx:**451-6926
(518) 292-5120 .. **LaPointe,** George A Jr. '83 %Dept Econ Dvlpmnt -30 S Pearl -Albany 12245 **Fx:**292-5807
(631) 756-4093 .. **LaPointe,** Laurence M '77 %State Ins Fund -8 Corp Ctr Dr -Melvll 11747 **Fx:**756-4060
(212) 382-0700 .. **LaPolla,** Chas P '86 (Ostrolenk FG&S,LLP) -1180 Av of Amer -NY 10036
(212) 461-2150 .. **LaPolla,** Regina Lee '90 -44 Wall -NY 10005
(914) 428-4787 .. **LaPorta,** Patricia A '93 Cnsl Skyline Title,LLC -199 Main -White Plns 10601
(518) 381-3871 .. **LaPorta,** Patrick J '90 Cnsl Trustco Bank -3 Sarnowski Dr -Glenvll 12302 **Fx:**381-3608
(212) 225-2000 .. **Laporte,** Leah M '09 %Cleary GS&H -1 Lbrty Plz -NY 10006
(212) 385-4949 .. **La Porte,** Nicholas A '94 %Associated Builders & Owners -80 Maiden Ln -NY 10038 **Fx:**385-1442
(516) 295-3344 .. **Lapp,** Chas E III '75 (Lapp & L) -100 Cedarhrst Av Bx435 -Cedarhrst 11516 **Fx:**295-3460
(845) 638-3012 .. **Lapp,** Ira H '98 %R Neimark & Assoc,LLP -37 Congers Rd -New Cty 10956 **Fx:**638-3093
(212) 998-6550 .. **Lapp,** Kevin D '05 %NYU Law Schl -245 Sullivan -NY 10012
(585) 428-5210 .. **Lapp,** Leanne G '99 %Pub Def -10 N Fitzhugh -Rchstr 14614 **Fx:**428-2234
(518) 792-2117 .. **Lapper,** Jonathan C '86 (Bartlett PS&R,PC) -1 Wshngtn Bx2168 -Glens Fls 12801
(212) 732-3200 .. **Lappert,** Stephen F '86 (Carter L&M LLP) -2 Wall -NY 10005
(914) 765-4062 .. **Lappin,** John C '89 IBM -1 New Orchrd Rd -Armonk 10504 **Fx:**765-7533
(516) 921-2525 .. **Lapping,** Robt K '77 (McHenry H&L,PC) -6800 Jericho Tpk -Syosset 11791
(585) 238-2000 .. **Laprade,** Steven E '98 %Phillips L LLP -1400 First Fed Plz -Rchstr 14614
(212) 818-8031 .. **Laptook,** Eric J '80 Itochu Intl -335 Mad Av -NY 10017 **Fx:**818-8493
(212) 973-0572 .. **Laptook,** Kenneth N '82 (Wolff & S PC) -140 Bway -NY 10005
(646) 291-7339 .. **Lapus,** Maria Rosario T O '06 -317 16th Av -Brklyn 11215
(212) 474-1000 .. **Lapushchik,** Tatiana '01 (Cravath S&M LLP) -825 8th Av -NY 10019
(212) 227-3333 .. **Laquercia,** Thos M '70 (Smith & L,LLP) -291 Bway -NY 10007
(212) 756-2000 .. **Lara,** Nelida '09 %Schulte R&Z LLP -919 3rd Av -NY 10022
(212) 836-8000 .. **Lara,** Stacey A '99 Kaye S LLP -425 Park Av -NY 10022
(212) 307-8226 .. **Laracuente-Sanchez,** Guidette '92 %Citibank -666 5th Av -NY 10103
(212) 609-6800 .. **Laracy,** Ward C '91 (McCarter & E,LLP) -245 Park Av -NY 10167
(585) 243-7028 .. **Laragy,** Christopher J '90 -6 Court -Geneseo 14454
(516) 571-3800 .. **Laraia,** Cynthia M '97 %DA -262 Old Cntry Rd -Mineola 11501 **Fx:**248-9479
(914) 682-0500 .. **LaRaus,** Lawr B '87 (Buonamici & L,LLP) -222 Bloomingdale Rd -White Plns 10605 **Fx:**997-2666
(212) 735-3000 .. **Larcombe,** Eleni '04 %Skadden ASM&F LLP -4 Times Sq -NY 10036
(212) 998-6077 .. **Larcombe,** Sarah K '02 NYU Law Schl -245 Sullivan -NY 10012
(516) 671-6815 .. **Lardi,** Paul F '58 -8 Jaegger Dr -Glen Head 11545 **Fx:**759-3280
(212) 906-1200 .. **Lardy,** Lillian H '08 %Latham & W -885 3rd Av -NY 10022
(516) 357-0056 .. **LaReddola Lester & Associates, LLP** -600 Old Cntry Rd -Gdn Cty 11530 **Fx:**357-0069
(516) 357-0056 .. **LaReddola,** Robt J '95 (LaReddola L & Assoc,LLP) -600 Old Cntry Rd -Gdn Cty 11530
(845) 362-3543 .. **Laredo,** Carolyn M '95 Laredo&Jaffe Mediatn Grp,LLC -978 Route 45 -Pomona 10970
(212) 803-3100 .. **Laremont,** Anita Webb '80 %Empire State Dvlmnt Corp -633 3rd Av -NY 10017
(212) 455-2000 .. **Laretto,** Jeffrey A '09 %Simpson T&B LLP -425 Lex Av -NY 10017
(212) 483-2323 .. **Largey,** James P '96 %JP Morgan Chase -345 Park Av -NY 10154
(212) 859-8000 .. **Lari,** Shahzeb '03 (Fried FHS&J LLP) -1 NY Plz -NY 10004
(585) 338-6800 .. **Larimer,** John D '02 %Bausch & Lomb -One Bausch & Lomb Pl -Rchstr 14604 **Fx:**338-8706
(212) 297-5800 .. **Lario,** Wendy Johnson '03 (Day P LLP) -7 Times Sq -NY 10036
(212) 661-5030 .. **Larizza,** Silvia Simpson '98 %Schoeman U&K,LLP -60 E 42nd -NY 10165
(212) 732-8700 .. **Lark,** Audrey A '99 %McAloon & F,PC -123 William -NY 10038
(212) 259-8000 .. **Lark,** Fredk J '99 (Dewey & L LLP) -1301 Av of Amer -NY 10019
(212) 986-6890 .. **Lark,** J Andrew '83 -501 5th Av -NY 10017
(631) 734-6807 .. **Lark,** Richd F '62 (Lark & F) -Main Rd Bx973 -Cutchogue 11935
(212) 788-1599 .. **Larkin,** Arthur G '90 Law Dept -100 Church -NY 10007 **Fx:**788-9776
(845) 566-5345 .. **Larkin Axelrod Ingrassia & Tetenbaum,LLP** -356 Meadow Av -Newburgh 12550 **Fx:**566-5148
(845) 562-3366 .. **Larkin Axelrod Ingrassia & Tetenbaum,LLP** -34 Route 17K -Newburgh 12550 **Fx:**562-0859
(845) 342-3366 .. **Larkin Axelrod Ingrassia & Tetenbaum,LLP** -626 E Main -Middletwn 10940
(631) 425-4100 .. **Larkin,** Bailey C '08 %Ré NH&C,LLP -36 N NY Av -Huntngtn 11743
(212) 513-3200 .. **Larkin,** Brian O '98 SrCnsl Holland & K LLP -31 W 52nd -NY 10019
(646) 435-9505 .. **Larkin,** Edw W '79 OfCnsl Baritz & C LLP -233 Bway -NY 10279
(585) 295-4400 .. **Larkin,** Edwin M '63 (Hiscock & B,LLP) -2000 HSBC Plz -Rchstr 14604
(212) 307-5500 .. **Larkin,** Edwin M III '91 (Venable LLP) -1270 Av of Amer -NY 10020
(516) 747-4082 .. **Larkin,** Hugh J '96 %Montfort HM&S LLP -1140 Franklin Av Bx7677 -Gdn Cty 11530
(212) 506-5000 .. **Larkin,** James M '03 %Orrick H&S LLP -51 W 52nd -NY 10019
(914) 627-3000 .. **Larkin,** James P '76 Diversified Invstmnt Advsrs -440 Mamaroneck Av -Harrison 10528
(516) 542-1000 .. **Larkin,** Jennifer L '02 %Geisler & G,LLP -100 Q Roosevelt Blvd -Gdn Cty 11530
(212) 261-8000 .. **Larkin,** John F III '66 OfCnsl Mendes & M,LLP -750 7th Av -NY 10019
(800) 416-5454 .. **Larkin,** Kenneth H '87 (Fusco B&R) -180 Froehlich Farm Blvd -Woodbury 11797
(800) 416-5454 .. **Larkin,** Kenneth H '87 (Fusco B&R) -2116 Wllmsbrdg Rd -Bronx 10461
(800) 416-5454 .. **Larkin,** Kenneth H '87 (Fusco B&R) -11 Penn Plz -NY 10001
(315) 425-2700 .. **Larkin,** Matthew J '97 (Hiscock & B,LLP) -One Park Pl -Syracuse 13202
(212) 490-3000 .. **Larkin,** Peter J '94 (Wilson EME&D LLP) -150 E 42nd -NY 10017
(914) 323-7000 .. **Larkin,** Peter J '94 (Wilson EME&D LLP) -3 Gannett Dr -White Plns 10604
(212) 532-0800 .. **Larkin,** Richd T '83 %AFTRA -260 Mad Av -NY 10016 **Fx:**545-1238
(607) 656-4515 .. **Larkin,** Robt M '74 -36 Genesee Bx570 -Greene 13778 **Fx:**656-9016
(631) 300-4960 .. **Larkin,** Robt X '81 (Bello & L) -150 Motor Pkwy -Hauppauge 11788
(718) 330-7861 .. **Larkin,** Sandra A '98 %ODAR-SSA -111 Lvngstn -Brklyn 11201 **Fx:**330-2009
(315) 448-0672 .. **Larkin,** Wm F '84 %US Atty -100 S Clinton Bx7198 -Syracuse 13261 **Fx:**448-0689
(845) 566-5345 .. **Larkin,** Wm J III '81 (Larkin AI&T,LLP) -356 Meadow Av -Newburgh 12550
(973) 315-4409 .. **Larner,** Henry A '87 (Budd L) -140 Bway -NY 10005

(212) 425-9300 .. **LaRobardier,** Genevieve K '85 (Bressler A&R,PC) -17 State -NY 10004
(212) 335-4500 .. **LaRocca,** Dianne R '05 %DLA Piper LLP -1251 Av of Amer -NY 10020
(212) 530-4822 .. **LaRocca Hornik Rosen Greenberg & Blaha LLP** -40 Wall -NY 10005 **Fx:**530-4815
(516) 571-3800 .. **Larocca,** Jos J '80 %DA -262 Old Cntry Rd -Mineola 11501 **Fx:**248-9479
(516) 759-9898 .. **LaRocca,** Lisa '89 -11 Chicken Valley Rd -Old Brookvll 11545 **Fx:**802-2069
(585) 987-2800 .. **LaRocca,** Lorisa D '03 %Woods OG LLP -2 State -Rchstr 14614
(917) 971-4606 .. **LaRocca,** Marco '03 -82 Arlyn Dr E -Massapequa 11758 **Fx:**(631) 574-3155
(914) 591-7722 .. **LaRocca,** Robt R '81 (Roy ML&R) -56 Main Bx108 -Irvngtn 10533
(718) 238-6800 .. **Larocca,** Stephen R '86 (DiConza LD&K) -478 Bay Ridge Pkwy -Brklyn 11209
(212) 785-8127 .. **LaRocca,** Stephen S '91 (SS LaRocca,PLLC) -11 Bway -NY 10004 **Fx:**248-2960
(973) 848-4014 .. **La Rocco,** Anthony P '83 (K&L Gates LLP) -599 Lex Av -NY 10022 **Fx:**848-4001
(212) 541-2000 .. **La Rocco,** Chris M '06 %Bryan C LLP -1290 Av of Amer -NY 10104
(212) 969-3000 .. **Laroche,** Rachelle L '09 %Proskauer R LLP -1585 Bway -NY 10036
(212) 218-2100 .. **LaRock,** Adam C '10 %Fitzpatrick CH&S -1290 Av of Amer -NY 10104
(212) 571-1112 .. **LaRock,** Allen L '97 (Zohar L&P,LLP) -42 Bway -NY 10004 **Fx:**571-1113
(315) 782-5871 .. **LaRock,** Jane Getman '88 -120 Wshngtn -Watertwn 13601 **Fx:**782-5489
(212) 848-4000 .. **Larocque,** Gabrielle J '06 %Shearman & S LLP -599 Lex Av -NY 10022
(212) 878-8000 .. **Larocque,** Michl W '09 %Clifford C LLP -31 W 52nd -NY 10019
(518) 483-2551 .. **La Rocque,** Thos C '67 -455 E Main -Malone 12953 **Fx:**483-5666
(212) 878-7900 .. **LaRosa,** Bridget '98 %Fox R LLP -100 Park Av -NY 10017
(212) 326-3939 .. **LaRosa,** Gasper J '02 %Jones D -222 E 41st -NY 10017
(516) 739-3090 .. **LaRosa,** Michl '03 %Mason & M,PC -394 Old Cntry Rd -Gdn Cty 11530 **Fx:**739-5060
(718) 987-1100 .. **LaRosa,** Richd A '73 (Passarello & L) -94 Lincoln Av -Staten Isl 10306
(718) 876-6300 .. **LaRosa,** Shara L '97 DA -130 Styvsnt Pl -Staten Isl 10301
(212) 536-3900 .. **Larose,** Catherine A '09 %K&L Gates LLP -599 Lex Av -NY 10022
(845) 454-2001 .. **LaRose,** Keith V '79 (LaRose & L) -510 Haight Av -Poughkeepsie 12603 **Fx:**454-2535
(212) 294-6700 .. **Larose,** Lawr A '84 (Winston & S) -200 Park Av -NY 10166
(718) 590-3799 .. **LaRose,** Peter J '83 %Hon M DeMarco -851 Grand Cncrs -Bronx 10451
(845) 331-2525 .. **LaRose,** Richd L Jr. '98 %Ryan R&R,LLP -115 Green Bx3153 -Kingston 12402
(845) 454-2001 .. **LaRose,** Shelley-Ann '81 (LaRose & L) -510 Haight Av -Poughkeepsie 12603 **Fx:**454-2535
(315) 428-1000 .. **LaRose,** Stuart J '93 -307 S Clinton -Syracuse 13202 **Fx:**428-1002
(212) 788-8734 .. **LaRose,** Timothy J '84 %Sheriff's Ofc -31 Chmbrs -NY 10007 **Fx:**766-9666
(845) 340-1723 .. **LaRose,** Wm C '02 NYS DOT -11 Quarry -Kingston 12401
(631) 439-5200 .. **Larounis,** Thos '85 -35 Pinelawn Rd -Melvll 11747
(212) 833-8159 .. **Larrabee,** Jennifer A '99 Sony BMG Music -550 Mad Av -NY 10022
(914) 251-0001 .. **Larrabee,** Susan B '87 (Lane S&L LLP) -106 Corp Park Dr -White Plns 10604
(315) 437-7600 .. **Larrison,** David W '71 (Ferrara FLB&R,PC) -5010 Campuswood Dr -E Syracuse 13057
(646) 723-7639 .. **Larry,** W James III '07 Partiarch Partners LLC -32 Av of Amer -NY 10013
(212) 855-9159 .. **Larsen,** Bryn K '96 Goldman Sachs & Co -180 Maiden Ln -NY 10038
(631) 737-4321 .. **Larsen,** Edw V '83 -5022 Expwy Dr S -Ronkonkoma 11779 **Fx:**737-4353
(212) 715-9100 .. **Larsen,** Elizabeth F '07 %Kramer LN&F,LLP -1177 Av of Amer -NY 10036
(212) 710-0000 .. **Larsen,** Kristian K '99 %Drohan L,LLP -489 5th Av -NY 10017
(212) 309-8402 .. **Larsen,** Lance D '97 ING -230 Park Av -NY 10169
(212) 336-2000 .. **Larsen,** Matthew B '05 %Patterson BW&T LLP -1133 Av of Amer -NY 10036
(518) 486-2926 .. **Larsen,** Petra M '95 %OPRHP -Agncy Bldg 1 ESP -Albany 12238 **Fx:**474-5106
(212) 269-0927 .. **Larsen,** Wm P III '80 (D'Amato & L,LLP) -2 World Fncl Ctr -NY 10281
(718) 761-5751 .. **Larson,** Allan G '91 -186 Merrymount -Staten Isl 10314 **Fx:**761-5751
(716) 483-0479 .. **Larson,** Fredk A '77 F Larson -408 W 5th -Jamestwn 14701 **Fx:**664-2132
(212) 880-6000 .. **Larson,** Gregg T '02 %Torys LLP -237 Park Av -NY 10017
(212) 310-8000 .. **Larson,** Jennifer D '09 %Weil G&M LLP -767 5th Av -NY 10153
(212) 715-1000 .. **Larson,** Jennifer L '00 %Arnold & P LLP -399 Park Av -NY 10022
(212) 403-1000 .. **Larson,** Jos D '95 (Wachtell LR&K) -51 W 52nd -NY 10019
(718) 590-2000 .. **Larson,** Lori Ann '97 %DA -198 E 161st -Bronx 10451 **Fx:**590-6477
(212) 528-0886 .. **Larson,** Michl J '03 M Larson,PC -321 Bway -NY 10007 **Fx:**529-0887
(212) 858-1000 .. **Larson,** Michl J '09 %Pillsbury WSP LLP -1540 Bway -NY 10036
(315) 448-8400 .. **Larson,** Nancy J '88 %Law Dept -233 E Wshngtn -Syracuse 13202 **Fx:**448-8381
(212) 836-8000 .. **Larson,** Patricia A '06 %Kaye S LLP -425 Park Av -NY 10022
(718) 494-8800 .. **Larson,** Remy '01 %HM File,PC -260 Christopher Ln -Staten Isl 10314 **Fx:**494-1776
(718) 490-3664 .. **Larson,** Robt S '80 -803 Jewett Av -Staten Isl 10314 **Fx:**273-6937
(212) 225-2000 .. **Larson,** Scott M '08 %Cleary GS&H -1 Lbrty Plz -NY 10006
(516) 393-2200 .. **Larson,** Shilpa Patel '07 %Garfunkel W,PC -111 Grt Nck Rd -Gt Neck 11021
(212) 854-3159 .. **Larson,** Sonja A '02 Columbia Law Schl -435 W 116th -NY 10027
(212) 336-0142 .. **Larson,** Stephen A '05 SEC -3 World Fncl Ctr -NY 10281 **Fx:**336-1323
(212) 310-8000 .. **Larson,** Todd D '05 %Weil G&M LLP -767 5th Av -NY 10153
(212) 225-2000 .. **Larson,** Wallace L Jr. '99 Cnsl Cleary GS&H -1 Lbrty Plz -NY 10006
(914) 478-2801 .. **LaRuffa,** Eric J '91 %R Greenspan,PC -220 Heatherdell Rd -Ardsley 10502 **Fx:**478-2913
(212) 318-6000 .. **Laruffa,** Erin E '08 %Paul HJ&W LLP -75 E 55th -NY 10022
(212) 773-3000 .. **Larusso,** Christine A '09 %Ernst & Young,LLP -5 Times Sq -NY 10036
(516) 248-3520 .. **LaRusso,** Robt P '71 (LaRusso & C) -300 Old Cntry Rd -Mineola 11501 **Fx:**248-3522
(212) 697-3122 .. **Larywon,** Kenneth R '79 (Martin C&B LLP) -220 E 42nd -NY 10017
(718) 793-5535 .. **LaSala,** Jake '86 -125-10 Qns Blvd -Kew Gdns 11415 **Fx:**261-3482
(917) 519-8666 .. **Lasala,** John P '96 Goldman Sachs & Co -32 Old Slip -NY 10005
(212) 483-9490 .. **LaSala,** Jos P '81 (McElroy DM&C,LLP) -88 Pine -NY 10005
(212) 756-2000 .. **LaSalle,** Frank J '05 %Schulte R&Z LLP -919 3rd Av -NY 10022
(212) 446-2300 .. **Lasalle,** John F '08 %Boies S&F LLP -575 Lex Av -NY 10022
(516) 328-2300 .. **LaSalle,** Lori A '92 (Abrams FFEGF&E,LLP) -1111 Marcus Av -Lk Success 11042
(718) 533-0033 .. **La Salle,** Richd '92 -88-01 Roosevelt Av -Jcksn Hts 11372 **Fx:**533-8749
(516) 535-1100 .. **La Salvia,** Lori A '99 %Valdebenito & A -1399 Franklin Av -Gdn Cty 11530 **Fx:**535-3936
(212) 421-6000 .. **La Sasso,** Mariel S '05 (LaSasso G Law Grp PLLC) -80 Maiden Ln -NY 10038 **Fx:**421-6006
(914) 644-9200 .. **La Scala,** Andrea T '98 %D Petshaft,PC -222 Bloomingdale Rd -White Plns 10605 **Fx:**644-9300
(718) 969-7039 .. **LaScala,** Raymond '57 -162-12 77th Av -Flushng 11366
(585) 232-6500 .. **Lascell,** David M '66 (Harter S&E LLP) -1600 Bausch & Lomb Pl -Rchstr 14604
(518) 462-5300 .. **Lasch,** Frank J '57 (DeGraff F&K LLP) -90 State -Albany 12207
(212) 980-9600 .. **Laschewer,** Heather L '97 %Kaufman B&R -120 Bway -NY 10271
(315) 724-1530 .. **Lascurettes,** Tod M '78 (McLane S and L,LLP) -20 Elizabeth Bx524 -Utica 13503 **Fx:**724-1852
(646) 602-5600 .. **Lasdon,** Douglas H '82 %Urban Justice Ctr -123 William -NY 10038 **Fx:**(212) 533-4598
(212) 636-5400 .. **Laserson,** Lillian J '84 %DC Comics -1700 Bway -NY 10019 **Fx:**636-5595
(212) 496-1300 .. **Lash,** Donald A '92 %Sinergia Inc -15 W 65th -NY 10023 **Fx:**496-5608
(716) 847-8400 .. **Lash,** Robt L '00 %Phillips L LLP -3400 HSBC Ctr -Buffalo 14203
(212) 701-3000 .. **Lashbrook,** Marc R '07 %Cahill G&R LLP -80 Pine -NY 10005 **Fx:**269-5420
(212) 474-1000 .. **Lasher,** Jos E '08 %Cravath S&M LLP -825 8th Av -NY 10019
(212) 940-3080 .. **Lasher,** Wm W III '80 SrCnsl Nixon P LLP -437 Mad Av -NY 10022
(212) 421-4100 .. **Lashin,** Jodi L '98 OfCnsl Pryor C LLP -7 Times Sq -NY 10036
(212) 407-4000 .. **Lashkari,** Leily '90 SrCnsl Loeb & L,LLP -345 Park Av -NY 10154
(212) 373-3000 .. **Lashko,** Oksana '08 %Paul WRW&G LLP -1285 Av of Amer -NY 10019
(718) 875-1128 .. **Lashley,** Allen '57 -16 Court -Brklyn 11241 **Fx:**797-4911
(718) 250-2000 .. **Lashley,** Deborah A '81 %DA -350 Jay -Brklyn 11201 **Fx:**250-2314
(212) 593-6700 .. **Lask,** Russell J '06 %Aaronson RF&D,LLP -757 3rd Av -NY 10017
(212) 358-5762 .. **Lask,** Susan C '89 -244 5th Av -NY 10001
(212) 808-7800 .. **Laska,** Alan J '85 (Kelley D&W LLP) -101 Park Av -NY 10178
(212) 735-8600 .. **Laska,** Jeffery H '97 Morrison C LLP -909 3rd Av -NY 10022
(212) 883-0015 .. **Laskay,** C Mark '99 (Benedetto L,LLC) -122 E 42nd -NY 10168 **Fx:**591-6904
(718) 326-3500 .. **Laske,** Arthur M '91 -65-06 Grand Av -Maspeth 11378 **Fx:**326-3500
(516) 571-0334 .. **Laske,** Carl A '90 Cnsl Dept of Assessment -240 Old Cntry Rd -Mineola 11501
(212) 225-2000 .. **Lasker,** Alida Y '08 %Cleary GS&H -1 Lbrty Plz -NY 10006
(716) 488-3090 .. **Lasker,** Kenneth M '87 (Burgett & R) -15 E 5th Bx3090 -Jamestwn 14702
(212) 238-3000 .. **Lasker,** Richd S '73 (Emmet M&M,LLP) -120 Bway -NY 10271
(212) 725-8566 .. **Laskin,** Andrew M '93 (Robinson & Y,PC) -232 Mad Av -NY 10016
(718) 250-2000 .. **Laskin,** Jonathan B '91 %DA -350 Jay -Brklyn 11201 **Fx:**250-2314
(516) 213-5151 .. **Laskin,** Michelle F '91 Laskin Law,PC -410 E Jericho Tpk -Mineola 11501 **Fx:**213-5152
(212) 233-0314 .. **Laskin,** Shira '09 %Wolfson & C -233 Bway -NY 10279 **Fx:**349-4911
(212) 808-2700 .. **Laskis,** Jamie L '05 %Pepper H LLP -620 8th Av -NY 10018
(212) 345-2144 .. **Lasko,** Richd P '71 Marsh & McLennan Cos -1166 Av of Amer -NY 10036 **Fx:**345-2045
(718) 579-2839 .. **Lasko,** Wm J '91 %City Sheriff -3030 3rd Av -Bronx 10455
(212) 837-9050 .. **Laskowitz,** Jedediah I M '02 JP Morgan Fleming Asset Mgmt -522 5th Av -NY 10036
(212) 736-4500 .. **Laskowitz,** Shari S '00 (Nesenoff & M,LLP) -363 7th Av -NY 10001
(718) 894-3966 .. **Laskowski,** Krystyna M '94 -57-38 64th -Maspeth 11378
(516) 227-0808 .. **Lasky,** Barry M '73 (Lasky & S,PC) -595 Stewart Av -Gdn Cty 11530 **Fx:**745-0769
(212) 446-4800 .. **Lasky,** Benjamin A '06 %Kirkland & E LLP -153 E 53rd -NY 10022
(212) 336-2000 .. **Lasky,** Brian N '01 %Patterson BW&T LLP -1133 Av of Amer -NY 10036
(212) 907-0800 .. **Lasky,** Leigh R '96 (Lasky & R,Ltd) -140 Bway -NY 10005
(212) 804-4200 .. **Lasky,** Matthew J '99 %Mound CW&G -One Bttry Pk Plz -NY 10004
(718) 286-6000 .. **Lasky,** Merri T '81 %DA -125-01 Qns Blvd -Kew Gdns 11415
(212) 468-4800 .. **Lasky,** Michl C '79 (Davis & G LLP) -1740 Bway -NY 10019
(212) 907-0800 .. **Lasky & Rifkind,Ltd** -140 Bway -NY 10005
(212) 972-2175 .. **Lasky,** Robt L '55 -99 Park Av -NY 10016
(212) 278-7086 .. **Lasky,** Robt S '93 %Societe Generale -1221 Av of Amer -NY 10020
(516) 747-1136 .. **Lasky,** Sean R '96 %Steinberg FB&F,PC -40 Crsswys Park Dr -Woodbury 11797
(212) 510-1400 .. **Laslo,** Christina Creek '03 %Spec Comm of Invstgtn -80 Maiden Ln -NY 10038 **Fx:**510-1550
(315) 463-4032 .. **Lasner,** Harvey R '71 %Koldin Law Ctr -6661 Kirkvll Rd Bx279 -E Syracuse 13057 **Fx:**463-6512
(914) 682-3300 .. **La Sorsa & Beneventano** -3 Barker Av -White Plns 10601 **Fx:**682-3740
(914) 682-3300 .. **La Sorsa,** Gregory M '84 (La Sorsa & B) -3 Barker Av -White Plns 10601
(631) 261-9709 .. **LaSpina,** Bruno J '90 -171 Scudder Av -Northprt 11768

(718) 767-3333 .. **LaSpina,** Gregory M '82 (Borchert GL&L,PC) -19-02 Whitestone Expy -Whitestone 11357
(212) 381-7000 .. **LaSpisa,** Vincent III '99 %Sabin B&G LLP -4 Times Sq -NY 10036
(212) 850-7500 .. **Lasry,** Marc L '85 %Ave Cptl Grp -535 Mad Av -NY 10022 **Fx:**850-7598
(212) 286-8585 .. **Lassalle,** Doralba '03 %Heidell PM&B,LLP -99 Park Av -NY 10016
(212) 695-5670 .. **Lassar,** Stephen D '70 (Goldfinger & L LLP) -750 3rd Av -NY 10017
(716) 664-9890 .. **Lasser,** Miles L '49 Ralph L Sheldon Fndtn,Inc -7 E 3rd Bx417 -Jamestwn 14702 **Fx:**483-6116
(607) 255-3383 .. **Lasser,** Mitchel '91 %Cornell Law Schl -Myron Taylor Hall -Ithaca 14853 **Fx:**255-7193
(718) 727-8900 .. **Lasser,** Myron G '59 -60 Bay -Staten Isl 10301 **Fx:**727-9837
(212) 279-9090 .. **Lasser,** Stephen M '02 (Stark & S) -One Penn Plz -NY 10119 **Fx:**279-9113
(212) 553-7742 .. **Lasseron,** Arnaud '00 Moodys Investors Srvc -99 Church -NY 10007
(718) 651-0500 .. **Lassin,** Byron '70 -39-18 63rd -Woodside 11377 **Fx:**651-0262
(718) 826-3760 .. **Lasson,** Lori B '87 (Goldberg & L) -215 Marlboro Rd -Brklyn 11226 **Fx:**826-3760
(212) 692-9666 .. **Last,** Bennett H '69 (Gilbride TL&S LLC) -708 3rd Av -NY 10017
(516) 222-2722 .. **Last,** Maxine K '89 -585 Stewart Av -Gdn Cty 11530 **Fx:**222-1060
(212) 859-8000 .. **Last,** Meyer '83 (Fried FHS&J LLP) -1 NY Plz -NY 10004
(212) 935-8880 .. **Last,** Richd S '82 (Foreht LL&K,LLP) -228 E 45th -NY 10017
(718) 298-1198 .. **Lastella,** Vito M '73 Supreme Ct -88-11 Sutphin Blvd -Jamaica 11435
(516) 357-3000 .. **Lastorino,** Carol D '92 (Rivkin R LLP) -926 RXR Plz -Uniondale 11556
(973) 228-5700 .. **Lastorino,** Kevin M '00 (Brach E LLC) -100 Park Av -NY 10017 **Fx:**228-7852
(212) 334-1871 .. **Lat,** David B '01 -262 Mott -NY 10012
(212) 277-9000 .. **Latack,** Andrew B '07 CAA Sports -162 5th Av -NY 10010
(585) 295-4400 .. **Latella,** Robt N '67 OfCnsl Hiscock & B,LLP -2000 HSBC Plz -Rchstr 14604
(212) 608-1600 .. **LaTerra,** Danl C '08 %Maggiano D&L,PC -521 5th Av -NY 10175
(518) 474-8211 .. **Latham,** Chilton B '80 %Law Reporting Bur -1 Commerce Plz -Albany 12210 **Fx:**463-6869
(718) 222-9800 .. **Latham,** Christopher D '80 (Brecher FPWT&Z,PC) -335 Adams -Brklyn 11201
(212) 819-8200 .. **Latham,** Danl M '98 (White & C LLP) -1155 Av of Amer -NY 10036
(716) 633-7860 .. **Latham,** Julie A '08 Ward B&D -5500 Main -Williamsvll 14221
(631) 727-2180 .. **Latham,** Stephen B '78 (Twomey LSKD&Q,LLP) -33 W 2nd Bx9398 -Rvrhead 11901
(212) 906-1200 .. **Latham & Watkins** -885 3rd Av -NY 10022 **Fx:**751-4864
(212) 850-6220 .. **Lathrop & Gage LC** -230 Park Av -NY 10169 **Fx:**850-6221
(718) 857-3663 .. **Lathrop,** Jaime '03 -641 Prsdnt -Brklyn 11215
(858) 314-1566 .. **Lathrop,** Mitchell L '81 (Mintz LCFG&P,PC) -666 3rd Av -NY 10017
(212) 770-7000 .. **Lathrop,** Peter K '69 %AIG -70 Pine -NY 10270 **Fx:**785-1468
(212) 472-6262 .. **Latifi,** Ali R '03 %Tucker & L,LLP -160 E 84th -NY 10028 **Fx:**744-6509
(212) 472-6262 .. **Latifi-M-Tehrani,** Afschineh '93 (Tucker & L,LLP) -160 E 84th -NY 10028 **Fx:**744-6509
(607) 753-4105 .. **Latimer,** Christopher P '00 SUNY-Poli Sci Dept -207 Old Main -Cortlnd 13045
(718) 520-7956 .. **Latimer,** Jonathan T '86 -80-02 Kew Grdns Rd -Kew Gdns 11415
(718) 286-2000 .. **Latimer,** Leigh E '88 %Leg Aid -120-46 Qns Blvd -Kew Gdns 11415 **Fx:**286-2286
(718) 286-0960 .. **Latimer,** Lucinda B '07 NYC Dept of Bldgs -120-55 Qns Blvd -Jamaica 11424
(518) 782-4900 .. **Latimer,** Suzanne L '93 (LaFave L&S,LLP) -951 Albany Shaker Rd -Latham 12110 **Fx:**785-9705
(646) 252-2819 .. **Latimer,** Thos P '82 %Transit Auth -2 Bway -NY 10004 **Fx:**252-5559
(518) 462-0110 .. **Latin,** Thos D '75 %Sheehan GCG&J LLP -54 State -Albany 12207
(914) 524-5600 .. **Latini,** Michl J '86 %L Fishman -303 S Bway -Tarrytwn 10591 **Fx:**524-5742
(914) 347-2300 .. **Latino,** Jos M '79 OfCnsl AJ Maiocchi PLLC -22 Saw Mill Rvr Rd -Hawthorne 10532 **Fx:**347-5047
(518) 474-6400 .. **Latino,** Melissa A '03 %Dept of Ed -89 Wshngtn Av -Albany 12234 **Fx:**473-2925
(845) 486-4200 .. **Latino,** Steven M '97 %Shaw PM&L,LLP -21 Van Wagner Rd -Poughkeepsie 12603
(718) 769-4282 .. **Latkovskaia,** Anna '02 (A Latkovskaia,LLC) -3820 Nostrand Av -Brklyn 11235 **Fx:**769-7337
(212) 318-3000 .. **Latman,** Marc D '98 (Fulbright & J LLP) -666 5th Av -NY 10103
(212) 592-1400 .. **Latner,** Irwin M '86 (Herrick,F LLP) -2 Park Av -NY 10016
(516) 227-2300 .. **Latner,** Jennifer R '97 Wright Risk Mgmt -333 Earle Ovngton Blvd -Uniondale 11553 **Fx:**227-2352
(631) 852-2500 .. **Lato,** Karla Aschmoneit '87 %DA -200 Center Dr -Rvrhead 11901 **Fx:**852-1769
(631) 853-4161 .. **Lato,** Leonard '86 %DA -N Cnty Cmplx Bldg 77 -Hauppauge 11788 **Fx:**853-4192
(716) 250-1800 .. **Latona,** Anthony J '72 (Jaeckle F&M,LLP) -400 Essjay Rd -Amherst 14221
(631) 234-1500 .. **Latona,** Jos A '80 %Rubin & R LLC -1787 Vets Hwy -Islandia 11749
(716) 842-0416 .. **LaTona,** Jos M '74 -403 Main -Buffalo 14203 **Fx:**853-2892
(914) 523-3004 .. **LaTorre,** Agatino Jr. '02 -419 E 78th -NY 10075 **Fx:**(212) 535-0564
(212) 272-9920 .. **LaTorre-Weiner,** Catherine '99 %JP Morgan Chase -383 Mad Av -NY 10179
(718) 721-5740 .. **Latos,** Andrew '89 (Latos L&D,PC) -22-15 31st -Astoria 11105 **Fx:**721-9645
(718) 721-5740 .. **Latos,** Peter '91 (Latos L&D,PC) -22-15 31st -Astoria 11105 **Fx:**721-9645
(718) 222-2315 .. **LaTour,** Jessica M '04 %Law Dept -350 Jay -Brklyn 11201 **Fx:**222-2373
(718) 330-7697 .. **LaTour,** Stephanie '95 %NLRB -2 Metrotech Ctr -Brklyn 11201 **Fx:**330-7579
(516) 342-2200 .. **LaTrace,** Anthony P '95 %Schwartzapfel Prtnrs -300 Jericho Quad -Jericho 11753
(212) 578-2211 .. **Latrenta,** Nicholas D '82 %MetLife -1095 Av of Amer -NY 10036 **Fx:**578-3916
(516) 796-9700 .. **Latronica,** Robt R Jr. '92 (Latronica Law Firm,PC) -64 Division Av -Levittwn 11756 **Fx:**796-9702
(646) 471-4000 .. **Lattanzio,** Christine A '99 %PricewaterhouseCoopers LLP -300 Mad Av -NY 10017
(631) 249-8200 .. **Lattanzio,** Diana '02 %DePinto N & Assoc,LLP -445 Broadhllw Rd -Melvll 11747 **Fx:**249-8209
(516) 354-7688 .. **Lattanzio,** Frank '79 -1143 Hempstd Tpk -Franklin Sq 11010 **Fx:**354-4890
(914) 472-6202 .. **Lattanzio,** Patricia M '09 %Clair & G -720 Wht Plns Rd -Scarsdale 10583 **Fx:**472-1936
(212) 756-2000 .. **Lattanzio,** Peter R '09 %Schulte R&Z LLP -919 3rd Av -NY 10022
(212) 264-8306 .. **Latterman,** Carol A '77 %US GSA -26 Fed Plz -NY 10278 **Fx:**264-1987
(212) 530-5000 .. **Latterner,** Matthew J '09 Milbank TH&M LLP -1 Chase Manh Plz -NY 10005
(516) 541-5069 .. **Lattime,** Suzanne Niedzwiecki '94 -126 Shoreham Rd -Massapequa 11758
(716) 845-7465 .. **Lattimore-Young,** Mary Jo '86 Family Ct -1 Niagara Plz -Buffalo 14202 **Fx:**858-6293
(212) 848-4000 .. **Lattman,** Laura J '06 %Shearman & S LLP -599 Lex Av -NY 10022
(212) 389-8223 .. **Lattman,** Peter T '97 Contra Capital Mgmt -350 Mad Av -NY 10017
(212) 363-1200 .. **Latto,** Douglas A '92 (Baumeister & S) -1 Exch Plz -NY 10006
(212) 815-1818 .. **Latty,** Carla Ann '84 %DC 37 MELS -125 Barclay -NY 10007 **Fx:**815-1343
(516) 294-1368 .. **Latuga,** Diane M '83 -146 Bengeyfld Dr -E Williston 11596 **Fx:**741-1292
(212) 806-5400 .. **Latza,** Wm D '82 (Stroock &S&L LLP) -180 Maiden Ln -NY 10038
(516) 944-5848 .. **Latzman,** Patricia '75 -51 Mackey Av -Pt Wash 11050 **Fx:**944-5848
(212) 532-3368 .. **Latzman,** Stephen '75 -276 5th Av -NY 10001 **Fx:**685-5731
(212) 757-5000 .. **Lau,** Alex Yook '01 %Sklover D&F,LLC -10 Rckfllr Plz -NY 10020 **Fx:**757-5002
(212) 661-9100 .. **Lau,** Benjamin W '91 OfCnsl Otterbourg SH&R,PC -230 Park Av -NY 10169
(212) 218-2100 .. **Lau,** Dana '07 %Fitzpatrick CH&S -1290 Av of Amer -NY 10104
(212) 635-1622 .. **Lau,** Estella M '81 %Bk Of NY -1 Wall -NY 10286
(718) 359-9700 .. **Lau,** Jay '04 Lau & Assoc,PC -133-47 Sanford Av -Flushng 11355 **Fx:**762-9385
(212) 277-4000 .. **Lau,** Joelle S L '09 %Freshfields BD LLP -520 Mad Av -NY 10022
(212) 417-3700 .. **Lau,** Kin-Hang '97 %MFY Legal Srvcs -299 Bway -NY 10007 **Fx:**417-3890
(212) 272-8716 .. **Lau,** Marisa K '96 %JP Morgan Chase -383 Mad Av -NY 10179
(516) 876-4213 .. **Lau,** Marissa C '05 %Hooper & W LLC -50 Jericho Tpk -Jericho 11753 **Fx:**876-6906
(212) 474-1000 .. **Lau,** Matthew Y O '10 %Cravath S&M LLP -825 8th Av -NY 10019
(845) 433-1161 .. **Lau,** Richd '91 %IBM -2455 South Rd -Poughkeepsie 12601
(516) 229-6000 .. **Lau,** Richd T '86 R Lau & Assoc -300 Jericho Quad Bx9040 -Jericho 11753 **Fx:**229-6167
(212) 622-5284 .. **Lau,** Sherman '95 JP Morgan Chase & Co -277 Park Av -NY 10172
(212) 720-2032 .. **Lau,** Stanley J '96 %Federal Reserve Bk -33 Lbrty -NY 10045
(914) 686-1700 .. **Lau,** Steven R '87 (O'Connor R,LLP) -200 Mamaroneck Av -White Plns 10601
(212) 742-8700 .. **Lau,** Yat Fai '06 Garson D&C LLP -110 Wall -NY 10005
(212) 635-2244 .. **Lau,** Yee Ling Elaine '05 %Rosner N&R LLP -110 Wall -NY 10005
(914) 683-1112 .. **Laub,** Alfred C '79 (Laub D,LLP) -3 Barker Av -White Plns 10601 **Fx:**683-8903
(914) 761-1300 .. **Laub,** Danl M '06 %Cuddy & F LLP -445 Hmltn Av -White Plns 10601
(716) 854-5333 .. **Laub,** David C '66 -438 Main -Buffalo 14202 **Fx:**856-0828
(914) 457-2300 .. **Laub,** Kenneth A '81 (Kanterman & S,LLP) -50 Main -White Plns 10606
(212) 326-3939 .. **Laub,** M Joel '92 OfCnsl Jones D -222 E 41st -NY 10017
(212) 834-0600 .. **Laub,** Michl J '80 (Gordon & S,PC) -355 Lex Av -NY 10017
(212) 644-0500 .. **Lauber,** Robyn H '06 %Jacobs R,LLC -777 3rd Av -NY 10017
(914) 725-9890 .. **Laubich,** Lori M '87 -19 Castle Walk -Scarsdale 10583
(516) 229-6000 .. **Laubis,** Christine M '93 %R Lau & Assoc -300 Jericho Quad Bx9040 -Jericho 11753 **Fx:**229-6167
(646) 386-5000 .. **Laubscher,** Jay C '97 %Surrogates Ct -31 Chmbrs -NY 10007
(315) 853-8399 .. **Laucello,** Michl J '78 -40 Chenango Av Bx272 -Clinton 13323
(212) 209-4800 .. **Lauchheimer,** Aaron B '07 %Brown R LLP -7 Times Sq -NY 10036
(619) 595-5419 .. **Lauchlan,** Robt J Jr. '89 (McKenna L&A) -230 Park Av -NY 10169 **Fx:**595-5450
(212) 655-3500 .. **Lauck,** Brian T '98 %Meister S&F LLP -140 E 45th -NY 10017
(585) 362-4700 .. **Laudadio,** Brian '97 (Bond S&K,PLLC) -350 Linden Oaks -Rchstr 14625
(646) 495-3065 .. **Laudadio,** Frank '94 Mark Bruce Intl -909 3rd Av -NY 10022
(212) 906-1200 .. **Lau Dan,** Jose A '95 OfCnsl Latham & W -885 3rd Av -NY 10022
(212) 848-4000 .. **Laudano,** Erica J '05 %Shearman & S LLP -599 Lex Av -NY 10022
(518) 486-2921 .. **Laudato,** Paul J '79 %OPRHP -Agncy Bldg 1 ESP -Albany 12238 **Fx:**474-5106
(585) 546-2500 .. **Laude,** Raquel B '09 %McConville CC&M,PC -25 E Main -Rchstr 14614
(914) 766-4320 .. **Lauderdale,** Ronald A '75 IBM -294 Route 100 -Somers 10589
(716) 856-7091 .. **Laudisio,** Mark C '96 %J Freedman -424 Main -Buffalo 14202 **Fx:**856-7097
(212) 676-6294 .. **Laudon,** Jack W '82 Business Integrity Comm -100 Church -NY 10007 **Fx:**676-6204
(212) 481-1312 .. **Laudonio,** Tara A '98 -271 Mad Av -NY 10016 **Fx:**481-1316
(212) 983-4141 .. **Laudor,** Richd S '87 Cnsl D Rozenholc & Assoc -400 Mad Av -NY 10017 **Fx:**983-4356
(212) 768-6700 .. **Lauer,** Abigail D '07 %Sonnenschein N&R LLP -1221 Av of Amer -NY 10020
(212) 960-0051 .. **Lauer,** Andrew J '91 %Yeshiva Univ -500 W 185th -NY 10033 **Fx:**960-5346
(212) 696-6000 .. **Lauer,** Eliot '75 (Curtis M-PC&M LLP) -101 Park Av -NY 10178
(212) 382-3211 .. **Lauer,** Herbert '67 -22 W 38th -NY 10018
(718) 252-1974 .. **Lauer,** Jos I '67 -876 E 28th -Brklyn 11210
(212) 421-4100 .. **Laufer,** Alan S '79 %Pryor C LLP -7 Times Sq -NY 10036
(212) 876-4030 .. **Laufer,** Albert L '87 -185 E 85th -NY 10028 **Fx:**876-4030
(212) 422-1020 .. **Laufer,** Andrew C '98 (A Laufer PLLC) -40 Exch Pl -NY 10005 **Fx:**422-1069
(212) 758-4700 .. **Laufer,** Barry '86 -489 5th Av -NY 10017 **Fx:**644-0544

(718) 331-7999 .. **Laufer,** Jacob '73 Laufer & Assoc -1660 60th -Brklyn 11204 **Fx:**259-2479
(212) 422-8500 .. **Laufer,** Jacob '75 J Laufer PC -65 Bway -NY 10006 **Fx:**422-9038
(212) 566-7188 .. **Laufer,** Laurence D '86 (Genova B&G) -115 Bway -NY 10006
(212) 309-6000 .. **Laufer,** Linda E '75 Morgan L&B LLP -101 Park Av -NY 10178
(212) 267-6770 .. **Laufer,** Michl M '74 (Laufer & Assoc,PLLC) -7 Dey -NY 10007 **Fx:**267-6773
(212) 373-3333 .. **Laufer,** Robt L '63 OfCnsl Paul WRW&G LLP -1285 Av of Amer -NY 10019
(516) 227-0700 .. **Laufer,** Rochelle '87 Cnsl Farrell F,PC -1320 RXR Plz -Uniondale 11556
(212) 626-1057 .. **Laufer,** Steven M '99 %Bank Leumi -564 5th Av -NY 10036
(212) 259-8000 .. **Laufgraben,** Eric '05 %Dewey & L LLP -1301 Av of Amer -NY 10019
(718) 694-5720 .. **Laughlin,** Brigid A '07 %Transit Auth -130 Lvngstn -Brklyn 11201 **Fx:**694-5726
(607) 264-9988 .. **Laughlin,** Dennis B '05 Tracys Law Ofc -77 Alden Bx217 -Cherry Vly 13320 **Fx:**264-9094
(212) 478-7200 .. **Laughlin,** James P '78 SpclCnsl Hahn & H LLP -488 Mad Av -NY 10022
(212) 483-2323 .. **Laughlin,** Robt J '93 %JP Morgan Chase -345 Park Av -NY 10154
(212) 223-6444 .. **Laughlin,** Thos L '07 Scott +S,LLP -500 5th Av -NY 10110 **Fx:**223-6334
(212) 625-0300 .. **Lau-Kee,** Glenn '75 (Kee & L-K,PLLC) -354 Broome -NY 10013
(212) 858-1000 .. **Laukenmann,** Christopher B '06 (Pillsbury WSP LLP) -1540 Bway -NY 10036
(212) 326-3939 .. **Laukitis,** Lisa G '00 (Jones D) -222 E 41st -NY 10017
(716) 484-7196 .. **Laumer,** J Kevin '79 (Fessenden L&D) -81 Forest Av Bx590 -Jamestwn 14702
(212) 335-9000 .. **Launay,** Jeanine M '90 %DA -1 Hogan Pl -NY 10013
(718) 966-5353 .. **Laura,** Jos M '87 (Laura & M) -236 Richmond Valley Rd -Staten Isl 10309
(718) 966-5353 .. **Laura & Matarrese** -236 Richmond Valley Rd -Staten Isl 10309 **Fx:**948-1966
(718) 588-8017 .. **Laureano,** Robt A '91 -910 Grnd Cncrs -Bronx 10451 **Fx:**588-8035
(212) 806-5400 .. **Lauredo,** Manuel E '01 SpclCnsl Stroock &S&L LLP -180 Maiden Ln -NY 10038
(212) 786-8829 .. **Lauren,** Amy DeJesus '00 %EMI Music NA -150 5th Av -NY 10011 **Fx:**786-8103
(212) 880-2070 .. **Laurence,** Elaine S '80 E Laurence Assoc,LLC -275 Mad Av -NY 10016
(212) 866-8654 .. **Laurence,** Stuart G '67 -285 Riverside Dr -NY 10025
(212) 754-9400 .. **Laurencell,** Marianne '04 %Todtman NS&J,PC -425 Park Av -NY 10022
(914) 421-2600 .. **Laurency,** Yan K '04 Nextel Inc -1 N Bway -White Plns 10601
(212) 547-5400 .. **Laurenson,** Edwin C '78 (McDermott W&E LLP) -340 Mad Av -NY 10173
(315) 423-4400 .. **Laurenti,** Carissa A '07 %Wolff G&G,LLP -217 Mntgmry -Syracuse 13202
(212) 836-8000 .. **Laurenzi,** Robt R '00 Cnsl Kaye S LLP -425 Park Av -NY 10022
(212) 696-6000 .. **Laurer,** Thos '01 %Curtis M-PC&M LLP -101 Park Av -NY 10178
(516) 747-1990 .. **Lauri,** Andrew M '95 (Cascone & K,LLP) -1399 Franklin Av -Gdn Cty 11530
(315) 458-5220 .. **Lauri,** Brian J '92 (Hall M&L,PLLC) -111 Church Bx278 -N Syracuse 13212
(631) 473-5550 .. **Lauri,** Kenneth J '89 -503 Main -Pt Jffrsn 11777 **Fx:**473-9330
(212) 545-4000 .. **Lauri,** Kevin G '91 (Jackson L LLP) -666 3rd Av -NY 10017
(646) 610-5400 .. **Lauriano,** Olga L '99 %NYPD -1 Police Plz -NY 10038
(212) 363-1380 .. **Lauricella,** Michl J '10 %Herten BSCBL&H,LLC -747 3rd Av -NY 10017
(518) 449-8893 .. **Lauricella,** Peter A '97 (Wilson EME&D LLP) -677 Bway -Albany 12207
(212) 837-6832 .. **Laurie,** Ashley J '10 %Hughes H&R LLP -1 Bttry Pk Plz -NY 10004 **Fx:**299-6832
(718) 699-8863 .. **Lauriello,** Adrian '93 -52-10 108th -Corona 11368
(914) 631-6900 .. **Lauriello,** Anthony '95 %Guttridge & C,PC -303 S Bway -Tarrytwn 10591 **Fx:**631-6644
(212) 946-2720 .. **Lauriello,** Valerie J '98 %Feren & F -11 Penn Plz -NY 10001
(518) 447-3200 .. **Laurilliard,** Kevin '86 (McNamee LT&W,PC) -677 Bway -Albany 12207
(212) 965-9081 .. **Laurin,** Jennifer E '05 %Neufeld S&B -99 Hudson -NY 10013
(212) 922-9700 .. **Laurin,** Kristin Kerrigan '94 %1st Amer Title -633 3rd Av -NY 10017 **Fx:**922-0881
(212) 789-3100 .. **Laurinaitis,** Denise E '99 %Riemer & B LLP -7 Times Sq -NY 10036 **Fx:**719-0140
(347) 296-1668 .. **Laurino,** Clare '91 %Supreme Ct Law Dept -360 Adams -Brklyn 11201 **Fx:**643-6114
(516) 393-6133 .. **Laurino,** Frank J '79 F Laurino -999 Stewart Av -Bethpage 11714 **Fx:**393-6130
(516) 248-4771 .. **Laurino,** Louis D '51 (Laurino & L) -229 7th -Gdn Cty 11530 **Fx:**248-4785
(516) 248-4771 .. **Laurino,** Louis M '86 (Laurino & L) -229 7th -Gdn Cty 11530 **Fx:**248-4785
(716) 200-5050 .. **Laurita,** Alan J '74 OfCnsl Harris B PLLC -726 Exchange -Buffalo 14210
(347) 273-1342 .. **Lauro,** Thos S '81 -1110 South Av -Staten Isl 10314
(212) 335-9000 .. **Lauscher,** David F '98 %DA -1 Hogan Pl -NY 10013
(516) 346-7788 .. **Laut,** Gregory C '05 Northrup Grumman -600 Grumman Rd W -Bethpage 11714
(212) 326-3939 .. **Lauter,** John J Jr. '75 OfCnsl Jones D -222 E 41st -NY 10017
(212) 302-2600 .. **Lauterbach Garfinkel Damast & Hollander LLP** -22 W 38th -NY 10018 **Fx:**764-3269
(914) 779-2211 .. **Lauterbach Garfinkel Damast & Hollander LLP** -35 E Grassy Sprain Rd -Ynkrs 10710 **Fx:**779-4791
(914) 779-2211 .. **Lauterbach,** Leon A '50 (Lauterbach GD&H LLP) -35 E Grassy Sprain Rd -Ynkrs 10710
(845) 639-1699 .. **Lauterbach,** R Spencer '93 -151 N Main Bx298 -New Cty 10956 **Fx:**639-5352
(631) 928-1430 .. **Lauto,** Paul A '91 (P Lauto,PLLC) -Bx554 -Miller Pl 11764 **Fx:**928-1431
(631) 864-4100 .. **Lauto,** Robt D '86 -218 Main -E Setauket 11733 **Fx:**864-3786
(212) 870-2320 .. **Lautt,** Ruth '93 Fair Witness -475 Riverside Dr -NY 10115
(212) 335-4500 .. **Lauvaux,** Alexandra '03 %DLA Piper LLP -1251 Av of Amer -NY 10020
(516) 229-4590 .. **Lauzon,** Gail S '90 -875 Merrick Av -Westbury 11590
(718) 505-1955 .. **Lava,** Brian R '93 -9131 Qns Blvd -Elmhrst 11373 **Fx:**505-9866
(516) 902-0574 .. **Lava,** Marvin S '63 -648 Balfour Pl -Melvll 11747
(212) 872-6820 .. **Lavadera,** Frank M '84 %KPMG LLP -345 Park Av -NY 10154
(212) 770-3665 .. **LaVaglia,** Frank A '95 %AIG -70 Pine -NY 10270
(212) 603-6300 .. **Lavaia,** Marc A '02 %Robinson BLGG&G PC -875 3rd Av -NY 10022
(212) 878-8000 .. **Lavail,** Sabrina '09 %Clifford C LLP -31 W 52nd -NY 10019
(315) 435-2470 .. **Lavalas,** Romana A '01 %DA -505 S State -Syracuse 13202 **Fx:**435-3969
(315) 488-0044 .. **LaValle,** Anthony C '84 -2103 Milton Av -Syracuse 13209
(516) 794-3500 .. **Lavalle,** Dennis P '74 (Brunetti A&T,PLLC) -170 Old Cntry Rd -Mineola 11501 **Fx:**794-3696
(631) 331-5800 .. **La Valle,** John J '94 (J La Valle,PC) -9 Eagle Lndg -Mt Sinai 11766 **Fx:**331-3550
(718) 848-4000 .. **LaValle,** Kenneth '91 -36-16 30th Av -Astoria 11103
(631) 727-2180 .. **LaValle,** Kenneth P '93 OfCnsl Twomey LSKD&Q,LLP -33 W 2nd Bx9398 -Rvrhead 11901
(718) 777-0078 .. **LaValle,** Rita Mougias '88 -36-16 30th Av -Astoria 11103 **Fx:**777-0177
(631) 569-2320 .. **LaValle,** Ronald F '92 -205 N Ocean Av -Patchogue 11772
(718) 777-0078 .. **LaValle,** Wm J '92 -36-16 30th Av -Astoria 11103 **Fx:**777-0177
(716) 855-5320 .. **LaVallee,** Diane M '84 NYS Dept of Taxation -77 Bway -Buffalo 14203
(516) 756-5100 .. **Lavallee,** Keith A '89 -4 West Gate Rd -Farmngdl 11735 **Fx:**756-4629
(516) 845-4900 .. **Lavallee,** Raymond G '60 -4 W Gate Rd -Farmngdl 11735 **Fx:**845-7089
(631) 851-9500 .. **Lavallee,** Thos J '89 -490 Wheeler Rd -Hauppauge 11788 **Fx:**851-9140
(212) 421-9630 .. **LaVallee,** Traci A '01 %Smythe Masterson & Judd -230 Park Av -NY 10169 **Fx:**421-9665
(212) 408-5100 .. **Lavallo,** Jocelyn E '06 %Chadbourne & P LLP -30 Rckfllr Plz -NY 10112
(212) 442-5884 .. **Lavandeira,** Barbara A '91 Dept Youth & Comm Dvlpmnt -156 William -NY 10038
(315) 422-7111 .. **LaVaute,** James R '73 (Blitman & K LLP) -443 N Franklin -Syracuse 13204
(516) 739-8111 .. **Lavelle,** Dominick W '91 -38 Willis Av -Mineola 11501 **Fx:**739-3917
(516) 739-8111 .. **Lavelle,** Emily K '07 D Lavelle -38 Willis Av -Mineola 11501 **Fx:**739-3917
(518) 869-6227 .. **Lavelle & Finn,LLP** -29 British Amer Blvd -Latham 12110 **Fx:**869-0572
(607) 432-3333 .. **Lavelle & Finn,LLP** -22-26 Watkins Av -Oneonta 13820 **Fx:**(518) 869-0572
(516) 739-8111 .. **Lavelle,** John E '05 %D Lavelle -38 Willis Av -Mineola 11501 **Fx:**739-3917
(518) 869-6227 .. **Lavelle,** John H '82 (Lavelle & F,LLP) -29 British Amer Blvd -Latham 12110
(212) 839-5300 .. **Lavelle,** John J '96 (Sidley A LLP) -787 7th Av -NY 10019
(212) 360-1335 .. **LaVelle,** Laura M '00 %Dept of Parks & Rec -The Arsenal Cntrl Pk -NY 10065 **Fx:**360-1373
(631) 475-0001 .. **LaVelle,** Wm T '88 (LaVelle & M,LLP) -57 E Main -Patchogue 11772 **Fx:**447-7150
(516) 513-1830 .. **Laveman,** Robin S '87 -445 Broadhllw Rd -Melvll 11747 **Fx:**827-5632
(212) 552-3939 .. **Lavena,** Maria S '06 J P Morgan Chase -1 Chase Manh Plz -NY 10005
(212) 541-2000 .. **Lavender,** Bradford B '95 (Bryan C LLP) -1290 Av of Amer -NY 10104
(718) 643-6555 .. **Lavender,** Philip J '96 %Marcus Attys -13 Greene Av -Brklyn 11238 **Fx:**643-9111
(585) 678-7231 .. **LaVerdi,** Barbara J '83 Constellation Brands,Inc -270 Hgh Pnt Dr -Victor 14564 **Fx:**678-7112
(212) 909-6000 .. **LaVerghetta,** Dino L '07 %Debevoise & P LLP -919 3rd Av -NY 10022
(212) 506-5000 .. **Laveris,** Nicholas A '89 %Orrick H&S LLP -51 W 52nd -NY 10019
(212) 715-9100 .. **LaVerne,** Darren A '05 %Kramer LN&F,LLP -1177 Av of Amer -NY 10036
(585) 546-5960 .. **Laverne & Hanks** -36 Main W -Rchstr 14614 **Fx:**546-6389
(212) 848-8172 .. **Laverriere,** Kenneth J '88 (Shearman & S LLP) -599 Lex Av -NY 10022
(212) 248-8800 .. **Lavery,** Jason J '03 %Callan KB&B LLP -1 Whitehall -NY 10004
(518) 357-2068 .. **Lavery,** Karen McKenzie '99 DEC -1150 N Westcott Rd -Schnctdy 12306 **Fx:**357-2087
(585) 428-2020 .. **Lavery,** Margaret J '08 Monroe Cnty Surrogates Ct -99 Exchange Blvd -Rchstr 14614
(212) 691-2356 .. **Lavery,** Michl J '73 -106 Perry -NY 10014 **Fx:**(801) 705-2574
(917) 922-6503 .. **Lavery,** Peter G '00 -Croton-On-Hud 10520 **Fx:**(309) 420-8278
(212) 351-4000 .. **Lavery,** Rachel A '07 %Gibson D&C LLP -200 Park Av -NY 10166
(516) 327-3000 .. **Lavery,** Thos E '78 Astoria Fed Svngs & Loan -1 Astoria Fed Plz -Lk Success 11042 **Fx:**327-7756
(518) 266-1000 .. **Lavery,** Thos E '97 %Pattison SG&G,PC -22 1st Bx208 -Troy 12181
(212) 425-7200 .. **Lavery,** Thos F '08 %Kenyon & K,LLP -1 Bway -NY 10004
(518) 402-6757 .. **Lavery,** Timothy E '93 %Workers Comp Bd -20 Park -Albany 12207
(212) 335-9000 .. **Laveson,** Sharon S '03 %DA -1 Hogan Pl -NY 10013
(212) 790-4500 .. **Lavie,** Jennifer Deitch '02 %Manatt P&P,LLP -7 Times Sq -NY 10036
(212) 697-3122 .. **Lavietes,** Steven A '86 (Martin C&B LLP) -220 E 42nd -NY 10017
(212) 412-1479 .. **LaVigne,** Angela Roxas '04 Barclays Capital -200 Park Av -NY 10166
(212) 637-2325 .. **Lavigne,** Christopher L '03 %US Atty -1 St Andrews Plz -NY 10007
(212) 735-3000 .. **Lavigne,** Christopher N '10 %Skadden ASM&F LLP -4 Times Sq -NY 10036
(212) 813-8800 .. **LaVigne,** Peter W '79 (Goodwin P LLP) -620 8th Av -NY 10018
(212) 891-0715 .. **Lavin,** Benjamin '79 %FOJP Srvc Corp -28 E 28th -NY 10016 **Fx:**308-3911
(212) 753-7500 .. **Lavin,** Brian C '03 %Hartman & C LLP -488 Mad Av -NY 10022
(212) 373-3000 .. **Lavin,** Brian C '08 %Paul WRW&G LLP -1285 Av of Amer -NY 10019

(212) 806-5400 .. **Lavin,** Howard S '83 (Stroock &S&L LLP) -180 Maiden Ln -NY 10038
(212) 728-8000 .. **Lavin,** Jamie L '08 %Willkie F&G LLP -787 7th Av -NY 10019
(716) 856-1289 .. **Lavin,** John J '79 (Lavin & K) -528 Brisbane Bldg -Buffalo 14203 **Fx:**856-8808
(212) 319-6898 .. **Lavin O'Neil Ricci Cedrone & DiSipio** -420 Lex Av -NY 10170 **Fx:**319-6932
(212) 603-6300 .. **Lavin,** Scott A '97 (Robinson BLGG&G PC) -875 3rd Av -NY 10022
(212) 483-9490 .. **Lavin,** Stanley '52 OfCnsl McElroy DM&C,LLP -88 Pine -NY 10005
(718) 829-7400 .. **Lavin,** Thos J Jr. '84 -2980 Bruckner Blvd -Bronx 10465 **Fx:**829-7356
(516) 498-8830 .. **Lavin,** Thos J '92 (Narotsky & L,LLP) -60 Cuttermill Rd -Gt Neck 11021
(518) 445-2311 .. **Lavine,** Amy M '08 Albany Law Schl -80 New Scotland Av -Albany 12208 **Fx:**445-2315
(516) 676-0050 .. **Lavine,** Chas D '73 NYS Assembly -70 Glen -Glen Cove 11542 **Fx:**676-0071
(315) 422-1391 .. **Lavine,** Gary J '79 OfCnsl Green & S,PLLC -One Lincoln Ctr #900 -Syracuse 13202
(212) 577-3688 .. **Lavine,** Jos '87 %Leg Aid -199 Water -NY 10038 **Fx:**509-8431
(212) 645-1849 .. **Lavine,** Rachel '99 -37 W 12th -NY 10011 **Fx:**675-1967
(212) 234-1999 .. **Lavinger,** Michl B '91 Medilex -69 E 130th -NY 10037 **Fx:**234-8999
(212) 227-2780 .. **Lavinsky,** Roger N '85 %Jaroslawicz & J -225 Bway -NY 10007
(631) 689-2950 .. **LaVita,** Ronald J '84 -194 Main -E Setauket 11733 **Fx:**751-1205
(212) 852-3543 .. **Lavner,** Steven '81 %US Trust Co,NA -114 W 47th -NY 10036 **Fx:**852-1310
(212) 506-3900 .. **Lavoie,** Danl R '95 (Steptoe & J LLP) -750 7th Av -NY 10019
(631) 232-0200 .. **Lavoie,** Suzanne '99 %Fumuso KDSS&F,LLP -110 Marcus Blvd -Hauppauge 11788
(212) 455-2000 .. **Lavon-Krein,** Danl '07 %Simpson T&B LLP -425 Lex Av -NY 10017
(518) 561-8657 .. **Lavorando,** Jos '81 -30 Clinton -Plattsbrgh 12901 **Fx:**561-1443
(631) 376-1301 .. **Lavorata,** Richd Jr. '85 -101 N Wellwood Av -Lindenhrst 11757 **Fx:**376-2347
(212) 362-2450 .. **Lavori,** Nora '77 -100 W 80th -NY 10024
(631) 737-4110 .. **Lavrenchik,** Peter G '96 %Gruenberg & K,PC -3275 Vets Mem'l Hwy -Ronkonkoma 11779 **Fx:**737-4155
(212) 848-4000 .. **Lavu,** Sheila '09 %Shearman & S LLP -599 Lex Av -NY 10022
(212) 883-4900 .. **Law,** Chas B '87 (Cozen O) -277 Park Av -NY 10172
(518) 381-4651 .. **Law,** Donna J '85 -1537 Grenoside Av -Niskayuna 12309
(212) 310-8000 .. **Law,** Erin J '00 %Weil G&M LLP -767 5th Av -NY 10153
(212) 294-6700 .. **Law,** Howard A IV '10 %Winston & S -200 Park Av -NY 10166
(917) 699-8796 .. **Law,** Jonathan K H '09 McKinsey & Co -55 E 52nd -NY 10055
(212) 474-1000 .. **Law,** Joyce Y M '98 %Cravath S&M LLP -825 8th Av -NY 10019
(646) 701-4680 .. **Law,** Karine '07 (Puygrenier & L LLP) -1699 Lex Av -NY 10029 **Fx:**(800) 616-0253
(212) 689-4800 .. **Law,** Katharine S '75 -150 E 37th -NY 10016 **Fx:**689-0926
(914) 755-6839 .. **Law,** Kenneth D '85 -240 North Av -New Rchll 10801
(212) 715-9100 .. **Law,** Kerri Ann '96 (Kramer LN&F,LLP) -1177 Av of Amer -NY 10036
(518) 457-2070 .. **Law,** Kevin R '96 %Dept of Tax & Fin -Bldg 9 State Campus -Albany 12227 **Fx:**457-6131
(516) 222-7700 .. **Law,** Kevin S '88 %LI Power Auth -333 Earle Ovngton Blvd -Uniondale 11553 **Fx:**222-9137
(585) 238-2000 .. **Law,** Michl R '76 (Phillips L LLP) -1400 First Fed Plz -Rchstr 14614
(212) 809-7800 .. **Law,** Raymond '06 %Jaffe & K,LLP -40 Wall -NY 10005
(914) 273-5125 .. **Law,** Robt H III '52 -80 Business Park Dr -Armonk 10504 **Fx:**273-5127
(518) 438-2858 .. **Law,** Robt T III '79 -3 Atrium Dr -Albany 12205 **Fx:**453-8385
(518) 761-9200 .. **Law,** Walter J '66 -266 South Bx2325 -Glens Fls 12801 **Fx:**761-9200
(585) 232-6500 .. **Law,** Wm L III '09 %Harter S&E LLP -1600 Bausch & Lomb Pl -Rchstr 14604
(212) 365-4406 .. **Lawal,** Fatai O '05 -233 5th Av -NY 10016 **Fx:**213-3152
(914) 948-7000 .. **Lawall,** Dara J '09 %Keidel W&C LLP -925 Wstchstr Av -White Plns 10604
(212) 297-5800 .. **Lawatsch,** Frank E Jr. '69 (Day P LLP) -7 Times Sq -NY 10036
(516) 741-2666 .. **Lawler,** Albert K '78 (Lally M&R LLP) -220 Old Cntry Rd -Mineola 11501
(212) 415-3600 .. **Lawler,** Andrea G '99 %Omnicom Group -437 Mad Av -NY 10022 **Fx:**415-3530
(212) 832-3160 .. **Lawler,** Andrew M '61 (A Lawler,PC) -641 Lex Av -NY 10022 **Fx:**832-3158
(212) 988-1130 .. **Lawler,** Patricia R '91 -234 E 72nd -NY 10021 **Fx:**988-7418
(212) 294-6700 .. **Lawler,** Richd F '74 (Winston & S) -200 Park Av -NY 10166
(212) 696-4848 .. **Lawler,** Ryan W '05 %Mintz & G LLP -470 Park Av S -NY 10016
(212) 576-7000 .. **Lawler Kilgallen,** Clare '98 NY Life Ins -51 Mad Av -NY 10010 **Fx:**576-4492
(212) 252-0300 .. **Lawless,** Fran I '87 (Kagan LLLG&C,LLP) -200 Mad Av -NY 10016
(718) 843-7584 .. **Lawless,** John J '76 %Ragano & R -110-15 Lbrty Av -S Richmond Hll 11419
(212) 754-0665 .. **Lawless,** Mark J '73 -250 W 57th -NY 10107
(631) 864-4460 .. **Lawless,** Meaghan '08 Primary Land Srvcs LLC -368 Vets Mem'l Hwy -Commack 11725
(212) 417-7018 .. **Lawless,** Monica R '91 %Brookfield Fncl Prop -3 World Fncl Ctr -NY 10281
(212) 490-3000 .. **Lawless,** Patrick J '01 OfCnsl Wilson EME&D LLP -150 E 42nd -NY 10017
(315) 445-8550 .. **Lawless,** Patrick T '94 %Widewaters Grp -5786 Widewaters Pkwy Bx3 -DeWitt 13214 **Fx:**445-8570
(516) 746-0707 .. **Lawless,** Paul '93 %Hammill OCDP&K,PC -6851 Jericho Tpk -Syosset 11791
(212) 759-8203 .. **Lawless,** Robt T '88 (Hedinger & L) -110 Wall -NY 10005
(212) 382-3300 .. **Lawlor,** James N '93 (Wollmuth M&D LLP) -500 5th Av -NY 10110
(516) 248-7700 .. **Lawlor,** John E '85 -129 3rd -Mineola 11501 **Fx:**742-7675
(315) 437-7600 .. **Lawlor,** Miles G '91 (Ferrara FLB&R,PC) -5010 Campuswood Dr -E Syracuse 13057
(518) 457-4380 .. **Lawlor,** Shannon J '08 Dept of Labor -State Campus Bldg 12 -Albany 12240 **Fx:**485-1819
(631) 844-2513 .. **Lawlor,** Susan W '88 %Vytra Health Plans -395 N Srvc Rd -Melvll 11747 **Fx:**719-0399
(516) 296-1000 .. **Lawlor,** Tammy R '97 (Miller & M,PC) -100 Q Roosevelt Blvd -Gdn Cty 11530 **Fx:**296-1030
(212) 875-7921 .. **Lawlor,** Todd D '99 (Lawlor & R LLP) -551 Fifth Av -NY 10176 **Fx:**712-8855
(201) 387-9090 .. **Lawn,** Lawr E '83 -236 Port Ben Rd Bx281 -Wawarsing 12489 **Fx:**387-9330
(914) 355-4151 .. **Lawner,** Ivan '83 -29 Lakevw Rd -New Rchll 10804 **Fx:**355-4152
(212) 715-1000 .. **Lawrence,** Alan W '91 (Arnold & P LLP) -399 Park Av -NY 10022
(518) 587-2100 .. **Lawrence,** Albert B '82 %Empire State Cllg -111 West Av -Saratoga Spgs 12866
(631) 423-7500 .. **Lawrence,** Andrew W '74 (Lawrence & L) -23 Green -Huntngtn 11743 **Fx:**423-7573
(212) 735-3000 .. **Lawrence,** Barbara J '94 Cnsl Skadden ASM&F LLP -4 Times Sq -NY 10036
(212) 806-5400 .. **Lawrence,** Brett '95 (Stroock &S&L LLP) -180 Maiden Ln -NY 10038
(718) 625-8940 .. **Lawrence,** Bruce A '85 -15 Metrotech Ctr N -Brklyn 11201 **Fx:**624-5756
(585) 232-5300 .. **Lawrence,** C Bruce '70 (Boylan BCV&W,LLP) -2400 Chase Sq -Rchstr 14604
(631) 423-7500 .. **Lawrence,** Carl M '83 (Lawrence & L) -23 Green -Huntngtn 11743 **Fx:**423-7573
(212) 859-8000 .. **Lawrence,** Carmen J '82 (Fried FHS&J LLP) -1 NY Plz -NY 10004
(212) 349-8173 .. **Lawrence,** David D F '88 (Durkin & D) -111 Bway -NY 10006 **Fx:**285-1968
(212) 416-8023 .. **Lawrence,** David III '98 %Dept of Law -120 Bway -NY 10271 **Fx:**416-8092
(718) 746-0500 .. **Lawrence,** David J '89 -25-77 F Lewis Blvd -Flushng 11358
(212) 902-0295 .. **Lawrence,** David N '81 Goldman Sachs -85 Broad -NY 10004
(347) 866-1243 .. **Lawrence,** David S '95 -110 Wall -NY 10005
(914) 725-4808 .. **Lawrence,** Donald L '59 -670 Post Rd -Scarsdale 10583
(631) 755-0101 .. **Lawrence,** Erin M '06 %Lewis JAA,LLP -425 Broad Hollow Rd -Melvll 11747
(718) 625-1620 .. **Lawrence,** Evelyn R '45 -1433 72nd -Brklyn 11228
(718) 746-1941 .. **Lawrence,** George P '91 -149-25 11th Av -Whitestone 11357
(914) 997-0500 .. **Lawrence,** Gerald '06 (Lowey DC&H,PC) -1 N Bway -White Plns 10601
(585) 243-7590 .. **Lawrence,** Gordon J II '85 Family Ct -2 Court -Geneseo 14454
(212) 599-0900 .. **Lawrence,** Guy A '83 (Bower & L,PC) -261 Mad Av -NY 10016
(212) 468-8000 .. **Lawrence,** J Alexander '02 (Morrison & F LLP) -1290 Av of Amer -NY 10104
(212) 547-5400 .. **Lawrence,** Jennifer B '09 %McDermott W&E LLP -340 Mad Av -NY 10173
(516) 746-6423 .. **Lawrence,** John '75 -190 Willis Av -Mineola 11501
(212) 351-4000 .. **Lawrence,** John E '09 %Gibson D&C LLP -200 Park Av -NY 10166
(716) 856-4000 .. **Lawrence,** Joshua K '08 %Hodgson R LLP -140 Pearl -Buffalo 14202
(718) 250-0400 .. **Lawrence,** Karen L '92 %R Tusa -1 MetroTech Ctr -Brklyn 11201 **Fx:**250-0591
(212) 872-1000 .. **Lawrence,** Kathleen O'Malley '10 -One Bryant Park -NY 10036 **Fx:**872-1002
(914) 946-5900 .. **Lawrence,** Kerry A '90 (Briccetti C&L,LLP) -81 Main -White Plns 10601
(518) 486-7815 .. **Lawrence,** Kerry-Ann N '06 Ins Dept -1 Commerce Plz -Albany 12257
(716) 855-2800 .. **Lawrence,** Kris E '96 %Mura & S,PLLC -14 Lafayette Sq #930 -Buffalo 14203
(516) 873-2000 .. **Lawrence,** Kyle '07 %Moritt HH&H LLP -400 Grdn City Plz -Gdn Cty 11530
(516) 538-2400 .. **Lawrence,** Lawr S '71 (Lawrence and W,PC) -215 Hilton Av Bx1200 -Hempstd 11551
(585) 325-7455 .. **Lawrence,** Martin L '58 OfCnsl Philippone Law Ofc,PC -31 E Main -Rchstr 14608 **Fx:**546-6565
(516) 764-7651 .. **Lawrence,** Maryann W '85 -33 Lincoln Ct -Rockvll Ctr 11570
(212) 340-0400 .. **Lawrence,** Meredith S '95 %Appllt Div 1st Dept -27 Mad Av -NY 10010 **Fx:**889-4412
(212) 298-5585 .. **Lawrence,** Mortimer A '86 NYS Senate -250 Bway -NY 10007
(917) 778-6600 .. **Lawrence,** Norman '98 %J Toomey -485 Lex Av -NY 10017 **Fx:**778-7048
(914) 232-1100 .. **Lawrence,** Randall G '87 (R Lawrence & Assoc,PC) -135 Bedford Rd -Katonah 10536 **Fx:**232-2150
(212) 504-6000 .. **Lawrence,** Robt C III '64 (Cadwalader W&T LLP) -1 World Fncl Ctr -NY 10281
(866) 348-5819 .. **Lawrence,** Robt H '77 %SSA-ODAR -50 Fountain Plz -Buffalo 14202 **Fx:**(716) 551-4078
(212) 541-6222 .. **Lawrence,** Robt L '81 (Kane K,PC) -1350 Av of Amer -NY 10019
(631) 694-0033 .. **Lawrence,** Roger B '79 (Lawrence WR&B,PC) -425 Broadhllw Rd -Melvll 11747
(518) 548-2771 .. **Lawrence,** Ronile '79 (Lawrence & S PLLC) -2917 State Route 30 Bx156 -Speculator 12164 **Fx:**548-2447
(212) 541-5996 .. **Lawrence,** Stuart W '07 %Housing Consrvtn Coordinators,Inc -777 10th Av -NY 10019 **Fx:**541-5966
(212) 848-7638 .. **Lawrence,** W Jeffrey '82 (Shearman & S LLP) -599 Lex Av -NY 10022
(516) 538-2400 .. **Lawrence and Walsh,PC** -215 Hilton Av Bx1200 -Hempstd 11551 **Fx:**538-2079
(866) 353-3310 .. **Lawrence,** Wm A '05 %Pannone LD&W LLC -81 Main -White Plns 10606
(212) 588-0800 .. **Lawrence,** Wm F '77 (Frommer L&H LLP) -745 5th Av -NY 10151
(212) 554-1234 .. **Lawrence,** Windy L '03 %AXA Financial Inc -1290 Av of Amer -NY 10104 **Fx:**707-3963
(631) 694-0033 .. **Lawrence Worden Rainis & Bard, PC** -425 Broadhllw Rd -Melvll 11747 **Fx:**694-9331
(212) 364-8221 .. **Lawrence-Apfelbaum,** Marc J '84 %Time Warner Cable -60 Columbus Av -NY 10023 **Fx:**364-8460
(212) 318-6000 .. **Lawrence Athey,** Ann '00 OfCnsl Paul HJ&W LLP -75 E 55th -NY 10022
(914) 686-1700 .. **Laws,** April J '05 %O'Connor R,LLP -200 Mamaroneck Av -White Plns 10601
(212) 973-0572 .. **Laws,** Keyana C '04 %Wolff & S PC -140 Bway -NY 10005
(718) 276-7867 .. **Laws,** Marlo Rene '80 -216-15 120th Av -Cambria Hts 11411
(212) 416-8000 .. **Lawsky,** Benjamin M '97 %Dept of Law -120 Bway -NY 10271

(212) 909-6000 .. **Lawson**, Benjamin T '10 %Debevoise & P LLP -919 3rd Av -NY 10022
(716) 847-0650 .. **Lawson**, Ellen M '85 %Leg Srvcs -237 Main -Buffalo 14203 **Fx**:847-0227
(212) 527-7575 .. **Lawson**, Ernest T '05 %Grover & F,PC -750 3rd Av -NY 10017
(212) 818-9200 .. **Lawson**, Jonathan S '07 %Satterlee SB&B LLP -230 Park Av -NY 10169
(212) 705-7000 .. **Lawson**, Matthew J '05 Cnsl Bingham M LLP -399 Park Av -NY 10022
(718) 928-3700 .. **Lawson**, Theresa D '06 %LSNYC-Bronx -579 Courtlandt Av -Bronx 10451 **Fx**:402-7586
(518) 798-4395 .. **Lawson**, Thos M '52 -62 Wincrest Dr -Queensbury 12804
(212) 267-2555 .. **Lawson**, Tracy J '09 %Bretz & C,LLP -305 Bway -NY 10007
(646) 313-8138 .. **Lawson**, Trisha L '99 Bnk of Amer -1 Bryant Pk -NY 10036
(716) 854-3015 .. **Lawson**, Wm E Jr. '54 (Aaron DS&L,LLP) -43 Court -Buffalo 14202
(315) 422-1391 .. **Lawson Hatch**, Emilee K '09 %Green & S,PLLC -One Lincoln Ctr #900 -Syracuse 13202
(212) 466-7700 .. **Lawton**, Catherine A '85 %Sandler O'Neill & Prtnrs,LP -919 3rd Av -NY 10022 **Fx**:466-7998
(212) 697-3122 .. **Lawton**, Jeff '82 (Martin C&B LLP) -220 E 42nd -NY 10017
(212) 735-3000 .. **Lawton**, Jerome J '68 Cnsl Skadden ASM&F LLP -4 Times Sq -NY 10036
(212) 456-2550 .. **Lawton-Thames**, Lynnore S '07 ABC,Inc -47 W 66th -NY 10023
(518) 694-3592 .. **Lawyer**, Kim C '01 Cnsl Cnty Pub Def -30 Clinton Av -Albany 12207 **Fx**:694-3628
(212) 696-1999 .. **Lax**, Barry R '94 (Lax & N LLP) -1412 Bway -NY 10018
(212) 922-0891 .. **Lax**, Emil '84 (Segal & L) -501 5th Av -NY 10017
(718) 368-5905 .. **Lax**, Jeffrey M '99 Kingsboro Cmmnty Cllg -2001 Oriental Blvd -Brklyn 11235 **Fx**:368-4874
(646) 452-9640 .. **Lax**, Orly '01 Man Investments -1 Rckfllr Plz -NY 10020
(212) 818-9150 .. **Lax**, Robt I '95 R Lax & Assoc -122 E 42nd -NY 10168 **Fx**:818-1266
(718) 250-2000 .. **Laxer**, Nancy E '85 %DA -350 Jay -Brklyn 11201 **Fx**:250-2314
(516) 794-5310 .. **Lay**, Clifford A '05 %Abrams GMB,LLP -125 Jericho Tpk -Jericho 11753
(212) 268-5136 .. **Lay**, Cynthia Molkenthin '07 %Harwood L -350 5th Av -NY 10118
(516) 659-3561 .. **Lay**, Wm D '93 -481 8th Av -NY 10001 **Fx**:(917) 591-9060
(518) 747-3881 .. **Layden**, Leon M '57 (Layden & L) -169 Main Bx168 -Hudson Fls 12839 **Fx**:747-0145
(518) 747-3881 .. **Layden**, Stephen M '95 %Layden & L -169 Main Bx168 -Hudson Fls 12839 **Fx**:747-0145
(212) 455-2000 .. **Layfield**, Danl J '08 %Simpson T&B LLP -425 Lex Av -NY 10017
(516) 354-6444 .. **Laykind**, Marc B '90 -1662 Old Cntry Rd Bx525 -Plainvw 11803 **Fx**:354-6471
(718) 692-4600 .. **Layne**, Alan N '58 -4716 Av N -Brklyn 11234
(212) 237-0000 .. **Layne**, Eliot Ramey '03 %Vinson & E LLP -666 5th Av -NY 10103
(718) 977-7045 .. **Layne**, Erika E '06 Verizon -1 Cross Isl Pkwy -Rosedale 11422
(516) 767-8857 .. **Layne**, Lester E '97 -33 Main -Pt Wash 11050 **Fx**:944-0310
(212) 606-7175 .. **Layne**, Tanya S '03 Sotheby's,Inc -1334 York Av -NY 10021 **Fx**:606-7574
(212) 631-8694 .. **Laytin**, Jeffrey L '70 (Laytin V LLP) -1 Penn Plz -NY 10119 **Fx**:273-4306
(212) 227-1104 .. **Layton**, Paul T '81 -30 Vesey -NY 10007 **Fx**:233-9713
(212) 846-8612 .. **Lazalde**, Virginia Anne '95 MTV Networks -1515 Bway -NY 10036 **Fx**:258-8358
(516) 621-8400 .. **Lazar**, Dennis S '73 -55 Hrbr Pk Dr -Pt Wash 11050
(212) 889-3500 .. **Lazar**, Ethan H '86 %Lazar Grp -419 Park Av S -NY 10016 **Fx**:889-5131
(212) 757-0007 .. **Lazar**, Janet G '80 -888 7th Av -NY 10106 **Fx**:757-0469
(212) 613-1900 .. **Lazar**, Jason M '97 Riese Org Corp Grp -560 5th Av -NY 10036 **Fx**:629-0942
(212) 785-9100 .. **Lazar**, Jillian A '06 %Paduano & W LLP -1251 Av of Amer -NY 10020
(212) 474-1000 .. **Lazar**, John E '05 %Cravath S&M LLP -825 8th Av -NY 10019
(845) 896-9651 .. **Lazar**, Kathryn S '76 (Lazar & S) -280 Route 82 -Hopewell Junct 12533
(212) 867-4488 .. **Lazar**, Larry Z '90 (Moss & K) -122 E 42nd -NY 10168
(212) 598-4520 .. **Lazar**, Melvin E '57 -442 E 20th -NY 10009 **Fx**:598-4520
(718) 265-1500 .. **Lazar**, Ron '95 (Aini & L,PLLC) -2615 Coney Isl Av -Brklyn 11223 **Fx**:265-1515
(212) 438-2000 .. **Lazar**, Ruth E '91 Standard & Poor's -55 Water -NY 10041
(718) 268-4155 .. **Lazar**, Scott A '79 (Barrett L,LLC) -109-01 72nd Rd -Frst Hlls 11375
(212) 245-1000 .. **Lazar**, Wendi '93 OfCnsl Outten & G LLP -3 Park Av -NY 10016
(516) 683-1313 .. **Lazar**, Yael N '96 Y Lazar,PC -585 Stewart Av -Gdn Cty 11530 **Fx**:683-0555
(212) 521-4322 .. **LaZare**, Jill A '00 JA LaZare,LLC -590 Mad Av -NY 10022 **Fx**:521-4099
(212) 758-9300 .. **Lazare Potter & Giacovas LLP** -950 3rd Av -NY 10022 **Fx**:888-0919
(212) 679-4666 .. **Lazare**, Shirley '01 %Frenkel H&S LLP -16 E 34th -NY 10016
(212) 758-9300 .. **Lazare**, Stephen M '86 (Lazare P&G LLP) -950 3rd Av -NY 10022
(212) 788-1203 .. **Lazar-Geliebter**, Stephanie '85 %Law Dept -100 Church -NY 10007 **Fx**:788-0367
(716) 847-0662 .. **Lazarin**, Jessica M '06 Erie Cnty Bar Assn -237 Main -Buffalo 14203
(718) 990-7627 .. **Lazaro**, Christine M '03 %St John's Law Schl -8000 Utopia Pkwy -Jamaica 11439 **Fx**:990-6931
(718) 720-2877 .. **Lazaro**, Debra Ann '95 %Votto & C,LLP -60 Bay -Staten Isl 10310
(212) 504-6000 .. **Lazaroff**, Michl S '97 SpclCnsl Cadwalader W&T LLP -1 World Fncl Ctr -NY 10281
(845) 856-5335 .. **Lazaroff**, Vern '85 -143 Pike Bx1108 -Pt Jervis 12771 **Fx**:856-5340
(518) 877-9250 .. **Lazarow**, Martin S '66 -Bx284 -Clifton Pk 12065 **Fx**:877-9250
(516) 483-4500 .. **Lazarowitz**, Harvey O '60 (Lazarowitz & M,PLLC) -33 Front -Hempstd 11550 **Fx**:483-4511
(718) 531-9700 .. **Lazarowitz & Manganillo,LLP** -2004 Ralph Av -Brklyn 11234 **Fx**:444-5768
(718) 531-9700 .. **Lazarowitz**, Michl S '96 (Lazarowitz & M,LLP) -2004 Ralph Av -Brklyn 11234
(212) 692-1000 .. **Lazaruk**, Kenneth H '83 (Duane M LLP) -1540 Bway -NY 10036
(845) 565-1100 .. **Lazarus**, Aryeh '08 %Tarshis CLM&M,PLLC -One Corwin Ct -Newburgh 12550
(866) 966-5115 .. **Lazarus**, Bruce J '90 -19 E 88th -NY 10128
(718) 590-2000 .. **Lazarus**, David G '06 DA -198 E 161st -Bronx 10451 **Fx**:590-6477
(212) 756-2000 .. **Lazarus**, Donna '07 %Schulte R&Z LLP -919 3rd Av -NY 10022
(845) 947-1100 .. **Lazarus**, Ellen D '09 %Phillips & M,LLP -148 Route 9W -Stony Pnt 10980
(212) 610-6300 .. **Lazarus**, Gary S '03 %Allen & O -1221 Av of Amer -NY 10020
(212) 889-7400 .. **Lazarus**, Gilbert A '89 %Lazarus & L,PC -240 Mad Av -NY 10016 **Fx**:684-0314
(212) 889-7400 .. **Lazarus**, Harlan M '80 (Lazarus & L,PC) -240 Mad Av -NY 10016 **Fx**:684-0314
(212) 557-3600 .. **Lazarus**, Howard J '74 %Tudor Realty -250 Park Av S -NY 10003
(716) 873-9111 .. **Lazarus**, James A '79 (J Lazarus,PLLC) -4242 Ridge Lea Rd -Amherst 14226 **Fx**:873-9119
(212) 836-1487 .. **Lazarus**, Julie M '05 UJA Fed of NY -130 E 59th -NY 10022
(718) 625-9600 .. **Lazarus**, Ksakousti '02 %PL Kamaras -26 Court -Brklyn 11242
(212) 889-7400 .. **Lazarus**, Lester A '46 (Lazarus & L,PC) -240 Mad Av -NY 10016 **Fx**:684-0314
(212) 599-0900 .. **Lazarus**, Lisa K '92 (Bower & L,PC) -261 Mad Av -NY 10016
(718) 881-5600 .. **Lazarus**, Mark D '83 (Lazarus L&W) -3699 Bainbrdg Av -Bronx 10467 **Fx**:881-5666
(212) 558-4000 .. **Lazarus**, Meredith L '10 %Sullivan & C LLP -125 Broad -NY 10004
(718) 298-1053 .. **Lazarus**, Richd H '78 Supreme Ct -88-11 Sutphin Blvd -Jamaica 11435
(212) 302-5252 .. **Lazarus**, Scott R '91 (Lazarus & H LLP) -561 7th Av -NY 10018 **Fx**:302-8181
(212) 381-5364 .. **Lazarus**, Theo P '02 DoubleClick -111 8th -NY 10011
(212) 969-3000 .. **Lazatin**, Christine Garin '06 %Proskauer R LLP -1585 Bway -NY 10036
(646) 312-8712 .. **Lazebnik**, Ron '06 %Fordham Law Schl -33 W 60th -NY 10023
(716) 847-7187 .. **Lazelle**, Jeanette '99 Dept Labor-Div Labor Stndrds -65 Court -Buffalo 14202
(716) 633-6500 .. **Lazenski**, David P Sr. '78 W Moran & Assoc,PC -6500 Main -Williamsvll 14221 **Fx**:633-3370
(631) 761-0800 .. **Lazer Aptheker Rosella & Yedid,PC** -225 Old Cntry Rd -Melvll 11747 **Fx**:761-0015
(631) 761-0800 .. **Lazer**, David '81 (Lazer AR&Y,PC) -225 Old Cntry Rd -Melvll 11747
(631) 761-0800 .. **Lazer**, Leon D '48 OfCnsl Lazer AR&Y,PC -225 Old Cntry Rd -Melvll 11747
(631) 761-7000 .. **Lazer**, Leon D '48 %Touro Cllg Law Ctr -225 Eastvw Dr -Central Islip 11722
(212) 361-1400 .. **Lazerson**, Vivian T '81 %Envrnmntl Cntrl Brd -66 John -NY 10038 **Fx**:361-1900
(212) 652-3783 .. **Lazetera**, Lianne '88 (Schlesinger G&L LLP) -535 Mad Av -NY 10022
(212) 270-7260 .. **Lazio**, Enrico A '84 JP Morgan Chase -270 Park Av -NY 10017
(212) 547-5400 .. **Lazo**, Christiana M '07 %McDermott W&E LLP -340 Mad Av -NY 10173
(212) 408-2500 .. **Lazo**, Jennifer A '09 %Baker B,LLP -30 Rckfllr Plz -NY 10112
(718) 531-1478 .. **Lazofsky**, Miriam '56 -103-14 Av M -Brklyn 11236 **Fx**:251-2155
(716) 856-8811 .. **Lazroe**, Jeffrey A '72 -410 Main -Buffalo 14202 **Fx**:408-5594
(716) 856-8811 .. **Lazroe**, Matthew A '06 -410 Main -Buffalo 14202
(518) 473-5671 .. **Lazzari**, Livio '83 %Div of Parole -97 Central Av -Albany 12206 **Fx**:473-6037
(212) 735-3000 .. **Lazzarini**, Shannon T '06 %Skadden ASM&F LLP -4 Times Sq -NY 10036
(718) 488-1900 .. **Lazzaro & Gregory,PC** -360 Court -Brklyn 11231 **Fx**:488-1927
(718) 488-1900 .. **Lazzaro**, Lance '88 (Lazzaro & G,PC) -360 Court -Brklyn 11231
(718) 488-1900 .. **Lazzaro**, Randall C '92 (Lazzaro & G,PC) -360 Court -Brklyn 11231
(212) 951-6400 .. **Lazzaro**, Stephen J '75 %Dept of Education -475 Park Av S -NY 10016 **Fx**:951-6465
(914) 328-0404 .. **Lazzarotti**, Jos J '03 (Jackson L LLP) -1 N Bway -White Plns 10601
(212) 773-3000 .. **Le**, Andy '06 Ernst & Young -5 Times Sq -NY 10036
(212) 878-8000 .. **Le**, Augustin H '08 %Clifford C LLP -31 W 52nd -NY 10019
(212) 883-1700 .. **Le**, Carol Kim '05 %Duval & S LLP -101 Park Av -NY 10178
(212) 565-3074 .. **Le**, Julia N '07 Google Inc -76 9th Av -NY 10011
(212) 310-8000 .. **Le**, Kathy '08 %Weil G&M LLP -767 5th Av -NY 10153
(914) 948-1200 .. **Le**, Lam Dinh '08 %Cerussi & S,PC -1 N Lex Av -White Plns 10601
(212) 269-0927 .. **Le**, Megan M '03 %D'Amato & L,LLP -2 World Fncl Ctr -NY 10281
(212) 218-2100 .. **Le**, Steven K '08 %Fitzpatrick CH&S -1290 Av of Amer -NY 10104
(212) 878-8000 .. **Le**, Taylor T '06 %Clifford C LLP -31 W 52nd -NY 10019
(212) 230-8800 .. **Le**, Tuongvy Thi '09 %WilmerHale -399 Park Av -NY 10022
(212) 506-1700 .. **Lea**, Deborah J '02 Kasowitz BT&F LLP -1633 Bway -NY 10019
(212) 662-3003 .. **Leach**, Brenda Lee '94 -2753 Bway -NY 10025
(212) 264-0336 .. **Leach**, David E III '77 %NLRB -26 Fed Plz -NY 10278 **Fx**:264-8427
(315) 413-5400 .. **Leach**, David E '91 (Goldberg S LLP) -5789 Widewaters Pkwy -Syracuse 13214
(516) 357-3700 .. **Leach**, Judith E '04 %Cullen and D LLP -100 Q Roosevelt Blvd -Gdn Cty 11530
(212) 416-8000 .. **Leach**, Leslie G '82 %Dept of Law -120 Bway -NY 10271
(212) 404-5777 .. **Leach**, Romelia S '07 %Littleton JUP&K LLP -39 Bway -NY 10006
(212) 593-6700 .. **Leacy**, Rosanne '87 OfCnsl Aaronson RF&D,LLP -757 3rd Av -NY 10017
(716) 631-0463 .. **Leader**, Bennett '57 -5792 Main -Williamsvll 14221 **Fx**:631-0477
(212) 486-2400 .. **Leader & Berkon LLP** -630 3rd Av -NY 10017 **Fx**:486-3099
(315) 287-2000 .. **Leader**, Henry J '88 (Case & L LLP) -107 E Main Bx13 -Gouverneur 13642
(212) 346-4675 .. **Leader**, Howard '82 -111 Bway -NY 10006
(212) 508-6700 .. **Leader**, Jaclyn J '08 %Tannenbaum HS&H LLP -900 3rd Av -NY 10022
(212) 486-2400 .. **Leader**, James K '72 (Leader & B LLP) -630 3rd Av -NY 10017
(212) 969-3000 .. **Leader**, Jordan B '00 %Proskauer R LLP -1585 Bway -NY 10036
(212) 486-2400 .. **Leader**, Joshua K '97 (Leader & B LLP) -630 3rd Av -NY 10017
(646) 246-3535 .. **Leader**, Rhonda E '87 DOC -249-04 60th Av -Little Neck 11362
(315) 287-2000 .. **Leader**, Robt J '63 (Case & L LLP) -107 E Main Bx13 -Gouverneur 13642
(212) 964-6611 .. **Leader**, Robyn J '01 %Lester SK&D -120 Bway -NY 10271
(212) 661-7300 .. **Leaderman**, Ian C '04 %Malapero & P LLP -295 Mad Av -NY 10017
(212) 408-2500 .. **Leaf**, Marc A '85 (Baker B,LLP) -30 Rckfllr Plz -NY 10112
(212) 728-8000 .. **Leaf**, Russell L '01 (Willkie F&G LLP) -787 7th Av -NY 10019

(212) 728-8000 .. **Leaf,** Saml M '98 %Willkie F&G LLP -787 7th Av -NY 10019
(212) 355-4390 .. **Leaf,** Shalom '89 -600 Mad Av -NY 10022
(718) 353-8830 .. **Leagh,** John J '88 Leagh & Assoc,PLLC -136-20 38th Av -Flushng 11354 **Fx:**353-6540
(631) 231-2183 .. **Leahey,** Anne E '79 %Dept of Law -300 Motor Pkwy -Hauppauge 11788 **Fx:**435-4757
(212) 269-7308 .. **Leahey & Johnson PC** -120 Wall -NY 10005 **Fx:**422-4751
(212) 326-3939 .. **Leahey,** Phineas E '03 %Jones D -222 E 41st -NY 10017
(212) 590-7798 .. **Leahey,** Shane E '01 Omnicommedia Grp -11 Mad Av -NY 10010
(516) 873-6200 .. **Leahy,** Diana M '81 %R Macchia & Assoc -98 Front -Mineola 11501 **Fx:**873-1611
(212) 852-3741 .. **Leahy,** Harriet F '76 %US Trust Co,NA -114 W 47th -NY 10036 **Fx:**852-1310
(212) 553-0300 .. **Leahy,** James M '90 %Moody's Invstr Srvc -250 Greenwich -NY 10007
(516) 762-0022 .. **Leahy,** Jennifer A '01 JA Leahy,PLLC -68 S Srvc Rd -Melvll 11747 **Fx:**977-1776
(718) 283-7019 .. **Leahy,** Joyce A '79 (Maimonides Med Ctr) -4802 10th Av -Brklyn 11219 **Fx:**283-7180
(212) 458-7040 .. **Leahy,** Michl W '99 AIG -175 Water -NY 10038
(212) 436-1146 .. **Leahy,** Patrick T '77 IRS -290 Bway -NY 10007 **Fx:**436-1063
(516) 229-4200 .. **Leahy,** Richd C '62 %Mendolia & S -875 Merrick Av -Westbury 11590
(718) 590-2000 .. **Leahy,** Thos L '81 %DA -198 E 161st -Bronx 10451 **Fx:**590-6477
(518) 474-7330 .. **Leahy-Scott,** Catherine E '88 %Dept of Law -The Cptl -Albany 12224
(718) 579-3047 .. **Leak,** Felicia G '84 Leg Aid -1020 Grnd Cncrs -Bronx 10451 **Fx:**588-2611
(212) 833-5088 .. **Leak,** G Wade '91 Sony BMG Music Entrtnmnt -550 Mad Av -NY 10022 **Fx:**833-8406
(212) 326-3939 .. **Leake,** Paul D '89 (Jones D) -222 E 41st -NY 10017
(212) 787-7760 .. **Leal,** Enrique A '95 -2463 Bway -NY 10025 **Fx:**787-6237
(718) 655-2900 .. **Leal,** Fernando M '01 %Belovin & F -2311 Wht Plns Rd -Bronx 10467
(518) 431-6700 .. **Leaman,** Alice W '04 %Manatt P&P,LLP -30 S Pearl -Albany 12207
(212) 504-6000 .. **Leamon,** James David '07 %Cadwalader W&T LLP -1 World Fncl Ctr -NY 10281
(631) 577-7770 .. **Leandre,** Jacques M '99 %K Dodson -100 Baylis Rd -Melvll 11747 **Fx:**577-7199
(212) 588-0022 .. **Leaness,** Chas G '84 OfCnsl Sanders OV&R -501 Mad Av -NY 10022
(212) 406-3911 .. **Leanza & Agrapidis,PC** -521 5th Av -NY 10175
(212) 406-3911 .. **Leanza,** Frank M '84 (Leanza & A,PC) -521 5th Av -NY 10175
(516) 747-9700 .. **Learn,** Jeffrey A '00 %Ryan & H,PC -1 Old Cntry Rd -Carle Pl 11514
(607) 734-9254 .. **Learned,** Norman J III '85 -928 W Gray -Elmira 14905
(607) 734-1519 .. **Learned,** Philip C '61 (Learned RL&H,LLP) -449 E Water -Elmira 14901
(607) 734-1519 .. **Learned Reilly Learned & Hughes,LLP** -449 E Water -Elmira 14901 **Fx:**734-1880
(607) 734-1519 .. **Learned,** Scott J '81 (Learned RL&H,LLP) -449 E Water -Elmira 14901
(845) 896-2229 .. **Leary,** Danl F '86 (Cuddy & F LLP) -300 Westage Business Ctr -Fishkill 12524
(518) 432-9700 .. **Leary,** Gerald P '97 (Balzer & L,PLLC) -275½ Lark -Albany 12210 **Fx:**432-9722
(518) 474-6740 .. **Leary,** James W '07 %Dept of State -41 State -Albany 12231 **Fx:**473-9211
(212) 967-1800 .. **Leary,** Jennifer C '03 OfCnsl Bryant BJ&R LLP -140 Bway -NY 10005
(518) 489-9423 .. **Leary,** Linda S '83 (D Zee,PC) -1 Winners Cir -Albany 12205 **Fx:**489-9429
(585) 392-3152 .. **Leary,** Mary G '93 -507 North Av -Hilton 14468
(518) 474-7154 .. **Leary,** Maureen F '83 %Dept of Law -The Cptl -Albany 12224
(212) 365-6565 .. **Leary,** Patrick W '99 %Promontory Fncl Grp -280 Park Av -NY 10017 **Fx:**365-6580
(716) 853-3801 .. **Leary,** Robt D '84 (Kenney SL&N,LLP) -14 Lafayette Sq -Buffalo 14203
(212) 309-8200 .. **Leary,** Robt G '87 ING Invstmnt Mgmt -230 Park Av -NY 10169
(212) 412-6720 .. **Leas,** Bret E '02 Barclays Capital Inc -200 Park Av -NY 10166
(212) 421-2150 .. **Leas,** Christine M '97 (Sive P&R,PC) -460 Park Av -NY 10022
(914) 723-7373 .. **Lease,** Michl M '82 -455 Cntrl Pk Av -Scarsdale 10583 **Fx:**723-7637
(914) 288-0022 .. **Leason,** David G '93 (Leason E LLP) -81 Main -White Plns 10601
(914) 288-0022 .. **Leason Ellis LLP** -81 Main -White Plns 10601 **Fx:**288-0023
(607) 748-7351 .. **Leasure Gow Munk & Rizzuto** -101 Jffrsn Av -Endicott 13760 **Fx:**748-2790
(315) 476-9433 .. **Leasure,** Virginia A '87 -401 Crossett -Syracuse 13207 **Fx:**471-5048
(212) 341-6256 .. **Leath,** Lisa C '98 %Liquidation Bur -123 William -NY 10038 **Fx:**608-3398
(212) 696-6000 .. **Leathley,** Christian '09 Cnsl Curtis M-PC&M LLP -101 Park Av -NY 10178
(212) 766-5222 .. **Leav,** Danl T '93 (Leav & S LLP) -120 Bway -NY 10271 **Fx:**693-2377
(212) 352-9251 .. **Leavin,** Paul '92 -113 Univ Pl 8th Fl -NY 10003
(718) 729-0986 .. **Leavitt Kerson & Duane** -45-29 47th -Woodside 11377 **Fx:**729-0623
(718) 793-8822 .. **Leavitt Kerson & Duane** -118-35 Qns Blvd -Frst Hlls 11375 **Fx:**261-5013
(212) 973-9339 .. **Leavitt Kerson & Duane** -228 E 45th -NY 10017 **Fx:**973-9494
(718) 729-0986 .. **Leavitt,** Marc C '77 (Leavitt K&D) -45-29 47th -Woodside 11377
(212) 902-5782 .. **Leavitt,** Matthew D '91 Goldman Sachs -85 Broad -NY 10004
(212) 267-2321 .. **Leavitt,** Michl L '83 (Cohen & L PC) -277 Bway -NY 10007
(212) 897-5852 .. **Leavitt,** Wm '97 -305 Bway -NY 10007
(732) 855-6049 .. **Leavitt-Gruberger,** Edwin '76 (Wilentz G&S) -110 William -NY 10038 **Fx:**726-6599
(212) 885-4000 .. **Leavy,** Keith C '79 BMO Nesbitt Burns -3 Times Sq -NY 10036
(631) 673-7555 .. **Leavy,** Michl G '85 -191 NY Av -Huntngtn 11743 **Fx:**425-7030
(212) 406-1919 .. **Leavy,** Michl S '94 %Gennet KA&R,PC -140 Bway -NY 10005
(212) 839-5562 .. **Leavy,** Richd A '97 (Sidley A LLP) -787 7th Av -NY 10019
(315) 343-3500 .. **Lebaudy,** Diego '02 -94 E Brdg -Oswego 13126 **Fx:**343-0069
(516) 829-0363 .. **Lebeaux,** Edw W '81 %Israel I&P,LLP -11 Grace Av -Gt Neck 11021 **Fx:**829-0366
(212) 370-1300 .. **Lebedev,** Svetlana E '08 %Ellenoff G&S LLP -150 E 42nd -NY 10017
(718) 634-5900 .. **Lebenbaum,** Alan G '77 -156 Beach 139th -Belle Hbr 11694
(212) 874-8282 .. **Lebenberg,** Margot T '93 Princeton Review -2315 Bway -NY 10024
(212) 431-5757 .. **Lebenger,** Aaron L '82 -401 Bway -NY 10013 **Fx:**431-5759
(516) 579-7700 .. **Lebensbaum,** Leon '54 (L Lebensbaum,PC) -3601 Hempstd Tpk -Levittwn 11756 **Fx:**579-7945
(212) 594-2030 .. **Lebensfeld,** Alan M '78 (Lebensfeld BS&S LLP) -31 South -Mt Vernon 10550
(212) 594-2030 .. **Lebensfeld Borker Sussman & Sharon LLP** -31 South -Mt Vernon 10550 **Fx:**594-6875
(212) 416-8000 .. **Lebensohn,** Alisa R '94 %Dept of Law -120 Bway -NY 10271
(212) 566-2113 .. **Lebensohn,** Rachel E '06 %Linowes Law Firm -150 Bway -NY 10038 **Fx:**566-2114
(845) 831-5367 .. **Lebensold,** Linda R '68 -7 Chatham Ct -Fishkill 12524 **Fx:**831-6406
(212) 318-9737 .. **Lebenstein,** David N '77 Colliers ABR -40 E 52nd -NY 10022
(212) 484-3900 .. **Leber,** Bernice K '79 (Arent F LLP) -1675 Bway -NY 10019
(212) 576-6095 .. **Leber,** Richd '75 %NYLIM -51 Mad Av -NY 10010
(315) 478-1334 .. **Leberman,** Wm J '82 -110 W Fayette -Syracuse 13202 **Fx:**424-1011
(212) 358-1000 .. **Lebewohl,** Jacob J '75 -157 E Houston -NY 10002 **Fx:**353-1836
(212) 813-8800 .. **Lebioda,** Lauren Troxclair '08 %Goodwin P LLP -620 8th Av -NY 10018
(212) 326-3939 .. **Lebioda,** Nathan P S '07 %Jones D -222 E 41st -NY 10017
(631) 406-6620 .. **Lebit,** Michl A '92 -191 Terry Rd -Smithtwn 11787
(518) 946-7058 .. **LeBlanc,** Nancy E '58 -Hardy Rd Bx60 -Wilmngtn 12997 **Fx:**946-7623
(212) 558-4000 .. **Leblanc-Lapointe,** Brigitte '09 %Sullivan & C LLP -125 Broad -NY 10004
(212) 715-9100 .. **LeBlang,** Kevin B '85 (Kramer LN&F,LLP) -1177 Av of Amer -NY 10036
(212) 271-0215 .. **LeBlang,** Skip Alan '80 -325 Bway -NY 10007 **Fx:**267-5813
(212) 872-1000 .. **Leblang,** Stuart E '91 -One Bryant Park -NY 10036 **Fx:**872-1002
(212) 909-6000 .. **Lebolt,** David S '03 %Debevoise & P LLP -919 3rd Av -NY 10022
(212) 806-5400 .. **Le Bouef,** Scott '00 (Stroock &S&L LLP) -180 Maiden Ln -NY 10038
(516) 626-9444 .. **LeBovici,** Jacqueline R '92 (LeBovici & L) -18 Ests Dr -Roslyn 11576
(516) 626-9444 .. **LeBovici,** Ronald S '59 (LeBovici & L) -18 Ests Dr -Roslyn 11576
(914) 962-0400 .. **LeBovit,** Lisa Ann '91 (Lieberman & L) -334 Underhill Av -Yorktwn Hts 10598
(212) 554-1400 .. **Lebovitch,** Mark '00 (Bernstein LB&G LLP) -1285 Av of Amer -NY 10019
(718) 438-2525 .. **Lebovits,** Allan '07 %NC Caller,PC -266 Bway -Brklyn 11211 **Fx:**972-4154
(516) 560-6400 .. **Lebovitz,** Linda I '83 %Leg Aid -1 Helen Keller Way -Hempstd 11550 **Fx:**565-3694
(212) 868-3311 .. **Lebow,** James B '85 -5 Penn Plz -NY 10001
(212) 449-1000 .. **Lebow,** Jonathan T '94 Merrill Lynch -4 World Fncl Ctr -NY 10080
(212) 935-6000 .. **Lebow,** Mark Denis '65 (Lebow & S LLP) -770 Lex Av -NY 10065
(516) 328-2300 .. **Lebow,** Ron '02 %Abrams FFEGF&E,LLP -1111 Marcus Av -Lk Success 11042
(212) 935-6000 .. **Lebow & Sokolow LLP** -770 Lex Av -NY 10065 **Fx:**935-4865
(631) 543-7667 .. **LeBow,** Susan M '64 (Sarisohn Law Prtnrs LLP) -350 Vets Mem'l Hwy -Commack 11725 **Fx:**543-7901
(212) 969-3000 .. **Lebowich,** Michl J '98 (Proskauer R LLP) -1585 Bway -NY 10036
(212) 557-4000 .. **Lebowitz,** Alan G '79 (Grunfeld DLS&K LLP) -399 Park Av -NY 10022
(718) 522-0666 .. **Lebowitz,** Alan L '61 Cnsl Sanders G&B,PC -26 Court -Brklyn 11242
(212) 669-7778 .. **Lebowitz,** Alan P '82 %Comptroller -1 Centre -NY 10007 **Fx:**669-2884
(212) 233-3079 .. **Lebowitz,** Alan R '85 (Maloof LC&O,PA) -299 Bway -NY 10007
(212) 272-5473 .. **Lebowitz,** David A '90 %JP Morgan Chase -383 Mad Av -NY 10179
(212) 619-2051 .. **Lebowitz,** Don '78 -277 Bway -NY 10007 **Fx:**619-6351
(212) 859-8000 .. **Lebowitz,** Henry C '97 (Fried FHS&J LLP) -1 NY Plz -NY 10004
(718) 250-0400 .. **Lebowitz,** Ira H '93 %R Tusa -1 MetroTech Ctr -Brklyn 11201 **Fx:**250-0591
(315) 422-1391 .. **Lebowitz,** Jack R '76 %Green & S,PLLC -One Lincoln Ctr #900 -Syracuse 13202
(914) 834-4848 .. **LeBowitz,** Jerome D '53 -60 Wildwood Rd -New Rchll 10804
(212) 935-6020 .. **Lebowitz,** Laurence J '79 Lebowitz & Assoc -485 Mad Av -NY 10022 **Fx:**753-8101
(212) 682-6818 .. **Lebowitz,** Marc A '93 Lebowitz Law Ofc -275 Mad Av -NY 10016
(518) 792-2117 .. **Lebowitz,** Mark A '73 (Bartlett PS&R,PC) -1 Wshngtn Bx2168 -Glens Fls 12801
(518) 792-1638 .. **Lebowitz,** Neil H '84 -288 Glen -Glens Fls 12801
(212) 553-5516 .. **Lebowitz,** Stephanie M '96 -1 Lbrty Plz -NY 10006
(516) 625-9400 .. **Lebowitz,** Stephen M '96 Topspin Prtnrs -3 Expwy Plz -Roslyn Hts 11577
(212) 309-5982 .. **Lebowitz Prager,** Wendy '93 %ING Asset Mngt -230 Park Av -NY 10169
(718) 298-8924 .. **LeBright,** JoAnn C '93 %Leg Aid -153-01 Jamaica Av -Jamaica 11432 **Fx:**657-0537
(212) 770-6151 .. **Lebron,** Kimberly A '03 AIG Global Inv Grp -70 Pine -NY 10270
(212) 961-4475 .. **Lebron,** Roberto G '88 %Dept of Law -163 W 125th -NY 10027 **Fx:**961-4003
(518) 886-4388 .. **LeBrou,** James J '92 AYCO -321 Bway Bx860 -Saratoga Spgs 12866
(212) 770-1079 .. **Lebson,** Danl P '90 %AIG -70 Pine -NY 10270
(212) 708-1800 .. **Lebson,** Scott J '99 %Ladas & P -26 W 61st -NY 10023
(212) 593-2155 .. **Lebson,** Sean E '94 %Scaffidi & Assoc -747 3rd Av -NY 10017 **Fx:**593-2257
(212) 259-8000 .. **Lebwohl,** Andrew Z '08 %Dewey & L LLP -1301 Av of Amer -NY 10019
(718) 520-3914 .. **Lebwohl,** Dennis '71 %Hon R McDonald -25-10 Court Sq -LIC 11101
(718) 544-7701 .. **Lebwohl,** Linda Salza '84 %Goldstein & G,LLP -118-35 Qns Blvd -Frst Hlls 11375

(518) 862-1090 .. **LeCain,** Sara L '05 NYSERDA -17 Columbia Cir -Albany 12203 **Fx:**862-1091
(518) 474-6530 .. **Lecakes,** Dakin D '99 %Dept Pub Srvc -3 ESP -Albany 12223
(518) 786-1800 .. **LeCakes,** Jennifer D '99 (Flink S LLC) -23 British Amer Blvd -Latham 12110 **Fx:**786-1969
(212) 449-6453 .. **Lecaros,** Melvina Carrick '02 Merrill Lynch -4 World Fncl Ctr -NY 10080
(518) 782-1929 .. **Lecce,** Louie '83 -40 British Amer Blvd -Latham 12110 **Fx:**782-3429
(212) 969-3000 .. **Leccese,** Jos M '86 (Proskauer R LLP) -1585 Bway -NY 10036
(212) 532-8100 .. **Lecci,** Kimberly A '08 %Stern & M,LLP -115 Bway -NY 10006
(516) 942-3700 .. **Lecci,** Salvatore A '75 -420 Jericho Tpk -Jericho 11753 **Fx:**942-3366
(212) 481-4801 .. **Lecciso,** Francesco A '97 %Trustforte Eductnl Srvcs -271 Mad Av -NY 10016
(914) 698-5296 .. **Lechleiter,** Gerard '65 -421 Waverly Av -Mamaroneck 10543
(212) 264-3650 .. **Lechleitner,** Andreea L '99 %SSA Ofc Genl Cnsl -26 Fed Plz -NY 10278 **Fx:**264-6372
(646) 392-9250 .. **Lechleitner,** Peter D '99 %M Klein & Assoc -200 Mad Av -NY 10016 **Fx:**(212) 779-1499
(212) 819-8200 .. **Lechner,** Alfred J Jr. '73 (White & C LLP) -1155 Av of Amer -NY 10036
(212) 808-7800 .. **Lechner,** Coleman T '06 %Kelley D&W LLP -101 Park Av -NY 10178
(718) 996-2386 .. **Lechowicz,** Gabriela Z '96 -3415 Neptune Av -Brklyn 11224
(631) 853-4318 .. **Lechtrecker,** Kerri N '93 Family Ct -400 Carleton Av -Central Islip 11722
(212) 219-8555 .. **Lechtzin,** Jeremy '00 The Knot, Inc -462 Bway -NY 10013
(518) 487-7600 .. **Leckerling,** Richd E '78 (Whiteman O&H LLP) -1 Commerce Plz -Albany 12260
(212) 610-6300 .. **Leckie,** Elizabeth '90 (Allen & O) -1221 Av of Amer -NY 10020
(212) 464-0889 .. **Leckie,** Gavin F '90 JP Morgan Chase Bk -345 Park Av -NY 10154
(607) 734-2271 .. **LeClair,** Lawr '81 (Sayles & E) -1 W Church -Elmira 14901
(585) 327-4100 .. **Leclair,** Paul L '88 (Leclair KGC,LLP) -150 State -Rchstr 14614 **Fx:**327-4200
(212) 430-8020 .. **LeClairRyan, PC** -830 3rd Av -NY 10022 **Fx:**430-8079
(212) 446-4800 .. **LeCointe,** Lisa V '07 %Kirkland & E LLP -153 E 53rd -NY 10022
(212) 425-7200 .. **Lecomte,** Linda Shudy '08 (Kenyon & K,LLP) -1 Bway -NY 10004
(315) 232-4551 .. **LeConey,** Ashley N '10 %McClusky Law Firm,LLC -8 Main Bx97 -Adams 13605 **Fx:**232-2562
(212) 349-5150 .. **Lecour,** Elina '04 %Galvano & X,PC -150 Bway -NY 10038
(518) 583-4600 .. **LeCours,** Alan R '84 (LeCours C&Y,LLP) -59 Church -Saratoga Spgs 12866 **Fx:**583-4642
(518) 458-6105 .. **LeCours,** Brian R '86 -125 Wolf Rd -Albany 12205
(518) 285-5050 .. **LeCours,** Lisa Anne '94 Hon V Graffeo -20 Eagle -Albany 12207
(212) 903-9000 .. **LeCren,** Danelle Vaudine '02 (Linklaters) -1345 Av of Amer -NY 10105
(212) 481-9866 .. **LeCrichia,** Anthony F '89 -245 E 33rd -NY 10016 **Fx:**481-9863
(315) 298-5192 .. **Ledden,** C Earl '71 -29 Broad -Pulaski 13142 **Fx:**298-3451
(315) 638-8283 .. **Ledden,** Jay H '71 -60 Oswego -Baldwinsvll 13027 **Fx:**638-8843
(718) 448-4735 .. **Leddy,** Danl D Jr. '66 -5 Parkvw Pl -Staten Isl 10310
(845) 783-4763 .. **Leddy,** Francis J Jr. '83 -1 Thornwood Ct -Monroe 10926
(212) 891-0799 .. **Leddy,** Joanne M '80 %FOJP Srvc Corp -28 E 28th -NY 10016 **Fx:**702-6382
(212) 349-0096 .. **Leddy,** Patrick J '60 -305 Bway -NY 10007 **Fx:**406-2271
(212) 449-1000 .. **Ledee,** Richd F '96 %Merrill Lynch -220 Bway -NY 10038
(212) 558-4000 .. **Ledenev,** Vasily A '08 %Sullivan & C LLP -125 Broad -NY 10004
(212) 547-5400 .. **Leder,** Amy B '93 (McDermott W&E LLP) -340 Mad Av -NY 10173
(516) 213-5000 .. **Leder,** Andrew R '92 -99 Q Roosevelt Blvd -Gdn Cty 11530
(212) 297-0056 .. **Leder,** Howard S '82 -319 Lafayette -NY 10012 **Fx:**(208) 441-9380
Leder, Jonathan L '08 -7 Ravine Rd -Gt Neck 11023
(212) 408-5100 .. **Leder,** Richd M '62 (Chadbourne & P LLP) -30 Rckfllr Plz -NY 10112
(718) 601-2314 .. **Leder,** Robt A '88 -3840 Greystone Av -Bronx 10463
(718) 851-6900 .. **Ledereich,** Leonard '85 -4920 15th Av -Brklyn 11219 **Fx:**851-4530
(212) 335-9000 .. **Lederer,** Elizabeth J '80 %DA -1 Hogan Pl -NY 10013
(212) 644-4420 .. **Lederer,** Irvin '77 SrCnsl Fabiani C&H,LLP -570 Lex Av -NY 10022
(212) 704-6319 .. **Lederer,** Karen F '79 (Troutman S LLP) -405 Lex Av -NY 10174
(212) 728-8000 .. **Lederer,** Marc J '04 Willkie F&G LLP -787 7th Av -NY 10019
(212) 799-5509 .. **Lederer,** Michl L '88 -185 W End Av -NY 10023 **Fx:**595-7859
(212) 969-3000 .. **Lederkramer,** David M '83 (Proskauer R LLP) -1585 Bway -NY 10036
(516) 541-8900 .. **Lederman & Abrahams, LLP** -567 Bway -Massapequa 11758 **Fx:**541-9232
(212) 554-7800 .. **Lederman,** Andrew P '85 OfCnsl Moses & S LLP -405 Lex Av -NY 10174
(212) 788-6485 .. **Lederman,** Barbara Ann '85 NY DoITT -75 Park Pl -NY 10007
(212) 754-9400 .. **Lederman,** Bruce '80 (Todtman NS&J,PC) -425 Park Av -NY 10022
(212) 564-9800 .. **Lederman,** Bruce H '85 (D'Agostino L&L,LLP) -345 7th Av -NY 10001
(914) 557-0181 .. **Lederman,** Chas O '93 -15 Avondale Rd -White Plns 10605
(212) 476-9000 .. **Lederman,** Diane E '84 %Neuberger Berman Trust Co -605 3rd Av -NY 10158 **Fx:**476-9090
(212) 310-8000 .. **Lederman,** Evan S '06 %Weil G&M LLP -767 5th Av -NY 10153
(212) 374-9160 .. **Lederman,** Georges G '86 -52 Duane -NY 10007 **Fx:**732-6323
(516) 541-8900 .. **Lederman,** Harold N '59 (Lederman & A,LLP) -567 Bway -Massapequa 11758
(718) 423-8100 .. **Lederman,** Laura J '93 %M Curri Middle Sch -46-35 Oceania -Bayside 11361
(212) 431-2100 .. **Lederman,** Lawr '68 %NY Law Schl -185 W Bway -NY 10013 **Fx:**406-0103
(212) 929-5876 .. **Lederman,** Nancy M '78 -55 W 14th -NY 10011
(212) 701-3000 .. **Ledermann,** Julie C '10 %Cahill G&R LLP -80 Pine -NY 10005 **Fx:**269-5420
(212) 790-9200 .. **Ledesma,** Roberto '09 %Cowan L&L,PC -1133 Av of Amer -NY 10036
(212) 848-4000 .. **Ledet,** Scott P '08 %Shearman & S LLP -599 Lex Av -NY 10022
(516) 747-1210 .. **Ledgin,** David H '80 -1539 Franklin Av -Mineola 11501 **Fx:**747-1211
(212) 986-6000 .. **Ledley,** James R '73 (Kleinberg KW&C,PC) -551 5th Av -NY 10176
(212) 382-3300 .. **Ledley,** Michl C '01 Cnsl Wollmuth M&D LLP -500 5th Av -NY 10110
(212) 588-0800 .. **LeDonne,** Eugene '98 (Frommer L&H LLP) -745 5th Av -NY 10151
(718) 276-6656 .. **Ledwidge,** Jos A '98 J Ledwidge,PC -170-26 Cedarcroft Rd -Jamaica 11432 **Fx:**701-3726
(914) 323-7000 .. **Ledwin,** Mark G '90 (Wilson EME&D LLP) -3 Gannett Dr -White Plns 10604
(516) 593-1771 .. **Ledwith,** Peter K '67 (Ledwith & A) -14 St James Pl -Lynbrk 11563 **Fx:**593-1816
(212) 261-8000 .. **Ledwith,** Thos W '00 %Mendes & M,LLP -750 7th Av -NY 10019
(212) 581-4540 .. **Ledy,** David M '74 %Realty Holdings Amer -1370 Av of Amer -NY 10019 **Fx:**581-4950
(212) 447-1111 .. **Ledy-Gurren Bass & Siff** -475 Park Av S -NY 10016 **Fx:**447-6686
(212) 447-1111 .. **Ledy-Gurren,** Nancy '76 (Ledy-Gurren B&S) -475 Park Av S -NY 10016
(212) 264-9253 .. **Lee,** Aimee '95 %US DOJ -26 Fed Plz -NY 10278 **Fx:**264-1916
(212) 564-9496 .. **Lee,** Alan '82 -408 8th Av -NY 10001 **Fx:**268-1679
(212) 506-5000 .. **Lee,** Alexandria V '08 %Orrick H&S LLP -51 W 52nd -NY 10019
(212) 474-1000 .. **Lee,** Alice Y '09 %Cravath S&M LLP -825 8th Av -NY 10019
(585) 381-3400 .. **Lee,** Alison M K '06 %Rupp BPC&C LLC -3300 Monroe Av -Rchstr 14618
(212) 909-6000 .. **Lee,** Allison A '09 %Debevoise & P LLP -919 3rd Av -NY 10022
(718) 983-8800 .. **Lee & Amtzis,LLP** -260 Christopher Ln -Staten Isl 10314 **Fx:**983-7078
(212) 271-0664 .. **Lee Anav Chung LLP** -350 5th Av -NY 10118 **Fx:**271-0665
(212) 859-8000 .. **Lee,** Andrea Y '10 %Fried FHS&J LLP -1 NY Plz -NY 10004
(212) 294-6700 .. **Lee,** Andrea Yoon '08 %Winston & S -200 Park Av -NY 10166
(212) 808-7800 .. **Lee,** Andrew H '94 %Kelley D&W LLP -101 Park Av -NY 10178
(212) 921-8399 .. **Lee,** Andrew S '08 %Lankler S&W LLP -500 5th Av -NY 10110
(212) 770-7729 .. **Lee,** Angela '94 AIG -70 Pine -NY 10270
(212) 272-8680 .. **Lee,** Anita J '99 %JP Morgan Chase -383 Mad Av -NY 10179
(212) 318-3000 .. **Lee,** Anna '95 Cnsl Fulbright & J LLP -666 5th Av -NY 10103
(845) 639-7800 .. **Lee,** Anna Chou '88 %Mandel K&B,LLP -210 Route 303 -Vly Cottage 10989
(718) 614-8339 .. **Lee,** Annette Anhwa '95 -903 Sheridan Av -Bronx 10451
(212) 225-2000 .. **Lee,** Annie Han '10 %Cleary GS&H -1 Lbrty Plz -NY 10006
(585) 454-1660 .. **Lee,** Anthony C '01 %Vasile Law Grp,PLLC -1200 Jffrsn Rd -Rchstr 14623
(585) 232-6500 .. **Lee,** Anthony T '85 (Harter S&E LLP) -1600 Bausch & Lomb Pl -Rchstr 14604
(212) 715-9100 .. **Lee,** Antonia S '09 %Kramer LN&F,LLP -1177 Av of Amer -NY 10036
(518) 762-3840 .. **Lee,** Barbara S '88 %Family Ct -11 N William -Johnstwn 12095
(212) 416-8300 .. **Lee,** Benjamin J '93 Atty Gen -120 Bway -NY 10271
(212) 619-2859 .. **Lee,** Benjamin S '97 %Gell & G -299 Bway -NY 10007 **Fx:**964-9485
(518) 449-3300 .. **Lee,** Benjamin W H '00 %Nolan & H,LLP -39 N Pearl -Albany 12207
(212) 474-1000 .. **Lee,** Bomi '10 %Cravath S&M LLP -825 8th Av -NY 10019
(212) 735-3000 .. **Lee,** Boong-Kyu '03 Cnsl Skadden ASM&F LLP -4 Times Sq -NY 10036
(518) 587-1380 .. **Lee,** Brian D '83 B Lee,PLLC -138 Church -Saratoga Spgs 12866 **Fx:**587-1393
(516) 326-2400 .. **Lee,** Brian E '77 (Ivone D&J,LLP) -2001 Marcus Av -Lk Success 11042
(212) 530-5000 .. **Lee,** Brian J '09 %Milbank TH&M LLP -1 Chase Manh Plz -NY 10005
(516) 572-2000 .. **Lee,** Brian S B '96 %DA -99 Main -Hempstd 11550 **Fx:**572-2606
(212) 421-2150 .. **Lee,** Bridget M '07 %Sive P&R,PC -460 Park Av -NY 10022
(212) 412-4000 .. **Lee,** Byung-Il '97 Barclays Capital -200 Park Av -NY 10166
(212) 400-7214 .. **Lee,** C K '98 (Kraselnik & L,PLLC) -40 Wall -NY 10005 **Fx:**400-7162
(212) 209-3117 .. **Lee,** Carol F '07 Taconic Cptl Advsrs LP -450 Park Av -NY 10022
(212) 617-3332 .. **Lee,** Carol Jung Min '03 Bloomberg LP -731 Lex Av -NY 10022
(718) 428-6367 .. **Lee,** Caroline A '87 -43-60 Douglstn Pkwy -Douglastn 11363
(212) 326-3939 .. **Lee,** Carolyn J '81 (Jones D) -222 E 41st -NY 10017
(607) 273-4200 .. **Lee,** Carolyn S '00 (Miller M,LLP) -202 E State -Ithaca 14850
(212) 225-2000 .. **Lee,** Catherine Haemin '05 %Cleary GS&H -1 Lbrty Plz -NY 10006
(845) 568-7599 .. **Lee,** Catherine I '00 -46 Alfred Pl -Walden 12586 **Fx:**778-2883
(718) 961-6355 .. **Lee,** Chanwoo '88 -35-20 147th -Flushng 11354 **Fx:**961-6343
(212) 278-1000 .. **Lee,** Chas T '77 (Anderson K&O,PC) -1251 Av of Amer -NY 10020
(212) 732-3366 .. **Lee,** Charlotte Cho-Lan '78 -277 Bway -NY 10007 **Fx:**742-1651
(914) 665-2440 .. **Lee,** Cheryl J '04 %DA -Roosevelt Sq -Mt Vernon 10550 **Fx:**668-2314
(212) 692-1000 .. **Lee,** Chester P '84 (Duane M LLP) -1540 Bway -NY 10036
(212) 670-0215 .. **Lee,** Chiek Chuin '01 Merrill Lynch -222 Bway -NY 10038
(212) 610-6300 .. **Lee,** Christina Y '03 %Allen & O -1221 Av of Amer -NY 10020
(212) 750-8300 .. **Lee,** Christopher B Y '98 KKR KPE LLC -9 W 57th -NY 10019
(914) 761-7190 .. **Lee,** Christopher P '81 %ODAR-SSA -75 S Bway -White Plns 10601 **Fx:**682-7006
(212) 682-2280 .. **Lee,** Cindy C '08 %Holm & O LLP -3 W 35th -NY 10001
(212) 902-0900 .. **Lee,** Craig A '02 Goldman Sachs & Co -85 Broad -NY 10004
(212) 859-8000 .. **Lee,** Dana E '10 %Fried FHS&J LLP -1 NY Plz -NY 10004
(212) 998-2319 .. **Lee,** Dana H '93 Acedemic & Hlth Affrs -70 Wshngtn Sq -NY 10012
(212) 357-1978 .. **Lee,** Danl H '03 Goldman Sachs -1 NY Plz -NY 10004
(718) 643-1334 .. **Lee,** Danl K '86 -39-01 Main -Flushng 11354
(212) 504-6000 .. **Lee,** Danl S '10 Cadwalader W&T LLP -1 World Fncl Ctr -NY 10281
(212) 643-7000 .. **Lee,** David Chunyi '08 %Sills C&G PC -One Rckfllr Plz -NY 10020
(212) 728-8000 .. **Lee,** David D '04 %Willkie F&G LLP -787 7th Av -NY 10019
(212) 940-3000 .. **Lee,** David H '07 %Nixon P LLP -437 Mad Av -NY 10022
(212) 226-6248 .. **Lee,** David J '94 (Lee & C,PLLC) -150 Bway -NY 10038
(212) 619-2330 .. **Lee,** David M '77 -120 Bway -NY 10271
(716) 851-4343 .. **Lee,** David M '10 Law Dept -65 Niagara Sq -Buffalo 14202 **Fx:**851-4105
(212) 698-4570 .. **Lee,** David S '80 (Stapper & V) -10 Rckfllr Plz -NY 10020
(212) 447-5599 .. **Lee,** David S '03 %Agins SR&B,LLP -386 Park Av S -NY 10016
(212) 373-3000 .. **Lee,** David U '09 %Paul WRW&G LLP -1285 Av of Amer -NY 10019
(212) 680-1055 .. **Lee,** David W '92 -2 Mott -NY 10013
(212) 974-6000 .. **Lee,** Delbert Victor '00 Elliott Mgmt Corp -712 5th Av -NY 10019
(212) 790-4500 .. **Lee,** Diana J '74 (Manatt P&P,LLP) -7 Times Sq -NY 10036
(646) 497-4810 .. **Lee,** Dina C '99 Neuberger Berman,LLC -605 3rd Av -NY 10158
(914) 472-5395 .. **Lee,** Donald B '75 -4 Westvw Ln -Scarsdale 10583

(212) 541-7800 .. **Lee,** Donna '98 %Planned Parenthood -434 W 33rd -NY 10001 **Fx:**868-4677
(212) 373-3000 .. **Lee,** Donna '07 %Paul WRW&G LLP -1285 Av of Amer -NY 10019
(718) 340-4200 .. **Lee,** Donna Hae Kyun '92 %CUNY Law Schl -65-21 Main -Flushng 11367 **Fx:**340-4482
(212) 277-4000 .. **Lee,** Donna Ju-Yun '05 %Freshfields BD LLP -520 Mad Av -NY 10022
(914) 640-8196 .. **Lee,** Doreen '00 Starwood Hotels & Resorts Wrldwde Inc -111 Wstchstr Av -White Plns 10601
(845) 353-2050 .. **Lee,** Duncan R II '88 -301 Highmount Ter -Upper Nyack 10960 **Fx:**353-5288
(212) 845-7500 .. **Lee,** Dyana '87 Thacher Assoc,LLC -330 W 42nd -NY 10036 **Fx:**845-7549
(212) 403-1000 .. **Lee,** Edw J '07 %Wachtell LR&K -51 W 52nd -NY 10019
(212) 407-4000 .. **Lee,** Edw K '09 %Loeb & L,LLP -345 Park Av -NY 10154
(718) 896-9335 .. **Lee,** Edwin W '85 -71 Brook Ct N -New Hyde Pk 11040
(212) 490-2277 .. **Lee,** Ellen '03 NY Land Srvcs -630 3rd Av -NY 10017 **Fx:**490-8012
(607) 334-2247 .. **Lee & Emerson** -35 W Main Bx711 -Norwich 13815 **Fx:**334-5999
(212) 446-4800 .. **Lee,** Emily C '09 %Kirkland & E LLP -153 E 53rd -NY 10022
(212) 790-4500 .. **Lee,** Emily H Y '07 %Manatt P&P,LLP -7 Times Sq -NY 10036
(212) 973-8000 .. **Lee,** Emma '99 %Schnader HS&L LLP -140 Bway -NY 10005
(516) 248-2234 .. **Lee,** Eric B '96 (Sackstein S&L,LLP) -1140 Franklin Av -Gdn Cty 11530
(212) 969-3000 .. **Lee,** Eric Grant '07 %Proskauer R LLP -1585 Bway -NY 10036
(212) 292-6658 .. **Lee,** Erica Cheng '00 Ziff Bros Invstmnts -350 Park Av -NY 10022
(212) 530-5000 .. **Lee,** Ethan Y '10 %Milbank TH&M LLP -1 Chase Manh Plz -NY 10005
(212) 318-6000 .. **Lee,** Eugene '04 %Paul HJ&W LLP -75 E 55th -NY 10022
(212) 221-6666 .. **Lee,** Eugene T '99 Apple Mortgage Corp -19 W 44th -NY 10036
(212) 272-7072 .. **Lee,** Eunice '05 %JP Morgan Chase -383 Mad Av -NY 10179
(212) 402-4100 .. **Lee,** Eunice C '97 %Ofc Appllt Def -11 Park Pl -NY 10007 **Fx:**402-4199
(212) 776-5153 .. **Lee,** Eva J '82 Housing Auth -250 Bway -NY 10007
(212) 728-2200 .. **Lee,** Evan T '09 %Axinn V&H LLP -114 W 47th -NY 10036
(212) 407-4000 .. **Lee,** Frank '88 (Loeb & L,LLP) -345 Park Av -NY 10154
(212) 872-1000 .. **Lee,** Fredk T '05 -One Bryant Park -NY 10036 **Fx:**872-1002
(212) 909-6000 .. **Lee,** Gary '08 %Debevoise & P LLP -919 3rd Av -NY 10022
(212) 468-8000 .. **Lee,** Gary S '91 (Morrison & F LLP) -1290 Av of Amer -NY 10104
(212) 492-1566 .. **Lee,** Gene Ming '98 Gensler -1230 Av of Amer -NY 10020 **Fx:**492-1472
(212) 596-9000 .. **Lee,** Gene W '93 (Ropes & G LLP) -1211 Av of Amer -NY 10036
(718) 709-3027 .. **Lee,** Gerald B '99 JetBlue Airways -118-29 Qns Blvd -Frst Hlls 11375
(212) 422-0202 .. **Lee,** Gilbert '02 %Sedgwick DM&A LLP -125 Broad -NY 10004
(718) 639-7764 .. **Lee,** Gisig '92 -30-53 69th -Woodside 11377
(212) 698-3500 .. **Lee,** Gowoon '09 %Dechert LLP -1095 Av of Amer -NY 10036
(212) 735-7456 .. **Lee,** Grace '08 Tremblant Capital Grp -767 5th Av -NY 10153
(212) 848-4000 .. **Lee,** Grace J '07 %Shearman & S LLP -599 Lex Av -NY 10022
(212) 683-4141 .. **Lee,** Grace Y '03 %Lynch & Assoc -462 7th Av -NY 10018 **Fx:**208-0948
(212) 902-7584 .. **Lee,** Gregory D '93 %Goldman Sachs -1 NY Plz -NY 10004
(212) 325-3630 .. **Lee,** Haewon '07 Credit Suisse Securities (USA) LLC -1 Mad Av -NY 10010
(212) 577-3444 .. **Lee,** Hamilton '07 Legal Aid -199 Water -NY 10038
(212) 596-9000 .. **Lee,** Hanyong '09 %Ropes & G LLP -1211 Av of Amer -NY 10036
(212) 455-2000 .. **Lee,** Ho Min '10 %Simpson T&B LLP -425 Lex Av -NY 10017
(212) 626-4100 .. **Lee,** Hoon '01 %Baker & M LLP -1114 Av of Amer -NY 10036
(212) 521-5400 .. **Lee,** Horim Kate '08 %Reed S LLP -599 Lex Av -NY 10022
(212) 450-4000 .. **Lee,** Hsien-Jay '09 %Davis P&W LLP -450 Lex Av -NY 10017
(212) 909-6174 .. **Lee,** Huey-Fun '95 Cnsl Debevoise & P LLP -919 3rd Av -NY 10022
(212) 577-3360 .. **Lee,** Hwan-Hui Helen '96 Leg Aid Civ Appls -199 Water -NY 10038
(212) 455-2000 .. **Lee,** Hyang Sook '95 SrCnsl Simpson T&B LLP -425 Lex Av -NY 10017
(212) 527-1000 .. **Lee,** Hyun Soo '04 %Jones HC&B PC -1 Bttry Pk Plz -NY 10004
(212) 629-6002 .. **Lee,** Inkyung '06 (I Lee,PC) -16 W 32nd -NY 10001 **Fx:**629-6005
(212) 547-5400 .. **Lee,** In-Young '87 (McDermott W&E LLP) -340 Mad Av -NY 10173
(914) 376-3757 .. **Lee,** Isabel K '04 Legal Srvcs of the Hudson Vlly -30 S Bway -Ynkrs 10701
(585) 530-3115 .. **Lee,** Ivan E '04 Appllt Div 4th Dept -50 East Av Ste 200 -Rchstr 14604 **Fx:**530-3247
(914) 765-4268 .. **Lee,** Jacob S '03 IBM -1 New Orchrd Rd -Armonk 10504 **Fx:**765-7533
(212) 710-0000 .. **Lee,** Jae W '98 (Drohan L,LLP) -489 5th Av -NY 10017
(718) 522-1477 .. **Lee,** James '00 -188 Montague -Brklyn 11201 **Fx:**522-1499
(212) 756-2000 .. **Lee,** James Chi-Ho '05 %Schulte R&Z LLP -919 3rd Av -NY 10022
(212) 808-9400 .. **Lee,** James H '98 Madison Title Agency LLC -100 Park Av -NY 10017 **Fx:**808-9420
(212) 594-5000 .. **Lee,** James J '06 %Togut S&S LLP -1 Penn Plz -NY 10119
(973) 596-4833 .. **Lee,** James M '88 (Gibbons PC) -1 Penn Plz -NY 10119 **Fx:**639-6264
(212) 428-2175 .. **Lee,** James M '90 %OCA -25 Beaver -NY 10004 **Fx:**428-2155
(516) 488-3300 .. **Lee,** James M '08 Shaub AC&S,LLP -1983 Marcus Av -Lk Success 11042
(212) 431-9059 .. **Lee,** James W '89 -100 Lafayette -NY 10013 **Fx:**431-9084
(212) 270-6255 .. **Lee,** James Y '95 JP Morgan Chase & Co -270 Park Av -NY 10017 **Fx:**270-7473
(518) 455-7797 .. **Lee,** Jane H '10 Ct of Appls -20 Eagle -Albany 12207
(212) 319-1000 .. **Lee,** Janet J '08 Quirk & B,PC -845 3rd Av -NY 10022
(212) 357-7507 .. **Lee,** Janet M '02 Goldman Sachs -1 NY Plz -NY 10004
(212) 697-3122 .. **Lee,** Janet O '07 %Martin C&B LLP -220 E 42nd -NY 10017
(212) 807-8199 .. **Lee,** Janice M '80 -62 Morton -NY 10014
(212) 701-3000 .. **Lee,** Jason Y-H '08 %Cahill G&R LLP -80 Pine -NY 10005 **Fx:**269-5420
(212) 889-7170 .. **Lee,** Jay Sung '95 -15 E 32nd -NY 10016 **Fx:**447-0968
(212) 594-5300 .. **Lee,** Jean '04 %Milberg LLP -1 Penn Plz -NY 10119
(212) 225-2000 .. **Lee,** Jean '07 %Cleary GS&H -1 Lbrty Plz -NY 10006
(212) 230-8800 .. **Lee,** Jeffrey C '08 %WilmerHale -399 Park Av -NY 10022
(212) 688-4000 .. **Lee,** Jeffrey T '06 NYS HFA -641 Lex Av -NY 10022 **Fx:**872-0362
(212) 259-8000 .. **Lee,** Jennifer '07 %Dewey & L LLP -1301 Av of Amer -NY 10019
(631) 439-4200 .. **Lee,** Jennifer E '96 %R Tusa -898 Vets Mem'l Hwy -Hauppauge 11788 **Fx:**439-4292
(212) 878-8000 .. **Lee,** Jennifer E '06 %Clifford C LLP -31 W 52nd -NY 10019
(212) 425-7200 .. **Lee,** Jeong-Ah '10 %Kenyon & K,LLP -1 Bway -NY 10004
(212) 262-5100 .. **Lee,** Jerome G Jr. '82 -350 5th Av -NY 10118 **Fx:**397-0047
(212) 735-3000 .. **Lee,** Jessica Blaine '06 %Skadden ASM&F LLP -4 Times Sq -NY 10036
(212) 903-9000 .. **Lee,** Jessica K '10 %Linklaters -1345 Av of Amer -NY 10105
(212) 453-3662 .. **Lee,** Jihee '06 Ace Westchester Specialty Grp -1325 Av of Amer -NY 10019
(212) 244-4664 .. **Lee,** Jin Hee '01 NY Lawyers Pub Intrst -151 W 30th -NY 10001 **Fx:**244-4570
(718) 876-6300 .. **Lee,** Jin P '06 %DA -130 Styvsnt Pl -Staten Isl 10301
(212) 858-4400 .. **Lee,** Jisook '00 %FINRA -1 Lbrty Plz -NY 10006
(212) 474-1000 .. **Lee,** Joanne J '08 %Cravath S&M LLP -825 8th Av -NY 10019
(718) 359-5520 .. **Lee,** John Hyuk '99 -188-06 Nrthrn Blvd -Flushng 11358
(212) 907-9700 .. **Lee,** John J '94 (Smith G&R,LLP) -250 Park Av -NY 10177
(212) 259-8000 .. **Lee,** John J '07 %Dewey & L LLP -1301 Av of Amer -NY 10019
(212) 880-3800 .. **Lee,** John J '08 %Akerman S -335 Mad Av -NY 10017
(212) 435-3571 .. **Lee,** John Jody '81 %Port Auth of NY/NJ -225 Park Av S -NY 10003 **Fx:**435-3555
(212) 596-9000 .. **Lee,** John King '07 %Ropes & G LLP -1211 Av of Amer -NY 10036
(212) 455-2000 .. **Lee,** Joia E '10 %Simpson T&B LLP -425 Lex Av -NY 10017
(212) 610-6300 .. **Lee,** Jonathan Hyui '05 %Allen & O -1221 Av of Amer -NY 10020
(212) 213-6393 .. **Lee,** Jong Gu '01 -1220 Bway -NY 10001
(212) 425-7200 .. **Lee,** Jong Hwa '92 Cnsl Kenyon & K,LLP -1 Bway -NY 10004
(718) 321-2250 .. **Lee,** Joonhee '02 NYPD -37-05 Union -Flushng 11354
(212) 373-3000 .. **Lee,** Jos IV '99 Paul WRW&G LLP -1285 Av of Amer -NY 10019
(212) 837-6000 .. **Lee,** Jos '06 %Hughes H&R LLP -1 Bttry Pk Plz -NY 10004
(516) 432-9229 .. **Lee,** Jos T '86 -265 E Beech -Long Bch 11561
(718) 250-2000 .. **Lee,** Joshua '06 %DA -350 Jay -Brklyn 11201 **Fx:**250-2314
(518) 474-6530 .. **Lee,** Judith Ann '82 %Dept Pub Srvc -3 ESP -Albany 12223
(212) 416-6234 .. **Lee,** Julia H '01 %Dept of Law -120 Bway -NY 10271
(212) 963-9075 .. **Lee,** Jun Hee '90 US Secretariat Ofc of Legal Affrs -1 UN Plz -NY 10017
(212) 401-0800 .. **Lee,** Jun Hwa '01 %Disciplinary Comm -61 Bway -NY 10006 **Fx:**287-1045
(212) 845-2000 .. **Lee,** June Hie '03 KBC Financl Prdcts -140 E 45th -NY 10017 **Fx:**845-2100
(212) 310-8000 .. **Lee,** June K '08 %Weil G&M LLP -767 5th Av -NY 10153
(212) 267-1900 .. **Lee,** Jung J '07 %Wade CM -111 Bway -NY 10006
(516) 571-3056 .. **Lee,** Jung-Hea '02 %Cnty Atty -1 West -Mineola 11501 **Fx:**571-6604
(212) 310-8000 .. **Lee,** Justin C '10 %Weil G&M LLP -767 5th Av -NY 10153
(212) 310-8000 .. **Lee,** Justin D '10 %Weil G&M LLP -767 5th Av -NY 10153
(212) 450-4000 .. **Lee,** Justine Z '02 %Davis P&W LLP -450 Lex Av -NY 10017
(914) 251-0603 .. **Lee,** Karen '01 %Gelardi & R,LLP -800 Wstchstr Av -Rye Brook 10573 **Fx:**253-0909
(212) 336-0120 .. **Lee,** Karen M '02 %SEC -3 World Fncl Ctr -NY 10281 **Fx:**336-1323
(212) 909-6000 .. **Lee,** Karl '05 %Debevoise & P LLP -919 3rd Av -NY 10022
(212) 733-0848 .. **Lee,** Katherine K '92 Pfizer Inc -235 E 42nd -NY 10017
(212) 756-2000 .. **Lee,** Kathleen E '05 %Schulte R&Z LLP -919 3rd Av -NY 10022
(585) 325-5150 .. **Lee,** Kathryn Kelleher '98 %Faraci L,LLP -28 E Main -Rchstr 14614
(212) 837-6000 .. **Lee,** Kenneth E '93 (Hughes H&R LLP) -1 Bttry Pk Plz -NY 10004
(212) 530-5000 .. **Lee,** Kevin B '10 Milbank TH&M LLP -1 Chase Manh Plz -NY 10005
(212) 903-9000 .. **Lee,** Kevin K '09 %Linklaters -1345 Av of Amer -NY 10105
(845) 486-6800 .. **Lee,** Kimberly Hunt '00 (McCabe & M LLP) -63 Wshngtn Bx509 -Poughkeepsie 12602
(212) 319-6898 .. **Lee,** Kirsten M '09 %Lavin ORC&D -420 Lex Av -NY 10170
(212) 450-4000 .. **Lee,** Kristina M-K '09 %Davis P&W LLP -450 Lex Av -NY 10017
(718) 358-5908 .. **Lee,** Kyong O L '96 -30-25 Parsons Blvd -Flushng 11354
(212) 504-6000 .. **Lee,** Lauren U '03 %Cadwalader W&T LLP -1 World Fncl Ctr -NY 10281
(212) 302-2400 .. **Lee,** Lawr G '02 %Lynch DE LLP -264 W 40th -NY 10018
(212) 957-7600 .. **Lee,** Lawr J '05 %Cohen & G LLP -800 3rd Av -NY 10022
(212) 715-9100 .. **Lee,** Lilias E '07 %Kramer LN&F,LLP -1177 Av of Amer -NY 10036
(212) 676-0934 .. **Lee,** Lisa '95 Hlth & Hsptl Corp -346 Bway -NY 10013
(718) 222-2359 .. **Lee,** Lucy '08 %Law Dept -350 Jay -Brklyn 11201 **Fx:**222-2373
(718) 522-0686 .. **Lee,** Margaret S '92 -188 Sackett -Brklyn 11231 **Fx:**858-5414
(212) 984-7868 .. **Lee,** Martin R '58 (Warshaw BCS&K,LLP) -555 5th Av -NY 10017
(212) 732-3200 .. **Lee,** Mary Beth Werner '00 %Carter L&M LLP -2 Wall -NY 10005
(212) 395-7010 .. **Lee,** Mary Jane '00 Verizon -1095 Av of Amer -NY 10036
(212) 286-0040 .. **Lee,** May Hung '04 %Younkins & S LLP -420 Lex Av -NY 10170 **Fx:**949-1920
(201) 447-5600 .. **Lee,** Melinda L '02 OfCnsl Johnson & C,LLP -307 7th Av -NY 10001 **Fx:**447-2080
(347) 404-9929 .. **Lee,** Melissa C '06 %MHLS -120 Schermerhorn -Brklyn 11201 **Fx:**(718) 243-2408
(212) 773-3518 .. **Lee,** Melissa L '03 Ernst & Young LLP -5 Times Sq -NY 10036
(212) 735-3000 .. **Lee,** Michl S H '09 %Skadden ASM&F LLP -4 Times Sq -NY 10036
(212) 530-5000 .. **Lee,** Michl S-Y '08 %Milbank TH&M LLP -1 Chase Manh Plz -NY 10005
(212) 944-6022 .. **Lee,** Michl Y '05 RECD -111 Division -NY 10002
(212) 751-2600 .. **Lee,** Min Jung '02 Random House -1745 Bway -NY 10019
(212) 968-4159 .. **Lee,** Minjoo '98 %GFI Grp -55 Water -NY 10041
(212) 919-3786 .. **Lee,** Mondo Ulysses '02 %Guardian Life Ins -7 Hanover Sq -NY 10004 **Fx:**919-2693
(718) 447-6054 .. **Lee,** Nichole E '99 N Lee,PC -291 Jewett Av -Staten Isl 10302 **Fx:**818-9896
(631) 761-7000 .. **Lee,** Nicola P '89 %Touro Cllg Law Ctr -225 Eastvw Dr -Central Islip 11722
(914) 288-9560 .. **Lee,** Padraic D '91 -57 Hathaway Ln -White Plns 10605
(212) 282-2000 .. **Lee,** Parkin '82 %Rockefeller Grp -1221 Av of Amer -NY 10020 **Fx:**282-2005
(212) 262-2390 .. **Lee,** Patricia A '07 (Connell F LLP) -888 7th Av -NY 10106
(212) 484-8000 .. **Lee,** Patricia Chung-Yen '98 Time Warner -1 Time Warner Ctr -NY 10019
(212) 808-7800 .. **Lee,** Patricia M '84 (Kelley D&W LLP) -101 Park Av -NY 10178
(212) 522-3383 .. **Lee,** Paul A '02 %Time Inc -1271 Av of Amer -NY 10020 **Fx:**522-0437
(212) 909-6000 .. **Lee,** Paul L '74 (Debevoise & P LLP) -919 3rd Av -NY 10022
(212) 350-7460 .. **Lee,** Paul S '01 %Korea Exchange Bk -460 Park Av -NY 10022
(212) 909-6000 .. **Lee,** Pou-I '09 %Debevoise & P LLP -919 3rd Av -NY 10022
(212) 609-6800 .. **Lee,** Priscilla '06 %McCarter & E,LLP -245 Park Av -NY 10167

(212) 675-8484 .. **Lee,** R May '91 Rowen Warren Inc -36 W 25th -NY 10010
(718) 983-8800 .. **Lee,** R Randy '69 (Lee & A,LLP) -260 Christopher Ln -Staten Isl 10314
(631) 342-6000 .. **Lee,** Rachel '99 Computer Assoc Intl -1 Computer Assoc Plz -Islandia 11749
(212) 331-2803 .. **Lee,** Rachel '06 Universal Music Grp,Inc -1755 Bway -NY 10019
(212) 468-4800 .. **Lee,** Randall H '03 %Davis & G LLP -1740 Bway -NY 10019
(212) 379-6988 .. **Lee,** Regina F '78 %Chinatwn Hlth Clinic Fndn -268 Canal -NY 10013 **Fx:**379-6936
(212) 849-7000 .. **Lee,** Rex '05 %Quinn EU&S,LLP -51 Mad Av -NY 10010
(518) 761-6547 .. **Lee,** Richd A '78 Supreme Ct -1340 State Route 9 -Lk George 12845 **Fx:**761-6465
(718) 886-8383 .. **Lee,** Richd H '96 -136-20 38th Av -Flushng 11354
(212) 909-6000 .. **Lee,** Richd S '06 %Debevoise & P LLP -919 3rd Av -NY 10022
(212) 250-8187 .. **Lee,** Robt Chuan-Jin '01 %Deutsche Bank -60 Wall -NY 10005
(212) 349-4300 .. **Lee,** Robt E Jr. '67 Lee & K,PC -225 Bway -NY 10007 **Fx:**766-8039
(716) 852-2611 .. **Lee,** Robt E Jr. '79 -17 Court -Buffalo 14202
(716) 853-8530 .. **Lee,** Robt J '84 %OCTF -350 Main Pl Twr -Buffalo 14202 **Fx:**853-8550
(212) 594-3656 .. **Lee,** Robt K '03 %SC Yom -38 W 32nd -NY 10001 **Fx:**594-3621
(631) 852-1696 .. **Lee,** Robt T '79 %Hon R Doyle -210 Center Dr -Rvrhead 11901
(212) 446-4800 .. **Lee,** Rochelle H '09 %Kirkland & E LLP -153 E 53rd -NY 10022
(212) 530-5000 .. **Lee,** Roger B '09 %Milbank TH&M LLP -1 Chase Manh Plz -NY 10005
(212) 648-0430 .. **Lee,** Rose J '05 %JP Morgan Chase -245 Park Av -NY 10167
(212) 608-8100 .. **Lee,** Sabrina L '82 -11 Mott -NY 10013
(212) 408-2500 .. **Lee,** Sandra Sohee '02 SpclCnsl Baker B,LLP -30 Rckfllr Plz -NY 10112
(212) 903-9000 .. **Lee,** Sarah B '08 %Linklaters -1345 Av of Amer -NY 10105
(718) 618-3683 .. **Lee,** Seon Jeong '05 Hon A Torres - Supreme Ct -265 E 161st -Bronx 10451
(212) 408-5100 .. **Lee,** Sey-Hyo '92 (Chadbourne & P LLP) -30 Rckfllr Plz -NY 10112
(212) 455-2000 .. **Lee,** Shinzong Florence '10 %Simpson T&B LLP -425 Lex Av -NY 10017
(631) 962-2000 .. **Lee,** Shu Muk '96 %OSI Pharm -41 Pinelawn Rd -Melvll 11747
(212) 227-5577 .. **Lee,** Simon '76 (Lee & C,PC) -7 Chatham Sq -NY 10038 **Fx:**732-2671
(212) 651-7500 .. **Lee,** Simon '07 %Segal MS&M -850 3rd Av -NY 10022
(212) 326-3939 .. **Lee,** Solyn '10 %Jones D -222 E 41st -NY 10017
(212) 310-2000 .. **Lee,** Song-Chu '06 Colgate-Palmolive -300 Park Av -NY 10022 **Fx:**310-3406
(212) 622-5624 .. **Lee,** Sonia '97 JP Morgan Chase & Co -277 Park Av -NY 10172
(212) 225-2000 .. **Lee,** Sonya Hyun Shik '02 Cleary GS&H -1 Lbrty Plz -NY 10006
(212) 656-5151 .. **Lee,** Soo Jee '92 %NYSE -11 Wall -NY 10005
(516) 294-1333 .. **Lee,** Soojung Christine '08 %DeMartini & Y LLP -264 Hillside Av -Williston Pk 11596
(212) 537-1244 .. **Lee,** Soo-Mi '91 Morgan Stanley -1633 Bway -NY 10019
(212) 483-9600 .. **Lee,** Sooyung T '00 %Costello S&G LLP -44 Wall -NY 10005
(212) 444-6357 .. **Lee,** Sophia '97 ITG Inc -380 Mad Av -NY 10017 **Fx:**444-6295
(212) 715-9100 .. **Lee,** Soyoung '01 %Kramer LN&F,LLP -1177 Av of Amer -NY 10036
(516) 432-8224 .. **Lee,** Stephen K '67 -415 E Penn Bx57 -Long Bch 11561
(212) 637-2413 .. **Lee,** Steve C '04 US Atty -1 St Andrews Plz -NY 10007
(212) 698-3500 .. **Lee,** Steve J '04 %Dechert LLP -1095 Av of Amer -NY 10036
(212) 319-1000 .. **Lee,** Steven A '88 (Quirk & B,PC) -845 3rd Av -NY 10022
(212) 425-7200 .. **Lee,** Steven J '85 (Kenyon & K,LLP) -1 Bway -NY 10004
(212) 495-0100 .. **Lee,** Stewart W '01 %Gottesman WMF&W,PC -11 Hanover Sq -NY 10005 **Fx:**480-9797
(212) 610-6300 .. **Lee,** Sue R '04 %Allen & O -1221 Av of Amer -NY 10020
(212) 412-4785 .. **Lee,** Sung-A '03 Eveready Ins Co -59 Maiden Ln -NY 10038
(914) 997-0500 .. **Lee,** Sung-Min '09 %Lowey DC&H,PC -1 N Bway -White Plns 10601
(518) 374-3373 .. **Lee,** Sunny '93 (Silverman S&S) -527 State -Schnctdy 12305
(212) 425-1900 .. **Lee,** Susan '08 %Freehill H&M LLP -80 Pine -NY 10005
(212) 566-6780 .. **Lee,** Susan '09 %D Moss & Assoc -15 Maiden Ln -NY 10038 **Fx:**766-3362
(718) 838-7878 .. **Lee,** Susan S '07 %Bronx Defenders -860 Crtlandt Av -Bronx 10451 **Fx:**665-0100
(212) 310-8000 .. **Lee,** Suzanne Min-Sung '07 %Weil G&M LLP -767 5th Av -NY 10153
(212) 848-4000 .. **Lee,** Sylvia '07 %Shearman & S LLP -599 Lex Av -NY 10022
(212) 483-9600 .. **Lee,** Sylvia E '95 Costello S&G LLP -44 Wall -NY 10005
(212) 454-3478 .. **Lee,** Tammie '97 %Deutsche Bank -60 Wall -NY 10005
(212) 957-0500 .. **Lee,** Tammy Mea Hwa '99 -145 W 57th -NY 10019 **Fx:**957-2020
(212) 572-4200 .. **Lee,** Teena Heejung '97 %Estee Lauder -767 5th Av -NY 10153 **Fx:**572-3989
(212) 421-4100 .. **Lee,** Teresa A '01 (Pryor C LLP) -7 Times Sq -NY 10036
(212) 806-5400 .. **Lee,** Terisa H '07 %Stroock &S&L LLP -180 Maiden Ln -NY 10038
(516) 564-4970 .. **Lee,** Thelma M '80 Dept of Social Srvcs -50 Clinton -Hempstd 11550
(718) 252-4467 .. **Lee,** Thos E '74 Lee & K,PC -2175 Flatbush Av -Brklyn 11234 **Fx:**338-3551
(212) 636-6000 .. **Lee,** Thos H '01 %Fordham Univ Sch of Law -140 W 62nd -NY 10023 **Fx:**636-6899
(212) 925-3060 .. **Lee,** Thos W '93 -48 Allen -NY 10002
(212) 449-1000 .. **Lee,** Thos W '95 %Merrill Lynch -220 Bway -NY 10038
(585) 263-6760 .. **Lee,** Tiffany Ho-Yan '98 %US Atty -620 Fed Bldg -Rchstr 14614 **Fx:**263-6226
(212) 761-2269 .. **Lee,** Todd R '96 Morgan Stanley -1585 Bway -NY 10036
(212) 223-3066 .. **Lee,** Victor H '86 Victory Grp Ltd -188 E 64th -NY 10065
(212) 596-9000 .. **Lee,** Vince S '08 %Ropes & G LLP -1211 Av of Amer -NY 10036
(212) 504-6000 .. **Lee,** Vinny '07 %Cadwalader W&T LLP -1 World Fncl Ctr -NY 10281
(212) 225-2000 .. **Lee,** Vivian S '10 %Cleary GS&H -1 Lbrty Plz -NY 10006
(212) 688-5151 .. **Lee,** Walter-Michael '04 %Gibney A&F,LLP -665 5th Av -NY 10022
(212) 556-2100 .. **Lee,** Wan Chieh '06 %King & S -1185 Av of Amer -NY 10036
(845) 639-7800 .. **Lee,** Wendy H '97 %Mandel K&B,LLP -210 Route 303 -Vly Cottage 10989
(718) 539-8448 .. **Lee,** Wm '85 ALJ -3056 Whitestone Expy -Flushng 11354
(212) 291-3747 .. **Lee,** Wm F '94 %Citigroup -125 Broad -NY 10004
(212) 370-1300 .. **Lee,** Wing Shing Brian '06 %Ellenoff G&S LLP -150 E 42nd -NY 10017
(212) 969-3000 .. **Lee,** Winnie '07 %Proskauer R LLP -1585 Bway -NY 10036
(212) 267-1911 .. **Lee,** Winston '78 -20 Vesey -NY 10007 **Fx:**964-2926
(718) 224-8174 .. **Lee,** Won J '04 -45-22 Sprngfld Blvd -Bayside 11361
(212) 425-7670 .. **Lee,** Woomee '04 %A Schreiber -40 Exch Pl -NY 10005 **Fx:**425-9237
(212) 617-6523 .. **Lee,** Yoomi '09 %Bloomberg LP -731 Lex Av -NY 10022
(212) 739-3229 .. **Lee,** Young '98 Allianz Global Invstrs -1345 Av of Amer -NY 10105
(646) 386-4405 .. **Lee,** Young Chun '94 Supreme Ct -111 Centre -NY 10013
(212) 506-5000 .. **Lee,** Young J '03 %Orrick H&S LLP -51 W 52nd -NY 10019
(631) 852-1686 .. **Lee,** Young Jun '05 Supreme Ct -210 Center Dr -Rvrhead 11901
(212) 909-6000 .. **Lee,** Young Kuk '07 %Debevoise & P LLP -919 3rd Av -NY 10022
(212) 636-6000 .. **Lee,** Youngjae '00 %Fordham Univ Sch of Law -140 W 62nd -NY 10023 **Fx:**636-6899
(212) 225-2000 .. **Lee,** Youngro '08 %Cleary GS&H -1 Lbrty Plz -NY 10006
(212) 596-9000 .. **Lee,** Yuan-Sea Janise '03 %Ropes & G LLP -1211 Av of Amer -NY 10036
(212) 417-8700 .. **Lee,** Yuanchung '97 %Fed Def of NY Inc -52 Duane -NY 10007 **Fx:**571-0392
(516) 921-8600 .. **Lee,** Yuichi Paul '93 %McAndrew C&P -95 Froehlich Farm Blvd -Woodbury 11797
(212) 770-5268 .. **Lee,** Yun Gyong '95 AIG -70 Pine -NY 10270
(718) 254-0700 .. **Lee,** Yung-Mi '93 Bklyn Defender Srvcs -177 Lvngstn -Brklyn 11201 **Fx:**254-0897
(212) 735-3000 .. **Lee,** Yvonne L '09 %Skadden ASM&F LLP -4 Times Sq -NY 10036
(518) 455-5091 .. **Leech,** Sandra M '99 Admin Reg Rev Comm -Agncy Bldg 4 -Albany 12248 **Fx:**455-4175
(518) 487-7600 .. **Leech,** Seth R '99 (Whiteman O&H LLP) -1 Commerce Plz -Albany 12260
(212) 777-4800 .. **Lee-Cunningham,** Bonda E '83 %Fed of ProtestantWelfareAgcy -281 Park Av S -NY 10010 **Fx:**982-0697
(716) 631-5700 .. **Leed,** Carolyn E '05 %Sargent & C,LLP -6245 Sheridan Dr -Williamsvll 14221 **Fx:**631-9120
(212) 566-4099 .. **Leeder,** Louis I '91 -277 Bway -NY 10007 **Fx:**346-0858
(607) 778-2423 .. **Leeds,** Brian T '08 %DA -45 Hawley Bx1766 -Bnghmtn 13902 **Fx:**778-8870
(212) 736-2870 .. **Leeds,** Craig S '93 -350 5th Av-Ste 3304 -NY 10118
(212) 835-2000 .. **Leeds,** Jeffrey T '86 (Leeds Weld & Co) -350 Park Av -NY 10022
(716) 873-7908 .. **Leeds,** Karen B '77 -265 Lincoln Pkwy -Buffalo 14216
(631) 941-4150 .. **Leeds,** Kenneth W '66 -61 Uppr Sheep Pasture Rd Bx61 -E Setauket 11733 **Fx:**941-4136
(516) 873-9550 .. **Leeds,** Lenard '75 (Leeds M&B) -1 Old Cntry Rd -Carle Pl 11514
(212) 361-1930 .. **Leeds,** Mark H '74 %Envrnmntl Cntrl Brd -66 John -NY 10038 **Fx:**361-1900
(212) 801-6947 .. **Leeds,** Mark H '85 (Greenberg T,LLP) -200 Park Av -NY 10166
(212) 922-9250 .. **Leeds,** Matthew J '78 (Ganfer & S LLP) -360 Lex Av -NY 10017
(212) 773-5613 .. **Leeds,** Maura B '93 %Ernst & Young LLP -5 Times Sq -NY 10036
(516) 873-9550 .. **Leeds Morelli & Brown** -1 Old Cntry Rd -Carle Pl 11514 **Fx:**747-5024
(212) 688-3200 .. **Leeds,** Rachel S '06 %Scheichet & D,PC -767 3rd Av -NY 10017
(718) 488-8255 .. **Leeds,** Spencer A '90 -26 Court -Brklyn 11242 **Fx:**488-8299
(212) 232-1300 .. **Leeds,** Suzanne B '07 %Lewis BB&S LLP -77 Water -NY 10005
(212) 563-4100 .. **Leeds,** Zachary N '05 %Cohen W&S LLP -330 W 42nd -NY 10036
(212) 450-4000 .. **Leef,** Catherine G '88 %Davis P&W LLP -450 Lex Av -NY 10017
(516) 561-5003 .. **Leef,** Joel L '49 -147 S Franklin Av -Vly Stream 11580
(212) 323-2250 .. **Leef-Hewitt,** Roxanne '85 %HHC-OLA-Medical Litigation -346 Bway -NY 10013 **Fx:**323-2251
(585) 325-4545 .. **Leegant,** Jo Anne '81 (Egger & L) -144 Exchange Blvd -Rchstr 14614 **Fx:**325-6716
(315) 265-2595 .. **Leek,** Jerry C '64 JC Leek,PLLC -107 S Canton Rd -Potsdam 13676 **Fx:**265-4909
(212) 906-1200 .. **Lee Lim,** Jiyeon '87 (Latham & W) -885 3rd Av -NY 10022
(212) 696-9111 .. **Leemon,** Scott E '96 (S Leemon,PC) -140 E 45th -NY 10017 **Fx:**(800) 856-9712
(845) 639-7800 .. **Leen,** Edw J '97 %Mandel K&B,LLP -210 Route 303 -Vly Cottage 10989
(914) 378-1010 .. **Leen,** John J C '01 %Fitzgerald & F -538 Riverdale Av -Ynkrs 10705
(718) 250-2000 .. **Leeper,** James K M '86 %DA -350 Jay -Brklyn 11201 **Fx:**250-2314
(914) 824-5070 .. **Lee-Renert,** Matthew A '95 %Atty Grievance Comm -399 Knollwood Rd -White Plns 10603 **Fx:**949-0997
(212) 403-1000 .. **Lees,** Alexander B '07 %Wachtell LR&K -51 W 52nd -NY 10019
(212) 477-1899 .. **Lees,** Aubrey '79 -799 Bway -NY 10003
(212) 669-4717 .. **Lees,** Ilene A '97 DCAS-DLS -1 Centre -NY 10007 **Fx:**669-2139
(212) 762-5171 .. **Lees,** Jason J '02 Morgan Stanley -1221 Av of Amer -NY 10020
(212) 480-2290 .. **Lees,** Martha Alexandra '94 %Insurance Dept -25 Beaver -NY 10004 **Fx:**480-5272
(212) 453-3649 .. **Leest,** Michl L '02 ACE -1325 Av of Amer -NY 10019
(212) 335-9000 .. **Leet,** Scott P '02 %DA -1 Hogan Pl -NY 10013
(212) 265-7600 .. **Lefcourt,** Blossom B '06 Broadway Video -1619 Bway -NY 10019
(212) 737-0400 .. **Lefcourt,** Gerald B '67 (G Lefcourt,PC) -148 E 78th -NY 10075 **Fx:**988-6192
(845) 359-2149 .. **Lefcourt,** Robyn H '92 (Lewis & L) -Bx219 -Blauvelt 10913
(203) 330-2265 .. **Lefebvre,** Edw B '09 %Pullman & C,LLC -50 Main -White Plns 10606
(518) 434-4553 .. **Lefebvre,** Kim F '80 %Justice Dept -74 Chapel -Albany 12207 **Fx:**434-4459
(914) 793-2874 .. **Leferovich,** John Jr. '58 -134 Siwanoy Blvd -Eastchstr 10709 **Fx:**793-5225
(212) 858-1000 .. **Lefever,** Anne C '08 %Pillsbury WSP LLP -1540 Bway -NY 10036
(212) 422-1200 .. **Leff,** Allison G '03 %Abrams GF&J,PC -1 Bttry Pk Plz -NY 10004
(516) 798-0900 .. **Leff,** Barry M '97 (Leff & L,LLP) -1022 Park Blvd -Massapequa Pk 11762 **Fx:**798-0751
(212) 384-1000 .. **Leff,** Douglas A '93 FBI -26 Fed Plz -NY 10278
(212) 416-8465 .. **Leff,** Eugene J '72 %Dept of Law -120 Bway -NY 10271
(516) 739-7500 .. **Leff,** Howard B '79 H Leff PC -1055 Franklin Av -Gdn Cty 11530 **Fx:**739-3587
(212) 674-5986 .. **Leff,** Katherine V G '91 -40 1st Av -NY 10009
(212) 416-8705 .. **Leff,** Marjorie S '92 %Dept of Law -120 Bway -NY 10271 **Fx:**416-6147
(914) 939-0002 .. **Leff,** Meredith Ann '98 %Gallo F&N,LLP -211 S Ridge -Rye Brook 10573

(212) 735-3000 .. **Leff,** Neil M '81 (Skadden ASM&F LLP) -4 Times Sq -NY 10036
(516) 798-0900 .. **Leff,** Richd A '92 Leff & L,LLP -1022 Park Blvd -Massapequa Pk 11762 **Fx:**798-0751
(212) 509-3456 .. **Leff,** Richd E '98 %McGivney & K,PC -80 Broad -NY 10004
(716) 854-3321 .. **Leff,** Richd I '74 -403 Main -Buffalo 14203 **Fx:**608-1313
(718) 793-1311 .. **Leff,** Richd R '71 -80-02 Kew Grdns Rd -Kew Gdns 11415 **Fx:**575-4070
(516) 798-0900 .. **Leff,** Robt M '60 (Leff & L,LLP) -1022 Park Blvd -Massapequa Pk 11762 **Fx:**798-0751
(914) 347-2600 .. **Leff,** Robt M '94 (Traub LS&S LLP) -7 Skyline Dr -Hawthorne 10532
(212) 474-1000 .. **Leff,** Ross M '08 %Cravath S&M LLP -825 8th Av -NY 10019
(718) 624-0154 .. **Leff,** Thos D '93 Cnsl Katz & Assoc -26 Court -Brklyn 11242 **Fx:**624-4212
(212) 982-0253 .. **Leffel,** Fredric J '75 -112 E 19th -NY 10003
(212) 765-3200 .. **Leffel,** Jonathan T '98 Nigro Karlin S&F -156 W 56th -NY 10019
(212) 373-3000 .. **Leffell,** Danl J '83 (Paul WRW&G LLP) -1285 Av of Amer -NY 10019
(212) 935-5500 .. **Lefferts,** Matthew C '93 (Franklin WR&V) -488 Mad Av -NY 10022
(212) 661-2900 .. **Leffler,** Andrew J '08 %Kriss & F LLP -360 Lex Av -NY 10017
(212) 891-9100 .. **Leffler,** Bruce S '77 (Goldfarb & F LLP) -345 Park Av -NY 10154
(212) 447-7575 .. **Leffler,** David J '82 (Leffler M&M LLC) -200 Mad Av -NY 10016 **Fx:**202-4229
(212) 969-3000 .. **Leffler,** Fredric C '78 SrCnsl Proskauer R LLP -1585 Bway -NY 10036
(845) 469-4900 .. **Leffler,** Marc R '98 -99 Brookside Av -Chester 10918 **Fx:**469-2022
(212) 292-4344 .. **Leffler,** Raymond G '58 -521 5th Av -NY 10175
(212) 944-2200 .. **Leffler,** Stanley S '61 (Ferber CE&C,LLP) -530 5th Av -NY 10036
(212) 951-6565 .. **Lefkarites,** Christopher P '59 %NYS Ed Dept-OLS -475 Park Av S -NY 10016 **Fx:**951-6573
(212) 557-6230 .. **Lefkort,** Leonard J '50 -221 W 82nd -NY 10024
(212) 728-8000 .. **Lefkort,** Maurice M '90 (Willkie F&G LLP) -787 7th Av -NY 10019
(212) 766-5665 .. **Lefkowicz,** Mark I '96 (Lefkowicz & G) -150 Bway -NY 10038 **Fx:**608-5201
(516) 295-9680 .. **Lefkowitz,** Aaron J '04 %A Katsman,PC -65 Roosevelt Av -Vly Stream 11581 **Fx:**295-9685
(516) 942-4700 .. **Lefkowitz,** Danl J '82 OfCnsl Lefkowitz H&C -500 N Bway -Jericho 11753
(212) 310-8850 .. **Lefkowitz,** David S '87 (Weil G&M LLP) -767 5th Av -NY 10153
(914) 285-9800 .. **Lefkowitz,** Elisa J '92 %Kurzman EC&L,LLP -1 N Bway -White Plns 10601
(212) 968-1001 .. **Lefkowitz,** Ellen '77 (Gwertzman LBS&M) -80 Broad -NY 10004
(212) 770-8815 .. **Lefkowitz,** Eric S '99 AIG -70 Pine -NY 10270
(518) 786-9069 .. **Lefkowitz,** Gary A '83 %Schiller & K LLP -950 New Loudon Rd -Latham 12110
(516) 942-4700 .. **Lefkowitz Hogan & Cassell** -500 N Bway -Jericho 11753 **Fx:**942-4705
(212) 551-7888 .. **Lefkowitz,** Howard M '89 -380 Lex Av #1700 -NY 10168 **Fx:**(914) 769-5437
(914) 769-7668 .. **Lefkowitz,** Howard M '89 -32 Flag Hill Rd -Chappaqua 10514 **Fx:**769-5437
(212) 682-1440 .. **Lefkowitz,** Jared M '99 -250 Park Av -NY 10177 **Fx:**(917) 591-8991
(212) 446-4800 .. **Lefkowitz,** Jay P '88 (Kirkland & E LLP) -153 E 53rd -NY 10022
(518) 457-2854 .. **Lefkowitz,** Jerome '55 PERB -80 Wolf Rd -Albany 12205 **Fx:**457-2664
(212) 566-3200 .. **Lefkowitz,** Jonathan B '99 %P Mann LLC -45 Bway -NY 10006 **Fx:**566-0220
(212) 837-6000 .. **Lefkowitz,** Kenneth A '84 (Hughes H&R LLP) -1 Bttry Pk Plz -NY 10004
(516) 280-2472 .. **Lefkowitz,** Lawr S '98 -575 Uniondale Av -Uniondale 11553 **Fx:**280-2473
(212) 645-1990 .. **Lefkowitz,** Lori M '91 %Levine & G -115 Christopher -NY 10014
(212) 732-4800 .. **Lefkowitz,** Mark D '73 -150 Bway -NY 10038 **Fx:**964-7919
(212) 867-6000 .. **Lefkowitz,** Michl E '90 (Rosenberg & E,PC) -733 3rd Av -NY 10017
(718) 923-4206 .. **Lefkowitz,** Michl I '75 %OTDA Fair Hearings -14 Boerum Pl -Brklyn 11201
(212) 267-3091 .. **Lefkowitz,** Michele C '05 %Wilentz G&S -110 William -NY 10038 **Fx:**(732) 726-6572
(212) 754-5100 .. **Lefkowitz,** Miriam '09 Shufro Rose & Co -745 5th Av -NY 10151 **Fx:**754-5111
(212) 471-8544 .. **Lefkowitz,** Natalie M '98 (Herzfeld & R,PC) -125 Broad -NY 10004
(631) 232-1130 .. **Lefkowitz & Poulos** -1770 Motor Pkwy -Hauppauge 11788 **Fx:**232-1938
(845) 627-1011 .. **Lefkowitz,** Richd A '67 -404 E Route 59 -Nanuet 10954 **Fx:**620-9390
(516) 228-2324 .. **Lefkowitz,** Richd B '83 (Fox & L,LLP) -666 Old Cntry Rd -Gdn Cty 11530 **Fx:**228-8990
(212) 759-1200 .. **Lefkowitz,** Richd S '85 (Lefkowitz & E) -444 Mad Av -NY 10022 **Fx:**317-8717
(212) 363-7500 .. **Lefkowitz,** Robt H '06 %Levi & K LLP -30 Broad -NY 10004
(845) 665-1968 .. **Lefkowitz,** Sol '49 -177 Old Route 17 -Monticello 12701
(212) 859-8000 .. **Lefkowitz,** Stephen A '65 (Fried FHS&J LLP) -1 NY Plz -NY 10004
(914) 428-1438 .. **Lefland,** Robt M '81 %T Bona,PC -123 Main -White Plns 10601 **Fx:**428-1413
(845) 639-9147 .. **Lefland,** Robt M '81 -19 Sundbury Dr -New Cty 10956
(212) 326-3939 .. **Lefont,** Stacey Nichols '93 OfCnsl Jones D -222 E 41st -NY 10017
(718) 230-8806 .. **Lefort,** Nicole '93 -345 Clinton Av -Brklyn 11238
(212) 708-6600 .. **LeFrak,** Harrison T '98 %LeFrak Org -40 W 57th -NY 10019 **Fx:**708-6681
(516) 364-7900 .. **Lefranc,** Tamara '04 Epstein F&G -45 Crsswys Park Dr W -Woodbury 11797
(212) 455-2000 .. **Lefranc,** Till I '09 %Simpson T&B LLP -425 Lex Av -NY 10017
(212) 352-3220 .. **Lefton,** Nicole R '90 American Confernece Inst -41 W 25th -NY 10010 **Fx:**352-3231
(212) 801-3159 .. **Lefton,** Ronald D '77 (Greenberg T,LLP) -200 Park Av -NY 10166
(212) 557-4190 .. **Leftt,** Andrew D '02 %D Kownacki,PC -420 Lex Av -NY 10170 **Fx:**557-4188
(212) 407-8383 .. **Leftwich,** Michelle A '94 NBA Properties -645 5th Av -NY 10022
(212) 442-1400 .. **Legagneur,** Vanessa C '06 Conflicts of Int Bd -2 Lafayette -NY 10007 **Fx:**442-1407
(631) 751-1464 .. **Legakis,** Peter P '82 (Legakis & V,PC) -60 Route 25A -E Setauket 11733 **Fx:**751-2264
(718) 321-1800 .. **Legan,** Stanley J '78 (Ross LRZ&F,LLP) -41-60 Main -Flushng 11355
(212) 967-8500 .. **Legan,** Stanley J '78 (Ross LRZ&F,LLP) -450 7th Av -NY 10123
(212) 577-3688 .. **Legano Ross,** Joanne '84 %Leg Aid -199 Water -NY 10038 **Fx:**509-8431
(212) 583-5000 .. **Legaspi,** Mark L N '08 Blackstone Grp -345 Park Av -NY 10154
(212) 504-6000 .. **Legault,** Jeffrey A '02 SpclCnsl Cadwalader W&T LLP -1 World Fncl Ctr -NY 10281
(212) 596-9000 .. **Leger,** Olivier A '09 %Ropes & G LLP -1211 Av of Amer -NY 10036
(212) 334-4466 .. **Legere,** Mark P '90 -350 Bway -NY 10013
(212) 803-5107 .. **Legeros,** Katherine R D '95 %NY Cnty Defender Srvcs -225 Bway -NY 10007 **Fx:**571-6035
(914) 946-6774 .. **Leggett,** Russell R '59 (Pilkington & L,PC) -222 Bloomingdale Rd -White Plns 10605
(518) 464-4080 .. **Leggiero-Grossman,** Heather J '06 (Dorfman-Robbie,CPAs,PC) -6 Wembley Ct -Albany 12205
(631) 754-0486 .. **Leggio,** Anthony J '92 -635 Pulaski Rd -Greenlawn 11740 **Fx:**754-9067
(518) 719-3590 .. **Leggio,** Sarah A '08 %DA -411 Main -Catskill 12414 **Fx:**719-3792
(212) 490-3000 .. **Leghorn,** Thos A '82 (Wilson EME&D LLP) -150 E 42nd -NY 10017
(914) 323-7000 .. **Leghorn,** Thos A '82 (Wilson EME&D LLP) -3 Gannett Dr -White Plns 10604
(518) 273-2201 .. **Legnard,** Jos F '74 Village of Green Island -20 Clinton -Green Island 12183
(212) 868-1010 .. **Lego,** John S '93 %Kudman TA LLP -350 5th Av -NY 10118
(212) 791-0613 .. **Legon,** Steven Z '96 -401 Bway -NY 10013 **Fx:**964-2926
(518) 474-0871 .. **Legorius,** Christine M '88 Cnsl DMV -6 ESP -Albany 12228 **Fx:**486-4485
(914) 422-8700 .. **Legow,** Amy K '87 %OCTF -101 E Post Rd -White Plns 10601 **Fx:**422-8795
(212) 851-8432 .. **Legros,** Evans J '97 Legros Law Firm LLC -116 W 23rd -NY 10011
(516) 873-9300 .. **Legum,** Steven G '76 -170 Old Cntry Rd -Mineola 11501 **Fx:**742-0571
(212) 344-3800 .. **Lehach,** Brian M '04 Christophe & Assoc,PC -2 Wall -NY 10005 **Fx:**344-3212
(212) 808-7800 .. **LeHane,** Robt L '99 (Kelley D&W LLP) -101 Park Av -NY 10178
(212) 708-6682 .. **Lehman,** Arnold S '84 LeFrak Org -40 W 57th -NY 10019 **Fx:**708-6681
(212) 697-2715 .. **Lehman,** Arthur '77 (Lehman & G,PC) -52 Vndrblt Av -NY 10017 **Fx:**697-2773
(516) 222-0888 .. **Lehman,** Bob E '85 (Lehman & E LLP) -50 Chas Lindbergh Blvd -Uniondale 11553
(315) 789-8480 .. **Lehman,** Bram S '91 (Bond M&L,PC) -91 Genesee -Geneva 14456
(212) 756-2000 .. **Lehman,** Burton '65 OfCnsl Schulte R&Z LLP -919 3rd Av -NY 10022
(212) 867-3636 .. **Lehman,** Douglas M '75 (Levin & G,PC) -420 Lex Av -NY 10170
(631) 366-3555 .. **Lehman,** Dudley L '65 -732 Smithtwn Bypass -Smithtwn 11787 **Fx:**366-3567
(516) 222-0888 .. **Lehman & Eilen LLP** -50 Chas Lindbergh Blvd -Uniondale 11553 **Fx:**222-0948
(718) 261-3047 .. **Lehman,** Gregory C '88 %Queens Law Assoc -118-21 Qns Blvd -Frst Hlls 11375 **Fx:**261-0798
(212) 785-4400 .. **Lehman,** Jeffrey M '92 -40 Exchange -NY 10005 **Fx:**(866) 634-4818
(212) 661-3535 .. **Lehman,** Margaret E '86 (Hodgson R LLP) -60 E 42nd -NY 10165
(212) 770-1625 .. **Lehman,** Robin G '95 %AIG -80 Pine -NY 10005 **Fx:**344-0972
(212) 576-8568 .. **Lehman,** Seth M '00 Marvel Enterprises,Inc -417 5th Av -NY 10016
(212) 889-4440 .. **Lehman,** Stanley P '83 %Scolari G&W -475 Park Av S -NY 10016
(212) 297-2665 .. **Lehman,** Stephanie F '97 (Cozen O) -277 Park Av -NY 10172 **Fx:**672-1149
(646) 223-4200 .. **Lehman,** Stephen P '93 %Reuters -3 Times Sq -NY 10036 **Fx:**223-4250
(315) 474-2911 .. **Lehman,** Suzanne K '07 %Smith SK&S,PC -250 S Clinton -Syracuse 13202
(518) 431-4164 .. **Lehmann,** Gregory C '01 NLRB -1 Clinton Av & N Pearl -Albany 12207
(212) 336-0184 .. **Lehmann,** John C Jr. '05 SEC -3 World Fncl Ctr -NY 10281 **Fx:**336-1323
(212) 790-4500 .. **Lehmann,** Michl A '88 (Manatt P&P,LLP) -7 Times Sq -NY 10036
(212) 848-4000 .. **Lehner,** Jason R '96 (Shearman & S LLP) -599 Lex Av -NY 10022
(212) 727-2700 .. **Lehner,** Peter H '86 NRDC -40 W 20th -NY 10011 **Fx:**727-1773
(716) 884-1122 .. **Lehner,** Richd J '56 -134 Highland Av -Buffalo 14222 **Fx:**884-1007
(718) 618-1418 .. **Lehnert,** Jack S '95 %Supreme Ct -851 Grnd Cncrs -Bronx 10451
(212) 455-2000 .. **Lehpamer,** Kevin J '04 %Simpson T&B LLP -425 Lex Av -NY 10017
(718) 876-6300 .. **Lehr,** David W '73 %DA -130 Styvsnt Pl -Staten Isl 10301
(516) 364-1095 .. **Lehr,** John '06 McBreen & K -500 N Bway -Jericho 11753
(212) 318-6000 .. **Lehr,** Jonathan M '72 Paul HJ&W LLP -75 E 55th -NY 10022
(212) 450-4000 .. **Lehr,** Matthew B '88 (Davis P&W LLP) -450 Lex Av -NY 10017
(212) 336-2000 .. **Lehrburger,** Robt W '90 (Patterson BW&T LLP) -1133 Av of Amer -NY 10036
(212) 722-2000 .. **Lehrer,** Andrew '79 %Leg Aid -230 E 106th -NY 10029 **Fx:**876-5365
(212) 996-6657 .. **Lehrer,** Gaby F '77 -12 E 88th -NY 10128
(212) 768-6700 .. **Lehrer,** Mark R '77 (Sonnenschein N&R LLP) -2 World Fncl Ctr -NY 10281
(212) 589-4200 .. **Lehrer,** Richd M '94 (Baker & H LLP) -45 Rckfllr Plz -NY 10111
(212) 735-8600 .. **Lehrer,** Rudolph F '05 %Morrison C LLP -909 3rd Av -NY 10022
(212) 763-4100 .. **Lehrer,** Sander '67 (Reavis PL LLP) -41 Mad Av -NY 10010
(212) 981-1070 .. **Lehrer,** Scott E '94 %RiskMetrics Grp -1 Chase Manh Plz -NY 10005
(212) 836-8000 .. **Lehrfield,** Aaron Y '96 (Kaye S LLP) -425 Park Av -NY 10022
(212) 752-1000 .. **Lehrhaupt,** Wayne R '75 (Eiseman LL&K,PC) -805 3rd Av -NY 10022
(914) 761-4488 .. **Lehrman,** Fredric M '74 (Lehrman & K) -199 Main -White Plns 10601
(914) 761-4488 .. **Lehrman & Kronick** -199 Main -White Plns 10601 **Fx:**761-4672
(516) 248-2552 .. **Lehrman,** Lewis H '68 -114 Old Cntry Rd -Mineola 11501 **Fx:**746-1924
(212) 980-0120 .. **Lehrman,** Mark D '88 Cnsl Frankfurt KK&S,PC -488 Mad Av -NY 10022
(212) 582-6500 .. **Lehrman,** Michl B '86 (Arshack H&L,PLLC) -1790 Bway -NY 10019
(646) 495-3123 .. **Lehrman,** Robt A '90 %Mark Bruce Intl -909 3rd Av -NY 10022

(212) 813-5900 .. **Lehrman,** Ronald J '58 (Fross ZL&Z,PC) -866 UN Plz -NY 10017
(914) 761-4488 .. **Lehrman,** Stephen J '70 (Lehrman & K) -199 Main -White Plns 10601
(212) 468-4800 .. **Lehv,** David G '74 (Davis & G LLP) -1740 Bway -NY 10019
(212) 813-5900 .. **Lehv,** Richd Z '73 (Fross ZL&Z,PC) -866 UN Plz -NY 10017
(212) 848-4000 .. **Lei,** Devin S '08 %Shearman & S LLP -599 Lex Av -NY 10022
(212) 275-1605 .. **Leib,** Howard D '85 %Atlantic Records -1290 Av of the Americas -NY 10104 **Fx:**405-5287
(716) 856-5500 .. **Leibeck,** Jeffrey J '07 %Damon M LLP -200 Delaware Av -Buffalo 14202
(631) 470-1883 .. **Leibell,** Jeffrey N '92 Garden City Grp Inc -105 Maxess Rd -Melvll 11747
(845) 225-5500 .. **Leibell,** Vincent L III '75 OfCnsl Curtiss & L,PC -20 Church -Carmel 10512
(212) 336-2000 .. **Leibensperger,** Kristen Karns '06 %Patterson BW&T LLP -1133 Av of Amer -NY 10036
(212) 728-8000 .. **Leibert,** Burton M '81 (Willkie F&G LLP) -787 7th Av -NY 10019
(212) 553-4073 .. **Leibert,** Marc A '01 Moody's Investor Srv -99 Church -NY 10007
(212) 564-6633 .. **Leibert,** Wayne S '80 White & M,PC -875 Av of Amer -NY 10001
(718) 775-3293 .. **Leibfreid,** Laura S '02 -93 Montague -Brklyn 11201
(212) 383-2508 .. **Leibler,** Danl I '99 State Dep Comptroller for NYC -59 Maiden Ln -NY 10038
(212) 609-6072 .. **Leibler,** Jack '65 URS -5 Penn Plz -NY 10001
(212) 755-5510 .. **Leibman,** David J '87 (Loeb B & Prtnrs) -505 Park Av -NY 10022
(914) 948-6800 .. **Leibman,** Leonard S '56 -8 Chester Av -White Plns 10601 **Fx:**948-2802
(212) 765-3040 .. **Leibner,** Adam H '94 %NS Bienstock,Inc -250 W 57th -NY 10107 **Fx:**757-6411
(516) 785-2796 .. **Leibner,** Jerry S '72 (JS Leibner,PC) -3061 Timothy Rd -Bellmore 11710 **Fx:**785-2796
(212) 765-3040 .. **Leibner,** Jonathan M '96 %NS Bienstock,Inc -250 W 57th -NY 10107 **Fx:**757-6411
(607) 272-2300 .. **Leibo,** Jeffrey G '04 %Anelli X,PC -202 E State -Ithaca 14850 **Fx:**272-2330
(212) 355-6182 .. **Leibow,** Sandra '81 %EP Dine Inc -115 E 57th -NY 10022 **Fx:**755-8486
(516) 829-4919 .. **Leibowicz,** Barry '73 -111 Grt Nck Rd -Gt Neck 11021 **Fx:**829-4911
(212) 233-5000 .. **Leibowitz,** Alan B '75 (Simonson HL&G,PC) -15 Maiden Ln -NY 10038
(516) 802-0630 .. **Leibowitz,** Allison C '04 %Simmons J,LLP -115 Eileen Way -Syosset 11791
(516) 877-5600 .. **Leibowitz,** Charlesa Rowan '94 %R Tusa -1225 Franklin Av -Gdn Cty 11530 **Fx:**877-5695
(212) 637-1947 .. **Leibowitz,** David S '01 US Atty -1 St Andrews Plz -NY 10007
(718) 951-7063 .. **Leibowitz,** Ephraim K '56 -2223 Av O -Brklyn 11210 **Fx:**951-6271
(212) 487-9700 .. **Leibowitz,** Eric R '06 %White F&F,LLP -61 Bway -NY 10006
(212) 416-6340 .. **Leibowitz,** Gary N '93 %Dept of Law -120 Bway -NY 10271 **Fx:**416-6147
(212) 969-3000 .. **Leibowitz,** Henry J '89 SrCnsl Proskauer R LLP -1585 Bway -NY 10036
(212) 764-1018 .. **Leibowitz,** Herman M '76 -56 W 45th -NY 10036 **Fx:**768-3081
(631) 928-1100 .. **Leibowitz,** Ira H '67 -5507-10 Nesconset Hwy 203 -Mt Sinai 11766 **Fx:**928-5022
(516) 228-9800 .. **Leibowitz,** Jason S '07 %CD Robins -180 Froehlich Farm Blvd -Woodbury 11797
(212) 669-7531 .. **Leibowitz,** Kenneth M '74 DCAS-DLS -1 Centre -NY 10007 **Fx:**669-8558
(516) 222-0888 .. **Leibowitz,** Lawr S '73 Cnsl Lehman & E LLP -50 Chas Lindbergh Blvd -Uniondale 11553
(917) 863-2897 .. **Leibowitz,** Leonard '65 -120 W 86th -NY 10024 **Fx:**(212) 877 1287
(212) 877-5882 .. **Leibowitz,** Margaret S '77 -120 W 86th -NY 10024
(212) 455-2000 .. **Leibowitz,** Noah M '00 %Simpson T&B LLP -425 Lex Av -NY 10017
(845) 295-0400 .. **Leibowitz,** Patti J '90 -6 N Main Bx306 -Liberty 12754 **Fx:**295-9040
(212) 587-3001 .. **Leibowitz,** Saml '91 (Leibowitz & B) -225 Bway -NY 10007 **Fx:**587-8699
(212) 715-9100 .. **Leibowitz,** Zoe D '07 %Kramer LN&F,LLP -1177 Av of Amer -NY 10036
(212) 225-2000 .. **Leibson,** Michele K '81 %Cleary GS&H -1 Lbrty Plz -NY 10006
(212) 227-4200 .. **Leiby,** Doron A '09 %J Miller & Assoc,PC -32 Bway -NY 10004 **Fx:**504-8369
(800) 595-5520 .. **Leiby,** Kenneth L Jr. '81 OfCnsl Shackleton & H -104 W 40th -NY 10018
(631) 777-5196 .. **Leicher,** Marvin H '58 (Hershman & L,LLP) -425 Broad Hollow Rd -Melvll 11747 **Fx:**777-3204
(212) 833-1188 .. **Leicht,** Chad M '04 %Friedman KS&A LLP -1633 Bway -NY 10019 **Fx:**373-7988
(212) 819-8200 .. **Leicht,** Eric F '95 (White & C LLP) -1155 Av of Amer -NY 10036
(914) 669-1062 .. **Leicht,** F Josiah '84 (FJL Assoc,LLC) -60 June Rd Bx665 -N Salem 10560
(212) 863-6300 .. **Leicht,** Holly M '98 %HPD -100 Gold -NY 10038 **Fx:**863-8201
(212) 809-1111 .. **Leicht,** Leonard C '95 (Morgan MA) -39 Bway -NY 10006
(212) 599-7575 .. **Leichter,** Henry O '58 OfCnsl Harnik & F LLP -645 5th Av -NY 10022 **Fx:**867-8120
(212) 704-6000 .. **Leichtling,** Michl A '69 (Troutman S LLP) -405 Lex Av -NY 10174
(212) 407-4000 .. **Leichtling,** Noah J '01 %Loeb & L,LLP -345 Park Av -NY 10154
(800) 553-9940 .. **Leichtman,** David L '97 (Robins KM&C LLP) -499 Park Av -NY 10022
(718) 547-7200 .. **Leid,** Ury A '78 (UA Leid & Assoc) -3274 Bstn Rd -Bronx 10469 **Fx:**547-4548
(212) 997-3810 .. **Leider,** Andrew B '77 -27 Downing -NY 10014 **Fx:**997-3819
(212) 530-5000 .. **Leider,** Jeffrey M '10 %Milbank TH&M LLP -1 Chase Manh Plz -NY 10005
(212) 966-6420 .. **Leider,** Mark B '94 Lwyrs For Children -110 Lafayette -NY 10013 **Fx:**966-0531
(631) 393-9400 .. **Leiderman,** Joel D '75 %Forster & G -500 Bi-Cnty Blvd Bx9030 -Farmngdl 11735
(212) 349-6009 .. **Leidholdt,** Dorchen A '89 %Sanctuary for Families -110 Wall -NY 10005 **Fx:**566-0344
(212) 473-7912 .. **Leifer,** Jane A '79 -7 Peter Cooper Rd -NY 10010
(212) 334-9699 .. **Leifer,** Max D '72 (M Leifer,PC) -214 Sullivan -NY 10012 **Fx:**966-9544
(212) 334-9699 .. **Leifer,** Seth M '04 %M Leifer,PC -214 Sullivan -NY 10012 **Fx:**966-9544
(212) 264-5916 .. **Leifer,** Wendy '95 DHS -26 Fed Plz -NY 10278
(914) 559-3100 .. **Leifert,** John L '97 %Heidell PM&B,LLP -81 Main -White Plns 10601
(212) 878-8000 .. **Leigh,** Audrey S '04 %Clifford C LLP -31 W 52nd -NY 10019
(516) 463-5851 .. **Leigh,** Cindie Chernack '93 HU Law Library -122 Hofstra Way -Hempstd 11549
(212) 538-6711 .. **Leigh,** Ellen M '95 %Credit Suisse First Boston -1 Mad Av -NY 10010
(718) 380-3708 .. **Leight,** Arnold '56 OfCnsl Colin & S -164-16 73rd Av -Fresh Mdws 11366 **Fx:**591-8535
(212) 619-6452 .. **Leight,** Jody '80 -150 Bway -NY 10038 **Fx:**240-0365
(212) 732-8368 .. **Leighton,** Barry B '65 (Caruso SLCU&S) -132 Nassau -NY 10038
(212) 421-2233 .. **Leighton,** Jeffrey A '83 (Wilk A LLP) -675 3rd Av -NY 10017
(212) 788-0407 .. **Leighton,** Maxwell D '08 %Law Dept -100 Church -NY 10007 **Fx:**788-0367
(212) 267-6019 .. **Leighton,** Robt P '62 -132 Nassau -NY 10038
(212) 208-3600 .. **Leighton,** Terence S '94 %Zurich Capital Mrkts -105 E 17th -NY 10003
(516) 688-1700 .. **Leighton,** Theo R '86 %IRS -1600 Stewart Av -Westbury 11590 **Fx:**688-1750
(315) 498-6673 .. **Leiker,** Jean E '98 Drescher Corp -200 Monarch Rd -Liverpool 13088
(212) 318-3000 .. **Leiman,** Leonard M '55 OfCnsl Fulbright & J LLP -666 5th Av -NY 10103
(212) 723-4899 .. **Leiman-Carbia,** Julius R '96 Citigroup Global Mrkts -390 Greenwich -NY 10013
(212) 223-0400 .. **Leinbach,** Bryan D '05 %Zeichner E&K LLP -575 Lex Av -NY 10022
(585) 263-1000 .. **Leinberg,** Gunnar G '94 (Nixon P LLP) -1100 Clinton Sq -Rchstr 14604
(212) 735-3000 .. **Leineweber,** Thos M '08 %Skadden ASM&F LLP -4 Times Sq -NY 10036
(212) 270-6506 .. **Leinhardt,** Jeanne E '85 JP Morgan Chase -245 Park Av -NY 10167
(212) 373-3000 .. **Leinhardt,** Walter F '56 OfCnsl Paul WRW&G LLP -1285 Av of Amer -NY 10019
(516) 746-8000 .. **Leinheardt,** Wallace L '63 OfCnsl Jaspan S LLP -300 Grdn City Plz -Gdn Cty 11530
(212) 907-9600 .. **Leinheiser,** Carly '10 %Ingram YGC&B,LLP -250 Park Av -NY 10177
(718) 979-5200 .. **Leininger,** Wm J '75 (W Leininger,PC) -34 Dumont Av -Staten Isl 10305 **Fx:**667-7128
(212) 841-1000 .. **Leino,** Natalie MacLean '10 %Covington & B LLP -620 8th Av -NY 10018
(914) 941-5500 .. **Leins,** Richd A '75 (Greene L&R) -500 Exec Blvd -Ossining 10562
(718) 720-5718 .. **Leinseider,** Seymour H '74 -720 Forest Av -Staten Isl 10310 **Fx:**720-1190
(516) 571-3056 .. **Lein-Taubenfeld,** Cheryl A '93 %Cnty Atty -1 West -Mineola 11501 **Fx:**571-6604
(212) 225-2000 .. **Leinwand,** David '93 (Cleary GS&H) -1 Lbrty Plz -NY 10006
(212) 850-7524 .. **Leinwand,** David S '92 Ave Cptl Grp -535 Mad Av -NY 10022 **Fx:**850-7584
(212) 725-7338 .. **Leinwand,** Harris D '69 -315 Mad Av -NY 10017
(212) 603-6300 .. **Leinwand,** Robt R '74 (Robinson BLGG&G PC) -875 3rd Av -NY 10022
(585) 232-6500 .. **Leipold,** Paul A '69 Cnsl Harter S&E LLP -1600 Bausch & Lomb Pl -Rchstr 14604
(212) 225-2000 .. **Leipsic,** Adrian R '07 %Cleary GS&H -1 Lbrty Plz -NY 10006
(718) 928-3700 .. **Leipziger,** Amy L '08 %LSNYC-Bronx -579 Courtlandt Av -Bronx 10451 **Fx:**402-7586
(212) 805-3900 .. **Leis,** Matthew '06 %Clausen M PC -1 Chase Manh Plz -NY 10005
(716) 853-0246 .. **Leising,** Wm E '79 -237 Main -Buffalo 14203 **Fx:**856-7226
(212) 788-0971 .. **Leist,** Alexis L '00 %Law Dept -100 Church -NY 10007 **Fx:**788-0367
(518) 427-2650 .. **Leistensnider,** Ruth E '89 (Nixon P LLP) -677 Bway -Albany 12207
(516) 747-6300 .. **Leistman,** Donald F '81 (Koeppel M&L,LLP) -155 First Bx863 -Mineola 11501
(212) 458-3386 .. **Leisz,** Christopher J '00 Natl Union Fire Ins Co -175 Water -NY 10038
(212) 225-2000 .. **Leitch,** Evan J '10 %Cleary GS&H -1 Lbrty Plz -NY 10006
(631) 421-4488 .. **Leitch,** Noel Eton '97 %Serpe A&K -149 Main Bx165 -Huntngtn 11743
(516) 794-9100 .. **Leiter,** David J '06 East Coast Abstract -100 Q Roosevelt Blvd -Gdn Cty 11530
(631) 859-0300 .. **Leiter,** Eric Z '04 %Zaklukiewicz P&M,LLP -2701 Sunrise Hwy Bx389 -Islip Terr 11752
(315) 453-7742 .. **Leiter,** James A '71 -4313 Lazybrook Cir -Liverpool 13088
(716) 636-7600 .. **Leiter,** Mark A '68 -1 JJ Audubon Pkwy -Amherst 14228 **Fx:**636-7606
(516) 747-0300 .. **Leiter,** Monica M C '05 %Meltzer LG&B,LLP -190 Willis Av -Mineola 11501
(212) 213-6996 .. **Leith,** Thos M '07 %Spears & I LLP -51 Mad Av -NY 10010
(212) 687-4499 .. **Leitman,** Genay A '82 -245 E 44th -NY 10017
(212) 218-5500 .. **Leitman,** Tracey A '85 (Seyfarth S LLP) -620 8th Av -NY 10018
(212) 588-5500 .. **Leitner,** Abraham '97 (Davies WP&V LLP) -625 Mad Av -NY 10022
(212) 725-2700 .. **Leitner,** Arthur M '73 -1430 Bway -NY 10018
(516) 466-6500 .. **Leitner,** Brett R '01 %Parker WA LLP -6 Hrbr Park Dr S -Pt Wash 11050
(212) 856-9600 .. **Leitner,** Curtis B '08 %Morvillo AGIA&B,PC -565 5th Av -NY 10017
(212) 635-0400 .. **Leitner & Getz LLP** -65 Bway -NY 10006 **Fx:**635-0449
(914) 824-5328 .. **Leitner,** Howard '66 Supreme Ct -111 Dr Martin Luther King Blvd -White Plns 10601
(212) 735-3000 .. **Leitner,** J J Harwayne '99 %Skadden ASM&F LLP -4 Times Sq -NY 10036
(212) 635-0400 .. **Leitner,** Jerome M '66 (Leitner & G LLP) -65 Bway -NY 10006
(212) 448-1800 .. **Leitner,** Justin R '07 %Roberts RLSC&F LLP -235 Park Av S -NY 10003

(212) 506-1700 .. **Leivick**, Sarah Gibbs '07 %Kasowitz BT&F LLP -1633 Bway -NY 10019
(212) 417-8700 .. **Leiwant**, Barry D '76 %Fed Def of NY Inc -52 Duane -NY 10007 **Fx:**571-0392
(212) 285-3038 .. **Leiwant**, Sherry J '76 %Better Balance -75 Maiden Ln -NY 10038 **Fx:**724-3535
(212) 596-9000 .. **Leiz**, James A '04 %Ropes & G LLP -1211 Av of Amer -NY 10036
(315) 425-2700 .. **Leja**, Andrew J '91 (Hiscock & B,LLP) -One Park Pl -Syracuse 13202
(631) 853-4161 .. **LeJava**, Nancy B '03 -N Cnty Cmplx Bldg 77 -Hauppauge 11788 **Fx:**853-4192
(718) 254-6096 .. **Lekakis**, Artemis '94 %US Atty -271 Cadman Plz E -Brklyn 11201 **Fx:**254-6479
(718) 590-2000 .. **Lekas**, Anthony '10 %DA -198 E 161st -Bronx 10451 **Fx:**590-6477
(212) 668-1900 .. **Lekas**, Paul N '04 %Brune & R LLP -80 Broad -NY 10004
(212) 872-1000 .. **Lekhel**, Arina '01 -One Bryant Park -NY 10036 **Fx:**872-1002
(315) 386-4583 .. **Lekki Hill Fischer & Duprey,PC** -21 Court Bx469 -Canton 13617 **Fx:**386-2365
(315) 764-0503 .. **Lekki Hill Fischer & Duprey,PC** -227 E Orvis -Massena 13662 **Fx:**764-0505
(315) 764-0503 .. **Lekki**, Peter B '74 (Lekki HF&D,PC) -227 E Orvis -Massena 13662
(315) 386-4583 .. **Lekki**, Peter B '74 (Lekki HF&D,PC) -21 Court Bx469 -Canton 13617
(718) 520-9311 .. **Lekos**, Ronald N '83 %Police Dept -68-40 Austin -Frst Hlls 11375
(212) 735-3000 .. **Lekstutis**, Carmine '07 %Skadden ASM&F LLP -4 Times Sq -NY 10036
(212) 669-0600 .. **Leland**, Kipp C '02 %Hill R LLP -45 Bway -NY 10006
(212) 859-8000 .. **Leland**, Richd G '75 (Fried FHS&J LLP) -1 NY Plz -NY 10004
(212) 906-1200 .. **Lele**, Abhay Diwakar '02 %Latham & W -885 3rd Av -NY 10022
(212) 450-4000 .. **Lele**, Ajay B '01 Cnsl Davis P&W LLP -450 Lex Av -NY 10017
(212) 554-7800 .. **Lellos**, Stella '00 (Moses & S LLP) -405 Lex Av -NY 10174
(212) 547-5400 .. **Lelonek**, Adam H '07 %McDermott W&E LLP -340 Mad Av -NY 10173
(212) 474-1000 .. **Lelutiu**, Radu A '04 %Cravath S&M LLP -825 8th Av -NY 10019
(212) 250-8260 .. **Lem**, Robt K '74 %Deutsche Bank -60 Wall -NY 10005
(212) 509-9400 .. **Lemagne**, Mariflor '97 Cozen O -45 Bway Atrium -NY 10006
(718) 722-3100 .. **Lemaire**, Janet M '90 %Leg Aid -111 Lvngstn -Brklyn 11201 **Fx:**722-3093
(212) 325-2000 .. **Leman**, Nora K '05 Credit Suisse -1 Mad Av -NY 10010
(646) 264-3650 .. **LeMar**, Harold W '88 %US Dept of Labor -201 Varick -NY 10014 **Fx:**264-3660
(212) 878-8000 .. **LeMaster**, Jefferey D '07 %Clifford C LLP -31 W 52nd -NY 10019
(212) 408-5100 .. **LeMay**, David M '82 (Chadbourne & P LLP) -30 Rckfllr Plz -NY 10112
(315) 386-8501 .. **LeMay**, Marcia L '96 (Nash P&L) -113 Main Bx529 -Canton 13617 **Fx:**386-8936
(718) 260-2300 .. **Lemberg**, Jennifer L '97 %Hon C Sifton -225 Cadman Plz E -Brklyn 11201
(917) 777-4200 .. **Lemberger**, Ephraim D '03 Cnsl Bingham M LLP -1 Bttry Pk Plz -NY 10004
(585) 454-3323 .. **Lembke**, Matthew R '94 (Cerulli M&L) -339 East Av -Rchstr 14604
(212) 735-3000 .. **Lembo**, Loren R '93 %Skadden ASM&F LLP -4 Times Sq -NY 10036
(212) 858-1000 .. **Lembrich**, Gregory T '05 %Pillsbury WSP LLP -1540 Bway -NY 10036
(212) 341-2715 .. **LeMelle**, Edw M '92 %Admin Children's Srvcs -150 William -NY 10038 **Fx:**341-2700
(212) 854-5796 .. **Le Melle**, Patrice M '86 Columbia Univ -535 W 116th 412 Low Mem'l Library -NY 10027
(718) 286-6000 .. **LeMelle**, Wilbert J '87 %DA -125-01 Qns Blvd -Kew Gdns 11415
(212) 578-2211 .. **Lemelman**, Bernard '82 %MetLife -27-01 Qns Plz N -LIC 11101
(212) 588-0800 .. **Lemere**, Mary Ann G '87 Frommer L&H LLP -745 5th Av -NY 10151
(518) 581-8800 .. **Lemery Greisler LLC** -60 Railroad Pl -Saratoga Spgs 12866 **Fx:**581-8823
(518) 433-8800 .. **Lemery Greisler LLC** -50 Beaver -Albany 12207 **Fx:**433-8823
(518) 581-8800 .. **Lemery**, John C '65 (Lemery G LLC) -60 Railroad Pl -Saratoga Spgs 12866
(212) 353-4115 .. **Lemiesz**, Linda M '07 Cooper Union -30 Cooper Sq -NY 10003
(516) 747-4399 .. **LeMieux**, Dianna '88 -200 Old Cntry Rd -Mineola 11501 **Fx:**741-7758
(718) 768-0927 .. **Lemily**, Thos J '58 -705 4th Av -Brklyn 11232
(518) 899-5700 .. **Lemire**, Christopher R '93 (Lemire J,LLC) -2534 Route 9 Bx2485 -Malta 12020 **Fx:**899-5487
(212) 637-2532 .. **Lemire**, Katherine A '98 US Atty -1 St Andrews Plz -NY 10007
(518) 899-5700 .. **Lemire**, Mark J '02 %Lemire J,LLC -2534 Route 9 Bx2485 -Malta 12020 **Fx:**899-5487
(516) 294-9200 .. **Lemke**, Dennis M '88 -114 Old Cntry Rd -Mineola 11501 **Fx:**746-1071
(914) 767-6772 .. **Lemke**, Judith A '02 Pepsi Bottling Group,Inc -1 Pepsi Way -Somers 10589
(212) 867-4100 .. **Lemkhen**, Izabell '09 %Furman K&B LLP -61 Bway -NY 10006
(516) 390-4775 .. **Lemle**, Robt S '79 -50 Chas Lindbergh Blvd -Uniondale 11553
(212) 382-6600 .. **Lemlek**, Adele F '84 %NYC Bar -42 W 44th -NY 10036 **Fx:**398-6634
(212) 848-4000 .. **Lemli**, Courtney E '08 %Shearman & S LLP -599 Lex Av -NY 10022
(646) 522-9082 .. **Lemmo**, Edw A '84 -19 W 74th -NY 10023
(518) 449-3900 .. **Lemmon**, Carolyn Snyder '96 OfCnsl Cooper E&S,LLP -39 N Pearl -Albany 12207
(631) 444-8250 .. **Le Moal-Gray**, Michele J '01 SUNY Univ Cnsl -221 Admin Bldg -Stony Brk 11794 **Fx:**444-6101
(718) 981-7500 .. **Lemole**, Jon E '92 -1492 Victory Blvd -Staten Isl 10301 **Fx:**720-1882
(718) 981-7500 .. **Lemole**, Paul A '64 (Lemole M & Assoc) -1492 Victory Blvd -Staten Isl 10301 **Fx:**720-1882
(518) 474-7700 .. **LéMon**, Pamela J '01 NYS OPWDD -44 Holland Av -Albany 12229 **Fx:**474-7382
(212) 788-0881 .. **Lemonedes**, James '80 %Law Dept -100 Church -NY 10007 **Fx:**788-0367
(212) 310-8000 .. **Lemons**, Robt J '00 (Weil G&M LLP) -767 5th Av -NY 10153
(212) 307-5500 .. **Le Moult**, Brendan J '99 (Venable LLP) -1270 Av of Amer -NY 10020
(914) 723-0097 .. **Lempel**, Steven '82 -6 Jffrsn Rd -Scarsdale 10583
(516) 719-0090 .. **Lempenski**, Robt J '80 (R Lempenski,PC) -1 Old Cntry Rd -Carle Pl 11514 **Fx:**719-0091
(212) 735-3000 .. **Lempert**, Eran '05 %Skadden ASM&F LLP -4 Times Sq -NY 10036
(518) 486-7815 .. **Len**, Tobias J '01 %Insurance Dept -99 Wshngtn Av -Albany 12257 **Fx:**473-4600
(212) 971-3175 .. **Lenaghan**, James M '85 OfCnsl d'Arcambal L&O LLP -40 Fulton -NY 10038 **Fx:**971-3176
(212) 947-9779 .. **Lenaghan**, Matthew '00 %Advocates for Chldrn of NY -151 W 30th -NY 10001 **Fx:**947-9790
(212) 826-0808 .. **Lenaghan**, Robt A '93 %MLB Players Assn -12 E 49th -NY 10017 **Fx:**752-3649
(212) 237-0000 .. **Lenahan**, Brenda K '01 (Vinson & E LLP) -666 5th Av -NY 10103
(212) 530-5000 .. **Lenahan**, Kathryn A '10 %Milbank TH&M LLP -1 Chase Manh Plz -NY 10005
(914) 946-0400 .. **Lenane**, Timothy J '90 (Schiavetti CDW&N,LLP) -709 Wstchstr Av -White Plns 10604
(212) 225-2000 .. **Lenas**, Elizabeth '01 Cnsl Cleary GS&H -1 Lbrty Plz -NY 10006
(914) 631-7202 .. **Lence**, George E '84 -14 Hemlock Dr -Sleepy Hollow 10591
(516) 747-5900 .. **Lenchner**, Mitchell J '84 (Kaye & L) -220 Mineola Blvd -Mineola 11501
(212) 471-6212 .. **Lenci**, Edw K '91 (Hinshaw & C LLP) -780 3rd Av -NY 10017
(212) 425-1900 .. **Lenck**, Eric E '74 (Freehill H&M LLP) -80 Pine -NY 10005
(212) 759-4600 .. **Lencyk**, Andrew E '93 (Wolf P LLP) -845 3rd Av -NY 10022
(315) 546-0068 .. **Lenczewski**, Mitchell P '87 %Sassani & S,PC -7767 Oswego Rd -Liverpool 13090
(212) 408-2500 .. **Lendaris**, Steven '09 %Baker B,LLP -30 Rckfllr Plz -NY 10112
(212) 310-8000 .. **Lender**, David J '94 (Weil G&M LLP) -767 5th Av -NY 10153
(212) 561-6420 .. **Lender**, Jeffrey S '02 Kensington Title Agency -39 W 37th -NY 10018
(718) 694-4757 .. **Lendino**, Michl A '89 %NYC Transit Auth -130 Lvngstn -Brklyn 11201 **Fx:**488-6515
(914) 921-1035 .. **Lendino**, Michl J '83 -350 Theo Fremd Av -Rye 10580
(718) 286-6000 .. **Lendino**, Therese M '83 %DA -125-01 Qns Blvd -Kew Gdns 11415
(212) 586-0088 .. **Lenefsky**, David '64 -1 Columbus Pl -NY 10019 **Fx:**586-0066
(718) 543-5861 .. **Lenes**, Marc S '96 %Kensington Intl Grp -3419 Irwin Av -Bronx 10463
(212) 768-6700 .. **Lenet**, Sara C '08 %Sonnenschein N&R LLP -2 World Fncl Ctr -NY 10281
(212) 481-4801 .. **Lengkong**, Ronald '09 %B Silberzweig -271 Mad Av -NY 10016 **Fx:**481-4971
(585) 381-3400 .. **Lenhard**, Matthew A '98 (Rupp BPC&C LLC) -3300 Monroe Av -Rchstr 14618
(716) 568-8200 .. **Lenhardt**, Clayton J '09 %J Adams & Assoc,PLLC -500 Essjay Rd -Williamsvll 14221 **Fx:**568-8292
(646) 827-0502 .. **Lenhardt**, Robt J B '88 ORIX Finance -245 Park Av -NY 10167 **Fx:**(469) 385-1353
(212) 636-7608 .. **Lenhardt**, Robin A '97 Fordham Univ Sch of Law -140 W 62nd -NY 10023 **Fx:**636-6899
(585) 899-1414 .. **Leni**, Robt S '96 %Harris COJW&L -300 Linden Oaks -Rchstr 14625
(718) 250-2000 .. **Lenich**, Tara F '04 DA -350 Jay -Brklyn 11201 **Fx:**250-2314
(212) 696-6000 .. **Lenihan**, Danl R '82 (Curtis M-PC&M LLP) -101 Park Av -NY 10178
(518) 402-0748 .. **Lenihan**, David A '78 Dept of Health -433 River -Troy 12180 **Fx:**402-0751
(914) 949-8855 .. **Lenihan**, James M '91 -235 Main -White Plns 10601
(917) 805-2004 .. **Lenihan**, Joan C '98 -9115 Colonial Rd -Brklyn 11209
(516) 328-2300 .. **Lenihan**, Sean P '09 %Abrams FFEGF&E,LLP -1111 Marcus Av -Lk Success 11042
(212) 576-7000 .. **Lenkiewicz**, Cynthia J '86 %NY Life Ins -51 Mad Av -NY 10010 **Fx:**447-0569
(212) 504-6000 .. **Lenkowsky**, Steven '77 Cnsl Cadwalader W&T LLP -1 World Fncl Ctr -NY 10281
(516) 228-8484 .. **Lenna**, Leo G '96 OfCnsl Dilworth & B,LLP -1000 Woodbury Rd -Woodbury 11797
(518) 487-5460 .. **Lennard**, Bruce D '03 %DA -6 Lodge -Albany 12207 **Fx:**487-5093
(212) 785-8300 .. **Lennard**, Ian J '03 Natl Cargo Bureau Inc -17 Battery Pl -NY 10004 **Fx:**785-8333
(212) 788-1193 .. **Lennard**, Kimberly A '91 %Law Dept -100 Church -NY 10007 **Fx:**788-0367
(518) 383-1600 .. **Lenney**, David M '84 -1 Barney Rd -Clifton Pk 12065
(315) 866-7709 .. **Lenney**, James R '72 -412 N Prospect Bx589 -Herkimer 13350 **Fx:**866-2351
(212) 446-4800 .. **Lennon**, Brian S '04 %Kirkland & E LLP -153 E 53rd -NY 10022
(914) 378-1010 .. **Lennon**, Christopher J '83 %Fitzgerald & F -538 Riverdale Av -Ynkrs 10705
(518) 573-7704 .. **Lennon**, Cristina Paone '96 -9 Anchor Dr -Waterfrd 12188 **Fx:**371-8201
(212) 792-5660 .. **Lennon**, David P '89 Lennon & K PC -245 Park Av -NY 10167 **Fx:**202-5337
(718) 875-1300 .. **Lennon**, Debra J '80 %Appllt Div 2nd Dept -45 Monroe Pl -Brklyn 11201 **Fx:**858-2446
(845) 778-2121 .. **Lennon**, Gerald A '78 (Jacobowitz & G,LLP) -158 Orange Av Bx367 -Walden 12586
(716) 854-2211 .. **Lennon**, J Michl '74 -525 Delaware Av -Buffalo 14202 **Fx:**854-8122
(716) 834-9181 .. **Lennon**, J Michl '04 %Blair & R,LLP -2645 Sheridan Dr -Tonawanda 14150
(212) 732-4858 .. **Lennon**, Janet J '80 -225 Bway -NY 10007
(716) 854-1300 .. **Lennon**, John Patrick '02 %Rosenthal S&M,LLP -300 Main -Buffalo 14202
(212) 490-6050 .. **Lennon**, Kevin J '97 (Lennon M&L LLC) -420 Lex Av -NY 10170 **Fx:**490-6070
(212) 425-7200 .. **Lennon**, Michl J '75 (Kenyon & K,LLP) -1 Bway -NY 10004
(212) 490-6050 .. **Lennon**, Patrick F '93 (Lennon M&L LLC) -420 Lex Av -NY 10170 **Fx:**490-6070
(646) 840-3638 .. **Lennon**, Robt G '93 Linden Advisors -590 Mad Av -NY 10022
(212) 310-8000 .. **Lennox**, Maria N '09 %Weil G&M LLP -767 5th Av -NY 10153
(212) 705-7000 .. **Lennox**, Regina A '08 %Bingham M LLP -399 Park Av -NY 10022
(516) 663-6600 .. **Leno**, David P '98 %Ruskin MF,PC -1425 RXR Plz -Uniondale 11556
(212) 756-2000 .. **Lenobel**, Jeffrey A '79 (Schulte R&Z LLP) -919 3rd Av -NY 10022

(212) 225-7700 .. **Lenoff,** Michl J '82 (Cartafalsa ST&L) -165 Bway -NY 10006
(212) 281-2833 .. **Lenoir,** J Kip '75 SrCnsl K Lenoir,PC -257 W 139th -NY 10030
(585) 627-2553 .. **Lenon,** Joshua A '09 Thomson Reuters -50 Broad -Rchstr 14694
(212) 336-2000 .. **Lenow,** Jared P '08 %Patterson BW&T LLP -1133 Av of Amer -NY 10036
(516) 294-6410 .. **Lenowitz,** Melissa A '04 S Cohn -1 Old Cntry Rd -Carle Pl 11514 **Fx:**294-0094
(631) 269-6969 .. **Lenowitz,** Neil '89 -1 Max Way -Commack 11725
(516) 364-3080 .. **Lenowitz,** Ronald A '75 -7600 Jericho Tpk -Woodbury 11797
(212) 225-2000 .. **Lens,** Molly Manning '04 %Cleary GS&H -1 Lbrty Plz -NY 10006
(631) 853-4600 .. **Lens,** Vicki '81 %Dept of Citizen Affairs -N Cnty Cmplx Bldg 340 -Hauppauge 11788 **Fx:**853-4825
(212) 806-5400 .. **Lenson,** Todd E '97 (Stroock &S&L LLP) -180 Maiden Ln -NY 10038
(212) 753-9692 .. **Lent & Abrams** -286 Mad Av -NY 10017 **Fx:**593-1990
(212) 461-7190 .. **Lent,** Brian S '85 (Fishman M,PC) -44 Wall -NY 10005
(212) 735-3000 .. **Lent,** Chas S '01 Cnsl Skadden ASM&F LLP -4 Times Sq -NY 10036
(518) 474-8211 .. **Lent,** Dennis M '84 %Law Reporting Bur -1 Commerce Plz -Albany 12210 **Fx:**463-6869
(845) 562-5005 .. **Lent,** John B '04 %ARCS -280 Bway -Newburgh 12550 **Fx:**562-5212
(212) 713-2273 .. **Lenti,** Frank A '77 PaineWebber Inc -1285 Av of Amer -NY 10019
(718) 286-6000 .. **Lenti,** Gregory M '05 %DA -125-01 Qns Blvd -Kew Gdns 11415
(718) 886-8508 .. **Lentini,** Malan '04 (M Lentini,PLLC) -41-25 Kissena Blvd -Flushng 11355 **Fx:**886-9761
(516) 228-3214 .. **Lentini,** Vincent M '91 -600 Old Cntry Rd -Gdn Cty 11530 **Fx:**228-9385
(845) 342-4866 .. **Lentino,** Richd N '78 -138 W Main -Middletwn 10940 **Fx:**344-5043
(518) 279-3183 .. **Lentivech,** Douglas E '92 -312 Old Rd -Cropseyville 12052 **Fx:**279-3183
(718) 383-8684 .. **Lentol,** Jos R '70 -152 Russell -Brklyn 11222
(516) 240-8900 .. **Lentz,** Benjamin D '77 (Torre LGG&R,LLP) -100 Jericho Quad -Jericho 11753
(518) 449-0044 .. **Lentz,** Edw T '03 SpclCnsl Hoffman W&D LLC -75 State -Albany 12207 **Fx:**449-0047
(718) 243-6816 .. **Lentz,** Marty '03 %Leg Aid -111 Lvngstn -Brklyn 11201 **Fx:**237-8737
(518) 842-3561 .. **Lenz,** Peter G '96 RCIL -347 W Main -Amsterdam 12010 **Fx:**842-0905
(212) 576-7000 .. **Lenz,** Scott L '90 %NY Life Ins -51 Mad Av -NY 10010 **Fx:**447-0569
(718) 370-7030 .. **Lenza,** Anthony A Jr. '99 %Amabile & E,PC -1000 South Av -Staten Isl 10314
(212) 310-8000 .. **Lenza,** Arielle G '09 %Weil G&M LLP -767 5th Av -NY 10153
(718) 285-6491 .. **Lenza,** Matthew '04 -24 Burbank Av -Staten Isl 10306
(212) 450-4000 .. **Lenzi,** David I '08 %Davis P&W LLP -450 Lex Av -NY 10017
(212) 335-9000 .. **Lenzner,** Jonathan F '05 %DA -1 Hogan Pl -NY 10013
(212) 336-2000 .. **Lenzner,** Lawr P '93 (Patterson BW&T LLP) -1133 Av of Amer -NY 10036
(212) 416-8963 .. **Leo,** Donald '93 %Dept of Law -120 Bway -NY 10271
(631) 698-2000 .. **Leo,** Donald W Jr. '93 D Leo & Assoc,PC -100 Patco Ct -Islandia 11749 **Fx:**698-4943
(845) 566-4400 .. **Leo,** Jeffrey C '99 -288 N Plnk Rd -Newburgh 12550
(631) 351-3042 .. **Leo,** John J '82 (Town Atty) -100 Main -Huntngtn 11743 **Fx:**351-3032
(212) 293-8668 .. **Leo,** Kathleen Anne '96 United Media -200 Mad Av -NY 10016
(212) 340-0400 .. **Leo,** Leona L '76 %Appllt Div 1st Dept -27 Mad Av -NY 10010 **Fx:**889-4412
(212) 442-4553 .. **Leo,** Matilde '89 Dept Probation -100 Centre -NY 10013 **Fx:**442-4555
(212) 855-5083 .. **Leo,** Nancy J '98 %Depository Trust Co -55 Water -NY 10041 **Fx:**855-4936
(914) 423-0505 .. **Leo,** Nicholas Jr. '95 -111 Lockwood Av -Ynkrs 10701 **Fx:**423-0606
(212) 949-7120 .. **Leo,** Robt J '84 %Meeks & S -330 Mad Av -NY 10017
(212) 446-4800 .. **Leon,** Eric F '94 (Kirkland & E LLP) -153 E 53rd -NY 10022
(212) 227-4848 .. **Leon,** Jos P '00 %Ceccarelli W PLLC -2 Wall -NY 10005
(212) 372-2000 .. **Leon,** Matthew T '95 %Newmark Knight Frank -125 Park Av -NY 10017 **Fx:**372-2386
(516) 746-8000 .. **Leon,** Michl A '05 %Jaspan S LLP -300 Grdn City Plz -Gdn Cty 11530
(212) 545-4000 .. **Leonard,** Alexander W '09 %Jackson L LLP -666 3rd Av -NY 10017
(516) 365-3999 .. **Leonard,** Angela M '97 %Marden Kane Inc -36 Maple Pl -Manhsst 11030
(212) 431-2156 .. **Leonard,** Arthur S '78 NY Law Schl -185 W Bway -NY 10013 **Fx:**431-1804
(213) 576-1153 .. **Leonard,** Carson M '94 (Alston & B LLP) -90 Park Av -NY 10016 **Fx:**576-1100
(212) 557-4000 .. **Leonard,** Christina M '10 %Grunfeld DLS&K LLP -399 Park Av -NY 10022
(315) 218-8000 .. **Leonard,** Colin M '02 (Bond S&K,PLLC) -1 Lincoln Ctr -Syracuse 13202
(212) 468-8000 .. **Leonard,** Craigh '70 SrCnsl Morrison & F LLP -1290 Av of Amer -NY 10104
(212) 450-4000 .. **Leonard,** Edwin Deane '57 SrCnsl Davis P&W LLP -450 Lex Av -NY 10017
(212) 986-6840 .. **Leonard,** Ethan Y '97 %N Brickman -317 Mad Av -NY 10017 **Fx:**986-7691
(585) 475-1222 .. **Leonard,** Gary H '80 -81 Doncaster Rd -Rchstr 14623
(212) 559-0233 .. **Leonard,** Harry P '79 %Citigroup Inc -909 3rd Av -NY 10292
(607) 772-9262 .. **Leonard,** Hugh B '88 (O'Connor GL&C,LLP) -84 Court -Bnghmtn 13901
(516) 746-8000 .. **Leonard,** James D '09 (Jaspan S LLP) -300 Grdn City Plz -Gdn Cty 11530
(212) 735-3000 .. **Leonard,** James L Jr. '06 %Skadden ASM&F LLP -4 Times Sq -NY 10036
(212) 218-2100 .. **Leonard,** Jason A '08 %Fitzpatrick CH&S -1290 Av of Amer -NY 10104
(973) 379-4800 .. **Leonard,** Jeffrey S '81 (Budd L) -140 Bway -NY 10005
(212) 338-0700 .. **Leonard,** Jessica L '06 %Hoffman P&F PLLC -220 E 42nd -NY 10017
(212) 809-9100 .. **Leonard,** John '81 OfCnsl Brunelle & H,PC -1 Whitehall -NY 10004 **Fx:**809-3219
(315) 336-1410 .. **Leonard,** John G '99 -301 N Wshngtn -Rome 13440 **Fx:**336-1434
(212) 557-4000 .. **Leonard,** Kevin W '99 %Grunfeld DLS&K LLP -399 Park Av -NY 10022
(212) 406-4400 .. **Leonard,** Lawr '81 -291 Bway -NY 10007
(607) 756-0255 .. **Leonard,** Mary E '86 -1 N Main Bx787 -Cortlnd 13045 **Fx:**756-0257
(212) 909-6000 .. **Leonard,** Matthew L '07 %Debevoise & P LLP -919 3rd Av -NY 10022
(212) 483-9490 .. **Leonard,** Nicole A '98 %McElroy DM&C,LLP -88 Pine -NY 10005
(518) 884-0080 .. **Leonard,** Patricia M '91 (Kelly & L,LLP) -199 Milton Av -Ballston Spa 12020 **Fx:**884-0083
(914) 654-8276 .. **Leonard,** Rhonda S '86 -110 Pondvw Ln -New Rchll 10804 **Fx:**654-8276
(516) 240-8900 .. **Leonard,** Robt B '74 OfCnsl Torre LGG&R,LLP -100 Jericho Quad -Jericho 11753
(917) 777-4200 .. **Leonard,** Robt G '86 (Bingham M LLP) -1 Bttry Pk Plz -NY 10004
(212) 248-3145 .. **Leonard,** Robt M '82 (Drinker B&R LLP) -140 Bway -NY 10005
(718) 447-2062 .. **Leonard,** Robt S '96 -93 W Cott Blvd -Staten Isl 10314
(212) 809-2663 .. **Leonard,** Sarah B '02 Bondholder Comm Grp -30 Broad -NY 10004
(800) 910-0529 .. **Leonard,** Shelly A '99 Blau B&L,LLC -224 W 30th -NY 10001 **Fx:**(212) 488-4848
(914) 730-3025 .. **Leonard,** Susan McInnis '93 %Leonard & S -48 Banksvll Rd -Armonk 10504 **Fx:**730-3026
(212) 546-4000 .. **Leonard,** Tanya F '00 Bristol-Myers Squibb -345 Park Av -NY 10154 **Fx:**546-9562
(914) 946-1030 .. **Leonard,** Thos J '85 (Barry M&M) -55 Church -White Plns 10601
(718) 967-2148 .. **Leonardi,** Dennis S '04 (D Leonardi & Assoc PLLC) -4218 Amboy Rd -Staten Isl 10308 **Fx:**228-9528
(516) 759-1212 .. **Leonardi,** Domenick P '04 %Mohen & T LLP -186 Birch Hill Rd -Locust Vly 11560
(716) 856-5500 .. **Leonardi,** Jennifer L '06 %Damon M LLP -200 Delaware Av -Buffalo 14202
(212) 859-8000 .. **Leonardi,** Joshua N '07 %Fried FHS&J LLP -1 NY Plz -NY 10004
(718) 250-2000 .. **Leonardi,** Maria A '89 %DA -350 Jay -Brklyn 11201 **Fx:**250-2314
(516) 747-9700 .. **Leonardis,** Lois A '98 %Ryan & H,PC -1 Old Cntry Rd -Carle Pl 11514
(845) 831-3233 .. **Leonardo,** Paul A '65 -1 Sandra Pl -Beacon 12508
(585) 546-6680 .. **Leonardo,** Stephen M '85 -30 W Broad -Rchstr 14614 **Fx:**546-4783
(631) 715-7900 .. **Leonardo-Beckmann,** Diane '89 %US Atty -610 Fed Plz -Central Islip 11722
(518) 822-9406 .. **Leonardson,** John M '78 -6 Willard Pl -Hudson 12534
(917) 454-1175 .. **Leonart,** Ralph A '90 %Police Dept -2 Lafayette -NY 10007
(212) 458-1090 .. **Leone,** Barbara A '99 AIG -175 Water -NY 10038
(516) 248-1700 .. **Leone,** Domenica R '08 %Forchelli CDSM&T,LLP -333 Earle Ovngton Blvd -Uniondale 11553
(315) 422-3466 .. **Leone,** Edw S '84 (Bottar L,PLLC) -120 Madison -Syracuse 13202
(212) 809-7600 .. **Leone,** Francis J '98 %Cheven K&H -40 Wall -NY 10005
(212) 782-4637 .. **Leone,** Fredk A '89 %Bk of Tokyo-Mitsubishi -1251 Av of Amer -NY 10020 **Fx:**782-6420
(315) 255-3854 .. **Leone,** James A '92 (Leone & B) -7 Court Bx188 -Auburn 13021 **Fx:**253-0091
(646) 857-8747 .. **Leone,** John '98 AIG Capital Prtnrs,Inc -277 Park Av -NY 10172
(716) 854-4300 .. **Leone,** John F '87 (Gross SB&G,PC) -465 Main -Buffalo 14203
(716) 285-9511 .. **Leone,** Jos L Jr. '74 -731 Third -Niagara Fls 14301 **Fx:**285-6618
(212) 416-8000 .. **Leone,** Kathryn E '03 %Dept of Law -120 Bway -NY 10271
(212) 791-4120 .. **Leone,** Matthew A '93 %Carreras & M PLLC -11 Park Pl -NY 10007
(585) 899-1414 .. **Leone,** Michl P '00 (Harris COJW&L) -300 Linden Oaks -Rchstr 14625
(212) 450-4000 .. **Leone,** Paul M '84 Davis P&W LLP -450 Lex Av -NY 10017
(716) 332-0842 .. **Leone,** Philip D '98 -403 Main -Buffalo 14203
(914) 592-7766 .. **Leone,** Richd J '72 -14 Salk Dr -Elmsfrd 10523
(914) 428-6742 .. **Leone,** Rita A '88 -137 Columbus Av -White Plns 10604
(585) 232-1020 .. **Leone,** Robt F '87 -36 W Main -Rchstr 14614
(516) 747-0300 .. **Leong,** Alexander '03 %Meltzer LG&B,LLP -190 Willis Av -Mineola 11501
(718) 886-2211 .. **Leong,** Andrew M '91 (Leong Law Grp,PC) -136-20 38th Av -Flushng 11354 **Fx:**886-2221
(516) 248-4714 .. **Leong,** Christopher G '96 -116 Fourth -New Hyde Pk 11040 **Fx:**873-1627
(212) 355-3636 .. **Leong,** Lilian Mee-Woon '84 %King Fook Co -673 5th Av -NY 10022
(212) 357-3314 .. **Leong,** Susan J '90 Goldman Sachs Asset Mgmt -32 Old Slip -NY 10005
(212) 416-8656 .. **Leong,** Vincent '86 %Dept of Law -120 Bway -NY 10271
(212) 504-6000 .. **Leonhardt,** Julie C '08 %Cadwalader W&T LLP -1 World Fncl Ctr -NY 10281
(212) 244-2999 .. **Leonhauser,** Barbara A '00 %Kopff N&D LLP -440 9th Av -NY 10001
(516) 674-4100 .. **Leonick,** James F '89 (Parisi & L) -58 Schl -Glen Cove 11542 **Fx:**674-3582
(631) 368-8490 .. **Leonick,** Lisa A '90 -382 Larkfld Rd -E Northprt 11731 **Fx:**368-8490
(516) 222-6200 .. **Leonti,** G Careccia '85 %Berkman HPP&F,PC -100 Grdn City Plz -Gdn Cty 11530
(212) 764-4222 .. **Leonti,** Jennifer A '07 %S Jeffries & Assoc -1560 Bway -NY 10036 **Fx:**764-4229
(212) 704-6000 .. **Leonti,** John J '02 %Troutman S LLP -405 Lex Av -NY 10174
(212) 506-1700 .. **Leopold,** Brett A '99 Kasowitz BT&F LLP -1633 Bway -NY 10019
(212) 512-2000 .. **Leopold,** George Wm Jr. '73 %McGraw-Hill -1221 Av of Amer -NY 10020 **Fx:**512-4827
(718) 625-2805 .. **Leopold Gross & Sommers,PC** -16 Court -Brklyn 11241 **Fx:**522-4280
(212) 967-8001 .. **Leopold,** Howard B '91 (Goodman & L LLP) -460 Park Av -NY 10022
(212) 259-8000 .. **Leopold,** Jacqueline Rose '02 Cnsl Dewey & L LLP -1301 Av of Amer -NY 10019
(845) 638-3938 .. **Leopold,** James F '67 -20 Squadron Blvd -New Cty 10956 **Fx:**638-3915
(212) 916-0600 .. **Leopold,** Kenneth E '84 Tweedy Browne Co -350 Park Av -NY 10022

(212) 442-0398 .. **Leopold**, Lynn M '87 %Law Dept -60 Lafayette -NY 10013 **Fx:**442-6865
(646) 454-9594 .. **Leopold**, Michl D '83 -405 E 54th -NY 10022
(718) 286-6000 .. **Leopold**, Robin D '91 %DA -125-01 Qns Blvd -Kew Gdns 11415
(212) 788-0462 .. **Leoussis**, Fay '80 %Law Dept -100 Church -NY 10007 **Fx:**788-0367
(800) 364-7132 .. **LePack**, Keith P '90 -211 W 71st -NY 10023
(585) 325-7515 .. **LePage**, Herbert J Jr. '63 SrCnsl Forsyth HOK&M,PC -1 Chase Sq -Rchstr 14604
(212) 935-4400 .. **LePatner**, Barry B '73 (LePatner & Assoc LLP) -600 Lex Av -NY 10022 **Fx:**935-4404
(212) 973-0572 .. **Lepelstat**, Marc R '85 Cnsl Wolff & S PC -140 Bway -NY 10005
(212) 509-3900 .. **Lepera**, Christine '83 (Mitchell S&K LLP) -12 E 49th -NY 10017
(516) 222-0500 .. **Leperides**, Constance '05 %Goodman J&P,LLP -1103 Stewart Av -Gdn Cty 11530
(315) 448-8400 .. **Lepiane**, Rosemary F '05 Law Dept -233 E Wshngtn -Syracuse 13202 **Fx:**448-8381
(518) 402-1871 .. **Lepicier**, Denise '79 %Dept of Health -Corning Twr 24th Fl -Albany 12237 **Fx:**473-4896
(716) 823-7634 .. **Lepkowski**, Kim M '96 -3422 McKinley Pkwy -Blasdell 14219
(212) 419-3983 .. **Lepore**, A Donald III '03 RNK Capital LLC -527 Mad Av -NY 10022
(914) 835-8847 .. **Lepore**, Claudia Teich '96 -54 Walker Av -Rye 10580 **Fx:**835-8847
(212) 688-5151 .. **Lepore**, Filomena '06 %Gibney A&F,LLP -665 5th Av -NY 10022
(212) 294-6700 .. **Lepore**, Lauren B '04 %Winston & S -200 Park Av -NY 10166
(718) 667-9090 .. **Lepore**, Louis P '92 %Menicucci V & Assoc -2040 Victory Blvd -Staten Isl 10314 **Fx:**667-0700
(585) 325-2350 .. **LePore**, Rudolph J '54 -1 E Main -Rchstr 14614 **Fx:**262-2610
(212) 756-2000 .. **Lepore**, Victoria A '03 %Schulte R&Z LLP -919 3rd Av -NY 10022
(516) 647-3807 .. **Leporin**, Sandra J '94 -8 Highland Pl -Sea Cliff 11579 **Fx:**609-3336
(718) 761-9300 .. **Lepowsky**, Richd A '86 (Vaslas LH&D LLP) -201 Edward Curry Av -Staten Isl 10314
(718) 613-2577 .. **Lepp**, Gerald P '62 %Dist Ct -225 Cadman Plz E -Brklyn 11201 **Fx:**613-2368
(212) 252-0300 .. **Lepper**, Jack E '91 (Kagan LLLG&C,LLP) -200 Mad Av -NY 10016
(212) 849-7000 .. **Lepri**, Thos J '05 %Quinn EU&S,LLP -51 Mad Av -NY 10010
(212) 474-1000 .. **Leraris**, Rory A '09 %Cravath S&M LLP -825 8th Av -NY 10019
(718) 470-1042 .. **Leras**, George P '90 -70-18 261st -Glen Oaks 11004 **Fx:**470-6264
(212) 836-8000 .. **Lerch**, Phillip R '06 %Kaye S LLP -425 Park Av -NY 10022
(212) 490-9505 .. **Lercher**, Monica S '83 %Sterling Natl Bk -145 E 40th -NY 10016
(800) 622-7078 .. **Lerer**, Bruno Dov '84 Spencer Trask & Co -535 Mad Av -NY 10022
(718) 254-6124 .. **Lerer**, Justin D '03 US Atty-EDNY -271 Cadman Plz E -Brklyn 11201
(718) 590-4667 .. **Lerman**, Adam '07 %Law Dept -198 E 161st -Bronx 10451 **Fx:**590-2686
(914) 834-5010 .. **Lerman**, Barbara '82 -5 Waller Av -White Plns 10601 **Fx:**834-5024
(212) 545-4765 .. **Lerman**, Ilan A '98 (Wolf HAF&H LLP) -270 Mad Av -NY 10016
(516) 742-9282 .. **Lerman**, Jeffrey G '81 -170 Old Cntry Rd -Mineola 11501 **Fx:**742-4105
(718) 252-7956 .. **Lerman**, Jos I '96 -1124 E 32nd -Brklyn 11210
(212) 288-7380 .. **Lerman**, Marvin S '67 (M Lerman,PC) -872 Mad Av -NY 10021 **Fx:**744-3678
(212) 351-4500 .. **Lerman**, Stephanie G '09 %Epstein B&G,PC -250 Park Av -NY 10177
(212) 272-7254 .. **Lerner**, Alla '00 %JP Morgan Chase -383 Mad Av -NY 10179
(212) 687-4900 .. **Lerner**, Andrew R '91 Cnsl Wormser KG&J LLP -825 3rd Av -NY 10022
(212) 325-2000 .. **Lerner**, Andrew S '99 Credit Suisse -11 Mad Av -NY 10010
(212) 805-0177 .. **Lerner**, Barbara Anne '93 US Dist Ct Pro Se Ofc -500 Pearl -NY 10007
(914) 967-8599 .. **Lerner**, Barry E '82 -59 Franklin Av -Rye 10580 **Fx:**(718) 543-3601
(212) 728-8000 .. **Lerner**, Caren E '07 %Willkie F&G LLP -787 7th Av -NY 10019
(631) 234-7900 .. **Lerner**, Clive D '60 (Lerner & P) -87 W Suffolk Av -Central Islip 11722 **Fx:**234-8026
(212) 735-8609 .. **Lerner**, David '81 (Morrison C LLP) -909 3rd Av -NY 10022
(212) 335-4500 .. **Lerner**, Eric A '02 %DLA Piper LLP -1251 Av of Amer -NY 10020
(212) 715-9100 .. **Lerner**, Eric M '83 (Kramer LN&F,LLP) -1177 Av of Amer -NY 10036
(212) 421-4100 .. **Lerner**, Eric S '05 %Pryor C LLP -7 Times Sq -NY 10036
(516) 333-3323 .. **Lerner**, Gary '81 -265 Post Av -Westbury 11590
(718) 972-6333 .. **Lerner**, Gary '99 -4121 18th Av -Brklyn 11218 **Fx:**972-9034
(718) 339-1100 .. **Lerner**, Gary '99 -1723 E 12th -Brklyn 11229 **Fx:**339-1101
(212) 557-7200 .. **Lerner**, Gary I '97 %Davidoff M&H,LLP -605 3rd Av -NY 10158
(212) 833-1110 .. **Lerner**, Gregg S '83 (Friedman KS&A LLP) -1633 Bway -NY 10019 **Fx:**373-7910
(516) 433-2808 .. **Lerner**, Irving '56 I Lerner,PC -32 Peter Ct -Jericho 11753 **Fx:**433-3778
(212) 259-8000 .. **Lerner**, James F '90 Cnsl Dewey & L LLP -1301 Av of Amer -NY 10019
(212) 479-6000 .. **Lerner**, Jennifer K '05 %Cooley LLP -1114 Av of Amer -NY 10036
(212) 686-4655 .. **Lerner**, Johnathan C '97 (Abraham L&A LLP) -292 Mad Av -NY 10017
(212) 735-3000 .. **Lerner**, Jonathan J '74 (Skadden ASM&F LLP) -4 Times Sq -NY 10036
(212) 681-0117 .. **Lerner**, Jonathan J '83 (Starr GD&R) -530 5th Av -NY 10036
(516) 741-4100 .. **Lerner**, Kimberly D '99 %Lerner & L PC -1 Old Cntry Rd Bx125 -Carle Pl 11514 **Fx:**741-7485
(212) 294-6700 .. **Lerner**, Lane H '90 Winston & S -200 Park Av -NY 10166
(212) 909-6000 .. **Lerner**, Linda '77 Cnsl Debevoise & P LLP -919 3rd Av -NY 10022
(212) 818-9200 .. **Lerner**, Mark A '95 (Satterlee SB&B LLP) -230 Park Av -NY 10169
(212) 506-1700 .. **Lerner**, Mark W '91 (Kasowitz BT&F LLP) -1633 Bway -NY 10019
(212) 455-2000 .. **Lerner**, Marni J '92 (Simpson T&B LLP) -425 Lex Av -NY 10017
(631) 425-9252 .. **Lerner**, Martin '57 -34 Cmbrdg Av -Melvll 11747 **Fx:**425-9263
(212) 684-7776 .. **Lerner**, Martin A '80 (Freed & L) -12 E 33rd -NY 10016
(212) 888-7100 .. **Lerner**, Martin L '97 OfCnsl Akabas & S -488 Mad Av -NY 10022 **Fx:**(646) 521-0663
(518) 463-5400 .. **Lerner**, Matthew S '00 (Goldberg S LLP) -8 Southwoods Blvd -Albany 12211
(212) 566-4530 .. **Lerner**, Nancy M '79 %Dept of Bldgs -280 Bway -NY 10007
(212) 632-6000 .. **Lerner**, Neal A '92 %Lazard Freres -30 Rckfllr Plz -NY 10112 **Fx:**632-6060
(212) 683-0286 .. **Lerner**, Olivia '06 -124 W 60th -NY 10023
(212) 381-7000 .. **Lerner**, Peter A '94 (Sabin B&G LLP) -4 Times Sq -NY 10036
(212) 922-2999 .. **Lerner**, Peter S '75 %The Kaufmann Fund -140 E 45th -NY 10017
(212) 269-8700 .. **Lerner**, Philip '58 -17 Battery Pl -NY 10004 **Fx:**269-8702
(516) 465-8090 .. **Lerner**, Philip '75 %North Shore-LIJ Hlth Systm -145 Community Dr -Gt Neck 11021 **Fx:**465-8105
(212) 593-6700 .. **Lerner**, Philip D '78 (Aaronson RF&D,LLP) -757 3rd Av -NY 10017
(212) 969-3000 .. **Lerner**, Rachel S '96 %Proskauer R LLP -1585 Bway -NY 10036
(212) 848-9800 .. **Lerner**, Ralph E '68 OfCnsl Withers B LLP -430 Park Av -NY 10022
(212) 490-3000 .. **Lerner**, Richd E '89 (Wilson EME&D LLP) -150 E 42nd -NY 10017
(516) 741-4100 .. **Lerner**, Richd W '70 (Lerner & L PC) -1 Old Cntry Rd Bx125 -Carle Pl 11514 **Fx:**741-7485
(718) 853-9300 .. **Lerner**, Robt N '86 -5313 8th Av -Brklyn 11220 **Fx:**853-9549
(516) 624-0179 .. **Lerner**, Sheryl P '88 -Bx904 -Syosset 11791 **Fx:**624-0026
(212) 407-0135 .. **Lerner**, Stephen D '86 (Squire S&D LLP) -30 Rckfllr Plz -NY 10112
(516) 766-7700 .. **Lerner**, Steven P '84 (Kassoff R&L) -100 Merrick Rd -Rockvll Ctr 11570
(212) 801-1440 .. **Lerner**, Suzanne Sage '92 HF Admin Srvcs -25 Bway -NY 10004
(631) 777-2358 .. **Lerose**, Douglas J '84 -445 Broadhllw Rd -Melvll 11747
(212) 757-5800 .. **LeRoux**, Carey '99 Titlevest Agncy -44 Wall -NY 10005
(732) 855-6458 .. **Lert**, Richd F '00 (Wilentz G&S) -110 William -NY 10038 **Fx:**726-6521
(212) 631-4371 .. **Lesane**, Jamaal T '02 MSG LP -2 Penn Av -NY 10121
(212) 808-0604 .. **Lesavoy**, Lisa '85 -333 E 43rd -NY 10017 **Fx:**808-0117
(518) 792-1174 .. **Lescault**, Melissa Dwyer '02 %McPhillips F&C,LLP -288 Glen Bx299 -Glens Fls 12801
(718) 292-1131 .. **Lesch**, David P '91 (Lesch & L,PC) -860 Grnd Cncrs -Bronx 10451 **Fx:**292-1148
(718) 292-1131 .. **Lesch**, Gary E '95 (Lesch & L,PC) -860 Grnd Cncrs -Bronx 10451 **Fx:**292-1148
(718) 292-1131 .. **Lesch**, Marjorie A '78 OfCnsl Lesch & L,PC -860 Grnd Cncrs -Bronx 10451 **Fx:**292-1148
(212) 259-8000 .. **Lesch**, Michl '61 OfCnsl Dewey & L LLP -1301 Av of Amer -NY 10019
(718) 292-1131 .. **Lesch**, Solomon I '66 OfCnsl Lesch & L,PC -860 Grnd Cncrs -Bronx 10451 **Fx:**292-1148
(212) 247-6000 .. **Leschins**, Preston A '82 (Anzalone & L) -888 7th Av -NY 10106 **Fx:**265-9582
(212) 779-7070 .. **Lescott**, Nadia Y '04 %Ronemus & V -112 Mad Av -NY 10016
(212) 984-7882 .. **Lese**, Peter L '86 (Warshaw BCS&K,LLP) -555 5th Av -NY 10017
(212) 632-1984 .. **Lese**, Shawn C '98 Lazard Freres -30 Rckfllr Plz -NY 10112 **Fx:**632-6060
(212) 732-7184 .. **Leser Hunter Taubman & Taubman** -17 State -NY 10004 **Fx:**202-6380
(212) 988-8653 .. **Lesh**, Michl D '81 -58 E 79th -NY 10075
(914) 375-0100 .. **Lesh**, Steven '91 %Novick ELRW&L,PC -733 Ynkrs Av -Ynkrs 10704
(718) 802-2746 .. **Leshaw**, Hannah '05 Admin Children's Srvcs -330 Jay -Brklyn 11201
(631) 422-0500 .. **Leshen**, Jos C '75 %P Alba,PC -1250 Montauk Hwy -W Islip 11795 **Fx:**422-0967
(718) 237-2000 .. **Lesher**, Adrian A '85 %Leg Aid -111 Lvngstn -Brklyn 11201 **Fx:**237-8737
(914) 681-9500 .. **Leshko**, Gary L '91 (Baker LS&B,LLP) -1 N Lex Av -White Plns 10601
(212) 532-5550 .. **Leshkowitz**, C H '78 (Leshkowitz & Co LLP) -270 Mad Av -NY 10016 **Fx:**532-4007
(212) 248-0880 .. **Leshkowitz**, Naftuli T '98 Leshkowitz Law,PLLC -45 Bway -NY 10006 **Fx:**248-0999
(516) 295-2885 .. **Leshnower**, Richd '67 -1215 E Bway -Hewlett 11557 **Fx:**295-4366
(212) 532-4000 .. **Leshnower**, Steven A '01 %Dobrish ZG LLP -757 3rd Av -NY 10017
(212) 859-8000 .. **Lesk**, Ann Berger '79 (Fried FHS&J LLP) -1 NY Plz -NY 10004
(212) 382-3300 .. **Leska**, Richd C '95 (Wollmuth M&D LLP) -500 5th Av -NY 10110
(212) 776-5092 .. **Leske**, Corina L '02 %NYC Housing Auth -250 Bway -NY 10007 **Fx:**776-5039
(212) 836-8541 .. **Leskin**, Lori B '93 (Kaye S LLP) -425 Park Av -NY 10022 **Fx:**836-7153
(607) 724-2421 .. **Lesko**, Gregory S '89 Lesko Fncl Srvcs,Inc -53 Chenango -Bnghmtn 13901
(845) 679-2561 .. **Lesko**, Jason M '95 -Bx1486 -Woodstock 12498
(716) 847-8400 .. **Leslie**, Craig A '98 (Phillips L LLP) -3400 HSBC Ctr -Buffalo 14203
(646) 386-3643 .. **Leslie**, Dean W M '03 %Supreme Ct-Law Dept -60 Centre -NY 10007
(212) 902-2054 .. **Leslie**, Felix S '03 Goldman Sachs -85 Broad -NY 10004
(631) 952-6400 .. **Leslie**, Karen G '83 %Medicaid Fraud Cntrl -300 Motor Pkwy -Hauppauge 11788 **Fx:**952-6382
(212) 790-0266 .. **Leslie**, Melanie B '92 %Benj N Cardozo Schl of Law -55 5th Av -NY 10003 **Fx:**790-0205
(518) 473-2728 .. **Leslie**, Robt P '92 %NY Dept of State -80 S Swan -Albany 12210
(914) 946-7902 .. **Leslie**, Rosalie C '94 -202 Mamaroneck Av -White Plns 10601 **Fx:**946-5090
(212) 474-1000 .. **Leslie**, Scott A '09 %Cravath S&M LLP -825 8th Av -NY 10019
(914) 286-2910 .. **Leslie**, Thos M '75 (Greenberg T,LLP) -445 Hmltn Av -White Plns 10601
(718) 625-2775 .. **Leslie-Hopkins**, Sonali '84 -32 Court -Brklyn 11201
(212) 504-6000 .. **Lesman**, Adam D '09 %Cadwalader W&T LLP -1 World Fncl Ctr -NY 10281
(212) 891-0888 .. **Lesman**, Michl S '83 Cnsl FOJP Srvc Corp -28 E 28th -NY 10016
(718) 243-6823 .. **Lesman**, Wm A '06 %Leg Aid -111 Lvngstn -Brklyn 11201 **Fx:**237-8737
(212) 909-6000 .. **Lesnak**, Benjamin P '09 %Debevoise & P LLP -919 3rd Av -NY 10022
(212) 564-2770 .. **Lesnevich**, Walter A '77 (Lesnevich & M) -350 5th Av -NY 10118
(518) 474-8211 .. **Lesniak**, John W '79 %Law Reporting Bur -1 Commerce Plz -Albany 12210 **Fx:**463-6869
(914) 949-9515 .. **Lesniak**, Laurie Ann '97 Crown Abstract LLC -399 Knollwood Rd -White Plns 10603 **Fx:**949-8999
(212) 574-1200 .. **Lesnick**, Adam D '97 Cnsl Seward & K LLP -1 Bttry Pk Plz -NY 10004
(914) 476-0600 .. **Lesnick**, Chas B S '86 -733 Ynkrs Av -Ynkrs 10704 **Fx:**476-0614
(212) 326-3939 .. **Lesnick**, Randi C '99 (Jones D) -222 E 41st -NY 10017
(212) 530-5000 .. **Lesovitz**, Jeffrey W '07 %Milbank TH&M LLP -1 Chase Manh Plz -NY 10005

(518) 885-2902 .. **Lesperance**, James B Jr. '92 -5 Sherman Way Bx139 -Ballston Spa 12020 **Fx**:885-2903
(845) 486-6800 .. **Lesperance**, Karen Folster '00 %McCabe & M LLP -63 Wshngtn Bx509 -Poughkeepsie 12602
(718) 590-3722 .. **Lespinasse**, Sandra '96 Supreme Ct -851 Grnd Cncrs -Bronx 10451
(212) 858-1000 .. **Lessard**, Mark N '02 %Pillsbury WSP LLP -1540 Bway -NY 10036
(212) 506-5000 .. **Lessard**, Stephen C '08 %Orrick H&S LLP -51 W 52nd -NY 10019
(212) 818-8798 .. **Lessem**, Jos H '87 OfCnsl Graubard M -405 Lex Av -NY 10174
(212) 935-3131 .. **Lesser**, Beatrice '82 (Gallet D&B,LLP) -845 3rd Av -NY 10022
(212) 735-8702 .. **Lesser**, Danielle C '92 (Morrison C LLP) -909 3rd Av -NY 10022
(212) 969-1429 .. **Lesser**, David M '04 %Alliance Bernstein LP -1345 Av of Amer -NY 10105 **Fx**:554-4639
(212) 230-8851 .. **Lesser**, David S '02 Cnsl WilmerHale -399 Park Av -NY 10022
(212) 683-3636 .. **Lesser**, Eric B '89 (Krass S&S,PC) -419 Park Av S -NY 10016
(212) 406-6000 .. **Lesser**, Gary J '96 (Semmel & L,LLP) -20 Vesey -NY 10007 **Fx**:406-6001
(914) 948-7000 .. **Lesser**, Jeffrey A '88 (Keidel W&C LLP) -925 Wstchstr Av -White Plns 10604
(212) 888-4042 .. **Lesser**, Jill C '77 -110 E 59th -NY 10022 **Fx**:935-0966
(212) 684-8535 .. **Lesser**, Jonathan A '92 -475 Park Av S -NY 10016 **Fx**:(917) 677-8774
(212) 599-5455 .. **Lesser**, Leonard F '92 (Simon Lesser,PC) -420 Lex Av -NY 10170 **Fx**:599-5459
(212) 382-0909 .. **Lesser**, Lisa H '94 (Peckar & A,PC) -41 Mad Av -NY 10154
(212) 455-2000 .. **Lesser**, Lori E '94 (Simpson T&B LLP) -425 Lex Av -NY 10017
(914) 699-5538 .. **Lesser**, Marc E '83 (Kronisch & L,PC) -6 Gramatan Av -Mt Vernon 10550 **Fx**:699-5603
(212) 459-1919 .. **Lesser**, Michl C '83 -630 9th Av -NY 10036 **Fx**:459-2707
(518) 402-9521 .. **Lesser**, Michl J '88 %DEC -625 Bway -Albany 12233 **Fx**:402-9018
(212) 259-8000 .. **Lesser**, Rebecca A '02 %Dewey & L LLP -1301 Av of Amer -NY 10019
(212) 599-5455 .. **Lesser**, Renee Simon '93 (Simon Lesser,PC) -420 Lex Av -NY 10170 **Fx**:599-5459
(845) 638-1433 .. **Lesser**, Robt H '86 -1 Rise Rd -New Cty 10956 **Fx**:638-1433
(212) 682-9832 .. **Lesser**, Robt I '82 (Greenblatt L LLP) -370 Lex Av -NY 10017 **Fx**:867-9319
(914) 934-9200 .. **Lesser**, Seth R '89 (Klafter O&L LLP) -2 Intl Dr -Rye Brook 10573 **Fx**:934-9220
(516) 791-5957 .. **Lesser**, Seymour S '49 -212 Hungry Hrbr Rd -Vly Stream 11581 **Fx**:791-1180
(845) 562-9020 .. **Lesser**, Sol '76 (Silver FS&L) -3250 Route 9W -New Windsor 12553
(315) 471-8111 .. **Lesser**, Susan Fortin '89 (Scolaro SCF&B,PC) -507 Plum -Syracuse 13204
(212) 609-6800 .. **Lesser**, Tracy J '00 %McCarter & E,LLP -245 Park Av -NY 10167
(212) 902-0870 .. **Lessing**, Alisa Gettenberg '98 %Goldman Sachs -1 NY Plz -NY 10004
(212) 446-7000 .. **Lessing**, David L '96 %McKinsey & Co -55 E 52nd -NY 10055 **Fx**:688-9521
(212) 490-4100 .. **Lessler**, Arthur L '66 OfCnsl Storch A&M,PC -140 E 45th -NY 10017
(212) 885-5000 .. **Lessler**, Jay P '98 (Blank R LLP) -405 Lex Av -NY 10174
(212) 219-9257 .. **Lessoff**, Jeffrey L '84 -350 Bway -NY 10013
(212) 664-5165 .. **Lestch**, David A '81 %NBC Universal -30 Rckfllr Plz -NY 10112
(212) 596-9000 .. **Lestelle**, Evan P '10 %Ropes & G LLP -1211 Av of Amer -NY 10036
(212) 688-8555 .. **Lestelle**, Karin C '83 OfCnsl Fragomen DB&L LLP -7 Hanover Sq -NY 10004
(212) 637-2416 .. **Lester**, Amy '03 %US Atty -1 St Andrews Plz -NY 10007
(631) 907-3500 .. **Lester**, Brian J '98 (Tarbet L&S) -524 Montauk Hwy Bx2635 -Amagansett 11930 **Fx**:907-3501
(212) 803-5100 .. **Lester**, C Sidney '88 %NY Cnty Defender Srvcs -225 Bway -NY 10007 **Fx**:571-6035
(516) 365-1400 .. **Lester**, David S '81 (Cooperman LM LLP) -1129 Nrthrn Blvd -Manhsst 11030
(585) 385-0465 .. **Lester**, Fredk P '96 -102 S Main -Pittsfrd 14534
(212) 964-6611 .. **Lester**, Howard '53 OfCnsl Lester SK&D -120 Bway -NY 10271
(212) 279-4490 .. **Lester**, Ian '05 %D Bleckner,PC -350 5th Av -NY 10118 **Fx**:279-4495
(212) 832-5357 .. **Lester**, Jack L '78 -261 Mad Av -NY 10016
(518) 472-1224 .. **Lester**, Kelly Mooney '94 (Phillips L LLP) -30 S Pearl -Albany 12207
(516) 773-3950 .. **Lester**, Kenneth J '80 -15 Fieldstone Ln -Gt Neck 11020
(516) 644-2494 .. **Lester**, Kyle F '99 -3601 Hempstd Tpk -Levittwn 11756 **Fx**:644-2495
(212) 984-7849 .. **Lester**, Marshall N '71 (Warshaw BCS&K,LLP) -555 5th Av -NY 10017
(516) 794-2323 .. **Lester Minsky & Berzak** -325 Merrick Av -E Meadow 11554 **Fx**:794-2431
(585) 637-8114 .. **Lester**, Nat O III '88 -64 Main Bx248 -Brockprt 14420 **Fx**:637-8657
(516) 357-9191 .. **Lester**, Roy J '85 (Lester & W,PC) -600 Old Cntry Rd -Gdn Cty 11530 **Fx**:357-9281
(212) 478-0000 .. **Lester**, Sara R '04 DE Shaw & Co -120 W 45th -NY 10036 **Fx**:478-0100
(212) 964-6611 .. **Lester Schwab Katz & Dwyer** -120 Bway -NY 10271 **Fx**:267-5916
(516) 357-0056 .. **Lester**, Steven M '89 (LaReddola L & Assoc,LLP) -600 Old Cntry Rd -Gdn Cty 11530
(212) 415-9200 .. **Lestrade**, Laura M '93 Dorsey & W LLP -250 Park Av -NY 10177
(914) 273-8999 .. **Lestz**, Alan M '70 -8 Carolyn Pl -Armonk 10504
(212) 839-5300 .. **Lestz**, David J '00 Cnsl Sidley A LLP -787 7th Av -NY 10019
(212) 508-6700 .. **LeSueur**, Carl D '05 %Tannenbaum HS&H LLP -900 3rd Av -NY 10022
(315) 379-2225 .. **Lesyk**, Alexander '83 DA -48 Court -Canton 13617 **Fx**:379-2301
(518) 673-3221 .. **Leszczynski**, Sarah J '04 S Leszczynski,PLLC -22 Church Bx180 -Canajoharie 13317 **Fx**:673-3110
(718) 894-4981 .. **Leszczynski**, Steven D '90 -64-17 Clinton Av -Maspeth 11378 **Fx**:894-4981
(212) 661-1151 .. **Leszkiewicz**, Margaret J '96 %Marin G LLP -40 Wall -NY 10005
(585) 872-6790 .. **Leszyk**, Richd A '89 -322 Ridge Rd -Ontario 14519 **Fx**:265-2670
(908) 352-5577 .. **LeTendre**, Jon P '96 -39 Bangor -Staten Isl 10314 **Fx**:352-2008
(212) 592-1400 .. **Leto**, Marisa A '04 %Herrick,F LLP -2 Park Av -NY 10016
(516) 742-1444 .. **Leto**, Salvatore J '88 (Wagner D&L,PC) -227 Mineola Blvd -Mineola 11501
(212) 308-0070 .. **LeTourneau**, Patrice E '10 %McCusker AR&C,PC -805 3rd Av -NY 10022
(516) 767-0607 .. **Letowsky**, Martin E '78 -170 Old Cntry Rd -Mineola 11501 **Fx**:741-0546
(212) 859-8000 .. **Letowsky**, Risa C '03 %Fried FHS&J LLP -1 NY Plz -NY 10004
(212) 903-9000 .. **Letrich**, Dylan A '09 %Linklaters -1345 Av of Amer -NY 10105
(716) 852-1234 .. **Letro**, Francis M '80 -110 Pearl -Buffalo 14202 **Fx**:853-2930
(914) 674-2505 .. **Letsen**, Royden A '53 -828 S Bway -Tarrytwn 10591
(212) 558-4000 .. **Letson**, Timothea G P '07 %Sullivan & C LLP -125 Broad -NY 10004
(212) 223-6700 .. **Letsou**, Thos C '94 %Zukerman GB&C,LLP -875 3rd Av -NY 10022
(631) 242-2020 .. **Lettera**, Frank L '95 %JS Caramagno -1641 Deer Prk Av -Deer Pk 11729 **Fx**:242-2034
(516) 783-1439 .. **Lettieri**, Jeanne M '86 -2081 Natalie Blvd -Seafrd 11783
(212) 532-3651 .. **Lettieri**, Jerry S '02 Marwood Grp -733 3rd Av -NY 10017
(716) 200-5050 .. **Lettieri**, Pietra Grazia '02 %Harris B PLLC -726 Exchange -Buffalo 14210
(347) 592-2200 .. **Lettman**, Antonette D '01 Leg Srvcs -89-00 Sutphin Blvd -Jamaica 11435 **Fx**:(718) 937-5350
(716) 636-7600 .. **Letty**, Doreen E '92 %HoganWillig -2410 N Forest Rd -Amherst 14068
(718) 243-6258 .. **Letwin**, Michl Z '86 %Leg Aid -111 Lvngstn -Brklyn 11201 **Fx**:237-8737
(212) 282-5000 .. **Leu**, Karen R '99 Avon Products -1345 Av of Amer -NY 10105
(212) 297-5800 .. **Leu**, Richd '03 %Day P LLP -7 Times Sq -NY 10036
(212) 663-0270 .. **Leubsdorf**, John D '89 -333 Cntrl Pk W -NY 10025 **Fx**:663-0270
(212) 596-9000 .. **Leuchtenburg**, Joshua A '85 (Ropes & G LLP) -1211 Av of Amer -NY 10036
(212) 259-8000 .. **Leung**, Brian J '09 %Dewey & L LLP -1301 Av of Amer -NY 10019
(212) 416-6389 .. **Leung**, Christopher K '06 NYS Atty Gen -120 Bway -NY 10271
(212) 880-6000 .. **Leung**, Darien G '97 (Torys LLP) -237 Park Av -NY 10017
(212) 627-2223 .. **Leung**, Edw '96 NY State -175 Varick -NY 10014
(212) 458-2540 .. **Leung**, Jeffrey '01 AIG Domestic Claims -175 Water -NY 10038
(212) 848-4000 .. **Leung**, Joanna P '07 %Shearman & S LLP -599 Lex Av -NY 10022
(212) 506-1700 .. **Leung**, Kanchana W '03 %Kasowitz BT&F LLP -1633 Bway -NY 10019
(212) 715-9100 .. **Leung**, Marissa S '06 %Kramer LN&F,LLP -1177 Av of Amer -NY 10036
(646) 442-2202 .. **Leung**, Nhadine '98 Living Cities,Inc -55 W 125th -NY 10027
(212) 446-2300 .. **Leung**, Robt W '95 (Boies S&F LLP) -575 Lex Av -NY 10022
(212) 546-4000 .. **Leung**, Sandra '85 %Bristol-Myers Squibb -345 Park Av -NY 10154 **Fx**:546-9562
(212) 964-9282 .. **Leung**, Stephen S '08 %N Weinrib & Assoc -305 Bway -NY 10007 **Fx**:964-9525
(718) 387-4000 .. **Leung**, Susan A '99 (Levin & L PC) -185 Marcy Av -Brklyn 11211
(212) 761-8034 .. **Leung**, Titus W '96 Morgan Stanley -1585 Bway -NY 10036
(212) 455-2000 .. **Leutner**, LeAnn S '97 %Simpson T&B LLP -425 Lex Av -NY 10017
(212) 728-8000 .. **Leutzinger**, Michelle K '09 %Willkie F&G LLP -787 7th Av -NY 10019
(212) 355-6030 .. **Leuzzi**, Bruce J '89 (Leuzzi & L LLP) -400 Park Av -NY 10022 **Fx**:317-1807
(212) 355-6030 .. **Leuzzi**, Jos P '59 (Leuzzi & L LLP) -400 Park Av -NY 10022 **Fx**:317-1807
(718) 390-5322 .. **Lev**, Jodi H '00 %Law Dept -60 Bay -Staten Isl 10301 **Fx**:390-5338
(914) 738-2032 .. **Leva**, Sabina Lepre '94 -19 Central Dr -Bronxvll 10708 **Fx**:667-6839
(212) 481-7338 .. **Levai**, Michl I '93 (M Levai PC) -332 E 29th -NY 10016 **Fx**:679-5336
(212) 686-9288 .. **Levan**, Patricia D '96 -310 E 46th -NY 10017 **Fx**:656-1756
(212) 698-3500 .. **Levander**, Andrew J '78 (Dechert LLP) -1095 Av of Amer -NY 10036
(516) 827-9236 .. **Levano**, Gerald A '93 -998-C Old Cntry Rd -Plainvw 11803 **Fx**:938-5773
(212) 762-7226 .. **Levarda**, Daniela '97 Axiom/Morgan Stanley -1221 Av of Amer -NY 10020 **Fx**:507-1446
(718) 428-7373 .. **Levas**, Chas A '82 -36-51 Bell Blvd -Bayside 11361 **Fx**:428-8020
(914) 684-0090 .. **Le Vasseur**, Anne Casey '05 %Diserio MO&C LLP -50 Main -White Plns 10606
(212) 490-3000 .. **Levasseur**, Guy J '93 (Wilson EME&D LLP) -150 E 42nd -NY 10017
(914) 323-7000 .. **Levasseur**, Guy J '93 (Wilson EME&D LLP) -3 Gannett Dr -White Plns 10604
(212) 809-8585 .. **Levasseur**, M Dru '07 Lambda Legal -120 Wall -NY 10005
(315) 386-4305 .. **Levato**, Michl L '86 -11 Main Bx252 -Canton 13617 **Fx**:386-1710
(212) 813-8800 .. **Levato**, Thos S '01 %Goodwin P LLP -620 8th Av -NY 10018
(212) 643-7000 .. **Leve**, Marc D '93 %Sills C&G PC -One Rckfllr Plz -NY 10020
(718) 643-5686 .. **Levell**, Vincent A '84 Family Ct -283 Adams -Brklyn 11201
(212) 873-6000 .. **Levelt**, Ursula '01 TWU Local 100 -80 W End Av -NY 10023
(212) 725-9800 .. **Leven**, Adrianne J '07 %Osborn Law,PC -295 Mad Av -NY 10017
(212) 768-3878 .. **Leven**, Andrew '88 (Smith SWH&B,LLP) -100 Park Av -NY 10017
(914) 738-1959 .. **Leven**, David C '69 -544 Manor Ridge Rd -Pelham 10803
(516) 295-4036 .. **Levenberg**, Jerome J '62 -251 Wshngtn Av -Cedarhrst 11516 **Fx**:295-4036
(212) 408-5100 .. **Levenberg**, Keith '03 %Chadbourne & P LLP -30 Rckfllr Plz -NY 10112
(631) 421-4200 .. **Levenbron**, Maurice '39 (Levenbron & S) -Bx2229 -Huntngtn 11743
(631) 421-4200 .. **Levenbron & Stern** -Bx2229 -Huntngtn 11743
(607) 763-9200 .. **Levene Gouldin & Thompson,LLP** -BxF-1706 -Bnghmtn 13902 **Fx**:763-9211
(607) 763-9200 .. **Levene Gouldin & Thompson,LLP** -71 State -Bnghmtn 13902
(212) 403-1000 .. **Levene**, Ralph M '88 (Wachtell LR&K) -51 W 52nd -NY 10019
(607) 763-9200 .. **Levene**, Saml K '62 (Levene G&T,LLP) -BxF-1706 -Bnghmtn 13902
(212) 269-4900 .. **Levene**, Stuart C '80 (Ford MEW&G,LLP) -Wall Street Plz -NY 10005
(212) 735-8600 .. **Levenglick**, Martin H '80 (Morrison C LLP) -909 3rd Av -NY 10022
(212) 935-1400 .. **Levenson**, Adam A '99 %Seiden & S,PC -570 Lex Av -NY 10022
(212) 961-7067 .. **Levenson**, Brian S '06 %The Inc Records -237 W 37th -NY 10018
(212) 474-1000 .. **Levenson**, David A '10 %Cravath S&M LLP -825 8th Av -NY 10019

(914) 681-6200 .. **Levenson,** Gary D '02 %NYPA -123 Main -White Plns 10601 **Fx:**390-8038
(212) 869-7000 .. **Levenson,** Heather M '04 %Feldman W&S LLP -420 Lex Av -NY 10170
(914) 824-5800 .. **Levenson,** Joan G '89 Judicial Institute -84 N Bway -White Plns 10603
(212) 732-0522 .. **Levenson,** Leonard J '57 -225 Bway -NY 10007 **Fx:**587-0570
(212) 809-7600 .. **Levenson,** Mark L '76 %Cheven K&H -40 Wall -NY 10005
(212) 988-5202 .. **Levenson,** Martin J '68 -155 E 77th -NY 10075 **Fx:**628-5225
(212) 799-2876 .. **Levenson,** Richd L '50 -277 West End Av -NY 10023 **Fx:**799-2876
(212) 533-6300 .. **Levenstien,** Damon S '02 %NYSUT -52 Bway -NY 10004 **Fx:**995-2347
(718) 286-6000 .. **Leventhal,** Brad A '89 %DA -125-01 Qns Blvd -Kew Gdns 11415
(718) 722-6463 .. **Leventhal,** Danl H '06 Appllt Div 2nd Dept -45 Monroe Pl -Brklyn 11201 **Fx:**858-2446
(718) 997-2860 .. **Leventhal,** David A '02 Queens College -6419 Kissena Blvd -Flushng 11367
(212) 983-9330 .. **Leventhal,** David H '94 %Faruqi & F,LLP -369 Lex Av -NY 10017 **Fx:**983-9331
(516) 569-7552 .. **Leventhal,** Donald C '88 -517 Saddle Rdg Rd -Woodmere 11598
(516) 482-4436 .. **Leventhal,** Gabriel A '02 %Gleich S&F -36 S Station Plz -Gt Neck 11021
(646) 386-3630 .. **Leventhal,** Howard G '71 Supreme Ct Spcl Referee -60 Centre -NY 10007
(718) 722-4100 .. **Leventhal,** Jason '98 (Leventhal & K,LLP) -45 Main -Brklyn 11201
(718) 556-9600 .. **Leventhal,** Jason '98 (Leventhal & K,LLP) -60 Bay -Staten Isl 10301
(718) 727-6608 .. **Leventhal,** Jason R '88 -60 Bay -Staten Isl 10301
(516) 622-9200 .. **Leventhal,** Joshua R '05 %Westerman BEM&S,LLP -1201 RXR Plz -Uniondale 11553
(718) 722-4100 .. **Leventhal & Klein,LLP** -45 Main -Brklyn 11201 **Fx:**522-3225
(718) 556-9600 .. **Leventhal & Klein,LLP** -60 Bay -Staten Isl 10301 **Fx:**448-8685
(212) 407-1200 .. **Leventhal,** Mara A '95 -485 Lex Av -NY 10017 **Fx:**407-1299
(212) 935-0800 .. **Leventhal,** Melvyn R '80 -488 Mad Av -NY 10022
(718) 590-2000 .. **Leventhal,** Nicole '97 %DA -198 E 161st -Bronx 10451 **Fx:**590-6477
(914) 375-0100 .. **Leventhal,** Robt H '74 (Novick ELRW&L,PC) -733 Ynkrs Av -Ynkrs 10704
(516) 222-0500 .. **Leventhal,** Roberta Ross '87 -1103 Stewart Av -Gdn Cty 11530 **Fx:**222-2462
(212) 670-0478 .. **Leventhal,** Samantha J '97 Merrill Lynch -222 Bway -NY 10038 **Fx:**670-4524
(212) 720-5026 .. **Leventhal,** Shari D '89 %Fed Reserve Bk -33 Lbrty -NY 10045 **Fx:**785-5748
(516) 484-5440 .. **Leventhal,** Steven G '81 (S Leventhal,PC) -15 Remsen Av -Roslyn 11576 **Fx:**484-2710
(347) 296-1682 .. **Leventhal-Quintero,** Ellen '82 %Supreme Ct Law Dept -360 Adams -Brklyn 11201 **Fx:**643-6114
(516) 357-3634 .. **Leventritt Lewittes & Bender** -1010 Nrthrn Blvd -Gt Neck 11021
(914) 288-9191 .. **Lever,** David B '90 (Lever & S,LLP) -303 Old Tarrytown Rd -White Plns 10603
(914) 285-9800 .. **Lever,** Joel S '77 (Kurzman EC&L,LLP) -1 N Bway -White Plns 10601
(914) 937-9032 .. **Lever,** Lawr G '75 -5 Greenhouse Cir -Rye Brook 10573 **Fx:**937-9032
(914) 288-9191 .. **Lever & Stolzenberg,LLP** -303 Old Tarrytown Rd -White Plns 10603 **Fx:**288-9197
(516) 538-2500 .. **Leverage,** Thos G '86 (Furey FLMW&D,PC) -600 Front -Hempstd 11550
(212) 878-8000 .. **Levere,** Colin J '08 %Clifford C LLP -31 W 52nd -NY 10019
(212) 773-4610 .. **Levere,** David G '81 Ernst & Young LLP -5 Times Sq -NY 10036
(516) 931-2323 .. **Levering,** Susan Dworkin '79 -183 Bway -Hicksvll 11801 **Fx:**938-9401
(585) 724-7255 .. **Leverone,** Jos D '03 Eastman Kodak Co -343 State -Rchstr 14650
(631) 329-9700 .. **Leverrier,** Dianne K '02 -23 Royal -E Hampton 11937
(718) 447-1687 .. **Levey,** Lila R '79 -46 Pelton Av -Staten Isl 10310
(212) 750-8585 .. **Levey,** Lisa D '82 %WP Stewart & Co,Inc -527 Mad Av -NY 10022 **Fx:**750-0768
(212) 626-4100 .. **Levey,** Marc M '85 (Baker & M LLP) -1114 Av of Amer -NY 10036
(585) 232-5300 .. **Levey,** Sherman F '59 OfCnsl Boylan BCV&W,LLP -2400 Chase Sq -Rchstr 14604
(212) 907-7300 .. **Levi,** Amit '10 %Golenbock EAB&P -437 Mad Av -NY 10022
(212) 373-3000 .. **Levi,** Danl H '99 %Paul WRW&G LLP -1285 Av of Amer -NY 10019
(718) 380-1122 .. **Levi,** Daniella '02 (Levi & M,LLP) -15916 Union Tpk -Fresh Mdws 11366 **Fx:**380-1124
(212) 816-3718 .. **Levi,** Elissa M '05 Citigroup -388 Greenwich -NY 10013
(212) 980-0404 .. **Levi,** Eric R '90 %J Dearie & Assoc -515 Mad Av -NY 10022 **Fx:**980-0555
(646) 878-0800 .. **Levi,** Guy '07 %Pearl CZL,LLP -1500 Bway -NY 10036
(212) 308-6100 .. **Levi,** Howard B '83 (Levi L&F LLP) -1185 Av of Amer -NY 10036
(212) 308-7400 .. **Levi,** Jill '83 (Todd & L,LLP) -444 Mad Av -NY 10022
(212) 363-7500 .. **Levi,** Jos E '96 (Levi & K LLP) -30 Broad -NY 10004
(212) 412-1405 .. **Levi,** Julie A '03 Baclays Capital Inc -200 Park Av -NY 10166
(212) 363-7500 .. **Levi & Korsinsky LLP** -30 Broad -NY 10004 **Fx:**363-7171
(212) 308-6100 .. **Levi Lubarsky & Feigenbaum LLP** -1185 Av of Amer -NY 10036 **Fx:**308-8830
(212) 964-7400 .. **Levi,** Mark D '77 Smith MDWY&Y,PC -111 John -NY 10038
(716) 693-9600 .. **Levi,** Robt E '60 (McKenna B&L) -126 Broad -Tonawanda 14150 **Fx:**693-0024
(518) 472-3330 .. **Levi,** Ross D '98 Empire State Pride Agenda -99 Wshngtn Av -Albany 12210
(718) 216-0404 .. **Levi,** Rusudan G '04 -71 W 47th -NY 10036
(212) 788-0670 .. **Levi,** Steven R '85 %Law Dept -100 Church -NY 10007 **Fx:**788-0367
(212) 735-3000 .. **Levi,** Stuart D '87 (Skadden ASM&F LLP) -4 Times Sq -NY 10036
(718) 965-6450 .. **Levi,** Walter E '93 -882 3rd Av -Brklyn 11232 **Fx:**965-6170
(212) 446-4053 .. **Leviant,** Shulamit '94 MH Davidson & Co -885 3rd Av -NY 10022
(212) 964-3290 .. **Levidow,** David J '51 (Levidow L&O) -299 Bway -NY 10007
(212) 964-3290 .. **Levidow Levidow & Oberman** -299 Bway -NY 10007 **Fx:**571-1053
(212) 553-0300 .. **Levidy,** Nicholas J '79 %Moody's Invstr Srvc -250 Greenwich -NY 10007
(212) 331-5133 .. **Levie,** Jessica R '07 HRA -180 Water -NY 10038
(212) 964-5570 .. **Levien,** Adam S '02 %Sacks & S -150 Bway -NY 10038 **Fx:**349-2141
(516) 939-9200 .. **Levien,** Bradley J '96 (Mintzer SZL&M LLP) -17 W John -Hicksvll 11801
(212) 922-9055 .. **Levien,** James R '62 -51 E 42nd -NY 10017 **Fx:**922-9057
(212) 267-7580 .. **Levien,** Jan F '74 (Adler & G) -155 E 55th -NY 10022
(212) 362-0976 .. **Levien,** Jane S '75 -6 W 77th -NY 10024 **Fx:**362-0976
(212) 981-1777 .. **Levien,** Jeffrey S '92 Scott-Lawrence -Bx599 -Armonk 10504
(212) 909-6306 .. **Levi Minzi,** Maurizio '94 (Debevoise & P LLP) -919 3rd Av -NY 10022
(516) 741-6565 .. **Levin,** A Thos '67 (Meyer SE&K,PC) -990 Stewart Av Bx9194 -Gdn Cty 11530
(718) 522-1972 .. **Levin,** Alan M '83 -26 Court -Brklyn 11242
(212) 813-8800 .. **Levin,** Andrew B '10 %Goodwin P LLP -620 8th Av -NY 10018
(516) 222-4500 .. **Levin,** Barry '85 -1055 Franklin Av -Gdn Cty 11530 **Fx:**228-8120
(718) 884-5892 .. **Levin,** Batya Schaefer '81 -5260 Sycamore -Bronx 10471
(718) 746-3440 .. **Levin,** Brad S '06 %Sacco & F,LLP -141-07 20th Av -Whitestone 11357
(212) 791-6060 .. **Levin,** Chaim A '85 Tradition Asiel Securities,Inc -75 Park Pl -NY 10007
(718) 387-4000 .. **Levin,** Chavie D '03 (Levin & L PC) -185 Marcy Av -Brklyn 11211
(718) 237-2000 .. **Levin,** Clifford D '86 %Leg Aid -111 Lvngstn -Brklyn 11201 **Fx:**237-8737
(585) 530-3050 .. **Levin,** Craig S '88 %MHLS -50 East Av -Rchstr 14604 **Fx:**530-3079
(718) 590-2000 .. **Levin,** Dana R '07 %DA -198 E 161st -Bronx 10451 **Fx:**590-6477
(212) 770-8640 .. **Levin,** David A '97 AIG -70 Pine -NY 10270
(212) 957-0900 .. **Levin,** David E '89 -200 W 57th -NY 10019
(718) 590-2000 .. **Levin,** Donald H '75 %DA -198 E 161st -Bronx 10451 **Fx:**590-6477
(718) 613-2542 .. **Levin,** Duncan P '03 %Hon N Garufis - USDC -225 Cadman Plz E -Brklyn 11201
(212) 384-1000 .. **Levin,** Edw '01 FBI -26 Fed Plz -NY 10278
(631) 439-4200 .. **Levin,** Edw C '77 %R Tusa -898 Vets Mem'l Hwy -Hauppauge 11788 **Fx:**439-4292
(212) 407-8312 .. **Levin,** Erik J '02 NBA Properties -645 5th Av -NY 10022 **Fx:**888-7931
(212) 878-8000 .. **Levin,** Erika B '05 %Clifford C LLP -31 W 52nd -NY 10019
(212) 715-9100 .. **Levin,** Ezra G '61 (Kramer LN&F,LLP) -1177 Av of Amer -NY 10036
(212) 756-1824 .. **Levin,** Frank S '90 Bernstein Glbl Wlth Mgmt -1345 Av of Amer -NY 10105
(212) 351-4000 .. **Levin,** Gabrielle '07 %Gibson D&C LLP -200 Park Av -NY 10166
(212) 732-2000 .. **Levin,** Galete J '04 %Cullen and D LLP -44 Wall -NY 10005
(212) 504-6000 .. **Levin,** Geoffrey W '94 (Cadwalader W&T LLP) -1 World Fncl Ctr -NY 10281
(212) 867-3636 .. **Levin & Glasser,PC** -420 Lex Av -NY 10170 **Fx:**661-2446
(212) 687-9006 .. **Levin,** Glenn I '86 -60 E 42nd -NY 10165 **Fx:**687-9010
(212) 833-1128 .. **Levin,** Hallie B '98 (Friedman KS&A LLP) -1633 Bway -NY 10019 **Fx:**373-7928
(212) 403-1000 .. **Levin,** Ian L '94 Cnsl Wachtell LR&K -51 W 52nd -NY 10019
(212) 924-1220 .. **Levin,** Israel Y '90 %Leg Srvcs Local 237 -216 W 14th -NY 10011 **Fx:**647-9421
(212) 841-1000 .. **Levin,** Jack P '72 (Covington & B LLP) -620 8th Av -NY 10018
(212) 788-0474 .. **Levin,** Jacob R '94 %Law Dept -100 Church -NY 10007 **Fx:**788-0367
(212) 666-2395 .. **Levin,** James B '79 -101 W 104th -NY 10025 **Fx:**666-5114
(212) 632-1963 .. **Levin,** Jared M '99 -30 Rckfllr Plz -NY 10112
(212) 490-4100 .. **Levin,** Jason B '05 %Storch A&M,PC -140 E 45th -NY 10017
(212) 541-2000 .. **Levin,** Jeffrey K '81 Cnsl Bryan C LLP -1290 Av of Amer -NY 10104
(914) 725-3468 .. **Levin,** Jeffrey L '76 -16 Rdgdl Rd -Scarsdale 10583 **Fx:**725-3468
(212) 872-9800 .. **Levin,** Jeffrey S '80 (Squire S&D LLP) -30 Rckfllr Plz -NY 10112
(212) 756-2000 .. **Levin,** Jessica R '08 %Schulte R&Z LLP -919 3rd Av -NY 10022
(914) 946-1400 .. **Levin,** Joan S '81 (Vouté LM&C,LLP) -170 Hmltn Av -White Plns 10601
(212) 541-2000 .. **Levin,** Joel A '78 (Bryan C LLP) -1290 Av of Amer -NY 10104
(914) 995-7714 .. **Levin,** Joshua '09 Westchester Cnty Human Rghts Cmmn -112 E Post Rd -White Plns 10601 **Fx:**995-7720
(212) 756-2000 .. **Levin,** Joshua D '10 %Schulte R&Z LLP -919 3rd Av -NY 10022
(845) 496-4492 .. **Levin,** Judith '74 -22 North -Washingtnvll 10992 **Fx:**496-7580
(212) 679-9895 .. **Levin,** Juliette S '85 (JS Levin,PC) -2 Park Av -NY 10016 **Fx:**679-9842
(518) 408-2805 .. **Levin,** Justin C '06 Dept of Law -The Cptl -Albany 12224
(516) 357-3700 .. **Levin,** Karen I '92 (Cullen and D LLP) -100 Q Roosevelt Blvd -Gdn Cty 11530
(917) 346-1971 .. **Levin,** Katrine A '96 IP Centric Law -270 W 17th -NY 10011
(914) 761-1300 .. **Levin,** Leslie '98 %Cuddy & F LLP -445 Hmltn Av -White Plns 10601
(718) 429-2021 .. **Levin,** M Jos '66 (Gross & L LLP) -86-26 Qns Blvd -Elmhrst 11373
(212) 592-1400 .. **Levin,** Mara B '86 (Herrick,F LLP) -2 Park Av -NY 10016
(212) 991-6119 .. **Levin,** Marc H '00 TNS -11 Mad Av -NY 10010
(212) 438-1831 .. **Levin,** Mark '04 Standard & Poor's -55 Water -NY 10041
(212) 790-9200 .. **Levin,** Martin P '84 OfCnsl Cowan L&L,PC -1133 Av of Amer -NY 10036
(516) 663-6600 .. **Levin,** Meeka S '09 %Ruskin MF,PC -1425 RXR Plz -Uniondale 11556
(212) 983-0331 .. **Levin,** Meir '89 -521 5th Av -NY 10175
(516) 775-7007 .. **Levin,** Melissa S '08 %Gutman MB&S,PC -813 Jericho Tpk -New Hyde Pk 11040
(212) 807-2297 .. **Levin,** Michl A '64 %Thomson Reuters/RIA -195 Bway -NY 10007
(212) 484-8525 .. **Levin,** Michl D '98 Time Warner Inc -1 Time Warner Ctr -NY 10019
(516) 338-2888 .. **Levin,** Michl G '96 (Levin & C,LLP) -265 Post Av -Westbury 11590 **Fx:**338-4343
(212) 557-2800 .. **Levin,** Michl J '73 OfCnsl Barger & W LLP -10 E 40th -NY 10016
(212) 715-1000 .. **Levin,** Michl K '09 %Arnold & P LLP -399 Park Av -NY 10022
(516) 931-1800 .. **Levin,** Michele R '97 (Catalano G&P LLP) -100 Jericho Quadrangle -Jericho 11753
(212) 506-3900 .. **Levin,** Michelle L '05 %Steptoe & J LLP -750 7th Av -NY 10019
(212) 735-3000 .. **Levin,** Noah D '08 %Skadden ASM&F LLP -4 Times Sq -NY 10036
(914) 813-7257 .. **Levin,** Owein C '08 %DA -3010 Wstchstr Av -Purchase 10577 **Fx:**813-7211
(212) 450-4000 .. **Levin,** Peter S W '82 (Davis P&W LLP) -450 Lex Av -NY 10017
(212) 473-9173 .. **Levin,** Rand J '94 %Razor & Tie Direct, LLC -214 Sullivan -NY 10012 **Fx:**473-9174

(212) 909-9500 .. **Levin,** Raymond H '85 OfCnsl Wachtel & M,LLP -885 2nd Av -NY 10017
(212) 460-4089 .. **Levin,** Richd A '75 Con Ed -4 Irving Pl -NY 10003
(212) 474-1000 .. **Levin,** Richd B '06 (Cravath S&M LLP) -825 8th Av -NY 10019
(585) 546-1383 .. **Levin,** Richd S '72 (Lubelle L & K) -19 W Main -Rchstr 14614 **Fx:**546-1385
(516) 656-5300 .. **Levin,** Robt G '80 Mullooly JR&F LLP -6851 Jericho Tpk Bx9036 -Syosset 11791
(212) 987-8000 .. **Levin,** Roger M '70 -15 E 90th -NY 10128 **Fx:**987-8001
(212) 753-7800 .. **Levin,** Sara B '96 -488 Mad Av -NY 10022
(914) 946-1400 .. **Levin,** Sarah R '10 %Vouté LM&C,LLP -170 Hmltn Av -White Plns 10601
(212) 483-9490 .. **Levin,** Scott A '05 %McElroy DM&C,LLP -88 Pine -NY 10005
(212) 654-3205 .. **Levin,** Seth I '92 VH1 -345 Hudson -NY 10014
(212) 479-6000 .. **Levin,** Shira Nadich '77 (Cooley LLP) -1114 Av of Amer -NY 10036
(212) 588-5500 .. **Levin,** Steven H '86 (Davies WP&V LLP) -625 Mad Av -NY 10022
(212) 867-3636 .. **Levin,** Steven I '75 (Levin & G,PC) -420 Lex Av -NY 10170
(212) 355-2497 .. **Levin,** Susan G '84 -141 E 55th -NY 10022
(516) 745-6000 .. **Levin,** Victor '60 V Levin,PC -585 Stewart Av -Gdn Cty 11530 **Fx:**745-6003
(212) 859-8000 .. **Levina,** Tatyana '08 %Fried FHS&J LLP -1 NY Plz -NY 10004
(212) 317-0211 .. **Levinbook,** David G '98 DBI Staffing -12 E 44th -NY 10017
(212) 223-3778 .. **Levinbook,** Neil S '99 (N Levinbook LLC) -222 E 56th -NY 10022
(212) 477-5118 .. **Levine,** A Barry '71 -320 E 23rd -NY 10010 **Fx:**477-5118
(212) 836-8000 .. **Levine,** Aaron H '08 %Kaye S LLP -425 Park Av -NY 10022
(631) 390-0010 .. **Levine,** Adam D '09 %Bruno G&S,LLP -445 Broad Hollow Rd -Melvll 11747
(516) 803-6347 .. **Levine,** Adam K '97 %Rainbow Media Holdings -200 Jericho Quad -Jericho 11753
(212) 878-8000 .. **Levine,** Adam S '09 %Clifford C LLP -31 W 52nd -NY 10019
(212) 715-9100 .. **Levine,** Adina C '07 %Kramer LN&F,LLP -1177 Av of Amer -NY 10036
(212) 971-3175 .. **Levine,** Aimee P '88 (d'Arcambal L&O LLP) -40 Fulton -NY 10038 **Fx:**971-3176
(212) 479-6000 .. **Levine,** Alan '74 (Cooley LLP) -1114 Av of Amer -NY 10036
(718) 793-6363 .. **Levine,** Alan D '81 -80-02 Kew Grdns Rd -Kew Gdns 11415 **Fx:**520-8751
(212) 735-8600 .. **Levine,** Alan M '97 (Morrison C LLP) -909 3rd Av -NY 10022
(212) 728-8000 .. **Levine,** Alison R '09 %Willkie F&G LLP -787 7th Av -NY 10019
(212) 701-3000 .. **Levine,** Aliza R '97 (Cahill G&R LLP) -80 Pine -NY 10005 **Fx:**269-5420
(516) 538-7640 .. **Levine,** Allan R '72 -225 Maple -W Hempstead 11552
(212) 944-0500 .. **Levine,** Allen M '07 %Hofheimer G&G,LLP -530 5th Av -NY 10036
(212) 506-2500 .. **Levine,** Allison K '06 %Mayer B LLP -1675 Bway -NY 10019
(914) 681-6200 .. **Levine,** Amy J '87 %NYPA -123 Main -White Plns 10601 **Fx:**390-8038
(914) 682-3900 .. **Levine,** Andrea '96 %Lawyers Title Ins -Ten Bank -White Plns 10606 **Fx:**682-3556
(212) 705-0118 .. **Levine,** Andrea C '79 %Natl Advertising Division -70 W 36th -NY 10018
(212) 833-1196 .. **Levine,** Andrew '07 %Friedman KS&A LLP -1633 Bway -NY 10019 **Fx:**373-7996
(212) 891-5702 .. **Levine,** Andrew B '89 CDC Ixis NA -9 W 57th -NY 10019
(212) 681-6150 .. **Levine,** Andrew C '80 -60 E 42nd -NY 10165 **Fx:**681-6137
(212) 859-8000 .. **Levine,** Andrew H '03 %Fried FHS&J LLP -1 NY Plz -NY 10004
(212) 268-3222 .. **Levine,** Andrew J '05 (Raphaelson & L,PC) -14 Penn Plz -NY 10122 **Fx:**268-3313
(212) 381-7000 .. **Levine,** Andrew M '81 (Sabin B&G LLP) -4 Times Sq -NY 10036
(212) 326-3939 .. **Levine,** Andrew M '99 (Jones D) -222 E 41st -NY 10017
(212) 909-6000 .. **Levine,** Andrew M '03 %Debevoise & P LLP -919 3rd Av -NY 10022
(212) 216-1615 .. **Levine,** Andrew Stuart '85 SL Green Rlty Corp -420 Lex Av -NY 10170 **Fx:**216-1785
(516) 466-5255 .. **Levine,** Arlene Kurlan '84 -5 Aspen Pl -Gt Neck 11021
(212) 969-3000 .. **Levine,** Arnold J '62 (Proskauer R LLP) -1585 Bway -NY 10036
(212) 732-5800 .. **Levine,** Arnold J '94 -233 Bway -NY 10279 **Fx:**608-3280
(212) 808-4270 .. **Levine,** Arthur '51 -211 E 43rd -NY 10017 **Fx:**687-6856
(516) 742-4545 .. **Levine,** Arthur '59 -300 Grdn City Plz -Gdn Cty 11530
(718) 979-3300 .. **LeVine,** Audrey M '91 %MHLS -777 Seaview Av -Staten Isl 10305 **Fx:**667-2666
(718) 876-6300 .. **Levine,** Autumn '05 DA -130 Styvsnt Pl -Staten Isl 10301
(516) 564-7791 .. **Levine,** Barbara Baum '84 (Sherman FS&L LLP) -175 Fulton Av -Hempstd 11550
(718) 438-0842 .. **Levine,** Barbara Pearlman '84 -820 Ocean Pkwy -Brklyn 11230
(212) 268-1177 .. **Levine,** Barton P '72 -260 Mad Av -NY 10016 **Fx:**268-6267
(315) 472-4481 .. **Levine,** Benjamin D '73 %Ali P&C -614 James -Syracuse 13203
(585) 262-4700 .. **Levine,** Bernard D '64 (Bilgore RLK&K) -950 Rynlds Arcd Bldg -Rchstr 14614
(718) 383-0111 .. **Levine,** Bert '64 (Bertman & L) -945 Manh Av -Brklyn 11222 **Fx:**383-3343
(212) 561-7700 .. **Levine,** Beth E '93 OfCnsl Pachulski SZ&J -780 3rd Av -NY 10017
(212) 584-5740 .. **Levine,** Beth Friedman '89 %Keryx Biopharm -750 Lex Av -NY 10022
(212) 967-3000 .. **Levine & Blit,PLLC** -350 5th Av -NY 10118 **Fx:**967-3010
(718) 351-4135 .. **Levine,** Brian D '89 -16 Flagg Pl -Staten Isl 10304 **Fx:**948-3552
(212) 509-9400 .. **Levine,** Brian S '03 %Cozen O -45 Bway Atrium -NY 10006
(212) 592-1400 .. **Levine,** Bruce P '86 (Herrick,F LLP) -2 Park Av -NY 10016
(212) 563-4100 .. **Levine,** Bruce S '87 (Cohen W&S LLP) -330 W 42nd -NY 10036
(212) 735-3000 .. **Levine,** Bryan J '05 %Skadden ASM&F LLP -4 Times Sq -NY 10036
(516) 222-2299 .. **Levine,** Bryce R '98 %J Schecter & Assoc -595 Stewart Av -Gdn Cty 11530 **Fx:**222-2303
(212) 480-3030 .. **Levine,** Carl F '70 %M Pressman -125 Maiden Ln -NY 10038 **Fx:**480-2590
(212) 627-8100 .. **Levine,** Carl J '98 (Levy R,PC) -80 8th Av -NY 10011
(212) 837-6000 .. **Levine,** Carolyn B '84 (Hughes H&R LLP) -1 Bttry Pk Plz -NY 10004
(212) 506-1700 .. **Levine,** Cindy M '05 %Kasowitz BT&F LLP -1633 Bway -NY 10019
(914) 276-0222 .. **Levine,** Cory A '94 CA Levine,PC -352 Route 202 -Somers 10589 **Fx:**276-3422
(845) 225-0111 .. **Levine,** Cory A '94 CA Levine,PC -1834 Route 6 -Carmel 10512 **Fx:**225-0110
(212) 940-8800 .. **Levine,** Dana B '94 SpclCnsl Katten MR LLP -575 Mad Av -NY 10022
(718) 417-1700 .. **Levine,** Danl '07 Deutsch & S LLP -79-37 Myrtle Av -Glendale 11385
(212) 373-3000 .. **Levine,** Danl B '06 %Paul WRW&G LLP -1285 Av of Amer -NY 10019
(212) 772-0688 .. **Levine,** Danl J '98 %Levine & F,LLC -645 5th Av -NY 10022 **Fx:**(732) 238-6055
(212) 761-2827 .. **Levine,** Danielle A '01 Morgan Stanley -1585 Bway -NY 10036
(212) 373-3000 .. **Levine,** David A '06 %Paul WRW&G LLP -1285 Av of Amer -NY 10019
(716) 284-2306 .. **Levine,** David E '82 -Bx456 -Niagara Fls 14302 **Fx:**284-2308
(718) 875-1212 .. **Levine,** David E '92 -186 Joralemon -Brklyn 11201 **Fx:**875-1717
(212) 889-0707 .. **Levine,** David E '93 (Platte KL&L,LLP) -10 E 40th -NY 10016
(212) 728-8000 .. **Levine,** David F '00 (Willkie F&G LLP) -787 7th Av -NY 10019
(212) 756-2000 .. **Levine,** David H '02 %Schulte R&Z LLP -919 3rd Av -NY 10022
(516) 248-0050 .. **Levine,** David I '90 -1565 Franklin Av -Mineola 11501
(212) 407-4000 .. **Levine,** David J '99 %Loeb & L,LLP -345 Park Av -NY 10154
(516) 775-5500 .. **Levine,** David J '01 Norse Realty Corp -2001 Marcus Av -New Hyde Pk 11042
(518) 474-4453 .. **LeVine,** David M '78 %MHLS -40 Steuben -Albany 12207 **Fx:**473-5849
(212) 250-7613 .. **Levine,** David M '94 %Deutsche Bank -60 Wall -NY 10005
(212) 530-5000 .. **Levine,** David M '09 %Milbank TH&M LLP -1 Chase Manh Plz -NY 10005
(516) 483-5161 .. **Levine,** Deborah Casper '89 -175 Fulton Av -Hempstd 11550 **Fx:**483-5168
(212) 431-2460 .. **Levine,** Diane '90 Sotheby's Intl Realty -379 W Bway -NY 10012
(212) 778-6911 .. **Levine,** Donald R '86 %Prudential Sec -One NY Plz -NY 10004
(516) 747-5566 .. **Levine,** Donna L '81 (Ezratty E&L) -80 E Old Cntry Rd -Mineola 11501
(516) 747-0300 .. **Levine,** Douglas L '08 %Meltzer LG&B,LLP -190 Willis Av -Mineola 11501
(631) 234-5484 .. **Levine,** Eliot S '78 (E Levine & Assoc) -1455 Vets Mem'l Hwy -Hauppauge 11749 **Fx:**234-5561
(212) 974-7474 .. **Levine,** Ellis B '63 (Cowan DA&S LLP) -41 Mad Av -NY 10010
(212) 545-4730 .. **Levine,** Eric B '78 (Wolf HAF&H LLP) -270 Mad Av -NY 10016
(212) 973-0572 .. **Levine,** Eric J '93 Cnsl Wolff & S PC -140 Bway -NY 10005
(212) 608-1009 .. **Levine,** Eric L '96 (Levine & S,PC) -132 Nassau -NY 10038
(212) 259-8000 .. **Levine,** Eric M '09 %Dewey & L LLP -1301 Av of Amer -NY 10019
(212) 752-1000 .. **Levine,** Eric R '87 (Eiseman LL&K,PC) -805 3rd Av -NY 10022
(607) 273-4611 .. **Levine,** Eric S '94 Alternatives FCU -125 N Fulton -Ithaca 14850 **Fx:**277-6391
(718) 442-2129 .. **Levine,** Frances Katz '82 -621 Clove Rd -Staten Isl 10310
(212) 352-3100 .. **Levine,** Fred A '77 Law & Public Policy Consltng -20 River Ter -NY 10282 **Fx:**352-3142
(718) 482-1382 .. **Levine,** Fredk '68 -110-20 71st Rd -Frst Hlls 11375
(917) 716-4773 .. **Levine,** Fredk N '94 F Levine,PE -111 John -NY 10038 **Fx:**(718) 549-2644
(516) 546-6751 .. **Levine,** Gary A '87 -794 Marilyn Ln -Baldwin 11510 **Fx:**546-6702
(516) 294-5775 .. **Levine,** Gary L '08 %Klee & W,LLP -350 Willis Av -Mineola 11501
(845) 452-2366 .. **Levine,** Gary M '80 (G Levine,PC) -290 Hooker Av -Poughkeepsie 12603 **Fx:**485-2771
(585) 327-3223 .. **Levine,** Gary M '84 %Dept of Law -144 Exchange Blvd -Rchstr 14614 **Fx:**546-7514
(212) 649-9700 .. **Levine,** Gary N '92 Greystone & Co -152 W 57th -NY 10019
(914) 693-0533 .. **Levine,** Gerald '63 -5 Sweetbriar Rd -Ardsley 10502
(212) 596-0580 .. **Levine,** Gerald M '76 (Levine S,LLP) -130 W 42nd -NY 10036
(212) 645-1990 .. **Levine & Gilbert** -115 Christopher -NY 10014
(516) 496-8981 .. **Levine,** Glenn D '83 -24 Roberta Ln -Syosset 11791 **Fx:**496-4994
(516) 746-5800 .. **Levine,** Glenn S '94 -114 Old Cntry Rd -Mineola 11501 **Fx:**294-9510
(212) 480-8800 .. **Levine,** Gregory '00 (Furnari L LLP) -11 Bway -NY 10004 **Fx:**480-4208
(212) 213-1285 .. **Levine,** Gregory S '01 -400 Park Av -NY 10022
(516) 248-7575 .. **Levine & Grossman** -114 Old Cntry Rd -Mineola 11501 **Fx:**294-0645
(212) 338-0700 .. **Levine,** Harlan L '94 (Hoffman P&F PLLC) -220 E 42nd -NY 10017
(212) 592-1400 .. **Levine,** Harold '84 (Herrick,F LLP) -2 Park Av -NY 10016
(212) 645-1990 .. **Levine,** Harvey A '61 (Levine & G) -115 Christopher -NY 10014
(212) 335-4500 .. **Levine,** Heidi L '97 (DLA Piper LLP) -1251 Av of Amer -NY 10020
(212) 506-5000 .. **Levine,** Herbert J '61 Cnsl Orrick H&S LLP -51 W 52nd -NY 10019
(212) 488-1598 .. **Levine,** Hilary R '07 %Havkins RR&V,LLP -11 Penn Plz -NY 10001
(212) 829-3206 .. **Levine,** Hirschell E '61 Eisner & Lubin LLP -444 Mad Av -NY 10022
(845) 473-2040 .. **Levine Hofstetter & Frangk** -316 Main -Poughkeepsie 12601
(607) 721-8440 .. **Levine,** Hollie S '86 %MHLS -44 Hawley -Bnghmtn 13901 **Fx:**721-8447
(518) 487-7600 .. **Levine,** Howard A '56 SrCnsl Whiteman O&H LLP -1 Commerce Plz -Albany 12260
(212) 223-3400 .. **Levine,** Howard S '97 %ER Gold -108-18 Qns Blvd -Frst Hlls 11375
(212) 885-7783 .. **Levine,** Ilyse D '97 %ADL -605 3rd Av -NY 10158 **Fx:**885-5881
(516) 829-7911 .. **Levine,** Ira '83 -320 Nrthrn Blvd -Gt Neck 11021 **Fx:**829-7913
(718) 855-2110 .. **Levine,** Ira S '66 -351 Court -Brklyn 11231
(212) 506-1733 .. **Levine,** Jack '94 Kasowitz BT&F LLP -1633 Bway -NY 10019
(518) 402-6969 .. **Levine,** James R '93 %Envrnmtl Facilities -625 Bway -Albany 12207 **Fx:**402-6972
(212) 468-4800 .. **Levine,** James R '02 (Davis & G LLP) -1740 Bway -NY 10019
(212) 894-1512 .. **Levine,** Jane A '86 Sotheby's,Inc -1334 York Av -NY 10021 **Fx:**606-7574
(212) 669-2020 .. **Levine,** Jane R '76 %Comptroller -1 Centre -NY 10007
(212) 728-8000 .. **Levine,** Janice E '85 SpclCnsl Willkie F&G LLP -787 7th Av -NY 10019
(212) 785-5115 .. **Levine,** Jared T '01 (Dervishi L&M,PC) -11 Bway -NY 10004 **Fx:**480-8560
(212) 532-5881 .. **Levine,** Jason R '95 %T Torto -419 Park Av S -NY 10016 **Fx:**481-5851
(212) 269-3988 .. **Levine,** Jeffrey E '87 -19 Rector -NY 10006
(516) 745-4565 .. **Levine,** Jeffrey H '89 %JP Morgan Chase & Co -900 Stewart Av -Gdn Cty 11530 **Fx:**745-4528
(212) 721-9600 .. **Levine,** Jeffrey K '93 -11 Riverside Dr -NY 10023
(212) 867-4466 .. **Levine,** Jeffrey S '94 (Belkin BW&G,LLP) -270 Mad Av -NY 10016
(212) 403-1000 .. **Levine,** Jenna E '09 %Wachtell LR&K -51 W 52nd -NY 10019

(631) 390-0010 .. **Levine,** Jennifer A '09 %Bruno G&S,LLP -445 Broad Hollow Rd -Melvll 11747
(718) 590-5438 .. **Levine,** Jennifer P '03 ACS-DLS -900 Sheridan Av -Bronx 10451
(718) 507-6464 .. **Levine,** Jerald '68 -73-19 Bway -Jcksn Hts 11372
(212) 482-8830 .. **Levine,** Jerold E '91 -5 Sunrise Plz -Vly Stream 11580
(212) 407-4000 .. **Levine,** Jerome L '75 (Loeb & L,LLP) -345 Park Av -NY 10154
(212) 442-3329 .. **Levine,** Jesse I '63 %Law Dept -100 Church -NY 10007 **Fx:**788-0367
(212) 221-6900 .. **Levine,** Jessica E '08 %Winget S&S,LLP -45 Bway -NY 10006
(516) 747-3222 .. **Levine,** Joel L '94 (Levine & W,PLLC) -259 Mineola Blvd -Mineola 11501
(914) 640-8100 .. **Levine,** Jonathan B '68 %Starwood Hotels & Resorts -1111 Wstchstr Av -White Plns 10604 **Fx:**640-8250
(212) 850-2800 .. **Levine,** Jonathan I '01 (Andrews K LLP) -450 Lex Av -NY 10017
(212) 697-9400 .. **Levine,** Jonathan M '97 %Cheifetz IM,PC -275 Mad Av -NY 10016
(212) 455-2000 .. **Levine,** Joshua A '96 (Simpson T&B LLP) -425 Lex Av -NY 10017
(212) 816-6114 .. **Levine,** Joshua E '00 Citigroup -388 Greenwich -NY 10013
(212) 693-0085 .. **Levine,** Joshua M '95 %Appellate Advocates -2 Rector -NY 10006 **Fx:**693-0878
(914) 948-1556 .. **Levine,** Joshua S '80 (Danziger & M LLP) -123 Main -White Plns 10601
(516) 482-0962 .. **Levine,** Joyce Celnik '89 Cnsl Kalin LW,LLC -185 Grt Nck Rd -Gt Neck 11021
(845) 562-0203 .. **Levine,** Jules P '66 OfCnsl Finkelstein & Prtnrs,LLP -1279 Route 300 Bx1111 -Newburgh 12550
(718) 992-9601 .. **Levine,** Justin '86 -859 Concord Vllg W -Bronx 10451 **Fx:**293-2891
(212) 693-0085 .. **Levine,** Katherine A '07 %Appellate Advocates -2 Rector -NY 10006 **Fx:**693-0878
(646) 473-3902 .. **Levine,** Kenneth A '90 Cnsl USPS -380 W 33rd -NY 10199
(212) 883-1700 .. **Levine,** Lance I '95 (Duval & S LLP) -101 Park Av -NY 10178
(212) 416-8000 .. **Levine,** Laura J '90 %Dept of Law -120 Bway -NY 10271
(516) 393-2200 .. **Levine,** Lauren M '03 Garfunkel W,PC -111 Grt Nck Rd -Gt Neck 11021
(718) 857-1348 .. **Levine,** Laurence '73 -232 Lincoln Pl -Brklyn 11217
(212) 679-0400 .. **Levine,** Lawr '61 -450 7th Av -NY 10123 **Fx:**679-1080
(631) 293-7800 .. **Levine,** Lawr A '74 -445 Broad Hollow Rd -Melvll 11747 **Fx:**293-7886
(212) 727-2700 .. **Levine,** Lawr M '02 %NRDC -40 W 20th -NY 10011 **Fx:**727-1773
(212) 967-3000 .. **Levine,** Les J '80 (Levine & B,PLLC) -350 5th Av -NY 10118
(914) 761-2033 .. **Levine,** Leslie I '58 -90 Bryant Av -White Plns 10605
(516) 829-6900 .. **Levine,** Leslie J '69 (Ackerman LCB&L,LLP) -1010 Nrthrn Blvd -Gt Neck 11021
(914) 481-5555 .. **Levine,** Linnea J '91 -32 Elm Pl -Rye 10580
(516) 433-6677 .. **Levine,** Lisa '89 %Stewart GM&B -6800 Jericho Tpk -Syosset 11791
(212) 922-6120 .. **Levine,** Lisa A '96 Bank of NY/Mellon -200 Park Av -NY 10166
(315) 422-1311 .. **Levine,** Louis '78 (Melvin & M,PLLC) -217 S Salina -Syracuse 13202
(845) 794-3000 .. **Levine,** Lynda G '90 Cnty Atty -100 North -Monticello 12701
(718) 359-4321 .. **Levine,** Marc E '92 %Grand Pacific Fin Corp -41-99 Main -Flushng 11355
(516) 825-0298 .. **Levine,** Marilyn M '78 -1057 Linden -Vly Stream 11580 **Fx:**825-6264
(212) 880-1330 .. **Levine,** Marjorie '86 Chicago Title -711 3rd Av -NY 10017
(212) 687-7230 .. **Levine,** Mark '82 Stull S&B -6 E 45th -NY 10017
(212) 592-1400 .. **Levine,** Mark A '71 (Herrick,F LLP) -2 Park Av -NY 10016
(718) 225-5531 .. **Levine,** Mark J '95 -2 Bay Club Dr -Bayside 11360
(212) 755-8555 .. **Levine,** Mark W '95 M Safra & Co,Inc -499 Park Av -NY 10022
(212) 557-4680 .. **Levine,** Marva M '84 %Verizon -245 Park Av -NY 10167
(212) 909-9500 .. **Levine,** Marvin J '75 OfCnsl Wachtel & M,LLP -885 2nd Av -NY 10017
(212) 765-5070 .. **Levine,** Matthew L '91 (Fish & R,PC) -153 E 53rd -NY 10022
(516) 734-3645 .. **Levine,** Matthew S '00 Dealer Track,Inc -1111 Marcus Av -New Hyde Pk 11042
(212) 902-1000 .. **Levine,** Matthew S '05 %Goldman Sachs -1 NY Plz -NY 10004
(518) 474-7330 .. **Levine,** Megan Lesser '83 %Dept of Law -The Cptl -Albany 12224
(516) 512-6333 .. **Levine,** Melissa B '91 %Gold SKB LLP -1025 Old Cntry Rd -Westbury 11590
(212) 351-4000 .. **Levine,** Meredith F '10 Gibson D&C LLP -200 Park Av -NY 10166
(718) 855-8404 .. **Levine,** Michl '66 -26 Court -Brklyn 11242
(212) 351-4500 .. **Levine,** Michl A '89 (Epstein B&G,PC) -250 Park Av -NY 10177
(516) 354-1570 .. **Levine,** Michl C '98 (Meyerson & L,LLP) -1040 Hempstd Tpk -Franklin Sq 11010 **Fx:**358-9673
(212) 564-9090 .. **Levine,** Michl G '95 %Altier & V,LLC -450 7th Av -NY 10123
(212) 564-9800 .. **Levine,** Michl J '81 (D'Agostino L&L,LLP) -345 7th Av -NY 10001
(914) 600-4288 .. **Levine,** Michl L '78 -15 Barclay Rd -Scarsdale 10583
(212) 455-9867 .. **Levine,** Michl S '81 %LISC -501 Fashion Av -NY 10018 **Fx:**682-5929
(631) 293-2300 .. **Levine,** Michl S '85 (Rappaport GG&L LLP) -1355 Motor Pkwy -Hauppauge 11749
(516) 741-6266 .. **Levine,** Michl S '92 (McCabe CM&F,LLP) -346 Westbury Av Bx9000 -Carle Pl 11514
(212) 986-6000 .. **Levine,** Michl S '98 OfCnsl Kleinberg KW&C,PC -551 5th Av -NY 10176
(212) 721-8284 .. **Levine,** Micheline '89 -139 W 82nd -NY 10024
(212) 461-7190 .. **Levine,** Mitchell B '93 (Fishman M,PC) -44 Wall -NY 10005
(716) 285-0626 .. **Levine,** Morree M '52 -665-669 Main MPO 456 -Niagara Fls 14302
(716) 645-3650 .. **Levine,** Murray '84 %Dept Psychology -SUNY -Buffalo 14260 **Fx:**645-3801
(212) 872-1000 .. **Levine,** Natalie E '08 -One Bryant Park -NY 10036 **Fx:**872-1002
(518) 487-7600 .. **Levine,** Neil L '83 (Whiteman O&H LLP) -1 Commerce Plz -Albany 12260
(212) 230-8800 .. **Levine,** Noah A '05 (WilmerHale) -399 Park Av -NY 10022
(212) 969-3000 .. **Levine,** Orrin '07 %Proskauer R LLP -1585 Bway -NY 10036
(518) 433-8800 .. **Levine,** Paul A '87 (Lemery G LLC) -50 Beaver -Albany 12207
(212) 806-5400 .. **Levine,** Penny L '87 SpclCnsl Stroock &S&L LLP -180 Maiden Ln -NY 10038
(212) 599-0009 .. **Levine,** Peter M '82 -99 Park Av -NY 10016 **Fx:**838-8663
(718) 763-2783 .. **Levine,** Philip I '83 -7302 Av M -Brklyn 11234 **Fx:**763-2783
(212) 245-6565 .. **Levine Plotkin & Menin,LLP** -1740 Bway -NY 10019 **Fx:**245-8683
(212) 859-8000 .. **Levine,** Rachel S '08 %Fried FHS&J LLP -1 NY Plz -NY 10004
(212) 872-1000 .. **Levine,** Randy L '81 -One Bryant Park -NY 10036 **Fx:**872-1002
(212) 685-4565 .. **Levine,** Randy M '95 (Schachter & L,LLP) -419 Park Av -NY 10016 **Fx:**685-5980
(212) 683-3645 .. **Levine,** Rebecca-Sue '83 -200 E 27th -NY 10016
(212) 651-6500 .. **Levine,** Renee J '03 Arch Ins Grp -1 Lbrty Plz -NY 10006
(212) 903-8700 .. **Levine,** Richd A '68 (Roberts & H,LLP) -825 8th Av -NY 10019
(212) 967-7508 .. **Levine,** Richd A '93 NY Real Estate Inst -132 W 36th -NY 10018
(631) 669-1710 .. **Levine,** Richd I '69 -512 Sunrise Hwy -W Babylon 11704 **Fx:**669-1714
(212) 310-8000 .. **Levine,** Richd L '84 (Weil G&M LLP) -767 5th Av -NY 10153
(212) 659-5246 .. **Levine,** Richd M '89 %Kerzner Intl -730 5th Av -NY 10019
(212) 476-5955 .. **Levine,** Richd S '81 %Neuberger Berman,LLC -605 3rd Av -NY 10158 **Fx:**476-9862
(212) 245-6565 .. **Levine,** Robt F '64 (Levine P&M,LLP) -1740 Bway -NY 10019
(914) 761-1300 .. **Levine,** Robt J '93 (Cuddy & F LLP) -445 Hmltn Av -White Plns 10601
(212) 450-4000 .. **Levine,** Robt Jay '76 SrCnsl Davis P&W LLP -450 Lex Av -NY 10017
(212) 472-8538 .. **Levine,** Robt Jonathan '72 -500 E 85th -NY 10028
(212) 315-3330 .. **Levine,** Robt M '76 -340 W 55th -NY 10019 **Fx:**315-1888
(917) 742-1586 .. **Levine,** Robt M '03 -Bx1005 -RYE 10580
(212) 288-6173 .. **Levine,** Robt P '56 -444 Park Av S -NY 10016 **Fx:**(860) 927-1539
(845) 452-2350 .. **Levine,** Robt S '75 Levine & L -2 Jffrsn Plz -Poughkeepsie 12601 **Fx:**473-2200
(212) 310-8000 .. **Levine,** Robt S '08 %Weil G&M LLP -767 5th Av -NY 10153
(718) 595-6586 .. **Levine,** Robin M '84 %DEP -59-17 Junction Blvd -Flushng 11373 **Fx:**595-6543
(212) 772-0688 .. **Levine,** Roger N '69 (Levine & F,LLC) -645 5th Av -NY 10022 **Fx:**(732) 238-6055
(212) 592-1400 .. **Levine,** Ronald J '78 (Herrick,F LLP) -2 Park Av -NY 10016
(845) 473-2040 .. **Levine,** Ronald R '63 (Levine H&F) -316 Main -Poughkeepsie 12601
(212) 485-9804 .. **Levine,** Ross M '04 (Schwartz L&K,PLLC) -60 E 42nd -NY 10165
(212) 753-3468 .. **Levine,** Roxanne H '85 (Wildes & W,PC) -515 Mad Av -NY 10022
(212) 688-6565 .. **Levine,** Sally Anne '74 -575 Mad Av -NY 10022
(212) 596-0580 .. **Levine Samuel,LLP** -130 W 42nd -NY 10036
(516) 647-7711 .. **Le Vine,** Saul S '60 -54 Center Ct -Roslyn Hts 11577 **Fx:**484-7505
(212) 836-8000 .. **Levine,** Scott B '08 %Kaye S LLP -425 Park Av -NY 10022
(212) 593-3000 .. **Levine,** Scott K '85 (Platzer SKLG&J,LLP) -1065 Av of Amer -NY 10018
(516) 228-9444 .. **Levine,** Seth A '99 (Richman & L,PC) -666 Old Cntry Rd -Gdn Cty 11530 **Fx:**228-9514
(212) 682-7474 .. **Levine,** Seth L '94 (Foley & L LLP) -90 Park Av -NY 10016
(212) 704-6000 .. **Levine,** Seymour '52 SrCnsl Troutman S LLP -405 Lex Av -NY 10174
(212) 773-2042 .. **Levine,** Shari M '08 Ernst & Young -5 Times Sq -NY 10036
(212) 657-0366 .. **Levine-Shea,** Sheri R '98 Salomon Smith Barney -77 Water -NY 10005
(212) 596-0580 .. **Levine,** Sheila J '84 OfCnsl Levine S,LLP -130 W 42nd -NY 10036
(516) 621-4519 .. **Levine,** Sherrie G '84 -29 Crescent Ln -Roslyn Hts 11577 **Fx:**621-2925
(212) 676-6312 .. **Levine,** Sheryl H '93 %Business Integrity Comm -100 Church -NY 10007 **Fx:**676-6204
(212) 768-6700 .. **Levine,** Shira P '04 %Sonnenschein N&R LLP -2 World Fncl Ctr -NY 10281
(212) 608-1009 .. **Levine & Siman,PC** -132 Nassau -NY 10038 **Fx:**608-1433
(212) 312-1400 .. **Levine,** Simone A '02 %NYS Assembly -250 Bway -NY 10007
(212) 687-2777 .. **Levine & Slavit** -60 E 42nd -NY 10165 **Fx:**983-4637
(516) 829-0363 .. **Levine,** Stacy Mandel '96 %Israel I&P,LLP -11 Grace Av -Gt Neck 11021 **Fx:**829-0366
(212) 824-5700 .. **Levine,** Stefanie Fishman '96 Practising Law Inst -810 7th Av -NY 10019
(631) 853-5212 .. **Levine,** Stephanie D '99 %Leg Aid -400 Carleton Av Bx9082 -Central Islip 11722 **Fx:**853-7798
(718) 855-5123 .. **Levine,** Stephen '76 (Levine & G) -32 Court -Brklyn 11201 **Fx:**522-0432
(914) 457-2300 .. **Levine,** Steven '83 (Kanterman & S,LLP) 60 Main -White Plns 10606
(914) 946-6641 .. **Levine,** Steven Jon '67 -50 Main -White Plns 10606 **Fx:**946-9637
(845) 486-2280 .. **Levine,** Steven W '92 %Pub Def -22 Market -Poughkeepsie 12601 **Fx:**486-2266
(914) 481-5555 .. **Levine,** Stuart M '67 L Levine,PC -32 Elm Pl -Rye 10580
(212) 850-6100 .. **Levine Sullivan Koch & Schulz,LLP** -321 W 44th -NY 10036 **Fx:**850-6299
(212) 552-6271 .. **Levine,** Susan A '80 JP Morgan Chase -1 Chase Manh Plz -NY 10081
(212) 247-2515 .. **Levine,** Susan C '76 -1650 Bway -NY 10019 **Fx:**247-5866
(212) 620-2680 .. **Levine,** Sydney R '06 %Starr Assoc LLP -245 5th Av -NY 10016 **Fx:**696-5013
(516) 365-1400 .. **Levine,** Syma Shulman '82 (Cooperman LM LLP) -1129 Nrthrn Blvd -Manhsst 11030
(516) 294-6852 .. **Levine,** Tedd S '88 -1010 Franklin Av -Gdn Cty 11530 **Fx:**294-4860
(212) 403-1000 .. **Levine,** Theo A '93 OfCnsl Wachtell LR&K -51 W 52nd -NY 10019
(212) 725-1610 .. **Levine,** Thos S '64 -470 Park Av S -NY 10016
(718) 853-8220 .. **Levine,** Wayne M '83 (Berman S&L) -4607 Ft Hmltn Pkwy -Brklyn 11219
(516) 248-7575 .. **Levine,** Wm F '61 (Levine & G) -114 Old Cntry Rd -Mineola 11501
(212) 421-4100 .. **Levine,** Wm M '87 (Pryor C LLP) -7 Times Sq -NY 10036
(212) 455-2000 .. **Levine,** Wm R '10 %Simpson T&B LLP -425 Lex Av -NY 10017
(516) 747-3222 .. **Levine & Wiss, PLLC** -259 Mineola Blvd -Mineola 11501 **Fx:**873-5166
(212) 407-4000 .. **Levin-Epstein,** Joshua D '09 %Loeb & L,LLP -345 Park Av -NY 10154
(914) 766-1900 .. **Leviner,** Ron '00 IBM -294 Route 100 -Somers 10589
(718) 520-1600 .. **Levine-Shapiro,** Lisa D '83 -80-02 Kew Grdns Rd -Kew Gdns 11415
(631) 351-3042 .. **Levine-Sorkin,** Heidi S '89 %Town Atty -100 Main -Huntngtn 11743 **Fx:**351-3032
(212) 759-7100 .. **LeViness,** Thos R '65 (Pell & L,PC) -260 Mad Av -NY 10016
(212) 909-6000 .. **Levin Mesard,** Nicole S '98 (Debevoise & P LLP) -919 3rd Av -NY 10022
(631) 261-7777 .. **Levins,** Amy B '99 %Bushell K&M -7 Bayview Av -Northprt 11768
(212) 575-7900 .. **Levins,** Will '64 (Ballon SB&N,PC) -729 7th Av -NY 10019

(718) 837-9700 .. **Levinsky,** Anatta '98 (A Levinsky,PC) -6924 Bay Pkwy -Brklyn 11204
(212) 262-1000 .. **Levinsohn & Arnay LLP** -1790 Bway -NY 10019 **Fx:**262-5022
(212) 984-7819 .. **Levinsohn,** Donna M '79 Cnsl Warshaw BCS&K,LLP -555 5th Av -NY 10017
(212) 262-1000 .. **Levinsohn,** Mark A '83 (Levinsohn & A LLP) -1790 Bway -NY 10019
(212) 969-3000 .. **Levinsohn,** Robt J '49 (Proskauer R LLP) -1585 Bway -NY 10036
(914) 323-7000 .. **Levinson,** Andrew C '07 %Wilson EME&D LLP -3 Gannett Dr -White Plns 10604
(518) 828-3410 .. **Levinson,** Arlene '78 (Pub Def) -610 State -Hudson 12534 **Fx:**828-4076
(718) 590-3758 .. **Levinson,** Brenda S '83 %Supreme Ct -851 Grnd Cncrs -Bronx 10451
(212) 750-9898 .. **Levinson,** Bruce H '80 -747 3rd Av -NY 10017 **Fx:**750-2536
(718) 520-9400 .. **Levinson,** Bryan F '57 -125-10 Qns Blvd -Kew Gdns 11415 **Fx:**520-0791
(845) 928-9444 .. **Levinson,** David L '69 (Levinson R&O,PC) -Bx244 -Centrl Vly 10917
(516) 812-0300 .. **Levinson,** Doreen '92 Hornell Brewing Co,Inc -60 Crsswys Park Dr W -Woodbury 11797
(212) 922-9250 .. **Levinson,** Gabriel '00 %Ganfer & S LLP -360 Lex Av -NY 10017
(516) 466-6030 .. **Levinson,** Harris E '83 Mirkin & G,PC -98 Cuttermill Rd -Gt Neck 11021
(516) 571-3432 .. **Levinson,** Harvey B '64 Dept of Assessment -240 Old Cntry Rd -Mineola 11501
(212) 335-9000 .. **Levinson,** Jeffrey M '02 %DA -1 Hogan Pl -NY 10013
(212) 704-6000 .. **Levinson,** Lawr M '78 (Troutman S LLP) -405 Lex Av -NY 10174
(212) 308-4411 .. **Levinson,** Leslie J '81 (Edwards AP&D LLP) -750 Lex Av -NY 10022
(212) 246-7100 .. **Levinson,** Lori Robin '87 Grtr NY Hsptl Assn -555 W 57th -NY 10019
(914) 377-6240 .. **Levinson,** Michl '98 %Law Dept -300 City Hall -Ynkrs 10701 **Fx:**964-0563
(212) 689-1113 .. **Levinson,** Myrna A '76 (Garbarini & S,PC) -432 Park Av S -NY 10016
(212) 448-1100 .. **Levinson,** Paul H '78 (McLaughlin & S,LLP) -260 Mad Av -NY 10016
(516) 486-5959 .. **Levinson,** Ralph W '47 -491 Bell -W Hempstead 11552
(845) 928-9444 .. **Levinson Reineke & Ornstein,PC** -Bx244 -Centrl Vly 10917 **Fx:**928-9941
(718) 286-2159 .. **Levinson,** Robin '90 %Leg Aid -120-46 Qns Blvd -Kew Gdns 11415 **Fx:**286-2286
(516) 489-5000 .. **Levinson,** Ronald J '63 -Town Hall -Hempstd 11550 **Fx:**489-5150
(516) 433-6403 .. **Levinson,** Ronald T '98 -998 Old Cntry Rd -Plainvw 11803 **Fx:**433-6404
(212) 460-4089 .. **Levinson,** Scott A '95 Con Ed -4 Irving Pl -NY 10003
(845) 526-1999 .. **Levinson,** Scott S '85 -269 Peekskill Hllw Rd -Putnam Vly 10579 **Fx:**526-1001
(718) 237-2900 .. **Levinson,** Seth N '85 -188 Montague -Brklyn 11201 **Fx:**522-3906
(212) 308-5363 .. **Levinson,** Stuart J '97 -343 E 51st -NY 10022
(585) 546-7830 .. **Levinson,** Wm S '86 (Culley MT&P,LLP) -36 W Main -Rchstr 14614
(212) 246-8045 .. **Levintoff,** Carina '83 (Bureau FL) -101 Park Av -NY 10178 **Fx:**246-2951
(516) 622-9200 .. **Levinton,** Jay H '99 (Westerman BEM&S,LLP) -1201 RXR Plz -Uniondale 11553
(212) 486-7272 .. **Levisohn Berger, LLP** -11 Bway -NY 10004 **Fx:**486-0323
(212) 506-1700 .. **Levison,** Harold G '73 (Kasowitz BT&F LLP) -1633 Bway -NY 10019
(212) 297-5800 .. **Levison,** Michl H '99 (Day P LLP) -7 Times Sq -NY 10036
(585) 641-8001 .. **Levison,** Stuart L '67 (Allen & O) -625 Panorama Trl -Rchstr 14625
(718) 340-4475 .. **Levister,** Degna P '93 CUNY Law Schl -65-21 Main -Flushng 11367 **Fx:**340-4482
(212) 279-5050 .. **Levit,** Lawr D '86 Cnsl Abraham F&T LLP -1 Penn Plz -NY 10119
(718) 769-1512 .. **Levit,** Oleg '05 -1804 Jerome Av -Brklyn 11235
(212) 432-3800 .. **Levitan & Frieland,PC** -111 E 35th -NY 10016 **Fx:**432-0151
(212) 969-3000 .. **Levitan,** Jeffrey W '83 (Proskauer R LLP) -1585 Bway -NY 10036
(631) 367-3111 .. **Levitan,** Katherine '56 OfCnsl Brettschneider & B,LLP -83 Prospect -Huntngtn 11743 **Fx:**427-6912
(212) 432-3800 .. **Levitan,** Philip I '81 (Levitan & F,PC) -111 E 35th -NY 10016
(914) 948-3111 .. **Levitan,** Shari J '82 Solomon Schechter Schl -30 Dellwood Rd -White Plns 10605
(917) 777-4200 .. **Levitan,** Steven W '87 (Bingham M LLP) -1 Bttry Pk Plz -NY 10004
(212) 547-5400 .. **Levitas,** Jessica '07 %McDermott W&E LLP -340 Mad Av -NY 10173
(212) 688-6400 .. **Levitas,** Phyllis B '91 -270 Mad Av -NY 10016 **Fx:**688-6457
(212) 400-6900 .. **Levites,** Paul C '87 Cnsl Gottbetter & Prtnrs -488 Mad Av -NY 10022 **Fx:**400-6901
(212) 688-0500 .. **Levites,** Raymond A '71 Levites & Assoc,LLC -1251 Av of Amer -NY 10020 **Fx:**688-0012
(212) 344-5210 .. **Levitin,** Eli '89 %South Ferry Bldg Co -1 State Street Plz -NY 10004
(212) 938-1213 .. **Levitin,** Jeffrey '99 (Levitin & Assoc,PC) -1430 Bway -NY 10018
(212) 701-3000 .. **Levitin,** Joel H '94 (Cahill G&R LLP) -80 Pine -NY 10005 **Fx:**269-5420
(212) 436-5040 .. **Levitin,** Martin '96 Deloitte & Touche LLP -2 World Fncl Ctr -NY 10281
(516) 328-2300 .. **Levitin,** Mitchell H '84 %Abrams FFEGF&E,LLP -1111 Marcus Av -Lk Success 11042
(516) 328-2300 .. **Levitin,** Nancy B '86 (Abrams FFEGF&E,LLP) -1111 Marcus Av -Lk Success 11042
(718) 382-4300 .. **Levitis,** Michl '00 Levitis & Assoc,PC -1729 E 12th -Brklyn 11229 **Fx:**382-4394
(212) 298-5107 .. **Leviton,** Renee K '95 %Leg Aid -49 Thomas -NY 10013 **Fx:**298-5252
(212) 930-9700 .. **Levitsky,** Asher S '68 Cnsl Sichenzia RFF LLP -61 Bway -NY 10006
(212) 909-6000 .. **Levitsky,** Jonathan E '98 (Debevoise & P LLP) -919 3rd Av -NY 10022
(585) 232-2225 .. **Levitsky,** Steven B '94 (Handelman W&L) -410 Rynlds Arcd -Rchstr 14614
(212) 259-8000 .. **Levitsky,** Steven E '78 Cnsl Dewey & L LLP -1301 Av of Amer -NY 10019
(212) 267-6456 .. **Levitt,** Amy '82 (Fischer Bros) -217 Bway -NY 10007 **Fx:**267-6468
(212) 425-1401 .. **Levitt,** Andrew C '96 Cnsl O'Hare P LLP -82 Wall -NY 10005 **Fx:**425-1421
(631) 549-8600 .. **Levitt,** Andrew J '94 AJ Levitt,PC -755 NY Av -Huntngtn 11743 **Fx:**549-7646
(315) 724-2194 .. **Levitt,** Caroline L '08 %Levitt & G -91 Genesee Bx97 -New Hartfrd 13413 **Fx:**724-2261
(212) 286-0099 .. **Levitt,** Danl P '76 -551 5th Av -NY 10176 **Fx:**286-0495
(631) 262-9780 .. **Levitt,** Eugene J '53 -6 Gina Dr -Centerprt 11721 **Fx:**262-9780
(914) 723-5842 .. **Levitt,** Ilene J '79 -32 Fenimore Rd -Scarsdale 10583
(212) 768-6700 .. **Levitt,** Jack B '53 (Sonnenschein N&R LLP) -1221 Av of Amer -NY 10020
(212) 468-8000 .. **Levitt,** Jamie A '93 (Morrison & F LLP) -1290 Av of Amer -NY 10104
(212) 577-3688 .. **Levitt,** Jane '92 %Leg Aid -199 Water -NY 10038 **Fx:**509-8431
(212) 801-3760 .. **Levitt,** Jeffrey A '86 (Michael L&R LLP) -60 Columbus Cir -NY 10023
(516) 799-3600 .. **Levitt,** Jeffrey M '68 -Bx306 -Massapequa 11758
(718) 250-2000 .. **Levitt,** Jeffrey R '83 %DA -350 Jay -Brklyn 11201 **Fx:**250-2314
(212) 218-2100 .. **Levitt,** Jeffrey S '08 %Fitzpatrick CH&S -1290 Av of Amer -NY 10104
(212) 992-8158 .. **Levitt,** Justin M '06 Cnsl Brennan Ctr for Justice -161 Av of Amer -NY 10013 **Fx:**995-4550
(212) 217-2837 .. **Levitt,** Kenneth W '74 -277 Bway -NY 10007
(212) 975-3633 .. **Levitt,** Mallory D '94 %CBS Inc -51 W 52nd -NY 10019 **Fx:**975-3930
(315) 724-2194 .. **Levitt,** Mark D '72 (Levitt & G) -91 Genesee Bx97 -New Hartfrd 13413 **Fx:**724-2261
(212) 859-8000 .. **Levitt,** Michl A '94 (Fried FHS&J LLP) -1 NY Plz -NY 10004
(212) 770-7075 .. **Levitt,** Michelle A '95 %AIG -70 Pine -NY 10270 **Fx:**344-6271
(212) 757-8438 .. **Levitt & Needleman, PC** -250 W 57th -NY 10107 **Fx:**713-0746
(631) 777-1700 .. **Levitt,** Paul E '81 (Vitale & L,PC) -445 Broad Hollow Rd -Melvll 11747
(212) 480-4000 .. **Levitt,** Richd W '79 (Levitt & K) -40 Fulton -NY 10038 **Fx:**480-4444
(516) 229-4200 .. **Levitt,** Robt W '92 %Mendolia & S -875 Merrick Av -Westbury 11590
(212) 872-6717 .. **Levitt,** Russell D '85 KPMG LLP -345 Park Av -NY 10154
(212) 878-8000 .. **Levitt,** Sarah R '10 %Clifford C LLP -31 W 52nd -NY 10019
(516) 248-9700 .. **Levitt,** Steven L '82 (S Levitt & Assoc,PC) -2 Hillside Av -Williston Pk 11596 **Fx:**741-9224
(914) 345-9001 .. **Levitt,** Tal Y '95 %Taro Pharmaceuticals USA Inc -5 Skyline Dr -Hawthorne 10532
(212) 302-6868 .. **Levitz,** Howard J '60 OfCnsl Flaster & W,PC -36 W 44th -NY 10036
(212) 228-1331 .. **Levitz,** Lonny R '92 (Kuharski L&G) -176 Hart Blvd -Staten Isl 10301
(516) 377-5954 .. **Levner,** Nathan '84 -186 Atl Av -Freeprt 11520 **Fx:**377-6822
(718) 823-6033 .. **LeVoci,** Vincent '93 -1590 Paulding Av -Bronx 10462
(631) 862-0814 .. **Levorchick,** Jos D '84 -Bx1276 -Smithtwn 11787
(718) 942-4004 .. **Levoritz,** Yonatan S '05 Y Levoritz,PC -2306 Coney Isl Av -Brklyn 11223 **Fx:**942-4152
(845) 695-2600 .. **Levson,** Sheri M '02 Mediacom Communications -100 Crystal Run Rd -Middletwn 10941
(212) 259-8000 .. **Levy,** Aaron D '06 %Dewey & L LLP -1301 Av of Amer -NY 10019
(845) 225-3641 .. **Levy,** Adam B '93 (DA) -40 Gleneida Av -Carmel 10512
(516) 802-0630 .. **Levy,** Adam M '04 %Simmons J,LLP -115 Eileen Way -Syosset 11791
(212) 949-8770 .. **Levy,** Alan '76 (Levy T&C,LLP) -630 3rd Av -NY 10017
(212) 514-7400 .. **Levy,** Alan R '01 %Buckley & C,PA -225 Bway -NY 10007
(212) 974-2400 .. **Levy,** Alexander M '02 %J Burstein -1790 Bway -NY 10019 **Fx:**974-2944
(212) 701-3000 .. **Levy,** Alison R '06 %Cahill G&R LLP -80 Pine -NY 10005 **Fx:**269-5420
(212) 661-5030 .. **Levy,** Alycia S '08 %Schoeman U&K,LLP -60 E 42nd -NY 10165
(212) 829-7300 .. **Levy,** Andrew A '73 -900 3rd Av -NY 10022
(212) 335-4500 .. **Levy,** Andrew H '84 (DLA Piper LLP) -1251 Av of Amer -NY 10020
(212) 688-6400 .. **Levy,** Arthur G '99 -270 Mad Av -NY 10016
(718) 797-0770 .. **Levy,** Arthur J '66 -40 Clinton -Brklyn 11201
(516) 357-3000 .. **Levy,** Barry I '92 (Rivkin R LLP) -926 RXR Plz -Uniondale 11556
(914) 225-4943 .. **Levy,** Benjamin M '75 %Morgan Stanley -2000 Wstchstr Av -Purchase 10577
(212) 969-6082 .. **Levy,** Benjamin M '02 Alliance Bernstein LP -1345 Av of Amer -NY 10105 **Fx:**554-4639
(914) 813-6883 .. **Levy,** Beth A '86 My Sisters' Place -100 E 1st -Mt Vernon 10550
(315) 448-4800 .. **Levy,** Bonnie Gail '77 Cnsl Dept of Law -615 Erie Blvd W -Syracuse 13204 **Fx:**448-4853
(212) 859-8000 .. **Levy,** Bradley B '08 %Fried FHS&J LLP -1 NY Plz -NY 10004
(631) 661-0672 .. **Levy,** Brian J '04 (Fields & L LLP) -112 Route 109 -W Babylon 11704 **Fx:**661-0676
(212) 725-2244 .. **Levy,** Brian M '85 -358 5th Av -NY 10001
(973) 596-4841 .. **Levy,** Bruce A '89 (Gibbons PC) -1 Penn Plz -NY 10119 **Fx:**639-6223
(212) 705-7000 .. **Levy,** Carol Weiner '87 OfCnsl Bingham M LLP -399 Park Av -NY 10022
(646) 295-4211 .. **Levy,** Carole M '92 -2790 Bway -NY 10025
(718) 643-7688 .. **Levy,** Carole Princer '84 Family Ct -283 Adams -Brklyn 11201 **Fx:**643-6358
(516) 942-2651 .. **Levy,** Caroline '81 %Amer Jewsh Cmte -3 Coach Hill Ln -Northprt 11768 **Fx:**942-4759
(516) 942-8514 .. **Levy,** Caroline Krass '94 -9 Lewis Av -Jericho 11753
(212) 345-5000 .. **Levy,** Cliona A '99 Marsh & McLennan -1166 Av of Amer -NY 10036 **Fx:**345-5627
(212) 259-8000 .. **Levy,** Corinne D '03 %Dewey & L LLP -1301 Av of Amer -NY 10019
(212) 661-2900 .. **Levy,** Danl '07 %Kriss & F LLP -360 Lex Av -NY 10017
(718) 832-2033 .. **Levy,** Danl H '87 -41 Schermerhorn -Brklyn 11201
(718) 684-2530 .. **Levy,** Danl H '05 (Rios & L LLP) -3140 E Tremont Av -Bronx 10461 **Fx:**684-2531
(212) 637-1062 .. **Levy,** Danl W '97 US Atty -1 St Andrews Plz -NY 10007
(516) 320-6627 .. **Levy,** David A '80 -880 Bellmore Av -N Bellmore 11710
(518) 426-4940 .. **Levy,** David J '01 (Levy & O PLLC) -350 Nrthrn Blvd -Albany 12204

(585) 232-1980 .. **Levy,** David M '48 OfCnsl Levy & L,PC -45 Exchange -Rchstr 14614
(212) 603-6300 .. **Levy,** David M '81 (Robinson BLGG&G PC) -875 3rd Av -NY 10022
(212) 371-0033 .. **Levy Davis & Maher,LLP** -29 Bway -NY 10006 **Fx:**371-0463
(212) 336-0123 .. **Levy,** Dina S '02 %SEC -3 World Fncl Ctr -NY 10281 **Fx:**336-1323
(212) 508-7283 .. **Levy,** Donald H '69 -770 Lex Av -NY 10065
(212) 788-1185 .. **Levy,** Edwin M '91 %Law Dept -100 Church -NY 10007 **Fx:**788-0367
(212) 643-2503 .. **Levy Ehrlich & Petriello,PC** -555 5th Av -NY 10017
(212) 558-4000 .. **Levy,** Ellis '08 %Sullivan & C LLP -125 Broad -NY 10004
(212) 341-2737 .. **Levy,** Emily N '97 %Admin Children's Srvcs -150 William -NY 10038 **Fx:**341-2700
(718) 579-3000 .. **Levy,** Eric D '97 %Leg Aid -1020 Grnd Cncrs -Bronx 10451 **Fx:**588-2611
(516) 428-1464 .. **Levy,** Eugene D '72 -1178 Mdwbrk Rd -N Merrick 11566 **Fx:**489-3759
(212) 735-3889 .. **Levy,** Evan R '96 (Skadden ASM&F LLP) -4 Times Sq -NY 10036
(718) 243-6490 .. **Levy,** Ezra C '99 %Leg Aid -111 Lvngstn -Brklyn 11201 **Fx:**237-8737
(516) 481-2302 .. **Levy,** Frederic J '79 (Hamilton Levy Miller) -644 Woodfld Rd -W Hempstead 11552 **Fx:**481-5107
(212) 451-2300 .. **Levy,** Fredrick J '87 OfCnsl Olshan GFR&W LLP -65 E 55th -NY 10022
(212) 768-6700 .. **Levy,** Gayle P '87 (Sonnenschein N&R LLP) -1221 Av of Amer -NY 10020
(845) 562-0203 .. **Levy,** George M '76 (Finkelstein & Prtnrs,LLP) -1279 Route 300 Bx1111 -Newburgh 12550
(212) 297-5800 .. **Levy,** Gerald '67 (Day P LLP) -7 Times Sq -NY 10036
(516) 921-1200 .. **Levy,** Gregory T '92 (Zavatsky M&L,LLP) -33 Qns Bx510 -Syosset 11791
(212) 446-2300 .. **Levy,** Harlan A '81 (Boies S&F LLP) -575 Lex Av -NY 10022
(212) 492-5807 .. **Levy,** Harold '80 Kaplan Inc -888 7th Av -NY 10106
(516) 745-1122 .. **Levy,** Harold J '91 Cnsl Quadrino & S,PC -666 Old Cntry Rd -Gdn Cty 11530
(718) 237-1900 .. **Levy,** Harold L '67 (Flamhaft LH&R) -16 Court -Brklyn 11241
(212) 863-6300 .. **Levy,** Helen Clancy '84 %HPD -100 Gold -NY 10038 **Fx:**863-8201
(212) 370-4950 .. **Levy,** Herbert Monte '46 -230 Park Av -NY 10169 **Fx:**873-0999
(212) 980-4200 .. **Levy Holm Pellegrino & Drath, LLP** -950 3rd Av -NY 10022 **Fx:**371-3215
(212) 587-0321 .. **Levy,** Howard Yale '87 -Peck Slip Station Bx1051 -NY 10272
(212) 488-1200 .. **Levy,** Ian N '05 %Kobre & K,LLP -800 3rd Av -NY 10022
(212) 643-2503 .. **Levy,** Ira A '74 (Levy E&P,PC) -555 5th Av -NY 10017
(212) 813-8800 .. **Levy,** Ira Jay '89 (Goodwin P LLP) -620 8th Av -NY 10018
(914) 329-0297 .. **Levy,** Ira S '93 -173 Ivy Hill Ln -Rye Brook 10573 **Fx:**939-5389
(212) 980-4200 .. **Levy,** Irwin '80 (Levy HP&D,LLP) -950 3rd Av -NY 10022
(212) 735-8764 .. **Levy,** Jack '77 (Morrison C LLP) -909 3rd Av -NY 10022
(212) 594-9412 .. **Levy,** Jack S '97 %Register.com -575 8th Av -NY 10018
(212) 935-5500 .. **Levy,** Jake M '08 %Franklin WR&V -488 Mad Av -NY 10022
(212) 766-1200 .. **Levy,** Jamie B '03 %Shestack & Y,LLP -233 Bway -NY 10279
(914) 323-7000 .. **Levy,** Jay W '76 (Wilson EME&D LLP) -3 Gannett Dr -White Plns 10604
(212) 448-1800 .. **Levy,** Jeffrey A '89 (Roberts RLSC&F LLP) -235 Park Av S -NY 10003
(516) 466-8005 .. **Levy,** Jeffrey N '78 (Tashlik KG&C PC) -40 Cuttermill Rd -Gt Neck 11021
(718) 237-5500 .. **Levy,** Jennifer L '97 %Leg Srvcs -105 Court -Brklyn 11201 **Fx:**855-0733
(212) 854-1389 .. **Levy,** Jennifer M '06 Columbia Univ -2920 Bway -NY 10027
(212) 225-2000 .. **Levy,** Jennifer R '05 Cleary GS&H -1 Lbrty Plz -NY 10006
(212) 692-1000 .. **Levy,** Jerome T '67 (Duane M LLP) -1540 Bway -NY 10036
(914) 701-0008 .. **Levy,** Jerrold G '99 Imperial Sterling Ltd -287 Bowman Av -Purchase 10577
(914) 964-5519 .. **Levy,** Jerrold M '72 Section & Outreach -20 S Bway -Ynkrs 10701
(212) 705-7000 .. **Levy,** Jill C '07 %Bingham M LLP -399 Park Av -NY 10022
(212) 820-7700 .. **Levy,** Jill M '94 (Boundas SW&B,LLC) -1 Bttry Pk Plz -NY 10004
(212) 594-9222 .. **Levy,** Joel '59 -224 W 35th -NY 10001 **Fx:**268-9441
(212) 452-3457 .. **Levy,** Joel F '65 Benefit & Comp Cnsltnts -401 E 80th -NY 10075 **Fx:**(866) 896-8656
(212) 686-6827 .. **Levy,** John A '06 Corporate Counseling Assoc -475 Park Av S -NY 10016
(212) 693-1250 .. **Levy,** John Corcos '62 -217 Bway -NY 10007 **Fx:**233-1060
(718) 928-3700 .. **Levy,** Jonathan L '97 %LSNYC-Bronx -579 Courtlandt Av -Bronx 10451 **Fx:**402-7586
(212) 428-6485 .. **Levy,** Jonathan S '99 RBC Capital Markets -165 Bway -NY 10006
(718) 279-7555 .. **Levy,** Jos D '04 %B Montague & Prtnrs -212-45 26th Av -Bayside 11360 **Fx:**279-8154
(516) 487-6655 .. **Levy,** Joshua '95 %Levy & L -12 Tulip Dr -Gt Neck 11021
(212) 973-0572 .. **Levy,** Joshua M '08 %Wolff & S PC -140 Bway -NY 10005
(212) 839-5300 .. **Levy,** Joshua S '10 %Sidley A LLP -787 7th Av -NY 10019
(212) 962-1965 .. **Levy,** Judith '59 (Levy & L) -40 E 10th -NY 10003
(212) 944-0500 .. **Levy,** Jules E '65 (Hofheimer G&G,LLP) -530 5th Av -NY 10036 **Fx:**897-4993
(212) 455-2000 .. **Levy,** Julie Ann '95 Cnsl Simpson T&B LLP -425 Lex Av -NY 10017
(212) 294-6700 .. **Levy,** Justin M '03 %Winston & S -200 Park Av -NY 10166
(646) 386-3211 .. **Levy,** Kelly O'Neill '93 Supreme Ct -60 Centre -NY 10007
(212) 448-1100 .. **Levy,** Laura V '09 %McLaughlin & S,LLP -260 Mad Av -NY 10016
(212) 583-4044 .. **Levy,** Lauren Blythe '03 %Perry Cptl LLC -767 5th Av -NY 10153
(212) 508-6100 .. **Levy,** Laurence A '76 Cnsl Bracewell & G,LLP -1251 Av of Amer -NY 10020
(516) 357-3000 .. **Levy,** Lawr A '86 (Rivkin R LLP) -926 RXR Plz -Uniondale 11556
(212) 759-4600 .. **Levy,** Lester L '67 (Wolf P LLP) -845 3rd Av -NY 10022
(212) 962-1965 .. **Levy & Levy** -40 E 10th -NY 10003 **Fx:**962-3711
(585) 232-1980 .. **Levy & Licata,PC** -45 Exchange -Rchstr 14614 **Fx:**232-2578
(607) 723-5341 .. **Levy,** Lillian L '84 (Hinman H&K,LLP) -80 Exchange Bx5250 -Bnghmtn 13902
(212) 859-8000 .. **Levy,** Lisa A '91 (Fried FHS&J LLP) -1 NY Plz -NY 10004
(212) 425-0055 .. **Levy,** Lori J '93 %Sharretts PC&B -75 Broad -NY 10004
(212) 425-0055 .. **Levy,** M Barry '61 (Sharretts PC&B) -75 Broad -NY 10004
(212) 448-1100 .. **Levy,** Magnolia D '04 (McLaughlin & S,LLP) -260 Mad Av -NY 10016
(212) 728-8000 .. **Levy,** Mara R '03 Willkie F&G LLP -787 7th Av -NY 10019
(212) 705-5660 .. **Levy,** Marc W '97 Island Cptl Grp LLC -717 5th Av -NY 10022
(212) 558-4000 .. **Levy,** Marcia N '85 SpclCnsl Sullivan & C LLP -125 Broad -NY 10004
(212) 551-1739 .. **Levy,** Marilyn W '52 -230 Park Av -NY 10169 **Fx:**808-3020
(212) 806-5400 .. **Levy,** Mark A '64 OfCnsl Stroock &S&L LLP -180 Maiden Ln -NY 10038
(607) 231-6991 .. **Levy,** Mark E '88 Hinman H&K,LLP -80 Exchange Bx5250 -Bnghmtn 13902
(212) 925-9100 .. **Levy,** Mark J '76 (Reddy L&Z,PC) -85 Worth -NY 10013
(516) 561-8740 .. **Levy,** Mathew '89 -350-11 N Corona Av -Vly Stream 11580
(516) 294-5432 .. **Levy,** Mathew J '98 (Kern AC&S,PC) -1325 Franklin Av -Gdn Cty 11530
(212) 683-7100 .. **Levy,** Matthew P '99 %Gallo V&K,LLP -90 Broad -NY 10004
(212) 728-8000 .. **Levy,** Meredith J '09 %Willkie F&G LLP -787 7th Av -NY 10019
(845) 291-2454 .. **Levy,** Meryl I '04 %Leg Aid -2 Court Ln Bx328 -Goshen 10924 **Fx:**294-2638
(516) 365-3000 .. **Levy,** Michl A '68 (Levy & S,PC) -1615 Nrthrn Blvd -Manhsst 11030
(212) 637-2346 .. **Levy,** Michl A '99 %US Atty -1 St Andrews Plz -NY 10007
(212) 907-9700 .. **Levy,** Michl C '02 %Smith G&R,LLP -250 Park Av -NY 10177
(212) 425-7200 .. **Levy,** Michl K '06 (Kenyon & K,LLP) -1 Bway -NY 10004
(516) 487-6655 .. **Levy,** Morton '57 (Levy & L) -12 Tulip Dr -Gt Neck 11021
(212) 484-7065 .. **Levy,** Nichelle N '02 Time Warner Glbl Mrktng -1 Time Warner Ctr -NY 10019
(212) 442-9298 .. **Levy,** Noam '09 %Law Dept -100 Church -NY 10007 **Fx:**788-0367
(212) 983-2661 .. **Levy,** Norman '68 -555 5th Av -NY 10017
(518) 426-4940 .. **Levy & Obstarczyk PLLC** -350 Nrthrn Blvd -Albany 12204 **Fx:**426-4957
(518) 306-4176 .. **Levy & Obstarczyk PLLC** -161 Lk Av -Saratoga Spgs 12866 **Fx:**426-4957
(212) 588-0800 .. **Levy,** Paul A '02 %Frommer L&H LLP -745 5th Av -NY 10151
(516) 292-6278 .. **Levy,** Paul S '84 -58 Hilton Av -Hempstd 11550 **Fx:**292-5821
(516) 822-5800 .. **Levy,** Peter H '86 -366 N Bway -Jericho 11753 **Fx:**822-5848
(212) 270-5951 .. **Levy,** Philip H '82 JP Morgan Chase -270 Park Av -NY 10017
(212) 605-6200 .. **Levy Phillips & Konigsberg,LLP** -800 3rd Av -NY 10022 **Fx:**605-6290
(212) 627-8100 .. **Levy Ratner,PC** -80 8th Av -NY 10011 **Fx:**627-8182
(212) 325-2000 .. **Levy,** Reuben J '03 Credit Suisse First Boston -11 Mad Av -NY 10010
(212) 421-4100 .. **Levy,** Richd Jr. '80 (Pryor C LLP) -7 Times Sq -NY 10036
(212) 627-8100 .. **Levy,** Richd A '68 (Levy R,PC) -80 8th Av -NY 10011
(212) 788-3300 .. **Levy,** Richd A '71 %Hlth & Hsptl Corp -125 Worth -NY 10013 **Fx:**267-6905
(312) 923-2648 .. **Levy,** Richd F '54 (Jenner & B LLP) -919 3rd Av -NY 10022 **Fx:**923-2748
(516) 379-7334 .. **Levy,** Richd M '78 -2448 Merrick Av -Merrick 11566 **Fx:**379-7392
(718) 627-7800 .. **Levy,** Richd M '78 -902 Kings Hwy -Brklyn 11223 **Fx:**627-2361
(718) 522-1020 .. **Levy,** Richd M '03 %Rubenstein & R -16 Court -Brklyn 11241
(718) 297-2800 .. **Levy,** Robt '85 -148-03 Hillside Av -Jamaica 11435 **Fx:**297-2885
(212) 307-5800 .. **Levy,** Robt A '65 (Friedman LG&G,PC) -250 W 57th -NY 10107
(212) 674-3000 .. **Levy,** Robt E '70 -611 Bway -NY 10012 **Fx:**674-4052
(212) 228-9666 .. **Levy,** Robt L '91 (Bantle & L LLP) -817 Bway -NY 10003 **Fx:**228-7654
(212) 264-6933 .. **Levy,** Robt P '04 DHS -26 Fed Plz -NY 10278
(516) 802-7007 .. **Levy,** Robt S '56 (Levy S&C,LLP) -1425 RXR Plz -Uniondale 11556
(631) 499-5400 .. **Levy,** Robt S '73 (Smith CL PC) -5036 Jericho Tpk Bx49 -Commack 11725
(212) 947-9166 .. **Levy,** Robyn M '94 OfCnsl G Statfeld -3 W 35th -NY 10001 **Fx:**594-0019
(212) 509-5050 .. **Levy,** Saml D '91 (Wuersch & G LLP) -100 Wall -NY 10005
(718) 254-7000 .. **Levy,** Sandra L '92 %US Atty -271 Cadman Plz E -Brklyn 11201 **Fx:**254-6479
(516) 365-3000 .. **Levy & Schneps, PC** -1615 Nrthrn Blvd -Manhsst 11030 **Fx:**365-3164
(212) 682-1818 .. **Levy,** Scott '06 %Murray F&S LLP -275 Mad Av -NY 10016
(718) 838-7878 .. **Levy,** Scott D '08 Bronx Defenders -860 Crtlandt Av -Bronx 10451 **Fx:**665-0100
(212) 968-2982 .. **Levy,** Shara L '07 GFI Grp Inc -55 Water -NY 10041
(212) 661-1212 .. **Levy Sonet & Siegel LLP** -630 3rd Av -NY 10017 **Fx:**661-1657
(212) 672-4700 .. **Levy,** Spencer G '96 %The Witkoff Group -220 E 42nd -NY 10017
(212) 605-6200 .. **Levy,** Stanley J '59 (Levy P&K,LLP) -800 3rd Av -NY 10022
(212) 479-6000 .. **Levy,** Stephane '04 %Cooley LLP -1114 Av of Amer -NY 10036
(518) 489-1098 .. **Levy,** Stephen G '94 -21 Everett Road Ext -Albany 12205 **Fx:**489-3304
(212) 483-9600 .. **Levy,** Stephen J '87 %Costello S&G LLP -44 Wall -NY 10005
(914) 285-9800 .. **Levy,** Stephen R '77 (Kurzman EC&L,LLP) -1 N Bway -White Plns 10601
(631) 666-6200 .. **Levy,** Steven A '89 %PF Adams,PC -49 5th Av Bx1089M -Bay Shr 11706 **Fx:**665-6739
(212) 599-0777 .. **Levy,** Stewart L '78 (Eisenberg T&L) -675 3rd Av -NY 10017
(516) 802-7007 .. **Levy Stopol & Camelo,LLP** -1425 RXR Plz -Uniondale 11556 **Fx:**802-7008
(718) 590-2000 .. **Levy,** Stuart P '84 %DA -198 E 161st -Bronx 10451 **Fx:**590-6477
(718) 590-3281 .. **Levy,** Sue B Schleifer '66 Family Ct -900 Sheridan Av -Bronx 10451 **Fx:**590-2681
(212) 962-1965 .. **Levy,** Susan Joan '91 %Levy & L -40 E 10th -NY 10003
(516) 487-6655 .. **Levy,** Susan Weinberg '92 (Levy & L) -12 Tulip Dr -Gt Neck 11021
(212) 869-3500 .. **Levy,** Suzanne B '93 -500 5th Av -NY 10110
(212) 688-6400 .. **Levy,** Thos R '61 -270 Mad Av -NY 10016
(212) 949-8770 .. **Levy Tolman & Costello,LLP** -630 3rd Av -NY 10017 **Fx:**661-9491
(212) 878-8000 .. **Levy,** Victor '04 %Clifford C LLP -31 W 52nd -NY 10019
(212) 357-2332 .. **Levy,** Yael K '09 Goldman Sachs -85 Broad -NY 10004
(516) 681-2636 .. **Levy,** Zachary '59 -9 Maxine Av -Plainvw 11803
(212) 310-8000 .. **Levy,** Zohar R '09 %Weil G&M LLP -767 5th Av -NY 10153
(212) 984-7725 .. **Lew,** Avi '95 %Warshaw BCS&K,LLP -555 5th Av -NY 10017
(718) 263-0080 .. **Lew,** Barbara M '91 -118-21 Qns Blvd -Frst Hlls 11375 **Fx:**793-1400
(212) 819-8200 .. **Lew,** David '07 %White & C LLP -1155 Av of Amer -NY 10036
(718) 575-0594 .. **Lew,** Elana Teitelman '97 -138-46 Jewel Av -Flushng 11367
(212) 274-8600 .. **Lew,** Kao Pin '86 -350 Bway -NY 10013 **Fx:**943-1940
(716) 675-4072 .. **Lew,** Marilyn E '92 -Bx301 -Orchard Pk 14127
(212) 714-0400 .. **Lew,** Mark I '85 Wellfleet Prtnrs -1 Penn Plz -NY 10119

(212) 422-0488 .. **Lew,** Raymond W '02 %Rick SF&B,LLP -90 Broad -NY 10004
(716) 674-4710 .. **Lewandowski,** Brian N '83 Lewandowski & Assoc -721 Center Rd -W Seneca 14224 **Fx:**674-5595
(212) 452-5300 .. **Lewandowski,** Michl T '99 Cnsl Darger & E,LLP -116 E 27th -NY 10016
(585) 423-1469 .. **Lewandowski,** Wm J '94 %Xerox -100 Clinton Av S -Rchstr 14644
(315) 866-0007 .. **Lewandrowski,** Lorraine H '94 -430 N Main -Herkimer 13350 **Fx:**866-1881
(212) 238-8900 .. **Lewbel,** Steven I '92 (Melito & A,PC) -233 Bway -NY 10279
(212) 468-4800 .. **Lewczak,** Jos J '94 (Davis & G LLP) -1740 Bway -NY 10019
(212) 530-5000 .. **Lewen,** Ulric M '09 %Milbank TH&M LLP -1 Chase Manh Plz -NY 10005
(718) 553-3273 .. **Lewerenz,** Christian L '98 %FAA -1 Aviation Plz -Jamaica 11434 **Fx:**995-5699
(914) 640-8228 .. **Lewers,** Cornett L '83 %Starwood Hotels & Resorts -1111 Wstchstr Av -White Plns 10604 **Fx:**640-8250
(212) 484-3900 .. **Lewertoff,** Katrin '04 %Arent F LLP -1675 Bway -NY 10019
(212) 446-2300 .. **Lewicky,** Christina M '93 %Boies S&F LLP -575 Lex Av -NY 10022
(315) 422-7000 .. **Lewien,** Kathryn E '04 Pyramid Mgmt Grp,Inc -4 Clinton Sq -Syracuse 13202
(212) 292-8100 .. **Lewin,** Andrew E '86 %Kaufman Bros LP -800 3rd Av -NY 10022
(212) 684-3900 .. **Lewin,** Barry R '08 %Gottlieb R&R,PC -270 Mad Av -NY 10016
(212) 609-6800 .. **Lewin,** Harley I '70 (McCarter & E,LLP) -245 Park Av -NY 10167
(212) 759-2600 .. **Lewin,** John J '79 (Irwin LC&L,PC) -845 3rd Av -NY 10022
(212) 295-6490 .. **Lewin,** Judith B '02 WilmerHale -399 Park Av -NY 10022
(631) 427-7790 .. **Lewin,** Lev J '03 (Lewin GB,LLP) -900 Walt Whitman Rd -Melvll 11747
(212) 735-8625 .. **Lewin,** Malcolm I '66 (Morrison C LLP) -909 3rd Av -NY 10022
(212) 625-5700 .. **Lewin,** Melissa E '04 Two Sigma Investments,LLC -379 W Bway -NY 10012 **Fx:**625-5800
(212) 617-8794 .. **Lewin,** Michelle '01 Bloomberg LP -731 Lex Av -NY 10022
(212) 637-2337 .. **Lewin,** Nicholas J '05 US Atty -1 St Andrews Plz -NY 10007
(212) 806-5400 .. **Lewin,** Robt '78 (Stroock &S&L LLP) -180 Maiden Ln -NY 10038
(212) 759-2600 .. **Lewin,** Stephen R '78 (Irwin LC&L,PC) -845 3rd Av -NY 10022
(315) 443-1222 .. **Lewin,** Travis H D '72 %Syracuse Univ Cllg of Law -Wht Hall -Syracuse 13244 **Fx:**443-4213
(212) 632-5501 .. **LeWine,** Jerome M '65 OfCnsl Salans LLP -620 5th Av -NY 10020
(718) 544-9219 .. **Lewine,** Stuart A '83 -68-07 Clyde -Frst Hlls 11375
(212) 355-7254 .. **Lewinger,** Robt J '81 -245 E 19th -NY 10003 **Fx:**355-7674
(212) 446-4800 .. **Lewinstein,** Marc A '07 %Kirkland & E LLP -153 E 53rd -NY 10022
(212) 260-5578 .. **LeWinter,** Jonathan S '89 -145 4th Av -NY 10003 **Fx:**260-5578
(212) 725-6100 .. **Lewinter,** Mark '84 (Amsterdam & L) -9 E 40th -NY 10016
(914) 784-6818 .. **Lewis,** Abigail A '95 IBM -19 Skyline Dr -Hawthorne 10532 **Fx:**241-4038
(212) 867-9140 .. **Lewis,** Adina '96 (Lewis & G,PC) -60 E 42nd -NY 10165 **Fx:**867-9143
(212) 732-3200 .. **Lewis,** Alan '87 (Carter L&M LLP) -2 Wall -NY 10005
(212) 649-2000 .. **Lewis,** Alan E '93 %Hearst Corp -300 W 57th -NY 10019 **Fx:**649-2035
(845) 561-2727 .. **Lewis,** Alan R '79 -425 Robnsn Av -Newburgh 12550 **Fx:**561-6961
(212) 269-0927 .. **Lewis,** Albert B '53 Cnsl D'Amato & L,LLP -2 World Fncl Ctr -NY 10281
(718) 246-5333 .. **Lewis,** Alden T '83 -26 Court -Brklyn 11242 **Fx:**230-7668
(716) 854-2100 .. **Lewis,** Allan M '69 (Lewis & L,PC) -37 Franklin -Buffalo 14202 **Fx:**854-0433
(212) 298-5181 .. **Lewis,** Allison M '06 Leg Aid -49 Thomas -NY 10013 **Fx:**298-5252
(212) 848-4000 .. **Lewis,** Amy G '08 %Shearman & S LLP -599 Lex Av -NY 10022
(212) 286-1666 .. **Lewis,** Andrew D '74 (Tonachel & L,PC) -276 5th Av -NY 10001
(212) 596-9000 .. **Lewis,** Ann E '74 Cnsl Ropes & G LLP -1211 Av of Amer -NY 10036
(212) 417-4357 .. **Lewis,** Anna Rose '84 %Dept of Health -90 Church -NY 10007 **Fx:**417-4392
(845) 359-2149 .. **Lewis,** Arleen '85 (Lewis & L) -Bx219 -Blauvelt 10913
(212) 471-8500 .. **Lewis,** Arlene E '00 %Herzfeld & R,PC -125 Broad -NY 10004
(212) 460-4250 .. **Lewis,** Arthur '82 Con Ed -4 Irving Pl -NY 10003
(800) 416-5454 .. **Lewis,** Bari M '87 %Fusco B&R -11 Penn Plz -NY 10001
(800) 416-5454 .. **Lewis,** Bari M '87 %Fusco B&R -2116 Wllmsbrdg Rd -Bronx 10461
(800) 416-5454 .. **Lewis,** Bari M '87 %Fusco B&R -626 RXR Plz -Uniondale 11553
(800) 416-5454 .. **Lewis,** Bari M '87 %Fusco B&R -180 Froehlich Farm Blvd -Woodbury 11797
(212) 859-8000 .. **Lewis,** Benjamin A '08 %Fried FHS&J LLP -1 NY Plz -NY 10004
(718) 590-6162 .. **Lewis,** Betty Lawr '81 %Law Dept -198 E 161st -Bronx 10451 **Fx:**590-2686
(212) 504-6000 .. **Lewis,** Brent A '02 %Cadwalader W&T LLP -1 World Fncl Ctr -NY 10281
(718) 243-9323 .. **Lewis,** Brett E '99 (Lewis & H) -45 Main -Brklyn 11201 **Fx:**243-9326
(212) 859-8000 .. **Lewis,** Brian M '09 %Fried FHS&J LLP -1 NY Plz -NY 10004
(212) 373-3000 .. **Lewis,** Brian W '10 %Paul WRW&G LLP -1285 Av of Amer -NY 10019
(212) 232-1300 .. **Lewis Brisbois Bisgaard & Smith LLP** -77 Water -NY 10005 **Fx:**232-1399
(631) 755-0101 .. **Lewis,** Bryan F '03 %Lewis JAA,LLP -425 Broad Hollow Rd -Melvll 11747
(212) 252-0300 .. **Lewis,** Burt A '65 (Kagan LLLG&C,LLP) -200 Mad Av -NY 10016
(212) 598-5900 .. **Lewis,** Cari A '07 %Alonso A&K PC -920 Bway -NY 10010
(585) 232-6500 .. **Lewis,** Carmen E '08 %Harter S&E LLP -1600 Bausch & Lomb Pl -Rchstr 14604
(718) 602-1115 .. **Lewis,** Carol Ann M '93 -589 Greene Av -Brklyn 11216 **Fx:**622-1666
(212) 735-3000 .. **Lewis,** Charlotte A '09 %Skadden ASM&F LLP -4 Times Sq -NY 10036
(212) 278-6207 .. **Lewis,** Cheryl L '01 Societe Generale -1221 Av of Amer -NY 10020
(212) 243-5241 .. **Lewis,** Christopher H '01 Cnsl ALARIC Compliance -800 3rd Av -NY 10022
(212) 419-1500 .. **Lewis Clifton & Nikolaidis,PC** -350 7th Av -NY 10001 **Fx:**419-1510
(212) 755-3200 .. **Lewis,** Courtney S '06 %S Silberfein,PC -1212 Av of Amer -NY 10036 **Fx:**944-6600
(212) 848-4000 .. **Lewis,** Danl C '02 %Shearman & S LLP -599 Lex Av -NY 10022
(212) 351-4500 .. **Lewis,** Danl R '02 (Epstein B&G,PC) -250 Park Av -NY 10177
(212) 316-0027 .. **Lewis,** Daulton J Jr. '76 -528 W 111th -NY 10025 **Fx:**865-4894
(718) 330-1200 .. **Lewis,** David A '76 %Fed Def of NY Inc -1 Pierrepont Plz -Brklyn 11201 **Fx:**855-0760
(212) 506-1700 .. **Lewis,** David A '02 Cnsl Kasowitz BT&F LLP -1633 Bway -NY 10019
(212) 285-2290 .. **Lewis,** David L '80 (Lewis & F) -225 Bway -NY 10007
(516) 933-7550 .. **Lewis,** David R '84 (D Lewis & Assoc) -998 Old Cntry Rd -Plainvw 11803 **Fx:**433-6404
(212) 637-2627 .. **Lewis,** David Raymond '85 US Atty -1 St Andrews Plz -NY 10007
(212) 259-8000 .. **Lewis,** Davina M '08 %Dewey & L LLP -1301 Av of Amer -NY 10019
(631) 577-7319 .. **Lewis,** Deborah '83 %Travelers -100 Baylis Rd Bx9093 -Melvll 11747
(646) 386-5700 .. **Lewis,** Debra K '83 Civil Ct -111 Centre -NY 10013
(212) 735-3000 .. **Lewis,** Donald D '02 %Skadden ASM&F LLP -4 Times Sq -NY 10036
(718) 286-2000 .. **Lewis,** Donna M '88 %Leg Aid -120-46 Qns Blvd -Kew Gdns 11415 **Fx:**286-2286
(212) 577-3530 .. **Lewis,** Dori A '76 %Leg Aid -199 Water -NY 10038 **Fx:**425-2465
(973) 848-4700 .. **Lewis,** Ebonee Hamilton '04 %Littler M,PC -900 3rd Av -NY 10022 **Fx:**643-5626
(585) 394-2513 .. **Lewis,** Edw G '76 -24 Bucknghm -Rchstr 14607
(212) 728-8000 .. **Lewis,** Elizabeth Buckley '92 %Willkie F&G LLP -787 7th Av -NY 10019
(585) 263-7930 .. **Lewis,** Ellen C '86 %Wilson Commencement Pk -251 Joseph Av -Rchstr 14605
(212) 962-1020 .. **Lewis,** Elliot L '95 %M Lamonsoff -80 Maiden Ln -NY 10038 **Fx:**962-3078
(646) 638-8435 .. **Lewis,** Emily C '05 in Demand LLC -345 Hudson -NY 10014
(212) 715-1000 .. **Lewis,** Emma Kelton '98 %Arnold & P LLP -399 Park Av -NY 10022
(212) 883-2507 .. **Lewis,** Erica '00 ING Clarion -230 Park Av -NY 10169
(718) 250-2000 .. **Lewis,** Esi M '06 DA -350 Jay -Brklyn 11201 **Fx:**250-2314
(212) 442-4900 .. **Lewis,** Faye Kessin '85 %Ofc Admin Trials -40 Rector -NY 10006 **Fx:**442-4947
(212) 285-2290 .. **Lewis & Fiore** -225 Bway -NY 10007 **Fx:**964-4506
(518) 257-3000 .. **Lewis,** Frances P '92 %Dormitory Auth -515 Bway -Albany 12207 **Fx:**257-3101
(212) 227-3900 .. **Lewis,** Fredric '55 -7 Dey -NY 10007 **Fx:**406-9571
(914) 559-3100 .. **Lewis,** Garrett P '77 (Heidell PM&B,LLP) -81 Main -White Plns 10601
(914) 766-4259 .. **Lewis,** Gary W '87 IBM -294 Route 100 -Somers 10589
(516) 485-0238 .. **Lewis,** Gerald P '80 -1576 Front -E Meadow 11554 **Fx:**485-0250
(845) 454-1200 .. **Lewis & Greer,PC** -510 Haight Av Bx2990 -Poughkeepsie 12603 **Fx:**454-3315
(718) 250-1100 .. **Lewis,** Gregory P '84 %E Garfinkel -12 Metrotech Ctr -Brklyn 11201 **Fx:**250-1168
(518) 374-3344 .. **Lewis,** H Richd '62 -650 Franklin -Schnctdy 12305 **Fx:**374-0828
(914) 328-8522 .. **Lewis,** Harold B '03 Coastal Recovery Corp -180 S Bway -White Plns 10605
(585) 225-3446 .. **Lewis,** Herbert J '68 (Darweesh LK&V,LLP) -1081 Long Pond Rd -Rchstr 14626
(212) 692-1000 .. **Lewis,** J Michl '01 (Duane M LLP) -1540 Bway -NY 10036
(212) 331-4982 .. **Lewis,** Jaime D '00 HRA -180 Water -NY 10038
(212) 623-6759 .. **Lewis,** James R '79 JP Morgan Chase & Co -4 NY Plz -NY 10004
(212) 474-1000 .. **Lewis,** Janet L '87 %Cravath S&M LLP -825 8th Av -NY 10019
(631) 420-2538 .. **Lewis,** Janice A '82 Farmingdale State Univ -2350 Broadhllw Rd -Farmngdl 11735
(212) 277-0455 .. **Lewis,** Jarret S '02 Hartford Fincl Products -2 Park Av -NY 10016
(212) 272-9462 .. **Lewis,** Jason A '98 %JP Morgan Chase -383 Mad Av -NY 10179
(212) 336-2000 .. **Lewis,** Jeffrey I D '87 (Patterson BW&T LLP) -1133 Av of Amer -NY 10036
(914) 472-9011 .. **Lewis,** Jeffrey S '78 -81 Brite Av -Scarsdale 10583
(212) 225-2000 .. **Lewis,** Jeffrey S '87 (Cleary GS&H) -1 Lbrty Plz -NY 10006
(212) 578-2211 .. **Lewis,** Jennifer Wynne '96 %MetLife -27-01 Qns Plz N -LIC 11101
(212) 277-6500 .. **Lewis,** Joan L '85 Cnsl Dickstein S LLP -1633 Bway -NY 10019
(212) 455-2000 .. **Lewis,** John F '08 %Simpson T&B LLP -425 Lex Av -NY 10017
(914) 332-8629 .. **Lewis,** John R '78 -36 Hemlock Dr -Sleepy Hollow 10591
(516) 501-9000 .. **Lewis,** John R Jr. '95 (JR Lewis Jr,PC) -4 West Gate Rd -Farmngdl 11735 **Fx:**845-7089
(631) 755-0101 .. **Lewis Johs Avallone Aviles, LLP** -425 Broad Hollow Rd -Melvll 11747 **Fx:**755-0117
(631) 369-7600 .. **Lewis Johs Avallone Aviles, LLP** -21 E 2nd -Rvrhead 11901 **Fx:**369-7680
(212) 233-7195 .. **Lewis Johs Avallone Aviles, LLP** -61 Bway -NY 10006 **Fx:**233-7196
(212) 319-0990 .. **Lewis,** Jon A '86 %Toby Spitz Assoc -110 E 59th -NY 10022 **Fx:**319-1555
(845) 336-4705 .. **Lewis,** Jon M '75 -120 Morey Hill Rd -Kingston 12401
(212) 909-6000 .. **Lewis,** Jonathan F '95 (Debevoise & P LLP) -919 3rd Av -NY 10022
(212) 218-7155 .. **Lewis,** Jonathan H '94 Special Cnsl Inc -60 E 42nd -NY 10165
(914) 437-7670 .. **Lewis,** Kenneth M '87 (Teitelbaum & B LLP) -3 Barker Av -White Plns 10601 **Fx:**437-7672
(516) 355-7901 .. **Lewis,** Kerri E '96 Paganini GCC&F -1979 Marcus Av -Lk Success 11042
(518) 372-1160 .. **Lewis,** Kirk M '86 Schenectady ARC -214 State Bx2236 -Schnctdy 12301 **Fx:**377-2189
(212) 504-6000 .. **Lewis,** L Alexander '95 %Cadwalader W&T LLP -1 World Fncl Ctr -NY 10281
(516) 739-0000 .. **Lewis,** Laurie M '03 %Martyn T&M -330 Old Cntry Rd -Mineola 11501
(716) 854-2100 .. **Lewis,** Lawr S '79 (Lewis & L,PC) -37 Franklin -Buffalo 14202 **Fx:**854-0433
(212) 689-4025 .. **Lewis,** Lawr S '83 -276 5th Av -NY 10001 **Fx:**683-2469
(845) 359-2149 .. **Lewis & Lefcourt** -Bx219 -Blauvelt 10913
(212) 869-3500 .. **Lewis,** Leslie L '01 %J Fuchsberg Law Firm,LLP -500 5th Av -NY 10110 **Fx:**398-1532
(315) 724-5149 .. **Lewis,** Leslie R '71 -23 Genesee -New Hartfrd 13413 **Fx:**724-0338
(212) 732-0707 .. **Lewis,** Lindsay A '08 J Dratel,PC -2 Wall -NY 10005 **Fx:**571-3792
(516) 463-6123 .. **Lewis,** Lisa '94 Hofstra University Law School -121 Hofstra Univ -Hempstd 11549
(212) 653-8700 .. **Lewis,** Lisa M '01 %Sheppard MR&H LLP -30 Rckfllr Plz -NY 10112
(212) 756-8911 .. **Lewis,** Loida Nicolas '75 -115 E 57th -NY 10022 **Fx:**756-8954

(914) 597-7800 .. **Lewis,** Lori B '02 %Lewis S&C,LLC -11 Martine Av -White Plns 10606 **Fx:**597-7801
(845) 454-1200 .. **Lewis,** Lou '69 (Lewis & G,PC) -510 Haight Av Bx2990 -Poughkeepsie 12603
(315) 474-1214 .. **Lewis,** Louise J '04 Syracuse Metro Abstract Co -6505A Basile Rowe -E Syracuse 13057
(718) 748-9482 .. **Lewis,** Lynn Ann '85 (LA Lewis & Assoc) -456 82nd -Brklyn 11209 **Fx:**238-0797
(212) 238-3000 .. **Lewis,** Marc C '86 OfCnsl Emmet M&M,LLP -120 Bway -NY 10271
(212) 833-6751 .. **Lewis,** Marc M '96 Sony Corp of America -555 Mad Av -NY 10022
(646) 386-3656 .. **Lewis,** Marian '79 Supreme Ct Spcl Referee -60 Centre -NY 10007
(631) 467-1711 .. **Lewis,** Mark W '74 -622 Hawkins Av Bx377 -Lk Ronkonkoma 11779 **Fx:**467-1930
(212) 336-0125 .. **Lewis,** Maureen F '04 %SEC -3 World Fncl Ctr -NY 10281 **Fx:**336-1323
(212) 772-0943 .. **Lewis & McKenna** -521 5th Av -NY 10175 **Fx:**758-0069
(516) 571-3751 .. **Lewis,** Melissa T '06 %DA -262 Old Cntry Rd -Mineola 11501 **Fx:**248-9479
(212) 558-4000 .. **Lewis,** Michl D '08 %Sullivan & C LLP -125 Broad -NY 10004
(516) 542-4900 .. **Lewis,** Michl G '95 Getty Petroleum Mrktng Inc -1500 Hempstd Tpk -E Meadow 11554
(917) 778-6600 .. **Lewis,** Michl H '76 %J Toomey -485 Lex Av -NY 10017 **Fx:**778-7048
(914) 683-3531 .. **Lewis,** Michelle Helene '98 %Kramer K,LLP -445 Hmltn Av -White Plns 10601
(212) 519-7848 .. **Lewis,** Mie '07 ACLU -125 Broad -NY 10004
(212) 878-7900 .. **Lewis,** Mord Michl '07 %Fox R LLP -100 Park Av -NY 10017
(914) 765-6354 .. **Lewis,** Nancy R '90 IBM Credit Corp -1 N Castle Dr -Armonk 10504 **Fx:**765-7533
(631) 963-5454 .. **Lewis,** Neal M '89 %Neighborhood Network -7180 Republic Airport -Farmngdl 11735 **Fx:**963-5466
(718) 590-2000 .. **Lewis,** Nicholas E '09 %DA -198 E 161st -Bronx 10451 **Fx:**590-6477
(212) 450-4000 .. **Lewis,** Ogden N '73 SrCnsl Davis P&W LLP -450 Lex Av -NY 10017
(914) 328-1500 .. **Lewis,** Pamela L '83 -81 Main -White Plns 10601 **Fx:**686-4824
(718) 520-3798 .. **Lewis,** Paul R '88 %Hon S Fisher -88-11 Sutphin Blvd -Jamaica 11435
(212) 772-0943 .. **Lewis,** Paul Z '63 (Lewis & M) -521 5th Av -NY 10175
(585) 753-4500 .. **Lewis,** Peter C '85 %DA -832 Watts Bldg -Rchstr 14614 **Fx:**753-4576
(518) 943-6667 .. **Lewis,** Ralph C Jr. '74 (Lewis & S) -287 Main Bx383 -Catskill 12414
(716) 484-7196 .. **Lewis,** Randall S '99 %Fessenden L&D -81 Forest Av Bx590 -Jamestwn 14702
(607) 723-5341 .. **Lewis,** Richd C '76 SpclCnsl Hinman H&K,LLP -80 Exchange Bx5250 -Bnghmtn 13902
(212) 252-0300 .. **Lewis,** Richd H '93 (Kagan LLLG&C,LLP) -200 Mad Av -NY 10016
(718) 680-7090 .. **Lewis,** Richd Klar '84 -8519 4th Av -Brklyn 11209
(212) 521-5400 .. **Lewis,** Richd P '97 (Reed S LLP) -599 Lex Av -NY 10022
(212) 265-8600 .. **Lewis,** Robt J '03 %MS Taub LLP -110 E 59th -NY 10022 **Fx:**581-8958
(212) 721-7353 .. **Lewis,** Robt L '72 -7 Penn Plz -NY 10001 **Fx:**818-0625
(212) 626-4100 .. **Lewis,** Robt P '80 (Baker & M LLP) -1114 Av of Amer -NY 10036
(845) 358-0048 .. **Lewis,** Robt P Jr. '69 (Mann M&L,PC) -17 S Bway Bx991 -Nyack 10960
(212) 752-5800 .. **Lewis,** Robt R '75 -1633 Bway -NY 10019
(845) 358-7100 .. **Lewis,** Robt S '87 (R Lewis,PC) -53 Burd -Nyack 10960 **Fx:**353-6943
(516) 487-7375 .. **Lewis,** Robt W '07 I Newman -98 Cuttermill Rd -Gt Neck 11021 **Fx:**487-0113
(212) 980-4084 .. **Lewis,** Robt Y '88 (Freeman L LLP) -228 E 45th -NY 10017
(212) 307-5858 .. **Lewis,** Robin A '84 -19 Fulton -NY 10038
(518) 561-3700 .. **Lewis & Rogers, PC** -53 Court -Plattsbrgh 12901 **Fx:**561-2080
(212) 935-9831 .. **Lewis,** Roland J '89 %Metro Waterfront Alliance -241 Water -NY 10038
(212) 556-7080 .. **Lewis,** Russell T '73 %The NY Times Co -620 8th Av -NY 10018
(212) 819-8200 .. **Lewis,** Sara N '10 %White & C LLP -1155 Av of Amer -NY 10036
(212) 273-7305 .. **Lewis,** Sarah A '04 Gleacher & Co Securities,Inc -677 Bway -Albany 12207 **Fx:**(800) 887-4129
(516) 357-3000 .. **Lewis,** Shari C '83 (Rivkin R LLP) -926 RXR Plz -Uniondale 11556
(212) 780-2845 .. **Lewis,** Stanley J '07 Con Ed -4 Irving Pl -NY 10003
(518) 943-6667 .. **Lewis & Stanzione** -287 Main Bx383 -Catskill 12414 **Fx:**943-5157
(914) 761-0300 .. **Lewis,** Stephen R '79 (Stephens BR&L) -175 Main -White Plns 10601
(212) 682-8811 .. **Lewis,** Steven E '76 (Dunnington B&M LLP) -1359 Bway -NY 10018
(212) 839-5317 .. **Lewis,** Susan D '78 (Sidley A LLP) -787 7th Av -NY 10019
(914) 993-1546 .. **Lewis,** Timothy W '87 Town Atty -177 Hillside Av -Greenburgh 10607 **Fx:**993-1656
(212) 785-7600 .. **Lewis,** Timothy W '03 TW Lewis & Co -370 7th Av -NY 10001
(212) 906-1200 .. **Lewis,** Toby D '10 %Latham & W -885 3rd Av -NY 10022
(212) 563-2200 .. **Lewis,** Willa I '79 (Brandt S&L LLP) -386 Park Av S -NY 10016
(516) 759-2722 .. **Lewis,** Wm E '96 (Ryan M&L,LLP) -90 Forest Av -Locust Vly 11560
(212) 233-7195 .. **Lewis,** Wm J '72 (Lewis JAA,LLP) -61 Bway -NY 10006
(914) 738-1794 .. **Lewis,** Wm J '91 -150 4th Av -Pelham 10803
(212) 715-9100 .. **Lewis,** Yehudis S '96 SpclCnsl Kramer LN&F,LLP -1177 Av of Amer -NY 10036
(518) 533-3000 .. **Lewis Belcher,** Sarah '90 SrCnsl Bond S&K,PLLC -111 Wshngtn Av -Albany 12210
(914) 668-4600 .. **Lewis-Burnett,** Carla '92 %Bozeman Law Firm,LLP -6 Gramatan Av -Mt Vernon 10550 **Fx:**668-4721
(212) 506-5000 .. **Lewis-Gruss,** Ayanna '03 %Orrick H&S LLP -51 W 52nd -NY 10019
(516) 374-1400 .. **Lewisohn,** Jeffrey L '78 -483 Chestnut -Cedarhrst 11516 **Fx:**374-7293
(516) 489-5000 .. **Lewis Sisun,** Alison '86 %Town Atty -Town Hall -Hempstd 11550 **Fx:**489-5150
(718) 230-7000 .. **Lewis-Williams,** Sharon '98 -890 Atl Av -Brklyn 11238
(718) 857-8564 .. **Lewis-Williams,** Yvette '95 -946 Fulton -Brklyn 11238
(845) 647-9800 .. **Lewit,** Guy M '81 -Bx586 -Ellenvll 12428 **Fx:**(718) 504-4221
(212) 230-5500 .. **Lewit,** Peter M '94 %Davis SLM&H LLP -689 5th Av -NY 10022
(212) 230-5500 .. **Lewit,** Vivian S '96 %Davis SLM&H LLP -689 5th Av -NY 10022
(212) 547-5400 .. **Lewittes,** Meir A '03 (McDermott W&E LLP) -340 Mad Av -NY 10173
(212) 403-8129 .. **Lewkonia,** Michl W '07 DE Shaw & Co,LP -120 W 45th -NY 10036
(212) 225-2000 .. **Lewkow,** Victor I '74 (Cleary GS&H) -1 Lbrty Plz -NY 10006
(315) 218-8000 .. **Lewkowicz,** Thaddeus J '81 (Bond S&K,PLLC) -1 Lincoln Ctr -Syracuse 13202
(212) 806-5400 .. **Lewner,** Andrew S '02 SpclCnsl Stroock &S&L LLP -180 Maiden Ln -NY 10038
(212) 854-0787 .. **Lewton,** Audra M '04 Barnard Cllg-Dvlpmnt Ofc -3009 Bway -NY 10027
(212) 344-0003 .. **Lewyckyj,** Boris J '77 -11 Bway -NY 10004 **Fx:**480-2809
(212) 440-2350 .. **Lewyn,** Alfred T '84 %C Siegel -40 Wall -NY 10005 **Fx:**440-2385
(212) 455-2000 .. **Lewyn,** Thos M '57 OfCnsl Simpson T&B LLP -425 Lex Av -NY 10017
(845) 357-0036 .. **Lexow Berbit & Associates, PC** -56 Park Av Bx239 -Suffern 10901 **Fx:**357-0297
(585) 428-5890 .. **Lexvold,** Timothy M '84 %Cnty Atty -300G Hall Of Justice -Rchstr 14614 **Fx:**428-2704
(516) 542-5900 .. **Leyden,** James J Jr. '78 %Congdon FORDT&F -333 Earle Ovngton Blvd -Uniondale 11553
(585) 728-5230 .. **Leyden,** John F Jr. '74 Sullivan & L -Bx396 -Wayland 14572 **Fx:**728-3612
(212) 872-1000 .. **Leyden,** Lauren H '06 -One Bryant Park -NY 10036 **Fx:**872-1002
(212) 683-9559 .. **Leyden,** Michl S '01 %Goldberg & C,PLLC -31 E 32nd -NY 10016 **Fx:**683-7901
(516) 393-2200 .. **Leyden,** Sean P '96 (Garfunkel W,PC) -111 Grt Nck Rd -Gt Neck 11021
(212) 558-4000 .. **Leydier,** Marion C '02 (Sullivan & C LLP) -125 Broad -NY 10004
(585) 419-9000 .. **Leyens,** E Adam '90 (Adair Law Firm LLP) -290 Linden Oaks -Rchstr 14625 **Fx:**419-8071
(718) 354-3200 .. **Leykam,** Wm A '76 %Battiste A&S,Inc -60 Bay -Staten Isl 10301
(718) 243-9323 .. **Leytes,** Dina '09 %Lewis & H -45 Main -Brklyn 11201 **Fx:**243-9326
(212) 530-5000 .. **Leyton,** Nicole P '08 %Milbank TH&M LLP -1 Chase Manh Plz -NY 10005
(646) 563-8930 .. **Leyva,** Leo V '89 (Cole SMF&L,PA) -900 3rd Av -NY 10022 **Fx:**521-2030
(914) 358-3261 .. **Lezcano,** Julissa '07 -500 Mamaroneck Av -Harrison 10528 **Fx:**517-5351
(212) 318-3000 .. **L'Helias,** Thos P '99 (Fulbright & J LLP) -666 5th Av -NY 10103
(585) 546-8170 .. **Lheron,** Peter A '89 -11 N Goodman -Rchstr 14607
(212) 425-7200 .. **Li,** Anne E '07 %Kenyon & K,LLP -1 Bway -NY 10004
(212) 966-5932 .. **Li,** Bethany Y '09 AALDEF -99 Hudson -NY 10013 **Fx:**966-4303
(212) 967-7690 .. **Li,** Bing '99 (B Li,LLC) -1350 Bway -NY 10018 **Fx:**(917) 591-9292
(212) 355-4141 .. **Li,** Bo '04 Stndrd Sec Life Ins -485 Mad Av -NY 10022
(212) 859-8000 .. **Li,** Bryan '08 %Fried FHS&J LLP -1 NY Plz -NY 10004
(212) 430-6810 .. **Li,** Cang '94 -65 Bway -NY 10006 **Fx:**430-6815
(212) 704-6000 .. **Li,** Dan '08 OfCnsl Troutman S LLP -405 Lex Av -NY 10174
(631) 501-5700 .. **Li,** Dan '09 Carter DF&S LLP -445 Broadhallow Rd -Melvll 11747
(212) 735-3000 .. **Li,** Danielle '07 %Skadden ASM&F LLP -4 Times Sq -NY 10036
(718) 759-9636 .. **Li,** David S '99 -6402 Ft Hmltn Pkwy -Brklyn 11219
(914) 961-0960 .. **Li,** Feng '04 -35 E Grassy Sprain Rd -Ynkrs 10710
(212) 226-3960 .. **Li,** Feng '06 %F Liu -2 Bway -NY 10038
(212) 610-6300 .. **Li,** Gary '09 %Allen & O -1221 Av of Amer -NY 10020
(718) 888-0882 .. **Li,** Han Jun '08 -39-07 Prince -Flushng 11354
(212) 849-7414 .. **Li,** Holly Y '04 -51 Mad Av -NY 10010
(718) 983-8800 .. **Li,** Jeffrey C '99 %Lee & A,LLP -260 Christopher Ln -Staten Isl 10314
(212) 558-4000 .. **Li,** Ji '08 %Sullivan & C LLP -125 Broad -NY 10004
(212) 903-9000 .. **Li,** Jiadong '09 %Linklaters -1345 Av of Amer -NY 10105
(212) 385-4003 .. **Li,** Jin '06 G Chen & Assoc PC -305 Bway -NY 10007
(212) 335-9000 .. **Li,** Joanne Y '01 %DA -1 Hogan Pl -NY 10013
(212) 351-4000 .. **Li,** Jonathan J '07 %Gibson D&C LLP -200 Park Av -NY 10166
(212) 596-9000 .. **Li,** Joy P '09 %Ropes & G LLP -1211 Av of Amer -NY 10036
(212) 841-2288 .. **Li,** Juliana C '05 BNP Paribas -787 7th Av -NY 10019
(212) 967-8100 .. **Li,** Kelly K '02 Primetime Intl -135 W 36th -NY 10018
(212) 885-5000 .. **Li,** Kim '09 %Blank R LLP -405 Lex Av -NY 10174
(212) 839-5300 .. **Li,** Lei '08 %Sidley A LLP -787 7th Av -NY 10019
(212) 436-4007 .. **Li,** Li '04 %Deloitte & Touche LLP -2 World Fncl Ctr -NY 10281
(212) 225-2000 .. **Li,** Liang '07 Cleary GS&H -1 Lbrty Plz -NY 10006 **Fx:**225-3999
(212) 226-3960 .. **Li,** Lin '05 %F Liu -2 Bway -NY 10038
(212) 645-9677 .. **Li,** Ling '03 Natl Comm on US China Relations -71 W 23rd -NY 10010
(212) 801-6775 .. **Li,** Matthias W '05 %Greenberg T,LLP -200 Park Av -NY 10166
(212) 906-1200 .. **Li,** Melinda '07 %Latham & W -885 3rd Av -NY 10022
(212) 805-6374 .. **Li,** P Patty '07 Hon V Marrero USDC -500 Pearl -NY 10007
(718) 888-1201 .. **Li,** Shuaiyu '00 -39-01 Main -Flushng 11354 **Fx:**888-1231
(646) 643-3098 .. **Li,** Ting I '98 -90 Bowery -NY 10013
(212) 373-3000 .. **Li,** Tong '09 %Paul WRW&G LLP -1285 Av of Amer -NY 10019
(212) 351-3400 .. **Li,** Xiao '09 Desmarais LLP -230 Park Av -NY 10169 **Fx:**351-3401
(212) 964-2461 .. **Li,** Yafang '99 -225 Bway -NY 10007
(212) 370-1300 .. **Li,** Ying '06 %Ellenoff G&S LLP -150 E 42nd -NY 10017
(212) 450-4000 .. **Li,** Yinjie '07 %Davis P&W LLP -450 Lex Av -NY 10017
(212) 225-2000 .. **Li,** Yisu '10 %Cleary GS&H -1 Lbrty Plz -NY 10006
(212) 450-4000 .. **Li,** Yue '08 %Davis P&W LLP -450 Lex Av -NY 10017
(212) 609-6800 .. **Li,** Zhenggui '05 %McCarter & E,LLP -245 Park Av -NY 10167
(212) 728-8000 .. **Li,** Zheyao '10 %Willkie F&G LLP -787 7th Av -NY 10019
(212) 596-9000 .. **Li,** Zhi Ying '03 %Ropes & G LLP -1211 Av of Amer -NY 10036
(212) 446-2300 .. **Lia,** Robt M '00 Cnsl Boies S&F LLP -575 Lex Av -NY 10022
(718) 229-0990 .. **Liametz,** Audie R '04 -2 Bay Club Dr -Bayside 11360 **Fx:**229-0990
(914) 576-1259 .. **Lian,** Albert W '55 -1273 North Av -New Rchll 10804
(718) 286-6000 .. **Liander,** James M '86 %DA -125-01 Qns Blvd -Kew Gdns 11415
(212) 848-9800 .. **Liang,** Chi-yu '06 %Withers B LLP -430 Park Av -NY 10022
(212) 475-8335 .. **Liang,** Edw P '94 Select Equity -380 Lafayette -NY 10003
(516) 733-1822 .. **Liang,** Eric G '06 Cnsl Rivers Edge Land Srvcs -77 Newbrdg Rd -Hicksvll 11801
(212) 592-1400 .. **Liang,** Regina M '10 %Herrick,F LLP -2 Park Av -NY 10016
(212) 425-7200 .. **Liang,** Stanley D '03 %Kenyon & K,LLP -1 Bway -NY 10004
(212) 765-5070 .. **Liang,** Wing Hay '07 %Fish & R,PC -153 E 53rd -NY 10022
(212) 455-2000 .. **Liang,** Yueting '08 %Simpson T&B LLP -425 Lex Av -NY 10017
(516) 802-0630 .. **Liantonio,** Stephanie '09 %Simmons J,LLP -115 Eileen Way -Syosset 11791

(516) 747-4082 .. **Liantonio-McBride,** Gaetana '89 %Montfort HM&S LLP -1140 Franklin Av Bx7677 -Gdn Cty 11530
(212) 624-4172 .. **Liao,** Edw Ho Tung '94 E Liao,PC -49 W 37th -NY 10018 **Fx:**624-4175
(914) 949-6996 .. **Liao,** Henry L P '06 %Penino & M,LLP -180 E Post Rd -White Plns 10601
(212) 504-6000 .. **Liao,** Jeffrey '05 %Cadwalader W&T LLP -1 World Fncl Ctr -NY 10281
(212) 517-4225 .. **Liapakis,** Pamela Anagnos '71 -515 E 79th -NY 10075
(212) 361-8290 .. **Liban,** Theo B '82 Dept of Finance Adjudication -66 John -NY 10038 **Fx:**361-8233
(201) 867-5070 .. **Libassi,** Mary '83 -350 Bway -NY 10013 **Fx:**867-0911
(516) 488-9860 .. **Libby,** Douglas E '75 Cnsl Sewanhaka Cntrl High Schl District -77 Landau Av -Floral Pk 11001 **Fx:**488-7738
(212) 344-3000 .. **Libby,** Douglas M '78 %Seneca Ins Co -160 Water -NY 10038
(516) 794-9460 .. **Libby,** Irene Castaldo '76 %O'Donnell SG&L,LLP -245 Hillside Av -Williston Pk 11596
(212) 836-8000 .. **Liben,** Deborah '07 %Kaye S LLP -425 Park Av -NY 10022
(585) 381-0660 .. **Libenson,** Amy '82 1st Data Debit Srvcs -1173 Pttsfrd-Vctr Rd -Pittsfrd 14534
Liberatore, Lina '86 -14 Hilldale Rd -Dobbs Ferry 10522
(914) 945-6000 .. **Liberchuk,** Larry '01 Phillips Electronics NA Corp -345 Scarborough Rd -Briarclff Mnr 10510
(212) 508-6700 .. **Liberman,** Enrique E '02 (Tannenbaum HS&H LLP) -900 3rd Av -NY 10022
(212) 872-1000 .. **Liberman,** Isabelle R '09 -One Bryant Park -NY 10036 **Fx:**872-1002
(212) 553-0300 .. **Liberman,** Jessica Brand '00 %Moody's Invstr Srvc -250 Greenwich -NY 10007
(212) 885-5000 .. **Liberman,** Lois J '89 (Blank R LLP) -405 Lex Av -NY 10174
(516) 627-3326 .. **Liberman,** Susan R '98 -1129 Nrthrn Blvd -Manhsst 11030 **Fx:**627-0530
(516) 650-5095 .. **Libert,** Jack L '75 J Libert,PC -164 Anstice -Oyster Bay 11771
(845) 565-1100 .. **Liberth,** Richd F '77 (Tarshis CLM&M,PLLC) -One Corwin Ct -Newburgh 12550
(212) 935-3000 .. **Liberto,** Muriel M '07 %Mintz LCFG&P,PC -666 3rd Av -NY 10017
(212) 876-6695 .. **Libes,** Deborah S '80 -45 E 89th -NY 10128
(212) 859-8000 .. **Libhart,** Gabriel A '10 %Fried FHS&J LLP -1 NY Plz -NY 10004
(212) 385-4410 .. **Libo,** Andrew L '83 (Gersowitz L&K,PC) -111 Bway -NY 10006
(914) 681-9065 .. **Libous,** Matthew T '04 (Libous & S) -399 Knollwood Rd -White Plns 10603
(212) 704-6000 .. **Libove,** Adam S '08 %Troutman S LLP -405 Lex Av -NY 10174
(212) 980-3500 .. **Libow,** Beata S '09 %Pavia & H LLP -600 Mad Av -NY 10022
(212) 735-3000 .. **Libow,** Beth Olohan '09 %Skadden ASM&F LLP -4 Times Sq -NY 10036
(212) 425-9300 .. **Libowsky,** David J '87 (Bressler A&R,PC) -17 State -NY 10004
(212) 259-8000 .. **Librera,** Kelly A '02 (Dewey & L LLP) -1301 Av of Amer -NY 10019
(516) 741-1040 .. **Librett Friedland & Lieberman,LLP** -1325 Franklin Av -Gdn Cty 11530 **Fx:**741-1592
(212) 683-3730 .. **Librett,** Martin F '83 OfCnsl Thomas & W -104 W 27th -NY 10001
(516) 741-1040 .. **Librett,** Richd A '74 (Librett F&L,LLP) -1325 Franklin Av -Gdn Cty 11530
(718) 615-0044 .. **LiBrizzi,** Russell L '97 %Lozner & M -1901 Emmons Av -Brklyn 11235
(914) 253-8300 .. **Libson,** Craig S '86 -5 Covent Pl -Hartsdale 10530
(212) 506-1700 .. **Libster,** Jacqueline B '01 Kasowitz BT&F LLP -1633 Bway -NY 10019
(212) 589-4200 .. **Liburd,** Essence '07 %Baker & H LLP -45 Rckfllr Plz -NY 10111
(212) 822-1435 .. **Liburd,** Marjorie A '79 (Scott & L) -305 Bway -NY 10007
(212) 233-7195 .. **Libutti,** Eileen H '92 (Lewis JAA,LLP) -61 Bway -NY 10006
(212) 509-3900 .. **LiCalsi,** Paul V '78 (Mitchell S&K LLP) -12 E 49th -NY 10017
(212) 762-7159 .. **LiCalzi,** Jacqueline O '88 Morgan Stanley -1221 Av of Amer -NY 10020
(516) 394-4200 .. **LiCalzi,** James N '94 (Duffy & D) -1370 RXR Plz -Uniondale 11556
(917) 207-9353 .. **Licandro,** Irina '09 -350 5th Av -NY 10118
(212) 336-0126 .. **Licardo,** Gwen A '99 %SEC -3 World Fncl Ctr -NY 10281 **Fx:**336-1323
(631) 581-2300 .. **Licari,** Thos B '78 -8 Laurel Av -E Islip 11730 **Fx:**581-2705
(845) 357-4242 .. **Licata & Conklin** -222 Route 59 -Suffern 10901 **Fx:**357-4574
(845) 357-4242 .. **Licata,** James D '85 (Licata & C) -222 Route 59 -Suffern 10901
(716) 636-7600 .. **Licata,** John B '93 %HoganWillig -2410 N Forest Rd -Amherst 14068
(718) 326-6200 .. **Licata,** JoMarie '02 (Sullivan & G) -73-42 68th Av -Middl Vllg 11379 **Fx:**228-7010
(516) 746-7780 .. **Licata,** Jos J III '96 (Rossillo & L,PC) -355 Post Av -Westbury 11590
(516) 221-7427 .. **Licata,** Rory C '96 (RC Licata,PC) -2185 Brookside Av -Wantagh 11793 **Fx:**221-7412
(212) 349-6565 .. **Licata,** Vincent J '92 -225 Bway -NY 10007 **Fx:**349-5781
(585) 232-1980 .. **Licata,** Walter J '63 (Levy & L,PC) -45 Exchange -Rchstr 14614
(516) 742-3470 .. **Licata-McCord,** Nicole J '03 %Kral CRRP&G,LLP -538 Broadhllw Rd -Melvll 11747
(516) 227-2662 .. **Licatesi,** Anthony J '88 (Rubin & L,PC) -591 Stewart Av -Gdn Cty 11530
(518) 477-7951 .. **Liccardi,** Jos B '79 (Maney M&L) -77 Troy Rd -E Greenbush 12061
(212) 790-9200 .. **Licciardi,** Maryann E '04 %Cowan L&L,PC -1133 Av of Amer -NY 10036
(516) 746-8000 .. **Liccione,** Maureen T '82 (Jaspan S LLP) -300 Grdn City Plz -Gdn Cty 11530
(212) 474-1000 .. **Lichman,** Rachael L '09 %Cravath S&M LLP -825 8th Av -NY 10019
(718) 250-2000 .. **Lichstein,** Toni C '73 %DA -350 Jay -Brklyn 11201 **Fx:**250-2314
(516) 227-8560 .. **Licht,** Alan B '93 %Dept Soc Srvcs -60 Chas Lindbergh Blvd -Uniondale 11553
(212) 986-4560 .. **Licht,** Steven M '66 %Special Funds -205 E 42nd -NY 10017 **Fx:**697-2474
(718) 834-8220 .. **Lichtash,** Terry '45 -215 Adams -Brklyn 11201
(212) 228-6320 .. **Lichten,** Stuart L '88 (Schwartz L&B,PC) -275 7th Av -NY 10001
(212) 389-7818 .. **Lichtenberg,** Barry E '82 (Schwartz L LLP) -420 Lex Av -NY 10170
(212) 969-3000 .. **Lichtenfeld,** Steven L '82 (Proskauer R LLP) -1585 Bway -NY 10036
(914) 666-3322 .. **Lichtenstein,** Alan D '77 -71 Smith Av -Mt Kisco 10549 **Fx:**666-3280
(212) 564-0757 .. **Lichtenstein,** Jack '52 -224 W 35th -NY 10001
(212) 834-0600 .. **Lichtenstein,** Jon D '91 (Gordon & S,PC) -355 Lex Av -NY 10017
(516) 873-6300 .. **Lichtenstein,** Jos M '87 -131 Mineola Blvd -Mineola 11501 **Fx:**873-7986
(212) 471-6201 .. **Lichtenstein,** Kari H '00 (Advocate & L,LLP) -780 3rd Av -NY 10017 **Fx:**935-1166
(212) 223-4000 .. **Lichtenstein,** Mark S '93 (Crowell & M LLP) -590 Mad Av -NY 10022
(646) 610-6322 .. **Lichtenstein,** Nancy J '00 %NYPD -1 Police Plz -NY 10038
(914) 698-3313 .. **Lichtenstein,** Sande E '65 (Lichtenstein & S) -158 W Bstn Post Rd -Mamaroneck 10543
(516) 328-2300 .. **Lichtenstein,** Sarah C '79 (Abrams FFEGF&E,LLP) -1111 Marcus Av -Lk Success 11042
(914) 698-3313 .. **Lichtenstein & Schindel** -158 W Bstn Post Rd -Mamaroneck 10543 **Fx:**698-3478
(212) 973-0572 .. **Lichtenstein,** Scott W '10 %Wolff&S,PC -140 Bway -NY 10005
(716) 849-1333 .. **Lichtenthal,** John M '06 %Lipsitz GSC LLP -42 Delaware Av -Buffalo 14202
(212) 859-8000 .. **Lichter,** Brian S '03 %Fried FHS&J LLP -1 NY Plz -NY 10004
(212) 310-8000 .. **Lichter,** Jason I '05 %Weil G&M LLP -767 5th Av -NY 10153
(212) 284-6617 .. **Lichter,** Jonathan M '76 %UJC -25 Bway -NY 10004 **Fx:**271-6709
(212) 345-9729 .. **Lichter,** Leon J '88 Marsh USA -1166 Av of Amer -NY 10036 **Fx:**345-4808
(212) 867-7750 .. **Lichter,** Leonard '55 (Lichter GO PC) -551 5th Av -NY 10176
(212) 941-4075 .. **Lichter,** Rosalind S '83 -375 Greenwich -NY 10013 **Fx:**941-4076
(718) 264-1420 .. **Lichtiger,** Ira '82 %Bluestone Orgn Inc -193-04 Horace Hrdng Expy -Fresh Mdws 11365 **Fx:**264-1507
(212) 384-0211 .. **Lichtman,** Gary A '82 -233 Bway -NY 10279 **Fx:**406-2313
(212) 750-1200 .. **Lichtman,** Jeffrey A '79 (Trolman G&L,PC) -777 3rd Av -NY 10017
(212) 581-1001 .. **Lichtman,** Jeffrey H '91 -750 Lex Av -NY 10022 **Fx:**581-4999
(212) 735-3000 .. **Lichtman,** Jeffrey S '83 (Skadden ASM&F LLP) -4 Times Sq -NY 10036
(212) 701-3000 .. **Lichtman,** Saml '01 Cnsl Cahill G&R LLP -80 Pine -NY 10005 **Fx:**269-5420
(212) 352-3220 .. **Lichtman,** Shari H '93 American Conference Inst -41 W 25th -NY 10010 **Fx:**352-3231
(718) 438-2525 .. **Lichtman,** Yehuda A '07 NC Caller,PC -4309 13th Av -Brklyn 11219 **Fx:**972-4154
(718) 354-3200 .. **Licitra,** Jos F '85 OfCnsl Battiste A&S,Inc -60 Bay -Staten Isl 10301
(914) 828-8842 .. **Licitra,** Lawr J '83 Swiss Re America -175 King -Armonk 10504 **Fx:**828-7842
(718) 261-3047 .. **Licitra,** Wanda L '86 %Queens Law Assoc -118-21 Qns Blvd -Frst Hlls 11375 **Fx:**261-0798
(212) 407-4000 .. **Licker,** Eugene R '80 (Loeb & L,LLP) -345 Park Av -NY 10154
(845) 638-0800 .. **Licker,** Mark B '84 (Kahn & L) -369 S Main -New Cty 10956 **Fx:**638-0707
(845) 371-4700 .. **Licker,** Melissa N '08 %Fein SK&S,PC -747 Chestnut Rdg Rd -Spg Vly 10977
(315) 422-1172 .. **Lickstein,** Scott A '81 (Newman & L) -235 E Water -Syracuse 13202 **Fx:**422-1400
(212) 403-7300 .. **Licul,** Valdi '96 (Vladeck WE&E,PC) -1501 Bway -NY 10036
(315) 425-2700 .. **Liddell,** David B '67 (Hiscock & B,LLP) -One Park Pl -Syracuse 13202
(315) 425-2700 .. **Liddell,** Robt B '91 (Hiscock & B,LLP) -One Park Pl -Syracuse 13202
(212) 237-8614 .. **Liddie,** Michl A '02 John Jay Cllg-Rikers Isl Prgm -899 10th Av -NY 10019
(212) 687-8500 .. **Liddle,** Jeffrey L '77 (Liddle & R,LLP) -800 3rd Av -NY 10022
(212) 687-8500 .. **Liddle & Robinson,LLP** -800 3rd Av -NY 10022 **Fx:**687-1505
(212) 309-8100 .. **Lidke,** Elizabeth '91 %Lexis/Nexis -125 Park Av -NY 10017 **Fx:**309-8187
(212) 872-1000 .. **Lidsky,** Isaac J '05 -One Bryant Park -NY 10036 **Fx:**872-1002
(718) 546-0950 .. **Lidz,** Linda M '86 Dept of Correction -75-20 Astoria Blvd -E Elmhrst 11370
(718) 250-2000 .. **Lieb,** Ann Goodman '82 %DA -350 Jay -Brklyn 11201 **Fx:**250-2314
(212) 969-3000 .. **Lieb,** Bruce L '80 (Proskauer R LLP) -1585 Bway -NY 10036
(631) 878-4455 .. **Lieb,** David K '77 DK Lieb,PC -376A Main -Ctr Moriches 11934 **Fx:**878-4460
(212) 873-7340 .. **Lieb,** Ellen M '86 -450 West End Av -NY 10024
(631) 758-3030 .. **Lieb,** Jos '78 -Bx1039 -Patchogue 11772 **Fx:**758-3882
(212) 643-7000 .. **Lieb,** Katherine M '06 %Sills C&G PC -One Rckfllr Plz -NY 10020
(212) 840-6695 .. **Lieb,** L Robt '70 -80 W 40th -NY 10018
(631) 738-4765 .. **Lieb,** Peter M '83 Symbol Tech -1 Symbol Plz -Holtsvll 11742
(212) 479-6000 .. **Lieb,** Richd '54 OfCnsl Cooley LLP -1114 Av of Amer -NY 10036
(212) 588-0800 .. **Lieb,** Stephen J '97 (Frommer L&H LLP) -745 5th Av -NY 10151
(716) 858-2200 .. **Liebenow,** Brian R '08 %Cnty Atty -95 Franklin -Buffalo 14202 **Fx:**858-2281
(212) 592-1400 .. **Liebenson,** Jeffrey M '79 Cnsl Herrick,F LLP -2 Park Av -NY 10016
(212) 659-7300 .. **Liebenstein,** David M '07 %Haynes & B,LLP -1221 Av of Amer -NY 10020
(212) 867-4466 .. **Liebenstein,** Seth A '06 %Belkin BW&G,LLP -270 Mad Av -NY 10016
(212) 599-1717 .. **Lieber,** Alan H '87 (Barnett EGK&L,PC) -122 E 42nd -NY 10168
(212) 949-5586 .. **Lieber,** Barbie D '88 (Lieber & L,LLP) -60 E 42nd -NY 10165 **Fx:**949-5587
(212) 949-5585 .. **Lieber,** Bruce J '86 (Lieber & L,LLP) -60 E 42nd -NY 10165 **Fx:**949-5587
(518) 374-2146 .. **Lieber,** Danl F '05 -36 Irving Rd -Scotia 12302
(212) 827-5400 .. **Lieber,** Edw B '01 %Disney Theatrical Grp -214 W 42nd -NY 10036
(212) 267-5333 .. **Lieber,** Erik '81 (Lieber & G) -11 Park Pl -NY 10007
(212) 267-5333 .. **Lieber & Gary** -11 Park Pl -NY 10007 **Fx:**267-6168
(212) 218-2100 .. **Lieber,** Natalie D '09 %Fitzpatrick CH&S -1290 Av of Amer -NY 10104
(212) 326-3939 .. **Lieber,** Sarah E '04 %Jones D -222 E 41st -NY 10017
(212) 668-8400 .. **Lieberman,** Ari R '10 %L Grandelli,PC -90 Broad -NY 10004 **Fx:**483-0918
(212) 922-9250 .. **Lieberman,** Arthur M '64 OfCnsl Ganfer & S LLP -360 Lex Av -NY 10017
(516) 222-0888 .. **Lieberman,** Audra T '07 %Lehman & E LLP -50 Chas Lindbergh Blvd -Uniondale 11553
(212) 788-1678 .. **Lieberman,** Brian D '02 Law Dept -100 Church -NY 10007 **Fx:**788-0367

(480) 607-9700 .. **Lieberman**, Bruce R '65 -Bx231244 -Gt Neck 11023 **Fx:**607-9424
(212) 483-1444 .. **Lieberman**, Danl J '91 %A Gross -50 Bway -NY 10004 **Fx:**483-1480
(212) 455-2000 .. **Lieberman**, David '90 (Simpson T&B LLP) -425 Lex Av -NY 10017
(212) 608-3500 .. **Lieberman**, David H '70 (Beckman L&B LLP) -116 John -NY 10038
(212) 607-3300 .. **Lieberman**, Donna E '74 %NYCLU -125 Broad -NY 10004
(212) 765-9100 .. **Lieberman**, Donna H '84 OfCnsl Halperin BR,LLP -555 Mad Av -NY 10022
(516) 935-2330 .. **Lieberman**, Douglas M '87 (Markotsis & L) -183 Bway -Hicksvll 11801
(516) 741-1040 .. **Lieberman**, Edw L '78 (Librett F&L,LLP) -1325 Franklin Av -Gdn Cty 11530
(914) 347-2213 .. **Lieberman**, Edw M '75 -114 Cedar Hill Rd -Bedfrd 10506
(914) 993-1546 .. **Lieberman**, Edw M '75 %Town Atty -177 Hillside Av -Greenburgh 10607 **Fx:**993-1656
(212) 909-6000 .. **Lieberman**, Ellen '81 Cnsl Debevoise & P LLP -919 3rd Av -NY 10022
(212) 254-1111 .. **Lieberman**, Eric M '74 (Rabinowitz BSK&L,PC) -111 Bway -NY 10006
(212) 552-1815 .. **Lieberman**, Frederic L '80 JP Morgan Chase & Co -1 Chase Manahttan Plz -NY 10081 **Fx:**552-1630
(212) 245-6754 .. **Lieberman**, Gary A '84 -7 Penn Plz -NY 10001 **Fx:**956-7549
(212) 471-6220 .. **Lieberman**, Hal R '71 (Hinshaw & C LLP) -780 3rd Av -NY 10017
(212) 878-8013 .. **Lieberman**, Jeffrey A '85 (Clifford C LLP) -31 W 52nd -NY 10019
(212) 661-1100 .. **Lieberman**, Jeremy A '03 %Pomerantz HG&G LLP -100 Park Av -NY 10017
(212) 431-2378 .. **Lieberman**, Jethro K '67 %NY Law Schl -185 W Bway -NY 10013 **Fx:**431-8193
(718) 499-6777 .. **Lieberman**, Joan A '91 -320 7th Av -Brklyn 11215 **Fx:**228-4808
(212) 339-8930 .. **Lieberman**, Joan Wiesen '82 Cnsl T Pieniek,PC -1 Old Cntry Rd -Carle Pl 11514 **Fx:**(516) 280-3405
(914) 686-6648 .. **Lieberman**, Joel B '67 -66 Richbell Rd -White Plns 10605 **Fx:**288-9887
(212) 333-1029 .. **Lieberman**, Jonathan A '92 %Polygram Holding,Inc -825 8th Av -NY 10019
(212) 455-2000 .. **Lieberman**, Jonathan A '09 %Simpson T&B LLP -425 Lex Av -NY 10017
(800) 333-6524 .. **Lieberman**, Kirsty M '02 Merrill Lynch -222 Bway -NY 10038
(212) 687-2770 .. **Lieberman**, Lance J '76 (Cohen PL&P) -551 5th Av -NY 10176
(914) 962-0400 .. **Lieberman & LeBovit** -334 Underhill Av -Yorktwn Hts 10598 **Fx:**962-0498
(315) 425-2700 .. **Lieberman**, Leigh A '05 %Hiscock & B,LLP -One Park Pl -Syracuse 13202
(718) 250-2000 .. **Lieberman**, Lewis E '95 %DA -350 Jay -Brklyn 11201 **Fx:**250-2314
(212) 317-1133 .. **Lieberman**, Marc N '06 Realex Capital -444 Mad Av -NY 10022
(516) 426-9500 .. **Lieberman**, Mark L '75 -900 Merchants Cncrs -Westbury 11590 **Fx:**228-6569
(516) 496-8300 .. **Lieberman**, Martin L '71 OfCnsl Santemma & D,LLC -575 Underhill Blvd -Syosset 11791 **Fx:**496-8303
(718) 783-0849 .. **Lieberman**, Marvin '59 -154 St Johns Pl -Brklyn 11217
(914) 347-2600 .. **Lieberman**, Meryl R '82 (Traub LS&S LLP) -7 Skyline Dr -Hawthorne 10532
(914) 962-0400 .. **Lieberman**, Mitchell P '85 (Lieberman & L) -334 Underhill Av -Yorktwn Hts 10598
(212) 735-3000 .. **Lieberman**, Nancy Ann '80 (Skadden ASM&F LLP) -4 Times Sq -NY 10036
(516) 227-0700 .. **Lieberman**, Nancy D '86 (Farrell F,PC) -1320 RXR Plz -Uniondale 11556
(212) 373-3000 .. **Lieberman**, Neil R '09 Paul WRW&G LLP -1285 Av of Amer -NY 10019
(212) 940-8800 .. **Lieberman**, Nina E Abraham '02 SpclCnsl Katten MR LLP -575 Mad Av -NY 10022
(718) 254-0700 .. **Lieberman**, Paul '80 %Bklyn Defender Srvcs -177 Lvngstn -Brklyn 11201 **Fx:**254-0897
(914) 328-0404 .. **Lieberman**, Penny Ann '86 (Jackson L LLP) -1 N Bway -White Plns 10601
(212) 947-3793 .. **Lieberman**, Saml J '01 OfCnsl Sadis & G LLP -551 5th Av -NY 10176
(212) 804-4200 .. **Lieberman**, Sara F '06 %Mound CW&G -One Bttry Pk Plz -NY 10004
(518) 242-3740 .. **Lieberman**, Scott '98 %Ct of Claims -Justice Bldg ESP Bx7344 -Albany 12224 **Fx:**432-3450
(212) 421-4100 .. **Lieberman**, Seth H '05 %Pryor C LLP -7 Times Sq -NY 10036
(718) 250-2000 .. **Lieberman**, Seth M '83 %DA -350 Jay -Brklyn 11201 **Fx:**250-2314
(212) 421-1700 .. **Lieberman**, Stefanie E '01 Janklow & Nesbit Assoc -445 Park Av -NY 10022
(212) 577-3688 .. **Lieberman Cohen**, Laura J '97 %Leg Aid -199 Water -NY 10038 **Fx:**509-8431
(716) 488-3090 .. **Liebers**, Robt A '84 (Burgett & R) -15 E 5th Bx3090 -Jamestwn 14702
(718) 544-0884 .. **Liebersohn**, Danl E '89 -45 Bramblebrook Rd -Ardsley 10502
(212) 931-1245 .. **Lieberson**, Miriam '92 Worldnow -747 3rd Av -NY 10017
(212) 589-4200 .. **Lieberstein**, Eugene '65 OfCnsl Baker & H LLP -45 Rckfllr Plz -NY 10111
(212) 775-8700 .. **Lieberstein**, Marc A '93 (Kilpatrick S,LLP) -31 W 52nd -NY 10019
(518) 761-6207 .. **Liebert**, Glenn B '06 Warren Cnty Pub Def -1340 State Route 9 -Lk George 12845
(212) 226-3292 .. **Liebert**, Lisa Kolb '77 -257 Church -NY 10013 **Fx:**246-0565
(212) 548-1550 .. **Lieberthal**, Keith L '01 Tommy Hilfiger USA,Inc -601 W 26th -NY 10001
(212) 806-2966 .. **Liebes**, Hal '90 Fred Aiger & Co,Inc -111 5th Av -NY 10003
(212) 804-5740 .. **Liebesman Martiniuk**, Ruth '89 -110 Wall -NY 10005 **Fx:**(201) 617-7710
(212) 335-9000 .. **Liebhafsky**, Douglas S '65 %DA -1 Hogan Pl -NY 10013
(212) 779-1414 .. **Liebhard**, Sandy A '90 (Bernstein L LLP) -10 E 40th -NY 10016
(212) 486-9494 .. **Liebhardt**, Nadine S '74 -488 Mad Av -NY 10022 **Fx:**486-0701
(212) 268-7535 .. **Liebhauser**, Lynda E '99 OfCnsl Bonner KT&C,LLP -350 5th Av -NY 10118
(315) 703-6600 .. **Liebler**, Lewis '86 %Leg Aid -472 S Salina -Syracuse 13202 **Fx:**671-0062
(914) 935-1249 .. **Lieblich**, Herman '47 -8 Meeting House Ln -Rye Brook 10573
(212) 944-0900 .. **Lieblich**, Kenneth M '83 (Mishaan D&L) -1370 Bway -NY 10018
(212) 237-1000 .. **Liebling**, Chas B '01 (Windels ML&M,LLP) -156 W 56th -NY 10019
(212) 309-8100 .. **Liebman**, Allyson Stemple '99 %Lexis/Nexis -125 Park Av -NY 10017 **Fx:**309-8187
(212) 545-7373 .. **Liebman**, Barry B '87 %K Wilhelm -445 Park Av -NY 10022 **Fx:**545-9093
(212) 854-0678 .. **Liebman**, Benjamin L '00 %Columbia Law Schl -435 W 116th -NY 10027 **Fx:**854-7946
(518) 445-2311 .. **Liebman**, Bennett '75 Albany Law Schl -80 New Scotland Av -Albany 12208 **Fx:**445-2315
(212) 854-8557 .. **Liebman**, Carol Bensinger '93 %Columbia Law Schl -435 W 116th -NY 10027 **Fx:**854-7946
(212) 619-6287 .. **Liebman**, Chas D '93 (Johnson L,LLP) -305 Bway -NY 10007 **Fx:**619-1358
(212) 213-6681 .. **Liebman**, David E '74 -350 Bway -NY 10013 **Fx:**625-3939
(518) 457-2153 .. **Liebman**, Deborah R '81 %Dept of Tax & Fin -Bldg 9 State Campus -Albany 12227 **Fx:**457-6131
(212) 969-3000 .. **Liebman**, Donald '85 SrCnsl Proskauer R LLP -1585 Bway -NY 10036
(516) 766-5426 .. **Liebman**, Jos I '70 -20 Strathmore Ln -Rockvll Ctr 11570 **Fx:**(815) 550-9691
(516) 747-7400 .. **Liebman**, Joshua M '09 %Rosenberg C&B LLP -100 Grdn City Plz -Gdn Cty 11530
(212) 854-5699 .. **Liebman**, Lance M '95 %Columbia Law Schl -435 W 116th -NY 10027 **Fx:**854-7946
(914) 698-3313 .. **Liebman**, Lynn Abelson '87 %Lichtenstein & S -158 W Bstn Post Rd -Mamaroneck 10543
(914) 323-7000 .. **Liebman**, Nicole B '09 %Wilson EME&D LLP -3 Gannett Dr -White Plns 10604
(718) 987-5070 .. **Liebman**, Raymond L '74 -43 New Dorp Plz -Staten Isl 10306 **Fx:**987-5046
(212) 653-8874 .. **Liebman**, Richd M '81 (Liebman & S LLC) -330 Mad Av -NY 10017 **Fx:**(646) 495-5006
(212) 265-6888 .. **Liebman**, Scott S '06 %Porzio B&N,PC -156 W 56th -NY 10019
(516) 328-5191 .. **Liebman**, Seymour E '89 %Canon USA -1 Canon Plz -Lk Success 11042 **Fx:**328-5193
(646) 386-3662 .. **Liebman**, Steven E '78 Supreme Ct Spcl Referee -60 Centre -NY 10007
(347) 404-9244 .. **Liebman**, Susan Ann '92 %Hon D Thomas-Supreme Ct -360 Adams -Brklyn 11201
(518) 445-3221 .. **Liebman-Alperson**, Laura A '09 Albany Law Schl -80 New Scotland Av -Albany 12208 **Fx:**445-2315
(212) 449-4353 .. **Liebmann**, Bradley N '90 %Merrill Lynch -220 Bway -NY 10038
(585) 425-0865 .. **Liebmann**, Felix G '51 -31 Dunbrdg Heights -Fairprt 14450
(212) 701-3000 .. **Liebmann**, Geoffrey E '87 (Cahill G&R LLP) -80 Pine -NY 10005 **Fx:**269-5420
(212) 839-5300 .. **Liebmann**, Jeff S '79 (Sidley A LLP) -787 7th Av -NY 10019
(516) 463-4736 .. **Liebmann**, Theodor S '96 %Hofstra Law Schl -121 Hofstra Univ -Hempstd 11549
(212) 286-1384 .. **Liebolt**, F Lee Jr. '68 -420 Lex Av -NY 10170
(212) 558-4000 .. **Liebov**, David '76 Sullivan & C LLP -125 Broad -NY 10004
(212) 767-8939 .. **Liebowitz**, Amy J '95 %Comedy Central -1775 Bway -NY 10019 **Fx:**767-8592
(212) 307-0440 .. **Liebowitz**, Elise G '85 -250 W 57th -NY 10107 **Fx:**977-7035
(212) 779-8600 .. **Liebowitz**, Jeffrey B '93 %Silverman SS&B PLLC -381 Park Av S -NY 10016
(212) 345-1739 .. **Liebowitz**, Marianne Ashley '96 Marsh & McLennan Cos -1166 Av of Amer -NY 10036 **Fx:**345-4808
(914) 995-3419 .. **Liebowitz**, Mary A '99 %DA -111 Martin Luther King Blvd -White Plns 10601 **Fx:**995-3363
(212) 790-9200 .. **Liebowitz**, Sidney I '47 (Cowan L&L,PC) -1133 Av of Amer -NY 10036
(518) 486-1895 .. **Liebschutz**, Elizabeth Hoffman '91 %Dept Pub Srvc -3 ESP -Albany 12223
(585) 987-2800 .. **Liebschutz**, John F '77 (Woods OG LLP) -2 State -Rchstr 14614
(718) 528-5800 .. **Liechtung**, Chas C '79 -30 S Central Av -Vly Stream 11580 **Fx:**528-0066
(212) 825-1212 .. **Liederman**, Arthur J '78 (Morrison M LLP) -17 State -NY 10004
(212) 752-9700 .. **Lief**, Jason A '96 (Gersten S LLP) -600 Lex Av -NY 10022
(212) 351-4500 .. **Lief**, Stephen J '83 Cnsl Epstein B&G,PC -250 Park Av -NY 10177
(212) 355-9500 .. **Lieff Cabraser Heimann & Bernstein, LLP** -250 Hudson -NY 10013 **Fx:**355-9592
(631) 360-7570 .. **Lieffrig**, Yvonne '85 %Town Atty -99 W Main -Smithtwn 11787 **Fx:**360-7719
(315) 472-6388 .. **Liegel**, Robt G '64 (Failmezger & L) -202 N Townsend -Syracuse 13203
(212) 474-1000 .. **Liekefett**, Kai Haakon E '08 %Cravath S&M LLP -825 8th Av -NY 10019
(212) 458-2910 .. **Liell**, James T '98 %AIG -175 Water -NY 10038
(718) 725-3200 .. **Lien**, Ferron A '09 Admin Children's Srvcs -151-20 Jamaica Av -Jamaica 11432
(212) 848-4000 .. **Lienau**, Odette '08 %Shearman & S LLP -599 Lex Av -NY 10022
(646) 602-5667 .. **Lienhard**, Wm G '98 %Urban Justice Ctr -123 William -NY 10038 **Fx:**(212) 533-4598
(973) 228-5700 .. **Lienhardt**, Debra C '98 (Brach E LLC) -100 Park Av -NY 10017 **Fx:**228-7852
(212) 848-4000 .. **Liersaph**, Gretchen D '05 %Shearman & S LLP -599 Lex Av -NY 10022
(631) 232-2400 .. **Liese**, Barbara '90 %Nassau/Sfflk Law Srv -1757 Vets Hwy -Islandia 11749 **Fx:**232-2489
(516) 248-6400 .. **Lieser**, David I '97 %Davidoff M&H,LLP -200 Grdn City Plz -Gdn Cty 11530
(212) 293-9400 .. **Lieu**, Susanne J '00 %Lawr Ruben Co -600 Mad Av -NY 10022 **Fx:**293-9401
(212) 345-3342 .. **Life**, Kevin J '89 Marsh USA Inc -1166 Av of the Americas -NY 10036
(212) 487-9701 .. **Liferiedge**, Brian S '93 %Robin HK&F -1 Bttry Pk Plz -NY 10014
(212) 336-0593 .. **Lifeso**, Catherine E '01 %SEC -3 World Fncl Ctr -NY 10281 **Fx:**336-1323
(212) 357-0232 .. **Liff**, Allison R '01 Goldman Sachs -1 NY Plz -NY 10004
(212) 768-6700 .. **Lifflander**, Matthew L '58 OfCnsl Sonnenschein N&R LLP -1221 Av of Amer -NY 10020
(212) 332-8820 .. **Lifflander & Reich LLP** -1221 Av of Amer -NY 10020 **Fx:**332-8821
(212) 751-2700 .. **Lifland**, John C '60 %JAMS -620 8th Av -NY 10018 **Fx:**751-4099

(516) 569-1687 .. **Lifland,** Thos A '69 -383 Donmoor Rd -Lawrence 11559 **Fx:**569-1929
(212) 788-7000 .. **Lifrak,** Saphora M '86 %City Cncl Leg Div -250 Bway -NY 10007 **Fx:**788-7034
(212) 592-1400 .. **Lifschitz,** I Nathaniel '06 %Herrick,F LLP -2 Park Av -NY 10016
(718) 286-6000 .. **Lifschitz,** Jeanette '80 %DA -125-01 Qns Blvd -Kew Gdns 11415
(518) 432-1200 .. **Lifset,** Marc J '79 (McGlinchey S PLLC) -194 Wshngtn Av -Albany 12210
(212) 227-4210 .. **Lifsey,** Susan V '00 %Weg & M,PC -52 Duane -NY 10007
(212) 832-9318 .. **Lifshey,** Deborah L '94 Pearl Meyer & Prtnrs -445 Park Av -NY 10022
(212) 863-6300 .. **Lifshey,** Robt '83 %HPD -100 Gold -NY 10038 **Fx:**863-8201
(845) 340-3888 .. **Lifshin-Clark,** Beth '98 Hon EM Kavanagh -1 Pearl -Kingston 12401 **Fx:**340-3893
(914) 448-0200 .. **Lifshitz,** Benai L '08 %Bartlett MB&M,LLP -81 Main -White Plns 10601
(212) 213-6222 .. **Lifshitz,** Joshua M '94 (Bull & L,LLP) -18 E 41st -NY 10017
(212) 949-8989 .. **Lifshutz,** Ian R '00 (Lifshutz & L,PC) -501 5th Av -NY 10017 **Fx:**922-9620
(212) 949-8989 .. **Lifshutz,** Marvin L '55 (Lifshutz & L,PC) -501 5th Av -NY 10017 **Fx:**922-9620
(914) 375-0100 .. **Lifson,** Peter A '77 (Novick ELRW&L,PC) -733 Ynkrs Av -Ynkrs 10704
(516) 571-2475 .. **Lifson,** Robt A '75 Hon D Martin -100 Supreme Ct Dr -Mineola 11501 **Fx:**571-0458
(212) 478-0000 .. **Liftin,** John M '67 DE Shaw & Co -120 W 45th -NY 10036 **Fx:**478-0100
(212) 837-6000 .. **Lifton,** Diane E '92 (Hughes H&R LLP) -1 Bttry Pk Plz -NY 10004
(212) 538-6278 .. **Lifton,** Mary Connell '05 Credit Suisse -11 Mad Av -NY 10010
(877) 725-5442 .. **Liga,** Salvatore J '95 Liga Law Grp PC -520 Wht Plns Rd -Tarrytwn 10591 **Fx:**(917) 591-8818
(716) 754-8046 .. **Ligammari,** Andrew A '86 -637 79th -Niagara Fls 14304
(212) 566-6880 .. **Ligansky,** Robt '83 -80 Maiden Ln -NY 10038
(212) 464-2350 .. **Ligas-Hadjandreas,** Katerina '02 JP Morgan Chase -345 Park Av -NY 10154
(212) 737-5754 .. **Ligelis,** Calliope K '79 (Ligelis & Associates) -501 E 79th -NY 10075 **Fx:**737-5754
(212) 474-1000 .. **Ligelis,** Gregory J Jr. '10 %Cravath S&M LLP -825 8th Av -NY 10019
(212) 619-0156 .. **Liggio,** Paul A '59 -111 John -NY 10038 **Fx:**406-3677
(212) 389-5000 .. **Ligh,** Peter '02 %Sutherland A&B LLP -1114 Av of Amer -NY 10036
(212) 751-1700 .. **Light,** Bill S '82 (Jaffe R&L LLP) -880 3rd Av -NY 10022
(914) 948-5525 .. **Light,** Dennis W '02 DW Light,PLLC -149 Grand -White Plns 10601 **Fx:**761-5444
(718) 237-5500 .. **Light,** Jennifer L '99 %Leg Srvcs -105 Court -Brklyn 11201 **Fx:**855-0733
(212) 446-4800 .. **Light,** Russell '09 (Kirkland & E LLP) -153 E 53rd -NY 10022
(212) 637-2774 .. **Light,** Sarah E '01 %US Atty -86 Chmbrs -NY 10007
(646) 315-7333 .. **Light,** Susan '82 %FINRA -14 Wall -NY 10005 **Fx:**315-7440
(718) 579-7912 .. **Light,** Vicki E '85 %Leg Aid -900 Sheridan Av -Bronx 10451 **Fx:**293-8744
(914) 235-3200 .. **Light,** Warren M '67 %Goldfarb Prop -524 North Av -New Rchll 10801 **Fx:**235-8760
(315) 682-9198 .. **Lightcap,** Kerry M '94 AFSCME Cncl 66 -8108 Cazenovia Rd -Manlius 13104 **Fx:**682-9254
(315) 453-3053 .. **Lightcap,** Victoria Lieb '90 %Finkelstein & Prtnrs,LLP -716 7th N -Liverpool 13088
(212) 906-1200 .. **Lightdale,** Sarah M '06 %Latham & W -885 3rd Av -NY 10022
(212) 371-8730 .. **Lighter,** Lawr '62 -488 Mad Av -NY 10022 **Fx:**753-3630
(646) 213-5100 .. **Lightman,** Douglas M '05 WTAS -452 5th Av -NY 10018
(212) 891-1600 .. **Lightner,** Mark A '09 %Jenner & B LLP -919 3rd Av -NY 10022
(585) 394-3930 .. **Lightsey,** Mary Walpole '95 -21 Sly -Canandaigua 14424 **Fx:**394-3276
(631) 853-4104 .. **Lightstone,** Jessica L '05 %DA -400 Carleton Av Bx9082 -Central Islip 11722 **Fx:**853-7838
(212) 669-2225 .. **Ligorio,** Mario E '77 %DCAS-DLS -1 Centre -NY 10007 **Fx:**669-8558
(718) 238-6800 .. **Ligresti,** Paul '99 %DiConza LD&K -478 Bay Ridge Pkwy -Brklyn 11209
(212) 763-1638 .. **Liguori,** Albert W '00 Alvarez & Marsal Taxand,LLC -125 Park Av -NY 10017
(518) 713-2144 .. **Liguori,** John W '93 (Rehfuss L & Assoc,PC) -40 British Amer Blvd -Latham 12110 **Fx:**713-2148
(646) 885-4786 .. **Liguori,** Madelynn '00 %Dept Sanitation -125 Worth -NY 10013 **Fx:**(212) 791-3824
(212) 303-1634 .. **Liguori,** Marcello '00 MSD Capital,LP -645 5th Av -NY 10022
(845) 279-2986 .. **Liguori,** Michl T '03 %Hogan & R -1441 Route 22 -Brewstr 10509
(315) 788-6984 .. **Liinve,** Mai L '77 -482 Bugbee Dr -Watertwn 13601
(212) 521-5400 .. **Liivak,** Andres '00 (Reed S LLP) -599 Lex Av -NY 10022
(732) 682-1403 .. **Lijoi,** Peter B '88 Cnsl Fairfield Residential,LLC -73 2nd Av -NY 10003 **Fx:**273-6926
(631) 669-3000 .. **Like,** Irving '50 (Reilly LT&M) -179 Little East Neck Rd N -Babylon 11702
(718) 590-3607 .. **Liker,** Howard '82 %Civil Ct -851 Grnd Cncrs -Bronx 10451 **Fx:**590-7294
(716) 565-2000 .. **Likoudis,** Michl '56 -17 Beresford Ct -Williamsvll 14221 **Fx:**565-2002
(631) 501-5700 .. **Likourezos,** George '96 (Carter DF&S LLP) -445 Broadhallow Rd -Melvll 11747
(716) 853-9555 .. **Lilac,** Dean E Jr. '05 %Leg Aid -237 Main -Buffalo 14203 **Fx:**853-3219
(212) 416-8490 .. **Lilien,** Jason R '96 %Dept of Law -120 Bway -NY 10271
(212) 906-1200 .. **Lilien,** Warren H '01 (Latham & W) -885 3rd Av -NY 10022
(212) 683-3344 .. **Lilienfeld,** Carol '72 -708 3rd Av -NY 10017 **Fx:**286-8481
(212) 848-4000 .. **Lilienfeld,** Doreen E '95 (Shearman & S LLP) -599 Lex Av -NY 10022
(716) 496-5568 .. **Lillenstein,** Mark A '73 (Lillenstein Law Ofcs) -22 Smith Av -Delevan 14042
(212) 554-7800 .. **Lillienstein,** Robt D '84 OfCnsl Moses & S LLP -405 Lex Av -NY 10174
(212) 872-1000 .. **Lilling,** Austin S '01 -One Bryant Park -NY 10036 **Fx:**872-1002
(516) 487-5800 .. **Lilling,** Caryn L '93 (Mauro G&L LLP) -60 Cuttermill Rd -Gt Neck 11021
(716) 633-3313 .. **Lilling,** Richd A '95 (Milber MP&S LLP) -2809 Wehrle Dr -Williamsvll 14221
(212) 430-0800 .. **Lillis,** John T Jr. '77 (Kennedy LS&E) -75 Maiden Ln -NY 10038
(212) 819-8200 .. **Lillis,** John T '81 (White & C LLP) -1155 Av of Amer -NY 10036
(716) 636-9181 .. **Lillis,** Tara B '88 -10 John James Audubon Pkwy -Buffalo 14228
(212) 841-4230 .. **Lillvis,** Matthew H '04 %Millennium Mgmt LLC -666 5th Av -NY 10103
(212) 687-6523 .. **Lilly,** Jos H III '89 -60 E 42nd -NY 10165 **Fx:**687-6526
(516) 742-7777 .. **Lilly,** Jos P '93 %Frazer & F,LLP -1415 Kellum Pl -Gdn Cty 11530
(631) 736-6633 .. **Lilly,** Lisa M '94 -396 Middle Cntry Rd -Coram 11727 **Fx:**736-6065
(516) 794-9460 .. **Lilly,** Thos J '62 SrCnsl O'Donnell SG&L,LLP -245 Hillside Av -Williston Pk 11596
(516) 794-9460 .. **Lilly,** Thos J Jr. '85 (O'Donnell SG&L,LLP) -245 Hillside Av -Williston Pk 11596
(212) 225-2000 .. **Lim,** Anna Francesca '08 %Cleary GS&H -1 Lbrty Plz -NY 10006
(212) 909-6000 .. **Lim,** Byungkwon '89 (Debevoise & P LLP) -919 3rd Av -NY 10022
(212) 629-8585 .. **Lim,** Chas '02 SrCnsl Ellenberg & Prtnrs LLP -575 8th Av -NY 10018
(212) 841-1139 .. **Lim,** Danl '04 -620 8th Av -NY 10018 **Fx:**841-1010
(718) 358-8935 .. **Lim,** Elisa '80 -171-12 Nrthrn Blvd -Flushng 11358
(212) 619-5355 .. **Lim,** Fidelio L '81 -65 Bway -NY 10006
(212) 761-2231 .. **Lim,** Fredk B '97 Morgan Stanley -1585 Bway -NY 10036
(212) 735-3000 .. **Lim,** Glen K '04 %Skadden ASM&F LLP -4 Times Sq -NY 10036
(212) 326-3939 .. **Lim,** Graham '06 %Jones D -222 E 41st -NY 10017
(212) 426-3091 .. **Lim,** Justin Jose RS '07 Leg Aid -230 E 106th -NY 10029 **Fx:**(646) 616-4091
(212) 813-5900 .. **Lim,** Karen Bee Geok '05 %Fross ZL&Z,PC -866 UN Plz -NY 10017
(212) 776-5027 .. **Lim,** Lisa S '93 NYC Housing Auth -250 Bway -NY 10007 **Fx:**776-5039
(212) 225-2000 .. **Lim,** Soo Yeun '09 %Cleary GS&H -1 Lbrty Plz -NY 10006
(212) 307-8000 .. **Lim,** Stanley W '01 Gelfand Rennert&Feldman -360 Hmltn Av -White Plns 10601
(845) 562-0203 .. **Lim,** Steven '84 (Finkelstein & Prtnrs,LLP) -1279 Route 300 Bx1111 -Newburgh 12550
(212) 601-9700 .. **Lim,** Thailary '07 %Ginarte OGG&W,LLP -225 Bway -NY 10007
(212) 260-2079 .. **Lim,** Thos E '87 -505 E 14th -NY 10009
(914) 332-5800 .. **Lim,** Tillie '85 Hitachi -50 Prospect Av -Tarrytwn 10591 **Fx:**332-5555
(212) 964-6611 .. **Lim,** Tomas B '97 %Lester SK&D -120 Bway -NY 10271
(718) 461-8787 .. **Lim,** Wonshick '88 -3812 150th -Flushng 11354 **Fx:**461-8488
(212) 735-3000 .. **Lima,** Augusto C '09 %Skadden ASM&F LLP -4 Times Sq -NY 10036
(914) 788-0990 .. **Lima & Baresich LLC** -30 Dickerson Rd -Cortlandt Manor 10567 **Fx:**788-0440
(718) 281-2700 .. **Lima & Baresich LLC** -210-12 32nd Av -Bayside 11361 **Fx:**281-2468
(718) 281-2700 .. **Lima,** Paul X '90 (Lima & B LLC) -210-12 32nd Av -Bayside 11361
(212) 309-1000 .. **Lima,** Paulo R '06 %Hunton & W -200 Park Av -NY 10166
(212) 225-2000 .. **Liman,** Lewis J '88 (Cleary GS&H) -1 Lbrty Plz -NY 10006
(718) 370-7030 .. **Limani,** Flutra '96 %Amabile & E,PC -1000 South Av -Staten Isl 10314
(212) 940-8800 .. **Limardo,** Mark A '88 (Katten MR LLP) -575 Mad Av -NY 10022
(212) 219-7655 .. **Limb,** Ben Q '85 -180 Prince -NY 10012
(212) 349-6009 .. **Limb,** Esther H '05 Sanctuary fo Families -67 Wall Bx1406 -NY 10268
(212) 458-3606 .. **Limb,** John J '02 AIG -175 Water -NY 10038
(212) 236-6077 .. **Limerick,** Robt C Jr. '95 %Merrill Lynch -250 Vesey South Twr -NY 10080 **Fx:**236-8758
(516) 877-8100 .. **Limmer,** Brian M '83 -114 Old Cntry Rd -Mineola 11501 **Fx:**877-8706
(212) 557-7292 .. **Limmer,** H Robt '60 -333 E 45th -NY 10017 **Fx:**983-6517
(212) 310-8000 .. **Limmer,** Sam C '10 %Weil G&M LLP -767 5th Av -NY 10153
(516) 742-2300 .. **Limmer,** Scott J '94 (Limmer & Assoc,PLLC) -200 Old Cntry Rd -Mineola 11501 **Fx:**742-1605
(516) 829-6900 .. **Limmer,** Stephen G '72 (Ackerman LCB&L,LLP) -1010 Nrthrn Blvd -Gt Neck 11021
(212) 460-2571 .. **Limmiatis,** Paul '99 %ConEd -4 Irving Pl -NY 10003
(516) 747-6400 .. **Limoncelli,** Gary L '89 NAI Claims Cnsltng,Inc -850 Fulton -Farmngdl 11735 **Fx:**741-1700
(212) 880-3800 .. **Limoncelli,** Gregory T '84 (Akerman S) -335 Mad Av -NY 10017
(516) 742-3777 .. **Limoncelli,** Jerry J '54 (Limoncelli & S) -229 7th -Gdn Cty 11530
(516) 742-3777 .. **Limoncelli & Sperendi** -229 7th -Gdn Cty 11530 **Fx:**742-1321
(516) 496-5822 .. **Limone,** Geraldine S '05 %T Spina -170 Froehlich Farm Blvd -Woodbury 11797 **Fx:**496-5420
(914) 632-4700 .. **Limongello,** Andrea '09 %McDonough Law Firm, LLP -145 Huguenot -New Rchll 10801
(212) 801-6574 .. **Limpert,** Nathan A '01 (Greenberg T,LLP) -200 Park Av -NY 10166
(631) 665-9547 .. **Limpert,** Philip A Jr. '64 -130 Orinoco Dr Bx336 -Brightwtrs 11718 **Fx:**666-4759
(212) 440-7428 .. **Limpus,** Andrea Johnson '02 CNA Global -40 Wall -NY 10005
(212) 940-8800 .. **Lin,** Aimee S '02 %Katten MR LLP -575 Mad Av -NY 10022
(212) 504-6000 .. **Lin,** Alexander T '98 SpclCnsl Cadwalader W&T LLP -1 World Fncl Ctr -NY 10281
(212) 468-4800 .. **Lin,** Allie '03 %Davis & G LLP -1740 Bway -NY 10019
(212) 735-8600 .. **Lin,** Alvin C '01 %Morrison C LLP -909 3rd Av -NY 10022
(212) 506-5000 .. **Lin,** Andrew '10 %Orrick H&S LLP -51 W 52nd -NY 10019
(212) 259-8000 .. **Lin,** Angela K '07 %Dewey & L LLP -1301 Av of Amer -NY 10019
(212) 545-6108 .. **Lin,** Anthony K '02 %IncisiveMedia /NYLJ -120 Bway -NY 10271
(718) 780-0339 .. **Lin,** Chih Wei '06 %Bklyn Law Schl -250 Joralemon -Brklyn 11201 **Fx:**780-0393
(212) 608-6500 .. **Lin,** David D '04 OfCnsl DeHeng C,LLC -225 Bway -NY 10007
(212) 728-2200 .. **Lin,** David X '10 %Axinn V&H LLP -114 W 47th -NY 10036
(212) 536-3900 .. **Lin,** Dean Chih '05 %K&L Gates LLP -599 Lex Av -NY 10022
(516) 938-3100 .. **Lin,** En-Chia Anna '08 %P Roach & Assoc,PC -125 Michl Dr -Syosset 11791 **Fx:**931-4403
(718) 579-3149 .. **Lin,** Felicia H '09 Legal Aid -1020 Grnd Cntrl -Bronx 10451
(917) 237-2900 .. **Lin,** Ivy '05 %Axiom Legal Solutions -75 Spring -NY 10012 **Fx:**(212) 343-7446
(718) 595-7405 .. **Lin,** James F '93 %DEP -59-17 Junction Blvd -Flushng 11373

(212) 335-9000 .. **Lin,** James S '90 %DA -1 Hogan Pl -NY 10013
(212) 906-1200 .. **Lin,** Jennie C '08 %Latham & W -885 3rd Av -NY 10022
(718) 875-1300 .. **Lin,** Jenny Yichun '97 %Appllt Div 2nd Dept -45 Monroe Pl -Brklyn 11201 **Fx:**858-2446
(212) 878-8000 .. **Lin,** Jing '07 %Clifford C LLP -31 W 52nd -NY 10019
(212) 833-1100 .. **Lin,** John C '09 %Friedman KS&A LLP -1633 Bway -NY 10019
(212) 343-9820 .. **Lin,** John Chia-Chang '93 -401 Bway -NY 10013
(212) 403-1000 .. **Lin,** Karen W '10 %Wachtell LR&K -51 W 52nd -NY 10019
(718) 321-3303 .. **Lin,** Kenny D '99 -136-21 Roosevelt Av -Flushng 11354 **Fx:**321-3067
(212) 450-4000 .. **Lin,** Kyoko Takahashi '97 (Davis P&W LLP) -450 Lex Av -NY 10017
(212) 558-4000 .. **Lin,** Li '09 %Sullivan & C LLP -125 Broad -NY 10004
(212) 220-3830 .. **Lin,** Linda D '03 (Nicoletti H&S) -88 Pine -NY 10005
(914) 422-4069 .. **Lin,** Linda M '03 Womens Justice Ctr -78 W Bway -White Plns 10603
(212) 819-8200 .. **Lin,** Lydia E '03 %White & C LLP -1155 Av of Amer -NY 10036
(718) 377-3500 .. **Lin,** Malvina '98 (M Lin,PC) -1203 Av J -Brklyn 11230
(212) 335-8916 .. **Lin,** Mao Yu '02 %DA -1 Hogan Pl -NY 10013
(212) 278-0400 .. **Lin,** Min Michl '08 %Cooper & D LLP -30 Rckfllr Plz -NY 10112
(212) 506-1700 .. **Lin,** Nelson C '04 Kasowitz BT&F LLP -1633 Bway -NY 10019
(212) 506-2500 .. **Lin,** Paula Garrett '03 %Mayer B LLP -1675 Bway -NY 10019
(212) 735-3000 .. **Lin,** Peter S '07 %Skadden ASM&F LLP -4 Times Sq -NY 10036
(212) 643-7000 .. **Lin,** Rachel J '01 %Sills C&G PC -One Rckfllr Plz -NY 10020
(212) 906-1200 .. **Lin,** Raymond Y '86 (Latham & W) -885 3rd Av -NY 10022
(212) 230-8800 .. **Lin,** Ronnie J '08 %WilmerHale -399 Park Av -NY 10022
(212) 596-9000 .. **Lin,** Sensen '09 %Ropes & G LLP -1211 Av of Amer -NY 10036
(718) 352-9800 .. **Lin,** Shiauh-Wei '88 -214-26 41st Av -Bayside 11361
(212) 245-1000 .. **Lin,** Sonia R '10 %Outten & G LLP -3 Park Av -NY 10016
(212) 548-7422 .. **Lin,** Susan L '05 %West Group -530 5th Av -NY 10036 **Fx:**867-2404
(212) 703-8484 .. **Lin,** Tao '97 %Wang & S -305 Mad Av -NY 10165 **Fx:**768-2766
(212) 841-1000 .. **Lin,** Terry H '08 %Covington & B LLP -620 8th Av -NY 10018
(212) 530-1800 .. **Lin,** Timothy E '00 %Richards K&O LLP -1 World Fncl Ctr -NY 10281
(212) 839-5300 .. **Lin,** Udele '09 %Sidley A LLP -787 7th Av -NY 10019
(212) 963-2293 .. **Lin,** Weicheng '95 UN Joint Appls Bd -880 E 44th -NY 10017
(718) 352-9800 .. **Lin,** Wei-Nuoo '88 %SW Lin -214-26 41st Av -Bayside 11361
(212) 808-8100 .. **Lin,** Wilda '04 %Kostelanetz & F,LLP -7 Wrld Trd Ctr -NY 10007
(212) 371-8008 .. **Lin,** Xiaofeng '08 %Guzov O,LLC -600 Mad Av -NY 10022
(212) 455-2000 .. **Lin,** Xiaohui '08 %Simpson T&B LLP -425 Lex Av -NY 10017
(212) 450-4000 .. **Lin,** Xiaoxi '10 %Davis P&W LLP -450 Lex Av -NY 10017
(212) 925-3242 .. **Lin,** Yi '93 -7 Chatham Sq -NY 10038
(718) 579-7900 .. **Linardi,** Michl F '10 Leg Aid -900 Sheridan Av -Bronx 10451 **Fx:**293-8744
(718) 473-0628 .. **Linares,** Boris H '99 (Linares & Assoc,PC) -4022 74th -Jcksn Hts 11372
(212) 504-6000 .. **Linares,** Francisco J '93 SpclCnsl Cadwalader W&T LLP -1 World Fncl Ctr -NY 10281
(212) 426-3000 .. **Linares,** Ivelices '02 Leg Aid -230 E 106th -NY 10029 **Fx:**876-5365
(718) 250-2000 .. **Linares,** Jacqueline M '95 %DA -350 Jay -Brklyn 11201 **Fx:**250-2314
(718) 250-2001 .. **Linares,** Maria Z '97 %DA -350 Jay -Brklyn 11201 **Fx:**250-2314
(718) 947-2490 .. **Lincer,** Brian A '05 -247 Prospect Av -Brklyn 11215 **Fx:**947-1483
(212) 225-2000 .. **Lincer,** Richd S '79 (Cleary GS&H) -1 Lbrty Plz -NY 10006
(212) 225-2000 .. **Linch,** Maureen E '09 %Cleary GS&H -1 Lbrty Plz -NY 10006
(212) 682-8811 .. **Lincoln,** Robt T '67 (Dunnington B&M LLP) -1359 Bway -NY 10018
(212) 360-2380 .. **Lincoln,** Simon J '96 (Lincoln B LLP) -110 E 59th -NY 10022 **Fx:**360-2381
(315) 781-1465 .. **Lind,** Darius K '08 Leg Assistance -361 S Main -Geneva 14456 **Fx:**781-2565
(917) 721-5155 .. **Lind,** Guy S '00 -245 E 84th -NY 10028 **Fx:**(212) 744-8191
(212) 940-3005 .. **Lind,** Kenneth C '78 (Nixon P LLP) -437 Mad Av -NY 10022
(914) 640-6400 .. **Lind,** Patricia Anne '84 %Nine West Group Inc -1129 Wstchstr Av -White Plns 10604
(212) 888-7725 .. **Lind,** Richd B '75 -745 5th Av -NY 10151 **Fx:**371-2961
(212) 931-7875 .. **Lind,** Sylvia E '96 MLB -245 Park Av -NY 10167 **Fx:**949-5657
(718) 548-4092 .. **Linda,** Donna S '84 -4555 H Hdsn Pkwy -Bronx 10471
(212) 450-4000 .. **Lindabury,** Jane '04 %Davis P&W LLP -450 Lex Av -NY 10017
(212) 855-9818 .. **Lindabury,** Jonathan H '01 Goldman Sachs -1 NY Plz -NY 10004
(212) 742-3390 .. **Lindabury McCormick Estabrook & Cooper,PC** -26 Bway -NY 10004 **Fx:**269-5016
(845) 486-6800 .. **Lindars,** Ian C '05 %McCabe & M LLP -63 Wshngtn Bx509 -Poughkeepsie 12602
(212) 558-4000 .. **Lindauer,** Erik D '82 (Sullivan & C LLP) -125 Broad -NY 10004
(315) 637-8307 .. **Lindauer,** John A '75 -4907 Briarwood Ln -Manlius 13104
(212) 323-0254 .. **Lindauer,** Mitchell J '77 OppenheimerFunds,Inc -225 Lbrty -NY 10281 **Fx:**323-4070
(518) 828-3414 .. **Lindauer,** Tracy J '03 %DA -325 Columbia -Hudson 12534 **Fx:**828-8491
(212) 418-8614 .. **Lindberg,** Marian E '83 -757 3rd Av -NY 10017
(718) 590-2000 .. **Lindblom,** Cynthia M '98 %DA -198 E 161st -Bronx 10451 **Fx:**590-6477
(212) 446-4800 .. **Lindblom,** Marjorie Press '95 (Kirkland & E LLP) -153 E 53rd -NY 10022
(518) 857-3901 .. **Lindburg,** Michl R '76 -45 Hills Rd -Loudonvll 12211 **Fx:**434-8457
(212) 488-1300 .. **Linde,** Stephen A '80 (Cohen & P LLP) -444 Mad Av -NY 10022
(212) 373-3000 .. **Linde,** Steven H '09 %Paul WRW&G LLP -1285 Av of Amer -NY 10019
(845) 638-1943 .. **Lindeman,** Devora L '96 SrCnsl Greenwald D LLP -30 Ramland Rd -Orangebrg 10962
(212) 354-8930 .. **Lindemann,** Eric T '96 (Lindemann & L) -25 W 43rd -NY 10036 **Fx:**764-7888
(516) 357-3000 .. **Lindemann,** Erik K '04 %Rivkin R LLP -926 RXR Plz -Uniondale 11556
(631) 853-4161 .. **Lindemann,** Marc A '02 %DA -N Cnty Cmplx Bldg 77 -Hauppauge 11788 **Fx:**853-4192
(212) 861-3331 .. **Linden,** Bella L '56 -165 E 72nd -NY 10021
(212) 264-3650 .. **Linden,** Jeremy A '08 %SSA Ofc Genl Cnsl -26 Fed Plz -NY 10278 **Fx:**264-6372
(212) 689-3929 .. **Linden,** Lawr M '78 -440 Park Av S -NY 10016 **Fx:**252-9991
(212) 344-0099 .. **Linden,** Leonard J '79 -140 Bway -NY 10005
(516) 393-6180 .. **Linden,** Nancy S '93 -Bx9040 -Bethpage 11714 **Fx:**393-6150
(212) 371-6600 .. **Linden,** Peter S '85 (Kirby M LLP) -825 3rd Av -NY 10022
(212) 564-8268 .. **Linden,** Rene M '86 OfCnsl Paparian & Assoc LLC -233 Bway -NY 10279 **Fx:**564-3864
(315) 386-4595 .. **Linden,** Roger B '78 (Oliver Law Firm) -117 Main -Canton 13617 **Fx:**379-1240
(315) 265-2747 .. **Linden,** Roger B '78 (Cappello L&L) -76 Market Bx5153 -Potsdam 13676
(212) 577-3349 .. **Lindenauer,** Susan B '65 Leg Aid -199 Water -NY 10038
(212) 984-7747 .. **Lindenbaum,** Adam J '04 %Warshaw BCS&K,LLP -555 5th Av -NY 10017
(631) 422-2130 .. **Lindenbaum,** Carolyn B '92 %V Berger Jr -133 E Main -Babylon 11702
(800) 782-8656 .. **Lindenbaum,** David G '01 (Cittone & L LLP) -122 W 27th -NY 10001 **Fx:**(212) 624-0244
(212) 532-0154 .. **Lindenbaum,** Herbert G '62 -110 E 59th -NY 10022 **Fx:**532-8221
(914) 941-5668 .. **Lindenbaum,** Jeffrey A '02 %Collen IP -80 S Highland Av -Ossining 10562 **Fx:**941-6091
(212) 891-2100 .. **Lindenbaum,** Philip A '02 Cerberus Capital Mgmnt -299 Park Av -NY 10171
(212) 715-9100 .. **Lindenbaum,** Saml H '60 Cnsl Kramer LN&F,LLP -1177 Av of Amer -NY 10036
(212) 553-3200 .. **Lindenbaum,** Sandford R '74 (Marulli LE&T,LLP) -5 Hanover Sq -NY 10004
(212) 867-4466 .. **Lindenberg,** Lewis A '81 (Belkin BW&G,LLP) -270 Mad Av -NY 10016
(212) 921-1600 .. **Lindenberg,** Mark '96 (Goldberg SL&B,PC) -45 W 45th -NY 10036
(646) 380-0472 .. **Lindenfeld,** Danl A '87 -345 7th Av -NY 10001 **Fx:**380-0473
(315) 655-8325 .. **Lindenfeld,** Harris N '87 (H Lindenfeld,PC) -11 Lincklaen Bx465 -Cazenovia 13035 **Fx:**655-3303
(212) 921-2236 .. **Lindenfelser,** Cecilia M E '93 -60 E 42nd -NY 10165
(212) 687-0100 .. **Lindenman,** Eric H '91 (Harris B PLLC) -100 Wall -NY 10005
(212) 554-7800 .. **Linder,** Alan E '79 (Moses & S LLP) -405 Lex Av -NY 10174
(212) 922-1080 .. **Linder,** Brian D '84 (Clayman & R,LLP) -305 Mad Av -NY 10165
(212) 416-3088 .. **Linder,** Craig A '08 Dow Jones & Co -1211 Av of Amer -NY 10036
(212) 488-1710 .. **Linder,** Herve N '02 (Ernst & L,LLC) -17 Battery Pl -NY 10004 **Fx:**488-1667
(212) 248-3140 .. **Linder,** Justin C '08 %Drinker B&R LLP -140 Bway -NY 10005
(212) 732-3665 .. **Linder,** Mark J '89 (Harmon L&R) -42 Bway -NY 10004
(718) 253-1100 .. **Linder,** Robt B '76 -1642 Coney Isl Av -Brklyn 11230
(516) 883-3856 .. **Linder,** Shari Alexander '94 -66 Barkers Pnt Rd -Sands Pnt 11050
(631) 661-6827 .. **Linder,** Susan S '87 -10 Michalis Ct -W Islip 11795
(212) 758-7600 .. **Linder,** Toby Holbreich '96 %Collazo C&M -747 3rd Av -NY 10017
(716) 632-1644 .. **Linderman,** Danl J '77 %UAW Lgl Srvcs Plan -307 Cayuga Rd -Cheektowaga 14225 **Fx:**632-1897
(212) 478-0000 .. **Lindholm,** J Andrew '98 DE Shaw & Co -120 W 45th -NY 10036
(845) 567-0100 .. **LindHolm,** John A Jr. '84 (Ouimette G&A) -843 Union Av -New Windsor 12553
(212) 530-5000 .. **Lindholm,** Robt L '09 %Milbank TH&M LLP -1 Chase Manh Plz -NY 10005
(845) 291-2454 .. **Lindine,** David A '80 %Leg Aid -2 Court Ln Bx328 -Goshen 10924 **Fx:**294-2638
(212) 858-1728 .. **Lindley,** David M '76 (Pillsbury WSP LLP) -1540 Bway -NY 10036
(212) 984-6670 .. **Lindman,** Linda E '86 CB Richard Ellis -200 Park Av -NY 10166 **Fx:**984-6655
(518) 453-4600 .. **Lindner,** Edw J '81 %Comm Judicial Cndct -ESP -Albany 12223 **Fx:**486-1850
(917) 663-2640 .. **Lindon,** Timothy J '92 Phillip Morris Latin Amer -120 Park Av -NY 10017
(212) 349-5550 .. **Lindover,** Donald I '67 -150 Bway -NY 10038 **Fx:**349-5578
(585) 530-3123 .. **Lindquist,** Christopher D '02 Appllt Div 4th Dept -50 East Av Ste 200 -Rchstr 14604 **Fx:**530-3247
(212) 480-4800 .. **Lindquist,** Eric '94 (Fox H&C LLP) -825 3rd Av -NY 10022
(212) 442-1569 .. **Lindsay,** Andre L '09 %Law Dept -100 Church -NY 10007 **Fx:**788-0367
(518) 274-4360 .. **Lindsay,** Christopher L '85 -15 Deerfld Dr -Brunswick 12180
(212) 412-2690 .. **Lindsay,** David J '99 Barclays Capital -222 Bway -NY 10038
(212) 455-2000 .. **Lindsay,** Emma L '04 %Simpson T&B LLP -425 Lex Av -NY 10017
(212) 660-3000 .. **Lindsay,** George P '74 (Sullivan & W LLP) -1290 Av of Amer -NY 10104
(212) 225-2000 .. **Lindsay,** Ira K '10 %Cleary GS&H -1 Lbrty Plz -NY 10006
(516) 409-6200 .. **Lindsay,** Kathleen '94 %Furey KWM&C,PC -2174 Jackson Av -Seafrd 11783
(212) 351-4000 .. **Lindsay,** Kimberly '09 Gibson D&C LLP -200 Park Av -NY 10166
(716) 285-9555 .. **Lindsay,** Lawr '92 (Viola C&L) -770 Main Bx948 -Niagara Fls 14302
(212) 268-5136 .. **Lindsay,** Robyn B '92 Cnsl Harwood L -350 5th Av -NY 10118
(518) 426-3877 .. **Lindsay-Gaddy,** Samantha J '04 Excelsior Advocates,LLC -403 Lvngstn Av -Albany 12206
(212) 314-4650 .. **Lindsay-Ochoa,** Elizabeth A '09 AXA Equitable -1290 Av of Amer -NY 10104
(631) 439-4200 .. **Lindsey,** Allison B '94 %R Tusa -898 Vets Mem'l Hwy -Hauppauge 11788 **Fx:**439-4292
(212) 342-8762 .. **Lindsey,** Catherine A '95 CSTV Networks -85 10th Av -NY 10011
(212) 257-6960 .. **Lindsey,** David M '99 (Chaffetz L LLP) -1350 Av of Amer -NY 10019
(607) 763-9200 .. **Lindsey,** Jamye L '02 (Levene G&T,LLP) -BxF-1706 -Bnghmtn 13902
(518) 386-2266 .. **Lindsey,** John J L '07 Pub Def -519 State -Schnctdy 12305 **Fx:**386-2814
(212) 421-1011 .. **Lindsey,** Jonathan A '76 (Major Lindsey & Africa) -551 5th Av -NY 10176 **Fx:**421-1042
(518) 445-2240 .. **Lindsey,** Mary A '81 Albany Intl Corp -Bx1907 -Albany 12201
(212) 306-7200 .. **Lindsey,** Michele R '00 %Mayors Ofc Labor Rel -40 Rector -NY 10006 **Fx:**306-7223
(212) 527-1000 .. **Lindsey,** Tonya M '97 (Jones HC&B PC) -1 Bttry Pk Plz -NY 10004
(631) 757-4175 .. **Lindsey,** Wendi A '96 -1 Marys Ln -Centerprt 11721 **Fx:**757-4215
(718) 792-4800 .. **Lindstadt,** Michl A '06 %A Bespechny -2931 Wstchstr Av -Bronx 10461
(518) 392-7451 .. **Lindstedt-Simmons,** Bethene '87 -Bx180 -Chatham 12037
(845) 291-3136 .. **Lindstrom,** John R '84 Hon J Alessandro -255-285 Main -Goshen 10924 **Fx:**291-2595

(212) 339-2365 .. **Lindstrom,** Lisa A '08 Allen & Co LLC -711 5th Av -NY 10022
(212) 490-3000 .. **Lindstrom,** Wendy J '99 %Wilson EME&D LLP -150 E 42nd -NY 10017
(212) 836-8000 .. **Lindvall,** Scott G '95 (Kaye S LLP) -425 Park Av -NY 10022
(212) 599-5799 .. **Lineen,** Caroline B '06 %Rutherford & C LLP -369 Lex Av -NY 10017
(212) 335-9000 .. **Linehan,** Chas F '02 %DA -1 Hogan Pl -NY 10013
(718) 590-2000 .. **Linehan,** Kieran J '08 %DA -198 E 161st -Bronx 10451 **Fx:**590-6477
(845) 807-0650 .. **Linen,** Karen L '84 Family Ct -100 North -Monticello 12701 **Fx:**794-0199
(212) 354-0600 .. **Liner,** Robt F '74 (Stark A&L,LLP) -7 Penn Plz -NY 10001
(212) 610-6300 .. **Ling,** Elicia I '05 %Allen & O -1221 Av of Amer -NY 10020
(718) 445-3472 .. **Ling,** Margaret T '86 -13935 35th Av -Flushng 11354
(212) 474-1000 .. **Lingard,** Nicholas P '10 %Cravath S&M LLP -825 8th Av -NY 10019
(212) 267-8297 .. **Lingas,** Elino B '86 -132 Nassau -NY 10038 **Fx:**267-5967
(212) 682-8811 .. **Lingelbach,** Albert L '67 (Dunnington B&M LLP) -1359 Bway -NY 10018
(315) 471-3151 .. **Linger,** David G '88 (Hancock & E,LLP) -1500 AXA Twr I Bx4976 -Syracuse 13221
(585) 272-0540 .. **Lingle,** Michl J '01 %Thomas & S LLP -693 East Av -Rchstr 14607
(718) 817-0769 .. **Lingner,** Eugene K '09 Fordham Univ -441 E Fordham Rd -Bronx 10458
(716) 852-8222 .. **Linhardt,** Kathleen Ann '96 %Paladino C&Q -295 Main -Buffalo 14203
(516) 255-4160 .. **Link,** Bonnie '81 (Kardisch L & Assoc PC) -80 E Old Cntry Rd -Mineola 11501 **Fx:**255-4163
(516) 482-3500 .. **Link,** Danl H '59 -98 Cuttermill Rd -Gt Neck 11021
(914) 828-8994 .. **Link,** Josephine Boccia '91 Swiss Re Life & Hlth -175 King -Armonk 10504
(516) 466-8005 .. **Link,** Mariya V '05 %Tashlik KG&C PC -40 Cuttermill Rd -Gt Neck 11021
(212) 450-4000 .. **Link,** Troland S '64 SrCnsl Davis P&W LLP -450 Lex Av -NY 10017
(212) 701-3000 .. **Linken,** Peter J '07 %Cahill G&R LLP -80 Pine -NY 10005 **Fx:**269-5420
(212) 940-7007 .. **Linker,** Arthur S '75 (Katten MR LLP) -575 Mad Av -NY 10022
(212) 578-2211 .. **Linker,** Ian S '99 Cnsl MetLife -1095 Av of Amer -NY 10036 **Fx:**578-3916
(212) 661-7300 .. **Linker,** Joni '81 %Malapero & P LLP -295 Mad Av -NY 10017
(212) 682-1818 .. **Linkh,** Gregory B '00 %Murray F&S LLP -275 Mad Av -NY 10016
(212) 578-2275 .. **Lin Kim,** Maria Y '98 MetLife -1095 Av of Amer -NY 10036 **Fx:**578-3916
(212) 903-9000 .. **Linklaters** -1345 Av of Amer -NY 10105 **Fx:**424-9100
(212) 592-1400 .. **Linkletter,** Kimberly J '10 %Herrick,F LLP -2 Park Av -NY 10016
(212) 506-2500 .. **Linley,** David A K '03 Cnsl Mayer B LLP -1675 Bway -NY 10019
(914) 949-4200 .. **Linn,** Chas B '74 -901 N Bway -N White Plns 10603 **Fx:**949-6897
(516) 466-4333 .. **Linn,** David A '96 -175 E Shore Rd -Gt Neck 11023 **Fx:**466-4336
(914) 949-2909 .. **Linn,** Janet B '78 (Eckert SC&M,LLC) -10 Bank -White Plns 10606
(585) 287-5080 .. **Linn,** Janice L '05 -36 W Main -Rchstr 14614
(516) 227-0700 .. **Linn,** Jordan S '00 %Farrell F,PC -1320 RXR Plz -Uniondale 11556
(718) 399-3310 .. **Linn,** Robt W '75 (Linn & Green Consulting) -24 Prospect Park W -Brklyn 11215
(518) 449-5400 .. **Linnan & Fallon,LLP** -61 Columbia #300 -Albany 12210 **Fx:**449-5262
(518) 449-5400 .. **Linnan,** James D '73 (Linnan & F,LLP) -61 Columbia #300 -Albany 12210
(914) 766-1900 .. **Linne,** Anna L '08 IBM -294 Route 100 -Somers 10589
(716) 853-6001 .. **Linneball,** Laura A '92 (Wilder & L,LLP) -403 Main at Court -Buffalo 14203
(914) 238-2318 .. **Linnehan,** Mary E '99 -320 King -Chappaqua 10514
(516) 829-0363 .. **Lino,** Regina A '90 %Israel I&P,LLP -11 Grace Av -Gt Neck 11021 **Fx:**829-0366
(212) 566-2113 .. **Linowes,** Michl J '99 (Linowes Law Firm) -150 Bway -NY 10038 **Fx:**566-2114
(212) 486-7272 .. **Linowitz,** Jane B '87 (Levisohn B,LLP) -11 Bway -NY 10004
(212) 309-8260 .. **Lins,** Gerald T '95 ING Furman Selz -230 Park Av -NY 10169
(212) 563-4100 .. **Linsey,** James L '82 (Cohen W&S LLP) -330 W 42nd -NY 10036
(516) 374-7393 .. **Linsky,** Jody K '86 -300 Pepperdg Rd -Hewlett Hbr 11557 **Fx:**374-0683
(212) 547-5400 .. **Linsky,** Lisa A '85 (McDermott W&E LLP) -340 Mad Av -NY 10173
(585) 346-0510 .. **Linsner,** Margaret Graf '92 -33 Main Bx550 -Livonia 14487 **Fx:**346-0531
(845) 239-1828 .. **Linson,** Camille S '97 -13 Parrot -Cold Spg 10516
(212) 661-8400 .. **Linson,** Danl B '05 J Chambers,PC -60 E 42nd -NY 10165 **Fx:**661-1242
(212) 336-2000 .. **Lintemuth,** Lynde F '08 %Patterson BW&T LLP -1133 Av of Amer -NY 10036
(212) 237-1000 .. **Linton,** Craig A '10 %Windels ML&M,LLP -156 W 56th -NY 10019
(518) 794-5218 .. **Linville,** Robt W '79 (Linville Law Firm) -1251 Route 13 -Old Chatham 12136 **Fx:**794-5233
(516) 328-3500 .. **Linwood,** Julie A '92 (McDonnell & A,PC) -401 Franklin Av -Gdn Cty 11530
(212) 298-5175 .. **Linzer,** Lawr '70 Leg Aid -49 Thomas -NY 10013
(516) 296-7000 .. **Linzer,** Paul Stuart '92 %Certilman BA&H,LLP -90 Merrick Av -E Meadow 11554
(212) 553-4786 .. **Lioce,** Stephen G '94 %Moody's Invstr Srvc -250 Greenwich -NY 10007
(212) 227-4210 .. **Liolis,** Harris '05 %Weg & M,PC -52 Duane -NY 10007
(212) 909-6000 .. **Lion,** Marilyn A '06 %Debevoise & P LLP -919 3rd Av -NY 10022
(212) 448-1100 .. **Lion,** Walter H '81 (McLaughlin & S,LLP) -260 Mad Av -NY 10016
(212) 474-1000 .. **Lione,** Francesco '06 %Cravath S&M LLP -825 8th Av -NY 10019
(516) 742-4700 .. **Lione,** Michl B '80 MKM Abstract Srvcs -238 Mineola Blvd Bx427 -Mineola 11501 **Fx:**742-0675
(516) 308-3760 .. **Liotta & Cantanno LLP** -519 Central Av -Massapequa 11758 **Fx:**308-3774
(516) 308-3760 .. **Liotta,** Christopher J '93 (Liotta & C LLP) -519 Central Av -Massapequa 11758
(914) 946-8900 .. **Liotta,** Denise P '85 OfCnsl Clark G&M -99 Court -White Plns 10601
(914) 524-5600 .. **Liotti,** Louis H '78 %L Fishman -303 S Bway -Tarrytwn 10591 **Fx:**524-5742
(516) 794-4700 .. **Liotti,** Thos F '77 -600 Old Cntry Rd -Gdn Cty 11530 **Fx:**794-2816
(212) 310-8000 .. **Liou,** Jessica '09 %Weil G&M LLP -767 5th Av -NY 10153
(646) 587-0188 .. **Liou,** Leta '05 (Liou & M,PLLC) -124 Nassau -NY 10038 **Fx:**587-0187
(516) 747-2000 .. **Lioz,** Lawr S '71 (Margolin Winer Evens,LLP) -400 Grdn City Plz -Gdn Cty 11530 **Fx:**747-6707
(212) 759-8203 .. **Lipari,** David P '01 %Hedinger & L -110 Wall -NY 10005
(212) 903-8700 .. **Lipari,** Jos '79 (Roberts & H,LLP) -825 8th Av -NY 10019
(212) 404-5777 .. **Lipari,** Jos '04 (Littleton JUP&K LLP) -39 Bway -NY 10006
(718) 254-7000 .. **Lipari,** Vincent '83 %US Atty -271 Cadman Plz E -Brklyn 11201 **Fx:**254-6479
(212) 559-6681 .. **Lipcan,** Natasha M '05 %Citigroup Inc -425 Park Av -NY 10043
(212) 581-3320 .. **Lipetz,** Andrew K '96 %Wasserman G&R,LLP -1700 Bway -NY 10019
(212) 846-4663 .. **Lipetz,** Cathy L '89 MTV Networks -1515 Bway -NY 10036
(212) 230-8827 .. **Lipez,** Julia M '07 %WilmerHale -399 Park Av -NY 10022
(718) 546-0950 .. **Lipford,** Audrey H '94 %Dept of Correction -75-20 Astoria Blvd -E Elmhrst 11370
(718) 330-7705 .. **Lipin,** Nancy B '96 %NLRB -2 Metrotech Ctr -Brklyn 11201 **Fx:**330-7579
(212) 331-2563 .. **Lipiner,** Marcus H '94 Universal Music Grp -1755 Bway -NY 10019
(518) 792-2117 .. **Lipinski,** Bruce O '89 (Bartlett PS&R,PC) -1 Wshngtn Bx2168 -Glens Fls 12801
(718) 643-8986 .. **Lipinsky,** Clara H '81 %Family Ct -283 Adams -Brklyn 11201
(516) 294-5432 .. **Lipitz Marder,** Stacey J '08 %Kern AC&S,PC -1325 Franklin Av -Gdn Cty 11530
(718) 896-7807 .. **Lipka,** Jordan L '85 -63-33 98th Pl -Rego Pk 11374
(718) 286-6000 .. **Lipkansky,** Maryam N'Ha Margo '96 %DA -125-01 Qns Blvd -Kew Gdns 11415
(212) 401-0800 .. **Lipkansky,** Vitaly '97 %Disciplinary Comm -61 Bway -NY 10006 **Fx:**287-1045
(212) 728-8000 .. **Lipkin,** Alan J '79 (Willkie F&G LLP) -787 7th Av -NY 10019
(212) 788-0704 .. **Lipkin,** Andrew G '90 %Law Dept -100 Church -NY 10007 **Fx:**788-0367
(212) 490-3000 .. **Lipkin,** Jason R '06 %Wilson EME&D LLP -150 E 42nd -NY 10017
(718) 229-8743 .. **Lipkin,** Leon B '65 -52-34 241st -Douglastn 11362
(914) 681-0645 .. **Lipkin,** Lewis F '77 (Mariano & L PLLC) -941 N Bway -White Plns 10603
(212) 456-7176 .. **Lipkind,** Alec M '89 %Walt Disney -77 W 66th -NY 10023 **Fx:**456-6565
(716) 633-4485 .. **Lipkind,** Andrew '80 -6225 Sheridan Dr -Williamsvll 14221 **Fx:**633-4509
(212) 533-6300 .. **Lipkind,** Stuart I '76 %NYSUT -52 Bway -NY 10004 **Fx:**995-2347
(212) 925-4023 .. **Lipkis,** Mordechai I '81 Shushana Co -50 Walker -NY 10013
(212) 319-8500 .. **Lipkowitz,** Eugene V '64 OfCnsl Stevens & L PC -485 Mad Av -NY 10022
(845) 294-7944 .. **Lipman,** Alan S '58 (Fabricant L&F,PLLC) -1 Harriman Sq Bx60 -Goshen 10924
(212) 806-5400 .. **Lipman,** Alex '92 (Stroock &S&L LLP) -180 Maiden Ln -NY 10038
(716) 633-3200 .. **Lipman,** Allan R '56 (Lipman B&J,LLP) -333 Intl Dr -Williamsvll 14221
(212) 293-8900 .. **Lipman,** Beth D '93 %EMMES Asset Mgt -420 Lex Av -NY 10170 **Fx:**293-8805
(716) 633-3200 .. **Lipman Biltekoff & Joy, LLP** -333 Intl Dr -Williamsvll 14221 **Fx:**633-0301
(212) 363-6969 .. **Lipman & Booth,LLC** -11 Bway #967 -NY 10004 **Fx:**363-6041
(212) 805-0262 .. **Lipman,** Eric S '01 Hon PK Castel -500 Pearl -NY 10007
(212) 661-3080 .. **Lipman,** Harry W '91 (Rottenberg LR,PC) -369 Lex Av -NY 10017
(716) 856-8004 .. **Lipman,** Howard S '81 (Cardarelli & L,LLP) -69 Delaware Av -Buffalo 14202
(212) 272-2559 .. **Lipman,** Jeffrey M '74 %JP Morgan Chase -383 Mad Av -NY 10179
(212) 891-2327 .. **Lipman,** Joshua N '05 Richemont NA Inc -645 5th Av -NY 10022
(212) 753-6116 .. **Lipman,** Lawr '94 %Manhattan Parking Systems -277 Park Av -NY 10172
(914) 235-8922 .. **Lipman,** Lisa R '87 -145 Huguenot -New Rchll 10801
(212) 953-6000 .. **Lipman,** Louise E '79 OfCnsl Katsky K LLP -605 3rd Av -NY 10158
(718) 260-9696 .. **Lipman,** Marylyn P '85 -32 Court -Brklyn 11201
(212) 751-7700 .. **Lipman,** Matthew E '89 %Faust & O,LLP -488 Mad Av -NY 10022
(212) 363-6969 .. **Lipman,** Noah '85 Lipman & B,LLC -11 Bway #967 -NY 10004
(516) 931-0050 .. **Lipman & Plesur,LLP** -500 N Bway -Jericho 11753 **Fx:**931-0030
(212) 661-0085 .. **Lipman & Plesur,LLP** -1350 Bway -NY 10018
(516) 938-6593 .. **Lipman,** Richd '76 -400 S Oyster Bay Rd -Hicksvll 11801 **Fx:**433-0467
(516) 931-0050 .. **Lipman,** Robt D '87 (Lipman & P,LLP) -500 N Bway -Jericho 11753
(212) 837-6898 .. **Lipman,** Ross '85 Cnsl Hughes H&R LLP -1 Bttry Pk Plz -NY 10004
(212) 640-2000 .. **Lipner,** Alan J '64 %Amer Exp -200 Vesey -NY 10285
(631) 656-2157 .. **Lipner,** Judith Rosen '90 Five Towns Cllg Bus Law -305 N Srvc Rd -Dix Hlls 11746
(212) 225-2000 .. **Lipner,** Louis A '10 %Cleary GS&H -1 Lbrty Plz -NY 10006
(516) 294-8899 .. **Lipner,** Seth E '81 (Deutsch & L) -1325 Franklin Av -Gdn Cty 11530
(212) 223-3900 .. **Lipofsky,** Jos '86 OfCnsl Zwerling S&Z,LLP -41 Mad Av -NY 10010
(212) 480-7472 .. **Lipovetsky,** Thos T '07 %DHCR -25 Beaver -NY 10004 **Fx:**480-7416
(212) 385-1772 .. **Lipp,** Amy F '82 %Posner & P -170 Bway -NY 10038 **Fx:**385-2061
(212) 838-7442 .. **Lipp,** Susan Rosenblum '85 Cmmnty Housing Imprvmnt Prog -377 Bway -NY 10013
(212) 863-6300 .. **Lippa,** Frances '82 %HPD -100 Gold -NY 10038 **Fx:**863-8201
(716) 565-2000 .. **Lippa,** Philip '51 -17 Beresford Ct -Williamsvll 14221
(516) 747-0300 .. **Lippe,** Richd A '64 (Meltzer LG&B,LLP) -190 Willis Av -Mineola 11501
(212) 233-1230 .. **Lippel,** Alan C '68 -299 Bway -NY 10007 **Fx:**(201) 488-4407
(212) 762-6007 .. **Lipper,** Howard '86 Morgan Stanley -1221 Av of Amer -NY 10020
(212) 558-4000 .. **Lippert,** Matthew L '09 %Sullivan & C LLP -125 Broad -NY 10004
(212) 937-7201 .. **Lippert,** Nels T '70 (WilmerHale) -399 Park Av -NY 10022
(716) 853-5100 .. **Lippes,** Gerald S '64 (Lippes MWF LLP) -665 Main -Buffalo 14203
(716) 884-4800 .. **Lippes,** Joshua R '05 -1260 Delaware Av -Buffalo 14209 **Fx:**884-6117
(716) 853-5100 .. **Lippes Mathias Wexler Friedman LLP** -665 Main -Buffalo 14203 **Fx:**853-5199
(716) 884-4800 .. **Lippes,** Richd J '70 -1260 Delaware Av -Buffalo 14209 **Fx:**884-6117

(212) 848-4000 .. **Lippett,** Sharon '99 Cnsl Shearman & S LLP -599 Lex Av -NY 10022
(718) 590-8378 .. **Lippiello,** Melissa F '04 ACS -900 Sheridan Av -Bronx 10451
(718) 817-5810 .. **Lippiello,** Vincenzo S '04 Fordham Univ-Ofc Legal Cnsl -441 E Fordham Rd -Bronx 10458 **Fx:**814-3115
(212) 788-0790 .. **Lippin,** Louise '92 %Law Dept -100 Church -NY 10007 **Fx:**788-0367
(212) 430-1034 .. **Lippin,** Saml D '83 -201 E 65th -NY 10065
(212) 381-7535 .. **Lippincott,** Amy N '04 Guggenheim Prtnrs -135 E 57th -NY 10022
(585) 231-1563 .. **Lippitt,** David W '87 -16 W Main -Rchstr 14614
(914) 824-5325 .. **Lippman,** Amy Fiedler '89 %Supreme Ct -111 Martin Luther King Blvd -White Plns 10601
(845) 338-8393 .. **Lippman,** Barry M '69 (B Lippman,PC) -110 Maiden Ln -Kingston 12401 **Fx:**338-6641
(212) 593-2022 .. **Lippman,** Harvey J '72 (Richardson & Assoc) -590 Mad Av -NY 10022 **Fx:**593-2087
(212) 272-3413 .. **Lippman,** Jay M '87 JP Morgan Chase -320 Park Av -NY 10022
(212) 259-8000 .. **Lippman,** Lindsay E '05 %Dewey & L LLP -1301 Av of Amer -NY 10019
(212) 724-7213 .. **Lippman,** Melvin M '66 -160 W 71st -NY 10023 **Fx:**724-7213
(718) 992-1428 .. **Lippman,** Michl M '69 -135 Southside Av -Hastings-On-Hud 10706
(212) 687-3747 .. **Lippman,** Michl R '91 (Tuchman KWL&G,LLP) -6 E 45th -NY 10017
(716) 854-4705 .. **Lippman O'Connor** -300 Pearl -Buffalo 14202 **Fx:**854-1932
(518) 581-8800 .. **Lippman,** Robt A '89 %Lemery G LLC -60 Railroad Pl -Saratoga Spgs 12866
(716) 854-4705 .. **Lippman,** Robt M '82 Lippman O -300 Pearl -Buffalo 14202
(212) 596-9000 .. **Lippman,** Russell L '02 %Ropes & G LLP -1211 Av of Amer -NY 10036
(212) 407-4000 .. **Lippmann,** Andrew E '84 (Loeb & L,LLP) -345 Park Av -NY 10154
(631) 591-2961 .. **Lippmann,** Jennifer S '99 (Lippmann & G) -1641 Deer Prk Av -Deer Pk 11729 **Fx:**242-2034
(718) 403-3613 .. **Lippman-Phillips,** Joyce '83 Dept of Finance -345 Adams -Brklyn 11201 **Fx:**403-3650
(212) 852-7166 .. **Lippner,** J Jordan '97 News Corp -1211 Av of Amer -NY 10036 **Fx:**852-7217
(212) 530-5000 .. **Lipps,** Tiara P '10 %Milbank TH&M LLP -1 Chase Manh Plz -NY 10005
(718) 403-8503 .. **Lipschitz,** Benjamin '97 %DOITT -11 Metrotech Ctr -Brklyn 11201 **Fx:**403-8504
(516) 741-4104 .. **Lipschitz,** Lawr B '74 %Cmmnwlth Land Title -330 Old Cntry Rd -Mineola 11501 **Fx:**741-4296
(845) 352-4448 .. **Lipschutz,** Florence '83 -101 Route 306 -Monsey 10952 **Fx:**356-9756
(212) 479-6000 .. **Lipschutz,** Mark W '87 OfCnsl Cooley LLP -1114 Av of Amer -NY 10036
(212) 415-5332 .. **Lipscomb,** Casey S '01 %McKinsey & Co -55 E 52nd -NY 10055 **Fx:**688-9521
(212) 578-2211 .. **Lipscomb,** James L '73 %MetLife -27-01 Qns Plz N -LIC 11101
(212) 230-8880 .. **Lipsett,** Christopher R '00 (WilmerHale) -399 Park Av -NY 10022
(212) 867-8280 .. **Lipsett,** John G '59 (Patton ELM&S) -420 Lex Av -NY 10170
(212) 259-8000 .. **Lipsey,** Kirk D '94 (Dewey & L LLP) -1301 Av of Amer -NY 10019
(212) 806-5400 .. **Lipshie,** Burton N '67 Stroock &S&L LLP -180 Maiden Ln -NY 10038
(212) 326-2000 .. **Lipshitz,** Doron '96 (O'Melveny & M LLP) -7 Times Sq -NY 10036
(212) 909-6000 .. **Lipshitz,** Michl Noam '10 %Debevoise & P LLP -919 3rd Av -NY 10022
(212) 848-4000 .. **Lipshitz,** Ruth '00 %Shearman & S LLP -599 Lex Av -NY 10022
(212) 207-8787 .. **Lipshutz,** Barbara J '96 Cnsl Jacobs & B LLP -445 Park Av -NY 10022
(212) 708-9868 .. **Lipshutz,** Patty '78 %MOMA -11 W 53rd -NY 10019
(212) 674-1111 .. **Lipsig,** Diana E '92 (Lipsig P,PLLC) -156 5th Av -NY 10010
(212) 674-1111 .. **Lipsig Price, PLLC** -156 5th Av -NY 10010 **Fx:**(646) 649-9650
(212) 285-3300 .. **Lipsig Shapey Manus & Moverman,PC** -40 Fulton -NY 10038 **Fx:**406-4544
(716) 849-1333 .. **Lipsitz Green Scime Cambria LLP** -42 Delaware Av -Buffalo 14202 **Fx:**855-1580
(716) 672-7004 .. **Lipsitz Green Scime Cambria LLP** -4 W Main -Fredonia 14063 **Fx:**672-7155
(716) 565-1200 .. **Lipsitz Green Scime Cambria LLP** -35 Maple Rd -Williamsvll 14221 **Fx:**565-1228
(716) 634-9918 .. **Lipsitz Green Scime Cambria LLP** -585 Aero Dr -Cheektowaga 14225 **Fx:**634-0381
(716) 849-0701 .. **Lipsitz,** John N '79 (Lipsitz & P LLC) -135 Delaware Av -Buffalo 14202
(716) 849-0701 .. **Lipsitz & Ponterio LLC** -135 Delaware Av -Buffalo 14202 **Fx:**849-0708
(212) 715-9100 .. **Lipsitz,** Randy '81 (Kramer LN&F,LLP) -1177 Av of Amer -NY 10036
(716) 849-1333 .. **Lipsitz,** Richd '43 OfCnsl Lipsitz GSC LLP -42 Delaware Av -Buffalo 14202
(212) 563-1710 .. **Lipsius,** Cheryl D '99 %Schindel FLG&R LLP -14 Penn Plz -NY 10122
(212) 563-1710 .. **Lipsius,** Ira S '80 (Schindel FLG&R LLP) -14 Penn Plz -NY 10122
(516) 227-2700 .. **Lipsky Bresky & Lowe,LLP** -585 Stewart Av -Gdn Cty 11530 **Fx:**227-2424
(212) 471-8500 .. **Lipsky,** Bryan D '09 %Herzfeld & R,PC -125 Broad -NY 10004
(212) 452-3449 .. **Lipsky,** Burton G '62 -254 E 68th -NY 10065 **Fx:**452-0043
(516) 488-7736 .. **Lipsky,** David E '92 -5 Dakota Dr -New Hyde Pk 11042
(212) 218-5500 .. **Lipsky,** Douglas B '05 %Seyfarth S LLP -620 8th Av -NY 10018
(212) 840-6444 .. **Lipsky,** Joel B '78 (Lipsky S&L,PC) -120 W 45th -NY 10036
(973) 228-5700 .. **Lipsky,** Leonard '09 %Brach E LLC -100 Park Av -NY 10017 **Fx:**228-7852
(212) 728-8000 .. **Lipsky,** Matthew Louis '10 %Willkie F&G LLP -787 7th Av -NY 10019
(845) 356-5500 .. **Lipsky,** Robt C '95 -2 Perlman Dr -Spg Vly 10977 **Fx:**352-8865
(212) 840-6444 .. **Lipsky Seidman & Lipsky,PC** -120 W 45th -NY 10036 **Fx:**921-7186
(516) 227-2700 .. **Lipsky,** Wendy L '86 (Lipsky B&L,LLP) -585 Stewart Av -Gdn Cty 11530
(914) 813-5020 .. **Lipsman,** Joshua B '06 %Westchester Cty Dept of Hlth -145 Huguenot -New Rchll 10801
(212) 532-7700 .. **Lipsman,** Richd M '73 -90 Park Av -NY 10016 **Fx:**986-4939
(212) 407-1200 .. **Lipsman,** Sandra Myndelle '84 -485 Lex Av -NY 10017 **Fx:**407-1299
(212) 848-4000 .. **Lipson,** Andrew Z '10 Shearman & S LLP -599 Lex Av -NY 10022
(845) 892-1509 .. **Lipson,** Gary N '09 IBM -2070 Route 52 -Hopewell Junct 12533
(585) 258-2800 .. **Lipson,** Gordon J '66 OfCnsl Underberg & K LLP -300 Bausch & Lomb Pl -Rchstr 14604
(212) 626-4100 .. **Lipson,** Jessica L '06 %Baker & M LLP -1114 Av of Amer -NY 10036
(518) 474-3920 .. **Lipson,** Karen B '89 %Dept of Health -Corning Twr 24th Fl -Albany 12237 **Fx:**473-2802
(212) 310-8000 .. **Lipson,** Lauren B '06 %Weil G&M LLP -767 5th Av -NY 10153
(516) 512-8939 .. **Lipson,** Michl E '75 -1225 Franklin Av -Gdn Cty 11530
(914) 328-5570 .. **Lipson,** Roy A '85 -108 Woodlnds Av -White Plns 10607
(212) 806-5400 .. **Lipstein,** Steven A '10 %Stroock &S&L LLP -180 Maiden Ln -NY 10038
(212) 227-9683 .. **Lipsyte,** Susannah '03 %HDC -110 William -NY 10038 **Fx:**227-6865
(212) 468-8000 .. **Lipsztein,** Leonardo '08 %Morrison & F LLP -1290 Av of Amer -NY 10104
(212) 836-8000 .. **Liptak,** Michl L '06 %Kaye S LLP -425 Park Av -NY 10022
(716) 853-3801 .. **Liptak,** Thos E '84 (Kenney SL&N,LLP) -14 Lafayette Sq -Buffalo 14203
(914) 225-5573 .. **Lipton,** Andrew H '03 Morgan Stanley -2000 Wstchstr Av -Purchase 10577
(212) 553-0300 .. **Lipton,** Andrew S '78 %Moody's Invstr Srvc -250 Greenwich -NY 10007
(212) 554-1400 .. **Lipton,** Ann M '01 %Bernstein LB&G LLP -1285 Av of Amer -NY 10019
(212) 233-7040 .. **Lipton,** Bella Kopf '54 (Lipton & L) -277 Bway -NY 10007 **Fx:**571-0276
(718) 436-5359 .. **Lipton,** Carol '86 -800 Greenwood Av -Brklyn 11218 **Fx:**436-5359
(212) 479-6000 .. **Lipton,** Chet F '80 (Cooley LLP) -1114 Av of Amer -NY 10036
(212) 446-2323 .. **Lipton,** Evan L '06 %G Shargel -570 Lex Av -NY 10022 **Fx:**446-2330
(914) 997-8100 .. **Lipton,** Gail R '82 (Burke LM&G) -10 Bank -White Plns 10606
(845) 624-0100 .. **Lipton,** Gary Lawr '77 -55 Old Tpk Rd -Nanuet 10954 **Fx:**624-0288
(212) 689-8808 .. **Lipton,** Ira J '81 (Hoguet NR&K,LLP) -10 E 40th -NY 10016
(212) 284-3431 .. **Lipton,** Jeffrey H '96 Jeffries & Co -520 Mad Av -NY 10022
(212) 323-1901 .. **Lipton,** Jody C '99 Cnsl Ofc Chief Med Examiner -421 E 26th -NY 10016 **Fx:**323-1920
(516) 571-3800 .. **Lipton,** Karen Kalbacher '80 %DA -262 Old Cntry Rd -Mineola 11501 **Fx:**248-9479
(718) 595-4730 .. **Lipton,** Leslie Mark '83 %DEP-BWT -96-05 Horace Hrdng Expy -Corona 11368 **Fx:**595-6950
(212) 403-1000 .. **Lipton,** Martin '56 (Wachtell LR&K) -51 W 52nd -NY 10019
(212) 765-2100 .. **Lipton,** Neil D '65 (Spivak L LLP) -1700 Bway -NY 10019
(212) 702-0858 .. **Lipton,** Norman D '88 -205 E 60th -NY 10022
(212) 558-4000 .. **Lipton,** Samantha D '10 %Sullivan & C LLP -125 Broad -NY 10004
(845) 485-8814 .. **Lipton,** Stephen M '76 -21 Adriance Av -Poughkeepsie 12601
(212) 223-0660 .. **Lipton,** Susan Lytle '84 -550 Park Av -NY 10065
(516) 222-2777 .. **Lira,** David M '82 -595 Stewart Av -Gdn Cty 11530 **Fx:**222-2971
(718) 592-3600 .. **Lisa,** Jos F '61 -Bx356167 -Jamaica 11435
(516) 877-1233 .. **Lisabeth,** Jeffrey S '81 -54 Willis Av -Mineola 11501 **Fx:**877-0235
(212) 735-3000 .. **Lisagar,** Matthew S '10 %Skadden ASM&F LLP -4 Times Sq -NY 10036
(716) 566-1300 .. **Lisandrelli,** Kathryn A '09 %Hiscock & B,LLP -1100 M&T Ctr -Buffalo 14203
(646) 386-5687 .. **Lisanti,** Melinda Phillips '94 %Hon M Shulman -111 Centre -NY 10013
(315) 479-3900 .. **Lischak,** John M '64 SSA-OHA -300 S State -Syracuse 13202
(212) 696-6000 .. **Lischin,** Matthew C '10 %Curtis M-PC&M LLP -101 Park Av -NY 10178
(212) 836-8000 .. **Liscio,** Mark F '84 (Kaye S LLP) -425 Park Av -NY 10022
(212) 460-3355 .. **Lisi,** Frank A '77 Con Ed -4 Irving Pl -NY 10003
(516) 678-7100 .. **Lisi,** Gregory S '93 -55 Front -Rockvll Ctr 11570 **Fx:**536-9548
(315) 798-5766 .. **Lisi,** Laurie '84 %DA -800 Park Av -Utica 13501 **Fx:**798-5582
(607) 763-9200 .. **Lisi-Murray,** Maria E '03 (Levene G&T,LLP) -BxF-1706 -Bnghmtn 13902
(212) 474-1000 .. **Lisk,** Danl T '06 %Cravath S&M LLP -825 8th Av -NY 10019
(212) 837-6000 .. **Lisk,** Francesca K '03 %Hughes H&R LLP -1 Bttry Pk Plz -NY 10004
(212) 408-5100 .. **Liskov,** Richd G '75 SpclCnsl Chadbourne & P LLP -30 Rckfllr Plz -NY 10112
(718) 761-7201 .. **Lisnow,** Jeffrey N '90 -416 Colon Av -Staten Isl 10308 **Fx:**948-0328
(212) 872-1000 .. **Liss,** Heidi T '93 -One Bryant Park -NY 10036 **Fx:**872-1002
(212) 450-4000 .. **Liss,** James D '77 Cnsl Davis P&W LLP -450 Lex Av -NY 10017
(973) 596-4569 .. **Liss,** Jonathan S '98 Cnsl Gibbons PC -1 Penn Plz -NY 10119 **Fx:**639-6237
(646) 386-4042 .. **Liss,** Marjorie A '78 Supreme Ct -111 Centre -NY 10013
(914) 682-2061 .. **Liss,** Michl '85 -50 Main -White Plns 10606 **Fx:**682-2177
(212) 980-2277 .. **Liss,** Michl S '81 Cipher Capital Prtnrs LLC -570 Mad Av -NY 10022
(212) 586-6165 .. **Liss,** Norman '55 (N Liss,PC) -200 W 57th -NY 10019 **Fx:**586-1194
(646) 298-7667 .. **Liss,** Randie M '83 -26 Court -Brklyn 11242 **Fx:**(718) 522-4208
(212) 683-7300 .. **Liss,** Solomon '73 (Klein & L) -470 Park Av S -NY 10016
(718) 837-4000 .. **Liss,** Stafford M '84 (Blay & L) -8778 Bay Pkwy -Brklyn 11214
(518) 455-5788 .. **Liss,** Stephen B '92 NYS Assembly -837 LOB -Albany 12248
(212) 819-8200 .. **Liss,** Zohar '04 %White & C LLP -1155 Av of Amer -NY 10036
(516) 496-5822 .. **Lissauer,** Danl S '03 %T Spina -170 Froehlich Farm Blvd -Woodbury 11797 **Fx:**496-5420
(845) 562-0203 .. **Lissauer,** Lawr D '87 (Finkelstein & Prtnrs,LLP) -1279 Route 300 Bx1111 -Newburgh 12550 **Fx:**569-9560
(212) 657-7527 .. **Lissemore,** Nancy C '91 Citigroup -111 Wall -NY 10043
(212) 752-8000 .. **Lissner,** Allison Lange '10 %Cole SMF&L,PA -900 3rd Av -NY 10022
(212) 307-1499 .. **Lissner,** Michl D '83 (Lissner & L LLP) -250 W 57th -NY 10107 **Fx:**757-1825
(212) 318-6000 .. **List,** Loren J '05 %Paul HJ&W LLP -75 E 55th -NY 10022
(212) 964-3840 .. **List,** Robt S '84 -80 Maiden Ln -NY 10038
(516) 822-4100 .. **List,** Roy A '77 -109 Newbrdg Rd -Hicksvll 11801 **Fx:**822-2178

(212) 259-8000 .. **Lister,** Amelia R S H '07 %Dewey & L LLP -1301 Av of Amer -NY 10019
(212) 821-0142 .. **Lister,** Robt D '94 %IMAX Corp -110 E 59th -NY 10022
(212) 269-2500 .. **Listhaus,** Bruce L '88 (Gorlick K&L,PC) -17 State -NY 10004
(212) 837-6000 .. **Liston,** David G '94 Cnsl Hughes H&R LLP -1 Bttry Pk Plz -NY 10004
(212) 450-4000 .. **Liston,** Joshua D '03 %Davis P&W LLP -450 Lex Av -NY 10017
(716) 858-2200 .. **Liszewski,** Michl J '84 %Cnty Atty -95 Franklin -Buffalo 14202 **Fx:**858-2281
(845) 228-4200 .. **Lita,** Giuseppina R '00 %W Sayegh,PC -65 Gleneida Av -Carmel 10512 **Fx:**228-4832
(516) 408-6314 .. **Litcher-Butler,** Barbara '87 (Butler & B) -377 Oak -Gdn Cty 11530 **Fx:**222-2508
(212) 434-0100 .. **Litchfield Cavo LLP** -420 Lex Av -NY 10170 **Fx:**434-0105
(845) 292-8083 .. **Litchman,** Ronald J '77 -96 N Main -Liberty 12754 **Fx:**(866) 480-3772
(631) 669-3710 .. **Lite,** Justin N '86 (Lite & R,PLLC) -212 Higbie Ln -W Islip 11795
(631) 669-3710 .. **Lite & Russell, PLLC** -212 Higbie Ln -W Islip 11795 **Fx:**669-3812
(718) 391-1720 .. **Litera,** Lisa S '86 %Dept Design & Cnstrctn -30-30 Thomson Av -LIC 11101 **Fx:**391-1894
(212) 402-3293 .. **Lites,** Barry D '87 %Tradecard Inc -75 Maiden Ln -NY 10038
(845) 778-2121 .. **Lithco,** George W '87 (Jacobowitz & G,LLP) -158 Orange Av Bx367 -Walden 12586
(516) 571-2506 .. **Litke,** Carol J '08 DA -262 Old Cntry Rd -Mineola 11501
(212) 728-8000 .. **Litke,** Gary S '86 %Willkie F&G LLP -787 7th Av -NY 10019
(212) 213-5577 .. **Litman,** Alfred I '73 (Litman & J) -1133 Bway -NY 10010
(212) 363-6900 .. **Litman,** Alyssa E '07 %Faust GS&B LLP -2 Rector -NY 10006
(212) 809-4500 .. **Litman Asche & Gioiella,LLP** -140 Bway -NY 10005 **Fx:**742-8757
(212) 336-2000 .. **Litman,** Benjamin S '07 %Patterson BW&T LLP -1133 Av of Amer -NY 10036
(516) 869-4000 .. **Litman,** Eugene '58 (Litman & L,PC) -209 Glenmore -Williston Pk 11596 **Fx:**908-4210
(212) 525-5563 .. **Litman,** Helena Dunica '81 -452 5th Av -NY 10018
(212) 213-5577 .. **Litman & Jacobs** -1133 Bway -NY 10010
(516) 869-4000 .. **Litman,** Jeffrey E '89 (Litman & L,PC) -209 Glenmore -Williston Pk 11596 **Fx:**908-4210
(516) 869-4000 .. **Litman,** Kenneth S '96 %Litman & L,PC -209 Glenmore -Williston Pk 11596 **Fx:**908-4210
(718) 252-3800 .. **Litman,** Robt A '93 -2917 Av P -Brklyn 11229
(212) 770-5954 .. **Litman,** Scott D '99 AIG Inc -70 Pine -NY 10270
(212) 789-2110 .. **Litner,** Jon D '89 %NHL -1251 Av of Amer -NY 10020
(718) 250-0400 .. **Litos,** Maria '03 %R Tusa -1 MetroTech Ctr -Brklyn 11201 **Fx:**250-0591
(212) 848-4000 .. **Litowitz,** Danl '00 Cnsl Shearman & S LLP -599 Lex Av -NY 10022
(631) 368-4747 .. **Litrel,** Christopher J '97 -467 Brook Av -Deer Pk 11729
(516) 352-0810 .. **Litroff,** Herman '52 -9 Wilben Ct -New Hyde Pk 11040
(718) 884-5070 .. **Litsky,** Ruth Ann '87 -3721 Riverdale Av -Bronx 10463 **Fx:**884-5070
(212) 416-6173 .. **Litsky,** Thos B '90 %Dept of Law -120 Bway -NY 10271 **Fx:**416-8962
(212) 363-1380 .. **Litt,** Arnold D '81 (Herten BSCBL&H,LLC) -747 3rd Av -NY 10017
(212) 902-1212 .. **Litt,** Bonnie S '90 %Goldman Sachs -1 NY Plz -NY 10004
(212) 735-3000 .. **Litt,** Gregory A '04 Cnsl Skadden ASM&F LLP -4 Times Sq -NY 10036
(212) 771-0818 .. **Litt,** Kenneth S '92 Wolters Kluwer Law & Business -76 9th Av -NY 10011
(212) 637-2295 .. **Litt,** Marc O '93 %US Atty -1 St Andrews Plz -NY 10007
(516) 764-0084 .. **Litt,** Marilyn K '79 -441 Anthony -Oceanside 11572
(212) 337-9770 .. **Litt,** Mikhail '06 %Tsyngauz & Assoc,PC -18 W 21st -NY 10010 **Fx:**337-9773
(516) 663-6600 .. **Litt,** Robt G '94 (Ruskin MF,PC) -1425 RXR Plz -Uniondale 11556
(212) 608-5300 .. **Litt,** Samantha B '10 %B D'Orazio,PC -100 Lafayette -NY 10013 **Fx:**608-5398
(718) 237-2000 .. **Litt,** Susan L '99 %Leg Aid -111 Lvngstn -Brklyn 11201 **Fx:**237-8737
(585) 538-2504 .. **Litteer,** Harold H Jr. '91 -3184 State Bx171 -Caledonia 14423 **Fx:**538-2811
(212) 756-2000 .. **Littenberg,** Michl R '91 (Schulte R&Z LLP) -919 3rd Av -NY 10022
(716) 853-5100 .. **Little,** Brendan H '08 Lippes MWF LLP -665 Main -Buffalo 14203
(518) 783-0200 .. **Little,** David A '87 NYS Schl Bds Assn -24 Century Hill Dr -Latham 12110
(212) 837-6000 .. **Little,** Edw J M '75 (Hughes H&R LLP) -1 Bttry Pk Plz -NY 10004
(518) 792-2113 .. **Little,** Elizabeth E '93 OfCnsl Little & O PC -19 W Notre Dame Bx898 -Glens Fls 12801
(212) 819-8200 .. **Little,** Gregory G '05 (White & C LLP) -1155 Av of Amer -NY 10036
(518) 792-2113 .. **Little,** J David '66 (Little & O PC) -19 W Notre Dame Bx898 -Glens Fls 12801
(518) 436-0344 .. **Little,** Jason A '07 %Deily M&G,LLP -8 Thurlow Ter -Albany 12203
(212) 715-9100 .. **Little,** Joshua R '08 %Kramer LN&F,LLP -1177 Av of Amer -NY 10036
(585) 753-4500 .. **Little,** Kristin M '07 DA -832 Watts Bldg -Rchstr 14614 **Fx:**753-4576
(631) 913-4444 .. **Little,** Melanie L '92 (Dell LT&V LLP) -5 Orvll Dr -Bohemia 11716
(212) 577-3688 .. **Little,** Nancy E '84 %Leg Aid -199 Water -NY 10038 **Fx:**509-8431
(518) 792-2113 .. **Little & O'Connor Attorneys PC** -19 W Notre Dame Bx898 -Glens Fls 12801 **Fx:**792-6972
(212) 277-4000 .. **Little,** Simon J '08 %Freshfields BD LLP -520 Mad Av -NY 10022
(212) 336-8471 .. **Little,** Tanisha M '01 Morrison & F LLP -1290 Av of Amer -NY 10104
(212) 940-8800 .. **Little,** Timothy G '86 (Katten MR LLP) -575 Mad Av -NY 10022
(518) 402-9185 .. **Little,** Wm G '82 %DEC -625 Bway -Albany 12233 **Fx:**402-9018
(518) 456-0082 .. **Little,** Wm T '06 %Bailey K&J,PC -5 Pine West Plz -Albany 12205 **Fx:**456-4767
(518) 862-2708 .. **Littlefield-Moreno,** Sheri '95 GE -319 Great Oaks Blvd -Albany 12203
(212) 902-7196 .. **Littlejohn,** Darren A '03 Goldman Sachs -1 NY Plz -NY 10004
(718) 549-1664 .. **Littlejohn,** Lamont H '03 -5440 Netherland Av -Bronx 10471 **Fx:**549-1664
(212) 583-9600 .. **Littler Mendelson,PC** -900 3rd Av -NY 10022 **Fx:**832-2719
(631) 293-4525 .. **Littler Mendelson,PC** -290 Broadhllw Rd -Melvll 11747 **Fx:**293-4546
(585) 203-3400 .. **Littler Mendelson,PC** -400 Linden Oaks -Rchstr 14625
(212) 404-5777 .. **Littleton Joyce Ughetta Park & Kelly LLP** -39 Bway -NY 10006 **Fx:**232-0088
(914) 417-3400 .. **Littleton Joyce Ughetta Park & Kelly LLP** -1 Manhattanvll Rd -Purchase 10577 **Fx:**417-3401
(212) 404-5777 .. **Littleton,** Robt W '84 (Littleton JUP&K LLP) -39 Bway -NY 10006
(646) 855-0841 .. **Littman,** Amy B '95 Bank of Amer -1 Bryant Pk -NY 10036
(845) 639-3800 .. **Littman,** Amy Baldwin '86 -20 Squadron Blvd -New Cty 10956 **Fx:**639-3801
(631) 755-0101 .. **Littman,** Judith N '95 %Lewis JAA,LLP -425 Broad Hollow Rd -Melvll 11747
(212) 490-2020 .. **Littman Krooks LLP** -655 3rd Av -NY 10017 **Fx:**490-2990
(914) 684-2100 .. **Littman Krooks LLP** -399 Knollwood Rd -White Plns 10603 **Fx:**684-9865
(212) 335-9000 .. **Littman,** Lauren S '02 %DA -1 Hogan Pl -NY 10013
(516) 712-4000 .. **Littman,** Matthew Ian '03 %Milber MP&S LLP -1000 Woodbury Rd -Woodbury 11797
(212) 490-2020 .. **Littman,** Mitchell C '84 (Littman K LLP) -655 3rd Av -NY 10017
(212) 201-4841 .. **Littman,** Owen S '98 Ramius Capital Grp LLC -599 Lex Av -NY 10022
(607) 277-7527 .. **Littman,** Peter N '79 (Littman & B) -308 N Tioga -Ithaca 14850 **Fx:**275-9141
(212) 692-9666 .. **Littman,** Robt '61 OfCnsl Gilbride TL&S LLC -708 3rd Av -NY 10017
(212) 532-6682 .. **Littman,** Robt '61 (Shlom & L) -370 Lex Av -NY 10017
(516) 571-3056 .. **Littman,** Saml '84 Cnty Atty -1 West -Mineola 11501 **Fx:**571-6604
(212) 532-6682 .. **Littman,** Thos W '99 (Shlom & L) -370 Lex Av -NY 10017
(212) 685-0530 .. **Litton,** Claude J '69 %Mnhttn Prop Co -295 5th Av -NY 10016 **Fx:**685-0857
(718) 250-2000 .. **Litton,** Lara Vittoria '02 %DA -350 Jay -Brklyn 11201 **Fx:**250-2314
(212) 764-6444 .. **Littwin,** Anne M '00 (Epstein & L,LLP) -450 7th Av -NY 10123 **Fx:**764-6445
(212) 735-3000 .. **Littzi,** John M '04 %Skadden ASM&F LLP -4 Times Sq -NY 10036
(212) 918-3000 .. **Litvack,** Sanford M '64 (Hogan L LLP) -875 3rd Av -NY 10022
(212) 398-0055 .. **Litvin,** Dan '07 %Garwin G&F,LLP -1501 Bway -NY 10036
(212) 407-8364 .. **Litvin,** Joel M '86 NBA -645 5th Av -NY 10022
(212) 310-8000 .. **Litvinoff,** Scott M '09 %Weil G&M LLP -767 5th Av -NY 10153
(718) 428-4806 .. **Litwack,** Kenneth D '77 (K Litwack,PC) -38-08 Bell Blvd -Bayside 11361 **Fx:**947-2794
(718) 428-6100 .. **Litwack,** Lawr M '69 Cnsl Big Apple Abstract Corp -42-40 Bell Blvd -Bayside 11361 **Fx:**428-2064
(718) 428-4605 .. **Litwack,** Robt '92 -42-40 Bell Blvd -Bayside 11361 **Fx:**428-2064
(718) 251-4000 .. **Litwak,** Harris '85 -1370 Ralph Av -Brklyn 11236
(914) 670-5746 .. **Litwer,** Susan '75 -303 Fairway Green -Mamaroneck 10543
(718) 590-2000 .. **Litwin,** Amy J '04 %DA -198 E 161st -Bronx 10451 **Fx:**590-6477
(212) 837-6000 .. **Litwin,** Ethan E '99 (Hughes H&R LLP) -1 Bttry Pk Plz -NY 10004
(212) 557-1854 .. **Litwin,** Gerald H '67 (Litwin & T,PA) -292 Mad Av -NY 10016 **Fx:**557-1856
(212) 355-0934 .. **Litwin,** Jay A '69 -412 E 55th -NY 10022
(716) 854-7525 .. **Litwin,** Jonathan C '07 %Serotte R&W -300 Delaware Av -Buffalo 14202
(518) 372-3329 .. **Litz,** Jos L '85 (Litz & L) -143 Clinton -Schnctdy 12305 **Fx:**372-3358
(518) 372-3329 .. **Litz,** Kenneth P '80 (Litz & L) -143 Clinton -Schnctdy 12305 **Fx:**372-3358
(212) 770-6918 .. **Litzky,** Eric N '90 %AIG -70 Pine -NY 10270 **Fx:**785-1584
(718) 261-7700 .. **Litzman,** Jay H '79 OfCnsl Rappaport HC&R,PC -118-35 Qns Blvd -Frst Hlls 11375
(646) 315-7300 .. **Liu,** Adeline '83 %FINRA -14 Wall -NY 10005 **Fx:**315-7440
(718) 522-3333 .. **Liu,** B B '09 %Children's Law Ctr -44 Court -Brklyn 11201 **Fx:**522-7376
(212) 790-0000 .. **Liu,** Bobby '97 Och-Ziff Capital Mgmt -9 W 57th -NY 10019
(212) 530-5000 .. **Liu,** Brian E '07 %Milbank TH&M LLP -1 Chase Manh Plz -NY 10005
(212) 403-1000 .. **Liu,** C Derek '09 %Wachtell LR&K -51 W 52nd -NY 10019
(347) 404-9133 .. **Liu,** Chas Y J '95 %Civil Ct -141 Lvngstn -Brklyn 11201 **Fx:**(718) 643-3733
(212) 264-5916 .. **Liu,** Chau-Yi '04 DHS -26 Fed Plz -NY 10278
(917) 777-4200 .. **Liu,** Derrick P '09 %Bingham M LLP -1 Bttry Pk Plz -NY 10004
(646) 386-3229 .. **Liu,** Edw '07 NYS Supreme CT -60 Centre -NY 10007
(718) 886-5100 .. **Liu,** Emanuel Weiran '03 -3901 Main -Flushng 11354
(212) 735-3000 .. **Liu,** Emily '09 %Skadden ASM&F LLP -4 Times Sq -NY 10036
(212) 225-2000 .. **Liu,** Emily Y '09 %Cleary GS&H -1 Lbrty Plz -NY 10006
(212) 309-6000 .. **Liu,** Emmeline S '07 %Morgan L&B LLP -101 Park Av -NY 10178
(718) 460-9768 .. **Liu,** Fei '91 -39-01 Main -Flushng 11354
(212) 226-3960 .. **Liu,** Fengling '00 -2 Bway -NY 10038
(212) 345-3020 .. **Liu,** Florence R '03 Marsh & McLennan Cos -1166 Av of Amer -NY 10036
(212) 941-5799 .. **Liu,** Frank Ruhua '00 -401 Bway -NY 10013
(212) 873-7063 .. **Liu,** Geofrey Chien '05 %Joelson & R -149 W 72nd -NY 10023
(212) 446-2300 .. **Liu,** George Y '96 (Boies S&F LLP) -575 Lex Av -NY 10022
(646) 442-3100 .. **Liu,** Gerald B '84 Legal Srvcs -90 John -NY 10038 **Fx:**(212) 227-9798
(212) 626-4100 .. **Liu,** Gilbert K S '96 (Baker & M LLP) -1114 Av of Amer -NY 10036
(914) 995-4457 .. **Liu,** Hae Jin '00 %DA -111 Martin Luther King Blvd -White Plns 10601 **Fx:**995-3363
(212) 335-4500 .. **Liu,** (Henry) Hong '91 (DLA Piper LLP) -1251 Av of Amer -NY 10020
(607) 974-9000 .. **Liu,** Hong '00 %Corning -1 Rvrfrnt Plz -Corning 14831 **Fx:**974-6135
(212) 468-8000 .. **Liu,** Hui '07 %Morrison & F LLP -1290 Av of Amer -NY 10104
(212) 849-7000 .. **Liu,** Jason L '07 %Quinn EU&S,LLP -51 Mad Av -NY 10010
(212) 245-1000 .. **Liu,** Jennifer L '10 %Outten & G LLP -3 Park Av -NY 10016
(212) 558-4000 .. **Liu,** Jiang '02 %Sullivan & C LLP -125 Broad -NY 10004
(212) 765-8370 .. **Liu,** Joanne A '99 -1400 Av of Amer -NY 10019
(212) 813-8800 .. **Liu,** Josephine '06 %Goodwin P LLP -620 8th Av -NY 10018
(212) 259-8000 .. **Liu,** Judy G Z '81 (Dewey & L LLP) -1301 Av of Amer -NY 10019
(212) 608-3103 .. **Liu,** Kelly C '94 %Rubert & G,PC -150 Bway -NY 10038
(212) 965-2250 .. **Liu,** Kimberly A '09 NAACP Legal Dfns & Educ Fund Inc -99 Hudson -NY 10013
(212) 558-4000 .. **Liu,** Kung-Wei '08 %Sullivan & C LLP -125 Broad -NY 10004
(212) 455-2000 .. **Liu,** Lulu Y J '09 %Simpson T&B LLP -425 Lex Av -NY 10017
(718) 243-6846 .. **Liu,** Paul '88 %Leg Aid -111 Lvngstn -Brklyn 11201 **Fx:**237-8737
(212) 762-3327 .. **Liu,** Renee Soniya '00 Morgan Stanley -750 7th Av -NY 10019

(212) 267-9878 .. **Liu,** Stella S '93 -225 Bway -NY 10007 **Fx:**267-1226
(845) 352-4080 .. **Liu,** Sue '06 %Barr P & Assoc PLLC -664 Chestnut Rdg Rd Bx664 -Spg Vly 10977 **Fx:**352-6777
(212) 608-3700 .. **Liu,** Therese Te-Lan '79 (Soong & L) -305 Bway -NY 10007
(212) 698-3500 .. **Liu,** Tina P '98 %Dechert LLP -1095 Av of Amer -NY 10036
(212) 446-2300 .. **Liu,** Vincent Y '07 %Boies S&F LLP -575 Lex Av -NY 10022
(212) 504-6000 .. **Liu,** Wm Y '08 %Cadwalader W&T LLP -1 World Fncl Ctr -NY 10281
(212) 318-3000 .. **Liu,** Xiusheng '08 %Fulbright & J LLP -666 5th Av -NY 10103
(212) 226-0182 .. **Liu,** Yu-Xi '05 -401 Bway -NY 10013 **Fx:**226-0835
(212) 373-3000 .. **Liu,** Zhiping '08 %Paul WRW&G LLP -1285 Av of Amer -NY 10019
(212) 530-5000 .. **Liubicic,** Robt J '99 (Milbank TH&M LLP) -1 Chase Manh Plz -NY 10005
(212) 836-8000 .. **Liubicic,** Sandra J '09 %Kaye S LLP -425 Park Av -NY 10022
(914) 967-3023 .. **Lium,** John D '71 -Bx 664 -Rye 10580
(212) 643-6400 .. **Liuzzo,** Annalisa '98 %Garganigo G&W -14 Penn Plz -NY 10122
(212) 885-5000 .. **Liuzzo,** Peter J '99 %Blank R LLP -405 Lex Av -NY 10174
(212) 825-0365 .. **Liuzzo,** Rosemary J '06 %AL Bailey,PC -120 Bway -NY 10271 **Fx:**825-0999
(518) 439-0375 .. **Livaditis,** Bess '08 %Friedman & M,PC -2 Normanskill Blvd Bx69 -Delmar 12054
(212) 768-6700 .. **Livanos,** Maria M '84 (Sonnenschein N&R LLP) -2 World Fncl Ctr -NY 10281
(212) 848-4000 .. **Lively,** Francis P '08 %Shearman & S LLP -599 Lex Av -NY 10022
(212) 504-6000 .. **Lively,** Jessica '03 %Cadwalader W&T LLP -1 World Fncl Ctr -NY 10281
(212) 839-8630 .. **Lively,** Susan D '09 Sidley A LLP -787 7th Av -NY 10019
(212) 728-8000 .. **Livermore,** Faith K '09 %Willkie F&G LLP -787 7th Av -NY 10019
(718) 624-6263 .. **Liverpool,** Colin A '09 Edwards & Assoc -188 Montague -Brklyn 11201 **Fx:**858-0411
(212) 772-5394 .. **Liveson,** Avi O '75 Hunter College -695 Park Av -NY 10065
(212) 373-3000 .. **Livingston,** Christopher W '10 %Paul WRW&G LLP -1285 Av of Amer -NY 10019
(914) 995-3420 .. **Livingston,** Edw H '88 %DA -111 Martin Luther King Blvd -White Plns 10601 **Fx:**995-3363
(315) 782-3201 .. **Livingston,** H Chas Jr. '82 (Wisner S&L) -1040 Bradley -Watertwn 13601 **Fx:**788-1157
(585) 987-2800 .. **Livingston,** Jason P '06 %Woods OG LLP -2 State -Rchstr 14614
(212) 556-2100 .. **Livingston,** Jeffrey E '73 King & S -1185 Av of Amer -NY 10036
(315) 797-9261 .. **Livingston,** John J '71 (Getnick LA&P,LLP) -258 Genesee -Utica 13502
(212) 267-4177 .. **Livingston,** Judith A '80 (Kramer DL&M) -217 Bway -NY 10007
(518) 455-2577 .. **Livingston,** Karen J '98 %Senate Majority Cnsl -430 The Cptl -Albany 12247
(212) 682-3454 .. **Livingston,** McKenzie A '06 %Rosenberg FS LLP -551 5th Av -NY 10176
(315) 546-0068 .. **Livingston,** Michl N '89 %Sassani & S,PC -7767 Oswego Rd -Liverpool 13090
(212) 687-7770 .. **Livingston,** Peter I '70 (Rosen L&C LLP) -275 Mad Av -NY 10016
(917) 406-4491 .. **Livingston,** Reginald Monroe II '00 -255 Huguenot -New Rchll 10801
(516) 742-6200 .. **Livingston,** Stephen W '07 %Lynn G&D,LLP -330 Old Cntry Rd -Mineola 11501 **Fx:**742-5294
(607) 272-5212 .. **Livingston,** Todd L '06 -401 E State -Ithaca 14850 **Fx:**272-0155
(914) 995-3497 .. **Livingston,** Valerie Anne '89 %DA -111 Martin Luther King Blvd -White Plns 10601 **Fx:**995-3363
(718) 206-0103 .. **Livingston-Corcoran,** Rachel A '99 %Law Dept -89-17 Sutphin Blvd -Jamaica 11435 **Fx:**206-4702
(646) 878-0800 .. **Livneh,** Keren '09 %Pearl CZL,LLP -1500 Bway -NY 10036
(315) 234-9900 .. **Livolsi,** Michl J '07 %F Miller -6575 Kirkvll Rd -E Syracuse 13057 **Fx:**234-9908
(718) 298-1105 .. **Livote,** Leonard '79 Supreme Ct Referee -88-11 Sutphin Blvd -Jamaica 11435
(212) 490-3944 .. **Livoti Bernstein & Moraco,PC** -122 E 42nd -NY 10168 **Fx:**661-5189
(516) 833-5630 .. **Livoti,** Frank J '79 (Beekman SK&L,LLP) -1050 Franklin Av -Gdn Cty 11530
(917) 703-4029 .. **Livoti,** Robt V '73 -47 Barry Rd -Scarsdale 10583
(212) 480-3030 .. **Livow,** Michl S '77 %M Pressman -125 Maiden Ln -NY 10038 **Fx:**480-2590
(631) 853-4377 .. **Livrieri,** Denise '85 %Family Ct -400 Carleton Av Bx9077 -Central Islip 11722
(212) 859-8000 .. **Livshits,** Aleksandr B '10 %Fried FHS&J LLP -1 NY Plz -NY 10004
(212) 225-2000 .. **Livshiz,** David Y '08 %Cleary GS&H -1 Lbrty Plz -NY 10006
(212) 248-3140 .. **Liwski,** Christopher D '10 %Drinker B&R LLP -140 Bway -NY 10005
(718) 230-3730 .. **Liz,** Maria E '88 -459 Vndrblt Av -Brklyn 11238
(914) 684-1700 .. **Lizarazo,** Luz A '09 %Delgado & D -300 Martine Av -White Plns 10601 **Fx:**684-1701
(212) 608-1600 .. **Lizzi,** Michl '92 (Maggiano D&L,PC) -521 5th Av -NY 10175
(212) 372-2000 .. **Lizzul,** John M '80 %Newmark Knight Frank -125 Park Av -NY 10017 **Fx:**372-2386
(212) 335-9000 .. **Llambelis,** Lillian '94 %DA -1 Hogan Pl -NY 10013
(212) 309-1000 .. **Llanes,** Katrina M '08 %Hunton & W -200 Park Av -NY 10166
(212) 819-8200 .. **Llano Oddone,** Rafael E '05 %White & C LLP -1155 Av of Amer -NY 10036
(212) 815-1818 .. **Llewellyn,** Admarie V '96 DC 37 MELS -125 Barclay -NY 10007 **Fx:**815-1343
(212) 782-4212 .. **Llewellyn,** Chas W '95 Bank of Tokyo -1251 Av of Amer -NY 10020
(516) 873-6200 .. **Llewellyn,** Jessica J '06 %R Macchia & Assoc -98 Front -Mineola 11501 **Fx:**873-1611
(212) 836-8000 .. **Llewellyn,** Paul C '96 (Kaye S LLP) -425 Park Av -NY 10022
(917) 620-7971 .. **Llewellyn,** Ron C '00 Cnsl Gray H LLP -845 3rd Av -NY 10022 **Fx:**(202) 218-3910
(718) 250-2000 .. **Llewellyn,** Terry-Ann N '05 DA -350 Jay -Brklyn 11201 **Fx:**250-2314
(212) 826-8200 .. **Llorca,** Manuel R '75 (Llorca & H LLP) -845 3rd Av -NY 10022 **Fx:**935-0671
(845) 353-1818 .. **Llorens,** Armando '89 OfCnsl Furgang & A,LLP -2 Crosfld Av -W Nyack 10994 **Fx:**353-1996
(212) 728-8000 .. **Lloyd,** Andrew R '10 %Willkie F&G LLP -787 7th Av -NY 10019
(914) 995-4172 .. **Lloyd,** Doreen M '97 %DA -111 Martin Luther King Blvd -White Plns 10601 **Fx:**995-3363
(646) 386-5700 .. **Lloyd,** Erin E '07 Civil Ct -111 Centre -NY 10013
(212) 220-3000 .. **Lloyd,** Hope M '00 Broadcast Music Inc -250 Greenwich -NY 10007
(212) 474-1000 .. **Lloyd,** John Clint '09 %Cravath S&M LLP -825 8th Av -NY 10019
(212) 781-4404 .. **Lloyd,** Michl K '85 -775 Riverside Dr -NY 10032
(212) 270-1954 .. **Lloyd,** Seth M '09 JP Morgan Chase & Co -270 Park Av -NY 10017
(212) 489-1600 .. **Lloyd,** Wm F '07 %Deloitte LLP -1633 Bway -NY 10019 **Fx:**492-4201
(718) 270-6495 .. **Lloyd-Bey,** Abdul A '03 Medgar Evers Cllg -1150 Carroll -Brklyn 11225
(212) 756-2000 .. **Lloyd-Davies,** Helen '02 SpclCnsl Schulte R&Z LLP -919 3rd Av -NY 10022
(212) 848-4000 .. **Lo,** Fung-Lum Mindy '09 %Shearman & S LLP -599 Lex Av -NY 10022
(212) 553-3200 .. **Lo,** Hope H '09 %Marulli LE&T,LLP -5 Hanover Sq -NY 10004
(212) 867-0088 .. **Lo,** James P '94 -50 E 42nd -NY 10017
(518) 474-0986 .. **Lo,** Hung Kay '93 %NYS ORPTS -WA Harriman State Campus -Albany 12227 **Fx:**474-3657
(718) 539-8082 .. **Lo,** Julie Y '84 %AO Realty -135-26 Roosevelt Av -Flushng 11354
(718) 463-5043 .. **Lo,** Lawr '85 -136-21 Roosevelt Av -Flushng 11354 **Fx:**939-6929
(212) 688-5447 .. **Lo,** Lawr J '89 %Tseyang Corp -34 E 51st -NY 10022 **Fx:**980-2081
(212) 373-3000 .. **Lo,** Po Ying '08 %Paul WRW&G LLP -1285 Av of Amer -NY 10019
(212) 336-8000 .. **Lo,** Saml '09 %Amster R&E -90 Park Av -NY 10016
(212) 225-2000 .. **Lo,** Shirley Marshall '10 %Cleary GS&H -1 Lbrty Plz -NY 10006
(212) 489-8230 .. **Loacker,** Lynn J '80 Davis WT LLP -1633 Bway -NY 10019
(718) 907-6220 .. **Loatman-Clark,** Tamara L '04 (Johnson L Law Grp LLC) -45 Main -Brklyn 11201 **Fx:**228-8425
(212) 742-8700 .. **Lobaito,** Jennifer M '08 %Garson D&C LLP -110 Wall -NY 10005
(518) 943-7500 .. **Lobb,** Jens G '76 -338 Main -Catskill 12414 **Fx:**943-7510
(518) 966-4355 .. **Lobb,** Jens G '76 -Route 32 Bx 583 -Greenvll 12083 **Fx:**943-7510
(716) 852-2323 .. **Lobban,** Loren D '76 -57 Wdbrdg Av -Buffalo 14214 **Fx:**852-4882
(631) 689-3621 .. **Lobben,** Kathleen F '84 -15 Cemetery Ln -Setauket 11733 **Fx:**689-3621
(212) 474-1000 .. **Lobe,** David R '07 %Cravath S&M LLP -825 8th Av -NY 10019
(212) 664-5016 .. **Lobel,** Beth R '90 %NBC -30 Rckfllr Plz -NY 10112
(212) 764-3757 .. **Lobel,** Douglas A '74 (D Lobel,PC) -28 W 44th -NY 10036 **Fx:**921-4988
(518) 431-0130 .. **Lobel,** Ira B '75 %Fed Medtn & Cncltn Srv -1 Clinton Sq -Albany 12207
(212) 289-5448 .. **Lobel,** Judith Stern '90 -1040 Park Av -NY 10028
(718) 286-6000 .. **Lobel,** Marnie B '99 %DA -125-01 Qns Blvd -Kew Gdns 11415
(212) 226-1133 .. **Lobel,** Peter D '92 -401 Bway -NY 10013 **Fx:**226-1805
(212) 699-0060 .. **Lobel,** Rhona J '78 Lobel Chemical Corp -1556 3rd Av -NY 10128 **Fx:**699-0056
(212) 725-2727 .. **Lobel,** Richd S '99 %S Lobel,PC -9 E 40th -NY 10016 **Fx:**725-3910
(212) 725-2727 .. **Lobel,** Sheldon '61 (S Lobel,PC) -9 E 40th -NY 10016 **Fx:**725-3910
(212) 208-3529 .. **Lobel,** Susan Jacobs '91 %Ambac Assurance -1 State Street Plz -NY 10004 **Fx:**785-1178
(212) 725-2727 .. **Lobel-Esrig,** Marci J '93 %S Lobel,PC -9 E 40th -NY 10016 **Fx:**725-3910
(212) 310-8000 .. **Lobell,** Carl D '62 (Weil G&M LLP) -767 5th Av -NY 10153
(212) 554-4522 .. **Lobell,** J Jay '90 Paramount BioSciences -787 7th Av -NY 10019
(516) 741-6565 .. **LoBello,** Edw J '82 (Meyer SE&K,PC) -990 Stewart Av Bx9194 -Gdn Cty 11530
(212) 239-4999 .. **LoBello,** Edw J '82 (Meyer SE&K,PC) -1350 Bway Bx822 -NY 10018
(516) 877-5600 .. **Lobelson,** Eileen S '86 %R Tusa -1225 Franklin Av -Gdn Cty 11530 **Fx:**877-5695
(212) 918-8202 .. **Lobenfeld,** Eric J '76 (Hogan L LLP) -875 3rd Av -NY 10022
(212) 677-5645 .. **Lobenthal,** Jos S Jr. '59 -440 E 23rd -NY 10010 **Fx:**677-8926
(212) 997-4400 .. **Lobenthal,** Nicholas W '91 (Teitler & T,LLP) -1114 Av of Amer -NY 10036 **Fx:**997-4949
(845) 569-7600 .. **LoBiondo,** Anthony R '92 -36 N Plnk Rd -Newburgh 12550 **Fx:**569-7601
(845) 569-7600 .. **LoBiondo,** Juliana '91 -36 N Plnk Rd -Newburgh 12550 **Fx:**569-7601
(212) 732-6460 .. **Lobl,** David '78 (Schwartz & S,PC) -225 Bway -NY 10007
(212) 450-4000 .. **Lobl,** Herbert M '60 SrCnsl Davis P&W LLP -450 Lex Av -NY 10017
(914) 235-8550 .. **Lobo,** Cynthia W '99 (Lobo Law Firm) -240 North Av -New Rchll 10801 **Fx:**235-8570
(718) 578-9963 .. **Lobosco,** Jos A '90 -118-21 Qns Blvd -Frst Hlls 11375
(212) 446-4800 .. **Lobovits,** Esty R '08 %Kirkland & E LLP -153 E 53rd -NY 10022
(718) 667-0001 .. **Lobraico-Reitano,** Gina-Marie '86 -1918 Victory Blvd -Staten Isl 10314 **Fx:**667-0610
(212) 455-2000 .. **Lobrano,** John D '84 (Simpson T&B LLP) -425 Lex Av -NY 10017
(212) 688-8555 .. **Lo Breglio,** Kiera '06 %Fragomen DB&L LLP -7 Hanover Sq -NY 10004
(718) 641-7538 .. **LoBue,** Jos K '87 -135-20 Lbrty Av -S Richmond Hll 11419
(212) 336-2000 .. **LoBue,** Robt P '79 (Patterson BW&T LLP) -1133 Av of Amer -NY 10036
(212) 545-1740 .. **LoBue,** Thos S '91 OfCnsl Ateshoglou & A,PC -381 Park Av S -NY 10016
(718) 341-2623 .. **Locantro,** James C '89 -1 Cross Isl Plz -Rosedale 11422
(215) 864-6364 .. **LoCasale,** Gregory T '89 (White and W LLP) -1 Penn Plz -NY 10119 **Fx:**789-7665
(914) 428-0505 .. **LoCascio,** Jos C '69 -200 E Post Rd -White Plns 10601 **Fx:**428-0519
(914) 478-0900 .. **LoCascio,** Jos R Jr. '77 -560 Warburton Av -Hastings-On-Hud 10706 **Fx:**478-1720
(315) 579-0273 .. **Locastro,** Beth A S '07 -100 Kreischer Rd -Syracuse 13212 **Fx:**422-3259
(212) 291-3672 .. **Locatelli,** Tina L '02 %Cirigroup -125 Broad -NY 10004
(631) 845-2600 .. **Lochner,** Christopher M '97 %Morenus CG&B -58 S Srvc Rd -Melvll 11747
(914) 773-1818 .. **Lochner,** Stephen '77 (Edelstein & L LLP) -343 Manvll Rd -Plsntvll 10570
(518) 486-4523 .. **Lochte,** Drew A '93 %Dept of Law -The Cptl -Albany 12224
(212) 336-8000 .. **LoCicero,** Anthony F '76 (Amster R&E) -90 Park Av -NY 10016
(716) 856-2626 .. **Locicero,** Michl J '10 %Tronolone & S,PC -298 Main -Buffalo 14202

(716) 856-2626 .. **Locicero,** Nicholas G '08 %Tronolone & S,PC -298 Main -Buffalo 14202
(716) 684-5123 .. **LoCicero,** Nicholas L '72 -25 Central Av -Lancaster 14086 **Fx:**684-5125
(718) 875-1300 .. **Locitzer,** Deborah J '85 %Appllt Div 2nd Dept -45 Monroe Pl -Brklyn 11201 **Fx:**858-2446
(212) 261-8000 .. **Lock,** George C '73 (Mendes & M,LLP) -750 7th Av -NY 10019
(212) 237-8000 .. **Lock,** Shmuel T '93 %John Jay Cllg -899 10th Av -NY 10019
(212) 578-3154 .. **Lockard,** Jessica L '04 %MetLife -27-01 Qns Plz N -LIC 11101
(212) 637-2193 .. **Lockard,** Michl D '04 %US Atty -1 St Andrews Plz -NY 10007
(212) 935-8787 .. **Locke,** Chas T '75 (Locke & H,LLP) -1114 Av of Amer -NY 10036 **Fx:**935-5663
(914) 632-8568 .. **Locke,** Gordon '63 -74 Sheldrake Pl -New Rchll 10804 **Fx:**654-8226
(718) 821-1943 .. **Locke,** Henry F Jr. '66 Locke & L -68-31 Fresh Pond Rd -Rdgwd 11385 **Fx:**821-1950
(585) 263-1000 .. **Locke,** James A III '67 SrCnsl Nixon P LLP -1100 Clinton Sq -Rchstr 14604
(716) 847-8400 .. **Locke,** James A '75 (Phillips L LLP) -3400 HSBC Ctr -Buffalo 14203
(212) 554-2600 .. **Locke,** Jeffrey B '02 Daylight Forensic -1 Rckfllr Plz -NY 10020
(212) 388-3000 .. **Locke,** Katchen A '00 %Local 32B-32J SEIU -101 Av of Amer -NY 10013
(212) 730-7750 .. **Locke,** Kevin S '96 %Nicoletti GS&O,LLP -555 5th Av -NY 10017
(212) 415-8600 .. **Locke Lord Bissell & Liddell LLP** -3 World Fncl Ctr -NY 10281 **Fx:**303-2754
(315) 733-0419 .. **Locke,** Merritt Sullivan '94 (Saunders K,LLP) -185 Genesee -Utica 13501
(212) 202-2600 .. **Locke,** Roy G '06 OfCnsl Sher LLP -41 Mad Av -NY 10010 **Fx:**202-4156
(212) 813-1600 .. **Locke,** Scott D '96 %Kalow & S -488 Mad Av -NY 10022
(212) 430-6400 .. **Locke,** Steven I '96 (Carabba L LLP) -100 William -NY 10038
(585) 266-7780 .. **Lockemeyer,** Jennifer L '97 Ayco Co -147 Chestnut Hill Dr -Rchstr 14617 **Fx:**266-8615
(212) 391-5200 .. **Locker,** Aaron '52 (Locker G&B,PC) -420 5th Av -NY 10018
(212) 757-6027 .. **Locker,** Alan N '64 -630 5th Av -NY 10111
(212) 391-5200 .. **Locker,** Fredk B '81 (Locker G&B,PC) -420 5th Av -NY 10018
(212) 391-5200 .. **Locker Greenberg & Brainin,PC** -420 5th Av -NY 10018 **Fx:**391-2035
(212) 391-5200 .. **Locker,** Jeffrey M '82 (Locker G&B,PC) -420 5th Av -NY 10018
(212) 442-3010 .. **Locker,** Katherine R '99 ACS -150 William -NY 10038
(516) 394-4200 .. **Lockhart,** Brian C '04 %Duffy & D -1370 RXR Plz -Uniondale 11556
(212) 807-5529 .. **Lockhart,** Dorothea '99 -305 Mad Av -NY 10165
(631) 495-5892 .. **Lockhart,** Harvey G '66 -755 Park Av -Huntngtn 11743 **Fx:**423-1201
(585) 243-4320 .. **Lockhart,** John M III '97 %Presutti Law Ofc,PC -32 Main Bx157 -Geneseo 14454 **Fx:**243-0420
(212) 732-3200 .. **Lockhart,** Judith A '86 (Carter L&M LLP) -2 Wall -NY 10005
(718) 250-2000 .. **Lockhart,** Lynnette N '08 %DA -350 Jay -Brklyn 11201 **Fx:**250-2314
(914) 632-1606 .. **Lockhart,** Ronald S '59 -6 Forbes Blvd -Eastchstr 10709 **Fx:**623-0649
(212) 668-5927 .. **Locklear,** Amber S '06 %Ropers MK&B -17 State -NY 10004
(716) 662-1900 .. **Locklear,** Cynthia E '84 %ITT Corp -7 Centre Dr -Orchard Pk 14127
(212) 838-3333 .. **Locks,** Gene '94 (Locks Law Firm,PLLC) -747 3rd Av -NY 10017 **Fx:**838-3735
(212) 577-3344 .. **Lockshin,** Amanda '07 Leg Aid -199 Water -NY 10038
(718) 875-1300 .. **Lockwood,** Jack W II '09 %Appllt Div 2nd Dept -45 Monroe Pl -Brklyn 11201 **Fx:**858-2446
(315) 635-9944 .. **Lockwood,** M June '63 OfCnsl Bucci Law Firm,PLLC -104 Syracuse Bx207 -Baldwinsvll 13027 **Fx:**638-1827
(631) 242-3369 .. **Lockwood,** Scott '96 -1476 Deer Prk Av -N Babylon 11703
(315) 724-5177 .. **Lockwood,** Stephen L '67 (S Lockwood,PC) -285 Genesee -Utica 13501 **Fx:**368-0084
(516) 572-3446 .. **Loconsolo,** Elizabeth J '85 Sheriff's Ofc -100 Carman Av -E Meadow 11554
(212) 370-5800 .. **Loconte,** Richd A '05 Assn for a Better NY -355 Lex Av -NY 10017 **Fx:**661-4304
(315) 376-5347 .. **Loconti,** Kathlene M '01 Supreme Ct -7660 State -Lowvll 13367 **Fx:**376-5398
(718) 590-6362 .. **Locorotondo,** Lucianna '89 Supreme Ct -851 Grand Cncrs -Bronx 10451 **Fx:**590-1011
(212) 340-0400 .. **LoCurto,** Laura T '81 %Appllt Div 1st Dept -27 Mad Av -NY 10010 **Fx:**889-4412
(516) 571-3033 .. **LoCurto,** Lisa Anne '96 %Cnty Atty -1 West -Mineola 11501 **Fx:**571-6604
(212) 773-6634 .. **Loda,** Katherine E '98 Ernst & Young LLP -5 Times Sq -NY 10036
(516) 571-3883 .. **Lodato,** James J '83 %Supreme Ct Law Lib -100 Supreme Ct Dr -Mineola 11501
(516) 794-1100 .. **Lodato,** Vincent J '93 (Russo D&L) -1975 Hempstd Tpk -E Meadow 11554
(845) 225-8155 .. **Lodes,** Carl F '73 -1717 Route 6 Bx806 -Carmel 10512 **Fx:**225-1303
(716) 484-7196 .. **Lodestro,** Lucian L '59 (Fessenden L&D) -81 Forest Av Bx590 -Jamestwn 14702
(914) 272-4017 .. **Lodewick,** Robt J Jr. '65 Gerber Life Ins Co -1311 Mamaroneck Av -White Plns 10605 **Fx:**272-4099
(212) 947-4999 .. **Lodge,** Suzanne O'Keefe '97 %Camacho MM,LLP -350 5th Av -NY 10118
(518) 402-9185 .. **Lodico,** Philip '76 %DEC -625 Bway -Albany 12233 **Fx:**402-9018
(607) 734-0500 .. **Lodico,** Wm J '80 -150 Lk Bx1176 -Elmira 14902
(518) 473-4596 .. **Lodovice,** Clay J '02 Employee Relations -Agncy Bldg 2 -Albany 12223
(212) 964-3290 .. **LoDuca,** Peter P '85 OfCnsl Levidow L&O -299 Bway -NY 10007
LoDuca, Salvatore '91 CLM Dvlpmnt Corp -653 152nd -Whitestone 11357
(212) 268-8707 .. **Loeb,** Andrew I '84 (A Loeb,PC) -50 W 17th -NY 10011 **Fx:**(917) 386-2275
(212) 755-5510 .. **Loeb Block & Partners** -505 Park Av -NY 10022 **Fx:**755-1777
(212) 744-0184 .. **Loeb,** Hadassah S '85 -133 E 64th -NY 10065
(914) 286-3400 .. **Loeb,** Harvey '81 Leg Aid -1 N Bway -White Plns 10601 **Fx:**682-4112
(845) 561-0550 .. **Loeb,** James R '58 (Drake LHKGG&R PLLC) -555 Hudson Valley Av -New Windsor 12553
(585) 264-1880 .. **Loeb,** Judith Holender '84 -290 Linden Oaks -Rchstr 14625 **Fx:**586-7393
(212) 649-2000 .. **Loeb,** Larry M '67 %Hearst Corp -300 W 57th -NY 10019 **Fx:**649-2035
(212) 407-4000 .. **Loeb & Loeb,LLP** -345 Park Av -NY 10154 **Fx:**407-4990
(212) 863-8060 .. **Loeb,** Stephen A '89 %HPD -100 Gold -NY 10038
(845) 371-4700 .. **Loeb,** Steven A '05 %Fein SK&S,PC -747 Chestnut Rdg Rd -Spg Vly 10977
(212) 225-2000 .. **Loeb,** Steven M '80 (Cleary GS&H) -1 Lbrty Plz -NY 10006
(718) 928-3700 .. **Loeb,** Wm A '81 LSNYC-Bronx -579 Courtlandt Av -Bronx 10451 **Fx:**402-7586
(609) 919-6672 .. **Loeber,** Christopher C '96 (Morgan L&B LLP) -101 Park Av -NY 10178 **Fx:**919-6600
(212) 446-4800 .. **Loebl,** Maurice '06 %Kirkland & E LLP -153 E 53rd -NY 10022
(212) 218-5500 .. **Loebl,** Richd I '03 OfCnsl Seyfarth S LLP -620 8th Av -NY 10018
(212) 343-5775 .. **Loecher,** Murray '65 -7 Wrld Trd Ctr -NY 10007
(212) 326-3939 .. **Loecker,** Matthew R '09 %Jones D -222 E 41st -NY 10017
(631) 853-4104 .. **Loeffler,** Catherine M '93 %DA -400 Carleton Av Bx9082 -Central Islip 11722 **Fx:**853-7838
(631) 232-4180 .. **Loeffler,** James M '96 (J Loeffler,PLLC) -320 Carleton Av -Central Islip 11722 **Fx:**342-8350
(718) 579-3000 .. **Loehr,** Melissa A '02 %Leg Aid -1020 Grnd Cncrs -Bronx 10451 **Fx:**588-2611
(212) 854-9869 .. **Loengard,** Philippa S M '04 Columbia Law Schl-Kernochan Ctr -435 W 116th -NY 10027
(212) 238-3000 .. **Loening,** Michl '59 OfCnsl Emmet M&M,LLP -120 Bway -NY 10271
(212) 376-6400 .. **Loesberg,** Matthew T '89 %Marshall DWC&G -88 Pine -NY 10005
(212) 661-9100 .. **Loesberg,** Michl J '93 %Otterbourg SH&R,PC -230 Park Av -NY 10169
(716) 362-2323 .. **Loesch,** Julie M '98 %Child & Fam Svcs-Ctr for Resolutn & Jstc -625 Delaware Av -Buffalo 14202 **Fx:**362-2324
(212) 481-5777 .. **Loesch,** Lawr F '83 Allied Barton Security Srvcs -330 W 34th -NY 10001
(212) 525-6170 .. **Loeser,** Doron I '87 %HSBC Bank -452 5th Av -NY 10018
(716) 632-4048 .. **Loeser,** Herbert W Jr. '53 -90 Stoneleigh Av -Buffalo 14223
(212) 880-3800 .. **Loeser,** Jessica T '07 %Akerman S -335 Mad Av -NY 10017
(212) 259-8000 .. **Loeshelle,** Steven R '74 (Dewey & L LLP) -1301 Av of Amer -NY 10019
(516) 543-4510 .. **Loew,** Albert '58 -25 Merrick Av -Merrick 11566
(607) 763-9200 .. **Loew,** Jeffrey A '94 (Levene G&T,LLP) -BxF-1706 -Bnghmtn 13902
(518) 462-1015 .. **Loew,** Jill A '89 %ODAR-SSA -74 N Pearl -Albany 12207
(631) 265-1700 .. **Loew,** Raymond M '66 OfCnsl Kenney GW&S,LLP -50 Route 111 -Smithtwn 11787
(914) 763-5619 .. **Loewald,** Francis A '70 -106 Boway Rd Bx200 -S Salem 10590 **Fx:**763-3870
(212) 335-4500 .. **Loewe,** Mads R '03 %DLA Piper LLP -1251 Av of Amer -NY 10020
(845) 638-3886 .. **Loewenberg,** Deborah Wolikow '80 (Loewenberg & Y,LLP) -155 N Main -New Cty 10956 **Fx:**638-3889
(845) 634-9500 .. **Loewenberg,** Deborah Wolikow '80 (Gribetz & L,PLLC) -155 N Main -New Cty 10956 **Fx:**639-9105
(212) 468-8000 .. **Loewenson,** Carl H Jr. '85 (Morrison & F LLP) -1290 Av of Amer -NY 10104
(646) 878-0800 .. **Loewenstein,** David A '88 (Pearl CZL,LLP) -1500 Bway -NY 10036
(518) 432-7861 .. **Loewenstein,** Nina '94 %Disability Advocates,Inc -5 Clinton Sq -Albany 12207 **Fx:**427-6561
(973) 315-4417 .. **Loewenstein,** Robt A '79 (Budd L) -140 Bway -NY 10005
(212) 684-3900 .. **Loewenthal,** Barbara H '91 Cnsl Gottlieb R&R,PC -270 Mad Av -NY 10016
(212) 335-9000 .. **Loewy,** E Elizabeth '85 %DA -1 Hogan Pl -NY 10013
(212) 940-8800 .. **Loewy,** Robt '99 SpclCnsl Katten MR LLP -575 Mad Av -NY 10022
(212) 609-6800 .. **Lofaro,** Adriana M '09 %McCarter & E,LLP -245 Park Av -NY 10167
(212) 878-1700 .. **Lofaro,** Christian D '03 %Marshall DWC&G -140 Bway -NY 10005
(914) 681-0200 .. **Lofaro,** Jennifer A '06 %DelBello DWW&W,LLP -1 N Lex Av -White Plns 10601
(315) 476-5280 .. **LoFaro,** John A '90 -307 S Clinton -Syracuse 13202 **Fx:**479-8847
(201) 498-0400 .. **LoFaro & Reiser,LLP** -100 Wall -NY 10005 **Fx:**498-0016
(212) 504-6000 .. **Lofchie,** Steven '90 (Cadwalader W&T LLP) -1 World Fncl Ctr -NY 10281
(212) 558-4000 .. **Lofdahl,** Lisa A '00 SpclCnsl Sullivan & C LLP -125 Broad -NY 10004
(212) 335-4500 .. **Loffman,** Leslie '79 (DLA Piper LLP) -1251 Av of Amer -NY 10020
(212) 805-3900 .. **Loffredo,** Michl T '99 %Clausen M PC -1 Chase Manh Plz -NY 10005
(718) 340-4200 .. **Loffredo,** Stephen J '82 %CUNY Law Schl -65-21 Main -Flushng 11367 **Fx:**340-4482
(212) 551-1192 .. **Lofredo,** Andrew V '04 (Capuano & L LLP) -380 Lex Av -NY 10168 **Fx:**(646) 558-0238
(914) 347-2600 .. **Lofrese,** James J '92 %Traub LS&S LLP -7 Skyline Dr -Hawthorne 10532
(516) 222-6500 .. **Lofrumento,** Michl F '02 (Galasso LC&L,LLP) -377 Oak -Gdn Cty 11530
(212) 460-1137 .. **Lofrumento,** Susan J '93 ConEd Co of NY,Inc -4 Irving Pl -NY 10003
(212) 474-1000 .. **Loft,** Duane L '06 %Cravath S&M LLP -825 8th Av -NY 10019
(516) 826-6500 .. **Loftin,** Jacqulyn S '08 %LaMonica H&M LLP -3305 Jerusalem Av -Wantagh 11793
(212) 364-5340 .. **Loftis,** David E '91 %Innocence Project -100 5th Av -NY 10011 **Fx:**364-5341
(716) 856-0600 .. **Loftis,** Tim C '81 (Jaeckle F&M,LLP) -12 Fountain Plz -Buffalo 14202
(212) 848-4000 .. **Loftus,** James G '05 %Shearman & S LLP -599 Lex Av -NY 10022
(585) 889-1180 .. **Loftus,** John M '59 -54 Main -Scottsvll 14546 **Fx:**889-1189
(716) 852-3600 .. **Loftus,** Kevin E '03 %Chelus HS&M,PC -438 Main -Buffalo 14202
(914) 948-4500 .. **Loftus,** Kevin M '84 (O'Connor MCD&O) -1 Barker Av -White Plns 10601
(845) 634-0888 .. **Loftus,** Patrick J '90 (Freeman & L RLLP) -4 Laurel Rd -New Cty 10956

(212) 756-2000 .. **Loga**, Karen J '99 SpclCnsl Schulte R&Z LLP -919 3rd Av -NY 10022
(212) 480-6297 .. **Logan**, Ann Hyatt '07 %Insurance Dept -25 Beaver -NY 10004 **Fx:**480-5272
(518) 437-1802 .. **Logan**, Brian E '92 Bryant & Stratton College -1259 Central Av -Albany 12205 **Fx:**437-1048
(212) 351-4000 .. **Logan**, Cedric D '09 %Gibson D&C LLP -200 Park Av -NY 10166
(212) 578-3117 .. **Logan**, Duncan J '90 %MetLife -27-01 Qns Plz N -LIC 11101
(914) 948-8373 .. **Logan**, Henry J '54 -925 Wstchstr Av -White Plns 10604 **Fx:**946-3708
(212) 806-1656 .. **Logan**, John F '80 %AMFAR -120 Wall -NY 10005 **Fx:**806-1601
(212) 455-2000 .. **Logan**, Kenneth R '73 OfCnsl Simpson T&B LLP -425 Lex Av -NY 10017
(716) 845-7455 .. **Logan**, Margaret L '87 Family Ct -1 Niagara Plz -Buffalo 14202 **Fx:**858-4739
(212) 547-5400 .. **Logan**, Molly A '09 %McDermott W&E LLP -340 Mad Av -NY 10173
(914) 231-2700 .. **Logan**, Richd H '83 %DA -104 S Bway -Ynkrs 10701 **Fx:**969-0574
(212) 735-3000 .. **Logan**, Thos D '89 Cnsl Skadden ASM&F LLP -4 Times Sq -NY 10036
(212) 481-1411 .. **Logan**, W Andrew P III '96 Donlin Recano -419 Park Av S -NY 10016 **Fx:**481-1416
(585) 232-2292 .. **Logan-Baldwin**, Emmelyn '69 -171 State -Rchstr 14614
(845) 638-3178 .. **Loganzo**, Rondi Kline '92 -7 Gregory -New Cty 10956 **Fx:**638-3179
(212) 651-9500 .. **Loggie**, Ryan P '09 Matlin Patterson Global Advisers LLC -520 Mad Av -NY 10022
(212) 486-2626 .. **Logigian**, John D '78 %Jean Doumanian Prdctns -595 Mad Av -NY 10022
(212) 486-1455 .. **LoGiudice**, Laura M '00 %Post PGM&S,PA -575 Mad Av -NY 10022
(212) 944-9009 .. **LoGiudice**, Michl '97 (M LoGiudice,LLP) -263 New Hcknsck Rd -Wappingers Fls 12590 **Fx:**(845) 463-5856
(516) 248-9880 .. **Loglisci**, David A '93 (Agovino & A,LLP) -330 Old Cntry Rd -Mineola 11501
(631) 462-6900 .. **Loglisci**, Marcus E '03 (Alber & L) -5036 Jericho Tpk -Commack 11725 **Fx:**462-6999
(212) 335-9000 .. **Logue**, Emily A '02 %DA -1 Hogan Pl -NY 10013
(212) 318-6000 .. **Logue**, Kevin C '85 (Paul HJ&W LLP) -75 E 55th -NY 10022
(212) 689-8808 .. **Logue**, Sarah K '08 Hoguet NR&K,LLP -10 E 40th -NY 10016
(212) 816-9347 .. **Logue**, Sofia '00 Citigroup -388 Greenwich -NY 10013 **Fx:**732-2982
(516) 248-3302 .. **Logue**, Toni E '87 %Dept of Law -200 Old Cntry Rd -Mineola 11501 **Fx:**747-6432
(631) 853-5160 .. **Loguercio**, Caren L '93 Hon E Pines -400 Carleton Av -Central Islip 11722
(516) 873-8000 .. **Loguidice**, Andrea D '06 %Kroll M&K,LLP -400 Grdn City Plz -Gdn Cty 11530
(212) 259-8000 .. **Loguidice**, Dana L '06 %Dewey & L LLP -1301 Av of Amer -NY 10019
(212) 349-0450 .. **LoGuidice**, Robin '90 (Grimble & L,LLC) -217 Bway -NY 10007
(646) 386-3365 .. **Logus**, Maria '81 %Hon J Carey -100 Centre -NY 10013
(212) 310-8000 .. **Loh**, Andrea Y '10 %Weil G&M LLP -767 5th Av -NY 10153
(212) 218-2100 .. **Loh**, Christopher E '99 %Fitzpatrick CH&S -1290 Av of Amer -NY 10104
(212) 509-9400 .. **Loh**, David Y '93 (Cozen O) -45 Bway Atrium -NY 10006
(212) 455-2000 .. **Lohia**, Swati '08 %Simpson T&B LLP -425 Lex Av -NY 10017
(212) 637-2235 .. **Lohier**, Raymond J Jr. '93 SpclCnsl US Atty -1 St Andrews Plz -NY 10007
(212) 325-2000 .. **Lohonen**, Dylan P '05 Credit Suisse -1 Mad Av -NY 10010
(516) 868-6737 .. **Lohr**, Donald R '78 -50 Chas Lindbergh Blvd -Uniondale 11553
(212) 633-5230 .. **Lohr**, Grace White '82 %Talent Partners -115 W 18th -NY 10011
(914) 946-1400 .. **Lohrfink**, Chas D Jr. '79 (Vouté LM&C,LLP) -170 Hmltn Av -White Plns 10601
(716) 626-1564 .. **Lohrman**, Chas Richd '97 %Simpson & S PLLC -5555 Main -Williamsvll 14221 **Fx:**626-0366
(718) 979-7114 .. **Loiacono**, Angelo R '01 (Martin & L) -274 Watchogue Rd -Staten Isl 10304 **Fx:**979-6657
(845) 566-5345 .. **Loiacono**, Dana M '00 %Larkin AI&T,LLP -356 Meadow Av -Newburgh 12550
(718) 370-7030 .. **Loiacono**, Nicholas J '07 %Amabile & E,PC -1000 South Av -Staten Isl 10314
(212) 849-7000 .. **Loigman**, Robt S '94 (Quinn EU&S,LLP) -51 Mad Av -NY 10010
(845) 471-4440 .. **Lois**, Dale J '90 (Quartararo & L PLLC) -1399 Route 52 -Fishkill 12524 **Fx:**471-7318
(212) 714-1720 .. **Lois**, Gregory '09 (Tompkins MW&B LLP) -140 Bway -NY 10005
(631) 853-4104 .. **Loiseau**, Latoya R '07 DA -400 Carleton Av Bx9082 -Central Islip 11722 **Fx:**853-7838
(212) 789-2688 .. **Loiselle**, Claude G '00 %NHL -1251 Av of Amer -NY 10020
(718) 335-3312 .. **Loiti**, Antonio '66 -30-21 72nd -Flushng 11370
(212) 909-6000 .. **Loizou**, Elaina '06 %Debevoise & P LLP -919 3rd Av -NY 10022
(516) 572-6818 .. **Loizzo**, Josephine A '84 %MHLS -2201 Hempstd Tpk -E Meadow 11554 **Fx:**572-4926
(212) 408-2500 .. **Lok**, Helen '09 %Baker B,LLP -30 Rckfllr Plz -NY 10112
(315) 234-8610 .. **Lok**, Lily K '02 Hon G Lowe -100 S Clinton Bx7346 -Syracuse 13261
(212) 455-2000 .. **Lok**, Mindy M '05 %Simpson T&B LLP -425 Lex Av -NY 10017
(631) 853-4049 .. **Lolis**, Gail M '86 %Cnty Atty -Dennison Bldg Bx6100 -Hauppauge 11788 **Fx:**853-5169
(212) 237-0000 .. **Lollo**, Stephanie '04 %Vinson & E LLP -666 5th Av -NY 10103
(516) 354-5454 .. **Loloey**, Aaron '96 -3000 Marcus Av -Lk Success 11042 **Fx:**354-2803
(212) 504-6000 .. **Lom**, Andrew J '06 %Cadwalader W&T LLP -1 World Fncl Ctr -NY 10281
(718) 334-2351 .. **Lomangino**, Vincent M '99 %MHLS -79-01 Bway -Elmhrst 11373 **Fx:**334-2353
(518) 725-7578 .. **Lomanto**, Angelo D '61 -36 Prospect Av -Gloversvll 12078
(518) 465-3553 .. **Lomanto**, Concetta R '87 (Maynard OS&C,LLP) -6 Twr Pl -Albany 12203
(518) 725-3111 .. **Lomanto**, Edw S '57 -6 Fremont -Gloversvll 12078 **Fx:**725-2746
(718) 286-7100 .. **Lomanto**, Salvatore '87 %FBI -80-02 Kew Grdns Rd -Kew Gdns 11415
(212) 525-6694 .. **LoMascolo**, Angelo R '81 HSBC Markets USA Inc -452 5th Av -NY 10018
(212) 682-7704 .. **Lomax**, Donald R '79 D Lomax,PC -386 Park Av S -NY 10016 **Fx:**682-2494
(212) 442-6860 .. **Lomazow**, Jillian P '02 %Law Dept -52 Duane -NY 10007 **Fx:**442-6868
(212) 530-5000 .. **Lomazow**, Tyson M '01 (Milbank TH&M LLP) -1 Chase Manh Plz -NY 10005
(585) 225-5110 .. **Lomb**, Gregory P '91 -39 Crab Apple Ln -Rchstr 14626
(212) 551-1755 .. **Lombard**, G Mathew III '97 (Lombard & G LLP) -230 Park Av -NY 10169 **Fx:**(646) 349-5567
(718) 793-2626 .. **Lombard**, Leonard '72 -1 Station Sq -Frst Hlls 11375
(718) 615-4550 .. **Lombard**, Leslie A '96 %S Hilsenrath -1803 Gravesend Neck Rd -Brklyn 11229 **Fx:**615-4557
(718) 359-2200 .. **Lombard**, Richd T Jr. '90 (Cullen and D LLP) -158-14 Nrthrn Blvd -Flushng 11358
(212) 285-3800 .. **Lombardi**, Brooke '06 %Subin Assoc LLP -150 Bway -NY 10007
(212) 880-2632 .. **Lombardi**, Christine '95 %R Warfield -100 Park Av -NY 10017 **Fx:**880-6499
(212) 619-8328 .. **Lombardi**, Dino J '90 (Lombardi & S PLLC) -52 Duane -NY 10007 **Fx:**732-6323
(212) 788-0667 .. **Lombardi**, Ellen '88 %Law Dept -100 Church -NY 10007 **Fx:**788-0367
(315) 476-3181 .. **Lombardi**, Francis T '61 -Bx11194 -Syracuse 13218
(845) 342-2299 .. **Lombardi**, Frank A '03 -38 Jordan Ln -Middletwn 10940
(718) 822-2203 .. **Lombardi**, Frank D '96 %Cavallo & C -3396 E Tremont Av -Bronx 10461 **Fx:**597-4617
(518) 438-2000 .. **Lombardi**, Gary L '73 (Lombardi WWHA&D PC) -III Winners Cir -Albany 12205
(914) 472-4242 .. **Lombardi**, Leonard E '67 (Maniatis D&L,LLP) -700 Wht Plns Rd -Scarsdale 10583 **Fx:**472-5074
(212) 964-1390 .. **Lombardi**, Matthew C '06 %Tolmage PH&F -20 Vesey -NY 10007
(914) 948-8180 .. **Lombardi**, Michl J '88 -81 Main -White Plns 10601 **Fx:**683-1279
(315) 442-0100 .. **Lombardi**, Tarky J Jr. '54 (Gilberti SH&S,PC) -555 E Genesee -Syracuse 13202
(212) 557-1818 .. **Lombardi**, Victoria A '82 (Silverson P&L) -192 Lex Av -NY 10016
(518) 438-2000 .. **Lombardi Walsh Wakeman Harrison Amodeo & Davenport PC** -III Winners Cir -Albany 12205 **Fx:**438-2471
(631) 265-4500 .. **Lombardi-Curtin**, Christina M '03 %Meyer M&K -28 Manor Rd -Smithtwn 11787
(718) 849-7272 .. **Lombardino**, Anthony V '60 -101-05 Lefferts Blvd -S Richmond Hll 11419
(212) 244-2999 .. **Lombardo**, Amy C '99 %Kopff N&D LLP -440 9th Av -NY 10001
(212) 859-8000 .. **Lombardo**, Christine M '09 %Fried FHS&J LLP -1 NY Plz -NY 10004
(212) 661-7300 .. **Lombardo**, Frank J '87 (Malapero & P LLP) -295 Mad Av -NY 10017
(518) 843-0043 .. **Lombardo**, James A '80 (Horigan H&L,PC) -49 E Main Bx520 -Amsterdam 12010
(212) 980-4500 .. **Lombardo**, Jennifer '03 %Cohen L LLP -885 3rd Av -NY 10022
(631) 287-3065 .. **Lombardo**, Jos '87 %Town Atty -116 Hmptn Rd -Southampton 11968 **Fx:**287-3662
(973) 596-4481 .. **Lombardo**, Lisa '00 Cnsl Gibbons PC -1 Penn Plz -NY 10119 **Fx:**639-6336
(212) 756-2093 .. **Lombardo**, Lisa L '95 -919 3rd Av -NY 10022
(212) 682-6935 .. **Lombardo**, Louis '96 (Lombardo D LLP) -275 Mad Av -NY 10016 **Fx:**619-1028
(716) 855-1111 .. **Lombardo**, Michl J '81 (Duke HP&G LLP) -350 Main -Buffalo 14202
(518) 474-7330 .. **Lombardo**, Richd '90 %Dept of Law -The Cptl -Albany 12224
(718) 250-2000 .. **Lombardo**, Tazio N '10 %DA -350 Jay -Brklyn 11201 **Fx:**250-2314
(646) 747-5234 .. **Lombardy**, Christopher M '99 (C Lombardy & Assoc,LLC) -546 5th Av -NY 10036
(212) 408-9000 .. **Lombardy**, David Y '04 AXA Advisors,LLC -1633 Bway -NY 10019
(212) 659-9680 .. **Lombillo**, Sybil A '00 Mt Sinai Schl of Med -1 Gustave Levy Pl Bx1675 -NY 10029
(212) 564-8500 .. **Lombino**, Annamaria A '94 -224 W 35th -NY 10001 **Fx:**564-3653
(212) 776-2032 .. **Lombino**, Richd M '98 Coalition for the Homeless -129 Fulton -NY 10038
(631) 271-2771 .. **Lomeli**, Gloria '91 %J Newman -82 Main -Huntngtn 11743 **Fx:**424-1060
(212) 483-9490 .. **Lomelo**, Lisa E '04 %McElroy DM&C,LLP -88 Pine -NY 10005
(212) 267-1900 .. **Lomena**, Edw '06 %Wade CM -111 Bway -NY 10006
(585) 546-1510 .. **Lomenzo**, John P Jr. '74 -144 Exchange Blvd -Rchstr 14614 **Fx:**546-6343
(212) 838-7797 .. **Lometti**, Christopher '87 Cohen MS&T,PLLC -88 Pine -NY 10005
(212) 458-5641 .. **Lomm**, Dana B '07 Chartis -175 Water -NY 10038
(212) 822-0516 .. **Lomm**, Jessica L '04 Apollo Mgmt -9 W 57th -NY 10019
(718) 250-2000 .. **Lomma**, Shea S '05 %DA -350 Jay -Brklyn 11201 **Fx:**250-2314
(212) 647-7300 .. **Lomolino**, Christina C '84 %Intl Photographers Guild -80 8th Av -NY 10011
(585) 244-6000 .. **LoMonaco**, Richd S '61 -2180 Monroe Av -Rchstr 14618
(718) 286-6000 .. **Lomp**, Peter V '93 %DA -125-01 Qns Blvd -Kew Gdns 11415
(718) 849-5314 .. **Lomtevas**, Peter C '00 (P Lomtevas,PC) -101-54 106th -Ozone Pk 11416 **Fx:**738-5314
(718) 262-7100 .. **Lomuscio**, Catherine '80 Civil Ct -89-17 Sutphin Blvd -Jamaica 11435 **Fx:**262-7107
(212) 267-6101 .. **Lomuscio**, Frank A Jr. '87 -305 Bway -NY 10007 **Fx:**(718) 225-1328
(518) 465-3484 .. **Lonano**, James E '09 %Carter CCBM&L,PC -20 Corp Wds Blvd -Albany 12211
(212) 504-6000 .. **Loncar**, Ivan B '00 (Cadwalader W&T LLP) -1 World Fncl Ctr -NY 10281
(518) 464-2419 .. **Loncto**, Deborah A '83 AYCO -1 Wall Bx15073 -Albany 12212
(212) 848-4000 .. **Lonczak**, Donald J '92 (Shearman & S LLP) -599 Lex Av -NY 10022
(212) 808-0700 .. **Londa**, Bruce S '89 (Norris M&M,PA) -875 3rd Av -NY 10022
(212) 449-3727 .. **Londin**, Cara Somach '90 %Merrill Lynch -220 Bway -NY 10038
(516) 746-8000 .. **Londin**, J Robt '87 (Jaspan S LLP) -300 Grdn City Plz -Gdn Cty 11530
(212) 753-6119 .. **London**, Allen F '74 -257 Park Av S -NY 10010
(212) 479-6000 .. **London**, Allison J '05 %Cooley LLP -1114 Av of Amer -NY 10036

(212) 788-0518 .. **London,** Amy Goldman '84 %Law Dept -100 Church -NY 10007 **Fx:**788-0367
(518) 402-9507 .. **London,** Anthony A '94 %DEC -625 Bway -Albany 12233 **Fx:**402-9018
(212) 343-1700 .. **London,** Benjamin C '06 %Cape Advsrs Inc -483 Bway -NY 10013 **Fx:**343-8510
(212) 972-1000 .. **London,** Bernard '78 (London F LLP) -59 Maiden Ln -NY 10038
(212) 972-1000 .. **London,** Danl W '06 %London F LLP -59 Maiden Ln -NY 10038
(212) 788-0755 .. **London,** Dara S '05 Admin Children's Srvcs -220 Church -NY 10013
(914) 965-7230 .. **London,** Donald H '83 -984 N Bway -Ynkrs 10701 **Fx:**965-7237
(212) 833-1199 .. **London,** Ellen M '08 %Friedman KS&A LLP -1633 Bway -NY 10019 **Fx:**373-7999
(518) 279-0088 .. **London,** Eric N '97 -52 Colehamer Av -Troy 12180
(212) 972-1000 .. **London Fischer LLP** -59 Maiden Ln -NY 10038 **Fx:**972-1030
(212) 841-1000 .. **London,** Frank S '02 %Covington & B LLP -620 8th Av -NY 10018
(212) 682-8811 .. **London,** Fredk W '77 OfCnsl Dunnington B&M LLP -1359 Bway -NY 10018
(212) 683-8000 .. **London,** Ira D '60 (London & R) -245 5th Av -NY 10016 **Fx:**683-9422
(212) 859-8000 .. **London,** Joel L '83 SpclCnsl Fried FHS&J LLP -1 NY Plz -NY 10004
(212) 558-4385 .. **London,** Joy E '88 Sullivan & C LLP -125 Broad -NY 10004 **Fx:**558-4155
(212) 964-3700 .. **London,** Joyce E '88 -20 Vesey -NY 10007 **Fx:**964-5911
(212) 490-3000 .. **London,** Kenneth L '02 %Wilson EME&D LLP -150 E 42nd -NY 10017
(631) 454-7070 .. **London,** Laquan M '06 Estee Lauder Co -350 S Srvc Rd -Melvll 11747
(716) 636-7600 .. **London,** Leonard G '67 OfCnsl HoganWillig -2410 N Forest Rd -Amherst 14068
(212) 753-6274 .. **London,** Margot Ross '74 London Mgmt -340 E 51st -NY 10022
(212) 373-3000 .. **London,** Martin '58 OfCnsl Paul WRW&G LLP -1285 Av of Amer -NY 10019
(212) 566-7500 .. **London,** Michl A '98 (Douglas & L) -111 John -NY 10038
(718) 681-3903 .. **London,** Paul S '91 -177 E 161st -Bronx 10451 **Fx:**588-1294
(718) 896-2000 .. **London,** Richd D '97 Taller & W,PC -118-35 Qns Blvd -Frst Hlls 11375
(212) 964-5543 .. **London,** Ronald S '97 %Eisenberg & Blau,CPA'S -150 Bway -NY 10038
(718) 746-3440 .. **London,** Scott A '05 %Sacco & F,LLP -141-07 20th Av -Whitestone 11357
(718) 222-9042 .. **London,** Steven S '90 -44 Court -Brklyn 11201
(212) 964-8038 .. **London,** Stuart '80 (Worth L&L,LLP) -111 John -NY 10038
(914) 288-9600 .. **London,** Wm D '65 -222 Bloomingdale Rd -White Plns 10605 **Fx:**997-2666
(347) 404-9133 .. **London,** Zoe '99 %Civil Ct -141 Lvngstn -Brklyn 11201 **Fx:**(718) 643-3733
(212) 267-6364 .. **Londoner,** Ranakdevi Chudasama '03 %Kossoff & U -217 Bway -NY 10007
(845) 338-5058 .. **Lonergan,** James S '90 (Lonergan & L) -25 Lucas Av -Kingston 12401 **Fx:**338-2596
(212) 801-6927 .. **Lonergan,** Kristen J '01 (Greenberg T,LLP) -200 Park Av -NY 10166
(212) 402-9400 .. **Lonergan,** Kyle A '01 SrCnsl McKool S,PC -1 Bryant Park -NY 10036
(212) 684-2500 .. **Lonergan,** Lawr R '93 -292 Mad Av -NY 10017 **Fx:**684-2512
(845) 338-5058 .. **Lonergan,** Michl J '84 (Lonergan & L) -25 Lucas Av -Kingston 12401 **Fx:**338-2596
(212) 836-7591 .. **Lonergan,** Saml N '02 %Kaye S LLP -425 Park Av -NY 10022 **Fx:**836-6406
(716) 853-8400 .. **Lonergan,** Wm D '83 %Dept of Law -350 Main Pl Twr -Buffalo 14202 **Fx:**853-8571
(212) 836-8000 .. **Lonergan,** Wm M '98 Cnsl Kaye S LLP -425 Park Av -NY 10022
(914) 763-6600 .. **Lonergan,** Wm R Jr. '69 -96 Spring Bx478 -S Salem 10590 **Fx:**763-6617
(212) 605-6200 .. **Long,** Amber R '06 %Levy P&K,LLP -800 3rd Av -NY 10022
(212) 450-4000 .. **Long,** Arthur S '95 (Davis P&W LLP) -450 Lex Av -NY 10017
(914) 761-1300 .. **Long,** Barry E '65 (Cuddy & F LLP) -445 Hmltn Av -White Plns 10601
(212) 325-2864 .. **Long,** Caitlin F '97 Credit Suisse -11 Mad Av -NY 10010
(212) 232-1300 .. **Long,** Christopher A '06 %Lewis BB&S LLP -77 Water -NY 10005
(718) 875-1300 .. **Long,** David C '09 %Appllt Div 2nd Dept -45 Monroe Pl -Brklyn 11201 **Fx:**858-2446
(718) 923-8282 .. **Long,** David S '93 Red Hook Comm Justice Ctr -88 Visitation Pl -Brklyn 11231
(718) 442-2022 .. **Long,** Geoffrey '85 -1942 Victory Blvd -Staten Isl 10314
(212) 416-8729 .. **Long,** Hannah Tischer Stith '01 %Dept of Law -120 Bway -NY 10271
(718) 442-1020 .. **Long,** J Steven '72 -1942 Victory Blvd -Staten Isl 10314 **Fx:**273-0132
(212) 681-1575 .. **Long,** James C Jr. '96 %Belluck & F LLP -546 5th Av -NY 10036
(518) 458-2444 .. **Long,** James E '79 -668 Central Av -Albany 12206 **Fx:**458-2448
(607) 778-2428 .. **Long,** Joan C '90 %Hon F Lebous-Supreme Ct -92 Court -Bnghmtn 13901
(631) 666-5766 .. **Long,** John E Jr. '64 (Long TBSWJ&S) -120 4th Av Bx5591 -Bay Shr 11706
(631) 423-3918 .. **Long,** Joyce D '77 -7 Marine -Huntngtn 11743
(718) 286-6000 .. **Long,** Marcia H '78 %DA -125-01 Qns Blvd -Kew Gdns 11415
(607) 639-2783 .. **Long,** Mary Jo '78 -197 Main Bx465 -Afton 13730 **Fx:**639-2768
(914) 286-3400 .. **Long,** Mary P '86 Leg Aid -1 N Bway -White Plns 10601 **Fx:**682-4112
(212) 661-5858 .. **Long,** Michl G '88 -30 W 26th -NY 10010 **Fx:**255-4285
(718) 590-2000 .. **Long,** Morgan M '08 %DA -198 E 161st -Bronx 10451 **Fx:**590-6477
(716) 853-3801 .. **Long,** Nancy A '07 %Kenney SL&N,LLP -14 Lafayette Sq -Buffalo 14203
(518) 474-2705 .. **Long,** Regina '09 Div of Human Rights -Bx2049 -Albany 12220
(212) 596-1105 .. **Long,** Richd A '76 Sybase,Inc -1114 Av of Amer -NY 10036
(607) 723-9511 .. **Long,** Richd B '57 OfCnsl Coughlin & G,LLP -19 Chenango Bx2039 -Bnghmtn 13902
(631) 585-4343 .. **Long,** Robin L '81 -160-2 Remngtn Blvd -Ronkonkoma 11779
(212) 371-1000 .. **Long,** Shauna R '02 Catholic Charities -1011 1st Av -NY 10022
(212) 490-8026 .. **Long,** Stephen P '80 (Karson & L LLP) -600 3rd Av -NY 10016 **Fx:**490-8413
(716) 689-4972 .. **Long,** Steven K '96 Mark IV Industries -Bx810 -Buffalo 14226
(212) 506-5000 .. **Long,** Susan P '07 %Orrick H&S LLP -51 W 52nd -NY 10019
(212) 909-6000 .. **Long,** Timothy S '01 %Debevoise & P LLP -919 3rd Av -NY 10022
(631) 666-5766 .. **Long Tuminello Besso Seligman Werner Johnston & Sullivan** -120 4th Av Bx5591 -Bay Shr 11706 **Fx:**666-8401
(631) 851-0604 .. **Long,** Walter D Jr. '78 -490 Wheeler Rd -Hauppauge 11788
(716) 362-1139 .. **Long,** Wm A Jr. '90 (Long Firm,LLP) -70 Niagara -Buffalo 14202
(212) 735-3000 .. **Longani,** Kapil '09 %Skadden ASM&F LLP -4 Times Sq -NY 10036
(718) 789-6541 .. **Longchamp,** Wiener '79 -132 6th Av -Brklyn 11217
(518) 486-9564 .. **Longden,** Keith '93 %Workers Comp Bd -20 Park -Albany 12207
(315) 866-3981 .. **Longe,** Francis T '49 -507 Henry -Herkimer 13350
(315) 735-6162 .. **Longeretta,** David A '94 %J Longeretta -298 Genesee -Utica 13502 **Fx:**735-0911
(315) 735-6162 .. **Longeretta,** John A '59 (J Longeretta) -298 Genesee -Utica 13502 **Fx:**735-0911
(315) 735-6162 .. **Longeretta,** Paul M '96 %J Longeretta -298 Genesee -Utica 13502 **Fx:**735-0911
(212) 687-7230 .. **Longman,** Howard T '83 Stull S&B -6 E 45th -NY 10017
(212) 336-2000 .. **Longman,** Jenny L '06 %Patterson BW&T LLP -1133 Av of Amer -NY 10036
(212) 506-1700 .. **Longman,** Robt A '57 OfCnsl Kasowitz BT&F LLP -1633 Bway -NY 10019
(212) 728-8000 .. **Longmire,** John C '96 (Willkie F&G LLP) -787 7th Av -NY 10019
(212) 689-1113 .. **Longo,** Andrew '91 %Garbarini & S,PC -432 Park Av S -NY 10016
(718) 855-5684 .. **Longo & D'Apice** -26 Court -Brklyn 11242 **Fx:**802-9495
(716) 853-8400 .. **Longo,** Darren R '97 %Dept of Law -350 Main Pl Twr -Buffalo 14202 **Fx:**853-8571
(212) 661-9000 .. **Longo,** Frank A '91 %D Golomb -230 Park Av -NY 10169 **Fx:**661-6181
(716) 845-7494 .. **Longo,** Frank J '97 Family Ct -1 Niagara Plz -Buffalo 14202 **Fx:**858-7757
(212) 227-2075 .. **Longo,** Jos J '55 J Longo,PC -321 Bway -NY 10007 **Fx:**349-4037
(212) 237-1000 .. **Longo,** Kim M '02 %Windels ML&M,LLP -156 W 56th -NY 10019
(631) 342-9664 .. **Longo,** Lance R '93 -43 Schneider Ln -Hauppauge 11788 **Fx:**342-9232
(845) 294-3361 .. **Longo,** Laurel A '85 (DeProspo P&L) -42 Park Pl -Goshen 10924
(718) 855-5684 .. **Longo,** Mark A '77 (Longo & D) -26 Court -Brklyn 11242
(716) 854-4080 .. **Longo,** Mark J '91 (Block C&L,PC) -1 Niagara Sq -Buffalo 14202
(914) 345-6510 .. **Longo,** Michl V '02 %Miranda SSSV LLP -570 Taxter Rd -Elmsfrd 10523
(212) 758-4311 .. **Longo,** Peter A '84 (Longo & B) -430 Park Av -NY 10022 **Fx:**758-4312
(914) 946-4777 .. **Longo,** Ronald A '81 (Keane & B,PC) -445 Hmltn Av -White Plns 10601
(631) 665-9274 .. **Longo,** Salvatore P '57 -2174 Pond Rd -Lk Ronkonkoma 11779
(718) 286-6000 .. **Longobardi,** Francis J '06 %DA -125-01 Qns Blvd -Kew Gdns 11415
(914) 681-6060 .. **Longobardi,** Gina M '04 S Owens -140 Grand -White Plns 10601
(914) 323-7000 .. **Longobardi,** Jessica F '07 %Wilson EME&D LLP -3 Gannett Dr -White Plns 10604
(718) 399-5900 .. **Longobardi,** Jo Ann M '91 FIEEF -75 Greene Av -Brklyn 11238
(212) 490-3600 .. **Longobardi,** Laura E '87 %Arenson D&K -295 Mad Av -NY 10017 **Fx:**490-7102
(212) 351-4000 .. **Longobardo,** John P '04 %Gibson D&C LLP -200 Park Av -NY 10166
(914) 761-6131 .. **Longobucco,** Pat '04 -44 Church -White Plns 10601 **Fx:**948-2255
(212) 258-6000 .. **Longoria,** Diane Marks '04 %Viacom -1515 Bway -NY 10036
(212) 705-8862 .. **Longoria,** Jose A '07 QVT Fncl LP -1177 Av of Amer -NY 10036
(973) 596-4629 .. **Longstaff,** Carrie A '06 %Gibbons PC -1 Penn Plz -NY 10119 **Fx:**639-8379
(315) 474-7571 .. **Longstreet,** Ami S '85 (Mackenzie H LLP) -101 S Salina Bx4967 -Syracuse 13221
(315) 422-9295 .. **Longstreet & Berry, LLP** -313 Mntgmry -Syracuse 13202 **Fx:**422-6955
(315) 422-9295 .. **Longstreet,** Michl J '85 (Longstreet & B,LLP) -313 Mntgmry -Syracuse 13202
(518) 766-5959 .. **Longstreet,** Scott P '82 -Bx142 -Old Chatham 12136
(212) 909-6000 .. **Longstreth,** Bevis '62 SrCnsl Debevoise & P LLP -919 3rd Av -NY 10022
(845) 246-9575 .. **Longtoe,** Mark E '00 %Murphy Law Ofc -1 W Brdg Bx300 -Saugerties 12477 **Fx:**246-1905
(212) 490-8003 .. **Longuet,** Pascale '90 -240 E 47th -NY 10017 **Fx:**687-3881
(516) 676-1630 .. **Longworth,** Cara A '93 City Atty -9 Glen -Glen Cove 11542 **Fx:**759-6791
(914) 479-5804 .. **Longworth,** George N '02 (Grant & L,LLP) -377 Ashford Av -Dobbs Ferry 10522 **Fx:**479-5808
(212) 964-8038 .. **Longworth,** Gregory M '93 (Worth L&L,LLP) -111 John -NY 10038
(212) 558-6668 .. **Longworth,** Peter T '80 %Foley SO&W -100 William -NY 10038
(212) 805-4852 .. **Longyear,** Michl D '09 USDC-Sthrn Dist -500 Pearl -NY 10007
(631) 812-6570 .. **LoNigro,** Vincent J '98 Leviton Manufacturing Co Inc -201 N Srvc Rd -Melvll 11747
(212) 935-5500 .. **Lonner,** Jonathan A '95 (Franklin WR&V) -488 Mad Av -NY 10022
(212) 264-5916 .. **Lonoff,** Michl S '94 %DHS -26 Fed Plz -NY 10278
(212) 547-0686 .. **Lonshein,** Alison D '02 Frick Collection -1 E 70th -NY 10021
(716) 856-8804 .. **Lonski,** Robt D '85 %Erie Cnty Bar Assn -170 Franklin -Buffalo 14202 **Fx:**856-0424
(845) 647-8500 .. **Lonstein,** Julie Cohen '91 -1 Terrace Hill Bx351 -Ellenvll 12428 **Fx:**647-6277
(845) 647-8500 .. **Lonstein,** Wayne D '87 -1 Terrace Hill Bx351 -Ellenvll 12428 **Fx:**647-6277
(212) 577-3001 .. **Lonsway,** Nicole S '09 HIV Law Project -15 Maiden Ln -NY 10038
(212) 481-0091 .. **Lontok,** Erwin F '99 (Sonn & Assoc,PC) -207 W 25th -NY 10001 **Fx:**481-0112
(718) 793-5100 .. **Lontos,** Drew R '82 (Young K&L,PC) -86-25 Lefferts Blvd -Richmnd Hll 11418
(718) 935-1010 .. **Lonuzzi,** John A '94 (Lonuzzi & W,LLP) -60 Sackett -Brklyn 11231 **Fx:**935-1935
(212) 848-4000 .. **Loo,** Alexa Jo C Y '09 %Shearman & S LLP -599 Lex Av -NY 10022

(212) 340-2362 .. **Loo,** Christine '90 %Metro-North -347 Mad Av -NY 10017 **Fx:**697-9079
(631) 270-7378 .. **Looby,** Eldon L '04 -68 S Srvc Rd -Melvll 11747
(718) 236-3800 .. **Looby,** Mary M '88 (Gravante & L) -1514 86th -Brklyn 11228
(716) 816-3742 .. **Looby,** Michl J '76 Buffalo Public Schls -713 City Hall -Buffalo 14202
(516) 408-1600 .. **Loock,** Kenneth W '03 %Heidell PM&B,LLP -1050 Franklin Av -Gdn Cty 11530
(212) 484-8000 .. **Look,** Yvonne K '94 %Time Warner -1 Time Warner Ctr -NY 10019
(212) 980-9600 .. **Lookstein,** Thos '01 %Kaufman B&R -120 Bway -NY 10271
(914) 323-7000 .. **Loomba,** Lalit K '92 OfCnsl Wilson EME&D LLP -3 Gannett Dr -White Plns 10604
(212) 465-9200 .. **Loomie,** Paul E '87 (Kolenda & L,LLP) -450 7th Av -NY 10001
(518) 457-2411 .. **Loomis,** Peter S '75 %DOT -50 Wolf Rd -Albany 12232 **Fx:**457-4021
(718) 254-7520 .. **Loonam,** James P '02 US Atty-EDNY -147 Pierrepont -Brklyn 11201
(212) 909-5438 .. **Loonan,** Jos I '79 %KPMG LLP -280 Park Av -NY 10017
(212) 382-3300 .. **Loone,** Piret '02 Cnsl Wollmuth M&D LLP -500 5th Av -NY 10110
(212) 733-1038 .. **Looney,** Adrian G '99 -150 E 42nd -NY 10017
(516) 571-3800 .. **Looney,** Danl G '82 %DA -262 Old Cntry Rd -Mineola 11501 **Fx:**248-9479
(631) 249-8258 .. **Looney,** Francis B '40 -4 Quaker Meeting House Rd -Farmngdl 11735
(716) 854-2020 .. **Looney,** John W '00 (Cellino & B,PC) -350 Main -Buffalo 14202
(212) 455-2000 .. **Looney,** Walter A Jr. '78 (Simpson T&B LLP) -425 Lex Av -NY 10017
(212) 384-1000 .. **Loonie,** Johanna M '89 %FBI -26 Fed Plz -NY 10278
(212) 732-3200 .. **Loop,** Jeffrey L '03 Cnsl Carter L&M LLP -2 Wall -NY 10005
(212) 408-5100 .. **Lootens,** Jennifer M '03 %Chadbourne & P LLP -30 Rckfllr Plz -NY 10112
(212) 267-3700 .. **LoPalo,** Christopher R '04 %Napoli BR LLP -350 5th Av -NY 10118
(212) 947-4999 .. **LoPalo,** Peter J '03 %Camacho MM,LLP -350 5th Av -NY 10118
(845) 486-2300 .. **LoPane,** Angela '99 %DA -236 Main -Poughkeepsie 12601 **Fx:**486-2324
(716) 200-5050 .. **Lopardi,** Tracie L '99 (Harris B PLLC) -726 Exchange -Buffalo 14210
(716) 836-5688 .. **Lopat,** Stanley M '62 -78 E Somerset Av -Tonawanda 14150
(212) 326-3939 .. **Lopata,** Christopher J '97 OfCnsl Jones D -222 E 41st -NY 10017
(973) 596-4611 .. **Lopata,** Pamela '04 %Gibbons PC -1 Penn Plz -NY 10119 **Fx:**639-6341
(914) 925-3440 .. **Lopatin,** Peter A '76 -411 Theo Fremd Av -Rye 10580
(212) 752-0007 .. **Lopeman,** Mark A '91 (Tofel & Prtnrs,LLP) -730 3rd Av -NY 10017 **Fx:**752-8881
(212) 756-2000 .. **Loper,** Robt B '93 (Schulte R&Z LLP) -919 3rd Av -NY 10022
(212) 735-3000 .. **Loper,** Timothy P '06 %Skadden ASM&F LLP -4 Times Sq -NY 10036
(917) 551-1300 .. **Lopera,** Omar D '82 %Koehler & I LLP -61 Bway -NY 10006
(718) 250-2000 .. **Lopes,** Celeste V '85 %DA -350 Jay -Brklyn 11201 **Fx:**250-2314
(212) 676-7920 .. **Lopez,** Anthony '00 %ACS - DLS Child Support -220 Church -NY 10013 **Fx:**676-7956
(212) 878-8000 .. **Lopez,** Anthony A III '02 (Clifford C LLP) -31 W 52nd -NY 10019
(718) 260-4750 .. **Lopez,** Armando '83 %Leg Aid -111 Lvngstn -Brklyn 11201 **Fx:**260-4744
(718) 478-5502 .. **Lopez,** Arturo '09 Emerald Isle Immigration Ctr -5926 Woodside Av 2nd Fl -Woodside 11377
(212) 836-8000 .. **Lopez,** Carlos L '09 %Kaye S LLP -425 Park Av -NY 10022
(212) 308-0070 .. **Lopez,** Catherine C '03 %McCusker AR&C,PC -805 3rd Av -NY 10022
(718) 725-3080 .. **Lopez,** Cynthia '02 ACS -151-20 Jamaica Av -Jamaica 11432 **Fx:**725-3124
(631) 287-5520 .. **Lopez,** David '66 -171 Edge of Woods Rd Bx323 -Southampton 11969 **Fx:**283-4735
(212) 225-2000 .. **Lopez,** David C '90 (Cleary GS&H) -1 Lbrty Plz -NY 10006
(631) 277-0300 .. **Lopez,** Elizabeth '09 %Bartlett MB&M,LLP -670 Main -Islip 11751
(212) 252-7300 .. **Lopez,** Felix '92 %Puerto Rico Fed Affairs Admin -475 Park Av S -NY 10016
(212) 969 3000 .. **Lopez,** Frank J '03 (Proskauer R LLP) -1585 Bway -NY 10036
(585) 325-6530 .. **Lopez,** Gloria '85 %Urban League -265 N Clinton Av -Rchstr 14605 **Fx:**325-4864
(718) 250-2000 .. **Lopez,** Grace J '01 %DA -350 Jay -Brklyn 11201 **Fx:**250-2314
(212) 964-4144 .. **Lopez,** Jason L '01 -325 Bway -NY 10007
(516) 741-4799 .. **Lopez,** Joaquin J '03 %Baker SBGFM&N,LLC -100 Grdn City Plz -Gdn Cty 11530
(212) 267-3091 .. **Lopez,** Julia A '06 %Wilentz G&S -110 William -NY 10038 **Fx:**(732) 726-4766
(718) 429-8469 .. **Lopez,** Leardo L '98 -82-11 37th Av -Jcksn Hts 11372 **Fx:**429-8459
(516) 739-0081 .. **Lopez,** Leslie '04 %Andrea & T -320 Old Cntry Rd -Gdn Cty 11530
(212) 349-6009 .. **Lopez,** Linda '94 %Sanctuary for Families -110 Wall -NY 10005 **Fx:**566-0344
(212) 264-6519 .. **Lopez,** Luz Adriana '04 DHS-Immigration & Customs Enfrcmnt -26 Fed Plz -NY 10278
(212) 446-7000 .. **Lopez,** Luz Mari '93 %McKinsey & Co -55 E 52nd -NY 10055 **Fx:**688-9521
(646) 386-4406 .. **Lopez,** Mayra Ivelisse '01 %Hon R Hayes -111 Centre -NY 10013
(585) 428-5210 .. **Lopez,** Michl C '98 %Pub Def -10 N Fitzhugh -Rchstr 14614 **Fx:**428-2234
(914) 995-4172 .. **Lopez,** Michelle '97 %DA -111 Martin Luther King Blvd -White Plns 10601 **Fx:**995-3363
(212) 557-0200 .. **Lopez,** Miguel A '01 (Quarto L,LLP) -501 5th Av -NY 10017 **Fx:**557-0205
(212) 669-3592 .. **Lopez,** Norma I '89 NYC Civil Serv Comm -1 Centre -NY 10007
(212) 213-8844 .. **Lopez,** Paula '04 %Allyn & F LLP -200 Mad Av -NY 10016
(212) 244-4307 .. **Lopez,** Peter J '87 Alloy,Inc -151 W 26th -NY 10001 **Fx:**244-4311
(212) 788-5020 .. **Lopez,** Robt '79 %Dept Hlth -125 Worth CN-30 -NY 10013 **Fx:**788-4300
(212) 661-3691 .. **Lopez Romero & Montelione,PC** -551 5th Av -NY 10176 **Fx:**370-7894
(212) 371-6600 .. **Lopez,** Sarah G '04 %Kirby M LLP -825 3rd Av -NY 10022
(585) 428-5210 .. **Lopez,** Silvia M '08 %Pub Def -10 N Fitzhugh -Rchstr 14614 **Fx:**428-2234
(212) 271-4256 .. **Lopez,** Sonia M '99 Richcourt Fund Advsrs -825 3rd Av -NY 10022
(212) 953-6000 .. **Lopez,** Thos M '80 (Katsky K LLP) -605 3rd Av -NY 10158
(607) 433-1038 .. **Lopez,** Victor D '84 -25 Ceperley Av -Oneonta 13820
(212) 788-5025 .. **Lopez,** Wilfredo '77 %Dept Hlth -125 Worth CN-30 -NY 10013 **Fx:**788-4300
(212) 770-7000 .. **Lopez,** Yvette '04 AIG -70 Pine -NY 10270
(914) 332-4700 .. **Lopez Gonzalez,** Sonia E '02 %Mirsky & B,PLLC -303 S Bway -Tarrytwn 10591 **Fx:**332-1671
(718) 672-4015 .. **Lopez-Martinez,** Elizabeth '94 -33-27 91st -Jcksn Hts 11372
(917) 338-7728 .. **Lopez-Paredes,** Eva '05 -122 Elizabeth -NY 10013
(212) 837-6000 .. **LoPiccolo,** Jos '04 %Hughes H&R LLP -1 Bttry Pk Plz -NY 10004
(516) 408-3666 .. **Lo Piccolo,** Jos A '98 %Hession BC&L,LLP -1103 Stewart Av -Gdn Cty 11530
(716) 856-4000 .. **Lopinski,** John D '03 %Hodgson R LLP -140 Pearl -Buffalo 14202
(212) 687-2900 .. **Lopkin,** Wayne M '81 (W Lopkin,LLC) -52 Vndrblt Av -NY 10017 **Fx:**687-2035
(212) 735-3000 .. **Lopo,** Diana M '84 (Skadden ASM&F LLP) -4 Times Sq -NY 10036
(212) 354-1166 .. **Lopoten,** Stuart A '03 %Triumph Srch Cnsltnts -130 W 42nd -NY 10036 **Fx:**354-1141
(212) 306-7100 .. **Loprest,** Amy M '96 %Campaign Finance Bd -40 Rector -NY 10006 **Fx:**306-7143
(212) 637-2728 .. **LoPrest,** F James Jr. '91 %US Atty -86 Chmbrs -NY 10007
(212) 425-0551 .. **LoPresti,** Anthony A '01 -30 Broad -NY 10004
(516) 739-2020 .. **LoPresti,** Anthony J '88 -310 Old Cntry Rd -Gdn Cty 11530 **Fx:**739-6643
(212) 481-9011 .. **LoPresti,** Danl S '91 %Shaw & B -9 E 40th -NY 10016
(516) 741-1167 .. **Lopresti,** Genevieve Lane '86 -219 Mineola Blvd -Mineola 11501
(718) 351-2656 .. **LoPresti,** John P Jr. '72 -2141 Richmond Rd -Staten Isl 10306
(212) 732-4029 .. **LoPresti,** Marc M '98 -45 Bway -NY 10006
(516) 571-9038 .. **LoPresti,** Robt '81 Family Ct -1200 Old Cntry Rd -Westbury 11590
(914) 698-8200 .. **LoPresti,** Stephen J '78 (Hayes & L,PC) -260 Harrison Av -Harrison 10528
(631) 265-6300 .. **LoPresti,** Thos A '88 -222 E Main -Smithtwn 11787
(718) 932-2800 .. **Lopresto,** Thos J '69 SpclCnsl Lopresto & B -4502 Ditmars Blvd -Astoria 11105 **Fx:**721-6846
(212) 325-2000 .. **LoPrete,** Corey Evan '01 Credit Suisse Securities -11 Mad Av -NY 10010
(212) 888-6106 .. **LoPreto,** Virginia A '83 -420 Lex Av -NY 10170 **Fx:**688-1611
(212) 761-4000 .. **Lorah,** Tim O'Neal '97 Morgan Stanley -1221 Av of Amer -NY 10020
(845) 357-7721 .. **Lorber,** Jos '70 (J Lorber,PC) -2 Exec Blvd -Suffern 10901 **Fx:**357-7820
(212) 969-3000 .. **Lorber,** Lawr Z '71 (Proskauer R LLP) -1585 Bway -NY 10036
(917) 297-4667 .. **Lorch,** Ernest H '58 -1015 Saw Mill Rvr Rd -Ardsley 10502
(212) 474-1000 .. **Lorch,** Steven J '10 %Cravath S&M LLP -825 8th Av -NY 10019
(212) 961-8342 .. **Lord,** Barbara J '67 Div of ABC -317 Lenox Av -NY 10027
(212) 672-4700 .. **Lord,** Bonnie '92 %The Witkoff Group -220 E 42nd -NY 10017 **Fx:**672-4726
(718) 222-6421 .. **Lord,** Cleston R '01 NYCHA Energy Dept -350 Lvngstn -Brklyn 11217
(212) 592-3502 .. **Lord,** Frank '93 -350 Canal PMB 1155 -NY 10013
(212) 592-1400 .. **Lord,** Frank K IV '04 %Herrick,F LLP -2 Park Av -NY 10016
(212) 631-2760 .. **Lord,** Lisa Terrell '95 Coach -516 W 34th -NY 10001
(646) 258-1761 .. **Lord,** Michl H '93 M Lord & Co LLC -245 5th Av -NY 10016
(518) 473-6992 .. **Lord,** Nancy Hershey '81 %Dept of Law -The Cptl -Albany 12224
(315) 946-3397 .. **Lord,** Nancy M '90 -88 William Bx86 -Lyons 14489 **Fx:**946-4818
(585) 492-2532 .. **Lord,** Steven J '03 %T Raszeja -26 West -Arcade 14009 **Fx:**(716) 496-5144
(212) 593-6700 .. **Lorde,** Janice '06 %Aaronson RF&D,LLP -757 3rd Av -NY 10017
(914) 766-3676 .. **Lorden,** Jessica E '87 IBM -294 Route 100 -Somers 10589
(631) 234-8585 .. **Lord-James,** Marilyn '03 %Bracken & M,LLP -1 Suffolk Sq -Islandia 11749
(212) 248-8800 .. **Lore,** David A '02 %Callan KB&B LLP -1 Whitehall -NY 10004
(212) 447-5599 .. **Lore,** Jillian H '08 %Agins SR&B,LLP -386 Park Av S -NY 10016
(212) 705-7000 .. **Lore,** Kenneth G '80 (Bingham M LLP) -399 Park Av -NY 10022
(716) 633-9853 .. **Loree,** James M '84 -77 McNair Rd -Williamsvll 14221
(212) 319-8500 .. **Loree,** Philip J Jr. '90 (Stevens & L PC) -485 Mad Av -NY 10022
(212) 269-5500 .. **Lorell,** Elizabeth F '03 (Gordon & R LLP) -90 Broad -NY 10004
(212) 461-2323 .. **Lorell,** Jeffrey W '84 (Saiber LLC) -44 Wall -NY 10005
(516) 785-3909 .. **Loren,** Bruce M '91 -3938 Jerusalem Av -Seafrd 11783
(845) 947-6401 .. **Lorenc,** Robt W '74 %MHLS -Letchworth Vllg Dvlpmntl Ctr Bx470 -Thiells 10984 **Fx:**947-6391
(212) 947-3793 .. **Lorence,** Roger D '77 (Sadis & G LLP) -551 5th Av -NY 10176
(212) 598-8000 .. **Lorenson,** David A '73 %Guardian Life Ins -7 Hanover Sq -NY 10004 **Fx:**919-2693
(212) 805-6374 .. **Lorentz,** Dayna K '04 %Hon V Marrero -40 Centre -NY 10007
(212) 656-5858 .. **Lorentz,** Karen '81 NYSE EuroNext -11 Wall -NY 10005
(914) 949-2700 .. **Lorenz,** Brian E '64 (Bleakley P&S,LLP) -1 N Lex Av -White Plns 10601
(212) 226-5054 .. **Lorenz,** David J '00 %Powley & G,PC -304 Hudson -NY 10013 **Fx:**266-5085
(607) 436-3478 .. **Lorenz,** Magdalena '05 %SUNY Cllg -320 Netzer Admin Bldg -Oneonta 13820
(212) 210-9528 .. **Lorenzo,** Alexander S '06 %Alston & B LLP -90 Park Av -NY 10016
(716) 632-7751 .. **Lorenzo,** Arthur A '51 -53 Hmptn Hill Dr -Williamsvll 14221
(212) 686-3838 .. **Lorenzo,** Eric F '08 %Barst M&K LLP -2 Park Av -NY 10016
(914) 824-5070 .. **Lorenzo,** Faith A '91 Atty Grievance Comm -399 Knollwood Rd -White Plns 10603 **Fx:**949-0997
(800) 636-6586 .. **Lorenzo,** Harry E '51 OfCnsl HoganWillig -2410 N Forest Rd -Getzvll 14068
(718) 250-1400 .. **Lorenzo,** Jos '89 %BZ Green -12 MetroTech Ctr -Brklyn 11201 **Fx:**250-1401
(212) 808-7800 .. **Lorenzo,** Marisa A '06 %Kelley D&W LLP -101 Park Av -NY 10178
(212) 661-1325 .. **Lorenzo,** Melissa M '05 Fortent -99 Park Av -NY 10016 **Fx:**661-4216
(212) 407-4000 .. **Lorenzo,** Richd M '79 (Loeb & L,LLP) -345 Park Av -NY 10154
(716) 853-9555 .. **Lorenzo,** Theresa M '84 %Leg Aid -237 Main -Buffalo 14203 **Fx:**853-3219
(212) 765-5070 .. **Loretto,** David '03 %Fish & R,PC -153 E 53rd -NY 10022
(716) 649-1571 .. **Loretto,** Terry D '02 (Magavern & L,PC) -71 Main -Hambrg 14075
(718) 875-1800 .. **Lorge,** Bernard '60 -3515 H Hdsn Pkwy -Bronx 10463
(718) 875-1800 .. **Lorge,** Evelyn '77 -3515 H Hdsn Pkwy -Bronx 10463 **Fx:**884-5497
(516) 228-0393 .. **Lorge,** Richd D '64 -900 Merchants Cncrs -Westbury 11590 **Fx:**227-6594

(718) 204-0656 .. **Loria,** Philip '05 (Loria & Assoc,PC) -37-20 Bway -Astoria 11103 **Fx:**204-0657
(585) 428-5151 .. **Loria-Dinolfo,** Cheryl '87 Cnty Clerk -39 W Main -Rchstr 14614
(212) 878-8000 .. **Lorido,** Alexander R '09 Clifford C LLP -31 W 52nd -NY 10019
(212) 632-5500 .. **Lorieau,** Pierre J '00 Cnsl Salans LLP -620 5th Av -NY 10020
(914) 261-0827 .. **LoRiggio,** Jos A '98 -520 Wht Plns Rd -Tarrytwn 10591
(716) 824-7200 .. **Lorigo,** Jos C '08 %R Lorigo -101 Slade Av -W Seneca 14224 **Fx:**824-8728
(716) 824-7200 .. **Lorigo,** Ralph C '74 -101 Slade Av -W Seneca 14224 **Fx:**824-8728
(212) 248-3168 .. **Lorin,** Andrew J '90 (Drinker B&R LLP) -140 Bway -NY 10005
(718) 596-1144 .. **Lorin,** Leonard '54 -26 Court -Brklyn 11242 **Fx:**596-1146
(212) 574-1200 .. **Lorin,** Susan Joy '82 %Seward & K LLP -1 Bttry Pk Plz -NY 10004
(212) 596-9000 .. **Loring,** Denise L '83 (Ropes & G LLP) -1211 Av of Amer -NY 10036
(212) 696-4848 .. **Loring,** Heath O '07 %Mintz & G LLP -470 Park Av S -NY 10016
(716) 649-9087 .. **Loring,** Joan E '74 -280 Maple Av -Hambrg 14075
(518) 474-6400 .. **Lorini,** Mary Ellen '83 %Dept of Ed -89 Wshngtn Av -Albany 12234 **Fx:**473-2925
(212) 559-8611 .. **Lorinsky,** Scott J '93 Citigroup Alternative Invstmnts -731 Lex Av -NY 10022
(516) 571-3310 .. **Lorintz,** Jos H '83 Supreme Ct -100 Supreme Ct Dr -Mineola 11501 **Fx:**571-1316
(518) 843-2080 .. **Lorman,** Lisa Weidel '89 (Lorman Law Firm) -123 Guy Park Av -Amsterdam 12010 **Fx:**843-8055
(518) 843-2080 .. **Lorman,** Wm E '89 (Lorman Law Firm) -123 Guy Park Av -Amsterdam 12010 **Fx:**843-8055
(212) 693-2222 .. **Lorme,** Peter J '94 %D Gallagher,PC -150 Bway -NY 10038 **Fx:**608-5977
(518) 388-4364 .. **Lorusso,** Jessica Dale '02 %DA -612 State -Schnctdy 12305 **Fx:**388-4569
(516) 921-4305 .. **LoRusso,** Michl G '88 M LoRusso PC -316 Jackson Av -Syosset 11791 **Fx:**921-0729
(212) 894-7429 .. **Lo Russo,** Ronald T '05 Vornado Realty Trust -888 7th Av -NY 10106
(212) 805-3900 .. **Lory,** Tyler J '89 (Clausen M PC) -1 Chase Manh Plz -NY 10005
(212) 640-2877 .. **LoSacco,** Mark '93 %Amer Exp -200 Vesey -NY 10285
(212) 867-4466 .. **Losardo,** Joshua G '99 (Belkin BW&G,LLP) -270 Mad Av -NY 10016
(212) 505-9080 .. **Loscalzo,** Anthony J '69 (Loscalzo & L,PC) -14 E 4th -NY 10012
(516) 972-3257 .. **Loscalzo,** Francis J '96 -223 Wall -Huntngtn 11743
(914) 935-5403 .. **Loscalzo,** Lisa M '88 Compass Grp USA Inc -3 Intl Dr -Rye Brook 10573 **Fx:**935-5696
(212) 505-9080 .. **Loscalzo & Loscalzo,PC** -14 E 4th -NY 10012 **Fx:**533-0067
(212) 551-4000 .. **Loscalzo,** Philip '00 %Sanofi-Synthelabo -90 Park Av -NY 10016 **Fx:**551-4919
(212) 221-5700 .. **LoSchiavo,** Robt W '84 (Goldberg WFG LLP) -1501 Bway -NY 10036
(518) 794-0431 .. **Loselle,** Arlen G '60 -875 Cnty Route 13 -Old Chatham 12136 **Fx:**794-0431
(212) 307-4400 .. **Loshak,** Eliot '57 -200 W 79th -NY 10024
(518) 485-7203 .. **Loshbaugh,** Chad M '02 Dept Civil Srvc -Harriman Campus Bldg 1 -Albany 12239 **Fx:**457-6654
(212) 536-3900 .. **Loshilov,** Alexander Y '08 (K&L Gates LLP) -599 Lex Av -NY 10022
(716) 856-1636 .. **Losi,** Colleen Rogers '88 OfCnsl Walsh R&G -14 Lafayette Sq -Buffalo 14203
(716) 854-1446 .. **Losi,** David P '82 (Losi & G) -170 Franklin -Buffalo 14202
(716) 854-1446 .. **Losi & Gangi** -170 Franklin -Buffalo 14202 **Fx:**854-6614
(212) 259-8000 .. **Losk,** Danl A '08 %Dewey & L LLP -1301 Av of Amer -NY 10019
(212) 538-0187 .. **Loskove,** Arthur Adam '00 CSFB -1 Mad Av -NY 10010
(212) 487-9700 .. **Losman,** Nathan '86 White F&F,LLP -61 Bway -NY 10006
(212) 422-0202 .. **Losquadro,** Christopher J '96 %Sedgwick DM&A LLP -125 Broad -NY 10004
(315) 234-8500 .. **Losquadro,** Melissa A '03 %US Dist Ct -100 S Clinton Bx7367 -Syracuse 13261
(212) 669-0600 .. **Losquadro,** Wm F '68 OfCnsl Hill R LLP -45 Bway -NY 10006
(212) 450-4000 .. **Loss,** Danl M '05 %Davis P&W LLP -450 Lex Av -NY 10017
(646) 386-4093 .. **Loss,** Frank J '90 %Hon E McLaughlin -100 Centre -NY 10013
(212) 408-5100 .. **Loss,** Gregory M '90 (Chadbourne & P LLP) -30 Rckfllr Plz -NY 10112
(716) 852-5533 .. **Loss,** John T '89 (Connors & V,LLP) -1000 Lbrty Bldg -Buffalo 14202
(212) 717-6132 .. **Loss,** Margaret R '73 -201 E 80th -NY 10075 **Fx:**842-0909
(212) 627-8100 .. **Lossia,** Dana E '06 %Levy R,PC -80 8th Av -NY 10011
(607) 256-3024 .. **Losurdo,** Francis '98 -409 Taughannock Blvd -Ithaca 14850
(716) 842-2558 .. **Lo Tempio,** Andrew C '89 -227 Niagara -Buffalo 14201
(716) 845-6000 .. **LoTempio,** David A '84 (Kavinoky C LLP) -726 Exchange -Buffalo 14210
(716) 855-3761 .. **LoTempio,** Frank III '98 %LoTempio & B,PC -181 Franklin -Buffalo 14202 **Fx:**855-3437
(716) 855-3761 .. **LoTempio,** Frank L '74 (LoTempio & B,PC) -181 Franklin -Buffalo 14202 **Fx:**855-3437
(716) 855-3761 .. **LoTempio,** Terri L '96 %LoTempio & B,PC -181 Franklin -Buffalo 14202 **Fx:**855-3437
(716) 853-1111 .. **LoTempio,** Vincent G '87 (Kloss S&L) -69 Delaware Av -Buffalo 14202 **Fx:**847-2924
(716) 851-4343 .. **LoTempio-Hoffman,** Melissa A '99 %Law Dept -65 Niagara Sq -Buffalo 14202 **Fx:**851-4105
(212) 537-2447 .. **Lotfy,** Ola El Shaer '95 Morgan Stanley -1633 Bway -NY 10019
(212) 692-1000 .. **Lotito,** James '00 %Duane M LLP -1540 Bway -NY 10036
(212) 735-3000 .. **Lott,** Ashley M '10 %Skadden ASM&F LLP -4 Times Sq -NY 10036
(631) 454-0606 .. **Lott,** Dawn A '97 (Dandeneau & L) -425 Broadhllw Rd -Melvll 11747 **Fx:**454-9250
(518) 761-4114 .. **Lotters,** Arlene J '89 -206 Glen -Glens Fls 12801
(212) 330-1000 .. **Lotti,** Diane L '81 %Buck Consultants -1 Penn Plz -NY 10119 **Fx:**695-4184
(973) 596-4547 .. **Lottinville,** Nancy A '81 Cnsl Gibbons PC -1 Penn Plz -NY 10119 **Fx:**639-6481
(212) 956-9500 .. **Lottman,** Andrew M '95 Hand B&A LLP -8 W 40th -NY 10018 **Fx:**376-6080
(212) 310-8000 .. **Lottmann,** Annelies '09 %Weil G&M LLP -767 5th Av -NY 10153
(845) 808-1150 .. **Lotto,** Adrienne '06 %Cnty Atty -48 Gleneida Av -Carmel 10512 **Fx:**808-1903
(631) 588-3000 .. **Lotto,** Gerald L '66 -3330 Vets Mem'l Hwy -Bohemia 11716
(212) 661-2900 .. **LoTurco,** Jennifer M '07 %Kriss & F LLP -360 Lex Av -NY 10017
(631) 427-9500 .. **LoTurco,** John H '93 (LoTurco & M) -434 NY Av -Huntngtn 11743 **Fx:**427-9501
(212) 458-1201 .. **Lotz,** James J '93 %AIG -175 Water -NY 10038 **Fx:**458-1259
(212) 455-2000 .. **Lotz,** Markus '08 %Simpson T&B LLP -425 Lex Av -NY 10017
(212) 237-1000 .. **Lotzof,** Kaylie S '10 %Windels ML&M,LLP -156 W 56th -NY 10019
(212) 903-9000 .. **Lou,** Elaine K '10 %Linklaters -1345 Av of Amer -NY 10105
(212) 231-1662 .. **Lou,** Lan '02 MacQuarie Holdings(USA)Inc -125 W 55th -NY 10019 **Fx:**231-1010
(212) 361-7996 .. **Louallen,** Keith E '05 Dept Homeless Srvcs -33 Beaver -NY 10004 **Fx:**361-8002
(212) 601-2680 .. **Louard,** Kenneth A '92 Gonzalez S&H LLP -350 5th Av -NY 10118
(212) 513-3200 .. **Loube,** Harmony I '07 %Holland & K LLP -31 W 52nd -NY 10019
(212) 272-6666 .. **Loubier,** Gabriel '90 %JP Morgan Chase -320 Park Av -NY 10022
(212) 788-5421 .. **Loubriel-Murdock,** Valerie A '86 NYC ACS -220 Church -NY 10013
(212) 867-4100 .. **Loucks,** Bain R '06 %Furman K&B LLP -61 Bway -NY 10006
(212) 572-3987 .. **Louden,** Nancy C '79 %Estee Lauder -767 5th Av -NY 10153 **Fx:**572-3989
(716) 852-5200 .. **Loudenslager,** Cory L '02 %Hamberger & W -700 Main Pl Twr -Buffalo 14202
(212) 969-3000 .. **Loughery,** Victoria L '09 %Proskauer R LLP -1585 Bway -NY 10036
(718) 802-6644 .. **Loughlin,** John E '93 %Workers Comp Bd -111 Lvngstn -Brklyn 11201
(845) 794-3833 .. **Loughlin,** Jos P '88 (Billig L&B LLP) -146 Rck Hll Rd Bx780 -Rck Hll 12775 **Fx:**794-3827
(908) 233-9000 .. **Loughlin,** Vincent K '81 (Johnstone SL&L) -225 Bway -NY 10007
(212) 536-3900 .. **Loughlin,** Walter P '99 (K&L Gates LLP) -599 Lex Av -NY 10022
(914) 636-5051 .. **Loughman,** Edw D III '81 (Muldoon H&L) -271 North Av -New Rchll 10801
(212) 607-2800 .. **Loughnan,** Alan B '77 %FTC -1 Bowling Grn -NY 10004 **Fx:**607-2822
(212) 637-2265 .. **Loughnane,** Joan M '00 %US Atty -1 St Andrews Plz -NY 10007
(212) 425-7200 .. **Loughnane,** Michl D '85 (Kenyon & K,LLP) -1 Bway -NY 10004
(518) 426-4600 .. **Loughney,** Robt M '87 (Couch W,LLP) -540 Bway Bx22222 -Albany 12201
(516) 775-4569 .. **Loughran,** Gerard V '74 -68 Dartmth -Gdn Cty 11530
(607) 723-2696 .. **Loughran,** Mark J '88 (Loughran & L) -89 Court -Bnghmtn 13901 **Fx:**723-2611
(516) 742-4343 .. **Loughran,** Matthew J '01 %Scully SM&P PC -400 Grdn City Plz -Gdn Cty 11530
(212) 909-6000 .. **Loughran,** Peter J '90 (Debevoise & P LLP) -919 3rd Av -NY 10022
(212) 510-1400 .. **Loughran,** Regina A '84 %Spec Comm of Invstgtn -80 Maiden Ln -NY 10038 **Fx:**510-1550
(212) 244-5500 .. **Loughran,** Regina A '91 Henry M Feiereisen LLC -708 3rd Av -NY 10017 **Fx:**244-2233
(607) 723-2696 .. **Loughran,** Sarah K '99 (Loughran & L) -89 Court -Bnghmtn 13901 **Fx:**723-2611
(212) 843-9400 .. **Loughran,** Sean P '03 Carnegie Assoc -1330 Av of Amer -NY 10019
(718) 855-9000 .. **Loughren,** Kristen L '08 %Cullen and D LLP -177 Montague -Brklyn 11201
(212) 834-5553 .. **Loughrey,** Jennifer A '01 JP Morgan Mortgage Capital -270 Park Av -NY 10017
(212) 357-6670 .. **Louie,** Stephen G '94 Cnsl Goldman Sachs -85 Broad -NY 10004 **Fx:**769-7142
(212) 272-6066 .. **Louie,** Virginia '04 %JP Morgan Chase -383 Mad Av -NY 10179
(845) 471-0058 .. **Louis,** C Benjie '93 %Leg Srvcs -29 N Hmltn -Poughkeepsie 12601 **Fx:**471-0244
(212) 319-5240 .. **Louis,** Danl J '10 %Flicker G & Assoc,LLP -45 Bway -NY 10006
(914) 287-7345 .. **Louis,** James G '92 J Louis,PLLC -445 Hmltn Av -White Plns 10601 **Fx:**946-2494
(212) 554-1400 .. **Louis,** Karine '04 %Bernstein LB&G LLP -1285 Av of Amer -NY 10019
(718) 260-4750 .. **Louis,** Kesha '05 %Leg Aid -111 Lvngstn -Brklyn 11201 **Fx:**260-4744
(212) 977-9001 .. **Louis,** Margaret '77 %RHI Entrtnmnt -1325 Av of Amer -NY 10019 **Fx:**977-9049
(212) 788-1079 .. **Louis,** Stephen E '81 %Law Dept -100 Church -NY 10007 **Fx:**788-0367
(212) 931-9986 .. **Louissaint,** Arthur O '10 -40 Exch Pl -NY 10005 **Fx:**(646) 434-0758
(718) 298-0500 .. **Loukides,** Daphne '84 %Surrogate's Ct -88-11 Sutphin Blvd -Jamaica 11435 **Fx:**520-5048
(212) 225-7700 .. **Loumeau,** Paul '00 %Cartafalsa ST&L -165 Bway -NY 10006
(212) 309-1000 .. **Loumiet,** Carlos E '78 (Hunton & W) -200 Park Av -NY 10166
(212) 259-8000 .. **Lounsbury,** Adam L '09 %Dewey & L LLP -1301 Av of Amer -NY 10019
(212) 867-9500 .. **Loura,** Erin E '09 %Kurzman K&F,LLP -230 Park Av -NY 10169
(718) 855-9000 .. **Lourenso,** Frank J '91 %Cullen and D LLP -177 Montague -Brklyn 11201
(518) 469-6449 .. **Louridas,** Aaron A '01 (Louridas & L) -3034 Patrick Rd -Schnctdy 12303
(518) 469-6449 .. **Louridas,** Jaime Czajka '02 %Louridas & L -3034 Patrick Rd -Schnctdy 12303
(212) 969-3000 .. **Lourie,** Gwen J '76 %Proskauer R LLP -1585 Bway -NY 10036
(212) 481-5275 .. **Louros,** Steven '81 -1261 Bway -NY 10001
(212) 265-1310 .. **Louttit,** Robt J '86 %5th Ave Business Imprvmnt Dist -16 E 52nd -NY 10022
(631) 756-2024 .. **Louttit,** Robt P '03 %Huenke & R -1 Huntngtn Quad -Melvll 11747
(212) 586-8699 .. **Louzoun,** H Malka '89 -250 W 57th -NY 10107 **Fx:**586-8753
(716) 854-1112 .. **Lovallo,** Timothy R '79 (Lovallo & W) -1088 Ellicott Sq Bldg -Buffalo 14203 **Fx:**854-1288
(516) 294-8844 .. **Lovas,** Claudia P '01 %L'Abbate BC&C,LLP -1001 Franklin Av -Gdn Cty 11530
(212) 947-9779 .. **Love,** Christie N '06 %Advocates for Chldrn -151 W 30th -NY 10001
(631) 277-8080 .. **Love,** Christopher A '95 (Cassidy R&L,PC) -70 W Main -E Islip 11730 **Fx:**277-4908
(585) 389-1210 .. **Love,** Diane '83 -350 Linden Oaks -Rchstr 14625 **Fx:**389-1212
(212) 230-5500 .. **Love,** Erin D '06 %Davis SLM&H LLP -689 5th Av -NY 10022
(212) 770-3976 .. **Love,** Francine E '92 %AIG -72 Wall -NY 10005 **Fx:**514-6099

(212) 848-4000 .. **Love,** Gina S '02 Cnsl Shearman & S LLP -599 Lex Av -NY 10022
(845) 436-9212 .. **Love,** J David '85 -6 Southbranch -Liberty 12754
(212) 354-6800 .. **Love,** J David '85 OfCnsl Silbowitz GSS&F,LLP -25 W 43rd -NY 10036
(716) 679-0034 .. **Love,** Jane E '85 -49 Maple Av -Fredonia 14063 **Fx:**753-4444
(212) 937-7233 .. **Love,** Jane M '99 (WilmerHale) -399 Park Av -NY 10022
(212) 891-5708 .. **Love,** Jonathan Andrew '96 CDC Mortg Capital -9 W 57th -NY 10019
(518) 456-0460 .. **Love,** Kara Conway '91 KC Love -450 New Karner Rd -Albany 12205 **Fx:**456-0922
(718) 575-0013 .. **Love,** Laurence L '93 -118-35 Qns Blvd -Flushng 11375 **Fx:**520-8544
(212) 790-0200 .. **Love,** Lela P '81 %Benj N Cardozo Schl of Law -55 5th Av -NY 10003 **Fx:**790-0345
(212) 306-1789 .. **Love,** Wm C Jr. '94 American Stock Exchange LLC -86 Trinity Pl -NY 10006
(716) 881-5800 .. **Love,** Wm J Jr. '68 OfCnsl Siegel K&K -426 Franklin -Buffalo 14202 **Fx:**881-0669
(716) 854-2020 .. **Lovecchio,** Michl J '01 (Cellino & B,PC) -350 Main -Buffalo 14202
(631) 669-4370 .. **Lovegrove,** Paul N '87 (P Lovegrove PC) -398 Route 111 -Smithtwn 11787 **Fx:**587-6347
(315) 729-5609 .. **Lovejoy,** Dianne S '81 -126 Main Bx412 -Penn Yan 14527
(212) 808-8100 .. **Lovejoy,** H Stow '79 %Kostelanetz & F,LLP -7 Wrld Trd Ctr -NY 10007
(212) 632-6000 .. **Lovejoy,** Jesse R '70 %Lazard Freres -30 Rckfllr Plz -NY 10112 **Fx:**632-6060
(315) 422-8191 .. **Lovejoy-Grinnell,** Bryn '09 %Leg Aid -351 S Warren -Syracuse 13202 **Fx:**472-2819
(716) 853-5100 .. **Lovelace,** Christian M '07 Lippes MWF LLP -665 Main -Buffalo 14203
(212) 521-5400 .. **Lovelace,** Othiamba N '10 %Reed S LLP -599 Lex Av -NY 10022
(716) 792-4123 .. **Loveland,** Chas R '65 (C Loveland,PC) -11 Lake Av BxC -Brocton 14716 **Fx:**792-4143
(718) 625-0987 .. **Loveless,** Chas A '02 Slochowsky & S -26 Court -Brklyn 11242 **Fx:**625-5628
(212) 608-1900 .. **Lovell,** Christopher '77 (Lovell SH LLP) -61 Bway -NY 10006
(718) 658-0500 .. **Lovell,** Faith S '07 %Law Dept -151-20 Jamaica Av -Jamaica 11432 **Fx:**658-4025
(212) 756-2000 .. **Lovell,** Nora '10 %Schulte R&Z LLP -919 3rd Av -NY 10022
(718) 835-9300 .. **Lovell,** Richd H '81 (R Lovell,PC) -107-48 Crossbay Blvd -Ozone Pk 11417 **Fx:**835-9700
(212) 483-9490 .. **Lovell,** Sandra D '04 %McElroy DM&C,LLP -88 Pine -NY 10005
(212) 608-1900 .. **Lovell Stewart Halebian LLP** -61 Bway -NY 10006
(585) 381-6830 .. **Lovenheim,** Peter C '79 -280 Sandringham Rd -Rchstr 14610
(212) 259-8000 .. **Lovenworth,** Stanton J '78 (Dewey & L LLP) -1301 Av of Amer -NY 10019
(212) 708-1800 .. **Lovera Riso,** Sebastian J '09 %Ladas & P -26 W 61st -NY 10023
(718) 293-2222 .. **Loverro,** Frank J '78 -944 Gerard Av -Bronx 10452
(718) 658-0500 .. **Lovett,** Andrea '88 %Law Dept -151-20 Jamaica Av -Jamaica 11432 **Fx:**658-4025
(914) 347-4500 .. **Lovett,** Jonathan '72 (Lovett & B, LLP) -37A Saw Mill Rvr Rd -Hawthorne 10532 **Fx:**347-4545
(212) 373-3000 .. **Lovett,** Saml E '08 %Paul WRW&G LLP -1285 Av of Amer -NY 10019
(212) 735-3000 .. **Lovett,** Suzanne D '92 %Skadden ASM&F LLP -4 Times Sq -NY 10036
(516) 545-5160 .. **Lovette,** Katherine E '10 Cnsl Natl Grid -175 E Old Cntry Rd -Hicksvll 11801 **Fx:**545-5029
(212) 506-3900 .. **Lovi,** John D '86 (Steptoe & J LLP) -750 7th Av -NY 10019
(212) 306-7120 .. **Loving,** Katharine G '98 %Campaign Finance Bd -40 Rector -NY 10006 **Fx:**306-7143
(917) 887-9399 .. **Loving,** Raymond L '87 -225 Bway -NY 10007
(212) 506-1700 .. **Lovinger,** Blythe E '96 (Kasowitz BT&F LLP) -1633 Bway -NY 10019
(212) 340-0400 .. **Lovinger,** Richd '83 %Appllt Div 1st Dept -27 Mad Av -NY 10010 **Fx:**889-4412
(212) 598-0760 .. **Lovit,** Neil S '71 -35 E 9th -NY 10003
(718) 409-6262 .. **Lovitch,** Steven K '78 -950 Morris Park Av -Bronx 10462 **Fx:**409-6323
(212) 326-3939 .. **Lovitt,** Traci L '98 (Jones D) -222 E 41st -NY 10017
(631) 853-4343 .. **Lovly,** Catherine L '05 Leg Aid -400 Carleton Av Bx9082 -Central Islip 11722 **Fx:**853-7798
(607) 773-2887 .. **Lovric,** Miroslav '86 %US Atty -15 Henry -Bnghmtn 13901 **Fx:**773-2901
(516) 883-5432 .. **Low,** Harold W '76 %Publishers Clearing House -382 Channel Dr -Pt Wash 11050
(518) 708-0645 .. **Low,** Jeffrey J '09 -Bx189 -Coxsackie 12051
(212) 741-9300 .. **Low,** Sean A '93 Preston Bailey Design -147 W 25th -NY 10001
(212) 259-8000 .. **Low,** Sean M '08 %Dewey & L LLP -1301 Av of Amer -NY 10019
(212) 788-1007 .. **Low-Beer,** John R '87 %Law Dept -100 Church -NY 10007 **Fx:**788-0367
(212) 806-5400 .. **Lowden,** David W '75 SpclCnsl Stroock &S&L LLP -180 Maiden Ln -NY 10038
(212) 689-8808 .. **Lowden,** Kathleen L '86 %Hoguet NR&K,LLP -10 E 40th -NY 10016
(716) 636-7600 .. **Lowe,** Amanda L '09 %HoganWillig -2410 N Forest Rd -Amherst 14068
(212) 218-5500 .. **Lowe,** Christopher H '01 (Seyfarth S LLP) -620 8th Av -NY 10018
(212) 657-2474 .. **Lowe,** Dana R '99 Citibank -111 Wall -NY 10043
(212) 762-6705 .. **Lowe,** Douglas '82 Morgan Stanley -1221 Av of Amer -NY 10020
(845) 225-7899 .. **Lowe,** E Nobles '36 -554 Gipsy Trl Rd -Carmel 10512 **Fx:**228-4479
(212) 415-8600 .. **Lowe,** Jeffrey D '04 %Locke LB&L LLP -3 World Fncl Ctr -NY 10281
(585) 295-4400 .. **Lowe,** John P Jr. '79 (Hiscock & B,LLP) -2000 HSBC Plz -Rchstr 14604
(585) 232-6500 .. **Lowe,** Kristin M '10 %Harter S&E LLP -1600 Bausch & Lomb Pl -Rchstr 14604
(212) 870-2623 .. **Lowe,** Leslie H '81 ICCR -475 Riverside Dr -NY 10115
(212) 839-7000 .. **Lowe,** Mark A '67 (Hill B&N LLP) -200 Lbrty -NY 10281
(516) 883-5575 .. **Lowe,** Martin T '94 -27A Millpond Rd -Pt Wash 11050
(631) 501-5700 .. **Lowe,** Matthew S '08 %Carter DF&S LLP -445 Broadhallow Rd -Melvll 11747
(516) 227-2700 .. **Lowe,** Michl '85 (Lipsky B&L,LLP) -585 Stewart Av -Gdn Cty 11530
(212) 862-8700 .. **Lowe,** Robt L '06 %JL Greenup & Assoc -205 W 137th -NY 10030 **Fx:**862-2664
(631) 231-2424 .. **Lowe,** Rose Farrell '77 %Dept of Law -300 Motor Pkwy -Hauppauge 11788 **Fx:**435-4757
(212) 935-3000 .. **Lowe,** Sarah A '07 %Mintz LCFG&P,PC -666 3rd Av -NY 10017
Lowe, Stephen B '76 -53 Old Route 304 -New Cty 10956
(585) 419-8800 .. **Lowe,** Wm Q '10 %Harris B PLLC -99 Garnsey Rd -Pittsfrd 14534
(917) 454-1100 .. **Lowell,** Arlynne '94 %Police Dept -2 Lafayette -NY 10007
(212) 662-0606 .. **Lowen,** Lawr T '73 (LT Lowen,PC) -340 W 57th -NY 10019 **Fx:**202-3687
(718) 352-7607 .. **Lowenberger,** Diane M '89 DM Lowenberger,PC -38-07 255th -Little Neck 11363 **Fx:**352-2992
(212) 735-3000 .. **Lowenbraun,** Leslie '77 Cnsl Skadden ASM&F LLP -4 Times Sq -NY 10036
(212) 307-3292 .. **Lowenbraun,** Renata D '90 -445 Park Av -NY 10022 **Fx:**202-5016
(516) 233-3414 .. **Lowenbraun,** Solomon M '50 -99 S Srvc Rd -New Hyde Pk 11040
(718) 286-6000 .. **Lowenburg,** Mary M '99 %DA -125-01 Qns Blvd -Kew Gdns 11415
(212) 998-6208 .. **Lowenfeld,** Andreas F '55 %NYU Law Schl -40 Wshngtn Sq S -NY 10012 **Fx:**995-4692
(718) 648-4888 .. **Lowenfeld,** Julia A '04 -1706 Sheepshead Bay Rd -Brklyn 11235
(917) 375-9996 .. **Lowenfeld,** Julian H '91 -350 Cntrl Pk W -NY 10025
(718) 243-6251 .. **Lowenfeld,** Marianna '92 %Leg Aid -111 Lvngstn -Brklyn 11201 **Fx:**237-8737
(914) 582-7217 .. **Lowenfeld,** Meg J '85 -33 Town Green Dr -Elmsfrd 10523
(212) 223-3200 .. **Lowenfels,** Fred M '69 Transammonia,Inc -320 Park Av -NY 10022 **Fx:**752-2137
(212) 421-1965 .. **Lowenfels,** Lewis D '61 (Tolins & L) -747 3rd Av -NY 10017
(315) 422-1391 .. **Lowengard,** Sara E '08 %Green & S,PLLC -One Lincoln Ctr #900 -Syracuse 13202
(631) 622-0600 .. **Lowenhar,** Steven F '75 -445 Broad Hollow Rd -Melvll 11747 **Fx:**390-5001
(518) 432-7861 .. **Lowenstein,** Amy E '05 %Disability Advocates,Inc -5 Clinton Sq -Albany 12207 **Fx:**427-6561
(212) 508-6700 .. **Lowenstein,** Arthur P '78 Cnsl Tannenbaum HS&H LLP -900 3rd Av -NY 10022
(646) 863-3533 .. **Lowenstein,** D Mara '97 (Obeid & L,LLP) -148 Duane -NY 10013 **Fx:**(917) 720-9089
(914) 253-2000 .. **Lowenstein,** Eric I '00 %Pepsico -700 Andrsn Hill Rd -Purchase 10577
(718) 548-4536 .. **Lowenstein,** Herbert '80 -4555 H Hdsn Pkwy -Bronx 10471
(212) 541-2000 .. **Lowenstein,** Kenneth K '75 Cnsl Bryan C LLP -1290 Av of Amer -NY 10104
(646) 386-3792 .. **Lowenstein,** Leslie S '78 Supreme Ct Spcl Referee -71 Thomas -NY 10013
(212) 262-6700 .. **Lowenstein Sandler PC** -1251 Av of Amer -NY 10020 **Fx:**262-7402
(212) 724-2646 .. **Lowenstern,** Barbara Ann '91 -205 West End Av -NY 10023 **Fx:**724-2646
(212) 662-5324 .. **Lowenthal,** Andrea '89 A Lowenthal PLLC -1120 Av of Amer -NY 10036
(212) 458-6314 .. **Lowenthal,** Craig L '01 AIG Commercial Ins -175 Water -NY 10038
(212) 336-2000 .. **Lowenthal,** Danl A III '88 (Patterson BW&T LLP) -1133 Av of Amer -NY 10036
(973) 315-4508 .. **Lowenthal,** Ellen Tchorni '79 %Budd L -140 Bway -NY 10005
(212) 806-5400 .. **Lowenthal,** Jeffrey S '84 (Stroock &S&L LLP) -180 Maiden Ln -NY 10038
(718) 758-2200 .. **Lowenthal & Kofman,PC** -2001 Flatbush Av -Brklyn 11234 **Fx:**758-2201
(212) 225-2000 .. **Lowenthal,** Mitchell A '82 (Cleary GS&H) -1 Lbrty Plz -NY 10006
(212) 832-0400 .. **Lowenthal,** Neil S '94 Berdon LLP -360 Mad Av -NY 10017
(718) 758-2200 .. **Lowenthal,** Steven '84 (Lowenthal & K,PC) -2001 Flatbush Av -Brklyn 11234
(212) 533-6300 .. **Lower,** Conrad W '88 %NYSUT -52 Bway -NY 10004 **Fx:**995-2347
(631) 262-0955 .. **Lowery,** Hugh Havener '92 -199 Main Bx63 -Northprt 11768 **Fx:**261-6431
(631) 666-0708 .. **Lowery,** Juliette S '93 -6 Ocean Av -Bay Shr 11706
(212) 474-1000 .. **Lowery,** Saml M '08 %Cravath S&M LLP -825 8th Av -NY 10019
(212) 977-9700 .. **Lowet,** Henry A '58 Cnsl Phillips N LLP -666 5th Av -NY 10103
(914) 997-0500 .. **Lowey Dannenberg Cohen & Hart,PC** -1 N Bway -White Plns 10601 **Fx:**997-0035
(914) 997-0500 .. **Lowey,** Stephen '59 (Lowey DC&H,PC) -1 N Bway -White Plns 10601
(518) 862-1200 .. **Low-Haviland,** Maryanne E '92 %Martin H&M LLP -Bx15141 -Albany 12212
(212) 696-6000 .. **Lowin,** Benjamin M '06 %Curtis M-PC&M LLP -101 Park Av -NY 10178
(212) 735-8600 .. **Lowin,** Jeffrey A '68 (Morrison C LLP) -909 3rd Av -NY 10022
(908) 315-3429 .. **Lowinger,** Edw '85 -72-14 136th -Flushng 11367 **Fx:**315-3428
(516) 569-5001 .. **Lowinger,** Faye '06 %Schonfeld & G,LLP -112 Spruce -Cedarhrst 11516
(718) 851-7227 .. **Lowinger,** Richd L '91 -571 E 9th -Brklyn 11218
(212) 687-3000 .. **Lowitt,** Jeffrey B '92 %Jaffe & A,LLP -600 3rd Av -NY 10016
(212) 228-9268 .. **Lowitt,** Peter D '82 -60 E 8th -NY 10003
(315) 422-2241 .. **Lowitz,** Burton '56 -120 E Wshngtn -Syracuse 13202
(716) 858-6410 .. **Lowman,** Albert V Jr. '79 %Soc Srvcs Cnsl -95 Franklin -Buffalo 14202 **Fx:**858-7342
(585) 238-2000 .. **Lown,** Ryan A '08 %Phillips L LLP -1400 First Fed Plz -Rchstr 14614
(212) 309-1000 .. **Lowney,** Karen Anne '89 Hunton & W -200 Park Av -NY 10166
(914) 995-3000 .. **Lowry,** Jennifer L '02 %DA -111 Martin Luther King Blvd -White Plns 10601 **Fx:**995-3363
(516) 678-2740 .. **Lowry,** Kevin '91 -89 Burtis Av -Rockvll Ctr 11570 **Fx:**608-5715
(212) 683-2210 .. **Lowry,** Marcia '69 %Childrens Rts Inc -330 7th Av -NY 10001 **Fx:**683-4015
(914) 220-1900 .. **Lowson,** Beth N '94 %Nelson Law Firm,LLC -1 N Bway -White Plns 10601
(212) 986-5500 .. **Lowson,** Steven R '88 %Sequa Corp -300 Blaisdell Rd -Orangebrg 10962
(718) 599-3500 .. **Lowy,** Abraham '05 (Treff & L PLLC) -342 Bedford Av -Brklyn 11211 **Fx:**387-6282
(718) 579-3000 .. **Lowy,** Allison K '91 %Leg Aid -1020 Grnd Cncrs -Bronx 10451 **Fx:**588-2611

(718) 520-2397 .. **Lowy,** Brian H '88 %Hon J Blumenfeld -125-01 Qns Blvd -Kew Gdns 11415 **Fx:**520-8603
(212) 474-1000 .. **Lowy,** George T '55 SrCnsl Cravath S&M LLP -825 8th Av -NY 10019
(212) 371-7799 .. **Lowy,** John B '80 (J Lowy,PC) -645 5th Av -NY 10022 **Fx:**371-8527
(212) 820-9340 .. **Lowy,** Lloyd S '86 (Hawkins D&W LLP) -One Chase Manh Plz -NY 10005
(212) 404-4072 .. **Lowy,** Lynn Feldman '93 Cnsl NYU Hosp Ctr -1 Park Av -NY 10016 **Fx:**404-4092
(212) 659-8105 .. **Lowy,** Marina O '90 %Mt Sinai Med Ctr -1 Gustave L Levy Pl Bx 1099 -NY 10029 **Fx:**348-2230
(212) 975-3406 .. **Lowy,** Susanna M '82 %CBS Inc -51 W 52nd -NY 10019 **Fx:**975-3930
(212) 848-4000 .. **Loxley,** Oliver D T '09 %Shearman & S LLP -599 Lex Av -NY 10022
(212) 446-4800 .. **Loy,** Jos A '05 %Kirkland & E LLP -153 E 53rd -NY 10022
(212) 880-1433 .. **Loyal,** Timothy M '06 Fidelity Natl Fncl,Inc -711 3rd Av -NY 10017
(631) 293-6060 .. **Loyd,** Wm J '06 (Cellino & B,PC) -445 Broad Hollow Rd -Melvll 11747
(212) 969-3000 .. **Lozada,** Charley E '09 %Proskauer R LLP -1585 Bway -NY 10036
(212) 267-1650 .. **Lozano,** Maria E '92 %Fine O&A,LLP -39 Bway -NY 10006
(212) 735-3000 .. **Lozano,** Paola '02 (Skadden ASM&F LLP) -4 Times Sq -NY 10036
(716) 282-5490 .. **Lozinsky,** Connie M '88 -2524 Pine Av Bx2145 MMS -Niagara Fls 14301 **Fx:**282-5493
(914) 282-3245 .. **Lozito,** Bruce R '07 -125 River -Sleepy Hollow 10591
(212) 947-1999 .. **Lozito,** Danielle M '03 %Methfessel & W,PC -450 7th Av -NY 10123
(631) 852-2781 .. **Lozito,** Leonard J '93 %Hon Emerson -235 Griffing Av -Rvrhead 11901
(718) 615-0044 .. **Lozner,** David V '95 (Lozner & M) -1901 Emmons Av -Brklyn 11235
(646) 723-7635 .. **Lozner,** Joshua J '02 Patriarch Prtnrs LLC -32 Av of Amer -NY 10013
(718) 615-0044 .. **Lozner & Mastropietro** -1901 Emmons Av -Brklyn 11235 **Fx:**615-0722
(973) 597-6128 .. **Lozner,** Melissa Toner '02 %Lowenstein S PC -1251 Av of Amer -NY 10020 **Fx:**597-6129
(212) 705-7000 .. **Lozner,** Steven W '03 Cnsl Bingham M LLP -399 Park Av -NY 10022
(212) 275-4048 .. **Lozow,** Chas S '87 Elektra Ent Grp -75 Rckfllr Plz -NY 10019 **Fx:**275-1800
(212) 254-2260 .. **Lozynskyj,** Askold S '77 -225 E 11th -NY 10003 **Fx:**979-1011
(212) 537-2428 .. **Lu,** Amy '02 Morgan Stanley -1633 Bway -NY 10019
(212) 719-0200 .. **Lu,** Andrea '99 BAR/BRI -1500 Bway -NY 10036 **Fx:**719-1421
(212) 547-5400 .. **Lu,** Audrey '09 %McDermott W&E LLP -340 Mad Av -NY 10173
(212) 838-4811 .. **Lu,** David '05 %AR Golub,PC -42 E 64th -NY 10065 **Fx:**838-4869
(212) 588-0800 .. **Lu,** Deborah L '05 %Frommer L&H LLP -745 5th Av -NY 10151
(212) 264-5916 .. **Lu,** Fen '92 %DHS -26 Fed Plz -NY 10278
(718) 939-4633 .. **Lu,** Haonian '07 KK Tung PC -38-21 Main -Flushng 11354 **Fx:**939-4468
(212) 839-5300 .. **Lu,** Jackie '07 %Sidley A LLP -787 7th Av -NY 10019
(212) 558-4000 .. **Lu,** Jingjing '07 %Sullivan & C LLP -125 Broad -NY 10004
(212) 258-8000 .. **Lu,** Karen C '98 %MTV Networks -1515 Bway -NY 10036 **Fx:**258-8358
(212) 224-1568 .. **Lu,** Kathryn A '87 %Mutual of America -320 Park Av -NY 10022
(212) 765-5070 .. **Lu,** Lawr T-W '08 Fish & R,PC -153 E 53rd -NY 10022
(212) 715-1307 .. **Lu,** Lily J '98 (Arnold & P LLP) -399 Park Av -NY 10022
(212) 596-9000 .. **Lu,** Margaret C '08 %Ropes & G LLP -1211 Av of Amer -NY 10036
(212) 389-5000 .. **Lu,** Phuc H '04 %Sutherland A&B LLP -1114 Av of Amer -NY 10036
(212) 529-1558 .. **Lu,** Tony Y '03 -225 Bway -NY 10007 **Fx:**786-7895
(516) 622-8378 .. **Lu,** Wei '09 Kylin TV Inc -1600 Old Cntry Rd -Plainvw 11803
(212) 906-1200 .. **Lu,** Wm '00 (Latham & W) -885 3rd Av -NY 10022
(212) 610-6300 .. **Lubarsky,** Jessica D '04 %Allen & O -1221 Av of Amer -NY 10020
(718) 787-1811 .. **Lubarsky,** Leon '02 (Lubarsky & T) -2699 Coney Isl Av -Brklyn 11223 **Fx:**787-1511
(914) 997-8558 .. **Lubarsky,** Neil R '81 N Lubarsky & Assoc -2900 Wstchstr Av -Purchase 10577 **Fx:**220-6183
(212) 308-6100 .. **Lubarsky,** Richd F '84 (Levi L&F LLP) -1185 Av of Amer -NY 10036
(212) 918-3000 .. **Lubart,** Mitchell R '80 (Hogan L LLP) -875 3rd Av -NY 10022
(516) 609-9170 .. **Lubasch,** Richd J '72 -168 Forest Av -Locust Vly 11560
(914) 328-0404 .. **Lubbe,** E Johannes '96 (Jackson L LLP) -1 N Bway -White Plns 10601
(973) 596-4649 .. **Lubben,** Michl J '97 (Gibbons PC) -1 Penn Plz -NY 10119 **Fx:**639-6236
(212) 859-8000 .. **Lubcher,** Fredk '55 OfCnsl Fried FHS&J LLP -1 NY Plz -NY 10004
(212) 701-3000 .. **Lubeley,** Michl Justin '03 %Cahill G&R LLP -80 Pine -NY 10005 **Fx:**269-5420
(212) 766-1888 .. **Lubell,** Allyson P '89 %Morris DA&F -2 Rector -NY 10006
(212) 837-6000 .. **Lubell,** Danl S '88 (Hughes H&R LLP) -1 Bttry Pk Plz -NY 10004
(212) 986-7714 .. **Lubell,** David G '58 (Propp L&J,LLP) -1500 Bway -NY 10036
(212) 541-2000 .. **Lubell,** Harold A '56 OfCnsl Bryan C LLP -1290 Av of Amer -NY 10104
(212) 848-4000 .. **Lubell,** Karina B '09 %Shearman & S LLP -599 Lex Av -NY 10022
(914) 375-0100 .. **Lubell,** Peter '74 (Novick ELRW&L,PC) -733 Ynkrs Av -Ynkrs 10704
(212) 242-7480 .. **Lubelsky,** Mark L '93 (M Lubelsky & Assoc) -123 W 18th -NY 10011
(212) 458-2019 .. **Lubenesky,** John S '01 AIG -175 Water -NY 10038
(914) 358-4934 .. **Luber,** Esta S '99 %Ferro L&Z LLC -1025 Wstchstr Av -White Plns 10604
(212) 506-1700 .. **Lubert,** Rachel E '07 %Kasowitz BT&F LLP -1633 Bway -NY 10019
(518) 385-0380 .. **Lubert,** Richd P '85 GE Co -1 River Rd -Schnctdy 12345
(212) 644-0515 .. **Lubetski,** Saul '95 Harbor Group Intl -150 E 58th -NY 10155
(212) 616-3006 .. **Lubetzky,** Danl '97 Peaceworks,LLC -Bx1393 -NY 10113 **Fx:**616-3005
(732) 855-6408 .. **Lubic,** Douglas W '85 (Wilentz G&S) -110 William -NY 10038 **Fx:**726-6526
(212) 252-0300 .. **Lubic,** Wm J '53 (Kagan LLLG&C,LLP) -200 Mad Av -NY 10016
(914) 995-2667 .. **Lubin,** Barbara A '87 %Cnty Atty -148 Martine Av -White Plns 10601 **Fx:**995-5858
(516) 887-8200 .. **Lubin,** David '90 (D Lubin & Assoc,PLLC) -5 N Vllg Av -Rockvll Ctr 11570 **Fx:**887-8250
(516) 354-0149 .. **Lubin,** Emmanuel A '00 (Lubin & S) -229 Jericho Tpk -Floral Pk 11001
(212) 909-6000 .. **Lubin,** Jonathan L '09 %Debevoise & P LLP -919 3rd Av -NY 10022
(212) 566-3529 .. **Lubin,** Julie Margot '94 %Dept of Bldgs -280 Bway -NY 10007
(646) 610-5305 .. **Lubin,** Kevin '84 %NYPD -1 Police Plz -NY 10038 **Fx:**610-7832
(212) 236-6009 .. **Lubin,** Mark L '83 %Merrill Lynch -225 Lbrty -NY 10080
(212) 806-5400 .. **Lubin,** Michl E '99 SpclCnsl Stroock &S&L LLP -180 Maiden Ln -NY 10038
(212) 363-1380 .. **Lubin,** Michl I '83 Cnsl Herten BSCBL&H,LLC -747 3rd Av -NY 10017
(914) 323-7000 .. **Lubin,** Rory L '96 (Wilson EME&D LLP) -3 Gannett Dr -White Plns 10604
(516) 354-0149 .. **Lubin & St Louis** -229 Jericho Tpk -Floral Pk 11001 **Fx:**354-3097
(212) 227-4100 .. **Lubiner,** Alan M '75 (Lubiner & S) -111 Bway -NY 10006 **Fx:**406-3244
(212) 788-1528 .. **Lubinof,** Faye '05 Law Dept -100 Church -NY 10007 **Fx:**788-0367
(845) 496-8885 .. **Lubinsky,** Judith L '80 -100 Egbertson Rd -Campbell Hall 10916 **Fx:**496-1013
(212) 752-1161 .. **Lubitz,** A Peter '73 OfCnsl Traiger & H LLP -501 5th Av -NY 10017 **Fx:**937-5229
(212) 309-8100 .. **Lubitz,** Dana B '91 %Lexis/Nexis -125 Park Av -NY 10017 **Fx:**309-8187
(212) 756-2000 .. **Lubitz,** David J '10 %Schulte R&Z LLP -919 3rd Av -NY 10022
(212) 941-1552 .. **Lubitz,** Leonard S '78 (Devereaux & L,PC) -277 Bway -NY 10007
(914) 948-2300 .. **Lubitz,** Murray S '73 -235 Main -White Plns 10601 **Fx:**948-4745
(914) 328-9625 .. **Lubitz,** Murray S '73 -295 Mill -Poughkeepsie 12601 **Fx:**948-4745
(845) 356-0700 .. **Lubitz,** Robt A '84 -747 Chestnut Rdg Rd -Chestnut Rdg 10977
(212) 878-8000 .. **Lubliner,** Barbara S '99 %Clifford C LLP -31 W 52nd -NY 10019
(212) 460-3302 .. **Lubling,** Chanoch '78 Con Ed -4 Irving Pl -NY 10003
(212) 264-9320 .. **Lublinski,** Melvin '72 %US DOJ Antitrust Div -26 Fed Plz Ste 3630 -NY 10278
(212) 517-3821 .. **Luboff,** Marvin '64 -1025 5th Av -NY 10028 **Fx:**517-8293
(212) 779-9800 .. **Luboja,** J Gary '81 (Luboja & T,LLP) -10 E 40th -NY 10016
(212) 779-9800 .. **Luboja & Thau, LLP** -10 E 40th -NY 10016 **Fx:**252-0457
(516) 571-4906 .. **Lubov,** Helane B '83 %Supreme Ct -100 Supreme Ct Dr -Mineola 11501
(516) 773-6075 .. **Lubov,** Perry L '80 -39 Olive -Gt Neck 11020
(718) 243-6383 .. **Lubow,** Adam M '08 Legal Aid -111 Lvngstn -Brklyn 11201
(518) 589-5723 .. **Lubow,** Greg D '76 -6026 Main Bx839 -Tannersvll 12485 **Fx:**589-6015
(212) 310-8566 .. **Lubowitz,** Michl E '91 (Weil G&M LLP) -767 5th Av -NY 10153
(914) 472-8069 .. **Lubowitz,** Steven I '84 -700 Wht Plns Rd -Scarsdale 10583 **Fx:**725-6160
(914) 472-8069 .. **Lubowitz,** Susan I '81 -700 Wht Plns Rd -Scarsdale 10583 **Fx:**725-6160
(516) 228-8600 .. **Luby,** Chester J '53 -333 Earle Ovngton Blvd -Uniondale 11553
(212) 697-4090 .. **Luca,** Patricia A '85 %Platzer L&P LLP -61 Bway -NY 10006
(212) 705-7000 .. **Lucan,** Andrea Wang '07 %Bingham M LLP -399 Park Av -NY 10022
(212) 218-5500 .. **Lucano,** Andrew '01 (Seyfarth S LLP) -620 8th Av -NY 10018
(718) 556-1800 .. **Lucarelli,** Thos A '90 (Lucarelli & C) -1491 Richmond Rd -Staten Isl 10304 **Fx:**556-1775
(212) 442-6855 .. **Lucas,** Andrew J '10 %Law Dept -100 Church -NY 10007 **Fx:**788-0367
(212) 308-9635 .. **Lucas,** Barbara N '85 -444 E 52nd -NY 10022
(718) 293-7003 .. **Lucas,** Carl '86 (Lucas & L) -Stadium Station Bx524617 -Bronx 10452
(212) 872-3606 .. **Lucas,** Dante D '92 %KPMG LLP -345 Park Av -NY 10154
(212) 715-9100 .. **Lucas,** Diane O '08 %Kramer LN&F,LLP -1177 Av of Amer -NY 10036
(212) 661-8000 .. **Lucas,** Donald C '84 (Lucas & M,LLP) -475 Park Av S -NY 10016
(914) 777-1134 .. **Lucas,** Emily J '05 %Ingerman S LLP -550 Mamaroneck Av -Harrison 10528
(718) 383-0432 .. **Lucas,** Henry P '53 -608 Humboldt -Brklyn 11222 **Fx:**383-2737
(212) 954-8981 .. **Lucas,** Kirstin M '06 KPMG LLP -345 Park Av -NY 10154
(212) 486-7738 .. **Lucas,** Magaly C '90 -259 Bennett Av -NY 10040
(914) 967-3867 .. **Lucas,** Margaret R '86 -4 Bird Ln -Rye 10580
(212) 859-8000 .. **Lucas,** Mark Hamilton '06 %Fried FHS&J LLP -1 NY Plz -NY 10004
(718) 293-7003 .. **Lucas,** Melissa '86 (Lucas & L) -Stadium Station Bx524617 -Bronx 10452
(212) 661-8000 .. **Lucas & Mercanti, LLP** -475 Park Av S -NY 10016 **Fx:**661-8002
(212) 513-3200 .. **Lucas,** Nancy K '03 %Holland & K LLP -31 W 52nd -NY 10019
(212) 688-1900 .. **Lucas,** Paul V '01 %Greenberg T&H,LLP -767 3rd Av -NY 10017
(212) 442-6851 .. **Lucas,** Peter Christopher '08 %Law Dept -100 Church -NY 10007 **Fx:**788-0367
(212) 504-6000 .. **Lucas,** Reginald D '08 %Cadwalader W&T LLP -1 World Fncl Ctr -NY 10281
(516) 676-6262 .. **Lucas,** Robt G '65 (Kelly L&P) -23 Birch Hill Rd -Locust Vly 11560
(212) 983-6000 .. **Lucas,** Scott A '95 -250 Park Av -NY 10177 **Fx:**286-9516
(212) 458-2125 .. **Lucas,** Tara L '04 -175 Water -NY 10038
(631) 288-2120 .. **Lucas,** Terry Z '90 Open Book -1 Glovers Ln -Westhmptn Bch 11978
(914) 347-7039 .. **Lucasey,** Jean M '01 Student Advocacy,Inc -3 W Main -Elmsfrd 10523
(212) 480-2125 .. **Lucashuk,** Joana M '07 %Insurance Dept -25 Beaver -NY 10004 **Fx:**480-5272
(631) 589-2895 .. **Lucca,** Heather A '05 Relative Abstract -3 Christine Ct -Bohemia 11716
(631) 589-2894 .. **Lucca,** Nicholas '07 Relative Abstract Corp -3 Christine Ct -Bohemia 11716
(914) 948-8600 .. **Lucchese & D'Ammora,LLP** -10 Bank -White Plns 10606 **Fx:**948-2972
(914) 948-8600 .. **Lucchese,** Robt J '84 (Lucchese & D,LLP) -10 Bank -White Plns 10606
(315) 471-0065 .. **Lucchesi,** Jos L '87 (Mangano L&C) -201 E Jffrsn -Syracuse 13202
(718) 967-3723 .. **Lucchesi Nolan,** Carol '87 -10 Buttonwood Rd -Staten Isl 10304
(212) 233-4700 .. **Lucciola,** Gerard A '83 (Rosato & L,PC) -233 Bway -NY 10279 **Fx:**233-6500
(212) 325-2000 .. **Luce,** David D '00 Credit Suisse -11 Mad Av -NY 10010

(607) 723-0600 .. **Luce,** Joshua M '08 %Gitto & N,LLP -71 State -Bnghmtn 13901 **Fx:**723-0634
(607) 723-9511 .. **Luce,** Kristen K '08 %Coughlin & G,LLP -19 Chenango Bx2039 -Bnghmtn 13902
(607) 687-0567 .. **Luce,** Kristen K '08 %Coughlin & G,LLP -27-29 Lk Bx250 -Owego 13827
(212) 728-8000 .. **Lucena-Pichardo,** Jodi A '09 %Willkie F&G LLP -787 7th Av -NY 10019
(914) 948-7700 .. **Luceno,** Chas E '85 OfCnsl E Campbell -2 Mad Av -Valhalla 10595 **Fx:**948-7795
(212) 577-3461 .. **Lucente,** Martin '90 %Leg Aid -199 Water -NY 10038 **Fx:**509-8431
(716) 881-3010 .. **Lucente,** Rocco II '86 (Cohen & L,PC) -343 Elmwood Av Bx5204 -Buffalo 14213
(607) 797-4839 .. **Lucenti,** Amy Jo '05 %Hogan SLS&D,LLP -Bx660 -Bnghmtn 13902
(212) 334-4577 .. **Lucentini,** Eric J '99 OfCnsl Jones C LLP -225 Bway -NY 10007 **Fx:**406-6890
(212) 334-4577 .. **Lucentini,** Sandra E '03 OfCnsl Jones C LLP -225 Bway -NY 10007 **Fx:**406-6890
(516) 557-2312 .. **Lucere,** Mary T '88 (M Lucere,PLLC) -4007 Merrick Rd -Seafrd 11783
(518) 487-7600 .. **Lucey,** Brian J '95 (Whiteman O&H LLP) -1 Commerce Plz -Albany 12260
(518) 465-4089 .. **Lucey,** John F Jr. '41 -345 Nrthrn Blvd -Albany 12204
(212) 335-9000 .. **Lucey,** Shannon G '01 %DA -1 Hogan Pl -NY 10013
(212) 384-1000 .. **Lucey,** Timothy K '02 %FBI -26 Fed Plz -NY 10278
(212) 451-1146 .. **Luchins,** Moshe A '97 %Zweig Companies -900 3rd Av -NY 10022
(212) 259-8000 .. **Luchs,** Bryan J '99 (Dewey & L LLP) -1301 Av of Amer -NY 10019
(212) 793-7852 .. **Luchs,** Erik C '96 Citigroup -425 Park Av -NY 10022
(516) 294-3400 .. **Lucia,** Alfred P '78 -100 Grdn City Plz -Gdn Cty 11530 **Fx:**248-8907
(585) 641-8000 .. **Lucia,** Steven A '89 (Fix SB&G,PC) -295 Woodcliff Dr -Fairprt 14450
(212) 373-3000 .. **Luciano,** Adriana T '10 %Paul WRW&G LLP -1285 Av of Amer -NY 10019
(212) 785-2577 .. **Luciano,** Elizabeth '93 %Rosner & N -26 Bway -NY 10004 **Fx:**785-5203
(718) 923-4206 .. **Luciano,** Kenneth J '87 %OTDA Fair Hearings -14 Boerum Pl -Brklyn 11201
(914) 995-3413 .. **Luciano,** Maryanne '81 %DA -111 Martin Luther King Blvd -White Plns 10601 **Fx:**995-3363
(516) 364-3333 .. **Luciano,** Nino V '92 %Mass Mutual -1000 Woodbury Rd -Woodbury 11797 **Fx:**364-3647
(212) 607-2829 .. **Luciano,** Susan M '95 FTC -1 Bowling Grn -NY 10004
(631) 224-5550 .. **Luciano,** Thos D '93 %Town Atty -655 Main -Islip 11751 **Fx:**224-5573
(718) 376-4766 .. **Luciano-Beras,** Juan Pablo '05 -1123 Av Z -Brklyn 11235
(212) 735-3000 .. **Lucibello,** Vincenzo P '06 %Skadden ASM&F LLP -4 Times Sq -NY 10036
(718) 250-2000 .. **Lucibello,** Wanda '82 %DA -350 Jay -Brklyn 11201 **Fx:**250-2314
(212) 818-8800 .. **Lucido,** Paul A '91 (Graubard M) -405 Lex Av -NY 10174
(716) 856-4000 .. **Lucinski,** Ryan J '06 %Hodgson R LLP -140 Pearl -Buffalo 14202
(631) 862-0751 .. **Lucivero,** Lucretia M '91 -Bx137 -St James 11780 **Fx:**862-0751
(212) 417-3736 .. **Luck,** Dinah M '05 MFY Legal Srvcs -299 Bway -NY 10007 **Fx:**417-3890
(607) 772-9671 .. **Luckanick,** Alexander W '67 -134 Front -Bnghmtn 13905 **Fx:**771-6103
(718) 558-8257 .. **Luckey,** Kimberly A '00 %LIRR -Jamaica Station -Jamaica 11435 **Fx:**558-8211
(518) 457-2070 .. **Luckina,** Anita K '00 %Dept of Tax & Fin -Bldg 9 State Campus -Albany 12227 **Fx:**457-6131
(212) 610-6300 .. **Lucking,** David G '07 SrCnsl Allen & O -1221 Av of Amer -NY 10020
(516) 479-6300 .. **Luckman,** Gerard R '94 (Silverman A LLP) -100 Jericho Quad -Jericho 11753
(516) 679-0008 .. **Luckman,** Gregg A '92 -16 Verbena Av -Floral Pk 11001 **Fx:**908-4391
(212) 483-0105 .. **Luckner,** Steven J '97 %Coughlin D LLP -88 Pine-Wall St Plz -NY 10005
(212) 702-0900 .. **Luckow,** Lance '04 %Axelrod F&D -260 Mad Av -NY 10016 **Fx:**355-7365
(516) 873-1511 .. **Lucks,** Ava S '08 %Fischetti & P -310 Old Cntry Rd -Gdn Cty 11530
(718) 793-9000 .. **Lucks,** Robt C '90 -118-35 Qns Blvd -Frst Hlls 11375
(212) 308-4411 .. **Lucks,** Steven M '05 %Edwards AP&D LLP -750 Lex Av -NY 10022
(845) 634-6291 .. **Lucrezia,** Angelo M '00 -151 S Main -New Cty 10956
(914) 377-6176 .. **Lucyk,** Brian M '76 City of Yonkers -40 S Bway -Ynkrs 10701 **Fx:**377-6940
(212) 450-4000 .. **Lucyk,** Brianne M '06 %Davis P&W LLP -450 Lex Av -NY 10017
(516) 496-6218 .. **Lucyk,** Ricky J '94 Geico -170 Froelich Farm Blvd -Woodbury 11797
(518) 429-4200 .. **Ludd,** Oksana M '80 (Hiscock & B,LLP) -50 Beaver -Albany 12207
(631) 749-2364 .. **Luddecke,** Hugh F Jr. '78 -3 Williette Rd Bx769 -Shelter Isl 11964
(212) 237-1000 .. **Luddy,** Robt J '92 (Windels ML&M,LLP) -156 W 56th -NY 10019
(518) 745-4343 .. **Ludemann,** Matthew R '85 (Stanclift L&M,PC) -3 Warren Bx358 -Glens Fls 12801 **Fx:**745-4344
(212) 609-6800 .. **Ludgin,** David A '82 (McCarter & E,LLP) -245 Park Av -NY 10167
(315) 592-7255 .. **Ludington,** Ramsey G '54 -217 Oneida -Fulton 13069
(315) 593-6278 .. **Ludington,** Spencer J '88 -217 Oneida -Fulton 13069 **Fx:**592-7205
(516) 997-7330 .. **Ludlam,** Margot L '95 %Baxter S&S,PC -99 N Bway -Hicksvll 11801
(315) 839-5037 .. **Ludlow,** G Kevin '84 -Bx452 -Sauquoit 13456
(518) 432-9220 .. **Ludman,** Kenneth '81 %Patricia Lynch Assoc Inc -677 Bway -Albany 12207 **Fx:**432-9186
(212) 450-4000 .. **Ludmerer,** Nancy B '81 Cnsl Davis P&W LLP -450 Lex Av -NY 10017
(315) 475-3127 .. **Ludovici,** Lyndsey '08 Leg Srvcs -472 S Salina -Syracuse 13202 **Fx:**475-2706
(718) 855-9122 .. **Ludwig,** Arnold J '74 -26 Court -Brklyn 11242
(716) 856-4000 .. **Ludwig,** Cynthia G '05 %Hodgson R LLP -140 Pearl -Buffalo 14202
(212) 735-3000 .. **Ludwig,** Erik K '07 %Skadden ASM&F LLP -4 Times Sq -NY 10036
(212) 431-4800 .. **Ludwig,** Gordon M '80 -30 W 26th -NY 10010
(212) 254-5500 .. **Ludwig,** John Toby '95 -853 Bway -NY 10003 **Fx:**254-4800
(212) 817-5423 .. **Ludwig,** Michl '92 CBS -555 W 57th -NY 10019 **Fx:**586-8291
(212) 264-8306 .. **Ludwig,** Nicole '04 %US GSA -26 Fed Plz -NY 10278 **Fx:**264-1987
(212) 765-5070 .. **Ludwig,** S Peter '69 Fish & R,PC -153 E 53rd -NY 10022
(212) 680-5100 .. **Ludwig,** Sarah I '93 NEDAP -176 Grand -NY 10013 **Fx:**680-5104
(212) 474-1000 .. **Ludwig,** Victor V '09 %Cravath S&M LLP -825 8th Av -NY 10019
(212) 537-1063 .. **Ludwigson,** Susan L '97 Morgan Stanley -1633 Bway -NY 10019
(914) 945-3667 .. **Ludwin,** Richd M '92 Thos J Watson Research Ctr -Bx218 -Yorktwn Hts 10598
(212) 449-1309 .. **Lue,** Alex J '04 Merrill Lynch -250 Vesey -NY 10080
(212) 578-2164 .. **Luecke,** George Anthony '96 MetLife Inc -2701 Qns Plz N -LIC 11101
(212) 770-3175 .. **Luedecker,** Warren A Jr. '81 %AIG -72 Wall -NY 10005 **Fx:**480-9146
(212) 903-8700 .. **Luehring,** JoAnn '83 (Roberts & H,LLP) -825 8th Av -NY 10019
(212) 672-5778 .. **Lueker,** Stephen R '04 HVB Grp -150 E 42nd -NY 10017
(212) 225-2000 .. **Luft,** Avram E '00 Cnsl Cleary GS&H -1 Lbrty Plz -NY 10006
(516) 794-2720 .. **Luft,** Beatrice Bloch '93 -1900 Hempstd Tpk -E Meadow 11554 **Fx:**794-6535
(631) 266-2703 .. **Luft,** Leslie '82 -15 Fenimore Ln -Huntngtn 11743
(212) 474-1000 .. **Luft,** Richd N '10 %Cravath S&M LLP -825 8th Av -NY 10019
(212) 450-4000 .. **Luftglass,** Karen L '05 %Davis P&W LLP -450 Lex Av -NY 10017
(212) 450-4000 .. **Luftglass,** Marc M '05 %Davis P&W LLP -450 Lex Av -NY 10017
(212) 450-4000 .. **Luftglass,** Scott B '05 %Davis P&W LLP -450 Lex Av -NY 10017
(212) 759-2600 .. **Luftig,** Andrew I '05 %Irwin LC&L,PC -845 3rd Av -NY 10022
(212) 325-4481 .. **Luftig,** Richd S '94 %Credit Suisse First Boston -11 Mad Av -NY 10010
(212) 255-4638 .. **Luftig,** Wendy J '89 -36 W 22nd -NY 10010
(212) 644-4420 .. **Lugara,** Antonino '05 %Fabiani C&H,LLP -570 Lex Av -NY 10022
(516) 542-2200 .. **Lugassy,** Guy '09 Healthplex Inc -333 Earle Ovngton Blvd -Uniondale 11553
(585) 428-5210 .. **Lugbill,** Ron G '07 Pub Def -10 N Fitzhugh -Rchstr 14614 **Fx:**428-2234
(212) 837-6000 .. **Luger,** A Stephen '81 (Hughes H&R LLP) -1 Bttry Pk Plz -NY 10004
(212) 244-6255 .. **Luger,** Arthur A '80 -450 7th Av -NY 10123 **Fx:**244-6256
(212) 645-6390 .. **Luger,** Wendy I '85 -511 Av of Amer PMB 20 -NY 10011 **Fx:**645-6390
(631) 667-1510 .. **Luglio,** Albert J '56 (Kelly L&A) -2023 Deer Prk Av -Deer Pk 11729
(917) 843-3880 .. **Lugo,** A Alberto '97 -64 Joyce Rd -Eastchstr 10709 **Fx:**(908) 378-1639
(212) 844-9251 .. **Lugo,** Adelfa Ann '77 -942 Burke Av -Bronx 10469
(718) 855-3000 .. **Lugo,** Betty '85 (Pacheco & L) -340 Atl Av -Brklyn 11201
(212) 508-8020 .. **Lugo,** Catherine A '03 Nippon Express USA,Inc -590 Mad Av -NY 10022
(212) 863-6300 .. **Lugo,** Edwin '95 %HPD -100 Gold -NY 10038
(516) 294-5433 .. **Lugo,** Jessica '07 %Ahmuty D&M -200 IU Willets Rd -Albertson 11507
(212) 306-1397 .. **Lugo Natal,** Ivonne '84 Amer Stock Exch -86 Trinity Pl -NY 10006 **Fx:**306-2139
(718) 993-1000 .. **Lugovina,** Carol N '84 %LRF Management -384 E 149th -Bronx 10455
(718) 546-0950 .. **Lugo-Wongsuwan,** Rosa '89 %Dept of Correction -75-20 Astoria Blvd -E Elmhrst 11370
(347) 269-4461 .. **Luhana,** Roopal P '03 (Chaffin L LLP) -330 Mad Av -NY 10017 **Fx:**(888) 499-1123
(518) 884-0000 .. **Luhn,** Christopher N '86 C Luhn,PC -199 Milton Av -Ballston Spa 12020 **Fx:**884-0009
(518) 388-1270 .. **Luhn,** V Jerome '76 %CQC -401 State -Schnctdy 12305 **Fx:**388-1275
(518) 295-8257 .. **Luhr,** Christopher '00 %DA -Bx888 -Schoharie 12157
(716) 856-1344 .. **Luhr,** John Paul '91 %Bouvier Prtnrshp,LLP -350 Main -Buffalo 14202 **Fx:**856-1369
(212) 925-3438 .. **Lui,** Alfred S H '92 -33 Bowery -NY 10002
(646) 442-3100 .. **Lui,** Saml W-L '08 Legal Srvcs -90 John -NY 10038 **Fx:**(212) 227-9798
(212) 626-2067 .. **Lui,** Suzanne Lee '97 %Pru Capital Grp -1114 Av of Amer -NY 10036
(518) 783-1100 .. **Luibrand,** Kevin A '84 (Luibrand Law Firm,PLLC) -950 New Loudon Rd -Latham 12110
(212) 592-1400 .. **Luick,** Jonathan E '09 %Herrick,F LLP -2 Park Av -NY 10016
(212) 323-7070 .. **Luis,** Anthony D '00 %Rawle & H LLP -14 Wall -NY 10005
(914) 813-5800 .. **Luis,** Francisco C '94 %DA -475 North Av -New Rchll 10801 **Fx:**813-5806
(212) 310-8000 .. **Luise,** Christopher T '09 %Weil G&M LLP -767 5th Av -NY 10153
(914) 761-1300 .. **Luisi,** Anthony P '09 %Cuddy & F LLP -445 Hmltn Av -White Plns 10601
(718) 442-3377 .. **Luisi,** John V '89 -110 Belmont Pl -Staten Isl 10301
(212) 687-3000 .. **Luisi,** Rocco '07 %Jaffe & A,LLP -600 3rd Av -NY 10016
(212) 268-0204 .. **Lujack,** Anthony M '00 %ETC Inc -240 W 35th -NY 10001
(212) 219-8686 .. **Luk,** Chas K '89 (Luk & L) -254 Canal -NY 10013 **Fx:**219-8817
(212) 464-2664 .. **Luk,** Elizabeth M '07 JP Morgan -345 Park Av -NY 10154
(212) 219-8686 .. **Luk,** Leon K '89 (Luk & L) -254 Canal -NY 10013 **Fx:**219-8817
(585) 424-2670 .. **Lukacher,** Kenneth J '95 -3136 Winton Rd S -Rchstr 14623
(212) 973-0572 .. **Lukanski,** John O '99 (Wolff & S PC) -140 Bway -NY 10005
(718) 243-6376 .. **Lukas,** Gabriela '98 %Leg Aid -111 Lvngstn -Brklyn 11201 **Fx:**237-8737
(212) 418-0500 .. **Lukas,** Karen B '80 Cnsl Morris & M LLP -767 3rd Av -NY 10017
(212) 699-8854 .. **Lukasewicz,** Michelle '02 Berdon LLP -360 Mad Av -NY 10017
(212) 681-4300 .. **Lukashok,** Edw '67 -122 E 42nd -NY 10168
(716) 847-8400 .. **Lukasiewicz,** Alisa Ann '96 SpclCnsl Phillips L LLP -3400 HSBC Ctr -Buffalo 14203
(716) 883-0355 .. **Lukasiewicz,** Marie L '93 %R Perk -995 Elmwood Av -Buffalo 14222
(716) 852-1888 .. **Lukasik,** Danl T '89 %Cantor LD&P,PC -350 Main -Buffalo 14202
(716) 852-1888 .. **Lukasik,** Kelsey D '99 %Cantor LD&P,PC -350 Main -Buffalo 14202
(212) 578-2211 .. **Lukaszewski,** Anthony S '88 %MetLife -27-01 Qns Plz N -LIC 11101
(516) 775-9400 .. **Lukaszewski,** Chester P '01 %Jeffrey Goldberg,PC -2001 Marcus Av -Lk Success 11042 **Fx:**775-4477
(212) 773-5790 .. **Luke,** Bing '09 Ernst & Young LLP -5 Times Sq -NY 10036

(212) 687-3000 .. **Luke,** Donald F '73 (Jaffe & A,LLP) -600 3rd Av -NY 10016
(212) 479-6000 .. **Luke,** Frances M '02 %Cooley LLP -1114 Av of Amer -NY 10036
(518) 486-7815 .. **Luke,** Kimberly B '04 %Insurance Dept -99 Wshngtn Av -Albany 12257 **Fx:**474-3397
(212) 859-5022 .. **Luke,** Neil C '02 -110 Wall -NY 10005
(212) 589-4200 .. **Luke,** Tarsha L T '08 %Baker & H LLP -45 Rckfllr Plz -NY 10111
(315) 867-1173 .. **Luke,** Thaddeus J '94 %Supreme Ct -301 N Wshngtn -Herkimer 13350
(212) 940-3104 .. **Lukeman,** Barbara A '01 %Nixon P LLP -437 Mad Av -NY 10022
(315) 735-7566 .. **Luker,** Mary Ellen '84 %Petrone & P,PC -1624 Genesee -Utica 13502
(212) 260-9905 .. **Lukievics,** Helen J '81 Branford Communications,Inc -611 Bway -NY 10012 **Fx:**260-9908
(315) 336-0772 .. **Lukin,** Paul M '79 %Hon J Grow -300 N James -Rome 13440 **Fx:**337-0846
(718) 268-8111 .. **Lukose,** Judy E '04 %D Mastrodomenico -107-19 71st Av -Frst Hlls 11375 **Fx:**268-7382
(631) 369-7600 .. **Lukoski,** Edw G '77 Cnsl Lewis JAA,LLP -21 E 2nd -Rvrhead 11901
(315) 475-3127 .. **Lukow,** Robt W '93 %Leg Srvcs -472 S Salina -Syracuse 13202 **Fx:**475-2706
(212) 406-2270 .. **Lukowicz,** Ronald J '78 -225 Bway -NY 10007 **Fx:**267-9726
(518) 462-4242 .. **Lukowski,** Scott D '09 %Colwell C&P,LLP -20 Corp Wds Blvd -Albany 12211
(718) 250-2000 .. **Lukowsky,** Jannette '99 %DA -350 Jay -Brklyn 11201 **Fx:**250-2314
(212) 626-1187 .. **Luks,** Gary M '86 Bank Leumi USA -562 5th Av -NY 10036 **Fx:**626-1195
(607) 936-9313 .. **Lull,** Robt E '49 -48 E Market -Corning 14830
(212) 628-3884 .. **Lulla,** Joel L '83 -12 E 86th -NY 10028 **Fx:**628-3713
(212) 269-4900 .. **Lullo,** Gregory J '09 %Ford MEW&G,LLP -Wall Street Plz -NY 10005
(212) 848-4000 .. **Lum,** Chune Loong '10 Shearman & S LLP -599 Lex Av -NY 10022
(212) 775-9002 .. **Lum Drasco & Positan,LLC** -325 Bway -NY 10007 **Fx:**(973) 403-9021
(212) 272-0595 .. **Lum,** Erin M '04 %JP Morgan Chase -383 Mad Av -NY 10179 **Fx:**(917) 849-2670
(212) 326-3939 .. **Lum,** Forewing '08 %Jones D -222 E 41st -NY 10017
(212) 490-3000 .. **Lum,** Larry H '87 (Wilson EME&D LLP) -150 E 42nd -NY 10017
(212) 801-2215 .. **Luma,** Daren A '97 %Greenberg T,LLP -200 Park Av -NY 10166
(914) 683-1800 .. **Luman,** Arthur E '65 (Luman H&T) -140 Grand -White Plns 10601
(914) 683-1800 .. **Luman Helfman & Tucker** -140 Grand -White Plns 10601 **Fx:**683-1897
(315) 379-2410 .. **Lumb,** Sharon M '77 %Family Ct -Cthse -Canton 13617 **Fx:**379-2386
(718) 522-1743 .. **Lumer,** Michl B '96 %Reibman & W -26 Court -Brklyn 11242 **Fx:**643-9297
(212) 435-3571 .. **Lum-Mazur,** Doris '84 %Port Auth of NY/NJ -225 Park Av S -NY 10003 **Fx:**435-3555
(718) 262-3420 .. **Luna,** Heidi '00 %Admin Children's Srvcs -92-31 Union Hall -Jamaica 11433
(716) 648-6666 .. **Luna,** Jason C '00 (J Luna,PLLC) -4535 Southwestern Blvd -Hambrg 14075 **Fx:**648-6665
(914) 997-0555 .. **Luna-Molé,** Rosa '01 %Quinn & M,LLP -399 Knollwood Rd -White Plns 10603
(212) 588-0800 .. **Lunasin,** Heidi '10 %Frommer L&H LLP -745 5th Av -NY 10151
(914) 422-4237 .. **Lund,** Andrew C W '04 Pace Law Schl -78 N Bway -White Plns 10603 **Fx:**422-4039
(631) 761-0800 .. **Lund,** Christopher J '08 %Lazer AR&Y,PC -225 Old Cntry Rd -Melvll 11747
(212) 259-8000 .. **Lund,** Steven P '76 (Dewey & L LLP) -1301 Av of Amer -NY 10019
(516) 545-4397 .. **Lundahl,** Walter J '84 %Natl Grid -175 E Old Cntry Rd -Hicksvll 11801 **Fx:**545-5029
(585) 263-1000 .. **Lundback,** B G Staffan '75 (Nixon P LLP) -1100 Clinton Sq -Rchstr 14604
(716) 664-2346 .. **Lundberg,** Dana Adam '01 (Lundberg & G,LLP) -202 W 4th -Jamestwn 14701
(716) 664-2346 .. **Lundberg & Gustafson, LLP** -202 W 4th -Jamestwn 14701 **Fx:**664-2439
(718) 802-2735 .. **Lundberg,** Molly S '07 ACS -330 Jay -Brklyn 11201
(631) 727-4100 .. **Lundberg,** Pierre G '50 (Smith FLI&Y) -456 Griffing Av Bx389 -Rvrhead 11901
(518) 392-4430 .. **Lunde,** Asbjorn R '49 (AR Lunde,PC) -135 La Brnche Rd -Hillsdale 12529 **Fx:**(718) 884-2919
(212) 746-1334 .. **Lunde,** Janice Kirsten '93 NY Presbyterian Hsptl -525 E 68th Bx88 -NY 10065 **Fx:**746-8603
(212) 735-8600 .. **Lundell,** Karin J '00 (Morrison C LLP) -909 3rd Av -NY 10022
(914) 789-5020 .. **Lundgren,** Kurt E '93 (Thwaites & L) -3 W Main -Elmsfrd 10523 **Fx:**789-5022
(631) 982-0130 .. **Lundgren,** Linda A '02 OfCnsl L Donato -180 E Main -Smithtwn 11787 **Fx:**982-0086
(212) 619-5000 .. **Lundgren,** Nicholas D '01 %EDC -110 William -NY 10038 **Fx:**312-3912
(212) 267-1900 .. **Lundi,** Katusia '09 %Wade CM -111 Bway -NY 10006
(212) 361-2980 .. **Lundin,** Ann '82 %Traffic Violations Bur -19 Rector -NY 10006
(914) 997-7980 .. **Lundin,** Diane M '93 SpclCnsl Hon J Lippman -140 Grand -White Plns 10601 **Fx:**997-7781
(212) 344-5400 .. **Lundin,** John M '98 (Schlam S&D LLP) -26 Bway -NY 10004
(718) 558-8246 .. **Lundin,** Priscilla '77 %LIRR -Jamaica Station -Jamaica 11435 **Fx:**558-8211
(212) 225-2330 .. **Lunding,** Christopher H '72 SrCnsl Cleary GS&H -1 Lbrty Plz -NY 10006
(212) 867-4100 .. **Lundman,** Jennie M '05 %Furman K&B LLP -61 Bway -NY 10006
(212) 538-7402 .. **Lundquist,** Tiffany C '05 Credit Suisse Securities LLC -11 Mad Av -NY 10010
(716) 439-7085 .. **Lundquist,** Timothy R '86 %DA -175 Hawley -Lockprt 14094 **Fx:**439-7102
(716) 856-4000 .. **Lundquist,** Wm A '81 (Hodgson R LLP) -140 Pearl -Buffalo 14202
(212) 230-5050 .. **Lundqvist,** Bertil '90 Cnsl CV Starr & Co,Inc -399 Park Av -NY 10022
(212) 536-3900 .. **Lundstrom,** Mandy '09 %K&L Gates LLP -599 Lex Av -NY 10022
(212) 691-0950 .. **Lundstrum,** Corinne E '03 Ctr for Family Representation,Inc -166 John -NY 10038 **Fx:**691-0951
(914) 824-5380 .. **Lundwall,** Colleen '84 Hon P Rosato -140 Grand -White Plns 10601 **Fx:**995-4396
(212) 686-3838 .. **Lundy,** Danl B '07 %Barst M&K LLP -2 Park Av -NY 10016
(845) 279-7051 .. **Lundy,** James P '57 -3951 Danbury Rd -Brewstr 10509 **Fx:**279-3518
(845) 279-7051 .. **Lundy,** James P II '95 -3951 Danbury Rd -Brewstr 10509 **Fx:**279-3518
(212) 478-3405 .. **Lundy,** James W Jr. '96 Syncora Guarantee Inc -825 8th Av -NY 10019
(212) 318-3000 .. **Lundy,** Kelli M '10 %Fulbright & J LLP -666 5th Av -NY 10103
(212) 218-2100 .. **Lundy,** Leisa Smith '94 (Fitzpatrick CH&S) -1290 Av of Amer -NY 10104
(516) 466-3100 .. **Lundy,** Mark H '88 %Gould Investors -60 Cuttermill Rd -Gt Neck 11021 **Fx:**466-3132
(845) 279-2986 .. **Lundy,** Marny E '92 %Hogan & R -1441 Route 22 -Brewstr 10509
(718) 999-2048 .. **Lundy,** Paulette A '97 %Fire Dept -9 Metrotech Ctr -Brklyn 11201 **Fx:**999-1290
(212) 320-3757 .. **Luneau,** John P '02 Palm Pictures, LLC -76 9th Av -NY 10011 **Fx:**(425) 955-4713
(212) 735-3000 .. **Luneau,** Peter D '04 %Skadden ASM&F LLP -4 Times Sq -NY 10036
(718) 459-5400 .. **Lunenfeld,** Richd C '94 %Farber R&K PC -97-77 Qns Blvd -Rego Pk 11374
(516) 627-5417 .. **Lunetta,** Andrew D '96 OfCnsl R Eredics -103 Plandome Rd -Manhsst 11030 **Fx:**627-5852
(718) 590-2000 .. **Lung,** Felicity '00 %DA -198 E 161st -Bronx 10451 **Fx:**590-6477
(516) 248-8253 .. **Lung,** Henry '00 -94 Willis Av -Mineola 11501 **Fx:**248-0136
(212) 852-7227 .. **Lung,** Michelle-Feng '01 News America Inc -1211 Av of Amer -NY 10036
(212) 506-1700 .. **Lungen,** Alan S '99 SpclCnsl Kasowitz BT&F LLP -1633 Bway -NY 10019
(718) 254-7000 .. **Lunger,** Richd T '94 %US Atty -271 Cadman Plz E -Brklyn 11201 **Fx:**254-6479
(212) 455-2000 .. **Lungstrum,** Justin M '01 (Simpson T&B LLP) -425 Lex Av -NY 10017
(212) 262-6699 .. **Lunin,** Scott B '75 (Tenzer & L LLP) -1775 Bway -NY 10019
(212) 450-4000 .. **Lunin,** Scott N '10 %Davis P&W LLP -450 Lex Av -NY 10017
(212) 859-8000 .. **Lunn,** Nicole M '10 %Fried FHS&J LLP -1 NY Plz -NY 10004
(212) 207-9009 .. **Lunn,** Renate J '04 %J Siegel -233 Bway -NY 10007
(585) 454-2181 .. **Lunn,** Robt J '75 (Trevett CS&A,PC) -2 State -Rchstr 14614
(914) 961-6202 .. **Lunney,** J Robt '55 -3 Locust Ln -Bronxvll 10708 **Fx:**961-6992
(212) 850-2988 .. **Luntz,** David S '94 %Intl Corp Consltnts -509 Mad Av -NY 10022 **Fx:**850-2987
(518) 436-0751 .. **Luntz,** David T '89 (Hinman S PC) -121 State -Albany 12207
(914) 833-1775 .. **Luntz Loebel,** Caryn S '93 -2005 Palmer Av -Larchmnt 10538
(212) 806-5400 .. **Luo,** Vivian '09 %Stroock &S&L LLP -180 Maiden Ln -NY 10038
(718) 518-1140 .. **Luongo,** Ann P '88 -2125 Wllmsbrdg Rd -Bronx 10461
(212) 319-6060 .. **Luongo,** Julia L '98 %Fairfield Greenwich Grp -919 3rd Av -NY 10022 **Fx:**319-0450
(212) 298-5058 .. **Luongo,** Justine M '03 Leg Aid -49 Thomas -NY 10013 **Fx:**298-5252
(914) 835-6122 .. **Luongo,** Nancy Anne '84 -350 Theo Fremd Av -Rye 10580
(516) 741-0700 .. **Luongo,** Philip J '86 -1325 Franklin Av -Gdn Cty 11530 **Fx:**742-9416
(631) 486-8508 .. **Luongo-DeVivo,** Maria R '90 M Luongo,PC -14 Meadow Rue Ln -E Northprt 11731 **Fx:**486-8508
(718) 590-8588 .. **Lupano,** Nancy L '99 ACS-DLS -900 Sheridan Av -Bronx 10451
(516) 942-4020 .. **Luparello,** Denise Winter '02 -76 N Bway -Hicksvll 11801
(914) 241-0017 .. **Lupatkin,** Andrew S '98 -15 Walden Hill -Chappaqua 10514 **Fx:**241-0017
(212) 586-2211 .. **Lupert,** Leslie A '71 (Orans EL&B LLP) -875 3rd Av -NY 10022
(212) 750-7800 .. **Lupesko-Persky,** Osnat '08 %Brafman & Assoc -767 3rd Av -NY 10017 **Fx:**750-3906
(516) 357-3700 .. **Lupetin,** Jocelyn E '09 %Cullen and D LLP -100 Q Roosevelt Blvd -Gdn Cty 11530
(212) 530-5000 .. **Lupfer,** Jennifer T '07 %Milbank TH&M LLP -1 Chase Manh Plz -NY 10005
(315) 798-5766 .. **Lupi,** Dawn A '87 %DA -800 Park Av -Utica 13501 **Fx:**798-5582
(315) 474-2829 .. **Lupia,** Chas E '92 -120 E Wshngtn -Syracuse 13202
(315) 656-9093 .. **Lupia,** Jos A Jr. '78 -108 Bxwood Ln -Minoa 13116 **Fx:**656-8811
(315) 735-7566 .. **Lupia,** Kathleen A '01 %Petrone & P,PC -1624 Genesee -Utica 13502
(315) 793-7000 .. **Lupia,** Paul J '79 %Leg Aid -255 Genesee -Utica 13501 **Fx:**732-3202
(716) 854-0700 .. **Lupiani,** Amy L '05 %J Feroleto -438 Main -Buffalo 14202 **Fx:**854-0265
(716) 783-9217 .. **Lupiani,** Scott M '05 -40 La Riviere Dr -Buffalo 14202
(631) 853-4161 .. **Lupinacci,** Brooke Ann '05 DA -N Cnty Cmplx Bldg 77 -Hauppauge 11788 **Fx:**853-4192
(212) 819-8200 .. **Lupinacci,** Francis E '08 %White & C LLP -1155 Av of Amer -NY 10036
(845) 294-1677 .. **Lupinetti,** Bernadette '80 -305 Main -Goshen 10924 **Fx:**294-3075
(212) 969-3000 .. **Lupion,** Adam M '02 %Proskauer R LLP -1585 Bway -NY 10036
(212) 735-8600 .. **Lupion,** Evan '07 %Morrison C LLP -909 3rd Av -NY 10022
(212) 506-5000 .. **Lupion,** Lisa B '07 %Orrick H&S LLP -51 W 52nd -NY 10019
(516) 829-0363 .. **Lupis,** Josephine M '01 %Israel I&P,LLP -11 Grace Av -Gt Neck 11021 **Fx:**829-0366
(212) 412-9500 .. **Lupkin,** Jonathan D '93 (Flemming ZWZ LLP) -1 Lbrty Plz -NY 10006
(212) 841-1000 .. **Lupkin,** Lorie E '07 %Covington & B LLP -620 8th Av -NY 10018
(516) 482-1223 .. **Lupkin,** Stanley N '66 -98 Cutter Mill Rd -Gt Neck 11021 **Fx:**466-2799
(646) 435-7815 .. **Lupo,** Jennifer '96 J Lupo PLLC -77 Bleecker -NY 10012
(718) 590-2000 .. **Lupo,** Jessica-Deanna '03 %DA -198 E 161st -Bronx 10451 **Fx:**590-6477
(212) 776-5000 .. **Lupo,** Josephine A '88 %NYC Housing Auth -250 Bway -NY 10007 **Fx:**776-5039
(718) 539-0622 .. **Lupoli,** Matthew M '74 -167-16 Nrthrn Blvd Bx580283 -Flushng 11358
(646) 610-5400 .. **Lupoli,** Tara M '06 NYPD -1 Police Plz -NY 10038
(631) 385-9354 .. **Lupoli,** Virginia E M '75 -Bx237 -Cold Spg Hbr 11724 **Fx:**385-4477
(212) 258-4000 .. **Lupone,** E Robt '85 %Siemens Corp -153 E 53rd -NY 10022 **Fx:**767-0580

(212) 309-1000 .. **Luppen,** Luppe B '09 %Hunton & W -200 Park Av -NY 10166
(516) 784-6101 .. **Lupu,** Andrew H '85 Axiom Legal -75 Spring -NY 10012 **Fx:**(212) 343-7446
(914) 476-0600 .. **Lupu,** Emanuela '00 %Smith B&J,LLP -733 Ynkrs Av -Ynkrs 10704
(631) 780-7057 .. **Luqman,** Elisa V '96 I Gambit Inc -1600 Calebs Path Ext -Hauppauge 11788
(914) 441-1856 .. **Luria,** Ann '85 -42 Rockldg Dr -Brewstr 10509 **Fx:**(845) 278-0625
(212) 468-4800 .. **Luria,** Mary M '68 (Davis & G LLP) -1740 Bway -NY 10019
(212) 739-1014 .. **Luria,** Roy S '01 %Comverse Tech -810 7th Av -NY 10019
(914) 834-6725 .. **Lurie,** Alvin D '44 (A Lurie,PC) -13 Cntry Clb Dr -Larchmnt 10538
(347) 404-9476 .. **Lurie,** Amy E '05 %Criminal Ct -120 Schermerhorn -Brklyn 11201 **Fx:**(718) 643-3538
(914) 468-8009 .. **Lurie,** Danl S '01 Endurance Srvcs Ltd -333 Wstchstr Av -White Plns 10604
(212) 687-1600 .. **Lurie & Flatow PC** -420 Lex Av -NY 10170 **Fx:**687-8710
(212) 867-5800 .. **Lurie,** James M '78 (Osler H&H LLP) -620 8th Av -NY 10018
(212) 310-8000 .. **Lurie,** Jamie '08 %Weil G&M LLP -767 5th Av -NY 10153
(212) 449-6364 .. **Lurie,** Keith E '96 %Merrill Lynch -220 Bway -NY 10038
(914) 834-2936 .. **Lurie,** Michl '72 -5 Leafy Ln Bx1045 -Larchmnt 10538 **Fx:**833-3506
(212) 902-4929 .. **Lurie,** R Thornton '77 Goldman Sachs & Co -85 Broad -NY 10004
(212) 685-7411 .. **Lurie,** Saml J '56 (Lurie IM&R,LLP) -475 Park Av S -NY 10016 **Fx:**685-9827
(212) 317-5469 .. **Lurie,** Todd F '94 Swiss Re -55 E 52nd -NY 10055
(212) 808-2103 .. **Lurie,** Wendy A '88 %ING Asset Mngt -230 Park Av -NY 10169
(212) 808-7800 .. **Lury,** Richd R '74 (Kelley D&W LLP) -101 Park Av -NY 10178
(845) 225-8404 .. **Lusardi,** Robt C '79 (Daniels & P,LLP) -102 Gleneida Av -Carmel 10512
(212) 943-9080 .. **Lusher,** LaDonna M '05 %Virginia & A -111 Bway -NY 10006
(212) 790-0268 .. **Lushing,** Peter '65 %Benj N Cardozo Schl of Law -55 5th Av -NY 10003 **Fx:**790-0345
(212) 222-6355 .. **Lushing,** Susan C '68 -740 West End Av -NY 10025 **Fx:**865-0006
(718) 238-6500 .. **Lushpenko,** Yelizaveta '10 Connors & S,PC -7408 5th Av -Brklyn 11209
(212) 664-4966 .. **Lusins,** Gillian M '91 %NBC -30 Rckfllr Plz -NY 10112
(914) 422-1241 .. **Lusita-Rich,** Doreen '01 %Law Dept -255 Main -White Plns 10601 **Fx:**422-1231
(585) 263-1000 .. **Lusk,** Jared C '99 %Nixon P LLP -1100 Clinton Sq -Rchstr 14604
(516) 829-6900 .. **Luskin,** Andrew J '86 (Ackerman LCB&L,LLP) -1010 Nrthrn Blvd -Gt Neck 11021
(212) 885-5000 .. **Luskin,** Martin '81 (Blank R LLP) -405 Lex Av -NY 10174
(212) 837-6110 .. **Luskin,** Michl '78 (Hughes H&R LLP) -1 Bttry Pk Plz -NY 10004 **Fx:**299-6110
(516) 832-3200 .. **Luskoff,** Allison L '02 %1st Amer Title -333 Earle Ovngton Blvd -Uniondale 11553 **Fx:**832-3299
(845) 638-5846 .. **Lussen,** Edw T '93 %Cnty Atty -Cnty Ofc Bldg -New Cty 10956 **Fx:**638-5676
(518) 523-2556 .. **Lussi,** Arthur S '89 %Crowne Plz Resort & Golf Club -101 Olympic Dr -Lk Placid 12946 **Fx:**523-9410
(518) 640-5000 .. **Lussier,** Brian D '98 AYCO -25 British Amer Blvd -Latham 12110
(212) 244-2999 .. **Lust,** Marc J '77 (Kopff N&D LLP) -440 9th Av -NY 10001
(212) 686-7700 .. **Lustbader,** Brian G '79 OfCnsl Mazur CR&S PC -1250 Bway -NY 10001
(212) 683-2210 .. **Lustbader,** Ira P '93 %Childrens Rts Inc -330 7th Av -NY 10001 **Fx:**683-4015
(973) 596-4731 .. **Lustberg,** Lawr S '84 (Gibbons PC) -1 Penn Plz -NY 10119 **Fx:**639-6285
(518) 792-4828 .. **Lustberg,** Robt M '78 (Lustberg & F) -5 Garrison Rd -Queensbury 12804 **Fx:**792-4896
(718) 854-1082 .. **Lustgarten,** Chester P '77 -81 Chester Av -Brklyn 11218
(212) 391-9500 .. **Lusthaus,** Julianne Cowan '96 (Einbinder & D,PC) -104 W 40th -NY 10018
(718) 488-7900 .. **Lusthaus,** Meredith A '97 (Coffinas & L,PC) -186 Joralemon -Brklyn 11201
(516) 937-1366 .. **Lusthaus,** Robt S '66 -497 S Oyster Bay Rd -Plainvw 11803 **Fx:**938-2915
(212) 268-6100 .. **Lusthaus,** Russell B '96 (Lusthaus & L,PLLC) -330 7th Av -NY 10001 **Fx:**268-6106
(212) 268-6100 .. **Lusthaus,** Stephen J '67 (Lusthaus & L,PLLC) -330 7th Av -NY 10001 **Fx:**268-0106
(518) 431-4761 .. **Lustick,** Marc W '71 %IRS -1 Clinton Av -Albany 12207
(212) 732-4992 .. **Lustig,** D Carl III '79 (Arye L&S,PC) -20 Vesey -NY 10007
(585) 232-3730 .. **Lustig,** Douglas J '75 (Chamberlain D LLP) -1600 Crssrds Bldg -Rchstr 14614
(212) 682-2800 .. **Lustig,** Gerald I '52 OfCnsl Silverman & W -50 E 42nd -NY 10017
(718) 858-4250 .. **Lustig,** Harvey '75 (Goldberg & L) -188 Montague -Brklyn 11201 **Fx:**522-2645
(631) 582-4000 .. **Lustig,** Leonard '63 (Tsunis G&L,LLP) -2929 Express Dr N -Islandia 11749
(631) 390-0010 .. **Lustig,** Mitchell S '82 %Bruno G&S,LLP -445 Broad Hollow Rd -Melvll 11747
(917) 587-5189 .. **Lustig,** Raymond J '82 -4519 243rd -Douglastn 11362 **Fx:**(718) 423-2093
(212) 683-9180 .. **Lustigman,** Andrew B '96 (Lustigman Firm,PC) -149 Mad Av -NY 10016 **Fx:**683-9181
(212) 683-9180 .. **Lustigman,** Sheldon S '65 (Lustigman Firm,PC) -149 Mad Av -NY 10016 **Fx:**683-9181
(212) 991-9590 .. **Lustrin,** Alan J '86 (Lustrin T,LLP) -28 W 44th -NY 10036 **Fx:**991-9595
(212) 510-0500 .. **Lustrin,** Pamela J '89 %US Trustees Ofc -33 Whitehall -NY 10004 **Fx:**668-2255
(212) 574-1200 .. **Lustrin,** Robt E '89 (Seward & K LLP) -1 Bttry Pk Plz -NY 10004
(516) 542-8800 .. **Lutfy,** Frances T '89 (Lutfy & L,PC) -595 Stewart Av -Gdn Cty 11530 **Fx:**542-0472
(718) 442-2272 .. **Lutfy,** James L '81 (Lutfy & S) -1405 Clove Rd -Staten Isl 10301
(516) 542-8800 .. **Lutfy,** John C '90 (Lutfy & L,PC) -595 Stewart Av -Gdn Cty 11530 **Fx:**542-0472
(718) 442-2272 .. **Lutfy & Santora** -1405 Clove Rd -Staten Isl 10301 **Fx:**442-1939
(212) 715-9100 .. **Lutgens,** Christine P '00 (Kramer LN&F,LLP) -1177 Av of Amer -NY 10036
(607) 565-2874 .. **Luther,** Fredk C '84 -441 Broad Bx31 -Waverly 14892 **Fx:**565-7919
(585) 272-7100 .. **Luther,** John G '95 %Nationwide Precision -200 Tech Park Dr -Rchstr 14623
(518) 402-6757 .. **Luther,** Lance S '98 %Workers Comp Bd -20 Park -Albany 12207
(212) 549-2500 .. **Luthra,** Namita '98 %ACLU -125 Broad -NY 10004 **Fx:**549-2652
(347) 592-2200 .. **Luthra,** Rashmi '01 Leg Srvcs -89-00 Sutphin Blvd -Jamaica 11435 **Fx:**(718) 937-5350
(516) 572-2000 .. **Lutinger,** Susan '09 %DA -99 Main -Hempstd 11550 **Fx:**572-2606
(212) 829-4770 .. **Lutnick,** Edith '83 Cantor Fitzgerald Relief Fund -199 Water -NY 10038 **Fx:**829-4895
(212) 450-4000 .. **Lutrin,** Jessica '10 %Davis P&W LLP -450 Lex Av -NY 10017
(212) 819-8200 .. **Lutt,** Steven M '92 Cnsl White & C LLP -1155 Av of Amer -NY 10036
(212) 829-0011 .. **Luttati,** Carol M '86 -150 E 58th -NY 10155 **Fx:**829-0055
(212) 957-1940 .. **Lutteral,** Margarita N '73 -301 W 45th -NY 10036
(516) 365-3218 .. **Luttinger,** David A '63 -100 Manhsst Woods Rd -Manhsst 11030 **Fx:**365-3218
(212) 309-6000 .. **Luttinger,** David A Jr. '92 (Morgan L&B LLP) -101 Park Av -NY 10178
(718) 645-3111 .. **Lutwak,** Diane E '87 %Leg Aid Society Ofc for the Aging -111 Lvngstn -Brklyn 11201 **Fx:**260-4722
(212) 964-6611 .. **Lutwin,** Erik B '00 %Lester SK&D -120 Bway -NY 10271
(212) 431-5757 .. **Lutwin,** Joel M '66 (Lutwin & J) -401 Bway -NY 10013 **Fx:**431-5759
(415) 393-8211 .. **Lutz,** Brian M '03 %Gibson D&C LLP -200 Park Av -NY 10166 **Fx:**374-8406
(212) 581-3320 .. **Lutz,** Douglas J '91 %Wasserman G&R,LLP -1700 Bway -NY 10019
(518) 474-7469 .. **Lutz,** Holly Nelson '87 %OCA -Agncy Bldg 4 ESP -Albany 12223 **Fx:**473-5514
(315) 637-2578 .. **Lutz,** James N '61 -60 Midlake Cir -E Syracuse 13057 **Fx:**637-2578
(212) 547-5400 .. **Lutz,** John T '91 (McDermott W&E LLP) -340 Mad Av -NY 10173
(914) 347-1200 .. **Lutz,** Kerry H '85 %Lutz Applt Srvcs -108 Corp Park Dr -White Plns 10604 **Fx:**347-1204
(585) 362-4700 .. **Lutz,** Peter C '91 (Bond S&K,PLLC) -350 Linden Oaks -Rchstr 14625
(212) 504-6000 .. **Lutz,** Regina M '02 %Cadwalader W&T LLP -1 World Fncl Ctr -NY 10281
(631) 617-5179 .. **Lutzen,** Fred '04 -110 Marcus Blvd -Hauppauge 11788 **Fx:**(866) 634-7632
(631) 234-2222 .. **Lutzer,** A Scott '74 Cnsl Siben & F -1455 Vets Mem'l Hwy -Hauppauge 11749
(631) 451-6500 .. **Lutzer,** Jennifer J '04 %Brookhaven Law Dept -1 Indpndnc Hill -Farmngvll 11738 **Fx:**698-4489
(212) 977-9700 .. **Lutzker,** Elliot H '79 (Phillips N LLP) -666 5th Av -NY 10103
(212) 310-8000 .. **Lutzker,** Stacey M '09 %Weil G&M LLP -767 5th Av -NY 10153
(212) 686-7700 .. **Lutzky,** Barry I '83 OfCnsl Mazur CR&S PC -1250 Bway -NY 10001
(718) 329-9500 .. **Lutzky,** Jayson '83 (J Lutzky,PC) -26 W 183rd -Bronx 10453 **Fx:**329-8760
(212) 838-1177 .. **Luu,** Quyen Vu Ha '07 Morse ZR&L LLP -405 Park Av -NY 10022
(212) 981-4500 .. **Lux,** Danl S '87 PeterSan Grp -1450 Bway -NY 10018 **Fx:**981-4560
(212) 687-3860 .. **Luxemburg,** Marc J '63 (Snow BK,PC) -605 3rd Av -NY 10158
(212) 558-5500 .. **Luxenberg,** Arthur M '85 (Weitz & L,PC) -700 Bway -NY 10003
(212) 681-8313 .. **Luz,** Thos J '86 (Karaahmet L&G LLP) -370 Lex Av -NY 10017 **Fx:**208-2917
(212) 903-9000 .. **Luzárraga,** Alberto '89 (Linklaters) -1345 Av of Amer -NY 10105
(212) 940-8800 .. **Luzarraga,** Jose I '98 SpclCnsl Katten MR LLP -575 Mad Av -NY 10022
(718) 749-4466 .. **Luzhansky,** Evelina '01 -8135 166th -Jamaica 11432
(315) 655-8325 .. **Luzinski,** Lauren M '08 %H Lindenfeld,PC -11 Lincklaen Bx465 -Cazenovia 13035 **Fx:**655-3303
(914) 698-4600 .. **Luzio,** Michele A '88 -875 Mamaroneck Av -Mamaroneck 10543 **Fx:**698-4646
(914) 995-3419 .. **Luzio,** Thos G '89 %DA -111 Martin Luther King Blvd -White Plns 10601 **Fx:**995-3363
(212) 496-6606 .. **Luzmore,** Loren Krause '84 -15 W 72nd -NY 10023 **Fx:**496-6606
(716) 847-8400 .. **Luzon,** David J '98 %Phillips L LLP -3400 HSBC Ctr -Buffalo 14203
(212) 669-0600 .. **Luzzatto,** Ernesto V '64 %Hill R LLP -45 Bway -NY 10006
(212) 788-0603 .. **Luzzi,** Saadia C '89 %Law Dept -100 Church -NY 10007 **Fx:**788-0367
(212) 274-8001 .. **Ly,** Susan '03 %C Chong PLLC 80 Bowery -NY 10013 **Fx:**274-8196
(212) 335-4500 .. **Lyakhovetskaya,** Yulia '10 %DLA Piper LLP -1251 Av of Amer -NY 10020
(212) 867-6000 .. **Lycoyannis,** Alexander '02 %Rosenberg & E,PC -733 3rd Av -NY 10017
(518) 755-6342 .. **Lyda,** Brian S '01 Lyda Law Firm,PLLC -97 Vly Rd -Albany 12205
(212) 697-3122 .. **Lyddane,** John L A '73 (Martin C&B LLP) -220 E 42nd -NY 10017
(212) 593-3000 .. **Lydell,** Sherri D '89 (Platzer SKLG&J,LLP) -1065 Av of Amer -NY 10018
(914) 722-4100 .. **Lyder,** James K '96 (Lyder & S LLP) -670 Wht Plns Rd -Scarsdale 10583 **Fx:**722-6586
(315) 425-2700 .. **Lydford,** Robt J '10 %Hiscock & B,LLP -One Park Pl -Syracuse 13202
(585) 265-3990 .. **Lydon,** Patrick D '74 Sutter S&L PC -20 W Main -Webster 14580
(631) 582-5100 .. **Lyell,** Geraldine '91 -1324 Motor Pkwy -Hauppauge 11749 **Fx:**582-6803
(212) 225-2000 .. **Lyerly,** S Brynn '10 %Cleary GS&H -1 Lbrty Plz -NY 10006
(212) 756-2000 .. **Lyerly,** Stephanie K '09 %Schulte R&Z LLP -919 3rd Av -NY 10022
(212) 435-3571 .. **Lyken-Fields,** Leslie '78 %Port Auth of NY/NJ -225 Park Av S -NY 10003 **Fx:**435-3555
(716) 373-1920 .. **Lyle,** Ethan M '00 (Dwyer B&L,LLP) -1616 W State Bx648 -Olean 14760
(212) 209-3080 .. **Lyman,** Gary M '77 (Reitler K&R LLC) -885 3rd Av -NY 10022
(585) 589-5623 .. **Lyman,** Nathan M '81 Lyman & L LLC -51 N Main -Albion 14411 **Fx:**589-5623
(212) 878-6641 .. **Lyman,** Robt G '69 -275 Mad Av -NY 10016 **Fx:**878-6642
(315) 422-7111 .. **Lyman,** Seamus P '03 (HDL Prprty Grp LLC) -7085 Manlius Ctr Rd -E Syracuse 13057 **Fx:**671-1501
(212) 808-7800 .. **Lynagh,** John J '72 (Kelley D&W LLP) -101 Park Av -NY 10178
(516) 496-0202 .. **Lynam,** Janine T '06 %Joseph & T,LLP -2 Roosevelt Av -Syosset 11791 **Fx:**921-7785
(212) 474-1000 .. **Lynaugh,** Margaret E '09 %Cravath S&M LLP -825 8th Av -NY 10019
(516) 541-1060 .. **Lynch,** Adrienne C '80 -1060 Park Blvd -Massapequa Pk 11762 **Fx:**541-1375
(212) 310-8000 .. **Lynch,** Alexander D '88 (Weil G&M LLP) -767 5th Av -NY 10153

(315) 793-2184 .. **Lynch,** Andrea '78 %Ct of Claims -207 E Genesee -Utica 13501 **Fx:**793-2217
(877) 222-1814 .. **Lynch,** Angel '92 %B Rothenberg -100 Duffy Av -Hicksvll 11801 **Fx:**(866) 894-2182
(585) 258-2800 .. **Lynch,** Anna E '87 (Underberg & K LLP) -300 Bausch & Lomb Pl -Rchstr 14604
(212) 259-8000 .. **Lynch,** Arthur J '88 (Dewey & L LLP) -1301 Av of Amer -NY 10019
(800) 656-9529 .. **Lynch,** Arthur V '88 (Lynch Law Firm,PC) -222 Route 59 -Suffern 10901 **Fx:**(888) 271-9726
(212) 227-4762 .. **Lynch,** B Alicia '96 (Giblin & L) -225 Bway -NY 10007 **Fx:**732-6703
(516) 683-1717 .. **Lynch,** Brenda M '98 (V Russo & Assoc,PC) -1600 Stewart Av -Westbury 11590 **Fx:**683-9393
(914) 366-7200 .. **Lynch,** Brian '79 %Stinnes Corp -120 Wht Plns Rd -Tarrytwn 10591 **Fx:**366-8226
(914) 921-3511 .. **Lynch,** Carol M '83 -10 Robert Crisfld Pl -Rye 10580
(315) 253-0326 .. **Lynch,** Chas H Jr. '74 (Boyle & A,PC) -110 Genesee -Auburn 13021
(631) 755-5175 .. **Lynch,** Christopher '96 JP Morgan Chase & Co -395 N Srvc Rd -Melvll 11747
(212) 521-5400 .. **Lynch,** Christopher A '04 %Reed S LLP -599 Lex Av -NY 10022
(212) 450-4000 .. **Lynch,** Christopher P '08 %Davis P&W LLP -450 Lex Av -NY 10017
(718) 250-2000 .. **Lynch,** Cynthia Ann '90 %DA -350 Jay -Brklyn 11201 **Fx:**250-2314
(518) 487-5460 .. **Lynch,** Danl C '04 %DA -6 Lodge -Albany 12207 **Fx:**487-5093
(212) 571-4888 .. **Lynch,** Danl F '89 -20 Vesey -NY 10007
(845) 353-2000 .. **Lynch,** Dennis E A '79 (Feerick LM PLLC) -96 S Bway -Nyack 10960
(212) 998-6696 .. **Lynch,** Elizabeth M '04 NYU Law Schl -110 W 3rd -NY 10012
(585) 232-6500 .. **Lynch,** Ellen P '01 (Harter S&E LLP) -1600 Bausch & Lomb Pl -Rchstr 14604
(212) 761-4000 .. **Lynch,** Gary G '90 Morgan Stanley -1585 Bway -NY 10036
(212) 683-4141 .. **Lynch,** H Michl '88 (Lynch & Assoc) -462 7th Av -NY 10018 **Fx:**208-0948
(347) 401-9945 .. **Lynch,** Harold J '66 Family Ct -330 Jay -Brklyn 11201
(212) 819-8200 .. **Lynch,** Helena A '06 %White & C LLP -1155 Av of Amer -NY 10036
(315) 685-3416 .. **Lynch,** J Richd '63 (Milford L&S) -2-4 Fennell Bx47 -Skaneateles 13152
(718) 469-8555 .. **Lynch,** James A Jr. '95 -1988 Bedford Av -Brklyn 11225
(516) 873-0100 .. **Lynch,** James D '79 (Lynch & L) -250 Old Cntry Rd -Mineola 11501 **Fx:**873-0108
(845) 878-4200 .. **Lynch,** James F '85 Natl Fire Sprinkler Assn -40 Jon Barrett Rd -Patterson 12563 **Fx:**878-4215
(516) 746-2072 .. **Lynch,** James J '69 (Lynch Legal Assoc,LLP) -26 Grove Bx598 -Glenwd Landing 11547 **Fx:**248-2972
(845) 876-4688 .. **Lynch,** James J '02 -6140 Route 9 -Rhinebeck 12572
(212) 302-2400 .. **Lynch,** James R '84 (Lynch DE LLP) -264 W 40th -NY 10018
(800) 656-9529 .. **Lynch,** James S '93 (Lynch Law Firm,PC) -222 Route 59 -Suffern 10901 **Fx:**(888) 271-9726
(516) 873-0100 .. **Lynch,** James W '50 (Lynch & L) -250 Old Cntry Rd -Mineola 11501 **Fx:**873-0108
(212) 848-4000 .. **Lynch,** Joanne L '08 %Shearman & S LLP -599 Lex Av -NY 10022
(212) 436-5926 .. **Lynch,** John A '00 Deloitte & Touche LLP -2 World Fncl Ctr -NY 10281
(212) 909-6000 .. **Lynch,** John C '04 %Debevoise & P LLP -919 3rd Av -NY 10022
(212) 403-1000 .. **Lynch,** John F '98 (Wachtell LR&K) -51 W 52nd -NY 10019
(631) 467-3233 .. **Lynch,** John H '84 -4250 Vets Mem'l Hwy -Holbrook 11741 **Fx:**467-4605
(212) 980-4919 .. **Lynch,** John J '51 -333 E 53rd -NY 10022
(212) 421-4100 .. **Lynch,** John J '84 (Pryor C LLP) -7 Times Sq -NY 10036
(607) 797-4839 .. **Lynch,** John P '90 (Hogan SLS&D,LLP) -Bx660 -Bnghmtn 13902
(631) 858-5800 .. **Lynch,** John R '64 -201 Moreland Rd -Hauppauge 11788
(212) 819-8200 .. **Lynch,** John T '09 %White & C LLP -1155 Av of Amer -NY 10036
(212) 940-3717 .. **Lynch,** Jos J '03 (Nixon P LLP) -437 Mad Av -NY 10022
(914) 948-4500 .. **Lynch,** Katherine A '00 %O'Connor MCD&O -1 Barker Av -White Plns 10601
(516) 949-4217 .. **Lynch,** Kathleen '91 FINRA -2 Jericho Plz -Jericho 11753
(716) 843-5700 .. **Lynch,** Kathleen Ann '87 %US Atty -138 Delaware Av -Buffalo 14202 **Fx:**551-3052
(212) 982-9800 .. **Lynch,** Kathleen M '97 -568 Bway -NY 10012 **Fx:**982-5499
(212) 509-2805 .. **Lynch,** Kathy M '93 (KM Lynch & Assoc,PLLC) -160 Bway -NY 10038 **Fx:**509-2808
(212) 789-2000 .. **Lynch,** Kelley A '10 %NHL Enterprises,LP -1185 Av of Amer -NY 10036 **Fx:**789-2020
(212) 400-6330 .. **Lynch,** Kenneth B '84 (Lynch & Co,PC) -420 Lex Av -NY 10170 **Fx:**400-6331
(315) 426-7403 .. **Lynch,** Kenneth P '89 %DEC -615 Erie Blvd W -Syracuse 13204 **Fx:**426-7408
(212) 593-2155 .. **Lynch,** Kevin B '82 OfCnsl Scaffidi & Assoc -747 3rd Av -NY 10017 **Fx:**593-2257
(516) 746-2072 .. **Lynch,** Kyle T '04 -26 Grove Bx598 -Glenwd Landing 11547 **Fx:**248-2972
(631) 325-1024 .. **Lynch,** Leslie Ann Evans '91 -Bx2018 -Remsenbrg 11960 **Fx:**325-8189
(718) 254-7000 .. **Lynch,** Loretta E '85 (US Atty) -271 Cadman Plz E -Brklyn 11201 **Fx:**254-6479
(212) 269-0927 .. **Lynch,** Luke D Jr. '70 (D'Amato & L,LLP) -2 World Fncl Ctr -NY 10281
(518) 433-8800 .. **Lynch,** Margaret Comard '83 Lemery G LLC -50 Beaver -Albany 12207
(518) 445-2311 .. **Lynch,** Mary '86 %Law Clinic & Justice Ctr -80 New Scotland Av -Albany 12208
(212) 770-1018 .. **Lynch,** Mary Ellen '96 AIG -80 Pine -NY 10005
(212) 277-0768 .. **Lynch,** Maureen E '02 Hartford Ins Co -2 Park Av -NY 10016
(585) 232-6500 .. **Lynch,** Meghan M '06 %Harter S&E LLP -1600 Bausch & Lomb Pl -Rchstr 14604
(518) 827-6619 .. **Lynch,** Michl '69 -Bx41 -Fultonham 12071
(212) 808-7800 .. **Lynch,** Michl C Jr. '98 (Kelley D&W LLP) -101 Park Av -NY 10178
(212) 697-3122 .. **Lynch,** Michl F '90 (Martin C&B LLP) -220 E 42nd -NY 10017
(212) 804-4200 .. **Lynch,** Michl T '04 %Mound CW&G -One Bttry Pk Plz -NY 10004
(516) 424-5407 .. **Lynch,** Michelle K '06 -Bx038388 -Elmont 11003
(212) 310-8000 .. **Lynch,** Nancy E '99 Cnsl Weil G&M LLP -767 5th Av -NY 10153
(516) 922-8030 .. **Lynch,** Paul W '61 (Murphy & L,PC) -1045 Oyster Bay Rd -E Norwich 11732
(518) 463-1252 .. **Lynch,** Peter A '80 (Lynch & H,PLLC) -111 State -Albany 12207 **Fx:**463-1255
(718) 420-3779 .. **Lynch,** R Johnston J II '71 -9 Purroy Pl -Staten Isl 10304
(212) 648-0584 .. **Lynch,** Robt B '74 JP Morgan Chase -245 Park Av -NY 10167
(516) 739-1212 .. **Lynch,** Robt P '81 -245 Hillside Av -Williston Pk 11596 **Fx:**294-1416
(212) 682-4001 .. **Lynch Rowin LLP** -630 3rd Av -NY 10017 **Fx:**682-4003
(516) 571-3020 .. **Lynch,** Sighle M '87 Cnty Atty -1 West -Mineola 11501 **Fx:**571-6604
(212) 382-2044 .. **Lynch,** Stacy R '05 Marshall Firm -271 Mad Av -NY 10016 **Fx:**382-3610
(631) 852-3166 .. **Lynch,** Stephen J '79 Hon W Rebolini -1 Court -Rvrhead 11901 **Fx:**852-3188
(718) 243-6209 .. **Lynch,** Steven E '07 Leg Aid -199 Water -NY 10038
(212) 326-3939 .. **Lynch,** Thos E '99 (Jones D) -222 E 41st -NY 10017
(315) 471-1318 .. **Lynch,** Thos J '73 -2700 Bellevue Av -Syracuse 13219 **Fx:**471-1409
(718) 590-6356 .. **Lynch,** Thos J '82 Supreme Ct -851 Grnd Cncrs -Bronx 10451
(212) 682-4001 .. **Lynch,** Thos P '73 (Lynch R LLP) -630 3rd Av -NY 10017
(716) 843-5700 .. **Lynch,** Timothy C '99 %US Atty -138 Delaware Av -Buffalo 14202 **Fx:**551-3052
(585) 724-4438 .. **Lynch,** Timothy M '88 Eastman Kodak Co -343 State -Rchstr 14650 **Fx:**724-9448
(718) 590-2000 .. **Lynch,** Timothy W '06 DA -198 E 161st -Bronx 10451 **Fx:**590-6477
(718) 491-9181 .. **Lynch,** Vincent J '74 -9011 5th Av -Brklyn 11209
(518) 402-0748 .. **Lynch,** Wm J '87 %Dept of Health -433 River -Troy 12180 **Fx:**402-0751
(585) 586-7110 .. **Lynd,** Deborah T '88 -91 Woodside Dr -Penfld 14526
(585) 262-6250 .. **Lynd,** Edw J III '91 -25 E Main -Rchstr 14614
(718) 990-6011 .. **Lyndon,** Mary L '76 %St John's Law Schl -8000 Utopia Pkwy -Jamaica 11439 **Fx:**591-1855
(212) 326-3939 .. **Lyne,** Scott D '01 %Jones D -222 E 41st -NY 10017
(914) 328-0404 .. **Lynett,** Jos J '96 %Jackson L LLP -1 N Bway -White Plns 10601
(212) 949-9022 .. **Lynfield,** Peter J '77 (Abelman F&S) -666 3rd Av -NY 10017
(212) 303-4814 .. **Lyng,** Catherine '79 Fortis Fincl Srvcs -520 Mad Av -NY 10022
(212) 512-1000 .. **Lyngklip,** Ole W III '93 %HBO -1100 Av of Amer -NY 10036 **Fx:**512-1986
(212) 465-6000 .. **Lynn,** Andrew S '83 %Madison Sq Grdn,LP -2 Penn Plz -NY 10121 **Fx:**465-6011
(212) 719-4400 .. **Lynn,** James P Jr. '88 (Lynn & C,LLP) -58 W 40th -NY 10018 **Fx:**719-4440
(212) 408-2500 .. **Lynn,** Jamie R '07 %Baker B,LLP -30 Rckfllr Plz -NY 10112
(212) 752-5255 .. **Lynn,** Jennifer B '97 %P Cannell & Co -645 Mad Av -NY 10022
(212) 702-4331 .. **Lynn,** Jesse A '97 Icahn Enterprises LP -767 5th Av -NY 10153 **Fx:**688-1158
(212) 335-9000 .. **Lynn,** Jessica R '98 %DA -1 Hogan Pl -NY 10013
(212) 670-0215 .. **Lynn,** Karim G '88 %Merrill Lynch -222 Bway -NY 10038
(315) 329-0349 .. **Lynn,** M Kathleen '86 -117 Highbrdg Bx544 -Fayettevll 13066 **Fx:**329-0369
(631) 853-4049 .. **Lynn,** Marcia J '79 %Cnty Atty -Dennison Bldg Bx6100 -Hauppauge 11788 **Fx:**853-5169
(315) 442-0100 .. **Lynn,** Martin A '05 %Gilberti SH&S,PC -555 E Genesee -Syracuse 13202
(212) 836-8000 .. **Lynn,** Michl A '84 Cnsl Kaye S LLP -425 Park Av -NY 10022
(212) 664-5165 .. **Lynn,** Richd W '79 %NBC Universal -30 Rckfllr Plz -NY 10112
(516) 742-6200 .. **Lynn,** Robt P Jr. '69 (Lynn G&D,LLP) -330 Old Cntry Rd -Mineola 11501 **Fx:**742-5294
(212) 538-4500 .. **Lynn,** Robt P '95 Credit Suisse -11 Mad Av -NY 10010
(212) 547-5400 .. **Lynn,** Robt W '02 (McDermott W&E LLP) -340 Mad Av -NY 10173
(212) 532-3200 .. **Lynn,** Suzanne M '72 %Manpower Demo Research -16 E 34th -NY 10016 **Fx:**684-0832
(315) 422-1391 .. **Lynn,** Timothy M '97 (Green & S,PLLC) -One Lincoln Ctr #900 -Syracuse 13202
(914) 241-4500 .. **Lynn,** Wendy R '86 -Bx512 -Bedfrd Hlls 10507
(315) 474-1267 .. **Lynn,** Wm F '60 (Lynn Law Firm,LLP) -101 S Salina -Syracuse 13202 **Fx:**474-4514
(315) 474-1267 .. **Lynn-Ford,** Patricia A '86 (Lynn Law Firm,LLP) -101 S Salina -Syracuse 13202 **Fx:**474-4514
(718) 590-2000 .. **Lynton,** Derek R '99 %DA -198 E 161st -Bronx 10451 **Fx:**590-6477
(212) 506-5000 .. **Lyon,** Carl F Jr. '69 (Orrick H&S LLP) -51 W 52nd -NY 10019
(212) 424-7000 .. **Lyon,** Elizabeth Ann '96 Lifetime TV -309 W 49th -NY 10019 **Fx:**957-4447
(716) 845-2101 .. **Lyon,** Gordon W '06 Hon EF Pigott Jr -438 Main -Buffalo 14202
(212) 274-1724 .. **Lyon,** Kara M '94 %Accessible Evidence -158 Hester -NY 10013 **Fx:**274-1634
(212) 484-3900 .. **Lyons,** Alan R '98 Cnsl Arent F LLP -1675 Bway -NY 10019
(212) 878-8000 .. **Lyons,** Alexis D '09 %Clifford C LLP -31 W 52nd -NY 10019
(212) 806-5400 .. **Lyons,** Amy E '10 %Stroock &S&L LLP -180 Maiden Ln -NY 10038
(518) 452-1800 .. **Lyons,** Christopher R '89 (Towne R & Prtnrs,PC) -450 New Karner Rd Bx15072 -Albany 12212
(607) 723-9404 .. **Lyons,** D Edwin '60 Lyons & L -188 Court -Bnghmtn 13901 **Fx:**771-6134
(212) 506-1700 .. **Lyons,** Dana Judeen '06 %Kasowitz BT&F LLP -1633 Bway -NY 10019
(516) 622-9200 .. **Lyons,** Danl G '04 (Westerman BEM&S,LLP) -1201 RXR Plz -Uniondale 11553
(212) 384-1000 .. **Lyons,** Danl J '95 %FBI -26 Fed Plz -NY 10278
(914) 631-1336 .. **Lyons,** Desmond C B '94 (Lyons M,LLP) -16 New Bway -Sleepy Hollow 10591
(212) 298-5179 .. **Lyons,** Douglas B '76 %Leg Aid -49 Thomas -NY 10013 **Fx:**298-5252
(212) 594-2400 .. **Lyons & Flood** -65 W 36th -NY 10018 **Fx:**594-4589
(212) 909-6000 .. **Lyons,** Gregory J '09 (Debevoise & P LLP) -919 3rd Av -NY 10022
(718) 595-6549 .. **Lyons,** Holly B '03 %DEP -59-17 Junction Blvd -Flushng 11373 **Fx:**595-6543
(212) 403-1000 .. **Lyons,** J Austin '91 %Wachtell LR&K -51 W 52nd -NY 10019
(212) 883-0379 .. **Lyons,** Jack '53 %Loeb Partners -521 5th Av -NY 10175 **Fx:**883-0388
(212) 248-8800 .. **Lyons,** Jessica J '07 %Callan KB&B LLP -1 Whitehall -NY 10004
(212) 328-2800 .. **Lyons,** John D '83 Savills LLC -599 Lex Av -NY 10022
(845) 876-2800 .. **Lyons,** John F '86 (Grant & L,LLP) -149 Wurtemburg Rd -Rhinebeck 12572

(212) 826-0100 .. **Lyons,** Kevin J '84 %FSA -31 W 52nd -NY 10019 **Fx:**893-2710
(212) 594-2400 .. **Lyons,** Kirk M H '85 (Lyons & F) -65 W 36th -NY 10018
(212) 267-4876 .. **Lyons,** Kristy K '03 %Hoagland LMD&D,LLP -1501 Bway -NY 10036
(212) 262-2390 .. **Lyons,** M Trevor '97 (Connell F LLP) -888 7th Av -NY 10106
(607) 778-6552 .. **Lyons,** Martha A '84 Hon R Connerton -Bx1766 -Bnghmtn 13902
(212) 768-6700 .. **Lyons,** Matthew J '03 %Sonnenschein N&R LLP -2 World Fncl Ctr -NY 10281
(914) 631-1336 .. **Lyons McGovern,LLP** -16 New Bway -Sleepy Hollow 10591 **Fx:**631-1161
(212) 416-8000 .. **Lyons,** Paul B '95 %Dept of Law -120 Bway -NY 10271
(315) 422-3466 .. **Lyons,** Paul G '10 %Bottar L,PLLC -120 Madison -Syracuse 13202
(212) 848-7666 .. **Lyons,** Peter D '81 (Shearman & S LLP) -599 Lex Av -NY 10022
(315) 488-0744 .. **Lyons,** Richd J '66 -4194 St John Dr -Syracuse 13215
(212) 506-1700 .. **Lyons,** Sean W '07 Kasowitz BT&F LLP -1633 Bway -NY 10019
(516) 877-1965 .. **Lyons,** Sheila M '84 -229 7th -Gdn Cty 11530 **Fx:**877-1955
(212) 255-8833 .. **Lyons,** Steven '82 (M Liu & Assoc PLLC) -107 Grand -NY 10013 **Fx:**255-4981
(845) 831-1234 .. **Lyons & Supple** -5 Cliff Bx510 -Beacon 12508 **Fx:**831-2268
(845) 297-0600 .. **Lyons & Supple** -92 E Main Bx 46 -Wappingers Fls 12590 **Fx:**297-8877
(516) 546-2003 .. **Lyons,** Susan B '85 -2504 Grand Av -Baldwin 11510 **Fx:**378-6124
(914) 686-1700 .. **Lyons,** Vincent M '96 (O'Connor R,LLP) -200 Mamaroneck Av -White Plns 10601
(631) 591-2457 .. **Lyons,** Vincent P '82 -37 Foxglove Row -Rvrhead 11901
(212) 808-3004 .. **Lysaght,** Deborah Martz '78 (Lysaght & L,PC) -230 Park Av -NY 10169 **Fx:**808-3020
(212) 808-3004 .. **Lysaght,** James D '02 (Lysaght & L,PC) -230 Park Av -NY 10169 **Fx:**808-3020
(914) 337-2010 .. **Lysaght,** James F '73 (Pease & L) -15 Park Pl -Bronxvll 10708
(212) 558-4000 .. **Lysenko,** Olga '08 %Sullivan & C LLP -125 Broad -NY 10004
(516) 294-8844 .. **Lyson,** Susannah C '03 %L'Abbate BC&C,LLP -1001 Franklin Av -Gdn Cty 11530
(518) 431-6700 .. **Lytle,** James W '79 (Manatt P&P,LLP) -30 S Pearl -Albany 12207
(212) 790-4500 .. **Lytle,** James W '79 (Manatt P&P,LLP) -7 Times Sq -NY 10036
(212) 237-1000 .. **Lyttle,** John W Jr. '66 (Windels ML&M,LLP) -156 W 56th -NY 10019
(518) 445-2311 .. **Lytton,** Timothy D '03 %Albany Law Schl -80 New Scotland Av -Albany 12208 **Fx:**445-2315
(845) 429-2922 .. **Lyubarskiy,** Igor '04 -196 Ramapo Rd -Garnervll 10923 **Fx:**(206) 600-5297
(732) 855-6038 .. **Lyubarsky,** Alex '03 %Wilentz G&S -110 William -NY 10038 **Fx:**726-6690
(212) 859-8000 .. **Lyznik,** Karolina J '10 %Fried FHS&J LLP -1 NY Plz -NY 10004
(212) 267-1650 .. **Ma,** Annie '02 %Fine O&A,LLP -39 Bway -NY 10006
(917) 596-0239 .. **Ma,** Beverly M '05 -46 Lincoln Av -Tuckahoe 10707
(718) 760-8518 .. **Ma,** Der-Long '92 %NY Intl Group -90-49 53rd Av -Elmhrst 11373
(212) 370-1770 .. **Ma,** Edw Y '77 (Ma & Assoc) -7 Brighton Rd S -Manhsst 11030
(212) 848-4000 .. **Ma,** Frances Y H '09 Shearman & S LLP -599 Lex Av -NY 10022
(212) 756-2000 .. **Ma,** Jie James '05 %Schulte R&Z LLP -919 3rd Av -NY 10022
(212) 431-6938 .. **Ma,** Richd J '97 -315 Bway -NY 10007
(212) 756-2000 .. **Ma,** Stacey Y K '10 %Schulte R&Z LLP -919 3rd Av -NY 10022
(716) 856-0600 .. **Ma,** Tehsheng Abby '01 %Jaeckle F&M,LLP -12 Fountain Plz -Buffalo 14202
(212) 940-8800 .. **Ma,** Tiffany '08 %Katten MR LLP -575 Mad Av -NY 10022
(212) 318-6000 .. **Ma,** Wayne W '05 %Paul HJ&W LLP -75 E 55th -NY 10022
(212) 622-5265 .. **Ma,** Wenyan '99 JP Morgan Sec -277 Park Av -NY 10172
(212) 237-8038 .. **Ma,** Yue '02 John Jay Cllg -899 10th Av -NY 10019
(212) 710-3900 .. **Maag,** Douglas R '86 SrCnsl Clyde & Co US LLP -405 Lex Av -NY 10174 **Fx:**710-3950
(212) 789-8709 .. **Maalouf,** John J '97 (Maalouf Law Firm,LLC) -500 5th Av -NY 10110 **Fx:**789-8718
(212) 449-9005 .. **Maanavi,** Dariush P '98 Merrill Lynch -4 World Fncl Ctr -NY 10080
(212) 980-0120 .. **Maas,** Brian E '78 (Frankfurt KK&S,PC) -488 Mad Av -NY 10022
(585) 419-8800 .. **Maas,** Bruce L '80 (Harris B PLLC) -99 Garnsey Rd -Pittsfrd 14534
(716) 856-5500 .. **Maas,** Gary R '80 (Damon M LLP) -200 Delaware Av -Buffalo 14202
(212) 309-1000 .. **Maas,** Harrison D '71 SrCnsl Hunton & W -200 Park Av -NY 10166
(212) 763-5000 .. **Maazel,** Ilann M '98 (Emery CB&A LLP) -75 Rckfllr Plz -NY 10019
(212) 363-3100 .. **Mabanta,** Katie A '10 %Bivona & C,PC -88 Pine -NY 10005
(585) 419-8800 .. **MacAdam,** Regina Ciccone '94 SrCnsl Harris B PLLC -99 Garnsey Rd -Pittsfrd 14534
(718) 643-7986 .. **MacAdams,** Monica '95 OCA-Supreme Ct -360 Adams -Brklyn 11201
(212) 384-0288 .. **Macadangdang,** Ann B '06 Serrins & Assoc LLC -233 Bway -NY 10279
(518) 463-1716 .. **MacAffer,** Kenneth S Jr. '56 -10 N Sage Hill Ln -Menands 12204
(718) 250-2000 .. **Macajoux,** Johanne A '06 DA -350 Jay -Brklyn 11201 **Fx:**250-2314
(212) 552-1716 .. **MacAllister,** Robt M '78 JP Morgan Chase -1 Chase Manh Plz -NY 10081
(315) 649-2182 .. **Macaluso,** Carmen J '56 -27901 Bayview Dr -Chaumont 13622 **Fx:**649-4299
(212) 903-9000 .. **Macaluso,** Danl J '03 %Linklaters -1345 Av of Amer -NY 10105
(212) 688-5151 .. **Macaluso,** John '91 (Gibney A&F,LLP) -665 5th Av -NY 10022
(718) 364-4000 .. **Macaluso,** Jos G '91 (MacAluso & F,PC) -1 Fordham Plz -Bronx 10458 **Fx:**364-6330
(914) 428-3313 .. **Macaluso,** Wendy L '96 %Curan AF&N,LLP -14 Mamaroneck Av -White Plns 10601 **Fx:**949-5800
(212) 458-1518 .. **MacAneney,** J Robt '92 AIG -175 Water -NY 10038
(914) 665-2440 .. **Macarchuk,** Patrick A '97 %DA -Roosevelt Sq -Mt Vernon 10550 **Fx:**668-2314
(718) 446-0100 .. **Macari,** Louis J '70 Exit Realty Lewis & Murphy -95-40 Roosevelt Av -Jcksn Hts 11372 **Fx:**457-8820
(518) 272-6565 .. **Macari,** Paul M '88 (Martin SWD&J) -279 River Bx1530 -Troy 12181
(516) 248-2400 .. **Macari,** Sharon A '97 (Ialenti & M) -170 Old Cntry Rd -Mineola 11501
(212) 609-6800 .. **Macarone,** Jessica J '02 %McCarter & E,LLP -245 Park Av -NY 10167
(212) 755-6000 .. **Macarthur,** Andrew P '08 %Aronauer R&Y,LLP -444 Mad Av -NY 10022
(315) 422-9039 .. **MacArthur,** Gordon T '54 -117 Woodlawn Ter -Syracuse 13203
(212) 962-1020 .. **MacArthur,** Seth Jesse '00 %M Lamonsoff -80 Maiden Ln -NY 10038 **Fx:**962-3078
(516) 214-4561 .. **MacAskill,** Andrew E '88 -1400 Old Cntry Rd -Westbury 11590
(585) 385-3100 .. **MacAulay,** Paul D '80 -290 Linden Oaks -Rchstr 14625 **Fx:**385-3340
(914) 232-0953 .. **Macaulay,** Zoe '80 -10 Birch Dr -Katonah 10536 **Fx:**232-9228
(973) 476-5417 .. **MacAvery,** J Terence '76 OfCnsl Goldstein J LLP -110 Wall -NY 10005 **Fx:**(212) 898-0386
(212) 232-2410 .. **MacAvery,** Meghan E '07 Goldstein J LLP -110 Wall -NY 10005 **Fx:**232-2412
(212) 598-5900 .. **MacAvoy,** Erin E '05 %Alonso A&K PC -920 Bway -NY 10010
(212) 859-8000 .. **MacAvoy,** Janice '89 (Fried FHS&J LLP) -1 NY Plz -NY 10004
(212) 903-9000 .. **MacBean,** Donald J '07 %Linklaters -1345 Av of Amer -NY 10105
(585) 753-4500 .. **MacBride,** Jason A '04 %DA -832 Watts Bldg -Rchstr 14614 **Fx:**753-4576
(716) 204-2400 .. **Maccagnano,** Michelle D '02 %SJ Baum,PC -220 Nrthpnte Pkwy Bx1291 -Buffalo 14240 **Fx:**204-4600
(212) 450-4000 .. **Maccallum,** Alexandra Y '10 %Davis P&W LLP -450 Lex Av -NY 10017
(716) 488-0758 .. **MacCallum,** James A '97 (Bly SBP&M) -3 Lakevw Av Bx3327 -Jamestwn 14702
(716) 845-9445 .. **Maccallum,** John M '81 %Supreme Ct -50 Delaware Av -Buffalo 14202
(212) 335-4500 .. **MacCallum,** R Kenneth '87 (DLA Piper LLP) -1251 Av of Amer -NY 10020
(845) 225-1504 .. **Maccarini,** Anthony G '75 -1699 Route 6 Bx330 -Carmel 10512 **Fx:**225-1295
(516) 942-0244 .. **Maccaro,** James A '91 %Office oDA&R -375 N Bway -Jericho 11753 **Fx:**942-0353
(516) 674-6782 .. **Maccarone,** John L '85 -41 Forest Av -Glen Cove 11542 **Fx:**671-7440
(518) 485-7692 .. **Maccarone,** Robt M '85 Probation & Alternatives -80 Wolf -Albany 12205
(516) 293-3955 .. **Maccarrone,** Eugene T '82 -8 Chapin Rd -Farmngdl 11735
(212) 752-6700 .. **MacCarthy,** Kevin '70 (K MacCarthy Assoc) -150 E 55th -NY 10022 **Fx:**319-7584
(845) 358-0074 .. **MacCartney,** Harold Y Jr. '68 (MacCartney MK&M) -13 N Bway Bx350 -Nyack 10960
(845) 353-2000 .. **MacCartney,** J David Jr. '94 (Feerick LM PLLC) -96 S Bway -Nyack 10960
(845) 358-0074 .. **MacCartney MacCartney Kerrigan & MacCartney** -13 N Bway Bx350 -Nyack 10960 **Fx:**358-0793
(212) 363-3100 .. **Macchia,** Robt G '88 (Bivona & C,PC) -88 Pine -NY 10005
(516) 873-6200 .. **Macchia,** Robt P '89 R Macchia & Assoc -98 Front -Mineola 11501 **Fx:**873-1611
(718) 522-2300 .. **Macchiarola,** Frank J '66 St Francis Cllg -180 Remsen -Brklyn 11201
(718) 446-6777 .. **Macchiarulo,** Louis '88 -40-06 Warren -Elmhrst 11373 **Fx:**779-6984
(718) 783-4799 .. **Macchio,** Nicholas R Jr. '62 -22 St Johns Pl -Brklyn 11217 **Fx:**783-6173
(631) 549-7900 .. **Macco,** Michl J '82 (Macco & S,LLP) -135 Pinelawn Rd -Melvll 11747
(631) 549-7900 .. **Macco & Stern,LLP** -135 Pinelawn Rd -Melvll 11747 **Fx:**549-7845
(212) 791-0285 .. **Maccone,** Maria N '07 %Malaby & B,LLC -150 Bway -NY 10038 **Fx:**791-0286
(845) 225-3641 .. **MacCrae,** Mary Jane '83 %DA -40 Gleneida Av -Carmel 10512
(212) 558-4000 .. **MacCrate,** Robt '49 SrCnsl Sullivan & C LLP -125 Broad -NY 10004
(516) 822-3550 .. **MacDavitt,** Sean R '08 %Hoffmann & B LLP -6900 Jericho Tpk -Syosset 11791 **Fx:**822-3582
(631) 952-6977 .. **MacDevitt,** Veronica Bindrim '89 %Medicaid Fraud Cntrl -300 Motor Pkwy -Hauppauge 11788 **Fx:**952-6382
(631) 232-0200 .. **MacDevitt,** Wm G '93 %Fumuso KDSS&F,LLP -110 Marcus Blvd -Hauppauge 11788
(212) 530-5000 .. **Macdonald,** Alastair J '10 %Milbank TH&M LLP -1 Chase Manh Plz NY 10005
(212) 836-8000 .. **Macdonald,** Andrew '78 (Kaye S LLP) -425 Park Av -NY 10022
(917) 385-1001 .. **MacDonald,** Angelo G '87 -200 W 60th -NY 10023 **Fx:**(212) 956-1009
(716) 853-3801 .. **MacDonald,** Brian A '92 (Kenney SL&N,LLP) -14 Lafayette Sq -Buffalo 14203
(914) 245-2277 .. **MacDonald,** Bruce B '74 -1940 Commerce -Yorktwn Hts 10598
(212) 728-8000 .. **Macdonald,** Colin C '09 %Willkie F&G LLP -787 7th Av -NY 10019
(212) 446-4800 .. **MacDonald,** David '98 (Kirkland & E LLP) -153 E 53rd -NY 10022
(212) 307-5500 .. **Macdonald,** Donald A 3rd '10 %Venable LLP -1270 Av of Amer -NY 10020
(212) 944-2948 .. **MacDonald,** Eleanor Sovern '67 %NLRB -120 W 45th -NY 10036
(212) 553-5400 .. **Mac Donald,** Holly '00 Zurich NA -1 Lbrty Plz -NY 10006
(845) 855-5900 .. **MacDonald,** Ian Scott '00 %Daniels & P,LLP -517 Route 22 -Pawling 12564
(212) 626-4100 .. **Macdonald,** J Ross '82 OfCnsl Baker & M LLP -1114 Av of Amer -NY 10036
(716) 854-5636 .. **MacDonald,** Janet Clark '95 -110 Pearl -Buffalo 14202
(212) 259-8000 .. **MacDonald,** Jeffrey S '99 (Dewey & L LLP) -1301 Av of Amer -NY 10019
(212) 588-5500 .. **MacDonald,** Jennifer H '98 %Davies WP&V LLP -625 Mad Av -NY 10022
(212) 403-3612 .. **MacDonald,** Judith R '76 Rothschild Inc -1251 Av of Amer -NY 10020
(212) 841-1000 .. **Macdonald,** Katharine C '10 %Covington & B LLP -620 8th Av -NY 10018
(518) 432-3425 .. **Macdonald,** Kevin J '99 %Ct of Claims -Justice Bldg ESP Bx7344 -Albany 12224 **Fx:**432-3450
(212) 659-8105 .. **Macdonald,** Michl G '68 %Mt Sinai Med Ctr -1 Gustave L Levy Pl Bx 1099 -NY 10029 **Fx:**348-2230
(212) 937-7223 .. **Macdonald,** Peter J '01 (WilmerHale) -399 Park Av -NY 10022
(212) 403-6700 .. **MacDonald,** Robt C '01 Gide LN LLP -120 W 45th -NY 10036
(212) 839-5300 .. **Macdonald,** Scott M '05 %Sidley A LLP -787 7th Av -NY 10019
(212) 259-8000 .. **MacDonald,** Stephen R '77 (Dewey & L LLP) -1301 Av of Amer -NY 10019
(212) 820-9333 .. **MacDonald,** W Cullen '70 (Hawkins D&W LLP) -One Chase Manh Plz -NY 10005

(585) 387-0220 .. **MacDonald,** Wm J '79 -2526 Browncroft Blvd -Rchstr 14625

(212) 259-8000 .. **MacDonald,** Wm R '99 %Dewey & L LLP -1301 Av of Amer -NY 10019

(516) 822-8900 .. **MacDonnell,** Patrick L '82 Fiedelman & M -2 Jericho Plz -Jericho 11753

(212) 685-7411 .. **MacDonnell,** Robt R '68 (Lurie IM&R,LLP) -475 Park Av S -NY 10016 **Fx:**685-9827

(212) 852-3655 .. **MacDonnell,** Robt R Jr. '95 %US Trust Co,NA -114 W 47th -NY 10036 **Fx:**852-1310

(212) 798-6100 .. **MacDougall,** Cameron D '02 Fortress Invsmnt Grp LLC -1345 Av of Amer -NY 10105

(917) 535-1817 .. **Macdougall,** Christopher D '07 -4129 46th -Sunnyside 11104

(347) 273-1288 .. **MacDougall,** Michl A '04 -1110 South Av -Staten Isl 10314 **Fx:**273-1388

(646) 557-9000 .. **MacDougall,** Michelle Yale '99 Fimat USA -630 5th Av -NY 10111

(347) 404-9133 .. **Mace,** Douglas W '04 %Civil Ct -141 Lvngstn -Brklyn 11201 **Fx:**(718) 643-3733

(212) 571-3980 .. **Mace,** Janet C '03 -30 Vesey -NY 10007

(212) 259-8000 .. **Mace,** Jeffrey H '84 (Dewey & L LLP) -1301 Av of Amer -NY 10019

(914) 248-6141 .. **Mace,** Valerie '67 -Somers Rd Bx636 -Somers 10589 **Fx:**248-8017

(212) 336-8000 .. **Macedo,** Chas R '90 (Amster R&E) -90 Park Av -NY 10016

(718) 279-3770 .. **Macedonio,** Elizabeth Edwards '94 (E Macedonio,PC) -42-40 Bell Blvd -Bayside 11361 **Fx:**281-0850

(212) 878-0295 .. **Macedonio,** Salvatore Jr. '98 %MTA -347 Mad Av -NY 10017

(212) 732-2929 .. **Maceira,** Raymond '96 %Dansker & A Assoc -30 Vesey -NY 10007 **Fx:**732-8795

(914) 969-5000 .. **Macellaro,** Chas J '59 CJ Macellaro,PC -570 Ynkrs Av -Ynkrs 10704 **Fx:**963-1772

(718) 520-2599 .. **MacEwen,** Elizabeth A '89 Hon S Golar -88-11 Stuphin Blvd -Jamaica 11435 **Fx:**520-6433

(212) 636-6000 .. **Macey,** Gregg P '07 Fordham Univ Sch of Law -140 W 62nd -NY 10023 **Fx:**636-6899

(516) 683-3516 .. **MacFall,** Timothy J '86 (Rigrodsky & L,PA) -585 Stewart Av -Gdn Cty 11530

(212) 532-8085 .. **MacFarlane,** Mina '97 -311 E 23rd -NY 10010

(212) 751-1640 .. **Mac Giollabhui,** Niall '07 -112 Mad Av -NY 10016

(212) 557-7700 .. **MacGrady,** Barbara L '98 OfCnsl Davidson D&C LLP -60 E 42nd -NY 10165

(212) 610-6300 .. **MacGrath,** Dana C '97 SrCnsl Allen & O -1221 Av of Amer -NY 10020

(212) 808-7800 .. **Mac Gregor,** Alison L '01 (Kelley D&W LLP) -101 Park Av -NY 10178

(212) 450-4000 .. **MacGregor,** Deborah L '04 %Davis P&W LLP -450 Lex Av -NY 10017

(212) 790-9200 .. **MacGregor,** Meichelle R '95 %Cowan L&L,PC -1133 Av of Amer -NY 10036

(212) 554-1234 .. **Mac Gregor,** Wm T '08 AXA Financial Inc -1290 Av of Amer -NY 10104 **Fx:**707-3963

(212) 474-1000 .. **Mach,** Kyle W '07 %Cravath S&M LLP -825 8th Av -NY 10019

(212) 490-9000 .. **Machado,** Dennis M '02 %TIAA-CREF -730 3rd Av -NY 10017

(585) 428-5755 .. **Machado,** Kerri E '04 Cnty Atty -50 W Main -Rchstr 14614 **Fx:**428-2031

(914) 949-4918 .. **Machado,** Manuel J '02 -445 Hmltn Av -White Plns 10601 **Fx:**206-3941

(718) 396-0300 .. **Machado,** Patricia M '96 -87-08 Justice Av -Elmhrst 11373

(212) 903-9000 .. **Machan,** Katherine Zupan '05 %Linklaters -1345 Av of Amer -NY 10105

(212) 825-9811 .. **Machcinski,** Victor A Jr. '79 SrCnsl Krebsbach & S,PC -55 Bway -NY 10006

(716) 852-5200 .. **Machelor,** Kristin M '99 %Hamberger & W -700 Main Pl Twr -Buffalo 14202

(212) 310 8000 .. **Machera,** Christopher R '06 %Weil G&M LLP -767 5th Av -NY 10153

(212) 218-3350 .. **Machinist,** Alexandra Hirschfeld '06 %L Chester Literary Agency -630 5th Av -NY 10111

(212) 719-0200 .. **Machione,** Joan M '95 %BAR/BRI -1500 Bway -NY 10036 **Fx:**719-1421

(518) 392-6960 .. **Machiz,** Larry H '79 -Tice Hill Rd -Ghent 12075

(212) 325-2000 .. **Machlis,** Roger M '87 Credit Suisse -11 Mad Av -NY 10010

(212) 259-8000 .. **Machnacki,** Christopher S '08 %Dewey & L LLP -1301 Av of Amer -NY 10019

(212) 859-8000 .. **Macholz,** Wm G Jr. '06 %Fried FHS&J LLP -1 NY Plz -NY 10004

(212) 685-2225 .. **Machson,** Robt A '85 %RA Machson & Assoc -271 Mad Av -NY 10016 **Fx:**685-7315

(315) 422-2255 .. **Macht Brenizer & Gingold** -510 State Twr Bldg -Syracuse 13202 **Fx:**422-6360

(212) 479-6724 .. **Macht,** Timothy A '03 (Macht SA&I LLP) -1114 Av of Amer -NY 10036 **Fx:**202-6417

(212) 984-6646 .. **Machuca,** Edwin A '05 Cnsl CB Richard Ellis -200 Park Av -NY 10166

(914) 493-2800 .. **Macias,** Xavier A '97 %Cnty Hlthcr Corp -95 Grasslands Rd -Valhalla 10595 **Fx:**493-2321

(212) 323-2250 .. **Macias-Itak,** Marianne V '86 %HHC-OLA-Medical Litigation -346 Bway -NY 10013 **Fx:**323-2251

(212) 821-0561 .. **Macielak,** Paul F '76 %NY Hsptl/Cornell Med Ctr -425 E 61st -NY 10065

(212) 558-4000 .. **Macikowski,** Kevin D '09 %Sullivan & C LLP -125 Broad -NY 10004

(212) 742-8700 .. **Macina,** Jessica A '08 %Garson D&C LLP -110 Wall -NY 10005

(914) 698-5188 .. **Macina,** Mary Beth '01 Srvc Statn Dealers of Grtr NY,Inc -421 Waverly Av -Mamaroneck 10543

(212) 841-2000 .. **MacInnes,** Jean L '03 BNP Paribas -787 7th Av -NY 10019

(631) 424-2525 .. **MacInnes,** John M '02 %Mandler & S,LLP -1609 NY Av -Huntngtn Sta 11746

(212) 250-2500 .. **MacInnis,** James H Jr. '01 %Deutsche Bank -60 Wall -NY 10005

(212) 558-5500 .. **MacIntyre,** Matthew T '05 %Weitz & L,PC -700 Bway -NY 10003

(212) 449-2940 .. **Macioce,** Frank M Jr. '73 %Merrill Lynch -220 Bway -NY 10038

(212) 596-9000 .. **Macioce,** Lauren Decker '10 %Ropes & G LLP -1211 Av of Amer -NY 10036

(845) 883-6754 .. **Maciocia,** Annamaria '91 -Bx472 -Modena 12548

(212) 267-0200 .. **Mack,** Anthony C '96 -20 Vesey -NY 10007 **Fx:**(973) 624-5005

(518) 758-2333 .. **Mack,** Barrett D '05 (Fitzsimmons & M,PC) -3223 Church Bx310 -Valatie 12184 **Fx:**758-2330

(315) 435-2170 .. **Mack,** Christopher M '78 %Cnty Atty -421 Mntgmry -Syracuse 13202 **Fx:**435-5729

(212) 362-6155 .. **Mack,** Dennis W '70 -180 Riverside Dr -NY 10024 **Fx:**769-2895

(650) 470-4500 .. **Mack,** Eric '08 %Skadden ASM&F LLP -4 Times Sq -NY 10036 **Fx:**470-4570

(212) 521-5400 .. **Mack,** Eulalia M '91 (Reed S LLP) -599 Lex Av -NY 10022

(212) 835-1572 .. **Mack,** Grace D '85 (Lampf LP&P) -5 Penn Plz 19th Fl -NY 10119

(518) 399-1200 .. **Mack,** Howard '73 -133 Saratoga Rd -Glenvll 12302 **Fx:**836-0230

(607) 773-0673 .. **Mack,** James A '82 -53 Chenango -Bnghmtn 13901 **Fx:**773-0672

(718) 361-2861 .. **Mack,** Kathryn R '05 -49-47 31st -LIC 11101

(518) 386-2266 .. **Mack,** Lauren '06 Pub Def -519 State -Schnctdy 12305 **Fx:**386-2814

(718) 250-2000 .. **Mack,** Lauren E '90 %DA -350 Jay -Brklyn 11201 **Fx:**250-2314

(518) 408-2555 .. **Mack,** Martin J '80 NYS Ofc Intergovernmental Affrs -State Cptl -Albany 12224

(212) 515-3233 .. **Mack,** Richd J '95 (Apollo Real Est Advsrs) -60 Columbus Cir -NY 10023 **Fx:**515-3284

(716) 852-5211 .. **Mack,** Stephanie A '08 %MA Bjork -350 Main -Buffalo 14202 **Fx:**852-8149

(212) 868-9300 .. **Mack,** Stuart A '84 -350 5th Av -NY 10118 **Fx:**736-8677

(585) 798-1000 .. **Mack,** Thos C '64 (Mack & P) -Cook Bldg-534 Main Bx248 -Medina 14103 **Fx:**798-1003

(212) 619-3730 .. **Mack,** Walter S Jr. '73 (Doar RK&M) -217 Bway -NY 10007

(212) 849-7000 .. **Mack,** Wm B III '04 %Quinn EU&S,LLP -51 Mad Av -NY 10010

(212) 735-3000 .. **Mack,** Wm H '04 %Skadden ASM&F LLP -4 Times Sq -NY 10036

(516) 357-3700 .. **Mackasek,** Thos C '75 (Cullen and D LLP) -100 Q Roosevelt Blvd -Gdn Cty 11530

(212) 943-1090 .. **Mackauf,** Stephen H '70 (Gair GCSMB&R) -80 Pine -NY 10005

(315) 472-5201 .. **Mackay Caswell & Callahan,PC** -103 E Water -Syracuse 13202 **Fx:**472-5002

(718) 254-7000 .. **Mackay,** Elizabeth J '05 %US Atty -271 Cadman Plz E -Brklyn 11201 **Fx:**254-6479

(845) 783-2216 .. **Mackay,** Hugh R '81 -47 James Rd -Monroe 10950

(631) 271-4945 .. **Mackay,** John F Jr. '70 -1 Woodfld Ct -Huntngtn 11743

(845) 462-0001 .. **MacKay,** Kevin M '93 (Serino M&B,PLLC) -12 Walker Rd -Poughkeepsie 12603

(914) 946-3700 .. **Mackay,** Kristen L '09 %McCarthy F LLP -11 Martine Av -White Plns 10606

(585) 243-7020 .. **MacKay,** Kyle D '93 %DA -2 Court -Geneseo 14454 **Fx:**243-7199

(914) 765-3630 .. **MacKay,** M Jennifer '96 MBIA -113 King -Armonk 10504

(212) 687-4900 .. **Mackay,** Michl W '79 Cnsl Wormser KG&J LLP -825 3rd Av -NY 10022

(718) 423-6800 .. **MacKay Wrynn & Brady LLP** -40-26 235th -Douglastn 11363 **Fx:**224-4782

(212) 909-6000 .. **Macke,** Jonathan J '09 %Debevoise & P LLP -919 3rd Av -NY 10022

(212) 416-8370 .. **MacKechnie,** Roseann B '79 %Dept of Law -120 Bway -NY 10271

(212) 788-3300 .. **MacKechnie,** Russell W Jr. '79 %Hlth & Hsptl Corp -125 Worth -NY 10013 **Fx:**267-6905

(212) 557-7700 .. **MacKenty,** John E '58 OfCnsl Davidson D&C LLP -60 E 42nd -NY 10165

(631) 439-2450 .. **Mackenzie,** Andrea S '89 %Leg Aid -320 Carleton Av -Central Islip 11722 **Fx:**439-2453

(516) 742-9200 .. **Mackenzie,** Donald N '96 %Edelman K&J PLLC -1 Old Cntry Rd -Carle Pl 11514

(212) 770-1518 .. **Mackenzie,** Gae V '91 %AIG -80 Pine -NY 10005 **Fx:**809-2452

(315) 474-7571 .. **Mackenzie Hughes LLP** -101 S Salina Bx4967 -Syracuse 13221 **Fx:**474-6409

(585) 381-2199 .. **MacKenzie,** Karen M '84 -730 Stone Rd -Pittsfrd 14534

(518) 266-9060 .. **Mackenzie,** Melody A '98 (Assaf & M PLLC) -427 River -Troy 12180 **Fx:**266-9064

(716) 856-3500 .. **MacKenzie,** Sean J '05 %Magavern MG LLP -1100 Rand Bldg -Buffalo 14203

(646) 250-0462 .. **Mackenzie,** Stephen P '09 Barclays Capital -745 7th Av -NY 10019

(845) 454-9611 .. **MacKenzie,** Tracy Cass '04 (Battistoni & M) -97 Cannon -Poughkeepsie 12601 **Fx:**471-2035

(518) 673-5656 .. **MacKenzie,** Wm B '51 OfCnsl MacKenzie & T -42 Church Bx330 -Canajoharie 13317 **Fx:**673-3501

(212) 506-5000 .. **Mackerron,** John A '88 (Orrick H&S LLP) -51 W 52nd -NY 10019

(212) 622-4215 .. **Mackey,** David H '03 JP Morgan Chase -277 Park Av -NY 10172

(518) 474-7700 .. **Mackey,** Donna L '84 %NYS OPWDD -44 Holland Av -Albany 12229 **Fx:**474-7382

(212) 772-0943 .. **Mackey,** George Foster '64 %Lewis & M -521 5th Av -NY 10175

(585) 295-4400 .. **Mackey,** George G '72 (Hiscock & B,LLP) -2000 HSBC Plz -Rchstr 14604

(212) 264-1595 .. **Mackey,** Gerard '94 %IRS Ofc Dist Cnsl -290 Bway -NY 10007

(845) 473-8100 .. **Mackey,** Joshua E '99 (Iseman CR&H,LLP) -2649 South Rd -Poughkeepsie 12601

(516) 328-4400 .. **Mackey,** Kirk W '91 Canon USA,Inc -1 Canon Plz -New Hyde Pk 11042

(518) 452-3710 .. **Mackey,** L Michl '82 (Feeney C&M) -116 Great Oaks Blvd -Albany 12203

(212) 878-8489 .. **Mackey,** Leonard B Jr. '76 (Clifford C LLP) -31 W 52nd -NY 10019

(631) 582-3700 .. **Mackey,** Lester W '84 -3075 Vets Mem'l Hwy -Ronkonkoma 11779

(646) 743-0376 .. **Mackey,** Meredith L '03 %Bk of Amer Merrill Lynch -1 Bryant Pk -NY 10036

(716) 849-1333 .. **Mackey,** Patrick J '07 %Lipsitz GSC LLP -42 Delaware Av -Buffalo 14202

(212) 753-5000 .. **Mackey,** Paul G '89 (Schiff H LLP) -900 3rd Av -NY 10022

(212) 455-2000 .. **Mackey,** Ursula '07 %Simpson T&B LLP -425 Lex Av -NY 10017

(212) 922-9722 .. **Mackiewicz,** Richd W Jr. '87 (Mackiewicz & Assoc,LLC) -60 E 42nd -NY 10165 **Fx:**922-9723

(607) 637-5400 .. **Mackin,** F Gerald '75 OfCnsl L Sienko Jr -12 E Main Bx579 -Hancock 13783

(315) 218-8000 .. **Mackin,** James E '70 (Bond S&K,PLLC) -1 Lincoln Ctr -Syracuse 13202

(914) 277-3993 .. **Mackin,** Ralph R '66 -112 Titicus Rd -N Salem 10560 **Fx:**277-8663

(212) 225-2000 .. **Mackinnon,** Ari D '07 %Cleary GS&H -1 Lbrty Plz -NY 10006

(212) 839-5300 .. **MacKinnon,** John A '75 (Sidley A LLP) -787 7th Av -NY 10019

(516) 676-4600 .. **Mac Kinnon,** Peter P '74 (Humes & W) -147 Forest Av Bx546 -Locust Vly 11560

(212) 762-3317 .. **Mackle,** Anne M '04 Morgan Stanley -750 7th Av -NY 10019

(718) 482-8585 .. **Mackle,** Robt J '93 SrCnsl Skyline CreditRide,Inc -52-29 35th -LIC 11101 **Fx:**482-7757
(212) 619-8119 .. **Mackler,** Camille J '07 T Napolitano -299 Bway -NY 10007
(212) 593-6700 .. **Macklin,** Hilary S '05 %Aaronson RF&D,LLP -757 3rd Av -NY 10017
(516) 741-2743 .. **Macklin,** John C '70 -5 Morris Dr -New Hyde Pk 11040
(516) 545-5160 .. **Macklin,** Ronald J '89 %Natl Grid -175 E Old Cntry Rd -Hicksvll 11801 **Fx:**545-5029
(212) 227-6655 .. **Macklowitz,** Michl L '74 -299 Bway -NY 10007 **Fx:**732-6972
(585) 454-5650 .. **MacKnight,** David D '76 %Lacy K LLP -130 E Main -Rchstr 14604
(212) 687-4900 .. **MacKnight,** Wm J Jr. '67 (Wormser KG&J LLP) -825 3rd Av -NY 10022
(212) 736-0500 .. **Mackoff,** Scot P '95 %Mitofsky SN&H LLP -152 Mad Av -NY 10016
(518) 828-5400 .. **Mackowski,** Vincent P '06 %Guterman S&A,PLLC -21 N 7th -Hudson 12534
(518) 463-2268 .. **MacKrell,** Patrick J '79 NY Business Dvlpmnt Corp -50 Beaver Bx738 -Albany 12201
(516) 623-1111 .. **Mackreth,** Patricia M '87 %Curtis V PC -2174 Hewlett Av Bx801 -Merrick 11566 **Fx:**623-0758
(212) 506-1700 .. **Mack Rosenberg,** Kimberly M '94 %Kasowitz BT&F LLP -1633 Bway -NY 10019
(212) 563-4100 .. **Mackson,** Tzvi N '08 %Cohen W&S LLP -330 W 42nd -NY 10036
(212) 715-9100 .. **Macksoud,** Lauren M '04 %Kramer LN&F,LLP -1177 Av of Amer -NY 10036
(212) 785-7520 .. **Macksoud,** Richd M Jr. '80 OfCnsl Coti & S -17 State -NY 10004
(646) 672-6262 .. **Mackzum,** Kent M '08 MHLS -600 E 125th -NY 10035
(631) 324-5909 .. **MacLachlan,** John A '96 (MacLachlan & E LLP) -241 Pantigo Rd -E Hampton 11937
(212) 278-7188 .. **Maclay,** John B III '95 %Societe Generale -1221 Av of Amer -NY 10020
(212) 603-6300 .. **MacLean,** Babcock '83 (Robinson BLGG&G PC) -875 3rd Av -NY 10022
(212) 483-9490 .. **MacLean,** Cora E '06 %McElroy DM&C,LLP -88 Pine -NY 10005
(585) 385-0860 .. **MacLean,** David C Jr. '92 -1 Burr Oak Dr -Pittsfrd 14534
(212) 449-6577 .. **MacLean,** Donald A '01 Merrill Lynch -4 World Fncl Ctr -NY 10080
(212) 682-1555 .. **MacLean,** Ian W '93 (MacLean Law Firm,LLC) -100 Park Av -NY 10017 **Fx:**682-6999
(631) 853-7855 .. **MacLean,** Jocelyn Anne '96 %District Ct Law Dept -400 Carleton Av Bx9075 -Central Islip 11722
(212) 801-3137 .. **MacLean,** Justin A '09 %Greenberg T,LLP -200 Park Av -NY 10166
(407) 342-9705 .. **MacLellan,** Jos D '08 -1247-A 79th -Brklyn 11228
(212) 530-5000 .. **MacLennan,** Jane L '86 -1 Chase Manh Plz -NY 10005 **Fx:**530-5219
(212) 474-1000 .. **Macleod,** Adam S '10 %Cravath S&M LLP -825 8th Av -NY 10019
(212) 450-4000 .. **Macleod,** Alexander N '08 %Davis P&W LLP -450 Lex Av -NY 10017
(516) 571-2770 .. **MacLeod,** Gordon L '73 %Supreme Ct -100 Supreme Ct Dr -Mineola 11501
(212) 878-7900 .. **MacLeod,** Janet M '99 (Fox R LLP) -100 Park Av -NY 10017
(212) 403-1000 .. **MacLeod,** Joshua M '09 %Wachtell LR&K -51 W 52nd -NY 10019
(212) 530-5000 .. **MacLeod,** Kevin A '04 %Milbank TH&M LLP -1 Chase Manh Plz -NY 10005
(845) 454-3250 .. **MacLeod,** Roderick J '94 (Gellert & K,PC) -75 Wshngtn -Poughkeepsie 12601
(518) 486-9564 .. **MacMaster,** Heather M '93 %Workers Comp Bd -20 Park -Albany 12207
(212) 571-5500 .. **MacMillan,** Kathleen E '09 %Rothman SS&S,LLP -100 Lafayette -NY 10013
(212) 571-0550 .. **MacMillan,** Kevin L '01 (Allegaert B&V LLP) -111 Bway -NY 10006
(212) 695-8100 .. **Macmull,** Joel G '05 %Goetz F,LLP -1 Penn Plz -NY 10119
(516) 431-0781 .. **MacMurray,** J Richd '62 -891 W Beech Bx538 -Long Bch 11561 **Fx:**431-0786
(212) 596-9000 .. **MacMurray,** John C '65 (Ropes & G LLP) -1211 Av of Amer -NY 10036
(845) 986-2669 .. **MacNamara,** Brian S '01 -70 Four Crnrs Rd -Warwick 10990
(732) 634-3700 .. **MacNaughton,** W James '77 -477 Mad Av -NY 10022
(718) 694-3862 .. **MacNeal,** Kelly D '90 %Transit Auth -130 Lvngstn -Brklyn 11201 **Fx:**694-5726
(518) 481-1544 .. **MacNeill,** Glenn '86 %DA -Ct Hse -Malone 12953 **Fx:**481-1545
(718) 233-2976 .. **Macner,** Esther A '87 E Macner,PC -26 Court -Brklyn 11242 **Fx:**233-4297
(845) 298-2000 .. **MacNish,** Karen P '99 OfCnsl Vergilis SRD&D,LLP -1136 Route 9 -Wappingers Fls 12590
(212) 506-5000 .. **Maco,** Katherine L '08 %Orrick H&S LLP -51 W 52nd -NY 10019
(516) 571-2854 .. **Maco,** Rhonda L '03 Cnsl Nassau Co Comptroller -240 Old Cntry Rd -Mineola 11501
(518) 218-7100 .. **Macomber,** Michl W '10 %Tully R,PLLC -441 New Karner Rd -Albany 12205
(212) 258-4908 .. **Macon,** Valencia N '96 Siemens Corp -153 E 53rd -NY 10022
(212) 765-5070 .. **Macphail,** Stuart '04 (Fish & R,PC) -153 E 53rd -NY 10022
(315) 448-4800 .. **MacPherson,** Maureen A '85 Dept of Law -615 Erie Blvd W -Syracuse 13204 **Fx:**448-4853
(212) 613-2000 .. **MacPherson,** Robt J '83 (Gibbons PC) -1 Penn Plz -NY 10119
(212) 259-8000 .. **MacRae,** Cameron F III '66 OfCnsl Dewey & L LLP -1301 Av of Amer -NY 10019
(718) 852-8888 .. **MacRae,** John Y '90 %LSNYC-Brooklyn -180 Lvngstn -Brklyn 11201 **Fx:**858-1786
(518) 474-7700 .. **MacRae,** Patrick F '80 %NYS OPWDD -44 Holland Av -Albany 12229 **Fx:**474-7382
(212) 788-8883 .. **Macrae,** Phebe Barber '95 %Law Dept -100 Church -NY 10007 **Fx:**788-0367
(212) 407-4000 .. **MacRae,** Warren K '93 (Loeb & L,LLP) -345 Park Av -NY 10154
(914) 232-8174 .. **Macreery,** John B '74 (Deren G&M) -28 Edgemont Rd -Katonah 10536
(914) 946-3700 .. **Macreery,** Wm F '75 Cnsl McCarthy F LLP -11 Martine Av -White Plns 10606
(518) 465-3524 .. **Macri,** Giovanna J '96 %NYS Defenders Assn -194 Wshngtn Av -Albany 12210 **Fx:**465-3249
(631) 342-6000 .. **Macri,** Glenn V '97 %CA,Inc -1 CA Plz -Islandia 11749 **Fx:**342-4866
(516) 338-5780 .. **Macri Greenspan & Moramarco** -393 Old Cntry Rd -Carle Pl 11514 **Fx:**338-5798
(516) 944-4544 .. **Macri,** Jos F '94 Cnsl Cedar Shopping Ctrs,Inc -44 S Bayles Av -Pt Wash 11050 **Fx:**767-6497
(212) 406-3911 .. **Macri,** Mia M '91 %Leanza & A,PC -521 5th Av -NY 10175
(315) 866-6144 .. **Macri,** Nicholas A '92 -203 N Prospect -Herkimer 13350 **Fx:**866-4007
(212) 682-0020 .. **Macri,** Stephen J '86 (Putney TH&H LLP) -521 5th Av -NY 10175
(212) 688-8555 .. **Macris,** Catherine A '04 %Fragomen DB&L LLP -7 Hanover Sq -NY 10004
(212) 701-3000 .. **Macris,** Michl '75 (Cahill G&R LLP) -80 Pine -NY 10005 **Fx:**269-5420
(718) 474-0111 .. **Macron & Cowhey, PC** -257 Beach 116th -Rckwy Pk 11694 **Fx:**945-0880
(212) 361-1515 .. **Macron,** James J '91 Envrnmntl Cntrl Brd -66 John -NY 10038 **Fx:**361-1900
(718) 474-0111 .. **Macron,** John J '89 (Macron & C, PC) -257 Beach 116th -Rckwy Pk 11694
(718) 889-3582 .. **Macron,** Mark A '88 -491 Bard Av -Staten Isl 10310 **Fx:**889-3584
(212) 548-2100 .. **MacSteel,** Genevieve '90 (McGuire W LLP) -1345 Av of Amer -NY 10105
(845) 343-3000 .. **MacVean Lewis Sherwin & McDermott,PC** -34 Grove Bx310 -Middletwn 10940 **Fx:**343-3866
(212) 339-9100 .. **MacWilliams,** John J '83 Beacon Grp -270 Park Av -NY 10017
(212) 370-7612 .. **Macy,** Jonathan P '05 UBS Fncl Srvcs -200 Park Av -NY 10166
(516) 222-6200 .. **Macy,** Jos E '84 (Berkman HPP&F,PC) -100 Grdn City Plz -Gdn Cty 11530
(716) 507-8630 .. **Macy,** Patricia M '93 Maximus,Inc -9548 Cobblestone Dr -Clarence 14031 **Fx:**833-0613
(212) 596-9000 .. **Maczka,** Arkadiusz M '10 %Ropes & G LLP -1211 Av of Amer -NY 10036
(212) 801-6576 .. **Maczko,** Jos R '09 %Greenberg T,LLP -200 Park Av -NY 10166
(212) 209-5450 .. **Madama,** Havona '98 (Madama GO LLP) -450 Park Av S -NY 10016 **Fx:**209-5460
(212) 992-8654 .. **Madar,** Josiah R '03 %NYU Law Schl -40 Wshngtn Sq S -NY 10012 **Fx:**995-4600
(718) 418-7690 .. **Madar,** Wm C '05 Make the Road by Walking -301 Grove -Brklyn 11237
(212) 486-5252 .. **Madariaga,** Elena G '01 K2 Advisors -570 Lex Av -NY 10022
(516) 498-2900 .. **Maday,** Ronald Chas '96 (Naidich WB&M,LLP) -80 Cuttermill Rd -Gt Neck 11021 **Fx:**466-3555
(212) 589-4200 .. **Madbak,** Hanna F '05 %Baker & H LLP -45 Rckfllr Plz -NY 10111
(212) 577-3688 .. **Maddalo,** Lorraine '81 %Leg Aid -199 Water -NY 10038 **Fx:**509-8431
(718) 351-2464 .. **Maddatu,** Nestor P '86 -105 Delaware Av -Staten Isl 10304
(718) 262-3410 .. **Madden,** Christina M '00 ACS-DLS -92-31 Union Hall -Jamaica 11433
(212) 875-5834 .. **Madden,** John B Jr. '80 Lincoln Cntr Dvlpmnt Project,Inc -1865 Bway -NY 10023
(212) 848-7055 .. **Madden,** John J '76 (Shearman & S LLP) -599 Lex Av -NY 10022
(212) 949-4646 .. **Madden,** John P '79 (Canfield M&R,LLP) -230 Park Av -NY 10169
(914) 261-7549 .. **Madden,** Jos D '80 -25 Bank -White Plns 10606
(914) 949-2700 .. **Madden,** Jos N '99 (Bleakley P&S,LLP) -1 N Lex Av -White Plns 10601
(212) 682-7900 .. **Madden,** Keith J '06 %Kreinik Assoc,LLC -275 Mad Av -NY 10016 **Fx:**682-0030
(718) 246-4330 .. **Madden,** Kenneth V '86 -186 Montague -Brklyn 11201 **Fx:**246-4691
(212) 788-0880 .. **Madden,** Kevin A '06 Law Dept -100 Church -NY 10007 **Fx:**788-0367
(212) 541-6741 .. **Madden,** Kimberly A '99 Fund for Modern Cts -351 W 54th -NY 10019
(716) 856-4000 .. **Madden,** Lance J '73 (Hodgson R LLP) -140 Pearl -Buffalo 14202
(212) 733-3451 .. **Madden,** Margaret M '94 %Pfizer Inc -235 E 42nd -NY 10017
(518) 473-0361 .. **Madden,** Maureen A '87 %State Comptroller -110 State -Albany 12236 **Fx:**473-9104
(212) 697-3122 .. **Madden,** Michl F '92 (Martin C&B LLP) -220 E 42nd -NY 10017
(212) 307-5500 .. **Madden,** Michl K '78 (Venable LLP) -1270 Av of Amer -NY 10020
(585) 232-6500 .. **Madden,** Neal D '72 (Harter S&E LLP) -1600 Bausch & Lomb Pl -Rchstr 14604
(718) 624-0964 .. **Madden,** Paul J '69 -26 Court -Brklyn 11242 **Fx:**237-1393
(212) 578-2211 .. **Madden,** Sandra I '96 %MetLife -27-01 Qns Plz N -LIC 11101
(315) 676-2222 .. **Madden,** Stephanie A '95 (O'Connell Law Firm) -3269 Fulton Av Bx567 -Centrl Sq 13036 **Fx:**676-2219
(518) 272-8289 .. **Madden,** Wm Patrick '84 %Troy Rehab -Bx1249 -Troy 12181
(212) 461-5505 .. **Maddi,** Thos W '96 CIT Group Inc -11 W 42nd -NY 10036
(718) 291-2100 .. **Maddiwar,** Rajesh '98 -167-18 Hillside Av -Jamaica 11432
(212) 416-8627 .. **Maddox,** Barbara Demchuk '86 %Dept of Law -120 Bway -NY 10271
(212) 696-1999 .. **Maddox,** Brian D '05 %Lax & N LLP -1412 Bway -NY 10018
(212) 450-4000 .. **Maddox,** Matthew R '09 %Davis P&W LLP -450 Lex Av -NY 10017
(212) 450-4000 .. **Maddox,** Zoe J G '06 %Davis P&W LLP -450 Lex Av -NY 10017
(212) 819-8200 .. **Maddrey,** Wendell C '83 (White & C LLP) -1155 Av of Amer -NY 10036
(518) 689-1412 .. **Madeiros,** Pamela A '84 (Greenberg T,LLP) -54 State -Albany 12207
(212) 791-7791 .. **Madeo,** Donald F '94 (Madeo & F) -299 Bway -NY 10007 **Fx:**791-9706
(212) 935-3000 .. **Madeo,** Jill M '09 %Mintz LCFG&P,PC -666 3rd Av -NY 10017
(212) 849-7000 .. **Mader,** David S '09 %Quinn EU&S,LLP -51 Mad Av -NY 10010
(212) 648-0588 .. **Mader,** Leanne M '98 JP Morgan Chase -245 Park Av -NY 10017
(845) 471-5053 .. **Madera,** Jeanette '93 -Bx1203 -Poughkeepsie 12602
(212) 461-2323 .. **Maderer,** Wm F '73 (Saiber LLC) -44 Wall -NY 10005
(212) 474-1000 .. **Mades,** Dean M '06 %Cravath S&M LLP -825 8th Av -NY 10019
(516) 248-6050 .. **Madey,** R Gregory Jr. '03 -114 Old Cntry Rd -Mineola 11501
(315) 866-6600 .. **Madia,** Frank L '99 %GF Aney -401 N Prospect -Herkimer 13350 **Fx:**866-7860
(212) 227-1980 .. **Madigan,** Edw J '86 (Meltzer FM&C) -225 Bway -NY 10007
(607) 763-9200 .. **Madigan,** Kathryn Grant '79 (Levene G&T,LLP) -BxF-1706 -Bnghmtn 13902
(212) 839-5300 .. **Madigan,** Michl '90 (Sidley A LLP) -787 7th Av -NY 10019
(516) 741-2121 .. **Madigan,** Richd M '77 %N Kanzer -1325 Franklin Av -Gdn Cty 11530 **Fx:**741-3930
(607) 723-9511 .. **Madigan,** Robt J Jr. '78 (Coughlin & G,LLP) -19 Chenango Bx2039 -Bnghmtn 13902

(607) 637-3707 .. **Madigan,** Robt J Jr. '78 (Coughlin & G,LLP) -125 Wheeler -Hancock 13783
(607) 467-4010 .. **Madigan,** Robt J Jr. '78 (Coughlin & G,LLP) -105 Front Bx147 -Deposit 13754
(607) 776-4031 .. **Madigan,** S A '96 -16 W Pulteney Sq Bx214 -Bath 14810
(212) 705-9300 .. **Madigan,** Sarah N '05 BBC Wrldwide Amer -747 3rd Av -NY 10017
(631) 852-6000 .. **Madigan,** Wm F '06 Suffolk Cnty Police Dept -30 Yaphank Av -Yaphank 11980
(212) 636-6000 .. **Madison,** Michl '67 %Fordham Univ Sch of Law -140 W 62nd -NY 10023 **Fx:**636-6899
(607) 652-2402 .. **Madison,** Paul G J '89 -31 Harper -Stamfrd 12167
(212) 514-8087 .. **Madison,** Peter J '71 -111 John -NY 10038
(212) 682-3161 .. **Madison,** Richd J '75 -708 3rd Av -NY 10017 **Fx:**661-6328
(718) 250-2000 .. **Madni,** Sabeeha I '05 %DA -350 Jay -Brklyn 11201 **Fx:**250-2314
(212) 759-4600 .. **Madoff,** Emily '80 (Wolf P LLP) -845 3rd Av -NY 10022
(646) 471-4000 .. **Madole,** Ewing '86 %PricewaterhouseCoopers LLP -300 Mad Av -NY 10017
(212) 947-9779 .. **Madon,** Meredith I '05 Advocates for Children -151 W 30th -NY 10001
(212) 759-9740 .. **Madon,** Roger H '73 (Madon M,PC) -260 Mad Av -NY 10016 **Fx:**759-7063
(518) 561-6800 .. **Madonna,** Carl J '78 -219 Champlain Dr -Plattsbrgh 12901 **Fx:**563-1196
(914) 843-4552 .. **Madonna,** Kevin J '99 (Kennedy & M LLP) -78 N Bway -White Plns 10603
(212) 750-1200 .. **Madonna,** Michl A '93 (Trolman G&L,PC) -777 3rd Av -NY 10017
(718) 518-1075 .. **Madonna,** Wm J '91 -991 Morris Park Av -Bronx 10462
(718) 780-7997 .. **Madow,** Michl P '83 %Bklyn Law Schl -250 Joralemon -Brklyn 11201 **Fx:**780-0393
(585) 387-7031 .. **Madrazo,** Brian P '93 Paychex Inc -911 Panorama Trl S -Rchstr 14625
(212) 404-6926 .. **Madrid,** Andres N '92 -1230 Av of Amer -NY 10020 **Fx:**(917) 536-9981
(646) 386-5136 .. **Madrid,** Jeanette '91 %Family Ct -60 Lafayette -NY 10013
(212) 603-6122 .. **Madrigano,** Jonathan '96 Citi Family Ofc -31 W 52nd -NY 10019 **Fx:**765-1057
(212) 806-5400 .. **Madris,** Richd G '95 (Stroock &S&L LLP) -180 Maiden Ln -NY 10038
(212) 637-2715 .. **Madsen,** Bertrand R '03 US Atty -86 Chmbrs -NY 10007
(518) 220-1850 .. **Madsen,** Jonathan M '05 %Schmeiser O&W -22 Century Hill Dr -Latham 12110
(631) 261-8834 .. **Madsen,** Jos E '88 %Ingerman S LLP -150 Motor Pkwy -Hauppauge 11788
(516) 465-8090 .. **Madsen,** Patricia '88 North Shore-LIJ Hlth Systm -145 Community Dr -Gt Neck 11021 **Fx:**465-8013
(212) 474-1000 .. **Madsen,** Stephen S '81 (Cravath S&M LLP) -825 8th Av -NY 10019
(212) 773-5061 .. **Madsen,** Steven W '82 Ernst & Young LLP -5 Times Sq -NY 10036
(212) 590-2414 .. **Madu Edozie & Madu,PC** -304 Park Av S -NY 10010 **Fx:**590-2413
(718) 379-3500 .. **Madu Edozie & Madu,PC** -3007 Eastchstr Rd -Bronx 10469 **Fx:**379-6246
(212) 918-4868 .. **Maduabum,** Peter A '04 (Cobos EM&M,LLC) -48 Wall -NY 10005 **Fx:**918-4801
(212) 547-5400 .. **Madubuko,** Obiamaka P '99 (McDermott W&E LLP) -340 Mad Av -NY 10173
(212) 232-0155 .. **Maduegbuna,** Saml O '93 (Maduegbuna C,LLP) -110 Wall -NY 10005
(212) 735-3000 .. **Madunic,** Jelena '10 %Skadden ASM&F LLP -4 Times Sq -NY 10036
(914) 238-8582 .. **Maduras,** John S '81 -190 S Bedford Rd -Chappaqua 10514
(212) 384-1000 .. **Maduro,** Denis B '80 %FBI -26 Fed Plz -NY 10278
(631) 265-2077 .. **Mady,** Matthew K '07 (Castrovinci & M) -1 Edgewood Av -Smithtwn 11787 **Fx:**265-0627
(212) 422-1200 .. **Maeglin,** Thos R '04 %Abrams GF&J,PC -1 Bttry Pk Plz -NY 10004
(516) 222-6200 .. **Mael,** Bruce D '90 %Berkman HPP&F,PC -100 Grdn City Plz -Gdn Cty 11530
(917) 921-9472 .. **Maemoto,** Mari '01 (M Maemoto,PC) -1178 Bway -NY 10001 **Fx:**(212) 202-3532
(212) 219-3360 .. **Maer,** Foster S '81 %Latino Justice PRLDEF -99 Hudson -NY 10013 **Fx:**431-4276
(212) 587-4112 .. **Maerov,** Michelle E '94 %Dept of Law -120 Bway -NY 10271
(516) 496-5822 .. **Maertz,** Jennifer J '06 Cnsl T Spina -170 Froehlich Farm Blvd -Woodbury 11797 **Fx:**496-5420
(212) 618-2060 .. **Maese,** Vivian A '83 BIDS Trading,LP -111 Bway -NY 10006 **Fx:**618-2031
(585) 546-5530 .. **Maess,** Jean E '83 %Thomson West -50 E Broad -Rchstr 14694
(315) 433-2629 .. **Maestri,** David G '99 %BOCES -6820 Thompson Rd -Syracuse 13211
(631) 360-0400 .. **Maffei,** Frank M Jr. '87 (Jakubowski RMG&T) -969 Jericho Tpk -St James 11780 **Fx:**360-0408
(914) 961-1515 .. **Maffei,** Lawr L '67 (Maffei M&K) -35 E Grassy Sprain Rd -Ynkrs 10710 **Fx:**961-2976
(516) 746-8000 .. **Maffei,** Steven '04 %Jaspan S LLP -300 Grdn City Plz -Gdn Cty 11530
(718) 491-9397 .. **Maffei,** Steven J '96 -544 Bay Ridge Pkwy -Brklyn 11209 **Fx:**745-2786
(212) 883-4900 .. **Maffeo,** J Bruce '80 (Cozen O) -277 Park Av -NY 10172
(516) 326-2400 .. **Maffia,** Anthony M '03 %Ivone D&J,LLP -2001 Marcus Av -Lk Success 11042
(212) 728-8000 .. **Maffucci,** Amy E '10 %Willkie F&G LLP -787 7th Av -NY 10019
(212) 250-8481 .. **Maffucci,** Marianna '84 %Deutsche Bank -60 Wall -NY 10005
(315) 699-3095 .. **Mafrici,** Thos B '92 Mafrici Law Ofc -8355 US Route 11 -Cicero 13039 **Fx:**699-3809
(646) 386-3168 .. **Magaldi,** Rose Ann '82 Hon A Schlesinger -60 Centre -NY 10007
(212) 710-3900 .. **Magali,** Nicholas L '95 %Clyde & Co US LLP -405 Lex Av -NY 10174 **Fx:**710-3950
(212) 594-5000 .. **Magaliff,** Howard P '85 %Togut S&S LLP -1 Penn Plz -NY 10119
(212) 909-6000 .. **Magaram,** Kate A '10 %Debevoise & P LLP -919 3rd Av -NY 10022
(212) 764-4222 .. **Magardichian,** Lucy '06 %S Jeffries & Assoc -1560 Bway -NY 10036 **Fx:**764-4229
(631) 581-1930 .. **Magarelli Giannone,** Kathreen A '94 Amer Lawyer Media -128 Carleton Av -E Islip 11730 **Fx:**581-7420
(212) 594-8870 .. **Magarian,** John J '03 %C Young & Assoc -104 W 40th -NY 10018
(212) 358-1500 .. **Magarik,** Larry '79 OfCnsl Kennedy J&M,PC -113 Univ Pl -NY 10003
(518) 443-2220 .. **Magaril,** Paul '85 Cnsl PCI -90 S Swan -Albany 12210 **Fx:**443-2237
(716) 856-3500 .. **Magavern,** James L '59 OfCnsl Magavern MG LLP -1100 Rand Bldg -Buffalo 14203
(716) 649-1571 .. **Magavern,** Jeffrey C '90 (Magavern & L,PC) -71 Main -Hambrg 14075
(716) 649-1571 .. **Magavern & Loretto, PC** -71 Main -Hambrg 14075 **Fx:**648-6187
(716) 856-3500 .. **Magavern Magavern Grimm LLP** -1100 Rand Bldg -Buffalo 14203 **Fx:**856-3390
(716) 874-2111 .. **Magavern Magavern Grimm LLP** -3080 Delaware Av -Kenmore 14217 **Fx:**874-0680
(716) 285-1550 .. **Magavern Magavern Grimm LLP** -810 Main -Niagara Fls 14301 **Fx:**285-1559
(716) 649-1571 .. **Magavern,** Willard J Jr. '62 (Magavern & L,PC) -71 Main -Hambrg 14075
(716) 856-3500 .. **Magavern,** Wm J II '62 OfCnsl Magavern MG LLP -1100 Rand Bldg -Buffalo 14203
(516) 741-7575 .. **Magbitang,** Myles J '00 %Vecchione V&C LLP -147 Hrrcks Rd -Gdn Cty Pk 11040 **Fx:**294-4636
(718) 389-4112 .. **Magda,** Romuald P '95 -776A Manh Av -Brklyn 11222 **Fx:**389-4685
(212) 820-7700 .. **Magedoff,** Ari R '04 %Boundas SW&B,LLC -1 Bttry Pk Plz -NY 10004
(212) 871-5711 .. **Magedoff,** Laura J '04 (Nissenbaum Law Grp,LLC) -140 Bway -NY 10005 **Fx:**871-5712
(516) 255-4616 .. **Magee,** Blane '79 -77 N Centre Av -Rockvll Ctr 11570 **Fx:**255-9183
(212) 422-1080 .. **Magee,** Deborah Ann '85 -70 West -NY 10006 **Fx:**422-1090
(718) 250-2000 .. **Magee,** James W '07 %DA -350 Jay -Brklyn 11201 **Fx:**250-2314
(585) 225-3080 .. **Magee,** Mary E '89 Parrs & P LLP -105 Canal Lndng Blvd -Rchstr 14626 **Fx:**225-0459
(212) 474-1000 .. **Magel,** Gina M '09 %Cravath S&M LLP -825 8th Av -NY 10019
(646) 264-3650 .. **Magenheimer,** James A '75 %US Dept of Labor -201 Varick -NY 10014 **Fx:**264-3660
(212) 732-2292 .. **Mager,** Matthew R '95 %Jasper & J -299 Bway -NY 10007 **Fx:**349-1724
(518) 426-4600 .. **Mager,** Michl B '91 (Couch W,LLP) -540 Bway Bx22222 -Albany 12201
(212) 733-7058 .. **Mages,** Rubie A '74 %Pfizer Inc -235 E 42nd -NY 10017
(212) 684-1911 .. **Magett,** Carol Elyse '83 (Magett & Assoc) -381 Park Av S -NY 10016 **Fx:**213-1092
(212) 756-2000 .. **Maggi,** Michl S '05 %Schulte R&Z LLP -919 3rd Av -NY 10022
(516) 365-1200 .. **Maggiani,** Euclid F '55 -1295 Nrthrn Blvd -Manhsst 11030 **Fx:**365-5668
(212) 608-1600 .. **Maggiano,** Michl Jos '76 (Maggiano D&L,PC) -521 5th Av -NY 10175
(914) 765-4083 .. **Maggin,** Bruce R '79 %IBM -North Castle Dr -Armonk 10504
(914) 835-3404 .. **Maggio,** Andrew J '01 (Maggio & Assoc) -141 E Bstn Post Rd -Mamaroneck 10543
(585) 232-3360 .. **Maggio,** Frank G '79 -One E Main -Rchstr 14614
(212) 490-9100 .. **Maggio,** John '97 (Condon & F LLP) -7 Times Sq -NY 10036
(212) 398-8881 .. **Maggioni,** Ilaria '02 %R Kunstadt,PC -875 6th Av -NY 10001 **Fx:**398-2922
(646) 502-2023 .. **Maggiora,** Cristiana I '02 Fila USA Inc -340 Mad Av -NY 10173
(914) 337-6300 .. **Maggiotto,** Louis J Jr. '74 OfCnsl Nobile M&D,LLP -111 Kraft Av -Bronxvll 10708
(631) 584-7144 .. **Maggipinto,** V Anthony '78 -Moriches Rd Bx471 -St James 11780
(518) 429-4200 .. **Maggs,** Amy J '03 OfCnsl Hiscock & B,LLP -50 Beaver -Albany 12207
(607) 733-4635 .. **Maggs,** Bryan J '01 %Davidson & O,PC -243 Lk -Elmira 14901
(518) 783-2704 .. **Magguilli,** Michl C '82 Colonie Town Atty -Mem'l Town Hall Bx508 -Newtonville 12128 **Fx:**786-7324
(518) 434-1121 .. **Magguilli,** Michl C '82 (Bloomberg & M) -Bx714 -Newtonville 12128
(212) 916-6328 .. **Maghlar,** Livia L '91 %TIAA CREF -730 3rd Av -NY 10017
(212) 558-4000 .. **Magid,** Adam K '09 %Sullivan & C LLP -125 Broad -NY 10004
(631) 845-2430 .. **Magid,** Patricia M '81 Zurich NA -58 S Srvc Rd -Melvll 11747
(718) 675-8589 .. **Magid,** Stephen H '85 %Supreme Ct -18 Richmond Ter -Staten Isl 10301
(212) 909-6000 .. **Magida,** Danl J '05 %Debevoise & P LLP -919 3rd Av -NY 10022
(646) 602-5649 .. **Magida,** Jennifer B '06 Urban Justice Ctr -123 William -NY 10038 **Fx:**(212) 533-4598
(516) 829-2929 .. **Magida,** Kenneth S '74 -98 Cuttermill Rd -Gt Neck 11021 **Fx:**466-2799
(212) 969-3000 .. **Magier,** Heather G '86 %Proskauer R LLP -1585 Bway -NY 10036
(212) 734-9500 .. **Magier,** Leora A '86 -156A E 83rd -NY 10028 **Fx:**628-8194
(212) 564-8525 .. **Magier,** Seymour '74 (Magier & S) -450 7th Av -NY 10123 **Fx:**967-0867
(631) 852-8600 .. **Magill,** Bradford S III '03 %DA -Feather Hill Shopping Ctr Main Rd -Southold 11971
(718) 624-1327 .. **Magill,** Goldah Brenner '84 -44 Court -Brklyn 11201 **Fx:**624-0198
(212) 752-5200 .. **Magill,** Robt T '00 Green Levin Snyder -150 E 58th -NY 10155 **Fx:**752-8245
(516) 773-1491 .. **Magilligan,** Eileen R '95 %Lakeville School -47-27 Jayson Av -Gt Neck 11020
(212) 403-1000 .. **Maginley,** Olivia A '10 %Wachtell LR&K -51 W 52nd -NY 10019
(212) 619-6000 .. **Magistre,** Dervis '96 (Fay K&M,LLP) -150 Bway -NY 10038 **Fx:**208-6879
(718) 260-2410 .. **Magliana,** Melissa Ann '05 Hon CB Amon -225 Cadman Plz E -Brklyn 11201
(212) 636-6000 .. **Magliano,** Carlynn R '03 Fordham Univ Sch of Law -140 W 62nd -NY 10023 **Fx:**636-6899
(212) 779-8600 .. **Magliano,** Wm A '92 %Silverman SS&B PLLC -381 Park Av S -NY 10016
(212) 819-8200 .. **Maglich,** Marko C '00 %White & C LLP -1155 Av of Amer -NY 10036
(518) 402-9188 .. **Maglienti,** Jennifer L '99 %DEC -625 Bway -Albany 12233 **Fx:**402-9018
(212) 248-2220 .. **Magliery,** John M '03 %Kennedy JG LLC -99 Wall -NY 10005 **Fx:**248-0170
(718) 383-5500 .. **Magliocco,** Antonio Jr. '78 %Peerless Importers -16 Brdgwtr -Brklyn 11222
(718) 383-5500 .. **Magliocco,** Jos J '83 %Peerless Importers -16 Brdgwtr -Brklyn 11222

(212) 962-1550 .. **Magliochetti,** Scott D '89 Starpoint Solutions -115 Bway -NY 10006
(718) 590-2926 .. **Magnani,** Linda A '84 %Criminal Ct -265 E 161st -Bronx 10451
(212) 428-2100 .. **Magnani,** Michl J '83 %OCA -25 Beaver -NY 10004 **Fx:**428-2188
(718) 250-2000 .. **Magnani,** Samantha '97 %DA -350 Jay -Brklyn 11201 **Fx:**250-2314
(973) 218-1161 .. **Magnanini,** Robt A '94 (Boies S&F LLP) -575 Lex Av -NY 10022 **Fx:**218-1106
(917) 534-4944 .. **Magnano,** Jos S '80 Centre Grp Holdings,LLC -105 E 17th -NY 10003
(315) 487-6650 .. **Magnarelli,** David J '78 -5111 W Genesee -Camillus 13031 **Fx:**487-2990
(315) 471-8111 .. **Magnarelli,** Wm B '74 (Scolaro SCF&B,PC) -507 Plum -Syracuse 13204
(212) 468-8000 .. **Magnas,** Jos R '00 %Morrison & F LLP -1290 Av of Amer -NY 10104
(212) 612-4365 .. **Magner,** Matthew A '98 Chubb Grp -55 Water -NY 10041
(914) 332-1800 .. **Magnetti,** Ralph E '87 (Cherry E&K,LLP) -150 Wht Plns Rd -Tarrytwn 10591
(718) 447-1810 .. **Magnotti,** Jos E '72 (Napolitano & M) -1492 Victory Blvd -Staten Isl 10301
(516) 299-5556 .. **Magnozzi,** Mark F '97 (Magnozzi & K,LLP) -1 Expwy Plz -Roslyn Hts 11577 **Fx:**299-5598
(212) 883-0007 .. **Magnus,** Ilysa M '94 I Magnus,PC -60 E 42nd -NY 10165 **Fx:**883-0040
(914) 949-3443 .. **Magnus,** Lee '53 -175 Main -White Plns 10601 **Fx:**948-6051
(716) 871-9050 .. **Magnuson,** Cory R '04 %Capital Mgmt Svcs -726 Exchange -Buffalo 14210
(212) 846-5963 .. **Magnuson,** Leah M '99 MTV Networks -1515 Bway -NY 10036
(315) 785-2239 .. **Magnuson,** Nels G '89 DEC -317 Wshngtn -Watertwn 13601 **Fx:**785-2242
(914) 964-8888 .. **Magoolaghan,** Joan M '79 (Koob & M) -221 Devoe Av -Ynkrs 10705
(212) 758-3838 .. **Magory,** Vallerie V '89 -160 E 56th -NY 10022
(212) 962-1450 .. **Magovern,** Fredk J '72 (Magovern & S) -111 John -NY 10038
(212) 223-0400 .. **Magovern,** John J '75 OfCnsl Zeichner E&K LLP -575 Lex Av -NY 10022
(212) 962-1450 .. **Magovern & Sclafani** -111 John -NY 10038 **Fx:**385-0235
(212) 966-5932 .. **Magpantay,** Glenn D '99 %AALDEF -99 Hudson -NY 10013 **Fx:**966-4303
(212) 688-5151 .. **Magrath,** Christopher W M '86 OfCnsl Gibney A&F,LLP -665 5th Av -NY 10022
(212) 859-8000 .. **Magri,** Eren '08 %Fried FHS&J LLP -1 NY Plz -NY 10004
(718) 286-7413 .. **Magri,** John F '92 %FBI -80-02 Kew Grdns Rd -Kew Gdns 11415
(212) 688-7267 .. **Magri,** Philip '96 Trump Entrtnmnt Resorts -725 5th Av -NY 10022
(212) 883-8833 .. **Magrino,** John W '05 %Tacopina & A -275 Mad Av -NY 10016
(845) 639-2411 .. **Magrino,** Robt V '93 -10 Esquire Rd -New Cty 10956 **Fx:**638-1912
(718) 728-4000 .. **Magriples,** George '84 -21-71 Steinway -LIC 11105 **Fx:**728-2002
(914) 779-5258 .. **Magro,** Richd D '53 -26 Ivanhoe Pl -Ynkrs 10710 **Fx:**779-5258
(914) 946-1400 .. **Magro,** Richd L '67 (Vouté LM&C,LLP) -170 Hmltn Av -White Plns 10601
(212) 788-8899 .. **Magsino,** Teresita V '07 %Law Dept -100 Church -NY 10007 **Fx:**788-0367
(212) 998-6430 .. **Maguigan,** Holly '92 %NYU Law Schl -245 Sullivan -NY 10012 **Fx:**995-4031
(914) 631-4419 .. **Maguill,** Geraldine P '00 -58 Rosehill Av -Tarrytwn 10591
(212) 819-8200 .. **Maguire,** Cecily P '87 Cnsl White & C LLP -1155 Av of Amer -NY 10036
(212) 848-4000 .. **Maguire,** Eileen '85 Cnsl Shearman & S LLP -599 Lex Av -NY 10022
(212) 909-6000 .. **Maguire,** George E B '87 (Debevoise & P LLP) -919 3rd Av -NY 10022
(516) 229-6000 .. **Maguire,** Jane M '76 %R Lau & Assoc -300 Jericho Quad Bx9040 -Jericho 11753 **Fx:**229-6167
(516) 627-5512 .. **Maguire,** Kate E '93 -10 Knolls Ln -Manhsst 11030 **Fx:**627-1113
(516) 357-3000 .. **Maguire,** Katherine M '10 %Rivkin R LLP -926 RXR Plz -Uniondale 11556
(516) 228-8400 .. **Maguire,** Kenneth R '82 (Shay & M LLP) -1900 Hempstd Tpk -E Meadow 11554
(914) 946-1030 .. **Maguire,** Kevin G '88 (Barry M&M) -55 Church -White Plns 10601
(585) 425-5280 .. **Maguire,** Lisa K '93 Maximus Chtd -50 Square Dr -Victor 14564
(518) 434-9807 .. **Maguire,** Richd R '90 (D'Agostino KM&C,PC) -16 Sage Estate -Menands 12204
(718) 590-5436 .. **Maguire,** Sebastian '04 ACS -900 Sheridan Av -Bronx 10451
(212) 660-3000 .. **Maguire,** Sharon C '86 %Sullivan & W LLP -1290 Av of Amer -NY 10104
(914) 251-1525 .. **Maguire,** Theresa N '88 (Pollock & M,LLP) -106 Corp Park Dr -White Plns 10604
(212) 837-6000 .. **Maguire,** Wm R '86 (Hughes H&R LLP) -1 Bttry Pk Plz -NY 10004
(516) 396-6648 .. **Magwood,** Derrick '04 D Magwood LLC -380 N Bway -Jericho 11753 **Fx:**977-3350
(845) 291-2050 .. **Magwood,** Monique F '08 %DA -255-275 Main -Goshen 10924 **Fx:**291-2085
(212) 233-2828 .. **Mah,** Suk Wah '88 -2 Mott -NY 10013 **Fx:**233-8889
(718) 250-2000 .. **Mahabir,** Indira M '10 %DA -350 Jay -Brklyn 11201 **Fx:**250-2314
(914) 358-0041 .. **Mahadeva,** Prassana '02 (Mahadeva,PLLC) -445 Hmltn Av -White Plns 10601
(518) 434-2341 .. **Mahady,** Frank T '69 -Bx1223 -Albany 12201 **Fx:**436-4992
(212) 490-1700 .. **Mahajan,** Sarvesh '00 %Wiggin & D -450 Lex Av -NY 10017
(212) 474-1000 .. **Mahan,** Brendan R '10 %Cravath S&M LLP -825 8th Av -NY 10019
(585) 546-2404 .. **Mahan,** Francis B '70 -16 E Main -Rchstr 14614 **Fx:**546-2431
(212) 343-9600 .. **Mahan,** Michl H '07 J Peikoff,PC -173 E Bway -NY 10002 **Fx:**343-3043
(631) 854-8300 .. **Mahan,** Patrick J '95 %Cnty Police Dept -1630 5th Av -Bay Shr 11706
(518) 474-1331 .. **Mahar,** Amy J '91 Ofc Mntl Health -44 Holland Av -Albany 12229 **Fx:**473-7863
(518) 399-0188 .. **Mahar,** Lawr J '78 -Bx451 -Burnt Hlls 12027 **Fx:**399-0188
(845) 486-6800 .. **Mahar,** Thos D Jr. '64 OfCnsl McCabe & M LLP -63 Wshngtn Bx509 -Poughkeepsie 12602
(518) 474-8266 .. **Mahar,** Timothy J '85 %Dept of Health -Corning Twr 24th Fl -Albany 12237 **Fx:**473-2430
(914) 572-3147 .. **Mahatme,** Ujwala R '90 (Mahatme B,PLLC) -50 Main -White Plns 10606 **Fx:**722-4468
(212) 438-2412 .. **Mahdavian,** Sharif '94 %Standard & Poor's -55 Water -NY 10041
(212) 762-5558 .. **Mahendran,** M Sharmini '93 Morgan Stanley -1221 Av of Amer -NY 10020
(212) 413-5155 .. **Maher,** Aleena B '88 %USA Cable -30 Rckfllr -NY 10112
(212) 446-4800 .. **Maher,** Alejandro '04 %Kirkland & E LLP -153 E 53rd -NY 10022
(845) 228-5100 .. **Maher,** Christopher X '86 C Maher,LLC -105 Gleneida Av -Carmel 10512 **Fx:**228-5103
(212) 371-0033 .. **Maher,** Damon R '81 (Levy D&M,LLP) -29 Bway -NY 10006
(646) 292-5555 .. **Maher,** Danl F Jr. '82 Excess Line Assn of NY -55 Bway -NY 10006 **Fx:**292-5505
(212) 830-7722 .. **Maher,** Deborah A '02 Cnsl Randalls Islnd Sports Fndn -24 W 61st -NY 10023 **Fx:**830-7710
(212) 618-1250 .. **Maher,** Donald E '82 (Maher & B) -14 Wall -NY 10005 **Fx:**618-1251
(212) 455-9800 .. **Maher,** Gregory G '87 %LISC -501 Fashion Av -NY 10018 **Fx:**682-5929
(914) 713-0563 .. **Maher,** Heidi '94 -82 Greentree Dr -Scarsdale 10583
(914) 749-8200 .. **Maher,** Helen M '99 (Boies S&F LLP) -333 Main -Armonk 10504
(518) 891-4671 .. **Maher,** James E '78 -Bx627 -Saranac Lk 12983 **Fx:**891-4671
(908) 277-2444 .. **Maher,** John A '81 -1 Lbrty Plz -NY 10006 **Fx:**277-6888
(718) 931-3131 .. **Maher,** John A '93 (Kravet H&M,PC) -1135A Morris Park Av -Bronx 10461
(212) 562-3893 .. **Maher,** John J '09 Bellevue Hospital Ctr -462 1st Av -NY 10016 **Fx:**562-2769
(212) 279-3500 .. **Maher,** John T '90 OfCnsl Russin VB&B,LLP -260 Mad Av -NY 10016
(212) 455-9861 .. **Maher,** Kenneth P '99 LIS Corp -501 7th Av -NY 10018
(212) 854-6699 .. **Maher,** Laila Moussa '97 Columbia Univ -535 W 116th -NY 10027
(212) 286-0225 .. **Maher,** Patricia '06 %Casey & B LLC -65 W 36th -NY 10018 **Fx:**286-0261
(516) 487-7460 .. **Maher,** Randa D '88 (Maher & P,LLP) -14 Bond -Gt Neck 11021 **Fx:**977-3003
(212) 876-5500 .. **Maher,** Sean M '02 %Neighborhood Def Srv -317 Lenox Av -NY 10027 **Fx:**876-5586
(516) 802-3690 .. **Maher,** Tara A '89 -251 Post Av -Westbury 11590
(718) 260-7501 .. **Maher,** Theresa A '84 %Cumberland Hosp -100 N Portlnd Av -Brklyn 11205
(631) 265-0134 .. **Maher,** Thos F '92 %Kral CRRP&G,LLP -538 Broadhllw Rd -Melvll 11747 **Fx:**265-4289
(914) 633-2192 .. **Maher,** Vincent F '88 Iona Cllg -715 North Av -New Rchll 10801 **Fx:**633-2091
(212) 382-3300 .. **Maher,** Wm A '86 (Wollmuth M&D LLP) -500 5th Av -NY 10110
(914) 328-0404 .. **Maheran,** Tarek M '08 %Jackson L LLP -1 N Bway -White Plns 10601
(718) 236-4242 .. **Mahfouz,** Richd L '85 Mahfouz Sollazzo & Marangelli,LLP -6606 17th Av -Brklyn 11204
(212) 290-1833 .. **Mahl,** Joel D '75 OTDA Fair Hearings -330 W 34th -NY 10001
(212) 527-1000 .. **Mahlan,** Wm C Jr. '86 %Jones HC&B PC -1 Bttry Pk Plz -NY 10004
(212) 351-4000 .. **Mahlberg,** Cindy Chang '07 %Gibson D&C LLP -200 Park Av -NY 10166
(212) 326-3939 .. **Mahle,** David M '69 OfCnsl Jones D -222 E 41st -NY 10017
(212) 357-8373 .. **Mahle,** Lisa R '05 Goldman Sachs -180 Maiden Ln -NY 10038
(212) 889-7600 .. **Mahler,** Barry A '74 -274 Mad Av -NY 10016 **Fx:**889-9568
(718) 268-6000 .. **Mahler & Harris,PC** -125-10 Qns Blvd -Kew Gdns 11415 **Fx:**263-0134
(516) 227-0700 .. **Mahler,** Lyle C '96 (Farrell F,PC) -1320 RXR Plz -Uniondale 11556
(516) 334-3500 .. **Mahler,** Paul W '97 %Malen & Assoc,PC -123 Frost -Westbury 11590
(212) 687-1230 .. **Mahler,** Peter A '83 (Farrell F,PC) -370 Lex Av -NY 10017
(212) 472-9569 .. **Mahler,** Robt A '90 -419 E 64th -NY 10065 **Fx:**472-9785
(718) 268-6000 .. **Mahler,** Stephen R '64 (Mahler & H,PC) -125-10 Qns Blvd -Kew Gdns 11415
(631) 673-8362 .. **Mahlstadt,** Theresa M '06 %R Ross -141 E Main -Huntngtn 11743 **Fx:**673-5690
(212) 909-6000 .. **Mahmoudov,** Vadim '00 (Debevoise & P LLP) -919 3rd Av -NY 10022
(212) 478-0257 .. **Mahon,** Christopher J '87 %DE Shaw & Co -120 W 45th -NY 10036
(212) 819-8000 .. **Mahon,** James F Jr. '89 %Hecht & Co -622 3rd Av -NY 10017 **Fx:**302-0973
(212) 584-2990 .. **Mahon,** James J '76 (Lally M&R LLP) -36 W 44th -NY 10036
(516) 538-1111 .. **Mahon,** John P '48 OfCnsl Mahon MK&O,LLC -254 Nassau Blvd -Garden City South 11530
(516) 538-1111 .. **Mahon,** Kenneth P '86 (Mahon MK&O,LLC) -254 Nassau Blvd -Garden City South 11530
(212) 766-1888 .. **Mahon,** Kevin F '86 (Morris DA&F) -2 Rector -NY 10006
(516) 538-1111 .. **Mahon,** Lawr T '86 (Mahon MK&O,LLC) -254 Nassau Blvd -Garden City South 11530
(516) 538-1111 .. **Mahon Mahon Kerins & O'Brien,LLC** -254 Nassau Blvd -Garden City South 11530 **Fx:**538-1957
(516) 463-5864 .. **Mahon,** Malachy T Sr. '60 Hofstra Law Schl -121 Hofstra Univ -Hempstd 11549
(631) 820-3605 .. **Mahon,** Malachy T Jr. '92 -1160 E Jericho Tpk -Huntngtn 11743 **Fx:**470-3630
(516) 489-5000 .. **Mahon,** Mary Elizabeth '87 Town Atty -Town Hall -Hempstd 11550 **Fx:**489-5150
(718) 558-8264 .. **Mahon,** Mary Jennings '76 LIRR -Jamaica Station -Jamaica 11435 **Fx:**558-8211
(845) 675-7070 .. **Mahon,** Michl J '81 (Mahon VH) -83 Main -Nyack 10960 **Fx:**675-7072
(212) 416-6497 .. **Mahon,** Pamela Lynam '92 %Dept of Law -120 Bway -NY 10271
(845) 565-1100 .. **Mahon,** Richd M II '87 (Tarshis CLM&M,PLLC) -One Corwin Ct -Newburgh 12550
(914) 946-4053 .. **Mahon,** Stephanie M '77 -112 Grandvw Av -White Plns 10605
(212) 872-9800 .. **Mahon,** Stephen C '89 (Squire S&D LLP) -30 Rckfllr Plz -NY 10112
(212) 759-5800 .. **Mahon,** Susan P '90 %Gartner + B,PC -801 2nd Av -NY 10017
(212) 450-4000 .. **Mahone,** Darren C '09 %Davis P&W LLP -450 Lex Av -NY 10017
(212) 903-9000 .. **Mahoney,** Anne R '90 %Linklaters -1345 Av of Amer -NY 10105
(716) 200-5050 .. **Mahoney,** Brian C '88 (Harris B PLLC) -726 Exchange -Buffalo 14210
(212) 385-1422 .. **Mahoney,** Cornelius A '69 SrCnsl Mahoney & K,LLP -76 Beaver -NY 10005

(845) 294-7287 .. **Mahoney,** Dana L '99 %MHLS -5 Coates Dr -Goshen 10924 **Fx:**294-6389
(585) 243-1870 .. **Mahoney,** David B '70 -152 Court -Geneseo 14454 **Fx:**243-1874
(516) 479-6300 .. **Mahoney,** David J '02 %Silverman A LLP -100 Jericho Quad -Jericho 11753
(845) 294-4080 .. **Mahoney,** Dennis J III '85 %Burke M&G -40 Matthews Bx216 -Goshen 10924
(516) 334-5200 .. **Mahoney,** Donal M '82 -Bx488 -Mineola 11501
(518) 792-2117 .. **Mahoney,** Elisabeth B '04 %Bartlett PS&R,PC -1 Wshngtn Bx2168 -Glens Fls 12801
(212) 661-7300 .. **Mahoney,** George L '94 (Malapero & P LLP) -295 Mad Av -NY 10017
(212) 335-4500 .. **Mahoney,** Ian T '09 %DLA Piper LLP -1251 Av of Amer -NY 10020
(631) 422-2130 .. **Mahoney,** Jacqueline M '94 %V Berger Jr -133 E Main -Babylon 11702
(716) 853-1616 .. **Mahoney,** James W '08 %Harter S&E LLP -12 Fountain Plz -Buffalo 14202
(845) 279-4989 .. **Mahoney,** John W '87 -4 Fair Meadow Dr -Brewstr 10509 **Fx:**279-5748
(845) 291-3150 .. **Mahoney,** Jos F '98 %Cnty Atty -255 Main -Goshen 10924 **Fx:**291-3167
(718) 254-6026 .. **Mahoney,** Kathleen A '83 %US Atty -271 Cadman Plz E -Brklyn 11201 **Fx:**254-6479
(631) 261-7777 .. **Mahoney,** Kathleen M '87 -7 Bayview Av -Northprt 11768
(212) 966-2707 .. **Mahoney,** Kaye '01 -543 Bway -NY 10012
(212) 385-1422 .. **Mahoney & Keane, LLP** -76 Beaver -NY 10005 **Fx:**385-1605
(212) 676-7826 .. **Mahoney,** Kevin P '98 %Admin Children's Srvcs -60 Lafayette -NY 10013
(716) 636-7600 .. **Mahoney,** Kevin S '97 %HoganWillig -2410 N Forest Rd -Amherst 14068
(212) 387-8400 .. **Mahoney,** Lauren E '08 %Goldfarb AS&K LLP -350 5th Av -NY 10118
(212) 644-4420 .. **Mahoney,** Marc M '98 %Fabiani C&H,LLP -570 Lex Av -NY 10022
(716) 853-3700 .. **Mahoney,** Mark J '75 (Harrington & M) -70 Niagara -Buffalo 14202
(914) 949-1305 .. **Mahoney,** Mary E '89 %Leg Srvcs -90 Maple Av -White Plns 10601 **Fx:**949-6213
(212) 573-1870 .. **Mahoney,** Michl G '96 %Pfizer Inc -235 E 42nd -NY 10017 **Fx:**808-6468
(585) 786-8450 .. **Mahoney,** Neal J '88 %Leg Aid -18 Linwood Av -Warsaw 14569 **Fx:**786-8478
(516) 229-6000 .. **Mahoney,** Patrick J '75 %R Lau & Assoc -300 Jericho Quad Bx9040 -Jericho 11753 **Fx:**229-6167
(212) 417-5300 .. **Mahoney,** Paul J '91 Medicaid Fraud Cntrl -120 Bway -NY 10271 **Fx:**417-5274
(212) 351-4000 .. **Mahoney,** Stacey Anne '95 (Gibson D&C LLP) -200 Park Av -NY 10166
(585) 344-7907 .. **Mahoney,** Stephen M '90 %Genesee Valley BOCES -80 Munson -Le Roy 14482 **Fx:**344-7909
(718) 898-9400 .. **Mahoney,** Thos P L '95 -62-87 Woodhvn Blvd -Rego Pk 11374 **Fx:**898-9823
(518) 827-8008 .. **Mahoney,** Thos R '72 -123 Middle Fort Rd Bx784 -Middleburgh 12122 **Fx:**827-8077
(646) 522-8520 .. **Mahoney,** Timothy M '04 -6531 Fitchett Bx6451 -Rego Pk 11374
(212) 530-5000 .. **Mahoney,** Wm J '79 (Milbank TH&M LLP) -1 Chase Manh Plz -NY 10005
(212) 335-9000 .. **Mahoney,** Wm P '86 %DA -1 Hogan Pl -NY 10013
(516) 746-8000 .. **Mahony,** Andrew M '91 (Jaspan S LLP) -300 Grdn City Plz -Gdn City 11530
(212) 806-5400 .. **Mahony,** Evelyn M '08 %Stroock &S&L LLP -180 Maiden Ln -NY 10038
(516) 248-6500 .. **Mahony,** Harold A '58 (Froehlich M&D) -34 Willis Av -Mineola 11501
(716) 204-9480 .. **Mahony,** Phillip '06 %SJ Baum,PC -900 Merchants Cncrs -Westbury 11590 **Fx:**204-9680
(646) 386-3359 .. **Mahowald,** Lisa M '03 Hon B Fried -60 Centre -NY 10007
(315) 471-8111 .. **Mahr,** Douglas J '91 (Scolaro SCF&B,PC) -507 Plum -Syracuse 13204
(518) 383-1182 .. **Mahserjian,** Jean M '86 J Mahserjian,PC -1741 Route 9 -Clifton Pk 12065 **Fx:**375-9348
(212) 425-7200 .. **Mahtani,** Amit M '09 %Kenyon & K,LLP -1 Bway -NY 10004
(212) 705-7000 .. **Mai,** Stephanie W '02 Cnsl Bingham M LLP -399 Park Av -NY 10022
(716) 845-6000 .. **Maibohm,** Danielle P '06 %Kavinoky C LLP -726 Exchange -Buffalo 14210
(716) 853-9555 .. **Maichle,** Danielle H '83 %Leg Aid -237 Main -Buffalo 14203 **Fx:**853-3219
(212) 964-6611 .. **Maida,** Rachel T '06 %Lester SK&D -120 Bway -NY 10271
(914) 769-4000 .. **Maida,** Toni Anne '91 (Wren & M,LLP) -343 Manvll Rd -Plsntvll 10570 **Fx:**769-4153
(516) 223-8553 .. **Maidenbaum,** Jeffrey A '85 (Maidenbaum & Assoc PLLC) -1 Broadcast Plz -Merrick 11566 **Fx:**223-7096
(516) 569-8100 .. **Maidenbaum,** Shalom S '87 (Rosenfeld & M) -132 Spruce -Cedarhrst 11516
(212) 732-4800 .. **Maidens,** Melinda B '86 %Jeffer H&V -150 Bway -NY 10038
(518) 436-0344 .. **Maider,** Richd C '96 %Deily M&G,LLP -8 Thurlow Ter -Albany 12203
(518) 725-7195 .. **Maider,** Robt L '58 (Maider & S) -37 E Fulton -Gloversvll 12078
(518) 725-7195 .. **Maider & Smith** -37 E Fulton -Gloversvll 12078 **Fx:**773-3343
(212) 755-0500 .. **Maidman,** Gregory L '93 (Maidman and M,LLP) -70 E 55th -NY 10022
(212) 755-0500 .. **Maidman,** Mitchel A '89 (Maidman and M,LLP) -70 E 55th -NY 10022
(212) 755-0500 .. **Maidman and Mittelman,LLP** -70 E 55th -NY 10022 **Fx:**319-4549
(212) 755-0500 .. **Maidman,** Richd H M '61 OfCnsl Maidman and M,LLP -70 E 55th -NY 10022
(518) 664-2951 .. **Maiello,** Matthew A '08 %Carola B&T,PLLC -215 Park Av -Mechanicvll 12118 **Fx:**664-1150
(212) 696-6000 .. **Maier,** Alexandra '06 %Curtis M-PC&M LLP -101 Park Av -NY 10178
(516) 746-6235 .. **Maier,** Betty Ann '87 -153 Andrews Rd -Mineola 11501 **Fx:**741-6717
(212) 230-8800 .. **Maier,** Cosmin '08 %WilmerHale -399 Park Av -NY 10022
(845) 340-0010 .. **Maier,** John III '74 -Bx2324 -Kingston 12402 **Fx:**340-0099
(516) 694-3000 .. **Maier,** Kathryn J '09 %Guercio & G,LLP -77 Conklin -Farmngdl 11735 **Fx:**694-4738
(914) 285-9800 .. **Maier,** Lynn J '77 (Kurzman EC&L,LLP) -1 N Bway -White Plns 10601
(212) 610-6300 .. **Maier,** Michl T '09 %Allen & O -1221 Av of Amer -NY 10020
(845) 782-3685 .. **Maier,** Mitchell B '92 -132 Stage Rd -Monroe 10950 **Fx:**782-6403
(212) 277-6500 .. **Maier,** Paul C '07 %Dickstein S LLP -1633 Bway -NY 10019
(718) 722-4545 .. **Maier,** Philip L '82 PERB -55 Hanson Pl -Brklyn 11217 **Fx:**722-4550
(212) 408-2500 .. **Maier,** Robt L '03 %Baker B,LLP -30 Rckfllr Plz -NY 10112
(845) 454-1919 .. **Maier-Lore,** Angela J '90 %V Catalano -4 Lbrty -Poughkeepsie 12601
(718) 720-3900 .. **Maietta,** Carl A '02 %Kuhn & O,LLP -1 Edgewtr Plz -Staten Isl 10305
(716) 843-5700 .. **Maigret,** Richd P '75 %US Atty -138 Delaware Av -Buffalo 14202 **Fx:**551-3052
(518) 765-4184 .. **Maikoff,** Timothy N '92 -2 Winding Ln -Voorheesvll 12186
(212) 592-1400 .. **Mailman,** Gary '67 Cnsl Herrick,F LLP -2 Park Av -NY 10016
(212) 832-4000 .. **Mailman,** Jay N '73 OfCnsl Eisen & S,LLP -18 E 48th -NY 10017
(718) 598-0609 .. **Mailman,** Jeffrey S '10 -217-22 82nd Av -Qns Vllg 11427
(212) 735-2692 .. **Mailman,** Kevin D '03 Skadden ASM&F LLP -4 Times Sq -NY 10036 **Fx:**735-2000
(518) 851-7744 .. **Mailman,** Stanley '53 -160 Lockwood Rd -Craryville 12521
(212) 336-3620 .. **Maiman,** Jessica Z '09 %EEOC -33 Whitehall -NY 10004
(212) 868-0690 .. **Maiman,** Melvin '56 -45 Sutton Pl S -NY 10022
(212) 637-2238 .. **Maimin,** Michl D '00 %US Atty -1 St Andrews Plz -NY 10007
(212) 605-6200 .. **Maimon,** Moishe '86 (Levy P&K,LLP) -800 3rd Av -NY 10022
(718) 357-1216 .. **Maimone,** Albert M '05 (Forcina & M PC) -148-29 Cross Isl Pkwy -Whitestone 11357 **Fx:**357-1219
(516) 390-9595 .. **Maimone,** Thos J '78 (Maimone & Assoc,PLLC) -170 Old Cntry Rd -Mineola 11501 **Fx:**877-0321
(212) 455-2000 .. **Maimone-Medwick,** Jennifer '07 %Simpson T&B LLP -425 Lex Av -NY 10017
(212) 808-2700 .. **Mainali,** Bipul K '07 %Pepper H LLP -620 8th Av -NY 10018
(518) 218-2088 .. **Mainello,** Mark A '90 (Ruffo TM&M PC) -300 Great Oaks Blvd -Albany 12203
(607) 273-6444 .. **Maines,** Russell E '01 %Harris B PLLC -119 E Seneca -Ithaca 14850
(845) 331-9434 .. **Mainetti,** Alfred B '73 (Mainetti M&O,PC) -303 Clinton Av Bx3058 -Kingston 12402
(845) 331-9434 .. **Mainetti Mainetti & O'Connor,PC** -303 Clinton Av Bx3058 -Kingston 12402 **Fx:**331-2004
(718) 488-0701 .. **Mainiero,** Francis A '76 -26 Court -Brklyn 11242
(212) 267-6611 .. **Mainiero,** Jos J '84 -305 Bway -NY 10007 **Fx:**732-0888
(212) 403-1000 .. **Mainland,** Grant R '08 %Wachtell LR&K -51 W 52nd -NY 10019
(716) 649-2064 .. **Maino,** Louis R '83 -125 Alxndr Way Bx452 -Orchard Pk 14127
(212) 225-2000 .. **Mainoo,** Abena Ayowa '10 %Cleary GS&H -1 Lbrty Plz -NY 10006
(518) 402-0205 .. **Mains,** Wm M '92 %UIA Bd -Troy Atrium Bx15126 -Albany 12212 **Fx:**402-6208
(607) 734-3380 .. **Maio,** Steven P '91 (Hutchison & M) -315 Lk -Elmira 14901 **Fx:**734-3398
(607) 937-8383 .. **Maio,** Steven P '91 (Hutchison & M) -9 W 1st -Corning 14830 **Fx:**936-2410
(914) 347-2300 .. **Maiocchi,** Anthony J '79 -22 Saw Mill Rvr Rd -Hawthorne 10532 **Fx:**347-5047
(212) 878-7251 .. **Maiocchi,** Christine T '75 %MTA -347 Mad Av -NY 10017
(203) 504-1809 .. **Maiocco,** Adam V '07 %Heidell PM&B,LLP -99 Park Av -NY 10016 **Fx:**353-1892
(516) 692-8888 .. **Maioli,** Jay H '82 (F Chau & Assoc,LLC) -130 Woodbury Rd -Woodbury 11797 **Fx:**692-8889
(718) 298-1670 .. **Maiolo,** Sally R '88 Hon T Raffaele -88-11 Stuphin Blvd -Jamaica 11435 **Fx:**298-1155
(212) 406-1700 .. **Maiorana,** Matthew J '98 %Queller FWF&K LLP -233 Bway -NY 10279
(516) 229-4200 .. **Maiorino,** Peter P '01 %Mendolia & S -875 Merrick Av -Westbury 11590
(518) 402-1144 .. **Mair,** Andrew B '80 %Workers Comp Bd -20 Park -Albany 12207
(212) 338-9100 .. **Mair,** David N '92 (Kaiser S&M,PC) -111 Bway -NY 10006
(212) 474-1000 .. **Mair,** Patrick '07 %Cravath S&M LLP -825 8th Av -NY 10019
(212) 735-3000 .. **Mair,** Peter '08 %Skadden ASM&F LLP -4 Times Sq -NY 10036
(718) 354-3200 .. **Mair,** Zoie T '92 %Battiste A&S,Inc -60 Bay -Staten Isl 10301
(718) 368-2322 .. **Maira,** Jos B '97 -1229 Av Y -Brklyn 11235 **Fx:**368-3938
(212) 521-5400 .. **Maira,** Thos G '97 Cnsl Reed S LLP -599 Lex Av -NY 10022
(212) 269-1000 .. **Mairanz,** Theo T '81 (Neiman & M PC) -39 Bway -NY 10006
(212) 265-6888 .. **Mairo,** John S '95 (Porzio B&N,PC) -156 W 56th -NY 10019
(212) 323-1903 .. **Mairs,** Mimi Clark '97 OCME -421 E 26th -NY 10016
(914) 472-7882 .. **Mairs,** Patricia Ann '84 -12 Rutland Rd -Scarsdale 10583 **Fx:**472-7858
(212) 810-5277 .. **Mairzadeh,** S Gabriel '97 BlackRock Invstmnt Mgmt,LLC -55 E 52nd -NY 10055 **Fx:**810-8745
(718) 206-2411 .. **Mais,** Anna-Kae A '09 %Vernon & Assoc -9004 161st -Jamaica 11432 **Fx:**297-4263
(646) 386-3614 .. **Mais,** Michl E '86 %Supreme Ct-Law Dept -60 Centre -NY 10007
(347) 594-4483 .. **Mais,** Rina M '01 -901 Sheridan Av -Bronx 10451
(212) 223-4000 .. **Maisano,** James '93 Cnsl Crowell & M LLP -590 Mad Av -NY 10022
(718) 625-5320 .. **Maisel,** Drew A '86 D Maisel,PC -186 Joralemon -Brklyn 11201 **Fx:**625-4177
(212) 506-1700 .. **Maisel,** Rebecca L '08 %Kasowitz BT&F LLP -1633 Bway -NY 10019
(212) 373-3000 .. **Maisel,** Susan R '08 %Paul WRW&G LLP -1285 Av of Amer -NY 10019
(716) 631-4772 .. **Maislin,** Sam '73 -6720 Main -Williamsvll 14221
(646) 587-0188 .. **Maisonet,** Dimitri A '04 (Liou & M,PLLC) -124 Nassau -NY 10038 **Fx:**587-0187
(845) 454-3250 .. **Maissel,** Raina E '77 OfCnsl Gellert & K,PC -75 Wshngtn -Poughkeepsie 12601
(212) 682-0020 .. **Maisto,** Barbara M '97 (Putney TH&H LLP) -521 5th Av -NY 10175
(516) 565-0872 .. **Maisto,** Ellen T '83 -623 Grdn Ln -E Meadow 11554
(917) 817-8007 .. **Maistrow,** Brad S '85 -17 Battery Pl -NY 10004
(212) 791-8400 .. **Mait Wang & Simmons** -110 Wall -NY 10005 **Fx:**571-0070
(212) 791-8400 .. **Mait,** Wm R '74 (Mait W&S) -110 Wall -NY 10005

(212) 629-4970 .. **Maitland**, Gary '79 (Kreisberg & M,LLP) -116 John -NY 10038
(212) 486-0042 .. **Maitland**, Guy E C '69 Intl Registries -437 Mad Av -NY 10022 **Fx**:486-5313
(212) 906-1200 .. **Maitland**, Peter S '06 %Latham & W -885 3rd Av -NY 10022
(718) 823-4000 .. **Maizes**, Howard '58 (Maizes & M,LLP) -2027 Wllmsbrdg Rd -Bronx 10461 **Fx**:828-7644
(718) 823-4000 .. **Maizes**, Michl H '85 (Maizes & M,LLP) -2027 Wllmsbrdg Rd -Bronx 10461 **Fx**:828-7644
(718) 823-4000 .. **Maizes**, Steven R '86 (Maizes & M,LLP) -2027 Wllmsbrdg Rd -Bronx 10461 **Fx**:828-7644
(212) 644-1010 .. **Maizner**, Michl Z '04 %Kauff M&M LLP -950 3rd Av -NY 10022
(718) 349-3434 .. **Maj**, B Tomasz '95 -94-98 Nassau Av Bx204 -Brklyn 11222 **Fx**:349-3462
(585) 428-4181 .. **Majchrzak**, Danl P Jr. '92 Hon D Egan -99 Exchange Blvd -Rchstr 14614
(914) 238-9226 .. **Majerfeld-Perlmutter**, Aitana '87 -6 Whippoorwill Close -Chappaqua 10514
(212) 621-6000 .. **Majeske**, Martin R '97 %ASCAP -1 Lincoln Plz -NY 10023 **Fx**:787-1381
(631) 577-7740 .. **Majewski**, Michl '79 St Paul Travelers -100 Baylis Rd Bx9093 -Melvll 11747 **Fx**:577-7575
(917) 777-4200 .. **Majewski**, Thos M '96 (Bingham M LLP) -1 Bttry Pk Plz -NY 10004
(631) 582-5558 .. **Majid**, Arshad '00 (Majid Assoc PC) -300 Rabro Dr -Hauppauge 11788
(212) 832-8000 .. **Majid**, Natasha Z '04 Allen & Co -711 5th Av -NY 10022
(212) 310-8000 .. **Majid**, Saima '06 %Weil G&M LLP -767 5th Av -NY 10153
(516) 357-3000 .. **Majkowski**, Paul V '95 (Rivkin R LLP) -926 RXR Plz -Uniondale 11556
(212) 683-3154 .. **Major**, A Edw Jr. '88 -135 E 38th -NY 10016 **Fx**:370-0387
(518) 584-3129 .. **Major**, Mark A '84 -324 West Av -Saratoga Spgs 12866
(212) 686-8663 .. **Major**, Martin S '73 -211 E 38th -NY 10016
(212) 310-8000 .. **Majors**, C Hayward '02 %Weil G&M LLP -767 5th Av -NY 10153
(845) 338-8900 .. **Majorski**, Davor N '96 %A Zweben -12 John -Kingston 12401 **Fx**:338-8947
(212) 450-4000 .. **Majumdar**, Devasish '09 %Davis P&W LLP -450 Lex Av -NY 10017
(212) 450-4000 .. **Majumdar**, Shakhi '09 %Davis P&W LLP -450 Lex Av -NY 10017
(315) 442-0100 .. **Majumdar**, Somendu B '89 OfCnsl Gilberti SH&S,PC -555 E Genesee -Syracuse 13202
(212) 230-1300 .. **Mak**, Angela '02 %Beigelman F&F,PC -100 Wall -NY 10005 **Fx**:230-1090
(212) 704-6000 .. **Mak**, Clara W Y '04 %Troutman S LLP -405 Lex Av -NY 10174
(212) 701-3000 .. **Mak**, Gordon Y '09 %Cahill G&R LLP -80 Pine -NY 10005 **Fx**:269-5420
(212) 436-4318 .. **Mak**, Ilene '88 Deloitte & Touche,LLP -2 World Fncl Ctr -NY 10281
(212) 848-4000 .. **Mak**, Justin R '08 %Shearman & S LLP -599 Lex Av -NY 10022
(212) 351-4500 .. **Mak**, Raymond T '84 (Epstein B&G,PC) -250 Park Av -NY 10177
(212) 353-9005 .. **Makachi**, Chas C '02 De Novo Legal -150 E 42nd -NY 10017
(914) 995-2670 .. **Makanju**, Winston O '06 %Cnty Atty -148 Martine Av -White Plns 10601 **Fx**:995-5858
(212) 419-9394 .. **Makarius**, Michl T '07 Schlossberg:Flynn -111 5th Av -NY 10003
(212) 872-9800 .. **Makarowitz**, Jonathan M '99 OfCnsl Squire S&D LLP -30 Rckfllr Plz -NY 10112
(718) 643-1922 .. **Makau**, Elena K '92 -26 Court -Brklyn 11242 **Fx**:643-2007
(516) 279-6970 .. **Makelele**, Miali A '06 Makelele & Assoc,LLC -552 Uniondale Av -Uniondale 11553
(585) 454-4060 .. **Maker**, Ruhi '86 %Empire Justice Ctr -1 W Main -Rchstr 14614 **Fx**:454-4019
(914) 834-3500 .. **Maker**, Wm Jr. '76 (McMillan CM&P LLP) -2180 Bstn Post Rd -Larchmnt 10538
(212) 474-1000 .. **Makhdumi**, Fareeha M '02 %Cravath S&M LLP -825 8th Av -NY 10019
(212) 326-3939 .. **Maki**, J Eric '87 (Jones D) -222 E 41st -NY 10017
(212) 701-3000 .. **Makich**, Ann Serina '98 (Cahill G&R LLP) -80 Pine -NY 10005 **Fx**:269-5420
(716) 853-4340 .. **Makin**, Patrick A '02 Getman & B -800 Rand Bldg -Buffalo 14203
(212) 425-7200 .. **Makin**, Thos R '01 (Kenyon & K,LLP) -1 Bway -NY 10004
(212) 310-8000 .. **Makinen**, Marita A '94 (Weil G&M LLP) -767 5th Av -NY 10153
(212) 964-9292 .. **Makis**, Maria C '95 %R Koenigsberg -305 Bway #800 -NY 10007 **Fx**:267-5183
(212) 660-3000 .. **Mako**, Mark D '00 %Sullivan & W LLP -1290 Av of Amer -NY 10104
(914) 765-3936 .. **Makode**, Gail Dave '00 %MBIA Ins Corp -113 King -Armonk 10504
(516) 228-6522 .. **Makofsky**, Ellen G '86 (Raskin & M) -600 Old Cntry Rd -Gdn Cty 11530 **Fx**:228-6525
(212) 330-8151 .. **Makoski**, Danl S '09 %Brinen & Assoc,LLC -7 Dey -NY 10007 **Fx**:202-5330
(212) 403-1000 .. **Makow**, Lawr S '95 (Wachtell LR&K) -51 W 52nd -NY 10019
(718) 624-1550 .. **Makow**, Tracy E '89 (Brickner M,LLP) -292 Warren -Brklyn 11201 **Fx**:855-1094
(212) 975-8979 .. **Makower**, Alissa D '93 %CBS Inc -51 W 52nd -NY 10019 **Fx**:975-3930
(516) 222-1233 .. **Makower**, David A '95 -1900 Hempstd Tpk -E Meadow 11554
(212) 754-9400 .. **Makower**, Jill L '94 Cnsl Todtman NS&J,PC -425 Park Av -NY 10022
(646) 562-3405 .. **Makower**, Sharon H '94 %PLC -747 3rd Av -NY 10017
(716) 853-5100 .. **Makowski**, Matthew J '08 %Lippes MWF LLP -665 Main -Buffalo 14203
(516) 712-4000 .. **Makris**, Harry J '86 (Milber MP&S LLP) -1000 Woodbury Rd -Woodbury 11797
(914) 632-0861 .. **Makris**, Helen '88 -107 Pondvw Ln -New Rchll 10804
(914) 323-7000 .. **Makris**, James S '98 %Wilson EME&D LLP -3 Gannett Dr -White Plns 10604
(646) 495-1661 .. **Maksin**, Natalie C '04 %Maksin Lgl Grp PLLC -350 5th Av -NY 10118
(646) 495-1661 .. **Maksin**, Steven V '01 (Maksin Lgl Grp PLLC) -350 5th Av -NY 10118
(212) 318-6000 .. **Makso**, David '07 %Paul HJ&W LLP -75 E 55th -NY 10022
(212) 791-0285 .. **Malaby**, Cori L '95 %Malaby & B,LLC -150 Bway -NY 10038 **Fx**:791-0286
(212) 791-0285 .. **Malaby**, Robt C '85 (Malaby & B,LLC) -150 Bway -NY 10038 **Fx**:791-0286
(212) 233-0350 .. **Malach**, David '73 (Sobel RF&S,LLP) -150 Bway -NY 10038
(212) 473-0255 .. **Malach**, Solomon '73 Seedco -915 Bway -NY 10010
(914) 428-3101 .. **Malach**, Therese R '81 -470 Mamaroneck Av -White Plns 10605 **Fx**:428-4317
(718) 477-1818 .. **Malachovsky**, Shachar S '02 S Malachovsky,PLLC -28 Braisted Av -Staten Isl 10314 **Fx**:477-6101
(212) 804-5770 .. **Malachovsky**, Shachar S '02 Cnsl S Malachovsky,PLLC -110 Wall -NY 10005 **Fx**:(718) 477-6101
(518) 285-8689 .. **Malaczynski**, Heidi A '88 %Family Ct -30 Clinton Av -Albany 12207 **Fx**:462-4240
(631) 853-4049 .. **Malafi**, Christine '91 Cnty Atty -Dennison Bldg Bx6100 -Hauppauge 11788 **Fx**:853-5169
(212) 879-5580 .. **Malagiere**, Richd '97 -17 Battery Pl -NY 10004 **Fx**:879-5583
(212) 227-1767 .. **Malagon**, Mauricio A '95 -30 Vesey -NY 10007
(631) 845-2600 .. **Malagreca**, Frank J '93 %Morenus CG&B -58 S Srvc Rd -Melvll 11747
(518) 462-6765 .. **Malak**, Anne-Marie Conron '95 %Leg Aid -55 Colvin Av -Albany 12206 **Fx**:427-8352
(212) 536-3900 .. **Malakoff**, Drew A '99 %K&L Gates LLP -599 Lex Av -NY 10022
(718) 763-1328 .. **Malakoff**, Harvey T '59 -108-19 Flatlands 9th -Brklyn 11236
(212) 940-3040 .. **Malali**, Prem N '97 (Nixon P LLP) -437 Mad Av -NY 10022
(212) 245-1000 .. **Malalis**, Carmelyn P '02 (Outten & G LLP) -3 Park Av -NY 10016
(212) 403-6700 .. **Malamed**, David Alexandre '96 Gide LN LLP -120 W 45th -NY 10036
(212) 495-0100 .. **Malamy**, Kenneth W '75 (Gottesman WMF&W,PC) -11 Hanover Sq -NY 10005
(718) 935-5858 .. **Malamy**, Marlene L '78 %Bd of Educ -65 Court -Brklyn 11201
(646) 842-0892 .. **Malanaphy**, Liam R '99 -506 Prospect Av -Brklyn 11215 **Fx**:(718) 965-6015
(212) 237-0000 .. **Malandra**, Emily H '09 %Vinson & E LLP -666 5th Av -NY 10103
(212) 509-6009 .. **Malang**, Elizabeth E '01 %Ryan & C LLP -2 Wall -NY 10005
(212) 351-4500 .. **Malanga**, Lauren A '99 (Epstein B&G,PC) -250 Park Av -NY 10177
(631) 854-4970 .. **Malanga**, Thos J Jr. '95 Dept of Parks -Bx144 -W Sayvll 11796
(212) 661-7300 .. **Malapero & Prisco LLP** -295 Mad Av -NY 10017 **Fx**:661-7640
(212) 661-7300 .. **Malapero**, Raymond J '81 (Malapero & P LLP) -295 Mad Av -NY 10017
(212) 373-3000 .. **Malaquin**, Didier '84 Cnsl Paul WRW&G LLP -1285 Av of Amer -NY 10019
(914) 946-2889 .. **Malara**, Francis J '06 (Penachio M LLP) -235 Main -White Plns 10601 **Fx**:946-2882
(914) 285-3732 .. **Malara**, Jos S '79 JS Malara,PC -Bx396 -S Salem 10590 **Fx**:285-3971
(585) 381-3820 .. **Malarney**, Michl W '73 OfCnsl Pearl Law Firm,PA -1159 Pttsfrd Victor Rd -Pittsfrd 14534 **Fx**:381-3886
(212) 813-8800 .. **Malaska**, Kimberlee A '08 %Goodwin P LLP -620 8th Av -NY 10018
(212) 412-4000 .. **Malaspina**, Elizabeth K '03 Barclays Capital Inc -200 Park Av -NY 10166
(212) 250-5387 .. **Malaspina**, Roxanne '94 %Deutsche Bank -60 Wall -NY 10005
(212) 478-7200 .. **Malatak**, Robt J '95 SpclCnsl Hahn & H LLP -488 Mad Av -NY 10022
(212) 670-0310 .. **Malawsky**, Donald N '73 %Merrill Lynch -222 Bway -NY 10038
(212) 526-7000 .. **Malbacho**, Brian M '08 Barclays Capital -745 7th Av -NY 10019
(646) 281-5915 .. **Malchman**, Robt E '90 -500 5th Av -NY 10110
(516) 887-8200 .. **Malcolm**, Patrice N '09 %D Lubin & Assoc,PLLC -5 N Vllg Av -Rockvll Ctr 11570 **Fx**:887-8250
(718) 618-2500 .. **Malcolm-Charles**, Carol E '02 %Civil Ct -851 Grnd Cncrs -Bronx 10451 **Fx**:590-7294
(212) 969-3000 .. **Malcolmson**, Hazel T '07 %Proskauer R LLP -1585 Bway -NY 10036
(716) 856-4000 .. **Malcomb**, Chas W II '10 %Hodgson R LLP -140 Pearl -Buffalo 14202
(516) 294-9400 .. **Maldonado**, Andrea L '05 (Eisenberg & M,LLP) -100 Q Roosevelt Blvd -Gdn Cty 11530 **Fx**:(631) 240-4165
(914) 526-7166 .. **Maldonado**, Danl P '96 -823 Terrace Pl -Cortlandt Manor 10567
(631) 724-6085 .. **Maldonado**, David '74 -102 Sheppard Ln -Nesconset 11767
(212) 652-3890 .. **Maldonado**, José '83 (Pitta & G LLP) -120 Bway -NY 10271
(917) 551-1300 .. **Maldonado**, Mercedes M '93 %Koehler & I LLP -61 Bway -NY 10006
(212) 306-8096 .. **Maldonado**, Migdalia '76 %Housing Authority -250 Bway -NY 10007 **Fx**:306-7997
(212) 278-0400 .. **Maldonado**, Robt T '94 (Cooper & D LLP) -30 Rckfllr Plz -NY 10112
(212) 246-2400 .. **Maldonado**, Roger J '82 (Balber PM&VDT,PC) -1370 Av of Amer -NY 10019
(212) 797-3544 .. **Maldonado**, Rosalyn '95 %French & C,LLP -29 Bway -NY 10006
(212) 237-8911 .. **Maldonado**, Rosemarie '83 John Jay College -899 10th Av -NY 10019
(914) 472-2300 .. **Maldonado**, Sarah Thos '94 OfCnsl Jones G,LLP -670 Wht Plns Rd -Scarsdale 10583
(718) 409-0109 .. **Maldonado Cruz**, Lumarie '03 Cnsl Asm N Rivera -1126 Pelham Pkwy S -Bronx 10461
(716) 853-8400 .. **Maldovan**, Wm D '78 %Dept of Law -350 Main Pl Twr -Buffalo 14202 **Fx**:853-8571
(718) 273-4046 .. **Maleady**, James A '92 %Bosco B&M -857 Forest Av -Staten Isl 10310
(212) 490-1700 .. **Malech**, Steven B '06 Cnsl Wiggin & D -450 Lex Av -NY 10017
(212) 943-1233 .. **Malecki**, Jenice L '92 Malecki Law -11 Bway -NY 10004 **Fx**:943-1238
(518) 373-1500 .. **Malecki**, Paul M '99 OfCnsl R Beebe LLC -514 Vischers Ferry Rd -Clifton Pk 12065 **Fx**:373-0030
(212) 849-7000 .. **Malek**, Kevin N '06 %Quinn EU&S,LLP -51 Mad Av -NY 10010
(212) 554-7800 .. **Malek**, Linda A '95 (Moses & S LLP) -405 Lex Av -NY 10174
(212) 754-1610 .. **Malek**, Paul D '94 Latigo Prtnrs LLP -590 Mad Av -NY 10022
(212) 589-4200 .. **Malek**, Sammi '03 %Baker & H LLP -45 Rckfllr Plz -NY 10111
(516) 334-3500 .. **Malen**, Dennis S '68 (Malen & Assoc,PC) -123 Frost -Westbury 11590
(516) 496-7904 .. **Maleno**, Barbara L '93 -180 Froehlich Farm Blvd -Woodbury 11797 **Fx**:496-7906
(631) 475-0644 .. **Maler**, Ernest R Jr. '82 -64 E Roe Blvd Bx377 -Patchogue 11772
(516) 357-3000 .. **Malerba**, Benjamin P III '02 (Rivkin R LLP) -926 RXR Plz -Uniondale 11556
(516) 663-6600 .. **Malerba**, Kimberly B '04 %Ruskin MF,PC -1425 RXR Plz -Uniondale 11556

(516) 832-7627 .. **Maleson,** Lindsay R '03 %Nixon P LLP -50 Jericho Quadrangle -Jericho 11753
(518) 487-7600 .. **Maleszweski,** Amanda A '08 %Whiteman O&H LLP -1 Commerce Plz -Albany 12260
(212) 938-5000 .. **Maletsky,** Richd A '04 %Cantor Fitzgerald -110 E 59th -NY 10022
(718) 389-7668 .. **Malewski,** Alexander J Jr. '80 (Malewski M&B LLP) -657 Manh Av -Brklyn 11222
(718) 389-7668 .. **Malewski Malewski & Boccio LLP** -657 Manh Av -Brklyn 11222 **Fx:**383-7972
(718) 389-7668 .. **Malewski,** Robt P '95 (Malewski M&B LLP) -657 Manh Av -Brklyn 11222
(716) 845-9487 .. **Maley,** Kevin M '97 Supreme Ct -25 Delaware Av -Buffalo 14202 **Fx:**851-3293
(914) 683-8030 .. **Maley,** Philip M '64 -10 Bank -White Plns 10606
(212) 490-3000 .. **Malfa,** Frances '95 (Wilson EME&D LLP) -150 E 42nd -NY 10017
(315) 218-8000 .. **Malfitano,** Larry P '82 (Bond S&K,PLLC) -1 Lincoln Ctr -Syracuse 13202
(315) 422-7000 .. **Malfitano,** Marc A '78 %Pyramid -4 Clinton Sq -Syracuse 13202 **Fx:**422-2717
(585) 419-8800 .. **Malgieri,** Patrick M '80 (Harris B PLLC) -99 Garnsey Rd -Pittsfrd 14534
(212) 593-7100 .. **Malgieri,** Phyllis A '09 (Fischetti & M LLP) -747 3rd Av -NY 10017 **Fx:**758-2809
(718) 250-2000 .. **Malhotra,** Anju '93 %DA -350 Jay -Brklyn 11201 **Fx:**250-2314
(212) 593-2284 .. **Malhotra,** Gaurav Gary '97 Malhotra & Assoc -54 E 11th -NY 10003
(212) 265-2171 .. **Malhotra,** Reena '02 %Solil Mgmt -640 5th Av -NY 10019 **Fx:**265-1669
(631) 844-7254 .. **Malhotra,** Sanjay '92 Adecco USA -175 Broad Hollow Rd -Melvll 11747
(914) 788-4126 .. **Malia,** Glen P '84 G Malia -2117 Crompond Rd -Cortlandt Manor 10567 **Fx:**788-5741
(585) 325-5703 .. **Malia,** Thos R '88 -301 Exchange Blvd -Rchstr 14608 **Fx:**325-4568
(212) 396-8764 .. **Maliagros,** Spiros '02 Tiedemann Invstmnt Grp -535 Mad Av -NY 10022
(716) 851-4343 .. **Malican,** Denise M '91 %Law Dept -65 Niagara Sq -Buffalo 14202 **Fx:**851-4105
(631) 761-7000 .. **Maligno,** Thos '79 %Touro Cllg Law Ctr -225 Eastvw Dr -Central Islip 11722
(212) 583-9600 .. **Malik,** Adam '08 %Littler M,PC -900 3rd Av -NY 10022
(516) 328-2300 .. **Malik,** Betsy R '88 (Abrams FFEGF&E,LLP) -1111 Marcus Av -Lk Success 11042
(212) 506-5000 .. **Malik,** C Anne '10 %Orrick H&S LLP -51 W 52nd -NY 10019
(212) 408-5100 .. **Malik,** Faryal Q '08 %Chadbourne & P LLP -30 Rckfllr Plz -NY 10112
(212) 545-7770 .. **Malik,** Jitesh '03 (Malik & P,PC) -347 5th Av -NY 10016
(212) 808-5167 .. **Malik,** Markus '05 The Grow Ntwrk/Mcgraw-Hill -2 Penn Plz -NY 10121
(718) 286-6000 .. **Malik,** Mina Quinto '00 %DA -125-01 Qns Blvd -Kew Gdns 11415
(212) 906-1200 .. **Malik,** Omeed '07 %Latham & W -885 3rd Av -NY 10022
(718) 446-5755 .. **Malik,** Pankaj '94 (Malik & Assoc,PC) -75-35 31st Av -E Elmhrst 11370 **Fx:**446-0665
(718) 250-2000 .. **Malikouzakis,** Joanna '10 %DA -350 Jay -Brklyn 11201 **Fx:**250-2314
(212) 313-3600 .. **Malikzay,** Sania '09 %Barry M&M -2 Rector -NY 10006
(845) 298-1600 .. **Malin,** Andrea B '91 (Genova & M) -1136 Route 9 -Wappingers Fls 12590 **Fx:**298-1265
(212) 450-2000 .. **Malin,** Danl A '03 NFL -280 Park Av -NY 10017 **Fx:**681-7599
(212) 685-7777 .. **Malin,** Gary L '94 %Citi Habitats,Inc -250 Park Av S -NY 10003 **Fx:**685-6154
(516) 482-6676 .. **Malin,** George L '64 -60 Cutter Mill Rd Bx386 -Gt Neck 11022 **Fx:**482-0429
(212) 294-6700 .. **Malin,** Jennifer L '98 (Winston & S) -200 Park Av -NY 10166
(716) 664-5210 .. **Malin,** Ronald W '59 (Price FM&W) -400 Key Bk Bldg Bx1219 -Jamestwn 14702
(631) 423-2176 .. **Malin,** Scott H '78 -23 Chrlstn Dr -Huntngtn 11743 **Fx:**424-0754
(212) 759-9740 .. **Malin,** Tyler D '06 (Madon M,PC) -260 Mad Av -NY 10016 **Fx:**759-7063
(212) 986-7410 .. **Malina,** Bernard '66 (Malina & Assoc) -444 Mad Av -NY 10022 **Fx:**983-8421
(212) 250-0677 .. **Malina,** Lynne '75 %Deutsche Bank -60 Wall -NY 10005 **Fx:**797-4561
(212) 794-5430 .. **Malina,** Richd '72 %CUNY -535 E 80th -NY 10075 **Fx:**794-5426
(516) 747-8000 .. **Malinaro,** Jason P '08 Marschhausen & F,PC -835 Old Cntry Rd -Westbury 11590 **Fx:**747-6439
(516) 229-6000 .. **Maline,** Jeremy R '90 %R Lau & Assoc -300 Jericho Quad Bx9040 -Jericho 11753 **Fx:**229-6167
(212) 813-8800 .. **Maline,** Michl D '95 (Goodwin P LLP) -620 8th Av -NY 10018
(212) 313-3600 .. **Malino,** Alex R '01 %Barry M&M -2 Rector -NY 10006
(212) 964-7400 .. **Malinow,** Stacy I '95 Smith MDWY&Y,PC -111 John -NY 10038
(212) 947-4999 .. **Malinowski,** Eric S '04 %Camacho MM,LLP -350 5th Av -NY 10118
(212) 906-1200 .. **Malionek,** Robt J '05 %Latham & W -885 3rd Av -NY 10022
(516) 572-4754 .. **Maliszewski,** Sandra C '01 Nassau Hlth Care Corp -2201 Hempstd Tpk -E Meadow 11554
(212) 944-0500 .. **Malito,** Nicholas B '07 %Hofheimer G&G,LLP -530 5th Av -NY 10036 **Fx:**897-4980
(516) 248-6400 .. **Malito,** Robt J '70 (Davidoff M&H,LLP) -200 Grdn City Plz -Gdn Cty 11530
(516) 248-6400 .. **Malito,** Stephen A '97 %Davidoff M&H,LLP -200 Grdn City Plz -Gdn Cty 11530
(631) 852-2326 .. **Malito,** Vincent A '67 %Hon P Henry -235 Griffing Av -Rvrhead 11901 **Fx:**852-2328
(212) 723-5875 .. **Malitzis,** John F '93 Citigroup Global Mrkts -390 Greenwich -NY 10013
(212) 766-2466 .. **Maliza,** Amy K '04 (DiSanto LLP) -15 Maiden Ln -NY 10038 **Fx:**(866) 746-0504
(212) 921-8399 .. **Malizia,** Kathryn E '10 %Lankler S&W LLP -500 5th Av -NY 10110
(212) 460-0618 .. **Malka,** Rafael '02 Prudential Douglas Elliman -51 E 10th -NY 10003
(716) 645-3909 .. **Malkan,** Jeffrey D '89 SUNY Buffalo Lw Schl -O'Brian Hall -Buffalo 14260
(212) 309-6000 .. **Malkani,** Geeta '09 %Morgan L&B LLP -101 Park Av -NY 10178
(212) 503-3569 .. **Malkani,** Shirin '99 Ziff Davis Media Inc -28 E 28th -NY 10016
(518) 449-3359 .. **Malkin,** Arthur N '79 (Malkin & R) -80 State -Albany 12207 **Fx:**449-5788
(212) 588-0800 .. **Malkin,** Brian J '05 %Frommer L&H LLP -745 5th Av -NY 10151
(212) 506-2500 .. **Malkin,** Cary J '01 (Mayer B LLP) -1675 Bway -NY 10019
(212) 486-8615 .. **Malkin,** David '68 -950 3rd Av -NY 10022
(212) 836-8000 .. **Malkin,** Jessica A '04 %Kaye S LLP -425 Park Av -NY 10022
(315) 448-4800 .. **Malkin,** Judith C '93 %Dept of Law -615 Erie Blvd W -Syracuse 13204 **Fx:**448-4853
(212) 829-4966 .. **Malkin,** Laurie Claire '00 Cantor Fitzgerald -110 E 59th -NY 10022
(212) 230-1425 .. **Malkin,** Lawr S '98 Riversville Capital,Inc -110 E 55th -NY 10022
(212) 687-8700 .. **Malkin,** Peter L '58 (Malkin Hldngs,LLC) -60 E 42nd -NY 10165 **Fx:**986-7679
(212) 335-9108 .. **Malkin,** Ryan D '07 DA -1 Hogan Pl -NY 10013
(607) 763-9200 .. **Malkin,** Sandra Ellen '02 OfCnsl Levene G&T,LLP -BxF-1706 -Bnghmtn 13902
(716) 852-5875 .. **Mallaber,** Randy C '03 %Feldman K LLP -110 Pearl -Buffalo 14202
(646) 442-3450 .. **Mallach,** Saville A '01 -228 E 45th -NY 10017
(347) 296-1545 .. **Mallafre,** Consuelo M '87 %Hon M Steinhardt -360 Adams -Brklyn 11201
(518) 455-4363 .. **Mallalieu,** Julia C '96 NYS Assembly -520 The Cptl -Albany 12248
(716) 285-1682 .. **Mallam,** Whitney W '66 -324 Pine -Niagara Fls 14301 **Fx:**285-3463
(718) 238-2400 .. **Mallas,** Kostantinos '98 (Georgaklis & M) -9118 5th Av -Brklyn 11209 **Fx:**238-2116
(212) 705-0121 .. **Mallen,** David G '93 Natl Advertising Division/CBBB -70 W 36th -NY 10018 **Fx:**705-0130
(212) 878-8000 .. **Mallen,** Renee M '01 %Clifford C LLP -31 W 52nd -NY 10019
(212) 801-2217 .. **Mallenbaum,** Stephan J '83 (Greenberg T,LLP) -200 Park Av -NY 10166
(212) 858-1000 .. **Maller,** Brant K '84 (Pillsbury WSP LLP) -1540 Bway -NY 10036
(212) 732-4818 .. **Maller,** Jay A '79 -30 Vesey -NY 10007 **Fx:**732-4923
(518) 234-3431 .. **Mallery,** Roger H '56 -545 Main Bx88 -Cobleskill 12043 **Fx:**234-2577
(518) 234-3431 .. **Mallery,** Susan J '94 -545 Main Bx88 -Cobleskill 12043 **Fx:**234-2577
(518) 640-5039 .. **Mallette,** Jason P '02 AYCO -25 British Amer Blvd -Latham 12110
(718) 250-1400 .. **Malley,** Brendan J '90 %BZ Green -12 MetroTech Ctr -Brklyn 11201 **Fx:**250-1401
(607) 330-4000 .. **Malley,** Danl P '99 (Bond S&K,PLLC) -10 Brown Rd -Ithaca 14850
(646) 522-6488 .. **Malley,** Edw J '92 TRC Environmental Corp -1430 Bway -NY 10018 **Fx:**(212) 221-7840
(212) 592-1400 .. **Malley,** John J '96 %Fidelity Natl Title Ins -711 3rd Av -NY 10017 **Fx:**592-1500
(718) 613-2170 .. **Malley,** Sean A '09 US Dist Ct - Eastern Dist -225 Cadman Plz E -Brklyn 11201
(716) 856-5500 .. **Mallia,** Molly L '06 %Damon M LLP -200 Delaware Av -Buffalo 14202
(718) 461-6633 .. **Mallilo,** Anthony '77 (Mallilo & G) -163-09 Nrthrn Blvd -Flushng 11358
(718) 461-6633 .. **Mallilo & Grossman** -163-09 Nrthrn Blvd -Flushng 11358 **Fx:**321-8636
(718) 951-7345 .. **Mallilo & Grossman** -1957 Flatbush Av -Brklyn 11234 **Fx:**951-7456
(212) 285-1200 .. **Mallin,** Barry K '70 (Mallin & Assoc,PC) -132 Nassau -NY 10038 **Fx:**285-1202
(212) 486-0511 .. **Mallin,** Joel '61 -110 E 59th -NY 10022
(212) 227-4210 .. **Mallin,** Joshua L '85 (Weg & M,PC) -52 Duane -NY 10007
(212) 832-3939 .. **Mallin,** Lauren N '06 %R Felder & Prtnrs,PC -437 Mad Av -NY 10022 **Fx:**838-1103
(212) 770-8381 .. **Mallinson,** John L '99 AIG Global Real Estate -70 Pine -NY 10270
(516) 228-9181 .. **Mallis,** Cheryl Y '03 %Gassman BB&T,PC -666 Old Cntry Rd -Gdn Cty 11530
(212) 818-8800 .. **Mallis,** Steven '74 (Graubard M) -405 Lex Av -NY 10174
(212) 897-5840 .. **Mallon,** Kevin C '04 OfCnsl Fishman & N -305 Bway -NY 10007 **Fx:**897-5841
(212) 306-1570 .. **Mallon,** Shawn R '02 %FINRA -65 Bway -NY 10006
(845) 756-3505 .. **Mallon,** Virginia D '83 -107 Mtnvw Dr -Elizaville 12523 **Fx:**756-5880
(212) 714-2277 .. **Mallonga,** Jose Teodoro S '88 (Abad C&M,LLC) -350 5th Av -NY 10118 **Fx:**714-9331
(917) 476-3925 .. **Mallow,** David M '94 (Dickinson & M) -321 Bway -NY 10007
(212) 964-7990 .. **Mallow,** Gerold M '67 (Mallow K&N,PC) -321 Bway -NY 10007
(212) 964-7990 .. **Mallow Konstam & Nisonoff,PC** -321 Bway -NY 10007 **Fx:**267-4080
(212) 735-3000 .. **Malloy,** Christopher P '94 (Skadden ASM&F LLP) -4 Times Sq -NY 10036
(212) 721-8476 .. **Malloy,** Emily C '99 -325 Riverside Dr -NY 10025
(718) 625-0330 .. **Malloy,** Frances '81 -446 State -Brklyn 11217 **Fx:**625-5794
(212) 458-5670 .. **Malloy,** James F '06 AIG Domestic Claims -175 Water -NY 10038
(631) 265-9650 .. **Malloy,** Kevin J '91 -742 Vets Mem'l Hwy -Hauppauge 11788
(212) 310-8000 .. **Malloy,** Lavell '03 %Weil G&M LLP -767 5th Av -NY 10153
(212) 336-3620 .. **Malloy,** Margaret A '00 %EEOC -33 Whitehall -NY 10004
(516) 255-1800 .. **Malloy,** Marybeth '99 %Rosenblum & B LLP -100 Merrick Rd -Rockvll Ctr 11570
(718) 286-6000 .. **Malloy,** Patricia Ann '97 %DA -125-01 Qns Blvd -Kew Gdns 11415
(212) 227-4492 .. **Malloy,** Peter G '04 -20 Vesey -NY 10007
(212) 551-3147 .. **Malloy-Curtis,** Tracy A '04 Intl Rescue Comm -122 E 42nd -NY 10168
(518) 449-3900 .. **Malloy-Pogoda,** Kelly L '95 (Cooper E&S,LLP) -39 N Pearl -Albany 12207
(212) 848-0276 .. **Malman,** Arthur B '68 (Malman & G) -645 5th Av -NY 10022
(212) 998-6166 .. **Malman,** Laurie L '72 %NYU Law Schl -40 Wshngtn Sq S -NY 10012 **Fx:**995-4075
(607) 778-2111 .. **Malmquist,** Rebecca A '05 Broome Cnty Surrogates Ct -Bx1766 -Bnghmtn 13902 **Fx:**778-2308
(212) 421-4100 .. **Malmud,** Thos J '64 (Pryor C LLP) -7 Times Sq -NY 10036
(718) 401-8595 .. **Maloff,** Lawr A '87 -840 Grnd Cncrs -Bronx 10451
(212) 483-9600 .. **Malon,** Henry C '57 -44 Wall -NY 10005
(516) 334-6727 .. **Malon,** Paul E '82 %Fidelity Natl Title Ins -900 Merchants Cncrs -Westbury 11590 **Fx:**334-7459
(845) 876-3024 .. **Malone,** Adeline P '79 Marvin & M PLLC -6369 Mill Bx151 -Rhinebeck 12572 **Fx:**876-5622

(516) 742-9743 .. **Malone,** Anne V '93 (Callahan & M) -263 Mineola Blvd -Mineola 11501
(516) 571-2475 .. **Malone,** Charlene '78 %Hon M Segal -100 Supreme Ct Dr -Mineola 11501
(212) 278-1382 .. **Malone,** Cort T '03 %Anderson K&O,PC -1251 Av of Amer -NY 10020
(212) 757-0007 .. **Malone,** Danl C '97 (Scarola E LLP) -888 7th Av -NY 10106
(315) 823-2720 .. **Malone,** David M '67 (Malone & M LLP) -45 W Main Bx276 -Little Fls 13365 **Fx:**823-2723
(516) 572-2800 .. **Malone,** Dianne E '90 Nassau Downs OTB -220 Fulton Av -Hempstd 11550
(516) 393-6143 .. **Malone,** Donald F '75 %F Laurino -999 Stewart Av -Bethpage 11714 **Fx:**393-6130
(646) 562-3405 .. **Malone,** Emily A '05 %PLC -747 3rd Av -NY 10017
(212) 350-2700 .. **Malone,** Gary J '83 (Constantine C,PC) -450 Lex Av -NY 10017
(212) 838-6888 .. **Malone,** Georgia J '79 -147 E 61st -NY 10065
(718) 531-6600 .. **Malone,** John A '87 Bergen Bch Youth Org -2335 Bergen Av -Brklyn 11234
(315) 823-2720 .. **Malone,** Joy A '77 (Malone & M LLP) -45 W Main Bx276 -Little Fls 13365 **Fx:**823-2723
(518) 426-4600 .. **Malone,** Lawr G '73 OfCnsl Couch W,LLP -540 Bway Bx22222 -Albany 12201
(914) 468-7600 .. **Malone,** Margaret '07 %Nordlicht & H -800 Wstchstr Av -Rye Brook 10573 **Fx:**468-7608
(914) 390-8026 .. **Malone,** Mark K '83 NYPA-Utilities -123 Main -White Plns 10601
(212) 556-2100 .. **Malone,** Michl J P III '78 (King & S) -1185 Av of Amer -NY 10036
(718) 250-2000 .. **Malone,** Michelle A '06 %DA -350 Jay -Brklyn 11201 **Fx:**250-2314
(516) 773-8300 .. **Malone,** Randall K '96 %Wisselman H & Assoc,PC -1010 Nrthrn Blvd -Gt Neck 11021 **Fx:**773-8304
(315) 823-2720 .. **Malone,** Robt J '78 (Malone & M LLP) -45 W Main Bx276 -Little Fls 13365 **Fx:**823-2723
(315) 867-1123 .. **Malone,** Robt J '78 Cnsl Cnty Atty -109 Mary -Herkimer 13350 **Fx:**867-1492
(631) 271-6596 .. **Malone,** Shaun M '95 %C Cassar,PC -13 E Carver -Huntngtn 11743
(212) 664-4444 .. **Malone,** Stephen J '00 %NBC -30 Rckfllr Plz -NY 10112
(585) 249-4800 .. **Malone,** Steven E '79 -1173 Pttsfrd-Vctr Rd -Pittsfrd 14534 **Fx:**249-4824
(516) 379-2500 .. **Malone Tauber & Sohn** -147 W Merrick Rd Bx589 -Freeprt 11520 **Fx:**379-2755
(212) 906-1200 .. **Malone,** Thos J '06 %Latham & W -885 3rd Av -NY 10022
(212) 867-0500 .. **Malone,** Thos P '97 -60 E 42nd -NY 10165 **Fx:**867-0511
(516) 379-2500 .. **Malone,** Wm J '57 %Malone T&S -147 W Merrick Rd Bx589 -Freeprt 11520
(516) 248-9168 .. **Maloney,** Alyce E '49 -257 Stewart Av -Gdn Cty 11530
(212) 906-1200 .. **Maloney,** Amy C '05 %Latham & W -885 3rd Av -NY 10022
(212) 687-8181 .. **Maloney,** Andrew J III '89 (Kreindler & K) -750 3rd Av -NY 10017
(212) 588-1670 .. **Maloney,** Brian G '93 (Ambrecht & M LLP) -245 Park Av -NY 10167
(212) 574-1200 .. **Maloney,** Brian P '06 %Seward & K LLP -1 Bttry Pk Plz -NY 10004
(716) 829-3176 .. **Maloney,** Brigid '99 SUNY Buffalo Schl of Medicine -3435 Main -Buffalo 14214 **Fx:**829-2799
(716) 842-2761 .. **Maloney,** Cathy Lovejoy '95 Child & Family Srvcs -330 Delaware Av -Buffalo 14202
(718) 286-6000 .. **Maloney,** Christine M '05 %DA -125-01 Qns Blvd -Kew Gdns 11415
(315) 699-3032 .. **Maloney,** Francis E Jr. '63 -Bx6507 -Syracuse 13217
(212) 207-8400 .. **Maloney,** James J '69 (Kavanagh M&O LLP) -415 Mad Av -NY 10017
(516) 767-1395 .. **Maloney,** James M '96 -Bx551 -Pt Wash 11050 **Fx:**767-1326
(716) 651-9663 .. **Maloney,** James R '92 -3291 Walden Av -Depew 14043
(631) 208-1063 .. **Maloney,** Jennifer M '89 Tellus Abstract -101 Colin Dr -Holbrook 11741
(716) 631-3871 .. **Maloney,** Joan Ellison '84 (Maloney & M) -5820 Main -Williamsvll 14221
(212) 297-5800 .. **Maloney,** John C Jr. '76 (Day P LLP) -7 Times Sq -NY 10036
(212) 973-0572 .. **Maloney,** John P '91 Cnsl Wolff & S PC -140 Bway -NY 10005
(716) 631-3871 .. **Maloney,** John T '57 (Maloney & M) -5820 Main -Williamsvll 14221
(518) 465-3484 .. **Maloney,** John T '74 (Carter CCBM&L,PC) -20 Corp Wds Blvd -Albany 12211
(607) 734-0990 .. **Maloney,** John W '95 (Keyser M&W LLP) -150 Lk -Elmira 14901
(212) 223-6700 .. **Maloney,** Jos E '93 (Zukerman GB&C,LLP) -875 3rd Av -NY 10022
(516) 299-2236 .. **Maloney,** Judith Mathers '86 Long Island Univ -700 Nrthrn Blvd -Brookvll 11548 **Fx:**299-2066
(718) 298-8925 .. **Maloney,** Kathleen M '05 %Leg Aid -153-01 Jamaica Av -Jamaica 11432 **Fx:**657-0537
(518) 455-7500 .. **Maloney,** Keeley A '06 %Legis Bill Drftng Comm -310 The Cptl -Albany 12224 **Fx:**455-7598
(212) 297-5800 .. **Maloney,** M Cassin Jr. '95 SrCnsl Day P LLP -7 Times Sq -NY 10036
(212) 458-2122 .. **Maloney,** Mari B '88 %AIG -175 Water -NY 10038
(516) 887-2255 .. **Maloney,** Maria '89 -211 Bway -Lynbrk 11563
(716) 282-2356 .. **Maloney,** Mary Ellen '95 (Maloney & M) -256 Third #21 -Niagara Fls 14303
(212) 683-7100 .. **Maloney,** Mary L '88 (Gallo V&K,LLP) -90 Broad -NY 10004
(516) 229-6000 .. **Maloney,** Matthew C '98 %R Lau & Assoc -300 Jericho Quad Bx9040 -Jericho 11753 **Fx:**229-6167
(212) 450-4000 .. **Maloney,** Meghan M '10 %Davis P&W LLP -450 Lex Av -NY 10017
(631) 208-9062 .. **Maloney,** Michl F '89 (MF Maloney,PC) -101 Colin Dr -Holbrook 11741 **Fx:**208-1064
(212) 808-7800 .. **Maloney,** Michl J '06 %Kelley D&W LLP -101 Park Av -NY 10178
(716) 282-2356 .. **Maloney,** Michl V '58 (Maloney & M) -256 Third #21 -Niagara Fls 14303
(716) 942-4255 .. **Maloney,** Moira N '90 US DOE -Bx191 -W Vly 14171
(716) 885-8645 .. **Maloney,** Patrick J '81 %Dempsey & D -561 Franklin -Buffalo 14202 **Fx:**885-8569
(212) 213-0700 .. **Maloney,** Paul H IV '83 P Maloney,PC -60 E 42nd -NY 10165 **Fx:**213-0711
(212) 422-1212 .. **Maloney,** Peter T '93 QBE The Americas -88 Pine -NY 10005
(516) 357-3000 .. **Maloney,** Robt A '04 %Rivkin R LLP -926 RXR Plz -Uniondale 11556
(212) 446-4800 .. **Maloney,** Sean P '93 (Kirkland & E LLP) -153 E 53rd -NY 10022
(212) 839-5300 .. **Maloney,** Sean P '05 %Sidley A LLP -787 7th Av -NY 10019
(212) 490-2020 .. **Maloney,** Timothy J '04 %Littman K LLP -655 3rd Av -NY 10017
(212) 944-7333 .. **Maloney,** Wm J '85 (Rode & Q) -55 W 39th -NY 10018
(631) 369-1700 .. **Maloney,** Wm P '66 (Esseks H&A,LLP) -108 E Main Bx279 -Rvrhead 11901
(518) 266-3000 .. **Maloney,** Winifred M '83 %Div Tax Appls -500 Fed -Troy 12180 **Fx:**272-5178
(212) 538-9685 .. **Maloni,** Jennifer J '97 CSFB -1 Mad Av -NY 10010
(914) 921-1200 .. **Maloof,** David T '84 (Maloof B&E LLC) -411 Theo Fremd Av -Rye 10580 **Fx:**921-1023
(212) 233-3079 .. **Maloof,** Jack A '86 (Maloof LC&O,PA) -299 Bway -NY 10007
(212) 233-3079 .. **Maloof Lebowitz Connahan & Oleske,PA** -299 Bway -NY 10007 **Fx:**233-3984
(516) 594-1866 .. **Maloof,** Lily A '93 -435 Wanamaker -Oceanside 11572 **Fx:**594-0727
(212) 480-5284 .. **Maloor,** Sapna S '06 %Insurance Dept -25 Beaver -NY 10004 **Fx:**480-5272
(212) 489-1600 .. **Maloul,** Lisa Gitnik '00 %Deloitte LLP -1633 Bway -NY 10019 **Fx:**492-4201
(716) 855-1118 .. **Maloy,** James M '80 %JE Morris -424 Main -Buffalo 14202 **Fx:**855-1119
(212) 460-1053 .. **Malpica,** Annette '00 Con Ed of NY -4 Irving Pl -NY 10003
(914) 287-7711 .. **Malsch,** Jeffrey M '96 (Pisciotti M&B,PC) -445 Hmltn Av -White Plns 10601 **Fx:**287-7715
(914) 764-1940 .. **Malsin,** Steven A '81 -237 Uppr Shad Rd -Pound Rdg 10576 **Fx:**764-1940
(212) 715-1000 .. **Maltbie,** John '97 %Arnold & P LLP -399 Park Av -NY 10022
(212) 688-5151 .. **Maltby,** Stephen J O '79 (Gibney A&F,LLP) -665 5th Av -NY 10022
(631) 543-8811 .. **Maltese,** Carl A '02 %C altese -1050 W Jericho Tpk -Smithtwn 11787 **Fx:**543-1718
(516) 747-5900 .. **Maltese,** Danl P '02 %Kaye & L -220 Mineola Blvd -Mineola 11501
(516) 877-9200 .. **Maltese,** Diane M '02 %S Kaplan -200 Willis Av -Mineola 11501 **Fx:**877-2554
(212) 557-1818 .. **Maltin,** Nancy I '01 %Silverson P&L -192 Lex Av -NY 10016
(212) 947-3793 .. **Maltser,** Yelena '04 %Sadis & G LLP -551 5th Av -NY 10176
(718) 694-3934 .. **Maltser,** Yury '01 Cnsl Transit Auth -130 Lvngstn -Brklyn 11201 **Fx:**694-5726
(718) 544-8840 .. **Maltz,** Judah '77 -125-10 Qns Blvd -Kew Gdns 11415 **Fx:**544-7112
(212) 468-4800 .. **Maltz,** Mark E '89 (Davis & G LLP) -1740 Bway -NY 10019
(212) 705-4804 .. **Maltz,** Richd M '80 Cnsl Frankfurt KK&S,PC -488 Mad Av -NY 10022 **Fx:**(347) 438-2087
(516) 791-7715 .. **Maltzman,** Carl B '79 -371 Hungry Hrbr Rd -N Woodmere 11581 **Fx:**791-7715
(212) 761-4753 .. **Maluenda,** Annette V '95 Morgan Stanley -1585 Bway -NY 10036
(212) 705-7000 .. **Maluf,** Edw F '91 (Bingham M LLP) -399 Park Av -NY 10022
(212) 839-5300 .. **Maluf,** Farid R '87 (Sidley A LLP) -787 7th Av -NY 10019
(646) 471-4000 .. **Malul,** Isaac '99 %PricewaterhouseCoopers LLP -300 Mad Av -NY 10017
(718) 741-3400 .. **Malunowicz,** Eileen '89 Childrens Law Ctr -2501 Grnd Cncrs -Bronx 10468
(212) 307-5500 .. **Maly,** Heather L '08 %Venable LLP -1270 Av of Amer -NY 10020
(607) 432-6932 .. **Malz,** Carol Ann '99 -554 Main Bx1446 -Oneonta 13820 **Fx:**432-2331
(212) 446-4800 .. **Malz,** Jordan Nathaniel '01 (Kirkland & E LLP) -153 E 53rd -NY 10022
(212) 210-1256 .. **Mamak,** Matthew W '04 %Alston & B LLP -90 Park Av -NY 10016
(212) 504-6000 .. **Maman,** Michele '07 %Cadwalader W&T LLP -1 World Fncl Ctr -NY 10281
(212) 705-7000 .. **Mamaysky,** Isaac '09 %Bingham M LLP -399 Park Av -NY 10022
(212) 326-3939 .. **Mamedova,** Kamilla '09 %Jones D -222 E 41st -NY 10017
(718) 238-9100 .. **Mammolito,** Jerome T '81 (Sands & M,PC) -7512 3rd Av -Brklyn 11209 **Fx:**238-9112
(516) 918-7821 .. **Mammone,** Carin Ann '95 Deloitte & Touche LLP -2 Jericho Plz -Jericho 11753
(914) 631-5050 .. **Mamo,** Anthony J '93 (Medina TSM&C PC) -95 Beekman Av -Sleepy Hollow 10591 **Fx:**703-6466
(212) 801-9336 .. **Mamorsky,** Jeffrey D '72 (Greenberg T,LLP) -200 Park Av -NY 10166
(516) 775-7007 .. **Mamos,** Fotina '06 %Gutman MB&S,PC -813 Jericho Tpk -New Hyde Pk 11040
(516) 877-0509 .. **Mamos,** George '80 (Mamos & M) -104 11th -Gdn Cty 11530
(718) 661-4008 .. **Mamos,** Philip '80 (Mamos & M) -334 E 79th -NY 10075 **Fx:**939-7825
(516) 229-6000 .. **Mamounis,** Nicholas P '88 %R Lau & Assoc -300 Jericho Quad Bx9040 -Jericho 11753 **Fx:**229-6167
(315) 946-7502 .. **Mamuscia,** Francis A '88 Hon H Nesbitt -54 Broad -Lyons 14489 **Fx:**946-7411
(212) 468-8000 .. **Man,** Arthur '05 %Morrison & F LLP -1290 Av of Amer -NY 10104
(212) 374-9600 .. **Man,** Yat T '86 -11 E Bway -NY 10038 **Fx:**964-8344
(212) 265-6888 .. **Manak,** Jos M '87 Cnsl Porzio B&N,PC -156 W 56th -NY 10019
(212) 973-0572 .. **Manalansan,** Carlos G '95 %Wolff & S PC -140 Bway -NY 10005
(212) 450-2000 .. **Manara,** Kevin K '07 %NFL -280 Park Av -NY 10017 **Fx:**681-7599
(212) 527-1000 .. **Manarel,** Michl R '89 %Jones HC&B PC -1 Bttry Pk Plz -NY 10004
(516) 379-2454 .. **Manas,** Lillyan J '85 -708 Seaman Av -Baldwin 11510 **Fx:**379-6208
(212) 735-3763 .. **Manasse,** Michl G '97 Tinicum Inc -800 3rd Av -NY 10022
(212) 371-8008 .. **Manasse,** Patrick E '09 %Guzov O,LLC -600 Mad Av -NY 10022
(212) 450-4000 .. **Manatad Dillen,** Noreen M P '03 Davis P&W LLP -450 Lex Av -NY 10017
(212) 790-4500 .. **Manatt Phelps & Phillips, LLP** -7 Times Sq -NY 10036 **Fx:**790-4545
(518) 431-6700 .. **Manatt Phelps & Phillips, LLP** -30 S Pearl -Albany 12207 **Fx:**431-6767
(212) 530-5000 .. **Manausa,** Jeanette L '07 %Milbank TH&M LLP -1 Chase Manh Plz -NY 10005
(212) 506-5000 .. **Manbeck,** Peter C '83 (Orrick H&S LLP) -51 W 52nd -NY 10019
(212) 619-3490 .. **Manca,** Jeffrey B '92 -30 Vesey -NY 10007 **Fx:**964-7441
(716) 847-8400 .. **Mancabelli,** Patricia A '99 %Phillips L LLP -3400 HSBC Ctr -Buffalo 14203
(315) 479-8660 .. **Mance,** Frances P '05 %Alexander & C,LLC -115 E Jffrsn -Syracuse 13202
(212) 643-8904 .. **Manchanda,** Nidhi Nina '98 %Assadi & M,LLP -200 W 57th -NY 10019 **Fx:**643-9192
(212) 968-8600 .. **Manchanda,** Rahul D '02 -80 Wall -NY 10005 **Fx:**968-8601
(631) 247-0404 .. **Mancher,** Mark S '77 (Jackson L LLP) -58 S Srvc Rd -Melvll 11747
(212) 541-9100 .. **Mancher,** Robt S '07 %Schiavetti CDW&N,LLP -575 8th Av -NY 10018

(607) 763-9200 .. **Manchester,** Cynthia Ann K '92 (Levene G&T,LLP) -BxF-1706 -Bnghmtn 13902
(212) 973-8000 .. **Manchester,** Edw D '05 %Schnader HS&L LLP -140 Bway -NY 10005
(212) 994-8401 .. **Manchester,** Jon H '91 -675 3rd Av -NY 10017 **Fx:**994-8404
(212) 490-3000 .. **Manchisi,** Francis P '82 (Wilson EME&D LLP) -150 E 42nd -NY 10017
(212) 244-2999 .. **Manci,** Michl L '78 (Kopff N&D LLP) -440 9th Av -NY 10001
(716) 853-1616 .. **Mancinelli,** Anthony D '77 (Harter S&E LLP) -12 Fountain Plz -Buffalo 14202
(212) 962-6525 .. **Mancinelli,** Steven '91 (Mancinelli & Assoc) -111 John -NY 10038 **Fx:**962-6791
(212) 506-2500 .. **Mancini,** A John P '90 (Mayer B LLP) -1675 Bway -NY 10019
(212) 456-5379 .. **Mancini,** Albert P '99 %ABC Radio Networks -125 W End Av -NY 10023
(917) 521-3900 .. **Mancini,** Dawn '03 Dept of Homeless Srvcs -346 Powers Av -Bronx 10454
(518) 452-0144 .. **Mancini and Hayko, PC** -2050 Wstrn Av -Guilderlnd 12084 **Fx:**452-0022
(518) 474-0491 .. **Mancini,** John A '03 %Executive Chamber -The Cptl -Albany 12224
(315) 330-2929 .. **Mancini,** Jos A '01 Air Force Research Lab/RIJ -26 Electronic Pkwy -Rome 13441
(518) 457-4951 .. **Mancini,** Leonard A '77 %Dept Correctional Srvcs -1220 Wshngtn Av -Albany 12226 **Fx:**457-7555
(646) 471-5443 .. **Mancini,** Louis A '05 %PricewaterhouseCoopers LLP -300 Mad Av -NY 10017
(518) 452-0144 .. **Mancini,** Ralph G '63 (Mancini and H,PC) -2050 Wstrn Av -Guilderlnd 12084
(914) 333-7420 .. **Mancini,** Ralph J '89 %Akzo Nobel -120 Wht Plns Rd -Tarrytwn 10591
(212) 902-1000 .. **Mancini,** Robt S '85 %Goldman Sachs -1 NY Plz -NY 10004
(212) 657-2171 .. **Mancini,** Susanna '91 %Citibank -111 Wall -NY 10043
(516) 393-2200 .. **Mancino,** Peter B '96 (Garfunkel W,PC) -111 Grt Nck Rd -Gt Neck 11021
(212) 728-8000 .. **Mancino,** Richd '83 (Willkie F&G LLP) -787 7th Av -NY 10019
(914) 684-2100 .. **Mancino,** Vincent P '99 (Littman K LLP) -399 Knollwood Rd -White Plns 10603
(585) 419-8800 .. **Mancuso,** John A '10 %Harris B PLLC -99 Garnsey Rd -Pittsfrd 14534
(315) 471-3151 .. **Mancuso,** Jos T '98 (Hancock & E,LLP) -1500 AXA Twr I Bx4976 -Syracuse 13221
(212) 447-8690 .. **Mancuso,** Karen W '80 OfCnsl Lamson & C,PC -9 E 40th -NY 10016 **Fx:**447-8691
(212) 872-1000 .. **Mancuso,** Mario '97 -One Bryant Park -NY 10036 **Fx:**872-1002
(212) 710-3900 .. **Mancuso,** Peter G '09 %Clyde & Co US LLP -405 Lex Av -NY 10174 **Fx:**710-3950
(516) 571-3800 .. **Mancuso,** Peter J '79 %DA -262 Old Cntry Rd -Mineola 11501 **Fx:**248-9479
(718) 983-1300 .. **Mancuso,** Philip '04 -201 Edward Curry Av -Staten Isl 10314 **Fx:**983-1308
(914) 761-9200 .. **Mancuso,** Robt J '74 (Mancuso R&F) -1 N Bway -White Plns 10601
(914) 761-9200 .. **Mancuso Rubin & Fufidio** -1 N Bway -White Plns 10601 **Fx:**686-3478
(716) 855-2800 .. **Mancuso,** Scott D '10 %Mura & S,PLLC -14 Lafayette Sq #930 -Buffalo 14203
(315) 793-9041 .. **Mancuso,** Steven P '02 -1331 Belle Av -Utica 13501
(212) 883-6500 .. **Mancuso,** Susan Anne '86 %Podell SS&B,LLP -605 3rd Av -NY 10158
(212) 902-9836 .. **Mandac,** Janice C '07 Goldman Sachs & Co -85 Broad -NY 10004
(516) 228-3908 .. **Manda-Flannery,** Roberta H '88 %UIA Bd -400 Oak -Gdn Cty 11530 **Fx:**794-1061
(212) 835-1514 .. **Mandal,** Paul H '96 %Dreifuss B&P,LLP -1 Penn Plz -NY 10019
(212) 754-5000 .. **Mandarano,** Elizabeth R '99 Yoga Effects,LLC -226 E 54th -NY 10022
(631) 724-6666 .. **Mandaro,** Gayle A '93 %P Gierer -400 Town Line Rd Bx5296 -Hauppauge 11788 **Fx:**724-6602
(212) 336-8000 .. **Mandaro,** Richd S '95 SrCnsl Amster R&E -90 Park Av -NY 10016
(516) 328-2300 .. **Mandato,** Albert L '94 %Abrams FFEGF&E,LLP -1111 Marcus Av -Lk Success 11042
(212) 422-0202 .. **Mandel,** Aaron F '06 %Sedgwick DM&A LLP -125 Broad -NY 10004
(212) 627-9898 .. **Mandel,** Adam D '06 %Sloss Law Ofc,PC -555 W 25th -NY 10001 **Fx:**627-9498
(718) 579-3000 .. **Mandel,** Andrew R '88 %Leg Aid -1020 Grnd Cncrs -Bronx 10451 **Fx:**588-2611
(212) 788-8148 .. **Mandel,** Barbara J '85 %Admin Children's Srvcs -220 Church -NY 10013
(212) 218-5500 .. **Mandel,** Barry H '70 (Seyfarth S LLP) -620 8th Av -NY 10018
(212) 338-3564 .. **Mandel,** Barry J '72 (Foley & L LLP) -90 Park Av -NY 10016
(718) 847-8985 .. **Mandel,** Barry S '92 -83-30 118th -Kew Gdns 11415 **Fx:**847-8035
(518) 283-9099 .. **Mandel Clemente,PC** -120 DeFreest Dr -North Greenbush 12180 **Fx:**283-0900
(212) 753-5000 .. **Mandel,** David A '66 OfCnsl Schiff H LLP -900 3rd Av -NY 10022
(212) 269-5600 .. **Mandel,** Evan M '04 (Mandel B LLP) -11 Bway -NY 10004 **Fx:**(646) 964-6667
(212) 595-3320 .. **Mandel,** Franklin B '73 -290 W End Av -NY 10023 **Fx:**595-3319
(212) 594-5200 .. **Mandel,** Fredk H '61 (Mandel & M,LLP) -1350 Bway -NY 10018 **Fx:**594-5236
(212) 455-2000 .. **Mandel,** Gary B '95 (Simpson T&B LLP) -425 Lex Av -NY 10017
(718) 471-0100 .. **Mandel,** Gary J '91 -1931 Mott Av -Far Rckwy 11691 **Fx:**471-0138
(212) 548-0600 .. **Mandel,** Harlan M '90 %Open Soc Jstc Initiative -400 W 59th -NY 10019 **Fx:**548-4679
(212) 533-3396 .. **Mandel,** Howard M '85 -541 E 20th -NY 10010
(212) 541-2000 .. **Mandel,** Jack '81 OfCnsl Bryan C LLP -1290 Av of Amer -NY 10104
(212) 692-1000 .. **Mandel,** Jamie B '01 (Duane M LLP) -1540 Bway -NY 10036
(718) 788-6800 .. **Mandel,** Jerome P '69 (J Mandel,PC) -26 Court -Brklyn 11242 **Fx:**643-0181
(718) 250-2000 .. **Mandel,** Jodi L '86 %DA -350 Jay -Brklyn 11201 **Fx:**250-2314
(718) 229-3600 .. **Mandel,** Jos M '40 -42-11 214th Pl -Bayside 11361 **Fx:**229-0975
(845) 639-7800 .. **Mandel Katz & Brosnan,LLP** -210 Route 303 -Vly Cottage 10989 **Fx:**639-7850
(212) 530-5076 .. **Mandel,** Lena '91 -1 Chase Manh Plz -NY 10005 **Fx:**530-5219
(516) 365-3000 .. **Mandel,** Lewis R '73 OfCnsl Levy & S,PC -1615 Nrthrn Blvd -Manhsst 11030
(212) 370-1300 .. **Mandel,** Marc H '07 %Ellenoff G&S LLP -150 E 42nd -NY 10017
(212) 949-6300 .. **Mandel,** Marc O '76 (Golden & M,LLP) -122 E 42nd -NY 10168
(212) 819-8200 .. **Mandel,** Mark L '95 (White & C LLP) -1155 Av of Amer -NY 10036
(212) 756-2000 .. **Mandel,** Mark S '88 (Schulte R&Z LLP) -919 3rd Av -NY 10022
(212) 687-4900 .. **Mandel,** Michl '02 %Wormser KG&J LLP -825 3rd Av -NY 10022
(212) 554-1400 .. **Mandel,** Noam N '04 %Bernstein LB&G LLP -1285 Av of Amer -NY 10019
(212) 594-5200 .. **Mandel,** Patricia C '76 (Mandel & M,LLP) -1350 Bway -NY 10018 **Fx:**594-5236
(212) 449-2440 .. **Mandel,** Philip M '73 %Merrill Lynch -220 Bway -NY 10038
(914) 946-5093 .. **Mandel,** Richd R '78 %LP Biondi -81 Main -White Plns 10601 **Fx:**946-7372
(212) 790-9200 .. **Mandel,** Richd S '86 (Cowan L&L,PC) -1133 Av of Amer -NY 10036
(914) 946-7430 .. **Mandel,** Robt '83 -300 Hmltn Av -White Plns 10601 **Fx:**946-5051
(212) 557-7200 .. **Mandel,** Ron J '06 %Davidoff M&H,LLP -605 3rd Av -NY 10158
(212) 366-2002 .. **Mandel,** Scott H '98 -375 Hudson -NY 10014
(516) 625-1700 .. **Mandel,** Scott J '00 %Salamon GB&S,PC -97 Powerhse Rd -Roslyn Hts 11577
(212) 697-7383 .. **Mandel,** Steven J '80 (Mandel Law Firm) -370 Lex Av -NY 10017 **Fx:**681-6157
(212) 356-7552 .. **Mandel,** Susan L '82 Ofc of Leg Srvcs -333 7th Av -NY 10001
(212) 668-1700 .. **Mandel,** Val '95 (V Mandel,PC) -80 Wall -NY 10005 **Fx:**668-1701
(914) 723-6180 .. **Mandel,** Veronica H '87 -340 Ardsley Rd -Scarsdale 10583 **Fx:**723-1424
(631) 396-5000 .. **Mandelbaum,** Adam I '00 Nu Horizons Electronics Corp -70 Maxess Rd -Melvll 11747
(212) 269-4900 .. **Mandelbaum,** Andrew I '05 %Ford MEW&G,LLP -Wall Street Plz -NY 10005
(718) 431-1166 .. **Mandelbaum,** Chas '87 -3910 14th Av -Brklyn 11218 **Fx:**633-0494
(212) 482-2190 .. **Mandelbaum,** David L '93 -88 Pine -NY 10005
(212) 657-1275 .. **Mandelbaum,** Elaine H '84 Citigroup Global Mrkts -77 Water -NY 10005
(914) 421-0500 .. **Mandelbaum,** Howard F '75 (Levine & M) -222 Bloomingdale Rd -White Plns 10605
(212) 864-4058 .. **Mandelbaum,** Joel I '77 -825 West End Av -NY 10025
(212) 757-0007 .. **Mandelbaum,** Sara L '88 Cnsl Scarola E LLP -888 7th Av -NY 10106
(914) 949-6400 .. **Mandelbaum,** Seth M '97 %McCullough G&S,LLP -1311 Mamaroneck Av -White Plns 10605
(212) 766-1888 .. **Mandelbaum,** Tara P '98 %Morris DA&F -2 Rector -NY 10006
(212) 784-5800 .. **Mandelbaum,** Thos I '85 (Hiscock & B,LLP) -7 Times Sq -NY 10036
(516) 624-0240 .. **Mandelbaum,** W Adam '81 -62 South -Oyster Bay 11771 **Fx:**624-8067
(718) 254-0700 .. **Mandelcorn,** Harvey S '73 %Bklyn Defender Srvcs -177 Lvngstn -Brklyn 11201 **Fx:**254-0897
(212) 682-8383 .. **Mandelker,** Lawr A '68 (Kantor DWMT&G,PC) -51 E 42nd -NY 10017
(212) 218-5500 .. **Mandelker,** Lawr D '04 %Seyfarth S LLP -620 8th Av -NY 10018
(212) 969-3000 .. **Mandelker,** Sigal P '03 SrCnsl Proskauer R LLP -1585 Bway -NY 10036
(718) 403-3600 .. **Mandelkorn,** Marcia '98 %Dept of Finance -345 Adams -Brklyn 11201 **Fx:**403-3650
(845) 246-3666 .. **Mandell,** Adam T '08 %Maynard OS&C,LLP -Bx180 -Saugerties 12477
(212) 768-6700 .. **Mandell,** Andrea N '93 (Sonnenschein N&R LLP) -2 World Fncl Ctr -NY 10281
(212) 331-4680 .. **Mandell,** Andrew '81 HRA -180 Water -NY 10038
(516) 688-1700 .. **Mandell,** Andrew J '86 %IRS -1600 Stewart Av -Westbury 11590 **Fx:**688-1750
(212) 459-0500 .. **Mandell,** Arnold '66 Mandell & M -1501 Bway -NY 10036 **Fx:**459-2896
(212) 213-8860 .. **Mandell,** Danl C '95 (Caraballo & M,LLC) -10 E 40th -NY 10016
(212) 676-6296 .. **Mandell,** David S '98 %Business Integrity Comm -100 Church -NY 10007 **Fx:**676-6204
(212) 704-6000 .. **Mandell,** Edw R '68 (Troutman S LLP) -405 Lex Av -NY 10174
(212) 225-2000 .. **Mandell,** Elizabeth Scarlett '05 %Cleary GS&H -1 Lbrty Plz -NY 10006
(212) 867-4777 .. **Mandell,** Howard L '88 -60 E 42nd -NY 10165
(516) 599-8822 .. **Mandell,** Irving '62 (Gellman & M) -29 Bway -Lynbrk 11563
(914) 741-6100 .. **Mandell,** Jacqueline '92 %Kaufman B&R -200 Summit Lk Dr -Valhalla 10595
(212) 883-4953 .. **Mandell,** Jill L '98 %Cozen O -277 Park Av -NY 10172 **Fx:**672-1153
(516) 599-8833 .. **Mandell,** Jonathan D '93 (Mandell & S) -29 Bway -Lynbrk 11563 **Fx:**599-6611
(718) 286-6000 .. **Mandell,** Joshua Scott '96 %DA -125-01 Qns Blvd -Kew Gdns 11415
(516) 354-2800 .. **Mandell Mandell Okin & Edelman,LLP** -3000 Marcus Av -Lk Success 11042 **Fx:**354-2803
(718) 281-0890 .. **Mandell,** Marie '79 -42-40 Bell Blvd -Bayside 11361
(516) 354-2800 .. **Mandell,** Mark J '74 (Mandell MO&E,LLP) -3000 Marcus Av -Lk Success 11042
(516) 354-2800 .. **Mandell,** Matthew M '00 (Mandell MO&E,LLP) -3000 Marcus Av -Lk Success 11042
(212) 695-8100 .. **Mandell,** Mordy '95 %Goetz F,LLP -1 Penn Plz -NY 10119
(845) 294-2616 .. **Mandell,** Richd '73 -60 Erie -Goshen 10924
(212) 839-5300 .. **Mandell,** Robt '95 (Sidley A LLP) -787 7th Av -NY 10019
(212) 593-6700 .. **Mandell,** Steven C '67 OfCnsl Aaronson RF&D,LLP -757 3rd Av -NY 10017
(212) 277-4000 .. **Mandelli,** Giorgio F '09 %Freshfields BD LLP -520 Mad Av -NY 10022
(212) 969-3000 .. **Mandelman,** Marc A '94 SrCnsl Proskauer R LLP -1585 Bway -NY 10036
(212) 478-7200 .. **Mandelsberg,** Steven J '79 (Hahn & H LLP) -488 Mad Av -NY 10022
(516) 997-0999 .. **Mandelup,** A Scott '78 (Pryor & M,LLP) -675 Old Cntry Rd -Westbury 11590
(212) 424-9556 .. **Mander,** Wm L '72 -59 Maiden Ln -NY 10038 **Fx:**262-2769
(516) 746-0180 .. **Mandera,** Cindy E '94 OfCnsl J Zenir,PC -114 Old Cntry Rd -Mineola 11501 **Fx:**741-7853

(212) 878-8000 .. **Manders**, Jonathan L B '07 %Clifford C LLP -31 W 52nd -NY 10019
(516) 741-6009 .. **Mandery**, Edw J '93 (Mandery & M) -332 Willis Av -Mineola 11501 **Fx:**747-3136
(212) 237-8000 .. **Mandery**, Evan J '93 %John Jay Cllg -899 10th Av -NY 10019
(516) 741-6009 .. **Mandery**, Melanie '94 (Mandery & M) -332 Willis Av -Mineola 11501 **Fx:**747-3136
(718) 263-3695 .. **Mandiberg**, Susan B '92 -123-20 82nd Av -Kew Gdns 11415 **Fx:**263-3697
(718) 237-2000 .. **Mandic**, Jean '91 %Leg Aid -111 Lvngstn -Brklyn 11201 **Fx:**237-8737
(718) 418-4150 .. **Mandija**, Alma '04 -66-57 Fresh Pond Rd -Rdgwd 11385 **Fx:**418-6447
(212) 833-7343 .. **Mandil**, Danl M '90 Sony BMG Music Corp -550 Mad Av -NY 10022
(718) 767-4165 .. **Mandina**, Constance M '68 -14-34 162nd -Beechurst 11357
(845) 639-7800 .. **Mandler**, John J '03 (Mandel K&B,LLP) -210 Route 303 -Vly Cottage 10989
(631) 424-2525 .. **Mandler**, Peter A '86 (Mandler & S,LLP) -1609 NY Av -Huntngtn Sta 11746
(212) 697-1111 .. **Mandler**, Ronald M '97 %L-3 Cmmnctns Corp -600 3rd Av -NY 10016 **Fx:**682-7959
(631) 424-2525 .. **Mandler & Sieger,LLP** -1609 NY Av -Huntngtn Sta 11746 **Fx:**424-4676
(718) 298-7300 .. **Mandleur**, Yvonne '92 Envrnmntl Cntrl Bd -144-06 94th Av -Jamaica 11435
(212) 577-3433 .. **Mandor**, Melissa C '06 Leg Aid Juv Rghts -199 Water -NY 10038 **Fx:**577-3520
(212) 218-2100 .. **Mandra**, Raymond R '91 (Fitzpatrick CH&S) -1290 Av of Amer -NY 10104
(845) 512-6000 .. **Mandracchia**, Stephen P '84 %Hudson Technologies -1 Blue Hill Plz Bx1541 -Pearl Rvr 10965 **Fx:**512-6070
(212) 336-2000 .. **Mandrgoc**, Melissa A '01 %Patterson BW&T LLP -1133 Av of Amer -NY 10036
(315) 479-8660 .. **Mandronico**, Timothy R '00 %Alexander & C,LLC -115 E Jffrsn -Syracuse 13202
(718) 253-5519 .. **Manela**, Chanie '87 -1476 E 21st -Brklyn 11210
(585) 473-2904 .. **Manello**, Seymour '66 -265 Warren Av -Rchstr 14618 **Fx:**442-6369
(516) 741-5252 .. **Manes**, Barbara E '79 %Sanders SBWV&G,PC -100 Hrrcks Rd -Mineola 11501
(845) 279-2995 .. **Manes**, Connie Anne '97 -Bx719 -Brewstr 10509
(212) 717-5358 .. **Manes**, Harvey R '05 -200 E 69th -NY 10021
(212) 806-5400 .. **Manes**, Janna '94 (Stroock &S&L LLP) -180 Maiden Ln -NY 10038
(212) 519-7847 .. **Manes**, Jonathan M '09 ACLU -125 Broad -NY 10004
(315) 422-1391 .. **Manes**, Sidney L '55 OfCnsl Green & S,PLLC -One Lincoln Ctr #900 -Syracuse 13202
(914) 762-0957 .. **Manes**, Victoria E '79 (Triad Grp,LLC) -185 Jordan Rd -Troy 12180 **Fx:**762-3726
(212) 947-8710 .. **Manesis**, Harry P '82 -224 W 30th -NY 10001 **Fx:**564-2543
(718) 461-6633 .. **Manessis**, John S '01 Mallilo & G -163-09 Nrthrn Blvd -Flushng 11358
(212) 408-5100 .. **Manetta**, Stephen J '95 Cnsl Chadbourne & P LLP -30 Rckfllr Plz -NY 10112
(914) 631-0280 .. **Manetti**, Renald A '57 -418 Bellwood Av -Tarrytwn 10591
(212) 545-4731 .. **Manevitz**, Ingrid C '03 %Wolf HAF&H LLP -270 Mad Av -NY 10016
(917) 733-5103 .. **Manewitz**, Mark L '74 (Manewitz & S LLC) -360 E 72nd -NY 10021 **Fx:**(609) 935-0567
(518) 477-7951 .. **Maney**, Anthony S '91 (Maney M&L) -77 Troy Rd -E Greenbush 12061
(518) 447-7110 .. **Maney**, John E '88 Cnty Atty -112 State -Albany 12207
(518) 463-1311 .. **Maney**, Kevin P '82 (Scheiberling R&M) -100 State -Albany 12207
(315) 471-3151 .. **Maney**, Maureen E '02 (Hancock & E,LLP) -1500 AXA Twr I Bx4976 -Syracuse 13221
(518) 477-7951 .. **Maney McConville & Liccardi** -77 Troy Rd -E Greenbush 12061 **Fx:**477-6851
(212) 558-4000 .. **Maney**, Michl M '66 SrCnsl Sullivan & C LLP -125 Broad -NY 10004
(212) 626-4100 .. **Maney**, Michele '03 %Baker & M LLP -1114 Av of Amer -NY 10036
(518) 477-7951 .. **Maney**, Patrick T '67 (Maney M&L) -77 Troy Rd -E Greenbush 12061
(212) 237-0000 .. **Manford**, L Price '08 (Vinson & E LLP) -666 5th Av -NY 10103
(212) 931-7811 .. **Manfred**, Robt D Jr. '99 MLB -245 Park Av -NY 10167 **Fx:**949-5657
(212) 839-5300 .. **Manfredi**, Dennis M '00 (Sidley A LLP) -787 7th Av -NY 10019
(914) 333-0510 .. **Manfredi**, Francis P '85 (Manfredi Assoc,PLLC) -35 Rosehill Av -Tarrytwn 10591
(631) 424-6100 .. **Manfredi**, Linda P '98 Advantage Title -410 NY Av -Huntngtn 11743 **Fx:**424-6049
(315) 435-2470 .. **Manfredi**, Michl J '09 DA -505 S State -Syracuse 13202 **Fx:**435-3969
(518) 462-0300 .. **Manfredo**, Robt F '09 %Girvin & F,PC -20 Corp Wds Blvd -Albany 12211
(914) 736-1918 .. **Manfredonia**, Albert W '83 -1200 Brown -Peekskill 10566
(631) 277-8080 .. **Manfredonia**, Andrew P '05 OfCnsl Cassidy R&L,PC -70 W Main -E Islip 11730 **Fx:**277-4908
(914) 345-3020 .. **Manfro**, Jordan J '07 %Knuckles K&E,LLP -565 Taxter Rd -Elmsfrd 10523
(718) 575-5145 .. **Manfro**, Lisa A '86 -80-02 Kew Grdns Rd -Kew Gdns 11415 **Fx:**268-4812
(212) 832-2049 .. **Manfro**, Melissa J '06 %Schreck RDA&H -1790 Bway -NY 10019 **Fx:**832-2969
(212) 813-8800 .. **Mang**, Jason C '08 Goodwin P LLP -620 8th Av -NY 10018
(718) 464-4448 .. **Mangal**, Yovendra '05 (DelCarmen & M,PC) -8787 F Lewis Blvd -Qns Vllg 11427
(646) 458-6865 .. **Mangalo**, Renee L '98 ACE USA -140 Bway -NY 10005
(212) 239-4922 .. **Mangalonzo**, Manuel V '85 -110 W 34th -NY 10001
(914) 576-7630 .. **Mangan**, J Warren '62 (O'Connor & M,PC) -271 North Av -New Rchll 10801
(716) 842-5400 .. **Mangan**, John G II '90 M&T Bank Corp -One M&T Plz -Buffalo 14203
(845) 268-2438 .. **Mangan**, John J Jr. '84 -25 N Conger Av -Congers 10920
(212) 834-1080 .. **Mangan**, Linda R '84 %GreenPoint Bk -90 Park Av -NY 10016 **Fx:**834-1402
(212) 823-2815 .. **Mangan**, Louis T '88 Alliance Bernstein LP -1345 Av of Amer -NY 10105 **Fx:**554-4639
(607) 748-7351 .. **Mangan**, Maureen A '01 %Leasure GM&R -101 Jffrsn Av -Endicott 13760
(212) 248-2171 .. **Mangan**, Michl P '99 -160 Pearl -NY 10005 **Fx:**248-2155
(516) 483-4500 .. **Manganillo**, Carlo '74 (Lazarowitz & M,PLLC) -33 Front -Hempstd 11550 **Fx:**483-4511
(516) 571-6000 .. **Mangano**, Edw P '88 County Exec -1550 Franklin Av -Mineola 11501
(631) 242-3690 .. **Mangano**, Frank V '74 -514 DeWitt Av -N Babylon 11703 **Fx:**242-3669
(212) 751-2700 .. **Mangano**, Guy J '55 %JAMS -620 8th Av -NY 10018 **Fx:**751-4099
(212) 244-7676 .. **Mangano**, Kenneth E '83 (Ferro KMS,PC) -424 W 33rd -NY 10001
(315) 471-0065 .. **Mangano Lucchesi & Collins** -201 E Jffrsn -Syracuse 13202 **Fx:**471-5759
(315) 471-0065 .. **Mangano**, Rocco J '82 (Mangano L&C) -201 E Jffrsn -Syracuse 13202
(646) 872-2067 .. **Mangaroo**, Charmaine Salama '02 (Firm Resolutns LLC) -125-28 Qns Blvd -Kew Gdns 11415
(212) 596-9000 .. **Mangasarian**, Karen '01 %Ropes & G LLP -1211 Av of Amer -NY 10036
(516) 319-6018 .. **Mangelli**, John J '96 -12 16th -Bayvll 11709
(212) 833-8151 .. **Manghisi**, Jos R '88 Sony Corp of Amer -550 Mad Av -NY 10022
(212) 336-2000 .. **Mangi**, Adeel Abdullah '01 (Patterson BW&T LLP) -1133 Av of Amer -NY 10036
(516) 294-1949 .. **Mangi**, Robt C '82 (Mangi & G LLP) -1400 Old Cntry Rd -Westbury 11590
(516) 364-0200 .. **Mangia**, Angelo J '79 Standard Funding Corp -335 Crsswys Park Dr -Woodbury 11797
(914) 686-1041 .. **Mangialardi**, Arlene Paregian '86 -111 N Central Av -Hartsdale 10530
(914) 686-1041 .. **Mangialardi**, John '84 (Mangialardi & B) -111 N Central Av -Hartsdale 10530 **Fx:**686-1043
(631) 582-4098 .. **Mangiaracina**, Anthony J '84 -1727 Vets Mem'l Hwy -Islandia 11749 **Fx:**582-4140
(516) 781-5515 .. **Mangiaracina**, Jos '68 -2169 Jones Av -Wantagh 11793 **Fx:**826-4391
(212) 808-7800 .. **Mangiardi**, Anne M '07 %Kelley D&W LLP -101 Park Av -NY 10178
(914) 235-7176 .. **Mangiatordi**, Frank P '60 -5 Wilputte Pl -New Rchll 10804 **Fx:**235-7176
(212) 308-1000 .. **Mangieri**, Frank J '91 RFR Holding LLC -390 Park Av -NY 10022 **Fx:**308-8510
(516) 294-5433 .. **Manginello**, Melissa '08 %Ahmuty D&M -200 IU Willets Rd -Albertson 11507
(212) 261-8000 .. **Mangino**, Robt M Jr. '85 (Mendes & M,LLP) -750 7th Av -NY 10019
(585) 423-0952 .. **Mangione**, Salvatore A '79 (Mangione & Assoc,PC) -205 St Paul -Rchstr 14604 **Fx:**546-8355
(212) 695-5454 .. **Mango**, Anthony G '94 (Mango & I,LLP) -14 Penn Plz -NY 10122
(518) 382-0203 .. **Mango**, Chas J '82 -207 Mohawk Av -Scotia 12302 **Fx:**382-0427
(212) 695-5454 .. **Mango & Iacoviello,LLP** -14 Penn Plz -NY 10122 **Fx:**695-0797
(914) 288-8052 .. **Mangold**, Christopher L '86 (Danziger & M LLP) -170 Hmltn Av -White Plns 10601 **Fx:**323-0369
(845) 486-6800 .. **Mangold**, Harold L '65 OfCnsl McCabe & M LLP -63 Wshngtn Bx509 -Poughkeepsie 12602
(212) 909-6000 .. **Mangold**, Rebecca G '09 %Debevoise & P LLP -919 3rd Av -NY 10022
(716) 645-2428 .. **Mangold**, Susan Vivian '94 %SUNY Buffalo Lw Schl -O'Brian Hall -Buffalo 14260 **Fx:**645-5968
(212) 832-0034 .. **Mangold**, Suzanne B '79 -575 Park Av -NY 10065
(914) 358-1380 .. **Mangone**, Anthony J '01 -399 Knollwood Rd -White Plns 10603 **Fx:**358-1381
(516) 520-1000 .. **Manheim**, Jason P '99 -650 Wantagh Av -Levittwn 11756
(212) 761-4000 .. **Manheimer**, Edw S '04 Morgan Stanley -1585 Bway -NY 10036
(516) 280-3065 .. **Manheimer**, Jeffrey A '75 -377 Oak -Gdn Cty 11530 **Fx:**280-3067
(212) 309-6000 .. **Mani**, Namita E '05 %Morgan L&B LLP -101 Park Av -NY 10178
(212) 635-6734 .. **Mani**, Nandini '98 Bank of NY-Mellon -1 Wall -NY 10286
(212) 351-4500 .. **Maniar**, Purvi Badiani '02 (Epstein B&G,PC) -250 Park Av -NY 10177
(716) 884-4202 .. **Manias**, Giles P '71 -295 Main -Buffalo 14203 **Fx:**362-3151
(212) 261-8000 .. **Maniatis**, George L '82 (Mendes & M,LLP) -750 7th Av -NY 10019
(212) 244-2999 .. **Maniatis**, Richd M '09 %Kopff N&D LLP -440 9th Av -NY 10001
(212) 594-5300 .. **Maniatis**, Victoria J '94 %Milberg LLP -1 Penn Plz -NY 10119
(212) 248-5060 .. **Maniatis**, Wm J '96 (Schlemmer & M LLP) -111 Bway -NY 10006 **Fx:**389-9793
(212) 896-6500 .. **Manice**, Chas D '08 %Howrey LLP -601 Lex Av -NY 10022
(315) 866-0006 .. **Manieri**, Jessica M '03 %K Bowers -209 N Wshngtn -Herkimer 13350 **Fx:**866-0689
(917) 237-2929 .. **Manierre**, Paul S '88 Axiom Law -75 Spring -NY 10012
(212) 545-4600 .. **Manifold**, Betsy C '87 (Wolf HAF&H LLP) -270 Mad Av -NY 10016
(973) 228-5700 .. **Manigan**, Mark E '04 (Brach E LLC) -100 Park Av -NY 10017 **Fx:**228-7852
(212) 626-6738 .. **Manigault**, L Monique '03 (M Manigault,PC) -1120 Av of Amer -NY 10036
(718) 250-2000 .. **Manigo**, Simone M '07 %DA -350 Jay -Brklyn 11201 **Fx:**250-2314
(585) 428-5210 .. **Manin**, J B Afoh '07 Pub Def -10 N Fitzhugh -Rchstr 14614 **Fx:**428-2234
(631) 389-0046 .. **Manin**, Mara S '91 -105 Maxess Rd -Melvll 11747
(585) 461-0195 .. **Manioci**, Gerald '66 -124 Wntrgrn Way -Rchstr 14618 **Fx:**461-1767
(518) 447-8500 .. **Manion**, Aaron T '04 1st Albany Mgmt Corp -677 Bway -Albany 12207
(315) 724-1800 .. **Manion**, Ann W '88 -2106 Genesee -Utica 13502 **Fx:**724-3817
(212) 478-7200 .. **Manion**, Christopher A '09 Hahn & H LLP -488 Mad Av -NY 10022
(212) 839-5300 .. **Manion**, Timothy J '08 %Sidley A LLP -787 7th Av -NY 10019
(212) 269-0927 .. **Manire**, Michl L '83 (D'Amato & L,LLP) -2 World Fncl Ctr -NY 10281
(212) 435-3571 .. **Maniscalco**, Ilea A '07 %Port Auth of NY/NJ -225 Park Av S -NY 10003 **Fx:**435-3555
(516) 826-6500 .. **Maniscalco**, Jos S '96 (LaMonica H&M LLP) -3305 Jerusalem Av -Wantagh 11793
(914) 681-8700 .. **Maniscalco**, Karen '97 %Milber MP&S LLP -3 Barker Av -White Plns 10601
(212) 213-1933 .. **Maniscalco**, Patricia '93 -276 5th Av -NY 10001
(212) 490-3000 .. **Manisero**, Thos R '83 (Wilson EME&D LLP) -150 E 42nd -NY 10017

(212) 382-2221 .. **Maniskas,** Richd A '09 %Glancy B&G LLP -1430 Bway -NY 10018 **Fx:**382-3944
(516) 942-7801 .. **Manister,** Todd J '84 (O'Brien & M,PC) -120 Bethpage Rd -Hicksvll 11801
(212) 490-3000 .. **Manjeshwar,** Sana A '08 %Wilson EME&D LLP -150 E 42nd -NY 10017
(716) 566-1300 .. **Manka,** Brian G '05 %Hiscock & B,LLP -1100 M&T Ctr -Buffalo 14203
(212) 790-0362 .. **Mankad,** Leena D '01 Benj N Cardozo Schl of Law -55 5th Av -NY 10003 **Fx:**790-0345
(518) 474-4367 .. **Mankes,** Karen Marcoux '75 %Dept of Law -The Cptl -Albany 12224
(212) 468-4800 .. **Manket,** Steven M '82 (Davis & G LLP) -1740 Bway -NY 10019
(516) 357-3000 .. **Manko,** David A '96 (Rivkin R LLP) -926 RXR Plz -Uniondale 11556
(212) 428-2105 .. **Mankos,** Rose M '01 %NYS Ofc of Cont Legal Edu -25 Beaver -NY 10004
(315) 866-7976 .. **Manley,** Donald F '04 Manley Law Firm,PC -109 Park Av Bx16 -Herkimer 13350 **Fx:**219-5453
(212) 483-9490 .. **Manley,** Fred A Jr. '79 OfCnsl McElroy DM&C,LLP -88 Pine -NY 10005
(212) 335-9000 .. **Manley,** Heather C '01 %DA -1 Hogan Pl -NY 10013
(631) 853-4161 .. **Manley,** Jonathan B '07 DA -N Cnty Cmplx Bldg 77 -Hauppauge 11788 **Fx:**853-4192
(518) 434-1493 .. **Manley,** Kathy E '01 %Kindlon & S,PC -74 Chapel -Albany 12207
(212) 219-1800 .. **Manley,** Linda Schechter '92 %Lawyers Alliance NY -171 Mad Av -NY 10016 **Fx:**941-7458
(845) 634-0888 .. **Manley,** Loring K '56 OfCnsl Freeman & L RLLP -4 Laurel Rd -New Cty 10956
(212) 684-4400 .. **Manley,** Marisa '83 %Commercial Tenant Rep -295 Mad Av -NY 10017 **Fx:**684-4403
(212) 969-1337 .. **Manley,** Mark R '90 %Alliance Bernstein LP -1345 Av of Amer -NY 10105 **Fx:**554-4639
(914) 949-2700 .. **Manley,** Mary Ellen '79 (Bleakley P&S,LLP) -1 N Lex Av -White Plns 10601
(718) 780-8619 .. **Manley,** Steve '94 %Pfizer Inc -630 Flushing Av -Brklyn 11206
(718) 250-2000 .. **Manley,** Tracy A '03 %DA -350 Jay -Brklyn 11201 **Fx:**250-2314
(212) 902-3878 .. **Mann,** Arline '79 %Goldman Sachs -1 NY Plz -NY 10004
(212) 728-8000 .. **Mann,** Carissa M '10 %Willkie F&G LLP -787 7th Av -NY 10019
(917) 684-8772 .. **Mann,** Carolyn A '07 -485 Mad Av -NY 10022 **Fx:**(212) 588-0471
(914) 939-2000 .. **Mann,** Carolyn H '94 (Mann & M,LLP) -316 Wstchstr Av -Pt Chester 10573 **Fx:**939-2162
(212) 558-4000 .. **Mann,** Christopher L '91 (Sullivan & C LLP) -125 Broad -NY 10004
(212) 715-1000 .. **Mann,** Cynthia D '91 (Arnold & P LLP) -399 Park Av -NY 10022
(518) 445-2311 .. **Mann,** Deborah A '80 Albany Law Schl -80 New Scotland Av -Albany 12208 **Fx:**445-2315
(212) 834-0600 .. **Mann,** Emily C '00 %Gordon & S,PC -355 Lex Av -NY 10017
(212) 351-4000 .. **Mann,** Eric N '08 %Gibson D&C LLP -200 Park Av -NY 10166
(212) 341-2734 .. **Mann,** Francene Arden '86 ACS -150 William -NY 10038 **Fx:**341-2700
(914) 682-2634 .. **Mann,** Francis B Jr. '81 (MannBent & Assoc,PC) -50 Main -White Plns 10606 **Fx:**682-7784
(212) 753-5000 .. **Mann,** Henry Lee '07 %Schiff H LLP -900 3rd Av -NY 10022
(845) 638-4070 .. **Mann,** Howard '78 H Mann Law Firm -10 Esquire Rd -New Cty 10956 **Fx:**638-2443
(914) 682-2632 .. **Mann,** Howard L '66 -50 Main -White Plns 10606 **Fx:**682-2633
(212) 489-8230 .. **Mann,** James H '07 (Davis WT LLP) -1633 Bway -NY 10019
(212) 885-5000 .. **Mann,** Janet R '08 %Blank R LLP -405 Lex Av -NY 10174
(212) 806-5400 .. **Mann,** Jeffrey M '02 %Stroock &S&L LLP -180 Maiden Ln -NY 10038
(212) 801-2111 .. **Mann,** Jeffrey R '69 (Greenberg T,LLP) -200 Park Av -NY 10166
(212) 899-5146 .. **Mann,** Jeffrey S '99 Little Bear Invstmnts -11 Penn Plz -NY 10001 **Fx:**(917) 463-3812
(212) 735-3000 .. **Mann,** Jordan E '06 %Skadden ASM&F LLP -4 Times Sq -NY 10036
(212) 941-1888 .. **Mann,** Jos C '84 (Mann M&S,PC) -153 Centre -NY 10013 **Fx:**941-0554
(917) 297-8370 .. **Mann,** June R '99 -305 Bway -NY 10007
(212) 455-2000 .. **Mann,** Linton III '08 %Simpson T&B LLP -425 Lex Av -NY 10017
(212) 460-2020 .. **Mann,** Lisa B '82 Con Ed -4 Irving Pl -NY 10003
(212) 941-1888 .. **Mann,** Lydia Y '08 (Mann M&S,PC) -153 Centre -NY 10013 **Fx:**941-0554
(845) 358-0048 .. **Mann Mann & Lewis,PC** -17 S Bway Bx991 -Nyack 10960 **Fx:**358-1810
(212) 766-4700 .. **Mann,** Matthew C '03 %Katz & R -116 John -NY 10038 **Fx:**766-4705
(518) 785-3300 .. **Mann,** Matthew J '94 Mann Law Firm PC -Bx143 -Latham 12110 **Fx:**783-5691
(212) 307-5500 .. **Mann,** Megan H '10 %Venable LLP -1270 Av of Amer -NY 10020
(212) 839-5300 .. **Mann,** Michl D '07 %Sidley A LLP -787 7th Av -NY 10019
(914) 939-2000 .. **Mann,** Monroe Yale '49 (Mann & M,LLP) -316 Wstchstr Av -Pt Chester 10573 **Fx:**939-2162
(212) 416-8666 .. **Mann,** Neal S '76 %Dept of Law -120 Bway -NY 10271
(845) 358-0048 .. **Mann,** Orville H Jr. '61 (Mann M&L,PC) -17 S Bway Bx991 -Nyack 10960
(212) 566-3200 .. **Mann,** Pamela A '77 -45 Bway -NY 10006 **Fx:**566-0220
(914) 872-4010 .. **Mann,** Robt E '78 Westchester Wealth Advisors,LLC -800 Wstchstr Av -Pt Chester 10573
(631) 952-6505 .. **Mann,** Scott E '92 %UIA Bd -NYS Ofc Bldg -Hauppauge 11788 **Fx:**952-3385
(212) 859-8000 .. **Mann,** Simeon G '09 %Fried FHS&J LLP -1 NY Plz -NY 10004
(212) 689-8400 .. **Mann,** Stephen '60 Prescott Capital -645 5th Av -NY 10022 **Fx:**689-8490
(347) 404-9600 .. **Mann,** Steven A '06 Hon K McGrath Jr - Criminal Ct -120 Schermerhorn -Brklyn 11201
(212) 670-0152 .. **Mann,** V James '75 %Merrill Lynch -222 Bway -NY 10038
(212) 526-4071 .. **Manna,** Chas A '98 %Barclays Capital Inc -399 Park Av -NY 10022
(718) 996-7732 .. **Manna,** John S '76 -198 Av U -Brklyn 11223
(716) 849-1333 .. **Manna,** Jos J '96 (Lipsitz GSC LLP) -42 Delaware Av -Buffalo 14202
(845) 735-0510 .. **Manna,** Michl A '81 (M Manna & Assoc,PC) -300 N Mddltwn Rd -Pearl Rvr 10965 **Fx:**(201) 447-6631
(212) 381-4364 .. **Manna,** Santo '99 Murex NA Inc -810 7th Av -NY 10019
(212) 715-9100 .. **Mannal,** Douglas H '01 (Kramer LN&F,LLP) -1177 Av of Amer -NY 10036
(212) 689-1131 .. **Mannarino,** Arthur A '69 (Mannarino & C,PC) -315 Mad Av -NY 10017
(212) 689-1131 .. **Mannarino & Candela, PC** -315 Mad Av -NY 10017 **Fx:**689-4772
(212) 994-9963 .. **Mannarino,** Peter J '10 %Federman S LLP -220 E 42nd -NY 10017 **Fx:**685-5199
(212) 553-3200 .. **Mannarino,** Richd O '95 (Marulli LE&T,LLP) -5 Hanover Sq -NY 10004
(212) 458-3230 .. **Manne,** Eric S '00 AIG -175 Water -NY 10038
(315) 866-7642 .. **Manne,** Karl E '93 -107 Court -Herkimer 13350 **Fx:**866-8332
(518) 325-1777 .. **Manne,** Letty J '94 -Bx455 -Craryville 12521
(845) 567-5700 .. **Manners,** Robt A '82 Prdctn Resource Grp LLC -539 Temple Hill Rd -New Windsor 12553
(516) 942-3900 .. **Manners,** Robt M '94 (Manners & Assoc,LLP) -950 Jericho Tpk -Westbury 11590 **Fx:**942-4330
(212) 490-3000 .. **Manners,** Tania '04 %Wilson EME&D LLP -150 E 42nd -NY 10017
(212) 682-0580 .. **Mannheimer Swartling** -101 Park Av -NY 10178 **Fx:**682-0982
(516) 802-4915 .. **Manniello,** Michl C '88 M Manniello,PC -1025 Old Cntry Rd -Westbury 11590 **Fx:**802-4917
(716) 541-8222 .. **Mannillo,** Jeffrey C '97 -300 Pearl -Buffalo 14202 **Fx:**854-8258
(212) 641-3888 .. **Manning,** Barbara Brooke '79 %Schroder Investment Mgmt NA -875 3rd Av -NY 10022 **Fx:**641-3804
(716) 856-4000 .. **Manning,** Brian D '10 %Hodgson R LLP -140 Pearl -Buffalo 14202
(212) 513-3200 .. **Manning,** Cassaundra L '05 %Holland & K LLP -31 W 52nd -NY 10019
(518) 873-3380 .. **Manning,** Danl T III '90 Cnty Atty -7551 Court Bx217 -Elizabethtwn 12932 **Fx:**873-3894
(212) 425-9300 .. **Manning,** Diana C '94 (Bressler A&R,PC) -17 State -NY 10004
(718) 366-3800 .. **Manning,** Donald E '97 Ridgewood Senior Citizens Cncl -217 Wyckoff Av -Brklyn 11237
(914) 793-0288 .. **Manning,** James J P '57 (Manning & R) -65 Pondfld Rd -Bronxvll 10708
(212) 474-1000 .. **Manning,** Jane K '10 %Cravath S&M LLP -825 8th Av -NY 10019
(518) 439-2911 .. **Manning,** Jeremiah F '66 -49 Oldox Rd -Delmar 12054 **Fx:**439-2562
(518) 439-2911 .. **Manning,** Jeremiah F '96 -49 Oldox Rd -Delmar 12054 **Fx:**439-2562
(212) 806-5400 .. **Manning,** Jerome A '53 OfCnsl Stroock &S&L LLP -180 Maiden Ln -NY 10038
(914) 962-0778 .. **Manning,** John B '88 -1820 Commerce -Yorktwn Hts 10598 **Fx:**245-2262
(518) 963-4510 .. **Manning,** John T '60 (Manning & S) -3665 Essex Rd Bx309 -Willsboro 12996 **Fx:**963-7557
(914) 524-7550 .. **Manning,** John W '79 (JW Manning,PC) -120 Wht Plns Rd -Tarrytwn 10591 **Fx:**524-9769
(716) 847-8400 .. **Manning,** Kenneth A '78 (Phillips L LLP) -3400 HSBC Ctr -Buffalo 14203
(718) 242-8115 .. **Manning,** Lawr W '85 %JP Morgan Chase -4 Metrotech Ctr -Brklyn 11201
(212) 558-4000 .. **Manning,** Lindsay M '07 %Sullivan & C LLP -125 Broad -NY 10004
(212) 442-0399 .. **Manning,** Lori A '89 %Law Dept -100 Church -NY 10007 **Fx:**788-0367
(212) 867-4100 .. **Manning,** Melissa A '06 %Furman K&B LLP -61 Bway -NY 10006
(631) 853-4104 .. **Manning,** Michl '07 %DA -400 Carleton Av Bx9082 -Central Islip 11722 **Fx:**853-7838
(631) 577-7201 .. **Manning,** Michl F X '78 -100 Baylis Rd Bx9093 -Melvll 11747
(518) 474-8211 .. **Manning,** Michl G '79 %Law Reporting Bur -1 Commerce Plz -Albany 12210 **Fx:**463-6869
(212) 801-6861 .. **Manning,** Michl P '84 OfCnsl Greenberg T,LLP -200 Park Av -NY 10166
(315) 265-0470 .. **Manning,** Richd V '70 -10 Cassidy Rd Bx273 -Parishvll 13672
(516) 433-6677 .. **Manning,** Robt W '84 (Stewart GM&B) -6800 Jericho Tpk -Syosset 11791
(914) 793-0288 .. **Manning & Russo** -65 Pondfld Rd -Bronxvll 10708 **Fx:**793-0670
(212) 689-0700 .. **Manning,** Thos A '65 TA Manning & Assoc -12 E 41st -NY 10017
(212) 407-4000 .. **Manning,** Wm J Jr. '83 SrCnsl Loeb & L,LLP -345 Park Av -NY 10154
(914) 328-0404 .. **Manning,** Wm J '87 (Jackson L LLP) -1 N Bway -White Plns 10601
(845) 794-3000 .. **Mannino,** Karen '97 Cnty Atty -100 North Bx5012 -Monticello 12701 **Fx:**794-4924
(212) 313-3600 .. **Mannino,** Laureen M '94 %Barry M&M -2 Rector -NY 10006
(315) 478-3500 .. **Mannion & Copani** -224 Harrison -Syracuse 13202 **Fx:**478-0204
(516) 747-7400 .. **Mannion,** David M '07 %Rosenberg C&B LLP -100 Grdn City Plz -Gdn Cty 11530
(607) 737-2969 .. **Mannion,** Elizabeth J '06 %Pub Def -163 Lk Bx588 -Elmira 14902 **Fx:**737-2853
(315) 478-3500 .. **Mannion,** Terence A J '84 (Mannion & C) -224 Harrison -Syracuse 13202
(518) 793-2535 .. **Mannix,** Danl J '00 (Muller & M,PLLC) -257 Bay Rd Bx143 -Glens Fls 12801 **Fx:**793-6238
(518) 581-9615 .. **Mannix,** John C Jr. '85 -198 Church -Saratoga Spgs 12866 **Fx:**580-0882
(845) 471-0058 .. **Mannix,** Kathleen R '90 %Leg Srvcs -29 N Hmltn -Poughkeepsie 12601 **Fx:**471-0244
(212) 633-6967 .. **Mannix,** Mary R '76 %Natl Ctr Law & Economic Justice -275 7th Av -NY 10001 **Fx:**633-6371
(212) 930-9700 .. **Manno,** David B '98 (Sichenzia RFF LLP) -61 Bway -NY 10006
(516) 485-6698 .. **Manno,** Salvatore A '77 -652 Blackstone -E Meadow 11554
(212) 356-0336 .. **Manno,** Theo P '75 %SBLI Fund -460 W 34th -NY 10001 **Fx:**356-0376
(716) 434-2685 .. **Manns,** Amy Zuba '93 -6301 Tonawanda Creek Rd -Lockprt 14094
(212) 610-1505 .. **Manocha,** Rohit '84 Tri-Artisan Prtnrs -110 E 59th -NY 10022
(212) 244-7676 .. **Manolakis,** Michl N '00 %Ferro KMS,PC -424 W 33rd -NY 10001
(212) 479-5855 .. **Manolas,** Nicholas '96 Eurohype AG -1114 Av of Amer -NY 10036
(212) 230-8800 .. **Manor,** Edw O '07 WilmerHale -399 Park Av -NY 10022
(516) 741-1032 .. **Manoussos,** Michl '93 (Manoussos & M,PLLC) -595 Stewart Av -Gdn Cty 11530 **Fx:**741-7510
(212) 860-1400 .. **Manove,** Emily E '98 Hunter College High School -71 E 94th -NY 10128
(212) 826-7060 .. **Manowitz,** David B '63 Stahl Real Estate -277 Park Av -NY 10172 **Fx:**223-4609
(845) 896-1400 .. **Manpel,** Dominique A '87 -155 Main -Beacon 12508 **Fx:**831-9507

(518) 408-2088 .. **Mans**, Jeffrey P '86 %Ofc of Secretary to Gov -The Cptl -Albany 12224
(212) 479-6000 .. **Mansbach**, Peter J '61 SrCnsl Cooley LLP -1114 Av of Amer -NY 10036
(212) 698-3500 .. **Mansdorf**, Rachel D '05 %Dechert LLP -1095 Av of Amer -NY 10036
(212) 530-5000 .. **Mansfield**, Abbey L '09 %Milbank TH&M LLP -1 Chase Manh Plz -NY 10005
(212) 801-9277 .. **Mansfield**, Alan E '79 (Greenberg T,LLP) -200 Park Av -NY 10166
(516) 794-6500 .. **Mansfield**, Christopher F '00 %Kennedy & G -1050 Franklin Av -Gdn Cty 11530 **Fx**:794-5171
(631) 234-1188 .. **Mansfield**, David A '78 -1 Suffolk Sq -Islandia 11749
(212) 863-6300 .. **Mansfield**, Deborah S '77 %HPD -100 Gold -NY 10038
(212) 335-9000 .. **Mansfield**, Gregory H '82 %DA -1 Hogan Pl -NY 10013
(212) 676-6219 .. **Mansfield**, Michl J '85 %Business Integrity Comm -100 Church -NY 10007 **Fx**:676-6204
(845) 758-9108 .. **Mansfield**, Thos C '86 Golden Rabbit -55 Old Post Rd N -Red Hook 12571 **Fx**:758-3118
(212) 854-2003 .. **Manshel**, Andrew M '83 Barnard College -3009 Bway -NY 10027 **Fx**:854-4052
(518) 372-1121 .. **Mansion**, Jodi L '96 -1346 Ruffner Rd -Niskayuna 12309
(518) 464-1077 .. **Mansion**, Michl P '94 -1528 Central Av -Albany 12205 **Fx**:464-0280
(585) 454-2020 .. **Manske**, Brett L '00 (Cellino & B,PC) -16 W Main -Rchstr 14614
(212) 373-8087 .. **Mansky**, Adam J '93 Ctr for Ct Innovation -520 8th Av -NY 10018 **Fx**:397-0985
(516) 747-1990 .. **Manso**, Gary A '81 %Cascone & K,LLP -1399 Franklin Av -Gdn Cty 11530
(716) 438-2939 .. **Manson**, Alexander R '62 -111 Grasmere Rd -Lockprt 14094 **Fx**:433-8026
(516) 482-2155 .. **Manson**, Barry '68 -310 Nrthrn Blvd -Gt Neck 11021 **Fx**:482-2167
(845) 692-9700 .. **Manson**, David B '96 (Damelio G&M) -90 Crystal Run Rd -Middletwn 10941 **Fx**:692-9704
(212) 415-9200 .. **Manson**, Robt G '88 OfCnsl Dorsey & W LLP -250 Park Av -NY 10177
(212) 488-1598 .. **Mansoor**, Dustin P '07 Havkins RR&V,LLP -11 Penn Plz -NY 10001
(716) 285-3463 .. **Mansour**, David J '83 -324 Pine -Niagara Fls 14301 **Fx**:285-3463
(716) 858-2424 .. **Mansour**, James W II '05 %DA -25 Delaware Av -Buffalo 14202 **Fx**:858-7425
(212) 468-8000 .. **Mansour**, Jana W '00 (Morrison & F LLP) -1290 Av of Amer -NY 10104
(585) 381-7749 .. **Mansour**, John P '63 -489 Harrogate Dr -Rchstr 14625 **Fx**:381-7749
(646) 471-4000 .. **Mansouri**, Margaret Mourvarid '03 PricewaterhouseCoopers LLP -300 Mad Av -NY 10017
(516) 365-1792 .. **Mansouri**, Milene '99 -111 Firestone Cir -Roslyn 11576
(212) 922-2200 .. **Manteau**, Philippe C M '07 OfCnsl Watson F&W LLP -1133 Av of Amer -NY 10036
(212) 599-1515 .. **Mantel**, Allan D '77 (Stein RM,LLP) -405 Lex Av -NY 10174
(212) 953-5500 .. **Mantel**, Arthur S '71 (Alter M LLP) -90 Park Av -NY 10016
(212) 451-2300 .. **Mantel**, Kenneth S '07 %Olshan GFR&W LLP -65 E 55th -NY 10022
(718) 286-6000 .. **Mantell**, Benjamin J '04 %DA -125-01 Qns Blvd -Kew Gdns 11415
(646) 386-5891 .. **Mantell**, Deborah P '08 MHLS -41 Mad Av -NY 10010
(914) 725-4882 .. **Mantell**, Edmund H '78 -5 Carthage Ln -Scarsdale 10583
(718) 254-6253 .. **Mantell**, Laura D '98 %US Atty -271 Cadman Plz E -Brklyn 11201 **Fx**:254-6479
(212) 750-3896 .. **Mantell**, Michl '69 -60 E 42nd -NY 10165 **Fx**:768-2766
(973) 596-4533 .. **Mantell**, Natalie H '06 %Gibbons PC -1 Penn Plz -NY 10119 **Fx**:639-8351
(845) 565-1100 .. **Mantello**, Rebecca Baldwin '08 Tarshis CLM&M,PLLC -One Corwin Ct -Newburgh 12550
(212) 878-8000 .. **Manthas**, Vicky '98 Cnsl Clifford C LLP -31 W 52nd -NY 10019
(212) 310-8000 .. **Manthei**, Christina M '08 %Weil G&M LLP -767 5th Av -NY 10153
(718) 579-7900 .. **Mantilla**, Ruth M '09 Leg Aid -900 Sheridan Av -Bronx 10451 **Fx**:293-8744
(315) 423-2932 .. **Mantione**, Chas J Jr. '99 Workers Comp Bd -935 James -Syracuse 13203 **Fx**:423-2938
(718) 206-4727 .. **Mantione**, Patrick J '95 %Law Dept -89-17 Sutphin Blvd -Jamaica 11435 **Fx**:206-4702
(516) 887-4881 .. **Mantione**, Steven K '83 -333 Hempstd Av -Malverne 11565 **Fx**:599-6316
(917) 622-8983 .. **Mantione**, Swati P '95 -12 Thadford -E Northprt 11731 **Fx**:(631) 266-1627
(212) 335-4500 .. **Manton**, Lauren E '06 %DLA Piper LLP -1251 Av of Amer -NY 10020
(718) 823-8600 .. **Mantovani**, Andrew P '76 -2622 E Tremont Av -Bronx 10461 **Fx**:518-8273
(718) 237-3100 .. **Mantri**, Resham '07 Leg Aid -111 Lvngstn -Brklyn 11201 **Fx**:250-4243
(631) 393-9400 .. **Mantyla**, Kristen S '06 %Forster & G -500 Bi-Cnty Blvd Bx9030 -Farmngdl 11735
(646) 216-2400 .. **Manuali**, Corrado '01 (Kranjac M&V LLP) -40 Wall -NY 10005 **Fx**:216-2373
(212) 792-0999 .. **Manuel**, Chas B Jr. '77 (Manuel & R LLP) -1 Penn Plz -NY 10119
(518) 464-2050 .. **Manuel**, Christine M '05 Ayco Co -1 Wall -Colonie 12205
(212) 421-2233 .. **Manuel**, Edw A '58 OfCnsl Wilk A LLP -675 3rd Av -NY 10017
(646) 471-2201 .. **Manuel**, Paul A '92 PricewaterhouseCoopers LLP -300 Mad Av -NY 10017
(716) 852-5875 .. **Manuele**, Stephen A '01 (Feldman K LLP) -110 Pearl -Buffalo 14202
(212) 735-8600 .. **Manuelian**, Matthew D '84 (Morrison C LLP) -909 3rd Av -NY 10022
(212) 664-4444 .. **Manuelian**, Michl D '92 %NBC -30 Rckfllr Plz -NY 10112
(516) 741-6266 .. **Manus**, Barry L '90 %McCabe CM&F,LLP -346 Westbury Av Bx9000 -Carle Pl 11514
(212) 819-8200 .. **Manus**, Justin A '57 OfCnsl White & C LLP -1155 Av of Amer -NY 10036
(212) 285-3300 .. **Manus**, Mark J '81 (Lipsig SM&M,PC) -40 Fulton -NY 10038
(518) 449-3375 .. **Manuta**, Louis '90 Pub Util Law Proj -194 Wshngtn Av -Albany 12210 **Fx**:449-1769
(646) 479-9830 .. **Many**, Kimberly J '98 -200 E 71st -NY 10021 **Fx**:(212) 933-1812
(212) 474-1000 .. **Manz**, Kevin E '10 %Cravath S&M LLP -825 8th Av -NY 10019
(718) 990-6655 .. **Manz**, Wm H '85 %St John's Law Schl -8000 Utopia Pkwy -Jamaica 11439 **Fx**:591-1855
(212) 225-2000 .. **Manzanares**, Robt T '10 %Cleary GS&H -1 Lbrty Plz -NY 10006
(315) 488-5120 .. **Manzano**, John G '89 Manzano Law Ofc -550 Charles Av -Syracuse 13209 **Fx**:488-4982
(914) 251-4881 .. **Manzella**, Stephen M '88 -777 Wstchstr Av -White Plns 10604
(631) 852-2500 .. **Manzello**, Caren J '91 %DA -200 Center Dr -Rvrhead 11901 **Fx**:852-1769
(212) 246-2400 .. **Manzi**, Michl T '93 (Balber PM&VDT,PC) -1370 Av of Amer -NY 10019
(718) 762-1991 .. **Manzi**, Ronald E '75 -33-70 Prince -Flushng 11354 **Fx**:762-1997
(212) 208-8033 .. **Manzi**, Rosaleen M '84 %Standard & Poor's -55 Water -NY 10041
(516) 538-2500 .. **Manzione**, Stuart J '88 (Furey FLMW&D,PC) -600 Front -Hempstd 11550
(212) 804-4200 .. **Manzo**, Deanna M '08 %Mound CW&G -One Bttry Pk Plz -NY 10004
(212) 735-3000 .. **Manzo**, Margaret Cregan '05 %Skadden ASM&F LLP -4 Times Sq -NY 10036
(516) 942-3457 .. **Manzo**, Patricia '94 -410 Jericho Tpk -Jericho 11753 **Fx**:942-3758
(631) 366-6361 .. **Manzo**, Valerie S '80 -16 DeMont -Smithtwn 11787
(718) 447-8841 .. **Manzulli**, Michl F '66 (Lahr DMK&P) -33 Decker Av -Staten Isl 10302
(212) 735-3000 .. **Mao**, Janson '08 %Skadden ASM&F LLP -4 Times Sq -NY 10036
(212) 373-3000 .. **Mao**, Melissa S '10 %Paul WRW&G LLP -1285 Av of Amer -NY 10019
(212) 538-7822 .. **Mao**, Xueli '01 Credit Suisse -1 Mad Av -NY 10010
(917) 534-5061 .. **Maoz**, Inbal '03 %AOL Inc -770 Bway -NY 10003
(212) 715-9100 .. **Maoz**, M Michl '03 %Kramer LN&F,LLP -1177 Av of Amer -NY 10036
(646) 562-3405 .. **Ma Patterson**, Miriam Ming-Wai '96 %PLC -747 3rd Av -NY 10017
(212) 460-4917 .. **Mapelli**, Paul F '90 Con Ed -4 Irving Pl -NY 10003
(212) 208-4100 .. **Mapes**, Christine A '05 Cnsl Liberty Intl -55 Water -NY 10041 **Fx**:208-4112
(646) 274-1356 .. **Maples**, Rashida J '05 -5 E 59th -NY 10022
(212) 953-2381 .. **Mapou**, Tracey D '02 %Rubin F&F,LLP -292 Mad Av -NY 10017
(212) 279-1343 .. **Mapp**, Donald '99 (D Mapp,PC) -15 W 34th -NY 10001 **Fx**:279-9656
(585) 214-5004 .. **Mapstone**, Heather C '02 Element K LLC -500 Canal Vw Blvd -Rchstr 14623
(516) 733-7000 .. **Maquilon**, Michl '09 Catholic Charities Diocese of Rockville Ctr -90 Cherry Ln -Hicksvll 11801
(212) 369-6368 .. **Mar**, Marie Ann '81 OfCnsl Friedberg CC&P,LLP -767 3rd Av -NY 10017
(718) 928-3700 .. **Mar**, Nelson '99 %LSNYC-Bronx -579 Courtlandt Av -Bronx 10451 **Fx**:402-7586
(800) 877-1373 .. **Mara**, John D '86 %Workers Comp Bd -168-46 91st Av -Jamaica 11432
(716) 878-8000 .. **Marabella**, Erika M '04 Rich Products -1 Robert Rich Way -Buffalo 14213 **Fx**:878-8767
(914) 276-4260 .. **Maracic**, Marilyn '86 -330A Heritage Hills Dr -Somers 10589
(914) 663-1500 .. **Marafino**, John J '90 -9 W Prospect Av -Mt Vernon 10550 **Fx**:663-2775
(212) 735-3000 .. **Marafioti**, Kayalyn A '80 (Skadden ASM&F LLP) -4 Times Sq -NY 10036
(518) 464-4400 .. **Maragno**, Anthony M '99 (Kelleher & M,LLP) -113 Great Oaks Blvd -Albany 12203 **Fx**:464-2620
(212) 248-0800 .. **Maragoudakis**, Michl G '07 %Martinez & R,PC -67 Wall -NY 10005
(212) 355-3225 .. **Maraia**, John A '87 Toyota Tsusho America,Inc -805 3rd Av -NY 10022
(845) 254-4095 .. **Maran**, Michl J '87 St Johns Univ -Tobin College of Business -Jamaica 11439 **Fx**:254-4095
(212) 999-5800 .. **Marando**, Michl J '04 %Wilson SG&R -1301 Av of Americas -NY 10019
(212) 268-5898 .. **Maranga**, Theophilus Fuseini '92 -16 E 34th -NY 10016 **Fx**:346-0019
(516) 747-0400 .. **Marangas**, Theodora A '84 (Tomao & M) -1225 Franklin Av -Gdn Cty 11530 **Fx**:248-8693
(518) 449-8893 .. **Marangas**, Theresa B '86 (Wilson EME&D LLP) -677 Bway -Albany 12207
(315) 497-1190 .. **Marangola**, Chas A '80 -141 Main Bx17 -Moravia 13118 **Fx**:497-1234
(585) 263-6760 .. **Marangola**, Robt A '99 %US Atty -620 Fed Bldg -Rchstr 14614 **Fx**:263-6226
(585) 232-6500 .. **Marangola**, Sara Holderle '06 %Harter S&E LLP -1600 Bausch & Lomb Pl -Rchstr 14604
(718) 273-8324 .. **Marangos**, Denise '04 %J Marangos -1134A Hylan Blvd -Staten Isl 10305 **Fx**:273-8096
(718) 273-8324 .. **Marangos**, John Z '84 -1134A Hylan Blvd -Staten Isl 10305 **Fx**:273-8096
(516) 564-8000 .. **Marano**, Antonio G '04 %J Hiebler & Assoc -901 Franklin Av -Gdn Cty 11530 **Fx**:564-1714
(631) 476-7577 .. **Marano**, Lori A '88 (Geisler & G,LLP) -417 E Main -Pt Jffrsn 11777
(212) 812-3136 .. **Marano**, Ricardo '02 King Street Capital Mgmt -65 E 55th -NY 10022
(212) 383-1386 .. **Marano**, Stacy A '98 %State Comptroller -59 Maiden Ln -NY 10038 **Fx**:383-3901
(716) 204-2400 .. **Marans**, Michelle C '94 %SJ Baum,PC -220 Nrthpnte Pkwy Bx1291 -Buffalo 14240 **Fx**:204-4600
(212) 968-0244 .. **Marans**, Richd D '88 (Marans & W,LLC) -29 Bway -NY 10006 **Fx**:785-1618
(914) 949-1070 .. **Marantis**, Zachary '58 (van N&M,LLP) -199 Main -White Plns 10601
(212) 225-2000 .. **Maranto**, Christopher F '09 %Cleary GS&H -1 Lbrty Plz -NY 10006
(716) 842-2200 .. **Maranto**, Robt J '93 (Andrews B&M,LLP) -69 Delaware Av -Buffalo 14202
(914) 925-6700 .. **Marantz**, Neil G '86 -150 Theo Fremd Av -Rye 10580 **Fx**:925-8800
(212) 239-5188 .. **Marasa**, Michl '88 %Div Of Parole -314 W 40th -NY 10018 **Fx**:239-6160
(516) 681-1100 .. **Marasciullo**, Janene M '07 (Kaufman DV&G,LLP) -135 Crsswys Park Dr -Woodbury 11797
(212) 237-3114 .. **Marasco**, Bernard A '78 -1633 Bway -NY 10019 **Fx**:237-3197
(212) 687-3000 .. **Marashlian**, Benjamin S '05 %Jaffe & A,LLP -600 3rd Av -NY 10016

(914) 993-1546 .. **Marasse,** Richd L '91 %Town Atty -177 Hillside Av -Greenburgh 10607 **Fx:**993-1656
(646) 822-1801 .. **Maratto,** Michelle '93 (Itkowitz & H) -305 Bway -NY 10007 **Fx:**(212) 822-1417
(718) 590-2000 .. **Maraynes,** Sean B '09 %DA -198 E 161st -Bronx 10451 **Fx:**590-6477
(212) 488-1300 .. **Marazzi,** Stefanie L '08 %Cohen & P LLP -444 Mad Av -NY 10022
(718) 494-7292 .. **Marazzo,** John J '81 -31 Kell Av -Staten Isl 10314
(212) 553-9215 .. **Marber,** Paul A '86 (Cochran Firm) -233 Bway -NY 10279
(716) 681-7190 .. **Marble,** Bradley D '06 %Brown C LLP -5775 Bway -Lancaster 14086
(646) 264-3678 .. **Marblestone,** Judith '06 %US Dept of Labor -201 Varick -NY 10014 **Fx:**264-3660
(518) 753-7700 .. **Marbot,** Karen L '95 -115 Stover Rd -Vly Fls 12185
(212) 295-5002 .. **Marc,** Patrick '07 Verizon -560 Lex Av -NY 10022
(518) 262-3828 .. **Marcantano,** Mark R '88 %Albany Med Ctr -43 New Scotland Av -Albany 12208 **Fx:**262-4184
(212) 286-9374 .. **Marcantonio,** Jan '82 OfCnsl E Weissman -60 E 42nd -NY 10165 **Fx:**937-1529
(212) 701-3950 .. **Marcantonio,** Nicholas '77 -80 Pine 16th Fl -NY 10005 **Fx:**269-5420
(212) 504-6000 .. **Marcantonio,** Stephanie L '05 %Cadwalader W&T LLP -1 World Fncl Ctr -NY 10281
(212) 351-4500 .. **Marcari,** Wendy G '94 (Epstein B&G,PC) -250 Park Av -NY 10177
(212) 554-2600 .. **Marcelle,** Kristen '00 %Daylight Forensic -1 Rckfllr Plz -NY 10020
(518) 427-1720 .. **Marcelle,** Thos J '89 -324 Bway -Albany 12207
(212) 596-9000 .. **Marcellino,** Carl P '00 %Ropes & G LLP -1211 Av of Amer -NY 10036
(516) 742-5645 .. **Marcellino,** Michl J '83 -245 Hillside Av -Williston Pk 11596
(914) 323-7000 .. **Marcellino,** Stephen M '76 (Wilson EME&D LLP) -3 Gannett Dr -White Plns 10604
(212) 490-3000 .. **Marcellino,** Stephen M '76 (Wilson EME&D LLP) -150 E 42nd -NY 10017
(585) 232-1940 .. **Marcera,** Salvatore J Jr. '99 -125 State -Rchstr 14614
(718) 725-3202 .. **March,** Andrew G '05 ACS -15120 Jamaica Av -Jamaica 11432
(212) 752-1161 .. **March,** Christopher J '88 OfCnsl Traiger & H LLP -501 5th Av -NY 10017 **Fx:**937-5229
(212) 553-5400 .. **March,** James W '82 %Zurich NA -1 Lbrty Plz -NY 10006
(914) 765-0719 .. **March,** Laurie '84 -9 Sniffen Rd -Armonk 10504
(212) 819-8200 .. **Marchand,** Jessica B '06 %White & C LLP -1155 Av of Amer -NY 10036
(212) 259-8000 .. **Marchant,** Eliot '08 %Dewey & L LLP -1301 Av of Amer -NY 10019
(716) 858-8058 .. **Marchant,** Scott D '98 Erie Cnty Legislature -92 Franklin -Buffalo 14202 **Fx:**858-8818
(716) 858-2424 .. **Marche,** Peter J '07 %DA -25 Delaware Av -Buffalo 14202 **Fx:**858-7425
(516) 229-6000 .. **Marchello,** Chas J '88 %R Lau & Assoc -300 Jericho Quad Bx9040 -Jericho 11753 **Fx:**229-6167
(516) 741-6161 .. **Marchelos,** Peter S '92 -87 Mineola Blvd -Mineola 11501 **Fx:**248-0282
(516) 248-0202 .. **Marchelos,** Steve J '88 -87 Mineola Blvd -Mineola 11501 **Fx:**248-0282
(212) 952-1111 .. **Marcheret,** Francis P '54 OfCnsl H Gladstein & Prtnrs LLC -110 Wall -NY 10005 **Fx:**943-7427
(518) 266-3000 .. **Marchese,** Andrew F '77 %Div Tax Appls -500 Fed -Troy 12180 **Fx:**272-5178
(212) 858-7710 .. **Marchese,** Anthony J '03 %Nowell AKB,PA -140 Bway PMB 46028 -NY 10005
(716) 845-6446 .. **Marchese,** Chas J '81 (Gleichenhaus M&F,PC) -43 Court -Buffalo 14202 **Fx:**845-6475
(212) 808-7800 .. **Marchese,** George J '69 (Kelley D&W LLP) -101 Park Av -NY 10178
(716) 853-4080 .. **Marchese,** John J '93 (Colucci & G,PC) -424 Main -Buffalo 14202
(212) 557-1818 .. **Marchese,** Jos C III '08 %Silverson P&L -192 Lex Av -NY 10016
(212) 848-4000 .. **Marchese,** Jos I '04 %Shearman & S LLP -599 Lex Av -NY 10022
(718) 904-0200 .. **Marchese,** Matthew '88 (M Marchese,PC) -2403 E Tremont Av -Bronx 10461 **Fx:**904-1142
(516) 869-1111 .. **Marchese,** Paul P '94 (Marchese & M,LLP) -47 Plandome Rd -Manhsst 11030 **Fx:**869-0697
(585) 753-1380 .. **Marchese,** Richd A Jr. '84 %Cnty Atty -307 Cnty Ofc Bldg -Rchstr 14614 **Fx:**753-1331
(718) 491-6555 .. **Marchese,** Robt K '87 (R Marchese,PC) -1275 81st -Brklyn 11228 **Fx:**491-0096
(914) 995-2660 .. **Marchese,** Shelly Miller '98 %Cnty Atty -148 Martine Av -White Plns 10601 **Fx:**995-5858
(516) 248-7141 .. **Marchesi,** Anthony P '85 -1415 Kellum Pl -Gdn Cty 11530
(646) 287-0451 .. **Marchetti,** Luke '01 -366 Amsterdan Av -NY 10024
(212) 597-1436 .. **Marchetti,** Peter V '01 Cnsl WestLB AG -1211 Av of Amer -NY 10036
(914) 205-3163 .. **Marchetti-Bruck,** Gloria M '92 -42 Quarry Ln -Bedfrd 10506
(718) 876-5723 .. **Marchi,** Louis J '80 %DA -67 Targee -Staten Isl 10304
(212) 361-1744 .. **Marchiano,** Maria L '93 Environmental Cntrl Bd -66 John -NY 10038
(212) 819-8200 .. **Marchica,** Nicholas V '04 %White & C LLP -1155 Av of Amer -NY 10036
(718) 222-8880 .. **Marchini,** Mario M '98 %Jones JO -45 Main -Brklyn 11201
(585) 272-7870 .. **Marchioni,** John D '98 SrCnsl Marchioni & Assoc,LLC -2024 W Henrietta Rd -Rchstr 14623 **Fx:**272-7871
(518) 471-4820 .. **Marchiony,** Robt W '07 Supreme Ct -Bx7350 -Albany 12224
(212) 341-6400 .. **Marchisello,** Mary Jo '78 (Liquidation Bur) -123 William -NY 10038 **Fx:**608-3398
(212) 541-6980 .. **Marchisio,** Juvenal L '66 -401 E 65th -NY 10065 **Fx:**541-6994
(212) 964-7400 .. **Marchisotto,** Paul A '08 %Smith MDWY&Y,PC -111 John -NY 10038
(718) 784-2727 .. **Marciano,** Anthony L '86 -21-77 31st -Astoria 11105 **Fx:**784-2777
(212) 808-7800 .. **Marciano,** Taraneh J '08 %Kelley D&W LLP -101 Park Av -NY 10178
(914) 995-4200 .. **Marciano,** Virginia A '06 DA -111 Martin Luther King Blvd -White Plns 10601 **Fx:**995-3363
(212) 220-3830 .. **Marcigliano,** Frank M '69 (Nicoletti H&S) -88 Pine -NY 10005
(212) 619-6000 .. **Marcin,** Michl J '98 (Fay K&M,LLP) -150 Bway -NY 10038 **Fx:**208-6879
(516) 227-0700 .. **Marcin,** Patricia C '86 Cnsl Farrell F,PC -1320 RXR Plz -Uniondale 11556
(631) 283-7007 .. **Marcincuk,** Robt E '91 (O'Shea M&B,LLP) -250 N Sea Rd -Southampton 11968
(518) 456-0082 .. **Marciniszyn,** Andrew T '05 %Bailey K&J,PC -5 Pine West Plz -Albany 12205 **Fx:**456-4767
(212) 596-9000 .. **Marcinkus,** David J '09 %Ropes & G LLP -1211 Av of Amer -NY 10036
(212) 589-4200 .. **Marck,** Michelle K '09 Baker & H LLP -45 Rckfllr Plz -NY 10111
(212) 648-0795 .. **Marckesano,** Patricia Ann '05 JP Morgan Chase & Co -245 Park Av -NY 10167
(212) 208-1435 .. **Marco,** George A '94 G Marco PLLC -140 Bway -NY 10005
(212) 883-6500 .. **Marco,** Lawr H '81 (Podell SS&B,LLP) -605 3rd Av -NY 10158
(212) 750-6776 .. **Marcoccia,** Rachel K '02 %Morgenstern & B,LLC -885 3rd Av -NY 10022
(212) 225-2000 .. **Marcogliese,** Pamela '03 %Cleary GS&H -1 Lbrty Plz -NY 10006
(516) 358-5690 .. **Marcoline,** Thos J '01 V Toomey -3000 Marcus Av -Lk Success 11042 **Fx:**775-0237
(212) 355-4149 .. **Marconi,** Dawn M '05 %Goldweber E LLP -635 Mad Av -NY 10022
(914) 251-8200 .. **Marconi,** Jos C '85 Greywolf Capital Mgmt -4 Manhattanvll Rd -Purchase 10577 **Fx:**251-8244
(212) 848-4000 .. **Marcopoulos,** Alexander J '09 %Shearman & S LLP -599 Lex Av -NY 10022
(631) 665-5884 .. **Marcos,** Jaime A '95 (Marcos N&A,LLP) -220 5th Av -Bay Shr 11706 **Fx:**968-0946
(212) 455-2000 .. **Marcos Sanchez,** Borja '07 %Simpson T&B LLP -425 Lex Av -NY 10017
(516) 280-2281 .. **Marcote,** Danl P '99 (Marcote & Assoc,PC) -403 Merrick Av -E Meadow 11554 **Fx:**280-2283
(212) 343-6386 .. **Marcotrigiano,** Paul F '86 Scholastic Inc -557 Bway -NY 10012
(212) 808-7800 .. **Marcotte,** Matthew D '03 %Kelley D&W LLP -101 Park Av -NY 10178
(516) 627-7460 .. **Marcotullio,** Jos P '56 -18 Knolls Dr -Manhsst Hlls 11040
(914) 335-4007 .. **Marcoux,** Thos A '81 Kraft Foods,Inc -555 S Bway -Tarrytwn 10591 **Fx:**335-4300
(212) 450-4000 .. **Marcovitz,** Jennifer E '09 %Davis P&W LLP -450 Lex Av -NY 10017
(212) 218-2100 .. **Marcovivi,** Leila Kaplus '08 %Fitzpatrick CH&S -1290 Av of Amer -NY 10104
(212) 385-8000 .. **Marcowitz,** Edw L C '92 %Barasch MS&P -11 Park Pl -NY 10007
(212) 277-4000 .. **Marcu,** Aaron R '81 (Freshfields BD LLP) -520 Mad Av -NY 10022
(607) 778-2117 .. **Marcus,** Aaron J '97 %Cnty Atty -Cnty Ofc Bldg Bx1766 -Bnghmtn 13902 **Fx:**778-6122
(718) 268-3900 .. **Marcus,** Alan '83 (Federman & M) -118-21 Qns Blvd -Frst Hlls 11375 **Fx:**268-3963
(212) 964-6611 .. **Marcus,** Allan M '86 Cnsl Lester SK&D -120 Bway -NY 10271
(212) 863-6050 .. **Marcus,** Amy L '01 %HPD -100 Gold -NY 10038
(212) 752-9700 .. **Marcus,** Arthur S '90 (Gersten S LLP) -600 Lex Av -NY 10022
(212) 878-8000 .. **Marcus,** B Russell '05 %Clifford C LLP -31 W 52nd -NY 10019
(212) 968-1001 .. **Marcus,** Barbara J '83 (Gwertzman LBS&M) -80 Broad -NY 10004
(914) 633-7400 .. **Marcus,** Barry D '66 (Marcus O&K LLP) -145 Huguenot -New Rchll 10801
(212) 818-8800 .. **Marcus,** Caryn L '90 %Graubard M -405 Lex Av -NY 10174
(212) 446-4800 .. **Marcus,** Christopher J '00 (Kirkland & E LLP) -153 E 53rd -NY 10022
(212) 535-3141 .. **Marcus,** Corinne S '77 -180 E End Av -NY 10128 **Fx:**535-3141
(212) 325-2000 .. **Marcus,** Cortney '00 Credit Suisse -1 Mad Av -NY 10010
(212) 336-1100 .. **Marcus,** Danl R '02 %SEC -3 World Fncl Ctr -NY 10281 **Fx:**336-1323
(212) 670-0311 .. **Marcus,** David '62 %Merrill Lynch -222 Bway -NY 10038
(212) 705-7000 .. **Marcus,** David M '95 %Bingham M LLP -399 Park Av -NY 10022
(646) 536-7602 .. **Marcus,** David M '96 -1650 Bway -NY 10019
(716) 565-3800 .. **Marcus,** David P '85 (Marcus & C LLP) -2821 Wehrle Dr -Buffalo 14221 **Fx:**565-3801
(212) 243-8234 .. **Marcus,** David R '77 -175 W 13th -NY 10011
(607) 432-2252 .. **Marcus,** Debra '82 Planned Parenthood -37 Dietz -Oneonta 13820 **Fx:**432-7206
(718) 375-5586 .. **Marcus,** Donald '62 -1936 E 24th -Brklyn 11229
(914) 328-9666 .. **Marcus,** Ellen A '94 %D Gladstone -1 Barker Av -White Plns 10601 **Fx:**328-7842
(212) 297-5800 .. **Marcus,** Elyse Adler '01 Cnsl Day P LLP -7 Times Sq -NY 10036
(212) 836-8000 .. **Marcus,** Eric P '77 (Kaye S LLP) -425 Park Av -NY 10022
(914) 472-4545 .. **Marcus,** Fred H '61 -32 Wilmot Cir -Scarsdale 10583 **Fx:**472-4004
(607) 652-7327 .. **Marcus,** George '50 (Rushmore MM&C) -11 Harper -Stamfrd 12167
(914) 683-0090 .. **Marcus Gould & Sussman,LLP** -222 Bloomingdale Rd -White Plns 10605 **Fx:**683-0098
(212) 708-1600 .. **Marcus,** H Gwen '82 %Showtime Networks Inc -1633 Bway -NY 10019 **Fx:**708-1391
(716) 634-2753 .. **Marcus,** H Jeffrey '91 -5888 Main -Williamsvll 14221
(212) 415-8600 .. **Marcus,** Harry C '65 (Locke LB&L LLP) -3 World Fncl Ctr -NY 10281
(212) 417-5544 .. **Marcus,** Hilton A '05 NYS Comm/Health Care Facilities -90 Church -NY 10007
(347) 404-9133 .. **Marcus,** Ilana J '05 Civil Ct -141 Lvngstn -Brklyn 11201 **Fx:**(718) 643-3733
(212) 667-9786 .. **Marcus,** Ilana R '88 Nomura Holdng Amer Inc -2 World Fncl Ctr -NY 10281
(212) 547-5400 .. **Marcus,** Isaac '98 (McDermott W&E LLP) -340 Mad Av -NY 10173
(716) 829-3451 .. **Marcus,** Isabel S '89 SUNY-Buffalo School of Law -527 O'Brian Hall -Buffalo 14260 **Fx:**829-3453
(212) 310-8000 .. **Marcus,** Jacqueline '83 (Weil G&M LLP) -767 5th Av -NY 10153
(212) 513-3200 .. **Marcus,** Jacqueline '10 %Holland & K LLP -31 W 52nd -NY 10019
(212) 790-9570 .. **Marcus,** Jason C '77 -1001 Av of Amer -NY 10018
(212) 425-9300 .. **Marcus,** Jed L '91 (Bressler A&R,PC) -17 State -NY 10004
(718) 643-6555 .. **Marcus,** Jed Shawn '77 (Marcus Attys) -13 Greene Av -Brklyn 11238 **Fx:**643-9111
(212) 949-2202 .. **Marcus,** Jeffrey '71 -260 Mad Av -NY 10016
(914) 835-1818 .. **Marcus,** Jennifer E '07 %E Vecchio & Assoc -550 Mamaroneck Av -Harrison 10528 **Fx:**835-1858
(212) 509-2800 .. **Marcus,** Jennifer M '05 %Ostrowitz & O -150 Bway -NY 10038 **Fx:**(732) 446-5837

(347) 592-2500 .. **Marcus,** Jessica E '02 %Bklyn Fam Def Proj -177 Lvngstn -Brklyn 11201 **Fx:**(718) 596-4704
(212) 815-1818 .. **Marcus,** Jill M '87 %DC 37 MELS -125 Barclay -NY 10007 **Fx:**815-1343
(212) 490-2900 .. **Marcus,** Joel R '77 (Marcus & P LLP) -708 3rd Av -NY 10017 **Fx:**599-3167
(516) 228-3131 .. **Marcus,** Joshua A '98 (Franklin G&C,PC) -666 Old Cntry Rd -Gdn Cty 11530
(914) 632-4700 .. **Marcus,** K Richd '54 (McDonough Law Firm, LLP) -145 Huguenot -New Rchll 10801
(212) 384-1000 .. **Marcus,** Kim E '93 FBI -26 Fed Plz -NY 10278
(212) 209-4800 .. **Marcus,** Linda B '99 (Brown R LLP) -7 Times Sq -NY 10036
(516) 496-5822 .. **Marcus,** Lisa M '00 T Spina -170 Froehlich Farm Blvd -Woodbury 11797 **Fx:**496-5420
(212) 664-0355 .. **Marcus,** Louis G '70 -1230 Av of Amer -NY 10020
(212) 636-6823 .. **Marcus,** Maria L '61 %Fordham Univ Sch of Law -140 W 62nd -NY 10023 **Fx:**636-6899
(212) 755-5757 .. **Marcus,** Michl '91 Marcus Law Firm LLC -110 E 59th -NY 10022 **Fx:**755-4666
(516) 889-2559 .. **Marcus,** Michl C '69 -452 W Beech -Long Bch 11561 **Fx:**889-4252
(866) 862-7348 .. **Marcus,** Michelle S '88 SSA-ODAR -74 N Pearl -Albany 12207
(914) 683-0090 .. **Marcus,** Myron '60 (Marcus G&S,LLP) -222 Bloomingdale Rd -White Plns 10605
(212) 833-8000 .. **Marcus,** Nancy C '92 Sony BMG Music Entrtnmnt -550 Mad Av -NY 10022 **Fx:**833-8406
(212) 889-3700 .. **Marcus,** Natalie S '05 %Abbey SR&A LLP -212 E 39th -NY 10016
(914) 633-7400 .. **Marcus Ollman & Kommer LLP** -145 Huguenot -New Rchll 10801 **Fx:**633-7445
(914) 741-5050 .. **Marcus,** Phyllis Knight '85 Marcus Law Grp PLLC -50 Bway -Hawthorne 10532 **Fx:**741-5850
(607) 273-6841 .. **Marcus,** Randall B '86 (Barney GDM&O,LLP) -119 E Seneca -Ithaca 14850
(631) 370-2800 .. **Marcus,** Randi D '91 -290 Broadhllw Rd -Melvll 11747 **Fx:**370-2996
(212) 734-0471 .. **Marcus,** Richd '54 -211 E 70th -NY 10021
(716) 875-6039 .. **Marcus,** Richd C '51 -155 Woodcrst Blvd -Buffalo 14223 **Fx:**875-6039
(718) 671-6161 .. **Marcus,** Richd S '65 -139 Dreiser Loop -Bronx 10475
(845) 638-1300 .. **Marcus,** Robt B '67 (RB Marcus,PC) -203 Strawtown Rd -New Cty 10956 **Fx:**638-3303
(516) 342-2200 .. **Marcus,** Robt B '80 (Schwartzapfel Prtnrs) -300 Jericho Quad -Jericho 11753
(212) 755-7500 .. **Marcus Rosenberg & Diamond LLP** -488 Mad Av -NY 10022 **Fx:**755-8713
(212) 267-3091 .. **Marcus,** Ruth D '88 Cnsl Wilentz G&S -110 William -NY 10038 **Fx:**(732) 726-6564
(212) 447-7575 .. **Marcus,** Seth L '95 (Leffler M&M LLC) -200 Mad Av -NY 10016 **Fx:**202-4229
(212) 521-5400 .. **Marcus,** Stacy K '06 %Reed S LLP -599 Lex Av -NY 10022
(212) 975-1870 .. **Marcus,** Stephanie R '97 Cnsl CBS Inc -51 W 52nd -NY 10019 **Fx:**(646) 792-6035
(212) 344-3100 .. **Marcus,** Stephen H '68 OfCnsl Frenkel LWW&G,LLP -1 Whitehall -NY 10004
(212) 989-6187 .. **Marcus,** Steven J '70 -431 W 22nd -NY 10011 **Fx:**989-7858
(212) 705-7000 .. **Marcus,** Todd B '90 (Bingham M LLP) -399 Park Av -NY 10022
(212) 906-1200 .. **Marcus,** Todd D '08 %Latham & W -885 3rd Av -NY 10022
(212) 665-6730 .. **Marcus,** Valerie '88 -801 W End Av -NY 10025
(212) 483-9600 .. **Marcus,** Walter R '75 %Costello S&G LLP -44 Wall -NY 10005
(914) 288-0022 .. **Marcus,** Yuval H '95 (Leason E LLP) -81 Main -White Plns 10601
(212) 836-8000 .. **Marcusa,** Fred H '71 (Kaye S LLP) -425 Park Av -NY 10022
(212) 363-3100 .. **Marcusa,** Stephen M '73 Bivona & C,PC -88 Pine -NY 10005
(212) 943-9000 .. **Marden,** David C '07 %Dewey P&K LLP -220 E 42nd -NY 10017
(212) 922-9250 .. **Marden,** Jonathan C '07 %Ganfer & S LLP -360 Lex Av -NY 10017
(718) 237-3100 .. **Marden,** Stephanie E '07 Leg Aid -111 Lvngstn -Brklyn 11201 **Fx:**250-4243
(516) 741-6565 .. **Marder,** Alan E '83 (Meyer SE&K,PC) -990 Stewart Av Bx9194 -Gdn Cty 11530
(212) 967-1134 .. **Marder Eskesen & Nass** -450 7th Av -NY 10123 **Fx:**967-2105
(212) 967-1134 .. **Marder,** Kenneth '80 (Marder E&N) -450 7th Av -NY 10123
(212) 693-0085 .. **Marder,** Reyna E '92 %Appellate Advocates -2 Rector -NY 10006 **Fx:**693-0878
(212) 277-5862 .. **Marderosian,** Mark D '92 -99 Park Av -NY 10016
(212) 852-3968 .. **Mardo,** David Peter '98 US Trust Co of NY -114 W 47th -NY 10036
(212) 425-3240 .. **Mardon,** Andre Mazzola '79 (Marrinan & MM,PC) -26 Bway -NY 10004
(718) 828-8200 .. **Mardon,** Brian C '06 %Spiegel & B,LLP -2622 E Tremont Av -Bronx 10461
(716) 204-2400 .. **Marecki,** Anthony G '04 %SJ Baum,PC -220 Nrthpnte Pkwy Bx1291 -Buffalo 14240 **Fx:**204-4600
(716) 626-0680 .. **Marecki,** Laura Konst '92 -5355 Main -Williamsvll 14221 **Fx:**626-0317
(212) 530-5000 .. **Marecki,** Patrick D '06 %Milbank TH&M LLP -1 Chase Manh Plz -NY 10005
(212) 687-8500 .. **Marek,** David M '00 (Liddle & R,LLP) -800 3rd Av -NY 10022
(212) 285-0510 .. **Marek,** Herbert J '86 %Wilkofsky FK&C -299 Bway -NY 10007
(212) 373-3000 .. **Marell,** Jeffrey D '94 (Paul WRW&G LLP) -1285 Av of Amer -NY 10019
(212) 309-6000 .. **Marenco,** Ruby '07 %Morgan L&B LLP -101 Park Av -NY 10178
(718) 829-3207 .. **Marengo,** Christopher J '86 -2116 Wllmsbrdg Rd -Bronx 10461 **Fx:**792-7645
(914) 245-7582 .. **Mareno,** Antonio '53 -3505 Tulip Dr -Yorktwn Hts 10598 **Fx:**245-7582
(718) 921-0916 .. **Maresca,** Ann M '82 -336 99th -Brklyn 11209
(212) 636-7952 .. **Maresca,** Elizabeth A '92 %Fordham Univ Sch of Law -140 W 62nd -NY 10023 **Fx:**636-6899
(914) 968-5800 .. **Maresca,** Gary F '00 %Sayegh & S,PC -615 Ynkrs Av -Ynkrs 10704 **Fx:**968-5950
(212) 513-3200 .. **Maresky,** Moira '06 %Holland & K LLP -31 W 52nd -NY 10019
(212) 684-1010 .. **Marett,** Louis Q '76 -404 Park Av S -NY 10016 **Fx:**689-3315
(212) 225-2000 .. **Marette,** Patrick G '93 %Cleary GS&H -1 Lbrty Plz -NY 10006
(914) 761-0381 .. **Marfeo,** Allison M '01 %A Hazen -30 Glenn -White Plns 10603 **Fx:**948-3371
(718) 409-0800 .. **Margand,** John P '90 Healthy Respect -3250 Wstchstr Av -Bronx 10461 **Fx:**409-1081
(212) 580-3122 .. **Margareten,** Lester J '66 -80 Cntrl Pk W -NY 10023
(212) 457-9569 .. **Margaretten,** Nancy A '83 %IncisiveMedia /NYLJ -120 Bway -NY 10271
(212) 852-1000 .. **Margaris,** Anastasia Grammenos '94 %US Trust Co,NA -114 W 47th -NY 10036 **Fx:**852-1310
(212) 691-8931 .. **Margello,** Michl '81 -404 Park Av S -NY 10016
(914) 289-2330 .. **Margenot,** Joan E '85 %Ct of Claims -140 Grand -White Plns 10601 **Fx:**289-2333
(212) 521-5400 .. **Marger,** Jos M '90 (Reed S LLP) -599 Lex Av -NY 10022
(212) 442-4507 .. **Margetanski,** Danl S '95 %Law Dept -100 Church -NY 10007 **Fx:**788-0367
(212) 435-3571 .. **Margetson,** Carole A '97 %Port Auth of NY/NJ -225 Park Av S -NY 10003 **Fx:**435-3555
(212) 237-1000 .. **Margiano,** Jeanine T '04 %Windels ML&M,LLP -156 W 56th -NY 10019
(212) 687-2770 .. **Margiano,** Richd D '01 %Cohen PL&P -551 5th Av -NY 10176
(212) 813-5900 .. **Margiotta,** John P '97 (Fross ZL&Z,PC) -866 UN Plz -NY 10017
(631) 957-3029 .. **Margiotta,** Paul J '03 Babylon Town Atty -200 E Sunrise Hwy -Lindenhrst 11757 **Fx:**957-3146
(631) 470-3574 .. **Margiotta & Ricigliano** -425 Broadhllw Rd -Melvll 11747
(914) 347-2600 .. **Margolies,** Brian M '99 (Traub LS&S LLP) -7 Skyline Dr -Hawthorne 10532
(212) 809-7600 .. **Margolies,** Carolyn S '81 %Cheven K&H -40 Wall -NY 10005
(212) 752-2196 .. **Margolies,** Jacob '87 Yomiuri News Inc -747 3rd Av -NY 10017
(212) 980-9600 .. **Margolies,** Melinda Bridie '99 %Kaufman B&R -120 Bway -NY 10271
(212) 756-2000 .. **Margolies,** Neil '06 %Schulte R&Z LLP -919 3rd Av -NY 10022
(212) 450-2000 .. **Margolies,** Rachel L '02 NFL -280 Park Av -NY 10017 **Fx:**681-7599
(212) 889-3700 .. **Margolies,** Richd B '02 %Abbey SR&A LLP -212 E 39th -NY 10016
(212) 867-9500 .. **Margolies,** Stanley E '61 Cnsl Kurzman K&F,LLP -230 Park Av -NY 10169
(631) 427-8100 .. **Margolin,** Brett K '08 %Margolin & M -52 Elm -Huntngtn 11743 **Fx:**427-8134
(212) 770-1735 .. **Margolin,** Bruce D '90 %AIG -80 Pine -NY 10005
(516) 921-3838 .. **Margolin,** C Lance '84 (Pitnick & M LLP) -6800 Jericho Tpk -Syosset 11791 **Fx:**921-3824
(212) 606-1592 .. **Margolin,** Constance B '73 %Hosp For Spec Surg -535 E 70th -NY 10021 **Fx:**517-8781
(914) 347-5624 .. **Margolin,** David V '92 (D Margolin,PC) -7 Skyline Dr -Hawthorne 10532
(212) 247-4844 .. **Margolin,** Errol F '72 (Margolin & P,LLP) -111 W 57th -NY 10019
(718) 522-6600 .. **Margolin,** Fredk A '71 -26 Court -Brklyn 11242 **Fx:**522-6602
(631) 427-8100 .. **Margolin,** James S '79 (Margolin & M) -52 Elm -Huntngtn 11743 **Fx:**427-8134
(212) 837-6000 .. **Margolin,** Jeffrey S '03 %Hughes H&R LLP -1 Bttry Pk Plz -NY 10004
(212) 697-2310 .. **Margolin,** Jesse '54 (Becker R LLP) -317 Mad Av -NY 10017
(212) 953-6000 .. **Margolin,** Joshua S '05 %Katsky K LLP -605 3rd Av -NY 10158
(212) 522-3890 .. **Margolin,** Judith R '91 %Time Inc -1271 Av of Amer -NY 10020 **Fx:**522-0437
(914) 476-0600 .. **Margolin,** Laurence S '85 OfCnsl Smith B&J,LLP -733 Ynkrs Av -Ynkrs 10704 **Fx:**457-0040
(631) 234-8585 .. **Margolin,** Linda U '76 (Bracken & M,LLP) -1 Suffolk Sq -Islandia 11749
(917) 494-1108 .. **Margolin,** Lisa K '95 (Margolin & M,LLP) -400 E 56th -NY 10022
(718) 643-3184 .. **Margolin,** Marcia '78 %Hon N Firetog -360 Adams -Brklyn 11201
(212) 742-8700 .. **Margolin,** Pamela B '09 Garson D&C LLP -110 Wall -NY 10005
(212) 247-4844 .. **Margolin & Pierce,LLP** -111 W 57th -NY 10019 **Fx:**247-1155
(212) 916-4219 .. **Margolin,** Randi Block '80 %TIAA-CREF -730 3rd Av -NY 10017
(631) 852-1737 .. **Margolin,** Robt A '73 Surrogate's Ct -320 Center Dr -Rvrhead 11901
(914) 681-7880 .. **Margolin,** Scott A '96 Carl Zeiss Intl -1 Zeiss Dr -Thornwd 10594
(212) 838-1033 .. **Margolin,** Seymour '62 (Margolin & M,LLP) -400 E 56th -NY 10022
(212) 458-3296 .. **Margolis,** Adam J '03 AIG -175 Water -NY 10038
(212) 735-7810 .. **Margolis,** Alexandra '86 Cnsl Skadden ASM&F LLP -4 Times Sq -NY 10036
(212) 201-1170 .. **Margolis,** Barry G '90 (Abrams GMB,LLP) -237 W 35th -NY 10001
(914) 323-7000 .. **Margolis,** Bernice E '02 %Wilson EME&D LLP -3 Gannett Dr -White Plns 10604
(212) 228-7727 .. **Margolis,** Beth M '84 (Gladstein R&M,LLP) -817 Bway -NY 10003
(315) 733-2889 .. **Margolis,** Brad S '84 -2600 Oneida -Utica 13501 **Fx:**735-2558
(212) 506-5000 .. **Margolis,** Brian B '92 (Orrick H&S LLP) -51 W 52nd -NY 10019
(212) 425-7200 .. **Margolis,** Danl P '07 %Kenyon & K,LLP -1 Bway -NY 10004
(212) 558-4000 .. **Margolis,** Danl R '05 %Sullivan & C LLP -125 Broad -NY 10004
(212) 728-8000 .. **Margolis,** Donna P '93 SpclCnsl Willkie F&G LLP -787 7th Av -NY 10019
(212) 804-4200 .. **Margolis,** Ellen G '85 (Mound CW&G) -One Bttry Pk Plz -NY 10004
(212) 770-1981 .. **Margolis,** Genna H '90 %AIG -80 Pine -NY 10005 **Fx:**344-2286
(516) 294-9400 .. **Margolis,** Ira M '66 (Eisenberg & M,LLP) -100 Q Roosevelt Blvd -Gdn Cty 11530 **Fx:**294-9137
(845) 267-4878 .. **Margolis,** Jay K '85 JK Margolis,PC -151 N Main -New Cty 10956 **Fx:**634-5979
(212) 490-0900 .. **Margolis,** Jeffrey A '72 (Margolis Law Firm) -11 E 44th -NY 10017
(212) 999-5800 .. **Margolis,** Jessica L '01 (Wilson SG&R) -1301 Av of Americas -NY 10019
(631) 578-1888 .. **Margolis,** Jonathan O '91 (Margolis & F,LLP) -41 Natcon Dr -Shirley 11967 **Fx:**410-1937
(212) 801-2105 .. **Margolis,** Jonathan S '80 (Greenberg T,LLP) -200 Park Av -NY 10166
(212) 644-1010 .. **Margolis,** Kenneth A '81 (Kauff M&M LLP) -950 3rd Av -NY 10022
(212) 267-6659 .. **Margolis,** Larry B '87 -305 Bway -NY 10007
(212) 859-5001 .. **Margolis,** Martin G '84 (Margolis Law Firm,LLC) -110 Wall -NY 10005 **Fx:**943-2300
(718) 459-6000 .. **Margolis,** Michl R '07 %Pennisi D&N LLP -97-77 Qns Blvd -Rego Pk 11374
(212) 541-5550 .. **Margolis,** Ronald J '66 -110 E 59th -NY 10022
(212) 310-8000 .. **Margolis,** Steven M '90 Cnsl Weil G&M LLP -767 5th Av -NY 10153
(212) 213-5800 .. **Margolis & Tisman LLP** -280 Mad Av -NY 10016 **Fx:**686-1544
(212) 279-5577 .. **Margolis Druyan,** Rosalie '92 %M Druyan -450 7th Av -NY 10123
(347) 296-1032 .. **Margolis Kleinberg,** Karen '82 Cnsl Supreme Ct -320 Jay -Brklyn 11201 **Fx:**296-1337

(212) 697-9846 .. **Margolius,** Edwin A '44 -51 E 42nd -NY 10017
(518) 943-5100 .. **Margolius,** Peter M '76 -7 Howard -Catskill 12414 **Fx:**943-4373
(516) 944-6277 .. **Margolius,** Richd P '77 -74 Davis Rd -Pt Wash 11050
(212) 820-2603 .. **Margraff,** Sandra Costa '05 %AIG -160 Water -NY 10038
(212) 599-1717 .. **Margro,** Nancy A '99 %Barnett EGK&L,PC -122 E 42nd -NY 10168
(212) 288-5597 .. **Margules,** Susan Beth '80 -791 Park Av -NY 10021 **Fx:**288-5597
(516) 571-3800 .. **Margulies,** Abigail S '03 %DA -262 Old Cntry Rd -Mineola 11501 **Fx:**248-9479
(212) 326-3939 .. **Margulies,** Arthur J '04 %Jones D -222 E 41st -NY 10017
(212) 382-6600 .. **Margulies,** Leah '86 %NYC Bar -42 W 44th -NY 10036 **Fx:**398-6634
(212) 506-1700 .. **Margulies,** Michl D '09 %Kasowitz BT&F LLP -1633 Bway -NY 10019
(516) 223-5617 .. **Margulies,** Neil A '83 -294 W Merrick Rd -Freeprt 11520
(212) 836-8000 .. **Margulies,** Paul I '08 %Kaye S LLP -425 Park Av -NY 10022
(516) 379-2500 .. **Margulies,** Paul J '98 %Malone T&S -147 W Merrick Rd Bx589 -Freeprt 11520
(212) 964-3400 .. **Margulies,** Robt W '83 (Drabkin & M) -120 Bway -NY 10271
(212) 644-4018 .. **Margulies,** Steven I '89 Shopkorn Mgmt -410 Park Av -NY 10022
(212) 668-5927 .. **Margulis,** Andrew L '89 (Ropers MK&B) -17 State -NY 10004
(212) 682-7474 .. **Margulis,** Howard L '99 (Foley & L LLP) -90 Park Av -NY 10016
(716) 505-2700 .. **Margulis,** Randy S '93 (Felle S&M,LLC) -6024 Main -Williamsvll 14221 **Fx:**506-2727
(212) 223-0200 .. **Margulis-Ohnuma,** Mary '98 %Stillman F&S,PC -425 Park Av -NY 10022
(212) 685-0999 .. **Margulis-Ohnuma,** Zachary A '00 -260 Mad Av -NY 10016 **Fx:**(845) 265-4628
(212) 506-5000 .. **Margulyan,** Igor '10 %Orrick H&S LLP -51 W 52nd -NY 10019
(646) 746-9700 .. **Marhamati,** Sheila L '02 US CFTC -140 Bway -NY 10005 **Fx:**746-9939
(914) 244-3131 .. **Marhoffer,** Susan Bloch '88 -344 Main -Mt Kisco 10549 **Fx:**(203) 431-7660
(212) 360-0876 .. **Mari,** Jacqueline '91 -16 E 98th -NY 10029
(914) 248-5297 .. **Mari,** John J '62 -Route 118 Bx940 -Baldwin Place 10505
(212) 227-5335 .. **Mari,** Mathew J '77 -110 Wall -NY 10005 **Fx:**(718) 836-2518
(914) 684-0333 .. **Maria,** Jos A '74 -301 Old Tarrytown Rd -White Plns 10603 **Fx:**684-9772
(914) 235-7884 .. **Maria,** Michl A III '85 -120 Woodlawn Av -New Rchll 10804
(212) 310-8000 .. **Marian,** Cynthia A '09 %Weil G&M LLP -767 5th Av -NY 10153
(212) 558-4000 .. **Marian,** Omri Y '10 %Sullivan & C LLP -125 Broad -NY 10004
(585) 753-1380 .. **Marianetti,** Brian E '09 Cnty Atty -307 Cnty Ofc Bldg -Rchstr 14614 **Fx:**753-1331
(914) 946-5100 .. **Mariani,** Alessia P '09 %Bashian & F,LLP -235 Main -White Plns 10601
(212) 335-9000 .. **Mariani,** Gilda I '77 %DA -1 Hogan Pl -NY 10013
(212) 474-1000 .. **Mariani,** Michl E '10 %Cravath S&M LLP -825 8th Av -NY 10019
(212) 632-3255 .. **Mariani,** Michl M '76 Fiduciary Trust Co Intl -600 5th Av -NY 10020 **Fx:**632-3198
(845) 430-5770 .. **Mariani,** Nicole M '05 -14 Lake Av -Middletwn 10940
(516) 832-7520 .. **Mariani,** Raymond L '88 (Nixon P LLP) -50 Jericho Quadrangle -Jericho 11753
(516) 775-7007 .. **Mariano,** Arthur G '95 (Gutman MB&S,PC) -813 Jericho Tpk -New Hyde Pk 11040
(914) 681-0645 .. **Mariano & Lipkin PLLC** -941 N Bway -White Plns 10603 **Fx:**681-0786
(716) 551-3341 .. **Mariano,** Marianne '95 %Fed Pub Def -300 Pearl -Buffalo 14202 **Fx:**551-3346
(516) 229-4400 .. **Mariano,** Theresa Penaflor '96 %Kay & G -875 Merrick Av -Westbury 11590
(914) 681-0645 .. **Mariano,** Wm E '59 (Mariano & L PLLC) -941 N Bway -White Plns 10603
(718) 779-5551 .. **Marichal,** Hector A '82 HA Marichal,PC -37-21 75th -Jcksn Hts 11372 **Fx:**779-5168
(212) 819-8200 .. **Mariconda,** Stephanie L '10 %White & C LLP -1155 Av of Amer -NY 10036
(212) 533-6300 .. **Mariette,** Yvonne M '92 %NYSUT -52 Bway -NY 10004 **Fx:**995-2347
(845) 225-3778 .. **Marin,** Carla L '90 -1762 Route 6 -Carmel 10512
(212) 661-1151 .. **Marin Goodman LLP** -40 Wall -NY 10005 **Fx:**661-1141
(631) 853-4343 .. **Marin,** Jennifer A '99 %Leg Aid -400 Carleton Av Bx9082 -Central Islip 11722 **Fx:**853-7798
(212) 655-6000 .. **Marin,** Kenneth P '93 (Chapman & C LLP) -330 Mad Av -NY 10017
(347) 404-9133 .. **Marin,** Laurie E '93 %Civil Ct -141 Lvngstn -Brklyn 11201 **Fx:**(718) 643-3733
(516) 565-5377 .. **Marin,** Nadia L '97 %Workplace Project -91 N Franklin -Hempstd 11550 **Fx:**565-5470
(212) 661-1151 .. **Marin,** Richd P '82 (Marin G LLP) -40 Wall -NY 10005
(212) 460-3530 .. **Marin,** Rita C '81 Con Ed -4 Irving Pl -NY 10003
(212) 788-1385 .. **Marin,** Yvonne R '04 ACS -220 Church -NY 10013
(212) 446-4800 .. **Marina,** James E '97 (Kirkland & E LLP) -153 E 53rd -NY 10022
(212) 294-6700 .. **Marina,** Lana C '94 OfCnsl Winston & S -200 Park Av -NY 10166
(914) 312-2806 .. **Marinaccio,** Anne M '96 %Verizon Business -2 Intl Dr -Rye Brook 10573
(718) 590-2000 .. **Marinaccio,** Jennifer A '05 %DA -198 E 161st -Bronx 10451 **Fx:**590-6477
(914) 761-0707 .. **Marinaccio,** Michl A '77 (Culleton & M) -245 Main -White Plns 10601 **Fx:**761-0795
(212) 504-6000 .. **Marinakis,** Maria '10 %Cadwalader W&T LLP -1 World Fncl Ctr -NY 10281
(917) 439-1916 .. **Marinangeli,** Michl G '84 MGM & Assoc -1646 1st Av -NY 10028
(212) 407-4000 .. **Marinaro,** Frank J '92 (Loeb & L,LLP) -345 Park Av -NY 10154
(716) 857-6161 .. **Marine,** Deborah L '97 %Health Care Plan -205 Park Club Ln -Buffalo 14221
(212) 335-9000 .. **Marinelli,** Christopher P '01 %DA -1 Hogan Pl -NY 10013
(914) 684-0333 .. **Marinelli,** Frances D '83 %J Maria -301 Old Tarrytown Rd -White Plns 10603 **Fx:**684-9772
(212) 697-3122 .. **Marinelli,** Francesca L '09 %Martin C&B LLP -220 E 42nd -NY 10017
(212) 455-2000 .. **Marinelli,** Francis C '90 Cnsl Simpson T&B LLP -425 Lex Av -NY 10017
(718) 250-2000 .. **Marinelli,** Gina M '98 %DA -350 Jay -Brklyn 11201 **Fx:**250-2314
(212) 506-2500 .. **Marinelli,** Josh S J '07 %Mayer B LLP -1675 Bway -NY 10019
(518) 474-6400 .. **Marinelli,** Kathleen '88 %Dept of Ed -89 Wshngtn Av -Albany 12234 **Fx:**473-2925
(212) 513-3200 .. **Marinelli,** Marisa A '88 (Holland & K LLP) -31 W 52nd -NY 10019
(845) 526-3899 .. **Marinelli,** Michl L '02 Aphrodite Construction Co Inc -9 Blueberry Ln -Putnam Vly 10579
(718) 624-9391 .. **Marinelli,** Robt J '93 (Cardinale H&M) -26 Court -Brklyn 11242
(716) 833-7910 .. **Marinelli,** Robt L '68 -946 Brighton Rd -Tonawanda 14150
(718) 492-3600 .. **Marinelli,** Scott M '02 -471 54th -Brklyn 11220 **Fx:**(908) 653-0079
(516) 678-1800 .. **Marinello,** Christopher A '88 (Marinello & Assoc) -100 Merrick Rd -Rockvll Ctr 11570 **Fx:**678-1885
(516) 747-1400 .. **Marinello,** Leonard P '91 %Bonchonsky & Z,LLP -226 7th -Gdn Cty 11530
(212) 233-4420 .. **Marinello,** Maria C '80 -220 5th Av -NY 10001 **Fx:**566-7158
(518) 581-8600 .. **Marinello,** Meghan A '09 %Fairbanks-Fletcher,PLLC -78 Church -Saratoga Spgs 12866 **Fx:**(888) 859-8140
(212) 705-0126 .. **Marinello,** Peter C '88 NAD -70 W 36th -NY 10018
(516) 877-2270 .. **Marinello,** Salvatore J '74 -55 Mineola Blvd -Mineola 11501 **Fx:**746-7691
(212) 446-4800 .. **Marines,** Jennifer L '05 %Kirkland & E LLP -153 E 53rd -NY 10022
(718) 314-5188 .. **Marinescu,** Venus Diana '07 -38-50 Bell Blvd -Bayside 11361
(212) 637-2402 .. **Maringer,** Elizabeth F '95 %US Atty -1 St Andrews Plz -NY 10007
(212) 728-8000 .. **Mariniello,** Andrew R '06 %Willkie F&G LLP -787 7th Av -NY 10019
(646) 471-4000 .. **Marini Fichera,** Catalina C '03 %PricewaterhouseCoopers LLP -300 Mad Av -NY 10017
(718) 392-8000 .. **Marinis,** Peter '90 (Kordas & M) -5-47 47th Rd -LIC 11101
(646) 610-5336 .. **Marin-Jordan,** Ruby '93 NYPD -1 Police Plz -NY 10038
(212) 435-3484 .. **Marinko,** Stephen '02 %Port Auth of NY/NJ -225 Park Av S -NY 10003 **Fx:**435-3555
(212) 635-0505 .. **Marino,** Angelo John '73 OfCnsl Cichanowicz CKV&T,LLP -61 Bway -NY 10006
(516) 922-9100 .. **Marino,** Anthony '95 %V McNamara -1045 Oyster Bay Rd -E Norwich 11732 **Fx:**922-9208
(212) 400-7177 .. **Marino,** Anthony J '87 (Garrity GMG&F) -40 Wall -NY 10005
(516) 922-4040 .. **Marino & Bernstein,PC** -Townsend Sq Bx180 -Oyster Bay 11771 **Fx:**922-4046
(315) 469-0062 .. **Marino,** Carl A '62 -4311 W Seneca Tpk -Syracuse 13215 **Fx:**469-0150
(646) 837-0100 .. **Marino,** Carla M '82 (Wenick & F,PC) -28 E 28th -NY 10016
(212) 486-2400 .. **Marino,** Caroline C '03 %Leader & B LLP -630 3rd Av -NY 10017
(914) 997-1380 .. **Marino & Chambers,PC** -1 Barker Av -White Plns 10601 **Fx:**997-1096
(516) 775-4100 .. **Marino,** Christina A '88 (Marino & S) -199 Jericho Tpk -Floral Pk 11001
(212) 974-7474 .. **Marino,** Christopher J '05 Cnsl Cowan DA&S LLP -41 Mad Av -NY 10010
(607) 746-2193 .. **Marino,** Douglas M '04 %Schimmerling Law Ofc -98 Main Bx168 -Delhi 13753 **Fx:**746-6057
(914) 997-1380 .. **Marino,** Frank P '72 (Marino & C,PC) -1 Barker Av -White Plns 10601
(845) 562-3366 .. **Marino,** Gerard J '81 %Larkin AI&T,LLP -34 Route 17K -Newburgh 12550
(212) 880-1200 .. **Marino,** Jack A Jr. '71 %Chicago Title/Ticor -711 3rd Av -NY 10017 **Fx:**880-1400
(585) 697-1825 .. **Marino,** James A '94 -1 S Wshngtn -Rchstr 14614 **Fx:**697-1826
(516) 795-1506 .. **Marino,** James G '83 -1 Wood Av -Massapequa 11758
(914) 288-9191 .. **Marino,** James M '82 Cnsl Lever & S,LLP -303 Old Tarrytown Rd -White Plns 10603
(212) 869-5030 .. **Marino,** James R '88 (Kucker & B,LLP) -747 3rd Av -NY 10017
(212) 268-5136 .. **Marino,** Jeanne O '80 Cnsl Harwood L -350 5th Av -NY 10118
(718) 746-0538 .. **Marino,** John J '66 -160-38 23rd Av -Whitestone 11357
(631) 750-5305 .. **Marin,** Jos '99 -700 Lakelnd Av -Bohemia 11716
(212) 431-2810 .. **Marino,** Jos L Jr. '76 %NY Law Schl -185 W Bway -NY 10013 **Fx:**966-1726
(516) 487-1850 .. **Marino,** Julio J '54 -175 E Shore Rd Bx454 -Gt Neck 11023 **Fx:**487-1851
(212) 318-6000 .. **Marino,** Justin R '08 %Paul HJ&W LLP -75 E 55th -NY 10022
(212) 504-6000 .. **Marino,** Kenneth J '86 Cadwalader W&T LLP -1 World Fncl Ctr -NY 10281
(212) 412-9500 .. **Marino,** Linda M '86 OfCnsl Flemming ZWZ LLP -1 Lbrty Plz -NY 10006
(212) 735-3000 .. **Marino,** Lisa K '05 %Skadden ASM&F LLP -4 Times Sq -NY 10036
(212) 748-9552 .. **Marino,** Mark A '04 Prudential Douglas Elliman -205 E 42nd -NY 10017
(718) 625-8940 .. **Marino,** Mary Frances G '91 %B Lawrence -15 Metrotech Ctr N -Brklyn 11201 **Fx:**624-5756
(631) 289-4600 .. **Marino,** Matthew S '98 Jacoby & J -1737 N Ocean Av -Medfrd 11763 **Fx:**654-5095
(212) 449-6825 .. **Marino,** Melanie '06 %Bk of Amer Merrill Lynch -4 World Fncl Ctr -NY 10080
(718) 447-6700 .. **Marino,** Michl D '74 -Bx100506 -Staten Isl 10310
(212) 218-5500 .. **Marino,** Michl F '76 (Seyfarth S LLP) -620 8th Av -NY 10018
(845) 535-3311 .. **Marino,** Michl J '81 -61 High Av -Nyack 10960 **Fx:**535-3313
(212) 363-6900 .. **Marino,** Nicholas J '05 %Faust GS&B LLP -2 Rector -NY 10006
(516) 829-8399 .. **Marino,** Nora Constance '96 -175 E Shore Rd -Gt Neck 11023 **Fx:**829-4699
(914) 368-4525 .. **Marino,** Paul J '01 (Marino & Assoc,PC) -30 Glenn -White Plns 10603 **Fx:**368-4527
(212) 297-5800 .. **Marino,** Paul R '03 Cnsl Day P LLP -7 Times Sq -NY 10036
(516) 489-5000 .. **Marino,** Philip R '77 %Town Atty -Town Hall -Hempstd 11550 **Fx:**489-5150
(516) 621-0600 .. **Marino,** Robt J '90 %Sontag & H -69 Roslyn Rd -Roslyn Hts 11577
(212) 593-2155 .. **Marino,** Robt M II '95 %Scaffidi & Assoc -747 3rd Av -NY 10017 **Fx:**593-2257
(516) 292-4700 .. **Marino,** Salvatore L '95 (Dalli & M,LLP) -231 Mineola Blvd -Mineola 11501 **Fx:**292-5198
(516) 801-9549 .. **Marino,** Sandra R '97 Pall Corp -2200 Nrthrn Blvd -Greenvale 11548
(718) 424-5850 .. **Marino & Scotti** -104-14 Roosevelt Av -Corona 11368 **Fx:**899-0825
(516) 775-4100 .. **Marino & Scotti** -199 Jericho Tpk -Floral Pk 11001 **Fx:**775-3965
(212) 682-8811 .. **Marino,** Thos V '82 (Dunnington B&M LLP) -1359 Bway -NY 10018
Marino, Wm '53 -7 Jill Ct -Greenlawn 11740

(212) 819-2107 .. **Marinoff,** Gara E '09 Iconix Brand Grp,Inc -1450 Bway -NY 10018
(212) 697-2323 .. **Marino Rojas,** Jennifer L '00 Childrens Defense Fund -15 Maiden Ln -NY 10038 **Fx:**697-0566
(212) 239-4999 .. **Marinovic,** Robt '00 (Meyer SE&K,PC) -1350 Bway Bx822 -NY 10018
(518) 274-5034 .. **Marinstein,** Edw R '86 (Marinstein & M,PLLC) -22 1st Bx155 -Troy 12181 **Fx:**274-5039
(518) 274-5034 .. **Marinstein,** Elliott F '55 (Marinstein & M,PLLC) -22 1st Bx155 -Troy 12181 **Fx:**274-5039
(518) 869-2152 .. **Marinucci,** David P '76 -423 New Karner Rd -Albany 12205
(914) 963-7892 .. **Marinucci,** Dominick E '81 -131 Kingston Av -Ynkrs 10701 **Fx:**963-7892
(212) 468-8000 .. **Marinuzzi,** Lorenzo '97 (Morrison & F LLP) -1290 Av of Amer -NY 10104
(718) 286-1500 .. **Mario,** Edw D '09 %Leg Srvcs -97-77 Qns Blvd -Rego Pk 11374 **Fx:**275-5352
(917) 687-8120 .. **Marion,** Edw R '93 -72-11 Austin PMB 295 -Frst Hlls 11375 **Fx:**(718) 504-7974
(716) 858-2424 .. **Marion,** J Michl '81 %DA -25 Delaware Av -Buffalo 14202 **Fx:**858-7425
(716) 565-2000 .. **Marion,** Jeffrey E '95 -17 Beresford Ct -Williamsvll 14221
(914) 333-9641 .. **Marion,** Michl E '85 %Philips Electronics -345 Scarborough Rd Bx3001 -Briarclff Mnr 10510 **Fx:**332-0615
(212) 506-2500 .. **Marion,** Michl K '05 %Mayer B LLP -1675 Bway -NY 10019
(212) 754-9400 .. **Marion,** Roger K '94 Cnsl Todtman NS&J,PC -425 Park Av -NY 10022
(718) 928-3700 .. **Maris,** Elizabeth A '95 %LSNYC-Bronx -579 Courtlandt Av -Bronx 10451 **Fx:**402-7586
(212) 819-8200 .. **Maris,** Marika '08 %White & C LLP -1155 Av of Amer -NY 10036
(315) 425-9000 .. **Marjama Muldoon Blasiak & Sullivan LLP** -250 S Clinton -Syracuse 13202 **Fx:**425-9114
(315) 425-9000 .. **Marjama,** Owen D '66 OfCnsl Marjama MB&S LLP -250 S Clinton -Syracuse 13202
(516) 466-0410 .. **Mark,** Bernard S '73 (Kestenbaum & M) -40 Cuttermill Rd -Gt Neck 11021
(516) 294-5433 .. **Mark,** Brian F '03 %Ahmuty D&M -200 IU Willets Rd -Albertson 11507
(914) 699-8600 .. **Mark,** Carol R '88 (Ross & M,LLP) -559 Gramatan Av -Mt Vernon 10552
(212) 836-8000 .. **Mark,** Dana L '85 Cnsl Kaye S LLP -425 Park Av -NY 10022
(212) 922-9250 .. **Mark,** Danielle L '01 %Ganfer & S LLP -360 Lex Av -NY 10017
(212) 506-1700 .. **Mark,** David J '78 OfCnsl Kasowitz BT&F LLP -1633 Bway -NY 10019
(212) 856-9600 .. **Mark,** Eli J '09 %Morvillo AGIA&B,PC -565 5th Av -NY 10017
(212) 785-9100 .. **Mark,** Gideon E '01 OfCnsl Paduano & W LLP -1251 Av of Amer -NY 10020
(718) 966-5345 .. **Mark,** Helene '87 -197 Shotwell Av -Staten Isl 10312 **Fx:**966-5345
(516) 333-1415 .. **Mark,** Jason A '00 (Mark & Assoc,PC) -626 RXR Plz -Uniondale 11556 **Fx:**333-1838
(212) 701-3000 .. **Mark,** Jonathan I '75 (Cahill G&R LLP) -80 Pine -NY 10005 **Fx:**269-5420
(585) 798-5555 .. **Mark,** Lance J '75 L Mark,PLLC -539-B Main Bx426 -Medina 14103 **Fx:**798-5559
(212) 506-5000 .. **Mark,** Richd W '81 (Orrick H&S LLP) -51 W 52nd -NY 10019
(518) 591-5232 .. **Mark,** Robt J '79 %NYS ORPTS -WA Harriman State Campus -Albany 12227 **Fx:**474-3657
(718) 338-0342 .. **Mark,** Saml J '76 -1901 Ocean Av -Brklyn 11230
(212) 966-5932 .. **Mark,** Stanley J '78 %AALDEF -99 Hudson -NY 10013 **Fx:**966-4303
(516) 227-6363 .. **Mark,** Steven H '93 %Amato & Assoc,PC -666 Old Cntry Rd -Gdn Cty 11530 **Fx:**227-6367
(212) 728-8000 .. **Mark,** Thos '03 %Willkie F&G LLP -787 7th Av -NY 10019
(718) 875-3675 .. **Mark,** Thos E '77 -423 Atl Av -Brklyn 11217
(718) 250-2000 .. **Markarian,** Arlene M '89 %DA -350 Jay -Brklyn 11201 **Fx:**250-2314
(716) 874-2111 .. **Markarian,** Edw J '86 (Magavern MG LLP) -3080 Delaware Av -Kenmore 14217
(212) 629-4648 .. **Markel,** Adam D '95 AD Markel,PC -11 Bway -NY 10004 **Fx:**(732) 577-8466
(212) 504-6000 .. **Markel,** Gregory A '72 (Cadwalader W&T LLP) -1 World Fncl Ctr -NY 10281
(716) 856-4000 .. **Markel,** Jason E '97 (Hodgson R LLP) -140 Pearl -Buffalo 14202
(212) 277-6500 .. **Markel,** Keith A '99 Cnsl Dickstein S LLP -1633 Bway -NY 10019
(212) 225-2000 .. **Markel,** Neil R '08 %Cleary GS&H -1 Lbrty Plz -NY 10006
(212) 940-8800 .. **Markel,** Robinson '62 OfCnsl Katten MR LLP -575 Mad Av -NY 10022
(212) 589-4200 .. **Markel,** Tatiana '09 %Baker & H LLP -45 Rckfllr Plz -NY 10111
(716) 655-0102 .. **Markello,** Jeffrey P '91 (Sakowski & M,LLP) -Bx399 -Elma 14059 **Fx:**655-1820
(716) 655-0102 .. **Markello,** Mia M '99 Sakowski & M,LLP -Bx399 -Elma 14059 **Fx:**655-1820
(917) 522-3250 .. **Markels,** Gail E '82 Entertainment Software Assn -317 Mad Av -NY 10017
(914) 682-6822 .. **Markenson,** Ari J '97 OfCnsl Benesch FC&A,LLP -50 Main -White Plns 10606
(845) 291-7661 .. **Markert,** Caryn A '02 %Family Ct -285 Main -Goshen 10924
(914) 949-2700 .. **Markert,** Richd F '81 (Bleakley P&S,LLP) -1 N Lex Av -White Plns 10601
(212) 804-4200 .. **Markewich,** Danl '65 (Mound CW&G) -One Bttry Pk Plz -NY 10004
(212) 542-3157 .. **Markewich,** Eve Rachel '88 (Markewich & R) -18 E 48th -NY 10017 **Fx:**308-7780
(212) 873-9346 .. **Markewich,** Robt '47 (Markewich F&M,PC) -175 Riverside Dr -NY 10024 **Fx:**873-9346
(212) 805-0220 .. **Markey,** Elizabeth K '05 Hon J Keenan -500 Pearl -NY 10007
(212) 692-1000 .. **Markey,** James G '87 (Duane M LLP) -1540 Bway -NY 10036
(212) 687-9359 .. **Markey,** Joan M '75 -711 3rd Av -NY 10017
(718) 430-2552 .. **Markey,** Nancy M '99 Einstein Medical -1300 Morris Park Av -Bronx 10461
(315) 432-3866 .. **Markey Clarkson,** Erin L '95 Carrier Corp -Bx4800 -Syracuse 13221
(212) 752-2800 .. **Markfield,** Robt S '68 (Markfield & S LLP) -805 3rd Av -NY 10022
(212) 752-2800 .. **Markfield & Solomon LLP** -805 3rd Av -NY 10022 **Fx:**752-0265
(212) 483-0105 .. **Markham,** Danl F '88 (Coughlin D LLP) -88 Pine-Wall St Plz -NY 10005
(212) 818-9200 .. **Markham,** Edwin T '85 (Satterlee SB&B LLP) -230 Park Av -NY 10169
(212) 462-5034 .. **Markham,** Jason A '00 DIRECTV Latin Amer LLC -1211 Av of Amer -NY 10036
(914) 948-1556 .. **Markhoff,** Harris '63 (Danziger & M LLP) -123 Main -White Plns 10601
(914) 948-1556 .. **Markhoff,** Michl '91 (Danziger & M LLP) -123 Main -White Plns 10601
(914) 946-1452 .. **Markhoff & Mittman PC** -14 Mamaroneck Av -White Plns 10601 **Fx:**946-0810
(914) 234-4002 .. **Markhoff,** Nancy Allen '91 -29 Brundage Ridge Rd -Bedfrd 10506
(914) 946-1452 .. **Markhoff,** Paul M '66 (Markhoff & M PC) -14 Mamaroneck Av -White Plns 10601
(914) 273-7300 .. **Markin,** Caryn D '80 %Schutz & M -6 Spruce Hill Rd -Armonk 10504
(914) 273-7300 .. **Markin,** Steven B '76 (Schutz & M) -6 Spruce Hill Rd -Armonk 10504
(716) 655-2885 .. **Markle,** Jane E '84 -Bx761 -E Aurora 14052
(718) 830-4583 .. **Marklein,** Walter R '84 -88-34 Rutledge Av -Glendale 11385 **Fx:**830-4584
(212) 701-3000 .. **Markley,** Brian T '01 (Cahill G&R LLP) -80 Pine -NY 10005 **Fx:**269-5420
(212) 895-1494 .. **Markman,** Jennifer R '04 %Clifford C LLP -31 W 52nd -NY 10019
(212) 532-2100 .. **Markman,** Jody E '87 J Markman,PLLC -1775 Bway -NY 10019 **Fx:**532-2198
(212) 979-9100 .. **Markman,** Ross G '93 %Suberi Bros -902 Bway -NY 10010 **Fx:**979-5331
(718) 858-9676 .. **Markman,** Stephen R '97 -105 Court -Brklyn 11201 **Fx:**625-2671
(212) 488-1200 .. **Markoe,** Zaharah R '01 %Kobre & K,LLP -800 3rd Av -NY 10022
(212) 664-4444 .. **Markoff,** Lisa Green '91 %NBC -30 Rckfllr Plz -NY 10112
(212) 964-7400 .. **Markoff,** Matthew E '09 Smith MDWY&Y,PC -111 John -NY 10038
(347) 401-9244 .. **Markoff,** Robt A '01 %Hon J Battaglia -141 Lvngstn -Brklyn 11201
(516) 599-1000 .. **Markos,** John Jaye '79 -128 B Hempstd Av -Lynbrk 11563 **Fx:**599-5355
(212) 785-7520 .. **Markos,** John P '79 OfCnsl Coti & S -17 State -NY 10004
(516) 935-2330 .. **Markotsis,** James C '87 (Markotsis & L) -183 Bway -Hicksvll 11801
(516) 935-2330 .. **Markotsis & Lieberman** -183 Bway -Hicksvll 11801 **Fx:**935-2260
(212) 878-7900 .. **Markou,** Damianos '96 (Fox R LLP) -100 Park Av -NY 10017
(516) 794-7340 .. **Markovic,** Mirsade '01 %Fager & A,LLP -90 Merrick Av -E Meadow 11554
(212) 841-4100 .. **Markovich,** Edw '98 %Millennium Ptnrs LP -666 5th Av -NY 10103 **Fx:**841-4141
(212) 422-0202 .. **Markovich,** Laura K '98 %Sedgwick DM&A LLP -125 Broad -NY 10004
(212) 805-3900 .. **Markovich,** Virginia M '04 %Clausen M PC -1 Chase Manh Plz -NY 10005
(212) 947-7534 .. **Markovitch,** Michl H '83 -250 W 57th -NY 10107 **Fx:**244-1845
(518) 587-4451 .. **Markovits,** Ilsa Pasciullo '80 -Bx795 -Saratoga Spgs 12866 **Fx:**587-4584
(845) 343-0505 .. **Markovits,** Robt L '62 (Markovits & M) -12 Evergreen Dr Bx2025 -Middletwn 10940 **Fx:**343-9008
(518) 464-0640 .. **Markovits,** Stephen R '81 (Devine M&S LLP) -52 Corp Cir -Albany 12203
(212) 227-4000 .. **Markovits,** Thos P '80 (Mirman M&L,PC) -291 Bway -NY 10007
(212) 451-2300 .. **Markovits,** Yehuda I '00 (Olshan GFR&W LLP) -65 E 55th -NY 10022
(212) 442-2028 .. **Markovitz,** Ruth '91 %Law Dept -100 Church -NY 10007 **Fx:**788-0367
(212) 481-1220 .. **Markowitz,** Alon M '91 (Markowitz & C LLP) -271 Mad Av -NY 10016 **Fx:**481-1221
(212) 692-1000 .. **Markowitz,** Brian J '02 %Duane M LLP -1540 Bway -NY 10036
(212) 888-8922 .. **Markowitz,** David A '96 LC Fiabane -947 2nd Av -NY 10022
(212) 416-8000 .. **Markowitz,** David A '97 %Dept of Law -120 Bway -NY 10271
(914) 358-3274 .. **Markowitz,** Gerald H '56 (Markowitz & P) -500 Mamaroneck Av -Harrison 10528
(845) 356-0938 .. **Markowitz,** Harry '77 -55 Remsen Av -Monsey 10952
(718) 590-7856 .. **Markowitz,** Jared S '04 %ACS -900 Sheridan Av -Bronx 10451
(718) 468-0068 .. **Markowitz,** Jay S '00 -15916 Union Tpke -Fresh Mdws 11366 **Fx:**261-5776
(631) 694-2300 .. **Markowitz,** Joel M '69 (Lamb & B,LLP) -534 Broadhllw Rd Bx9034 -Melvll 11747
(212) 589-4200 .. **Markowitz,** Laurence S '77 (Baker & H LLP) -45 Rckfllr Plz -NY 10111
(914) 347-1292 .. **Markowitz,** Linda '89 (Rosenthal & M,LLP) -45 Knollwood Rd -Elmsfrd 10523
(212) 988-2916 .. **Markowitz,** Martin '69 -525 E 86th -NY 10028
(516) 295-9061 .. **Markowitz,** Michl A '89 -1553 Bway -Hewlett 11557 **Fx:**374-3314
(212) 418-4726 .. **Markowitz,** Michl E '07 ICON Capital Corp -100 5th Av -NY 10011
(212) 382-0700 .. **Markowitz,** Michl I '99 %Ostrolenk FG&S,LLP -1180 Av of Amer -NY 10036
(212) 553-1012 .. **Markowitz,** Murray R '96 %Moody's Invstr Srvc -250 Greenwich -NY 10007
(718) 590-6025 .. **Markowitz,** Nicole Gerber '09 %Law Dept -900 Sheridan Av -Bronx 10451 **Fx:**590-2699
(212) 790-0200 .. **Markowitz,** Peter L '02 Benj N Cardozo Schl of Law -55 5th Av -NY 10003 **Fx:**790-0345
(914) 358-3274 .. **Markowitz & Piro** -500 Mamaroneck Av -Harrison 10528 **Fx:**946-7468
(631) 427-7888 .. **Markowitz & Rabbach LLP** -290 Broadhllw Rd -Melvll 11747
(212) 486-9494 .. **Markowitz,** Richd H '73 -488 Mad Av -NY 10022
(212) 382-0909 .. **Markowitz,** Roger S '68 (Peckar & A,PC) -41 Mad Av -NY 10154
(914) 273-3959 .. **Markowitz,** Ronald A '75 -355 maij -Armonk 10504 **Fx:**273-4008
(212) 869-6000 .. **Markowitz & Roshco, LLP** -530 5th Av -NY 10036
(212) 216-8000 .. **Markowitz,** Scott S '90 (Tarter K&D LLP) -1350 Bway -NY 10018
(212) 869-6000 .. **Markowitz,** Seth P '95 (Markowitz & R,LLP) -530 5th Av -NY 10036
(516) 935-3500 .. **Markowitz,** Stuart D '80 -575 Jericho Tpk -Jericho 11753 **Fx:**935-3599
(212) 949-8700 .. **Markowitz Savitt,** Shari H '96 %Eisner LLP -750 3rd Av -NY 10017 **Fx:**891-4100
(212) 506-1700 .. **Marks,** Aaron H '94 (Kasowitz BT&F LLP) -1633 Bway -NY 10019

(212) 227-4300 .. **Marks,** Alfred M '53 OfCnsl Schwartz & T LLP -15 Maiden Ln -NY 10038 **Fx:**227-4311
(212) 593-1700 .. **Marks,** Alfred M '53 OfCnsl Kaplan L LLP -1065 Av of Amer -NY 10018
(212) 297-5800 .. **Marks,** Alfred W J '87 (Day P LLP) -7 Times Sq -NY 10036
(212) 333-8452 .. **Marks,** Amanda M '94 %Universal Music Grp -825 8th Av -NY 10019 **Fx:**333-8296
(212) 583-9600 .. **Marks,** Andrew P '85 (Littler M,PC) -900 3rd Av -NY 10022
(212) 310-8000 .. **Marks,** Benjamin E '98 (Weil G&M LLP) -767 5th Av -NY 10153
(212) 769-4040 .. **Marks,** Burton H '57 -115 Cntrl Pk W -NY 10023 **Fx:**769-4244
(212) 370-4477 .. **Marks,** Cabot J '92 -485 Mad Av -NY 10022 **Fx:**588-0471
(716) 362-0170 .. **Marks,** Christopher M '94 Jensen ML&V LLC -360 Delaware Av -Buffalo 14202
(212) 964-7400 .. **Marks,** Darren R '07 %Smith MDWY&Y,PC -111 John -NY 10038
(212) 326-3939 .. **Marks,** David G '10 %Jones D -222 E 41st -NY 10017
(212) 505-2880 .. **Marks,** Ellen '73 (Raphael & M) -276 Park Av S -NY 10010
(631) 385-5100 .. **Marks,** George L '53 %Marks & M -1160 E Jericho Tpk -Huntngtn 11743
(732) 747-7100 .. **Marks,** Gerald A '70 (Marks & K,LLP) -55 Wall -NY 10005 **Fx:**219-0625
(212) 953-6000 .. **Marks,** Gregory K '75 (Katsky K LLP) -605 3rd Av -NY 10158
(585) 232-3464 .. **Marks,** Homer H '51 (Traynor S&M) -45 Exchange -Rchstr 14614
(201) 541-4551 .. **Marks,** James V '95 Dassault Falcon Jet Corp -Rockvll Ctr 11570
(585) 232-3464 .. **Marks,** Jeffrey H '82 (Traynor S&M) -45 Exchange -Rchstr 14614
(212) 571-4878 .. **Marks,** Jeffrey Ian '80 -277 Bway -NY 10007 **Fx:**571-0468
(212) 318-3000 .. **Marks,** Jeffrey M '83 (Fulbright & J LLP) -666 5th Av -NY 10103
(585) 546-5530 .. **Marks,** Jill M '93 %Thomson West -50 E Broad -Rchstr 14694
(212) 545-8008 .. **Marks,** Jonathan '73 (J Marks,PC) -220 5th Av -NY 10001 **Fx:**889-3595
(716) 847-8400 .. **Marks,** Kelly E '07 %Phillips L LLP -3400 HSBC Ctr -Buffalo 14203
(212) 949-8700 .. **Marks,** Lester A '71 %Eisner LLP -750 3rd Av -NY 10017 **Fx:**891-4100
(212) 943-3400 .. **Marks,** Lionel Alan '55 -61 Bway -NY 10006 **Fx:**943-3495
(212) 586-7799 .. **Marks,** Lisa J '93 %Chesky Records -355 W 52nd -NY 10019
(718) 613-3500 .. **Marks,** Manuel S '83 %UIA Bd -Bx29002 -Brklyn 11201 **Fx:**613-3566
(212) 756-2000 .. **Marks,** Mary K '94 SpclCnsl Schulte R&Z LLP -919 3rd Av -NY 10022
(212) 453-3687 .. **Marks,** Matia R '04 ACE Westchester Specialty -1325 Av of Amer -NY 10019
(212) 730-8133 .. **Marks,** Melissa B '07 %Gunderson DSVF&H,LLP -220 W 42nd -NY 10036
(646) 386-4072 .. **Marks,** Michl B '81 %Hon R Uviller -100 Centre -NY 10013
(212) 630-5004 .. **Marks,** Michl S '06 East Rock Cptl LLC -10 E 53rd -NY 10022
(212) 582-0970 .. **Marks,** Michl V '76 St Nicholas Music Inc -1619 Bway -NY 10019 **Fx:**582-1097
(914) 949-0962 .. **Marks,** Morton '54 -47 Lawrence Dr -N White Plns 10603 **Fx:**949-0962
(212) 727-2700 .. **Marks,** Nancy S '87 %NRDC -40 W 20th -NY 10011 **Fx:**727-1773
(914) 345-3701 .. **Marks O'Neill O'Brien & Courtney, PC** -530 Saw Mill Rvr Rd -Elmsfrd 10523 **Fx:**345-3743
(212) 259-8000 .. **Marks,** Patti J '93 Cnsl Dewey & L LLP -1301 Av of Amer -NY 10019
(212) 788-0884 .. **Marks,** Paul F '84 %Law Dept -100 Church -NY 10007 **Fx:**788-0367
(845) 562-9550 .. **Marks,** Paul L '82 -5020 Route 9W -Newburgh 12550 **Fx:**562-9525
(845) 561-6917 .. **Marks,** Paul L '82 -155 N Plnk Rd -Newburgh 12550 **Fx:**561-1540
(516) 571-3800 .. **Marks,** Rachel R '04 %DA -262 Old Cntry Rd -Mineola 11501 **Fx:**248-9479
(212) 715-1000 .. **Marks,** Ramon P '77 (Arnold & P LLP) -399 Park Av -NY 10022
(212) 564-9515 .. **Marks,** Roger '88 (Marks & M,LLC) -350 5th Av -NY 10118 **Fx:**629-5759
(212) 441-1776 .. **Marks,** Roger M Jr. '89 Aon Risk Srvcs -199 Water -NY 10038
(516) 349-6100 .. **Marks,** Roger N '74 %Episcopal Health Srvcs -700 Hicksvll Rd -Bethpage 11714
(212) 872-1000 .. **Marks,** Ryan N '07 -One Bryant Park -NY 10036 **Fx:**872-1002
(212) 484-3900 .. **Marks,** Sarah I '07 %Arent F LLP -1675 Bway -NY 10019
(212) 564-9515 .. **Marks,** Seymour '57 (Marks & M,LLC) -350 5th Av -NY 10118 **Fx:**629-5759
(212) 735-8600 .. **Marks,** Theo L '59 OfCnsl Morrison C LLP -909 3rd Av -NY 10022
(212) 735-3000 .. **Marks,** Thos R '10 %Skadden ASM&F LLP -4 Times Sq -NY 10036
(631) 385-5100 .. **Marks,** Wayne T '83 %Marks & M -1160 E Jericho Tpk -Huntngtn 11743
(212) 451-2300 .. **Marks-Esterman,** Lori '99 (Olshan GFR&W LLP) -65 E 55th -NY 10022
(212) 408-5100 .. **Markson,** Edouard S '97 (Chadbourne & P LLP) -30 Rckfllr Plz -NY 10112
(212) 310-8000 .. **Markson,** Johanna Lowry '91 Weil G&M LLP -767 5th Av -NY 10153
(845) 359-0737 .. **Markstein,** Paul L '82 (Menschik & M) -574 Rt 303 -Blauvelt 10913
(212) 223-3200 .. **Markstein,** Wm E '94 Transammonia,Inc -350 Park Av -NY 10022
(212) 608-4140 .. **Marku,** Isejn '95 -299 Bway -NY 10007 **Fx:**608-6256
(212) 907-0700 .. **Markunas,** Michl '08 %Labaton S LLP -140 Bway -NY 10005
(212) 697-3250 .. **Markus,** Alexander '04 Goldberg & R PLLC -115 Bway -NY 10006 **Fx:**227-4533
(914) 241-6300 .. **Markus,** Anthony C '86 (Markus & S,LLP) -116 Radio Cir -Mt Kisco 10549 **Fx:**241-6308
(212) 298-5585 .. **Markus,** David E '02 SpclCnsl Senate Majority Leaders Ofc -250 Bway -NY 10007 **Fx:**298-5605
(212) 580-4556 .. **Markus,** Frank '70 -290 West End Av -NY 10023
(203) 672-3212 .. **Markus,** Ilan '03 (LeClairRyan,PC) -830 3rd Av -NY 10022
(212) 593-8000 .. **Markus,** Shay M '04 %Warner Prtnrs,PC -950 3rd Av -NY 10022 **Fx:**593-9058
(917) 815-9017 .. **Markus,** Stacy M '03 S Markus PLLC -1760 2nd Av -NY 10128 **Fx:**(646) 478-9396
(516) 408-9000 .. **Markus,** Stephen P '85 (Walsh MM&D LLP) -229 Seventh -Gdn Cty 11530
(212) 530-5000 .. **Markus,** Taisa '89 (Milbank TH&M LLP) -1 Chase Manh Plz -NY 10005
(914) 472-5600 .. **Markuson,** Gloria Crowley '54 -185 Summerfld -Scarsdale 10583 **Fx:**472-5605
(212) 578-2211 .. **Markussen,** Christine Nels '89 %MetLife -27-01 Qns Plz N -LIC 11101
(716) 652-7134 .. **Marky,** Douglas W '79 -204 Hllcrst Rd -E Aurora 14052
(716) 847-8400 .. **Marky,** James D '10 %Phillips L LLP -3400 HSBC Ctr -Buffalo 14203
(212) 735-3000 .. **Marlaire,** Sean C '08 %Skadden ASM&F LLP -4 Times Sq -NY 10036
(212) 935-3000 .. **Marlar,** Tricia C '05 %Mintz LCFG&P,PC -666 3rd Av -NY 10017
(212) 468-8000 .. **Marlatt,** Jerry R '85 SrCnsl Morrison & F LLP -1290 Av of Amer -NY 10104
(212) 983-9330 .. **Marlborough,** Christopher '04 %Faruqi & F,LLP -369 Lex Av -NY 10017 **Fx:**983-9331
(212) 687-4900 .. **Marlborough,** Jennifer L '99 %Wormser KG&J LLP -825 3rd Av -NY 10022
(631) 786-1210 .. **Marlek,** Marilyn A '78 -Bx477 -Northprt 11768
(212) 269-4900 .. **Marler,** John C '06 %Ford MEW&G,LLP -Wall Street Plz -NY 10005
(212) 225-2000 .. **Marler,** Melissa K '04 %Cleary GS&H -1 Lbrty Plz -NY 10006
(716) 856-5500 .. **Marlette,** Peter S '85 (Damon M LLP) -200 Delaware Av -Buffalo 14202
(631) 853-4049 .. **Marletti-Schifano,** Marisa G '97 %Cnty Atty -Dennison Bldg Bx6100 -Hauppauge 11788 **Fx:**853-5169
(607) 778-2423 .. **Marley,** Allison L '09 %DA -45 Hawley Bx1766 -Bnghmtn 13902 **Fx:**778-8870
(212) 318-3000 .. **Marlin,** James P '71 (Fulbright & J LLP) -666 5th Av -NY 10103
(212) 719-0200 .. **Marlin,** Mary K '01 %BAR/BRI -1500 Bway -NY 10036 **Fx:**719-1421
(718) 596-3300 .. **Marlin,** Michl C '75 P Schneider & Assoc PLLC -335 Adams -Brklyn 11201
(212) 715-9100 .. **Marlin,** Richd '59 Cnsl Kramer LN&F,LLP -1177 Av of Amer -NY 10036
(718) 720-0047 .. **Marlin,** Ruth Sacks '92 -80 Bay Street Lndg -Staten Isl 10301
(212) 277-0433 .. **Marlin,** Timothy L '01 Hartford Fncl Products -2 Park Av -NY 10016
(212) 584-6151 .. **Marlow,** Chad A '00 Public Advocacy Grp -75 Maiden Ln -NY 10038
(212) 521-5400 .. **Marlow,** Danielle J '97 (Reed S LLP) -599 Lex Av -NY 10022
(845) 454-3250 .. **Marlow,** George D '67 Cnsl Gellert & K,PC -75 Wshngtn -Poughkeepsie 12601
(212) 858-7200 .. **Marlow,** Joshua R '99 RBC Dominion Sec -165 Bway -NY 10006
(516) 222-0101 .. **Marlow,** Lenard '59 (Divorce Mdtn Prof) -585 Stewart Av -Gdn Cty 11530 **Fx:**745-5745
(212) 233-0113 .. **Marlow,** Martin '66 -111 John -NY 10038
(315) 369-2245 .. **Marlow,** Tracy A '85 -133 Garmon Av Bx554 -Old Forge 13420 **Fx:**369-2245
(212) 460-3445 .. **Marlowe,** Charmaine L '90 Con Ed -4 Irving Pl -NY 10003
(212) 318-6000 .. **Marlowe,** Keith D '09 %Paul HJ&W LLP -75 E 55th -NY 10022
(212) 572-6210 .. **Marlowe,** Mary Ann C '87 (Keane & M) -300 Park Av -NY 10022
(315) 422-1152 .. **Marlow-Jones,** Nicole M '98 (Costello C&F,PLLC) -500 Plum -Syracuse 13204
(631) 261-7778 .. **Marmanillo,** Nicole U '04 %Brody O&O -7 Bayview Av -Northprt 11768
(516) 742-8340 .. **Marmann,** Diane Pacifico '91 %Pacifico D&P -136 Willis Av -Mineola 11501
(315) 793-2225 .. **Marmelstein,** Joel L '75 %Dept of Law -207 Genesee -Utica 13501 **Fx:**793-2228
(718) 403-9629 .. **Marmer,** Melanie M '89 -44 Court -Brklyn 11201 **Fx:**403-9501
(212) 891-1600 .. **Marmer,** Ronald L '06 (Jenner & B LLP) -919 3rd Av -NY 10022
(212) 373-3000 .. **Marmon,** Nathaniel E '07 %Paul WRW&G LLP -1285 Av of Amer -NY 10019
(973) 848-4016 .. **Marmora,** John M '85 (K&L Gates LLP) -599 Lex Av -NY 10022 **Fx:**848-4001
(914) 995-2660 .. **Marmorato,** Antonietta U '07 %Cnty Atty -148 Martine Av -White Plns 10601 **Fx:**995-5858
(914) 948-4700 .. **Marmorato,** Gino A '06 %Kent HWCV&F,LLP -111 Church -White Plns 10601
(646) 386-4520 .. **Marmorek,** Kay '78 %Criminal Ct -100 Centre -NY 10013
(212) 286-8585 .. **Marmorek,** Keri S '99 %Heidell PM&B,LLP -99 Park Av -NY 10016
(212) 223-0200 .. **Marmur,** Nathaniel Z '95 (Stillman F&S,PC) -425 Park Av -NY 10022
(212) 482-2320 .. **Marnel,** Sara '07 Justice Ctr -100 Wall -NY 10005
(516) 542-9000 .. **Marnell,** Russell I '85 -90 Merrick Av -E Meadow 11554 **Fx:**542-2039
(631) 271-3095 .. **Marnell,** Susan P '85 -Bx20576 -Huntngtn Sta 11746
(212) 436-4446 .. **Marnin,** Gil '91 Deloitte & Touche,LLP -2 World Fncl Ctr -NY 10281 **Fx:**436-5971
(212) 245-1000 .. **Marnin,** Seth M '08 %Outten & G LLP -3 Park Av -NY 10016
(212) 819-8200 .. **Marnin,** Tal '97 Cnsl White & C LLP -1155 Av of Amer -NY 10036
(914) 948-1410 .. **Marocco,** Frank '85 -175 Main -White Plns 10601 **Fx:**761-1871
(646) 530-1158 .. **Maroko,** Richd Alexander '98 NY Hotel & Motel Trades Cncl -708 8th Av -NY 10036
(518) 393-2476 .. **Marola,** Lydia Rocissano '89 -8 Irving Rd -Scotia 12302 **Fx:**393-2476
(212) 735-8600 .. **Maron,** Evan I '95 (Morrison C LLP) -909 3rd Av -NY 10022
(914) 946-7200 .. **Maron,** Leslie B '78 (Maron & M) -1 N Bway -White Plns 10601 **Fx:**993-0251
(212) 922-9250 .. **Maron,** Matthew R '06 %Ganfer & S LLP -360 Lex Av -NY 10017
(212) 298-5165 .. **Maron,** Maud J '99 %Leg Aid -49 Thomas -NY 10013 **Fx:**298-5252
(718) 855-7515 .. **Maron,** Sheila K '81 -16 Court -Brklyn 11241 **Fx:**855-7521
(631) 367-8312 .. **Maroney,** John P '90 %Cld Srng Hrbr Lab -1 Bungtown Rd Bx100 -Cold Spg Hbr 11724
(631) 881-0888 .. **Maroney,** Matthew J '95 -445 Broad Hollow Rd #25 -Melvll 11747 **Fx:**(516) 908-5007
(212) 992-8839 .. **Maroney,** Terry A '99 NYU Law Schl -40 Wshngtn Sq S -NY 10012
(315) 443-2524 .. **Maroney,** Thos J '63 %Syracuse Univ Cllg of Law -Wht Hall -Syracuse 13244 **Fx:**443-4213
(212) 509-2009 .. **Maroney,** Thos J '81 (Maroney O LLP) -11 Bway -NY 10004 **Fx:**504-2754
(212) 556-2100 .. **Marooney,** Richd T Jr. '95 (King & S) -1185 Av of Amer -NY 10036
(718) 402-1990 .. **Marothy,** Christopher A '80 Dubow & S -860 Grnd Cncrs -Bronx 10451
(315) 408-8907 .. **Marotta,** Andrea D '03 -Bx139 -Sackets Hbr 13685
(718) 390-0555 .. **Marotta,** Danl C '93 (Gabor & M LLC) -1878 Victory Blvd -Staten Isl 10314
(516) 364-7900 .. **Marotta,** Frank J '91 Epstein F&G -45 Crsswys Park Dr W -Woodbury 11797

(518) 431-5062 .. **Marotta,** James F Jr. '02 Farm Family Ins -Bx656 -Albany 12201 **Fx:**431-5979
(718) 224-6664 .. **Marotta,** John J '72 -242-03 Nrthrn Blvd -Douglastn 11362 **Fx:**224-6628
(212) 593-6700 .. **Marotta,** Nicholas J '86 (Aaronson RF&D,LLP) -757 3rd Av -NY 10017
(212) 854-4083 .. **Marotta,** Susan M '90 Columbia Univ -535 W 116th 412 Low Mem'l Library -NY 10027
(516) 432-7111 .. **Marotti,** Regina M '94 (R Marotti,PC) -532 E Olive -Long Bch 11561 **Fx:**432-7171
(716) 854-4080 .. **Marotto,** Melanie C '93 %Block C&L,PC -1 Niagara Sq -Buffalo 14202
(845) 471-6050 .. **Maroulis,** Peter L '62 -104 Hooker Av -Poughkeepsie 12601
(212) 608-0600 .. **Marous,** Gabriel J '01 (Marous & M,PC) -1674 Bway -NY 10019 **Fx:**608-2901
(212) 608-0600 .. **Marous,** Justine A '01 (Marous & M,PC) -1674 Bway -NY 10019 **Fx:**608-2901
(914) 743-1468 .. **Marquardt,** Jeanmarie A '97 -88 Wild Birch Farms -Cortlandt Manor 10567 **Fx:**743-1467
(212) 816-6128 .. **Marquardt,** Karl L '99 %Citigroup -388 Greenwich -NY 10013
(315) 466-4444 .. **Marquardt,** Wm J '93 (Trespasz & M) -251 W Fayette -Syracuse 13202 **Fx:**466-5555
(212) 848-4000 .. **Marques,** Angela R Early '06 %Shearman & S LLP -599 Lex Av -NY 10022
(212) 385-1400 .. **Marques Jackson,** Stacey A '01 -299 Bway -NY 10007 **Fx:**385-0098
(718) 725-3062 .. **Marquez,** Ann M '06 %ACS -15120 Jamaica Av -Jamaica 11432
(914) 989-6650 .. **Marquez,** John R '86 (Eustace & M) -1133 Wstchstr Av -White Plns 10604
(718) 742-6550 .. **Marquez,** Lisa Ann '98 NYC Dept of Ed -501 Courtlandt Av -Bronx 10451
(212) 309-6000 .. **Marquez,** Priscilla '09 %Morgan L&B LLP -101 Park Av -NY 10178
(212) 594-5300 .. **Marquez,** Rolando G '05 %Milberg LLP -1 Penn Plz -NY 10119
(718) 293-1000 .. **Marquez,** Sergio '87 -1015 Grnd Cncrs -Bronx 10452 **Fx:**293-3337
(212) 888-3033 .. **Marquez-Bottome,** Andrea '04 %Becker GM&M LLP -299 Park Av -NY 10171
(212) 560-9590 .. **Marquez-Melecio,** Michelle '91 %SG Komen Breast Cancer Fndn -341 W 38th -NY 10018
(845) 638-6045 .. **Marquith,** Susan '83 -105 Shetland Dr -New Cty 10956
(212) 201-7110 .. **Marr,** Amelia Porricelli '91 Cnsl Allan Riley Co -645 Fifth Av -NY 10022 **Fx:**661-1955
(718) 649-4989 .. **Marra,** Alessandro F '84 -1142 E 92nd -Brklyn 11236 **Fx:**649-4990
(212) 264-5916 .. **Marra,** Angela T '95 %DHS -26 Fed Plz -NY 10278
(516) 759-8469 .. **Marra,** Anthony J '92 OfCnsl M Montesano,PC -40 Glen -Glen Cove 11542 **Fx:**759-3801
(716) 845-7465 .. **Marra,** Catherine E '93 Family Ct -1 Niagara Plz -Buffalo 14202 **Fx:**858-6293
(718) 923-4206 .. **Marra,** Gerard J '75 %OTDA Fair Hearings -14 Boerum Pl -Brklyn 11201
(914) 964-6806 .. **Marra,** Jos A '84 (J Marra) -909 Mdlnd Av -Ynkrs 10704 **Fx:**964-0137
(212) 704-1216 .. **Marra,** Michl R '96 Interpublic Grp -1114 Av of Amer -NY 10036
(212) 431-5588 .. **Marra,** Nicole S '97 -25 N Moore -NY 10013
(718) 390-5356 .. **Marra,** Ralph P '83 NYS Unified Ct Sys -18 Richmond Ter -Staten Isl 10301
(212) 363-1380 .. **Marra,** Susan M '83 (Herten BSCBL&H,LLC) -747 3rd Av -NY 10017
(516) 746-7799 .. **Marrali,** Josephine '03 %Reisman P&R LLP -1305 Franklin Av -Gdn Cty 11530
(716) 362-1177 .. **Marranca,** Mindy L '00 -70 Niagara -Buffalo 14202
(212) 244-3333 .. **Marrano,** Douglas M '00 (Donovan H LLP) -1350 Bway -NY 10018
(716) 827-6677 .. **Marrano,** Frederic J '79 -714 Ridge Rd -Lackawanna 14218
(718) 654-2800 .. **Marrano,** Leon D III '89 %Marson Construction -414 E 203rd -Bronx 10467
(716) 856-4000 .. **Marrapese,** Arthur A III '82 (Hodgson R LLP) -140 Pearl -Buffalo 14202
(718) 983-8000 .. **Marrazzo & Dollard** 1265 Richmond Av -Staten Isl 10314 **Fx:**983-7899
(631) 844-7800 .. **Marrazzo,** Kevin '83 %Olsten Corp -175 Broadhllw Rd -Melvll 11747 **Fx:**844-7414
(518) 449-8893 .. **Marrello,** Lisa M '93 (Wilson EME&D LLP) -677 Bway -Albany 12207
(212) 848-4000 .. **Marren,** Anne E '10 Shearman & S LLP -599 Lex Av -NY 10022
(914) 835-0840 .. **Marren,** Bernard D Jr. '79 -15 John Jay Pl -Rye 10580
(716) 845-9439 .. **Marren,** Danl J '86 (Supreme Ct) -25 Delaware Av -Buffalo 14202 **Fx:**851-3293
(914) 967-6420 .. **Marren,** Joan P '82 -5 Crawford Rd -Harrison 10528
(914) 967-6420 .. **Marren,** Jos H '80 -5 Crawford Rd -Harrison 10528
(212) 788-4888 .. **Marrero,** Ernesto Jr. '83 %HHC/Correctional Hlth Srvcs -125 Worth -NY 10013
(718) 855-5252 .. **Marrero,** Jesus M '86 -311 Court -Brklyn 11231 **Fx:**625-5370
(212) 331-5063 .. **Marrero,** Luisa Petrin '99 %NYC HRA -180 Water -NY 10038
(631) 773-6467 .. **Marrero,** Wilson '02 -510 Broad Hollow Rd -Melvll 11747 **Fx:**773-6468
(516) 935-0739 .. **Marri,** Alfonse '91 -390 Bway -Bethpage 11714
(212) 269-4900 .. **Marrin,** Richd B '71 (Ford MEW&G,LLP) -Wall Street Plz -NY 10005
(212) 269-4900 .. **Marrin,** Richd B Jr. '97 -Wall Street Plz -NY 10005 **Fx:**344-4294
(212) 425-3240 .. **Marrinan,** Kevin J '81 (Marrinan & MM,PC) -26 Bway -NY 10004
(212) 425-3240 .. **Marrinan & Mazzola Mardon, PC** -26 Bway -NY 10004 **Fx:**943-6649
(518) 457-5162 .. **Marriner,** Tina M '03 Educ Dept -80 Wolf Rd -Albany 12205
(212) 576-5925 .. **Marrion,** Catherine A '96 %NY Life Ins -51 Mad Av -NY 10010 **Fx:**576-7991
(212) 474-1000 .. **Marriott,** David R '95 (Cravath S&M LLP) -825 8th Av -NY 10019
(518) 473-2998 .. **Marriott,** Deborah A '86 NYS Ed Dept -89 Wshngtn Av -Albany 12234 **Fx:**402-5940
(716) 847-8400 .. **Marriott,** Susan M '08 %Phillips L LLP -3400 HSBC Ctr -Buffalo 14203
(315) 472-6417 .. **Marris & Bartholomae** -317 Mntgmry -Syracuse 13202 **Fx:**472-2909
(716) 684-0001 .. **Marris,** Jos M '94 PCB Grp,Inc -3425 Walden Av -Depew 14043
(315) 472-6417 .. **Marris,** Karin Huntley '89 %Marris & B -317 Mntgmry -Syracuse 13202
(315) 472-6417 .. **Marris,** Margaret A '81 (Marris & B) -317 Mntgmry -Syracuse 13202
(315) 472-6417 .. **Marris,** Richd F '83 (Marris & B) -317 Mntgmry -Syracuse 13202
(315) 453-6530 .. **Marris,** Susan B '93 State Ins Fund -1045 7th N -Liverpool 13088 **Fx:**453-6540
(585) 263-1000 .. **Marro,** Nicole M '96 Cnsl Nixon P LLP -1100 Clinton Sq -Rchstr 14604
(212) 314-3882 .. **Marron,** Edw A '78 %AXA Financial Inc -1290 Av of Amer -NY 10104 **Fx:**707-7963
(585) 232-3730 .. **Marron,** George D '00 (Chamberlain D LLP) -1600 Crssrds Bldg -Rchstr 14614
(315) 474-7541 .. **Marrone,** Anthony A II '10 %Menter R&T,PC -308 Maltbie -Syracuse 13204
(516) 676-0126 .. **Marrone,** Anthony E '85 -44 Smith -Glen Cove 11542
(718) 892-0400 .. **Marrone,** David V '00 %W Gallina -1180 Morris Park Av -Bronx 10461 **Fx:**892-0033
(718) 261-1711 .. **Marrone,** Gerard M '01 -66-85 73rd Pl -Middl Vllg 11379 **Fx:**458-2181
(718) 250-2000 .. **Marrone,** John R '99 %DA -350 Jay -Brklyn 11201 **Fx:**250-2314
(914) 376-3757 .. **Marrone,** Nancy J '98 %Leg Srvcs -30 S Bway -Ynkrs 10701 **Fx:**376-8739
(212) 878-8000 .. **Marrouk,** Leyla '03 %Clifford C LLP -31 W 52nd -NY 10019
(914) 666-8033 .. **Marrow,** Paul B '69 OfCnsl Banks SG&W,LLP -118 N Bedford Rd Bx320 -Mt Kisco 10549
(914) 263-0780 .. **Marrow,** Robt V '65 OfCnsl Salon MDN&B,LLP -292 Mad Av -NY 10017 **Fx:**560-2111
(718) 254-6790 .. **Marrus,** Melissa B '04 %US Atty -271 Cadman Plz E -Brklyn 11201 **Fx:**254-6479
(631) 979-3000 .. **Mars,** Fredk M '53 (Certilman BA&H,LLP) -1393 Vets Mem'l Hwy -Hauppauge 11788
(212) 765-4300 .. **Mars,** Harvey S '86 H Mars,LLC -322 W 48th -NY 10036 **Fx:**765-2775
(212) 833-5604 .. **Mars,** Heather R '02 Sony BMG Music -550 Mad Av -NY 10022
(914) 703-6300 .. **Marsala,** Wm E '94 %Pillinger MT,LLP -570 Taxter Rd -Elmsfrd 10523
(516) 747-8000 .. **Marschhausen,** Dirk '90 (Marschhausen & F,PC) -835 Old Cntry Rd -Westbury 11590 **Fx:**747-6439
(212) 480-4800 .. **Marschner,** Edw C '71 (Fox H&C LLP) -825 3rd Av -NY 10022
(212) 526-2920 .. **Marsh,** Benjamin K '00 %Barclays Capital Inc -745 7th Av -NY 10019
(212) 808-1170 .. **Marsh,** Bridget K '01 LSTA -360 Mad Av -NY 10017 **Fx:**808-1183
(212) 480-5284 .. **Marsh,** D Monica '99 %Insurance Dept -25 Beaver -NY 10004 **Fx:**480-5272
(212) 705-7000 .. **Marsh,** E Marcus III '06 %Bingham M LLP -399 Park Av -NY 10022
(212) 643-0044 .. **Marsh,** Eileen Melody '86 (Eisbrouch & M,PC) -950 3rd Av -NY 10022 **Fx:**(201) 342-3211
(212) 689-1600 .. **Marsh,** Gordon H '64 (Marsh V&D LLP) -500 5th Av -NY 10110 **Fx:**689-0210
(516) 741-1818 .. **Marsh,** James G '76 (O'Reilly M&C,PC) -222 Old Cntry Rd -Mineola 11501
(914) 686-4456 .. **Marsh,** James R '91 (Marsh M&W PLLC) -81 Main -White Plns 10601 **Fx:**206-3998
(518) 436-6000 .. **Marsh,** Kerry D '71 (Marsh Wassmermann & McHugh,LLC) -677 Bway -Albany 12207 **Fx:**436-6009
(212) 867-1955 .. **Marsh,** Kirke Wright '98 (KW Marsh,PC) -501 5th Av -NY 10017 **Fx:**504-8252
(315) 788-3400 .. **Marsh,** Leonard '57 Cnsl RL Renzi -1201 Wshngtn -Watertwn 13601 **Fx:**788-3466
(716) 636-7600 .. **Marsh,** Linda J '79 HoganWillig -2410 N Forest Rd -Amherst 14068
(212) 425-7200 .. **Marsh,** Michelle Mancino '97 (Kenyon & K,LLP) -1 Bway NY 10004
(516) 829-8140 .. **Marsh,** Patricia J '87 (Marsh & G,PC) -350 Nrthrn Blvd -Gt Neck 11021 **Fx:**829-7431
(518) 447-3401 .. **Marsh,** Peter L '94 Bank of Amer -Peter Kiernan Plz -Albany 12207 **Fx:**447-5182
(646) 862-7909 .. **Marsh,** Steven P '06 Marsh IP Law -9 W 20th -NY 10011
(315) 471-3151 .. **Marsh,** Wendy A '95 (Hancock & E,LLP) -1500 AXA Twr I Bx4976 -Syracuse 13221
(212) 788-1354 .. **Marshack,** Morton J '77 %Law Dept -100 Church -NY 10007 **Fx:**788-0367
(516) 829-8265 .. **Marshak,** Linda Faith '03 (Brady & M,LLP) -4523 Arcadia Ln -Gt Neck 11020 **Fx:**482-2688
(718) 254-0700 .. **Marshak,** Martin M '74 %Bklyn Defender Srvcs -177 Lvngstn -Brklyn 11201 **Fx:**254-0897
(845) 782-8355 .. **Marshak,** Morton '67 -1 Stage Rd -Monroe 10950 **Fx:**783-4985
(212) 557-4000 .. **Marshak,** Ned H '76 OfCnsl Grunfeld DLS&K LLP -399 Park Av -NY 10022
(516) 357-3700 .. **Marshall,** Adam M '10 %Cullen and D LLP -100 Q Roosevelt Blvd -Gdn Cty 11530
(212) 440-2481 .. **Marshall,** Amy '02 CNA -40 Wall -NY 10005
(914) 333-0825 .. **Marshall,** Anita Lubetsky '82 -660 Wht Plns Rd -Tarrytwn 10591 **Fx:**524-7070
(315) 423-7100 .. **Marshall,** Anthony P '83 (Harris B PLLC) -300 S State -Syracuse 13202
(516) 741-8005 .. **Marshall & Bellard** -1305 Franklin Av -Gdn Cty 11530 **Fx:**741-9213
(212) 265-1103 .. **Marshall,** Betty Keil '84 -55 West End Av -NY 10023 **Fx:**265-1103
(212) 259-8000 .. **Marshall,** Claudene A '09 %Dewey & L LLP -1301 Av of Amer -NY 10019
(212) 619-4444 .. **Marshall Conway Wright & Bradley,PC** -116 John -NY 10038 **Fx:**962-2647
(516) 997-6000 .. **Marshall,** Craig B '87 (Marshall & M) -30 Jericho Exec Plz -Jericho 11753 **Fx:**997-0860
(212) 558-5500 .. **Marshall,** Curt D '93 %Weitz & L,PC -700 Bway -NY 10003
(954) 356-0011 .. **Marshall,** Damien J '02 (Boies S&F LLP) -575 Lex Av -NY 10022 **Fx:**356-0022
(212) 571-3030 .. **Marshall,** Darrell Andrew '95 -225 Bway -NY 10007 **Fx:**571-1441
(518) 561-1055 .. **Marshall,** David J '76 -40 Clinton -Plattsbrgh 12901
(212) 309-1072 .. **Marshall,** David J '07 %Hunton & W -200 Park Av -NY 10166
(212) 308-4411 .. **Marshall,** David R '83 (Edwards AP&D LLP) -750 Lex Av -NY 10022

(845) 574-4169 .. **Marshall,** Deborah V '91 Rockland Comm Cllg -145 Cllg Rd -Suffern 10901
(914) 378-1010 .. **Marshall,** Delsia G '83 %Fitzgerald & F -538 Riverdale Av -Ynkrs 10705
(212) 878-1700 .. **Marshall Dennehey Warner Coleman & Goggin** -140 Bway -NY 10005 **Fx:**878-1701
(212) 376-6400 .. **Marshall Dennehey Warner Coleman & Goggin** -88 Pine -NY 10005 **Fx:**376-6494
(212) 888-3033 .. **Marshall,** Edw A '03 %Becker GM&M LLP -299 Park Av -NY 10171
(516) 997-6000 .. **Marshall,** Edw S '50 (Marshall & M) -30 Jericho Exec Plz -Jericho 11753 **Fx:**997-0860
(212) 837-6000 .. **Marshall,** Gabrielle S '06 %Hughes H&R LLP -1 Bttry Pk Plz -NY 10004
(718) 248-0023 .. **Marshall,** Gary S '82 Citibank NA -1 Court Sq -LIC 11101
(212) 971-3113 .. **Marshall,** Glenn R '75 G Marshall & Assoc -444 Mad Av -NY 10022 **Fx:**563-5287
(917) 453-9294 .. **Marshall,** Gordon '53 G Marshall,PC -521 5th Av -NY 10175
(718) 250-2000 .. **Marshall,** Gregory A '05 %DA -350 Jay -Brklyn 11201 **Fx:**250-2314
(212) 530-5000 .. **Marshall,** James W '10 %Milbank TH&M LLP -1 Chase Manh Plz -NY 10005
(516) 228-8530 .. **Marshall,** Jay A '77 -585 Stewart Av -Gdn Cty 11530 **Fx:**228-8534
(212) 619-4444 .. **Marshall,** Jeffrey A '77 (Marshall CW&B,PC) -116 John -NY 10038
(718) 522-3333 .. **Marshall,** Jennifer A '07 Children's Law Ctr -44 Court -Brklyn 11201 **Fx:**522-7376
(516) 561-3229 .. **Marshall,** John J Jr. '81 -Bx1023 -Rockvll Ctr 11571 **Fx:**908-4733
(212) 765-5070 .. **Marshall,** Jonathan A '64 SrCnsl Fish & R,PC -153 E 53rd -NY 10022
(212) 488-1200 .. **Marshall,** Katharine E '03 %Kobre & K,LLP -800 3rd Av -NY 10022
(516) 364-6006 .. **Marshall,** Keisha N '09 %Cohen & S,LLP -199 Crsswys Park Dr Bx9004 -Woodbury 11797
(212) 749-8972 .. **Marshall,** Kenneth R '75 -22 W 95th -NY 10025
(212) 790-9200 .. **Marshall,** Laurie B '97 %Cowan L&L,PC -1133 Av of Amer -NY 10036
(914) 428-1040 .. **Marshall,** Lorraine '81 -21 Cleveland -Valhalla 10595 **Fx:**949-4220
(212) 535-4440 .. **Marshall,** Marcia K '64 -140 E 81st -NY 10028 **Fx:**535-7171
(212) 572-3740 .. **Marshall,** Marilu '82 Estee Lauder -767 5th Av -NY 10153 **Fx:**571-6737
(631) 329-2520 .. **Marshall,** Nancy J '90 -10 Dorset Rd -E Hampton 11937
(845) 592-7000 .. **Marshall,** Natalie J '95 OfCnsl Donoghue TA&D LLP -2517 Route 52 -Hopewell Junct 12533
(212) 382-2044 .. **Marshall,** Paul G '52 (Marshall Firm) -271 Mad Av -NY 10016 **Fx:**382-3610
(716) 852-1300 .. **Marshall,** Philip M '73 OfCnsl Amigone S&M,LLP -350 Main -Buffalo 14202
(631) 421-4330 .. **Marshall,** Regina '90 -6 Casey -Huntngtn 11743 **Fx:**421-5336
(212) 596-9000 .. **Marshall,** Richd D '81 (Ropes & G LLP) -1211 Av of Amer -NY 10036
(212) 619-5000 .. **Marshall,** Richd E '74 %EDC -110 William -NY 10038 **Fx:**312-3912
(212) 909-9500 .. **Marshall,** Robt S Jr. '04 %Wachtel & M,LLP -885 2nd Av -NY 10017
(800) 877-1373 .. **Marshall,** Rohan M '91 Workers Comp Bd -215 W 125th -NY 10027
(212) 557-0002 .. **Marshall,** S Pitkin '70 -331 Mad Av -NY 10017
(585) 232-4090 .. **Marshall,** Sarah Ellen '03 %Leg Aid -1 W Main -Rchstr 14614 **Fx:**232-2352
(212) 981-4500 .. **Marshall,** Sarah G '00 PeterSan Grp -1450 Bway -NY 10018 **Fx:**981-4560
(212) 336-2000 .. **Marshall,** Sean R '09 %Patterson BW&T LLP -1133 Av of Amer -NY 10036
(845) 735-1700 .. **Marshall,** Sharon P '86 %Active Intl -1 Blue Hill Plz -Pearl Rvr 10965
(212) 259-8000 .. **Marshall,** Sheila H '64 OfCnsl Dewey & L LLP -1301 Av of Amer -NY 10019
(212) 768-6700 .. **Marshall,** Stephen A '68 (Sonnenschein N&R LLP) -1221 Av of Amer -NY 10020
(315) 423-7100 .. **Marshall,** Steven A '10 %Harris B PLLC -300 S State -Syracuse 13202
(212) 259-8000 .. **Marshall,** Susan Ann '89 (Dewey & L LLP) -1301 Av of Amer -NY 10019
(646) 216-2400 .. **Marshall,** Thos R '87 OfCnsl Kranjac M&V LLP -40 Wall -NY 10005 **Fx:**216-2373
(212) 705-7000 .. **Marshall,** Torsten M '92 (Bingham M LLP) -399 Park Av -NY 10022
(212) 223-0400 .. **Marshall,** Wm T Jr. '72 (Zeichner E&K LLP) -575 Lex Av -NY 10022
(718) 969-9200 .. **Marshburn,** Carlyet D '81 (C Marshburn,PC) -160-29 Union Tpk -Fresh Mdws 11366 **Fx:**969-0707
(212) 801-9362 .. **Marsico,** Anthony J '95 (Greenberg T,LLP) -200 Park Av -NY 10166
(914) 921-6480 .. **Marsico,** James '94 -350 Theo Fremd Av -Rye 10580 **Fx:**921-0186
(212) 431-2180 .. **Marsico,** Richd D '86 %NY Law Schl -185 W Bway -NY 10013 **Fx:**966-2053
(516) 378-1700 .. **Marsigliano,** John L '79 (Chesney & M) -2305 Grand Av -Baldwin 11510
(914) 749-8200 .. **Marsillo,** Wm D '98 (Boies S&F LLP) -333 Main -Armonk 10504
(914) 946-4666 .. **Marson,** Jay D '93 %Ctr For Behavior Therapy -222 Wstchstr Av -White Plns 10604
(212) 841-1000 .. **Marson,** Jonas A '02 %Covington & B LLP -620 8th Av -NY 10018
(212) 201-9218 .. **Marston,** Sara E '05 EMusic.com,Inc -535 5th Av -NY 10017
(716) 856-5500 .. **Marszalkowski,** Michl E '84 SpclCnsl Damon M LLP -200 Delaware Av -Buffalo 14202
(914) 241-0022 .. **Martabano,** Christina M '89 -269 N Bedford Rd -Mt Kisco 10549 **Fx:**241-0187
Martarella, Jos M '01 %Transit Auth -2 Bway -NY 10004 **Fx:**(646) 252-5559
(845) 565-4646 .. **Marte-Indzonka,** Michele M '89 -46 S Plnk Rd -Newburgh 12550
(518) 640-5522 .. **Martel,** James E '97 AYCO -25 British Amer Blvd -Latham 12110
(212) 640-5759 .. **Martel,** Jeffrey A '83 %Amer Exp -200 Vesey -NY 10285
(212) 944-0600 .. **Martel,** Sarah E '08 %Hafif & Assoc,PLLC -275 Mad Av -NY 10016 **Fx:**944-7747
(212) 872-1000 .. **Martell,** Alana S '04 -One Bryant Park -NY 10036 **Fx:**872-1002
(212) 317-2672 .. **Martell,** Alice E '77 (Martell Agncy) -1350 Av of Amer -NY 10019
(718) 546-0950 .. **Martell,** Angie I '90 %Dept of Correction -75-20 Astoria Blvd -E Elmhrst 11370
(518) 465-2333 .. **Martell,** Christopher M '05 %Hodgson R LLP -677 Bway -Albany 12207
(631) 694-0033 .. **Martell,** James '88 (Lawrence WR&B,PC) -425 Broadhllw Rd -Melvll 11747
(518) 581-8800 .. **Martell,** Karen S '87 (Lemery G LLC) -60 Railroad Pl -Saratoga Spgs 12866
(914) 592-6044 .. **Martell,** Keith J '06 %W Martell -33 W Main -Elmsfrd 10523 **Fx:**592-4091
(212) 735-8600 .. **Martell,** Michl L '74 (Morrison C LLP) -909 3rd Av -NY 10022
(516) 572-2000 .. **Martell,** Richd R '08 %DA -99 Main -Hempstd 11550 **Fx:**572-2606
(914) 592-6044 .. **Martell,** Wayne R '72 -33 W Main -Elmsfrd 10523 **Fx:**592-4091
(212) 455-2000 .. **Martelli,** Peter '02 (Simpson T&B LLP) -425 Lex Av -NY 10017
(516) 228-3333 .. **Martello,** Greg P '89 (Martello & L,PC) -666 Old Cntry Rd -Gdn Cty 11530
(718) 585-6551 .. **Martello,** John M '04 %Pena & K,PLLC -1200 Waters Pl -Bronx 10461 **Fx:**585-6618
(516) 228-3333 .. **Martello & LaMagna, PC** -666 Old Cntry Rd -Gdn Cty 11530 **Fx:**228-3339
(212) 715-1000 .. **Martemucci,** Marco J '09 %Arnold & P LLP -399 Park Av -NY 10022
(212) 617-1878 .. **Marten,** Catherine '99 Bloomberg LP -731 Lex Av -NY 10022
(516) 747-5800 .. **Marten,** Kenneth L '79 -200 Old Cntry Rd -Mineola 11501 **Fx:**739-5800
(212) 909-6000 .. **Martens,** Carol B '09 %Debevoise & P LLP -919 3rd Av -NY 10022
(518) 486-2921 .. **Martens,** Kathleen L '85 %OPRHP -Agncy Bldg 1 ESP -Albany 12238 **Fx:**474-5106
(914) 242-7020 .. **Martensson,** Barbara '00 -10 Deveau Rd -N Salem 10560 **Fx:**242-7485
(718) 220-4892 .. **Marth,** John D '03 %POTS -2763 Webster Av -Bronx 10458
(315) 798-5870 .. **Marthage,** Patrick J '87 %Pub Def -321 Main -Utica 13501 **Fx:**798-6419
(212) 584-9258 .. **Marthaller,** Ellise M '02 -1700 Bway -NY 10019
(518) 869-5552 .. **Marthy,** Paul C '92 %Breakell PC -10 Airline Dr -Albany 12205 **Fx:**869-4222
(212) 878-9493 .. **Marti,** Harsha G '03 Cnsl Warburg Pincus LLC -450 Lex Av -NY 10017 **Fx:**878-9351
(917) 778-6500 .. **Marti,** Jerry '99 %K Dodson -485 Lex Av -NY 10017
(718) 875-1300 .. **Marti,** Maria Esperanza '94 %Appllt Div 2nd Dept -45 Monroe Pl -Brklyn 11201 **Fx:**858-2446
(212) 295-6359 .. **Marti,** Meera Malhotra '07 %WilmerHale -399 Park Av -NY 10022
(516) 522-2585 .. **Martial,** Marie A '03 -626 RXR Plz -Uniondale 11556
(212) 310-8000 .. **Martialay,** Elizabeth A '96 %Weil G&M LLP -767 5th Av -NY 10153
(631) 728-2654 .. **Martielli,** Marina M '98 -15 Woodfld Av -E Quogue 11942 **Fx:**728-2257
(212) 567-5680 .. **Martignetti,** Anthony '93 -90 Park Ter E -NY 10034
(516) 484-8211 .. **Martin,** Alan Jay '62 -415 Chestnut Dr -Roslyn 11576 **Fx:**484-1084
(212) 248-3140 .. **Martin,** Alvin C '58 OfCnsl Drinker B&R LLP -140 Bway -NY 10005
(212) 756-2000 .. **Martin,** Andrea '04 %Schulte R&Z LLP -919 3rd Av -NY 10022
(516) 571-2042 .. **Martin,** Andrew L '86 %Surrogate's Ct -262 Old Cntry Rd -Mineola 11501 **Fx:**571-3864
(518) 279-1217 .. **Martin,** Andrew M '98 OfCnsl Bruno Law Ofc PLLC -3991 NY Rte 2 Bx159 -Cropseyville 12052 **Fx:**279-9434
(212) 530-1800 .. **Martin,** Andrew M '99 %Richards K&O LLP -1 World Fncl Ctr -NY 10281
(631) 874-7337 .. **Martin,** Anna '96 -250 Montauk Hwy -E Moriches 11940 **Fx:**878-5685
(718) 875-1300 .. **Martin,** Anna M '93 Appllt Div 2nd Dept -45 Monroe Pl -Brklyn 11201 **Fx:**858-2446
(212) 355-9500 .. **Martin,** Annika K '05 %Lieff CH&B,LLP -250 Hudson -NY 10013
(212) 458-1559 .. **Martin,** Atea '91 AIGTS -175 Water -NY 10038
(212) 541-2000 .. **Martin,** Benson V '01 %Bryan C LLP -1290 Av of Amer -NY 10104
(212) 312-2272 .. **Martin,** Brad '85 %Leg Aid -60 Lafayette -NY 10013 **Fx:**349-0874
(631) 427-9500 .. **Martin,** Bradford J '94 (LoTurco & M) -434 NY Av -Huntngtn 11743 **Fx:**427-9501
(631) 844-9555 .. **Martin,** Brian M '06 %Dodge & M,PC -175 Pinelawn Rd -Melvll 11747 **Fx:**844-9666
(212) 906-1200 .. **Martin,** Catherine M '08 %Latham & W -885 3rd Av -NY 10022
(516) 241-5658 .. **Martin,** Chas A '02 -343 Marylnd Av -Massapequa Pk 11762
(718) 983-8000 .. **Martin,** Christine R '85 %Marrazzo & D -1265 Richmond Av -Staten Isl 10314
(212) 803-5100 .. **Martin,** Christopher H '83 %NY Cnty Defender Srvcs -225 Bway -NY 10007 **Fx:**571-6035
(212) 627-2020 .. **Martin,** Christopher W '94 %Hudson Rvr Pk Trust -353 West St at W Houston -NY 10014 **Fx:**627-2021
(718) 250-0400 .. **Martin,** Claire '91 %R Tusa -1 MetroTech Ctr -Brklyn 11201 **Fx:**250-0591
(212) 697-3122 .. **Martin Clearwater & Bell LLP** -220 E 42nd -NY 10017 **Fx:**949-7054
(516) 222-8500 .. **Martin Clearwater & Bell LLP** -90 Merrick Av -E Meadow 11554 **Fx:**222-8513
(914) 328-2969 .. **Martin Clearwater & Bell LLP** -245 Main -White Plns 10601 **Fx:**328-4056
(212) 407-4000 .. **Martin,** Corey N '00 (Loeb & L,LLP) -345 Park Av -NY 10154
(212) 907-0700 .. **Martin,** Craig A '05 %Labaton S LLP -140 Bway -NY 10005
(516) 775-2236 .. **Martin,** Danl '99 %Santangelo B&S -1800 Nrthrn Blvd -Roslyn 11576
(212) 756-2000 .. **Martin,** Danl '06 %Schulte R&Z LLP -919 3rd Av -NY 10022
(646) 471-0263 .. **Martin,** David '00 PricewaterhouseCoopers LLP -300 Mad Av -NY 10017
(212) 762-5259 .. **Martin,** David A '99 Morgan Stanley -1221 6th Av -NY 10020
(914) 683-1800 .. **Martin,** David H '02 -140 Grand -White Plns 10601 **Fx:**683-8231
(516) 294-8886 .. **Martin,** David L '87 (D Martin,PC) -1539 Franklin Av -Mineola 11501 **Fx:**294-8668
(718) 590-3777 .. **Martin,** David M '76 %Hon L Wilkins -851 Grnd Cncrs -Bronx 10451
(315) 423-7100 .. **Martin,** David P '79 (Harris B PLLC) -300 S State -Syracuse 13202
(845) 486-2280 .. **Martin,** David S '88 %Pub Def -22 Market -Poughkeepsie 12601 **Fx:**486-2266
(212) 870-4592 .. **Martin,** David W '95 %Metropolitan Opera -Lincoln Ctr -NY 10023 **Fx:**870-7681
(212) 849-7000 .. **Martin,** Deborah L '07 Quinn EU&S,LLP -51 Mad Av -NY 10010

(585) 546-7430 .. **Martin,** Debra A '81 Dept of Law -144 Exchange Blvd -Rchstr 14614 **Fx:**546-7514
(315) 423-7100 .. **Martin,** Donald J '68 (Harris B PLLC) -300 S State -Syracuse 13202
(212) 961-8327 .. **Martin,** Donald T '71 NYS Liquor Auth -317 Lenox Av -NY 10027 **Fx:**961-8316
(212) 307-5500 .. **Martin,** Doreen S '02 %Venable LLP -1270 Av of Amer -NY 10020
(516) 393-2200 .. **Martin,** Doris L '88 (Garfunkel W,PC) -111 Grt Nck Rd -Gt Neck 11021
(212) 286-0038 .. **Martin,** Edw H '64 -279 E 44th -NY 10017
(716) 434-2010 .. **Martin,** Edw J '96 %J Wilson -111 Ontario -Lockprt 14094 **Fx:**433-0502
(212) 431-7200 .. **Martin,** Edwina F '94 %Legal Srvcs NYC -350 Bway -NY 10013 **Fx:**966-9571
(716) 856-4000 .. **Martin,** Eileen M '93 (Hodgson R LLP) -140 Pearl -Buffalo 14202
(212) 336-2000 .. **Martin,** Ellen M '78 (Patterson BW&T LLP) -1133 Av of Amer -NY 10036
(718) 855-0400 .. **Martin,** Elliot S '81 -16 Court -Brklyn 11241
(212) 549-2500 .. **Martin,** Emily J '00 %ACLU -125 Broad -NY 10004 **Fx:**549-2651
(516) 328-2300 .. **Martin,** Eugene J '06 %Abrams FFEGF&E,LLP -1111 Marcus Av -Lk Success 11042
(631) 421-1211 .. **Martin Fallon & Mullé** -100 E Carver -Huntngtn 11743 **Fx:**421-5439
(914) 949-2700 .. **Martin,** Fredk J '57 (Bleakley P&S,LLP) -1 N Lex Av -White Plns 10601
(315) 449-2616 .. **Martin Ganotis Brown Mould & Currie,PC** -5790 Widewaters Pkwy -DeWitt 13214 **Fx:**449-4315
(716) 635-3730 .. **Martin,** Gina Marie '95 %Independent Hlth -511 Farber Lks Dr -Buffalo 14221 **Fx:**635-3838
(718) 979-7114 .. **Martin,** Graig C '01 -274 Watchogue Rd -Staten Isl 10304 **Fx:**979-6657
(518) 862-1200 .. **Martin Harding & Mazzotti LLP** -Bx15141 -Albany 12212 **Fx:**862-0180
(845) 485-6800 .. **Martin,** Jacqueline T '82 (JT Martin,PLLC) -2 Cannon -Poughkeepsie 12601 **Fx:**485-6835
(845) 331-5200 .. **Martin,** Jacqueline T '82 (JT Martin,PLLC) -159 Green -Kingston 12401 **Fx:**331-5329
(212) 704-6000 .. **Martin,** James G '97 OfCnsl Troutman S LLP -405 Lex Av -NY 10174
(718) 809-7093 .. **Martin,** James V '00 -372 Dekalb Av -Brklyn 11205
(518) 626-9000 .. **Martin,** Jay B '78 (Dewey & L LLP) -99 Wshngtn Av -Albany 12210
(914) 766-4620 .. **Martin,** Jaye B '80 IBM Corp -Route 100 -Somers 10589 **Fx:**766-4851
(845) 876-4047 .. **Martin,** Jeffrey C '86 -187 E Market Bx649 -Rhinebeck 12572 **Fx:**876-3906
(212) 784-8872 .. **Martin,** Jeffrey I '98 Rho Capital Prtnrs -152 W 57th -NY 10019
(585) 638-6331 .. **Martin,** Jeffrey R '82 (Heath & M) -66 Vllg Sq Bx200 -Holley 14470 **Fx:**638-7221
(516) 227-2300 .. **Martin,** Jennifer A '04 %Wright Risk Mgmt -333 Earle Ovngton Blvd -Uniondale 11553 **Fx:**227-2352
(212) 398-6565 .. **Martin,** Jennifer K '02 %Cncl of Senior Ctrs -49 W 45th -NY 10036 **Fx:**398-8398
(212) 981-6540 .. **Martin,** Jennifer R '04 %Stroz Friedberg LLC -32 Av of Amer -NY 10013 **Fx:**981-6545
(212) 373-8673 .. **Martin,** Jessica Nagle '00 Friedman KS&A LLP -1633 Bway -NY 10019 **Fx:**833-1250
(631) 329-3563 .. **Martin,** Joan K '88 -16 Bay View Av -E Hampton 11937
(212) 335-9000 .. **Martin,** John B '09 %DA -1 Hogan Pl -NY 10013
(212) 733-6872 .. **Martin,** John C '00 %Pfizer Inc -150 E 42nd -NY 10017
(212) 340-0400 .. **Martin,** John F '88 %Appllt Div 1st Dept -27 Mad Av -NY 10010 **Fx:**889-4412
(516) 393-2200 .. **Martin,** John G '85 %Garfunkel W,PC -111 Grt Nck Rd -Gt Neck 11021
(914) 686-5600 .. **Martin,** John M Jr. '86 %All NY Title Agency -180 E Post Rd -White Plns 10601 **Fx:**686-1440
(212) 883-0000 .. **Martin,** John S Jr. '61 (Martin & O) -565 5th Av -NY 10017
(212) 450-4000 .. **Martin,** Jonathan D '04 %Davis P&W LLP -450 Lex Av -NY 10017
(212) 483-9490 .. **Martin,** Jonathan D '09 %McElroy DM&C,LLP -88 Pine -NY 10005
(914) 328-0404 .. **Martin,** Jos M '92 (Jackson L LLP) -1 N Bway -White Plns 10601
(212) 998-1302 .. **Martin,** Jules A '85 NYU -7 Wshngtn Pl -NY 10003
(212) 596-9000 .. **Martin,** Julie S '09 %Ropes & G LLP -1211 Av of Amer -NY 10036
(315) 446-7093 .. **Martin,** K Kelly '84 -5013 Woodside Rd -Fayettevll 13066
(315) 422-2052 .. **Martin,** Karen Karhar '02 R Dague,PLLC -472 S Salina -Syracuse 13202 **Fx:**474-4334
(716) 852-1234 .. **Martin,** Kathleen J '00 %F Letro -110 Pearl -Buffalo 14202 **Fx:**853-2930
(212) 309-6000 .. **Martin,** Kathleen M '99 %Morgan L&B LLP -101 Park Av -NY 10178
(914) 993-1963 .. **Martin,** Kathryn M '04 US Atty -300 Quarropas -White Plns 10601 **Fx:**993-9036
(518) 457-2411 .. **Martin,** Keith D '85 %DOT -50 Wolf Rd -Albany 12232 **Fx:**457-4021
(631) 329-9017 .. **Martin,** Kenneth '81 -31 Oak Hill Ln Ext -E Hampton 11937
(607) 687-2121 .. **Martin,** Kirk O '97 Century 21 -444 Front -Owego 13827
(315) 734-2917 .. **Martin,** Kristen Holly '95 Utica Natl Ins Grp -Bx530 -Utica 13503
(212) 610-6300 .. **Martin,** Laura A '01 %Allen & O -1221 Av of Amer -NY 10020
(212) 231-1582 .. **Martin,** Laura G '03 MacQuarie Capital Invstmnt Mgmt LLC -125 W 55th -NY 10019
(212) 876-7700 .. **Martin,** Lauren M '09 %ASPCA -424 E 92nd -NY 10128 **Fx:**860-3560
(212) 788-1009 .. **Martin,** Lawr M '82 %Law Dept -100 Church -NY 10007 **Fx:**788-0367
(516) 222-0900 .. **Martin,** Leslie '70 -595 Stewart Av -Gdn Cty 11530 **Fx:**222-2971
(718) 409-8215 .. **Martin,** Linda '05 %Morningside Hse -1000 Pelham Pkwy S -Bronx 10461
(212) 455-2000 .. **Martin,** Linda H '97 (Simpson T&B LLP) -425 Lex Av -NY 10017
(716) 856-4000 .. **Martin,** Lizabeth A '92 (Hodgson R LLP) -140 Pearl -Buffalo 14202
(212) 295-6412 .. **Martin,** Lori A '92 (WilmerHale) -399 Park Av -NY 10022
(585) 232-5756 .. **Martin,** M Kathleen '83 Comm Judicial Cndct -400 Andrews -Rchstr 14604 **Fx:**232-7834
(914) 276-3223 .. **Martin,** M Linda '87 -352 Route 202 -Somers 10589 **Fx:**276-2429
(212) 408-5100 .. **Martin,** Malcolm E '63 OfCnsl Chadbourne & P LLP -30 Rckfllr Plz -NY 10112
(212) 577-3500 .. **Martin,** Margaret West '93 %Leg Aid -199 Water -NY 10038 **Fx:**809-1370
(212) 426-4970 .. **Martin,** Marjorie A '80 Traffic Violation Bur -159 E 125th -NY 10035
(212) 526-7697 .. **Martin,** Mary Shannon '03 Barclays Capital Inc -745 7th Av -NY 10019
(718) 442-4424 .. **Martin,** Marylou V '88 (Corash & H,PC) -1200 South Av -Staten Isl 10314
(212) 782-9881 .. **Martin,** Matthew E '88 Random House -1540 Bway -NY 10036
(212) 867-8280 .. **Martin,** Matthew J '99 (Patton ELM&S) -420 Lex Av -NY 10170
(212) 770-1760 .. **Martin,** Maureen P '93 %AIG -80 Pine -NY 10005 **Fx:**344-2286
(212) 332-8300 .. **Martin,** Megan L '02 %Dunnegan LLC -350 5th Av -NY 10118 **Fx:**332-8301
(212) 310-6915 .. **Martin,** Michl E '83 Brklyn NY Holdings,LLC -717 5th Av -NY 10022
(212) 636-6000 .. **Martin,** Michl M '66 %Fordham Univ Sch of Law -140 W 62nd -NY 10023 **Fx:**636-6899
(518) 745-0511 .. **Martin,** Michl S '93 -511 Glen -Glens Fls 12801 **Fx:**745-0514
(212) 636-7781 .. **Martin,** Michl W '93 %Fordham Univ Sch of Law -140 W 62nd -NY 10023 **Fx:**636-6899
(212) 455-2000 .. **Martin,** Natalia '88 %Simpson T&B LLP -425 Lex Av -NY 10017
(646) 831-6391 .. **Martin,** Nicholas B '03 %AIG -555 Taxter Rd -Elmsfrd 10523
(212) 640-2000 .. **Martin,** Nicolette A '98 %Amer Exp -200 Vesey -NY 10285
(716) 856-9090 .. **Martin,** Patrick E '86 (Kennedy S&M) -1100 Lbrty Bldg -Buffalo 14202
(315) 458-5220 .. **Martin,** Patrick E '88 (Hall M&L,PLLC) -111 Church Bx278 -N Syracuse 13212
(315) 635-3222 .. **Martin,** Paul N '81 (Farrell M&B) -44 Oswego Bx199 -Baldwinsvll 13027
(212) 809-0000 .. **Martin,** Paul P '90 (Preston WM&E,PLLC) -65 Bway -NY 10006 **Fx:**809-4753
(212) 801-6906 .. **Martin,** Paul T II '10 %Greenberg T,LLP -200 Park Av -NY 10166
(516) 431-1000 .. **Martin,** Peter A '97 City Ct -1 W Chester -Long Bch 11561
(718) 979-7114 .. **Martin,** Peter F '01 (Martin & L) -274 Watchogue Rd -Staten Isl 10304 **Fx:**979-6657
(716) 856-1344 .. **Martin,** Peter J '64 (Bouvier Prtnrshp,LLP) -350 Main -Buffalo 14202 **Fx:**856-1369
(212) 286-8585 .. **Martin,** Rachelle Barjon '05 %Heidell PM&B,LLP -99 Park Av -NY 10016
(212) 848-4000 .. **Martin,** Randy L '04 %Shearman & S LLP -599 Lex Av -NY 10022
(212) 637-2714 .. **Martin,** Rebecca C '94 %US Atty -86 Chmbrs -NY 10007
(212) 839-5300 .. **Martin,** Renwick D '74 (Sidley A LLP) -787 7th Av -NY 10019
(212) 506-5000 .. **Martin,** Richd A '75 (Orrick H&S LLP) -51 W 52nd -NY 10019
(516) 378-5700 .. **Martin,** Richd B '72 (Martin & M) -148 Lng Bch Av -Freeprt 11520 **Fx:**623-5281
(212) 815-1818 .. **Martin,** Robt A '81 %DC 37 MELS -125 Barclay -NY 10007 **Fx:**815-1343
(516) 742-3470 .. **Martin,** Robt D '91 (Kral CRRP&G,LLP) -538 Broadhllw Rd -Melvll 11747
(212) 686-4401 .. **Martin,** Robt F '60 %Abramson Law Grp PLLC -570 Lex Av -NY 10022 **Fx:**686-6515
(212) 415-9200 .. **Martin,** Robt F '97 OfCnsl Dorsey & W LLP -250 Park Av -NY 10177
(212) 416-8000 .. **Martin,** Roberta L '94 %Dept of Law -120 Bway -NY 10271
(212) 661-3535 .. **Martin,** Roy I '72 (Hodgson R LLP) -60 E 42nd -NY 10165
(518) 725-0676 .. **Martin,** Russell P '85 -11 Church -Gloversvll 12078 **Fx:**725-4002
(212) 468-8000 .. **Martin,** Samantha L '08 %Morrison & F LLP -1290 Av of Amer -NY 10104
(212) 783-3731 .. **Martin,** Saml L '97 Citi Smith Barney -485 Lex Av -NY 10017
(212) 801-2231 .. **Martin,** Scott A '91 (Greenberg T,LLP) -200 Park Av -NY 10166
(518) 474-0871 .. **Martin,** Sean J '85 DMV -6 ESP -Albany 12228 **Fx:**486-4485
(716) 849-8900 .. **Martin,** Shawn P '94 (Hurwitz & F,PC) -1300 Lbrty Bldg -Buffalo 14202
(518) 272-6565 .. **Martin Shudt Wallace DiLorenzo & Johnson** -279 River Bx1530 -Troy 12181 **Fx:**272-5587
(631) 421-1211 .. **Martin,** Stanley G '68 (Martin F&M) -100 E Carver -Huntngtn 11743
(212) 486-0581 .. **Martin,** Steven D '94 -4541 39th Pl -Sunnyside 11104
(212) 321-8119 .. **Martin,** Steven M '82 Verizon Communications -140 West -NY 10007
(212) 269-7308 .. **Martin,** Steven M '92 (Leahey & J PC) -120 Wall -NY 10005
(631) 421-1211 .. **Martin,** Susan Lorde '88 %Martin F&M -100 E Carver -Huntngtn 11743
(212) 354-0600 .. **Martin,** Tara J '98 (Stark A&L,LLP) -7 Penn Plz -NY 10001
(212) 701-0460 .. **Martin,** Tara K '06 Travelex Srvcs Inc -29 Bway -NY 10006
(646) 216-2145 .. **Martin,** Teresa R '01 T Martin,PC -260 Mad Av -NY 10016
(212) 682-0020 .. **Martin,** Thos A '73 (Putney TH&H LLP) -521 5th Av -NY 10175
(212) 878-6630 .. **Martin,** Thos A '93 -275 Mad Av -NY 10016
(914) 993-4567 .. **Martin,** Thos J '70 %NY Medical Cllg -Sunshine Cottage -Valhalla 10595 **Fx:**993-4328
(212) 224-1562 .. **Martin,** Thos L '05 Mutual of America -320 Park Av -NY 10022 **Fx:**224-2518
(212) 572-8600 .. **Martin,** Timothy S '02 MacAndrews & Forbes -35 E 62nd -NY 10065
(212) 813-5900 .. **Martin,** Todd E '01 %Fross ZL&Z,PC -866 UN Plz -NY 10017
(518) 745-0511 .. **Martin,** Trinidad Martinez '91 -511 Glen -Glens Fls 12801 **Fx:**745-0514
(585) 530-3050 .. **Martin,** Walter F '77 %MHLS -50 East Av -Rchstr 14604 **Fx:**530-3079
(212) 788-4285 .. **Martin,** Wm G '80 %Dept Hlth & Mental Hygiene -125 Worth Bx 30B -NY 10013 **Fx:**788-4296
(914) 328-8028 .. **Martin,** Wm G '89 (Martin & C,PC) -44 Church -White Plns 10601 **Fx:**206-3619
(212) 403-1000 .. **Martin,** Wm J '06 %Wachtell LR&K -51 W 52nd -NY 10019
(347) 843-8655 .. **Martin,** Wm T '77 (W Martin & Assoc) -945 E 226th -Bronx 10466
(212) 701-3000 .. **Martin,** Zachary J '10 %Cahill G&R LLP -80 Pine -NY 10005 **Fx:**269-5420
(914) 737-2554 .. **Martin-Crowley,** Rita '87 %Engelhard Corp -1057 Lwr South -Peekskill 10566
(518) 402-0205 .. **Martindale,** Christine Patka '92 %UIA Bd -Troy Atrium Bx15126 -Albany 12212 **Fx:**402-6208
(212) 577-3449 .. **Martindale,** Conway C II '05 %Leg Aid -199 Water -NY 10038
(518) 746-2216 .. **Martindale,** Danl S '97 %Cnty Atty -383 Bway -Ft Edward 12828 **Fx:**746-2137
(212) 747-1230 .. **Martine,** Anthony D '95 (McMahon M&G LLP) -55 Washington -Brklyn 11201

(212) 747-1230 .. **Martine,** Louis J '58 (McMahon M&G LLP) -55 Washington -Brklyn 11201
(914) 285-9797 .. **Martineau,** Ellen Werfel '82 %Kitson LLP -50 Main -White Plns 10606
(914) 769-1726 .. **Martineau,** Jacqueline A '96 (Martineau & M) -444 Bedford Rd -Plsntvll 10570 **Fx:**769-1442
(518) 647-8877 .. **Martineau,** James E Jr. '99 -15 Schl Ln Bx187 -Au Sable Frks 12912 **Fx:**647-8316
(914) 769-1726 .. **Martineau,** Paul A '61 (Martineau & M) -444 Bedford Rd -Plsntvll 10570 **Fx:**769-1442
(518) 383-5192 .. **Martineau,** Paul W Jr. '89 -Bx1511 -Clifton Pk 12065
(212) 326-3939 .. **Martinek,** Sebastian '07 %Jones D -222 E 41st -NY 10017
(914) 345-0601 .. **Martinelli,** Michl A Jr. '09 Westchester Magazine -100 Clearbrook Rd -Elmsfrd 10523
(518) 474-7700 .. **Martinelli,** Patricia '80 %NYS OPWDD -44 Holland Av -Albany 12229 **Fx:**474-7382
(212) 506-5000 .. **Martinelli,** Richd F '01 %Orrick H&S LLP -51 W 52nd -NY 10019
(718) 667-0500 .. **Martinelli,** Vincent J '93 -2040 Victory Blvd -Staten Isl 10314 **Fx:**667-5526
(212) 309-6000 .. **Martinez,** Adriana M '05 %Morgan L&B LLP -101 Park Av -NY 10178
(914) 271-0165 .. **Martinez,** Antonia J '83 A Martinez,LLC -Bx883 -Croton-On-Hud 10520 **Fx:**470-1074
(212) 989-0404 .. **Martinez,** Antonia J '83 OfCnsl P Polastri,PC -63-56 Saunders Bx740155 -Rego Pk 11374 **Fx:**633-0190
(973) 454-0028 .. **Martinez,** Antonio C II '96 -7 Howe -Warwick 10990 **Fx:**(202) 318-2361
(212) 989-0404 .. **Martinez,** Antonio C II '96 OfCnsl P Polastri,PC -63-56 Saunders Bx740155 -Rego Pk 11374 **Fx:**633-0190
(212) 969-3000 .. **Martinez,** Carlos E '88 (Proskauer R LLP) -1585 Bway -NY 10036
(718) 590-2000 .. **Martinez,** Carmen E '99 %DA -198 E 161st -Bronx 10451 **Fx:**590-6477
(212) 661-7121 .. **Martinez,** Cristina Baiata '96 %Hon C Ciparick -122 E 42nd -NY 10168
(212) 973-0572 .. **Martinez,** Cristina L '09 %Wolff & S PC -140 Bway -NY 10005
(917) 417-3448 .. **Martinez,** Dario A '99 (Martinez & Assoc) -589 Amstrdm Av -NY 10024
(212) 891-9600 .. **Martinez,** David A '09 %Stanfield Cptl Ptnrs -430 Park Av -NY 10022
(212) 225-2000 .. **Martinez,** David F '10 %Cleary GS&H -1 Lbrty Plz -NY 10006
(212) 683-1153 .. **Martinez,** Diana '89 -347 5th Av -NY 10016
(718) 681-9333 .. **Martinez,** Elias Jr. '64 -903F Sheridan Av -Bronx 10451
(718) 218-0242 .. **Martinez,** Emily M '98 Family Ct -151-20 Jamaica Av -Jamaica 11432
(631) 583-3000 .. **Martinez,** Eric S '96 -10 Erland Rd -Stony Brk 11790
(212) 460-6671 .. **Martinez,** Eva L '97 Con Ed -4 Irving Pl -NY 10003
(212) 790-4500 .. **Martinez,** Gabriel T '09 %Manatt P&P,LLP -7 Times Sq -NY 10036
(585) 454-0700 .. **Martinez,** Heidi S '91 Cnsl Ward GH&R LLP -300 State -Rchstr 14614
(212) 805-0177 .. **Martinez,** I Alexei '92 %USDC -500 Pearl -NY 10007
(718) 722-3100 .. **Martinez,** Jocelyne G '90 %Leg Aid -111 Lvngstn -Brklyn 11201 **Fx:**722-3093
(212) 428-2961 .. **Martinez,** Jorge '94 %OCA -25 Beaver -NY 10004 **Fx:**428-2974
(212) 566-4500 .. **Martinez,** Jose Jr. '95 -325 E 41st -NY 10017 **Fx:**566-4542
(646) 315-7300 .. **Martinez,** Josefina '87 %FINRA -14 Wall -NY 10005 **Fx:**315-7440
(518) 436-6000 .. **Martinez,** Juan A '08 Marsh Wassmermann & McHugh,LLC -677 Bway -Albany 12207 **Fx:**436-6009
(212) 882-6983 .. **Martinez,** Judith D '00 UBS Wealth Mgmt -51 W 52nd -NY 10019
(917) 637-3600 .. **Martinez,** Katherine Hall '93 %Ctr for Reproductive Rts -120 Wall -NY 10005 **Fx:**637-3666
(212) 788-3153 .. **Martinez,** Larry R '08 %Law Dept -100 Church -NY 10007 **Fx:**700-0367
(212) 248-0800 .. **Martinez,** Louis R '85 (Martinez & R,PC) -67 Wall -NY 10005
(212) 277-4000 .. **Martinez,** Lucy E '04 %Freshfields BD LLP -520 Mad Av -NY 10022
(212) 716-5800 .. **Martinez,** Luis M '98 %Amer Arbtrtn Assn -1633 Bway -NY 10019
(212) 841-1000 .. **Martinez,** M Beatriz '07 %Covington & B LLP -620 8th Av -NY 10018
(718) 579-7953 .. **Martinez,** Mariella '06 %Leg Aid -900 Sheridan Av -Bronx 10451 **Fx:**293-8744
(631) 796-2745 .. **Martinez,** Matthew J '02 -Bx185 -Deer Pk 11729
(212) 964-8038 .. **Martinez,** Michl A '97 %Worth L&L,LLP -111 John -NY 10038
(212) 506-5000 .. **Martinez,** Michelle M '04 %Orrick H&S LLP -51 W 52nd -NY 10019
(212) 765-5070 .. **Martinez,** Miriam London '04 Cnsl Fish & R,PC -153 E 53rd -NY 10022
(917) 534-4780 .. **Martinez,** Mirna E '96 Zurich Ins -105 E 17th -NY 10003
(212) 229-6227 .. **Martinez,** Paul H '84 Turner Construction Co -375 Hudson -NY 10014 **Fx:**229-6247
(718) 487-1300 .. **Martinez,** Rafael '78 %Leg Srvcs Corp A -80 Jamaica Av -Brklyn 11207 **Fx:**342-1780
(718) 255-5800 .. **Martinez,** Ramon A Jr. '03 (Martinez Law Grp,PC) -10603 Corona Av -Corona 11368
(585) 325-5150 .. **Martinez,** Raul E '91 %Faraci L,LLP -28 E Main -Rchstr 14614
(516) 222-7700 .. **Martinez,** Raymond P '94 %LI Power Auth -333 Earle Ovngton Blvd -Uniondale 11553 **Fx:**222-9137
(212) 243-1313 .. **Martinez,** Renee D '04 Leg Action Ctr -225 Varick -NY 10014 **Fx:**675-0286
(212) 610-6300 .. **Martinez,** Ricardo S '99 SrCnsl Allen & O -1221 Av of Amer -NY 10020
(212) 248-0800 .. **Martinez & Ritorto,PC** -67 Wall -NY 10005 **Fx:**248-0990
(914) 358-4844 .. **Martinez,** Robt E '98 R Martinez,PLLC -81 Main -White Plns 10601
(212) 317-6000 .. **Martinez,** Rodrigo '05 CEMEX -590 Mad Av -NY 10022
(914) 225-5535 .. **Martinez,** Sarah Tyson '02 Morgan Stanley -2000 Wstchstr Av -Purchase 10577
(516) 463-4739 .. **Martinez,** Serge A '01 Hofstra Law Schl -121 Hofstra Univ -Hempstd 11549
(516) 803-2535 .. **Martinez,** Ululy '00 Cablevision -1111 Stewart Av -Bethpage 11714 **Fx:**803-2667
(212) 610-6300 .. **Martinez,** Yara M '06 %Allen & O -1221 Av of Amer -NY 10020
(212) 998-6436 .. **Martinez,** Yumari L '02 Ctr for Cmmnty Problem Solving -245 Sullivan -NY 10012
(718) 590-3760 .. **Martinez Borges,** Rosemary '91 %Hon J Moore -851 Grnd Cncrs -Bronx 10451
(516) 393-2200 .. **Martinez-Cipolla,** Lourdes '93 (Garfunkel W,PC) -111 Grt Nck Rd -Gt Neck 11021
(212) 348-7449 .. **Martinez-Gunter,** Maribel '96 %Legal Srvcs -1 W 125th -NY 10027 **Fx:**348-4093
(212) 819-8200 .. **Martinez-Herrera,** Manuel '07 %White & C LLP -1155 Av of Amer -NY 10036
(212) 431-2115 .. **Martinez Rubio,** Angelina '05 Ctr for NYC Law -57 Worth -NY 10013
(718) 797-7153 .. **Martin-Gibbons,** Patricia L '89 -26 Court -Brklyn 11242 **Fx:**797-7152
(315) 339-7670 .. **Martin-Grande,** Diane M '91 (Corp Cnsl) -City Hall 198 N Wshngtn -Rome 13440 **Fx:**838-1166
(845) 569-0787 .. **Martini,** Carolyn L '95 -26 Route 17K -Newburgh 12550 **Fx:**569-7171
(212) 308-0210 .. **Martini,** Jaclyn A '08 %C Kutner,LLP -110 E 59th -NY 10022 **Fx:**308-0213
(212) 216-1214 .. **Martini,** Jessica M '98 Human Rights Watch -350 5th Av -NY 10118
(845) 486-2220 .. **Martini,** Jude T '94 Hon C Sproat -10 Market -Poughkeepsie 12601
(516) 364-5127 .. **Martinico,** John M '83 -11 Underhill Av -Syosset 11791
(212) 821-3000 .. **Martino,** Anthony L '03 UBS Investment Bk -299 Park Av -NY 10171
(914) 381-5658 .. **Martino,** Antonio '91 -617 Willow -Mamaroneck 10543
(212) 705-7000 .. **Martino,** Brett L '08 %Bingham M LLP -399 Park Av -NY 10022
(914) 668-5506 .. **Martino,** Douglas J '85 (Martino & W) -22 W 1st -Mt Vernon 10550
(516) 538-7780 .. **Martino,** Jos V '96 %N Pellegrini,LLC -320 Nassau Blvd -Garden City South 11530 **Fx:**564-0906
(914) 668-5506 .. **Martino,** Louis J '54 (Martino & W) -22 W 1st -Mt Vernon 10550
(212) 735-3000 .. **Martino,** Matthew M '03 %Skadden ASM&F LLP -4 Times Sq -NY 10036
(607) 936-3739 .. **Martino,** Michl J '87 (Rossettie R&M) -269 W Pulteney -Corning 14830
(718) 605-7360 .. **Martino,** Nicholas Jr. '88 -7448 Amboy Rd -Staten Isl 10307 **Fx:**605-7363
(212) 849-7000 .. **Martino,** Peter D '08 %Quinn EU&S,LLP -51 Mad Av -NY 10010
(518) 640-5000 .. **Martino,** Richd F '98 AYCO -25 British Amer Blvd -Latham 12110
(914) 668-5506 .. **Martino & Weiss** -22 W 1st -Mt Vernon 10550 **Fx:**668-5219
(631) 467-7922 .. **Martins,** Cristine S '96 Martins & Assoc -Bx255 -Mineola 11501
(212) 218-5500 .. **Martins,** Eric D '63 (Seyfarth S LLP) -620 8th Av -NY 10018
(516) 294-5614 .. **Martins,** Jack M '92 (Martins & S) -221 Mineola Blvd -Mineola 11501
(516) 248-5027 .. **Martins,** Louis L '99 (L Martins,PC) -321 Willis Av -Mineola 11501 **Fx:**414-4447
(516) 294-5614 .. **Martins & Silva** -221 Mineola Blvd -Mineola 11501 **Fx:**294-5709
(212) 583-2000 .. **Martinson,** Linda S '80 Baron Capital -767 5th Av -NY 10153
(631) 361-9494 .. **Martinson,** Rosemary E '92 %A Vardaro,PC -732 Smithtwn Bypass -Smithtwn 11787 **Fx:**361-8752
(914) 944-0960 .. **Martin-Valiquette,** Louise '90 -1 Rockldg Av -Ossining 10562 **Fx:**941-7245
(914) 773-3675 .. **Martirano,** Maryellen '80 Pace Univ -861 Bedford Rd -Plsntvll 10570
(212) 310-8000 .. **Martire,** Frank III '08 %Weil G&M LLP -767 5th Av -NY 10153
(201) 585-0852 .. **Martire,** Liliana '00 L Martire,LLC -155 W 85th -NY 10024 **Fx:**585-0853
(518) 474-1310 .. **Martland,** Luke '93 %Gov's Cnsls Ofc -242 State Cptl -Albany 12224
(716) 649-5372 .. **Martnshin,** Edw J '92 -12 Norwood Av -Hambrg 14075 **Fx:**312-9239
(914) 328-2969 .. **Marto,** Brian T '05 %Martin C&B LLP -245 Main -White Plns 10601
(315) 424-1105 .. **Martoccia,** Anthony R '03 %McMahon K&S,PC -500 S Salina -Syracuse 13202
(716) 852-5533 .. **Martoche,** Amy C '00 (Connors & V,LLP) -1000 Lbrty Bldg -Buffalo 14202
(716) 845-2560 .. **Martoche,** Mary Dee '77 %Surrogates Ct -92 Franklin -Buffalo 14202 **Fx:**853-3741
(212) 243-1313 .. **Marton,** Anita R '83 %Leg Action Ctr -225 Varick -NY 10014 **Fx:**675-0286
(518) 455-4387 .. **Marton,** Elana S '99 Assembly Prog -522 The Cptl -Albany 12248
(585) 787-0474 .. **Marton,** Marie Ducie '85 -947 Dibbles Trl -Webster 14580
(212) 735-3000 .. **Marton,** Miriam H '07 %Skadden ASM&F LLP -4 Times Sq -NY 10036
(646) 471-4000 .. **Martone,** Andrew C '93 %PricewaterhouseCoopers LLP -300 Mad Av -NY 10017
(718) 520-7956 .. **Martone,** Anthony J '88 -80-02 Kew Grdns Rd -Kew Gdns 11415 **Fx:**793-0165
(212) 577-3688 .. **Martone,** Katheryne M '87 %Leg Aid -199 Water -NY 10038 **Fx:**509-8431
(212) 508-6100 .. **Martone,** Laura S '08 %Bracewell & G,LLP -1251 Av of Amer -NY 10020
(516) 747-6300 .. **Martone,** Michl R '59 (Koeppel M&L,LLP) -155 First Bx863 -Mineola 11501
(212) 596-9000 .. **Martone,** Patricia A '74 (Ropes & G LLP) -1211 Av of Amer -NY 10036
(716) 566-1300 .. **Martorana,** Chas C '81 (Hiscock & B,LLP) -1100 M&T Ctr -Buffalo 14203
(212) 351-4000 .. **Martorana,** Keith R '08 %Gibson D&C LLP -200 Park Av -NY 10166
(212) 425-9300 .. **Martorana,** Regina P '04 %Bressler A&R,PC -17 State -NY 10004
(212) 916-3461 .. **Martorana,** Robt D Jr. '98 LexisNexis -125 Park Av -NY 10017
(718) 649-2000 .. **Martorana,** Vincent J '78 -9207 Flatlands Av -Brklyn 11236 **Fx:**649-2104
(212) 521-5400 .. **Martorana,** Vincent R '03 %Reed S LLP -599 Lex Av -NY 10022
(718) 579-3111 .. **Martorano,** James J '75 %Leg Aid -1020 Grnd Cncrs -Bronx 10451 **Fx:**588-2611
(718) 491-0431 .. **Martorell,** Fredk J '95 (F Martorell,PC) -1275 81st -Brklyn 11228 **Fx:**491-0096
(516) 249-3450 .. **Martorella,** John P '08 %Carman C&I,LLP -266 Main -Farmngdl 11735
(516) 922-1359 .. **Martorelli,** Nancy '92 (N Martorelli & Assoc,PC) -980 Seaview Dr -Oyster Bay 11771
(212) 984-0706 .. **Martori Dunlap,** Nancy '95 OfCnsl Nadborny & B LLP -100 Park Av -NY 10017
(212) 468-4800 .. **Martucci,** Angela M '05 %Davis & G LLP -1740 Bway -NY 10019

(845) 236-4411 .. **Martuscello,** Danl M '77 (Rusk WH&M,LLP) -1390 Route 9W Bx727 -Marlboro 12542
(212) 267-7944 .. **Martuscello,** Henry A '82 -108 Greenwich -NY 10006 **Fx:**267-8279
(212) 385-9424 .. **Martuscello,** Mary Mihalakos '84 -108 Greenwich -NY 10006 **Fx:**267-8279
(518) 829-7778 .. **Martuscello,** Wm F '89 -154 2nd Av -Fonda 12068 **Fx:**829-7772
(315) 425-2700 .. **Marty,** Fredk S '71 (Hiscock & B,LLP) -One Park Pl -Syracuse 13202
(315) 474-7571 .. **Marty,** Fredk W '04 %Mackenzie H LLP -101 S Salina Bx4967 -Syracuse 13221
(516) 739-0000 .. **Martyn,** Catherine M '81 (Martyn T&M) -330 Old Cntry Rd -Mineola 11501
(212) 559-5558 .. **Martyn,** Thos C '96 Citigroup Trust -485 Lex Av -NY 10017
(516) 739-0000 .. **Martyn,** Thos M '89 (Martyn T&M) -330 Old Cntry Rd -Mineola 11501
(516) 739-0000 .. **Martyn Toher & Martyn** -330 Old Cntry Rd -Mineola 11501 **Fx:**739-0329
(718) 923-6300 .. **Martynetz,** Myron '77 %Atty Grievance Comm -335 Adams -Brklyn 11201 **Fx:**624-2978
(212) 558-4000 .. **Martz,** Eric A '09 %Sullivan & C LLP -125 Broad -NY 10004
(212) 553-3200 .. **Marulli,** Gerard J '77 (Marulli LE&T,LLP) -5 Hanover Sq -NY 10004
(212) 553-3200 .. **Marulli Lindenbaum Edelman & Tomaszewski, LLP** -5 Hanover Sq -NY 10004 **Fx:**406-7590
(516) 479-6300 .. **Marullo,** Peter '87 Silverman A LLP -100 Jericho Quad -Jericho 11753
(716) 852-1000 .. **Marusak,** Jos J '82 %PW Beltz,PC -36 Church -Buffalo 14202 **Fx:**852-5887
(585) 546-6844 .. **Marvald,** Kenneth A '88 %Jasco Tools -1001 Lex Av Bx60620 -Rchstr 14606
(914) 366-5700 .. **Marvel,** Loretta Benedetto '81 MA Bjork -660 Wht Plns Rd -Tarrytwn 10591 **Fx:**366-5759
(212) 676-8348 .. **Marville,** Colin '85 %Law Dept -100 Church -NY 10007 **Fx:**788-0367
(212) 903-9000 .. **Marvin,** Christopher M '05 %Linklaters -1345 Av of Amer -NY 10105
(212) 532-8100 .. **Marvin,** Danl S '01 %Stern & M,LLP -115 Bway -NY 10006
(845) 876-3024 .. **Marvin,** John R '88 (Marvin & M PLLC) -6369 Mill Bx151 -Rhinebeck 12572 **Fx:**876-5622
(212) 455-2000 .. **Marvin,** Kristin M '09 %Simpson T&B LLP -425 Lex Av -NY 10017
(212) 326-3939 .. **Marvin,** Lynn M '05 %Jones D -222 E 41st -NY 10017
(845) 876-3024 .. **Marvin,** Robt J '53 (Marvin & M PLLC) -6369 Mill Bx151 -Rhinebeck 12572 **Fx:**876-5622
(845) 855-1555 .. **Marvin,** Robt J Jr. '84 (Marvin & M PLLC) -3 W Main Bx420 -Pawling 12564 **Fx:**855-9526
(914) 995-2660 .. **Marvin,** Stefanie L '99 Cnty Atty -148 Martine Av -White Plns 10601 **Fx:**995-5858
(631) 477-9277 .. **Marvin,** Valerie '89 -218 Front -Greenprt 11944
(718) 237-6389 .. **Marvinny,** Jonathan A '05 %Leg Aid -111 Lvngstn -Brklyn 11201 **Fx:**237-8737
(914) 666-5600 .. **Marwell,** John S '74 (Shamberg MD&H,PC) -55 Smith Av -Mt Kisco 10549
(212) 779-9910 .. **Marx,** Brendan R '84 Eaton & V LLP -3 Park Av -NY 10016
(516) 741-4720 .. **Marx,** Bruce E '84 -300 Grdn City Plz -Gdn Cty 11530 **Fx:**294-5208
(718) 380-8882 .. **Marx,** David E '86 -158-13 72nd Av -Flushng 11365
(212) 713-8818 .. **Marx,** Edw '78 UBS Fncl Srvcs,Inc -1285 Av of Amer -NY 10019
(212) 515-7028 .. **Marx,** Francine '82 Dexia Credit Local -445 Park Av -NY 10022
(212) 262-2390 .. **Marx,** Jason E '99 %Connell F LLP -888 7th Av -NY 10106
(914) 287-0888 .. **Marx,** Kenneth A '98 %J Sena Jr -55 Church -White Plns 10601 **Fx:**997-1204
(212) 415-9200 .. **Marx,** Owen C '75 (Dorsey & W LLP) -250 Park Av -NY 10177
(914) 949-4760 .. **Marx,** Paul I '83 -1 N Lex Av -White Plns 10601 **Fx:**949-4141
(212) 450-4000 .. **Marx,** Rachel S '10 %Davis P&W LLP -450 Lex Av -NY 10017
(718) 843-3300 .. **Marx,** Richd S '76 (Gusmorino & M) -104-21 Lefferts Blvd -S Richmond Hll 11419
(718) 380-8882 .. **Marx,** Robt '60 -158-13 72nd Av -Flushng 11365
(212) 382-2044 .. **Marx,** Robt O '84 %Marshall Firm -271 Mad Av -NY 10016 **Fx:**382-3610
(516) 624-6372 .. **Marx,** Steven J '97 Town Supervisors Ofc -54 Audrey Av -Oyster Bay 11771
(212) 475-5883 .. **Maryanov,** Linda '86 (Zimmerman & M) -304 Park Av S -NY 10010 **Fx:**677-5835
(212) 810-5097 .. **Maryles,** David B '01 BlackRock -40 E 52nd -NY 10022
(212) 983-6975 .. **Maryles,** Naomi T '01 American Friends of Nishmat -271 Mad Av -NY 10016
(646) 225-6549 .. **Marzano,** Elvira '05 (Marzano & S) -65 Bway -NY 10006 **Fx:**349-2053
(212) 267-0200 .. **Marzec,** Darius A '07 Marzec Law Firm,PC -225 Bway -NY 10007 **Fx:**587-0755
(212) 676-0968 .. **Marzick,** Abbey M '08 %Law Dept -60 Lafayette -NY 10013 **Fx:**442-6865
(212) 245-1000 .. **Marzigliano,** Tammy T '02 (Outten & G LLP) -3 Park Av -NY 10016
(203) 375-4803 .. **Marzik,** Robt K '62 R Marzik,PC -380 Lex Av -NY 10168 **Fx:**386-0136
(518) 272-2110 .. **Marzitelli,** Thos S '89 -64 2nd -Troy 12180 **Fx:**272-2345
(315) 422-0314 .. **Marzocchi,** John J '85 %Germain & G -314 E Fayette -Syracuse 13202 **Fx:**478-6544
(315) 445-8550 .. **Marzocchi,** Marco '88 %Widewaters Grp -5786 Widewaters Pkwy Bx3 -DeWitt 13214 **Fx:**445-8570
(845) 353-2000 .. **Marzolla,** Mary E '96 %Feerick LM PLLC -96 S Bway -Nyack 10960
(631) 757-0747 .. **Marzuk,** George C '86 -5 Bway -Greenlawn 11740
(212) 848-4000 .. **Marzulli,** John A Jr. '79 (Shearman & S LLP) -599 Lex Av -NY 10022
(914) 723-4300 .. **Marzullo,** Henry A Jr. '62 OfCnsl Lackenbach S LLP -1 Chase Rd -Scarsdale 10583
(212) 872-4443 .. **Masaitis,** Scott M '99 %KPMG LLP -345 Park Av -NY 10154
(718) 595-4716 .. **Masalski,** Emily N '06 DEP-BWT -96-05 Horace Hrdng Expy -Corona 11368 **Fx:**595-6950
(212) 450-4000 .. **Masanzu,** Shingira Samantha '10 %Davis P&W LLP -450 Lex Av -NY 10017
(212) 274-9100 .. **Mascali,** Arnold F Jr. '92 AON Horizon -199 Water -NY 10038 **Fx:**274-8575
(518) 464-1300 .. **Mascali,** Robt P '77 OfCnsl Roemer WG&M LLP -13 Columbia Cir -Albany 12203
(212) 357-0376 .. **Mascarello,** John A '92 Goldman Sachs -1 NY Plz -NY 10004
(212) 848-4000 .. **Mascarenhas,** Ignatius Anthony Jr. '10 Shearman & S LLP -599 Lex Av -NY 10022
(212) 277-4000 .. **Mascarenhas,** Viren M '06 %Freshfields BD LLP -520 Mad Av -NY 10022
(315) 366-2236 .. **Mascari,** Robt A '82 DA -Cnty Cthse Bx578 -Wampsville 13163 **Fx:**366-2503
(315) 841-3131 .. **Mascaro,** Jos '58 -7315 Calif Rd -Deansboro 13328 **Fx:**841-3131
(212) 728-8000 .. **Mascera,** Carol R '97 (Willkie F&G LLP) -787 7th Av -NY 10019
(845) 639-8100 .. **Masch,** Julia L '91 (Masch C & Assoc,LLP) -254 S Main -New Cty 10956 **Fx:**639-8104
(212) 790-9200 .. **Maschio,** Michl F '66 (Cowan L&L,PC) -1133 Av of Amer -NY 10036
(212) 940-3000 .. **Maschio,** Patrick '08 Cnsl Nixon P LLP -437 Mad Av -NY 10022
(212) 692-1000 .. **Mascia,** Jos A '92 %Duane M LLP -1540 Bway -NY 10036
(212) 278-1000 .. **Mascia,** Raymond A '10 %Anderson K&O,PC -1251 Av of Amer -NY 10020
(212) 801-9355 .. **Mascialino,** John L '96 (Greenberg T,LLP) -200 Park Av -NY 10166
(212) 259-8000 .. **Mascio,** Pamela A '07 %Dewey & L LLP -1301 Av of Amer -NY 10019
(585) 263-1000 .. **Mascitti,** Gregory J '97 (Nixon P LLP) -1100 Clinton Sq -Rchstr 14604
(718) 250-4230 .. **Masco,** Lori A '04 %Leg Aid -111 Lvngstn -Brklyn 11201 **Fx:**250-4243
(646) 458-7000 .. **Mascola,** Michl J '96 Ace USA -140 Bway -NY 10005
(845) 353-4909 .. **Mascola,** Susanne '94 -45 N Greenbush Rd -W Nyack 10994 **Fx:**353-4909
(845) 638-5180 .. **Mascola,** Thos M '82 %Cnty Atty -Cnty Ofc Bldg -New Cty 10956 **Fx:**638-5676
(845) 627-6161 .. **Mascola,** Thos M '82 -161 N Mddltwn Rd -Pearl Rvr 10965
(914) 318-3725 .. **Mascoll,** Dawn H '91 -902 Old Cntry Rd -Elmsfrd 10523
(718) 273-4046 .. **Mascolo,** Anthony A '81 (Bosco B&M) -857 Forest Av -Staten Isl 10310
(718) 261-2215 .. **Mascolo,** Anthony L '85 -123-60 83rd Av -Kew Gdns 11415 **Fx:**261-1062
(718) 261-2215 .. **Mascolo,** Anthony P '06 %A Mascolo -123-60 83rd Av -Kew Gdns 11415 **Fx:**261-1062
(212) 980-9600 .. **Mascolo,** Mark L '09 %Kaufman B&R -120 Bway -NY 10271
(516) 877-2900 .. **Mascolo,** Neil C Jr. '92 (Bartlett MB&M,LLP) -300 Old Cntry Rd -Mineola 11501
(718) 797-5700 .. **Masef,** Steven J '91 OfCnsl Wenig S LLP -26 Court -Brklyn 11242
(212) 885-5000 .. **Masella,** James V III '93 (Blank R LLP) -405 Lex Av -NY 10174
(212) 637-2288 .. **Masella,** Jessica A '01 %US Atty -1 St Andrews Plz -NY 10007
(845) 469-9541 .. **Masella,** Peter J '57 Town Justice -1786 Kings Hwy -Chester 10918
(212) 455-2000 .. **Mash,** Stephanie R '10 %Simpson T&B LLP -425 Lex Av -NY 10017
(212) 922-9600 .. **Mashaal,** David R '97 (Mashaal & Assoc PLLC) -245 Park Av -NY 10167 **Fx:**792-4001
(212) 969-3000 .. **Mashberg,** Gregg M '78 (Proskauer R LLP) -1585 Bway -NY 10036
(212) 969-3000 .. **Masheb,** Craig A '95 SrCnsl Proskauer R LLP -1585 Bway -NY 10036
(315) 539-1300 .. **Mashewske,** David G '98 %DA -48 W Williams -Waterloo 13165 **Fx:**539-0531
(631) 852-8800 .. **Mashhadian,** Shahin Y '07 %DA -116 Hmptn Rd -Southampton 11968 **Fx:**852-8806
(518) 452-5600 .. **Mashmann,** Garth H '10 %Heslin RF&M PC -5 Columbia Cir -Albany 12203
(516) 596-0390 .. **Masi,** Gary R '84 -14 St James Pl -Lynbrk 11563 **Fx:**593-1240
(718) 987-6008 .. **Masi,** Jos III '09 -78 Allison Av -Staten Isl 10306
(212) 587-0550 .. **Masi,** Marialaina L '92 (DiRaimondo & M,LLP) -120 Bway -NY 10271 **Fx:**587-0545
(631) 777-5557 .. **Masi,** Marialaina L '92 (DiRaimondo & M,LLP) -445 Broadhllw Rd -Melvll 11747 **Fx:**777-5114
(516) 873-0795 .. **Masiakos,** Jordan '92 (Golan & M,LLP) -200 Willis Av -Mineola 11501 **Fx:**873-6686
(718) 386-0342 .. **Masiello,** Dominick J '62 -66-10 Forest Av -Rdgwd 11385 **Fx:**386-5029
(631) 414-6089 .. **Masilamani,** Mekalaradha '05 Estee Lauder -155 Pinelawn Rd -Melvll 11747
(212) 417-3700 .. **Masimore,** Christin J '05 %MFY Legal Srvcs -299 Bway -NY 10007 **Fx:**417-3890
(212) 637-2580 .. **Masimore,** Jason A '03 %US Atty -1 St Andrews Plz -NY 10007
(212) 521-5400 .. **Masin,** Adam M '01 (Reed S LLP) -599 Lex Av -NY 10022
(631) 422-0500 .. **Masin,** Linda Lori Alba '92 %P Alba,PC -1250 Montauk Hwy -W Islip 11795 **Fx:**422-0967
(516) 921-1282 .. **Masini,** Mark I '01 M Masini,PC -825 E Gate Blvd -Gdn Cty 11530 **Fx:**706-4003
(631) 736-2424 .. **Masino,** Dennis '75 (D Masino,PC) -760 Horseblock Rd -Farmngvll 11738 **Fx:**736-2058
(585) 419-8800 .. **Masino,** Michl J '92 (Harris B PLLC) -99 Garnsey Rd -Pittsfrd 14534
(212) 820-9602 .. **Maskai,** Shyam '00 %Hawkins D&W LLP -One Chase Manh Plz -NY 10005
(212) 724-8669 .. **Maskaleris,** Stephen N '80 -123 Bank -NY 10014
(212) 326-3939 .. **Maskel,** Gregory S '08 %Jones D -222 E 41st -NY 10017
(914) 251-3287 .. **Masket,** Steven N '79 WJ Deutsch & Sons,Ltd -108 Corp Park Dr -White Plns 10604 **Fx:**251-0283
(212) 310-8000 .. **Maskin,** Arvin '84 (Weil G&M LLP) -767 5th Av -NY 10153
(914) 997-1420 .. **Maslansky,** Harris J '69 %Jaris Entertainment -4 Middle Rd -White Plns 10605
(212) 925-3405 .. **Maslansky,** Michl F '97 Luntz Maslansky Strategic Research -200 Varick -NY 10014
(718) 250-4213 .. **Maslauskas,** Laura M '08 Legal Aid -111 Lvngstn -Brklyn 11201
(516) 822-8900 .. **Masler,** Ross P '91 Fiedelman & M -2 Jericho Plz -Jericho 11753
(212) 227-9390 .. **Masliah,** Noemi E '80 (Masliah & S,PC) -225 Bway -NY 10007 **Fx:**227-9564
(212) 644-0303 .. **Maslin,** Scott H '07 E Hayes,PC -515 Mad Av -NY 10022 **Fx:**644-4818
(518) 388-1270 .. **Masline,** Gary W '75 %CQC -401 State -Schnctdy 12305 **Fx:**388-1275
(212) 556-2100 .. **Maslo,** Paul B '09 %King & S -1185 Av of Amer -NY 10036
(718) 375-8211 .. **Maslow,** Aaron D '81 -1761 Stuart -Brklyn 11229

(585) 520-2188 .. **Maslow**, Lisa J '97 -1039 Monroe Av -Rchstr 14620
(585) 381-2557 .. **Maslow**, Louis II '96 -9 Devonwood Ln -Pittsfrd 14534 **Fx:**(208) 330-2557
(585) 295-7315 .. **Maslyn**, James E '79 (Cellino & B,PC) -16 W Main -Rchstr 14614
(518) 457-2070 .. **Maslyn**, Robt A '77 %Dept of Tax & Fin -Bldg 9 State Campus -Albany 12227 **Fx:**457-6131
(212) 477-3002 .. **Masnyj**, Zenon B '80 -29 E 7th -NY 10003 **Fx:**254-5875
(212) 788-3764 .. **Mason**, Abra S '09 %Law Dept -100 Church -NY 10007 **Fx:**788-0367
(212) 558-4000 .. **Mason**, Andrew S '82 (Sullivan & C LLP) -125 Broad -NY 10004
(212) 578-2211 .. **Mason**, Ann-Marie '00 %MetLife -27-01 Qns Plz N -LIC 11101
(518) 324-4667 .. **Mason**, Ashley Beck '04 %MHLS -186 US Oval -Plattsbrgh 12903
(212) 455-2000 .. **Mason**, Brandon C '10 %Simpson T&B LLP -425 Lex Av -NY 10017
(212) 536-3900 .. **Mason**, Bronwen Charters '07 %K&L Gates LLP -599 Lex Av -NY 10022
Mason, Carrie M '09 -2 Helmsford Way -Penfld 14526
(914) 833-1805 .. **Mason**, Chas A '81 -482 Weaver -Larchmnt 10538 **Fx:**834-8179
(212) 808-7800 .. **Mason**, Christina M '89 (Kelley D&W LLP) -101 Park Av -NY 10178
(212) 940-3017 .. **Mason**, Christopher M '85 (Nixon P LLP) -437 Mad Av -NY 10022
(315) 699-8475 .. **Mason**, Christopher R '93 NY Compensation Mgr -6250 S Bay Rd -Syracuse 13220
(212) 541-9100 .. **Mason**, D Christopher '04 %Schiavetti CDW&N,LLP -575 8th Av -NY 10018
(212) 335-4500 .. **Mason**, David A '01 %DLA Piper LLP -1251 Av of Amer -NY 10020
(212) 596-9000 .. **Mason**, Deborah E '09 %Ropes & G LLP -1211 Av of Amer -NY 10036
(646) 836-6466 .. **Mason**, Elisa '06 US DOJ -150 Park Row -NY 10007
(212) 332-7590 .. **Mason**, Elizabeth A '89 -45 Rckfllr Plz -NY 10111
(212) 388-3600 .. **Mason**, Evelyn I '88 %32B-J Leg Srvcs -101 Av of Amer -NY 10013 **Fx:**388-3061
(212) 481-9011 .. **Mason**, Geoffrey A '95 %Shaw & B -9 E 40th -NY 10016
(516) 746-5498 .. **Mason**, Gregory J '86 -220 Old Cntry Rd -Mineola 11501 **Fx:**746-6397
(914) 995-4172 .. **Mason**, Heide E '88 %DA -111 Martin Luther King Blvd -White Plns 10601 **Fx:**995-3363
(914) 698-1350 .. **Mason**, Joyce J '84 -309 Carroll Av -Mamaroneck 10543 **Fx:**698-0319
(516) 710-6200 .. **Mason**, Julie A '04 Mason & M PC -27 Cynthia Ct -Hempstd 11550
(631) 756-4370 .. **Mason**, Katherine Ann '93 %State Ins Fund -199 Church -NY 10007 **Fx:**(212) 385-9199
(212) 836-8000 .. **Mason**, Kenneth G M '98 (Kaye S LLP) -425 Park Av -NY 10022
(203) 255-6560 .. **Mason**, Kevin M '94 (Ryan M&L,LLP) -90 Forest Av -Locust Vly 11560 **Fx:**255-6570
(212) 697-3122 .. **Mason**, Kimberly A '09 %Martin C&B LLP -220 E 42nd -NY 10017
(516) 333-1228 .. **Mason**, Lola H '78 -98 Store Hill Rd -Old Westbury 11568
(212) 633-8033 .. **Mason**, Lori '00 Klee Brasserie -200 9th Av -NY 10011
(212) 208-8000 .. **Mason**, M Scott '95 %Standard & Poor's -55 Water -NY 10041
(516) 742-0009 .. **Mason**, Madelynn Russell '88 (Mason & A,LLC) -377 Oak -Gdn Cty 11530 **Fx:**742-0908
(718) 544-8492 .. **Mason**, Marilyne '79 -119-20 80th Rd -Kew Gdns 11415 **Fx:**544-0605
(516) 739-3090 .. **Mason**, Michaelangelo V '97 (Mason & M,PC) -394 Old Cntry Rd -Gdn Cty 11530 **Fx:**739-5060
(212) 455-2000 .. **Mason**, Omari L R '10 %Simpson T&B LLP -425 Lex Av -NY 10017
(518) 457-5807 .. **Mason**, Paul H W '91 Dept of Labor -WA Harriman Campus -Albany 12240
(212) 682-7050 .. **Mason**, Pauline A '89 %Geringer & D -5 Hanover Sq -NY 10004
(212) 326-7139 .. **Mason**, Peter D C '89 UNICEF -3 UN Plz -NY 10017 **Fx:**303-7938
(212) 325-8661 .. **Mason**, Reese Fredrick '96 CSFB -11 Mad Av -NY 10010
(212) 403-1000 .. **Mason**, Richd G '88 (Wachtell LR&K) -51 W 52nd -NY 10019
(212) 715-1000 .. **Mason**, Robt C '88 (Arnold & P LLP) -399 Park Av -NY 10022
(212) 361-7996 .. **Mason**, S Scott '93 %Dept Homeless Srvcs -33 Beaver -NY 10004 **Fx:**361-8002
(718) 990-1595 .. **Mason**, Sara A '02 St Johns Univ Law Schl -8000 Utopia Pkwy -Jamaica 11439
(212) 717-6540 .. **Mason**, Stephen L '74 -31 Garrisons Lndng -Garrison 10524 **Fx:**(845) 424-4158
(516) 747-5930 .. **Mason**, Stephen R '78 -485 Jericho Tpk -Mineola 11501 **Fx:**248-6615
(516) 627-7572 .. **Mason**, Thos J '65 -227 Munsey Pl -Manhsst 11030 **Fx:**627-7578
(212) 935-3000 .. **Mason**, Todd E '05 (Mintz LCFG&P,PC) -666 3rd Av -NY 10017
(212) 661-9100 .. **Mason**, Valerie S '84 (Otterbourg SH&R,PC) -230 Park Av -NY 10169
(212) 335-9000 .. **Mason**, Wm B '09 %DA -1 Hogan Pl -NY 10013
(516) 739-3090 .. **Mason**, Wm M '95 (Mason & M,PC) -394 Old Cntry Rd -Gdn Cty 11530 **Fx:**739-5060
(718) 250-2000 .. **Masone**, Diana L '05 %DA -350 Jay -Brklyn 11201 **Fx:**250-2314
(718) 639-1100 .. **Masone**, Leonard '73 (Masone WP&C) -69-34 Grand Av -Maspeth 11378
(631) 853-4544 .. **Masone**, Linda Ann '90 %District Ct Law Dept -400 Carleton Av Bx9075 -Central Islip 11722
(718) 639-1100 .. **Masone**, Lisa J '05 (Masone WP&C) -69-34 Grand Av -Maspeth 11378
(718) 625-2300 .. **Masone**, Matthew '06 Severance B&S,PC -16 Court -Brklyn 11241
(212) 723-5875 .. **Masone**, Michl J '02 %Citigroup Global Mrkts -390 Greenwich -NY 10013
(718) 639-1100 .. **Masone**, Michelle A '09 %Masone WP&C -69-34 Grand Av -Maspeth 11378
(718) 222-8880 .. **Masone**, Richd G '00 %Jones JO -45 Main -Brklyn 11201
(718) 639-1100 .. **Masone White Penkava & Cristofari** -69-34 Grand Av -Maspeth 11378 **Fx:**899-6875
(212) 228-2253 .. **Masonson**, Nina '83 -511 E 20th -NY 10010
(212) 373-3000 .. **Masotti**, Marco V '93 (Paul WRW&G LLP) -1285 Av of Amer -NY 10019
(212) 640-7138 .. **Masotti-Pagano**, Jennifer A '04 Amer Exp -200 Vesey -NY 10285
(516) 747-0300 .. **Masri**, Michl H '97 (Meltzer LG&B,LLP) -190 Willis Av -Mineola 11501
(212) 819-8200 .. **Masri**, Michl J '07 %White & C LLP -1155 Av of Amer -NY 10036
(347) 404-9400 .. **Mass**, Alan H '84 %Criminal Ct -120 Schermerhorn -Brklyn 11201 **Fx:**(718) 643-3538
(212) 682-4001 .. **Mass**, Allen R '76 OfCnsl Lynch R LLP -630 3rd Av -NY 10017
(212) 753-8700 .. **Mass**, Arthur '65 -1173A 2nd Av PMB 123 -NY 10065 **Fx:**753-8940
(212) 708-1800 .. **Mass**, Clifford J '88 (Ladas & P) -26 W 61st -NY 10023
(212) 788-1618 .. **Mass**, Marian '86 %Law Dept -100 Church -NY 10007 **Fx:**788-0367
(212) 247-6100 .. **Mass**, Mitchell R '68 (M Mass,PC) -500 E 85th -NY 10028 **Fx:**956-7549
(212) 902-9771 .. **Mass**, Robt A '79 Goldman Sachs -1 NY Plz -NY 10004
(212) 659-7300 .. **Mass**, Stuart '84 (Haynes & B,LLP) -1221 Av of Amer -NY 10020
(631) 470-9662 .. **Massa**, Amel '88 -780 NY Av -Huntngtn 11743
(212) 935-3131 .. **Massa**, Peter R '05 %Gallet D&B,LLP -845 3rd Av -NY 10022
(212) 922-0450 .. **Massamillo**, Eugene '81 (Kaplan M&A,LLC) -70 E 55th -NY 10022
(212) 448-1100 .. **Massand**, Dilip N '93 (McLaughlin & S,LLP) -260 Mad Av -NY 10016
(585) 454-3323 .. **Massare**, Edw J '66 (Cerulli M&L) -339 East Av -Rchstr 14604
(914) 694-1880 .. **Massarelli**, Crystal M '00 (Greenberg & M,LLP) -2929 Purchase -Purchase 10577
(716) 285-9338 .. **Massaro**, Angelo '62 (Hovey & M) -631 Main -Niagara Fls 14301
(914) 767-6000 .. **Massaro**, Carlo '97 Pepsi Bottling Grp -1 Pepsi Way -Somers 10589
(212) 244-3998 .. **Massaro**, Frank R '81 -303 5th Av -NY 10016 **Fx:**629-9656
(212) 733-6513 .. **Massaro**, Jane A '86 %Pfizer Inc -150 E 42nd -NY 10017
(516) 394-4200 .. **Massaro**, Jay J '05 %Duffy & D -1370 RXR Plz -Uniondale 11556
(212) 536-3900 .. **Massaro**, Lorraine '78 (K&L Gates LLP) -599 Lex Av -NY 10022
(716) 286-4121 .. **Massaro**, Maria A '94 City School Dist -630 66th -Niagara Fls 14304
(516) 832-7500 .. **Massaro**, Peter S '10 %Nixon P LLP -50 Jericho Quadrangle -Jericho 11753
(518) 447-3200 .. **Massaroni**, Christopher '83 (McNamee LT&W,PC) -677 Bway -Albany 12207
(518) 374-1800 .. **Massaroni**, John R '80 (Capasso & M LLP) -215 State Bx1088 -Schnctdy 12301
(718) 239-0395 .. **Massas**, Jose L '93 (J Massas,PC) -1136 Castle Hill Av -Bronx 10462 **Fx:**239-0631
(212) 867-3810 .. **Massel**, Elihu S '66 -122 E 42nd -NY 10168 **Fx:**687-8158
(212) 455-2000 .. **Massel**, Morris J '00 %Simpson T&B LLP -425 Lex Av -NY 10017
(716) 662-1900 .. **Masselli**, Cheryl L '05 ITT Enidine Inc -7 Centre Dr -Orchard Pk 14127
(914) 328-0404 .. **Massen**, Nina '94 %Jackson L LLP -1 N Bway -White Plns 10601
(212) 766-1700 .. **Massena**, Alain V '02 -305 Bway -NY 10007 **Fx:**766-1701
(212) 373-3000 .. **Masser**, Adam L '10 %Paul WRW&G LLP -1285 Av of Amer -NY 10019
(315) 471-3151 .. **Massett**, Marguerite A '95 (Hancock & E,LLP) -1500 AXA Twr I Bx4976 -Syracuse 13221
(212) 637-2283 .. **Massey**, David B '98 %US Atty -1 St Andrews Plz -NY 10007
(212) 363-1220 .. **Massey**, Ellen M '80 -26 Bway -NY 10004
(845) 628-5339 .. **Massey**, George E '60 -21 Kia Ora Blvd -Mahopac 10541 **Fx:**628-5339
(212) 297-5800 .. **Massey**, Henry Nelson '80 (Day P LLP) -7 Times Sq -NY 10036
(212) 698-3500 .. **Massey**, Kathleen N '90 (Dechert LLP) -1095 Av of Amer -NY 10036
(718) 928-3700 .. **Massey**, Randi '97 %LSNYC-Bronx -1118 Grnd Cncrs -Bronx 10456 **Fx:**590-1129
(212) 807-2180 .. **Massey**, Wm E '80 Thomson Reuters -195 Bway -NY 10007
(212) 839-5300 .. **Massey**, Wm R '87 (Sidley A LLP) -787 7th Av -NY 10019
(212) 228-7727 .. **Massey**, Wm S '05 %Gladstein R&M,LLP -817 Bway -NY 10003
(212) 244-4664 .. **Massie**, Miranda K S '97 NY Lawyers Pub Intrst -151 W 30th -NY 10001 **Fx:**244-4570
(212) 227-9390 .. **Massie**, Tanisha L '02 OfCnsl Masliah & S,PC -225 Bway -NY 10007 **Fx:**227-9564
(516) 683-8880 .. **Massimo**, Nicholas J '94 (Massimo & P,PC) -99 Q Roosevelt Blvd -Gdn Cty 11530
(516) 683-8880 .. **Massimo & Panetta,PC** -99 Q Roosevelt Blvd -Gdn Cty 11530 **Fx:**794-9039
(631) 844-7071 .. **Massina**, Barbra Ann '93 %Olsten Corp -175 Broadhllw Rd -Melvll 11747 **Fx:**844-7266
(607) 273-7200 .. **Masson**, Robin Abrahamson '78 -120 E Buffalo -Ithaca 14850 **Fx:**273-7240
(212) 577-3916 .. **Masson-Churin**, Bobette M '83 %Leg Aid -199 Water -NY 10038 **Fx:**577-3520
(212) 207-6771 .. **Massoud**, Ahmed Aly '86 (Massoud & P,LLP) -99 Park Av -NY 10016 **Fx:**207-6774
(315) 797-1940 .. **Massoud**, George J '96 G Massoud,PC -2434 Chenango Rd -Utica 13502 **Fx:**797-0361
(212) 806-5400 .. **Massouh**, Naji '98 SpclCnsl Stroock &S&L LLP -180 Maiden Ln -NY 10038
(917) 237-1113 .. **Massucci**, Thos V '96 -401 Bway -NY 10013
(212) 554-0622 .. **Mast**, Jennifer L '05 Economist Grp -111 W 15th -NY 10019
(646) 943-5909 .. **Mast**, Stuart N '02 Beazkey USA Srvcs,Inc -400 Mad Av -NY 10017
(516) 357-3700 .. **Mastaglio**, Peter J '68 (Cullen and D LLP) -100 Q Roosevelt Blvd -Gdn Cty 11530
(518) 487-5460 .. **Mastaitis**, Benjamin M '05 %DA -6 Lodge -Albany 12207 **Fx:**487-5093
(518) 587-5188 .. **Mastaitis**, Katherine L '05 %Leg Aid -112 Spring -Saratoga Spgs 12866 **Fx:**587-0959
(518) 583-9497 .. **Mastaitis**, Stephen J '80 (SJ Mastaitis,PC) -151 Franklin Beach Rd -Saratoga Spgs 12866 **Fx:**583-9481
(718) 281-0300 .. **Mastakouris**, Theo '96 -39-25 Bell Blvd -Bayside 11361
(212) 310-8000 .. **Mastando**, John P III '97 (Weil G&M LLP) -767 5th Av -NY 10153
(212) 824-5700 .. **Mastandrea**, John '97 %Practising Law Inst -810 7th Av -NY 10019
(516) 571-3800 .. **Mastanduono**, Jennifer A '07 %DA -262 Old Cntry Rd -Mineola 11501 **Fx:**248-9479
(212) 687-6262 .. **Mastbaum**, Abe '07 Cnsl Barton B&P,LLP -420 Lex Av -NY 10170
(212) 801-6814 .. **Mastbaum**, Steve '78 (Greenberg T,LLP) -200 Park Av -NY 10166
(212) 566-7188 .. **Mastellone**, Dina M '99 %Genova B&G -115 Bway -NY 10006
(914) 323-7000 .. **Mastellone**, Janine A '96 OfCnsl Wilson EME&D LLP -3 Gannett Dr -White Plns 10604
(718) 667-7175 .. **Master**, Danl L Jr. '86 -135 Circle Rd -Staten Isl 10304
(212) 637-2248 .. **Master**, Howard S '05 US Atty -1 St Andrews Plz -NY 10007
(212) 252-8113 .. **Master**, John J III '97 MSG -2 Penn Plz -NY 10121
(718) 923-6300 .. **Master**, Susan B '02 %Atty Grievance Comm -335 Adams -Brklyn 11201 **Fx:**624-2978

(212) 244-4664 .. **Masters,** Amanda '97 %NY Lawyers Pub Intrst -151 W 30th -NY 10001 **Fx:**244-4570
(518) 474-1010 .. **Masters,** Jonathan D '00 %Ofc Inspector Genl -ESP Agncy Bldg 2 -Albany 12223 **Fx:**486-3745
(718) 282-2500 .. **Masters,** Kathleen A '79 %CAMBA Lgl Srvcs -884 Flatbush Av -Brklyn 11226 **Fx:**282-8329
(212) 859-8000 .. **Masters,** Keriann '03 %Fried FHS&J LLP -1 NY Plz -NY 10004
(516) 747-6442 .. **Masters,** R Thos Jr. '87 -125 Brook -Gdn Cty 11530
(914) 288-8139 .. **Masters,** Robt '74 %Acadia Realty Trust -1311 Mamaroneck Av -White Plns 10605
(718) 286-6000 .. **Masters,** Robt J '81 %DA -125-01 Qns Blvd -Kew Gdns 11415
(212) 448-9570 .. **Masterson,** Brian R '08 %Callahan & F,LLC -40 Exch Pl -NY 10005
(845) 297-8904 .. **Masterson,** K E '80 -21 Clapp Av -Wappingers Fls 12590
(845) 568-2759 .. **Masterson,** Lori E '98 St Lukes Cornwall Hsptl -70 Dubois -Newburgh 12550 **Fx:**568-2095
(212) 357-0634 .. **Masterson,** Michl L '04 Goldman Sachs -1 NY Plz -NY 10004
(516) 627-7403 .. **Masterson,** Richd G '77 -185 Manhsst Woods Rd -Manhsst 11030
(631) 427-2099 .. **Maston,** Bruce M '88 (Spencer M&M,LLP) -Bx128 -Huntngtn Sta 11746 **Fx:**427-2996
(212) 259-8000 .. **Mastoris,** George E '04 %Dewey & L LLP -1301 Av of Amer -NY 10019
(212) 319-7125 .. **Mastracchio,** James N '97 (Caplin & D) -375 Park Av -NY 10152
(518) 474-7330 .. **Mastracco,** Marcus J '95 %Dept of Law -The Cptl -Albany 12224
(516) 693-0330 .. **Mastrangelo,** Dean S '99 -1101 Stewart Av -Gdn Cty 11530 **Fx:**693-0331
(212) 924-3414 .. **Mastrangelo,** Jos N '42 -72 Barrow -NY 10014
(212) 804-4200 .. **Mastrangelo,** Raymond S '94 %Mound CW&G -One Bttry Pk Plz -NY 10004
(212) 593-6700 .. **Mastrantonio,** John J Jr. '06 %Aaronson RF&D,LLP -757 3rd Av -NY 10017
(631) 434-1000 .. **Mastrantonio,** Robt '93 -308 W Main -Smithtwn 11787
(212) 858-1000 .. **Mastrapa,** Carlos M '01 %Pillsbury WSP LLP -1540 Bway -NY 10036
(585) 232-8810 .. **Mastrella,** Danl J '81 -16 W Main -Rchstr 14614 **Fx:**232-6804
(516) 741-2585 .. **Mastriano,** Danielle '05 %Rosicki R & Assoc,PC -51 E Bethpage Rd -Plainvw 11803 **Fx:**741-4748
(518) 869-6227 .. **Mastro,** Arkley L Jr. '72 OfCnsl Lavelle & F,LLP -29 British Amer Blvd -Latham 12110
(718) 675-8752 .. **Mastro,** Eva '06 Richmond Cnty Sup Ct -18 Richmond Ter -Staten Isl 10301
(212) 351-4000 .. **Mastro,** Randy M '82 (Gibson D&C LLP) -200 Park Av -NY 10166
(718) 761-9300 .. **Mastro,** Wm F '03 %Vaslas LH&D LLP -201 Edward Curry Av -Staten Isl 10314
(631) 225-4220 .. **Mastroberti,** Brian T '94 -151 S 14th -Lindenhrst 11757
(631) 694-0033 .. **Mastrocinque,** Michl '05 %Lawrence WR&B,PC -425 Broadhllw Rd -Melvll 11747
(212) 816-8247 .. **Mastrocola,** Dimitri G '90 Citigroup Global Mrkts -388 Greenwich -NY 10013
(585) 428-4280 .. **Mastrocola,** Robt A '84 Unified Ct Sys -161 Hall of Justice -Rchstr 14614
(718) 545-5518 .. **Mastrocola,** Stephanie '99 %Stefanidis & M LLP -31-10 37th Av -LIC 11101 **Fx:**545-5087
(212) 563-4100 .. **Mastroddi,** Travis M '02 (Cohen W&S LLP) -330 W 42nd -NY 10036
(718) 268-8111 .. **Mastrodomenico,** Donald E '81 -107-19 71st Av -Frst Hlls 11375 **Fx:**268-7382
(585) 325-7440 .. **Mastrodonato,** Anthony J '76 (Kaman BMJ&G LLP) -135 Corp Woods -Rchstr 14623
(212) 551-8500 .. **Mastrogiacomo,** Robt J '89 %Israel Discount Bk -511 5th Av -NY 10017 **Fx:**551-8916
(646) 447-0080 .. **Mastrogiacomo,** Wm F '79 Emblem Hlth Srvcs Co LLC -55 Water -NY 10041
(212) 308-5858 .. **Mastrogiovanni,** Jessica '04 %Bragar WE&S,PC -885 3rd Av -NY 10022
(516) 333-1711 .. **Mastroianni,** Anthony '76 (Mastroianni & M) -355 Post Av -Westbury 11590 **Fx:**997-5920
(516) 333-1711 .. **Mastroianni,** Tomasina Cuda '88 %Mastroianni & M -355 Post Av -Westbury 11590 **Fx:**997-5920
(315) 218-8000 .. **Mastroleo,** Adam P '07 %Bond S&K,PLLC -1 Lincoln Ctr -Syracuse 13202
(315) 823-2324 .. **Mastromoro,** Norman L '81 -104 Lyle Rd -Little Fls 13365 **Fx:**823-2523
(212) 458-5744 .. **Mastronardo,** Richd G '00 AIG -175 Water -NY 10038
(212) 669-4719 .. **Mastropaolo,** Mary M '89 Public Advocate Ofc -1 Centre -NY 10007 **Fx:**669-4701
(212) 940-3141 .. **Mastropieri,** Nicole F '05 %Nixon P LLP -437 Mad Av -NY 10022
(718) 615-0044 .. **Mastropietro,** Donato '88 (Lozner & M) -1901 Emmons Av -Brklyn 11235
(518) 226-0700 .. **Mastropietro,** John P '96 (Mastropietro & F,LLC) -63 Franklin -Saratoga Spgs 12866 **Fx:**226-0701
(212) 836-8000 .. **Mastrosimone,** Salvatore J '95 (Kaye S LLP) -425 Park Av -NY 10022
(212) 949-9022 .. **Mastrovito,** Marie Anne '93 (Abelman F&S) -666 3rd Av -NY 10017
(212) 770-1288 .. **Masucci,** Deborah '81 AIG -80 Pine -NY 10005
(516) 832-7573 .. **Masucci,** Michele A '88 (Nixon P LLP) -50 Jericho Quadrangle -Jericho 11753
(212) 258-3333 .. **Masuda,** Junji '95 (Masuda Intl) -152 W 57th -NY 10019 **Fx:**957-3939
(212) 201-1170 .. **Masuko,** Karen Michi '05 %Abrams GMB,LLP -237 W 35th -NY 10001
(845) 586-3533 .. **Masullo,** Peter G '80 -Miller Rd Bx244 -New Kingston 12459 **Fx:**586-3533
(212) 931-8220 .. **Masur,** Steven R '94 (Masur & Assoc) -101 E 15th -NY 10003
(631) 501-5700 .. **Masure,** Eric B '06 %Carter DF&S LLP -445 Broadhallow Rd -Melvll 11747
(718) 942-7777 .. **Masure,** Fredric S '83 -1352 Penn Av -Brklyn 11239 **Fx:**942-2222
(212) 474-1000 .. **Maswoswe,** Rumbidzayishe K '09 %Cravath S&M LLP -825 8th Av -NY 10019
(212) 223-4000 .. **Maswoswe,** Shamiso K '08 %Crowell & M LLP -590 Mad Av -NY 10022
(212) 909-9500 .. **Masyr,** Jesse '75 (Wachtel & M,LLP) -885 2nd Av -NY 10017
(212) 230-8800 .. **Masys,** Jeremy A '07 %WilmerHale -399 Park Av -NY 10022
(518) 474-7330 .. **Matalavage,** Joan '84 %Dept of Law -The Cptl -Albany 12224
(516) 931-8100 .. **Matalon,** Gregory L '99 (Capell BM&S,LLP) -100 Jericho Quadrangle -Jericho 11753
(212) 244-9000 .. **Matalon,** Jos Lee '90 Matalon SE -450 7th Av -NY 10123 **Fx:**244-4615
(201) 287-1500 .. **Matano,** Gary R '90 (J Samel & Partners) -150 Bway -NY 10038 **Fx:**287-1555
(212) 530-5000 .. **Matar,** Neda '04 %Milbank TH&M LLP -1 Chase Manh Plz -NY 10005
(212) 967-3322 .. **Matarangas,** Dennis S '94 (Bournazos & M,PC) -111 Bway -NY 10006 **Fx:**268-5012
(212) 652-3890 .. **Mataraso,** Matthew H '58 OfCnsl Pitta & G LLP -120 Bway -NY 10271
(518) 449-3320 .. **Mataraso,** Matthew H '58 OfCnsl Pitta BD&G LLP -111 Wshngtn Av -Albany 12210
(914) 346-8088 .. **Matarazzo,** Barbara A '84 -925 Wstchstr Av -White Plns 10604 **Fx:**681-0013
(212) 558-5500 .. **Matarazzo,** Hadley L '06 %Weitz & L,PC -700 Bway -NY 10003
(516) 624-0400 .. **Matarazzo,** Mark '92 -127 South -Oyster Bay 11771
(212) 277-4000 .. **Matarese,** Christian A '08 %Freshfields BD LLP -520 Mad Av -NY 10022
(212) 558-4000 .. **Matarese,** Richd Scott '09 %Sullivan & C LLP -125 Broad -NY 10004
(718) 966-5353 .. **Matarrese,** Gregory P '87 (Laura & M) -236 Richmond Valley Rd -Staten Isl 10309
(212) 421-4100 .. **Matase,** Jeanne C '88 OfCnsl Pryor C LLP -7 Times Sq -NY 10036
(212) 213-5000 .. **Matays,** Chas '72 (Matays & K) -271 Mad Av -NY 10016
(212) 213-5000 .. **Matays & Kretschmann** -271 Mad Av -NY 10016 **Fx:**725-6677
(212) 272-2273 .. **Matays,** Michl B '01 -383 Mad Av -NY 10179
(212) 735-3000 .. **Matays,** Steven J '01 (Skadden ASM&F LLP) -4 Times Sq -NY 10036
(646) 452-1600 .. **Mate,** Jonathan L '70 -845 3rd Av -NY 10022 **Fx:**(201) 457-1987
(516) 222-0002 .. **Mate,** Jonathan L '70 -131 Jericho Tpk -Jericho 11753 **Fx:**(201) 457-1987
(516) 536-1411 .. **Matejka,** Regina A '88 -1122 Franklin Av -Gdn Cty 11530 **Fx:**536-1411
(212) 254-4646 .. **Matera,** Alessio F '55 -54 W 10th -NY 10011
(516) 409-6200 .. **Matera,** Glenn J '85 (Furey KWM&C,PC) -2174 Jackson Av -Seafrd 11783
(212) 785-2929 .. **Matera,** Matthew S '02 %Conway FC&K,PC -48 Wall -NY 10005
(516) 741-6700 .. **Matera,** Michaelangelo '97 -560 Broadhllw Rd -Melvll 11747 **Fx:**741-6797
(845) 384-6544 .. **Matera,** Peter F '86 -Bx95 -W Pk 12493 **Fx:**384-6560
(845) 340-3315 .. **Matera,** Peter F '86 %DA -285 Wall -Kingston 12401 **Fx:**340-3185
(845) 384-6544 .. **Matera,** Peter Francis '59 -Bx95 -W Pk 12493
(845) 352-8800 .. **Matera,** Rosemarie E '81 (Kurtzman M PC) -664 Chestnut Rdg Rd -Spg Vly 10977
(718) 777-7070 .. **Materassi,** Marco '95 -2809 Ditmars Blvd -Astoria 11105
(516) 931-2600 .. **Materazo,** Jos A '94 (Churbuck CJ&M PC) -43A E Barclay -Hicksvll 11801
(212) 267-7600 .. **Materna,** Jos A '75 (Solomon PBH&S LLP) -40 Wall -NY 10005
(631) 589-3322 .. **Mates,** Donald A Jr. '88 -4875 Sunrise Hwy -Bohemia 11716
(212) 242-8457 .. **Mates,** Irving I '55 -341 W 24th -NY 10011 **Fx:**333-0763
(212) 922-9250 .. **Matetsky,** Ira B '87 (Ganfer & S LLP) -360 Lex Av -NY 10017
(212) 259-8000 .. **Mateyaschuk,** Douglas W II '05 %Dewey & L LLP -1301 Av of Amer -NY 10019
(212) 489-1600 .. **Mathe,** Steven T '04 Deloitte Touche Tohmatsu -1633 Bway -NY 10019 **Fx:**489-1687
(212) 775-9002 .. **Matheke,** Cynthia A '86 (Lum D&P,LLC) -325 Bway -NY 10007
(516) 946-4567 .. **Mathers,** Allen S '74 -349 Stewart Av -Gdn Cty 11530 **Fx:**746-4513
(212) 259-8000 .. **Mathes,** Apryl '07 %Dewey & L LLP -1301 Av of Amer -NY 10019
(518) 487-7600 .. **Mathes,** Todd M '05 %Whiteman O&H LLP -1 Commerce Plz -Albany 12260
(212) 943-1233 .. **Mathew,** Julie K '03 %Malecki Law -11 Bway -NY 10004 **Fx:**943-1238
(631) 204-1981 .. **Mathew,** Richd M '81 -295 N Sea Rd -Southampton 11968 **Fx:**204-1986
(212) 403-1000 .. **Mathew,** Shaun J '08 %Wachtell LR&K -51 W 52nd -NY 10019
(631) 234-1500 .. **Mathew,** Suby '06 %Rubin & R LLC -1787 Vets Hwy -Islandia 11749
(631) 694-2300 .. **Mathews,** Alyson '05 %Lamb & B,LLP -534 Broadhllw Rd Bx9034 -Melvll 11747
(718) 838-7878 .. **Mathews,** Ann H '03 %Bronx Defenders -860 Crtlandt Av -Bronx 10451 **Fx:**665-0100
(212) 776-5000 .. **Mathews,** Blondine '93 NYC Housing Auth -250 Bway -NY 10007 **Fx:**776-5039
(212) 506-5000 .. **Mathews,** Danl A '76 (Orrick H&S LLP) -51 W 52nd -NY 10019
(315) 471-2188 .. **Mathews,** Danl F III '94 -913 Univ Bldg -Syracuse 13202 **Fx:**471-2138
(212) 225-2000 .. **Mathews,** James D '04 %Cleary GS&H -1 Lbrty Plz -NY 10006
(718) 250-1400 .. **Mathews,** Jeffrey A '04 %BZ Green -12 MetroTech Ctr -Brklyn 11201 **Fx:**250-1401
(315) 422-1152 .. **Mathews,** Jennifer E '97 SpclCnsl Costello C&F,PLLC -500 Plum -Syracuse 13204
(315) 477-7319 .. **Mathews,** Jos R '72 DMV -4671 Onondaga Blvd -Syracuse 13219
(716) 204-3300 .. **Mathews,** Karen L '81 MakMax HD LLC/Birdair,Inc -500 Essjay Rd -Amherst 14221 **Fx:**204-3302
(212) 351-4000 .. **Mathews,** Kristen '09 Gibson D&C LLP -200 Park Av -NY 10166
(212) 969-3000 .. **Mathews,** Kristen J '99 (Proskauer R LLP) -1585 Bway -NY 10036
(212) 504-6000 .. **Mathews,** Lambrina '00 %Cadwalader W&T LLP -1 World Fncl Ctr -NY 10281
(212) 310-8000 .. **Mathews,** Marie L '04 %Weil G&M LLP -767 5th Av -NY 10153
(212) 506-5000 .. **Mathews,** Nikiforos '97 OfCnsl Orrick H&S LLP -51 W 52nd -NY 10019
(315) 682-7585 .. **Mathewson,** George A '63 (G Mathewson,PC) -224 Fayette -Manlius 13104
(212) 998-0789 .. **Mathewson,** Rosemary '79 Stern School of Business -44 W 4th -NY 10012
(607) 778-2201 .. **Mathey,** Mary Beth '79 %Hon P Monserrate -Cthse -Bnghmtn 13901 **Fx:**778-2398
(716) 856-0041 .. **Mathias,** Paul W '78 -225 Bannard Av -Tonawanda 14150 **Fx:**856-1955

(516) 522-2565 .. **Mathias,** Scott L '90 %Greenfield & R -626 RXR Plz -Uniondale 11556 **Fx:**522-2566
(716) 853-5100 .. **Mathias,** Wm E II '71 (Lippes MWF LLP) -665 Main -Buffalo 14203
(518) 793-0722 .. **Mathias,** Wilson S '75 -726 Bay Rd -Queensbury 12804 **Fx:**793-0741
(212) 667-9046 .. **Mathies,** Blair H Jr. '91 Nomura Sec Intl -2 World Fncl Ctr -NY 10281
(212) 909-6000 .. **Mathieu,** Emily J '07 %Debevoise & P LLP -919 3rd Av -NY 10022
(718) 923-3329 .. **Mathieu,** Richd T '88 OTDA Fair Hearings -14 Boerum Pl -Brklyn 11201
(917) 658-0701 .. **Mathis,** Kimberly M '02 -515 Split Rock Rd -Syosset 11791
(212) 943-0280 .. **Mathis,** Sarah Marr '05 %McCanliss & E LLP -88 Pine -NY 10005
(212) 878-8000 .. **Mathis-McCullough,** Malora S '97 %Clifford C LLP -31 W 52nd -NY 10019
(914) 345-0005 .. **Mathless,** Scott L '96 Nesci K,PLLC -40 Saw Mill Rvr Rd -Hawthorne 10532
(212) 596-9000 .. **Mathrani,** Vikram A '09 %Ropes & G LLP -1211 Av of Amer -NY 10036
(212) 850-2800 .. **Mathur,** Abhishek '06 %Andrews K LLP -450 Lex Av -NY 10017
(212) 547-5400 .. **Mathus,** David L '87 (McDermott W&E LLP) -340 Mad Av -NY 10173
(212) 490-3000 .. **Mathwich,** Mary C '04 %Wilson EME&D LLP -150 E 42nd -NY 10017
(516) 705-5263 .. **Matiash,** Mark '03 -3115 Lng Bch Rd -Oceanside 11572 **Fx:**706-1659
(212) 702-3567 .. **Matin,** Esmat B '05 Rochdale Invstmnt Mgmt LLC -570 Lex Av -NY 10022
(212) 613-5000 .. **Matiychenko,** Irina '97 %Leg Assist Grp -450 W 33rd -NY 10001 **Fx:**750-0820
(212) 549-4508 .. **Matlin,** David F '93 Scripps Ntwrk -1180 Av of Amer -NY 10036
(212) 536-3900 .. **Matlin,** Robt S '86 (K&L Gates LLP) -599 Lex Av -NY 10022
(212) 803-3100 .. **Matlin,** Steven J '81 %Empire State Dvlmnt Corp -633 3rd Av -NY 10017
(212) 964-1890 .. **Matlin,** Wm S '98 %Hoffman & R,LLP -505 8th Av -NY 10018
(212) 424-0434 .. **Matorin,** Carol M '77 Limited Brands Inc -666 5th Av -NY 10103
(212) 277-5830 .. **Matorin,** Peter S '73 (Beldock L&H LLP) -99 Park Av -NY 10016
(212) 964-0499 .. **Matos,** Arturo W '83 -132 Nassau -NY 10038 **Fx:**619-2340
(212) 455-2000 .. **Matos,** Berta A '07 %Simpson T&B LLP -425 Lex Av -NY 10017
(516) 745-8310 .. **Matos,** Edgar '02 %Perez & V -333 Earle Ovngton Blvd Bx9372 -Uniondale 11553
(212) 340-0400 .. **Matos,** Maria '94 %Appllt Div 1st Dept -27 Mad Av -NY 10010 **Fx:**889-4412
(516) 931-8100 .. **Matos,** Renato N '09 %Capell BM&S,LLP -100 Jericho Quadrangle -Jericho 11753
(631) 845-2600 .. **Matozzo,** Francesco R '93 %Morenus CG&B -58 S Srvc Rd -Melvll 11747
(212) 980-9600 .. **Matra,** Rocco P '98 (Kaufman B&R) -120 Bway -NY 10271
(212) 610-6300 .. **Matras,** Todd A '01 %Allen & O -1221 Av of Amer -NY 10020
(914) 232-4921 .. **Matschke,** Sara Schepps '85 -1 Merritt Ct -Katonah 10536 **Fx:**232-6253
(516) 791-9642 .. **Matsil,** Melvin I '68 -756 Mulberry Pl -N Woodmere 11581
(212) 836-8000 .. **Matsis,** Vanessa G '08 %Kaye S LLP -425 Park Av -NY 10022
(845) 562-9100 .. **Matsler,** Michl J '84 (Rider W&F,PC) -655 Little Britain Rd -New Windsor 12553
(646) 252-2932 .. **Matson,** Regina R '82 NYC Transit Ofc of Labor Relatns -2 Bway -NY 10004
(212) 688-1408 .. **Matsoukas,** Amelia '70 (Matsoukas & M) -505 Park Av -NY 10022 **Fx:**688-1741
(212) 688-1408 .. **Matsoukas,** Peter N '70 (Matsoukas & M) -505 Park Av -NY 10022 **Fx:**688-1741
(212) 468-8000 .. **Matsubara,** Odessa L R '10 %Morrison & F LLP -1290 Av of Amer -NY 10104
(212) 670-0267 .. **Matsumoto,** Fumiko '96 Merrill Lynch -222 Bway -NY 10038
(212) 667-1627 .. **Matsumoto,** Miyuki '04 Nomura Resrch Inst Amer,Inc -2 World Fncl Ctr -NY 10281
(212) 705-7000 .. **Matsunaga,** Len '87 (Bingham M LLP) -399 Park Av -NY 10022
(212) 705-7000 .. **Matsuo,** Gene Y '66 OfCnsl Bingham M LLP -399 Park Av -NY 10022
(212) 796-8848 .. **Matsuo,** Joanne Aiko '02 %Klasko RS&S,LLP -317 Mad Av -NY 10017 **Fx:**297-1799
(315) 425-2700 .. **Matt,** Francis X III '02 OfCnsl Hiscock & B,LLP -One Park Pl -Syracuse 13202
(607) 722-5000 .. **Matt,** Ryan R '08 %C Garufi -68 Oak -Bnghmtn 13905 **Fx:**722-5626
(315) 334-5050 .. **Mattacola,** Gregory A '99 (Sammarco M&S,LLP) -217 N Wshngtn Bx725 -Rome 13442
(718) 389-2427 .. **Mattaliano,** Michl P '08 %Agostino & Assoc,PC -500 Kngslnd Av -Brklyn 11222
(716) 856-4022 .. **Mattar,** Brenda Ann '93 (Mattar D&G,LLP) -17 Court -Buffalo 14202
(716) 856-4022 .. **Mattar D'Agostino & Gottlieb,LLP** -17 Court -Buffalo 14202 **Fx:**856-5814
(716) 856-4022 .. **Mattar,** Lawr J '59 (Mattar D&G,LLP) -17 Court -Buffalo 14202
(716) 633-4300 .. **Mattar,** Norman J '61 -5792 Main -Williamsvll 14221
(716) 633-3535 .. **Mattar,** Wm K '89 (W Mattar,PC) -6720 Main -Williamsvll 14221 **Fx:**631-9804
(718) 590-2104 .. **Mattaway,** Lisa R '89 %DA -198 E 161st -Bronx 10451 **Fx:**590-6477
(518) 793-3843 .. **Matte,** Jeffrey C '89 (Matte & N,PC) -444 Glen -Glens Fls 12801
(518) 793-3843 .. **Matte & Nenninger,PC** -444 Glen -Glens Fls 12801 **Fx:**793-6963
(212) 506-5000 .. **Mattei,** Andrew '88 (Orrick H&S LLP) -51 W 52nd -NY 10019
(718) 983-8555 .. **Mattei,** Grace V '84 -1265 Richmond Av -Staten Isl 10314 **Fx:**983-7899
(212) 909-6000 .. **Mattei,** Ivan E '87 (Debevoise & P LLP) -919 3rd Av -NY 10022
(516) 505-0600 .. **Mattei,** Kevin A '03 (J McCormack,PC) -1035 Stewart Av -Gdn Cty 11530 **Fx:**505-0632
(718) 482-4965 .. **Mattei,** Suzanne Y '92 %DEC -1 Hunters Pnt Plz -LIC 11101 **Fx:**482-4962
(212) 848-4000 .. **Mattei,** Tania A '03 %Shearman & S LLP -599 Lex Av -NY 10022
(716) 852-2500 .. **Matteliano,** Jos A '77 (Augello & M LLP) -17 Court -Buffalo 14202
(212) 735-3000 .. **Matteo,** Jos A '06 %Skadden ASM&F LLP -4 Times Sq -NY 10036
(212) 698-1147 .. **Matteozzi,** Maria Soledad '06 %Alfaro-Abogados -150 E 58th -NY 10155 **Fx:**698-1143
(516) 712-4000 .. **Mattera,** Frank '92 (Milber MP&S LLP) -1000 Woodbury Rd -Woodbury 11797
(212) 730-7750 .. **Mattera,** Laura M '79 %Nicoletti GS&O,LLP -555 5th Av -NY 10017
(845) 942-1317 .. **Mattera,** Louis E '50 -19 Waldron -Stony Pnt 10980
(212) 728-8000 .. **Mattera,** Marshall J '09 %Willkie F&G LLP -787 7th Av -NY 10019
(212) 504-6000 .. **Mattern,** Elizabeth D '09 %Cadwalader W&T LLP -1 World Fncl Ctr -NY 10281
(212) 592-1400 .. **Mattes,** Dylan B '09 %Herrick,F LLP -2 Park Av -NY 10016
(914) 632-4150 .. **Mattesi,** Anthony '01 (A Mattesi,PC) -240 North Av -New Rchll 10801 **Fx:**632-4159
(315) 422-2052 .. **Matteson,** Adam R '00 -472 S Salina -Syracuse 13202
(212) 485-9600 .. **Mattessich,** Kevin M '86 (Kaufman DV&G,LLP) -100 William -NY 10038
(914) 376-3757 .. **Mattessich,** Sandra C '02 %Leg Srvcs -30 S Bway -Ynkrs 10701 **Fx:**376-8739
(516) 621-0222 .. **Matthes,** Julie '98 %GosmanLaw PC -55 Bryant Av -Roslyn 11576 **Fx:**621-3322
(212) 250-8180 .. **Matthew,** Keri N '99 %Deutsche Bank -60 Wall -NY 10005
(212) 569-1692 .. **Matthew,** Rubylette A '94 -148 Post Av -NY 10034 **Fx:**569-1969
(212) 848-4000 .. **Matthews,** Ann S '08 %Shearman & S LLP -599 Lex Av -NY 10022
(631) 324-5909 .. **Matthews,** Brian E '05 %MacLachlan & E LLP -241 Pantigo Rd -E Hampton 11937
(914) 323-7000 .. **Matthews,** Brian J '07 %Wilson EME&D LLP -3 Gannett Dr -White Plns 10604
(212) 336-0132 .. **Matthews,** Cynthia Anne '89 %SEC -3 World Fncl Ctr -NY 10281 **Fx:**336-1323
(212) 425-7200 .. **Matthews,** Danl S '07 %Kenyon & K,LLP -1 Bway -NY 10004
(212) 626-4100 .. **Matthews,** Edwin S Jr. '63 OfCnsl Baker & M LLP -1114 Av of Amer -NY 10036
(212) 696-6000 .. **Matthews,** Eileen P '86 (Curtis M-PC&M LLP) -101 Park Av -NY 10178
(518) 439-8311 .. **Matthews,** Elizabeth K '03 NYSARC,Inc -393 Delaware Av -Delmar 12054
(212) 258-7122 .. **Matthews,** Elizabeth M '94 %MTV Networks -1515 Bway -NY 10036 **Fx:**258-8358
(718) 254-7000 .. **Matthews,** Gail A '88 %US Atty -271 Cadman Plz E -Brklyn 11201 **Fx:**254-6479
(631) 283-2400 .. **Matthews & Ham** -38 Nugent -Southampton 11968 **Fx:**287-1076
(631) 351-3042 .. **Matthews,** James F '83 (Town Atty) -100 Main -Huntngtn 11743 **Fx:**351-3032
(718) 590-2000 .. **Matthews,** Janelle C L '08 %DA -198 E 161st -Bronx 10451 **Fx:**590-6477
(518) 402-9184 .. **Matthews,** Joan Leary '84 DEC -625 Bway -Albany 12233 **Fx:**402-9018
(516) 678-6500 .. **Matthews,** John A Jr. '81 Gallagher & M -55 Maple Av -Rockvll Ctr 11570 **Fx:**536-9593
(212) 277-6500 .. **Matthews,** John C '07 %Dickstein S LLP -1633 Bway -NY 10019
(518) 457-2070 .. **Matthews,** John E '90 %Dept of Tax & Fin -Bldg 9 State Campus -Albany 12227 **Fx:**457-6131
(212) 578-7422 .. **Matthews,** Jonathan F '02 %MetLife -27-01 Qns Plz N -LIC 11101
(212) 684-3900 .. **Matthews,** Joshua R '08 %Gottlieb R&R,PC -270 Mad Av -NY 10016
(212) 617-3525 .. **Matthews,** Kathryn E '99 Bloomberg LP -731 Lex Av -NY 10022
(212) 530-1800 .. **Matthews,** Kiowa Taos '06 Richards K&O LLP -1 World Fncl Ctr -NY 10281
(646) 557-5100 .. **Matthews,** Laurie Droughton '97 %Patton B LLP -1185 Av of Amer -NY 10036
(845) 733-2727 .. **Matthews,** Marcelle D '87 -60 Main Bx243 -Bloomngbrg 12721 **Fx:**733-2777
(212) 351-4000 .. **Matthews,** Marques B '09 %Gibson D&C LLP -200 Park Av -NY 10166
(631) 673-7555 .. **Matthews,** Patricia Loftus '88 -191 NY Av -Huntngtn 11743
(212) 267-6659 .. **Matthews,** Paul W '93 -305 Bway -NY 10007 **Fx:**732-2191
(516) 746-6000 .. **Matthews,** Russell G '79 Albanese Devlpmnt Corp -1050 Franklin Av -Gdn Cty 11530
(212) 237-1000 .. **Matthews,** Scott R '00 %Windels ML&M,LLP -156 W 56th -NY 10019
(212) 788-8107 .. **Matthews,** Terri C '86 Mayors Ofc of Ops -253 Bway -NY 10007
(516) 408-7030 .. **Matthews,** Victor L '05 %T Sherwood,LLC -300 Grdn City Plz -Gdn Cty 11530 **Fx:**408-7032
(212) 872-9800 .. **Mattiaccio,** Richd L '79 (Squire S&D LLP) -30 Rckfllr Plz -NY 10112
(914) 232-2242 .. **Mattice,** Jamie Kuflik '02 %PD Hoffman,PC -200 Katonah Av -Katonah 10536 **Fx:**232-2245
(607) 763-9200 .. **Matties,** Richd N '66 OfCnsl Levene G&T,LLP -BxF-1706 -Bnghmtn 13902
(716) 551-4931 .. **Mattimore,** Mary E '89 %NLRB -130 S Elmwood Av -Buffalo 14202 **Fx:**551-4972
(516) 241-7343 .. **Mattimore,** Timothy J '72 -Bx772 -E Islip 11730 **Fx:**(631) 277-8697
(716) 847-7958 .. **Mattina,** Jacqueline '86 Crime Victims Bd -65 Court -Buffalo 14202
(718) 720-5630 .. **Mattina,** Philip J '83 -334 Forest Av -Staten Isl 10301 **Fx:**720-8491
(716) 849-1333 .. **Mattingly,** Christopher S '92 (Lipsitz GSC LLP) -42 Delaware Av -Buffalo 14202
(212) 880-6000 .. **Mattingly,** Glen D '07 %Torys LLP -237 Park Av -NY 10017
(212) 536-3900 .. **Mattioli,** Eli R '72 (K&L Gates LLP) -599 Lex Av -NY 10022
(212) 345-1218 .. **Mattis,** J Michelle '04 Marsh & McLennan -1166 Av of Amer -NY 10036
(718) 275-1012 .. **Mattis,** Lawr W '91 Circle Of Confusion Ltd -10723 71st Rd -Frst Hlls 11375
(212) 323-0322 .. **Mattisinko,** Susan C '96 OppenheimerFunds,Inc -225 Lbrty -NY 10281
(718) 797-7380 .. **Mattiske,** Kristin A '04 Hon K Matsumoto -225 Cadman Plz E -Brklyn 11201
(212) 916-5615 .. **Mattison,** Chas E '84 %TIAA-CREF -730 3rd Av -NY 10017
(585) 419-8800 .. **Mattison,** Glenn D '90 %Harris B PLLC -99 Garnsey Rd -Pittsfrd 14534
(607) 734-5204 .. **Mattison,** Timothy K '84 (Personius MP&B) -150 Lk Bx146 -Elmira 14902
(315) 471-3151 .. **Mattison,** Zachary M '07 %Hancock & E,LLP -1500 AXA Twr I Bx4976 -Syracuse 13221
(212) 836-8000 .. **Mattli,** Corinne A '09 %Kaye S LLP -425 Park Av -NY 10022
(212) 808-6848 .. **Mattner,** Richd A '76 Rabobank Nederland -245 Park Av -NY 10167

(718) 353-5500 .. **Mattone,** Irene M '83 (Mattone MMMMM&T) -134-01 20th Av -Cllg Pnt 11356
(718) 747-6600 .. **Mattone,** James V '90 (Mattone & M) -214-20 41st Av -Bayside 11361
(718) 353-5500 .. **Mattone,** Jos M '55 (Mattone MMMMM&T) -134-01 20th Av -Cllg Pnt 11356
(718) 353-5500 .. **Mattone,** Jos M Jr. '87 (Mattone MMMMM&T) -134-01 20th Av -Cllg Pnt 11356
(718) 353-5500 .. **Mattone Mattone Mattone Mattone Megna & Todd** -134-01 20th Av -Cllg Pnt 11356 **Fx:**353-0704
(718) 353-5500 .. **Mattone,** Michl X '92 (Mattone MMMMM&T) -134-01 20th Av -Cllg Pnt 11356
(718) 353-5500 .. **Mattone,** Teresa A '89 (Mattone MMMMM&T) -134-01 20th Av -Cllg Pnt 11356
(718) 747-6600 .. **Mattone-McCabe,** Grovine Y '98 (Mattone & M) -214-20 41st Av -Bayside 11361
(212) 269-4900 .. **Mattoon,** John A Jr. '08 %Ford MEW&G,LLP -Wall Street Plz -NY 10005
(716) 856-5500 .. **Mattrey,** Colleen K '05 %Damon M LLP -200 Delaware Av -Buffalo 14202
(716) 852-1300 .. **Mattrey,** Wm H '71 (Amigone S&M,LLP) -350 Main -Buffalo 14202
(718) 579-3000 .. **Mattson,** Julia L '02 %Leg Aid -1020 Grnd Cncrs -Bronx 10451 **Fx:**588-2611
(585) 546-5530 .. **Mattson,** Rebecca A '07 Thomson West -50 Broad -Rchstr 14694
(914) 241-3026 .. **Mattson,** Robt N '64 -Cottage Rd -Mt Kisco 10549
(516) 742-2400 .. **Matturro,** Anthony '62 (Matturro & Assoc) -1025 Old Cntry Rd -Westbury 11590 **Fx:**742-2233
(516) 742-2400 .. **Matturro,** Anthony Jr. '98 (Matturro & Assoc) -1025 Old Cntry Rd -Westbury 11590 **Fx:**742-2233
(212) 697-3122 .. **Matty,** Jeffrey S '05 %Martin C&B LLP -220 E 42nd -NY 10017
(212) 813-5900 .. **Matty,** Lesley J '08 Fross ZL&Z,PC -866 UN Plz -NY 10017
(800) 416-5454 .. **Matty,** Rosaria C '90 (Fusco B&R) -180 Froehlich Farm Blvd -Woodbury 11797
(800) 416-5454 .. **Matty,** Rosaria C '90 (Fusco B&R) -3253 Route 112 -Medfrd 11763
(518) 449-3900 .. **Matula,** Brian W '03 (Cooper E&S,LLP) -39 N Pearl -Albany 12207
(845) 340-4300 .. **Matula-Evans,** Anna J '97 Matula-Evans Law Firm,PC -656 Aaron Ct -Kingston 12401 **Fx:**340-4310
(631) 499-9100 .. **Matura,** Marijana F '09 %Shulman K,LLP -510 Broadhllw Rd -Melvll 11747
(212) 653-8700 .. **Matus,** Gabriel G '01 %Sheppard MR&H LLP -30 Rckfllr Plz -NY 10112
(212) 858-1000 .. **Matus,** Wayne C '76 (Pillsbury WSP LLP) -1540 Bway -NY 10036
(212) 506-1700 .. **Matushaj,** Teresa '93 %Kasowitz BT&F LLP -1633 Bway -NY 10019
(516) 869-6344 .. **Matusiak,** James J '85 -1615 Nrthrn Blvd -Manhsst 11030 **Fx:**869-6345
(212) 741-4851 .. **Matusiak,** Wm J '97 Police Dept -130 Av C -NY 10009
(716) 854-1111 .. **Matusick,** Mitchell '53 (Spadafora & V) -2 Symphony Cir -Buffalo 14201
(518) 584-5050 .. **Matusik,** Donald M '73 -Bx464 -Saratoga Spgs 12866 **Fx:**432-3025
(518) 584-5050 .. **Matusik,** Donald M '73 -60 Loudonvll Rd -Albany 12204 **Fx:**432-3025
(716) 887-7902 .. **Matuszak,** Russell J '93 Healthnow NY Inc -Bx80' -Buffalo 14240
(718) 746-3440 .. **Matuza,** Albert R Jr. '10 %Sacco & F,LLP -141-07 20th Av -Whitestone 11357
(212) 935-3000 .. **Matvenko,** Boris '02 %Mintz LCFG&P,PC -666 3rd Av -NY 10017
(212) 456-0563 .. **Matyas,** Elena M '97 %Walt Disney -77 W 66th -NY 10023 **Fx:**456-6565
(914) 747-0543 .. **Matystik,** Walter F '82 -314 Marietta Av -Hawthorne 10532
(212) 492-3912 .. **Matz,** Deborah J '05 Deloitte & Touche LLP -1633 Bway -NY 10019
(914) 682-6884 .. **Matz,** Kevin '94 -50 Main -White Plns 10606 **Fx:**682-6887
(212) 279-2795 .. **Matz,** Nolan '88 -989 Av of Amer -NY 10018 **Fx:**378-2054
(646) 414-6816 .. **Matz,** Robt '98 Cnsl Lowenstein S PC -1251 Av of Amer -NY 10020 **Fx:**(973) 422-6879
(212) 244-4630 .. **Matz,** Steven J '01 (Katz & M,PC) -1350 Av of Amer -NY 10019 **Fx:**(646) 219-5717
(212) 530-5000 .. **Matz,** Thos J '00 OfCnsl Milbank TH&M LLP -1 Chase Manh Plz -NY 10005
(516) 742-4949 .. **Matza,** Chas '81 OfCnsl R Reisch -1 Old Cntry Rd -Carle Pl 11514 **Fx:**742-1977
(516) 594-8150 .. **Matza,** Jack D '80 (Ross & M) -265 Sunrise Hwy -Rockvll Ctr 11570 **Fx:**594-8108
(631) 656-8511 .. **Matza,** Jos '94 -20 Strongs Ct -Smithtwn 11787
(212) 227-5550 .. **Matza,** Morris E '55 -110 Wall -NY 10005 **Fx:**267-0402
(212) 478-7200 .. **Matzat,** Rosanne Thos '86 (Hahn & H LLP) -488 Mad Av -NY 10022
(212) 732-3200 .. **Matzye,** Patricia '89 Cnsl Carter L&M LLP -2 Wall -NY 10005
(845) 339-0729 .. **Mauceri,** Michl C '90 -195 Wall Bx3651 -Kingston 12402
(914) 682-7800 .. **Mauch,** Helen Collier '92 OfCnsl Zarin & S -81 Main -White Plns 10601
(585) 232-3730 .. **Maue,** Carol S '81 (Chamberlain D LLP) -1600 Crssrds Bldg -Rchstr 14614
(516) 248-5803 .. **Mauer,** Robt '66 -1325 Franklin Av -Gdn Cty 11530 **Fx:**877-7760
(212) 547-2640 .. **Mauer,** Sharon K '03 Northstar Realty Finance -399 Park Av -NY 10022
(845) 486-2209 .. **Maugeri,** Juliana '86 Hon G Marlow -10 Market -Poughkeepsie 12601
(212) 909-6000 .. **Maugue,** Pierre '96 (Debevoise & P LLP) -919 3rd Av -NY 10022
(212) 852-6092 .. **Mauhs,** Frederic M '88 WestLB AG -250 Greenwich -NY 10007 **Fx:**852-6148
(518) 234-3525 .. **Mauhs,** Peter M '59 -105 Union Bx129 -Cobleskill 12043 **Fx:**234-3525
(212) 661-1100 .. **Maul,** Anthony F '05 Pomerantz HG&G LLP -100 Park Av -NY 10017
(212) 638-1903 .. **Mauler,** Marilyn S '78 %Chase Manhattan Bk -55 Water -NY 10041
(516) 294-8844 .. **Maunz,** Danl M '05 %L'Abbate BC&C,LLP -1001 Franklin Av -Gdn Cty 11530
(212) 951-6561 .. **Maupin,** Diane G '81 %NYS Ed Dept-OLS -475 Park Av S -NY 10016 **Fx:**951-6573
(631) 852-1745 .. **Maurelli,** Theresa '88 %Surrogates Ct -320 Center Dr -Rvrhead 11901
(212) 838-4128 .. **Maurer,** Chas D '65 -75 Rckfllr Plz -NY 10019 **Fx:**697-2521
(516) 773-8585 .. **Maurer,** Ellen W '84 (Goldman & M,LLP) -475 Nrthrn Blvd -Gt Neck 11021
(212) 791-9730 .. **Maurer,** Gregory M '85 %PF Adams,PC -30 Vesey -NY 10007
(845) 896-5295 .. **Maurer,** Ira M '80 Maurer Law Firm,PLLC -300 Westage Business Ctr Dr -Fishkill 12524 **Fx:**896-5299
(212) 852-1000 .. **Maurer,** Jeffrey S '77 %US Trust Co,NA -114 W 47th -NY 10036 **Fx:**852-1310
(518) 445-2311 .. **Maurer,** Nancy M '79 %Law Clinic & Justice Ctr -80 New Scotland Av -Albany 12208
(212) 244-9500 .. **Maurer,** Richd H '94 (White and W LLP) -1 Penn Plz -NY 10119
(585) 753-4500 .. **Maurer,** Zachary S '08 DA -832 Watts Bldg -Rchstr 14614 **Fx:**753-4576
(212) 303-7100 .. **Maurice,** Guy '05 MKP Capital Mgmt LLC -600 Lex Av -NY 10022
(212) 529-5131 .. **Mauriel,** Michl J '99 (Mauriel K&T LLP) -151 1st Av -NY 10003 **Fx:**529-5132
(718) 442-8727 .. **Mauriello,** Louis J '66 -1 Edgewtr Plz -Staten Isl 10305 **Fx:**816-5483
(914) 242-9724 .. **Mauriello,** Mark A '85 (M Mauriello,PC) -Bx604 -Bedfrd Hlls 10507
(516) 671-2038 .. **Maurino,** Anthony J '73 -1 Schl -Glen Cove 11542 **Fx:**759-3419
(212) 947-4999 .. **Mauro,** Christopher C '93 (Camacho MM,LLP) -350 5th Av -NY 10118
(212) 644-4420 .. **Mauro,** Craig P '98 %Fabiani C&H,LLP -570 Lex Av -NY 10022
(516) 739-2900 .. **Mauro,** George '85 -72 Jericho Tpk -Mineola 11501
(516) 487-5800 .. **Mauro Goldberg & Lilling LLP** -60 Cuttermill Rd -Gt Neck 11021 **Fx:**487-5811
(631) 669-0921 .. **Mauro,** Jos M '96 -306 W McCall Av -W Islip 11795
(516) 487-5800 .. **Mauro,** Kenneth '80 (Mauro G&L LLP) -60 Cuttermill Rd -Gt Neck 11021
(212) 526-6356 .. **Mauro,** Maria R '03 Barclays Capital -745 7th Av -NY 10019
(718) 426-0698 .. **Mauro,** Michl A '85 -80-00 Cooper Av -Glendale 11385
(516) 328-8899 .. **Mauro,** Michl J '00 %Milman L Law Grp PLLC -3000 Marcus Av -Lk Success 11042 **Fx:**328-0082
(212) 335-9000 .. **Mauro,** Nicholas J '05 %DA -1 Hogan Pl -NY 10013
(631) 543-3663 .. **Mauro,** Reynold A '70 -353 Vets Mem'l Hwy -Commack 11725
(315) 793-8807 .. **Mauro,** Ricardo J '94 -Bx336 -Utica 13503
(516) 221-2266 .. **Mauro,** Russell D '89 -1414 Wantagh Av -Wantagh 11793 **Fx:**221-7272
(516) 328-2300 .. **Mauro,** Susan '97 %Abrams FFEGF&E,LLP -1111 Marcus Av -Lk Success 11042
(718) 466-3000 .. **Maury,** Rafael '94 %Civil Ct -1118 Grnd Cncrs -Bronx 10456 **Fx:**466-3006
(212) 683-3800 .. **Mauser,** Marc R '87 OfCnsl Dinkes & S,PC -112 Mad Av -NY 10016
(518) 587-5700 .. **Mausert,** Kurt G '89 -376 Bway -Saratoga Spgs 12866 **Fx:**587-0269
(518) 473-6873 .. **Mausler,** Craig R '84 %Div of Parole -97 Central Av -Albany 12206 **Fx:**473-6037
(212) 732-3665 .. **Mausolf,** Eric W '04 %Harmon L&R -42 Bway -NY 10004
(212) 705-7000 .. **Mautner,** Erin Kate '06 %Bingham M LLP -399 Park Av -NY 10022
(212) 909-9500 .. **Mautner,** Jordan H '03 %Wachtel & M,LLP -885 2nd Av -NY 10017
(212) 807-4758 .. **Mautner,** Scott A '92 Cnsl ImpreMedia LLC -1 Metrotech Ctr -Brklyn 11201
(607) 674-2191 .. **Mavady,** Kayphet '00 (Taylor & M) -5 N Main Bx713 -Sherburne 13460 **Fx:**674-4744
(631) 370-1100 .. **Mavashev,** Roman '03 %Eqty Sttlmnt Srvs -444 Route 111 -Smithtwn 11787
(585) 753-1380 .. **Maves,** Mark E '86 %Cnty Atty -307 Cnty Ofc Bldg -Rchstr 14614 **Fx:**753-1331
(212) 592-1400 .. **Mavica,** Gina M '03 %Herrick,F LLP -2 Park Av -NY 10016
(718) 777-1717 .. **Mavrelis,** Bill '92 -30-05 30th Av -Astoria 11102 **Fx:**204-2655
(516) 358-7200 .. **Mavrides,** Dean '96 (Mavrides M & Assoc,LLP) -3000 Marcus Av -Lk Success 11042 **Fx:**358-7250
(917) 777-4200 .. **Mavrides,** Michl F '93 (Bingham M LLP) -1 Bttry Pk Plz -NY 10004
(212) 742-1851 .. **Mavrides,** Pavlos Lazaros '97 Provident Grp -654 Mad Av -NY 10065
(212) 872-3650 .. **Mavridis-Sales,** Panayiota '87 KPMG LLP -345 Park Av -NY 10154
(212) 973-3886 .. **Mavrikos,** Zaharoula '05 USCR LLC -99 Park Av -NY 10016
(718) 777-0400 .. **Mavromihalis,** Theo '99 (Mavromihalis & P) -3403 Bway -Astoria 11106
(212) 253-6040 .. **Mavronicolas,** Anthony J '79 -915 Bway -NY 10010
(516) 596-4400 .. **Mavroudis,** Frank N '87 -146 N Central Av -Vly Stream 11580 **Fx:**596-4411
(315) 425-2700 .. **Mawhinney,** Donald M '52 OfCnsl Hiscock & B,LLP -One Park Pl -Syracuse 13202
(212) 848-1100 .. **Mawhinney,** Tamara Ann '94 %Perm Mission of Canada to UN -1 Dag Hmmrskjld Plz -NY 10017
(212) 506-1700 .. **Max,** David M '06 %Kasowitz BT&F LLP -1633 Bway -NY 10019
(212) 653-8700 .. **Max,** Theo C '85 (Sheppard MR&H LLP) -30 Rckfllr Plz -NY 10112
(212) 788-0987 .. **Maxey,** Brian G '01 %Law Dept -100 Church -NY 10007 **Fx:**788-0367
(212) 998-6164 .. **Maxfield,** Guy B '59 %NYU Law Schl -40 Wshngtn Sq S -NY 10012 **Fx:**995-4407
(212) 902-4087 .. **Maxfield,** Karen I '00 Goldman Sachs & Co -85 Broad -NY 10004
(212) 576-7000 .. **Maxfield,** Sandra E '96 %NY Life Ins -51 Mad Av -NY 10010 **Fx:**447-0569
(716) 692-2342 .. **Maxian,** Thos J '04 Twin City Ambulance -365 Fillmore Av -Tonawanda 14150
(845) 291-2670 .. **Maxim,** Cheryl E '87 %Childrens Rts Society -213 W Main Bx1002 -Goshen 10924 **Fx:**291-2679
(212) 801-3766 .. **Maxman,** Joel '84 %Michael L&R LLP -60 Columbus Cir -NY 10023
(607) 547-8772 .. **Maxson,** Bruce E '90 Pub Def -197 Main -Cooperstwn 13326
(631) 694-2400 .. **Maxson,** Lane T '88 (Hamburger MYK&M,LLP) -225 Broadhllw Rd -Melvll 11747
(914) 472-2300 .. **Maxwell,** Alexandra M '06 %Jones G,LLP -670 Wht Plns Rd -Scarsdale 10583
(518) 563-5945 .. **Maxwell,** Cheryl L '89 -30 Clinton -Plattsbrgh 12901 **Fx:**563-9363
(212) 909-6000 .. **Maxwell,** Elizabeth J '05 %Debevoise & P LLP -919 3rd Av -NY 10022
(631) 665-4512 .. **Maxwell,** George S '71 -60 Maple Av -Bay Shr 11706 **Fx:**665-4535
(716) 874-2111 .. **Maxwell,** Gregg S '90 -3080 Delaware Av -Buffalo 14217 **Fx:**874-0680

(212) 209-3050 .. **Maxwell,** Jaime M '09 %Reitler K&R LLC -885 3rd Av -NY 10022
(315) 435-2470 .. **Maxwell,** James P '82 %DA -505 S State -Syracuse 13202 **Fx:**435-3969
(212) 782-4632 .. **Maxwell,** James S '86 Mitsubishi UFJ Fncl Grp,Inc -1251 Av of Amer -NY 10020
(212) 319-1000 .. **Maxwell,** Joel M '05 %Quirk & B,PC -845 3rd Av -NY 10022
(518) 475-0016 .. **Maxwell,** John F '79 (Maxwell & V) -2 Normanskill Blvd -Delmar 12054
(716) 885-1300 .. **Maxwell,** John F '93 (Maxwell & M) -1230 Delaware Av -Buffalo 14209
(914) 457-2300 .. **Maxwell,** Judith H '99 (Kanterman & S,LLP) -50 Main -White Plns 10606
(212) 466-3753 .. **Maxwell,** Michl '91 1st Fncl Funding & Invstmnt Corp -142 W 57th -NY 10019
(716) 856-4000 .. **Maxwell,** Michl E '89 (Hodgson R LLP) -140 Pearl -Buffalo 14202
(212) 279-9200 .. **Maxwell,** Neil S '80 (Abrams FFEGF&E,LLP) -630 3rd Av -NY 10017
(212) 903-9000 .. **Maxwell,** Robin J H '87 (Linklaters) -1345 Av of Amer -NY 10105
(716) 845-3628 .. **Maxwell,** Suzanne M '88 Supreme Ct -92 Franklin -Buffalo 14202 **Fx:**851-3293
(518) 475-0016 .. **Maxwell & Van Ryn** -2 Normanskill Blvd -Delmar 12054 **Fx:**475-7576
(518) 463-3647 .. **Maxwell,** Woodrow J '71 -2017 10th -Rensselaer 12144
(516) 869-8201 .. **May,** Anne K '78 -26 Knolls Dr -New Hyde Pk 11040
(212) 819-8200 .. **May,** Chas D '10 %White & C LLP -1155 Av of Amer -NY 10036
(212) 455-2000 .. **May,** Christopher R '03 %Simpson T&B LLP -425 Lex Av -NY 10017
(212) 286-8585 .. **May,** Danl G '96 (Heidell PM&B,LLP) -99 Park Av -NY 10016
(718) 548-1717 .. **May,** Debra M '97 SAR Academy -655 W 254th -Bronx 10471
(718) 459-6000 .. **May,** Denise M '98 %Pennisi D&N LLP -97-77 Qns Blvd -Rego Pk 11374
(212) 277-4000 .. **May,** Gregory E '88 (Freshfields BD LLP) -520 Mad Av -NY 10022
(212) 318-6000 .. **May,** Jacqueline A '88 OfCnsl Paul HJ&W LLP -75 E 55th -NY 10022
(212) 201-2894 .. **May,** Jason D '02 Cnsl JD May,LLC -1 Lbrty Plz -NY 10006 **Fx:**201-6109
(212) 497-2804 .. **May,** Jennifer A '99 Fortress Invstmnt Grp LLC -1345 Av of Amer -NY 10105
(516) 746-8000 .. **May,** John F '01 OfCnsl Jaspan S LLP -300 Grdn City Plz -Gdn Cty 11530
(212) 752-8000 .. **May,** Laurence '76 (Cole SMF&L,PA) -900 3rd Av -NY 10022
(212) 966-6420 .. **May,** Lisa Dale '00 %Lwyrs For Children -110 Lafayette -NY 10013 **Fx:**966-0531
(845) 486-4200 .. **May,** Margo L '77 (Shaw PM&L,LLP) -21 Van Wagner Rd -Poughkeepsie 12603
(212) 509-9400 .. **May,** Marianne Gaul '08 (Cozen O) -45 Bway Atrium -NY 10006
(607) 272-3442 .. **May,** Michl R '85 (Adams TM&M) -301 Clinton Hse -Ithaca 14850
(516) 763-3200 .. **May,** Mitchel K '89 %S May & Assoc -255 Merrick Rd -Rockvll Ctr 11570 **Fx:**763-3243
(212) 998-9494 .. **May,** Patricia Ann '97 %NYU Cllg of Dentistry -345 E 24th -NY 10010
(212) 858-7107 .. **May,** Paul V '91 RBC Capital Mrkts Corp -1 Lbrty Plz -NY 10006
(718) 706-7114 .. **May,** Peter I '96 Fiduciary Ins Co of Amer -45-07 Davis -LIC 11101 **Fx:**729-7833
(212) 689-8808 .. **May,** Randi B '99 (Hoguet NR&K,LLP) -10 E 40th -NY 10016
(716) 433-5921 .. **May,** Richd F '72 (Smith SF&M) -131 East Av Bx540 -Lockprt 14095
(518) 581-8800 .. **May,** Robt J Jr. '88 (Lemery G LLC) -60 Railroad Pl -Saratoga Spgs 12866
(212) 805-0238 .. **May,** Robt W '08 Hon R Patterson Jr -500 Pearl -NY 10007
(716) 693-2335 .. **May,** Sabrina M '07 %Brick B&E,PC -91 Tremont Bx604 -N Tonawanda 14120
(212) 294-6700 .. **May,** Shannon G '10 %Winston & S -200 Park Av -NY 10166
(518) 449-5400 .. **May,** Shawn T '04 %Linnan & F,LLP -61 Columbia #300 -Albany 12210
(516) 763-3200 .. **May,** Sheldon '60 (S May & Assoc) -255 Merrick Rd -Rockvll Ctr 11570 **Fx:**763-3243
(516) 763-3200 .. **May,** Ted E '97 %S May & Assoc -255 Merrick Rd -Rockvll Ctr 11570 **Fx:**763-3243
(212) 553-0300 .. **May,** Wm L '89 %Moody's Invstr Srvc -250 Greenwich -NY 10007
(315) 749-7021 .. **Maya,** John A '93 -510 Bleecker -Utica 13501 **Fx:**749-7022
(212) 682-5700 .. **Maya,** Jos '91 (Maya M,PC) -261 Mad Av -NY 10016 **Fx:**697-4432
(212) 682-5700 .. **Maya,** Susan M '02 (Maya M,PC) -261 Mad Av -NY 10016 **Fx:**697-4432
(516) 296-7000 .. **Mayall,** Jaspreet '92 (Certilman BA&H,LLP) -90 Merrick Av -E Meadow 11554
(212) 297-6220 .. **Maybaum,** Gregory B '91 -420 Lex Av -NY 10170 **Fx:**479-2520
(518) 471-4800 .. **Mayberger,** Robt D '79 %Appllt Div 3rd Dept -Capitol Station Bx7288 -Albany 12224 **Fx:**471-4750
(212) 207-5100 .. **Mayberry,** Michl R '93 Conti Group Cos,Inc -277 Park Av -NY 10172 **Fx:**207-2980
(212) 293-9400 .. **Mayblum,** Jonathan I '88 %Lawr Ruben Co -600 Mad Av -NY 10022 **Fx:**293-9401
(212) 580-6500 .. **Maycher,** Dennis A '73 (DA Maycher,PC) -204 W 84th -NY 10024
(315) 471-5533 .. **Maye,** Hurclee '72 -3532 James -Syracuse 13206 **Fx:**478-4643
(212) 521-3500 .. **Mayefsky,** Allan E '79 (Aronson M&S, LLP) -485 Lex Av -NY 10017
(212) 836-8000 .. **Mayell,** Manvin '86 (Kaye S LLP) -425 Park Av -NY 10022
(212) 735-8600 .. **Mayer,** Alyssa J '07 Morrison C LLP -909 3rd Av -NY 10022
(718) 643-6555 .. **Mayer,** Amy J '97 %Marcus Attys -13 Greene Av -Brklyn 11238 **Fx:**643-9111
(631) 853-4161 .. **Mayer,** Anne E '06 %DA -N Cnty Cmplx Bldg 77 -Hauppauge 11788 **Fx:**853-4192
(212) 506-2500 .. **Mayer Brown LLP** -1675 Bway -NY 10019 **Fx:**262-1910
(212) 382-4686 .. **Mayer,** Carl J '89 Mayer Law Grp -1040 Av of Amer -NY 10018 **Fx:**382-4687
(914) 846-7000 .. **Mayer,** Carol S '85 %NY Life Ins -1 Rockwood Rd -Sleepy Hollow 10591 **Fx:**846-4755
(212) 450-4000 .. **Mayer,** Christopher '75 (Davis P&W LLP) -450 Lex Av -NY 10017
(518) 445-2311 .. **Mayer,** Connie '86 %Albany Law Schl -80 New Scotland Av -Albany 12208 **Fx:**445-2315
(212) 980-4500 .. **Mayer,** Daniella T '01 %Cohen L LLP -885 3rd Av -NY 10022
(585) 899-1414 .. **Mayer,** David F '85 (Harris COJW&L) -300 Linden Oaks -Rchstr 14625
(212) 964-5570 .. **Mayer,** David H '06 %Sacks & S -150 Bway -NY 10038 **Fx:**349-2141
(212) 557-6376 .. **Mayer,** Deborah A '83 -300 E 33rd -NY 10016
(718) 254-7000 .. **Mayer,** Deborah S '02 %US Atty -271 Cadman Plz E -Brklyn 11201 **Fx:**254-6479
(212) 684-3000 .. **Mayer,** Debra A '87 (Shatzkin & M,PC) -1776 Bway -NY 10019 **Fx:**684-5333
(212) 403-1000 .. **Mayer,** Douglas K '87 (Wachtell LR&K) -51 W 52nd -NY 10019
(516) 385-6595 .. **Mayer,** Douglas P '06 (Mayer & M LLP) -114 Old Cntry Rd -Mineola 11501 **Fx:**294-9510
(518) 533-3000 .. **Mayer,** Frank C '97 (Bond S&K,PLLC) -111 Wshngtn Av -Albany 12210
(914) 337-3033 .. **Mayer,** George R '74 -65 Pondfld Rd -Bronxvll 10708 **Fx:**337-1038
(212) 785-0282 .. **Mayer,** Gregory J '90 Ringler Assoc,Inc -50 Broad -NY 10004 **Fx:**785-0209
(631) 348-7600 .. **Mayer,** Harold B Jr. '78 %Cashin Assoc -1200 Vets Mem'l Hwy -Hauppauge 11788
(716) 877-4434 .. **Mayer,** James R '84 -1066 Englewood Av -Kenmore 14223 **Fx:**877-8243
(212) 684-6920 .. **Mayer,** Joel B '64 -295 Mad Av -NY 10017 **Fx:**972-8572
(516) 670-3200 .. **Mayer,** Joel R '97 Plant Payment -670 Lng Bch Blvd -Long Bch 11561
(646) 386-4408 .. **Mayer,** John-Paul V '94 %Hon B Allen -111 Centre -NY 10013
(212) 449-6847 .. **Mayer,** Juno A H '04 Merrill Lynch -4 World Fncl Ctr -NY 10080
(212) 355-7570 .. **Mayer,** Matthew W '73 %Park Twr Rlty -499 Park Av -NY 10022
(516) 557-2639 .. **Mayer,** Michl C '95 Darbian Media LLC -2487 Natta Blvd -Bellmore 11710
(914) 723-4182 .. **Mayer,** Michl F '42 -50 Popham Rd -Scarsdale 10583
(716) 849-6500 .. **Mayer,** Nicole Schreib '00 %Brown & T,LLC -14 Lafayette Sq -Buffalo 14203
(212) 272-7124 .. **Mayer,** Pamela A '91 %JP Morgan Chase -383 Mad Av -NY 10179
(585) 338-6353 .. **Mayer,** Patricia A '87 Bausch & Lomb -One Bausch & Lomb Pl -Rchstr 14604
(631) 853-4104 .. **Mayer,** Peter H '08 %DA -400 Carleton Av Bx9082 -Central Islip 11722 **Fx:**853-7838
(212) 318-3000 .. **Mayer,** Randolph J '82 (Fulbright & J LLP) -666 5th Av -NY 10103
(631) 864-7700 .. **Mayer,** Robt J '77 -142 Joralemon -Brklyn 11201 **Fx:**864-9298
(212) 969-3000 .. **Mayer,** Robt S '95 %Proskauer R LLP -1585 Bway -NY 10036
(631) 654-5134 .. **Mayer,** Robt W '75 (Mayer R&H PC) -178 E Main -Patchogue 11772 **Fx:**654-5252
(212) 971-7766 .. **Mayer,** Ronald C '75 SelfHelp Community Srvcs Inc -520 8th Av -NY 10018
(607) 273-4200 .. **Mayer,** Rosanne '79 (Miller M,LLP) -202 E State -Ithaca 14850
(914) 487-7330 .. **Mayer,** Saml B '73 Cnsl White and W LLP -427 Bedford Rd -Plsntvll 10570
(914) 487-7330 .. **Mayer,** Saml B '73 Cnsl White and W LLP -427 Bedford Rd -Plsntvll 10570
(212) 837-6000 .. **Mayer,** Theodor V H '78 (Hughes H&R LLP) -1 Bttry Pk Plz -NY 10004
(212) 715-9100 .. **Mayer,** Thos Moers '82 (Kramer LN&F,LLP) -1177 Av of Amer -NY 10036
(518) 474-5607 .. **Mayer,** Wm G '78 %Ofc Gnl Srvcs -Corning Twr ESP -Albany 12242 **Fx:**473-4973
(212) 735-3000 .. **Mayer-Cesiano,** Maxim O '07 %Skadden ASM&F LLP -4 Times Sq -NY 10036
(585) 815-0288 .. **Mayer-Dorociak,** Danielle M '04 %Rosicki R & Assoc,PC -26 Harvester Av -Batavia 14020 **Fx:**815-0299
(212) 715-9100 .. **Mayerfeld,** J Michl '94 (Kramer LN&F,LLP) -1177 Av of Amer -NY 10036
(516) 505-7715 .. **Mayerhofer,** Tara '06 FA DeSousa -24 Main -Hempstd 11550
(212) 593-6700 .. **Mayeri,** David A '95 (Aaronson RF&D,LLP) -757 3rd Av -NY 10017
(718) 643-8190 .. **Mayeri,** Israella F '91 %Family Ct -283 Adams -Brklyn 11201
(212) 227-9220 .. **Mayers,** Abraham J '00 -110 Wall -NY 10005
(212) 305-3279 .. **Mayers,** Beth Friedman '97 %Columbia PresbyterianMed Ctr -3959 Bway Babies Hsptl 2-N -NY 10032
(212) 975-2927 .. **Mayers,** Hazel-Ann F '00 CBS Inc -51 W 52nd -NY 10019 **Fx:**975-3930
(212) 250-5032 .. **Mayers,** Jonathan M '01 %Deutsche Bank -60 Wall -NY 10005
(212) 265-7200 .. **Mayerson,** Gary S '80 (Mayerson & Assoc) -330 W 38th -NY 10018 **Fx:**265-1735
(212) 685-7474 .. **Mayerson,** Harold A '67 (Mayerson SA LLP) -292 Mad Av -NY 10017
(212) 872-9800 .. **Mayerson,** Sandra E '97 (Squire S&D LLP) -30 Rckfllr Plz -NY 10112
(212) 685-7474 .. **Mayerson Stutman Abramowitz LLP** -292 Mad Av -NY 10017 **Fx:**685-1176
(212) 608-1900 .. **Mayes,** Adam C '01 Lovell SH LLP -61 Bway -NY 10006
(212) 922-1800 .. **Mayes,** Jessica H '09 %McKenna L&A -230 Park Av -NY 10169
(914) 995-3460 .. **Mayes,** Robt E '06 %DA -111 Martin Luther King Blvd -White Plns 10601 **Fx:**995-3363
(212) 836-8000 .. **Mayesh,** Jay P '73 (Kaye S LLP) -425 Park Av -NY 10022
(212) 270-2543 .. **Mayfield,** A Edw '00 JP Morgan Chase -245 Park Av -NY 10167
(518) 474-0871 .. **Mayhew,** Everett A Jr. '87 %DMV -6 ESP -Albany 12228 **Fx:**486-4485
(212) 225-2000 .. **Mayhle,** Timothy D '09 %Cleary GS&H -1 Lbrty Plz -NY 10006
(212) 278-1000 .. **Maylor,** Carrie L '09 %Anderson K&O,PC -1251 Av of Amer -NY 10020
(718) 339-7777 .. **Maylov,** Dinara G '00 -2370 Coney Isl Av -Brklyn 11223
(516) 681-1038 .. **Maymudes,** Carol Sue '82 -608 Woodbury Rd -Plainvw 11803 **Fx:**681-1038
(212) 239-5900 .. **Maynard,** Ava R '84 %Sabatini & Assoc -237 W 35th -NY 10001 **Fx:**279-1265
(914) 323-7000 .. **Maynard,** Cary '80 OfCnsl Wilson EME&D LLP -3 Gannett Dr -White Plns 10604
(212) 872-1000 .. **Maynard,** Douglass B '87 -One Bryant Park -NY 10036 **Fx:**872-1002
(212) 373-3000 .. **Maynard,** Edwin S '85 (Paul WRW&G LLP) -1285 Av of Amer -NY 10019
(212) 596-9000 .. **Maynard,** John '67 (Ropes & G LLP) -1211 Av of Amer -NY 10036
(917) 454-1100 .. **Maynard,** Lonene C '01 Police Dept -2 Lafayette -NY 10007
(518) 465-3553 .. **Maynard O'Connor Smith & Catalinotto,LLP** -6 Twr Pl -Albany 12203 **Fx:**465-5845

(845) 246-3666 .. **Maynard O'Connor Smith & Catalinotto,LLP** -Bx180 -Saugerties 12477 **Fx:**246-0390
(516) 869-1111 .. **Maynard,** Robin S '03 (Marchese & M,LLP) -47 Plandome Rd -Manhsst 11030 **Fx:**869-0697
(212) 735-3000 .. **Mayne,** James B '08 %Skadden ASM&F LLP -4 Times Sq -NY 10036
(212) 490-3000 .. **Mayo,** Celena R '01 OfCnsl Wilson EME&D LLP -150 E 42nd -NY 10017
(212) 373-3000 .. **Mayo,** David W '88 (Paul WRW&G LLP) -1285 Av of Amer -NY 10019
(518) 477-4025 .. **Mayo,** Gordon R '74 -139 Horizon Vw Dr -E Greenbush 12061 **Fx:**477-4025
(212) 962-5757 .. **Mayo,** Margaret H '78 (Gaffin & M,PC) -225 Bway -NY 10007
(914) 220-1900 .. **Mayo,** Mary Anne '82 (Nelson Law Firm,LLC) -1 N Bway -White Plns 10601
(914) 806-0904 .. **Mayo,** Stephen I '79 Cnsl Mayo Linoleum Works,LLC -721 E 133rd -Bronx 10454 **Fx:**813-2798
(347) 401-9580 .. **Mayo,** Steven D '88 %Appllt Term -141 Lvngstn -Brklyn 11201 **Fx:**(718) 643-7889
(718) 909-8538 .. **Mayol,** Anthony Jr. '95 -147 W 35th -NY 10001
(646) 220-8694 .. **Mayol,** Beatrice '99 -7839 147th -Flushng 11367
(212) 297-5800 .. **Mayor,** J Andres '06 %Day P LLP -7 Times Sq -NY 10036
(718) 554-0482 .. **Mayora,** Margaret '94 -20 Bay Street Lndng -Staten Isl 10301 **Fx:**887-8570
(212) 834-0600 .. **Mayouhas,** Eldar '05 %Gordon & S,PC -355 Lex Av -NY 10017
(718) 286-2000 .. **Mayr,** Edw G '76 %Leg Aid -120-46 Qns Blvd -Kew Gdns 11415 **Fx:**286-2286
(516) 593-0828 .. **Mayr,** John '63 -16 Cmbrdg -Malverne 11565 **Fx:**593-0828
(212) 513-3200 .. **Mays,** C Parkhill Jr. '01 (Holland & K LLP) -31 W 52nd -NY 10019
(212) 213-6996 .. **Mays,** Charlita '98 (Spears & I LLP) -51 Mad Av -NY 10010
(212) 250-7123 .. **Mays,** Sonya S '09 Deutsche Bk -60 Wall -NY 10005
(631) 273-8822 .. **Mays,** Tammy Renea '92 NYSUT -150 Motor Pkwy -Hauppauge 11788
(518) 786-2880 .. **May-Skinner,** Nancy E '90 %Fager & A,LLP -8 British Amer Blvd -Latham 12110
(212) 556-5187 .. **Maytal,** Itai '09 NY Times -620 8th Av -NY 10018
(212) 416-8000 .. **Mayuga,** Vilda I '04 %Dept of Law -120 Bway -NY 10271
(315) 428-5187 .. **Maywalt,** Roxane E '92 Natl Grid Srvc Co Inc -300 Erie Blvd W -Syracuse 13202
(212) 336-0133 .. **Maza,** Alan S '90 SEC -3 World Fncl Ctr -NY 10281 **Fx:**336-1323
(212) 872-9800 .. **Mazanec,** Danl C '09 %Squire S&D LLP -30 Rckfllr Plz -NY 10112
(212) 756-2000 .. **Mazarakis,** Akrivi '04 %Schulte R&Z LLP -919 3rd Av -NY 10022
(212) 227-9008 .. **Mazarin,** Brad E '91 -277 Bway -NY 10007 **Fx:**693-0368
(212) 267-8480 .. **Mazaroli,** David L '80 -11 Park Pl -NY 10007 **Fx:**732-7352
(212) 566-7188 .. **Mazawey,** Jennifer '99 Cnsl Genova B&G -115 Bway -NY 10006
(212) 742-1400 .. **Mazeau,** Robt G '88 -110 Wall -NY 10005 **Fx:**(866) 230-2001
(516) 683-5225 .. **Mazek,** Susan Chapman '89 IRS -107 Charles Lindberg Blvd -Gdn Cty 11530 **Fx:**683-5124
(212) 221-5700 .. **Mazel,** Arnold '68 (Goldberg WFG LLP) -1501 Bway -NY 10036
(212) 349-1668 .. **Mazel,** Geoffrey R '87 (Hankin & M,PLLC) -7 Penn Plz -NY 10001
(212) 335-4072 .. **Mazel,** Jos W '98 %DA -1 Hogan Pl -NY 10013 **Fx:**335-4152
(212) 906-1200 .. **Mazer,** Chas J G '07 %Latham & W -885 3rd Av -NY 10022
(212) 344-5400 .. **Mazer,** Jonathan '94 (Schlam S&D LLP) -26 Bway -NY 10004
(212) 299-2000 .. **Mazer,** Neil M '09 NYMEX -1 North End Av -NY 10282 **Fx:**301-4700
(516) 783-1050 .. **Mazer,** Peter M '79 -2437 5th Av -E Meadow 11554 **Fx:**783-4547
(212) 545-4722 .. **Mazer,** Rachel B '05 %Wolf HAF&H LLP -270 Mad Av -NY 10016
(516) 433-0830 .. **Mazer,** Steven H '81 -18 Fair Ln -Jericho 11753
(516) 741-6565 .. **Mazer-Marino,** Jil '91 OfCnsl Meyer SE&K,PC -990 Stewart Av Bx9194 -Gdn Cty 11530
(212) 859-8000 .. **Mazgalev,** Victoria T '10 %Fried FHS&J LLP -1 NY Plz -NY 10004
(646) 471-6181 .. **Mazhar,** Usman A '03 PricewaterhouseCoopers LLP -300 Mad Av -NY 10017
(914) 834-6363 .. **Mazin,** Donald S '60 -1415 Bstn Post Rd Bx308 -Larchmnt 10538 **Fx:**834-6417
(212) 698-3500 .. **Mazin,** George J '82 (Dechert LLP) -1095 Av of Amer -NY 10036
(914) 834-6363 .. **Mazin,** Lynne S '01 -1415 Bstn Post Rd Bx308 -Larchmnt 10538
(212) 506-1700 .. **Mazin,** Zachary W '04 %Kasowitz BT&F LLP -1633 Bway -NY 10019
(718) 855-9000 .. **Mazlin,** Margaret '97 %Cullen and D LLP -177 Montague -Brklyn 11201
(716) 855-2800 .. **Mazur,** Bethany L '09 %Mura & S,PLLC -14 Lafayette Sq #930 -Buffalo 14203
(212) 233-5340 .. **Mazur & Bocketti** -225 Bway -NY 10007 **Fx:**233-5346
(212) 686-7700 .. **Mazur Carp Rubin & Schulman PC** -1250 Bway -NY 10001 **Fx:**532-1425
(716) 286-4420 .. **Mazur,** Christopher M '97 %Law Dept -745 Main Bx69 -Niagara Fls 14302 **Fx:**286-4424
(212) 313-9012 .. **Mazur,** Danielle Greene '91 Law Journal Press -120 Bway -NY 10271
(212) 878-8000 .. **Mazur,** Joan B '82 Cnsl Clifford C LLP -31 W 52nd -NY 10019
(212) 683-7999 .. **Mazur,** Marilyn C '73 Legal Srvcs for Children Inc -271 Mad Av -NY 10016 **Fx:**683-5544
(518) 371-8888 .. **Mazur,** Matthew I '83 %Ianniello A&R,PC -805 Route 146 -Clifton Pk 12065
(212) 402-4100 .. **Mazur,** Matthew L '10 Ofc Appllt Def -11 Park Pl -NY 10007 **Fx:**402-4199
(212) 403-1000 .. **Mazur,** Robt B '74 OfCnsl Wachtell LR&K -51 W 52nd -NY 10019
(212) 686-7700 .. **Mazur,** Sayward '64 (Mazur CR&S PC) -1250 Bway -NY 10001
(212) 506-2500 .. **Mazur,** Terri A '06 (Mayer B LLP) -1675 Bway -NY 10019
(212) 233-5340 .. **Mazur,** Wayne J '86 (Mazur & B) -225 Bway -NY 10007
(212) 752-3380 .. **Mazura,** Bethany F '04 %NYC Dept Educ -52 Chmbrs -NY 10007
(866) 288-1271 .. **Mazurczyk,** Monika '90 -80 Broad -NY 10004 **Fx:**(732) 222-0388
(212) 964-7400 .. **Mazure,** David E '63 Smith MDWY&Y,PC -111 John -NY 10038
(212) 922-1080 .. **Mazurek,** Henry E Jr. '94 Cnsl Clayman & R,LLP -305 Mad Av -NY 10165
(212) 617-2503 .. **Mazyck,** Desmond Spencer '02 Bloomberg LP -731 Lex Av -NY 10022
(845) 565-9261 .. **Mazza,** Alison H '99 B Kulak -484 Temple Hill Rd -New Windsor 12553
(212) 688-5151 .. **Mazza,** Angelo E P '88 (Gibney A&F,LLP) -665 5th Av -NY 10022
(607) 273-6000 .. **Mazza,** Bruno A Jr. '52 %Mazza & M -307 N Tioga -Ithaca 14850 **Fx:**273-4110
(212) 284-7192 .. **Mazza,** Christina M '07 Enterprise Comm Partners,Inc -1 Whitehall -NY 10004
(607) 273-6000 .. **Mazza,** Edw A '78 (Mazza & M) -307 N Tioga -Ithaca 14850 **Fx:**273-4110
(518) 474-6530 .. **Mazza,** Guy R '90 %Dept Pub Srvc -3 ESP -Albany 12223
(212) 669-8349 .. **Mazza,** Karen M '83 %Comptroller-Bur Asst Mgt -1 Centre -NY 10007 **Fx:**669-3837
(212) 728-8000 .. **Mazza,** Leslie M '78 (Willkie F&G LLP) -787 7th Av -NY 10019
(585) 419-8800 .. **Mazza,** Monique F '09 %Harris B PLLC -99 Garnsey Rd -Pittsfrd 14534
(518) 886-4000 .. **Mazza,** Ral J '07 Ayco Co,LP -321 Bway -Saratoga Spgs 12866 **Fx:**886-4444
(646) 644-9597 .. **Mazzaferro,** Donna M '85 -1942 Richmond Ter -Staten Isl 10302 **Fx:**(718) 524-1003
(914) 225-4679 .. **Mazzagetti,** Elizabeth A '03 Morgan Stanley -2000 Wstchstr Av -Purchase 10577
(212) 788-0590 .. **Mazzalonga,** Stephen '05 %Law Dept -100 Church -NY 10007 **Fx:**788-0367
(718) 792-0444 .. **Mazzanobile,** Aiga N '89 %MHLS -1500 Waters Pl -Bronx 10461 **Fx:**597-7385
(914) 946-7200 .. **Mazzanti,** Diane M '80 (Maron & M) -1 N Bway -White Plns 10601 **Fx:**993-0251
(516) 571-3800 .. **Mazzapica,** Elizabeth H '08 %DA -262 Old Cntry Rd -Mineola 11501 **Fx:**248-9479
(212) 964-6611 .. **Mazzara,** Lauren M '02 %Lester SK&D -120 Bway -NY 10271
(631) 360-0600 .. **Mazzara,** Timothy F '87 (Mazzara & S,PC) -800 Vets Mem'l Hwy -Hauppauge 11788 **Fx:**360-0669
(866) 348-5819 .. **Mazzarella,** Bruce R '74 %SSA-ODAR -50 Fountain Plz -Buffalo 14202 **Fx:**(716) 551-4078
(585) 454-7145 .. **Mazzarella,** Frank III '08 %Gallo & I,LLP -39 State -Rchstr 14614
(516) 796-3150 .. **Mazzarella,** James '76 -734 Franklin Av -Gdn Cty 11530
(585) 428-5210 .. **Mazzarella,** Julie M '07 %Pub Def -10 N Fitzhugh -Rchstr 14614 **Fx:**428-2234
(212) 335-9000 .. **Mazzarelli,** Frank D '02 %DA -1 Hogan Pl -NY 10013
(845) 567-6406 .. **Mazzariello,** Michl '91 -Main Bx506 -Wallkill 12589
(718) 439-2901 .. **Mazzarisi,** Leonard J Jr. '86 -1203 Bay Ridge Pkwy -Brklyn 11228 **Fx:**439-2907
(718) 236-6600 .. **Mazzarisi,** Leonard J Sr. '51 -7302 18th Av -Brklyn 11204
(212) 906-1200 .. **Mazzaro,** Eugene P '00 %Latham & W -885 3rd Av -NY 10022
(212) 346-0045 .. **Mazzatto,** Kim E '99 %P Weitz & Assoc,PC -233 Bway -NY 10279 **Fx:**346-0876
(631) 363-8600 .. **Mazzei & Blair** -9B Montauk Hwy -Blue Pnt 11715
(914) 725-6060 .. **Mazzei,** Mary Ann Longobucco '02 New Age Title Agency Inc -700 Wht Plns Rd -Scarsdale 10583 **Fx:**725-2634
(212) 514-9190 .. **Mazzei,** Robt M '08 %Downing & P,PC -17 Battery Pl -NY 10004
(631) 363-8600 .. **Mazzei,** Timothy P '80 (Mazzei & B) -9B Montauk Hwy -Blue Pnt 11715
(212) 374-9495 .. **Mazzella,** John F '90 -979 Bay -Staten Isl 10305
(718) 236-9365 .. **Mazzella,** Nancy A '89 -69 Bay 7th -Brklyn 11228
(212) 599-0700 .. **Mazzeo,** Robt L '83 (Mazzeo S&B LLP) -708 3rd Av -NY 10017 **Fx:**599-8400
(516) 356-6508 .. **Mazzer,** Mark B '86 -2969 Post Av -Wantagh 11793
(212) 808-0444 .. **Mazzitelli,** Ricardo F '04 %Robbins & Assoc,PC -60 E 42nd -NY 10165 **Fx:**808-4150
(212) 768-4343 .. **Mazzola,** Bryan J '00 (Cantor E&M,LLP) -49 W 37th -NY 10018
(212) 490-3000 .. **Mazzola,** Jean-Claude '97 (Wilson EME&D LLP) -150 E 42nd -NY 10017
(516) 571-3800 .. **Mazzola,** Jennine B '04 %DA -262 Old Cntry Rd -Mineola 11501 **Fx:**248-9479
(212) 633-4209 .. **Mazzola,** Justin J '04 %Amnesty Intl -5 Penn Plz -NY 10001
(631) 853-7770 .. **Mazzola,** Louis E '68 %Leg Aid -400 Carlton Av -Central Islip 11722 **Fx:**853-4336
(212) 482-0001 .. **Mazzola,** Matthew P '08 %Russo K&T LLP -33 Whitehall -NY 10004
(212) 698-3500 .. **Mazzone,** Danl W '09 %Dechert LLP -1095 Av of Amer -NY 10036
(718) 780-7514 .. **Mazzone,** Jason D '98 %Bklyn Law Schl -250 Joralemon -Brklyn 11201 **Fx:**780-0393
(516) 433-1300 .. **Mazzone,** Lewis A '72 -420 Jericho Tpk -Jericho 11753 **Fx:**433-1341
(212) 701-3000 .. **Mazzone,** Peter T '10 %Cahill G&R LLP -80 Pine -NY 10005 **Fx:**269-5420
(646) 386-3935 .. **Mazzotta,** Rosanna E '03 Supreme Ct -100 Centre -NY 10013
(518) 452-0941 .. **Mazzotta,** Thos G '87 (Segel GM&S,PC) -9 Wshngtn Sq -Albany 12205
(518) 862-1200 .. **Mazzotti,** Victor L '83 (Martin H&M LLP) -Bx15141 -Albany 12212
(212) 606-4111 .. **Mazzucco,** David '91 Sotheby's Intl Realty -38 E 61st -NY 10065 **Fx:**606-7574
(718) 816-0700 .. **Mazzucco,** Ronald '74 -686 Forest Av -Staten Isl 10310 **Fx:**981-7388
(516) 746-3500 .. **Mazzuchin,** Robt S '97 (Brand G&B,PC) -600 Old Cntry Rd -Gdn Cty 11530
(518) 434-4377 .. **Mazzullo,** Donald S '78 (Harter S&E LLP) -111 Wshngtn Av -Albany 12210
(585) 232-6500 .. **Mazzullo,** Donald S '78 (Harter S&E LLP) -1600 Bausch & Lomb Pl -Rchstr 14604
(585) 428-2888 .. **Mazzullo,** Michl J '81 %Hon K Fisher -545 Hall of Justice -Rchstr 14614
(718) 519-0828 .. **Mbamali,** Ikechukwu A '93 (Mbamali & M) -4634 Wht Plns Rd -Bronx 10470 **Fx:**994-5652
(718) 519-0828 .. **Mbamali,** Olufunke Ayoku '96 (Mbamali & M) -4634 Wht Plns Rd -Bronx 10470 **Fx:**994-5652
(718) 923-4246 .. **Mbamara,** Oliver Obioma '00 %OTDA Fair Hearings -14 Boerum Pl -Brklyn 11201
(212) 713-1270 .. **Mbiti,** John M '99 UBS AG -1285 Av of Amer -NY 10019
(212) 773-4784 .. **Mbwa-Mboma,** Marcellin N '09 Ernst & Young LLP -5 Times Sq -NY 10036
(212) 326-3939 .. **McAchran,** Kathleen L '10 OfCnsl Jones D -222 E 41st -NY 10017
(845) 778-7588 .. **McAdam & Fallon,PC** -90 Scofld Bx500 -Walden 12586 **Fx:**778-2501
(845) 778-7588 .. **McAdam,** Gregory '72 (McAdam & F,PC) -90 Scofld Bx500 -Walden 12586
(845) 778-7588 .. **McAdam,** Timothy S '86 (McAdam & F,PC) -90 Scofld Bx500 -Walden 12586

(212) 406-5145 .. **McAdams,** Jeffrey C '90 -305 Bway -NY 10007 **Fx:**619-0714

(212) 909-5000 .. **McAdoo,** Nina E '99 KPMG LLP -757 3rd Av -NY 10017

(518) 452-8700 .. **McAlary,** John J '92 Board of Law Examiners -254 Wshngtn Av Ext -Albany 12203 **Fx:**452-5729

(516) 229-6000 .. **McAleavey,** Barbie T '00 %R Lau & Assoc -300 Jericho Quad Bx9040 -Jericho 11753 **Fx:**229-6167

(212) 825-1212 .. **McAleavey,** Jamie K '09 %Morrison M LLP -17 State -NY 10004

(212) 859-8000 .. **McAleavey,** Russell P '09 %Fried FHS&J LLP -1 NY Plz -NY 10004

(212) 331-4100 .. **McAlevey,** Catherine B '81 Family Independence Admin -180 Water -NY 10038 **Fx:**331-6295

(518) 647-5608 .. **McAlevey,** John F '51 -Bx309 -Jay 12941

(212) 701-3000 .. **McAlister,** Erin R '10 %Cahill G&R LLP -80 Pine -NY 10005 **Fx:**269-5420

(518) 402-0205 .. **McAlister,** Joyce P '84 %UIA Bd -Troy Atrium Bx15126 -Albany 12212 **Fx:**402-6208

(212) 674-0355 .. **McAlister,** Phroska L '83 -116 W 23rd -NY 10011

(845) 292-1128 .. **McAllister,** Elizabeth '81 -Bx261 -Liberty 12754 **Fx:**292-1128

(315) 701-0030 .. **McAllister,** G Robt '58 -Bx443 -Cazenovia 13035

(718) 731-7253 .. **McAllister,** Kevin L '93 -909 Sheridan Av -Bronx 10451

(347) 404-9133 .. **McAllister,** Lorna J '95 Civil Ct -141 Lvngstn -Brklyn 11201 **Fx:**(718) 643-3733

(845) 434-8200 .. **McAllister,** Michl D '92 %Resnick Supermarket Equipment -BxQ -Mtn Dale 12763

(212) 818-9200 .. **McAllister,** Michl J '66 (Satterlee SB&B LLP) -230 Park Av -NY 10169

(212) 751-2700 .. **McAllister,** Michl T '91 %JAMS -620 8th Av -NY 10018 **Fx:**751-4099

(585) 728-2110 .. **McAllister,** Patrick F '82 -31 Main Bx338 -Wayland 14572 **Fx:**728-2715

(212) 274-0920 .. **McAllister,** Paul J '76 -401 Bway -NY 10013 **Fx:**941-7108

(585) 728-2110 .. **McAllister,** Robt L '48 -31 Main Bx338 -Wayland 14572 **Fx:**728-2715

(516) 571-3800 .. **McAllister,** Ryan H '07 %DA -262 Old Cntry Rd -Mineola 11501 **Fx:**248-9479

(518) 434-0600 .. **McAllister,** Ryan T '03 %Boies S&F LLP -10 N Pearl -Albany 12207

(212) 243-1856 .. **McAlonan,** John P '81 Old Europe -315 Bleecker -NY 10014

(516) 536-0900 .. **McAlonan,** Raymond E '76 %Jacobson & S -510 Merrick Rd Bx46 -Rockvll Ctr 11571

(212) 732-8700 .. **McAloon & Friedman,PC** -123 William -NY 10038 **Fx:**227-2903

(516) 357-3000 .. **McAloon,** Sean '07 %Rivkin R LLP -926 RXR Plz -Uniondale 11556

(631) 665-3400 .. **McAlpine,** Bruce J '95 %Siben & S,LLP -90 E Main Bx149P -Bay Shr 11706

(212) 816-6000 .. **McAlpine,** Matthew J '02 Citigroup -388 Greenwich -NY 10013

(631) 261-8834 .. **McAlvin,** Michl G '01 %Ingerman S LLP -150 Motor Pkwy -Hauppauge 11788

(212) 302-2810 .. **McAnaney,** Edw G '64 -240 Mad Av -NY 10016

(516) 921-8600 .. **McAndrew Conboy & Prisco** -95 Froehlich Farm Blvd -Woodbury 11797 **Fx:**921-5728

(585) 987-2800 .. **McAndrew,** John K '91 (Woods OG LLP) -2 State -Rchstr 14614

(516) 921-8600 .. **McAndrew,** Kevin B '83 (McAndrew C&P) -95 Froehlich Farm Blvd -Woodbury 11797

(914) 946-1400 .. **McAndrew,** Mark F '95 (Vouté LM&C,LLP) -170 Hmltn Av -White Plns 10601

(315) 349-8666 .. **McAndrew,** Michl R '97 Oswego Cnty Ct -39 Churchill Rd -Oswego 13126 **Fx:**349-8669

(516) 481-3121 .. **McAndrews & Christiansen** -141 Jackson -Hempstd 11550

(212) 261-8000 .. **McAndrews,** John G '75 (Mendes & M,LLP) -750 7th Av -NY 10019

(212) 244-4664 .. **McAnnany,** Kelly J '06 NY Lawyers Pub Intrst -151 W 30th -NY 10001 **Fx:**244-4570

(718) 340-4348 .. **McArdle,** Andrea L '79 CUNY Schl of Law -6521 Main -Flushng 11367

(718) 237-3400 .. **McArdle,** Casey A '98 %J Barrett & Assoc -353 2nd -Brklyn 11215 **Fx:**222-5858

(212) 210-9542 .. **McArdle,** Christopher L '10 %Alston & B LLP -90 Park Av -NY 10016

(315) 448-4800 .. **McArdle,** Edw F '84 %Dept of Law -615 Erie Blvd W -Syracuse 13204 **Fx:**448-4853

(877) 711-3994 .. **McArdle,** Gia C '93 -300 Grdn City Plz -Gdn Cty 11530

(212) 964-6611 .. **McArdle,** Kevin J '04 %Lester SK&D -120 Bway -NY 10271

(315) 376-5366 .. **McArdle,** Kevin M '83 %Hon C Merrell -7660 N State -Lowvll 13367

(518) 481-5000 .. **McArdle,** Matthew H '03 Fischer B&M -Cntry Clb Rd Bx420 -Malone 12953

(212) 633-3952 .. **McArdle,** Maureen '82 Elsevier Inc -360 Park Av S -NY 10010

(718) 923-4206 .. **McArdle,** Thos J '91 %OTDA Fair Hearings -14 Boerum Pl -Brklyn 11201

(212) 891-1600 .. **McArn,** Heather Dolan '93 SpclCnsl Jenner & B LLP -919 3rd Av -NY 10022

(718) 739-6400 .. **McArthur,** Charmaine M A '06 DHCR -92-31 Union Hall -Jamaica 11433 **Fx:**262-7938

(212) 558-4000 .. **McArthur,** Kathleen S '08 %Sullivan & C LLP -125 Broad -NY 10004

(631) 577-7724 .. **McArthur,** Richd P '70 K Dodson -100 Baylis Rd -Melvll 11747 **Fx:**577-7199

(212) 474-1000 .. **McArthur,** Stephen C '08 %Cravath S&M LLP -825 8th Av -NY 10019

(212) 474-1000 .. **McAtee,** Darin P '93 (Cravath S&M LLP) -825 8th Av -NY 10019

(212) 790-9217 .. **McAulay,** Lloyd '60 Cnsl Cowan L&L,PC -1133 Av of Amer -NY 10036

(212) 335-4500 .. **McAuley,** Beth K '05 %DLA Piper LLP -1251 Av of Amer -NY 10020

(716) 676-5524 .. **McAuley,** James A I IV '05 -4 S Main -Franklinvll 14737 **Fx:**676-3541

(212) 807-5838 .. **McAuley,** Jolene M '03 Disney Publishing -114 5th Av -NY 10011

(212) 490-3000 .. **McAuley-Parrish,** Yashana F '02 %Wilson EME&D LLP -150 E 42nd -NY 10017

(212) 319-5240 .. **McAuliffe,** Chas H '70 OfCnsl Flicker G & Assoc,LLP -45 Bway -NY 10006

(516) 663-6600 .. **McAuliffe,** Danl L '02 %Ruskin MF,PC -1425 RXR Plz -Uniondale 11556

(212) 418-0525 .. **McAuliffe,** E Timothy '67 OfCnsl Morris & M LLP -767 3rd Av -NY 10017 **Fx:**755-4476

(212) 553-9232 .. **McAuliffe,** E Timothy Jr. '99 Cochran Firm -233 Bway -NY 10279

(518) 762-0106 .. **McAuliffe,** J Gerard Jr. '89 -55 E Main -Johnstwn 12095 **Fx:**762-0122

(315) 425-2700 .. **McAuliffe,** Kevin R '77 (Hiscock & B,LLP) -One Park Pl -Syracuse 13202

(631) 465-0044 .. **McAuliffe,** Michl G '92 -48 S Srvc Rd -Melvll 11747 **Fx:**465-0045

(718) 204-0440 .. **McAuliffe,** Patrick J '99 -40-16 31st Av -Astoria 11103 **Fx:**204-0440

(315) 422-1391 .. **McAuliffe,** Sharon A '93 (Green & S,PLLC) -One Lincoln Ctr #900 -Syracuse 13202

(212) 878-8000 .. **McAvan,** Debbie '06 %Clifford C LLP -31 W 52nd -NY 10019

(631) 243-4516 .. **McAvey,** Joanne S '82 -1641 Deer Prk Av -Deer Pk 11729

(212) 452-9188 .. **McAvoy & Banta** -322 E 86th -NY 10028 **Fx:**452-9190

(212) 940-3112 .. **McAvoy,** Danl L '04 %Nixon P LLP -437 Mad Av -NY 10022

(212) 643-4760 .. **McAvoy,** Jerome V '77 NYS Ed Dept -116 W 32nd -NY 10001

(718) 763-0275 .. **McBain,** Alexander R '92 -1409 E 99th -Brklyn 11236 **Fx:**763-0275

(914) 235-3200 .. **McBain,** Chas E '06 %Pelican Mgmt -524 North Av -New Rchll 10801

(212) 656-6805 .. **McBennett,** Cindy M '98 NYSE Euronext -20 Broad -NY 10005

(212) 751-9800 .. **McBrayer,** Martha Martin '97 (Morelli R PC) -950 3rd Av -NY 10022

(212) 972-1000 .. **McBrearty,** Russell J '09 %London F LLP -59 Maiden Ln -NY 10038

(516) 364-1095 .. **McBreen & Kopko** -500 N Bway -Jericho 11753 **Fx:**364-0612

(212) 326-3939 .. **McBride,** Alexander P '09 %Jones D -222 E 41st -NY 10017

(518) 474-4552 .. **McBride,** Ann E '04 %Insurance Dept -99 Wshngtn Av -Albany 12257 **Fx:**473-4600

(516) 296-7000 .. **McBride,** Corinne D '06 %Certilman BA&H,LLP -90 Merrick Av -E Meadow 11554

(212) 306-1000 .. **McBride,** Courtney A '03 %Amer Stock Exch -86 Trinity Pl -NY 10006

(212) 268-5136 .. **McBride,** David F '83 (Harwood L) -350 5th Av -NY 10118

(212) 258-4000 .. **McBride,** Douglas J '86 %Siemens Corp -153 E 53rd -NY 10022 **Fx:**767-0580

(212) 267-8135 .. **McBride,** H Colin '75 -74 Reade -NY 10007 **Fx:**(914) 499-7693

(914) 862-4400 .. **McBride,** John B '93 -132 Old Post Rd N -Croton-On-Hud 10520 **Fx:**271-2184

(212) 578-2211 .. **McBride,** Jos '88 %MetLife -27-01 Qns Plz N -LIC 11101

(607) 337-1745 .. **McBride,** Jos A '84 DA -5 Court -Norwich 13815 **Fx:**337-1746

(518) 402-9011 .. **McBride,** Mary T '88 %DEC -625 Bway -Albany 12233 **Fx:**402-9018

(212) 455-2000 .. **McBride,** Matthew G '07 %Simpson T&B LLP -425 Lex Av -NY 10017

(516) 747-1080 .. **McBride,** Maureen '93 -114 Old Cntry Rd -Mineola 11501

(212) 248-8800 .. **McBride,** Meredith F '09 %Callan KB&B LLP -1 Whitehall -NY 10004

(212) 262-2390 .. **McBride,** Michl X '79 (Connell F LLP) -888 7th Av -NY 10106

(631) 845-2600 .. **McBride,** Paul '90 Morenus CG&B -58 S Srvc Rd -Melvll 11747

(607) 336-1070 .. **McBride,** Peter J '64 -16 Front -Norwich 13815 **Fx:**336-1078

(631) 852-1749 .. **McBride,** Scott P '86 %Surrogates Ct -320 Center Dr -Rvrhead 11901

(212) 906-1200 .. **McBride,** Stephen P '07 %Latham & W -885 3rd Av -NY 10022

(845) 562-3262 .. **McBride Gaillard,** Jacqueline '97 (Cocchia & G) -3262 Route 9W -New Windsor 12553 **Fx:**562-6272

(212) 661-1151 .. **McBurney,** Margret M '06 %Marin G LLP -40 Wall -NY 10005

(212) 720-3402 .. **McCabe,** Alison R '05 Dept City Planning -22 Reade -NY 10007

(212) 980-9600 .. **McCabe,** Allison T '09 %Kaufman B&R -120 Bway -NY 10271

(716) 858-2200 .. **McCabe,** Amy M '00 %Cnty Atty -95 Franklin -Buffalo 14202 **Fx:**858-2281

(212) 447-5500 .. **McCabe,** Christopher Patrick '96 (Quinn M LLP) -274 Mad Av -NY 10016 **Fx:**880-2081

(516) 741-6266 .. **McCabe Collins McGeough & Fowler,LLP** -346 Westbury Av Bx9000 -Carle Pl 11514 **Fx:**873-9496

(716) 674-1000 .. **McCabe,** Dale J '73 -976-A Union Rd -W Seneca 14224 **Fx:**674-1005

(845) 454-3441 .. **McCabe,** Danl J '81 -42 Catharine -Poughkeepsie 12601

(516) 741-6266 .. **McCabe,** Danl P '03 %McCabe CM&F,LLP -346 Westbury Av Bx9000 -Carle Pl 11514

(212) 728-8000 .. **McCabe,** David J '84 (Willkie F&G LLP) -787 7th Av -NY 10019

(607) 721-8778 .. **McCabe,** Dennis C '82 %Dept of Law -44 Hawley -Bnghmtn 13901 **Fx:**721-8789

(516) 228-1300 .. **McCabe,** Edw G '89 SpclCnsl Sahn WC&B,PLLC -333 Earle Ovngton Blvd -Uniondale 11553

(718) 520-3740 .. **McCabe,** Eileen J '77 %Supreme Ct -88-11 Sutphin Blvd -Jamaica 11435

(212) 261-8000 .. **McCabe,** Eileen T '88 (Mendes & M,LLP) -750 7th Av -NY 10019

(917) 237-2904 .. **McCabe,** Elizabeth Crutcher '02 Axiom Legal Solutions -75 Spring -NY 10012

(212) 373-3000 .. **McCabe,** Elizabeth Gallagher '07 %Paul WRW&G LLP -1285 Av of Amer -NY 10019

(212) 458-3262 .. **McCabe,** Eric A '06 AIG Domestic Claims Inc -175 Water -NY 10038

(800) 416-5454 .. **McCabe,** Erin K '94 (Fusco B&R) -626 RXR Plz -Uniondale 11553

(800) 416-5454 .. **McCabe,** Erin K '94 (Fusco B&R) -3253 Route 112 -Medfrd 11763

(800) 416-5454 .. **McCabe,** Erin K '94 (Fusco B&R) -80-02 Kew Grdns Rd -Kew Gdns 11415

(800) 416-5454 .. **McCabe,** Erin K '94 (Fusco B&R) -180 Froehlich Farm Blvd -Woodbury 11797

(800) 416-5454 .. **McCabe,** Erin K '94 (Fusco B&R) -353 Vets Mem'l Hwy -Commack 11725

(212) 248-7200 .. **McCabe & Flynn,LLP** -1 Whitehall -NY 10004 **Fx:**248-2365

(212) 757-6233 .. **McCabe,** Gerard G '91 -10 Rckfllr Plz -NY 10020

(212) 371-1000 .. **McCabe,** James P '87 Cnsl NY Archdiocese -1011 1st Av -NY 10022 **Fx:**371-3288

(516) 739-0000 .. **McCabe,** Jos F '01 Martyn T&M -330 Old Cntry Rd -Mineola 11501

(212) 635-6601 .. **McCabe,** Kathleen Blake '02 %Bk of NY Mellon -1 Wall -NY 10286

(212) 916-3455 .. **McCabe,** Kevin P '93 %Lexis/Nexis -125 Park Av -NY 10017 **Fx:**309-8187

(845) 486-6800 .. **McCabe & Mack LLP** -63 Wshngtn Bx509 -Poughkeepsie 12602 **Fx:**486-7621

(716) 858-2424 .. **McCabe,** Mara L '04 %DA -25 Delaware Av -Buffalo 14202 **Fx:**858-7425
(212) 408-7713 .. **McCabe,** Mary Ellen '85 %Bk Of NY -1290 Av of Amer -NY 10104
(585) 880-9828 .. **McCabe,** Mary M '89 -674 Quaker Meeting House Rd -Honeoye Fls 14472
(315) 689-7256 .. **McCabe,** Matthew C '88 %North Main Cnsltng -20 N Main Bx921 -Jordan 13080
(716) 843-5700 .. **McCabe,** Michl L '00 %US Atty -138 Delaware Av -Buffalo 14202 **Fx:**551-3052
(212) 763-6800 .. **McCabe,** Monica P '86 (Vandenberg & F,LLP) -60 E 42nd -NY 10165
(212) 728-8000 .. **McCabe,** Nancy Kessler '94 %Willkie F&G LLP -787 7th Av -NY 10019
(212) 697-6555 .. **McCabe,** Orla J '08 %Biedermann RH&R -570 Lex Av -NY 10022
(212) 696-5500 .. **McCabe,** Peter M '61 -112 Mad Av -NY 10016
(716) 566-1300 .. **McCabe,** Raymond N '84 (Hiscock & B,LLP) -1100 M&T Ctr -Buffalo 14203
(212) 270-8484 .. **McCabe,** Robt O '79 JP Morgan Chase & Co -270 Park Av -NY 10017
(212) 335-9000 .. **McCabe,** Robin A '90 %DA -1 Hogan Pl -NY 10013
(516) 741-6266 .. **McCabe,** Stephen M '65 (McCabe CM&F,LLP) -346 Westbury Av Bx9000 -Carle Pl 11514
(718) 325-4200 .. **McCabe,** Terrence M '67 (Blauman & M) -4234 Vireo Av -Bronx 10470
(212) 696-6000 .. **McCabe,** Timothy N '02 %Curtis M-PC&M LLP -101 Park Av -NY 10178
(212) 349-6460 .. **McCabe,** Tracy Lynn '91 %NYPIRG -9 Murray -NY 10007 **Fx:**349-1366
(914) 636-8900 .. **McCabe Weisberg & Conway,PC** -145 Huguenot -New Rchll 10801 **Fx:**636-8901
(516) 571-2684 .. **McCabe,** Wm '02 %Hon E McCabe -100 Supreme Ct Dr -Mineola 11501
(718) 897-2211 .. **McCabe,** Wm G '00 %N Kalra -100-15 Qns Blvd -Frst Hlls 11375
(212) 596-9000 .. **McCabe,** Wm J '89 (Ropes & G LLP) -1211 Av of Amer -NY 10036
(212) 668-2808 .. **McCabe,** Wm J '98 Openheimer & Co,Inc -125 Broad -NY 10004
(716) 856-3500 .. **McCafferty,** Brendan P '93 SpclCnsl Magavern MG LLP -1100 Rand Bldg -Buffalo 14203
(212) 248-8800 .. **McCafferty,** Jessica '09 %Callan KB&B LLP -1 Whitehall -NY 10004
(716) 845-2657 .. **McCafferty,** Karen M '81 Buffalo City Ct -50 Delaware Av -Buffalo 14202
(315) 781-1465 .. **McCafferty,** Keith '86 %Leg Assistance -361 S Main -Geneva 14456 **Fx:**781-2565
(212) 859-8000 .. **McCafferty,** Todd '08 %Fried FHS&J LLP -1 NY Plz -NY 10004
(718) 326-6300 .. **McCafferty,** Wm '64 %Crosscounty Federal Svngs Bk -79-21 Metro Av -Middl Vllg 11379 **Fx:**326-6347
(212) 730-8133 .. **McCaffery,** Margaret C '03 %Gunderson DSVF&H,LLP -220 W 42nd -NY 10036
(631) 549-1938 .. **McCaffery,** Suzanne Liberti '04 Follick & B,PC -33 Walt Whitman Rd -Huntngtn Sta 11746
(516) 294-8844 .. **McCaffery,** Wm T '97 (L'Abbate BC&C,LLP) -1001 Franklin Av -Gdn Cty 11530
(212) 447-7575 .. **McCaffrey,** Brian '85 (Leffler M&M LLC) -200 Mad Av -NY 10016 **Fx:**202-4229
(212) 310-8000 .. **McCaffrey,** Carlyn S '74 (Weil G&M LLP) -767 5th Av -NY 10153
(585) 243-0313 .. **McCaffrey,** Gregory J '02 %Jones & S -31 Main -Geneseo 14454 **Fx:**243-3625
(212) 992-8182 .. **McCaffrey,** John C '95 New York Univ School of Law -40 Wshngtn Sq S -NY 10012
(607) 273-3339 .. **McCaffrey,** John S '88 %Williamson C&S -317 N Tioga Bx126 -Ithaca 14850
(718) 855-9000 .. **McCaffrey,** Kevin C '01 %Cullen and D LLP -177 Montague -Brklyn 11201
(212) 265-6888 .. **McCaffrey,** Kevin J '85 Cnsl Porzio B&N,PC -156 W 56th -NY 10019
(718) 558-8352 .. **McCaffrey,** Kevin P '89 %LIRR -Jamaica Station -Jamaica 11435 **Fx:**558-8211
(845) 634-3696 .. **McCaffrey,** M Lynn '85 OfCnsl I Becker,LLC -49 Maple Av Bx796 -New Cty 10956 **Fx:**634-3019
(212) 336-8000 .. **McCaffrey,** Norajean '03 %Amster R&E -90 Park Av -NY 10016
(212) 227-0347 .. **McCaffrey,** Patrick J '91 %Weiss W&W,PC -25 Park Pl -NY 10007
(212) 446-4800 .. **McCaffrey,** Ryan A '07 %Kirkland & E LLP -153 E 53rd -NY 10022
(718) 423-4200 .. **McCaffrey,** Sean F '92 -38-50 Bell Blvd -Bayside 11361
(718) 403-1172 .. **McCaffrey,** Stephen W '88 %National Grid -1 MetroTech Ctr -Brklyn 11201
(212) 506-1700 .. **McCaffrey,** Thos D '08 %Kasowitz BT&F LLP -1633 Bway -NY 10019
(212) 520-6089 .. **McCaffrey,** Thos P '85 (Meloni & M,PC) -1515 Bway -NY 10036 **Fx:**(917) 210-3758
(718) 444-5010 .. **Mc Cahey,** John P '59 -2640 E 63rd -Brklyn 11234
(212) 478-7200 .. **McCahey,** John P '80 (Hahn & H LLP) -488 Mad Av -NY 10022
(718) 361-1514 .. **McCall,** Brian J '92 %N Isserlis -36-01 43rd Av -LIC 11101 **Fx:**(347) 418-3839
(212) 450-4000 .. **McCall,** Christopher L '08 %Davis P&W LLP -450 Lex Av -NY 10017
(347) 404-9133 .. **McCall,** James P '76 %Civil Ct -141 Lvngstn -Brklyn 11201 **Fx:**(718) 643-3733
(212) 858-1000 .. **McCall,** Jennifer Jordan '83 (Pillsbury WSP LLP) -1540 Bway -NY 10036
(212) 506-1700 .. **McCall,** Katrina R '05 Kasowitz BT&F LLP -1633 Bway -NY 10019
(212) 474-1000 .. **McCall,** Vicki '09 %Cravath S&M LLP -825 8th Av -NY 10019
(212) 728-8000 .. **McCallen,** Benjamin P '06 %Willkie F&G LLP -787 7th Av -NY 10019
(516) 877-2900 .. **McCallen,** Grace Carreras '86 (Bartlett MB&M,LLP) -300 Old Cntry Rd -Mineola 11501
(212) 732-3640 .. **McCallen,** Thos J '96 (Carreras & M PLLC) -11 Park Pl -NY 10007
(212) 237-1000 .. **McCalley,** Priscilla P '07 %Windels ML&M,LLP -156 W 56th -NY 10019
(914) 328-8484 .. **McCallion,** Donald G Jr. '78 -222 Bloomingdale Rd -White Plns 10605 **Fx:**328-8663
(212) 527-1000 .. **McCallion,** Gail K '95 (Jones HC&B PC) -1 Bttry Pk Plz -NY 10004
(646) 366-0880 .. **McCallion,** Kenneth F '73 (McCallion & Assoc,LLP) -100 Park Av -NY 10017 **Fx:**366-1384
(212) 765-5070 .. **McCallion,** Kristen A '06 %Fish & R,PC -153 E 53rd -NY 10022
(914) 964-6806 .. **McCallion,** Lauren J '07 %J Marra -909 Mdlnd Av -Ynkrs 10704 **Fx:**964-0137
(212) 957-7600 .. **McCallion,** Sandra C '94 (Cohen & G LLP) -800 3rd Av -NY 10022
(718) 286-6000 .. **McCallum,** Howard D '04 %DA -125-01 Qns Blvd -Kew Gdns 11415
(212) 277-4000 .. **McCallum,** Robt J '08 %Freshfields BD LLP -520 Mad Av -NY 10022
(212) 637-2200 .. **McCallum,** Sarah Eddy '03 US Atty -1 St Andrews Plz -NY 10007
(631) 755-0101 .. **McCally,** Danl W '97 %Lewis JAA,LLP -425 Broad Hollow Rd -Melvll 11747
(212) 558-4000 .. **McCammon,** Melanie A '10 %Sullivan & C LLP -125 Broad -NY 10004
(212) 264-2819 .. **McCandless,** Scott C '98 %Hon RK Musgrave -1 Fed Plz -NY 10278
(212) 969-3000 .. **McCane,** Julie A '07 %Proskauer R LLP -1585 Bway -NY 10036
(518) 449-2245 .. **McCane,** Kevin F '89 (Erwin M&D) -23 Elk -Albany 12207 **Fx:**449-7890
(212) 943-0280 .. **McCanliss & Early LLP** -88 Pine -NY 10005 **Fx:**943-0283
(212) 458-1294 .. **McCann,** Amy E '07 Chartis Ins -175 Water -NY 10038
(518) 457-2070 .. **McCann,** Brian J '84 %Dept of Tax & Fin -Bldg 9 State Campus -Albany 12227 **Fx:**485-6607
(212) 742-9280 .. **McCann,** Brian Matthew '00 %Waterfront Comm -39 Bway -NY 10006 **Fx:**480-0587
(212) 953-6000 .. **McCann,** Christine A '95 %Katsky K LLP -605 3rd Av -NY 10158
(315) 218-8000 .. **McCann,** Danielle M '02 %Bond S&K,PLLC -1 Lincoln Ctr -Syracuse 13202
(212) 829-9819 .. **McCann,** Doris J '49 -1040 1st Av -NY 10022
(212) 687-3272 .. **McCann,** Dorothy E '96 (Blum & M) -271 Mad Av -NY 10016 **Fx:**949-0469
(718) 273-6677 .. **McCann,** Eileen Agnes '96 %Leg Aid -60 Bay -Staten Isl 10301 **Fx:**442-2679
(585) 226-2040 .. **McCann,** James '63 -9 Genesee Bx88 -Avon 14414 **Fx:**226-3830
(212) 262-2390 .. **McCann,** James C '88 (Connell F LLP) -888 7th Av -NY 10106
(212) 986-6000 .. **McCann,** James D '98 (Kleinberg KW&C,PC) -551 5th Av -NY 10176
(516) 794-4700 .. **McCann,** Jennifer L '07 %T Liotti -600 Old Cntry Rd -Gdn Cty 11530 **Fx:**794-2816
(716) 631-9981 .. **McCann,** Jennifer M '05 %Labin & B -531 Farber Lks Dr -Williamsvll 14221
(315) 471-3151 .. **McCann,** John T '83 (Hancock & E,LLP) -1500 AXA Twr I Bx4976 -Syracuse 13221
(516) 766-3131 .. **McCann,** Jos D '85 (Murray & M) -100 Merrick Rd -Rockvll Ctr 11570
(518) 486-9545 .. **McCann,** Jos G '00 State Comptroller -110 State -Albany 12236 **Fx:**473-9104
(607) 797-2315 .. **McCann,** Jos T '95 -31 Beethoven -Bnghmtn 13905 **Fx:**797-2315
(212) 417-8362 .. **McCann,** Margaret E '00 Research Fndtn CUNY -230 W 41st -NY 10036 **Fx:**417-8379
(212) 701-3000 .. **McCann,** Mary '06 %Cahill G&R LLP -80 Pine -NY 10005 **Fx:**269-5420
(718) 556-1919 .. **McCann,** Maryanne T '93 -136 Bay -Staten Isl 10301
(212) 269-4900 .. **McCann,** Matthew C '06 %Ford MEW&G,LLP -Wall Street Plz -NY 10005
(212) 788-0861 .. **McCann,** Max O '09 %Law Dept -100 Church -NY 10007 **Fx:**788-0367
(212) 975-1799 .. **McCann,** Melissa C '95 CBS -51 W 52nd -NY 10019
(718) 894-4080 .. **McCann,** Michl F '82 -61-66 67th -Middl Vllg 11379
(845) 615-8500 .. **McCann,** Michl P '98 (O'Keeffe & M LLP) -25 Main -Goshen 10924
(212) 850-1412 .. **McCann,** Michelle L '97 %Seligman Fncl Srvcs -100 Park Av -NY 10017
(716) 855-1111 .. **McCann,** Stephen J '05 %Duke HP&G LLP -350 Main -Buffalo 14202
(212) 460-2164 .. **McCann,** Timothy M '85 Con Ed -4 Irving Pl -NY 10003
(518) 474-2063 .. **McCann,** Wm J Jr. '92 %Bd of Elections -40 Steuben -Albany 12207
(212) 262-2390 .. **McCann,** Wm Novins '98 (Connell F LLP) -888 7th Av -NY 10106
(212) 416-8000 .. **McCants,** Nakisha '09 %Dept of Law -120 Bway -NY 10271
(212) 972-1000 .. **McCarey,** Danl J '05 %London F LLP -59 Maiden Ln -NY 10038
(845) 457-9413 .. **McCarl,** James R '83 J McCarl & Assoc -18 Brdg -Montgmry 12549 **Fx:**457-5097
(212) 653-8700 .. **McCarney,** James G '82 (Sheppard MR&H LLP) -30 Rckfllr Plz -NY 10112
(212) 456-7777 .. **McCarren,** Dana Dorgan '98 ABC,Inc -77 W 66th -NY 10023 **Fx:**456-7753
(212) 385-1422 .. **McCarren,** Edw J '63 -111 Bway -NY 10006 **Fx:**385-1605
(516) 825-6240 .. **McCarren,** Maureen M '88 -147 S Franklin Av -Vly Stream 11580 **Fx:**825-1318
(646) 386-5206 .. **McCarrick,** Dorothy '81 %Family Ct -60 Lafayette -NY 10013
(212) 521-4430 .. **McCarrick,** James M '95 (Becker M LLC) -590 Mad Av -NY 10022
(631) 580-4279 .. **McCarrick,** James P '01 -22 Charles -Centereach 11720
(212) 244-9500 .. **McCarrick,** John F '86 (White and W LLP) -1 Penn Plz -NY 10119
(914) 487-7330 .. **McCarrick,** John F '96 (White and W LLP) -427 Bedford Rd -Plsntvll 10570
(212) 553-3664 .. **McCarroll,** Elizabeth M '01 Moodys Investors Srvc -99 Church -NY 10007
(212) 521-5400 .. **McCarroll,** James C '00 (Reed S LLP) -599 Lex Av -NY 10022
(718) 694-5712 .. **McCarroll,** Walter J '66 %Transit Auth -130 Lvngstn -Brklyn 11201 **Fx:**694-5726
(212) 683-3520 .. **McCarron,** Catherine F '09 %Jager S,PC -485 Mad Av -NY 10022
(631) 694-6500 .. **McCarron,** John T '91 -445 Broadhllw Rd -Melvll 11747 **Fx:**694-6504
(845) 359-5400 .. **McCarron,** Lawr B '86 Rogers M&H,PC -100 Dutch Hill Rd -Orangebrg 10962 **Fx:**359-5577
(718) 286-6000 .. **McCarron,** Leslie A '88 %DA -125-01 Qns Blvd -Kew Gdns 11415
(212) 609-6800 .. **McCarter & English,LLP** -245 Park Av -NY 10167 **Fx:**609-6921
(212) 214-5139 .. **McCarter,** Susan Austin '98 Wachovia -375 Park Av -NY 10152
(212) 309-6000 .. **McCarthy,** Alice L '06 %Morgan L&B LLP -101 Park Av -NY 10178
(212) 909-6000 .. **McCarthy,** Alicia '85 Cnsl Debevoise & P LLP -919 3rd Av -NY 10022
(212) 669-3536 .. **McCarthy,** Anne J '85 Dept Admin Srvcs -1 Centre -NY 10007
(212) 399-1600 .. **McCarthy,** Anne M '01 %Mutual of America -320 Park Av -NY 10022

(212) 408-5100 .. **McCarthy,** Bernard W '69 Cnsl Chadbourne & P LLP -30 Rckfllr Plz -NY 10112
(516) 767-3600 .. **McCarthy,** Brian T '01 %Chalos O&D -366 Main -Pt Wash 11050
(914) 588-4480 .. **McCarthy,** Bryan C '78 -282 Katonah Av -Katonah 10536
(631) 979-9800 .. **McCarthy & Carbone,PC** -400 Townline Rd -Hauppauge 11788 **Fx:**979-3384
(212) 471-8500 .. **McCarthy,** Carl B '98 (Herzfeld & R,PC) -125 Broad -NY 10004
(914) 738-5173 .. **McCarthy,** Catherine F '43 -134 Harmon Av -Pelham 10803 **Fx:**738-4626
(716) 858-2424 .. **McCarthy,** Christopher M '03 %DA -25 Delaware Av -Buffalo 14202 **Fx:**858-7425
(518) 402-9223 .. **McCarthy,** Colleen Anne '89 %DEC -625 Bway -Albany 12233 **Fx:**402-9018
(212) 571-0550 .. **McCarthy,** Cornelius P '88 (Allegaert B&V LLP) -111 Bway -NY 10006
(914) 271-2828 .. **McCarthy,** Danl F '86 (McCarthy Law Firm,PC) -1 Croton Pnt Av -Croton-On-Hud 10520 **Fx:**271-2880
(212) 968-8300 .. **McCarthy,** Danl J '99 (Mintzer SZL&M LLP) -39 Bway -NY 10006
(718) 590-2000 .. **McCarthy,** Danl T '80 %DA -198 E 161st -Bronx 10451 **Fx:**590-6477
(914) 683-5900 .. **McCarthy,** Danl W '76 %Statewide Abstract -202 Mamaroneck Av -White Plns 10601 **Fx:**683-5905
(607) 763-9200 .. **McCarthy,** David F '87 (Levene G&T,LLP) -BxF-1706 -Bnghmtn 13902
(212) 615-2200 .. **McCarthy,** David J '87 (Butler FF&M,PC) -36 W 44th -NY 10036
(516) 802-0880 .. **McCarthy,** David W '69 -100 Crsswys Park Dr W -Woodbury 11797 **Fx:**802-0838
(212) 416-8397 .. **McCarthy,** Deborah Yurchuk '86 Dept of Law -120 Bway -NY 10271
(212) 272-4729 .. **McCarthy,** Denis J '90 %JP Morgan Chase -1 Metrotech Ctr N -Brklyn 11201
(212) 221-6900 .. **McCarthy,** Dianna L '97 (Winget S&S,LLP) -45 Bway -NY 10006
(516) 627-7136 .. **McCarthy,** Donal F '61 -22 Shorehaven Ln -Manhsst 11030
(315) 475-6952 .. **McCarthy,** Donald P '56 -2112 Erie Blvd E -Syracuse 13224
(631) 451-6500 .. **Mc Carthy,** Edw Hornidge '99 Brookhaven Law Dept -1 Indpndnc Hill -Farmngvll 11738 **Fx:**698-4489
(718) 981-7500 .. **McCarthy,** Edw P '63 (Lemole M & Assoc) -1492 Victory Blvd -Staten Isl 10301 **Fx:**720-1882
(718) 709-2272 .. **McCarthy,** Eileen P '94 JetBlue Airways Corp -118-29 Qns Blvd -Frst Hlls 11375
(914) 995-4287 .. **McCarthy,** Eileen Songer '96 Westchester Cnty Clerk -110 Dr Martin Luther King Jr Blvd -White Plns 10601
(212) 986-1200 .. **McCarthy,** Elisabeth S '85 (Gordon HR&C LLP) -355 Lex Av -NY 10017
(516) 571-3800 .. **McCarthy,** Elise C '83 %DA -262 Old Cntry Rd -Mineola 11501 **Fx:**248-9479
(646) 315-7374 .. **McCarthy,** Ellen R '89 %FINRA -14 Wall -NY 10005 **Fx:**315-7440
(914) 946-3700 .. **McCarthy Fingar LLP** -11 Martine Av -White Plns 10606 **Fx:**946-0134
(212) 557-5040 .. **McCarthy Fingar LLP** -747 3rd Av -NY 10017 **Fx:**557-5065
(631) 846-6754 .. **McCarthy,** Gary J '92 -38 Hyde Ln -Coram 11727
(212) 732-6000 .. **McCarthy,** Gerald T '92 (McCarthy & K LLP) -52 Duane -NY 10007
(516) 733-9200 .. **McCarthy,** Gerard M '86 Allied NA -390 N Bway -Jericho 11753 **Fx:**681-7390
(212) 669-3011 .. **McCarthy,** Gianna M '98 Comptroller-Asset Mgmt -1 Centre -NY 10007
(631) 427-2099 .. **McCarthy,** Glenn C '96 (Spencer M&M,LLP) -Bx128 -Huntngtn Sta 11746 **Fx:**427-2996
(631) 806-0073 .. **McCarthy,** Glenn J '02 -60 Ripley Dr -Northprt 11768
(718) 472-8000 .. **McCarthy,** Hugh T '68 %Schl Cnstrctn Auth -30-30 Thomson Av -LIC 11101 **Fx:**472-8088
(212) 922-9700 .. **McCarthy,** J Brian '91 %1st Amer Title -633 3rd Av -NY 10017 **Fx:**922-0881
(315) 475-8461 .. **McCarthy,** J Mark '70 (Coulter V&M,LLP) -636 Old Liverpool Rd -Liverpool 13088
(518) 462-0300 .. **McCarthy,** James A P '82 OfCnsl Girvin & F,PC -20 Corp Wds Blvd -Albany 12211
(516) 741-3900 .. **McCarthy,** James D '88 -170 Old Cntry Rd -Mineola 11501 **Fx:**741-3383
(718) 505-6650 .. **McCarthy,** James P '96 (Kaplan & M) -75-20 Astoria Blvd -E Elmhrst 11370
(718) 544-7977 .. **McCarthy,** James S '84 (JS McCarthy,PC) -106-19 Metro Av -Frst Hlls 11375
(516) 746-8100 .. **McCarthy,** James S '92 (D Buttafuoco & Assoc) -144 Woodbury Rd -Woodbury 11797 **Fx:**746-6473
(646) 441-1304 .. **McCarthy,** Jennie M '02 McCarthy/CapSquires,LLC -240 W 40th -NY 10018
(845) 486-2512 .. **McCarthy,** Joan H '81 %Sup Ct Law Dept -50 Market -Poughkeepsie 12601 **Fx:**473-5403
(212) 682-7050 .. **McCarthy,** John A '86 (Geringer & D) -5 Hanover Sq -NY 10004
(315) 475-1626 .. **McCarthy,** John B '91 %Coyne Textile Srvcs -140 Crtland Av -Syracuse 13202 **Fx:**475-0057
(212) 558-4000 .. **McCarthy,** John G '10 %Sullivan & C LLP -125 Broad -NY 10004
(212) 907-9700 .. **McCarthy,** John Gerard '92 (Smith G&R,LLP) -250 Park Av -NY 10177
(212) 468-8000 .. **McCarthy,** John J Jr. '71 (Morrison & F LLP) -1290 Av of Amer -NY 10104
(212) 450-4000 .. **McCarthy,** John J Jr. '81 (Davis P&W LLP) -450 Lex Av -NY 10017
(212) 626-6755 .. **McCarthy,** John J III '98 -1120 Av of Amer -NY 10036
(212) 635-4340 .. **McCarthy,** John J '99 NYS Moreland Comm -61 Bway -NY 10006
(607) 776-3389 .. **McCarthy,** John K '75 -12 W Pulteney Sq Bx528 -Bath 14810 **Fx:**776-2876
(212) 230-8800 .. **McCarthy,** John Kevin '91 (WilmerHale) -399 Park Av -NY 10022
(212) 869-5300 .. **McCarthy,** John M '78 %CPC -28 E 28th -NY 10016 **Fx:**683-2909
(914) 779-2080 .. **McCarthy,** Jolianne '78 -41 Algonquin -Ynkrs 10710
(718) 250-2000 .. **McCarthy,** Jos J Jr. '82 %DA -350 Jay -Brklyn 11201 **Fx:**250-2314
(716) 852-0400 .. **McCarthy,** Jos V '70 (Roach BM&G,PC) -424 Main -Buffalo 14202
(212) 310-2550 .. **McCarthy,** Joyce M '97 %Colgate-Palmolive -300 Park Av -NY 10022 **Fx:**310-3230
(914) 422-8755 .. **McCarthy,** Judith C '92 %Dept of Law -101 E Post Rd -White Plns 10601 **Fx:**422-8706
(212) 336-2000 .. **McCarthy,** Karen M '94 Cnsl Patterson BW&T LLP -1133 Av of Amer -NY 10036
(516) 357-3000 .. **McCarthy,** Karin M '93 %Rivkin R LLP -926 RXR Plz -Uniondale 11556
(212) 556-2100 .. **McCarthy,** Kathleen E '87 (King & S) -1185 Av of Amer -NY 10036
(212) 657-1292 .. **McCarthy,** Kathleen M '96 Citigroup Global Mrkts -77 Water -NY 10005
(212) 398-9238 .. **McCarthy,** Kathleen Norah '98 %D Guerin -315 Mad Av -NY 10017 **Fx:**869-0944
(212) 455-2000 .. **McCarthy,** Kathryn A '96 %Simpson T&B LLP -425 Lex Av -NY 10017
(212) 735-3000 .. **McCarthy,** Keira H '08 %Skadden ASM&F LLP -4 Times Sq -NY 10036
(585) 423-4977 .. **McCarthy,** Kelly Ann '91 Xerox Corp -100 Clinton Av S -Rchstr 14604
(212) 732-6000 .. **McCarthy & Kelly LLP** -52 Duane -NY 10007 **Fx:**732-6323
(716) 852-0400 .. **McCarthy,** Kevin D '95 %Roach BM&G,PC -424 Main -Buffalo 14202
(718) 324-8900 .. **McCarthy,** Kevin T '94 (McMahon M&V) -147 E 233rd -Bronx 10470
(315) 785-3152 .. **McCarthy,** Laurel A '99 %Pub Def -175 Arsenal -Watertwn 13601 **Fx:**785-5060
(914) 632-8382 .. **McCarthy,** Layne Carlough '82 %Goodstein & Assoc -270 North Av -New Rchll 10801 **Fx:**632-1833
(607) 274-5603 .. **McCarthy,** Margaret '90 %Cnty DSS -320 W State -Ithaca 14850 **Fx:**274-5020
(516) 357-3700 .. **McCarthy,** Marianne '85 OfCnsl Cullen and D LLP -100 Q Roosevelt Blvd -Gdn Cty 11530
(518) 427-9700 .. **McCarthy,** Mark J '86 (Harris B PLLC) -677 Bway -Albany 12207
(212) 787-3202 .. **McCarthy,** Martin N '63 (McCarthy & S) -2095 Bway -NY 10023
(585) 262-5130 .. **McCarthy,** Martin P II '04 %Muldoon & G -144 Exchange Blvd -Rchstr 14614
(212) 223-0400 .. **McCarthy,** Mary Gately '03 %Zeichner E&K LLP -575 Lex Av -NY 10022
(718) 553-3285 .. **McCarthy,** Mary M '91 %FAA -1 Aviation Plz -Jamaica 11434 **Fx:**995-5699
(518) 402-0205 .. **McCarthy,** Maryann K '96 UIA Bd -Troy Atrium Bx15126 -Albany 12212 **Fx:**402-6208
(607) 776-3389 .. **McCarthy,** Mathew K '05 %McCarthy Law Ofc -12 W Pulteney Sq Bx528 -Bath 14810 **Fx:**776-2876
(607) 776-9631 .. **McCarthy,** Mathew K '05 %DA -3 E Pulteney Sq -Bath 14810 **Fx:**776-7052
(212) 475-4378 .. **McCarthy,** Maureen W '88 -126 Waverly Pl -NY 10011 **Fx:**674-3916
(212) 233-0130 .. **McCarthy,** Meghan '01 %Nelson Ld&H -120 Bway -NY 10271
(914) 323-7000 .. **McCarthy,** Melissa '02 %Wilson EME&D LLP -3 Gannett Dr -White Plns 10604
(631) 360-5600 .. **McCarthy,** Michl C '07 %Grabie & G,LLP -162 Terry Rd -Smithtwn 11787 **Fx:**360-3370
(631) 898-2080 .. **McCarthy,** Michl E '90 -180 Oser Av -Hauppauge 11788 **Fx:**435-4751
(212) 659-7300 .. **McCarthy,** Michl J '05 %Haynes & B,LLP -1221 Av of Amer -NY 10020
(212) 225-2000 .. **McCarthy,** Michl J '10 %Cleary GS&H -1 Lbrty Plz -NY 10006
(716) 851-5053 .. **McCarthy,** Michl L '68 %Urban Renewal Agency -65 Niagara Sq -Buffalo 14202
(631) 351-4000 .. **McCarthy,** Michl L '86 -7 E Carver -Huntngtn 11743 **Fx:**351-4024
(631) 864-2307 .. **McCarthy,** Michl N '98 M McCarthy,PC -7 Pine Rdg Dr -Smithtwn 11787 **Fx:**543-2083
(315) 435-2170 .. **McCarthy,** Michl P '94 Cnty Atty -421 Mntgmry -Syracuse 13202 **Fx:**435-5729
(212) 431-2384 .. **McCarthy,** Michl T '88 %NY Law Schl -185 W Bway -NY 10013 **Fx:**963-8839
(315) 448-0526 .. **McCarthy,** Michl W '80 %US District Ct for Northern District of NY -100 S Clinton -Syracuse 13261
(212) 306-7244 .. **McCarthy,** Michele C '04 NY Ofc of Labor Relations -40 Rector -NY 10006
(631) 853-5212 .. **McCarthy,** Michelle K '03 %Leg Aid -400 Carleton Av Bx9082 -Central Islip 11722 **Fx:**853-7798
(212) 325-7072 .. **McCarthy,** Noreen P '97 CSFB-Leg Dept -1 Mad Av -NY 10010
(212) 262-2390 .. **McCarthy,** Owen C '09 Cnsl Connell F LLP -888 7th Av -NY 10106
(212) 848-4000 .. **McCarthy,** Owen W '09 %Shearman & S LLP -599 Lex Av -NY 10022
(212) 357-4704 .. **McCarthy,** Patricia M '97 Goldman Sachs -1 NY Plz -NY 10004
(631) 979-9800 .. **McCarthy,** Patrick C '94 (McCarthy & C,PC) -400 Townline Rd -Hauppauge 11788
(716) 852-3540 .. **McCarthy,** Patrick D '10 %Watson BCJ&S -12 Fountain Plz -Buffalo 14202
(631) 852-2365 .. **McCarthy,** Patrick T '89 Hon T Whelan -1 Court -Rvrhead 11901
(716) 853-8438 .. **McCarthy,** Paul F '75 %Dept of Law -350 Main Pl Twr -Buffalo 14202 **Fx:**853-8571
(212) 732-2000 .. **McCarthy,** Peter M '86 (Cullen and D LLP) -44 Wall -NY 10005
(212) 338-6207 .. **McCarthy,** Philip E II '90 Merrill Lynch -200 Park Av -NY 10166
(914) 763-2466 .. **McCarthy,** Randy Costa '85 %Natl Cnsltnts Assoc -46 Church Tvrn Rd -S Salem 10590
(718) 383-5152 .. **McCarthy,** Richd H '00 SIAC -2 Metrotech Ctr -Brklyn 11201
(518) 473-4310 .. **McCarthy,** Richd J '80 %State Comptroller -110 State -Albany 12236 **Fx:**473-9104
(914) 997-8100 .. **McCarthy,** Robt A '83 (Burke LM&G) -10 Bank -White Plns 10606
(212) 768-6700 .. **McCarthy,** Robt E '87 (Sonnenschein N&R LLP) -2 World Fncl Ctr -NY 10281
(518) 785-3841 .. **McCarthy,** Robt F '91 (McCarthy Law Firm) -Bx11-383 -Albany 12211 **Fx:**785-0125
(212) 248-9100 .. **McCarthy,** Robt F '94 %Epstein M&M -1 Whitehall -NY 10004
(585) 232-3730 .. **McCarthy,** Robt G '04 %Chamberlain D LLP -1600 Crssrds Bldg -Rchstr 14614
(716) 631-7025 .. **McCarthy,** Robt P '99 %Town of Amherst -5583 Main -Williamsvll 14221
(212) 878-8000 .. **McCarthy,** Ryan P '05 %Clifford C LLP -31 W 52nd -NY 10019
(212) 808-8100 .. **McCarthy,** Sharon L '90 (Kostelanetz & F,LLP) -7 Wrld Trd Ctr -NY 10007
(212) 551-0701 .. **McCarthy,** Stephen E '92 Mutual Marine Ofc,Inc -919 3rd Av -NY 10022 **Fx:**986-1310
(212) 925-5901 .. **McCarthy,** Stephen G Jr. '86 -35 Worth -NY 10013 **Fx:**226-5904
(212) 787-3202 .. **McCarthy & Sullivan** -2095 Bway -NY 10023 **Fx:**362-7656

(212) 370-5100 .. **McCarthy,** Suzanne M '99 OfCnsl O'Donnell SG&L,LLP -60 E 42nd -NY 10165
(212) 785-6410 .. **McCarthy Tetrault LLP** -1 NY Plz -NY 10004 **Fx:**785-6438
(718) 250-0400 .. **McCarthy,** Thos J '79 %R Tusa -1 MetroTech Ctr -Brklyn 11201 **Fx:**250-0591
(516) 797-5500 .. **McCarthy,** Thos J '92 -678 Bway -Massapequa 11758 **Fx:**798-0568
(315) 451-1010 .. **McCarthy,** Thos R '91 -602 Vine -Liverpool 13088 **Fx:**457-1354
(518) 371-6651 .. **McCarthy,** Thos R '94 Justice Ct -1 Town Hall Plz -Clifton Pk 12065
(716) 883-7800 .. **McCarthy,** Timothy A '76 (Burd & M) -78 Bryant -Buffalo 14209
(585) 343-1423 .. **McCarthy,** Timothy A '76 %OTB -700 Ellicott -Batavia 14020 **Fx:**343-6873
(212) 649-5600 .. **McCarthy,** Timothy J '00 %Rockefeller & Co,Inc -30 Rckfllr Plz -NY 10112 **Fx:**649-5977
(212) 612-3270 .. **McCarthy,** Timothy J '01 (Mishcon de R NY LLP) -200 Park Av -NY 10166
(718) 624-0154 .. **McCarthy,** Timothy M '83 Cnsl Katz & Assoc -26 Court -Brklyn 11242 **Fx:**624-4212
(315) 474-1511 .. **McCarthy,** Tracey B '99 %National Grid -300 Erie Blvd W -Syracuse 13202 **Fx:**428-6149
(518) 436-2840 .. **McCarthy,** Vanessa A '92 %Thruway Auth -200 Southrn Blvd Bx189 -Albany 12201 **Fx:**471-4340
(716) 854-5333 .. **McCarthy,** W Donn '51 -438 Main -Buffalo 14202 **Fx:**856-0828
(716) 439-7172 .. **McCarthy,** Wm F '75 %Family Ct -Cthse -Lockprt 14094 **Fx:**439-7170
(518) 434-6141 .. **McCarthy,** Wm M '66 -60 S Swan -Albany 12210 **Fx:**434-6140
(518) 782-4900 .. **McCarthy-Cerrito,** Vida L '09 %LaFave L&S,LLP -951 Albany Shaker Rd -Latham 12110 **Fx:**785-9705
(212) 808-8300 .. **McCarthy Lapham,** Lynne M '90 %Rosensteel Law -90 Park Av -NY 10016
(518) 486-9718 .. **McCartin,** Michl G '91 %Dept of Law -The Cptl -Albany 12224
(212) 682-2288 .. **McCartin,** Wm F '78 (Sankel S&M,LLP) -750 3rd Av -NY 10017
(518) 486-7003 .. **McCartney,** Brian P '86 Div of Housing -3840 State -Albany 12207
(212) 909-0761 .. **McCartney,** George F '75 %Nippon Life Ins -521 5th Av -NY 10175
(518) 436-2840 .. **McCartney,** Katherine A '85 %Thruway Auth -200 Southrn Blvd Bx189 -Albany 12201 **Fx:**471-4340
(607) 776-9631 .. **McCartney,** Michl D '75 %DA -3 E Pulteney Sq -Bath 14810 **Fx:**776-7052
(212) 238-3000 .. **McCartney,** Patrick A '85 (Emmet M&M,LLP) -120 Bway -NY 10271
(212) 684-1880 .. **McCartney,** Terrence E '95 (Rheingold VRS&M LLP) -113 E 37th -NY 10016
(914) 995-3387 .. **McCarty,** James A Jr. '80 %DA -111 Martin Luther King Blvd -White Plns 10601 **Fx:**995-3363
(914) 698-1110 .. **McCarty,** Martha Sokol '81 MS McCarty,PC -910 E Bstn Post Rd -Mamaroneck 10543 **Fx:**698-9156
(585) 244-8910 .. **McCarty,** Terence '97 %Fiandach & F -100 Allens Crk Rd -Rchstr 14618 **Fx:**244-4863
(718) 969-2686 .. **McCarville,** Carol L '85 -154-78 71st Av -Flushng 11367
(518) 377-6489 .. **McCary & Huff, LLP** -107 N Ballston Av -Scotia 12302 **Fx:**377-6521
(518) 377-6489 .. **McCary,** Kathryn '82 (McCary & H,LLP) -107 N Ballston Av -Scotia 12302
(973) 491-3565 .. **McCaskey,** Anthony S '03 (LeClairRyan,PC) -830 3rd Av -NY 10022 **Fx:**491-3555
(607) 257-0121 .. **McCauley,** James N '93 -701 W State -Ithaca 14850
(585) 292-3371 .. **McCauley,** Jos J '88 Monroe Commnty Cllg -1000 E Henrietta Rd -Rchstr 14623
(212) 649-2000 .. **McCauley,** Kevin J '80 %Hearst Corp -300 W 57th -NY 10019 **Fx:**649-2035
(212) 422-9424 .. **McCauley,** Mark R '00 %Gogick B&O,LLP -11 Bway -NY 10004
(516) 466-6500 .. **McCauley,** Matthew J '02 %Parker WA LLP -6 Hrbr Park Dr S -Pt Wash 11050
(518) 474-6530 .. **McCauley,** Maureen J '77 %Dept Pub Srvc -3 ESP -Albany 12223
(212) 406-1855 .. **McCauley,** Michl B '91 (Palmer B&H) -140 Bway -NY 10005
(716) 861-4132 .. **McCauley,** Rebecca Ziebarth '04 -231 Willardshire Rd -Orchard Pk 14127
(212) 679-3124 .. **McCauley,** Todd M '94 -274 Mad Av -NY 10016 **Fx:**679-3105
(518) 434-6195 .. **McCauley Belokopitsky,** Kyle R '06 NYS Catholic Conference -465 State -Albany 12203 **Fx:**434-9796
(845) 794-3000 .. **McCausland,** Cheryl A '87 Cnty Atty -100 North Bx5012 -Monticello 12701 **Fx:**794-4924
(845) 791-6600 .. **McCausland,** Timothy S '86 Cnsl Gaffken & Barriger Co,Inc -198 Brdgvll Rd -Monticello 12701 **Fx:**791-6603
(212) 373-3000 .. **McCavitt,** Stephanie R '93 Cnsl Paul WRW&G LLP -1285 Av of Amer -NY 10019
(212) 230-8810 .. **McCaw,** Robt B '00 SrCnsl WilmerHale -399 Park Av -NY 10022
(212) 622-6717 .. **McCaw,** Vandana G '91 JP Morgan Chase -277 Park Av -NY 10172
(212) 756-2000 .. **McCawley,** Brian '07 %Schulte R&Z LLP -919 3rd Av -NY 10022
(212) 836-8000 .. **McCay,** Frank J '88 Cnsl Kaye S LLP -425 Park Av -NY 10022
(718) 472-8070 .. **McClain,** Terry K '83 %Schl Cnstrctn Auth -30-30 Thomson Av -LIC 11101 **Fx:**472-8600
(212) 878-8000 .. **McClain,** Treasure L '02 %Clifford C LLP -31 W 52nd -NY 10019
(212) 450-4000 .. **McClammy,** James I '99 Cnsl Davis P&W LLP -450 Lex Av -NY 10017
(631) 853-4343 .. **McClancy,** Kevin G '82 %Leg Aid -400 Carleton Av Bx9082 -Central Islip 11722 **Fx:**853-7798
(212) 756-2000 .. **McClane,** Janna Gabriel '06 Schulte R&Z LLP -919 3rd Av -NY 10022
(716) 842-2800 .. **McClaren,** Michl '92 (Webster S LLP) -1400 Lbrty Bldg -Buffalo 14202
(716) 842-2800 .. **McClaren,** Susan M '92 (Webster S LLP) -484 Main -E Aurora 14052
(845) 732-7500 .. **McClarnon,** Wm T '96 %Medicaid Fraud Cntrl -1 Blue Hill Plz Bx1557 -Pearl Rvr 10965 **Fx:**732-7555
(718) 546-0950 .. **McClary,** Dawn J '93 %Dept of Correction -75-20 Astoria Blvd -E Elmhrst 11370
(212) 763-6800 .. **McClary,** Eichakeem L '07 %Vandenberg & F,LLP -60 E 42nd -NY 10165
(607) 255-5124 .. **McClary,** Patricia A '83 %Cornell Univ -300 CCC Bldg-Grdn Av -Ithaca 14853 **Fx:**255-2794
(212) 839-5300 .. **McClay,** Adam '10 %Sidley A LLP -787 7th Av -NY 10019
(585) 232-6500 .. **McClean,** Alexander R '07 %Harter S&E LLP -1600 Bausch & Lomb Pl -Rchstr 14604
(212) 947-6555 .. **McClean,** Anne-Marie '98 OfCnsl S Tashman -3 W 35th -NY 10001 **Fx:**594-0019
(631) 232-1130 .. **McClellan,** Michl M '89 -1770 Motor Pkwy -Hauppauge 11749
(212) 459-7749 .. **McClellan,** Wm J '84 Dept of Tax & Fin -1740 Bway -NY 10019
(585) 473-8723 .. **McClelland,** Helvi '82 %Mediation Srvcs -16 N Goodman -Rchstr 14607
(585) 394-7220 .. **McClelland,** Neal P '74 -45 Ontario -Canandaigua 14424 **Fx:**394-0822
(212) 489-1600 .. **McClelland,** Scott M '04 %Deloitte LLP -1633 Bway -NY 10019 **Fx:**492-4201
(585) 641-8000 .. **McClenathan,** Edw W '08 Fix SB&G,PC -295 Woodcliff Dr -Fairprt 14450
(212) 421-0031 .. **McClendon,** J Stewart '53 -200 E 66th -NY 10065
(212) 387-6560 .. **McClimon,** Timothy J '87 %AT&T Foundation -32 Av of Amer -NY 10013
(212) 768-6700 .. **McClintock,** Douglas J '76 (Sonnenschein N&R LLP) -2 World Fncl Ctr -NY 10281
(212) 455-2000 .. **McCloskey,** Brian P '06 %Simpson T&B LLP -425 Lex Av -NY 10017
(516) 572-2000 .. **McCloskey,** Gerard C '09 %DA -99 Main -Hempstd 11550 **Fx:**572-2606
(518) 486-1336 .. **McCloskey,** Jane '84 %Dept of Health -Corning Twr 24th Fl -Albany 12237 **Fx:**486-4834
(585) 247-9000 .. **McCloskey,** Karen R '91 Shapiro D&B,LLP -250 Mile Xing Blvd -Rchstr 14624
(718) 250-2000 .. **McCloskey,** Meredith '07 %DA -350 Jay -Brklyn 11201 **Fx:**250-2314
(516) 747-8448 .. **McCloskey,** Patrick L '68 Nassau Cnty Bar Assn -15th & West -Mineola 11501 **Fx:**873-8032
(212) 277-6500 .. **McCloskey,** Patrick T '00 %Dickstein S LLP -1633 Bway -NY 10019
(914) 328-0404 .. **McCloskey,** Rebecca M '03 %Jackson L LLP -1 N Bway -White Plns 10601
(718) 845-4444 .. **McCloskey,** Thos P '72 (Aliazzo M&G) -94-03 101st Av -Ozone Pk 11416
(845) 291-2650 .. **McCloud,** Tina M '81 %Cnty Atty -285 Main -Goshen 10924 **Fx:**291-3014
(516) 571-2092 .. **McCloy,** Danl J '86 %Cnty Treasurer -240 Old Cntry Rd -Mineola 11501
(212) 349-2722 .. **McCloy,** Rosemarie R '82 -225 Bway -NY 10007
(518) 713-2144 .. **McClung,** Jessica A '09 %Rehfuss L & Assoc,PC -40 British Amer Blvd -Latham 12110 **Fx:**713-2148
(212) 735-3000 .. **McClung,** Katherine S '05 %Skadden ASM&F LLP -4 Times Sq -NY 10036
(212) 735-3000 .. **McClure,** Andrew P '08 %Skadden ASM&F LLP -4 Times Sq -NY 10036
(914) 495-3050 .. **McClure,** Christopher W '00 (Reisman R&M,LLP) -151 Bway -Hawthorne 10532 **Fx:**495-3051
(212) 576-7000 .. **McClure,** Monique Anne '91 %NYLIM -51 Mad Av -NY 10010
(212) 268-7535 .. **McClure,** Stephanie '08 %Bonner KT&C,LLP -350 5th Av -NY 10118
(212) 819-8200 .. **McCluskey,** Casey M '10 %White & C LLP -1155 Av of Amer -NY 10036
(212) 373-3000 .. **McCluskey,** Jerome P '07 %Paul WRW&G LLP -1285 Av of Amer -NY 10019
(315) 232-4551 .. **McClusky,** James P '89 (McClusky Law Firm,LLC) -8 Main Bx97 -Adams 13605 **Fx:**232-2562
(315) 387-3433 .. **McClusky,** Timothy M '89 (McClusky Law Firm,LLC) -2089 Lk Bx697 -Sandy Crk 13145 **Fx:**387-5738
(518) 402-9003 .. **McClymonds,** James T '93 DEC -625 Bway -Albany 12233 **Fx:**402-9037
(845) 331-5330 .. **McColgan,** Timothy P '02 -Bx3034 -Kingston 12402
(212) 664-4444 .. **McCollester,** Lauren Ellis '92 %NBC -30 Rckfllr Plz -NY 10112
(212) 373-3000 .. **McColm,** Elizabeth R '99 (Paul WRW&G LLP) -1285 Av of Amer -NY 10019
(585) 343-2250 .. **McComb,** Danl R '79 -435 E Main -Batavia 14020
(212) 558-4000 .. **McCombs,** Theo A B '09 %Sullivan & C LLP -125 Broad -NY 10004
(631) 753-4200 .. **McConaghy,** Elizabeth A '87 NIC Holding Corp -25 Melvll Park Rd -Melvll 11747 **Fx:**390-5421
(212) 571-7100 .. **McCone,** Cody K '85 (O'Dwyer & B,LLP) -52 Duane -NY 10007
(585) 781-9064 .. **McConnaughey,** Jan R '89 %Eastman Kodak -343 State -Rchstr 14650
(212) 474-1000 .. **McConnell,** Ashley E '06 -825 8th Av -NY 10019
(212) 925-2800 .. **McConnell,** Dennis P '90 (Dolgenos N&C LLP) -271 Mad Av -NY 10016
(212) 218-8760 .. **McConnell,** James D Jr. '93 (Hargraves M&C,PC) -420 Lex Av -NY 10170
(212) 335-9000 .. **McConnell,** John A '05 %DA -1 Hogan Pl -NY 10013
(212) 218-8760 .. **McConnell,** John P '91 (Hargraves M&C,PC) -420 Lex Av -NY 10170
(212) 349-3000 .. **McConnell,** Kevin R '77 (Himmelstein MGD&J) -15 Maiden Ln -NY 10038
(212) 239-4999 .. **McConnell,** Patricia '79 (Meyer SE&K,PC) -1350 Bway Bx822 -NY 10018
(917) 778-6600 .. **McConnell,** Patrick J '89 %J Toomey -485 Lex Av -NY 10017 **Fx:**778-7048
(212) 345-9755 .. **McConney,** Jean M '98 %Marsh USA -1166 Av of Amer -NY 10036 **Fx:**345-4808
(212) 343-5658 .. **McConnon,** Jos M '03 J McConnon & Assoc PC -35 Worth -NY 10013 **Fx:**343-5690
(718) 233-3785 .. **McConvery,** Sharon '96 %Tansey T&C -221 Jffrsn Av -Staten Isl 10306
(516) 624-0744 .. **McConville,** Bernard R '63 -233 Pond Vw Dr -Pt Wash 11050
(585) 546-2500 .. **McConville Considine Cooman & Morin,PC** -25 E Main -Rchstr 14614 **Fx:**546-7218
(518) 477-7951 .. **McConville,** Edw '58 (Maney M&L) -77 Troy Rd -E Greenbush 12061
(516) 627-9088 .. **McConville,** Kimberly Anne '95 -47 Valley Rd -Manhsst 11030
(518) 383-4000 .. **McConville,** Kris M '99 (Overton RD&D,LLP) -19 Halfmoon Exec Park Dr Bx437 -Clifton Pk 12065
(585) 546-2500 .. **McConville,** Michl F '75 (McConville CC&M,PC) -25 E Main -Rchstr 14614

(212) 681-6500 .. **McCoobery,** Dennis H '98 %Stempel BC&H,PC -675 3rd Av -NY 10017
(212) 509-2100 .. **McCooey,** Michl Pierce '96 Griswold Co -55 Bway -NY 10006
(212) 801-3760 .. **McCool,** Jennifer Ann '98 %Michael L&R LLP -60 Columbus Cir -NY 10023
(212) 512-1000 .. **McCool,** Judith M '09 %HBO -1100 Av of Amer -NY 10036 **Fx:**512-1986
(914) 323-7000 .. **McCord,** Morgan R '10 %Wilson EME&D LLP -3 Gannett Dr -White Plns 10604
(516) 296-7000 .. **McCord,** Richd J '80 (Certilman BA&H,LLP) -90 Merrick Av -E Meadow 11554
(315) 798-5870 .. **McCormac,** Leland D III '90 %Pub Def -321 Main -Utica 13501 **Fx:**798-6419
(212) 335-4500 .. **McCormack,** Aidan M '93 (DLA Piper LLP) -1251 Av of Amer -NY 10020
(212) 735-3000 .. **McCormack,** Alexandra J '04 %Skadden ASM&F LLP -4 Times Sq -NY 10036
(212) 546-4000 .. **McCormack,** Douglas J '91 %Bristol-Myers Squibb -345 Park Av -NY 10154 **Fx:**546-9562
(845) 896-1108 .. **McCormack,** Edw T '82 -1003 Main -Fishkill 12524 **Fx:**896-1109
(631) 470-3574 .. **McCormack,** Ellen Savino '89 (Margiotta & R) -425 Broadhllw Rd -Melvll 11747
(212) 683-7999 .. **McCormack,** Erin K '06 Ptnrshp for Chldrns Rts -271 Mad Av -NY 10016
(212) 335-4500 .. **McCormack,** Garry P '82 (DLA Piper LLP) -1251 Av of Amer -NY 10020
(212) 354-3820 .. **McCormack,** Howard M '62 OfCnsl Burke & P -100 Park Av -NY 10017
(516) 505-0600 .. **McCormack,** John E '94 (J McCormack,PC) -1035 Stewart Av -Gdn Cty 11530 **Fx:**505-0632
(718) 590-2100 .. **McCormack,** Jos A '87 %DA -198 E 161st -Bronx 10451 **Fx:**590-6477
(718) 855-9000 .. **McCormack,** Kathleen M '87 (Cullen and D LLP) -177 Montague -Brklyn 11201
(315) 478-0933 .. **McCormack,** Kevin E '82 -333 E Onondaga -Syracuse 13202
(516) 741-2948 .. **McCormack,** Marie F '86 (MF McCormack,PC) -138 Mineola Blvd -Mineola 11501
(212) 770-1258 .. **McCormack,** Marie Judith '93 Amer Intl Underwriters -80 Pine -NY 10005
(631) 853-4161 .. **McCormack,** Maureen Anne '93 %DA -N Cnty Cmplx Bldg 77 -Hauppauge 11788 **Fx:**853-4192
(212) 504-6000 .. **McCormack,** Michl A '97 SpclCnsl Cadwalader W&T LLP -1 World Fncl Ctr -NY 10281
(718) 286-6000 .. **McCormack,** Peter J III '86 %DA -125-01 Qns Blvd -Kew Gdns 11415
(845) 353-0100 .. **McCormack & Phillips** -51 N Bway #2 -Nyack 10960 **Fx:**358-7466
(518) 436-4077 .. **McCormack,** R Christopher Jr. '87 -111 Wshngtn Av -Albany 12210 **Fx:**432-4267
(845) 353-0100 .. **McCormack,** Ronald G '71 (McCormack & P) -51 N Bway #2 -Nyack 10960
(212) 878-8000 .. **McCormack,** Shannon M '08 %Clifford C LLP -31 W 52nd -NY 10019
(212) 408-5100 .. **McCormack,** Thos J '83 (Chadbourne & P LLP) -30 Rckfllr Plz -NY 10112
(212) 596-9000 .. **McCormack,** Wm F '73 (Ropes & G LLP) -1211 Av of Amer -NY 10036
(716) 881-8056 .. **McCormick,** Amanda Fantauzzo '02 Univ of Buffalo -672 Delaware Av -Buffalo 14209
(212) 229-2953 .. **McCormick,** Andrew G '91 (Winslett SM&B LLP) -6 E 39th -NY 10016 **Fx:**(646) 390-2115
(585) 546-4900 .. **McCormick,** Ann Schnepp '82 %Home Leasing Corp -850 Clinton Sq -Rchstr 14604 **Fx:**546-5433
(718) 707-9997 .. **McCormick,** Barbara A '00 %Dornan & Assoc,PLLC -10-40 Jackson Av -LIC 11101 **Fx:**228-5940
(212) 918-3000 .. **McCormick,** Brian R '09 %Hogan L LLP -875 3rd Av -NY 10022
(516) 294-5106 .. **McCormick,** Carole E '82 OfCnsl W Boccio,PC -22 Jericho Tpk -Mineola 11501 **Fx:**294-1657
(212) 286-4471 .. **McCormick,** Chas F '96 (McCormick & O,LLP) -9 E 40th -NY 10016 **Fx:**504-9574
(631) 289-0303 .. **McCormick,** Danl P '91 (Devine & M) -Bx580 -Manorvll 11949
(845) 291-2454 .. **McCormick,** Dennis B '73 Leg Aid -2 Court Ln Bx328 -Goshen 10924 **Fx:**294-2638
(914) 301-5925 .. **McCormick Dunne & Foley** -51 Bedford Rd -Katonah 10536 **Fx:**301-5924
(212) 692-1000 .. **McCormick,** Eric W '94 SpclCnsl Duane M LLP -1540 Bway -NY 10036
(315) 443-1310 .. **McCormick,** Heidi W '05 %Syracuse Univ Cllg of Law -Wht Hall -Syracuse 13244 **Fx:**443-4213
(212) 259-8000 .. **McCormick,** Hugh T '77 OfCnsl Dewey & L LLP -1301 Av of Amer -NY 10019
(315) 946-5905 .. **Mc Cormick,** Jacqueline A '93 %DA -54 Broad -Lyons 14489 **Fx:**946-5911
(914) 925-1143 .. **McCormick,** James G '84 Tremont Capital Mgmt -555 Theo Fremd Av -Rye 10580
(212) 688-9200 .. **McCormick,** James H '03 Empire Search Partners,LLC -445 Park Av -NY 10022
(212) 446-8167 .. **McCormick,** John P '96 McKinsey & Co -55 E 52nd -NY 10055 **Fx:**688-9521
(212) 373-3000 .. **McCormick,** Katherine L '02 %Paul WRW&G LLP -1285 Av of Amer -NY 10019
(212) 630-5615 .. **McCormick,** Marisa '04 Conde Nast -750 3rd Av -NY 10017
(516) 571-3800 .. **McCormick,** Maureen M '87 %DA -262 Old Cntry Rd -Mineola 11501 **Fx:**248-9479
(518) 834-7700 .. **McCormick,** Michl D '90 (Russell & M) -101 Clinton Bx549 -Keesevll 12944 **Fx:**834-9300
(315) 793-2370 .. **McCormick,** Michl H '05 %MHLS -207 Genesee -Utica 13501 **Fx:**793-2371
(518) 457-2449 .. **McCormick,** Michl R '75 %Agriculture & Mrkts -10B Airline Dr -Albany 12235 **Fx:**457-8842
(631) 738-9100 .. **McCormick,** Patrick '89 (Campolo M&M,LLP) -3340 Vets Mem'l Hwy -Bohemia 11716 **Fx:**738-0659
(716) 566-5400 .. **McCormick,** Paul D '94 %Goldberg S LLP -665 Main -Buffalo 14203
(212) 835-1514 .. **McCormick,** Paul M '03 %Dreifuss B&P,LLP -1 Penn Plz -NY 10019
(917) 658-3714 .. **McCormick,** Richd J '02 -210 W 70th -NY 10023
(914) 377-6240 .. **McCormick,** Rory '91 %Law Dept -300 City Hall -Ynkrs 10701 **Fx:**964-0563
(212) 696-4848 .. **McCormick,** Terence W '93 %Mintz & G LLP -470 Park Av S -NY 10016
(518) 383-4000 .. **McCormick,** Thos R '04 (Overton RD&D,LLP) -19 Halfmoon Exec Park Dr Bx437 -Clifton Pk 12065
(212) 751-3001 .. **McCormick,** Timothy R '05 (Thompson & K LLP) -919 3rd Av -NY 10022
(518) 843-3717 .. **McCoski,** Kelli P '86 -123 Guy Park Av -Amsterdam 12010 **Fx:**843-3188
(718) 380-2435 .. **McCotter,** James V '92 -169-11 81st Av -Jamaica 11432
(212) 837-6782 .. **McCoubrey,** Saml C III '08 %Hughes H&R LLP -1 Bttry Pk Plz -NY 10004 **Fx:**299-6782
(212) 532-0500 .. **McCourt,** Lawr C '96 (Heiberger & Assoc,PC) -205 Lex Av -NY 10016 **Fx:**532-2040
(212) 793-1598 .. **McCourt,** Timothy J '89 Citigroup -425 Park Av -NY 10022
(212) 775-8700 .. **McCoy,** Amanda L '09 %Kilpatrick S,LLP -31 W 52nd -NY 10019
(212) 688-5151 .. **McCoy,** Amy R '04 %Gibney A&F,LLP -665 5th Av -NY 10022
(718) 286-6000 .. **McCoy,** Christine A '04 %DA -125-01 Qns Blvd -Kew Gdns 11415
(631) 360-5600 .. **McCoy,** Dennis C '07 Grabie & G,LLP -162 Terry Rd -Smithtwn 11787 **Fx:**360-3370
(716) 566-1300 .. **McCoy,** Dennis R '78 (Hiscock & B,LLP) -1100 M&T Ctr -Buffalo 14203
(212) 839-7000 .. **McCoy,** Elizabeth A '89 (Hill B&N LLP) -200 Lbrty -NY 10281
(212) 687-6523 .. **McCoy,** Henry D II '63 -60 E 42nd -NY 10165
(212) 272-6378 .. **McCoy,** John Scott '87 JP Morgan Chase -383 Mad Av -NY 10179
(518) 477-4575 .. **McCoy,** Jos M '81 (Corrigan M&B) -220 Columbia Tpk -Rensselaer 12144
(516) 867-5100 .. **McCoy,** Margaret F '88 Seaport Title Agency -106 Woodcleft Av -Freeprt 11520
(631) 853-4161 .. **McCoy,** Michl G '02 %DA -N Cnty Cmplx Bldg 77 -Hauppauge 11788 **Fx:**853-4192
(914) 225-5540 .. **McCoy,** Wm F '85 Morgan Stanley -2000 Wstchstr Av -Purchase 10577
(516) 877-7000 .. **McCoyd,** Edw A '68 (McCoyd P&R,LLP) -1100 Franklin Av -Gdn Cty 11530
(516) 877-7000 .. **McCoyd Parkas & Ronan,LLP** -1100 Franklin Av -Gdn Cty 11530 **Fx:**248-8550
(845) 565-9261 .. **McCoy-Evans,** Tara J '04 B Kulak -484 Temple Hill Rd -New Windsor 12553
(716) 542-5413 .. **McCracken,** Alan P '84 %Nicholas PSB&Z -12364 Main Rd Bx176 -Akron 14001
(212) 922-9250 .. **McCracken,** Wm D '01 %Ganfer & S LLP -360 Lex Av -NY 10017
(212) 837-6000 .. **McCracken,** Windy B '06 %Hughes H&R LLP -1 Bttry Pk Plz -NY 10004
(212) 275-4952 .. **McCrady,** Wm Tucker '02 Warner Music Group -75 Rckfllr Plz -NY 10019
(212) 556-4031 .. **McCraw,** David E '93 %The NY Times Co -620 8th Av -NY 10018 **Fx:**556-4634
(212) 374-7930 .. **McCray,** Danl '96 %NYC Dept Educ-OLS -52 Chmbrs -NY 10007 **Fx:**374-0423
(718) 237-2000 .. **McCrea,** Arlene F '99 %Leg Aid -111 Lvngstn -Brklyn 11201 **Fx:**237-8737
(347) 404-9133 .. **Mc Cready,** Jeffrey D '99 %Civil Ct -141 Lvngstn -Brklyn 11201 **Fx:**(718) 643-3733
(716) 882-2300 .. **McCready,** Maureen A '73 (McCready & T) -6 N Pearl -Buffalo 14202
(718) 250-2000 .. **Mc Cready,** Roger L '97 %DA -350 Jay -Brklyn 11201 **Fx:**250-2314
(631) 852-8600 .. **McCready,** Shaun K '09 %DA -Feather Hill Shopping Ctr Main Rd -Southold 11971
(716) 882-2300 .. **McCready & Todaro** -6 N Pearl -Buffalo 14202 **Fx:**882-2322
(347) 472-3502 .. **McCreanor,** Robt D '03 Catholic Migration-Immigrant Tenant Advocacy -47-01 Qns Blvd -Sunnyside 11104 **Fx:**(718) 392-5170
(585) 263-1000 .. **McCreary,** Jean H '85 (Nixon P LLP) -1100 Clinton Sq -Rchstr 14604
(315) 788-2888 .. **McCreary,** Stuart A '87 -Bx772 -Watertwn 13601 **Fx:**782-0880
(212) 816-5874 .. **McCreary,** Tracy H '93 Salomon Smith Barney -388 Greenwich -NY 10013
(212) 547-5400 .. **McCreay,** Frank '01 (McDermott W&E LLP) -340 Mad Av -NY 10173
(212) 297-6175 .. **McCreery,** Wm '59 -420 Lex Av -NY 10170
(212) 458-5890 .. **McCreesh,** Patrick J '91 AIG Domestic Claims -175 Water -NY 10038
(917) 602-3837 .. **McCrink,** Christine Loughlin '99 -20 Terrace Pl -Tuckahoe 10707
(212) 661-7300 .. **McCrink,** Katherine L '10 %Malapero & P LLP -295 Mad Av -NY 10017
(212) 264-8583 .. **McCrohan,** Eileen M '98 DHS-Immgrtn -26 Fed Plz -NY 10278
(315) 471-8111 .. **McCrohan,** Shane M '03 %Scolaro SCF&B,PC -507 Plum -Syracuse 13204
(212) 957-0700 .. **McCrorie,** James J '93 (J McCrorie,PC) -1 Penn Plz -NY 10119 **Fx:**459-1340
(716) 853-9555 .. **McCrory,** Athena E '04 Leg Aid -237 Main -Buffalo 14203 **Fx:**853-3219
(212) 578-5152 .. **McCrory,** Hugh G Jr. '87 %MetLife -27-01 Qns Plz N -LIC 11101
(516) 222-8500 .. **McCrory,** Rosaleen T '89 (Martin C&B LLP) -90 Merrick Av -E Meadow 11554
(212) 980-1900 .. **McCrossen,** Bryan P '02 %Donovan & G,LLP -261 Mad Av -NY 10016
(631) 751-5757 .. **McCrosson,** Kimberly R '02 %Glynn M&P,LLP -57 North Cntry Rd Bx712 -Stony Brk 11790
(914) 592-8422 .. **McCue,** Florence '92 -1518 Old Cntry Rd -Elmsfrd 10523 **Fx:**592-8422
(845) 496-3669 .. **McCue,** Frank T Jr. '71 -45 E Main Bx173 -Washingtnvll 10992
(212) 931-5500 .. **McCue,** John W III '03 (McCue S&Z,PC) -521 5th Av -NY 10175
(212) 858-7706 .. **McCue,** Kurt E '89 (Slowinski A,LLP) -140 Bway PMB 46039 -NY 10005
(845) 565-5900 .. **McCue,** Leonard J '66 -367 Windsor Hwy -New Windsor 12553 **Fx:**565-0713
(585) 746-0138 .. **McCue,** Martin T '03 -14 Fall Meadow Dr -Pittsfrd 14534 **Fx:**248-2111

(212) 931-5500 .. **McCue Sussmane & Zapfel,PC** -521 5th Av -NY 10175
(845) 638-5660 .. **McCue Cincotta,** Clare F '81 %Pub Def -11 New Hempstd Rd -New Cty 10956
(646) 610-6347 .. **McCullagh,** Paul G '97 %NYPD -1 Police Plz -NY 10038
(716) 845-3680 .. **McCulley,** Nancy B '79 Erie Cnty FJC -237 Main -Buffalo 14203
(212) 270-5922 .. **McCulloch,** Kathryn V '76 JP Morgan Chase -270 Park Av -NY 10017
(212) 398-9508 .. **McCulloch,** Kenneth '68 -111 John -NY 10038 **Fx:**398-9512
(212) 388-3843 .. **McCulloch,** Kevin O '74 %Local 32B-32J -101 6th Av -NY 10013
(212) 488-1200 .. **McCulloch,** Scott K '07 %Kobre & K,LLP -800 3rd Av -NY 10022
(631) 422-1500 .. **McCulloh,** Wm C '01 (W McCulloh,PC) -868 Little East Neck Rd -W Babylon 11704 **Fx:**422-1559
(315) 234-8570 .. **McCullough,** Annelle '78 Hon N Mordue -100 S Clinton Bx7367 -Syracuse 13261
(212) 558-4000 .. **McCullough,** Austin F '08 %Sullivan & C LLP -125 Broad -NY 10004
(718) 453-2051 .. **McCullough,** Danl '96 -683 Putnam Av -Brklyn 11221
(914) 422-8757 .. **McCullough,** Dian Kerr '90 %Dept of Law -101 E Post Rd -White Plns 10601 **Fx:**422-8706
(845) 826-3705 .. **McCullough,** Doreen M '03 (DM McCullough,LLC) -30 Ramland Rd -Orangebrg 10962
(914) 949-6400 .. **McCullough,** Frank S Jr. '68 (McCullough G&S,LLP) -1311 Mamaroneck Av -White Plns 10605
(646) 435-0300 .. **McCullough Ginsberg Montano & Partners,LLP** -320 E 53rd -NY 10022 **Fx:**349-2217
(914) 949-6400 .. **McCullough Goldberger & Staudt,LLP** -1311 Mamaroneck Av -White Plns 10605 **Fx:**949-2510
(212) 635-1188 .. **McCullough,** Mary M '01 Bk of NY Mellon -1 Wall -NY 10286
(585) 328-3210 .. **McCullough,** Monica C '06 Providence Hsing Dvlpmt Corp -1136 Buffalo Rd -Rchstr 14624
(212) 676-4875 .. **McCullough,** Roseanne M '96 %Zurich NA -1 Lbrty Plz -NY 10006
(646) 747-4647 .. **McCullough,** Theo V III '01 (McCullough GM&P,LLP) -320 E 53rd -NY 10022
(718) 898-6969 .. **McCullough,** Thos E '76 -37-06 82nd -Jcksn Hts 11372 **Fx:**335-4468
(518) 690-4410 .. **McCullough Day,** Kathy M '07 %R Croak & Assoc -314 Great Oaks Blvd -Albany 12203 **Fx:**690-4435
(212) 348-7449 .. **McCune,** Mary P '94 %Legal Srvcs -1 W 125th -NY 10027 **Fx:**348-4093
(212) 259-8000 .. **McCune,** Shawn R '99 Cnsl Dewey & L LLP -1301 Av of Amer -NY 10019
(212) 819-8200 .. **McCurdy,** Meghan '00 %White & C LLP -1155 Av of Amer -NY 10036
(315) 379-1466 .. **McCurn,** Neal P Jr. '92 (Oot & Assoc,PLLC) -63 Main -Canton 13617 **Fx:**379-1433
(315) 471-6687 .. **McCurn,** Neal P Jr. '92 (Oot & Assoc,PLLC) -503 E Wshngtn -Syracuse 13202 **Fx:**476-7603
(212) 504-6000 .. **McCurrach,** Branden K '07 %Cadwalader W&T LLP -1 World Fncl Ctr -NY 10281
(212) 558-4000 .. **McCurrach,** Duncan C '85 (Sullivan & C LLP) -125 Broad -NY 10004
(212) 308-0070 .. **McCusker Anselmi Rosen & Carvelli, PC** -805 3rd Av -NY 10022 **Fx:**(917) 677-8978
(212) 308-0070 .. **McCusker,** John B '83 (McCusker AR&C,PC) -805 3rd Av -NY 10022
(212) 308-0070 .. **McCusker,** Paul G '97 (McCusker AR&C,PC) -805 3rd Av -NY 10022
(585) 454-7145 .. **McCusker,** Timothy K '76 %Gallo & I,LLP -39 State -Rchstr 14614
(212) 705-7000 .. **McCusker-Concannon,** Elizabeth Fitts '09 %Bingham M LLP -399 Park Av -NY 10022
(718) 851-9065 .. **McCutcheon,** James H '95 -195 E 2nd -Brklyn 11218
(212) 224-1570 .. **McCutcheon,** James K '86 %Mutual of America -320 Park Av -NY 10022
(212) 538-9712 .. **McCutcheon,** John Casey '01 Credit Suisse -1 Mad Av -NY 10010
(518) 388-4364 .. **McCutcheon,** Katie Q '07 DA -612 State -Schnctdy 12305 **Fx:**388-4569
(585) 344-1994 .. **McCutcheon,** Robt B '81 (Bonarigo & M) -18 Ellicott -Batavia 14020 **Fx:**344-1996
(516) 939-9200 .. **McDaid,** Thos P '01 %Mintzer SZL&M LLP -17 W John -Hicksvll 11801
(212) 613-5033 .. **McDaniel,** David R '05 Leg Assist Grp -450 W 33rd -NY 10001 **Fx:**750-0820
(212) 373-3000 .. **McDaniel,** Geneva B '10 Paul WRW&G LLP -1285 Av of Amer -NY 10019
(917) 254-4670 .. **McDaniel,** Jay R '92 (McDaniel & C,LLP) -350 5th Av -NY 10018 **Fx:**(201) 845-3777
(718) 596-7457 .. **McDaniel,** K C '82 KC McDaniel PLLC -100 Jay -Brklyn 11201
(212) 446-4800 .. **McDaniel,** Katherine L '07 %Kirkland & E LLP -153 E 53rd -NY 10022
(212) 270-2611 .. **McDavid,** Wm H '73 JP Morgan Chase -270 Park Av -NY 10017
(212) 351-3400 .. **McDavit,** Jonas R '07 Desmarais LLP -230 Park Av -NY 10169 **Fx:**351-3401
(631) 475-5272 .. **McDay,** Temple '89 -2717 Sipp Av -Medfrd 11763
(315) 471-8113 .. **McDermott & Britt,PC** -103 E Water -Syracuse 13202 **Fx:**471-0446
(212) 504-6000 .. **McDermott,** Christopher M '87 (Cadwalader W&T LLP) -1 World Fncl Ctr -NY 10281
(212) 376-6400 .. **McDermott,** Danl G '76 (Marshall DWC&G) -88 Pine -NY 10005
(212) 250-6855 .. **McDermott,** Douglas J '96 %Deutsche Bk -60 Wall -NY 10005
(212) 609-6800 .. **McDermott,** Edw T '74 (McCarter & E,LLP) -245 Park Av -NY 10167
(914) 276-2747 .. **McDermott,** Fausta R L '86 (McDermott & M) -293 Route 100 -Somers 10589 **Fx:**276-7608
(212) 816-8631 .. **McDermott,** Glen M '94 Salomon Smith Barney -388 Greenwich -NY 10013
(646) 610-6880 .. **McDermott,** James P '81 %NYPD -1 Police Plz -NY 10038
(516) 536-2418 .. **McDermott,** John F Jr. '74 -3520 Anchor Pl -Oceanside 11572 **Fx:**536-4805
(212) 513-3200 .. **McDermott,** John J '53 (Holland & K LLP) -31 W 52nd -NY 10019
(212) 449-7270 .. **McDermott,** John J '82 Merrill Lynch -4 World Fncl Ctr -NY 10080
(315) 471-8113 .. **McDermott,** John R Jr. '79 (McDermott & B,PC) -103 E Water -Syracuse 13202
(212) 268-5136 .. **McDermott,** John W '09 %Harwood L -350 5th Av -NY 10118
(212) 474-1000 .. **McDermott,** Kathleen H '08 %Cravath S&M LLP -825 8th Av -NY 10019
(516) 822-3550 .. **McDermott,** Kevin E '90 %Hoffmann & B LLP -6900 Jericho Tpk -Syosset 11791 **Fx:**822-3582
(516) 742-3662 .. **McDermott,** Kevin M '87 (Patacca & Assoc) -392 Hillside Av -Williston Pk 11596 **Fx:**742-5767
(845) 298-2000 .. **McDermott,** Kevin T '95 %Vergilis SRD&D,LLP -1136 Route 9 -Wappingers Fls 12590
(845) 294-7287 .. **McDermott,** Laurie Tieder '90 %MHLS -5 Coates Dr -Goshen 10924 **Fx:**294-6389
(212) 735-3000 .. **McDermott,** Mark A '07 (Skadden ASM&F LLP) -4 Times Sq -NY 10036
(212) 335-4500 .. **McDermott,** Matthew B '10 %DLA Piper LLP -1251 Av of Amer -NY 10020
(914) 798-5400 .. **McDermott,** Matthew J '96 %Goldberg S LLP -11 Martine Av -White Plns 10606
(212) 425-7854 .. **Mc Dermott,** Michl '97 %Georgoulis & Assoc PLLC -45 Bway -NY 10006 **Fx:**422-5360
(516) 227-0700 .. **McDermott,** Michl E '82 Cnsl Farrell F,PC -1320 RXR Plz -Uniondale 11556
(315) 458-8090 .. **McDermott,** Michl J '80 (McDermott Law Firm) -5860 S Bay Rd -Cicero 13039 **Fx:**458-8098
(914) 276-2747 .. **McDermott,** Michl J '85 (McDermott & M) -293 Route 100 -Somers 10589 **Fx:**276-7608
(212) 557-5055 .. **McDermott,** Michl J '85 %Semetis Law Firm -286 Mad Av -NY 10017 **Fx:**557-5051
(518) 462-5601 .. **McDermott,** Michl P '90 OfCnsl O'Connell & A -54 State -Albany 12207
(212) 418-8600 .. **McDermott,** Mikaela A '03 Kornstein VW&P,LLP -757 3rd Av -NY 10017
(315) 393-1111 .. **McDermott,** Mindy E '07 %Carlisle C&C,PC -602 State Bx757 -Ogdensbrg 13669 **Fx:**393-1181
(845) 343-3000 .. **McDermott,** Paul T '65 (MacVean LS&M,PC) -34 Grove Bx310 -Middletwn 10940
(631) 414-0094 .. **McDermott,** Robt G '92 -110 Marcus Blvd -Hauppauge 11788 **Fx:**414-0098
(212) 547-5400 .. **McDermott,** Robt J '71 OfCnsl McDermott W&E LLP -340 Mad Av -NY 10173
(646) 471-4241 .. **McDermott,** Robt J '98 PriceWaterhouseCoopers LLP -300 Mad Av -NY 10017
(212) 578-2211 .. **McDermott,** Sheila M '01 %MetLife -1095 Av of Amer -NY 10036 **Fx:**578-3916
(212) 335-4500 .. **McDermott,** Stanley III '88 (DLA Piper LLP) -1251 Av of Amer -NY 10020
(718) 254-7000 .. **McDermott,** Suzanne '96 %US Atty -271 Cadman Plz E -Brklyn 11201 **Fx:**254-6479
(516) 317-9002 .. **McDermott,** Thos F '75 -315 Old Salt Rd Bx343 -Mattituck 11952 **Fx:**(631) 298-7293
(607) 273-8410 .. **McDermott,** Wesley E '70 -405 N Tioga -Ithaca 14850 **Fx:**273-3802
(212) 547-5400 .. **McDermott Will & Emery LLP** -340 Mad Av -NY 10173 **Fx:**547-5444
(716) 284-0435 .. **McDermott,** Wm J '76 Sevenson Envir Svcs -2749 Lockport Rd -Niagara Fls 14305 **Fx:**284-7645
(516) 465-9100 .. **McDermott,** Wm J '89 -499 Jericho Tpk -Mineola 11501 **Fx:**465-9105
(718) 237-2000 .. **McDermott,** Zachary M '09 %Leg Aid -111 Lvngstn -Brklyn 11201 **Fx:**237-8737
(212) 819-8200 .. **McDevitt,** Heather K '94 (White & C LLP) -1155 Av of Amer -NY 10036
(212) 578-7418 .. **McDevitt,** Molly D '99 %MetLife -27-01 Qns Plz N -LIC 11101
(518) 463-3200 .. **McDevitt,** Pamela M '96 NYS Bar Assn -1 Elk -Albany 12207
(607) 535-4528 .. **McDivitt,** Stewart E '74 -Route 14 & Ayers Bx359 -Montour Fls 14865 **Fx:**535-7646
(212) 695-5670 .. **McDonagh,** Janis Cowhey '91 (Goldfinger & L LLP) -750 3rd Av -NY 10017
(212) 964-6611 .. **McDonagh,** Michl E '87 (Lester SK&D) -120 Bway -NY 10271
(212) 964-7556 .. **McDonagh,** Michl J '92 -30 Vesey -NY 10007
(516) 229-4325 .. **McDonagh,** Patricia M '96 %J Bilello & Assoc -875 Merrick Av -Westbury 11590
(718) 261-6863 .. **McDonald,** Christopher D '00 %M Mund & Assoc -100-15 Qns Blvd -Frst Hlls 11375 **Fx:**261-5709
(212) 907-0700 .. **McDonald,** Christopher J '93 (Labaton S LLP) -140 Bway -NY 10005
(518) 487-7600 .. **McDonald,** Christopher M '06 %Whiteman O&H LLP -1 Commerce Plz -Albany 12260
(212) 701-3000 .. **McDonald,** Collin D '09 %Cahill G&R LLP -80 Pine -NY 10005 **Fx:**269-5420
(585) 464-3894 .. **McDonald,** Danl R '76 Hahn Automtv Warehse -415 W Main -Rchstr 14608 **Fx:**235-3108
(212) 859-8000 .. **McDonald,** David M '95 %Fried FHS&J LLP -1 NY Plz -NY 10004
(212) 833-4202 .. **McDonald,** Deirdre M '90 Sony BMG Music Entrtnmnt -550 Mad Av -NY 10022 **Fx:**833-8406
(718) 579-3000 .. **McDonald,** Dorothy K '05 %Leg Aid -1020 Grnd Cncrs -Bronx 10451 **Fx:**588-2611
(212) 698-3500 .. **McDonald,** Edw A '72 (Dechert LLP) -1095 Av of Amer -NY 10036
McDonald, Elizabeth J '79 -8 Austin Park -Pittsfrd 14534
(518) 474-3517 .. **McDonald,** Ellen M '79 %State Comptroller -110 State -Albany 12236 **Fx:**473-9104
(212) 869-3200 .. **McDonald,** Geoffrey K '03 %Molod S&D,PC -104 W 40th -NY 10018
(315) 336-4500 .. **McDonald,** Gerald T '58 OfCnsl O'Shea M&S,LLP -107 W Lbrty Bx4310 -Rome 13442
(585) 362-4700 .. **McDonald,** Gregory J '96 (Bond S&K,PLLC) -350 Linden Oaks -Rchstr 14625
(518) 783-4767 .. **McDonald,** Harry W '41 -930 Albany Shaker Rd -Latham 12110 **Fx:**783-3077
(212) 733-0412 .. **McDonald,** Heather A '97 Pfizer -150 E 42nd -NY 10017
(212) 589-4200 .. **McDonald,** Heather J '87 (Baker & H LLP) -45 Rckfllr Plz -NY 10111
(212) 768-6700 .. **McDonald,** Hugh M '91 (Sonnenschein N&R LLP) -1221 Av of Amer -NY 10020
(212) 558-4000 .. **McDonald,** Ian D '07 %Sullivan & C LLP -125 Broad -NY 10004

(212) 715-9100 .. **McDonald,** Izabel P '93 SpclCnsl Kramer LN&F,LLP -1177 Av of Amer -NY 10036
(212) 297-1357 .. **McDonald,** James W Jr. '74 Santandea Ctrl Hispano -45 E 53rd -NY 10022
(315) 655-8325 .. **McDonald,** Jana K '01 %H Lindenfeld,PC -11 Lincklaen Bx465 -Cazenovia 13035 **Fx:**655-3303
(212) 310-8000 .. **McDonald,** Jane E '97 (Weil G&M LLP) -767 5th Av -NY 10153
(212) 608-1911 .. **McDonald,** John B Jr. '70 OfCnsl Stockschlaeder M&S,PC -110 William -NY 10038
(518) 585-2631 .. **McDonald,** John C '60 -Bx391 -Ticonderoga 12883 **Fx:**585-2631
(845) 563-4602 .. **McDonald,** John H '02 Cnsl Twn of New Windsor -555 Union Av -New Windsor 12553 **Fx:**563-4602
(212) 309-6000 .. **McDonald,** Jos F '66 SrCnsl Morgan L&B LLP -101 Park Av -NY 10178
(212) 335-9000 .. **McDonald,** Karen F '02 %DA -1 Hogan Pl -NY 10013
(212) 953-3400 .. **McDonald,** Kathryn Ann '79 (Robinson & M) -61 Bway -NY 10006
(212) 848-4000 .. **McDonald,** Kelly E '08 %Shearman & S LLP -599 Lex Av -NY 10022
(315) 789-8480 .. **McDonald,** Kevin J '81 (Bond M&L,PC) -91 Genesee -Geneva 14456
(212) 406-1700 .. **McDonald,** Kevin S '75 (Queller FWF&K LLP) -233 Bway -NY 10279
(212) 656-2626 .. **McDonald,** Kevin T '88 NYSE -14 Wall -NY 10005
(212) 360-2380 .. **McDonald,** Kristin T '05 %Lincoln B LLP -110 E 59th -NY 10022 **Fx:**360-2381
(585) 464-9400 .. **McDonald,** Lee Ann D '96 %Wilmorite -1265 Scottsvll Rd -Rchstr 14624 **Fx:**328-1784
(518) 266-9060 .. **McDonald,** Marissa C '06 %Assaf & M PLLC -427 River -Troy 12180 **Fx:**266-9064
(315) 789-8480 .. **McDonald,** Mark M '85 (Bond M&L,PC) -91 Genesee -Geneva 14456
(212) 687-8500 .. **McDonald,** Matthew J '09 %Liddle & R,LLP -800 3rd Av -NY 10022
(212) 335-9000 .. **McDonald,** Megan M '09 %DA -1 Hogan Pl -NY 10013
(516) 294-0300 .. **McDonald,** Robt A '84 (Collins M&G) -138 Mineola Blvd -Mineola 11501
(315) 218-8000 .. **McDonald,** Roderick C '97 (Bond S&K,PLLC) -1 Lincoln Ctr -Syracuse 13202
(716) 853-9555 .. **McDonald,** Shawn P '03 %Leg Aid -237 Main -Buffalo 14203 **Fx:**853-3219
(212) 373-3000 .. **McDonald,** Stacy F '09 %Paul WRW&G LLP -1285 Av of Amer -NY 10019
(845) 534-7200 .. **McDonald,** T Bruce B Jr. '87 -286 Main -Cornwall 12518 **Fx:**534-2008
(585) 641-8000 .. **McDonald,** T Mary '77 (Fix SB&G,PC) -295 Woodcliff Dr -Fairprt 14450
(315) 445-0600 .. **McDonald,** Timothy F '98 (McDonald & K PC) -120 E Wshngtn -Syracuse 13202
(212) 248-9100 .. **McDonald,** Virginia E '81 (Epstein M&M) -1 Whitehall -NY 10004
(315) 789-8480 .. **McDonald,** Wm J Jr. '78 (Bond M&L,PC) -91 Genesee -Geneva 14456
(516) 663-6600 .. **McDonald,** Wm J '98 %Ruskin MF,PC -1425 RXR Plz -Uniondale 11556
(631) 226-2100 .. **McDonaugh,** James A '95 (Phillips WAC&M) -165 S Wellwood Av -Lindenhrst 11757
(212) 415-9200 .. **McDonell,** Neil E '84 (Dorsey & W LLP) -250 Park Av -NY 10177
(516) 328-3500 .. **McDonnell & Adels, PC** -401 Franklin Av -Gdn Cty 11530 **Fx:**328-3697
(212) 227-0347 .. **McDonnell,** Brian B '97 %Weiss W&W,PC -25 Park Pl -NY 10007
(631) 577-2400 .. **McDonnell,** J Pearse '84 (Tromello M&K) -25 Melvll Park Rd Bx9038 -Melvll 11747
(212) 504-6000 .. **McDonnell,** James T '08 %Cadwalader W&T LLP -1 World Fncl Ctr -NY 10281
(718) 250-2000 .. **McDonnell,** Janet M '99 %DA -350 Jay -Brklyn 11201 **Fx:**250-2314
(518) 266-3036 .. **McDonnell,** Jean A '93 %Tax Appls Tribunal -500 Fed -Troy 12180 **Fx:**271-0886
(212) 669-7400 .. **McDonnell,** Jennifer E '07 NYC Media Grp -1 Centre -NY 10007
(315) 793-3622 .. **McDonnell,** Jennifer M '00 %Estate Planning Law Ctr -555 French Rd -New Hartfrd 13413
(631) 913-4444 .. **McDonnell,** John S '94 (Dell LT&V LLP) -5 Orvll Dr -Bohemia 11716
(646) 515-4652 .. **McDonnell,** Keith B '07 Philips Electronics -1251 Av of Amer -NY 10020
(516) 496-1919 .. **McDonnell,** Laurence G '88 (Keller O&W,PC) -242 Crsswys Park Dr W -Woodbury 11797
(212) 909-6000 .. **McDonnell,** Michl K '04 %Debevoise & P LLP -919 3rd Av -NY 10022
(516) 328-3500 .. **McDonnell,** Patrick J '85 (McDonnell & A,PC) -401 Franklin Av -Gdn Cty 11530
(585) 530-3144 .. **McDonnell,** Patrick J '04 Appellate Div 4th Dept -50 East Av -Rchstr 14604 **Fx:**530-3247
(212) 428-2150 .. **McDonnell,** Paul '82 OCA -25 Beaver -NY 10004
(914) 422-4381 .. **McDonnell,** Thos M '76 %Pace Law Schl -78 N Bway -White Plns 10603 **Fx:**422-4039
(646) 328-0120 .. **McDonnell,** Timothy J '94 (Bennett GM&P,LLP) -494 8th Av -NY 10001
(607) 772-6070 .. **McDonough & Artz,PC** -89 Court Bx1740 -Bnghmtn 13902 **Fx:**772-0173
(212) 538-7303 .. **McDonough,** Brennan S '02 Credit Suisse Securities LLC -1 Mad Av -NY 10010
(212) 248-3160 .. **McDonough,** Brian F '81 (Drinker B&R LLP) -140 Bway -NY 10005
(516) 229-4400 .. **McDonough,** Brian P '01 %Kay & G -875 Merrick Av -Westbury 11590
(516) 496-5822 .. **McDonough,** Brian P '07 %T Spina -170 Froehlich Farm Blvd -Woodbury 11797 **Fx:**496-5420
(212) 785-2929 .. **McDonough,** Caitlin B '04 %Conway FC&K,PC -48 Wall -NY 10005
(631) 673-6670 .. **McDonough,** Chris G '88 (McDonough & M) -115 Broad Hollow Rd -Melvll 11747 **Fx:**673-7023
(518) 474-7700 .. **McDonough,** Cynthia Elwell '94 %NYS OPWDD -44 Holland Av -Albany 12229 **Fx:**474-7382
(212) 785-2929 .. **McDonough,** Danl K '00 %Conway FC&K,PC -48 Wall -NY 10005
(631) 673-6670 .. **McDonough,** Diana Brusca '85 (McDonough & M) -115 Broad Hollow Rd -Melvll 11747 **Fx:**673-7023
(212) 259-8000 .. **McDonough,** Ffiona M '02 %Dewey & L LLP -1301 Av of Amer -NY 10019
(516) 294-6670 .. **McDonough,** Francis J '77 McDonough & M -55 Hilton Av -Gdn Cty 11530 **Fx:**248-0630
(914) 276-3933 .. **McDonough,** J Edw '62 -440C Heritage Hls -Somers 10589 **Fx:**276-3377
(315) 471-6687 .. **McDonough,** John F Jr. '84 SrCnsl Oot & Assoc,PLLC -503 E Wshngtn -Syracuse 13202 **Fx:**476-7603
(212) 509-9400 .. **McDonough,** John J III '80 (Cozen O) -45 Bway Atrium -NY 10006
(212) 435-3541 .. **McDonough,** John P '09 Port Auth of NY/NJ -225 Park Av S -NY 10003 **Fx:**435-3555
(212) 208-3280 .. **McDonough,** Kathleen A '83 %AMBAC -1 State Street Plz -NY 10004
(607) 844-8211 .. **McDonough,** Kathleen P '85 Tompkins Cortland CC -Bx139 -Dryden 13053
(212) 326-2000 .. **McDonough,** Kelly E '10 %O'Melveny & M LLP -7 Times Sq -NY 10036
(607) 772-6070 .. **McDonough,** Kevin F '70 (McDonough & A,PC) -89 Court Bx1740 -Bnghmtn 13902
(212) 599-1515 .. **McDonough,** Kevin M '96 (Stein RM,LLP) -405 Lex Av -NY 10174
(212) 906-1200 .. **McDonough,** Kevin M '06 %Latham & W -885 3rd Av -NY 10022
(516) 592-6800 .. **McDonough,** Kevin P '89 (Spellman RSGM&P,LLP) -229 Seventh -Gdn Cty 11530
(212) 373-3000 .. **McDonough,** Krista A '06 %Paul WRW&G LLP -1285 Av of Amer -NY 10019
(914) 632-4700 .. **The McDonough Law Firm, LLP** -145 Huguenot -New Rchll 10801 **Fx:**632-3329
(212) 461-7113 .. **The McDonough Law Firm, LLP** -44 W Wall -NY 10005 **Fx:**461-2223
(516) 496-1919 .. **McDonough,** Matthew M '85 (Keller O&W,PC) -242 Crsswys Park Dr W -Woodbury 11797
(914) 358-4934 .. **McDonough,** Michl A '01 %Ferro L&Z LLC -1025 Wstchstr Av -White Plns 10604
(212) 509-2050 .. **McDonough,** Paul S '78 -50 Broad -NY 10004 **Fx:**344-5163
(212) 684-0199 .. **McDonough,** Robt F '88 Polsinelli S PC -7 Penn Plz -NY 10001
(212) 732-3200 .. **McDonough,** Theo Y '08 %Carter L&M LLP -2 Wall -NY 10005
(518) 792-0915 .. **McDonough,** Thos J '62 -1088 State Route 9 -Queensbury 12804 **Fx:**792-2003
(914) 328-0404 .. **McDonough,** Thos P '96 (Jackson L LLP) -1 N Bway -White Plns 10601
(212) 756-2000 .. **McDoom,** Leah V '09 %Schulte R&Z LLP -919 3rd Av -NY 10022
(516) 408-9000 .. **McDougal,** Paul R '85 (Walsh MM&D LLP) -229 Seventh -Gdn Cty 11530
(212) 530-5000 .. **McDougall,** Eliza W '02 %Milbank TH&M LLP -1 Chase Manh Plz -NY 10005
(716) 847-8400 .. **McDougall,** Lisa '87 (Phillips L LLP) -3400 HSBC Ctr -Buffalo 14203
(718) 923-4206 .. **McDougall,** Robt D '72 %OTDA Fair Hearings -14 Boerum Pl -Brklyn 11201
(631) 423-4390 .. **McDow,** Alicia M '02 %Mincone & M,PC -110 Walt Whitman Rd -South Huntington 11746 **Fx:**423-4408
(212) 545-4600 .. **McDowell,** Alan A B '07 %Wolf HAF&H LLP -270 Mad Av -NY 10016
(607) 737-3735 .. **McDowell,** Boyd II '51 -1 Chemung Canal Plz -Elmira 14901 **Fx:**737-3850
(914) 249-5367 .. **McDowell,** David L '97 MasterCard Intl -2000 Purchase -Purchase 10577
(718) 778-9100 .. **McDowell,** Derek P '79 -1476A Fulton -Brklyn 11216 **Fx:**778-6064
(212) 848-9800 .. **McDowell,** Jay H '64 OfCnsl Withers B LLP -430 Park Av -NY 10022
(914) 220-1900 .. **McDowell,** Sean W '09 (Nelson Law Firm,LLC) -1 N Bway -White Plns 10601
(212) 688-9112 .. **McDuffie,** Tanya D '02 %EP Dine Inc -115 E 57th -NY 10022 **Fx:**755-8486
(631) 853-5761 .. **McEachin,** Samantha N '02 %Cnty Atty -400 Carleton Av -Central Islip 11722 **Fx:**853-7788
(716) 856-5500 .. **McEldowney,** Virginia C '86 SpclCnsl Damon M LLP -200 Delaware Av -Buffalo 14202
(845) 561-0550 .. **McElduff,** Timothy P Jr. '98 %Drake LHKGG&R PLLC -555 Hudson Valley Av -New Windsor 12553
(212) 297-5800 .. **McEleney,** Sumy '08 %Day P LLP -7 Times Sq -NY 10036
(212) 307-5100 .. **McElfish,** Raymond D '92 (McElfish & Assoc,LLC) -350 5th Av -NY 10118 **Fx:**307-5200
(212) 735-3000 .. **McElhaney,** Christy L '88 Cnsl Skadden ASM&F LLP -4 Times Sq -NY 10036
(516) 281-9800 .. **McElhenny,** Brian W '81 (Goldberg S LLP) -200 Old Cntry Rd -Mineola 11501
(212) 801-3165 .. **McElhenny,** Shaun D '09 %Greenberg T,LLP -200 Park Av -NY 10166
(585) 987-2800 .. **McElheny,** James P '78 (Woods OG LLP) -2 State -Rchstr 14614
(646) 282-2500 .. **McElhinney,** Danl C '98 Epiq Systems -757 3rd Av -NY 10017
(631) 473-5100 .. **McElhone,** James E '87 (Barbera & M,PC) -428 Route 25A Bx5595 -Miller Pl 11764 **Fx:**473-2648
(631) 231-2424 .. **McElligott,** Denis J '86 %Dept of Law -300 Motor Pkwy -Hauppauge 11788 **Fx:**435-4757
(212) 340-0400 .. **McElligott,** John K '76 %Appllt Div 1st Dept -27 Mad Av -NY 10010 **Fx:**889-4412
(212) 552-3131 .. **McElligott,** Valerie B '04 Cnsl JP Morgan Chase & Co -1 Chase Manh Plz -NY 10005 **Fx:**383-0246
(212) 210-9595 .. **McElreath,** Mark F '02 (Alston & B LLP) -90 Park Av -NY 10016
(914) 961-6100 .. **McElroen,** Lawr J '92 Hudson Valley Bank -21 Scarsdale Rd -Ynkrs 10707
(716) 852-1000 .. **McElroy,** Carrie R '09 %PW Beltz,PC -36 Church -Buffalo 14202 **Fx:**852-5887
(212) 483-9490 .. **McElroy Deutsch Mulvaney & Carpenter,LLP** -88 Pine -NY 10005 **Fx:**483-9129
(516) 248-7007 .. **McElroy,** Eugene F '84 (McElroy & M) -114 Old Cntry Rd -Mineola 11501
(212) 980-0120 .. **McElroy,** Gavin D '86 (Frankfurt KK&S,PC) -488 Mad Av -NY 10022
(718) 990-5699 .. **McElroy,** Kathleen M '94 %St Johns Univ -8000 Utopia Pkwy -Jamaica 11439
(516) 463-5858 .. **McElroy,** Kevin '87 %Hofstra Law Schl -121 Hofstra Univ -Hempstd 11549
(516) 248-7007 .. **McElroy,** Kristen M '00 (McElroy & M) -114 Old Cntry Rd -Mineola 11501

(212) 474-1000 .. **McElroy,** Thos H '10 %Cravath S&M LLP -825 8th Av -NY 10019
(716) 854-2620 .. **McElvein,** Thos I Jr. '62 -1500 Lbrty Bldg -Buffalo 14202 **Fx:**854-0082
(607) 274-5461 .. **McElwee,** Andrew M '04 %DA -320 N Tioga -Ithaca 14850 **Fx:**274-5429
(631) 225-6675 .. **McElwee,** Craig E '95 -1476 Deer Pa -N Babylon 11703
(212) 302-5101 .. **McElyea,** Wm D '92 (Silverstein LN&M,LLP) -500 5th Av -NY 10110
(718) 349-4709 .. **McEnaney,** Timothy M '01 Nouveau Elevator Industries,Inc -74 Calyer -Brklyn 11222
(212) 637-2571 .. **McEnany,** John M '87 %US Atty -1 St Andrews Plz -NY 10007
(718) 324-4333 .. **McEneney,** Michl F '60 -91 E 236th -Bronx 10470 **Fx:**324-4333
(718) 885-1234 .. **McEnery,** Cormac '79 -562 City Isl Av -Bronx 10464 **Fx:**885-1112
(212) 839-5300 .. **McEnroe,** Diane Crosson '89 Cnsl Sidley A LLP -787 7th Av -NY 10019
(718) 901-6600 .. **McEnroe,** Gerard J '92 %Schl Cnstrctn Auth -188 W 230th -Bronx 10463 **Fx:**901-6649
(212) 373-3000 .. **McEnroe,** John P '65 OfCnsl Paul WRW&G LLP -1285 Av of Amer -NY 10019
(914) 833-8000 .. **McEnroe,** Mark T '90 Cedar St Grp,LLC -1890 Palmer Av -Larchmnt 10538
(212) 599-8200 .. **McEnroe,** Michele L '02 %Shaub AC&S,LLP -655 3rd Av -NY 10017
(212) 297-0075 .. **McEnroe,** Paul J '97 Sidoti & Co -317 Mad Av -NY 10017
(516) 227-0700 .. **McEntee,** John P '86 (Farrell F,PC) -1320 RXR Plz -Uniondale 11556
(718) 353-2250 .. **McEntee,** John R '80 -33-21 F Lewis Blvd -Flushng 11358
(718) 961-4497 .. **McEntee,** Linda A '80 -33-21 F Lewis Blvd -Flushng 11358
(914) 765-1900 .. **McEvily,** Ann C '88 IBM -1 New Orchrd Rd -Armonk 10504 **Fx:**765-7533
(516) 222-0202 .. **McEvily,** Chas J '74 (DaSilva H&M LLP) -585 Stewart Av -Gdn Cty 11530 **Fx:**222-1669
(516) 766-7993 .. **McEvily,** Stephanie '80 -68 Roxen Rd -Rockvll Ctr 11570 **Fx:**766-7993
(518) 457-2070 .. **McEvoy,** Andrew T Jr. '63 Dept of Tax & Fin -Bldg 9 State Campus -Albany 12227 **Fx:**457-6131
(212) 637-2309 .. **McEvoy,** Deirdre A '99 %US Atty -1 St Andrews Plz -NY 10007
(518) 828-9985 .. **McEvoy,** Dennis W '85 (Koweek C&M,PC) -445 Warren -Hudson 12534
(212) 598-1450 .. **McEvoy,** Gerald W '86 Guardian Trust Co -7 Hanover Sq -NY 10004
(212) 436-5856 .. **McEvoy,** Helen T '08 Deloitte & Touche,LLP -2 World Fncl Ctr -NY 10281
(212) 857-8272 .. **McEvoy,** John P '95 (Baker MM&M,PC) -330 W 34th -NY 10001 **Fx:**857-8238
(212) 344-5680 .. **McEvoy,** Lauren M '09 %Thompson H LLP -335 Mad Av -NY 10017
(585) 232-6500 .. **McEvoy,** Michl R '82 (Harter S&E LLP) -1600 Bausch & Lomb Pl -Rchstr 14604
(212) 673-1769 .. **McEvoy,** Patrick J '58 -510 E 23rd -NY 10010
(212) 308-4411 .. **McEvoy,** Rory J '78 (Edwards AP&D LLP) -750 Lex Av -NY 10022
(716) 842-5001 .. **McEvoy,** Timothy G '87 %M&T Bk -1 M & T Plz -Buffalo 14203 **Fx:**842-5376
(914) 698-2880 .. **McEvoy-Derrico,** Christie L '97 -910 E Bstn Post Rd -Mamaroneck 10543 **Fx:**698-9156
(518) 372-1008 .. **McEwan,** Robt S Jr. '85 -514 State -Schnctdy 12305 **Fx:**372-1009
(973) 848-4700 .. **McEwan,** Russell J '96 (Littler M,PC) -900 3rd Av -NY 10022 **Fx:**643-5626
(212) 281-4887 .. **McEwen,** Lucille Leta '93 Harlem Congregations -2854 Fredrck Douglass Blvd -NY 10039
(585) 396-4411 .. **McFadden,** Barry D '91 %Cnty Atty -27 N Main -Canandaigua 14424 **Fx:**396-4481
(212) 856-9600 .. **McFadden,** JoAnna G '07 %Morvillo AGIA&B,PC -565 5th Av -NY 10017
(518) 431-1000 .. **McFadden,** John R '09 %Siegal,LLC -16 Corp Wds Blvd -Albany 12211 **Fx:**465-7200
(212) 891-1600 .. **McFadden,** Jos J '06 %Jenner & B LLP -919 3rd Av -NY 10022
(585) 232-6500 .. **McFadden,** Langston D '04 %Harter S&E LLP -1600 Bausch & Lomb Pl -Rchstr 14604
(212) 854-0287 .. **McFadden,** Laurie '00 %Columbia Univ -535 W 116th 412 Low Mem'l Library -NY 10027
(212) 319-6898 .. **McFadden,** Leona C '94 (Lavin ORC&D) -420 Lex Av -NY 10170
(646) 610-6347 .. **McFadden,** Lisa M '01 NYPD -One Police Plz -NY 10038
(585) 232-6500 .. **McFadden,** Shaleeya B '05 %Harter S&E LLP -1600 Bausch & Lomb Pl -Rchstr 14604
(718) 813-2155 .. **McFadin,** Mary Diane '98 -490 Warren -Brklyn 11217
(212) 848-4000 .. **McFadyen,** Douglas R A '96 (Shearman & S LLP) -599 Lex Av -NY 10022
(518) 402-6757 .. **McFarland,** Andrew P '95 %Workers Comp Bd -20 Park -Albany 12207
(716) 875-8664 .. **McFarland,** James T '56 OfCnsl Bartlo H&W -22 Victoria Blvd -Kenmore 14217 **Fx:**447-0067
(718) 963-5774 .. **McFarland,** Janet Lynn '02 %MHLS -760 Bway -Brklyn 11206 **Fx:**384-2702
(518) 464-6770 .. **McFarland,** Mandy M '01 (Thorn GT&B,LLP) -5 Wembley Ct Bx15054 -Albany 12212
(212) 216-1208 .. **McFarland,** Maria '02 %Human Rights Watch -350 5th Av -NY 10118 **Fx:**736-1300
(212) 857-8815 .. **McFarland,** Michl G '08 US Ct of Appls -233 Bway -NY 10279
(631) 715-7900 .. **McFarland,** Thos A '82 %US Atty -610 Fed Plz -Central Islip 11722
(585) 262-2860 .. **McFarland,** Timothy J '87 %Medicaid Fraud Cntrl -144 Exchange Blvd -Rchstr 14614 **Fx:**262-2866
(718) 286-6000 .. **McFarlane,** Alicia A '09 %DA -125-01 Qns Blvd -Kew Gdns 11415
(212) 416-8000 .. **McFarlane,** Amy E '08 %Dept of Law -120 Bway -NY 10271
(212) 594-5300 .. **McFarlane,** John R '06 %Milberg LLP -1 Penn Plz -NY 10119
(212) 487-9701 .. **McFarlane,** Karen W '83 %Robin HK&F -1 Bttry Pk Plz -NY 10014
(212) 806-5400 .. **McFarlane,** Matthew B '06 %Stroock &S&L LLP -180 Maiden Ln -NY 10038
(646) 536-3883 .. **McFarlane,** R Naomi '01 -545 8th Av -NY 10018 **Fx:**546-5993
(212) 975-3552 .. **McFarlin,** Patricia A '84 %CBS Inc -51 W 52nd -NY 10019 **Fx:**975-3930
(914) 668-6622 .. **McFarquhar,** Joan L '84 -105 Stevens Av -Mt Vernon 10550 **Fx:**668-7763
(212) 442-4900 .. **McFaul,** Chas D '71 %Ofc Admin Trials -40 Rector -NY 10006 **Fx:**442-4947
(516) 294-8844 .. **McFaul,** Danl A Jr. '04 %L'Abbate BC&C,LLP -1001 Franklin Av -Gdn Cty 11530
(516) 624-6700 .. **McFaul,** John M '76 JM McFaul,PC -19 W Main -Oyster Bay 11771 **Fx:**922-7173
(212) 541-6222 .. **McFeely,** Brendan P '99 %Kane K,PC -1350 Av of Amer -NY 10019
(646) 414-6914 .. **McFerrin-Clancy,** John '89 (Lowenstein S PC) -1251 Av of Amer -NY 10020 **Fx:**(973) 422-6897
(212) 340-0400 .. **McFerrin-Clancy,** Sylvia Starr '92 %Appllt Div 1st Dept -27 Mad Av -NY 10010 **Fx:**889-4412
(212) 670-0186 .. **McGaffey,** Fredk C '69 %Merrill Lynch -222 Bway -NY 10038
(516) 681-3100 .. **McGahan,** James M '85 (Donohue MC&B) -555 N Bway Bx350 -Jericho 11753
(212) 351-3768 .. **McGahan,** Michl F '76 (Epstein B&G,PC) -250 Park Av -NY 10177
(518) 873-3335 .. **McGahay,** Allison M '05 %DA -Cthse -Elizabethtwn 12932 **Fx:**873-3788
(914) 665-3417 .. **McGahran,** Kathleen T '99 Pelham Assoc,Inc -29 Alameda Pl -Mt Vernon 10552 **Fx:**665-6797
(914) 476-3409 .. **McGahren,** Eugene D Jr. '55 -225 Kneeland Av -Ynkrs 10705 **Fx:**476-0994
(212) 449-3462 .. **McGahren,** Thos J '93 Merrill Lynch -250 Vesey -NY 10080
(212) 935-5700 .. **McGann,** Kathleen M '99 %Colucci & U -218 E 50th -NY 10022
(212) 819-8200 .. **McGann,** Kevin X '97 (White & C LLP) -1155 Av of Amer -NY 10036
McGann, Thos J Jr. '77 -1225 Franklin Av -Gdn Cty 11530 **Fx:**(516) 873-8881
(516) 294-5200 .. **McGannon,** Christian M '91 %Picciano & S -900 Merchants Cncrs -Westbury 11590
(212) 384-1000 .. **McGarrity,** Michl C '96 %FBI -26 Fed Plz -NY 10278
(914) 684-0200 .. **McGarrity,** Thos F '73 (Rosenblatt & M LLP) -200 Mamaroneck Av -White Plns 10601
(914) 939-7420 .. **McGarry,** Ann '90 -75 Hllcrst Av -Rye Brook 10573
(212) 867-0100 .. **McGarry,** James '55 (McGarry & S) -317 Mad Av -NY 10017 **Fx:**867-3243
(212) 385-8000 .. **McGarry,** James P '81 OfCnsl Barasch MS&P -11 Park Pl -NY 10007
(212) 735-3000 .. **McGarry,** Martha E '78 (Skadden ASM&F LLP) -4 Times Sq -NY 10036
(212) 455-2000 .. **McGarry,** Mary Elizabeth '83 (Simpson T&B LLP) -425 Lex Av -NY 10017
(518) 435-8092 .. **McGarry,** Michl T '83 %Finkelstein & Prtnrs,LLP -80 Wolf Rd -Albany 12205
(315) 218-8000 .. **McGarry,** Wm L Jr. '75 OfCnsl Bond S&K,PLLC -1 Lincoln Ctr -Syracuse 13202
(516) 623-7862 .. **McGarvey,** Chas A '57 -19 Meadow Ln -Rockvll Ctr 11570
(646) 733-3200 .. **McGarvey-DePuy,** Mary B '00 US Customs -1 Penn Plz -NY 10119
(212) 513-0981 .. **McGaughey,** Lawr H '69 -217 Bway -NY 10007 **Fx:**732-5546
(212) 547-5400 .. **McGavin,** Thos A Jr. '74 (McDermott W&E LLP) -340 Mad Av -NY 10173
(315) 386-5732 .. **McGaw,** Maureen C '89 -51 Miner Bx671 -Canton 13617
(845) 451-4091 .. **McGaw,** Ronald J '88 %City Court -62 Civic Ctr Plz -Poughkeepsie 12601 **Fx:**451-4094
(516) 822-8900 .. **McGaw,** Susan D '85 (Fiedelman & M) -2 Jericho Plz -Jericho 11753
(212) 705-7000 .. **McGay,** Jennifer Hurley '99 (Bingham M LLP) -399 Park Av -NY 10022
(631) 749-2518 .. **McGayhey,** Donald M '86 -55A N Ferry Rd Bx1946 -Shelter Isl 11964
(212) 670-0362 .. **McGeachy,** Joycelyn E '94 %Merrill Lynch -222 Bway -NY 10038
(212) 455-2000 .. **McGee,** Bryan K '06 %Simpson T&B LLP -425 Lex Av -NY 10017
(516) 238-0474 .. **McGee,** Denis T '88 -6 Flower Hill Pl -Pt Wash 11050
(212) 354-4500 .. **McGee,** Erin V '06 %Friedman & W -1500 Bway -NY 10036
(716) 648-4368 .. **McGee,** John P '84 -155 Oliver Pl -Hambrg 14075
(718) 876-6300 .. **McGee,** Karen Fisher '77 %DA -130 Styvsnt Pl -Staten Isl 10301
(212) 788-7140 .. **McGee,** Kathleen A '02 Ofc of Special Enforcement -1 Centre -NY 10007
(212) 232-1300 .. **McGee,** Kelly A '02 (Lewis BB&S LLP) -77 Water -NY 10005
(212) 872-2172 .. **McGee,** Mark D '08 KPMG LLP -345 Park Av -NY 10154
(716) 883-7272 .. **McGee,** Michl R '70 (McGee & G) -200 Summer -Buffalo 14222
(718) 544-0041 .. **McGee,** Nancy M '06 %J Wisell -80-02 Kew Grdns Rd -Kew Gdns 11415 **Fx:**261-0316
(631) 723-2110 .. **McGeehan,** John R '90 Hampton Bays High Schl -88 E Argonne Rd -Hampton Bays 11946
(212) 318-6000 .. **McGeeney,** John S '60 OfCnsl Paul HJ&W LLP -75 E 55th -NY 10022
(845) 429-2080 .. **McGeorge,** Alan B '82 -109 Clove Av Bx114 -Haverstraw 10927 **Fx:**429-5066
(212) 819-8200 .. **McGeorge,** Randall C '03 Cnsl White & C LLP -1155 Av of Amer -NY 10036
(516) 741-6266 .. **McGeough,** Brian J '81 (McCabe CM&F,LLP) -346 Westbury Av Bx9000 -Carle Pl 11514
(212) 757-0400 .. **McGerity,** Margaret A '82 (Folkenflik & M) -1500 Bway -NY 10036 **Fx:**757-2010
(646) 386-3975 .. **McGevna,** James P '72 %Hon B Goodman -100 Centre -NY 10013
(315) 379-1466 .. **McGevna,** James P '93 (Oot & Assoc,PLLC) -63 Main -Canton 13617 **Fx:**379-1433
(315) 471-6687 .. **McGevna,** James P '93 (Oot & Assoc,PLLC) -503 E Wshngtn -Syracuse 13202 **Fx:**476-7603
(631) 730-8686 .. **McGiff,** Stephen J '91 -96 S Ocean Av -Patchogue 11772 **Fx:**730-8661
(212) 859-8000 .. **McGill,** Christina M '04 %Fried FHS&J LLP -1 NY Plz -NY 10004
(212) 506-2500 .. **McGill,** David H '05 %Mayer B LLP -1675 Bway -NY 10019
(212) 848-4000 .. **McGill,** Geoffrey J '09 %Shearman & S LLP -599 Lex Av -NY 10022
(516) 671-2671 .. **McGill,** Gilbert W '76 -203 Glen Cove Av Bx176 -Sea Cliff 11579
(212) 882-5367 .. **McGill,** Jos M '94 UBS Global Asset Mgmt -51 W 52nd -NY 10019
(212) 687-7410 .. **McGill,** Kevin J '69 (Clifton B&D,LLP) -420 Lex Av -NY 10170
(212) 688-4000 .. **McGill,** M Lauren '87 %NYS HFA -641 Lex Av -NY 10022 **Fx:**872-0362
(212) 294-6700 .. **McGill,** Patrick M '10 %Winston & S -200 Park Av -NY 10166
(914) 253-3448 .. **McGill,** Sarah L '88 %Pepsico -700 Andrsn Hill Rd -Purchase 10577
(585) 381-7470 .. **McGill,** Timothy R '76 -248 Willow Brook Office Park -Fairprt 14450 **Fx:**381-7498

(212) 779-9910 .. **McGill,** Vincent J '81 (Eaton & V LLP) -3 Park Av -NY 10016
(716) 648-3502 .. **McGillicuddy,** Jacquelyn A '83 -Bx522 -Hambrg 14075 **Fx:**648-3508
(718) 780-0696 .. **McGillion,** Ines '01 %Bklyn Law Schl -250 Joralemon -Brklyn 11201 **Fx:**780-0393
(212) 705-7000 .. **McGillycuddy,** Danl '81 (Bingham M LLP) -399 Park Av -NY 10022
(845) 369-2114 .. **McGillycuddy,** Joan M '89 Avon Products -Avon Pl -Suffern 10901
(212) 770-7688 .. **McGilvery,** Cheri M '96 %AIG -70 Pine -NY 10270
(212) 839-7000 .. **Mc Ginis,** Kenneth F '09 %Hill B&N LLP -200 Lbrty -NY 10281
(516) 227-6000 .. **McGinity,** Leo F '54 (McGinity & M) -1225 Franklin Av -Gdn Cty 11530 **Fx:**432-7490
(516) 227-6000 .. **McGinity,** Leo F Jr. '89 (McGinity & M) -1225 Franklin Av -Gdn Cty 11530 **Fx:**432-7490
(646) 538-4846 .. **McGinley,** Alexandra C '02 Credit Suisse -1 Mad Av -NY 10010
(845) 340-0355 .. **McGinley,** Brigid K '81 -271 Thomas -Hurley 12443
(212) 508-6100 .. **McGinley,** Elizabeth Lavelle '97 (Bracewell & G,LLP) -1251 Av of Amer -NY 10020
(212) 450-4000 .. **McGinley,** Joanna Aitken '07 %Davis P&W LLP -450 Lex Av -NY 10017
(212) 710-5501 .. **McGinley,** Lisa E '05 FNF Title Intl -140 E 45th -NY 10017
(212) 325-2000 .. **McGinley,** Marybeth '97 Credit Suisse -11 Mad Av -NY 10010
(212) 458-1917 .. **McGinley,** Patrick J '99 AIG -175 Water -NY 10038
(212) 448-9933 .. **McGinley,** Patrick W '60 OfCnsl Finder & C LLP -9 E 38th -NY 10016
(315) 426-7405 .. **McGinn,** Barbara Ann '04 DEC -615 Erie Blvd W -Syracuse 13204 **Fx:**426-7408
(518) 474-6538 .. **McGinn,** Danl C '04 Dept of Temp & Disability Assistance -99 Wshngtn -Albany 12210
(631) 715-7871 .. **McGinn,** Denise '99 %US Atty -610 Fed Plz -Central Islip 11722
(212) 490-9100 .. **McGinn,** Laura A '96 %Condon & F LLP -7 Times Sq -NY 10036
(518) 449-5131 .. **McGinn,** Mary Ann '84 %McGinn Smith & Co -99 Pine -Albany 12207 **Fx:**449-4894
(718) 698-4884 .. **McGinn,** Sheila T '91 (Sargente & M,LLC) -900 South Av -Staten Isl 10314
(212) 728-8000 .. **McGinn,** Timothy J '10 %Willkie F&G LLP -787 7th Av -NY 10019
(585) 327-5043 .. **McGinn,** Wm D '77 -125 State -Rchstr 14614 **Fx:**454-1254
(212) 487-9701 .. **McGinnis,** Kevin J '02 %Robin HK&F -1 Bttry Pk Plz -NY 10014
(212) 865-1566 .. **McGinnis,** Michl '64 -285 Riverside Dr -NY 10025 **Fx:**865-1566
(845) 471-5721 .. **McGinnis,** Peter C '69 -515 Haight Av -Poughkeepsie 12603 **Fx:**559-0068
(315) 448-8400 .. **McGinty,** James P '68 %Law Dept -233 E Wshngtn -Syracuse 13202 **Fx:**448-8381
(845) 658-7145 .. **McGinty,** Sara W '85 (McGinty & M) -Bx354 -Rosendale 12472 **Fx:**658-9574
(212) 621-6000 .. **McGivern,** Joan M '85 %ASCAP -1 Lincoln Plz -NY 10023 **Fx:**787-1381
(518) 346-4249 .. **McGivern Shaw & O'Connor** -207 Mohawk Av -Scotia 12302 **Fx:**346-4253
(212) 509-3456 .. **McGivney,** Chas M Jr. '97 (McGivney & K,PC) -80 Broad -NY 10004
(518) 758-2255 .. **McGivney,** Douglas K '65 -4 Orchrd Dr -Kinderhook 12106 **Fx:**758-6385
(212) 688-5151 .. **McGivney,** James H '73 (Gibney A&F,LLP) -665 5th Av -NY 10022
(212) 879-5666 .. **McGivney,** Jos H '92 (JH McGivney & Assoc) -425 E 79th -NY 10075
(212) 509-3456 .. **McGivney & Kluger,PC** -80 Broad -NY 10004 **Fx:**509-4420
(315) 473-9648 .. **McGivney & Kluger,PC** -110 W Fayette -Syracuse 13202 **Fx:**473-9654
(212) 509-3456 .. **McGivney,** Lawr J T '05 (McGivney & K,PC) -80 Broad -NY 10004
(212) 345-9470 .. **McGlarry,** Paula Collins '99 %Marsh USA -1166 Av of Amer -NY 10036 **Fx:**345-4808
(212) 931-7800 .. **McGlarry,** Robt E '99 %Baseball Cmmssnr -245 Park Av -NY 10167
(212) 558-4000 .. **McGlashan,** Patrick A '07 %Sullivan & C LLP -125 Broad -NY 10004
(607) 734-8161 .. **McGlenn,** John R '72 (Buck DR&M) -100 Baldwin -Elmira 14901
(518) 432-1200 .. **McGlinchey Stafford PLLC** -194 Wshngtn Av -Albany 12210 **Fx:**432-8711
(718) 590-5438 .. **McGloin,** Eugene P '05 ACS -900 Sheridan Av -Bronx 10451
(212) 454-2339 .. **McGloin,** Paul E '88 %Deutsche Bk -280 Park Av -NY 10017
(212) 536-9755 .. **McGloin,** Tracy L '02 Cumberland Assoc,LLC -1114 Av of Amer -NY 10036
(212) 262-2390 .. **McGloin,** Wm T '92 (Connell F LLP) -888 7th Av -NY 10106
(212) 506-1700 .. **McGloin-King,** Jamie W '06 %Kasowitz BT&F LLP -1633 Bway -NY 10019
(716) 886-1242 .. **McGlone,** Janet Greene '85 %Mental Hlth Assn -999 Delaware Av -Buffalo 14209 **Fx:**881-6428
(212) 318-6000 .. **McGlyn,** Michele B '07 %Paul HJ&W LLP -75 E 55th -NY 10022
(718) 446-1313 .. **McGlynn,** Bradley M '79 McGlynn & M -62-07 Woodside Av -Woodside 11377 **Fx:**672-6523
(516) 766-6200 .. **McGlynn,** James A '03 J McGlynn,LLC -100 N Centre Av -Rockvll Ctr 11570
(315) 474-7571 .. **McGlynn,** Maureen Dunn '97 (Mackenzie H LLP) -101 S Salina Bx4967 -Syracuse 13221
(914) 376-4902 .. **McGlynn,** Richd M '88 -707 Ynkrs Av -Ynkrs 10704 **Fx:**476-2950
(212) 850-6220 .. **McGlynn Reilly,** Bernadette '00 %Lathrop & G LC -230 Park Av -NY 10169
(914) 377-0590 .. **McGoey,** Barry B '03 -656 Ynkrs Av -Ynkrs 10704
(914) 633-5593 .. **McGoey,** Chas K '81 -271 North Av -New Rchll 10801
(914) 907-7393 .. **McGoey,** Gillian E '93 -336 E 77th -NY 10075 **Fx:**592-3213
(212) 837-6776 .. **McGoey,** John T '06 %Hughes H&R LLP -1 Bttry Pk Plz -NY 10004
(914) 636-3300 .. **McGoey,** Robt J '67 -271 North Av -New Rchll 10801
(718) 237-2000 .. **McGoldrick,** Edna T '00 %Leg Aid -111 Lvngstn -Brklyn 11201 **Fx:**237-8737
(718) 286-6000 .. **McGoldrick,** John F '05 %DA -125-01 Qns Blvd -Kew Gdns 11415
(212) 401-0800 .. **McGoldrick,** Stephen P '95 %Disciplinary Comm -61 Bway -NY 10006 **Fx:**287-1045
(516) 872-8300 .. **McGoldrick,** Wm M '82 -Bx626 -Vly Stream 11582
(212) 481-7007 .. **McGonigle,** Ryan A '02 %Baker & R -1350 Bway -NY 10018
(212) 689-6700 .. **McGorry,** Mark W '87 -286 Mad Av -NY 10017 **Fx:**689-7010
(716) 854-6495 .. **McGorry,** Michl P J '84 (Silverberg YS&M) -515 Brisbane Bldg -Buffalo 14203
(716) 854-6495 .. **McGorry,** Pamela M '96 %Silverberg YS&M -515 Brisbane Bldg -Buffalo 14203
(212) 637-2505 .. **McGorty,** Glen G '99 %US Atty -1 St Andrews Plz -NY 10007
(914) 332-0927 .. **McGough,** James A '62 -12 Highland Av -N Tarrytwn 10591
(212) 805-4616 .. **McGough,** Matthew J '02 Hon D Batts -500 Pearl -NY 10007
(315) 471-8111 .. **McGough,** Stewart M '80 (Scolaro SCF&B,PC) -507 Plum -Syracuse 13204
(212) 318-6000 .. **McGovern,** Adam J '10 %Paul HJ&W LLP -75 E 55th -NY 10022
(212) 298-5286 .. **McGovern,** Amelia P '91 %Leg Aid -49 Thomas -NY 10013 **Fx:**298-5252
(516) 437-4385 .. **McGovern,** Bernard F '74 (Vishnick MM LLP) -3000 Marcus Av -Lk Success 11042
(212) 966-3308 .. **McGovern,** Brian J '98 -15 Maiden Ln -NY 10038 **Fx:**966-3341
(212) 504-6000 .. **McGovern,** Brian T '85 (Cadwalader W&T LLP) -1 World Fncl Ctr -NY 10281
(914) 289-1961 .. **McGovern,** Cecilia J '83 (McGovern & A) -2 William -White Plns 10601 **Fx:**289-1962
(914) 632-9300 .. **McGovern Connelly & Davidson** -145 Huguenot -New Rchll 10801 **Fx:**632-1615
(914) 686-1055 .. **McGovern & Dawson** -111 Church -White Plns 10601 **Fx:**948-4721
(212) 576-4698 .. **McGovern,** Deborah A '04 %NYLIM -51 Mad Av -NY 10010
(212) 816-0224 .. **McGovern,** Hugh M '81 Citigroup -388 Greenwich -NY 10013
(631) 715-7900 .. **McGovern,** James G '93 US Atty -610 Fed Plz -Central Islip 11722
(212) 336-0134 .. **McGovern,** James M '93 %SEC -3 World Fncl Ctr -NY 10281 **Fx:**336-1323
(212) 825-1774 .. **McGovern,** James V '69 -26 Bway -NY 10004
(212) 810-3240 .. **McGovern,** Jennifer M '08 Black Rock,Inc -40 E 52nd -NY 10022
(212) 279-6200 .. **McGovern,** John M '94 (McGovern & Assoc) -16 W 32nd -NY 10001
(914) 323-7000 .. **McGovern,** Jos A H '00 (Wilson EME&D LLP) -3 Gannett Dr -White Plns 10604
(518) 427-2933 .. **McGovern,** Jos P '90 -5 Wilson -Albany 12207 **Fx:**427-2933
(212) 310-8000 .. **McGovern,** Katherine J '08 Weil G&M LLP -767 5th Av -NY 10153
(518) 783-2200 .. **McGovern,** Kathleen F '88 %Brown & B -11 Century Hill Dr -Latham 12110 **Fx:**783-2225
(607) 273-3666 .. **McGovern,** Kelly I '07 Leg Srvcs -215 N Cayuga -Ithaca 14850 **Fx:**273-5521
(212) 688-9840 .. **McGovern,** Kevin M '93 McGovern & Assoc,LLC -14 E 60th -NY 10022
(914) 631-1336 .. **McGovern,** Kyle C '92 (Lyons M,LLP) -16 New Bway -Sleepy Hollow 10591
(914) 686-1055 .. **McGovern,** Lawr F '81 (McGovern & D) -111 Church -White Plns 10601
(212) 450-4000 .. **McGovern,** Michl E '09 %Davis P&W LLP -450 Lex Av -NY 10017
(212) 596-9000 .. **McGovern,** Michl G '06 (Ropes & G LLP) -1211 Av of Amer -NY 10036
(212) 449-0336 .. **McGovern,** Michl M '75 %Merrill Lynch -220 Bway -NY 10038
(212) 384-1000 .. **McGovern,** Pamela A '97 %FBI -26 Fed Plz -NY 10278
(212) 566-7188 .. **McGovern,** Patrick W '80 (Genova B&G) -115 Bway -NY 10006
(212) 415-3756 .. **McGovern,** Raymond E Jr. '84 %Omnicom Group -437 Mad Av -NY 10022 **Fx:**415-3530
(631) 249-6565 .. **McGovern,** Robt T '87 OfCnsl Archer BG&L,LLP -425 Broadhllw Rd -Melvll 11747
(212) 908-0722 .. **McGovern,** Stacey A '97 Fitch Ratings -1 State Street Plz -NY 10004
(212) 468-8000 .. **McGovern,** Thos P '05 %Morrison & F LLP -1290 Av of Amer -NY 10104
(212) 762-4949 .. **McGovern,** Wm F '94 Morgan Stanley -1221 Av of Amer -NY 10020
(212) 302-5559 .. **McGowan,** Carter Anne '96 %RFPNY -729 7th Av -NY 10019
(914) 493-5667 .. **McGowan,** Coreen '96 Westchester Medical Ctr -Taylor Care Ctr C-2 -Valhalla 10595
(631) 661-4415 .. **McGowan,** Douglas E '98 -325 Paumanake Av -W Islip 11795 **Fx:**661-4416
(845) 486-6800 .. **McGowan,** J Jos '61 (McCabe & M LLP) -63 Wshngtn Bx509 -Poughkeepsie 12602
(518) 474-7642 .. **McGowan,** James B '82 %Dept of Law -The Cptl -Albany 12224 **Fx:**473-1572
(315) 474-7541 .. **McGowan,** James H III '66 (Menter R&T,PC) -308 Maltbie -Syracuse 13204
(718) 898-8013 .. **McGowan,** James J '73 -69-34 60th Dr -Maspeth 11378 **Fx:**898-5897
(315) 218-8000 .. **McGowan,** John G '82 (Bond S&K,PLLC) -1 Lincoln Ctr -Syracuse 13202
(631) 324-4977 .. **McGowan,** John T '73 (Osborne & M) -135 Main Bx5011 -E Hampton 11937
(646) 386-3352 .. **McGowan,** Jon M '04 Unified Ct Sys -111 Centre -NY 10013
McGowan, Judy L '04 -227 Steers Rd -Amsterdam 12010
(212) 408-4268 .. **McGowan,** Margaret E '97 Bank of NY -1290 Av of Amer -NY 10104
(315) 343-2451 .. **McGowan,** Mary E '86 (Reynolds & M,PLLC) -138 W 4th -Oswego 13126 **Fx:**343-1125
(914) 686-0500 .. **McGowan,** Matthew J '02 -111 Church -White Plns 10601 **Fx:**686-0505
(212) 416-8000 .. **McGowan,** Meredith J '00 %Dept of Law -120 Bway -NY 10271
(212) 220-3830 .. **McGowan,** Michl F '88 (Nicoletti H&S) -88 Pine -NY 10005
(212) 839-5741 .. **McGowan,** Peter B '02 Sidley A LLP -787 7th Av -NY 10019
(518) 474-6530 .. **McGowan,** Peter M '88 %Dept Pub Srvc -3 ESP -Albany 12223
(718) 651-7360 .. **McGowan,** Regina M '03 (R McGowan,LLP) -68-15 Borden Av -Maspeth 11378 **Fx:**446-0796
(516) 747-0300 .. **McGowan,** Thos J '85 (Meltzer LG&B,LLP) -190 Willis Av -Mineola 11501
(315) 789-9191 .. **McGowan,** Wm F '64 W McGowan,PC -37 Seneca -Geneva 14456 **Fx:**789-9192
(212) 813-8800 .. **McGowen,** Fredk R '93 SrCnsl Goodwin P LLP -620 8th Av -NY 10018
(212) 506-5000 .. **McGowen,** Lorraine S '87 (Orrick H&S LLP) -51 W 52nd -NY 10019
(212) 388-3600 .. **McGowen,** Steven C '87 %32B-J Leg Srvcs -101 Av of Amer -NY 10013 **Fx:**388-3061
(212) 788-8743 .. **McGowin,** Kevin A '09 %NYC Bd Stndrds & Appls -40 Rector -NY 10006
(518) 474-5201 .. **McGown,** Fredk H III '78 %Dept of Law -The Cptl -Albany 12224

(607) 547-8967 .. **McGown**, Margaret E '90 -Bx105 -Cooperstwn 13326 **Fx**:547-1034
(718) 298-0239 .. **McGrady**, Jane A '88 %Family Ct -151-20 Jamaica Av -Jamaica 11432 **Fx**:297-2530
(646) 290-6496 .. **McGrail**, David C '01 -676A 9th Av -NY 10036
(646) 471-0124 .. **McGrail**, David W '98 %PricewaterhouseCoopers LLP -300 Mad Av -NY 10017
(212) 825-9811 .. **McGrail**, Katherine M '06 %Krebsbach & S,PC -55 Bway -NY 10006
(718) 390-5383 .. **McGrail**, Kenneth R '79 %Supreme Ct Law Dept -18 Richmond Ter -Staten Isl 10301
(585) 218-8610 .. **McGrain**, Craig L '86 Durham Ltd -101 Sullys Trl -Pittsfrd 14534
(212) 906-1200 .. **McGrane**, Bryan A '10 %Latham & W -885 3rd Av -NY 10022
(516) 229-6000 .. **McGrane**, John K '66 %R Lau & Assoc -300 Jericho Quad Bx9040 -Jericho 11753 **Fx**:229-6167
(212) 487-9700 .. **McGrane**, Virginia L '88 (White F&F,LLP) -61 Bway -NY 10006
(516) 560-6400 .. **McGrath**, Amber '09 %Leg Aid -1 Helen Keller Way -Hempstd 11550 **Fx**:565-3694
(315) 431-0736 .. **McGrath**, Ann '88 (Esce & M) -10 Adler Dr -E Syracuse 13057 **Fx**:437-9462
(914) 244-0029 .. **McGrath**, Beverly T '08 %Quaranta & Assoc -121 Smith Av -Mt Kisco 10549 **Fx**:244-0031
(914) 995-2660 .. **McGrath**, Brendan J '01 %Cnty Atty -148 Martine Av -White Plns 10601 **Fx**:995-5858
(718) 579-3000 .. **McGrath**, Caroline M '88 %Leg Aid -1020 Grnd Cncrs -Bronx 10451 **Fx**:588-2611
(212) 318-6000 .. **McGrath**, Casey J '08 %Paul HJ&W LLP -75 E 55th -NY 10022
(212) 417-8300 .. **McGrath**, Catherine F '84 %Research Fndtn CUNY -230 W 41st -NY 10036 **Fx**:417-8379
(212) 682-7474 .. **McGrath**, Catherine M '86 (Foley & L LLP) -90 Park Av -NY 10016
(212) 608-1900 .. **McGrath**, Christopher M '05 Lovell SH LLP -61 Bway -NY 10006
(212) 732-9000 .. **McGrath**, Christopher T '84 (Sullivan PBM&C PC) -120 Bway -NY 10271
(516) 742-0707 .. **McGrath**, Christopher T '84 (Sullivan PBM&C PC) -55 Mineola Blvd -Mineola 11501
(212) 306-1885 .. **McGrath**, Claire P '87 %Amer Stock Exch -86 Trinity Pl -NY 10006
(212) 735-3000 .. **McGrath**, Coleen M '03 %Skadden ASM&F LLP -4 Times Sq -NY 10036
(212) 355-5781 .. **McGrath**, Diahn W '88 -110 E 59th -NY 10022 **Fx**:826-0776
(716) 632-3600 .. **McGrath**, Donald G '63 -17 Beresford Ct -Buffalo 14221
(718) 590-2000 .. **McGrath**, Elizabeth '07 %DA -198 E 161st -Bronx 10451 **Fx**:590-6477
(212) 408-2500 .. **McGrath**, Fredk H II '81 (Baker B,LLP) -30 Rckfllr Plz -NY 10112
(631) 574-2221 .. **McGrath**, Gregg M '94 %D Tetlak,PC -315 Walt Whitman Rd -Huntngtn Sta 11746 **Fx**:963-9020
(718) 558-8352 .. **McGrath**, J Dennis '68 %LIRR -Jamaica Station -Jamaica 11435 **Fx**:558-8211
(212) 682-0020 .. **McGrath**, James E III '87 (Putney TH&H LLP) -521 5th Av -NY 10175
(315) 343-1181 .. **McGrath**, James P '52 -38 E Utica -Oswego 13126
(518) 457-1260 .. **McGrath**, John J '92 %DCJS -4 Twr Pl -Albany 12203 **Fx**:457-3089
(718) 441-5460 .. **McGrath**, John P '95 (Kazmierczuk & M) -103-16 Metro Av -Frst Hlls 11375 **Fx**:441-5537
(212) 752-6664 .. **McGrath**, John W '60 -380 Lex Av -NY 10168 **Fx**:983-9701
(718) 441-5460 .. **McGrath**, Katherine M '96 (Kazmierczuk & M) -103-16 Metro Av -Frst Hlls 11375 **Fx**:441-5537
(212) 977-9700 .. **McGrath**, Kevin B '61 (Phillips N LLP) -666 5th Av -NY 10103
(212) 907-9600 .. **McGrath**, Kevin J '06 %Ingram YGC&B,LLP -250 Park Av -NY 10177
(212) 336-0533 .. **McGrath**, Kevin P '81 SEC -3 World Fncl Ctr -NY 10281 **Fx**:336-1323
(845) 207-3093 .. **McGrath**, Leo T '88 -3871 Danbury Rd -Brewstr 10509
(212) 682-8811 .. **McGrath**, Luke A '97 (Dunnington B&M LLP) -1359 Bway -NY 10018
(212) 808-7800 .. **McGrath**, Mark E '02 %Kelley D&W LLP -101 Park Av -NY 10178
(516) 536-6912 .. **McGrath**, Mary Jane '91 -561 Wateredge Av -Baldwin 11510 **Fx**:536-6912
(607) 284-2654 .. **McGrath**, Matthew T '83 ALSTOM Trans -1 Transit Dr -Hornell 14843 **Fx**:324-2252
(585) 753-4500 .. **McGrath**, Matthew T '09 %DA -832 Watts Bldg -Rchstr 14614 **Fx**:753-4576
(518) 431-5406 .. **McGrath**, Melissa G '96 %Farm Family Ins -Bx656 -Albany 12201 **Fx**:431-5979
(212) 768-6700 .. **McGrath**, Michl C '90 (Sonnenschein N&R LLP) -2 World Fncl Ctr -NY 10281
(212) 261-8000 .. **McGrath**, Michl P '05 %Mendes & M,LLP -750 7th Av -NY 10019
(212) 682-0020 .. **McGrath**, Michl T '81 (Putney TH&H LLP) -521 5th Av -NY 10175
(716) 774-3522 .. **McGrath**, Patricia M '81 Cannon Design -2170 Whitehaven Rd -Grand Isl 14072 **Fx**:773-5909
(518) 455-7780 .. **McGrath**, Paul J '86 %Ct of Appls -20 Eagle -Albany 12207
(212) 661-9100 .. **McGrath**, R Brian '01 %Otterbourg SH&R,PC -230 Park Av -NY 10169
(212) 848-4000 .. **McGrath**, Sean D '10 Shearman & S LLP -599 Lex Av -NY 10022
(212) 530-1800 .. **McGrath**, Stefan '97 Richards K&O LLP -1 World Fncl Ctr -NY 10281
(212) 788-1056 .. **McGrath**, Stephen J '75 %Law Dept -100 Church -NY 10007 **Fx**:788-0367
(212) 903-9000 .. **McGrath**, Thos A III '95 (Linklaters) -1345 Av of Amer -NY 10105
(212) 355-2232 .. **McGrath**, Thos J '60 -110 E 59th -NY 10022 **Fx**:826-0776
(212) 264-5916 .. **McGrath**, Thos P '89 %DHS -26 Fed Plz -NY 10278
(914) 949-5361 .. **McGrath**, Wayne J '74 -15 Steward Pl -White Plns 10603 **Fx**:428-1262
(315) 474-2943 .. **McGraw**, Charlene E '82 (Sugarman Law Firm,LLP) -211 W Jffrsn -Syracuse 13202
(518) 462-4106 .. **McGraw**, Danl J '88 %IUOE Local #106 -111 Wshngtn Av -Albany 12210
(315) 422-7725 .. **McGraw**, James R '73 -333 E Onondaga -Syracuse 13202 **Fx**:422-7741
(914) 273-2273 .. **McGraw**, John J '65 -3 Arrowhead Ln -Armonk 10504 **Fx**:765-0922
(212) 218-2100 .. **McGraw**, Michl P '01 (Fitzpatrick CH&S) -1290 Av of Amer -NY 10104
(315) 464-4700 .. **McGraw**, Regina S '99 %SUNY Univ Cnsl -60 Prsdntl Plz -Syracuse 13202 **Fx**:464-4706
(607) 753-5008 .. **McGraw**, Robt P '00 %DA -46 Greenbush -Cortlnd 13045 **Fx**:756-3477
(212) 825-1212 .. **McGraw**, Stephanie S '10 %Morrison M LLP -17 State -NY 10004
(212) 483-2323 .. **McGraw**, Thos C '82 %JP Morgan Chase -345 Park Av -NY 10154
(212) 450-4000 .. **McGreal**, Michelle M '08 %Davis P&W LLP -450 Lex Av -NY 10017
(917) 848-1099 .. **McGreevy**, John J '92 Prosiris Capital Mgmt LLC -529 5th Av -NY 10017
(631) 298-1720 .. **McGreevy**, Peter R '97 (McGreevy & H,LLP) -455 Lloyds Ln Bx18 -Mattituck 11952 **Fx**:614-4500
(914) 533-2608 .. **McGreevy**, Robt P '70 -21 Glen Dr -S Salem 10590
(607) 638-5570 .. **McGregor**, Bruce C '61 -64 Main Bx56 -Schenevus 12155 **Fx**:638-4236
(607) 264-8051 .. **McGregor**, Bruce C '61 -8 Main Bx151 -Cherry Vly 13320 **Fx**:638-4236
(212) 857-5324 .. **McGregor**, Frank A '07 Cnsl Health Mgmt Systems,Inc -401 Park Av S -NY 10016
(212) 594-5300 .. **McGregor**, Kristi Stahnke '03 (Milberg LLP) -1 Penn Plz -NY 10119
(718) 324-2982 .. **McGregor**, Lorna Ann '95 -769A E 236th -Bronx 10466 **Fx**:324-1725
(718) 298-1212 .. **McGregor**, Nicole A '97 %Hon M Grays -88-11 Sutphin Blvd -Jamaica 11435
(212) 326-3939 .. **McGrew**, Jennifer M '10 %Jones D -222 E 41st -NY 10017
(212) 225-2000 .. **McGrory**, Glenn P '01 (Cleary GS&H) -1 Lbrty Plz -NY 10006
(518) 463-0770 .. **McGrory**, Karen E '01 %P Scagnelli -48 Columbia -Albany 12207
(516) 746-1392 .. **McGrory**, Patrick J '92 -300 Old Cntry Rd -Mineola 11501 **Fx**:746-2683
(212) 747-9311 .. **McGruder**, David N '97 -65 Bway -NY 10006 **Fx**:809-4753
(212) 909-6000 .. **McGuigan**, Michl P '05 %Debevoise & P LLP -919 3rd Av -NY 10022
(516) 573-7100 .. **McGuigan**, Robt W '81 Nassau Cnty Police Dept -1490 Franklin Av -Mineola 11501
(212) 753-5000 .. **McGuinness**, Christine Ann '89 (Schiff H LLP) -900 3rd Av -NY 10022
(845) 695-6811 .. **McGuinness**, Denis E '91 %MA Bjork -100 Crystal Run Rd -Middletwn 10941 **Fx**:695-6818
(716) 858-6866 .. **McGuinness**, Edw J '70 DSS-Ofc of Cnsl -478 Main -Buffalo 14202
(631) 423-5500 .. **McGuinness**, Edw P III '91 -70 Main -Huntngtn 11743
(212) 859-8000 .. **McGuinness**, John P '03 %Fried FHS&J LLP -1 NY Plz -NY 10004
(718) 990-8018 .. **McGuinness**, Margaret E '00 St John's Law Schl -8000 Utopia Pkwy -Jamaica 11439 **Fx**:591-1855
(518) 745-4343 .. **McGuinness**, Martin J '09 %Stanclift L&M,PC -3 Warren Bx358 -Glens Fls 12801 **Fx**:745-4344
(212) 848-4000 .. **McGuinness**, Michl J '98 (Shearman & S LLP) -599 Lex Av -NY 10022
(212) 752-2609 .. **McGuinness**, Peter J '85 -FDR Station Bx7219 -NY 10150
(607) 763-9200 .. **McGuinness**, Terrance M '09 %Levene G&T,LLP -BxF-1706 -Bnghmtn 13902
(212) 576-7000 .. **McGuinness**, Thos E '02 %NY Life Ins -51 Mad Av -NY 10010 **Fx**:447-0569
(212) 859-8000 .. **McGuinness**, Wm G '80 (Fried FHS&J LLP) -1 NY Plz -NY 10004
(914) 497-4766 .. **McGuinness**, Wm T Jr. '03 -Bx457 -Brewstr 10509
(212) 644-1010 .. **McGuire**, Aislinn S '02 %Kauff M&M LLP -950 3rd Av -NY 10022
(212) 431-5000 .. **McGuire**, Arthur H '79 %BlumbergExcelsior,Inc -62 White -NY 10013 **Fx**:431-5111
(212) 637-2220 .. **McGuire**, Brendan R '03 US Atty -1 St Andrews Plz -NY 10007
(212) 588-0800 .. **McGuire**, Brian M '05 %Frommer L&H LLP -745 5th Av -NY 10151
(516) 466-7900 .. **McGuire**, Catherine Kiley '90 %Kiley K&K,PLLC -107 Nrthrn Blvd -Gt Neck 11021
(315) 218-8000 .. **McGuire**, Chas S '71 OfCnsl Bond S&K,PLLC -1 Lincoln Ctr -Syracuse 13202
(800) 281-1515 .. **McGuire**, Christine M '00 (Power Law Firm LLP) -590 Mad Av -NY 10022 **Fx**:903-1993
(631) 348-1702 .. **McGuire**, Christopher P '95 -100 Carleton Av -Central Islip 11722 **Fx**:348-3628
(845) 620-9606 .. **McGuire**, Francine M '95 -221 Rockland Rd -Pearl Rvr 10965 **Fx**:620-9606
(315) 218-8000 .. **McGuire**, George R '97 (Bond S&K,PLLC) -1 Lincoln Ctr -Syracuse 13202
(212) 894-7200 .. **McGuire**, Harold F Jr. '62 (Entwistle & C LLP) -280 Park Av -NY 10017
(212) 261-8000 .. **McGuire**, James A III '76 (Mendes & M,LLP) -750 7th Av -NY 10019
(212) 612-3270 .. **McGuire**, James J '84 (Mishcon de R NY LLP) -200 Park Av -NY 10166
(516) 877-0117 .. **McGuire**, James J '90 J McGuire PC -8 Kilburn Rd -Gdn Cty 11530
(212) 668-5036 .. **McGuire**, John T '81 Oppenheimer & Co,Inc -125 Broad -NY 10004
(631) 421-8600 .. **McGuire**, Karen D '86 (McGuire C,PC) -775 Park Av -Huntngtn 11743 **Fx**:427-5106
(212) 545-4773 .. **McGuire**, Kate Marietta '00 %Wolf HAF&H LLP -270 Mad Av -NY 10016
(585) 987-2800 .. **McGuire**, Katherine H '90 (Woods OG LLP) -2 State -Rchstr 14614
(518) 279-4292 .. **McGuire**, Kenneth J Jr. '90 -710 Brnswck Rd -Troy 12180
(212) 506-5000 .. **McGuire**, Kirsty G '04 %Orrick H&S LLP -51 W 52nd -NY 10019
(914) 478-4293 .. **McGuire**, Matthew G '97 (Brady M&S,PC) -603 Warburton Av -Hastings-On-Hud 10706
(845) 292-6800 .. **McGuire**, Michl F '02 -111 Sullivan Av -Ferndale 12734 **Fx**:292-6860
(212) 706-0248 .. **McGuire**, Michl H '01 (Hollyer B LLP) -60 E 42nd -NY 10165 **Fx**:(646) 652-5336
(516) 229-4300 .. **McGuire**, Michele A '97 %J Bilello & Assoc -875 Merrick Av -Westbury 11590
(516) 593-6210 .. **McGuire**, Mildred A '00 -30 S Central Av -Vly Stream 11580 **Fx**:593-6209
(914) 767-6000 .. **McGuire**, Pamela C '74 %Pepsi Bottling Grp -1 Pepsi Way -Somers 10589
(212) 644-1010 .. **McGuire**, Raymond G '64 (Kauff M&M LLP) -950 3rd Av -NY 10022
(212) 817-6734 .. **McGuire**, Robt J '61 -415 Mad Av -NY 10017
(212) 591-1308 .. **McGuire**, Ronald B '88 -PMB199-511 Av of Amer -NY 10011 **Fx**:(201) 795-5571
(631) 493-0909 .. **McGuire**, Susan C '93 (Annunziata & R) -300 Commack Rd -Commack 11725 **Fx**:493-3081

(212) 351-4500 .. **McGuire,** Terence H '04 %Epstein B&G,PC -250 Park Av -NY 10177
(718) 941-4400 .. **McGuire,** Thaeddeus J '84 -2809 Church Av -Brklyn 11226
(518) 402-9223 .. **McGuire,** Thos J '92 %DEC -625 Bway -Albany 12233 **Fx:**402-9018
(212) 714-1720 .. **McGuire,** Wm B '82 (Tompkins MW&B LLP) -140 Bway -NY 10005
(212) 548-2100 .. **McGuire Woods LLP** -1345 Av of Amer -NY 10105 **Fx:**548-2150
(914) 377-8100 .. **McGuirk,** G Scott '81 Smith-Cairns Ford Lincoln Mercury -900 Cntrl Pk Av -Ynkrs 10704 **Fx:**377-8118
(516) 683-4284 .. **McGuirk,** Gerard Hugh '96 %CFS Bank -615 Merrick Av -Westbury 11590 **Fx:**683-8385
(212) 735-2336 .. **McGuirk,** J Bruce '85 %Skadden ASM&F LLP -4 Times Sq -NY 10036
(585) 263-1000 .. **McGuirk,** Richd A '92 (Nixon P LLP) -1100 Clinton Sq -Rchstr 14604
(518) 382-5073 .. **McGuirl,** Katherine A '05 %Law Dept -201 City Hall -Schnctdy 12305 **Fx:**382-5074
(212) 415-9200 .. **McGunigle,** Brian E '74 (Dorsey & W LLP) -250 Park Av -NY 10177
(315) 435-2470 .. **McGunnigle,** Melinda H '01 %DA -505 S State -Syracuse 13202 **Fx:**435-3969
(212) 596-9000 .. **McGurk,** Kenneth C '09 %Ropes & G LLP -1211 Av of Amer -NY 10036
(212) 979-8228 .. **McGurn,** Danl E '96 %The A Consulting Team,Inc -200 Park Av S -NY 10003 **Fx:**979-8272
(212) 323-2250 .. **McHale,** Ann Marie '84 %HHC-OLA-Medical Litigation -346 Bway -NY 10013 **Fx:**323-2251
(212) 579-1172 .. **McHale,** Elaine Robinson '81 (Bevan MG&Z,PC) -200 Mad Av -NY 10016
(646) 386-4053 .. **McHale,** Katherine J '84 Hon R Carruthers -100 Centre -NY 10013
(212) 279-4777 .. **McHale,** Kim I '96 K McHale & Assoc -302 5th Av -NY 10001
(516) 622-9200 .. **McHale,** Kristen B '03 %Westerman BEM&S,LLP -1201 RXR Plz -Uniondale 11553
(212) 637-3219 .. **McHale,** Mary C '84 %EPA -290 Bway -NY 10007 **Fx:**637-3096
(716) 845-9463 .. **McHale,** Michl J '94 Supreme Ct -25 Delaware Av -Buffalo 14202 **Fx:**851-3293
(631) 878-1373 .. **McHeffey,** Jos W '82 -43 Montauk Hwy -Ctr Moriches 11934 **Fx:**878-6101
(212) 483-9490 .. **McHeffey,** Laurence M '86 (McElroy DM&C,LLP) -88 Pine -NY 10005
(212) 417-4960 .. **McHenry,** Barnabas '57 -164 E 72nd -NY 10021 **Fx:**417-4956
(516) 921-2525 .. **McHenry Horan & Lapping,PC** -6800 Jericho Tpk -Syosset 11791 **Fx:**921-5697
(347) 325-1366 .. **McHenry,** Loretta '91 -Brklyn 11229
(212) 756-2000 .. **McHenry,** Patrick R '10 %Schulte R&Z LLP -919 3rd Av -NY 10022
(516) 921-2525 .. **McHenry,** Robt J '74 (McHenry H&L,PC) -6800 Jericho Tpk -Syosset 11791
(212) 522-0695 .. **McHugh,** Catharine Michele '91 %Time Inc -1271 Av of Amer -NY 10020 **Fx:**522-0437
(212) 839-5300 .. **McHugh,** Charlene C '02 Cnsl Sidley A LLP -787 7th Av -NY 10019
(718) 246-2030 .. **McHugh,** Donald J Jr. '00 %NYPD -700 Columbia -Brklyn 11231
(518) 756-6700 .. **McHugh,** George D '98 (McHugh,PC) -149 Main -Ravena 12143 **Fx:**756-9753
(516) 267-6300 .. **McHugh,** Hilary L '10 %Bond S&K,PLLC -1399 Franklin Av -Gdn Cty 11530
(516) 918-3032 .. **McHugh,** Jeanine L '97 Luxottica Grp -44 Hrbr Park Dr -Pt Wash 11050
(845) 567-1002 .. **McHugh,** John A '99 -1161 Little Britain Rd -New Windsor 12553 **Fx:**567-0025
(212) 483-0875 .. **McHugh,** John F '68 (JF McHugh) -6 Water -NY 10004 **Fx:**483-0876
(212) 849-7000 .. **McHugh,** John M '10 %Quinn EU&S,LLP -51 Mad Av -NY 10010
(631) 853-5761 .. **McHugh,** Keith R '89 %Cnty Atty -400 Carleton Av -Central Islip 11722 **Fx:**853-7788
(718) 250-1100 .. **McHugh,** Kevin Barry '86 Cnsl E Garfinkel -12 Metrotech Ctr -Brklyn 11201 **Fx:**250-1168
(516) 939-9200 .. **McHugh,** Leslie Ann '88 %Mintzer SZL&M LLP -17 W John -Hicksvll 11801
(646) 386-3259 .. **McHugh,** Megan '00 Hon R Lowe III -100 Centre -NY 10013
(518) 370-4645 .. **McHugh,** Peter B '73 (Englert CM&F,LLP) -224 State Bx1092 -Schnctdy 12301
(212) 608-5657 .. **McHugh,** Peter J '76 (Keating & M) -132 Nassau -NY 10038 **Fx:**(866) 408-1843
(917) 604-6600 .. **McHugh,** Peter J '76 (Keating & M) -204-54 8th Av -Breezy Point 11697 **Fx:**(866) 408-1843
(516) 741-6296 .. **McHugh,** Russell T '87 (McHugh & L LLP) -1 Old Cntry Rd -Carle Pl 11514 **Fx:**741-2458
(212) 319-6898 .. **McHugh,** Timothy J '95 (Lavin ORC&D) -420 Lex Av -NY 10170
(917) 327-2900 .. **McIlroy,** Kerry D '03 Axiom Legal Solutions -75 Spring -NY 10012
(516) 671-5300 .. **McIlveen,** Sandra Lee '98 %Polin P&V -1 Schl -Glen Cove 11542
(212) 225-2000 .. **McIlwain,** Knox L '08 %Cleary GS&H -1 Lbrty Plz -NY 10006
(212) 371-6600 .. **McInerney,** Alice '77 (Kirby M LLP) -825 3rd Av -NY 10022
(212) 576-5803 .. **McInerney,** Barbara '86 NY Life Ins -51 Mad Av -NY 10010
(631) 200-1278 .. **McInerney,** Christine '87 Cnsl NBTY Inc -2100 Smithtown Av -Ronkonkoma 11779
(212) 735-3000 .. **McInerney,** Colm P '06 %Skadden ASM&F LLP -4 Times Sq -NY 10036
(631) 654-0750 .. **McInerney,** Francis M Jr. '65 -Bx681 -Bellprt 11713 **Fx:**286-6323
(212) 723-3371 .. **McInerney,** John L '71 Citigroup Global Mrkts -388 Greenwich -NY 10013
(212) 504-6000 .. **McInerney,** Wm P '85 (Cadwalader W&T LLP) -1 World Fncl Ctr -NY 10281
(212) 292-4573 .. **McInnis,** Timothy J '85 -521 5th Av -NY 10175 **Fx:**292-4574
(212) 450-4000 .. **McIntire,** Keith E '08 Davis P&W LLP -450 Lex Av -NY 10017
(518) 792-2117 .. **McIntire,** Philip C '68 (Bartlett PS&R,PC) -1 Wshngtn Bx2168 -Glens Fls 12801
(585) 889-5481 .. **McIntosh,** Candace R '80 -16 Brook Valley Dr -Rchstr 14624 **Fx:**889-5191
(518) 719-3590 .. **McIntosh,** Danielle D '02 %DA -411 Main -Catskill 12414 **Fx:**719-3792
(518) 473-5671 .. **McIntosh,** Elliott A '99 %Div of Parole -97 Central Av -Albany 12206 **Fx:**473-6037
(212) 858-8265 .. **McIntosh,** Joanne P '92 First Investors Life Ins Co -110 Wall -NY 10005 **Fx:**858-8219
(212) 335-9000 .. **McIntosh,** Michl A '88 %DA -1 Hogan Pl -NY 10013
(212) 693-0085 .. **McIntosh,** Winston L '79 %Appellate Advocates -2 Rector -NY 10006 **Fx:**693-0878
(518) 434-0600 .. **McIntyre,** Andrew D '07 Boies S&F LLP -10 N Pearl -Albany 12207 **Fx:**434-0665
(212) 972-5560 .. **McIntyre,** Ann Teresa '83 (Zichello & M,LLP) -60 E 42nd -NY 10165
(212) 435-3571 .. **McIntyre,** Carlene V '88 %Port Auth of NY/NJ -225 Park Av S -NY 10003 **Fx:**435-3555
(631) 665-0609 .. **McIntyre,** Edw T '95 %Sherman FS&L LLP -8 E Main -Bay Shr 11706
(212) 450-4000 .. **McIntyre,** James P '78 Cnsl Davis P&W LLP -450 Lex Av -NY 10017
(212) 244-2999 .. **McIntyre,** Kelly D '09 %Kopff N&D LLP -440 9th Av -NY 10001
(212) 735-3000 .. **McIntyre,** Laura A '09 %Skadden ASM&F LLP -4 Times Sq -NY 10036
(212) 227-9987 .. **McIntyre,** Margaret E '96 -225 Bway -NY 10007 **Fx:**227-9987
(914) 738-7262 .. **McIntyre,** Marie J '86 -205 Monterey Av -Pelham 10803 **Fx:**712-0337
(212) 788-3015 .. **Mc Intyre,** Mark P '97 Ofc of Envrnmntl Coordination -100 Gold -NY 10038
(212) 558-4000 .. **McIntyre,** Nina F '07 %Sullivan & C LLP -125 Broad -NY 10004
(716) 631-8310 .. **McIntyre,** Philip H '81 Superior Grp -Bx9057 -Williamsvll 14231
(315) 376-5535 .. **McIntyre,** Todd W '92 Family Ct Support Magistrate -7660 State -Lowvll 13367 **Fx:**376-5189
(212) 407-4000 .. **McIsaac,** Michl J '03 %Loeb & L,LLP -345 Park Av -NY 10154
(607) 272-5212 .. **McKain,** Carla N '08 %Coughlin & G,LLP -401 E State -Ithaca 14850
(212) 385-1215 .. **McKay,** Alison L '01 %P Lange -445 Park Av -NY 10022 **Fx:**608-1215
(212) 458-6018 .. **McKay,** Allen R '97 AIG Tech Srvcs -175 Water -NY 10038
(631) 756-4256 .. **McKay,** Chas J '92 %State Ins Fund -8 Corp Ctr Dr -Melvll 11747 **Fx:**756-4060
(212) 265-6888 .. **McKay,** Diane Dunn '90 (Porzio B&N,PC) -156 W 56th -NY 10019
(212) 460-2158 .. **McKay,** Douglas J '90 Con Ed -4 Irving Pl -NY 10003 **Fx:**780-6483
(212) 331-6167 .. **McKay,** Jack Gaines '98 %HRA -180 Water -NY 10038
(516) 328-9201 .. **McKay,** John F III '86 (Ruffo TM&M PC) -3000 Marcus Av -Lk Success 11042
(845) 565-1100 .. **McKay,** Jos G '92 SpclCnsl Tarshis CLM&M,PLLC -One Corwin Ct -Newburgh 12550
(212) 558-8912 .. **McKay,** Kevin J '75 Dominick & Dominick LLC -150 E 52nd -NY 10022
(212) 509-9400 .. **McKay,** Lorraine G '08 %Cozen O -45 Bway Atrium -NY 10006
(212) 237-0000 .. **McKay,** Michl V '83 (Vinson & E LLP) -666 5th Av -NY 10103
(518) 285-8301 .. **McKay,** Michele A '87 %Appllt Div 3rd Dept -Capitol Station Bx7288 -Albany 12224 **Fx:**471-4750
(212) 586-7074 .. **McKay,** Peter Albert '74 -250 W 57th -NY 10107 **Fx:**581-9819
(845) 639-2454 .. **McKay,** Ricardo A '72 -4 Greendale Rd -New Cty 10956 **Fx:**639-4409
(516) 742-6600 .. **McKay,** Robt B '70 (Carney & M) -1050 Franklin Av -Gdn Cty 11530
(212) 808-6846 .. **McKay,** Terance C '90 Rabobank -245 Park Av -NY 10167
(914) 762-3639 .. **McKean,** Gordon A '69 -40 Justamere Dr -Ossining 10562
(845) 557-8656 .. **McKean,** Michl E '82 -Route 97 Bx182 -Barryvll 12719 **Fx:**557-6992
(716) 847-3698 .. **McKeating,** Michl P '89 %OTDA -295 Main -Buffalo 14203 **Fx:**847-3699
(212) 698-3500 .. **McKechnie,** Blair F '08 %Dechert LLP -1095 Av of Amer -NY 10036
(212) 921-7171 .. **McKechnie,** Jos R Jr. '97 GCAM LLC -214 W 39th -NY 10018 **Fx:**921-7112
(212) 422-9424 .. **McKee,** Albert Wesley '01 %Gogick B&O,LLP -11 Bway -NY 10004
(212) 506-2500 .. **McKee,** Hugh T '09 %Mayer B LLP -1675 Bway -NY 10019
(914) 921-5294 .. **McKee,** James E '90 %Gamco Investors -1 Corp Ctr -Rye 10580
(212) 319-6060 .. **McKeefry,** Mark J '00 Fairfield Greenwich -55 E 52nd -NY 10055
(607) 746-2295 .. **McKeegan,** Bruce J '83 (McKeegan & M) -127 129 Main Bx188 -Delhi 13753
(212) 661-4200 .. **McKeegan,** George P '73 (McKeegan & S,PC) -192 Lex Av -NY 10016
(607) 746-2295 .. **McKeegan,** Robt J '48 (McKeegan & M) -127-129 Main Bx188 -Delhi 13753
(212) 661-4200 .. **McKeegan & Shearer,PC** -192 Lex Av -NY 10016 **Fx:**661-4813
(212) 909-6000 .. **McKeever,** Brooke Monahan '06 %Debevoise & P LLP -919 3rd Av -NY 10022
(718) 990-6028 .. **McKeever,** Claire C '94 %St John's Law Schl -8000 Utopia Pkwy -Jamaica 11439 **Fx:**990-5998
(212) 468-8000 .. **McKellar,** Crystal D '04 %Morrison & F LLP -1290 Av of Amer -NY 10104
(212) 277-4000 .. **McKellar,** Justin R G '08 %Freshfields BD LLP -520 Mad Av -NY 10022
(716) 934-2600 .. **McKelvey,** Thos H '74 (Pelletter M & P) -271 Central Av Bx29 -Silver Crk 14136 **Fx:**934-2623
(212) 930-8920 .. **McKendry,** Kevin P '78 %Lloyds Bk -1251 Av of Amer -NY 10020
(212) 867-4004 .. **McKenna,** Anita F '82 (Jaffe & M) -100 Park Av -NY 10017
(212) 259-8000 .. **McKenna,** Anne '05 %Dewey & L LLP -1301 Av of Amer -NY 10019
(516) 599-2020 .. **McKenna,** Brian E '76 OfCnsl A Chianese & Assoc -100 Merrick Rd -Rockvll Ctr 11570 **Fx:**599-6476
(716) 856-4000 .. **McKenna,** Britta L '05 %Hodgson R LLP -140 Pearl -Buffalo 14202
(516) 739-3395 .. **McKenna,** Bryan A '94 (Murphy & M,LLC) -1461 Franklin Av -Gdn Cty 11530 **Fx:**742-5278
(585) 325-5150 .. **McKenna,** Carol A '91 %Faraci L,LLP -28 E Main -Rchstr 14614
(914) 686-0500 .. **McKenna,** Danl J '99 DJ McKenna PC -111 Church -White Plns 10601 **Fx:**686-0505
(716) 852-8368 .. **McKenna,** Donald F '55 -295 Main -Buffalo 14203 **Fx:**852-8381
(347) 296-1667 .. **McKenna,** Eileen M '98 %Supreme Ct Law Dept -360 Adams -Brklyn 11201 **Fx:**643-6114
(212) 594-5300 .. **McKenna,** Elizabeth A '99 %Milberg LLP -1 Penn Plz -NY 10119
(516) 294-8844 .. **McKenna,** John D '96 (L'Abbate BC&C,LLP) -1001 Franklin Av -Gdn Cty 11530
(631) 728-0258 .. **McKenna,** John J Jr. '70 -37 Shinnecock Rd -Hampton Bays 11946
(914) 946-8200 .. **McKenna,** John J II '89 %R Peirce & Assoc -8 Cottage Pl -White Plns 10601
(212) 969-3000 .. **McKenna,** Kathleen M '80 (Proskauer R LLP) -1585 Bway -NY 10036

(212) 506-1700 .. **McKenna,** Keith '98 (Kasowitz BT&F LLP) -1633 Bway -NY 10019
(973) 596-4729 .. **McKenna,** Kevin J '83 (Gibbons PC) -1 Penn Plz -NY 10119 **Fx:**639-6279
(212) 922-1800 .. **McKenna Long & Aldridge** -230 Park Av -NY 10169 **Fx:**922-1819
(518) 462-1800 .. **McKenna Long & Aldridge** -111 Wshngtn Av -Albany 12210 **Fx:**462-4875
(212) 318-6000 .. **McKenna,** Mary '91 Paul HJ&W LLP -75 E 55th -NY 10022
(914) 253-2000 .. **McKenna,** Matthew M '76 %Pepsico -700 Andrsn Hill Rd -Purchase 10577
(718) 222-2107 .. **McKenna,** Meghan E '10 %Law Dept -350 Jay -Brklyn 11201 **Fx:**222-2393
(212) 772-0943 .. **McKenna,** Michl F '81 (Lewis & M) -521 5th Av -NY 10175
(646) 386-5700 .. **McKenna,** Myles P '06 Civil Ct -111 Centre -NY 10013
(518) 437-7841 .. **McKenna,** Patrick J '94 Amer Cancer Society -260 Osborne Rd -Albany 12211
(516) 561-7766 .. **McKenna,** Patrick M '77 (McKenna & S) -Bx250 -Vly Stream 11582 **Fx:**561-7793
(718) 967-0124 .. **McKenna,** Robt F '80 -1720 Drumgoole Rd W -Staten Isl 10309
(518) 456-0460 .. **McKenna,** Rosemary Weaver '90 KC Love -450 New Karner Rd -Albany 12205 **Fx:**456-0922
(718) 557-6547 .. **McKenna,** Sandra M '00 OHA-SSA -155-10 Jamaica Av -Jamaica 11432
(212) 250-8430 .. **McKenna,** Sean L '92 Deutsche Bk -60 Wall -NY 10005
(914) 948-0999 .. **McKenna,** Thos H '79 -17 Pheasant Ridge Rd -Ossining 10562
(212) 983-1300 .. **McKenna,** Thos J '85 (Gainey & M) -295 Mad Av -NY 10017
(212) 983-1300 .. **McKenna,** Thos J '85 -291 Crestwood Av -Tuckahoe 10707 **Fx:**983-0383
(315) 424-0513 .. **McKenna,** Whitney K '01 Carrols Corp -968 James -Syracuse 13203 **Fx:**475-9616
(315) 733-3167 .. **McKennan,** John T '46 -15 Foxcroft Rd -New Hartfrd 13413
(212) 532-8100 .. **McKenney,** James A '01 %Stern & M,LLP -115 Bway -NY 10006
(212) 277-4000 .. **McKenney,** Raquel Azevedo '09 %Freshfields BD LLP -520 Mad Av -NY 10022
(212) 918-3000 .. **McKenney,** Victoria '03 %Hogan L LLP -875 3rd Av -NY 10022
(212) 807-2925 .. **McKenny,** Betsy B '77 %Thomson Reuters/RIA -195 Bway -NY 10007
(212) 702-5400 .. **McKenzie,** Christopher J '93 (Beveridge & D,PC) -477 Mad Av -NY 10022
(315) 788-3400 .. **McKenzie,** Cynthia M '96 %RL Renzi -1201 Wshngtn -Watertwn 13601 **Fx:**788-3466
(212) 862-5512 .. **McKenzie,** Daphne D '85 -230 W 135th -NY 10030 **Fx:**862-5324
(212) 808-7800 .. **McKenzie,** Gregory M '92 (Kelley D&W LLP) -101 Park Av -NY 10178
(212) 424-8234 .. **McKenzie,** Lorna M '92 Jazz at Lincoln Ctr -33 W 60th -NY 10023
(212) 335-9000 .. **McKenzie,** Matthew J '10 %DA -1 Hogan Pl -NY 10013
(646) 225-4163 .. **McKenzie,** Michl A '95 Microsoft Corp -1290 Av of Amer -NY 10104
(212) 909-6000 .. **McKenzie,** Naila Bayo '09 %Debevoise & P LLP -919 3rd Av -NY 10022
(212) 918-4868 .. **McKenzie,** Peter A '05 (Cobos EM&M,LLC) -48 Wall -NY 10005 **Fx:**918-4801
(718) 222-9803 .. **McKenzie,** Ransford B '92 -16 Court -Brklyn 11241
(718) 420-5636 .. **McKenzie,** Sharon '03 NYC Dept Educ -715 Ocean Ter -Staten Isl 10301
(212) 998-6756 .. **McKenzie,** Troy A '01 %NYU Law Schl -40 Wshngtn Sq S -NY 10012 **Fx:**995-3156
(718) 741-8412 .. **McKenzie,** Veanka S '93 %Div of Human Rights -1 Fordham Plz -Bronx 10458 **Fx:**741-8102
(718) 250-2000 .. **McKenzie,** Wayne S '90 %DA -350 Jay -Brklyn 11201 **Fx:**250-2314
(212) 724-1835 .. **McKeon,** Agnes C '87 -10 W 65th -NY 10023 **Fx:**724-1835
(212) 319-5240 .. **McKeon,** Brendan E '07 %Flicker G & Assoc,LLP -45 Bway -NY 10006
(718) 505-2236 .. **McKeon,** Kenneth Edw '96 -51-27 Hillyer -Elmhrst 11373 **Fx:**898-7846
(212) 259-8000 .. **McKeon,** Marianne '81 Cnsl Dewey & L LLP -1301 Av of Amer -NY 10019
(518) 486-8283 .. **McKeon,** Matthew J '96 %Key Equipment Finance -54 State -Albany 12207
(212) 735-3000 .. **McKeon,** Peter '79 Cnsl Skadden ASM&F LLP -4 Times Sq -NY 10036
(585) 396-9627 .. **McKeown,** John F '85 -70 N Main Bx611 -Canandaigua 14424 **Fx:**396-9264
(914) 432-5103 .. **McKeown,** Mary A '95 -Bx161 -Briarclff Mnr 10510
(516) 512-6590 .. **McKeown,** Patrick B '86 %Pieret & Assoc -400 Grdn City Plz -Gdn Cty 11530 **Fx:**742-4116
(718) 220-6850 .. **McKeown,** Wm B '75 %Wildlife Conservation Soc -2300 Southrn Blvd -Bronx 10460 **Fx:**220-2573
(212) 326-3939 .. **McKernan,** Jos T '98 OfCnsl Jones D -222 E 41st -NY 10017
(718) 317-5007 .. **McKernan,** Kevin P '78 -7583 Amboy Rd -Staten Isl 10307 **Fx:**317-2996
(607) 723-9511 .. **McKertich,** Robt H '09 %Coughlin & G,LLP -19 Chenango Bx2039 -Bnghmtn 13902
(718) 298-1000 .. **McKetney Butler,** LaurenTina S '95 Supreme Ct -89-17 Sutphin Blvd -Jamaica 11435
(516) 228-1300 .. **McKevitt,** Thos '97 SpclCnsl Sahn WC&B,PLLC -333 Earle Ovngton Blvd -Uniondale 11553
(718) 995-3206 .. **McKew,** Mark L '00 Top Line Logistics -147-70 184th -Jamaica 11413
(845) 359-5486 .. **McKie,** Ronald H '67 -1 Lawrence Pk -Piermont 10968
(212) 373-3000 .. **McKiernan,** Donald J '99 Paul WRW&G LLP -1285 Av of Amer -NY 10019
(518) 487-7600 .. **McKiernan,** M Alanna '03 %Whiteman O&H LLP -1 Commerce Plz -Albany 12260
(914) 949-9042 .. **McKiernan,** Peter G '83 -12 Hillside Ter -White Plns 10601
(212) 758-0050 .. **McKillop,** Jos J '01 %Title Assoc -825 3rd Av -NY 10022 **Fx:**758-8223
(607) 273-0733 .. **McKinley,** Erin E '97 -309 N Aurora -Ithaca 14850 **Fx:**330-2631
(212) 691-0950 .. **McKinley,** Tenee S '08 Ctr for Family Representation -116 John -NY 10038
(212) 735-8600 .. **McKinney,** Carl Derek '05 %Morrison C LLP -909 3rd Av -NY 10022
(212) 909-6000 .. **McKinney,** Laura A '07 %Debevoise & P LLP -919 3rd Av -NY 10022
(914) 793-9215 .. **McKinnis,** George C '67 -12 Locust Ln -Bronxvll 10708
(516) 746-2300 .. **McKinnon,** Alita P '00 %A Capetola -2C Hillside Av -Williston Pk 11596 **Fx:**746-2318
(631) 444-8250 .. **McKinnon,** M Veronica '91 %SUNY Univ Cnsl -221 Admin Bldg -Stony Brk 11794 **Fx:**444-6101
(716) 849-0701 .. **McKinnon,** Neil J '90 (Lipsitz & P LLC) -135 Delaware Av -Buffalo 14202
(212) 775-2975 .. **McKniff,** Jos W '94 Ernst & Young LLP -5 Times Sq -NY 10036
(212) 935-3000 .. **McKnight,** James M '91 (Mintz LCFG&P,PC) -666 3rd Av -NY 10017
(212) 762-8031 .. **McKnight,** Riche T '04 Morgan Stanley -1221 Av of Amer -NY 10020
(212) 558-4000 .. **McKnight,** S Neal '97 (Sullivan & C LLP) -125 Broad -NY 10004
(212) 577-3444 .. **McKnight,** Tanisha S '05 Leg Aid -199 Water -NY 10038 **Fx:**809-1370
(347) 401-9752 .. **McKnight,** Toshia M '96 Family Ct Referee -330 Jay -Brklyn 11201
(212) 402-9400 .. **McKool Smith, PC** -1 Bryant Park -NY 10036 **Fx:**402-9444
(212) 245-7300 .. **McKoy,** Michl L '98 (Serling R&F,LLP) -119 5th Av -NY 10003
(518) 457-2411 .. **McLachlan,** Janice '91 %DOT -50 Wolf Rd -Albany 12232 **Fx:**457-4021
(212) 782-4624 .. **McLachlin,** Harry D '97 %Bk of Tokyo-Mitsubishi -1251 Av of Amer -NY 10020 **Fx:**782-6420
(212) 557-4000 .. **McLafferty,** Mika M '08 %Grunfeld DLS&K LLP -399 Park Av -NY 10022
(212) 395-5997 .. **McLamore-Holmes,** Glenda '98 %Verizon -140 West -NY 10007
(516) 589-3121 .. **McLane,** Danl S '93 -Bx1436 -Bayvll 11709
(315) 253-0326 .. **McLane,** John P '68 (Boyle & A,PC) -110 Genesee -Auburn 13021
(315) 724-1530 .. **McLane,** Mark W '80 (McLane S and L,LLP) -20 Elizabeth Bx524 -Utica 13503 **Fx:**724-1852
(212) 975-6020 .. **McLane,** Molly Hart '97 %CBS News -555 W 57th -NY 10019
(212) 705-7000 .. **McLane,** Noreen E '09 %Bingham M LLP -399 Park Av -NY 10022
(973) 848-4700 .. **McLane,** Wm P '97 (Littler M,PC) -900 3rd Av -NY 10022 **Fx:**643-5626
(718) 935-2000 .. **McLaren,** Candace R '00 %NYC Dept Educ -65 Court -Brklyn 11201
(212) 878-8000 .. **McLaren,** Laura J '04 %Clifford C LLP -31 W 52nd -NY 10019
(718) 816-0247 .. **McLaughlin,** Alan M '84 (O'Donnell & M) -390 Manor Rd -Staten Isl 10314
(716) 858-6506 .. **McLaughlin,** Bonnie A '87 Dept Soc Srvcs -95 Franklin -Buffalo 14202 **Fx:**858-6506
(212) 610-6300 .. **McLaughlin,** Cathleen E '91 (Allen & O) -1221 Av of Amer -NY 10020
(212) 434-0100 .. **McLaughlin,** Christopher A '88 (Litchfield C LLP) -420 Lex Av -NY 10170
(212) 839-5300 .. **Mc Laughlin,** Danl A '97 Cnsl Sidley A LLP -787 7th Av -NY 10019
(518) 761-7678 .. **McLaughlin,** Denise H '79 Hon JT Breen -1340 State Route 9 -Lk George 12845
(212) 225-2000 .. **McLaughlin,** Duane '99 (Cleary GS&H) -1 Lbrty Plz -NY 10006
(914) 765-6033 .. **McLaughlin,** Edw F '76 %IBM Credit Corp -North Castle Dr -Armonk 10504
(212) 698-3500 .. **McLaughlin,** Ethan B '08 %Dechert LLP -1095 Av of Amer -NY 10036
(212) 732-2000 .. **McLaughlin,** Frank C Jr. '62 (Cullen and D LLP) -44 Wall -NY 10005
(914) 642-6574 .. **McLaughlin,** Gregory M '03 IBM -1133 Wstchstr Av -White Plns 10604
(516) 358-5300 .. **McLaughlin,** Harold B '65 OfCnsl Giuffre,PC -99 Tulip Av -Floral Pk 11001 **Fx:**358-0400
(631) 665-6661 .. **McLaughlin,** J Stewart '62 -21 Maple Av Bx5230 -Bay Shr 11706 **Fx:**665-2552
(631) 758-0303 .. **McLaughlin,** Jane M '90 %H Goldstein -1719 N Ocean Av -Medfrd 11763 **Fx:**758-0309
(516) 357-3700 .. **McLaughlin,** Jennifer A '00 (Cullen and D LLP) -100 Q Roosevelt Blvd -Gdn Cty 11530
(212) 839-5300 .. **McLaughlin,** Jos '66 (Sidley A LLP) -787 7th Av -NY 10019
(212) 455-2000 .. **McLaughlin,** Jos '89 (Simpson T&B LLP) -425 Lex Av -NY 10017
(212) 705-7000 .. **McLaughlin,** Jos T '68 OfCnsl Bingham M LLP -399 Park Av -NY 10022
(212) 477-1846 .. **McLaughlin,** Kathryn A '93 (McLaughlin & W,PC) -276 5th Av -NY 10001 **Fx:**477-1731
(914) 946-5100 .. **McLaughlin,** Liam J '97 %Bashian & F,LLP -235 Main -White Plns 10601
(212) 307-5500 .. **McLaughlin,** Matthew T '95 (Venable LLP) -1270 Av of Amer -NY 10020
(617) 345-6154 .. **McLaughlin,** Matthew T '05 %Nixon P LLP -437 Mad Av -NY 10022 **Fx:**(866) 440-6480
(212) 530-5000 .. **McLaughlin,** Melanie A '08 %Milbank TH&M LLP -1 Chase Manh Plz -NY 10005
(845) 357-6494 .. **McLaughlin,** Michl J '85 -4 Evergreen Ct -Suffern 10901
(212) 333-0200 .. **McLaughlin,** Michl J '06 %Arkin KR LLP -590 Mad Av -NY 10022
(212) 278-0400 .. **McLaughlin,** Neal J '09 %Cooper & D LLP -30 Rckfllr Plz -NY 10112
(716) 536-0589 .. **McLaughlin,** Patrick J '99 -55 Koenig Rd -Tonawanda 14150 **Fx:**832-5680
(718) 515-7500 .. **McLaughlin,** Randolph M '79 (McLaughlin G&C) -959 E 233rd -Bronx 10466 **Fx:**515-5557
(212) 243-2424 .. **McLaughlin,** Richd D '83 OfCnsl Schepisi & M,PA -200 Park Av S -NY 10003
(516) 229-4400 .. **McLaughlin,** Richd G '86 Kay & G -875 Merrick Av -Westbury 11590
(518) 465-2333 .. **McLaughlin,** Robt J '86 (Hodgson R LLP) -677 Bway -Albany 12207
(212) 859-8000 .. **McLaughlin,** Robt M '84 (Fried FHS&J LLP) -1 NY Plz -NY 10004
(516) 385-6595 .. **McLaughlin,** Robt O '08 (Mayer & M LLP) -114 Old Cntry Rd -Mineola 11501 **Fx:**294-9510
(315) 218-8000 .. **McLaughlin,** Robt S '88 (Bond S&K,PLLC) -1 Lincoln Ctr -Syracuse 13202
(718) 816-4480 .. **McLaughlin,** Rory M '77 -1444 Clove Rd -Staten Isl 10301
(914) 682-2068 .. **McLaughlin,** Stephen P '93 (Ansa A,LLP) -50 Main -White Plns 10606
(212) 448-1100 .. **McLaughlin & Stern,LLP** -260 Mad Av -NY 10016 **Fx:**448-0066
(845) 677-5700 .. **McLaughlin & Stern,LLP** -3304 Franklin Av Bx1369 -Millbrook 12545 **Fx:**677-0097

(212) 947-8800 .. **McLaughlin,** Susan A '07 ThyssenKrupp Elevator -519 8th Av -NY 10018
(212) 728-8000 .. **Mc Laughlin,** Terence K '97 (Willkie F&G LLP) -787 7th Av -NY 10019
(716) 852-1380 .. **McLaughlin,** Wm F '69 (Abbarno M&K) -314 Brisbane Bldg -Buffalo 14203
(516) 599-6000 .. **McLaughlin,** Wm J '84 -81 Hempstd Av -Lynbrk 11563 **Fx:**599-0419
(212) 859-8000 .. **McLean,** Adrian A '97 %Fried FHS&J LLP -1 NY Plz -NY 10004
(212) 735-3000 .. **McLean,** Andrew J '09 %Skadden ASM&F LLP -4 Times Sq -NY 10036
(718) 206-4733 .. **McLean,** Barbara '79 %Law Dept -89-17 Sutphin Blvd -Jamaica 11435 **Fx:**206-4702
(518) 273-6133 .. **McLean,** Barbara M '89 -Bx1087 -Troy 12181
(212) 696-6000 .. **McLean,** Chelsea R '09 %Curtis M-PC&M LLP -101 Park Av -NY 10178
(212) 708-8115 .. **McLean,** D Benjamin '05 Sundance Channel -1633 Bway -NY 10019
(585) 263-1000 .. **McLean,** Deborah J '79 (Nixon P LLP) -1100 Clinton Sq -Rchstr 14604
(718) 557-6585 .. **McLean,** Gil '01 SSA-ODAR -155-10 Jamaica Av -Jamaica 11432
(212) 416-8435 .. **McLean,** Hugh L '87 %Dept of Law -120 Bway -NY 10271 **Fx:**416-8931
(212) 850-1864 .. **McLean,** John E '98 %J&W Seligman & Co -100 Park Av -NY 10017 **Fx:**922-5731
(212) 227-3636 .. **McLean,** Laura J '08 %Spar & B,PC -225 Bway -NY 10007
(518) 449-8893 .. **McLean,** Mary Ann '79 (Wilson EME&D LLP) -677 Bway -Albany 12207
(212) 949-5666 .. **McLean,** Mora L '83 African-Amer Inst -420 Lex Av -NY 10170
(212) 522-4907 .. **McLean,** Rhonda J '87 %Time Inc -1271 Av of Amer -NY 10020 **Fx:**522-0437
(585) 436-6664 .. **McLean,** Robt F II '99 OMMI Fncl Grp -1099 Jay -Rchstr 14611
(212) 513-3200 .. **McLean,** Tiana M '10 %Holland & K LLP -31 W 52nd -NY 10019
(315) 461-4277 .. **McLean,** Tracey A '91 (Falge & M,PC) -3300 Vickery Rd -N Syracuse 13212
(212) 859-3460 .. **McLellan & Bialkowski** -110 Wall -NY 10005 **Fx:**943-2300
(212) 859-3460 .. **McLellan,** Harry E III '89 (McLellan & B) -110 Wall -NY 10005
(212) 221-6900 .. **McLellan,** Kenneth A '96 %Winget S&S,LLP -45 Bway -NY 10006
(212) 309-1000 .. **McLellan,** Melinda L '06 %Hunton & W -200 Park Av -NY 10166
(315) 425-6161 .. **McLellan,** Peter E '93 -1117 E Genesee -Syracuse 13210 **Fx:**475-8498
(607) 721-8356 .. **McLellan,** Scott D '98 Workers Comp Bd -44 Hawley -Bnghmtn 13901
(212) 446-2300 .. **McLelland,** Andrew S '08 %Boies S&F LLP -575 Lex Av -NY 10022
(212) 455-2000 .. **McLendon,** Kathrine A '85 SrCnsl Simpson T&B LLP -425 Lex Av -NY 10017
(212) 349-6009 .. **McLeod,** Blyth M '09 Sanctuary for Families -110 Wall -NY 10005 **Fx:**566-0344
(212) 310-2979 .. **McLeod,** Brigette R '94 %Colgate-Palmolive -300 Park Av -NY 10022 **Fx:**310-3230
(914) 995-5435 .. **McLeod,** Donald N '89 %Cnty Atty -148 Martine Av -White Plns 10601 **Fx:**995-5858
(212) 337-4276 .. **McLeod,** Elizabeth '83 RIAA -195 Bway -NY 10007
(212) 403-1000 .. **McLeod,** Ryan A '09 %Wachtell LR&K -51 W 52nd -NY 10019
(212) 839-5300 .. **McLeod,** Stephanie '07 %Sidley A LLP -787 7th Av -NY 10019
(718) 250-2000 .. **McLeod,** Stephen M '99 %DA -350 Jay -Brklyn 11201 **Fx:**250-2314
(914) 993-9393 .. **McLeron,** Timothy W '93 %Stewart Title Ins -707 Wstchstr Av -White Plns 10604 **Fx:**997-1698
(914) 613-9806 .. **McLoone,** Kevin D '85 -1 Exec Blvd -Ynkrs 10701
(845) 486-2300 .. **McLoughlin,** Edw T '92 %DA -236 Main -Poughkeepsie 12601 **Fx:**486-2324
(212) 450-4000 .. **McLoughlin,** Jean M '95 (Davis P&W LLP) -450 Lex Av -NY 10017
(516) 873-1511 .. **McLoughlin,** John E '88 %Fischetti & P -310 Old Cntry Rd -Gdn Cty 11530
(212) 891-1600 .. **McLoughlin,** Luke P '06 %Jenner & B LLP -919 3rd Av -NY 10022
(212) 701-3000 .. **McLoughlin,** Maura A '91 Cahill G&R LLP -80 Pine -NY 10005 **Fx:**269-5420
(212) 468-4800 .. **McLoughlin,** Maureen A '95 (Davis & G LLP) -1740 Bway -NY 10019
(516) 227-8076 .. **McLoughlin,** Maureen L '04 Dept Soc Srvcs -60 Chas Lindbergh Blvd -Uniondale 11553
(212) 788-0654 .. **McLoughlin,** Michl J '64 %Law Dept -100 Church -NY 10007 **Fx:**788-0367
(212) 521-5400 .. **McLoughlin,** Michl W '90 (Reed S LLP) -599 Lex Av -NY 10022
(845) 294-5717 .. **McLoughlin,** Patrick '79 -12 N Church Bx94 -Goshen 10924
(845) 486-2300 .. **McLoughlin,** Sinead M '04 DA -236 Main -Poughkeepsie 12601 **Fx:**486-2324
(718) 447-0933 .. **McLoughlin,** Stephen J '87 -501 Forest Rd -Staten Isl 10304 **Fx:**442-4507
(646) 333-9808 .. **McLoughlin,** Wm P '99 %Barclays Capital Inc -745 7th Av -NY 10019
(212) 768-4343 .. **McMahan,** Crystal M '07 %Cantor E&M,LLP -49 W 37th -NY 10018
(212) 335-4500 .. **McMahan,** Michl P '10 %DLA Piper LLP -1251 Av of Amer -NY 10020
(212) 455-2000 .. **McMahon,** Anthony J '07 %Simpson T&B LLP -425 Lex Av -NY 10017
(212) 940-3181 .. **McMahon,** Arthur F Jr. '74 (Nixon P LLP) -437 Mad Av -NY 10022
(212) 450-4000 .. **McMahon,** Brett M '07 %Davis P&W LLP -450 Lex Av -NY 10017
(516) 465-8090 .. **McMahon,** Colleen C '00 %North Shore-LIJ Hlth Systm -145 Community Dr -Gt Neck 11021 **Fx:**465-8013
(518) 584-5030 .. **McMahon & Coseo,PC** -16 Lake Av Bx587 -Saratoga Spgs 12866 **Fx:**584-0238
(518) 654-9011 .. **McMahon & Coseo,PC** -215 Main -Corinth 12822 **Fx:**654-9012
(315) 424-1105 .. **McMahon,** Danl A '60 (McMahon K&S,PC) -500 S Salina -Syracuse 13202
(315) 424-1105 .. **McMahon,** Danl G '95 (McMahon K&S,PC) -500 S Salina -Syracuse 13202
(518) 463-3200 .. **McMahon,** Danl J '86 %NYS Bar Assn -1 Elk -Albany 12207 **Fx:**487-5544
(212) 218-2100 .. **McMahon,** Dennis J '10 %Fitzpatrick CH&S -1290 Av of Amer -NY 10104
(518) 584-6515 .. **McMahon,** Edw J '56 -98 Adams -Saratoga Spgs 12866
(212) 637-6100 .. **McMahon,** Edw J '96 %US Marshal's Ofc -500 Pearl -NY 10007 **Fx:**637-6142
(212) 797-1877 .. **McMahon,** Gerald J '80 -26 Bway -NY 10004 **Fx:**797-1419
(845) 621-2596 .. **McMahon,** Gilbert K '91 -33 Highland Vw Rd -Mahopac 10541 **Fx:**621-2596
(212) 839-5300 .. **McMahon,** Gregory J '91 Cnsl Sidley A LLP -787 7th Av -NY 10019
(315) 336-4700 .. **McMahon & Grow** -301 N Wshngtn Bx4350 -Rome 13442 **Fx:**336-5851
(212) 326-3939 .. **McMahon,** J S Terry '09 %Jones D -222 E 41st -NY 10017
(516) 825-1000 .. **McMahon,** James A Jr. '83 (JA McMahon,PC) -20 W Lincoln Av -Vly Stream 11580 **Fx:**568-1723
(917) 592-4779 .. **McMahon,** James C Jr. '78 (McMahon & K,LLP) -545 W 45TH -NY 10036
(516) 433-7026 .. **McMahon,** James F '60 -71 Hay Path Rd -Plainvw 11803 **Fx:**433-7026
(718) 254-7000 .. **McMahon,** James F '88 %US Atty -271 Cadman Plz E -Brklyn 11201 **Fx:**254-6479
(212) 772-0943 .. **McMahon,** James M '04 %Lewis & M -521 5th Av -NY 10175
(212) 264-3650 .. **McMahon,** Jennifer S '02 SSA Ofc Genl Cnsl -26 Fed Plz -NY 10278 **Fx:**264-6372
(716) 204-4999 .. **McMahon,** Joel A '01 Cnsl Allcare Dental Mgmt,LLC -8205 Main -Buffalo 14221
(845) 577-2500 .. **McMahon,** John D '77 Orange/Rcklnd Util -1 Blue Hill Plz -Pearl Rvr 10965
(914) 948-5544 .. **McMahon,** John J '81 -175 Main -White Plns 10601 **Fx:**948-5695
(518) 584-5030 .. **McMahon,** John L '56 (McMahon & C,PC) -16 Lake Av Bx587 -Saratoga Spgs 12866
(212) 233-0440 .. **McMahon,** John P '67 (McMahon & C,PC) -132 Nassau -NY 10038
(718) 299-7000 .. **McMahon,** Jos J '94 Procida Construction Co -456 E 173rd -Bronx 10457
(518) 462-5601 .. **McMahon,** Joshua E '09 O'Connell & A -54 State -Albany 12207
(646) 586-9470 .. **McMahon,** Judith A '92 Supreme Ct -100 Centre -NY 10013
(716) 551-4221 .. **McMahon,** Karen M '87 %Hon J Curtin USDC -68 Court -Buffalo 14202
(917) 592-4779 .. **McMahon & Kelly, LLP** -545 W 45TH -NY 10036 **Fx:**(212) 664-8550
(315) 424-1105 .. **McMahon Kublick & Smith,PC** -500 S Salina -Syracuse 13202 **Fx:**478-4843
(718) 237-3100 .. **McMahon,** Lena M '07 Leg Aid -111 Lvngstn -Brklyn 11201 **Fx:**250-4243
(212) 747-1230 .. **McMahon Martine & Gallagher LLP** -55 Washington -Brklyn 11201 **Fx:**747-1239
(718) 324-8900 .. **McMahon,** Matthew J '84 (McMahon M&V) -147 E 233rd -Bronx 10470
(718) 324-8900 .. **McMahon McCarthy & Verrelli** -147 E 233rd -Bronx 10470 **Fx:**324-2614
(212) 648-0289 .. **McMahon,** Melissa '84 JP Morgan Chase -245 Park Av -NY 10167
(212) 808-7800 .. **McMahon,** Michl H II '09 %Kelley D&W LLP -101 Park Av -NY 10178
(212) 541-2000 .. **McMahon,** Michelle K '05 %Bryan C LLP -1290 Av of Amer -NY 10104
(518) 402-4582 .. **McMahon,** Pamela A '82 %State Comptroller -110 State -Albany 12236 **Fx:**473-9104
(917) 903-3639 .. **McMahon,** Patrick J '99 Mariner Invstmnt Grp -500 Mamaroneck Av -Harrison 10528
(718) 654-8988 .. **McMahon,** Patrick J '06 Koors & J -4234 Viero Av -Bronx 10470
(631) 543-7676 .. **McMahon,** Paul M '02 P McMahon & Assoc -356 Vets Mem'l Hwy -Commack 11725
(845) 703-3101 .. **McMahon,** Peter C '93 (Bonacic KCM&B,LLP) -90 Crystal Run Rd -Middletwn 10941
(315) 336-7300 .. **McMahon,** Richd H Jr. '91 %Rome Savings Bk -100 On The Mall -Rome 13440
(914) 946-1030 .. **McMahon,** Robt C '80 %Barry M&M -55 Church -White Plns 10601
(315) 448-8400 .. **McMahon,** Rory A '97 Law Dept -233 E Wshngtn -Syracuse 13202 **Fx:**448-8381
(212) 382-0700 .. **McMahon,** Sean P '06 %Ostrolenk FG&S,LLP -1180 Av of Amer -NY 10036
(315) 487-3724 .. **McMahon,** Stephen T '86 -5214 W Genesee -Camillus 13031 **Fx:**487-4517
(315) 635-6845 .. **McMahon,** Timothy F '84 -60 Oswego -Baldwinsvll 13027 **Fx:**638-8843
(315) 424-1105 .. **McMahon,** Timothy J '87 (McMahon K&S,PC) -500 S Salina -Syracuse 13202
(315) 422-1152 .. **McMahon,** Timothy N '07 %Costello C&F,PLLC -500 Plum -Syracuse 13204
(631) 727-3002 .. **McManmon,** James '87 -123 Maple Av -Rvrhead 11901
(718) 741-8446 .. **McManus,** Bellew S '89 Div of Human Rights -1 Fordham Plz -Bronx 10458 **Fx:**741-8102
(212) 425-3100 .. **McManus Collura & Richter, PC** -48 Wall -NY 10005 **Fx:**425-3175
(914) 765-3533 .. **McManus,** Danl E Jr. '94 %MBIA Ins Corp -113 King -Armonk 10504
(212) 309-6824 .. **McManus,** David A '93 (Morgan L&B LLP) -101 Park Av -NY 10178
(516) 734-3646 .. **McManus,** Donna Giarratano '99 Dealertrack Inc -1111 Marcus Av -New Hyde Pk 11042
(518) 641-0500 .. **McManus,** Elizabeth Dailey '97 %West Firm,PLLC -677 Bway -Albany 12207 **Fx:**615-1500
(212) 696-8284 .. **McManus,** Heather Ribar '93 %Amer Kennel Club,Inc -260 Mad Av -NY 10016
(914) 945-6055 .. **McManus,** Jill A '87 Philips Electronics -345 Scarborough Rd -Briarclff Mnr 10510
(212) 425-3100 .. **McManus,** John A '76 (McManus C&R,PC) -48 Wall -NY 10005
(212) 818-8274 .. **McManus,** John F '95 Itochu Intl -335 Mad Av -NY 10017 **Fx:**818-8493
(212) 382-6698 .. **McManus,** John T '70 NYC Bar -42 W 44th -NY 10036 **Fx:**768-1433
(518) 427-9700 .. **McManus,** John T '98 (Harris B PLLC) -677 Bway -Albany 12207
(212) 908-0739 .. **McManus,** Katherine Sherwood '83 %Fitch Investor's Service -1 State Street Plz -NY 10004 **Fx:**480-4421
(212) 425-9300 .. **McManus,** Keith P '08 %Bressler A&R,PC -17 State -NY 10004
(516) 742-0707 .. **McManus,** Kerry A '92 %Sullivan PBM&C PC -55 Mineola Blvd -Mineola 11501
(212) 697-3122 .. **McManus,** Kevin P '96 (Martin C&B LLP) -220 E 42nd -NY 10017

(718) 237-2000 .. **McManus,** Kevin P '02 %Leg Aid -111 Lvngstn -Brklyn 11201 **Fx:**237-8737
(212) 455-2000 .. **McManus,** Krista B '99 %Simpson T&B LLP -425 Lex Av -NY 10017
(518) 457-4380 .. **McManus,** Mary E '98 %Dept of Labor -State Campus Bldg 12 -Albany 12240 **Fx:**485-1819
(631) 694-9555 .. **McManus,** Michl A '68 Misonix -1938 New Hwy -Farmngdl 11735
(516) 294-5433 .. **McManus,** Philip J '72 (Ahmuty D&M) -200 IU Willets Rd -Albertson 11507
(845) 986-7660 .. **McManus,** Robt F '87 -14 Oaklnd Av -Warwick 10990 **Fx:**986-2388
(212) 732-9000 .. **McManus,** Thos J '06 %Sullivan PBM&C PC -120 Bway -NY 10271
(212) 761-3733 .. **McManus,** Thos N '93 Morgan Stanley -1585 Bway -NY 10036
(716) 633-5432 .. **Mc Master,** Christopher W '01 %D Brody -5547 Main -Williamsvll 14221
(646) 562-3405 .. **McMaster,** Heather M '99 %PLC -747 3rd Av -NY 10017
(212) 916-7800 .. **McMaster,** Michl G '97 Rabobank Nederland -245 Park Av -NY 10167
(212) 984-7700 .. **McMenamin,** Paul R '93 (Warshaw BCS&K,LLP) -555 5th Av -NY 10017
(212) 661-5000 .. **McMennamin,** M Breeze '82 %Frankel & A -230 Park Av -NY 10169
(718) 596-4877 .. **McMickens,** Jacqueline '90 (J McMickens & Assoc,PLLC) -26 Court -Brklyn 11242 **Fx:**596-5009
(212) 259-6355 .. **Mc Millan,** Andrew D '99 -1301 Av of Amer -NY 10019 **Fx:**259-6333
(212) 926-0231 .. **McMillan,** Bridgett '98 -445 Park Av -NY 10022
(212) 841-1000 .. **McMillan,** Christine A '06 %Covington & B LLP -620 8th Av -NY 10018
(914) 834-3500 .. **McMillan Constabile Maker & Perone LLP** -2180 Bstn Post Rd -Larchmnt 10538 **Fx:**834-0620
(516) 877-7000 .. **McMillan,** David M '10 %McCoyd P&R,LLP -1100 Franklin Av -Gdn Cty 11530
(212) 986-6262 .. **McMillan,** James Edw '99 J McMillan,PC -19 Fulton -NY 10038 **Fx:**986-1551
(914) 684-9100 .. **McMillan,** Keith J '80 (Bailly & M,LLP) -244 Wstchstr Av -White Plns 10604
(212) 234-7958 .. **McMillan,** L Benet '74 -716 Schl Dr -Baldwin 11510
(212) 259-8000 .. **McMillan,** L Londell '91 (Dewey & L LLP) -1301 Av of Amer -NY 10019
(212) 732-8700 .. **McMillan,** Linda Plona '86 (McAloon & F,PC) -123 William -NY 10038
(212) 715-1000 .. **McMillan,** Lucy S '05 %Arnold & P LLP -399 Park Av -NY 10022
(718) 286-3000 .. **McMillan,** Mark '02 %Boro Pres Ofc -120-55 Qns Blvd -Kew Gdns 11424 **Fx:**286-2885
(516) 255-1800 .. **McMillan,** Mark A '91 %Rosenblum & B LLP -100 Merrick Rd -Rockvll Ctr 11570
(212) 333-8170 .. **McMillan,** Randall Eugene '96 Island DEF Jam Music Grp -825 8th Av -NY 10019
(516) 746-5599 .. **McMillan,** Robt R '60 OfCnsl Bee RFH&D,LLP -170 Old Cntry Rd -Mineola 11501
(516) 571-2870 .. **McMillan,** Robin E '97 %Hon G Kohn -100 Supreme Ct Dr -Mineola 11501
(914) 834-3500 .. **McMillan,** Stewart A '95 OfCnsl McMillan CM&P LLP -2180 Bstn Post Rd -Larchmnt 10538
(914) 834-3500 .. **McMillan,** Stewart J '67 (McMillan CM&P LLP) -2180 Bstn Post Rd -Larchmnt 10538
(845) 454-1200 .. **McMillan,** Veronica Ann '99 (Lewis & G,PC) -510 Haight Av Bx2990 -Poughkeepsie 12603
(212) 554-1400 .. **McMillen,** Lauren A '01 %Bernstein LB&G LLP -1285 Av of Amer -NY 10019
(518) 792-2117 .. **McMillen,** Robt S '69 (Bartlett PS&R,PC) -1 Wshngtn Bx2168 -Glens Fls 12801
(212) 804-4200 .. **McMonagle,** Diana E '06 %Mound CW&G -One Bttry Pk Plz -NY 10004
(212) 313-9024 .. **McMorris,** Frances A '94 %The Daily Deal -105 Mad Av -NY 10016
(518) 745-4343 .. **McMorris,** Jeffrey E '88 (Stanclift L&M,PC) -3 Warren Bx358 -Glens Fls 12801 **Fx:**745-4344
(212) 349-7020 .. **McMorris,** Wm J Jr. '88 (Slutsky M&M, LLP) -100 Park Av -NY 10017 **Fx:**(203) 762-9864
(716) 853-8440 .. **McMorrow,** Roseanne '02 %Dept of Law -350 Main Pl Twr -Buffalo 14202 **Fx:**853-8571
(212) 786-8120 .. **McMullan,** Alasdair J '88 EMI Music NA -150 5th Av -NY 10011 **Fx:**786-8123
(212) 506-1700 .. **McMullan,** Leigh F '07 Kasowitz BT&F LLP -1633 Bway -NY 10019
(212) 735-3000 .. **McMullan,** Todd J '09 %Skadden ASM&F LLP -4 Times Sq -NY 10036
(212) 370-3744 .. **McMullan,** Wm R '76 (Danow M&P,PC) -275 Mad Av -NY 10016
(607) 763-9200 .. **McMullen,** Karen J '10 %Levene G&T,LLP -BxF-1706 -Bnghmtn 13902
(631) 261-6679 .. **McMullen,** Kevin P '73 -139A Fox Ln -Northprt 11768
(585) 295-5762 .. **McMullen Reston,** Margaret B '04 Leg Aid -1 W Main -Rchstr 14614
(212) 214-6062 .. **McMullin,** James F '00 Wachovia -375 Park Av -NY 10152
(646) 300-6167 .. **McMurdo,** Matthew C '99 -501 Mad Av -NY 10022 **Fx:**390-7090
(212) 878-7900 .. **McMurdy,** Keith R '03 (Fox R LLP) -100 Park Av -NY 10017
(212) 236-1000 .. **McMurray,** Locke R '95 %Merrill Lynch -225 Lbrty -NY 10080
(716) 645-8141 .. **McMurray,** Thad G '06 Univ at Buffalo -1576 Sweet Home Rd -Amherst 14228
(212) 532-4000 .. **McMurray-Killelea,** Erin E '06 %Dobrish ZG LLP -757 3rd Av -NY 10017
(212) 261-8000 .. **McMurrer,** Edw J '72 OfCnsl Mendes & M,LLP -750 7th Av -NY 10019
(212) 474-1000 .. **McMurrough,** Micaela R H '08 %Cravath S&M LLP -825 8th Av -NY 10019
(212) 608-5444 .. **McMurry,** Ralph L '71 -30 Vesey -NY 10007
(516) 408-1600 .. **McNaboe,** John P '98 (Heidell PM&B,LLP) -1050 Franklin Av -Gdn Cty 11530
(212) 837-6000 .. **McNair,** Karin '01 %Hughes H&R LLP -1 Bttry Pk Plz -NY 10004
(845) 634-7909 .. **McNair,** Pamela J '93 %Esbin & A,LLP -497 S Main -New Cty 10956 **Fx:**634-4160
(716) 372-5655 .. **McNall,** Carole B '94 -807 Irving -Olean 14760 **Fx:**372-5655
(212) 819-8200 .. **McNallen,** Brendan M '07 %White & C LLP -1155 Av of Amer -NY 10036
(212) 710-3900 .. **McNally,** Daren S '93 (Clyde & Co US LLP) -405 Lex Av -NY 10174 **Fx:**710-3950
(212) 248-2220 .. **McNally,** Derek A '04 %Kennedy JG LLC -99 Wall -NY 10005 **Fx:**248-0170
(631) 694-2400 .. **McNally,** Douglas K '78 (Hamburger MYK&M,LLP) -225 Broadhllw Rd -Melvll 11747
(631) 694-0033 .. **McNally,** Gail J '96 %Lawrence WR&B,PC -425 Broadhllw Rd -Melvll 11747
(212) 325-2000 .. **McNally,** Keith '04 Credit Suisse -1 Mad Av -NY 10010
(631) 547-4277 .. **McNally,** Kristine M '98 Nikon Inc -1300 Walt Whitman Rd -Melvll 11747 **Fx:**547-6261
(518) 270-4040 .. **McNally,** Richd J Jr. '88 DA -80 2nd -Troy 12180 **Fx:**270-4025
(518) 668-5412 .. **McNally,** Robt P '84 (Stafford C&M,PC) -175 Ottawa -Lk George 12845
(973) 300-4260 .. **McNally,** Stephen B '88 SrCnsl Wuersch & G LLP -100 Wall -NY 10005 **Fx:**300-4264
(516) 745-8310 .. **McNally,** Thos M '98 %Perez & V -333 Earle Ovngton Blvd Bx9372 -Uniondale 11553
(516) 228-8484 .. **McNally,** Thos W '03 %Dilworth & B,LLP -1000 Woodbury Rd -Woodbury 11797
(212) 490-9100 .. **McNamar,** Eric C '05 %Condon & F LLP -7 Times Sq -NY 10036
(716) 845-3650 .. **McNamara,** Aileen M '91 %MHLS -438 Main -Buffalo 14202 **Fx:**874-7794
(212) 277-0453 .. **McNamara,** Brendon M '98 Hartford Fncl -2 Park Av -NY 10016
(716) 858-2424 .. **McNamara,** Brian P '93 %DA -25 Delaware Av -Buffalo 14202 **Fx:**858-7425
(516) 829-0363 .. **McNamara,** Catherine '04 %Israel I&P,LLP -11 Grace Av -Gt Neck 11021 **Fx:**829-0366
(212) 447-1222 .. **McNamara,** Danl J '80 (DeCicco G&M,PC) -14 E 38th -NY 10016
(212) 759-4888 .. **McNamara,** David J '87 (Phillips L LLP) -437 Mad Av -NY 10022
(716) 847-8400 .. **McNamara,** David J '87 (Phillips L LLP) -3400 HSBC Ctr -Buffalo 14203
(212) 907-4000 .. **McNamara,** Dennis P '88 %Josephthal & Co,Inc -200 Park Av -NY 10166
(212) 489-8230 .. **McNamara,** Elizabeth A '82 (Davis WT LLP) -1633 Bway -NY 10019
(716) 655-2029 .. **McNamara,** Elizabeth C '84 %Aurora Waldorf School -525 W Fls Rd -W Fls 14170
(212) 344-0464 .. **McNamara,** Francis H '68 OfCnsl Cardillo & C -29 Bway -NY 10006
(845) 306-1000 .. **McNamara,** Francis J III '80 %Watchtower -100 Watchtower Dr -Patterson 12563 **Fx:**306-0709
(212) 710-3900 .. **McNamara,** James P '06 %Clyde & Co US LLP -405 Lex Av -NY 10174 **Fx:**710-3950
(516) 377-6499 .. **McNamara,** Jennifer A '91 -8 Euston Rd -Merrick 11566 **Fx:**377-6499
(631) 853-4049 .. **McNamara,** Jennifer K '97 %Cnty Atty -Dennison Bldg Bx6100 -Hauppauge 11788 **Fx:**853-5169
(212) 682-7050 .. **McNamara,** John T '91 (Geringer & D) -5 Hanover Sq -NY 10004
(212) 237-1000 .. **Mcnamara,** Kevin T '09 (Windels ML&M,LLP) -156 W 56th -NY 10019
(212) 840-0097 .. **McNamara,** Kristin J '04 Novozymes NA,Inc -500 5th Av -NY 10110
(716) 566-1300 .. **McNamara,** Mark R '80 (Hiscock & B,LLP) -1100 M&T Ctr -Buffalo 14203
(518) 464-6770 .. **McNamara,** Matthew H '00 (Thorn GT&B,LLP) -5 Wembley Ct Bx15054 -Albany 12212
(518) 436-0751 .. **McNamara,** Meghan K '08 %Hinman S PC -121 State -Albany 12207
(212) 574-1200 .. **McNamara,** Michl J '84 (Seward & K LLP) -1 Bttry Pk Plz -NY 10004
(631) 249-4939 .. **McNamara,** Michl T '00 (McNamara & Z PC) -560 Broadhllw Rd -Melvll 11747 **Fx:**249-4943
(212) 935-0900 .. **McNamara,** Patrick '85 Cnsl Rubln & B,LLP -501 Mad Av -NY 10022
(516) 357-3000 .. **McNamara,** Peter P '82 (Rivkin R LLP) -926 RXR Plz -Uniondale 11556
(518) 386-2266 .. **McNamara,** Robt G '06 %Pub Def -519 State -Schnctdy 12305 **Fx:**386-2814
(315) 798-5766 .. **McNamara,** Scott D '92 DA -800 Park Av -Utica 13501 **Fx:**798-5582
(212) 742-8700 .. **McNamara,** Susan M '07 %Garson D&C LLP -110 Wall -NY 10005
(516) 296-7000 .. **McNamara,** Thos J '81 (Certilman BA&H,LLP) -90 Merrick Av -E Meadow 11554
(914) 347-2600 .. **McNamara,** Timothy G '86 %Traub LS&S LLP -7 Skyline Dr -Hawthorne 10532
(212) 279-9090 .. **McNamara,** Timothy J '87 (Stark & S) -One Penn Plz -NY 10119 **Fx:**279-9113
(516) 781-9797 .. **McNamara,** Timothy W '75 -3330 Park Av -Wantagh 11793
(516) 922-9100 .. **McNamara,** Vincent D P '78 -1045 Oyster Bay Rd -E Norwich 11732 **Fx:**922-9208
(212) 530-5000 .. **McNamara,** Wm J '08 %Milbank TH&M LLP -1 Chase Manh Plz -NY 10005
(516) 627-7768 .. **McNamara-Riley,** Sheila '95 -54 Sherry Hill Ln -Manhsst 11030
(516) 873-3900 .. **McNamee,** Glenn P '98 %C Connick,PLLC -114 Old Cntry Rd -Mineola 11501 **Fx:**873-3904
(212) 504-6000 .. **McNamee,** Kevin J '02 %Cadwalader W&T LLP -1 World Fncl Ctr -NY 10281
(518) 447-3200 .. **McNamee Lochner Titus & Williams,PC** -677 Bway -Albany 12207 **Fx:**426-4260
(212) 373-3000 .. **McNary,** Colin C '07 Paul WRW&G LLP -1285 Av of Amer -NY 10019
(516) 759-6800 .. **McNaughton,** Donna M '95 -40 Kirkwood Dr -Glen Cove 11542 **Fx:**759-9034
(212) 698-3500 .. **McNaughton,** Ryan D '06 %Dechert LLP -1095 Av of Amer -NY 10036
(212) 371-6600 .. **McNeela,** Andrew M '99 %Kirby M LLP -825 3rd Av -NY 10022
(631) 271-5200 .. **McNeely,** Lori A '00 %Horn & H -780 NY Av -Huntngtn 11743 **Fx:**271-5216
(212) 762-4767 .. **McNeil,** Alex R '02 Morgan Stanley -1221 Av of Amer -NY 10020
(212) 964-6611 .. **McNeil,** Kate B '10 %Lester SK&D -120 Bway -NY 10271
(607) 266-8090 .. **McNeil,** Susan B '03 -410 E Upland Rd -Ithaca 14850 **Fx:**266-8091
(212) 578-8154 .. **McNeil,** Tracey L '01 MetLife -27-01 Qns Plz N -LIC 11101
(585) 678-1851 .. **McNeill,** Martha R '09 -144 Fairprt Vllg Lndg -Fairprt 14450
(718) 250-2000 .. **McNeill,** Patricia M '95 %DA -350 Jay -Brklyn 11201 **Fx:**250-2314

(212) 558-4000 .. **McNeill,** Ryan M '06 %Sullivan & C LLP -125 Broad -NY 10004
(212) 310-8000 .. **McNeill,** Walter G '60 (Weil G&M LLP) -767 5th Av -NY 10153
(914) 472-2420 .. **McNenney,** Edw J '57 -240 Garth Rd -Scarsdale 10583
(914) 259-6060 .. **McNerney,** Carolyn A '02 Malubi-Kahlua Intl -777 Wstchstr Av -White Plns 10604
(631) 265-1355 .. **McNichol,** Joan E '80 (Coffman & M) -4 Tiffany Ln -Smithtwn 11787
(212) 553-5400 .. **McNicholas,** Colleen Anne '97 %Zurich NA -1 Lbrty Plz -NY 10006
(718) 261-0033 .. **McNicholas,** Sean A '99 -125-10 Qns Blvd -Kew Gdns 11415 **Fx:**261-1919
(212) 486-4446 .. **McNicol,** Paul M '83 %Pilot Grp -75 Rckfllr Plz -NY 10019
(212) 218-4119 .. **McNiff,** Joann '96 %Morgens Waterfall -600 5th Av -NY 10020
(718) 250-2000 .. **McNiff,** John J '98 %DA -350 Jay -Brklyn 11201 **Fx:**250-2314
(516) 248-1200 .. **McNiff,** Kevin R '96 %Mulholland M&R -374 Hillside Av -Williston Pk 11596
(212) 331-5130 .. **McNish,** Robyn L '03 HRA-OLA -180 Water -NY 10038
(212) 692-2952 .. **McNulty,** Ann M '82 Smith Barney -450 Lex Av -NY 10017 **Fx:**697-0569
(212) 363-3100 .. **McNulty,** Anthony J '67 %Bivona & C,PC -88 Pine -NY 10005
(212) 458-1520 .. **McNulty,** Christopher J '00 AIG -175 Water -NY 10038
(212) 250-8667 .. **McNulty,** Derek E '96 Deutsche Bk Sec -60 Wall -NY 10005
(631) 727-8200 .. **McNulty,** John R '58 (McNulty-Spiess,PC) -214 Roanoke Av Bx757 -Rvrhead 11901
(212) 252-0004 .. **McNulty,** Jos P Jr. '85 (Carroll M&K LLC) -570 Lex Av -NY 10022
(973) 596-4873 .. **McNulty,** Kevin '85 (Gibbons PC) -1 Penn Plz -NY 10119 **Fx:**639-6242
(212) 460-3483 .. **McNulty,** Michl J '77 Con Ed -4 Irving Pl -NY 10003
(212) 735-3000 .. **McNulty,** Patricia A '86 %Skadden ASM&F LLP -4 Times Sq -NY 10036
(518) 452-7008 .. **McNulty,** Sharon Lee '77 -111 Knollwood Ter -Albany 12203 **Fx:**456-4739
(631) 727-8200 .. **McNulty-Spiess, PC** -214 Roanoke Av Bx757 -Rvrhead 11901 **Fx:**727-8262
(212) 344-0272 .. **McNulty,** Thos P '90 -347 5th Av -NY 10016
(212) 816-4678 .. **McNulty,** Thos P '09 %Citigrp -388 Greenwich -NY 10013
(212) 788-3312 .. **McNulty,** Wayne A '03 Hlth & Hsptl Corp -125 Worth -NY 10013 **Fx:**267-6905
(914) 949-2909 .. **McNutt,** Briar L '95 Eckert SC&M,LLC -10 Bank -White Plns 10606
(212) 259-8000 .. **McNutt,** Cynthia P '08 %Dewey & L LLP -1301 Av of Amer -NY 10019
(315) 255-3414 .. **McOmber,** Maggie Wetherby '07 %Bentkofsky & C,LLC -144 Genesee -Auburn 13021 **Fx:**255-2262
(212) 335-4500 .. **McOwen,** Micah J B '08 %DLA Piper LLP -1251 Av of Amer -NY 10020
(347) 401-9096 .. **McPadden,** John N '04 %Hon C Heffernan Jr -320 Jay -Brklyn 11201
(212) 506-1700 .. **McParland,** Christopher R '05 %Kasowitz BT&F LLP -1633 Bway -NY 10019
(716) 773-2442 .. **McPartlan,** Michl F '05 M Frentzel -1763 Baseline Rd -Grand Isl 14072 **Fx:**773-4750
(718) 548-7240 .. **McPartland,** Anne T '87 -3816 Review Pl -Bronx 10463
(631) 853-4161 .. **McPartland,** Christopher A '91 %DA -N Cnty Cmplx Bldg 77 -Hauppauge 11788 **Fx:**853-4192
(914) 328-3661 .. **McPartland,** Matthew G '87 -175 Main -White Plns 10601
(212) 530-4837 .. **McPartland,** Patrick T '98 %LaRocca HRG&B LLP -40 Wall -NY 10005
(212) 373-3000 .. **McPhail,** Stuart C '09 %Paul WRW&G LLP -1285 Av of Amer -NY 10019
(518) 854-9111 .. **McPhee,** Donald P '95 -192 Main Bx577 -Salem 12865 **Fx:**854-9114
(212) 884-6225 .. **McPhee,** Jaime M '02 Guggenheim Advisors LLC -135 E 57th -NY 10022 **Fx:**756-9997
(716) 847-8400 .. **McPhee,** Sean C '06 %Phillips L LLP -3400 HSBC Ctr -Buffalo 14203
(718) 590-3246 .. **McPheeters,** Lindsey M '10 %Law Dept -900 Sheridan Av -Bronx 10451 **Fx:**590-2699
(716) 853-0907 .. **McPherson,** Darryl N '93 SrCnsl BFSA -617 Main -Buffalo 14203 **Fx:**853-9052
(212) 468-8000 .. **McPherson,** Guy W '05 %Morrison & F LLP -1290 Av of Amer -NY 10104
(212) 261-7000 .. **McPherson,** James C '06 %Calyon -1301 Av of Amer -NY 10019
(212) 335-4500 .. **McPherson,** Jermaine L '08 %DLA Piper LLP -1251 Av of Amer -NY 10020
(212) 227-7878 .. **McPherson,** Kenneth D Jr. '83 (Waters MM) -233 Bway -NY 10279
(212) 258-8000 .. **McPherson,** Lance G '97 %MTV Networks -1515 Bway -NY 10036 **Fx:**258-8358
(212) 885-5000 .. **McPherson,** Laurie J '91 (Blank R LLP) -405 Lex Av -NY 10174
(212) 468-8000 .. **McPherson,** Mark D '00 (Morrison & F LLP) -1290 Av of Amer -NY 10104
(718) 491-9270 .. **McPherson,** Mary Jane '87 -579 74th -Brklyn 11209
(518) 473-0620 .. **McPherson,** Sybil A '92 Governor's Ofc Reg Reform -ESP Bx2107 -Albany 12220 **Fx:**473-9962
(212) 969-3000 .. **McPherson,** Valarie H '01 %Proskauer R LLP -1585 Bway -NY 10036
(212) 371-3141 .. **McPheters & Dankin,PC** -260 Mad Av -NY 10016 **Fx:**371-6753
(516) 294-5433 .. **McPhilliamy,** John A '91 (Ahmuty D&M) -200 IU Willets Rd -Albertson 11507
(518) 792-1174 .. **McPhillips Fitzgerald & Cullum, LLP** -288 Glen Bx299 -Glens Fls 12801 **Fx:**792-1675
(518) 798-9531 .. **McPhillips,** Jos W '77 -55 Saratoga Av Bx1391 -S Glens Fls 12803 **Fx:**798-9532
(212) 689-3819 .. **McPolin,** Gregory S '00 Pangea3 LLC -18 E 41st -NY 10017 **Fx:**820-9784
(631) 232-2400 .. **McQuade,** Carolyn '94 Nassau/Sfflk Law Srv -1757 Vets Hwy -Islandia 11749 **Fx:**232-2489
(516) 431-6255 .. **McQuade,** Francis X '95 McQuade & S -116 E Park Av -Long Bch 11561 **Fx:**431-1664
(212) 506-5000 .. **McQuade,** James H '96 OfCnsl Orrick H&S LLP -51 W 52nd -NY 10019
(212) 599-3644 .. **McQuade,** Jos F '70 (McQuade & M) -390 5th Av -NY 10018 **Fx:**599-3116
(631) 853-4343 .. **McQuade,** Maryellen '99 %Leg Aid -400 Carleton Av Bx9082 -Central Islip 11722 **Fx:**853-7798
(212) 599-3644 .. **McQuade,** Michl D '69 (McQuade & M) -390 5th Av -NY 10018 **Fx:**599-3116
(212) 306-7204 .. **McQuade,** Stephen M '03 Ofc Cllctv Brgn -40 Rector -NY 10006 **Fx:**306-7168
(518) 694-0910 .. **McQuade,** Thos P '93 (Owens M,PLLC) -41 State -Albany 12207
(212) 458-1058 .. **McQuaid,** James J '95 AIG -175 Water -NY 10038
(914) 993-1936 .. **McQuaid,** Nicholas L '06 US Atty -300 Quarropas -White Plns 10601 **Fx:**993-9036
(516) 759-5101 .. **McQuair,** Chas G '93 -325 Glen Cove Av -Sea Cliff 11579 **Fx:**759-5102
(585) 263-1000 .. **McQueen,** John R '78 (Nixon P LLP) -1100 Clinton Sq -Rchstr 14604
(917) 454-1100 .. **McQueen,** Marjorie Pascale '98 NYPD -2 Lafayette -NY 10007
(212) 859-8000 .. **McQueen,** Robt B '07 %Fried FHS&J LLP -1 NY Plz -NY 10004
(516) 688-1700 .. **McQueeney,** Theresa G '94 %IRS -1600 Stewart Av -Westbury 11590 **Fx:**688-1750
(518) 686-9600 .. **McQuerrey,** J Mark '90 -5 Main -Hoosick Fls 12090
(518) 765-2105 .. **McQuide,** Stephen '67 -88 Deer Cliff Rd -Voorheesvll 12186
(516) 222-2434 .. **McQuillan,** Arthur T '91 %White Q&S -377 Oak Bx9304 -Gdn Cty 11530
(212) 310-2834 .. **McQuillan,** Elizabeth A '86 %Colgate-Palmolive -300 Park Av -NY 10022 **Fx:**310-3230
(914) 779-7171 .. **McQuillan,** John Q '59 -125 Crestwood Av -Tuckahoe 10707 **Fx:**779-5055
(212) 841-7500 .. **McQuillan,** Michele '99 Cushman & Wakefield -1290 Av of Amer -NY 10104
(212) 692-1000 .. **McQuillen,** Brian P '96 (Duane M LLP) -1540 Bway -NY 10036
(585) 475-2935 .. **McQuiller,** Laverne Lee '96 %RIT -93 Lomb Mem'l Dr -Rchstr 14623
(212) 430-0800 .. **McQuilling,** Lenore E '80 Cnsl Kennedy LS&E -75 Maiden Ln -NY 10038
(212) 238-3000 .. **McQuiston,** Julian A '83 (Emmet M&M,LLP) -120 Bway -NY 10271
(315) 343-9116 .. **McRae,** Douglas M '05 %Bond S&K,PLLC -130 E 2nd -Oswego 13126
(212) 820-9300 .. **McRae,** Kathryn B '99 -1 Chase Manh Plz -NY 10005 **Fx:**514-8425
(718) 487-1300 .. **McRae,** Leander E '87 %Leg Srvcs Corp A -80 Jamaica Av -Brklyn 11207 **Fx:**342-1780
(212) 310-8000 .. **McRae,** Peter J '09 %Weil G&M LLP -767 5th Av -NY 10153
(212) 225-2000 .. **McRae,** Wm L '98 (Cleary GS&H) -1 Lbrty Plz -NY 10006
(631) 853-5212 .. **McRedmond,** Mark D '01 %Leg Aid -400 Carleton Av Bx9082 -Central Islip 11722 **Fx:**853-7798
(516) 227-0700 .. **McRoberts,** Franklin C IV '06 %Farrell F,PC -1320 RXR Plz -Uniondale 11556
(212) 536-3900 .. **McRobie,** Katherine A '08 %K&L Gates LLP -599 Lex Av -NY 10022
(516) 294-0430 .. **McRory,** Raymond J '73 -124 Cherry Vlly Av -Gdn Cty 11530 **Fx:**742-6160
(212) 603-6300 .. **McRory,** Russell P '94 (Robinson BLGG&G PC) -875 3rd Av -NY 10022
(718) 618-1365 .. **McShan,** Eddie J '95 Bronx Supreme Ct -851 Grnd Cncrs -Bronx 10451
(716) 847-8400 .. **McShane,** Amy E '07 %Phillips L LLP -3400 HSBC Ctr -Buffalo 14203
(212) 387-8457 .. **McShane,** James F '86 -400 E 20th -NY 10009
(973) 596-4637 .. **McShane,** Sheila F '00 (Gibbons PC) -1 Penn Plz -NY 10119 **Fx:**639-6482
(212) 817-6709 .. **McShane,** Thos A '83 Safir Rosetti -415 Mad Av -NY 10017
(212) 679-9090 .. **McShea,** Sarah Diane '80 -26 Bway -NY 10004 **Fx:**683-5840
(315) 476-8450 .. **McSherry,** Jonathan P '08 %DeLaney & O,LLP -1 Lincoln Ctr -Syracuse 13202
(718) 237-2000 .. **McSherry,** Meighan Marie '96 %Leg Aid -111 Lvngstn -Brklyn 11201 **Fx:**237-8737
(212) 223-4000 .. **McSherry,** Wm J Jr. '74 (Crowell & M LLP) -590 Mad Av -NY 10022
(212) 837-6000 .. **McSloy,** Steven Paul '89 Cnsl Hughes H&R LLP -1 Bttry Pk Plz -NY 10004
(914) 835-2213 .. **McSorley,** Wm C '98 -236 Union Av -Harrison 10528 **Fx:**835-4340
(518) 482-1755 .. **McSparron,** James G '73 -Bx8509 -Albany 12208
(212) 564-6633 .. **McSpedon,** Jos '82 (White & M,PC) -875 Av of Amer -NY 10001
(212) 788-1333 .. **McSpiritt,** James W '87 %Law Dept -100 Church -NY 10007 **Fx:**788-0367
(212) 768-6700 .. **McSwain,** Shannon E '03 %Sonnenschein N&R LLP -2 World Fncl Ctr -NY 10281
(516) 739-8111 .. **Mc Sweeney,** Lauren E '97 %D Lavelle -38 Willis Av -Mineola 11501 **Fx:**739-3917
(212) 669-8898 .. **McSweeney,** Michl M '00 City Clerks Ofc -141 Worth -NY 10013 **Fx:**669-3300
(718) 224-4746 .. **McSweeney,** Michelle A '06 %AM Carrozza -213-38 40th Av -Bayside 11361 **Fx:**224-4794
(212) 306-3357 .. **McSweeney,** Robt J '81 NYC Housing Auth -250 Bway -NY 10007 **Fx:**776-5039
(212) 930-9700 .. **Mc Sweeney,** Siobhain A '08 %Sichenzia RFF LLP -61 Bway -NY 10006
(212) 885-5000 .. **McSweeney,** Stephen P '84 (Blank R LLP) -405 Lex Av -NY 10174
(516) 747-8877 .. **McSweeney,** Theresa M '87 %Spizz & C,LLP -114 Old Cntry Rd -Mineola 11501
(212) 732-3200 .. **McSwiggan,** Danl J '84 (Carter L&M LLP) -2 Wall -NY 10005
(212) 418-8600 .. **McTaggart,** David T '03 %Kornstein VW&P,LLP -757 3rd Av -NY 10017
(212) 295-6368 .. **McTague,** Alexandra B '05 %WilmerHale -399 Park Av -NY 10022
(518) 465-3553 .. **Mc Tague,** Anne-Jo Pennock '01 (Maynard OS&C,LLP) -6 Twr Pl -Albany 12203
(212) 382-0909 .. **McTague,** Eugene J Jr. '91 (Peckar & A,PC) -41 Mad Av -NY 10154
(212) 732-3200 .. **McTamaney,** Robt A '71 (Carter L&M LLP) -2 Wall -NY 10005
(516) 490-4047 .. **McTeigue,** Neil '98 %Bookspan -501 Franklin Av -Gdn Cty 11530 **Fx:**490-4284
(212) 460-2432 .. **McTiernan,** Chas E Jr. '72 Con Ed -4 Irving Pl -NY 10003
(973) 596-4739 .. **McTiernan,** Edw F '88 (Gibbons PC) -1 Penn Plz -NY 10119 **Fx:**639-6246
(914) 946-1030 .. **McTiernan,** Patricia A '88 %Barry M&M -55 Church -White Plns 10601
(212) 313-3600 .. **McTiernan,** Roger P '58 (Barry M&M) -2 Rector -NY 10006
(212) 313-3600 .. **McTiernan,** Roger P Jr. '81 (Barry M&M) -2 Rector -NY 10006

(516) 229-4300 .. **McTiernan,** Wm B '92 J Bilello & Assoc -875 Merrick Av -Westbury 11590
(212) 770-7000 .. **McTigue,** Michl P '02 %AIG -70 Pine -NY 10270
(631) 288-6500 .. **McVann,** Thos T Jr. '72 -100 Mill Rd Bx827 -Westhmptn Bch 11978 **Fx:**288-6546
(718) 442-4424 .. **McVay,** George E '66 (Corash & H,PC) -1200 South Av -Staten Isl 10314
(212) 730-8133 .. **McVay,** Kenneth R '03 %Gunderson DSVF&H,LLP -220 W 42nd -NY 10036
(212) 829-0454 .. **McVeety,** Kristen J '99 (Gabler & M LLP) -209 E 56th -NY 10022 **Fx:**829-0455
(914) 921-4820 .. **McVeigh,** Catherine M '99 OfCnsl Bonnist & C,LLP -800 Wstchstr Av -Rye Brook 10573 **Fx:**921-4823
(212) 237-3147 .. **McVeigh,** Maeve T '05 Paramount Grp -1633 Bway -NY 10019
(631) 543-2900 .. **McVey,** David M '01 %Davis & H,LLP -1345 Motor Pkwy -Islandia 11749
(631) 654-4900 .. **McVicker,** Christine L '06 %Cartier BA&D,PC -100 Austin -Patchogue 11772
(607) 432-1922 .. **McVinney,** Richd W '83 (Van Woert & M) -50 Dietz -Oneonta 13820 **Fx:**432-7517
(212) 480-6787 .. **McVoy,** Cullen S '73 %DHCR -25 Beaver -NY 10004 **Fx:**480-7416
(516) 296-7000 .. **McWalters,** Susan L '96 (Certilman BA&H,LLP) -90 Merrick Av -E Meadow 11554
(212) 625-1400 .. **McWeeney,** John J Jr. '97 %Putumayo World Music -411 Lafayette -NY 10003
(212) 297-5800 .. **McWha,** Keith J '03 Cnsl Day P LLP -7 Times Sq -NY 10036
(212) 436-1136 .. **McWilliams,** Alissa '87 IRS -290 Bway -NY 10007
(518) 765-2866 .. **Meacham,** Donald D '62 -26 Orchrd Path Bx313 -Voorheesvll 12186 **Fx:**765-2867
(518) 487-7600 .. **Meacham,** Norma G '78 (Whiteman O&H LLP) -1 Commerce Plz -Albany 12260
(212) 316-0872 .. **Meacham,** Thornton J Jr. '43 -320 Manh Av -NY 10026
(518) 464-6770 .. **Mead,** Erin P '03 %Thorn GT&B,LLP -5 Wembley Ct Bx15054 -Albany 12212
(212) 839-5300 .. **Mead,** Francesca '10 %Sidley A LLP -787 7th Av -NY 10019
(315) 788-6700 .. **Mead,** George E III '81 %Schwerzmann & W,PC -215 Wshngtn Bx704 -Watertwn 13601
(914) 899-3100 .. **Mead Hecht Conklin & Gallagher** -109 Spencer Pl -Mamaroneck 10543 **Fx:**899-3101
(212) 558-4000 .. **Mead,** John P '78 (Sullivan & C LLP) -125 Broad -NY 10004
(607) 723-9511 .. **Mead,** Lars P '03 %Coughlin & G,LLP -19 Chenango Bx2039 -Bnghmtn 13902
(518) 435-1919 .. **Mead,** Matthew R '87 (Stockton B&M,LLP) -2 Twr Pl -Albany 12203
(607) 723-5341 .. **Mead,** Ryan M '08 %Hinman H&K,LLP -80 Exchange Bx5250 -Bnghmtn 13902
(718) 306-2107 .. **Mead,** Wesley R '03 -23-10 Steinway -Astoria 11105
(212) 797-3544 .. **Meade,** Barry '98 (French & C,LLP) -29 Bway -NY 10006
(718) 242-2519 .. **Meade,** Colleen Anne '96 JP Morgan Chase Bk,NA -4 MetroTech Ctr -Brklyn 11201
(212) 969-3000 .. **Meade,** James D '92 (Proskauer R LLP) -1585 Bway -NY 10036
(516) 487-6500 .. **Meade,** James G '74 (Munley & M PLLC) -160 Middle Nck Rd -Gt Neck 11021
(212) 310-8000 .. **Meade,** Kevin F '05 %Weil G&M LLP -767 5th Av -NY 10153
(845) 567-5700 .. **Meade,** Kimberly E '95 %Production Resource Grp,LLC -539 Temple Hill Rd -New Windsor 12553 **Fx:**567-5800
(646) 386-3005 .. **Meade,** Robt C Jr. '74 Supreme Ct Civil -60 Centre -NY 10007
(914) 949-2700 .. **Meade,** Robt D '72 (Bleakley P&S,LLP) -1 N Lex Av -White Plns 10601
(518) 827-7770 .. **Meade,** Teresa '84 -124 Mill Valley Rd -Middleburgh 12122
(518) 877-8338 .. **Meader,** John D '63 -271 Round Lk Rd -Ballston Lk 12019
(212) 883-9111 .. **Meaders Duckworth & Moore** -551 5th Av -NY 10176 **Fx:**883-9114
(212) 745-5845 .. **Meaders,** Leigh Mozelle '95 IBM -590 Mad Av -NY 10022 **Fx:**745-5868
(914) 834-6472 .. **Meadow,** Claire Samuelson '63 -35 N Chatsworth Av -Larchmnt 10538 **Fx:**834-9092
(914) 834-6472 .. **Meadow,** Myron J '59 -35 N Chatsworth Av -Larchmnt 10538 **Fx:**630-4044
(212) 421-2800 .. **Meadow,** Richd D '85 Lanier Law Firm,PLLC -126 E 56th -NY 10022 **Fx:**421-2878
(212) 335-9000 .. **Meadows,** James B '05 %DA -1 Hogan Pl -NY 10013
(212) 861-9683 .. **Meadows,** Laura Lou '67 Cnsl Captions for Literacy -351 E 84th -NY 10028 **Fx:**861-0030
(716) 853-9555 .. **Meadows,** Sherree '91 %Leg Aid -237 Main -Buffalo 14203 **Fx:**853-3219
(315) 436-5567 .. **Meadvin,** Anne C S '76 -333 E Onondaga -Syracuse 13202
(914) 381-6508 .. **Meadvin,** Michl M '76 Castle Oil Corp -440 Mamaroneck Av -Harrison 10528 **Fx:**381-6501
(718) 250-2000 .. **Meagher,** Brian C '00 %DA -350 Jay -Brklyn 11201 **Fx:**250-2314
(914) 328-8844 .. **Meagher,** Christopher B '93 (Meagher & M) -175 Main -White Plns 10601 **Fx:**328-8570
(631) 501-5700 .. **Meagher,** Edw C '96 (Carter DF&S LLP) -445 Broadhallow Rd -Melvll 11747
(607) 722-3660 .. **Meagher,** Fredk J '39 (Meagher & M) -15 Hawley -Bnghmtn 13901 **Fx:**722-3628
(607) 722-3660 .. **Meagher,** Fredk J Jr. '72 (Meagher & M) -15 Hawley -Bnghmtn 13901 **Fx:**722-3628
(212) 533-6300 .. **Meagher,** J Christopher '74 %NYSUT -52 Bway -NY 10004 **Fx:**995-2347
(607) 754-0410 .. **Meagher,** Jos B '73 (Thomas C&M) -1201 Monroe Bx329 -Endicott 13761
(212) 825-0400 .. **Meagher,** Justin P '01 %Clinton Grp Inc -9 W 57th -NY 10019
(212) 474-1000 .. **Meagher,** Patrick A '09 %Cravath S&M LLP -825 8th Av -NY 10019
(518) 320-1746 .. **Meagher,** Terése P '98 State Univ Cnstrctn Fund -353 Bway -Albany 12246 **Fx:**689-2634
(315) 471-3151 .. **Meagher,** Walter L Jr. '66 (Hancock & E,LLP) -1500 AXA Twr I Bx4976 -Syracuse 13221
(212) 702-0900 .. **Mealey,** Ronald P '56 OfCnsl Axelrod F&D -260 Mad Av -NY 10016 **Fx:**355-7365
(516) 832-7597 .. **Mealiffe,** Thos M '06 %Nixon P LLP -50 Jericho Quadrangle -Jericho 11753
(212) 434-0100 .. **Meaney,** James M '05 %Litchfield C LLP -420 Lex Av -NY 10170
(516) 571-3800 .. **Meaney,** Martin D '89 %DA -262 Old Cntry Rd -Mineola 11501 **Fx:**248-9479
(212) 732-3200 .. **Meara,** Karen E '10 %Carter L&M LLP -2 Wall -NY 10005
(516) 249-0040 .. **Meares,** Jos D '89 J Meares,PC -320 Conklin -Farmngdl 11735 **Fx:**249-0045
(212) 224-6810 .. **Mears,** Rachel B '03 Forest Labs -909 3rd Av -NY 10022
(212) 493-8494 .. **Mears,** Wm H Jr. '69 Brown Bros Harriman -140 Bway -NY 10005 **Fx:**493-8206
(914) 962-3700 .. **Measter,** Barbara Perdiue '81 Measter & S -1961 Commerce -Yorktwn Hts 10598 **Fx:**962-5515
(585) 396-7600 .. **Meath,** Brian P '82 %Canandaigua Wine Co -235 N Blmfld Rd -Canandaigua 14424 **Fx:**396-7831
(518) 792-2657 .. **Meath,** Richd V '82 -2 Apple Ln -Queensbury 12804
(315) 468-4149 .. **Mecca,** Andrew A '69 -5410 W Genesee -Camillus 13031
(845) 770-3510 .. **Mecchella,** John N '85 %Tech Traffic Cnsltnt -30 Hemlock Dr -Congers 10920
(212) 859-8000 .. **Mechanic,** Jonathan L '78 (Fried FHS&J LLP) -1 NY Plz -NY 10004
(718) 579-3000 .. **Mechanic,** Steven L '71 Leg Aid -1020 Grnd Cncrs -Bronx 10451 **Fx:**588-2611
(212) 735-3000 .. **Mechcatie,** Anthony P '94 Cnsl Skadden ASM&F LLP -4 Times Sq -NY 10036
(212) 806-5400 .. **Mechling,** Curtis C '76 (Stroock &S&L LLP) -180 Maiden Ln -NY 10038
(212) 530-5000 .. **Mechlowicz,** Freyda H '05 %Milbank TH&M LLP -1 Chase Manh Plz -NY 10005
(914) 654-8217 .. **Mechmann,** John R '83 -1498 North Av -New Rchll 10804
(585) 232-5300 .. **Mechur,** Robt F '69 (Boylan BCV&W,LLP) -2400 Chase Sq -Rchstr 14604
(716) 855-7300 .. **Meckler,** Lawr M '77 %NFTA -181 Ellicott -Buffalo 14203 **Fx:**855-7657
(518) 561-3700 .. **Meconi,** Wm T '79 WT Meconi,PC -53 Court -Plattsbrgh 12901 **Fx:**561-2080
(646) 201-9302 .. **Medabalmi,** Venkata '03 BMI Pacific -247 W 122nd -NY 10027
(212) 735-3000 .. **Medalie,** Danl B '07 %Skadden ASM&F LLP -4 Times Sq -NY 10036
(631) 968-7600 .. **Medalie,** Randolph M '69 (Flower M&M) -24 E Main -Bay Shr 11706
(315) 478-3587 .. **Medcraf,** James H '74 -614 James -Syracuse 13203 **Fx:**472-8299
(607) 272-2314 .. **Medeiros,** Katrina Thaler '00 (Thaler & T) -309 N Tioga Bx266 -Ithaca 14851 **Fx:**272-8466
(212) 710-2643 .. **Medenica,** Olivera '01 (Wahab & M,LLC) -1115 Bway -NY 10011 **Fx:**(646) 619-4195
(718) 625-0202 .. **Mederos,** Paul G '93 (Clark C&M,LLP) -Bx26515 -Brklyn 11202 **Fx:**625-2644
(212) 819-8200 .. **Mederos,** Rudy R '03 White & C LLP -1155 Av of Amer -NY 10036
(212) 573-7748 .. **Medford-Rosow,** Traci '81 %Pfizer Inc -150 E 42nd -NY 10017
(212) 385-1772 .. **Medic,** Jos '03 %Posner & P -170 Bway -NY 10038 **Fx:**385-2061
(845) 610-3431 .. **Medican,** Wm A '83 -Bx102 -Chester 10918 **Fx:**469-9670
(212) 732-8700 .. **Medici,** Jos F '08 %McAloon & F,PC -123 William -NY 10038
(914) 286-3400 .. **Medina,** Ada D '03 Leg Aid -1 N Bway -White Plns 10601 **Fx:**682-4112
(914) 448-0200 .. **Medina,** Adonaid Casado '07 %Bartlett MB&M,LLP -81 Main -White Plns 10601
(914) 941-4485 .. **Medina,** Amanda '92 (Medina TSM&C PC) -31 Croton Av -Ossining 10562 **Fx:**941-4513
(718) 286-6000 .. **Medina,** Andrea A '05 %DA -125-01 Qns Blvd -Kew Gdns 11415
(516) 742-7777 .. **Medina,** Christie R '07 %Frazer & F,LLP -1415 Kellum Pl -Gdn Cty 11530
(212) 456-7777 .. **Medina,** Derek M '96 %ABC -47 W 66th -NY 10023
(212) 404-1742 .. **Medina,** Eric S '05 (Medina Law Firm,LLC) -1040 Av of Amer -NY 10018 **Fx:**(888) 833-9534
(718) 782-0100 .. **Medina,** Gustavo '82 -5758 58th Pl -Maspeth 11378
(212) 339-2433 .. **Medina,** Kevin T '06 Allen & Co -711 5th Av -NY 10022
(845) 300-2113 .. **Medina,** Mars A '95 -785 Sequoia Dr -Vly Cottage 10989 **Fx:**268-6344
(212) 241-6447 .. **Medina,** Mary E '93 %Mt Sinai Med Ctr -1 Gustave L Levy Pl -NY 10029
(914) 333-0700 .. **Medina,** Nicole '97 %Snyder & S -94 Wht Plns Rd -Tarrytwn 10591 **Fx:**333-0743
(212) 416-8464 .. **Medina,** Pedro Jr. '90 %Dept of Law -120 Bway -NY 10271
(718) 590-0200 .. **Medina,** Rene '85 -901 Sheridan Av -Bronx 10451 **Fx:**588-8443
(212) 846-8449 .. **Medina,** Rhonda Adams '94 %MTV Networks -1515 Bway -NY 10036 **Fx:**258-8358
(212) 742-0256 .. **Medina,** Richd A '85 -111 Bway -NY 10006 **Fx:**363-6978
(212) 830-9274 .. **Medina,** Tomas E '92 Smart Money -1755 Bway -NY 10019
(212) 259-8000 .. **Medina,** Virginia '99 %Dewey & L LLP -1301 Av of Amer -NY 10019
(716) 847-0662 .. **Medina-Zelazny,** Lillian '06 %Volunteer Lwyrs Prjt -237 Main -Buffalo 14203 **Fx:**847-0307
(212) 227-0640 .. **Medinets,** Dov B '10 %Ginsberg & W,PC -225 Bway -NY 10007
(212) 323-2250 .. **Mediodia,** Lisa M '93 %HHC-OLA-Medical Litigation -346 Bway -NY 10013 **Fx:**323-2251
(212) 557-2800 .. **Medley,** Kyle M '04 %Barger & W LLP -10 E 40th -NY 10016
(212) 515-3200 .. **Medley,** Laurie D '02 Apollo Mgt LP -9 W 57th -NY 10019
(585) 641-8001 .. **Medley,** Mary Lou '84 (Allen & O) -625 Panorama Trl -Rchstr 14625
(718) 403-3677 .. **Medley,** Ronald J '82 Dept of Finance OLA -345 Adams -Brklyn 11201
(212) 278-7505 .. **Medlicott,** Natalie R '00 Societe Generale -1221 Av of Amer -NY 10020
(212) 848-4000 .. **Medlin,** Phil S II '06 %Shearman & S LLP -599 Lex Av -NY 10022
(212) 336-2000 .. **Medlow,** Jill-Ann F '05 Patterson BW&T LLP -1133 Av of Amer -NY 10036
(631) 424-3597 .. **Mednick,** Ian S '04 %B Salamone & Assoc,PC -8 Ford Pl -Dix Hlls 11746 **Fx:**424-5023
(518) 370-2211 .. **Mednick,** Kevin S '79 (Bendall & M) -836 Plymouth Av -Schnctdy 12308 **Fx:**370-3840
(347) 296-1842 .. **Mednick,** Meira C '97 %Supreme Ct -360 Adams -Brklyn 11201
(845) 794-5200 .. **Mednick,** Michl B '93 -18 Prince Bx612 -Monticello 12701 **Fx:**794-7784
(718) 250-2000 .. **Medow,** Kori A '06 DA -350 Jay -Brklyn 11201 **Fx:**250-2314
(212) 228-1675 .. **Medows,** Joel S '71 -530 Grand -NY 10002
(212) 351-4000 .. **Medrano,** Kevin A '10 Gibson D&C LLP -200 Park Av -NY 10166

(212) 650-6620 .. **Medrano,** Luz E '06 %CUNY Citizenshp & Immig Prjct -138th & Convent Av -NY 10031 **Fx:**650-6643
(212) 295-6410 .. **Medrano,** Pedro A '04 Cnsl WilmerHale -399 Park Av -NY 10022
(212) 264-2041 .. **Medve,** Marianna '94 US GSA -26 Fed Plz -NY 10278 **Fx:**264-1987
(212) 878-8149 .. **Medvinsky,** Larry P '94 (Clifford C LLP) -31 W 52nd -NY 10019
(212) 878-8168 .. **Medwick,** Craig S '78 (Clifford C LLP) -31 W 52nd -NY 10019
(212) 578-5883 .. **Medwid,** Nancy E '99 AIG -80 Pine -NY 10005
(212) 626-4100 .. **Medynskaya,** Julia '05 %Baker & M LLP -1114 Av of Amer -NY 10036
(212) 335-4500 .. **Medzhibovsky,** Leon '98 (DLA Piper LLP) -1251 Av of Amer -NY 10020
(212) 218-2100 .. **Mee,** Brendan S '00 %Fitzpatrick CH&S -1290 Av of Amer -NY 10104
(716) 761-6723 .. **Meeder,** Clinton C '65 -155 E Main Bx 470 -Sherman 14781
(716) 673-1361 .. **Meeder,** Curt N '96 %Schaack WCN PC -2 W Main Bx109 -Fredonia 14063
(212) 297-5800 .. **Meehan,** Aileen C '82 (Day P LLP) -7 Times Sq -NY 10036
(212) 872-1000 .. **Meehan,** Andrew M '09 -One Bryant Park -NY 10036 **Fx:**872-1002
(718) 250-2000 .. **Meehan,** Christopher J '10 %DA -350 Jay -Brklyn 11201 **Fx:**250-2314
(914) 493-2800 .. **Meehan,** Gregory F '82 %Cnty Hlthcr Corp -95 Grasslands Rd -Valhalla 10595 **Fx:**493-2321
(212) 326-3939 .. **Meehan,** Kevin A '09 %Jones D -222 E 41st -NY 10017
(516) 334-4500 .. **Meehan,** Kiera J '04 %Sokoloff S LLP -355 Post Av -Westbury 11590 **Fx:**334-4501
(845) 732-7547 .. **Meehan,** Laura J '85 %Medicaid Fraud Cntrl -1 Blue Hill Plz Bx1557 -Pearl Rvr 10965 **Fx:**732-7555
(718) 278-2678 .. **Meehan,** Louis '78 -22-46 79th -E Elmhrst 11370
(212) 954-3755 .. **Meehan,** Meghan V '05 KPMG LLP -345 Park Av -NY 10154
(516) 822-4142 .. **Meehan,** Michl John '96 -73 Sackett -Hicksvll 11801 **Fx:**620-6843
(914) 747-2532 .. **Meehan,** Robt F '74 -232 Myrtle -Hawthorne 10532
(212) 824-5700 .. **Meehan,** Seema Lal '06 Practising Law Inst -810 7th Av -NY 10019
(646) 424-6243 .. **Meehan,** Timothy M '97 ING Financial Srvcs LLC -1325 Av of Amer -NY 10019
(212) 425-1900 .. **Meehan,** Wayne D '85 (Freehill H&M LLP) -80 Pine -NY 10005
(212) 349-7020 .. **Meehan,** Wm A '82 (Slutsky M&M, LLP) -100 Park Av -NY 10017 **Fx:**(203) 762-9864
(212) 528-1332 .. **Meeker,** Fredk W '73 -7 Dey -NY 10007 **Fx:**528-1341
(212) 682-6616 .. **Meekins,** Susan L '84 -570 Lex Av -NY 10022 **Fx:**682-6026
(718) 237-3100 .. **Meeks,** Alexandra W '08 Leg Aid -111 Lvngstn -Brklyn 11201 **Fx:**250-4243
(845) 956-1380 .. **Meeks,** David E '92 (PATBAR.COM) -195 South -Middletwn 10940
(212) 949-7120 .. **Meeks & Sheppard** -330 Mad Av -NY 10017 **Fx:**949-7271
(845) 454-4244 .. **Meenagh,** John P Jr. '81 (Kelly & M,LLP) -135 N Water -Poughkeepsie 12601
(212) 226-7334 .. **Meenan,** Colleen M '92 (Meenan & Assoc,LLC) -64 Fulton -NY 10038 **Fx:**226-7716
Meenan, Michl J '92 -5 Doe Run -Manorvll 11949
(212) 867-6000 .. **Meer,** Jolie E '06 %Rosenberg & E,PC -733 3rd Av -NY 10017
(212) 945-2080 .. **Meer,** Jonah M '80 -50 Battery Pl -NY 10280 **Fx:**(508) 629-0074
(212) 490-3000 .. **Meer,** Jonathan E '07 %Wilson EME&D LLP -150 E 42nd -NY 10017
(212) 614-6432 .. **Meeropol,** Rachel A '03 Ctr Cnstnl Rights -666 Bway -NY 10012 **Fx:**614-6499
(212) 940-8800 .. **Meerovitch,** Shelly '01 (Katten MR LLP) -575 Mad Av -NY 10022
(212) 720-5026 .. **Meertens,** Michelle A '99 %Fed Reserve Bk -33 Lbrty -NY 10045 **Fx:**785-5748
(914) 251-1618 .. **Meese,** Gregory D '89 (Price MS&D,PC) -106 Corp Park Dr -White Plns 10604
(585) 753-4500 .. **Meetze,** Melissa M '05 DA -832 Watts Bldg -Rchstr 14614 **Fx:**753-4576
(845) 291-2650 .. **Meffert,** David S '02 %Cnty Atty -285 Main -Goshen 10924 **Fx:**291-3014
(516) 481-8000 .. **Megale,** Jos R '86 -250 Fulton Av -Hempstd 11550 **Fx:**485-4855
(212) 446-7000 .. **Megalli,** Mark '02 %McKinsey & Co -55 E 52nd -NY 10055 **Fx:**688-9521
(516) 317-6660 .. **Megaro,** Patrick M '03 -215 Hilton Av Bx1200 -Hempstd 11551
(212) 651-7500 .. **Megerian,** Talene N '03 %Segal MS&M -850 3rd Av -NY 10022
(212) 468-8000 .. **Megevick,** Wm F Jr. '86 SrCnsl Morrison & F LLP -1290 Av of Amer -NY 10104
(315) 471-1664 .. **Meggesto Crossett & Valerino,LLP** -313 E Willow -Syracuse 13203 **Fx:**471-7882
(315) 471-1664 .. **Meggesto,** James A '74 (Meggesto C&V,LLP) -313 E Willow -Syracuse 13203
(718) 237-2000 .. **Meggett,** Eric D '88 %Leg Aid -111 Lvngstn -Brklyn 11201 **Fx:**237-8737
(718) 286-6000 .. **Megias,** Dianna L '90 %DA -125-01 Qns Blvd -Kew Gdns 11415
(212) 228-7727 .. **Meginniss,** Walter M Jr. '78 (Gladstein R&M,LLP) -817 Bway -NY 10003
(718) 359-5555 .. **Meglio,** John J '61 -33-28 191st -Flushng 11358 **Fx:**939-9563
(212) 436-6616 .. **Megna,** Dominic '09 Deloitte Tax LLP -2 World Fncl Ctr -NY 10281
(718) 353-5500 .. **Megna,** Philip W '77 (Mattone MMMMM&T) -134-01 20th Av -Cllg Pnt 11356
(716) 832-2420 .. **Megna,** Ralph '79 -12 Cleveland Dr -Buffalo 14215 **Fx:**836-4272
(212) 692-0367 .. **Megna,** Rebecca K '93 %Hack POMW&M -600 3rd Av -NY 10016
(631) 473-1000 .. **Meguin,** Robt R '75 J Ray & Assoc -122 N Cntry Rd Bx5440 -Miller Pl 11764
(585) 419-8800 .. **Mehalick,** David M '82 (Harris B PLLC) -99 Garnsey Rd -Pittsfrd 14534
(212) 450-4000 .. **Mehar,** Jason '10 %Davis P&W LLP -450 Lex Av -NY 10017
(516) 623-1111 .. **Mehary,** Michl G '84 -2174 Hewlett Av Bx801 -Merrick 11566 **Fx:**623-0758
(212) 406-0069 .. **Mehl,** Fredk '76 -277 Bway -NY 10007 **Fx:**385-2545
(718) 758-0300 .. **Mehl,** Jeffrey E '87 J Mehl,PC -3003 Av K -Brklyn 11210 **Fx:**758-0301
(212) 239-1100 .. **Mehl,** Spence '87 %Retail Cnsltng Srvcs -460 W 34th -NY 10001 **Fx:**268-5484
(212) 962-4688 .. **Mehler & Buscemi** -305 Bway -NY 10007 **Fx:**964-0643
(212) 969-3000 .. **Mehler,** Fern R '95 %Proskauer R LLP -1585 Bway -NY 10036
(212) 527-7503 .. **Mehler,** Gordon '83 -575 Lex Av -NY 10022 **Fx:**527-7504
(212) 962-4688 .. **Mehler,** Martin P '74 (Mehler & B) -305 Bway -NY 10007
(212) 532-0333 .. **Mehler,** Phyllis '52 %Seavey Org -3 Park Av -NY 10016 **Fx:**481-3390
(212) 343-0834 .. **Mehling,** Elizabeth D '02 -51 White -NY 10013
(212) 592-1400 .. **Mehlman,** Avery S '92 %Herrick,F LLP -2 Park Av -NY 10016
(212) 407-4000 .. **Mehlman,** Barry T '82 (Loeb & L,LLP) -345 Park Av -NY 10154
(516) 374-2239 .. **Mehlman,** Beth R '96 -949 Nrthfld Rd -Woodmere 11598
(718) 459-9021 .. **Mehlman,** Chas J '75 Mid-State Mgmt Corp -97-77 Qns Blvd -Rego Pk 11374
(212) 455-2000 .. **Mehlman,** Nancy Lynn '00 (Simpson T&B LLP) -425 Lex Av -NY 10017
(718) 459-9000 .. **Mehlman,** Rashel M '91 %Sweeney GR&B,LLP -95-25 Qns Blvd -Rego Pk 11374
(212) 269-2500 .. **Mehlsack,** Barbara S '76 (Gorlick K&L,PC) -17 State -NY 10004
(518) 447-7150 .. **Mehm,** George F '93 %Pub Def -60 S Pearl -Albany 12207 **Fx:**447-5533
(877) 222-1814 .. **Mehm,** Michl A '00 %B Rothenberg -100 Duffy Av -Hicksvll 11801 **Fx:**(866) 894-2182
(631) 694-2300 .. **Mehnert,** Matthew J '05 %Lamb & B,LLP -534 Broadhllw Rd Bx9034 -Melvll 11747
(212) 237-1000 .. **Mehno,** Christopher D '90 %Windels ML&M,LLP -156 W 56th -NY 10019
(212) 287-3365 .. **Mehra,** Ajay '97 Penella Weinberg Prtnrs -767 5th Av -NY 10153
(212) 715-9100 .. **Mehra,** Benu '03 %Kramer LN&F,LLP -1177 Av of Amer -NY 10036
(212) 351-4000 .. **Mehraban,** Darius Jos '99 (Gibson D&C LLP) -200 Park Av -NY 10166
(212) 336-0591 .. **Mehraban,** Lara S '00 %SEC -3 World Fncl Ctr -NY 10281 **Fx:**336-1323
(212) 455-2000 .. **Mehrara,** Sasan '98 (Simpson T&B LLP) -425 Lex Av -NY 10017
(212) 268-7777 .. **Mehrfar,** Arman Adam '96 -358 5th Av -NY 10001 **Fx:**268-7778
(212) 379-1250 .. **Mehrfar,** Edw Omid '92 Strategic Captial Sltns LLC -61 Bway -NY 10006
(212) 922-1599 .. **Mehring,** Marc J '93 -12 W 37th -NY 10018 **Fx:**661-5564
(212) 848-4000 .. **Mehrjou,** Navid '07 %Shearman & S LLP -599 Lex Av -NY 10022
(914) 643-6517 .. **Mehrtens,** Thos E '82 -107 Lk Av -Tuckahoe 10707
(212) 237-0000 .. **Mehta,** Anuragh R '10 %Vinson & E LLP -666 5th Av -NY 10103
(212) 425-0555 .. **Mehta,** Cyrus D '89 C Mehta & Assoc,PLLC -2 Wall -NY 10005 **Fx:**425-3282
(212) 504-6000 .. **Mehta,** Dorothy D '05 %Cadwalader W&T LLP -1 World Fncl Ctr -NY 10281
(718) 590-2000 .. **Mehta,** Isha M '09 %DA -198 E 161st -Bronx 10451 **Fx:**590-6477
(212) 735-2627 .. **Mehta,** Kamine '03 Skadden ASM&F LLP -4 Times Sq -NY 10036 **Fx:**735-2000
(212) 906-1200 .. **Mehta,** Parul '07 %Latham & W -885 3rd Av -NY 10022
(212) 839-5300 .. **Mehta,** Prabhat Kumar '96 (Sidley A LLP) -787 7th Av -NY 10019
(212) 872-1000 .. **Mehta,** Prakash H '10 -One Bryant Park -NY 10036 **Fx:**872-1002
(845) 796-2100 .. **Mehta,** Raj R '84 %Frontier Ins Group -195 Lk Louise Marie Dr -Rck Hll 12775
(845) 794-4094 .. **Mehta,** Raj R '84 %Leg Aid -11 Bank -Monticello 12701 **Fx:**794-0119
(516) 466-4446 .. **Mehta,** Rashmin '83 -475 Nrthrn Blvd -Gt Neck 11021 **Fx:**466-3867
(212) 578-2211 .. **Mehta,** Sandhya '97 %MetLife -27-01 Qns Plz N -LIC 11101
(212) 839-5300 .. **Mehta,** Swati D '07 %Sidley A LLP -787 7th Av -NY 10019
(212) 761-7169 .. **Mehta,** Vikram '01 Morgan Stanley -1585 Bway -NY 10036
(516) 624-6150 .. **Mei,** Fredk E '85 %Town Atty -Town Hall -Oyster Bay 11771 **Fx:**624-6196
(212) 416-8305 .. **Meier,** Andrew H '03 %Dept of Law -120 Bway -NY 10271
(585) 798-2250 .. **Meier,** Andrew W '05 (Webster S&M,LLP) -343 Main Bx606 -Medina 14103 **Fx:**798-0776
(212) 305-0047 .. **Meier,** Benjamin M '02 Columbia Univ -617 W 168th -NY 10032 **Fx:**305-3659
(518) 688-2846 .. **Meier,** Christina W '05 (Toombs & M,PLLC) -157 Barrett -Schnctdy 12305 **Fx:**688-2849
(516) 393-2200 .. **Meier,** Danl M '07 %Garfunkel W,PC -111 Grt Nck Rd -Gt Neck 11021
(212) 759-9770 .. **Meier Franzino & Scher,LLP** -570 Lex Av -NY 10022 **Fx:**644-2298
(518) 437-8100 .. **Meier,** Henry C '97 %Credit Union Assn -1021 Watervliet-Shaker Rd Bx15118 -Albany 12212 **Fx:**437-8500
(845) 486-3048 .. **Meier,** James D '82 %Cnty Atty -60 Market -Poughkeepsie 12601 **Fx:**486-2796
(315) 738-1223 .. **Meier,** Raymond A '77 OfCnsl Bond S&K,PLLC -501 Main -Utica 13501
(212) 759-9770 .. **Meier,** Steven K '71 (Meier F&S,LLP) -570 Lex Av -NY 10022
(718) 762-8200 .. **Meier,** Wm G '61 -4240 Bell Blvd -Bayside 11361 **Fx:**463-0241
(212) 599-3322 .. **Meierhofer,** George F Jr. '87 %Becker P,LLP -45 Bway -NY 10006
(212) 848-4000 .. **Meiers,** Christine A '06 %Shearman & S LLP -599 Lex Av -NY 10022
(914) 698-0100 .. **Meighan,** Jefferson D '67 (Meighan & N) -100 Mamaroneck Av -Mamaroneck 10543
(914) 698-0100 .. **Meighan & Necarsulmer** -100 Mamaroneck Av -Mamaroneck 10543 **Fx:**698-6984
(518) 573-1865 .. **Meigher,** Jessica R '06 -Bx182 -Slingerlnds 12159 **Fx:**914-1184
(212) 233-3079 .. **Meikle,** Christopher G '89 (Maloof LC&O,PA) -299 Bway -NY 10007
(212) 558-4000 .. **Meiklejohn,** D Stuart '76 SrCnsl Sullivan & C LLP -125 Broad -NY 10004
(212) 264-0654 .. **Meiklejohn,** Rebecca '76 %US DOJ Antitrust Div -26 Fed Plz Ste 3630 -NY 10278
(718) 369-6904 .. **Meilen,** Gerhard '73 -108 Prospect Park W -Brklyn 11215
(212) 801-9364 .. **Meili,** Barbara C '84 (Greenberg T,LLP) -200 Park Av -NY 10166
(212) 918-3000 .. **Meilman,** Derek B '03 %Hogan L LLP -875 3rd Av -NY 10022
(212) 277-6500 .. **Meilman,** Edw A '67 (Dickstein S LLP) -1633 Bway -NY 10019
(212) 218-5500 .. **Meilman,** Roy K '80 (Seyfarth S LLP) -620 8th Av -NY 10018
(201) 615-3220 .. **Meimaris,** Alkistis G '03 -612 E Grassy Sprain Rd -Ynkrs 10710 **Fx:**886-2810
(212) 748-1733 .. **Meinwald,** Barbara J '88 -168 2nd Av -NY 10003 **Fx:**385-1932
(516) 829-0363 .. **Meir,** Abraham J '09 %Israel I&P,LLP -11 Grace Av -Gt Neck 11021 **Fx:**829-0366
(212) 764-1261 .. **Meirowitz,** Alexandra Jacobs '02 %C Meirowitz,PLLC -36 W 44th -NY 10036 **Fx:**221-0999
(212) 764-1261 .. **Meirowitz,** Clifford A '91 -36 W 44th -NY 10036 **Fx:**221-0999
(212) 385-9190 .. **Meirowitz,** Lewis A '95 (Finkelstein M&E) -11 Park Pl -NY 10007

(212) 576-5683 .. **Meirowitz**, Mark '81 NY Life Ins -51 Mad Av -NY 10010 **Fx**:447-0569
(212) 558-5500 .. **Meirowitz**, Saml M '01 Weitz & L,PC -700 Bway -NY 10003
(718) 838-7878 .. **Meis**, V Marika '01 %Bronx Defenders -860 Crtlandt Av -Bronx 10451 **Fx**:665-0100
(516) 571-3800 .. **Meisel**, Brad J '09 %DA -262 Old Cntry Rd -Mineola 11501 **Fx**:248-9479
(718) 590-2000 .. **Meisel**, Douglas S '08 %DA -198 E 161st -Bronx 10451 **Fx**:590-6477
(212) 753-5599 .. **Meisel**, Elliott '72 (Brill & M) -845 3rd Av -NY 10022
(212) 735-3000 .. **Meisel**, Jane W '82 Cnsl Skadden ASM&F LLP -4 Times Sq -NY 10036
(212) 521-4430 .. **Meisel**, Stacey L '03 (Becker M LLC) -590 Mad Av -NY 10022
(212) 984-5400 .. **Meisel**, Susan A '87 %Inst of Intl Educ -809 UN Plz -NY 10017
(212) 554-0400 .. **Meiselas**, Kenneth R '82 (Grubman I&S,PC) -152 W 57th -NY 10019
(914) 997-9550 .. **Meiseles**, Howard '87 %UIA Bd -120 Bloomingdale Rd -White Plns 10605 **Fx**:997-0014
(646) 855-0850 .. **Meiselman**, Abby '87 Bank of Amer -1 Bryant Pk -NY 10036
(914) 517-5000 .. **Meiselman**, David J '74 (Meiselman DPC&E,PC) -1311 Mamaroneck Av -White Plns 10605
(914) 517-5000 .. **Meiselman Denlea Packman Carton & Eberz,PC** -1311 Mamaroneck Av -White Plns 10605 **Fx**:517-5055
(212) 766-2200 .. **Meiselman & Gordon, LLP** -80 Maiden Ln -NY 10038 **Fx**:766-2222
(212) 766-2200 .. **Meiselman**, Michl L '92 (Meiselman & G,LLP) -80 Maiden Ln -NY 10038
(516) 471-1900 .. **Meiselman**, Michelle L '00 %Havkins RR&V,LLP -114 Old Cntry Rd -Mineola 11501
(212) 401-3200 .. **Meisels**, David M '92 Royal Bank of Scotland -101 Park Av -NY 10178
(212) 953-2381 .. **Meisels**, Grant M '88 %Rubin F&F,LLP -292 Mad Av -NY 10017
(212) 589-4200 .. **Meisels**, Naomi P '84 Baker & H LLP -45 Rckfllr Plz -NY 10111
(914) 323-7000 .. **Meisels**, Peter A '71 (Wilson EME&D LLP) -3 Gannett Dr -White Plns 10604
(718) 741-8418 .. **Meisels**, Robt A '96 %Div of Human Rights -1 Fordham Plz -Bronx 10458 **Fx**:741-8102
(631) 234-8585 .. **Meisenheimer**, Patricia McKennay '85 %Bracken & M,LLP -1 Suffolk Sq -Islandia 11749
(212) 922-6775 .. **Meiser**, Maria C '98 Dreyfus -200 Park Av -NY 10166
(212) 310-8000 .. **Meises**, Michele J '92 Cnsl Weil G&M LLP -767 5th Av -NY 10153
(518) 447-3200 .. **Meislahn**, Harry P '66 OfCnsl McNamee LT&W,PC -677 Bway -Albany 12207
(516) 229-6000 .. **Meisler**, Linda '81 %R Lau & Assoc -300 Jericho Quad Bx9040 -Jericho 11753 **Fx**:229-6167
(212) 773-3579 .. **Meisler**, Michl A '99 Ernst & Young LLP -5 Times Sq -NY 10036
(914) 345-3701 .. **Meisner**, Brian D '08 %Marks OO&C,PC -530 Saw Mill Rvr Rd -Elmsfrd 10523
(516) 747-4437 .. **Meisner**, Steven A '79 -400 Grdn City Plz -Gdn Cty 11530 **Fx**:248-8155
(212) 689-8600 .. **Meissner**, George S '52 (Meissner K&F,LLP) -275 Mad Av -NY 10016
(212) 689-8600 .. **Meissner Kleinberg & Finkel,LLP** -275 Mad Av -NY 10016 **Fx**:686-0252
(212) 689-8600 .. **Meissner**, Philip M '92 %Meissner K&F,LLP -275 Mad Av -NY 10016
(212) 764-3100 .. **Meissner**, Stuart D '89 (S Meissner LLC) -450 7th Av -NY 10123 **Fx**:(646) 843-4964
(212) 735-3000 .. **Meister**, David '88 (Skadden ASM&F LLP) -4 Times Sq -NY 10036
(212) 468-8000 .. **Meister**, Gabriel E '00 (Morrison & F LLP) -1290 Av of Amer -NY 10104
(212) 593-6700 .. **Meister**, Jonathan A '95 %Aaronson RF&D,LLP -757 3rd Av -NY 10017
(212) 554-1400 .. **Meister**, Kristin Ann '05 Bernstein LB&G LLP -1285 Av of Amer -NY 10019
(212) 403-7330 .. **Meister**, Robt A '63 (Pedowitz & M LLP) -1501 Bway -NY 10036 **Fx**:354-6614
(212) 681-3026 .. **Meister**, Robin S '07 %Charter Atlantic Corp -200 Park Av -NY 10166
(212) 790-9200 .. **Meister**, Ronald W '70 (Cowan L&L,PC) -1133 Av of Amer -NY 10036
(212) 655-3500 .. **Meister Seelig & Fein LLP** -140 E 45th -NY 10017 **Fx**:655-3535
(212) 655-3500 .. **Meister**, Stephen B '81 (Meister S&F LLP) -140 E 45th -NY 10017
(212) 701-3000 .. **Meistrell**, Gerard M '66 (Cahill G&R LLP) -80 Pine -NY 10005 **Fx**:269-5420
(718) 927-2600 .. **Meitlis**, Erit S '97 Prestige Label -960 Alabama Av -Brklyn 11207
(631) 265-0134 .. **Mejia**, David M '00 %Kral CRRP&G,LLP -538 Broadhllw Rd -Melvll 11747 **Fx**:265-4289
(212) 335-9000 .. **Mejia**, Daysi M '02 %DA -1 Hogan Pl -NY 10013
(212) 225-2000 .. **Mejia**, Frances K '07 %Cleary GS&H -1 Lbrty Plz -NY 10006
(212) 728-8728 .. **Mejia**, Van V '00 -787 7th Av -NY 10019 **Fx**:728-9728
(212) 688-5151 .. **Mejia-Opaciuch**, Maria '88 %Gibney A&F,LLP -665 5th Av -NY 10022
(516) 333-7777 .. **Mejias**, David L '96 (Mejias M&A,PC) -1 Dosoris Ln -Glen Cove 11542 **Fx**:333-7878
(516) 869-7613 .. **Mejias**, Linda K '05 %Town Atty -220 Plandome Rd -Manhsst 11030 **Fx**:869-7605
(718) 339-6668 .. **Melamed**, Abraham '55 (A Melamed,PC) -1580 Dahill Rd -Brklyn 11204 **Fx**:336-1389
(212) 371-5700 .. **Melamed**, Gary '06 %Jankoff & G,PC -575 Lex Av -NY 10022
(212) 227-6821 .. **Melamed**, Martin '77 (Roura & M) -233 Bway -NY 10279
(516) 829-0363 .. **Melamed**, Neda '97 Israel I&P,LLP -11 Grace Av -Gt Neck 11021 **Fx**:829-0366
(212) 319-6888 .. **Melamed**, Peter B '07 Kim & B PC -110 E 59th -NY 10022
(718) 375-5078 .. **Melamed**, Robt '97 -1502 Kings Hwy -Brklyn 11229 **Fx**:375-5109
(845) 897-5199 .. **Melanson**, Elizabeth L '05 %Feldman K&C,LLP -995 Main BxA -Fishkill 12524
(212) 845-7500 .. **Melanson**, Thos J '05 Thacher Assoc,LLC -330 W 42nd -NY 10036 **Fx**:845-7549
(631) 751-1100 .. **Melbardis**, W Alexander '72 -194 Main -E Setauket 11733 **Fx**:751-1205
(716) 855-1050 .. **Melber**, Brian M '97 (Personius M LLP) -2100 Main Place Twr -Buffalo 14202
(845) 255-0403 .. **Melbert**, James L '68 (Tully & M) -176 Main Bx574 -New Paltz 12561 **Fx**:255-0858
(212) 980-8470 .. **Melcer**, Jeffrey B '94 -39 Bway -NY 10006 **Fx**:980-8256
(212) 259-8000 .. **Melcher**, Victoria L '05 %Dewey & L LLP -1301 Av of Amer -NY 10019
(315) 218-8000 .. **Melchor**, Henry H '75 (Bond S&K,PLLC) -1 Lincoln Ctr -Syracuse 13202
(212) 269-0061 .. **Mele**, Armand P '92 (Junge & M,LLP) -250 W 57th -NY 10107 **Fx**:269-0515
(845) 894-7050 .. **Mele**, Carmine Jos '93 IBM -2070 Route 52 -Hopewell Junct 12533
(212) 571-7100 .. **Mele**, Joy K '01 %O'Dwyer & B,LLP -52 Duane -NY 10007
(718) 254-7000 .. **Mele**, Toni M '98 %US Atty -271 Cadman Plz E -Brklyn 11201 **Fx**:254-6479
(212) 285-3800 .. **Melendez**, Frank M '87 Subin Assoc LLP -150 Bway -NY 10007
(212) 931-7403 .. **Melendez**, Louis '79 %MLB -245 Park Av -NY 10167 **Fx**:949-5657
(212) 458-1193 .. **Melendez**, Magali '94 %AIG -175 Water -NY 10038
(212) 839-5300 .. **Melendez**, Maria De Los Angeles '93 (Sidley A LLP) -787 7th Av -NY 10019
(315) 443-3437 .. **Melendez**, Suzette M '91 Syracuse Univ Cllg of Law -Wht Hall -Syracuse 13244 **Fx**:443-4213
(212) 705-7000 .. **Melendi**, Christina Edling '04 (Bingham M LLP) -399 Park Av -NY 10022
(212) 806-5400 .. **Melendres**, Linda M '08 %Stroock &S&L LLP -180 Maiden Ln -NY 10038
(518) 861-6477 .. **Melewski**, Bernard C '84 -32 Fryer Ln -Altamont 12009
(315) 218-8000 .. **Melfi**, Patrick V '05 (Bond S&K,PLLC) -1 Lincoln Ctr -Syracuse 13202
(212) 504-6000 .. **Melgar**, Tod M '97 SpclCnsl Cadwalader W&T LLP -1 World Fncl Ctr -NY 10281
(212) 403-1000 .. **Meli**, Graham W '06 %Wachtell LR&K -51 W 52nd -NY 10019
(212) 448-9933 .. **Meli**, Paul L '81 OfCnsl Finder & C LLP -9 E 38th -NY 10016
(212) 692-9666 .. **Meli**, Sal '01 (Gilbride TL&S LLC) -708 3rd Av -NY 10017
(718) 886-4660 .. **Meli**, Salvatore A '76 -189-05 Crocheron Av -Flushng 11358 **Fx**:461-5906
(212) 969-3000 .. **Melican**, Amy F '97 %Proskauer R LLP -1585 Bway -NY 10036
(212) 272-2542 .. **Melican**, John W '97 %JP Morgan Chase -383 Mad Av -NY 10179
(212) 292-6534 .. **Melican**, Marlane E '95 Ziff Bros Invstmnts,LLC -350 Park Av -NY 10022
(212) 474-1000 .. **Melikjanian**, Margarita '06 %Cravath S&M LLP -825 8th Av -NY 10019
(718) 353-5500 .. **Melillo**, Denise R '91 %Mattone MMMMM&T -134-01 20th Av -Cllg Pnt 11356
(914) 789-8878 .. **Melillo**, Judy A '02 Cnsl Fujifilm -200 Summit Lk Dr -Valhalla 10595
(212) 732-2000 .. **Melillo**, Nicholas P '07 %Cullen and D LLP -44 Wall -NY 10005
(516) 674-3330 .. **Melillo**, Robt A '69 -108 Forest Av Bx447 -Locust Vly 11560
(716) 565-0070 .. **Melin**, Peter P '91 -2956 Union Rd -Cheektowaga 14227
(212) 460-5757 .. **Melinger**, Michl W '75 (Gellis & M,LLP) -137 5th Av -NY 10010
(212) 867-1117 .. **Melino**, Jean K '97 Innovative Philanthropy LLC -5 Hanover Sq -NY 10004
(212) 279-6818 .. **Melis**, Demetrios G '94 D Melis,PC -259 W 29th -NY 10001 **Fx**:279-9024
(716) 848-5943 .. **Melisz**, Rosalie Ann '98 M&T Bank -465 Main -Buffalo 14203
(212) 238-8900 .. **Melito & Adolfsen,PC** -233 Bway -NY 10279 **Fx**:238-8999
(212) 238-8900 .. **Melito**, Ignatius J '77 (Melito & A,PC) -233 Bway -NY 10279
(518) 455-2597 .. **Melkonian**, Michl H '91 %Senate Majority Cnsl -The Cptl -Albany 12247
(315) 336-0200 .. **Mellace**, Frank Jr. '89 -314 N James -Rome 13440 **Fx**:336-3701
(315) 366-2236 .. **Mellace**, Jos A '99 %DA -Cnty Cthse Bx578 -Wampsville 13163 **Fx**:366-2503
(914) 997-0555 .. **Mellea**, Philip J '90 (Quinn & M,LLP) -399 Knollwood Rd -White Plns 10603
(718) 590-2000 .. **Mellem**, Megan S '09 %DA -198 E 161st -Bronx 10451 **Fx**:590-6477
(212) 221-6900 .. **Mellen**, Steven E '00 (Winget S&S,LLP) -45 Bway -NY 10006
(212) 363-3100 .. **Meller**, Alan R '83 (Bivona & C,PC) -88 Pine -NY 10005
(212) 382-0909 .. **Meller**, Bruce D '75 (Peckar & A,PC) -41 Mad Av -NY 10154
(212) 973-0572 .. **Meller**, June S '85 Cnsl Wolff & S PC -140 Bway -NY 10005
(212) 788-0677 .. **Meller**, Lauren E '91 ACS-DLS -220 Church -NY 10013
(212) 421-4100 .. **Mellevold**, Christopher G '93 (Pryor C LLP) -7 Times Sq -NY 10036
(212) 518-8679 .. **Mellevold**, Linda Loving '93 -800 3rd Av -NY 10022 **Fx**:752-8881
(845) 876-4057 .. **Melley**, Steven M '76 -24 Closs Dr -Rhinebeck 12572 **Fx**:876-5745
(212) 250-7560 .. **Mellgard**, David M '85 %Deutsche Bank -60 Wall -NY 10005
(212) 509-6300 .. **Melli Guerin Wall & Messineo** -17 Battery Pl -NY 10004 **Fx**:509-6996
(212) 549-2500 .. **Melling**, Louise F '88 %ACLU -125 Broad -NY 10004 **Fx**:549-2651
(845) 638-5001 .. **Mellion**, James H '75 %DA -1 S Main -New Cty 10956 **Fx**:638-5070
(212) 485-3452 .. **Mellis**, Michl J '92 MLB Advanced Media LP -75 9th Av -NY 10011
(631) 247-0404 .. **Mellk**, Wendy J '94 (Jackson L LLP) -58 S Srvc Rd -Melvll 11747
(914) 967-2114 .. **Mello**, Ellen M '89 %Tyre & D -150 Purchase -Rye 10580
(212) 294-6700 .. **Mello**, H Jos '67 OfCnsl Winston & S -200 Park Av -NY 10166
(212) 310-8000 .. **Mello**, Laura S '96 Weil G&M LLP -767 5th Av -NY 10153
(212) 782-4638 .. **Mellon**, Amy A '99 %Bk of Tokyo-Mitsubishi -1251 Av of Amer -NY 10020 **Fx**:782-6420
(212) 682-6800 .. **Mellon**, Raymond T '82 (Zetlin & D LLP) -801 2nd Av -NY 10017
(212) 909-6000 .. **Mellon**, Ryan S '10 %Debevoise & P LLP -919 3rd Av -NY 10022
(212) 705-7000 .. **Mellor**, Thos C '95 (Bingham M LLP) -399 Park Av -NY 10022
(646) 415-8492 .. **Mellow**, Ariana M '09 Property Holdings,Inc -Bx166 -Mill Neck 11765
(212) 826-0100 .. **Mellstrom**, Brian H '85 %FSA -31 W 52nd -NY 10019 **Fx**:893-2710
(212) 552-1422 .. **Mellusi**, Caroline A '84 JP Morgan Chase -1 Chase Manh Plz -NY 10081
(212) 962-1590 .. **Mellusi**, Ralph J '75 (Tabak M&S) -29 Bway -NY 10006
(631) 765-3016 .. **Melly**, Francis P '51 -330 Dayton Rd Bx617 -Southold 11971
(516) 535-1100 .. **Melly**, Venessa Deneen '05 %Valdebenito & A -1399 Franklin Av -Gdn Cty 11530 **Fx**:535-3936
(212) 504-6000 .. **Melman**, Danl J '02 %Cadwalader W&T LLP -1 World Fncl Ctr -NY 10281
(212) 408-5100 .. **Melmed**, Jonathan M A '99 (Chadbourne & P LLP) -30 Rckfllr Plz -NY 10112
(212) 702-5400 .. **Melnick**, Adam M '09 %Beveridge & D,PC -477 Mad Av -NY 10022

(212) 489-7100 .. **Melnick,** Andrew B '78 The James Mintz Grp -32 Av of Amer -NY 10013 **Fx:**489-7037
(516) 746-8000 .. **Melnick,** Carol Ann '94 (Jaspan S LLP) -300 Grdn City Plz -Gdn Cty 11530
(212) 756-2000 .. **Melnick,** Katharine R '08 %Schulte R&Z LLP -919 3rd Av -NY 10022
(212) 490-0100 .. **Melnick,** Matthew G '04 %Schuman & Assoc -1536 3rd Av -NY 10028 **Fx:**490-0156
(718) 590-2000 .. **Melnick,** Michele L '06 %DA -198 E 161st -Bronx 10451 **Fx:**590-6477
(212) 903-9000 .. **Melnick,** Noah P '06 %Linklaters -1345 Av of Amer -NY 10105
(212) 239-4999 .. **Melnick,** Randi B '07 %Meyer SE&K,PC -1350 Bway Bx822 -NY 10018
(212) 593-6700 .. **Melnick,** Robt S '82 (Aaronson RF&D,LLP) -757 3rd Av -NY 10017
(718) 298-8960 .. **Melnick,** Stanley H '73 %Leg Aid -153-01 Jamaica Av -Jamaica 11432 **Fx:**657-0537
(212) 319-4200 .. **Melnick,** Stuart L '88 -100 Park Av -NY 10017
(718) 474-6400 .. **Melnicke,** Briendy F '89 -1637 50th -Brklyn 11204
(315) 422-5564 .. **Melnicoff,** Joel N '65 -120 E Wshngtn -Syracuse 13202 **Fx:**474-7484
(212) 308-4411 .. **Melnik,** Selinda A '85 (Edwards AP&D LLP) -750 Lex Av -NY 10022
(631) 761-7000 .. **Melniker,** Heather K '82 %Touro Cllg Law Ctr -225 Eastvw Dr -Central Islip 11722
(212) 259-8000 .. **Melniker,** Sophie I '10 %Dewey & L LLP -1301 Av of Amer -NY 10019
(212) 880-1270 .. **Melnikoff,** Marcy J '96 Fidelity Natl Fncl -711 3rd Av -NY 10017
(914) 381-6700 .. **Melnikoff,** Ruth M '84 Judicial Title Ins Agncy LLC -800 Wstchstr Av -Rye Brook 10573 **Fx:**381-3131
(212) 480-6789 .. **Melnitsky,** Sheldon D '79 %DHCR -25 Beaver -NY 10004 **Fx:**480-7416
(718) 728-3616 .. **Melnyk,** Ronald S '75 -25-65 45th -Astoria 11103
(212) 732-2000 .. **Melnyk Tripp,** Suzanne '00 %Cullen and D LLP -44 Wall -NY 10005
(718) 899-6881 .. **Melo,** David J '84 -37-32 75th -Jcksn Hts 11372 **Fx:**899-6919
(914) 323-7000 .. **Melo,** George M '01 (Wilson EME&D LLP) -3 Gannett Dr -White Plns 10604
(212) 596-9000 .. **Melogy,** John R '10 %Ropes & G LLP -1211 Av of Amer -NY 10036
(212) 787-2500 .. **Melohn,** Leon '87 (Melohn Properties) -1995 Bway -NY 10023
(212) 806-5400 .. **Melone,** Leah A '06 SpclCnsl Stroock &S&L LLP -180 Maiden Ln -NY 10038
(212) 309-6000 .. **Melone,** Michl J '03 %Morgan L&B LLP -101 Park Av -NY 10178
(212) 520-6089 .. **Meloni,** Robt S '81 (Meloni & M,PC) -1515 Bway -NY 10036 **Fx:**(917) 210-3758
(516) 227-0700 .. **Melore,** Stephen F '88 (Farrell F,PC) -1320 RXR Plz -Uniondale 11556
(212) 728-8000 .. **Meloro,** Thos J Jr. '90 (Willkie F&G LLP) -787 7th Av -NY 10019
(212) 668-1900 .. **Melrose,** Kendra L '09 %Brune & R LLP -80 Broad -NY 10004
(212) 592-6711 .. **Melson,** Mark D '81 %Bovis Lend Lease Hldngs -200 Park Av -NY 10166 **Fx:**592-6997
(212) 513-3200 .. **Melton,** Howell W Jr. '07 (Holland & K LLP) -31 W 52nd -NY 10019
(718) 286-6000 .. **Melton,** Jessica L '02 %DA -125-01 Qns Blvd -Kew Gdns 11415
(516) 647-6867 .. **Melton,** Timothy M '03 Oceanic House -256 Montauk Hwy -Moriches 11955
(914) 997-1346 .. **Meltz,** Louis S '89 (Seham SM&P,LLP) -445 Hmltn Av -White Plns 10601
(516) 393-2200 .. **Meltzer,** Allison B '08 %Garfunkel W,PC -111 Grt Nck Rd -Gt Neck 11021
(212) 676-7858 .. **Meltzer,** Arthur '84 NYC HRA -180 Water -NY 10038 **Fx:**385-8418
(718) 237-5500 .. **Meltzer,** Brent N '03 %Leg Srvcs -105 Court -Brklyn 11201 **Fx:**855-0733
(212) 592-1400 .. **Meltzer,** Bryan C '10 %Herrick,F LLP -2 Park Av -NY 10016
(212) 717-2993 .. **Meltzer,** Carol '92 -200 E 84th -NY 10028
(212) 575-0847 .. **Meltzer,** Craig F '79 -60 E 42nd -NY 10165
(646) 224-6969 .. **Meltzer,** Curt '80 -555 8th Av -NY 10018
(212) 267-9020 .. **Meltzer,** David D '85 (Shapiro B&A LLP) -225 Bway -NY 10007
(646) 562-1267 .. **Meltzer,** Donald '85 Cowen & Co -1221 Av of Amer -NY 10020
(212) 227-1980 .. **Meltzer Fishman Madigan & Campbell** -225 Bway -NY 10007 **Fx:**791-5912
(516) 747-0300 .. **Meltzer,** Gary M '92 (Meltzer LG&B,LLP) -190 Willis Av -Mineola 11501
(212) 788-1585 .. **Meltzer,** Hilary M '93 %Law Dept -100 Church -NY 10007 **Fx:**788-0367
(212) 455-2000 .. **Meltzer,** Jason R '06 %Simpson T&B LLP -425 Lex Av -NY 10017
(516) 747-0300 .. **Meltzer,** Lewis S '65 (Meltzer LG&B,LLP) -190 Willis Av -Mineola 11501
(516) 747-0300 .. **Meltzer Lippe Goldstein & Breitstone, LLP** -190 Willis Av -Mineola 11501 **Fx:**747-0653
(212) 867-4466 .. **Meltzer,** Martin '89 (Belkin BW&G,LLP) -270 Mad Av -NY 10016
(914) 712-2000 .. **Meltzer,** Michl A '63 (Meltzer & P,LLP) -145 Huguenot -New Rchll 10801
(914) 922-2580 .. **Meltzer,** Michl I '76 Sirota Consulting -1 Manhattanvll Rd -Purchase 10577 **Fx:**696-3401
(845) 794-6700 .. **Meltzer,** Perry E '70 -547 Bway Bx1130 -Monticello 12701 **Fx:**794-6754
(914) 712-2000 .. **Meltzer & Pravetz,LLP** -145 Huguenot -New Rchll 10801 **Fx:**654-3068
(212) 335-4500 .. **Meltzer,** Roger '78 (DLA Piper LLP) -1251 Av of Amer -NY 10020
(212) 822-1443 .. **Meltzer,** Ronald J '90 -305 Bway -NY 10007 **Fx:**822-1407
(212) 504-6000 .. **Meltzer,** Stephanie J '95 (Cadwalader W&T LLP) -1 World Fncl Ctr -NY 10281
(718) 532-4300 .. **Meltzer,** Stuart E '89 S Meltzer & Assoc,PC -32 Court -Brklyn 11201
(212) 705-7000 .. **Meltzer,** Wm A '84 OfCnsl Bingham M LLP -399 Park Av -NY 10022
(212) 373-3000 .. **Meltzer Meshkov,** Jesse L '08 %Paul WRW&G LLP -1285 Av of Amer -NY 10019
(212) 244-6222 .. **Melucci,** Danl '92 (Melucci C&S,LLP) -26 Bway -NY 10004 **Fx:**244-7165
(315) 422-1152 .. **Melvin,** Edw G '97 (Costello C&F,PLLC) -500 Plum -Syracuse 13204
(914) 666-5506 .. **Melvin,** Edw T '75 -47 Taylor Rd -Mt Kisco 10549 **Fx:**242-6232
(315) 422-1311 .. **Melvin & Melvin,PLLC** -217 S Salina -Syracuse 13202 **Fx:**479-7612
(315) 422-1311 .. **Melvin,** Merle D '59 OfCnsl Melvin & M,PLLC -217 S Salina -Syracuse 13202
(212) 506-2500 .. **Melvin,** Virginia A '87 Cnsl Mayer B LLP -1675 Bway -NY 10019
(212) 688-0782 .. **Melwani,** Gloria Kui '06 %Barrack R&B -1350 Bway -NY 10018
(646) 723-2453 .. **Melzer,** Andrew C '04 %Sanford W&H,LLP -1350 Av of Amer -NY 10019
(716) 270-2431 .. **Melzer,** Anne '84 %IRS -300 Pearl -Buffalo 14202
(212) 753-3468 .. **Melzer,** Marnie L '06 %Wildes & W,PC -515 Mad Av -NY 10022
(718) 520-6652 .. **Memblatt,** Judith B '85 %Hon J Rios -125-01 Qns Blvd -Kew Gdns 11415
(646) 792-2256 .. **Membrado,** Michl M '90 -115 E 57th -NY 10022
(718) 590-6227 .. **Meminger,** Diane C '97 %Law Dept -900 Sheridan Av -Bronx 10451 **Fx:**590-2699
(516) 794-2800 .. **Memmoli,** Diane '80 OfCnsl M Devack,PLLC -90 Merrick Av -E Meadow 11554 **Fx:**794-2900
(212) 336-2000 .. **Mena,** Amy Carper '03 %Patterson BW&T LLP -1133 Av of Amer -NY 10036
(212) 521-5400 .. **Menachemi,** Efrat '06 %Reed S LLP -599 Lex Av -NY 10022
(800) 563-3428 .. **Menack,** Steven Boyd '88 -280 Park Av S #8M -NY 10010 **Fx:**(973) 402-6237
(212) 532-3850 .. **Menagh,** Douglas D '78 (Menagh & F,PC) -386 Park Av S -NY 10016
(212) 532-3850 .. **Menagh & Falcone,PC** -386 Park Av S -NY 10016 **Fx:**481-0972
(718) 694-3891 .. **Menaker,** Francine E '93 %Transit Auth -130 Lvngstn -Brklyn 11201 **Fx:**694-5726
(212) 545-1900 .. **Menaker & Herrmann LLP** -10 E 40th -NY 10016 **Fx:**545-1656
(212) 848-4000 .. **Menaker,** Mitchell E '76 (Shearman & S LLP) -599 Lex Av -NY 10022
(212) 545-1900 .. **Menaker,** Richd G '75 (Menaker & H LLP) -10 E 40th -NY 10016
(212) 310-8000 .. **Menaldino,** Janeane R '10 %Weil G&M LLP -767 5th Av -NY 10153
(212) 446-4800 .. **Mena Ortiz,** Andres '01 (Kirkland & E LLP) -153 E 53rd -NY 10022
(585) 267-0314 .. **Menard,** John I '04 -1630 Empire Blvd -Webster 14580
(716) 649-4053 .. **Menard,** Michl '78 -206 Lk -Hambrg 14075
(516) 482-4530 .. **Menard,** Shirley J '96 -27 Edgewood Pl -Gt Neck 11024 **Fx:**482-4879
(518) 690-2828 .. **Menard,** Trudy A '03 %F Altman & Assoc -6 Walker Way -Albany 12205 **Fx:**690-2809
(212) 848-4000 .. **Menasché,** Nicholas M '07 %Shearman & S LLP -599 Lex Av -NY 10022
(212) 310-8000 .. **Mencaroni,** Danl '04 %Weil G&M LLP -767 5th Av -NY 10153
(212) 836-8000 .. **Menchel,** David '05 Kaye S LLP -425 Park Av -NY 10022
(212) 488-1200 .. **Menchel,** Matthew I '88 (Kobre & K,LLP) -800 3rd Av -NY 10022
(646) 837-0100 .. **Menchel,** Rita S '97 %Wenick & F,PC -28 E 28th -NY 10016
(516) 873-2000 .. **Mencher,** Eric M '85 (Moritt HH&H LLP) -400 Grdn City Plz -Gdn Cty 11530
(516) 227-2221 .. **Mencher,** Jules M '77 -666 Old Cntry Rd -Gdn Cty 11530 **Fx:**227-2224
(212) 425-1401 .. **Menchini,** Richd A '84 (O'Hare P LLP) -82 Wall -NY 10005 **Fx:**425-1421
(212) 813-5900 .. **Mende,** Craig S '93 (Fross ZL&Z,PC) -866 UN Plz -NY 10017
(212) 736-4430 .. **Mendel,** Alan A '68 (Blecher M&F) -1501 Bway -NY 10036
(212) 972-5430 .. **Mendel,** Rebecca L '99 (Rosin SM) -801 2nd Av -NY 10017
(212) 370-1300 .. **Mendelberg,** Gabriel P '98 (Ellenoff G&S LLP) -150 E 42nd -NY 10017
(212) 629-4970 .. **Mendelberg,** Jill L '02 %Kreisberg & M,LLP -116 John -NY 10038
(212) 310-8000 .. **Mendelowitz,** Adam S '09 %Weil G&M LLP -767 5th Av -NY 10153
(516) 921-1200 .. **Mendelsohn,** Allan B '83 (Zavatsky M&L,LLP) -33 Qns Bx510 -Syosset 11791
(212) 872-1000 .. **Mendelsohn,** Bruce S '06 -One Bryant Park -NY 10036 **Fx:**872-1002
(631) 648-6182 .. **Mendelsohn,** Jennifer Ann '92 -500 Portion Rd -Ronkonkoma 11779
(212) 756-2000 .. **Mendelsohn,** Justin A '08 %Schulte R&Z LLP -919 3rd Av -NY 10022
(212) 972-1000 .. **Mendelsohn,** Richd L '88 %London F LLP -59 Maiden Ln -NY 10038
(718) 286-6000 .. **Mendelsohn,** Scott I '09 DA -125-01 Qns Blvd -Kew Gdns 11415
(212) 468-8000 .. **Mendelson,** Barbara R '82 (Morrison & F LLP) -1290 Av of Amer -NY 10104
(914) 698-5986 .. **Mendelson,** Barry L '67 -14 Fairway Dr -Mamaroneck 10543 **Fx:**698-8656
(718) 852-8849 .. **Mendelson,** Cindy J '85 (Mendelson & M) -26 Court -Brklyn 11242 **Fx:**852-1489
(212) 416-8115 .. **Mendelson,** Ellen S '86 %Dept of Law -120 Bway -NY 10271
(212) 885-5000 .. **Mendelson,** Eric C '93 %Blank R LLP -405 Lex Av -NY 10174
(718) 852-8849 .. **Mendelson,** Hyman J '59 (Mendelson & M) -26 Court -Brklyn 11242 **Fx:**852-1489
(516) 873-2000 .. **Mendelson,** Lee J '93 (Moritt HH&H LLP) -400 Grdn City Plz -Gdn Cty 11530
(516) 482-8228 .. **Mendelson,** Norman '68 (Mendelson & Assoc PLLC) -101 Atl Av -Lynbrk 11563 **Fx:**482-8271
(212) 309-6000 .. **Mendelson,** Robt C '85 (Morgan L&B LLP) -101 Park Av -NY 10178
(212) 902-1000 .. **Mendelson,** Sharon '97 Goldman Sachs -180 Maiden Ln -NY 10038
(212) 653-8700 .. **Mendenhall,** Greggory B '05 SpclCnsl Sheppard MR&H LLP -30 Rckfllr Plz -NY 10112
(212) 261-8000 .. **Mendes & Mount,LLP** -750 7th Av -NY 10019 **Fx:**261-8750
(212) 279-9200 .. **Mendez,** Alfredo F '79 (Abrams FFEGF&E,LLP) -630 3rd Av -NY 10017
(212) 859-8000 .. **Mendez,** Cynthia C '06 %Fried FHS&J LLP -1 NY Plz -NY 10004
(516) 294-5100 .. **Mendez,** Diane K '86 OfCnsl Murphy B&O,LLP -22 Jericho Tpk -Mineola 11501
(718) 435-5200 .. **Mendez,** Hector '81 %Port Realty -4601 6th Av -Brklyn 11220 **Fx:**435-7994
(212) 788-8688 .. **Mendez,** Ivan A Jr. '07 %Law Dept -100 Church -NY 10007 **Fx:**788-0367
(212) 455-2000 .. **Mendez,** Juan F '99 %Simpson T&B LLP -425 Lex Av -NY 10017
(315) 435-2170 .. **Mendez,** Luis A '83 %Cnty Atty -421 Mntgmry -Syracuse 13202 **Fx:**435-5729

(516) 571-9241 .. **Mendez,** Margaret '95 %Cnty Atty -1 West -Mineola 11501 **Fx:**571-6604
(212) 450-4000 .. **Mendez,** Mark M '01 (Davis P&W LLP) -450 Lex Av -NY 10017
(212) 614-8751 .. **Mendez,** Rosaura '97 -237 1st Av -NY 10003
(212) 880-3800 .. **Mendez-Penate,** Carlos E '77 (Akerman S) -335 Mad Av -NY 10017
(212) 436-1034 .. **Mendiburt,** Oleida '97 %IRS -290 Bway -NY 10007
(585) 381-2620 .. **Mendick,** Diane O'Hara '83 -55 Sully's Trl -Pittsfrd 14534 **Fx:**381-2626
(212) 788-3122 .. **Mendik,** Julie B '94 Office of the Mayor -City Hall -NY 10007
(518) 449-3107 .. **Mendleson,** Ira III '69 (Buckley M&C,PC) -29 Wards Ln -Albany 12204
(212) 610-6111 .. **Mendola,** Jos A '88 %Nikko Securities -535 Mad Av -NY 10022
(516) 489-9373 .. **Mendola,** Jos V '86 -24 Rhoda -W Hempstead 11552 **Fx:**(212) 692-0098
(716) 841-2094 .. **Mendola,** Michl R '93 %HSBC Bank -1 HSBC Ctr -Buffalo 14203 **Fx:**841-5087
(212) 222-3639 .. **Mendola,** Sally '74 -785 West End Av -NY 10025 **Fx:**222-3639
(212) 698-3500 .. **Mendola,** Sarah E '08 %Dechert LLP -1095 Av of Amer -NY 10036
(631) 852-2500 .. **Mendola-D'Andrea,** Lisabeth A '06 %DA -200 Center Dr -Rvrhead 11901 **Fx:**852-1769
(212) 225-2000 .. **Mendolaro,** Mario S '08 %Cleary GS&H -1 Lbrty Plz -NY 10006
(516) 229-4200 .. **Mendolia,** Lonnie M '94 (Mendolia & S) -875 Merrick Av -Westbury 11590
(516) 229-4200 .. **Mendolia & Stenz** -875 Merrick Av -Westbury 11590 **Fx:**229-4203
(212) 483-9490 .. **Mendoza,** Alexis P '02 %McElroy DM&C,LLP -88 Pine -NY 10005
(212) 351-4000 .. **Mendoza,** Christian P '04 Gibson D&C LLP -200 Park Av -NY 10166
(516) 742-8058 .. **Mendoza,** Jos P '00 %Abamont & Assoc -200 Grdn City Plz Bx9250 -Gdn Cty 11530 **Fx:**742-7308
(212) 455-2000 .. **Mendoza,** Riley C '08 %Simpson T&B LLP -425 Lex Av -NY 10017
(516) 222-7700 .. **Mendoza,** Tamika S '03 %LI Power Auth -333 Earle Ovngton Blvd -Uniondale 11553 **Fx:**222-9137
(917) 363-4993 .. **Mendrala,** Edmund J '83 -2 Stonewall Cir -West Harrison 10604 **Fx:**591-6189
(585) 232-6500 .. **Mendrick,** Ronald J '84 (Harter S&E LLP) -1600 Bausch & Lomb Pl -Rchstr 14604
(212) 455-2000 .. **Mendrzycki,** Edw C '68 OfCnsl Simpson T&B LLP -425 Lex Av -NY 10017
(845) 928-7076 .. **Mendrzycki,** Wm J '94 -Bx1009 -Highland Mills 10930
(212) 213-1220 .. **Mendys,** Alissa A '06 %Weiner MM&B,LLC -220 5th Av -NY 10001
(718) 590-2000 .. **Mendys,** L Newton Jr. '05 %DA -198 E 161st -Bronx 10451 **Fx:**590-6477
(631) 475-0001 .. **Menechino,** Alicia M '00 LaVelle & M,LLP -57 E Main -Patchogue 11772 **Fx:**447-7150
(212) 776-5000 .. **Menegakis,** Byron S '88 %NYC Housing Auth -250 Bway -NY 10007 **Fx:**776-5039
(212) 351-4000 .. **Menendez,** Matthew J '09 %Gibson D&C LLP -200 Park Av -NY 10166
(212) 489-8230 .. **Menendez,** Maya N '03 %Davis WT LLP -1633 Bway -NY 10019
(212) 460-2916 .. **Mener,** Leon Z '75 Con Ed -4 Irving Pl -NY 10003
(212) 969-3000 .. **Menes,** Caroline Kim '98 %Proskauer R LLP -1585 Bway -NY 10036
(718) 741-8419 .. **Menes,** Matthew A '96 %Div of Human Rights -1 Fordham Plz -Bronx 10458 **Fx:**741-8102
(212) 216-9029 .. **Meneses,** Jorge Obed V '92 -70 Bowery -NY 10013 **Fx:**216-9025
(212) 687-4900 .. **Meng,** Cristina L '09 %Wormser KG&J LLP -825 3rd Av -NY 10022
(212) 584-0058 .. **Meng,** Grace '04 (Yoon & K LLP) -11 E 44th -NY 10017
(212) 925-0101 .. **Meng,** Grace Sung Ehn '05 C Slovinsky -401 Bway -NY 10013 **Fx:**219-9412
(516) 683-0901 .. **Meng,** M Kathryn '67 (Cianciulli M&P) -Bx246 -Uniondale 11553
(212) 474-1000 .. **Menge,** Benjamin R '09 %Cravath S&M LLP -825 8th Av -NY 10019
(212) 458-1455 .. **Menger,** Andrew F '96 %AIG -175 Water -NY 10038 **Fx:**458-1475
(212) 318-3000 .. **Mengwall,** Erik L '04 %Fulbright & J LLP -666 5th Av -NY 10103
(718) 667-9090 .. **Menicucci,** Michl M '88 (Menicucci V & Assoc) -2040 Victory Blvd -Staten Isl 10314 **Fx:**667-0700
(914) 654-0227 .. **Menillo,** Gregory '83 G Menillo,PC -703 Pelham Rd -New Rchll 10805
(212) 989-3611 .. **Menillo,** Michl A '65 -10 Sheridan Sq -NY 10014
(212) 245-6565 .. **Menin,** Geoffrey D '78 (Levine P&M,LLP) -1740 Bway -NY 10019
(212) 580-3136 .. **Menin,** Lisa '83 %Jacobson Prop -150 Columbus Av -NY 10023
(212) 735-3000 .. **Menitove,** Michl H '09 %Skadden ASM&F LLP -4 Times Sq -NY 10036
(845) 291-0011 .. **Menke,** Mindy '07 %Blustein SR&B,LLP -10 Matthews -Goshen 10924
(212) 509-1616 .. **Menken,** Bruce E '87 (Beranbaum M LLP) -80 Pine -NY 10005
(914) 686-4456 .. **Menken,** David A '82 (Marsh M&W PLLC) -81 Main -White Plns 10601 **Fx:**206-3998
(212) 883-1700 .. **Menkes,** Eric G '86 (Duval & S LLP) -101 Park Av -NY 10178
(212) 460-2741 .. **Menkes,** Lawr S '82 Con Ed -4 Irving Pl -NY 10003 **Fx:**677-5850
(212) 285-0900 .. **Menkes,** Sheryl R '90 -319 Bway -NY 10007 **Fx:**658-9408
(212) 876-7700 .. **Menkin,** Cori Ann '02 %ASPCA -424 E 92nd -NY 10128 **Fx:**860-3560
(315) 425-1212 .. **Menkin,** Edw Z '77 -555 E Genesee -Syracuse 13202 **Fx:**425-7164
(516) 294-8844 .. **Menna,** Jillian '06 %L'Abbate BC&C,LLP -1001 Franklin Av -Gdn Cty 11530
(716) 839-7777 .. **Menna,** John '07 %O'Brien B PC -40 N Forest Rd -Williamsvll 14221
(914) 948-8490 .. **Menna,** Philip F '77 -235 Mamaroneck Av -White Plns 10605 **Fx:**948-3811
(212) 608-8840 .. **Menna,** Philip G '91 %Bamundo Z&S,LLP -111 John -NY 10038
(718) 260-5124 .. **Mennella,** Concetta I '90 %NYC Techincal Cllg -300 Jay -Brklyn 11201 **Fx:**260-5387
(646) 315-7423 .. **Mennella,** Jennifer '04 %FINRA -14 Wall -NY 10005 **Fx:**315-7440
(718) 320-3326 .. **Mennen,** Sally S '87 %Riverbay Corp -2049 Bartow Av -Bronx 10475 **Fx:**320-3397
(518) 456-0082 .. **Mennillo,** Crystal R '07 %Bailey K&J,PC -5 Pine West Plz -Albany 12205 **Fx:**456-4767
(212) 698-3500 .. **Mennitt,** Gary J '91 (Dechert LLP) -1095 Av of Amer -NY 10036
(718) 987-2000 .. **Mennona,** Virginia M '89 %John Gulino,PC -85 New Dorp Ln -Staten Isl 10306
(212) 687-4900 .. **Menon,** Appen P '87 Wormser KG&J LLP -825 3rd Av -NY 10022
(718) 590-2000 .. **Menon,** Chandra Simonton '06 DA -198 E 161st -Bronx 10451 **Fx:**590-6477
(212) 312-2312 .. **Menon,** Nisha '03 %Leg Aid -60 Lafayette -NY 10013 **Fx:**349-0874
(212) 967-8202 .. **Menon,** Priyanka Gopinath '06 %Pagan Law Firm,PC -245 5th Av -NY 10016 **Fx:**967-8794
(212) 693-1058 .. **Menon,** Ruby '05 SpclCnsl Coughlin SGR&R LLP -52 Duane -NY 10007
(516) 538-7476 .. **Menoudakos,** Peter '66 -220 Nassau Blvd S -Garden City South 11530 **Fx:**538-7459
(516) 538-7476 .. **Menoudakos,** Peter '97 -220 Nassau Blvd S -Garden City South 11530 **Fx:**538-7459
(718) 457-2400 .. **Menowitz,** Fredk A '61 -91-31 Qns Blvd -Elmhrst 11373 **Fx:**458-2561
(212) 578-2211 .. **Mensch,** Andrew B '98 %MetLife -27-01 Qns Plz N -LIC 11101
(212) 448-1100 .. **Mensch,** Hannah W '04 %McLaughlin & S,LLP -260 Mad Av -NY 10016
(845) 359-0737 .. **Menschik,** Judith M '81 (Menschik & M) -574 Rt 303 -Blauvelt 10913
(845) 359-0737 .. **Menschik & Markstein** -574 Rt 303 -Blauvelt 10913 **Fx:**359-2572
(518) 462-5601 .. **Mensh,** Aaron S '10 %O'Connell & A -54 State -Albany 12207
(716) 532-2602 .. **Menshel,** Denny '85 -Bx71 -Gowanda 14070
(516) 551-4424 .. **Mensher,** Mark D '92 -3255 Lawson Blvd -Oceanside 11572
(212) 972-6161 .. **Mensi,** Dennis W '99 (Cassin & C LLP) -711 3rd Av -NY 10017
(212) 530-1800 .. **Mensing,** Ryan E '05 %Richards K&O LLP -1 World Fncl Ctr -NY 10281
(212) 841-1000 .. **Ment,** Andrew W '99 (Covington & B LLP) -620 8th Av -NY 10018
(212) 816-4445 .. **Ment,** Jason '03 Citi Private Equity -388 Greenwich -NY 10013
(315) 474-7541 .. **Menter Rudin & Trivelpiece,PC** -308 Maltbie -Syracuse 13204 **Fx:**474-4040
(315) 786-7950 .. **Menter Rudin & Trivelpiece,PC** -120 Wshngtn -Watertwn 13601 **Fx:**786-7852
(212) 558-4000 .. **Menting,** Mark J '85 (Sullivan & C LLP) -125 Broad -NY 10004
(516) 571-3800 .. **Mention-Lewis,** Risco D '94 %DA -262 Old Cntry Rd -Mineola 11501 **Fx:**248-9479
(212) 728-8000 .. **Menton,** Francis J Jr. '76 (Willkie F&G LLP) -787 7th Av -NY 10019
(212) 521-5400 .. **Mentone,** Kristina M '04 %Reed S LLP -599 Lex Av -NY 10022
(212) 595-9127 .. **Mentz,** Barbara A '74 -140 W 86th -NY 10024 **Fx:**595-1628
(212) 922-0450 .. **Mentz,** Lawr '73 (Kaplan M&A,LLC) -70 E 55th -NY 10022
(212) 489-1600 .. **Mentz,** Lawr G '10 %Deloitte LLP -1633 Bway -NY 10019 **Fx:**492-4201
(212) 819-8200 .. **Mentzer,** Stefan M '02 %White & C LLP -1155 Av of Amer -NY 10036
(631) 225-3784 .. **Menu,** Susan '92 -Bx2309 -Amagansett 11930 **Fx:**604-5138
(914) 592-1919 .. **Meny,** Laura L '08 %FG Cottrell -5 W Main -Elmsfrd 10523 **Fx:**592-2987
(212) 223-2100 .. **Menz Bonner & Komar LLP** -444 Mad Av -NY 10022 **Fx:**223-2185
(212) 848-4000 .. **Menz,** James U '06 %Shearman & S LLP -599 Lex Av -NY 10022
(212) 223-2100 .. **Menz,** John R '86 (Menz B&K LLP) -444 Mad Av -NY 10022
(212) 909-6000 .. **Menza,** Marjorie J '03 %Debevoise & P LLP -919 3rd Av -NY 10022
(212) 536-3900 .. **Menzi,** Aaron W '06 %K&L Gates LLP -599 Lex Av -NY 10022
(716) 204-1055 .. **Menzie,** Laurie L '96 (Pfalzgraf B&M LLP) -455 Cayuga Rd -Buffalo 14225 **Fx:**204-1080
(212) 971-5606 .. **Meola,** Michl N '06 HYDC -225 W 34th -NY 10122
(518) 713-2030 .. **Meola,** Rudolph J '92 -950 New Loudon Rd -Latham 12110 **Fx:**713-2032
(716) 856-4000 .. **Meosky,** Paul D '89 (Hodgson R LLP) -140 Pearl -Buffalo 14202
(631) 232-6130 .. **Mer,** Julie L '04 %Weiner L LLP -888 Vets Mem'l Hwy -Hauppauge 11788
(212) 629-9690 .. **Merani,** Peter C '92 -298 5th Av -NY 10001 **Fx:**629-9664
(585) 235-4229 .. **Merante,** Rosemaria '93 (Merante & M) -1411 Chili Av -Rchstr 14624 **Fx:**436-9706
(585) 235-4229 .. **Merante,** Vincent E '92 (Merante & M) -1411 Chili Av -Rchstr 14624 **Fx:**436-9706
(718) 796-8568 .. **Meranus,** Philip '66 -3240 H Hdsn Pkwy -Bronx 10463
(212) 248-8800 .. **Merber,** Kenneth S '89 (Callan KB&B LLP) -1 Whitehall -NY 10004
(212) 506-5000 .. **Mercadante,** James A '88 (Orrick H&S LLP) -51 W 52nd -NY 10019
(212) 226-0350 .. **Mercader,** Manuel A '99 (Mercader & B PLLC) -100 Church -NY 10007 **Fx:**226-0391
(516) 794-7340 .. **Mercado,** Alphonso A '93 %Fager & A,LLP -90 Merrick Av -E Meadow 11554
(212) 490-3000 .. **Mercado,** Anna L Robles '06 %Wilson EME&D LLP -150 E 42nd -NY 10017
(212) 474-1000 .. **Mercado,** David '85 (Cravath S&M LLP) -825 8th Av -NY 10019
(212) 848-4000 .. **Mercado,** Grissel A '08 %Shearman & S LLP -599 Lex Av -NY 10022
(212) 455-2000 .. **Mercado,** Jaime '96 (Simpson T&B LLP) -425 Lex Av -NY 10017
(718) 549-3952 .. **Mercado,** Josephine '84 -314 W 231st -Bronx 10463 **Fx:**549-3952
(212) 309-1000 .. **Mercado,** Lalaine '07 %Hunton & W -200 Park Av -NY 10166
(212) 277-0428 .. **Mercado,** Raymond A '97 Hartford Fncl -2 Park Av -NY 10016
(212) 483-0105 .. **Mercado-Washington,** Kim V '07 %Coughlin D LLP -88 Pine-Wall St Plz -NY 10005
(631) 232-1950 .. **Mercaldi,** Robt L '02 -320 Carleton Av -Central Islip 11722 **Fx:**232-5343
(212) 953-2381 .. **Mercante,** James E '86 (Rubin F&F,LLP) -292 Mad Av -NY 10017
(212) 661-8000 .. **Mercanti,** Michl N '90 (Lucas & M,LLP) -475 Park Av S -NY 10016
(212) 573-0944 .. **Merced,** Deusdedi '96 (D Merced,PC) -330 Mad Av -NY 10017
(347) 296-1665 .. **Mercedes,** Jeanette M '96 %Supreme Ct Law Dept -360 Adams -Brklyn 11201 **Fx:**643-6114
(212) 310-8000 .. **Mercedes,** Ramon E '09 %Weil G&M LLP -767 5th Av -NY 10153
(631) 751-5757 .. **Mercep,** Anthony W '81 (Glynn M&P,LLP) -57 North Cntry Rd Bx712 -Stony Brk 11790
(888) 637-2370 .. **Mercer,** Brian P '95 -90 Crandon Way -Rchstr 14618
(212) 264-0155 .. **Mercer,** James E '87 %Army Corps Engrs -26 Fed Plz -NY 10278 **Fx:**264-8171
(212) 532-2100 .. **Mercer,** Samara M '07 %J Markman,PLLC -1775 Bway -NY 10019 **Fx:**532-2198
(212) 446-4800 .. **Mercer,** Wm C '01 OfCnsl Kirkland & E LLP -153 E 53rd -NY 10022
(631) 952-6400 .. **Merchan,** Lara B '94 Medicaid Fraud Cntrl -300 Motor Pkwy -Hauppauge 11788 **Fx:**952-6382

(845) 201-8090 .. **Merchant**, Joy D '01 (Diviny & M,PC) -39 E Central Av -Pearl Rvr 10965 **Fx**:201-8092
(585) 424-3333 .. **Mercier**, Sarah Lawless '90 -99 Ridgeland Rd -Rchstr 14623
(845) 300-4088 .. **Merck**, Norbert J '91 -126 Moehring Dr -Blauvelt 10913
(212) 449-4968 .. **Mercogliano**, Theresa L '93 Merrill Lynch -4 World Fncl Ctr -NY 10080
(212) 490-5387 .. **Mercorella**, Anthony J '52 -150 E 42nd -NY 10017 **Fx**:490-3038
(518) 798-1758 .. **Mercure**, Michl J '00 %R Newell -1 South Wstrn Plz Bx2152 -Glens Fls 12801 **Fx**:798-0740
(716) 849-1333 .. **Mercure**, Thos M '97 (Lipsitz GSC LLP) -42 Delaware Av -Buffalo 14202
(631) 277-4300 .. **Mercurio**, Jos R '94 %Shlimbaum & S -265 Main Bx8 -Islip 11751 **Fx**:277-4350
(516) 877-2751 .. **Mercurio**, Laureen '88 -626 Willis Av -Williston Pk 11596
(631) 852-1431 .. **Mercurio**, Michl P '85 Suffolk Cnty Ct -210 Center Dr -Rvrhead 11901
(212) 237-1000 .. **Mercurio**, Robt D '74 (Windels ML&M,LLP) -156 W 56th -NY 10019
(631) 547-0951 .. **Mercuris**, Bret L '86 -223 Wall #383 -Huntngtn 11743
(585) 238-2000 .. **Mercury**, Albert M '81 (Phillips L LLP) -1400 First Fed Plz -Rchstr 14614
(518) 280-8872 .. **Mercy**, Brian D '01 B Mercy PLLC -514 State -Schnctdy 12305 **Fx**:280-8831
(518) 213-6000 .. **Mercy**, Megan M '05 NYSUT -800 Troy-Schnctdy Rd -Latham 12110 **Fx**:213-6488
(585) 258-2800 .. **Mereau**, Jennifer A '00 %Underberg & K LLP -300 Bausch & Lomb Pl -Rchstr 14604
(212) 240-0020 .. **Meredith Cohen Greenfogel & Skirnick** -1 Lbrty Plz -NY 10006 **Fx**:240-0021
(212) 270-2178 .. **Meredith**, Gregory S '75 JP Morgan Chase -270 Park Av -NY 10017
(212) 760-0098 .. **Meredith**, Jennifer M '02 (Meredith & K,PLLC) -330 Mad Av -NY 10017 **Fx**:202-3819
(212) 373-3000 .. **Meredith**, Nathan D '10 %Paul WRW&G LLP -1285 Av of Amer -NY 10019
(212) 373-3000 .. **Meredith-Goujon**, Claudine K '99 Cnsl Paul WRW&G LLP -1285 Av of Amer -NY 10019
(718) 286-2000 .. **Merenstein**, Fern R '88 %Leg Aid -120-46 Qns Blvd -Kew Gdns 11415 **Fx**:286-2286
(212) 683-2525 .. **Merer**, Todd M '65 -575 Lex Av -NY 10022 **Fx**:213-9786
(518) 474-3654 .. **Mereson**, Julie S '80 %Dept of Law -The Cptl -Albany 12224
(212) 867-6000 .. **Mergentime**, Larry R '01 (Rosenberg & E,PC) -733 3rd Av -NY 10017
(518) 487-5460 .. **Merges**, Renee Z '84 %DA -6 Lodge -Albany 12207 **Fx**:487-5093
(212) 679-3600 .. **Meriam**, Harold A III '76 Helmsley Entrprs,Inc -230 Park Av -NY 10169 **Fx**:867-7570
(212) 813-8800 .. **Meriam**, Thos C '77 (Goodwin P LLP) -620 8th Av -NY 10018
(212) 450-4000 .. **Meriggi**, Jeffrey G '08 %Davis P&W LLP -450 Lex Av -NY 10017
(212) 632-6388 .. **Merimee**, John D '04 %Lazard Freres -30 Rckfllr Plz -NY 10112 **Fx**:632-6060
(212) 848-4000 .. **Meringolo**, Colleen M '07 %Shearman & S LLP -599 Lex Av -NY 10022
(631) 499-3800 .. **Meringolo**, John A '91 (Kalb & R,PC) -283 Commack Rd -Commack 11725
(212) 336-2000 .. **Merino**, Carl A '05 %Patterson BW&T LLP -1133 Av of Amer -NY 10036
(212) 854-0284 .. **Merino**, Gonzalo '02 %Columbia Univ -535 W 116th 412 Low Mem'l Library -NY 10027
(212) 735-3000 .. **Meriweather**, Tiffany N '09 %Skadden ASM&F LLP -4 Times Sq -NY 10036
(212) 645-8111 .. **Merjian**, Armen H '90 Housing Works,Inc -320 W 13th -NY 10014
(212) 455-2000 .. **Merjian**, Mardi R '88 Cnsl Simpson T&B LLP -425 Lex Av -NY 10017
(585) 454-4400 .. **Merkel**, David A '61 (Merkel & M) -701 Mt Hope Av -Rchstr 14620 **Fx**:454-5500
(585) 263-1000 .. **Merkel**, Edwin V '97 Cnsl Nixon P LLP -1100 Clinton Sq -Rchstr 14604
(585) 325-8000 .. **Merkel**, Sarah E '01 %Wolford Law LLP -16 E Main -Rchstr 14614 **Fx**:325-8009
(212) 829-4829 .. **Merkel**, Stephen M '85 Cantor Fitzgerald -110 E 59th -NY 10022 **Fx**:829-4708
(212) 318-6000 .. **Merkelson**, Randall A '06 %Paul HJ&W LLP -75 E 55th -NY 10022
(212) 307-1122 .. **Merkelson**, Wayne P '76 %Sandoz Corp -608 5th Av -NY 10020
(646) 386-4520 .. **Merker**, Peter L '80 %Criminal Ct -100 Centre -NY 10013
(212) 838-7200 .. **Merkin**, J Ezra '80 Gabriel Capital Grp -450 Park Av -NY 10022
(212) 577-3505 .. **Merkine**, Claire V '04 %Leg Aid -199 Water -NY 10038 **Fx**:577-3520
(718) 630-2900 .. **Merkl**, Kathleen A '92 %VA -800 Poly Pl -Brklyn 11209 **Fx**:630-2917
(718) 445-4235 .. **Merkl**, Neil M '55 -35-35 161st -Flushng 11358 **Fx**:445-4310
(212) 808-7811 .. **Merkl**, Neil M '84 (Kelley D&W LLP) -101 Park Av -NY 10178
(718) 254-7000 .. **Merkl**, Taryn A '02 %US Atty -271 Cadman Plz E -Brklyn 11201 **Fx**:254-6479
(212) 922-6711 .. **Merkle**, Mary L '68 Dreyfus Corp -200 Park Av -NY 10166
(212) 474-1000 .. **Merkle**, Matthew C '09 %Cravath S&M LLP -825 8th Av -NY 10019
(518) 339-9036 .. **Merkle**, Sharon A '00 -358 Bway -Saratoga Spgs 12866 **Fx**:(800) 546-7601
(518) 485-9373 .. **Merklen**, Wendy A '00 Ofc of State Review -80 Wolf Rd -Albany 12205
(718) 671-2793 .. **Merklen**, Wm A '84 -1464 Hammersley Av -Bronx 10469 **Fx**:671-4311
(516) 357-3000 .. **Merkrebs**, Howard M '91 (Rivkin R LLP) -926 RXR Plz -Uniondale 11556
(212) 806-5400 .. **Merkt**, Bonnie A '06 %Stroock &S&L LLP -180 Maiden Ln -NY 10038
(914) 684-0090 .. **Merkt**, Dixon M Jr. '06 %Diserio MO&C LLP -50 Main -White Plns 10606
(212) 268-9001 .. **Merkur**, Bruce D '76 (B Merkur,PC) -225 W 35th -NY 10001
(212) 715-9100 .. **Merl**, Seth R '03 %Kramer LN&F,LLP -1177 Av of Amer -NY 10036
(212) 471-2990 .. **Merle Brown & Nakamura,PC** -90 Broad -NY 10004 **Fx**:471-2997
(631) 288-4005 .. **Merle**, Hugh M '87 -44 Mill Rd Bx1226 -Westhmptn Bch 11978 **Fx**:288-4577
(212) 805-4659 .. **Merle**, Natasha C '09 US Dist Ct -500 Pearl -NY 10007
(212) 471-2990 .. **Merle**, Pierre F V '76 (Merle B&N,PC) -90 Broad -NY 10004
(212) 763-4100 .. **Merlen**, Deena R '97 (Reavis PL LLP) -41 Mad Av -NY 10010
(212) 446-2300 .. **Merley**, Michl M '07 %Boies S&F LLP -575 Lex Av -NY 10022
(212) 408-2500 .. **Merling**, Jeremy P '06 %Baker B,LLP -30 Rckfllr Plz -NY 10112
(212) 341-7900 .. **Merlino**, Giovanni C '99 %Brecher FPWT&Z,PC -233 Bway -NY 10279
(212) 530-3900 .. **Merlino**, James M '96 (Hannum FP&M, LLC) -55 Bway -NY 10006
(212) 742-3390 .. **Merlino**, Jeffrey R '02 Lindabury ME&C,PC -26 Bway -NY 10004
(718) 698-2200 .. **Merlino**, John R Jr. '99 (Merlino & G) -1259 Richmond Av -Staten Isl 10314 **Fx**:698-0024
(212) 969-3000 .. **Merlino**, Silvana M '96 %Proskauer R LLP -1585 Bway -NY 10036
(585) 987-2800 .. **Merlo**, Saml P '62 (Woods OG LLP) -2 State -Rchstr 14614
(516) 570-4000 .. **Mermel**, Mark D '75 -98 Cuttermill Rd -Gt Neck 11021 **Fx**:570-4333
(516) 487-7792 .. **Mermelstein**, Bernard B '79 -11 Oak Dr -Gt Neck 11021
(718) 376-5071 .. **Mermelstein**, Beth '87 -2053 E 35th -Brklyn 11234
(212) 213-3818 .. **Mermelstein**, Edw A '96 E Mermelstein & Assoc,PC -302 5th Av -NY 10001 **Fx**:213-3747
(212) 859-8000 .. **Mermelstein**, Joshua '81 (Fried FHS&J LLP) -1 NY Plz -NY 10004
(718) 692-1013 .. **Mermelstein**, Laurie E '92 (Seidemann & M) -974 E 27th -Brklyn 11210
(516) 328-2300 .. **Mermelstein**, Lee N '04 %Abrams FFEGF&E,LLP -1111 Marcus Av -Lk Success 11042
(212) 490-3000 .. **Mermelstein**, Richd T '86 (Wilson EME&D LLP) -150 E 42nd -NY 10017
(914) 323-7000 .. **Mermelstein**, Richd T '86 (Wilson EME&D LLP) -3 Gannett Dr -White Plns 10604
(718) 436-8098 .. **Mermelstein**, Sol '81 -5521 New Utrecht Av -Brklyn 11219 **Fx**:436-8174
(516) 295-3575 .. **Mernick**, Paul M '85 -337R Central Av -Lawrence 11559 **Fx**:295-0722
(212) 474-1000 .. **Merns**, Jillian E '09 %Cravath S&M LLP -825 8th Av -NY 10019
(212) 484-8000 .. **Mero**, Norma Drelich '94 %Time Warner -1 Time Warner Ctr -NY 10019
(212) 661-2111 .. **Mero**, Steven C '89 -551 5th Av -NY 10176 **Fx**:573-9852
(212) 593-6111 .. **Merola**, Jerry A '86 (Greenberg & M) -521 5th Av -NY 10175 **Fx**:(516) 887-1720
(212) 333-8800 .. **Merola**, Michl J '97 UBS Fncl Srvcs -590 Mad Av -NY 10022
(716) 856-4000 .. **Merola**, Michelle '06 (Hodgson R LLP) -140 Pearl -Buffalo 14202
(212) 742-8700 .. **Merolesi**, Kari A '01 (Garson D&C LLP) -110 Wall -NY 10005
(718) 921-6601 .. **Merolesi**, Marc A '99 %T Beinert -155 Bay Ridge Av -Brklyn 11220 **Fx**:921-6609
(212) 430-8020 .. **Merolla**, Paul A '75 (LeClairRyan,PC) -830 3rd Av -NY 10022
(212) 998-6191 .. **Meron**, Theodor '84 %NYU Law Schl -40 Wshngtn Sq S -NY 10012 **Fx**:995-3055
(914) 699-6052 .. **Merovitch**, Alan '74 -153 Stevens Av -Mt Vernon 10550 **Fx**:699-1769
(212) 558-4000 .. **Merow**, John E '58 SrCnsl Sullivan & C LLP -125 Broad -NY 10004
(914) 949-0333 .. **Merran**, Harold '59 -100 E Hartsdale Av -Hartsdale 10530
(315) 376-8214 .. **Merrell**, Edgar S K 3rd '79 Merrell & M -Bx151 -Lowvll 13367 **Fx**:376-8216
(716) 854-2620 .. **Merrick**, Andrew D '66 (Brown & K,LLP) -1500 Lbrty Bldg -Buffalo 14202
(631) 852-2500 .. **Merrifield**, Denise '87 %DA -200 Center Dr -Rvrhead 11901 **Fx**:852-1769
(914) 961-4441 .. **Merrigan**, Kathleen M '01 %Begos H&B LLP -7 Pondfld Rd Bx369 -Bronxvll 10708
(212) 841-1000 .. **Merrill**, Gina R '06 %Covington & B LLP -620 8th Av -NY 10018
(212) 425-0700 .. **Merrill**, Monica Risi '78 %Kelner & K -140 Bway -NY 10005
(212) 374-6770 .. **Merrill**, Robin '96 %NYC Dept Educ-OLS -52 Chmbrs -NY 10007 **Fx**:374-5596
(212) 705-7000 .. **Merrill**, Susan L '88 (Bingham M LLP) -399 Park Av -NY 10022
(212) 794-5280 .. **Merrill**, Suzanne E '95 -402 E 69th -NY 10021 **Fx**:794-5280
(212) 788-5025 .. **Merrill**, Thos C '87 %Dept Hlth -125 Worth CN-30 -NY 10013 **Fx**:788-4300
(212) 938-5000 .. **Merriman**, Christine O '88 %Cantor Fitzgerald -110 E 59th -NY 10022
(315) 425-2700 .. **Merriman**, Courtney M '07 %Hiscock & B,LLP -One Park Pl -Syracuse 13202
(914) 251-7922 .. **Merriman**, James D IV '94 %Charter Schls Inst/SUNY -735 Andrsn Hill -Purchase 10577
(716) 551-4741 .. **Merriman**, Joy A '93 %US DHS -130 Delaware Av -Buffalo 14202
(585) 454-0700 .. **Merriman**, Kevin T '93 (Ward GH&R LLP) -300 State -Rchstr 14614
(212) 980-0120 .. **Merriman**, Mark A '05 %Frankfurt KK&S,PC -488 Mad Av -NY 10022
(212) 451-2300 .. **Merrit**, Manes M '78 (Olshan GFR&W LLP) -65 E 55th -NY 10022
(212) 244-9500 .. **Merritt**, Jaime M '05 %White and W LLP -1 Penn Plz -NY 10119
(631) 412-5526 .. **Merritt**, Richd J '82 -2 Birs Av -Lindenhrst 11757
(212) 374-9101 .. **Merritt**, Shawn '09 %Brill & Assoc,PC -111 John -NY 10038 **Fx**:374-9108
(631) 231-2424 .. **Merritt**, Tracey A '90 %Dept of Law -300 Motor Pkwy -Hauppauge 11788 **Fx**:435-4757
(212) 269-3200 .. **Merritt**, Wm A Jr. '65 McAllister Transprtn & Towing -17 Battery Pl -NY 10004 **Fx**:509-1147
(516) 992-3485 .. **Merritts**, George R '95 -1225 Franklin Av -Gdn Cty 11530 **Fx**:214-4157
(212) 454-6866 .. **Merry**, E Vincent III '03 Deutsche Bank AG -280 Park Av -NY 10017
(607) 324-1104 .. **Merry**, Joan D '98 %Shults & S -9 Seneca -Hornell 14843 **Fx**:324-7983
(585) 377-5487 .. **Mersereau**, Julie V '85 -9 Farmingham Dr -Penfld 14526
(212) 863-6300 .. **Mershon**, Michele '90 %HPD -100 Gold -NY 10038 **Fx**:863-8201
(212) 594-3656 .. **Mershon**, Stuart Y '97 %SC Yom -38 W 32nd -NY 10001 **Fx**:594-3621
(718) 330-7861 .. **Mersich**, Edith M '92 %ODAR-SSA -111 Lvngstn -Brklyn 11201 **Fx**:330-2009
(646) 935-4058 .. **Mersky**, Craig M '00 Ketchum Inc -1285 Av of Amer -NY 10019
(212) 553-5601 .. **Merson**, Jacqueline M '87 Zurich NA -1 Lbrty Plz -NY 10006
(212) 257-6800 .. **Merson**, Jordan K '06 %Thompson W&G LLP -85 5th Av -NY 10003
(212) 502-4300 .. **Merson**, Mark A '81 Ruback & M -462 7th Av -NY 10018 **Fx**:502-0540
(212) 326-3939 .. **Mersten**, Sean D '10 %Jones D -222 E 41st -NY 10017

(315) 422-6154 .. **Mertell**, Lorraine Rann '81 (Greene H&S) -1 Lincoln Ctr -Syracuse 13202
(607) 687-0567 .. **Mertens**, Richd W '74 (Coughlin & G,LLP) -27-29 Lk Bx250 -Owego 13827
(607) 723-9511 .. **Mertens**, Richd W '74 (Coughlin & G,LLP) -19 Chenango Bx2039 -Bnghmtn 13902
(914) 422-4333 .. **Merton**, Vanessa H '74 %John Jay Lgl Srvcs -80 N Bway -White Plns 10603 **Fx**:422-4391
(516) 574-6142 .. **Mertz**, Christine R '99 %JP Morgan Chase -1985 Marcus Av -New Hyde Pk 11040
(518) 455-4131 .. **Mertz**, John R '01 NY State Assembly -80 S Swan -Albany 12210
(212) 226-7700 .. **Mertzel**, Nancy J '89 (Donovan & Y LLP) -161 Av of Amer -NY 10013
(212) 742-9870 .. **Meruelo**, Raul P '82 -42 Bway -NY 10004 **Fx**:571-1113
(315) 207-8036 .. **Mervine**, Edw A '87 Pathfinder Bank -214 W 1st -Oswego 13126 **Fx**:207-8047
(607) 723-5341 .. **Mervis**, Harvey D '86 (Hinman H&K,LLP) -80 Exchange Bx5250 -Bnghmtn 13902
(212) 969-3000 .. **Mervis**, Michl T '91 (Proskauer R LLP) -1585 Bway -NY 10036
(646) 610-5917 .. **Mervish**, Amy B '95 %NYPD -1 Police Plz -NY 10038
(212) 381-7000 .. **Merwin**, Nancy L '02 %Sabin B&G LLP -4 Times Sq -NY 10036
(585) 454-3030 .. **Merzbach**, Ralph K '78 -73 State -Rchstr 14614 **Fx**:454-3044
(212) 956-2054 .. **Merzer**, Stuart L '04 Paulson & Co -1251 Av of Amer -NY 10020
(607) 432-4242 .. **Merzig**, David S '78 Kehoe & M,PC -8-12 Dietz -Oneonta 13820
(212) 335-9000 .. **Merzon**, Antonia M '99 %DA -1 Hogan Pl -NY 10013
(212) 225-2000 .. **Mesa**, Gabriel J '96 SpclCnsl Cleary GS&H -1 Lbrty Plz -NY 10006
(716) 852-1544 .. **Mescall**, Dennis P '87 (Smith M&S,LLC) -786 Ellicott Sq Bldg -Buffalo 14203
(212) 509-9400 .. **Mescall**, Kevin G '83 (Cozen O) -45 Bway Atrium -NY 10006
(212) 577-3300 .. **Mescon**, Cory E '10 %Leg Aid -199 Water -NY 10038
(212) 577-3515 .. **Meselson**, Amy Valor '04 Legal Aid -199 Water -NY 10038
(585) 325-3400 .. **Meserve**, James A '87 Montemaggi & Assoc -130 W Main -Rchstr 14614 **Fx**:325-4161
(585) 262-2667 .. **Mesh**, Christopher M '00 (Connors & F,LLP) -3445 Winton Pl -Rchstr 14623
(212) 382-0505 .. **Mesh**, Dana J '87 %Hank-Kross -500 5th Av -NY 10110 **Fx**:328-0987
(212) 816-7866 .. **Meshel**, Adam R '96 Citigroup -388 Greenwich -NY 10013
(516) 466-4422 .. **Meshnick**, Stacey J '97 %R Fatoullah & Assoc -425 Nrthrn Blvd -Gt Neck 11021 **Fx**:466-2219
(516) 489-6959 .. **Mesidor**, Marjorie '05 %F Brewington -556 Peninsula Blvd -Hempstd 11550 **Fx**:489-6958
(212) 770-1532 .. **Mesita**, Anthony Jos '96 AIGTS -80 Pine -NY 10005
(518) 452-5600 .. **Mesiti**, Nicholas '89 (Heslin RF&M PC) -5 Columbia Cir -Albany 12203
(212) 384-1000 .. **Meskill**, James J '00 %FBI -26 Fed Plz -NY 10278
(718) 246-1725 .. **Meskin**, Benjamin M '95 -5403 5th Av -Brklyn 11220 **Fx**:765-0365
(212) 888-3033 .. **Mesler**, Stacey-Anne '03 Becker GM&M LLP -299 Park Av -NY 10171
(212) 697-9280 .. **Mesorana**, Carmen A '97 %Rosenberg MF&W -122 E 42nd -NY 10168
(914) 333-0300 .. **Mesrop**, Alden '57 OfCnsl Ryan & S,LLP -1 Neperan Rd -Tarrytwn 10591 **Fx**:333-0301
(518) 464-2306 .. **Messa**, Frank L '77 AYCO -1 Wall Bx15073 -Albany 12212
(212) 841-1244 .. **Messado**, Tanya '05 -620 8th Av -NY 10018 **Fx**:841-1010
(716) 831-1800 .. **Messana-Morrow**, Carolyn '84 %Health Management Group -3020 Bailey Av -Buffalo 14215 **Fx**:831-1818
(914) 385-6000 .. **Messemer**, Cynthia Kulas '96 (Hodges W&S LLP) -55 Church -White Plns 10601 **Fx**:385-6060
(315) 422-3030 .. **Messenger & Elliott** -441 S Salina -Syracuse 13202 **Fx**:422-4554
(315) 422-3030 .. **Messenger**, James H Jr. '81 (Messenger & E) -441 S Salina -Syracuse 13202
(212) 558-4000 .. **Messenger**, Trevor J '10 %Sullivan & C LLP -125 Broad -NY 10004
(718) 858-1474 .. **Messer**, Gregory '78 -26 Court -Brklyn 11242 **Fx**:797-5360
(646) 654-6000 .. **Messer**, Heidi S '97 %Linkshare Corp -215 Park Av S -NY 10003
(516) 741-1032 .. **Messer**, John A '98 (Manoussos & M,PLLC) -595 Stewart Av -Gdn Cty 11530 **Fx**:741-7510
(212) 450-4000 .. **Messer**, Michelle '08 %Davis P&W LLP -450 Lex Av -NY 10017
(212) 481-5600 .. **Messer**, Peter M '68 (P Messer,PC) -60 E 42nd -NY 10165 **Fx**:697-0877
(646) 654-6000 .. **Messer**, Stephen D '98 %Linkshare Corp -215 Park Av S -NY 10003
(315) 218-8000 .. **Messer**, Suzanne M '07 %Bond S&K,PLLC -1 Lincoln Ctr -Syracuse 13202
(212) 398-2900 .. **Messi**, Michl A '96 (Swidler & M LLP) -57 W 38th -NY 10018 **Fx**:398-0405
(212) 259-8000 .. **Messiah**, Lucericia T '05 %Dewey & L LLP -1301 Av of Amer -NY 10019
(646) 378-2292 .. **Messian**, Joshua A '10 %Stark & S -One Penn Plz -NY 10119 **Fx**:378-2293
(718) 232-5559 .. **Messiana**, Laura '93 -1714 Benson Av -Brklyn 11214 **Fx**:232-5884
(212) 719-6335 .. **Messier**, Judith C '04 IRS -110 W 44th -NY 10036
(212) 446-4800 .. **Messika**, Galia '02 (Kirkland & E LLP) -153 E 53rd -NY 10022
(631) 547-0300 .. **Messina**, Albert V Jr. '07 %Novick & Assoc,PC -202 E Main -Huntngtn 11743 **Fx**:547-0212
(914) 949-9440 .. **Messina**, Anthony J '82 (Messina & Assoc,PC) -81 Main -White Plns 10601 **Fx**:949-9470
(212) 455-2000 .. **Messina**, Brandon L '08 %Simpson T&B LLP -425 Lex Av -NY 10017
(716) 634-7777 .. **Messina**, Chas A '05 -1301 N Forest Rd -Williamsvll 14221
(212) 759-5800 .. **Messina**, Christine M '98 (Gartner + B,PC) -801 2nd Av -NY 10017
(518) 443-5400 .. **Messina**, Ellen Lacy '77 %SUNY Univ Cnsl -S333 SUNY Plz -Albany 12246 **Fx**:443-5409
(212) 261-8000 .. **Messina**, Francis J '10 %Mendes & M,LLP -750 7th Av -NY 10019
(718) 446-0566 .. **Messina**, Frank G '82 -40-06 Warren -Elmhrst 11373 **Fx**:779-6984
(212) 425-7200 .. **Messina**, Gerard A '91 (Kenyon & K,LLP) -1 Bway -NY 10004
(585) 987-2800 .. **Messina**, Harry P Jr. '57 (Woods OG LLP) -2 State -Rchstr 14614
(212) 250-5763 .. **Messina**, John J '02 Deutsche Bank AG -60 Wall -NY 10005
(212) 791-1284 .. **Messina**, Jos '60 -110 William -NY 10038 **Fx**:732-1826
(646) 252-6210 .. **Messina**, Jos A '81 %Transit Auth -2 Bway -NY 10004
(914) 381-2728 .. **Messina**, Jos C '77 -424 Mamaroneck Av -Mamaroneck 10543 **Fx**:381-0907
(518) 455-2342 .. **Messina**, Jos R '73 SrCnsl NYS Senate Majority -The Cptl -Albany 12247 **Fx**:426-6815
(212) 286-8585 .. **Messina**, Matthew F '98 %Heidell PM&B,LLP -99 Park Av -NY 10016
(585) 396-7600 .. **Messina**, Michl H '94 %Canandaigua Wine Co -235 N Blmfld Rd -Canandaigua 14424 **Fx**:396-7831
(631) 676-3880 .. **Messina**, Michele R '95 -2395 Ocean Av -Ronkonkoma 11779 **Fx**:676-3881
(516) 364-6006 .. **Messina**, Steven J '10 %Cohen & S,LLP -199 Crsswys Park Dr Bx9004 -Woodbury 11797
(212) 735-3000 .. **Messina**, Steven M '98 Cnsl Skadden ASM&F LLP -4 Times Sq -NY 10036
(646) 207-4705 .. **Messina**, Toni M '89 -100 Lafayette -NY 10013 **Fx**:(212) 571-5507
(212) 760-2554 .. **Messina**, Victoria A '06 Pro Bono Net -151 W 30th -NY 10001
(631) 650-1200 .. **Messina**, Vincent J Jr. '89 (Sinnreich K&M LLP) -267 Carleton Av -Central Islip 11722
(212) 770-1726 .. **Messineo**, Barbara G '95 %AIG -80 Pine -NY 10005
(212) 310-8000 .. **Messineo**, Robt L '79 (Weil G&M LLP) -767 5th Av -NY 10153
(631) 281-9521 .. **Messinetti**, John E '69 (Batt & M,PC) -210 Wm Floyd Pkwy -Shirley 11967 **Fx**:281-1451
(631) 281-9521 .. **Messinetti**, John E Jr. '94 (Batt & M,PC) -210 Wm Floyd Pkwy -Shirley 11967 **Fx**:281-1451
(212) 576-3425 .. **Messing**, Jos A '91 NY Life Investment Mgmt LLC -51 Mad Av -NY 10010
(212) 230-8800 .. **Messinger**, Andrew H '07 %WilmerHale -399 Park Av -NY 10022
(212) 302-6868 .. **Messinger**, Barry W '70 Cnsl Flaster & W,PC -36 W 44th -NY 10036
(212) 873-7732 .. **Messinger**, Gloria '55 -27 W 86th -NY 10024
(212) 594-5300 .. **Messinger**, Jeffrey R '85 (Milberg LLP) -1 Penn Plz -NY 10119
(212) 728-8000 .. **Messinger**, Jordan A '04 %Willkie F&G LLP -787 7th Av -NY 10019
(718) 858-3100 .. **Messinger**, Jules G '86 (Weinstein CM&P) -26 Court -Brklyn 11242
(212) 975-3779 .. **Messinger**, Martin P '75 %CBS Inc -51 W 52nd -NY 10019 **Fx**:975-3930
(718) 793-7800 .. **Messinger**, Scott '96 (Gladstein & M) -118-21 Qns Blvd -Frst Hlls 11375 **Fx**:793-0524
(914) 682-8444 .. **Messinger**, Stanley '64 -50 Main -White Plns 10606 **Fx**:682-9018
(212) 521-5400 .. **Messite**, Andrew B '90 (Reed S LLP) -599 Lex Av -NY 10022
(212) 464-1244 .. **Messner**, Mary E '84 JP Morgan Chase & Co -345 Park Av -NY 10154
(516) 694-3000 .. **Mestecky**, Christopher F '06 %Guercio & G,LLP -77 Conklin -Farmngdl 11735 **Fx**:694-4738
(212) 223-3562 .. **Mester**, Chas L '92 (Turek RM LLP) -377 5th Av -NY 10016
(646) 237-7875 .. **Mesterman**, Dan '98 -369 Lex Av -NY 10017
(212) 472-6107 .. **Mestler**, Gilbert E '89 -205 E 78th -NY 10075 **Fx**:472-0183
(212) 558-4000 .. **Mestres**, Ricardo A Jr. '62 SrCnsl Sullivan & C LLP -125 Broad -NY 10004
(212) 272-4105 .. **Mesuk**, Lynn B '94 %JP Morgan Chase -383 Mad Av -NY 10179
(631) 300-4960 .. **Meszaros**, John C '90 %Bello & L -150 Motor Pkwy -Hauppauge 11788
(718) 424-3331 .. **Metalios**, M Evan '85 -71-19 Nrthrn Blvd -Jcksn Hts 11372
(212) 632-3023 .. **Metallo**, Eric C '04 Franklin Templeton -600 5th Av -NY 10020
(914) 413-4788 .. **Metaxas**, John C '84 -16 Ridge Rd -Katonah 10536
(203) 672-1631 .. **Metaxas**, Victoria '87 Cnsl LeClairRyan,PC -830 3rd Av -NY 10022
(212) 556-2100 .. **Metcalf**, Andrew M '01 (King & S) -1185 Av of Amer -NY 10036
(212) 594-5300 .. **Metcalf**, Elizabeth S '09 %Milberg LLP -1 Penn Plz -NY 10119
(212) 751-3001 .. **Metcalf**, Jerry L '07 (Thompson & K LLP) -919 3rd Av -NY 10022
(212) 918-3000 .. **Metcalf**, Slade R '74 (Hogan L LLP) -875 3rd Av -NY 10022
(518) 455-4191 .. **Metcalfe**, Amy A '01 %Ofc Cnsl to Majority -448M State Cptl -Albany 12248 **Fx**:455-4103
(607) 721-8440 .. **Metcalfe**, Chas H '85 %MHLS -44 Hawley -Bnghmtn 13901 **Fx**:721-8447
(718) 855-9000 .. **Metcalfe**, David T '84 (Cullen and D LLP) -177 Montague -Brklyn 11201
(516) 357-3700 .. **Metcalfe**, David T '84 (Cullen and D LLP) -100 Q Roosevelt Blvd Gdn Cty 11530
(718) 296-5126 .. **Metellus**, Sonia '96 -8613 75th -Woodhvn 11421
(212) 336-8000 .. **Metelski**, Marion P '03 SrCnsl Amster R&E -90 Park Av -NY 10016
(212) 858-4000 .. **Meth**, Elissa M '01 FINRA -1 Lbrty Plz -NY 10006 **Fx**:858-4389
(917) 597-5647 .. **Meth**, Israel Z '06 -44 Bennett Av -NY 10033
(212) 454-6913 .. **Meth**, Stephanie K '79 Deutsche Bank AG -280 Park Av -NY 10017
(845) 783-3728 .. **Meth**, Warren E '75 -28 Peter Bush Dr -Monroe 10950
(212) 947-1999 .. **Methfessel & Werbel,PC** -450 7th Av -NY 10123 **Fx**:947-3332
(914) 288-9700 .. **Metis**, Peter '96 (Schnaufer & M,LLP) -280 N Central Av -Hartsdale 10530 **Fx**:288-9717
(212) 548-2100 .. **Metjahic**, Safet '05 %McGuire W LLP -1345 Av of Amer -NY 10105
(516) 294-8844 .. **Metli**, Richd '75 OfCnsl L'Abbate BC&C,LLP -1001 Franklin Av -Gdn Cty 11530
(845) 586-2070 .. **Metnick**, Dennis '87 -835 Main Bx1011 -Margaretvll 12455 **Fx**:586-2815
(212) 902-0441 .. **Metrailler**, Edouard W '05 Goldman Sachs & Co -85 Broad -NY 10004
(914) 965-4221 .. **Metrena**, Silvia M '04 -20 S Bway -Ynkrs 10701
(914) 694-9500 .. **Metrick**, Allan S '73 OfCnsl Trokie L LLP -1133 Wstchstr Av -White Plns 10604
(718) 262-3673 .. **Mets**, Denis E '88 %Admin Children's Srvcs -89-14 Parsons Blvd -Jamaica 11432
(212) 848-4000 .. **Metsch**, Richd H '84 Cnsl Shearman & S LLP -599 Lex Av -NY 10022
(212) 584-5241 .. **Metsch**, Seth A '99 %Sirius Satellite Radio -1221 Av of Amer -NY 10020 **Fx**:584-5353
(212) 753-7500 .. **Metsch**, Victor M '69 (Hartman & C LLP) -488 Mad Av -NY 10022
(212) 966-6420 .. **Metsch-Ampel**, Glenn '89 %Lwyrs For Children -110 Lafayette -NY 10013 **Fx**:966-0531
(716) 204-9001 .. **Metschl**, Danl R '82 (DiNardo & M,PC) -2813 Wehrle Dr -Williamsvll 14221
(212) 679-1166 .. **Metselaar**, Paul A '83 The Lawyers' Travel Srvc -71 5th Av -NY 10003 **Fx**:329-7373
(212) 310-8000 .. **Mette**, Danl J '84 (Weil G&M LLP) -767 5th Av -NY 10153
(718) 331-7700 .. **Mettlach**, Justin L '09 %Frekhtman & Assoc -60 Bay 26th -Brklyn 11214

(585) 295-4400 .. **Mettler,** Danielle E '07 %Hiscock & B,LLP -2000 HSBC Plz -Rchstr 14604
(914) 242-1778 .. **Mettler,** Jeanne E '78 -20 Woodsbrdg Rd -Katonah 10536 **Fx:**242-2004
(518) 329-2006 .. **Mettler,** Jeanne E '78 -1647 Church Bx6 -Copake 12516 **Fx:**329-0700
(212) 697-3122 .. **Mettu,** Nithin R '09 %Martin C&B LLP -220 E 42nd -NY 10017
(718) 739-4444 .. **Metu,** Chijioke '07 Placid & E PC -161-10 Jamaica Av -Jamaica 11432 **Fx:**739-4440
(212) 684-1111 .. **Metz,** Alfred N '82 (Deutsch M&D,LLP) -18 East 41st -NY 10017
(212) 825-0365 .. **Metz,** Jeffrey R '80 (AL Bailey,PC) -120 Bway -NY 10271 **Fx:**825-0999
(212) 338-6405 .. **Metz,** Jeremy '83 %Verizon -12 Hall Av -Goldens Bridge 10526
(718) 899-8479 .. **Metz,** Martin M '73 -80-15 41st Av -Elmhrst 11373
(914) 243-5563 .. **Metz,** Matthew P '87 -3535 Hill Blvd -Yorktwn Hts 10598 **Fx:**243-0296
(718) 286-6000 .. **Metz,** Shlomit L '99 %DA -125-01 Qns Blvd -Kew Gdns 11415
(914) 243-5563 .. **Metz,** Susan L '89 -3535 Hill Blvd -Yorktwn Hts 10598
(212) 259-8000 .. **Metzger,** Amy J '05 %Dewey & L LLP -1301 Av of Amer -NY 10019
(646) 471-4000 .. **Metzger,** Avram S '87 %PricewaterhouseCoopers LLP -300 Mad Av -NY 10017
(914) 457-2300 .. **Metzger,** David L '95 (Kanterman & S,LLP) -50 Main -White Plns 10606
(212) 454-2777 .. **Metzger,** Elisa D '07 Deutsche Asset Mgmt -345 Park Av -NY 10154
(212) 758-5400 .. **Metzger,** Ellen '81 %MacKayShields LLC -9 W 57th -NY 10019
(212) 854-2675 .. **Metzger,** Gillian E '97 %Columbia Law Schl -435 W 116th -NY 10027 **Fx:**854-7946
(212) 681-6500 .. **Metzger,** Jordan J '84 (Stempel BC&H,PC) -675 3rd Av -NY 10017
(212) 506-5000 .. **Metzger,** Laura D '04 %Orrick H&S LLP -51 W 52nd -NY 10019
(914) 640-6811 .. **Metzger,** Margot J '90 Starwood Hotels & Resorts -1111 Wstchstr Av -White Plns 10604 **Fx:**640-8250
(845) 473-7000 .. **Metzger,** Mark J '81 (Goldstein & M,LLP) -40 Grdn -Poughkeepsie 12601
(516) 374-1741 .. **Metzger,** Melvin '51 -2 Ivy Ln -Lawrence 11559 **Fx:**374-0945
(212) 783-4384 .. **Metzger,** Michl J '07 Citigroup -485 Lex Av -NY 10017
(212) 732-2000 .. **Metzger,** Peter '83 (Cullen and D LLP) -44 Wall -NY 10005
(212) 683-7100 .. **Metzger,** Ronni P '84 OfCnsl Gallo V&K,LLP -90 Broad -NY 10004
(718) 601-7960 .. **Metzger,** Sania A '92 -3226 Tibbett Av -Bronx 10463
(212) 775-6680 .. **Metzger,** Steve H '06 2 Sigma Invstmnts,LLC -379 W Bway -NY 10012
(646) 473-6039 .. **Metzger,** Suzanne A '04 SEIU Natl Benefit Fund -330 W 42nd -NY 10036
(212) 980-4200 .. **Metzger,** Theo J '79 (Levy HP&D,LLP) -950 3rd Av -NY 10022
(646) 351-5562 .. **Metzger,** Wendy J '99 Yahoo! Inc -45 W 18th -NY 10011
(212) 808-7800 .. **Metzinger,** Jaclyn M '09 %Kelley D&W LLP -101 Park Av -NY 10178
(212) 446-4800 .. **Metzl,** Alexandra Fidler '09 %Kirkland & E LLP -153 E 53rd -NY 10022
(212) 514-9190 .. **Metzler,** Alison D '92 (Downing & P,PC) -17 Battery Pl -NY 10004
(212) 944-7722 .. **Metzler,** Arthur A '95 AMA Cnsltng Engnrs,PC -250 W 39th -NY 10018 **Fx:**944-2363
(585) 343-3090 .. **Metzler,** David L '72 (Rybak M&G,LLP) -104 Bank -Batavia 14020
(585) 232-3730 .. **Metzler,** Eric J '88 (Chamberlain D LLP) -1600 Crssrds Bldg -Rchstr 14614
(585) 232-5300 .. **Metzler,** James E '84 (Boylan BCV&W,LLP) -2400 Chase Sq -Rchstr 14604
(212) 803-3222 .. **Metzler,** Jeffrey P '03 Empire State Development Corp -633 3rd Av -NY 10017
(585) 428-4549 .. **Metzler,** Paula Casey '94 OCA -545 Hall of Justice -Rchstr 14614 **Fx:**428-2990
(212) 859-8000 .. **Meuller,** Markus '09 %Fried FHS&J LLP -1 NY Plz -NY 10004
(518) 474-7668 .. **Meunier,** Lydia Hoffman '01 %Insurance Dept -99 Wshngtn Av -Albany 12257 **Fx:**473-4600
(315) 476-6487 .. **Mevec & Cognetti** -206 N Townsend -Syracuse 13203 **Fx:**476-6618
(315) 476-6487 .. **Mevec,** Danny Louis '92 (Mevec & C) -206 N Townsend -Syracuse 13203
(212) 239-5714 .. **Mevec,** Edw R '90 NYS Div of Parole -314 W 40th -NY 10018
(212) 683-7100 .. **Mevorach,** Danl P '07 %Gallo V&K,LLP -90 Broad -NY 10004
(516) 295-7655 .. **Mevorach,** Jack '89 -132 Spruce -Cedarhrst 11516 **Fx:**295-7656
(516) 487-0175 .. **Mevorach,** Lisa T '05 %E Schwartz -343 Grt Nck Rd -Gt Neck 11021 **Fx:**773-7706
(516) 747-0720 .. **Mevorah,** Victor '83 (V Mevorah,PC) -100 Grdn City Plz -Gdn Cty 11530 **Fx:**742-4106
(212) 308-0210 .. **Mevs,** Patrick P '06 %C Kutner,LLP -110 E 59th -NY 10022 **Fx:**308-0213
(212) 808-8300 .. **Meyenschein,** Heiko P '92 SrCnsl Rosensteel Law -90 Park Av -NY 10016
(212) 861-0879 .. **Meyer,** Alfred A '61 -138 E 78th -NY 10075
(212) 325-2000 .. **Meyer,** Allen '89 Credit Suisse -1 Mad Av -NY 10010
(212) 218-5500 .. **Meyer,** Allison E '08 Seyfarth S LLP -620 8th Av -NY 10018
(212) 909-6000 .. **Meyer,** Anne C '99 Cnsl Debevoise & P LLP -919 3rd Av -NY 10022
(212) 247-5153 .. **Meyer,** Brian A '87 -350 Park Av -NY 10022
(631) 293-5000 .. **Meyer,** Bruce A '75 -1200 Vets Hwy -Hauppauge 11788 **Fx:**234-4272
(212) 310-8000 .. **Meyer,** Bruce S '87 (Weil G&M LLP) -767 5th Av -NY 10153
(212) 431-2194 .. **Meyer,** Carlin '75 %NY Law Schl -185 W Bway -NY 10013 **Fx:**431-1864
(212) 417-7156 .. **Meyer,** Carol A '80 Brookfield Properties Mgmt,LLC -200 Vesey -NY 10285
(631) 265-0010 .. **Meyer,** Caryn L '02 %Cohen & W,PC -80 Maple Av Bx768 -Smithtwn 11787
(518) 465-2488 .. **Meyer,** Christopher P '86 %E Ryan -38 Eagle -Albany 12207 **Fx:**465-6612
(518) 487-7600 .. **Meyer,** Christopher W '05 %Whiteman O&H LLP -1 Commerce Plz -Albany 12260
(212) 541-1873 .. **Meyer,** Cynthia B '91 %AXA Advisors,LLC -1633 Bway -NY 10019
(212) 310-8000 .. **Meyer,** Damon P '06 %Weil G&M LLP -767 5th Av -NY 10153
(212) 446-4800 .. **Meyer,** David S '08 %Kirkland & E LLP -153 E 53rd -NY 10022
(212) 430-8020 .. **Meyer,** Deborah I '99 Cnsl LeClairRyan,PC -830 3rd Av -NY 10022
(845) 343-0839 .. **Meyer & Diesenhouse** -Dolsontown Rd Bx2106 -Middletwn 10940 **Fx:**344-8349
(518) 562-0803 .. **Meyer,** Edw D '93 -Bx3021 -Plattsbrgh 12901 **Fx:**562-0878
(845) 343-0839 .. **Meyer,** Edw J '64 (Meyer & D) -Dolsontown Rd Bx2106 -Middletwn 10940
(212) 909-6000 .. **Meyer,** Eric D '04 %Debevoise & P LLP -919 3rd Av -NY 10022
(212) 668-2700 .. **Meyer,** Franklin N '70 (FN Meyer,PC) -61 Bway -NY 10006
(631) 728-8775 .. **Meyer,** Fredk C '75 -10 Sagamore Rd -Hampton Bays 11946 **Fx:**728-7383
(631) 694-2929 .. **Meyer,** Henry T III '77 SrCnsl Fonar Corp -110 Marcus Dr -Melvll 11747 **Fx:**753-5150
(212) 223-4000 .. **Meyer,** Herbert I '77 SrCnsl Crowell & M LLP -590 Mad Av -NY 10022
(212) 809-8585 .. **Meyer,** Hilary '06 Lambda Legal -120 Wall -NY 10005
(631) 853-5212 .. **Meyer,** Holly C '03 %Leg Aid -400 Carleton Av Bx9082 -Central Islip 11722 **Fx:**853-7798
(845) 735-9400 .. **Meyer,** Irwin S '66 -Bx1606 -Pearl Rvr 10965 **Fx:**735-8908
(212) 661-3900 .. **Meyer,** J Edw '63 -230 Park Av -NY 10169 **Fx:**661-2153
(212) 751-4300 .. **Meyer,** Jacqueline I '85 (Hodgson R LLP) -1540 Bway -NY 10036
(914) 238-2860 .. **Meyer,** James T '89 (Meyer & S LLP) -27 S Greeley Av -Chappaqua 10514 **Fx:**238-2833
(201) 862-9500 .. **Meyer,** Jan '95 -50 E 42nd -NY 10017 **Fx:**862-9400
(212) 768-6700 .. **Meyer,** Jane A '94 (Sonnenschein N&R LLP) -2 World Fncl Ctr -NY 10281
(212) 259-8000 .. **Meyer,** Janis M '82 (Dewey & L LLP) -1301 Av of Amer -NY 10019
(212) 455-2000 .. **Meyer,** Jayma M '79 Cnsl Simpson T&B LLP -425 Lex Av -NY 10017
(516) 681-1100 .. **Meyer,** Jeffery A '05 %Kaufman DV&G,LLP -135 Crsswys Park Dr -Woodbury 11797
(518) 745-1400 .. **Meyer,** Jeffrey R '05 %FitzGerald MBF -16 Pearl Bx2017 -Glens Fls 12801
(212) 208-3543 .. **Meyer,** Jennifer Anne '96 Ambac Assurance Corp -1 State Street Plz -NY 10004
(212) 479-6724 .. **Meyer,** Jennifer C '01 %Macht SA&I LLP -1114 Av of Amer -NY 10036 **Fx:**202-6417
(866) 353-3310 .. **Meyer,** Josh J '97 SrCnsl Pannone LD&W LLC -81 Main -White Plns 10606
(518) 561-4400 .. **Meyer,** Justin R '07 %Stafford OC&T,PLLC -1 Cumberland Av Bx2947 -Plattsbrgh 12901
(212) 523-2162 .. **Meyer,** Kathryn C '74 %Beth Israel Med Ctr -555 W 57th -NY 10019
(212) 373-3000 .. **Meyer,** Kenneth B '09 %Paul WRW&G LLP -1285 Av of Amer -NY 10019
(212) 265-6888 .. **Meyer,** Kenneth R '89 (Porzio B&N,PC) -156 W 56th -NY 10019
(516) 222-2333 .. **Meyer,** Lance H '06 %Barbara Law Firm -401 Franklin Av -Gdn Cty 11530 **Fx:**222-2935
(212) 349-9100 .. **Meyer,** Lisa E '90 -41 Mad Av -NY 10010 **Fx:**(866) 655-8465
(212) 953-6000 .. **Meyer,** Lori Kathleen '02 %Katsky K LLP -605 3rd Av -NY 10158
(212) 471-8453 .. **Meyer,** Mark A '72 (Herzfeld & R,PC) -125 Broad -NY 10004
(315) 422-9538 .. **Meyer,** Mary C '00 CNY Cmmnty Fndtn,Inc -500 S Salina -Syracuse 13202 **Fx:**471-6031
(518) 471-4813 .. **Meyer,** Matthew J '06 Appllt Div 3rd Dept -Capitol Station Bx7288 -Albany 12224 **Fx:**471-4750
(631) 242-5006 .. **Meyer,** Melvin P '68 -24 Sarah Dr -Huntngtn Sta 11746 **Fx:**667-5792
(631) 265-4500 .. **Meyer Meyer & Keneally** -28 Manor Rd -Smithtwn 11787 **Fx:**265-4560
(718) 935-1781 .. **Meyer,** Monique '92 -175 Adams -Brklyn 11201 **Fx:**935-1781
(212) 902-0860 .. **Meyer,** Patricia J '00 Goldman Sachs -1 NY Plz -NY 10004
(212) 878-8176 .. **Meyer,** Paul C '79 (Clifford C LLP) -31 W 52nd -NY 10019
(585) 546-2350 .. **Meyer,** Paul E '84 (Biernbaum & M LLP) -19 W Main -Rchstr 14614
(914) 961-3000 .. **Meyer,** Paul W Jr. '83 -35 E Grassy Sprain Rd -Ynkrs 10710 **Fx:**961-4993
(212) 515-2800 .. **Meyer,** Rachel '00 Hedgeop Compliance -3 Park Av -NY 10016
(585) 243-1010 .. **Meyer,** Randolph A '74 -29 Main -Geneseo 14454 **Fx:**243-4833
(516) 684-2900 .. **Meyer,** Rhonda L '89 %Pegalis & E,LLC -1 Hllw Ln -Lk Success 11042
(212) 885-5000 .. **Meyer,** Richd S '01 (Blank R LLP) -405 Lex Av -NY 10174
(518) 285-8692 .. **Meyer,** Robt J '82 %Family Ct -30 Clinton -Albany 12207
(973) 290-2323 .. **Meyer,** Robt O '86 VanBeuren Mgmt,Inc -650 Mad Av -NY 10022 **Fx:**993-5780
(718) 254-7000 .. **Meyer,** Stephen J '03 US Atty -271 Cadman Plz E -Brklyn 11201 **Fx:**254-6479
(212) 415-8600 .. **Meyer,** Steven F '90 (Locke LB&L LLP) -3 World Fncl Ctr -NY 10281
(212) 757-1905 .. **Meyer,** Stuart S '91 -530 5th Av -NY 10036 **Fx:**944-7630
(212) 239-4999 .. **Meyer Suozzi English & Klein,PC** -1350 Bway Bx822 -NY 10018 **Fx:**239-1311
(516) 741-6565 .. **Meyer Suozzi English & Klein,PC** -990 Stewart Av Bx9194 -Gdn Cty 11530 **Fx:**741-6706
(518) 465-5551 .. **Meyer Suozzi English & Klein,PC** -One Commerce Plz -Albany 12260 **Fx:**465-2033
(631) 249-6565 .. **Meyer Suozzi English & Klein,PC** -425 Broadhllw Rd Bx9064 -Melvll 11747 **Fx:**777-6906
(716) 851-2711 .. **Meyer,** Susan J '90 %UIA Bd -290 Main -Buffalo 14202 **Fx:**851-2795
(212) 696-6000 .. **Meyer,** Tammy L '03 %Curtis M-PC&M LLP -101 Park Av -NY 10178
(631) 265-4500 .. **Meyer,** Terence X '82 (Meyer M&K) -28 Manor Rd -Smithtwn 11787
(212) 474-1000 .. **Meyer,** Timothy C '10 Cravath S&M LLP -825 8th Av -NY 10019
(516) 227-0700 .. **Meyer,** Willets S '94 (Farrell F,PC) -1320 RXR Plz -Uniondale 11556
(716) 832-1118 .. **Meyer,** Wm C '96 %N Saia -1925 Kensngtn Av -Buffalo 14215 **Fx:**832-7074
(212) 768-6700 .. **Meyerhoff,** Gary '94 (Sonnenschein N&R LLP) -1221 Av of Amer -NY 10020
(212) 415-3759 .. **Meyerowitz,** Eric P '96 Omnicom Group -437 Mad Av -NY 10022 **Fx:**415-3530
(212) 686-7008 .. **Meyerowitz,** Ira Scot '96 (Meyerowitz J,PLLC) -295 Mad Av -NY 10017 **Fx:**542-8883
(212) 225-2000 .. **Meyers,** Aaron J '09 %Cleary GS&H -1 Lbrty Plz -NY 10006
(518) 464-1300 .. **Meyers,** Adam W '03 %Roemer WG&M LLP -13 Columbia Cir -Albany 12203
(212) 252-1212 .. **Meyers,** Allan S '58 (Meyers Law Firm PLLC) -1123 Bway -NY 10010
(516) 487-8131 .. **Meyers,** Barbara '90 -32 Vndrblt Dr -Gt Neck 11020

(212) 226-4106 .. **Meyers,** Danl L '67 -299 Bway -NY 10007 **Fx:**431-0107
(212) 508-6100 .. **Meyers,** Danl S '04 %Bracewell & G,LLP -1251 Av of Amer -NY 10020
(518) 465-0400 .. **Meyers,** Danielle N '06 %O'Connor OB&F,PC -20 Corp Wds Blvd -Albany 12211
(518) 464-9075 .. **Meyers,** David W '97 (Meyers & M,LLP) -1734 Wstrn Av -Albany 12203 **Fx:**464-9078
(212) 708-1448 .. **Meyers,** Deborah L '92 %Showtime Networks Inc -1633 Bway -NY 10019 **Fx:**654-4719
(212) 373-3000 .. **Meyers,** Diane '92 Cnsl Paul WRW&G LLP -1285 Av of Amer -NY 10019
(212) 230-8800 .. **Meyers,** Emily M '08 %WilmerHale -399 Park Av -NY 10022
(315) 703-6600 .. **Meyers,** Gigi E '07 Leg Aid -472 S Salina -Syracuse 13202 **Fx:**671-0062
(212) 252-1212 .. **Meyers,** Glenn R '97 (Meyers Law Firm PLLC) -1123 Bway -NY 10010
(212) 509-2500 .. **Meyers,** Howard G Jr. '67 (Meyers M&T) -5 Hanover Sq -NY 10004 **Fx:**509-2424
(212) 509-2500 .. **Meyers,** Howard G III '93 (Meyers M&T) -5 Hanover Sq -NY 10004 **Fx:**509-2424
(212) 431-2338 .. **Meyers,** Howard S '95 (NY Law Schl) -185 W Bway -NY 10013 **Fx:**431-1830
(718) 339-3330 .. **Meyers,** Irwin '70 (Meyers S&C) -3620 Quentin Rd -Brklyn 11234
(718) 273-2525 .. **Meyers,** Jay A '91 -1688 Victory Blvd -Staten Isl 10314
(518) 486-2921 .. **Meyers,** Jeffrey A '96 %OPRHP -Agncy Bldg 1 ESP -Albany 12238 **Fx:**474-5106
(212) 806-5400 .. **Meyers,** Jeffrey W '80 (Stroock &S&L LLP) -180 Maiden Ln -NY 10038
(212) 366-8900 .. **Meyers,** Jonathan E '03 Forbes.com -90 5th Av -NY 10011
(845) 724-2278 .. **Meyers,** Jonathan P '92 %Active Intl -1 Blue Hill Plz Bx1705 -Pearl Rvr 10965
(212) 736-0600 .. **Meyers,** Jos L '86 -224 W 30th -NY 10001
(212) 258-4000 .. **Meyers,** Kenneth R '88 %Siemens Corp -153 E 53rd -NY 10022 **Fx:**767-0580
(212) 267-3091 .. **Meyers,** Laurie E '91 (Wilentz G&S) -110 William -NY 10038 **Fx:**(732) 726-6597
(716) 854-2907 .. **Meyers,** Lisa P '84 %Chicago Title Ins -424 Main -Buffalo 14202 **Fx:**852-7346
(212) 218-5500 .. **Meyers,** Lori M '83 OfCnsl Seyfarth S LLP -620 8th Av -NY 10018
(212) 735-3000 .. **Meyers,** Lucas V '09 %Skadden ASM&F LLP -4 Times Sq -NY 10036
(212) 859-8000 .. **Meyers,** Melanie E '88 (Fried FHS&J LLP) -1 NY Plz -NY 10004
(212) 521-5400 .. **Meyers,** Michl A '64 (Reed S LLP) -599 Lex Av -NY 10022
(212) 506-5000 .. **Meyers,** Michl R '99 (Orrick H&S LLP) -51 W 52nd -NY 10019
(212) 406-1500 .. **Meyers,** Milton L '71 -305 Bway -NY 10007
(212) 859-8000 .. **Meyers,** Mindy P '06 %Fried FHS&J LLP -1 NY Plz -NY 10004
(631) 784-7722 .. **Meyers,** Natasha '03 (N Meyers,PC) -55 Elm -Huntngtn 11743 **Fx:**784-5154
(518) 464-9075 .. **Meyers,** Richd M '60 (Meyers & M,LLP) -1734 Wstrn Av -Albany 12203 **Fx:**464-9078
(631) 969-7777 .. **Meyers,** Robt I '03 %Frenkel LWW&G,LLP -20 W Main -Bay Shr 11706 **Fx:**206-0540
(718) 225-5505 .. **Meyers,** Robt S '88 -46-40 Sprngfld Blvd -Bayside 11361 **Fx:**225-2164
(845) 727-4000 .. **Meyers,** Ron L '00 %B Cane -50 Piermont Av -Nyack 10960 **Fx:**727-4023
(212) 481-3780 .. **Meyers,** Sara E '96 Sadin Law Inst -425 E 25th -NY 10010 **Fx:**481-3791
(718) 339-3330 .. **Meyers Saxon & Cole** -3620 Quentin Rd -Brklyn 11234
(516) 572-2381 .. **Meyers,** Stephanie S '78 Nassau Cnty Dist Ct-Law Dept -99 Main -Hempstd 11550
(212) 422-1500 .. **Meyers Tersigni Feldman & Gray LLP** -14 Wall -NY 10005 **Fx:**422-1650
(518) 828-9444 .. **Meyers,** Victor M '69 (Rapport MWS&R,LLP) -436 Union -Hudson 12534
(212) 366-5125 .. **Meyers,** Wm V '90 -460 W 24th -NY 10011 **Fx:**929-4050
(716) 853-2888 .. **Meyers-Buth,** Cheryl '94 %T Burton -716 Brisbane Bldg -Buffalo 14203 **Fx:**853-2892
(212) 578-0494 .. **Meyers Moss,** Beth R '00 MetLife -1 MetLife Plz -LIC 11101
(212) 728-8000 .. **Meyerson,** Andrew R '10 %Willkie F&G LLP -787 7th Av -NY 10019
(212) 505-8400 .. **Meyerson,** Barry A '96 B Meyerson,PC -200 Park Av S -NY 10003 **Fx:**505-6690
(516) 354-1570 .. **Meyerson,** Brian J '94 (Meyerson & L,LLP) -1040 Hempstd Tpk -Franklin Sq 11010 **Fx:**358-9673
(212) 878-5132 .. **Meyerson,** Bruce '80 (Goulston & S,PC) -750 3rd Av -NY 10017 **Fx:**878-5532
(518) 785-7440 .. **Meyerson,** Craig A '99 -17 British Amer Blvd -Latham 12110 **Fx:**786-6446
(646) 674-2044 .. **Meyerson,** Howard L '90 %Liquidnet -498 7th Av -NY 10018
(212) 226-3310 .. **Meyerson,** James I '71 -64 Fulton -NY 10038
(212) 455-2000 .. **Meyerson,** Lee '82 (Simpson T&B LLP) -425 Lex Av -NY 10017
(516) 354-1570 .. **Meyerson,** Marvin I '60 (Meyerson & L,LLP) -1040 Hempstd Tpk -Franklin Sq 11010 **Fx:**358-9673
(718) 745-0880 .. **Meyerson,** Michl C '89 (Bisogno & M) -7018 Ft Hmltn Pkwy -Brklyn 11228 **Fx:**680-3891
(718) 579-3034 .. **Meyerson,** Richd A '84 %Leg Aid -1020 Grnd Cncrs -Bronx 10451 **Fx:**588-3375
(212) 697-5200 .. **Meyerson,** Stanley F '85 Sands Bros & Co -90 Park Av -NY 10016
(631) 390-7150 .. **Meyland,** Sarah J '92 %Citizen Cmpgn -225A Main -Farmngdl 11735 **Fx:**390-7160
(212) 686-3300 .. **Meyrowitz,** David H '71 (Simon M&M,PC) -470 Park Av S -NY 10016
(212) 310-8000 .. **Meyrowitz,** Melissa A '99 %Weil G&M LLP -767 5th Av -NY 10153
(212) 859-8000 .. **Meza,** Catherine '07 %Fried FHS&J LLP -1 NY Plz -NY 10004
(212) 371-7771 .. **Mezan,** Richd S '73 -488 Mad Av -NY 10022 **Fx:**836-4979
(914) 524-2722 .. **Mezey,** Laura '89 Bayer HealthCare,LLC -511 Benedict Av -Tarrytwn 10591
(212) 909-6000 .. **Mezhburd,** Serge '03 %Debevoise & P LLP -919 3rd Av -NY 10022
(212) 735-3000 .. **Mezo,** Alberto Abraham '10 %Skadden ASM&F LLP -4 Times Sq -NY 10036
(518) 473-7322 .. **Mezoff,** Arieh '89 %OTDA -40 N Pearl -Albany 12243 **Fx:**474-9389
(718) 627-9100 .. **Mezrahi,** Jos I '71 -449 Quentin Rd -Brklyn 11223
(212) 804-4200 .. **Mezzacappa,** John '79 (Mound CW&G) -One Bttry Pk Plz -NY 10004
(212) 756-2000 .. **Mezzacappa,** Michl M '99 (Schulte R&Z LLP) -919 3rd Av -NY 10022
(914) 741-6100 .. **Mezzacappa,** Michl P '89 (Kaufman B&R) -200 Summit Lk Dr -Valhalla 10595
(718) 520-4737 .. **Mezzina,** Maryjean '81 %Supreme Ct Criminal -125-01 Qns Blvd -Kew Gdns 11415
(718) 444-0213 .. **Mgbada,** Perpetua N '95 -1151 E 101st -Brklyn 11236
(212) 636-6000 .. **Mgbako,** Chito A '08 %Fordham Univ Sch of Law -140 W 62nd -NY 10023 **Fx:**636-6899
(212) 373-3000 .. **Mi,** Frances Fang-Yi '96 Cnsl Paul WRW&G LLP -1285 Av of Amer -NY 10019
(212) 776-5000 .. **Mialkowski,** Meredith G '05 %NYC Housing Auth -250 Bway -NY 10007 **Fx:**776-5039
(212) 297-5800 .. **Miani,** Jennifer M '96 %Day P LLP -7 Times Sq -NY 10036
(914) 328-1844 .. **Miano & Colangelo, LLP** -550 Mamaroneck Av -Harrison 10528 **Fx:**328-7243
(914) 328-1844 .. **Miano,** Jos R '79 (Miano & C,LLP) -550 Mamaroneck Av -Harrison 10528
(212) 323-0200 .. **Miao,** Wei Wayne '00 OppenheimerFunds,Inc -225 Lbrty -NY 10281
(212) 355-9500 .. **Miarmi,** Michl J '06 %Lieff CH&B,LLP -250 Hudson -NY 10013
(212) 809-7800 .. **Miasnikova,** Natalja '08 %Jaffe & K,LLP -40 Wall -NY 10005
(212) 245-1000 .. **Miazad,** Ossai '05 %Outten & G LLP -3 Park Av -NY 10016
(716) 856-1536 .. **Mical,** Alison L '00 %D Seeger -69 Delaware Av -Buffalo 14202 **Fx:**856-1408
(607) 723-9511 .. **Micale,** Emily C '08 %Coughlin & G,LLP -19 Chenango Bx2039 -Bnghmtn 13902
(212) 446-4800 .. **Micallef,** Ryan '07 %Kirkland & E LLP -153 E 53rd -NY 10022
(212) 909-6000 .. **Micarelli,** Carl J '92 Cnsl Debevoise & P LLP -919 3rd Av -NY 10022
(585) 899-6031 .. **Micca,** Louis J '89 -11 State -Pittsfrd 14534
(518) 442-3887 .. **Miccio,** G Kristian '86 %CWIG Rckflr Cllg SUNY -135 Wstrn Av Draper Hall -Albany 12222
(914) 834-3500 .. **Micek,** Patricia G '78 (McMillan CM&P LLP) -2180 Bstn Post Rd -Larchmnt 10538
(914) 989-6650 .. **Miceli,** Diane '87 (Eustace & M) -1133 Wstchstr Av -White Plns 10604
(585) 637-8155 .. **Miceli,** James S '78 -24 Union -Brockprt 14420 **Fx:**637-8156
(716) 677-3560 .. **Miceli,** Patricia W '99 %West Seneca Central Schools -1415 Ctr Rd -W Seneca 14224
(212) 885-8007 .. **Mich,** Brian J '86 BDO Seidman,LLP -330 Mad Av -NY 10017
(718) 391-6037 .. **Micha,** Emil T III '93 Dept of Ed -2811 Qns Plz -LIC 11101
(212) 318-6000 .. **Michael,** Anthony N '02 %Paul HJ&W LLP -75 E 55th -NY 10022
(212) 801-3760 .. **Michael,** Bernard J '85 (Michael L&R LLP) -60 Columbus Cir -NY 10023
(212) 668-1900 .. **Michael,** Chas A '04 %Brune & R LLP -80 Broad -NY 10004
(212) 301-4081 .. **Michael,** Evan A '03 National Fncl Prtnrs -340 Mad Av -NY 10173
(718) 286-6000 .. **Michael,** Jennifer S '05 DA -125-01 Qns Blvd -Kew Gdns 11415
(212) 247-0848 .. **Michael,** Jill A '90 (Bienstock & M,PC) -250 W 57th -NY 10107
(212) 735-3000 .. **Michael,** Justin M '04 %Skadden ASM&F LLP -4 Times Sq -NY 10036
(212) 557-7700 .. **Michael,** Kelly M '03 %Davidson D&C LLP -60 E 42nd -NY 10165
(212) 819-8200 .. **Michael,** Kevin C '09 %White & C LLP -1155 Av of Amer -NY 10036
(212) 847-7900 .. **Michael,** Kim L '03 %Wechsler & C,LLP -17 State -NY 10004
(518) 828-6113 .. **Michael,** Leann L '07 -118 Green -Hudson 12534
(212) 801-3760 .. **Michael Levitt & Rubenstein LLP** -60 Columbus Cir -NY 10023 **Fx:**801-3762
(718) 380-1122 .. **Michael,** Lisa '04 (Levi & M,LLP) -15916 Union Tpk -Fresh Mdws 11366 **Fx:**380-1124
(718) 590-8932 .. **Michael,** Marsha D '03 Hon T Webber -851 Grnd Cncrs -Bronx 10451
(212) 768-6700 .. **Michael,** Martin P '75 (Sonnenschein N&R LLP) -1221 Av of Amer -NY 10020
(718) 339-1400 .. **Michael,** Michl H '93 (Michael & S,LLC) -2226 Ocean Av -Brklyn 11229
(212) 704-6318 .. **Michael,** Philip R '73 OfCnsl Troutman S LLP -405 Lex Av -NY 10174 **Fx:**704-5996
(212) 278-0400 .. **Michael,** Rakesh J '09 %Cooper & D LLP -30 Rckfllr Plz -NY 10112
(212) 758-4606 .. **Michael,** Robt E '75 (R Michael & Assoc,PLLC) -950 3rd Av -NY 10022 **Fx:**319-8922
(914) 592-8784 .. **Michael,** Roberta L '97 -45 Knollwood Rd -Elmsfrd 10523
(212) 878-8000 .. **Michael,** Sheelyn Marker '00 %Clifford C LLP -31 W 52nd -NY 10019
(212) 524-5000 .. **Michael,** Wendy '94 Cnsl Jacob M&F -1270 Av of Amer -NY 10020
(212) 373-3000 .. **Michael,** Wm B '05 %Paul WRW&G LLP -1285 Av of Amer -NY 10019
(212) 412-9500 .. **Michaeli,** David R '10 %Flemming ZWZ LLP -1 Lbrty Plz -NY 10006
(212) 403-1000 .. **Michaelis,** Carrie Z '05 %Wachtell LR&K -51 W 52nd -NY 10019
(212) 808-2700 .. **Michaels,** Adam B '03 OfCnsl Pepper H LLP -620 8th Av -NY 10018
(518) 474-6530 .. **Michaels,** Alan T '98 %Dept Pub Srvc -3 ESP -Albany 12223
(315) 474-7808 .. **Michaels,** Beverly A '53 (Michaels & M) -902 State Twr Bldg -Syracuse 13202
(607) 256-2000 .. **Michaels,** Christopher A '94 (Brown & M,PC) -118 N Tioga -Ithaca 14850
(212) 878-8000 .. **Michaels,** Danl '08 %Clifford C LLP -31 W 52nd -NY 10019
(518) 392-9150 .. **Michaels,** David Seth '81 -Route 203 at Beale Rd Bx96 -Spencertown 12165 **Fx:**392-9130
(845) 348-0001 .. **Michaels,** Dennis D '92 -3 Main -Nyack 10960 **Fx:**675-3131
(315) 474-7808 .. **Michaels,** Edw A '88 (Michaels & M) -902 State Twr Bldg -Syracuse 13202
(516) 741-1130 .. **Michaels,** Elene '08 %Herman KC&C,LLP -400 Grdn City Plz -Gdn Cty 11530
(973) 992-4800 .. **Michaels,** Eric J '83 (Fox R LLP) -100 Park Av -NY 10017 **Fx:**992-9125
(518) 562-3291 .. **Michaels,** Glen F '01 %Dept of Law -43 Durkee -Plattsbrgh 12901 **Fx:**562-3294
(516) 295-4886 .. **Michaels,** Harold '61 -Bx386 -Woodmere 11598

(718) 585-6551 .. **Michaels,** Jonathan O '96 Pena & K,PLLC -1200 Waters Pl -Bronx 10461 **Fx:**585-6618
(212) 682-8811 .. **Michaels,** Jos IV '71 (Dunnington B&M LLP) -1359 Bway -NY 10018
(212) 635-3150 .. **Michaels,** Kenneth '94 Ofc Inspector Genl -61 Bway -NY 10006 **Fx:**809-6287
(315) 253-3293 .. **Michaels,** Lee S '67 (Michaels & S,PC) -71 South -Auburn 13021
(914) 962-1374 .. **Michaels,** Mark A '86 -1992 Commerce -Yorktwn Hts 10598
(212) 578-0910 .. **Michaels,** Matthew A '00 %MetLife -1095 Av of Amer -NY 10036 **Fx:**578-3916
(212) 318-3000 .. **Michaels,** Philip J '77 (Fulbright & J LLP) -666 5th Av -NY 10103
(212) 245-0900 .. **Michaels,** Robt S '82 -150 E 52nd -NY 10022 **Fx:**245-5459
(315) 253-3293 .. **Michaels & Smolak,PC** -71 South -Auburn 13021 **Fx:**252-6970
(212) 909-6000 .. **Michaels,** Steven S '85 Cnsl Debevoise & P LLP -919 3rd Av -NY 10022
(212) 779-7977 .. **Michaels,** Theodora K '98 Carlin America Inc -126 E 38th -NY 10016
(631) 495-6905 .. **Michaels,** Wm W Jr. '89 -425 NY Av -Huntngtn 11743
(212) 336-0031 .. **Michaelson,** Andrew Z '04 SEC -3 World Fncl Ctr -NY 10281 **Fx:**336-1323
(212) 944-0500 .. **Michaelson,** Arthur M '50 Cnsl Hofheimer G&G,LLP -530 5th Av -NY 10036 **Fx:**869-4930
(212) 816-3529 .. **Michaelson,** Dory S '03 Citigroup -388 Greenwich -NY 10013
(917) 974-9815 .. **Michaelson,** Jay M '98 Metatronics Inc -189 Canopus Hllw Rd -Putnam Vly 10579
(718) 286-2428 .. **Michaelson,** Jennifer J '89 %Leg Aid -120-46 Qns Blvd -Kew Gdns 11415 **Fx:**286-2286
(212) 918-3000 .. **Michaelson,** Martin '68 (Hogan L LLP) -875 3rd Av -NY 10022
(212) 536-3900 .. **Michaelson,** Robt '83 (K&L Gates LLP) -599 Lex Av -NY 10022
(212) 687-3860 .. **Michailidis,** Evangelos '08 %Snow BK,PC -605 3rd Av -NY 10158
(718) 725-3187 .. **Michajlo,** Susan R '99 %Admin Childrens Srvcs -15120 Jamaica Av -Jamaica 11432
(212) 319-4900 .. **Michal,** Robt P '91 %Frishauf HG&C -220 5th Av -NY 10001
(716) 633-1500 .. **Michalak & Dobson** -6225 Sheridan Dr -Williamsvll 14221 **Fx:**633-4806
(716) 679-1011 .. **Michalak,** Donald H '80 -11 E Main -Fredonia 14063 **Fx:**679-9740
(716) 633-1500 .. **Michalak,** Robt W '76 (Michalak & D) -6225 Sheridan Dr -Williamsvll 14221
(212) 530-5000 .. **Michalchuk,** Danl J '01 %Milbank TH&M LLP -1 Chase Manh Plz -NY 10005
(212) 530-5000 .. **Michalczak,** Jeffrey T '05 %Milbank TH&M LLP -1 Chase Manh Plz -NY 10005
(631) 752-2996 .. **Michalczyk,** Mildred J '84 -16 E Walnut Av -Farmngdl 11735 **Fx:**420-9604
(212) 264-6423 .. **Michalec,** Laura Ann '94 %DHS -26 Fed Plz -NY 10278
(518) 474-7330 .. **Michalec,** Ronald J '74 %Dept of Law -The Cptl -Albany 12224
(716) 826-6677 .. **Michalek,** Paul M '72 (Michalek & H) -300 Center Rd -Buffalo 14224
(716) 858-2424 .. **Michalek,** Paul M Jr. '03 %DA -25 Delaware Av -Buffalo 14202 **Fx:**858-7425
(212) 553-0300 .. **Michalek,** Richd J '94 %Moody's Invstr Srvc -250 Greenwich -NY 10007
(212) 909-6000 .. **Michalik,** Peter J '10 %Debevoise & P LLP -919 3rd Av -NY 10022
(845) 359-7700 .. **Michalos,** Peter C '78 (Notaro M&Z PC) -100 Dutch Hill Rd -Orangebrg 10962
(212) 698-3500 .. **Michalovsky,** Evan D '05 %Dechert LLP -1095 Av of Amer -NY 10036
(718) 497-1012 .. **Michalovsky,** Joel '71 -53-01 Grand Av -Maspeth 11378
(516) 822-4100 .. **Michalske,** Courtney Ann '05 %R List -109 Newbrdg Rd -Hicksvll 11801 **Fx:**822-2178
(585) 275-6740 .. **Michalski,** Jeannie D '99 Univ of Rochester -300 Crittenden Blvd -Rchstr 14642
(315) 353-7398 .. **Michaud,** Paula A '06 (Sassone & M) -40 S Main -Norwd 13668 **Fx:**353-9957
(212) 640-2000 .. **Michaud,** Steven J '84 %Amer Exp -200 Vesey -NY 10285
(212) 657-2194 .. **Michaux,** Denise A '96 Citibank -111 Wall -NY 10005 **Fx:**657-1616
(212) 515-3200 .. **Michel,** Cindy Zee '01 %Apollo Mgmt LP -9 W 57th -NY 10022
(212) 506-5000 .. **Michel,** Clifford R '97 OfCnsl Orrick H&S LLP -51 W 52nd -NY 10019
(516) 374-5707 .. **Michel,** Craig R '82 -591 Malvin Mall -Cedarhrst 11516
(585) 454-1130 .. **Michel,** F Robt '70 Cnsl FR Michel -28 E Main -Rchstr 14614 **Fx:**454-6118
(212) 770-6040 .. **Michel,** Jacqueline E '96 %AIG -70 Pine -NY 10270
(212) 836-8000 .. **Michel,** Patrick A '97 %Kaye S LLP -425 Park Av -NY 10022
(212) 506-5000 .. **Michel,** Robt B '94 (Orrick H&S LLP) -51 W 52nd -NY 10019
(212) 872-1646 .. **Michel,** Tiffany Taylor '93 Renaissance Technologies -800 3rd Av -NY 10022
(516) 564-8000 .. **Michelakos,** Stamatis T '06 %J Hiebler & Assoc -901 Franklin Av -Gdn Cty 11530 **Fx:**564-1714
(516) 248-8000 .. **Michelen,** Oscar '86 (Sandback B&M) -200 Old Cntry Rd -Mineola 11501
(212) 326-3939 .. **Micheletto,** Robt C '04 (Jones D) -222 E 41st -NY 10017
(212) 938-0600 .. **Michel-Garcia,** Gildardo '98 %Schwartz LLC -90 Broad -NY 10004 **Fx:**938-0601
(212) 964-6611 .. **Michell,** Robt M '00 %Lester SK&D -120 Bway -NY 10271
(212) 730-7700 .. **Michelman & Robinson, LLP** -114 W 47th -NY 10036 **Fx:**730-7725
(212) 619-1250 .. **Michel-Roache,** Mootze '90 -225 Bway -NY 10007
(212) 819-8200 .. **Michels,** Jonathan S '08 %White & C LLP -1155 Av of Amer -NY 10036
(212) 732-2000 .. **Michels,** Paul A '83 (Cullen and D LLP) -44 Wall -NY 10005
(516) 766-2270 .. **Michelson,** Allen '58 -91 Murray Dr -Oceanside 11572
(212) 588-0880 .. **Michelstein,** Steven D '93 (Michelstein & Assoc) -485 Mad Av -NY 10022 **Fx:**588-0811
(212) 559-2189 .. **Michelutti,** Marina '04 %Citibank -485 Lex Av -NY 10017
(718) 240-4500 .. **Michetti,** Felice L '85 Grenadier Realty Corp -1230 Penn Av -Brklyn 11239 **Fx:**642-8690
(212) 701-3000 .. **Michetti,** Michl E '89 (Cahill G&R LLP) -80 Pine -NY 10005 **Fx:**269-5420
(212) 801-9218 .. **Michigan,** Mark I '91 (Greenberg T,LLP) -200 Park Av -NY 10166
(315) 382-0530 .. **Micho,** P Scott '97 -307 S Clinton -Syracuse 13202 **Fx:**479-8847
(212) 354-1166 .. **Mickelson,** Lauren B '05 %Triumph Srch Cnsltnts -130 W 42nd -NY 10036 **Fx:**354-1141
(212) 735-3000 .. **Mickisch,** Sven G '06 %Skadden ASM&F LLP -4 Times Sq -NY 10036
(716) 856-5500 .. **Micklus,** Ryan K '07 %Damon M LLP -200 Delaware Av -Buffalo 14202
(585) 218-9051 .. **Micros,** Anthony T '52 -2 Sandy Ln -Pittsfrd 14534 **Fx:**218-0457
(607) 734-3384 .. **Middaugh,** Kimberlee Balok '00 -311 Lk -Elmira 14901
(212) 610-6300 .. **Middelkoop,** Katinka I '09 %Allen & O -1221 Av of Amer -NY 10020
(914) 798-5400 .. **Middlebrook,** Brian E '06 %Goldberg S LLP -11 Martine Av -White Plns 10606
(914) 997-1346 .. **Middlebrook,** Lucas K '06 %Seham SM&P,LLP -445 Hmltn Av -White Plns 10601
(212) 233-8080 .. **Middleman,** Patricia Misasi '85 -305 Bway -NY 10007
(212) 670-0222 .. **Middlemiss,** Paul '87 Merrill Lynch -222 Bway -NY 10038 **Fx:**670-4501
(845) 291-2050 .. **Middlemiss,** Robt H '07 %DA -255-275 Main -Goshen 10924 **Fx:**291-2085
(718) 528-7274 .. **Middleton,** Cathy M '92 -225-16 Merrick Blvd -Laurelton 11413 **Fx:**528-2633
(212) 521-4068 .. **Middleton,** Matthew J '96 -590 Mad Av -NY 10022
(631) 738-9100 .. **Middleton,** Scott D '89 (Campolo M&M,LLP) -3340 Vets Mem'l Hwy -Bohemia 11716 **Fx:**738-0659
(315) 568-5861 .. **Midey & Mirras** -54 Fall Bx299 -Seneca Fls 13148 **Fx:**568-2324
(212) 336-2000 .. **Midha,** Abja Uttam '06 %Patterson BW&T LLP -1133 Av of Amer -NY 10036
(212) 785-4100 .. **Midonick,** Millard L '37 OfCnsl Fensterstock & Prtnrs LLP -30 Wall -NY 10005
(212) 370-1300 .. **Midura,** Michl A '00 %Ellenoff G&S LLP -150 E 42nd -NY 10017
(212) 735-3000 .. **Midvidy,** David H '91 (Skadden ASM&F LLP) -4 Times Sq -NY 10036
(212) 616-3042 .. **Miedel,** Florian '94 -111 Bway -NY 10006
(212) 687-0100 .. **Miedel,** Wm T '00 %Harris B PLLC -100 Wall -NY 10005
(212) 246-8045 .. **Miedzianogora,** Yves '83 Bureau FL -101 Park Av -NY 10178 **Fx:**246-2951
(516) 357-3000 .. **Miehl,** Christopher F '07 Rivkin R LLP -926 RXR Plz -Uniondale 11556
(212) 553-5758 .. **Miele,** Anthony M '82 %Zurich NA -1 Lbrty Plz -NY 10006 **Fx:**225-7027
(914) 798-5400 .. **Miele,** Carmela '07 %Goldberg S LLP -11 Martine Av -White Plns 10606
(718) 745-2222 .. **Miele,** Chas D '81 -425 74th -Brklyn 11209 **Fx:**630-5065
(212) 269-7308 .. **Miele,** Marc D '07 %Leahey & J PC -120 Wall -NY 10005
(845) 294-4080 .. **Miele,** Robt M '85 (Burke M&G) -40 Matthews Bx216 -Goshen 10924
(845) 357-7500 .. **Miele,** Robt M '85 (Burke M&G) -Bx397 -Suffern 10901
(631) 425-4155 .. **Mielo,** Patrick S '87 (Mielo & S,LLP) -61 Chichester Rd -Huntngtn 11743
(631) 425-4155 .. **Mielo & Stasko,LLP** -61 Chichester Rd -Huntngtn 11743 **Fx:**425-1509
(212) 816-5802 .. **Mierswa,** Thos M Jr. '84 Smith Barney -388 Greenwich -NY 10013
(212) 519-7412 .. **Mierzwa,** Craig T '97 SrCnsl Simon G&F,PLC -750 3rd Av -NY 10017 **Fx:**519-7413
(315) 735-0844 .. **Mierzwa,** Nancy J '77 -1303 City -Utica 13502
(212) 259-8000 .. **Miesowitz,** Sabrina A '09 %Dewey & L LLP -1301 Av of Amer -NY 10019
(212) 931-7402 .. **Mifsud,** Paul V '99 MLB -245 Park Av -NY 10167 **Fx:**949-5657
(315) 724-4545 .. **Miga,** Brian M '75 Miga Law Firm -2106 Genesee -Utica 13502 **Fx:**724-3817
(212) 725-3846 .. **Migally,** Angela F '05 %O Mohammedi,LLC -233 Bway -NY 10279 **Fx:**202-7621
(212) 837-6553 .. **Migally,** Christina F '07 %Hughes H&R LLP -1 Bttry Pk Plz -NY 10004 **Fx:**422-4726
(516) 248-7000 .. **Migatz,** Bruce W '76 (Albanese & A LLP) -1050 Franklin Av -Gdn Cty 11530
(212) 418-0554 .. **Migdal,** David '87 Morris & M LLP -767 3rd Av -NY 10017
(212) 408-5100 .. **Migdal,** Jean M '99 %Chadbourne & P LLP -30 Rckfllr Plz -NY 10112
(212) 832-4900 .. **Migdal,** Lester C '42 -770 Lex Av -NY 10065
(212) 357-1963 .. **Migdal,** Samantha D '05 Goldman Sachs & Co -85 Broad -NY 10004
(516) 357-3000 .. **Migdalen,** Jeffrey '02 %Rivkin R LLP -926 RXR Plz -Uniondale 11556
(212) 442-8599 .. **Migdalis,** Paraskevi V '03 %Law Dept -100 Church -NY 10007 **Fx:**788-0367
(212) 344-1444 .. **Migdol,** Gerald S '80 %GFC Management Srvcs -50 Bway -NY 10004 **Fx:**344-9720
(212) 891-9100 .. **Migdon,** Andrew H '98 (Goldfarb & F LLP) -345 Park Av -NY 10154
(212) 969-3000 .. **Migdon,** Michelle R '98 %Proskauer R LLP -1585 Bway -NY 10036
(212) 891-9100 .. **Migdon,** Sidney A '65 (Goldfarb & F LLP) -345 Park Av -NY 10154
(212) 836-8000 .. **Migliaccio,** Christopher M '09 Kaye S LLP -425 Park Av -NY 10022
(716) 856-1010 .. **Migliaccio,** Domenic J '79 -69 Delaware Av -Buffalo 14202 **Fx:**856-1008
(914) 285-8500 .. **Migliaccio,** Nick '91 %TK Moore -701 Wstchstr Av -White Plns 10604 **Fx:**285-8510
(718) 888-8880 .. **Migliaccio,** Richd J '75 %Dai & Assoc,PC -136-20 38th Av -Flushng 11354 **Fx:**888-9270
(516) 296-4600 .. **Miglino,** Michl P '75 %Chicago Title/Ticor -330 Old Cntry Rd -Mineola 11501
(718) 746-3839 .. **Miglino,** Nicholas J '75 -146-06 20th Av -Whitestone 11357
(631) 543-3663 .. **Migliore & Infranco,PC** -353 Vets Mem'l Hwy -Commack 11725 **Fx:**543-3682
(631) 543-3663 .. **Migliore,** Rudolph F X '77 (Migliore & I,PC) -353 Vets Mem'l Hwy -Commack 11725
(212) 335-9000 .. **Mignola,** Gina M '89 %DA -1 Hogan Pl -NY 10013
(315) 361-8037 .. **Mignone,** Bryan M '04 Cnsl Oneida Indian Nation Enterprises -5218 Patrick Rd -Verona 13478 **Fx:**361-8009
(347) 296-1489 .. **Mignone,** Elizabeth M '00 Law Clerk -320 Jay -Brklyn 11201
(212) 768-6700 .. **Mignone,** Peter J '97 (Sonnenschein N&R LLP) -2 World Fncl Ctr -NY 10281
(212) 735-3000 .. **Mihailova,** Anna '08 %Skadden ASM&F LLP -4 Times Sq -NY 10036
(516) 739-5100 .. **Mihalick,** Andrew J '91 %Farber B&Z LLP -51 Charles -Mineola 11501

(718) 204-2060 .. **Mihalios**, George N '97 -29-25 24th Av -LIC 11102 **Fx**:932-6316
(212) 977-9700 .. **Mihalos**, Athena M '04 %Phillips N LLP -666 5th Av -NY 10103
(212) 417-8300 .. **Mihas**, Joanne '94 %Research Fndtn CUNY -230 W 41st -NY 10036 **Fx**:417-8379
(718) 229-6000 .. **Mihos**, Evangelos '93 -214-07 39th Av -Bayside 11361 **Fx**:229-6001
(518) 465-1451 .. **Mihuta**, Lucas G '05 C Rutnik -270 Mt Hope Dr -Albany 12202 **Fx**:465-1458
(718) 522-1020 .. **Mijuca**, Robt '00 %Rubenstein & R -16 Court -Brklyn 11241
(866) 348-5819 .. **Mikan**, Mary L '91 %SSA-ODAR -50 Fountain Plz -Buffalo 14202 **Fx**:(716) 551-4078
(212) 373-3000 .. **Mikel**, Issa F '06 %Paul WRW&G LLP -1285 Av of Amer -NY 10019
(516) 822-7700 .. **Mikelinich**, Mario B '85 (M Mikelinich,PC) -6800 Jericho Tpk -Syosset 11791 **Fx**:822-7714
(718) 739-6400 .. **Mikelson**, Jeanne M '89 %DHCR -92-31 Union Hall -Jamaica 11433 **Fx**:262-7938
(212) 558-4000 .. **Mikes**, Jordan S '10 %Sullivan & C LLP -125 Broad -NY 10004
(212) 644-0440 .. **Mikhailov**, Michl '98 (M Mikhailov,PC) -425 Mad Av -NY 10017 **Fx**:644-9802
(646) 386-3671 .. **Mikhaleva**, Anna '09 Supreme Ct-Law Dept -60 Centre -NY 10007
(718) 450-0682 .. **Mikhlin**, Sergey '05 -626 RexCorp Plz -Uniondale 11556
(212) 661-1010 .. **Miki**, Katsumi '92 (Ogihara & Assoc,PLLC) -122 E 42nd -NY 10168 **Fx**:661-6116
(716) 633-9922 .. **Mikienis**, Christopher J '00 (Mikienis & M PC) -5838 Main -Williamsvll 14221
(914) 378-2091 .. **Mikkelsen**, Erika K '01 Consumers Union -101 Truman Av -Ynkrs 10703
(212) 909-6000 .. **Mikkor**, Alison M '03 %Debevoise & P LLP -919 3rd Av -NY 10022
(516) 565-4123 .. **Miklacki**, Joel M '81 -119 Jackson -Hempstd 11550 **Fx**:565-4123
(212) 351-4500 .. **Miklave**, Matthew T '94 (Epstein B&G,PC) -250 Park Av -NY 10177
(845) 638-5300 .. **Miklitsch**, Catherine M '79 %Family Ct -1 S Main -New Cty 10956 **Fx**:638-5319
(516) 832-7777 .. **Miklos**, Danl P '05 %Silberstein A&M,PC -600 Old Cntry Rd -Gdn Cty 11530
(516) 832-7777 .. **Miklos**, Jos '77 (Silberstein A&M,PC) -600 Old Cntry Rd -Gdn Cty 11530
(914) 834-9220 .. **Miklus**, Paul J '71 -7 Woodlnd Av -Larchmnt 10538 **Fx**:834-9224
(212) 736-2624 .. **Mikofsky**, Anton J '86 -236 W 26th -NY 10001 **Fx**:981-0528
(516) 222-2050 .. **Mikolay**, Adam E '87 (A Mikolay,PC) -90 Merrick Av -E Meadow 11554 **Fx**:222-0450
(914) 428-8800 .. **Mikulak**, Kelley T '03 %Stern KP&W,LLP -1025 Wstchstr Av -White Plns 10604
(518) 462-5601 .. **Mikullitz**, Kelly J '06 %O'Connell & A -54 State -Albany 12207
(914) 995-3481 .. **Milaccio**, Wm C '96 %DA -111 Martin Luther King Blvd -White Plns 10601 **Fx**:995-3363
(212) 446-7585 .. **Milam**, Derrick S '00 %McKinsey & Co -55 E 52nd -NY 10055 **Fx**:688-9521
(212) 259-8000 .. **Milam**, Shane M '07 %Dewey & L LLP -1301 Av of Amer -NY 10019
(212) 458-3326 .. **Milana**, Robt A '86 AIGTS,Inc -175 Water -NY 10038
(718) 590-2000 .. **Milanes**, Michelle O '08 %DA -198 E 161st -Bronx 10451 **Fx**:590-6477
(212) 504-6000 .. **Milani**, Homan H '07 %Cadwalader W&T LLP -1 World Fncl Ctr -NY 10281
(212) 351-4500 .. **Milani**, Wm J '82 (Epstein B&G,PC) -250 Park Av -NY 10177
(212) 278-6985 .. **Milankov**, Steve '01 Societe Generale -1221 Av of Amer -NY 10020
(212) 309-6000 .. **Milano**, Andrew L '09 %Morgan L&B LLP -101 Park Av -NY 10178
(315) 455-6668 .. **Milano**, Gary V '82 %Transportation Security Admin -Syracuse-Hancock Intl Airport -N Syracuse 13212 **Fx**:455-7222
(212) 922-0700 .. **Milano**, Jos '75 -71 Vndrblt Av -NY 10169
(718) 222-2314 .. **Milano**, Karen E '07 %Law Dept -350 Jay -Brklyn 11201 **Fx**:222-2373
(516) 741-2585 .. **Milas**, Lisa '95 %Rosicki R & Assoc,PC -51 E Bethpage Rd -Plainvw 11803 **Fx**:741-4748
(518) 457-2070 .. **Milavec**, Michelle Wendt '02 %Dept of Tax & Fin -Bldg 9 State Campus -Albany 12227 **Fx**:457-6131
(212) 930-9700 .. **Milazzo**, Christopher P '97 Cnsl Sichenzia RFF LLP -61 Bway -NY 10006
(631) 589-5200 .. **Milazzo**, John C '95 %Water Auth -4060 Sunrise Hwy -Oakdale 11769
(212) 621-7991 .. **Milazzo**, Michele L '03 Associated Press -450 W 33rd -NY 10001
(212) 261-8000 .. **Milazzo**, Richd C '81 (Mendes & M,LLP) -750 7th Av -NY 10019
(212) 530-5000 .. **Milbank Tweed Hadley & McCloy LLP** -1 Chase Manh Plz -NY 10005 **Fx**:530-5219
(646) 458-7025 .. **Milbauer**, Kenneth D '84 ACE USA Diversified Risk -140 Bway -NY 10005
(212) 227-8007 .. **Milbauer**, Paul E '78 -90 John -NY 10038 **Fx**:227-2948
(212) 685-8500 .. **Milbauer**, Seth '93 (Greenstein & M,LLP) -1825 Park Av -NY 10035
(516) 712-4000 .. **Milber**, Dean L '88 (Milber MP&S LLP) -1000 Woodbury Rd -Woodbury 11797
(516) 712-4000 .. **Milber Makris Plousadis & Seiden LLP** -1000 Woodbury Rd -Woodbury 11797 **Fx**:712-4013
(914) 681-8700 .. **Milber Makris Plousadis & Seiden LLP** -3 Barker Av -White Plns 10601 **Fx**:681-8709
(716) 633-3313 .. **Milber Makris Plousadis & Seiden LLP** -2809 Wehrle Dr -Williamsvll 14221 **Fx**:633-3318
(212) 251-5067 .. **Milberg**, Frances '71 %The Segal Co -1 Park Av -NY 10016 **Fx**:251-5490
(212) 594-5300 .. **Milberg LLP** -1 Penn Plz -NY 10119 **Fx**:868-1229
(716) 566-1300 .. **Milbrand**, James P '95 (Hiscock & B,LLP) -1100 M&T Ctr -Buffalo 14203
(631) 447-6500 .. **Milburn**, Eric E Jr. '98 (Gilbert B&M,LLP) -440 Waverly Av -Patchogue 11772
(212) 715-1000 .. **Milburn**, Nancy Gordon '85 (Arnold & P LLP) -399 Park Av -NY 10022
(212) 837-6349 .. **Milburn**, Nicholas J '09 %Hughes H&R LLP -1 Bttry Pk Plz -NY 10004
(212) 227-8140 .. **Milcetic**, Antonette M '03 %Taubman K&S LLP -30 Vesey -NY 10007
(212) 344-3800 .. **Milch**, Aleksander B '98 %Christophe & Assoc,PC -2 Wall -NY 10005 **Fx**:344-3212
(212) 964-7400 .. **Milch**, Angela L '95 Smith MDWY&Y,PC -111 John -NY 10038
(716) 856-4200 .. **Milch**, Chas E '67 (Gibson M&C,LLP) -69 Delaware Av -Buffalo 14202
(212) 346-0045 .. **Milch**, Douglas A '92 %P Weitz & Assoc,PC -233 Bway -NY 10279 **Fx**:346-0876
(716) 634-3320 .. **Milch**, Philip A '74 %Pope Law Firm,PLLC -6580 Main -Williamsvll 14221 **Fx**:204-2770
(212) 697-3122 .. **Milch**, Stewart G '94 %Martin C&B LLP -220 E 42nd -NY 10017
(631) 755-0101 .. **Milchan**, Michl '96 %Lewis JAA,LLP -425 Broad Hollow Rd -Melvll 11747
(646) 458-6850 .. **Milch-Cardarelli**, Stefanie R '99 ACE USA -140 Bway -NY 10005
(914) 286-2819 .. **Milde**, Karl F Jr. '70 -10 Bank -White Plns 10606
(914) 693-9116 .. **Mildner**, Esther E '84 E Mildner,PC -54 Prospect Av -Ardsley 10502 **Fx**:674-4218
(212) 619-4501 .. **Mildworm**, Saul '38 -11 Park Pl -NY 10007
(212) 504-6000 .. **Milenkevich**, Christopher '04 %Cadwalader W&T LLP -1 World Fncl Ctr -NY 10281
(914) 493-2800 .. **Mileo-Drohan**, Toni '92 %Cnty Hlthcr Corp -95 Grasslands Rd -Valhalla 10595 **Fx**:493-2321
(212) 906-1200 .. **Miles**, Benjamin J '07 %Latham & W -885 3rd Av -NY 10022
(212) 820-9419 .. **Miles**, C Todd '81 (Hawkins D&W LLP) -One Chase Manh Plz -NY 10005
(718) 324-2715 .. **Miles**, Charmaine L '84 -1757 Edenwald Av -Bronx 10466 **Fx**:324-2717
(718) 250-2000 .. **Miles**, Gavin W '90 %DA -350 Jay -Brklyn 11201 **Fx**:250-2314
(212) 730-8133 .. **Miles**, Heather '09 %Gunderson DSVF&H,LLP -220 W 42nd -NY 10036
(212) 808-7800 .. **Miles**, Jacob J '80 (Kelley D&W LLP) -101 Park Av -NY 10178
(845) 352-3975 .. **Miles**, Jerrold W '00 -313 N Main -Spg Vly 10977 **Fx**:352-8457
(212) 382-3300 .. **Miles**, Kenneth J '03 %Wollmuth M&D LLP -500 5th Av -NY 10110
(347) 418-3830 .. **Miles**, Lawr R '80 -36-01 43rd Av -LIC 11101 **Fx**:418-3838
(212) 801-6890 .. **Miles**, Maria C '99 %Greenberg T,LLP -200 Park Av -NY 10166
(212) 813-8800 .. **Miles**, Michl W '07 %Goodwin P LLP -620 8th Av -NY 10018
(716) 836-5530 .. **Miles**, Raymond T III '73 -2777 Sheridan Dr -Tonawanda 14150 **Fx**:836-5530
(212) 508-6100 .. **Miles**, Robin J '04 (Bracewell & G,LLP) -1251 Av of Amer -NY 10020
(914) 249-2000 .. **Miles**, Shawn A '01 %MasterCard Intl -2000 Purchase -Purchase 10577
(212) 374-5475 .. **Miles**, Suzanne E '03 %NYC Dept Educ -52 Chmbrs -NY 10007
(212) 989-4472 .. **Miles**, Wm M '46 -290 9th Av -NY 10001
(212) 408-5100 .. **Miletic**, Jennifer M '06 %Chadbourne & P LLP -30 Rckfllr Plz -NY 10112
(212) 808-0020 .. **Miletsky**, Robt J '81 -53 Legend Cir -White Plns 10603 **Fx**:808-0862
(212) 657-8587 .. **Milevo**, Doris J '04 Citigroup -111 Wall -NY 10043
(718) 590-3254 .. **Milevoj**, Melissa K '00 %Law Dept -900 Sheridan Av -Bronx 10451 **Fx**:590-2699
(315) 685-3416 .. **Milford Lynch & Shannon** -2-4 Fennell Bx47 -Skaneateles 13152 **Fx**:685-2460
(212) 992-8871 .. **Milgram**, Anne M '97 NYU Law Schl -40 Wshngtn Sq S -NY 10012 **Fx**:995-4894
(516) 409-6200 .. **Milgrim**, Brett J '09 %Furey KWM&C,PC -2174 Jackson Av -Seafrd 11783
(212) 698-3500 .. **Milgrim**, Joshua Y '04 %Dechert LLP -1095 Av of Amer -NY 10036
(212) 732-9000 .. **Milgrim**, Liza '03 %Sullivan PBM&C PC -120 Bway -NY 10271
(516) 333-7777 .. **Milgrim**, Randi M '96 (Mejias M&A,PC) -1 Dosoris Ln -Glen Cove 11542 **Fx**:333-7878
(610) 438-4418 .. **Milgrim**, Roger M '61 -75 E 55th -NY 10022 **Fx**:438-3606
(212) 205-7000 .. **Milgrom**, Matthieu L '06 %Ashurst LLP -7 Times Sq -NY 10036
(516) 222-6200 .. **Milgrom**, Miriam R '84 (Berkman HPP&F,PC) -100 Grdn City Plz -Gdn Cty 11530
(212) 374-7868 .. **Milgrom-Elcott**, Talia '03 Dept of Ed -52 Chmbrs -NY 10007
(518) 213-6000 .. **Milham**, Deborah A '98 %NYSUT -800 Troy-Schnctdy Rd -Latham 12110 **Fx**:213-6488
(914) 253-2549 .. **Milhoua**, Karen C '96 %Pepsico -700 Andrsn Hill Rd -Purchase 10577
(212) 312-7408 .. **Miliano**, Michl J '96 %State Ins Fund -199 Church -NY 10007 **Fx**:385-9199
(914) 428-4200 .. **Milianta**, Dorothy J '89 -7-11 S Bway -White Plns 10601 **Fx**:428-1241
(518) 474-6740 .. **Milillo**, Antonio '89 Dept of State -41 State -Albany 12231 **Fx**:473-9211
(212) 594-5000 .. **Milin**, Richd K '89 %Togut S&S LLP -1 Penn Plz -NY 10119
(212) 610-6300 .. **Milin**, Zorka '06 %Allen & O -1221 Av of Amer -NY 10020
(212) 836-8000 .. **Milina**, Svetlana '04 %Kaye S LLP -425 Park Av -NY 10022
(718) 590-2000 .. **Militano**, Alexandra A '96 %DA -198 E 161st -Bronx 10451 **Fx**:590-6477
(518) 393-1594 .. **Militano**, Mary Cosgrove '81 -7 Cornell Blvd -Scotia 12302
(315) 734-2358 .. **Militello**, Christopher M '01 %Utica Natl Ins -180 Genesee Bx530 -Utica 13502 **Fx**:734-2662
(631) 423-7755 .. **Militello**, Jos P '10 %Bragoli & Assoc,PC -999 Walt Whitman Rd -Melvll 11747 **Fx**:423-5299
(716) 672-2164 .. **Militello**, Laurie L '91 (Eades & M,PC) -11 E Main Bx149 -Fredonia 14063
(585) 454-5050 .. **Militello**, P Adam '08 %Brown & H -2 State -Rchstr 14614
(212) 219-0890 .. **Militello**, Saml '85 -16 Court -Brklyn 11241
(315) 435-2170 .. **Militi**, Jos M '91 %Cnty Atty -421 Mntgmry -Syracuse 13202 **Fx**:435-5729
(212) 682-2900 .. **Milito**, Christopher '00 %Braverman & Assoc,PC -331 Mad Av -NY 10017 **Fx**:682-7718
(631) 852-2500 .. **Milito**, Jennifer A '02 %DA -200 Center Dr -Rvrhead 11901 **Fx**:852-1769
(516) 437-4385 .. **Milizio**, Jos G '84 (Vishnick MM LLP) -3000 Marcus Av -Lk Success 11042
(212) 596-9000 .. **Milkes**, Jay G '95 (Ropes & G LLP) -1211 Av of Amer -NY 10036
(212) 880-9515 .. **Milkov**, Kristy Watson '03 %Morvillo AGIA&B,PC -565 5th Av -NY 10017
(716) 492-2204 .. **Milks**, Bryan R '84 -36 N Main Bx249 -Delevan 14042 **Fx**:492-5156
(716) 689-4449 .. **Millane**, John V III '88 -17 Beresford Ct -Williamsvll 14221 **Fx**:408-8811

(212) 295-6411 .. **Millar,** James H '01 (WilmerHale) -399 Park Av -NY 10022
(212) 922-1080 .. **Millard,** Amy E '84 (Clayman & R,LLP) -305 Mad Av -NY 10165
(212) 325-2000 .. **Millard,** Elizabeth W '80 Credit Suisse -11 Mad Av -NY 10010
(212) 832-7900 .. **Millard Greene & Udell** -15 E 62nd -NY 10065
(212) 455-2000 .. **Millard,** John Alden Jr. '00 (Simpson T&B LLP) -425 Lex Av -NY 10017
(914) 993-9393 .. **Millas,** Stephen D '98 Stewart Title Ins -707 Wstchstr Av -White Plns 10604 **Fx:**997-1698
(646) 826-5704 .. **Millen,** Jeffrey A '97 Och-Ziff -9 W 57th -NY 10019
(585) 263-1000 .. **Miller,** A Darren '08 %Nixon P LLP -1100 Clinton Sq -Rchstr 14604
(718) 706-7114 .. **Miller,** Aaron D '10 Fiduciary Ins Co of Amer -4507 Davis -LIC 11101
(631) 537-1155 .. **Miller,** Adam M '99 A Miller Grp,PC -2462 Main Bx1947 -Brdghmptn 11932 **Fx:**537-1255
(212) 335-9000 .. **Miller,** Adam S '00 %DA -1 Hogan Pl -NY 10013
(212) 310-8000 .. **Miller,** Alan B '62 SrCnsl Weil G&M LLP -767 5th Av -NY 10153
(212) 336-8000 .. **Miller,** Alan D '00 SrCnsl Amster R&E -90 Park Av -NY 10016
(212) 326-3939 .. **Miller,** Alan S '07 (Jones D) -222 E 41st -NY 10017
(212) 940-8800 .. **Miller,** Alfred '52 Cnsl Katten MR LLP -575 Mad Av -NY 10022
(212) 446-4800 .. **Miller,** Alison C '08 %Kirkland & E LLP -153 E 53rd -NY 10022
(518) 828-2100 .. **Miller,** Allen C Jr. '80 -32 Courts Ln -Hudson 12534
(914) 846-7000 .. **Miller,** Amy '05 NY Life Ins -1 Rockwood Rd -Sleepy Hollow 10591 **Fx:**846-4755
(212) 335-9990 .. **Miller,** Amy E '06 NY County District Attorneys Ofc -1 Hogan Pl -NY 10013
(212) 554-1400 .. **Miller,** Amy J '02 %Bernstein LB&G LLP -1285 Av of Amer -NY 10019
(516) 561-6645 .. **Miller,** Andrea E '96 %E Schlissel -479 Merrick Rd -Lynbrk 11563 **Fx:**561-6716
(973) 315-4412 .. **Miller,** Andrew J '81 (Budd L) -140 Bway -NY 10005
(716) 849-1333 .. **Miller,** Andrew O '05 %Lipsitz GSC LLP -42 Delaware Av -Buffalo 14202
(718) 522-0023 .. **Miller,** Andrew R '93 -26 Court -Brklyn 11242 **Fx:**522-0024
(716) 847-8400 .. **Miller,** Angela Z '99 (Phillips L LLP) -3400 HSBC Ctr -Buffalo 14203
(585) 232-3730 .. **Miller,** Anita C '74 OfCnsl Chamberlain D LLP -1600 Crssrds Bldg -Rchstr 14614
(212) 252-2932 .. **Miller,** Anita L '99 NYC Transit Authority -2 Bway -NY 10004
(212) 416-8000 .. **Miller,** Anthony P '88 %Dept of Law -120 Bway -NY 10271
(631) 586-1111 .. **Miller Apfel & Curran PLLC** -900 Grand Blvd -Deer Pk 11729 **Fx:**586-1113
(212) 699-7000 .. **Miller,** Arlyn B '90 %Charmer Sunbelt Grp -60 E 42nd -NY 10165
(718) 997-0641 .. **Miller,** Arthur L '83 -67-05 Alderton -Rego Pk 11374
(212) 992-8147 .. **Miller,** Arthur R '59 %NYU Law Schl -40 Wshngtn Sq S -NY 10012 **Fx:**995-4590
(212) 594-5300 .. **Miller,** Arthur R '59 SpclCnsl Milberg LLP -1 Penn Plz -NY 10119
(516) 365-1400 .. **Miller,** Asher H '78 (Cooperman LM LLP) -1129 Nrthrn Blvd -Manhsst 11030
(212) 421-2150 .. **Miller,** Ashley S '05 %Sive P&R,PC -460 Park Av -NY 10022
(212) 530-5000 .. **Miller,** Atara '03 %Milbank TH&M LLP -1 Chase Manh Plz -NY 10005
(845) 677-3494 .. **Miller & Aubin** -110 Church BxC -Millbrook 12545 **Fx:**677-6641
(518) 464-1300 .. **Miller,** Aurelia M '10 %Roemer WG&M LLP -13 Columbia Cir -Albany 12203
(212) 893-8262 .. **Miller,** Berton '74 Starlite Media LLC -825 3rd Av -NY 10022 **Fx:**838-4533
(845) 343-0505 .. **Miller,** Brenda J '88 %Markovits & M -12 Evergreen Dr Bx2025 -Middletwn 10940 **Fx:**343-9008
(212) 468-8000 .. **Miller,** Brett H '92 (Morrison & F LLP) -1290 Av of Amer -NY 10104
(914) 995-5446 .. **Miller,** Brian D '09 %Cnty Atty -148 Martine Av -White Plns 10601 **Fx:**995-5858
(212) 730-8133 .. **Miller,** Brian J '06 %Gunderson DSVF&H,LLP -220 W 42nd -NY 10036
(718) 361-8080 .. **Miller,** Brian L '95 %J Werlin -45-10 Court Sq -LIC 11101 **Fx:**361-0344
(914) 347-2600 .. **Miller,** Brian L '06 %Traub LS&S LLP -7 Skyline Dr -Hawthorne 10532
(631) 586-1111 .. **Miller,** Bruce J '60 (Miller A&C PLLC) -900 Grand Blvd -Deer Pk 11729
(516) 357-3700 .. **Miller,** Bruce V '75 SpclCnsl Cullen and D LLP -100 Q Roosevelt Blvd -Gdn Cty 11530
(716) 879-4182 .. **Miller,** Bryan E '99 US Army Corps of Engineers -1776 Niagara -Buffalo 14207
(212) 704-4400 .. **Miller Canfield Paddock & Stone,PLLC** -500 5th Av -NY 10110 **Fx:**704-4410
(212) 258-4419 .. **Miller,** Carla M '96 Siemens Corp -153 E 53rd -NY 10022 **Fx:**767-0580
(212) 403-1000 .. **Miller,** Carol '81 %Wachtell LR&K -51 W 52nd -NY 10019
(518) 465-1500 .. **Miller,** Carolyn A '10 %Cannon H&W,LLP -54 State -Albany 12207
(212) 318-3753 .. **Miller,** Carolyn Ann '96 Galleon Grp -590 Mad Av -NY 10022 **Fx:**371-0092
(212) 442-1400 .. **Miller,** Carolyn L '96 %Conflicts of Int Bd -2 Lafayette -NY 10007 **Fx:**442-1407
(212) 815-1818 .. **Miller,** Carrie S '05 %DC 37 MELS -125 Barclay -NY 10007 **Fx:**815-1343
(212) 670-0216 .. **Miller,** Caryn A '77 %Merrill Lynch -222 Bway -NY 10038
(212) 264-2842 .. **Miller,** Catherine D S '05 Hon G Carman -1 Fed Plz -NY 10278
(631) 231-1199 .. **Miller,** Catherine E '94 %Reynolds CGHL&Q,LLP -35 Arkay Dr -Hauppauge 11788
(212) 277-6500 .. **Miller,** Chas E '71 SrCnsl Dickstein S LLP -1633 Bway -NY 10019
(212) 762-7244 .. **Miller,** Chas L '00 Morgan Stanley & Co Inc -1221 Av of Amer -NY 10020
(716) 845-5500 .. **Miller,** Chas L II '04 -424 Main -Buffalo 14202 **Fx:**845-5516
(212) 506-1700 .. **Miller,** Chas M '98 (Kasowitz BT&F LLP) -1633 Bway -NY 10019
(315) 568-0911 .. **Miller,** Christi L '04 %Bradshaw -69 Fall -Seneca Fls 13148 **Fx:**568-0910
(212) 455-2000 .. **Miller,** Christian L '10 %Simpson T&B LLP -425 Lex Av -NY 10017
(212) 336-2000 .. **Miller,** Christine H '79 Cnsl Patterson BW&T LLP -1133 Av of Amer -NY 10036
(516) 627-5417 .. **Miller,** Christopher L '07 %R Eredics -103 Plandome Rd -Manhsst 11030 **Fx:**627-5852
(212) 336-2000 .. **Miller,** Christopher Y '01 %Patterson BW&T LLP -1133 Av of Amer -NY 10036

(718) 815-2003 .. **Miller,** Claire Cody '88 -1 Edgewtr Plz -Staten Isl 10305 **Fx:**815-2012
(212) 458-2510 .. **Miller,** Colin M '99 AIG -175 Water -NY 10038
(607) 535-9354 .. **Miller,** Connie Fern '77 -601 N Decatur -Watkins Glen 14891 **Fx:**535-4218
(212) 644-6160 .. **Miller,** Courtlandt G '81 %Diagnostek Inc -405 Park Av -NY 10022 **Fx:**644-6161
(212) 859-8000 .. **Miller,** Craig F '83 (Fried FHS&J LLP) -1 NY Plz -NY 10004
(716) 853-8190 .. **Miller,** Craig L '76 -14 Lafayette Sq -Buffalo 14203 **Fx:**853-8197
(212) 572-4200 .. **Miller,** Cynthia Rana '96 %Estee Lauder -767 5th Av -NY 10153 **Fx:**572-3989
(607) 776-8492 .. **Miller,** Danette E '88 Hon M Furfure -13 E Pulteney Sq -Bath 14810 **Fx:**776-4921
(845) 429-5371 .. **Miller,** Danl '77 (Miller M&S,PC) -90 New Main Bx360 -Haverstraw 10927
(212) 556-2100 .. **Miller,** Danl C '04 %King & S -1185 Av of Amer -NY 10036
(212) 259-8000 .. **Miller,** Danl E '05 %Dewey & L LLP -1301 Av of Amer -NY 10019
(585) 247-7340 .. **Miller,** Danl Lincoln '59 -2648 Chili Av -Rchstr 14624 **Fx:**247-7340
(718) 369-2026 .. **Miller,** Danl R '85 -503 4th Av -Brklyn 11215 **Fx:**369-2029
(516) 328-3500 .. **Miller,** Danny J '98 %McDonnell & A,PC -401 Franklin Av -Gdn Cty 11530
(212) 818-8800 .. **Miller,** David A '81 (Graubard M) -405 Lex Av -NY 10174
(212) 839-5300 .. **Miller,** David C '76 (Sidley A LLP) -787 7th Av -NY 10019
(212) 259-8000 .. **Miller,** David C '00 %Dewey & L LLP -1301 Av of Amer -NY 10019
(516) 877-2424 .. **Miller,** David E '92 (Weinberg G&P LLP) -400 Grdn City Plz -Gdn Cty 11530
(212) 660-5550 .. **Miller,** David E '01 %MC Rakower,PC -747 3rd Av -NY 10017 **Fx:**660-5551
(212) 906-1200 .. **Miller,** David J '07 %Latham & W -885 3rd Av -NY 10022
(585) 374-2130 .. **Miller,** David P '82 -111 N Main Bx356 -Naples 14512
(212) 504-6000 .. **Miller,** David S '91 (Cadwalader W&T LLP) -1 World Fncl Ctr -NY 10281
(607) 229-3828 .. **Miller,** Deborah Wolf '98 -109 E Seneca -Ithaca 14850
(516) 571-2070 .. **Miller,** Denise B '76 %Cnty Ct -262 Old Cntry Rd -Mineola 11501 **Fx:**571-2160
(212) 306-3283 .. **Miller,** Desiree V '95 Housing Auth-Ofc of Impartial Hearings -250 Bway -NY 10007
(212) 225-2000 .. **Miller,** Diana Claybon '09 %Cleary GS&H -1 Lbrty Plz -NY 10006
(631) 712-5721 .. **Miller,** Dina T '90 Hon A Lindsay -100 Fed Plz Bx9014 -Central Islip 11722
(716) 852-7628 .. **Miller,** Donald Lang '55 %Miller Gesko Inc -237 Main -Buffalo 14203
(516) 394-4200 .. **Miller,** Dorothy R '10 %Duffy & D -1370 RXR Plz -Uniondale 11556
(518) 465-7591 .. **Miller & Dubuc,PC** -14 Corp Wds Blvd -Albany 12211 **Fx:**426-3309
(212) 732-6710 .. **Miller,** Edw G '67 -277 Bway -NY 10007 **Fx:**566-4780
(718) 531-9700 .. **Miller,** Edw S '83 %Lazarowitz & M,LLP -2004 Ralph Av -Brklyn 11234
(212) 758-1625 .. **Miller,** Edw W '95 -350 5th Av -NY 10118
(631) 265-3960 .. **Miller,** Edwin '59 (Campbell & M) -94 Maple Av Bx901 -Smithtwn 11787 **Fx:**265-4603
(212) 679-0400 .. **Miller & Eisenman,LLP** -450 7th Av -NY 10123 **Fx:**679-1080
(516) 829-8222 .. **Miller,** Elaine '58 -98 Cuttermill Rd -Gt Neck 11021 **Fx:**829-8665
(212) 872-1000 .. **Miller,** Eli N '09 -One Bryant Park -NY 10036 **Fx:**872-1002
(212) 489-8230 .. **Miller,** Elisa L '05 %Davis WT LLP -1633 Bway -NY 10019
(631) 852-2500 .. **Miller,** Elizabeth L '06 %DA -200 Center Dr -Rvrhead 11901 **Fx:**852-1769
(212) 408-5100 .. **Miller,** Elizabeth M '97 %Chadbourne & P LLP -30 Rckfllr Plz -NY 10112
(212) 566-2266 .. **Miller,** Elyse D '10 %J Orlian,PC -277 Bway -NY 10007 **Fx:**566-4780
(718) 854-1400 .. **Miller,** Eric '96 %Parkway Realty Assoc LLC -1205 47th -Brklyn 11219
(212) 259-8000 .. **Miller,** Eric C '08 %Dewey & L LLP -1301 Av of Amer -NY 10019
(516) 489-8536 .. **Miller,** Ernest '71 -306 Lester Ct -W Hempstead 11552 **Fx:**489-8536
(718) 875-1888 .. **Miller,** Ernest J '52 -26 Court -Brklyn 11242 **Fx:**797-0558
(212) 884-7221 .. **Miller,** Esther D '85 GMAC Commercial Credit -1290 Av of Amer -NY 10104 **Fx:**884-7372
(914) 592-4167 .. **Miller,** Evelyn '77 %Hitsman H&O LLC -220 Wht Plns Rd -Tarrytwn 10591
(914) 681-0200 .. **Miller,** Faith G '81 (DelBello DWW&W,LLP) -1 N Lex Av -White Plns 10601
(212) 566-3296 .. **Miller,** Felicia R '87 %Dept of Bldgs -280 Bway -NY 10007
(315) 234-9900 .. **Miller,** Frank W '79 (F Miller) -6575 Kirkvll Rd -E Syracuse 13057 **Fx:**234-9908
(212) 661-6844 .. **Miller,** Frederica L '88 -299 Bway -NY 10007 **Fx:**661-5844
(518) 465-8682 .. **Miller,** Fredk '65 -5 Chestnut Hill South Rd -Albany 12211
(914) 699-5798 .. **Miller,** Fredk J '49 -22 W 1st -Mt Vernon 10550
(516) 393-2200 .. **Miller,** Fredrick I '77 (Garfunkel W,PC) -111 Grt Nck Rd -Gt Neck 11021
(212) 669-3483 .. **Miller,** Fredrika V '79 NYC Comptrollers Ofc -1 Centre -NY 10007
(212) 657-2150 .. **Miller,** Frettra Monay '91 %Citibank NA -111 Wall -NY 10005
(585) 271-1500 .. **Miller,** G Michl '82 (Dibble & M,PC) -55 Canterbury Rd -Rchstr 14607
(212) 264-0482 .. **Miller,** Gardner B Jr. '03 US DOJ -26 Fed Plz -NY 10278 **Fx:**264-1916
(212) 924-2174 .. **Miller,** Gary R '75 -195 W 10th -NY 10014
(631) 666-3300 .. **Miller,** Gary S '88 (Askinas & M) -1991 Union Blvd -Bay Shr 11706 **Fx:**666-3392
(516) 374-0080 .. **Miller,** Gary S '89 Trident Grp -77 Spruce -Cedarhrst 11516
(212) 998-6329 .. **Miller,** Geoffrey P '02 %NYU Law Schl -40 Wshngtn Sq S -NY 10012 **Fx:**995-4590
(212) 506-2500 .. **Miller,** George K '84 (Mayer B LLP) -1675 Bway -NY 10019
(516) 296-1000 .. **Miller,** George T '65 (Miller & M,PC) -100 Q Roosevelt Blvd -Gdn Cty 11530
(212) 349-0300 .. **Miller,** Glenn D '85 (Sivin & M LLP) -170 Bway -NY 10038
(212) 699-2200 .. **Miller,** Glenn F '02 TowerBrook Cptl Prtnrs -430 Park Av -NY 10022
(212) 629-0123 .. **Miller,** Glenn Martin '93 -875 6th Av -NY 10001 **Fx:**629-8982
(212) 788-0599 .. **Miller,** Gordon D '66 Law Dept -100 Church -NY 10007 **Fx:**788-0367

(212) 318-6000 .. **Miller**, Gregg S '88 OfCnsl Paul HJ&W LLP -75 E 55th -NY 10022
(212) 432-7419 .. **Miller**, Gregory D '00 (Podvey MCHC&C) -400 Park Av -NY 10022
(716) 853-8426 .. **Miller**, Gregory P '83 %Dept of Law -350 Main Pl Twr -Buffalo 14202 **Fx**:853-8571
(716) 852-0400 .. **Miller**, Gregory T '98 (Roach BM&G,PC) -424 Main -Buffalo 14202
(212) 357-1975 .. **Miller**, Guy M '97 %Goldman Sachs -1 NY Plz -NY 10004
(518) 465-7581 .. **Miller**, Harry V B '75 (Herzog Law Firm,PC) -7 Southwoods Blvd -Albany 12211
(212) 310-8000 .. **Miller**, Harvey R '59 (Weil G&M LLP) -767 5th Av -NY 10153
(607) 723-5341 .. **Miller**, Heather V '08 %Hinman H&K,LLP -80 Exchange Bx5250 -Bnghmtn 13902
(914) 946-8900 .. **Miller**, Henry G '59 (Clark G&M) -99 Court -White Plns 10601
(516) 267-6300 .. **Miller**, Howard M '91 (Bond S&K,PLLC) -1399 Franklin Av -Gdn Cty 11530
(718) 875-2191 .. **Miller**, Ira K '80 -26 Court -Brklyn 11242 **Fx**:797-0558
(212) 422-1200 .. **Miller**, Irwin D '78 (Abrams GF&J,PC) -1 Bttry Pk Plz -NY 10004
(212) 408-5100 .. **Miller**, J Allen '80 (Chadbourne & P LLP) -30 Rckfllr Plz -NY 10112
(845) 624-6248 .. **Miller**, Jaclyn M '99 -120 N Main -New Cty 10956 **Fx**:634-2444
(914) 428-1438 .. **Miller**, James C '85 %T Bona,PC -123 Main -White Plns 10601 **Fx**:428-1413
(212) 878-8254 .. **Miller**, James D '93 Cnsl Clifford C LLP -31 W 52nd -NY 10019
(585) 394-7370 .. **Miller**, James F '74 -Bx129 -Ionia 14475
(631) 852-1650 .. **Miller**, James H III '79 %Leg Aid -300 Center Dr -Rvrhead 11901 **Fx**:852-1655
(607) 936-4341 .. **Miller**, James P '88 -347 E 2nd -Corning 14830 **Fx**:936-4189
(212) 839-5300 .. **Miller**, Janet E '02 %Sidley A LLP -787 7th Av -NY 10019
(212) 752-5200 .. **Miller**, Janice R '99 %Greene Levin Snyder LLC -150 E 58th -NY 10155
(800) 742-9696 .. **Miller**, Jason A '02 %Binder & B,PC -33-00 Nrthrn Blvd -LIC 11101 **Fx**:(212) 677-0423
(212) 806-5174 .. **Miller**, Jason E '96 %IIG Capital LLC -1500 Bway -NY 10036
(212) 885-5000 .. **Miller**, Jason I '07 %Blank R LLP -405 Lex Av -NY 10174
(212) 758-5577 .. **Miller**, Jay J '58 -430 E 57th -NY 10022 **Fx**:758-0624
(212) 751-2700 .. **Miller**, Jeanne C '80 %JAMS -620 8th Av -NY 10018 **Fx**:751-4099
(212) 504-6000 .. **Miller**, Jed B '07 %Cadwalader W&T LLP -1 World Fncl Ctr -NY 10281
(516) 622-9200 .. **Miller**, Jeffrey A '93 (Westerman BEM&S,LLP) -1201 RXR Plz -Uniondale 11553
(212) 752-9200 .. **Miller**, Jeffrey Craig '77 (Miller KS LLP) -488 Mad Av -NY 10022 **Fx**:688-3996
(516) 248-6755 .. **Miller**, Jeffrey H '98 -350 Willis Av -Mineola 11501
(518) 377-2225 .. **Miller**, Jeffrey N '77 (Friedman H&M,LLP) -100 Great Oaks Blvd Bx38279 -Albany 12203
(212) 227-4200 .. **Miller**, Jeffrey R '96 (J Miller & Assoc,PC) -32 Bway -NY 10004 **Fx**:504-8369
(914) 703-6300 .. **Miller**, Jeffrey T '90 (Pillinger MT,LLP) -570 Taxter Rd -Elmsfrd 10523
(631) 577-7344 .. **Miller**, Jennifer E '04 Travelers -100 Baylis Rd -Melvll 11747
(212) 897-0996 .. **Miller**, Jennifer Kasmin '94 -60 E 42nd -NY 10165
(212) 909-9500 .. **Miller**, Jennifer L '96 %Wachtel & M,LLP -885 2nd Av -NY 10017
(212) 557-7700 .. **Miller**, Jennifer L '05 %Davidson D&C LLP -60 E 42nd -NY 10165
(212) 832-7400 .. **Miller**, Jennifer R '09 Weidenbaum & H,LLP -708 3rd Av -NY 10017
(516) 674-3700 .. **Miller**, Jessica Bier '97 TM Bier & Assoc -79 Hazel -Glen Cove 11542
(518) 561-4400 .. **Miller**, Jessica L '04 %Stafford OC&T,PLLC -1 Cumberland Av Bx2947 -Plattsbrgh 12901
(212) 788-8285 .. **Miller**, Jessica L '09 %Law Dept -100 Church -NY 10007 **Fx**:788-0367
(212) 813-8800 .. **Miller**, Jessica W '03 %Goodwin P LLP -620 8th Av -NY 10018
(212) 601-2425 .. **Miller**, Jill L '92 (J Miller & Assoc,PC) -61 Bway -NY 10006 **Fx**:809-3660
(212) 468-8000 .. **Miller**, Jodi K '03 %Morrison & F LLP -1290 Av of Amer -NY 10104
(718) 454-2632 .. **Miller**, Joel E '57 -73-11 184th -Flushng 11366
(212) 336-3500 .. **Miller**, Joel M '67 (Miller & W,PC) -570 Lex Av -NY 10022
(212) 607-3300 .. **Miller**, Johanna E '09 NYCLU -125 Broad -NY 10004
(518) 533-3000 .. **Miller**, John A '96 (Bond S&K,PLLC) -111 Wshngtn Av -Albany 12210
(518) 457-2070 .. **Miller**, John C '94 %Dept of Tax & Fin -Bldg 9 State Campus -Albany 12227 **Fx**:457-6131
(516) 887-4433 .. **Miller**, John D '65 %Improved Fndng Techniques -211 Bway Bx720 -Lynbrk 11563 **Fx**:887-1470
(845) 306-1000 .. **Miller**, John O III '96 %Watchtower -100 Watchtower Dr -Patterson 12563 **Fx**:306-0709
(212) 839-5300 .. **Miller**, Jonathan B '88 (Sidley A LLP) -787 7th Av -NY 10019
(518) 483-8400 .. **Miller**, Jonathan J '91 (Cnty Atty) -436 E Main -Malone 12953 **Fx**:483-2054
(212) 259-8000 .. **Miller**, Jonathan W '81 (Dewey & L LLP) -1301 Av of Amer -NY 10019
(212) 838-3333 .. **Miller**, Jonathan W '97 (Locks Law Firm,PLLC) -747 3rd Av -NY 10017 **Fx**:838-3735
(212) 578-2079 .. **Miller**, Jory E '91 %MetLife -27-01 Qns Plz N -LIC 11101 **Fx**:578-3916
(718) 855-9000 .. **Miller**, Jos '95 (Cullen and D LLP) -177 Montague -Brklyn 11201
(631) 563-1188 .. **Miller**, Jos A III '74 -213-1 Montauk Hwy -W Sayvll 11796 **Fx**:563-0896
(718) 793-2801 .. **Miller**, Jos B '72 J Miller,PC -125-10 Qns Blvd -Kew Gdns 11415 **Fx**:263-0134
(585) 808-5100 .. **Miller**, Jos P '09 -37 South Bx53 -Cuba 14727 **Fx**:(888) 355-9130
(585) 325-7455 .. **Miller**, Jos T '73 OfCnsl Philippone Law Ofc,PC -31 E Main -Rchstr 14608 **Fx**:546-6565
(212) 969-3000 .. **Miller**, Joshua M '06 %Proskauer R LLP -1585 Bway -NY 10036
(212) 455-2000 .. **Miller**, Julia A '07 %Simpson T&B LLP -425 Lex Av -NY 10017
(212) 309-6000 .. **Miller**, Julia N '03 %Morgan L&B LLP -101 Park Av -NY 10178
(212) 264-7090 .. **Miller**, Justin R '05 Hon LM Gordon -1 Fed Plz -NY 10278
(518) 427-9700 .. **Miller**, Justin S '99 (Harris B PLLC) -677 Bway -Albany 12207
(917) 778-6500 .. **Miller**, Kalman '93 %K Dodson -485 Lex Av -NY 10017
(212) 442-4900 .. **Miller**, Kara J '89 %Ofc Admin Trials -40 Rector -NY 10006 **Fx**:442-4947
(212) 684-1000 .. **Miller**, Kara K Kathan '03 %Slade & N LLP -245 5th Av -NY 10016 **Fx**:684-0646
(212) 487-4444 .. **Miller**, Karen '78 %Dept Cnsmr Affrs -42 Bway -NY 10004 **Fx**:487-4197
(718) 923-4206 .. **Miller**, Karen '84 %OTDA Fair Hearings -14 Boerum Pl -Brklyn 11201
(516) 371-1818 .. **Miller**, Karen Singer '84 %LI Ctr for Child Devel -385 Pearsall Av -Cedarhrst 11516
(516) 374-0080 .. **Miller**, Karla L '89 %Excalibur Land Srvcs -77 Spruce -Cedarhrst 11516 **Fx**:374-0284
(212) 872-1000 .. **Miller**, Kassia E '07 -One Bryant Park -NY 10036 **Fx**:872-1002
(212) 435-3571 .. **Miller**, Kathleen G '75 %Port Auth of NY/NJ -225 Park Av S -NY 10003 **Fx**:435-3555
(718) 302-7900 .. **Miller**, Keith A '01 NYC Dept of Ed -215 Heyward -Brklyn 11206
(315) 701-5768 .. **Miller**, Keith D '93 -1000 7th N -Liverpool 13088 **Fx**:701-5770
(212) 318-6000 .. **Miller**, Keith W '91 (Paul HJ&W LLP) -75 E 55th -NY 10022
(212) 661-9100 .. **Miller**, Kenneth J '76 OfCnsl Otterbourg SH&R,PC -230 Park Av -NY 10169
(212) 401-4028 .. **Miller**, Kenneth N '76 -350 5th Av -NY 10118
(212) 351-4000 .. **Miller**, Kenneth W '07 %Gibson D&C LLP -200 Park Av -NY 10166
(212) 210-9520 .. **Miller**, Kevin '91 (Alston & B LLP) -90 Park Av -NY 10016
(212) 964-6611 .. **Miller**, Kimberly A '03 %Lester SK&D -120 Bway -NY 10271
(646) 386-5700 .. **Miller**, Kisha L '98 %Civil Ct -111 Centre -NY 10013
(212) 701-3000 .. **Miller**, Kyle I '09 %Cahill G&R LLP -80 Pine -NY 10005 **Fx**:269-5420
(212) 326-3939 .. **Miller**, Lance E '10 %Jones D -222 E 41st -NY 10017
(212) 888-8200 .. **Miller**, Larry B '94 %Feder K LLP -845 3rd Av -NY 10022
(315) 492-3000 .. **Miller**, Lauren M '96 (Cramer S&M,PC) -3175 E Genesee -Syracuse 13224
(212) 259-8000 .. **Miller**, Lawr E '72 OfCnsl Dewey & L LLP -1301 Av of Amer -NY 10019
(646) 375-2247 .. **Miller**, Lawr R '80 Identrust,Inc -116 W 23rd -NY 10011
(212) 733-5841 .. **Miller**, Lawr R '94 Cnsl Pfizer Inc -235 E 42nd -NY 10017
(212) 679-0400 .. **Miller**, Lee '71 (Miller & E,LLP) -450 7th Av -NY 10123
(212) 750-1333 .. **Miller**, Lindsay A '05 %I Garr,PC -777 3rd Av -NY 10017 **Fx**:486-2978
(212) 759-0700 .. **Miller**, Lisa C '00 %ESR Bd -317 Mad Av -NY 10017
(646) 471-4000 .. **Miller**, Lisa M '03 %PricewaterhouseCoopers LLP -300 Mad Av -NY 10017
(518) 481-1593 .. **Miller**, Lorelei B '03 Franklin Cnty Conflict Def -355 W Main -Malone 12953
(631) 853-7605 .. **Miller**, Lorraine R '82 %District Ct Law Dept -400 Carleton Av Bx9075 -Central Islip 11722
(585) 232-7210 .. **Miller**, Luther W '58 (Cooke & M) -183 Main E -Rchstr 14604
(631) 878-6729 .. **Miller**, M Raye '93 -250 Montauk Hwy -E Moriches 11940 **Fx**:878-5685
(518) 793-6611 .. **Miller Mannix Schachner & Hafner,LLC** -451 Glen Bx765 -Glens Fls 12801 **Fx**:793-6690
(516) 422-8814 .. **Miller**, Marc E '92 Reliance 1st Cptl LLC -100 Baylis Rd -Melvll 11747
(845) 331-7330 .. **Miller**, Marc W '75 (Miller W & Assoc,PC) -270 Fair Bx4030 -Kingston 12402 **Fx**:331-7596
(631) 852-7684 .. **Miller**, Marcia Soraya '05 %NYS Supreme Court -210 Center Dr -Rvrhead 11901
(914) 747-1253 .. **Miller**, Marilyn '08 -653 Bellevw Av Bx206 -Thornwd 10594 **Fx**:449-6491
(585) 263-6760 .. **Miller**, Marisa J '06 US Atty -620 Fed Bldg -Rchstr 14614 **Fx**:263-6226
(516) 569-8100 .. **Miller**, Mark H '95 %Rosenfeld & M -132 Spruce -Cedarhrst 11516
(914) 273-1300 .. **Miller**, Mark P '76 %Veneziano & Assoc -84 Business Park Dr -Armonk 10504 **Fx**:273-1303
(646) 654-5040 .. **Miller**, Mark S '86 %VNU USA -770 Bway -NY 10003
(718) 254-7000 .. **Miller**, Marshall L '99 %US Atty -271 Cadman Plz E -Brklyn 11201 **Fx**:254-6479
(212) 398-1260 .. **Miller**, Martin B '89 (Miller & M LLP) -529 5th Av -NY 10017
(212) 728-8000 .. **Miller**, Martin R '83 OfCnsl Willkie F&G LLP -787 7th Av -NY 10019
(845) 482-4200 .. **Miller**, Martin S '75 -4861 State Route 52 Bx658 -Jffrsnvll 12748 **Fx**:794-1009
(845) 794-4440 .. **Miller**, Martin S '75 -10 St John -Monticello 12701 **Fx**:794-1009
(212) 294-6700 .. **Miller**, Marvin J Jr. '94 (Winston & S) -200 Park Av -NY 10166
(516) 248-9500 .. **Miller**, Mary A '97 %S Kobrick,PC -1305 Franklin Av -Gdn Cty 11530 **Fx**:248-7606
(212) 771-4241 .. **Miller**, Matthew A '94 %Trust Co of the West -1251 Av of Amer -NY 10020 **Fx**:771-4089
(585) 258-2800 .. **Miller**, Matthew D '06 %Underberg & K LLP -300 Bausch & Lomb Pl -Rchstr 14604
(646) 855-1052 .. **Miller**, Matthew I '96 %Bank of Amer Securities LLC -1 Bryant Pk -NY 10036
(212) 661-9100 .. **Miller**, Matthew J '89 OfCnsl Otterbourg SH&R,PC -230 Park Av -NY 10169
(212) 506-1700 .. **Miller**, Matthew R '97 Kasowitz BT&F LLP -1633 Bway -NY 10019
(212) 558-4000 .. **Miller**, Maura E '04 %Sullivan & C LLP -125 Broad -NY 10004
(718) 935-5924 .. **Miller**, Maurice L '81 Educ Dept-Ofc Compliance Srvcs -131 Lvngstn -Brklyn 11201 **Fx**:935-5944
(607) 273-4200 .. **Miller Mayer, LLP** -202 E State -Ithaca 14850 **Fx**:272-6694
(631) 761-7000 .. **Miller**, Meredith R '01 %Touro Cllg Law Ctr -225 Eastvw Dr -Central Islip 11722
(212) 545-7000 .. **Miller**, Michl '84 -1250 Bway -NY 10001 **Fx**:532-8800
(212) 468-8000 .. **Miller**, Michl B '92 (Morrison & F LLP) -1290 Av of Amer -NY 10104
(631) 756-0000 .. **Miller**, Michl B '94 SrCnsl M Miller,PC -100 Broadhllw Rd -Farmngdl 11735 **Fx**:756-0004
(212) 506-3900 .. **Miller**, Michl C '86 (Steptoe & J LLP) -750 7th Av -NY 10019
(631) 738-5362 .. **Miller**, Michl C '98 SrCnsl Symbol Technologies,Inc -1 Symbol Plz -Holtsvll 11742 **Fx**:738-4110
(718) 875-1300 .. **Miller**, Michl E '81 %Appllt Div 2nd Dept -45 Monroe Pl -Brklyn 11201 **Fx**:858-2446
(585) 232-3730 .. **Miller**, Michl J '63 OfCnsl Chamberlain D LLP -1600 Crssrds Bldg -Rchstr 14614
(631) 852-2500 .. **Miller**, Michl J '82 %DA -200 Center Dr -Rvrhead 11901 **Fx**:852-1769
(212) 903-8700 .. **Miller**, Michl J '92 (Roberts & H,LLP) -825 8th Av -NY 10019
(315) 697-2288 .. **Miller**, Michl J '05 (Taylor & M LLP) -133 S Peterboro -Canastota 13032 **Fx**:697-8428
(315) 331-1919 .. **Miller**, Michl R '93 -211 West Av -Newark 14513 **Fx**:331-8140
(212) 714-1720 .. **Miller**, Michl S '86 (Tompkins MW&B LLP) -140 Bway -NY 10005
(845) 429-5371 .. **Miller Miller & Shandler,PC** -90 New Main Bx360 -Haverstraw 10927 **Fx**:429-5375

(516) 296-1000 .. **Miller & Milone,PC** -100 Q Roosevelt Blvd -Gdn Cty 11530
(516) 484-4010 .. **Miller Montiel & Strano** -99 Powerhse Rd -Roslyn Hts 11577 **Fx:**484-2130
(718) 254-7000 .. **Miller,** Nancy A '88 %US Atty -271 Cadman Plz E -Brklyn 11201 **Fx:**254-6479
(718) 522-0023 .. **Miller,** Natalie M '94 -26 Court -Brklyn 11242 **Fx:**522-0024
(516) 746-7633 .. **Miller,** Neil A '82 -200 Old Cntry Rd -Mineola 11501 **Fx:**741-7758
(212) 953-6000 .. **Miller,** Neil S '95 (Katsky K LLP) -605 3rd Av -NY 10158
(516) 571-9030 .. **Miller,** Neil T '82 Family Ct -1200 Old Cntry Rd -Westbury 11590
(212) 440-3432 .. **Miller,** Neil T '88 CNA Pro -40 Wall -NY 10005
(212) 909-6000 .. **Miller,** Nicholas W '09 %Debevoise & P LLP -919 3rd Av -NY 10022
(718) 286-6000 .. **Miller,** Noliesa A '06 %DA -125-01 Qns Blvd -Kew Gdns 11415
(212) 715-1000 .. **Miller,** Pamela Addison '98 (Arnold & P LLP) -399 Park Av -NY 10022
(212) 788-0876 .. **Miller,** Patricia B '90 %Law Dept -100 Church -NY 10007 **Fx:**788-0367
(212) 836-8000 .. **Miller,** Paul S '63 SpclCnsl Kaye S LLP -425 Park Av -NY 10022
(212) 636-6901 .. **Miller,** Paul S '00 Fordham Law Library -140 W 62nd -NY 10023
(631) 979-6666 .. **Miller,** Paula Ann '93 (PA Miller,PC) -308 W Main -Smithtwn 11787 **Fx:**979-6701
(212) 969-3000 .. **Miller,** Paula L '06 %Proskauer R LLP -1585 Bway -NY 10036
(212) 448-1800 .. **Miller,** Peggy A '78 Cnsl Roberts RLSC&F LLP -235 Park Av S -NY 10003
(914) 337-0154 .. **Miller,** Percy S '68 -219 Grandvw Blvd -Ynkrs 10710
(646) 264-3650 .. **Miller,** Percy S '68 %US Dept of Labor -201 Varick -NY 10014 **Fx:**264-3660
(212) 872-1000 .. **Miller,** Peter A '85 -One Bryant Park -NY 10036 **Fx:**872-1002
(607) 272-3442 .. **Miller,** Peter J '86 (Adams TM&M) -301 Clinton Hse -Ithaca 14850
(315) 478-4832 .. **Miller,** Philip C '78 -201 E Jffrsn -Syracuse 13202 **Fx:**475-4835
(518) 459-1803 .. **Miller,** Philip C '83 -17 Computer Dr E -Albany 12205 **Fx:**459-2048
(212) 725-9800 .. **Miller,** Philip J '90 %Osborn Law,PC -295 Mad Av -NY 10017
(718) 641-8380 .. **Miller,** Phyllis D '90 -86-11 151 Av -Howard Bch 11414
(914) 668-9600 .. **Miller & Platt,PC** -175 Main -White Plns 10601 **Fx:**668-6646
(607) 273-4200 .. **Miller,** R James '79 (Miller M,LLP) -202 E State -Ithaca 14850
(212) 373-3000 .. **Miller,** Rachale C '07 %Paul WRW&G LLP -1285 Av of Amer -NY 10019
(212) 770-1919 .. **Miller,** Rachel '89 %AIG -80 Pine -NY 10005
(212) 512-1000 .. **Miller,** Rachel A '96 HBO -1100 Av of Amer -NY 10036 **Fx:**512-1986
(212) 566-1000 .. **Miller,** Raina F '09 %Sullivan & B LLP -115 Bway -NY 10006 **Fx:**566-1068
(718) 461-6633 .. **Miller,** Randall P '85 %Mallilo & G -163-09 Nrthrn Blvd -Flushng 11358
(347) 563-0162 .. **Miller,** Randi S '93 OfCnsl Bains Law Grp,PC -12 East 8th -NY 10003 **Fx:**(212) 674-1827
(585) 232-6500 .. **Miller,** Raymond P '90 (Harter S&E LLP) -1600 Bausch & Lomb Pl -Rchstr 14604
(212) 455-2000 .. **Miller,** Richd A '70 OfCnsl Simpson T&B LLP -425 Lex Av -NY 10017
(631) 543-3030 .. **Miller,** Richd A '70 (Miller & S,LLP) -356 Vets Mem'l Hwy -Commack 11725 **Fx:**543-2888
(718) 596-7789 .. **Miller,** Richd A '86 -186 Montague -Brklyn 11201
(212) 460-3389 .. **Miller,** Richd B '88 Con Ed -4 Irving Pl -NY 10003
(518) 464-9700 .. **Miller,** Richd C Jr. '79 Cnsl RC Miller Jr,PLLC -Bx12155 -Albany 12212 **Fx:**292-1635
(212) 867-9500 .. **Miller,** Richd E '62 Cnsl Kurzman K&F,LLP -230 Park Av -NY 10169
(607) 785-7160 .. **Miller,** Richd H II '94 -2304 North -Endicott 13760 **Fx:**785-7168
(212) 596-6245 .. **Miller,** Richd I '73 American Inst CPA's -1211 Av of Amer -NY 10036 **Fx:**596-6104
(518) 465-7591 .. **Miller,** Richd J '72 (Miller & D,PC) -14 Corp Wds Blvd -Albany 12211
(212) 418-0570 .. **Miller,** Richd J Jr. '90 (Morris & M LLP) -767 3rd Av -NY 10017
(518) 426-8111 .. **Miller,** Richd J Jr. '90 (Morris & M LLP) -19 Dove -Albany 12210
(212) 536-3900 .. **Miller,** Richd S '78 (K&L Gates LLP) -599 Lex Av -NY 10022
(516) 877-5600 .. **Miller,** Richd W '74 %R Tusa -1225 Franklin Av -Gdn Cty 11530 **Fx:**877-5695
(914) 834-3500 .. **Miller,** Rita J '86 OfCnsl McMillan CM&P LLP -2180 Bstn Post Rd -Larchmnt 10538
(716) 894-0235 .. **Miller,** Robt '57 (Miller & M) -1332 Walden Av -Buffalo 14211
(212) 770-5810 .. **Miller,** Robt A '90 AIG Global Srvcs,Inc -72 Wall -NY 10005
(212) 557-7700 .. **Miller,** Robt C '65 (Davidson D&C LLP) -60 E 42nd -NY 10165
(518) 371-2320 .. **Miller,** Robt C '69 %Windsor Dvlpmnt -Bx1549 -Clifton Pk 12065
(518) 371-2320 .. **Miller,** Robt C Jr. '00 Cnsl Windsor Dvlpmnt -5 South Dr Bx1549 -Clifton Pk 12065
(212) 723-6020 .. **Miller,** Robt D '95 Salomon Smith Barney -390 Greenwich -NY 10013
(718) 261-7700 .. **Miller,** Robt I '85 (Rappaport HC&R,PC) -118-35 Qns Blvd -Frst Hlls 11375
(845) 454-5909 .. **Miller,** Robt Irving '94 (Sholes & M,LLP) -327 Mill -Poughkeepsie 12601
(212) 689-5933 .. **Miller,** Robt J '69 -16 E 34th -NY 10016 **Fx:**532-3206
(212) 297-5800 .. **Miller,** Robt J '71 (Day P LLP) -7 Times Sq -NY 10036
(212) 593-7399 .. **Miller,** Robt M '78 -535 Mad Av -NY 10022
(212) 328-6180 .. **Miller,** Robin S '82 %CMW Lgl Search -845 3rd Av -NY 10022 **Fx:**328-6181
(212) 310-8000 .. **Miller,** Rodney D '02 (Weil G&M LLP) -767 5th Av -NY 10153
(212) 585-3425 .. **Miller,** Ryan O '07 %B Kishner & Assoc -420 Lex Av -NY 10170 **Fx:**752-1810
(212) 562-4961 .. **Miller,** Sally J '86 %MHLS -Bellevue Hsptl 27th & 1st Av -NY 10016
(212) 506-5000 .. **Miller,** Sam S '66 (Orrick H&S LLP) -51 W 52nd -NY 10019
(518) 782-4900 .. **Miller,** Samantha '07 %LaFave L&S,LLP -951 Albany Shaker Rd -Latham 12110 **Fx:**785-9705
(212) 245-1000 .. **Miller,** Saml R '08 OfCnsl Outten & G LLP -3 Park Av -NY 10016
(516) 887-6607 .. **Miller,** Saml W '84 -381 Sunrise Hwy -Lynbrk 11563 **Fx:**887-3372
(607) 723-9511 .. **Miller,** Scot G '00 (Coughlin & G,LLP) -19 Chenango Bx2039 -Bnghmtn 13902
(718) 797-0700 .. **Miller,** Scott A '88 -16 Court -Brklyn 11241 **Fx:**855-2427
(607) 273-5475 .. **Miller,** Scott A '96 (Holmberg GV&M) -200 E Buffalo -Ithaca 14850
(716) 841-4230 .. **Miller,** Scott D '84 %HSBC Bank -1 HSBC Ctr -Buffalo 14203 **Fx:**841-5087
(212) 527-1000 .. **Miller,** Scott E '82 (Jones HC&B PC) -1 Bttry Pk Plz -NY 10004
(631) 756-9530 .. **Miller,** Scott J '09 Milcon Construction Corp -142 Dale -W Babylon 11704
(212) 869-7000 .. **Miller,** Scott M '86 (Feldman W&S LLP) -420 Lex Av -NY 10170
(212) 333-1502 .. **Miller,** Scott M '99 Trident Media Grp -41 Mad Av -NY 10010
(212) 259-8000 .. **Miller,** Sebastian L '09 %Dewey & L LLP -1301 Av of Amer -NY 10019
(212) 587-2400 .. **Miller,** Seth A '87 (Collins D&M,LLP) -277 Bway -NY 10007
(212) 686-0783 .. **Miller,** Seymour '56 -Murray Hill Station Bx1102 -NY 10156 **Fx:**779-1918
(212) 801-3131 .. **Miller,** Simon '94 (Greenberg T,LLP) -200 Park Av -NY 10166
(914) 946-3700 .. **Miller,** Sondra '55 Cnsl McCarthy F LLP -11 Martine Av -White Plns 10606
(212) 488-3417 .. **Miller,** Sonia E '99 -244 5th Av -NY 10001 **Fx:**432-7600
(631) 692-4322 .. **Miller,** Stacey Rabine '93 %Bristol-Myers Squibb Co -31 Garnett Pl -Melvll 11747 **Fx:**692-9166
(212) 698-3500 .. **Miller,** Stefan M '09 %Dechert LLP -1095 Av of Amer -NY 10036
(212) 815-1818 .. **Miller,** Stefanie A '07 DC 37 MELS -125 Barclay -NY 10007 **Fx:**815-1343
(631) 853-4545 .. **Miller,** Stephen B '78 %District Ct Law Dept -400 Carleton Av Bx9075 -Central Islip 11722
(716) 373-8010 .. **Miller,** Stephen D '82 Cnty Dept Soc Srvcs -1701 Lincoln Av -Olean 14760
(212) 558-4000 .. **Miller,** Stephen E '10 %Sullivan & C LLP -125 Broad -NY 10004
(516) 484-4010 .. **Miller,** Steven '79 (Miller M&S) -99 Powerhse Rd -Roslyn Hts 11577
(516) 747-8830 .. **Miller,** Steven E '91 %Jaghab & J -176 Mineola Blvd -Mineola 11501 **Fx:**747-8770
(718) 330-7861 .. **Miller,** Steven G '92 Ofc of Hearings & Appls -111 Lvngstn -Brklyn 11201
(914) 333-7420 .. **Miller,** Steven J '84 %Akzo Nobel -120 Wht Plns Rd -Tarrytwn 10591
(718) 250-2000 .. **Miller,** Steven R '89 %DA -350 Jay -Brklyn 11201 **Fx:**250-2314
(212) 552-0671 .. **Miller,** Steven S '71 JP Morgan Chase -1 Chase Manh Plz -NY 10081
(212) 581-5005 .. **Miller,** Stuart '87 (Lankenau & M LLP) -132 Nassau -NY 10038
(914) 323-7000 .. **Miller,** Stuart A '97 (Wilson EME&D LLP) -3 Gannett Dr -White Plns 10604
(212) 490-3000 .. **Miller,** Stuart A '97 (Wilson EME&D LLP) -150 E 42nd -NY 10017
(315) 568-9841 .. **Miller,** Stuart O '64 Miller & M -Bx364 -Seneca Fls 13148 **Fx:**568-9842
(845) 677-3494 .. **Miller,** Susan '76 (Miller & A) -110 Church BxC -Millbrook 12545
(516) 248-6000 .. **Miller,** Susan '91 %Kaufman B&R -1205 Franklin Av -Gdn Cty 11530
(212) 408-1136 .. **Miller,** Suzanna C '95 -30 Rckfllr Plz -NY 10112
(212) 607-8636 .. **Miller,** Tamar E '06 US Dept of Labor-EBSA -33 Whitehall -NY 10004
(716) 894-0235 .. **Miller,** Terence W '87 (Miller & M) -1332 Walden Av -Buffalo 14211
(607) 722-4934 .. **Miller,** Thos '79 -Bx11472 -Albany 12211 **Fx:**(800) 546-7601
(607) 758-5588 .. **Miller,** Thos H '95 Cnty Conflict Atty -60 Central Av -Cortlnd 13045 **Fx:**753-5325
(315) 448-0126 .. **Miller,** Thos J '82 -314 E Fayette -Syracuse 13202 **Fx:**448-0246
(914) 457-2300 .. **Miller,** Thos J '86 (Kanterman & S,LLP) -50 Main -White Plns 10606
(212) 941-0792 .. **Miller,** Thos K '85 (Miller & C) -377 Bway -NY 10013 **Fx:**431-4460
(212) 880-3800 .. **Miller,** Todd A '06 (Akerman S) -335 Mad Av -NY 10017
(631) 821-7700 .. **Miller,** Todd C '95 (Miller & C,LLP) -3400 Vets Mem'l Hwy -Bohemia 11716 **Fx:**821-8700
(607) 565-8181 .. **Miller,** Todd H '03 -447 Fulton -Waverly 14892
(212) 267-6703 .. **Miller,** Tracey J '85 -170 Bway -NY 10038
(212) 241-6868 .. **Miller,** Tracy E '83 %Mt Sinai Dept Health Policy -1 Gustave A Levy Pl Bx 1077 -NY 10029
(914) 725-0300 .. **Miller,** W Rowland '59 (Judy M&O,PC) -700 Wht Plns Rd -Scarsdale 10583
(516) 294-5775 .. **Miller,** Wayne G '95 (Klee & W,LLP) -350 Willis Av -Mineola 11501
(212) 278-0400 .. **Miller,** Wendy E '90 (Cooper & D LLP) -30 Rckfllr Plz -NY 10112
(516) 248-6568 .. **Miller,** Willard F '85 WF Miller,LLP -350 Old Cntry Rd -Gdn Cty 11530 **Fx:**248-2427
(212) 312-6704 .. **Miller,** Wm '97 Benchmark Co -40 Fulton -NY 10038
(631) 727-2818 .. **Miller,** Wm C '87 -312 Roanoke Av -Rvrhead 11901 **Fx:**727-0636
(212) 557-7700 .. **Miller,** Wm H Jr. '67 (Davidson D&C LLP) -60 E 42nd -NY 10165
(585) 343-6362 .. **Miller,** Wm H '76 -205 Naramore Dr -Batavia 14020
(212) 788-1006 .. **Miller,** Wm H '05 Law Dept -100 Church -NY 10007 **Fx:**788-0367
(212) 701-3000 .. **Miller,** Wm J '01 (Cahill G&R LLP) -80 Pine -NY 10005 **Fx:**269-5420
(212) 450-4000 .. **Miller,** Wm R Jr. '07 %Davis P&W LLP -450 Lex Av -NY 10017
(212) 336-3500 .. **Miller & Wrubel,PC** -570 Lex Av -NY 10022 **Fx:**336-3555
(212) 972-4900 .. **Miller,** Yoram J '99 (Shapiro FA&S LLP) -380 Mad Av -NY 10017
(212) 909-6000 .. **Millerman,** Elena M '01 %Debevoise & P LLP -919 3rd Av -NY 10022
(212) 450-4000 .. **Millerman,** James M '00 %Davis P&W LLP -450 Lex Av -NY 10017
(212) 735-3000 .. **Miller-Ojeda Hagglund,** Cristina I '08 %Skadden ASM&F LLP -4 Times Sq -NY 10036
(212) 644-4420 .. **Miller Ostrover,** Marla '90 OfCnsl Fabiani C&H,LLP -570 Lex Av -NY 10022
(212) 931-7482 .. **Miller-Wachtel,** Ellen '78 %MLB Properties -245 Park Av -NY 10167 **Fx:**949-5697
(718) 624-2482 .. **Millet,** Michl A '67 -32 Court -Brklyn 11201 **Fx:**625-6837
(212) 993-3481 .. **Millet,** Ronald '92 %FSA -31 W 52nd -NY 10019 **Fx:**893-2710
(212) 351-4500 .. **Millett,** Eileen D '78 Cnsl Epstein B&G,PC -250 Park Av -NY 10177
(212) 218-2100 .. **Millett,** Fredk C '09 %Fitzpatrick CH&S -1290 Av of Amer -NY 10104
(212) 903-9000 .. **Millett,** Jessica M '07 %Linklaters -1345 Av of Amer -NY 10105
(607) 397-1111 .. **Millias,** Paul J '98 -222 Main -Worcester 12197 **Fx:**397-1001
(212) 640-1219 .. **Millien,** Raymond '04 Amer Exp -200 Vesey -NY 10285
(212) 869-2300 .. **Milligan,** Connie L '08 %Toback B&R,LLP -15 W 44th -NY 10036
(212) 732-3200 .. **Milligan,** Emily L '04 %Carter L&M LLP -2 Wall -NY 10005
(631) 422-8400 .. **Milligan,** Jos A '59 -200 W Main Bx328 -Babylon 11702 **Fx:**422-8483
(212) 310-8000 .. **Milligan,** Peter M '10 %Weil G&M LLP -767 5th Av -NY 10153
(212) 558-4000 .. **Milligan,** Stephen T '09 %Sullivan & C LLP -125 Broad -NY 10004

(845) 565-1100 .. **Milligram,** Steven I '82 (Tarshis CLM&M,PLLC) -One Corwin Ct -Newburgh 12550
(585) 753-3485 .. **Milliken,** David R '83 Conflict Def Ofc -30 W Broad -Rchstr 14614 **Fx:**324-4245
(315) 453-3053 .. **Milliman,** Christopher T '91 %Finkelstein & Prtnrs,LLP -716 7th N -Liverpool 13088
(716) 858-2424 .. **Milling,** Donna A '88 %DA -25 Delaware Av -Buffalo 14202 **Fx:**858-7425
(212) 506-5000 .. **Milling,** R King Jr. '01 (Orrick H&S LLP) -51 W 52nd -NY 10019
(212) 423-3500 .. **Millinger,** Donald M '01 %Guggenheim Msm -1071 5th Av -NY 10128
(518) 668-5491 .. **Millington,** Susan E '99 -377 Canada -Lk George 12845 **Fx:**668-5492
(518) 668-5491 .. **Millington,** Wm W '53 -377 Canada -Lk George 12845 **Fx:**668-5492
(212) 902-9408 .. **Millis,** Wm D '01 Goldman Sachs -1 NY Plz -NY 10004
(631) 367-7100 .. **Millkey,** Mark T '90 Coughlin SGR&R LLP -58 S Srvc Rd -Melvll 11747
(212) 583-9600 .. **Millman,** Bruce R '74 (Littler M,PC) -900 3rd Av -NY 10022
(212) 969-3000 .. **Millman,** Claude '89 (Proskauer R LLP) -1585 Bway -NY 10036
(516) 677-9400 .. **Millman,** Danl L '93 %Goldstein & A -575 Underhill Blvd -Syosset 11791
(212) 406-4700 .. **Millman,** Debra '89 -60 E 42nd -NY 10165
(845) 947-1100 .. **Millman,** Jeffrey T '92 (Phillips & M,LLP) -148 Route 9W -Stony Pnt 10980
(212) 554-7800 .. **Millman,** Jenna R '04 %Moses & S LLP -405 Lex Av -NY 10174
(845) 471-1775 .. **Millman,** Jode Susan '80 (JS Millman,PC) -97-99 Cannon -Poughkeepsie 12601 **Fx:**471-2035
(212) 735-8600 .. **Millman,** Marissa L '05 %Morrison C LLP -909 3rd Av -NY 10022
(212) 288-7933 .. **Millman,** Mary Zitwer '82 -342 E 67th -NY 10065
(212) 575-1292 .. **Millman,** Matthew B '08 %Uncyk B&N,LLP -555 5th Av -NY 10017
(914) 684-6518 .. **Millman,** Paul M '81 -1 N Bway -White Plns 10601 **Fx:**684-0196
(212) 261-1000 .. **Millman,** Raquel A '03 Elizabeth Arden Inc -200 Park Av S -NY 10003
(212) 806-5400 .. **Millman,** Sherry J '85 %Stroock &S&L LLP -180 Maiden Ln -NY 10038
(212) 922-2200 .. **Millman,** Stephen L '79 (Watson F&W LLP) -1133 Av of Amer -NY 10036
(212) 983-1221 .. **Millman,** Valerie '96 %Ochs & G,LLP -60 E 42nd -NY 10165
(718) 222-0719 .. **Millman,** Warren L '84 -189 Montague -Brklyn 11201 **Fx:**875-6797
(212) 261-8000 .. **Millman,** Wendy B '83 SrCnsl Mendes & M,LLP -750 7th Av -NY 10019
(212) 213-1220 .. **Millo,** Frank R '82 (Weiner MM&B,LLC) -220 5th Av -NY 10001
(518) 427-2650 .. **Millock,** Peter J '74 (Nixon P LLP) -677 Bway -Albany 12207
(718) 325-5000 .. **Millon,** Steven E '85 %M Pfeifer -714 E 241st -Bronx 10470 **Fx:**324-0333
(845) 331-8350 .. **Millouras-Lettre,** Rebecca '00 R Millouras-Lettre,PLLC -736 Bway -Kingston 12401 **Fx:**331-1132
(212) 308-4411 .. **Mills,** Amber S M '09 %Edwards AP&D LLP -750 Lex Av -NY 10022
(212) 837-6000 .. **Mills,** Carl W '06 %Hughes H&R LLP -1 Bttry Pk Plz -NY 10004
(516) 759-4300 .. **Mills,** Chas G IV '67 -56 Schl -Glen Cove 11542 **Fx:**759-4329
(518) 373-9900 .. **Mills,** Christopher K '05 (Mills Law Firm,LLP) -1520 Crescent Rd -Clifton Pk 12065 **Fx:**383-7162
(212) 732-9000 .. **Mills,** Donte O '06 %Sullivan PBM&C PC -120 Bway -NY 10271
(518) 402-6757 .. **Mills,** Douglas J '93 %Workers Comp Bd -20 Park -Albany 12207
(212) 637-3198 .. **Mills,** Flaire Hope '87 %EPA -290 Bway -NY 10007 **Fx:**637-3199
(212) 788-0300 .. **Mills,** G Foster '79 %Law Dept -100 Church -NY 10007 **Fx:**788-0367
(518) 377-3096 .. **Mills,** George R '60 -524 Engleman Av -Scotia 12302
(518) 373-9900 .. **Mills,** Gregory S '76 (Mills Law Firm,LLP) -1520 Crescent Rd -Clifton Pk 12065 **Fx:**383-7162
(518) 487-5460 .. **Mills,** Jasper L '07 %DA -6 Lodge -Albany 12207 **Fx:**487-5093
(212) 504-6000 .. **Mills,** Jessica V '10 %Cadwalader W&T LLP -1 World Fncl Ctr -NY 10281
(212) 554-1400 .. **Mills,** John J '03 %Bernstein LB&G LLP -1285 Av of Amer -NY 10019
(315) 785-3053 .. **Mills,** Kristyna S '96 %DA -175 Arsenal -Watertwn 13601 **Fx:**785-3371
(518) 758-9200 .. **Mills,** Lisa M '99 -2880 Route 9 Bx811 -Valatie 12184 **Fx:**758-9201
(212) 264-2719 .. **Mills,** Marguerite Clymene '94 %DHS -26 Fed Plz -NY 10278
(718) 928-3700 .. **Mills,** Maura McHugh '05 LSNYC-Bronx -579 Courtlandt Av -Bronx 10451 **Fx:**402-7586
(212) 450-4264 .. **Mills,** Michl '76 -450 Lex Av -NY 10017 **Fx:**450-5742
(212) 450-4000 .. **Mills,** Phillip R '87 (Davis P&W LLP) -450 Lex Av -NY 10017
(212) 483-9490 .. **Mills,** Richd S '87 (McElroy DM&C,LLP) -88 Pine -NY 10005
(516) 333-4526 .. **Mills,** Richd Scott '98 %RTP Environmental Assoc -400 Post Av -Westbury 11590
(716) 854-2620 .. **Mills,** Ryan J '04 (Brown & K,LLP) -1500 Lbrty Bldg -Buffalo 14202
(212) 309-1000 .. **Mills,** Sara K '09 %Hunton & W -200 Park Av -NY 10166
(212) 309-1000 .. **Mills,** Sharon M '08 %Hunton & W -200 Park Av -NY 10166
(212) 813-8800 .. **Mills,** Stephen G '85 (Goodwin P LLP) -620 8th Av -NY 10018
(516) 484-4010 .. **Mills,** Tanisha N '10 %Miller M&S -99 Powerhse Rd -Roslyn Hts 11577
(212) 504-6000 .. **Mills,** Wm P III '92 (Cadwalader W&T LLP) -1 World Fncl Ctr -NY 10281
(212) 431-2380 .. **Mills,** Wm R '83 %NY Law Schl -185 W Bway -NY 10013 **Fx:**965-8839
(212) 474-1000 .. **Millson,** Rory O '78 (Cravath S&M LLP) -825 8th Av -NY 10019
(212) 468-8000 .. **Mills-Robertson,** Richd B '02 %Morrison & F LLP -1290 Av of Amer -NY 10104
(212) 310-8000 .. **Millstein,** Ira M '49 (Weil G&M LLP) -767 5th Av -NY 10153
(212) 632-1940 .. **Millstein,** James E '83 Lazard Freres & Co -30 Rckfllr Plz -NY 10112
(212) 468-8000 .. **Millstein,** Julian S '79 SrCnsl Morrison & F LLP -1290 Av of Amer -NY 10104
(212) 888-3133 .. **Millstein,** Mona R '82 -150 E 58th -NY 10155 **Fx:**317-2946
(607) 723-5341 .. **Millus,** Albert J Jr. '83 (Hinman H&K,LLP) -80 Exchange Bx5250 -Bnghmtn 13902
(212) 317-8500 .. **Millus,** Paul F '87 (Snitow KH&M,LLP) -575 Lex Av -NY 10022
(914) 428-9098 .. **Milman,** Harvey F '66 Drew Indstrs -200 Mamaroneck Av -White Plns 10601
(516) 328-8899 .. **Milman,** Lawr I '63 (Milman L Law Grp PLLC) -3000 Marcus Av -Lk Success 11042 **Fx:**328-0082
(718) 625-1015 .. **Milman,** Leon A '66 -26 Court -Brklyn 11242 **Fx:**858-5144
(516) 328-8899 .. **Milman,** Richd I '95 %Milman L Law Grp PLLC -3000 Marcus Av -Lk Success 11042 **Fx:**328-0082
(516) 328-8899 .. **Milman,** Robt F '89 %Milman L Law Grp PLLC -3000 Marcus Av -Lk Success 11042 **Fx:**328-0082
(212) 819-8200 .. **Milmed,** Paul K '76 OfCnsl White & C LLP -1155 Av of Amer -NY 10036
(212) 735-3000 .. **Milmoe,** J Gregory Jr. '76 (Skadden ASM&F LLP) -4 Times Sq -NY 10036
(212) 848-4000 .. **Milne,** Gregory B '05 %Shearman & S LLP -599 Lex Av -NY 10022
(212) 373-3000 .. **Milne,** Julia Bartolf '10 %Paul WRW&G LLP -1285 Av of Amer -NY 10019
(718) 725-3048 .. **Milne,** Lois A '00 %ACS-DLS -151-20 Jamaica Av -Jamaica 11432 **Fx:**725-3124
(212) 819-8200 .. **Milne,** Robt A '90 (White & C LLP) -1155 Av of Amer -NY 10036
(718) 523-6622 .. **Milne,** Thos W '73 -Bx1407 -Montauk 11954
(212) 935-3131 .. **Milner,** David N '76 (Gallet D&B,LLP) -845 3rd Av -NY 10022
(315) 797-5200 .. **Milner,** David R '87 %Cmmrcl Trvlrs Mtl -70 Genesee -Utica 13502 **Fx:**797-3198
(516) 561-6622 .. **Milner,** Eric M '08 %Simon & M -99 W Hawthorne Av -Vly Stream 11580
(212) 841-1000 .. **Milner,** Jessica S '07 %Covington & B LLP -620 8th Av -NY 10018
(718) 766-5242 .. **Milner,** Julie M '09 (Milner & Z) -8302 Bway -Elmhrst 11373
(516) 561-6622 .. **Milner,** Martin L '77 (Simon & M) -99 W Hawthorne Av -Vly Stream 11580
(212) 475-3673 .. **Milner,** Michl M '83 (Tese & M) -1 Minetta Ln -NY 10012
(212) 278-0400 .. **Milner,** Richd S '91 (Cooper & D LLP) -30 Rckfllr Plz -NY 10112
(212) 603-6300 .. **Milner,** Robt M '65 (Robinson BLGG&G PC) -875 3rd Av -NY 10022
(917) 626-0366 .. **Milo,** Chas '84 -327 Cntrl Pk W -NY 10025
(212) 758-9927 .. **Milonas,** Chas G '85 -239 E 51st -NY 10022 **Fx:**583-0003
(212) 858-1000 .. **Milonas,** E Leo '60 (Pillsbury WSP LLP) -1540 Bway -NY 10036
(585) 428-4302 .. **Milonas,** Valerie J '99 Hon J Valentino -545 Hall of Justice -Rchstr 14614 **Fx:**428-1885
(516) 296-1000 .. **Milone,** Christina Miller '93 (Miller & M,PC) -100 Q Roosevelt Blvd -Gdn Cty 11530
(631) 390-0010 .. **Milone,** Kristina L '09 %Bruno G&S,LLP -445 Broad Hollow Rd -Melvll 11747
(516) 766-3644 .. **Milone,** Louis J Jr. '72 (L Milone Jr,PC) -Bx1523 -Baldwin 11510 **Fx:**766-5770
(914) 997-2500 .. **Milone,** Lydia A '90 (Bodnar & M LLP) -140 Grand -White Plns 10601 **Fx:**997-8155
(516) 633-1308 .. **Milone,** Mary D '96 -8 Elm Av -Farmngdl 11735
(516) 280-2895 .. **Milone,** Philip S '83 -1055 Franklin Av -Gdn Cty 11530 **Fx:**280-2879
(718) 262-7993 .. **Milone,** Ralph P '88 Div of Housing & Cmmnty Renewal -9231 Union Hall -Jamaica 11433
(518) 862-1090 .. **Milonovich,** Valerie S '93 %NYSERDA -17 Columbia Cir -Albany 12203 **Fx:**862-1091
(212) 465-1110 .. **Miloski,** Darlene S '94 %Bader Y&N LLP -350 5th Av -NY 10118
(212) 444-8084 .. **Milovansky,** Bistra '05 -381 Park Av S -NY 10016 **Fx:**889-8688
(716) 878-9413 .. **Milovich,** Erin M '06 Benderson Dvlpmnt Co -570 Delaware Av -Buffalo 14202
(212) 849-7000 .. **Milowic,** Jos '08 %Quinn EU&S,LLP -51 Mad Av -NY 10010
(212) 804-4200 .. **Milrad,** Joshua L '96 %Mound CW&G -One Bttry Pk Plz -NY 10004
(718) 797-5166 .. **Milsap,** Michl R '86 -283 Adams -Brklyn 11201
(212) 350-2700 .. **Milstein,** Abby S '78 (Constantine C,PC) -450 Lex Av -NY 10017
(212) 259-8000 .. **Milstein,** Ariel '06 %Dewey & L LLP -1301 Av of Amer -NY 10019
(212) 801-6495 .. **Milstein,** Danl R '93 %Greenberg T,LLP -200 Park Av -NY 10166
(518) 408-2491 .. **Milstein,** David E '85 %Ofc for Technology -State Cptl ESP Bx2062 -Albany 12220
(212) 751-8000 .. **Milstein,** Edw P '75 (Dankner & M,PC) -41 E 57th -NY 10022
(212) 708-0830 .. **Milstein,** Howard P '78 -335 Mad Av -NY 10017
(518) 462-6433 .. **Milstein,** James P '84 (Milstein & M) -293 Wshngtn Av -Albany 12206 **Fx:**462-6436
(212) 643-8904 .. **Milstein,** Rakhel S '04 %Assadi & M,LLP -200 W 57th -NY 10019 **Fx:**643-9192
(518) 462-6433 .. **Milstein,** Susan B '82 (Milstein & M) -293 Wshngtn Av -Albany 12206 **Fx:**462-6436
(212) 736-4500 .. **Miltenberg,** Andrew T '91 (Nesenoff & M,LLP) -363 7th Av -NY 10001
(212) 857-8700 .. **Milton,** Karen Greve '82 %US Cts for the 2nd Circuit -40 Foley Sq -NY 10007 **Fx:**857-8680
(212) 624-1200 .. **Milton,** Robt C III '00 CIFC -250 Park Av -NY 10177 **Fx:**624-1199
(845) 291-2050 .. **Milza,** Michl E '97 %DA -255-275 Main -Goshen 10924 **Fx:**291-2085
(212) 370-1300 .. **Mimeles,** Adam S '97 (Ellenoff G&S LLP) -150 E 42nd -NY 10017
(347) 404-9133 .. **Mimes,** Sherveal R '10 Civil Ct -141 Lvngstn -Brklyn 11201 **Fx:**(718) 643-3733
(631) 627-3923 .. **Mims,** Jerry M '97 J Mims PC -130 Barton Av -Patchogue 11772
(212) 736-0650 .. **Min,** Dae-Ki '85 -38 W 32nd -NY 10001 **Fx:**465-8648
(212) 310-8000 .. **Min,** Eric H '08 %Weil G&M LLP -767 5th Av -NY 10153
(212) 766-1100 .. **Min,** Esther Kyong '87 (Ragues & M,LLP) -11 Bway -NY 10004
(718) 875-1300 .. **Min,** Kyong-Ah Evelyn '01 %Appllt Div 2nd Dept -45 Monroe Pl -Brklyn 11201 **Fx:**858-2446
(212) 297-6114 .. **Min,** Richd '08 (Camhi & M LLC) -420 Lex Av -NY 10170 **Fx:**479-2521
(212) 586-9830 .. **Min,** Saml K '93 -146 W 57th -NY 10019 **Fx:**754-0038
(212) 506-5000 .. **Min,** Sie Ne Chris '07 %Orrick H&S LLP -51 W 52nd -NY 10019
(914) 640-8100 .. **Min,** Wm E '91 %Starwood Hotels & Resorts -1111 Wstchstr Av -White Plns 10604 **Fx:**640-8250
(212) 533-0415 .. **Mina,** F V '67 FV Mina,PC -624 E 20th -NY 10009
(212) 818-8062 .. **Minami,** Eri '97 Itochu Intl -335 Mad Av -NY 10017 **Fx:**818-8493
(845) 834-2555 .. **Minard,** Jason D '06 (Minard Law,PLLC) -3665 Route 9W Bx817 -Highlnd 12528 **Fx:**834-2559
(212) 610-6300 .. **Minas,** Jacob A '98 SrCnsl Allen & O -1221 Av of Amer -NY 10020
(631) 261-7777 .. **Minasi,** Jos P '83 (Bushell K&M) -7 Bayview Av -Northprt 11768
(212) 481-1900 .. **Minasian,** Lawr D '00 (Del Valle & Assoc) -445 Park Av -NY 10022 **Fx:**481-4853
(212) 631-0880 .. **Minasz,** Michl '72 -111 John -NY 10038

(212) 697-9280 .. **Minc,** Danl C '78 (Rosenberg MF&W) -122 E 42nd -NY 10168
(631) 462-5888 .. **Mincer,** Jane Dillof '81 %Rubin & R, PLLC -6080 Jericho Tpk -Commack 11725
(212) 226-5600 .. **Minchenberg,** Alfred '53 (Minchenberg & W) -401 Bway -NY 10013 **Fx:**941-5963
(718) 727-7700 .. **Minchew,** Jamie M '87 (Minchew S&B,LLP) -1741 Victory Blvd -Staten Isl 10314
(631) 423-4390 .. **Mincone,** Eugene J '01 %Mincone & M,PC -110 Walt Whitman Rd -South Huntington 11746 **Fx:**423-4408
(631) 423-4390 .. **Mincone,** John V '91 (Mincone & M,PC) -110 Walt Whitman Rd -South Huntington 11746 **Fx:**423-4408
(631) 423-4390 .. **Mincone,** Jos '87 (Mincone & M,PC) -110 Walt Whitman Rd -South Huntington 11746 **Fx:**423-4408
(718) 780-7956 .. **Minda,** Gary '88 %Bklyn Law Schl -250 Joralemon -Brklyn 11201 **Fx:**780-0393
(516) 773-2000 .. **Mindel,** Alan M '99 -30 Cuttermill Rd -Gt Neck 11021
(212) 596-9000 .. **Mindell,** David W '09 %Ropes & G LLP -1211 Av of Amer -NY 10036
(315) 448-4800 .. **Mindell,** James J '86 %OCTF -615 Erie Blvd W -Syracuse 13204 **Fx:**448-4858
(212) 416-8323 .. **Mindell,** Stephen E '59 %Dept of Law -120 Bway -NY 10271
(212) 245-6565 .. **Mindell,** Susan '96 (Levine P&M,LLP) -1740 Bway -NY 10019
(212) 757-8112 .. **Minder,** David J '74 Sterling National Bnk -650 5th Av -NY 10019
(914) 232-2433 .. **Mindich,** Bernard '61 -189 Waccabuc Rd -Goldens Bridge 10526 **Fx:**232-0323
(212) 821-1533 .. **Mindich,** Mark J '97 Renaissance Tech -800 3rd Av -NY 10022
(212) 805-0184 .. **Mindlin,** Danielle Posen '09 Hon H Baer -500 Pearl -NY 10007
(607) 257-8075 .. **Mindlin,** Mindy '94 -112 Midway Rd -Ithaca 14850
(212) 403-1000 .. **Mindlin,** Philip '85 (Wachtell LR&K) -51 W 52nd -NY 10019
(518) 562-0600 .. **Mindoro,** Erin R '08 %O'Connell & A -206 W Bay Plz -Plattsbrgh 12901
(585) 263-1000 .. **Mindy,** Steven C '09 %Nixon P LLP -1100 Clinton Sq -Rchstr 14604
(518) 464-1300 .. **Mineaux,** John R '85 (Roemer WG&M LLP) -13 Columbia Cir -Albany 12203
(631) 724-0200 .. **Minella,** Adam A '88 -199 E Main -Smithtwn 11787 **Fx:**265-2832
(718) 824-7600 .. **Minella,** Alexander '52 -2815 Mddltwn Rd -Bronx 10461
(212) 264-2842 .. **Minella,** Nicholas J '04 %Hon G Carman -1 Fed Plz -NY 10278
(631) 724-0200 .. **Minella,** Tracey A '88 -199 E Main -Smithtwn 11787 **Fx:**265-2832
(631) 777-1700 .. **Mineo,** Gregory M '06 %Vitale & L,PC -445 Broad Hollow Rd -Melvll 11747
(716) 635-5169 .. **Mineo,** John '87 Tops Markets -Bx1027 -Buffalo 14240
(716) 854-3400 .. **Mineo,** Nicholas L '05 %Rupp BPC&C LLC -1600 Lbrty Bldg -Buffalo 14202
(516) 248-1700 .. **Mineo,** Peter R '75 (Forchelli CDSM&T,LLP) -333 Earle Ovngton Blvd -Uniondale 11553
(516) 489-5000 .. **Mineo,** Raymond F '76 %City of Hempstead -Town Hall -Hempstd 11550 **Fx:**438-2908
(516) 775-7844 .. **Mineo,** Raymond F '76 -446 Lucille Av -Elmont 11003 **Fx:**775-6417
(212) 836-8000 .. **Miner,** Aaron F '08 %Kaye S LLP -425 Park Av -NY 10022
(914) 933-6038 .. **Miner,** Emily B '04 Navigators Grp Inc -6 Intl Dr -Pt Chester 10573
(518) 828-0327 .. **Miner,** Lance R '79 (Miner & M) -6 W Court -Hudson 12534
(212) 668-0059 .. **Miner,** Marc H '91 %Zalman & S -61 Bway -NY 10006
(212) 513-3200 .. **Miner,** Martin P '65 (Holland & K LLP) -31 W 52nd -NY 10019
(518) 828-8327 .. **Miner,** Maryellen C '80 (Miner & M) -6 W Court -Hudson 12534
(607) 749-7296 .. **Miner,** Natalie B '92 -25 S Main Bx310 -Homer 13077 **Fx:**749-4313
(716) 855-3611 .. **Miner,** R Chas '76 (Smith MO&S,LLP) -69 Delaware Av -Buffalo 14202
(315) 476-0876 .. **Miner,** Stephanie A '00 -Bx11455 -Syracuse 13218
(212) 335-4114 .. **Miner,** Tara Christie '91 %DA -1 Hogan Pl -NY 10013
(585) 268-9410 .. **Miner,** Thos A '80 %Cnty Atty -7 Court -Belmont 14813 **Fx:**268-9651
(516) 681-1100 .. **Minero,** Matthew J '00 %Kaufman DV&G,LLP -135 Crsswys Park Dr -Woodbury 11797
(516) 872-7400 .. **Minerva & D'Agostino** -107 S Central Av -Vly Stream 11580
(631) 712-5713 .. **Minerva,** Deanna L '03 %Hon ET Boyle -834 Fed Plz -Central Islip 11722
(646) 722-8500 .. **Minerva,** Domenico G '07 %Grant & E,PA -485 Lex Av -NY 10017
(516) 872-7400 .. **Minerva,** Dominick J '03 %Minerva & D -107 S Central Av -Vly Stream 11580
(516) 872-7400 .. **Minerva,** Dominick M '67 (Minerva & D) -107 S Central Av -Vly Stream 11580
(212) 705-7000 .. **Minerva,** Matthew '04 %Bingham M LLP -399 Park Av -NY 10022
(631) 439-1720 .. **Minerva,** Steven W '82 %MHLS -320 Carleton Av -Central Islip 11722 **Fx:**951-2562
(646) 755-3304 .. **Mines,** Steven J '80 %Shanker & S,PC -420 Lex Av -NY 10170
(212) 416-8726 .. **Minett,** Jeff W '89 %Dept of Law -120 Bway -NY 10271
(212) 299-2000 .. **Minett,** Nancy M '83 %NYMEX -1 North End Av -NY 10282 **Fx:**301-4700
(212) 839-5300 .. **Minetti,** Ryan B '01 %Sidley A LLP -787 7th Av -NY 10019
(973) 494-0603 .. **Minetto,** Pamela J '88 %Mound CW&G -One Bttry Pk Plz -NY 10004 **Fx:**242-4244
(718) 250-2000 .. **Ming,** Maritza A '99 %DA -350 Jay -Brklyn 11201 **Fx:**250-2314
(212) 878-4000 .. **Minger,** Teresa D '04 %Mitsui & Co -200 Park Av -NY 10166 **Fx:**878-4800
(718) 720-3300 .. **Mingino,** Michl J '88 (Romagnolo & M,LLP) -400 St Marks Pl -Staten Isl 10301 **Fx:**720-2995
(212) 885-5000 .. **Mingione,** Anthony A '04 %Blank R LLP -405 Lex Av -NY 10174
(212) 964-7650 .. **Mingione,** Ernest R '90 -77 Baxter -NY 10013
(607) 255-3903 .. **Mingle,** James J '96 %Cornell Univ -300 CCC Bldg-Grdn Av -Ithaca 14853 **Fx:**255-2794
(212) 770-1938 .. **Mingoia,** Frances S '00 AIG -80 Pine -NY 10005
(212) 592-6700 .. **Mingoia,** Lisa Schuminsky '95 %Bovis Lend Lease Hldngs -200 Park Av -NY 10166 **Fx:**592-6997
(315) 466-1492 .. **Mingolelli,** Ralph A '87 -120 E Wshngtn -Syracuse 13202 **Fx:**475-6287
(212) 728-8000 .. **Minias,** Jos G '03 (Willkie F&G LLP) -787 7th Av -NY 10019
(516) 832-7527 .. **Minicucci,** Richd F '78 (Nixon P LLP) -50 Jericho Quadrangle -Jericho 11753
(914) 733-7715 .. **Minihan,** Michl J '95 (Worldwide Trade Prtnrs LLC) -1 N Bway -White Plns 10601
(212) 983-1199 .. **Minikes,** Jonathan Z '86 (Cutler M&A,LLP) -708 3rd Av -NY 10017
(212) 218-2100 .. **Minion,** Danl J '07 %Fitzpatrick CH&S -1290 Av of Amer -NY 10104
(516) 248-1200 .. **Minion,** Robt C '60 (Mulholland M&R) -374 Hillside Av -Williston Pk 11596
(646) 414-6815 .. **Minion,** Robt G '87 (Lowenstein S PC) -1251 Av of Amer -NY 10020 **Fx:**(973) 597-2425
(716) 853-9555 .. **Ministero,** Susan C '89 Leg Aid -237 Main -Buffalo 14203 **Fx:**853-3219
(212) 425-9300 .. **Miniter,** Scott A '06 %Bressler A&R,PC -17 State -NY 10004
(518) 583-7367 .. **Minkel,** Wm J '84 -192 Woodlawn Av -Saratoga Spgs 12866 **Fx:**583-7367
(212) 732-3200 .. **Minkin,** George '51 Cnsl Carter L&M LLP -2 Wall -NY 10005
(212) 972-1000 .. **Minkin,** Gregg D '94 (London F LLP) -59 Maiden Ln -NY 10038
(212) 725-2727 .. **Minkin,** Irving E '85 %S Lobel,PC -9 E 40th -NY 10016 **Fx:**725-3910
(718) 222-2023 .. **Minkina,** Olga '06 %Law Dept -350 Jay -Brklyn 11201 **Fx:**222-2088
(212) 736-5300 .. **Minko,** Anthony J '06 %Block O&M LLP -1 Penn Plz -NY 10119
(914) 949-2826 .. **Minkoff,** Bruce '83 %Robinowitz CD&D,LLP -199 Main -White Plns 10601
(212) 318-6000 .. **Minkoff,** Chas G '04 %Paul HJ&W LLP -75 E 55th -NY 10022
(212) 480-4240 .. **Minkoff,** Jonathan A '01 %Fuchsberg & F -29 Bway -NY 10006
(212) 284-2300 .. **Minkoff,** Robt K '89 Jeffries & Co,Inc -520 Mad Av -NY 10022
(212) 980-0120 .. **Minkoff,** Ronald C '81 (Frankfurt KK&S,PC) -488 Mad Av -NY 10022
(212) 259-8000 .. **Minkovich,** Alexandra D '05 %Dewey & L LLP -1301 Av of Amer -NY 10019
(212) 806-5400 .. **Minkowitz,** Martin '63 OfCnsl Stroock &S&L LLP -180 Maiden Ln -NY 10038
(212) 788-0862 .. **Minnah-Donkoh,** Kuuku A '07 %Law Dept -100 Church -NY 10007 **Fx:**788-0367
(212) 389-5000 .. **Minnear,** Norman E B '09 (Sutherland A&B LLP) -1114 Av of Amer -NY 10036
(212) 619-3730 .. **Minnefor,** Eileen A '90 Cnsl Doar RK&M -217 Bway -NY 10007
(212) 835-1514 .. **Minnefor,** Michl R '09 %Dreifuss B&P,LLP -1 Penn Plz -NY 10019
(212) 619-3730 .. **Minnefor,** Paul E '02 OfCnsl Doar RK&M -217 Bway -NY 10007
(212) 839-5300 .. **Minnerop,** Henry F '64 SrCnsl Sidley A LLP -787 7th Av -NY 10019
(212) 626-4100 .. **Minnis,** Lindsay A '08 %Baker & M LLP -1114 Av of Amer -NY 10036
(212) 521-5400 .. **Minniti,** Cindy S '00 (Reed S LLP) -599 Lex Av -NY 10022
(914) 698-9300 .. **Minniti,** Jos A '58 -100 Mamaroneck Av -Mamaroneck 10543 **Fx:**381-7517
(212) 556-2100 .. **Minniti,** Kathleen Sina '96 %King & S -1185 Av of Amer -NY 10036
(212) 839-5300 .. **Minoff,** Debra Weinstein '10 %Sidley A LLP -787 7th Av -NY 10019
(212) 840-2778 .. **Minoff,** Jack '61 -36 W 44th -NY 10036
(718) 816-0066 .. **Minogue,** Robt '86 -471 Bement Av -Staten Isl 10310
(212) 326-3939 .. **Minoli,** Eugenio '02 %Jones D -222 E 41st -NY 10017
(518) 220-1850 .. **Minor,** Autondria Shir'Nae '05 %Schmeiser O&W -22 Century Hill Dr -Latham 12110
(212) 801-3090 .. **Minor,** C Randall '09 %Greenberg T,LLP -200 Park Av -NY 10166
(646) 315-7377 .. **Minor,** Marc B '02 %FINRA -14 Wall -NY 10005 **Fx:**315-7440
(212) 639-1136 .. **Minot,** Jeffrey R '64 -440 E 79th -NY 10075 **Fx:**249-5729
(866) 683-4200 .. **Minott,** Alyson E '93 %O Minott,PC -50 Court -Brklyn 11201 **Fx:**227-0456
(866) 683-4200 .. **Minott,** Oliver C '97 (O Minott,PC) -50 Court -Brklyn 11201 **Fx:**227-0456
(212) 355-6182 .. **Minott,** Roxanne T '04 EP Dine Inc -115 E 57th -NY 10022 **Fx:**755-8486
(631) 543-7667 .. **Minott,** Terri P '93 OfCnsl Sarisohn Law Prtnrs LLP -350 Vets Mem'l Hwy -Commack 11725 **Fx:**543-7901
(845) 878-4120 .. **Minotti,** Thos J '90 -Bx374 -Stormvll 12582
(212) 506-1700 .. **Minsker,** Jonathan E '98 (Kasowitz BT&F LLP) -1633 Bway -NY 10019
(646) 234-7006 .. **Minsky,** Bruce W '90 (BW Minsky,PC) -112 Brick Church Rd -New Hempstead 10977 **Fx:**(702) 973-6607
(845) 247-3621 .. **Minsky,** Eleanor '87 -Bx1117 -Saugerties 12477
(516) 794-2323 .. **Minsky,** Howard A '73 (Lester M&B) -325 Merrick Av -E Meadow 11554
(212) 682-6800 .. **Minsky,** Jenifer Blake '99 %Zetlin & D LLP -801 2nd Av -NY 10017
(516) 794-2327 .. **Minsky,** Leigh A '04 %Lester M&B -325 Merrick Av -E Meadow 11554 **Fx:**794-2431
(212) 605-6274 .. **Minsky,** Martin '86 -800 3rd Av -NY 10022
(212) 346-0849 .. **Minsley,** Morton S '83 -101 Lafayette -NY 10013 **Fx:**766-9798
(212) 599-1515 .. **Minson,** Edw R '03 %Stein RM,LLP -405 Lex Av -NY 10174
(718) 824-5281 .. **Minter,** Carolyn V '77 -411 E 160th -Bronx 10451
(914) 762-1458 .. **Minter,** Carolyn V '77 -79 Croton Av -Ossining 10562
(212) 643-0966 .. **Minter,** Rachel J '86 -345 7th Av -NY 10001 **Fx:**643-0980
(631) 981-0192 .. **Minto,** John R '89 -22 High -Lk Ronkonkoma 11779 **Fx:**981-0192
(212) 751-8334 .. **Minton,** Edw '60 Koeppel Management Co -Bx287146 -NY 10128 **Fx:**751-8834
(212) 756-2000 .. **Minton,** Peter I '07 %Schulte R&Z LLP -919 3rd Av -NY 10022
(516) 742-7525 .. **Minton,** Richd I '58 -259 Mineola Blvd -Mineola 11501 **Fx:**873-5166
(212) 836-8000 .. **Mintz,** Benjamin '96 (Kaye S LLP) -425 Park Av -NY 10022
(212) 609-6800 .. **Mintz,** Bryan H '00 %McCarter & E,LLP -245 Park Av -NY 10167
(631) 952-3500 .. **Mintz,** Cheryl Rosenthal '94 (Rosenthal & M,LLP) -330 Vndrblt Motor Pkwy -Hauppauge 11788 **Fx:**952-5600
(212) 354-1779 .. **Mintz,** Danl H '86 %W 39th St Co -205 W 39th -NY 10018 **Fx:**354-3711
(212) 509-0918 .. **Mintz,** David A '85 (Weissman & M LLC) -80 Pine -NY 10005
(212) 504-6000 .. **Mintz,** Douglas S '00 SpclCnsl Cadwalader W&T LLP -1 World Fncl Ctr -NY 10281
(212) 486-2500 .. **Mintz & Fraade,PC** -488 Mad Av -NY 10022 **Fx:**486-0701
(212) 486-2500 .. **Mintz,** Fredk M '60 (Mintz & F,PC) -488 Mad Av -NY 10022
(212) 696-4848 .. **Mintz & Gold LLP** -470 Park Av S -NY 10016 **Fx:**696-1231
(315) 471-0524 .. **Mintz,** Jason '07 %Kenny & K PLLC -W 315 Fayette -Syracuse 13202 **Fx:**471-4238
(516) 775-7007 .. **Mintz,** Kenneth '75 (Gutman MB&S,PC) -813 Jericho Tpk -New Hyde Pk 11040
(516) 222-1350 .. **Mintz,** Laura A '07 %Barrocas & R -100 Q Roosevelt Blvd -Gdn Cty 11530
(212) 935-3000 .. **Mintz Levin Cohn Ferris Glovsky & Popeo,PC** -666 3rd Av -NY 10017 **Fx:**983-3115

(631) 725-9199 .. **Mintz,** Linda S '88 LCP Advsrs,LLC -3330 Noyac Rd -Sag Hbr 11963
(212) 447-1800 .. **Mintz,** Marshall A '00 (Mintz & O LLP) -260 Mad Av -NY 10016
(212) 832-0400 .. **Mintz,** Meyer '00 Berdon LLP -360 Mad Av -NY 10017
(212) 935-3131 .. **Mintz,** Perry L '84 (Gallet D&B,LLP) -845 3rd Av -NY 10022
(718) 250-2000 .. **Mintz,** Phyllis R '95 %DA -350 Jay -Brklyn 11201 **Fx:**250-2314
(212) 836-8000 .. **Mintz,** Roxanne J '10 Kaye S LLP -425 Park Av -NY 10022
(516) 379-1311 .. **Mintz & Schaffer** -30 S Ocean Av -Freeprt 11520 **Fx:**623-4299
(212) 349-4494 .. **Mintz,** Seymour D '85 -299 Bway -NY 10007 **Fx:**608-6392
(212) 532-9131 .. **Mintz,** Sidney W '55 -3 Richbourne Ln Bx1262 -Melvll 11747 **Fx:**(631) 491-1908
(212) 227-4016 .. **Mintz,** Sol '50 (Bloom & M) -225 Bway -NY 10007
(914) 967-7787 .. **Mintz,** Stephen A '69 %Stemin Assoc -11 Eve Ln -Rye 10580 **Fx:**967-7787
(212) 696-4848 .. **Mintz,** Steven G '89 (Mintz & G LLP) -470 Park Av S -NY 10016
(516) 228-6658 .. **Mintz,** Susan G '92 %Gervase & V,PC -377 Oak -Gdn Cty 11530
(212) 551-0345 .. **Mintz,** Victor '84 Govt of Israel -800 2nd Av -NY 10017
(212) 887-6817 .. **Mintzer,** Jonathan C '75 Hearst-Angyle TV -888 7th Av -NY 10106
(212) 715-9100 .. **Mintzer,** Karen '94 SpclCnsl Kramer LN&F,LLP -1177 Av of Amer -NY 10036
(212) 403-7300 .. **Mintzer,** Kevin T '98 (Vladeck WE&E,PC) -1501 Bway -NY 10036
(212) 393-9070 .. **Mintzer,** Maureen I '81 %LegalEase -139 Fulton -NY 10038 **Fx:**393-9796
(212) 637-3168 .. **Mintzer,** Michl A '69 %EPA -290 Bway -NY 10007 **Fx:**637-3096
(212) 968-8300 .. **Mintzer Sarowitz Zeris Ledva & Meyers LLP** -39 Bway -NY 10006 **Fx:**968-9840
(516) 939-9200 .. **Mintzer Sarowitz Zeris Ledva & Meyers LLP** -17 W John -Hicksvll 11801 **Fx:**939-9201
(212) 857-8800 .. **Minuse,** Catherine J '76 %US Ct of Appls -40 Foley Sq -NY 10007
(212) 483-0105 .. **Minuskin,** Heidi S '87 OfCnsl Coughlin D LLP -88 Pine-Wall St Plz -NY 10005
(212) 225-2000 .. **Minvielle,** Emilio '10 %Cleary GS&H -1 Lbrty Plz -NY 10006
(212) 790-0200 .. **Minzer,** Max J '03 Benj N Cardozo Schl of Law -55 5th Av -NY 10003 **Fx:**790-0345
(212) 944-1000 .. **Minzner,** Edw S '52 %M Pfeifer -714 E 241st -Bronx 10470 **Fx:**(718) 324-0333
(516) 281-8550 .. **Mionis,** Gary M '95 (Gianfortune & M,PC) -231 Mineola Blvd -Mineola 11501 **Fx:**281-8552
(607) 432-5331 .. **Miosek,** Ryan W '09 %Hinman H&K,LLP -Five Ford Av -Oneonta 13820
(607) 723-5341 .. **Miosek,** Ryan W '09 %Hinman H&K,LLP -80 Exchange Bx5250 -Bnghmtn 13902
(212) 819-8200 .. **Mir,** Imraan Rashid '05 %White & C LLP -1155 Av of Amer -NY 10036
(212) 610-6300 .. **Mir,** Sami A '04 %Allen & O -1221 Av of Amer -NY 10020
(212) 944-1529 .. **Mir,** Samiya Nilofar '01 (Katona & M) -49 W 37th -NY 10018 **Fx:**553-7370
(516) 794-7340 .. **Mirabel,** Catherine A '83 %Fager & A,LLP -90 Merrick Av -E Meadow 11554
(516) 280-7700 .. **Mirabella,** David P '98 (Mirabella & Q,LLC) -400 Grdn City Plz -Gdn Cty 11530 **Fx:**280-7701
(877) 222-1814 .. **Mirabella,** Elke E '07 %B Rothenberg -100 Duffy Av -Hicksvll 11801 **Fx:**(866) 894-2182
(631) 281-8724 .. **Mirabella,** Jos D '93 -1235 Montauk Hwy -Mastic 11950 **Fx:**281-2050
(212) 676-6312 .. **Mirabella,** Michl E '04 %Business Integrity Comm -100 Church -NY 10007 **Fx:**676-6204
(516) 714-7094 .. **Mirabelli,** Maryann S '04 %T Spina -170 Froehlich Farm Blvd -Woodbury 11797 **Fx:**496-5420
(718) 254-7000 .. **Mirabile,** Catherine M '98 %US Atty -271 Cadman Plz E -Brklyn 11201 **Fx:**254-6479
(845) 486-6800 .. **Mirabile,** Matthew V '93 (McCabe & M LLP) -63 Wshngtn Bx509 -Poughkeepsie 12602
(212) 915-7000 .. **Mirabile,** Russell M '75 XL Aerospace -200 Lbrty -NY 10281
(516) 688-1709 .. **Mirabito,** Diane R '86 %IRS -1600 Stewart Av -Westbury 11590 **Fx:**688-1750
(315) 592-3100 .. **Mirabito,** Jerome A '80 Fulton Svngs Bk -75 S 1st -Fulton 13069 **Fx:**592-2990
(516) 676-9055 .. **Mirabito,** Nicholas '82 -5 Orchrd Ln -Sea Cliff 11579
(212) 564-9800 .. **Miraglia,** Bettina M '97 (D'Agostino L&L,LLP) -345 7th Av -NY 10001
(516) 747-4770 .. **Miraglia,** Nicholas F '97 %Hopkins & K -100 Q Roosevelt Blvd -Gdn Cty 11530
(212) 577-3688 .. **Miraglia,** Steven J '91 %Leg Aid -199 Water -NY 10038 **Fx:**509-8431
(212) 395-3776 .. **Miragliotta,** Bernadette '92 %Verizon -140 West -NY 10007
(212) 972-1000 .. **Miragliotta,** Jeffrey D '09 %London F LLP -59 Maiden Ln -NY 10038
(212) 205-7000 .. **Miran,** Michl '84 Cnsl Ashurst LLP -7 Times Sq -NY 10036
(518) 452-5600 .. **Miranda,** David P '89 (Heslin RF&M PC) -5 Columbia Cir -Albany 12203
(212) 785-7400 .. **Miranda,** Denise M '98 (Harris & M,LLP) -11 Bway -NY 10004
(716) 881-8165 .. **Miranda,** Elizabeth G Everett '96 D'Youville College -320 Porter Av -Buffalo 14201
(516) 572-2000 .. **Miranda,** Jos C '58 %DA -99 Main -Hempstd 11550 **Fx:**572-2606
(516) 229-4200 .. **Miranda,** Katherine '01 %Mendolia & S -875 Merrick Av -Westbury 11590
(212) 939-9535 .. **Miranda,** Laura M '91 L Miranda,PLLC -100 Church -NY 10007 **Fx:**939-9533
(212) 728-8000 .. **Miranda,** Manuel A '06 %Willkie F&G LLP -787 7th Av -NY 10019
(914) 694-3300 .. **Miranda,** Marisa '99 %DiSciullo & Assoc -2975 Wstchstr Av -Purchase 10577 **Fx:**694-2244
(516) 741-7676 .. **Miranda,** Michl A '87 (Miranda SSSV LLP) -240 Mineola Blvd -Mineola 11501
(845) 688-7127 .. **Miranda,** Michl J '75 -62 Andrew Ln -Mt Tremper 12457
(845) 357-8957 .. **Miranda,** Mirella C '02 -85 Lafayette Av -Suffern 10901
(212) 880-1237 .. **Miranda,** Neal J '81 Chicago Title Ins Co -711 3rd Av -NY 10017 **Fx:**880-9649
(212) 776-5055 .. **Miranda,** Raquel '98 Housing Auth -250 Bway -NY 10007
(212) 937-4000 .. **Miranda,** Roberta '05 %Fitzpatrick & HTCPA,LLP -12 E 49th -NY 10017
(516) 741-7676 .. **Miranda Sambursky Slone Sklarin Verveniotis LLP** -240 Mineola Blvd -Mineola 11501 **Fx:**741-9060
(914) 345-6510 .. **Miranda Sambursky Slone Sklarin Verveniotis LLP** -570 Taxter Rd -Elmsfrd 10523 **Fx:**345-6514
(212) 201-1170 .. **Miranda Sambursky Slone Sklarin Verveniotis LLP** -237 W 35th -NY 10001 **Fx:**201-1171
(716) 856-5500 .. **Miranda,** Taylor M '09 %Damon M LLP -200 Delaware Av -Buffalo 14202
(212) 725-6530 .. **Miranda,** Zulma '05 SrCnsl Global Justice Ctr -25 E 21st -NY 10010 **Fx:**725-6536
(212) 530-5000 .. **Miranda-Schmidt,** Gail '88 %Milbank TH&M LLP -1 Chase Manh Plz -NY 10005
(516) 883-6419 .. **Miranne,** Jos J III '77 -4 Wyndham Way -Pt Wash 11050
(212) 474-1000 .. **Miranne,** Robt A '09 %Cravath S&M LLP -825 8th Av -NY 10019
(212) 318-6000 .. **Miranowski,** Elisabeth '10 %Paul HJ&W LLP -75 E 55th -NY 10022
(212) 856-4000 .. **Mirarchi,** Saverio '80 Canadian Imperial Bank -425 Lex -NY 10017
(718) 590-2000 .. **Miras,** John C '08 %DA -198 E 161st -Bronx 10451 **Fx:**590-6477
(212) 318-6000 .. **Miras,** Mary P '03 %Paul HJ&W LLP -75 E 55th -NY 10022
(212) 629-6265 .. **Mirasol,** Manuel E '89 -370 7th Av -NY 10001 **Fx:**643-8083
(212) 455-2000 .. **Mirbagheri,** Sonya M '08 %Simpson T&B LLP -425 Lex Av -NY 10017
(212) 277-4000 .. **Mirchandani,** Dolly '97 (Freshfields BD LLP) -520 Mad Av -NY 10022
(212) 305-4891 .. **Mirchandani,** Navin '05 Columbia Univ Med Ctr -622 W 168th -NY 10032
(718) 887-9484 .. **Mirel,** Robt J '74 OfCnsl Weitz Law Firm,PA -777 Kent Av -Brklyn 11205 **Fx:**865-0909
(212) 473-8700 .. **Mirer,** Jeanne E '07 (Eisner & M,PC) -113 Univ Pl -NY 10003 **Fx:**473-8705
(718) 274-6900 .. **Miret,** Gary F '87 G Miret -31-17 Ditmars Blvd -Astoria 11105 **Fx:**274-7500
(718) 260-4750 .. **Mirhosseini,** Bahar '08 Leg Aid -111 Lvngstn -Brklyn 11201 **Fx:**260-4744
(212) 504-6000 .. **Mirick,** Christopher R '08 (Cadwalader W&T LLP) -1 World Fncl Ctr -NY 10281
(212) 233-2100 .. **Mirisola,** Chas J Jr. '88 (Oshman & M,LLP) -42 Bway -NY 10004
(914) 422-1241 .. **Mirisola,** Elizabeth C '88 Law Dept -255 Main -White Plns 10601 **Fx:**422-1231
(212) 728-8000 .. **Miritello,** Christopher J '09 %Willkie F&G LLP -787 7th Av -NY 10019
(631) 957-3467 .. **Miritello,** Stephanie A '85 %Sanj Realty -10 Horse Hill Rd -Brookvll 11545
(516) 466-6030 .. **Mirkin & Gordon, PC** -98 Cuttermill Rd -Gt Neck 11021 **Fx:**(718) 895-7164
(212) 940-8800 .. **Mirkin,** Saml M '08 %Katten MR LLP -575 Mad Av -NY 10022
(718) 250-2000 .. **Mirman,** Danl S '08 %DA -350 Jay -Brklyn 11201 **Fx:**250-2314
(718) 286-6000 .. **Mirman,** Julie '07 DA -125-01 Qns Blvd -Kew Gdns 11415
(212) 227-4000 .. **Mirman Markovits & Landau, PC** -291 Bway -NY 10007
(212) 227-4000 .. **Mirman,** Michele S '77 (Mirman M&L,PC) -291 Bway -NY 10007
(212) 227-4000 .. **Mirman,** Paul '69 OfCnsl Mirman M&L,PC -291 Bway -NY 10007
(212) 684-3900 .. **Mirman Broome,** Donna '92 %Gottlieb R&R,PC -270 Mad Av -NY 10016
(212) 382-0700 .. **Miro,** Douglas A '86 (Ostrolenk FG&S,LLP) -1180 Av of Amer -NY 10036
(212) 558-4000 .. **Miro,** Sara '08 %Sullivan & C LLP -125 Broad -NY 10004
(718) 390-5422 .. **Mirocznik,** Menachem Mendy '98 %Civil Ct -927 Castleton Av -Staten Isl 10310 **Fx:**390-8108
(212) 526-0678 .. **Mirocznik,** Yakov D '05 Barclays Capital -745 7th Av -NY 10019
(212) 876-5500 .. **Miron,** Annalisa '05 %Neighborhood Def Srv -317 Lenox Av -NY 10027 **Fx:**876-5586
(212) 689-6153 .. **Miron,** Louis H '01 -30 Waterside Plz -NY 10010
(845) 336-6000 .. **Miron,** Stephen E '71 -PO Bx 1598 -Kingston 12402
(631) 271-7043 .. **Mironenko,** Nina '89 (N Mironenko,PC) -191 NY Av -Huntngtn 11743 **Fx:**425-7030
(212) 940-8910 .. **Mironer,** Merril A '66 (Katten MR LLP) -575 Mad Av -NY 10022
(718) 545-5518 .. **Mironis,** Peter '93 (Stefanidis & M LLP) -31-10 37th Av -LIC 11101 **Fx:**545-5087
(212) 250-4297 .. **Mirostaw,** Jay T '04 %Deutsche Bank -60 Wall -NY 10005
(516) 794-7780 .. **Mirotznik,** Bernard '53 -2115 Hempstd Tpk -E Meadow 11554
(212) 242-3022 .. **Mirotznik,** Carol J '86 -10 W 15th -NY 10011
(212) 826-2787 .. **Mirotznik,** Chas M '82 -420 Lex Av -NY 10170 **Fx:**826-2852
(516) 794-8827 .. **Mirotznik,** Michl B '92 Mirotznik & Assoc,LLC -2115 Hempstd Tpk -E Meadow 11554 **Fx:**794-7971
(718) 667-9090 .. **Mirra,** Maria A '03 Menicucci V & Assoc -2040 Victory Blvd -Staten Isl 10314 **Fx:**667-0700
(315) 568-5861 .. **Mirras,** Michl J '95 (Midey & M) -54 Fall Bx299 -Seneca Fls 13148
(631) 852-1872 .. **Mirro,** Adrienne M '81 %Supreme Ct Law Dept -210 Center Dr -Rvrhead 11901 **Fx:**852-2020
(845) 294-5401 .. **Mirro & Bennett** -176 Main BxB -Goshen 10924 **Fx:**294-3894
(845) 294-5401 .. **Mirro,** Donald W '62 (Mirro & B) -176 Main BxB -Goshen 10924
(212) 361-7720 .. **Mirro,** Michele '88 Dept Cnsmr Affrs -66 John -NY 10038
(516) 739-6000 .. **Mirro,** Roy J '87 RJ Mirro & Assoc PC -300 Grdn City Plz -Gdn Cty 11530 **Fx:**739-6006
(516) 741-4350 .. **Mirsky,** David M '91 -114 Old Cntry Rd -Mineola 11501
(914) 332-4700 .. **Mirsky,** Ellis R '77 (Mirsky & B,PLLC) -303 S Bway -Tarrytwn 10591 **Fx:**332-1671
(516) 931-0700 .. **Mirsky,** H Wayne '69 (Gastwirth & M,LLP) -479 S Oyster Bay Rd -Plainvw 11803
(718) 739-7522 .. **Mirsky,** Morris '54 -130-30 31st Av -Flushng 11354
(212) 686-2340 .. **Mirsky,** Moshe Z '81 -9 E 40th -NY 10016 **Fx:**686-6413
(516) 349-0540 .. **Mirsky,** Steven '87 (Alexander Wolf & Co) -1 Dupont -Plainvw 11803
(212) 586-5100 .. **Mirvis,** Morgan O '05 William Morris Entertainment LLC -1325 Av of Amer -NY 10019
(212) 403-1000 .. **Mirvis,** Theo N '78 (Wachtell LR&K) -51 W 52nd -NY 10019
(718) 934-4141 .. **Mirvis,** Tony '05 -2753 Coney Isl Av -Brklyn 11235
(914) 995-4172 .. **Mirza,** Adeel '04 %DA -111 Martin Luther King Blvd -White Plns 10601 **Fx:**995-3363
(212) 640-9279 .. **Mirza,** Aisha Y '03 Amer Express -200 Vesey -NY 10285
(716) 695-9110 .. **Mis,** Jeffrey N '85 -27 Main -Tonawanda 14150 **Fx:**692-0446
(585) 621-4210 .. **Misch,** Michl H '91 %Century Liquor -3349 Monroe Av -Rchstr 14618
(212) 425-5191 .. **Mischel & Horn,PC** -1 Whitehall -NY 10004 **Fx:**425-5890

(212) 788-2830 .. **Mischel,** Jason R '03 %NY MOPD -100 Gold -NY 10038 **Fx:**341-9843
(212) 425-5191 .. **Mischel,** Richd E '74 (Mischel & H,PC) -1 Whitehall -NY 10004
(914) 697-2330 .. **Mischel,** Staciellen Stevenson '00 US Tennis Assoc Inc -70 W Red Oak Ln -White Plns 10604
(718) 260-2430 .. **Mischel Eisner,** Linda C '93 Hon R Dearie -225 Cadman Plz E -Brklyn 11201
(212) 530-5000 .. **Mischner,** Sara H '10 %Milbank TH&M LLP -1 Chase Manh Plz -NY 10005
(716) 854-1002 .. **Miserendino Celniker Seegert & Estoff,PC** -295 Main -Buffalo 14203 **Fx:**854-6748
(716) 854-1002 .. **Miserendino,** Joy E '88 (Miserendino CS&E,PC) -295 Main -Buffalo 14203
(716) 854-1002 .. **Miserendino,** Saml R Jr. '92 (Miserendino CS&E,PC) -295 Main -Buffalo 14203
(516) 742-4525 .. **Miserendino,** Sandy A '92 -58 Hillside Av -Williston Pk 11596 **Fx:**747-2445
(212) 758-7600 .. **Mish,** Risa M '90 SrCnsl Collazo C&M -747 3rd Av -NY 10017
(212) 506-1700 .. **Mishaan,** Albert Shemmy '95 (Kasowitz BT&F LLP) -1633 Bway -NY 10019
(212) 944-0900 .. **Mishaan Dayon & Lieblich** -1370 Bway -NY 10018 **Fx:**944-4301
(212) 560-9100 .. **Mishaan,** Michl A '89 (M Mishaan,PC) -150 42nd -NY 10017 **Fx:**560-9108
(212) 944-0900 .. **Mishaan,** Saul A '83 (Mishaan D&L) -1370 Bway -NY 10018
(212) 782-4415 .. **Mishal,** Nadia L '05 Mitsubishi UFJ -1251 Av of Amer -NY 10020
(212) 541-9100 .. **Mishara,** Eric R '86 (Schiavetti CDW&N,LLP) -575 8th Av -NY 10018
(212) 612-3270 .. **Mishcon de Reya New York LLP** -200 Park Av -NY 10166
(212) 836-8000 .. **Misher,** Jeffrey A '04 %Kaye S LLP -425 Park Av -NY 10022
(212) 903-8700 .. **Misher,** Norman J '77 (Roberts & H,LLP) -825 8th Av -NY 10019
(212) 609-6800 .. **Misher,** Sheldon E '66 SpclCnsl McCarter & E,LLP -245 Park Av -NY 10167
(212) 354-5650 .. **Mishev,** Milena S '03 %Graham C PC -36 W 44th -NY 10036
(212) 798-6100 .. **Mishkin,** Alexander V '95 Fortress Invstmnt Grp -1345 Av of Amer -NY 10105
(212) 357-0362 .. **Mishkin,** Bruce L '66 Goldman Sachs -85 Broad -NY 10004
(212) 728-8000 .. **Mishkin,** Douglas W '10 %Willkie F&G LLP -787 7th Av -NY 10019
(212) 225-2000 .. **Mishkin,** Edwin B '61 SrCnsl Cleary GS&H -1 Lbrty Plz -NY 10006
(718) 643-4680 .. **Mishkin,** Ellen C '85 -120 Schermerhorn -Brklyn 11201
(646) 386-5100 .. **Mishkin,** Janet S '73 Surrogates Ct -31 Chmbrs -NY 10007
(212) 735-3000 .. **Mishkin,** Jeffrey A '73 (Skadden ASM&F LLP) -4 Times Sq -NY 10036
(212) 310-8000 .. **Mishkin,** Jessie B '07 %Weil G&M LLP -767 5th Av -NY 10153
(917) 515-5600 .. **Mishkin,** Marion S '93 -155 E 77th -NY 10075 **Fx:**(212) 585-1800
(212) 752-1181 .. **Mishkin,** Paul '49 -870 UN Plz -NY 10017
(212) 450-4000 .. **Mishkin,** Paul S '05 %Davis P&W LLP -450 Lex Av -NY 10017
(631) 234-1154 .. **Mishkin,** Scott M '93 (S Mishkin,PC) -1 Suffolk Sq -Islandia 11749 **Fx:**234-5048
(516) 222-6200 .. **Mishkin,** Stanley '49 Cnsl Berkman HPP&F,PC -100 Grdn City Plz -Gdn Cty 11530
(914) 576-2088 .. **Mishkoff,** Coleman '78 -370 Pinebrook Blvd -New Rchll 10804
(518) 462-6753 .. **Mishler,** Mark S '82 M Mishler,PC -750 Bway -Albany 12207 **Fx:**432-7325
(212) 336-2000 .. **Mishra,** Anjan '07 %Patterson BW&T LLP -1133 Av of Amer -NY 10036
(212) 218-5500 .. **Mishra,** Devjani '98 (Seyfarth S LLP) -620 8th Av -NY 10018
(315) 732-5121 .. **Misiaszek,** Michl J '84 (Helmer JM&K) -405 Court -Utica 13502
(516) 741-2666 .. **Misir,** Deborah N '05 (Lally M&R LLP) -220 Old Cntry Rd -Mineola 11501
(516) 248-9880 .. **Misir,** Parshhueram T '99 %Agovino & A,LLP -330 Old Cntry Rd -Mineola 11501
(516) 357-3000 .. **Misiti,** Frank M '05 %Rivkin R LLP -926 RXR Plz -Uniondale 11556
(212) 968-8600 .. **Misiti,** Nicklaus J '09 %Manchanda Law Ofc,PLLC -80 Wall -NY 10005 **Fx:**968-8601
(718) 468-0500 .. **Misk,** Gerard N '91 (Ginsburg & M) -215-48 Jamaica Av -Qns Vllg 11428
(718) 468-0500 .. **Misk,** Jos N '92 (Ginsburg & M) -215-48 Jamaica Av -Qns Vllg 11428
(716) 433-1344 .. **Miskell,** Allen D '75 (Miskell & M) -280 East Av Bx464 -Lockprt 14095
(716) 433-1344 .. **Miskell,** Laura A '05 %Miskell & M -280 East Av Bx464 -Lockprt 14095
(716) 433-1344 .. **Miskell & Moxham** -280 East Av Bx464 -Lockprt 14095
(631) 715-7900 .. **Miskiewicz,** James L '89 %US Atty -610 Fed Plz -Central Islip 11722
(212) 268-0900 .. **Miskin,** Howard C '56 (Miskin & T-Y) -1350 Bway -NY 10018 **Fx:**268-0904
(212) 458-3685 .. **Miskovich,** Paul '99 AIG -175 Water -NY 10038
(718) 286-6000 .. **Misorek,** Mark E '04 %DA -125-01 Qns Blvd -Kew Gdns 11415
(212) 504-6000 .. **Misra,** Anup '09 %Cadwalader W&T LLP -1 World Fncl Ctr -NY 10281
(212) 244-1064 .. **Misra,** Arun '97 -110 W 34th -NY 10001 **Fx:**244-1085
(212) 806-5400 .. **Misra,** Seema A '98 (Stroock &S&L LLP) -180 Maiden Ln -NY 10038
(516) 825-3025 .. **Misrok,** Kenneth I '90 (Misrok Law Firm,LLP) -30 S Central Av -Vly Stream 11580 **Fx:**825-3531
(516) 825-3025 .. **Misrok,** Lawr J '68 (Misrok Law Firm,LLP) -30 S Central Av -Vly Stream 11580 **Fx:**825-3531
(585) 544-7090 .. **Missal,** Paul T '63 (Pirrello MP&F) -2040 E Ridge Rd -Rchstr 14622
(212) 628-9180 .. **Missan,** Richd S '59 -301 E 78th -NY 10075 **Fx:**628-9223
(516) 741-2585 .. **Missick,** Jacqueline C '09 %Rosicki R & Assoc,PC -51 E Bethpage Rd -Plainvw 11803 **Fx:**741-4748
(212) 298-2085 .. **Missry,** Michelle A '87 %IRS -290 Bway -NY 10007
(212) 909-9500 .. **Missry,** Morris '91 (Wachtel & M,LLP) -885 2nd Av -NY 10017
(212) 684-3900 .. **Misthal,** Marc P '00 (Gottlieb R&R,PC) -270 Mad Av -NY 10016
(518) 462-6765 .. **Mistishen,** Barbara B '04 %Leg Aid -55 Colvin Av -Albany 12206 **Fx:**427-8352
(607) 723-3551 .. **Mistretta,** F David '79 %Security Mutual Life -Bx1625 -Bnghmtn 13902 **Fx:**772-2114
(631) 366-0498 .. **Mistretta,** Jos '57 -58 Kristin Ln -Hauppauge 11788 **Fx:**366-6071
(212) 458-1239 .. **Mistretta,** Pauline T '80 AIG -175 Water -NY 10038 **Fx:**458-1349
(607) 723-3551 .. **Mistretta,** Susan E '86 %Security Mutual Life -Bx1625 -Bnghmtn 13902 **Fx:**772-2114
(516) 222-1350 .. **Misuraca,** Khadija A '06 %Barrocas & R -100 Q Roosevelt Blvd -Gdn Cty 11530
(718) 923-4206 .. **Misurelli,** Christine '84 %OTDA Fair Hearings -14 Boerum Pl -Brklyn 11201
(516) 357-3700 .. **Mitacek,** Deirdre M '97 %Cullen and D LLP -100 Q Roosevelt Blvd -Gdn Cty 11530
(718) 250-2000 .. **Mitchel,** Gregory P '89 %DA -350 Jay -Brklyn 11201 **Fx:**250-2314
(914) 997-7100 .. **Mitchel,** Tamara A '83 (Berman BF&G pc) -123 Main -White Plns 10601
(845) 454-9460 .. **Mitchell,** Anne Elizabeth '77 MHLS -10 Ross Cir -Poughkeepsie 12601 **Fx:**471-9308
(212) 213-5005 .. **Mitchell,** Bartly '86 (Carro C&M,LLP) -475 Park Av S -NY 10016
(212) 319-8500 .. **Mitchell,** Bradley L '92 (Stevens & L PC) -485 Mad Av -NY 10022
(212) 450-4000 .. **Mitchell,** Bradley W '07 %Davis P&W LLP -450 Lex Av -NY 10017
(631) 853-4049 .. **Mitchell,** Brian C '89 %Cnty Atty -Dennison Bldg Bx6100 -Hauppauge 11788 **Fx:**853-5169
(914) 946-0600 .. **Mitchell,** Brian P '08 %Pino & Assoc -50 Main -White Plns 10606 **Fx:**946-0650
(212) 557-4000 .. **Mitchell,** Bruce M '76 (Grunfeld DLS&K LLP) -399 Park Av -NY 10022
(212) 294-6700 .. **Mitchell,** C MacNeil '68 (Winston & S) -200 Park Av -NY 10166
(212) 288-3650 .. **Mitchell,** Carol '00 -784 Park Av -NY 10021 **Fx:**288-4635
(212) 765-9100 .. **Mitchell,** Carrie E '05 %Halperin BR,LLP -555 Mad Av -NY 10022
(212) 909-6000 .. **Mitchell,** Chandra J '02 %Debevoise & P LLP -919 3rd Av -NY 10022
(212) 385-8036 .. **Mitchell,** Chas L '06 %J Fleming,PC -22 Crtlandt -NY 10007 **Fx:**406-2045
(212) 521-5400 .. **Mitchell,** Cheryl A '95 (Reed S LLP) -599 Lex Av -NY 10022
(212) 425-2200 .. **Mitchell,** Clyde '80 (Claugus & M) -110 Wall -NY 10005
(212) 704-6000 .. **Mitchell,** Cynthia J '03 %Troutman S LLP -405 Lex Av -NY 10174
(212) 227-0347 .. **Mitchell,** Danl E Jr. '09 %Weiss W&W,PC -25 Park Pl -NY 10007
(212) 794-5382 .. **Mitchell,** Daphna H '87 %CUNY -535 E 80th -NY 10075 **Fx:**794-5426
(518) 270-4606 .. **Mitchell,** David B '96 Corp Cnsl -1 Monument Sq -Troy 12180 **Fx:**270-4609
(212) 859-8000 .. **Mitchell,** David S '80 (Fried FHS&J LLP) -1 NY Plz -NY 10004
(718) 579-7940 .. **Mitchell,** Dawne A '95 %Leg Aid -900 Sheridan Av -Bronx 10451 **Fx:**293-8744
(212) 825-0365 .. **Mitchell,** Donald B '10 %AL Bailey,PC -120 Bway -NY 10271 **Fx:**825-0999
(212) 872-1000 .. **Mitchell,** Donna '99 -One Bryant Park -NY 10036 **Fx:**872-1002
(212) 885-5000 .. **Mitchell,** Dylan Sinclair '96 (Blank R LLP) -405 Lex Av -NY 10174
(914) 337-6300 .. **Mitchell,** Edw J '85 %Nobile M&D,LLP -111 Kraft Av -Bronxvll 10708
(518) 257-1443 .. **Mitchell,** Ellen M '99 %CSEA,Inc -143 Wshngtn Av Bx7125 -Albany 12224 **Fx:**449-1525
(607) 272-5840 .. **Mitchell,** Emerson W '99 -309 N Tioga -Ithaca 14850
(518) 464-2000 .. **Mitchell,** Erin A '06 Ayco Co -1 Wall -Albany 12205
(212) 574-1200 .. **Mitchell,** Franklin L '10 %Seward & K LLP -1 Bttry Pk Plz -NY 10004
(716) 843-5700 .. **Mitchell,** Gail Y '86 %US Atty -138 Delaware Av -Buffalo 14202 **Fx:**551-3052
(315) 655-3463 .. **Mitchell Goris & Stokes,LLC** -5 Mill Bx312 -Cazenovia 13035 **Fx:**655-4544
(212) 961-4475 .. **Mitchell,** Guy H '92 Dept of Law -163 W 125th -NY 10027 **Fx:**961-4003
(212) 558-4000 .. **Mitchell,** Heather Celeste '09 %Sullivan & C LLP -125 Broad -NY 10004
(718) 997-1000 .. **Mitchell & Incantalupo** -98-20 Metro Av -Frst Hlls 11375 **Fx:**575-1600
(212) 655-5000 .. **Mitchell,** Jaclyn D '03 %Gannon R&M -120 Bway -NY 10271
(212) 223-0200 .. **Mitchell,** James A '90 (Stillman F&S,PC) -425 Park Av -NY 10022
(212) 553-1913 .. **Mitchell,** Jason A '04 Moody's Invstr Srvc -250 Greenwich -NY 10007
(212) 756-2000 .. **Mitchell,** Jason T '07 %Schulte R&Z LLP -919 3rd Av -NY 10022
(212) 613-2009 .. **Mitchell,** Jeffrey A '82 (Gibbons PC) -1 Penn Plz -NY 10119 **Fx:**554-9696
(718) 997-1000 .. **Mitchell,** John A '69 (Mitchell & I) -98-20 Metro Av -Frst Hlls 11375
(212) 813-9359 .. **Mitchell,** John D '86 (JD Mitchell Assoc,PC) -745 5th Av -NY 10151 **Fx:**813-9546
(518) 464-6770 .. **Mitchell,** John T '67 OfCnsl Thorn GT&B,LLP -5 Wembley Ct Bx15054 -Albany 12212
(212) 696-9500 .. **Mitchell,** John W '76 -30 Broad -NY 10004 **Fx:**334-5412
(212) 239-3030 .. **Mitchell,** Jos C '74 %Samuels Fndtn -350 5th Av -NY 10118 **Fx:**239-3039
(518) 640-5000 .. **Mitchell,** Jos D '85 AYCO -25 British Amer Blvd -Latham 12110
(631) 725-2820 .. **Mitchell,** Judith '77 -43 Lincoln -Sag Hbr 11963 **Fx:**725-2820
(212) 538-1485 .. **Mitchell,** Karen M '00 Credit Suisse -1 Mad Av -NY 10010
(718) 643-2004 .. **Mitchell,** Kenneth C '98 %Hon M Brennan -120 Schermerhorn -Brklyn 11201
(718) 876-6300 .. **Mitchell,** Kirstin L '09 DA -130 Styvsnt Pl -Staten Isl 10301
(518) 465-3553 .. **Mitchell,** Lia B '07 %Maynard OS&C,LLP -6 Twr Pl -Albany 12203
(716) 839-9656 .. **Mitchell,** Lisa L '95 -309 Eggert Rd -Buffalo 14215
(845) 291-2050 .. **Mitchell,** Lynda J '90 %DA -255-275 Main -Goshen 10924 **Fx:**291-2085
(212) 841-8000 .. **Mitchell,** Marc L '03 %SRC/Universal -1755 Bway -NY 10019
(212) 859-8000 .. **Mitchell,** Maya A '09 %Fried FHS&J LLP -1 NY Plz -NY 10004
(212) 847-4539 .. **Mitchell,** Michl J '90 Shipowners Claim Bureau,Inc -1 Bttry Pk Plz -NY 10004
(212) 848-4000 .. **Mitchell,** Michl P '06 %Shearman & S LLP -599 Lex Av -NY 10022
(212) 619-5000 .. **Mitchell,** Michl R '99 %EDC -110 William -NY 10038 **Fx:**312-3912
(518) 358-2272 .. **Mitchell,** Michele F '00 St Regis Mohawk Tribal Cncl -412 State Route 37 -Hogansburg 13655
(212) 801-3085 .. **Mitchell,** Nancy A '07 (Greenberg T,LLP) -200 Park Av -NY 10166
(212) 619-2800 .. **Mitchell,** Neville '91 (Mitchell Law Ofc PC) -225 Bway -NY 10007 **Fx:**619-2929
(212) 610-6300 .. **Mitchell,** Nicholas E '08 %Allen & O -1221 Av of Amer -NY 10020
(212) 770-1780 .. **Mitchell,** Nneka I '01 AIG -80 Pine -NY 10005
(716) 853-5100 .. **Mitchell,** Paul A '89 (Lippes MWF LLP) -665 Main -Buffalo 14203
(914) 592-4275 .. **Mitchell,** Peter J '97 %MHLS -100 Clearbrook Rd -Elmsfrd 10523 **Fx:**592-2634
(212) 298-5071 .. **Mitchell,** Peter R '99 %Leg Aid -49 Thomas -NY 10013 **Fx:**298-5252

(315) 655-3463 .. **Mitchell**, Peter W '62 (Mitchell G&S,LLC) -5 Mill Bx312 -Cazenovia 13035
(212) 351-4500 .. **Mitchell**, Philip D '95 (Epstein B&G,PC) -250 Park Av -NY 10177
(845) 473-8100 .. **Mitchell**, Richd A '75 (Iseman CR&H,LLP) -2649 South Rd -Poughkeepsie 12601
(315) 343-3866 .. **Mitchell**, Richd C Jr. '70 -52 E Cayuga -Oswego 13126 **Fx**:342-8815
(315) 349-8296 .. **Mitchell**, Richd C '96 (Cnty Atty) -46 E Brdg -Oswego 13126 **Fx**:349-8298
(212) 728-8000 .. **Mitchell**, Rita D '08 %Willkie F&G LLP -787 7th Av -NY 10019
(631) 853-7770 .. **Mitchell**, Robt C '64 %Leg Aid -400 Carlton Av -Central Islip 11722 **Fx**:853-4336
(212) 440-3377 .. **Mitchell**, Sandra M '05 CNA -40 Wall -NY 10005
(212) 878-8000 .. **Mitchell**, Sherry L '03 %Clifford C LLP -31 W 52nd -NY 10019
(212) 509-3900 .. **Mitchell Silberberg & Knupp LLP** -12 E 49th -NY 10017 **Fx**:509-7239
(845) 358-4300 .. **Mitchell**, Stuart M '57 -81 First Av Bx779 -Nyack 10960 **Fx**:358-4386
(718) 625-5297 .. **Mitchell**, Susan E '94 -32 Court -Brklyn 11201
(518) 432-4318 .. **Mitchell**, Thos A '77 -27 Elk -Albany 12207 **Fx**:434-9093
(212) 943-0280 .. **Mitchell**, Thos J '75 (McCanliss & E LLP) -88 Pine -NY 10005
(212) 875-6247 .. **Mitchell**, Valerie E '93 Sesame Workshop -1 Lincoln Plz -NY 10023
(516) 294-5433 .. **Mitchell**, Wm J '00 %Ahmuty D&M -200 IU Willets Rd -Albertson 11507
(347) 401-9910 .. **Mitek**, Jennifer T '01 Kings Cnty Fam Ct -330 Jay -Brklyn 11201
(518) 465-7933 .. **Mithen-Demasi**, Lori Ann '93 %Assn of Towns of NYS -146 State -Albany 12207 **Fx**:465-0724
(212) 619-4444 .. **Mitkoff**, Marci D '89 %Marshall CW&B,PC -116 John -NY 10038
(914) 428-3313 .. **Mitlitzky**, Steven R '92 %Curan AF&N,LLP -14 Mamaroneck Av -White Plns 10601 **Fx**:949-5800
(212) 336-2000 .. **Mitnick**, Carrie L '04 %Patterson BW&T LLP -1133 Av of Amer -NY 10036
(212) 336-8000 .. **Mitnick**, David K '01 %Amster R&E -90 Park Av -NY 10016
(516) 746-8000 .. **Mitnick**, Jack '61 OfCnsl Jaspan S LLP -300 Grdn City Plz -Gdn Cty 11530
(212) 512-3179 .. **Mitnick**, Jeffrey L '88 %McGraw-Hill -1221 Av of Amer -NY 10020 **Fx**:512-4827
(212) 839-5300 .. **Mitnick**, Joel '88 (Sidley A LLP) -787 7th Av -NY 10019
(212) 450-4000 .. **Mitnick**, Scott D '04 %Davis P&W LLP -450 Lex Av -NY 10017
(718) 780-7906 .. **Mitnick Benjamin**, Alana D '04 Bklyn Law Schl -250 Joralemon -Brklyn 11201 **Fx**:780-0393
(212) 736-0500 .. **Mitofsky Shapiro Neville & Hazen LLP** -152 Mad Av -NY 10016 **Fx**:736-1177
(631) 231-3775 .. **Mitola**, Danl M '94 %Atty Grievance Comm -150 Motor Pkwy -Hauppauge 11788
(516) 393-5555 .. **Mitola**, Ryan D '02 %Schneider M LLP -666 Old Cntry Rd -Gdn Cty 11530 **Fx**:393-5556
(516) 229-4501 .. **Mitola**, Susan J '96 %Russo A&T -875 Merrick Av -Westbury 11590
(212) 921-2200 .. **Mitra**, Ghobadi '00 Update Leg Staffing -1140 Av of Amer -NY 10036
(212) 819-8200 .. **Mitra**, Jayashree '09 %White & C LLP -1155 Av of Amer -NY 10036
(212) 661-5100 .. **Mitrani**, Morris K '82 (M Mitrani,PC) -100 Park Av -NY 10017 **Fx**:661-7867
(585) 293-9171 .. **Mitrano**, Gerard A '68 -10 Hutton Cir -Churchville 14428
(607) 277-1023 .. **Mitrano**, Tracy B '96 -20 Chase Ln -Ithaca 14850
(585) 425-2542 .. **Mitrano**, Vincent P '60 -43 E Pnte -Fairprt 14450
(516) 432-8917 .. **Mitrany**, Leon D '52 -19 Georgia Av -Long Bch 11561
(718) 979-4459 .. **Mitri**, Michl F '88 -263 Bryant Av -Staten Isl 10306
(716) 856-5500 .. **Mitri**, Serafina M '02 SpclCnsl Damon M LLP -200 Delaware Av -Buffalo 14202
(212) 415-9200 .. **Mitrione**, Gianfranco G '03 %Dorsey & W LLP -250 Park Av -NY 10177
(585) 924-9537 .. **Mitris**, George '87 -1 E Main -Victor 14564 **Fx**:924-9966
(212) 701-3000 .. **Mitrovich**, Mark P '10 %Cahill G&R LLP -80 Pine -NY 10005 **Fx**:269-5420
(212) 705-7000 .. **Mitry**, Danl F '06 %Bingham M LLP -399 Park Av -NY 10022
(718) 809-5111 .. **Mitsel**, Jacqueline G '08 -104 Hewlett Neck Rd -Woodmere 11598
(212) 782-4400 .. **Mitsuishi**, Motoi '93 %Bk of Tokyo-Mitsubishi -1251 Av of Amer -NY 10020 **Fx**:782-6420
(212) 455-0940 .. **Mittal**, Nikhil '00 JANA Partners,LLC -767 5th Av -NY 10153
(516) 326-0808 .. **Mittel**, Todd W '96 Jzanus,Ltd -170 Jericho Tpk -Floral Pk 11001 **Fx**:326-0998
(212) 714-3524 .. **Mittelman**, Sonya F '84 %M Goodwin -292 5th Av -NY 10001
(516) 482-8422 .. **Mittenthal**, Lawr J '51 -525 Nrthrn Blvd -Gt Neck 11021 **Fx**:482-8422
(212) 701-3000 .. **Mittin**, Jamie L '10 %Cahill G&R LLP -80 Pine -NY 10005 **Fx**:269-5420
(212) 332-2041 .. **Mittleman**, April S '94 %Millburn Corp -1270 Av of Amer -NY 10020
(212) 509-3456 .. **Mittleman**, Michele J '85 %McGivney & K,PC -80 Broad -NY 10004
(718) 409-1016 .. **Mittleman**, Philip A '75 -500 Brush Av -Bronx 10465 **Fx**:931-6426
(585) 232-6460 .. **Mittleman**, Ronald A '69 (Scolaro SCF&B,PC) -16 W Main -Rchstr 14614
(212) 622-6592 .. **Mittler**, Patricia E '09 JP Morgan Securities Inc -383 Mad Av -NY 10017
(212) 312-2335 .. **Mittler**, Renee F '88 %Leg Aid -60 Lafayette -NY 10013 **Fx**:349-0874
(212) 697-9500 .. **Mittman**, Barbara R '86 (Grushko & M,PC) -551 5th Av -NY 10176 **Fx**:697-3575
(914) 946-1452 .. **Mittman**, Brian M '95 (Markhoff & M PC) -14 Mamaroneck Av -White Plns 10601
(212) 821-4835 .. **Mittman**, Dan A '91 UBS -299 Park Av -NY 10171
(212) 759-7656 .. **Mittman**, Ellyn Roth '78 -110 E 59th -NY 10022
(212) 969-3000 .. **Mittman**, Jeremy M '04 %Proskauer R LLP -1585 Bway -NY 10036
(212) 659-7300 .. **Mittman**, Lawr '76 (Haynes & B,LLP) -1221 Av of Amer -NY 10020
(212) 885-5000 .. **Mittman**, Robt '66 (Blank R LLP) -405 Lex Av -NY 10174
(212) 492-3691 .. **Mitts**, Sean '85 Deloitte & Touche,LLP -1633 Bway -NY 10019
(212) 980-3500 .. **Mitzner**, Adam D '90 (Pavia & H LLP) -600 Mad Av -NY 10022
(212) 564-1250 .. **Mitzner**, Albert D '00 %Karp & K -370 7th Av -NY 10001
(845) 794-3344 .. **Mitzner**, Bonnie M '83 %DA -414 Bway -Monticello 12701 **Fx**:794-3646
(646) 825-3026 .. **Mitzner**, Marvin B '74 -405 Lex Av -NY 10174
(914) 946-4777 .. **Mitzner**, Melvyn '62 OfCnsl Keane & B,PC -445 Hmltn Av -White Plns 10601
(212) 624-5858 .. **Miuccio**, James J '04 -140 Bway -NY 10005 **Fx**:401-8128
(585) 232-3730 .. **Mix**, Matthew J '02 %Chamberlain D LLP -1600 Crssrds Bldg -Rchstr 14614
(212) 277-4000 .. **Miyamoto**, Ken '02 -520 Mad Av -NY 10022 **Fx**:277-4001
(212) 809-7600 .. **Miyashita**, Mayu '00 %Cheven K&H -40 Wall -NY 10005 **Fx**:344-4936
(212) 484-3900 .. **Miyazaki**, Marianna F '08 %Arent F LLP -1675 Bway -NY 10019
(212) 474-1000 .. **Mize**, James D '09 %Cravath S&M LLP -825 8th Av -NY 10019
(212) 559-3924 .. **Mizerik**, Ocean E '02 Citigroup Inc -425 Park Av -NY 10022
(212) 962-3638 .. **Mizio**, Domenic J '59 -321 Bway -NY 10007 **Fx**:571-4309
(212) 476-9000 .. **Mizrachi**, Avi Mark '95 %Neuberger Berman,LLC -605 3rd Av -NY 10158 **Fx**:476-9862
(212) 576-7000 .. **Mizrachi**, Ron J '96 %NY Life Ins -51 Mad Av -NY 10010 **Fx**:447-0569
(212) 582-8000 .. **Mizrack**, Richd '67 Cnsl Feingold & A,LLP -1330 Av of Amer -NY 10019
(917) 637-3600 .. **Mizrahi**, Celine '09 Ctr for Reproductive Rts -120 Wall -NY 10005 **Fx**:637-3666
(212) 686-4600 .. **Mizrahi**, Jason A '04 %H Felcher -347 5th Av -NY 10016 **Fx**:686-4686
(212) 906-1200 .. **Mizrahi**, Oded '05 %Latham & W -885 3rd Av -NY 10022
(212) 514-7400 .. **Mizrahi**, Robt N '07 %Buckley & C,PA -225 Bway -NY 10007
(212) 237-1000 .. **Mizrahi**, Saml M '93 %Windels ML&M,LLP -156 W 56th -NY 10019
(718) 981-4747 .. **Mizrahi**, Wm W '52 -9 Borman Av -Staten Isl 10314
(212) 757-8438 .. **Mizrahi**, Yael '05 %Levitt & N,PC -250 W 57th -NY 10107
(212) 705-7000 .. **Mizuki**, Fumiaki '76 (Bingham M LLP) -399 Park Av -NY 10022
(212) 679-1500 .. **Mlawski**, Jack D '78 (Galvin & M) -470 Park Av S -NY 10016
(212) 360-5581 .. **Mliakoff**, Alexander Y '89 -4 E 89th -NY 10128 **Fx**:369-0240
(646) 386-5891 .. **Mlinac**, Melinda M '85 %MHLS -41 Mad Av -NY 10010
(631) 843-5500 .. **Mlotek**, Mark E '81 Henry Schein,Inc -135 Duryea Rd -Melvll 11747
(212) 755-4895 .. **Mlott**, Agnes '73 -220 E 60th -NY 10022 **Fx**:755-4895
(212) 918-3000 .. **Mlynar**, Theo J '95 (Hogan L LLP) -875 3rd Av -NY 10022
(212) 331-5127 .. **Mo**, Chi '88 HRA -180 Water -NY 10038 **Fx**:331-4370
(212) 385-1500 .. **Mo**, Hugh H '77 -225 Bway -NY 10007 **Fx**:385-1870
(212) 318-6000 .. **Mo**, Jennifer A '03 %Paul HJ&W LLP -75 E 55th -NY 10022
(212) 969-3000 .. **Mo**, Karen Y '07 %Proskauer R LLP -1585 Bway -NY 10036
(212) 822-8300 .. **Mo**, Lourdes Rodriguez '84 %NMIC -76 Wadsworth Av -NY 10033 **Fx**:740-9645
(212) 530-5000 .. **Mo**, Richd Z '10 %Milbank TH&M LLP -1 Chase Manh Plz -NY 10005
(212) 472-4847 .. **Moak**, Roger M '74 -930 5th Av -NY 10021
(845) 306-1000 .. **Moake**, Richd D '97 %Watchtower -100 Watchtower Dr -Patterson 12563 **Fx**:306-0709
(212) 410-7296 .. **Moan**, Terrence A '73 DDM Dvlpmt & Svcs -2080 Lex Av -NY 10035
(716) 566-5400 .. **Moar**, Danl B '08 Goldberg S LLP -665 Main -Buffalo 14203
(212) 891-9100 .. **Moattar**, Kamran '92 (Goldfarb & F LLP) -345 Park Av -NY 10154
(212) 969-3000 .. **Moawad**, Rima R '00 (Proskauer R LLP) -1585 Bway -NY 10036
(212) 317-8500 .. **Mobayen**, Leila '08 %Snitow KH&M,LLP -575 Lex Av -NY 10022
(212) 530-5000 .. **Moberg**, Anders '05 %Milbank TH&M LLP -1 Chase Manh Plz -NY 10005
(516) 247-7010 .. **Moberg**, Michl J '99 (Moberg & Assoc) -333 Earle Ovngton Blvd -Uniondale 11553 **Fx**:247-7031
(518) 634-2350 .. **Moberly**, Marlene '97 -Bx395 -Freehold 12431
(212) 701-3000 .. **Mobilia**, Athy A '90 (Cahill G&R LLP) -80 Pine -NY 10005 **Fx**:269-5420
(212) 697-3122 .. **Mobilia**, Thos A '90 (Martin C&B LLP) -220 E 42nd -NY 10017
(212) 541-2000 .. **Mobley**, Charla Beth R '99 %Bryan C LLP 1290 Av of Amer -NY 10104
(718) 493-3136 .. **Mobley**, Paula L '99 -1141 Eastern Pkwy -Brklyn 11213 **Fx**:774-7845
(212) 668-5663 .. **Moburg**, Mark B '94 %Hon B Lifland -1 Bowling Grn -NY 10004
(212) 909-6000 .. **Mocanu**, Alexandru '09 %Debevoise & P LLP 919 3rd Av -NY 10022
(516) 248-9500 .. **Moccia**, Anthony M '08 %S Kobrick,PC -1305 Franklin Av -Gdn Cty 11530 **Fx**:248-7606
(914) 242-1995 .. **Moccia**, Christine '92 -Bx93 -Chappaqua 10514 **Fx**:241-3437
(203) 330-2128 .. **Mocciolo**, Adam S '07 %Pullman & C,LLC -50 Main -White Plns 10606
(518) 270-3779 .. **Mocerine**, Jessica Brooke '05 %Hon R Jacon-Cnty Ct -80 2nd -Troy 12180
(212) 403-1000 .. **Mock**, Jasand P '06 %Wachtell LR&K -51 W 52nd -NY 10019
(718) 490-7177 .. **Mock**, Judy S '00 -26 Court -Brklyn 11242 **Fx**:237-1425
(516) 489-5397 .. **Mock**, Kenneth B '94 -891 Nassau Rd -Uniondale 11553 **Fx**:564-8834
(212) 318-3000 .. **Mock**, Travis J '10 %Fulbright & J LLP -666 5th Av -NY 10103
(718) 875-1300 .. **Mockerman**, Jennifer L '07 %Appllt Div 2nd Dept -45 Monroe Pl -Brklyn 11201 **Fx**:858-2446
(212) 788-1652 .. **Modafferi**, Matthew J '10 %Law Dept -100 Church -NY 10007 **Fx**:788-0367
(212) 363-3100 .. **Modansky**, Michl C '75 (Bivona & C,PC) -88 Pine -NY 10005
(212) 793-2403 .. **Mode**, Paul J Jr. '05 Citigroup Inc -399 Park Av -NY 10022
(716) 855-3761 .. **Modeas**, Harry G Jr. '94 %LoTempio & B,PC -181 Franklin -Buffalo 14202 **Fx**:855-3437
(973) 848-4700 .. **Model**, Alan I '99 (Littler M,PC) -900 3rd Av -NY 10022 **Fx**:643-5626
(212) 724-4861 .. **Model**, Renate H '53 -525 West End Av -NY 10024 **Fx**:724-0395
(631) 423-8989 .. **Modelewski**, Christopher '90 -44 Elm -Huntngtn 11743 **Fx**:421-5134
(212) 373-1919 .. **Modell**, Gerald '69 (Krusch & M) -10 Rckfllr Plz -NY 10020
(718) 423-5900 .. **Modena**, Robt S '70 -242-03 Nrthrn Blvd -Little Neck 11362
(718) 250-2000 .. **Modest**, Virginia C '87 %DA -350 Jay -Brklyn 11201 **Fx**:250-2314
(212) 833-3669 .. **Modeste**, Petal Nevella '01 Weil G&M LLP -767 5th Av -NY 10153 **Fx**:310-8007
(315) 474-7541 .. **Modesti**, Julian B '95 (Menter R&T,PC) -308 Maltbie -Syracuse 13204
(212) 351-3400 .. **Modi**, Ameet A '09 Desmarais LLP -230 Park Av -NY 10169 **Fx**:351-3401
(212) 756-2000 .. **Modi**, Nina R '09 %Schulte R&Z LLP -919 3rd Av -NY 10022

(718) 590-3750 .. **Modica,** Ann Marie '95 %Hon M Gross -851 Grand Cncrs -Bronx 10451
(716) 838-0400 .. **Modica,** Francine E '92 -2655 Sheridan Dr -Tonawanda 14150
(585) 227-2070 .. **Modica,** Lorrie Walsh '87 OfCnsl Modica & Assoc -2430 Ridgeway Av -Rchstr 14626 **Fx:**368-1100
(212) 269-5500 .. **Modica,** Robt '01 SrCnsl Gordon & R LLP -90 Broad -NY 10004
(585) 227-2070 .. **Modica,** Steven V '87 (Modica & Assoc) -2430 Ridgeway Av -Rchstr 14626 **Fx:**368-1100
(914) 271-9595 .. **Modica-Snow,** Maria '82 -104 Grand -Croton-On-Hud 10520 **Fx:**271-2889
(212) 218-5500 .. **Modlin,** Chas M '83 (Seyfarth S LLP) -620 8th Av -NY 10018
(212) 371-5400 .. **Modlin,** Howard S '56 (Weisman CS&M PC) -445 Park Av -NY 10022
(212) 837-6000 .. **Modlin,** James M '86 (Hughes H&R LLP) -1 Bttry Pk Plz -NY 10004
(212) 483-9490 .. **Modugno,** Louis A '96 (McElroy DM&C,LLP) -88 Pine -NY 10005
(212) 964-7552 .. **Modupe,** Rueben O '99 -139 Fulton -NY 10038 **Fx:**693-1663
(212) 262-2390 .. **Mody,** Neil V '05 %Connell F LLP -888 7th Av -NY 10106
(212) 259-8000 .. **Modzelesky,** Amy M '10 %Dewey & L LLP -1301 Av of Amer -NY 10019
(516) 487-7300 .. **Modzelewski,** James '99 -98 Cuttermill Rd -Gt Neck 11021 **Fx:**504-6390
(212) 788-0768 .. **Moed,** Louise A '90 %Law Dept -100 Church -NY 10007 **Fx:**788-0367
(718) 250-2000 .. **Moehle,** Elizabeth M '07 %DA -350 Jay -Brklyn 11201 **Fx:**250-2314
(585) 271-3249 .. **Moehle,** Wm W '80 -2425 Clover -Rchstr 14618 **Fx:**271-0847
(212) 907-0700 .. **Moehlman,** Matthew C '05 %Labaton S LLP -140 Bway -NY 10005
(718) 728-6100 .. **Moehring,** John J '90 (Papadopoulos-Vlantes & M,PC) -901 Sheridan Av -Bronx 10451 **Fx:**728-9701
(212) 504-6000 .. **Moehringer,** John T '97 (Cadwalader W&T LLP) -1 World Fncl Ctr -NY 10281
(212) 431-5000 .. **Moel,** Marc D '89 %BlumbergExcelsior,Inc -62 White -NY 10013 **Fx:**431-5111
(516) 569-1995 .. **Moelis,** Laurence S '87 %Lastrada Entertainment -1315-B Bway -Hewlett 11557 **Fx:**569-1464
(516) 569-1995 .. **Moelis,** Stephen N '92 %Lastrada Entertainment -1315-B Bway -Hewlett 11557 **Fx:**569-1464
(716) 332-7825 .. **Moeller,** Andrew W '00 US Dist Ct -68 Court -Buffalo 14202
(315) 474-1285 .. **Moeller,** Elizabeth D '08 %DJ & JA Cirando -101 S Salina -Syracuse 13202
(716) 823-6556 .. **Moeller,** Robt A '70 -2732 Seneca -W Seneca 14224
(718) 286-2242 .. **Moeller,** Robt W '88 Leg Aid -120-46 Qns Blvd -Kew Gdns 11415 **Fx:**286-2286
(212) 692-9666 .. **Moeller,** Sheila A '89 OfCnsl Gilbride TL&S LLC -708 3rd Av -NY 10017
(315) 701-0379 .. **Moen,** Andrew T '97 (Moen & T) -5100 W Genesee -Camillus 13031
(716) 634-3776 .. **Moen,** Christopher P '77 Moen Law Ofcs -210 Capen Blvd -Buffalo 14226
(315) 701-0379 .. **Moen & Thurston** -5100 W Genesee -Camillus 13031 **Fx:**455-7150
(212) 248-3140 .. **Moench,** Matthew C '08 %Drinker B&R LLP -140 Bway -NY 10005
(212) 806-5400 .. **Moerdler,** Chas G '56 (Stroock &S&L LLP) -180 Maiden Ln -NY 10038
(212) 435-3571 .. **Moerdler,** Jeffrey A '82 Port Auth of NY/NJ -225 Park Av S -NY 10003 **Fx:**435-3555
(212) 935-3000 .. **Moerdler,** Jeffrey A '82 %Mintz LCFG&P,PC -666 3rd Av -NY 10017
(917) 608-2278 .. **Moerdler,** Sharon M '94 Supreme Ct -4640 Lvngstn Av -Bronx 10471
(212) 425-7200 .. **Moersfelder,** Matthew E M '06 %Kenyon & K,LLP -1 Bway -NY 10004
(212) 294-6700 .. **Moetell,** Michl C '07 (Winston & S) -200 Park Av -NY 10166
(212) 625-0700 .. **Moezinia,** Francis S '93 -81 Franklin -NY 10013 **Fx:**625-0900
(212) 715-9100 .. **Moff,** Jason M '06 %Kramer LN&F,LLP -1177 Av of Amer -NY 10036
(212) 259-8000 .. **Moffat,** Laurie A '08 %Dewey & L LLP -1301 Av of Amer -NY 10019
(212) 723-6906 .. **Moffat,** Michele J '92 Citigroup Global Mrkts -390 Greenwich -NY 10013
(212) 922-1800 .. **Moffat,** S Jane '07 %McKenna L&A -230 Park Av -NY 10169
(212) 632-5500 .. **Moffatt,** Lora A '91 (Salans LLP) -620 5th Av -NY 10020
(631) 694-2300 .. **Moffet,** Diane J '90 Cnsl Lamb & B,LLP -534 Broadhllw Rd Bx9034 -Melvll 11747
(718) 250-1400 .. **Moffett,** Christine M '93 %BZ Green -12 MetroTech Ctr -Brklyn 11201 **Fx:**250-1401
(518) 285-8435 .. **Moffett,** Jennifer E '05 %Hon J Assini -620 State -Schnctdy 12305
(518) 462-0300 .. **Moffett,** Tara Lynn '00 %Girvin & F,PC -20 Corp Wds Blvd -Albany 12211
(845) 565-3700 .. **Moffit,** Kathleen '90 Med Excel USA Inc -484 Temple Hill Rd -New Windsor 12553
(212) 297-5800 .. **Moffitt,** Brian E '95 SrCnsl Day P LLP -7 Times Sq -NY 10036
(212) 449-7179 .. **Moffitt,** David J '97 Merrill Lynch -250 Vesey -NY 10080
(212) 530-1800 .. **Mogan,** Grant J '06 %Richards K&O LLP -1 World Fncl Ctr -NY 10281
(518) 455-4265 .. **Mogan,** Heather A '02 Ofc of Minority Cnsl -440 The Cptl -Albany 12248
(716) 854-5636 .. **Mogavero,** Albert J '70 -110 Pearl -Buffalo 14202 **Fx:**854-0806
(914) 969-5514 .. **Mogavero,** Bruce K '85 BK Mogavero,PC -7070 Xavier Dr -Ynkrs 10704 **Fx:**969-1630
(716) 523-9979 .. **Mogavero,** Robt F '73 -4517 Parker Rd -Hambrg 14075
(212) 351-4000 .. **Mogck,** Brian D '07 %Gibson D&C LLP -200 Park Av -NY 10166
(212) 323-8255 .. **Mogel,** David L '85 (Sims MK&D LLP) -67 Wall -NY 10005
(212) 213-6996 .. **Mogel,** Jason T '99 (Spears & I LLP) -51 Mad Av -NY 10010
(845) 791-7676 .. **Mogel,** Steven N '02 %Shawn Law Ofcs -30 North Bx1320 -Monticello 12701 **Fx:**791-4660
(212) 231-1000 .. **Mogg,** Katherine A M '00 MacQuarie Securities(USA)Inc -125 W 55th -NY 10019 **Fx:**231-1010
(718) 331-7700 .. **Mogg,** Richd R '90 %Frekhtman & Assoc -60 Bay 26th -Brklyn 11214
(212) 344-7941 .. **Moghadassi,** Ramyar '92 (Moghadassi & Assoc) -405 Lex Av -NY 10174
(212) 344-7941 .. **Moghadassi-Weiss,** Roya '97 (Moghadassi & Assoc) -405 Lex Av -NY 10174
(212) 318-6000 .. **Moghal,** Saleem N '04 %Paul HJ&W LLP -75 E 55th -NY 10022
(212) 873-2118 .. **Moghrabi,** Zuhayr A '67 (Moghrabi & L) -54 Riverside Dr -NY 10024 **Fx:**873-5852
(212) 687-2770 .. **Mogil,** Darren S '02 %Cohen PL&P -551 5th Av -NY 10176
(212) 983-9330 .. **Mogil,** Jamie R '06 Faruqi & F,LLP -369 Lex Av -NY 10017 **Fx:**983-9331
(212) 854-8382 .. **Moglen,** Eben '88 %Columbia Law Schl -435 W 116th -NY 10027 **Fx:**854-7946
(212) 622-2669 .. **Moglia,** Mary M '94 %JP Morgan Chase & Co -277 Park Av -NY 10172
(518) 474-5228 .. **Mogor,** Cornelia '81 %Dept of Law -The Cptl -Albany 12224
(212) 225-2000 .. **Mogul,** Elliott C '09 %Cleary GS&H -1 Lbrty Plz -NY 10006
(212) 880-9478 .. **Mogul,** Judith L '87 (Morvillo AGIA&B,PC) -565 5th Av -NY 10017
(212) 298-5029 .. **Mogulescu,** Kate A '04 Leg Aid -49 Thomas -NY 10013 **Fx:**298-5252
(212) 376-3157 .. **Mogulescu,** Sara E '99 Vera Inst of Justice -233 Bway -NY 10279 **Fx:**941-9407
(212) 558-4021 .. **Mohajer,** Ramin Afshar '09 %Sullivan & C LLP -125 Broad -NY 10004
(718) 738-5150 .. **Mohamed,** Kaiumullah '94 -103-18 Lefferts Blvd -S Richmond Hll 11419 **Fx:**738-8515
(212) 808-8100 .. **Mohammad,** Usman '00 %Kostelanetz & F,LLP -7 Wrld Trd Ctr -NY 10007
(718) 858-3230 .. **Mohammed,** T S M '94 Harlowtown -352 Classon Av -Brklyn 11238 **Fx:**858-1991
(212) 725-3846 .. **Mohammedi,** Omar Tarik '97 -233 Bway -NY 10279 **Fx:**202-7621
(212) 819-8200 .. **Mohan,** Patrick R '08 %White & C LLP -1155 Av of Amer -NY 10036
(914) 766-4344 .. **Mohan,** Theresa K '91 IBM -294 Route 100 -Somers 10589
(212) 306-7100 .. **Mohandoss,** Veena '06 %Campaign Finance Bd -40 Rector -NY 10006 **Fx:**306-7143
(212) 209-3096 .. **Mohanty,** Namrata '07 %Reitler K&R LLC -885 3rd Av -NY 10022
(718) 590-6168 .. **Mohbat,** Jos E '80 %Law Dept -198 E 161st -Bronx 10451 **Fx:**590-2686
(212) 872-1000 .. **Mohemad Amin,** M Amrin '09 -One Bryant Park -NY 10036 **Fx:**872-1002
(516) 759-1212 .. **Mohen,** Thos P '83 (Mohen & T LLP) -186 Birch Hill Rd -Locust Vly 11560
(516) 759-1212 .. **Mohen & Treacy LLP** -186 Birch Hill Rd -Locust Vly 11560 **Fx:**759-3234
(845) 291-2050 .. **Mohl,** Julie M '02 %DA -255-275 Main -Goshen 10924 **Fx:**291-2085
(212) 396-8850 .. **Mohl Abrahams,** Rachel '95 Avi Chai Fndtn -1015 Park Av -NY 10028 **Fx:**396-8833
(516) 747-6300 .. **Mohlenhoff,** Edw C '88 %Koeppel M&L,LLP -155 First Bx863 -Mineola 11501
(212) 421-4100 .. **Mohler,** Bryan T '08 %Pryor C LLP -7 Times Sq -NY 10036
(914) 323-7000 .. **Mohnach,** Mary E '01 %Wilson EME&D LLP -3 Gannett Dr -White Plns 10604
(212) 859-8000 .. **Mohney,** Trent H J '09 %Fried FHS&J LLP -1 NY Plz -NY 10004
(212) 736-2624 .. **Mohr,** Bonnie L '04 -236 W 26th -NY 10001 **Fx:**981-0528
(518) 408-0469 .. **Mohr,** Bradley C '75 %Workers Comp Bd -20 Park -Albany 12207
(845) 510-4088 .. **Mohr,** J Gary '93 -3 Lisa Ln -Goshen 10924
(212) 310-9578 .. **Mohr,** Karen P '92 Instinet Corp -3 Times Sq -NY 10036
(718) 293-1542 .. **Mohr,** Martin J '00 Mohr & M -901 Sheridan Av -Bronx 10451 **Fx:**293-5395
(716) 681-3305 .. **Mohr,** Ralph M '80 -5622 Bway -Lancaster 14086
(212) 230-8800 .. **Mohr,** Sarah K '09 %WilmerHale -399 Park Av -NY 10022
(212) 246-6080 .. **Mohrer,** Fruma '94 %YIVO Inst -15 W 16th -NY 10011
(631) 851-0700 .. **Mohrman,** Jacqueline '99 1st Land Title Agncy of NY,Inc -267 Carleton Av -Central Islip 11722 **Fx:**851-9622
(212) 295-6405 .. **Mohtashemi,** Mark '02 WilmerHale -399 Park Av -NY 10022
(585) 937-8987 .. **Mohun,** Michl M '81 -344 Kern Rd -Cowlesville 14037 **Fx:**937-8988
(212) 836-8000 .. **Moilanen,** Lindsay S '10 Kaye S LLP -425 Park Av -NY 10022
(212) 558-4000 .. **Moin,** Andrew D '09 %Sullivan & C LLP -125 Broad -NY 10004
(212) 668-6000 .. **Moin,** Cheryl Eisberg '81 (Hill & M LLP) -2 Wall -NY 10005
(631) 549-3131 .. **Moir,** Maria '87 (Moir & S,LLP) -155 W Carver -Huntngtn 11743 **Fx:**549-3601
(516) 942-9100 .. **Moisan,** Matthew J '09 %P Birzon & Assoc -400 Jericho Tpk -Jericho 11753 **Fx:**942-0596
(212) 375-6659 .. **Moise,** David J '82 OfCnsl Hass & H,LLP -135 W 50th -NY 10020 **Fx:**375-6888
(212) 697-6555 .. **Moise Cassetta,** Madeleine E '09 %Biedermann RH&R -570 Lex Av -NY 10022
(914) 636-2648 .. **Moise-Stone,** Florence '91 (Moise & S,PC) -30 Church -New Rchll 10801 **Fx:**626-2528
(212) 906-1200 .. **Mojtabaee-Zamani,** Reza K '10 %Latham & W -885 3rd Av -NY 10022
(212) 468-8000 .. **Mok,** Man-Ni Judy '08 %Morrison & F LLP -1290 Av of Amer -NY 10104
(212) 704-6000 .. **Mok,** Roger '08 %Troutman S LLP -405 Lex Av -NY 10174
(917) 721-2544 .. **Mok,** Saml I '04 -350 Bway -NY 10013 **Fx:**(212) 226-3224
(212) 226-5520 .. **Mok,** Winnie '83 -101 Lafayette -NY 10013
(212) 474-1000 .. **Mokas,** Alysa D '03 Cravath S&M LLP -825 8th Av -NY 10019
(212) 815-0844 .. **Moked,** Neely '03 %Hon S Evans -71 Thomas -NY 10013
(212) 425-7200 .. **Moken,** Merri C '05 %Kenyon & K,LLP -1 Bway -NY 10004
(516) 248-1500 .. **Mokotoff & Mondshine** -1200 King -Rye Brook 10573 **Fx:**873-8700
(516) 248-1500 .. **Mokotoff,** Shirley '42 (Mokotoff & M) -1200 King -Rye Brook 10573
(646) 330-4547 .. **Molander,** Garth A '95 (Molander & Assoc) -9 E 38th -NY 10016 **Fx:**452-3567
(631) 256-8495 .. **Molander,** Garth A '95 (Molander & Assoc) -4875 Sunrise Hwy -Bohemia 11716 **Fx:**256-8496
(631) 501-3100 .. **Molano,** Paul '85 %J Humphreys -3 Huntngtn Quad Bx9028 -Melvll 11747 **Fx:**501-3085
(212) 806-5400 .. **Molaro,** Giuseppe '04 %Stroock &S&L LLP -180 Maiden Ln -NY 10038
(516) 746-6505 .. **Molbegott,** Elinor D '78 -419 Latham Ln -E Williston 11596 **Fx:**294-8435
(212) 233-2400 .. **Molbert,** Andrew M '90 -325 Bway -NY 10007 **Fx:**233-6746
(212) 878-8384 .. **Moldenhauer,** David T '87 (Clifford C LLP) -31 W 52nd -NY 10019
(716) 566-2800 .. **Moldenhauer,** Mark A '02 (Bond S&K,PLLC) -40 Fountian Plz -Buffalo 14202
(212) 563-4100 .. **Moldof,** Stephen B '70 (Cohen W&S LLP) -330 W 42nd -NY 10036

(212) 504-6000 .. **Moldovan**, Elena V '06 %Cadwalader W&T LLP -1 World Fncl Ctr -NY 10281
(212) 735-8603 .. **Moldovan**, Jos T '83 (Morrison C LLP) -909 3rd Av -NY 10022
(516) 294-3300 .. **Moldovan**, Neil '84 -1 Old Cntry Rd -Carle Pl 11514 **Fx**:294-4019
(212) 219-1800 .. **Moldover**, Judith A '79 Lawyers Alliance NY -171 Mad Av -NY 10016 **Fx**:941-7458
(212) 563-3370 .. **Moldovsky**, Brem '03 (B Moldovsky,LLC) -110 Wall -NY 10005 **Fx**:563-3371
(212) 450-4000 .. **Moldowan**, Gillian D E '08 %Davis P&W LLP -450 Lex Av -NY 10017
(212) 450-4000 .. **Moldowan**, Michl J '09 %Davis P&W LLP -450 Lex Av -NY 10017
(845) 628-1100 .. **Molé**, Anthony R '01 (Herodes & M,PC) -888 Route 6 -Mahopac 10541 **Fx**:628-1110
(212) 637-2275 .. **Molé**, Marissa B '00 %US Atty -1 St Andrews Plz -NY 10007
(914) 862-5140 .. **Molea**, Anthony J '95 %DA -1940 Commerce -Yorktwn Hts 10598 **Fx**:862-5146
(212) 891-1600 .. **Molenda**, John J '99 (Jenner & B LLP) -919 3rd Av -NY 10022
(212) 218-2100 .. **Molenda**, Victoria Silcott '05 %Fitzpatrick CH&S -1290 Av of Amer -NY 10104
(516) 496-5822 .. **Molesso**, Peter J '07 %T Spina -170 Froehlich Farm Blvd -Woodbury 11797 **Fx**:496-5420
(845) 279-9049 .. **Molesworth**, Lynda Nunziato '97 -76 Sunset Dr Bx654 -Brewstr 10509
(212) 728-8000 .. **Molesworth**, Rita M '96 (Willkie F&G LLP) -787 7th Av -NY 10019
(212) 805-5116 .. **Moletteri**, Andrea F '92 %NY Cnty Defender Srvcs -225 Bway -NY 10007 **Fx**:571-6035
(212) 969-3000 .. **Moletto**, Susan A '05 %Proskauer R LLP -1585 Bway -NY 10036
(212) 460-6671 .. **Molfetta**, Michele A '02 Con Ed -4 Irving Pl -NY 10003
(212) 479-4165 .. **Molho**, Robin S '86 AON Risk Srvcs -199 Water -NY 10038
(212) 416-8422 .. **Molic**, Robt R '68 %Dept of Law -120 Bway -NY 10271
(518) 486-3190 .. **Molik**, David '79 NYSOCFS -52 Wshngtn Av -Rensselaer 12144 **Fx**:474-9218
(716) 937-7562 .. **Molik**, Edw J '55 -12943 W Main -Alden 14004
(212) 208-3361 .. **Molin**, Karl T II '84 Ambac Assurance Corp -1 State Street Plz -NY 10004 **Fx**:785-1178
(212) 745-5826 .. **Molina**, Ana L '98 IBM -590 Mad Av -NY 10022 **Fx**:745-5868
(718) 579-7929 .. **Molina**, Cesar '86 %Leg Aid -900 Sheridan Av -Bronx 10451 **Fx**:293-8744
(212) 455-2000 .. **Molina**, Danl '09 %Simpson T&B LLP -425 Lex Av -NY 10017
(212) 335-9000 .. **Molina**, Jeannette L '94 %DA -1 Hogan Pl -NY 10013
(212) 425-1900 .. **Molina**, Manuel A '89 %Freehill H&M LLP -80 Pine -NY 10005
(212) 770-7000 .. **Molina**, Roxana M '01 %AIG -80 Pine -NY 10005 **Fx**:344-2286
(718) 401-1600 .. **Molina**, Victor J '99 -247 E 149th -Bronx 10451 **Fx**:401-1600
(212) 363-6900 .. **Molinares**, Jessica '05 %Faust GS&B LLP -2 Rector -NY 10006
(516) 542-1000 .. **Molinares-Emanuel**, Ivette P '97 %Geisler & G,LLP -100 Q Roosevelt Blvd -Gdn Cty 11530
(212) 351-4500 .. **Molinari**, Brian M '99 %Epstein B&G,PC -250 Park Av -NY 10177
(718) 442-0900 .. **Molinari**, Guy V '53 Russo S&D,PC -1010 Forest Av -Staten Isl 10310
(516) 378-5700 .. **Molinari**, John E '72 (Martin & M) -148 Lng Bch Av -Freeprt 11520 **Fx**:623-5281
(212) 946-4703 .. **Molinari**, John F '77 Legal Content,Inc -11 Penn Plz -NY 10001
(631) 907-3500 .. **Molinari**, Laura Anne '98 OfCnsl Tarbet L&S -524 Montauk Hwy Bx2635 -Amagansett 11930 **Fx**:907-3501
(718) 873-4708 .. **Molinari**, Ralph J '72 -74 Lincoln Av -Staten Isl 10306
(212) 451-2900 .. **Molinari**, Saml L '78 Cnsl Robinson & C LLP -885 3rd Av -NY 10022
(646) 660-4923 .. **Molinaro**, Valerie A '82 -445 Park Av -NY 10022 **Fx**:(917) 322-2395
(516) 747-1822 .. **Moline**, Alfred P Jr. '64 -26 Cary Rd -New Hyde Pk 11040 **Fx**:747-1822
(212) 964-7400 .. **Molinelli**, Stephen J '93 Smith MDWY&Y,PC -111 John -NY 10038
(212) 408-2500 .. **Molino**, J Elizabeth Cogan '05 %Baker B,LLP -30 Rckfllr Plz -NY 10112
(212) 446-8432 .. **Molino**, Virginia L '84 %McKinsey & Co -55 E 52nd -NY 10055 **Fx**:688-9521
(914) 834-6000 .. **Molinoff**, Danl D '75 -2039 Palmer Av -Larchmnt 10538 **Fx**:834-6222
(516) 296-9234 .. **Molins**, Arthur J '81 %Lufthansa -1640 Hempstd Tpk -E Meadow 11554 **Fx**:296-9399
(518) 439-0375 .. **Molinsek**, Stephen L '91 (Friedman & M,PC) -2 Normanskill Blvd Bx69 -Delmar 12054
(716) 858-2424 .. **Molisani**, Seth T '09 %DA -25 Delaware Av -Buffalo 14202 **Fx**:858-7425
(212) 468-8000 .. **Molison**, Stacy L W '09 %Morrison & F LLP -1290 Av of Amer -NY 10104
(914) 722-6922 .. **Moliterno**, Jos V '74 -670 Wht Plns Rd -Scarsdale 10583
(212) 944-0500 .. **Moliver**, Marianna '08 %Hofheimer G&G,LLP -530 5th Av -NY 10036
(212) 846-6075 .. **Molko**, Jos R '98 %MTV Networks -1515 Bway -NY 10036 **Fx**:258-8358
(212) 756-2000 .. **Moll**, Kelli L '95 (Schulte R&Z LLP) -919 3rd Av -NY 10022
(212) 878-1036 .. **Moll**, Rhonda J '86 %MTA -347 Mad Av -NY 10017 **Fx**:878-0147
(212) 889-7111 .. **Moll**, Robt M '68 -9 E 40th -NY 10016 **Fx**:481-6757
(716) 566-5400 .. **Moll**, Thos M '86 (Goldberg S LLP) -665 Main -Buffalo 14203
(315) 422-4323 .. **Molldrem**, Bernhard P Jr. '78 -224 Harrison -Syracuse 13202 **Fx**:422-4318
(212) 859-8000 .. **Molle**, Mark '05 %Fried FHS&J LLP -1 NY Plz -NY 10004
(607) 778-2423 .. **Mollen**, Gerald F '78 (DA) -45 Hawley Bx1766 -Bnghmtn 13902 **Fx**:778-8870
(212) 592-1400 .. **Mollen**, Milton '50 Cnsl Herrick,F LLP -2 Park Av -NY 10016
(212) 751-2700 .. **Mollen**, Milton '50 %JAMS -620 8th Av -NY 10018 **Fx**:751-4099
(212) 592-1400 .. **Mollen**, Scott E '72 (Herrick,F LLP) -2 Park Av -NY 10016
(212) 799-2400 .. **Moller**, Allan S '71 (AS Moller,LLC) -110 W 78th -NY 10024 **Fx**:799-2444
(845) 383-3839 .. **Moller**, Christian D '04 %MHLS -173 Boices Ln -Kingston 12401
(212) 506-2500 .. **Moller**, Elizabeth Ann '05 %Mayer B LLP -1675 Bway -NY 10019
(212) 687-8181 .. **Moller**, Marc S '63 (Kreindler & K) -750 3rd Av -NY 10017
(718) 549-1452 .. **Moller**, Shelah S '82 -4701 Grosvenor Av -Bronx 10471
(212) 450-4000 .. **Mollerus**, Michl T '97 (Davis P&W LLP) -450 Lex Av -NY 10017
(914) 993-5505 .. **Mollica**, Donna M '06 HRH Construction LLC -50 Main -White Plns 10606
(212) 294-6700 .. **Mollica**, Patricia A '95 (Winston & S) -200 Park Av -NY 10166
(845) 485-5353 .. **Mollica**, Paul L '83 -4 Lbrty -Poughkeepsie 12601
(718) 996-5600 .. **Mollica**, Raymond J '00 (Arze & M,LLP) -2352 80th -Brklyn 11214 **Fx**:996-5800
(718) 426-1709 .. **Molligo**, Anthony J '79 TSA-LaGuardia -7520 Astoria Blvd -E Elmhrst 11370
(212) 306-1000 .. **Mollin**, Danl Z '96 %Amer Stock Exch -86 Trinity Pl -NY 10006
(631) 608-4100 .. **Mollins**, Kenneth M '82 (K Mollins,PC) -425 Broadhllw Rd -Melvll 11747 **Fx**:608-4107
(516) 822-1599 .. **Mollins**, Mindy R '90 -114 Bounty Ln -Jericho 11753
(631) 361-7810 .. **Mollo**, Douglas J '88 -51 E Main -Smithtwn 11787 **Fx**:361-7851
(212) 758-7600 .. **Mollo**, Farah '98 %Collazo C&M -747 3rd Av -NY 10017
(718) 858-3401 .. **Mollo**, Peter J '89 -266 Smith -Brklyn 11231 **Fx**:858-3035
(212) 661-9100 .. **Mollod**, Jonathan '97 Otterbourg SH&R,PC -230 Park Av -NY 10169
(212) 867-1100 .. **Molloy**, Cindy E '89 (Tratner & M) -551 5th Av -NY 10176
(914) 948-8829 .. **Molloy**, John G '83 (J Molloy,PC) -305 Old Tarrytown Rd -White Plns 10603 **Fx**:948-8890
(716) 675-5050 .. **Molloy**, John J '78 -4268 Seneca -W Seneca 14224
(516) 334-1000 .. **Molloy**, John L Jr. '64 -346 Maple Av -Westbury 11590
(212) 261-8000 .. **Molloy**, Jos K '78 (Mendes & M,LLP) -750 7th Av -NY 10019
(716) 856-1600 .. **Molloy**, Kathleen A '92 (Hurwitz & D) -424 Main -Buffalo 14202
(631) 415-4808 .. **Molloy**, Kenneth J '89 -320 Carleton Av -Central Islip 11722 **Fx**:415-4809
(212) 807-8355 .. **Molloy**, Laurence B III '91 -365 W 20th -NY 10011
(716) 853-8100 .. **Molloy**, Mark A '97 (Nixon P LLP) -40 Fountain Plz -Buffalo 14202
(516) 741-5050 .. **Molloy**, Peter C '82 %Fidelity Natl Title Ins -1415 Kellum Pl -Gdn Cty 11530 **Fx**:741-5363
(518) 213-6060 .. **Molloy**, Robt E '93 -22 Century Hill Dr -Latham 12110 **Fx**:213-6055
(212) 867-1100 .. **Molloy**, Sean A '88 OfCnsl Tratner & M -551 5th Av -NY 10176
(516) 775-3300 .. **Molloy**, Therese M '92 OfCnsl M Kovit -248-52 Jericho Tpk -Floral Pk 11001 **Fx**:775-3320
(212) 906-1200 .. **Molluzzo**, John C Jr. '07 %Latham & W -885 3rd Av -NY 10022
(315) 474-6448 .. **Molnar**, F Scott '92 (Byrne C&P PC) -100 Madison -Syracuse 13202
(212) 247-0848 .. **Molnar**, Lindsay D '07 %Bienstock & M,PC -250 W 57th -NY 10107
(212) 715-9100 .. **Molner**, Thos E '89 (Kramer LN&F,LLP) -1177 Av of Amer -NY 10036
(212) 607-8160 .. **Molo**, Steven F '04 (MoloLamken) -540 Mad Av -NY 10022 **Fx**:607-8161
(212) 869-3200 .. **Molod**, Fredk M '51 (Molod S&D,PC) -104 W 40th -NY 10018
(212) 888-2485 .. **Molod**, Irene '85 -400 E 56th -NY 10022
(212) 869-3200 .. **Molod**, Julie E '95 %Molod S&D,PC -104 W 40th -NY 10018
(212) 869-3200 .. **Molod Spitz & DeSantis,PC** -104 W 40th -NY 10018 **Fx**:869-4242
(212) 468-8000 .. **Moloff**, Leda A K '10 %Morrison & F LLP -1290 Av of Amer -NY 10104
(212) 224-0354 .. **Molofsky**, Nan '87 City Invstmt Fund -299 Park Av -NY 10171
(518) 433-4300 .. **Moloney**, Danl P '05 GE Co RESO -12 Corp Wds Blvd -Albany 12211
(914) 472-9709 .. **Moloney**, Kevin D '63 -281 Garth Rd -Scarsdale 10583 **Fx**:472-9709
(212) 408-5100 .. **Moloney**, Lori F '92 Chadbourne & P LLP -30 Rckfllr Plz -NY 10112
(212) 225-2000 .. **Moloney**, Thos J '77 (Cleary GS&H) -1 Lbrty Plz -NY 10006
(212) 279-7575 .. **Molot**, Valery '87 -225 W 34th -NY 10122 **Fx**:643-2346
(212) 425-9300 .. **Moltner**, Kenneth M '86 Cnsl Bressler A&R,PC -17 State -NY 10004
(212) 529-2880 .. **Moltner**, Steven '85 -435 E 14th -NY 10009
(212) 209-4800 .. **Molton**, David J '83 (Brown R LLP) -7 Times Sq -NY 10036
(212) 840-2644 .. **Molumby**, Ronan J '87 (Sioris & M) -350 5th Av -NY 10118 **Fx**:921-0163
(212) 756-2000 .. **Momborquette**, David K '92 (Schulte R&Z LLP) -919 3rd Av -NY 10022
(718) 286-2450 .. **Mombrun**, Marie I '92 %Leg Aid -120-46 Qns Blvd -Kew Gdns 11415 **Fx**:263-4234
(212) 554-1234 .. **Momen**, Matin '04 AXA Financial Inc -1290 Av of Amer -NY 10104 **Fx**:707-3903
(212) 735-8600 .. **Momin**, Karim N '99 %Morrison C LLP -909 3rd Av -NY 10022
(646) 428-3763 .. **Momo**, Jane Tobey '78 %Dept of Educ -32 Old Slip -NY 10005 **Fx**:428-3890
(212) 878-8000 .. **Mon**, Kathleen C '10 %Clifford C LLP -31 W 52nd -NY 10019
(585) 325-2040 .. **Monacelli**, Don W '77 -1 E Main -Rchstr 14614
(585) 757-2547 .. **Monachino**, Catherine M Ohl '87 -45 Church -Elba 14058
(212) 218-5500 .. **Monachino**, David M '91 (Seyfarth S LLP) -620 8th Av -NY 10018
(607) 763-9200 .. **Monachino**, Sam P '85 (Levene G&T,LLP) -BxF-1706 -Bnghmtn 13902
(212) 687-3000 .. **Monack**, Mark P '94 %Jaffe & A,LLP -600 3rd Av -NY 10016
(585) 254-8191 .. **Monaco**, Anthony '87 %Rochester Colonial Mfg -1794 Lyell Av -Rchstr 14606
(718) 872-0533 .. **Monaco**, Antonietta M '90 (Monaco & M,LLP) -7610 13th Av -Brklyn 11228 **Fx**:872-0536
(718) 872-0533 .. **Monaco**, Antonio Jr. '91 (Monaco & M,LLP) -7610 13th Av -Brklyn 11228 **Fx**:872-0536
(518) 641-0500 .. **Monaco**, Cindy M '95 %West Firm,PLLC -677 Bway -Albany 12207 **Fx**:615-1500
(212) 278-1000 .. **Monaco**, Cynthia '93 (Anderson K&O,PC) -1251 Av of Amer -NY 10020
(212) 422-1200 .. **Monaco**, Dennis J '01 %Abrams GF&J,PC -1 Bttry Pk Plz -NY 10004
(212) 259-8000 .. **Monaco**, Francis R '97 (Dewey & L LLP) -1301 Av of Amer -NY 10019
(718) 440-2923 .. **Monaco**, Joann R '98 -1812 Forest Hll Rd -Staten Isl 10314
(212) 486-4244 .. **Monaco**, Jos D III '96 -1500 Bway -NY 10036 **Fx**:317-2946
(585) 777-7537 .. **Monaco**, Lynne A '91 Frontier Comm Corp -111 Field -Rchstr 14620
(518) 465-3484 .. **Monaco**, Mackenzie C '05 %Carter CCBM&L,PC -20 Corp Wds Blvd -Albany 12211
(212) 748-2241 .. **Monaco**, Marie L '91 %Zurich Amer Ins Grp -1 Lbrty Plz -NY 10006
(212) 788-7103 .. **Monaco**, Philip A '95 City Cncl of NY -City Hall -NY 10007
(203) 894-8306 .. **Monaco**, Richd G '87 -80 Wstchstr Sq -Bronx 10461 **Fx**:894-4621
(607) 843-2951 .. **Monaco**, Roger '75 -20 Lafayette Pk Bx391 -Oxfrd 13830 **Fx**:843-2961

(914) 961-1448 .. **Monaco,** Stephen C '80 -35 E Grassy Sprain Rd -Ynkrs 10710 **Fx:**961-1339
(631) 231-1450 .. **Monaco,** Wm '89 (Feldman K&M,PC) -330 Vndrblt Motor Pkwy -Hauppauge 11788
(518) 270-3761 .. **Monagan,** Joanne P '90 Family Ct -1504 5th Av -Troy 12180
(516) 280-1328 .. **Monaghan,** Edw W '02 -445 Broad Hollow Rd -Melvll 11747 **Fx:**798-4704
(585) 704-9810 .. **Monaghan,** Jane E '97 -6062 Burke Hill Rd -Warsaw 14569 **Fx:**786-8639
(518) 271-7704 .. **Monaghan,** Jos F '57 -616 19th Bx23 -Watervliet 12189 **Fx:**271-7704
(212) 564-9800 .. **Monaghan,** Kellyann '01 %D'Agostino L&L,LLP -345 7th Av -NY 10001
(212) 980-1900 .. **Monaghan,** Kevin J '01 %Donovan & G,LLP -261 Mad Av -NY 10016
(585) 454-3960 .. **Monaghan,** Lori Robb '02 -1 E Main -Rchstr 14614
(585) 753-4500 .. **Monaghan,** Mark E '00 %DA -832 Watts Bldg -Rchstr 14614 **Fx:**753-4576
(212) 909-6000 .. **Monaghan,** Maura K '00 (Debevoise & P LLP) -919 3rd Av -NY 10022
(212) 751-4300 .. **Monaghan,** Maureen R '99 %Hodgson R LLP -1540 Bway -NY 10036
(718) 579-3000 .. **Monaghan,** Michl J '74 %Leg Aid -1020 Grnd Cncrs -Bronx 10451 **Fx:**588-2611
(212) 541-6980 .. **Monaghan Monaghan Lamb & Marchisio** -401 E 65th -NY 10019 **Fx:**541-6994
(212) 541-6980 .. **Monaghan,** Patrick J Jr. '71 (Monaghan ML&M) -401 E 65th -NY 10019
(516) 877-2900 .. **Monaghan,** Peter G '78 (Bartlett MB&M,LLP) -300 Old Cntry Rd -Mineola 11501
(631) 298-5071 .. **Monaghan,** Richd F '68 Cnsl Monaghan ML&M -3055 Camp Mineola Rd -Mattituck 11952 **Fx:**(201) 802-9066
(718) 474-4955 .. **Monaghan,** Thos C '75 -609 Cross Bay Blvd -Broad Channel 11693 **Fx:**474-8402
(212) 506-1700 .. **Monahan,** Aileen K '05 Kasowitz BT&F LLP -1633 Bway -NY 10019
(516) 294-8844 .. **Monahan,** Amy M '01 %L'Abbate BC&C,LLP -1001 Franklin Av -Gdn Cty 11530
(631) 234-3030 .. **Monahan,** Anne-Marie L '93 OfCnsl Davidow DS&S,LLP -1601 Vets Mem'l Hwy -Islandia 11749
(212) 935-5700 .. **Monahan,** Courtney Wilson '90 (Colucci & U) -218 E 50th -NY 10022
(212) 953-2381 .. **Monahan,** Crystal D '03 %Rubin F&F,LLP -292 Mad Av -NY 10017
(716) 856-0600 .. **Monahan,** John M '97 (Jaeckle F&M,LLP) -12 Fountain Plz -Buffalo 14202
(212) 819-8200 .. **Monahan,** Katherine C '09 %White & C LLP -1155 Av of Amer -NY 10036
(212) 408-4271 .. **Monahan,** Kevin J '69 Bk of NY -1290 Av of Amer -NY 10104
(718) 965-7300 .. **Monahan,** Michl J '93 %RC Diocese of Brklyn -310 Prospect Park W -Brklyn 11215 **Fx:**965-7363
(631) 482-1187 .. **Monahan,** Pamela '97 -Bx963 -Hampton Bays 11946
(718) 680-8400 .. **Monahan,** Thos M '89 (Simon M&S,LLC) -7504 5th Av -Brklyn 11209
(518) 464-6000 .. **Monahan,** Todd G '03 %Arroyo Copland & Assoc,PLLC -300 Great Oaks Blvd -Albany 12203 **Fx:**464-6014
(212) 558-4000 .. **Monahan,** Wm B '04 %Sullivan & C LLP -125 Broad -NY 10004
(212) 922-9700 .. **Monasebian,** Leila '06 %1st Amer Title -633 3rd Av -NY 10017 **Fx:**922-0881
(315) 422-2458 .. **Monashefsky,** Gregory I '89 -300 S State -Syracuse 13202 **Fx:**579-0186
(212) 451-2900 .. **Monassebian,** David Y '00 Cnsl Robinson & C LLP -885 3rd Av -NY 10022
(516) 932-4300 .. **Monassebian,** Jeff '83 Technology Practice Grp LLC -1010 Nrthrn Blvd -Gt Neck 11021
(516) 445-0411 .. **Monasterio,** Viviana G '98 -56 Dail -New Hyde Pk 11040 **Fx:**591-9549
(631) 853-5212 .. **Monastero,** Deborah A '04 Leg Aid -400 Carleton Av Bx9082 -Central Islip 11722 **Fx:**853-7798
(212) 735-3000 .. **Monastyrskaya,** Tatiana '05 %Skadden ASM&F LLP -4 Times Sq -NY 10036
(631) 234-4411 .. **Monat,** Lawr M '67 -150 Motor Pkwy -Hauppauge 11788
(212) 310-8000 .. **Moncada,** Alcira C '04 Weil G&M LLP -767 5th Av -NY 10153
(716) 856-3646 .. **Moncher,** Jeffrey K '92 %Cole SHH&G,PC -37 Franklin -Buffalo 14202
(716) 853-9555 .. **Moncher,** Michelle L '95 %Leg Aid -237 Main -Buffalo 14203 **Fx:**853-3219
(718) 780-0322 .. **Monck-Marcellino,** Caitlin A '03 Bklyn Law Schl -250 Joralemon -Brklyn 11201 **Fx:**780-0393
(212) 406-5551 .. **Moncrief,** John L Jr. '74 -70 Lafayette -NY 10013 **Fx:**962-5311
(212) 788-1160 .. **Moncure,** Albert F Jr. '76 %Law Dept -100 Church -NY 10007 **Fx:**788-0367
(212) 697-1200 .. **Mond,** Jerry '76 -401 E 34th -NY 10016 **Fx:**697-1100
(516) 627-9200 .. **Mond,** Jerry '76 -170 Old Cntry Rd -Mineola 11501
(718) 984-4096 .. **Mondella,** Lauren A '93 -12 Figurea Av -Staten Isl 10312
(631) 755-0101 .. **Mondelli,** Greg M '96 %Lewis JAA,LLP -425 Broad Hollow Rd -Melvll 11747
(516) 542-5900 .. **Mondelli,** Heather J '01 %Congdon FORDT&F -333 Earle Ovngton Blvd -Uniondale 11553
(516) 222-6200 .. **Mondello,** Jos N '71 Cnsl Berkman HPP&F,PC -100 Grdn City Plz -Gdn Cty 11530
(914) 591-7722 .. **Mondello,** Philip J '74 (Roy ML&R) -56 Main Bx108 -Irvngtn 10533
(347) 296-1474 .. **Mondesir,** Alix '83 Ct Atty-Referee -360 Adams -Brklyn 11201 **Fx:**401-9131
(212) 262-5540 .. **Mondora,** Gerald J '68 -800 Wstchstr Av -Pt Chester 10573
(212) 841-1000 .. **Mondschein,** Lisa '01 SpclCnsl Covington & B LLP -620 8th Av -NY 10018
(718) 968-9000 .. **Mondschein,** Michl J '74 -1684 Remsen Av -Brklyn 11236 **Fx:**251-7471
(914) 422-0010 .. **Mondschein,** Morris A '61 Borenkind & M -399 Knollwood Rd -White Plns 10603 **Fx:**946-6301
(718) 965-4746 .. **Mondschein,** Stacey B '88 -358 7th Av -Brklyn 11215
(516) 364-8100 .. **Mondshein,** Lee J '70 -7600 Jericho Tpk -Woodbury 11797 **Fx:**364-8518
(607) 547-1369 .. **Mone,** Carmela '87 %Cnty Law Guardian -21 Railroad Av -Cooperstwn 13326 **Fx:**547-7003
(631) 244-1278 .. **Mone,** Jennifer M '94 NBTY -90 Orvll Dr -Bohemia 11716
(212) 661-9321 .. **Mone,** Mary C '76 Chambers of Chief Judge -230 Park Av -NY 10169
(845) 561-8000 .. **Monell,** James L '50 OfCnsl Northrop & S,PC -1 Corwin Ct Bx2395 -Newburgh 12550
(212) 619-4949 .. **Monell,** Natasha R '04 Record Press Inc -229 W 36th -NY 10018 **Fx:**608-3141
(212) 298-5291 .. **Moner,** Curtis L '01 %Leg Aid -49 Thomas -NY 10013 **Fx:**298-5252
(585) 789-1529 .. **Monette,** Leigh M '08 Monette,LLC -Bx1056 -Pittsfrd 14534
(212) 765-5070 .. **Monfredo,** Leonard A '09 %Fish & R,PC -153 E 53rd -NY 10022
(212) 474-1000 .. **Monga,** Anish '09 %Cravath S&M LLP -825 8th Av -NY 10019
(718) 206-4729 .. **Monge,** Brandy M '05 %Law Dept -89-17 Sutphin Blvd -Jamaica 11435 **Fx:**206-4702
(212) 506-2500 .. **Monge,** Katherine Scollard '09 %Mayer B LLP -1675 Bway -NY 10019
(516) 694-3000 .. **Mongelli,** Jeffrey '96 %Guercio & G,LLP -77 Conklin -Farmngdl 11735 **Fx:**694-4738
(718) 463-7333 .. **Mongelli,** Michl F II '87 -41-07 162nd -Flushng 11358 **Fx:**358-4872
(732) 549-9800 .. **Mongelli,** Richd '90 -261 Mad Av -NY 10016 **Fx:**549-9802
(631) 853-4104 .. **Mongeluzzi,** John A '86 %DA -400 Carleton Av Bx9082 -Central Islip 11722 **Fx:**853-7838
(516) 248-1700 .. **Mongioi,** Mary E '83 Cnsl Forchelli CDSM&T,LLP -333 Earle Ovngton Blvd -Uniondale 11553
(718) 728-4646 .. **Mongitore,** Lillian J '02 PS 70Q -30-45 42nd -Astoria 11103
(212) 589-4200 .. **Monier,** Christy A '09 %Baker & H LLP -45 Rckfllr Plz -NY 10111
(212) 605-6200 .. **Monier,** Philip III '92 %Levy P&K,LLP -800 3rd Av -NY 10022
(212) 728-8000 .. **Monin,** Katharine N '07 %Willkie F&G LLP -787 7th Av -NY 10019
(646) 429-7500 .. **Monitz,** Jay L '83 %Macys,Inc -11 Penn Plz -NY 10001 **Fx:**429-7521
(212) 258-6000 .. **Moniz,** Henry T A '00 Viacom -1515 Bway -NY 10036
(212) 225-2000 .. **Moniz,** J Webb '71 (Cleary GS&H) -1 Lbrty Plz -NY 10006
(718) 590-6215 .. **Moniz,** Jade A '09 Law Dept -198 E 161st -Bronx 10451 **Fx:**590-2686
(518) 474-7330 .. **Monjeau,** Thos R '83 %Dept of Law -The Cptl -Albany 12224
(212) 598-8000 .. **Monjoy,** Michl A '71 %Guardian Life Ins -7 Hanover Sq -NY 10004 **Fx:**919-2693
(212) 538-1017 .. **Monk,** David A '99 Credit Suisse -11 Mad Av -NY 10010
(914) 686-4800 .. **Monk,** Glenn A '81 (Harrington O&M,LLP) -81 Main -White Plns 10601
(212) 663-0724 .. **Monk,** Stan '84 -600 W 111th -NY 10025
(212) 664-7421 .. **Monkarsh,** Randy I '95 %NBC -30 Rckfllr Plz -NY 10112
(585) 232-3900 .. **Monks,** Thos R '83 -183 E Main -Rchstr 14604
(718) 739-6205 .. **Monn,** Fredda J '86 Family Ct -151-20 Jamaica Av -Jamaica 11432
(914) 949-6996 .. **Monn,** Steven Jay '83 %Penino & M,LLP -180 E Post Rd -White Plns 10601
(516) 466-0410 .. **Monoson,** Jill S '92 %Kestenbaum & M -40 Cuttermill Rd -Gt Neck 11021
(718) 590-2000 .. **Monoson,** Tama S '05 %DA -198 E 161st -Bronx 10451 **Fx:**590-6477
(914) 347-2600 .. **Monosov,** Jeremy P '08 %Traub LS&S LLP -7 Skyline Dr -Hawthorne 10532
(212) 331-5038 .. **Monroe,** Barbara J '00 NYC HRA-Ofc Lgl Affrs -180 Water -NY 10038
(212) 420-7536 .. **Monroe,** Eve E '90 (E Monroe PC) -625 E 11th -NY 10009 **Fx:**420-7536
(845) 294-8900 .. **Monroe,** James E '97 (Dupee & M,PC) -211 Main Bx470 -Goshen 10924
(315) 379-9890 .. **Monroe,** James L '92 -1 Park Pl -Canton 13617 **Fx:**379-9891
(212) 421-2233 .. **Monroe,** Karen A '84 (Wilk A LLP) -675 3rd Av -NY 10017
(518) 455-9952 .. **Monroe,** Kelly M '05 %Thuillez FGB&Y,LLP -20 Corp Wds Blvd -Albany 12211
(212) 558-4000 .. **Monroe,** Kendyl K '01 SrCnsl Sullivan & C LLP -125 Broad -NY 10004
(212) 756-2000 .. **Monroe,** Kimberly M '99 SpclCnsl Schulte R&Z LLP -919 3rd Av -NY 10022
(212) 689-6009 .. **Monroe,** Matthew C '09 %Gentile & Assoc -233 5th Av -NY 10016 **Fx:**213-1093
(212) 345-5923 .. **Monroe,** Steven M '91 Marsh & McLennan Cos -1166 Av of Amer -NY 10036
(518) 434-0600 .. **Monroe,** Teresa A '06 %Boies S&F LLP -10 N Pearl -Albany 12207
(212) 270-5919 .. **Monroe-Koatz,** Carolyn Lee '85 JP Morgan Chase & Co -270 Park Av -NY 10017
(631) 844-9555 .. **Monroy,** Alejandro '99 (Dodge & M,PC) -175 Pinelawn Rd -Melvll 11747 **Fx:**844-9666
(516) 393-2200 .. **Monroy,** Marianne '98 %Garfunkel W,PC -111 Grt Nck Rd -Gt Neck 11021
(518) 465-0400 .. **Monserrate,** Michele M '90 (O'Connor OB&F,PC) -20 Corp Wds Blvd -Albany 12211
(212) 326-1590 .. **Monsky,** John R '86 (Oak Hill Cptl Ptnrs) -65 E 55th -NY 10022 **Fx:**527-8450
(212) 855-9156 .. **Monson,** Nicole S '04 Goldman Sachs & Co -32 Old Slip -NY 10005
(212) 918-3000 .. **Monsour,** Franklin G Jr. '05 %Hogan L LLP -875 3rd Av -NY 10022
(516) 775-1414 .. **Monsour Winn Kurland & Warner,LLP** -3000 Marcus Av -Lk Success 11042 **Fx:**354-4731
(914) 681-8700 .. **Montag,** David J '98 (Milber MP&S LLP) -3 Barker Av -White Plns 10601
(212) 626-4100 .. **Montag,** Hans Dieter '96 (Baker & M LLP) -1114 Av of Amer -NY 10036
(212) 218-5500 .. **Montag,** Jerry A '85 OfCnsl Seyfarth S LLP -620 8th Av -NY 10018
(212) 609-6800 .. **Montagna,** Veronica H '07 %McCarter & E,LLP -245 Park Av -NY 10167
(914) 995-4607 .. **Montagnino,** James '89 %Unified Ct Sys -111 Martin Luther King Blvd -White Plns 10601 **Fx:**995-5078
(518) 447-9664 .. **Montagnino,** Nancy K '89 %MHLS -75 New Scotland Av -Albany 12208 **Fx:**447-9697
(212) 996-1287 .. **Montagu,** Alexandre A '92 Cnsl MontaguLaw,PC -1120 Av of Amer -NY 10036 **Fx:**996-9579
(212) 787-3669 .. **Montague,** Andrea M '90 -205 West End Av -NY 10023
(212) 735-3000 .. **Montague,** Autumn M '07 %Skadden ASM&F LLP -4 Times Sq -NY 10036

(718) 279-7555 .. **Montague,** Bruce '87 (B Montague & Prtnrs) -212-45 26th Av -Bayside 11360 **Fx:**279-8154
(212) 790-9200 .. **Montague,** Mark '93 (Cowan L&L,PC) -1133 Av of Amer -NY 10036
(914) 674-4858 .. **Montague,** Michele L '92 -9 Lookout Pl -Ardsley 10502 **Fx:**674-0206
(718) 424-1233 .. **Montaigne,** Kerry E '97 KE O'Shaughnessy LLC -62-57 Woodhvn Blvd -Rego Pk 11374 **Fx:**424-1626
(845) 634-7010 .. **Montalbano,** Anthony '65 (Montalbano C&F,PC) -67 N Main Bx1070 -New Cty 10956
(845) 634-7010 .. **Montalbano Condon & Frank,PC** -67 N Main Bx1070 -New Cty 10956 **Fx:**634-8993
(646) 471-5463 .. **Montalbano,** Nicholas W '06 PricewaterhouseCoopers LLP -300 Mad Av -NY 10017
(718) 520-2218 .. **Montalbano,** Rosemarie '92 Supreme Ct -125-01 Qns Blvd -Kew Gdns 11415
(212) 880-0845 .. **Montalette,** Nicole '70 -60 E 42nd -NY 10165 **Fx:**682-1965
(718) 273-3100 .. **Montalto,** Nicholas T '67 -888 Forest Av -Staten Isl 10310 **Fx:**442-5088
(845) 639-6944 .. **Montalto,** Patrice S '05 Jewel Abstract,Inc -151 S Main -New Cty 10956
(518) 436-3461 .. **Montalto,** Stacey Mahany '03 ACOG -152 Wshngtn Av -Albany 12210 **Fx:**426-4728
(212) 248-3140 .. **Montalto,** Vincent J '08 %Drinker B&R LLP -140 Bway -NY 10005
(646) 386-5700 .. **Montalvo,** Jennifer '98 %Civil Ct -111 Centre -NY 10013
(914) 965-9486 .. **Montalvo,** Marta M '81 NY Dept of Motor Vehicles -1 Larkin Plz -Ynkrs 10701
(212) 332-4488 .. **Montan,** Sylvia M '95 -45 Rckfllr Plz -NY 10111
(212) 732-6000 .. **Montana,** Aileen L '06 %McCarthy & K LLP -52 Duane -NY 10007
(914) 737-3515 .. **Montana,** Lewis '77 (Levine & M) -1019 Park Bx668 -Peekskill 10566 **Fx:**737-1041
(212) 335-4186 .. **Montana,** Matthew P '09 DA -80 Centre -NY 10013
(718) 990-1389 .. **Montana,** Patricia Grande '00 %St John's Law Schl -8000 Utopia Pkwy -Jamaica 11439 **Fx:**591-1855
(212) 532-8100 .. **Montana,** Richd 2nd '89 (Stern & M,LLP) -115 Bway -NY 10006
(718) 923-0690 .. **Montana-Marson,** Helen T '84 %R Santoriella PC -335 Adams -Brklyn 11201 **Fx:**923-0683
(212) 788-0645 .. **Montana-O'Connor,** Jenny A '97 Law Dept -100 Church -NY 10007 **Fx:**788-8919
(212) 346-1274 .. **Montanaro,** Lisa A '96 %Pace Univ -156 William -NY 10038 **Fx:**346-1682
(718) 326-8526 .. **Montanez,** Danny '91 -66-66 79th -Middl Vllg 11379
(212) 755-5510 .. **Montanez,** Yuisa G '99 %Loeb B & Prtnrs -505 Park Av -NY 10022
(646) 375-2109 .. **Montanile,** Jos A '95 (Hausner & M,PLLC) -116 W 23rd -NY 10011
(646) 375-2109 .. **Montanile,** Leslie Hausner '92 (Hausner & M,PLLC) -116 W 23rd -NY 10011
(516) 294-5200 .. **Montano,** Annmarie C '02 %Picciano & S -900 Merchants Cncrs -Westbury 11590
(718) 822-2400 .. **Montano,** Armando '77 -181 E 161st -Bronx 10451 **Fx:**(347) 591-3436
(646) 435-0300 .. **Montano,** James S '07 (McCullough GM&P,LLP) -320 E 53rd -NY 10022
(716) 834-5000 .. **Montante,** Carl J '67 %Uniland Dvlpmnt -100 Corp Pkwy -Amherst 14226 **Fx:**834-5034
(716) 834-5000 .. **Montante,** Carl J Jr. '93 %Uniland Dvlpmnt -100 Corp Pkwy -Amherst 14226
(585) 225-3080 .. **Montante,** Jennifer L '06 %Parrs & P LLP -105 Canal Lndng Blvd -Rchstr 14626 **Fx:**225-0459
(212) 986-6000 .. **Montaruli,** Anthony F '07 %Kleinberg KW&C,PC -551 5th Av -NY 10176
(631) 582-1200 .. **Montas,** Stéphane M '98 %DeHaan B LLP -300 Rabro Dr -Hauppauge 11788
(212) 804-4200 .. **Montbach,** Francis A '71 (Mound CW&G) -One Bttry Pk Plz -NY 10004
(212) 425-2200 .. **Montclare,** Jason S '00 -110 Wall -NY 10005
(212) 509-3900 .. **Montclare,** Paul D '75 (Mitchell S&K LLP) -12 E 49th -NY 10017
(212) 599-0900 .. **Monte,** Anina H '00 (Bower & L,PC) -261 Mad Av -NY 10016
(718) 250-2000 .. **Monte,** Kendra K '97 %DA -350 Jay -Brklyn 11201 **Fx:**250-2314
(716) 856-4000 .. **Monte,** Laura A '93 (Hodgson R LLP) -140 Pearl -Buffalo 14202
(212) 931-8300 .. **Monte,** Marc J '02 %Strongin R&A,LLP -5 Hanover Sq -NY 10004
(212) 382-0909 .. **Monte,** Paul G '88 (Peckar & A,PC) -41 Mad Av -NY 10154
(716) 852-3600 .. **Monte,** Rebecca E '86 (Chelus HS&M,PC) -438 Main -Buffalo 14202
(716) 608-7664 .. **Monte,** Rebecca E '86 (Chelus HS&M,PC) -2448 Union Rd -Cheektowaga 14225
(516) 228-5999 .. **Montefinise,** Michl R '82 %DCMC Long Island -605 Stewart Av -Gdn Cty 11530 **Fx:**228-3647
(914) 761-2689 .. **Monteforte,** Danl M '87 -142 Harrison E -White Plns 10604
(212) 541-2000 .. **Monteforte,** Steven '84 (Bryan C LLP) -1290 Av of Amer -NY 10104
(631) 543-3700 .. **Montefusco,** Robt H '98 %A Firestone,PC -612 Vets Mem'l Hwy -Hauppauge 11788 **Fx:**543-3737
(212) 226-7700 .. **Monteiro,** Christina Santos '05 %Donovan & Y LLP -161 Av of Amer -NY 10013
(212) 573-5000 .. **Monteiro,** Kenneth T '89 Ford Fndtn -320 E 43rd -NY 10017
(516) 280-4600 .. **Monteiro,** Marcus '03 (Monteiro & F LLP) -91 N Franklin -Hempstd 11550 **Fx:**280-4530
(212) 754-9400 .. **Montejo,** Felipe '96 Cnsl Todtman NS&J,PC -425 Park Av -NY 10022
(212) 427-0667 .. **Montejo,** Ruben T '85 -238 E 89th -NY 10128 **Fx:**349-1246
(516) 739-3066 .. **Monteleone,** Andrew A '00 -114 Old Cntry Rd -Mineola 11501 **Fx:**741-7853
(914) 666-2118 .. **Monteleone,** Anthony J '64 (Monteleone & M) -19 N Moger Av -Mt Kisco 10549 **Fx:**666-0509
(212) 475-9764 .. **Monteleone,** Frank J '87 -27 Union Sq W -NY 10003 **Fx:**475-1638
(914) 666-2118 .. **Monteleone,** Gregory A '91 (Monteleone & M) -19 N Moger Av -Mt Kisco 10549 **Fx:**666-0509
(718) 522-1786 .. **Monteleone,** John A '43 -16 Court -Brklyn 11241
(718) 522-3633 .. **Monteleone,** John J '64 -32 Court -Brklyn 11201
(646) 833-0900 .. **Monteleone,** Jos P '81 (Tressler LLP) -One Penn Plz -NY 10119
(212) 825-1300 .. **Monteleone,** Jos P '88 Somerset Prtnrs,LLC -450 Park Av -NY 10022 **Fx:**825-1129
(212) 363-3100 .. **Monteleone,** Marlene '79 (Bivona & C,PC) -88 Pine -NY 10005
(212) 564-6633 .. **Monteleone,** Sally A '95 %White & M,PC -875 Av of Amer -NY 10001
(212) 374-1493 .. **Monteleone,** Tara Koenig '92 Supreme Ct 1st Dept -60 Centre -NY 10007
(212) 661-3691 .. **Montelione,** Richd J '84 (Lopez R&M,PC) -551 5th Av -NY 10176
(718) 746-4600 .. **Montell,** Edw C '58 -154-15 Powells Cove Blvd -Whitestone 11357 **Fx:**746-4552
(212) 218-5500 .. **Montellaro,** Randell '86 (Seyfarth S LLP) -620 8th Av -NY 10018
(585) 325-3400 .. **Montemaggi,** Lewis F '74 Montemaggi & Assoc -130 W Main -Rchstr 14614 **Fx:**325-4161
(585) 546-7830 .. **Montemalo,** Frank G '91 %Culley MT&P,LLP -36 W Main -Rchstr 14614
(718) 847-7880 .. **Montemarano,** Eugenia A '93 (E Montemarano,PC) -81-67 Lefferts Blvd -Kew Gdns 11415 **Fx:**847-7735
(212) 506-1700 .. **Montenegro,** Christine A '01 (Kasowitz BT&F LLP) -1633 Bway -NY 10019
(212) 416-8000 .. **Montenegro,** Veronica V '09 %Dept of Law -120 Bway -NY 10271
(516) 333-4200 .. **Monter,** Marilyn B '77 %Holiday Mgt Assoc -400 Post Av -Westbury 11590
(631) 231-1313 .. **Montera,** Kevin D '94 Bayshore Storage -1 Corp Dr -Hauppauge 11788
(617) 739-4224 .. **Monterisi,** John Jr. '81 (Deily M&G,LLP) -8 Thurlow Ter -Albany 12203 **Fx:**232-2302
(212) 268-5695 .. **Montero,** Christhie M '09 Paradocs,Inc -1 Penn Plz -NY 10119
(212) 940-3714 .. **Montes,** Jim '01 %Nixon P LLP -437 Mad Av -NY 10022
(516) 487-5800 .. **Montes,** Richd J '03 %Mauro G&L LLP -60 Cuttermill Rd -Gt Neck 11021
(516) 741-6565 .. **Montesano,** Carmela T '84 OfCnsl Meyer SE&K,PC -990 Stewart Av Bx9194 -Gdn Cty 11530
(212) 732-9000 .. **Montesano,** Elizabeth '01 %Sullivan PBM&C PC -120 Bway -NY 10271
(212) 852-7713 .. **Montesano,** Katherine Garcia '03 News Corp -1211 Av of Amer -NY 10036 **Fx:**852-7147
(212) 373-3000 .. **Montesano,** Liza '10 %Paul WRW&G LLP -1285 Av of Amer -NY 10019
(516) 759-8469 .. **Montesano,** Michl A '89 (M Montesano,PC) -40 Glen -Glen Cove 11542 **Fx:**759-3801
(716) 648-2806 .. **Montesano,** Michl Jos '91 (Montesano & W,PC) -4255 Clark -Hambrg 14075
(212) 732-3200 .. **Monte-Sano,** Vincent '68 (Carter L&M LLP) -2 Wall -NY 10005
(716) 648-2806 .. **Montesano & Winokur,PC** -4255 Clark -Hambrg 14075 **Fx:**648-2012
(212) 363-7500 .. **Monteverde,** Juan E '07 %Levi & K LLP -30 Broad -NY 10004
(973) 849-1894 .. **Monteyne,** Renee L '06 %Gibbons PC -1 Penn Plz -NY 10119 **Fx:**639-6494
(212) 636-7955 .. **Montez,** Abel P '92 Fordham Univ Sch of Law -140 W 62nd -NY 10023 **Fx:**636-7167
(516) 747-4082 .. **Montfort Healy McGuire & Salley LLP** -1140 Franklin Av Bx7677 -Gdn Cty 11530 **Fx:**746-0748
(516) 572-2000 .. **Montgomery,** April N '08 %DA -99 Main -Hempstd 11550 **Fx:**572-2606
(212) 416-8000 .. **Montgomery,** Brian H '07 %Dept of Law -120 Bway -NY 10271
(718) 643-8989 .. **Montgomery,** Cheryl Lee '91 %Hon S Weinstein -283 Adams -Brklyn 11201
(914) 766-4925 .. **Montgomery,** Christina Mary '94 IBM -294 Route 100 -Somers 10589
(212) 632-5500 .. **Montgomery,** Claude D '84 (Salans LLP) -620 5th Av -NY 10020
(212) 973-8000 .. **Montgomery,** David E '62 SrCnsl Schnader HS&L LLP -140 Bway -NY 10005
(212) 245-7779 .. **Montgomery,** Franklin '80 -30 Vesey -NY 10007
(212) 889-9828 .. **Montgomery,** James A '99 J Montgomery,PLLC -267 5th Av -NY 10016 **Fx:**889-9818
(718) 403-9261 .. **Montgomery,** Kenneth J '99 K Montgomery PLLC -55 Washington -Brklyn 11201 **Fx:**403-9851
(212) 848-4000 .. **Montgomery,** Malcolm K '90 (Shearman & S LLP) -599 Lex Av -NY 10022
(212) 728-8000 .. **Montgomery,** Marc E '10 %Willkie F&G LLP -787 7th Av -NY 10019
(631) 588-2900 .. **Montgomery,** Michl J '95 (Wolinsky P&M,LLP) -329 Hawkins Av -Lk Ronkonkoma 11779
(518) 434-1311 .. **Montgomery,** Paul C '84 %Mercer Cos -Three E-Comm 2 -Albany 12207 **Fx:**434-6157
(718) 286-2000 .. **Montgomery,** Paul S '91 %Leg Aid -120-46 Qns Blvd -Kew Gdns 11415 **Fx:**286-2286
(516) 393-6116 .. **Montgomery,** Stephanie O '02 S Rubin -999 Stewart Av -Bethpage 11714 **Fx:**393-6150
(212) 323-7070 .. **Montgomery,** Steven R '04 %Rawle & H LLP -14 Wall -NY 10005
(212) 310-8000 .. **Montgomery,** Tamika R '08 %Weil G&M LLP -767 5th Av -NY 10153
(518) 798-6885 .. **Montgomery,** Wm E III '83 -130 Maple Bx228 -Glens Fls 12801 **Fx:**798-5974
(212) 969-3000 .. **Montgomery,** Yolanda D '04 %Proskauer R LLP -1585 Bway -NY 10036
(212) 632-6314 .. **Month,** Stephan C '87 %Lazard Freres -30 Rckfllr Plz -NY 10112 **Fx:**632-6060
(518) 432-7861 .. **Monthie,** Jennifer J '04 Disability Advocates,Inc -5 Clinton Sq -Albany 12207 **Fx:**427-6561
(518) 786-3534 .. **Monthie,** Stephen P '85 -623 New Loudon Rd Bx966 -Latham 12110
(631) 847-5452 .. **Monti,** Beatriz M '94 %Arrow Electronics -50 Marcus Dr -Melvll 11747
(516) 484-4010 .. **Montiel,** Catherine M '93 (Miller M&S) -99 Powerhse Rd -Roslyn Hts 11577
(516) 747-9500 .. **Montiglio,** Anthony J '77 -300 Old Cntry Rd -Mineola 11501 **Fx:**747-9502
(516) 294-5433 .. **Montiglio,** Thos A Jr. '02 %Ahmuty D&M -200 IU Willets Rd -Albertson 11507
(212) 408-5100 .. **Montmarquet,** Nancy L '87 Cnsl Chadbourne & P LLP -30 Rckfllr Plz -NY 10112
(212) 863-8260 .. **Montminy,** David A '06 NYC DHP&D -100 Gold -NY 10038
(718) 590-2000 .. **Montminy,** Renee A '06 %DA -198 E 161st -Bronx 10451 **Fx:**590-6477
(646) 471-4000 .. **Montone,** David G '00 %PricewaterhouseCoopers LLP -300 Mad Av -NY 10017

(914) 225-4771 .. **Montone,** John J '97 Morgan Stanley -2000 Wstchstr Av -Purchase 10577
(716) 655-7100 .. **Montour,** Mark A '84 -Bx393 -Elma 14059
(212) 582-3881 .. **Montoya,** Amy L '98 -112 W 56th -NY 10019
(718) 579-3000 .. **Montoya,** Claudia E '91 %Leg Aid -1020 Grnd Cncrs -Bronx 10451 **Fx:**588-2611
(212) 471-6228 .. **Montoya,** Concepcion A '02 (Hinshaw & C LLP) -780 3rd Av -NY 10017
(212) 774-3655 .. **Montoya,** David S '98 (Seaview Capital Advisors,LLC) -260 Mad Av -NY 10016
(212) 980-9660 .. **Montrose,** Barry '74 -16 Penn Plz -NY 10001 **Fx:**571-4846
(212) 980-9600 .. **Montrose,** Samantha R '10 %Kaufman B&R -120 Bway -NY 10271
(716) 392-0327 .. **Montroy,** Carla J Miller '06 -88 W Utica -Buffalo 14209 **Fx:**883-8415
(716) 662-2401 .. **Montroy,** Clair A III '78 -4240 N Buffalo Rd Bx816 -Orchard Pk 14127 **Fx:**662-2498
(516) 338-4714 .. **Montuori,** Paul A '02 (P Montuori,PC) -265 Post Av -Westbury 11590
(607) 756-7501 .. **Monty,** Victoria J '03 (Pomeroy AC&M,LLP) -16 Tompkins Bx828 -Cortlnd 13045
(212) 301-4000 .. **Moo,** Veronica Ei Chun '05 Natl Fncl Ptnrs -340 Mad Av -NY 10173 **Fx:**301-4001
(212) 909-6241 .. **Moodhe,** Jos P '82 (Debevoise & P LLP) -919 3rd Av -NY 10022
(212) 408-2500 .. **Moodie,** Colin B '08 %Baker B,LLP -30 Rckfllr Plz -NY 10112
(212) 403-1000 .. **Moodie,** Gordon S '05 %Wachtell LR&K -51 W 52nd -NY 10019
(212) 715-7573 .. **Moody,** Anna C '00 Interfor Inc -575 Mad Av -NY 10022
(516) 877-2900 .. **Moody,** Brian S '02 %Bartlett MB&M,LLP -300 Old Cntry Rd -Mineola 11501
(212) 431-7129 .. **Moody,** David K '92 (Purrington MW LLP) -320 W 13th -NY 10014
(212) 230-5504 .. **Moody,** Elizabeth J '00 Davis SLM&H LLP -689 5th Av -NY 10022
(212) 450-4000 .. **Moody,** Gerald M Jr. '10 %Davis P&W LLP -450 Lex Av -NY 10017
(646) 345-8446 .. **Moody,** Gwendolyn '90 -305 Bway -NY 10007
(315) 349-3200 .. **Moody,** Mark M '96 %DA -Pub Safety Ctr -Oswego 13126 **Fx:**349-3212
(212) 298-5191 .. **Moody,** Sharon Maquita '90 Leg Aid -49 Thomas -NY 10013
(315) 253-4050 .. **Moody,** Simon K '93 (Williams HM&B) -11 Court -Auburn 13021 **Fx:**253-4223
(212) 940-3000 .. **Moolsintong,** Peerapa Joann '08 %Nixon P LLP -437 Mad Av -NY 10022
(516) 937-5900 .. **Moomjian,** Gary T '78 (Moomjian WW&C LLP) -100 Jericho Quad -Jericho 11753
(516) 937-5900 .. **Moomjian Waite Wactlar & Coleman LLP** -100 Jericho Quad -Jericho 11753 **Fx:**937-5050
(212) 858-1000 .. **Moon,** Alexander P '86 (Pillsbury WSP LLP) -1540 Bway -NY 10036
(646) 200-6300 .. **Moon,** Brian T '08 %Park & J LLP -630 3rd Av -NY 10017 **Fx:**200-6301
(212) 848-4000 .. **Moon,** Hee Won '10 Shearman & S LLP -599 Lex Av -NY 10022
(315) 234-8577 .. **Moon,** Janet E '09 US Dist Ct-Northern Dist -100 S Clinton -Syracuse 13203
(212) 574-1200 .. **Moon,** Je Jun '99 %Seward & K LLP -1 Bttry Pk Plz -NY 10004
(212) 422-0202 .. **Moon,** Jessika J '00 %Sedgwick DM&A LLP -125 Broad -NY 10004
(212) 821-2827 .. **Moon,** John G '01 UBS Investment Bk -299 Park Av -NY 10171
(212) 225-2000 .. **Moon,** Kenneth H '09 %Cleary GS&H -1 Lbrty Plz -NY 10006
(212) 682-0020 .. **Moon,** M Christopher '06 %Putney TH&H LLP -521 5th Av -NY 10175
(516) 972-0472 .. **Moon,** Nicholas J '70 -15 Factory -Union Spgs 13160
(212) 314-2120 .. **Moon,** Sun Jin '06 AXA Financial Inc -1290 Av of Amer -NY 10104 **Fx:**707-3963
(914) 642-3847 .. **Moon,** Tina Kyunghi '96 IBM Americas -1133 Wstchstr Av -White Plns 10604
(212) 326-3939 .. **Moon,** Yeah S '04 %Jones D -222 E 41st -NY 10017
(607) 255-9933 .. **Mooney,** Andrea J '93 %Cornell Law Schl -Myron Taylor Hall -Ithaca 14853 **Fx:**255-7193
(315) 442-0100 .. **Mooney,** Brendan J '09 %Gilberti SH&S,PC -555 E Genesee -Syracuse 13202
(212) 943-0280 .. **Mooney,** Chas D '75 (McCanliss & E LLP) -88 Pine -NY 10005
(718) 281-5404 .. **Mooney,** Christine A '07 Queensborough Comm College -22205 56th Av -Oakland Gdns 11364
(212) 232-1300 .. **Mooney,** Ellen E '08 %Lewis BB&S LLP -77 Water -NY 10005
(212) 682-8811 .. **Mooney,** Francis J Jr. '64 OfCnsl Dunnington B&M LLP -1359 Bway -NY 10018
(716) 849-8900 .. **Mooney,** Harry F '76 (Hurwitz & F,PC) -1300 Lbrty Bldg -Buffalo 14202
(212) 407-4000 .. **Mooney,** Jennie E '01 %Loeb & L,LLP -345 Park Av -NY 10154
(212) 232-1300 .. **Mooney,** Jessica L '08 %Lewis BB&S LLP -77 Water -NY 10005
(716) 566-5400 .. **Mooney,** Jos L '94 (Goldberg S LLP) -665 Main -Buffalo 14203
(212) 468-8000 .. **Mooney,** Kyle W K '01 %Morrison & F LLP -1290 Av of Amer -NY 10104
(518) 436-0344 .. **Mooney,** Martin A '90 (Deily M&G,LLP) -8 Thurlow Ter -Albany 12203
(212) 456-7532 .. **Mooney,** Mary A '96 ABC -77 W 66th -NY 10023 **Fx:**456-6202
(212) 267-0011 .. **Mooney,** Mika M '08 %Shafer G,LLP -90 John -NY 10038
(914) 220-0038 .. **Mooney,** Patricia M '82 %Pattison & F -1 N Lex Av -White Plns 10601
(585) 232-5300 .. **Mooney,** Scott M '05 %Boylan BCV&W,LLP -2400 Chase Sq -Rchstr 14604
(716) 856-5500 .. **Mooney,** Sheri L '97 (Damon M LLP) -200 Delaware Av -Buffalo 14202
(212) 335-9000 .. **Mooney,** Thos J '83 %DA -1 Hogan Pl -NY 10013
(631) 360-2207 .. **Moonis,** Tom L '91 T Moonis,PC -135 W Main -Smithtwn 11787 **Fx:**360-2208
(845) 679-9166 .. **Moor,** Gideon A '97 Miller Howard Inv -Bx549 -Woodstock 12498
(718) 805-1500 .. **Moore,** A Patricia '75 (Harding & M) -80-59 Lefferts Blvd -Kew Gdns 11415
(212) 403-6700 .. **Moore,** Alison L '02 %Gide LN LLP -120 W 45th -NY 10036
(212) 806-5400 .. **Moore,** Amanda K '03 %Stroock &S&L LLP -180 Maiden Ln -NY 10038
(716) 849-3110 .. **Moore,** Andrea Polvino '84 %Merchants Ins Group -250 Main -Buffalo 14202 **Fx:**849-3107
(212) 335-9000 .. **Moore,** Audrey S '90 %DA -1 Hogan Pl -NY 10013
(212) 732-0002 .. **Moore,** Benjamin D T '08 %Cohen F&R,LLP -20 Vesey -NY 10007
(212) 265-6888 .. **Moore,** Brett S '02 (Porzio B&N,PC) -156 W 56th -NY 10019
(212) 594-5000 .. **Moore,** Brian F '99 %Togut S&S LLP -1 Penn Plz -NY 10119
(914) 422-8700 .. **Moore,** Brian J '88 %OCTF -101 E Post Rd -White Plns 10601 **Fx:**422-8795
(518) 583-5340 .. **Moore,** Carol Ann '90 %Ct of Claims -65 S Bway -Saratoga Spgs 12866 **Fx:**583-5345
(212) 264-6518 .. **Moore,** Carol Ann '96 US DHS -26 Fed Plz -NY 10278
(631) 852-3888 .. **Moore,** Carol L '93 Hon PJ Baisley Jr -One Court -Rvrhead 11901 **Fx:**852-3745
(212) 735-3000 .. **Moore,** Cason A '08 %Skadden ASM&F LLP -4 Times Sq -NY 10036
(212) 530-5000 .. **Moore,** Chantel D '97 -1 Chase Manh Plz 47th Fl -NY 10005 **Fx:**530-5219
(212) 506-5000 .. **Moore,** Christopher J '91 (Orrick H&S LLP) -51 W 52nd -NY 10019
(212) 225-2000 .. **Moore,** Christopher P '01 (Cleary GS&H) -1 Lbrty Plz -NY 10006
(212) 474-1000 .. **Moore,** Christopher R '09 %Cravath S&M LLP -825 8th Av -NY 10019
(518) 445-2311 .. **Moore,** Dale L '87 %Albany Law Schl -80 New Scotland Av -Albany 12208 **Fx:**445-2315
(585) 419-8800 .. **Moore,** Danl J '89 (Harris B PLLC) -99 Garnsey Rd -Pittsfrd 14534
(212) 577-3457 .. **Moore,** David L III '06 Legal Aid -199 Water -NY 10038
(315) 234-8564 .. **Moore,** Deborah E '92 %Hon F Scullin Jr -100 S Clinton Bx7255 -Syracuse 13261
(718) 409-2410 .. **Moore,** Deidra R '01 DR Moore PC -2253 Esplanade Av -Bronx 10469
(212) 819-8200 .. **Moore,** Derrick F '10 %White & C LLP -1155 Av of Amer -NY 10036
(212) 373-3000 .. **Moore,** Donald F '62 OfCnsl Paul WRW&G LLP -1285 Av of Amer -NY 10019
(212) 559-2057 .. **Moore,** Douglas K '81 Citigroup Private Bk -666 5th Av -NY 10103 **Fx:**793-3219
(646) 613-2000 .. **Moore,** Emerson S II '00 TMP Worldwide -205 Hudson -NY 10013
(212) 761-4000 .. **Moore,** Frank C III '00 Morgan Stanley -1221 Av of Amer -NY 10020
(212) 733-7195 .. **Moore,** Geoffrey P '04 %Pfizer Inc -235 E 42nd -NY 10017
(212) 615-2200 .. **Moore,** Grail Anne '88 Butler FF&M,PC -36 W 44th -NY 10036
(718) 590-2000 .. **Moore,** Hannah E C '08 %DA -198 E 161st -Bronx 10451 **Fx:**590-6477
(212) 735-3000 .. **Moore,** Harold F '81 (Skadden ASM&F LLP) -4 Times Sq -NY 10036
(212) 906-1200 .. **Moore,** Hayley J '10 %Latham & W -885 3rd Av -NY 10022
(607) 273-4200 .. **Moore,** Heather L '08 Miller M,LLP -202 E State -Ithaca 14850
(518) 257-3000 .. **Moore,** J Matthew '97 %Dormitory Auth -515 Bway -Albany 12207 **Fx:**257-3101
(631) 234-3111 .. **Moore,** J Stewart '00 (JS Moore,PC) -320 Carleton Av -Central Islip 11722 **Fx:**234-3341
(212) 809-9100 .. **Moore,** James A Jr. '03 %Brunelle & H,PC -1 Whitehall -NY 10004 **Fx:**809-3219
(585) 232-6500 .. **Moore,** James C '64 Cnsl Harter S&E LLP -1600 Bausch & Lomb Pl -Rchstr 14604
(212) 309-8100 .. **Moore,** James C II '88 %Lexis/Nexis -125 Park Av -NY 10017 **Fx:**309-8187
(212) 385-3555 .. **Moore,** James J '80 (Greenbaum & M) -225 Bway -NY 10007 **Fx:**385-2875
(212) 698-3500 .. **Moore,** James O '05 %Dechert LLP -1095 Av of Amer -NY 10036
(718) 369-3200 .. **Moore,** Jason Arthur '96 -450 7th Av -Brklyn 11215
(518) 474-1310 .. **Moore,** Jennifer M '95 %Gov's Cnsls Ofc -242 State Cptl -Albany 12224
(212) 836-8000 .. **Moore,** Jennifer R '06 %Kaye S LLP -425 Park Av -NY 10022
(516) 496-5822 .. **Moore,** Joel S '10 T Spina -170 Froehlich Farm Blvd -Woodbury 11797 **Fx:**496-5420
(718) 469-9009 .. **Moore,** John A '90 -2705 Church Av -Brklyn 11226 **Fx:**469-9071
(518) 452-1800 .. **Moore,** John F '99 OfCnsl Towne R & Prtnrs,PC -450 New Karner Rd Bx15072 -Albany 12212
(212) 313-3600 .. **Moore,** John J '61 OfCnsl Barry M&M -2 Rector -NY 10006
(212) 761-5416 .. **Moore,** John J Jr. '95 Morgan Stanley -1585 Bway -NY 10036
(212) 407-7347 .. **Moore,** John R '00 %Swiss Re Fncl Products -55 E 52nd -NY 10055
(516) 571-2684 .. **Moore,** John T '72 %Hon I McGinity -100 Supreme Ct Dr -Mineola 11501
(607) 734-6191 .. **Moore,** John V '65 (Moore & W,LLP) -150 Lk -Elmira 14901
(516) 682-8286 .. **Moore,** Jonathan A '85 -35 Roosevelt Av -Syosset 11791 **Fx:**682-8272
(212) 277-5835 .. **Moore,** Jonathan C '85 (Beldock L&H LLP) -99 Park Av -NY 10016
(212) 952-6200 .. **Moore,** Julia M '90 %Nourse & B,LLP -55 Bway -NY 10006
(212) 310-8000 .. **Moore,** Julian D '09 %Weil G&M LLP -767 5th Av -NY 10153
(212) 637-2473 .. **Moore,** Julian J '02 US Atty -1 St Andrews Plz -NY 10007
(212) 578-2211 .. **Moore,** Katanya '05 MetLife -27-01 Qns Plz N -LIC 11101
(212) 309-6000 .. **Moore,** Kelly '92 (Morgan L&B LLP) -101 Park Av -NY 10178
(212) 682-5702 .. **Moore,** Kenneth I '69 (Hutton & S) -475 5th Av -NY 10017
(718) 876-5723 .. **Moore,** Kenneth N Jr. '06 DA -67 Targee -Staten Isl 10304
(315) 468-0490 .. **Moore,** Kevin M '87 -4182 St John Dr -Syracuse 13215
(914) 288-8018 .. **Moore,** Kevin O '78 -220 Wht Plns Rd -Tarrytwn 10591
(212) 969-3000 .. **Moore,** Latoya S '10 %Proskauer R LLP -1585 Bway -NY 10036
(646) 610-5400 .. **Moore,** Lesa K '07 NYPD -1 Police Plz -NY 10038
(212) 763-4100 .. **Moore,** Mark H '83 (Reavis PL LLP) -41 Mad Av -NY 10010
(212) 656-3000 .. **Moore,** Matthew L '96 NYSE Regulation -14 Wall -NY 10005
(212) 554-7800 .. **Moore,** Matthew P '09 %Moses & S LLP -405 Lex Av -NY 10174
(212) 530-5000 .. **Moore,** Megan P '04 %Milbank TH&M LLP -1 Chase Manh Plz -NY 10005
(212) 848-4000 .. **Moore,** Meghan L '10 Shearman & S LLP -599 Lex Av -NY 10022
(518) 438-9907 .. **Moore,** Michl J '78 (Young SWRB&M,LLC) -5 Palisades Dr -Albany 12205
(212) 388-2176 .. **Moore,** Mikhael R '04 32BJ SEIU -101 6th Av -NY 10013
(212) 450-4000 .. **Moore,** Nadia E '10 %Davis P&W LLP -450 Lex Av -NY 10017
(212) 907-6638 .. **Moore,** Nicholas C '03 -405 Lex Av -NY 10174
(845) 373-9338 .. **Moore,** Norman '71 -Main Bx36 -Amenia 12501
(585) 454-1310 .. **Moore,** Pamela Ann '91 -25 E Main -Rchstr 14614
(631) 765-4330 .. **Moore,** Patrica C '87 -51020 Main Rd -Southold 11971 **Fx:**765-4643
(212) 506-1700 .. **Moore,** Patrick D '02 Kasowitz BT&F LLP -1633 Bway -NY 10019
(845) 473-7773 .. **Moore,** Patrick F '81 -299 Main -Poughkeepsie 12601 **Fx:**473-5548
(914) 995-3420 .. **Moore,** Patrick P '88 %DA -111 Martin Luther King Blvd -White Plns 10601 **Fx:**995-3363

(718) 590-2000 .. **Moore,** Pearl N '07 %DA -198 E 161st -Bronx 10451 **Fx:**590-6477
(212) 704-1289 .. **Moore,** Randi M '05 Cnsl Interpublic Grp of Companies,Inc -1114 Av of Amer -NY 10036
(212) 244-2999 .. **Moore,** Rebecca S '06 %Kopff N&D LLP -440 9th Av -NY 10001
(800) 742-9696 .. **Moore,** Rene Stevenson '91 %Binder & B,PC -33-00 Nrthrn Blvd -LIC 11101 **Fx:**(718) 512-2424
(212) 965-2200 .. **Moore,** ReNika C '04 %NAACP/LDF -99 Hudson -NY 10013 **Fx:**226-7592
(718) 494-5000 .. **Moore,** Rhonda M '02 Merrill Lynch -900 South Av -Staten Isl 10314
(716) 856-3500 .. **Moore,** Richd A '86 (Magavern MG LLP) -1100 Rand Bldg -Buffalo 14203
(212) 883-9111 .. **Moore,** Richd W '76 (Meaders D&M) -551 5th Av -NY 10176
(518) 882-7180 .. **Moore,** Robt A '68 -Bx323 -Galway 12074
(516) 486-7307 .. **Moore,** Robt L '74 (Quesada & M,LLP) -128 Avon Pl -W Hempstead 11552
(607) 734-4291 .. **Moore,** Robt S '92 (Perry & Carroll,Inc) -100 W Church Bx307 -Elmira 14902 **Fx:**737-2627
(518) 457-2771 .. **Moore,** Ruth A '84 %Agriculture & Mrkts -10B Airline Dr -Albany 12235 **Fx:**457-8842
(212) 506-1700 .. **Moore,** Saml K '05 %Kasowitz BT&F LLP -1633 Bway -NY 10019
(607) 734-6191 .. **Moore,** Scott D '99 (Moore & W,LLP) -150 Lk -Elmira 14901
(607) 277-4080 .. **Moore,** Shawn M '99 Cnsl Human Rights Comm -120 W State -Ithaca 14850 **Fx:**277-4106
(212) 225-2000 .. **Moore,** Stacey R '09 %Cleary GS&H -1 Lbrty Plz -NY 10006
(845) 638-5001 .. **Moore,** Stephen '84 %DA -1 S Main -New Cty 10956 **Fx:**638-5070
(716) 847-7632 .. **Moore,** Tasha E '99 %Div of Human Rights -65 Court -Buffalo 14202 **Fx:**847-7625
(212) 267-4177 .. **Moore,** Thos A '73 (Kramer DL&M) -217 Bway -NY 10007
(631) 852-2176 .. **Moore,** Thos F '88 %Hon G Weber -210 Center Dr -Rvrhead 11901 **Fx:**852-3857
(914) 285-8500 .. **Moore,** Thos K '84 -701 Wstchstr Av -White Plns 10604 **Fx:**285-8510
(518) 464-9958 .. **Moore,** Thos P '05 %Bosman & Assoc,PLLC -1 Exec Centre Dr -Albany 12203 **Fx:**464-0968
(212) 333-8630 .. **Moore,** Thos R '58 -445 Park Av -NY 10022 **Fx:**977-5932
(212) 227-8150 .. **Moore,** Thos W III '72 (Treacy SM&M) -111 Bway -NY 10006
(315) 474-2981 .. **Moore,** Timothy A '75 (Tisdell M&W) -120 E Wshngtn -Syracuse 13202
(212) 964-7400 .. **Moore,** Trina L '01 Smith MDWY&Y,PC -111 John -NY 10038
(212) 698-3500 .. **Moore,** Valerie Diden '05 %Dechert LLP -1095 Av of Amer -NY 10036
(516) 571-2736 .. **Moore,** Victoria Gumbs '00 NYS Supreme Ct -100 Supreme Ct Dr -Mineola 11501 **Fx:**571-2170
(716) 856-5500 .. **Moore,** Vincent J '70 (Damon M LLP) -200 Delaware Av -Buffalo 14202
(212) 218-5500 .. **Moore,** Willard S '88 (Seyfarth S LLP) -620 8th Av -NY 10018
(716) 849-1333 .. **Moore,** Wm P '04 %Lipsitz GSC LLP -42 Delaware Av -Buffalo 14202
(607) 734-6191 .. **Moore & Woodhouse, LLP** -150 Lk -Elmira 14901 **Fx:**734-9282
(212) 564-6633 .. **Moore-McSpedon,** Sheila A '82 OfCnsl White & M,PC -875 Av of Amer -NY 10001
(212) 295-8510 .. **Moores,** Patricia A '88 Integro Ins Brokers -1 State Street Plz -NY 10004
(212) 309-1000 .. **Moorhead,** Bruce W Jr. '06 (Hunton & W) -200 Park Av -NY 10166
(585) 288-2710 .. **Moorhead,** Gaye L '81 Sisters of Mercy -1437 Blossom Rd -Rchstr 14610
(212) 596-9000 .. **Moorman,** John W '08 %Ropes & G LLP -1211 Av of Amer -NY 10036
(212) 966-6420 .. **Moorman,** Michl V '96 %Lwyrs For Children -110 Lafayette -NY 10013 **Fx:**966-0531
(914) 640-1838 .. **Moorman,** Michele Pinder '96 Starwood Hotels & Resorts -1111 Wstchstr Av -White Plns 10604 **Fx:**640-8250
(212) 846-7628 .. **Moorman,** Yasmin S '04 MTV Networks -1515 Bway -NY 10036
(212) 733-8207 .. **Moorthy,** Hemamalini '03 %Pfizer Inc -235 E 42nd -NY 10017
(212) 436-1712 .. **Moorthy,** Nancy M '86 IRS -290 Bway -NY 10007
(212) 272-8642 .. **Moosally,** Michelle Y '02 %JP Morgan Chase -383 Mad Av -NY 10179
(212) 846-7691 .. **Moosnick,** Heather L '00 %MTV Networks -1515 Bway -NY 10036
(716) 856-5500 .. **Moot,** Richd E '49 SpclCnsl Damon M LLP -200 Delaware Av -Buffalo 14202
(914) 761-0241 .. **Moo Young,** Joan A '87 (JA Moo Young PC) -19 Court -White Plns 10601 **Fx:**761-1432
(212) 204-6555 .. **Mor,** Ifat '02 -215 E 68th -NY 10065
(212) 858-6090 .. **Mor,** Shai Avihu '98 RBC Capital Mrkts Corp -1 Lbrty Plz -NY 10006
(845) 454-6672 .. **Mora,** Frank M '97 -90 Market -Poughkeepsie 12601 **Fx:**454-4492
(585) 586-5770 .. **Morabito,** David R '81 -117 W Cmmrcial Bx187 -E Rchstr 14445
(718) 590-2000 .. **Morabito,** John M '81 %DA -198 E 161st -Bronx 10451 **Fx:**590-6477
(585) 586-5770 .. **Morabito,** Kevin A '89 -117 W Cmmrcial Bx187 -E Rchstr 14445 **Fx:**383-1496
(585) 586-5770 .. **Morabito,** Nicholas '53 -117 W Cmmrcial Bx187 -E Rchstr 14445
(585) 385-3845 .. **Morabito,** Ralph '68 -120 W Cmmrcial -E Rchstr 14445 **Fx:**586-4792
(212) 264-5958 .. **Morace,** Philip L '81 %DOJ Immigration Ct -26 Fed Plz -NY 10278
(212) 846-8939 .. **Morachnick,** Tami L '91 MTV Networks -1515 Bway -NY 10036
(212) 490-3944 .. **Moraco,** Robt F '72 (Livoti B&M,PC) -122 E 42nd -NY 10168
(718) 579-3000 .. **Moradoff,** Mara B '89 %Leg Aid -1020 Grnd Cncrs -Bronx 10451 **Fx:**588-2611
(212) 225-2000 .. **Morag,** Boaz S '93 SpclCnsl Cleary GS&H -1 Lbrty Plz -NY 10006
(585) 263-1000 .. **Moragne,** John D '08 %Nixon P LLP -1100 Clinton Sq -Rchstr 14604
(212) 547-5400 .. **Morain,** Malinda '06 %McDermott W&E LLP -340 Mad Av -NY 10173
(212) 221-6900 .. **Morais,** Melissa L '05 %Winget S&S,LLP -45 Bway -NY 10006
(212) 226-7098 .. **Morak,** Glenn H '82 (Abramson & M) -35 Worth -NY 10013
(516) 229-6000 .. **Morale,** John T '03 %R Lau & Assoc -300 Jericho Quad Bx9040 -Jericho 11753 **Fx:**229-6167
(516) 229-4300 .. **Morale,** Patrick J '02 J Bilello & Assoc -875 Merrick Av -Westbury 11590
(212) 364-5340 .. **Morales,** Alba R '02 Innocence Project -100 5th Av -NY 10011 **Fx:**364-5341
(212) 596-9000 .. **Morales,** Carl A '10 %Ropes & G LLP -1211 Av of Amer -NY 10036
(212) 753-5000 .. **Morales,** Carlos M '80 Cnsl Schiff H LLP -900 3rd Av -NY 10022
(212) 636-6000 .. **Morales,** Carmen A '91 Fordham Univ Sch of Law -140 W 62nd -NY 10023 **Fx:**636-6899
(718) 618-1200 .. **Morales,** Connie '01 Supreme Ct -851 Grnd Cncrs -Bronx 10451
(646) 386-5700 .. **Morales,** Emily '02 %Civil Ct -111 Centre -NY 10013
(212) 264-6373 .. **Morales,** Fernando '96 %HHS -26 Fed Plz -NY 10278 **Fx:**264-6364
(212) 819-8554 .. **Morales,** Gladys M '03 -1155 Av of Amer -NY 10036 **Fx:**354-8113
(631) 493-3444 .. **Morales,** Grace M '89 -35 Crooked Hill Rd -Commack 11725
(212) 222-3448 .. **Morales,** Iris '80 -220 Manh Av -NY 10025
(212) 735-3000 .. **Morales,** Jose R '10 %Skadden ASM&F LLP -4 Times Sq -NY 10036
(212) 216-8000 .. **Morales,** Melissa Bobe '05 %Tarter K&D LLP -1350 Bway -NY 10018
(516) 750-0024 .. **Morales,** Orlando '02 Morales & Assoc,PC -280 Main -Farmngdl 11735
(212) 428-2150 .. **Morales,** Pedro A Jr. '92 %OCA -25 Beaver -NY 10004 **Fx:**428-2155
(516) 488-3300 .. **Morales,** Ralph V '98 %Shaub AC&S,LLP -1983 Marcus Av -Lk Success 11042
(212) 506-2500 .. **Morales,** Rosa M '07 %Mayer B LLP -1675 Bway -NY 10019
(212) 850-6220 .. **Morales,** Suzanna M M '05 %Lathrop & G LC -230 Park Av -NY 10169
(718) 298-0235 .. **Morales,** Teresita A '00 Family Ct -151-20 Jamaica Av -Jamaica 11432
(212) 696-6000 .. **Morales,** Valentina M '05 %Curtis M-PC&M LLP -101 Park Av -NY 10178
(212) 232-1300 .. **Morales,** Vanessa M '03 %Lewis BB&S LLP -77 Water -NY 10005
(914) 995-3339 .. **Morales,** Yvonne '98 %DA -111 Martin Luther King Blvd -White Plns 10601 **Fx:**995-3363
(212) 687-0100 .. **Morales Marquez,** Rosevelie '03 %Harris B PLLC -100 Wall -NY 10005
(212) 351-4000 .. **Morales Singh,** Mary E '09 Gibson D&C LLP -200 Park Av -NY 10166
(516) 338-5780 .. **Moramarco,** Eugene R '65 (Macri G&M) -393 Old Cntry Rd -Carle Pl 11514
(212) 210-9532 .. **Moran,** Adrienne D '09 %Alston & B LLP -90 Park Av -NY 10016
(845) 339-5556 .. **Moran,** Andrea '72 (Moran & G) -60 Pearl -Kingston 12401 **Fx:**339-5671
(212) 318-6000 .. **Moran,** Brian P '94 Paul HJ&W LLP -75 E 55th -NY 10022
(516) 741-3060 .. **Moran Brodrick & Elliot** -300 Grdn City Plz -Gdn Cty 11530 **Fx:**741-0782
(718) 250-2000 .. **Moran,** Carol L '83 %DA -350 Jay -Brklyn 11201 **Fx:**250-2314
(212) 803-5100 .. **Moran,** Cheryl J '96 %NY Cnty Defender Srvcs -225 Bway -NY 10007 **Fx:**571-6035
(212) 819-8200 .. **Moran,** Christine '09 %White & C LLP -1155 Av of Amer -NY 10036
(607) 723-5341 .. **Moran,** Christopher J '65 SpclCnsl Hinman H&K,LLP -80 Exchange Bx5250 -Bnghmtn 13902
(516) 227-0700 .. **Moran,** Domenique Camacho '94 (Farrell F,PC) -1320 RXR Plz -Uniondale 11556
(212) 436-6839 .. **Moran,** Edw K '90 Deloitte Srvcs -2 World Fncl Ctr -NY 10281
(516) 678-1294 .. **Moran,** Eugene J '58 -20 Ardsley Pl -Rockvll Ctr 11570
(516) 678-6660 .. **Moran,** Grace D '79 (Moran K LLP) -265 Sunrise Hwy -Rockvll Ctr 11570
(607) 722-3495 .. **Moran,** James F '83 (Aswad & I) -46 Front -Bnghmtn 13905
(914) 946-1030 .. **Moran,** James L '80 (Barry M&M) -55 Church -White Plns 10601
(718) 590-2000 .. **Moran,** Jamie H '06 %DA -198 E 161st -Bronx 10451 **Fx:**590-6477
(914) 345-3701 .. **Moran,** John J '80 %Marks OO&C,PC -530 Saw Mill Rvr Rd -Elmsfrd 10523
(718) 779-3567 .. **Moran,** John T '76 -35 30 73rd -Jcksn Hts 11372
(212) 442-4383 .. **Moran,** Jonathan D '09 %Law Dept -100 Church -NY 10007 **Fx:**788-0367
(212) 793-7613 .. **Moran,** Julia E '96 Citigroup -425 Park Av -NY 10022
(718) 274-6910 .. **Moran,** Justine C '97 -31-12 38th -Astoria 11103 **Fx:**204-2914
(516) 678-6660 .. **Moran Karamouzis LLP** -265 Sunrise Hwy -Rockvll Ctr 11570 **Fx:**678-6661
(212) 425-2125 .. **Moran Karamouzis LLP** -475 Park Av -NY 10016 **Fx:**425-2126
(212) 770-5030 .. **Moran,** Kate E '00 AIG -70 Pine -NY 10270
(845) 369-8130 .. **Moran,** Kenneth '78 -321 Route 59 Bx27 -Tallman 10982 **Fx:**369-1233
(212) 810-2331 .. **Moran,** Kevin P '03 FRM Research -888 7th Av -NY 10106
(212) 428-2517 .. **Moran,** Kristie Macchio '90 %OCA -25 Beaver -NY 10004
(917) 548-3822 .. **Moran,** Lisa V '96 -73 Worth -NY 10013
(315) 448-4800 .. **Moran,** Maria '91 %OCTF -615 Erie Blvd W -Syracuse 13204 **Fx:**448-4858
(212) 231-7100 .. **Moran,** Mark E '95 24/7 Media -132 W 31st -NY 10001 **Fx:**760-1774
(212) 669-4834 .. **Moran,** Martin J Jr. '87 Comptrollers Ofc -1 Centre -NY 10007
(718) 446-1789 .. **Moran,** Matthew E '92 %NY Walks Inc -33-52 81st -Jcksn Hts 11372 **Fx:**478-3036
(845) 634-6126 .. **Moran,** Maureen A '94 -169 S Main-PMB 387 -New Cty 10956 **Fx:**634-5890
(212) 450-4000 .. **Moran,** Michl J S '09 %Davis P&W LLP -450 Lex Av -NY 10017
(518) 474-8211 .. **Moran,** Michl S '80 %Law Reporting Bur -1 Commerce Plz -Albany 12210 **Fx:**463-6869
(212) 735-3000 .. **Moran,** Patricia '04 (Skadden ASM&F LLP) -4 Times Sq -NY 10036
(212) 670-0196 .. **Moran,** Patrick J '94 %Merrill Lynch -222 Bway -NY 10038
(212) 261-8000 .. **Moran,** Paul E '78 (Mendes & M,LLP) -750 7th Av -NY 10019
(212) 382-0909 .. **Moran,** Peter E '02 %Peckar & A,PC -41 Mad Av -NY 10154
(845) 638-5001 .. **Moran,** Richd K '02 %DA -1 S Main -New Cty 10956 **Fx:**638-5070
(516) 741-3060 .. **Moran,** Robt A '60 (Moran B&E) -300 Grdn City Plz -Gdn Cty 11530
(516) 498-8830 .. **Moran,** Robt A '04 -60 Cuttermill Rd -Gt Neck 11021 **Fx:**498-8998
(315) 435-2470 .. **Moran,** Robt E '06 DA -505 S State -Syracuse 13202 **Fx:**435-3969
(718) 590-8148 .. **Moran,** Rosemary C '00 %Admin Children's Srvcs -900 Sheridan Av -Bronx 10451 **Fx:**992-0084
(212) 259-8000 .. **Moran,** Sean M '89 (Dewey & L LLP) -1301 Av of Amer -NY 10019
(212) 425-2125 .. **Moran,** Siobhan E '87 (Moran K LLP) -475 Park Av -NY 10016
(516) 678-6660 .. **Moran,** Siobhan E '87 (Moran K LLP) -265 Sunrise Hwy -Rockvll Ctr 11570

(212) 225-2000 .. **Moran,** Siobhan F '10 %Cleary GS&H -1 Lbrty Plz -NY 10006
(585) 243-7020 .. **Moran,** Thos E '85 (DA) -2 Court -Geneseo 14454 **Fx:**243-7199
(212) 797-4362 .. **Moran,** Thos J '99 %Rafter & Assoc,PLLC -29 Bway -NY 10006 **Fx:**797-4363
(585) 591-1800 .. **Moran,** Timothy F '76 Kibbe K&M -2 Main Bx268 -Attica 14011
(212) 438-2440 .. **Moran,** Timothy J '00 %Standard & Poor's -55 Water -NY 10041
(716) 633-6500 .. **Moran,** Wm C '82 (W Moran & Assoc,PC) -6500 Main -Williamsvll 14221 **Fx:**633-3370
(212) 609-6800 .. **Moran,** Wm M '90 (McCarter & E,LLP) -245 Park Av -NY 10167
(646) 400-4822 .. **Morancy,** Kersuze '10 -133 W 118th -NY 10026
(516) 593-8883 .. **Morandi,** Danielle M '95 -265 Sunrise Hwy -Rockvll Ctr 11570 **Fx:**593-8891
(212) 786-6046 .. **Morandi,** Dominic P '92 Morandi Taub & Sarnoff,LLC -1325 Av of Amer -NY 10019 **Fx:**786-6045
(845) 896-2229 .. **Morando,** Anthony F '09 %Cuddy & F LLP -300 Westage Business Ctr -Fishkill 12524
(516) 692-8888 .. **Morano,** Michl F '99 (F Chau & Assoc,LLC) -130 Woodbury Rd -Woodbury 11797 **Fx:**692-8889
(518) 370-4793 .. **Morano,** Regina G '96 %MVP Health Plan -111 Lbrty Bx2207 -Schnctdy 12301
(516) 712-4000 .. **Morante,** Heather A '07 %Milber MP&S LLP -1000 Woodbury Rd -Woodbury 11797
(212) 335-4500 .. **Morante,** Paolo '05 (DLA Piper LLP) -1251 Av of Amer -NY 10020
(315) 483-6936 .. **Moraski,** Christina Potter '86 %WCTA Fed Credit Union -10 Benton Pl Bx40 -Sodus 14551 **Fx:**483-9716
(716) 852-5533 .. **Morath,** Jos D Jr. '06 %Connors & V,LLP -1000 Lbrty Bldg -Buffalo 14202
(716) 847-8400 .. **Moravec,** Michl R '75 (Phillips L LLP) -3400 HSBC Ctr -Buffalo 14203
(212) 998-6430 .. **Morawetz,** Nancy '82 %NYU Law Schl -245 Sullivan -NY 10012 **Fx:**995-4031
(315) 701-9998 .. **Morawski,** Jos P '03 %R Gordon -1 Lincoln Ctr -Syracuse 13202
(716) 853-8476 .. **Morcio,** Wendy E '88 %Dept of Law -350 Main Pl Twr -Buffalo 14202 **Fx:**853-8571
(716) 773-9433 .. **Mordaunt,** Timothy J '88 -5888 Main -Buffalo 14221 **Fx:**773-9438
(718) 969-9200 .. **Mordente,** Anthony R '83 Mordente Law Firm -160-29 Union Tpk -Fresh Mdws 11366 **Fx:**969-0707
(212) 776-5000 .. **Mordi,** Sam '91 %NYC Housing Auth -250 Bway -NY 10007 **Fx:**776-5039
(516) 228-9246 .. **Mordini,** Cora Amelia '97 DHS -711 Stewart Av -Gdn Cty 11530
(716) 681-0600 .. **Mordino,** Jos M '70 -2478 George Urban Blvd -Depew 14043
(212) 969-3000 .. **Mordkoff,** David S '09 %Proskauer R LLP -1585 Bway -NY 10036
(212) 683-3750 .. **Mordowitz,** Abraham M '77 (Mordowitz & L,LLP) -118 E 28th -NY 10016 **Fx:**679-5216
(212) 294-6700 .. **Morduchowitz,** Daphne P '06 %Winston & S -200 Park Av -NY 10166
(315) 435-2470 .. **Mordue,** Michl J '96 %DA -505 S State -Syracuse 13202 **Fx:**435-3969
(212) 888-8200 .. **More,** R Jeffrey '76 %Feder K LLP -845 3rd Av -NY 10022
(212) 730-7700 .. **Morea,** Douglas M '78 (Michelman & R,LLP) -114 W 47th -NY 10036
(516) 942-0244 .. **Morea,** Grace L '91 %Office oDA&R -375 N Bway -Jericho 11753 **Fx:**942-0353
(718) 263-2400 .. **Morea,** Russell C '67 -123-60 83rd Av -Kew Gdns 11415
(212) 822-9525 .. **Morehead,** Shawn V '01 Advocates for Chldrn of NY -151 W 30th -NY 10001
(914) 681-0200 .. **Morehouse,** Susan Currie '80 %DelBello DWW&W,LLP -1 N Lex Av -White Plns 10601
(212) 398-8600 .. **Moreira,** Jorge W '85 (Moreira & Assoc,PLLC) -130 W 42nd -NY 10036 **Fx:**398-9425
(212) 398-8600 .. **Moreira,** Sheila '04 %Moreira & Assoc,PLLC -130 W 42nd -NY 10036 **Fx:**398-9425
(646) 315-7378 .. **Moreiro,** Roberto '08 FINRA -14 Wall -NY 10005 **Fx:**315-7440
(914) 785-5300 .. **Morejon,** Manna '02 %A Lamer -555 Taxter Rd -Elmsfrd 10523 **Fx:**347-4269
(212) 670-0217 .. **Morel,** James C '69 %Merrill Lynch -222 Bway -NY 10038
(212) 382-6600 .. **Morel,** Ramona M '06 %NYC Bar -42 W 44th -NY 10036 **Fx:**398-6634
(212) 687-7410 .. **Moreland,** Danl C '96 %Clifton B&D,LLP -420 Lex Av -NY 10170
(212) 509-0500 .. **Moreland,** Sharon B '96 (Schoenfeld M,PC) -61 Bway -NY 10006
(212) 969-3000 .. **Morell,** Avram E '94 %Proskauer R LLP -1585 Bway -NY 10036
(646) 392-9250 .. **Morell,** Carol A '89 %M Klein & Assoc -200 Mad Av -NY 10016 **Fx:**(212) 779-1499
(315) 597-5337 .. **Morell,** John P '97 %Converse & M,LLP -224 E Main Bx215 -Palmyra 14522
(646) 414-6954 .. **Morelle,** Marissa L '00 Cnsl Lowenstein S PC -1251 Av of Amer -NY 10020 **Fx:**(973) 422-6819
(718) 250-2000 .. **Morelli,** Angelo M '86 %DA -350 Jay -Brklyn 11201 **Fx:**250-2314
(212) 751-9800 .. **Morelli,** Benedict P '77 (Morelli R PC) -950 3rd Av -NY 10022
(212) 972-1100 .. **Morelli,** Carl J '71 (Morelli & G,LLP) -380 Lex Av -NY 10168
(212) 972-1100 .. **Morelli & Gold,LLP** -380 Lex Av -NY 10168 **Fx:**983-5271
(516) 741-4104 .. **Morelli,** Janice M '82 %Cmmnwlth Land Title -330 Old Cntry Rd -Mineola 11501 **Fx:**741-4296
(718) 250-2000 .. **Morelli,** Michl A '93 %DA -350 Jay -Brklyn 11201 **Fx:**250-2314
(212) 506-2500 .. **Morelli,** Michl V '98 (Mayer B LLP) -1675 Bway -NY 10019
(212) 751-9800 .. **Morelli Ratner PC** -950 3rd Av -NY 10022 **Fx:**751-0046
(516) 248-1200 .. **Morelli,** Ronald J '73 %Mulholland M&R -374 Hillside Av -Williston Pk 11596
(212) 286-8585 .. **Morelli,** Rosary '79 (Heidell PM&B,LLP) -99 Park Av -NY 10016
(516) 873-9550 .. **Morelli,** Steven A '82 (Leeds M&B) -1 Old Cntry Rd -Carle Pl 11514
(212) 577-3688 .. **Morello,** Lorca '96 %Leg Aid -199 Water -NY 10038 **Fx:**509-8431
(212) 586-0700 .. **Morello,** Maurizio J '02 (Fulton R&H,LLP) -1 Rckfllr Plz -NY 10020
(516) 378-1700 .. **Morello,** Stephen V '90 %Chesney & M -2305 Grand Av -Baldwin 11510
(516) 873-6600 .. **Moreno,** Amanda J '97 %Sharinn & L -333 Earle Ovngton Blvd -Uniondale 11553
(718) 802-1616 .. **Moreno,** Angelicque M '94 (Avanzino & M,PC) -26 Court -Brklyn 11242 **Fx:**802-0189
(212) 631-7555 .. **Moreno,** Carlos '92 -352 7th Av -NY 10001 **Fx:**947-5069
(518) 431-0247 .. **Moreno,** Carlos A '94 %US Atty -445 Bway -Albany 12207 **Fx:**431-0249
(718) 273-4046 .. **Moreno,** David L '04 %Bosco B&M -857 Forest Av -Staten Isl 10310
(716) 836-5307 .. **Moreno,** Jos G '84 -90 Homesgarth Av -Cheektowaga 14225
(845) 306-1000 .. **Moreno,** Mario F '94 %Watchtower -100 Watchtower Dr -Patterson 12563 **Fx:**306-0709
(347) 401-9580 .. **Moreno,** Meghan M '00 %Appllt Term -141 Lvngstn -Brklyn 11201 **Fx:**(718) 643-7889
(212) 560-7348 .. **Moreno,** Patricia '89 -184 E 161st -Bronx 10451
(212) 596-9000 .. **Moreno,** Raul '09 %Ropes & G LLP -1211 Av of Amer -NY 10036
(646) 541-2000 .. **Moreno-Paz,** Alejandro '91 -730 5th Av -NY 10019
(631) 845-2600 .. **Morenus Conway Goren & Brandman** -58 S Srvc Rd -Melvll 11747 **Fx:**845-2626
(631) 777-2330 .. **Morenus,** Eugene O Jr. '84 (O'Connor OH&D,LLP) -1 Huntngtn Quad -Melvll 11747
(631) 845-2600 .. **Morenus,** Linda L '81 (Morenus CG&B) -58 S Srvc Rd -Melvll 11747
(212) 551-3630 .. **Moreschi-Galvao,** Carla Cilento '05 -230 Park Av -NY 10169 **Fx:**913-9243
(718) 390-5383 .. **Moresco,** Judith F '88 %Supreme Ct Law Dept -18 Richmond Ter -Staten Isl 10301
(212) 922-9700 .. **Moretta,** Anthony '04 1st Amer Title -633 3rd Av -NY 10017 **Fx:**922-0881
(212) 440-4300 .. **Moretti,** Amanda '92 %Leg Aid -199 Water -NY 10038
(212) 788-0434 .. **Moretti,** Barbara M '94 %Law Dept -100 Church -NY 10007 **Fx:**788-0367
(914) 761-7190 .. **Moretti,** Celeste P '96 %SSA-OHA -75 S Bway -White Plns 10601
(212) 801-9273 .. **Moretti,** Christian '03 %Greenberg T,LLP -200 Park Av -NY 10166
(212) 238-4800 .. **Moretti,** Danl S '85 (Landman CB&F,PC) -120 Bway -NY 10271
(585) 238-2000 .. **Moretti,** Mark J '79 (Phillips L LLP) -1400 First Fed Plz -Rchstr 14614
(212) 863-6300 .. **Moretti,** Valentine J '78 %HPD -100 Gold -NY 10038 **Fx:**863-8201
(212) 446-4800 .. **Morettini,** Ryan M '04 %Kirkland & E LLP -153 E 53rd -NY 10022
(212) 382-6600 .. **Morey,** Alice Ann '77 %NYC Bar -42 W 44th -NY 10036 **Fx:**398-6634
(716) 849-1333 .. **Morey,** Matthew B '08 %Lipsitz GSC LLP -42 Delaware Av -Buffalo 14202
(516) 679-7731 .. **Morezzi,** Eugenia J '92 -2957 Wilson Av -Wantagh 11793 **Fx:**679-7731
(212) 551-1800 .. **Morgado,** Jos M III '99 Westpac Banking Corp -575 5th Av -NY 10017
(212) 450-2000 .. **Morgado,** Matthew D '06 %NFL -280 Park Av -NY 10017 **Fx:**681-7599
(212) 258-6000 .. **Morgado,** R Gregory '01 %Viacom -1515 Bway -NY 10036
(716) 858-2424 .. **Morgan,** Ashley M '08 %DA -25 Delaware Av -Buffalo 14202 **Fx:**858-7425
(914) 793-1010 .. **Morgan Bagg & Persons** -274 Wht Plns Rd -Eastchstr 10707 **Fx:**793-1068
(212) 637-2699 .. **Morgan,** Brian K '05 US Atty -86 Chmbrs -NY 10007
(212) 248-3140 .. **Morgan,** Brian P '09 %Drinker B&R LLP -140 Bway -NY 10005
(716) 824-2221 .. **Morgan,** Carl W '93 -2221 Abbott Rd -Buffalo 14218
(845) 331-5777 .. **Morgan,** Carol K '03 %M Spinac -325 Wall Bx3748 -Kingston 12402 **Fx:**331-0108
(212) 509-9400 .. **Morgan,** Caroline A '08 %Cozen O -45 Bway Atrium -NY 10006
(212) 294-6700 .. **Morgan,** Catriona M '99 %Winston & S -200 Park Av -NY 10166
(212) 454-5521 .. **Morgan,** Christine M '95 %Deutsche Bank -60 Wall -NY 10005
(516) 627-9350 .. **Morgan,** Claude D '99 %Greater NY Conference -7 Shelter Rock Rd Bx5029 -Manhsst 11030 **Fx:**627-9272
(212) 918-3000 .. **Morgan,** Claudia T '99 Hogan L LLP -875 3rd Av -NY 10022
(212) 529-5358 .. **Morgan,** Colleen '05 Thor Equities LLC -15 W 39th -NY 10081
(212) 725-0200 .. **Morgan,** Cortney O'Toole '02 %Barnes R&C -475 Park Av S -NY 10016
(315) 798-5742 .. **Morgan,** Denise J '01 Dept Soc Srvcs -800 Park Av -Utica 13501
(212) 741-3510 .. **Morgan,** Diana '00 %R Olshever,PC -148 W 24th -NY 10011 **Fx:**741-3549
(212) 785-5115 .. **Morgan,** Duane R '04 (Dervishi L&M,PC) -11 Bway -NY 10004 **Fx:**480-8560
(516) 433-8050 .. **Morgan,** Eileen Ann '91 (Stouges M&P LLC) -115 N Bway -Hicksvll 11801
(718) 286-2000 .. **Morgan,** Florence '87 %Leg Aid -120-46 Qns Blvd -Kew Gdns 11415 **Fx:**286-2286
(845) 451-4065 .. **Morgan,** G Brian '83 Corp Cnsl -62 Civic Ctr Plz -Poughkeepsie 12601 **Fx:**451-4070
(212) 310-8000 .. **Morgan,** Gabriel A '09 %Weil G&M LLP -767 5th Av -NY 10153
(212) 756-2000 .. **Morgan,** J R '10 %Schulte R&Z LLP -919 3rd Av -NY 10022
(212) 656-2417 .. **Morgan,** James C '07 NYSE -20 Broad -NY 10005
(518) 439-7734 .. **Morgan,** James E '73 (Galvin & M) -217 Delaware Av -Delmar 12054
(212) 446-4800 .. **Morgan,** Jennifer M '02 (Kirkland & E LLP) -153 E 53rd -NY 10022
(646) 524-9076 .. **Morgan,** Jennifer P '08 Gilt Groupe,Inc -2 Park Av -NY 10016
(516) 764-0303 .. **Morgan,** John D '75 Morgan & M -55 Front -Rockvll Ctr 11570 **Fx:**536-9548
(212) 474-1000 .. **Morgan,** Kanika A '99 Cravath S&M LLP -825 8th Av -NY 10019
(212) 803-5100 .. **Morgan,** Kevin E '02 %NY Cnty Defender Srvcs -225 Bway -NY 10007 **Fx:**571-6035
(212) 512-1000 .. **Morgan,** Lasherelle R '03 %HBO -1100 Av of Amer -NY 10036 **Fx:**512-1986
(212) 309-6000 .. **Morgan Lewis & Bockius LLP** -101 Park Av -NY 10178 **Fx:**309-6273
(718) 262-3674 .. **Morgan,** Margaret '03 ACS -8914 Parsons Blvd -Jamaica 11432
(212) 809-1111 .. **Morgan Melhuish Abrutyn** -39 Bway -NY 10006 **Fx:**509-3422
(716) 373-2165 .. **Morgan,** Michl A '07 %DiCerbo & P -201 N Union -Olean 14760
(518) 443-5886 .. **Morgan,** Michl D '75 %SUNY Univ Cnsl -S333 SUNY Plz -Albany 12246 **Fx:**443-5409
(646) 264-3650 .. **Morgan,** Mychelle '98 %US Dept of Labor -201 Varick -NY 10014 **Fx:**264-3660
(845) 562-0203 .. **Morgan,** Nancy Y '87 (Finkelstein & Prtnrs,LLP) -1279 Route 300 Bx1111 -Newburgh 12550
(585) 530-3100 .. **Morgan,** Patricia L '81 %Appllt Div 4th Dept -50 East Av Ste 200 -Rchstr 14604 **Fx:**530-3247
(518) 442-4978 .. **Morgan,** Paul V '69 Schl of Business -1400 Wshngtn Av -Albany 12222
(518) 285-6100 .. **Morgan,** Paul V Jr. '91 Surrogates Ct -80 2nd -Troy 12180 **Fx:**272-5452
(212) 940-3703 .. **Morgan,** Paulette J '06 Cnsl Nixon P LLP -437 Mad Av -NY 10022

(914) 941-2515 .. **Morgan,** Penelope W '77 -75 S Highland Av -Ossining 10562 **Fx:**762-8327
(212) 768-5342 .. **Morgan,** Peter S '98 (Sonnenschein N&R LLP) -2 World Fncl Ctr -NY 10281
(212) 705-7000 .. **Morgan,** Raleigh B '09 %Bingham M LLP -399 Park Av -NY 10022
(212) 596-9000 .. **Morgan,** Robt C '70 (Ropes & G LLP) -1211 Av of Amer -NY 10036
(212) 238-3000 .. **Morgan,** Robt L '85 OfCnsl Emmet M&M,LLP -120 Bway -NY 10271
(718) 487-1300 .. **Morgan,** Rose M '90 %Leg Srvcs Corp A -80 Jamaica Av -Brklyn 11207 **Fx:**342-1780
(716) 353-4108 .. **Morgan,** Schavon R '05 -Bx472 -Machias 14101
(212) 213-1220 .. **Morgan,** Scott F '81 (Weiner MM&B,LLC) -220 5th Av -NY 10001
(212) 819-8200 .. **Morgan,** Shamia G '10 %White & C LLP -1155 Av of Amer -NY 10036
(212) 839-9468 .. **Morgan,** Tonya D '04 %Dept of Transportation -55 Water -NY 10041
(516) 229-4200 .. **Morgan,** Tracy Ann '94 %Mendolia & S -875 Merrick Av -Westbury 11590
(315) 476-2945 .. **Morgan,** Wm R '76 Morgan Law Firm,PC -120 E Wshngtn -Syracuse 13202 **Fx:**476-5208
(631) 239-6817 .. **Morganelli,** Patrick J '79 %E Troy -44 Bway -Greenlawn 11740 **Fx:**239-6816
(212) 586-5905 .. **Morganroth,** Jeffrey B '97 -110 E 42nd -NY 10017 **Fx:**(248) 864-4001
(516) 739-8300 .. **Morganstern,** Allen R '70 AR Morganstern,PC -355 Post Av -Westbury 11590 **Fx:**739-8390
(516) 741-2585 .. **Morganstern,** Andrew C '75 SrCnsl Rosicki R & Assoc,PC -51 E Bethpage Rd -Plainvw 11803 **Fx:**470-0972
(212) 944-0500 .. **Morganstern,** Gerald H '67 (Hofheimer G&G,LLP) -530 5th Av -NY 10036 **Fx:**897-4990
(212) 610-6300 .. **Morgenbesser,** Henry I '81 (Allen & O) -1221 Av of Amer -NY 10020
(716) 847-0650 .. **Morgenheim,** Keith A '76 %Leg Srvcs -237 Main -Buffalo 14203 **Fx:**847-0227
(718) 694-5713 .. **Morgenroth,** Diane J '78 %Transit Auth -130 Lvngstn -Brklyn 11201 **Fx:**694-5726
(718) 777-9595 .. **Morgenstern,** Ami '94 -40-17 Bway Bx3223 -Astoria 11103
(212) 816-7544 .. **Morgenstern,** Beth R '80 Smith Barney -388 Greenwich -NY 10013
(212) 750-6776 .. **Morgenstern & Blue, LLC** -885 3rd Av -NY 10022 **Fx:**750-3128
(516) 739-5908 .. **Morgenstern,** Jeff '85 (J Morgenstern,PLLC) -1 Old Cntry Rd -Carle Pl 11514 **Fx:**719-7280
(585) 641-8000 .. **Morgenstern,** Jordan E '05 %Fix SB&G,PC -295 Woodcliff Dr -Fairprt 14450
(212) 259-8000 .. **Morgenstern,** Mathew M '10 %Dewey & L LLP -1301 Av of Amer -NY 10019
(212) 906-1200 .. **Morgenstern,** Orly C '09 %Latham & W -885 3rd Av -NY 10022
(212) 750-6776 .. **Morgenstern,** Peter D '83 (Morgenstern & B,LLC) -885 3rd Av -NY 10022
(212) 836-8000 .. **Morgenstern,** Saul P '82 (Kaye S LLP) -425 Park Av -NY 10022
(631) 265-8000 .. **Morgenthal,** Eric L '02 (E Morgenthal,PLLC) -50 Rte 111 -Smithtwn 11787
(212) 888-2005 .. **Morgenthau & Greenes, LLP** -575 Lex Av -NY 10022 **Fx:**486-4035
(212) 888-2005 .. **Morgenthau,** Joel L '70 (Morgenthau & G,LLP) -575 Lex Av -NY 10022
(212) 403-1000 .. **Morgenthau,** Robt M '49 OfCnsl Wachtell LR&K -51 W 52nd -NY 10019
(212) 682-6800 .. **Morgenweck,** Eric R '00 %Zetlin & D LLP -801 2nd Av -NY 10017
(212) 975-8150 .. **Morgeson,** Matthew D '97 %CBS Inc -51 W 52nd -NY 10019 **Fx:**975-3930
(518) 474-6740 .. **Morgiewicz,** Riele Jessica '00 %Dept of State -41 State -Albany 12231 **Fx:**473-9211
(631) 244-2043 .. **Morgillo,** Robt M '79 %Vitamin World -4320 Vets Hwy -Holbrook 11741
(718) 252-0174 .. **Morginshteren,** Alla '01 -106 Av I -Brklyn 11230 **Fx:**377-1042
(212) 883-6500 .. **Morgulis,** Meir '00 %Podell SS&B,LLP -605 3rd Av -NY 10158
(212) 259-8000 .. **Morhouse,** Sanford W '69 OfCnsl Dewey & L LLP -1301 Av of Amer -NY 10019
(716) 854-1300 .. **Moriarity,** Erin M '09 %Rosenthal S&M,LLP -300 Main -Buffalo 14202
(518) 445-2311 .. **Moriarty,** Danl G '68 Albany Law Schl -80 New Scotland Av -Albany 12208 **Fx:**445-2315
(212) 715-9100 .. **Moriarty,** James J '96 (Kramer LN&F,LLP) -1177 Av of Amer -NY 10036
(646) 372-0450 .. **Moriarty,** James T '75 -110 E 59th -NY 10022
(212) 940-8800 .. **Moriarty,** Kathleen H '81 (Katten MR LLP) -575 Mad Av -NY 10022
(718) 741-3400 .. **Moriarty,** Meredith A '04 %Childrens Law Ctr -2501 Grnd Cncrs -Bronx 10468
(212) 973-8000 .. **Moriarty,** Michl J '76 Cnsl Schnader HS&L LLP -140 Bway -NY 10005
(212) 237-1000 .. **Moriarty,** Michl M '84 (Windels ML&M,LLP) -156 W 56th -NY 10019
(845) 635-2547 .. **Moriarty,** Patrick E '70 -22 W Gretna Rd -Plsnt Vlly 12569
(212) 474-1000 .. **Moriarty,** Patrick J '87 Cravath S&M LLP -825 8th Av -NY 10019
(212) 967-3000 .. **Moriarty,** Russell S '05 %Levine & B,PLLC -350 5th Av -NY 10118
(518) 357-2887 .. **Moriarty,** Stephanie E '97 -420 Danna Joelle Dr -Schnctdy 12303
(212) 250-4993 .. **Moriarty,** Tracey A '02 %Deutsche Bank -60 Wall -NY 10005
(516) 571-5810 .. **Moriates,** Tricia A '03 %Hon R Bruno -400 Cnty Seat Dr -Mineola 11501
(212) 788-0734 .. **Moriber,** Saml A '91 %Law Dept -100 Church -NY 10007 **Fx:**788-0367
(212) 446-7415 .. **Moricca,** David S '03 McKinsey & Co -55 E 52nd -NY 10055 **Fx:**688-9521
(585) 352-0803 .. **Morich,** Michl S '94 -353 Gallup Rd -Spencerprt 14559
(212) 261-8000 .. **Morici,** Gerard C '04 %Mendes & M,LLP -750 7th Av -NY 10019
(516) 873-1902 .. **Morici,** Michl D '74 (Morici & M) -1399 Franklin Av -Gdn Cty 11530 **Fx:**873-3948
(212) 687-6050 .. **Morici,** Michl D '00 (Morici & M) -600 3rd Av -NY 10016 **Fx:**557-9610
(718) 946-0111 .. **Morici,** Robt '85 (Morici & M) -262 Smith -Brklyn 11231
(516) 873-1902 .. **Morici,** Robt '85 (Morici & M) -1399 Franklin Av -Gdn Cty 11530 **Fx:**873-3948
(845) 691-7292 .. **Moriello,** Jos M '77 (DiStasi M&M PLLC) -400 Uppr North Rd Bx915 -Highlnd 12528
(845) 338-6600 .. **Moriello,** Michl A '92 (Riseley & M,PLLC) -111 Green Bx4465 -Kingston 12402
(212) 593-7600 .. **Moriello,** Michl L '03 %S Harris & Assoc -110 E 59th -NY 10022
(518) 455-7518 .. **Morigerato,** Erin C '07 Cnsl NYS Legislature -310 Cptl Bldg -Albany 12224
(212) 962-5757 .. **Morik,** Christopher '91 %Gaffin & M,PC -225 Bway -NY 10007
(212) 891-1898 .. **Morikawa,** Duane M '96 Natixis Capital Mrkts -9 W 57th -NY 10019
(212) 225-2000 .. **Morimura,** Kana '08 %Cleary GS&H -1 Lbrty Plz -NY 10006
(315) 349-3350 .. **Morin,** Bobette Jean '83 %Family Ct -39 Churchill Rd -Oswego 13126 **Fx:**349-3457
(914) 422-8755 .. **Morin,** Doris K '79 %Dept of Law -101 E Post Rd -White Plns 10601 **Fx:**422-8706
(212) 687-4900 .. **Morin,** John T '72 (Wormser KG&J LLP) -825 3rd Av -NY 10022
(212) 237-8751 .. **Morin,** Jose L '85 %John Jay College -445 W 59th -NY 10019
(585) 546-2500 .. **Morin,** Lucien A II '75 (McConville CC&M,PC) -25 E Main -Rchstr 14614
(212) 357-7128 .. **Morina,** J Thos '90 Goldman Sachs -85 Broad -NY 10004
(212) 623-5730 .. **Moring,** Ellen R '90 JP Morgan Chase Bk NA -4 NY Plz -NY 10004
(212) 490-3000 .. **Morio,** John D '85 (Wilson EME&D LLP) -150 E 42nd -NY 10017
(914) 323-7000 .. **Morio,** John D '85 (Wilson EME&D LLP) -3 Gannett Dr -White Plns 10604
(212) 819-8200 .. **Morioka,** Leslie '94 (White & C LLP) -1155 Av of Amer -NY 10036
(718) 447-2620 .. **Morisano,** Anthony J Jr. '89 -432 Forest Av -Staten Isl 10301
(212) 406-9686 .. **Morisco,** Angela M '90 %E D'Elia,PC -120 Bway -NY 10271 **Fx:**406-9688
(212) 808-4195 .. **Morishita,** Junya '01 Norinchukin Bank -245 Park Av -NY 10167
(212) 355-1794 .. **Morisi,** Chas R '88 -800 5th Av -NY 10065
(718) 287-8762 .. **Morisset,** David '04 -123 Linden Blvd -Brklyn 11226 **Fx:**287-8917
(516) 873-2000 .. **Moritt Hock Hamroff & Horowitz LLP** -400 Grdn City Plz -Gdn Cty 11530 **Fx:**873-2010
(516) 873-2000 .. **Moritt,** Neil J '64 (Moritt HH&H LLP) -400 Grdn City Plz -Gdn Cty 11530
(212) 403-1000 .. **Moritz,** Garrett B '04 %Wachtell LR&K -51 W 52nd -NY 10019
(212) 675-2378 .. **Moritz,** Kirk D '78 -10 W 15th -NY 10011
(212) 635-1513 .. **Moritz,** Margaret E '87 Bk of NY Mellon -1 Wall -NY 10286
(631) 749-0233 .. **Moritz,** Sharon A '86 -25 N Ferry Rd Bx580 -Shelter Isl 11964 **Fx:**749-0945
(212) 867-0677 .. **Moritz,** Victor R '90 -134 Johnson Rd -Scarsdale 10583
(212) 878-7900 .. **Moriwaki,** Gary S '77 (Fox R LLP) -100 Park Av -NY 10017
(212) 887-7708 .. **Morizio,** Lawr '93 Keefe Bruyette & Woods,Inc -787 7th Av -NY 10019
(516) 681-1100 .. **Morken,** Debbie '02 Kaufman DV&G,LLP -135 Crsswys Park Dr -Woodbury 11797
(516) 227-0700 .. **Morken,** John R '78 (Farrell F,PC) -1320 RXR Plz -Uniondale 11556
(518) 234-2621 .. **Morlang,** Craig T '94 -117 Granite Dr -Cobleskill 12043 **Fx:**234-2621
(212) 578-2211 .. **Morledge,** Jos W '00 %MetLife -27-01 Qns Plz N -LIC 11101
(212) 822-8300 .. **Morley,** Alan G '90 NMIC -76 Wadsworth Av -NY 10033 **Fx:**740-9645
(718) 590-3722 .. **Morley,** Christopher T '82 %Supreme Ct -851 Grnd Cncrs -Bronx 10451
(212) 644-4420 .. **Morley,** Debbie-Ann '00 %Fabiani C&H,LLP -570 Lex Av -NY 10022
(212) 372-3425 .. **Morley,** Jeremy D '75 -230 Park Av -NY 10169 **Fx:**(815) 301-6742
(212) 261-8000 .. **Morley,** Michl E '90 (Mendes & M,LLP) -750 7th Av -NY 10019
(518) 272-6565 .. **Morley,** Scott M '02 %Martin SWD&J -279 River Bx1530 -Troy 12181
(212) 578-2473 .. **Morley,** Seamus M '07 MetLife -27-01 Qns Plz N -LIC 11101
(212) 666-1076 .. **Morley,** Wm H Jr. '70 -382 Cntrl Pk W -NY 10025
(212) 310-8000 .. **Morneau,** Jeffrey M '05 %Weil G&M LLP -767 5th Av -NY 10153
(212) 943-0280 .. **Morning,** Ingrid '85 OfCnsl McCanliss & E LLP -88 Pine -NY 10005
(212) 537-1571 .. **Morningstar,** Matthew E '02 Morgan Stanley & Co Inc -1585 Bway -NY 10036
(914) 762-0776 .. **Moro,** Patricia L '91 -573 N State Rd -Briarclff Mnr 10510 **Fx:**762-6877
(631) 852-2500 .. **Moroff,** Laurie I '00 %DA -200 Center Dr -Rvrhead 11901 **Fx:**852-1769
(646) 278-2000 .. **Moroff,** Margaret C '91 Vera Inst of Justice -636 Bway -NY 10012
(212) 473-3372 .. **Moroff,** Shelley S '90 -150 E 18th -NY 10003 **Fx:**473-1570
(718) 855-2522 .. **Morofsky,** Allan M '84 -7 Douglass -Brklyn 11231 **Fx:**855-2523
(914) 385-6000 .. **Moroknek,** Harold L '89 (Hodges W&S LLP) -55 Church -White Plns 10601 **Fx:**385-6060
(516) 864-6835 .. **Moroknek,** Mark '85 -175 The Vale -Syosset 11791 **Fx:**584-9264
(516) 223-8553 .. **Morokoff,** Carol G '87 %Maidenbaum & Assoc PLLC -1 Broadcast Plz -Merrick 11566 **Fx:**223-7096
(212) 376-6400 .. **Moroney,** Crystal G '08 %Marshall DWC&G -88 Pine -NY 10005
(516) 997-6130 .. **Moroney,** Francis X '77 -497 Westbury Av -Carle Pl 11514 **Fx:**997-6018
(631) 501-3100 .. **Moroney,** John P '89 %J Humphreys -3 Huntngtn Quad Bx9028 -Melvll 11747 **Fx:**501-3085
(718) 261-6069 .. **Moroney,** Karen L '92 Hon S Rotker -125-01 Qns Blvd -Kew Gdns 11415
(212) 326-3939 .. **Moroney,** Kathleen '08 %Jones D -222 E 41st -NY 10017
(212) 883-1700 .. **Moros,** Heather L '09 %Duval & S LLP -101 Park Av -NY 10178
(212) 698-3500 .. **Morosanu,** Nicole S R '07 %Dechert LLP -1095 Av of Amer -NY 10036
(212) 640-2000 .. **Moros-Nahim,** Jorge C '03 Amer Express -3 World Fncl Ctr -NY 10285
(212) 468-4800 .. **Moross,** Jeffrey A '66 (Davis & G LLP) -1740 Bway -NY 10019
(212) 688-8555 .. **Morowitz,** Nancy H '98 %Fragomen DB&L LLP -7 Hanover Sq -NY 10004
(212) 407-4000 .. **Moroz,** Eugene '68 %Loeb & L,LLP -345 Park Av -NY 10154
(212) 790-9200 .. **Morozova,** Yelena '08 %Cowan L&L,PC -1133 Av of Amer -NY 10036
(212) 558-4000 .. **Morphy,** James C '80 (Sullivan & C LLP) -125 Broad -NY 10004
(518) 473-0951 .. **Morphy,** Patrick T '78 %Dept of Law -The Cptl -Albany 12224
(212) 916-2875 .. **Morpurgo,** Alison D '00 UBS Intl,Inc -101 Park Av -NY 10178
(212) 583-9478 .. **Morra,** Maria G '87 -239 E 61st -NY 10065

(516) 294-5100 .. **Morra,** Peter '95 OfCnsl Murphy B&O,LLP -22 Jericho Tpk -Mineola 11501
(212) 238-3000 .. **Morreale,** Leonard J Jr. '80 OfCnsl Emmet M&M,LLP -120 Bway -NY 10271
(212) 474-1000 .. **Morreale,** Matthew G '98 %Cravath S&M LLP -825 8th Av -NY 10019
(212) 782-4838 .. **Morreale,** Monique L '99 %Bk of Tokyo-Mitsubishi -1251 Av of Amer -NY 10020 **Fx:**782-6420
(607) 723-0600 .. **Morreall,** Edmond F '00 (Gitto & N,LLP) -71 State -Bnghmtn 13901 **Fx:**723-0634
(718) 613-3500 .. **Morrell,** Lynn A '77 %UIA Bd -Bx29002 -Brklyn 11201 **Fx:**613-3566
(315) 568-5221 .. **Morrell,** Patrick J '98 (Morrell & S) -102 Fall -Seneca Fls 13148
(315) 539-1300 .. **Morrell,** Patrick J '98 %DA -48 W Williams -Waterloo 13165 **Fx:**539-0531
(315) 568-5221 .. **Morrell & Sipos** -102 Fall -Seneca Fls 13148 **Fx:**568-2265
(631) 264-0303 .. **Morrell,** Wm C '67 (VanNostrand & M) -53 Bway Bx307 -Amityvll 11701
(212) 361-1400 .. **Morrick,** Clive I '82 Envrnmntl Cntrl Brd -66 John -NY 10038 **Fx:**361-1900
(212) 836-8000 .. **Morriello,** Henry G '84 (Kaye S LLP) -425 Park Av -NY 10022
(212) 450-4000 .. **Morril,** Jane M '08 %Davis P&W LLP -450 Lex Av -NY 10017
(212) 258-6000 .. **Morril,** Mark C '72 %Viacom -1515 Bway -NY 10036
(212) 592-3539 .. **Morrill,** Aaron R '89 -244 5th Av -NY 10001 **Fx:**591-6157
(212) 714-2904 .. **Morris,** Aaron C '06 Immigration Equality -40 Exch Pl -NY 10005
(212) 486-0426 .. **Morris,** Alan R '56 -501 Mad Av -NY 10022
(212) 236-6008 .. **Morris,** Allan I '81 Merrill Lynch -225 Lbrty -NY 10080
(212) 259-8000 .. **Morris,** Andrew L '07 %Dewey & L LLP -1301 Av of Amer -NY 10019
(212) 326-3939 .. **Morris,** Brandon T '09 %Jones D -222 E 41st -NY 10017
(716) 674-9100 .. **Morris & Bray,PC** -1299 Union Rd -Buffalo 14224 **Fx:**674-7116
(646) 733-3200 .. **Morris,** Brian D '00 US Dept Homeland Sec -1 Penn Plz -NY 10119
(315) 379-0326 .. **Morris,** Cecily '85 %Supreme Ct -48 Court -Canton 13617
(518) 859-5544 .. **Morris,** Christian P '05 -Bx1 -Schuylrvll 12871
(203) 330-2109 .. **Morris,** D Robt '75 (Pullman & C,LLC) -50 Main -White Plns 10606
(914) 945-3217 .. **Morris,** Danl P '85 IBM -Bx218 -Yorktwn Hts 10598 **Fx:**241-4038
(212) 687-7410 .. **Morris,** Danl W '00 %Clifton B&D,LLP -420 Lex Av -NY 10170
(585) 468-2770 .. **Morris,** David J '82 -6 1st Bx610 -Nunda 14517 **Fx:**468-5375
(212) 859-8000 .. **Morris,** David M '90 (Fried FHS&J LLP) -1 NY Plz -NY 10004
(518) 583-3500 .. **Morris,** David W '61 -43 Brookside Dr -Saratoga Spgs 12866 **Fx:**583-9793
(212) 298-9194 .. **Morris,** David W '06 PBA of the City of New York -40 Fulton -NY 10038
(607) 535-8121 .. **Morris,** Dennis J '79 %Cnty Atty -105 9th -Watkins Glen 14891 **Fx:**535-8123
(212) 788-1233 .. **Morris,** Dona B '91 %Law Dept -100 Church -NY 10007 **Fx:**788-0367
(718) 330-1200 .. **Morris,** Douglas G '84 %Fed Def of NY Inc -1 Pierrepont Plz -Brklyn 11201 **Fx:**855-0760
(212) 766-1888 .. **Morris Duffy Alonso & Faley** -2 Rector -NY 10006 **Fx:**766-3252
(212) 513-3200 .. **Morris,** Francesca A '99 (Holland & K LLP) -31 W 52nd -NY 10019
(212) 449-4969 .. **Morris,** Fredk D '97 %Merrill Lynch -4 World Fncl Ctr -NY 10080
(212) 709-3540 .. **Morris,** Gia L '96 %Banking Dept -1 State -NY 10004 **Fx:**709-1655
(212) 446-4800 .. **Morris,** Gregory A '05 %Kirkland & E LLP -153 E 53rd -NY 10022
(212) 696-9308 .. **Morris,** Henry '79 Morris & Carrick Inc -271 Mad Av -NY 10016
(914) 834-2595 .. **Morris,** J Robt '50 -8 Pine Rdg Rd -Larchmnt 10538
(585) 292-5750 .. **Morris,** James E '67 (Morris and M) -120 Corp Woods -Rchstr 14623 **Fx:**292-5793
(716) 855-1118 .. **Morris,** James E '80 -424 Main -Buffalo 14202 **Fx:**855-1119
(212) 220-3830 .. **Morris,** James E '10 %Nicoletti H&S -88 Pine -NY 10005
(518) 485-1781 .. **Morris,** James J Jr. '77 Dept of Tax & Fin -Bldg 9 State Campus -Albany 12227
(914) 793-5060 .. **Morris,** James S '67 70 Millard Av -Bronxvll 10708 **Fx:**793-5062
(212) 474-1000 .. **Morris,** Jared '09 %Cravath S&M LLP -825 8th Av -NY 10019
(212) 708-1515 .. **Morris,** Jennie H '99 %Showtime Networks Inc -1633 Bway -NY 10019
(212) 310-8000 .. **Morris,** Jesse L '10 %Weil G&M LLP -767 5th Av -NY 10153
(212) 561-7700 .. **Morris,** John A '91 (Pachulski SZ&J) -780 3rd Av -NY 10017
(516) 739-0400 .. **Morris,** John J '83 %Kelly R&K,LLP -330 Old Cntry Rd -Mineola 11501
(212) 483-9490 .. **Morris,** John W '95 (McElroy DM&C,LLP) -88 Pine -NY 10005
(212) 944-8000 .. **Morris,** Jonathan B '94 %Bluefly,Inc -42 W 39th -NY 10018
(212) 309-6000 .. **Morris,** Jonathan D '99 (Morgan L&B LLP) -101 Park Av -NY 10178
(212) 526-1614 .. **Morris,** Jonathan R '82 Barclays Capital Inc -399 Park Av -NY 10022
(718) 588-5200 .. **Morris,** Julia C '09 Law Dept -198 E 161st -Bronx 10451 **Fx:**590-2686
(718) 826-8401 .. **Morris,** L Blake '88 -Box 3289 Church St Sta -NY 10008
(585) 621-1930 .. **Morris,** Lisa B '85 -1577 Ridge Rd W -Rchstr 14615
(518) 489-8424 .. **Morris,** Maria B '98 %AFSCME Council 82 -63 Colvin Av -Albany 12206 **Fx:**435-1523
(718) 520-3801 .. **Morris,** Marian B '81 %Supreme Ct -88-11 Sutphin Blvd -Jamaica 11435
(518) 862-0676 .. **Morris,** Mark D '74 -217 Great Oaks Ofc Pk -Albany 12203 **Fx:**862-0706
(212) 298-5013 .. **Morris,** Martin H Jr. '05 %Leg Aid -49 Thomas -NY 10013 **Fx:**298-5252
(516) 825-0468 .. **Morris,** Mary Lee '86 -193 Cedar Av -Hewlett 11557
(212) 969-3000 .. **Morris,** Matthew J '00 %Proskauer R LLP -1585 Bway -NY 10036
(212) 918-3000 .. **Morris,** Matthew P '92 (Hogan L LLP) -875 3rd Av -NY 10022
(212) 418-0500 .. **Morris & McVeigh LLP** -767 3rd Av -NY 10017 **Fx:**421-0922
(518) 426-8111 .. **Morris & McVeigh LLP** -19 Dove -Albany 12210 **Fx:**426-5111
(212) 483-9600 .. **Morris,** Michl J '90 (Costello S&G LLP) -44 Wall -NY 10005
(212) 425-7200 .. **Morris,** Michelle C '06 %Kenyon & K,LLP -1 Bway -NY 10004
(518) 474-5586 .. **Morris,** Mitchell S '77 %State Comptroller -110 State -Albany 12236 **Fx:**473-9104
(845) 638-8000 .. **Morris,** Nancy B '91 -20 Squadron Blvd -New Cty 10956 **Fx:**638-8002
(718) 527-7676 .. **Morris,** Narissa '98 -229-02 Merrick Blvd -Laurelton 11413 **Fx:**341-1085
(212) 349-0600 .. **Morris,** Peter D '83 -60 E 42nd -NY 10165
(914) 681-8700 .. **Morris,** Peter J '96 %Milber MP&S LLP -3 Barker Av -White Plns 10601
(212) 318-6000 .. **Morris,** Pheabe S '07 %Paul HJ&W LLP -75 E 55th -NY 10022
(518) 783-0200 .. **Morris,** Quinn M '08 %NYS Schl Bds Assn -24 Century Hill Dr -Latham 12110
(585) 292-5750 .. **Morris,** Richd D '61 (Morris and M) -120 Corp Woods -Rchstr 14623 **Fx:**292-5793
(212) 837-3628 .. **Morris,** Richd F '81 %JP Morgan Chase -530 5th Av -NY 10036
(212) 592-1400 .. **Morris,** Richd M '91 (Herrick,F LLP) -2 Park Av -NY 10016
(212) 227-7200 .. **Morris,** Richd P '74 (Klein W&M) -277 Bway -NY 10007
(518) 745-1400 .. **Morris,** Robt Chas '66 %FitzGerald MBF -16 Pearl Bx2017 -Glens Fls 12801
(212) 715-9100 .. **Morris,** Robt W '96 (Kramer LN&F,LLP) -1177 Av of Amer -NY 10036
(212) 903-8781 .. **Morris,** Ronald A '59 OfCnsl Roberts & H,LLP -825 8th Av -NY 10019
(212) 728-8000 .. **Morris,** Russell D '00 %Willkie F&G LLP -787 7th Av -NY 10019
(212) 980-0404 .. **Morris,** Saml '41 %J Dearie & Assoc -515 Mad Av -NY 10022 **Fx:**980-0555
(212) 267-3550 .. **Morris,** Scott A '05 %S Einstein & Assoc,PC -20 Vesey -NY 10007 **Fx:**267-3803
(212) 613-5000 .. **Morris,** Shari M '09 Leg Assist Grp -450 W 33rd -NY 10001 **Fx:**750-0820
(718) 237-2428 .. **Morris,** Stephanie R '96 AM Only,Inc -55 Washington -Brklyn 11201
(585) 292-5750 .. **Morris,** Stephen P '58 (Morris and M) -120 Corp Woods -Rchstr 14623 **Fx:**292-5793
(212) 762-4000 .. **Morris,** Stephen R '99 %Morgan Stanley -1221 Av of Amer -NY 10020
(914) 747-9500 .. **Morris,** Susan Wilf '84 OfCnsl AL Berman -50 Bway -Hawthorne 10532 **Fx:**747-0935
(212) 406-4993 .. **Morris,** Wade T '95 -225 Bway -NY 10007 **Fx:**406-4996
(516) 883-2427 .. **Morris,** Wm H Jr. '86 -4 Cmbrdg Av -Pt Wash 11050
(718) 258-3726 .. **Morrisey,** Wm C '56 -1448 E 28th -Brklyn 11210
(212) 687-2770 .. **Morrison,** Alan J '93 (Cohen PL&P) -551 5th Av -NY 10176
(212) 536-3900 .. **Morrison,** Andrew L '88 (K&L Gates LLP) -599 Lex Av -NY 10022
(914) 592-8282 .. **Morrison,** Arthur '64 -11 Skyline Dr -Hawthorne 10532 **Fx:**592-3482
(212) 278-7854 .. **Morrison,** Carol A '98 Societe Generale -1221 Av of Amer -NY 10020
(212) 317-5309 .. **Morrison,** Christopher P '92 Swiss Re America Corp -55 E 52nd -NY 10055
(212) 735-8600 .. **Morrison Cohen LLP** -909 3rd Av -NY 10022 **Fx:**735-8708
(914) 949-2700 .. **Morrison,** Danl W III '85 (Bleakley P&S,LLP) -1 N Lex Av -White Plns 10601
(212) 254-0897 .. **Morrison,** Diane M '83 -113 Stanton -NY 10002
(845) 756-5254 .. **Morrison,** Edw A '58 -54 Weaver Rd -Elizaville 12523 **Fx:**756-2870
(212) 343-8000 .. **Morrison,** Eric H '85 (Morrison & W) -49 W 38th -NY 10018
(212) 468-8000 .. **Morrison & Foerster LLP** -1290 Av of Amer -NY 10104 **Fx:**468-7900
(212) 848-4000 .. **Morrison,** John A '91 Cnsl Shearman & S LLP -599 Lex Av -NY 10022
(212) 655-3500 .. **Morrison,** Lawr F '98 (Meister S&F LLP) -140 E 45th -NY 10017
(212) 825-0365 .. **Morrison,** Leni P '09 %AL Bailey,PC -120 Bway -NY 10271 **Fx:**825-0999
(914) 636-7117 .. **Morrison,** Leonard M '85 -196 Elm -New Rchll 10805 **Fx:**636-7146
(631) 232-1818 .. **Morrison,** Linda S '89 -350 Vets Mem'l Hwy -Commack 11725
(212) 825-1212 .. **Morrison Mahoney LLP** -17 State -NY 10004 **Fx:**825-1313
(212) 576-7000 .. **Morrison,** Marguerite '83 %NYLIM -51 Mad Av -NY 10010
(212) 818-0400 .. **Morrison,** Michl E '04 %M Wolk -515 Mad Av -NY 10022 **Fx:**818-0440
(212) 269-0927 .. **Morrison,** Neil R '91 (D'Amato & L,LLP) -2 World Fncl Ctr -NY 10281
(212) 364-5340 .. **Morrison,** Nina R '00 %Innocence Project -100 5th Av -NY 10011 **Fx:**364-5341
(585) 263-1000 .. **Morrison,** Patrice B '83 (Nixon P LLP) -1100 Clinton Sq -Rchstr 14604
(631) 724-7600 .. **Morrison,** Richd W '84 (Grundfast & M) -8 Manor Rd -Smithtwn 11787 **Fx:**724-7812
(212) 864-5520 .. **Morrison,** Ron '83 -230 W 105th -NY 10025
(212) 637-2691 .. **Morrison,** Ross E '95 %US Atty -86 Chmbrs -NY 10007
(212) 922-9700 .. **Morrison,** Susan '87 1st Amer Title -633 3rd Av -NY 10017 **Fx:**922-0881
(718) 720-7292 .. **Morrison,** Susan A '97 -28 Moody Pl -Staten Isl 10310 **Fx:**720-7292
(212) 790-4500 .. **Morrison,** Thos C '66 (Manatt P&P,LLP) -7 Times Sq -NY 10036
(518) 487-7600 .. **Morrison,** Timothy P '00 %Whiteman O&H LLP -1 Commerce Plz -Albany 12260
(212) 343-8000 .. **Morrison & Wagner** -49 W 38th -NY 10018 **Fx:**343-2621
(716) 847-8400 .. **Morrison-Taylor,** Paul '81 (Phillips L LLP) -3400 HSBC Ctr -Buffalo 14203
(212) 408-5100 .. **Morrisroe,** Garyowen P '83 (Chadbourne & P LLP) -30 Rckfllr Plz -NY 10112
(212) 588-0800 .. **Morrissey,** Barbara Zafonte '96 OfCnsl Frommer L&H LLP -745 5th Av -NY 10151
(516) 742-2500 .. **Morrissey,** Brian P '88 (Gallagher & F) -1050 Franklin Av -Gdn Cty 11530
(212) 857-8230 .. **Morrissey,** Colin F '97 (Baker MM&M,PC) -330 W 34th -NY 10001
(315) 342-7214 .. **Morrissey,** Craig S '97 %Rodak & K -55 W 2nd -Oswego 13126
(914) 271-0920 .. **Morrissey,** Eugene '49 (Steckler GM&M) -6 Cook Ln -Croton-On-Hud 10520 **Fx:**271-0942
(212) 779-3500 .. **Morrissey,** J Jos III '93 OfCnsl Morrissey & M,LLP -60 E 42nd -NY 10165 **Fx:**779-2995
(845) 256-0550 .. **Morrissey,** J Jos III '93 -243 Main -New Paltz 12561 **Fx:**256-0041
(212) 779-3500 .. **Morrissey,** James J Jr. '65 (Morrissey & M,LLP) -60 E 42nd -NY 10165 **Fx:**779-2995
(718) 335-5139 .. **Morrissey,** James M '76 -62-10 Woodside Av -Woodside 11377 **Fx:**335-0106
(716) 853-8471 .. **Morrissey,** James M '79 %Dept of Law -350 Main Pl Twr -Buffalo 14202 **Fx:**853-8571
(716) 854-3333 .. **Morrissey,** James T '77 -578 McKinley Pkwy -Buffalo 14220
(212) 792-9576 .. **Morrissey,** John J '78 %Aon Fncl Srvcs Grp -199 Water -NY 10038
(212) 574-1200 .. **Morrissey,** Jos M '04 %Seward & K LLP -1 Bttry Pk Plz -NY 10004
(718) 643-5760 .. **Morrissey,** Kevin R '91 %Hon M Schneier -360 Adams -Brklyn 11201

(212) 454-6890 .. **Morrissey,** Kim Hae Shil '01 Deutsche Asset Mgmt -345 Park Av -NY 10154
(914) 762-1260 .. **Morrissey,** Lauren Spector '87 -11 Watson Av Bx1455 -Ossining 10562 **Fx:**762-1260
(516) 333-9331 .. **Morrissey,** Michl R '94 -220 Westbury Av -Carle Pl 11514 **Fx:**333-9605
(212) 237-1000 .. **Morrissey,** Rachel A '06 %Windels ML&M,LLP -156 W 56th -NY 10019
(212) 510-0500 .. **Morrissey,** Richd C '88 %US Trustees Ofc -33 Whitehall -NY 10004 **Fx:**668-2255
(518) 271-7883 .. **Morrissey,** Richd T '95 -64 2nd -Troy 12180 **Fx:**271-7897
(212) 779-3500 .. **Morrissey,** Sabrina E '95 (Morrissey & M,LLP) -60 E 42nd -NY 10165 **Fx:**779-2995
(631) 859-0300 .. **Morrissey,** Wm E Jr. '90 (Zaklukiewicz P&M,LLP) -2701 Sunrise Hwy Bx389 -Islip Terr 11752
(212) 252-0300 .. **Morrissy,** John D '08 %Kagan LLLG&C,LLP -200 Mad Av -NY 10016
(212) 310-8000 .. **Morrissy,** Stuart A '01 %Weil G&M LLP -767 5th Av -NY 10153
(631) 852-2584 .. **Morro,** Frank Jr. '89 %Hon R Gazzillo -200 Center Dr -Rvrhead 11901 **Fx:**852-3854
(212) 753-5000 .. **Morron,** Kelly L '87 Cnsl Schiff H LLP -900 3rd Av -NY 10022
(631) 422-3901 .. **Morrone,** Jos A Jr. '81 -155 Farmngdl Rd -W Babylon 11704
(631) 852-1749 .. **Morrone,** Linda '81 Surrogates Ct Law Dept -320 Center Dr -Rvrhead 11901 **Fx:**852-1777
(516) 571-3800 .. **Morrone,** Melissa M '01 %DA -262 Old Cntry Rd -Mineola 11501 **Fx:**248-9479
(212) 754-8000 .. **Morrow,** Donna M '02 Morrow & Co -445 Park Av -NY 10022
(585) 428-5210 .. **Morrow,** Jeffery R '05 %Pub Def -10 N Fitzhugh -Rchstr 14614 **Fx:**428-2234
(212) 683-2210 .. **Morrow,** Kara E '03 %Childrens Rts Inc -330 7th Av -NY 10001 **Fx:**683-4015
(212) 474-3218 .. **Morrow,** Kiisha J B '03 Cravath S&M LLP -825 8th Av -NY 10019 **Fx:**474-3700
(212) 964-4140 .. **Morrow,** Leonard '61 -225 Bway -NY 10007
(716) 204-1105 .. **Morrow,** R Peter III '75 -455 Cayuga Rd -Buffalo 14225 **Fx:**204-1080
(212) 916-3773 .. **Morrow,** Rebecca O '78 Rabo Bank Intl -245 Park Av -NY 10167
(212) 593-7177 .. **Morrow,** Rizpah Ann '83 -233 Bway -NY 10279 **Fx:**732-1339
(212) 309-1000 .. **Morrow,** Robt J '83 (Hunton & W) -200 Park Av -NY 10166
(212) 292-5074 .. **Morrow,** T J '87 -2 Penn Plz -NY 10121
(518) 654-6540 .. **Morrow,** Todd W '00 -709 Main -Corinth 12822
(518) 891-7003 .. **Morrow,** Virginia James '95 -50 Kiwassa Rd -Saranac Lk 12983 **Fx:**891-6943
(914) 244-3100 .. **Morschhauser-Bosshart,** Karen A '85 -116 Radio Cir -Mt Kisco 10549 **Fx:**244-3242
(212) 992-8648 .. **Morse,** Adam H '03 Brennan Ctr for Justice -161 Av of Amer -NY 10013
(718) 720-4000 .. **Morse,** Andrea S '86 (Morse & M) -358 St Marks Pl -Staten Isl 10301 **Fx:**720-4172
(212) 724-3069 .. **Morse,** Barbara S '80 -201 W 86th -NY 10024
(212) 326-3939 .. **Morse,** Chas R A '98 (Jones D) -222 E 41st -NY 10017
(212) 969-2201 .. **Morse,** Christina A '03 %Alliance Bernstein LP -1345 Av of Amer -NY 10105 **Fx:**554-4639
(212) 237-8000 .. **Morse,** Christopher J '89 %John Jay Cllg -899 10th Av -NY 10019
(212) 490-3000 .. **Morse,** Danl J '01 %Wilson EME&D LLP -150 E 42nd -NY 10017
(212) 610-6300 .. **Morse,** Danl J '06 %Allen & O -1221 Av of Amer -NY 10020
(212) 536-3900 .. **Morse,** David Evan '81 (K&L Gates LLP) -599 Lex Av -NY 10022
(212) 661-9100 .. **Morse,** David W '84 (Otterbourg SH&R,PC) -230 Park Av -NY 10169
(212) 335-9263 .. **Morse,** Deborah L '81 %DA -1 Hogan Pl -NY 10013
(212) 651-2000 .. **Morse,** Elisabeth A '04 Oxygen Media LLC -75 9th Av -NY 10011
(212) 838-1177 .. **Morse,** Howard L '65 (Morse ZR&L LLP) 405 Park Av -NY 10022
(212) 230-8800 .. **Morse,** Jodie '07 %WilmerHale -399 Park Av -NY 10022
(315) 475-3127 .. **Morse,** Julie B '06 Leg Srvcs -472 S Salina -Syracuse 13202 **Fx:**475-2706
(516) 487-1446 .. **Morse,** Lester '50 (Morse & M,PLLC) -1400 Old Cntry Rd -Westbury 11590
(607) 734-2271 .. **Morse,** Lewis W Jr. '63 OfCnsl Sayles & E -1 W Church -Elmira 14901
(212) 878-8000 .. **Morse,** Mackenzie B '08 %Clifford C LLP -31 W 52nd -NY 10019
(716) 854-3861 .. **Morse,** Michl O '86 -534 Delaware Av -Buffalo 14202
(914) 747-4511 .. **Morse,** Robt C '74 -84 Pierce Dr -Plsntvll 10570
(212) 816-5871 .. **Morse,** Robt R '83 Citigroup -388 Greenwich -NY 10013
(212) 848-4000 .. **Morse,** Robt R Jr. '90 %Shearman & S LLP -599 Lex Av -NY 10022
(516) 487-1446 .. **Morse,** Steven A '82 (Morse & M,PLLC) -1400 Old Cntry Rd -Westbury 11590
(718) 720-4000 .. **Morse,** Thos K '83 (Morse & M) -358 St Marks Pl -Staten Isl 10301 **Fx:**720-4172
(212) 838-1177 .. **Morse Zelnick Rose & Lander LLP** -405 Park Av -NY 10022 **Fx:**838-9190
(212) 333-5552 .. **Morsellino,** John P '89 -340 W 57th -NY 10019
(212) 333-5552 .. **Morsellino,** Jos P '63 -340 W 57th -NY 10019 **Fx:**333-5553
(516) 759-4221 .. **Morsello,** Cara '87 -22 Meadow Ln -Glen Head 11545
(518) 438-9907 .. **Morss,** Elizabeth M '88 OfCnsl Young SWRB&M,LLC -5 Palisades Dr -Albany 12205
(212) 869-4646 .. **Mort,** Geoffrey A '87 Cnsl Kraus & Z LLP -500 5th Av -NY 10110
(518) 457-6137 .. **Mortati,** Julie '92 %State Police -1220 Wshngtn Av -Albany 12226 **Fx:**485-1164
(631) 368-1360 .. **Mortati,** Nicholas C J '94 -25 Fenimore Ln -Huntngtn 11743
(518) 862-1386 .. **Mortati,** Thos J '92 (Burke SM&H,LLP) -302 Wshngtn Av Ext Bx15085 -Albany 12212
(212) 909-6000 .. **Mortazavi,** Melissa D '06 %Debevoise & P LLP -919 3rd Av -NY 10022
(212) 425-7200 .. **Mortazavi,** Sheila '00 (Kenyon & K,LLP) -1 Bway -NY 10004
(646) 378-2192 .. **Mortensen,** Bradley J '82 (Christie PM&Y,PC) -5 Penn Plz -NY 10001
(212) 231-1820 .. **Mortensen,** Heidi Lee '95 Macquarie Holdings Inc -125 W 55th -NY 10019
(718) 250-2000 .. **Mortensen,** Hilda '91 %DA -350 Jay -Brklyn 11201 **Fx:**250-2314
(212) 687-6262 .. **Mortensen,** Philip S '73 (Barton B&P,LLP) -420 Lex Av -NY 10170
(646) 312-8791 .. **Mortenson,** Julian D '06 %Fordham Univ Sch of Law -140 W 62nd -NY 10023 **Fx:**(212) 636-6899
(212) 709-8073 .. **Morth,** Karen '90 -110 Wall 11th Fl -NY 10005
(212) 806-5400 .. **Mortimer,** Marianne S '06 %Stroock &S&L LLP -180 Maiden Ln -NY 10038
(914) 945-2789 .. **Mortinger,** Alison Douty '95 TJ Watson Resrch Ctr -Bx218 -Yorktwn Hts 10598
(917) 294-3907 .. **Mortinger,** Christian '98 Heinrich & Mortinger GMBH -1035 5th Av -NY 10028
(914) 766-3348 .. **Mortinger,** Stephen A '90 %IBM -Route 100 -Somers 10589
(516) 334-0583 .. **Mortis,** Doris E '70 -604 Powells Ln -Westbury 11590
(212) 669-8400 .. **Mortman,** Steven M '83 %DCAS-DLS -1 Centre -NY 10007 **Fx:**669-2139
(212) 530-5000 .. **Morton,** Andrew H '10 %Milbank TH&M LLP -1 Chase Manh Plz -NY 10005
(631) 761-7154 .. **Morton,** Christine E '00 Touro College of Law -255 Eastvw Dr -Central Islip 11722
(212) 848-4000 .. **Morton,** Jennifer Dill '08 %Shearman & S LLP -599 Lex Av -NY 10022
(212) 667-9300 .. **Morton,** Katherine M '06 Nomura Securities Intl -2 World Fncl Ctr -NY 10281
(212) 819-8200 .. **Morton,** Kellie M '07 %White & C LLP -1155 Av of Amer -NY 10036
(212) 813-8800 .. **Morton,** Larkin Moore '08 %Goodwin P LLP -620 8th Av -NY 10018
(212) 557-9600 .. **Morton,** Leonard P '95 -600 3rd Av -NY 10016 **Fx:**557-9610
(716) 432-2764 .. **Morton,** M Rogan '98 -21 Rugby Rd -Buffalo 14216
(212) 513-9300 .. **Morton,** Margaret Seay '91 NYC Dept of Cultural Affrs -31 Chmbrs -NY 10007
(716) 849-0701 .. **Morton,** Mathew J '08 %Lipsitz & P LLC -135 Delaware Av -Buffalo 14202
(716) 856-4200 .. **Morton,** Melissa M '08 %Gibson M&C,LLP -69 Delaware Av -Buffalo 14202
(718) 428-6388 .. **Morton,** Peter G '74 -39-09 Cpl Stone -Bayside 11361
(914) 286-3400 .. **Morton,** Roberta Elise '82 %Leg Aid -1 N Bway -White Plns 10601 **Fx:**682-4112
(518) 471-4803 .. **Morton,** Sean M '02 %Appllt Div 3rd Dept -Capitol Station Bx7288 -Albany 12224 **Fx:**471-4750
(212) 755-3100 .. **Morton,** Susan H '76 (Kaufmann GR&O LLP) -777 3rd Av -NY 10017
(212) 440-3933 .. **Morvay,** Lilian Adel '88 CNA Ins -40 Wall -NY 10005
(212) 856-9600 .. **Morvillo Abramowitz Grand Iason Anello & Bohrer, PC** -565 5th Av -NY 10017 **Fx:**856-9494
(212) 880-9495 .. **Morvillo,** Christopher J '93 (Morvillo AGIA&B,PC) -565 5th Av -NY 10017
(212) 880-9494 .. **Morvillo,** E Scott '98 Cnsl Morvillo AGIA&B,PC -565 5th Av -NY 10017
(212) 880-9435 .. **Morvillo,** Gregory R '03 Cnsl Morvillo AGIA&B,PC -565 5th Av -NY 10017
(516) 844-8800 .. **Morvillo,** Marialana M '88 Sleepys Inc -1000 S Oyster Bay Rd -Hicksvll 11801
(212) 856-9600 .. **Morvillo,** Robt C '09 Cnsl Morvillo AGIA&B,PC -565 5th Av -NY 10017
(212) 880-9400 .. **Morvillo,** Robt G '64 (Morvillo AGIA&B,PC) -565 5th Av -NY 10017
(646) 597-6386 .. **Morway,** Debra S '98 OfCnsl Curley & M LLP -5 Penn Plz -NY 10001 **Fx:**378-2232
(718) 243-0994 .. **Mosaku,** Adewale A '98 A Mosaku,PC -25 Bond -Brklyn 11201 **Fx:**243-9148
(845) 462-2700 .. **Mosbacher,** Stuart W '91 Cnsl DG Ellis -2076 South Rd -Poughkeepsie 12601 **Fx:**462-4895
(212) 521-3500 .. **Mosberg,** Michl A '98 (Aronson M&S, LLP) -485 Lex Av -NY 10017
(914) 899-3100 .. **Mosca,** Sharon A '07 %Mead HC&G -109 Spencer Pl -Mamaroneck 10543
(585) 383-7475 .. **Moscarelli,** J Beth '05 Paychex -911 Panorama Trl S -Rchstr 14625
(212) 541-2000 .. **Moscarello,** Erica L '01 Cnsl Bryan C LLP -1290 Av of Amer -NY 10104
(716) 852-3540 .. **Moscati,** John A Jr. '93 (Watson BCJ&S) -12 Fountain Plz -Buffalo 14202
(716) 843-5700 .. **Moscati,** Robt C '85 %US Atty -138 Delaware Av -Buffalo 14202 **Fx:**551-3052
(212) 696-6000 .. **Moscato,** Michl '82 (Curtis M-PC&M LLP) -101 Park Av -NY 10178
(212) 233-3800 .. **Moschella,** James M '97 (Karasyk & M,LLP) -225 Bway -NY 10007
(212) 688-8555 .. **Moschetta,** Francesca M '04 %Fragomen DB&L LLP -7 Hanover Sq -NY 10004
(646) 386-5700 .. **Moschetta,** Michl '82 %Civil Ct -111 Centre -NY 10013
(516) 229-6000 .. **Moschetti,** Guy A '96 %R Lau & Assoc -300 Jericho Quad Bx9040 -Jericho 11753 **Fx:**229-6167
(518) 785-4900 .. **Moschetti,** Peter J Jr. '85 (Anderson M&T,PLLC) -26 Century Hill Dr -Latham 12110
(212) 589-4200 .. **Moscow,** John '73 (Baker & H LLP) -45 Rckfllr Plz -NY 10111
(212) 701-3000 .. **Moscowitz,** Martha '09 %Cahill G&R LLP -80 Pine -NY 10005 **Fx:**269-5420
(212) 707-3020 .. **Moscowitz,** Todd E '97 Asylum Records -1290 Av of Amer -NY 10104
(516) 741-1717 .. **Mose,** Fredk P '74 (Hirsch B&M) -1225 Franklin Av -Gdn Cty 11530
(212) 341-2748 .. **Moseley-Jones,** Michele C '06 ACS -150 William -NY 10038
(315) 831-3581 .. **Moseman,** James W '76 (Kohn & M) -9580 Main Bx248 -Remsen 13438
(212) 621-6000 .. **Mosenkis,** Saml '94 %ASCAP -1 Lincoln Plz -NY 10023 **Fx:**787-1381
(212) 947-5770 .. **Mosenson,** Steven H '83 %Untd Cerebral Palsy -330 W 34th -NY 10001 **Fx:**594-4538
(212) 530-5000 .. **Moser,** Eric K '91 (Milbank TH&M LLP) -1 Chase Manh Plz -NY 10005
(212) 536-3900 .. **Moser,** Eric T '06 (K&L Gates LLP) -599 Lex Av -NY 10022
(212) 705-7749 .. **Moser,** Joel H '84 (Bingham M LLP) -399 Park Av -NY 10022 **Fx:**593-8972
(718) 390-5422 .. **Moser,** Kimberley Slade '91 %Civil Ct -927 Castleton Av -Staten Isl 10310 **Fx:**390-8108
(315) 376-5390 .. **Moser,** Leanne K '92 DA -7660 N State -Lowvll 13367 **Fx:**376-5873
(212) 294-6700 .. **Moser,** Michl A '95 (Winston & S) -200 Park Av -NY 10166
(718) 786-0300 .. **Moser,** Nathan F '79 %Natl Envelope Corp -29-10 Hunterspoint Av -LIC 11101
(212) 577-3284 .. **Moser,** Theresa B '97 %Leg Aid -199 Water -NY 10038 **Fx:**577-3520
(212) 685-7600 .. **Mosery,** Amy E '99 Heller H&F,PC -292 Mad Av -NY 10017

(212) 688-8555 .. **Moses,** Adam W '10 %Fragomen DB&L LLP -7 Hanover Sq -NY 10004
(315) 379-2269 .. **Moses,** Andrew S '91 Cnty Atty -48 Court -Canton 13617 **Fx:**379-2254
(212) 559-7206 .. **Moses,** Anne E '82 Citibank NA -425 Park Av -NY 10043 **Fx:**793-4400
(212) 880-9540 .. **Moses,** Barbara '94 (Morvillo AGIA&B,PC) -565 5th Av -NY 10017
(212) 373-3000 .. **Moses,** Bruce C '00 Paul WRW&G LLP -1285 Av of Amer -NY 10019
(914) 273-9445 .. **Moses,** Danl '84 -Bx799 -Armonk 10504
(914) 674-0913 .. **Moses,** Donald S '82 -11 Morningside Rd -Ardsley 10502
(315) 474-7571 .. **Moses,** Edw J '68 (Mackenzie H LLP) -101 S Salina Bx4967 -Syracuse 13221
(518) 810-6052 .. **Moses,** Gilah R '03 G Moses,PC -Bx9266 -Schnctdy 12309 **Fx:**393-0062
(718) 604-3925 .. **Moses,** Herbert J '93 HJ Moses,PC -1100 Lincoln Pl -Brklyn 11213
(212) 732-5800 .. **Moses,** I Bryce '95 (Friedman & M LLP) -233 Bway -NY 10279
(212) 403-1000 .. **Moses,** Jonathan M '97 (Wachtell LR&K) -51 W 52nd -NY 10019
(914) 993-0600 .. **Moses,** Jonathan S '93 (Keogh T&M) -1 N Bway -White Plns 10601 **Fx:**993-0251
(212) 736-2624 .. **Moses,** Manuel B '01 -236 W 26th -NY 10001
(212) 715-9100 .. **Moses,** Matthew B '07 %Kramer LN&F,LLP -1177 Av of Amer -NY 10036
(212) 373-3000 .. **Moses,** Matthew J '09 Paul WRW&G LLP -1285 Av of Amer -NY 10019
(212) 474-1000 .. **Moses,** Nicholas D '10 %Cravath S&M LLP -825 8th Av -NY 10019
(212) 354-0808 .. **Moses Preston & Ziegelman, LLP** -1065 Av of Amer -NY 10018 **Fx:**354-8429
(516) 741-6601 .. **Moses Preston & Ziegelman, LLP** -114 Old Cntry Rd -Mineola 11501
(315) 218-8352 .. **Moses,** Robt E '61 -1 Lincoln Ctr -Syracuse 13202 **Fx:**218-8100
(212) 354-0808 .. **Moses,** Robt H '90 (Moses P&Z,LLP) -1065 Av of Amer -NY 10018
(212) 292-3834 .. **Moses,** Robt J '93 %First Allied Securities -565 5th Av -NY 10017 **Fx:**697-2748
(212) 292-3834 .. **Moses,** Robt J '07 First Allied Sec -565 5th Av -NY 10017
(917) 519-2000 .. **Moses,** Scott I '02 -299 Park Av -NY 10171
(212) 554-7800 .. **Moses & Singer LLP** -405 Lex Av -NY 10174 **Fx:**554-7700
(716) 882-4890 .. **Mosey,** Acea M '95 (Mosey P,LLP) -625 Delaware Av -Buffalo 14202 **Fx:**882-5240
(212) 822-2268 .. **Moshan,** Michl J '96 (Gold SM PLLC) -134 Spring -NY 10012 **Fx:**966-2322
(212) 244-3333 .. **Moshe,** Michelle L '01 OfCnsl Donovan H LLP -1350 Bway -NY 10018
(212) 768-6700 .. **Moshe,** Mirella '04 %Sonnenschein N&R LLP -1221 Av of Amer -NY 10020
(516) 466-1100 .. **Moshell,** Susan Stein '78 %D Brownstein -98 Cutter Mill Rd -Gt Neck 11021 **Fx:**466-1286
(914) 995-5428 .. **Mosher,** Allison E '04 %Cnty Atty -148 Martine Av -White Plns 10601 **Fx:**995-5858
(315) 682-9880 .. **Mosher,** Barbara E '86 -Bx173 -Manlius 13104 **Fx:**682-0869
(212) 756-2000 .. **Mosher,** Donald J '92 (Schulte R&Z LLP) -919 3rd Av -NY 10022
(607) 535-6400 .. **Mosher,** Holly L '06 Pub Def -105 9th -Watkins Glen 14891 **Fx:**535-6404
(845) 758-8773 .. **Mosher,** Kelly J '85 -29 Grandmour Dr -Red Hook 12571 **Fx:**758-1503
(716) 285-9555 .. **Mosher,** Matthew T '05 %Viola C&L -770 Main Bx948 -Niagara Fls 14302
(607) 271-9262 .. **Moshier,** Kevin '82 %MHLS -100 Wshngtn -Elmira 14901
(914) 663-1131 .. **Mosiello,** Jodi A '99 Mosiello & M -15 S MacQuesten Pkwy -Mt Vernon 10550 **Fx:**663-1137
(716) 856-7800 .. **Moskal,** Paul M '80 FBI -1 FBI Plz -Buffalo 14202
(866) 348-5819 .. **Moskal,** Stanley A Jr. '54 %SSA-ODAR -50 Fountain Plz -Buffalo 14202 **Fx:**(716) 551-4078
(716) 984-2490 .. **Moskel,** Benjamin D '05 -108 Fishers Rd -Pittsfrd 14534
(212) 682-7474 .. **Moskin,** Jonathan E '84 (Foley & L LLP) -90 Park Av -NY 10016
(845) 354-1555 .. **Moskoff,** Miriam Federman '87 -12 Halley Dr -Pomona 10970
(212) 223-3562 .. **Moskovic,** Etan '07 %Turek RM LLP -377 5th Av -NY 10016
(516) 239-6382 .. **Moskovic,** Jeffrey '91 -73 Muriel Av -Lawrence 11559 **Fx:**239-7259
(212) 857-8230 .. **Moskovits,** Ronit Z '88 (Baker MM&M,PC) -330 W 34th -NY 10001
(212) 752-1206 .. **Moskovitz,** Stuart J '81 -15 Maiden Ln -NY 10038 **Fx:**(732) 431-0798
(212) 483-9490 .. **Moskow,** Robt S II '97 OfCnsl McElroy DM&C,LLP -88 Pine -NY 10005
(212) 294-6700 .. **Moskowitz,** Alan '10 %Winston & S -200 Park Av -NY 10166
(212) 401-3652 .. **Moskowitz,** Amy A '89 Royal Bank of Scotland -101 Park Av -NY 10178
(212) 221-7999 .. **Moskowitz,** Avraham C '81 (Moskowitz B&W,LLP) -345 7th Av -NY 10001
(212) 704-6000 .. **Moskowitz,** Bennet J '09 %Troutman S LLP -405 Lex Av -NY 10174
(212) 221-7999 .. **Moskowitz Book & Walsh, LLP** -345 7th Av -NY 10001 **Fx:**398-8835
(631) 608-4114 .. **Moskowitz,** Brian M '95 -532 Broadhllw Rd -Melvll 11747
(718) 969-7829 .. **Moskowitz,** Carole R '61 -182-16 80 Dr -Jamaica 11432
(212) 373-3331 .. **Moskowitz,** Dana L '00 -1285 Av of Amer -NY 10019 **Fx:**757-3990
(718) 812-8248 .. **Moskowitz,** Danl P '76 -15301 Jamaica Av -Jamaica 11432
(516) 569-5001 .. **Moskowitz,** Deena L '93 %Schonfeld & G,LLP -112 Spruce -Cedarhrst 11516
(212) 438-2000 .. **Moskowitz,** Dina J '88 %Standard & Poor's -55 Water -NY 10041
(212) 969-3000 .. **Moskowitz,** Ellen H '87 SrCnsl Proskauer R LLP -1585 Bway -NY 10036
(212) 333-3810 .. **Moskowitz,** Ellen M '89 (Brunswick Grp LLC) -140 W 45th -NY 10017 **Fx:**333-3811
(212) 450-4000 .. **Moskowitz,** Elliot '02 (Davis P&W LLP) -450 Lex Av -NY 10017
(212) 849-7000 .. **Moskowitz,** Eve Samara '06 %Quinn EU&S,LLP -51 Mad Av -NY 10010
(516) 560-6400 .. **Moskowitz,** Hani M '07 Leg Aid -1 Helen Keller Way -Hempstd 11550 **Fx:**565-3694
(212) 490-3000 .. **Moskowitz,** Harold J '65 (Wilson EME&D LLP) -150 E 42nd -NY 10017
(212) 759-9322 .. **Moskowitz,** Harvey D '60 -200 E 57th -NY 10022
(212) 753-5000 .. **Moskowitz,** Ivan W '74 (Schiff H LLP) -900 3rd Av -NY 10022
(212) 869-1990 .. **Moskowitz,** Jay S '81 %Fischer Inc -1212 Av of Amer -NY 10036 **Fx:**354-9775
(212) 223-4000 .. **Moskowitz,** Jonathan A '00 Cnsl Crowell & M LLP -590 Mad Av -NY 10022
(212) 506-5000 .. **Moskowitz,** Kara Fay '06 %Orrick H&S LLP -51 W 52nd -NY 10019
(212) 986-9700 .. **Moskowitz,** Keith M '89 (Eilenberg & K LLP) -11 E 44th -NY 10017
(212) 474-1000 .. **Moskowitz,** Lauren A '06 %Cravath S&M LLP -825 8th Av -NY 10019
(212) 670-0314 .. **Moskowitz,** Marla '01 Merrill Lynch -222 Bway -NY 10038
(212) 655-5000 .. **Moskowitz,** Martin J '88 (Gannon R&M) -120 Bway -NY 10271
(212) 889-7111 .. **Moskowitz,** Marvin '65 -9 E 40th -NY 10016 **Fx:**779-2365
(212) 382-0700 .. **Moskowitz,** Max '82 (Ostrolenk FG&S,LLP) -1180 Av of Amer -NY 10036
(845) 434-3162 .. **Moskowitz,** Melody '83 -Bx157 -Woodbourne 12788
(212) 684-7800 .. **Moskowitz,** Michl L '82 (Weltman & M,LLP) -270 Mad Av -NY 10016
(516) 931-4088 .. **Moskowitz,** Michl L '82 (Weltman & M,LLP) -575 Underhill Blvd -Syosset 11791
(212) 227-0430 .. **Moskowitz Passman & Edelman** -225 Bway -NY 10007 **Fx:**227-2278
(212) 679-1166 .. **Moskowitz,** Paul I '82 %The Lawyer's Travel Srvc -71 5th Av -NY 10003 **Fx:**448-0452
(212) 545-4000 .. **Moskowitz,** Peter C '91 (Jackson L LLP) -666 3rd Av -NY 10017
(212) 806-5400 .. **Moskowitz,** Ross F '85 (Stroock &S&L LLP) -180 Maiden Ln -NY 10038
(212) 530-5000 .. **Moskowitz,** Ruth A '10 %Milbank TH&M LLP -1 Chase Manh Plz -NY 10005
(212) 506-1700 .. **Moskowitz,** Seth A '98 (Kasowitz BT&F LLP) -1633 Bway -NY 10019
(212) 806-5400 .. **Moskowitz,** Steven P '92 (Stroock &S&L LLP) -180 Maiden Ln -NY 10038
(914) 499-6148 .. **Moskowitz,** Stuart S '82 IBM -1 New Orchrd Rd -Armonk 10504 **Fx:**765-7533
(516) 409-0769 .. **Moskowitz,** Stuart W '91 -2876 Merrick Rd -Bellmore 11710 **Fx:**221-1746
(212) 609-6800 .. **Moskowitz,** Theo D '91 SpclCnsl McCarter & E,LLP -245 Park Av -NY 10167
(212) 896-8600 .. **Moskowitz,** Wendy Finkel '82 %The Argo Corp -50 W 17th -NY 10011 **Fx:**896-8667
(212) 474-1000 .. **Mosley,** Danl L '82 (Cravath S&M LLP) -825 8th Av -NY 10019
(212) 631-7000 .. **Mosley,** Kevin L '87 (Shafran & M,PC) -350 5th Av -NY 10118
(212) 357-2510 .. **Mosley,** Michl S '89 Goldman Sachs -85 Broad -NY 10004
(845) 344-4855 .. **Moson,** Robt F '89 (Finkelstein & Prtnrs,LLP) -726 E Main -Middletwn 10940
(212) 837-6000 .. **Mosquera,** Dietmar Anthony '03 %Hughes H&R LLP -1 Bttry Pk Plz -NY 10004
(914) 333-0700 .. **Moss,** Adam M '08 %Snyder & S -94 Wht Plns Rd -Tarrytwn 10591 **Fx:**333-0743
(212) 209-3898 .. **Moss & Boris** -708 3rd Av -NY 10017 **Fx:**209-7108
(212) 257-6960 .. **Moss,** Cecilia Froelich '97 (Chaffetz L LLP) -1350 Av of Amer -NY 10019
(212) 655-3500 .. **Moss,** David G '00 %Meister S&F LLP -140 E 45th -NY 10017
(212) 566-6780 .. **Moss,** David L '96 (D Moss & Assoc) -15 Maiden Ln -NY 10038 **Fx:**766-3362
(212) 644-1000 .. **Moss,** Dena S '70 (Moss & M LLP) -220 5th Av -NY 10001 **Fx:**644-2590
(212) 417-4586 .. **Moss,** Devin E '76 NYS Ofc Medicaid Insp Gen -217 Bway -NY 10007 **Fx:**417-4259
(212) 644-1000 .. **Moss,** Donald C '71 (Moss & M LLP) -220 5th Av -NY 10001 **Fx:**644-2590
(212) 450-4000 .. **Moss,** Edw N '04 %Davis P&W LLP -450 Lex Av -NY 10017
(212) 267-1650 .. **Moss,** Edw R '73 %Fine O&A,LLP -39 Bway -NY 10006
(631) 981-9110 .. **Moss,** Francine H '79 (Judd & M,PC) -3505 Vets Mem'l Hwy -Ronkonkoma 11779 **Fx:**981-9004
(212) 765-2100 .. **Moss,** Franklin '79 (Spivak L LLP) -1700 Bway -NY 10019
(212) 867-4488 .. **Moss,** Gary N '76 (Moss & K) -122 E 42nd -NY 10168
(718) 268-0882 .. **Moss,** George E '73 -108-28 68th Dr -Frst Hlls 11375
(917) 543-4888 .. **Moss,** Glenn R '81 Moss Media -161 W 86th -NY 10024
(212) 246-2400 .. **Moss,** James A '74 (Balber PM&VDT,PC) -1370 Av of Amer -NY 10019
(212) 225-2000 .. **Moss,** Joel S '02 %Cleary GS&H -1 Lbrty Plz -NY 10006
(315) 673-2092 .. **Moss,** John A Jr. '71 (Moss & P) -8 W Main Bx195 -Marcellus 13108 **Fx:**673-9247
(516) 873-8000 .. **Moss,** John K '88 (Kroll M&K,LLP) -400 Grdn City Plz -Gdn Cty 11530
(212) 644-1000 .. **Moss,** John O C '03 (Moss & M LLP) -220 5th Av -NY 10001 **Fx:**644-2590
(212) 867-4488 .. **Moss & Kalish** -122 E 42nd -NY 10168 **Fx:**983-5276
(518) 861-6014 .. **Moss,** Kevin A '73 -462 Bond Rd -Altamont 12009 **Fx:**861-6014
(212) 715-9100 .. **Moss,** Kevin M '85 Cnsl Kramer LN&F,LLP -1177 Av of Amer -NY 10036
(212) 756-2000 .. **Moss,** Laurence M '97 (Schulte R&Z LLP) -919 3rd Av -NY 10022
(212) 228-5525 .. **Moss,** Lawr C '80 -41 Bleecker -NY 10012
(518) 846-7759 .. **Moss,** Marcia J '96 -9587 Route 9 -Chazy 12921
(212) 867-5800 .. **Moss,** Michele C '84 (Osler H&H LLP) -620 8th Av -NY 10018
(212) 594-5000 .. **Moss,** Naomi '09 %Togut S&S LLP -1 Penn Plz -NY 10119
(212) 506-5000 .. **Moss,** Patricia Quinn '87 (Orrick H&S LLP) -51 W 52nd -NY 10019
(585) 232-4090 .. **Moss,** Patti W '84 %Leg Aid -1 W Main -Rchstr 14614 **Fx:**232-2352
(212) 545-4000 .. **Moss,** Peter N '92 (Jackson L LLP) -666 3rd Av -NY 10017
(212) 715-9100 .. **Moss,** Richd L '90 SpclCnsl Kramer LN&F,LLP -1177 Av of Amer -NY 10036
(212) 209-3898 .. **Moss,** Robt J '58 (Moss & B) -708 3rd Av -NY 10017
(914) 478-7100 .. **Moss,** Ronald Scott '84 -93 Cochrane Av -Hastings-On-Hud 10706
(212) 572-4200 .. **Moss,** Sara E '75 Estee Lauder -767 5th Av -NY 10153 **Fx:**572-3989
(212) 317-1717 .. **Moss,** Susan M '95 (Chemtob MF&T LLP) -3 E 54th -NY 10022
(212) 421-4100 .. **Moss,** Tina Niehold '03 (Pryor C LLP) -7 Times Sq -NY 10036
(718) 848-8122 .. **Mossa,** Michl '02 -105-30 Crossbay Blvd -Ozone Pk 11417
(212) 417-2063 .. **Mossberg,** David A '08 Dept of State -123 William -NY 10038 **Fx:**417-5805
(212) 577-9710 .. **Mossberg,** Michl P '70 (White M,PLLP) -225 Bway -NY 10007 **Fx:**577-9715

(516) 921-2077 .. **Mosscrop,** Kimberly A '04 %M Angiulo & Assoc LLC -6800 Jericho Tpk -Syosset 11791 **Fx:**921-1223
(516) 228-3131 .. **Mosscrop,** Michl S '04 %Franklin G&C,PC -666 Old Cntry Rd -Gdn Cty 11530
(212) 451-3000 .. **Mosse,** David I '98 Trian Fund Mgmt,LP -280 Park Av -NY 10017 **Fx:**451-3216
(212) 696-6000 .. **Mosse,** Julia B '10 %Curtis M-PC&M LLP -101 Park Av -NY 10178
(212) 397-2000 .. **Mosse,** Richd H '73 -142 E 71st -NY 10021
(212) 935-5700 .. **Mossop,** W Brant '91 (Colucci & U) -218 E 50th -NY 10022
(914) 997-9181 .. **Most,** Carol W '93 (Most & K LLC) -222 Bloomingdale Rd -White Plns 10605 **Fx:**997-9180
(212) 695-8100 .. **Most,** Jack L '60 (Goetz F,LLP) -1 Penn Plz -NY 10119
(212) 725-2727 .. **Most,** Jordan F '97 %S Lobel,PC -9 E 40th -NY 10016 **Fx:**725-3910
(212) 806-5400 .. **Mostel,** Jon R '86 (Stroock &S&L LLP) -180 Maiden Ln -NY 10038
(718) 246-0863 .. **Mostofsky,** Steven Z '83 S Mostofsky,PC -26 Court -Brklyn 11242 **Fx:**855-2057
(516) 560-6400 .. **Moston,** Kent V '76 %Leg Aid -1 Helen Keller Way -Hempstd 11550 **Fx:**565-3694
(212) 788-0767 .. **Moston,** Rachel K '09 %Law Dept -100 Church -NY 10007 **Fx:**788-0367
(718) 389-8841 .. **Moszczynski,** Antoni '88 (Stevens & M) -835 Manh Av -Brklyn 11222
(212) 474-1000 .. **Moszkowski,** Melissa A '09 %Cravath S&M LLP -825 8th Av -NY 10019
(212) 587-9690 .. **Mota,** Gail '82 %J Samel & Partners -150 Bway -NY 10038 **Fx:**587-9673
(212) 806-5400 .. **Motelow,** Danielle S '06 %Stroock &S&L LLP -180 Maiden Ln -NY 10038
(212) 468-4800 .. **Motelson,** Glenn E '99 (Davis & G LLP) -1740 Bway -NY 10019
(212) 227-0430 .. **Motelson,** Jeffrey M '80 (Moskowitz P&E) -225 Bway -NY 10007
(718) 984-7077 .. **Motelson,** Michl J '93 -101 Tyrellan Av -Staten Isl 10309 **Fx:**984-7770
(212) 574-1200 .. **Mothersele,** Laura B '10 %Seward & K LLP -1 Bttry Pk Plz -NY 10004
(212) 399-3622 .. **Motherway,** Wm D '01 Tishman Rlty & Constrctn -666 5th Av -NY 10103 **Fx:**399-3657
(212) 450-4000 .. **Motley,** Warren '90 (Davis P&W LLP) -450 Lex Av -NY 10017
(212) 964-6611 .. **Motola,** David H '87 (Lester SK&D) -120 Bway -NY 10271
(914) 995-3617 .. **Motola,** Renee S '89 %Hon B Tolbert -111 Martin Luther King Blvd -White Plns 10601 **Fx:**285-4675
(212) 261-8000 .. **Mott,** Anna L '08 %Mendes & M,LLP -750 7th Av -NY 10019
(212) 701-3000 .. **Mott,** Christine L '08 %Cahill G&R LLP -80 Pine -NY 10005 **Fx:**269-5420
(585) 546-6448 .. **Mott,** Gregory J '73 (Davidson F LLP) -28 E Main -Rchstr 14614
(212) 661-3080 .. **Mott,** Hanno D '59 OfCnsl Rottenberg LR,PC -369 Lex Av -NY 10017
(631) 727-2180 .. **Mott,** Peter M '83 (Twomey LSKD&Q,LLP) -33 W 2nd Bx9398 -Rvrhead 11901
(518) 463-1183 .. **Mott,** Richd L '82 -600 Bway -Albany 12207 **Fx:**463-1480
(212) 791-7360 .. **Motta,** Anthony '80 -50 Bway -NY 10004
(518) 233-2444 .. **Motta,** Michele A '99 GE -260 Hudson Rvr Rd -Waterfrd 12188
(212) 530-5000 .. **Mottesi,** Marcelo A '95 (Milbank TH&M LLP) -1 Chase Manh Plz -NY 10005
(631) 581-1700 .. **Mottola,** Adam '05 %AP Mottola -137 Carleton Av -Islip Terr 11752 **Fx:**581-2798
(631) 581-1700 .. **Mottola,** Andrea Plavin '79 -137 Carleton Av -Islip Terr 11752 **Fx:**581-2798
(718) 250-2000 .. **Mottola,** Lawr G '09 %DA -350 Jay -Brklyn 11201 **Fx:**250-2314
(518) 374-3399 .. **Mottolese,** Maura C '92 (Higgins RB&C,PC) -1430 Balltown Rd -Niskayuna 12309
(212) 355-5200 .. **Motulsky,** John A '83 %Stonehill Invstmnt -110 E 59th -NY 10022 **Fx:**644-4264
(631) 653-5476 .. **Motz,** Kittric Daniels '80 -Bx131 -Quogue 11959
(212) 432-7419 .. **Motzenbecker,** Douglas E '02 (Podvey MCHC&C) -400 Park Av -NY 10022
(212) 556-2100 .. **Mouawad,** Caline '02 Cnsl King & S -1185 Av of Amer -NY 10036
(212) 259-8000 .. **Moubarak,** Danielle '09 %Dewey & L LLP -1301 Av of Amer -NY 10019
(212) 503-3500 .. **Moubarak,** Waleed A '99 Ziff Davis Media -28 E 28th -NY 10016
(212) 489-1400 .. **Mouchette,** Eric D '10 %Bickel & B -767 5th Av -NY 10153
(212) 940-8800 .. **Mouhadeb,** Raymond '04 %Katten MR LLP -575 Mad Av -NY 10022
(212) 355-6182 .. **Moukad,** Rosemary '81 %EP Dine Inc -115 E 57th -NY 10022 **Fx:**755-8486
(212) 820-7700 .. **Moukides,** Maria '97 OfCnsl Boundas SW&B,LLC -1 Bttry Pk Plz -NY 10004
(315) 449-2616 .. **Mould,** George F '76 Martin GBM&C,PC -5790 Widewaters Pkwy -DeWitt 13214
(212) 537-3035 .. **Moulin,** A Edw III '81 Morgan Stanley -1633 Bway -NY 10019 **Fx:**(646) 519-5480
(718) 545-2600 .. **Moulinos,** Andrew '86 -23-52 31st -Astoria 11105
(212) 832-5981 .. **Moulinos,** Peter '95 (Moulinos & Assoc LLC) -445 Park Av -NY 10022 **Fx:**832-5982
(646) 571-3676 .. **Moulon,** Marcia B '09 MB Moulon,PC -11 Bway -NY 10004
(212) 863-6300 .. **Moulterie,** Ulysses T '95 %HPD -100 Gold -NY 10038 **Fx:**863-8201
(212) 804-4200 .. **Mound Cotton Wollan & Greengrass** -One Bttry Pk Plz -NY 10004 **Fx:**344-8066
(518) 641-0500 .. **Mountain,** Gregory A '00 (West Firm,PLLC) -677 Bway -Albany 12207 **Fx:**615-1500
(716) 373-3363 .. **Mountain,** Robt E Jr. '72 (Mountain & S) -70 W Main Bx99 -Allegany 14706 **Fx:**372-3251
(212) 450-4000 .. **Mountainspring,** Elisabeth K '08 %Davis P&W LLP -450 Lex Av -NY 10017
(212) 506-5000 .. **Mountainspring,** Orion '07 %Orrick H&S LLP -51 W 52nd -NY 10019
(914) 777-1134 .. **Mountanos,** Gus '98 (Ingerman S LLP) -550 Mamaroneck Av -Harrison 10528
(212) 849-7000 .. **Mount-Namson,** Zena '09 %Quinn EU&S,LLP -51 Mad Av -NY 10010
(914) 682-8100 .. **Mountroukas,** Dino J '90 -111 N Central Av -Hartsdale 10530 **Fx:**686-1043
(212) 504-6000 .. **Mourning,** Paul W '84 (Cadwalader W&T LLP) -1 World Fncl Ctr -NY 10281
(631) 273-8822 .. **Mouscardy,** Lisa R '97 %NYS United Teachers -150 Motor Pkwy -Hauppauge 11788
(212) 506-5000 .. **Moussa,** Rhanda K '97 %Orrick H&S LLP -51 W 52nd -NY 10019
(212) 349-6009 .. **Moussavian,** Avideh '02 %Sanctuary for Families -110 Wall -NY 10005 **Fx:**566-0344
(518) 447-7372 .. **Mousseau,** Carly Murnane '06 Cnty DCYF -112 State -Albany 12207
(212) 872-1000 .. **Mousserie,** Sharon '00 -One Bryant Park -NY 10036 **Fx:**872-1002
(212) 809-7800 .. **Moussourakis,** Jason W '08 %Jaffe & K,LLP -40 Wall -NY 10005
(631) 853-4161 .. **Moustakas,** Spiros A '04 %DA -N Cnty Cmplx Bldg 77 -Hauppauge 11788 **Fx:**853-4192
(212) 909-6000 .. **Moustakis,** Caroline H '00 %Debevoise & P LLP -919 3rd Av -NY 10022
(212) 336-0542 .. **Moustakis,** Philip R '00 %SEC -3 World Fncl Ctr -NY 10281 **Fx:**336-1323
(718) 250-2000 .. **Moustapha,** Donna '07 %DA -350 Jay -Brklyn 11201 **Fx:**250-2314
(212) 742-8700 .. **Moutal,** Sara J '04 %Garson D&C LLP -110 Wall -NY 10005
(212) 788-8681 .. **Mouton,** Gregory P '09 %Law Dept -100 Church -NY 10007 **Fx:**788-0367
(212) 704-1362 .. **Moutsatsos,** Maria P '96 Interpublic Grp -1114 Av of Amer -NY 10036 **Fx:**704-1201
(212) 848-4000 .. **Mouynes,** Erika A '06 %Shearman & S LLP -599 Lex Av -NY 10022
(212) 506-5000 .. **Mouzakis,** Mache M '06 %Orrick H&S LLP -51 W 52nd -NY 10019
(516) 542-5900 .. **Mouzakitis,** Michl '04 %Congdon FORDT&F -333 Earle Ovngton Blvd -Uniondale 11553
(212) 309-8100 .. **Mouzon,** Danl G '92 %Lexis/Nexis -125 Park Av -NY 10017 **Fx:**309-8187
(212) 728-8000 .. **Movafaghi,** Matthew A J '10 %Willkie F&G LLP -787 7th Av -NY 10019
(917) 637-3628 .. **Movahed,** Michelle Pallak '07 %Ctr for Reproductive Rts -120 Wall -NY 10005 **Fx:**637-3666
(718) 590-7806 .. **Movasseghi,** Pashan '05 ACS -900 Sheridan Av -Bronx 10451
(212) 285-3300 .. **Moverman,** Thos J '79 (Lipsig SM&M,PC) -40 Fulton -NY 10038
(212) 509-3900 .. **Movit,** Jeffrey M '04 %Mitchell S&K LLP -12 E 49th -NY 10017
(718) 990-5650 .. **Movsesian,** Mark L '89 St John's Law Schl -8000 Utopia Pkwy -Jamaica 11439 **Fx:**591-1855
(212) 446-4800 .. **Movsovich,** Michl '93 (Kirkland & E LLP) -153 E 53rd -NY 10022
(646) 471-8757 .. **Movtady,** Gisoo '08 PricewaterhouseCoopers -300 Mad Av -NY 10017
(585) 423-3286 .. **Mowry,** David R '00 %Xerox -100 Clinton Av S -Rchstr 14644
(315) 963-7266 .. **Mowry,** John Michl '65 Mowry & M -Main Bx310 -Mexico 13114 **Fx:**963-7268
(716) 433-1344 .. **Moxham,** Walter E Jr. '74 (Miskell & M) -280 East Av Bx464 -Lockprt 14095
(212) 687-1980 .. **Moxley,** Chas J Jr. '69 OfCnsl Kaplan F&K LLP -850 3rd Av -NY 10022
(212) 661-6194 .. **Moxley,** Danny C '05 NYS Ct of Appeals -230 Park Av -NY 10169
(516) 488-6100 .. **Moy,** Donald R '78 Medical Society -865 Merrick Av Bx9007 -Westbury 11590 **Fx:**488-8389
(212) 245-1000 .. **Moy,** Laurence S '86 (Outten & G LLP) -3 Park Av -NY 10016
(518) 462-6765 .. **Moy,** Lillian M '97 %Leg Aid -55 Colvin Av -Albany 12206 **Fx:**427-8352
(212) 708-1800 .. **Moy,** Mary A '91 (Ladas & P) -26 W 61st -NY 10023
(718) 630-7000 .. **Moy,** Ping C '85 Lutheran Med Ctr -150 55th -Brklyn 11220
(212) 696-2116 .. **Moy,** Robt B '89 (Bennett & M LLP) -575 Lex Av -NY 10022 **Fx:**696-2115
(212) 925-7700 .. **Moy,** Robt J '93 -168 Canal -NY 10013 **Fx:**334-9418
(212) 244-2999 .. **Moy,** Selma '94 (Kopff N&D LLP) -440 9th Av -NY 10001
(212) 325-2000 .. **Moy,** Wm T '88 Credit Suisse -1 Mad Av -NY 10010
(516) 358-7200 .. **Moyal,** Douglas D '94 (Mavrides M & Assoc,LLP) -3000 Marcus Av -Lk Success 11042 **Fx:**358-7250
(212) 224-6424 .. **Moyer,** Connie L '89 %Apple Bk -122 E 42nd -NY 10168
(716) 284-0119 .. **Moyer,** George S '64 -Bx253 -Niagara Fls 14305
(518) 486-1336 .. **Moyer,** Leslie J '93 %Dept of Health -Corning Twr 24th Fl -Albany 12237 **Fx:**486-4834
(585) 458-2800 .. **Moyer Russi & Randall, PC** -2300 W Ridge Rd -Rchstr 14626 **Fx:**368-9703
(585) 458-2800 .. **Moyer,** Vincent M '87 (Moyer R&R,PC) -2300 W Ridge Rd -Rchstr 14626
(718) 788-7850 .. **Moylan,** Richd J '86 Green-Wood Cemetery -500 25th -Brklyn 11232 **Fx:**788-7782
(212) 210-9454 .. **Moyle,** James F '92 (Alston & B LLP) -90 Park Av -NY 10016
(212) 506-5000 .. **Moyle,** Robt B '06 %Orrick H&S LLP -51 W 52nd -NY 10019
(212) 316-6000 .. **Moyles,** Philip V '61 -720 West End Av -NY 10025
(646) 386-3255 .. **Moyne,** Nicholas W '99 Hon M Diamond -60 Centre -NY 10007
(212) 637-2510 .. **Moyne,** Parvin D '03 US Atty -1 St Andrews Plz -NY 10007
(585) 263-6760 .. **Moynihan,** Chas E '00 %US Atty -620 Fed Bldg -Rchstr 14614 **Fx:**263-6226
(518) 457-6137 .. **Moynihan,** Danl S '95 %State Police -1220 Wshngtn Av -Albany 12226 **Fx:**485-1164
(718) 474-5155 .. **Moynihan,** Dennis J '87 -431 Beach 125th -Rckwy Pk 11694
(518) 388-4364 .. **Moynihan,** Edw C III '86 %DA -612 State -Schnctdy 12305 **Fx:**388-4569
(585) 753-4500 .. **Moynihan,** Holly L '98 %DA -832 Watts Bldg -Rchstr 14614 **Fx:**753-4576
(315) 424-4944 .. **Moynihan,** Kenneth M '95 -120 E Wshngtn -Syracuse 13202 **Fx:**424-8014
(212) 670-0218 .. **Moynihan,** Kevin J '84 %Merrill Lynch -222 Bway -NY 10038
(518) 346-4291 .. **Moynihan,** Neil W '55 (Moynihan H&M) -704 Union -Schnctdy 12305 **Fx:**346-4292
(914) 949-6996 .. **Moynihan,** Patrick J '64 (Penino & M,LLP) -180 E Post Rd -White Plns 10601
(212) 964-5570 .. **Moynihan,** Peter T '85 %Sacks & S -150 Bway -NY 10038 **Fx:**349-2141
(212) 935-6020 .. **Moynihan,** Sean A '89 (Klein ZR LLP) -485 Mad Av -NY 10022
(212) 728-8000 .. **Moyseyenko,** Irene '01 %Willkie F&G LLP -787 7th Av -NY 10019
(516) 741-0003 .. **Moza,** Meir '97 -217 Willis Av -Mineola 11501 **Fx:**741-0033
(212) 512-1000 .. **Mozarsky,** Peter '87 %HBO -1100 Av of Amer -NY 10036 **Fx:**512-1986
(516) 562-5703 .. **Mozarsky,** Scott M '94 %CMP Media LLC -600 Community Dr -Manhsst 11030 **Fx:**562-7123

(315) 266-6100 .. **Mozden,** Martha S '83 %Pub Def -235 Elizabeth -Utica 13501 **Fx:**266-6105
(845) 362-6951 .. **Mozes,** Ted T '91 -16 Gladwyne Ct -Spg Vly 10977 **Fx:**362-6785
(212) 450-4000 .. **Mparadzi,** Andrea S '09 %Davis P&W LLP -450 Lex Av -NY 10017
(718) 928-3700 .. **Mpi,** Oroma '08 %LSNYC-Bronx -579 Courtlandt Av -Bronx 10451 **Fx:**402-7586
(518) 218-7580 .. **Mraz,** Mary J '89 -3 Wembley Ct -Albany 12205 **Fx:**218-7586
(212) 237-0000 .. **Mrazik,** David M '05 %Vinson & E LLP -666 5th Av -NY 10103
(914) 765-3923 .. **Mrosek,** Wendy E '85 %MBIA Ins Corp -113 King -Armonk 10504
(212) 683-0010 .. **Mrsich,** John Michl '96 (Taylor & M,LLP) -305 Mad Av -NY 10165
(212) 705-7000 .. **Muaddi,** Jawad B '08 %Bingham M LLP -399 Park Av -NY 10022
(212) 845-2344 .. **Muallem,** Jos '05 -62 William -NY 10005
(212) 374-6774 .. **Muallem,** Victor E '96 NYC Dept Educ -49-51 Chmbrs -NY 10007
(716) 566-1300 .. **Mucci,** Gary L '72 OfCnsl Hiscock & B,LLP -1100 M&T Ctr -Buffalo 14203
(607) 772-8440 .. **Mucci,** Michl J II '96 %R Perot -20-24 Wall -Bnghmtn 13901 **Fx:**772-8339
(212) 598-8000 .. **Mucci,** Michele A '96 %Guardian Life Ins -7 Hanover Sq -NY 10004 **Fx:**919-2693
(212) 344-5680 .. **Muccia,** Jos W '74 (Thompson H LLP) -335 Mad Av -NY 10017
(212) 440-2327 .. **Muccifori,** John C '98 CNA -40 Wall -NY 10005
(212) 482-0007 .. **Muccigrosso,** Mark R '94 (Talkin M&R,LLP) -40 Exch Pl -NY 10005 **Fx:**482-1303
(212) 231-8132 .. **Muccini,** Edw J '91 (Sacks & M LLC) -410 Park Av -NY 10022
(914) 765-1900 .. **Muccio,** Gina M '09 IBM -1 New Orchrd Rd -Armonk 10504 **Fx:**765-7533
(716) 856-4000 .. **Mucha,** Jennifer A '08 %Hodgson R LLP -140 Pearl -Buffalo 14202
(631) 467-1340 .. **Mucha,** Jos A '00 -622 Hawkins Av -Lk Ronkonkoma 11779 **Fx:**467-1930
(716) 851-7190 .. **Mucha,** Teresa J '96 %DEC -270 Mich Av -Buffalo 14203 **Fx:**851-7211
(516) 498-1000 .. **Muchmore,** Andrew M '09 %Hollander & S,LLP -40 Cuttermill Rd -Gt Neck 11021
(212) 315-5575 .. **Muchnick Golieb & Golieb,PC** -200 Park Av S -NY 10003 **Fx:**977-5133
(212) 315-5575 .. **Muchnick,** Howard W '70 (Muchnick G&G,PC) -200 Park Av S -NY 10003
(716) 857-7991 .. **Mucilli,** Antoinetta D '00 %Natl Fuel Gas -6363 Main -Williamsvll 14221 **Fx:**857-7614
(585) 454-5650 .. **Muck,** Timothy C '03 %Lacy K LLP -130 E Main -Rchstr 14604
(716) 681-7190 .. **Mucklewee,** James M '79 (Brown C LLP) -5775 Bway -Lancaster 14086
(718) 261-3400 .. **Mudd,** Robt F '73 -125-10 Qns Blvd -Kew Gdns 11415 **Fx:**261-5969
(845) 677-8342 .. **Mudge,** G A '70 -123 Kennel Rd -Wassaic 12592 **Fx:**677-4169
(212) 373-3000 .. **Mudho,** Sarah A '02 %Paul WRW&G LLP -1285 Av of Amer -NY 10019
(212) 793-7855 .. **Mudick,** Stephanie B '82 %Citigroup -153 E 53rd -NY 10043
(585) 232-6500 .. **Mudrick,** Benjamin E '08 %Harter S&E LLP -1600 Bausch & Lomb Pl -Rchstr 14604
(585) 394-0564 .. **Muehe,** Martin E '79 (Muehe & N,LLP) -48 N Main -Canandaigua 14424 **Fx:**396-9678
(607) 547-4249 .. **Muehl,** John M '96 DA -197 Main -Cooperstwn 13326 **Fx:**547-4373
(212) 272-2547 .. **Muehlgay,** Jeffrey L '95 %JP Morgan Chase -383 Mad Av -NY 10179
(212) 756-2000 .. **Muehlhausen,** Amanda J '09 %Schulte R&Z LLP -919 3rd Av -NY 10022
(212) 261-8000 .. **Mueller,** Alexander J '01 %Mendes & M,LLP -750 7th Av -NY 10019
(212) 974-7474 .. **Mueller,** Alexis N '07 %Cowan DA&S LLP -41 Mad Av -NY 10010
(914) 948-9864 .. **Mueller,** Anne R '86 -26 High Ridge Rd -West Harrison 10604 **Fx:**948-8998
(212) 640-2000 .. **Mueller,** Arthur C '98 Amer Exp -200 Vesey -NY 10285
(212) 227-8150 .. **Mueller,** Gary J '80 (Treacy SM&M) -111 Bway -NY 10006
(212) 268-5136 .. **Mueller,** Geoffrey D '07 %Harwood L -350 5th Av -NY 10118
(212) 995-5445 .. **Mueller,** Gregory K '93 (Lebson & M,PC) -381 Park Av S -NY 10016
(716) 853-1616 .. **Mueller,** John A '09 %Harter S&E LLP -12 Fountain Plz -Buffalo 14202
(212) 373-3000 .. **Mueller,** Jos D '09 Paul WRW&G LLP -1285 Av of Amer -NY 10019
(716) 645-3176 .. **Mueller,** Lisa M '93 %Buffalo Schl of Law -417 O'Brian Hall -Buffalo 14260 **Fx:**645-5940
(212) 858-1000 .. **Mueller,** Michl J '08 %Pillsbury WSP LLP -1540 Bway -NY 10036
(212) 649-5600 .. **Mueller,** Paula J '74 %Rockefeller & Co,Inc -30 Rckfllr Plz -NY 10112 **Fx:**649-5977
(518) 388-4364 .. **Mueller,** Philip W '90 %DA -612 State -Schnctdy 12305 **Fx:**388-4569
(212) 244-4664 .. **Mueller,** Roberta L '01 %NY Lawyers Pub Intrst -151 W 30th -NY 10001 **Fx:**244-4570
(212) 468-8000 .. **Mueller,** Thos M '87 (Morrison & F LLP) -1290 Av of Amer -NY 10104
(212) 425-5005 .. **Mueller,** Wm F '80 (Clemente M&T,PA) -14 Wall -NY 10005
(212) 326-3939 .. **Muenkel,** Jonathan A '02 %Jones D -222 E 41st -NY 10017
(716) 854-1300 .. **Muenkel,** Jos P '71 (Rosenthal S&M,LLP) -300 Main -Buffalo 14202
(212) 839-5300 .. **Muenz,** Jonathan W '09 %Sidley A LLP -787 7th Av -NY 10019
(212) 888-3033 .. **Muffly,** Robt C '83 (Becker GM&M LLP) -299 Park Av -NY 10171
(212) 969-3000 .. **Mufson,** Harris '07 %Proskauer R LLP -1585 Bway -NY 10036
(212) 335-4500 .. **Mugabi,** Frank I '04 %DLA Piper LLP -1251 Av of Amer -NY 10020
(212) 637-3108 .. **Mugdan,** Walter E '82 %EPA -290 Bway -NY 10007 **Fx:**637-3096
(716) 856-4000 .. **Mugel,** Jonathan A '91 (Hodgson R LLP) -140 Pearl -Buffalo 14202
(716) 446-2213 .. **Mugel,** Richd L '90 Williams Advanced Materials -2978 Main -Buffalo 14214
(716) 857-7991 .. **Mugel,** Sarah J '92 %Natl Fuel Gas -6363 Main -Williamsvll 14221 **Fx:**857-7614
(716) 667-9700 .. **Muggia,** Frank C '98 (F Muggia & Assoc,PLLC) -6438 W Quaker -Orchard Pk 14127 **Fx:**667-9711
(212) 909-6000 .. **Mughal,** Irfan '08 %Debevoise & P LLP -919 3rd Av -NY 10022
(518) 474-7403 .. **Mugno,** Cheryl A '84 %NYS OPWDD -44 Holland Av -Albany 12229 **Fx:**474-7382
(212) 925-3474 .. **Mugno,** John R '91 -350 Bway -NY 10013 **Fx:**925-3665
(718) 286-6000 .. **Muhammad-Starling,** Khadijah '88 %DA -125-01 Qns Blvd -Kew Gdns 11415
(212) 290-4700 .. **MuhammedAlly,** Sahr '03 %Human Rights Watch -350 5th Av -NY 10118 **Fx:**736-1300
(212) 446-4800 .. **Muheim,** Philipp M '08 %Kirkland & E LLP -153 E 53rd -NY 10022
(716) 633-3200 .. **Muhlbauer,** Deborah J '92 (Bluestein & M,PC) -333 Intl Dr -Williamsvll 14221
(212) 641-3890 .. **Muhlbaum,** Carin F '89 Schroder Invstmnt Mgmt -875 3rd Av -NY 10022
(212) 972-9600 .. **Muhlstock,** Arthur C '59 -10 E 40th -NY 10016 **Fx:**972-9605
(516) 294-5433 .. **Muhlstock,** Gary P '87 (Ahmuty D&M) -200 IU Willets Rd -Albertson 11507
(516) 466-6500 .. **Muhlstock,** Melanie Haberman '98 Cnsl Parker WA LLP -6 Hrbr Park Dr S -Pt Wash 11050
(212) 297-5800 .. **Muhlstock,** Steven A '01 %Day P LLP -7 Times Sq -NY 10036
(516) 741-4799 .. **Muhlstock,** Todd D '97 (Baker SBGFM&N,LLC) -100 Grdn City Plz -Gdn Cty 11530
(646) 392-9250 .. **Mui,** Kwok Lai '89 %M Klein & Assoc -200 Mad Av -NY 10016 **Fx:**(212) 779-1499
(212) 702-9000 .. **Mui,** Michl H '04 %Sack & S -110 E 59th -NY 10022 **Fx:**702-9702
(212) 336-0138 .. **Mui,** Sheldon '00 %SEC -3 World Fncl Ctr -NY 10281 **Fx:**336-1323
(518) 474-7330 .. **Muia,** Jos Jr. '80 %Dept of Law -The Cptl -Albany 12224
(212) 264-4036 .. **Muir,** Bonnie E '94 Social Security Admin -26 Fed Plz -NY 10278
(347) 592-2244 .. **Muir,** Maurice E '98 Leg Srvcs -89-00 Sutphin Blvd -Jamaica 11435 **Fx:**592-2244
(212) 458-1912 .. **Muir,** Robt '87 %AIG Tech Srvcs -175 Water -NY 10038
(212) 759-0900 .. **Muirhead,** Sophia A '93 Conference Board,Inc -845 3rd Av -NY 10022 **Fx:**980-7014
(716) 854-1400 .. **Mujahid-Moore,** Andrea A '94 %HOME,Inc -700 Main -Buffalo 14202 **Fx:**854-1140
(212) 848-4000 .. **Mujalovic,** Ilir '04 %Shearman & S LLP -599 Lex Av -NY 10022
(212) 837-3616 .. **Mukamal,** Adam S '99 JP Morgan Chase -530 5th Av -NY 10036
(212) 906-1200 .. **Mukamal,** Betsy J '02 OfCnsl Latham & W -885 3rd Av -NY 10022
(212) 484-1327 .. **Mukamal,** Deborah A '99 John Jay Cllg -555 W 57th -NY 10019
(212) 686-3838 .. **Mukamal,** Steven S '66 OfCnsl Barst M&K LLP -2 Park Av -NY 10016
(212) 705-5085 .. **Mukamal,** Thos S '01 Island Global Yachting -717 5th Av -NY 10022
(646) 602-5600 .. **Mukarji-Connolly,** Anya '03 Urban Justice Ctr -123 William -NY 10038 **Fx:**(212) 533-4598
(212) 508-6100 .. **Mukasey,** Marc L S '94 (Bracewell & G,LLP) -1251 Av of Amer -NY 10020
(212) 909-6000 .. **Mukasey,** Michl B '67 (Debevoise & P LLP) -919 3rd Av -NY 10022
(212) 210-9501 .. **Mukerjee,** Deepro R '02 (Alston & B LLP) -90 Park Av -NY 10016
(914) 946-4777 .. **Mukerji,** Deepankar '96 OfCnsl Keane & B,PC -445 Hmltn Av -White Plns 10601
(212) 705-7000 .. **Mukherjee,** Siddhartha K '08 %Bingham M LLP -399 Park Av -NY 10022
(212) 225-2000 .. **Mukhi,** Rahul '06 %Cleary GS&H -1 Lbrty Plz -NY 10006
(212) 878-8000 .. **Mukundan,** Anisha '08 %Clifford C LLP -31 W 52nd -NY 10019
(212) 909-2543 .. **Mularadelis,** Chris '94 Cnsl Unison Site Mgmt -340 Mad Av -NY 10173 **Fx:**755-4080
(646) 728-4109 .. **Mulcahy,** Anne Marie '04 KIND -767 5th Av -NY 10153
(212) 653-8700 .. **Mulcahy,** Benjamin R '06 (Sheppard MR&H LLP) -30 Rckfllr Plz -NY 10112
(212) 483-0105 .. **Mulcahy,** Conor T '06 %Coughlin D LLP -88 Pine-Wall St Plz -NY 10005
(212) 504-6000 .. **Mulcahy,** Danl J '72 SrCnsl Cadwalader W&T LLP -1 World Fncl Ctr -NY 10281
(212) 267-1900 .. **Mulcahy,** John '79 (Wade CM) -111 Bway -NY 10006
(212) 600-1868 .. **Mulcahy,** Rachel I '00 -2444 Bway -NY 10024
(212) 458-1941 .. **Mulcahy,** Richd P '03 AIG -175 Water -NY 10038 **Fx:**602-0069
(212) 506-2500 .. **Mulcare,** Monique J '92 %Mayer B LLP -1675 Bway -NY 10019
(212) 309-1136 .. **Mulder,** Bradford C '96 -150 Joralemon -Brklyn 11201 **Fx:**309-1100
(845) 294-7287 .. **Mulder,** Dawn M '99 %MHLS -5 Coates Dr -Goshen 10924 **Fx:**294-6389
(518) 792-7355 .. **Mulder,** Delwyn J '77 -1 South Wstrn Plz -Glens Fls 12801 **Fx:**793-1924
(212) 599-5799 .. **Mulderig,** L Diana '02 %Rutherford & C LLP -369 Lex Av -NY 10017
(518) 458-2705 .. **Mulderry,** Francis P '58 -125 Wolf Rd -Albany 12205
(845) 638-5341 .. **Muldoon,** Bruce A '79 Hon W Nelson -1 S Main -New Cty 10956 **Fx:**708-7236
(585) 262-5130 .. **Muldoon,** Gary '77 (Muldoon & G) -144 Exchange Blvd -Rchstr 14614
(585) 262-5130 .. **Muldoon & Getz** -144 Exchange Blvd -Rchstr 14614 **Fx:**262-3474
(914) 636-5051 .. **Muldoon Horgan & Loughman** -271 North Av -New Rchll 10801 **Fx:**636-5082
(315) 425-9000 .. **Muldoon,** James R '93 (Marjama MB&S LLP) -250 S Clinton -Syracuse 13202
(516) 671-5208 .. **Muldoon,** Jos W '53 -1 Schl -Glen Cove 11542 **Fx:**759-5516
(315) 253-4050 .. **Muldoon,** Ryan J '09 %Williams HM&B -11 Court -Auburn 13021 **Fx:**253-4223
(914) 946-1030 .. **Muldoon,** Thos E '98 %Barry M&M -55 Church -White Plns 10601
(518) 481-5000 .. **Muldowney,** John J '89 (Fischer B&M) -Cntry Clb Rd Bx420 -Malone 12953
(212) 940-8800 .. **Muldrew,** Brian L '06 %Katten MR LLP -575 Mad Av -NY 10022
(212) 872-1000 .. **Muldrow,** Ackneil M III '98 -One Bryant Park -NY 10036 **Fx:**872-1002
(646) 386-3500 .. **Mule,** Barbara M '88 %OCA -25 Beaver -NY 10004 **Fx:**(212) 748-5085
(631) 858-5800 .. **Mulé,** Jos A '75 (Reilly & M PLLC) -201 Moreland Rd -Hauppauge 11788
(516) 328-3500 .. **Mulé,** Linda A '79 %McDonnell & A,PC -401 Franklin Av -Gdn Cty 11530
(516) 357-3000 .. **Mulé,** Michl C '96 (Rivkin R LLP) -926 RXR Plz -Uniondale 11556
(585) 454-4060 .. **Mule,** Michl J '06 %Empire Justice Ctr -1 W Main -Rchstr 14614 **Fx:**454-4019
(212) 488-1200 .. **Mulgrave,** Alcides E '05 Kobre & K,LLP -800 3rd Av -NY 10022
(845) 639-4664 .. **Mulgrew,** Alexander Stuart '99 (Mulgrew & S,PC) -22 S Main -New Cty 10956
(845) 639-4664 .. **Mulgrew & Sassone,PC** -22 S Main -New Cty 10956 **Fx:**639-1159

(212) 848-4000 .. **Mulhall**, Marjorie A '09 %Shearman & S LLP -599 Lex Av -NY 10022
(845) 398-0361 .. **Mulhearn**, Kevin T '91 (K Mulhearn,PC) -60 Dutch Hill Rd -Orangebrg 10962 **Fx:**398-3836
(212) 710-3900 .. **Mulhearn**, Mary H '06 %Clyde & Co US LLP -405 Lex Av -NY 10174 **Fx:**710-3950
(516) 294-8000 .. **Mulhern**, Edwin J '54 -1 Old Cntry Rd -Carle Pl 11514 **Fx:**877-1195
(516) 354-8500 .. **Mulhern**, Edwin T '80 (Huwel & M) -11 New Hyde Pk Rd -Franklin Sq 11010
(646) 654-4898 .. **Mulhern**, Frank K '84 VNU Inc -770 Bway -NY 10003
(516) 328-2300 .. **Mulhern**, James P '03 %Abrams FFEGF&E,LLP -1111 Marcus Av -Lk Success 11042
(212) 259-8000 .. **Mulhern**, John P '83 (Dewey & L LLP) -1301 Av of Amer -NY 10019
(212) 237-0000 .. **Mulhern**, Lance A '09 %Vinson & E LLP -666 5th Av -NY 10103
(516) 783-0380 .. **Mulhern**, Patrick J Jr. '78 (Mulhern & K) -3330 Park Av -Wantagh 11793
(631) 853-5761 .. **Mulholland**, Brian '77 %Cnty Atty -400 Carleton Av -Central Islip 11722 **Fx:**853-7788
(212) 702-9027 .. **Mulholland**, Edwin M '72 (Mulholland & K,LLP) -641 Lex Av -NY 10022 **Fx:**702-9092
(631) 728-6436 .. **Mulholland**, Ellin M '55 -4 Cottage Ln -Hampton Bays 11946
(518) 886-4000 .. **Mulholland**, Heather L G '06 %AYCO -321 Bway Bx860 -Saratoga Spgs 12866
(516) 932-9569 .. **Mulholland**, John F '50 -3 Mayflower Dr -Hicksvll 11801 **Fx:**935-2965
(718) 739-6400 .. **Mulholland**, John J '90 %DHCR -92-31 Union Hall -Jamaica 11433 **Fx:**262-7938
(212) 947-4999 .. **Mulholland**, Kathleen M '93 (Camacho MM,LLP) -350 5th Av -NY 10118
(516) 663-6600 .. **Mulholland**, Mark S '85 (Ruskin MF,PC) -1425 RXR Plz -Uniondale 11556
(585) 647-6400 .. **Mulholland**, Maureen E '97 Monro Muffler Brake Inc -200 Holleder Pkwy -Rchstr 14615 **Fx:**647-0943
(516) 248-1200 .. **Mulholland Minion & Roe** -374 Hillside Av -Williston Pk 11596 **Fx:**248-1225
(718) 834-4850 .. **Mulholland**, Rory T '99 Gerber & G LLP -26 Court -Brklyn 11242 **Fx:**858-8119
(212) 599-8200 .. **Mulic**, Milja '07 %Shaub AC&S,LLP -655 3rd Av -NY 10017
(212) 836-8000 .. **Mulitz**, Michl C '93 (Kaye S LLP) -425 Park Av -NY 10022
(718) 243-6412 .. **Mull**, Nicole M '97 %Leg Aid -111 Lvngstn -Brklyn 11201 **Fx:**237-8737
(518) 758-6330 .. **Mullady**, John B '74 -57 Hennett Rd -Valatie 12184 **Fx:**758-6330
(212) 980-9600 .. **Mullahy**, John B '98 (Kaufman B&R) -120 Bway -NY 10271
(516) 677-4731 .. **Mullahy**, Pamela R '98 Hub Intl NE -100 Sunnyside Blvd -Woodbury 11797 **Fx:**(917) 934-9559
(518) 462-0300 .. **Mullahy**, Ryan P '08 %Girvin & F,PC -20 Corp Wds Blvd -Albany 12211
(631) 232-2400 .. **Mullahy**, Sheila A '09 %Nassau/Sfflk Law Srv -1757 Vets Hwy -Islandia 11749 **Fx:**232-2489
(212) 837-6089 .. **Mullaj**, Gentian '09 %Hughes H&R LLP -1 Bttry Pk Plz -NY 10004
(718) 965-6623 .. **Mullally**, Claire '88 -619 8th Av -Brklyn 11215 **Fx:**965-6624
(212) 918-3000 .. **Mullally**, M Veronica '97 (Hogan L LLP) -875 3rd Av -NY 10022
(631) 423-4390 .. **Mullan**, Jeannine M '00 %Mincone & M,PC -110 Walt Whitman Rd -South Huntington 11746 **Fx:**423-4408
(516) 294-5050 .. **Mullan**, John A '94 Cassisi & C,PC -114 Old Cntry Rd -Mineola 11501
(646) 284-8935 .. **Mullane**, Christopher J '05 Cnsl Professional Indemnity Agency -37 Radio Cir -Mt Kisco 10549
(718) 286-6000 .. **Mullaney**, Anne-Marie '87 %DA -125-01 Qns Blvd -Kew Gdns 11415
(518) 584-8000 .. **Mullaney**, Eleanor K '83 (Mullaney & M) -480 Bway -Saratoga Spgs 12866 **Fx:**584-0146
(718) 727-0547 .. **Mullaney**, James F '56 -61 Cebra Av -Staten Isl 10304
(914) 241-7917 .. **Mullaney**, Julie '82 -69 S Moger Av -Mt Kisco 10549 **Fx:**241-0380
(212) 689-1113 .. **Mullaney**, Laura M '07 Garbarini & S,PC -432 Park Av S -NY 10016
(518) 869-6227 .. **Mullaney**, Michl P '75 OfCnsl Lavelle & F,LLP -29 British Amer Blvd -Latham 12110
(518) 584-8000 .. **Mullaney**, Richd F '59 (Mullaney & M) -480 Bway -Saratoga Spgs 12866 **Fx:**584-0146
(212) 670-0335 .. **Mullaney**, Thos J '71 Bank of Amer - Legal Dept -222 Bway -NY 10038 **Fx:**670-4530
(212) 223-0800 .. **Mullaney**, Thos M '97 -500 5th Av -NY 10110
(716) 684-8060 .. **Mullaney-Westfall**, Colleen C '98 %Ecology & Envrnmnt -368 Plsntvw Dr -Lancaster 14086 **Fx:**684-0844
(212) 574-1200 .. **Mulle**, David R '05 %Seward & K LLP -1 Bttry Pk Plz -NY 10004
(917) 454-1100 .. **Mulle**, Laura M '08 Police Dept -2 Lafayette -NY 10007
(631) 421-1211 .. **Mullé**, Richd C '75 (Martin F&M) -100 E Carver -Huntngtn 11743
(718) 254-6825 .. **Mullee**, Bryan T '98 US Marshal's Srvc -225 Cadman Plz E -Brklyn 11201
(718) 447-5499 .. **Mullen**, Brian P '68 (Berel & M) -358 St Marks Pl -Staten Isl 10301
(212) 867-8989 .. **Mullen**, Catherine A '90 %Northwestern Mutual Life Ins -875 3rd Av -NY 10022
(516) 357-3700 .. **Mullen**, Corinne M '86 %Cullen and D LLP -100 Q Roosevelt Blvd -Gdn Cty 11530
(212) 530-5000 .. **Mullen**, Elisabeth O '08 %Milbank TH&M LLP -1 Chase Manh Plz -NY 10005
(212) 449-6980 .. **Mullen**, Erin Sian '01 Merrill Lynch -4 World Fncl Ctr -NY 10080
(631) 361-7050 .. **Mullen & Iannarone, PC** -300 E Main -Smithtwn 11787 **Fx:**361-7354
(212) 766-1177 .. **Mullen**, Jos T Jr. '83 -30 Vesey -NY 10007 **Fx:**766-1131
(718) 709-3032 .. **Mullen**, Karen Smith '02 JetBlue Airways -118-29 Qns Blvd -Frst Hlls 11375
(718) 250-4204 .. **Mullen**, Katherine E '89 %Leg Aid -111 Lvngstn -Brklyn 11201 **Fx:**250-4243
(631) 342-8070 .. **Mullen**, Mary Catherine Teresa '96 %Tinari OO&K,LLP -320 Carleton Av -Central Islip 11722
(631) 694-2300 .. **Mullen**, Michl F '63 Cnsl Lamb & B,LLP -534 Broadhllw Rd Bx9034 -Melvll 11747
(212) 735-3000 .. **Mullen**, Peter P '51 OfCnsl Skadden ASM&F LLP -4 Times Sq -NY 10036
(212) 530-5000 .. **Mullen**, Robt W Jr. '81 (Milbank TH&M LLP) -1 Chase Manh Plz -NY 10005
(212) 839-5300 .. **Mullen**, Sophia Park '08 %Sidley A LLP -787 7th Av -NY 10019
(212) 450-4000 .. **Mullen**, Wesley M '08 %Davis P&W LLP -450 Lex Av -NY 10017
(631) 591-2961 .. **Mullen-Garcia**, Nancy '03 (Lippmann & G) -1641 Deer Prk Av -Deer Pk 11729 **Fx:**242-2034
(212) 271-0214 .. **Muller**, Alex '78 -325 Bway -NY 10007
(212) 474-1000 .. **Muller**, Alexander '03 %Cravath S&M LLP -825 8th Av -NY 10019
(212) 593-3000 .. **Muller**, Andrew S '94 %Platzer SKLG&J,LLP -1065 Av of Amer -NY 10018
(212) 674-1071 .. **Muller**, Chas W '56 -14 Styvsnt Oval -NY 10009 **Fx:**505-3423
(607) 326-4204 .. **Muller**, Chas W '56 -1181 Vega Mtn Rd Bx18 -Denver 12421 **Fx:**326-2835
(212) 788-1121 .. **Muller**, Christopher J '98 %Law Dept -100 Church -NY 10007 **Fx:**788-0367
(212) 558-4000 .. **Muller**, Danl J '09 %Sullivan & C LLP -125 Broad -NY 10004
(212) 592-1400 .. **Muller**, Daniella Machnikoff '02 %Herrick,F LLP -2 Park Av -NY 10016
(516) 489-5000 .. **Muller**, Diana L '03 %Town Atty -Town Hall -Hempstd 11550 **Fx:**489-5150
(518) 587-0559 .. **Muller**, Emily G '99 -480 Bway -Saratoga Spgs 12866 **Fx:**587-0575
(212) 705-0142 .. **Muller**, Eric D '01 Cypress Grp LLC -65 E 55th -NY 10022
(718) 923-4433 .. **Muller**, Gregory H '98 -55 Hanson Pl -Brklyn 11217
(212) 349-0020 .. **Muller**, Henry H '59 -217 Bway -NY 10007
(212) 609-6800 .. **Muller**, Jeffrey Scott '04 %McCarter & E,LLP -245 Park Av -NY 10167
(518) 402-0205 .. **Muller**, John F '91 %UIA Bd -Troy Atrium Bx15126 -Albany 12212 **Fx:**402-6208
(585) 428-7033 .. **Muller**, John F '93 Police Dept -185 Exchange Blvd -Rchstr 14614
(646) 857-1365 .. **Muller**, John P '02 Risk Specialists Co of NY,Inc -30 Old Slip -NY 10005
(718) 237-2000 .. **Muller**, Luanne M '06 Leg Aid -111 Lvngstn -Brklyn 11201 **Fx:**237-8737
(212) 553-0300 .. **Muller**, Maria I '97 %Moody's Invstr Srvc -250 Greenwich -NY 10007
(212) 425-1900 .. **Muller**, Mark F '79 (Freehill H&M LLP) -80 Pine -NY 10005
(518) 793-2535 .. **Muller**, Michl J '77 (Muller & M,PLLC) -257 Bay Rd Bx143 -Glens Fls 12801 **Fx:**793-6238
(212) 250-8184 .. **Muller**, Nathan '89 %Deutsche Bk Sec -60 Wall -NY 10005
(212) 921-1600 .. **Muller**, Nathaniel '99 %Goldberg SL&B,PC -45 W 45th -NY 10036
(718) 389-2427 .. **Muller**, Reuben G '07 %Agostino & Assoc,PC -500 Kngslnd Av -Brklyn 11222
(718) 595-5964 .. **Muller**, Richd L '96 DEP -59-17 Junction Blvd -Flushng 11373 **Fx:**595-6543
(212) 450-4000 .. **Muller**, Scott W '77 (Davis P&W LLP) -450 Lex Av -NY 10017
(212) 559-6147 .. **Muller**, Susanne M '01 Citigroup -425 Park Av -NY 10022
(718) 254-7000 .. **Muller**, Wm J '73 %US Atty -271 Cadman Plz E -Brklyn 11201 **Fx:**254-6479
(516) 489-5000 .. **Muller**, Wm J '03 %Town Atty -Town Hall -Hempstd 11550 **Fx:**489-5150
(718) 876-6300 .. **Muller-Mondi**, Tuesday L '01 %DA -130 Styvsnt Pl -Staten Isl 10301
(212) 922-6780 .. **Mullery**, Robt R '80 Dreyfus -200 Park Av -NY 10166
(585) 530-3165 .. **Mulley**, James P Jr. '84 %Appllt Div 4th Dept -50 East Av Ste 200 -Rchstr 14604 **Fx:**530-3247
(212) 504-6000 .. **Mulligan**, Bryon J '00 SpclCnsl Cadwalader W&T LLP -1 World Fncl Ctr -NY 10281
(212) 244-9500 .. **Mulligan**, Howard F '89 Cnsl White and W LLP -1 Penn Plz -NY 10119
(212) 336-3748 .. **Mulligan**, Jean E '05 EEOC -33 Whitehall -NY 10004
(212) 696-6000 .. **Mulligan**, Jeremiah T '71 (Curtis M-PC&M LLP) -101 Park Av -NY 10178
(718) 403-3600 .. **Mulligan**, John J III '88 %Dept of Finance -345 Adams -Brklyn 11201 **Fx:**403-3650
(212) 833-1123 .. **Mulligan**, Mary E '90 (Friedman KS&A LLP) -1633 Bway -NY 10019 **Fx:**373-7923
(914) 243-4913 .. **Mulligan**, Patricia M '91 -3535 Hill Blvd -Yorktwn Hts 10598 **Fx:**243-0241
(518) 372-6473 .. **Mulligan**, Paul K '72 -705 Union -Schnctdy 12305 **Fx:**370-1613
(516) 334-2320 .. **Mulligan**, Robt F '60 (Kraemer & M) -342 Post Av -Westbury 11590
(718) 816-0005 .. **Mulligan**, Robt F '68 %Angiuli K&G,LLP -60 Bay -Staten Isl 10301
(212) 214-6236 .. **Mulligan**, Robt J '96 Wachovia Bk NA -375 Park Av -NY 10152
(212) 733-6666 .. **Mulligan**, Sarah J '97 %Pfizer Inc -235 E 42nd -NY 10017
(917) 454-1040 .. **Mulligan**, Thos J '83 US Immigration Ct -26 Fed Plz -NY 10278
(212) 788-5910 .. **Mulligan**, Timothy F '98 NYC Ofc Mgmt & Budget -75 Park Pl -NY 10007
(585) 243-3100 .. **Mulligan**, Wm A '81 -42 Oak -Geneseo 14454
(212) 515-2800 .. **Mulligan**, Wm G '96 Hedgeop Comp LLC -3 Park Av -NY 10016 **Fx:**515-2820
(914) 949-2700 .. **Mulligan**, Wm H Jr. '75 (Bleakley P&S,LLP) -1 N Lex Av -White Plns 10601
(212) 906-1200 .. **Mulliken**, David W '09 %Latham & W -885 3rd Av -NY 10022
(718) 875-9264 .. **Mullin**, Ashley L '10 %Warren & W,PC -185 Montague -Brklyn 11201 **Fx:**852-3069
(212) 931-7889 .. **Mullin**, Danl T '93 %MLB -245 Park Av -NY 10167 **Fx:**949-5657
(212) 219-2100 .. **Mullin**, Kathleen M '92 -110 William -NY 10038 **Fx:**226-7554
(212) 762-4000 .. **Mullin**, Mary E '94 Morgan Stanley -1221 Av of Amer -NY 10020
(212) 580-8985 .. **Mullin**, Monica H '82 -205 W 86th -NY 10024
(212) 639-1600 .. **Mullin**, Patrick A '90 -10 Rckfllr Plz -NY 10020
(315) 474-2943 .. **Mullin**, Paul V '86 (Sugarman Law Firm,LLP) -211 W Jffrsn -Syracuse 13202
(212) 906-1200 .. **Mullin**, Sarah R '09 %Latham & W -885 3rd Av -NY 10022
(585) 678-7100 .. **Mullin**, Thos J '77 %Constellation Brands -207 Hgh Pnt Dr -Victor 14564
(212) 671-1179 .. **Mullin**, Wm J '78 (Graham MNM&R,PC) -2350 Bway -NY 10024
(315) 479-9139 .. **Mullin**, Wm P '75 -215 E Water -Syracuse 13202
(516) 481-0400 .. **Mullings**, K Yasmin M '90 -1197 N Bway -N Massapequa 11758
(212) 487-4326 .. **Mullings**, Pansy D '76 %Dept Cnsmr Affrs -42 Bway -NY 10004 **Fx:**487-4197
(646) 312-3596 .. **Mullings**, Sandra J '81 Baruch College -1 Bernard Baruch Way -NY 10010 **Fx:**312-3571
(914) 828-8760 .. **Mullins**, Elizabeth '83 SwissRe Life & Hlth America -175 King -Armonk 10504

(914) 723-0333 .. **Mullins,** George J '66 -193 Brook -Scarsdale 10583
(212) 767-1775 .. **Mullins,** Kerry A '04 Fergus Prtnrshp -1325 Av of Amer -NY 10019
(914) 997-8529 .. **Mullins,** Kevin J '93 -336 West -White Plns 10605 **Fx:**997-0091
(516) 296-9579 .. **Mullins,** Lawr E '05 Lufthansa German Airlines -1640 Hempstd Tpk -E Meadow 11554
(914) 834-4400 .. **Mullins,** Mary Beth '87 -2001 Palmer Av -Larchmnt 10538 **Fx:**834-6064
(716) 856-4200 .. **Mullins,** Robt J II '98 (Gibson M&C,LLP) -69 Delaware Av -Buffalo 14202
(716) 851-3404 .. **Mullins,** Tearah G '89 %Hon R Sconiers -77 W Eagle -Buffalo 14202
(212) 421-1011 .. **Mullman,** Lawr N '78 Major L&A -551 5th Av -NY 10176 **Fx:**421-1042
(212) 885-5000 .. **Mullman,** Michl S '72 (Blank R LLP) -405 Lex Av -NY 10174
(212) 250-7417 .. **Mullock,** Cynthia L '05 Deutsche Bank AG -60 Wall -NY 10005
(516) 656-5300 .. **Mullooly Jeffrey Rooney & Flynn LLP** -6851 Jericho Tpk Bx9036 -Sysoset 11791 **Fx:**921-2131
(212) 306-7450 .. **Mulqueen,** Cliff S '90 %Comm on Human Rights -40 Rector -NY 10006 **Fx:**306-7414
(212) 563-2330 .. **Mulqueen,** Michl A '81 Barr & B Inc -460 W 34th -NY 10001 **Fx:**967-2297
(212) 790-0000 .. **Mulreed,** Shaun P '08 Och-Ziff Cap Mgt -9 W 57th -NY 10019
(718) 590-0268 .. **Mulrooney,** Margaret M '88 Family Ct -900 Sheridan Av -Bronx 10451
(212) 907-9600 .. **Mulrooney,** Tara B '02 Ingram YGC&B,LLP -250 Park Av -NY 10177
(516) 641-0725 .. **Mulry,** Harry J Jr. '73 -One Toms Pnt Ln -Pt Wash 11050 **Fx:**883-0020
(516) 536-0376 .. **Mulry,** Jeanne Farnan '90 -8 Arlngtn Av -Rockvll Ctr 11570
(718) 254-7000 .. **Mulry,** Kevin P '88 %US Atty -271 Cadman Plz E -Brklyn 11201 **Fx:**254-6479
(631) 853-7770 .. **Mulry,** Laurette D '01 Leg Aid -400 Carlton Av -Central Islip 11722 **Fx:**853-4336
(212) 818-9019 .. **Multer,** Andrew J '88 (Bahn H&M,LLP) -555 5th Av -NY 10017 **Fx:**986-5316
(716) 847-2523 .. **Multerer,** Mark R '87 %Sugarman Law Firm,LLP -14 Lafayette Sq -Buffalo 14203
(718) 643-7080 .. **Multer Kapusta,** Sharon J '97 %Hon GC Aronin -360 Adams -Brklyn 11201
(607) 255-5436 .. **Mulvanerton,** Mary R '99 Cornell Univ -102 Space Sciences Bldg -Ithaca 14853 **Fx:**255-5907
(212) 483-9490 .. **Mulvaney,** James M '82 (McElroy DM&C,LLP) -88 Pine -NY 10005
(518) 462-7448 .. **Mulvaney,** Richd E '94 NYS Troopers PBA -120 State -Albany 12207
(631) 862-8889 .. **Mulvehill,** John H '59 -220 Cambon Av -St James 11780 **Fx:**862-0535
(716) 847-8400 .. **Mulvehill,** Kevin J '07 %Phillips L LLP -3400 HSBC Ctr -Buffalo 14203
(585) 238-2000 .. **Mulvehill,** Kevin J '07 %Phillips L LLP -1400 First Fed Plz -Rchstr 14614
(212) 267-5556 .. **Mulvehill,** Urban S '70 (O'Neill D&K) -15 Beekman -NY 10038
(718) 694-3864 .. **Mulvenna,** Bridget '83 %Transit Auth -130 Lvngstn -Brklyn 11201 **Fx:**694-5726
(518) 486-1841 .. **Mulvey,** Jude Brearton '91 %Dept of Health -Corning Twr 24th Fl -Albany 12237 **Fx:**473-2430
(212) 458-1625 .. **Mulvey,** Michl B Jr. '91 %AIG -175 Water -NY 10038
(716) 883-7272 .. **Mulvey,** Michl B '03 %McGee & G -200 Summer -Buffalo 14222
(516) 599-6420 .. **Mulvey,** Robt J '67 OfCnsl Kruman & K -353 Hempstd Av -Malverne 11565
(315) 448-4800 .. **Mulvey,** Timothy P '85 %Dept of Law -615 Erie Blvd W -Syracuse 13204 **Fx:**448-4853
(212) 819-8200 .. **Mulvey,** Timothy V '97 Cnsl White & C LLP -1155 Av of Amer -NY 10036
(212) 416-8000 .. **Mulvihill,** Christopher B '00 %Dept of Law -120 Bway -NY 10271
(212) 972-5430 .. **Mulvihill,** Kerry B '04 %Rosin SM -801 2nd Av -NY 10017
(212) 698-3500 .. **Mulvihill,** Roger '63 (Dechert LLP) -1095 Av of Amer -NY 10036
(212) 455-2000 .. **Mulvihill,** Timothy J '01 %Simpson T&B LLP -425 Lex Av -NY 10017
(518) 584-1991 .. **Mumford,** Brian F '68 OfCnsl Cahill/Wink LLP -60 Railroad Pl -Saratoga Spgs 12866
(315) 524-5000 .. **Mumford,** Christopher B '67 (Lacy K LLP) -1276 Ridge Rd -Ontario 14519
(585) 454-5650 .. **Mumford,** Christopher B '67 (Lacy K LLP) -130 E Main -Rchstr 14604
(516) 229-4400 .. **Mumford,** Roger E '79 %Kay & G -875 Merrick Av -Westbury 11590
(212) 732-8700 .. **Mumm,** Lawr W '80 (McAloon & F,PC) -123 William -NY 10038
(212) 373-3000 .. **Mun,** Yeung Yin Danl '08 %Paul WRW&G LLP -1285 Av of Amer -NY 10019
(212) 536-3900 .. **Munafo,** Megan B '07 %K&L Gates LLP -599 Lex Av -NY 10022
(347) 404-9680 .. **Mund,** Gary R '77 Kings Cnty Surrogate's Ct -2 Johnson -Brklyn 11201 **Fx:**(718) 643-4512
(718) 261-6863 .. **Mund,** Mitchell '79 (M Mund & Assoc) -100-15 Qns Blvd -Frst Hlls 11375 **Fx:**261-5709
(718) 250-2000 .. **Mundaca,** Francisco E '09 %DA -350 Jay -Brklyn 11201 **Fx:**250-2314
(518) 884-0200 .. **Munday,** Belinda '93 %Donnellan & K,PLLC -20 Prospect -Ballston Spa 12020 **Fx:**884-0343
(212) 848-4000 .. **Mundheim,** Robt H '58 OfCnsl Shearman & S LLP -599 Lex Av -NY 10022
(212) 946-2714 .. **Mundie,** Steven A '96 S Mundie,PA -11 Penn Plz -NY 10001 **Fx:**946-2808
(212) 728-8000 .. **Mundiya,** Tariq '90 (Willkie F&G LLP) -787 7th Av -NY 10019
(718) 591-2000 .. **Mundo,** Vito V '83 Joint Indstry Bd of the Electrical Indstry -158-11 Harry Van Arsdale Jr Av -Flushng 11365 **Fx:**969-2292
(607) 642-3235 .. **Mundt,** George J Jr. '64 -5 Park Av Bx187 -Newark Vly 13811
(718) 858-1030 .. **Mundy,** Nicholas J '95 -26 Court -Brklyn 11242 **Fx:**679-9794
(212) 512-0500 .. **Muney,** Todd S '98 NYAT Inc -1040 6th Av -NY 10018
(845) 486-2280 .. **Mungavin,** Susan Mraz '99 %Pub Def -22 Market -Poughkeepsie 12601 **Fx:**486-2266
(716) 856-4201 .. **Munger,** Judith K '86 %Assn Rtrd Children -101 Oak -Buffalo 14203 **Fx:**856-3312
(212) 474-1000 .. **Mungovan,** Kara L '09 %Cravath S&M LLP -825 8th Av -NY 10019
(516) 741-3400 .. **Munier,** Noel '07 %A Colleluori & Assoc -180 Froehlich Farm Blvd -Woodbury 11797 **Fx:**921-8845
(212) 947-1000 .. **Munitz,** Martin '69 (M Munitz,PC) -3 W 35th -NY 10001 **Fx:**947-1901
(212) 964-3736 .. **Muniz,** Jose A '86 J Muniz,PC -277 Bway -NY 10007 **Fx:**227-0397
(212) 259-8000 .. **Muniz,** Krystal A '08 %Dewey & L LLP -1301 Av of Amer -NY 10019
(212) 688-8555 .. **Muniz,** Luisa Giuliana '98 %Fragomen DB&L LLP -7 Hanover Sq -NY 10004
(212) 632-2240 .. **Muniz,** Nicolas J '90 WPP -125 Park Av -NY 10017
(212) 863-6300 .. **Muniz,** Wm A '99 HPD -100 Gold -NY 10038 **Fx:**863-8201
(212) 981-4500 .. **Munk,** Barry S '97 PeterSan Grp -1450 Bway -NY 10018 **Fx:**981-4560
(607) 748-7351 .. **Munk,** Joe B '59 OfCnsl Leasure GM&R -101 Jffrsn Av -Endicott 13760
(518) 486-4603 .. **Munkwitz,** Kelly L '99 %Dept of Law -The Cptl -Albany 12224
(516) 487-6500 .. **Munley & Meade PLLC** -160 Middle Nck Rd -Gt Neck 11021 **Fx:**487-6539
(716) 672-4371 .. **Munley,** Michl L '72 Loguidice Educ Cntr -9520 Fredonia Stockton Rd -Fredonia 14063
(212) 989-0076 .. **Munn,** Martin S '71 -330 W 28th -NY 10001 **Fx:**989-0076
(718) 246-2828 .. **Munn,** Richd A '91 -270 Jay -Brklyn 11201
(631) 669-4917 .. **Munno,** Irene A '03 -158 Blvd Av -W Islip 11795 **Fx:**669-3459
(212) 574-1200 .. **Munno,** M Wm '74 (Seward & K LLP) -1 Bttry Pk Plz -NY 10004
(212) 698-3500 .. **Munno,** Thos F '69 (Dechert LLP) -1095 Av of Amer -NY 10036
(718) 320-3326 .. **Munns,** Michl J '82 %Riverbay Corp -2049 Bartow Av -Bronx 10475 **Fx:**320-3397
(718) 286-6000 .. **Munoz,** Andres A '06 %DA -125-01 Qns Blvd -Kew Gdns 11415
(212) 330-5442 .. **Munoz,** Evelyn '09 USPS -90 Church -NY 10007
(518) 486-1765 .. **Munoz,** Frank '80 NYS Ed Dept -89 Wshngtn -Albany 12234 **Fx:**474-3863
(212) 903-9000 .. **Munoz,** Jennifer P '06 %Linklaters -1345 Av of Amer -NY 10105
(212) 490-1409 .. **Munoz,** Kenneth W '76 Sports Captl Ptnrs -200 Park Av -NY 10166
(212) 907-7300 .. **Munoz,** Michl M '04 %Golenbock EAB&P -437 Mad Av -NY 10022
(212) 277-4000 .. **Munoz,** Priscilla J '07 %Freshfields BD LLP -520 Mad Av -NY 10022
(212) 695-3800 .. **Munoz,** Sandra M '02 InMotion -70 W 36th -NY 10018
(212) 319-2787 .. **Munoz-Sarmiento,** Sergio '07 VLA -1 E 53rd -NY 10022 **Fx:**752-6575
(718) 596-3800 .. **Munoz-Shivers,** Rachel I '04 Tenenbaum & B LLP -26 Court -Brklyn 11242
(518) 862-1090 .. **Munro,** David A '78 NYSERDA -17 Columbia Cir -Albany 12203 **Fx:**862-1091
(516) 876-9600 .. **Munro,** Dawn Ann '92 %Rovegno & T,PC -1010 Nrthrn Blvd -Gt Neck 11021
(212) 258-7800 .. **Munro,** Erika D '97 VH1-MTV Networks -1633 Bway -NY 10019
(212) 344-3900 .. **Munro,** Michl P '96 %Belair & E LLP -61 Bway -NY 10006
(718) 286-2000 .. **Munro,** Sarah A '07 Leg Aid -120-46 Qns Blvd -Kew Gdns 11415 **Fx:**286-2286
(718) 875-8882 .. **Munroe,** George D '94 -263 Monroe -Brklyn 11216
(585) 295-5771 .. **Munsaf,** Rachel '07 Leg Aid -1 W Main -Rchstr 14614
(212) 258-4424 .. **Munsell,** Elizabeth Sanders '97 Siemens Corp -153 E 53rd -NY 10022
(212) 839-5300 .. **Munsell,** James C '97 (Sidley A LLP) -787 7th Av -NY 10019
(212) 225-2000 .. **Munsell,** James F '69 SrCnsl Cleary GS&H -1 Lbrty Plz -NY 10006
(212) 687-7410 .. **Munsky,** Stefanie R '07 %Clifton B&D,LLP -420 Lex Av -NY 10170
(914) 249-2000 .. **Munson,** Carl J Jr. '83 %MasterCard Intl -2000 Purchase -Purchase 10577
(315) 986-8221 .. **Munson,** Denise R '92 -2100 Penfld Rd Bx29 -Walworth 14568 **Fx:**986-7048
(516) 877-5600 .. **Munson,** Donald M '91 %R Tusa -1225 Franklin Av -Gdn Cty 11530 **Fx:**877-5695
(212) 649-5905 .. **Munson,** Elizabeth P '84 Rockefeller Trust -30 Rckfllr Plz -NY 10112
(212) 298-5112 .. **Munson,** Gabriel R '04 Leg Aid -49 Thomas -NY 10013
(315) 598-8552 .. **Munson,** Pamela Anne '93 -163 S 1st -Fulton 13069
(212) 869-5030 .. **Munson,** Patrick K '82 (Kucker & B,LLP) -747 3rd Av -NY 10017
(315) 782-8800 .. **Munson,** Steven G '81 -200 Wshngtn -Watertwn 13601 **Fx:**782-0053
(212) 953-6633 .. **Munster,** Melissa L '09 %Cox PS&S LLP -630 3rd Av -NY 10017
(212) 490-4100 .. **Munves,** Russell D '74 (Storch A&M,PC) -140 E 45th -NY 10017
(212) 310-8000 .. **Munz,** Naomi '06 %Weil G&M LLP -767 5th Av -NY 10153
(516) 222-0676 .. **Munz,** Tina M '02 %G Haggerty & Assoc,PC -500 N Bway -Jericho 11753 **Fx:**222-8011
(631) 727-7345 .. **Munzel,** John J '65 -548 Roanoke Av -Rvrhead 11901 **Fx:**727-3575
(212) 213-8844 .. **Muoio,** Megan J '05 %Allyn & F LLP -200 Mad Av -NY 10016
(585) 262-5140 .. **Mura,** Paul E '64 -2 State -Rchstr 14614 **Fx:**232-3164
(716) 855-2800 .. **Mura,** Roy A '87 (Mura & S,PLLC) -14 Lafayette Sq #930 -Buffalo 14203
(716) 855-2800 .. **Mura & Storm, PLLC** -14 Lafayette Sq #930 -Buffalo 14203 **Fx:**855-2816
(212) 770-5820 .. **Murabito,** Matthew J '92 AIG -70 Pine -NY 10270
(516) 739-3322 .. **Muraca,** Felice J '88 -106 3rd -Mineola 11501
(516) 739-3322 .. **Muraca,** Gary '90 -106 3rd -Mineola 11501
(315) 733-2396 .. **Murad,** Anthony A '84 (Brindisi MBPJ&P,LLP) -2713 Genesee -Utica 13501
(315) 792-8000 .. **Murad,** Fredk W '79 (Murad & M) -291 Genesee -Utica 13501 **Fx:**792-8005
(315) 792-8000 .. **Murad,** George C '78 (Murad & M) -291 Genesee -Utica 13501 **Fx:**792-8005
(315) 792-8000 .. **Murad,** Gregory M '75 Murad & M -291 Genesee -Utica 13501 **Fx:**792-8005
(315) 471-3151 .. **Murad,** John L Jr. '84 (Hancock & E,LLP) -1500 AXA Twr I Bx4976 -Syracuse 13221
(716) 847-8400 .. **Murak,** Katherine A '10 %Phillips L LLP -3400 HSBC Ctr -Buffalo 14203
(716) 853-2050 .. **Murak,** Paul F '83 %Sliwa & L -237 Main -Buffalo 14203
(585) 232-6830 .. **Murante,** David A '74 -700 Wilder Bldg -Rchstr 14614
(212) 705-7000 .. **Murase,** Jiro '59 (Bingham M LLP) -399 Park Av -NY 10022
(212) 705-7000 .. **Murase,** Satoru '84 (Bingham M LLP) -399 Park Av -NY 10022
(631) 320-0157 .. **Muraskin,** Matthew '62 -646 Main -Pt Jffrsn 11777 **Fx:**320-0159

(212) 735-3000 .. **Murata,** Alessandra K '01 Cnsl Skadden ASM&F LLP -4 Times Sq -NY 10036
(212) 326-2000 .. **Murata,** Ken '01 Cnsl O'Melveny & M LLP -7 Times Sq -NY 10036
(212) 573-2323 .. **Muratore,** Andrew J '01 %Pfizer Inc -235 E 42nd -NY 10017
(212) 353-8280 .. **Muratore,** Anthony J '81 -104 E 25th -NY 10010
(646) 724-0416 .. **Muratore,** Christa L '05 -300 E 39th -NY 10016
(914) 846-7000 .. **Muratore,** Jos F '94 %NY Life Ins -1 Rockwood Rd -Sleepy Hollow 10591 **Fx:**846-4755
(212) 340-4936 .. **Murawski,** Jane M '97 %Metro-North -345 Mad Av -NY 10017 **Fx:**340-2391
(585) 671-4473 .. **Murch,** David R '78 (Murch & W,PC) -674 Ridge Rd -Webster 14580 **Fx:**671-1342
(212) 845-4336 .. **Murcia,** Alma J '00 AEA Investors LLC -55 E 52nd -NY 10055
(212) 336-2000 .. **Murdica,** James F '05 %Patterson BW&T LLP -1133 Av of Amer -NY 10036
(212) 788-0480 .. **Murdoch,** Christopher J '93 %Law Dept -100 Church -NY 10007 **Fx:**788-0367
(646) 557-5100 .. **Murdock,** Danl R '63 (Patton B LLP) -1185 Av of Amer -NY 10036
(212) 446-4800 .. **Murdock,** Hunter R '06 %Kirkland & E LLP -153 E 53rd -NY 10022
(212) 450-4000 .. **Murdock,** Mork '05 %Davis P&W LLP -450 Lex Av -NY 10017
(212) 715-9100 .. **Murdock,** Randal D '96 SpclCnsl Kramer LN&F,LLP -1177 Av of Amer -NY 10036
(315) 738-0600 .. **Murdock,** Viola Ann '94 SrCnsl PAR Technology Corp -8383 Seneca Tpk -New Hartfrd 13413
(631) 761-0800 .. **Murdock,** Zachary '85 (Lazer AR&Y,PC) -225 Old Cntry Rd -Melvll 11747
(516) 766-3200 .. **Murdy,** Paul J '86 (Murtagh C&B) -100 N Park Av -Rockvll Ctr 11570
(718) 852-9100 .. **Mure,** Jos Jr. '87 -26 Court -Brklyn 11242 **Fx:**797-5554
(212) 334-2393 .. **Murga,** Alfredo '05 (Hua & M,LLP) -350 Bway -NY 10013
(212) 339-5129 .. **Murgio,** David P '00 %Harbinger Captl Ptnrs -450 Park Av -NY 10022
(718) 817-3020 .. **Muriana,** Jos P '90 SpclCnsl Fordham Univ -441 E Fordham Rd Admin Bldg 117 -Bronx 10458 **Fx:**817-5722
(212) 407-4000 .. **Murillo,** C Christopher '06 %Loeb & L,LLP -345 Park Av -NY 10154
(212) 223-6700 .. **Murnane,** Brian T '88 OfCnsl Zukerman GB&C,LLP -875 3rd Av -NY 10022
(315) 733-4671 .. **Murnane,** Don P '60 (Rossi & M) -587 Main -NY Mlls 13417
(212) 425-1900 .. **Murnane,** Don P Jr. '87 (Freehill H&M LLP) -80 Pine -NY 10005
(212) 218-2100 .. **Murnane,** John D '80 (Fitzpatrick CH&S) -1290 Av of Amer -NY 10104
(518) 561-4400 .. **Murnane,** Thos M '87 Stafford OC&T,PLLC -1 Cumberland Av Bx2947 -Plattsbrgh 12901
(212) 754-7000 .. **Muro,** Bradley J '95 (Danziger D&M) -405 Park Av -NY 10022 **Fx:**758-0143
(718) 590-2000 .. **Muroff,** Jos J '85 %DA -198 E 161st -Bronx 10451 **Fx:**590-6477
(914) 946-1452 .. **Muroff,** Stuart S '93 (Markhoff & M PC) -14 Mamaroneck Av -White Plns 10601
(718) 250-2000 .. **Muros-Bishoff,** Amanda E '07 DA -350 Jay -Brklyn 11201 **Fx:**250-2314
(631) 957-6400 .. **Murov,** Yale M '65 Y Murov,PLLC -215 W Hoffman Av Bx504 -Lindenhrst 11757 **Fx:**957-6456
(716) 847-3438 .. **Murphy,** Amy J '88 %Ct of Claims -125 Main -Buffalo 14203 **Fx:**515-4813
(631) 283-0200 .. **Murphy,** Amy McShea '03 %Gilmartin & B -320 Hmptn Rd Bx5071 -Southampton 11969
(212) 669-4501 .. **Murphy,** Anne W '81 %Tax Appls Tribunal -1 Centre -NY 10007 **Fx:**669-4503
(518) 434-2622 .. **Murphy,** Anthony J '80 (Pozefsky B&M) -90 State -Albany 12207
(718) 423-6800 .. **Murphy,** Austin P Jr. '00 %MacKay W&D LLP -40-26 235th -Douglastn 11363
(212) 825-3507 .. **Murphy,** Ayana E '05 Dept of Bldgs -83 Maiden Ln -NY 10038
(516) 294-5100 .. **Murphy Bartol & O'Brien,LLP** -22 Jericho Tpk -Mineola 11501 **Fx:**294-5385
(518) 436-4781 .. **Murphy,** Brandy B '05 Comm Indp Cllg & Univ 17 Elk Bx7289 -Albany 12224
(212) 585-6452 .. **Murphy,** Brian A '95 NY Presbyterian Hospital -525 E 68th Bx 253 -NY 10065
(914) 674-4100 .. **Murphy,** Brian D '78 (Stecich M&L,LLP) -828 S Bway -Tarrytwn 10591
(212) 859-8000 .. **Murphy,** Brian D '79 (Fried FHS&J LLP) -1 NY Plz -NY 10004
(212) 218-5500 .. **Murphy,** Brian D '05 %Seyfarth S LLP -620 8th Av -NY 10018
(212) 980-0120 .. **Murphy,** Brian G '93 (Frankfurt KK&S,PC) -488 Mad Av -NY 10022
(518) 455-3121 .. **Murphy,** Brian M '69 %NYS Senate -806 Lgsltv Ofc Bldg -Albany 12247
(212) 532-4826 .. **Murphy,** Brian M '82 -1 Bttry Pk Plz -NY 10004 **Fx:**(201) 930-9191
(212) 308-4411 .. **Murphy,** Brian P '86 (Edwards AP&D LLP) -750 Lex Av -NY 10022
(516) 267-6300 .. **Murphy,** Brian P '07 %Bond S&K,PLLC -1399 Franklin Av -Gdn Cty 11530
(212) 530-5000 .. **Murphy,** Brian P '10 %Milbank TH&M LLP -1 Chase Manh Plz -NY 10005
(212) 237-0000 .. **Murphy,** Bryan D '09 %Vinson & E LLP -666 5th Av -NY 10103
(518) 690-0096 .. **Murphy Burns Barber & Murphy,LLP** -226 Great Oaks Blvd -Albany 12203 **Fx:**690-0053
(845) 778-2121 .. **Murphy,** Carmee G '06 %Jacobowitz & G,LLP -158 Orange Av Bx367 -Walden 12586
(607) 337-1724 .. **Murphy,** Catherine F '96 Supreme Ct -6 E Main -Norwich 13815 **Fx:**377-1722
(516) 299-3981 .. **Murphy,** Catherine M '94 Long Island Univ -Univ Ctr Bush Brown Hall -Brookvll 11548 **Fx:**299-2072
(212) 490-6050 .. **Murphy,** Chas Edmund '99 (Lennon M&L LLC) -420 Lex Av -NY 10170 **Fx:**490-6070
(646) 386-5700 .. **Murphy,** Christena M '00 Civil Ct -111 Centre -NY 10013
(585) 454-0700 .. **Murphy,** Christin M '07 %Ward GH&R LLP -300 State -Rchstr 14614
(212) 940-8800 .. **Murphy,** Christine M '05 %Katten MR LLP -575 Mad Av -NY 10022
(716) 884-2000 .. **Murphy,** Christopher M '94 (Doran & M) -1234 Delaware Av -Buffalo 14209
(845) 486-2300 .. **Murphy,** Cindy '97 %DA -236 Main -Poughkeepsie 12601 **Fx:**486-2324
(716) 884-2000 .. **Murphy,** Colleen '07 %Doran & M -1234 Delaware Av -Buffalo 14209
(716) 566-5400 .. **Murphy,** Colleen M '91 (Goldberg S LLP) -665 Main -Buffalo 14203
(646) 227-4200 .. **Murphy,** Connor '99 Navigant Cnsltng -666 3rd Av -NY 10017 **Fx:**227-4299
(212) 262-2390 .. **Murphy,** Conor F '09 %Connell F LLP -888 7th Av -NY 10106
(212) 805-3900 .. **Murphy,** Courtney E '95 (Clausen M PC) -1 Chase Manh Plz -NY 10005
(212) 237-1000 .. **Murphy,** Craig P '77 (Windels ML&M,LLP) -156 W 56th -NY 10019
(716) 845-9481 .. **Murphy,** Danl C '84 Supreme Ct -50 Delaware Av -Buffalo 14202
(212) 574-1200 .. **Murphy,** Danl C '94 Cnsl Seward & K LLP -1 Bttry Pk Plz -NY 10004
(212) 682-0020 .. **Murphy,** Danl F Jr. '76 (Putney TH&H LLP) -521 5th Av -NY 10175
(631) 852-2389 .. **Murphy,** Danl J '73 %Hon PF Cohalan -235 Griffing Av Bx321 -Rvrhead 11901 **Fx:**852-2719
(212) 308-4411 .. **Murphy,** Danl P '01 %Edwards AP&D LLP -750 Lex Av -NY 10022
(212) 210-2100 .. **Murphy,** Danl P '04 %Daily News,LP -450 W 33rd -NY 10001 **Fx:**643-7855
(585) 248-3800 .. **Murphy,** David L '78 (WeinsteinMurphy) -290 Linden Oaks -Rchstr 14625 **Fx:**248-4961
(212) 557-4000 .. **Murphy,** David M '86 (Grunfeld DLS&K LLP) -399 Park Av -NY 10022
(212) 403-1000 .. **Murphy,** David M '92 (Wachtell LR&K) -51 W 52nd -NY 10019
(518) 783-3843 .. **Murphy,** David R '76 (Hacker & M,LLP) -7 Airport Park Blvd -Latham 12110
(631) 584-2262 .. **Murphy,** Dawn '93 -1300 Vets Hwy -Hauppauge 11788
(516) 294-0777 .. **Murphy,** Denis J '58 -245 Hillside Av -Williston Pk 11596 **Fx:**294-1416
(914) 948-8392 .. **Murphy,** Dennis D '02 %J Stuttman,PC -44 S Bway -White Plns 10601 **Fx:**948-6973
(212) 577-7954 .. **Murphy,** Dennis R '97 %Leg Aid -199 Water -NY 10038
(315) 735-0026 .. **Murphy,** Donald J '76 -1017 Park Av -Utica 13501
(212) 776-5244 .. **Murphy,** Donna M '89 %NYC Housing Auth -250 Bway -NY 10007 **Fx:**776-5039
(212) 309-1000 .. **Murphy,** Douglas '02 Cnsl Hunton & W -200 Park Av -NY 10166
(212) 309-1000 .. **Murphy,** Edmond P '78 SrCnsl Hunton & W -200 Park Av -NY 10166
(716) 856-7091 .. **Murphy,** Edw J III '85 %J Freedman -424 Main -Buffalo 14202 **Fx:**856-7097
(516) 296-1000 .. **Murphy,** Elizabeth '07 %Miller & M,PC -100 Q Roosevelt Blvd -Gdn Cty 11530
(718) 243-4122 .. **Murphy,** Ellen D '93 %TA Dept of Buses -370 Jay -Brklyn 11201
(212) 880-9405 .. **Murphy,** Ellen M '04 %Morvillo AGIA&B,PC -565 5th Av -NY 10017
(212) 373-3000 .. **Murphy,** Erin '01 %Paul WRW&G LLP -1285 Av of Amer -NY 10019
(212) 902-9982 .. **Murphy,** Erin P '00 %Goldman Sachs -1 NY Plz -NY 10004
(212) 309-6000 .. **Murphy,** Finnbarr D '02 (Morgan L&B LLP) -101 Park Av -NY 10178
(516) 545-5160 .. **Murphy,** Francis J '91 SrCnsl Natl Grid -175 E Old Cntry Rd -Hicksvll 11801 **Fx:**545-5029
(631) 244-7434 .. **Murphy,** Francis P '80 -32 Bohack Ct -Sayvll 11782 **Fx:**244-8206
(212) 808-7800 .. **Murphy,** Francis T '52 OfCnsl Kelley D&W LLP -101 Park Av -NY 10178
(212) 909-6000 .. **Murphy,** Gary E '99 Cnsl Debevoise & P LLP -919 3rd Av -NY 10022
(518) 789-4442 .. **Murphy,** Gary L '87 (Downey H&M PLLC) -1 John BxZ -Millerton 12546
(212) 397-5529 .. **Murphy,** Gavin D '00 Soros Fund Mgmt LLC -888 7th Av -NY 10106
(914) 591-6162 .. **Murphy,** Gerald J '86 -14 S Bway -Irvngtn 10533
(585) 325-7515 .. **Murphy,** Gerald N '90 (Forsyth HOK&M,PC) -1 Chase Sq -Rchstr 14604
(631) 666-6200 .. **Murphy,** Gerald T Jr. '02 %PF Adams,PC -49 5th Av Bx1089M -Bay Shr 11706 **Fx:**665-6739
(646) 315-7379 .. **Murphy,** Gerard F '96 %FINRA -14 Wall -NY 10005 **Fx:**315-7440
(914) 286-2918 .. **Murphy,** Gregory P '93 OfCnsl Greenberg T,LLP -445 Hmltn Av -White Plns 10601
(914) 712-1100 .. **Murphy & Higgins,LLP** -1 Radisson Plz -New Rchll 10801 **Fx:**633-0512
(212) 556-2100 .. **Murphy,** J Emmett '07 %King & S -1185 Av of Amer -NY 10036
(212) 561-0255 .. **Murphy,** Jamal E '07 -244 5th Av -NY 10001 **Fx:**591-6689
(518) 584-2276 .. **Murphy,** James A Jr. '61 -Bx32 -Middl Grv 12850
(518) 885-2263 .. **Murphy,** James A III '87 (DA) -25 W High -Ballston Spa 12020 **Fx:**884-8627
(212) 943-9080 .. **Murphy,** James E '05 %Virginia & A -111 Bway -NY 10006
(631) 755-0101 .. **Murphy,** James F '90 %Lewis JAA,LLP -425 Broad Hollow Rd -Melvll 11747
(212) 318-6000 .. **Murphy,** James G '89 OfCnsl Paul HJ&W LLP -75 E 55th -NY 10022
(845) 652-5600 .. **Murphy & James, LLC** -275 N Mddltwn Rd -Pearl Rvr 10965 **Fx:**(212) 208-4423
(516) 922-8030 .. **Murphy,** James M '71 (Murphy & L,PC) -1045 Oyster Bay Rd -E Norwich 11732
(516) 747-4082 .. **Murphy,** James M '83 (Montfort HM&S LLP) -1140 Franklin Av Bx7677 -Gdn Cty 11530
(212) 765-2100 .. **Murphy,** James M '90 (Spivak L LLP) -1700 Bway -NY 10019
(315) 734-2000 .. **Murphy,** James P '92 %Utica Natl Ins -180 Genesee Bx530 -Utica 13502 **Fx:**734-2662
(516) 794-1900 .. **Murphy,** James R '79 (Bechtle & M) -100 Grdn City Plz -Gdn Cty 11530
(607) 753-1134 .. **Murphy,** James T '77 %Leg Srvcs -111 Port Watson -Cortlnd 13045 **Fx:**753-7257
(516) 775-7008 .. **Murphy,** James T '85 -40 Woodbine Ct -Floral Pk 11001 **Fx:**775-7794
(212) 474-1000 .. **Murphy,** Jarrod D '09 %Cravath S&M LLP -825 8th Av -NY 10019
(518) 220-1850 .. **Murphy,** Jason A '10 %Schmeiser O&W -22 Century Hill Dr -Latham 12110
(516) 746-8100 .. **Murphy,** Jason M '07 %D Buttafuoco & Assoc -144 Woodbury Rd -Woodbury 11797 **Fx:**746-6473
(212) 851-8374 .. **Murphy,** Jeanne M '82 Actimize Inc -1359 Bway -NY 10018 **Fx:**643-4193
(212) 768-6700 .. **Murphy,** Jeffrey J '84 (Sonnenschein N&R LLP) -2 World Fncl Ctr -NY 10281
(212) 318-6000 .. **Murphy,** Jeffrey R '09 %Paul HJ&W LLP -75 E 55th -NY 10022

(518) 457-2070 .. **Murphy,** Jennifer A '01 %Dept of Tax & Fin -Bldg 9 State Campus -Albany 12227 **Fx:**457-6131
(516) 378-1700 .. **Murphy,** Jerome C '82 (Chesney & M) -2305 Grand Av -Baldwin 11510
(866) 348-5819 .. **Murphy,** Jessica Vrooman '00 %SSA-ODAR -50 Fountain Plz -Buffalo 14202 **Fx:**(716) 551-4078
(212) 285-1200 .. **Murphy,** Jill G '09 %Mallin & Assoc,PC -132 Nassau -NY 10038 **Fx:**285-1202
(518) 436-0751 .. **Murphy,** Joan S '78 Hinman S PC -121 State -Albany 12207
(845) 298-9400 .. **Murphy,** John F '80 -11 Marshall Rd -Wappingers Fls 12590 **Fx:**298-9402
(914) 949-2700 .. **Murphy,** John J '81 %Bleakley P&S,LLP -1 N Lex Av -White Plns 10601
(718) 442-4052 .. **Murphy,** John M Jr. '79 -60 Bay -Staten Isl 10301 **Fx:**448-8685
(315) 695-3359 .. **Murphy,** John M Jr. '89 (J Murphy Jr,PC) -440 Main -Phoenix 13135 **Fx:**695-4037
(732) 372-9088 .. **Murphy,** John M III '06 -60 Bay -Staten Isl 10301
(212) 903-9000 .. **Murphy,** John O '03 %Linklaters -1345 Av of Amer -NY 10105
(212) 578-3095 .. **Murphy,** John R '76 %MetLife -27-01 Qns Plz N -LIC 11101
(914) 949-2700 .. **Murphy,** Jonathan A '87 (Bleakley P&S,LLP) -1 N Lex Av -White Plns 10601
(212) 259-8000 .. **Murphy,** Jos A '08 %Dewey & L LLP -1301 Av of Amer -NY 10019
(212) 909-6000 .. **Murphy,** Jos D '09 %Debevoise & P LLP -919 3rd Av -NY 10022
(716) 372-2853 .. **Murphy,** Jos P '77 (Murphy & M) -208 N Clinton -Olean 14760
(518) 459-6450 .. **Murphy,** Jos T '61 -1058 Wshngtn Av -Albany 12203 **Fx:**459-6451
(212) 245-1000 .. **Murphy,** Julia Griffin '10 OfCnsl Outten & G LLP -3 Park Av -NY 10016
(315) 363-5285 .. **Murphy,** Justin R '88 -248 Main Bx673 -Oneida 13421
(518) 392-6471 .. **Murphy,** Karen A '89 (Bonstrom & M) -76 Phelps Rd -Old Chatham 12136
(212) 553-5400 .. **Murphy,** Kathleen A '04 %Zurich NA -1 Lbrty Plz -NY 10006
(212) 310-8000 .. **Murphy,** Kathleen E '04 %Weil G&M LLP -767 5th Av -NY 10153
(212) 651-7500 .. **Murphy,** Katrina H '04 %Segal MS&M -850 3rd Av -NY 10022
(212) 947-1999 .. **Murphy,** Keith J '06 %Methfessel & W,PC -450 7th Av -NY 10123
(212) 589-4200 .. **Murphy,** Keith R '97 Cnsl Baker & H LLP -45 Rckfllr Plz -NY 10111
(212) 878-8000 .. **Murphy,** Kelly A '07 %Clifford C LLP -31 W 52nd -NY 10019
(212) 332-8900 .. **Murphy,** Kenneth C '96 (Simon & Prtnrs LLP) -551 5th Av -NY 10176 **Fx:**332-8909
(914) 328-3661 .. **Murphy,** Kenneth D '84 -175 Main -White Plns 10601
(845) 639-1320 .. **Murphy,** Kenneth J '83 (Samimi & M) -616 S Main -New Cty 10956 **Fx:**639-8069
(212) 588-0800 .. **Murphy,** Kevin '96 (Frommer L&H LLP) -745 5th Av -NY 10151
(315) 445-1700 .. **Murphy,** Kevin C '80 Wladis Law Firm,PC -5795 Widewaters Pkwy -Syracuse 13214 **Fx:**251-1073
(914) 824-5645 .. **Murphy,** Kevin G '91 %Surrogates Ct -111 Dr MLK Jr Blvd -White Plns 10601 **Fx:**995-3728
(212) 820-9300 .. **Murphy,** Kevin H '06 %Hawkins D&W LLP -One Chase Manh Plz -NY 10005
(716) 270-2431 .. **Murphy,** Kevin M '89 %IRS -300 Pearl -Buffalo 14202
(716) 853-8477 .. **Murphy,** Kim S '90 %Dept of Law -350 Main Pl Twr -Buffalo 14202 **Fx:**853-8571
(212) 683-7100 .. **Murphy,** Kristen A '00 %Gallo V&K,LLP -90 Broad -NY 10004
(845) 291-7100 .. **Murphy & Lambiase** -1997 State Route 17M -Goshen 10924 **Fx:**291-7171
(212) 455-2000 .. **Murphy,** Laura D '03 %Simpson T&B LLP -425 Lex Av -NY 10017
(914) 995-3000 .. **Murphy,** Laura M '89 %DA -111 Martin Luther King Blvd -White Plns 10601 **Fx:**995-3363
(516) 408-1600 .. **Murphy,** Laura Sheridan '05 %Heidell PM&B,LLP -1050 Franklin Av -Gdn Cty 11530
(516) 538-1111 .. **Murphy,** Lawr P Jr. '71 OfCnsl Mahon MK&O,LLC -254 Nassau Blvd -Garden City South 11530
(914) 234-6363 .. **Murphy,** Leah Lennon '91 (Kuntz S&M,PC) -444 Old Post Rd -Bedfrd 10506 **Fx:**234-6249
(585) 268-5800 .. **Murphy,** Leo J Jr. '72 Cnty Ct -7 Court -Belmont 14813 **Fx:**268-7090
(607) 898-3190 .. **Murphy,** Liam G B '89 (Ward & M) -170 Main -Groton 13073
(518) 885-2263 .. **Murphy,** Lyn A '96 %DA -25 W High -Ballston Spa 12020 **Fx:**884-8627
(516) 922-8030 .. **Murphy & Lynch,PC** -1045 Oyster Bay Rd -E Norwich 11732 **Fx:**624-8264
(716) 842-1100 .. **Murphy,** Lynn Archer '93 (Palmer M&T) -288 Linwood Av -Buffalo 14209 **Fx:**842-1104
(212) 836-8000 .. **Murphy,** M Thos '08 %Kaye S LLP -425 Park Av -NY 10022
(716) 853-4080 .. **Murphy,** Margaret A '04 %Colucci & G,PC -424 Main -Buffalo 14202
(212) 490-3000 .. **Murphy,** Margaret Marie '02 %Wilson EME&D LLP -150 E 42nd -NY 10017
(914) 846-5871 .. **Murphy,** Marijo Ford '95 NY Life Ins -1 Rockwood Rd -Sleepy Hollow 10591
(716) 551-4741 .. **Murphy,** Mark P '91 %US DHS -130 Delaware Av -Buffalo 14202
(914) 633-0901 .. **Murphy,** Martin J '79 -110 Wellngtn Rd -New Rchll 10804 **Fx:**633-0901
(516) 574-6150 .. **Murphy,** Martin J '83 %JP Morgan Chase -1985 Marcus Av -New Hyde Pk 11040
(315) 435-2170 .. **Murphy,** Martin J '87 %Cnty Atty -421 Mntgmry -Syracuse 13202 **Fx:**435-5729
(212) 436-1105 .. **Murphy,** Mary C '87 IRS -290 Bway -NY 10007 **Fx:**436-1063
(212) 309-6000 .. **Murphy,** Matthew B '08 %Morgan L&B LLP -101 Park Av -NY 10178
(716) 439-7085 .. **Murphy,** Matthew J III '78 (DA) -175 Hawley -Lockprt 14094 **Fx:**439-7102
(212) 779-9910 .. **Murphy,** Maura '88 (Eaton & V LLP) -3 Park Av -NY 10016
(914) 686-5600 .. **Murphy,** Maura L '03 All NY Title Agency -180 E Post Rd -White Plns 10601 **Fx:**686-1440
(212) 788-8939 .. **Murphy,** Maureen Ann '96 %Mayor's Ofc of Contracts -253 Bway -NY 10007
(212) 260-6412 .. **Murphy,** Meaghean C '05 -233 E 9th -NY 10003
(516) 357-3000 .. **Murphy,** Melissa M '03 %Rivkin R LLP -926 RXR Plz -Uniondale 11556
(212) 248-3140 .. **Murphy,** Meredith R '07 %Drinker B&R LLP -140 Bway -NY 10005
(212) 702-5400 .. **Murphy,** Michl '98 (Beveridge & D,PC) -477 Mad Av -NY 10022
(716) 847-8400 .. **Murphy,** Michl C '07 %Phillips L LLP -3400 HSBC Ctr -Buffalo 14203
(212) 810-5849 .. **Murphy,** Michl E '97 Black Rock Inc -40 E 52nd -NY 10022
(518) 465-3484 .. **Murphy,** Michl J '83 (Carter CCBM&L,PC) -20 Corp Wds Blvd -Albany 12211
(718) 579-3000 .. **Murphy,** Michl J '86 %Leg Aid -1020 Grnd Cncrs -Bronx 10451 **Fx:**588-2611
(518) 689-1411 .. **Murphy,** Michl J '92 (Greenberg T,LLP) -54 State -Albany 12207
(516) 328-9201 .. **Murphy,** Michl J '06 %Ruffo TM&M PC -3000 Marcus Av -Lk Success 11042
(212) 335-4500 .. **Murphy,** Michl P '88 (DLA Piper LLP) -1251 Av of Amer -NY 10020
(718) 267-1717 .. **Murphy,** Michl S '98 -25-28 Bway -Astoria 11106 **Fx:**204-5565
(315) 457-1422 .. **Murphy,** Michl W '76 -115 Colony Park Dr -Liverpool 13088
(212) 455-2000 .. **Murphy,** Michele '08 %Simpson T&B LLP -425 Lex Av -NY 10017
(212) 885-7232 .. **Murphy,** Michelle L '02 BDO USA,LLP -330 Mad Av -NY 10017
(212) 788-9111 .. **Murphy,** Molly R '02 NYC Council-Govt Affrs Div -250 Bway -NY 10007 **Fx:**341-0363
(212) 997-4400 .. **Murphy,** Nancy Anne '98 %Teitler & T,LLP -1114 Av of Amer -NY 10036 **Fx:**997-4949
(212) 297-5800 .. **Murphy,** Natalia '01 SrCnsl Day P LLP -7 Times Sq -NY 10036
(718) 250-2000 .. **Murphy,** Nicole A '06 %DA -350 Jay -Brklyn 11201 **Fx:**250-2314
(518) 762-3103 .. **Murphy Niles & Greco** -8 S William Bx687 -Johnstwn 12095 **Fx:**736-1170
(518) 862-7300 .. **Murphy,** Norah M '88 T Puleo -900 Watervliet Shaker Rd Bx12699 -Albany 12212 **Fx:**862-7322
(212) 839-5300 .. **Murphy,** Patricia A '82 (Sidley A LLP) -787 7th Av -NY 10019
(845) 652-5600 .. **Murphy,** Patricia A '84 (Murphy & J,LLC) -275 N Mddltwn Rd -Pearl Rvr 10965
(914) 681-0113 .. **Murphy,** Patricia A '91 -2 William -White Plns 10601
(914) 995-4172 .. **Murphy,** Patricia M '84 %DA -111 Martin Luther King Blvd -White Plns 10601 **Fx:**995-3363
(914) 238-6200 .. **Murphy,** Patricia M '86 (Murphy Law Firm) -140 King -Chappaqua 10514 **Fx:**238-8141
(212) 425-3600 .. **Murphy,** Patrick J '64 (Murphy & O) -40 Wall -NY 10005 **Fx:**425-3201
(212) 286-8585 .. **Murphy,** Patrick J '04 %Heidell PM&B,LLP -99 Park Av -NY 10016
(516) 741-6266 .. **Murphy,** Patrick M '84 (McCabe CM&F,LLP) -346 Westbury Av Bx9000 -Carle Pl 11514
(516) 489-0800 .. **Murphy,** Patrick N '05 %T Restivo,PC -100 Q Roosevelt Blvd -Gdn Cty 11530 **Fx:**683-8732
(212) 859-8000 .. **Murphy,** Patrick R '09 %Fried FHS&J LLP -1 NY Plz -NY 10004
(516) 498-8830 .. **Murphy,** Paul A '83 -60 Cuttermill Rd -Gt Neck 11021 **Fx:**498-8998
(631) 787-8452 .. **Murphy,** Pearl Olwen '99 (PO Murphy,PC) -150 Motor Pkwy -Hauppauge 11788 **Fx:**342-0069
(516) 352-3383 .. **Murphy,** Peter J '85 -390 Hillside Av -New Hyde Pk 11040 **Fx:**352-3721
(518) 436-0751 .. **Murphy,** Philip J '95 (Hinman S PC) -121 State -Albany 12207
(631) 665-3400 .. **Murphy,** Philip M '73 %Siben & S,LLP -90 E Main Bx149P -Bay Shr 11706
(845) 639-6600 .. **Murphy,** Phillip J '90 -10 Esquire Rd -New Cty 10956 **Fx:**639-6620
(212) 806-5400 .. **Murphy,** Quinlan '04 %Stroock &S&L LLP -180 Maiden Ln -NY 10038
(914) 684-6900 .. **Murphy,** Raymond W '77 -Bx768 -Armonk 10504
(716) 634-6750 .. **Murphy,** Richd H '77 (Sheffer M&W) -6461 Main -Williamsvll 14221
(518) 402-6757 .. **Murphy,** Robt A Jr. '80 %Workers Comp Bd -20 Park -Albany 12207
(607) 722-2122 .. **Murphy,** Robt C '87 -20 Hawley Bx430 -Bnghmtn 13902 **Fx:**722-0202
(917) 836-7532 .. **Murphy,** Robt E '82 -119 Rockland Ctr, Rte 59 -Nanuet 10954
(305) 982-6388 .. **Murphy,** Robt H '98 %SEC -3 World Fncl Ctr -NY 10281 **Fx:**(212) 336-1323
(516) 739-3395 .. **Murphy,** Robt S '81 (Murphy & M,LLC) -1461 Franklin Av -Gdn Cty 11530 **Fx:**742-5278
(716) 565-1100 .. **Murphy,** Ryan M '09 %Andreozzi F LLP -9145 Main -Clarence 14031
(212) 302-2400 .. **Murphy,** Sara T '03 %Lynch DE LLP -264 W 40th -NY 10018
(516) 742-5600 .. **Murphy,** Scott A '97 OfCnsl J Wallenstein -1100 Franklin Av -Gdn Cty 11530 **Fx:**742-5040
(631) 952-7962 .. **Murphy,** Seamus S '94 %Workers Comp Bd -220 Rabro Rd -Hauppauge 11788 **Fx:**738-1553
(845) 691-7292 .. **Murphy,** Sean '92 (DiStasi M&M PLLC) -400 Uppr North Rd Bx915 -Highlnd 12528
(212) 436-5706 .. **Murphy,** Sean K '97 Deloitte & Touche,LLP -2 World Fncl Ctr -NY 10281
(212) 530-5000 .. **Murphy,** Sean M '95 (Milbank TH&M LLP) -1 Chase Manh Plz -NY 10005
(212) 455-2000 .. **Murphy,** Sean P M '07 %Simpson T&B LLP -425 Lex Av -NY 10017
(212) 578-7057 .. **Murphy,** Sheila M '89 %MetLife -27-01 Qns Plz N -LIC 11101
(212) 736-5300 .. **Murphy,** Stephen J '98 (Block O&M LLP) -1 Penn Plz -NY 10119
(212) 308-0070 .. **Murphy,** Suzanne M '92 OfCnsl McCusker AR&C,PC -805 3rd Av -NY 10022
(845) 639-1415 .. **Murphy,** Terese Bartucci '86 Natl Granite Title Ins Agncy -155 N Main -New Cty 10956 **Fx:**638-4753
(914) 997-1346 .. **Murphy,** Theresa Anne '96 %Seham SM&P,LLP -445 Hmltn Av -White Plns 10601
(516) 764-2800 .. **Murphy,** Theresa Brennan '96 %Goldberg & C -66 N Vllg Av -Rockvll Ctr 11570
(845) 331-0702 .. **Murphy,** Thos A '87 (Cook NCK&M,PC) -85 Main Bx3939 -Kingston 12402
(212) 430-0800 .. **Murphy,** Thos C '92 Cnsl Kennedy LS&E -75 Maiden Ln -NY 10038
(315) 492-8424 .. **Murphy,** Thos G '82 -4632 Bloomsbury Dr -Syracuse 13215 **Fx:**492-4660
(315) 422-6154 .. **Murphy,** Thos J '88 (Greene H&S) -1 Lincoln Ctr -Syracuse 13202
(845) 562-1515 .. **Murphy,** Thos James '79 (T Murphy & Assoc) -717 Bway -Newburgh 12550 **Fx:**562-1160
(518) 690-0096 .. **Murphy,** Thos K '92 (Murphy BB&M,LLP) -226 Great Oaks Blvd -Albany 12203
(516) 622-0606 .. **Murphy,** Thos P '99 %P Rizzuto,PC -1 Old Cntry Rd -Carle Pl 11514 **Fx:**622-2112
(845) 246-9575 .. **Murphy,** Timothy '74 Murphy Law Ofc -1 W Brdg Bx300 -Saugerties 12477 **Fx:**246-1905
(914) 249-6379 .. **Murphy,** Timothy H '96 %MasterCard Intl -2000 Purchase -Purchase 10577

(315) 471-3151 .. **Murphy,** Timothy P '90 (Hancock & E,LLP) -1500 AXA Twr I Bx4976 -Syracuse 13221
(716) 853-9555 .. **Murphy,** Timothy P '95 %Leg Aid -237 Main -Buffalo 14203 **Fx:**853-3219
(212) 819-8200 .. **Murphy,** Toren J '08 %White & C LLP -1155 Av of Amer -NY 10036
(518) 447-7110 .. **Murphy,** Tracy A '93 Cnty Atty -112 State -Albany 12207
(845) 297-6670 .. **Murphy,** Tracy J '98 (TJ Murphy,PLLC) -169 Myers Crnrs Rd -Wappingers Fls 12590 **Fx:**(509) 351-9586
(315) 474-4431 .. **Murphy,** Tracy L '99 Rosewood Hghts Hlth Ctr -614 S Crouse Av -Syracuse 13210 **Fx:**703-1310
(212) 839-5300 .. **Murphy,** Victoria E '08 %Sidley A LLP -787 7th Av -NY 10019
(212) 656-6556 .. **Murphy,** Vincent F '70 NYSE -20 Broad -NY 10005
(716) 885-1300 .. **Murphy,** Wm D '99 (Maxwell & M) -1230 Delaware Av -Buffalo 14209
(212) 269-7308 .. **Murphy,** Wm G '69 OfCnsl Leahey & J PC -120 Wall -NY 10005
(914) 949-2700 .. **Murphy,** Wm M '82 (Bleakley P&S,LLP) -1 N Lex Av -White Plns 10601
(212) 222-7277 .. **Murphy & Zissu** -375 Riverside Dr -NY 10025 **Fx:**864-5284
(212) 423-1030 .. **Murphy Biondo,** Marcia '98 Murphy & Associates -103 E 125th -NY 10035 **Fx:**722-4966
(212) 805-3900 .. **Murphy-Petros,** Melissa A '96 %Clausen M PC -1 Chase Manh Plz -NY 10005
(718) 298-8946 .. **Murphy-Zadoff,** Eileen M '88 %Leg Aid -153-01 Jamaica Av -Jamaica 11432 **Fx:**657-0537
(212) 619-1250 .. **Murrain,** Godfrey H '55 -225 Bway -NY 10007 **Fx:**619-1253
(631) 844-7214 .. **Murray,** Adele Kittredge '97 %Olsten Corp -175 Broadhllw Rd -Melvll 11747 **Fx:**844-7414
(718) 222-2311 .. **Murray,** Alice '95 %Law Dept -350 Jay -Brklyn 11201 **Fx:**222-2373
(718) 264-3340 .. **Murray,** Andrew F '08 %MHLS -80-45 Wnchstr Blvd -Qns Vllg 11427 **Fx:**264-3559
(516) 357-3000 .. **Murray,** Anne M '93 (Rivkin R LLP) -926 RXR Plz -Uniondale 11556
(914) 762-7179 .. **Murray,** Barbara A '80 -35 Cherry Hill Ct -Briarclff Mnr 10510
(212) 732-2000 .. **Murray,** Brian E '94 (Cullen and D LLP) -44 Wall -NY 10005
(516) 229-4200 .. **Murray,** Brian J '03 Mendolia & S -875 Merrick Av -Westbury 11590
(212) 682-1818 .. **Murray,** Brian P '91 (Murray F&S LLP) -275 Mad Av -NY 10016
(212) 805-6715 .. **Murray,** Christine M '93 %Hon R Berman -40 Foley Sq -NY 10007
(212) 238-3000 .. **Murray,** Christopher '96 (Emmet M&M,LLP) -120 Bway -NY 10271
(212) 458-1512 .. **Murray,** Christopher J '95 AIU Holdings -175 Water -NY 10038
(718) 547-3403 .. **Murray,** Clinvern Delroy '03 D Murray & Assoc -4323 Brnx Blvd -Bronx 10466 **Fx:**547-3406
(518) 462-5601 .. **Murray,** Cornelius D '69 (O'Connell & A) -54 State -Albany 12207
(212) 973-8000 .. **Murray,** Cynthia A '04 %Schnader HS&L LLP -140 Bway -NY 10005
(518) 644-3353 .. **Murray,** Danl P '89 -964 Trout Lk Rd Bx1189 -Bolton Landing 12814 **Fx:**644-3353
(716) 847-8400 .. **Murray,** David J '87 (Phillips L LLP) -3400 HSBC Ctr -Buffalo 14203
(212) 859-5001 .. **Murray,** Dean P '07 %Margolis Law Firm,LLC -110 Wall -NY 10005 **Fx:**943-2300
(212) 788-1278 .. **Murray,** Diana M '88 %Law Dept -100 Church -NY 10007 **Fx:**788-0367
(718) 268-2171 .. **Murray,** Don A '92 (Shalley & M) -118-35 Qns Blvd -Frst Hlls 11375 **Fx:**520-8544
(212) 259-8000 .. **Murray,** Donald J '85 (Dewey & L LLP) -1301 Av of Amer -NY 10019
(516) 663-6600 .. **Murray,** E Christopher '88 (Ruskin MF,PC) -1425 RXR Plz -Uniondale 11556
(518) 455-7700 .. **Murray,** Elizabeth F '92 %Ct of Appls -20 Eagle -Albany 12207
(212) 790-4500 .. **Murray,** Elizabeth K '05 %Manatt P&P,LLP -7 Times Sq -NY 10036
(516) 365-9191 .. **Murray,** Erin D '03 The Hartford -1 Hllw Ln -New Hyde Pk 11042
(212) 373-3000 .. **Murray,** Francine N '03 Paul WRW&G LLP -1285 Av of Amer -NY 10019
(516) 766-3131 .. **Murray,** Francis J '71 (Murray & M) -100 Merrick Rd -Rockvll Ctr 11570
(845) 339-5550 .. **Murray,** Francis T '72 -23 Crown Bx3716 -Kingston 12402 **Fx:**339-5721
(212) 682-1818 .. **Murray Frank & Sailer LLP** -275 Mad Av -NY 10016 **Fx:**682-1892
(516) 767-3600 .. **Murray,** George E '02 %Chalos O&D -366 Main -Pt Wash 11050
(888) 204-2038 .. **Murray,** Gerald '60 -144 Woodbury Rd -Woodbury 11797 **Fx:**(623) 584-2392
(716) 884-0139 .. **Murray,** Glenn E '81 -484 Delaware Av -Buffalo 14202 **Fx:**884-0927
(914) 275-8019 .. **Murray,** Hwesu S '93 Dahomean Co,Inc -81 Pondfld Rd -Bronxvll 10708
(845) 647-4000 .. **Murray,** James J '56 OfCnsl Collier & B,PLLC -130 S Main Bx509 -Ellenvll 12428
(914) 789-2038 .. **Murray,** James V '67 Union Carbide Corp -771 Old Saw Mill Rvr Rd -Tarrytwn 10591
(212) 941-9266 .. **Murray,** JaneAnne '91 -233 Bway -NY 10279 **Fx:**571-9149
(585) 241-5999 .. **Murray,** Jeremy V '10 %Evans & F LLP -95 Allens Crk Rd -Rchstr 14618
(585) 295-4400 .. **Murray,** Jessica R '89 (Hiscock & B,LLP) -2000 HSBC Plz -Rchstr 14604
(212) 425-7200 .. **Murray,** John '07 %Kenyon & K,LLP -1 Bway -NY 10004
(914) 478-5842 .. **Murray,** John L '55 -172 High -Hastings-On-Hud 10706 **Fx:**478-5845
(516) 627-8910 .. **Murray,** John T '73 %Associated Global Services -3333 New Hyde Pk Rd -New Hyde Pk 11042
(212) 336-0034 .. **Murray,** John W R '00 %SEC -3 World Fncl Ctr -NY 10281 **Fx:**336-1323
(212) 909-6000 .. **Murray,** Jordan C '01 (Debevoise & P LLP) -919 3rd Av -NY 10022
(845) 371-7680 .. **Murray,** Jos G '86 (Zimmerer MC&K) -10 Esquire Rd -New Cty 10956
(212) 791-7200 .. **Murray,** Jos T '94 %Hart BD&H -90 John -NY 10038
(718) 514-3855 .. **Murray,** Jos W '07 -6123 190th -Fresh Mdws 11365
(212) 264-0777 .. **Murray,** Julia Marie '96 HUD -26 Fed Plz -NY 10278
(716) 636-9462 .. **Murray,** Karen E '91 %CGU Ins -Bx302 -Buffalo 14240
(631) 287-3065 .. **Murray,** Kathleen '00 %Town Atty -116 Hmptn Rd -Southampton 11968 **Fx:**287-3662
(212) 904-6493 .. **Murray,** Kathleen E '01 MacMillan McGraw Hill Co -2 Penn Plz -NY 10121
(212) 210-2885 .. **Murray,** Kay A '89 Tribune Co -220 E 42nd -NY 10017
(212) 663-4104 .. **Murray,** Kay C '77 -100 LaSalle -NY 10027
(718) 242-2758 .. **Murray,** Keith L '93 %Chase Manhattan Bk -4 Chase Metrotech Ctr -Brklyn 11245 **Fx:**242-3839
(212) 999-5800 .. **Murray,** Kenneth M '02 %Wilson SG&R -1301 Av of Americas -NY 10019
(845) 483-8200 .. **Murray,** Linda M '98 City Ct -62 Civic Ctr Plz -Poughkeepsie 12601 **Fx:**485-6795
(718) 389-9721 .. **Murray,** Loretta H '89 -907 Manh Av -Brklyn 11222 **Fx:**383-4252
(212) 766-4000 .. **Murray,** Marcie Waterman '85 (Deutsch TW&W,PC) -120 Bway -NY 10271
(646) 708-8088 .. **Murray,** Marianne Fusto '84 Fidelity Natl Law Grp -350 5th Av -NY 10118 **Fx:**(212) 594-8378
(631) 234-0909 .. **Murray,** Mark A '89 (Murray & H) -132 Clyde -W Sayvll 11796 **Fx:**234-2524
(516) 747-4770 .. **Murray,** Mark A '89 (Murray & H) -100 Q Roosevelt Blvd -Gdn Cty 11530 **Fx:**747-3928
(631) 853-4161 .. **Murray,** Mark J '99 %DA -N Cnty Cmplx Bldg 77 -Hauppauge 11788 **Fx:**853-4192
(212) 331-5155 .. **Murray,** Marsha E '01 HRA-OLA -180 Water -NY 10038
(212) 764-4062 .. **Murray,** Martin J '88 -475 Park Av S -NY 10016
(914) 636-2588 .. **Murray,** Mary Jane '60 -206 Overlook Rd -New Rchll 10804 **Fx:**632-0359
(716) 852-5211 .. **Murray,** Matthew T III '95 %MA Bjork -350 Main -Buffalo 14202 **Fx:**852-8149
(516) 766-3131 .. **Murray & McCann** -100 Merrick Rd -Rockvll Ctr 11570 **Fx:**678-4578
(518) 402-9188 .. **Murray,** Meta R '78 %DEC -625 Bway -Albany 12233 **Fx:**402-9018
(718) 579-3000 .. **Murray,** Michl J '89 %Leg Aid -1020 Grnd Cncrs -Bronx 10451 **Fx:**588-2611
(212) 530-5000 .. **Murray,** Michl M '96 (Milbank TH&M LLP) -1 Chase Manh Plz -NY 10005
(914) 310-7508 .. **Murray,** Nicola R '04 -9525 Seaview Ct -Brklyn 11236 **Fx:**(866) 541-4975
(212) 895-0260 .. **Murray,** P Susanne Mast '88 %Alliant Insurance Srvcs -99 Park Av -NY 10016
(518) 474-6367 .. **Murray,** Patricia L '83 %Bd of Elections -40 Steuben -Albany 12207
(212) 278-0400 .. **Murray,** Peter D '68 (Cooper & D LLP) -30 Rckfllr Plz -NY 10112
(518) 688-0755 .. **Murray,** Peter D '98 -10 Maxwell Dr -Clifton Pk 12065 **Fx:**688-0297
(315) 671-1106 .. **Murray,** R Michl '74 %Hon C Major -Cthse -Syracuse 13202 **Fx:**671-1184
(212) 879-5500 .. **Murray,** Rebecca L '99 %Metropolitan Museum -1000 5th Av -NY 10028 **Fx:**570-3850
(917) 207-1250 .. **Murray,** Richd H B '79 -30 Vesey -NY 10007 **Fx:**(718) 796-4457
(518) 285-8600 .. **Murray,** Rika '85 Family Ct -30 Clinton Av -Albany 12207
(716) 200-5050 .. **Murray,** Robt G '01 (Harris B PLLC) -726 Exchange -Buffalo 14210
(914) 523-4063 .. **Murray,** Robt W '65 -1181 Post Rd -Scarsdale 10583
(212) 408-2500 .. **Murray,** Robt W Jr. '81 (Baker B,LLP) -30 Rckfllr Plz -NY 10112
(212) 385-1422 .. **Murray,** Stephen J '68 OfCnsl Mahoney & K,LLP -76 Beaver -NY 10005
(212) 571-0111 .. **Murray,** Stephen P '05 %Hardin KM&P,PA -110 William -NY 10038
(716) 881-3010 .. **Murray,** Terrie Benson '80 (Cohen & L,PC) -343 Elmwood Av Bx5204 -Buffalo 14213
(212) 358-1500 .. **Murray,** Thos M '98 (Kennedy J&M,PC) -113 Univ Pl -NY 10003
(718) 923-4206 .. **Murray,** Thora M '91 %OTDA Fair Hearings -14 Boerum Pl -Brklyn 11201
(212) 880-2683 .. **Murray,** Timothy J '84 -100 Park Av -NY 10017 **Fx:**880-6499
(212) 335-9000 .. **Murray,** Warren J Jr. '70 %DA -1 Hogan Pl -NY 10013
(518) 388-3408 .. **Murray,** Wm J '82 -Bx7500 -Schnctdy 12301
(718) 206-4726 .. **Murrell,** Eric T '08 Law Dept -89-17 Sutphin Blvd -Jamaica 11435 **Fx:**206-4702
(845) 567-0177 .. **Murrell,** Patricia L '98 -572 Riley Rd -New Windsor 12553
(716) 856-4000 .. **Murrer,** Christopher G '10 %Hodgson R LLP -140 Pearl -Buffalo 14202
(716) 854-2020 .. **Murrett,** John C Jr. '82 (Cellino & B,PC) -350 Main -Buffalo 14202
(716) 842-6988 .. **Murrett,** Peter J Jr. '49 -237 Main -Buffalo 14203 **Fx:**852-0271
(212) 319-6898 .. **Murski,** Karina E '04 %Lavin ORC&D -420 Lex Av -NY 10170
(716) 839-1526 .. **Murszewski,** Sue Dealy '62 -84 Harper Rd -Snyder 14226
(516) 766-3200 .. **Murtagh Cohen & Byrne** -100 N Park Av -Rockvll Ctr 11570 **Fx:**766-3402
(631) 777-2330 .. **Murtagh,** Kevin J '78 (O'Connor OH&D,LLP) -1 Huntngtn Quad -Melvll 11747
(516) 931-0064 .. **Murtagh,** Kevin T '02 %Kingsley K&C -91 W Cherry -Hicksvll 11801 **Fx:**931-4313
(914) 967-4655 .. **Murtagh,** Martin J '55 -6 Mendota Av -Rye 10580
(518) 445-6050 .. **Murtagh-Monks,** Karen L '86 %Prisoners' Leg Srvcs -41 State -Albany 12207 **Fx:**445-6053
(845) 471-6320 .. **Murtaugh,** Edw J '49 -35 Market -Poughkeepsie 12601 **Fx:**471-4593
(212) 635-6725 .. **Murtha,** Eugenia K '02 Bank of NY-Mellon -1 Wall -NY 10005
(631) 747-0356 .. **Murtha,** James D '08 (Murtha & M,PLLC) -26 Railroad Av -Babylon 11702 **Fx:**991-7168
(212) 717-0196 .. **Murtha,** James J '58 -10 E 85th -NY 10028
(212) 984-7700 .. **Murtha,** Janet R '00 (Warshaw BCS&K,LLP) -555 5th Av -NY 10017
(212) 964-9640 .. **Murtha,** Kelly L '98 %Cascione P&G,PC -20 Vesey -NY 10007
(631) 747-0356 .. **Murtha,** Michelle '05 (Murtha & M,PLLC) -26 Railroad Av -Babylon 11702 **Fx:**991-7168
(212) 966-6906 .. **Murtha,** Robt A Jr. '86 -401 Bway -NY 10013 **Fx:**966-6392
(516) 997-4800 .. **Murtha,** T Kevin '84 (TK Murtha & Assoc,PC) -45 Post Av -Westbury 11590 **Fx:**997-9027
(516) 938-3100 .. **Murtha,** Timothy J '02 %P Roach & Assoc,PC -125 Michl Dr -Syosset 11791 **Fx:**931-4403
(212) 408-5100 .. **Murthy,** Divya '06 %Chadbourne & P LLP -30 Rckfllr Plz -NY 10112
(212) 833-1125 .. **Murzyn,** Jessica A '00 %Friedman KS&A LLP -1633 Bway -NY 10019 **Fx:**373-7925
(212) 474-1000 .. **Musa,** Derek D '10 %Cravath S&M LLP -825 8th Av -NY 10019
(716) 532-3351 .. **Musacchio,** James A '96 Musacchio & P -215 W Main Bx230 -Gowanda 14070 **Fx:**532-3022
(631) 242-5026 .. **Musachio,** Mark A '90 -1641 Deer Prk Av -Deer Pk 11729
(212) 752-2100 .. **Musa-Obregon,** S Michl '93 -5521 69th -Maspeth 11378 **Fx:**752-8677

(716) 856-7330 .. **Musarra,** Arthur F '48 -14 Lafayette Sq -Buffalo 14203 **Fx:**856-7331
(716) 836-7083 .. **Musarra,** Arthur F '87 -468 Lebrun -Eggertsvll 14226
(716) 856-7330 .. **Musarra,** Claudette R M '75 -14 Lafayette Sq -Buffalo 14203 **Fx:**856-7331
(516) 364-7900 .. **Musarra,** Michele A '99 Epstein F&G -45 Crsswys Park Dr W -Woodbury 11797
(212) 265-6888 .. **Muscalino,** Katharine A '08 %Porzio B&N,PC -156 W 56th -NY 10019
(516) 873-1902 .. **Muscara,** Allison '04 %Morici & M -1399 Franklin Av -Gdn Cty 11530 **Fx:**873-3948
(516) 485-0400 .. **Muscarella & DiRaimo** -42 Nassau Blvd -Gdn Cty 11530 **Fx:**485-0444
(516) 571-2427 .. **Muscarella,** Ignatius L '81 %Hon T Phelan -100 Supreme Ct Dr -Mineola 11501
(212) 358-6574 .. **Muscarella,** Lisa M '95 %Empire Ins Co -315 Park Av S -NY 10010
(516) 485-0400 .. **Muscarella,** Paul J '89 (Muscarella & D) -42 Nassau Blvd -Gdn Cty 11530
(516) 328-1188 .. **Muscarella & Tomasone** -1040 Hempstd Tpk -Franklin Sq 11010 **Fx:**358-9673
(516) 328-1188 .. **Muscarella,** Vincent T '80 (Muscarella & T) -1040 Hempstd Tpk -Franklin Sq 11010
(212) 326-2000 .. **Muscat,** Melissa J '07 %O'Melveny & M LLP -7 Times Sq -NY 10036
(718) 575-5145 .. **Muscatello,** Danielle M '07 %R DiDio -80-02 Kew Grdns Rd -Kew Gdns 11415 **Fx:**793-0165
(212) 735-3000 .. **Muscato,** Andrew '84 Cnsl Skadden ASM&F LLP -4 Times Sq -NY 10036
(716) 434-9177 .. **Muscato DiMillo & Vona** -107 East Av -Lockprt 14094 **Fx:**434-9196
(716) 434-9177 .. **Muscato,** George V C '73 (Muscato D&V) -107 East Av -Lockprt 14094
(518) 438-9907 .. **Muscato,** James A II '02 %Young SWRB&M,LLC -5 Palisades Dr -Albany 12205
(716) 435-4755 .. **Muscato,** Jos A '00 -210 Voorhees Av -Buffalo 14214
(212) 253-5833 .. **Muschel,** Meyer '89 -340 Bowery -NY 10012
(212) 442-0573 .. **Muschenheim,** Mark W '93 %Law Dept -100 Church -NY 10007 **Fx:**788-0367
(516) 378-2000 .. **Musco,** Mary Beth '89 %United CerebralPalsy -380 Wshngtn Av -Roosevelt 11575 **Fx:**378-0357
(518) 388-4276 .. **Muse,** Keith A '05 Cnty Atty -620 State -Schnctdy 12305 **Fx:**388-4493
(718) 250-2000 .. **Muse,** Kelli M '04 DA -350 Jay -Brklyn 11201 **Fx:**250-2314
(516) 228-8484 .. **Musella,** Michl J '95 %Dilworth & B,LLP -1000 Woodbury Rd -Woodbury 11797
(212) 687-7410 .. **Muser,** Richd K '80 (Clifton B&D,LLP) -420 Lex Av -NY 10170
(212) 302-8989 .. **Muserlian,** Chas A '62 Cnsl Hedman & C,PC -1185 Av of Amer -NY 10036
(917) 421-4725 .. **Muset,** Mihai '99 IRS -33 Maiden Ln -NY 10038
(212) 474-1000 .. **Mushkin,** Mark '10 %Cravath S&M LLP -825 8th Av -NY 10019
(212) 779-1980 .. **Musico,** Philip N '04 (Gannes & M,LLP) -325 Bway -NY 10007 **Fx:**779-1981
(914) 948-1200 .. **Musicus,** Andrew N '94 %Cerussi & S,PC -1 N Lex Av -White Plns 10601
(718) 725-4646 .. **Musikar,** Illana Tova '99 -116-10 Jamaica Av -Jamaica 11418
(716) 282-1712 .. **Musitano,** Angelo '89 -1520 Pine Av Bx2127 -Niagara Fls 14301 **Fx:**282-5693
(212) 858-7492 .. **Muskatel,** Josef '91 %RBC Capital Mrkts Corp -3 World Fncl Ctr -NY 10281
(212) 688-3200 .. **Muskin,** Victor P '69 OfCnsl Scheichet & D,PC -767 3rd Av -NY 10017
(718) 520-3183 .. **Muskus,** Helen Anna '98 %Family Ct -89-14 Parsons Blvd -Jamaica 11432
(516) 829-7270 .. **Musman,** Marc J '95 %M Weinberger,PC -50 Merrick Rd -Rockvll Ctr 11570 **Fx:**829-0102
(212) 506-5000 .. **Musoff,** Jay K '94 (Orrick H&S LLP) -51 W 52nd -NY 10019
(212) 735-3000 .. **Musoff,** Scott D '95 (Skadden ASM&F LLP) -4 Times Sq -NY 10036
(646) 755-3304 .. **Musoke,** Nabisubi N '01 %Shanker & S,PC -420 Lex Av -NY 10170
(212) 458-1140 .. **Musolino,** Teresa '02 AIG Domestic Claims,Inc -175 Water -NY 10038
(718) 263-3800 .. **Muss,** Jason A '98 %Muss & M -118-35 Qns Blvd -Frst Hlls 11375
(718) 263-3800 .. **Muss,** Joshua L '65 (Muss & M) -118-35 Qns Blvd -Frst Hlls 11375
(315) 324-6119 .. **Musselman,** Francis H '54 -Oak Pnt Bx289 -Hammond 13646 **Fx:**324-5215
(212) 848-4000 .. **Musselman,** Matthew F '01 %Shearman & S LLP -599 Lex Av -NY 10022
(716) 829-2861 .. **Mussenden,** Maureen R '85 %SUNY@Buffalo -3435 Main -Buffalo 14214
(212) 859-8000 .. **Mussio,** Donna F '95 %Fried FHS&J LLP -1 NY Plz -NY 10004
(718) 855-6840 .. **Musso,** Robt J '77 (Rosenberg M&W LLP) -26 Court -Brklyn 11242 **Fx:**625-1966
(516) 487-0100 .. **Musso,** Victor A '86 (Musso & W) -111 Grt Nck Rd -Gt Neck 11021 **Fx:**487-5524
(631) 543-3663 .. **Mustacchia,** Bartholomew '56 OfCnsl Migliore & I,PC -353 Vets Mem'l Hwy -Commack 11725
(315) 793-7000 .. **Mustard,** Danielle M '06 %Leg Aid -255 Genesee -Utica 13501 **Fx:**732-3202
(212) 935-3000 .. **Mustelier,** Victor F '90 (Mintz LCFG&P,PC) -666 3rd Av -NY 10017
(212) 642-1734 .. **Mustello,** Randi J '97 Intl Trademark Assn -655 3rd Av -NY 10017
(212) 259-8000 .. **Mustes,** George W '10 %Dewey & L LLP -1301 Av of Amer -NY 10019
(607) 271-9270 .. **Mustico,** Donald W '77 -221 W Church -Elmira 14901 **Fx:**271-9414
(607) 739-6702 .. **Mustico,** John P '76 -106 N Main -Horseheads 14845 **Fx:**739-8651
(607) 733-7770 .. **Mustico,** Michl W '98 %Mustico & Company -303 William -Elmira 14901
(212) 326-3939 .. **Mustillo,** Anthony D '05 %Jones D -222 E 41st -NY 10017
(212) 532-1973 .. **Musumeci,** Carmine V '82 (Krinsky & M) -274 Mad Av -NY 10016 **Fx:**545-7211
(212) 446-4800 .. **Musumeci,** Sandra L '01 %Kirkland & E LLP -153 E 53rd -NY 10022
(914) 470-0001 .. **Musurca,** James E '91 OfCnsl Babchik & Y,LLP -200 E Post Rd -White Plns 10601
(716) 853-2330 .. **Muth,** Peter A '80 SrCnsl Buchanan I&R PC -50 Fountain Plz -Buffalo 14202
(212) 560-9012 .. **Mutharika,** Monique E '04 Legal Options, Inc -875 Av of Amer -NY 10001
(212) 628-1434 .. **Muthuchidambaram,** Uma '90 %Muthu Consulting -308 E 79th -NY 10075
(914) 946-8800 .. **Mutino,** Peter J '63 (Smith RC&M,PC) -235 Main -White Plns 10601
(212) 250-2500 .. **Muttana,** Nilima D '01 %Deutsche Bk -345 Park Av -NY 10154
(914) 640-2257 .. **Mutterperl,** Laura B '03 Starwood Hotels & Resorts -1111 Wstchstr Av -White Plns 10604
(212) 318-3000 .. **Mutterperl,** Mark N '99 (Fulbright & J LLP) -666 5th Av -NY 10103
(212) 326-3939 .. **Muttreja,** Rajeev '09 %Jones D -222 E 41st -NY 10017
(716) 645-2873 .. **Mutua,** Athena D '88 -55 Woodley Rd -Buffalo 14215
(716) 645-2093 .. **Mutua,** Makau W '88 %SUNY Buffalo Lw Schl -O'Brian Hall -Buffalo 14260 **Fx:**645-5968
(718) 590-2000 .. **Mutz,** Larry R '08 %DA -198 E 161st -Bronx 10451 **Fx:**590-6477
(212) 834-0600 .. **Mutz,** Steven H '83 (Gordon & S,PC) -355 Lex Av -NY 10017
(516) 832-7777 .. **Muzio,** Jos C '99 %Silberstein A&M,PC -600 Old Cntry Rd -Gdn Cty 11530
(212) 351-4000 .. **Muzumdar,** Saee M '09 Gibson D&C LLP -200 Park Av -NY 10166
(212) 310-8000 .. **Muzzy,** Lucy E '07 %Weil G&M LLP -767 5th Av -NY 10153
(212) 351-4000 .. **Myatt,** Jason W '06 %Gibson D&C LLP -200 Park Av -NY 10166
(718) 468-3588 .. **Myatt,** Rene '85 -204-04 Hillside Av -Hollis 11423 **Fx:**468-5731
(518) 843-2900 .. **Mycek,** Wm H '82 (Mycek Law Firm) -146 Market -Amsterdam 12010 **Fx:**843-0234
(518) 843-2900 .. **Mycek,** Wm J '07 %Mycek Law Firm -146 Market -Amsterdam 12010 **Fx:**843-0234
(718) 250-2000 .. **Myco,** Christopher A '08 %DA -350 Jay -Brklyn 11201 **Fx:**250-2314
(718) 222-9800 .. **Myer,** Heather L A '08 %Brecher FPWT&Z,PC -335 Adams -Brklyn 11201
(631) 692-9116 .. **Myer,** Jill A '92 -49 Greenmeadow Ln -Cold Spring Hills 11743 **Fx:**692-5587
(212) 788-0869 .. **Myerberg,** Andrew T '09 %Law Dept -100 Church -NY 10007 **Fx:**788-0367
(212) 944-9457 .. **Myerberg,** Susan S '80 Helen Hayes Theatre -240 W 44th -NY 10036 **Fx:**302-3584
(845) 634-5694 .. **Myerowitz,** Howard '00 (Myerowitz J&G) -132 Buena Vista Rd -New Cty 10956 **Fx:**634-0917
(212) 735-3000 .. **Myers,** Alan C '76 (Skadden ASM&F LLP) -4 Times Sq -NY 10036
(212) 412-2662 .. **Myers,** Ann C '89 Barclays Cptl Inc -200 Park Av -NY 10166
(212) 417-8300 .. **Myers,** April '04 Research Fndtn CUNY -230 W 41st -NY 10036 **Fx:**417-8379
(516) 873-3900 .. **Myers,** Barbara A '84 -114 Old Cntry Rd -Mineola 11501 **Fx:**873-3904
(212) 998-6445 .. **Myers,** Caren M '99 NYU Law Schl -245 Sullivan -NY 10012 **Fx:**995-4031
(212) 450-4000 .. **Myers,** Courtenay U '98 Cnsl Davis P&W LLP -450 Lex Av -NY 10017
(212) 468-4800 .. **Myers,** Curt C '92 (Davis & G LLP) -1740 Bway -NY 10019
(212) 596-9000 .. **Myers,** Dana L '09 %Ropes & G LLP -1211 Av of Amer -NY 10036
(212) 267-6364 .. **Myers,** Dawn R '97 %Kossoff & U -217 Bway -NY 10007
(585) 428-5210 .. **Myers,** Grazina '07 Pub Def -10 N Fitzhugh -Rchstr 14614 **Fx:**428-2234
(716) 634-8400 .. **Myers,** James I '68 -5500 Main -Williamsvll 14221
(845) 679-2455 .. **Myers,** James R '64 -Cuan Slan Route 375 Bx188 -Woodstock 12498 **Fx:**679-2456
(212) 619-4350 .. **Myers,** Jan Kevin '84 (Newman MKGH,PC) -14 Wall -NY 10005
(516) 470-1661 .. **Myers,** Jane M '80 (J Myers,PC) -267 Carleton Av -Central Islip 11722 **Fx:**470-1657
(212) 878-8000 .. **Myers,** Jason D '01 %Clifford C LLP -31 W 52nd -NY 10019
(516) 505-0600 .. **Myers,** Jason M '09 %J McCormack,PC -1035 Stewart Av -Gdn Cty 11530 **Fx:**505-0632
(518) 402-0205 .. **Myers,** Jayson S '76 %UIA Bd -Troy Atrium Bx15126 -Albany 12212 **Fx:**402-6208
(212) 573-5061 .. **Myers,** Jeffrey N '00 %Pfizer Inc -150 E 42nd -NY 10017
(212) 526-0500 .. **Myers,** Jenna M '03 Barclays Capital Inc -745 7th Av -NY 10019
(212) 838-4120 .. **Myers,** Joanne J '85 %Carnegie Cncl -170 E 64th -NY 10065 **Fx:**752-2432
(212) 855-2276 .. **Myers,** John B '83 Bk of America -1 Bryant Pk -NY 10036
(718) 884-6600 .. **Myers,** Jonathan E '76 (KF Ross,PC) -5683 Riverdale Av #203 Bx900 -Bronx 10471 **Fx:**601-1099
(518) 782-9100 .. **Myers,** Justin D '08 Barbaruolo Law Firm PC -12 Cornell Rd -Latham 12110 **Fx:**782-9101
(845) 229-7597 .. **Myers,** Kelly S '99 -Bx805 -Hyde Pk 12538
(212) 558-4000 .. **Myers,** Ken S '07 %Sullivan & C LLP -125 Broad -NY 10004
(212) 513-3200 .. **Myers,** Lance D '77 (Holland & K LLP) -31 W 52nd -NY 10019
(585) 454-0700 .. **Myers,** Laura A '06 %Ward GH&R LLP -300 State -Rchstr 14614
(518) 374-8494 .. **Myers,** Mark A '08 %DeLorenzo Law Firm -201 Nott Ter -Schnctdy 12307 **Fx:**374-5906
(212) 986-5900 .. **Myers,** Matthew D '91 (Myers S&G) -299 Bway -NY 10007 **Fx:**986-6250
(516) 832-7604 .. **Myers,** Medea A '04 %Nixon P LLP -437 Mad Av -NY 10022
(518) 402-2594 .. **Myers,** Michl J '94 %Dept of Law -The Cptl -Albany 12224
(718) 780-7961 .. **Myers,** Minor III '04 %Bklyn Law Schl -250 Joralemon -Brklyn 11201 **Fx:**780-0393
(212) 318-6000 .. **Myers,** Rebecca K '99 %Paul HJ&W LLP -75 E 55th -NY 10022
(212) 259-8000 .. **Myers,** Robt C '70 (Dewey & L LLP) -1301 Av of Amer -NY 10019
(718) 722-3100 .. **Myers,** Stephen '72 %Leg Aid -111 Lvngstn -Brklyn 11201 **Fx:**722-3093
(631) 777-2330 .. **Myers,** Teresa M '04 %O'Connor OH&D,LLP -1 Huntngtn Quad -Melvll 11747
(212) 613-2005 .. **Myers,** Terry '75 (Gibbons PC) -1 Penn Plz -NY 10119 **Fx:**554-9670
(315) 218-8000 .. **Myers,** Thos E '75 (Bond S&K,PLLC) -1 Lincoln Ctr -Syracuse 13202
(212) 506-5000 .. **Myers,** Thos E '87 (Orrick H&S LLP) -51 W 52nd -NY 10019
(315) 424-0513 .. **Myers,** Wm E '82 Carrols Corp -968 James Bx6969 -Syracuse 13217
(315) 488-2667 .. **Myers,** Wm Jeff '90 (Welch & M LLP) -307 Kasson Rd Bx326 -Camillus 13031 **Fx:**488-6031
(845) 338-2770 .. **Myers,** Wm R S '91 -Bx3118 -Kingston 12402 **Fx:**338-4192

(518) 473-4076 .. **Myers,** Wm S '78 NYS DMV -224-260 S Pearl -Albany 12202 **Fx:**486-5198
(516) 625-9850 .. **Myers,** Wm T Sr. '87 (Shapiro U&M,PC) -Expwy Plz 1-#120 -Roslyn Hts 11577
(914) 834-9600 .. **Myerson,** David J '64 -2039 Palmer Av -Larchmnt 10538 **Fx:**834-4247
(718) 650-4087 .. **Myerson,** Matthew '02 Bureau of AT&F -241 37th -Brklyn 11232
(718) 983-6682 .. **Myerson,** Shoshana A '91 -182 Paulding Av -Staten Isl 10314 **Fx:**370-8203
(212) 373-3000 .. **Myerson,** Toby S '77 (Paul WRW&G LLP) -1285 Av of Amer -NY 10019
(607) 231-5900 .. **Myette,** Suzanne S '09 %Leg Aid -30 Fayette -Bnghmtn 13901 **Fx:**724-7211
(917) 881-6851 .. **Mykolajtchuk,** Jurij '94 -61 Bway -NY 10006
(212) 980-0120 .. **Myler,** Cameron A '02 %Frankfurt KK&S,PC -488 Mad Av -NY 10022
(212) 794-5382 .. **Myles,** Linda M '83 %CUNY -535 E 80th -NY 10075 **Fx:**794-5426
(585) 327-2685 .. **Myles,** Scott M '09 Thomson-Reuters -50 E Broad -Rchstr 14694
(718) 855-4266 .. **Myles,** Seth A '89 -186 Montague -Brklyn 11201
(212) 820-4541 .. **Mylott,** Raymond L Jr. '77 %AIG -160 Water -NY 10038
(212) 645-5909 .. **Myman,** Robt H '79 -1 Union Sq W -NY 10003 **Fx:**645-4830
(212) 223-6700 .. **Mynhier,** Rachel Anne '02 %Zukerman GB&C,LLP -875 3rd Av -NY 10022
(516) 326-4799 .. **Myrick,** Maria Scorcia '83 -62 Argyle Rd -Stewart Mnr 11530 **Fx:**326-3485
(212) 755-6100 .. **Myrill,** Christian P '83 -445 Park Av -NY 10022
(718) 286-6000 .. **Myrill,** Donna M '84 %DA -125-01 Qns Blvd -Kew Gdns 11415
(516) 864-3876 .. **Myron,** Suzanne M '08 -7669 Jericho Tpk -Woodbury 11797 **Fx:**496-9052
(845) 291-0011 .. **Myrow,** Jay R '85 (Blustein SR&B,LLP) -10 Matthews -Goshen 10924
(212) 788-9391 .. **Myrvold,** Barry K '85 %Law Dept -100 Church -NY 10007 **Fx:**788-0367
(212) 446-2300 .. **Myslinska,** Dagmar R '05 %Boies S&F LLP -575 Lex Av -NY 10022
(212) 732-0707 .. **Mysliwiec,** Aaron J '03 %J Dratel,PC -2 Wall -NY 10005 **Fx:**571-3792
(212) 245-2202 .. **Mysliwiec,** Ronald P '74 -1740 Bway -NY 10019
(716) 847-0650 .. **Myszka,** Dawn M '96 %Leg Srvcs -237 Main -Buffalo 14203 **Fx:**847-0227
(212) 878-8000 .. **Na,** Nari Haeseung '09 %Clifford C LLP -31 W 52nd -NY 10019
(315) 568-4975 .. **Nabinger,** John J '97 Pub Def Ofc -Bx702 -Seneca Fls 13148 **Fx:**568-2324
(518) 474-6400 .. **Nabozny,** Richd L '82 %Dept of Ed -89 Wshngtn Av -Albany 12234 **Fx:**473-2925
(585) 453-7730 .. **Nacca,** John '86 -30 W Broad -Rchstr 14614 **Fx:**453-0895
(585) 362-4700 .. **Nacca,** Jos S '09 %Bond S&K,PLLC -350 Linden Oaks -Rchstr 14625
(518) 485-9379 .. **Naccarato,** Susan Ann '97 Prof Asst Program-Dept of Ed -80 Wolf Rd -Albany 12205
(516) 678-7110 .. **Nachamie,** Andrew S '88 -7 Smith -Merrick 11566 **Fx:**678-6288
(212) 754-9400 .. **Nachamie,** Barton '60 (Todtman NS&J,PC) -425 Park Av -NY 10022
(516) 678-7110 .. **Nachamie,** Bonnie S '85 -7 Smith -Merrick 11566 **Fx:**678-6288
(914) 774-0156 .. **Nachamie,** Robt M '02 -1015 Park -Peekskill 10566 **Fx:**930-1115
(516) 678-7110 .. **Nachamie,** Stuart W '53 -7 Smith -Merrick 11566 **Fx:**678-6288
(212) 343-6734 .. **Nachbar,** Karen L '98 Scholastic Inc -557 Bway -NY 10012
(212) 267-1157 .. **Nachimovsky,** Yoram M '88 -299 Bway -NY 10007 **Fx:**267-1199
(914) 935-5375 .. **Nachimson,** Steven G '86 Compass Grp USA -3 Intl Dr -Rye Brook 10573 **Fx:**935-5550
(212) 326-3939 .. **Nachlis,** Warren L '98 (Jones D) -222 E 41st -NY 10017
(212) 335-4500 .. **Nachman,** David E '82 OfCnsl DLA Piper LLP -1251 Av of Amer -NY 10020
(914) 968-4915 .. **Nachman,** Eric P '77 -245 Rumsey Rd -Ynkrs 10701
(718) 852-8888 .. **Nachman,** Fraidy '91 %LSNYC-Brooklyn -180 Lvngstn -Brklyn 11201 **Fx:**858-1786
(212) 756-2000 .. **Nachman,** Meredith W '06 %Schulte R&Z LLP -919 3rd Av -NY 10022
(212) 983-8490 .. **Nachman,** Steven M '83 -675 3rd Av -NY 10017 **Fx:**949-1923
(212) 480-6082 .. **Nachman,** Steven N '92 %Insurance Dept -25 Beaver -NY 10004 **Fx:**480-5272
(212) 265-6600 .. **Nachman,** Steven Z '97 RD Mgmt Corp -810 7th Av -NY 10019
(718) 935-1055 .. **Nacht,** Brad M '90 -26 Court -Brklyn 11242 **Fx:**855-5937
(631) 853-5761 .. **Nacht,** Steven B '77 %Cnty Atty -400 Carleton Av -Central Islip 11722 **Fx:**853-7788
(212) 267-6364 .. **Nachtome,** Michl D '01 %Kossoff & U -217 Bway -NY 10007
(718) 928-3700 .. **Nacinovich,** Anne C '00 %LSNYC-Bronx -579 Courtlandt Av -Bronx 10451 **Fx:**402-7586
(315) 445-1700 .. **Nackley,** Justin M '06 %Wladis Law Firm,PC -5795 Widewaters Pkwy -Syracuse 13214 **Fx:**251-1073
(646) 733-3200 .. **Nackman,** Mark G '90 %US Customs -1 Penn Plz -NY 10119
(631) 366-2700 .. **Nackman,** Robin E '89 -191 Terry Rd -Smithtwn 11787 **Fx:**366-0062
(914) 824-5413 .. **Naclerio,** Alphonse M '76 Hon G Loehr -111 Martin Luther King Blvd -White Plns 10601 **Fx:**457-2664
(516) 742-4646 .. **Naclerio,** Frank A '78 -1205 Franklin Av -Gdn Cty 11530
(516) 663-6600 .. **Naclerio,** Gregory J '72 (Ruskin MF,PC) -1425 RXR Plz -Uniondale 11556
(646) 471-4000 .. **Nacron,** Robt A '78 %PricewaterhouseCoopers LLP -300 Mad Av -NY 10017
(845) 338-6088 .. **Nadan,** Marshall '72 -Bx4091 -Kingston 12402
(212) 869-5070 .. **Nadaner,** Glenn R '93 Alexander Nadaner Imports -37 W 47th -NY 10036
(914) 682-2604 .. **Nadborny & Brinberg LLP** -50 Main -White Plns 10606
(212) 984-0706 .. **Nadborny & Brinberg LLP** -100 Park Av -NY 10017
(914) 682-2604 .. **Nadborny,** Danl A '76 (Nadborny & B LLP) -50 Main -White Plns 10606 **Fx:**(212) 202-4207
(212) 755-3100 .. **Nadborny,** Felicia A '07 %Kaufmann GR&O LLP -777 3rd Av -NY 10017
(212) 455-2000 .. **Nadborny,** Jennifer L '05 %Simpson T&B LLP -425 Lex Av -NY 10017
(212) 619-5000 .. **Naddeo,** Richd J '03 %EDC -110 William -NY 10038 **Fx:**312-3912
(518) 792-6172 .. **Nadeau,** Edw L '54 -29 Windy Hill Rd -Glens Fls 12801
(212) 225-2000 .. **Nadeau,** Mark C '10 Cleary GS&H -1 Lbrty Plz -NY 10006
(718) 838-7856 .. **Nadel,** Amanda N '05 Bronx Defenders -860 Crtlandt Av -Bronx 10451 **Fx:**665-0100
(212) 891-7000 .. **Nadel,** David A '93 %Douglas Elliman,LLC -575 Mad Av -NY 10022
(516) 877-2200 .. **Nadel,** Lloyd J '76 -170 Old Cntry Rd -Mineola 11501
(212) 317-9500 .. **Nadel,** Lorraine '89 (Nadel & Assoc,PC) -3 E 54th -NY 10022 **Fx:**317-9849
(212) 532-2786 .. **Nadel,** Norman '56 -286 Mad Av -NY 10017 **Fx:**947-0907
(516) 829-2572 .. **Nadel & Pearlman** -287 Nrthrn Blvd -Gt Neck 11021 **Fx:**829-1334
(212) 940-7010 .. **Nadel,** Peter F '65 OfCnsl Katten MR LLP -575 Mad Av -NY 10022
(718) 855-6840 .. **Nadel,** Robt N '94 %Rosenberg M&W LLP -26 Court -Brklyn 11242 **Fx:**625-1966
(607) 722-5533 .. **Nadel,** Scott B '84 -34 Chenango Bx1221 -Bnghmtn 13902 **Fx:**722-5106
(212) 574-1200 .. **Nadel,** Steven B '92 (Seward & K LLP) -1 Bttry Pk Plz -NY 10004
(212) 801-2116 .. **Nadel,** Steven M '10 %Greenberg T,LLP -200 Park Av -NY 10166
(212) 806-5400 .. **Nadell,** Bernhardt M '96 (Stroock &S&L LLP) -180 Maiden Ln -NY 10038
(718) 590-2000 .. **Nadell,** Jaimee M '08 %DA -198 E 161st -Bronx 10451 **Fx:**590-6477
(212) 504-6000 .. **Nadelman,** Cary '99 %Cadwalader W&T LLP -1 World Fncl Ctr -NY 10281
(212) 752-3380 .. **Nadelman,** Richd '61 -880 3rd Av -NY 10022 **Fx:**688-0066
(212) 224-5026 .. **Nadelmann,** Deborah M '94 %Sumitomo Bk -277 Park Av -NY 10172 **Fx:**224-5111
(718) 595-5285 .. **Nadelson,** Jane J '04 DEP Envrnmntl Engineering -59-17 Junction Blvd -Flushng 11373
(516) 487-7510 .. **Nadelson,** Stuart R '74 -1 Bowers Ln -Gt Neck 11020 **Fx:**487-0526
(914) 968-2020 .. **Nader,** George D III '83 -50 Riverdale Av -Ynkrs 10701 **Fx:**968-2050
(212) 474-1000 .. **Nadile,** Janet M '88 Cravath S&M LLP -825 8th Av -NY 10019
(212) 400-7177 .. **Nadipuram,** Naveen M '08 %Garrity GMG&F -40 Wall -NY 10005
(631) 385-8900 .. **Nadjar,** Mark E '91 SrCnsl M Nadjar,PC -366 Vets Mem'l Hwy -Commack 11725 **Fx:**543-5899
(516) 222-2330 .. **Nadjari,** Douglas M '84 Jacobson G&K,LLP -585 Stewart Av -Gdn Cty 11530
(212) 756-2000 .. **Nadler,** Batya M '09 %Schulte R&Z LLP -919 3rd Av -NY 10022
(212) 575-7900 .. **Nadler,** Brett A '10 %Ballon SB&N,PC -729 7th Av -NY 10019
(585) 232-6900 .. **Nadler,** Christian M '05 %Gates & A,PC -28 E Main -Rchstr 14614
(212) 713-2000 .. **Nadler,** Laura L '97 UBS Financial Srvcs Inc -1285 Av of Amer -NY 10019
(631) 369-1112 .. **Nadler,** Meridith A '88 %Nassau/Sflk Law Srvc -313 W Main -Rvrhead 11901 **Fx:**369-1612
(718) 709-2275 .. **Nadler,** Mitchell J '00 JetBlue Airways -11829 Qns Blvd -Frst Hlls 11375
(212) 575-1292 .. **Nadler,** Myron R '62 (Uncyk B&N,LLP) -555 5th Av -NY 10017
(516) 832-7777 .. **Nadler,** Paul N '94 %Silberstein A&M,PC -600 Old Cntry Rd -Gdn Cty 11530
(212) 227-2780 .. **Nadoff,** Rena '89 Jaroslawicz & J -225 Bway -NY 10007
(212) 458-5729 .. **Nadolna,** Andrew S '97 AIG -175 Water -NY 10038 **Fx:**458-5679
(631) 755-0101 .. **Nador,** Jos M '93 %Lewis JAA,LLP -425 Broad Hollow Rd -Melvll 11747
(212) 373-3000 .. **Nadritch,** Brett D '04 %Paul WRW&G LLP -1285 Av of Amer -NY 10019
(212) 451-2300 .. **Nadritch,** Jordanna L '04 %Olshan GFR&W LLP -65 E 55th -NY 10022
(718) 340-4200 .. **Nadvorney,** David M C '96 %CUNY Law Schl -65-21 Main -Flushng 11367 **Fx:**340-4482
(212) 318-6000 .. **Nadworny,** Matthew E '09 %Paul HJ&W LLP -75 E 55th -NY 10022
(212) 574-1200 .. **Naeder,** Walter A '02 %Seward & K LLP -1 Bttry Pk Plz -NY 10004
(212) 309-6000 .. **Naeem,** Shawmir '03 %Morgan L&B LLP -101 Park Av -NY 10178
(716) 856-5500 .. **Naegely,** Eric C '99 (Damon M LLP) -200 Delaware Av -Buffalo 14202
(585) 546-5530 .. **Naffky,** Jeanne M '86 %Thomson West -50 E Broad -Rchstr 14694
(212) 529-0975 .. **Naftalis,** Alan R '75 -145 E 16th -NY 10003 **Fx:**529-0975
(212) 637-2456 .. **Naftalis,** Benjamin A '05 US Atty -1 St Andrews Plz -NY 10007
(212) 715-9100 .. **Naftalis,** Gary P '67 (Kramer LN&F,LLP) -1177 Av of Amer -NY 10036
(212) 403-1000 .. **Naftalis,** Joshua A '04 %Wachtell LR&K -51 W 52nd -NY 10019
(212) 820-2602 .. **Naftolin,** Michl E '89 AIG -160 Water -NY 10038
(212) 928-4402 .. **Naftulin,** Lois J '77 -180 Cabrini Blvd -NY 10033
(585) 889-1180 .. **Nafus,** Matthew D '92 -54 Main -Scottsvll 14546
(212) 782-6988 .. **Nagai,** Sara '00 Bank of Tokyo -1251 Av of Amer -NY 10020
(212) 225-2000 .. **Nagalski,** Beth E '09 %Cleary GS&H -1 Lbrty Plz -NY 10006
(212) 558-4000 .. **Nagano,** Aaron A '06 %Sullivan & C LLP -125 Broad -NY 10004
(212) 310-8000 .. **Nagar,** Roshelle A '89 %Weil G&M LLP -767 5th Av -NY 10153
(212) 805-0152 .. **Nagaraj,** Sheila '07 Hon A Hellerstein - USDC -500 Pearl -NY 10007
(212) 492-6750 .. **Nagarajan,** Kamesh '97 Smith Barney -787 7th Av -NY 10019
(212) 230-8800 .. **Nagel,** Andrew E '95 (WilmerHale) -399 Park Av -NY 10022
(716) 875-2503 .. **Nagel,** Catherine E '99 %J Nuchereno -2503 Niagara -Buffalo 14207 **Fx:**873-1780
(212) 383-2596 .. **Nagel,** Jason I '01 State Comptroller -59 Maiden Ln -NY 10038 **Fx:**383-3901
(212) 613-2061 .. **Nagel,** Jeffrey L '95 (Gibbons PC) -1 Penn Plz -NY 10119 **Fx:**554-9661
(212) 766-1177 .. **Nagel,** Martin I '89 %J Mullen Jr -30 Vesey -NY 10007 **Fx:**766-1131
(212) 904-1139 .. **Nagel,** Wm E III '99 (Nagel Law Ofc,PLLC) -224 W 35th -NY 10001 **Fx:**813-3241
(914) 478-2981 .. **Nager,** Arnold H '64 -79 Cliff -Hastings-On-Hud 10706 **Fx:**478-4370
(212) 839-5300 .. **Nager,** Benjamin L '97 Cnsl Sidley A LLP -787 7th Av -NY 10019
(516) 292-4700 .. **Nager,** George '58 -231 Mineola Blvd -Mineola 11501 **Fx:**292-5198
(212) 686-0100 .. **Nager,** Jocelyn R '88 (Frank FG&N,LLP) -1430 Bway -NY 10018
(212) 859-8000 .. **Naghi,** Nicole S '10 %Fried FHS&J LLP -1 NY Plz -NY 10004
(212) 684-0199 .. **Nagi,** Jason A '01 (Polsinelli S PC) -7 Penn Plz -NY 10001
(212) 762-1232 .. **Nagiel,** Melissa Agata '98 Morgan Stanley -750 7th Av -NY 10019
(212) 839-5300 .. **Nagin,** Benjamin R '97 (Sidley A LLP) -787 7th Av -NY 10019
(212) 645-3444 .. **Nagin,** Danl L '01 Partnership for the Homeless -305 7th Av -NY 10001
(917) 202-2247 .. **Nagin,** Jason H '05 -50 Bank -NY 10014
(212) 243-7757 .. **Nagin,** Kenneth L '78 %Superior Mgmt -50 Bank -NY 10014
(212) 243-7757 .. **Nagin,** Laurance W '72 %Superior Mgmt -50 Bank -NY 10014

(585) 218-9537 .. **Nagle,** Kelly A '86 -12 Sunset Blvd -Pittsfrd 14534 **Fx:**218-9537
(212) 859-8000 .. **Nagle,** Shannon Lowry '07 (Fried FHS&J LLP) -1 NY Plz -NY 10004
(518) 474-0594 .. **Nagle,** Stephen M '86 %Dept of Law -The Cptl -Albany 12224 **Fx:**408-2057
(212) 446-4800 .. **Nagler,** Christian O '98 (Kirkland & E LLP) -153 E 53rd -NY 10022
(212) 735-3000 .. **Nagler,** David L '93 (Skadden ASM&F LLP) -4 Times Sq -NY 10036
(646) 471-4000 .. **Nagler,** Marvin I '92 %PricewaterhouseCoopers LLP -300 Mad Av -NY 10017
(914) 995-4172 .. **Nagler,** Nadine C '88 %DA -111 Martin Luther King Blvd -White Plns 10601 **Fx:**995-3363
(212) 354-5900 .. **Nagler,** Stanley M '64 -1500 Bway -NY 10036 **Fx:**354-5924
(212) 779-9910 .. **Nagler,** Stephen M '65 (Eaton & V LLP) -3 Park Av -NY 10016
(212) 248-8800 .. **Nagler,** Vincent A '87 (Callan KB&B LLP) -1 Whitehall -NY 10004
(212) 596-9000 .. **Nagley,** Jared P '02 %Ropes & G LLP -1211 Av of Amer -NY 10036
(518) 943-2171 .. **Nagle-Zaik,** Kellyann G '96 %Hon G Pulver Jr -320 Main -Catskill 12414 **Fx:**943-1864
(212) 710-3900 .. **Nagorski,** Adam A '08 %Clyde & Co US LLP -405 Lex Av -NY 10174 **Fx:**710-3950
(212) 735-3000 .. **Nagorsky,** Mindy E '04 %Skadden ASM&F LLP -4 Times Sq -NY 10036
(631) 361-9494 .. **Nagosky,** Kelly L '97 %A Vardaro,PC -732 Smithtwn Bypass -Smithtwn 11787 **Fx:**361-8752
(516) 684-2900 .. **Nagrotsky,** Sanford S '82 (Pegalis & E,LLC) -1 Hllw Ln -Lk Success 11042
(845) 638-5180 .. **Nagubandi,** Radhika S '82 %Cnty Atty -Cnty Ofc Bldg -New Cty 10956 **Fx:**638-5676
(845) 634-4666 .. **Nagubandi,** Radhika S '82 -49 Maple Av -New Cty 10956
(212) 735-3000 .. **Nagy,** Anna '04 %Skadden ASM&F LLP -4 Times Sq -NY 10036
(518) 274-3510 .. **Nagy,** Jill '85 OfCnsl Bartle MD&J,LLP -251 River Bx448 -Troy 12181
(516) 759-9362 .. **Nagy,** John D '76 -4 Orchrd Ln -Sea Cliff 11579
(212) 336-8330 .. **Nagy,** Tibor L '07 (Susman G LLP) -560 Lex Av -NY 10022
(607) 974-4192 .. **Nah,** Kevin J '03 %Corning -1 Rvrfrnt Plz -Corning 14831 **Fx:**974-6135
(212) 408-5100 .. **Nah,** Soo-Ah '10 %Chadbourne & P LLP -30 Rckfllr Plz -NY 10112
(518) 429-4200 .. **Nahal,** Henry J '73 OfCnsl Hiscock & B,LLP -50 Beaver -Albany 12207
(212) 909-6000 .. **Nahar-Brown,** Zahra '08 %Debevoise & P LLP -919 3rd Av -NY 10022
(212) 855-3295 .. **Nahari,** Mihal '90 Depository Trust & Clearing Corp -55 Water -NY 10041
(877) 222-1814 .. **Nahas,** Christopher M '05 %B Rothenberg -100 Duffy Av -Hicksvll 11801 **Fx:**(866) 894-2182
(212) 686-0855 .. **Nahas,** Edmund A '58 (Zraick N&R) -303 5th Av -NY 10016
(212) 446-4800 .. **Nahas,** Newman A '08 %Kirkland & E LLP -153 E 53rd -NY 10022
(212) 335-9000 .. **Nahas,** Richd '95 %DA -1 Hogan Pl -NY 10013
(212) 686-0855 .. **Nahas,** Stuart E '94 (Zraick N&R) -303 5th Av -NY 10016
(212) 431-1300 .. **Nahins,** Todd I '78 (Borah GAN&G PC) -377 Bway -NY 10013
(212) 775-8700 .. **Nahitchevansky,** Georges H '92 (Kilpatrick S,LLP) -31 W 52nd -NY 10019
(212) 554-7800 .. **Nahley,** Stephen J '98 (Moses & S LLP) -405 Lex Av -NY 10174
(212) 837-6000 .. **Nahm,** Nathan I '83 SrCnsl Hughes H&R LLP -1 Bttry Pk Plz -NY 10004
(212) 221-5700 .. **Nahmias,** Gil I '02 %Goldberg WFG LLP -1501 Bway -NY 10036
(914) 245-0172 .. **Nahmias,** Louis '65 -2406 Mark Rd -Yorktwn Hts 10598
(212) 715-9100 .. **Nahoum,** Gariel S '09 %Kramer LN&F,LLP -1177 Av of Amer -NY 10036
(212) 859-8000 .. **Nahr,** J Christian '95 (Fried FHS&J LLP) -1 NY Plz -NY 10004
(212) 728-8000 .. **Nahum,** Joshua M '09 %Willkie F&G LLP -787 7th Av -NY 10019
(631) 979-7777 .. **Naiburg,** Eric W '72 (Naiburg & W,LLP) -320 Carleton Av -Central Islip 11722
(718) 286-6000 .. **Naiburg,** Jennifer L '94 %DA -125-01 Qns Blvd -Kew Gdns 11415
(212) 632-5500 .. **Naidech,** Alison G '97 Cnsl Salans LLP -620 5th Av -NY 10020
(212) 408-5100 .. **Naidech,** Scott W '02 (Chadbourne & P LLP) -30 Rckfllr Plz -NY 10112
(516) 498-2900 .. **Naidich,** Richd S '70 (Naidich WB&M,LLP) -80 Cuttermill Rd -Gt Neck 11021 **Fx:**466-3555
(917) 591-9828 .. **Naidoo,** Nishani D '99 -Bx282 -Bedfrd 10506
(212) 536-3900 .. **Naidu,** Bablu David '99 OfCnsl K&L Gates LLP -599 Lex Av -NY 10022
(212) 909-6000 .. **Naifeh,** Stuart C '10 %Debevoise & P LLP -919 3rd Av -NY 10022
(212) 508-6100 .. **Naik,** Soham D '04 %Bracewell & G,LLP -1251 Av of Amer -NY 10020
(212) 707-2000 .. **Nails,** Odell III '01 %Atlantic Recording Corp -1290 Av of Amer -NY 10104
(516) 746-6766 .. **Naima,** Theo A '98 %G Alweiss -229 7th -Gdn Cty 11530 **Fx:**741-9276
(212) 578-2211 .. **Naiman,** Mayer '93 %MetLife -27-01 Qns Plz N -LIC 11101
(212) 840-7188 .. **Naiman,** Steven Z '83 -485 Mad Av -NY 10022
(718) 528-3700 .. **Naimark,** Michl J '96 OfCnsl Naimark & T -169-95 137th Av -Jamaica 11434 **Fx:**528-3809
(718) 528-3700 .. **Naimark,** Sol '83 (Naimark & T) -169-95 137th Av -Jamaica 11434 **Fx:**528-3809
(518) 433-8800 .. **Naimo-Fredette,** Leesa '01 %Lemery G LLC -50 Beaver -Albany 12207
(914) 939-0002 .. **Naishtut,** Norman B '81 (Gallo F&N,LLP) -211 S Ridge -Rye Brook 10573
(212) 558-4000 .. **Naismith,** Peter G '07 %Sullivan & C LLP -125 Broad -NY 10004
(212) 554-7800 .. **Naito,** Hirohisa '04 OfCnsl Moses & S LLP -405 Lex Av -NY 10174
(845) 433-8571 .. **Najamy,** Johanna T '03 IBM -2455 South Rd -Poughkeepsie 12601
(845) 562-9020 .. **Najork,** Karl E '07 %Silver FS&L -3250 Route 9W -New Windsor 12553
(212) 697-3122 .. **Nakahara,** Yuko A '05 Martin C&B LLP -220 E 42nd -NY 10017
(212) 688-1500 .. **Nakamichi,** Mari '99 Gruss & Co -667 Mad Av -NY 10065
(212) 207-7658 .. **Nakamura,** Kanako '04 HarperCollins Publishers -10 E 53rd -NY 10022
(212) 269-0927 .. **Nakamura,** Maxine Kinue '00 %D'Amato & L,LLP -2 World Fncl Ctr -NY 10281
(212) 471-2990 .. **Nakamura,** Stephen H '01 (Merle B&N,PC) -90 Broad -NY 10004
(212) 331-5141 .. **Nakanishi,** Lisa Emiko '90 %HRA-Lgl Affrs -180 Water -NY 10038
(212) 450-4000 .. **Nakano,** Rhiannon N '10 %Davis P&W LLP -450 Lex Av -NY 10017
(212) 510-0500 .. **Nakano,** Serene K '83 %US Trustees Ofc -33 Whitehall -NY 10004 **Fx:**668-2255
(212) 735-3000 .. **Nakar,** Josseph '08 %Skadden ASM&F LLP -4 Times Sq -NY 10036
(212) 318-6000 .. **Nakhasi,** Smriti S '08 %Paul HJ&W LLP -75 E 55th -NY 10022
(212) 335-4500 .. **Nalavala,** Meherab N '07 %DLA Piper LLP -1251 Av of Amer -NY 10020
(516) 938-3888 .. **Naletova,** Eugenia '09 %JS Schwartz -410 E Jericho Tpk -Mineola 11501 **Fx:**938-3887
(877) 222-1814 .. **Nallan,** Anthony '96 %B Rothenberg -100 Duffy Av -Hicksvll 11801 **Fx:**(866) 894-2182
(212) 406-9257 .. **Nallaseth,** Cyrus S '88 -41-43 Beekman -NY 10038 **Fx:**406-9481
(212) 559-6139 .. **Nalle,** Graham D '04 Citigroup -909 3rd Av -NY 10022
(212) 848-8414 .. **Nallengara,** Lona S '99 (Shearman & S LLP) -599 Lex Av -NY 10022
(718) 816-9060 .. **Nalley,** Christopher P '83 (Sampel & N) -432 Forest Av -Staten Isl 10301 **Fx:**816-7669
(518) 993-4486 .. **Nalli,** Jos '85 -121 Honey Hill Rd Bx150 -Ft Plain 13339 **Fx:**993-4486
(516) 292-1818 .. **Nally,** James P '92 (White C&N,LLP) -58 Hilton Av -Hempstd 11550
(212) 616-5540 .. **Nalven,** Paul R '84 (Nalven & S) -350 5th Av -NY 10118 **Fx:**616-5543
(212) 878-8000 .. **Nam,** Alice J-Y '07 %Clifford C LLP -31 W 52nd -NY 10019
(212) 819-8200 .. **Nam,** Danl Ung Doo '99 (White & C LLP) -1155 Av of Amer -NY 10036
(212) 372-1540 .. **Nam,** Elizabeth E '98 Am Ex Tax Bus Srvcs -1185 Av of the AMericas -NY 10036
(212) 687-1980 .. **Nam,** Hae Sung '98 (Kaplan F&K LLP) -850 3rd Av -NY 10022
(212) 310-8000 .. **Nam,** Hoyoon '07 %Weil G&M LLP -767 5th Av -NY 10153
(212) 735-3000 .. **Nam,** J Stephanie '98 (Skadden ASM&F LLP) -4 Times Sq -NY 10036
(718) 353-5396 .. **Nam,** Janggeun '01 (J Nam,PC) -14209 37th Av -Flushng 11354
(212) 403-1000 .. **Nam,** Jennifer S '09 %Wachtell LR&K -51 W 52nd -NY 10019
(212) 725-7360 .. **Nam,** Soo U '96 (S Nam & Assoc) -386 Park Av S -NY 10016 **Fx:**725-7362
(212) 326-3939 .. **Nam,** Steven S '10 %Jones D -222 E 41st -NY 10017
(718) 590-2000 .. **Namani,** Burim '08 %DA -198 E 161st -Bronx 10451 **Fx:**590-6477
(212) 220-3830 .. **Namazi,** Nooshin '94 (Nicoletti H&S) -88 Pine -NY 10005
(914) 831-6440 .. **Namba,** Melissa R '99 City Ct -2 Roosevelt Sq N -Mt Vernon 10550 **Fx:**699-1230
(212) 808-7800 .. **Nambiar,** Deepak '02 %Kelley D&W LLP -101 Park Av -NY 10178
(516) 745-1331 .. **Namm,** David M '80 -600 Old Cntry Rd -Gdn Cty 11530 **Fx:**745-0456
(718) 283-6839 .. **Namm,** Sheila J '96 %Maimonides Med Ctr -4802 10th Av -Brklyn 11219 **Fx:**283-6553
(212) 696-6000 .. **Namnum,** Susana M '96 %Curtis M-PC&M LLP -101 Park Av -NY 10178
(212) 809-9491 .. **Nanavati,** Rajkumar Harit '96 IBG -1 Bttry Pk Plz -NY 10004
(212) 298-5143 .. **Nance,** Anyika K '04 Leg Aid -49 Thomas -NY 10013 **Fx:**298-5252
(212) 583-9600 .. **Nance,** Diana R '07 %Littler M,PC -900 3rd Av -NY 10022
(212) 506-2500 .. **Nance,** Russell E '99 (Mayer B LLP) -1675 Bway -NY 10019
(212) 808-8300 .. **Nanchahal,** Neha '10 %Rosensteel Law -90 Park Av -NY 10016
(718) 254-6409 .. **Nandan,** Kathleen Anne '96 %US Atty -271 Cadman Plz E -Brklyn 11201 **Fx:**254-6479
(516) 827-4300 .. **Naness Chaiet & Naness LLC** -375 N Bway -Jericho 11753 **Fx:**827-0202
(516) 827-4300 .. **Naness,** Jeffrey N '93 (Naness C&N LLC) -375 N Bway -Jericho 11753
(516) 827-4300 .. **Naness,** Richd M '61 (Naness C&N LLC) -375 N Bway -Jericho 11753
(718) 222-5300 .. **Nangia,** Aashish K '99 (Nangia & K LLP) -26 Court -Brklyn 11242
(212) 705-7000 .. **Nangiana,** Amrita K '10 %Bingham M LLP -399 Park Av -NY 10022
(516) 931-1800 .. **Nanis,** Maria Massucci '96 %Catalano G&P LLP -100 Jericho Quadrangle -Jericho 11753
(718) 777-8887 .. **Nanis & Rinaldi,LLP** -30-97 Steinway -Astoria 11103 **Fx:**777-8452
(718) 777-8887 .. **Nanis,** Wm C '93 (Nanis & R,LLP) -30-97 Steinway -Astoria 11103
(212) 589-4200 .. **Nann,** Alissa M '07 %Baker & H LLP -45 Rckfllr Plz -NY 10111
(212) 504-6000 .. **Nanni,** Anthony V '68 SpclCnsl Cadwalader W&T LLP -1 World Fncl Ctr -NY 10281
(212) 336-2000 .. **Nanni,** Ryan C '09 %Patterson BW&T LLP -1133 Av of Amer -NY 10036
(212) 351-4500 .. **Nanos,** Ian G '09 %Epstein B&G,PC -250 Park Av -NY 10177
(516) 486-4600 .. **Nanos,** Linda G '81 (Bendik & N) -250 Fulton Av -Hempstd 11550
(212) 310-9500 .. **Nanos,** Rania '98 %Instinet Corp -3 Times Square -NY 10036
(718) 643-2500 .. **Nanton,** Gregory '97 -890 Atl Av -Brklyn 11238
(516) 487-5800 .. **Naparty,** Matthew W '02 (Mauro G&L LLP) -60 Cuttermill Rd -Gt Neck 11021
(585) 232-4474 .. **Napier,** James A '87 (Napier & N) -100 Exec Ofc Bldg -Rchstr 14614 **Fx:**232-5368
(585) 232-4474 .. **Napier,** Robt A '85 (Napier & N) -100 Exec Ofc Bldg -Rchstr 14614 **Fx:**232-5368
(212) 785-2577 .. **Napierala,** Natalie A '92 (Rosner & N) -26 Bway -NY 10004 **Fx:**785-5203
(518) 862-9292 .. **Napierski,** Christine M '90 (Napierski V&N,LLP) -296 Wshngtn Av Ext -Albany 12203
(518) 862-9292 .. **Napierski,** Eugene D '92 (Napierski V&N,LLP) -296 Wshngtn Av Ext -Albany 12203
(518) 862-9292 .. **Napierski,** Eugene E '68 (Napierski V&N,LLP) -296 Wshngtn Av Ext -Albany 12203
(518) 862-9292 .. **Napierski Vandenburgh & Napierski,LLP** -296 Wshngtn Av Ext -Albany 12203 **Fx:**862-1519
(914) 701-0800 .. **Napior,** Leo K '06 %Friedman HK&P -2975 Wstchstr Av -Purchase 10577
(212) 906-1200 .. **Naples,** Clement J '04 %Latham & W -885 3rd Av -NY 10022
(716) 856-5222 .. **Naples,** James P '67 -43 Court -Buffalo 14202
(212) 728-8000 .. **Naples,** Nicole M '10 %Willkie F&G LLP -787 7th Av -NY 10019
(646) 610-6354 .. **Naples,** Pamela J '04 NYPD -1 Police Plz -NY 10038
(516) 560-6400 .. **Naples,** Timothy N '04 Leg Aid -1 Helen Keller Way -Hempstd 11550 **Fx:**565-3694
(716) 884-0077 .. **Naples,** Wm N '60 -215 Hmpshr -Buffalo 14213 **Fx:**881-2906
(212) 224-1450 .. **Napoleon,** Roger '80 %Mutual of America -320 Park Av -NY 10022
(212) 227-3333 .. **Napoles,** Robt W '90 %Smith & L,LLP -291 Bway -NY 10007
(718) 522-1377 .. **Napoletano,** Domenick '81 -351 Court -Brklyn 11231 **Fx:**596-6137

(845) 294-1612 .. **Napoletano,** Lisa Marie '96 -1787 Route 17M -Goshen 10924 **Fx:**294-7459
(914) 428-1438 .. **Napoli,** Anthony M '89 %T Bona,PC -123 Main -White Plns 10601 **Fx:**428-1413
(212) 267-3700 .. **Napoli Bern Ripka LLP** -350 5th Av -NY 10118 **Fx:**587-0031
(631) 543-4300 .. **Napoli,** Frank N '91 -357 Vets Mem'l Hwy -Commack 11725 **Fx:**543-4234
(718) 987-8444 .. **Napoli,** George V Jr. '84 %Chelli & B -149 New Dorp Ln -Staten Isl 10306
(212) 226-2100 .. **Napoli,** James C '84 (Caesar & N) -350 Bway -NY 10013
(212) 422-1200 .. **Napoli,** Jessica F '06 %Abrams GF&J,PC -1 Bttry Pk Plz -NY 10004
(212) 218-5500 .. **Napoli,** John P '83 (Seyfarth S LLP) -620 8th Av -NY 10018
(212) 693-0085 .. **Napoli,** Lisa Marie '96 %Appellate Advocates -2 Rector -NY 10006 **Fx:**693-0878
(516) 408-1600 .. **Napoli,** Michl J Jr. '07 %Heidell PM&B,LLP -1050 Franklin Av -Gdn Cty 11530
(212) 267-3700 .. **Napoli,** Paul J '92 (Napoli BR LLP) -350 5th Av -NY 10118
(212) 388-0850 .. **Napolitano,** Anthony '77 -19 E 9th Bx1025 -NY 10276 **Fx:**388-0843
(646) 855-5992 .. **Napolitano,** Catherine '02 Bank of America -1 Bryant Park -NY 10036
(516) 571-3027 .. **Napolitano,** Donna A '03 %Cnty Atty -1 West -Mineola 11501 **Fx:**571-3058
(718) 845-3070 .. **Napolitano,** John '84 J Napolitano -94-09 101st Av -Ozone Pk 11416 **Fx:**835-7126
(201) 447-5600 .. **Napolitano,** John A '86 (Johnson & C,LLP) -307 7th Av -NY 10001 **Fx:**447-2080
(631) 727-7345 .. **Napolitano,** Karen C '92 -619 Roanoke Av -Rvrhead 11901 **Fx:**727-3575
(585) 232-4724 .. **Napolitano,** Lorenzo '04 %Elliott S&C,LLP -1 E Main -Rchstr 14614
(718) 447-1810 .. **Napolitano & Magnotti** -1492 Victory Blvd -Staten Isl 10301 **Fx:**720-1882
(914) 946-5100 .. **Napolitano,** Michl A '87 %Bashian & F,LLP -235 Main -White Plns 10601
(516) 741-6565 .. **Napolitano,** Michl D '90 %Meyer SE&K,PC -990 Stewart Av Bx9194 -Gdn Cty 11530
(212) 915-8888 .. **Napolitano,** Nicole '01 Willis NA Inc -200 Lbrty -NY 10281
(718) 447-1810 .. **Napolitano,** Peter J '62 (Napolitano & M) -1492 Victory Blvd -Staten Isl 10301
(718) 845-3070 .. **Napolitano,** Peter N '96 OfCnsl J Napolitano -94-09 101st Av -Ozone Pk 11416 **Fx:**835-7126
(718) 409-0200 .. **Napolitano,** Phil '96 -1519 Castle Hill Av -Bronx 10462 **Fx:**239-0256
(516) 802-0630 .. **Napolitano,** Ryan S '10 %Simmons J,LLP -115 Eileen Way -Syosset 11791
(212) 735-3000 .. **Napolitano,** Steven F '89 (Skadden ASM&F LLP) -4 Times Sq -NY 10036
(212) 735-3000 .. **Napolitano,** Vincent J '10 %Skadden ASM&F LLP -4 Times Sq -NY 10036
(718) 738-2300 .. **Napolitano,** Vito A '78 -163-33 Crossbay Blvd -Howard Bch 11414 **Fx:**738-9785
(718) 273-9000 .. **Nappa,** Jos A '91 (Helbock N&G) -2550 Victory Blvd -Staten Isl 10314 **Fx:**816-0718
(631) 271-0505 .. **Nappi,** John T '59 -49 E 9th -Huntngtn Sta 11746 **Fx:**271-0512
(516) 333-3322 .. **Naqvi,** Sakeena B '00 %Jafri & J -143 Post Av -Westbury 11590 **Fx:**333-3342
(212) 506-1700 .. **Naqvi,** Zehra '08 %Kasowitz BT&F LLP -1633 Bway -NY 10019
(212) 858-1000 .. **Nara,** Fusae '92 (Pillsbury WSP LLP) -1540 Bway -NY 10036
(718) 845-5840 .. **Narain,** Camy T '98 (Narain Law Firm,PC) -110-23 Rockaway Blvd -S Ozone Pk 11420 **Fx:**845-5940
(516) 739-7403 .. **Narain,** Sharmila G '99 %Savran Law,PLLC -1 Old Cntry Rd -Carle Pl 11514 **Fx:**739-7408
(646) 234-9500 .. **Narang,** Charu '98 -101 W 55th -NY 10019
(516) 742-3400 .. **Naranjo,** Carolyn R '82 Naranjo & Assoc,PC -1225 Franklin Av -Gdn Cty 11530
(212) 557-8038 .. **Narayan,** Preeti '01 Cnsl Tata Cnsltncy Srvcs Ltd -101 Park Av -NY 10178
(212) 701-3000 .. **Narayan,** Shilpa A '10 %Cahill G&R LLP -80 Pine -NY 10005 **Fx:**269-5420
(212) 758-9700 .. **Narbaitz,** Lisa Anne '95 %KPMG LLP -345 Park Av -NY 10154
(716) 855-2324 .. **Narby,** George W '69 -509 Lbrty Bldg -Buffalo 14202 **Fx:**835-6969
(716) 481-2510 .. **Narby,** Mark W '90 Bridge Settlement Corp -525 Aero Dr -Buffalo 14225
(914) 725-1767 .. **Narcisi,** Vincent '84 -13 Dickel Rd -Scarsdale 10583
(518) 434-0600 .. **Nardacci,** Anne M '03 %Boies S&F LLP -10 N Pearl -Albany 12207
(212) 735-8600 .. **Nardella,** Nancy S '87 SrCnsl Morrison C LLP -909 3rd Av -NY 10022
(718) 884-4236 .. **Nardelli,** Alfred L '79 -4473 Douglas Av -Bronx 10471 **Fx:**548-3269
(212) 209-4800 .. **Nardi,** Diane M '01 (Brown R LLP) -7 Times Sq -NY 10036
(212) 407-4000 .. **Nardi,** Richd A '80 (Loeb & L,LLP) -345 Park Av -NY 10154
(212) 682-6800 .. **Nardiello,** Jaimee L '04 %Zetlin & D LLP -801 2nd Av -NY 10017
(212) 415-8600 .. **Nardiello,** Jason '02 %Locke LB&L LLP -3 World Fncl Ctr -NY 10281
(917) 320-2500 .. **Nardino,** Marie D '85 FDIC -350 5th Av -NY 10118 **Fx:**320-2917
(718) 803-3782 .. **Nardizzi,** Steven F '99 EPVA -75-20 Astoria Blvd -E Elmhrst 11370
(516) 248-2121 .. **Nardo,** Raymond '91 R Nardo PC -129 3rd -Mineola 11501 **Fx:**742-7675
(518) 462-5601 .. **Nardolillo,** David E '10 O'Connell & A -54 State -Albany 12207
(917) 318-7739 .. **Nardone,** Diane C '92 -11 5th Av -NY 10003
(914) 287-0900 .. **Nardone,** Peter K '91 -50 Main -White Plns 10606 **Fx:**287-7386
(845) 691-7611 .. **Nardone,** Richd '74 (Nardone & N) -1 N Roberts Rd Bx896 -Highlnd 12528
(646) 471-4463 .. **Nardozzi,** Thos C '80 %PricewaterhouseCoopers LLP -300 Mad Av -NY 10017
(212) 506-5000 .. **Narducci,** John '89 (Orrick H&S LLP) -51 W 52nd -NY 10019
(516) 296-7000 .. **Narendran,** Jothy '97 (Certilman BA&H,LLP) -90 Merrick Av -E Meadow 11554
(914) 712-0529 .. **Nargi,** Ernest L '97 -982 Grant Av -Pelham Mnr 10803
(212) 272-6057 .. **Nargolwala,** Christina L '93 %JP Morgan Chase -383 Mad Av -NY 10179
(212) 635-1166 .. **Narin,** Alvin A '90 Bk of NY Mellon -1 Wall -NY 10286
(845) 452-4200 .. **Narmore,** Jeff W '01 US Bankruptcy Ct-SDNY -355 Main -Poughkeepsie 12601
(516) 498-8830 .. **Narotsky & Lavin,LLP** -60 Cuttermill Rd -Gt Neck 11021 **Fx:**498-8998
(516) 498-8830 .. **Narotsky,** Lori '95 Narotsky & L,LLP -60 Cuttermill Rd -Gt Neck 11021 **Fx:**498-8998
(516) 498-8830 .. **Narotsky,** Louis A '71 (Narotsky & L,LLP) -60 Cuttermill Rd -Gt Neck 11021
(212) 355-2460 .. **Narotzky,** Philip L '89 Counsel Abstract,Inc -400 Park Av -NY 10022
(212) 627-0001 .. **Narov,** Hilla '99 Full Picture -915 Bway -NY 10010
(646) 383-7647 .. **Narra,** Shanti '95 -22 Crtland -NY 10007
(845) 358-1354 .. **Narral,** Raymond F '62 -5 Alleghany Av -Nyack 10960
(518) 563-5600 .. **Narrow,** Edw F '01 -18 Brinkerhoff Bx3006 -Plattsbrgh 12901 **Fx:**563-5623
(212) 408-5100 .. **Narvaez,** J Patrick '08 %Chadbourne & P LLP -30 Rckfllr Plz -NY 10112
(631) 324-8787 .. **Narvilas,** Madeleine A '04 %Town Atty -159 Pantigo Rd -E Hampton 11937 **Fx:**329-5371
(212) 474-1000 .. **Nasab,** Omid H '07 %Cravath S&M LLP -825 8th Av -NY 10019
(212) 506-1700 .. **Nasar,** Alice R '09 Kasowitz BT&F LLP -1633 Bway -NY 10019
(212) 335-9000 .. **Nasar,** David A '04 %DA -1 Hogan Pl -NY 10013
(718) 590-3973 .. **Nasar,** Omar '08 %Law Dept -198 E 161st -Bronx 10451 **Fx:**590-2686
(212) 903-9000 .. **Nasatir,** Justin F '10 %Linklaters -1345 Av of Amer -NY 10105
(718) 590-6024 .. **Nasca,** Carly M '04 %Law Dept -900 Sheridan Av -Bronx 10451 **Fx:**590-2699
(716) 875-0210 .. **Nasca,** Jos M '54 -Bx307 -Buffalo 14223
(585) 428-5432 .. **Nasca,** Kevin M '00 %Cnty Sheriffs Ofc -130 S Plymouth Av -Rchstr 14614
(716) 851-5054 .. **Nasca,** Sandra Ann '89 Neigborhood Revitalization Corp -65 Niagara Sq -Buffalo 14202
(315) 339-9080 .. **Nasci,** John T '95 -105 W Court Bx115 -Rome 13442 **Fx:**339-9082
(315) 671-2019 .. **Nasci,** Susan Hamlin '90 %Family Ct -401 Mntgmry -Syracuse 13202
(212) 244-3333 .. **Nash,** Andrea L '08 %Donovan H LLP -1350 Bway -NY 10018
(212) 450-4000 .. **Nash,** Andrew H M '09 %Davis P&W LLP -450 Lex Av -NY 10017
(212) 344-5400 .. **Nash,** Bradley J '03 OfCnsl Schlam S&D LLP -26 Bway -NY 10004
(315) 386-8501 .. **Nash,** Chas B '74 (Nash P&L) -113 Main Bx529 -Canton 13617 **Fx:**386-8936
(212) 940-3000 .. **Nash,** Deirdre E '10 %Nixon P LLP -437 Mad Av -NY 10022
(315) 425-2700 .. **Nash,** Douglas J '02 (Hiscock & B,LLP) -One Park Pl -Syracuse 13202
(212) 864-6497 .. **Nash,** Fred '39 -245 W 104th -NY 10025
(212) 721-3533 .. **Nash,** George W '68 -185 West End Av -NY 10023 **Fx:**721-3633
(212) 799-7734 .. **Nash,** J Newton '56 -230 Park Av -NY 10169 **Fx:**874-6349
(716) 881-3010 .. **Nash,** James J '05 %Cohen & L,PC -343 Elmwood Av Bx5204 -Buffalo 14213
(212) 986-6000 .. **Nash,** Jamie L '02 (Kleinberg KW&C,PC) -551 5th Av -NY 10176
(212) 889-3700 .. **Nash,** Jeremy N '08 Abbey SR&A LLP -212 E 39th -NY 10016
(212) 732-9000 .. **Nash,** John F '78 (Sullivan PBM&C PC) -120 Bway -NY 10271
(516) 742-0707 .. **Nash,** John F '78 (Sullivan PBM&C PC) -55 Mineola Blvd -Mineola 11501
(212) 221-5700 .. **Nash,** Kevin J '84 (Goldberg WFG LLP) -1501 Bway -NY 10036
(203) 876-0487 .. **Nash,** Laura E '94 -38 Euclid Av -Ardsley 10502
(716) 858-2424 .. **Nash,** Lauren '06 %DA -25 Delaware Av -Buffalo 14202 **Fx:**858-7425
(518) 408-0265 .. **Nash,** Marc S '94 Workers Comp Bd -20 Park -Albany 12207
(845) 291-3150 .. **Nash,** Mark S '90 %Cnty Atty -255 Main -Goshen 10924 **Fx:**291-3167
(607) 273-5787 .. **Nash,** Ralph W '78 %Crossmore Law Ofc -115 W Green -Ithaca 14850 **Fx:**273-0291
(914) 457-2300 .. **Nash,** Robt M '06 %Kanterman & S,LLP -50 Main -White Plns 10606
(212) 756-2000 .. **Nash,** Robt S '77 (Schulte R&Z LLP) -919 3rd Av -NY 10022
(518) 862-9292 .. **Nash,** Shawn T '00 %Napierski V&N,LLP 296 Wshngtn Av Ext -Albany 12203
(718) 386-4345 .. **Nashak,** George J Jr. '61 (Ramo N&B) -75-19 Myrtle Av -Glendale 11385
(718) 510-8820 .. **Nashak,** Michl G '88 -15 Metrotech Ctr -Brklyn 11201
(212) 408-5100 .. **Nashat,** Kessar '03 %Chadbourne & P LLP -30 Rckfllr Plz -NY 10112
(212) 232-1300 .. **Nashban,** Stephanie Alix '01 (Lewis BB&S LLP) -77 Water -NY 10005
(212) 468-8000 .. **Nashelsky,** Larren M '92 (Morrison & F LLP) -1290 Av of Amer -NY 10104
(212) 221-5700 .. **Nasiak,** Lisa C '97 %Goldberg WFG LLP -1501 Bway -NY 10036
(631) 236-9877 .. **Nasis,** Elbert F '96 (Dornfeld & N,LLP) -145 Marcus Blvd -Hauppauge 11788
(212) 883-1700 .. **Naso,** Chad A '09 %Duval & S LLP -101 Park Av -NY 10178
(914) 241-2531 .. **Naso,** James V '84 -Bx210 -New Rchll 10804
(845) 679-9376 .. **Naso,** Michl A '85 -Bx305 -Woodstock 12498
(212) 691-8700 .. **Naso-Kushner,** Jake A '07 %Almazan & Assoc,PC -27 Union Sq W -NY 10003 **Fx:**691-8701
(212) 848-4000 .. **Nasr,** Assaad Y '08 %Shearman & S LLP -599 Lex Av -NY 10022
(212) 967-1134 .. **Nass,** Eric M '96 (Marder E&N) -450 7th Av -NY 10123
(212) 370-0777 .. **Nass,** Herbert E '85 (H Nass & Assoc) -420 Lex Av -NY 10170 **Fx:**370-0707
(212) 715-9100 .. **Nassau,** Michl J '60 Cnsl Kramer LN&F,LLP -1177 Av of Amer -NY 10036
(914) 378-1010 .. **Nassau,** Randy B '93 %Fitzgerald & F -538 Riverdale Av -Ynkrs 10705
(585) 232-5300 .. **Nassau,** Robt G '86 OfCnsl Boylan BCV&W,LLP -2400 Chase Sq -Rchstr 14604
(212) 673-6669 .. **Nasser,** Nathan C '80 Ventura R&S -280 Park Av S -NY 10010
(212) 788-7100 .. **Nasser,** Terzah N '93 NYC Council -250 Bway -NY 10007
(212) 878-8000 .. **Nasser,** Zeinab '00 %Clifford C LLP -31 W 52nd -NY 10019
(212) 308-4411 .. **Nassi,** Pejman '04 %Edwards AP&D LLP -750 Lex Av -NY 10022
(518) 474-8211 .. **Nassif,** Gail A '81 %Law Reporting Bur -1 Commerce Plz -Albany 12210 **Fx:**463-6869
(212) 584-0700 .. **Nassif,** Valere Laurence '00 %Seeger W LLP -1 William -NY 10004

(212) 643-8080 .. **Nassimi,** Oliver '99 %Clifpass Development Inc -370 7th Av -NY 10001
(718) 247-7294 .. **Nassiripour,** Ali R '04 (Nassiripour & S,PC) -4027 74th -Elmhrst 11373
(212) 850-1368 .. **Nasta,** Frank J '90 %J&W Seligman & Co -100 Park Av -NY 10017 **Fx:**922-5731
(516) 775-2236 .. **Nasta,** Paul S '90 %Santangelo B&S -1800 Nrthrn Blvd -Roslyn 11576
(914) 253-3271 .. **Nastanski,** Cynthia Ann '96 Pepsico -700 Andrsn Hill Rd -Purchase 10577
(212) 261-8000 .. **Nastase,** Laura C '10 %Mendes & M,LLP -750 7th Av -NY 10019
(212) 907-7300 .. **Nastasi,** Ancela R '92 SpclCnsl Golenbock EAB&P -437 Mad Av -NY 10022
(646) 333-8725 .. **Nastasi,** John C '03 Lehman Bros -1271 Av of Amer -NY 10020
(212) 581-3100 .. **Nastaskin,** Natalia '95 Agency Group Ltd -142 W 57th -NY 10019 **Fx:**581-0015
(212) 808-7000 .. **Nasti,** Richd T '83 %HJ Kalikow & Co, Inc -101 Park Av -NY 10178
(315) 738-1000 .. **Nasto,** John A Jr. '78 Nasto Law Firm -4957 Cmmrcial Dr -Yorkville 13495 **Fx:**736-1932
(516) 374-2321 .. **Nastre,** Arthur J '73 -1253 Colonial Rd -Hewlett 11557 **Fx:**374-2635
(212) 425-1900 .. **Nastro,** Justin T '99 %Freehill H&M LLP -80 Pine -NY 10005
(516) 561-6645 .. **Nat,** Hilary I '07 %E Schlissel -479 Merrick Rd -Lynbrk 11563 **Fx:**561-6716
(516) 877-2900 .. **Natale,** Kevin R '90 %Bartlett MB&M,LLP -300 Old Cntry Rd -Mineola 11501
(845) 634-3627 .. **Natale,** Mary Ellen '94 Leg Aid -2 Congers Rd -New Cty 10956 **Fx:**634-8505
(212) 461-2323 .. **Natale,** Melissa A '04 %Saiber LLC -44 Wall -NY 10005
(212) 374-3407 .. **Natale,** Neil S '00 Dept of Ed - Lgl Srvcs -52 Chmbrs -NY 10007
(631) 501-3100 .. **Natale,** Victor J '84 %J Humphreys -3 Huntngtn Quad Bx9028 -Melvll 11747 **Fx:**501-3085
(585) 258-8691 .. **Natalie,** Jennifer R '01 Preferred Care -259 Monroe Av -Rchstr 14607 **Fx:**258-8060
(631) 853-4049 .. **Natalie,** Lawr J Jr. '93 %Cnty Atty -Dennison Bldg Bx6100 -Hauppauge 11788 **Fx:**853-5169
(212) 613-5000 .. **Nataneli,** Rachel '07 Leg Assist Grp -450 W 33rd -NY 10001 **Fx:**750-0820
(315) 458-3905 .. **Natanson,** Leroy '58 -218 Park Ln -N Syracuse 13212 **Fx:**458-0253
(212) 603-6300 .. **Natarajan,** Brenda B '06 %Robinson BLGG&G PC -875 3rd Av -NY 10022
(212) 504-6000 .. **Natbony,** Wm J '85 Cnsl Cadwalader W&T LLP -1 World Fncl Ctr -NY 10281
(914) 377-6240 .. **Natchev-Maertens,** Alain '85 Law Dept -300 City Hall -Ynkrs 10701 **Fx:**964-0563
(212) 801-9322 .. **Natelson,** Abby H '09 %Greenberg T,LLP -200 Park Av -NY 10166
(716) 433-3704 .. **Natemeier,** David P '72 -89 Regent Av -Lockprt 14094
(212) 548-4367 .. **Nath,** Aninda '97 Barclays Global Invstrs -200 Park Av -NY 10166
(212) 636-6000 .. **Nathan,** Alison J '03 %Fordham Univ Sch of Law -140 W 62nd -NY 10023 **Fx:**636-6899
(914) 723-3533 .. **Nathan,** Andrew J '82 Meritage Properties -2 Overhill Rd -Scarsdale 10583
(631) 231-9565 .. **Nathan,** Bernard A '79 (B Nathan,PC) -325 Wireless Blvd -Hauppauge 11788 **Fx:**273-9685
(212) 587-3448 .. **Nathan,** Betsey '87 -100 Lafayette -NY 10013 **Fx:**343-1375
(212) 204-8686 .. **Nathan,** Bruce S '81 (Lowenstein S PC) -1251 Av of Amer -NY 10020 **Fx:**(973) 422-6851
(212) 906-1200 .. **Nathan,** Chas M '67 (Latham & W) -885 3rd Av -NY 10022
(212) 279-7810 .. **Nathan,** Claude '75 -225 W 34th -NY 10122
(212) 867-3636 .. **Nathan,** David J '83 (Levin & G,PC) -420 Lex Av -NY 10170
(212) 545-4630 .. **Nathan,** Edgar J 3rd '48 (Wolf HAF&H LLP) -270 Mad Av -NY 10016
(212) 808-7840 .. **Nathan,** Frederic S '48 (Kelley D&W LLP) -101 Park Av -NY 10178
(212) 753-5000 .. **Nathan,** Harold S '77 (Schiff H LLP) -900 3rd Av -NY 10022
(516) 766-1619 .. **Nathan,** Heather B '03 %Dergarabedian D & Assoc -11 Clinton Av -Rockvll Ctr 11570 **Fx:**766-6121
(212) 688-8555 .. **Nathan,** Jennifer R '03 %Fragomen DB&L LLP -7 Hanover Sq -NY 10004
(212) 373-3000 .. **Nathan,** John E '67 (Paul WRW&G LLP) -1285 Av of Amer -NY 10019
(212) 560-1313 .. **Nathan,** Joshua C '92 %EBC -450 W 33rd -NY 10001 **Fx:**560-3191
(212) 374-2993 .. **Nathan,** Judy E '85 %NYC Dept Educ-OLS -52 Chmbrs -NY 10007 **Fx:**374-5596
(212) 986-3859 .. **Nathan,** Larry '63 -521 5th Av -NY 10175
(212) 341-9001 .. **Nathan,** Leora '04 ACS-DLS -150 William -NY 10038
(212) 575-7900 .. **Nathan,** Lindsay M '09 %Ballon SB&N,PC -729 7th Av -NY 10019
(212) 298-5042 .. **Nathan,** Lorin B '72 %Leg Aid -49 Thomas -NY 10013 **Fx:**298-5252
(212) 455-2000 .. **Nathan,** Michl D '82 (Simpson T&B LLP) -425 Lex Av -NY 10017
(516) 747-1100 .. **Nathan,** Naomi R '90 %Shayne DCS&D -114 Old Cntry Rd -Mineola 11501
(518) 474-4785 .. **Nathan,** Sandra M '77 Industrial Bd of Appls -ESP -Albany 12223
(212) 595-4035 .. **Nathan,** Sara E '81 -37 Riverside Dr -NY 10023
(718) 268-9226 .. **Nathan,** Stephen B '72 -98-20 Metro Av -Frst Hlls 11375
(212) 606-7175 .. **Nathan,** Susan J '04 %Sotheby's,Inc -1334 York Av -NY 10021 **Fx:**606-7574
(845) 986-1136 .. **Nathans,** Wm '79 (Stage N&Z,LLP) -23 West -Warwick 10990
(212) 831-2677 .. **Nathanson,** Carl J '60 -305 E 86th -NY 10028 **Fx:**831-2697
(212) 421-4100 .. **Nathanson,** Eli B '97 (Pryor C LLP) -7 Times Sq -NY 10036
(212) 608-6771 .. **Nathanson,** Eugene B '78 -30 Vesey -NY 10007 **Fx:**608-0479
(212) 988-0593 .. **Nathanson,** Eugenia S '89 -203 E 72nd -NY 10021 **Fx:**570-5036
(718) 793-1986 .. **Nathanson,** Fred I '80 -123-33 83rd Av -Kew Gdns 11415
(212) 848-4000 .. **Nathanson,** John A '94 Cnsl Shearman & S LLP -599 Lex Av -NY 10022
(212) 603-6300 .. **Nathanson,** Leonard B '70 (Robinson BLGG&G PC) -875 3rd Av -NY 10022
(212) 608-6771 .. **Nathanson,** Malvina '65 -30 Vesey -NY 10007 **Fx:**500-2729
(516) 568-0000 .. **Nathanson,** Mark '66 (Nathanson Law Firm,LLP) -81 Hempstd Av -Lynbrk 11563 **Fx:**568-9456
(516) 568-0000 .. **Nathanson,** Mitchell A '92 (Nathanson Law Firm,LLP) -81 Hempstd Av -Lynbrk 11563 **Fx:**568-9456
(212) 659-7300 .. **Nathanson,** Stacy E '04 %Haynes & B,LLP -1221 Av of Amer -NY 10020
(212) 501-7899 .. **Natiello,** Michl F '92 %FJ DeVito,PA -150 Bway -NY 10038
(516) 621-0900 .. **Natiss & Gordon, PC** -277 Willis Av -Roslyn Hts 11577 **Fx:**621-1304
(516) 621-0900 .. **Natiss,** Marvin '61 (Natiss & G,PC) -277 Willis Av -Roslyn Hts 11577
(212) 837-6841 .. **Natividad,** Kim F '10 %Hughes H&R LLP -1 Bttry Pk Plz -NY 10004 **Fx:**299-6841
(212) 465-5530 .. **Natkins,** Burt P '01 Parsons Brinckerhoff,Inc -1 Penn Plz -NY 10119
(212) 312-3000 .. **Natko,** Steven P '85 %FGIC -125 Park Av -NY 10017 **Fx:**312-3221
(631) 501-5700 .. **Natof,** Paul J '05 %Carter DF&S LLP -445 Broadhallow Rd -Melvll 11747
(212) 619-8087 .. **Natoli,** Albert A '82 -233 Bway -NY 10279 **Fx:**619-8097
(212) 949-9022 .. **Natoli,** Anthony J F '93 %Abelman F&S -666 3rd Av -NY 10017
(212) 537-4436 .. **Natoli,** Frank A '08 (Natoli-Lapin,LLC) -304 Park Av S -NY 10010
(607) 336-8200 .. **Natoli,** Lisa A '02 (Natoli & N,LLP) -27 W Main -Norwich 13815 **Fx:**336-8203
(917) 778-6600 .. **Natoli,** Rose G '93 %J Toomey -485 Lex Av -NY 10017 **Fx:**778-7048
(607) 336-8200 .. **Natoli,** Steven G '01 (Natoli & N,LLP) -27 W Main -Norwich 13815 **Fx:**336-8203
(212) 788-1033 .. **Natrella,** Elizabeth S '84 %Law Dept -100 Church -NY 10007 **Fx:**788-0367
(212) 840-8300 .. **Natter,** Benjamin '10 Natter & N -501 5th Av -NY 10017 **Fx:**302-0295
(212) 768-6700 .. **Natter,** David L '00 %Sonnenschein N&R LLP -2 World Fncl Ctr -NY 10281
(212) 865-5399 .. **Natter,** David M '91 -417 Riverside Dr -NY 10025
(212) 840-8300 .. **Natter,** Howard '65 (Natter & N) -501 5th Av -NY 10017 **Fx:**302-0295
(212) 840-8300 .. **Natter,** Seth '66 (Natter & N) -501 5th Av -NY 10017 **Fx:**302-0295
(607) 687-0338 .. **Natwick,** Karen Lee '97 Cnty Ct -Bx10 -Owego 13827
(212) 733-9483 .. **Nau,** Annabel '98 Pfizer,Inc -150 E 42nd -NY 10017
(718) 622-8149 .. **Nau,** Enealia S '97 -854 Fulton -Brklyn 11238
(212) 819-1928 .. **Naudon,** Carlos P '82 (Allister & N) -1430 Bway -NY 10018 **Fx:**819-1904
(212) 533-6300 .. **Naughton,** Aileen Calcagni '07 %NYSUT -52 Bway -NY 10004 **Fx:**995-2347
(716) 875-8664 .. **Naughton,** Chas J '89 Bartlo H&W -22 Victoria Blvd -Kenmore 14217
(518) 438-9907 .. **Naughton,** J Michl Jr. '85 (Young SWRB&M,LLC) -5 Palisades Dr -Albany 12205
(914) 674-7787 .. **Naughton,** Joanne '85 %Mercy College -555 Bway -Dobbs Ferry 10522 **Fx:**674-7542
(212) 450-4000 .. **Naughton,** John M '08 %Davis P&W LLP -450 Lex Av -NY 10017
(212) 788-1270 .. **Naughton,** Kathleen E '08 %Law Dept -100 Church -NY 10007 **Fx:**788-0367
(718) 254-7000 .. **Naughton,** Kathleen M '99 %US Atty -271 Cadman Plz E -Brklyn 11201 **Fx:**254-6479
(845) 294-4080 .. **Naughton,** Kelly M '07 %Burke M&G -40 Matthews Bx216 -Goshen 10924
(212) 515-7140 .. **Naughton,** Leo F '88 Dexia Global -445 Park Av -NY 10022
(212) 455-2000 .. **Naughton,** Michl C '95 SrCnsl Simpson T&B LLP -425 Lex Av -NY 10017
(518) 402-9188 .. **Naughton,** Michl P '98 DEC -625 Bway -Albany 12233 **Fx:**402-9018
(212) 983-8500 .. **Naughton,** Michl P '00 %Brown G&F LLP -355 Lex Av -NY 10017
(315) 442-0100 .. **Naughton,** Patricia Serventi '94 OfCnsl Gilberti SH&S,PC -555 E Genesee -Syracuse 13202
(212) 858-1000 .. **Naughton-Carr,** Jeanne '93 Cnsl Pillsbury WSP LLP -1540 Bway -NY 10036
(315) 785-3152 .. **Naumiec,** Richd V '09 %Pub Def -175 Arsenal -Watertwn 13601 **Fx:**785-5060
(212) 533-6300 .. **Naun,** John J '75 %NYSUT -52 Bway -NY 10004 **Fx:**995-2347
(212) 846-7883 .. **Naunton,** Heidi L '04 %Viacom -1515 Bway -NY 10036
(212) 704-9600 .. **Naunton,** Shawn P '01 Cnsl Zuckerman S,LLP -1540 Bway -NY 10036
(716) 856-4000 .. **Nauth,** Danl D '08 %Hodgson R LLP -140 Pearl -Buffalo 14202
(212) 581-4800 .. **Nautiyal,** Deviyani '95 %Arjay Telecom -995 Hempstd Tpk -Franklin Sq 11010
(716) 845-6000 .. **Navagh,** James J '86 Kavinoky C LLP -726 Exchange -Buffalo 14210
(516) 364-6444 .. **Navaretta,** John F '89 (Navaretta & H,LLP) -567 Jericho Tpk -Syosset 11791 **Fx:**364-5005
(212) 909-6000 .. **Navarino,** Jason D '08 %Debevoise & P LLP -919 3rd Av -NY 10022
(845) 562-0203 .. **Navarra,** Francis '90 (Finkelstein & Prtnrs,LLP) -1279 Route 300 Bx1111 -Newburgh 12550
(212) 228-5200 .. **Navarra,** Sebastian J '55 -19 E 9th -NY 10003 **Fx:**388-0843
(718) 224-2828 .. **Navarrete,** Priscilla J '06 -4506 Little Neck Pkwy -Little Neck 11362
(212) 801-6896 .. **Navarro,** Danl J '10 %Greenberg T,LLP -200 Park Av -NY 10166
(212) 488-1200 .. **Navarro,** Francisco J '04 %Kobre & K,LLP -800 3rd Av -NY 10022
(212) 286-8585 .. **Navarro,** James '01 %Heidell PM&B,LLP -99 Park Av -NY 10016
(631) 544-1500 .. **Navarro,** Leonor '02 -412 Larkfld Rd -E Northprt 11731 **Fx:**544-1250
(212) 440-4300 .. **Navarro,** Maria E '93 %Leg Aid -199 Water -NY 10038
(212) 309-6000 .. **Navarro,** Steven A '88 (Morgan L&B LLP) -101 Park Av -NY 10178
(716) 854-4080 .. **Navarro,** Thos J Jr. '94 (Notaro L&N,PC) -1 Niagara Sq -Buffalo 14202 **Fx:**854-0059
(212) 839-5300 .. **Navazio,** Michele F '04 %Sidley A LLP -787 7th Av -NY 10019
(212) 446-4800 .. **Naveh,** Keren '07 %Kirkland & E LLP -153 E 53rd -NY 10022
(212) 455-2000 .. **Naveira,** Juan M '08 %Simpson T&B LLP -425 Lex Av -NY 10017
(315) 337-6930 .. **Navelli,** Julia Markus '65 -Bx905 -Rome 13442 **Fx:**336-7921
(212) 455-2000 .. **Navia,** Ana M '07 %Simpson T&B LLP -425 Lex Av -NY 10017
(212) 408-5100 .. **Navia,** Talbert I '82 (Chadbourne & P LLP) -30 Rckfllr Plz -NY 10112
(518) 370-4743 .. **Naviasky,** Laurence '89 (Hoffman & N,PLLC) -1802 Eastern Pkwy -Schnctdy 12309 **Fx:**370-4870
(718) 254-7000 .. **Navickas,** Jo Ann M '85 %US Atty -271 Cadman Plz E -Brklyn 11201 **Fx:**254-6479
(212) 888-3413 .. **Navidi,** Sandra O '02 Muzinich & Co -450 Park Av -NY 10022
(212) 845-2159 .. **Navo,** Aviam E '04 KBC Fncl Products -140 W 45th -NY 10017
(212) 984-2576 .. **Navo,** Caylin E '04 Tiger Mgmt -101 Park Av -NY 10178
(718) 237-0825 .. **Navon,** Ira D '71 -32 Court -Brklyn 11201 **Fx:**(973) 993-0862

(718) 821-2201 .. **Navon,** Yuval '04 Knitwork Prdctns Corp -16-39 Centre -Rdgwd 11385
(607) 737-1944 .. **Navone,** Joshua C '02 -2854 Wstnghse Rd -Horseheads 14845 **Fx:**737-1946
(212) 637-2528 .. **Nawaday,** Jaimie L '05 US Atty -86 Chmbrs -NY 10007
(212) 637-2311 .. **Nawaday,** Kan M '04 %US Atty -1 St Andrews Plz -NY 10007
(516) 564-8000 .. **Nawaz,** Usman '05 %J Hiebler & Assoc -901 Franklin Av -Gdn Cty 11530 **Fx:**564-1714
(212) 596-9000 .. **Nawyn,** Marc D '09 %Ropes & G LLP -1211 Av of Amer -NY 10036
(212) 506-5000 .. **Nayak,** Sushila '00 %Orrick H&S LLP -51 W 52nd -NY 10019
(212) 903-9000 .. **Nayar,** Vivek '10 %Linklaters -1345 Av of Amer -NY 10105
(516) 746-5040 .. **Nayberg,** Robt S '85 %Scher Law Firm,LLP -1 Old Cntry Rd -Carle Pl 11514 **Fx:**747-9100
(203) 226-4515 .. **Nayer,** Stanley M '59 -98 Cuttermill Rd -Gt Neck 11021
(212) 999-5800 .. **Nayini,** Deepa R '06 %Wilson SG&R -1301 Av of Americas -NY 10019
(585) 295-5400 .. **Naylon,** Patrick B '83 (Goldberg S LLP) -2 State -Rchstr 14614
(607) 723-5341 .. **Naylor,** Colin T III '58 OfCnsl Hinman H&K,LLP -80 Exchange Bx5250 -Bnghmtn 13902
(518) 792-6516 .. **Naylor,** David '91 %Kenneally & T -470 Glen Bx379 -Glens Fls 12801
(212) 819-8200 .. **Naylor,** Jeremy M '07 (White & C LLP) -1155 Av of Amer -NY 10036
(212) 937-7249 .. **Nayman,** Stuart R '93 (WilmerHale) -399 Park Av -NY 10022
(718) 852-9694 .. **Nazar,** Debra Monaghan '88 -82 Schermerhorn -Brklyn 11201 **Fx:**852-9694
(212) 541-2000 .. **Nazarenko,** Anna '09 %Bryan C LLP -1290 Av of Amer -NY 10104
(212) 450-4000 .. **Nazareth,** Annette L '82 %Davis P&W LLP -450 Lex Av -NY 10017
(716) 856-9704 .. **Nazarian,** Armen J '08 %Feuerstein & S,LLP -17 St Louis Pl -Buffalo 14202 **Fx:**856-9707
(212) 261-7000 .. **Nazarian,** Nyieri '03 %Calyon -1301 Av of Amer -NY 10019
(516) 357-3000 .. **Nazarian,** Ruth '03 %Rivkin R LLP -926 RXR Plz -Uniondale 11556
(646) 290-5145 .. **Nazario,** Edwin J '99 Nazario Legal Grp,PLLC -845 3rd Av -NY 10022
(212) 705-7000 .. **Nazarov,** Vasiliy '09 %Bingham M LLP -399 Park Av -NY 10022
(646) 331-9378 .. **Nazrali,** Rehan '00 -73-20 Austin -Frst Hlls 11375
(718) 759-9777 .. **Nazrisho,** Russ M '05 (Nazrisho & Assoc,PC) -8023 7th Av -Brklyn 11228 **Fx:**759-9700
(718) 825-7719 .. **Ndanusa,** Mustapha Lakpene '02 -26 Court -Brklyn 11242
(212) 728-8000 .. **Ndukwe,** Joshua B '10 %Willkie F&G LLP -787 7th Av -NY 10019
(212) 536-3900 .. **Ndumele,** Uche D '05 %K&L Gates LLP -599 Lex Av -NY 10022
(212) 259-8000 .. **Nduom,** Papa Wassa Chiefy '08 %Dewey & L LLP -1301 Av of Amer -NY 10019
(914) 253-2000 .. **Neafsey,** Mara '92 %Pepsico -700 Andrsn Hill Rd -Purchase 10577
(212) 504-6000 .. **Neal,** Amber M '08 %Cadwalader W&T LLP -1 World Fncl Ctr -NY 10281
(718) 558-5725 .. **Neal,** Andrew G E '94 -137-32 Jamaica Av -Jamaica 11435 **Fx:**558-4277
(212) 455-2000 .. **Neal,** Joshua B '09 %Simpson T&B LLP -425 Lex Av -NY 10017
(212) 361-7971 .. **Neal,** Mark L '05 %NYC DHS Commissioners Ofc -33 Beaver -NY 10004 **Fx:**361-7977
(917) 715-8323 .. **Neal,** Wm S '88 -83-77 Woodhvn Blvd -Woodhvn 11421 **Fx:**(718) 849-5579
(212) 878-7176 .. **Neale,** Barbara C '73 %MTA -347 Mad Av -NY 10017
(914) 997-7575 .. **Neale,** J Henry Jr. '72 -222 Mamaroneck Av -White Plns 10605 **Fx:**288-0058
(212) 318-3000 .. **Neale,** James H '82 (Fulbright & J LLP) -666 5th Av -NY 10103
(212) 450-1273 .. **Neale,** JoAnn '95 %Major League Soccer -420 5th Av -NY 10018
(212) 728-8000 .. **Neale,** Margery K '84 (Willkie F&G LLP) -787 7th Av -NY 10019
(518) 462-6765 .. **Neale,** Rebecca G '08 %Leg Aid -55 Colvin Av -Albany 12206 **Fx:**427-8352
(518) 474-8211 .. **Neale,** Thos W '08 Law Reporting Bur -1 Commerce Plz -Albany 12210 **Fx:**463-6869
(212) 894-7200 .. **Nealon,** Arthur V '73 (Entwistle & C LLP) -280 Park Av -NY 10017
(718) 549-8438 .. **Nealon,** Kathryn D '76 -384 W 253rd -Bronx 10471
(718) 885-2110 .. **Nealon,** Linda Kay '75 -81 Fordham -Bronx 10464
(212) 779-9910 .. **Nealon,** Matthew P '94 %Eaton & V LLP -3 Park Av -NY 10016
(914) 517-5000 .. **Nealon,** Richd J '73 (Meiselman DPC&E,PC) -1311 Mamaroneck Av -White Plns 10605
(585) 473-3446 .. **Nealon,** Wm F '74 -214 Ashbourne Rd -Rchstr 14618
(518) 798-1727 .. **Nealon,** Wm J III '75 -591 Glen Bx151 -Glens Fls 12801 **Fx:**798-1774
(212) 671-1179 .. **Neandross,** Jeffrey L '73 (Graham MNM&R,PC) -2350 Bway -NY 10024
(212) 618-6395 .. **Nearenberg,** Mark L '85 -1230 Av of Amer -NY 10020 **Fx:**618-6309
(212) 270-6000 .. **Nearing,** Henry L S '00 JP Morgan Chase & Co -270 Park Av -NY 10017
(585) 273-2580 .. **Nearpass,** Catherine C '05 %Univ of Rochester Med Ctr -Bx278979 -Rchstr 14627 **Fx:**272-9311
(585) 263-1000 .. **Nearpass,** Gregory R '04 %Nixon P LLP -1100 Clinton Sq -Rchstr 14604
(212) 233-4995 .. **Neary,** Brian J '83 -15 Maiden Ln -NY 10038
(631) 421-2500 .. **Neary,** Brian P '87 (Caputi W&N) -50 Elm -Huntngtn 11743
(914) 949-2700 .. **Neary,** Claudia A '05 %Bleakley P&S,LLP -1 N Lex Av -White Plns 10601
(212) 788-9045 .. **Neary,** Elizabeth Buxton '94 City Cncl Finance Div -250 Bway -NY 10007
(631) 421-2500 .. **Neary,** Francis M '58 OfCnsl Caputi W&N -50 Elm -Huntngtn 11743
(914) 422-6265 .. **Neary,** Keary Downey '83 %DA -77 S Lex Av -White Plns 10601
(914) 666-2525 .. **Neary,** Mary C '84 (Arons & N LLP) -126 Barker -Mt Kisco 10549
(212) 903-9000 .. **Neary,** Michl J '98 %Linklaters -1345 Av of Amer -NY 10105
(212) 428-2150 .. **Neary,** Virginia M '91 %OCA -25 Beaver -NY 10004 **Fx:**428-2155
(212) 450-4000 .. **Neata,** Stefan A '09 %Davis P&W LLP -450 Lex Av -NY 10017
(212) 682-0020 .. **Neave,** Alexander '63 Cnsl Putney TH&H LLP -521 5th Av -NY 10175
(212) 659-7300 .. **Neave,** April L '06 %Haynes & B,LLP -1221 Av of Amer -NY 10020
(212) 682-0020 .. **Neave,** E Parker '93 (Putney TH&H LLP) -521 5th Av -NY 10175
(845) 758-8700 .. **Nebel,** Donna M '85 -87 E Market -Red Hook 12571 **Fx:**758-8704
(315) 798-5870 .. **Nebush,** Frank J Jr. '75 (Pub Def) -321 Main -Utica 13501 **Fx:**798-6419
(315) 798-5870 .. **Nebush,** Luke A '08 %Pub Def -321 Main -Utica 13501 **Fx:**798-6419
(212) 536-3900 .. **Nececkas,** Derek T '07 %K&L Gates LLP -599 Lex Av -NY 10022
(212) 997-7595 .. **Necheles,** Susan R '86 (Hafetz N&R) -500 5th Av -NY 10110
(212) 449-9036 .. **Neches,** Alon '03 Merrill Lynch -250 Vesey -NY 10080
(347) 296-1443 .. **Neckles,** Derefim B '01 Kings Cnty Supreme Ct -360 Adams -Brklyn 11201
(212) 319-5351 .. **Neckles,** Nicole A '01 %HP Fahringer PLLC -120 E 56th -NY 10022 **Fx:**319-6657
(212) 735-3000 .. **Neckles,** Peter J '78 (Skadden ASM&F LLP) -4 Times Sq -NY 10036
(212) 918-3000 .. **Nedd,** Omeca N '05 %Hogan L LLP -875 3rd Av -NY 10022
(315) 782-5898 .. **Neddo,** Anthony M '98 (Doldo & N,PC) -230 Franklin -Watertwn 13601 **Fx:**782-5482
(212) 840-5577 .. **Nederlander,** Robt '90 %Nederlander Orgn -1450 Bway -NY 10018
(718) 665-9533 .. **Nedick,** Michl J '74 -888 Grnd Cncrs -Bronx 10451 **Fx:**665-9147
(845) 628-3342 .. **Nedjoika-Jennings,** Linda Ann '91 -2 Weber Hill Rd -Mahopac 10541 **Fx:**621-1023
(917) 375-8267 .. **Nedow,** Beth R '98 %Law Dept -60 Lafayette -NY 10013 **Fx:**(212) 442-6865
(212) 225-2000 .. **Nee,** Ann B '09 Cleary GS&H -1 Lbrty Plz -NY 10006
(212) 243-4430 .. **Nee,** Lisa M '01 Vastardis Cap Svcs -41 Mad Av -NY 10010
(212) 326-3939 .. **Nee,** Owen D Jr. '74 OfCnsl Jones D -222 E 41st -NY 10017
(212) 735-3000 .. **Needell,** Benj F '67 (Skadden ASM&F LLP) -4 Times Sq -NY 10036
(212) 756-2000 .. **Needelman,** Jenny K '96 Schulte R&Z LLP -919 3rd Av -NY 10022
(718) 487-2322 .. **Needelman,** Martin S '70 Leg Srvcs Corp -256-260 Bway -Brklyn 11211 **Fx:**782-6790
(212) 474-1000 .. **Needham,** Andrew W '95 (Cravath S&M LLP) -825 8th Av -NY 10019
(315) 218-8000 .. **Needham,** Douglas P '08 %Bond S&K,PLLC -1 Lincoln Ctr -Syracuse 13202
(516) 742-0101 .. **Needham,** John A '53 (Pasta N&T) -436 Willis Av -Williston Pk 11596
(718) 579-3000 .. **Needham,** John C '82 %Leg Aid -1020 Grnd Cncrs -Bronx 10451 **Fx:**588-2611
(315) 671-2000 .. **Needham,** Margaret D '04 Family Ct -401 Mntgmry -Syracuse 13202
(718) 250-2000 .. **Needle,** Michelle L '05 %DA -350 Jay -Brklyn 11201 **Fx:**250-2314
(212) 226-1094 .. **Needle,** Sol '72 (Wyetzner & N) -401 Bway -NY 10013
(212) 407-4000 .. **Needleman,** Brad S '92 (Loeb & L,LLP) -345 Park Av -NY 10154
(518) 486-4511 .. **Needleman,** David V '68 %Dept of Law -The Cptl -Albany 12224
(212) 402-6000 .. **Needleman,** Harry '76 American Ind Fin Srvcs -335 Mad Av -NY 10017
(718) 295-5598 .. **Needleman,** Ira J '97 %Bronx AIDS Srvcs -540 E Fordham Rd -Bronx 10458 **Fx:**733-3429
(914) 286-3400 .. **Needleman,** Karen R '84 %Leg Aid -1 N Bway -White Plns 10601 **Fx:**682-4112
(212) 757-8438 .. **Needleman,** Marcia N '83 (Levitt & N,PC) -250 W 57th -NY 10107
(631) 979-3200 .. **Needleman,** Mark S '76 -222 E Main -Smithtwn 11787 **Fx:**979-4367
(212) 972-1000 .. **Needleman,** Myra '86 %London F LLP -59 Maiden Ln -NY 10038
(646) 837-0471 .. **Neel,** Matthew J '02 -350 5th Av -NY 10118
(212) 866-2037 .. **Neel,** Richd '64 -276 Riverside Dr -NY 10025
(212) 450-4000 .. **Neel,** Rosa M '08 %Davis P&W LLP -450 Lex Av -NY 10017
(212) 521-5400 .. **Neel,** Wallace B '03 %Reed S LLP -599 Lex Av -NY 10022
(718) 579-7900 .. **Neeley,** Zachary C '08 Leg Aid -900 Sheridan Av -Bronx 10451 **Fx:**293-8744
(212) 310-8000 .. **Neely,** Christopher M '09 %Weil G&M LLP -767 5th Av -NY 10153
(212) 455-2000 .. **Neely,** Wilson S '83 (Simpson T&B LLP) -425 Lex Av -NY 10017
(212) 909-6000 .. **Neenan,** Sean P '09 %Debevoise & P LLP -919 3rd Av -NY 10022
(607) 753-5046 .. **Neerbasch,** Lenore M '95 %Pub Def -60 Central Av -Cortlnd 13045 **Fx:**753-0781
(212) 468-8138 .. **Neesemann,** Carroll E '70 SrCnsl Morrison & F LLP -1290 Av of Amer -NY 10104
(212) 819-8200 .. **Neeser,** Renata Tonon '01 White & C LLP -1155 Av of Amer -NY 10036
(212) 323-7070 .. **Neeson,** Peter J '90 (Rawle & H LLP) -14 Wall -NY 10005
(518) 862-9292 .. **Neff,** Asa S '07 %Napierski V&N,LLP -296 Wshngtn Av Ext -Albany 12203
(212) 753-5000 .. **Neff,** Brian J '05 Cnsl Schiff H LLP -900 3rd Av -NY 10022
(212) 438-2556 .. **Neff,** Carl J '98 %Standard & Poor's -55 Water -NY 10041
(212) 403-1000 .. **Neff,** Danl A '78 (Wachtell LR&K) -51 W 52nd -NY 10019
(315) 448-8400 .. **Neff,** David H '85 %Law Dept -233 E Wshngtn -Syracuse 13202 **Fx:**448-8381
(212) 799-3394 .. **Neff,** Michl A '67 (M Neff,PC) -5 W 86th -NY 10024 **Fx:**873-0875
(212) 885-5000 .. **Neff,** Robyn A '07 %Blank R LLP -405 Lex Av -NY 10174
(212) 705-7000 .. **Neger,** Peter C '82 (Bingham M LLP) -399 Park Av -NY 10022
(516) 357-3700 .. **Neglia,** Patrick '94 (Cullen and D LLP) -100 Q Roosevelt Blvd -Gdn Cty 11530
(212) 421-4100 .. **Negrin,** Barry E '93 (Pryor C LLP) -7 Times Sq -NY 10036
(914) 834-1920 .. **Negrin,** Joel '71 (J Negrin,PC) -1865 Palmer Av -Larchmnt 10538 **Fx:**(877) 596-9325
(631) 390-5000 .. **Negrin-Wiener,** Melissa '02 (Genser DG&C,LLP) -445 Broad Hollow Rd -Melvll 11747
(718) 567-2990 .. **Negri Stathopoulos,** Kathleen E '89 -6917 Ft Hmltn Pkwy -Brklyn 11228
(845) 808-1150 .. **Negro,** Andrew W '02 %Cnty Atty -48 Gleneida Av -Carmel 10512 **Fx:**808-1903
(646) 216-2400 .. **Negron,** Hector M '08 %Kranjac M&V LLP -40 Wall -NY 10005 **Fx:**216-2373
(718) 643-2652 .. **Negron,** Mildred T '92 Family Ct -283 Adams -Brklyn 11201
(631) 451-6500 .. **Negron,** Raymond D '02 %Brookhaven Law Dept -1 Indpndnc Hill -Farmngvll 11738 **Fx:**698-4489
(212) 578-2211 .. **Negron,** Robt Jr. '02 %MetLife -27-01 Qns Plz N -LIC 11101
(914) 378-0963 .. **Negron,** Wanda Y '01 (Soto S&N,LLP) -281 S Bway -Ynkrs 10705
(212) 541-2000 .. **Nehama,** Serge D '91 Cnsl Bryan C LLP -1290 Av of Amer -NY 10104
(718) 482-6472 .. **Nehila,** John W '87 %DEC -1 Hunters Pnt Plz -LIC 11101 **Fx:**482-4962
(212) 753-3468 .. **Nehmad,** Tracey E '92 %Wildes & W,PC -515 Mad Av -NY 10022
(212) 446-4800 .. **Nehme,** Alexandra '04 %Kirkland & E LLP -153 E 53rd -NY 10022

(212) 551-8500 .. **Nehro,** Diana J '04 %Israel Discount Bk -511 5th Av -NY 10017 **Fx:**551-8916
(212) 562-1942 .. **Nehro,** Gregory P '02 Cowen & Co LLC -1221 Av of Amer -NY 10020
(212) 806-5400 .. **Neidell,** Martin H '72 (Stroock &S&L LLP) -180 Maiden Ln -NY 10038
(212) 451-2300 .. **Neidell,** Michl R '97 (Olshan GFR&W LLP) -65 E 55th -NY 10022
(607) 871-2329 .. **Neiderbach,** Michl A '90 Alfred Univ -1 Saxon Dr -Alfred 14802
(518) 449-8893 .. **Neidl,** Benjamin F '01 %Wilson EME&D LLP -677 Bway -Albany 12207
(518) 689-1435 .. **Neidl,** Cynthia Evans '02 (Greenberg T,LLP) -54 State -Albany 12207
(212) 294-6700 .. **Neier,** David '86 (Winston & S) -200 Park Av -NY 10166
(212) 833-1111 .. **Neier,** Hal '87 (Friedman KS&A LLP) -1633 Bway -NY 10019 **Fx:**373-7911
(212) 779-1414 .. **Neier,** Hanna R '06 %Bernstein L LLP -10 E 40th -NY 10016
(212) 483-1080 .. **Neifeld,** Marjorie '89 -74 Trinity Pl -NY 10006
(718) 222-8880 .. **Neiger,** Agnes '03 %Jones JO -45 Main -Brklyn 11201
(212) 267-7342 .. **Neiger,** Edw E '05 (Neiger LLP) -317 Mad Av -NY 10017 **Fx:**406-3677
(718) 538-6100 .. **Neiger,** Robin G '84 R Neiger -895 Sheridan Av -Bronx 10451 **Fx:**538-5101
(718) 251-2500 .. **Neihaus,** Alan S '77 %Mr Pickle -44 Bklyn Trmnl Market -Brklyn 11236 **Fx:**763-0503
(212) 859-8000 .. **Neihaus,** Randi S '08 %Fried FHS&J LLP -1 NY Plz -NY 10004
(914) 366-5700 .. **Neil,** David L '82 %MA Bjork -660 Wht Plns Rd -Tarrytwn 10591 **Fx:**366-5759
(212) 691-1500 .. **Neil,** Steven A '83 Westbeth Inc -463 West -NY 10014
(585) 546-5600 .. **Neilans,** Lisa Ann '96 (Pheterson SCN&S,LLP) -1 E Main -Rchstr 14614
(585) 377-4650 .. **Neild,** Wm J '75 -6 Cnty Clare Cres -Fairprt 14450 **Fx:**377-5907
(212) 667-5620 .. **Neilinger,** Brian J '95 %CIBC World Markets -300 Mad Av -NY 10017
(212) 403-1000 .. **Neill,** David S '85 (Wachtell LR&K) -51 W 52nd -NY 10019
(914) 764-9200 .. **Neill,** H Robt '92 -73 Wstchstr Av Bx117 -Pound Rdg 10576 **Fx:**764-8310
(716) 937-3353 .. **Neill,** Nathan S '75 (Neill & S,PLLC) -13166 Main Bx395 -Alden 14004 **Fx:**937-7222
(516) 229-4300 .. **Neill,** Peter T '83 %J Bilello & Assoc -875 Merrick Av -Westbury 11590
(212) 506-2500 .. **Neils,** Lynn A '90 (Mayer B LLP) -1675 Bway -NY 10019
(718) 357-3400 .. **Neilson,** James W '03 -1449 150th -Whitestone 11357
(718) 928-3700 .. **Neilson,** Kathryn '07 %LSNYC-Bronx -579 Courtlandt Av -Bronx 10451 **Fx:**402-7586
(212) 735-3000 .. **Neilson,** Sigrid E '09 %Skadden ASM&F LLP -4 Times Sq -NY 10036
(212) 714-2904 .. **Neilson,** Victoria F '95 Immigration Equality -40 Exch Pl -NY 10005 **Fx:**714-2973
(585) 263-9221 .. **Neilson,** Wm A '77 High Falls Brewing Co,LLC -445 St Paul -Rchstr 14605 **Fx:**546-8928
(212) 375-6196 .. **Neiman,** Jeffrey C '81 -111 John -NY 10038
(212) 269-1000 .. **Neiman & Mairanz PC** -39 Bway -NY 10006 **Fx:**635-9302
(212) 687-2770 .. **Neiman,** Marilyn S '80 SrCnsl Cohen PL&P -551 5th Av -NY 10176
(212) 269-1000 .. **Neiman,** Marvin '81 (Neiman & M PC) -39 Bway -NY 10006
(718) 377-2496 .. **Neiman,** Mitchell M '79 -811 E 19th -Brklyn 11230
(212) 295-6487 .. **Neiman,** Peter '92 SpclCnsl WilmerHale -399 Park Av -NY 10022
(212) 637-2576 .. **Neiman,** Shirah '69 %US Atty -1 St Andrews Plz -NY 10007
(718) 720-3900 .. **Neiman,** Yael '05 %Kuhn & O,LLP -1 Edgewtr Plz -Staten Isl 10305
(845) 638-3012 .. **Neimark,** Marshall A '98 %R Neimark & Assoc,LLP -37 Congers Rd -New Cty 10956 **Fx:**638-3093
(212) 259-8000 .. **Neimark,** Matthew A '09 %Dewey & L LLP -1301 Av of Amer -NY 10019
(845) 638-3012 .. **Neimark,** Richd P '76 (R Neimark & Assoc,LLP) -37 Congers Rd -New Cty 10956 **Fx:**638-3093
(212) 801-9383 .. **Neimeth,** Clifford E '86 (Greenberg T,LLP) -200 Park Av -NY 10166
(212) 841-1000 .. **Neira,** Christian '96 OfCnsl Covington & B LLP -620 8th Av -NY 10018
(631) 351-3042 .. **Neira,** Thelma '84 %Town Atty -100 Main -Huntngtn 11743 **Fx:**351-3032
(212) 704-9600 .. **Neish,** Laura E '03 %Zuckerman S,LLP -1540 Bway -NY 10036
(718) 548-4245 .. **Neiss,** Moshe S '78 -4619 Lvngstn Av -Bronx 10471 **Fx:**548-4245
(212) 361-1707 .. **Neisser,** Alison Juliet '82 %Envrnmntl Cntrl Brd -66 John -NY 10038 **Fx:**361-1900
(718) 204-4633 .. **Neitzel,** Warren J '80 %Bulova Corp -1 Bulova Av -Woodside 11377 **Fx:**204-3507
(518) 449-8893 .. **NeJame,** Samir S '99 (Wilson EME&D LLP) -677 Bway -Albany 12207
(518) 474-6740 .. **NeJame,** Scott '88 %Dept of State -41 State -Albany 12231 **Fx:**473-9211
(212) 596-9000 .. **Nejatian,** Kasra '09 %Ropes & G LLP -1211 Av of Amer -NY 10036
(212) 450-4000 .. **Nel,** Phoebe '09 %Davis P&W LLP -450 Lex Av -NY 10017
(631) 853-5212 .. **Neldner-Ratuszny,** Agnes B '04 Leg Aid -400 Carleton Av Bx9082 -Central Islip 11722 **Fx:**853-7798
(212) 819-8200 .. **Nelivigi,** Nandan S '96 (White & C LLP) -1155 Av of Amer -NY 10036
(212) 509-6300 .. **Nelke,** Richd A '00 %Melli GW&M -17 Battery Pl -NY 10004
(516) 378-1700 .. **Nelkin,** Henry D '79 (Chesney & M) -2305 Grand Av -Baldwin 11510
(212) 558-4000 .. **Nelles,** Sharon L '94 (Sullivan & C LLP) -125 Broad -NY 10004
(518) 474-7668 .. **Nelligan,** Kathleen '80 %Insurance Dept -99 Wshngtn Av -Albany 12257 **Fx:**486-2218
(212) 576-7000 .. **Nellis,** Nora P '05 %NY Life Ins -51 Mad Av -NY 10010 **Fx:**447-0569
(585) 546-1700 .. **Nellist,** Roger G '79 Advocacy Ctr -590 South Av -Rchstr 14620 **Fx:**546-7069
(212) 408-5100 .. **Nellos,** Alexandra K '04 %Chadbourne & P LLP -30 Rckfllr Plz -NY 10112
(212) 859-8000 .. **Nelms,** Jason R '06 %Fried FHS&J LLP -1 NY Plz -NY 10004
(516) 877-5600 .. **Nelsen,** Deirdre '79 %R Tusa -1225 Franklin Av -Gdn Cty 11530 **Fx:**877-5695
(212) 468-4800 .. **Nelson,** A Derek '00 Cnsl Davis & G LLP -1740 Bway -NY 10019
(516) 328-6200 .. **Nelson,** Alan M '80 -3000 Marcus Av -Lk Success 11042 **Fx:**328-6354
(315) 343-1939 .. **Nelson,** Allison J '99 (Caraccioli & N,PLLC) -120 E 1st -Oswego 13126 **Fx:**343-1822
(212) 509-9400 .. **Nelson,** Amanda L '05 %Cozen O -45 Bway Atrium -NY 10006
(212) 305-5883 .. **Nelson,** Angela D '02 Columbia Univ-IRB -722 W 168th -NY 10032
(845) 569-7335 .. **Nelson,** Bernis E '82 Law Dept -83 Bway -Newburgh 12550 **Fx:**569-7338
(914) 741-6055 .. **Nelson,** Beth S '84 -427 Bedford Rd -Plsntvll 10570 **Fx:**769-9252
(718) 709-2239 .. **Nelson,** Brandon W '01 JetBlue Airway -118-29 Qns Blvd -Frst Hlls 11375
(718) 590-8586 .. **Nelson,** Christopher '01 Admin Chldrns Srvcs -900 Sheridan Av -Bronx 10451
(212) 250-8181 .. **Nelson,** Christopher P '90 Deutsch Bk -60 Wall -NY 10005
(212) 484-7364 .. **Nelson,** Cindy E '81 Warner Bros -1 Time Warner Ctr -NY 10019
(914) 925-0022 .. **Nelson,** Clifford S '91 -555 Theo Fremd Av -Rye 10580
(212) 907-6677 .. **Nelson,** Danial A '07 (Nelson & M) -405 Lex Av -NY 10174 **Fx:**(646) 308-1178
(212) 648-0766 .. **Nelson,** Danl B '00 JPMorgan Chase Bk NA -245 Park -NY 10167
(212) 880-3800 .. **Nelson,** Danl Z '54 OfCnsl Akerman S -335 Mad Av -NY 10017
(212) 804-4200 .. **Nelson,** David A '98 %Mound CW&G -One Bttry Pk Plz -NY 10004
(585) 591-1100 .. **Nelson,** David H '83 (Dadd N&W) -11 Exchange Bx238 -Attica 14011
(212) 207-0463 .. **Nelson,** David I '01 Sumitomo Corp of America -600 3rd Av -NY 10016
(315) 785-2444 .. **Nelson,** Deanna R '94 %Dept of Law -317 Wshngtn -Watertwn 13601 **Fx:**785-2294
(516) 571-2408 .. **Nelson,** Debra M '91 %Hon D Palmieri -262 Old Cntry Rd -Mineola 11501 **Fx:**571-1491
(716) 753-2128 .. **Nelson,** Dustin D '83 (Schaack WCN PC) -31 S Erie Bx152 -Mayvll 14757
(212) 903-9000 .. **Nelson,** Elizabeth A '08 %Linklaters -1345 Av of Amer -NY 10105
(718) 356-0566 .. **Nelson,** Eric '86 -54 Florence -Staten Isl 10308 **Fx:**356-6069
(212) 294-6700 .. **Nelson,** Eric M '75 (Winston & S) -200 Park Av -NY 10166
(212) 354-3666 .. **Nelson,** Eric M '86 -112 Mad Av -NY 10016 **Fx:**354-2555
(607) 334-9323 .. **Nelson & Flanagan** -42 S Broad -Norwich 13815 **Fx:**336-2017
(212) 788-8714 .. **Nelson,** Genevieve '98 %Law Dept -100 Church -NY 10007 **Fx:**788-0367
(212) 766-1888 .. **Nelson,** Gregory S '83 %Morris DA&F -2 Rector -NY 10006
(212) 687-1980 .. **Nelson,** Gwendolyn S '09 %Kaplan F&K LLP -850 3rd Av -NY 10022
(212) 267-9222 .. **Nelson,** Helene W '85 %Gorayeb & Assoc,PC -100 William -NY 10038 **Fx:**962-5418
(646) 562-3405 .. **Nelson,** Ian R '00 %PLC -747 3rd Av -NY 10017
(845) 452-5900 .. **Nelson,** James E '74 (Van DeWater & V,LLP) -85 Civic Ctr Plz Bx112 -Poughkeepsie 12602
(212) 307-5500 .. **Nelson,** James E '05 (Venable LLP) -1270 Av of Amer -NY 10020
(212) 655-6000 .. **Nelson,** James Reid '04 (Chapman & C LLP) -330 Mad Av -NY 10017
(718) 990-2082 .. **Nelson,** Janai S '98 %St John's Law Schl -8000 Utopia Pkwy -Jamaica 11439 **Fx:**591-1855
(518) 463-3200 .. **Nelson,** Jean E II '78 %NYS Bar Assn -1 Elk -Albany 12207 **Fx:**487-5544
(212) 597-8305 .. **Nelson,** Jeff V '85 West LB AG -1211 Av of Amer -NY 10036
(914) 244-3241 .. **Nelson,** Jennifer F '90 -6 Deer Ridge Rd -Mt Kisco 10549
(646) 429-7500 .. **Nelson,** JoAnn '03 %Macys,Inc -11 Penn Plz -NY 10001 **Fx:**429-7521
(631) 269-1550 .. **Nelson,** John H '64 -28 Broadvw Av -Kings Pk 11754
(516) 524-8494 .. **Nelson,** John R '90 (J Nelson,PC) -99 S Park -Rockvll Ctr 11570
(914) 381-7600 .. **Nelson,** Jonathan B '93 Cnsl Dorf Law Firm,LLP -740 W Bstn Post Rd -Mamaroneck 10543 **Fx:**381-7608
(212) 593-5775 .. **Nelson,** Jonathan R '88 -111 Bway -NY 10006 **Fx:**593-5115
(516) 223-5500 .. **Nelson,** Kimberly I '03 %R Nelson -2249 Derby Rd -Baldwin 11510 **Fx:**223-5505
(212) 326-3939 .. **Nelson,** Laird E '10 %Jones D -222 E 41st -NY 10017
(212) 596-9000 .. **Nelson,** Laurie C '83 %Ropes & G LLP -1211 Av of Amer -NY 10036
(212) 373-3000 .. **Nelson,** Leila J '09 %Paul WRW&G LLP -1285 Av of Amer -NY 10019
(212) 286-0276 .. **Nelson,** Lester '53 -60 E 42nd -NY 10165 **Fx:**697-0877
(212) 233-0130 .. **Nelson Levine deLuca & Horst** -120 Bway -NY 10271 **Fx:**233-0172
(212) 417-3700 .. **Nelson,** Lycette '03 %MFY Legal Srvcs -299 Bway -NY 10007 **Fx:**417-3890
(212) 670-0189 .. **Nelson,** Margaret E '85 -222 Bway -NY 10038
(212) 323-2250 .. **Nelson,** Marianne B '79 %HHC-OLA-Medical Litigation -346 Bway -NY 10013 **Fx:**323-2251
(212) 969-2388 .. **Nelson,** Mark A '88 Alliance Bernstein LP -1345 Av of Amer -NY 10105 **Fx:**554-4639
(212) 998-6730 .. **Nelson,** Marta E '91 %The Brennan Ctr for Justice -161 Av of Amer -NY 10013
(212) 428-6490 .. **Nelson,** Michl D '96 Royal Bk of Canada -1 Lbrty Plz -NY 10006 **Fx:**968-1295
(212) 667-7000 .. **Nelson,** Michl D '98 CIBC World Markets -425 Lex Av -NY 10017
(212) 233-0130 .. **Nelson,** Michl R '03 (Nelson Ld&H) -120 Bway -NY 10271
(212) 720-5026 .. **Nelson,** Michl S '90 %Fed Reserve Bk -33 Lbrty -NY 10045 **Fx:**785-5748
(212) 796-8174 .. **Nelson,** Mitchell J '74 %FX Real Est & Entertnmnt -650 Mad Av -NY 10022
(516) 935-9487 .. **Nelson,** Moses '49 -90 Palo Alto Dr -Plainvw 11803
(212) 809-2663 .. **Nelson,** Nicole E '02 Bondholder Comm Grp -30 Broad -NY 10004
(212) 612-9200 .. **Nelson,** Norman R '69 %The Clearing House -450 W 33rd -NY 10001 **Fx:**612-9253
(212) 474-1000 .. **Nelson,** Pawan '10 %Cravath S&M LLP -825 8th Av -NY 10019
(585) 232-2282 .. **Nelson,** Peter C '74 -2 State -Rchstr 14614 **Fx:**232-7575
(212) 318-3000 .. **Nelson,** R Stephen Jr. '92 SrCnsl Fulbright & J LLP -666 5th Av -NY 10103
(212) 230-8864 .. **Nelson,** Rachel L '03 Cnsl WilmerHale -399 Park Av -NY 10022
(212) 657-9740 .. **Nelson,** Rebecca J '97 Citigroup -77 Water -NY 10005
(646) 654-7761 .. **Nelson,** Richd S '96 Buzzmetrics Inc -770 Bway -NY 10003
(516) 223-5500 .. **Nelson,** Robt N '72 -2249 Derby Rd -Baldwin 11510 **Fx:**223-5505
(212) 935-3000 .. **Nelson,** Ronald G '04 %Mintz LCFG&P,PC -666 3rd Av -NY 10017

(212) 938-1141 .. **Nelson**, Ronald J '89 (R Nelson,PC) -21 E 40th -NY 10016 **Fx:**(732) 748-8592
(212) 310-2285 .. **Nelson**, Rosemary '83 %Colgate-Palmolive -300 Park Av -NY 10022 **Fx:**310-3274
(212) 664-2593 .. **Nelson**, Sandra L '99 NBC Universal -30 Rckfllr Plz -NY 10112
(212) 940-3052 .. **Nelson**, Sarah A '01 Cnsl Nixon P LLP -437 Mad Av -NY 10022
(914) 220-1900 .. **Nelson**, Stephen J '87 (Nelson Law Firm,LLC) -1 N Bway -White Plns 10601
(212) 509-4000 .. **Nelson**, Steven G '75 %Cntntl Stck Trnsfr -17 Battery Pl -NY 10004 **Fx:**509-5750
(716) 856-4000 .. **Nelson**, Thos W '85 (Hodgson R LLP) -140 Pearl -Buffalo 14202
(212) 735-3000 .. **Nelson**, Timothy G '00 (Skadden ASM&F LLP) -4 Times Sq -NY 10036
(212) 440-2350 .. **Nelson**, Timothy S '03 %C Siegel -40 Wall -NY 10005 **Fx:**440-2385
(718) 254-7000 .. **Nelson**, Varuni '85 %US Atty -271 Cadman Plz E -Brklyn 11201 **Fx:**254-6479
(212) 722-2000 .. **Nelson**, Wm P '95 %Leg Aid -230 E 106th -NY 10029 **Fx:**876-5365
(347) 404-9133 .. **Nelson**, Yvens '01 %Civil Ct -141 Lvngstn -Brklyn 11201 **Fx:**(718) 643-3733
(212) 366-6100 .. **Nelson-Cashman**, Marilyn '99 %Weiss & R,PC -27 Union Sq W -NY 10003
(914) 835-6900 .. **Nemarow**, Jeryl L '82 (Piscionere & N,PC) -363 Bstn Post Rd -Rye 10580 **Fx:**835-6931
(212) 351-4000 .. **Nematzadeh**, Justin S '09 Gibson D&C LLP -200 Park Av -NY 10166
(212) 508-6100 .. **Nemazee**, Kamyar M '08 %Bracewell & G,LLP -1251 Av of Amer -NY 10020
(631) 232-0200 .. **Nembach**, Paul A '95 %Fumuso KDSS&F,LLP -110 Marcus Blvd -Hauppauge 11788
(718) 262-7100 .. **Nembhard**, Clifton A '99 %Civil Ct -89-17 Sutphin Blvd -Jamaica 11435 **Fx:**262-7107
(212) 878-8000 .. **Nembhard**, Shani K '04 %Clifford C LLP -31 W 52nd -NY 10019
(718) 238-6500 .. **Nemcik**, Donald M '81 -7408 5th Av -Brklyn 11209
(607) 544-1042 .. **Nemec**, Alicia M '93 -177 Watt Rd -Cooperstwn 13326
(212) 735-3000 .. **Nemec**, Douglas R '97 (Skadden ASM&F LLP) -4 Times Sq -NY 10036
(718) 250-2000 .. **Nemec**, Shulamit Rosenblum '78 %DA -350 Jay -Brklyn 11201 **Fx:**250-2314
(212) 940-8800 .. **Nemecek**, Philip A '92 (Katten MR LLP) -575 Mad Av -NY 10022
(718) 875-1300 .. **Nemeckova**, Zdena '89 Applt Div 2nd Dept -45 Monroe Pl -Brklyn 11201 **Fx:**858-2446
(212) 696-9100 .. **Nemerov**, Jeffrey A '67 (Segan N&S PC) -112 Mad Av -NY 10016
(212) 417-4357 .. **Nemerson**, Roy P '82 %Dept of Health -90 Church -NY 10007 **Fx:**417-4392
(212) 701-3000 .. **Nemes**, Mordechai '09 %Cahill G&R LLP -80 Pine -NY 10005 **Fx:**269-5420
(631) 234-4400 .. **Nemeth**, Jos G Jr. '75 (Pinks A&N) -140 Fell Ct -Hauppauge 11788
(212) 981-1076 .. **Nemeth**, Karen D '97 Riskmetrics Grp -1 Chase Plz -NY 10005
(716) 852-5875 .. **Nemeth**, Mark S '94 (Feldman K LLP) -110 Pearl -Buffalo 14202
(315) 363-3440 .. **Nemeti McDermott Eppolito & Hedglon** -112 Farrier Av -Oneida 13421 **Fx:**361-4112
(516) 775-7007 .. **Nemetsky**, Howard M '87 (Gutman MB&S,PC) -813 Jericho Tpk -New Hyde Pk 11040
(212) 408-2500 .. **Nemetz**, Leigh M '04 %Baker B,LLP -30 Rckfllr Plz -NY 10112
(607) 723-9511 .. **Nemia**, Frank '57 OfCnsl Coughlin & G,LLP -19 Chenango Bx2039 -Bnghmtn 13902
(212) 697-7383 .. **Nemia**, James F '89 %Mandel Law Firm -370 Lex Av -NY 10017 **Fx:**681-6157
(212) 619-4444 .. **Nemia**, Thos J '90 %Marshall CW&B,PC -116 John -NY 10038
(212) 883-4900 .. **Nemiroff**, Andrew P '05 %Cozen O -277 Park Av -NY 10172
(212) 705-7000 .. **Nemirovsky**, Dimitri '01 Cnsl Bingham M LLP -399 Park Av -NY 10022
(212) 346-5305 .. **Nemmers**, Barry H '77 %SAP America,Inc -95 Morton -NY 10014
(212) 710-0211 .. **Nemo**, Danl A '96 -519 8th Av -NY 10018
(516) 747-1230 .. **Nemser**, Alan '36 (Nemser & N) -320 Old Cntry Rd -Gdn Cty 11530 **Fx:**747-7356
(212) 698-3500 .. **Nemser**, Earl H '71 SpclCnsl Dechert LLP -1095 Av of Amer -NY 10036
(516) 747-1230 .. **Nemser**, Kathy S '79 (Nemser & N) -320 Old Cntry Rd -Gdn Cty 11530 **Fx:**747-7356
(212) 513-3200 .. **Nemsick**, Judith R '94 SrCnsl Holland & K LLP -31 W 52nd -NY 10019
(914) 476-0600 .. **Nenadich**, Peter A Jr. '05 %Smith B&J,LLP -733 Ynkrs Av -Ynkrs 10704
(518) 793-3843 .. **Nenninger**, Christopher S '86 (Matte & N,PC) -444 Glen -Glens Fls 12801
(518) 793-3843 .. **Nenninger**, Patricia Collopy '86 -444 Glen -Glens Fls 12801 **Fx:**793-6963
(212) 455-2000 .. **Nentchev**, Nentcho Petrov '06 %Simpson T&B LLP -425 Lex Av -NY 10017
(516) 935-2330 .. **Neofitos**, George '97 %Markotsis & L -183 Bway -Hicksvll 11801
(212) 728-8000 .. **Neos**, Theo A '07 %Willkie F&G LLP -787 7th Av -NY 10019
(631) 365-3599 .. **Nepf**, Barbara J '05 -Bx101 -E Setauket 11733
(212) 344-5680 .. **Nepf**, Ruthe A '90 OfCnsl Thompson H LLP -335 Mad Av -NY 10017
(212) 891-2100 .. **Neporent**, Mark A '83 Cerberus Capital Mgt LP -299 Park Av -NY 10171
(212) 770-1596 .. **Neptune**, Kharyne '87 %AIG -80 Pine -NY 10005 **Fx:**809-2793
(518) 474-4402 .. **Nepveu**, Kate Han '03 %Dept of Law -The Cptl -Albany 12224
(212) 661-1212 .. **Nerangis**, James T '88 (Levy S&S LLP) -630 3rd Av -NY 10017
(718) 913-0360 .. **Nerboso**, Robt Wright '79 -1719 68th -Brklyn 11204
(212) 676-6292 .. **Neren**, Leigh M '95 %Business Integrity Comm -100 Church -NY 10007 **Fx:**676-6204
(212) 779-9230 .. **Nerenberg**, Mark Eli '82 (ME Nerenberg,PC) -825 W End Av -NY 10025 **Fx:**779-9325
(212) 269-2500 .. **Nerenberg**, Michl R '07 Gorlick K&L,PC -17 State -NY 10004
(212) 848-8735 .. **Nergaard**, Diane M '84 -1 Chase Manh Plz -NY 10005
(315) 474-8844 .. **Neri**, Gerard J '90 Neri Law Ofcs -217 Mntgmry -Syracuse 13202 **Fx:**424-6826
(212) 335-4500 .. **Neri**, Leeanne S '05 %DLA Piper LLP -1251 Av of Amer -NY 10020
(518) 457-2070 .. **Neri**, Margaret Morovich '83 %Dept of Tax & Fin -Bldg 9 State Campus -Albany 12227 **Fx:**457-6131
(212) 246-8045 .. **Nerinck-Seltzer**, Ambre L '04 CMS Bureau Francis Lefebvre -101 Park Av -NY 10178
(212) 808-0700 .. **Neritani**, Adrian '05 (Norris M&M,PA) -875 3rd Av -NY 10022
(212) 326-2000 .. **Nerko**, Chas J '10 %O'Melveny & M LLP -7 Times Sq -NY 10036
(516) 741-7469 .. **Nerko**, Katherine Perrera '84 -58 Transverse Rd -Gdn Cty 11530
(718) 761-9300 .. **Nerlfi**, Ian M '10 %Vaslas LH&D LLP -201 Edward Curry Av -Staten Isl 10314
(212) 436-2164 .. **Nerlich**, Carl S '00 Deloitte & Touche LLP -2 World Fncl Ctr -NY 10281
(516) 504-2164 .. **Nero**, Gregory P '98 Sterling Equities -111 Grt Nck Rd S -Gt Neck 11021
(212) 468-8000 .. **Nero**, Roberta Moseley '80 OfCnsl Morrison & F LLP -1290 Av of Amer -NY 10104
(607) 746-6203 .. **Neroni**, Fredk J '74 -203 Main -Delhi 13753 **Fx:**746-6226
(607) 746-6203 .. **Neroni**, Tatiana '09 -203 Main -Delhi 13753 **Fx:**746-6226
(914) 949-2700 .. **Neroulias**, Jason G '07 %Bleakley P&S,LLP -1 N Lex Av -White Plns 10601
(212) 277-4000 .. **Nersesian**, Anna '10 %Freshfields BD LLP -520 Mad Av -NY 10022
(212) 415-7420 .. **Nersesian**, Richd A '78 %Merrill Lynch -717 5th Av -NY 10022 **Fx:**415-8005
(518) 725-8733 .. **Nershi**, Michl T '51 -16 Lee Av -Gloversvll 12078
(212) 869-7000 .. **Nertney**, Michl F '00 (Feldman W&S LLP) -420 Lex Av -NY 10170
(212) 447-7070 .. **Nesbitt**, Joy A '05 %Whatley D&K LLC -1540 Bway -NY 10036
(315) 461-4235 .. **Nesbitt**, Stephanie R '98 Penn Traffic -Bx4737 -Syracuse 13221
(914) 644-9200 .. **Neschis**, Benjamin B '99 %D Petshaft,PC -222 Bloomingdale Rd -White Plns 10605 **Fx:**644-9300
(212) 448-1100 .. **Neschis**, Janet C '80 (McLaughlin & S,LLP) -260 Mad Av -NY 10016
(914) 345-0005 .. **Nesci Keane, PLLC** -40 Saw Mill Rvr Rd -Hawthorne 10532 **Fx:**345-0811
(914) 345-0005 .. **Nesci**, Vincent P '72 (Nesci K,PLLC) -40 Saw Mill Rvr Rd -Hawthorne 10532
(516) 248-3302 .. **Nese**, Dorothy Oehler '83 %Dept of Law -200 Old Cntry Rd -Mineola 11501 **Fx:**747-6432
(212) 736-4500 .. **Nesenoff**, Ira S '86 (Nesenoff & M,LLP) -363 7th Av -NY 10001
(212) 736-4500 .. **Nesenoff & Miltenberg,LLP** -363 7th Av -NY 10001 **Fx:**736-2260
(212) 530-5000 .. **Nesgos**, Peter D '85 (Milbank TH&M LLP) -1 Chase Manh Plz -NY 10005
(845) 473-4500 .. **Nesheiwat**, Firas E '99 -303 Mill -Poughkeepsie 12601
(914) 337-3541 .. **Nesheiwat**, Neveen M '90 -598 Tuckahoe Rd -Ynkrs 10710
(718) 590-2000 .. **Nesheiwat**, Sharif '07 %DA -198 E 161st -Bronx 10451 **Fx:**590-6477
(212) 885-8000 .. **Nesi**, Nicholas A '79 %BDO USA,LLP -330 Mad Av -NY 10017 **Fx:**697-1299
(212) 878-8000 .. **Neslin**, Jenny B '08 %Clifford C LLP -31 W 52nd -NY 10019
(212) 221-5700 .. **Nesoff**, Mark '76 (Smith & N PLLC) -1501 Bway -NY 10036 **Fx:**221-6350
(716) 688-3800 .. **Nesper Ferber & DiGiacomo,LLP** -501 JJ Audobon Pkwy -Amherst 14228 **Fx:**688-3891
(716) 688-3800 .. **Nesper**, James M '55 (Nesper F&D,LLP) -501 JJ Audobon Pkwy -Amherst 14228
(716) 688-3800 .. **Nesper**, Paul T '85 (Nesper F&D,LLP) -501 JJ Audobon Pkwy -Amherst 14228
(212) 545-4657 .. **Nespole**, Gregory M '94 (Wolf HAF&H LLP) -270 Mad Av -NY 10016
(212) 318-3000 .. **Nespole**, James J '64 OfCnsl Fulbright & J LLP -666 5th Av -NY 10103
(212) 554-7800 .. **Ness**, Shari A '98 OfCnsl Moses & S LLP -405 Lex Av -NY 10174
(212) 947-3793 .. **Nessan**, Micah D '03 %Sadis & G LLP -551 5th Av -NY 10176
(212) 626-4100 .. **Nessel**, Mary Ann Burniske '96 %Baker & M LLP -1114 Av of Amer -NY 10036
(212) 687-3000 .. **Nessenson**, Lawr M '86 (Jaffe & A,LLP) -600 3rd Av -NY 10016
(212) 849-7000 .. **Nesser**, Isaac '04 %Quinn EU&S,LLP -51 Mad Av -NY 10010
(212) 593-6700 .. **Nessim**, Danl N '91 (Aaronson RF&D,LLP) -757 3rd Av -NY 10017
(212) 259-8000 .. **Nessler**, Richd A '92 Cnsl Dewey & L LLP -1301 Av of Amer -NY 10019
(914) 725-4050 .. **Nesson**, Barry E '82 -700 Wht Plns Rd -Scarsdale 10583 **Fx:**725-6160
(212) 855-3200 .. **Nesson**, Richd B '85 %Depository Trust -55 Water -NY 10041 **Fx:**855-3279
(212) 309-6000 .. **Nesspor**, Stephen W '09 %Morgan L&B LLP -101 Park Av -NY 10178
(212) 455-2000 .. **Nester**, Minta J '10 %Simpson T&B LLP -425 Lex Av -NY 10017
(212) 513-3200 .. **Nesterova**, Anna '08 %Holland & K LLP -31 W 52nd -NY 10019
(212) 816-9607 .. **Nestler**, Gary J '93 Citigroup -388 Greenwich -NY 10013
(518) 438-3620 .. **Nestler**, Roy K '01 (Nestler & G) -18 Corp Wds Blvd -Albany 12211 **Fx:**438-6955
(212) 326-3939 .. **Nestler**, Timothy J '07 %Jones D -222 E 41st -NY 10017
(212) 272-2085 .. **Nestor**, Francis J '70 %JP Morgan Chase -383 Mad Av -NY 10179
(212) 450-4000 .. **Nestor**, Julia '07 %Davis P&W LLP -450 Lex Av -NY 10017
(212) 533-8400 .. **Netburn**, Mitchell '93 Project Renewal -8 E 3rd -NY 10003 **Fx:**505-8890
(212) 763-5000 .. **Netburn**, Sarah '02 %Emery CB&A LLP -75 Rckfllr Plz -NY 10019
(888) 809-3269 .. **Nethersole**, Karen E '01 Full Circle NY -954 Lex Av -NY 10021 **Fx:**356-3269
(518) 439-9123 .. **Netter**, Miriam M '73 -28 Devon Rd -Delmar 12054
(845) 331-0702 .. **Netter**, Robt E '67 (Cook NCK&M,PC) -85 Main Bx3939 -Kingston 12402
(212) 310-8000 .. **Nettleton**, Stacy '03 %Weil G&M LLP -767 5th Av -NY 10153
(212) 728-8000 .. **Netzer**, Roger D '83 (Willkie F&G LLP) -787 7th Av -NY 10019
(212) 895-1838 .. **Neu**, Harold A '93 Miller Buckfire & Co Inc -153 E 53rd -NY 10022
(914) 681-0444 .. **Neubardt**, Andrew M '88 (Rende R&D,LLP) -202 Mamaroneck Av -White Plns 10601
(914) 948-7733 .. **Neubardt**, Saundra '85 -50 Main -White Plns 10606
(716) 937-3381 .. **Neubauer**, Hildegard '84 %Alden State Bk -13216 Bway -Alden 14004 **Fx:**937-9662
(212) 574-1200 .. **Neubauer**, Kevin M '10 %Seward & K LLP -1 Bttry Pk Plz -NY 10004
(718) 250-2000 .. **Neubauer**, Laura J '90 %DA -350 Jay -Brklyn 11201 **Fx:**250-2314
(716) 853-9555 .. **Neubeck**, Pamela L '88 %Leg Aid -237 Main -Buffalo 14203 **Fx:**853-3219

(917) 777-4200 .. **Neuberg,** Elisabeth A '03 Cnsl Bingham M LLP -1 Bttry Pk Plz -NY 10004
(718) 236-8700 .. **Neuberger,** Ari S '89 -5918 18th Av -Brklyn 11204 **Fx:**236-7403
(718) 447-1243 .. **Neuberger,** Jerome M '53 (Neuberger & N,LLP) -350 St Marks Pl -Staten Isl 10301 **Fx:**816-1353
(718) 447-5124 .. **Neuberger,** Ned C '89 (Neuberger & N,LLP) -350 St Marks Pl -Staten Isl 10301 **Fx:**816-1353
(212) 936-5100 .. **Neuberger,** Yehuda Leib '01 American Stock Transfer & Trust -59 Maiden Ln -NY 10038
(212) 998-6172 .. **Neuborne,** Burt '65 %NYU Law Schl -40 Wshngtn Sq S -NY 10012 **Fx:**995-4341
(212) 573-5000 .. **Neuborne,** Helen Redleaf '75 Ford Fndtn -320 E 43rd -NY 10017
(212) 310-8000 .. **Neubort,** Chayim D '03 %Weil G&M LLP -767 5th Av -NY 10153
(718) 250-3485 .. **Neubort,** Solomon '97 %DA -350 Jay -Brklyn 11201 **Fx:**250-2314
(212) 969-3000 .. **Neuburger,** Jeffrey D '87 (Proskauer R LLP) -1585 Bway -NY 10036
(347) 401-9580 .. **Neufeld,** Amos '94 %Appllt Term -141 Lvngstn -Brklyn 11201 **Fx:**(718) 643-7889
(718) 596-8886 .. **Neufeld,** David '80 -80 Lvngstn -Brklyn 11201
(631) 549-1717 .. **Neufeld,** David S J '74 (Neufeld & O) -225 Old Cntry Rd -Melvll 11747
(212) 986-0999 .. **Neufeld,** David S J '74 (Neufeld & O) -230 Park Av -NY 10169
(845) 306-1000 .. **Neufeld,** Erna '02 %Watchtower -100 Watchtower Dr -Patterson 12563 **Fx:**306-0709
(718) 596-8886 .. **Neufeld,** Lisa G '86 %D Neufeld -80 Lvngstn -Brklyn 11201
(212) 986-0999 .. **Neufeld & O'Leary** -230 Park Av -NY 10169 **Fx:**986-6341
(631) 549-1717 .. **Neufeld & O'Leary** -225 Old Cntry Rd -Melvll 11747
(212) 965-9081 .. **Neufeld,** Peter J '77 (Neufeld S&B) -99 Hudson -NY 10013
(646) 613-8359 .. **Neufeld,** Russell T '83 -99 Hudson -NY 10013 **Fx:**(212) 965-9084
(212) 965-9081 .. **Neufeld Scheck & Brustin** -99 Hudson -NY 10013 **Fx:**965-9084
(212) 788-1035 .. **Neufeld,** Sheryl R '00 %Law Dept -100 Church -NY 10007 **Fx:**788-0367
(212) 278-1840 .. **Neufeld,** Thos '78 (Anderson K&O,PC) -1251 Av of Amer -NY 10020
(718) 260-0965 .. **Neufeld,** Todd A '01 -49 Carroll -Brklyn 11231
(718) 920-4991 .. **Neugarten,** Joel '94 %Montefiore Med Ctr -111 E 210th -Bronx 10467 **Fx:**920-6658
(212) 577-7700 .. **Neugebauer,** Lynn '80 %Safe Horizon -2 Lafayette -NY 10007 **Fx:**385-0331
(914) 681-6060 .. **Neugebauer,** Paul L '90 %S Owens -140 Grand -White Plns 10601
(212) 446-2300 .. **Neuhardt,** Amy L '99 (Boies S&F LLP) -575 Lex Av -NY 10022
(212) 558-4000 .. **Neuhaus,** Jos E '86 (Sullivan & C LLP) -125 Broad -NY 10004
(212) 370-1300 .. **Neuhauser,** Stuart '89 (Ellenoff G&S LLP) -150 E 42nd -NY 10017
(914) 681-6200 .. **Neuman,** Andrew F '94 NYPA -123 Main -White Plns 10601 **Fx:**390-8038
(212) 504-6000 .. **Neuman,** Bonnie A '07 %Cadwalader W&T LLP -1 World Fncl Ctr -NY 10281
(315) 423-2949 .. **Neuman,** Ezequiel '95 -201 E Jffrsn -Syracuse 13202
(212) 818-9200 .. **Neuman,** Howard A '76 (Satterlee SB&B LLP) -230 Park Av -NY 10169
(212) 966-5612 .. **Neuman,** James '89 -100 Lafayette -NY 10013
(718) 436-6400 .. **Neuman,** Jerome '82 (J Neuman,PC) -1205 47th -Brklyn 11219 **Fx:**436-2833
(718) 614-3901 .. **Neuman,** Judah '03 -1252 E 8th -Brklyn 11230
(212) 969-3000 .. **Neuman,** Kristin Hackett '90 SrCnsl Proskauer R LLP -1585 Bway -NY 10036
(315) 696-8918 .. **Neuman,** Matthew R '01 (Riehlman S&S) -397 Route 281 Bx430 -Tully 13159
(607) 756-4006 .. **Neuman,** Matthew R '01 (Riehlman S&S) -39 Church -Cortlnd 13045
(845) 534-4440 .. **Neuman,** Peter X '63 -9 Braden Pl -Cornwall-On-Hud 12520 **Fx:**534-1397
(914) 833-5100 .. **Neuman,** Susan Cley '84 %Envrnmntl Ins Agncy -138 Chatsworth Av -Larchmnt 10538
(212) 435-3571 .. **Neumann,** Christopher J '91 %Port Auth of NY/NJ -225 Park Av S -NY 10003 **Fx:**435-3555
(315) 479-3900 .. **Neumann,** David F '79 %SSA-ODAR -300 S State -Syracuse 13202 **Fx:**479-3933
(516) 747-4082 .. **Neumann,** Donald S Jr. '73 (Montfort HM&S LLP) -1140 Franklin Av Bx7677 -Gdn Cty 11530
(877) 269-3277 .. **Neumann,** Elizabeth A '01 CNA -40 Wall -NY 10005
(315) 735-7566 .. **Neumann,** Janet F '99 %Petrone & P,PC -1624 Genesee -Utica 13502
(631) 725-5050 .. **Neumann,** Patricia F '88 P Neumann,PC -15 Cliff Dr -Sag Hbr 11963 **Fx:**725-3110
(516) 463-5881 .. **Neumann,** Richd K '81 %Hofstra Law Schl -121 Hofstra Univ -Hempstd 11549 **Fx:**463-4962
(212) 223-0400 .. **Neumann,** Ronald M '77 OfCnsl Zeichner E&K LLP -575 Lex Av -NY 10022
(718) 250-2000 .. **Neumann,** Stacey J '97 %DA -350 Jay -Brklyn 11201 **Fx:**250-2314
(212) 787-5335 .. **Neumark,** Avery E '78 -15 W 72nd -NY 10023 **Fx:**877-1327
(212) 715-9127 .. **Neunder,** Lisa C '06 Kramer LN&F,LLP -1177 Av of Amer -NY 10036
(212) 232-1300 .. **Neuner,** Jennifer Leah '98 %Lewis BB&S LLP -77 Water -NY 10005
(212) 455-2000 .. **Neuner,** Lynn K '94 (Simpson T&B LLP) -425 Lex Av -NY 10017
(516) 822-3550 .. **Neuner,** Robt '65 SrCnsl Hoffmann & B LLP -6900 Jericho Tpk -Syosset 11791 **Fx:**822-3582
(845) 627-0127 .. **Neuren,** Meryl R '83 %EB Holtzman -101 N Mddltwn Rd -Nanuet 10954 **Fx:**627-1231
(212) 397-5540 .. **Neus,** Michl C '88 %Soros Mgmt LLC -888 7th Av -NY 10106
(845) 838-6323 .. **Neusch,** Michele Lee '93 -380 Main -Beacon 12508 **Fx:**836-6325
(212) 636-6000 .. **Neustadt,** Frederic L '80 %Fordham Univ Sch of Law -140 W 62nd -NY 10023 **Fx:**636-6899
(914) 592-0003 .. **Neustadt,** Paul '56 Metropolis Abstract Corp -570 Taxter Rd -Elmsfrd 10523 **Fx:**592-1560
(212) 348-6469 .. **Neustadter,** Stanley E '67 -122 E 42nd -NY 10168
(718) 522-3333 .. **Neustaetter,** Janet '82 %Children's Law Ctr -44 Court -Brklyn 11201 **Fx:**522-7376
(212) 442-0456 .. **Neustein,** Cathy J '87 %Law Dept -100 Church -NY 10007 **Fx:**788-0367
(914) 693-8242 .. **Neustein,** Tammy '77 -175 Main -White Plns 10601 **Fx:**693-8242
(212) 715-9100 .. **Neuthaler,** Howard J '99 %Kramer LN&F,LLP -1177 Av of Amer -NY 10036
(212) 593-8800 .. **Neuwelt,** Klari '72 -110 E 59th -NY 10022 **Fx:**593-9131
(212) 309-6000 .. **Neuwirth,** Alan J '70 (Morgan L&B LLP) -101 Park Av -NY 10178
(212) 330-6060 .. **Neuwirth,** Francis '53 (Rosenberg N&K,PC) -2 Penn Plz -NY 10121 **Fx:**643-1951
(212) 557-7700 .. **Neuwirth,** Gloria S '59 (Davidson D&C LLP) -60 E 42nd -NY 10165
(212) 586-0906 .. **Neuwirth,** Jessica A '87 %Equality Now -250 W 57th -NY 10107 **Fx:**586-1611
(212) 310-8000 .. **Neuwirth,** John A '97 (Weil G&M LLP) -767 5th Av -NY 10153
(212) 688-1980 .. **Neuwirth,** Karen F '93 -18 E 48th -NY 10017 **Fx:**688-9374
(212) 651-8523 .. **Neuwirth,** Richd H '03 Ideasphere Inc -632 Bway -NY 10012
(212) 849-7000 .. **Neuwirth,** Stephen R '88 (Quinn EU&S,LLP) -51 Mad Av -NY 10010
(516) 741-4799 .. **Neuwirth,** Steven J '93 (Baker SBGFM&N,LLC) -100 Grdn City Plz -Gdn Cty 11530
(585) 546-1190 .. **Nevarez,** Juan A '78 (Nevarez & N) -144 Exchange Blvd -Rchstr 14614 **Fx:**546-6343
(585) 546-1190 .. **Nevarez,** Kathrine Noecker '79 (Nevarez & N) -144 Exchange Blvd -Rchstr 14614 **Fx:**546-6343
(212) 710-3900 .. **Nevarez,** Suhey I '08 Clyde & Co US LLP -405 Lex Av -NY 10174 **Fx:**710-3950
(212) 755-5510 .. **Nevas,** Susan R '89 SpclCnsl Loeb B & Prtnrs -505 Park Av -NY 10022
(212) 964-2066 .. **Neveloff,** Danl I '93 Neveloff Law Firm -111 John -NY 10038
(212) 715-9100 .. **Neveloff,** Jay A '75 (Kramer LN&F,LLP) -1177 Av of Amer -NY 10036
(212) 836-8000 .. **Neveloff,** Kevin J '09 %Kaye S LLP -425 Park Av -NY 10022
(518) 561-4931 .. **Neverett,** Meredith Ann '93 -10 Oak -Plattsbrgh 12901 **Fx:**563-5229
(718) 579-7931 .. **Nevergold,** Patricia '81 %Leg Aid -900 Sheridan Av -Bronx 10451 **Fx:**293-8744
(516) 877-5716 .. **Neves,** Edw E '95 %R Tusa -1225 Franklin Av -Gdn Cty 11530 **Fx:**877-5695
(516) 599-1375 .. **Nevias,** Lori '95 -24 Prnctn -Rockvll Ctr 11570
(212) 696-1999 .. **Neville,** Brian J '94 (Lax & N LLP) -1412 Bway -NY 10018
(212) 768-6700 .. **Neville,** Carole '91 (Sonnenschein N&R LLP) -1221 Av of Amer -NY 10020
(516) 883-5905 .. **Neville,** James C '85 -14 Vanderventer Av Bx1711 -Pt Wash 11050 **Fx:**883-9508
(212) 285-3300 .. **Neville,** James D '99 %Lipsig SM&M,PC -40 Fulton -NY 10038
(212) 806-5400 .. **Neville,** M Katherine '86 %Stroock &S&L LLP -180 Maiden Ln -NY 10038
(212) 907-9700 .. **Neville,** Mark K Jr. '75 Cnsl Smith G&R,LLP -250 Park Av -NY 10177
(347) 404-9920 .. **Neville,** Michl D '94 %MHLS -120 Schermerhorn -Brklyn 11201 **Fx:**(718) 243-2410
(212) 635-2730 .. **Neville Peterson LLP** -17 State -NY 10004 **Fx:**635-2734
(212) 989-5300 .. **Neville,** Richd '66 -399 Knollwood Rd -White Plns 10603 **Fx:**(914) 206-4825
(212) 736-0500 .. **Neville,** Wm J '85 (Mitofsky SN&H LLP) -152 Mad Av -NY 10016
(212) 589-4200 .. **Nevin,** Douglas M '06 %Baker & H LLP -45 Rckfllr Plz -NY 10111
(212) 406-2062 .. **Nevins,** Arthur G Jr. '75 A Nevins Jr & Assoc LLC -111 John -NY 10038 **Fx:**(908) 713-6658
(516) 877-7300 .. **Nevins,** David C '00 -500 N Bway -Jericho 11753
(212) 992-8931 .. **Nevins,** Elizabeth M '99 NYU Law Schl -40 Wshngtn Sq S -NY 10012 **Fx:**995-3156
(718) 793-1311 .. **Nevins,** Jamie Beth '00 %Cooper PC&C -80-02 Kew Grdns Rd -Kew Gdns 11415 **Fx:**575-4070
(716) 373-1995 .. **Nevins,** Mary Jane '79 -703 Community Bk Bldg -Olean 14760
(212) 504-6000 .. **Nevins,** Richd L '88 (Cadwalader W&T LLP) -1 World Fncl Ctr -NY 10281
(212) 278-1508 .. **Nevius,** John G '98 (Anderson K&O,PC) -1251 Av of Amer -NY 10020
(212) 308-6100 .. **Nevling,** J Kelley Jr. '70 OfCnsl Levi L&F LLP -1185 Av of Amer -NY 10036
(212) 589-4200 .. **New,** Jonathan B '98 (Baker & H LLP) -45 Rckfllr Plz -NY 10111
(212) 578-2078 .. **New,** Leslie J '04 Metlife -2701 Qns Plz N -LIC 11101
(718) 286-2450 .. **Newbauer,** April Anne '84 %Leg Aid -120-46 Qns Blvd -Kew Gdns 11415 **Fx:**263-4234
(914) 684-6800 .. **Newberg,** David A '80 (Collier HNN&B,LLP) -1 N Lex Av -White Plns 10601
(845) 794-8415 .. **Newberg,** Marvin N '75 -33 North -Monticello 12701 **Fx:**794-9701
(845) 794-8410 .. **Newberg,** Richd A '67 -33 North -Monticello 12701
(516) 328-8899 .. **Newberger,** Netanel '03 %Milman L Law Grp PLLC -3000 Marcus Av -Lk Success 11042 **Fx:**328-0082
(212) 230-8800 .. **Newberry,** B Matthew '06 WilmerHale -399 Park Av -NY 10022
(212) 577-3350 .. **Newbery,** John A '86 %Leg Aid -199 Water -NY 10038 **Fx:**577-3520
(212) 530-1800 .. **Newbold,** Tamala E '00 %Richards K&O LLP -1 World Fncl Ctr -NY 10281
(718) 930-6104 .. **Newbold Araya,** Russell O '00 -110 Wall -NY 10005
(914) 238-1000 .. **Newborn,** Andrea R '88 Reader's Digest -Readers Digest Rd -Plsntvll 10570 **Fx:**241-5644
(914) 633-1970 .. **Newborn,** Deborah W '83 -55 Lovell Rd -New Rchll 10804
(212) 758-7666 .. **Newborn,** Saml R '80 4 Kids Ent -1414 Av of Amer -NY 10019
(718) 332-2333 .. **Newborough,** Bruce A '83 (B Newborough,PC) -2625 E 14th -Brklyn 11235 **Fx:**332-7334
(212) 355-3135 .. **Newburger,** Cary L '85 -600 Mad Av -NY 10022 **Fx:**317-0725
(212) 302-5101 .. **Newburgh,** Morton '79 (Silverstein LN&M,LLP) -500 5th Av -NY 10110
(914) 376-3757 .. **Newcomb,** Brendan J '89 %Leg Srvcs -30 S Bway -Ynkrs 10701 **Fx:**376-8739
(212) 813-8800 .. **Newcomb,** Christopher R '10 Goodwin P LLP -620 8th Av -NY 10018
(212) 848-4000 .. **Newcomb,** Danforth '68 (Shearman & S LLP) -599 Lex Av -NY 10022
(716) 856-1344 .. **Newcomb,** Paula M Eade '91 SpclCnsl Bouvier Prtnrshp,LLP -350 Main -Buffalo 14202 **Fx:**856-1369
(716) 867-1627 .. **Newcomb,** Terence B '91 -Bx78 -Buffalo 14205 **Fx:**677-6766
(212) 455-2000 .. **Newcombe,** George M '76 (Simpson T&B LLP) -425 Lex Av -NY 10017

(631) 852-2500 .. **Newcombe,** Laura P '04 %DA -200 Center Dr -Rvrhead 11901 **Fx:**852-1769
(212) 310-8000 .. **Newell,** Ariane N '09 %Weil G&M LLP -767 5th Av -NY 10153
(212) 664-4444 .. **Newell,** Elizabeth A '01 %NBC -30 Rckfllr Plz -NY 10112
(518) 798-1758 .. **Newell,** Ronald L '69 -1 South Wstrn Plz Bx2152 -Glens Fls 12801 **Fx:**798-0740
(212) 541-2000 .. **Newell,** Tara B '01 (Bryan C LLP) -1290 Av of Amer -NY 10104
(516) 515-9744 .. **Newfeld,** Mark L '81 (Newfeld & F,PLLC) -1900 Hempstd Tpk -E Meadow 11554 **Fx:**222-7722
(212) 888-8001 .. **Newfield,** James S '95 (Rosenblum & T LLC) -405 Lex Av -NY 10174
(914) 686-6100 .. **Newfield,** James S '95 (Rosenblum & T LLC) -50 Main -White Plns 10606
(516) 222-1600 .. **Newfield,** Jason Adam '96 (Frankel & N,PC) -585 Stewart Av -Gdn Cty 11530
(516) 773-8035 .. **Newfield,** Jill E '84 (J Newfield,PC) -135 Wooleys Ln -Gt Neck 11023 **Fx:**773-0137
(914) 946-3700 .. **Newfield,** Lisa M '96 (McCarthy F LLP) -11 Martine Av -White Plns 10606
(212) 661-1344 .. **Newfield,** Meyer '58 %Newfield & B -60 E 42nd -NY 10165 **Fx:**661-2385
(518) 402-6019 .. **Newhouse,** Carol Hamilton '01 %Workers Comp Bd -20 Park -Albany 12207
(212) 259-8000 .. **Newhouse,** Jeffrey H '08 %Dewey & L LLP -1301 Av of Amer -NY 10019
(212) 661-1200 .. **Newhouse,** John '80 (Newhouse & S LLP) -3 W 35th -NY 10001
(212) 661-1200 .. **Newhouse & Shey LLP** -3 W 35th -NY 10001 **Fx:**599-6675
(212) 695-3666 .. **Newirth,** Eleanor B '82 -450 7th Av -NY 10123 **Fx:**279-1239
(212) 752-1515 .. **Newirth,** Jerold '84 -110 E 59th -NY 10022
(212) 750-7800 .. **Newirth,** Karen A '03 %Brafman & Assoc -767 3rd Av -NY 10017 **Fx:**750-3906
(212) 701-3000 .. **Newitz,** Noah B '95 (Cahill G&R LLP) -80 Pine -NY 10005 **Fx:**269-5420
(212) 446-7008 .. **Newkirk,** Christopher T '01 %McKinsey & Co -55 E 52nd -NY 10055 **Fx:**688-9521
(212) 536-3900 .. **Newkirk,** Harvey K '03 %K&L Gates LLP -599 Lex Av -NY 10022
(518) 452-1000 .. **Newkirk & Salada** -15 Corp Cir -Albany 12203
(212) 267-7600 .. **Newkofsky,** Lynne R '92 OfCnsl Solomon PBH&S LLP -40 Wall -NY 10005
(212) 468-8000 .. **Newland,** Taureen H '10 %Morrison & F LLP -1290 Av of Amer -NY 10104
(212) 355-5575 .. **Newman,** Adam T '95 (Smith & N,LLP) -363 7th Av -NY 10001 **Fx:**486-3150
(212) 301-3055 .. **Newman,** Adina M '97 %Fox News Channel -1211 Av of Amer -NY 10036
(212) 479-6000 .. **Newman,** Alison S '87 (Cooley LLP) -1114 Av of Amer -NY 10036
(718) 340-4200 .. **Newman,** Alizabeth '92 %CUNY Law Schl -65-21 Main -Flushng 11367 **Fx:**340-4482
(718) 849-1816 .. **Newman,** Ann '82 -82-35 Beverly Rd -Kew Gdns 11415
(212) 756-2000 .. **Newman,** Benjamin A '10 %Schulte R&Z LLP -919 3rd Av -NY 10022
(212) 756-2000 .. **Newman,** Beth Lehrman '05 %Schulte R&Z LLP -919 3rd Av -NY 10022
(212) 230-8835 .. **Newman,** Bruce H '92 (WilmerHale) -399 Park Av -NY 10022
(212) 506-2500 .. **Newman,** Cara L '06 %Mayer B LLP -1675 Bway -NY 10019
(212) 332-3321 .. **Newman,** Chas M '74 -386 Park Av S -NY 10016 **Fx:**447-5549
(212) 883-8833 .. **Newman,** Cindy '90 %Tacopina & A -275 Mad Av -NY 10016
(607) 337-1740 .. **Newman,** Claudette Y '95 %Supreme Ct -Chenango Cnty Cthse -Norwich 13815 **Fx:**336-3648
(212) 530-1800 .. **Newman,** Craig A '87 (Richards K&O LLP) -1 World Fncl Ctr -NY 10281
(718) 238-8322 .. **Newman,** Craig L '92 -8212 3rd Av -Brklyn 11209 **Fx:**238-8212
(212) 551-0305 .. **Newman,** Danl E '92 Govt of Israel -800 2nd Av -NY 10017
(718) 972-1273 .. **Newman,** Danl G '91 -2903 Ft Hmltn Pkwy -Brklyn 11218 **Fx:**435-6591
(516) 565-4123 .. **Newman,** Danielle '85 (Newman & G) -230 Hilton Av -Hempstd 11550
(212) 297-5800 .. **Newman,** David B '79 (Day P LLP) -7 Times Sq -NY 10036
(845) 362-2420 .. **Newman,** David B '86 -3 Bedford Rd -Monsey 10952 **Fx:**362-2420
(212) 450-4000 .. **Newman,** David C '08 %Davis P&W LLP -450 Lex Av -NY 10017
(607) 770-7565 .. **Newman,** David J '97 %United Structures,Inc -3101 Shippers Rd -Vestal 13850
(212) 872-1000 .. **Newman,** Deborah J '03 -One Bryant Park -NY 10036 **Fx:**872-1002
(212) 229-1516 .. **Newman,** Donna R '90 (Buttermore ND&F,LLP) -111 Bway -NY 10006
(516) 741-5650 .. **Newman,** Edw '55 E Newman,PLLC -1 Old Cntry Rd -Carle Pl 11514 **Fx:**741-9673
(212) 826-0100 .. **Newman,** Edw M '85 %FSA -31 W 52nd -NY 10019 **Fx:**893-2710
(585) 428-5210 .. **Newman,** Eric A '05 Pub Def -10 N Fitzhugh -Rchstr 14614 **Fx:**428-2234
(718) 523-0100 .. **Newman,** Erwin B '53 (Newman & N) -148-55 Hillside Av -Jamaica 11435 **Fx:**523-9477
(917) 776-7529 .. **Newman,** Eve Lynn '84 -900 South Av -Staten Isl 10314 **Fx:**(973) 379-2437
(212) 619-5400 .. **Newman Ferrara LLP** -1250 Bway -NY 10001 **Fx:**619-3090
(212) 689-8808 .. **Newman,** Fredric S '71 (Hoguet NR&K,LLP) -10 E 40th -NY 10016
(212) 669-2070 .. **Newman,** Glenn '79 %Tax Appls Tribunal -1 Centre -NY 10007 **Fx:**669-2211
(212) 669-4410 .. **Newman,** Glenn '79 Tax Commission -1 Centre -NY 10007 **Fx:**669-2003
(212) 308-7900 .. **Newman & Greenberg** -950 3rd Av -NY 10022 **Fx:**826-3273
(718) 523-0100 .. **Newman,** Gregory J '89 (Newman & N) -148-55 Hillside Av -Jamaica 11435 **Fx:**523-9477
(718) 896-2700 .. **Newman,** Gregory S '07 %Newman A & Assoc LLP -97-45 Qns Blvd -Rego Pk 11374 **Fx:**896-2560
(212) 308-7900 .. **Newman,** Gustave H '52 (Newman & G) -950 3rd Av -NY 10022
(212) 973-9797 .. **Newman,** Howard J '76 (Saretsky KD&G,LLP) -475 Park Av S -NY 10016
(516) 622-2341 .. **Newman,** Howard W '74 -1979 Marcus Av -New Hyde Pk 11042
(212) 962-1190 .. **Newman,** Ira M '83 (Sanocki N&T,LLP) -225 Bway -NY 10007
(516) 487-7375 .. **Newman,** Ira S '67 -98 Cuttermill Rd -Gt Neck 11021 **Fx:**487-0113
(212) 867-9123 .. **Newman,** Jacqueline '99 (Berkman BN&R,LLP) -521 5th Av -NY 10175
(718) 823-3122 .. **Newman,** James '80 (J Newman,PC) -2815 Waterbury Av -Bronx 10461 **Fx:**823-3172
(212) 735-3000 .. **Newman,** James B '08 %Skadden ASM&F LLP -4 Times Sq -NY 10036
(718) 834-8671 .. **Newman,** James M '70 -302 Atl Av -Brklyn 11201
(212) 490-3000 .. **Newman,** Jarrod B '98 Merrill Lynch -222 Bway -NY 10038
(212) 506-2999 .. **Newman,** Jay H '76 Elliott Assoc,LP -712 5th Av -NY 10019
(212) 371-9400 .. **Newman,** Jay M '78 (Newman & N,PC) -460 Park Av -NY 10022 **Fx:**371-8022
(212) 925-2800 .. **Newman,** Jeffrey A '71 (Dolgenos N&C LLP) -271 Mad Av -NY 10016
(212) 643-7000 .. **Newman,** Jeffrey H '70 (Sills C&G PC) -One Rckfllr Plz -NY 10020
(585) 919-3000 .. **Newman,** Jeffrey K '77 Infotonics Tech Ctr -5450 Campus Dr -Canandaigua 14424
(585) 336-1000 .. **Newman,** Jeremy D '05 ESL Fed Credit Union -225 Chestnut -Rchstr 14604 **Fx:**336-1014
(516) 783-8567 .. **Newman,** Joan E '79 -1663 Little Neck Av -N Bellmore 11710
(212) 995-0875 .. **Newman,** Joel A '67 -201 E 17th -NY 10003
(631) 271-2771 .. **Newman,** John '91 -82 Main -Huntngtn 11743 **Fx:**424-1060
(212) 839-5300 .. **Newman,** John H '70 SrCnsl Sidley A LLP -787 7th Av -NY 10019
(212) 265-6888 .. **Newman,** John M '83 OfCnsl Porzio B&N,PC -156 W 56th -NY 10019
(212) 599-5799 .. **Newman,** Jon E '93 OfCnsl Rutherford & C LLP -369 Lex Av -NY 10017
(212) 619-5400 .. **Newman,** Jonathan H '86 (Newman F LLP) -1250 Bway -NY 10001
(212) 558-4000 .. **Newman,** Julie A '06 %Sullivan & C LLP -125 Broad -NY 10004
(212) 345-5000 .. **Newman,** Justin E '02 Marsh & McLennan -1166 Av of Amer -NY 10036 **Fx:**345-5627
(212) 732-9450 .. **Newman,** Karen B '05 N Rosenberg -9 Murray -NY 10007 **Fx:**571-9893
(212) 264-8268 .. **Newman,** Karen M '87 %NLRB -26 Fed Plz -NY 10278 **Fx:**264-8427
(212) 456-6080 .. **Newman,** Kenneth E '72 %Walt Disney -77 W 66th -NY 10023 **Fx:**456-6180
(315) 474-7541 .. **Newman,** Kevin M '87 (Menter R&T,PC) -308 Maltbie -Syracuse 13204
(718) 823-3122 .. **Newman,** Kyle G '09 %J Newman,PC -2815 Waterbury Av -Bronx 10461 **Fx:**823-3172
(212) 833-1185 .. **Newman,** Lawr '56 -1633 Bway -NY 10019
(212) 335-9000 .. **Newman,** Lawr H '03 %DA -1 Hogan Pl -NY 10013
(212) 626-4100 .. **Newman,** Lawr W '65 (Baker & M LLP) -1114 Av of Amer -NY 10036
(212) 790-0253 .. **Newman,** Leslie S '86 %Benj N Cardozo Schl of Law -55 5th Av -NY 10003 **Fx:**790-0345
(212) 661-5030 .. **Newman,** Linda T '70 (Schoeman U&K,LLP) -60 E 42nd -NY 10165
(212) 684-1000 .. **Newman,** Louis I '68 (Slade & N LLP) -245 5th Av -NY 10016 **Fx:**684-0646
(718) 991-4600 .. **Newman,** Lucy C '00 %Leg Aid -953 Southrn Blvd -Bronx 10459 **Fx:**842-2867
(718) 375-8080 .. **Newman,** Marc Z '73 -3119 Quentin Rd -Brklyn 11234 **Fx:**375-3060
(914) 323-7000 .. **Newman,** Mark T '06 %Wilson EME&D LLP -3 Gannett Dr -White Plns 10604
(212) 558-4000 .. **Newman,** Mary Elizabeth K '09 %Sullivan & C LLP -125 Broad -NY 10004
(646) 709-9997 .. **Newman,** Michl B '92 -110 Wall -NY 10005
(212) 566-2240 .. **Newman,** Michl J '90 (Ranieri & N) -11 Park Pl -NY 10007 **Fx:**566-2249
(718) 237-1465 .. **Newman,** Michele M '88 -32 Willow Pl -Brklyn 11201
(718) 789-9559 .. **Newman,** Miriam G '47 -34 Plz E -Brklyn 11238
(718) 667-9194 .. **Newman,** Mitchell P '86 -94 Hancock -Staten Isl 10305
(212) 788-1025 .. **Newman,** Mordecai '91 %Law Dept -100 Church -NY 10007 **Fx:**788-0367
(718) 896-2700 .. **Newman,** Morris J '77 (Newman A & Assoc LLP) -97-45 Qns Blvd -Rego Pk 11374 **Fx:**896-2560
(212) 619-4350 .. **Newman Myers Kreines Gross Harris,PC** -14 Wall -NY 10005 **Fx:**619-3622
(212) 969-3000 .. **Newman,** Natalie M '06 %Proskauer R LLP -1585 Bway -NY 10036
(212) 691-6464 .. **Newman,** Nathan '90 %Dentorium Products -18 W 21st -NY 10010 **Fx:**242-6931
(212) 642-0950 .. **Newman & Okun,PC** -8 W 38th -NY 10018 **Fx:**642-0953
(212) 233-1050 .. **Newman O'Malley & Epstein,LLC** -217 Bway -NY 10007 **Fx:**233-1060
(315) 422-1172 .. **Newman,** Paul I '67 (Newman & L) -235 E Water -Syracuse 13202 **Fx:**422-1400
(212) 530-5000 .. **Newman,** Peter K '05 %Milbank TH&M LLP -1 Chase Manh Plz -NY 10005
(718) 585-3512 .. **Newman,** Philip '76 (Gallin & N) -860 Grnd Cncrs -Bronx 10451 **Fx:**993-3712
(212) 806-5400 .. **Newman,** Rachael A '07 %Stroock &S&L LLP -180 Maiden Ln -NY 10038
(212) 797-3737 .. **Newman,** Randall S '02 (Newman & Assoc,PC) -80 Wall -NY 10005
(516) 256-7737 .. **Newman,** Randy S '89 OfCnsl Weisman Law Grp,PC -140 Spruce -Cedarhrst 11516 **Fx:**256-7738
(212) 566-7500 .. **Newman,** Rebecca G '09 Douglas & L -111 John -NY 10038
(212) 986-0947 .. **Newman,** Richd '83 -122 E 42nd -NY 10168 **Fx:**972-1061
(516) 692-8888 .. **Newman,** Robt J '06 %F Chau & Assoc,LLC -130 Woodbury Rd -Woodbury 11797 **Fx:**692-8889
(212) 788-9098 .. **Newman,** Robt Jeffrey '95 %City Cncl Leg Div -250 Bway -NY 10007 **Fx:**788-7034
(212) 771-0818 .. **Newman,** Robin '97 Aspen Publishers -111 8th Av -NY 10011
(845) 634-2288 .. **Newman,** Saml L '73 -20 Squadron Blvd -New Cty 10956 **Fx:**638-0034
(212) 536-3900 .. **Newman,** Scott D '74 (K&L Gates LLP) -599 Lex Av -NY 10022
(212) 728-8000 .. **Newman,** Scott L '98 %Willkie F&G LLP -787 7th Av -NY 10019
(516) 562-7798 .. **Newman,** Shara J '01 United Business Media LLC -600 Community Dr -Manhsst 11030
(212) 223-9188 .. **Newman & Simpson, LLP** -845 3rd Av -NY 10022 **Fx:**(201) 487-8570
(212) 371-9400 .. **Newman,** Stephanie Graff '80 (Newman & N,PC) -460 Park Av -NY 10022 **Fx:**371-8022
(212) 431-2875 .. **Newman,** Stephen A '71 %NY Law Schl -185 W Bway -NY 10013 **Fx:**431-9205

(716) 853-8100 .. **Newman,** Stephen M '70 (Nixon P LLP) -40 Fountain Plz -Buffalo 14202
(212) 405-1000 .. **Newman,** Steve '91 -65 Bway -NY 10006 **Fx:**405-1001
(212) 953-6000 .. **Newman,** Steven H '91 (Katsky K LLP) -605 3rd Av -NY 10158
(212) 661-7100 .. **Newman,** Stuart B '64 (Salon MDN&B,LLP) -292 Mad Av -NY 10017
(518) 427-1600 .. **Newman,** Thos A '83 -316 Delaware Av -Delmar 12054 **Fx:**462-1925
(845) 357-2660 .. **Newman,** Thos J '51 OfCnsl Kornfeld RN&S -46 Wshngtn Av Bx177 -Suffern 10901
(845) 357-2660 .. **Newman,** Thos J Jr. '80 (Kornfeld RN&S) -46 Wshngtn Av Bx177 -Suffern 10901
(212) 692-1000 .. **Newman,** Thos R '61 OfCnsl Duane M LLP -1540 Bway -NY 10036
(212) 660-3000 .. **Newman,** Wm A '74 (Sullivan & W LLP) -1290 Av of Amer -NY 10104
(212) 478-7200 .. **Newman,** Zachary G '95 (Hahn & H LLP) -488 Mad Av -NY 10022
(914) 238-4668 .. **Newmark,** Allan J '53 -11 Laurel Ln -Chappaqua 10514
(718) 797-5200 .. **Newmark,** Jacqueline A '01 Riverfront Abstract -45 Main -Brklyn 11201
(518) 785-1900 .. **Newmark,** Lisa '92 %PEF -1168-70 Troy-Schnctdy Rd Bx12414 -Albany 12212 **Fx:**785-1323
(718) 403-3626 .. **Newmark,** Michl B '79 %Dept of Finance -345 Adams -Brklyn 11201 **Fx:**403-3650
(212) 468-8103 .. **Newmark,** Mitchell A '04 OfCnsl Morrison & F LLP -1290 Av of Amer -NY 10104
(212) 776-5000 .. **Newmark,** Richd D '77 %NYC Housing Auth -250 Bway -NY 10007 **Fx:**776-5039
(212) 655-3500 .. **Newmark,** Scott A '93 (Meister S&F LLP) -140 E 45th -NY 10017
(212) 506-5000 .. **Newmark,** Steven R '04 %Orrick H&S LLP -51 W 52nd -NY 10019
(212) 261-8000 .. **Newsom,** Anna R '98 (Mendes & M,LLP) -750 7th Av -NY 10019
(718) 815-5800 .. **Newstad,** Wm J '97 -3884 Amboy Rd -Staten Isl 10308 **Fx:**317-6183
(212) 450-4000 .. **Newstead,** Jennifer Gillian '97 (Davis P&W LLP) -450 Lex Av -NY 10017
(212) 935-3000 .. **Newton,** Andowah '08 %Mintz LCFG&P,PC -666 3rd Av -NY 10017
(212) 870-3206 .. **Newton,** Blake T III '70 %The Roothbert Fund -475 Riverside Dr -NY 10115
(718) 876-6300 .. **Newton,** David C '09 %DA -130 Styvsnt Pl -Staten Isl 10301
(718) 643-4407 .. **Newton,** Deirdre C '88 %Hon C Chambers -360 Adams -Brklyn 11201
(585) 394-0564 .. **Newton,** George F '99 (Muehe & N,LLP) -48 N Main -Canandaigua 14424 **Fx:**396-9678
(718) 991-4600 .. **Newton,** John P '03 Leg Aid -953 Southrn Blvd -Bronx 10459 **Fx:**842-2867
(212) 450-4000 .. **Newton,** Jonathan D '08 %Davis P&W LLP -450 Lex Av -NY 10017
(845) 454-4700 .. **Newton,** Mark T '85 Dra Imaging -1 Columbia -Poughkeepsie 12601
(212) 725-8001 .. **Newton,** Michl F '74 -286 Mad Av -NY 10017
(716) 858-2424 .. **Newton,** Rachel Lee '01 %DA -25 Delaware Av -Buffalo 14202 **Fx:**858-7425
(315) 435-2470 .. **Newtown,** Cynthia S '02 %DA -505 S State -Syracuse 13202 **Fx:**435-3969
(718) 855-9000 .. **Neyman,** Diana '07 %Cullen and D LLP -177 Montague -Brklyn 11201
(212) 846-4418 .. **Nezhad,** Janet F '91 %Nickelodeon -1515 Bway -NY 10036 **Fx:**846-1764
(212) 790-9464 .. **Nezu,** Victor A '99 (V Nezu,PC) -1001 Av of Amer -NY 10018 **Fx:**790-9465
(718) 260-8757 .. **Ng,** Amy '95 %Admin for Family Srvcs -345 Adams -Brklyn 11201
(212) 227-4848 .. **Ng,** Anna M K Belan '08 %Ceccarelli W PLLC -2 Wall -NY 10005
(212) 335-9000 .. **Ng,** Carey W '03 %DA -1 Hogan Pl -NY 10013
(212) 406-3070 .. **Ng,** David '75 (Karlsson & N,PC) -305 Bway -NY 10007
(212) 776-5000 .. **Ng,** Dennis J '89 %NYC Housing Auth -250 Bway -NY 10007 **Fx:**776-5039
(212) 310-8000 .. **Ng,** Eugene Jun-Yih '09 %Weil G&M LLP -767 5th Av -NY 10153
(212) 788-1034 .. **Ng,** Fay S '83 %Law Dept -100 Church -NY 10007 **Fx:**788-0367
(212) 442-4900 .. **Ng,** Frank K '02 %Ofc Admin Trials -40 Rector -NY 10006 **Fx:**442-4947
(646) 386-3433 .. **Ng,** Johnson C '91 %Supreme Ct-Law Dept -60 Centre -NY 10007
(212) 819-8200 .. **Ng,** Jonathan Y '08 %White & C LLP -1155 Av of Amer -NY 10036
(212) 259-8000 .. **Ng,** Julia '06 %Dewey & L LLP -1301 Av of Amer -NY 10019
(212) 450-4000 .. **Ng,** Katherine '08 %Davis P&W LLP -450 Lex Av -NY 10017
(718) 250-2000 .. **Ng,** Kin Wang '92 %DA -350 Jay -Brklyn 11201 **Fx:**250-2314
(212) 770-7838 .. **Ng,** Laura Ann '92 %AIG -70 Pine -NY 10270
(212) 732-9000 .. **Ng,** Marie '78 (Sullivan PBM&C PC) -120 Bway -NY 10271
(845) 794-2121 .. **Ng,** Peter J '78 (Willis & N) -444 Bway Bx874 -Monticello 12701 **Fx:**794-8412
(212) 858-1000 .. **Ng,** Priscilla Si Yip '06 %Pillsbury WSP LLP -1540 Bway -NY 10036
(212) 490-3000 .. **Ng,** Richd '00 %Wilson EME&D LLP -150 E 42nd -NY 10017
(212) 605-3100 .. **Ng,** Rita Ki Ying '95 Perelson Weiner -1 Dag Hammerskjold Plz -NY 10017
(718) 403-8557 .. **Ng,** Sylvia See-Wai '97 %DOITT -11 Metrotech Ctr -Brklyn 11201
(212) 770-1254 .. **Ng,** Tony H '98 AIG -80 Pine -NY 10005
(212) 483-9600 .. **Ng,** Wanda Yuk-Yun '05 %Costello S&G LLP -44 Wall -NY 10005
(718) 206-4712 .. **Ng,** Wm H '08 %Law Dept -89-17 Sutphin Blvd -Jamaica 11435 **Fx:**206-4702
(212) 310-8000 .. **Ng,** Wing Fu '06 %Weil G&M LLP -767 5th Av -NY 10153
(718) 357-8718 .. **Ngai,** Elaine '94 -17501 Peck Av -Fresh Mdws 11365
(212) 949-4700 .. **Ngai,** Jeannie '95 %Bushell SO&G LLP -60 E 42nd -NY 10165 **Fx:**286-0513
(718) 466-3000 .. **Ngai,** Lisa S '97 %Civil Ct -1118 Grnd Cncrs -Bronx 10456 **Fx:**466-3006
(212) 272-6251 .. **Ngalikpima,** Jean-Michel '03 %JP Morgan Chase -383 Mad Av -NY 10179
(718) 735-0008 .. **Ngati,** S Felix '98 -1203 Nostrand Av -Brklyn 11225 **Fx:**735-4889
(212) 490-3000 .. **Ngeo,** Tiffany L '98 AIGTS -175 Water -NY 10038
(212) 735-3000 .. **Ng'ethe,** Norbert M '09 %Skadden ASM&F LLP -4 Times Sq -NY 10036
(212) 259-8000 .. **Ngo,** John '08 %Dewey & L LLP -1301 Av of Amer -NY 10019
(212) 474-1000 .. **Ngo,** Minh Van '03 (Cravath S&M LLP) -825 8th Av -NY 10019
(718) 590-2000 .. **Ngomuo,** Meagan '09 %DA -198 E 161st -Bronx 10451 **Fx:**590-6477
(585) 423-2477 .. **Nguti,** Tallam I '87 %Xerox -100 Clinton Av S -Rchstr 14644
(212) 413-0827 .. **Nguyen,** Adam V '03 -750 Lex Av -NY 10022
(212) 640-9815 .. **Nguyen,** Angel Pendleton '02 %Amer Exp -200 Vesey -NY 10285
(212) 907-0700 .. **Nguyen,** Angelina '04 %Labaton S LLP -140 Bway -NY 10005
(212) 530-5000 .. **Nguyen,** Bich-Nga H '03 %Milbank TH&M LLP -1 Chase Manh Plz -NY 10005
(212) 272-9879 .. **Nguyen,** Diane '01 JP Morgan -383 Mad Av -NY 10179
(212) 341-9848 .. **Nguyen,** Diep '09 %Law Dept -100 Church -NY 10007 **Fx:**788-0367
(718) 590-2000 .. **Nguyen,** Don H '10 %DA -198 E 161st -Bronx 10451 **Fx:**590-6477
(718) 222-2033 .. **Nguyen,** Don Hanh '08 %Law Dept -350 Jay -Brklyn 11201 **Fx:**222-2088
(212) 259-8000 .. **Nguyen,** Hai Nhu '08 %Dewey & L LLP -1301 Av of Amer -NY 10019
(212) 294-6700 .. **Nguyen,** Hiep Huu '08 %Winston & S -200 Park Av -NY 10166
(212) 418-6622 .. **Nguyen,** Kendrick D '06 Permal Asset Mgt -900 3rd Av -NY 10022
(212) 715-9100 .. **Nguyen,** Leslie K '05 %Kramer LN&F,LLP -1177 Av of Amer -NY 10036
(212) 576-7000 .. **Nguyen,** Lien-Ha Thi '01 %NYLIM -51 Mad Av -NY 10010
(212) 326-3939 .. **Nguyen,** Lynda Q '04 %Jones D -222 E 41st -NY 10017
(718) 892-9500 .. **Nguyen,** Peter Thanh '99 (Park & N) -1809 Paulding Av -Bronx 10462
(212) 370-1300 .. **Nguyen,** Phi H D '03 %Ellenoff G&S LLP -150 E 42nd -NY 10017
(212) 736-9721 .. **Nguyen,** Richd D '02 R Blanch,PC -350 5th Av -NY 10118
(646) 288-1847 .. **Nguyen,** Thao Phuong '98 -1040 Av of Amer -NY 10018
(212) 878-8000 .. **Nguyen,** Thien Huong Ngoc '07 %Clifford C LLP -31 W 52nd -NY 10019
(212) 788-0496 .. **Nguyen,** Thuyvu Le '10 %Law Dept -100 Church -NY 10007 **Fx:**788-0367
(347) 404-9400 .. **Nguyen,** Tony D '04 %Criminal Ct -120 Schermerhorn -Brklyn 11201 **Fx:**(718) 643-3538
(212) 788-1644 .. **Nguyen,** Uyen '07 %Law Dept -100 Church -NY 10007 **Fx:**788-0367
(518) 462-0110 .. **Nguyen-Clark,** Thien-Nga '05 %Sheehan GCG&J LLP -54 State -Albany 12207
(212) 326-2000 .. **Nhaissi,** Orly '07 %O'Melveny & M LLP -7 Times Sq -NY 10036
(212) 318-6000 .. **Ni,** Angela C '07 %Paul HJ&W LLP -75 E 55th -NY 10022
(212) 848-4000 .. **Ni,** Dawei '09 %Shearman & S LLP -599 Lex Av -NY 10022
(212) 274-6191 .. **Nianwan,** Madonna L '92 ACS -220 Church -NY 10013
(914) 347-4500 .. **Nicaj,** Drita '97 %Lovett & B, LLP -37A Saw Mill Rvr Rd -Hawthorne 10532 **Fx:**347-4545
(845) 577-7418 .. **Nicastri,** Christopher '87 %Intl Paper Co -1422 Long Mdw Rd -Tuxedo Pk 10987
(212) 406-9686 .. **Nicastri,** Jamie K '87 %E D'Elia,PC -120 Bway -NY 10271 **Fx:**406-9688
(518) 891-2420 .. **Nicastro,** Chas J '75 Nicastro & C -163 Olive Bx508 -Saranac Lk 12983 **Fx:**891-2522
(212) 526-1375 .. **Nicastro,** Frances M '02 Barclays Capital -745 7th Av -NY 10019
(516) 248-8660 .. **Nicchia,** Bernadette M '90 -29 Milford Pl -Rockvll Ctr 11570
(716) 694-7800 .. **Nicely,** Robt E '62 -148 Old Falls Blvd -N Tonawanda 14120 **Fx:**694-7802
(212) 259-8000 .. **Nicenko,** Vladimir '97 (Dewey & L LLP) -1301 Av of Amer -NY 10019
(212) 577-2523 .. **Nichinsky,** Robin J '83 %Ctr for Appllt Litigation -74 Trinity Pl -NY 10006 **Fx:**577-2535
(845) 778-2121 .. **Nichol,** Donald G '82 (Jacobowitz & G,LLP) -158 Orange Av Bx367 -Walden 12586
(607) 722-8889 .. **Nicholas,** Cecilia A '84 -52 Lathrop Av -Bnghmtn 13905
(516) 378-1700 .. **Nicholas,** Chas C '86 (Chesney & M) -2305 Grand Av -Baldwin 11510
(718) 793-1919 .. **Nicholas,** Christopher A '97 (Taylor N & Assoc,PC) -125-10 Qns Blvd -Kew Gdns 11415 **Fx:**793-4504
(212) 389-5000 .. **Nicholas,** Christopher P '75 OfCnsl Sutherland A&B LLP -1114 Av of Amer -NY 10036
(212) 233-2300 .. **Nicholas,** Darryl L '71 -225 Bway -NY 10007 **Fx:**233-6319
(315) 422-1152 .. **Nicholas,** Donald L '66 Cnsl Costello C&F,PLLC -500 Plum -Syracuse 13204
(516) 255-3716 .. **Nicholas,** George E '84 -61 Cedar Av -Rockvll Ctr 11570
(716) 542-5413 .. **Nicholas,** John E Jr. '75 (Nicholas PSB&Z) -12364 Main Rd Bx176 -Akron 14001
(716) 542-5413 .. **Nicholas Perot Smith Bernhardt & Zosh** -12364 Main Rd Bx176 -Akron 14001
(315) 453-9426 .. **Nicholas Perot Smith Welch & Smith** -219 1st Bx720 -Liverpool 13088 **Fx:**453-9436
(212) 521-5400 .. **Nicholas,** Robt A '81 (Reed S LLP) -599 Lex Av -NY 10022
(212) 751-1000 .. **Nicholas,** Socrates Scott L '83 -100 Wall -NY 10005
(212) 450-4000 .. **Nicholas,** Stevan R B '08 %Davis P&W LLP -450 Lex Av -NY 10017
(212) 312-2276 .. **Nicholas,** Wm F '84 %Leg Aid -60 Lafayette -NY 10013 **Fx:**349-0874
(914) 774-8105 .. **Nicholls,** Declan A '01 -180 E Post Rd -White Plns 10601
(212) 455-2000 .. **Nicholls,** Margaret H '07 %Simpson T&B LLP -425 Lex Av -NY 10017
(212) 943-1090 .. **Nicholls,** Mary '80 (Gair GCSMB&R) -80 Pine -NY 10005
(585) 428-6990 .. **Nichols,** Amy Hartman '92 %Law Dept -30 Church -Rchstr 14614 **Fx:**428-6950
(914) 697-4870 .. **Nichols,** Andrew T '77 (Rosenstock L&N) -800 Wstchstr Av -Rye Brook 10573
(212) 715-1000 .. **Nichols,** Annette E '08 %Arnold & P LLP -399 Park Av -NY 10022
(516) 677-0066 .. **Nichols & Cane,LLP** -6800 Jericho Tpk -Syosset 11791 **Fx:**677-9363
(716) 847-0650 .. **Nichols,** Cheryl L '08 Leg Srvcs -237 Main -Buffalo 14203 **Fx:**847-0227
(315) 445-8762 .. **Nichols,** Craig K '91 Nichols Law Ofc -333 Butternut Dr -Dewitt 13214 **Fx:**445-9573
(646) 434-1661 .. **Nichols,** David G Jr. '85 OfCnsl Cahill/Wink LLP -5 Penn Plz -NY 10001
(914) 761-1300 .. **Nichols,** Eon S '04 %Cuddy & F LLP -445 Hmltn Av -White Plns 10601
(716) 634-2497 .. **Nichols,** F Harris '62 (Kelly & S) -5678 Main -Williamsvll 14221

(716) 688-3800 .. **Nichols**, Gretchen M '03 %Nesper F&D,LLP -501 JJ Audobon Pkwy -Amherst 14228
(516) 877-2900 .. **Nichols**, Jeffrey R '95 (Bartlett MB&M,LLP) -300 Old Cntry Rd -Mineola 11501
(518) 462-5300 .. **Nichols**, John H III '03 %DeGraff F&K LLP -90 State -Albany 12207
(315) 425-2700 .. **Nichols**, John M '08 %Hiscock & B,LLP -One Park Pl -Syracuse 13202
(212) 909-6000 .. **Nichols**, John M H '10 %Debevoise & P LLP -919 3rd Av -NY 10022
(716) 649-0161 .. **Nichols**, Jon A '72 -20 Buffalo Bx240 -Hambrg 14075
(518) 793-5026 .. **Nichols**, Jos E '93 -163 Haviland Rd -Queensbury 12804 **Fx**:793-3422
(518) 483-1440 .. **Nichols**, Jos P '83 (Poissant NG&V,PC) -367 W Main -Malone 12953
(518) 483-2200 .. **Nichols**, Kevin F '93 Nichols Law Firm PLLC -465 E Main -Malone 12953 **Fx**:483-0099
(212) 428-6236 .. **Nichols**, Laurel A '73 %Royal Bk of Canada -1 Lbrty Plz -NY 10006 **Fx**:968-1295
(516) 877-1426 .. **Nichols**, Leonard J '55 -31 Woodlnd Dr -Roslyn 11576
(518) 462-5601 .. **Nichols**, Pamela Ann '91 (O'Connell & A) -54 State -Albany 12207
(631) 244-3155 .. **Nichols**, Peter L '78 %Dowling Cllg - Poli Sci Dept -Idle Hour Dr -Oakdale 11769
(716) 858-6410 .. **Nichols**, Peter W '78 %Soc Srvcs Cnsl -95 Franklin -Buffalo 14202 **Fx**:858-7342
(212) 819-8200 .. **Nichols**, Philip J '05 %White & C LLP -1155 Av of Amer -NY 10036
(516) 677-0066 .. **Nichols**, Regina Cane '91 (Nichols & C,LLP) -6800 Jericho Tpk -Syosset 11791
(716) 852-1000 .. **Nichols**, Robt B '74 %PW Beltz,PC -36 Church -Buffalo 14202 **Fx**:852-5887
(212) 587-5394 .. **Nichols**, Rosanne M '95 %State Ins Fund -199 Church -NY 10007 **Fx**:385-9199
(518) 273-8746 .. **Nichols**, Rosemary G '73 R Nichols Law Firm -1241 19th -Watervliet 12189 **Fx**:271-1110
(212) 406-7363 .. **Nichols**, Sandra Parnell '96 -225 Bway -NY 10007 **Fx**:566-1033
(914) 697-4870 .. **Nichols**, Suzanne B '86 (Rosenstock L&N) -800 Wstchstr Av -Rye Brook 10573
(212) 489-8230 .. **Nicholson**, Alexandra '88 (Davis WT LLP) -1633 Bway -NY 10019
(212) 412-9500 .. **Nicholson**, Anne B '09 %Flemming ZWZ LLP -1 Lbrty Plz -NY 10006
(718) 852-5900 .. **Nicholson**, Danielle J '09 %Wingate K&C -45 Main -Brklyn 11201
(516) 741-4682 .. **Nicholson**, Diana L '77 (Corner FN&C) -35 Hilton Av -Gdn Cty 11530
(718) 330-0577 .. **Nicholson**, Frederic A '92 -26 Court -Brklyn 11242 **Fx**:625-3855
(315) 342-5552 .. **Nicholson**, James M '99 -34 E Brdg -Oswego 13126 **Fx**:342-5553
(212) 728-8000 .. **Nicholson**, Jared B '10 %Willkie F&G LLP -787 7th Av -NY 10019
(212) 554-7800 .. **Nicholson**, Joanna R '09 %Moses & S LLP -405 Lex Av -NY 10174
(914) 669-5224 .. **Nicholson**, Margaret A '84 -293 Route 100 -Somers 10589 **Fx**:276-0795
(845) 897-1600 .. **Nicholson**, Marie T '08 %Rosicki R & Assoc,PC -2 Summit Ct -Fishkill 12524 **Fx**:897-2648
(516) 741-4682 .. **Nicholson**, Michl '71 (Corner FN&C) -35 Hilton Av -Gdn Cty 11530
(212) 841-1000 .. **Nicholson**, Michl C '93 SpclCnsl Covington & B LLP -620 8th Av -NY 10018
(585) 232-6500 .. **Nicholson**, Michl E '09 %Harter S&E LLP -1600 Bausch & Lomb Pl -Rchstr 14604
(646) 428-3882 .. **Nicholson**, Ramona J '02 %Dept of Educ -32 Old Slip -NY 10005 **Fx**:428-3890
(212) 541-9100 .. **Nicholson**, Richd W '84 (Schiavetti CDW&N,LLP) -575 8th Av -NY 10018
(718) 246-0288 .. **Nicholson**, Robt E '92 -26 Court -Brklyn 11242
(212) 651-7500 .. **Nicholson**, W Simone '01 %Segal MS&M -850 3rd Av -NY 10022
(914) 235-2917 .. **Nichtberger**, Cindy L '90 -60 Amherst Dr -New Rchll 10804
(914) 993-9639 .. **Nichter**, Mark L '75 -44 S Bway -White Plns 10601
(212) 715-9100 .. **Nick**, Andrew B '10 %Kramer LN&F,LLP -1177 Av of Amer -NY 10036
(212) 901-9402 .. **Nick**, Kenneth A '97 Guggenheim Prtnrs -135 E 57th -NY 10022
(718) 261-5260 .. **Nickelberg**, Diane L '99 -108-18 Qns Blvd -Frst Hlls 11375 **Fx**:261-5740
(212) 653-8700 .. **Nickelsberg**, Jessica E '08 %Sheppard MR&H LLP -30 Rckfllr Plz -NY 10112
(718) 931-6300 .. **Nickelsberg**, John L '75 (Rabine & N) -993 Morris Park Av -Bronx 10462
(914) 633-2697 .. **Nickerson**, Brian J '94 %Iona Cllg -715 North Av -New Rchll 10801 **Fx**:633-2019
(516) 571-3800 .. **Nickerson**, Lauren M '07 %DA -262 Old Cntry Rd -Mineola 11501 **Fx**:248-9479
(585) 899-3970 .. **Nickerson**, Michl J '01 (Basch & N) -1777 Penfld Rd -Penfld 14526
(646) 855-0861 .. **Nickerson**, Sarah Soames '99 Banc of Amer Securities -1 Bryant Park -NY 10036
(716) 692-2983 .. **Nickerson**, Shawn P '92 -324 Wheatfld -N Tonawanda 14120
(716) 695-8590 .. **Nickerson**, Shawn P '92 City Atty -216 Payne Av -N Tonawanda 14120 **Fx**:695-8592
(212) 980-0120 .. **Nickin**, Amy D S '98 (Frankfurt KK&S,PC) -488 Mad Av -NY 10022
(212) 354-5650 .. **Nickols**, Gail E '91 Graham Campaign -36 W 44th -NY 10036
(716) 853-6001 .. **Nickson**, Christopher S '99 %Wilder & L,LLP -403 Main at Court -Buffalo 14203
(518) 626-9000 .. **Nickson**, Gregory G '05 %Dewey & L LLP -99 Wshngtn Av -Albany 12210
(716) 845-9472 .. **Nickson**, Melissa H '98 Supreme Ct -92 Franklin -Buffalo 14202 **Fx**:851-3293
(516) 741-2405 .. **Niclas**, Samantha A '95 %Geoghan C&B LLC -250 Mineola Blvd -Mineola 11501
(914) 285-8500 .. **Nico**, Jos M '85 %TK Moore -701 Wstchstr Av -White Plns 10604 **Fx**:285-8510
(212) 474-1000 .. **Nicol**, Andrew K '09 %Cravath S&M LLP -825 8th Av -NY 10019
(845) 628-4669 .. **Nicolais**, John L '92 -12 Mahopac Grdns -Mahopac 10541
(212) 682-9200 .. **Nicolakis**, Nikitas E '07 %Ostrow K&F LLP -405 Lex Av -NY 10174
(914) 682-2636 .. **Nicolaou**, Carmen A '01 Cnsl Havkins RR&V,LLP -50 Main -White Plns 10606
(212) 735-3000 .. **Nicolas**, Andrea L '99 (Skadden ASM&F LLP) -4 Times Sq -NY 10036
(914) 995-3648 .. **Nicolas-Brewster**, Mary L '93 %Cnty Atty -148 Martine Av -White Plns 10601 **Fx**:995-5858
(914) 997-9550 .. **Nicolato**, Elizabeth Thompson '95 %UIA Bd -120 Bloomingdale Rd -White Plns 10605 **Fx**:997-0014
(212) 777-5032 .. **Nicolau**, George A '51 (G Nicolau,PC) -240 E 39th -NY 10016
(914) 684-6800 .. **Nicolay**, Harry J Jr. '86 (Collier HNN&B,LLP) -1 N Lex Av -White Plns 10601
(718) 250-2000 .. **Nicolazzi**, Anna-Sigga '96 %DA -350 Jay -Brklyn 11201 **Fx**:250-2314
(516) 542-5900 .. **Nicolello**, Richd J '86 %Congdon FORDT&F -333 Earle Ovngton Blvd -Uniondale 11553
(914) 312-2133 .. **Nicolello**, Stephen W '91 %MCI -2 Intl Dr -Rye Brook 10573
(315) 895-0442 .. **Nicolette**, Alan T '91 -Bx175 -Ilion 13357
(201) 488-9080 .. **Nicolette**, David A Jr. '85 -1711 Route 9D -Cold Spg 10516 **Fx**:488-5580
(518) 463-1269 .. **Nicolette**, Sean F '02 %Walsh & H -18 Corp Wds Blvd -Albany 12211
(212) 730-7750 .. **Nicoletti**, Frank M '72 (Nicoletti GS&O,LLP) -555 5th Av -NY 10017
(212) 730-7750 .. **Nicoletti Gonson Spinner & Owen, LLP** -555 5th Av -NY 10017 **Fx**:730-7850
(212) 220-3830 .. **Nicoletti Hornig & Sweeney** -88 Pine -NY 10005 **Fx**:220-3780
(212) 220-3830 .. **Nicoletti**, John A V '78 (Nicoletti H&S) -88 Pine -NY 10005
(212) 259-8000 .. **Nicolich**, John G '81 (Dewey & L LLP) -1301 Av of Amer -NY 10019
(516) 741-6355 .. **Nicolini**, John J '91 (Nicolini PF&S) -114 Old Cntry Rd Bx9006 -Mineola 11501
(516) 741-6355 .. **Nicolini Paradise Ferretti & Sabella** -114 Old Cntry Rd Bx9006 -Mineola 11501 **Fx**:741-1659
(631) 853-4161 .. **Nicolino**, Christopher A '89 %DA -N Cnty Cmplx Bldg 77 -Hauppauge 11788 **Fx**:853-4192
(516) 222-7700 .. **Nicolino**, Lynda '90 %LI Power Auth -333 Earle Ovngton Blvd -Uniondale 11553 **Fx**:222-9137
(212) 756-2000 .. **Nicoll**, James '02 %Schulte R&Z LLP -919 3rd Av -NY 10022
(212) 478-0000 .. **Nicoll**, Jason A '00 DE Shaw & Co -120 W 45th -NY 10036 **Fx**:478-0100
(718) 923-4250 .. **Nicoll**, Jerilyn Angeli '73 %OTDA Fair Hearings -14 Boerum Pl -Brklyn 11201
(212) 455-2000 .. **Nicoll**, Kristin M '04 %Simpson T&B LLP -425 Lex Av -NY 10017
(718) 537-4958 .. **Nicoll**, Michelle Lee '97 US SSA-DAR -226 E 161st -Bronx 10451
(516) 869-6900 .. **Nicolosi**, Maura '91 (Nicolosi & N,LLP) -111 Plandome Rd -Manhsst 11030 **Fx**:869-6500
(516) 869-6900 .. **Nicolosi**, Vincent F '66 (Nicolosi & N,LLP) -111 Plandome Rd -Manhsst 11030 **Fx**:869-6500
(212) 872-9848 .. **Nicols**, Howard J C '00 (Squire S&D LLP) -30 Rckfllr Plz -NY 10112
(212) 756-2000 .. **Nicolson**, John '08 %Schulte R&Z LLP -919 3rd Av -NY 10022
(716) 853-3087 .. **Nicolson**, Karen L '90 %Leg Srvcs -237 Main -Buffalo 14203 **Fx**:856-5317
(212) 935-1400 .. **Nicosia**, Christopher A '97 %Seiden & S,PC -570 Lex Av -NY 10022
(585) 232-8314 .. **Nicosia**, Edw G '94 (Buckner & K) -1 S Wshngtn -Rchstr 14614
(716) 565-2000 .. **Nicosia**, Frank R '59 -17 Beresford Ct -Williamsvll 14221 **Fx**:635-5025
(212) 801-2265 .. **Nicosia**, John A Jr. '98 %Greenberg T,LLP -200 Park Av -NY 10166
(212) 509-5050 .. **Nicosia**, Lisa R '95 OfCnsl Wuersch & G LLP -100 Wall -NY 10005
(845) 986-9596 .. **Nicosia**, Nicholas '05 (Donohue & N LLP) -11 Oaklnd Av -Warwick 10990 **Fx**:986-9479
(716) 565-2000 .. **Nicosia**, Ralph A '55 -17 Beresford Ct -Williamsvll 14221 **Fx**:635-5025
(516) 249-4444 .. **Nicosia**, Salvatore J '62 -145 Merritt Rd -Farmngdl 11735 **Fx**:249-4445
(914) 253-6563 .. **Nicotera**, Raymond V '91 -2975 Wstchstr Av -Purchase 10577 **Fx**:253-6815
(212) 702-5443 .. **Nicotra**, Elisabetta '95 -477 Mad Av -NY 10022
(212) 261-8000 .. **Nicotra**, Jaime M '04 %Mendes & M,LLP -750 7th Av -NY 10019
(212) 370-1300 .. **Nicotra**, Jos S '88 (Ellenoff G&S LLP) -150 E 42nd -NY 10017
(212) 448-1100 .. **Nicotra**, Rachel D '07 %McLaughlin & S,LLP -260 Mad Av -NY 10016
(718) 875-1300 .. **Nicotra-Bednar**, Nancy '97 %Appllt Div 2nd Dept -45 Monroe Pl -Brklyn 11201 **Fx**:858-2446
(212) 412-9500 .. **Nicyper**, Dean R '86 (Flemming ZWZ LLP) -1 Lbrty Plz -NY 10006
(212) 765-7000 .. **Nidel**, Richd O '77 -250 W 57th -NY 10107 **Fx**:956-4374
(212) 637-1063 .. **Nidiry**, Rosemary '98 %US Atty -1 St Andrews Plz -NY 10007
(212) 474-1000 .. **Nie**, Y Elizabeth '07 %Cravath S&M LLP -825 8th Av -NY 10019
(212) 703-5094 .. **Niebisch**, Stefanie A '97 Cncl for Intl Bus -1212 Av of Amer -NY 10036
(212) 776-5259 .. **Niederhoffer**, Jeffrey '86 NYC Housing Auth -250 Bway -NY 10007 **Fx**:776-5039
(212) 267-1900 .. **Niederman**, Alex N '09 %Wade CM -111 Bway -NY 10006
(315) 445-8670 .. **Niederpruem**, Craig '87 %MA Bjork -5784 Widewaters Pkwy -DeWitt 13214 **Fx**:445-8688
(212) 688-8555 .. **Niedzwiecki**, Tina R '09 %Fragomen DB&L LLP -7 Hanover Sq -NY 10004
(607) 723-0600 .. **Niefer**, David L '95 (Gitto & N,LLP) -71 State -Bnghmtn 13901 **Fx**:723-0634
(212) 328-7923 .. **Niehaus**, Kimberly Z '98 DiMaio Ahmad Cptl,LLC -277 Park Av -NY 10172
(212) 631-0223 .. **Niehaus**, Paul R '98 (Niehaus LLP) -1359 Bway -NY 10018 **Fx**:624-0223
(212) 559-0619 .. **Niehoff**, Edw E II '78 %Citibank -909 3rd Av -NY 10022
(212) 479-6724 .. **Nieland**, Andrew E '09 Macht SA&I LLP -1114 Av of Amer -NY 10036 **Fx**:202-6417
(518) 745-1400 .. **Nield**, Laura V '87 Cnsl FitzGerald MBF -16 Pearl Bx2017 -Glens Fls 12801
(516) 684-2900 .. **Nielsen**, Gerhardt M '83 %Pegalis & E,LLC -1 Hllw Ln -Lk Success 11042
(212) 848-4000 .. **Nielsen**, Jessica L '06 %Shearman & S LLP -599 Lex Av -NY 10022
(212) 696-6000 .. **Nielsen**, John D '99 Cnsl Curtis M-PC&M LLP -101 Park Av -NY 10178
(516) 532-5816 .. **Nielsen**, K L '95 Island Mediation & Legal Solutions -75 Wilton Rd -Cold Spg Hbr 11724 **Fx**:(631) 367-0275
(718) 625-3655 .. **Nielsen**, Robt C '70 -227 Warren -Brklyn 11201

(607) 723-5341 .. **Nielsen,** Robt N Jr. '84 SpclCnsl Hinman H&K,LLP -80 Exchange Bx5250 -Bnghmtn 13902
(631) 425-4100 .. **Nielsen,** Wm J '68 (Ré NH&C,LLP) -36 N NY Av -Huntngtn 11743
(212) 714-2277 .. **Nielson,** Jason A '06 %Abad C&M,LLC -350 5th Av -NY 10118 **Fx:**714-9331
(516) 249-3450 .. **Niemczyk,** Jos A '09 %Carman C&I,LLP -266 Main -Farmngdl 11735
(716) 693-2845 .. **Niemel,** Roger J '67 -82 Webster -N Tonawanda 14120
(212) 626-4100 .. **Niemeth,** Chas F '84 (Baker & M LLP) -1114 Av of Amer -NY 10036
(212) 713-8394 .. **Niemeyer,** Richd '01 UBS -1285 Av of the Americas -NY 10019
(631) 608-2103 .. **Niemi,** Elizabeth M '98 -Bx109 -Amityvll 11701
(516) 803-2599 .. **Niemir,** Gary J '04 Cablevision Sys -1111 Stewart Av -Bethpage 11714
(212) 888-0991 .. **Nierenberg,** Gerard I '46 -330 E 38th -NY 10016
(516) 741-2585 .. **Nierer,** Cynthia A '94 (Rosicki R & Assoc,PC) -51 E Bethpage Rd -Plainvw 11803 **Fx:**741-4748
(212) 819-8200 .. **Nierling,** Rebecca C '08 %White & C LLP -1155 Av of Amer -NY 10036
(516) 371-2800 .. **Nierman,** Jos H '99 -366 Pearsall Av -Cedarhrst 11516
(631) 968-4500 .. **Nieroda,** Barbara L '99 (Nieroda & N,PC) -260 W Main -Bay Shr 11706 **Fx:**968-6523
(631) 968-4500 .. **Nieroda,** Danl W '90 OfCnsl Nieroda & N,PC -260 W Main -Bay Shr 11706 **Fx:**968-6523
(631) 968-4500 .. **Nieroda,** Danl W Jr. '98 (Nieroda & N,PC) -260 W Main -Bay Shr 11706 **Fx:**968-6523
(718) 668-1450 .. **Nierva,** Julian R '96 -159 New Dorp Plz -Staten Isl 10306 **Fx:**504-4103
(718) 505-1010 .. **Nieto,** Alejandro '00 A Nieto,PC -40-47 75th -Elmhrst 11373 **Fx:**879-6439
(716) 483-7561 .. **Nieto,** Robt D '84 %City Ct -200 E 3rd -Jamestwn 14701 **Fx:**483-7519
(516) 739-0400 .. **Nieves,** Camille '87 %Kelly R&K,LLP -330 Old Cntry Rd -Mineola 11501
(212) 688-8555 .. **Nieves,** Jenny '99 %Fragomen DB&L LLP -7 Hanover Sq -NY 10004
(718) 250-2000 .. **Nieves,** Jose L '02 %DA -350 Jay -Brklyn 11201 **Fx:**250-2314
(718) 366-3800 .. **Nieves,** Marilyn '05 Bushwick Housing & Legal Assistance -217 Wyckoff Av -Brklyn 11237
(212) 728-8000 .. **Nieves,** Michl S '10 %Willkie F&G LLP -787 7th Av -NY 10019
(212) 839-5300 .. **Nieves,** Miguel A '09 %Sidley A LLP -787 7th Av -NY 10019
(212) 278-7254 .. **Nieves,** Sonia M '89 %Societe Generale -1221 Av of Amer -NY 10020
(516) 545-5160 .. **Nifora,** Kristina '03 Natl Grid -175 E Old Cntry Rd -Hicksvll 11801 **Fx:**545-5029
(518) 462-6765 .. **Nigam,** Shubh '05 %Leg Aid -55 Colvin Av -Albany 12206 **Fx:**427-8352
(347) 294-0661 .. **Nigen,** Lee M '91 L Nigen & Assoc,PC -26 Court -Brklyn 11242 **Fx:**291-4002
(607) 724-4328 .. **Night,** Wm E '38 Night & K -89 Court -Bnghmtn 13901 **Fx:**724-0608
(212) 455-2000 .. **Nightingale,** Andrew C '10 %Simpson T&B LLP -425 Lex Av -NY 10017
(516) 656-3353 .. **Nightingale,** Michl S '98 -300 Glen -Glen Cove 11542 **Fx:**656-3354
(914) 366-8800 .. **Nigrelli,** David A '05 (D Nigrelli,PLLC) -465 Columbus Av -Valhalla 10595 **Fx:**366-8808
(516) 539-6770 .. **Nigro D'Anna & Utrecht** -215 Uniondale Av -Uniondale 11553
(516) 539-6770 .. **Nigro,** Frank M '58 (Nigro D&U) -215 Uniondale Av -Uniondale 11553
(212) 554-7800 .. **Nigro,** Jennifer P '02 %Moses & S LLP -405 Lex Av -NY 10174
(518) 584-3900 .. **Nigro,** Kyran D '93 (Ferrara & N,PLLC) -358 Bway -Saratoga Spgs 12866
(631) 265-0134 .. **Nigro,** Richd C '82 (Kral CRRP&G,LLP) -538 Broadhllw Rd -Melvll 11747 **Fx:**265-4289
(516) 571-3800 .. **Nigro,** Robt M '77 %DA -262 Old Cntry Rd -Mineola 11501 **Fx:**248-9479
(516) 432-3881 .. **Nigro,** Scott K '80 -20 W Park Av -Long Bch 11561
(516) 296-7000 .. **Nigro,** Stacey Ramis '03 %Certilman BA&H,LLP -90 Merrick Av -E Meadow 11554
(800) 890-3090 .. **Nihalani,** Ashok '08 Jacoby & M,LLP -39 Bway -NY 10002 **Fx:**(212) 344-9400
(212) 502-4868 .. **Nihamin,** Felix '96 (F Nihamin & Assoc,PC) -65 W 36th -NY 10018 **Fx:**502-4869
(212) 963-5340 .. **Niihara,** Akiko '95 UN Ofc of Leg Affrs -318 Mad Av -NY 10017 **Fx:**963-6430
(212) 450-4000 .. **Niit,** Erik J '10 %Davis P&W LLP -450 Lex Av -NY 10017
(212) 225-2000 .. **Nijenhuis,** Erika W '88 (Cleary GS&H) -1 Lbrty Plz -NY 10006
(212) 735-3000 .. **Nijjar,** Sonia K '08 %Skadden ASM&F LLP -4 Times Sq -NY 10036
(518) 434-0600 .. **Nikas,** Luke W '07 %Boies S&F LLP -10 N Pearl -Albany 12207
(518) 747-4169 .. **Nikas,** Wm L '76 -116 Oak Bx267 -Hudson Fls 12839 **Fx:**747-8459
(718) 554-0523 .. **Nikhman,** Boris '07 B Nikhman -2903 Ocean Av -Brklyn 11235 **Fx:**928-9701
(212) 599-8200 .. **Nikiciuk,** Olga '00 %Shaub AC&S,LLP -655 3rd Av -NY 10017
(716) 648-3020 .. **Nikiel,** Heather E '08 %Shaw & S -4819 S Park Av -Hambrg 14075 **Fx:**648-3730
(914) 286-7010 .. **Nikischer,** Karen A '93 %Con Edison Solutions -100 Summit Lk Dr -Valhalla 10595
(718) 333-0898 .. **Nikishin,** Olga L '02 -2171 86th -Brklyn 11214 **Fx:**333-0887
(518) 640-5000 .. **Nikodem,** Bryant '09 AYCO Co,LP -25 British Amer Blvd -Latham 12110
(212) 419-1500 .. **Nikolaidis,** Louie D '85 (Lewis C&N,PC) -350 7th Av -NY 10001
(212) 909-6000 .. **Nikolaieva,** Iryna '01 %Debevoise & P LLP -919 3rd Av -NY 10022
(516) 747-2440 .. **Nikolis,** Phillip P '85 (Pugatch & N) -1205 Franklin Av -Gdn Cty 11530
(212) 401-1484 .. **Nikolis,** Theo P '87 Royal Bk of Scotland -101 Park Av -NY 10178 **Fx:**401-3627
(212) 488-1300 .. **Nikolovienis,** Matia S '01 %Cohen & P LLP -444 Mad Av -NY 10022
(212) 609-6800 .. **Nikolsky,** Mark E '02 %McCarter & E,LLP -245 Park Av -NY 10167
(716) 839-8397 .. **Niland,** Bridget E '99 Daemen College -4380 Main -Amherst 14226
(212) 528-1500 .. **Niler,** Marjorie Z '94 %M Berman & Assoc,PC -15 Maiden Ln -NY 10038 **Fx:**349-1887
(212) 307-0023 .. **Niles,** Ian A '94 I Niles,PC -145 Hudson -NY 10013
(518) 561-1980 .. **Niles,** John F '74 (Niles P&B) -46-48 Cornelia Bx2729 -Plattsbrgh 12901
(518) 561-1980 .. **Niles Piller & Bracy** -46-48 Cornelia Bx2729 -Plattsbrgh 12901 **Fx:**561-7567
(212) 403-1000 .. **Niles,** Sabastian V '07 %Wachtell LR&K -51 W 52nd -NY 10019
(212) 328-4602 .. **Nilsen,** Martin J '76 Arch Ins Grp -1 Lbrty Plz -NY 10006 **Fx:**651-6499
(212) 687-1155 .. **Nilson,** Deborah A '85 (Rozan & N,LLP) -420 Lex Av -NY 10170 **Fx:**687-1118
(212) 566-8120 .. **Nilva,** Stephanie M '95 Day One -Church Street Station Bx1507 -NY 10013
(212) 837-6000 .. **Nimaroff,** Carole '87 %Hughes H&R LLP -1 Bttry Pk Plz -NY 10004
(212) 964-6611 .. **Nimaroff,** Ellen '91 Cnsl Lester SK&D -120 Bway -NY 10271
(718) 520-1100 .. **Nimetz,** Everett N '77 -125-10 Qns Blvd -Kew Gdns 11415 **Fx:**575-4062
(212) 894-8940 .. **Nimetz,** Marshall A '76 CT Corp System -111 8th Av -NY 10011
(212) 318-3000 .. **Nimetz,** Warren J '80 (Fulbright & J LLP) -666 5th Av -NY 10103
(212) 286-8585 .. **Nimick,** Virginia J '08 %Heidell PM&B,LLP -99 Park Av -NY 10016
(212) 868-8100 .. **Nimkoff,** Ronald A '84 (Nimkoff Firm) -1 Penn Plz -NY 10119 **Fx:**868-0227
(212) 849-7000 .. **Nimrod,** Raymond N '07 (Quinn EU&S,LLP) -51 Mad Av -NY 10010
(212) 450-4000 .. **Nims,** Barbara '84 (Davis P&W LLP) -450 Lex Av -NY 10017
(212) 702-4349 .. **Ninivaggi,** Danl A '95 Icahn Enterprises LP -757 5th Av -NY 10153
(718) 858-0931 .. **Niosi,** Valerie '75 -143 Adelphi -Brklyn 11205
(212) 403-1000 .. **Nippert,** Corinne C '10 %Wachtell LR&K -51 W 52nd -NY 10019
(718) 544-3970 .. **Nir,** Ronald S '88 (R Nir,PC) -125-10 Qns Blvd -Kew Gdns 11415 **Fx:**575-4085
(212) 205-7000 .. **Nirenberg,** David Z '86 (Ashurst LLP) -7 Times Sq -NY 10036
(718) 966-6530 .. **Nirenberg,** Stanley S '71 -58 Lion -Staten Isl 10307
(212) 735-3000 .. **Nisa,** Jos P '88 Cnsl Skadden ASM&F LLP -4 Times Sq -NY 10036
(585) 546-2500 .. **Nischal,** Rita '05 %McConville CC&M,PC -25 E Main -Rchstr 14614
(212) 664-3564 .. **Nisco,** Cira Limoli '98 -30 Rockafeller Plz -NY 10112
(716) 250-1800 .. **Nisengard,** Michl L '08 %Jaeckle F&M,LLP -400 Essjay Rd -Amherst 14221
(212) 858-1000 .. **Nishawala,** Vipul N '96 (Pillsbury WSP LLP) -1540 Bway -NY 10036
(718) 694-6253 .. **Nishman,** Robt W '60 -35 Pierrepont -Brklyn 11201
(646) 471-4027 .. **Nisi,** Robt A '88 %PricewaterhouseCoopers -300 Mad Av -NY 10017
(212) 792-8484 .. **Nisim,** Francine N '01 (Stern T&B LLP) -380 Lex Av -NY 10168
(516) 358-5690 .. **Nisirios,** Irene '04 %V Toomey -3000 Marcus Av -Lk Success 11042 **Fx:**775-0237
(718) 631-0800 .. **Nisnewitz,** Craig M '82 (Feinstein & N,PC) -42-40 Bell Blvd -Bayside 11361
(718) 261-3000 .. **Nisonoff,** Bert H '60 -118-21 Qns Blvd -Frst Hlls 11375 **Fx:**793-0385
(212) 964-7990 .. **Nisonoff,** Madeleine '92 (Mallow K&N,PC) -321 Bway -NY 10007
(212) 361-7770 .. **Nisonoff,** Mitchell B '82 Dept Cnsmr Affrs -66 John -NY 10038
(212) 839-5300 .. **Nisonson,** Leigh H '08 Sidley A LLP -787 7th Av -NY 10019
(212) 222-2934 .. **Niss,** James '81 -400 Riverside Dr -NY 10025 **Fx:**(815) 301-8986
(212) 326-2000 .. **Nissan,** Ilan S '89 (O'Melveny & M LLP) -7 Times Sq -NY 10036
(212) 852-6000 .. **Nissan,** Limor '92 %Westdeutsch Landesbank -1211 Av of Amer -NY 10036
(212) 310-8169 .. **Nissan,** Michl '81 (Weil G&M LLP) -767 5th Av -NY 10153
(631) 665-3400 .. **Nissan,** Randy S '80 %Siben & S,LLP -90 E Main Bx149P -Bay Shr 11706
(212) 237-1000 .. **Nisselson,** Alan '76 (Windels ML&M,LLP) -156 W 56th -NY 10019
(212) 685-3539 .. **Nissen,** Elaine H '80 -500 5th Av -NY 10110 **Fx:**685-7135
(212) 267-5949 .. **Nissen,** Irwin K '55 -233 Bway -NY 10279 **Fx:**406-9843
(914) 723-4300 .. **Nissen,** J Harold '51 OfCnsl Lackenbach S LLP -1 Chase Rd -Scarsdale 10583
(212) 878-8000 .. **Nissen,** Lynne S '06 %Clifford C LLP -31 W 52nd -NY 10019
(914) 939-1111 .. **Nissen,** Nancy C '94 %MS Goldstein -62 Bowman Av -Rye Brook 10573 **Fx:**939-2369
(212) 756-2000 .. **Nissenbaum,** David '94 (Schulte R&Z LLP) -919 3rd Av -NY 10022
(212) 871-5711 .. **Nissenbaum,** Gary D '92 (Nissenbaum Law Grp,LLC) -140 Bway -NY 10005 **Fx:**871-5712
(212) 382-0700 .. **Nissenbaum,** Israel '75 OfCnsl Ostrolenk FG&S,LLP -1180 Av of Amer -NY 10036
(212) 636-7609 .. **Nissenbaum,** Robt J '07 %Fordham Univ Sch of Law -140 W 62nd -NY 10023 **Fx:**636-6899
(646) 502-7001 .. **Nisser,** Loan T '99 (JSBarkats PLLC) -100 Church -NY 10007 **Fx:**607-5544
(212) 407-7700 .. **Nissim,** Michl C '86 (Vedder P,PC) -1633 Bway -NY 10019
(212) 309-6000 .. **Nissim,** Michl E '06 %Morgan L&B LLP -101 Park Av -NY 10178
(212) 763-8041 .. **Nissim,** Norris '92 Luxor Capital Grp,LP -767 5th Av -NY 10153
(212) 750-1276 .. **Nissman,** Peter M '90 -111 Bway -NY 10006 **Fx:**346-7719
(212) 468-8000 .. **Niswander,** Rex L '83 OfCnsl Morrison & F LLP -1290 Av of Amer -NY 10104
(212) 490-3000 .. **Nitka,** Abigail '06 %Wilson EME&D LLP -150 E 42nd -NY 10017
(212) 732-9500 .. **Nitkewicz,** Andrew P '99 (Avelino N LLP) -225 Bway -NY 10007 **Fx:**732-4580
(516) 741-4799 .. **Nitkewicz,** Edw J '92 OfCnsl Baker SBGFM&N,LLC -100 Grdn City Plz -Gdn Cty 11530
(518) 473-8418 .. **Nitsche,** Jos E '81 %OCFS -52 Wshngtn -Rensselaer 12144 **Fx:**486-6361
(716) 855-5710 .. **Nitterauer,** Wm E '70 -60 Lakefront Blvd -Buffalo 14202 **Fx:**855-5722
(518) 473-5423 .. **Nitti,** Gino M '89 Div of Parole -97 Central Av -Albany 12206 **Fx:**473-6037
(212) 872-3574 .. **Niunoya,** Keiko '01 %KPMG, LLP -345 Park Av -NY 10154
(212) 805-5318 .. **Nivala,** Gregg R '06 L-3 Communications -600 3rd Av -NY 10016
(212) 361-7996 .. **Niveknand,** Amreeta '05 %Dept Homeless Srvcs -33 Beaver -NY 10004 **Fx:**361-8002
(212) 698-3500 .. **Nix,** James H '88 (Dechert LLP) -1095 Av of Amer -NY 10036
(212) 728-8000 .. **Nix,** Kelsey I '88 (Willkie F&G LLP) -787 7th Av -NY 10019
(212) 259-8000 .. **Nixon,** Benjamin '09 %Dewey & L LLP -1301 Av of Amer -NY 10019
(212) 351-4000 .. **Nixon,** Brett A '05 %Gibson D&C LLP -200 Park Av -NY 10166

(212) 351-4000 .. **Nixon,** Dianna M '96 OfCnsl Gibson D&C LLP -200 Park Av -NY 10166
(212) 425-0055 .. **Nixon,** Duncan A '76 %Sharretts PC&B -75 Broad -NY 10004
(315) 736-6787 .. **Nixon,** James E II '99 Nixon Law Firm,PLLC -105 Main -Whitesboro 13492
(212) 940-3000 .. **Nixon Peabody LLP** -437 Mad Av -NY 10022 **Fx:**940-3111
(585) 263-1000 .. **Nixon Peabody LLP** -1100 Clinton Sq -Rchstr 14604 **Fx:**263-1600
(516) 832-7500 .. **Nixon Peabody LLP** -50 Jericho Quadrangle -Jericho 11753 **Fx:**832-7555
(716) 853-8100 .. **Nixon Peabody LLP** -40 Fountain Plz -Buffalo 14202 **Fx:**853-8109
(518) 427-2650 .. **Nixon Peabody LLP** -677 Bway -Albany 12207 **Fx:**427-2666
(518) 465-3553 .. **Nizer,** Mark D '03 %Maynard OS&C,LLP -6 Twr Pl -Albany 12203
(212) 732-0030 .. **Nizewitz,** Robt M '77 %S Seung -2 Mott -NY 10013 **Fx:**227-5097
(718) 263-2411 .. **Nizin,** Leslie S '64 -125-10 Qns Blvd -Kew Gdns 11415 **Fx:**263-2911
(516) 227-6363 .. **Nizzo,** Amy J '04 %Amato & Assoc,PC -666 Old Cntry Rd -Gdn Cty 11530 **Fx:**227-6367
(212) 351-4500 .. **Nizzo,** Brett J '02 %Epstein B&G,PC -250 Park Av -NY 10177
(212) 398-9400 .. **Nkansah-Siriboe,** Danl K '97 (Siriboe & A) -110 W 40th -NY 10018 **Fx:**398-9411
(718) 855-1834 .. **Nnebe,** Okechukwu V '03 -255 Lvngstn -Brklyn 11217 **Fx:**855-1835
(845) 485-3904 .. **Nneji,** Emmanuel C '91 %Dept of Law -235 Main -Poughkeepsie 12601 **Fx:**452-3303
(716) 856-4200 .. **Noah,** Jennifer L '99 %Gibson M&C,LLP -69 Delaware Av -Buffalo 14202
(718) 250-4218 .. **Noah,** Michelle I '83 %Leg Aid -111 Lvngstn -Brklyn 11201 **Fx:**250-4243
(845) 808-1150 .. **Noah,** Robt A '95 %Cnty Atty -48 Gleneida Av -Carmel 10512 **Fx:**808-1903
(212) 864-3776 .. **Noam,** Eli M '77 -450 Riverside Dr -NY 10027
(516) 248-7000 .. **Nobel,** Debora G '80 %Albanese & A LLP -1050 Franklin Av -Gdn Cty 11530
(212) 335-9000 .. **Nobel,** Julie B '98 %DA -1 Hogan Pl -NY 10013
(914) 347-2600 .. **Nobel,** Robt S '93 (Traub LS&S LLP) -7 Skyline Dr -Hawthorne 10532
(516) 229-6000 .. **Nobile,** Anthony D '87 %R Lau & Assoc -300 Jericho Quad Bx9040 -Jericho 11753 **Fx:**229-6167
(914) 337-6300 .. **Nobile, Magarian & DiSalvo,LLP** -111 Kraft Av -Bronxvll 10708 **Fx:**337-6913
(585) 546-5964 .. **Nobile,** Michelle R '97 -36 W Main -Rchstr 14614 **Fx:**546-5966
(914) 337-6300 .. **Nobile,** Ralph R '56 (Nobile M&D,LLP) -111 Kraft Av -Bronxvll 10708
(212) 218-5500 .. **Nobile,** Robt J '85 (Seyfarth S LLP) -620 8th Av -NY 10018
(212) 783-1153 .. **Noble,** A Marie '99 CItigroup Invstmnts -731 Lex Av -NY 10022
(718) 896-7700 .. **Noble,** Igor '03 -68-60 Austin -Frst Hlls 11375
(716) 851-4343 .. **Noble,** Ilo Nwabugwu '91 %Law Dept -65 Niagara Sq -Buffalo 14202 **Fx:**851-4105
(212) 479-1505 .. **Noble,** James K III '85 Fortress Investment Grp -1345 Av of Amer -NY 10105
(212) 940-8800 .. **Noble,** Kenneth E '02 (Katten MR LLP) -575 Mad Av -NY 10022
(212) 819-8200 .. **Noble,** Roger W '74 (White & C LLP) -1155 Av of Amer -NY 10036
(646) 837-0100 .. **Noble,** Susan D '89 (Wenick & F,PC) -28 E 28th -NY 10016
(631) 470-1633 .. **Nobles,** Andre T '92 -7 Fifflers Green Dr -Lloyd Hbr 11743 **Fx:**425-1449
(585) 546-1260 .. **Nobles,** Jamie Lee '03 -45 Exchange Blvd -Rchstr 14614 **Fx:**546-7803
(212) 676-8158 .. **Nobles,** Russell Ann '77 Dept Youth & Comm Dvlpmnt -156 William -NY 10038
(212) 310-8000 .. **Nocco,** Frank P '89 (Weil G&M LLP) -767 5th Av -NY 10153
(585) 415-0964 .. **Noce,** Chas T '74 -40 Humboldt -Rchstr 14609 **Fx:**292-5580
(212) 421-6492 .. **Noce,** Gregory '07 %Squitieri & F,LLP -32 E 57th -NY 10022 **Fx:**421-6553
(718) 250-2000 .. **Nocella,** Jennifer A '00 %DA -350 Jay -Brklyn 11201 **Fx:**250-2314
(212) 828-6000 .. **Nocenti,** David M '84 Union Settlement Assn -237 E 104th -NY 10029
(212) 635-2244 .. **Nocera,** John A '79 (Rosner N&R LLP) -110 Wall -NY 10005
(518) 374-8200 .. **Nocera,** Ralph A '61 -224 State -Schnctdy 12305 **Fx:**374-1432
(212) 685-8500 .. **Nocerino,** Alex '06 %Greenstein & M,LLP -1825 Park Av -NY 10035
(315) 218-8000 .. **Nocilly,** David L '01 (Bond S&K,PLLC) -1 Lincoln Ctr -Syracuse 13202
(212) 872-1000 .. **Nock,** Louis L '92 -One Bryant Park -NY 10036 **Fx:**872-1002
(212) 801-2168 .. **Noda,** Masahiro '05 %Greenberg T,LLP -200 Park Av -NY 10166
(212) 839-5300 .. **Noda,** Reiko '02 %Sidley A LLP -787 7th Av -NY 10019
(917) 364-9340 .. **Noda,** Samantha M '06 -Bx1027 -NY 10008
(212) 468-8000 .. **Nodel,** Jordan '09 %Morrison & F LLP -1290 Av of Amer -NY 10104
(212) 536-3900 .. **Nodeland,** Knut L '07 %K&L Gates LLP -599 Lex Av -NY 10022
(212) 252-0415 .. **Nodjoumi,** Ebrahim Ali '01 -35 Park Av -NY 10016
(212) 732-2799 .. **Nodroff,** James J '71 -22 Howard -NY 10013
(585) 325-4140 .. **Noe,** Barbra Pohl '96 %Howe & Rusling,Inc -120 East Av -Rchstr 14604 **Fx:**325-7361
(716) 876-9218 .. **Noe,** Danl A '95 %Mueller Corp -789 Colvin Blvd -Kenmore 14217
(516) 759-5373 .. **Noe,** Mary '89 -35 Broad -Williston Pk 11596 **Fx:**759-8649
(845) 469-4900 .. **Noe,** Robt E '93 %Greenwald Law Ofc -99 Brookside Av -Chester 10918 **Fx:**469-2022
(516) 803-2516 .. **Noel,** Rochelle Marie '96 %Cablevision Sys -1111 Stewart Av -Bethpage 11714
(212) 841-2215 .. **Noero,** Francesco '06 BNP Paribas -787 7th Av -NY 10019
(212) 310-8000 .. **Noethen,** Kirsten A '05 %Weil G&M LLP -767 5th Av -NY 10153
(212) 259-8000 .. **Noferi,** Mark L '06 %Dewey & L LLP -1301 Av of Amer -NY 10019
(631) 427-5050 .. **Nofi,** Vincent J '80 (Scalzi & N) -150 Broad Hollow Rd -Melvll 11747
(516) 741-6266 .. **Nogan,** Thos J '86 (McCabe CM&F,LLP) -346 Westbury Av Bx9000 -Carle Pl 11514
(516) 677-9310 .. **Noga-Walker,** Shelly '85 -32 Beatrice Av -Syosset 11791 **Fx:**677-9312
(212) 431-1300 .. **Nogee,** Jeffrey L '78 Cnsl Borah GAN&G PC -377 Bway -NY 10013
(212) 808-2700 .. **Noggle,** Laura L '07 %Pepper H LLP -620 8th Av -NY 10018
(212) 468-8000 .. **Nogid,** Amy F '83 OfCnsl Morrison & F LLP -1290 Av of Amer -NY 10104
(716) 853-8100 .. **Nogueras-Trummer,** Lynnette '06 %Nixon P LLP -40 Fountain Plz -Buffalo 14202
(212) 415-8600 .. **Noh,** Peter H '09 %Locke LB&L LLP -3 World Fncl Ctr -NY 10281
(212) 848-4000 .. **Noh,** Solomon J '01 %Shearman & S LLP -599 Lex Av -NY 10022
(212) 613-5000 .. **Noh,** Sunny W '09 %Leg Assist Grp -450 W 33rd -NY 10001 **Fx:**750-0820
(646) 319-9764 .. **Nohavicka,** Jos D '94 -1121 Ellsworth Av -Bronx 10465 **Fx:**(718) 828-0193
(914) 421-7519 .. **Nohe,** Richd E '99 %Metromedia Fiber Ntwrk -360 Hmltn Av -White Plns 10601
(631) 853-5212 .. **Nohilly,** Kim E '97 %Leg Aid -400 Carleton Av Bx9082 -Central Islip 11722 **Fx:**853-7798
(212) 876-5500 .. **Noisette,** Leonard E '85 %Neighborhood Def Srv -317 Lenox Av -NY 10027 **Fx:**876-5586
(585) 295-4400 .. **Nojay,** Wm R '83 OfCnsl Hiscock & B,LLP -2000 HSBC Plz -Rchstr 14604
(212) 536-3900 .. **Nolan,** Anthony R G '98 (K&L Gates LLP) -599 Lex Av -NY 10022
(212) 506-2500 .. **Nolan,** Brian W '00 Cnsl Mayer B LLP -1675 Bway -NY 10019
(631) 236-4105 .. **Nolan,** Cathleen Quinn '93 (Goldson NC,PC) -145 Marcus Blvd -Hauppauge 11788 **Fx:**236-4110
(212) 872-3772 .. **Nolan,** Christopher J '89 Cnsl Magazine Publishers of Amer -810 7th Av -NY 10019
(212) 513-3200 .. **Nolan,** Christopher R '02 (Holland & K LLP) -31 W 52nd -NY 10019
(518) 641-6860 .. **Nolan,** Danl P '79 Johnson Illington Advisors -677 Bway -Albany 12207 **Fx:**641-6856
(212) 278-1000 .. **Nolan,** Dennis J '07 %Anderson K&O,PC -1251 Av of Amer -NY 10020
(212) 237-1000 .. **Nolan,** Edw P '74 (Windels ML&M,LLP) -156 W 56th -NY 10019
(212) 341-3076 .. **Nolan,** Esther R '94 %Admin Children's Srvcs -220 Church -NY 10013 **Fx:**676-0206
(212) 407-7700 .. **Nolan,** Francis X III '75 (Vedder P,PC) -1633 Bway -NY 10019
(914) 328-2969 .. **Nolan,** Francis X IV '09 %Martin C&B LLP -245 Main -White Plns 10601
(718) 243-2171 .. **Nolan,** Gerard P '86 -26 Court -Brklyn 11242
(212) 416-8478 .. **Nolan,** Gregory J '78 %Dept of Law -120 Bway -NY 10271
(518) 449-3300 .. **Nolan & Heller,LLP** -39 N Pearl -Albany 12207 **Fx:**432-3123
(518) 449-3300 .. **Nolan,** Howard C Jr. '58 SrCnsl Nolan & H,LLP -39 N Pearl -Albany 12207
(212) 402-7840 .. **Nolan,** James C '85 -65 Bway -NY 10006
(212) 872-5631 .. **Nolan,** James V '01 %KPMG LLP -345 Park Av -NY 10154
(212) 297-5800 .. **Nolan,** John B '81 (Day P LLP) -7 Times Sq -NY 10036
(718) 250-2000 .. **Nolan,** John P '76 %DA -350 Jay -Brklyn 11201 **Fx:**250-2314
(212) 906-1200 .. **Nolan,** Katharine E '03 %Latham & W -885 3rd Av -NY 10022
(212) 661-0011 .. **Nolan,** Kenneth P '78 (Speiser KN&G) -140 E 45th -NY 10017
(212) 340-0400 .. **Nolan,** Kevin J '83 %Applt Div 1st Dept -27 Mad Av -NY 10010 **Fx:**889-4412
(718) 694-5720 .. **Nolan,** Kristen M '04 %Transit Auth -130 Lvngstn -Brklyn 11201 **Fx:**694-5726
(631) 261-2200 .. **Nolan,** Laure Collins '93 -10 Laurel Av -Northprt 11768 **Fx:**261-6159
(516) 877-0800 .. **Nolan,** Lynne M '99 %Cartiglia C&R -1050 Franklin Av -Gdn Cty 11530
(212) 408-2500 .. **Nolan,** Margaret Dooley '01 %Baker B,LLP -30 Rckfllr Plz -NY 10112
(718) 240-7007 .. **Nolan,** Melanie Bauer '09 %Brookdale Hosp Med Ctr -1 Brookdale Plz -Brklyn 11212
(518) 692-8298 .. **Nolan,** Michl F '89 %Thruway Beverages -1184 Route 29 -Greenwich 12834
(585) 428-4373 .. **Nolan,** Michl J '93 %Hon S Lindley -461 Hall of Justice -Rchstr 14614
(315) 798-5766 .. **Nolan,** Michl R '06 DA -800 Park Av -Utica 13501 **Fx:**798-5582
(212) 838-5555 .. **Nolan,** Michl T '92 (Grenier H&N LLP) -60 E 42nd -NY 10165
(631) 694-2626 .. **Nolan,** Michl T '92 (Grenier H&N LLP) -445 Broadhllw Rd -Melvll 11747
(212) 779-9800 .. **Nolan,** Michelle A '03 %Luboja & T,LLP -10 E 40th -NY 10016
(718) 816-0005 .. **Nolan,** Nancy E '06 %Angiuli K&G,LLP -60 Bay -Staten Isl 10301
(631) 928-6500 .. **Nolan,** Richd T '58 -101 Rustic Rd -Pt Jffrsn 11777 **Fx:**928-6536
(212) 838-5555 .. **Nolan,** Robt F '49 (Grenier H&N LLP) -60 E 42nd -NY 10165
(631) 694-2626 .. **Nolan,** Robt F '49 (Grenier H&N LLP) -445 Broadhllw Rd -Melvll 11747
(212) 998-2257 .. **Nolan,** Terrance J '75 %NYU Ofc Leg Cnsl -70 Wshngtn Sq S -NY 10012 **Fx:**995-3048
(631) 727-8410 .. **Nolan,** Thos G '84 -One Union Sq Bx826 -Aquebogue 11931 **Fx:**727-1943
(718) 858-7440 .. **Nolan,** Thos J '73 (Gardiner & N) -142 Joralemon -Brklyn 11201 **Fx:**624-2455
(516) 248-2002 .. **Nolan,** Wm P '95 (Gallagher WB&P) -98 Willis Av -Mineola 11501
(212) 308-3456 .. **Nolan,** Wm Paul '73 (Nolan Law Firm) -444 E 75th -NY 10021 **Fx:**879-6806
(518) 487-7600 .. **Nolan,** Wm S '02 %Whiteman O&H LLP -1 Commerce Plz -Albany 12260
(212) 636-6000 .. **Nolan-Haley,** Jacqueline M '77 %Fordham Univ Sch of Law -140 W 62nd -NY 10023 **Fx:**636-6899
(212) 864-4724 .. **Nolan-Lee Sang,** Sharon '84 %DMV -159 E 125th -NY 10035
(212) 735-3000 .. **Nolens,** Olivier '08 %Skadden ASM&F LLP -4 Times Sq -NY 10036
(212) 608-4400 .. **Nolet,** Chas Jr. '85 (Wilson GD&N) -233 Bway -NY 10279
(518) 455-2891 .. **Nolfo,** Judith M '93 %NYS Senate -500G Cptl Bldg -Albany 12247 **Fx:**432-5419
(212) 286-9499 .. **Nolfo,** Matthew J '92 -275 Mad Av -NY 10016 **Fx:**286-8881
(518) 383-9400 .. **Noll,** Carrie McLoughlin '92 (Pennock B&N) -1407 Route 9 -Clifton Pk 12065
(212) 805-0256 .. **Noll,** David L '09 Hon R Holwell -500 Pearl -NY 10007
(914) 517-5000 .. **Noll,** Jerome '95 OfCnsl Meiselman DPC&E,PC -1311 Mamaroneck Av -White Plns 10605
(212) 906-1200 .. **Noll,** Jocelyn F '02 %Latham & W -885 3rd Av -NY 10022
(212) 504-6000 .. **Noll,** Rebekka C '10 %Cadwalader W&T LLP -1 World Fncl Ctr -NY 10281
(516) 741-1116 .. **Noll,** Richd E '94 (Bloom & N,LLP) -170 Old Cntry Rd -Mineola 11501 **Fx:**741-0546
(212) 573-8966 .. **Noll,** Ronald U '77 -330 E 38th -NY 10016
(914) 684-6800 .. **Nolletti,** James J '79 (Collier HNN&B,LLP) -1 N Lex Av -White Plns 10601
(914) 422-4353 .. **Nolon,** Jennie C '09 %Pace Law Schl -78 N Bway -White Plns 10603 **Fx:**422-4039

(914) 422-4090 .. **Nolon,** John R '71 %Pace Law Schl -78 N Bway -White Plns 10603 **Fx:**422-4039
(518) 587-6846 .. **Nolte,** Andrew J '83 -124 East Av -Saratoga Spgs 12866
(516) 365-9802 .. **Nolte Nolte & Hunter** -1077 Nrthrn Blvd -Roslyn 11576 **Fx:**365-9805
(212) 808-0448 .. **Nomberg,** Brett J '94 (Brand BN&R,LLP) -286 Mad Av -NY 10017
(212) 818-8000 .. **Nomura,** Keisuke '05 Itochu Intl -335 Mad Av -NY 10017 **Fx:**818-8493
(585) 419-8800 .. **Nonkes,** James P '04 %Harris B PLLC -99 Garnsey Rd -Pittsfrd 14534
(585) 419-8800 .. **Nonkes,** Steven P '10 %Harris B PLLC -99 Garnsey Rd -Pittsfrd 14534
(212) 259-8000 .. **Nonna,** John M '76 (Dewey & L LLP) -1301 Av of Amer -NY 10019
(212) 465-1110 .. **Nonnenmacher,** John J '89 (Bader Y&N LLP) -350 5th Av -NY 10118
(631) 476-6158 .. **Nonnenmann,** Gregory J '83 -3 Clinton -Mt Sinai 11766 **Fx:**476-6139
(212) 305-2036 .. **Noonan,** Brian J '94 NY Presbyterian Hsptl -525 E 68th Bx88 -NY 10065 **Fx:**746-8603
(212) 836-8000 .. **Noonan,** Danielle A '08 %Kaye S LLP -425 Park Av -NY 10022
(212) 372-2000 .. **Noonan,** David L '88 %Newmark Knight Frank -125 Park Av -NY 10017 **Fx:**372-2386
(914) 378-1010 .. **Noonan,** Michl J '85 %Fitzgerald & F -538 Riverdale Av -Ynkrs 10705
(716) 856-4000 .. **Noonan,** Timothy P '00 (Hodgson R LLP) -140 Pearl -Buffalo 14202
(585) 546-2434 .. **Noone,** Christopher S '87 %Hirsch & T PC -1000 Rynlds Arcd Bldg -Rchstr 14614
(212) 968-9573 .. **Noone,** James '97 Robeco -909 3rd Av -NY 10022
(212) 450-4000 .. **Noone,** Thos M '07 %Davis P&W LLP -450 Lex Av -NY 10017
(212) 461-2323 .. **Noorlander,** John H '05 %Saiber LLC -44 Wall -NY 10005
(212) 608-0808 .. **Nooter,** Thos H '75 (Freeman N&G) -30 Vesey -NY 10007 **Fx:**962-9696
(631) 271-7500 .. **Nora,** Karen Ellis '96 (Smyth N LLP) -143 Main -Huntngtn 11743
(585) 325-2520 .. **Noras,** Natasha L '08 %Leg Assistance -1 W Main -Rchstr 14614 **Fx:**325-2559
(212) 770-5235 .. **Norat,** Cecilia E '87 %AIG -70 Pine -NY 10270 **Fx:**509-1887
(212) 836-8000 .. **Norber,** Dan '93 Kaye S LLP -425 Park Av -NY 10022
(212) 848-4000 .. **Norberg,** Jane Ann '98 %Shearman & S LLP -599 Lex Av -NY 10022
(212) 682-7474 .. **Norbitz,** Todd C '91 (Foley & L LLP) -90 Park Av -NY 10016
(212) 248-3140 .. **Norcross,** Kenneth J '83 (Drinker B&R LLP) -140 Bway -NY 10005
(315) 422-7000 .. **Norcross,** Sarah K '00 -4 Clinton Sq -Syracuse 13202
(516) 568-2404 .. **Nord,** Amy S '82 -71 S Central Av -Vly Stream 11580 **Fx:**825-2752
(212) 455-2000 .. **Nord,** Jos S '10 %Simpson T&B LLP -425 Lex Av -NY 10017
(212) 351-4000 .. **Nordahl,** Stephen D '95 (Gibson D&C LLP) -200 Park Av -NY 10166
(315) 477-9900 .. **Nordby,** Eric C '93 (Porter NH LLP) -316 S Clinton -Syracuse 13202 **Fx:**477-9923
(212) 998-6730 .. **Norden,** Lawr D '97 Brennan Ctr for Jstc -161 Av of Amer -NY 10013 **Fx:**995-4550
(212) 876-7700 .. **Norden,** Melissa S '00 %ASPCA -424 E 92nd -NY 10128 **Fx:**860-3560
(212) 218-3316 .. **Norden,** Wm B '70 (Seyfarth S LLP) -620 8th Av -NY 10018 **Fx:**(917) 344-1289
(212) 692-1000 .. **Nordin,** H Bertil '86 (Duane M LLP) -1540 Bway -NY 10036
(914) 468-7600 .. **Nordlicht,** Ira S '73 (Nordlicht & H) -800 Wstchstr Av -Rye Brook 10573 **Fx:**468-7608
(315) 472-4500 .. **Nordone,** August J '74 -201 E Jffrsn -Syracuse 13202 **Fx:**472-4572
(212) 349-6009 .. **Norejko,** Amanda B '02 Sanctuary for Families -110 Wall -NY 10005 **Fx:**566-0344
(212) 839-5300 .. **Norell,** Mark O '95 Cnsl Sidley A LLP -787 7th Av -NY 10019
(516) 338-7520 .. **Norelli,** George H '84 (Daniels & N,PC) -900 Merchants Cncrs -Westbury 11590
(718) 459-6000 .. **Norelli,** George H '84 (Pennisi D&N LLP) -97-77 Qns Blvd -Rego Pk 11374
(914) 636-2612 .. **Noren,** Teri L '83 -285 Pinebrook Blvd -New Rchll 10804
(212) 848-4000 .. **Noreuil,** Andrew J '00 %Shearman & S LLP -599 Lex Av -NY 10022
(212) 218-2100 .. **Norey,** Erica L '08 %Fitzpatrick CH&S -1290 Av of Amer -NY 10104
(315) 343-4016 .. **Norfleet,** Doren P '69 -89 E 1st -Oswego 13126 **Fx:**343-0017
(315) 349-3350 .. **Norfleet,** Eben C '97 Family Ct -39 Churchill Rd -Oswego 13126 **Fx:**349-3457
(315) 474-2911 .. **Norfleet,** Kristin Lewis '00 (Smith SK&S,PC) -250 S Clinton -Syracuse 13202
(518) 523-5555 .. **Norfolk,** Matthew D '99 (Briggs N LLP) -2296 Saranac Av -Lk Placid 12946 **Fx:**523-5559
(201) 871-1333 .. **Norgaard,** Gary K '81 (Stern LF&N,LLC) -399 Knollwood Rd -White Plns 10603 **Fx:**871-3161
(518) 429-4200 .. **Norgrove,** Jessica A '02 %Hiscock & B,LLP -50 Beaver -Albany 12207
(845) 750-6386 .. **Nori,** Rekha '99 (Lahiri & N) -254 Fair -Kingston 12401 **Fx:**255-9039
(516) 364-0200 .. **Nori,** Robt '92 Standard Funding Corp -335 Crsswys Park Dr Bx9011 -Syosset 11791
(212) 759-0700 .. **Noriega,** Claude J Jr. '01 %ESR Bd -317 Mad Av -NY 10017
(212) 248-3140 .. **Norin,** Andy S '02 %Drinker B&R LLP -140 Bway -NY 10005
(212) 277-5882 .. **Norins,** Clare R '04 %Beldock L&H LLP -99 Park Av -NY 10016
(212) 791-5396 .. **Norinsberg,** Jon L '92 -225 Bway -NY 10007 **Fx:**406-6890
(718) 254-7000 .. **Norkin,** Walter M '01 US Atty -271 Cadman Plz E -Brklyn 11201 **Fx:**254-6479
(518) 449-3375 .. **Norlander,** Gerald A '73 %Pub Util Law Proj -194 Wshngtn Av -Albany 12210 **Fx:**449-1769
(518) 462-0300 .. **Norlander,** Karen '82 OfCnsl Girvin & F,PC -20 Corp Wds Blvd -Albany 12211
(718) 254-7000 .. **Norling,** Peter A '75 %US Atty -271 Cadman Plz E -Brklyn 11201 **Fx:**254-6479
(518) 449-3900 .. **Norman,** Craig H '78 (Cooper E&S,LLP) -39 N Pearl -Albany 12207
(716) 759-5689 .. **Norman,** Ernest J '71 Wilson Greatbatch Tech -10000 Wehrle Dr -Clarence 14031 **Fx:**759-5672
(718) 261-3047 .. **Norman,** Jennifer R '09 %Queens Law Assoc -118-21 Qns Blvd -Frst Hlls 11375 **Fx:**261-0798
(212) 735-3000 .. **Norman,** Katie '09 %Skadden ASM&F LLP -4 Times Sq -NY 10036
(646) 839-4631 .. **Norman,** Kevin T '06 Shelowitz & Assoc,PLLC -11 Penn Plz -NY 10001
(212) 801-9259 .. **Norman,** Laura S '78 (Greenberg T,LLP) -200 Park Av -NY 10166
(212) 425-1111 .. **Norman,** Milton '48 -61 Bway -NY 10006 **Fx:**425-0422
(212) 455-2000 .. **Norman,** Rise B '89 (Simpson T&B LLP) -425 Lex Av -NY 10017
(212) 640-5583 .. **Norman,** Stephen P '67 %Amer Exp -200 Vesey -NY 10285
(212) 753-5599 .. **Normand,** Ashley E '04 %Brill & M -845 3rd Av -NY 10022
(914) 749-8200 .. **Normand,** Edw J '96 (Boies S&F LLP) -333 Main -Armonk 10504
(212) 637-2709 .. **Normand,** Sarah Sheive '96 %US Atty -86 Chmbrs -NY 10007
(212) 421-4100 .. **Normandin,** Edw C '98 (Pryor C LLP) -7 Times Sq -NY 10036
(716) 687-4270 .. **Norman-Lane,** Deborah '81 %Moog Inc -Seneca & Jamison Rds -E Aurora 14052 **Fx:**687-4457
(516) 560-6400 .. **Normil,** Marie-Andree '06 Leg Aid -1 Helen Keller Way -Hempstd 11550 **Fx:**565-3694
(212) 294-6700 .. **Normile,** James S '77 (Winston & S) -200 Park Av -NY 10166
(212) 326-3939 .. **Normile,** John J '89 (Jones D) -222 E 41st -NY 10017
(607) 763-9200 .. **Normile,** John R Jr. '65 OfCnsl Levene G&T,LLP -BxF-1706 -Bnghmtn 13902
(212) 405-2677 .. **Nornberg,** Eran A '02 C&K Real Properties -675 3rd Av -NY 10017
(631) 249-8200 .. **Nornes,** Pamela J '89 (DePinto N & Assoc,LLP) -445 Broadhllw Rd -Melvll 11747 **Fx:**249-8209
(845) 291-3035 .. **Noroian,** Lisa B '96 %Hon C Klein -285 Main -Goshen 10924 **Fx:**291-4405
(212) 596-9000 .. **Norris,** Anthony J '94 (Ropes & G LLP) -1211 Av of Amer -NY 10036
(914) 428-3313 .. **Norris,** Chas B '86 (Curan AF&N,LLP) -14 Mamaroneck Av -White Plns 10601 **Fx:**949-5800
(718) 254-6376 .. **Norris,** Evan M '03 %US Atty -271 Cadman Plz E -Brklyn 11201 **Fx:**254-6479
(585) 275-2758 .. **Norris,** Gail M '84 %Univ of Rochester Med Ctr -Bx278979 -Rchstr 14627 **Fx:**272-9311
(212) 808-0700 .. **Norris McLaughlin & Marcus,PA** -875 3rd Av -NY 10022 **Fx:**808-0844
(585) 598-7511 .. **Norris,** Michl D '84 Sentry Grp -900 Linden Av -Rchstr 14625
(716) 433-5907 .. **Norris,** Michl J '06 %Seaman JH&B,LLP -76 West Av -Lockprt 14094
(518) 257-3120 .. **Norris,** S Monica '96 Dormitory Auth -515 Bway -Albany 12207 **Fx:**257-3101
(646) 562-3405 .. **Norris,** Sarah '08 %PLC -747 3rd Av -NY 10017
(631) 577-7740 .. **Norris-Poole,** Nicole '94 St Paul Travelers -100 Baylis Rd Bx9093 -Melvll 11747 **Fx:**577-7575
(518) 402-0566 .. **Norrix,** Pamela '86 Cnsl Frshwtr Wtlnds Appls Bd -625 Bway -Albany 12233
(585) 271-4800 .. **Norry,** Lewis A '87 (L Norry,PC) -1465 Monroe Av -Rchstr 14618
(212) 456-7777 .. **North,** Barbara C '78 %ABC -77 W 66th -NY 10023 **Fx:**456-6202
(212) 815-1818 .. **North,** Carol M '83 %DC 37 MELS -125 Barclay -NY 10007 **Fx:**815-1343
(585) 396-4056 .. **North,** Clyde C '81 -27 N Main -Canandaigua 14424
(516) 791-5740 .. **North,** Herbert W '55 -606 Nutley Pl -Vly Stream 11581
(212) 474-1000 .. **North,** Julie A '90 (Cravath S&M LLP) -825 8th Av -NY 10019
(212) 880-9565 .. **North,** Sarah J '05 %Morvillo AGIA&B,PC -565 5th Av -NY 10017
(212) 861-5000 .. **North,** Steven E '67 S North,PC -148 E 74th -NY 10021 **Fx:**861-4055
(914) 761-5628 .. **North,** Wendy L '92 %Underweiser & U LLP -1 Water -White Plns 10601 **Fx:**761-8927
(212) 226-2100 .. **Northcraft,** Dana M '05 %Caesar & N -350 Bway -NY 10013
(718) 596-5168 .. **Northern,** Ann C '85 -26 Court -Brklyn 11242 **Fx:**596-5342
(212) 545-1900 .. **Northey,** Rebecca '79 (Menaker & H LLP) -10 E 40th -NY 10016
(212) 416-8391 .. **Northrop,** Patricia Taibo '99 %Dept of Law -120 Bway -NY 10271
(845) 561-8000 .. **Northrop & Stradar, PC** -1 Corwin Ct Bx2395 -Newburgh 12550 **Fx:**561-2083
(914) 644-9200 .. **Northrup,** Gregory '08 %D Petshaft,PC -222 Bloomingdale Rd -White Plns 10605 **Fx:**644-9300
(518) 402-6723 .. **Northrup,** Kristen H '99 %Ofc of Chldrn & Family Srvcs -52 Wshngtn -Rensselaer 12144
(607) 664-2097 .. **Northrup,** Mary T '09 %DA -3 E Pulteney Sq -Bath 14810 **Fx:**664-2540
(607) 746-3557 .. **Northrup,** Richd D Jr. '84 DA -1 Cthse Sq -Delhi 13753 **Fx:**746-2297
(917) 637-3600 .. **Northup,** Nancy J '89 %Ctr for Reproductive Rts -120 Wall -NY 10005 **Fx:**637-3666
(212) 755-3333 .. **Northwood,** Edw C '82 (SC Ruchelman) -150 E 58th -NY 10155 **Fx:**755-5898
(212) 806-5400 .. **Norton,** Beth A '06 %Stroock &S&L LLP -180 Maiden Ln -NY 10038
(845) 294-7949 .. **Norton & Christensen** -60 Erie Bx308 -Goshen 10924 **Fx:**294-7791
(607) 763-9200 .. **Norton,** Danl R '09 %Levene G&T,LLP -BxF-1706 -Bnghmtn 13902
(716) 852-1000 .. **Norton,** Debra A '80 %PW Beltz,PC -36 Church -Buffalo 14202 **Fx:**852-5887
(585) 271-1500 .. **Norton,** Gerard F Jr. '62 SrCnsl Dibble & M,PC -55 Canterbury Rd -Rchstr 14607
(212) 279-9200 .. **Norton,** Jeanne Anne '97 %Abrams FFEGF&E,LLP -630 3rd Av -NY 10017
(212) 903-9000 .. **Norton,** Jeffrey L '93 (Linklaters) -1345 Av of Amer -NY 10105
(212) 935-7400 .. **Norton,** Jeffrey M '98 (Harwood F LLP) -488 Mad Av -NY 10022
(212) 661-7300 .. **Norton,** Keith J '03 %Malapero & P LLP -295 Mad Av -NY 10017
(631) 328-5040 .. **Norton,** Kyle E '03 -1551 Montauk Hwy -Oakdale 11769
(631) 728-7624 .. **Norton,** Lisa M '94 -51 Palo Alto Dr -Hampton Bays 11946
(212) 297-0100 .. **Norton,** Michl E '76 (Norton & Assoc LLC) -8 W 40th -NY 10018 **Fx:**376-6080
(914) 271-5115 .. **Norton,** Michl J '03 Prudential Albert Real Estate -2 Croton Pnt Av -Croton-On-Hud 10520
(212) 335-4500 .. **Norton,** Miles D '09 %DLA Piper LLP -1251 Av of Amer -NY 10020
(212) 839-5300 .. **Norton,** Patricia V '01 %Sidley A LLP -787 7th Av -NY 10019
(315) 853-4161 .. **Norton,** Paul A '82 -9 E Park Row -Clinton 13323 **Fx:**853-4489
(914) 967-0119 .. **Norton,** Peter J '66 -25 Seneca -Rye 10580
(212) 468-4800 .. **Norton,** Ralph W '87 (Davis & G LLP) -1740 Bway -NY 10019
(212) 309-1000 .. **Norton,** Richd P '01 Cnsl Hunton & W -200 Park Av -NY 10166
(914) 249-2000 .. **Norton,** Robt E Jr. '73 %MasterCard Intl -2000 Purchase -Purchase 10577
(212) 297-5800 .. **Norton,** Robt L '03 Cnsl Day P LLP -7 Times Sq -NY 10036

(212) 872-3351 ..**Norton,** Virginia A '02 KPMG LLP -345 Park Av -NY 10154
(510) 874-1007 ..**Norton,** Wm Fred '03 (Boies S&F LLP) -333 Main -Armonk 10504 **Fx:**874-1460
(518) 428-6771 ..**Nortz,** Scott R '87 -Bx558 -Clayton 13624
(212) 419-1550 ..**Norum,** M Christina '84 CWA Legal Dept -350 7th Av -NY 10001 **Fx:**419-1555
(212) 874-0280 ..**Norwalk,** L Jeffrey '93 -211 W 92nd -NY 10025
(212) 751-4440 ..**Norwick,** Kenneth P '66 Norwick & S -110 E 59th -NY 10022 **Fx:**604-9997
(212) 403-1000 ..**Norwitz,** Trevor S '91 (Wachtell LR&K) -51 W 52nd -NY 10019
(212) 313-1130 ..**Norwood,** Leslie M '99 SIFMA -360 Mad Av -NY 10017
(212) 264-3650 ..**Norwood,** Vernon '06 Cnsl SSA Ofc Genl Cnsl -26 Fed Plz -NY 10278 **Fx:**264-6372
(716) 881-3010 ..**Nosek,** Anthony M '72 OfCnsl Cohen & L,PC -343 Elmwood Av Bx5204 -Buffalo 14213
(516) 479-6300 ..**Nosek,** Robt D '99 %Silverman A LLP -100 Jericho Quad -Jericho 11753
(716) 858-7833 ..**Nosek,** Walter A '81 Dept Soc Srvcs -95 Franklin -Buffalo 14202
(716) 632-5591 ..**Nosenchuck,** Sharon L '95 -Bx1764 -Amherst 14226 **Fx:**632-5591
(212) 218-2100 ..**Nosher,** Todd M '07 %Fitzpatrick CH&S -1290 Av of Amer -NY 10104
(845) 635-5300 ..**Nosonowitz,** Stevan A '86 -1539 Main Bx671 -Plsnt Vlly 12569 **Fx:**635-5100
(212) 964-6611 ..**Noss,** Thos A '08 %Lester SK&D -120 Bway -NY 10271
(212) 715-9100 ..**Nossel,** Deon J '94 %Kramer LN&F,LLP -1177 Av of Amer -NY 10036
(518) 473-7051 ..**Nostramo,** Philip T '77 %OTDA-Fair Hearings -40 N Pearl -Albany 12243 **Fx:**473-6735
(212) 578-8820 ..**Nostramo,** Robt F '91 %MetLife -27-01 Qns Plz N -LIC 11101
(718) 258-3434 ..**Notarbartolo,** Jeffrey R '83 -1978 Flatbush Av -Brklyn 11234 **Fx:**252-3678
(212) 752-3602 ..**Notaris,** James A '95 %Notaris & Assoc -122 E 42nd -NY 10168 **Fx:**688-7519
(212) 967-2229 ..**Notarius,** Milton '49 -1220 Bway -NY 10001 **Fx:**967-2053
(845) 359-7700 ..**Notaro,** Angelo '76 (Notaro M&Z PC) -100 Dutch Hill Rd -Orangebrg 10962
(716) 854-4080 ..**Notaro,** Chas R '86 (Notaro L&N,PC) -1 Niagara Sq -Buffalo 14202 **Fx:**854-0059
(212) 966-7277 ..**Notaro,** Felicia G '85 -350 Bway -NY 10013 **Fx:**966-1302
(914) 698-5700 ..**Notaro,** Jos A '60 -100 Mamaroneck Av -Mamaroneck 10543
(212) 370-4900 ..**Notaro,** Mary G '92 %Rosenthal & H,PC -420 Lex Av -NY 10170
(845) 359-7700 ..**Notaro Michalos & Zaccaria PC** -100 Dutch Hill Rd -Orangebrg 10962 **Fx:**359-7798
(212) 278-8600 ..**Notaro Michalos & Zaccaria PC** -1270 Bway -NY 10001 **Fx:**278-8687
(716) 677-0337 ..**Notaro,** Paul '95 -4268 Seneca -W Seneca 14224
(212) 709-1640 ..**Notaro,** Rosanne '91 %Banking Dept -1 State -NY 10004 **Fx:**709-1655
(716) 845-9439 ..**Notaro,** Thos P '86 %Supreme Ct -25 Delaware Av -Buffalo 14202 **Fx:**851-3293
(212) 788-0771 ..**Noteboom,** Carrie E '04 %Law Dept -100 Church -NY 10007 **Fx:**788-0367
(518) 891-1649 ..**Noth,** Chas J '75 -115 Main -Saranac Lk 12983
(212) 683-2210 ..**Nothenberg,** Shirim '98 %Childrens Rts Inc -330 7th Av -NY 10001 **Fx:**683-4015
(845) 291-3150 ..**Nothnagle,** Matthew J '89 %Cnty Atty -255 Main -Goshen 10924 **Fx:**291-3167
(718) 542-9300 ..**Notice,** James U '03 OfCnsl Rodriguez & F -644 Soundvw Av -Bronx 10473
(212) 686-3838 ..**Notkin,** Deborah J '87 (Barst M&K LLP) -2 Park Av -NY 10016
(212) 541-6222 ..**Notkin,** Ethan '07 %Kane K,PC -1350 Av of Amer -NY 10019
(585) 232-1780 ..**Noto,** Anthony C '63 -1 E Main -Rchstr 14614 **Fx:**232-2134
(516) 498-3670 ..**Noto,** Dino G '88 1st Quality Entrprs,Inc -80 Cuttermill Rd -Gt Neck 11021 **Fx:**498-2444
(631) 666-8755 ..**Noto,** Janis M '90 -134 4th Av -Bay Shr 11706 **Fx:**666-0025
(585) 263-6760 ..**Noto,** Jennifer M '03 US Atty -620 Fed Bldg -Rchstr 14614 **Fx:**263-6226
(585) 263-1000 ..**Noto,** Jos M '01 (Nixon P LLP) -1100 Clinton Sq -Rchstr 14604
(585) 232-1815 ..**Noto,** Louis C '70 -16 Main E -Rchstr 14614 **Fx:**325-4559
(718) 723-5954 ..**Noto,** Marie C '03 DHS -1 Cross Isl Plz -Rosedale 11422
(718) 605-3100 ..**Noto,** Michl A '81 (Noto & Assoc,PC) -4041 Hylan Blvd -Staten Isl 10308 **Fx:**605-3400
(914) 698-9331 ..**Noto,** Paul J '81 -650 Halstead Av -Mamaroneck 10543 **Fx:**698-2148
(718) 237-2323 ..**Noto,** Peter J '82 %Noto & N PLLC -326 Atl Av -Brklyn 11201 **Fx:**237-2904
(212) 595-4028 ..**Noto,** Sabato J '83 -147 W 80th -NY 10024 **Fx:**787-5601
(718) 237-2323 ..**Noto,** Steven '09 %Noto & N PLLC -326 Atl Av -Brklyn 11201 **Fx:**237-2904
(718) 254-7000 ..**Notopoulos,** Patricia E '82 %US Atty -271 Cadman Plz E -Brklyn 11201 **Fx:**254-6479
(718) 250-2000 ..**Nottage,** Aaron M '95 %DA -350 Jay -Brklyn 11201 **Fx:**250-2314
(212) 431-1300 ..**Notte,** Craig M '97 %Borah GAN&G PC -377 Bway -NY 10013
(212) 325-7229 ..**Nottebohm,** Barbara H '95 CSFB -1 Mad Av -NY 10010
(914) 333-0700 ..**Nottes,** Danl B '09 %Snyder & S -94 Wht Plns Rd -Tarrytwn 10591 **Fx:**333-0743
(212) 969-2242 ..**Notto,** Danl A '99 %Alliance Bernstein LP -1345 Av of Amer -NY 10105 **Fx:**554-4639
(212) 577-2800 ..**Noumair,** James J '96 %Sexter & W -115 Bway -NY 10006
(212) 952-6200 ..**Nourse & Bowles, LLP** -55 Bway -NY 10006 **Fx:**952-0345
(212) 952-6200 ..**Nourse,** David A '65 (Nourse & B,LLP) -55 Bway -NY 10006
(914) 276-3720 ..**Nourse,** Hazel W '83 -376 Route 202 -Somers 10589
(914) 749-8200 ..**Nousek,** Lisa M '07 %Boies S&F LLP -333 Main -Armonk 10504
(212) 553-5523 ..**Nousias,** Olga '04 Zurich Ins NA -1 Lbrty Plz -NY 10006
(212) 852-7724 ..**Nova,** Janet Lapidus '93 %News America Inc -1211 Av of Amer -NY 10036
(212) 682-4002 ..**Novack Burnbaum Crystal LLP** -300 E 42nd -NY 10017 **Fx:**986-2907
(212) 536-3900 ..**Novack,** Gerald A '70 (K&L Gates LLP) -599 Lex Av -NY 10022
(212) 728-8000 ..**Novack,** Jeffrey A '09 %Willkie F&G LLP -787 7th Av -NY 10019
(212) 682-4002 ..**Novack,** Martin '54 (Novack BC LLP) -300 E 42nd -NY 10017
(518) 471-4777 ..**Novack,** Michl J '72 %Appllt Div 3rd Dept -Capitol Station Bx7288 -Albany 12224 **Fx:**471-4750
(212) 682-8800 ..**Novack,** Mindy C '85 %Brooks Bros Inc -346 Mad Av -NY 10017
(212) 308-4411 ..**Novack,** Robt '85 (Edwards AP&D LLP) -750 Lex Av -NY 10022
(585) 722-9349 ..**Novais,** David A '99 Eastman Kodak -343 State -Rchstr 14650
(212) 810-5462 ..**Novak,** Andrew S '94 %BlackRock Inc -40 E 52nd -NY 10022
(212) 422-0202 ..**Novak,** Christopher C '95 (Sedgwick DM&A LLP) -125 Broad -NY 10004
(914) 271-6633 ..**Novak,** Dale M '90 -1 Baltic Pl -Croton-On-Hud 10520 **Fx:**827-8270
(718) 286-6000 ..**Novak,** Danl A '03 DA -125-01 Qns Blvd -Kew Gdns 11415
(212) 588-5500 ..**Novak,** Darren W T '00 Cnsl Davies WP&V LLP -625 Mad Av -NY 10022
(718) 250-2000 ..**Novak,** Diana '93 %DA -350 Jay -Brklyn 11201 **Fx:**250-2314
(212) 944-0500 ..**Novak,** Edwin A '79 (Hofheimer G&G,LLP) -530 5th Av -NY 10036 **Fx:**897-6931
(585) 232-6500 ..**Novak,** Frank A III '95 (Harter S&E LLP) -1600 Bausch & Lomb Pl -Rchstr 14604
(516) 569-3030 ..**Novak,** G Alexander '80 (Novak J&S) -483 Chestnut -Cedarhrst 11516
(585) 442-7084 ..**Novak,** George J '70 (Novak & N) -100 Harvard -Rchstr 14607
(212) 782-4633 ..**Novak,** Jane Cotton '88 %Bk of Tokyo-Mitsubishi -1251 Av of Amer -NY 10020 **Fx:**782-6420
(631) 725-3785 ..**Novak,** John P '75 -24 Palmer Ter Bx990 -Sag Hbr 11963 **Fx:**725-3874
(516) 569-3030 ..**Novak Juhase & Stern** -483 Chestnut -Cedarhrst 11516 **Fx:**569-3039
(516) 240-8900 ..**Novak,** Lawr S '90 (Torre LGG&R,LLP) -100 Jericho Quad -Jericho 11753
(212) 833-5031 ..**Novak,** Linda '83 %Sony Music Entrtnmnt,Inc -550 Mad Av -NY 10022
(585) 442-7084 ..**Novak,** Margo H '72 (Novak & N) -100 Harvard -Rchstr 14607
(212) 867-4100 ..**Novak,** Maria '08 %Furman K&B LLP -61 Bway -NY 10006
(212) 681-2901 ..**Novak,** Richd E '90 -244 Mad Av -NY 10016
(212) 220-3830 ..**Novak,** Robt A '91 (Nicoletti H&S) -88 Pine -NY 10005
(917) 637-3600 ..**Novak,** Suzanne I '98 %Ctr for Reproductive Rts -120 Wall -NY 10005 **Fx:**637-3666
(212) 761-0147 ..**Novak,** Tasneem S '08 %Morgan Stanley -1585 Bway -NY 10036
(718) 590-2000 ..**Novak,** Wm P '07 %DA -198 E 161st -Bronx 10451 **Fx:**590-6477
(212) 723-3036 ..**Novakova,** Jelena '05 Citigroup -250 West -NY 10013
(212) 431-2355 ..**Noveck,** Beth Simone '98 NY Law Schl -185 W Bway -NY 10013 **Fx:**791-2144
(212) 431-1300 ..**Novella,** Anthony J '04 %Borah GAN&G PC -377 Bway -NY 10013
(212) 962-0732 ..**November,** Philip R '74 -291 Bway -NY 10007 **Fx:**349-2837
(914) 241-2400 ..**Novenstern Fabriani & Gaudio** -69 S Bedford Rd -Mt Kisco 10549 **Fx:**241-2402
(914) 241-2400 ..**Novenstern,** Kenneth J '85 (Novenstern F&G) -69 S Bedford Rd -Mt Kisco 10549
(212) 836-8000 ..**Novetsky,** Terry D '85 (Kaye S LLP) -425 Park Av -NY 10022
(212) 989-9100 ..**Novick,** Andrea T '78 (Finder NK LLP) -276 Park Av S -NY 10010
(631) 547-0300 ..**Novick,** Donald '78 (Novick & Assoc,PC) -202 E Main -Huntngtn 11743 **Fx:**547-0212
(914) 375-0100 ..**Novick Edelstein Lubell Reisman Wasserman & Leventhal, PC** -733 Ynkrs Av -Ynkrs 10704 **Fx:**375-0699
(516) 224-5100 ..**Novick,** Jeffrey M '68 J Novick -100 Crsswys Park W -Woodbury 11797 **Fx:**422-6199
(914) 636-7100 ..**Novick & Kaner** -56 Harrison -New Rchll 10801 **Fx:**636-7791
(718) 596-7800 ..**Novick,** Marc A '95 %Peters BK&G,PC -26 Court -Brklyn 11242
(845) 896-9600 ..**Novick,** Philip B '93 -1065 Main -Fishkill 12524 **Fx:**896-9652
(212) 474-1000 ..**Novick,** Robt E '77 %Cravath S&M LLP -825 8th Av -NY 10019
(212) 506-1700 ..**Novick,** Robt M '94 (Kasowitz BT&F LLP) -1633 Bway -NY 10019
(212) 687-0188 ..**Novick,** Shana R '82 Hebrew Free Loan Society -205 E 42nd -NY 10017
(914) 288-9595 ..**Novick,** Ted A '90 (Gaines GP&N,LLP) -1 N Bway -White Plns 10601
(845) 225-4004 ..**Noviello,** Matthew A '85 (Noviello & N) -77 Hughson Rd -Carmel 10512
(212) 458-1078 ..**Novik,** Svetlana '02 AIG -175 Water -NY 10038
(212) 909-6000 ..**Novik,** Vadim '10 %Debevoise & P LLP -919 3rd Av -NY 10022
(212) 594-5000 ..**Novikoff,** Elyse F '09 %Togut S&S LLP -1 Penn Plz -NY 10119
(212) 403-1000 ..**Novikoff,** Harold S '76 (Wachtell LR&K) -51 W 52nd -NY 10019
(516) 357-3000 ..**Novikoff,** Kenneth A '91 (Rivkin R LLP) -926 RXR Plz -Uniondale 11556
(212) 801-6718 ..**Novikoff,** Neil '80 (Greenberg T,LLP) -200 Park Av -NY 10166
(212) 552-3131 ..**Novikov,** Vladimir '00 JP Morgan Chase -1 Chase Manh Plz -NY 10005
(212) 601-9700 ..**Novins,** Gary R '93 %Ginarte OGG&W,LLP -225 Bway -NY 10007
(718) 544-8665 ..**Novitt,** Donald S '81 (Novitt S&S,LLP) -118-35 Qns Blvd -Frst Hlls 11375
(718) 544-8665 ..**Novitt Sahr & Snow, LLP** -118-35 Qns Blvd -Frst Hlls 11375 **Fx:**544-5703
(631) 539-0375 ..**Novitz,** Rondiene E '97 (Cruser M&N,LLP) -175 Pinelawn Rd -Melvll 11747
(914) 948-6764 ..**Novo,** Guy P '78 -14 Townsend Av -Hartsdale 10530 **Fx:**761-3382
(212) 209-4800 ..**Novod,** Gordon Z '02 (Brown R LLP) -7 Times Sq -NY 10036
(212) 233-6686 ..**Novofastovsky,** Ilya '03 (Novo Law Firm,PC) -299 Bway -NY 10007 **Fx:**233-6687
(212) 715-9100 ..**Novogrod,** John C '68 (Kramer LN&F,LLP) -1177 Av of Amer -NY 10036
(212) 318-6000 ..**Novomisle,** Wm A '06 %Paul HJ&W LLP -75 E 55th -NY 10022
(518) 449-8893 ..**Novotny,** F Douglas '80 (Wilson EME&D LLP) -677 Bway -Albany 12207
(716) 845-2560 ..**Novotny,** Linda C '77 %Surrogates Ct -92 Franklin -Buffalo 14202 **Fx:**853-3741
(212) 551-5476 ..**Nowack,** Andrew P '94 %Royal Alliance Assoc -1 World Fncl Ctr -NY 10281 **Fx:**551-5620
(212) 264-1963 ..**Nowadly,** Kristen M '99 %US GSA -26 Fed Plz -NY 10278 **Fx:**264-1987
(631) 726-8000 ..**Nowak,** Ann L '89 -Montauk Hwy Bx1290 -Water Mill 11976
(718) 590-2000 ..**Nowak,** Christina '06 DA -198 E 161st -Bronx 10451 **Fx:**590-6477
(716) 853-3801 ..**Nowak,** James S '92 (Kenney SL&N,LLP) -14 Lafayette Sq -Buffalo 14203
(212) 720-3700 ..**Nowak,** Jeremy L '82 %Foot Locker,Inc -112 W 34th -NY 10120 **Fx:**720-4116

(212) 732-3200 .. **Nowak**, Keith D '79 (Carter L&M LLP) -2 Wall -NY 10005
(973) 623-1822 .. **Nowak**, Kenneth I '81 (Zazzali FNK&F) -15 W 72nd -NY 10023 **Fx**:(212) 875-8275
(518) 374-3399 .. **Nowak**, Matthew T '09 %Higgins RB&C,PC -1430 Balltown Rd -Niskayuna 12309
(716) 845-1802 .. **Nowak**, Michl S '73 Supreme Ct -25 Delaware Av -Buffalo 14202 **Fx**:851-3293
(212) 450-4000 .. **Nowak**, Rafal A '04 %Davis P&W LLP -450 Lex Av -NY 10017
(516) 487-8200 .. **Nowak**, Robt E '65 -107 Nrthrn Blvd -Gt Neck 11021 **Fx**:487-4923
(585) 263-5812 .. **Nowak**, Trudy A '80 %US Trustees Ofc -100 State -Rchstr 14614 **Fx**:263-5862
(518) 473-5671 .. **Nowak**, Wm A III '91 %Div of Parole -97 Central Av -Albany 12206 **Fx**:473-6037
(716) 848-1100 .. **Nowakowski**, Wm E '85 -63 Hallam Rd -Buffalo 14216
(212) 858-7710 .. **Nowell Amoroso Klein Bierman,PA** -140 Bway PMB 46028 -NY 10005 **Fx**:858-7750
(212) 837-6000 .. **Nowell**, Tiffany M '06 %Hughes H&R LLP -1 Bttry Pk Plz -NY 10004
(212) 753-0300 .. **Nowick**, Neil A '75 (Dahan & N LLP) -1700 Bway -NY 10019
(212) 733-2113 .. **Nowicki**, Edw J Jr. '00 Pfizer -150 E 42nd -NY 10017
(518) 474-6026 .. **Nowicki**, Heather J '91 %State Comptroller -110 State -Albany 12236 **Fx**:473-9104
(212) 736-4201 .. **Nowokunski**, Joanne E '07 Ross & A LLC -270 Mad Av -NY 10016 **Fx**:736-2873
(518) 792-1880 .. **Nowotny**, Maria G '83 -16 Pearl -Glens Fls 12801 **Fx**:743-8204
(212) 538-4579 .. **Nowrojee**, Eruch P '98 Credit Suisse -11 Mad Av -NY 10010
(212) 662-0249 .. **Nowve**, Donald '80 -225 W 106th -NY 10025
(212) 832-5001 .. **Noy**, Isaac I '92 -336 E 59th -NY 10022 **Fx**:832-6990
(212) 832-1117 .. **Noy**, Jack '97 %DeBaron Assoc,Ltd -336 E 59th -NY 10022
(315) 363-6580 .. **Noyes**, Paul V '58 -131 Sherrill Rd -Sherrill 13461 **Fx**:363-4166
(212) 509-5050 .. **Noyes**, Peter C '91 SrCnsl Wuersch & G LLP -100 Wall -NY 10005
(718) 694-3887 .. **Noymer**, Carol '75 %Transit Auth -130 Lvngstn -Brklyn 11201 **Fx**:694-5726
(718) 382-4300 .. **Nozzolillo**, Anthony A '04 (A Nozzolillo,PC) -1729 E 12th -Brklyn 11229 **Fx**:943-6752
(585) 419-8800 .. **Nozzolio**, Michl F '80 OfCnsl Harris B PLLC -99 Garnsey Rd -Pittsfrd 14534
(212) 735-3000 .. **Ntonme**, Saml K '09 %Skadden ASM&F LLP -4 Times Sq -NY 10036
(518) 828-4065 .. **Nucci**, Georgia F '97 -46 Green -Hudson 12534
(347) 296-1016 .. **Nuccio**, Paul V '94 %Hon J Starkey-Supreme Ct -320 Jay -Brklyn 11201
(212) 907-0700 .. **Nuccitelli**, Tina '06 %Labaton S LLP -140 Bway -NY 10005
(716) 858-8148 .. **Nuchereno**, Barbara S '88 %Family Ct -1 Niagara Plz -Buffalo 14202
(716) 875-2503 .. **Nuchereno**, John R '78 -2503 Niagara -Buffalo 14207 **Fx**:873-1780
(212) 269-0927 .. **Nudel**, Rachel '06 %D'Amato & L,LLP -2 World Fncl Ctr -NY 10281
(212) 701-3000 .. **Nudelman**, Michele A '10 %Cahill G&R LLP -80 Pine -NY 10005 **Fx**:269-5420
(212) 891-9100 .. **Nudelman**, Nathan C '99 %Goldfarb & F LLP -345 Park Av -NY 10154
(212) 677-7171 .. **Nudelman**, Phyllis R '86 (Trst for Public Land) -666 Bway -NY 10012 **Fx**:353-2052
(631) 499-3015 .. **Nudelman**, Susan R '80 -92 Stonehurst Ln -Dix Hlls 11746 **Fx**:499-4727
(518) 402-6057 .. **Nuding**, Kathryn M '94 %Workers Comp Bd -20 Park -Albany 12207
(631) 689-7223 .. **Nudo**, Nicholas M III '84 -5 Glenrdg Av -Stony Brk 11790 **Fx**:689-2978
(845) 353-2000 .. **Nugent**, Brian D '05 %Feerick LM PLLC -96 S Bway -Nyack 10960
(716) 885-1150 .. **Nugent**, Carolyn M '06 %Drew & D,LLP -159 Linwood Av -Buffalo 14209 **Fx**:884-3707
(212) 326-2000 .. **Nugent**, Christian C '00 (O'Melveny & M LLP) -7 Times Sq -NY 10036
(516) 355-0050 .. **Nugent**, Colum P '70 -882 Hempstd Tpk -Franklin Sq 11010 **Fx**:355-5086
(212) 735-3000 .. **Nugent**, Eileen '79 (Skadden ASM&F LLP) -4 Times Sq -NY 10036
(315) 425-2700 .. **Nugent**, Gabriel M '99 (Hiscock & B,LLP) -One Park Pl -Syracuse 13202
(631) 691-0100 .. **Nugent**, Glenn T '90 %B Kennedy,PC -31 Greene Av -Amityvll 11701 **Fx**:691-1029
(631) 853-5212 .. **Nugent**, Jos M II '94 %Leg Aid -400 Carleton Av Bx9082 -Central Islip 11722 **Fx**:853-7798
(718) 250-2000 .. **Nugent**, Lisa A '08 %DA -350 Jay -Brklyn 11201 **Fx**:250-2314
(631) 587-3398 .. **Nugent**, Raymond J '59 -461 E Bay 4th -W Islip 11795
(212) 504-6000 .. **Nugent**, Richd M '96 (Cadwalader W&T LLP) -1 World Fncl Ctr -NY 10281
(518) 479-1405 .. **Nugent**, Timothy '82 -579 Columbia Tpk -E Greenbush 12061 **Fx**:477-2165
(516) 248-7000 .. **Nugent**, Wm J III '99 %Albanese & A LLP -1050 Franklin Av -Gdn Cty 11530
(315) 422-1152 .. **Nuhfer**, Jennifer L '05 %Costello C&F,PLLC -500 Plum -Syracuse 13204
(212) 574-1200 .. **Nuland**, Anthony C J '69 (Seward & K LLP) -1 Bttry Pk Plz -NY 10004
(212) 521-5400 .. **Null**, James S H '09 %Reed S LLP -599 Lex Av -NY 10022
(914) 761-1300 .. **Null**, Wm S '81 (Cuddy & F LLP) -445 Hmltn Av -White Plns 10601
(646) 428-3900 .. **Nunberg**, Miriam Augusta '98 Dept of Educ -32 Old Slip -NY 10005 **Fx**:428-3890
(516) 294-8844 .. **Nunberg**, Noah '78 (L'Abbate BC&C,LLP) -1001 Franklin Av -Gdn Cty 11530
(212) 570-0749 .. **Nunberg**, Rebecca Citron '79 -535 E 86th -NY 10028
(516) 229-6000 .. **Nunemaker**, James P Jr. '75 %R Lau & Assoc -300 Jericho Quad Bx9040 -Jericho 11753 **Fx**:229-6167
(212) 626-4100 .. **Nunes**, Jerry M '05 %Baker & M LLP -1114 Av of Amer -NY 10036
(212) 906-1200 .. **Nunes**, Jonathan A '02 %Latham & W -885 3rd Av -NY 10022
(585) 258-2800 .. **Nunes**, Paul V '78 (Underberg & K LLP) -300 Bausch & Lomb Pl -Rchstr 14604
(212) 509-6888 .. **Nunez**, Altagracia M '04 %J Getreu,PC -132 Nassau -NY 10038
(718) 590-3584 .. **Nunez**, Anthony M '96 Supreme Ct -851 Grnd Cncrs -Bronx 10451
(212) 442-1400 .. **Núñez**, Dinorah S '02 Conflicts of Int Bd -2 Lafayette -NY 10007 **Fx**:442-1407
(212) 446-2300 .. **Nunez**, Francisco R '09 %Boies S&F LLP -575 Lex Av -NY 10022
(718) 515-6000 .. **Nunez**, Richd E '86 %Corpina PK&P,LLP -2344 Eastchstr Rd -Bronx 10469
(845) 223-6993 .. **Nunez**, Richd J '02 Liberty Hall Family -1075 Route 82 -Hopewell Junct 12533
(718) 250-2000 .. **Nunez**, Victoria A '06 %DA -350 Jay -Brklyn 11201 **Fx**:250-2314
(212) 269-5500 .. **Nungesser**, Donald M '05 %Gordon & R LLP -90 Broad -NY 10004
(718) 590-2000 .. **Nunley**, Michl G '09 %DA -198 E 161st -Bronx 10451 **Fx**:590-6477
(516) 571-2915 .. **Nunn**, Christina V '06 %DA -262 Old Cntry Rd -Mineola 11501 **Fx**:571-1119
(585) 546-5270 .. **Nunn**, Mark S '82 (Fitzsimmons NF&P,LLP) -16 E Main -Rchstr 14614
(212) 558-4000 .. **Nunn**, Robin '07 %Sullivan & C LLP -125 Broad -NY 10004
(718) 261-7700 .. **Nunziata**, Marianne '03 %Rappaport HC&R,PC -118-35 Qns Blvd -Frst Hlls 11375
(212) 408-5100 .. **Nurgaziyeva**, Saule A '06 %Chadbourne & P LLP -30 Rckfllr Plz -NY 10112
(212) 351-4000 .. **Nurhussein**, Siham '07 %Gibson D&C LLP -200 Park Av -NY 10166
(212) 637-3195 .. **Nurkin**, Gary H '83 %EPA -290 Bway -NY 10007 **Fx**:637-3096
(212) 878-8000 .. **Nurmohamed**, Lateef '08 %Clifford C LLP -31 W 52nd -NY 10019
(212) 848-4000 .. **Nurmohamed**, Nadir '07 %Shearman & S LLP -599 Lex Av -NY 10022
(212) 294-6700 .. **Nurnberg**, Peter M '07 %Winston & S -200 Park Av -NY 10166
(212) 541-6222 .. **Nurnberg**, Ronald L '71 (Kane K,PC) -1350 Av of Amer -NY 10019
(914) 253-2000 .. **Nurse**, Brian M '97 %Pepsico -700 Andrsn Hill Rd -Purchase 10577
(212) 662-9034 .. **Nurse**, Eloise M '97 -208 W 119th -NY 10026
(718) 838-7878 .. **Nurse**, Jenay A '07 %Bronx Defenders -860 Crtlandt Av -Bronx 10451 **Fx**:665-0100
(212) 402-4100 .. **Nursey**, Jos M '93 %Ofc Appllt Def -11 Park Pl -NY 10007 **Fx**:402-4199
(212) 808-7800 .. **Nuruddin**, Nafees '09 %Kelley D&W LLP -101 Park Av -NY 10178
(914) 332-1500 .. **Nurzia**, Peter L '92 (Berry & N,LLP) -660 Wht Plns Rd -Tarrytwn 10591 **Fx**:332-1777
(212) 837-6000 .. **Nusbacher**, Gloria W '76 Cnsl Hughes H&R LLP -1 Bttry Pk Plz -NY 10004
(585) 987-2800 .. **Nusbaum**, Beryl '58 (Woods OG LLP) -2 State -Rchstr 14614
(212) 728-8000 .. **Nusbaum**, Jack H '65 (Willkie F&G LLP) -787 7th Av -NY 10019
(212) 768-6700 .. **Nusbaum**, Keith C '09 %Sonnenschein N&R LLP -1221 Av of Amer -NY 10020
(914) 654-0100 .. **Nusbaum**, Lawr G Jr. '56 -230 Pelham Rd -New Rchll 10805 **Fx**:654-1190
(212) 269-1400 .. **Nusbaum**, Lawr G III '87 (Gusrae KB&N PLLC) -120 Wall -NY 10005
(212) 592-1400 .. **Nusbaum**, Matt A D '09 %Herrick,F LLP -2 Park Av -NY 10016
(585) 987-2800 .. **Nusbaum**, Mitchell S '89 (Woods OG LLP) -2 State -Rchstr 14614
(212) 969-3000 .. **Nussbaum**, Amanda H '99 (Proskauer R LLP) -1585 Bway -NY 10036
(212) 403-1000 .. **Nussbaum**, Andrew J '93 (Wachtell LR&K) -51 W 52nd -NY 10019
(212) 403-1000 .. **Nussbaum**, Bernard W '62 (Wachtell LR&K) -51 W 52nd -NY 10019
(212) 545-4770 .. **Nussbaum**, Brett D '91 (Wolf HAF&H LLP) -270 Mad Av -NY 10016
(585) 263-1000 .. **Nussbaum**, Carolyn G '82 (Nixon P LLP) -1100 Clinton Sq -Rchstr 14604
(212) 571-7100 .. **Nussbaum**, Craig R '03 OfCnsl O'Dwyer & B,LLP -52 Duane -NY 10007
(212) 661-4202 .. **Nussbaum**, David M '81 Early Bird Cptl -275 Mad Av -NY 10016 **Fx**:661-4936
(212) 582-3636 .. **Nussbaum**, Donald M '74 -250 W 57th -NY 10107
(212) 790-9200 .. **Nussbaum**, Jeremy '68 (Cowan L&L,PC) -1133 Av of Amer -NY 10036
(212) 687-1980 .. **Nussbaum**, Linda P '78 (Kaplan F&K LLP) -850 3rd Av -NY 10022
(212) 344-8000 .. **Nussbaum**, Mark J '09 %Altman & S LLP -225 Bway -NY 10007
(212) 698-3500 .. **Nussbaum**, Martin '71 (Dechert LLP) -1095 Av of Amer -NY 10036
(212) 788-1178 .. **Nussbaum**, Martin '78 %Law Dept -100 Church -NY 10007 **Fx**:788-0367
(212) 407-4000 .. **Nussbaum**, Mitchell S '94 (Loeb & L,LLP) -345 Park Av -NY 10154
(718) 884-8203 .. **Nussbaum**, Robin Lynn '88 DEP -66 John -NY 10038 **Fx**:543-6541
(212) 363-2900 .. **Nussbaum**, Ronald J '72 OfCnsl Krieger & P LLP -39 Bway -NY 10006
(212) 318-3000 .. **Nussbaum**, Sheldon G '83 (Fulbright & J LLP) -666 5th Av -NY 10103
(212) 635-8203 .. **Nussbaum**, Stacey B '03 Bank of NY Capl Mrkts -1 Wall -NY 10005
(845) 255-0743 .. **Nussbaum**, Steven '88 -108 Main -New Paltz 12561 **Fx**:255-0987
(212) 582-3826 .. **Nussbaum**, Theo S '61 -575 Mad Av -NY 10022
(212) 272-4339 .. **Nussbaum**, Yosef M '03 %JP Morgan Chase -383 Mad Av -NY 10179
(212) 617-3473 .. **Nussbaum Fisher**, Leana B '99 Bloomberg LP -731 Lex Av -NY 10022
(718) 286-6000 .. **Nussdorf**, Harry '79 %DA -125-01 Qns Blvd -Kew Gdns 11415
(212) 370-1300 .. **Nutman**, Midge J '85 OfCnsl Ellenoff G&S LLP -150 E 42nd -NY 10017
(212) 421-9100 .. **Nutovic**, Isaac '80 -488 Mad Av -NY 10022
(716) 375-2260 .. **Nuttall**, Steven R '83 %Philosophy Department -St Bonaventure Univ Bx92 -St Bonaventure 14778
(212) 925-5040 .. **Nutter**, Caitlin N '09 %R Darby -20 Vesey -NY 10007 **Fx**:732-4648
(585) 327-4100 .. **Nutter**, John C '07 %Leclair KGC,LLP -150 State -Rchstr 14614 **Fx**:327-4200
(585) 272-0540 .. **Nutter-Singal**, Hannah '07 %Thomas & S LLP -693 East Av -Rchstr 14607
(212) 682-0655 .. **Nuwesra**, Lee S '92 -1623 Unionport Rd -Bronx 10462
(212) 436-2000 .. **Nuyen**, Julie T '10 Deloitte & Touche,LLP -2 World Fncl Ctr -NY 10281
(212) 903-9000 .. **Nuzbach**, Carly K '09 %Linklaters -1345 Av of Amer -NY 10105
(212) 682-3025 .. **Nuzov**, Ilya '05 %Weiss & L -551 5th Av -NY 10176
(212) 335-9000 .. **Nuzzi**, Steven A '83 %DA -1 Hogan Pl -NY 10013
(516) 328-6500 .. **Nuzzolese**, Gus P '86 %Sutton & Edwards -1981 Marcus Av -Lk Success 11042 **Fx**:328-6749
(212) 455-2000 .. **Nwabuzor**, Ekwutozia U '09 %Simpson T&B LLP -425 Lex Av -NY 10017
(718) 629-5888 .. **Nwachukwu**, Grace '99 -4703 Av D -Brklyn 11203

(516) 481-6082 .. **Nwadiogbu,** C Angela '00 %A Denaro,PC -62 Nichols Ct -Hempstd 11550 **Fx:**481-6302
(718) 703-3200 .. **Nwaigwe,** Josephine C '97 -2135 Caton Av -Brklyn 11226
(607) 974-3455 .. **Nwaneri,** Angela Ngozi '99 Corning Inc - Patent Dept -SP-TI-3 -Corning 14831
(516) 565-2004 .. **Nwanyanwu,** Anele O '98 Anele & Assoc -33 Main Bx146 -Hempstd 11551 **Fx:**565-2006
(212) 318-6000 .. **Nwaobi,** Debbie E '00 %Paul HJ&W LLP -75 E 55th -NY 10022
(212) 629-8979 .. **Nwauwa,** Ngozi A '92 -307 7th Av -NY 10001 **Fx:**629-8909
(718) 743-9333 .. **Nwele,** Kenneth F '00 -1209 Av Z -Brklyn 11235 **Fx:**743-4334
(718) 876-6300 .. **Nwikpo-Oppong,** Maurice K '05 DA -130 Styvsnt Pl -Staten Isl 10301
(212) 330-9137 .. **Nwogu,** Tiwa A '09 -1133 Bway -NY 10010 **Fx:**330-9138
(212) 964-7400 .. **Nwokoro,** Chukwuemeka '98 %Smith MDWY&Y,PC -111 John -NY 10038
(212) 373-3000 .. **Nyarady,** Catherine '97 (Paul WRW&G LLP) -1285 Av of Amer -NY 10019
(212) 869-3500 .. **Nyberg,** Christopher M '09 %J Fuchsberg Law Firm,LLP -500 5th Av -NY 10110 **Fx:**398-1532
(518) 487-7600 .. **Nye,** Jonathan P '83 (Whiteman O&H LLP) -1 Commerce Plz -Albany 12260
(516) 739-0000 .. **Nyear,** Jodi M '03 %Martyn T&M -330 Old Cntry Rd -Mineola 11501
(212) 819-8200 .. **Nyer,** Damien P X '08 %White & C LLP -1155 Av of Amer -NY 10036
(212) 806-5400 .. **Nygard,** James O '99 SpclCnsl Stroock &S&L LLP -180 Maiden Ln -NY 10038
(212) 768-6700 .. **Nygard,** Stephanie G '97 (Sonnenschein N&R LLP) -2 World Fncl Ctr -NY 10281
(212) 350-2700 .. **Nyhan,** Adam T '05 %Constantine C,PC -450 Lex Av -NY 10017
(718) 694-3859 .. **Nyhus-O'Shea,** Barbara A '83 %Transit Auth -130 Lvngstn -Brklyn 11201 **Fx:**694-5726
(718) 254-7000 .. **Nyiendo,** Licha M '04 US Atty -271 Cadman Plz E -Brklyn 11201 **Fx:**254-6479
(716) 675-1066 .. **Nyitrai,** Thos A '00 E Snyder -3976 Seneca -W Seneca 14224 **Fx:**674-4772
(631) 727-2180 .. **Nykamp,** Philip D '96 OfCnsl Twomey LSKD&Q,LLP -33 W 2nd Bx9398 -Rvrhead 11901
(914) 337-4469 .. **Nyland,** W Donald '58 -81 Pondfld Rd -Bronxvll 10708 **Fx:**337-4581
(716) 355-2740 .. **Nyweide,** Crandall G '93 -562 Clymer-Sherman Rd Bx369 -Clymer 14724 **Fx:**355-6167
(718) 522-3333 .. **Oakes,** Anamary L '95 %Children's Law Ctr -44 Court -Brklyn 11201 **Fx:**522-7376
(585) 419-8800 .. **Oakes,** David W '85 (Harris B PLLC) -99 Garnsey Rd -Pittsfrd 14534
(315) 349-3200 .. **Oakes,** Gregory S '01 %DA -Pub Safety Ctr -Oswego 13126 **Fx:**349-3212
(607) 231-5900 .. **Oakes,** Susan '01 %Leg Aid -30 Fayette -Bnghmtn 13901 **Fx:**724-7211
(646) 746-9700 .. **Oakland,** David W '00 CFTC -140 Bway -NY 10005 **Fx:**746-9938
(631) 474-3116 .. **Oakley,** Brian G '98 -Bx628 -Stony Brk 11790 **Fx:**474-3116
(518) 431-6700 .. **Oakley,** David J '81 Cnsl Manatt P&P,LLP -30 S Pearl -Albany 12207
(718) 780-3620 .. **Oami,** Emily R '01 NYM Fed Credit Union -501 6th -Brklyn 11215
(315) 788-5100 .. **Oastler,** Bradley W '10 %Conboy MB&K,LLP -407 Sherman -Watertwn 13601
(212) 854-2210 .. **Oates,** Anne Louise '78 %Columbia Univ -535 W 116th 412 Low Mem'l Library -NY 10027
(212) 446-4800 .. **Oates,** M Mitchell '06 %Kirkland & E LLP -153 E 53rd -NY 10022
(585) 428-5210 .. **Oathout,** Bryan '07 %Pub Def -10 N Fitzhugh -Rchstr 14614 **Fx:**428-2234
(631) 420-9300 .. **Obasanjo,** Olumuyiwa G '05 (Obasanjo & S LLP) -445 Broadhllw Rd -Melvll 11747 **Fx:**465-7052
(212) 905-7500 .. **Obasi,** Obasi Okafor '04 DeNovo Legal LLC -150 E 42nd -NY 10017
(212) 274-6003 .. **Obayi,** Nenna M '95 %ACS-Foster Care Litgtn Unit -220 Church -NY 10013
(631) 232-3400 .. **Obedin,** Glenn A '88 -320 Carleton Av -Central Islip 11722 **Fx:**232-5343
(212) 616-3040 .. **Obeid,** Fran '96 (Obeid & L,LLP) -111 Bway -NY 10006 **Fx:**(917) 720-9089
(315) 422-4967 .. **Obeid,** Omar A '09 -109 S Warren -Syracuse 13202
(212) 664-5433 .. **Obel,** David I '66 %NBC -30 Rckfllr Plz -NY 10112
(212) 753-5000 .. **Oberdier,** Carl W '91 (Schiff H LLP) -900 3rd Av -NY 10022
(212) 833-1174 .. **Oberdorfer,** Kevin L '06 %Friedman KS&A LLP -1633 Bway -NY 10019 **Fx:**373-7974
(914) 241-2696 .. **Oberfest,** Bruce D '73 -20 Cardinal Pl -Mt Kisco 10549
(212) 364-5340 .. **Oberfield,** Gabriel S '05 %Innocence Project -100 5th Av -NY 10011 **Fx:**364-5341
(212) 225-2000 .. **Oberg,** Amanda T '02 %Cleary GS&H -1 Lbrty Plz -NY 10006
(212) 238-3000 .. **Obergfell,** Brian D '86 (Emmet M&M,LLP) -120 Bway -NY 10271
(212) 425-7670 .. **Oberhauser,** Kimberly Y '08 A Schreiber -40 Exch Pl -NY 10005 **Fx:**425-9237
(212) 446-2300 .. **Oberkampff De Dabrun,** Camille '09 %Boies S&F LLP -575 Lex Av -NY 10022
(516) 747-1177 .. **Oberlander,** Benita '96 (Oberlander & O) -100 Q Roosevelt Blvd -Gdn Cty 11530
(212) 587-7977 .. **Oberlander,** Bert M '02 (Gonzalez O&H LLP) -841 Bway -NY 10013
(516) 747-1177 .. **Oberlander,** Gary '98 (Oberlander & O) -100 Q Roosevelt Blvd -Gdn Cty 11530 **Fx:**741-9497
(212) 664-2152 .. **Oberlander,** Lynn B '92 %NBC -30 Rckfllr Plz -NY 10112 **Fx:**664-3650
(516) 239-8870 .. **Oberlander,** Melvyn S '57 -42 Herrick Dr -Lawrence 11559 **Fx:**371-3458
(212) 883-0000 .. **Obermaier,** Otto G '60 (Martin & O) -565 5th Av -NY 10017
(212) 751-7480 .. **Oberman,** Brian '68 -160 E 56th -NY 10022 **Fx:**935-8425
(347) 404-9133 .. **Oberman,** Elissa N '79 %Civil Ct -141 Lvngstn -Brklyn 11201 **Fx:**(718) 643-3733
(718) 376-8888 .. **Oberman,** Igor S '98 -1051 Ocean Vw Av -Brklyn 11235 **Fx:**228-3590
(212) 790-0368 .. **Oberman,** Jonathan H '83 %Benj N Cardozo Schl of Law -55 5th Av -NY 10003 **Fx:**790-0345
(212) 715-9100 .. **Oberman,** Michl S '73 (Kramer LN&F,LLP) -1177 Av of Amer -NY 10036
(212) 964-3290 .. **Oberman,** Richd S '72 (Levidow L&O) -299 Bway -NY 10007
(315) 866-7401 .. **Oberman,** Scott H '83 M Castle -110 W Albany -Herkimer 13350 **Fx:**866-6960
(212) 934-1585 .. **Oberoi,** Navdeep Singh '99 Goldman Sachs & Co -1 NY Plz -NY 10004
(516) 227-2662 .. **Oberster,** Jeanine A '00 %Rubin & L,PC -591 Stewart Av -Gdn Cty 11530
(212) 790-9200 .. **Obert,** Don M '99 Cowan L&L,PC -1133 Av of Amer -NY 10036
(518) 272-0402 .. **Oberting,** Victor A III '91 -Bx607 -Troy 12181 **Fx:**272-7299
(518) 473-3782 .. **Obertubbesing,** Edw '89 %Medicaid Inspctr Gen -15 Bway -Albany 12204
(212) 922-9700 .. **Oberweger,** Timothy D '07 %1st Amer Title -633 3rd Av -NY 10017 **Fx:**922-0881
(212) 587-7478 .. **Obiajulu,** Anthony '88 %State Ins Fund -199 Church -NY 10007 **Fx:**385-9199
(646) 746-9766 .. **Obie,** Stephen Jay '92 CFTC -140 Bway -NY 10005 **Fx:**746-9940
(516) 678-9797 .. **Obiol,** Richd C '97 (Civardi O&B,LLP) -23 S Main -Freeprt 11520 **Fx:**678-2266
(212) 849-7000 .. **Oblak,** Jonathan B '00 %Quinn EU&S,LLP -51 Mad Av -NY 10010
(212) 360-2380 .. **O-Blanquet,** V Wynter W '07 %Lincoln B LLP -110 E 59th -NY 10022 **Fx:**360-2381
(212) 969-3000 .. **O'Blenes,** Carole '77 (Proskauer R LLP) -1585 Bway -NY 10036
(607) 746-7717 .. **Obolensky,** Larisa '93 -127 Main Bx494 -Delhi 13753 **Fx:**746-8032
(212) 418-8700 .. **Obolensky,** Michl N '76 Fortis Finl Srvcs LLC -520 Mad Av -NY 10022 **Fx:**(203) 705-5906
(718) 579-7967 .. **Oboma-Layat,** Grace '03 %Leg Aid -900 Sheridan Av -Bronx 10451 **Fx:**293-8744
(212) 558-6668 .. **O'Boyle,** Hugh P '66 OfCnsl Foley SO&W -100 William -NY 10038
(718) 359-2200 .. **O'Boyle,** James D '76 Cullen and D LLP -158-14 Nrthrn Blvd -Flushng 11358
(631) 363-8060 .. **O'Boyle,** Kevin F '86 -80 Montauk Hwy -Blue Pnt 11715 **Fx:**363-8062
(212) 351-4000 .. **O'Boyle,** Laura K '07 %Gibson D&C LLP -200 Park Av -NY 10166
(212) 668-2870 .. **O'Boyle,** Una M '92 US Bankruptcy Ct -1 Bowling Grn -NY 10004
(718) 817-4945 .. **Obregon,** Conrad J '67 %Fordham Univ -441 E Fordham Rd -Bronx 10458 **Fx:**817-5574
(212) 450-4000 .. **Obregon,** Juliana '06 %Davis P&W LLP -450 Lex Av -NY 10017
(845) 534-9500 .. **Obremski,** Chas P '72 -321 Main Bx547 -Cornwall 12518 **Fx:**534-9509
(212) 259-8000 .. **O'Brian,** Adam R '09 %Dewey & L LLP -1301 Av of Amer -NY 10019
(516) 229-4300 .. **O'Brien,** Aaron W '01 J Bilello & Assoc -875 Merrick Av -Westbury 11590
(718) 590-8584 .. **O'Brien,** Anne L '99 %Admin Children's Srvcs -900 Sheridan Av -Bronx 10451 **Fx:**992-0084
(516) 766-0539 .. **O'Brien,** Anne Patricia '95 -89 Fenway -Rockvll Ctr 11570
(716) 839-7777 .. **O'Brien Boyd PC** -40 N Forest Rd -Williamsvll 14221 **Fx:**839-9959
(212) 820-9409 .. **O'Brien,** Brendan '66 (Hawkins D&W LLP) -One Chase Manh Plz -NY 10005
(516) 294-5100 .. **O'Brien,** Catherine Z '93 OfCnsl Murphy B&O,LLP -22 Jericho Tpk -Mineola 11501
(212) 795-8643 .. **O'Brien,** Chas '85 -900 W 190th -NY 10040
(518) 465-3524 .. **O'Brien,** Chas F '84 %NYS Defenders Assn -194 Wshngtn Av -Albany 12210 **Fx:**465-3249
(518) 457-2070 .. **O'Brien,** Christopher '96 Dept of Tax & Fin -Bldg 9 State Campus -Albany 12227 **Fx:**457-6131
(716) 839-7777 .. **O'Brien,** Christopher J '89 (O'Brien B PC) -40 N Forest Rd -Williamsvll 14221
(212) 557-7700 .. **O'Brien,** Claire F '84 (Davidson D&C LLP) -60 E 42nd -NY 10165
(212) 596-9000 .. **O'Brien,** Clara '04 %Ropes & G LLP -1211 Av of Amer -NY 10036
(212) 848-8966 .. **O'Brien,** Clare '86 (Shearman & S LLP) -599 Lex Av -NY 10022
(212) 728-8000 .. **O'Brien,** Colleen M '08 %Willkie F&G LLP -787 7th Av -NY 10019
(585) 613-4000 .. **O'Brien,** Connor J '87 %US Dist Ct -100 State -Rchstr 14614
(631) 265-6660 .. **O'Brien,** Danl P '83 (O'Brien & O) -168 Smithtown Blvd -Nesconset 11767 **Fx:**265-3991
(212) 687-7410 .. **O'Brien,** Danl P '08 %Clifton B&D,LLP -420 Lex Av -NY 10170
(631) 324-3942 .. **O'Brien,** David K '83 %Ackerman OP&B,LLP -34 Pantigo Rd -E Hampton 11937
(518) 459-0183 .. **O'Brien,** Deborah Damm '78 DePaul Housing Mgmt -41 N Main Av -Albany 12203
(718) 539-4044 .. **O'Brien,** Debra E '87 -3901 Main -Flushng 11354
(631) 283-4111 .. **O'Brien,** Denise Burke '89 OfCnsl Burke & S,PLLC -41 Meeting House Ln -Southampton 11968
(212) 559-7753 .. **O'Brien,** Denise O '79 Citibank NA -399 Park Av -NY 10022
(516) 877-2055 .. **O'Brien,** Dennis P '04 (Prime & O,LLP) -1000 Franklin Av -Gdn Cty 11530 **Fx:**877-2894
(585) 987-2800 .. **O'Brien,** Donald W Jr. '78 (Woods OG LLP) -2 State -Rchstr 14614
(212) 315-7090 .. **O'Brien,** Douglas G '04 WINS Radio -345 Hudson -NY 10014
(212) 940-3139 .. **O'Brien,** E Vincent '63 SrCnsl Nixon P LLP -437 Mad Av -NY 10022
(212) 681-6500 .. **O'Brien,** Edmond P '98 (Stempel BC&H,PC) -675 3rd Av -NY 10017
(585) 899-1414 .. **O'Brien,** Edw M '83 (Harris COJW&L) -300 Linden Oaks -Rchstr 14625
(914) 995-2660 .. **O'Brien,** Eileen Campbell '99 %Cnty Atty -148 Martine Av -White Plns 10601 **Fx:**995-5858
(212) 972-5430 .. **O'Brien,** Emily Shain '03 %Rosin SM -801 2nd Av -NY 10017
(212) 804-4200 .. **O'Brien,** Erika B '06 %Mound CW&G -One Bttry Pk Plz -NY 10004
(516) 747-7800 .. **O'Brien,** Erin A '06 %Cronin C&H,PC -200 Old Cntry Rd -Mineola 11501
(914) 323-7000 .. **O'Brien,** H Michl '80 (Wilson EME&D LLP) -3 Gannett Dr -White Plns 10604
(212) 490-3000 .. **O'Brien,** H Michl '80 (Wilson EME&D LLP) -150 E 42nd -NY 10017
(212) 571-6111 .. **O'Brien,** J David '90 -20 Vesey -NY 10007 **Fx:**571-6166
(607) 734-2017 .. **O'Brien,** J Wm II '79 -200 William -Elmira 14901 **Fx:**734-2018
(212) 584-0700 .. **O'Brien,** James A III '00 Cnsl Seeger W LLP -1 William -NY 10004
(516) 822-9000 .. **O'Brien,** James F '79 -500 N Bway -Jericho 11753 **Fx:**822-1050
(212) 490-3000 .. **O'Brien,** James F '90 (Wilson EME&D LLP) -150 E 42nd -NY 10017

(914) 323-7000 .. **O'Brien,** James F '90 (Wilson EME&D LLP) -3 Gannett Dr -White Plns 10604
(212) 813-9300 .. **O'Brien,** James F '97 -410 Park Av -NY 10022 **Fx:**813-1907
(716) 839-9800 .. **O'Brien,** James J '55 -3960 Harlem Rd -Amherst 14226
(607) 723-9511 .. **O'Brien,** James P '81 (Coughlin & G,LLP) -19 Chenango Bx2039 -Bnghmtn 13902
(516) 248-1700 .. **O'Brien,** James P Jr. '95 (Forchelli CDSM&T,LLP) -333 Earle Ovngton Blvd -Uniondale 11553
(516) 935-2330 .. **O'Brien,** James P '95 %Markotsis & L -183 Bway -Hicksvll 11801
(212) 421-4100 .. **O'Brien,** James S Jr. '87 (Pryor C LLP) -7 Times Sq -NY 10036
(212) 403-1000 .. **O'Brien,** Jeannemarie '95 (Wachtell LR&K) -51 W 52nd -NY 10019
(212) 259-8000 .. **O'Brien,** Jennifer M '08 %Dewey & L LLP -1301 Av of Amer -NY 10019
(212) 326-3939 .. **O'Brien,** Jerome F Jr. '09 %Jones D -222 E 41st -NY 10017
(212) 252-1212 .. **O'Brien,** Joanne M '97 %Meyers Law Firm PLLC -1123 Bway -NY 10010
(646) 414-1055 .. **O'Brien,** John A '68 -860 UN Plz -NY 10017 **Fx:**414-1056
(212) 286-8585 .. **O'Brien,** John C '09 %Heidell PM&B,LLP -99 Park Av -NY 10016
(518) 462-8231 .. **O'Brien,** John J '48 -24 Park Hill -Albany 12204
(631) 725-2020 .. **O'Brien,** John M '90 -3330 Noyac Rd Bx3147 -Sag Hbr 11963 **Fx:**725-9511
(212) 698-3500 .. **O'Brien,** John P '09 %Dechert LLP -1095 Av of Amer -NY 10036
(212) 889-2121 .. **O'Brien,** Jordan M '06 %Kellner HG&F -470 Park Av S -NY 10016
(914) 722-1118 .. **O'Brien,** Jos F '99 -1001 Post Rd -Scarsdale 10583 **Fx:**722-1119
(914) 429-5743 .. **O'Brien,** Jos John Jr. '88 -31 Croton Av -Ossining 10562
(518) 833-6000 .. **O'Brien,** Juliane Massarelli '04 %Dept Soc Srvcs -127 Bloomingrove Dr -Troy 12180 **Fx:**833-6121
(212) 824-5700 .. **O'Brien,** Kara L '02 Practising Law Inst -810 7th Av -NY 10019
(212) 820-9473 .. **O'Brien,** Karen J '99 %Hawkins D&W LLP -One Chase Manh Plz -NY 10005
(212) 267-1650 .. **O'Brien,** Karen M '93 (Fine O&A,LLP) -39 Bway -NY 10006
(212) 891-0868 .. **O'Brien,** Katherine A '91 %FOJP Srvc Corp -28 E 28th -NY 10016 **Fx:**308-3911
(212) 318-6000 .. **O'Brien,** Katherine G '10 %Paul HJ&W LLP -75 E 55th -NY 10022
(914) 741-6100 .. **O'Brien,** Katherine J '03 %Kaufman B&R -200 Summit Lk Dr -Valhalla 10595
(212) 576-3994 .. **O'Brien,** Katherine R '83 NY Life Ins -51 Mad Av -NY 10010
(845) 360-5503 .. **O'Brien,** Kelli M '95 KM O'Brien,PC -Bx562 -Goshen 10924 **Fx:**360-5507
(212) 698-3500 .. **O'Brien,** Kevin J '80 (Dechert LLP) -1095 Av of Amer -NY 10036
(516) 294-5100 .. **O'Brien,** Kevin J '85 (Murphy B&O,LLP) -22 Jericho Tpk -Mineola 11501
(315) 655-3463 .. **O'Brien,** Kevin J '91 %Mitchell G&S,LLC -5 Mill Bx312 -Cazenovia 13035
(315) 473-0899 .. **O'Brien,** Kevin K '06 %Anelli X,PC -441 S Salina -Syracuse 13202 **Fx:**473-0530
(518) 427-7000 .. **O'Brien,** Kevin L '89 (O'Brien & Assoc) -18 Corp Wds Blvd -Albany 12211 **Fx:**463-1721
(212) 426-8650 .. **O'Brien,** Kevin T '84 -201 E 87th -NY 10128 **Fx:**426-8381
(518) 402-0748 .. **O'Brien,** Kimberly A '91 %Dept of Health -433 River -Troy 12180 **Fx:**402-0751
(212) 474-1000 .. **O'Brien,** Leslie A '08 %Cravath S&M LLP -825 8th Av -NY 10019
(212) 286-4471 .. **O'Brien,** Liam '92 (McCormick & O,LLP) -9 E 40th -NY 10016 **Fx:**504-9574
(212) 277-4000 .. **O'Brien,** Lisa M '94 (Freshfields BD LLP) -520 Mad Av -NY 10022
(516) 942-7801 .. **O'Brien & Manister,PC** -120 Bethpage Rd -Hicksvll 11801 **Fx:**871-0053
(718) 613-3500 .. **O'Brien,** Margaret B '79 %UIA Bd -Bx29002 -Brklyn 11201 **Fx:**613-3566
(347) 840-0906 .. **O'Brien,** Margaret I '02 -21 W 76th -NY 10023
(212) 297-1489 .. **O'Brien,** Margaret J '99 Dewitt Stern Grp,Inc -420 Lex Av -NY 10170
(212) 345-5120 .. **O'Brien,** Margaret Mary '87 %Marsh USA -1166 Av of Amer -NY 10036 **Fx:**345-4808
O'Brien, Mary Ellen E '99 -50 Poplar -Gdn Cty 11530
(718) 836-6551 .. **O'Brien,** Maureen E '81 -267 Dahlgren Pl -Brklyn 11228 **Fx:**836-6551
(516) 367-1204 .. **O'Brien,** Michl '77 -17 Woodgreen Way Bx581 -Syosset 11791
(212) 574-1200 .. **O'Brien,** Michl E '99 Cnsl Seward & K LLP -1 Bttry Pk Plz -NY 10004
(212) 230-8800 .. **O'Brien,** Michl J '81 (WilmerHale) -399 Park Av -NY 10022
(315) 471-0003 .. **O'Brien,** Michl J '82 -506 E Wshngtn -Syracuse 13202 **Fx:**471-3705
(212) 336-3620 .. **O'Brien,** Michl J '90 %EEOC -33 Whitehall -NY 10004
(518) 473-8411 .. **O'Brien,** Michl J '00 %OCFS -52 Wshngtn -Rensselaer 12144 **Fx:**486-7219
(212) 415-3640 .. **O'Brien,** Michl J L '89 (Omnicom Group) -437 Mad Av -NY 10022 **Fx:**415-3530
(516) 802-4746 .. **O'Brien,** Michl P '01 Palm Bay Intl -48 Hrbr Pk Dr -Pt Wash 11050 **Fx:**802-4813
(212) 269-2209 .. **O'Brien,** Michl P '03 (O'Brien & J,PLLC) -110 Wall -NY 10005
(212) 966-3730 .. **O'Brien,** Monica M '94 %Kelman W&V -2 Rector -NY 10006
(212) 736-3250 .. **O'Brien,** Patricia Ann '91 %Toberoff T&S,LLP -330 7th Av -NY 10001
(631) 224-4600 .. **O'Brien,** Patricia Ann '93 -265 E Main -E Islip 11730
(212) 779-9800 .. **O'Brien,** Patricia E '97 %Luboja & T,LLP -10 E 40th -NY 10016
(212) 967-8433 .. **O'Brien,** Patrick A '77 -350 5th Av -NY 10118 **Fx:**967-8443
(212) 326-3939 .. **O'Brien,** Patrick B '05 %Jones D -222 E 41st -NY 10017
(914) 828-8000 .. **O'Brien,** Patrick J '75 Swiss Re Life & Hlth Amer Inc -175 King -Armonk 10504 **Fx:**828-7000
(212) 888-3033 .. **O'Brien,** Patrick J '98 %Becker GM&M LLP -299 Park Av -NY 10171
(516) 766-0158 .. **O'Brien,** Paul V '69 -325 Morris Av -Rockvll Ctr 11570
(516) 742-5201 .. **O'Brien,** Paul V '97 SpclCnsl Phillips L LLP -1100 Franklin Av -Gdn Cty 11530
(212) 759-4888 .. **O'Brien,** Paul V '97 SpclCnsl Phillips L LLP -437 Mad Av -NY 10022
(585) 325-5760 .. **O'Brien,** Paul W '75 -45 East Av -Rchstr 14604 **Fx:**325-5813
(518) 474-2257 .. **O'Brien,** Paula J '06 %Consumer Protection Bd -5 ESP -Albany 12223 **Fx:**474-2474
(212) 259-8000 .. **O'Brien,** Peter K '92 (Dewey & L LLP) -1301 Av of Amer -NY 10019
(212) 794-5386 .. **O'Brien,** Raymond F '82 %CUNY -535 E 80th -NY 10075
(914) 686-1700 .. **O'Brien,** Richd T '06 %O'Connor R,LLP -200 Mamaroneck Av -White Plns 10601
(212) 362-0048 .. **O'Brien,** Robt G '66 -140 Riverside Dr -NY 10024 **Fx:**580-5539
(646) 252-7000 .. **O'Brien,** Robt M '72 %TBTA -2 Bway -NY 10004
(516) 538-1111 .. **O'Brien,** Robt P '88 (Mahon MK&O,LLC) -254 Nassau Blvd -Garden City South 11530
(516) 256-1800 .. **O'Brien,** Robt W '79 -877 N Corona Av -N Vly Strm 11580 **Fx:**256-1803
(518) 402-0748 .. **O'Brien,** Sean D '90 %Dept of Health -433 River -Troy 12180 **Fx:**402-0751
(212) 333-0200 .. **O'Brien,** Sean R '95 (Arkin KR LLP) -590 Mad Av -NY 10022
(518) 452-5600 .. **O'Brien,** Shanna K '06 %Heslin RF&M PC -5 Columbia Cir -Albany 12203
(631) 265-6660 .. **O'Brien,** Stephen L '86 (O'Brien & O) -168 Smithtown Blvd -Nesconset 11767 **Fx:**265-3991
(585) 753-4500 .. **O'Brien,** Stephen X '82 %DA -832 Watts Bldg -Rchstr 14614 **Fx:**753-4576
(212) 857-0000 .. **O'Brien,** Tama '05 Intl Ctr of Photography -1114 Av of Amer -NY 10036
(718) 250-2000 .. **O'Brien,** Taryen R '03 %DA -350 Jay -Brklyn 11201 **Fx:**250-2314
(212) 819-8200 .. **O'Brien,** Terence G '96 %White & C LLP -1155 Av of Amer -NY 10036
(607) 936-8737 .. **O'Brien,** Thos C '72 -36 W 5th -Corning 14830
(212) 351-7065 .. **O'Brien,** Thos D '03 Monster Worldwide Inc -622 3rd Av -NY 10017
(716) 839-9800 .. **O'Brien,** Thos E '56 -3960 Harlem Rd -Amherst 14226
(315) 853-2912 .. **O'Brien,** Thos F '78 -9 E Park Row -Clinton 13323 **Fx:**853-4489
(212) 577-3551 .. **O'Brien,** Thos M '82 %Leg Aid -199 Water -NY 10038
(212) 973-0572 .. **O'Brien,** Thos R '85 (Wolff & S PC) -140 Bway -NY 10005
(607) 732-1928 .. **O'Brien,** Timothy R '00 -26 Fairway Ln -Horseheads 14845
(212) 373-3000 .. **O'Brien,** Wm '87 Cnsl Paul WRW&G LLP -1285 Av of Amer -NY 10019
(212) 940-3043 .. **O'Brien,** Wm F Jr. '73 (Nixon P LLP) -437 Mad Av -NY 10022
(212) 479-6000 .. **O'Brien,** Wm H '78 (Cooley LLP) -1114 Av of Amer -NY 10036
(212) 735-3000 .. **O'Brien,** Wm J III '97 Cnsl Skadden ASM&F LLP -4 Times Sq -NY 10036
(212) 661-2490 .. **O'Brien,** Wm J '04 (Delany & O) -80 Broad -NY 10004
(518) 270-3751 .. **O'Brien-Aram,** Janet H '77 %Family Ct -105 3rd -Troy 12180
(212) 966-6420 .. **O'Brien-Gans,** Dawn '04 %Lwyrs For Children -110 Lafayette -NY 10013 **Fx:**966-0531
(518) 473-9009 .. **O'Brien-Nejame,** Kathleen M '04 State Comptroller -110 State -Albany 12236 **Fx:**473-9104
(212) 980-9600 .. **O'Brien Totten,** Elizabeth '01 %Kaufman B&R -120 Bway -NY 10271
(212) 527-1000 .. **O'Bryan,** Chas E '79 (Jones HC&B PC) -1 Bttry Pk Plz -NY 10004
(518) 426-4940 .. **Obstarczyk,** Christopher J '01 (Levy & O PLLC) -350 Nrthrn Blvd -Albany 12204
(585) 724-4255 .. **Obstarczyk,** Patricia A '86 %Eastman Kodak -343 State -Rchstr 14650
(212) 696-1212 .. **Obstfeld,** Harold B '71 (HB Obstfeld,PC) -100 Park Av -NY 10017 **Fx:**867-7369
(718) 358-8114 .. **O'Buckley,** Donal A '99 D O'Buckley,PC -16717 45th Av -Flushng 11358 **Fx:**353-0938
(212) 969-3000 .. **Obus,** Steven '74 (Proskauer R LLP) -1585 Bway -NY 10036
(631) 766-0398 .. **O'Byrne,** Ana M '96 -Bx1698 -Brdghmptn 11932 **Fx:**614-3830
(212) 848-9800 .. **O'Byrne,** Deidre G '98 (Withers B LLP) -430 Park Av -NY 10022
(585) 546-3340 .. **O'Byrne,** Joan de R '68 -19 W Main -Rchstr 14614
(212) 261-8000 .. **O'Byrne,** John D '92 (Mendes & M,LLP) -750 7th Av -NY 10019
(215) 446-6293 .. **O'Byrne,** Wm P '98 %Gibbons PC -1 Penn Plz -NY 10119 **Fx:**446-6329
(212) 222-4200 .. **O'Callaghan,** Danl J '76 -7 Dey -NY 10007
(212) 940-3754 .. **O'Callaghan,** Edw C '95 (Nixon P LLP) -437 Mad Av -NY 10022
(212) 848-4000 .. **O'Callaghan,** Erin M '07 %Shearman & S LLP -599 Lex Av -NY 10022
(516) 542-5900 .. **O'Callaghan,** Jane M '95 (Congdon FORDT&F) -333 Earle Ovngton Blvd -Uniondale 11553
(212) 450-4000 .. **O'Callaghan,** John A '09 %Davis P&W LLP -450 Lex Av -NY 10017
(973) 520-2328 .. **O'Callaghan,** Kirstin K '06 %Edwards AP&D LLP -750 Lex Av -NY 10022 **Fx:**(866) 204-2941
(914) 779-3558 .. **O'Callahan,** Mary A '92 -32 Gramatan Ct -Bronxvll 10708 **Fx:**779-5183
(212) 219-3279 .. **Ocampo,** Victor D '93 -139 Canal -NY 10002 **Fx:**219-0315
(716) 842-2800 .. **O'Carroll,** Donall G '06 %Webster S LLP -1400 Lbrty Bldg -Buffalo 14202
(212) 930-9700 .. **Ocasio,** Darrin M '03 (Sichenzia RFF LLP) -61 Bway -NY 10006
(718) 579-7922 .. **Ocasio,** Judy '88 %Leg Aid -900 Sheridan Av -Bronx 10451 **Fx:**293-8744
(718) 275-3660 .. **Ocasio,** Myrna '87 Harris Law Grp,LLP -96-14 63rd Dr -Rego Pk 11374 **Fx:**275-3405
(212) 719-2821 .. **Ocasio-Douglas,** Maria del Pilar '92 MD Ocasio-Douglas,PC -111 John -NY 10038
(212) 564-2770 .. **O'Cathain,** Domhnall M '06 Lesnevich &M-L,LLC -350 5th Av -NY 10118
(718) 237-2000 .. **Occhetti,** Richd A '70 %Leg Aid -111 Lvngstn -Brklyn 11201 **Fx:**237-8737
(212) 343-6646 .. **Occhini,** Lorraine '93 Scholastic Inc -557 Bway -NY 10012
(212) 834-1081 .. **Occhino,** Andy '84 %GreenPoint Bk -90 Park Av -NY 10016 **Fx:**834-1402
(516) 229-4300 .. **Occhiogrosso,** Frank J '96 %J Bilello & Assoc -875 Merrick Av -Westbury 11590
(212) 650-8276 .. **Occhiogrosso,** Paul F '89 City College of NY -160 Convent Av -NY 10031 **Fx:**650-8277
(212) 435-3571 .. **Occhiogrosso,** Scott C '00 Port Auth of NY/NJ -225 Park Av S -NY 10003 **Fx:**435-3555
(845) 354-1710 .. **Occhipinti,** Anthony J Jr. '73 -1593 Rt 202 Bx3100 -Pomona 10970 **Fx:**354-8193
(212) 239-5500 .. **Occhipinti,** Frank S '86 (Stewart O,LLP) -65 W 36th -NY 10018
(518) 694-8216 .. **Ochacher,** Perry M '89 Empire Strategic Planning -111 Wshngtn Av -Albany 12210
(914) 238-5800 .. **Ochman,** Evelyn L '86 OfCnsl T Krouner -93 N Greeley Av -Chappaqua 10514
(516) 659-5533 .. **Ochman,** Marshall L '79 -510 Merrick Rd -Rockvll Ctr 11570

(212) 310-8000 .. **Odoner,** Ellen J '78 (Weil G&M LLP) -767 5th Av -NY 10153
(518) 473-5096 .. **O'Donnell,** Brian J '76 %Dept of Law -The Cptl -Albany 12224
(212) 907-9600 .. **O'Donnell,** Cherish A '09 %Ingram YGC&B,LLP -250 Park Av -NY 10177
(212) 852-3388 .. **O'Donnell,** Christine L '98 Bank of America -1 Bryant Park -NY 10036
(212) 732-3320 .. **O'Donnell,** Christopher E '97 %Short & B,PC -217 Bway -NY 10007
(516) 624-6366 .. **O'Donnell,** Colin F '88 Cnsl Town Supervisor -54 Audrey Av -Oyster Bay 11771
(212) 530-5000 .. **O'Donnell,** Dennis C '92 OfCnsl Milbank TH&M LLP -1 Chase Manh Plz -NY 10005
(212) 728-8000 .. **O'Donnell,** Dianne E '03 SpclCnsl Willkie F&G LLP -787 7th Av -NY 10019
(212) 527-3723 .. **O'Donnell,** Edw J '00 Bank of NY -1 Wall -NY 10005
(212) 237-8388 .. **O'Donnell,** Eugene J '89 %John Jay Cllg -899 10th Av -NY 10019
(212) 319-0600 .. **O'Donnell & Fox,PC** -29 Bway -NY 10006 **Fx:**319-3597
(212) 460-2552 .. **O'Donnell,** Geraldine '78 Con Ed -4 Irving Pl -NY 10003
(914) 864-7122 .. **O'Donnell,** Grant D '08 %DA -25 Moore Av -Mt Kisco 10549
(718) 816-0247 .. **O'Donnell,** James M '60 (O'Donnell & M) -390 Manor Rd -Staten Isl 10314
(516) 877-5600 .. **O'Donnell,** John F '95 %R Tusa -1225 Franklin Av -Gdn Cty 11530 **Fx:**877-5695
(212) 637-2490 .. **O'Donnell,** John J '76 US Atty-SDNY -1 St Andrews Plz -NY 10007
(212) 637-2490 .. **O'Donnell,** John J '90 %US Atty -1 St Andrews Plz -NY 10007
(212) 825-0783 .. **O'Donnell,** John P '79 (J O'Donnell,PC) -130 Water -NY 10005 **Fx:**825-0890
(212) 872-6652 .. **O'Donnell,** Jonathan C '99 KPMG LLP -345 Park Av -NY 10154
(716) 856-0277 .. **O'Donnell,** Jos E '86 (Reden & O LLP) -135 Delaware Av -Buffalo 14202
(212) 308-8500 .. **O'Donnell,** Jos S '04 Investigative Mgmt Corp -825 3rd Av -NY 10022
(315) 470-1441 .. **O'Donnell,** Jos V '87 Diocese of Syracuse -240 E Onondaga -Syracuse 13201
(631) 421-2386 .. **O'Donnell,** Karen Anne '86 -6 Bennington -Melvll 11747
(646) 610-5400 .. **O'Donnell,** Kenneth W '02 NYPD -1 Police Plz -NY 10038
(718) 250-2000 .. **O'Donnell,** Kevin J '98 %DA -350 Jay -Brklyn 11201 **Fx:**250-2314
(212) 422-6111 .. **O'Donnell,** Kevin J '06 %Kenny S&Z -26 Bway -NY 10004
(718) 261-4500 .. **O'Donnell,** Kevin P '95 -125-10 Qns Blvd -Kew Gdns 11415 **Fx:**261-4509
(212) 373-3000 .. **O'Donnell,** Lindsay Nielsen '07 %Paul WRW&G LLP -1285 Av of Amer -NY 10019
(212) 837-6000 .. **O'Donnell,** Matthew P '07 %Hughes H&R LLP -1 Bttry Pk Plz -NY 10004
(716) 843-5700 .. **O'Donnell,** Maura K '04 %US Atty -138 Delaware Av -Buffalo 14202 **Fx:**551-3052
(718) 816-0247 .. **O'Donnell & McLaughlin** -390 Manor Rd -Staten Isl 10314 **Fx:**816-6137
(631) 853-4161 .. **O'Donnell,** Megan E '99 %DA -N Cnty Cmplx Bldg 77 -Hauppauge 11788 **Fx:**853-4192
(914) 649-3675 .. **O'Donnell,** Michl K '84 -81 Main -White Plns 10601
(914) 961-1300 .. **O'Donnell,** Nancy V '05 %Griffin CB&S,PC -51 Pondfld Rd -Bronxvll 10708
(631) 329-2843 .. **O'Donnell,** Patricia Ann '91 -157 N Main -E Hampton 11937 **Fx:**329-6743
(212) 819-8200 .. **O'Donnell,** Patricia U '03 %White & C LLP -1155 Av of Amer -NY 10036
(315) 866-3621 .. **O'Donnell,** Philip D '50 (O'Donnell & O) -115 W German Bx229 -Herkimer 13350 **Fx:**866-3624
(315) 866-3621 .. **O'Donnell,** Philip D Jr. '89 (O'Donnell & O) -115 W German Bx229 -Herkimer 13350 **Fx:**866-3624
(914) 761-1600 .. **O'Donnell,** Robt G '72 (R O'Donnell,PC) -50 Main -White Plns 10606 **Fx:**761-4016
(718) 816-0247 .. **O'Donnell,** Rosemary A '98 %O'Donnell & M -390 Manor Rd -Staten Isl 10314
(212) 370-5100 .. **O'Donnell Schwartz Glanstein & Lilly,LLP** -60 E 42nd -NY 10165 **Fx:**697-6299
(516) 794-9460 .. **O'Donnell Schwartz Glanstein & Lilly,LLP** -245 Hillside Av -Williston Pk 11596 **Fx:**794-9466
(212) 872-1000 .. **O'Donnell,** Sean E '98 -One Bryant Park -NY 10036 **Fx:**872-1002
(845) 534-8900 .. **O'Donnell,** Sheila '77 -257 Main Bx484 -Cornwall 12518 **Fx:**534-4652
(518) 242-3733 .. **O'Donnell,** Simon F '84 %Ct of Claims -Justice Bldg ESP Bx7344 -Albany 12224 **Fx:**242-3731
(315) 738-4838 .. **O'Donnell,** Thos F '77 %Utica Svgs Bnk -233 Genesee -Utica 13501
(212) 319-0600 .. **O'Donnell,** Thos G '78 (O'Donnell & F,PC) -29 Bway -NY 10006
(716) 286-4409 .. **O'Donnell,** Thos M '83 %Law Dept -745 Main Bx69 -Niagara Fls 14302 **Fx:**286-4424
(212) 598-9660 .. **O'Donnell,** Timothy '84 -632 Bway -NY 10012
(212) 319-0600 .. **O'Donnell,** Wm G '57 (O'Donnell & F,PC) -29 Bway -NY 10006
(212) 319-0600 .. **O'Donnell,** Wm G Jr. '84 (O'Donnell & F,PC) -29 Bway -NY 10006
(212) 859-8000 .. **O'Donoghue,** James D '05 Fried FHS&J LLP -1 NY Plz -NY 10004
(718) 618-3642 .. **O'Donoghue,** Lorraine D '07 Supreme Ct -88-11 Sutphin Blvd -Jamaica 11435
(212) 696-6000 .. **O'Donoghue,** Mark H '78 (Curtis M-PC&M LLP) -101 Park Av -NY 10178
(718) 520-3363 .. **O'Donoghue,** Virginia P '89 %Criminal Ct -125-01 Qns Blvd -Kew Gdns 11415
(718) 442-1700 .. **O'Donovan,** Timothy M '94 %Connors & C,PC -766 Castleton Av -Staten Isl 10310 **Fx:**442-1717
(585) 381-4320 .. **Odorisi,** Frank N '63 (Odorisi Law Firm) -311 S Wshngtn Bx69 -E Rchstr 14445 **Fx:**586-5624
(585) 381-4320 .. **Odorisi,** J Scott '94 (Odorisi Law Firm) -311 S Wshngtn Bx69 -E Rchstr 14445 **Fx:**586-5624
(585) 258-2800 .. **Odorisi,** Kelly L '97 (Underberg & K LLP) -300 Bausch & Lomb Pl -Rchstr 14604
(718) 273-2500 .. **O'Dowd,** John M Jr. '85 -1164 Victory Blvd -Staten Isl 10301 **Fx:**447-9908
(212) 554-1400 .. **O'Dowd,** Sean K '06 %Bernstein LB&G LLP -1285 Av of Amer -NY 10019
(212) 858-1000 .. **Odrich,** David G '87 (Pillsbury WSP LLP) -1540 Bway -NY 10036
(212) 576-4798 .. **O'Driscoll,** Carol M '89 %NY Life Ins -51 Mad Av -NY 10010 **Fx:**447-0569
(212) 506-5000 .. **O'Driscoll,** Peter S '88 (Orrick H&S LLP) -51 W 52nd -NY 10019
(212) 684-3366 .. **O'Driscoll,** Sean M '05 Irish Voice -875 Av of Amer -NY 10001
(716) 856-3300 .. **Odrobina,** Marc J '85 %Lumsden & McCormick -403 Main -Buffalo 14203 **Fx:**856-2524
(646) 386-5700 .. **Odunlami,** Anthony O '95 %Civil Ct -111 Centre -NY 10013
(718) 875-1611 .. **Odwak,** Barbara S '81 -32 Court -Brklyn 11201 **Fx:**875-0103
(914) 323-7000 .. **O'Dwyer,** Alison C '00 %Wilson EME&D LLP -3 Gannett Dr -White Plns 10604
(212) 571-7100 .. **O'Dwyer & Bernstien, LLP** -52 Duane -NY 10007 **Fx:**571-7124
(212) 571-7100 .. **O'Dwyer,** Brian '71 (O'Dwyer & B,LLP) -52 Duane -NY 10007
(585) 325-7515 .. **O'Dwyer,** Duncan W '67 (Forsyth HOK&M,PC) -1 Chase Sq -Rchstr 14604
(516) 542-5900 .. **O'Dwyer,** John T '86 (Congdon FORDT&F) -333 Earle Ovngton Blvd -Uniondale 11553
(646) 230-7444 .. **O'Dwyer,** Paul J '90 -134 W 26th -NY 10001
(212) 819-8200 .. **Odynski,** Kirsten J '09 %White & C LLP -1155 Av of Amer -NY 10036
(917) 428-3817 .. **Odza,** Brian J '95 -Bx431 -Bronx 10467
(716) 856-0600 .. **Odza,** Randall M '67 (Jaeckle F&M,LLP) -12 Fountain Plz -Buffalo 14202
(212) 408-5100 .. **Oechler,** Henry J Jr. '72 OfCnsl Chadbourne & P LLP -30 Rckfllr Plz -NY 10112
(518) 474-4567 .. **Oechsner,** Troy J '91 %Insurance Dept -99 Wshngtn Av -Albany 12257 **Fx:**473-4600
(585) 255-1402 .. **Oehlbeck,** Julianne A '99 Global Crossing -225 Kenneth Dr -Rchstr 14623 **Fx:**(877) 769-9844
(516) 829-0363 .. **Oehrlein,** Lance R '00 %Israel I&P,LLP -11 Grace Av -Gt Neck 11021 **Fx:**829-0366
(212) 819-8200 .. **Oelke,** Jeffrey J '93 (White & C LLP) -1155 Av of Amer -NY 10036
(212) 490-3000 .. **Oelsner,** Richd S '81 (Wilson EME&D LLP) -150 E 42nd -NY 10017
(914) 323-7000 .. **Oelsner,** Richd S '81 (Wilson EME&D LLP) -3 Gannett Dr -White Plns 10604
(212) 675-7955 .. **Oeser-Sweat,** Jamel L '02 -419 Lafayette -NY 10003
(212) 637-2698 .. **Oestericher,** Jeff '90 %US Atty -86 Chmbrs -NY 10007
(212) 894-7200 .. **Oestreich,** Stephen D '68 SrCnsl Entwistle & C LLP -280 Park Av -NY 10017
(914) 428-9330 .. **Oestreicher Ennis Dalrymple & Dalrymple, LLP** -235 Mamaroneck Av -White Plns 10605 **Fx:**428-9419
(914) 428-9330 .. **Oestreicher,** Julius Y '58 (Oestreicher ED&D,LLP) -235 Mamaroneck Av -White Plns 10605
(516) 803-2300 .. **Oetken,** James Paul '02 Cablevision Sys -1111 Stewart Av -Bethpage 11714
(212) 343-2662 .. **Ofeck,** Ron Z '92 (Ofeck & H LLP) -130 Madison -NY 10002 **Fx:**(201) 488-4475
(212) 607-3300 .. **Ofer,** Udi '02 NYCLU -125 Broad -NY 10004 **Fx:**344-3318
(212) 818-9200 .. **O'Ferrall,** Kirk H '85 (Satterlee SB&B LLP) -230 Park Av -NY 10169
(585) 249-0510 .. **Offen,** Alan L '69 -290 Linden Oaks -Rchstr 14625 **Fx:**419-8061
(212) 351-4000 .. **Offenhartz,** Adam H '90 (Gibson D&C LLP) -200 Park Av -NY 10166
(212) 666-9770 .. **Offenhartz,** Gilbert L '58 -884 West End Av -NY 10025
(212) 867-7750 .. **Offenkrantz,** Ronald J '61 (Lichter GO PC) -551 5th Av -NY 10176
(212) 626-4100 .. **Offerman,** Suzanne Ina '01 %Baker & M LLP -1114 Av of Amer -NY 10036
(716) 510-3724 .. **Offermann,** Francis J Jr. '54 -290 Beard Av -Buffalo 14214 **Fx:**381-9114
(516) 627-4468 .. **Offner,** Eric D '52 -20 Joy Dr -Manhsst Hlls 11040 **Fx:**742-5368
(212) 935-3000 .. **Offner,** Stuart A '78 (Mintz LCFG&P,PC) -666 3rd Av -NY 10017
(212) 825-0126 .. **Offsey,** Michelle A '06 Cnsl Dept of Invstgtn -80 Maiden Ln -NY 10038 **Fx:**825-5596
(718) 243-6279 .. **O'Flaherty,** Niamh P '90 %Leg Aid -111 Lvngstn -Brklyn 11201 **Fx:**237-8737
(718) 286-2000 .. **O'Flaherty,** Oona '90 %Leg Aid -120-46 Qns Blvd -Kew Gdns 11415 **Fx:**286-2286
(212) 788-0886 .. **O'Flynn,** Mary T '00 %Law Dept -100 Church -NY 10007 **Fx:**788-0367
(718) 852-8300 .. **Ofodile,** Anthony C '94 -498 Atl Av -Brklyn 11217 **Fx:**852-7361
[Civil Rights Law] [Discrimination Law] [Employment Law]
(212) 661-6787 .. **O'Friel,** Jennifer A '01 %Hon J Lippman-Ct of Appeals -230 Park Av -NY 10169
(845) 928-9708 .. **O'Friel,** John T '68 -2 Buena Vista Ter Bx94 -Centrl Vly 10917
(212) 676-3910 .. **Ofsevit,** Saml M '81 (Butzel L,PC) -380 Mad Av -NY 10017
(212) 371-8008 .. **Ofsink,** Darren L '95 (Guzov O,LLC) -600 Mad Av -NY 10022
(914) 225-5594 .. **Ofuya,** Temietan O '03 %Morgan Stanley -2000 Wstchstr Av -Purchase 10577
(212) 815-1818 .. **Ogaldez,** Elswith F '86 DC 37 MELS -125 Barclay -NY 10007 **Fx:**815-1343
(212) 683-0015 .. **O'Gara,** Debra S '05 Connect -Greeley Sq Station Bx20217 -NY 10001
(212) 808-7800 .. **O'Gara,** James V '79 (Kelley D&W LLP) -101 Park Av -NY 10178
(212) 481-8679 .. **O'Gara,** John M '96 -270 Mad Av -NY 10016 **Fx:**684-7995
(212) 837-6000 .. **O'Gara,** Patrick F '04 %Hughes H&R LLP -1 Bttry Pk Plz -NY 10004
(718) 286-2306 .. **O'Gara,** Scott H '87 %Leg Aid -120-46 Qns Blvd -Kew Gdns 11415 **Fx:**286-2286
(585) 473-3100 .. **O'Gara,** Thos K '10 %Ernstrom & D,LLP -180 Canal Vw Blvd -Rchstr 14623
(212) 474-1000 .. **Ogbara,** Helen O '09 %Cravath S&M LLP -825 8th Av -NY 10019
(716) 855-5710 .. **Ogden,** Laurie G '81 %L Ogden -60 Lakefront Blvd -Buffalo 14202
(716) 858-2424 .. **Ogden,** Sara N '06 %DA -25 Delaware Av -Buffalo 14202 **Fx:**858-7425
(212) 450-4000 .. **Ogden,** Thos P '84 (Davis P&W LLP) -450 Lex Av -NY 10017
(585) 786-8822 .. **O'Geen,** Donald G '98 %DA -147 N Main -Warsaw 14569 **Fx:**786-8842
(631) 288-3200 .. **Ogeka,** Chas J '94 -110 Mill Rd -Westhmptn Bch 11978
(212) 344-3440 .. **Ogen,** Eitan A '97 (Ogen & S,PC) -202 E 35th -NY 10016
(718) 207-6579 .. **Oghomienor Isaac,** Maurice O '01 -145-83 177th -Jamaica 11434
(212) 661-1010 .. **Ogihara,** Shigetaka '87 (Ogihara & Assoc,PLLC) -122 E 42nd -NY 10168 **Fx:**661-6116
(212) 845-7909 .. **Ogilvie,** Ian M '96 %Ramius Securities -599 Lex Av -NY 10022

(212) 845-7909 .. **Ogilvie,** Marran Humphrey '96 %Ramius Capital Grp,LLC -599 Lex Av -NY 10022 **Fx:**845-7999
(607) 732-0392 .. **Ogilvie,** Wm M '81 -124 W Franklin -Horseheads 14845 **Fx:**739-6242
(516) 487-8207 .. **Oginski,** Gerald M '89 (GM Oginski,LLC) -25 Grt Nck Rd -Gt Neck 11021 **Fx:**487-8472
(718) 250-2000 .. **Ogiste,** Lance P '90 %DA -350 Jay -Brklyn 11201 **Fx:**250-2314
(718) 725-6590 .. **Ogle,** Andrea S '97 -90-50 Parsons Blvd -Jamaica 11432 **Fx:**725-6595
(212) 558-4000 .. **Ogle,** Trevor '05 %Sullivan & C LLP -125 Broad -NY 10004
(716) 853-1616 .. **Ognibene,** Mary F '04 %Harter S&E LLP -12 Fountain Plz -Buffalo 14202
(718) 876-7770 .. **Ogorek,** Elky '84 %Supreme Ct -355 Front -Staten Isl 10304
(718) 604-6954 .. **Ogorek,** Maria Anne '89 %Transit Adjudication Bur -505 Fulton -Brklyn 11201
(212) 698-3593 .. **O'Gorman,** Debra D '91 Cnsl Dechert LLP -1095 Av of Amer -NY 10036
(914) 323-7000 .. **O'Gorman,** Edw J '89 (Wilson EME&D LLP) -3 Gannett Dr -White Plns 10604
(631) 756-4023 .. **O'Gorman,** Wm G '86 %State Ins Fund -8 Corp Ctr Dr -Melvll 11747 **Fx:**756-4060
(914) 683-1333 .. **O'Grady,** Anne '05 My Sisters Place -1 Water -White Plns 10601
(212) 351-4000 .. **O'Grady,** James B C '08 %Gibson D&C LLP -200 Park Av -NY 10166
(212) 661-0011 .. **O'Grady,** Jeanne Marie '02 %Speiser KN&G -140 E 45th -NY 10017
(212) 504-6000 .. **O'Grady,** John J III '58 SrCnsl Cadwalader W&T LLP -1 World Fncl Ctr -NY 10281
(845) 359-5890 .. **O'Grady,** John J '59 -74 Dederer Bx284 -Sparkill 10976
(516) 263-4421 .. **O'Grady,** John J '85 -1205 Franklin Av -Gdn Cty 11530 **Fx:**706-3048
(212) 998-6397 .. **O'Grady,** Paul M '95 NYU Law Schl -110 W 3rd -NY 10012 **Fx:**995-4032
(718) 590-3487 .. **O'Grady,** Siobhan T '05 %Law Dept -900 Sheridan Av -Bronx 10451 **Fx:**590-2699
(212) 715-1000 .. **O'Grady,** Timothy P '06 %Arnold & P LLP -399 Park Av -NY 10022
(518) 474-6400 .. **O'Grady-Parent,** Erin M '90 %Dept of Ed -89 Wshngtn Av -Albany 12234 **Fx:**473-2925
(212) 383-1558 .. **Oguagha,** Ifeyinwa O '97 State Comptroller -59 Maiden Ln -NY 10038 **Fx:**383-3901
(212) 326-3939 .. **Ogulluk,** Sevan '00 (Jones D) -222 E 41st -NY 10017
(718) 923-5200 .. **Ogunleye,** Abimbola D '08 NYC Dept Edn -335 Adams -Brklyn 11201 **Fx:**923-5145
(212) 474-1000 .. **Ogunmefun,** Olufunmilola O '10 %Cravath S&M LLP -825 8th Av -NY 10019
(212) 735-3000 .. **Ogunsanya,** Gregory O '04 %Skadden ASM&F LLP -4 Times Sq -NY 10036
(212) 878-0000 .. **Oh,** Amy Jung Hyun '02 %MTA -2 Penn Plz -NY 10121
(718) 813-5025 .. **Oh,** Andy S '02 A Oh,PLLC -9509 69th Av -Frst Hlls 11375
(631) 852-2500 .. **Oh,** Anne E '00 %DA -200 Center Dr -Rvrhead 11901 **Fx:**852-1769
(718) 250-2000 .. **Oh,** Eunyung T '06 DA -350 Jay -Brklyn 11201 **Fx:**250-2314
(212) 233-8100 .. **Oh,** H Susan '98 %Pollack Pl&D -225 Bway -NY 10007
(516) 294-1333 .. **Oh,** Jae Young '07 (DeMartini & Y LLP) -264 Hillside Av -Williston Pk 11596
(212) 447-7220 .. **Oh,** Jay Joonseok '93 (Choe & O,PC) -15 E 32nd -NY 10016 **Fx:**447-0968
(315) 443-5196 .. **Oh,** Jeong '98 %Syracuse Univ-Tech Transfer -2-220 Ctr Sci & Tech -Syracuse 13244 **Fx:**443-8469
(212) 612-9550 .. **Oh,** John R '96 %Dombroff & G,PC -40 Broad -NY 10004
(212) 286-0747 .. **Oh,** Kenneth C '98 %D Brecher -99 Park Av -NY 10016 **Fx:**808-4155
(718) 250-2000 .. **Oh,** Lawr P '95 %DA -350 Jay -Brklyn 11201 **Fx:**250-2314
(212) 277-4000 .. **Oh,** Patrick D '07 %Freshfields BD LLP -520 Mad Av -NY 10022
(212) 661-6886 .. **Oh,** Richd C '88 Taglich Bros,Inc -275 Mad Av -NY 10016 **Fx:**661-6824
(212) 531-3110 .. **Oh,** Seung Jin '02 -212 Canal -NY 10013 **Fx:**(201) 342-9101
(718) 605-4700 .. **Oh,** Sumee '01 -3453 Richmond Av -Staten Isl 10312
(212) 872-6836 .. **Oh,** Won K '01 KPMG LLP -345 Park Av -NY 10154
(212) 264-2921 .. **Oh,** Yongmin '04 %US Ct of Intl Trade -1 Fed Plz -NY 10278
(212) 701-3000 .. **Oh,** Yoon Ah '08 %Cahill G&R LLP -80 Pine -NY 10005 **Fx:**269-5420
(212) 484-8000 .. **O'Hagan,** Cindy J '94 %Time Warner -1 Time Warner Ctr -NY 10019
(212) 833-1153 .. **O'Hagan,** Eamonn J '06 %Friedman KS&A LLP -1633 Bway -NY 10019 **Fx:**373-7953
(212) 227-4000 .. **O'Hagan,** Michl J '90 %Mirman M&L,PC -291 Bway -NY 10007
(631) 852-2500 .. **O'Halloran,** Andrea L '01 %DA -200 Center Dr -Rvrhead 11901 **Fx:**852-1769
(718) 727-9303 .. **O'Halloran,** Brian S '87 -17 Seneca Av -Staten Isl 10301 **Fx:**273-1420
(718) 727-9303 .. **O'Halloran,** James K '85 -17 Seneca Av -Staten Isl 10301 **Fx:**273-1420
(718) 829-7400 .. **O'Halloran,** John J '96 %T Lavin Jr -2980 Bruckner Blvd -Bronx 10465 **Fx:**829-7356
(212) 360-3041 .. **O'Halloran,** Margaret R '02 TBTA -1 Randalls Isl -NY 10035
(212) 953-1856 .. **O'Halloran,** Neil J '98 (O'Halloran R LLP) -711 3rd Av -NY 10017
(212) 331-6167 .. **O'Halloran,** Richd J '78 HRA -180 Water -NY 10038
(212) 848-4000 .. **O'Halloran,** Rory B '06 %Shearman & S LLP -599 Lex Av -NY 10022
(718) 273-7799 .. **O'Halloran,** Wm T '61 -17 Seneca Av -Staten Isl 10301
(718) 727-9303 .. **O'Halloran,** Wm T '84 -17 Seneca Av -Staten Isl 10301
(212) 490-4949 .. **O'Hanlon,** Edw P '69 (Kieffer & H LLP) -230 Park Av -NY 10169
(212) 824-5700 .. **O'Hanlon,** Grace E '02 Practising Law Inst -810 7th Av -NY 10019
(631) 928-8000 .. **O'Hanlon,** Janet L '93 %Winkler KW&K,LLP -310 Hallock Av -Pt Jffrsn Sta 11776
(845) 528-4100 .. **O'Hanlon,** John P '72 McDermott & O PC -80 Mill -Putnam Vly 10579 **Fx:**528-7539
(914) 273-9114 .. **O'Hanlon,** John R '60 -6 Kavey Ln -Armonk 10504
(212) 417-5300 .. **O'Hanlon,** Thos E '96 %Medicaid Fraud Cntrl -120 Bway -NY 10271 **Fx:**417-5274
(646) 471-1154 .. **O'Hanrahan,** Ellenore '87 PricewaterhouseCoopers LLP -300 Mad Av -NY 10017
(914) 684-2100 .. **O'Hara,** Amy C '03 %Littman K LLP -399 Knollwood Rd -White Plns 10603
(516) 248-5757 .. **O'Hara,** Christopher P '87 (Colleran O&M,LLP) -1225 Franklin Av -Gdn Cty 11530
(212) 532-0500 .. **O'Hara,** Danl M '09 %Heiberger & Assoc,PC -205 Lex Av -NY 10016 **Fx:**532-2040
(315) 451-3810 .. **O'Hara,** Dennis G '65 (O'Hara O&C,PC) -7207 E Genesee -Fayettevll 13066
(315) 422-4742 .. **O'Hara,** Edw A III '73 -304 S Franklin -Syracuse 13202 **Fx:**478-6503
(516) 593-3028 .. **O'Hara,** Eileen Lynch '95 Malverne Realty -304 Hempstd Av -Malverne 11565 **Fx:**536-2881
(212) 219-1800 .. **O'Hara,** Hedwig '92 %Lawyers Alliance NY -171 Mad Av -NY 10016 **Fx:**941-7458
(631) 673-6670 .. **O'Hara,** James M '93 %Speyer & P,LLP -115 Broadhllw Rd -Melvll 11747
(914) 684-6800 .. **O'Hara,** Jennifer J '03 %Collier HNN&B,LLP -1 N Lex Av -White Plns 10601
(716) 858-8476 .. **O'Hara,** Kathleen E '85 Div of Labor Relations -95 Franklin -Buffalo 14202
(607) 723-9511 .. **O'Hara,** Keith A '91 (Coughlin & G,LLP) -19 Chenango Bx2039 -Bnghmtn 13902
(518) 792-2117 .. **O'Hara,** Malcolm B '82 (Bartlett PS&R,PC) -1 Wshngtn Bx2168 -Glens Fls 12801
(212) 209-5450 .. **O'Hara,** Mary Payton '93 (Madama GO LLP) -450 Park Av S -NY 10016 **Fx:**209-5460
(718) 854-5658 .. **O'Hara,** Michl J '71 -651 Vndrblt -Brklyn 11218
(315) 451-3810 .. **O'Hara O'Connell & Ciotoli,PC** -7207 E Genesee -Fayettevll 13066 **Fx:**451-5585
(212) 330-1144 .. **O'Hara,** Peter M '03 %Buck Consultants -1 Penn Plz -NY 10119 **Fx:**330-1349
(516) 248-5757 .. **O'Hara,** Richd L '58 (Colleran O&M,LLP) -1225 Franklin Av -Gdn Cty 11530
(212) 530-5006 .. **O'Hara,** Robt S Jr. '64 -1 Chase Manh Plz -NY 10005 **Fx:**530-5219
(518) 886-4000 .. **O'Hara,** Timothy D '97 AYCO -321 Bway Bx860 -Saratoga Spgs 12866
(212) 682-2280 .. **O'Hara,** Vincent F '81 (Holm & O LLP) -3 W 35th -NY 10001
(718) 739-2523 .. **O'Hara,** Wm B '03 Chapin Home for the Aging -16501 Chapin Pkwy -Jamaica 11432
(212) 336-2000 .. **O'Hare,** Bernard F '81 (Patterson BW&T LLP) -1133 Av of Amer -NY 10036
(718) 291-3400 .. **O'Hare,** James H '76 Shaevitz & S -148-55 Hillside Av -Jamaica 11435 **Fx:**739-5654
(917) 657-8802 .. **O'Hare,** Jean A '80 -408 W 57th -NY 10019
(212) 425-1401 .. **O'Hare,** Robt A Jr. '94 (O'Hare P LLP) -82 Wall -NY 10005 **Fx:**425-1421
(212) 903-8000 .. **O'Hare,** Robt J '83 %Amer Mgmt Assn -1601 Bway -NY 10019 **Fx:**903-8033
(845) 452-4090 .. **O'Hare,** Stephen P '86 SP O'Hare,PLLC -488 Freedom Plains Rd -Poughkeepsie 12603 **Fx:**452-4615
(718) 286-6000 .. **O'Hare,** Suzanne D '06 %DA -125-01 Qns Blvd -Kew Gdns 11415
(212) 446-4800 .. **O'Hargan,** Shawn P '07 %Kirkland & E LLP -153 E 53rd -NY 10022
(212) 806-5400 .. **Ohayon,** Lior J '03 %Stroock &S&L LLP -180 Maiden Ln -NY 10038
(212) 762-5380 .. **Ohayon,** Melissa R '05 Morgan Stanley -1221 Av of Amer -NY 10020
(718) 250-2000 .. **Ohayon,** Sharon '10 %DA -350 Jay -Brklyn 11201 **Fx:**250-2314
(212) 836-7785 .. **O'Hea,** June A '84 %Kaye S LLP -425 Park Av -NY 10022
(212) 422-1255 .. **O'Hearn,** Walter D Jr. '61 %Keane Securities -17 Battery Pl -NY 10004
(212) 947-1900 .. **Ohebshalom,** David J '95 (D Ohebshalom,PLLC) -347 5th Av -NY 10016
(212) 856-9600 .. **O'Hegarty,** Niall E '02 %Morvillo AGIA&B,PC -565 5th Av -NY 10017
(718) 727-6607 .. **Ohene,** Philip O '92 -805 Castleton Av -Staten Isl 10310 **Fx:**273-7546
(518) 456-6456 .. **O'Hern,** Thos J '86 (Gerstenzang OH&G) -210 Great Oaks Blvd -Albany 12203
(212) 285-4904 .. **O'Hern,** Wm F '82 -225 Bway -NY 10007
(212) 455-2000 .. **Ohiorhenuan,** Zara I '10 %Simpson T&B LLP -425 Lex Av -NY 10017
(585) 582-2330 .. **Ohl & Alexson** -Bx668 -Mendon 14506
(585) 582-2330 .. **Ohl,** Wayne I '74 (Ohl & A) -Bx668 -Mendon 14506
(914) 337-3260 .. **Ohlandt,** John F '56 -900 Palmer Rd -Bronxvll 10708
(212) 681-6500 .. **Ohlberg,** Heather R '06 %Stempel BC&H,PC -675 3rd Av -NY 10017
(212) 446-2300 .. **Ohlemeyer,** Wm S '01 Boies S&F LLP -575 Lex Av -NY 10022
(212) 701-3000 .. **Ohler,** Michl J '98 (Cahill G&R LLP) -80 Pine -NY 10005 **Fx:**269-5420
(631) 266-3535 .. **Ohlig,** Barbara B '83 -514 Larkfld Rd -E Northprt 11731 **Fx:**266-3536
(212) 856-9600 .. **Ohlig,** Gretchan R '95 %Morvillo AGIA&B,PC -565 5th Av -NY 10017
(212) 530-1800 .. **Ohlig,** James J '95 %Richards K&O LLP -1 World Fncl Ctr -NY 10281
(631) 266-1446 .. **Ohlig,** Louis J '62 -514 Larkfld Rd -E Northprt 11731 **Fx:**266-3536
(212) 732-3200 .. **Ohliger,** Lee A '82 Cnsl Carter L&M LLP -2 Wall -NY 10005
(212) 455-2000 .. **Ohlweiler,** John W '69 OfCnsl Simpson T&B LLP -425 Lex Av -NY 10017
(212) 335-9000 .. **Ohm,** Michl W '01 %DA -1 Hogan Pl -NY 10013
(212) 763-6800 .. **Ohman,** John C '93 (Vandenberg & F,LLP) -60 E 42nd -NY 10165
(212) 776-5209 .. **Ohmstedt,** Marguerite R '94 NYC Housing Auth -250 Bway -NY 10007 **Fx:**776-5039
(315) 386-4595 .. **O'Horo,** Cathleen E '74 (Oliver Law Firm) -117 Main -Canton 13617 **Fx:**379-1240
(516) 873-6334 .. **Ohrenstein & Brown,LLP** -1010 Franklin Av Bx9243 -Gdn Cty 11530 **Fx:**873-8912
(516) 873-6334 .. **Ohrenstein,** Manfred '51 (Ohrenstein & B,LLP) -1010 Franklin Av Bx9243 -Gdn Cty 11530
(212) 236-6011 .. **Ohrn,** Jon C '99 %Merrill Lynch -2 World Fncl Ctr -NY 10281
(914) 428-7338 .. **Oisher,** Jack '52 -200 Hgh Pnt Dr -Hartsdale 10530 **Fx:**949-3691
(212) 351-4000 .. **Ojea,** Mildred Milian '01 %Gibson D&C LLP -200 Park Av -NY 10166

(212) 766-0600 .. **Okada,** George '98 Seelig Law Ofc,LLC -299 Bway -NY 10007 **Fx:**766-2616
(212) 687-5252 .. **Okada,** Kyoho A '96 -60 E 42nd -NY 10165
(212) 661-0810 .. **Okada,** Masaharu '93 %Nippon Tel & Tel -101 Park Av -NY 10178
(212) 312-9813 .. **Okafor,** Isaac Guy '00 %State Ins Fund -199 Church -NY 10007 **Fx:**385-9199
(212) 674-5151 .. **Okamoto,** Yasuko '99 Macmillan -175 5th Av -NY 10010 **Fx:**529-0594
(212) 837-6000 .. **Okamoto,** Yasuo '77 (Hughes H&R LLP) -1 Bttry Pk Plz -NY 10004
(315) 689-9512 .. **O'Kane,** Darlene M '96 -Bx124 -Memphis 13112 **Fx:**689-9512
(718) 822-6800 .. **Okasi,** Brenda P '01 (Okasi & O,PC) -1106 Wht Plns Rd -Bronx 10472 **Fx:**822-6890
(718) 822-6800 .. **Okasi,** Steve N '01 (Okasi & O,PC) -1106 Wht Plns Rd -Bronx 10472 **Fx:**822-6890
(212) 859-8000 .. **Okasmaa,** Viktor '06 %Fried FHS&J LLP -1 NY Plz -NY 10004
(585) 344-3161 .. **Okay,** Mehmet Kemal '94 -Bx622 -Batavia 14021
(212) 438-2516 .. **O'Keefe,** Brian E '95 Standard & Poor's -55 Water -NY 10041
(631) 361-8115 .. **O'Keefe,** Brian L '93 (Sweeney & O) -742 Vets Mem'l Hwy -Hauppauge 11788 **Fx:**361-6404
(516) 249-1342 .. **O'Keefe,** Brian P '95 (Grey & G,LLP) -360 Main -Farmngdl 11735
(516) 463-5270 .. **O'Keefe,** Claire T '94 %Hofstra Law Schl -121 Hofstra Univ -Hempstd 11549
(212) 335-9000 .. **O'Keefe,** David '97 %DA -1 Hogan Pl -NY 10013
(716) 694-8404 .. **O'Keefe,** Dennis P '72 -282 Crkside Dr -Tonawanda 14150
(212) 586-0088 .. **O'Keefe,** Georgeanne M '92 %D Lenefsky -1 Columbus Pl -NY 10019 **Fx:**586-0066
(716) 854-3400 .. **O'Keefe,** James M '08 %Rupp BPC&C LLC -1600 Lbrty Bldg -Buffalo 14202
(516) 877-2424 .. **O'Keefe,** Jane F '02 %Weinberg G&P LLP -400 Grdn City Plz -Gdn Cty 11530
(212) 969-3000 .. **O'Keefe,** Jos C Jr. '93 SrCnsl Proskauer R LLP -1585 Bway -NY 10036
(212) 527-1000 .. **O'Keefe,** Kevin Patrick '96 (Jones HC&B PC) -1 Bttry Pk Plz -NY 10004
(631) 321-7938 .. **O'Keefe,** Maeghan Harper '05 -57 W Main -Babylon 11702
(212) 605-0518 .. **O'Keefe,** Margaret M '93 Proxy Adv Grp LLc -575 Mad Av -NY 10022
(585) 798-6406 .. **O'Keefe,** Michl D '03 -549-A N Main -Medina 14103
(914) 682-3970 .. **O'Keefe,** Richd M '77 -300 Main -White Plns 10601 **Fx:**761-2902
(585) 248-0140 .. **O'Keefe,** Shannon Joy '05 Barney & A,LLP -130 D Linden Oaks -Rchstr 14625 **Fx:**248-0175
(202) 872-5041 .. **O'Keefe,** Thos Andrew '86 Cnsl Mercosur Consulting Grp,Ltd -13 Hendrick Hills -Peekskill 10566
(212) 554-4046 .. **O'Keefe,** Thos C '74 -1285 Av of Amer -NY 10019 **Fx:**554-4089
(914) 232-9221 .. **O'Keefe,** Thos F '79 %Rosenberg & O'Keefe -200 Katonah Av -Katonah 10536 **Fx:**232-0574
(518) 285-8571 .. **O'Keefe,** Timothy P '97 Appllt Div 3rd Dept -Capitol Station Bx7288 -Albany 12224 **Fx:**463-1970
(516) 431-1000 .. **O'Keefe-Costello,** Noreen '79 %Corp Cnsl -1 W Chester -Long Bch 11561 **Fx:**431-1016
(518) 591-5232 .. **O'Keeffe,** James J '79 %NYS ORPTS -WA Harriman State Campus -Albany 12227 **Fx:**474-3657
(845) 615-8500 .. **O'Keeffe & McCann LLP** -25 Main -Goshen 10924 **Fx:**615-8501
(518) 367-6153 .. **O'Keeffe,** Patrick J '04 Empire BlueCross/Blue Shield -11 Corp Wds Blvd -Albany 12211
(914) 948-5300 .. **O'Keeffe,** Richd J '59 -2005 Palmer Av PMB 308 -Larchmnt 10538
(845) 615-8500 .. **O'Keeffe,** Wm T '94 (O'Keeffe & M LLP) -25 Main -Goshen 10924
(212) 848-4000 .. **Okehie,** Pamela N '10 Shearman & S LLP -599 Lex Av -NY 10022
(718) 940-3855 .. **Okeke,** Benjamin O '95 -3312 Church Av -Brklyn 11203 **Fx:**940-3862
(718) 855-9595 .. **O'Keke,** Patrick I '99 -255 Lvngstn -Brklyn 11217 **Fx:**855-9494
(718) 653-2650 .. **Okeke,** Victor N '99 -3921 Dyre Av -Bronx 10466 **Fx:**653-2649
(914) 946-2822 .. **O'Kelley & Faller,PC** -445 Hmltn Av -White Plns 10601 **Fx:**946-7950
(718) 923-3382 .. **Okello,** Joab O '97 OTDA Fair Hearings -14 Boerum Pl -Brklyn 11201
(212) 259-8000 .. **O'Kelly,** Eamon '00 (Dewey & L LLP) -1301 Av of Amer -NY 10019
(212) 725-0200 .. **O'Kelly,** James S '64 (Barnes R&C) -475 Park Av S -NY 10016
(516) 248-3338 .. **O'Kelly,** John L '85 Utility Audit Grp -127 Bengeyfld Dr -E Williston 11596 **Fx:**248-4187
(212) 922-9700 .. **Oken,** Howard '63 %1st Amer Title -633 3rd Av -NY 10017 **Fx:**922-0881
(718) 627-7800 .. **Okenwa,** Chuka Steve '01 C Okenwa,PC -902 Kings Hwy -Brklyn 11223 **Fx:**627-2361
(212) 788-9790 .. **Okereke,** Amy N '07 %Law Dept -100 Church -NY 10007 **Fx:**788-0367
(212) 416-8746 .. **Okereke,** Christina C '09 %Dept of Law -120 Bway -NY 10271
(212) 735-3000 .. **Okike,** Christine A '09 %Skadden ASM&F LLP -4 Times Sq -NY 10036
(718) 624-0675 .. **Okin,** Avery Eli '84 Bklyn Bar Assn -123 Remsen -Brklyn 11201 **Fx:**797-1713
(516) 354-2800 .. **Okin,** Lynn S '83 (Mandell MO&E,LLP) -3000 Marcus Av -Lk Success 11042
(212) 309-1000 .. **Okinaka,** Leslie A '98 (Hunton & W) -200 Park Av -NY 10166
(212) 709-8143 .. **Okocha,** Osita E '98 -110 Wall -NY 10005 **Fx:**943-2300
(212) 509-3456 .. **Okoh,** Okwede N '09 %McGivney & K,PC -80 Broad -NY 10004
(212) 564-8152 .. **Okoli,** Kenechukwu C '80 -330 7th Av -NY 10001
(212) 650-7226 .. **Okoro,** Heather Gresham '02 City College of NY -138th & Convent Av -NY 10031
(718) 262-9382 .. **Okoro,** Isaac N '96 -169-13 Jamaica Av -Jamaica 11432 **Fx:**262-9381
(212) 415-9200 .. **Okoro,** Onyinyechi '09 %Dorsey & W LLP -250 Park Av -NY 10177
(917) 804-9585 .. **Okoronkwo,** Kanu David '94 -104-15 198th -St Albans 11412
(212) 940-8800 .. **Okoshi,** Marilyn Selby '90 (Katten MR LLP) -575 Mad Av -NY 10022
(212) 925-5040 .. **Okoye,** Adaobi O '04 R Darby -20 Vesey -NY 10007 **Fx:**732-4648
(646) 315-7300 .. **Okpaku,** Jos Ohifeme '98 %FINRA -14 Wall -NY 10005 **Fx:**315-7440
(212) 474-1000 .. **Okpala,** Jane A '08 %Cravath S&M LLP -825 8th Av -NY 10019
(212) 732-2000 .. **Okrent,** Cynthia B '76 (Cullen and D LLP) -44 Wall -NY 10005
(516) 292-8088 .. **Okrent,** Danl A '96 Nassau/Sfflk Law Srv -1 Helen Keller Way -Hempstd 11550 **Fx:**292-6529
(631) 427-4600 .. **Okrent,** David R '92 -33 Walt Whitman Rd -Dix Hlls 11746 **Fx:**423-0476
(212) 213-4666 .. **Oksenhendler,** Guy M '94 -419 Park Av S -NY 10016
(212) 217-7637 .. **Okubo,** Lisa G '81 FIT -7th Av at 27th -NY 10001
(212) 918-3000 .. **Okuda,** Takashi '05 Hogan L LLP -875 3rd Av -NY 10022
(914) 993-1961 .. **Okula,** Stanley J Jr. '88 %US Atty -300 Quarropas -White Plns 10601 **Fx:**993-9036
(212) 688-5151 .. **Okulski,** Robt V '78 (Gibney A&F,LLP) -665 5th Av -NY 10022
(212) 770-7072 .. **Okum,** Gina B '99 %AIG -72 Wall -NY 10005
(212) 907-0700 .. **Okun,** Barry Michl '82 %Labaton S LLP -140 Bway -NY 10005
(212) 326-2000 .. **Okun,** Brad R '86 (O'Melveny & M LLP) -7 Times Sq -NY 10036
(212) 869-5030 .. **Okun,** Ivan B '99 %Kucker & B,LLP -747 3rd Av -NY 10017
(646) 695-0207 .. **Okun,** Jacob S '01 PLC Partners -20 E 46th -NY 10017
(212) 218-2100 .. **Okun,** Jason M '01 (Fitzpatrick CH&S) -1290 Av of Amer -NY 10104
(212) 619-2723 .. **Okun,** Jeffrey M '98 (J Okun,PC) -321 Bway -NY 10007
(212) 487-9700 .. **Okun,** Marisa J '05 %White F&F,LLP -61 Bway -NY 10006
(212) 642-0950 .. **Okun,** Wm A '76 (Newman & O,PC) -8 W 38th -NY 10018
(718) 923-4206 .. **Okwesa-Zachery,** Chinwe Chika '02 OTDA Fair Hearings -14 Boerum Pl -Brklyn 11201
(718) 250-2000 .. **Okyne,** Ira '07 %DA -350 Jay -Brklyn 11201 **Fx:**250-2314
(516) 812-4500 .. **Olam,** Haley E '08 %Stagg TC&W LLP -401 Franklin Av -Gdn Cty 11530
(212) 584-5100 .. **Olan,** Jennifer M '00 Sirius Satellite Radio -1221 Av of Amer -NY 10020
(212) 986-2390 .. **Olanoff,** Jeffrey '77 -551 5th Av -NY 10176 **Fx:**986-6607
(212) 351-4000 .. **Olanoff,** Oliver M '03 %Gibson D&C LLP -200 Park Av -NY 10166
(212) 267-7565 .. **Olarsch,** S David '95 -160 Bway -NY 10038 **Fx:**267-7571
(212) 763-8417 .. **Olasov,** David M '71 (Olasov & H LLP) -1325 Av of Amer -NY 10019 **Fx:**763-8414
(718) 618-2500 .. **Olaya,** Jennifer L '05 %Civil Ct -851 Grnd Cncrs -Bronx 10451 **Fx:**590-7294
(212) 790-4500 .. **Olberg,** Peter F '80 (Manatt P&P,LLP) -7 Times Sq -NY 10036
(212) 286-5037 .. **Olbrys,** Brooks A '97 (Ion Partners LLC) -521 5th Av -NY 10175 **Fx:**681-7442
(212) 964-6171 .. **Olch,** Norman A '68 -233 Bway -NY 10279 **Fx:**964-7634
(212) 878-8000 .. **Old,** Gareth F '08 (Clifford C LLP) -31 W 52nd -NY 10019
(212) 306-7100 .. **Oldenburg,** Christopher D '01 %Campaign Finance Bd -40 Rector -NY 10006 **Fx:**306-7143
(212) 547-5400 .. **Older,** Stephen E '89 (McDermott W&E LLP) -340 Mad Av -NY 10173
(718) 838-7878 .. **Olderman,** Justine J '99 %Bronx Defenders -860 Crtlandt Av -Bronx 10451 **Fx:**665-0100
(585) 419-8800 .. **Oldfield,** Linda '83 (Harris B PLLC) -99 Garnsey Rd -Pittsfrd 14534
(914) 997-0900 .. **Oldi,** Christopher M '09 Wormser KG&J LLP -399 Knollwood Rd -White Plns 10603
(914) 741-6100 .. **Oldis,** Andrew E '08 %Kaufman B&R -200 Summit Lk Dr -Valhalla 10595
(718) 206-4711 .. **Olds,** Dara A '04 %Law Dept -89-17 Sutphin Blvd -Jamaica 11435 **Fx:**206-4702
(845) 306-1000 .. **Olds,** Gregory D '85 %Watchtower -100 Watchtower Dr -Patterson 12563 **Fx:**306-0709
(315) 479-3380 .. **Olds,** Marjorie Z '77 %UIA Bd -450 S Salina -Syracuse 13202 **Fx:**479-3418
(718) 636-1155 .. **Olds,** Victor '78 %Leg Srvcs -1368 Fulton -Brklyn 11216 **Fx:**398-6414
(212) 506-2500 .. **Olds,** Victor O '09 %Mayer B LLP -1675 Bway -NY 10019
(212) 336-2000 .. **O'Leary,** Argiroula Krypotos '02 %Patterson BW&T LLP -1133 Av of Amer -NY 10036
(212) 319-6888 .. **O'Leary,** Arthur M '80 %Kim & B PC -110 E 59th -NY 10022
(212) 504-6000 .. **O'Leary,** Brendan D '07 %Cadwalader W&T LLP -1 World Fncl Ctr -NY 10281
(212) 664-2227 .. **O'Leary,** Brian J Jr. '94 NBC -30 Rckfllr Plz -NY 10112
(212) 210-9429 .. **Oleary,** Carolyn R '09 %Alston & B LLP -90 Park Av -NY 10016
(718) 894-1496 .. **O'Leary,** Catherine '94 -66-60 80th -Middl Vllg 11379 **Fx:**894-1303
(212) 267-1900 .. **O'Leary,** Christopher D '09 %Wade CM -111 Bway -NY 10006
(212) 837-6049 .. **O'Leary,** Colleen M '05 Hughes H&R LLP -1 Bttry Pk Plz -NY 10004 **Fx:**299-6049
(718) 286-6000 .. **O'Leary,** Danl J '87 %DA -125-01 Qns Blvd -Kew Gdns 11415
(518) 860-1444 .. **O'Leary,** Danl P '99 (Persing & O,LLP) -10 Century Hill Dr -Latham 12110 **Fx:**860-1448
(631) 549-1717 .. **O'Leary,** Denis P '86 (Neufeld & O) -225 Old Cntry Rd -Melvll 11747
(212) 986-0999 .. **O'Leary,** Denis P '86 (Neufeld & O) -230 Park Av -NY 10169
(516) 741-8203 .. **O'Leary,** Dennis A '84 %O'Leary & O -320 Old Cntry Rd -Gdn Cty 11530 **Fx:**741-8206
(718) 643-5121 .. **O'Leary,** Dennis J '84 %Hon LP Hall -360 Adams -Brklyn 11201
(518) 463-4481 .. **O'Leary,** Dennis M '74 -4 Pine -Albany 12207 **Fx:**426-3183
(845) 486-4300 .. **O'Leary,** Diane M '84 (Ostertag OB&F) -17 Cllgvw Av -Poughkeepsie 12603
(212) 563-4100 .. **O'Leary,** Elizabeth '97 (Cohen W&S LLP) -330 W 42nd -NY 10036
(212) 809-1111 .. **O'Leary,** Erin A '96 OfCnsl Morgan MA -39 Bway -NY 10006
(718) 894-1496 .. **O'Leary,** John '54 -66-60 80th -Middl Vllg 11379 **Fx:**894-1303
(718) 448-8400 .. **O'Leary,** John G '83 (O'Leary & S) -25 Manor Rd -Staten Isl 10310
(718) 706-9796 .. **O'Leary,** John M '88 -39-51 46th -Sunnyside 11104
(718) 629-9272 .. **O'Leary,** Jos T '51 -515 E 43rd -Brklyn 11203
(631) 390-0010 .. **O'Leary,** Kevin W '95 (Bruno G&S,LLP) -445 Broad Hollow Rd -Melvll 11747
(212) 406-1884 .. **O'Leary,** Linda E '81 %American Waterway Operators -241 Water -NY 10038
(516) 496-1903 .. **O'Leary,** Marina '98 Fazio R & Assoc LLP -175 Eileen Way -Syosset 11791 **Fx:**496-0912
(845) 343-6227 .. **O'Leary,** Michl '78 (Hayward PO&P) -225 Dolson Av Bx929 -Middletwn 10940 **Fx:**343-1927
(212) 747-1230 .. **O'Leary,** Michl T '95 (McMahon M&G LLP) -55 Washington -Brklyn 11201
(718) 657-5757 .. **O'Leary & O'Leary** -88-14 Sutphin Blvd -Jamaica 11435 **Fx:**526-3363
(212) 609-6800 .. **O'Leary,** Richd P '82 (McCarter & E,LLP) -245 Park Av -NY 10167
(718) 546-0950 .. **O'Leary,** Robt M '75 %Dept of Correction -75-20 Astoria Blvd -E Elmhrst 11370

(315) 682-9131 .. **O'Leary,** Robt P '83 -104 Plsnt Bx57 -Manlius 13104 **Fx:**682-4992
(516) 741-8203 .. **O'Leary,** Sean '86 %O'Leary & O -320 Old Cntry Rd -Gdn Cty 11530 **Fx:**741-8206
(718) 448-8400 .. **O'Leary & Spero** -25 Manor Rd -Staten Isl 10310 **Fx:**448-8448
(718) 657-5757 .. **O'Leary,** Stephen W Jr. '72 (O'Leary & O) -88-14 Sutphin Blvd -Jamaica 11435
(212) 815-0103 .. **O'Leary,** Terence J '03 %DA -1 Hogan Pl -NY 10013
(607) 865-7671 .. **O'Leary,** Terence P '74 -49 North Bx177 -Walton 13856 **Fx:**865-7672
(212) 208-9130 .. **O'Leary,** Teresa '96 Chapdelaine & Co -199 Water -NY 10038
(212) 262-2390 .. **O'Leary,** Thos J '99 (Connell F LLP) -888 7th Av -NY 10106
(518) 463-9284 .. **O'Leary,** Wm V '87 -5 Clinton Sq -Albany 12207
(315) 476-8450 .. **Olech,** Carol Currie '92 (DeLaney & O,LLP) -1 Lincoln Ctr -Syracuse 13202
(716) 881-5800 .. **Olena,** Kenneth A '81 %Siegel K&K -426 Franklin -Buffalo 14202
(212) 624-4300 .. **Olenick,** Donald J '83 BLDG Mgmt Co,Inc -417 5th Av -NY 10016 **Fx:**557-2531
(845) 471-0944 .. **Olenik,** Marilyn Bambeck '80 -26 Hornbeck Rd -Poughkeepsie 12603
(212) 371-4500 .. **Olenko,** Mariana '96 %Seiff K&A -444 Mad Av -NY 10022
(718) 468-3108 .. **Olesh,** Martin H '75 -75-06 192nd -Flushng 11366 **Fx:**740-4599
(212) 233-3079 .. **Oleske,** Jerald F '01 (Maloof LC&O,PA) -299 Bway -NY 10007
(212) 592-1400 .. **Oleske,** John P '02 Cnsl Herrick,F LLP -2 Park Av -NY 10016
(212) 416-8596 .. **Oleske,** Mary E L '85 %Dept of Law -120 Bway -NY 10271
(212) 576-7000 .. **Oleske,** Michl M '78 %NY Life Ins -51 Mad Av -NY 10010 **Fx:**447-0569
(914) 948-4500 .. **Oleson,** Richd C '79 (O'Connor MCD&O) -1 Barker Av -White Plns 10601
(718) 858-0722 .. **Olevsky,** Irina A '98 I Olevsky,PC -360 Court -Brklyn 11231
(718) 742-9717 .. **Olewuenyi,** Chris Chukolems '99 (CC Olewuenyi PC) -594 Grnd Cncrs -Bronx 10451 **Fx:**(908) 206-0514
(212) 249-0326 .. **Olick,** Alice D '78 -860 5th Av -NY 10065
(212) 278-1716 .. **Olick,** Arthur S '56 OfCnsl Anderson K&O,PC -1251 Av of Amer -NY 10020
(212) 692-1000 .. **Olick,** Jonathan A '88 (Duane M LLP) -1540 Bway -NY 10036
(212) 554-7891 .. **Olick,** Philip S '61 (Moses & S LLP) -405 Lex Av -NY 10174 **Fx:**554-7828
(212) 538-0839 .. **Olidge,** Darilyn T '94 Credit Suisse -1 Mad Av -NY 10010
(212) 584-0961 .. **Oliker,** Sarah M '04 Procure Treatment Ctrs,Inc -192 Lex Av -NY 10016 **Fx:**584-0950
(716) 886-5437 .. **Olin,** Judith G '86 Child Advocacy Ctr -556 Franklin -Buffalo 14202
(212) 574-1200 .. **Olin,** Kathleen M '02 %Seward & K LLP -1 Bttry Pk Plz -NY 10004
(212) 768-6700 .. **Olin,** Robt B '98 (Sonnenschein N&R LLP) -2 World Fncl Ctr -NY 10281
(212) 810-3860 .. **Oliner,** Harris '98 Black Rock,Inc -40 E 52nd -NY 10022
(212) 406-9710 .. **Oliner,** Jerome S '89 (Kral CRRP&G,LLP) -170 Bway -NY 10038
(516) 239-1418 .. **Oliner,** Martin '71 M Oliner,PC -195 Central Av -Lawrence 11559
(718) 923-4206 .. **Olinger,** Bruce S '83 %OTDA Fair Hearings -14 Boerum Pl -Brklyn 11201
(315) 701-5780 .. **Olinsky,** Howard D '86 (Olinsky & S) -300 S State -Syracuse 13202
(212) 250-5760 .. **Olinsky,** Jeffrey M '06 Deutsche Bank -60 Wall -NY 10005
(315) 701-5780 .. **Olinsky & Shurtliff** -300 S State -Syracuse 13202 **Fx:**701-5781
(518) 447-9664 .. **Olinzock,** Wayne E '89 %MHLS -75 New Scotland Av -Albany 12208 **Fx:**447-9697
(212) 524-5000 .. **Oliva,** Beth G '05 %Jacob M&F -1270 Av of Amer -NY 10020
(914) 286-3400 .. **Oliva,** Jacqueline F '81 %Leg Aid -1 N Bway -White Plns 10601 **Fx:**682-4112
(212) 765-9000 .. **Oliva,** John E '90 %Gazes,LLC -32 Av of Amer -NY 10013 **Fx:**765-9675
(914) 798-5400 .. **Oliva,** Jos A '94 (Goldberg S LLP) -11 Martine Av -White Plns 10606
(718) 990-6421 .. **Oliva,** Jos E '95 St Johns Univ -8000 Utopia Pkwy -Jamaica 11439
(516) 684-2900 .. **Oliva,** Linda M '89 %Pegalis & E,LLC -1 Hllw Ln -Lk Success 11042
(718) 482-4965 .. **Oliva,** Louis P '91 %DEC -1 Hunters Pnt Plz -LIC 11101 **Fx:**482-4962
(914) 286-3610 .. **Oliva,** Nicholas J '04 Mitsubishi Chemical Amer -1 N Lex Av -White Plns 10601
(212) 335-9000 .. **Oliva,** Stephanie D '09 %DA -1 Hogan Pl -NY 10013
(212) 986-7353 .. **Oliva,** Thos M '89 %Wingate R&S -420 Lex Av -NY 10170
(516) 876-0800 .. **Olivari,** Maria T '88 %Druckman Law Grp PLLC -242 Drexel Av -Westbury 11590 **Fx:**876-0888
(212) 610-6300 .. **Oliva Sainz de Aja,** Margarita '98 SrCnsl Allen & O -1221 Av of Amer -NY 10020
(212) 608-1818 .. **Olive,** Laurence H '90 -128 Mott -NY 10013 **Fx:**608-0505
(212) 357-2755 .. **Oliveira,** Carla M '99 Goldman Sachs -1 NY Plz -NY 10004
(212) 553-5671 .. **Oliveira,** Henrique J '99 %Zurich NA -1 Lbrty Plz -NY 10006
(212) 715-9210 .. **Oliveira,** Juliana Pereira '06 Kramer LN&F,LLP -1177 Av of Amer -NY 10036
(212) 566-7188 .. **Oliveira,** Michl J '90 Cnsl Genova B&G -115 Bway -NY 10006
(585) 275-5144 .. **Oliveiri,** David J '74 Univ of Rochester-Simon Grad Schl of Bsns -Bx270100E -Rchstr 14627
(716) 854-1111 .. **Oliver,** Abby E '09 %Spadafora & V -2 Symphony Cir -Buffalo 14201
(212) 554-7800 .. **Oliver,** Andrew J '03 (Moses & S LLP) -405 Lex Av -NY 10174
(914) 381-7400 .. **Oliver,** Arlene Gordon '94 (Rattet P&G,LLP) -550 Mamaroneck Av -Harrison 10528
(631) 293-6060 .. **Oliver,** Christian R '08 (Cellino & B,PC) -445 Broad Hollow Rd -Melvll 11747
(315) 422-7111 .. **Oliver,** Donald D '80 (Blitman & K LLP) -443 N Franklin -Syracuse 13204
(518) 408-4863 .. **Oliver,** Erin D '03 OCFS -52 Wshngtn -Rensselaer 12144 **Fx:**486-6361
(212) 568-7738 .. **Oliver,** Fernando J '90 -803 W 180th -NY 10033 **Fx:**568-5181
(646) 263-3495 .. **Oliver,** Gideon O '04 -200 E 10th -NY 10003
(516) 334-2500 .. **Oliver,** Ishelli L '03 %Feldman RK&F,PC -410 Jericho Tpk -Jericho 11753
(212) 589-4200 .. **Oliver,** Jason S '04 %Baker & H LLP -45 Rckfllr Plz -NY 10111
(718) 896-2500 .. **Oliver,** Jennifer Clapperton '99 -97-45 Qns Blvd -Flushng 11374 **Fx:**275-2094
(585) 248-3800 .. **Oliver,** Jeremy R '09 %WeinsteinMurphy -290 Linden Oaks -Rchstr 14625 **Fx:**248-4961
(518) 434-1022 .. **Oliver,** John M '95 (Sullivan KO&V, LLP) -152 Central Av -Albany 12206
(212) 530-5000 .. **Oliver,** Kathleen '10 %Milbank TH&M LLP -1 Chase Manh Plz -NY 10005
(518) 285-6000 .. **Oliver,** Kelly M '03 MapInfo Corp -1 Global Vw -Troy 12180 **Fx:**285-6060
(845) 562-0203 .. **Oliver,** Kenneth L '79 (Finkelstein & Prtnrs,LLP) -1279 Route 300 Bx1111 -Newburgh 12550
(914) 448-0200 .. **Oliver,** Kenneth S '80 (Bartlett MB&M,LLP) -81 Main -White Plns 10601
(212) 541-2000 .. **Oliver,** Kristina P '08 %Bryan C LLP -1290 Av of Amer -NY 10104
(315) 478-3500 .. **Oliver,** Laurie Colton '93 %Mannion & C -224 Harrison -Syracuse 13202
(518) 463-7962 .. **Oliver,** Lewis B Jr. '67 (Oliver & O) -156 Mad Av -Albany 12202
(716) 284-8831 .. **Oliver,** Mary Ann '89 %Leg Aid -775 3rd Bx844 -Niagara Fls 14302 **Fx:**284-8040
(212) 504-6000 .. **Oliver,** Matthew J '10 %Cadwalader W&T LLP -1 World Fncl Ctr -NY 10281
(212) 450-4000 .. **Oliver,** Melissa A '08 %Davis P&W LLP -450 Lex Av -NY 10017
(212) 259-8000 .. **Oliver,** Nabavi A '08 %Dewey & L LLP -1301 Av of Amer -NY 10019
(212) 450-4000 .. **Oliver,** Ross A '05 %Davis P&W LLP -450 Lex Av -NY 10017
(718) 286-6000 .. **Oliveri,** Christine M '07 %DA -125-01 Qns Blvd -Kew Gdns 11415
(914) 750-5933 .. **Oliveri,** Claudia '99 (Kissel H&W LLP) -580 Wht Plns Rd -Tarrytwn 10591
(212) 987-1100 .. **Oliveri,** Paul F '79 (Oliveri & S,PC) -1825 Park Av -NY 10035 **Fx:**297-0504
(716) 856-4200 .. **Oliveri,** Victor A '72 (Gibson M&C,LLP) -69 Delaware Av -Buffalo 14202
(716) 852-1300 .. **Oliverio,** B P '79 (Amigone S&M,LLP) -350 Main -Buffalo 14202
(716) 856-4000 .. **Oliverio,** Danl C '83 (Hodgson R LLP) -140 Pearl -Buffalo 14202
(914) 725-2567 .. **Oliverio,** Susan Guarino '93 -717 Wht Plns Rd -Scarsdale 10583 **Fx:**725-1547
(212) 848-8593 .. **Olivier,** Jeanne C '80 (Shearman & S LLP) -599 Lex Av -NY 10022
(718) 782-5500 .. **Olivier,** Karla A '94 Kupfer & Assoc,PLLC -190 N 10th -Brklyn 11211 **Fx:**782-5577
(718) 286-6000 .. **Olivier,** Vanessa A '09 %DA -125-01 Qns Blvd -Kew Gdns 11415
(212) 360-1313 .. **Olivieri,** Alessandro G '93 %Dept of Parks & Rec -The Arsenal Cntrl Pk -NY 10065 **Fx:**360-1373
(516) 470-0704 .. **Olivieri,** Danl R '83 D Olivieri,PC -100 Jericho Quad -Jericho 11753 **Fx:**931-8101
(212) 517-7880 .. **Olivieri,** Frances R '83 (Johnston & O) -36 E 72nd -NY 10021 **Fx:**517-7889
(212) 819-8200 .. **Olivieri,** John M '95 (White & C LLP) -1155 Av of Amer -NY 10036
(845) 256-3031 .. **Olivieri,** Lara Q '01 DEC -21 S Putt Crnrs Rd -New Paltz 12561 **Fx:**255-4659
(585) 647-3010 .. **Olivieri,** Leonard P '90 %Peko Precision Prod -1400 Emerson -Rchstr 14606 **Fx:**647-1366
(212) 962-0888 .. **Olivieri,** Richd J '95 -305 Bway -NY 10007 **Fx:**(646) 349-1768
(716) 856-4000 .. **Olivieri,** Robt J '76 (Hodgson R LLP) -140 Pearl -Buffalo 14202
(718) 340-1409 .. **Oliviero,** James F '72 Cnsl KSW,Inc -37-16 23rd -LIC 11101 **Fx:**361-5210
(516) 267-6300 .. **Olivo,** Craig L '95 (Bond S&K,PLLC) -1399 Franklin Av -Gdn Cty 11530
(212) 335-9000 .. **Olivo,** Jeanne A '87 %DA -1 Hogan Pl -NY 10013
(212) 697-6262 .. **Olivo,** John W Jr. '89 (Ward & O) -380 Mad Av -NY 10017
(212) 267-7900 .. **Olivo,** M Robbie '94 (Stamm & O,LLP) -295 Mad Av -NY 10017
(212) 867-4727 .. **Olivo,** Paul J '69 -300 E 40th -NY 10016
(212) 225-2000 .. **Oliwenstein,** David '09 %Cleary GS&H -1 Lbrty Plz -NY 10006
(212) 486-6060 .. **Olk,** Barbara E '77 (Trief & O) -150 E 58th -NY 10155
(212) 619-1245 .. **Ollen,** Danl J '83 -805 3rd Av -NY 10022 **Fx:**619-1248
(212) 525-2774 .. **Ollendorff,** Scott H '97 HSBC Securities -452 5th Av -NY 10018
(212) 536-3900 .. **Ollendorff,** Stephen A '64 OfCnsl K&L Gates LLP -599 Lex Av -NY 10022
(212) 728-8000 .. **Oller,** John R '83 (Willkie F&G LLP) -787 7th Av -NY 10019
(716) 856-0600 .. **Ollinick,** Christopher N '09 Jaeckle F&M,LLP -12 Fountain Plz -Buffalo 14202
(716) 854-3400 .. **Ollinick,** Elizabeth A '03 %Rupp BPC&C LLC -1600 Lbrty Bldg -Buffalo 14202
(516) 946-6111 .. **Ollivierre,** Dawn D '95 -46 Wedgewood Dr -Westbury 11590
(212) 596-9000 .. **Ollivierre,** Scott C '10 %Ropes & G LLP -1211 Av of Amer -NY 10036
(914) 633-7400 .. **Ollman,** Robt C '71 (Marcus O&K LLP) -145 Huguenot -New Rchll 10801
(516) 626-2470 .. **Olman,** Donald D '61 (Rassner R&O) -14 Twr Pl -Roslyn 11576
(631) 754-3200 .. **Olmstead,** Arthur E '83 -514 Larkfld Rd -E Northprt 11731 **Fx:**754-3003
(212) 848-4000 .. **Olmstead,** Clarence W Jr. '70 OfCnsl Shearman & S LLP -599 Lex Av -NY 10022
(212) 751-7700 .. **Olmstead,** John C '76 OfCnsl Faust & O,LLP -488 Mad Av -NY 10022
(212) 479-6724 .. **Olney,** Eric Saml '04 Macht SA&I LLP -1114 Av of Amer -NY 10036 **Fx:**202-6417
(212) 670-0364 .. **Olney,** Michl E '83 %Merrill Lynch -222 Bway -NY 10038
(631) 427-7888 .. **Olnowich,** Heath B '98 %Markowitz & R LLP -290 Broadhllw Rd -Melvll 11747
(212) 490-0704 .. **Oloko,** Shamsey '99 Thorgood Law Firm -100 Park Av -NY 10017 **Fx:**490-0706
(212) 705-7000 .. **O'Loughlin,** Colleen J '01 Cnsl Bingham M LLP -399 Park Av -NY 10022
(917) 937-3000 .. **O'Loughlin,** Darcy L '03 Guy Carpenter & Co,Inc -1166 Av of Amer -NY 10036
(212) 836-8000 .. **O'Loughlin,** David S '08 %Kaye S LLP -425 Park Av -NY 10022
(914) 524-5600 .. **O'Loughlin,** Edw G '76 %L Fishman -303 S Bway -Tarrytwn 10591 **Fx:**524-5742
(716) 566-1300 .. **O'Loughlin,** Sandra S '79 (Hiscock & B,LLP) -1100 M&T Ctr -Buffalo 14203
(212) 940-3007 .. **Olsen,** Abigail S '98 %Nixon P LLP -437 Mad Av -NY 10022
(518) 220-1850 .. **Olsen,** Arlen L '94 (Schmeiser O&W) -22 Century Hill Dr -Latham 12110
(631) 543-3663 .. **Olsen,** David W '91 OfCnsl Migliore & I,PC -353 Vets Mem'l Hwy -Commack 11725
(631) 734-7666 .. **Olsen,** David W '99 -Bx706 -Cutchogue 11935
(212) 806-5400 .. **Olsen,** Deborah M '00 SpclCnsl Stroock &S&L LLP -180 Maiden Ln -NY 10038

(631) 734-7666 .. **Olsen,** Gary F '65 -Bx706 -Cutchogue 11935
(212) 577-2600 .. **Olsen,** George L '86 (G Olsen,PC) -299 Bway -NY 10007 **Fx:**577-2606
(212) 806-5400 .. **Olsen,** Harold A '98 SpclCnsl Stroock &S&L LLP -180 Maiden Ln -NY 10038
(718) 875-1300 .. **Olsen,** Jeffrey J '89 %Appllt Div 2nd Dept -45 Monroe Pl -Brklyn 11201 **Fx:**858-2446
(212) 770-1686 .. **Olsen,** Marcy S '91 %AIG -80 Pine -NY 10005 **Fx:**809-2452
(646) 472-5169 .. **Olsen,** Marissa '99 -40 Clinton -Brklyn 11201 **Fx:**(212) 659-3249
(212) 940-8800 .. **Olsen,** Matthew W '03 (Katten MR LLP) -575 Mad Av -NY 10022
(516) 746-2300 .. **Olsen,** Michele R '02 %A Capetola -2C Hillside Av -Williston Pk 11596 **Fx:**746-2318
(212) 318-6000 .. **Olsen,** Peter C '90 (Paul HJ&W LLP) -75 E 55th -NY 10022
(845) 986-8600 .. **Olsen,** Priscilla Almquist '81 -37 Pumpkin Hill Rd Bx7 -Warwick 10990 **Fx:**987-1999
(716) 645-2052 .. **Olsen,** R Nils '93 %SUNY Buffalo Lw Schl -O'Brian Hall -Buffalo 14260 **Fx:**645-5968
(516) 676-7362 .. **Olsen,** Rosemary Anne '89 %City of Glen Cove -9 Glen -Glen Cove 11542 **Fx:**676-0108
(800) 358-2550 .. **Olsen,** Shelley Rossoff '83 NAM -990 Stewart Av -Gdn Cty 11530
(212) 770-7000 .. **Olsen,** Thos J IV '95 %AIG -80 Pine -NY 10005
(607) 753-5299 .. **Olsen-Tjensvold,** Ingrid '88 %Dept Soc Srvcs -60 Central Av Bx5590 -Cortlnd 13045 **Fx:**753-5392
(347) 448-8531 .. **Olshaker,** Clifford B '99 -4047 75th -Elmhrst 11373
(212) 451-2300 .. **Olshan Grundman Frome Rosenzweig & Wolosky LLP** -65 E 55th -NY 10022 **Fx:**451-2222
(212) 451-2300 .. **Olshan,** Marvin L '52 OfCnsl Olshan GFR&W LLP -65 E 55th -NY 10022
(212) 735-3000 .. **Olshan,** Regina '94 (Skadden ASM&F LLP) -4 Times Sq -NY 10036
(212) 526-0461 .. **Olshan,** Wm A '87 Cnsl Lehman Bros -1271 Av of Amer -NY 10020
(212) 505-2100 .. **Olshansky,** Barbara J '87 %Envrnmntl Def Fund -257 Park Av S -NY 10010 **Fx:**505-2375
(718) 590-2000 .. **Olsher,** Dahlia D '07 %DA -198 E 161st -Bronx 10451 **Fx:**590-6477
(212) 741-3510 .. **Olshever,** Robt M '77 -148 W 24th -NY 10011 **Fx:**741-3549
(212) 977-9700 .. **Olshin,** Ira C '94 Cnsl Phillips N LLP -666 5th Av -NY 10103
(212) 230-8800 .. **Olsky,** David '09 Cnsl WilmerHale -399 Park Av -NY 10022
(212) 606-7432 .. **Olsoff,** Jonathan A '86 %Sotheby's,Inc -1334 York Av -NY 10021 **Fx:**606-7574
(716) 488-0991 .. **Olson,** Avery S '09 -106 Forest Av -Jamestwn 14701
(516) 572-0585 .. **Olson,** Carolyn Cairns '78 Nassau Health Care Corp -2001 Hempstd Tpk -E Meadow 11554
(212) 450-4000 .. **Olson,** Christine L '10 %Davis P&W LLP -450 Lex Av -NY 10017
(631) 423-0001 .. **Olson,** Christopher S '82 -34 Dewey -Huntngtn 11743 **Fx:**271-0656
(212) 545-4880 .. **Olson,** David R '99 America Media Inc -1 Park Av -NY 10016
(716) 681-7190 .. **Olson,** David W '97 %Brown C LLP -5775 Bway -Lancaster 14086
(212) 880-3800 .. **Olson,** Eric W '93 OfCnsl Akerman S -335 Mad Av -NY 10017
(718) 966-3543 .. **Olson,** Joanne D '04 -136 Bay -Staten Isl 10301 **Fx:**815-1872
(212) 669-0600 .. **Olson,** John E '78 (Hill R LLP) -45 Bway -NY 10006
(914) 345-3020 .. **Olson,** Karen B '96 %Knuckles K&E,LLP -565 Taxter Rd -Elmsfrd 10523
(212) 416-8000 .. **Olson,** Kevin G W '00 %Dept of Law -120 Bway -NY 10271
(585) 352-8900 .. **Olson,** Richd J '78 -24 West Av Bx130 -Spencerprt 14559
(845) 486-6800 .. **Olson,** Richd J '85 (McCabe & M LLP) -63 Wshngtn Bx509 -Poughkeepsie 12602
(716) 884-5371 .. **Olson,** Roger A '63 -267 Linwood Av -Buffalo 14209
(212) 986-6200 .. **Olson,** Roger D '77 -230 Park Av -NY 10169 **Fx:**661-2153
(212) 553-0300 .. **Olson,** Ruth E '99 %Moody's Invstr Srvc -250 Greenwich -NY 10007
(518) 449-3900 .. **Olson,** Scott P '94 (Cooper E&S,LLP) -39 N Pearl -Albany 12207
(212) 838-7797 .. **Olson,** Steig D '04 %Cohen MS&T,PLLC -88 Pine -NY 10005
(212) 839-5300 .. **Olson,** Steven I '08 %Sidley A LLP -787 7th Av -NY 10019
(212) 225-2000 .. **Olson,** Wanda J '82 (Cleary GS&H) -1 Lbrty Plz -NY 10006
(516) 747-2000 .. **Olson,** Wayne M '85 (Margolin Winer Evens,LLP) -400 Grdn City Plz -Gdn Cty 11530 **Fx:**747-6707
(585) 473-1180 .. **Olsson,** Hope W '95 -1580 Elmwood Av -Rchstr 14620
(212) 558-4000 .. **Olsson,** John E '07 Sullivan & C LLP -125 Broad -NY 10004
(212) 819-8200 .. **Olsson,** Marten Matshans '00 %White & C LLP -1155 Av of Amer -NY 10036
(212) 259-8000 .. **Olstein,** David C '95 Cnsl Dewey & L LLP -1301 Av of Amer -NY 10019
(716) 284-8831 .. **Olszowka,** Deborah A '86 %Leg Aid -775 3rd Bx844 -Niagara Fls 14302 **Fx:**284-8040
(212) 420-4351 .. **Olt,** Felicia Ann '90 %Beth Israel Med Ctr -10 Fierman Hall -NY 10003 **Fx:**420-2467
(212) 944-9420 .. **Oltarsh,** David E '54 (Oltarsh & Assoc,PC) -494 8th Av -NY 10001 **Fx:**944-9120
(212) 944-9420 .. **Oltarsh,** Jennifer Maude '94 (Oltarsh & Assoc,PC) -494 8th Av -NY 10001 **Fx:**944-9120
(212) 944-9420 .. **Oltarsh,** Wm H '56 (Oltarsh & Assoc,PC) -494 8th Av -NY 10001 **Fx:**944-9120
(516) 931-8100 .. **Olteanu,** Andreea '06 %Capell BM&S,LLP -100 Jericho Quadrangle -Jericho 11753
(212) 720-5005 .. **Oltman,** James H '60 %Fed Reserve Bk -33 Lbrty -NY 10045 **Fx:**720-8742
(212) 587-5360 .. **Olugbodi,** Ojediji A '00 -116 John -NY 10038
(212) 225-2000 .. **Olupona,** Michelle Busayo '07 %Cleary GS&H -1 Lbrty Plz -NY 10006
(718) 585-2700 .. **Oluwasusi,** Adewunmi Ade '96 (A Oluwasusi,PC) -594 Grnd Cncrs -Bronx 10451 **Fx:**585-1627
(585) 387-0500 .. **Olver Korts LLP** -100 Ofc Park Way -Pittsfrd 14534 **Fx:**387-9234
(585) 387-0500 .. **Olver,** Melvin L '82 (Olver K LLP) -100 Ofc Park Way -Pittsfrd 14534
(516) 745-1122 .. **O'Mahony,** Wm J '94 (Quadrino & S,PC) -666 Old Cntry Rd -Gdn Cty 11530
(914) 765-4351 .. **O'Malia,** Scott A '01 IBM -1 N Castle Dr -Armonk 10504
(212) 770-1615 .. **O'Malley,** Barbara Ann '84 AIG -80 Pine -NY 10005
(212) 770-2698 .. **O'Malley,** Barbara J '91 %AIG -80 Pine -NY 10005 **Fx:**344-2357
(212) 218-2100 .. **O'Malley,** Brendan M '08 %Fitzpatrick CH&S -1290 Av of Amer -NY 10104
(212) 681-6500 .. **O'Malley,** Christopher P '06 %Stempel BC&H,PC -675 3rd Av -NY 10017
(212) 650-1126 .. **O'Malley,** Cormac K H '71 -156 E 79th -NY 10075 **Fx:**396-4662
(315) 442-0100 .. **O'Malley,** Deborah S '08 %Gilberti SH&S,PC -555 E Genesee -Syracuse 13202
(212) 669-8171 .. **O'Malley,** Edw F '81 %Ofc of the City Clerk -265 Mncpl Bldg -NY 10007
(212) 637-0136 .. **O'Malley,** George C '76 %USDC -500 Pearl -NY 10007
(212) 619-8387 .. **O'Malley,** James A '87 (J O'Malley,PC) -299 Bway -NY 10007 **Fx:**406-2967
(212) 318-6000 .. **O'Malley,** Jos M Jr. '93 (Paul HJ&W LLP) -75 E 55th -NY 10022
(212) 220-3830 .. **O'Malley,** Kevin J B '00 %Nicoletti H&S -88 Pine -NY 10005
(845) 359-0777 .. **O'Malley,** Kevin P '73 -155 Washington Bx40 -Tappan 10983 **Fx:**359-0913
(212) 953-2381 .. **O'Malley,** Michl C '98 %Rubin F&F,LLP -292 Mad Av -NY 10017
(518) 473-5671 .. **O'Malley,** Patricia E '93 %Div of Parole -97 Central Av -Albany 12206 **Fx:**473-6037
(718) 250-0400 .. **O'Malley,** Patrick T '94 %R Tusa -1 MetroTech Ctr -Brklyn 11201 **Fx:**250-0591
(212) 819-8200 .. **O'Malley,** Sean P '07 (White & C LLP) -1155 Av of Amer -NY 10036
(212) 944-0500 .. **O'Malley,** Suzanne M '04 %Hofheimer G&G,LLP -530 5th Av -NY 10036 **Fx:**897-4983
(212) 446-6273 .. **O'Malley,** Terrance J '98 Blue Ridge Capital,LLC -120 Wht Plns Rd -Tarrytwn 10591
(518) 783-0493 .. **O'Malley,** Thos K '88 -4093 Rvr Rd -Latham 12110 **Fx:**783-0493
(212) 233-2100 .. **O'Malley,** Thos P '93 (Oshman & M,LLP) -42 Bway -NY 10004
(212) 230-8800 .. **Oman,** Tabitha R '07 %WilmerHale -399 Park Av -NY 10022
(212) 571-6658 .. **Omansky,** Lawr A '75 -305 Bway -NY 10007 **Fx:**385-1977
(212) 621-1500 .. **Omar,** Riyad Ali '99 Assoc Press -450 W 33rd -NY 10001
(212) 848-4000 .. **O'Mara,** Coleen A '01 Cnsl Shearman & S LLP -599 Lex Av -NY 10022
(212) 735-3000 .. **O'Mara,** David M '10 %Skadden ASM&F LLP -4 Times Sq -NY 10036
(607) 733-4635 .. **O'Mara,** John F '58 (Davidson & O,PC) -243 Lk -Elmira 14901
(718) 250-2000 .. **O'Mara,** John P Jr. '79 %DA -350 Jay -Brklyn 11201 **Fx:**250-2314
(718) 270-4628 .. **O'Mara,** Kevin P '95 -450 Clarkson Av -Brklyn 11203
(212) 326-3939 .. **O'Mara,** L Kevin '88 (Jones D) -222 E 41st -NY 10017
(607) 738-7419 .. **O'Mara,** Marilyn Pina '92 -62 Quail Run -Elmira 14903
(914) 941-9262 .. **O'Mara,** Patrick J '74 -6 Somerstown Rd -Ossining 10562
(607) 733-4635 .. **O'Mara,** Thos F '92 (Davidson & O,PC) -243 Lk -Elmira 14901
(716) 633-5700 .. **O'Mara,** Timothy M '67 -5820 Main -Williamsvll 14221 **Fx:**632-1908
(212) 596-9000 .. **O'Mary,** Jessica Taylor '08 %Ropes & G LLP -1211 Av of Amer -NY 10036
(914) 328-0404 .. **Ombok,** Otieno B '02 %Jackson L LLP -1 N Bway -White Plns 10601
(718) 767-7667 .. **Ombres,** Teresa '81 (T Ombres LLC) -38-39 Bell Blvd -Bayside 11361 **Fx:**767-5488
(212) 983-8500 .. **O'Mea,** Patrick R '08 Brown G&F LLP -355 Lex Av -NY 10017
(718) 585-2315 .. **O'Meara,** Brendan T '00 -304 Grnd Cncrs -Bronx 10451 **Fx:**585-2048
(212) 530-1800 .. **O'Meara,** Eric M '95 %Richards K&O LLP -1 World Fncl Ctr -NY 10281
(718) 250-2000 .. **O'Meara,** Meghan A '08 %DA -350 Jay -Brklyn 11201 **Fx:**250-2314
(716) 858-2424 .. **Omel,** Kelley Anne '90 %DA -25 Delaware Av -Buffalo 14202 **Fx:**858-7425
(212) 554-7800 .. **O'Melia,** Joshua M '07 %Moses & S LLP -405 Lex Av -NY 10174
(212) 326-2000 .. **O'Melveny & Myers LLP** -7 Times Sq -NY 10036 **Fx:**326-2061
(716) 873-2900 .. **Omerhodzic,** Ibrahim '88 -601 Hertel Av -Buffalo 14207
(212) 416-8000 .. **Ommen,** Todd D '00 %Dept of Law -120 Bway -NY 10271
(212) 735-3000 .. **Omoregie,** Osahon O '08 %Skadden ASM&F LLP -4 Times Sq -NY 10036
(212) 599-5550 .. **Omrani,** Alex A '98 (Omrani & T,PC) -909 3rd Av -NY 10022
(212) 599-5550 .. **Omrani & Taub,PC** -909 3rd Av -NY 10022 **Fx:**599-5551
(212) 968-8300 .. **Omundson,** Erika L '98 %Mintzer SZL&M LLP -39 Bway -NY 10006
(212) 344-5400 .. **O'Murchadha,** Niall D '04 %Schlam S&D LLP -26 Bway -NY 10004
(212) 949-0100 .. **Onaga,** Grace S '81 %Cmmnwlth Land Title -140 E 45th -NY 10017 **Fx:**983-8430
(212) 371-1011 .. **Oncioiu,** Raluca Yidrica '99 %Catholic Charities -1011 1st Av -NY 10022
(212) 279-9090 .. **Onder,** Thos S '03 (Stark & S) -One Penn Plz -NY 10119 **Fx:**279-9113
(518) 285-8600 .. **Onderdonk,** Marne L '97 Family Ct -30 Clinton Av -Albany 12207
(914) 761-2252 .. **Ondrovic,** Robt S '86 (Boeggeman G&C,PC) -1 Water -White Plns 10601
(212) 225-2000 .. **O'Neal,** Sean A '01 (Cleary GS&H) -1 Lbrty Plz -NY 10006
(347) 296-1470 .. **O'Neale,** Inga M '02 %Hon MR Jackson -360 Adams -Brklyn 11201
(212) 610-6300 .. **O'Neil,** Brandon D '09 %Allen & O -1221 Av of Amer -NY 10020
(845) 452-6400 .. **O'Neil & Burke** -301 Mnchstr Rd -Poughkeepsie 12603
(845) 452-6400 .. **O'Neil,** D James '77 (O'Neil & B) -301 Mnchstr Rd -Poughkeepsie 12603
(212) 637-2533 .. **O'Neil,** David A '03 US Atty-SDNY -1 St Andrews Plz -NY 10007
(212) 326-3939 .. **O'Neil,** Jennifer J '09 %Jones D -222 E 41st -NY 10017
(518) 785-5252 .. **O'Neil,** Jennifer Tocci '87 -Bx6 -Latham 12110 **Fx:**785-7332
(212) 373-3379 .. **O'Neil,** John J '69 (Paul WRW&G LLP) -1285 Av of Amer -NY 10019
(914) 995-2660 .. **O'Neil,** John J '84 %Cnty Atty -148 Martine Av -White Plns 10601 **Fx:**995-5858
(212) 446-4800 .. **O'Neil,** John R '06 (Kirkland & E LLP) -153 E 53rd -NY 10022
(212) 859-8000 .. **O'Neil,** Lauren E '08 %Fried FHS&J LLP -1 NY Plz -NY 10004
(212) 556-2100 .. **O'Neil,** Margaret E '89 (King & S) -1185 Av of Amer -NY 10036
(212) 705-7000 .. **O'Neil,** Michl B '08 %Bingham M LLP -399 Park Av -NY 10022
(212) 940-8800 .. **O'Neil,** Patience J '84 SpclCnsl Katten MR LLP -575 Mad Av -NY 10022
(212) 268-8935 .. **O'Neil,** Paul '85 Human Rights in China -350 5th Av -NY 10118 **Fx:**239-2561
(914) 235-1525 .. **O'Neil,** Sean M '04 Leadership Designs -434 Pelhamdale Av -Pelham 10803
(516) 267-6300 .. **O'Neil,** Terence M '71 (Bond S&K,PLLC) -1399 Franklin Av -Gdn Cty 11530
(914) 846-7000 .. **O'Neill,** Brian M '83 %NY Life Ins -1 Rockwood Rd -Sleepy Hollow 10591 **Fx:**846-4755
(212) 848-4000 .. **O'Neill,** Casey T '09 %Shearman & S LLP -599 Lex Av -NY 10022

(212) 408-5100 .. **O'Neill**, Chas K '73 (Chadbourne & P LLP) -30 Rckfllr Plz -NY 10112
(646) 315-7382 .. **O'Neill**, Christopher R '06 FINRA -14 Wall -NY 10005
(914) 761-2252 .. **O'Neill**, Danl E '94 %Boeggeman G&C,PC -1 Water -White Plns 10601
(212) 408-5100 .. **O'Neill**, Danl J '62 OfCnsl Chadbourne & P LLP -30 Rckfllr Plz -NY 10112
(212) 850-8500 .. **O'Neill**, Danl J '75 OfCnsl Bruckmann & V,LLP -420 Lex Av -NY 10170
(212) 450-4000 .. **O'Neill**, Danl J '04 %Davis P&W LLP -450 Lex Av -NY 10017
(212) 267-5556 .. **O'Neill DiManno & Kelly** -15 Beekman -NY 10038 **Fx**:227-3235
(914) 833-2607 .. **O'Neill**, Eileen M '84 -129 Carleon Av -Larchmnt 10538
(212) 230-8800 .. **O'Neill**, Emily Penney '04 Cnsl WilmerHale -399 Park Av -NY 10022
(212) 695-5670 .. **O'Neill**, Eugene Jr. '81 %Goldfinger & L LLP -750 3rd Av -NY 10017
(212) 839-7000 .. **O'Neill**, Gregory W '73 (Hill B&N LLP) -200 Lbrty -NY 10281
(212) 779-3500 .. **O'Neill**, Heather J '97 %Morrissey & M,LLP -60 E 42nd -NY 10165 **Fx**:779-2995
(914) 390-4146 .. **O'Neill**, James F '98 %Hon C McMahon -300 Quarropas -White Plns 10601
(914) 949-2700 .. **O'Neill**, John I '79 OfCnsl Bleakley P&S,LLP -1 N Lex Av -White Plns 10601
(212) 977-4422 .. **O'Neill**, Judith D '01 (Nakhota,LLC) -2 Columbus Av -NY 10023 **Fx**:312-2134
(914) 251-0300 .. **O'Neill**, Kathleen M '92 CareNext Grp -2500 Wstchstr Av -Purchase 10577
(212) 225-2000 .. **O'Neill**, Kathleen M '07 %Cleary GS&H -1 Lbrty Plz -NY 10006
(914) 253-4883 .. **O'Neill**, Kelly Anne '93 %State Ins Fund -105 Corp Park Dr -White Plns 10604
(516) 593-5189 .. **O'Neill**, Kevin F '82 -426 Vincent Av -Lynbrk 11563
(212) 422-9424 .. **O'Neill**, Kevin J '88 (Gogick B&O,LLP) -11 Bway -NY 10004
(716) 854-4055 .. **O'Neill**, Kevin M '86 (O'Neill & B) -298 Main -Buffalo 14202 **Fx**:854-4062
(518) 474-1331 .. **O'Neill**, Kristin A '01 %Ofc Mntl Health -44 Holland Av -Albany 12229 **Fx**:473-7863
(718) 579-7900 .. **O'Neill**, Kristy A '10 Leg Aid -900 Sheridan Av -Bronx 10451 **Fx**:293-8744
(212) 719-9393 .. **O'Neill**, Laura Casarano '97 %Roundabout Theatre Co -231 W 39th -NY 10018
(212) 486-1455 .. **O'Neill**, Lauren Koffler '95 (Post PGM&S,PA) -575 Mad Av -NY 10022
(212) 819-8200 .. **O'Neill**, Louis F '97 Cnsl White & C LLP -1155 Av of Amer -NY 10036
(212) 909-6000 .. **O'Neill**, Margaret M '99 Cnsl Debevoise & P LLP -919 3rd Av -NY 10022
(212) 335-9000 .. **O'Neill**, Meghan '09 %DA -1 Hogan Pl -NY 10013
(212) 336-2000 .. **O'Neill**, Melissa J '06 %Patterson BW&T LLP -1133 Av of Amer -NY 10036
(716) 856-4000 .. **O'Neill**, Michl C '99 (Hodgson R LLP) -140 Pearl -Buffalo 14202
(212) 581-0990 .. **O'Neill**, Michl G '83 -30 Vesey -NY 10007 **Fx**:581-5897
(315) 448-4809 .. **O'Neill**, Michl R '78 %Dept of Law -615 Erie Blvd W -Syracuse 13204 **Fx**:448-4853
(212) 788-0904 .. **O'Neill**, Olivia Ann '81 %Law Dept -100 Church -NY 10007 **Fx**:788-0367
(212) 715-9100 .. **O'Neill**, P Bradley '91 (Kramer LN&F,LLP) -1177 Av of Amer -NY 10036
(845) 362-6493 .. **O'Neill**, Patrick J '80 %Intl Business -18 S Ridge Rd -Pomona 10970
(212) 419-1743 .. **O'Neill**, Paul T '94 Cnsl Edison Schls -485 Lex Av -NY 10017
(585) 641-8001 .. **O'Neill**, Raymond B Jr. '78 (Allen & O) -625 Panorama Trl -Rchstr 14625
(212) 697-3050 .. **O'Neill**, Robt P '67 (Sherry & O) -305 Mad Av -NY 10165
(212) 907-9600 .. **O'Neill**, Shane '87 (Ingram YGC&B,LLP) -250 Park Av -NY 10177
(718) 286-6000 .. **O'Neill**, Shanise J '08 %DA -125-01 Qns Blvd -Kew Gdns 11415
(212) 610-6300 .. **O'Neill**, Shawn L '09 %Allen & O -1221 Av of Amer -NY 10020
(718) 672-1939 .. **O'Neill**, Sheila '89 URS Corp -8211 57th Av -Elmhrst 11373
(518) 465-4413 .. **O'Neill**, Terrence B '83 Constantine Institute -102 Willett -Albany 12210 **Fx**:465-3200
(845) 462-6500 .. **O'Neill & Thatcher LLP** -15 Davis Av -Poughkeepsie 12603 **Fx**:462-6542
(845) 462-6500 .. **O'Neill**, Thos J '77 (O'Neill & T LLP) -15 Davis Av -Poughkeepsie 12603
(212) 902-7023 .. **O'Neill**, Timothy J '82 Goldman Sachs -85 Broad -NY 10004
(212) 237-1000 .. **O'Neill**, Timothy J '86 (Windels ML&M,LLP) -156 W 56th -NY 10019
(845) 452-6400 .. **O'Neill**, Wm J '71 OfCnsl O'Neil & B -301 Mnchstr Rd -Poughkeepsie 12603
(718) 556-3800 .. **O'Neill**, Wm J '82 O'Neill & O -328 Manor Rd -Staten Isl 10314 **Fx**:556-5838
(716) 887-7550 .. **O'Neil-White**, Alphonso '99 Healthnow NY -257 W Genesee -Buffalo 14202
(212) 374-6888 .. **Onek**, Matthew M '04 NYC Dept Educ-OLS -52 Chmbrs -NY 10007 **Fx**:374-5596
(212) 450-4000 .. **Ong**, Emmet P '08 %Davis P&W LLP -450 Lex Av -NY 10017
(212) 816-6191 .. **Ong**, George '98 Citigroup Global Mrkts -388 Greenwich -NY 10013
(212) 733-3528 .. **Ong**, Helen Chua '95 Pfizer Inc -235 E 42nd -NY 10017
(631) 324-5209 .. **Ongioni**, Marie '82 (Ongioni & B) -15 Railroad Av -E Hampton 11937 **Fx**:324-7521
(718) 859-9155 .. **Oni**, Olufunlola O '04 %A Chambers & Assoc -1721 Bklyn Av -Brklyn 11210 **Fx**:421-7687
(718) 388-3330 .. **Oniszczuk-Zawisny**, Marta '02 %Zawisny & Z,PC -578 Driggs Av -Brklyn 11211 **Fx**:338-3877
(212) 779-1779 .. **Onne**, Steven G '97 Appellate Div -41 Mad Av -NY 10010
(212) 229-6453 .. **Onnembo**, John D Jr. '04 Turner Construction Co -375 Hudson -NY 10014
(212) 578-2211 .. **Ono**, Lisa '98 %MetLife -27-01 Qns Plz N -LIC 11101
(845) 613-0880 .. **Onofrio**, Dara L '90 (Onofrio Law) -15 N Mill -Nyack 10960 **Fx**:613-0398
(845) 291-2050 .. **Onofry**, Jennifer P '06 %DA -255-275 Main -Goshen 10924 **Fx**:291-2085
(845) 856-4444 .. **Onofry**, Wm A '06 (Bavoso P&O) -19 E Main Bx3139 -Pt Jervis 12771
(718) 250-4267 .. **Onoge**, Forabo Bamidele '97 %Leg Aid -111 Lvngstn -Brklyn 11201 **Fx**:250-4243
(718) 299-0434 .. **Ononaji**, Francis N '93 -1777 Grand Cncrs -Bronx 10453
(212) 382-0909 .. **Onorata**, Gerard J '91 (Peckar & A,PC) -41 Mad Av -NY 10154
(212) 506-3900 .. **Onorato**, Anthony A '08 %Steptoe & J LLP -750 7th Av -NY 10019
(212) 277-4000 .. **Onorato**, David J '88 (Freshfields BD LLP) -520 Mad Av -NY 10022
(718) 292-1266 .. **Onorato**, Fredk J '90 Urban Architectural Interiors,Inc -375 E 163rd -Bronx 10451 **Fx**:665-3210
(516) 571-3800 .. **Onorato**, Jos R '74 %DA -262 Old Cntry Rd -Mineola 11501 **Fx**:248-9479
(718) 636-8000 .. **Onorato**, Philip J '91 (Wood R&W,LLP) -394-396 Waverly Av -Brklyn 11238 **Fx**:857-5628
(516) 560-6400 .. **Onorato**, Tara Marie '02 Leg Aid -1 Helen Keller Way -Hempstd 11550 **Fx**:565-3694
(212) 637-2721 .. **Onozawa**, Tomoko '03 US Atty -86 Chmbrs -NY 10007
(212) 279-9200 .. **Ontell**, Robt J '08 %Abrams FFEGF&E,LLP -630 3rd Av -NY 10017
(718) 881-2086 .. **Onua**, Anthony O '92 -3343 Paulding Av -Bronx 10469
(212) 969-3000 .. **Onufer**, Pamela A '98 %Proskauer R LLP -1585 Bway -NY 10036
(212) 808-7800 .. **Onuma**, Susan J '83 (Kelley D&W LLP) -101 Park Av -NY 10178
(212) 859-8000 .. **Onyango**, Stephen Joshua Ayugi '05 %Fried FHS&J LLP -1 NY Plz -NY 10004
(718) 923-4206 .. **Onyekaba**, Ogechukwu Nwamaka '97 %OTDA Fair Hearings -14 Boerum Pl -Brklyn 11201
(212) 859-5008 .. **Onyeobia**, Kelechi O '04 -110 Wall -NY 10005
(212) 938-0600 .. **Onyia**, Jos I '08 %Schwartz LLC -90 Broad -NY 10004 **Fx**:938-0601
(914) 813-2739 .. **Onyido**, John Chike '05 -39 Davenport Av -New Rchll 10805
(315) 471-6687 .. **Oot**, Leah A '00 (Oot & Assoc,PLLC) -503 E Wshngtn -Syracuse 13202 **Fx**:476-7603
(315) 379-1466 .. **Oot**, Leah A '00 (Oot & Assoc,PLLC) -63 Main -Canton 13617 **Fx**:379-1433
(315) 449-4306 .. **Oot**, Michl P '77 (Oot & S) -4983 Brittonfld Pkwy -E Syracuse 13057 **Fx**:449-4358
(315) 656-2265 .. **Oot**, Suzanne E '92 Oot Law Ofcs,PLLC -5900 N Burdick -E Syracuse 13057 **Fx**:656-5239
(315) 471-6687 .. **Oot**, Thaddeus B '52 Oot & Assoc,PLLC -503 E Wshngtn -Syracuse 13202 **Fx**:476-7603
(315) 379-1466 .. **Oot**, Thaddeus B '52 Oot & Assoc,PLLC -63 Main -Canton 13617 **Fx**:379-1433
(585) 724-6638 .. **Ooyama**, Clara Michiko '90 %Eastman Kodak -343 State -Rchstr 14650
(212) 848-4000 .. **Opar**, John L '81 (Shearman & S LLP) -599 Lex Av -NY 10022
(212) 889-4171 .. **Opatrny**, Robt B '82 -234 5th Av -NY 10001 **Fx**:889-4043
(212) 232-1300 .. **Opatut Rubin**, Sarah B '01 %Lewis BB&S LLP -77 Water -NY 10005
(212) 270-8763 .. **Opel**, Andrew R '03 JP Morgan Chase & Co -270 Park Av -NY 10017
(718) 855-9000 .. **Opell**, Glenn A '05 %Cullen and D LLP -177 Montague -Brklyn 11201
(212) 259-8000 .. **Opell**, Jill A '01 %Dewey & L LLP -1301 Av of Amer -NY 10019
(914) 472-1859 .. **Oper**, Felice B '88 -76 Huntngtn Av -Scarsdale 10583
(212) 286-8585 .. **Operman**, Dena '05 %Heidell PM&B,LLP -99 Park Av -NY 10016
(212) 244-4111 .. **Ophir-Harel**, Shlomit '00 %Shiboleth YR&Z,LLP -1 Penn Plz -NY 10119
(212) 318-6000 .. **Opich**, Jos P '88 (Paul HJ&W LLP) -75 E 55th -NY 10022
(212) 972-8533 .. **Opinsky**, Heidi E '86 -305 Mad Av -NY 10165 **Fx**:(203) 227-0786
(631) 852-2500 .. **Opisso**, Lawr N '06 %DA -200 Center Dr -Rvrhead 11901 **Fx**:852-1769
(212) 967-8270 .. **Opoku**, Kwadwo Amoako '96 -450 7th Av -NY 10123 **Fx**:967-8276
(212) 382-6620 .. **Opotowsky**, Barbara B '72 %NYC Bar -42 W 44th -NY 10036 **Fx**:398-6634
(212) 521-2400 .. **Opotowsky**, Stuart B '72 %Loews Corp -655 Mad Av -NY 10065 **Fx**:521-2360
(212) 226-7700 .. **Opp**, Amy C '04 %Donovan & Y LLP -161 Av of Amer -NY 10013
(518) 218-3750 .. **Oppedisano**, David J '03 Ayco Company,LLP -2 Wall -Albany 12205
(212) 589-4200 .. **Oppenheim**, Adam B '01 Cnsl Baker & H LLP -45 Rckfllr Plz -NY 10111
(212) 755-3100 .. **Oppenheim**, David W '00 %Kaufmann GR&O LLP -777 3rd Av -NY 10017
(212) 223-4050 .. **Oppenheim**, Jeffrey A '76 -845 3rd Av -NY 10022
(212) 935-8770 .. **Oppenheim**, Jerry '63 -510 Park Av -NY 10022 **Fx**:935-0290
(212) 407-4000 .. **Oppenheim**, Lanny A '72 (Loeb & L,LLP) -345 Park Av -NY 10154
(212) 447-1800 .. **Oppenheim**, Laura A '96 (Mintz & O LLP) -260 Mad Av -NY 10016
(212) 728-2000 .. **Oppenheim**, Louis J '83 %Athletes & Artists -220 W 42nd -NY 10036
(914) 683-8998 .. **Oppenheim**, Lucille C '85 (Gutterman & O) -202 Mamaroneck Av -White Plns 10601 **Fx**:948-1320
(516) 498-3692 .. **Oppenheim**, Moshe R '96 1st Quality Enterprise,Inc -80 Cuttermill Rd -Gt Neck 11021
(212) 228-1957 .. **Oppenheim**, Robt P '80 -200 Park Av S -NY 10003
(212) 967-4100 .. **Oppenheim**, Sarah Harris '02 HIAS Inc -333 7th Av -NY 10001
(212) 353-8556 .. **Oppenheim**, Stephanie E '88 -40 E 9th -NY 10003
(212) 673-5887 .. **Oppenheim**, Stephen L '56 -20 E 9th -NY 10003 **Fx**:598-0502
(212) 751-7700 .. **Oppenheim**, Steven D '65 (Faust & O,LLP) -488 Mad Av -NY 10022
(716) 858-2424 .. **Oppenheimer**, Andrew D '10 %DA -25 Delaware Av -Buffalo 14202 **Fx**:858-7425
(914) 801-3070 .. **Oppenheimer**, Brooke J '09 %CT Summation CaseVault -400 Columbus Av -Valhalla 10595
(914) 834-1900 .. **Oppenheimer**, Gordon S '66 -50 Howell Av Bx197 -Larchmnt 10538 **Fx**:206-3822
(518) 689-1459 .. **Oppenheimer**, Joshua L '07 %Greenberg T,LLP -54 State -Albany 12207
(716) 566-1300 .. **Oppenheimer**, Laurence B '81 (Hiscock & B,LLP) -1100 M&T Ctr -Buffalo 14203
(516) 466-2200 .. **Oppenheimer**, Lori Segal '84 -69 Susquehanna Av -Gt Neck 11021 **Fx**:466-4141
(212) 969-3000 .. **Oppenheimer**, Martin J '57 (Proskauer R LLP) -1585 Bway -NY 10036
(212) 832-1080 .. **Oppenheimer**, Martin J '63 -767 3rd Av -NY 10017 **Fx**:755-4476

(716) 856-5500 .. **Oppenheimer,** Randolph C '80 (Damon M LLP) -200 Delaware Av -Buffalo 14202
(585) 232-3730 .. **Oppenheimer,** Robt '52 OfCnsl Chamberlain D LLP -1600 Crssrds Bldg -Rchstr 14614
(212) 451-2300 .. **Oppenheimer,** Robt J '79 OfCnsl Olshan GFR&W LLP -65 E 55th -NY 10022
(585) 381-1988 .. **Oppenlander,** Judith A '91 %TD Cook -7 State -Pittsfrd 14534
(718) 946-2679 .. **Opper,** Edw '87 -2780 W 5th -Brklyn 11224
(212) 398-0055 .. **Opper,** Jos '76 (Garwin G&F,LLP) -1501 Bway -NY 10036
(518) 690-4410 .. **Oppy,** James D '05 Macy Law Firm -314 Great Oaks Blvd -Albany 12203 **Fx:**690-4435
(212) 530-1800 .. **O'Prey,** Patricia C '02 %Richards K&O LLP -1 World Fncl Ctr -NY 10281
(212) 599-1744 .. **Opton Handler & Feiler,LLP** -295 Mad Av -NY 10017 **Fx:**972-2219
(212) 557-7200 .. **Oquendo,** Ricardo E '90 (Davidoff M&H,LLP) -605 3rd Av -NY 10158
(212) 751-9800 .. **Orakwusi,** Ada N '10 %Morelli R PC -950 3rd Av -NY 10022
(212) 969-3000 .. **Oram,** Jonathan H '00 (Proskauer R LLP) -1585 Bway -NY 10036
(212) 661-8888 .. **Oram,** Peter D '64 -420 Lex Av -NY 10170 **Fx:**370-5637
(212) 938-0600 .. **Oramasionwu,** Linda N '08 %Schwartz LLC -90 Broad -NY 10004 **Fx:**938-0601
(212) 571-7100 .. **Oranga,** Mary Gladys T '03 %O'Dwyer & B,LLP -52 Duane -NY 10007
(516) 487-7300 .. **Orange,** Jan H '87 (Podlofsky & O,LLP) -98 Cuttermill Rd -Gt Neck 11021
(212) 227-0347 .. **Orange,** Margaret M '04 %Weiss W&W,PC -25 Park Pl -NY 10007
(212) 586-2211 .. **Orans Elsen Lupert & Brown LLP** -875 3rd Av -NY 10022 **Fx:**765-3662
(914) 347-1292 .. **Orbach,** Adrienne J '00 %Rosenthal & M,LLP -45 Knollwood Rd -Elmsfrd 10523
(212) 478-7200 .. **Orbach,** Jos '08 %Hahn & H LLP -488 Mad Av -NY 10022
(315) 218-8000 .. **Orbach,** Louis '94 (Bond S&K,PLLC) -1 Lincoln Ctr -Syracuse 13202
(212) 576-7000 .. **Orban,** Rachel A '98 %NYLIM -51 Mad Av -NY 10010
(607) 723-5341 .. **Orband,** James W '86 (Hinman H&K,LLP) -80 Exchange Bx5250 -Bnghmtn 13902
(212) 530-1800 .. **Orbe,** Wm Q '83 (Richards K&O LLP) -1 World Fncl Ctr -NY 10281
(212) 801-3780 .. **Orbison,** Michl H '85 -60 Columbus Cir -NY 10023 **Fx:**801-3781
(718) 370-7030 .. **Orbon,** John A '89 (Amabile & E,PC) -1000 South Av -Staten Isl 10314
(212) 754-7358 .. **Orbuch,** Steven E '93 %The Blackstone Grp -345 Park Av -NY 10154 **Fx:**754-8730
(212) 701-3000 .. **Orce,** Kenneth W '69 (Cahill G&R LLP) -80 Pine -NY 10005 **Fx:**269-5420
(212) 558-4000 .. **Orchowski,** Michl '09 %Sullivan & C LLP -125 Broad -NY 10004
(917) 375-8257 .. **Orcutt,** John E '07 %Law Dept -198 E 161st -Bronx 10451 **Fx:**(718) 590-2686
(212) 406-4100 .. **Orden,** Jeremy F '85 -225 Bway -NY 10007 **Fx:**566-8165
(212) 406-1200 .. **Orden,** Stewart L '80 -225 Bway -NY 10007
(518) 474-1010 .. **Ordman,** Robt S '74 %Ofc Inspector Genl -ESP Agncy Bldg 2 -Albany 12223 **Fx:**486-3745
(212) 335-9000 .. **Ordonez,** Bernice '03 %DA -1 Hogan Pl -NY 10013
(212) 479-6000 .. **Ordonez,** Gustavo A '99 %Cooley LLP -1114 Av of Amer -NY 10036
(718) 855-9000 .. **Ordover,** Marilyn '55 Cnsl Cullen and D LLP -177 Montague -Brklyn 11201
(212) 450-1251 .. **Ordower,** Wm Z '97 %Major League Soccer -420 5th Av -NY 10018 **Fx:**450-1305
(212) 310-8000 .. **Ordway,** Eric '87 (Weil G&M LLP) -767 5th Av -NY 10153
(315) 422-1391 .. **Ordway,** Lawr M Jr. '98 %Green & S,PLLC -One Lincoln Ctr #900 -Syracuse 13202
(585) 530-3140 .. **Ordyk,** Amanda L '07 %Appllt Div 4th Dept -50 East Av Ste 200 -Rchstr 14604 **Fx:**530-3247
(212) 918-3000 .. **Orecchio,** Maria '00 %Hogan L LLP -875 3rd Av -NY 10022
(518) 408-3019 .. **Orederu,** Omotayo A '89 %State Comptroller -110 State -Albany 12236 **Fx:**473-9104
(212) 227-3550 .. **O'Regan,** Francis M '64 OfCnsl Waesche S&O,PC -111 Bway -NY 10006
(212) 537-2449 .. **O'Regan,** Jeanne E '98 Morgan Stanley -1633 Bway -NY 10019
(212) 225-2000 .. **O'Reilly,** Benet John '00 (Cleary GS&H) -1 Lbrty Plz -NY 10006
(212) 218-2100 .. **O'Reilly,** Brian D '03 %Fitzpatrick CH&S -1290 Av of Amer -NY 10104
(212) 558-4000 .. **O'Reilly,** Brian P '03 %Sullivan & C LLP -125 Broad -NY 10004
(212) 909-6000 .. **O'Reilly,** Christine M '03 %Debevoise & P LLP -919 3rd Av -NY 10022
(212) 818-9200 .. **O'Reilly,** Erin A '05 (Satterlee SB&B LLP) -230 Park Av -NY 10169
(845) 621-1255 .. **O'Reilly,** Francis J '89 -10 McMahon Pl -Mahopac 10541 **Fx:**621-1686
(914) 592-4167 .. **O'Reilly,** John F '77 (Hitsman H&O LLC) -220 Wht Plns Rd -Tarrytwn 10591
(212) 294-6700 .. **O'Reilly,** Kenneth D '99 %Winston & S -200 Park Av -NY 10166
(516) 496-1919 .. **O'Reilly,** Kevin W '82 (Keller O&W,PC) -242 Crsswys Park Dr W -Woodbury 11797
(212) 986-4343 .. **O'Reilly,** Lillian '83 %Berkeley College -3 E 43rd -NY 10017
(516) 741-1818 .. **O'Reilly Marsh & Corteselli,PC** -222 Old Cntry Rd -Mineola 11501 **Fx:**741-1818
(212) 318-3000 .. **O'Reilly,** Mary E '04 %Fulbright & J LLP -666 5th Av -NY 10103
(212) 655-6000 .. **O'Reilly,** Meghan '03 %Chapman & C LLP -330 Mad Av -NY 10017
(212) 613-2055 .. **O'Reilly,** Michl S '99 (Gibbons PC) -1 Penn Plz -NY 10119 **Fx:**554-9655
(716) 849-1333 .. **O'Reilly,** Patrick C '81 (Lipsitz GSC LLP) -42 Delaware Av -Buffalo 14202
(516) 741-1818 .. **O'Reilly,** Philip J '63 (O'Reilly M&C,PC) -222 Old Cntry Rd -Mineola 11501
(212) 857-8230 .. **O'Reilly,** Richd G '91 %Baker MM&M,PC -330 W 34th -NY 10001
(845) 621-4100 .. **O'Reilly,** Terrence P '67 (O'Reilly Law Assoc) -880 S Lk Blvd -Mahopac 10541 **Fx:**621-4210
(212) 872-1000 .. **O'Reilly,** Thos J '09 -One Bryant Park -NY 10036 **Fx:**872-1002
(212) 262-2390 .. **O'Reilly,** Tricia Bevelock '93 (Connell F LLP) -888 7th Av -NY 10106
(212) 545-4649 .. **Orel,** Stephen H '85 OfCnsl Wolf HAF&H LLP -270 Mad Av -NY 10016
(718) 453-4238 .. **Orellana,** Joaquin E '05 -876 Bushwick Av -Brklyn 11221
(585) 428-5210 .. **Oren,** Amanda L '02 %Pub Def -10 N Fitzhugh -Rchstr 14614 **Fx:**428-2234
(212) 735-3000 .. **Oren,** Dvir '06 %Skadden ASM&F LLP -4 Times Sq -NY 10036
(212) 941-5025 .. **Oren,** Peninna Hanna '06 %Gabay-Rafiy & B LLP -299 Bway -NY 10007 **Fx:**202-3883
(212) 816-7186 .. **Orenbach,** Kenneth B '76 Citigroup Global Mrkts -388 Greenwich -NY 10013
(212) 669-8299 .. **Orengo,** Jose L '97 %Borough Pres -19 Fl S Mncpl Bldg -NY 10007 **Fx:**669-3380
(212) 687-0100 .. **Orenstein,** Andrew J '97 (Harris B PLLC) -100 Wall -NY 10005
(212) 552-4673 .. **Orenstein,** Babette V E '93 -1 Chase Manh Plz -NY 10005
(585) 586-4165 .. **Orenstein,** Barbara J '82 -Bx18263 -Rchstr 14618 **Fx:**383-1818
(212) 773-4485 .. **Orenstein,** Benjamin P '02 Ernst & Young LLP -5 Times Sq -NY 10036
(718) 819-0200 .. **Orenstein,** Dena '01 (Orenstein & K PC) -217-04 Nrthrn Blvd -Bayside 11361 **Fx:**819-0201
(212) 867-6000 .. **Orenstein,** Eric S '06 %Rosenberg & E,PC -733 3rd Av -NY 10017
(315) 696-5141 .. **Orenstein,** Gary L '56 -1285 Woodmancy Rd -Tully 13159 **Fx:**696-5141
(212) 754-6300 .. **Orenstein,** Keith S '83 (Orenstein & O,LLC) -425 Park Av -NY 10022 **Fx:**754-7141
(212) 436-4094 .. **Orenstein,** Lawr C '82 Deloitte & Touche,LLP -2 World Fncl Ctr -NY 10281 **Fx:**436-3642
(212) 779-9910 .. **Orenstein,** Mark '75 Cnsl Eaton & V LLP -3 Park Av -NY 10016
(212) 754-6300 .. **Orenstein,** Maryanne B '80 %Orenstein & O,LLC -425 Park Av -NY 10022 **Fx:**754-7141
(212) 209-4800 .. **Orenstein,** May '84 Brown R LLP -7 Times Sq -NY 10036
(212) 878-7900 .. **Ores,** Rhonda E '91 (Fox R LLP) -100 Park Av -NY 10017
(716) 645-2527 .. **Oreskovic,** Johanna '98 %SUNY Buffalo Lw Schl -O'Brian Hall -Buffalo 14260 **Fx:**645-2064
(718) 993-9999 .. **Oresky,** Jacob '87 (J Oresky & Assoc,PLLC) -155 E 149th -Bronx 10451 **Fx:**993-0142
(212) 455-2000 .. **Oresman,** Donald '58 OfCnsl Simpson T&B LLP -425 Lex Av -NY 10017
(212) 512-2511 .. **Orey,** Michl '85 -1221 Av of Amer -NY 10020
(212) 765-2100 .. **Orfan,** Elizabeth A '86 (Spivak L LLP) -1700 Bway -NY 10019
(518) 377-2225 .. **Orfan,** John L '95 %Friedman H&M,LLP -100 Great Oaks Blvd Bx38279 -Albany 12203
(516) 869-8200 .. **Organek,** Harry '74 -1225 Franklin Av -Gdn Cty 11530 **Fx:**977-1220
(516) 997-5191 .. **Organisciak,** Richd E '90 -845 Westbury Rd -Westbury 11590
(212) 944-1377 .. **Orgel,** Ephrat S '02 %M Kassimir & Assoc,PC -1065 Av of Amer -NY 10018 **Fx:**790-5868
(212) 791-3230 .. **Orgel,** Jane '02 -111 John -NY 10038
(212) 317-8500 .. **Orgel,** Scott I '05 %Snitow KH&M,LLP -575 Lex Av -NY 10022
(646) 878-0800 .. **Or Hof,** Dan '08 %Pearl CZL,LLP -1500 Bway -NY 10036
(212) 878-8000 .. **Origlia,** Danl L '99 %Clifford C LLP -31 W 52nd -NY 10019
(315) 792-0171 .. **Orilio,** John P '86 %Law Dept -1 Knndy Plz -Utica 13502 **Fx:**792-0175
(212) 596-9000 .. **Oringer,** Andrew L '85 (Ropes & G LLP) -1211 Av of Amer -NY 10036
(212) 756-5225 .. **Oriol,** Peter A '97 %Largo Music,Inc -425 Park Av -NY 10022
Orioli, Susan M '96 -22 Roberta Ln -Syosset 11791
(914) 422-1260 .. **Oristano,** Kerry M '83 City Personnel Ofc -255 Main -White Plns 10601
(212) 964-5858 .. **Orizal,** Joanne '93 -111 Bway -NY 10006 **Fx:**609-3734
(607) 273-6841 .. **Orkin,** Jonathan A '83 (Barney GDM&O,LLP) -119 E Seneca -Ithaca 14850
(212) 489-8230 .. **Orkin,** Leonard '58 (Davis WT LLP) -1633 Bway -NY 10019
(631) 361-6483 .. **Orlacchio,** DawnMarie '93 -Bx206 -Smithtwn 11787
(212) 820-9454 .. **Orlandi,** Kathleen J '85 (Hawkins D&W LLP) -One Chase Manh Plz -NY 10005
(212) 836-8000 .. **Orlandi,** Marisa A '07 %Kaye S LLP -425 Park Av -NY 10022
(212) 683-9700 .. **Orlando,** Francis B '83 GNY Mutual Ins -200 Mad Av -NY 10016 **Fx:**843-1962
(914) 949-1522 .. **Orlando,** Geoffrey K '71 -301 Old Tarrytown Rd -White Plns 10603 **Fx:**684-9772
(631) 231-1450 .. **Orlando,** James E '96 %Feldman K&M,PC -330 Vndrblt Motor Pkwy -Hauppauge 11788
(718) 238-0020 .. **Orlando,** John J '93 -8118 13th Av -Brklyn 11228 **Fx:**238-0031
(914) 686-1700 .. **Orlando,** Jos A '98 (O'Connor R,LLP) -200 Mamaroneck Av -White Plns 10601
(212) 449-0326 .. **Orlando,** Justin A '97 %Merrill Lynch -4 Wrld Fncl Ctr -NY 10080
(518) 862-1200 .. **Orlando,** Ronald B '83 %Martin H&M LLP -Bx15141 -Albany 12212
(203) 330-2129 .. **Orleans,** Jonathan B '85 (Pullman & C,LLC) -50 Main -White Plns 10606
(212) 566-2266 .. **Orlian,** Jos I '93 -277 Bway -NY 10007 **Fx:**566-4780
(212) 538-4265 .. **Orlich,** Todd M '93 %Credit Suisse -11 Mad Av -NY 10010
(212) 826-6747 .. **Orlikoff,** Steven '93 -Bx6225 -NY 10150 **Fx:**355-3978
(212) 237-1000 .. **Orlin,** David '50 (Windels ML&M,LLP) -156 W 56th -NY 10019
(212) 788-3963 .. **Orlin,** Robt '87 Dept Sanitation -125 Worth -NY 10013 **Fx:**791-3824
(212) 973-3070 .. **Orlin,** Robt K '91 %AECOM Tech Corp -605 3rd Av -NY 10158 **Fx:**973-3070
(315) 792-3267 .. **Orlin,** Theo S '74 %Utica Cllg/Syra Univ -Burrstone Rd -Utica 13502 **Fx:**792-3292
(212) 298-5129 .. **Orlins,** Eliza M '09 Leg Aid -49 Thomas -NY 10013 **Fx:**(646) 616-4379
(212) 931-7900 .. **Orlinsky,** Ethan G '90 %MLB Properties -245 Park Av -NY 10167 **Fx:**949-5697
(845) 294-8974 .. **Orloff,** Marc D '77 M Orloff,PC -55 Main Bx386 -Goshen 10924 **Fx:**294-6372
(646) 386-3359 .. **Orlofsky,** Benjamin T '04 Hon B Fried -111 Centre -NY 10013
(212) 888-7300 .. **Orlofsky,** Marc S '79 OfCnsl A Garfunkel -444 Mad Av -NY 10022 **Fx:**888-7306
(212) 285-1600 .. **Orlofsky,** Michl J '90 (Orlofsky & O) -14 Wall -NY 10005 **Fx:**285-1661
(718) 544-4100 .. **Orlow,** Adam M '98 (Orlow Firm) -71-18 Main -Flushng 11367 **Fx:**544-6485

(718) 544-4100 .. **Orlow,** Alexander '59 OfCnsl Orlow Firm -71-18 Main -Flushng 11367 **Fx:**544-6485
(212) 319-6898 .. **Orlow,** Barri A '09 %Lavin ORC&D -420 Lex Av -NY 10170
(718) 544-4100 .. **Orlow,** Brian S '97 (Orlow Firm) -71-18 Main -Flushng 11367 **Fx:**544-6485
(718) 544-4100 .. **Orlow,** Steven S '69 (Orlow Firm) -71-18 Main -Flushng 11367 **Fx:**544-6485
(212) 448-1100 .. **Orlowski,** Michelle Laitres '95 OfCnsl McLaughlin & S,LLP -260 Mad Av -NY 10016
(212) 964-6611 .. **Orlowski,** Steven P '96 (Lester SK&D) -120 Bway -NY 10271
(212) 408-5100 .. **Orman,** Gavin '05 %Chadbourne & P LLP -30 Rckfllr Plz -NY 10112
(585) 263-1000 .. **Orman,** Michl F '88 Cnsl Nixon P LLP -1100 Clinton Sq -Rchstr 14604
(212) 558-4000 .. **Orme,** Camille L '01 (Sullivan & C LLP) -125 Broad -NY 10004
(212) 530-5000 .. **Orme,** James A '08 %Milbank TH&M LLP -1 Chase Manh Plz -NY 10005
(212) 761-4706 .. **Orme,** Maria B '89 Morgan Stanley -1585 Bway -NY 10036
(212) 849-7000 .. **Ormond,** Hilary Ritter '07 %Quinn EU&S,LLP -51 Mad Av -NY 10010
(212) 474-1000 .. **Ormsby,** David G '61 SrCnsl Cravath S&M LLP -825 8th Av -NY 10019
(516) 223-9666 .. **Ormsten,** Franklin D '65 -165 Woodbine Av -Merrick 11566 **Fx:**623-4696
(716) 852-3600 .. **Orndoff,** Scott R '04 %Chelus HS&M,PC -438 Main -Buffalo 14202
(212) 839-5300 .. **Ornelas,** Ariana I '08 %Sidley A LLP -787 7th Av -NY 10019
(646) 424-6691 .. **Orner,** David S '95 %ING Capital LLC -1325 Av of Amer -NY 10019
(718) 575-9600 .. **Orner,** Philip E '91 -72-29 137th -Flushng 11367
(212) 461-2339 .. **Ornest,** Lisa '05 -44 Wall -NY 10005
(212) 335-4500 .. **Ornitz,** Richd M '71 (DLA Piper LLP) -1251 Av of Amer -NY 10020
(212) 891-2148 .. **Ornstein,** Alexander J '94 %Ceberus Capital Mgt LLP -299 Park Av -NY 10171
(212) 373-8089 .. **Ornstein,** Beth A '01 Ctr for Ct Innovation -520 8th Av -NY 10018
(631) 283-4842 .. **Ornstein,** J Alan '53 -414 Cnty Rd 39A -Southampton 11968 **Fx:**283-5148
(212) 903-1574 .. **Ornstein,** James K '97 Wm Morris Agency -1325 Av of Amer -NY 10019
(718) 778-5456 .. **Ornstein,** Sheldon S '58 (Ornstein & O,PC) -496 Clarkson Av -Brklyn 11203 **Fx:**756-0028
(212) 757-8438 .. **Orochena,** Rebecca A '06 %Levitt & N,PC -250 W 57th -NY 10107
(914) 933-6027 .. **Orol,** Elliot S '81 Navigators Grp,Inc -6 Intl Dr -Rye Brook 10573
(212) 687-6900 .. **Orol,** Harriet L '83 (Connell & W) -555 5th Av -NY 10017 **Fx:**687-6999
(315) 425-2831 .. **Oropallo,** Michl A '89 (Hiscock & B,LLP) -One Park Pl -Syracuse 13202 **Fx:**703-7367
(212) 735-3000 .. **O'Rorke,** James F Jr. '62 OfCnsl Skadden ASM&F LLP -4 Times Sq -NY 10036
(914) 997-2555 .. **Oros,** George '85 -2 Gannett Dr -White Plns 10604 **Fx:**997-7011
(212) 969-3000 .. **O'Rourke,** Brendan J '85 (Proskauer R LLP) -1585 Bway -NY 10036
(212) 384-1000 .. **O'Rourke,** Brian E '95 %FBI -26 Fed Plz -NY 10278
(212) 450-4000 .. **O'Rourke,** Catheryn A '00 Cnsl Davis P&W LLP -450 Lex Av -NY 10017
(516) 677-9785 .. **O'Rourke,** Chas M '88 -2 Swenson Dr -Woodbury 11797
(212) 251-8220 .. **O'Rourke,** Christopher J '94 Schieffelin & Co -85 10th Av -NY 10011
(212) 227-4530 .. **O'Rourke & Degen,PLLC** -225 Bway -NY 10007 **Fx:**385-9813
(607) 723-5341 .. **O'Rourke,** Delphine '02 SpclCnsl Hinman H&K,LLP -80 Exchange Bx5250 -Bnghmtn 13902
(516) 873-2000 .. **O'Rourke,** Dennis C '95 OfCnsl Moritt HH&H LLP -400 Grdn City Plz -Gdn Cty 11530
(914) 632-5000 .. **O'Rourke,** Eileen M '04 Sound Shore Med Ctr -16 Guion Pl -New Rchll 10801
(315) 471-4629 .. **O'Rourke,** Fredk H '88 (Hunt & O) -250 Harrison -Syracuse 13202 **Fx:**471-5098
(631) 361-3400 .. **O'Rourke,** James J III '75 (O'Rourke & H,PLLC) -235 Brooksite Dr -Hauppauge 11788 **Fx:**361-7324
(631) 853-4104 .. **O'Rourke,** James J '09 %DA -400 Carleton Av Bx9082 -Central Islip 11722 **Fx:**853-7838
(631) 852-4569 .. **O'Rourke,** Jeanne C '79 Bd of Elections -Bx700 -Yaphank 11980 **Fx:**852-4504
(516) 466-5291 .. **O'Rourke,** John C '95 (Gassler & O,PC) -1 Nrthrn Blvd -Gt Neck 11021 **Fx:**466-5290
(516) 822-2980 .. **O'Rourke,** John P '50 (O'Rourke S LLP) -6800 Jericho Tpk -Syosset 11791
(914) 995-4172 .. **O'Rourke,** John W '97 %DA -111 Martin Luther King Blvd -White Plns 10601 **Fx:**995-3363
(212) 422-0202 .. **O'Rourke,** Katelin B '07 %Sedgwick DM&A LLP -125 Broad -NY 10004
(516) 571-3056 .. **O'Rourke,** Maureen T '87 %Cnty Atty -1 West -Mineola 11501 **Fx:**571-6604
(212) 335-9000 .. **O'Rourke,** Melissa M '81 %DA -1 Hogan Pl -NY 10013
(716) 849-0328 .. **O'Rourke,** Michl G '74 -112 Franklin -Buffalo 14202 **Fx:**849-0592
(718) 258-9000 .. **O'Rourke,** Michl J '69 MJ O'Rourke,PC -2055 Flatbush Av -Brklyn 11234 **Fx:**258-9744
(212) 944-7333 .. **O'Rourke,** Michl S '73 (Rode & Q) -55 W 39th -NY 10018
(212) 504-6000 .. **O'Rourke,** Mollie E '06 %Cadwalader W&T LLP -1 World Fncl Ctr -NY 10281
(607) 273-2202 .. **O'Rourke,** Patricia M '06 %Schlather SP&S -200 E Buffalo Bx353 -Ithaca 14851
(212) 632-6000 .. **O'Rourke,** Pearl Y '04 Lazard Freres -30 Rckfllr Plz -NY 10112 **Fx:**632-6060
(212) 232-1300 .. **O'Rourke,** Philip J '93 (Lewis BB&S LLP) -77 Water -NY 10005
(914) 946-4777 .. **O'Rourke,** Richd L '82 (Keane & B,PC) -445 Hmltn Av -White Plns 10601
(516) 822-2980 .. **O'Rourke Seaman LLP** -6800 Jericho Tpk -Syosset 11791 **Fx:**822-1974
(718) 330-2853 .. **O'Rourke,** Tara A '01 %NLRB -2 Metrotech Ctr -Brklyn 11201 **Fx:**330-7579
(631) 249-7500 .. **O'Rourke,** Thos A '77 (Bodner & O LLP) -425 Broadhllw Rd -Melvll 11747 **Fx:**249-4508
(516) 822-2980 .. **O'Rourke,** Timothy C '88 (O'Rourke S LLP) -6800 Jericho Tpk -Syosset 11791
(516) 248-5757 .. **O'Rourke Pennington,** Carol '90 (Colleran O&M,LLP) -1225 Franklin Av -Gdn Cty 11530
(212) 384-1000 .. **Orphanos,** Peter P '91 %FBI -26 Fed Plz -NY 10278
(212) 468-8000 .. **Orr,** Dennis P '79 (Morrison & F LLP) -1290 Av of Amer -NY 10104
(914) 428-7700 .. **Orr,** Ian Douglas '98 (ID Orr,PC) -175 Main -White Plns 10601 **Fx:**428-7701
(212) 504-6000 .. **Orr,** Jennifer B '08 %Cadwalader W&T LLP -1 World Fncl Ctr -NY 10281
(212) 972-3000 .. **Orr,** Patrick J '03 %Klestadt & W,LLP -292 Mad Av -NY 10017
(212) 309-6000 .. **Orr,** Sheryl L '03 %Morgan L&B LLP -101 Park Av -NY 10178
(212) 455-2000 .. **Orr,** Stephen R G '06 %Simpson T&B LLP -425 Lex Av -NY 10017
(212) 506-5000 .. **Orrick Herrington & Sutcliffe LLP** -51 W 52nd -NY 10019 **Fx:**506-5151
(212) 594-5300 .. **Orrico,** Christopher J '10 %Milberg LLP -1 Penn Plz -NY 10119
(212) 756-2000 .. **Orrico,** Elizabeth G '10 %Schulte R&Z LLP -919 3rd Av -NY 10022
(212) 683-7050 .. **Orsatti,** Dawn M '02 %JM Abramson -375 5th Av -NY 10016 **Fx:**683-7076
(212) 704-0360 .. **Orseck,** Donald I '68 -530 5th Av -NY 10036 **Fx:**575-1170
(845) 292-5800 .. **Orseck,** Gerald '57 -1924 State Route 52 Bx469 -Liberty 12754 **Fx:**292-6749
(845) 292-5800 .. **Orseck,** Kirk O '03 -1924 State Route 52 Bx469 -Liberty 12754 **Fx:**292-6749
(866) 809-3391 .. **Orsetti,** Stephen M '05 -227 Tremont Rd -Lindenhrst 11757 **Fx:**809-3391
(212) 535-7763 .. **Orsher,** Stuart '83 -9 E 79th -NY 10075
(212) 833-1186 .. **Orsini,** John N '03 %Friedman KS&A LLP -1633 Bway -NY 10019 **Fx:**373-7986
(212) 474-1000 .. **Orsini,** Kevin J '04 %Cravath S&M LLP -825 8th Av -NY 10019
(212) 530-5000 .. **Ortblad,** Vanessa M '10 %Milbank TH&M LLP -1 Chase Manh Plz -NY 10005
(212) 388-3600 .. **Ortecho,** Elizabeth '97 %32B-J Leg Srvcs -101 Av of Amer -NY 10013 **Fx:**388-3061
(212) 962-1333 .. **Ortega,** Hugo G '88 (Tanner & O) -30 Vesey -NY 10007 **Fx:**962-1778
(516) 496-5822 .. **Ortega,** Jeanne M '95 %T Spina -170 Froehlich Farm Blvd -Woodbury 11797 **Fx:**496-5420
(718) 815-7754 .. **Ortega,** Manuel '87 -404 Manor Rd -Staten Isl 10314 **Fx:**815-7758
(212) 297-5800 .. **Ortega,** Rene A '04 %Day P LLP -7 Times Sq -NY 10036
(516) 832-7564 .. **Ortego,** Jos J '80 (Nixon P LLP) -50 Jericho Quadrangle -Jericho 11753
(516) 431-4441 .. **Ortego,** Shirley Bedor '80 Lancer Ins Co -370 W Park Av -Long Bch 11561
(585) 641-8000 .. **Ortenberg,** Reuben '65 OfCnsl Fix SB&G,PC -295 Woodcliff Dr -Fairprt 14450
(212) 446-2300 .. **Orthwein,** James B III '09 %Boies S&F LLP -575 Lex Av -NY 10022
(212) 664-5433 .. **Ortiz,** Angel L '98 %NBC -30 Rckfllr Plz -NY 10112
(973) 491-3365 .. **Ortiz,** Carlos F '87 (LeClairRyan,PC) -830 3rd Av -NY 10022 **Fx:**491-3395
(212) 836-8000 .. **Ortiz,** Christopher B '10 Kaye S LLP -425 Park Av -NY 10022
(646) 386-5700 .. **Ortiz,** Frances A '98 %Civil Ct -111 Centre -NY 10013
(718) 760-6540 .. **Ortiz,** Francisco D '99 %Dept of Parks & Rec -Olmsted Ctr -Flushng 11368 **Fx:**760-6730
(718) 522-1117 .. **Ortiz,** Frank A '59 (Ortiz and O,LLP) -127 Lvngstn -Brklyn 11201 **Fx:**596-1302
(212) 558-5500 .. **Ortiz,** Frank M '88 %Weitz & L,PC -700 Bway -NY 10003
(347) 703-2069 .. **Ortiz,** George A '08 -88 Charles -NY 10014 **Fx:**703-2069
(212) 310-8000 .. **Ortiz,** Heather L '03 Weil G&M LLP -767 5th Av -NY 10153
(212) 878-8000 .. **Ortiz,** Jame C '07 %Clifford C LLP -31 W 52nd -NY 10019
(212) 637-2398 .. **Ortiz,** Jessica '06 US Atty -1 St Andrews Plz -NY 10007
(212) 599-8200 .. **Ortiz,** John A '89 %Shaub AC&S,LLP -655 3rd Av -NY 10017
(718) 590-2000 .. **Ortiz,** Jonathan B '07 %DA -198 E 161st -Bronx 10451 **Fx:**590-6477
(718) 424-4848 .. **Ortiz,** Juan U '71 -82-11 37th Av -Jcksn Hts 11372 **Fx:**424-4420
(212) 264-3650 .. **Ortiz,** Karen M '00 %SSA Ofc Genl Cnsl -26 Fed Plz -NY 10278 **Fx:**264-6372
(516) 333-1972 .. **Ortiz,** Laura M '96 -265 Post Av -Westbury 11590 **Fx:**333-5972
(518) 270-3761 .. **Ortiz,** Leslie A '05 Rensselaer Cnty Fam Ct -1504 5th Av -Troy 12180
(518) 257-1443 .. **Ortiz,** Miguel Genaro '89 %CSEA,Inc -143 Wshngtn Av Bx7125 -Albany 12224 **Fx:**449-1525
(718) 522-1117 .. **Ortiz,** Norma E '88 (Ortiz and O,LLP) -127 Lvngstn -Brklyn 11201 **Fx:**596-1302
(516) 488-3300 .. **Ortiz,** Robt '96 %Shaub AC&S,LLP -1983 Marcus Av -Lk Success 11042
(718) 931-2575 .. **Ortiz-Hausmann,** Jeannette '03 %Codelia & S PC -1967 Turnbull Av -Bronx 10473
(845) 563-9374 .. **Ortiz-Lesh,** Leitha M '96 NY Life Ins Co -460 Temple Hill Rd -New Windsor 12553 **Fx:**569-0057
(516) 764-2800 .. **Ortmann,** Erik A '95 %Goldberg & C -66 N Vllg Av -Rockvll Ctr 11570
(212) 445-4567 .. **Ortner,** Carrie L '04 Newsweek -395 Hudson -NY 10014
(212) 969-3000 .. **Ortner,** Chas B '72 (Proskauer R LLP) -1585 Bway -NY 10036
(212) 335-9000 .. **Ortner,** Craig J '00 %DA -1 Hogan Pl -NY 10013
(212) 949-9022 .. **Ortner,** Melvin L '74 OfCnsl Abelman F&S -666 3rd Av -NY 10017
(212) 723-7355 .. **Ortner,** Wm G '94 Citigroup -390 Greenwich -NY 10013
(845) 225-3641 .. **Ortolano,** Lisa '91 %DA -40 Gleneida Av -Carmel 10512
(212) 588-0022 .. **Ortoli,** Richd J F '83 (Sanders OV&R) -501 Mad Av -NY 10022
(212) 335-9000 .. **Ortsman-Dauer,** Nicole A '98 %DA -1 Hogan Pl -NY 10013
(607) 770-1007 .. **Orville,** Peter '81 P Orville,PC -30 Riverside Dr -Bnghmtn 13905 **Fx:**770-1110
(212) 585-3305 .. **Orwasher,** Abram H '76 -308 E 78th -NY 10075
(212) 687-7410 .. **Orwel,** Sheryl A '04 %Clifton B&D,LLP -420 Lex Av -NY 10170
(212) 826-0808 .. **Orza,** Eugene '74 %MLB Players Assn -12 E 49th -NY 10017 **Fx:**752-3649
(212) 819-8200 .. **Orzechowski,** Daren M '00 (White & C LLP) -1155 Av of Amer -NY 10036
(631) 862-7500 .. **Orzechowski,** Stanley E '79 (S Orzechowski,PC) -38 Southrn Blvd -Nesconset 11767 **Fx:**862-7183
(716) 438-9848 .. **Orzechowski,** Victor J '74 -76 West Av Bx391 -Lockprt 14095 **Fx:**438-9848
(212) 252-0004 .. **Orzel,** John A '89 (Carroll M&K LLC) -570 Lex Av -NY 10022

(212) 431-0962 .. **Orzick,** Eric S '81 (Orzick & H) -350 Bway -NY 10013
(212) 431-0962 .. **Orzick & Hupert** -350 Bway -NY 10013
(212) 236-0533 .. **Osaki,** Isaac S '97 Merrill Lynch -225 Lbrty -NY 10281
(914) 761-1300 .. **Osar,** Robt L '73 %Cuddy & F LLP -445 Hmltn Av -White Plns 10601
(212) 756-2000 .. **Osayimwese,** Omozuwa '01 (Schulte R&Z LLP) -919 3rd Av -NY 10022
(607) 723-5341 .. **Osber,** Keith E '61 OfCnsl Hinman H&K,LLP -80 Exchange Bx5250 -Bnghmtn 13902
(212) 725-9800 .. **Osborn,** Danl A '91 (Osborn Law,PC) -295 Mad Av -NY 10017
(212) 558-4000 .. **Osborn,** Donald R '57 SrCnsl Sullivan & C LLP -125 Broad -NY 10004
(585) 454-6480 .. **Osborn,** John C '50 (Osborn R&B,LLP) -45 Exchange Blvd -Rchstr 14614
(212) 576-2670 .. **Osborn,** John E '77 (J Osborn,PC) -841 Bway -NY 10003 **Fx:**686-4023
(212) 735-3000 .. **Osborn,** John W '80 (Skadden ASM&F LLP) -4 Times Sq -NY 10036
(585) 454-6480 .. **Osborn Reed & Burke,LLP** -45 Exchange Blvd -Rchstr 14614 **Fx:**232-4877
(212) 728-8000 .. **Osborn,** Sarah C '92 (Willkie F&G LLP) -787 7th Av -NY 10019
(631) 342-8070 .. **Osborn,** Thos A '79 (Tinari OO&K,LLP) -320 Carleton Av -Central Islip 11722
(585) 262-2667 .. **Osborne,** Alexander M '03 OfCnsl Connors & F,LLP -3445 Winton Pl -Rchstr 14623
(207) 993-2444 .. **Osborne,** Bruce D '94 (Braunschweig & O) -99 Main -Nyack 10960 **Fx:**993-2444
(212) 944-0500 .. **Osborne,** Damon T '06 %Hofheimer G&G,LLP -530 5th Av -NY 10036 **Fx:**897-4991
(845) 462-2700 .. **Osborne,** David W '02 %DG Ellis -2076 South Rd -Poughkeepsie 12601 **Fx:**462-4895
(212) 373-3000 .. **Osborne,** Elizabeth Veit '09 %Paul WRW&G LLP -1285 Av of Amer -NY 10019
(212) 742-3390 .. **Osborne,** Jennifer A '07 %Lindabury ME&C,PC -26 Bway -NY 10004
(212) 415-8600 .. **Osborne,** John W '91 (Locke LB&L LLP) -3 World Fncl Ctr -NY 10281
(631) 324-4977 .. **Osborne & McGowan** -135 Main Bx5011 -E Hampton 11937 **Fx:**324-4578
(212) 403-7300 .. **Osborne,** Rebecca J '02 %Vladeck WE&E,PC -1501 Bway -NY 10036
(518) 485-2312 .. **Osborne,** Sara E '00 OASAS -1450 Wstrn Av -Albany 12203 **Fx:**485-2335
(646) 386-5700 .. **Osborne,** Stacy E '95 %Civil Ct -111 Centre -NY 10013
(631) 324-4977 .. **Osborne,** Thos J '84 (Osborne & M) -135 Main Bx5011 -E Hampton 11937
(607) 348-0433 .. **Osburn,** Judith E '95 -133 Main -Bnghmtn 13905 **Fx:**348-0392
(607) 763-9200 .. **Osburn,** Michl E '96 (Levene G&T,LLP) -BxF-1706 -Bnghmtn 13902
(718) 250-2000 .. **Oseep,** Lesley Cobb '08 %DA -350 Jay -Brklyn 11201 **Fx:**250-2314
(212) 782-7000 .. **O'Seep,** Nathaniel '03 Moore Capital Mgmt,Inc -1251 Av of Amer -NY 10020
(518) 474-3219 .. **Osei,** Kingsley Sarfo '02 %NYSHESC -99 Wshngtn Av -Albany 12255 **Fx:**486-6515
(212) 310-8000 .. **Osendarp,** Joanne E '05 (Weil G&M LLP) -767 5th Av -NY 10153
(718) 246-7200 .. **Oseni,** Adetokunbo Adelani '01 -26 Court -Brklyn 11242
(518) 474-7288 .. **Oser,** Andrea '90 %Dept of Law -The Cptl -Albany 12224
(212) 720-8136 .. **Oser,** Janice A '85 %Fed Reserve Bk -33 Lbrty -NY 10045
(212) 245-0105 .. **Oser,** Roy B '89 (Greenberg & O) -150 W 51st -NY 10019
(716) 856-5500 .. **Osgood,** Helen '75 SpclCnsl Damon M LLP -200 Delaware Av -Buffalo 14202
(646) 610-5400 .. **Osgood,** James J '90 %NYPD -1 Police Plz -NY 10038
(716) 856-0236 .. **Osgood,** Sharon Anscombe '80 -69 Delaware Av -Buffalo 14202 **Fx:**856-0237
(845) 623-0808 .. **Osgood,** Suzanne '87 -167 Route 304 -Nanuet 10954
(212) 450-4000 .. **Osha,** Jay A '10 %Davis P&W LLP -450 Lex Av -NY 10017
(914) 249-5711 .. **Oshatz,** Suzanne B '94 %MasterCard Intl -2000 Purchase -Purchase 10577
(631) 360-7333 .. **O'Shaughnessy,** Shawn P '98 %De Sena & S -1383 Vets Mem'l Hwy -Hauppauge 11788
(718) 442-1700 .. **O'Shaughnessy,** Susan E '92 %Connors & C,PC -766 Castleton Av -Staten Isl 10310 **Fx:**442-1717
(212) 732-8700 .. **O'Shaughnessy,** Timothy J '83 (McAloon & F,PC) -123 William -NY 10038
(212) 609-6800 .. **O'Shaughnessy,** Wm J '63 (McCarter & E,LLP) -245 Park Av -NY 10167
(212) 762-6813 .. **O'Shaughnessy,** Wm J Jr. '04 %Morgan Stanley -1221 Av of Amer -NY 10020
(518) 432-7511 .. **O'Shea,** Brendan C '81 (Gleason DW&O) -40 Beaver -Albany 12207
(212) 474-1000 .. **O'Shea,** Danl A '96 Cravath S&M LLP -825 8th Av -NY 10019
(914) 995-3632 .. **O'Shea,** Erin M '06 %Cnty Atty -148 Martine Av -White Plns 10601 **Fx:**995-2495
(212) 999-5800 .. **O'Shea,** Gerard D '05 %Wilson SG&R -1301 Av of Americas -NY 10019
(315) 336-4500 .. **O'Shea,** J Kevin '70 (O'Shea M&S,LLP) -107 W Lbrty Bx4310 -Rome 13442
(315) 471-3151 .. **O'Shea,** James J '10 %Hancock & E,LLP -1500 AXA Twr I Bx4976 -Syracuse 13221
(631) 283-7007 .. **O'Shea,** James M '82 (O'Shea M&B,LLP) -250 N Sea Rd -Southampton 11968
(718) 816-1110 .. **O'Shea,** Jos A '74 -698 Forest Av -Staten Isl 10310 **Fx:**876-0841
(212) 682-4426 .. **O'Shea,** Julie S '93 %O'Shea Prtnrs LLP -521 5th Av -NY 10175 **Fx:**682-4437
(212) 610-6300 .. **O'Shea,** Kevin J '85 (Allen & O) -1221 Av of Amer -NY 10020
(607) 737-2944 .. **O'Shea,** Kevin M '78 %DA -226 Lk Bx588 -Elmira 14902 **Fx:**737-2965
(718) 816-1110 .. **O'Shea,** Laurie '01 JA O'Shea -698 Forest Av -Staten Isl 10310 **Fx:**876-0841
(631) 283-7007 .. **O'Shea Marcincuk & Bruyn,LLP** -250 N Sea Rd -Southampton 11968 **Fx:**287-9480
(718) 592-3666 .. **O'Shea,** Martin T '79 -90-60 Corona Av -Elmhrst 11373
(914) 241-2188 .. **O'Shea,** Mary E '60 -268 McLain -Bedfrd Hlls 10507 **Fx:**241-2188
(315) 336-4500 .. **O'Shea McDonald & Stevens,LLP** -107 W Lbrty Bx4310 -Rome 13442 **Fx:**336-4618
(516) 296-7000 .. **O'Shea,** Michl F '83 (Certilman BA&H,LLP) -90 Merrick Av -E Meadow 11554
(212) 314-4350 .. **O'Shea,** Patricia Lane '09 AXA Distributors,LLC -1290 Av of Amer -NY 10104
(716) 855-3611 .. **O'Shea,** Philip J Jr. '73 (Smith MO&S,LLP) -69 Delaware Av -Buffalo 14202
(212) 682-4426 .. **O'Shea,** Sean F '88 (O'Shea Prtnrs LLP) -521 5th Av -NY 10175 **Fx:**682-4437
(845) 359-4016 .. **O'Shea,** Timothy '79 -100 Route 303 -Tappan 10983 **Fx:**359-0093
(315) 336-4500 .. **O'Shea,** Timothy B '70 (O'Shea M&S,LLP) -107 W Lbrty Bx4310 -Rome 13442
(914) 422-6076 .. **O'Shea,** Wm M '97 City Ct -77 S Lex Av -White Plns 10601
(212) 682-2288 .. **O'Shea-Maloney,** Carmel H '04 Sankel S&M,LLP -750 3rd Av -NY 10017
(212) 450-4000 .. **Oshen,** Ona A N '10 %Davis P&W LLP -450 Lex Av -NY 10017
(716) 204-2400 .. **Osher,** Jacob W '04 %SJ Baum,PC -220 Nrthpnte Pkwy Bx1291 -Buffalo 14240 **Fx:**204-4600
(212) 351-4000 .. **Osher,** L Mark '99 (Gibson D&C LLP) -200 Park Av -NY 10166
(718) 217-6242 .. **Oshikanlu,** Oluremilekun A '99 Oshikanlu & Assoc,PLLC -211-07 Jamaica Av -Qns Vllg 11428
(212) 224-4000 .. **Oshima,** Hiro '00 %Sumitomo Mitsui -277 Park Av -NY 10172 **Fx:**593-9522
(212) 576-7000 .. **Oshins,** Alice H '03 %NY Life Ins -51 Mad Av -NY 10010 **Fx:**447-0569
(718) 649-6000 .. **Oshins,** Jason A '93 -8623 Flatlands Av -Brklyn 11236 **Fx:**649-7003
(315) 738-1000 .. **Oshins,** Michl B '92 %Nasto Law Firm -4957 Cmmrcial Dr -Yorkville 13495 **Fx:**736-1932
(212) 756-2000 .. **Oshinsky,** Danl V '96 (Schulte R&Z LLP) -919 3rd Av -NY 10022
(585) 343-6320 .. **Oshlag,** Jeffrey D '61 OfCnsl Oshlag S&E -216 E Main -Batavia 14020
(585) 343-6320 .. **Oshlag Saleh & Earl** -216 E Main -Batavia 14020 **Fx:**343-6602
(212) 233-2100 .. **Oshman,** Matthew '72 (Oshman & M,LLP) -42 Bway -NY 10004
(212) 233-2100 .. **Oshman & Mirisola,LLP** -42 Bway -NY 10004 **Fx:**964-8656
(212) 233-2100 .. **Oshman,** Theo '82 (Oshman & M,LLP) -42 Bway -NY 10004
(631) 232-0200 .. **Oshrin,** Adam M '01 %Fumuso KDSS&F,LLP -110 Marcus Blvd -Hauppauge 11788
(212) 687-4900 .. **Oshrin,** Gayle S '97 %Wormser KG&J LLP -825 3rd Av -NY 10022
(212) 609-6800 .. **Osias,** Brian J '01 (McCarter & E,LLP) -245 Park Av -NY 10167
(516) 466-3434 .. **Osias,** Rosalie '84 -175 Grt Nck Rd -Gt Neck 11021 **Fx:**466-3490
(212) 701-3000 .. **Osipoff,** Melissa J '07 %Cahill G&R LLP -80 Pine -NY 10005 **Fx:**269-5420
(631) 232-2400 .. **Osk,** Victoria A '82 %Nassau/Sfflk Law Srv -1757 Vets Hwy -Islandia 11749 **Fx:**232-2489
(212) 867-5800 .. **Osler Hoskin & Harcourt LLP** -620 8th Av -NY 10018 **Fx:**867-5802
(212) 582-9526 .. **Osman,** Steve Dale '90 %Corbett & R -250 W 57th -NY 10019
(212) 207-8400 .. **Osnato,** John E '74 (Kavanagh M&O LLP) -415 Mad Av -NY 10017
(212) 336-0156 .. **Osnato,** Michl J Jr. '98 SEC -3 World Fncl Ctr -NY 10281 **Fx:**336-1323
(212) 326-3939 .. **Osner,** Miriam E '08 %Jones D -222 E 41st -NY 10017
(718) 286-6000 .. **Osnowitz,** Mark A '87 %DA -125-01 Qns Blvd -Kew Gdns 11415
(718) 922-6968 .. **Osoba,** Stella Olufunmilola '98 -41 Schermerhorn -Brklyn 11201
(518) 485-8822 .. **Osofisan,** Olatubosun O '98 %OCFS -52 Wshngtn -Rensselaer 12144 **Fx:**486-6361
(518) 398-8003 .. **Osofsky,** Richd A '70 -2990 E Church Bx677 -Pine Plns 12567 **Fx:**398-6464
(516) 877-0900 .. **Osojnak,** Danl J '87 -14 Front -Hempstd 11550 **Fx:**877-2008
(516) 877-0900 .. **Osojnak,** David J '97 %D Osojnak -14 Front -Hempstd 11550 **Fx:**877-2008
(646) 562-3400 .. **Osorio,** Nathalia '07 Practical Law Co,Inc -747 3rd Av -NY 10017
(718) 992-1900 .. **Ospina,** Leonard '99 (Rosenthal & O) -909-C Sheridan Av -Bronx 10451 **Fx:**992-5296
(718) 855-9000 .. **Ossa,** Edwin A '01 %Cullen and D LLP -177 Montague -Brklyn 11201
(914) 377-9000 .. **Ossentjuk,** Eric D '03 %Wieder & W,PC -35 E Grassy Sprain Rd -Ynkrs 10710 **Fx:**377-1007
(212) 538-2988 .. **Osserman,** Eric K '85 Credit Suisse -11 Mad Av -NY 10010
(212) 480-6790 .. **Ossi,** Christina S '88 %DHCR -25 Beaver -NY 10004 **Fx:**480-7416
(518) 474-6530 .. **Ossias,** Brian P '96 %Dept Pub Srvc -3 ESP -Albany 12223
(212) 891-0700 .. **Ossi Vega,** Joanne '89 %FOJP Srvc Corp -28 E 28th -NY 10016 **Fx:**308-3911
(718) 546-2045 .. **Ossohou,** Andre A '03 DOC Law Lib -1111 Hazen -E Elmhrst 11370
(718) 735-8871 .. **Osson,** Ronald E '86 -873 St Marks Av -Brklyn 11213
(518) 292-5120 .. **Osta,** Wm G '90 %Dept Econ Dvlpmnt -30 S Pearl -Albany 12245 **Fx:**292-5807
(212) 468-8000 .. **Ostad,** Karen '89 (Morrison & F LLP) -1290 Av of Amer -NY 10104
(516) 678-2956 .. **Ostar,** Wm L '77 -53 N Park Av -Rockvll Ctr 11570 **Fx:**536-5936
(212) 735-3000 .. **Ostendorff,** Rebecca L '08 %Skadden ASM&F LLP -4 Times Sq -NY 10036
(212) 696-4848 .. **Ostensen,** Paul '00 %Mintz & G LLP -470 Park Av S -NY 10016
(516) 248-7000 .. **Oster,** Barry A '79 %Albanese & A LLP -1050 Franklin Av -Gdn Cty 11530
(212) 418-6126 .. **Oster,** Ellen '89 %GM -767 5th Av -NY 10153 **Fx:**418-6123
(585) 247-9000 .. **Oster,** Ellis M '07 %Shapiro D&B,LLP -250 Mile Xing Blvd -Rchstr 14624
(212) 457-9568 .. **Oster,** Sean B '06 IncisiveMedia /NYLJ -120 Bway -NY 10271
(631) 439-1720 .. **Oster,** Shari G '85 %MHLS -320 Carleton Av -Central Islip 11722 **Fx:**273-9365
(212) 752-2100 .. **Osterbye,** Raymond C '02 %SM Musa-Obregon -5521 69th -Maspeth 11378 **Fx:**752-8677
(212) 635-3150 .. **Osterer,** Arlene S '78 %Ofc Inspector Genl -61 Bway -NY 10006 **Fx:**809-6287
(609) 986-1300 .. **Osterman,** David S '89 (Goldberg S LLP) -1200 Av of Amer -NY 10036 **Fx:**986-1301
(212) 363-6900 .. **Osterman,** Diana L '97 %Faust GS&B LLP -2 Rector -NY 10006
(212) 310-8000 .. **Osterman,** Jeffrey D '96 (Weil G&M LLP) -767 5th Av -NY 10153
(631) 853-4332 .. **Ostermann,** Gregory '79 %Hon M McNulty -400 Carleton Av -Central Islip 11722

(212) 421-4100 .. **Ostertag,** Juergen R '99 (Pryor C LLP) -7 Times Sq -NY 10036
(845) 486-4300 .. **Ostertag O'Leary Barrett & Faulkner** -17 Cllgvw Av -Poughkeepsie 12603 **Fx:**486-4080
(845) 486-4300 .. **Ostertag,** Robt L '57 (Ostertag OB&F) -17 Cllgvw Av -Poughkeepsie 12603
(212) 931-7800 .. **Ostertag,** Thos J '82 %Baseball Cmmssnr -245 Park Av -NY 10167
(212) 325-6901 .. **Ostfeld,** Scott D '03 Credit Suisse First Boston -11 Mad Av -NY 10010
(212) 608-2700 .. **Ostheimer,** David R '74 (Lamb & L) -233 Bway -NY 10279
(718) 250-4528 .. **Ostheimer,** Kimberlee A '09 Leg Aid -111 Lvngstn -Brklyn 11201 **Fx:**250-4243
(212) 403-1000 .. **Ostling,** Gregory E '99 (Wachtell LR&K) -51 W 52nd -NY 10019
(212) 773-5680 .. **Ostling,** Paul J '74 Ernst & Young LLP -5 Times Sq -NY 10036
(212) 909-6000 .. **Ostner,** Steven M '79 (Debevoise & P LLP) -919 3rd Av -NY 10022
(212) 906-1200 .. **Ostoya,** Kama C '10 %Latham & W -885 3rd Av -NY 10022
(212) 455-2000 .. **Ostrager,** Barry R '73 (Simpson T&B LLP) -425 Lex Av -NY 10017
(212) 681-0600 .. **Ostrager Chong Flaherty & Broitman,PC** -570 Lex Av -NY 10022 **Fx:**681-0300
(718) 222-8880 .. **Ostrager,** Eric W '97 (Jones JO) -45 Main -Brklyn 11201
(212) 681-0600 .. **Ostrager,** Glenn F '78 (Ostrager CF&B,PC) -570 Lex Av -NY 10022
(212) 696-6000 .. **Ostrager,** Jeffrey N '81 (Curtis M-PC&M LLP) -101 Park Av -NY 10178
(585) 987-2800 .. **Ostrander,** Francis M '05 %Woods OG LLP -2 State -Rchstr 14614
(631) 754-9300 .. **Ostrander,** George W '83 -168 Laurel Av -Northprt 11768 **Fx:**754-2618
(212) 762-5346 .. **Ostrander,** Richd A '96 Morgan Stanley -1221 Av of Amer -NY 10020
(212) 751-2700 .. **Ostrau,** Stanley S '51 %JAMS -620 8th Av -NY 10018 **Fx:**751-4099
(516) 296-7000 .. **Ostreicher,** David '05 %Certilman BA&H,LLP -90 Merrick Av -E Meadow 11554
(845) 469-7577 .. **Ostrer,** Benjamin '77 (Ostrer R,LLP) -111 Main Bx509 -Chester 10918
(718) 250-2000 .. **Ostrer,** Evan A '09 %DA -350 Jay -Brklyn 11201 **Fx:**250-2314
(845) 469-7577 .. **Ostrer Rosenwasser, LLP** -111 Main Bx509 -Chester 10918 **Fx:**469-8690
(845) 457-4646 .. **Ostrer Rosenwasser, LLP** -201 Ward Bx69 -Montgmry 12549 **Fx:**457-9007
(212) 604-9170 .. **Ostrin,** Zvi '01 -1900 51st -Brklyn 11204
(212) 541-6222 .. **Ostroff,** Gary E '97 %Kane K,PC -1350 Av of Amer -NY 10019
(212) 382-0700 .. **Ostrolenk Faber Gerb & Soffen,LLP** -1180 Av of Amer -NY 10036 **Fx:**382-0888
(518) 357-2048 .. **Ostrov,** Richd E '89 %DEC -1150 N Westcott Rd -Schnctdy 12306 **Fx:**357-2087
(212) 297-5800 .. **Ostrove,** Elliot D '98 (Day P LLP) -7 Times Sq -NY 10036
(212) 728-8000 .. **Ostrove,** Norman P '07 %Willkie F&G LLP -787 7th Av -NY 10019
(212) 208-1428 .. **Ostrovski,** Vitaly '98 -140 Bway -NY 10005
(718) 596-1787 .. **Ostrow,** Alan '80 -150 Oceana Dr W -Brklyn 11235
(212) 888-3033 .. **Ostrow,** Alec P '81 (Becker GM&M LLP) -299 Park Av -NY 10171
(212) 504-6000 .. **Ostrow,** Danl T '06 %Cadwalader W&T LLP -1 World Fncl Ctr -NY 10281
(212) 335-9000 .. **Ostrow,** Eleanor J '82 %DA -1 Hogan Pl -NY 10013
(212) 439-8768 .. **Ostrow,** Elizabeth S '88 -Yorkvll Finance Station Bx6446 -NY 10128
(212) 682-9200 .. **Ostrow Kaufman & Frankl LLP** -405 Lex Av -NY 10174 **Fx:**682-9222
(917) 868-1900 .. **Ostrow,** Marc D '90 -11 Bway -NY 10004 **Fx:**(347) 269-4470
(516) 877-1800 .. **Ostrow,** Michl J '58 (Schlissel OK,PLLC) -200 Grdn City Plz -Gdn Cty 11530
(212) 682-9200 .. **Ostrow,** Seth H '93 (Ostrow K&F LLP) -405 Lex Av -NY 10174
(212) 227-3620 .. **Ostrow,** Seymour '52 S Ostrow,PC -680 West End Av -NY 10025 **Fx:**269-8950
(516) 626-1960 .. **Ostrower,** Donald A '72 -50 Field Ln -Roslyn Hts 11577 **Fx:**626-1996
(212) 545-4000 .. **Ostrower,** Melissa Kotlow '00 %Jackson L LLP -666 3rd Av -NY 10017
(212) 455-2000 .. **Ostrower,** Silvia Noemi '05 %Simpson T&B LLP -425 Lex Av -NY 10017
(212) 509-2800 .. **Ostrowitz,** Alan R '78 (Ostrowitz & O) -150 Bway -NY 10038 **Fx:**(732) 446-5837
(212) 509-2800 .. **Ostrowitz,** Martha D '90 (Ostrowitz & O) -150 Bway -NY 10038 **Fx:**(732) 446-5837
(631) 439-2960 .. **Ostrowski,** George T Jr. '96 (Cavalier & Assoc) -144-1 Remngtn Blvd -Ronkonkoma 11779 **Fx:**439-2961
(212) 230-8800 .. **Ostrowski,** Izabela '03 WilmerHale -399 Park Av -NY 10022
(716) 854-1440 .. **Ostrowski,** James M '84 -295 Main -Buffalo 14203 **Fx:**853-1303
(212) 225-2000 .. **Ostrowski,** Tristan '07 %Cleary GS&H -1 Lbrty Plz -NY 10006
(212) 878-8000 .. **Ostrowsky,** Adam L '07 %Clifford C LLP -31 W 52nd -NY 10019
(718) 522-1358 .. **Ostrowsky,** Jos '84 -32 Court -Brklyn 11201
(212) 530-5000 .. **Ostrzega,** Jonathan R '10 %Milbank TH&M LLP -1 Chase Manh Plz -NY 10005
(212) 770-1035 .. **Ostuni,** Christopher J '03 AIG Tech Srvcs -80 Pine -NY 10005
(516) 624-6312 .. **Ostuni,** Lisa R '05 Oyster Bay -54 Audrey Av -Oyster Bay 11771
(212) 244-6600 .. **Ostwald,** David H '83 (Schechter & B,PC) -350 5th Av -NY 10118
(518) 457-2070 .. **Ostwald,** Peter B '94 %Dept of Tax & Fin -Bldg 9 State Campus -Albany 12227 **Fx:**457-6131
(718) 537-4958 .. **O'Sullivan,** Allan T '75 %ODAR-SSA -226 E 161st -Bronx 10451 **Fx:**590-1673
(212) 506-2500 .. **O'Sullivan,** Brian J '91 (Mayer B LLP) -1675 Bway -NY 10019
(212) 980-9600 .. **O'Sullivan,** Cara A '01 %Kaufman B&R -120 Bway -NY 10271
(212) 848-4000 .. **O'Sullivan,** Danl B '03 %Shearman & S LLP -599 Lex Av -NY 10022
(631) 361-6900 .. **O'Sullivan,** Dennis B '99 %A Ross -320 Carleton Av -Central Islip 11722
(718) 352-7600 .. **O'Sullivan,** Dennis J '90 -210-13 35th Av -Bayside 11361 **Fx:**352-7755
(212) 391-9552 .. **O'Sullivan,** Donald '84 -470 Park Av -NY 10016 **Fx:**391-9554
(516) 822-8900 .. **O'Sullivan,** James K '82 Fiedelman & M -2 Jericho Plz -Jericho 11753
(518) 745-1400 .. **O'Sullivan,** Jill E '94 %FitzGerald MBF -16 Pearl Bx2017 -Glens Fls 12801
(914) 559-3100 .. **O'Sullivan,** John P '88 OfCnsl Heidell PM&B,LLP -81 Main -White Plns 10601
(212) 401-0800 .. **O'Sullivan,** Kevin E F '77 %Disciplinary Comm -61 Bway -NY 10006 **Fx:**287-1045
(212) 566-4811 .. **O'Sullivan,** Kevin M '03 NYC Dept Bldgs -280 Bway -NY 10007
(212) 788-1003 .. **O'Sullivan,** Mary M '96 %Law Dept -100 Church -NY 10007 **Fx:**788-0367
(212) 848-7897 .. **O'Sullivan,** Maura E '86 (Shearman & S LLP) -599 Lex Av -NY 10022
(516) 921-1200 .. **O'Sullivan,** Michl J '86 (Zavatsky M&L,LLP) -33 Qns Bx510 -Syosset 11791
(718) 590-2000 .. **O'Sullivan,** Michl J '01 %DA -198 E 161st -Bronx 10451 **Fx:**590-6477
(212) 521-5400 .. **O'Sullivan,** Nicole K '09 %Reed S LLP -599 Lex Av -NY 10022
(914) 946-4777 .. **O'Sullivan,** Patrick J '90 (Keane & B,PC) -445 Hmltn Av -White Plns 10601
(315) 655-3463 .. **O'Sullivan,** Patrick J '94 (Mitchell G&S,LLC) -5 Mill Bx312 -Cazenovia 13035
(212) 312-3883 .. **O'Sullivan,** Patrick J Jr. '02 %EDC -110 William -NY 10038 **Fx:**312-3912
(212) 326-2000 .. **O'Sullivan,** Sarah S '07 %O'Melveny & M LLP -7 Times Sq -NY 10036
(516) 294-5433 .. **O'Sullivan,** Sean J '88 %Ahmuty D&M -200 IU Willets Rd -Albertson 11507
(718) 650-4700 .. **O'Sullivan,** Sean P '01 -84 New Dorp Plz -Staten Isl 10306 **Fx:**727-2976
(212) 455-2000 .. **O'Sullivan,** Shannon M '08 %Simpson T&B LLP -425 Lex Av -NY 10017
(518) 434-1935 .. **O'Sullivan,** Timothy J '87 %NY Lawyers Fund -119 Wshngtn Av -Albany 12210 **Fx:**434-5641
(212) 765-5070 .. **O'Sullivan,** Wm P '07 %Fish & R,PC -153 E 53rd -NY 10022
(212) 233-1033 .. **Osuna,** Robt A '95 -11 Park Pl -NY 10007
(212) 506-5000 .. **Oswald,** Edwin G '89 (Orrick H&S LLP) -51 W 52nd -NY 10019
(212) 594-5000 .. **Oswald,** Frank A '87 (Togut S&S LLP) -1 Penn Plz -NY 10119
(518) 854-3777 .. **Oswald,** Henry P '67 -Rexleigh Rd Bx482 -Salem 12865
(646) 471-4000 .. **Oswald,** James A '90 PricewaterhouseCoopers LLP -300 Mad Av -NY 10017
(518) 692-8619 .. **Oswald,** John K '99 -181 Main -Greenwich 12834
(212) 277-1015 .. **Oswald,** John P '85 (CT Capital Intl Inc) -655 Madison -NY 10065
(212) 848-4000 .. **Oswald,** Judson A '07 %Shearman & S LLP -599 Lex Av -NY 10022
(212) 819-8200 .. **Oswald,** Victoria L '04 %White & C LLP -1155 Av of Amer -NY 10036
(212) 530-5000 .. **Ota,** Candice P '07 %Milbank TH&M LLP -1 Chase Manh Plz -NY 10005
(212) 836-8000 .. **Otchin,** Jos W '10 Kaye S LLP -425 Park Av -NY 10022
(914) 965-1515 .. **Otero,** Antonio J '99 J Romano -703 Ynkrs Av -Ynkrs 10704 **Fx:**965-0410
(212) 309-1000 .. **Otero,** Brian V '02 (Hunton & W) -200 Park Av -NY 10166
(212) 297-5800 .. **Otero,** Camille V '99 Cnsl Day P LLP -7 Times Sq -NY 10036
(914) 798-5400 .. **Otero,** Rafael '82 SpclCnsl Goldberg S LLP -11 Martine Av -White Plns 10606
(212) 435-3571 .. **Otero,** Sandra B '83 %Port Auth of NY/NJ -225 Park Av S -NY 10003 **Fx:**435-3555
(718) 836-6700 .. **Otey,** Chas F '68 -366 72nd -Brklyn 11209 **Fx:**491-9097
(718) 250-2000 .. **Othman,** Yaser R '10 %DA -350 Jay -Brklyn 11201 **Fx:**250-2314
(212) 696-6000 .. **Otis,** Andrew D '99 (Curtis M-PC&M LLP) -101 Park Av -NY 10178
(212) 901-2272 .. **Otis,** Krista J '99 Equilend Holdings LLC -17 State -NY 10004
(516) 794-2800 .. **Otis,** Nicholas P '86 %M Devack,PLLC -90 Merrick Av -E Meadow 11554 **Fx:**794-2900
(315) 489-8407 .. **Otis,** Scott A '03 -Bx344 -Watertwn 13601
(914) 967-7404 .. **Otis,** Steven '86 (Mayor's Ofc) -1051 Bstn Post Rd -Rye 10580
(718) 923-4206 .. **Oto,** Darla Phillips '83 %OTDA Fair Hearings -14 Boerum Pl -Brklyn 11201
(212) 449-7056 .. **O'Toole,** Andrea S '99 Merrill Lynch -4 Wrld Fncl Ctr -NY 10080
(212) 736-5300 .. **O'Toole,** Danl P '93 (Block O&M LLP) -1 Penn Plz -NY 10119
(212) 307-5500 .. **O'Toole,** Edmund M '92 (Venable LLP) -1270 Av of Amer -NY 10020
(212) 697-6555 .. **O'Toole,** Edw L '08 %Biedermann RH&R -570 Lex Av -NY 10022
(212) 838-1153 .. **O'Toole,** Eileen '84 -270 Mad Av -NY 10016 **Fx:**949-0966
(914) 636-4848 .. **O'Toole,** Electa B '81 (O'Toole & O) -65 Rodman Oval -New Rchll 10805 **Fx:**636-4848
(585) 352-7300 .. **O'Toole,** Keith E '91 -24 West Av Bx130 -Spencerprt 14559 **Fx:**352-8709
(914) 232-1511 .. **O'Toole,** Marianne T '90 M O'Toole,LLC -20 Valley Rd -Katonah 10536 **Fx:**232-1599
(585) 232-6500 .. **O'Toole,** Martin W '87 (Harter S&E LLP) -1600 Bausch & Lomb Pl -Rchstr 14604
(718) 720-3900 .. **O'Toole,** Maureen A '87 (Kuhn & O,LLP) -1 Edgewtr Plz -Staten Isl 10305
(212) 839-5300 .. **O'Toole,** Meaghan M '97 Cnsl Sidley A LLP -787 7th Av -NY 10019
(914) 636-4848 .. **O'Toole,** Neil D '89 (O'Toole & O) -65 Rodman Oval -New Rchll 10805 **Fx:**636-4848
(716) 731-1771 .. **O'Toole,** Robt J '78 -Bx255 -Niagara Fls 14304 **Fx:**731-3377
(212) 867-6000 .. **O'Toole,** Sara A '06 %Rosenberg & E,PC -733 3rd Av -NY 10017
(646) 610-5400 .. **O'Toole,** Sean M '93 %NYPD -1 Police Plz -NY 10038
(646) 610-5400 .. **O'Toole,** Sean P '02 NYPD -1 Police Plz -NY 10038
(212) 666-5789 .. **Otos,** Sally '96 -250 W 99th -NY 10025 **Fx:**666-5674
(212) 663-3277 .. **Ott,** Gloria W '80 -801 West End Av -NY 10025
(212) 974-2400 .. **Ott,** Lara P '99 %J Burstein -1790 Bway -NY 10019 **Fx:**974-2944
(845) 486-3048 .. **Ott,** Richd A '94 %Cnty Atty -60 Market -Poughkeepsie 12601 **Fx:**486-2796
(212) 770-7678 .. **Ottaviano,** Anne T '87 %AIG -70 Pine -NY 10270
(716) 438-0488 .. **Ottaviano,** John J '86 (Ottaviano & S,LLP) -172 East Av Bx1230 -Lockprt 14095 **Fx:**438-0489
(212) 338-7664 .. **Ottaviano,** Mario '04 %Verizon -240 E 38th -NY 10016
(212) 541-7800 .. **Otten,** Barbara E '83 %Planned Parenthood -434 W 33rd -NY 10001 **Fx:**868-4677
(212) 259-8000 .. **Ottenberg,** Jill D '09 %Dewey & L LLP -1301 Av of Amer -NY 10019
(212) 371-8855 .. **Ottenbreit,** Kenneth G '91 (Stikeman E LLP) -445 Park Av -NY 10022
(212) 902-1000 .. **Ottensoser,** Danl A '97 %Goldman Sachs -1 NY Plz -NY 10004
(212) 481-7500 .. **Ottensoser,** Milton D '79 -275 Mad Av -NY 10016 **Fx:**481-5909

(212) 809-5568 .. **Ottensoser**, Saml F '68 Legend Merchant Grp -30 Broad -NY 10004 **Fx**:809-5567
(212) 779-1414 .. **Ottensoser**, Uri Seth '96 (Bernstein L LLP) -10 E 40th -NY 10016
(516) 739-0000 .. **Ottenwalder**, Irma J '92 %Martyn T&M -330 Old Cntry Rd -Mineola 11501
(212) 858-1000 .. **Otterbeck**, Charlotta '97 (Pillsbury WSP LLP) -1540 Bway -NY 10036
(718) 967-3737 .. **Otterbeck**, Christopher H '05 %Otterbeck Law Firm -939 Huguenot Av -Staten Isl 10312 **Fx**:967-9374
(718) 967-3737 .. **Otterbeck**, Harold J '77 (Otterbeck Law Firm) -939 Huguenot Av -Staten Isl 10312 **Fx**:967-9374
(212) 661-9100 .. **Otterbourg Steindler Houston & Rosen,PC** -230 Park Av -NY 10169 **Fx**:682-6104
(203) 255-6560 .. **Otterstedt**, Paul J '95 Cnsl Ryan M&L,LLP -90 Forest Av -Locust Vly 11560 **Fx**:255-6570
(212) 571-2000 .. **Ottinger**, Robt W '96 (Ottinger Firm,PC) -19 Fulton -NY 10038 **Fx**:571-0505
(212) 986-6000 .. **Otto**, Jason A '00 %Kleinberg KW&C,PC -551 5th Av -NY 10176
(718) 389-2427 .. **Otto**, John A '02 %Agostino & Assoc,PC -500 Kngslnd Av -Brklyn 11222
(212) 804-4200 .. **Otto**, Mitchell D '95 (Mound CW&G) -One Bttry Pk Plz -NY 10004
(315) 422-1311 .. **Otto**, Susan E '87 (Melvin & M,PLLC) -217 S Salina -Syracuse 13202
(212) 490-3000 .. **Ottombrino**, Lois K '82 (Wilson EME&D LLP) -150 E 42nd -NY 10017
(516) 222-2434 .. **Otton**, Christopher M '02 %White Q&S -377 Oak Bx9304 -Gdn Cty 11530
(212) 422-0202 .. **Oubre**, Brian M '04 %Sedgwick DM&A LLP -125 Broad -NY 10004
(212) 267-5353 .. **Ouchterloney**, Robt D '62 (Chamberlain WO&W) -575 8th Av -NY 10018
(315) 474-7447 .. **Oudemool**, Dirk J '65 -333 E Onondaga -Syracuse 13202 **Fx**:474-0425
(518) 445-2311 .. **Ouellette**, Alicia R '95 %Albany Law Schl -80 New Scotland Av -Albany 12208 **Fx**:445-2315
(518) 445-2028 .. **Ouellette**, Margaret A '88 %Citizens Bk -833 Bway -Albany 12207
(518) 473-8418 .. **Ouimet**, John A '76 %OCFS -52 Wshngtn -Rensselaer 12144 **Fx**:486-6361
(845) 454-9700 .. **Ouimette Goldstein & Andrews** -88 Market Bx192 -Poughkeepsie 12601 **Fx**:454-8743
(845) 342-2272 .. **Ouimette Goldstein & Andrews** -402 E Main Bx548 -Middletwn 10940 **Fx**:342-2032
(845) 567-0100 .. **Ouimette Goldstein & Andrews** -843 Union Av -New Windsor 12553 **Fx**:567-0139
(718) 726-6200 .. **Oummih**, Amal '96 -25-84 Steinway -Astoria 11103 **Fx**:721-9892
(607) 547-7580 .. **Oursler**, Mark N '89 Cnsl OCA -197 Main -Cooperstwn 13326
(212) 801-6788 .. **Ourvan**, Jeffrey A '03 %Greenberg T,LLP -200 Park Av -NY 10166
(212) 971-3175 .. **Ousley**, Jodie L '99 (d'Arcambal L&O LLP) -40 Fulton -NY 10038 **Fx**:971-3176
(516) 248-7900 .. **Oussani**, Rita C '83 OfCnsl Sweeny & S -510 Broad Hollow Rd -Melvll 11747 **Fx**:248-8730
(718) 768-3059 .. **Oussani**, Rita C '83 -777 5th Av -Brklyn 11232 **Fx**:965-0750
(212) 596-9000 .. **Oussayef**, Karim Z '09 %Ropes & G LLP -1211 Av of Amer -NY 10036
(718) 590-2000 .. **Oustatcher**, Adam S '99 %DA -198 E 161st -Bronx 10451 **Fx**:590-6477
(718) 651-5121 .. **Outeda**, Laura S '08 -82-11 37th Av -Jcksn Hts 11372
(212) 278-0128 .. **Outmezguine**, Avi '00 Scanbuy Inc -54 W 39th -NY 10018
(212) 669-8300 .. **Outram**, Denise A '86 %Manhattan Boro President Ofc -1 Centre -NY 10007
(212) 245-1000 .. **Outten & Golden LLP** -3 Park Av -NY 10016 **Fx**:977-4005
(212) 245-1000 .. **Outten**, Wayne N '79 (Outten & G LLP) -3 Park Av -NY 10016
(315) 866-6600 .. **Outtrim**, Garry L '94 %GF Aney -401 N Prospect -Herkimer 13350 **Fx**:866-7860
(212) 998-3700 .. **OuYang**, Elizabeth R '92 NYU A/P/A Studies Prgrm -41-51 E 11th -NY 10003
(212) 558-4000 .. **Ouyang**, Y Vivian '07 %Sullivan & C LLP -125 Broad -NY 10004
(631) 913-4444 .. **Ovadia**, Stephanie G '85 (Dell LT&V LLP) -5 Orvll Dr -Bohemia 11716
(212) 226-2376 .. **Oved**, Darren '95 (Oved & O LLP) -101 Av of Amer -NY 10013 **Fx**:226-7555
(212) 226-2376 .. **Oved**, Terrence A '92 (Oved & O LLP) -101 Av of Amer -NY 10013 **Fx**:226-7555
(585) 266-0430 .. **Ovejero**, Frank J '92 Everest Institute -1630 Portlnd Av -Rchstr 14621
(212) 996-5244 .. **Overall**, Martha R '76 -345 E 86th -NY 10028
(585) 546-9101 .. **Overbeck**, Danl '75 Fleet Private Clients Grp -1 East Av -Rchstr 14638 **Fx**:546-9114
(716) 648-1800 .. **Overdorf**, James R '88 -1 Bills Dr -Orchard Pk 14127
(585) 869-5111 .. **Overholt**, Judy M '90 -160 Linden Oaks -Rchstr 14625 **Fx**:869-5112
(212) 481-9600 .. **Overland**, John L Jr. '05 %Wagner D,PC -99 Mad Av -NY 10016
(718) 590-2000 .. **Overland**, Vanessa D '08 %DA -198 E 161st -Bronx 10451 **Fx**:590-6477
(212) 436-3817 .. **Overman**, Eric M '96 Deloitte & Touche LLP -2 World Fncl Ctr -NY 10281 **Fx**:653-3894
(845) 353-9747 .. **Overn**, Michl P '99 -305 N Bway -Nyack 10960
(212) 572-5410 .. **Overs**, Kimberley Anne D '93 Estee Lauder -767 5th Av -NY 10153
(212) 935-7400 .. **Overs**, Peter W Jr. '94 %Harwood F LLP -488 Mad Av -NY 10022
(518) 383-4000 .. **Overton**, Jack A Jr. '77 (Overton RD&D,LLP) -19 Halfmoon Exec Park Dr Bx437 -Clifton Pk 12065
(585) 419-8800 .. **Overton**, Kevin L '04 %Harris B PLLC -99 Garnsey Rd -Pittsfrd 14534
(518) 383-4000 .. **Overton Russell Doerr & Donovan,LLP** -19 Halfmoon Exec Park Dr Bx437 -Clifton Pk 12065 **Fx**:383-4282
(212) 751-9800 .. **Overzat**, Peter K '77 %Morelli R PC -950 3rd Av -NY 10022
(212) 361-7996 .. **Ovesey**, Michele M '80 %Dept Homeless Srvcs -33 Beaver -NY 10004 **Fx**:361-8002
(516) 739-1514 .. **Oviasu**, Thelma Nkem '94 -400 Grdn City Plz -Gdn Cty 11530 **Fx**:742-5967
(516) 357-3000 .. **Ovicher**, Julie '07 %Rivkin R LLP -926 RXR Plz -Uniondale 11556
(585) 263-6201 .. **Ovsiovitch**, Jay S '99 %Fed Pub Def -28 E Main -Rchstr 14614 **Fx**:263-5871
(516) 746-8000 .. **Oweis**, Joanne L '00 %Jaspan S LLP -300 Grdn City Plz -Gdn Cty 11530
(212) 596-9000 .. **Owen**, Andrew J '04 %Ropes & G LLP -1211 Av of Amer -NY 10036
(212) 725-7969 .. **Owen**, Christopher T '88 -200 Mad Av -NY 10016 **Fx**:213-3318
(212) 474-1000 .. **Owen**, David E '09 %Cravath S&M LLP -825 8th Av -NY 10019
(212) 701-3000 .. **Owen**, David R '98 (Cahill G&R LLP) -80 Pine -NY 10005 **Fx**:269-5420
(212) 730-7750 .. **Owen**, Edw L III '81 (Nicoletti GS&O,LLP) -555 5th Av -NY 10017
(585) 546-6010 .. **Owen**, Elizabeth J '96 %Beckerman & B -1 W Main -Rchstr 14614 **Fx**:546-7035
(646) 386-3217 .. **Owen**, Guy E '93 %Hon C Huff -60 Centre -NY 10007
(212) 326-3939 .. **Owen**, John T '02 %Jones D -222 E 41st -NY 10017
(845) 294-5001 .. **Owen**, Jos A '90 Owen Law Firm -Bx1000 -Goshen 10924 **Fx**:294-6355
(845) 294-4499 .. **Owen**, Patrick S '97 -160 Main Bx431 -Goshen 10924 **Fx**:294-4431
(914) 949-0109 .. **Owen**, R Christopher '80 (Owen & E) -1 Water -White Plns 10601 **Fx**:949-9223
(212) 967-4778 .. **Owen**, Richd K '83 -350 5th Av -NY 10118
(212) 318-3000 .. **Owen**, Robt D '74 (Fulbright & J LLP) -666 5th Av -NY 10103
(212) 489-8230 .. **Owens**, Andrew E '04 %Davis WT LLP -1633 Bway -NY 10019
(347) 529-7168 .. **Owens**, Arthur J '96 -1608 Beverley Rd -Brklyn 11226
(212) 773-2643 .. **Owens**, Brolota Shea '99 Ernst & Young LLP -5 Times Sq -NY 10036
(718) 250-2000 .. **Owens**, Charlotte C '09 %DA -350 Jay -Brklyn 11201 **Fx**:250-2314
(212) 309-6000 .. **Owens**, Christopher A '03 %Morgan L&B LLP -101 Park Av -NY 10178
(585) 244-8910 .. **Owens**, Clifford P '91 %Fiandach & F -100 Allens Crk Rd -Rchstr 14618 **Fx**:244-4863
(212) 267-7767 .. **Owens**, David B '88 %Gess G&S,PC -30 Vesey -NY 10007
(585) 262-1374 .. **Owens**, David L '91 -45 Exchange Blvd -Rchstr 14614 **Fx**:325-5536
(718) 875-1300 .. **Owens**, Dennis L '95 Appllt Div 2nd Dept -45 Monroe Pl -Brklyn 11201 **Fx**:858-2446
(516) 228-8484 .. **Owens**, Douglas M '01 %Dilworth & B,LLP -1000 Woodbury Rd -Woodbury 11797
(212) 858-1000 .. **Owens**, F Jos Jr. '71 (Pillsbury WSP LLP) -1540 Bway -NY 10036
(212) 259-8000 .. **Owens**, Gregory M '83 (Dewey & L LLP) -1301 Av of Amer -NY 10019
(716) 633-6597 .. **Owens**, J Eldon '70 -5050 Mdwbrk Rd -Williamsvll 14221
(716) 692-6530 .. **Owens**, J Eldon '70 (Owens & O) -21 Main -Tonawanda 14150
(718) 590-2000 .. **Owens**, Jasmine L '09 %DA -198 E 161st -Bronx 10451 **Fx**:590-6477
(212) 264-6116 .. **Owens**, Jessica Dahlin '03 DHS -26 Fed Plz -NY 10278
(914) 517-5000 .. **Owens**, Jill C '89 SpclCnsl Meiselman DPC&E,PC -1311 Mamaroneck Av -White Plns 10605
(212) 909-6000 .. **Owens**, Jillian M '09 %Debevoise & P LLP -919 3rd Av -NY 10022
(518) 694-0910 .. **Owens McQuade,PLLC** -41 State -Albany 12207 **Fx**:694-0912
(212) 728-8000 .. **Owens**, Rachel A '07 %Willkie F&G LLP -787 7th Av -NY 10019
(585) 477-4653 .. **Owens**, Raymond L '64 %Eastman Kodak -343 State -Rchstr 14650
(212) 906-1200 .. **Owens**, Richd D '90 (Latham & W) -885 3rd Av -NY 10022
(516) 571-3800 .. **Owens**, Robt J '81 %DA -262 Old Cntry Rd -Mineola 11501 **Fx**:248-9479
(914) 681-6060 .. **Owens**, Susan B '85 -140 Grand -White Plns 10601
(518) 862-1200 .. **Owens**, Susan Biggins '08 %Martin H&M LLP -Bx15141 -Albany 12212
(212) 252-0300 .. **Owens**, Tanya M '05 %Kagan LLLG&C,LLP -200 Mad Av -NY 10016
(518) 463-8763 .. **Owens**, Thos M '98 Albany Port Dist Commission -106 Smith Blvd -Albany 12202
(518) 561-4400 .. **Owens**, Wm L '75 Stafford OC&T,PLLC -1 Cumberland Av Bx2947 -Plattsbrgh 12901
(212) 306-7302 .. **Owh**, Michl I '04 Deferred Corp Plan -40 Rector -NY 10006
(585) 428-1838 .. **Owlett**, Deborah K '92 %Family Ct -301 Hall of Justice -Rchstr 14614
(212) 902-5729 .. **Owodunni**, Precious C '03 Goldman Sachs & Co -85 Broad -NY 10004
(212) 626-4100 .. **Owoo**, Olumide '07 %Baker & M LLP -1114 Av of Amer -NY 10036
(718) 447-9306 .. **Owotomo**, Dayo '91 -805 Castleton Av -Staten Isl 10310
(212) 307-0023 .. **Oxamendi**, David '97 %DeSimone AS&O LLP -145 Hudson -NY 10013
(516) 876-2200 .. **Oxenberg**, Jonathan J '86 -3 Meadowood Dr -Jericho 11753 **Fx**:333-4264
(212) 837-6000 .. **Oxford**, Neil J '02 (Hughes H&R LLP) -1 Bttry Pk Plz -NY 10004
(212) 546-9255 .. **Oxley**, Jos W '92 (Scarinci H) -107 Grand -NY 10013
(212) 455-2000 .. **Oxman**, Ariel '08 %Simpson T&B LLP -425 Lex Av -NY 10017
(212) 450-4000 .. **Oxman**, David C '70 SrCnsl Davis P&W LLP -450 Lex Av -NY 10017
(212) 232-1300 .. **Oxman**, Jennifer R '96 (Lewis BB&S LLP) -77 Water -NY 10005
(914) 422-3900 .. **Oxman**, Marc '69 (Oxman TKW&G LLP) -120 Bloomingdale Rd -White Plns 10605
(212) 259-8000 .. **Oxman**, Matthew C '07 %Dewey & L LLP -1301 Av of Amer -NY 10019
(212) 521-4430 .. **Oxman**, Michl A '91 %Becker M LLC -590 Mad Av -NY 10022
(212) 761-7753 .. **Oxman**, Stephen '74 Morgan Stanley -1585 Bway -NY 10036
(212) 481-5020 .. **Oxman**, Stephen A Jr. '02 Film Sales Co -165 Mad Av -NY 10016 **Fx**:481-5021
(914) 422-3900 .. **Oxman Tulis Kirkpatrick Whyatt & Geiger LLP** -120 Bloomingdale Rd -White Plns 10605 **Fx**:422-3636
(212) 885-5000 .. **Oxton**, Glen T '73 (Blank R LLP) -405 Lex Av -NY 10174
(212) 578-4829 .. **Oyen**, Elizabeth A '04 MetLife -27-01 Qns Plz N -LIC 11101
(212) 290-1833 .. **Oyeneye**, Kingsley Tunde '01 %OTDA Fair Hearings -330 W 34th -NY 10001 **Fx**:290-1926
(718) 549-2272 .. **Oz**, Shlomit J '96 -3333 H Hdsn Pkwy -Bronx 10463 **Fx**:432-1280
(212) 310-9311 .. **Ozarow**, Alan '80 -444 Mad Av -NY 10022
(212) 336-0144 .. **Ozaruk**, Bohdan S '83 SEC -3 World Fncl Ctr -NY 10281 **Fx**:336-1323
(212) 906-1200 .. **Ozawa**, Austin T '08 %Latham & W -885 3rd Av -NY 10022
(212) 848-4000 .. **Ozawa**, Joji '07 %Shearman & S LLP -599 Lex Av -NY 10022
(212) 949-7300 .. **Ozdural**, Sanem '06 %Vernon & G,LLP -261 Mad Av -NY 10016
(914) 238-6090 .. **Ozer**, Alyzza C '94 -412 Whippoorwill Rd -Chappaqua 10514 **Fx**:238-5949

(212) 949-4700 .. **Ozer,** Cem '93 %Bushell SO&G LLP -60 E 42nd -NY 10165 **Fx:**286-0513
(914) 665-2414 .. **Ozer,** Ivy M '90 %City Ct -2 Roosevelt Sq -Mt Vernon 10550
(718) 859-4686 .. **Ozeri,** Mitchell M '90 -1542 Flatbush Av -Brklyn 11210 **Fx:**859-5682
(212) 686-3838 .. **Ozgu,** Emre '98 (Barst M&K LLP) -2 Park Av -NY 10016
(212) 788-0895 .. **Ozgu,** Pinar '08 Law Dept -100 Church -NY 10007 **Fx:**788-0367
(516) 746-1111 .. **Oziel,** Michl J '05 -170 Old Cntry Rd -Mineola 11501
(718) 250-2000 .. **Oziemblewski,** Jill K '05 %DA -350 Jay -Brklyn 11201 **Fx:**250-2314
(212) 210-9533 .. **Ozim,** Frances Tola '09 %Alston & B LLP -90 Park Av -NY 10016
(516) 328-2300 .. **Ozimkowski,** Lester E '89 (Abrams FFEGF&E,LLP) -1111 Marcus Av -Lk Success 11042
(212) 446-7000 .. **Ozir,** Gil S '03 McKinsey & Co -55 E 52nd -NY 10055 **Fx:**688-9521
(212) 509-0099 .. **Ozisik,** Sevil '97 (Haker & O,LLP) -29 Bway -NY 10006 **Fx:**506-0488
(845) 778-7777 .. **Ozman,** Brandon '89 (Ozman Law Ofc) -130 W Main -Walden 12586
(845) 778-7700 .. **Ozman,** Raynard A '92 -130 W Main -Walden 12586
(607) 273-4200 .. **Ozmun,** Kristal J '09 Miller M,LLP -202 E State -Ithaca 14850
(212) 455-2000 .. **Ozner,** Jonathan R '08 %Simpson T&B LLP -425 Lex Av -NY 10017
(212) 735-7404 .. **Ozols,** Amy '01 -500 Park Av -NY 10022
(212) 723-3391 .. **Oztan,** Omer S '99 Citigroup -250 West -NY 10013
(212) 589-4200 .. **Ozturk,** Ferve E '09 %Baker & H LLP -45 Rckfllr Plz -NY 10111
(718) 643-8045 .. **Ozzi,** Wayne M '78 %Hon R Gigante -120 Schermerhorn -Brklyn 11201
(212) 489-8230 .. **Pa,** Monica '03 %Davis WT LLP -1633 Bway -NY 10019
(212) 506-1700 .. **Paar,** Randy '76 (Kasowitz BT&F LLP) -1633 Bway -NY 10019
(212) 453-2086 .. **Paasche,** Franz '88 Communications Cnsltng Wrldwd -220 E 42nd -NY 10017 **Fx:**453-2083
(212) 535-8942 .. **Pabon,** Pedro Jr. '89 -Bx1302 -NY 10028 **Fx:**517-5823
(212) 617-3362 .. **Pacchia,** Anthony L '07 Bloomberg LP -731 Lex Av -NY 10022
(212) 940-8800 .. **Paccione,** Anthony L '86 (Katten MR LLP) -575 Mad Av -NY 10022
(212) 533-6300 .. **Pace,** Angela E '03 %NYSUT -52 Bway -NY 10004 **Fx:**995-2347
(631) 661-6500 .. **Pace,** Anthony '52 (Pace & P,LLP) -400 Montauk Hwy -W Islip 11795 **Fx:**661-6678
(212) 506-5000 .. **Pace,** Damon C '99 (Orrick H&S LLP) -51 W 52nd -NY 10019
(716) 662-9808 .. **Pace,** Edw A '78 (Berkowitz & P) -4513 S Buffalo Bx639 -Orchard Pk 14127
(212) 819-8200 .. **Pace,** Jack E III '99 (White & C LLP) -1155 Av of Amer -NY 10036
(631) 661-6500 .. **Pace,** John '58 (Pace & P,LLP) -400 Montauk Hwy -W Islip 11795 **Fx:**661-6678
(212) 837-6000 .. **Pace,** Jordan E '08 %Hughes H&R LLP -1 Bttry Pk Plz -NY 10004
(212) 502-2140 .. **Pace,** Mark N '99 OCE Business Srvcs,Inc -460 W 34th -NY 10001
(212) 592-1400 .. **Pace,** Matthew D '86 Cnsl Herrick,F LLP -2 Park Av -NY 10016
(585) 798-1000 .. **Pace,** Nathan D '05 (Mack & P) -Cook Bldg-534 Main Bx248 -Medina 14103 **Fx:**798-1003
(212) 864-7955 .. **Pace,** Paula P '82 -180 W 93rd -NY 10025
(631) 543-9000 .. **Pace,** Rinaldo A '80 -398 Route 111 -Smithtwn 11787 **Fx:**543-9001
(516) 489-9600 .. **Pace,** Ronald E '70 -145 Hunters Dr -Syosset 11791 **Fx:**489-3782
(212) 318-6000 .. **Pace,** Vincent A '07 %Paul HJ&W LLP -75 E 55th -NY 10022
(212) 818-9600 .. **Paceleo,** Lorraine '99 %Greenfield S&S,LLP -600 3rd Av -NY 10016
(845) 359-8540 .. **Pacella,** Danl J '92 -16 Spruce -Orangebrg 10962
(212) 848-4000 .. **Pacella,** Jennifer M '09 %Shearman & S LLP -599 Lex Av -NY 10022
(212) 509-4600 .. **Pacella,** Richd B '69 -80 Broad -NY 10004 **Fx:**509-0406
(212) 858-1000 .. **Pacelli,** Albert P '82 (Pillsbury WSP LLP) -1540 Bway -NY 10036
(212) 556-2100 .. **Pacelli,** Andrea '09 King & S -1185 Av of Amer -NY 10036
(716) 847-0680 .. **Pacer,** Walter R Jr. '74 %W Pacer Jr -298 Main -Buffalo 14202
(212) 325-2000 .. **Pacewicz Hill,** Anna K '02 Credit Suisse -1 Mad Av -NY 10010
(631) 462-5888 .. **Pach,** Nicolette M '75 OfCnsl Rubin & R, PLLC -6080 Jericho Tpk -Commack 11725
(718) 855-3000 .. **Pacheco,** Carmen A '87 (Pacheco & L) -340 Atl Av -Brklyn 11201
(732) 855-6189 .. **Pacheco,** Deirdre Woulfe '89 Cnsl Wilentz G&S -110 William -NY 10038 **Fx:**726-6627
(315) 424-7209 .. **Pacheco,** Jos R II '92 Cnsl T Puleo -441 S Salina -Syracuse 13202 **Fx:**424-5553
(212) 407-0953 .. **Pacheco,** Mercedes M '93 %Santander Investments -45 E 53rd -NY 10022 **Fx:**407-7830
(212) 815-1818 .. **Pacheco,** Miranda '85 %DC 37 MELS -125 Barclay -NY 10007 **Fx:**815-1343
(212) 272-2000 .. **Pacheco,** Richd J '03 JP Morgan Chase -383 Mad Av -NY 10179
(631) 462-0014 .. **Pachilakis,** Billy D '05 B Pachilakis,PC -5921 74th -Middl Vllg 11379
(631) 324-3942 .. **Pachman,** Matthew E '85 (Ackerman OP&B,LLP) -34 Pantigo Rd -E Hampton 11937
(212) 907-9600 .. **Pachnanda,** Amol K '04 %Ingram YGC&B,LLP -250 Park Av -NY 10177
(914) 286-3400 .. **Pachnanda,** Ellen K '04 Leg Aid -1 N Bway -White Plns 10601 **Fx:**682-4112
(516) 773-3900 .. **Pacht,** Robt A '83 -525 Nrthrn Blvd -Gt Neck 11021 **Fx:**482-7327
(212) 435-3571 .. **Pachter,** Milton H '57 %Port Auth of NY/NJ -225 Park Av S -NY 10003 **Fx:**435-3555
(212) 561-7700 .. **Pachulski Stang Ziehl & Jones** -780 3rd Av -NY 10017 **Fx:**561-7777
(315) 724-9810 .. **Pachura,** Jos B Jr. '81 -7 Hopper Bx4247 -Utica 13504 **Fx:**724-5468
(212) 335-4500 .. **Paci,** Christopher C '89 (DLA Piper LLP) -1251 Av of Amer -NY 10020
(516) 742-8340 .. **Pacifico,** Chas L '65 (Pacifico D&P) -136 Willis Av -Mineola 11501
(212) 735-3000 .. **Pacifico,** Dawn M '99 %Skadden ASM&F LLP -4 Times Sq -NY 10036
(516) 742-8340 .. **Pacifico Di Gregorio & Pacifico** -136 Willis Av -Mineola 11501
(516) 676-6262 .. **Pacifico,** Jos H Jr. '90 (Kelly L&P) -23 Birch Hill Rd -Locust Vly 11560
(716) 853-9555 .. **Pacifico,** Michl J '08 %Leg Aid -237 Main -Buffalo 14203 **Fx:**853-3219
(845) 294-1895 .. **Pacione,** Albert P Jr. '75 A Pacione Jr,PLLC -45 Webster Av -Goshen 10924 **Fx:**294-1887
(516) 505-2300 .. **Pack,** Eric A '09 %Sharifov & R -50 Main -Hempstd 11550 **Fx:**505-2379
(212) 857-1418 .. **Pack,** Holly R '04 Fncl Info Srvcs Agency -450 W 33rd -NY 10001
(212) 847-7900 .. **Pack,** Leonard B '71 OfCnsl Wechsler & C,LLP -17 State -NY 10004
(631) 231-2177 .. **Pack,** Lori L '92 Atty Gen -300 Motor Pkwy -Hauppauge 11788
(845) 338-0500 .. **Packard,** Janet '82 -167 Green Bx4242 -Kingston 12402 **Fx:**331-0531
(212) 402-4100 .. **Packard,** Lisa A '09 %Ofc Applt Def -11 Park Pl -NY 10007 **Fx:**402-4199
(212) 631-7533 .. **Packard,** Stephen L '63 -352 7th Av -NY 10001
(646) 471-4000 .. **Packer,** Deborah '82 %PricewaterhouseCoopers LLP -300 Mad Av -NY 10017
(212) 730-7750 .. **Packer,** Jamie T '96 %Nicoletti GS&O,LLP -555 5th Av -NY 10017
(212) 735-3000 .. **Packer,** Marc R '85 (Skadden ASM&F LLP) -4 Times Sq -NY 10036
(212) 558-4000 .. **Packer,** Rachel A '08 %Sullivan & C LLP -125 Broad -NY 10004
(212) 310-8000 .. **Packer,** Tlalit '08 %Weil G&M LLP -767 5th Av -NY 10153
(212) 508-7456 .. **Packes,** Nancy '71 Feathered Nest -770 Lex Av -NY 10065
(212) 837-6000 .. **Packman,** Harry Jr. '85 Cnsl Hughes H&R LLP -1 Bttry Pk Plz -NY 10004
(212) 649-2000 .. **Packman,** Kenan '96 %Hearst Corp -300 W 57th -NY 10019 **Fx:**649-2035
(914) 517-5000 .. **Packman,** Myra I '80 (Meiselman DPC&E,PC) -1311 Mamaroneck Av -White Plns 10605
(516) 358-7200 .. **Packman,** Scott J '05 %Mavrides M & Assoc,LLP -3000 Marcus Av -Lk Success 11042 **Fx:**358-7250
(518) 937-2123 .. **Paczkowski,** Wm F '97 RPI -110 8th -Troy 12180
(718) 330-1200 .. **Padden,** Michl P '79 %Fed Def of NY Inc -1 Pierrepont Plz -Brklyn 11201 **Fx:**855-0760
(315) 287-7057 .. **Paddock,** Fredk E '94 -123 E Main -Gouverneur 13642 **Fx:**287-7058
(914) 478-0134 .. **Padegs,** Juris '59 -22 Minturn -Hastings-On-Hud 10706 **Fx:**478-3243
(212) 957-0900 .. **Padell,** Bert '59 Padell NFW & Co -59 Maiden Ln -NY 10038
(518) 257-3000 .. **Paden,** Deborah J '88 %Dormitory Auth -515 Bway -Albany 12207 **Fx:**257-3101
(914) 934-9844 .. **Padernacht,** Sheri S '96 -219 Treetop Cres -Rye Brook 10573
(212) 859-8000 .. **Padgett,** Amanda D '08 %Fried FHS&J LLP -1 NY Plz -NY 10004
(212) 558-4000 .. **Padgett,** Jason D '04 %Sullivan & C LLP -125 Broad -NY 10004
(212) 345-6000 .. **Padgett,** Kenneth M '71 %Marsh USA -1166 Av of Amer -NY 10036 **Fx:**345-4808
(212) 903-9000 .. **Padgett,** Kristin L '09 %Linklaters -1345 Av of Amer -NY 10105
(212) 319-9800 .. **Padian,** Gerald '89 (Tashjian & P) -729 7th Av -NY 10019
(516) 616-4440 .. **Padian,** Lauren A '10 %Brea Y,PC -35 N Tyson Av -Floral Pk 11001
(718) 262-7100 .. **Padilla,** Claribel Rosado '98 %Civil Ct -89-17 Sutphin Blvd -Jamaica 11435 **Fx:**262-7107
(212) 382-6600 .. **Padilla,** Damaris Solis '85 %NYC Bar -42 W 44th -NY 10036 **Fx:**398-6634
(212) 848-4000 .. **Padilla,** Hernando A '01 %Shearman & S LLP -599 Lex Av -NY 10022
(212) 377-2158 .. **Padilla,** Jeffrey W '95 (Padilla & Assoc,PLLC) -555 5th Av -NY 10017
(212) 848-4000 .. **Padilla,** John M '06 %Shearman & S LLP -599 Lex Av -NY 10022
(914) 366-4842 .. **Padilla,** Lisa Ayn '99 Estates for Life Mates -560 Wht Plns Rd -Tarrytwn 10591
(212) 222-5035 .. **Padilla,** Lydia E '93 -70 W 93rd -NY 10025 **Fx:**222-5035
(212) 576-9690 .. **Padilla-Diaz,** Linda '94 Medical Library Mutual -2 Park Av -NY 10016
(212) 446-4800 .. **Padlan,** Christine '05 %Kirkland & E LLP -153 E 53rd -NY 10022
(212) 488-1300 .. **Padnick,** Jennifer C '99 (Cohen & P LLP) -444 Mad Av -NY 10022
(212) 475-3699 .. **Padoch,** Jaroslaw '56 -71 E 7th -NY 10003
(212) 848-4000 .. **Padres,** Alexandro M '03 %Shearman & S LLP -599 Lex Av -NY 10022
(845) 485-2664 .. **Padron,** Carol Ann '91 -16 Tanglewood Ln -Poughkeepsie 12603 **Fx:**485-2664
(718) 250-1400 .. **Padua,** Charmagne A '06 %BZ Green -12 MetroTech Ctr -Brklyn 11201 **Fx:**250-1401
(212) 785-9100 .. **Paduano,** Anthony '84 (Paduano & W LLP) -1251 Av of Amer -NY 10020
(212) 785-9100 .. **Paduano & Weintraub LLP** -1251 Av of Amer -NY 10020 **Fx:**785-9099
(518) 565-4770 .. **Padula,** Domenica '06 %DA -137 Margaret -Plattsbrgh 12901 **Fx:**565-4777
(518) 474-8211 .. **Padula,** Rocco J '98 %Law Reporting Bur -1 Commerce Plz -Albany 12210 **Fx:**463-6869
(212) 616-3030 .. **Padurano,** Christopher '99 %C Ross & Assoc -111 Bway -NY 10006 **Fx:**616-3031
(212) 462-1536 .. **Padwa,** Sabrina I '96 %@Radical Media -435 Hudson -NY 10014
(212) 310-8000 .. **Pae,** Joon Beom '08 %Weil G&M LLP -767 5th Av -NY 10153
(631) 755-2020 .. **Paek,** Hyung D '99 Marchon Eyewear,Inc -35 Hub Dr -Melvll 11747
(212) 626-4100 .. **Paek,** John C '08 %Baker & M LLP -1114 Av of Amer -NY 10036
(212) 756-2000 .. **Paek,** Kyu Mike '09 %Schulte R&Z LLP -919 3rd Av -NY 10022
(718) 254-6023 .. **Paes,** Winston M '04 US Atty-EDNY -271 Cadman Plz E -Brklyn 11201
(212) 747-1230 .. **Paessler,** Robt N '96 (McMahon M&G LLP) -55 Washington -Brklyn 11201
(212) 474-1000 .. **Paetzold,** Claudia '06 %Cravath S&M LLP -825 8th Av -NY 10019
(212) 326-3939 .. **Paez,** Mauricio F '97 (Jones D) -222 E 41st -NY 10017
(212) 858-7700 .. **Paff,** Michl A '04 (Budd L) -140 Bway -NY 10005
(212) 709-8285 .. **Pagan,** Anthony '98 (Campos-Marquetti & P,PLLC) -110 Wall -NY 10005 **Fx:**943-2300
(631) 369-7373 .. **Pagan,** Luis A '97 -113 Griffing Av -Rvrhead 11901 **Fx:**369-2838
(718) 792-5103 .. **Pagan,** Marcos A III '87 -2622 E Tremont Av -Bronx 10461 **Fx:**792-5218
(718) 993-1598 .. **Pagan,** Ramon A '02 %RW Pagan -2116 Wllmsbrdg Rd -Bronx 10461 **Fx:**792-7645
(718) 993-1598 .. **Pagan,** Ramon W '77 RW Pagan -2116 Wllmsbrdg Rd -Bronx 10461 **Fx:**792-7645
(212) 967-8202 .. **Pagan,** Tania M '90 (Pagan Law Firm,PC) -245 5th Av -NY 10016 **Fx:**967-8794
(212) 967-8202 .. **Pagan,** Wm '88 (Pagan Law Firm,PC) -245 5th Av -NY 10016 **Fx:**967-8794
(516) 355-7901 .. **Paganini Gambeski Cioci Cusumano & Farole** -1979 Marcus Av -Lk Success 11042 **Fx:**355-7807

(516) 355-7901 .. **Paganini,** Kenneth '77 (Paganini GCC&F) -1979 Marcus Av -Lk Success 11042
(607) 734-2271 .. **Pagano,** Anthony F '03 %Sayles & E -1 W Church -Elmira 14901
(718) 515-4500 .. **Pagano,** Christopher '95 (Slingsby S&P) -3199 Bainbrdg Av -Bronx 10467
(845) 437-3142 .. **Pagano,** Danl A '87 %Vassar Bros Hsptl -Reade Pl -Poughkeepsie 12601 **Fx:**437-3196
(914) 734-4180 .. **Pagano,** Danl L '93 Peekskill Cnsl Ofc -840 Main -Peekskill 10566
(914) 830-5288 .. **Pagano,** Danl L '93 -2649 Strang Blvd -Yorktwn Hts 10598 **Fx:**788-4050
(516) 496-1919 .. **Pagano,** Denine C '06 %Keller O&W,PC -242 Crsswys Park Dr W -Woodbury 11797
(516) 624-8987 .. **Pagano,** Eugene S R '77 -200 Lex Av -Oyster Bay 11771 **Fx:**624-0813
(212) 940-8800 .. **Pagano,** George J '04 %Katten MR LLP -575 Mad Av -NY 10022
(212) 732-4740 .. **Pagano,** James P '76 -277 Bway -NY 10007 **Fx:**385-2545
(212) 223-4000 .. **Pagano,** Jeffrey W '85 (Crowell & M LLP) -590 Mad Av -NY 10022
(315) 343-3211 .. **Pagano,** Jos D '89 (Pagano Law Ofc) -271 E 10th -Oswego 13126 **Fx:**343-7960
(716) 945-1790 .. **Pagano,** Maria E '94 %Seneca Nation -Dept of Justice Bx231 -Salamanca 14779 **Fx:**945-6869
(718) 250-2000 .. **Pagano,** Natalie C '04 %DA -350 Jay -Brklyn 11201 **Fx:**250-2314
(212) 766-0600 .. **Pagano,** Paul A '10 %Seelig Law Ofc,LLC -299 Bway -NY 10007 **Fx:**766-2616
(212) 937-4000 .. **Pagano,** Ralph V '94 (Fitzpatrick & HTCPA,LLP) -12 E 49th -NY 10017
(914) 761-4200 .. **Pagano,** Robt P '92 %Steinberg & C,LLP -50 Main -White Plns 10606
(212) 455-2000 .. **Pagano,** Vincent Jr. '80 (Simpson T&B LLP) -425 Lex Av -NY 10017
(212) 972-6161 .. **Pagan-Ortiz,** Carmen I '04 %Cassin & C LLP -711 3rd Av -NY 10017
(212) 752-5258 .. **Paganucci,** Jennifer '06 %Schwartz SE&C LLC -845 3rd Av -NY 10022
(212) 883-5800 .. **Paganuzzi,** O Stephen Jr. '80 -261 Mad Av -NY 10016 **Fx:**(646) 365-8771
(212) 450-4000 .. **Page,** Aaron '07 %Davis P&W LLP -450 Lex Av -NY 10017
(212) 309-7803 .. **Page,** Alexis L '05 Lexis Nexis -125 Park Av -NY 10017
(914) 798-5400 .. **Page,** Alfred E Jr. '75 SpclCnsl Goldberg S LLP -11 Martine Av -White Plns 10606
(212) 909-6000 .. **Page,** Alison J '06 %Debevoise & P LLP -919 3rd Av -NY 10022
(914) 737-5419 .. **Page,** Claire R '94 -233 Tate Av -Buchanan 10511
(212) 859-8000 .. **Page,** Jenny '07 %Fried FHS&J LLP -1 NY Plz -NY 10004
(212) 878-7387 .. **Page,** Jerome F III '82 %MTA -347 Mad Av -NY 10017
(212) 837-6000 .. **Page,** Kenneth R '72 (Hughes H&R LLP) -1 Bttry Pk Plz -NY 10004
(212) 763-4100 .. **Page,** Nicole S '94 (Reavis PL LLP) -41 Mad Av -NY 10010
(718) 590-2000 .. **Page,** Raasheja N '07 %DA -198 E 161st -Bronx 10451 **Fx:**590-6477
(518) 455-5143 .. **Page,** Yolande '95 %NYS Assembly -104 LOB -Albany 12248
(718) 939-6400 .. **Pager,** Clark Jay '85 %Restaurant Depot -18-30 132nd -Cllg Pnt 11356 **Fx:**939-2680
(718) 998-1010 .. **Pager,** Wm '94 -203-205 Kings Hwy -Brklyn 11223 **Fx:**998-8046
(212) 421-2150 .. **Paget,** David '64 (Sive P&R,PC) -460 Park Av -NY 10022
(917) 579-1937 .. **Paget,** Mindy R '99 -110 Wall -NY 10005 **Fx:**(212) 504-3217
(631) 666-6200 .. **Pagliarello,** Gary '88 (PF Adams,PC) -49 5th Av Bx1089M -Bay Shr 11706 **Fx:**665-6739
(212) 819-8200 .. **Pagliarulo,** Kara P '07 %White & C LLP -1155 Av of Amer -NY 10036
(212) 267-3700 .. **Paglinawan,** James S '05 %Napoli BR LLP -350 5th Av -NY 10118
(631) 737-4110 .. **Paglino,** Michl J '87 Gruenberg & K,PC -3275 Vets Mem'l Hwy -Ronkonkoma 11779 **Fx:**737-4155
(718) 250-2000 .. **Pagliuco,** Mark L '99 DA -350 Jay -Brklyn 11201 **Fx:**250-2314
(212) 455-2000 .. **Pagliughi,** Andrew J '97 %Simpson T&B LLP -425 Lex Av -NY 10017
(631) 367-7000 .. **Pagliughi,** Jean M '88 (Baron & P) -85 Main -Cold Spg Hbr 11724
(516) 327-2732 .. **Pagliughi,** Kenneth J '05 BWD Grp LLC -113 S Srvc Rd -Jericho 11753
(914) 967-8871 .. **Pagnani,** Fredk J '58 -99 Biltmore Av -Rye 10580
(212) 558-4000 .. **Pagnani,** Keith A '90 (Sullivan & C LLP) -125 Broad -NY 10004
(212) 297-5800 .. **Pagnillo,** Jennifer M '01 SrCnsl Day P LLP -7 Times Sq -NY 10036
(914) 997-8888 .. **Pagnotta,** Deborah Volberg '82 Interfacet,Inc -81 Main -White Plns 10601 **Fx:**683-6240
(845) 838-3400 .. **Pagones,** Anthony L '58 (Pagones & C,PC) -355 Main Bx550 -Beacon 12508
(845) 838-3400 .. **Pagones & Cross,PC** -355 Main Bx550 -Beacon 12508 **Fx:**838-3412
(631) 577-7740 .. **Pagones,** Peter L '77 St Paul Travelers -100 Baylis Rd Bx9093 -Melvll 11747 **Fx:**577-7575
(845) 298-7246 .. **Pagones,** Steven A '87 Pagones-O'Neill,Inc -8 Barristers Row -Wappingers Fls 12590
(516) 229-6000 .. **Pagowska,** Grazyna M '01 %R Lau & Assoc -300 Jericho Quad Bx9040 -Jericho 11753 **Fx:**229-6167
(212) 221-5700 .. **Pahl,** Annyrose '09 %Goldberg WFG LLP -1501 Bway -NY 10036
(212) 259-8000 .. **Pahl,** Mitchel C '85 (Dewey & L LLP) -1301 Av of Amer -NY 10019
(212) 872-9800 .. **Pahlavan,** Arman '92 (Squire S&D LLP) -30 Rckfllr Plz -NY 10112
(516) 621-0222 .. **Pahlavan,** Atefeh Saatchi '02 %GosmanLaw PC -55 Bryant Av -Roslyn 11576 **Fx:**621-3322
(212) 806-5400 .. **Pahmer,** Michele L '94 SpclCnsl Stroock &S&L LLP -180 Maiden Ln -NY 10038
(212) 446-4800 .. **Pai,** Priya P '09 %Kirkland & E LLP -153 E 53rd -NY 10022
(212) 833-1156 .. **Pai,** Sheela V '06 %Friedman KS&A LLP -1633 Bway -NY 10019 **Fx:**373-7956
(212) 704-6522 .. **Paice,** Richd C '96 Sojitz Corp -1211 Av of Amer -NY 10036
(718) 888-9500 .. **Paick,** Ieback '07 %Kim & C,LLP -158-14 Nrthrn Blvd -Flushng 11358
(516) 742-3662 .. **Paidoussis,** George '93 (Patacca & Assoc) -392 Hillside Av -Williston Pk 11596 **Fx:**742-5767
(914) 234-4613 .. **Paige,** Danl F '96 DF Paige & Assoc,LLC -520 Pea Pond Rd -Katonah 10536
(212) 233-6000 .. **Paige,** Jeffrey R '85 -100 Park Av -NY 10017
(212) 349-5926 .. **Paige,** John M '75 -233 Bway -NY 10279 **Fx:**608-1072
(845) 639-0981 .. **Paige,** Mark S '88 -37 Congers Rd -New Cty 10956
(631) 501-7210 .. **Paige,** Stephen '98 Gentiva Hlth Srvcs -3 Huntngtn Quadrangle -Melvll 11747
(212) 474-1000 .. **Paik,** Jeffrey G '07 %Cravath S&M LLP -825 8th Av -NY 10019
(516) 496-3868 .. **Paik,** Susan '99 %Keusey T&B,PC -20 Crsswys Park Dr N -Woodbury 11797
(212) 682-9090 .. **Paikin,** Michl L '71 (M Paikin,PC) -551 5th Av -NY 10176 **Fx:**682-9040
(212) 643-7000 .. **Pailet,** Albert D '00 %Sills C&G PC -One Rckfllr Plz -NY 10020
(212) 969-3000 .. **Paine,** Jenifer DeWolf '97 SrCnsl Proskauer R LLP -1585 Bway -NY 10036
(315) 793-2370 .. **Paine,** Lisa L '89 %MHLS -207 Genesee -Utica 13501 **Fx:**793-2371
(212) 225-2000 .. **Paine,** Peter S Jr. '61 OfCnsl Cleary GS&H -1 Lbrty Plz -NY 10006
(212) 325-5438 .. **Paine,** Stephen T '90 CSFB -1 Mad Av -NY 10010
(212) 672-5300 .. **Paine,** Susan D '92 %Hypo and Vereinsbank -150 E 42nd -NY 10017
(516) 572-2000 .. **Painter,** Jed L '08 %DA -99 Main -Hempstd 11550 **Fx:**572-2606
(212) 732-2000 .. **Painter,** Kristen M '08 %Cullen and D LLP -44 Wall -NY 10005
(646) 386-5700 .. **Paioff,** Jared E '09 Civil Ct -111 Centre -NY 10013
(718) 875-1300 .. **Pairis,** Vanessa M '09 %Appllt Div 2nd Dept -45 Monroe Pl -Brklyn 11201 **Fx:**858-2446
(212) 649-2140 .. **Paisner,** Bruce L '69 %Hearst Entertainment -300 W 57th -NY 10019
(718) 250-2000 .. **Paisner,** Elisa '87 %DA -350 Jay -Brklyn 11201 **Fx:**250-2314
(716) 630-0400 .. **Pajak,** David J '83 -13179 Bway -Alden 14004
(716) 854-2020 .. **Pajak,** Gregory V '93 Cellino & B,PC -350 Main -Buffalo 14202
(212) 833-1195 .. **Pak,** Andrew S '07 %Friedman KS&A LLP -1633 Bway -NY 10019 **Fx:**373-7995
(212) 596-9000 .. **Pak,** Anneliese Hesun '02 %Ropes & G LLP -1211 Av of Amer -NY 10036
(212) 239-2378 .. **Pak,** Byongchae '86 (Pak & W LLC) -16 W 32nd -NY 10001 **Fx:**239-8732
(212) 999-5800 .. **Pak,** Chul '90 (Wilson SG&R) -1301 Av of Americas -NY 10019
(212) 490-3000 .. **Pak,** Dennis J '00 (Wilson EME&D LLP) -150 E 42nd -NY 10017
(212) 735-3000 .. **Pak,** James Y '08 %Skadden ASM&F LLP -4 Times Sq -NY 10036
(212) 872-1000 .. **Pak,** Jennifer Bartels '07 -One Bryant Park -NY 10036 **Fx:**872-1002
(212) 454-6818 .. **Pak,** John S '94 %Deutsche Bank -60 Wall -NY 10005
(212) 277-4000 .. **Pak,** Kay Kyungmin '05 %Freshfields BD LLP -520 Mad Av -NY 10022
(877) 222-1814 .. **Pak,** Mitchell E '91 %B Rothenberg -100 Duffy Av -Hicksvll 11801 **Fx:**(866) 894-2182
(718) 463-7790 .. **Pak,** Richd U '92 -39-01 Main -Flushng 11354 **Fx:**463-2475
(212) 326-2000 .. **Pak,** Sung '01 (O'Melveny & M LLP) -7 Times Sq -NY 10036
(212) 735-3000 .. **Pak,** Thos '93 Cnsl Skadden ASM&F LLP -4 Times Sq -NY 10036
(315) 673-2770 .. **Pakan,** Donna M '00 -5013 Surrey Dr -Syracuse 13215 **Fx:**673-2770
(516) 883-2090 .. **Pakel,** Edw D '79 -20 Guilford Rd -Pt Wash 11050 **Fx:**883-2090
(212) 479-6000 .. **Pakenham,** Kathleen M '96 (Cooley LLP) -1114 Av of Amer -NY 10036
(845) 634-9500 .. **Pakola,** Richd S '95 %Gribetz & L,PLLC -155 N Main -New Cty 10956 **Fx:**639-9105
(212) 714-1720 .. **Pakrul,** Marc C '03 %Tompkins MW&B LLP -140 Bway -NY 10005
(212) 298-9225 .. **Pakstis,** Karen A '85 PBA -40 Fulton -NY 10038
(212) 490-1700 .. **Pal,** Andrew J '90 (Wiggin & D) -450 Lex Av -NY 10017
(718) 875-4653 .. **Pal,** Indra '77 -50 Court -Brklyn 11201
(212) 705-7000 .. **Pal,** Monica '06 %Bingham M LLP -399 Park Av -NY 10022
(212) 848-4000 .. **Palach,** Randal D '06 %Shearman & S LLP -599 Lex Av -NY 10022
(718) 250-2000 .. **Palacio,** Andres F '06 %DA -350 Jay -Brklyn 11201 **Fx:**250-2314
(516) 869-7233 .. **Palacio,** Deborah I '93 %Kimco Realty Corp -3333 New Hyde Pk Rd -New Hyde Pk 11042 **Fx:**336-5619
(718) 250-4225 .. **Palacios,** Erin L '08 Leg Aid -111 Lvngstn -Brklyn 11201 **Fx:**250-4243
(212) 705-7000 .. **Palacios,** Joanna I '05 %Bingham M LLP -399 Park Av -NY 10022
(516) 873-8783 .. **Palacios,** Xavier A '98 -114 Old Cntry Rd -Mineola 11501 **Fx:**873-8790
(716) 852-8222 .. **Paladino,** Carl P '72 (Paladino C&Q) -295 Main -Buffalo 14203
(716) 852-8222 .. **Paladino Cavan & Quinlivan** -295 Main -Buffalo 14203 **Fx:**852-2829
(516) 538-7780 .. **Paladino,** Frank M '98 %N Pellegrini,LLC -320 Nassau Blvd -Garden City South 11530 **Fx:**564-0906
(212) 559-0114 .. **Paladino,** James N '93 %Citibank -153 E 53rd -NY 10022
(914) 967-8400 .. **Paladino,** Robt C '81 %Jasper Energy -93 Taylor Ln -Harrison 10528 **Fx:**967-2227
(518) 473-4321 .. **Paladino,** Victor G '88 %Dept of Law -The Cptl -Albany 12224
(212) 230-3300 .. **Palame,** David A '03 Colony Capital LLC -660 Mad Av -NY 10065
(914) 946-6774 .. **Palamidy,** Michele '83 %Pilkington & L,PC -222 Bloomingdale Rd -White Plns 10605
(212) 903-9000 .. **Palaniswamy,** Vijaya R '04 %Linklaters -1345 Av of Amer -NY 10105
(212) 608-1140 .. **Palant,** Boris '84 -225 Bway -NY 10007 **Fx:**608-0101
(914) 472-4786 .. **Palat,** Pamela '80 -15 Hillvw Dr -Scarsdale 10583
(718) 250-0400 .. **Palatianos,** John E '88 %R Tusa -1 MetroTech Ctr -Brklyn 11201 **Fx:**250-0591
(516) 572-2000 .. **Palatiello,** Jordan S '09 %DA -99 Main -Hempstd 11550 **Fx:**572-2606
(212) 425-4343 .. **Palatnik,** Eric S '98 E Palatnik,PC -32 Bway -NY 10004 **Fx:**968-7129
(212) 483-9490 .. **Palatucci,** Scott M '04 %McElroy DM&C,LLP -88 Pine -NY 10005
(914) 961-7800 .. **Palazzo,** Debra '02 (D Palazzo,LLC) -295 Main -Eastchstr 10709 **Fx:**793-8902
(585) 427-5400 .. **Palazzo,** Eugene O '86 %Xerox -100 Clinton Av S -Rchstr 14644
(212) 481-0091 .. **Palazzo-Fairweather,** Tina '94 -207 W 25th -NY 10001
(718) 286-6000 .. **Palazzolo,** Jos T II '06 %DA -125-01 Qns Blvd -Kew Gdns 11415
(212) 250-4290 .. **Palazzolo,** Salvatore P '85 %Deutsche Bank -60 Wall -NY 10005
(212) 406-3110 .. **Palces,** Jude Tadeo '96 %Albano Law Ofc -139 Fulton -NY 10038 **Fx:**406-3114
(212) 688-8555 .. **Paldino,** F Jos '99 %Fragomen DB&L LLP -7 Hanover Sq -NY 10004
(212) 664-2388 .. **Paldino,** Kara R '02 NBC Universal -30 Rckfllr Plz -NY 10112
(212) 459-7700 .. **Paldy,** David L '89 Dept of Tax & Fin -1740 Bway -NY 10019 **Fx:**459-7897

(212) 973-9797 .. **Palefski,** Jacob J '07 %Saretsky KD&G,LLP -475 Park Av S -NY 10016
(212) 867-9500 .. **Palella,** Chas '79 (Kurzman K&F,LLP) -230 Park Av -NY 10169
(212) 867-9500 .. **Palella,** Louis C '50 Cnsl Kurzman K&F,LLP -230 Park Av -NY 10169
(718) 524-5334 .. **Palemine,** Meredith C '06 -Bx60202 -Staten Isl 10306
(718) 993-9911 .. **Palen,** Marion A '82 (Fraiden & P) -327 E 149th -Bronx 10451
(212) 872-5650 .. **Paleologos,** Nicholas C '99 KPMG,LLP -345 Park Av -NY 10154
(212) 484-8000 .. **Palerm,** Silda '90 %Warner Music Grp -75 Rckfllr Plz -NY 10019 **Fx:**489-3342
(585) 987-2800 .. **Palermo,** Anthony R '57 OfCnsl Woods OG LLP -2 State -Rchstr 14614
(315) 955-6700 .. **Palermo,** Catherine J '94 %Leg Aid -44 Pub Sq -Watertwn 13601 **Fx:**785-9118
(212) 808-7789 .. **Palermo,** Christopher C '88 (Kelley D&W LLP) -101 Park Av -NY 10178
(631) 265-1051 .. **Palermo,** Christopher N '02 (Palermo P&T) -1300 Vets Mem'l Hwy -Hauppauge 11788
(631) 265-1051 .. **Palermo,** Edw R '94 (Palermo P&T) -1300 Vets Mem'l Hwy -Hauppauge 11788
(585) 362-4700 .. **Palermo,** Ingrid S '97 SrCnsl Bond S&K,PLLC -350 Linden Oaks -Rchstr 14625
(212) 750-9700 .. **Palermo,** Joan '86 -546 5th Av -NY 10036 **Fx:**750-8297
(585) 454-7145 .. **Palermo,** John C '97 %Gallo & I,LLP -39 State -Rchstr 14614
(212) 269-4900 .. **Palermo,** Lissa A '09 %Ford MEW&G,LLP -Wall Street Plz -NY 10005
(212) 621-8356 .. **Palermo,** Mark H '91 %ASCAP -1 Lincoln Plz -NY 10023 **Fx:**(718) 788-3646
(212) 636-5400 .. **Palermo,** Richd P '00 DC Comics -1700 Bway -NY 10019 **Fx:**636-5595
(914) 921-6168 .. **Palermo,** Rose C '88 -6 Wht Birch Dr -Rye 10580
(718) 866-5541 .. **Palermo,** Roseann '94 -80 Gaynor -Staten Isl 10309
(631) 265-1052 .. **Palermo,** Steven J '98 (Palermo P&T) -1300 Vets Mem'l Hwy -Hauppauge 11788
(212) 697-3122 .. **Paleudis,** Michl J '06 %Martin C&B LLP -220 E 42nd -NY 10017
(315) 736-3699 .. **Palewski,** Peter S '69 -1 Campbell Av -NY Mlls 13417 **Fx:**736-4199
(212) 909-6000 .. **Paley,** Alan H '76 (Debevoise & P LLP) -919 3rd Av -NY 10022
(212) 425-0055 .. **Paley,** Donald W '51 (Sharretts PC&B) -75 Broad -NY 10004
(585) 263-1000 .. **Paley,** Eric R '95 (Nixon P LLP) -1100 Clinton Sq -Rchstr 14604
(585) 238-2000 .. **Paley,** Gerald L '64 OfCnsl Phillips L LLP -1400 First Fed Plz -Rchstr 14614
(212) 425-0055 .. **Paley,** Kenneth R '81 %Sharretts PC&B -75 Broad -NY 10004
(718) 237-3100 .. **Paley,** Laura M '10 Leg Aid -111 Lvngstn -Brklyn 11201 **Fx:**250-4243
(212) 545-4705 .. **Paley,** Marc B '96 %Wolf HAF&H LLP -270 Mad Av -NY 10016
(212) 336-0145 .. **Paley,** Michl D '93 %SEC -3 World Fncl Ctr -NY 10281 **Fx:**336-1323
(212) 689-1113 .. **Paley,** Paul M '82 (Garbarini & S,PC) -432 Park Av S -NY 10016
(212) 492-1175 .. **Paley,** Richd J '82 WP Carey & Co,LLC -50 Rckfllr Plz -NY 10020
(212) 250-2686 .. **Palfrey,** Anne Marie '96 Deutsche Bk AG -60 Wall -NY 10005
(212) 841-1000 .. **Palgon,** Ira M '89 (Covington & B LLP) -620 8th Av -NY 10018
(631) 439-2316 .. **Paliani,** Alfred R '84 Cnsl Quality King Distributors,Inc -35 Sawgrss Dr -Bellprt 11713 **Fx:**439-2262
(212) 506-2500 .. **Palikovic,** Tiasha '09 %Mayer B LLP -1675 Bway -NY 10019
(212) 227-1640 .. **Palillo,** Frank W '83 -299 Bway -NY 10007 **Fx:**349-1724
(212) 608-8959 .. **Palillo,** Michl B '84 (M Palillo,PC) -277 Bway -NY 10007 **Fx:**608-0304
(716) 853-1616 .. **Palisano,** Saml J '72 (Harter S&E LLP) -12 Fountain Plz -Buffalo 14202
(212) 964-7400 .. **Paliseno,** Robt J '01 Smith MDWY&Y,PC -111 John -NY 10038
(914) 241-4687 .. **Palitz,** B Gregory Jr. '79 -431 Haines Rd -Mt Kisco 10549 **Fx:**241-1265
(212) 232-2055 .. **Palitz,** Stephen H '86 (Bierman & P LLP) -74 Trinity Pl -NY 10006 **Fx:**232-2056
(212) 852-7284 .. **Palker,** Jeffrey E '01 News Corp -1211 Av of Amer -NY 10036
(718) 250-2000 .. **Palkhiwala,** Michl P '03 %DA -350 Jay -Brklyn 11201 **Fx:**250-2314
(212) 541-5800 .. **Pall,** Jonathan S '06 Laurus Captl Mgmt -335 Mad Av -NY 10017 **Fx:**541-4434
(866) 311-1649 .. **Pall,** Lori A '88 (Pall & P,LLP) -26 Court -Brklyn 11242
(866) 311-1649 .. **Pall,** Roni S '87 (Pall & P,LLP) -26 Court -Brklyn 11242
(212) 836-8000 .. **Palla,** Sapna W '01 Cnsl Kaye S LLP -425 Park Av -NY 10022
(631) 752-7100 .. **Pallaci,** Vincent T '06 %Kushnick & Assoc,PC -445 Broad Hollow Rd -Melvll 11747 **Fx:**777-7732
(212) 849-7000 .. **Palladino,** Marc A '07 %Quinn EU&S,LLP -51 Mad Av -NY 10010
(718) 876-6300 .. **Palladino,** Mark A '93 %DA -130 Styvsnt Pl -Staten Isl 10301
(516) 712-4000 .. **Palladino,** Patrick F '04 %Milber MP&S LLP -1000 Woodbury Rd -Woodbury 11797
(212) 340-0400 .. **Palladino,** Rosemary F '85 %Appllt Div 1st Dept -27 Mad Av -NY 10010 **Fx:**889-4412
(716) 636-7600 .. **Palladino,** Stephanie M '08 %HoganWillig -2410 N Forest Rd -Amherst 14068
(212) 596-9000 .. **Palladino,** Vincent N '76 (Ropes & G LLP) -1211 Av of Amer -NY 10036
(518) 474-0571 .. **Pallante,** Frank P '95 %Ofc Gnl Srvcs -Corning Twr ESP -Albany 12242 **Fx:**473-4973
(212) 272-0140 .. **Pallante,** Sandra M '00 %JP Morgan Chase -383 Mad Av -NY 10179
(212) 918-3000 .. **Pallares,** Christine M '89 (Hogan L LLP) -875 3rd Av -NY 10022
(212) 425-1900 .. **Pallas,** Wm J '95 (Freehill H&M LLP) -80 Pine -NY 10005
(212) 412-9500 .. **Pallen,** Kimberly A '08 %Flemming ZWZ LLP -1 Lbrty Plz -NY 10006
(212) 902-7242 .. **Pallesen,** Edw S '01 Goldman Sachs & Co -85 Broad -NY 10004
(914) 472-7232 .. **Pallone,** Marjorie A '87 -144 Webster Rd -Scarsdale 10583
(212) 902-9477 .. **Pallone,** Philip T '99 Goldman Sachs & Co -85 Broad -NY 10004
(212) 889-6565 .. **Pallonetti,** Steven J '08 %Schwartz & P LLP -295 Mad Av -NY 10017
(631) 549-2000 .. **Pally,** Mitchell H '78 %Weber Law Grp,LLP -290 Broad Hollow Rd -Melvll 11747 **Fx:**549-2015
(212) 902-4762 .. **Palm,** Gregory K '77 %Goldman Sachs -1 NY Plz -NY 10004
(212) 326-2000 .. **Palm,** Katherine '08 %O'Melveny & M LLP -7 Times Sq -NY 10036
(212) 388-3600 .. **Palma,** Kirk K '98 %32B-J Leg Srvcs -101 Av of Amer -NY 10013 **Fx:**388-3061
(212) 455-2000 .. **Palma,** Laura '85 (Simpson T&B LLP) -425 Lex Av -NY 10017
(212) 858-7710 .. **Palma,** Michl J '96 (Nowell AKB,PA) -140 Bway PMB 46028 -NY 10005
(212) 686-8111 .. **Palma,** Richd '85 -381 Park Av S -NY 10016
(516) 571-3800 .. **Palma,** Stefanie M '08 %DA -262 Old Cntry Rd -Mineola 11501 **Fx:**248-9479
(212) 687-1736 .. **Palmadessa,** Joyce M '91 %R Schwartzberg & Assoc,PLLC -60 E 42nd -NY 10165
(518) 591-4636 .. **Palmateer,** Lee Allen '96 -90 State -Albany 12207 **Fx:**694-0527
(518) 432-1100 .. **Palmer,** Amanda N '00 Prosecutors Training Inst -107 Columbia -Albany 12210
(718) 738-9800 .. **Palmer,** Andrea R '00 %S Baron & Assoc,PC -159-49 Cross Bay Blvd -Howard Bch 11414 **Fx:**738-3912
(516) 410-3594 .. **Palmer,** Arlynn B '80 Coldwell Banker Claire Sobel -27 Powerhse Rd -Roslyn Hts 11577 **Fx:**621-7249
(516) 745-4526 .. **Palmer,** Belinda L '85 Chase Auto Finance -900 Stewart Av -Gdn Cty 11530
(212) 406-1855 .. **Palmer Biezup & Henderson** -140 Bway -NY 10005 **Fx:**858-7651
(212) 436-3461 .. **Palmer,** Calvin L '86 Deloitte & Touche,LLP -2 World Fncl Ctr -NY 10281
(518) 462-6765 .. **Palmer,** Carlotta L '07 %Leg Aid -55 Colvin Av -Albany 12206 **Fx:**427-8352
(212) 906-1200 .. **Palmer,** Catherine E '81 (Latham & W) -885 3rd Av -NY 10022
(212) 732-2000 .. **Palmer,** Christopher H '95 (Cullen and D LLP) -44 Wall -NY 10005
(212) 504-6000 .. **Palmer,** Deryck A '84 (Cadwalader W&T LLP) -1 World Fncl Ctr -NY 10281
(585) 232-5300 .. **Palmer,** Devin L '02 %Boylan BCV&W,LLP -2400 Chase Sq -Rchstr 14604
(212) 947-9779 .. **Palmer,** Erika J '05 Advocates for Chldrn of NY -151 W 30th -NY 10001
(315) 655-3009 .. **Palmer,** Fred G III '81 -26 Albany Bx410 -Cazenovia 13035 **Fx:**655-4830
(516) 365-5100 .. **Palmer,** Ivy M '89 Excel Realty Advisors LP -333 Earle Ovngton Blvd -Uniondale 11553
(212) 888-3833 .. **Palmer,** Jennifer A '06 %Gerber Finance -488 Mad Av -NY 10022
(516) 747-0022 .. **Palmer,** John W '69 -323 Willis Av -Mineola 11501 **Fx:**747-0026
(212) 682-0020 .. **Palmer,** Lansing R '73 (Putney TH&H LLP) -521 5th Av -NY 10175
(212) 563-1710 .. **Palmer,** Lorienton N A '90 (Schindel FLG&R LLP) -14 Penn Plz -NY 10122
(212) 508-6100 .. **Palmer,** Mark E '96 (Bracewell & G,LLP) -1251 Av of Amer -NY 10020
(212) 351-4000 .. **Palmer,** Mary P '90 Cnsl Gibson D&C LLP -200 Park Av -NY 10166
(212) 688-5640 .. **Palmer,** Michl D '05 %Joseph & H LLP -757 3rd Av -NY 10017
(212) 583-5974 .. **Palmer,** Rebecca M '98 The Blackstone Group -345 Park Av -NY 10154
(212) 318-3000 .. **Palmer,** Richd A '68 OfCnsl Fulbright & J LLP -666 5th Av -NY 10103
(315) 343-3866 .. **Palmer,** Richd B '73 -52 E Cayuga -Oswego 13126 **Fx:**342-8815
(212) 406-1855 .. **Palmer,** Richd W '50 OfCnsl Palmer B&H -140 Bway -NY 10005
(212) 669-4731 .. **Palmer,** Robt D '81 %Comptroller -1 Centre -NY 10007 **Fx:**669-4002
(845) 454-5300 .. **Palmer,** Robt N '72 -90 Market Bx5249 -Poughkeepsie 12602
(212) 725-1818 .. **Palmer,** Sheldon '69 OfCnsl Furgang & A,LLP -1325 Av of Amer -NY 10019 **Fx:**941-9711
(315) 733-2396 .. **Palmer,** Stephanie Ann '95 %Brindisi MBPJ&P,LLP -2713 Genesee -Utica 13501
(585) 436-9583 .. **Palmer,** Stephen L '99 %FedEx -2580 Maintou Rd -Rchstr 14624
(716) 842-1100 .. **Palmer,** Thos A '72 (Palmer M&T) -288 Linwood Av -Buffalo 14209 **Fx:**842-1104
(716) 250-1800 .. **Palmer,** Thos A '75 (Jaeckle F&M,LLP) -400 Essjay Rd -Amherst 14221
(212) 269-0927 .. **Palmer,** Walter '71 (D'Amato & L,LLP) -2 World Fncl Ctr -NY 10281
(607) 734-5204 .. **Palmer,** Wm R '68 (Personius MP&B) -150 Lk Bx146 -Elmira 14902
(212) 221-6900 .. **Palmeri,** Brian J '08 %Winget S&S,LLP -45 Bway -NY 10006
(212) 953-2381 .. **Palmeri,** Denise Anne '94 %Rubin F&F,LLP -292 Mad Av -NY 10017
(212) 608-1717 .. **Palmeri & Gaven** -80 Maiden Ln -NY 10038 **Fx:**732-0908
(212) 608-1717 .. **Palmeri,** John J '64 (Palmeri & G) -80 Maiden Ln -NY 10038
(631) 470-4070 .. **Palmeri,** Kevin C '99 K Palmeri,LLC -2100 Deer Prk Av -Deer Pk 11729
(516) 378-1700 .. **Palmeri,** Michl '89 (Chesney & M) -2305 Grand Av -Baldwin 11510
(516) 741-8400 .. **Palmeri,** Patrica E '88 %R Brook -114 Old Cntry Rd -Mineola 11501
(716) 635-1900 .. **Palmerton,** Nicole B '02 %Kaplan HMAF&F -20 Lawrence Bell Dr -Buffalo 14214 **Fx:**634-0431
(212) 508-6100 .. **Palmese,** Marco E '96 (Bracewell & G,LLP) -1251 Av of Amer -NY 10020
(212) 425-7200 .. **Palmese,** Maria L '91 (Kenyon & K,LLP) -1 Bway -NY 10004
(212) 969-3000 .. **Palmese,** Ronald Jr. '04 %Proskauer R LLP -1585 Bway -NY 10036
(585) 223-6021 .. **Palmiere,** David M '86 -17 Center Xing -Fairprt 14450
(585) 262-4360 .. **Palmiere,** Mark J '93 -16 E Main -Rchstr 14614
(585) 232-6144 .. **Palmiere,** Norman Andrew '86 Palmiere,PC -205 St Paul -Rchstr 14604 **Fx:**232-5215
(516) 248-9595 .. **Palmieri Castiglione & Associates, PC** -250 Mineola Blvd -Mineola 11501 **Fx:**248-7897
(212) 548-1801 .. **Palmieri,** Christian T '04 Tommy Hilfiger USA,Inc -601 W 26th -NY 10001
(212) 687-8500 .. **Palmieri,** Christine Ann '96 (Liddle & R,LLP) -800 3rd Av -NY 10022
(516) 746-8000 .. **Palmieri,** Christopher D '06 %Jaspan S LLP -300 Grdn City Plz -Gdn Cty 11530
(516) 496-1919 .. **Palmieri,** Dana K '86 (Keller O&W,PC) -242 Crsswys Park Dr W -Woodbury 11797
(212) 755-5510 .. **Palmieri,** Gabriela E '04 %Loeb B & Prtnrs -505 Park Av -NY 10022
(516) 622-0031 .. **Palmieri,** Ginamarie M '03 -9308 Linden Blvd -Ozone Pk 11417
(516) 526-3571 .. **Palmieri,** Laura '97 -11 Sherwood Dr -Huntngtn 11743
(516) 535-1809 .. **Palmieri,** Neil J '01 %Ahmuty D&M -200 IU Willets Rd -Albertson 11507
(516) 248-9595 .. **Palmieri,** Vito A '90 (Palmieri C & Assoc,PC) -250 Mineola Blvd -Mineola 11501

(516) 873-0011 .. **Palmiotto,** Anthony '83 (S Goldstein,LLP) -1 Old Cntry Rd -Carle Pl 11514 **Fx:**873-0120
(212) 766-9669 .. **Palmiotto,** Jos M '90 -111 John -NY 10038
(518) 370-4567 .. **Palmiotto,** Michl J '59 -39 Oakmont -Schnctdy 12309
(212) 785-2929 .. **Palmore,** Heather M '96 (Conway FC&K,PC) -48 Wall -NY 10005
(212) 857-2150 .. **Palmore,** Jos R '99 %Hon D Jacobs -40 Foley Sq -NY 10007
(212) 230-5319 .. **Palomba,** Tarz F '98 %Tiffany & Co -600 Mad Av -NY 10022 **Fx:**230-5323
(212) 788-0515 .. **Palomino,** Mark F '88 %Law Dept -100 Church -NY 10007 **Fx:**788-0367
(646) 386-5206 .. **Palos,** Nicholas J '90 %Family Ct -60 Lafayette -NY 10013
(212) 688-4000 .. **Palozzola,** Jos R '99 NYS HFA -641 Lex Av -NY 10022 **Fx:**872-0362
(212) 957-7600 .. **Paltiel,** Ellen L '96 %Cohen & G LLP -800 3rd Av -NY 10022
(516) 798-2421 .. **Paltrow,** Barbara L '54 -21 Ocean Av -Massapequa 11758 **Fx:**798-1414
(212) 556-2100 .. **Paltrowitz,** Adam '09 King & S -1185 Av of Amer -NY 10036
(518) 792-2117 .. **Paltrowitz,** J Lawr '75 (Bartlett PS&R,PC) -1 Wshngtn Bx2168 -Glens Fls 12801
(914) 251-0001 .. **Paltrowitz,** Julie H '03 %Lane S&L LLP -106 Corp Park Dr -White Plns 10604
(315) 471-9686 .. **Paltz,** Robt C '68 Allegiance House -7767 Oswego Rd -Liverpool 13090 **Fx:**471-9691
(516) 794-4700 .. **Paltzik,** Edw A '07 %T Liotti -600 Old Cntry Rd -Gdn Cty 11530 **Fx:**794-2816
(631) 298-4200 .. **Palumbo,** Anthony H '99 (Goggins & P) -13105 Main Rd Bx65 -Mattituck 11952 **Fx:**298-4214
(718) 556-4100 .. **Palumbo,** Anthony P '98 -236 Morningstar Rd -Staten Isl 10303 **Fx:**556-4103
(212) 563-6557 .. **Palumbo,** Brian M '85 %Broadwall Mgmt Corp -370 7th Av -NY 10001
(585) 232-4090 .. **Palumbo,** Carla Maria '83 %Leg Aid -1 W Main -Rchstr 14614 **Fx:**232-2352
(716) 373-2165 .. **Palumbo,** Danl R '76 (DiCerbo & P) -201 N Union -Olean 14760
(212) 735-3000 .. **Palumbo,** Gregory T '07 %Skadden ASM&F LLP -4 Times Sq -NY 10036
(212) 941-7100 .. **Palumbo,** James P '84 (Hornstein P&K) -350 Bway -NY 10013
(716) 759-9759 .. **Palumbo,** Jeffrey D '80 (Damon M LLP) -9276 Main -Clarence 14031
(212) 216-8000 .. **Palumbo,** Joann T '85 Cnsl Tarter K&D LLP -1350 Bway -NY 10018
(607) 936-3739 .. **Palumbo,** Judith Ann '95 %Rossettie R&M -269 W Pulteney -Corning 14830
(212) 465-5000 .. **Palumbo,** Lisa M '83 Parsons Brinckerhoff -1 Penn Plz -NY 10119 **Fx:**465-5096
(585) 227-7330 .. **Palumbo,** Marilyn J '95 -550 Latona Rd -Rchstr 14626 **Fx:**227-7334
(212) 819-8200 .. **Palumbo,** Nicholas A '05 %White & C LLP -1155 Av of Amer -NY 10036
(631) 563-2082 .. **Palumbo,** Nicole A '01 -25 Candee Av -Sayvll 11782
(212) 357-2191 .. **Palumbo,** Regina S '88 Goldman Sachs -1 NY Plz -NY 10004
(212) 677-7171 .. **Palumbo,** Richd E '87 Trust for Public Land -666 Bway -NY 10012 **Fx:**353-2052
(516) 783-6565 .. **Palumbo,** Steven F '94 (Rapuzzi P&R,PC) -3361 Park Av -Wantagh 11793 **Fx:**783-6868
(212) 771-0746 .. **Palumbo,** Terese L '97 Aspen Law & Business -76 9th Av -NY 10011
(212) 669-8400 .. **Paluszek,** Mitchell J '85 DCAS-DLS -1 Centre -NY 10007 **Fx:**669-2139
(212) 449-1936 .. **Palzer,** Keith A '89 %Merrill Lynch -220 Bway -NY 10038
(516) 292-1817 .. **Pam,** Jeffrey F '76 -529 May Ln -E Meadow 11554 **Fx:**292-1817
(212) 250-4986 .. **Pam,** Simone A '97 %Deutsche Bank -60 Wall -NY 10005
(212) 935-5700 .. **Pampalone,** Michl J III '05 %Colucci & U -218 E 50th -NY 10022
(212) 431-7129 .. **Pampush,** Stephen L '01 (Purrington MW LLP) -320 W 13th -NY 10014
(212) 813-8800 .. **Pan,** Catherine '05 %Goodwin P LLP -620 8th Av -NY 10018
(914) 819-5350 .. **Pan,** Chiahua '90 Virtual Law Prtnrs -97 Argyll Av -New Rchll 10804
(212) 391-4697 .. **Pan & Chu,LLP** -500 5th Av -NY 10110 **Fx:**391-9780
(212) 790-0831 .. **Pan,** Eric Juien-Yi '99 %Benj N Cardozo Schl of Law -55 5th Av -NY 10003 **Fx:**790-0345
(212) 446-7000 .. **Pan,** Lincoln '02 %McKinsey & Co -55 E 52nd -NY 10055 **Fx:**688-9521
(212) 391-4697 .. **Pan,** Mark '84 (Pan & C,LLP) -500 5th Av -NY 10110
(212) 506-1700 .. **Pan,** Peggy Liu '06 Kasowitz BT&F LLP -1633 Bway -NY 10019
(212) 406-5533 .. **Pan,** Ren Rong '90 -11 E Bway -NY 10038 **Fx:**964-5030
(212) 455-2000 .. **Pan,** Shih-Chi '10 %Simpson T&B LLP -425 Lex Av -NY 10017
(914) 681-8700 .. **Panagiotopoulos,** Georgios K '07 %Milber MP&S LLP -3 Barker Av -White Plns 10601
(516) 357-3000 .. **Panagopoulos,** John J '87 %Rivkin R LLP -926 RXR Plz -Uniondale 11556
(718) 222-2004 .. **Panagos,** Harry P '00 %Law Dept -350 Jay -Brklyn 11201 **Fx:**222-2088
(212) 578-5943 .. **Panarella,** Christopher C '95 %MetLife -27-01 Qns Plz N -LIC 11101
(212) 808-7800 .. **Panarella,** Nicholas J '95 (Kelley D&W LLP) -101 Park Av -NY 10178
(516) 541-4100 .. **Panaro,** Peter '77 -4216 Merrick Rd -Massapequa 11758 **Fx:**541-7559
(212) 225-2000 .. **Panas,** Joshua O '04 %Cleary GS&H -1 Lbrty Plz -NY 10006
(212) 946-4748 .. **Panas,** Peter '00 P Panas,PC -11 Penn Plz -NY 10001
(631) 853-4104 .. **Panasci,** Jeffrey S '08 %DA -400 Carleton Av Bx9082 -Central Islip 11722 **Fx:**853-7838
(518) 438-9907 .. **Panasci,** Robt A '02 %Young SWRB&M,LLC -5 Palisades Dr -Albany 12205
(212) 269-2500 .. **Panasci,** Thos J '05 %Gorlick K&L,PC -17 State -NY 10004
(212) 238-8900 .. **Panayotou,** Michl F '05 %Melito & A,PC -233 Bway -NY 10279
(516) 745-0066 .. **Pancella Haupt,** April '93 OfCnsl Karol H&S,PC -600 Old Cntry Rd -Gdn Cty 11530
(516) 576-0841 .. **Pancer,** Robin Getlan '88 -Bx69 -Jericho 11753
(212) 610-6300 .. **Panchal,** Chintan V '04 %Allen & O -1221 Av of Amer -NY 10020
(212) 374-2990 .. **Pancholy,** Ritu '07 %NYC Dept Educ -52 Chmbrs -NY 10007
(845) 567-0100 .. **Panchyshyn,** Eva M '00 %Ouimette G&A -843 Union Av -New Windsor 12553
(212) 922-9700 .. **Panciera,** Jennifer D '06 %1st Amer Title -633 3rd Av -NY 10017 **Fx:**922-0881
(716) 851-3742 .. **Pancoe,** Patricia A '77 Buffalo Bd of Educ -725 City Hall -Buffalo 14202 **Fx:**851-3935
(212) 867-6000 .. **Pancotti,** Danl G '04 %Rosenberg & E,PC -733 3rd Av -NY 10017
(718) 920-7787 .. **Panczner,** Christopher S '98 Montefiore Med Ctr -111 E 210th -Bronx 10467 **Fx:**920-2637
(212) 309-1000 .. **Pande,** Raj '88 (Hunton & W) -200 Park Av -NY 10166
(718) 286-6000 .. **Pandit-Durant,** Ushir '88 %DA -125-01 Qns Blvd -Kew Gdns 11415
(212) 458-2995 .. **Pandolfini,** Erika '99 AIG -175 Water -NY 10038
(516) 794-2323 .. **Pandolfo,** Debra A '92 %Lester M&B -325 Merrick Av -E Meadow 11554
(516) 222-0500 .. **Pandolfo,** Gregory '92 OfCnsl Goodman J&P,LLP -1103 Stewart Av -Gdn Cty 11530
(212) 425-5566 .. **Pandolfo,** Mara G '09 %S Shainwald,PC -200 W 57th -NY 10019 **Fx:**608-5863
(212) 670-0330 .. **Pandolfo,** Sebastian L '69 Cnsl Merrill Lynch -222 Bway -NY 10038 **Fx:**670-4521
(212) 940-6451 .. **Pandya,** Palash I '03 %Katten MR LLP -575 Mad Av -NY 10022
(212) 269-2511 .. **Pandya,** Sushrut K '99 -202 E 35th -NY 10016 **Fx:**269-2512
(718) 993-1553 .. **Pane,** Andrew M '81 -809 E 140th -Bronx 10454 **Fx:**402-0828
(716) 664-7354 .. **Panebianco,** George '90 (Lewis & L,PC) -208 Pine Bx0340 -Jamestwn 14702 **Fx:**664-7356
(718) 291-6500 .. **Panebianco,** Thos A '55 -146-08 Hillside Av -Jamaica 11435 **Fx:**291-6678
(212) 318-6000 .. **Panek,** Jonathan P '09 %Paul HJ&W LLP -75 E 55th -NY 10022
(516) 229-4400 .. **Panek,** Leigh Ann '97 %Kay & G -875 Merrick Av -Westbury 11590
(315) 472-1425 .. **Panels,** Peter P '75 (Harris & P) -120 E Wshngtn -Syracuse 13202
(212) 221-6900 .. **Panensky,** Howard E '07 %Winget S&S,LLP -45 Bway -NY 10006
(212) 306-7179 .. **Panepento,** Susan J '93 %Ofc Cllctv Brgn -40 Rector -NY 10006 **Fx:**306-7167
(585) 272-7007 .. **Panepinto,** Amy A '88 (Stoner & Assoc,PC) -2540 Brighton Henrietta Town Line Rd -Rchstr 14623 **Fx:**272-7011
(716) 852-1888 .. **Panepinto,** Marc C '98 (Cantor LD&P,PC) -350 Main -Buffalo 14202
(914) 948-2222 .. **Panero,** Douglas A '84 (Rabin P&H) -44 Church -White Plns 10601 **Fx:**948-2255
(212) 935-3555 .. **Panero,** Douglas A '84 (Rabin P&H) -675 3rd Av -NY 10017
(718) 769-9700 .. **Paneth,** Thos '81 -3900 Shore Pkwy -Brklyn 11235
(516) 683-8880 .. **Panetta,** Frank C '99 (Massimo & P,PC) -99 Q Roosevelt Blvd -Gdn Cty 11530
(718) 738-9800 .. **Panettiere,** Thos G '89 %S Baron & Assoc,PC -159-49 Cross Bay Blvd -Howard Bch 11414 **Fx:**738-3912
(518) 734-4344 .. **Panfel,** Bernard R '54 -Main Bx279 -Windham 12496 **Fx:**734-5162
(212) 683-7999 .. **Pang,** Aeri '04 Legal Srvcs for Children Inc -271 Mad Av -NY 10016
(212) 848-4000 .. **Pang,** Wesley H '09 %Shearman & S LLP -599 Lex Av -NY 10022
(212) 439-6132 .. **Pangalos,** Helene '89 (H Pangalos,PC) -44 Wall -NY 10005 **Fx:**439-6661
(518) 393-1341 .. **Pangburn,** Donald S '78 -2000 Bway -Schnctdy 12306
(646) 708-8088 .. **Pangilinan,** Liezl Irene Que '05 Fidelity Natl Law Grp -350 5th Av -NY 10118 **Fx:**(212) 594-8378
(212) 776-5000 .. **Pani,** Renu P '02 %NYC Housing Auth -250 Bway -NY 10007 **Fx:**776-5039
(607) 724-2385 .. **Paniccia,** Alfred Jr. '80 (Paniccia & B,LLP) -53 Chenango -Bnghmtn 13901
(518) 435-1919 .. **Paniccia,** John B '98 (Stockton B&M,LLP) -2 Twr Pl -Albany 12203
(518) 402-6092 .. **Paniccia,** Michelle L '99 %Workers Comp Bd -20 Park -Albany 12207
(212) 269-0927 .. **Paniccia,** Saml F '89 (D'Amato & L,LLP) -2 World Fncl Ctr -NY 10281
(518) 474-7330 .. **Panichi,** Candice M '01 %Dept of Law -The Cptl -Albany 12224
(212) 506-2500 .. **Paniewski,** Christopher A '08 %Mayer B LLP -1675 Bway -NY 10019
(516) 826-4632 .. **Panish,** Sam '49 -2788 Judith Dr -Bellmore 11710
(212) 363-3100 .. **Panitz,** Danl A '09 Bivona & C,PC -88 Pine -NY 10005
(877) 498-7050 .. **Panitz,** David J '92 %J Kasdon -112 E 19th -NY 10003 **Fx:**(201) 498-7051
(212) 222-3882 .. **Panjwani,** Andrea D '92 African Srvcs Comm -429 W 127th -NY 10027 **Fx:**222-7067
(212) 858-1000 .. **Panjwani,** M Ali '03 Cnsl Pillsbury WSP LLP -1540 Bway -NY 10036
(914) 428-8800 .. **Panken,** Andrew I '78 (Stern KP&W,LLP) -1025 Wstchstr Av -White Plns 10604
(212) 351-4500 .. **Panken,** Peter M '62 (Epstein B&G,PC) -250 Park Av -NY 10177
(718) 233-2751 .. **Panken,** Rhonda J '94 Inmohon,Inc -2432 Grnd Cncrs -Bronx 10458
(718) 243-2444 .. **Pankin,** David I '93 (D Pankin,PC) -48 Willoughby -Brklyn 11201 **Fx:**243-1144
(718) 222-8880 .. **Pankowski,** Sara '03 %Jones JO -45 Main -Brklyn 11201
(718) 833-9433 .. **Pannitto,** Rosa A '93 (Stanton & P) -457 77th -Brklyn 11209 **Fx:**680-8572
(212) 766-1888 .. **Pannone,** James A '96 %Morris DA&F -2 Rector -NY 10006
(718) 388-2661 .. **Pannone,** John A '50 -865 Bay Av -Mattituck 11952 **Fx:**388-2661
(866) 353-3310 .. **Pannone Lopes Devereaux & West LLC** -81 Main -White Plns 10606 **Fx:**353-5020
(716) 648-3020 .. **Pannozzo,** Christopher M '04 %Shaw & S -4819 S Park Av -Hambrg 14075 **Fx:**648-3730
(631) 231-4455 .. **Pannullo,** Thos P '00 %Long Island Vision -601 Suffolk Av -Brentwd 11717
(718) 672-8000 .. **Pannun,** Gurpatwant S '03 -7520 Astoria Blvd -E Elmhrst 11370
(718) 852-6600 .. **Panny,** Christopher J '81 -76 Court -Brklyn 11201 **Fx:**852-6447
(212) 370-3744 .. **Panoff,** Arthur J '74 (Danow M&P,PC) -275 Mad Av -NY 10016
(516) 683-0901 .. **Panos,** James '82 (Cianciulli M&P) -Bx246 -Uniondale 11553
(212) 403-1000 .. **Panovka,** Robin '93 (Wachtell LR&K) -51 W 52nd -NY 10019
(212) 298-5440 .. **Panovski,** Damjan '05 Leg Aid -49 Thomas -NY 10013 **Fx:**298-5252
(212) 558-4000 .. **Panse,** Shaunik R '10 %Sullivan & C LLP -125 Broad -NY 10004
(212) 836-8000 .. **Pant,** Navin Kumud '06 %Kaye S LLP -425 Park Av -NY 10022

(914) 251-1115 .. **Pantaleo,** Frances M '80 (Walsh & A LLP) -2900 Wstchstr Av -Purchase 10577
(212) 335-4500 .. **Pantaleo,** Peter S '06 (DLA Piper LLP) -1251 Av of Amer -NY 10020
(212) 455-2000 .. **Pantaleo,** Peter V '83 (Simpson T&B LLP) -425 Lex Av -NY 10017
(718) 774-5079 .. **Pantaleon,** Rawle '93 -175 Crown -Brklyn 11225
(212) 318-3000 .. **Pantaleoni,** Anthony '64 OfCnsl Fulbright & J LLP -666 5th Av -NY 10103
(914) 948-7000 .. **Pantaleoni,** Danielle M '08 %Keidel W&C LLP -925 Wstchstr Av -White Plns 10604
(607) 432-2950 .. **Pantaleoni,** Patricia '79 (Pantaleoni & B) -28 Watkins Av -Oneonta 13820
(212) 858-7710 .. **Pantano,** Anthony '94 (Nowell AKB,PA) -140 Bway PMB 46028 -NY 10005
(212) 349-5150 .. **Pantazis,** Konstantinos '97 %Galvano & X,PC -150 Bway -NY 10038
(212) 732-9450 .. **Pantel,** Jenna L '08 %N Rosenberg -9 Murray -NY 10007 **Fx:**571-9893
(516) 746-5599 .. **Pantelis,** Thos V '85 OfCnsl Bee RFH&D,LLP -170 Old Cntry Rd -Mineola 11501
(212) 922-0450 .. **Pantelopoulos,** Nicholas E '91 (Kaplan M&A,LLC) -70 E 55th -NY 10022
(212) 446-4800 .. **Panter,** Benjamin D '08 %Kirkland & E LLP -153 E 53rd -NY 10022
(718) 281-2154 .. **Panteris,** Alexia I '97 (Panteris & P LLP) -3516 Bell Blvd -Bayside 11361 **Fx:**281-4746
(718) 281-2154 .. **Panteris,** George '96 (Panteris & P LLP) -3516 Bell Blvd -Bayside 11361 **Fx:**281-4746
(212) 909-6000 .. **Pantin,** Lynnise Phillips '04 %Debevoise & P LLP -919 3rd Av -NY 10022
(212) 937-4000 .. **Pantino,** Thos R '93 Fitzpatrick & HTCPA,LLP -12 E 49th -NY 10017
(212) 592-1400 .. **Pantirer,** David M '08 %Herrick,F LLP -2 Park Av -NY 10016
(212) 574-1200 .. **Pantirer,** Marc H '10 %Seward & K LLP -1 Bttry Pk Plz -NY 10004
(212) 637-2785 .. **Pantoja,** Jos A '96 %US Atty -86 Chmbrs -NY 10007
(914) 333-0610 .. **Pantuliano,** Michl J '57 N Jain,PC -560 Wht Plns Rd -Tarrytwn 10591
(914) 666-7700 .. **Pantzer,** Tricia Cohen '99 Buckingham Prop -116 Radio Cir -Mt Kisco 10549
(212) 974-1111 .. **Panush,** Don B '67 -250 W 57th -NY 10107 **Fx:**974-2436
(718) 585-2511 .. **Panza,** Christine T '03 %Gold & R -840 Grnd Cncrs -Bronx 10451
(585) 338-6025 .. **Panzarella,** Angela J '83 %Bausch & Lomb -One Bausch & Lomb Pl -Rchstr 14604
(516) 889-0800 .. **Panzarella,** Christina M '00 (Aramanda & P,PC) -166 E Park Av -Long Bch 11561 **Fx:**889-2888
(516) 776-9494 .. **Panzavecchia,** Mark A '97 (Panzavecchia & Assoc) -1050 Franklin Av -Gdn Cty 11530 **Fx:**776-9406
(212) 995-5353 .. **Panzella,** Bernadette '82 B Panzella,PC -655 Av of Amer -NY 10010
(212) 269-7722 .. **Panzella,** Jeremy '07 %Rosabianca & Assoc,PLLC -14 Wall -NY 10005 **Fx:**269-7799
(212) 514-5335 .. **Panzer,** Edw S '62 -111 Bway -NY 10006 **Fx:**363-6978
(631) 789-1909 .. **Panzini,** Nicholas J '86 (N Panzini,PC) -365 Bway -Amityvll 11701 **Fx:**789-0961
(315) 896-2974 .. **Panzone,** John A '90 JA Panzone,PC -8021 Route 12 Bx352 -Barneveld 13304
(212) 294-6700 .. **Paolella,** Christopher J '01 OfCnsl Winston & S -200 Park Av -NY 10166
(212) 264-5916 .. **Paoli,** James D '96 DHS-Bur of Immigration -26 Fed Plz -NY 10278
(212) 735-3000 .. **Paoli,** Jessenia '05 %Skadden ASM&F LLP -4 Times Sq -NY 10036
(516) 545-5160 .. **Paoli,** Michele A '97 %Natl Grid -175 E Old Cntry Rd -Hicksvll 11801 **Fx:**545-5029
(212) 605-6200 .. **Paolicelli,** Diane M '82 (Levy P&K,LLP) -800 3rd Av -NY 10022
(212) 762-5366 .. **Paolillo,** James G '05 Morgan Stanley -1221 Av of Amer -NY 10020
(212) 250-0382 .. **Paolini,** Steven M '03 Deutsche Bk AG -60 Wall -NY 10005
(315) 798-5766 .. **Paolozzi,** Stacey L '98 %DA -800 Park Av -Utica 13501 **Fx:**798-5582
(631) 979-3828 .. **Paolucci,** Marylou A '95 -16 Trent Ln -Smithtwn 11787 **Fx:**265-8982
(718) 892-5846 .. **Paone,** Anthony J '88 -1076 Neill Av -Bronx 10461 **Fx:**892-6903
(212) 487-9700 .. **Paone,** Nicholas L '93 OfCnsl White F&F,LLP -61 Bway -NY 10006
(516) 766-1619 .. **Papa,** Danielle M '03 %Dergarabedian D & Assoc -11 Clinton Av -Rockvll Ctr 11570 **Fx:**766-6121
(718) 236-6100 .. **Papa,** Gerard J '76 -Bx140297 -Brklyn 11214
(516) 746-6200 .. **Papa,** Gino C '58 -114 Old Cntry Rd -Mineola 11501 **Fx:**746-6201
(718) 281-4000 .. **Papa,** John P '83 (Papa D&B) -42-40 Bell Blvd -Bayside 11361 **Fx:**281-4030
(518) 365-9711 .. **Papa,** Jos A Jr. '94 -11 Par Cir -Albany 12208
(516) 488-3300 .. **Papa,** Laura Miller '83 (Shaub AC&S,LLP) -1983 Marcus Av -Lk Success 11042
(315) 423-1026 .. **Papa,** Louis F '89 %Workers Comp Bd -935 James -Syracuse 13203 **Fx:**423-2938
(347) 404-9133 .. **Papa,** Margaret K '07 Civil Ct -141 Lvngstn -Brklyn 11201 **Fx:**(718) 643-3733
(518) 736-2900 .. **Papa,** Mario J '71 (Hodgson R LLP) -55 E Main -Johnstwn 12095
(518) 486-9564 .. **Papa,** Michl '98 %Workers Comp Bd -20 Park -Albany 12207
(212) 969-3000 .. **Papa,** Ronald R '81 (Proskauer R LLP) -1585 Bway -NY 10036
(518) 766-4732 .. **Papa,** Salvatore F '75 -Route 32 Bx 97 -N Chatham 12132
(518) 434-2454 .. **Papa,** Salvatore F '75 -90 State -Albany 12207 **Fx:**463-6046
(212) 319-3569 .. **Papa,** Vincent J '75 %Energy Merchant -126 E 56th -NY 10022 **Fx:**319-3587
(212) 701-3000 .. **Papachristos,** John '95 (Cahill G&R LLP) -80 Pine -NY 10005 **Fx:**269-5420
(212) 641-3200 .. **Papachristou,** Alexander '86 %NCH Capital -712 5th Av -NY 10019 **Fx:**641-3201
(212) 446-4800 .. **Papacostas,** Simeon G '09 %Kirkland & E LLP -153 E 53rd -NY 10022
(646) 345-3394 .. **Papadakis,** Felix N '91 -75 West End Av -NY 10023 **Fx:**(212) 957-6113
(718) 745-9799 .. **Papadakis,** Katerina '91 (K Nikiforou,PLLC) -269 86th -Brklyn 11209 **Fx:**745-5545
(212) 943-8940 .. **Papadatos,** Caroline '87 %Crisci W&H -17 State -NY 10004 **Fx:**425-3428
(212) 906-1200 .. **Papadima,** Raluca '07 %Latham & W -885 3rd Av -NY 10022
(718) 721-1250 .. **Papadopoulos,** Anthony C '03 (TCP Law Group) -3501 30th Av -Astoria 11103 **Fx:**721-1270
(516) 488-3300 .. **Papadopoulos,** Christina R '01 %Shaub AC&S,LLP -1983 Marcus Av -Lk Success 11042
(516) 741-4799 .. **Papadopoulos,** Poly '07 %Baker SBGFM&N,LLC -100 Grdn City Plz -Gdn Cty 11530
(718) 728-6100 .. **Papadopoulos-Vlantes,** Aglaia '93 (Papadopoulos-Vlantes & M,PC) -901 Sheridan Av -Bronx 10451 **Fx:**728-9701
(212) 938-5000 .. **Papageorgiou,** Antonio '03 %Cantor Fitzgerald -110 E 59th -NY 10022
(516) 620-1072 .. **Papagianakis,** Peter '01 Amer Home Mtg -538 Broadhllw Rd -Melvll 11747
(718) 274-1600 .. **Papagianopoulos,** Michl N '91 (Karabelas & P LLP) -31-10 37th Av -LIC 11101 **Fx:**204-7100
(212) 732-9000 .. **Papain,** Nicholas '79 (Sullivan PBM&C PC) -120 Bway -NY 10271
(516) 535-1700 .. **Papaioannou,** Georgia A '92 %Horing W&R,PC -11 Hillside Av -Williston Pk 11596
(716) 635-0290 .. **Papaj,** Ronald L '91 %Advantage Professionals -5110 Main -Williamsvll 14221
(212) 769-4644 .. **Papakhin,** Anton G '05 Chldrns Advsry Grp -155 W 72nd -NY 10023
(212) 259-8000 .. **Papalaskaris,** Angela M '04 %Dewey & L LLP -1301 Av of Amer -NY 10019
(646) 861-0135 .. **Papaleo,** Sebastian J '01 -99 John -NY 10038
(212) 363-1380 .. **Papalia,** Patrick '02 (Herten BSCBL&H,LLC) -747 3rd Av -NY 10017
(212) 461-2323 .. **Papalia,** Vincent F '85 (Saiber LLC) -44 Wall -NY 10005
(718) 558-8352 .. **Papandon,** Stephen N '92 %LIRR -Jamaica Station -Jamaica 11435 **Fx:**558-8211
(212) 867-3600 .. **Papano,** Susan G '84 -369 Lex Av -NY 10017 **Fx:**867-1914
(212) 479-6000 .. **Papantoniou,** Andreas Panagiotis '06 %Cooley LLP -1114 Av of Amer -NY 10036
(718) 392-9348 .. **Papapanayotou,** Jerasimos '78 -13-15 37th Av -LIC 11101 **Fx:**729-4160
(212) 687-8500 .. **Paparella,** Andrea M '05 %Liddle & R,LLP -800 3rd Av -NY 10022
(212) 837-6000 .. **Paparella,** Christopher M '88 (Hughes H&R LLP) -1 Bttry Pk Plz -NY 10004
(212) 788-0445 .. **Paparella,** Robt J '00 %Law Dept -100 Church -NY 10007 **Fx:**788-0367
(212) 564-8268 .. **Paparian,** Glenn T '88 (Paparian & Assoc LLC) -233 Bway -NY 10279 **Fx:**564-3864
(212) 969-3000 .. **Paparo,** Vincenzo '96 (Proskauer R LLP) -1585 Bway -NY 10036
(212) 732-3200 .. **Paparone,** Melissa E '04 %Carter L&M LLP -2 Wall -NY 10005
(718) 622-6767 .. **Papas,** Demetrios N '00 -195 Prospect Pl -Brklyn 11238
(914) 328-0404 .. **Papas,** Jennifer '09 %Jackson L LLP -1 N Bway -White Plns 10601
(646) 467-7378 .. **Papastrat,** John H '01 -122 W 27th -NY 10001 **Fx:**(888) 491-6883
(212) 314-5504 .. **Papazicos,** George '83 %Equitable Life Assurance -1290 Av of Amer -NY 10104
(212) 670-0270 .. **Pape,** Dennis M '67 -222 Bway -NY 10038
(516) 873-6334 .. **Pape,** Lauren M '03 Cnsl Ohrenstein & B,LLP -1010 Franklin Av Bx9243 -Gdn Cty 11530
(516) 355-7901 .. **Pape,** Robt J Jr. '83 Paganini GCC&F -1979 Marcus Av -Lk Success 11042
(845) 943-6400 .. **Pape,** Wm Phipps '01 -Bx26 -Cottekill 12419 **Fx:**(866) 465-1129
(212) 530-5000 .. **Papeika,** Gregory R '08 %Milbank TH&M LLP -1 Chase Manh Plz -NY 10005
(631) 725-4836 .. **Pape Murphree,** Kieran '95 -1 Bayberry Ln -Sag Hbr 11963
(212) 259-8000 .. **Papendick,** Ian L '08 %Dewey & L LLP -1301 Av of Amer -NY 10019
(212) 935-3000 .. **Papernik,** Joel I '69 (Mintz LCFG&P,PC) -666 3rd Av -NY 10017
(585) 428-5210 .. **Paperno,** Jill L '85 %Pub Def -10 N Fitzhugh -Rchstr 14614 **Fx:**428-2234
(212) 536-3900 .. **Papir,** Ryan M '02 %K&L Gates LLP -599 Lex Av -NY 10022
(212) 474-1000 .. **Papish,** Pamela J '98 %Cravath S&M LLP -825 8th Av -NY 10019
(631) 667-1510 .. **Papol,** Sheela M '92 %Kelly L&A -2023 Deer Prk Av -Deer Pk 11729
(914) 997-0500 .. **Papp,** Scott V '03 %Lowey DC&H,PC -1 N Bway -White Plns 10601
(212) 726-6500 .. **Pappa,** Kristina K '00 Atari,Inc -417 5th Av -NY 10016 **Fx:**726-4214
(212) 548-7255 .. **Pappachen,** George V '97 Millward Brown,Inc -909 3rd Av -NY 10022 **Fx:**548-7201
(585) 325-7515 .. **Pappal,** Nancy Ann '98 (Forsyth HOK&M,PC) -1 Chase Sq -Rchstr 14604
(212) 676-0987 .. **Pappalardo,** Amanda M '10 %Law Dept -60 Lafayette -NY 10013 **Fx:**442-6865
(585) 377-1310 .. **Pappalardo,** Fauna M '94 (Pappalardo & P) -115 N Main -Fairprt 14450
(315) 793-2370 .. **Pappalardo,** Frank S '98 MHLS -207 Genesee -Utica 13501 **Fx:**793-2371
(914) 592-3400 .. **Pappalardo,** Gregory J '89 (Pappalardo T&W LLP) -500 Mamaroneck Av -Harrison 10528
(914) 761-9400 .. **Pappalardo,** John A '87 (Farber P&C) -200 E Post Rd -White Plns 10601
(914) 725-7000 .. **Pappalardo,** John D '94 (Pappalardo & P LLP) -700 Wht Plns Rd -Scarsdale 10583 **Fx:**725-1700
(914) 725-7000 .. **Pappalardo,** John J '69 (Pappalardo & P LLP) -700 Wht Plns Rd -Scarsdale 10583 **Fx:**725-1700
(585) 377-1310 .. **Pappalardo,** P Frank '65 (Pappalardo & P) -115 N Main -Fairprt 14450
(914) 592-3400 .. **Pappalardo Tombini & Wolff LLP** -500 Mamaroneck Av -Harrison 10528 **Fx:**592-0733
(716) 847-8400 .. **Pappano,** John A '84 (Phillips L LLP) -3400 HSBC Ctr -Buffalo 14203
(914) 225-5600 .. **Pappas,** Alexa B '00 %Morgan Stanley -2000 Wstchstr Av -Purchase 10577
(718) 987-5100 .. **Pappas,** Andrew '95 -182 Rose Av -Staten Isl 10306 **Fx:**987-7282
(315) 472-4481 .. **Pappas,** C Andrew '67 (Ali P&C) -614 James -Syracuse 13203
(212) 466-1430 .. **Pappas,** Chris '57 (C Pappas & Assoc) -375 South End Av -NY 10280 **Fx:**466-1430
(718) 545-3614 .. **Pappas,** Christina S '89 (Pappas & P) -33-20 Bway -Astoria 11106 **Fx:**726-6545

(718) 229-5390 .. **Pappas,** Christos '01 %P Tischler -38-39 Bell Blvd -Bayside 11361 **Fx:**229-5759
(914) 773-3798 .. **Pappas,** George R '92 -152 Commerce -Hawthorne 10532
(212) 885-5000 .. **Pappas,** Harold N '66 OfCnsl Blank R LLP -405 Lex Av -NY 10174
(212) 264-3063 .. **Pappas,** Jeannette D '88 %IRS -290 Bway -NY 10007
(585) 232-1292 .. **Pappas,** Jordan E '55 -5914 Terrace Ln -Farmington 14425
(718) 545-3614 .. **Pappas,** Leah P '86 (Pappas & P) -33-20 Bway -Astoria 11106 **Fx:**726-6545
(212) 583-9600 .. **Pappas,** Michl P '90 (Littler M,PC) -900 3rd Av -NY 10022
(212) 310-8000 .. **Pappas,** Nicholas J '89 (Weil G&M LLP) -767 5th Av -NY 10153
(212) 735-8600 .. **Pappas,** Perry A '89 (Morrison C LLP) -909 3rd Av -NY 10022
(631) 666-6200 .. **Pappas,** Steven J '90 %PF Adams,PC -49 5th Av Bx1089M -Bay Shr 11706 **Fx:**665-6739
(212) 559-5481 .. **Papper,** Richd N '77 Citigroup Intl -399 Park Av -NY 10022
(212) 819-8200 .. **Pappy,** Susan J '07 %White & C LLP -1155 Av of Amer -NY 10036
(212) 754-1500 .. **Paprin,** Seth '79 -555 Mad Av -NY 10022 **Fx:**318-9435
(212) 867-0103 .. **Papson,** Costa L '62 -75 Rckfllr Plz -NY 10019 **Fx:**697-2521
(315) 474-2911 .. **Paquette,** Aimee M '10 %Smith SK&S,PC -250 S Clinton -Syracuse 13202
(718) 590-2000 .. **Paquette,** Cristina '98 %DA -198 E 161st -Bronx 10451 **Fx:**590-6477
(315) 422-1391 .. **Paquette,** Steven A '80 (Green & S,PLLC) -One Lincoln Ctr #900 -Syracuse 13202
(212) 210-9556 .. **Para,** Noel J '81 (Alston & B LLP) -90 Park Av -NY 10016
(914) 864-7122 .. **Parab,** Amit '08 %DA -25 Moore Av -Mt Kisco 10549
(718) 618-2500 .. **Parache-Brito,** Cynthia '02 %Civil Ct -851 Grnd Cncrs -Bronx 10451 **Fx:**590-7294
(212) 644-4420 .. **Paradeis,** Todd A '98 %Fabiani C&H,LLP -570 Lex Av -NY 10022
(212) 626-4100 .. **Paradis,** Margaret R A '76 (Baker & M LLP) -1114 Av of Amer -NY 10036
(212) 986-4500 .. **Paradis,** Paul O '91 (Horwitz H&P) -405 Lex Av -NY 10174
(212) 819-8200 .. **Paradise,** Jennifer A '05 Cnsl White & C LLP -1155 Av of Amer -NY 10036
(212) 836-4967 .. **Paradise,** Melvin '52 (Hartman & C LLP) -488 Mad Av -NY 10022 **Fx:**223-9911
(212) 448-1100 .. **Paradise,** Michl S '88 (McLaughlin & S,LLP) -260 Mad Av -NY 10016
(212) 237-0000 .. **Paradise,** Steven R '91 (Vinson & E LLP) -666 5th Av -NY 10103
(516) 741-6355 .. **Paradise,** Vincent J '64 (Nicolini PF&S) -114 Old Cntry Rd Bx9006 -Mineola 11501
(212) 680-1331 .. **Paragon,** Donald '65 D Paragon,PC -70 Bowery -NY 10013 **Fx:**226-9707
(914) 793-2626 .. **Parandian,** Kamran '02 -1 Barker Av -White Plns 10601 **Fx:**239-4678
(212) 768-6700 .. **Parang,** Zhubin '07 %Sonnenschein N&R LLP -1221 Av of Amer -NY 10020
(212) 770-7000 .. **Parangi,** Mahsa '98 %AIG -70 Pine -NY 10270
(212) 805-6730 .. **Paras,** Rachel R '05 Hon F Maas -500 Pearl -NY 10007
(212) 781-2111 .. **Paras,** Suzan Dawn '93 %Fotopoulos R&G -4160 Bway -NY 10033
(718) 935-1884 .. **Parascandola,** Blaise F '62 -16 Court -Brklyn 11241 **Fx:**855-5101
(212) 688-8555 .. **Parascandola,** Ciro A '08 %Fragomen DB&L LLP -7 Hanover Sq -NY 10004
(212) 227-4210 .. **Parash,** Wm H '92 (Weg & M,PC) -52 Duane -NY 10007
(516) 463-7053 .. **Parasidis,** Efthimios '01 %Hofstra Law Schl -121 Hofstra Univ -Hempstd 11549
(212) 724-0150 .. **Paraskevas,** Theo H '86 (US Corporate Ventures Grp) -48 Wall -NY 10005
(212) 583-9600 .. **Paraskevas-Thadani,** Elena '98 %Littler M,PC -900 3rd Av -NY 10022
(212) 889-3700 .. **Parasmo,** Grace E '07 %Abbey SR&A LLP -212 E 39th -NY 10016
(212) 455-2000 .. **Parasuraman,** Rohith A '09 %Simpson T&B LLP -425 Lex Av -NY 10017
(212) 640-4449 .. **Parauda,** John E '86 %Amer Exp -200 Vesey -NY 10285
(315) 735-6481 .. **Paravati Karl Green & DeBella** -12 Steuben Pk -Utica 13501 **Fx:**735-6406
(315) 735-6481 .. **Paravati,** Peter P Jr. '79 (Paravati KG&D) -12 Steuben Pk -Utica 13501
(516) 358-1409 .. **Parazzelli,** Janis A '78 -99 Tulip Av -Floral Pk 11001 **Fx:**775-0352
(212) 790-4500 .. **Parcher,** L Peter '62 (Manatt P&P,LLP) -7 Times Sq -NY 10036
(718) 777-0400 .. **Pardalis,** Anastasi '05 (Mavromihalis & P) -3403 Bway -Astoria 11106
(212) 940-8800 .. **Pardini,** Merritt A '02 %Katten MR LLP -575 Mad Av -NY 10022
(212) 547-5400 .. **Pardo,** James A '99 (McDermott W&E LLP) -340 Mad Av -NY 10173
(212) 496-1300 .. **Pardo,** Maria L '01 Sinergia Inc -15 W 65th -NY 10023
(212) 267-9020 .. **Pardo,** Marisa E '94 %Shapiro B&A LLP -225 Bway -NY 10007
(212) 252-8500 .. **Pardo,** Michl R '93 Public Investigations -38 E 29th -NY 10016 **Fx:**252-8700
(212) 773-0550 .. **Pardo,** Sheri Gilbert '96 %Ernst & Young,LLP -5 Times Sq -NY 10036
(212) 808-0448 .. **Pardo,** Thos S '95 %Brand BN&R,LLP -286 Mad Av -NY 10017
(585) 746-3600 .. **Pardyjak,** Patrick W '81 -7 State -Pittsfrd 14534
(212) 952-6200 .. **Pare,** Armand M Jr. '75 (Nourse & B,LLP) -55 Bway -NY 10006
(585) 394-1350 .. **Paré,** Teresa M '99 -20 Gorham -Canandaigua 14424 **Fx:**394-1351
(212) 836-8000 .. **Paredes,** Denise D '01 %Kaye S LLP -425 Park Av -NY 10022
(212) 601-8042 .. **Paredes,** Laurence D '97 Porter Novelli,Inc -75 Varick -NY 10013
(212) 538-2593 .. **Paredes,** Lourdes E '03 Credit Suisse -1 Mad Av -NY 10010
(212) 816-3571 .. **Parekattil,** Tina J '03 Citigroup -388 Greenwich -NY 10013
(212) 813-8800 .. **Parekh,** Ankur P '06 %Goodwin P LLP -620 8th Av -NY 10018
(212) 969-3000 .. **Parekh,** Megha H '10 %Proskauer R LLP -1585 Bway -NY 10036
(212) 984-2377 .. **Parekh,** Neel P '04 Tiger Consumer Mgmt -101 Park Av -NY 10178
(212) 336-2000 .. **Parekh,** Niraj J '05 %Patterson BW&T LLP -1133 Av of Amer -NY 10036
(212) 310-8000 .. **Parel,** S Scott '06 (Weil G&M LLP) -767 5th Av -NY 10153
(718) 990-6623 .. **Parella,** Robt E '63 %St John's Law Schl -8000 Utopia Pkwy -Jamaica 11439 **Fx:**591-1855
(212) 940-8800 .. **Parella,** Sharon '89 (Katten MR LLP) -575 Mad Av -NY 10022
(646) 471-4000 .. **Parello,** Laura J '91 %PricewaterhouseCoopers LLP -300 Mad Av -NY 10017
(212) 610-3644 .. **Parello,** Michl J '09 Cantor Fitzgerald -110 E 59th -NY 10022
(516) 742-4700 .. **Parendo,** Mark J '91 %MKM Abstract Srvcs -238 Mineola Blvd -Mineola 11501
(212) 640-5789 .. **Parent,** Louise M '76 %Amer Exp -200 Vesey -NY 10285
(212) 763-4100 .. **Parent,** Neil P '82 (Reavis PL LLP) -41 Mad Av -NY 10010
(516) 221-1748 .. **Parente,** Alan M '71 -2574 Neptune Av -Seafrd 11783 **Fx:**679-3244
(631) 843-3935 .. **Parente,** Bonnie Lou Santosus '95 Newsday -235 Pinelawn Rd -Melvll 11747
(518) 432-8000 .. **Parente,** Clemente J '89 (Crane & P) -48 Howard -Albany 12207
(516) 522-2695 .. **Parente,** Danl '96 (Callaghan P LLP) -626 RXR Plz -Uniondale 11556 **Fx:**(866) 269-3969
(212) 558-4000 .. **Parente,** Kathryn A '05 %Sullivan & C LLP -125 Broad -NY 10004
(212) 557-1818 .. **Pareres,** Jos T '87 (Silverson P&L) -192 Lex Av -NY 10016
(718) 741-8255 .. **Pares,** Migdalia '86 Div of Human Rights -1 Fordham Plz -Bronx 10458 **Fx:**741-8104
(716) 204-1055 .. **Pares,** Thos C '70 Pfalzgraf B&M LLP -455 Cayuga Rd -Buffalo 14225 **Fx:**204-1080
(716) 843-8486 .. **Paresi,** Christopher T '03 US DHS -726 Exhange -Buffalo 14210
(212) 975-3398 .. **Paretsky,** Danl '07 CBS -51 W 52nd -NY 10019
(212) 587-9690 .. **Paretsky,** Peter H '02 %J Samel & Partners -150 Bway -NY 10038 **Fx:**587-9673
(212) 746-1171 .. **Parham,** Cheryl A '88 %NY Presbyterian Hsptl -525 E 68th Bx88 -NY 10065 **Fx:**746-8603
(516) 692-8888 .. **Parham,** Eric M '01 OfCnsl F Chau & Assoc,LLC -130 Woodbury Rd -Woodbury 11797 **Fx:**692-8889
(212) 558-4000 .. **Parham,** Matthew A '06 %Sullivan & C LLP -125 Broad -NY 10004
(845) 638-5001 .. **Parietti,** Jennifer S '03 %DA -1 S Main -New Cty 10956 **Fx:**638-5070
(212) 335-4500 .. **Parikh,** Carrie S '06 %DLA Piper LLP -1251 Av of Amer -NY 10020
(212) 710-2643 .. **Parikh,** Jigar S '99 -110 Wall -NY 10005 **Fx:**(646) 619-4195
(212) 637-1071 .. **Parikh,** Michelle '05 US Atty -1 St Andrews Plz -NY 10007
(212) 788-5605 .. **Parikh,** Monica Debki '01 Dept for the Aging -2 Lafayette -NY 10007
(631) 499-5400 .. **Parikh,** Pragna '02 %Smith CL PC -5036 Jericho Tpk Bx49 -Commack 11725
(212) 566-7188 .. **Parikh,** Rajiv D '08 %Genova B&G -115 Bway -NY 10006
(212) 239-6603 .. **Parikh,** Rita Dharmesh '95 -330 7th Av -NY 10001
(212) 230-2802 .. **Parikh,** Tanya '03 %Fragomen DB&L LLP -7 Hanover Sq -NY 10004 **Fx:**319-5236
(212) 490-3331 .. **Parilla,** John G '66 (Parilla & G,PC) -60 E 42nd -NY 10165 **Fx:**986-4269
(718) 590-6364 .. **Parillo,** Denise L '79 %Hon M Marcus -851 Grnd Cncrs -Bronx 10451
(212) 964-0166 .. **Paris,** Jason L '96 JL Paris,PLLC -270 Mad Av -NY 10016 **Fx:**(917) 720-9819
(212) 756-2000 .. **Paris,** Lauren D '06 %Schulte R&Z LLP -919 3rd Av -NY 10022
(212) 841-3044 .. **Paris,** Morela L '94 BNP Paribas -787 7th Av -NY 10019
(607) 255-5124 .. **Parise,** Anthony F '77 %Cornell Univ -300 CCC Bldg-Grdn Av -Ithaca 14853 **Fx:**255-2794
(212) 318-3000 .. **Parise,** Jessica S '03 %Fulbright & J LLP -666 5th Av -NY 10103
(212) 553-6314 .. **Parise,** Laurie Anne '07 Youth Represent -346 Bway -NY 10013 **Fx:**964-3653
(212) 715-9100 .. **Parise,** Mark F '03 %Kramer LN&F,LLP -1177 Av of Amer -NY 10036
(718) 855-1720 .. **Pariser,** Danl W '78 -75 Lvngstn -Brklyn 11201 **Fx:**694-0733
(212) 225-7700 .. **Pariser,** Gail P '92 %Cartafalsa ST&L -165 Bway -NY 10006
(212) 398-7007 .. **Pariser,** Howard D '77 -114 W 47th -NY 10036
(212) 833-4117 .. **Pariser,** Jennifer L '90 Sony BMG Music Entrtnmnt -550 Mad Av -NY 10022 **Fx:**833-8406
(212) 490-3000 .. **Pariser,** Robt J '02 %Wilson EME&D LLP -150 E 42nd -NY 10017
(646) 602-5600 .. **Parish,** Jennifer J '97 %Urban Justice Ctr -123 William -NY 10038 **Fx:**(212) 533-4598
(212) 478-0664 .. **Parish,** John B '99 DE Shaw & Co -120 W 45th -NY 10036 **Fx:**478-0100
(212) 450-4000 .. **Parish,** Julie E '07 %Davis P&W LLP -450 Lex Av -NY 10017
(212) 225-2000 .. **Parish,** T David '93 Cleary GS&H -1 Lbrty Plz -NY 10006
(585) 232-8000 .. **Parisi,** Albert '89 (Parisi & B) -16 W Main -Rchstr 14614 **Fx:**232-7245
(631) 328-1335 .. **Parisi,** Anthony III '89 -11 Penn Plz -NY 10001
(845) 486-2300 .. **Parisi,** Anthony P '95 %DA -236 Main -Poughkeepsie 12601 **Fx:**486-2324
(516) 674-4100 .. **Parisi,** Chas E '85 (Parisi & L) -58 Schl -Glen Cove 11542 **Fx:**674-3582
(212) 848-4000 .. **Parisi,** Donna M '94 (Shearman & S LLP) -599 Lex Av -NY 10022
(518) 377-9096 .. **Parisi,** Frank N '57 SrCnsl Parisi C&S,PLLC -376 Bway Bx1087 -Schnctdy 12305 **Fx:**377-9108
(212) 244-7676 .. **Parisi,** George J '93 %Ferro KMS,PC -424 W 33rd -NY 10001
(518) 377-9096 .. **Parisi,** Gerard F '99 (Parisi C&S,PLLC) -376 Bway Bx1087 -Schnctdy 12305 **Fx:**377-9108
(516) 542-2100 .. **Parisi,** Gregory J '63 -600 Old Cntry Rd -Gdn Cty 11530 **Fx:**542-2114
(914) 921-5533 .. **Parisi,** Guy T '72 -720 Milton Rd -Rye 10580
(914) 949-2700 .. **Parisi,** Matthew G '94 (Bleakley P&S,LLP) -1 N Lex Av -White Plns 10601
(716) 858-2424 .. **Parisi,** Paul C '07 %DA -25 Delaware Av -Buffalo 14202 **Fx:**858-7425
(212) 545-4000 .. **Parisi,** Paul P '04 %Jackson L LLP -666 3rd Av -NY 10017
(631) 853-7913 .. **Parisi,** Rachel J '96 %Suffolk Cnty Fam Ct -400 Carleton Av -Central Islip 11722
(718) 761-3333 .. **Parisi Rampulla & Lenza PC** -78 Martin Av -Staten Isl 10314
(212) 458-1126 .. **Parisi,** Robt A Jr. '90 %AIG -175 Water -NY 10038 **Fx:**458-1100
(646) 386-4070 .. **Parisien,** Michelle B '89 Supreme Ct -100 Centre -NY 10013
(212) 728-8000 .. **Park,** Adeline C '10 %Willkie F&G LLP -787 7th Av -NY 10019
(212) 279-3883 .. **Park,** Andrew D '99 -16 W 32nd -NY 10001
(718) 762-9503 .. **Park,** Andrew I '94 (Park & P,PC) -3833 150th -Flushng 11354 **Fx:**762-9474
(212) 702-9027 .. **Park,** Ann M '08 %Mulholland & K,LLP -641 Lex Av -NY 10022 **Fx:**702-9092
(212) 223-0400 .. **Park,** Anna S '05 %Zeichner E&K LLP -575 Lex Av -NY 10022
(212) 401-2990 .. **Park,** Anthony S '03 -1 Rckfllr Plz -NY 10020
(212) 373-3000 .. **Park,** Benjamin D '06 Paul WRW&G LLP -1285 Av of Amer -NY 10019
(646) 386-3176 .. **Park,** Cathy S '98 Hon D Ling-Cohan -80 Centre -NY 10013
(718) 298-8900 .. **Park,** Chai Ri '09 %Leg Aid -153-01 Jamaica Av -Jamaica 11432 **Fx:**657-0537

(718) 590-2000 .. **Park,** Cristina Sun Woo '99 %DA -198 E 161st -Bronx 10451 **Fx:**590-6477
(212) 728-8000 .. **Park,** David K '97 SpclCnsl Willkie F&G LLP -787 7th Av -NY 10019
(212) 986-6000 .. **Park,** David Y '04 %Kleinberg KW&C,PC -551 5th Av -NY 10176
(212) 455-2000 .. **Park,** Diona N '10 %Simpson T&B LLP -425 Lex Av -NY 10017
(212) 312-2260 .. **Park,** E Grace '01 %Leg Aid -60 Lafayette -NY 10013 **Fx:**349-0874
(212) 816-0199 .. **Park,** Edw J '97 Citigroup Global Mrkts -388 Greenwich -NY 10013
(212) 450-4000 .. **Park,** Eilleen J '08 %Davis P&W LLP -450 Lex Av -NY 10017
(212) 559-2456 .. **Park,** Eugene J '98 Citigroup NA -485 Lex Av -NY 10017
(718) 640-9223 .. **Park,** Euna '03 %CUNY Citizenshp & Immig Prjct -39-07 Prince -Flushng 11354
(516) 742-4343 .. **Park,** Eunhee '98 (Scully SM&P PC) -400 Grdn City Plz -Gdn Cty 11530
(212) 867-6000 .. **Park,** Fredk E '88 (Rosenberg & E,PC) -733 3rd Av -NY 10017
(212) 474-1000 .. **Park,** G Young '09 %Cravath S&M LLP -825 8th Av -NY 10019
(212) 684-1422 .. **Park,** Gary S '92 -60 E 42nd -NY 10165 **Fx:**684-1428
(212) 736-9430 .. **Park,** Gi Heun '89 -1270 Bway -NY 10001 **Fx:**564-1649
(212) 683-8563 .. **Park,** Grace Serena '96 %Oaktree Capital Mngt -1301 Av of Amer -NY 10019
(212) 588-0800 .. **Park,** Haejin Sarah '03 %Frommer L&H LLP -745 5th Av -NY 10151
(212) 848-4000 .. **Park,** Hee Yeon '10 Shearman & S LLP -599 Lex Av -NY 10022
(212) 530-1800 .. **Park,** Hellen '09 Richards K&O LLP -1 World Fncl Ctr -NY 10281
(212) 449-0331 .. **Park,** Hyesun Grace '05 Merrill Lynch -4 World Fncl Ctr -NY 10080
(212) 239-3680 .. **Park,** Inho A '97 (Sim & P,LLP) -450 7th Av -NY 10123 **Fx:**239-3683
(212) 999-5800 .. **Park,** J Andrea '07 %Wilson SG&R -1301 Av of Americas -NY 10019
(212) 848-4000 .. **Park,** Jae Woo '06 %Shearman & S LLP -599 Lex Av -NY 10022
(718) 625-2200 .. **Park,** James J '01 Bklyn Law Schl -250 Joralemon -Brklyn 11201 **Fx:**780-0393
(212) 310-8000 .. **Park,** Jay Hyun '02 %Weil G&M LLP -767 5th Av -NY 10153
(718) 613-2554 .. **Park,** Jean Hee '05 US Dist Ct-EDNY -225 Cadman Plz E -Brklyn 11201
(718) 590-2000 .. **Park,** Jean Soo '03 DA -198 E 161st -Bronx 10451 **Fx:**590-6477
(212) 808-7800 .. **Park,** Jean Y '96 (Kelley D&W LLP) -101 Park Av -NY 10178
(212) 450-4000 .. **Park,** Jeeyeon '04 %Davis P&W LLP -450 Lex Av -NY 10017
(212) 878-8000 .. **Park,** Jennifer '07 %Clifford C LLP -31 W 52nd -NY 10019
(212) 771-9508 .. **Park,** Jennifer K '03 CIT Grp,Inc -505 5th Av -NY 10017
(212) 490-3000 .. **Park,** Jenny M '07 %Wilson EME&D LLP -150 E 42nd -NY 10017
(212) 696-9494 .. **Park,** Jill SunJung '94 (Park WC&N,LLP) -15 E 32nd -NY 10016 **Fx:**447-0968
(646) 471-0395 .. **Park,** Jin Woo '05 %PricewaterhouseCoopers LLP -300 Mad Av -NY 10017
(212) 474-1000 .. **Park,** Jisun '06 %Cravath S&M LLP -825 8th Av -NY 10019
(212) 373-3000 .. **Park,** JiYoung '09 %Paul WRW&G LLP -1285 Av of Amer -NY 10019
(212) 375-2050 .. **Park,** Joanne J '05 ACA Capital Holdings -140 Bway -NY 10005
(212) 271-0664 .. **Park,** John K '98 (Lee AC LLP) -350 5th Av -NY 10118
(718) 892-9500 .. **Park,** John S '94 (Park & N) -1809 Paulding Av -Bronx 10462
(585) 396-4411 .. **Park,** John W '74 (Cnty Atty) -27 N Main -Canandaigua 14424 **Fx:**396-4481
(212) 446-4800 .. **Park,** Joung Youl '09 %Kirkland & E LLP -153 E 53rd -NY 10022
(212) 839-5300 .. **Park,** Judie '07 %Sidley A LLP -787 7th Av -NY 10019
(201) 777-0349 .. **Park,** Julia Yong-hee '06 J Park LLC -250 W 57th -NY 10107 **Fx:**731-5176
(212) 335-9000 .. **Park,** Jung A '02 %DA -1 Hogan Pl -NY 10013
(212) 668-5927 .. **Park,** Jung Hyun '99 (Ropers MK&B) -17 State -NY 10004
(212) 756-2000 .. **Park,** Karen S '08 %Schulte R&Z LLP -919 3rd Av -NY 10022
(718) 250-2000 .. **Park,** Maria Y '96 %DA -350 Jay -Brklyn 11201 **Fx:**250-2314
(212) 530-1800 .. **Park,** Mary H '08 %Richards K&O LLP -1 World Fncl Ctr -NY 10281
(718) 788-1703 .. **Park,** Maxine H '94 -155 Water -Brklyn 11201 **Fx:**788-6311
(212) 909-6000 .. **Park,** Mee Ae '09 %Debevoise & P LLP -919 3rd Av -NY 10022
(718) 445-0652 .. **Park,** Miae '92 -34-25 149th -Flushng 11354 **Fx:**445-8155
(718) 892-9500 .. **Park & Nguyen** -1809 Paulding Av -Bronx 10462 **Fx:**892-4666
(212) 264-1174 .. **Park,** Rachel H '94 %HHS -26 Fed Plz -NY 10278 **Fx:**264-6364
(212) 735-3000 .. **Park,** Rose '09 %Skadden ASM&F LLP -4 Times Sq -NY 10036
(212) 891-5700 .. **Park,** Sandra Jiyoung '02 %Ixis -9 W 57th -NY 10019
(212) 698-3500 .. **Park,** Sang Hyuk '96 (Dechert LLP) -1095 Av of Amer -NY 10036
(212) 837-6844 .. **Park,** Sarah S '10 %Hughes H&R LLP -1 Bttry Pk Plz -NY 10004 **Fx:**299-6844
(212) 455-2000 .. **Park,** Seojung '07 %Simpson T&B LLP -425 Lex Av -NY 10017
(212) 294-6700 .. **Park,** Soyun '07 %Winston & S -200 Park Av -NY 10166
(212) 765-9100 .. **Park,** Stephanie S '09 %Halperin BR,LLP -555 Mad Av -NY 10022
(646) 386-5700 .. **Park,** Steven S '94 %Civil Ct -111 Centre -NY 10013
(212) 617-3652 .. **Park,** Sue J '04 Bloomberg Finance LP -731 Lex Av -NY 10022
(212) 801-2246 .. **Park,** Sun-Young '09 %Greenberg T,LLP -200 Park Av -NY 10166
(212) 756-2000 .. **Park,** Sung Uk '01 %Schulte R&Z LLP -919 3rd Av -NY 10022
(212) 451-5457 .. **Park,** Sunny S H '03 Saks Inc -12 E 49th -NY 10017
(212) 562-4961 .. **Park,** Susan '96 %MHLS -Bellevue Hsptl 27th & 1st Av -NY 10016
(718) 250-2000 .. **Park,** Susan E '07 %DA -350 Jay -Brklyn 11201 **Fx:**250-2314
(646) 200-6300 .. **Park,** Tai H '87 (Park & J LLP) -630 3rd Av -NY 10017 **Fx:**200-6301
(212) 336-2000 .. **Park,** Teresa Sanghee '05 %Patterson BW&T LLP -1133 Av of Amer -NY 10036
(212) 483-9600 .. **Park,** Woong C '02 %Costello S&G LLP -44 Wall -NY 10005
(212) 225-2000 .. **Park,** Yeora Song '07 %Cleary GS&H -1 Lbrty Plz -NY 10006
(914) 948-9500 .. **Park,** Yi-Hwa Jessica '09 %J Killerlane -175 Main -White Plns 10601 **Fx:**948-3004
(212) 404-5777 .. **Park,** Yong Jin '89 (Littleton JUP&K LLP) -39 Bway -NY 10006
(212) 808-7800 .. **Park,** Yong Sung '06 %Kelley D&W LLP -101 Park Av -NY 10178
(212) 442-1379 .. **Park,** Yonhi '89 %Dept For Aging -2 Lafayette -NY 10007
(212) 474-1000 .. **Park,** YouJung '09 %Cravath S&M LLP -825 8th Av -NY 10019
(212) 446-4800 .. **Park,** Young J '01 (Kirkland & E LLP) -153 E 53rd -NY 10022
(212) 816-3379 .. **Park,** Youngjoon '01 Citigroup Global Mrkts,Inc -388 Greenwich -NY 10013
(516) 877-7000 .. **Parkas,** Bill P '95 (McCoyd P&R,LLP) -1100 Franklin Av -Gdn Cty 11530
(718) 286-6000 .. **Parke,** Elizabeth D '84 %DA -125-01 Qns Blvd -Kew Gdns 11415
(212) 588-0800 .. **Parke,** Richd E '91 (Frommer L&H LLP) -745 5th Av -NY 10151
(860) 541-3318 .. **Parker,** Alan S '80 (Pullman & C,LLC) -50 Main -White Plns 10606
(212) 559-0483 .. **Parker,** Allen K '03 Citigroup NA -485 Lex Av -NY 10017
(212) 785-6410 .. **Parker,** Andrew C '04 (McCarthy T LLP) -1 NY Plz -NY 10004
(914) 683-8484 .. **Parker,** Anna B '84 OfCnsl Goodrich & B -5 Old Rd -Elmsfrd 10523
(212) 474-1000 .. **Parker,** C Allen '85 (Cravath S&M LLP) -825 8th Av -NY 10019
(518) 456-2722 .. **Parker & Castillo** -3 Wembley Ct -Albany 12205 **Fx:**456-2323
(212) 335-9000 .. **Parker,** Chauncey G IV '87 %DA -1 Hogan Pl -NY 10013
(914) 347-3440 .. **Parker,** Christian Kellogg '00 Cavalry Portfolio Srvcs -7 Skyline Dr -Hawthorne 10532
(212) 238-9497 .. **Parker,** Christina M '00 Platinum Underwriters -2 World Fncl Ctr -NY 10281
(212) 558-4000 .. **Parker,** Christine Trent '07 %Sullivan & C LLP -125 Broad -NY 10004
(212) 310-8000 .. **Parker,** Christopher M '98 %Weil G&M LLP -767 5th Av -NY 10153
(212) 421-4100 .. **Parker,** Colleen E '04 %Pryor C LLP -7 Times Sq -NY 10036
(914) 242-2090 .. **Parker,** Craig R '87 -52 Main -Bedfrd Hlls 10507
(212) 536-3900 .. **Parker,** Dana B '04 %K&L Gates LLP -599 Lex Av -NY 10022
(212) 239-9777 .. **Parker,** Danl S '85 (Parker & C,LLP) -331 Mad Av -NY 10017 **Fx:**239-9175
(718) 624-0154 .. **Parker,** Daryl L '93 Cnsl Katz & Assoc -26 Court -Brklyn 11242 **Fx:**624-4212
(212) 986-6000 .. **Parker,** David '74 (Kleinberg KW&C,PC) -551 5th Av -NY 10176
(212) 519-7832 .. **Parker,** Dennis D '81 %ACLU -125 Broad -NY 10004 **Fx:**549-2651
(212) 628-5566 .. **Parker,** Diana Davis '81 -162 E 80th -NY 10075 **Fx:**(646) 349-2030
(212) 361-1733 .. **Parker,** Douglas A '76 Envrnmntl Cntrl Brd -66 John -NY 10038 **Fx:**361-1900
(631) 853-5761 .. **Parker,** Edw A '78 %Cnty Atty -400 Carleton Av -Central Islip 11722 **Fx:**853-7788
(212) 599-1744 .. **Parker,** Eugene '55 OfCnsl Opton H&F,LLP -295 Mad Av -NY 10017
(585) 244-1040 .. **Parker,** George L '80 -267 Mulberry -Rchstr 14620 **Fx:**244-1040
(212) 612-4200 .. **Parker,** Glen H '96 %Hoey KT&E -55 Water -NY 10041
(585) 244-8910 .. **Parker,** Heather A '97 %Fiandach & F -100 Allens Crk Rd -Rchstr 14618 **Fx:**244-4863
(585) 244-8910 .. **Parker,** Heather R '09 Fiandach & F -100 Allens Crk Rd -Rchstr 14618 **Fx:**244-4863
(716) 851-2711 .. **Parker,** James S '85 %UIA Bd -290 Main -Buffalo 14202 **Fx:**851-2795
(212) 258-7299 .. **Parker,** Jennifer J '93 %MTV Networks -1515 Bway -NY 10036 **Fx:**258-8358
(212) 267-6700 .. **Parker,** Jerrold S '84 (Parker WA LLP) -111 John -NY 10038
(516) 466-6500 .. **Parker,** Jerrold S '84 (Parker WA LLP) -6 Hrbr Park Dr S -Pt Wash 11050
(212) 804-4200 .. **Parker,** John F '90 (Mound CW&G) -One Bttry Pk Plz -NY 10004
(914) 345-0432 .. **Parker,** John L '97 %Assblymn R Brodsky -5 W Main -Elmsfrd 10523 **Fx:**345-0436
(908) 782-9458 .. **Parker,** John R '00 JR Parker,LLC -11 Bway -NY 10004 **Fx:**782-4264
(315) 478-1229 .. **Parker,** John W III '74 Onondaga Cnty Bar Assn -527 Bucknghm Av -Syracuse 13210
(585) 419-8800 .. **Parker,** Joyce R '81 (Harris B PLLC) -99 Garnsey Rd -Pittsfrd 14534
(212) 458-3415 .. **Parker,** Karen A '93 AIG Tech Srvcs -175 Water -NY 10038 **Fx:**458-1660
(212) 969-3000 .. **Parker,** Katharine H '93 (Proskauer R LLP) -1585 Bway -NY 10036
(212) 373-3000 .. **Parker,** Kelley D '94 (Paul WRW&G LLP) -1285 Av of Amer -NY 10019
(518) 533-3000 .. **Parker,** Kimberlee S '94 (Bond S&K,PLLC) -111 Wshngtn Av -Albany 12210
(914) 333-7420 .. **Parker,** Lainie E '93 %Akzo Nobel -120 Wht Plns Rd -Tarrytwn 10591
(212) 538-6126 .. **Parker,** Lara M '03 Credit Suisse -1 Mad Av -NY 10010
(631) 589-1846 .. **Parker,** Laura J '95 -172 Edgewood Av -Oakdale 11769
(212) 373-8671 .. **Parker,** Lizbeth Ann '95 Friedman KS&A LLP -1633 Bway -NY 10019
(585) 758-7601 .. **Parker,** Louis C III '09 %Univ of Rochester Med Ctr -Bx278979 -Rchstr 14627 **Fx:**272-9311
(212) 863-8263 .. **Parker,** Lynette P '92 %HPD -100 Gold -NY 10038
(212) 221-7999 .. **Parker,** M Todd '06 %Moskowitz B&W,LLP -345 7th Av -NY 10001
(716) 855-5312 .. **Parker,** Melvin A '85 %Dept Taxation & Fin -77 Bway -Buffalo 14203 **Fx:**855-5318
(212) 458-5761 .. **Parker,** Michl H '94 AIG -175 Water -NY 10038
(716) 856-5012 .. **Parker,** Michelle M '94 (Anspach ME,LLP) -2400 Main Pl Twr -Buffalo 14202
(212) 670-0306 .. **Parker,** Patrick L '00 Merrill Lynch -222 Bway -NY 10038
(718) 239-7910 .. **Parker,** Philip E '60 -3318 Wht Plns Rd -Bronx 10467 **Fx:**(914) 961-0503
(212) 819-8200 .. **Parker,** R Gregory '07 %White & C LLP -1155 Av of Amer -NY 10036
(518) 532-7167 .. **Parker,** Randolph E '77 -Main Bx116 -Schroon Lk 12870 **Fx:**532-7311
(212) 508-6100 .. **Parker,** Raphael A '09 %Bracewell & G,LLP -1251 Av of Amer -NY 10020
(212) 768-6700 .. **Parker,** Rebecca Hughes '05 %Sonnenschein N&R LLP -1221 Av of Amer -NY 10020
(315) 736-5555 .. **Parker,** Richd G '75 -587 Main -NY Mlls 13417 **Fx:**736-5872
(646) 280-8411 .. **Parker,** Robt H '02 -410 Park Av -NY 10022
(212) 639-5800 .. **Parker,** Roger N '98 %Sloan-Kettering -1275 York Av -NY 10065 **Fx:**717-3079
(212) 835-1514 .. **Parker,** Ronald I '86 (Dreifuss B&P,LLP) -1 Penn Plz -NY 10019
(845) 647-2777 .. **Parker,** Saml R '65 -10 Tamarach Rd -Greenfield Pk 12435 **Fx:**647-1700
(212) 317-2883 .. **Parker,** Sandra D '80 -477 Mad Av -NY 10022 **Fx:**317-1383
(212) 382-3300 .. **Parker,** Serena M '02 %Wollmuth M&D LLP -500 5th Av -NY 10110
(914) 323-7000 .. **Parker,** Sheryl T '07 %Wilson EME&D LLP -3 Gannett Dr -White Plns 10604
(212) 458-1090 .. **Parker,** Stacy B '91 (AIGTS) -175 Water -NY 10038 **Fx:**458-0852
(518) 456-2722 .. **Parker,** Stephen W '81 (Parker & C) -3 Wembley Ct -Albany 12205
(212) 225-2000 .. **Parker,** Susanna E '10 %Cleary GS&H -1 Lbrty Plz -NY 10006
(516) 626-7776 .. **Parker,** Suzanne G '88 S Parker -99 Powerhse Rd -Roslyn Hts 11577 **Fx:**626-0111
(212) 210-9529 .. **Parker,** Thos J '92 (Alston & B LLP) -90 Park Av -NY 10016
(716) 633-5050 .. **Parker,** Venita A '97 %Gelber & O,LLC -6512 Main -Amherst 14221 **Fx:**633-9052
(516) 466-6500 .. **Parker Waichman Alonso LLP** -6 Hrbr Park Dr S -Pt Wash 11050 **Fx:**466-6665

(212) 267-6700 .. **Parker Waichman Alonso LLP** -111 John -NY 10038 **Fx:**227-8175
(716) 834-3735 .. **Parker-Feliciano,** Katherine '93 -521 Highgate Av -Buffalo 14215 **Fx:**834-3735
(718) 206-7687 .. **Parker-Norman,** Safiya J '08 %Law Dept -89-17 Sutphin Blvd -Jamaica 11435 **Fx:**206-4702
(631) 421-9300 .. **Parkes,** Thos J Jr. '98 -1 Huntngtn Quad -Melvll 11747 **Fx:**421-9303
(646) 315-7300 .. **Parkhurst,** Janet K '97 %FINRA -14 Wall -NY 10005 **Fx:**315-7440
(212) 868-6300 .. **Parkhurst,** Joshua S C '97 %Cary K LLP -1350 Bway -NY 10018
(212) 221-6900 .. **Parkin,** Christopher T '09 %Winget S&S,LLP -45 Bway -NY 10006
(212) 722-3993 .. **Parkin,** Todd R '91 -4 E 89th -NY 10128 **Fx:**722-3993
(315) 428-7261 .. **Parkinson,** John T '84 %National Grid -300 Erie Blvd W -Syracuse 13202 **Fx:**428-6149
(718) 875-1300 .. **Parkman,** Lori E '05 %Appllt Div 2nd Dept -45 Monroe Pl -Brklyn 11201 **Fx:**858-2446
(516) 487-6790 .. **Parkoff,** Adam L '09 Parkoff Org -98 Cuttermill Rd -Gt Neck 11021
(212) 296-6226 .. **Parks,** Andrew L '00 Morgan Stanley -522 5th Av -NY 10036
(212) 288-1999 .. **Parks,** David C '93 Mautner-Glick Corp -1345 3rd Av -NY 10075 **Fx:**535-1808
(607) 273-2202 .. **Parks,** David M '97 (Schlather SP&S) -200 E Buffalo Bx353 -Ithaca 14851
(212) 859-8000 .. **Parks,** Lee S '86 (Fried FHS&J LLP) -1 NY Plz -NY 10004
(212) 772-8681 .. **Parks,** Mitchell '94 -233 E 81st -NY 10028 **Fx:**772-8681
(212) 640-2000 .. **Parks,** Robt Benjamin '87 %Amer Exp -200 Vesey -NY 10285
(631) 271-5200 .. **Parlante,** Philip E '95 %Horn & H -780 NY Av -Huntngtn 11743 **Fx:**271-5216
(716) 270-0750 .. **Parlato,** Anthony C '90 -3343 Harlem Rd -Buffalo 14225
(716) 270-0750 .. **Parlato,** Beth Ann '94 -3343 Harlem Rd -Buffalo 14225 **Fx:**270-0751
(716) 834-2066 .. **Parlato,** Frank R '54 -209 Sweet Briar Rd -Tonawanda 14150 **Fx:**835-1586
(716) 639-9220 .. **Parlato,** Lucian C '74 -Bx4 -Getzvll 14068
(631) 732-7789 .. **Parlatore,** Anthony M '70 -290 Main -E Setauket 11733
(212) 355-2200 .. **Parlatore,** Timothy C '09 %E Franz,PLLC -747 3rd Av -NY 10017 **Fx:**937-2217
(212) 326-3939 .. **Parlikad,** Mahesh V '09 %Jones D -222 E 41st -NY 10017
(212) 513-3200 .. **Parlin,** Barbra R '94 (Holland & K LLP) -31 W 52nd -NY 10019
(212) 309-6000 .. **Parlo,** Christopher A '89 (Morgan L&B LLP) -101 Park Av -NY 10178
(718) 254-6228 .. **Parlovecchio,** Gina M '03 %US Atty -271 Cadman Plz E -Brklyn 11201 **Fx:**254-6479
(212) 483-8266 .. **Parmar,** Narinder S '94 %G Wright & Assoc,LLC -88 Pine -NY 10005 **Fx:**483-0971
(212) 225-2000 .. **Parmar,** Simrin K '09 %Cleary GS&H -1 Lbrty Plz -NY 10006
(585) 352-8801 .. **Parmele,** Thos H '73 -5500 Ridge Rd W -Spencerprt 14559 **Fx:**352-8918
(212) 801-3181 .. **Parmelee,** Mark L '97 %Greenberg T,LLP -200 Park Av -NY 10166
(212) 298-5062 .. **Parmenter,** Sean T '00 %Leg Aid -49 Thomas -NY 10013 **Fx:**298-5252
(212) 819-0555 .. **Parmet,** Wendy J '78 (Parmet & G,LLC) -60 E 42nd -NY 10165 **Fx:**840-2288
(315) 786-1758 .. **Parmeter,** John Jr. '84 -215 Wshngtn -Watertwn 13601 **Fx:**785-5537
(212) 425-1401 .. **Parnagian,** Christopher P '94 (O'Hare P LLP) -82 Wall -NY 10005 **Fx:**425-1421
(718) 824-8100 .. **Parnas,** Ilya E '98 -2190 Bstn Rd -Bronx 10462 **Fx:**824-4099
(212) 370-1300 .. **Parnass,** Geoffrey W '80 (Ellenoff G&S LLP) -150 E 42nd -NY 10017
(212) 416-2113 .. **Parnass,** Jeffrey D '00 Dow Jones & Co,Inc -1211 Av of Amer -NY 10036
(212) 909-6000 .. **Parnass,** Steven Zev '04 %Debevoise & P LLP -919 3rd Av -NY 10022
(631) 588-2900 .. **Parnell,** Bruce F '82 (Wolinsky P&M,LLP) -329 Hawkins Av -Lk Ronkonkoma 11779
(212) 808-0700 .. **Parnell,** George F '86 (Norris M&M,PA) -875 3rd Av -NY 10022
(212) 969-3000 .. **Parnes,** Alan P '78 (Proskauer R LLP) -1585 Bway -NY 10036
(212) 335-5835 .. **Parnes,** Jennifer L '09 %Fidelity Invstmnts -200 Lbrty -NY 10281
(718) 356-2422 .. **Parnes,** Mitchell H '87 -236 Richmond Valley Rd -Staten Isl 10309 **Fx:**966-2592
(518) 561-1113 .. **Parnes,** Omshanti H '80 -92 Brinkerhoff -Plattsbrgh 12901
(212) 909-6000 .. **Parnes,** Shelby E '09 %Debevoise & P LLP -919 3rd Av -NY 10022
(718) 227-3003 .. **Parnese,** John S '94 -4308 Richmond Av -Staten Isl 10312 **Fx:**227-2113
(718) 966-4927 .. **Parnese,** Ted V '00 -45 Page Av -Staten Isl 10309 **Fx:**966-4928
(212) 504-6000 .. **Parness,** Alan M '71 Cnsl Cadwalader W&T LLP -1 World Fncl Ctr -NY 10281
(212) 558-4000 .. **Parness,** Brian S '09 %Sullivan & C LLP -125 Broad -NY 10004
(212) 506-1700 .. **Parness,** Evan D '08 Kasowitz BT&F LLP -1633 Bway -NY 10019
(800) 553-9940 .. **Parness,** Hillel I '96 (Robins KM&C LLP) -499 Park Av -NY 10022
(212) 806-5400 .. **Parness,** Stanley '55 OfCnsl Stroock &S&L LLP -180 Maiden Ln -NY 10038
(315) 379-2103 .. **Paro,** Laurie L '92 %Dept Soc Srvcs -6 Judson -Canton 13617 **Fx:**386-2782
(212) 728-8000 .. **Parodi,** Michl R '10 %Willkie F&G LLP -787 7th Av -NY 10019
(212) 874-0100 .. **Parodneck,** Lloyd S '88 %Bellmarc Realty -424 Columbus Av -NY 10024
(646) 386-3982 .. **Paroff,** Melvin D '78 %NYS Supreme Ct -100 Centre -NY 10013 **Fx:**(212) 374-1953
(718) 793-1311 .. **Paroff,** Philip S '75 (Cooper PC&C) -80-02 Kew Grdns Rd -Kew Gdns 11415 **Fx:**575-4070
(718) 896-9600 .. **Paroff,** Sean M '02 Algin Mgmt Co,LLC -6435 Yllwstn Blvd -Frst Hlls 11375
(516) 579-3700 .. **Parola,** Fredk E Jr. '72 (Parola & G) -775 Wantagh Av -Wantagh 11793
(516) 579-3700 .. **Parola & Gross** -775 Wantagh Av -Wantagh 11793 **Fx:**579-3877
(716) 282-1242 .. **Parone,** Anthony D '60 OfCnsl Roscetti & D -730 Main -Niagara Fls 14301
(212) 480-6728 .. **Parpas,** Jason G '00 %DHCR -25 Beaver -NY 10004 **Fx:**480-7416
(212) 848-4000 .. **Parr,** D David Jr. '00 %Shearman & S LLP -599 Lex Av -NY 10022
(516) 746-3726 .. **Parra,** Cynthia D '92 -3000 Marcus Av -New Hyde Pk 11042
(212) 788-8681 .. **Parra,** Elan D '06 %Law Dept -100 Church -NY 10007 **Fx:**788-0367
(914) 995-4172 .. **Parra,** Wendy '02 %DA -111 Martin Luther King Blvd -White Plns 10601 **Fx:**995-3363
(212) 683-7100 .. **Parra,** Wm '00 %Gallo V&K,LLP -90 Broad -NY 10004
(212) 415-9253 .. **Parravani,** James V '90 OfCnsl Dorsey & W LLP -250 Park Av -NY 10177
(212) 573-6909 .. **Parrella,** Jeffrey M '98 -10 Oaklnd Av -Warwick 10990 **Fx:**(866) 541-9926
(718) 590-2507 .. **Parriman,** Ashley E '08 Cnsl Dept of Probation -215 E 161st -Bronx 10451 **Fx:**590-2988
(212) 947-0101 .. **Parrinelli,** Robt T '04 %JJ Appell -3 W 35th -NY 10001
(585) 454-2321 .. **Parrinello,** J Matthew '98 (Redmond & P,LLP) -36 W Main -Rchstr 14614
(585) 454-2321 .. **Parrinello,** John R '65 (Redmond & P,LLP) -36 W Main -Rchstr 14614
(212) 326-3939 .. **Parrinello,** Stephen P '08 %Jones D -222 E 41st -NY 10017
(212) 937-7295 .. **Parrington,** Lisa A '07 %WilmerHale -399 Park Av -NY 10022
(914) 422-8111 .. **Parrino,** Christopher F '95 C Parrino,PC -50 Main -White Plns 10606 **Fx:**422-0540
(212) 980-6833 .. **Parrino,** Irene F '93 -1350 Av of Amer -NY 10019
(212) 460-4931 .. **Parris,** Brian C '97 Con Ed -4 Irving Pl -NY 10003
(718) 722-6376 .. **Parris,** Colette M '09 Unified Ct Sys - Appellate Div, 2nd Dept -195 Montague -Brklyn 11201
(212) 837-6000 .. **Parris,** Collette A '09 %Hughes H&R LLP -1 Bttry Pk Plz -NY 10004
(212) 234-7823 .. **Parris,** Fay Y '92 -255 W 139th -NY 10030
(718) 246-5050 .. **Parris,** Gilbert C '00 -26 Court -Brklyn 11242 **Fx:**246-0910
(914) 253-4881 .. **Parris,** Gwendolyn A '97 %State Ins Fund -105 Corp Park Dr -White Plns 10604
(212) 902-8187 .. **Parrish,** Michl J '02 %Goldman Sachs -1 NY Plz -NY 10004
(212) 648-0868 .. **Parrish,** Pamela K '90 JP Morgan Chase -245 Park Av -NY 10167
(212) 474-1000 .. **Parrott,** Matthew C '09 %Cravath S&M LLP -825 8th Av -NY 10019
(212) 940-8800 .. **Parrott,** Matthew D '97 (Katten MR LLP) -575 Mad Av -NY 10022
(585) 647-6400 .. **Parrotta,** Gary M '88 %Monro Muffler Brake Inc -200 Holleder Pkwy -Rchstr 14615
(718) 366-3440 .. **Parrotta,** Jos M '49 -6106 Myrtle Av -Glendale 11385
(718) 556-9800 .. **Parrotta,** Patrick V '92 -1492 Victory Blvd -Staten Isl 10301 **Fx:**720-1882
(585) 225-3080 .. **Parrs,** Eugene '74 (Parrs & P LLP) -105 Canal Lndng Blvd -Rchstr 14626 **Fx:**225-0459
(212) 657-1361 .. **Parry,** Ann '87 Citigroup Global Mrkts -77 Water -NY 10005
(212) 770-0656 .. **Parry,** Carolyn M '96 %AIG -80 Pine -NY 10005
(212) 373-3000 .. **Parry,** Christine M '10 Paul WRW&G LLP -1285 Av of Amer -NY 10019
(631) 853-4049 .. **Parry,** Cynthia '75 %Cnty Atty -Dennison Bldg Bx6100 -Hauppauge 11788 **Fx:**853-5169
(212) 318-6000 .. **Parry,** Danl T '04 %Paul HJ&W LLP -75 E 55th -NY 10022
(315) 424-6115 .. **Parry,** Jeffrey R '95 -120 E Wshngtn -Syracuse 13202 **Fx:**234-5774
(607) 778-2423 .. **Parry,** Joann R '80 %DA -45 Hawley Bx1766 -Bnghmtn 13902 **Fx:**778-8870
(315) 337-3450 .. **Parry,** Kurt D '94 -410 W Court -Rome 13440 **Fx:**337-0813
(212) 554-7800 .. **Parry,** Mark N '83 (Moses & S LLP) -405 Lex Av -NY 10174
(516) 869-7210 .. **Parry,** Michl E '76 %Kimco Realty Corp -3333 New Hyde Pk Rd -New Hyde Pk 11042 **Fx:**869-7201
(212) 574-1200 .. **Parsadaian,** Christine L '07 %Seward & K LLP -1 Bttry Pk Plz -NY 10004
(516) 488-2828 .. **Parsard,** Keston O '03 -398 Penn Av -Floral Pk 11001
(212) 483-9490 .. **Parsells,** George H III '89 (McElroy DM&C,LLP) -88 Pine -NY 10005
(212) 336-3500 .. **Parsels,** Amanda F '08 %Miller & W,PC -570 Lex Av -NY 10022
(518) 296-8844 .. **Parshall,** Marvin D '60 (Parshall & W) -2668 State Route 7 -Cobleskill 12043
(607) 397-8062 .. **Parshall,** Marvin D '60 (Parshall & W) -153 Main Bx276 -Worcester 12197
(607) 397-8062 .. **Parshall,** Marvin D Jr. '91 (Parshall & W) -153 Main Bx276 -Worcester 12197
(518) 296-8844 .. **Parshall,** Marvin D Jr. '91 (Parshall & W) -2668 State Route 7 -Cobleskill 12043
(607) 397-8062 .. **Parshall & West** -153 Main Bx276 -Worcester 12197 **Fx:**397-8773
(518) 296-8844 .. **Parshall & West** -2668 State Route 7 -Cobleskill 12043
(212) 617-4431 .. **Parsio,** Anthony F '08 %Bloomberg LP -731 Lex Av -NY 10022
(212) 962-2877 .. **Parsley,** Monica L '06 %M Friedlander -15 Maiden Ln -NY 10038 **Fx:**571-4613
(212) 421-4100 .. **Parsly,** David E '08 %Pryor C LLP -7 Times Sq -NY 10036
(212) 308-0210 .. **Parsoff,** Carlie E '04 %C Kutner,LLP -110 E 59th -NY 10022 **Fx:**308-0213
(631) 777-3200 .. **Parsoff,** Neil M '75 (N Parsoff & Assoc,PC) -425 Broad Hollow Rd -Melvll 11747 **Fx:**777-3204
(212) 483-2323 .. **Parson,** Chadwick S '96 %JP Morgan Chase -345 Park Av -NY 10154
(718) 286-6000 .. **Parson,** Lauren R '06 %DA -125-01 Qns Blvd -Kew Gdns 11415
(631) 853-4161 .. **Parson,** Ming Liu '90 %DA -N Cnty Cmplx Bldg 77 -Hauppauge 11788 **Fx:**853-4192
(607) 734-2271 .. **Parsons,** Alan '56 OfCnsl Sayles & E -1 W Church -Elmira 14901
(212) 969-3000 .. **Parsons,** Chas H '99 (Proskauer R LLP) -1585 Bway -NY 10036
(212) 596-9000 .. **Parsons,** Christopher B '04 %Ropes & G LLP -1211 Av of Amer -NY 10036
(212) 757-8438 .. **Parsons,** Justin D '05 Levitt & N,PC -250 W 57th -NY 10107
(212) 218-2100 .. **Parsons,** Michl S '09 %Fitzpatrick CH&S -1290 Av of Amer -NY 10104
(212) 450-4000 .. **Parsons,** Wm Jr. '68 SrCnsl Davis P&W LLP -450 Lex Av -NY 10017
(212) 558-4000 .. **Parsont,** Jason W '08 %Sullivan & C LLP -125 Broad -NY 10004
(716) 674-1590 .. **Partacz,** James A '81 -3890 Seneca -W Seneca 14224 **Fx:**674-1591
(212) 259-8000 .. **Partain,** Rachel L '04 %Dewey & L LLP -1301 Av of Amer -NY 10019
(212) 309-1000 .. **Partee,** Peter S Sr. '07 (Hunton & W) -200 Park Av -NY 10166
(212) 808-2700 .. **Parten,** Michelle M '07 %Pepper H LLP -620 8th Av -NY 10018
(212) 867-1717 .. **Parter,** Alan S '69 (Parter Intl, Inc) -286 Mad Av -NY 10017 **Fx:**541-5934
(914) 834-0895 .. **Parter,** Alan S '69 -51 Circle Av -Larchmnt 10538 **Fx:**(212) 541-5934
(212) 788-0713 .. **Parthasarathy,** Madhu '09 %Law Dept -100 Church -NY 10007 **Fx:**788-0367

(716) 645-3616 .. **Parthasarathy,** Remla '95 %SUNY Buffalo Lw Schl -O'Brian Hall -Buffalo 14260 **Fx:**645-5968
(716) 858-2424 .. **Partridge,** Eugene T '08 %DA -25 Delaware Av -Buffalo 14202 **Fx:**858-7425
(914) 250-2400 .. **Partridge,** Jean M '87 Cnsl Benchmark Title -222 Bloomingdale Rd -White Plns 10605 **Fx:**422-1500
(518) 842-5640 .. **Partyka,** Fredk A II '78 -5 Hibbard -Amsterdam 12010 **Fx:**842-5640
(631) 761-0800 .. **Parvaneh,** Maryam '09 %Lazer AR&Y,PC -225 Old Cntry Rd -Melvll 11747
(212) 764-4222 .. **Parvatiyar,** Survi '05 %S Jeffries & Assoc -1560 Bway -NY 10036 **Fx:**764-4229
(212) 213-5800 .. **Parver,** James F '67 Cnsl Margolis & T LLP -280 Mad Av -NY 10016
(212) 836-8000 .. **Parver,** Jane W '74 (Kaye S LLP) -425 Park Av -NY 10022
(212) 218-2100 .. **Parvulescu,** Monica C '10 %Fitzpatrick CH&S -1290 Av of Amer -NY 10104
(212) 629-9400 .. **Parwani,** Vidya '07 %Yaskhi IC&R LLP -315 5th Av -NY 10016
(718) 410-3430 .. **Parziale,** Roberta A '99 Bronx Schl for Law -244 E 163rd -Bronx 10451
(212) 506-5000 .. **Pasacreta,** Amy G '00 %Orrick H&S LLP -51 W 52nd -NY 10019
(718) 876-6300 .. **Pasacreta,** Rick J '95 DA -130 Styvsnt Pl -Staten Isl 10301
(718) 391-1724 .. **Pasagiannis,** Efithia '04 NYC Dept of Design & Construction -3030 Thomson Av -LIC 11101
(631) 369-1700 .. **Pasca,** Anthony C '96 (Esseks H&A,LLP) -108 E Main Bx279 -Rvrhead 11901
(716) 856-4000 .. **Pascal,** Elizabeth '09 %Hodgson R LLP -140 Pearl -Buffalo 14202
(212) 532-7354 .. **Pascal,** Stephen C '69 -222 E 35th -NY 10016 **Fx:**532-7354
(516) 741-6800 .. **Pascale,** Brian C '06 %K Ready & Assoc -1565 Franklin Av -Mineola 11501
(718) 590-2000 .. **Pascale,** Danielle A '02 %DA -198 E 161st -Bronx 10451 **Fx:**590-6477
(212) 530-5000 .. **Pascale,** James V III '03 %Milbank TH&M LLP -1 Chase Manh Plz -NY 10005
(212) 451-2900 .. **Pascale,** Jeffrey '05 %Robinson & C LLP -885 3rd Av -NY 10022
(845) 565-1100 .. **Pascale,** Nicholas A '03 %Tarshis CLM&M,PLLC -One Corwin Ct -Newburgh 12550
(718) 967-1600 .. **Pascarella,** Ann Marie M '00 %J D'Agostino & Assoc -3309 Richmond Av -Staten Isl 10312 **Fx:**967-8677
(516) 227-0700 .. **Pascarella,** Darren A '03 %Farrell F,PC -1320 RXR Plz -Uniondale 11556
(518) 452-5600 .. **Pascarella,** David A '92 %Heslin RF&M PC -5 Columbia Cir -Albany 12203
(718) 448-1544 .. **Pascarella,** David A '00 Legal Advocacy Prog -100 Park Av -Staten Isl 10302
(516) 741-3476 .. **Pascarella,** James A '02 -1551 Franklin Av -Mineola 11501
(212) 669-7598 .. **Pascariu,** Corinne E '00 NYC Comptrollers Ofc -1 Centre -NY 10007
(914) 245-7000 .. **Paschkes,** Danl S '88 -1929 Commerce -Yorktwn Hts 10598 **Fx:**245-7075
(212) 446-4800 .. **Paschoal,** Carolina H '07 %Kirkland & E LLP -153 E 53rd -NY 10022
(212) 521-4430 .. **Pascoe,** Danl L '05 %Becker M LLC -590 Mad Av -NY 10022
(646) 610-6425 .. **Pascucci,** Michl '87 %NYPD -1 Police Plz -NY 10038
(315) 218-8000 .. **Pascucci,** Raymond J '88 (Bond S&K,PLLC) -1 Lincoln Ctr -Syracuse 13202
(516) 487-0052 .. **Pascucci,** Robt M '80 -277 Nrthrn Blvd -Gt Neck 11021
(631) 665-7400 .. **Pasculli,** Felicia '94 (F Pasculli,PC) -1 E Main -Bay Shr 11706 **Fx:**665-9262
(516) 746-8000 .. **Paseltiner,** David E '88 (Jaspan S LLP) -300 Grdn City Plz -Gdn Cty 11530
(212) 249-2718 .. **Pasewark,** Kyle A '02 Advise-in Solutions -1562 1st Av -NY 10028
(212) 670-0345 .. **Pash,** Jos J Jr. '86 SrCnsl Merrill Lynch -222 Bway -NY 10038 **Fx:**670-4521
(631) 351-1047 .. **Pashkin,** Mitchell L '92 -25 Harriet Ln -Huntngtn 11743 **Fx:**824-9328
(212) 207-6771 .. **Pashkoff,** Lisa '91 (Massoud & P,LLP) -99 Park Av -NY 10016 **Fx:**207-6774
(212) 455-2000 .. **Pashler,** Bryce A '05 %Simpson T&B LLP -425 Lex Av -NY 10017
(646) 442-6688 .. **Pashman,** David J '98 Meetup Inc -632 Bway -NY 10012
(212) 479-6000 .. **Pashman,** Scott J '01 %Cooley LLP -1114 Av of Amer -NY 10036
(212) 558-4000 .. **Pasini,** Lawr A '88 SpclCnsl Sullivan & C LLP -125 Broad -NY 10004
(212) 332-3334 .. **Pasinkoff,** Eric M '78 -260 Mad Av -NY 10016 **Fx:**486-7064
(718) 590-6026 .. **Paska,** Christine M '09 %Law Dept -900 Sheridan Av -Bronx 10451 **Fx:**590-2699
(212) 819-8200 .. **Paskal,** Ivan '09 %White & C LLP -1155 Av of Amer -NY 10036
(212) 474-1000 .. **Paskin,** Michl A '96 (Cravath S&M LLP) -825 8th Av -NY 10019
(212) 643-5454 .. **Paskoff,** Adam '92 (Paskoff & T) -225 W 34th -NY 10122
(212) 643-5454 .. **Paskoff & Tamber** -225 W 34th -NY 10122 **Fx:**643-2346
(212) 685-0969 .. **Paskowitz,** Laurence D '84 (Paskowitz & Assoc) -60 E 42nd -NY 10165 **Fx:**685-2306
(716) 852-8188 .. **Paskowitz,** Michl '75 -403 Main -Buffalo 14203 **Fx:**608-1313
(212) 839-5300 .. **Paskowitz,** Thos A '06 %Sidley A LLP -787 7th Av -NY 10019
(518) 443-5400 .. **Pasley,** Carolyn '77 %SUNY Univ Cnsl -S333 SUNY Plz -Albany 12246 **Fx:**443-5409
(212) 225-2000 .. **Pasniewski,** Justine '06 %Cleary GS&H -1 Lbrty Plz -NY 10006
(212) 216-6645 .. **Pasnik,** Michl James '95 UnitedHealthcare -One Penn Plz -NY 10119
(518) 481-1544 .. **Pasqua,** Gary M '07 %DA -Ct Hse -Malone 12953 **Fx:**481-1545
(845) 462-0001 .. **Pasquale,** Conrad '09 %Serino M&B,PLLC -12 Walker Rd -Poughkeepsie 12603
(516) 431-6744 .. **Pasquale,** John J '67 -86 Lynbrook Av Bx747 -Point Lookout 11569 **Fx:**431-6744
(212) 806-5400 .. **Pasquale,** Kenneth '90 (Stroock &S&L LLP) -180 Maiden Ln -NY 10038
(315) 334-4600 .. **Pasqualetti,** Gerald J '07 -312 N James -Rome 13440
(914) 400-6567 .. **Pasquantonio,** Anthony '56 -915 Wynnenwood Rd Bx327 -Pelham Mnr 10803 **Fx:**813-0004
(914) 632-6990 .. **Pasquantonio,** Jennifer A '91 -201 Wolfs Ln -Pelham 10803 **Fx:**632-8560
(516) 622-0099 .. **Pasquariello,** Antonio '00 (Carlinsky D&P,PLLC) -8 Duffy Av -Hicksvll 11801
(518) 689-0323 .. **Pasquariello,** Arthur A '72 (Pasquariello,LLP) -One Marcus Blvd -Albany 12205 **Fx:**689-0329
(212) 770-2326 .. **Pasquerella,** Anna '97 %AIG -80 Pine -NY 10005
(212) 858-4163 .. **Pasquerella,** Jeffrey M '97 FINRA -1 Lbrty Plz -NY 10006
(212) 558-4000 .. **Pasricha,** Anshu '08 %Sullivan & C LLP -125 Broad -NY 10004
(212) 268-2920 .. **Pasricha,** Gary S '95 OfCnsl Chatrath Law Firm,PC -494 8th Av -NY 10001 **Fx:**268-2921
(212) 806-5400 .. **Pass,** Jennifer L '10 %Stroock &S&L LLP -180 Maiden Ln -NY 10038
(212) 532-8100 .. **Pass,** Robin K '08 %Stern & M,LLP -115 Bway -NY 10006
(716) 366-3677 .. **Passafaro,** Jeffrey G '78 (Foley F&P) -93-95 E 4th Bx50 -Dunkirk 14048
(716) 853-9555 .. **Passafiume,** Frank R '09 Leg Aid -237 Main -Buffalo 14203 **Fx:**853-3219
(212) 278-1328 .. **Passannante,** Wm G '90 (Anderson K&O,PC) -1251 Av of Amer -NY 10020
(631) 321-8500 .. **Passarelli,** Robt J '82 (R Passarelli & Assoc) -One John -Babylon 11702 **Fx:**321-8591
(646) 654-8322 .. **Passarello,** Darya M '98 %Nielsen Media Research,Inc -770 Bway -NY 10003
(718) 987-1100 .. **Passarello,** John A Jr. '74 (Passarello & L) -94 Lincoln Av -Staten Isl 10306
(718) 987-1100 .. **Passarello & LaRosa** -94 Lincoln Av -Staten Isl 10306 **Fx:**667-8936
(212) 261-8000 .. **Passarello,** Pamela M '07 %Mendes & M,LLP -750 7th Av -NY 10019
(518) 833-1300 .. **Passaretti,** Linda J '96 Emma Willard Schl -285 Pawling Av -Troy 12180
(212) 735-3000 .. **Passaretti-Wu,** Rachel B '02 %Skadden ASM&F LLP -4 Times Sq -NY 10036
(212) 481-5555 .. **Passe,** Michl D '73 -18 E 41st -NY 10017 **Fx:**981-1790
(212) 558-4000 .. **Passer,** Alison L '08 %Sullivan & C LLP -125 Broad -NY 10004
(718) 625-2300 .. **Passer,** Noah H '08 Severance B&S,PC -16 Court -Brklyn 11241
(585) 325-1410 .. **Passero,** Ronald J '60 -45 Exchange Blvd -Rchstr 14614 **Fx:**325-1426
(516) 705-0100 .. **Passet,** Michl S '77 -1728 Sunrise Hwy -Merrick 11566 **Fx:**536-2501
(212) 558-4000 .. **Passey,** David J '00 %Sullivan & C LLP -125 Broad -NY 10004
(646) 386-5151 .. **Passidomo,** Peter J '87 %Family Ct -60 Lafayette -NY 10013
(212) 819-1212 .. **Passin,** Allan '50 -36 W 44th -NY 10036 **Fx:**827-0120
(845) 357-1071 .. **Passman,** Eugene Alan '75 -222 Route 59 -Suffern 10901 **Fx:**357-4574
(212) 935-3000 .. **Passner,** Jonathan M '07 %Mintz LCFG&P,PC -666 3rd Av -NY 10017
(212) 233-0400 .. **Passonneau,** Polly N '86 (P Passonneau,PC) -20 Vesey -NY 10007 **Fx:**964-2926
(212) 225-2000 .. **Passos,** Carla Raynal '01 %Cleary GS&H -1 Lbrty Plz -NY 10006
(516) 742-0101 .. **Pasta Needham & Taylor** -436 Willis Av -Williston Pk 11596
(212) 728-8000 .. **Pastakia,** Ketan '08 %Willkie F&G LLP -787 7th Av -NY 10019
(212) 715-9100 .. **Pastarnack,** Jennifer B '08 %Kramer LN&F,LLP -1177 Av of Amer -NY 10036
(607) 277-5907 .. **Pastel,** Christopher R '90 -8 Perry Ln -Ithaca 14850 **Fx:**697-0432
(518) 462-4715 .. **Pastel,** Robt S '85 (Pastel & R) -130 Wshngtn Av -Albany 12210 **Fx:**462-4756
(646) 337-7700 .. **Paster,** Darrell L '76 -321 W 89th -NY 10024 **Fx:**304-2862
(212) 868-6300 .. **Paster,** Rachel S '01 %Cary K LLP -1350 Bway -NY 10018
(212) 691-4283 .. **Paster-Michtom,** Paula L '74 %Michtom Cellars -32 Bethune -NY 10014
(212) 551-0728 .. **Pasternack,** Beth I '84 NY Marine & Gen Ins -919 3rd Av -NY 10022
(718) 281-8924 .. **Pasternack,** Michl P '93 St Marys Hsptl for Chldrn -29-01 216th -Bayside 11360
(516) 742-3636 .. **Pasternack,** Victor '76 (Brecher FPWT&Z,PC) -1325 Franklin Av -Gdn Cty 11530
(718) 875-7545 .. **Pasternak,** David S '81 -26 Court -Brklyn 11242
(914) 381-7400 .. **Pasternak,** Jonathan S '90 (Rattet P&G,LLP) -550 Mamaroneck Av -Harrison 10528
(212) 688-5151 .. **Pasternak,** Laura A '10 %Gibney A&F,LLP -665 5th Av -NY 10022
(212) 421-4100 .. **Pasternak,** Rachel J '07 %Pryor C LLP -7 Times Sq -NY 10036
(212) 596-9000 .. **Pastor,** Anthony A '01 %Ropes & G LLP -1211 Av of Amer -NY 10036
(212) 455-2000 .. **Pastor,** Louis J '10 %Simpson T&B LLP -425 Lex Av -NY 10017
(212) 297-6121 .. **Pastor,** Max B '04 -420 Lex Av -NY 10170
(212) 788-0756 .. **Pastor,** Michl J '03 %Law Dept -100 Church -NY 10007 **Fx:**788-0367
(212) 609-6800 .. **Pastor,** Sherilyn '89 (McCarter & E,LLP) -245 Park Av -NY 10167
(212) 637-2418 .. **Pastore,** James J Jr. '05 %US Atty -1 St Andrews Plz -NY 10007
(518) 383-5300 .. **Pastore,** John P '69 (Pentkowski P&F) -646 Plnk Rd -Clifton Pk 12065
(212) 418-8600 .. **Pastore,** Mariana C '03 %Kornstein VW&P,LLP -757 3rd Av -NY 10017
(518) 447-3200 .. **Pastore,** Paul C '91 (McNamee LT&W,PC) -677 Bway -Albany 12207
(518) 447-3200 .. **Pastore,** Peter A '81 (McNamee LT&W,PC) -677 Bway -Albany 12207
(212) 883-1700 .. **Pastore,** Timothy J '97 (Duval & S LLP) -101 Park Av -NY 10178
(212) 489-1400 .. **Pastrikos,** Catherine M '05 %Bickel & B -767 5th Av -NY 10153
(212) 805-3900 .. **Pastuszak,** Mark J '00 %Clausen M PC -1 Chase Manh Plz -NY 10005
(212) 751-3001 .. **Pasupulati,** Murali K '05 %Thompson & K LLP -919 3rd Av -NY 10022
(646) 386-5700 .. **Paszkowska,** Catherine '01 %Civil Ct -111 Centre -NY 10013
(212) 269-6000 .. **Paszynsky,** Salvatore M '00 Paszynsky Assoc,PC -110 Wall -NY 10005 **Fx:**937-5271
(516) 742-3662 .. **Patacca,** Paul '86 (Patacca & Assoc) -392 Hillside Av -Williston Pk 11596 **Fx:**742-5767
(631) 691-4000 .. **Patafio,** John T '90 J Patafio,PC -171 Park Av -Amityvll 11701 **Fx:**691-1715
(212) 408-5100 .. **Pataki,** George E '72 Cnsl Chadbourne & P LLP -30 Rckfllr Plz -NY 10112
(212) 762-5553 .. **Patalino,** Patrick M '01 Morgan Stanley -1221 Av of Amer -NY 10020

(315) 697-2288 .. **Patane,** John A '68 OfCnsl Taylor & M LLP -133 S Peterboro -Canastota 13032 **Fx:**697-8428
(212) 837-6275 .. **Patchen,** Alex G '04 Hughes H&R LLP -1 Bttry Pk Plz -NY 10004 **Fx:**299-8375
(212) 340-0400 .. **Patchen,** Robt J '94 %Appllt Div 1st Dept -27 Mad Av -NY 10010 **Fx:**889-4412
(914) 834-0747 .. **Patchen,** Stanley D '56 -14 N Chatsworth Av -Larchmnt 10538 **Fx:**630-0444
(212) 345-6000 .. **Patchke,** Carl W '92 %Marsh USA -1166 Av of Amer -NY 10036 **Fx:**345-4808
(212) 784-5800 .. **Patel,** Alpa Vinodchandra '05 %Hiscock & B,LLP -7 Times Sq -NY 10036
(212) 349-0230 .. **Patel,** Andrew G '82 -111 Bway -NY 10006 **Fx:**346-4665
(212) 836-8000 .. **Patel,** Ankan S '07 %Kaye S LLP -425 Park Av -NY 10022
(212) 809-1866 .. **Patel,** Chandra R '93 -Bx3335 -NY 10008
(212) 286-8585 .. **Patel,** Darshan I '98 (Heidell PM&B,LLP) -99 Park Av -NY 10016
(212) 302-6574 .. **Patel,** Dilip B '97 Cnsl Riker DSH&P LLP -500 5th Av -NY 10110
(646) 386-5700 .. **Patel,** Hemalee J '92 %Civil Ct -111 Centre -NY 10013
(212) 558-4000 .. **Patel,** Henrik P '02 %Sullivan & C LLP -125 Broad -NY 10004
(212) 381-7000 .. **Patel,** Ketul A '07 %Sabin B&G LLP -4 Times Sq -NY 10036
(212) 230-8800 .. **Patel,** Lipi M '10 %WilmerHale -399 Park Av -NY 10022
(212) 259-8000 .. **Patel,** Mayur Rajendra '05 %Dewey & L LLP -1301 Av of Amer -NY 10019
(585) 419-8800 .. **Patel,** Munesh '03 (Harris B PLLC) -99 Garnsey Rd -Pittsfrd 14534
(212) 859-8000 .. **Patel,** Naitik '10 %Fried FHS&J LLP -1 NY Plz -NY 10004
(212) 848-4000 .. **Patel,** Neeraj N '05 %Shearman & S LLP -599 Lex Av -NY 10022
(212) 325-2225 .. **Patel,** Neha F '02 Credit Suisse -11 Mad Av -NY 10010
(212) 279-3230 .. **Patel,** Pravinchandra J '79 (P Patel,PC) -1270 Bway -NY 10001 **Fx:**279-3280
(212) 735-3000 .. **Patel,** Priya D '10 %Skadden ASM&F LLP -4 Times Sq -NY 10036
(718) 286-6000 .. **Patel,** Purvi '03 %DA -125-01 Qns Blvd -Kew Gdns 11415
(212) 504-6000 .. **Patel,** Rajal B '07 %Cadwalader W&T LLP -1 World Fncl Ctr -NY 10281
(845) 735-2323 .. **Patel,** Rajan '95 -1 Blue Hill Plz Bx1566 -Pearl Rvr 10965 **Fx:**818-3698
(718) 767-7667 .. **Patel,** Riddhi S '10 OfCnsl T Ombres LLC -38-39 Bell Blvd -Bayside 11361 **Fx:**767-5488
(212) 482-0001 .. **Patel,** Rima C '08 %Russo K&T LLP -33 Whitehall -NY 10004
(212) 574-1200 .. **Patel,** Sagar J '10 %Seward & K LLP -1 Bttry Pk Plz -NY 10004
(212) 629-8585 .. **Patel,** Samir B '08 %Ellenberg & Prtnrs LLP -575 8th Av -NY 10018
(212) 902-0927 .. **Patel,** Sandeep Harji '02 Goldman Sachs & Co -85 Broad -NY 10004
(212) 761-0004 .. **Patel,** Sapna C '07 %Morgan Stanley -1585 Bway -NY 10036
(646) 602-5600 .. **Patel,** Sapna K '03 Urban Justice Ctr -123 William -NY 10038 **Fx:**(212) 533-4598
(212) 903-9000 .. **Patel,** Seema N '08 %Linklaters -1345 Av of Amer -NY 10105
(212) 259-8000 .. **Patel,** Sheel A '09 %Dewey & L LLP -1301 Av of Amer -NY 10019
(212) 547-5400 .. **Patel,** Shilpa V '08 %McDermott W&E LLP -340 Mad Av -NY 10173
(212) 335-4500 .. **Patel,** Sonal '02 %DLA Piper LLP -1251 Av of Amer -NY 10020
(212) 450-4000 .. **Patel,** Sonali D '10 %Davis P&W LLP -450 Lex Av -NY 10017
(212) 854-2640 .. **Patel,** T Natasha '01 Columbia Law Career Srvcs -435 William -NY 10027
(212) 909-6000 .. **Patel,** Vipul M '08 %Debevoise & P LLP -919 3rd Av -NY 10022
(212) 458-1526 .. **Patel,** Yera '02 AIG Tech Srvcs -175 Water -NY 10038
(212) 832-2797 .. **Patel,** Yogendra '07 %Shebitz B&C,PC -1325 Av of Amer -NY 10019
(212) 850-2800 .. **Patella,** Jos A '97 %Andrews K LLP -450 Lex Av -NY 10017
(212) 708-9120 .. **Patenaude,** Robt D '03 Bessemer Trst Co -630 5th Av -NY 10111 **Fx:**265-5826
(212) 336-0057 .. **Pater,** Joshua R '06 SEC -3 World Fncl Ctr -NY 10281 **Fx:**336-1323
(212) 733-9778 .. **Pater,** Matthew A '05 Pfizer Inc -150 E 42nd -NY 10017
(516) 488-3300 .. **Paterniti,** John D '97 %Shaub AC&S,LLP -1983 Marcus Av -Lk Success 11042
(212) 513-3200 .. **Paterno,** Adam J '09 %Holland & K LLP -31 W 52nd -NY 10019
(212) 416-8099 .. **Paterno,** Jos '00 %Dept of Law -120 Bway -NY 10271
(914) 921-1200 .. **Paterno,** Randie P '02 OfCnsl Maloof B&E LLC -411 Theo Fremd Av -Rye 10580 **Fx:**921-1023
(212) 986-5300 .. **Paterno,** Sandro S '90 -225 Bway -NY 10007
(212) 770-6920 .. **Paternostro,** Peter J '80 %AIG -70 Pine -NY 10270
(516) 741-6565 .. **Paterson,** Basil A '52 (Meyer SE&K,PC) -990 Stewart Av Bx9194 -Gdn Cty 11530
(212) 373-3000 .. **Paterson,** Paul A '10 %Paul WRW&G LLP -1285 Av of Amer -NY 10019
(212) 335-9000 .. **Pathak,** Rachana '05 %DA -1 Hogan Pl -NY 10013
(516) 931-3533 .. **Paticoff,** Sheila R '85 -167 High Pond Dr -Jericho 11753 **Fx:**931-3533
(516) 222-0099 .. **Patigalia,** Michl A '99 %Stanton & G,LLP -585 Stewart Av -Gdn Cty 11530 **Fx:**222-0079
(212) 733-1743 .. **Patil,** Neena M '01 Pfizer Inc -150 E 42nd -NY 10017
(212) 574-1200 .. **Patin,** Anne Cottrell '95 (Seward & K LLP) -1 Bttry Pk Plz -NY 10004
(212) 269-1600 .. **Patino,** Ryan '07 %Teigland-Hunt LLP -127 W 24th -NY 10011 **Fx:**269-1580
(212) 417-8300 .. **Patitucci,** Wendy E '88 %Research Fndtn CUNY -230 W 41st -NY 10036 **Fx:**417-8379
(518) 356-6000 .. **Patka,** Carl F '90 NYISO -10 Krey Blvd -Rensselaer 12144 **Fx:**356-6118
(518) 387-5286 .. **Patnode,** Patrick K '96 GE -1 Rsrch Cir -Schnctdy 12309 **Fx:**387-7751
(518) 561-5460 .. **Patnode,** Susan L '91 %Rural Law Ctr of NY, Inc -22 US Oval -Plattsbrgh 12903 **Fx:**561-5468
(212) 909-6000 .. **Patnode,** Terrianne M '05 %Debevoise & P LLP -919 3rd Av -NY 10022
(518) 447-3200 .. **Paton,** Scott C '95 (McNamee LT&W,PC) -677 Bway -Albany 12207
(212) 213-2326 .. **Patouris,** Nicholas '86 -1350 Bway -NY 10018 **Fx:**643-1882
(212) 921-8399 .. **Patrice,** Jos A '02 %Lankler S&W LLP -500 5th Av -NY 10110
(716) 856-1344 .. **Patricia,** Kenneth A '81 SpclCnsl Bouvier Prtnrshp,LLP -350 Main -Buffalo 14202 **Fx:**856-1369
(212) 651-1722 .. **Patrick,** Andrew D '00 D Patrick Law,PLLC -29 E 19th -NY 10003
(212) 788-1575 .. **Patrick,** Bradford C '08 %Law Dept -100 Church -NY 10007 **Fx:**788-0367
(212) 787-3351 .. **Patrick,** Bruce D '85 -127 W 80th -NY 10024
(516) 944-8973 .. **Patrick,** Casimir C II '67 -18 Bogart Av -Pt Wash 11050 **Fx:**767-3795
(607) 776-9631 .. **Patrick,** Craig A '07 %Cnty Atty -3 E Pulteney Sq -Bath 14810 **Fx:**776-4930
(518) 427-9700 .. **Patrick,** Harrie C III '73 (Harris B PLLC) -677 Bway -Albany 12207
(585) 232-6500 .. **Patrick,** Jessica Myers '09 %Harter S&E LLP -1600 Bausch & Lomb Pl -Rchstr 14604
(212) 688-8555 .. **Patrick,** Michl D '79 (Fragomen DB&L LLP) -7 Hanover Sq -NY 10004
(914) 285-0700 .. **Patrick,** Michl R '05 %Renzulli Law Firm,LLP -81 Main -White Plns 10601 **Fx:**285-1213
(212) 720-5026 .. **Patrick,** Michl Rhein '00 Fed Reserve Bk -33 Lbrty -NY 10045 **Fx:**785-5748
(212) 869-8500 .. **Patrick,** Shari L '83 Rockefeller Fndtn -420 5th Av -NY 10018 **Fx:**852-8203
(212) 669-2525 .. **Patricof,** Rochelle Weinstein '87 %Dept Finance -1 Centre -NY 10007
(212) 819-8200 .. **Patrikis,** Ernest T '69 (White & C LLP) -1155 Av of Amer -NY 10036
(914) 328-8844 .. **Patrissi,** Jennifer C '02 %Meagher & M -175 Main -White Plns 10601 **Fx:**328-8570
(845) 291-2454 .. **Patrizio,** Maria Ann '96 %Leg Aid -2 Court Ln Bx328 -Goshen 10924 **Fx:**294-2638
(212) 530-5000 .. **Patron,** Raisa E '09 %Milbank TH&M LLP -1 Chase Manh Plz -NY 10005
(845) 457-1131 .. **Patruno,** Frank S '96 -79 W Corbett Rd -Montgmry 12549
(212) 375-6702 .. **Patrusky,** Bernard '62 Weiser,LLP -135 W 50th -NY 10020 **Fx:**375-6888
(212) 565-0000 .. **Patry,** Wm F '01 Google Inc -76 9th Av -NY 10011 **Fx:**565-0001
(212) 837-6000 .. **Patryk,** Robb W '90 (Hughes H&R LLP) -1 Bttry Pk Plz -NY 10004
(845) 291-2581 .. **Patsalos,** Jeanne M '91 Support Magistrate -285 Main -Goshen 10924
(631) 225-4601 .. **Patsis,** George E '00 G Patsis,PLLC -152 N Wellwood Av -Lindenhrst 11757 **Fx:**225-4602
(212) 940-8800 .. **Patsos,** Catherine G '00 SpclCnsl Katten MR LLP -575 Mad Av -NY 10022
(212) 949-8080 .. **Patsos,** Christopher J '83 -122 E 42nd -NY 10168 **Fx:**949-9088
(212) 715-9100 .. **Patt,** Eileen M '09 %Kramer LN&F,LLP -1177 Av of Amer -NY 10036
(212) 701-3000 .. **Patt,** Jennifer A '08 %Cahill G&R LLP -80 Pine -NY 10005 **Fx:**269-5420
(212) 725-2967 .. **Patt,** Raymond M '39 -136 E 39th -NY 10016 **Fx:**684-6327
(212) 490-0400 .. **Pattarozzi,** Joani '09 %Beldock L&H LLP -99 Park Av -NY 10016
(607) 589-4232 .. **Patte,** George D Jr. '76 -140 N Main -Spencer 14883
(607) 272-3484 .. **Patte,** George D Jr. '76 -121 E Buffalo Bx174 -Ithaca 14851 **Fx:**277-2112
(212) 408-5100 .. **Patten,** Jeffrey W T '01 %Chadbourne & P LLP -30 Rckfllr Plz -NY 10112
(212) 962-1295 .. **Patten,** John D '70 -30 Vesey -NY 10007
(518) 435-1770 .. **Pattenaude,** Susan S '86 %The Legal Project -6 Exec Park Dr -Albany 12203 **Fx:**435-1773
(212) 564-7560 .. **Patterson,** Abigail Burns '08 S Klein -99 Mad Av -NY 10016 **Fx:**564-7845
(585) 383-8521 .. **Patterson,** Ann L '87 -27 Winding Rd -Rchstr 14618
(212) 336-2000 .. **Patterson Belknap Webb & Tyler LLP** -1133 Av of Amer -NY 10036 **Fx:**336-2222
(212) 682-6800 .. **Patterson,** Carol J '82 (Zetlin & D LLP) -801 2nd Av -NY 10017
(718) 466-3000 .. **Patterson,** Chas T '87 %Civil Ct -1118 Grnd Cncrs -Bronx 10456 **Fx:**466-3006
(212) 267-6364 .. **Patterson,** David J '81 OfCnsl Kossoff & U -217 Bway -NY 10007
(212) 396-9752 .. **Patterson,** David S '62 -165 E 65th -NY 10065
(212) 455-2000 .. **Patterson,** Ellen R '99 (Simpson T&B LLP) -425 Lex Av -NY 10017
(718) 250-2000 .. **Patterson,** Enetra H '03 %DA -350 Jay -Brklyn 11201 **Fx:**250-2314
(914) 448-0200 .. **Patterson,** Gary W Jr. '00 %Bartlett MB&M,LLP -81 Main -White Plns 10601
(212) 836-8000 .. **Patterson,** Jennifer B '95 (Kaye S LLP) -425 Park Av -NY 10022
(718) 428-4949 .. **Patterson,** Jerome D '92 (Kim P&S,PC) -42-40 Bell Blvd -Bayside 11361 **Fx:**428-1316
(518) 854-7250 .. **Patterson,** John R Jr. '76 -190 Main Bx427 -Salem 12865 **Fx:**854-9641
(646) 502-7001 .. **Patterson,** Kendrick P '06 (JSBarkats PLLC) -100 Church -NY 10007 **Fx:**607-5544
(718) 248-2506 .. **Patterson,** Kevin '87 %Citibank -1 Court Sq -LIC 11101
(212) 351-4000 .. **Patterson,** Krista L '07 %Gibson D&C LLP -200 Park Av -NY 10166
(315) 488-0044 .. **Patterson,** Larry '88 %Heritage -2103 Milton Av -Syracuse 13209
(212) 430-5400 .. **Patterson,** Maria M '83 SrCnsl Diamond M LLP -620 8th Av -NY 10018
(212) 464-2565 .. **Patterson,** Michl E '68 JP Morgan Chase & Co -345 Park Av -NY 10154
(716) 853-9555 .. **Patterson,** Nadine E '04 %Leg Aid -237 Main -Buffalo 14203 **Fx:**853-3219
(212) 640-3463 .. **Patterson,** Patricia A '74 %Amer Exp -200 Vesey -NY 10285
(212) 768-1000 .. **Patterson,** Philip C '02 %De Feis O&R,PC -500 5th Av -NY 10110
(212) 878-8000 .. **Patterson,** Rachael M '08 %Clifford C LLP -31 W 52nd -NY 10019
(716) 856-0600 .. **Patterson,** Robt W '84 (Jaeckle F&M,LLP) -12 Fountain Plz -Buffalo 14202
(212) 279-9090 .. **Patterson,** Stacey R '00 OfCnsl Stark & S -One Penn Plz -NY 10119 **Fx:**279-9113
(845) 838-6601 .. **Patterson,** Steven K '88 -33 Henry Bx910 -Beacon 12508 **Fx:**831-0744
(518) 398-9857 .. **Patterson,** Steven K '88 -2990 Church Bx21 -Pine Plns 12567 **Fx:**398-5297
(212) 248-3140 .. **Patterson,** Tonia A '09 %Drinker B&R LLP -140 Bway -NY 10005
(212) 909-6000 .. **Patterson,** W Barton '07 %Debevoise & P LLP -919 3rd Av -NY 10022
(914) 287-7374 .. **Patti,** Clement S Jr. '82 -470 Mamaroneck Av -White Plns 10605 **Fx:**287-7384
(212) 504-6000 .. **Patti,** Gregory P Jr. '93 (Cadwalader W&T LLP) -1 World Fncl Ctr -NY 10281
(914) 238-6146 .. **Patti-Cacace,** Palma B '81 -74 Old Lyme Rd -Chappaqua 10514
(518) 424-6392 .. **Pattison,** Brian D '88 -2508 Wstrn Av -Altamont 12009

(914) 220-0038 .. **Pattison & Flannery** -1 N Lex Av -White Plns 10601 **Fx:**220-0039
(585) 232-6500 .. **Pattison,** John T '77 (Harter S&E LLP) -1600 Bausch & Lomb Pl -Rchstr 14604
(518) 266-1000 .. **Pattison Sampson Ginsberg & Griffin,PC** -22 1st Bx208 -Troy 12181 **Fx:**274-6034
(914) 220-0038 .. **Pattison,** Thos R '70 (Pattison & F) -1 N Lex Av -White Plns 10601
(212) 547-5400 .. **Pattiz,** Keith M '78 (McDermott W&E LLP) -340 Mad Av -NY 10173
(212) 680-5150 .. **Patton,** Aaron D '03 %Friedman Law Grp LLP -270 Lafayette -NY 10012
(646) 557-5100 .. **Patton Boggs LLP** -1185 Av of Amer -NY 10036 **Fx:**557-5101
(516) 571-0764 .. **Patton,** Cara Anne '97 %Hon D Sher -400 Cnty Seat Dr -Mineola 11501
(315) 449-2616 .. **Patton,** Chas E '95 Martin GBM&C,PC -5790 Widewaters Pkwy -DeWitt 13214
(212) 474-1000 .. **Patton,** Christopher W '09 %Cravath S&M LLP -825 8th Av -NY 10019
(212) 867-8280 .. **Patton Eakins Lipsett Martin & Savage** -420 Lex Av -NY 10170 **Fx:**370-5637
(516) 431-7309 .. **Patton,** Eileen A '98 -662 W Beech -Long Bch 11561
(212) 867-8280 .. **Patton,** Frank Jr. '56 (Patton ELM&S) -420 Lex Av -NY 10170
(212) 341-6400 .. **Patton,** Kimara I '99 %Liquidation Bur -123 William -NY 10038 **Fx:**608-3398
(212) 762-6639 .. **Patton,** Paul D '90 Morgan Stanley -1221 Av of the Americas -NY 10020
(212) 858-1000 .. **Patton,** Shaileen E '09 %Pillsbury WSP LLP -1540 Bway -NY 10036
(516) 424-1466 .. **Paturi,** Kumar Sri Satya '99 -89 Nottnghm Rd -New Hyde Pk 11040
(516) 535-1700 .. **Patwa,** Ashka S '09 %Horing W&R,PC -11 Hillside Av -Williston Pk 11596
(212) 478-7200 .. **Patwardhan,** Huria S '06 %Hahn & H LLP -488 Mad Av -NY 10022
(518) 473-6107 .. **Patwell,** Patricia J '96 %Insurance Dept -99 Wshngtn Av -Albany 12257 **Fx:**473-5311
(315) 218-8000 .. **Patyi,** Frank J '99 (Bond S&K,PLLC) -1 Lincoln Ctr -Syracuse 13202
(212) 715-9100 .. **Pauer,** Janelle M '95 %Kramer LN&F,LLP -1177 Av of Amer -NY 10036
(347) 529-4604 .. **Pauk,** Edgar '77 -27 8th Av -Brklyn 11217
(212) 849-8843 .. **Pauker,** Stacey E '03 Westbrook Partners -645 Mad Av -NY 10022
(718) 736-4050 .. **Paukman,** Jos '05 -1421 Sheepshead Bay Rd -Brklyn 11235
(212) 819-8200 .. **Paul,** Abraham '05 White & C LLP -1155 Av of Amer -NY 10036
(212) 340-3269 .. **Paul,** Andrew J '86 %Metro-North -345 Mad Av -NY 10017 **Fx:**340-2391
(212) 371-1000 .. **Paul,** Andrew J '90 -1011 1st Av -NY 10022
(212) 667-9300 .. **Paul,** C Robt '81 Nomura Securities Intl -2 World Fncl Ctr -NY 10281
(518) 565-4630 .. **Paul,** Catherine M '90 %Surrogates Ct -137 Margaret -Plattsbrgh 12901 **Fx:**565-4769
(212) 547-5400 .. **Paul,** Christopher H '95 %McDermott W&E LLP -340 Mad Av -NY 10173
(212) 486-2400 .. **Paul,** David A '03 %Leader & B LLP -630 3rd Av -NY 10017
(718) 261-7700 .. **Paul,** David I '83 %Rappaport HC&R,PC -118-35 Qns Blvd -Frst Hlls 11375
(212) 361-7770 .. **Paul,** David S '89 %Dept Consumer Affrs -66 John -NY 10038
(212) 403-1000 .. **Paul,** Deborah L '91 (Wachtell LR&K) -51 W 52nd -NY 10019
(212) 319-2787 .. **Paul,** Elena M '01 VLA -1 E 53rd -NY 10022 **Fx:**752-6575
(212) 412-9500 .. **Paul,** Gerald G '71 (Flemming ZWZ LLP) -1 Lbrty Plz -NY 10006
(505) 983-2794 .. **Paul,** Harold W '76 H Paul,LLC -444 Mad Av -NY 10022
(212) 318-6000 .. **Paul Hastings Janofsky & Walker LLP** -75 E 55th -NY 10022 **Fx:**319-4090
(212) 752-3700 .. **Paul,** Herbert '58 -450 7th Av -NY 10123
(212) 878-8227 .. **Paul,** James W '71 (Clifford C LLP) -31 W 52nd -NY 10019
(212) 702-5400 .. **Paul,** John H '04 %Beveridge & D,PC -477 Mad Av -NY 10022
(718) 250-2000 .. **Paul,** Jonathan A '08 %DA -350 Jay -Brklyn 11201 **Fx:**250-2314
(800) 553-9940 .. **Paul,** Jordan S '08 %Robins KM&C LLP -499 Park Av -NY 10022
(914) 761-1549 .. **Paul,** Joshua '85 -2 Collyer Pl -White Plns 10605
(212) 506-1700 .. **Paul,** Joshua N '09 %Kasowitz BT&F LLP -1633 Bway -NY 10019
(212) 587-8000 .. **Paul,** Kenneth A '74 -111 Bway -NY 10006 **Fx:**374-1506
(716) 667-0061 .. **Paul,** Kim Kenna '80 (Bender & P) -6459 W Quaker -Orchard Pk 14127
(212) 547-5400 .. **Paul,** Kumar S '05 (McDermott W&E LLP) -340 Mad Av -NY 10173
(212) 489-8230 .. **Paul,** Marcia B '73 (Davis WT LLP) -1633 Bway -NY 10019
(212) 318-6000 .. **Paul,** Matthew R '99 %Paul HJ&W LLP -75 E 55th -NY 10022
(212) 815-1818 .. **Paul,** Max J '08 DC 37 MELS -125 Barclay -NY 10007 **Fx:**815-1343
(718) 793-7285 .. **Paul,** Michl '86 -90-11 35th Av -Jcksn Hts 11372 **Fx:**898-0093
(845) 356-0656 .. **Paul,** Michl G '92 -49 Maple Av -New Cty 10956 **Fx:**(732) 906-2344
(212) 632-6000 .. **Paul,** Nathan A '98 %Lazard Freres -30 Rckfllr Plz -NY 10112 **Fx:**632-6060
(718) 222-2330 .. **Paul,** Patricia E '10 %Law Dept -350 Jay -Brklyn 11201 **Fx:**222-2373
(315) 425-2700 .. **Paul,** Richd J '91 (Hiscock & B,LLP) -One Park Pl -Syracuse 13202
(212) 282-2536 .. **Paul,** Robt C '79 %Rockefeller Grp -1221 Av of Amer -NY 10020 **Fx:**282-2005
(212) 552-8847 .. **Paul,** Robt H '61 %JP Morgan Chase & Co -270 Park Av -NY 10017
(518) 863-8090 .. **Paul,** Roger L '78 -363 Cnty Hwy 113 Bx629 -Northvll 12134 **Fx:**863-2041
(212) 885-5000 .. **Paul,** Rustin I '03 %Blank R LLP -405 Lex Av -NY 10174
(212) 735-3000 .. **Paul,** Sarah E '88 OfCnsl Skadden ASM&F LLP -4 Times Sq -NY 10036
(212) 213-6996 .. **Paul,** Sarah E '06 %Spears & I LLP -51 Mad Av -NY 10010
(212) 416-8906 .. **Paul,** Shuva J '09 %Dept of Law -120 Bway -NY 10271
(585) 546-5530 .. **Paul,** Subrata '98 %Thomson West -50 E Broad -Rchstr 14694
(518) 346-8650 .. **Paul,** Sven R '86 -1334 Union -Schnctdy 12308 **Fx:**374-3466
(212) 373-3000 .. **Paul Weiss Rifkind Wharton & Garrison LLP** -1285 Av of Amer -NY 10019 **Fx:**757-3990
(212) 730-7700 .. **Paul,** Wesley J '97 (Michelman & R,LLP) -114 W 47th -NY 10036
(212) 474-1000 .. **Paula-Molina,** Rene '05 %Cravath S&M LLP -825 8th Av -NY 10019
(516) 944-6139 .. **Paulding,** Judith '89 -20 Marwood Rd S -Pt Wash 11050 **Fx:**883-4972
(212) 761-5641 .. **Paule,** Adrienne C '98 Morgan Stanley -1585 Bway -NY 10036
(718) 237-3100 .. **Paule,** Sarah P B '10 Leg Aid -111 Lvngstn -Brklyn 11201 **Fx:**250-4243
(212) 636-6000 .. **Paul-Emile,** Kimani C '97 %Fordham Univ Sch of Law -140 W 62nd -NY 10023 **Fx:**636-6899
(212) 728-8000 .. **Pauley,** Kristin McNamara '07 %Willkie F&G LLP -787 7th Av -NY 10019
(212) 416-8000 .. **Pauley,** Rachel S '01 %Dept of Law -120 Bway -NY 10271
(212) 635-8203 .. **Pauley,** Travis M '97 %BNY Capital Mrkts -1 Wall -NY 10286
(518) 458-2444 .. **Paulino,** Alejandra N '04 %J Long -668 Central Av -Albany 12206 **Fx:**458-2448
(718) 923-4206 .. **Paulino,** Edw '97 %OTDA Fair Hearings -14 Boerum Pl -Brklyn 11201
(585) 454-0700 .. **Paulino,** James M II '08 %Ward GH&R LLP -300 State -Rchstr 14614
(212) 858-1000 .. **Paull,** Davison C '07 %Pillsbury WSP LLP -1540 Bway -NY 10036
(716) 854-4300 .. **Paull,** Joel H '97 OfCnsl Gross SB&G,PC -465 Main -Buffalo 14203
(212) 733-6832 .. **Paulmann,** Fredk H IV '97 %Pfizer Inc -235 E 42nd -NY 10017 **Fx:**573-1824
(718) 370-3464 .. **Paulo,** Catherine M '79 -1140 Victory Blvd -Staten Isl 10301 **Fx:**370-3462
(718) 986-2596 .. **Paulonis,** Michl S '99 -287 Prospect Av -Brklyn 11215 **Fx:**228-3732
(212) 872-1000 .. **Paulos,** Danl J '06 -One Bryant Park -NY 10036 **Fx:**872-1002
(917) 551-1300 .. **Paulose,** Mathew Jr. '99 %Koehler & I LLP -61 Bway -NY 10006
(212) 906-1200 .. **Paulovic,** Stefan '10 %Latham & W -885 3rd Av -NY 10022
(212) 574-1200 .. **Paulsen,** Bruce G '86 (Seward & K LLP) -1 Bttry Pk Plz -NY 10004
(315) 785-3088 .. **Paulsen,** David J '90 %Cnty Atty -175 Arsenal -Watertwn 13601 **Fx:**785-5178
(212) 450-4000 .. **Paulsen,** Erik D '08 %Davis P&W LLP -450 Lex Av -NY 10017
(212) 788-1362 .. **Paulson,** Susan '04 Law Dept -100 Church -NY 10007 **Fx:**788-0367
(212) 998-6316 .. **Paulus-Jagric,** Deborah K '95 %NYU Law Schl -40 Wshngtn Sq S -NY 10012 **Fx:**995-3477
(716) 856-4000 .. **Pauly,** Dylan A '05 %Hodgson R LLP -140 Pearl -Buffalo 14202
(212) 715-9100 .. **Paupeck,** Gabrielle A '03 %Kramer LN&F,LLP -1177 Av of Amer -NY 10036
(518) 474-6400 .. **Paupini,** Sara E '04 %Dept of Ed -89 Wshngtn Av -Albany 12234 **Fx:**473-2925
(212) 504-6000 .. **Pauquette,** Lisa Johnston '97 (Cadwalader W&T LLP) -1 World Fncl Ctr -NY 10281
(212) 986-8282 .. **Paur,** Ira A '69 %Cohen & S -360 Lex Av -NY 10017
(518) 435-1919 .. **Pausley,** Wm M '94 (Stockton B&M,LLP) -2 Twr Pl -Albany 12203
(212) 583-9600 .. **Pauta,** George B '03 %Littler M,PC -900 3rd Av -NY 10022
(315) 218-8000 .. **Pautz,** Danl J '09 %Bond S&K,PLLC -1 Lincoln Ctr -Syracuse 13202
(607) 739-8763 .. **Pautz,** Scott J '88 Cooper P&W,LLP -2854 Wstnghse Rd -Horseheads 14845 **Fx:**739-9373
(718) 624-8423 .. **Pavalon,** Lynn S '99 %Osborne Assoc -175 Remsen -Brklyn 11201
(212) 687-2770 .. **Pavane,** Martin B '76 (Cohen PL&P) -551 5th Av -NY 10176
(718) 553-3052 .. **Paveglio,** David J '88 FAA -1 Aviation Plz -Jamaica 11434 **Fx:**995-5699
(845) 434-4988 .. **Pavelchak-Swift,** Lisa A '94 -5208 Main Bx1293 -S Fallsbrg 12779 **Fx:**434-2410
(718) 613-3500 .. **Paver,** Laurance I '76 %UIA Bd -Bx29002 -Brklyn 11201 **Fx:**613-3566
(516) 621-6599 .. **Paverman,** Lester M '75 -Bx322 -Roslyn Hts 11577
(585) 454-3377 .. **Pavia,** Dara R '93 (Brown & T,LLC) -19 Prince -Rchstr 14607
(718) 967-1600 .. **Pavia,** Edw J Jr. '93 %J D'Agostino & Assoc -3309 Richmond Av -Staten Isl 10312 **Fx:**967-8677
(585) 419-8800 .. **Pavia,** Frank C '93 (Harris B PLLC) -99 Garnsey Rd -Pittsfrd 14534
(212) 980-3500 .. **Pavia,** George M '51 (Pavia & H LLP) -600 Mad Av -NY 10022
(212) 980-3500 .. **Pavia & Harcourt LLP** -600 Mad Av -NY 10022 **Fx:**980-3185
(212) 294-6700 .. **Pavin,** Gregory G '90 (Winston & S) -200 Park Av -NY 10166
(718) 442-0800 .. **Pavis,** Matthew S '87 -370 St Marks Pl -Staten Isl 10301 **Fx:**442-2781
(718) 836-6032 .. **Pavlakos,** Olga '86 -Bx090512 -Brklyn 11209 **Fx:**836-4780
(212) 335-4500 .. **Pavlenishvili,** Georgiy D '07 %DLA Piper LLP -1251 Av of Amer -NY 10020
(212) 872-1000 .. **Pavlich,** Jonathan R '09 -One Bryant Park -NY 10036 **Fx:**872-1002
(212) 506-1700 .. **Pavlico,** Anitra '06 %Kasowitz BT&F LLP -1633 Bway -NY 10019
(212) 292-9679 .. **Pavlides,** Anne '97 Calvin Klein,Inc -205 W 39th -NY 10018
(718) 286-6000 .. **Pavlides,** Gregory C '91 %DA -125-01 Qns Blvd -Kew Gdns 11415
(718) 454-4040 .. **Pavlides,** Paul '61 (Campos & P,PC) -186-09 Union Tpk -Flushng 11366
(516) 542-5900 .. **Pavlides,** Paula '96 %Congdon FORDT&F -333 Earle Ovngton Blvd -Uniondale 11553
(212) 484-3900 .. **Pavlidis,** Nicholas P '05 %Arent F LLP -1675 Bway -NY 10019
(631) 853-4161 .. **Pavlik,** Craig D '94 %DA -N Cnty Cmplx Bldg 77 -Hauppauge 11788 **Fx:**853-4192
(516) 739-5100 .. **Pavloff,** Sherri N '90 (Farber B&Z LLP) -51 Charles -Mineola 11501
(212) 490-3000 .. **Pavlos,** Constantine '03 %Wilson EME&D LLP -150 E 42nd -NY 10017
(718) 787-1430 .. **Pavlounis,** Theo '95 -172 Gravesend Neck Rd -Brklyn 11223 **Fx:**336-8466
(845) 291-2670 .. **Pavlovic,** Kim '90 %Childrens Rts Society -213 W Main Bx1002 -Goshen 10924 **Fx:**291-2679
(516) 745-5605 .. **Pavlovic,** Nancy '01 T Bailey & Assoc,PC -175 W Old Cntry Rd -Hicksvll 11801
(212) 610-6300 .. **Pavlovic,** Vladimir '08 %Allen & O -1221 Av of Amer -NY 10020
(212) 770-2483 .. **Pavlow,** Peter '97 AIG -80 Pine -NY 10005
(516) 742-0888 .. **Pavone,** Michl D '83 (Schupbach W&P LLP) -1010 Franklin Av -Gdn Cty 11530
(315) 682-4040 .. **Pavone,** Salvatore '94 -Bx60 -Manlius 13104 **Fx:**682-0993
(315) 682-4040 .. **Pavone,** Sherene '95 -122 E Seneca Bx60 -Manlius 13104 **Fx:**682-0993
(914) 734-8800 .. **Pavon Simon,** Maria G '02 Hudson River Hlthcr -1037 Main -Peekskill 10566
(212) 759-2300 .. **Paw,** Elizabeth A '08 Carroll G&G,LLP -1790 Bway -NY 10019
(212) 557-3000 .. **Pawa,** Jack A '79 (Rivelis P&B,LLP) -286 Mad Av -NY 10017
(212) 878-8000 .. **Pawar,** Marshall '09 %Clifford C LLP -31 W 52nd -NY 10019
(716) 851-5265 .. **Pawarski,** Richd C '87 %City Auditor -City Hall -Buffalo 14202 **Fx:**851-4358
(518) 436-8408 .. **Pawelko,** Ronora M '01 Family Planning Advocates of NYS -17 Elk -Albany 12207

(212) 527-5531 .. **Pawlak,** Mark W '96 Revlon -237 Park Av -NY 10017
(212) 526-9498 .. **Pawlicki,** Dana C '97 Neuberger Berman Inc -1271 6th Av -NY 10020
(845) 457-7702 .. **Pawliczek,** Andrea Durgin '91 -18 Brdg -Montgmry 12549
(845) 651-2000 .. **Pawliczek,** James R '89 -62 N Main -Florida 10921 **Fx:**651-2040
(212) 471-8489 .. **Pawlow,** Wm P '97 (Herzfeld & R,PC) -125 Broad -NY 10004
(212) 819-8200 .. **Pawlowski,** Radoslaw '09 %White & C LLP -1155 Av of Amer -NY 10036
(518) 474-3324 .. **Pawson,** Kenneth '75 Dept of Ed & Voc Srvcs -1 Commerce Plz -Albany 12260
(914) 559-3100 .. **Paxson,** Daryl '92 %Heidell PM&B,LLP -81 Main -White Plns 10601
(212) 788-1037 .. **Payer,** Cheryl '92 %Law Dept -100 Church -NY 10007 **Fx:**788-0367
(212) 725-4423 .. **Paykin,** Jos N '90 (Paykin K&A LLP) -185 Mad Av -NY 10016
(212) 725-4423 .. **Paykin Krieg & Adams LLP** -185 Mad Av -NY 10016 **Fx:**684-9022
(212) 635-1092 .. **Paylago,** Stanley U '01 Bk of NY Mellon -1 Wall -NY 10286
(585) 232-6500 .. **Payment,** Kenneth A '66 (Harter S&E LLP) -1600 Bausch & Lomb Pl -Rchstr 14604
(212) 756-2000 .. **Payne,** Arlene M '08 %Schulte R&Z LLP -919 3rd Av -NY 10022
(718) 837-5000 .. **Payne,** Brian K '87 -314 Bay 14th -Brklyn 11214 **Fx:**234-2656
(212) 335-9000 .. **Payne,** Christine M '00 %DA -1 Hogan Pl -NY 10013
(607) 432-3769 .. **Payne,** Danl G '85 -5 Carson Rd -Oneonta 13820
(212) 264-9108 .. **Payne,** Deirdre J '86 %Army Corps Engrs -26 Fed Plz -NY 10278 **Fx:**264-8171
(212) 219-0090 .. **Payne,** Douglas B '80 -401 Bway -NY 10013 **Fx:**941-8525
(631) 547-6731 .. **Payne,** Janette O '88 Literacy Suffolk,Inc -1335 NY Av -Huntngtn Sta 11746
(212) 577-9100 .. **Payne,** Jeffrey A '96 (Vaccaro P,LLP) -225 W 14th -NY 10011 **Fx:**659-0760
(212) 682-7474 .. **Payne,** John B '08 %Foley & L LLP -90 Park Av -NY 10016
(212) 306-8242 .. **Payne,** Judith E '85 Housing Auth -250 Bway -NY 10007
(212) 687-0100 .. **Payne,** Konrad F '93 %Harris B PLLC -100 Wall -NY 10005
(212) 417-5300 .. **Payne,** Larissa U '05 %Medicaid Fraud Cntrl -120 Bway -NY 10271 **Fx:**417-5274
(518) 221-4491 .. **Payne,** Lisa A '84 -3744 Lk Shr Dr -Diamond Pt 12824
(607) 231-5900 .. **Payne,** Willa S '10 %Leg Aid -30 Fayette -Bnghmtn 13901 **Fx:**724-7211
(212) 374-2998 .. **Payne Garvey,** Maxine '96 %NYC Dept Educ-OLS -52 Chmbrs -NY 10007 **Fx:**374-5596
(212) 607-2800 .. **Paynter,** Carole A '89 %FTC -1 Bowling Grn -NY 10004 **Fx:**607-2822
(212) 259-8000 .. **Payson,** Andrianne S '02 %Dewey & L LLP -1301 Av of Amer -NY 10019
(914) 328-0404 .. **Payson,** Martin F '67 (Jackson L LLP) -1 N Bway -White Plns 10601
(914) 946-4808 .. **Payton,** Marcia L '97 OfCnsl Riebling P&S,LLP -1 N Bway -White Plns 10601 **Fx:**287-7578
(845) 778-2581 .. **Paz,** Francis B '96 (Jacobowitz & P) -156 Orange Av Bx366 -Walden 12586 **Fx:**778-5074
(212) 885-5000 .. **Paz,** Inbal '05 %Blank R LLP -405 Lex Av -NY 10174
(516) 621-0222 .. **Paz,** Marc A '02 %GosmanLaw PC -55 Bryant Av -Roslyn 11576 **Fx:**621-3322
(718) 760-6540 .. **Pazan,** Mary F '86 %Dept of Parks & Rec -Olmsted Ctr -Flushng 11368 **Fx:**760-6730
(212) 577-3546 .. **Pazar,** Diane '87 %Leg Aid -199 Water -NY 10038 **Fx:**577-3520
(212) 227-1212 .. **Pazer Epstein & Jaffe, PC** -20 Vesey -NY 10007 **Fx:**374-1778
(212) 227-1212 .. **Pazer,** Jonathan N '95 (Pazer E&J,PC) -20 Vesey -NY 10007
(212) 227-1212 .. **Pazer,** Perry '54 (Pazer E&J,PC) -20 Vesey -NY 10007
(212) 735-3000 .. **Pazich,** Nicholas L '09 %Skadden ASM&F LLP -4 Times Sq -NY 10036
(212) 839-5300 .. **Pe,** Jesselyn C '08 %Sidley A LLP -787 7th Av -NY 10019
(212) 788-1269 .. **Peabody,** Barbara W '79 %Law Dept -100 Church -NY 10007 **Fx:**788-0367
(212) 225-2000 .. **Peace,** Breon S '97 (Cleary GS&H) -1 Lbrty Plz -NY 10006
(516) 294-9200 .. **Peace,** Ernest J '60 -114 Old Cntry Rd -Mineola 11501 **Fx:**746-1071
(914) 633-5630 .. **Peace,** Jeffrey P '02 Sidney Frank Importing Co -20 Cedar -New Rchll 10801
(315) 955-6700 .. **Peace,** Robt T '94 %Leg Aid -44 Pub Sq -Watertwn 13601 **Fx:**785-9118
(212) 225-2000 .. **Peacock,** Lauren L '06 %Cleary GS&H -1 Lbrty Plz -NY 10006
(212) 325-1729 .. **Peacock,** Olga Igorevna '99 -11 Mad Av -NY 10010
(212) 264-4089 .. **Peacock,** Robin Longaker '99 %IRS -290 Bway -NY 10007 **Fx:**264-4089
(212) 713-7680 .. **Peacocke,** Teresa A R '04 3 Stone Bldg -10 Rckfllr Plz -NY 10020
(212) 340-0400 .. **Peake,** Robt F '82 %Appllt Div 1st Dept -27 Mad Av -NY 10010 **Fx:**889-4412
(212) 541-2000 .. **Pearce,** Alan S '66 (Bryan C LLP) -1290 Av of Amer -NY 10104
(607) 776-9631 .. **Pearce,** Braddock S '80 Pub Def -3 E Pulteney Sq -Bath 14810 **Fx:**664-2496
(212) 221-8733 .. **Pearce,** Donald '77 -1500 Bway -NY 10036 **Fx:**221-8468
(212) 552-2852 .. **Pearce,** Michl A '92 JP Morgan Chase -1 Chase Manh Plz -NY 10081
(212) 612-5409 .. **Pearce,** Renee C '06 %NYC Teachers Rtrmnt System -55 Water -NY 10041 **Fx:**612-5420
(914) 745-4000 .. **Pearce,** Rosemary E '86 %Towers Watson -100 Summit Lk Dr -Valhalla 10595
(212) 636-6834 .. **Pearce,** Russell G '82 %Fordham Univ Sch of Law -140 W 62nd -NY 10023 **Fx:**636-6899
(212) 766-1001 .. **Pearce,** Russell J Jr. '08 %W Rita -291 Bway -NY 10007 **Fx:**608-6802
(607) 723-9511 .. **Pearis,** Stuart M '62 OfCnsl Coughlin & G,LLP -19 Chenango Bx2039 -Bnghmtn 13902
(516) 921-6645 .. **Pearl,** Alan B '68 (A Pearl & Assoc,PC) -6800 Jericho Tpk -Syosset 11791 **Fx:**921-6774
(516) 294-9200 .. **Pearl,** Anthony A '95 -114 Old Cntry Rd -Mineola 11501
(718) 590-3673 .. **Pearl,** Bruce J '82 %Hon C Cirigliano -851 Grand Cncrs -Bronx 10451
(646) 878-0800 .. **Pearl Cohen Zedek Latzer,LLP** -1500 Bway -NY 10036 **Fx:**878-0801
(631) 694-2400 .. **Pearl,** David H '95 %Hamburger MYK&M,LLP -225 Broadhllw Rd -Melvll 11747
(212) 391-8300 .. **Pearl,** Judson W '46 -230 W 41st -NY 10036 **Fx:**391-8318
(212) 468-8000 .. **Pearl,** Michl A '66 OfCnsl Morrison & F LLP -1290 Av of Amer -NY 10104
(914) 461-0280 .. **Pearl,** Michl R '72 (Rothschild & P,LLP) -245 Main -White Plns 10601
(718) 250-2000 .. **Pearl,** Peter N '96 %DA -350 Jay -Brklyn 11201 **Fx:**250-2314
(631) 852-2500 .. **Pearl,** Raphael Augustus '98 %DA -200 Center Dr -Rvrhead 11901 **Fx:**852-1769
(585) 381-3820 .. **Pearl,** Robt J '74 (Pearl Law Firm,PA) -1159 Pttsfrd Victor Rd -Pittsfrd 14534 **Fx:**381-3886
(212) 262-4810 .. **Pearl,** Sara Lynn '84 Trident Media Grp LLC -41 Mad Av -NY 10010 **Fx:**262-4849
(212) 697-4090 .. **Pearl,** Scott W '89 %Platzer L&P LLP -61 Bway -NY 10006
(212) 632-6575 .. **Pearl,** Steven J '00 %Lazard Freres -30 Rckfllr Plz -NY 10112 **Fx:**632-6060
(845) 628-3891 .. **Pearle,** Howard D '67 -RD 2 Somerset Dr -Mahopac 10541 **Fx:**628-3993
(917) 237-2900 .. **Pearle,** Lauren C '02 Axiom Legal -75 Spring -NY 10012
(914) 697-2554 .. **Pearlin,** Marc A '87 Cnsl TAL Intl Container Corp -100 Manhattanvll Rd -Purchase 10577 **Fx:**697-2526
(646) 827-4257 .. **Pearlman,** Allan R '93 -116 W 23rd -NY 10011
(718) 261-9460 .. **Pearlman Apat Futterman Sirotkin & Seinfeld,LLP** -80-02 Kew Grdns Rd -Kew Gdns 11415 **Fx:**261-0479
(212) 455-2000 .. **Pearlman,** Brett A '08 %Simpson T&B LLP -425 Lex Av -NY 10017
(212) 455-2000 .. **Pearlman,** Chad S '10 %Simpson T&B LLP -425 Lex Av -NY 10017
(315) 733-2396 .. **Pearlman,** Eva Brindisi '97 (Brindisi MBPJ&P,LLP) -2713 Genesee -Utica 13501
(516) 829-2572 .. **Pearlman,** Fred David '80 (Nadel & P) -287 Nrthrn Blvd -Gt Neck 11021
(914) 995-3241 .. **Pearlman,** Henry S '86 %Cnty Atty -148 Martine Av -White Plns 10601 **Fx:**995-5858
(914) 683-5599 .. **Pearlman,** Jay W '84 (JW Pearlman PC) -445 Hmltn Av -White Plns 10601 **Fx:**428-1660
(518) 474-8494 .. **Pearlman,** Jeffrey H '01 Governors Ofc -State Cptl -Albany 12224
(212) 593-9155 .. **Pearlman,** Kenneth D '53 -200 E 64th -NY 10065
(212) 733-6466 .. **Pearlman,** Marina '99 %Pfizer Inc -235 E 42nd -NY 10017
(718) 217-9095 .. **Pearlman,** Morton I '59 -80-39 223rd -Qns Vllg 11427 **Fx:**217-9095
(212) 715-9100 .. **Pearlman,** Paul S '79 (Kramer LN&F,LLP) -1177 Av of Amer -NY 10036
(212) 277-6500 .. **Pearlman,** Rachel L '08 %Dickstein S LLP -1633 Bway -NY 10019
(212) 872-6084 .. **Pearlman,** Sharon Katz '85 KPMG LLP -757 3rd Av -NY 10017 **Fx:**872-6720
(212) 742-3390 .. **Pearlmutter,** Fredi L '72 (Lindabury ME&C,PC) -26 Bway -NY 10004
(212) 335-4500 .. **Pearlstein,** Ellyn M '08 %DLA Piper LLP -1251 Av of Amer -NY 10020
(212) 382-6600 .. **Pearlstein,** Lisa C '86 %NYC Bar -42 W 44th -NY 10036 **Fx:**398-6634
(212) 907-7300 .. **Pearlstein,** Wm G '85 Cnsl Golenbock EAB&P -437 Mad Av -NY 10022
(212) 264-0300 .. **Pearlstone,** Burt '79 %NLRB -26 Fed Plz -NY 10278 **Fx:**264-8427
(716) 831-0138 .. **Pearman,** Robt '75 -175 DePew Av -Buffalo 14214
(718) 250-1100 .. **Pearsall,** Michl J '86 %E Garfinkel -12 Metrotech Ctr -Brklyn 11201 **Fx:**250-1168
(212) 715-1000 .. **Pearsall,** Otis Pratt '57 (Arnold & P LLP) -399 Park Av -NY 10022
(718) 725-3032 .. **Pearson,** Beth '97 ACS-DLS -151-20 Jamaica Av -Jamaica 11432
(315) 682-4017 .. **Pearson,** Elijah A '53 CNY Legal Clinic -4635 Slippery Rock -Manlius 13104
(212) 335-9000 .. **Pearson,** Heather N '00 %DA -1 Hogan Pl -NY 10013
(516) 541-1800 .. **Pearson,** Henry W '54 -519 Hicksvll Rd -Massapequa 11758 **Fx:**921-3985
(212) 574-1200 .. **Pearson,** Jennifer J '99 %Seward & K LLP -1 Bttry Pk Plz -NY 10004
(212) 897-5840 .. **Pearson,** Laurence H '65 -305 Bway -NY 10007 **Fx:**897-5841
(917) 237-2900 .. **Pearson,** Laurice A '99 Axiom Legal Solutions -75 Spring -NY 10012
(212) 775-8700 .. **Pearson,** Lisa S '81 (Kilpatrick S,LLP) -31 W 52nd -NY 10019
(914) 323-7000 .. **Pearson,** Malik K '09 %Wilson EME&D LLP -3 Gannett Dr -White Plns 10604
(212) 244-2999 .. **Pearson,** Mary E '88 (Kopff N&D LLP) -440 9th Av -NY 10001
(212) 308-4411 .. **Pearson,** Neil R '77 (Edwards AP&D LLP) -750 Lex Av -NY 10022
(716) 632-2728 .. **Pearson,** Paul D '87 -1301 N Forest Rd -Williamsvll 14221 **Fx:**565-1575
(212) 326-3939 .. **Pearson,** Stephen J '08 (Jones D) -222 E 41st -NY 10017
(212) 310-8000 .. **Pearson,** Tashanna B '09 %Weil G&M LLP -767 5th Av -NY 10153
(212) 336-3620 .. **Peart,** Andree M '89 %EEOC -33 Whitehall -NY 10004
(585) 383-0580 .. **Peartree,** Audrey P '88 (Peartree & P LLP) -110 Linden Oaks -Rchstr 14625 **Fx:**383-0159
(585) 383-0580 .. **Peartree,** David S '84 (Peartree & P LLP) -110 Linden Oaks -Rchstr 14625 **Fx:**383-0159
(585) 473-3100 .. **Peartree,** Kevin F '91 (Ernstrom & D,LLP) -180 Canal Vw Blvd -Rchstr 14623
(315) 769-3898 .. **Pease,** Danl S '87 (Pease & G) -40 Main -Massena 13662 **Fx:**769-5018
(212) 584-5622 .. **Pease,** Kendell D '04 Stone Tower Cptl -152 W 57th -NY 10019
(212) 755-0100 .. **Pease,** Molly L '04 %Grais & E LLP -40 E 52nd -NY 10022
(914) 337-2010 .. **Pease,** Robt E '72 (Pease & L) -15 Park Pl -Bronxvll 10708
(212) 849-7000 .. **Pease,** Thos D '95 (Quinn EU&S,LLP) -51 Mad Av -NY 10010
(315) 448-0672 .. **Pease,** Wm H '73 %US Atty -100 S Clinton Bx7198 -Syracuse 13261 **Fx:**448-0689
(212) 225-2000 .. **Peaslee,** James M '77 (Cleary GS&H) -1 Lbrty Plz -NY 10006
(518) 473-4014 .. **Peaslee,** Maurice K '77 %State Comptroller -110 State -Albany 12236 **Fx:**473-9104
(646) 602-5600 .. **Peay,** Charlyne Brumskine '03 %Urban Justice Ctr -123 William -NY 10038 **Fx:**(212) 533-4598
(518) 877-7539 .. **Peca,** Gina M '87 -27 Southwood Dr -Ballston Lk 12019
(716) 566-1300 .. **Pechaitis,** Scott M '06 %Hiscock & B,LLP -1100 M&T Ctr -Buffalo 14203
(212) 836-8000 .. **Pechenik,** Graham M '09 %Kaye S LLP -425 Park Av -NY 10022
(518) 270-2950 .. **Pechenik,** Stephen A '79 (Cnty Atty) -1600 7th Av -Troy 12180 **Fx:**270-2954
(212) 940-8800 .. **Pechersky,** Julie '00 (Katten MR LLP) -575 Mad Av -NY 10022

(212) 713-2000 .. **Pechersky,** Yana '09 UBS Fincl Srvcs Inc -1285 Av of the Americas -NY 10019

(212) 867-3200 .. **Pechinski,** Matthew J '96 %Westwood Cptl LLC -489 5th Av -NY 10017 **Fx:**867-7515

(212) 583-9500 .. **Pechman,** Louis '84 (Berke-Weiss & P LLP) -488 Mad Av -NY 10022 **Fx:**308-8582

(516) 625-8250 .. **Pechnik-Schwartz,** Pamela K '82 -125 E Bway -Roslyn 11576 **Fx:**621-4397

(718) 237-2000 .. **Peck,** Alan L '71 %Leg Aid -111 Lvngstn -Brklyn 11201 **Fx:**237-8737

(516) 571-3800 .. **Peck,** Barbara E '93 %DA -262 Old Cntry Rd -Mineola 11501 **Fx:**248-9479

(518) 562-1446 .. **Peck,** Dana D '86 %Hon J Lahtinen -36 Oak Bx38 -Plattsbrgh 12901 **Fx:**562-1792

(212) 252-9550 .. **Peck,** David E '96 (Freiberg & P) -49 W 37th -NY 10018

(914) 381-2525 .. **Peck,** David J '78 (Brodsky & P) -550 Mamaroneck Av -Harrison 10528

(212) 318-6000 .. **Peck,** Edw L '70 OfCnsl Paul HJ&W LLP -75 E 55th -NY 10022

(212) 514-9190 .. **Peck,** Ernest J '94 (Downing & P,PC) -17 Battery Pl -NY 10004

(212) 468-8000 .. **Peck,** Geoffrey R '99 %Morrison & F LLP -1290 Av of Amer -NY 10104

(212) 704-0515 .. **Peck,** Gregory '57 -350 5th Av -NY 10118 **Fx:**704-0945

(212) 758-5230 .. **Peck & Heller** -845 3rd Av -NY 10022 **Fx:**758-5945

(212) 998-0302 .. **Peck,** Hilary Frank '04 NYU Ctr for Law & Business -44 W 4th -NY 10012 **Fx:**995-4202

(347) 404-9133 .. **Peck,** Holly E '96 %Civil Ct -141 Lvngstn -Brklyn 11201 **Fx:**(718) 643-3733

(516) 487-0317 .. **Peck,** Jeffrey C '70 -28 Jayson Av -Gt Neck 11021

(212) 310-8000 .. **Peck,** Joshua E '08 %Weil G&M LLP -767 5th Av -NY 10153

(212) 735-3000 .. **Peck,** Julia Jordan '05 %Skadden ASM&F LLP -4 Times Sq -NY 10036

(212) 408-9529 .. **Peck,** Lawr J '93 -1633 Bway -NY 10019 **Fx:**408-9530

(212) 514-9190 .. **Peck,** Marguerite D '87 (Downing & P,PC) -17 Battery Pl -NY 10004

(212) 839-5300 .. **Peck,** Michl P '82 SrCnsl Sidley A LLP -787 7th Av -NY 10019

(718) 237-2000 .. **Peck,** Robt '69 %Leg Aid -111 Lvngstn -Brklyn 11201 **Fx:**237-8737

(516) 627-0300 .. **Peck,** Robt G '64 -19 Park Av -Manhsst 11030 **Fx:**627-0300

(212) 858-1000 .. **Peck,** Rodney R '03 (Pillsbury WSP LLP) -1540 Bway -NY 10036

(516) 229-2715 .. **Peck,** Steven H '84 -50 Chas Lindbergh Blvd -Uniondale 11553 **Fx:**227-2350

(718) 254-0700 .. **Peck,** Sydney T '08 Cnsl Bklyn Defender Srvcs -177 Lvngstn -Brklyn 11201 **Fx:**254-0897

(212) 382-0909 .. **Peckar & Abramson,PC** -41 Mad Av -NY 10154 **Fx:**382-3456

(212) 382-0909 .. **Peckar,** Robt S '72 (Peckar & A,PC) -41 Mad Av -NY 10154

(914) 665-0100 .. **Pecker,** Elliot R '84 Pecker Iron Works -555 S Columbus Av -Mt Vernon 10550 **Fx:**665-0112

(212) 577-3378 .. **Peckerman,** Rachel M '05 Leg Aid -199 Water -NY 10038

(518) 929-5302 .. **Peckham,** Danl W '91 -279 Peckham Rd -Prattsville 12468 **Fx:**299-3536

(607) 778-2402 .. **Peckham,** Jos T '96 %Cnty Ofc of Risk & Ins -Cnty Ofc Bldg Bx1766 -Bnghmtn 13902

(585) 475-0260 .. **Pecora,** Alan J '94 %Insero Kasperski & Ciaccia -100 Chestnut -Rchstr 14604

(845) 486-6800 .. **Pecora,** Noelle M '06 %McCabe & M LLP -63 Wshngtn Bx509 -Poughkeepsie 12602

(716) 681-5200 .. **Pecoraro,** Anthony S '99 -69 Delaware Av -Buffalo 14202

(718) 224-7000 .. **Pecoraro,** Nunzio G '58 -42-24 Douglstn Pkwy -Douglastn 11363 **Fx:**(516) 628-8710

(718) 256-8200 .. **Pecoraro,** Raymond G '55 -7512 18th Av -Brklyn 11214

(212) 344-5053 .. **Pecoraro,** Steven J '86 (Pecoraro & S) -41 Mad Av -NY 10010 **Fx:**743-8120

(516) 294-5433 .. **Pecorelli,** Frank J Jr. '88 (Ahmuty D&M) -200 IU Willets Rd -Albertson 11507

(631) 271-4777 .. **Pecorino,** Janice '93 %D Kritzer & Assoc,PC -187 E Main -Huntngtn 11743 **Fx:**271-2530

(718) 595-6531 .. **Pecunies,** Russell P '85 %DEP -59-17 Junction Blvd -Flushng 11373 **Fx:**595-6543

(212) 759-8203 .. **Pedalino,** Jason P '99 %Hedinger & L -110 Wall -NY 10005

(718) 237-2900 .. **Pedalino,** Peter J '02 ACES -188 Montague -Brklyn 11201

(516) 222-6200 .. **Peddy,** Steven J '77 (Berkman HPP&F,PC) -100 Grdn City Plz -Gdn Cty 11530

(516) 747-6300 .. **Peddy,** Tracie P '77 OfCnsl Koeppel M&L,LLP -155 First Bx863 -Mineola 11501

(212) 768-6700 .. **Pedersen,** Barbara L '97 (Sonnenschein N&R LLP) -1221 Av of Amer -NY 10020

(212) 252-0004 .. **Pedersen,** Erik J '99 %Carroll M&K LLC -570 Lex Av -NY 10022

(212) 837-6058 .. **Pedersen,** Hali R '05 %Hughes H&R LLP -1 Bttry Pk Plz -NY 10004 **Fx:**299-6058

(212) 227-5748 .. **Pedersen,** Jorden N Jr. '81 (Baker P&R) -44 Court -Brklyn 11201 **Fx:**(201) 659-1400

(585) 613-4050 .. **Pedersen,** Mark W '82 USDC-WDNY -100 State -Rchstr 14614 **Fx:**613-4055

(212) 885-8398 .. **Pedersen,** Robt C '92 %BDO USA,LLP -330 Mad Av -NY 10017 **Fx:**697-1299

(212) 541-2000 .. **Pedersen,** Robt E '77 (Bryan C LLP) -1290 Av of Amer -NY 10104

(718) 558-8352 .. **Pedersen,** Roberta O '86 %LIRR -Jamaica Station -Jamaica 11435 **Fx:**558-8211

(212) 214-8138 .. **Pederson,** Alexis S '04 Wachovia Bank -375 Park Av -NY 10152

(212) 558-5500 .. **Pederson,** Michl E '90 %Weitz & L,PC -700 Bway -NY 10003

(518) 474-5794 .. **Pedicone,** Henry L Jr. '76 OTDA-Fair Hearings -40 N Pearl -Albany 12243 **Fx:**473-6735

(315) 671-1090 .. **Pedone,** Kimberly Jordan '94 %Hon J Lawton -Onondaga Cnty Cthse -Syracuse 13202 **Fx:**671-1180

(212) 664-4444 .. **Pedorella,** Marni Beck '95 %NBC -30 Rckfllr Plz -NY 10112

(212) 403-7321 .. **Pedowitz,** Arnold H '77 (Pedowitz & M LLP) -1501 Bway -NY 10036 **Fx:**354-6614

(212) 476-9000 .. **Pedowitz,** David R '85 %Neuberger Berman,LLC -605 3rd Av -NY 10158 **Fx:**476-9862

(516) 222-6200 .. **Pedowitz,** James M '38 OfCnsl Berkman HPP&F,PC -100 Grdn City Plz -Gdn Cty 11530

(212) 403-1000 .. **Pedowitz,** Lawr B '73 (Wachtell LR&K) -51 W 52nd -NY 10019

(516) 822-1600 .. **Pedranghelu,** John P Jr. '82 (Russo & P) -16 E Old Cntry Rd -Hicksvll 11801

(212) 821-3158 .. **Pedreira,** Jorge '94 UBS -299 Park Av -NY 10171

(212) 969-3000 .. **Pedreira,** Massiel '10 %Proskauer R LLP -1585 Bway -NY 10036

(212) 521-5400 .. **Pedretti,** Mark G '93 (Reed S LLP) -599 Lex Av -NY 10022

(315) 218-8000 .. **Pedro,** Patrick J '85 (Bond S&K,PLLC) -1 Lincoln Ctr -Syracuse 13202

(212) 909-6000 .. **Pedro,** Portia D '10 %Debevoise & P LLP -919 3rd Av -NY 10022

(973) 596-4713 .. **Pedro,** Verne A '02 %Gibbons PC -1 Penn Plz -NY 10119 **Fx:**639-6369

(212) 878-8000 .. **Pedrotty,** Simon P '07 %Clifford C LLP -31 W 52nd -NY 10019

(315) 701-0080 .. **Peebles,** Lisa A '93 %Fed Pub Def -4 Clinton Sq -Syracuse 13202 **Fx:**701-0081

(212) 239-4999 .. **Peek,** Barry J '78 (Meyer SE&K,PC) -1350 Bway Bx822 -NY 10018

(516) 229-4200 .. **Peek,** Jonathan D '02 %Mendolia & S -875 Merrick Av -Westbury 11590

(212) 839-5300 .. **Peel,** Kristen D '09 %Sidley A LLP -787 7th Av -NY 10019

(718) 809-0509 .. **Peel,** Tracy A '05 -208 Prospect Park W -Brklyn 11215

(212) 484-3900 .. **Peeler,** M Scott '98 (Arent F LLP) -1675 Bway -NY 10019

(718) 243-6844 .. **Peeples,** Arthur N '96 %Leg Aid -111 Lvngstn -Brklyn 11201 **Fx:**237-8737

(516) 570-4343 .. **Peeples,** Genevieve E '09 %Greenberg BG PC -3000 Marcus Av -New Hyde Pk 11042 **Fx:**570-4348

(212) 756-2000 .. **Pe'er,** Tomer A '06 %Schulte R&Z LLP -919 3rd Av -NY 10022

(212) 223-0200 .. **Peerce,** Marjorie J '84 (Stillman F&S,PC) -425 Park Av -NY 10022

(212) 872-1000 .. **Pees,** Robt H '88 -One Bryant Park -NY 10036 **Fx:**872-1002

(212) 277-4000 .. **Peet,** Chas D Jr. '62 OfCnsl Freshfields BD LLP -520 Mad Av -NY 10022

(315) 764-0569 .. **Peets,** Randy Lee '84 -1970 St Regis Blvd -Massena 13662 **Fx:**764-0921

(516) 684-2900 .. **Pegalis & Erickson,LLC** -1 Hllw Ln -Lk Success 11042 **Fx:**684-2939

(516) 684-2900 .. **Pegalis,** Steven E '66 (Pegalis & E,LLC) -1 Hllw Ln -Lk Success 11042

(716) 856-5500 .. **Pegnia,** Anthony F Jr. '98 (Damon M LLP) -200 Delaware Av -Buffalo 14202

(212) 943-9000 .. **Pegno,** David S '91 (Dewey P&K LLP) -220 E 42nd -NY 10017

(212) 765-5070 .. **Pegram,** John B '65 SrCnsl Fish & R,PC -153 E 53rd -NY 10022

(212) 506-1700 .. **Peguese,** Marvin C '99 %Kasowitz BT&F LLP -1633 Bway -NY 10019

(212) 827-7474 .. **Pehowski,** Carla M '84 TD Securities -31 W 52nd -NY 10019

(212) 593-1412 .. **Pei,** Liane '88 -434 E 52nd -NY 10022

(212) 841-1000 .. **Pei,** Rucia '08 %Covington & B LLP -620 8th Av -NY 10018

(212) 880-9455 .. **Peikin,** Jodi Misher '92 (Morvillo AGIA&B,PC) -565 5th Av -NY 10017

(212) 558-4000 .. **Peikin,** Steven R '92 (Sullivan & C LLP) -125 Broad -NY 10004

(212) 343-9600 .. **Peikoff,** Jodi '90 -173 E Bway -NY 10002 **Fx:**343-3043

(212) 530-5000 .. **Peinado,** Arnold B III '83 (Milbank TH&M LLP) -1 Chase Manh Plz -NY 10005

(716) 849-8900 .. **Peiper,** Steven E '05 %Hurwitz & F,PC -1300 Lbrty Bldg -Buffalo 14202

(212) 775-6648 .. **Peirce,** Elizabeth W '05 Two Sigma Invstmnts,LLC -379 W Bway -NY 10012

(212) 859-8000 .. **Peirce,** Jonathan '03 Fried FHS&J LLP -1 NY Plz -NY 10004

(914) 946-8200 .. **Peirce,** Robt A '83 (R Peirce & Assoc) -8 Cottage Pl -White Plns 10601

(516) 746-7799 .. **Peirez,** David H '62 (Reisman P&R LLP) -1305 Franklin Av -Gdn Cty 11530

(631) 425-2441 .. **Peirez,** Gregory B '95 -Bx536 -Windham 12496 **Fx:**425-9617

(914) 249-5903 .. **Peirez,** Joshua L '97 %MasterCard Intl -2000 Purchase -Purchase 10577

(718) 263-3606 .. **Peisak,** Steven A '76 -69-39 Yllwstn Blvd -Frst Hlls 11375

(212) 541-2000 .. **Peiser,** James F '08 %Bryan C LLP -1290 Av of Amer -NY 10104

(718) 229-1782 .. **Peiser,** Richd J '78 -38-17 Cpl Knndy -Bayside 11361

(212) 964-5000 .. **Peisner,** Kathi '81 (Peisner GS&S) -225 Bway -NY 10007

(917) 664-0200 .. **Peison,** David M '95 -520 W 19th -NY 10011

(212) 225-2000 .. **Pek,** Jane '09 %Cleary GS&H -1 Lbrty Plz -NY 10006

(212) 799-2872 .. **Pekelner,** Alan D '61 -336 W End Av -NY 10023

(212) 956-9500 .. **Peken,** Andrew M '03 Hand B&A LLP -8 W 40th -NY 10018 **Fx:**376-6080

(917) 778-6500 .. **Peker,** Alla '03 %K Dodson -485 Lex Av -NY 10017

(516) 432-9400 .. **Peknic,** Brian M '98 (Peknic P&S LLC) -1005 W Beech -Long Bch 11561 **Fx:**432-5396

(516) 432-9400 .. **Peknic,** Chas M '94 (Peknic P&S LLC) -1005 W Beech -Long Bch 11561 **Fx:**432-5396

(212) 527-1000 .. **Peknic,** Maureen E '06 %Jones HC&B PC -1 Bttry Pk Plz -NY 10004

(212) 808-7800 .. **Pekor,** Adam '09 %Kelley D&W LLP -101 Park Av -NY 10178

(212) 336-8000 .. **Pekowsky,** Holly Anne '96 %Amster R&E -90 Park Av -NY 10016

(212) 218-2100 .. **Pelaez,** Andrea '02 %Fitzpatrick CH&S -1290 Av of Amer -NY 10104

(212) 558-4000 .. **Pelaez,** Carlos A '09 %Sullivan & C LLP -125 Broad -NY 10004

(212) 785-0900 .. **Pelaez,** Monica '98 Winmill & Co -11 Hanover Sq -NY 10005

(518) 889-5000 .. **Pelagalli,** Paul '84 P Pelagalli,PLLC -20 Prospect -Ballston Spa 12020

(212) 526-0306 .. **Pelayo,** Carlos M '00 %Barclays Cptl Inc -399 Park Av -NY 10022

(718) 251-1200 .. **Peldman,** Jonathan '08 (J Peldman PC) -2054 Ralph Av -Brklyn 11234 **Fx:**233-2714

(212) 209-4800 .. **Peled,** Natalie Nola '10 Brown R LLP -7 Times Sq -NY 10036

(212) 701-3000 .. **Peleg,** Maya '09 %Cahill G&R LLP -80 Pine -NY 10005 **Fx:**269-5420

(518) 782-2511 .. **Pelersi,** Mark S '76 M Pelersi,CPA -1568 Central Av -Albany 12205 **Fx:**220-1444

(212) 455-2000 .. **Pelgrift,** Robt Y Jr. '75 Cnsl Simpson T&B LLP -425 Lex Av -NY 10017

(212) 776-5000 .. **Pelikow,** Alan '78 %NYC Housing Auth -250 Bway -NY 10007 **Fx:**776-5039

(516) 599-6700 .. **Pelinsky,** Michl '66 -29 Bway -Lynbrk 11563 **Fx:**599-6611

(212) 661-1151 .. **Pelissier,** Cassandre H '00 %Marin G LLP -40 Wall -NY 10005

(585) 544-3440 .. **Pelkey,** Bryan R '81 (Pelkey & P) -1134 Titus Av -Rchstr 14617 **Fx:**544-0132

(212) 408-5100 .. **Pelkowski,** Robt J '06 %Chadbourne & P LLP -30 Rckfllr Plz -NY 10112

(315) 343-6363 .. **Pelky,** Paul L '78 OfCnsl Amdursky PF&W,PC -26 E Oneida -Oswego 13126

(212) 373-3000 .. **Pell,** Annette Worden '09 %Paul WRW&G LLP -1285 Av of Amer -NY 10019
(518) 462-6160 .. **Pell,** Frank M '79 -329 Albany-Shaker Rd -Loudonvll 12211 **Fx:**462-6161
(212) 446-2300 .. **Pell,** Gabriel A '09 %Boies S&F LLP -575 Lex Av -NY 10022
(212) 880-6000 .. **Pell,** James Craig '05 %Torys LLP -237 Park Av -NY 10017
(212) 759-7100 .. **Pell & Le Viness, PC** -260 Mad Av -NY 10016 **Fx:**922-0133
(212) 819-8200 .. **Pell,** Owen C '84 (White & C LLP) -1155 Av of Amer -NY 10036
(716) 858-5421 .. **Pella,** Susan A '99 Delaware North Cos,Inc -40 Fountain Plz -Buffalo 14202 **Fx:**858-5793
(315) 638-0122 .. **Pelland,** David W '75 -8354 Dunham Rd -Baldwinsvll 13027 **Fx:**638-0122
(516) 799-0880 .. **Pelle,** David D '85 (Pelle & P) -5240 Merrick Rd -Massapequa 11758 **Fx:**799-0236
(516) 799-0880 .. **Pelle,** Domenick A '53 (Pelle & P) -5240 Merrick Rd -Massapequa 11758 **Fx:**799-0236
(518) 455-4757 .. **Pellegri,** Michelle S '04 Assembly Minority Cnsls Ofc -440 State Cptl -Albany 12248 **Fx:**455-5930
(845) 359-0606 .. **Pellegrin,** Danl S '85 %MHLS -140 Old Orangebrg Rd -Orangebrg 10962 **Fx:**365-1773
(212) 819-8200 .. **Pellegrini,** Enrico A '00 %White & C LLP -1155 Av of Amer -NY 10036
(212) 219-8312 .. **Pellegrini,** Frank L '93 (Pellegrini & Assoc,LLC) -336 W 37th -NY 10018 **Fx:**925-1702
(212) 548-2100 .. **Pellegrini,** John B '70 (McGuire W LLP) -1345 Av of Amer -NY 10105
(516) 538-7780 .. **Pellegrini,** Nicholas A '89 -320 Nassau Blvd -Garden City South 11530 **Fx:**564-0906
(518) 474-4090 .. **Pellegrini,** Walter J '77 Ofc Emp Rltns -Agncy Bldg 2 ESP -Albany 12223
(518) 473-8266 .. **Pellegrino,** Carmela '82 %OTDA -40 N Pearl -Albany 12243 **Fx:**474-9389
(315) 733-0417 .. **Pellegrino,** D Victor '75 -2627 Genesee -Utica 13501 **Fx:**792-8075
(212) 508-6700 .. **Pellegrino,** David A '91 (Tannenbaum HS&H LLP) -900 3rd Av -NY 10022
(585) 423-2230 .. **Pellegrino,** Dominic '75 -144 Exchange Blvd -Rchstr 14614 **Fx:**423-8245
(212) 384-1000 .. **Pellegrino,** Francis J '93 %FBI -26 Fed Plz -NY 10278
(212) 318-6000 .. **Pellegrino,** Jeffrey J '92 (Paul HJ&W LLP) -75 E 55th -NY 10022
(212) 637-2689 .. **Pellegrino,** Louis A III '00 US Atty-SDNY -86 Chmbrs -NY 10007
(718) 698-2200 .. **Pellegrino,** Michl '02 -1259 Richmond Av -Staten Isl 10314 **Fx:**698-0024
(212) 848-4000 .. **Pellegrino,** Michl J '06 %Shearman & S LLP -599 Lex Av -NY 10022
(718) 478-7484 .. **Pellegrino,** Richd II '91 -4006 Warren -Elmhrst 11373
(212) 980-4200 .. **Pellegrino,** Robt M '82 (Levy HP&D,LLP) -950 3rd Av -NY 10022
(917) 572-9999 .. **Pellegrino,** Thos J '01 -1650 Coney Isl Av -Brklyn 11230 **Fx:**(718) 998-0685
(518) 348-1000 .. **Peller,** Joel P '94 (Block CS&P,LLP) -9 Exec Park Dr -Clifton Pk 12065
(212) 558-4000 .. **Peller,** Matthew A '07 %Sullivan & C LLP -125 Broad -NY 10004
(212) 428-6211 .. **Peller,** Michl S '85 %Royal Bk of Canada -1 Lbrty Plz -NY 10006 **Fx:**968-1295
(212) 775-0055 .. **Pellerito,** Alexander Jr. '98 %Simon G&K LLP -1700 Bway -NY 10019
(518) 765-5783 .. **Pelletier,** Andrew T '86 -65 Altamont Rd -Voorheesvll 12186 **Fx:**765-2051
(585) 263-1000 .. **Pelletier,** Anita L '02 %Nixon P LLP -1100 Clinton Sq -Rchstr 14604
(212) 715-9320 .. **Pelletier,** Danl J '87 -1177 Av of Amer -NY 10036 **Fx:**715-8000
(908) 879-6600 .. **Pelletier,** Michl C '77 -666 3rd Av -NY 10017 **Fx:**879-6677
(716) 934-2600 .. **Pelletter,** James J '80 (Pelletter M & P) -271 Central Av Bx29 -Silver Crk 14136 **Fx:**934-2623
(212) 261-8000 .. **Pellettier,** Vanessa L '09 %Mendes & M,LLP -750 7th Av -NY 10019
(315) 733-3271 .. **Pelli,** Christopher J '00 CJ Pelli,PLLC -3 Derbyshire Pl -Utica 13501 **Fx:**(877) 397-3654
(315) 476-2191 .. **Pelligra,** Ronald J '81 -205 S Townsend -Syracuse 13202
(212) 313-3600 .. **Pellini,** John T '73 %Barry M&M -2 Rector -NY 10006
(212) 521-5400 .. **Pellis,** Mark D '92 Reed S LLP -599 Lex Av -NY 10022
(585) 388-3339 .. **Pellittiere,** Timothy '99 T Pellittiere,PLLC -481 Penbrooke Dr -Penfld 14526 **Fx:**388-3335
(315) 439-9248 .. **Pellow,** David M '76 -108 Dewitt Rd -Syracuse 13214 **Fx:**(866) 580-5868
(315) 435-2470 .. **Pelosi,** Frank B '03 %DA -505 S State -Syracuse 13202 **Fx:**435-3969
(212) 334-3599 .. **Pelosi,** John A '89 (Pelosi WE&S LLP) -233 Bway -NY 10279 **Fx:**965-1488
(607) 721-8332 .. **Pelosi,** Sharon M '04 Workers Comp Bd -44 Hawley -Bnghmtn 13901
(716) 282-1936 .. **Pelosino,** Nicholas A Jr. '90 -800 Main -Niagara Fls 14301 **Fx:**284-0539
(914) 231-1689 .. **Peloso,** Matthew T '96 Cnty Emergency Srvcs -4 Dana Rd -Valhalla 10595
(212) 259-8000 .. **Peloza,** Scott T '08 %Dewey & L LLP -1301 Av of Amer -NY 10019
(607) 776-4126 .. **Pels,** David Barry '88 %Leg Srvcs -104 E Steuben -Bath 14810 **Fx:**776-4029
(646) 386-4073 .. **Pels,** Valerie Anne '91 Hon M Corriero -111 Centre -NY 10013
(212) 737-5192 .. **Pelster,** Terry C '77 -201 E 79th -NY 10075 **Fx:**737-5282
(516) 292-8100 .. **Pelt,** Rita Ann '97 %Nassau/Sfflk Law Srv -1 Helen Keller Way -Hempstd 11550 **Fx:**292-6529
(585) 256-8760 .. **Pelta,** Edw J '89 %Gleason Works -Bx22970 -Rchstr 14692
(585) 232-6500 .. **Pelta,** Lisa G '88 Cnsl Harter S&E LLP -1600 Bausch & Lomb Pl -Rchstr 14604
(212) 385-9700 .. **Pelton,** Brent E '02 Pelton & Assoc,PC -111 Bway -NY 10006 **Fx:**385-0800
(585) 325-4300 .. **Pelton,** David C '64 (Pelton DDD&B) -45 Exchange Blvd -Rchstr 14614 **Fx:**325-6075
(212) 278-0400 .. **Pelton,** Wm E '69 (Cooper & D LLP) -30 Rckfllr Plz -NY 10112
(212) 349-6775 .. **Peltz,** Alexander '69 (Peltz & W) -222 Bway -NY 10038
(212) 906-1200 .. **Peltz,** Brynn D '89 (Latham & W) -885 3rd Av -NY 10022
(516) 798-2436 .. **Peltz,** Fillmore K '89 -34 Adam Rd W Bx299 -Massapequa 11758
(516) 433-2000 .. **Peltz,** Harry '67 -366 N Bway -Jericho 11753 **Fx:**922-5712
(212) 686-0707 .. **Peltz,** Howard J '78 -60 Mad Av -NY 10010 **Fx:**686-1851
(718) 625-0800 .. **Peltz,** Jeffrey B '84 (J Peltz,PC) -26 Court -Brklyn 11242 **Fx:**624-5386
(212) 422-8500 .. **Peltz,** Shulamis '04 J Laufer PC -65 Bway -NY 10006 **Fx:**422-9038
(212) 349-6775 .. **Peltz & Walker** -222 Bway -NY 10038 **Fx:**227-4002
(212) 608-1234 .. **Peluso,** Carl T '85 (Peluso & T) -70 Lafayette -NY 10013
(914) 738-2220 .. **Peluso,** Frank N '82 (FN Peluso,PC) -5 5th Av Bx327 -Pelham 10803
(518) 463-7784 .. **Peluso,** James R '01 %Dreyer B LLP -75 Columbia -Albany 12210
(212) 598-8000 .. **Peluso,** John U '87 %Guardian Life Ins -7 Hanover Sq -NY 10004 **Fx:**919-2693
(212) 790-4500 .. **Peluso,** Kimo Salvay '00 (Manatt P&P,LLP) -7 Times Sq -NY 10036
(518) 487-5460 .. **Peluso,** Matthew C '07 DA -6 Lodge -Albany 12207 **Fx:**487-5093
(718) 792-3119 .. **Peluso,** Peter J '58 -2885 Philip Av -Bronx 10465 **Fx:**518-9888
(212) 763-8105 .. **Peluso,** Rachelle A '92 %Sagen Asset Mgmt -1325 Av of Amer -NY 10019 **Fx:**763-8135
(212) 891-2100 .. **Peluso,** Sheila M '02 Cerberus Capital Mgmt LP -299 Park Av -NY 10171
(212) 870-3188 .. **Peluso,** Steven T '92 %Prof Examiner Srv -475 Riverside Dr -NY 10115
(516) 739-1950 .. **Peluso,** Tina A '81 %R Bogucki,PC -666 Old Cntry Rd -Gdn Cty 11530 **Fx:**227-1126
(212) 608-1234 .. **Peluso & Touger** -70 Lafayette -NY 10013 **Fx:**513-1989
(607) 324-6111 .. **Pelych,** Jos G '83 -211 Main -Hornell 14843 **Fx:**324-6255
(516) 627-2551 .. **Pelzer,** James E '71 -91 Dennis -Manhsst 11030
(212) 997-4400 .. **Pelzer,** Mary E '03 %Teitler & T,LLP -1114 Av of Amer -NY 10036 **Fx:**997-4949
(212) 748-8770 .. **Pelzer-Cabrera,** Mary E '04 S St Seaport Museum -12 Fulton -NY 10038
(917) 826-1776 .. **Pelzman,** Adam J '93 Pelzman & Co,LLC -2 W 67th -NY 10023
(518) 372-5689 .. **Pemberton,** James L '51 (Pemberton & B) -202 Union -Schnctdy 12305 **Fx:**372-5768
(516) 364-1095 .. **Pena,** Anneris M '98 %McBreen & K -500 N Bway -Jericho 11753
(718) 244-8157 .. **Pena,** Fernando C '02 Port Auth of NY/NJ -JFK Airport Bldg 14 -Jamaica 11430
(212) 376-3066 .. **Pena,** Jessica '03 Vera Inst of Justice -233 Bway -NY 10279 **Fx:**941-9407
(718) 585-6551 .. **Pena,** Jesus J '87 (Pena & K,PLLC) -1200 Waters Pl -Bronx 10461 **Fx:**585-6618
(718) 779-6961 .. **Pena,** Jesus J '87 Pena & K,PLLC -88-19 Roosevelt Av -Jcksn Hts 11372 **Fx:**779-6865
(212) 903-9000 .. **Pena,** Juan L '08 %Linklaters -1345 Av of Amer -NY 10105
(914) 664-6784 .. **Pena,** Matilde R '92 (Pena & Assoc) -336 Hutchison Blvd -Mt Vernon 10552
(212) 808-0700 .. **Peña,** Melissa A '04 %Norris M&M,PA -875 3rd Av -NY 10022
(718) 250-5111 .. **Pena-Chavez,** Amairis '03 %Family Justice Ctr -350 Jay -Brklyn 11201
(718) 661-2808 .. **Penache,** Perry P '87 -36-11 Bowne -Flushng 11354 **Fx:**661-2818
(914) 946-2889 .. **Penachio,** Anne J '92 (Penachio M LLP) -235 Main -White Plns 10601 **Fx:**946-2882
(212) 554-0400 .. **Penachio,** Jos D '94 (Grubman I&S,PC) -152 W 57th -NY 10019
(212) 701-3000 .. **Penalver,** Luis R '95 (Cahill G&R LLP) -80 Pine -NY 10005 **Fx:**269-5420
(718) 330-7861 .. **Penalver,** Moises '90 %ODAR-SSA -111 Lvngstn -Brklyn 11201 **Fx:**330-2009
(212) 210-9460 .. **Penaro,** Steven L '10 %Alston & B LLP -90 Park Av -NY 10016
(718) 618-2500 .. **Pena-Segura,** Eva M '03 %Civil Ct -851 Grnd Cncrs -Bronx 10451 **Fx:**590-7294
(631) 231-0222 .. **Penate-Perla,** Rafael '92 R Penate-Perla -1215 Suffolk Av -Brentwd 11717 **Fx:**231-0630
(212) 450-4000 .. **Penberthy,** Katherine C '09 %Davis P&W LLP -450 Lex Av -NY 10017
(212) 536-3900 .. **Penchina,** Dianne Greenberg '00 (K&L Gates LLP) -599 Lex Av -NY 10022
(212) 850-6100 .. **Penchina,** Robt '89 (Levine SK&S,LLP) -321 W 44th -NY 10036
(516) 746-0707 .. **Pender,** Michl J '81 (Hammill OCDP&K,PC) -6851 Jericho Tpk -Syosset 11791
(201) 692-8078 .. **Pendleton,** Edmond V '89 -Bx874 -NY 10030
(212) 310-8000 .. **Pendleton,** Megan '10 %Weil G&M LLP -767 5th Av -NY 10153
(516) 357-3000 .. **Pendola,** Chas J '03 OfCnsl Rivkin R LLP -926 RXR Plz -Uniondale 11556
(718) 447-8841 .. **Penett,** Thos K '77 (Lahr DMK&P) -33 Decker Av -Staten Isl 10302
(212) 335-9000 .. **Penfold,** Nicholas Halliday '05 %DA -1 Hogan Pl -NY 10013
(212) 788-5072 .. **Peng,** Gitte '02 Ofc of the Mayor -City Hall -NY 10007
(212) 935-3101 .. **Peng,** Haiyan '99 Bank of China -410 Mad Av -NY 10017
(212) 455-2000 .. **Peng,** Lesley C M '00 (Simpson T&B LLP) -425 Lex Av -NY 10017
(646) 746-9700 .. **Peng,** Linda Y '89 CFTC -140 Bway -NY 10005 **Fx:**746-9938
(212) 421-4100 .. **Peng,** Michl '04 %Pryor C LLP -7 Times Sq -NY 10036
(212) 918-3000 .. **Peng-Sue,** Collin J '09 %Hogan L LLP -875 3rd Av -NY 10022
(914) 997-7600 .. **Penichet,** Luis A '80 (Penichet Firm,PC) -140 Grand -White Plns 10601 **Fx:**997-8155
(516) 747-6300 .. **Penighetti,** Jason M '03 %Koeppel M&L,LLP -155 First Bx863 -Mineola 11501
(914) 949-6996 .. **Penino & Moynihan,LLP** -180 E Post Rd -White Plns 10601 **Fx:**949-6203
(914) 949-6996 .. **Penino,** Stephen J '86 (Penino & M,LLP) -180 E Post Rd -White Plns 10601
(718) 639-1100 .. **Penkava,** Eric A '80 (Masone WP&C) -69-34 Grand Av -Maspeth 11378
(212) 216-9708 .. **Penkovsky,** Nicholas A '94 N Penkovsky,PC -112 Mad Av -NY 10016 **Fx:**216-9491
(212) 637-2725 .. **Penn,** Allison D '99 %US Atty -86 Chmbrs -NY 10007
(212) 833-1172 .. **Penn,** Amy K '08 %Friedman KS&A LLP -1633 Bway -NY 10019 **Fx:**373-7972
(212) 661-5700 .. **Penn,** Craig E '84 (Penn & Assoc,LLP) -230 Park Av -NY 10169 **Fx:**751-4055
(914) 428-2288 .. **Penn,** Craig E '84 (Penn & Assoc,LLP) -1 N Bway -White Plns 10601 **Fx:**328-4178
(718) 969-5535 .. **Penn,** Cyril C '84 -147-42 Vllg Rd -Jamaica 11435 **Fx:**969-5535
(212) 801-6767 .. **Penn,** Denise J '05 %Greenberg T,LLP -200 Park Av -NY 10166
(212) 801-6493 .. **Penn,** H Richd '60 -200 Park Av -NY 10166 **Fx:**805-9493

(718) 358-2918 .. **Penn,** Ira '99 -7118 Main -Flushng 11367 **Fx:**504-6112
(212) 225-2000 .. **Penn,** Jeffrey R '09 %Cleary GS&H -1 Lbrty Plz -NY 10006
(212) 858-7116 .. **Penn,** John C '05 RBC Cptl Mkts Corp -1 Lbrty Pl -NY 10038
(212) 785-0157 .. **Penn,** Lois M '93 %NYS Nurses Assn -120 Wall -NY 10005 **Fx:**785-0429
(716) 636-7600 .. **Penn,** Mary Moorman '00 %HoganWillig -2410 N Forest Rd -Amherst 14068
(212) 354-7700 .. **Penn Proefriedt Schwarzfeld & Schwartz** -114 W 47th -NY 10036 **Fx:**997-5070
(212) 354-7700 .. **Penn,** Stephen H '62 (Penn PS&S) -114 W 47th -NY 10036
(585) 232-8314 .. **Penna,** Jacklyn M '96 %Buckner & K -1 S Wshngtn -Rchstr 14614
(585) 263-1000 .. **Penna,** Jonathan S '02 %Nixon P LLP -1100 Clinton Sq -Rchstr 14604
(212) 878-9000 .. **Pennachio,** Anthony '84 %A-L Associates -546 5th Av -NY 10036 **Fx:**878-9096
(212) 538-2794 .. **Pennay,** Lori J '01 Credit Suisse -11 Mad Av -NY 10010
(518) 781-4452 .. **Pennell,** Wm B '63 -Bx249 -Canaan 12029
(212) 692-7696 .. **Penner,** Chas G '01 Cnsl JANA Ptnrs LLC -767 5th Av -NY 10153
(212) 759-4888 .. **Penner,** Kimberly '87 (Phillips L LLP) -437 Mad Av -NY 10022
(212) 848-4000 .. **Penner,** Stephen N '06 %Shearman & S LLP -599 Lex Av -NY 10022
(914) 286-2929 .. **Pennessi,** Danl J '07 %Greenberg T,LLP -445 Hmltn Av -White Plns 10601
(716) 433-2524 .. **Penney,** Chas R '58 -538 Bewley Bldg -Lockprt 14094 **Fx:**434-6498
(212) 922-6757 .. **Pennfield,** Edw B '71 SrCnsl BNY Mellon Wealth Mgmt -200 Park Av -NY 10166
(212) 593-6700 .. **Pennie,** Nancy L '90 (Aaronson RF&D,LLP) -757 3rd Av -NY 10017
(212) 969-3000 .. **Pennington,** Christopher L '98 (Proskauer R LLP) -1585 Bway -NY 10036
(212) 682-4900 .. **Pennington,** David L '86 (Harvey P Ltd) -230 Park Av -NY 10169
(212) 487-9700 .. **Pennington,** Gregory S '98 (White F&F,LLP) -61 Bway -NY 10006
(718) 508-1249 .. **Pennington,** Hannah M '02 Sanctuary for Families -198 E 161st -Bronx 10451
(716) 858-2424 .. **Pennington,** Jaharr S '07 DA -25 Delaware Av -Buffalo 14202 **Fx:**858-7425
(212) 580-7480 .. **Pennington,** Jean Zimmer '71 -160 W 77th -NY 10024 **Fx:**769-2369
(212) 345-6333 .. **Pennington,** Louise W '96 %Marsh USA -1166 Av of Amer -NY 10036 **Fx:**345-4808
(917) 546-0747 .. **Pennington,** Mark C '89 -841 Bway -NY 10003
(212) 335-9000 .. **Pennington,** Melissa A '05 %DA -1 Hogan Pl -NY 10013
(516) 775-7546 .. **Pennington,** Ralph L Jr. '94 -249-02 Jericho Tpk -Floral Pk 11001
(212) 782-4679 .. **Pennington,** Thos A '83 Bk of Tokyo-Mitsubishi UFJ -1251 Av of Amer -NY 10020
(718) 459-6000 .. **Pennisi,** Albert F '67 (Pennisi D&N LLP) -97-77 Qns Blvd -Rego Pk 11374
(718) 459-6000 .. **Pennisi Daniels & Norelli LLP** -97-77 Qns Blvd -Rego Pk 11374 **Fx:**459-6875
(518) 383-9400 .. **Pennock Breedlove & Noll** -1407 Route 9 -Clifton Pk 12065 **Fx:**383-1959
(518) 383-9400 .. **Pennock,** John H Jr. '80 (Pennock B&N) -1407 Route 9 -Clifton Pk 12065
(212) 558-5500 .. **Pennock,** Paul J '89 %Weitz & L,PC -700 Bway -NY 10003
(212) 336-2000 .. **Pennoyer,** Robt M '51 OfCnsl Patterson BW&T LLP -1133 Av of Amer -NY 10036
(914) 472-5664 .. **Penny,** Wm E '87 -10 Forest Ln -Scarsdale 10583
(518) 452-0941 .. **Penpraze,** Lisa M '99 %Segel GM&S,PC -9 Wshngtn Sq -Albany 12205
(212) 208-8124 .. **Penrose,** James F '83 %Standard & Poor's -55 Water -NY 10041
(212) 715-9100 .. **Penry-Williams,** Susan J '77 (Kramer LN&F,LLP) -1177 Av of Amer -NY 10036
(212) 612-4200 .. **Pensabene,** Angela P '98 %Hoey KT&E -55 Water -NY 10041
(212) 218-2100 .. **Pensabene,** Lisa Barons '92 (Fitzpatrick CH&S) -1290 Av of Amer -NY 10104
(212) 218-2100 .. **Pensabene,** Marc J '95 (Fitzpatrick CH&S) -1290 Av of Amer -NY 10104
(212) 867-6000 .. **Pensabene,** Michl A '01 (Rosenberg & E,PC) -733 3rd Av -NY 10017
(212) 940-3124 .. **Penski,** Frank H '75 (Nixon P LLP) -437 Mad Av -NY 10022
(212) 530-5000 .. **Penski,** Rachel F '06 %Milbank TH&M LLP -1 Chase Manh Plz -NY 10005
(212) 385-8000 .. **Penson,** Dominique A '90 (Barasch MS&P) -11 Park Pl -NY 10007
(631) 698-0459 .. **Penstein,** Marvin H '72 -1123 Old Town Rd -Coram 11727 **Fx:**698-4934
(212) 504-6000 .. **Pensyl,** Bradley S '09 %Cadwalader W&T LLP -1 World Fncl Ctr -NY 10281
(518) 383-5300 .. **Pentkowski,** David H '79 (Pentkowski P&F) -646 Plnk Rd -Clifton Pk 12065
(518) 383-5300 .. **Pentkowski Pastore & Freestone** -646 Plnk Rd -Clifton Pk 12065 **Fx:**383-5347
(212) 940-8800 .. **Pentlow,** David A '01 (Katten MR LLP) -575 Mad Av -NY 10022
(212) 373-3000 .. **Penza,** Moira K '09 %Paul WRW&G LLP -1285 Av of Amer -NY 10019
(212) 230-8800 .. **Penzell,** Abigail J '08 %WilmerHale -399 Park Av -NY 10022
(516) 227-0700 .. **Penzer,** Eric W '97 (Farrell F,PC) -1320 RXR Plz -Uniondale 11556
(212) 675-2997 .. **Penzer,** Jason R '96 Manhattan Colorectal Assoc -36 7th Av -NY 10011
(212) 906-1200 .. **Penzer,** Michele Olivier '94 (Latham & W) -885 3rd Av -NY 10022
(631) 761-0800 .. **Penzer,** Russell L '99 %Lazer AR&Y,PC -225 Old Cntry Rd -Melvll 11747
(212) 621-5671 .. **Pepe,** Christine A '00 %ASCAP -1 Lincoln Plz -NY 10023 **Fx:**787-1381
(212) 407-1200 .. **Pepe,** Douglas J '00 -485 Lex Av -NY 10017 **Fx:**407-1299
(516) 293-5600 .. **Pepe,** James Patrick '74 -1067 NY Dr -N Massapequa 11758
(518) 474-1331 .. **Pepe,** Nancy J '97 Ofc Mntl Health -44 Holland Av -Albany 12229 **Fx:**473-7863
(212) 268-5136 .. **Pepe,** Russell A '80 (Harwood L) -350 5th Av -NY 10118
(212) 596-9000 .. **Pepe,** Steven '97 (Ropes & G LLP) -1211 Av of Amer -NY 10036
(212) 582-6430 .. **Pepe,** Steven J '96 -350 Bway -NY 10013 **Fx:**965-9375
(718) 388-8633 .. **Pepe,** Thos A '69 -85 Kngslnd Av -Brklyn 11222
(212) 615-3456 .. **Pepe-Robbins,** Suzanne '92 LS Power Dvlpmt LLC -1700 Bway -NY 10019 **Fx:**615-3440
(212) 306-8664 .. **Pepe-Souvenir,** Rodney L '95 Housing Auth -250 Bway -NY 10007
(212) 455-2000 .. **Pepin,** Jennifer M '09 %Simpson T&B LLP -425 Lex Av -NY 10017
(212) 348-7449 .. **Pepitone,** Danl F '07 Legal Srvcs -1 W 125th -NY 10027 **Fx:**348-4093
(212) 770-2489 .. **Pepitone,** Susan R '99 AIG Tech Srvcs -80 Pine -NY 10005
(212) 323-2250 .. **Pepkin,** Cari E '88 %HHC-OLA-Medical Litigation -346 Bway -NY 10013 **Fx:**323-2251
(212) 661-7300 .. **Peplinski,** John J '93 %Malapero & P LLP -295 Mad Av -NY 10017
(212) 225-2000 .. **Peponis,** Margaret E '97 (Cleary GS&H) -1 Lbrty Plz -NY 10006
(718) 792-2847 .. **Peppard,** Ellen P '93 OfCnsl H Hertzberg -1526 Wllmsbrdg Rd -Bronx 10461 **Fx:**892-6886
(212) 335-4500 .. **Peppas,** Rand Boyers '89 (DLA Piper LLP) -1251 Av of Amer -NY 10020
(212) 836-8000 .. **Pepper,** Allan M '68 (Kaye S LLP) -425 Park Av -NY 10022
(718) 990-6094 .. **Pepper,** Elyse '94 %St John's Law Schl -8000 Utopia Pkwy -Jamaica 11439 **Fx:**591-1855
(212) 351-4000 .. **Pepper,** Farrah L '02 %Gibson D&C LLP -200 Park Av -NY 10166
(212) 808-2700 .. **Pepper Hamilton LLP** -620 8th Av -NY 10018 **Fx:**286-9806
(212) 728-8000 .. **Pepper,** Jeni S '03 %Willkie F&G LLP -787 7th Av -NY 10019
(212) 416-8000 .. **Pepper,** Joshua B '01 %Dept of Law -120 Bway -NY 10271
(212) 259-8000 .. **Pepper,** Lee '10 %Dewey & L LLP -1301 Av of Amer -NY 10019
(516) 248-1638 .. **Pepper,** Lisa R '88 -821 Franklin Av -Gdn Cty 11530 **Fx:**877-0095
(845) 894-4713 .. **Pepper,** Margaret A '99 IBM -2070 Route 52 -Hopewell Junct 12533
(631) 470-1681 .. **Pepper,** Paul R '05 PR Pepper,LLC -18 W Carver -Huntngtn 11743
(516) 747-0300 .. **Pepper,** Phillip S '03 %Meltzer LG&B,LLP -190 Willis Av -Mineola 11501
(212) 450-4000 .. **Pepper,** Stephen M '01 Cnsl Davis P&W LLP -450 Lex Av -NY 10017
(212) 558-4000 .. **Pepperman,** Richd C II '93 (Sullivan & C LLP) -125 Broad -NY 10004
(212) 957-1780 .. **Pepperman,** Steven C '87 -60 E 42nd -NY 10165 **Fx:**983-1006
(212) 858-1000 .. **Peppers,** Jerry P '72 (Pillsbury WSP LLP) -1540 Bway -NY 10036
(718) 579-3000 .. **Peppito,** Mary B '92 %Leg Aid -1020 Grnd Cncrs -Bronx 10451 **Fx:**588-2611
(212) 973-9100 .. **Peragine,** Paul F '86 OfCnsl Rose & K LLP -757 3rd Av -NY 10017 **Fx:**973-9101
(516) 248-7141 .. **Peraino,** Joann '85 -1415 Kellum Pl -Gdn Cty 11530
(212) 705-4824 .. **Perala,** Brett T '06 %Rosenberg & G PC -488 Mad Av -NY 10022 **Fx:**593-9175
(212) 219-3360 .. **Perales,** Cesar A '66 Latino Justice PRLDEF -99 Hudson -NY 10013 **Fx:**431-4276
(212) 430-6660 .. **Peralta-Millan,** Edwin '83 -65 Bway -NY 10006
(212) 695-9595 .. **Perano,** Anthony J '88 -75 West End Av -NY 10023
(212) 245-1000 .. **Peratis,** Kathleen '79 (Outten & G LLP) -3 Park Av -NY 10016
(212) 994-6351 .. **Peraza,** Frank J '90 %Concrete Stories -55 White -NY 10013 **Fx:**(646) 613-8272
(212) 906-1200 .. **Perazzelli,** Jessica L '07 Latham & W -885 3rd Av -NY 10022
(914) 945-3145 .. **Percello,** Louis J '92 IBM -Bx218 -Yorktwn Hts 10598 **Fx:**945-3281
(212) 981-0519 .. **Perchekly,** Alexander '99 A Perchekly,PC -747 3rd Av -NY 10017
(845) 536-1800 .. **Perciballi,** Mario J '98 -34 Germonds Rd -New Cty 10956
(212) 416-8050 .. **Percoco,** Jos '05 %Dept of Law -120 Bway -NY 10271 **Fx:**416-4942
(845) 469-4900 .. **Perdikologos,** Constantina '10 %Greenwald Law Ofc -99 Brookside Av -Chester 10918 **Fx:**469-2022
(516) 466-0090 .. **Perdomo,** Francelina M '05 Yerushalmi & Assoc -17 Barstow Rd -Gt Neck 11021 **Fx:**466-8988
(212) 969-3000 .. **Perdue,** Abigail L '08 %Proskauer R LLP -1585 Bway -NY 10036
(516) 426-8700 .. **Pere,** Tammi D '91 -24 NY Av -W Hempstead 11552 **Fx:**279-4478
(212) 977-7033 .. **Perecman,** David H '79 (Perecman Firm PLLC) -250 W 57th -NY 10107
(212) 977-7033 .. **Perecman Firm PLLC** -250 W 57th -NY 10107 **Fx:**977-7035
(718) 447-1962 .. **Perednia,** Julia Hall '94 (Hall & H,LLP) -57 Beach -Staten Isl 10304 **Fx:**447-2761
(212) 382-0909 .. **Pereira,** Cesar F '06 %Peckar & A,PC -41 Mad Av -NY 10154
(718) 484-0865 .. **Pereira,** Herb '92 -1229 Flatbush Av -Brklyn 11226
(212) 758-5777 .. **Pereira,** John S '75 (Pereira & S,LLP) -150 E 58th -NY 10155 **Fx:**751-6950
(212) 953-1010 .. **Pereira,** Nathan P '09 %Henderson & K -420 Lex Av -NY 10170 **Fx:**953-1025
(212) 713-8207 .. **Pereira,** Steven M '87 College Bd -45 Columbus Av -NY 10023
(212) 506-3900 .. **Perel,** Andrew J '87 (Steptoe & J LLP) -750 7th Av -NY 10019
(716) 842-2800 .. **Perel,** Nelson '87 (Webster S LLP) -1400 Lbrty Bldg -Buffalo 14202
(212) 310-8000 .. **Perelman,** Sabrina A '07 %Weil G&M LLP -767 5th Av -NY 10153
(516) 571-3800 .. **Peress,** Diane M '80 %DA -262 Old Cntry Rd -Mineola 11501 **Fx:**248-9479
(212) 248-8800 .. **Peress,** Janine L '06 %Callan KB&B LLP -1 Whitehall -NY 10004
(212) 732-3320 .. **Peress,** Naim Moshe '99 %Short & B,PC -217 Bway -NY 10007
(718) 667-8785 .. **Peretore,** Frank '92 (Peretore & P,PC) -110 Park -Staten Isl 10306 **Fx:**(973) 729-8913
(718) 667-8785 .. **Peretore,** Janis Migliorise '86 (Peretore & P,PC) -110 Park -Staten Isl 10306 **Fx:**(973) 729-8913
(212) 744-3557 .. **Peretz,** Blossom Audrey '59 -1441 3rd Av -NY 10028
(917) 974-7744 .. **Peretz,** Danl S '05 -205 W 88th -NY 10024 **Fx:**(646) 678-3665
(212) 809-1166 .. **Perez,** Aileen '02 %Brunnock & F,PC -204 W 84th -NY 10024 **Fx:**809-1155
(212) 558-4000 .. **Perez,** Alex '09 %Sullivan & C LLP -125 Broad -NY 10004
(212) 250-2500 .. **Perez,** Alexander R '03 %Deutsche Bank -60 Wall -NY 10005
(212) 571-4900 .. **Perez,** Amanda E '04 %M Harris & Assoc LLC -5 Hanover Sq -NY 10004 **Fx:**571-0965
(315) 733-0455 .. **Perez,** Carole Calli '76 %Calli C&C -510 Bleecker -Utica 13501
(212) 939-1544 .. **Perez,** Cesar A '99 Columbia Univ/Harlem Hospital -506 Lenox Av -NY 10037
(212) 659-7300 .. **Perez,** Christopher J '10 %Haynes & B,LLP -1221 Av of Amer -NY 10020
(212) 530-5000 .. **Perez,** Danl J '10 %Milbank TH&M LLP -1 Chase Manh Plz -NY 10005
(212) 529-0223 .. **Perez,** Danl M '96 (Kuby & P,LLP) -119 W 23rd -NY 10011
(212) 571-1127 .. **Perez,** Dario '90 (Zohar L&P,LLP) -42 Bway -NY 10004 **Fx:**571-1113
(212) 504-6000 .. **Perez,** Diana M '08 %Cadwalader W&T LLP -1 World Fncl Ctr -NY 10281

(212) 385-0603 .. **Perez,** Edw '00 E Perez,PC -233 Bway -NY 10279 **Fx:**385-0617
(212) 219-1800 .. **Perez,** Elizabeth C '06 %Lawyers Alliance NY -171 Mad Av -NY 10016 **Fx:**941-7458
(212) 259-8000 .. **Perez,** Eridania '00 (Dewey & L LLP) -1301 Av of Amer -NY 10019
(718) 518-4154 .. **Perez,** Franklyn '80 Hostos Comm Cllg CUNY -475 Grnd Cncrs -Bronx 10451 **Fx:**518-4198
(212) 242-3740 .. **Perez,** Gil V '04 -55 W 14th -NY 10011 **Fx:**242-4725
(585) 325-4732 .. **Perez,** Gilbert R '86 -30 W Broad -Rchstr 14614 **Fx:**454-4026
(212) 998-6686 .. **Perez,** Ivan '99 NYU Pub Intrst Law Ctr -245 Sullivan -NY 10012 **Fx:**995-4529
(212) 504-6000 .. **Perez,** Jared J '06 %Cadwalader W&T LLP -1 World Fncl Ctr -NY 10281
(212) 833-6065 .. **Perez,** Jeannette M '04 Sony Bmg -550 Mad Av -NY 10022 **Fx:**833-6119
(315) 474-2911 .. **Perez,** Jose E '08 %Smith SK&S,PC -250 S Clinton -Syracuse 13202
(212) 739-7575 .. **Perez,** Jose L '86 %Latino Justice PRLDEF -99 Hudson -NY 10013 **Fx:**431-4276
(718) 918-0327 .. **Perez,** Jos C '87 -216 Pennyfld Av -Bronx 10465
(518) 432-9700 .. **Perez,** Julie Norine '05 %Balzer & L,PLLC -275½ Lark -Albany 12210 **Fx:**432-9722
(212) 607-8625 .. **Perez,** Kevin J '04 Dept of Labor -33 Whitehall -NY 10004 **Fx:**337-2112
(516) 390-9595 .. **Perez,** Lance '97 %Maimone & Assoc,PLLC -170 Old Cntry Rd -Mineola 11501 **Fx:**877-0321
(718) 250-2000 .. **Perez,** Leigh Ann '10 %DA -350 Jay -Brklyn 11201 **Fx:**250-2314
(718) 797-5700 .. **Perez,** Leslie '07 %Wenig S LLP -26 Court -Brklyn 11242
(716) 285-9631 .. **Perez,** Louis J '57 -324 Pine Av -Niagara Fls 14301 **Fx:**285-3463
(212) 951-6400 .. **Perez,** Lydia '88 %Dept of Education -475 Park Av S -NY 10016 **Fx:**951-6465
(212) 654-6716 .. **Perez,** Maria M '89 %Perez Minton Prdctns -1633 Bway -NY 10019 **Fx:**654-4735
(516) 745-8310 .. **Perez,** Milagros '87 (Perez & V) -333 Earle Ovngton Blvd Bx9372 -Uniondale 11553
(212) 742-3390 .. **Perez,** Monica '06 %Lindabury ME&C,PC -26 Bway -NY 10004
(212) 788-7000 .. **Perez,** Nelson '98 %City Cncl Leg Div -250 Bway -NY 10007 **Fx:**788-7034
(212) 610-6300 .. **Perez,** Nicole A '01 SrCnsl Allen & O -1221 Av of Amer -NY 10020
(212) 765-2100 .. **Pérez,** Nicole Cuda '01 %Spivak L LLP -1700 Bway -NY 10019
(718) 410-7230 .. **Perez,** Pablo '03 NYCHA -1220 Gerard Av -Bronx 10452
(212) 326-2000 .. **Perez,** Patricia M '98 (O'Melveny & M LLP) -7 Times Sq -NY 10036
(212) 872-1000 .. **Perez,** Rachel E '08 -One Bryant Park -NY 10036 **Fx:**872-1002
(914) 323-7000 .. **Perez,** Raymond '00 %Wilson EME&D LLP -3 Gannett Dr -White Plns 10604
(212) 930-9700 .. **Perez,** Robt '74 Cnsl Sichenzia RFF LLP -61 Bway -NY 10006
(718) 544-2600 .. **Perez,** Sandra '96 (Perez Law Ofc,PC) -125-10 Qns Blvd -Kew Gdns 11415 **Fx:**544-0714
(718) 250-1100 .. **Perez,** Scott C '01 %E Garfinkel -12 Metrotech Ctr -Brklyn 11201 **Fx:**250-1168
(212) 506-1700 .. **Perez,** Simone M '04 Kasowitz BT&F LLP -1633 Bway -NY 10019
(914) 995-3647 .. **Perez,** Stephanie '96 %Cnty Atty -148 Martine Av -White Plns 10601 **Fx:**995-5858
(212) 318-3000 .. **Perez,** Tania S '02 %Fulbright & J LLP -666 5th Av -NY 10103
(914) 993-4212 .. **Perez,** Valorie S '03 NYS Judicial Inst -84 N Bway -White Plns 10603
(516) 745-8310 .. **Perez & Varvaro** -333 Earle Ovngton Blvd Bx9372 -Uniondale 11553 **Fx:**745-8259
(212) 735-3000 .. **Perez Caldas,** Ralph E '09 %Skadden ASM&F LLP -4 Times Sq -NY 10036
(212) 310-8000 .. **Perez De Alejo,** Alfredo A '07 %Weil G&M LLP -767 5th Av -NY 10153
(212) 431-1300 .. **Perez-Hall,** Carlos C '04 %Borah GAN&G PC -377 Bway -NY 10013
(518) 455-7602 .. **Perez Jaquith,** Rosemarie '94 Legislative Bill Drafting Comm -55 Elk -Albany 12210 **Fx:**455-7689
(914) 422-8746 .. **Perez-Maldonado,** Wanda '97 %Dept of Law -101 E Post Rd -White Plns 10601 **Fx:**422-8706
(212) 450-4000 .. **Perez-Marques,** Antonio J '03 %Davis P&W LLP -450 Lex Av -NY 10017
(212) 308-7355 .. **Perez-Porter,** Melinda '91 Brookdale Fndtn -950 3rd Av -NY 10022
(212) 436-1114 .. **Perez-Vazquez,** Rafael L '80 IRS -290 Bway -NY 10007
(212) 752-5258 .. **Perez-Vellios,** Melanie J '07 %Schwartz SE&C LLC -845 3rd Av -NY 10022
(212) 969-3000 .. **Perez-Zarraga,** Yvonne M '06 %Proskauer R LLP -1585 Bway -NY 10036
(518) 426-3300 .. **Perfetti,** Carrie Anne '00 IPRO -20 Corp Wds Blvd -Albany 12211
(607) 753-3327 .. **Perfetti,** David W '67 SrCnsl Perfetti Law Ofc -62 N Main -Cortlnd 13045 **Fx:**753-3328
(607) 753-3327 .. **Perfetti,** Patrick A '95 Cnsl Perfetti Law Ofc -62 N Main -Cortlnd 13045 **Fx:**753-3328
(212) 488-1300 .. **Perfetto,** Louis A '94 (Cohen & P LLP) -444 Mad Av -NY 10022
(212) 238-2420 .. **Pergadia,** Viren Ramanand '95 %UIA Bd -59 Maiden Ln -NY 10038 **Fx:**238-2451
(212) 589-4200 .. **Pergament,** Benjamin D '00 (Baker & H LLP) -45 Rckfllr Plz -NY 10111
(516) 877-2424 .. **Pergament,** Marc A '81 (Weinberg G&P LLP) -400 Grdn City Plz -Gdn Cty 11530
(631) 499-4977 .. **Pergolizzi,** James J Jr. '57 -6500 Jericho Tpk -Commack 11725
(315) 218-8000 .. **Pergolizzi,** James J '10 %Bond S&K,PLLC -1 Lincoln Ctr -Syracuse 13202
(718) 236-6008 .. **Pergolizzi,** Jason S '02 -8208 18th Av Bx140504 -Brklyn 11214 **Fx:**236-6008
(718) 236-6008 .. **Pergolizzi,** Jos V '71 -8208 18th Av Bx140504 -Brklyn 11214 **Fx:**(631) 661-3569
(718) 627-1215 .. **Pergolizzi,** Stephen R '87 -911 Av U -Brklyn 11223 **Fx:**627-1082
(212) 868-6300 .. **Pergue,** Chas '92 (Cary K LLP) -1350 Bway -NY 10018
(212) 310-8000 .. **Perheentupa,** Ilkka I '01 %Weil G&M LLP -767 5th Av -NY 10153
(516) 889-4431 .. **Peri,** John Jr. '74 -314 NY Av -Long Bch 11561
(212) 692-6516 .. **Peri,** Steven B '75 Tandberg,Inc -1212 Av of Amer -NY 10036
(585) 387-0500 .. **Pericak,** John G '83 (Olver K LLP) -100 Ofc Park Way -Pittsfrd 14534
(212) 213-5500 .. **Periconi,** James J '78 (Periconi,LLC) -708 3rd Av -NY 10017 **Fx:**213-5030
(212) 770-1782 .. **Perides,** Maria H '80 %AIG -80 Pine -NY 10005 **Fx:**344-2286
(212) 636-6824 .. **Perillo,** Jos '55 %Fordham Univ Sch of Law -140 W 62nd -NY 10023 **Fx:**636-6899
(631) 232-2224 .. **Perini,** Raymond G '74 (Perini & H) -1770 Motor Pkwy -Hauppauge 11788 **Fx:**232-2344
(518) 455-7500 .. **Perino,** David '00 %Legislative Bill Drafting Comm -55 Elk -Albany 12210
(518) 285-8598 .. **Perino,** Justina Cintron '01 Hon KA O'Connor -112 State -Albany 12207
(718) 990-1928 .. **Perino,** Michl A '89 %St John's Law Schl -8000 Utopia Pkwy -Jamaica 11439 **Fx:**591-1855
(646) 747-0102 .. **Peristeris,** Apostolos A '04 Aris Cptl Mgmt,LLC -152 W 57th -NY 10019
(716) 883-0355 .. **Perk,** Robt H '83 -995 Elmwood Av -Buffalo 14222
(212) 832-7400 .. **Perkel,** Alyssa B '06 %Weidenbaum & H,LLP -708 3rd Av -NY 10017
(914) 684-9835 .. **Perkel,** Gordon B '74 Cnsl Land Trnsfr Ltd -188 E Post Rd -White Plns 10601 **Fx:**684-9802
(212) 372-5224 .. **Perkel,** Jonathan E '93 Travelocity.com LP -325 Hudson -NY 10013
(212) 704-6016 .. **Perkiel,** Mitchel H '75 (Troutman S LLP) -405 Lex Av -NY 10174
(212) 797-1007 .. **Perkins,** Blake '81 -26 Bway -NY 10004
(518) 584-4191 .. **Perkins,** Cindy Leadley '84 OfCnsl Perkins & P -267 Bway -Saratoga Spgs 12866 **Fx:**587-8175
(212) 474-1000 .. **Perkins,** David J '06 %Cravath S&M LLP -825 8th Av -NY 10019
(516) 705-0591 .. **Perkins,** David L '07 -40 E Merrick Rd -Vly Stream 11580
(718) 429-6993 .. **Perkins,** Donald J '78 -62-27 84th -Middl Vllg 11379
(212) 408-5100 .. **Perkins,** Francesca J E '09 %Chadbourne & P LLP -30 Rckfllr Plz -NY 10112
(212) 735-8647 .. **Perkins,** Fred H '85 (Morrison C LLP) -909 3rd Av -NY 10022
(212) 801-3188 .. **Perkins,** James W '88 (Greenberg T,LLP) -200 Park Av -NY 10166
(212) 906-1200 .. **Perkins,** Jennifer Silber '98 (Latham & W) -885 3rd Av -NY 10022
(518) 449-8893 .. **Perkins,** Jos T '92 (Wilson EME&D LLP) -677 Bway -Albany 12207
(607) 844-9111 .. **Perkins,** Mahlon R '75 (M Perkins,PC) -11 South Bx27 -Dryden 13053 **Fx:**844-8961
(585) 325-2520 .. **Perkins,** Margaret Skemp '92 %Leg Assistance -1 W Main -Rchstr 14614 **Fx:**325-2559
(718) 250-2000 .. **Perkins,** Michl '95 %DA -350 Jay -Brklyn 11201 **Fx:**250-2314
(845) 265-2820 .. **Perkins,** Patrick T '94 -1711 Route 9D -Cold Spg 10516 **Fx:**265-2819
(212) 909-6000 .. **Perkins,** Roswell B '49 Debevoise & P LLP -919 3rd Av -NY 10022
(212) 259-8000 .. **Perkins,** Russel G III '03 %Dewey & L LLP -1301 Av of Amer -NY 10019
(518) 584-4191 .. **Perkins,** S Scott '81 (Perkins & P) -267 Bway -Saratoga Spgs 12866 **Fx:**587-8175
(212) 218-5500 .. **Perkins,** Wm P '97 (Seyfarth S LLP) -620 8th Av -NY 10018
(212) 415-9200 .. **Perkovich,** Jos J '07 %Dorsey & W LLP -250 Park Av -NY 10177
(212) 686-3838 .. **Perkul,** Elise L '02 %Barst M&K LLP -2 Park Av -NY 10016
(212) 558-4000 .. **Perl,** Alynn C '08 %Sullivan & C LLP -125 Broad -NY 10004
(212) 261-7000 .. **Perl,** David A '97 Calyon -1301 Av of Amer -NY 10019
(914) 835-4346 .. **Perl,** Else '56 -365 West -Harrison 10528
(516) 496-5822 .. **Perl,** Michl J '07 %T Spina -170 Froehlich Farm Blvd -Woodbury 11797 **Fx:**496-5420
(212) 877-8546 .. **Perl,** Richd B '85 -1 W 67th -NY 10023
(716) 886-1257 .. **Perla,** Cynthia L '80 %Perla & P,LLP -367 Linwood Av -Buffalo 14209 **Fx:**886-2720
(716) 886-1257 .. **Perla,** Gregory J '75 (Perla & P,LLP) -367 Linwood Av -Buffalo 14209 **Fx:**886-2720
(716) 886-1257 .. **Perla,** Jeffrey A '76 (Perla & P,LLP) -367 Linwood Av -Buffalo 14209 **Fx:**886-2720
(716) 886-1257 .. **Perla,** Keith D '85 (Perla & P,LLP) -367 Linwood Av -Buffalo 14209 **Fx:**886-2720
(212) 816-4295 .. **Perla,** Mark B '98 Citigroup -388 Greenwich -NY 10013
(716) 886-1257 .. **Perla,** Mark S '78 (Perla & P,LLP) -367 Linwood Av -Buffalo 14209 **Fx:**886-2720
(716) 855-7300 .. **Perla,** Mary E '87 %NFTA -181 Ellicott -Buffalo 14203 **Fx:**855-7657
(716) 883-6415 .. **Perla,** Russell T '55 -367 Linwood Av -Buffalo 14209 **Fx:**882-1896
(914) 997-2500 .. **Perlberg,** Brandon M '07 %Bodnar & M LLP -140 Grand -White Plns 10601 **Fx:**997-8155
(631) 673-6670 .. **Perlberg,** Dennis M '73 (Speyer & P,LLP) -115 Broadhllw Rd -Melvll 11747
(310) 859-1511 .. **Perlberger,** Martin '80 (Perlberger Law Ofcs) -225 Bway #304 -NY 10007 **Fx:**859-1512
(212) 233-3676 .. **Perlberger,** Ralph '57 -225 Bway -NY 10007 **Fx:**233-3678
(212) 441-1150 .. **Perle,** Ellen R '84 Aon Grp,Inc -199 Water -NY 10038 **Fx:**441-1929
(212) 318-6000 .. **Perle,** Jonathan B '06 %Paul HJ&W LLP -75 E 55th -NY 10022
(716) 849-8900 .. **Perley,** Michl F '77 (Hurwitz & F,PC) -1300 Lbrty Bldg -Buffalo 14202
(212) 701-3000 .. **Perlgut,** Lauren B '06 %Cahill G&R LLP -80 Pine -NY 10005 **Fx:**269-5420
(845) 338-0510 .. **Perlin,** Jan '88 Zwiebel & F,LLP -72 Maiden Ln Bx3907 -Kingston 12402
(212) 431-2183 .. **Perlin,** Michl L '85 %NY Law Schl -185 W Bway -NY 10013 **Fx:**966-2053
(516) 739-0400 .. **Perlin,** Michele A '08 %Kelly R&K,LLP -330 Old Cntry Rd -Mineola 11501
(212) 840-3878 .. **Perlitsh,** Stephen M '83 (S Perlitsh,PC) -110 W 34th -NY 10001 **Fx:**(917) 510-0872
(212) 655-3500 .. **Perlman,** Barry M '95 (Meister S&F LLP) -140 E 45th -NY 10017
(212) 889-0575 .. **Perlman,** Clifford '88 (Perlman & P) -41 Mad Av -NY 10010 **Fx:**743-8120
(212) 684-1466 .. **Perlman,** Danl S '77 -2 Rector -NY 10006 **Fx:**684-1468
(718) 855-8708 .. **Perlman,** David H '64 -186 Montague -Brklyn 11201 **Fx:**855-4478
(212) 789-2025 .. **Perlman,** Douglas L '94 %NHL -1251 Av of Amer -NY 10020
(716) 285-1550 .. **Perlman,** Edw P '80 (Magavern MG LLP) -810 Main -Niagara Fls 14301
(516) 535-6666 .. **Perlman,** Ira M '85 -55 Bryant Av -Roslyn 11576 **Fx:**626-6696
(516) 385-4105 .. **Perlman,** Irving '53 -805 Preston Rd -E Meadow 11554
(212) 788-9587 .. **Perlman,** Jeffrey M '07 Cnsl Ofc Mgmt & Budget -75 Park Pl -NY 10007 **Fx:**788-9197
(212) 592-0731 .. **Perlman,** Jodi L '90 %Maiden Form Inc -200 Mad Av -NY 10016

(212) 612-3270 .. **Perlman,** Julian D '07 Mishcon de R NY LLP -200 Park Av -NY 10166
(212) 269-4310 .. **Perlman,** Lori J '94 OfCnsl Frankenthaler KS&K -420 Lex Av -NY 10170
(212) 223-7555 .. **Perlman,** Louis M '02 Lazam Prop -9 E 62nd -NY 10065 **Fx:**223-8297
(718) 206-4720 .. **Perlman,** Magdalena M '09 %Law Dept -89-17 Sutphin Blvd -Jamaica 11435 **Fx:**206-4702
(212) 438-3658 .. **Perlman,** Marc S '02 Standard & Poors -55 Water -NY 10041
(212) 537-1386 .. **Perlman,** Noah B '98 Morgan Stanley -1633 Bway -NY 10019
(716) 856-4000 .. **Perlman,** Paul I '80 (Hodgson R LLP) -140 Pearl -Buffalo 14202
(212) 889-0575 .. **Perlman,** Seth '85 (Perlman & P) -41 Mad Av -NY 10010 **Fx:**743-8120
(212) 376-8000 .. **Perlman,** Steven E '90 (Perlman & Assoc,PLLC) -551 5th Av -NY 10176 **Fx:**376-8070
(212) 529-1659 .. **Perlman,** Susan D '86 -753 9th Av -NY 10019
(212) 605-6200 .. **Perlman Raphael,** Audrey M '90 %Levy P&K,LLP -800 3rd Av -NY 10022
(212) 679-1990 .. **Perlmutter,** Adam D '93 A Perlmutter -260 Mad Av -NY 10016 **Fx:**679-1995
(516) 792-0732 .. **Perlmutter,** Beth '95 -200 Hempstd Av -Lynbrk 11563 **Fx:**792-0732
(845) 436-4109 .. **Perlmutter,** Bruce '74 -51 Bway Bx425 -Woodrdg 12789 **Fx:**436-9398
(212) 922-9250 .. **Perlmutter,** David M '64 (Ganfer & S LLP) -360 Lex Av -NY 10017
(718) 725-3058 .. **Perlmutter,** Eric B '03 %ACS -151-20 Jamaica Av -Jamaica 11432 **Fx:**725-3124
(914) 762-8639 .. **Perlmutter,** Joyce M '81 -63 Law Rd -Briarclff Mnr 10510
(212) 373-3000 .. **Perlmutter,** Marc E '78 (Paul WRW&G LLP) -1285 Av of Amer -NY 10019
(212) 541-2000 .. **Perlmutter,** Margery H '00 (Bryan C LLP) -1290 Av of Amer -NY 10104
(646) 563-8945 .. **Perlmutter,** Michl A '03 %Cole SMF&L,PA -900 3rd Av -NY 10022 **Fx:**521-2045
(845) 356-2570 .. **Perlmutter,** Randy J '01 (Kantrowitz G&G,PC) -747 Chestnut Rdg Rd -Chestnut Rdg 10977
(212) 248-1079 .. **Perlmutter,** Stephen D '73 -67 Wall -NY 10005
(516) 248-6400 .. **Perlmutter,** Stuart '70 (Davidoff M&H,LLP) -200 Grdn City Plz -Gdn Cty 11530
(212) 442-5132 .. **Perlmutter,** Wendy H '03 Admin Childrens Srvcs -150 William -NY 10038
(212) 902-1000 .. **Perloff,** Michl J '99 Goldman Sachs -180 Maiden Ln -NY 10038
(212) 592-1400 .. **Perlov,** Laura S '08 %Herrick,F LLP -2 Park Av -NY 10016
(212) 349-5618 .. **Perlowitz,** Alan J '89 (Chaves & P LLP) -116 John -NY 10038
(212) 450-8606 .. **Perlowitz,** Marc H '81 %Barneys' New York -575 5th Av -NY 10017
(212) 788-7022 .. **Perlson,** Douglas J '94 %Cncl Member N Dear -250 Bway -NY 10007 **Fx:**788-8964
(718) 686-3275 .. **Perlstein,** Abraham J '96 %Lifetime Care Fndtn -4510 16th Av -Brklyn 11204 **Fx:**851-2772
(516) 355-9600 .. **Perlstein,** Allen '87 (Friedman HK&P) -3000 Marcus Av -Lk Success 11042
(212) 832-9951 .. **Perlstein,** Robt S '74 -1501 Bway -NY 10036
(212) 488-1200 .. **Perlstein,** Steven W '99 (Kobre & K,LLP) -800 3rd Av -NY 10022
(212) 766-1888 .. **Permakoff,** Patricia E '80 (Morris DA&F) -2 Rector -NY 10006
(631) 731-4172 .. **Permenter,** Danelle M '04 D Permenter,PC -61 Pauls Path -Coram 11727 **Fx:**696-5409
(516) 746-8000 .. **Permut,** Michl '55 (Jaspan S LLP) -300 Grdn City Plz -Gdn Cty 11530
(914) 725-5005 .. **Permutt,** Judith E '80 Permutt & P -111 Brook -Scarsdale 10583 **Fx:**725-5065
(914) 725-5005 .. **Permutt,** Neal A '67 (Permutt & P) -111 Brook -Scarsdale 10583 **Fx:**725-5065
(914) 378-3900 .. **Permutt,** Robt J '97 Kaplan & M -1 Exec Blvd -Ynkrs 10701
(914) 725-5005 .. **Permutt,** Wm M '79 (Permutt & P) -111 Brook -Scarsdale 10583 **Fx:**725-5065
(718) 578-7785 .. **Perna,** Michl '02 -345 E Grand -Mt Vernon 10552
(716) 853-5700 .. **Perna,** Philip A '78 -460 Niagara -Buffalo 14201
(718) 667-5000 .. **Perniciaro,** Wm P '87 -84 New Dorp Plz -Staten Isl 10306 **Fx:**667-0798
(516) 248-3302 .. **Pernick,** Ralph '75 %Dept of Law -200 Old Cntry Rd -Mineola 11501 **Fx:**747-6432
(516) 759-8720 .. **Pernick,** Susan G '75 -4 Todd Ct -Glen Head 11545
(212) 490-3000 .. **Pernicone,** Carl J '84 (Wilson EME&D LLP) -150 E 42nd -NY 10017
(212) 640-5709 .. **Pero,** Anjli G '00 AMex -200 Vesey -NY 10285
(212) 770-7160 .. **Pero,** Richd '02 Chartis -70 Pine -NY 10270
(212) 553-8300 .. **Pero,** Scott B '91 %Cohen K & Assoc -2 Park Av -NY 10016 **Fx:**553-8721
(212) 784-5800 .. **Peroff,** Mark I '77 (Hiscock & B,LLP) -7 Times Sq -NY 10036
(914) 834-3500 .. **Perone,** John M '71 (McMillan CM&P LLP) -2180 Bstn Post Rd -Larchmnt 10538
(631) 501-3100 .. **Perone,** Peter A '80 %J Humphreys -3 Huntngtn Quad Bx9028 -Melvll 11747 **Fx:**501-3085
(914) 997-8100 .. **Perone,** Susan R '85 %Burke LM&G -10 Bank -White Plns 10606
(212) 842-8013 .. **Peronti,** Maryann '88 -380 Rector Pl -NY 10280 **Fx:**842-0675
(716) 542-5413 .. **Perot,** Lawr A '81 (Nicholas PSB&Z) -12364 Main Rd Bx176 -Akron 14001
(607) 772-8440 .. **Perot,** Remy R '68 SrCnsl R Perot -20-24 Wall -Bnghmtn 13901 **Fx:**772-8339
(585) 225-3080 .. **Perotto,** Gay B '87 (Parrs & P LLP) -105 Canal Lndng Blvd -Rchstr 14626 **Fx:**225-0459
(212) 969-3000 .. **Perra,** Kevin J '96 (Proskauer R LLP) -1585 Bway -NY 10036
(585) 232-4090 .. **Perrault,** Kathleen Lynd '01 Leg Aid -1 W Main -Rchstr 14614 **Fx:**232-2352
(212) 310-8000 .. **Perrault,** Kristen D '00 Weil G&M LLP -767 5th Av -NY 10153
(518) 457-2411 .. **Perreault,** Thos D '93 %DOT -50 Wolf Rd -Albany 12232 **Fx:**457-4021
(212) 953-1505 .. **Perrella,** Nicholas R '78 -260 Mad Av -NY 10016 **Fx:**953-3060
(914) 472-2300 .. **Perreten,** Paul F '66 OfCnsl Jones G,LLP -670 Wht Plns Rd -Scarsdale 10583
(914) 478-1127 .. **Perreten,** Paul F '66 -139 Southside Av -Hastings-On-Hud 10706 **Fx:**(860) 388-4721
(914) 251-1115 .. **Perretta,** Josephine P '06 %Walsh & A LLP -2900 Wstchstr Av -Purchase 10577
(718) 823-4416 .. **Perretta,** Maria '84 -1933 Wllmsbrdg Rd -Bronx 10461
(212) 259-8000 .. **Perri,** Adam B '00 %Dewey & L LLP -1301 Av of Amer -NY 10019
(516) 628-8888 .. **Perri,** Anthony D '75 -46 Bayvll Park Blvd -Bayvll 11709
(315) 781-1465 .. **Perri,** C Kenneth '88 %Leg Assistance -361 S Main -Geneva 14456 **Fx:**781-2565
(212) 805-3900 .. **Perri,** Carl M Jr. '00 (Clausen M PC) -1 Chase Manh Plz -NY 10005
(212) 506-3900 .. **Perri,** Justin B '04 %Steptoe & J LLP -750 7th Av -NY 10019
(212) 819-8200 .. **Perri,** Kerry O'Rourke '08 %White & C LLP -1155 Av of Amer -NY 10036
(212) 326-3939 .. **Perricone,** Anthony L '94 (Jones D) -222 E 41st -NY 10017
(585) 968-5292 .. **Perrigo,** Karen M '94 -Bx65 -Cuba 14727 **Fx:**968-6271
(518) 257-1443 .. **Perrin,** Leslie C '97 Civil Srvc Employees Assn -143 Wshngtn Av -Albany 12210 **Fx:**449-1525
(315) 683-5655 .. **Perrin,** Maureen A '75 (Perrin & D,PC) -Main -Fabius 13063 **Fx:**683-5479
(315) 677-3117 .. **Perrin,** Maureen A '75 (Perrin & D,PC) -6006 Route 20 Bx130 -LaFayette 13084 **Fx:**677-3530
(212) 676-0910 .. **Perrine,** Jean G '85 %Hlth & Hsptl Corp -346 Bway -NY 10013
(516) 221-7900 .. **Perrini,** Jos J III '92 -2876 Merrick Rd -Bellmore 11710 **Fx:**221-1746
(212) 801-6857 .. **Perron,** Stephanie F '03 %Greenberg T,LLP -200 Park Av -NY 10166
(516) 505-0600 .. **Perrone,** Christina N '08 %J McCormack,PC -1035 Stewart Av -Gdn Cty 11530 **Fx:**505-0632
(718) 258-5167 .. **Perrone,** Danl J '05 -1890 E 53rd -Brklyn 11234
(347) 404-9133 .. **Perrone,** Dejana M '09 %Civil Ct -141 Lvngstn -Brklyn 11201 **Fx:**(718) 643-3733
(516) 248-6400 .. **Perrone,** Frank L Jr. '97 %Davidoff M&H,LLP -200 Grdn City Plz -Gdn Cty 11530
(516) 248-8610 .. **Perrone,** Jos '74 (Ryan P&H,PC) -200 Old Cntry Rd -Mineola 11501
(646) 328-0120 .. **Perrone,** Jos J '89 (Bennett GM&P,LLP) -494 8th Av -NY 10001
(212) 949-5500 .. **Perrone,** Laura M '94 (L Perrone,PLLC) -60 E 42nd -NY 10165 **Fx:**949-0049
(212) 363-3100 .. **Perrone,** Marc A '01 %Bivona & C,PC -88 Pine -NY 10005
(212) 536-3900 .. **Perrone,** Patrick J '89 (K&L Gates LLP) -599 Lex Av -NY 10022
(914) 995-4172 .. **Perrone,** Perry P '87 %DA -111 Martin Luther King Blvd -White Plns 10601 **Fx:**995-3363
(212) 483-9490 .. **Perrone,** Rosalie J '08 %McElroy DM&C,LLP -88 Pine -NY 10005
(212) 596-9000 .. **Perron-Savard,** Philippe '10 %Ropes & G LLP -1211 Av of Amer -NY 10036
(718) 347-5921 .. **Perrotta,** Carmine '51 -82-14 Little Neck Pkwy -Floral Pk 11004
(718) 522-1910 .. **Perrotta,** Chas F X '58 -32 Court -Brklyn 11201
(718) 426-0444 .. **Perrotta,** Lyn A '90 %J Aiello -69-06 Grand Av -Maspeth 11378 **Fx:**803-9764
(516) 222-2434 .. **Perrotta,** Melissa A '04 %White Q&S -377 Oak Bx9304 -Gdn Cty 11530
(631) 424-2727 .. **Perrotta,** Michl F '77 -775 Park Av -Huntngtn 11743 **Fx:**385-7664
(914) 249-2000 .. **Perrotti,** Brenda '91 %MasterCard Intl -2000 Purchase -Purchase 10577
(315) 253-0361 .. **Perrotto,** Michaela '09 %BOCES -1879 W Genesee Street Rd -Auburn 13021
(516) 739-1500 .. **Perrucci,** Christine M '09 %Weiss & W -300 Old Cntry Rd -Mineola 11501 **Fx:**739-2189
(646) 742-0547 .. **Perruzzi,** Sean O '98 -137 E 28th -NY 10016
(716) 856-4000 .. **Perry,** Adam W '95 (Hodgson R LLP) -140 Pearl -Buffalo 14202
(212) 310-8000 .. **Perry,** Adrian J '09 %Weil G&M LLP -767 5th Av -NY 10153
(518) 270-8254 .. **Perry,** Alexander B '94 -1835 5th Av -Troy 12180
(212) 856-9600 .. **Perry,** Anne Cortina '07 %Morvillo AGIA&B,PC -565 5th Av -NY 10017
(212) 848-4000 .. **Perry,** C Jones Jr. '85 (Shearman & S LLP) -599 Lex Av -NY 10022
(212) 265-7711 .. **Perry,** Carol C '98 IF Mgmt -810 7th Av -NY 10019
(212) 330-0547 .. **Perry,** Christopher L '97 Covenant House -460 W 41st -NY 10036
(212) 292-6155 .. **Perry,** Chrystie Hale '05 Ziff Bros Investments LLC -350 Park Av -NY 10022
(212) 530-5000 .. **Perry,** Danl M '00 (Milbank TH&M LLP) -1 Chase Manh Plz -NY 10005
(212) 637-2434 .. **Perry,** Danya E '97 %US Atty -1 St Andrews Plz -NY 10007
(212) 889-6565 .. **Perry,** Davida S '86 (Schwartz & P LLP) -295 Mad Av -NY 10017
(212) 661-9100 .. **Perry,** Denaka L '08 %Otterbourg SH&R,PC -230 Park Av -NY 10169
(212) 788-0917 .. **Perry,** Devor D '08 %Law Dept -100 Church -NY 10007 **Fx:**788-0367
(212) 977-9700 .. **Perry,** Donald P '68 (Phillips N LLP) -666 5th Av -NY 10103
(631) 265-0134 .. **Perry,** Douglas P '79 (Kral CRRP&G,LLP) -538 Broadhllw Rd -Melvll 11747 **Fx:**265-4289
(315) 435-2170 .. **Perry,** Eileen P '85 %Cnty Atty -421 Mntgmry -Syracuse 13202 **Fx:**435-5729
(315) 218-8000 .. **Perry,** Elizabeth L '05 %Bond S&K,PLLC -1 Lincoln Ctr -Syracuse 13202
(212) 697-3122 .. **Perry,** Erin M '08 %Martin C&B LLP -220 E 42nd -NY 10017
(212) 375-6290 .. **Perry,** Gally '05 Oddcast,Inc -134 W 37th -NY 10018
(716) 743-0044 .. **Perry,** James M '74 -248 Meadow Dr -N Tonawanda 14120 **Fx:**743-1644
(212) 325-4367 .. **Perry,** James M '97 Credit Suisse -11 Mad Av -NY 10010
(212) 261-1133 .. **Perry,** James T '89 Elizabeth Arden Inc -200 Park Av S -NY 10003
(212) 450-4000 .. **Perry,** John W '08 %Davis P&W LLP -450 Lex Av -NY 10017
(212) 698-3500 .. **Perry,** Jonathan D '02 %Dechert LLP -1095 Av of Amer -NY 10036
(212) 698-3500 .. **Perry,** Jonathan P '02 %Dechert LLP -1095 Av of Amer -NY 10036
(212) 335-4096 .. **Perry,** Jos C '06 DA -1 Hogan Pl -NY 10013
(212) 599-0911 .. **Perry,** Kathy R '80 Perry Law Grp -305 Mad Av -NY 10165 **Fx:**599-5911
(212) 566-1770 .. **Perry,** Kenneth M '89 -395 South End Av -NY 10280 **Fx:**267-1846
(212) 924-1220 .. **Perry,** Kenneth R '89 %Leg Srvc Plan Lcl 237 -216 W 14th -NY 10011 **Fx:**647-9421
(212) 218-2100 .. **Perry,** Lawr S '89 (Fitzpatrick CH&S) -1290 Av of Amer -NY 10104
(914) 949-2826 .. **Perry,** Linda L '05 -199 Main -White Plns 10601 **Fx:**949-2822
(212) 962-1450 .. **Perry,** Marion C '06 %Magovern & S -111 John -NY 10038
(212) 848-4000 .. **Perry,** Mark S '96 %Shearman & S LLP -599 Lex Av -NY 10022

(718) 881-9008 .. **Perry,** Mitchell L '95 -2566 Wilson Av -Bronx 10469
(212) 605-6200 .. **Perry,** Nancy A '95 %Levy P&K,LLP -800 3rd Av -NY 10022
(212) 757-4800 .. **Perry,** Novalie Indira '00 -1841 Bway -NY 10023
(518) 377-6700 .. **Perry,** Pamela L '09 %Cioffi SW PC -2310 Nott E -Niskayuna 12309
(646) 386-5700 .. **Perry,** Phaedra Fane '03 %Civil Ct -111 Centre -NY 10013
(516) 496-5822 .. **Perry,** Rachel '00 %T Spina -170 Froehlich Farm Blvd -Woodbury 11797 **Fx:**496-5420
(315) 471-7604 .. **Perry,** Richd '90 -333 E Onondaga -Syracuse 13202 **Fx:**471-9476
(212) 607-3300 .. **Perry,** Robt A '99 %NYCLU -125 Broad -NY 10004
(212) 556-2100 .. **Perry,** Robt F '89 (King & S) -1185 Av of Amer -NY 10036
(914) 328-0404 .. **Perry,** Robt R '87 (Jackson L LLP) -1 N Bway -White Plns 10601
(212) 259-8000 .. **Perry,** Ryan '07 %Dewey & L LLP -1301 Av of Amer -NY 10019
(212) 696-6000 .. **Perry,** Shafiq R '09 %Curtis M-PC&M LLP -101 Park Av -NY 10178
(212) 558-5500 .. **Perry,** Stuart S '80 %Weitz & L,PC -700 Bway -NY 10003
(518) 436-7837 .. **Perry,** Suzanne E '81 -4 Chestnut Hill Rd S -Loudonvll 12211
(212) 506-5000 .. **Perry,** Tamia '00 Orrick H&S LLP -51 W 52nd -NY 10019
(716) 858-2200 .. **Perry,** Tiffany R '01 %Cnty Atty -95 Franklin -Buffalo 14202 **Fx:**858-2281
(315) 474-2943 .. **Perry,** Timothy J '78 (Sugarman Law Firm,LLP) -211 W Jffrsn -Syracuse 13202
(212) 258-8000 .. **Perry,** Tina M '00 %MTV Networks -1515 Bway -NY 10036 **Fx:**258-8358
(212) 926-6685 .. **Perry,** Twila L '77 -435 Convent Av -NY 10031
(646) 386-5700 .. **Perry,** Wm F '89 %Civil Ct -111 Centre -NY 10013
(315) 701-5780 .. **Perry-Shurtliff,** Jaya '97 %Olinsky & S -300 S State -Syracuse 13202
(518) 462-0300 .. **Pers,** Elaine M '88 OfCnsl Girvin & F,PC -20 Corp Wds Blvd -Albany 12211
(914) 961-4400 .. **Persanis,** Claire H '95 %Elefante & P,LLP -141 Hillside Pl -Eastchstr 10709
(914) 961-4400 .. **Persanis,** Matthew N '94 (Elefante & P,LLP) -141 Hillside Pl -Eastchstr 10709
(212) 403-1000 .. **Persaud,** Amanda N '00 Cnsl Wachtell LR&K -51 W 52nd -NY 10019
(718) 558-9188 .. **Persaud,** C Sonia '02 -8767 148th -Jamaica 11435
(718) 558-9188 .. **Persaud,** Horace H '93 -87-63 148th -Jamaica 11435 **Fx:**558-9187
(718) 231-6737 .. **Persaud,** Mahandra '99 -4200 Wht Plns Rd -Bronx 10466
(212) 318-6000 .. **Persaud,** Marcia N '09 %Paul HJ&W LLP -75 E 55th -NY 10022
(212) 826-0808 .. **Persaud,** Melissa A '99 %MLB Players Assn -12 E 49th -NY 10017 **Fx:**752-3649
(212) 839-5300 .. **Persaud,** Nadia N '04 Sidley A LLP -787 7th Av -NY 10019
(212) 872-1000 .. **Persaud,** Nyron J '08 -One Bryant Park -NY 10036 **Fx:**872-1002
(718) 850-0900 .. **Persaud,** Ravi B '94 (R Persaud,PC) -125-07 101st Av -S Richmond Hll 11419 **Fx:**850-1188
(631) 777-5440 .. **Persaud,** Sharmine '90 -1105 Route 110 -Farmngdl 11735 **Fx:**777-5443
(315) 793-8111 .. **Persbacker,** Sharon M '93 %US Bankruptcy Ct -10 Broad -Utica 13501
(212) 756-2000 .. **Perschetz,** Martin L '78 (Schulte R&Z LLP) -919 3rd Av -NY 10022
(212) 684-4289 .. **Perseo,** Mariann G '81 -340 W 28th -NY 10001 **Fx:**217-9950
(212) 603-6300 .. **Pershan,** Lee S '85 Cnsl Robinson BLGG&G PC -875 3rd Av -NY 10022
(212) 660-3000 .. **Pershan,** Richd H '56 OfCnsl Sullivan & W LLP -1290 Av of Amer -NY 10104
(718) 264-7808 .. **Pershay,** Barbara Emmanuel '84 -111-36 Farmers Blvd -St Albans 11412 **Fx:**264-7411
(212) 964-9282 .. **Pershman,** Sergei '08 %N Weinrib & Assoc -305 Bway -NY 10007 **Fx:**964-9525
(631) 491-9200 .. **Persichilli,** Thos '79 -2137 Deer Prk Av -Deer Pk 11729 **Fx:**360-8935
(716) 882-4890 .. **Persico,** Jennifer C '99 (Mosey P,LLP) -625 Delaware Av -Buffalo 14202 **Fx:**882-5240
(212) 887-1300 .. **Persico,** Marian T '81 %Arbitron Ratings Co -142 W 57th -NY 10019
(212) 969-3000 .. **Persily,** Marc A '96 (Proskauer R LLP) -1585 Bway -NY 10036
(914) 328-0674 .. **Persily,** Sarah Deitch '00 Pro Bono Prtnrshp,Inc -237 Mamaroneck Av -White Plns 10605 **Fx:**328-0538
(518) 860-1444 .. **Persing,** Danl J '82 (Persing & O,LLP) -10 Century Hill Dr -Latham 12110 **Fx:**860-1448
(201) 531-8000 .. **Persing,** David A '88 Metromedia Co -810 7th Av -NY 10019 **Fx:**531-2803
(212) 530-5000 .. **Persinger,** Jos M '79 OfCnsl Milbank TH&M LLP -1 Chase Manh Plz -NY 10005
(718) 875-7584 .. **Perskin,** Brian D '91 -105 Court -Brklyn 11201
(631) 665-3400 .. **Perskin,** Richd K '91 %Siben & S,LLP -90 E Main Bx149P -Bay Shr 11706
(718) 279-8800 .. **Perskin,** Robt S '76 R Perskin,PC -42-40 Bell Blvd -Bayside 11361 **Fx:**(201) 871-2129
(718) 875-7584 .. **Perskin,** Stephanie J '92 -105 Court -Brklyn 11201
(212) 907-0868 .. **Persky,** Bernard '69 (Labaton S LLP) -140 Bway -NY 10005
(718) 250-1100 .. **Persky,** David '83 %E Garfinkel -12 Metrotech Ctr -Brklyn 11201 **Fx:**250-1168
(516) 922-8228 .. **Persky,** Jamie L '91 J Persky & Assoc,PC -26 Hickman -Syosset 11791 **Fx:**922-3168
(516) 294-3370 .. **Persoff,** Stephan '68 -1 Old Cntry Rd -Carle Pl 11514 **Fx:**747-6384
(212) 307-4444 .. **Person,** Carl E '62 -325 W 45th -NY 10036 **Fx:**307-0247
(607) 734-5204 .. **Personius Mattison Palmer & Bocek** -150 Lk Bx146 -Elmira 14902 **Fx:**734-5206
(716) 855-1050 .. **Personius Melber LLP** -2100 Main Place Twr -Buffalo 14202 **Fx:**855-1052
(716) 855-1050 .. **Personius,** Rodney O '77 (Personius M LLP) -2100 Main Place Twr -Buffalo 14202
(516) 747-4082 .. **Persons,** John W '81 %Montfort HM&S LLP -1140 Franklin Av Bx7677 -Gdn Cty 11530
(585) 544-7090 .. **Personte,** Michl J '81 (Pirrello MP&F) -2040 E Ridge Rd -Rchstr 14622
(315) 735-6097 .. **Perta,** Alan E '87 -10 Morgan Ln -New Hartfrd 13413
(607) 763-9200 .. **Perticone,** John L '80 (Levene G&T,LLP) -BxF-1706 -Bnghmtn 13902
(585) 482-1120 .. **Perticone,** Maria '93 -Bx10401 -Rchstr 14610
(718) 923-4206 .. **Pertsas,** Konstantinos '87 %OTDA Fair Hearings -14 Boerum Pl -Brklyn 11201
(315) 733-2396 .. **Pertz,** Richd '77 (Brindisi MBPJ&P,LLP) -2713 Genesee -Utica 13501
(212) 819-0089 .. **Perusse,** Catherine V '89 %Edmonds & Co,PC -112 Mad Av -NY 10016 **Fx:**819-0189
(212) 693-0085 .. **Pervukhin,** Anna '05 Appellate Advocates -2 Rector -NY 10006 **Fx:**693-0878
(518) 566-0584 .. **Peryer,** Kevin L '84 K Peryer,PC -29 Trackside Bx3050 -Plattsbrgh 12901
(631) 730-1063 .. **Pesa,** Helena '07 -Patchogue 11772 **Fx:**228-0911
(585) 546-5530 .. **Pesando,** Marie K '92 %Thomson West -50 E Broad -Rchstr 14694
(212) 819-8200 .. **Pesant,** Chas J '03 %White & C LLP -1155 Av of Amer -NY 10036
(315) 474-2943 .. **Pesarchick,** Stephen G '89 (Sugarman Law Firm,LLP) -211 W Jffrsn -Syracuse 13202
(315) 479-3900 .. **Pesaresi-Jones,** Gina A '98 %SSA-ODAR -300 S State -Syracuse 13202 **Fx:**479-3933
(212) 752-9700 .. **Pescaru,** Paula '07 %Gersten S LLP -600 Lex Av -NY 10022
(516) 873-1511 .. **Pesce,** Frank V '81 (Fischetti & P) -310 Old Cntry Rd -Gdn Cty 11530
(631) 281-4444 .. **Pesce,** Rocco V '75 -519 Willaim Floyd Pkwy Bx689 -Shirley 11967 **Fx:**281-4440
(212) 872-6272 .. **Pesce,** Teresa Anne '88 (KPMG LLP) -345 Park Av -NY 10154
(718) 590-3730 .. **Pesce-Fusto,** Eleanor L '88 %Supreme Ct -851 Grnd Cncrs -Bronx 10451
(212) 265-5273 .. **Peschiera,** Alan E '83 -437 W 44th -NY 10036
(212) 504-6000 .. **Pescovitz,** Aliza '09 %Cadwalader W&T LLP -1 World Fncl Ctr -NY 10281
(212) 513-1988 .. **Pesetsky & Bookman** -325 Bway -NY 10007 **Fx:**385-0564
(212) 513-1988 .. **Pesetsky,** Warren B '69 (Pesetsky & B) -325 Bway -NY 10007
(516) 466-0090 .. **Peshkin,** Kenneth F '90 OfCnsl Yerushalmi & Assoc -17 Barstow Rd -Gt Neck 11021 **Fx:**466-8988
(914) 686-5042 .. **Peska,** Adam M '98 Cnsl Peska & Assoc -235 Main -White Plns 10601 **Fx:**428-1159
(914) 632-4700 .. **Peske,** Jeffrey S '03 %McDonough Law Firm, LLP -145 Huguenot -New Rchll 10801
(212) 867-2468 .. **Peskin,** Richd S '79 -319 Mad Av -NY 10017 **Fx:**867-2466
(212) 964-1390 .. **Peskin,** Stephan H '68 (Tolmage PH&F) -20 Vesey -NY 10007
(212) 907-7300 .. **Peskoe,** Andrew C '83 (Golenbock EAB&P) -437 Mad Av -NY 10022
(212) 592-1400 .. **Peskoe,** Howard E '75 Cnsl Herrick,F LLP -2 Park Av -NY 10016
(212) 839-5300 .. **Peskowitz,** Michl H '86 (Sidley A LLP) -787 7th Av -NY 10019
(212) 872-1000 .. **Pesner,** Steven M '72 -One Bryant Park -NY 10036 **Fx:**872-1002
(516) 488-3300 .. **Pessah-Bloom,** Lisa A '04 %Shaub AC&S,LLP -1983 Marcus Av -Lk Success 11042
(516) 822-1600 .. **Pessala,** John Ben '79 -16 E Old Cntry Rd -Hicksvll 11801 **Fx:**822-6160
(212) 961-0668 .. **Pessen,** Abigail J '73 Mediation Srvcs -80 Broad -NY 10004 **Fx:**961-0669
(212) 403-1000 .. **Pessin,** Gregory E '06 %Wachtell LR&K -51 W 52nd -NY 10019
(212) 878-8000 .. **Pesso,** Mark S '98 Cnsl Clifford C LLP -31 W 52nd -NY 10019
(212) 244-9500 .. **Pesso,** Maurice '01 (White and W LLP) -1 Penn Plz -NY 10119
(718) 701-1611 .. **Pessolano,** Clare M '09 -1110 South Av -Staten Isl 10314 **Fx:**701-1265
(212) 425-0555 .. **Pestaina,** Cora-Ann V '06 %C Mehta & Assoc,PLLC -2 Wall -NY 10005 **Fx:**425-3282
(212) 788-0862 .. **Pestana,** Georgia M '89 %Law Dept -100 Church -NY 10007 **Fx:**788-0367
(716) 855-1921 .. **Peszko,** Mark J '86 -515 Brisbane Bldg -Buffalo 14203 **Fx:**854-5080
(212) 688-3200 .. **Petchesky,** Harry J '62 Cnsl Scheichet & D,PC -767 3rd Av -NY 10017
(212) 848-4000 .. **Petepiece,** Scott D '01 (Shearman & S LLP) -599 Lex Av -NY 10022
(202) 361-2745 .. **Peter,** Alexander F '05 -244 5th Av -NY 10001 **Fx:**361-2745
(315) 425-2700 .. **Peterman,** Alan R '86 (Hiscock & B,LLP) -One Park Pl -Syracuse 13202
(212) 715-1000 .. **Peterman,** Cara M '10 %Arnold & P LLP -399 Park Av -NY 10022
(212) 336-2000 .. **Peterman,** Chad J '00 (Patterson BW&T LLP) -1133 Av of Amer -NY 10036
(212) 310-8000 .. **Peterman,** Eric J '89 (Weil G&M LLP) -767 5th Av -NY 10153
(212) 310-8000 .. **Peterman,** N Damali '09 %Weil G&M LLP -767 5th Av -NY 10153
(845) 225-5171 .. **Peterman,** Thos C '93 -Bx89 -Carmel 10512
(718) 515-6000 .. **Peterman,** Wm K III '86 (Corpina PK&P,LLP) -2344 Eastchstr Rd -Bronx 10469
(718) 596-7800 .. **Peters Berger Koshel & Goldberg,PC** -26 Court -Brklyn 11242
(518) 565-3390 .. **Peters,** Christine G '01 Dept Social Srvcs -13 Durkee -Plattsbrgh 12901 **Fx:**565-3626
(212) 728-8000 .. **Peters,** Christopher J '98 (Willkie F&G LLP) -787 7th Av -NY 10019
(585) 442-0540 .. **Peters,** David W '99 (Ashcraft FY&P,LLP) -150 Allens Crk Rd -Rchstr 14618
Peters, Delia L '90 -340 E 74th -NY 10021
(212) 207-0700 .. **Peters,** Elizabeth '78 Sumitomo Corp -600 3rd Av -NY 10016
(212) 484-8135 .. **Peters,** Elliott F '96 %Warner Music Grp -75 Rckfllr Plz -NY 10019 **Fx:**489-3342
(914) 762-5840 .. **Peters,** Frank J '92 -520 N State Rd -Briarclff Mnr 10510 **Fx:**762-9025
(516) 621-1517 .. **Peters,** Gary D '75 N Peters,PC -1500 Old Nrthrn Blvd -Roslyn 11576 **Fx:**621-1537
(347) 692-8891 .. **Peters,** George T '05 -26 Court -Brklyn 11242
(646) 610-6353 .. **Peters,** Harry '78 SrCnsl NYPD -1 Police Plz -NY 10038 **Fx:**610-6366
(212) 854-2472 .. **Peters,** Julie Stone '99 Columbia Univ -1150 Amstrdm Av -NY 10027
(212) 691-7070 .. **Peters,** Kelly P '09 %J Simermeyer,PC -148 Mad Av -NY 10016 **Fx:**691-7097
(518) 408-3976 .. **Peters,** Mark G '91 %NYS Comm Pub Integrity -540 Bway -Albany 12207
(212) 761-4699 .. **Peters,** Mary Lou '95 Morgan Stanley -1585 Bway -NY 10036
(518) 449-3125 .. **Peters,** Michl W '89 (Stockli GS&P,LLP) -90 State -Albany 12207
(212) 461-4240 .. **Peters,** Michele A '01 Weichert Rltrs-Peters Assoc -545 8th Av -NY 10018 **Fx:**461-4279
(212) 350-2700 .. **Peters,** Michelle A '00 %Constantine C,PC -450 Lex Av -NY 10017

(516) 621-1517 .. **Peters,** Nancy '96 -1500 Old Nrthrn Blvd -Roslyn 11576 **Fx:**621-1537
(212) 577-3688 .. **Peters,** Pamela A '88 %Leg Aid -199 Water -NY 10038 **Fx:**509-8431
(212) 907-9600 .. **Peters,** Paulette Lemay '87 Cnsl Ingram YGC&B,LLP -250 Park Av -NY 10177
(212) 237-0000 .. **Peters,** Robt D '08 %Vinson & E LLP -666 5th Av -NY 10103
(716) 699-2355 .. **Peters,** Ross A '76 (Peters & P) -1 Wshngtn Bx628 -Ellicottvll 14731 **Fx:**699-4248
(646) 473-3948 .. **Peters,** Susan L '98 %USPS -380 W 33rd -NY 10199 **Fx:**473-3914
(212) 558-4000 .. **Peterseil,** Yakob M '10 %Sullivan & C LLP -125 Broad -NY 10004
(914) 723-2366 .. **Petersen,** Abigail I '80 -101 Greenacres Av -Scarsdale 10583
(212) 820-9401 .. **Petersen,** Eric S '74 (Hawkins D&W LLP) -One Chase Manh Plz -NY 10005
(212) 775-8700 .. **Petersen,** Jos E '97 (Kilpatrick S,LLP) -31 W 52nd -NY 10019
(212) 401-0800 .. **Petersen,** Kim '00 %Disciplinary Comm -61 Bway -NY 10006 **Fx:**287-1045
(315) 625-5321 .. **Petersen,** Maureen H '98 -Bx336 -Parish 13131 **Fx:**625-7189
(718) 680-3230 .. **Petersen,** Michl '83 -231 67th -Brklyn 11220
(718) 254-7584 .. **Petersen,** Paige M '02 US Atty -1 Pierrepont Plz -Brklyn 11201
(212) 434-0100 .. **Petersen,** Richd H '94 %Litchfield C LLP -420 Lex Av -NY 10170
(914) 997-1346 .. **Petersen,** Scott C '94 (Seham SM&P,LLP) -445 Hmltn Av -White Plns 10601
(718) 590-5438 .. **Petersen-Talley,** Marie '85 %Admin Children's Srvcs -900 Sheridan Av -Bronx 10451
(203) 504-2050 .. **Peters-Hamlin,** Kristan '00 (Peters Hamlin,LLC) -100 Park Av -NY 10017 **Fx:**341-9816
(877) 581-8498 .. **Peters-Lawston,** Bonnie S '94 -Bx317 -Ridge 11961 **Fx:**(866) 431-0045
(212) 335-9000 .. **Peterson,** Alfred F '97 %DA -1 Hogan Pl -NY 10013
(212) 239-3322 .. **Peterson,** Amy L '90 -545 8th Av -NY 10018
(914) 328-0404 .. **Peterson,** Andrew A '81 (Jackson L LLP) -1 N Bway -White Plns 10601
(716) 841-1597 .. **Peterson,** Anne M '98 %HSBC Bank -1 HSBC Ctr -Buffalo 14203 **Fx:**841-5087
(732) 528-4411 .. **Peterson,** Chas F '67 -900 South Av -Staten Isl 10314 **Fx:**528-4411
(716) 849-1333 .. **Peterson,** Cherie L '85 (Lipsitz GSC LLP) -42 Delaware Av -Buffalo 14202
(212) 259-8000 .. **Peterson,** Christopher P '98 (Dewey & L LLP) -1301 Av of Amer -NY 10019
(518) 457-2070 .. **Peterson,** Clifford M '99 %Dept of Tax & Fin -Bldg 9 State Campus -Albany 12227 **Fx:**457-6131
(212) 541-2000 .. **Peterson,** Courtney J '08 %Bryan C LLP -1290 Av of Amer -NY 10104
(585) 530-3151 .. **Peterson,** Craig D '77 %Appllt Div 4th Dept -50 East Av Ste 200 -Rchstr 14604 **Fx:**530-3247
(716) 665-2000 .. **Peterson,** Cynthia Howard '79 %Bush Ind -1 Mason Dr Bx460 -Jamestwn 14702 **Fx:**665-2618
(315) 423-5019 .. **Peterson,** Danl J '00 US DODIG Crim Investigative Srvcs -441 S Salina -Syracuse 13202
(212) 766-1888 .. **Peterson,** Danielle M '01 %Morris DA&F -2 Rector -NY 10006
(212) 558-6884 .. **Peterson,** David M '91 (D Peterson,PC) -65 Bway -NY 10006 **Fx:**480-3617
(212) 755-0100 .. **Peterson,** Dianne M '91 %Grais & E LLP -40 E 52nd -NY 10022
(516) 482-1214 .. **Peterson,** Fran '78 (F Peterson,PC) -15 Oaks Hunt Rd -Gt Neck 11020
(212) 697-2424 .. **Peterson,** Gary E '79 %Imag Inc -1270 Av of the Americas -NY 10020 **Fx:**697-1494
(212) 553-5643 .. **Peterson,** George R '99 %Zurich NA -1 Lbrty Plz -NY 10006
(716) 664-3906 .. **Peterson,** Gregory L '77 (Phillips L LLP) -8 E 3rd Bx1279 -Jamestwn 14702
(516) 222-6200 .. **Peterson,** Gregory P '71 (Berkman HPP&F,PC) -100 Grdn City Plz -Gdn Cty 11530
(212) 583-6063 .. **Peterson,** Harold B Jr. '83 %Martin Geller CPA PC -800 3rd Av -NY 10022 **Fx:**421-4275
(212) 605-6200 .. **Peterson,** Holly C '04 %Levy P&K,LLP -800 3rd Av -NY 10022
(716) 857-7991 .. **Peterson,** James R '77 %Natl Fuel Gas -6363 Main -Williamsvll 14221 **Fx:**857-7614
(732) 528-4411 .. **Peterson,** Jennifer Ann '85 %C Peterson -900 South Av -Staten Isl 10314 **Fx:**528-4411
(212) 635-2730 .. **Peterson,** John M '78 (Neville P LLP) -17 State -NY 10004
(212) 826-0100 .. **Peterson,** Jonathan M '88 FSA -31 W 52nd -NY 10019 **Fx:**893-2710
(845) 679-4830 .. **Peterson,** Karen Alice '92 %Global Action Plan -Bx428 -Woodstock 12498
(716) 483-4498 .. **Peterson,** Karen Rene '99 Jamestown Schl Dist -201 E 4th -Jamestwn 14701
(212) 363-2500 .. **Peterson,** Keith H '85 %Finkelstein & V PC -90 Broad -NY 10004
(718) 354-4104 .. **Peterson,** Kevin C '85 -17 Tracy Ln -E Islip 11730
(212) 972-2929 .. **Peterson,** Kirstin R '96 %Trachtenberg R&F LLP -545 5th Av -NY 10017 **Fx:**972-7581
(718) 261-3047 .. **Peterson,** Laurie '81 %Queens Law Assoc -118-21 Qns Blvd -Frst Hlls 11375 **Fx:**261-0798
(212) 767-7800 .. **Peterson,** Lowell '87 Writers Guild -250 Hudson -NY 10013 **Fx:**582-1909
(315) 266-2098 .. **Peterson,** Margaret Murphy '84 -23 Oxford Rd -New Hartfrd 13413 **Fx:**266-2099
(631) 366-3555 .. **Peterson,** Mark A '82 -732 Smithtwn Bypass -Smithtwn 11787 **Fx:**366-3567
(212) 728-8000 .. **Peterson,** Matthew J '00 %Willkie F&G LLP -787 7th Av -NY 10019
(716) 839-1489 .. **Peterson,** Melanie M '99 %Sanders & S -401 Maryvale Dr -Cheektowaga 14225 **Fx:**839-1512
(212) 259-8000 .. **Peterson,** Melissa A '05 %Dewey & L LLP -1301 Av of Amer -NY 10019
(212) 490-9100 .. **Peterson,** Michl J '99 %Condon & F LLP -7 Times Sq -NY 10036
(516) 733-5469 .. **Peterson,** Nicholas H '09 Davis Vision Inc -159 Express -Plainvw 11803
(212) 713-9021 .. **Peterson,** Pamela W '00 UBS Securities LLC -1285 Av of Amer -NY 10019
(516) 466-4680 .. **Peterson,** R Bertil '67 (RB Peterson,PC) -15 Oaks Hunt Rd -Lk Success 11020
(518) 862-9292 .. **Peterson,** Scott M '05 %Napierski V&N,LLP -296 Wshngtn Av Ext -Albany 12203
(518) 899-1518 .. **Peterson & Thomas, PC** -49 Burlngtn Av Bx578 -Round Lk 12151 **Fx:**899-1561
(518) 899-1518 .. **Peterson,** Thos W '86 (Peterson & T,PC) -49 Burlngtn Av Bx578 -Round Lk 12151
(212) 308-4411 .. **Peterson,** Todd J '91 (Edwards AP&D LLP) -750 Lex Av -NY 10022
(212) 682-2900 .. **Peterson,** Tracy M '01 %Braverman & Assoc,PC -331 Mad Av -NY 10017 **Fx:**682-7718
(716) 372-8997 .. **Peterson,** Wendy G '98 Peterson Law -304 Community Bk Bldg -Olean 14760 **Fx:**372-8586
(212) 762-4763 .. **Peterson,** Wm B '85 Morgan Stanley -1221 Av of Amer -NY 10020
(212) 998-6467 .. **Peters-Quintero,** Mayra L '02 NYU Law Schl -245 Sullivan -NY 10012
(718) 996-0705 .. **Petersson,** Everett J '96 E Petersson,PC -32 Court -Brklyn 11201 **Fx:**996-1932
(212) 530-5000 .. **Petherbridge,** Dima '08 %Milbank TH&M LLP -1 Chase Manh Plz -NY 10005
(212) 310-8000 .. **Petherbridge,** Vaughan D '08 %Weil G&M LLP -767 5th Av -NY 10153
(973) 596-4751 .. **Peticolas,** Susanne '07 (Gibbons PC) -1 Penn Plz -NY 10119 **Fx:**639-6340
(845) 592-7000 .. **Petigrow,** Danl '90 (Donoghue TA&D LLP) -2517 Route 52 -Hopewell Junct 12533
(212) 835-1572 .. **Petigrow,** Paul M '81 (Lampf LP&P) -5 Penn Plz 19th Fl -NY 10119
(516) 682-8282 .. **Petillo,** Christopher M '95 (V Russo & Assoc,PC) -7600 Jericho Tpk -Woodbury 11797 **Fx:**682-8088
(516) 571-6190 .. **Petillo,** Diane C '95 %Cnty Atty -1 West -Mineola 11501 **Fx:**571-6604
(212) 803-3100 .. **Petillo,** Jos C '79 %Empire State Dvlmnt Corp -633 3rd Av -NY 10017
(212) 592-1400 .. **Petillo,** Kimberly C '06 %Herrick,F LLP -2 Park Av -NY 10016
(212) 609-6800 .. **Petit,** Jeffrey A '99 (McCarter & E,LLP) -245 Park Av -NY 10167
(845) 454-5586 .. **Petito,** Bruce A '74 -2 Austin Ct -Poughkeepsie 12603 **Fx:**454-5585
(212) 885-4103 .. **Petito,** Dominic A '81 BMO Cptl Mkts Inc -3 Times Sq -NY 10036
(212) 309-5485 .. **Petito,** Fredrick T '94 %Lexis/Nexis -125 Park Av -NY 10017 **Fx:**309-8187
(845) 454-5586 .. **Petito,** Jos P '08 -2 Austin Ct -Poughkeepsie 12603 **Fx:**454-5585
(516) 358-2023 .. **Petiton,** John E '85 -35 Harvard -Gdn Cty 11530 **Fx:**775-6285
(718) 590-2000 .. **Petitt,** Adam J '09 %DA -198 E 161st -Bronx 10451 **Fx:**590-6477
(718) 522-1020 .. **Petitt,** Robt H II '92 %Rubenstein & R -16 Court -Brklyn 11241
(212) 422-2660 .. **Petitti,** Danielle R '06 %Family Law Ctr -11 Bway -NY 10004 **Fx:**422-2666
(212) 430-8020 .. **Petkanics,** Bryan G '86 (LeClairRyan,PC) -830 3rd Av -NY 10022
(212) 582-6500 .. **Petkos,** Kevin C '05 %Arshack H&L,PLLC -1790 Bway -NY 10019
(212) 773-6833 .. **Petkova,** Radena V '09 Ernst & Young LLP -5 Times Sq -NY 10036
(212) 728-8000 .. **Petkun,** Emily L '10 %Willkie F&G LLP -787 7th Av -NY 10019
(315) 488-4411 .. **Petosa,** John J '96 Deli-Boy,Inc -100 Mathews -Syracuse 13209 **Fx:**488-4155
(516) 357-3000 .. **Petraglia,** Albert W '74 (Rivkin R LLP) -926 RXR Plz -Uniondale 11556
(518) 473-1416 .. **Petragnani,** Amy M '95 %Gvnr's Ofc Employee Relations -Agncy Bldg 2 ESP 13th Fl -Albany 12223 **Fx:**486-7303
(212) 381-7000 .. **Petraitis,** Martin F '91 (Sabin B&G LLP) -4 Times Sq -NY 10036
(646) 252-2935 .. **Petrak,** John Jr. '91 Transit Auth -2 Bway -NY 10004 **Fx:**252-5559
(718) 250-4263 .. **Petrakopoulos,** Polixene '03 %Leg Aid -111 Lvngstn -Brklyn 11201 **Fx:**250-4243
(212) 545-1900 .. **Petrakov,** Albena I '10 %Menaker & H LLP -10 E 40th -NY 10016
(585) 454-4460 .. **Petralia,** Arnold R '60 (Petralia W&O,PC) -16 E Main -Rchstr 14614
(914) 949-5797 .. **Petralia,** Louis M '80 -222 Mamaroneck Av -White Plns 10605 **Fx:**949-5909
(585) 454-4460 .. **Petralia Webb & O'Connell,PC** -16 E Main -Rchstr 14614 **Fx:**232-5079
(212) 770-5236 .. **Petralito,** Frank II '64 %AIG -70 Pine -NY 10270 **Fx:**785-1468
(845) 486-2300 .. **Petramale,** Frank R '97 %DA -236 Main -Poughkeepsie 12601 **Fx:**486-2324
(516) 227-0700 .. **Petraro,** Nina '07 %Farrell F,PC -1320 RXR Plz -Uniondale 11556
(212) 736-0525 .. **Petraro,** Vincent L '81 V Petraro,PLLC -350 7th Av -NY 10001
(516) 869-8866 .. **Petras,** Nicholas G '56 (Petras Law Firm) -60 Hillside Av -Manhsst 11030 **Fx:**869-8001
(516) 869-8866 .. **Petras,** Paul J '96 (Petras Law Firm) -60 Hillside Av -Manhsst 11030 **Fx:**869-8001
(718) 344-5374 .. **Petre,** Mark '00 -3730 Nautilus -Brklyn 11224
(212) 880-6000 .. **Petree,** Pamela Susan '01 %Torys LLP -237 Park Av -NY 10017
(212) 259-8000 .. **Petrella,** Christina M '09 %Dewey & L LLP -1301 Av of Amer -NY 10019
(212) 682-4426 .. **Petrella,** Michl E '01 (O'Shea Prtnrs LLP) -521 5th Av -NY 10175 **Fx:**682-4437
(212) 735-3000 .. **Petrella,** Russell C Jr. '10 %Skadden ASM&F LLP -4 Times Sq -NY 10036
(631) 424-3597 .. **Petrello,** Kathleen '91 %B Salamone & Assoc,PC -8 Ford Pl -Dix Hlls 11746 **Fx:**424-5023
(212) 519-8824 .. **Petrello,** Kevin A '97 Lava Trading Inc -95 Morton -NY 10014
(212) 309-6000 .. **Petretti,** Richd S '81 (Morgan L&B LLP) -101 Park Av -NY 10178
(212) 487-9700 .. **Petrey,** Ann Marie C '84 OfCnsl White F&F,LLP -61 Bway -NY 10006
(516) 489-5000 .. **Petri,** Cheryl E '86 %Town Atty -Town Hall -Hempstd 11550 **Fx:**489-5150
(718) 590-2000 .. **Petri,** Jason P '03 %DA -198 E 161st -Bronx 10451 **Fx:**590-6477
(716) 823-7111 .. **Petricca,** Arcangelo J '57 -605 Ridge Rd -Lackawanna 14218
(716) 823-7111 .. **Petricca-Reszel,** Catherine A '89 %A Petricca -605 Ridge Rd -Lackawanna 14218
(212) 504-6000 .. **Petrick,** Gregory M '83 (Cadwalader W&T LLP) -1 World Fncl Ctr -NY 10281
(212) 643-2503 .. **Petriello,** John J '80 (Levy E&P,PC) -555 5th Av -NY 10017
(631) 878-1700 .. **Petrigliano,** Lorraine '86 (Petrigliano & P,LLP) -Bx637 -Manorvll 11949
(631) 878-1700 .. **Petrigliano,** Victor G '86 (Petrigliano & P,LLP) -Bx637 -Manorvll 11949
(646) 227-2742 .. **Petrilli,** Jennifer A '97 Memorial Sloan-Kettering Cancer Ctr -633 3rd Av -NY 10017
(516) 431-6092 .. **Petrilli,** John A '82 -370 W Park Av -Long Bch 11561 **Fx:**889-8904
(212) 356-4475 .. **Petrilli,** Susan M '91 St Vincent Med Ctr -450 W 33rd -NY 10001

(718) 590-2000 .. **Petrillo,** Concetta '92 %DA -198 E 161st -Bronx 10451 **Fx:**590-6477
(516) 837-6285 .. **Petrillo,** Ellen M '00 Cnsl Sutton Alliance -515 Rockaway Av -Vly Stream 11581 **Fx:**837-6585
(212) 637-2519 .. **Petrillo,** Guy T '87 %US Atty -1 St Andrews Plz -NY 10007
(914) 686-5600 .. **Petrillo,** Jos S '80 %All NY Title Agency -180 E Post Rd -White Plns 10601 **Fx:**686-1440
(914) 946-0600 .. **Petrillo,** Richd T '94 %Pino & Assoc -50 Main -White Plns 10606 **Fx:**946-0650
(516) 766-1619 .. **Petrillo,** Wm S '95 -11 Clinton Av -Rockvll Ctr 11570
(845) 294-3361 .. **Petrizzo,** Jos P '84 (DeProspo P&L) -42 Park Pl -Goshen 10924
(631) 669-6400 .. **Petrizzo,** Louis J '71 -200 W Main -Babylon 11702 **Fx:**669-6482
(845) 338-1162 .. **Petro,** Thos K '86 -71 Maiden Ln -Kingston 12401 **Fx:**338-5662
(518) 462-4242 .. **Petroccione,** Emilio A F '83 (Colwell C&P,LLP) -20 Corp Wds Blvd -Albany 12211
(212) 906-1200 .. **Petrocelli,** Gina M '03 %Latham & W -885 3rd Av -NY 10022
(516) 466-4790 .. **Petrocelli,** Lisa M '95 -14 Bond PMB 111 -Gt Neck 11021
(917) 541-0595 .. **Petrocelli,** Louis A III '96 -8652 25th Av -Brklyn 11214
(212) 571-7000 .. **Petrocelli,** Michl R '02 %Petrocelli & C -217 Bway -NY 10007 **Fx:**571-6454
(212) 571-7000 .. **Petrocelli,** Richd N '75 (Petrocelli & C) -217 Bway -NY 10007 **Fx:**571-6454
(212) 736-1940 .. **Petroff,** David '98 Cnsl Davidson D&K LLC -485 7th Av -NY 10018
(212) 679-5800 .. **Petroff,** Martin '86 M Petroff & Assoc,PC -270 Mad Av -NY 10016 **Fx:**679-5801
(718) 336-4200 .. **Petroff,** Serge F '09 -1795 Coney Isl Av -Brklyn 11230
(212) 685-5509 .. **Petroff,** Svetlana V '82 (Rowland & P) -2 Park Av -NY 10016
(212) 855-7634 .. **Petrofsky,** John J '04 Depository Trust -55 Water -NY 10041 **Fx:**855-3279
(518) 391-2893 .. **Petromelis,** Chris P '06 -Bx29 -Latham 12110
(917) 589-5926 .. **Petromelis,** Simeone '90 -110 Wall -NY 10005
(315) 422-8191 .. **Petrone,** Danl J '07 %Leg Aid -351 S Warren -Syracuse 13202 **Fx:**472-2819
(914) 285-9500 .. **Petrone,** Evelyn '81 (Beck LP,PC) -399 Knollwood Rd -White Plns 10603
(800) 521-1260 .. **Petrone,** John R II '86 (Petrone & P,PC) -108 W Jffrsn -Syracuse 13202
(315) 735-7566 .. **Petrone,** John R II '86 (Petrone & P,PC) -1624 Genesee -Utica 13502
(800) 521-1260 .. **Petrone,** John R II '86 (Petrone & P,PC) -465 New Karner Rd -Albany 12205
(800) 521-1260 .. **Petrone,** Lori E '90 (Petrone & P,PC) -108 W Jffrsn -Syracuse 13202
(315) 735-7566 .. **Petrone,** Lori E '90 (Petrone & P,PC) -1624 Genesee -Utica 13502
(315) 735-7566 .. **Petrone & Petrone,PC** -1624 Genesee -Utica 13502 **Fx:**735-5368
(800) 521-1260 .. **Petrone & Petrone,PC** -465 New Karner Rd -Albany 12205 **Fx:**(315) 735-5368
(800) 521-1260 .. **Petrone & Petrone,PC** -205 St Paul -Rchstr 14614 **Fx:**(315) 735-5368
(800) 521-1260 .. **Petrone & Petrone,PC** -108 W Jffrsn -Syracuse 13202 **Fx:**(315) 476-0107
(800) 521-1260 .. **Petrone & Petrone,PC** -5500 Main -Williamsvll 14221 **Fx:**(716) 852-6216
(315) 789-2657 .. **Petronio,** Arthur A '73 -4067 W Lake Rd -Geneva 14456 **Fx:**789-1938
(212) 506-5000 .. **Petronio,** Michl C '97 (Orrick H&S LLP) -51 W 52nd -NY 10019
(516) 931-1800 .. **Petropoulos,** A Gary '89 (Catalano G&P LLP) -100 Jericho Quadrangle -Jericho 11753
(212) 770-1973 .. **Petropoulos,** Michl '92 %AIG TS -80 Pine -NY 10005 **Fx:**344-0972
(718) 250-2000 .. **Petrosino,** Jos A '76 %DA -350 Jay -Brklyn 11201 **Fx:**250-2314
(585) 454-7145 .. **Petrosino,** Paul V '06 %Gallo & I,LLP -39 State -Rchstr 14614
(631) 337-1977 .. **Petroske,** Clifford J '90 -4875 Sunrise Hwy -Bohemia 11716 **Fx:**337-1966
(212) 839-5300 .. **Petrosky,** Edw F Jr. '88 (Sidley A LLP) -787 7th Av -NY 10019
(212) 953-5300 .. **Petrossian,** Catherine '87 -28 W 44th -NY 10036
(212) 530-1800 .. **Petrou,** Alexia '08 Richards K&O LLP -1 World Fncl Ctr -NY 10281
(212) 455-2000 .. **Petrova,** Irina Nikolaeva '05 %Simpson T&B LLP -425 Lex Av -NY 10017
(212) 883-1700 .. **Petrova,** Violeta '07 %Duval & S LLP -101 Park Av -NY 10178
(212) 839-5300 .. **Petrow,** George J '88 (Sidley A LLP) -787 7th Av -NY 10019
(212) 405-1603 .. **Petrow-Cohen,** Julie '93 %Christopher Street Fncl -215 Park Av S -NY 10003
(631) 853-4049 .. **Petrowski,** John R '94 %Cnty Atty -Dennison Bldg Bx6100 -Hauppauge 11788 **Fx:**853-5169
(718) 585-2315 .. **Petrozza,** Melissa '05 %O'Meara Law Ofc -304 Grnd Cncrs -Bronx 10451 **Fx:**585-2048
(516) 496-1919 .. **Petrozzo,** Vincent J Jr. '85 (Keller O&W,PC) -242 Crsswys Park Dr W -Woodbury 11797
(212) 402-9400 .. **Petrsoric,** John F '01 %McKool S,PC -1 Bryant Park -NY 10036
(212) 613-2069 .. **Petrucci,** James J '02 (Gibbons PC) -1 Penn Plz -NY 10119 **Fx:**554-9669
(212) 696-5124 .. **Petrucci,** Robt M '89 -12 W 27th -NY 10001 **Fx:**696-5772
(212) 554-1400 .. **Petrusic,** Michl '08 %Bernstein LB&G LLP -1285 Av of Amer -NY 10019
(718) 921-1303 .. **Petrusky,** John T '93 (J Petrusky,PC) -417 Bay Ridge Pkwy -Brklyn 11209 **Fx:**921-6514
(585) 726-7522 .. **Petruzzelli,** Justin D '03 %Eastman Kodak -343 State -Rchstr 14650
(518) 473-1403 .. **Petruzzelli,** Michele A '93 %Dept of Health -Corning Twr 24th Fl -Albany 12237 **Fx:**473-2019
(212) 964-1070 .. **Petruzzi,** Minerva R '93 %K Ramseur -299 Bway -NY 10007 **Fx:**385-2742
(516) 378-1700 .. **Petruzzi,** Rudolph P '97 (Chesney & M) -2305 Grand Av -Baldwin 11510
(212) 554-1234 .. **Petruzzo,** Raffaele A '98 AXA Financial Inc -1290 Av of Amer -NY 10104 **Fx:**707-3963
(347) 592-2200 .. **Petsche,** Randolph '90 %Leg Srvcs -89-00 Sutphin Blvd -Jamaica 11435 **Fx:**(718) 937-5350
(914) 644-9200 .. **Petshaft,** David B '95 -222 Bloomingdale Rd -White Plns 10605 **Fx:**644-9300
(914) 249-2000 .. **Petta,** Paul G '00 MasterCard Intl -2000 Purchase -Purchase 10577
(212) 768-6700 .. **Pettapiece,** Karen J '05 Sonnenschein N&R LLP -1221 Av of Amer -NY 10020
(212) 923-6234 .. **Pette,** Elmer D '65 -131 Bennett Av -NY 10033
(631) 673-3855 .. **Pettersen,** Andrew M '92 -13 Hrbr Crest Ct -Huntngtn 11743
(212) 698-3500 .. **Petti,** Anna DiGabriele '04 %Dechert LLP -1095 Av of Amer -NY 10036
(212) 310-4647 .. **Petti,** Maria J '98 %Instinet Corp -3 Times Sq -NY 10036
(212) 918-3000 .. **Pettibone,** Peter J '68 (Hogan L LLP) -875 3rd Av -NY 10022
(212) 360-4105 .. **Pettiford,** Garnethia '94 Harlem Cmmnty Justice Ctr -170 E 121st -NY 10035 **Fx:**360-4996
(585) 586-1430 .. **Pettig,** David C '77 D Pettig & Assoc,PC -65A Monroe Av -Pittsfrd 14534 **Fx:**586-0245
(315) 253-0722 .. **Pettigrass,** Jos E '96 -39 William -Auburn 13021 **Fx:**253-0723
(631) 852-2500 .. **Pettigrew,** Todd A '02 %DA -200 Center Dr -Rvrhead 11901 **Fx:**852-1769
(718) 894-6417 .. **Pettinato,** Jos J '53 -63-23 77th -Middl Vllg 11379 **Fx:**894-6417
(212) 250-5579 .. **Pettinato,** Robt W Jr. '94 Deutsche Bank Securities -60 Wall -NY 10005
(914) 713-0505 .. **Pettinella,** John P '96 -800 Wstchstr Av -Rye Brook 10573 **Fx:**713-0606
(212) 547-5400 .. **Pettingill,** Michl '95 (McDermott W&E LLP) -340 Mad Av -NY 10173
(315) 298-2520 .. **Pettit,** Chas E '02 -1 James -Pulaski 13142 **Fx:**298-7770
(212) 626-4100 .. **Pettit,** Laurence '90 (Baker & M LLP) -1114 Av of Amer -NY 10036
(212) 489-1600 .. **Pettit,** Philip J '98 %Deloitte LLP -1633 Bway -NY 10019 **Fx:**492-4201
(518) 285-8585 .. **Pettit,** Stacy L '85 Surrogates Ct -30 Clinton Av -Albany 12207
(914) 232-8903 .. **Pettitt,** Ivan Satoshi '06 Pro Dialogue LLC -2 Lakevw Dr -Katonah 10536
(212) 566-2424 .. **Pettus,** Marvin K '88 (Pettus & W,PLLC) -150 Bway -NY 10038 **Fx:**566-2443
(212) 556-2100 .. **Pettus,** Richd C '97 (King & S) -1185 Av of Amer -NY 10036
(212) 852-1923 .. **Petty,** Robin L '01 US Trust Co,NA -114 W 47th -NY 10036 **Fx:**852-1310
(212) 682-7474 .. **Petukhova,** Olya '06 %Foley & L LLP -90 Park Av -NY 10016
(212) 895-6721 .. **Petzinger,** Walter F '82 Commerz Bk AG -2 World Fncl Ctr -NY 10281
(315) 376-5390 .. **Petzoldt,** Caleb J '08 %DA -7660 N State -Lowvll 13367 **Fx:**376-5873
(212) 756-2000 .. **Pevarnek,** Katherine '09 %Schulte R&Z LLP -919 3rd Av -NY 10022
(212) 609-2634 .. **Pevzner,** Bella '05 %Gibson & B,PC -14 Wall -NY 10005
(516) 463-5858 .. **Pew,** Curtis E '79 %Hofstra Law Schl -121 Hofstra Univ -Hempstd 11549
(516) 877-2900 .. **Pewarski,** Glen T '81 (Bartlett MB&M,LLP) -300 Old Cntry Rd -Mineola 11501
(212) 272-3455 .. **Peyer,** Sibyl C '84 %JP Morgan Chase -383 Mad Av -NY 10179
(914) 249-5173 .. **Peyron,** Marie R '88 %MasterCard Intl -2000 Purchase -Purchase 10577
(212) 593-6700 .. **Peysakhovich,** Sofya '06 %Aaronson RF&D,LLP -757 3rd Av -NY 10017
(212) 442-6814 .. **Peyton,** Rosemarie '91 %Law Dept -100 Church -NY 10007 **Fx:**788-0367
(212) 750-8700 .. **Pezo,** Marissa '09 %Friedman & W,PC -600 Lex Av -NY 10022
(631) 427-0100 .. **Pezold,** George C '62 (Pezold SH&S,LLC) -120 Main -Huntngtn 11743
(631) 427-0100 .. **Pezold Smith Hirschmann & Selvaggio,LLC** -120 Main -Huntngtn 11743 **Fx:**549-8962
(212) 504-6000 .. **Pezzano,** Tony V '90 (Cadwalader W&T LLP) -1 World Fncl Ctr -NY 10281
(212) 410-1758 .. **Pezzaro,** Edw R '82 -200 E 90th -NY 10128
(631) 351-3042 .. **Pezzino,** Margaret L '85 %Town Atty -100 Main -Huntngtn 11743 **Fx:**351-3032
(718) 273-6662 .. **Pezzoli,** Raymond J '71 -698 Forest Av -Staten Isl 10310
(718) 980-1464 .. **Pezzullo,** Nikole A '96 -60 Bay -Staten Isl 10301 **Fx:**448-8685
(585) 546-7830 .. **Pezzulo,** Glenn E '77 (Culley MT&P,LLP) -36 W Main -Rchstr 14614
(212) 621-6501 .. **Pfadenhauer,** Diane M '97 %ASCAP -1 Lincoln Plz -NY 10023
(716) 652-2260 .. **Pfaff,** E Peter '91 -673 Main -E Aurora 14052 **Fx:**652-2366
(212) 819-8200 .. **Pfaff,** Oliver '04 %White & C LLP -1155 Av of Amer -NY 10036
(212) 629-7744 .. **Pfahl,** Charlotte W '79 (Schneider P&R LLP) -2 Park Av -NY 10016
(716) 204-1055 .. **Pfalzgraf,** David R '68 (Pfalzgraf B&M LLP) -455 Cayuga Rd -Buffalo 14225 **Fx:**204-1080
(716) 854-3400 .. **Pfalzgraf,** David R Jr. '98 (Rupp BPC&C LLC) -1600 Lbrty Bldg -Buffalo 14202
(607) 273-4200 .. **Pfann,** George R Jr. '61 (Miller M,LLP) -202 E State -Ithaca 14850
(212) 425-7200 .. **Pfeffer,** A Anthony '98 (Kenyon & K,LLP) -1 Bway -NY 10004
(518) 475-1226 .. **Pfeffer,** Alan A '74 -38 Hancock Dr -Glenmont 12077
(212) 333-0200 .. **Pfeffer,** Alan I '81 %Arkin KR LLP -590 Mad Av -NY 10022
(212) 415-8600 .. **Pfeffer,** David H '61 OfCnsl Locke LB&L LLP -3 World Fncl Ctr -NY 10281
(212) 216-8000 .. **Pfeffer,** David J '97 (Tarter K&D LLP) -1350 Bway -NY 10018
(212) 661-3080 .. **Pfeffer,** Eric R '90 (Rottenberg LR,PC) -369 Lex Av -NY 10017
(212) 589-4200 .. **Pfeffer,** James E '02 %Baker & H LLP -45 Rckfllr Plz -NY 10111
(212) 448-1100 .. **Pfeffer,** Lindsay R '09 %McLaughlin & S,LLP -260 Mad Av -NY 10016
(212) 382-0700 .. **Pfeffer,** Martin '62 OfCnsl Ostrolenk FG&S,LLP -1180 Av of Amer -NY 10036
(212) 826-0100 .. **Pfeffer,** Nancy S '85 %FSA -31 W 52nd -NY 10019 **Fx:**893-2710
(212) 408-5100 .. **Pfeffer,** Philip A '01 (Chadbourne & P LLP) -30 Rckfllr Plz -NY 10112
(212) 849-7000 .. **Pfeffer,** Walter C '10 %Quinn EU&S,LLP -51 Mad Av -NY 10010
(315) 682-9198 .. **Pfeifer,** Fredk J '80 %AFSCME Cncl 66 -8108 Cazenovia Rd -Manlius 13104 **Fx:**682-9254
(315) 424-7209 .. **Pfeifer,** John F '93 Cnsl T Puleo -441 S Salina -Syracuse 13202 **Fx:**424-5553
(718) 325-5000 .. **Pfeifer,** Maxwell S '49 -714 E 241st -Bronx 10470 **Fx:**324-0333
(516) 222-1773 .. **Pfeifer,** Michl L '87 (ML Pfeifer,PC) -350 Old Cntry Rd -Gdn Cty 11530 **Fx:**222-7745
(718) 287-3050 .. **Pfeiffer,** Andrea J '83 -468 E 16th -Brklyn 11226
(212) 839-5300 .. **Pfeiffer,** Ashley Collins '09 %Sidley A LLP -787 7th Av -NY 10019
(212) 756-2000 .. **Pfeiffer,** Brian D '00 (Schulte R&Z LLP) -919 3rd Av -NY 10022

(518) 473-1403 .. **Pfeiffer,** Justin D '08 %Dept of Health -Corning Twr 24th Fl -Albany 12237 **Fx:**473-2019
(716) 847-0003 .. **Pfeiffer,** Raymond M '89 Pfeiffer & P,PC -Bx2355 -Blasdell 14219
(518) 462-0300 .. **Pfeiffer,** Wm D '93 Girvin & F,PC -20 Corp Wds Blvd -Albany 12211
(212) 335-9000 .. **Pfetsch,** Jeremy M '08 DA -1 Hogan Pl -NY 10013
(212) 790-4500 .. **Pfister,** Helen R '97 %Manatt P&P,LLP -7 Times Sq -NY 10036
(212) 660-3000 .. **Pfister,** Timothy J '79 (Sullivan & W LLP) -1290 Av of Amer -NY 10104
(212) 577-3465 .. **Pfitsch,** Hollis V '06 %Leg Aid -199 Water -NY 10038
(718) 875-1300 .. **Pflanz,** Karl E '92 %Appllt Div 2nd Dept -45 Monroe Pl -Brklyn 11201 **Fx:**858-2446
(212) 455-2000 .. **Pflug,** Mark D '96 (Simpson T&B LLP) -425 Lex Av -NY 10017
(212) 732-9000 .. **Pfluger,** George J '78 OfCnsl Sullivan PBM&C PC -120 Bway -NY 10271
(518) 443-5400 .. **Pfluger,** Janna '92 %SUNY Univ Cnsl -S333 SUNY Plz -Albany 12246 **Fx:**443-5409
(315) 448-0420 .. **Pfohl,** Lillian A '00 Hon R Pooler -Bx7395 -Syracuse 13261
(631) 265-0134 .. **Pforr,** Geoffrey H '87 Kral CRRP&G,LLP -538 Broadhllw Rd -Melvll 11747 **Fx:**265-4289
(212) 230-8800 .. **Pfuhl,** Sarah '03 Cnsl WilmerHale -399 Park Av -NY 10022
(718) 442-1700 .. **Pfuhler,** Robt J '95 %Connors & C,PC -766 Castleton Av -Staten Isl 10310 **Fx:**442-1717
(516) 328-2300 .. **Phair,** Barbara Stegun '99 (Abrams FFEGF&E,LLP) -1111 Marcus Av -Lk Success 11042
(212) 735-3000 .. **Phair,** Ida '10 %Skadden ASM&F LLP -4 Times Sq -NY 10036
(212) 741-8192 .. **Pham,** Bichha Thi '00 %Hunger Action Ntwrk of NYS -75 Varick -NY 10013 **Fx:**741-7236
(212) 463-2000 .. **Pham,** Chuong H '05 Deloitte & Touche LLP -2 World Fncl Ctr -NY 10281
(212) 325-4418 .. **Pham,** Hieu T '02 Credit Suisse Securities LLC -1 Mad Av -NY 10010
(212) 336-2000 .. **Pham,** Myriam Linh '96 %Patterson BW&T LLP -1133 Av of Amer -NY 10036
(212) 259-8000 .. **Pham-Quang,** Stephanie N '05 %Dewey & L LLP -1301 Av of Amer -NY 10019
(212) 506-1700 .. **Phanos,** Spiro A '06 %Kasowitz BT&F LLP -1633 Bway -NY 10019
(516) 622-9200 .. **Phanumas,** Joy '94 (Westerman BEM&S,LLP) -1201 RXR Plz -Uniondale 11553
(212) 336-2000 .. **Phares,** Gloria C '88 (Patterson BW&T LLP) -1133 Av of Amer -NY 10036
(716) 887-9888 .. **Pharr,** Robyn G '75 -460 Franklin -Buffalo 14202 **Fx:**887-9889
(716) 699-5455 .. **Phelan,** Andrew F '63 -Bx1181 -Ellicottvll 14731
(212) 335-4500 .. **Phelan,** John C '85 (DLA Piper LLP) -1251 Av of Amer -NY 10020
(516) 571-9041 .. **Phelan,** John F '89 %Cnty Atty -1200 Old Cntry Rd -Westbury 11590
(518) 640-6900 .. **Phelan,** John J '83 (Phelan P&D,LLP) -302 Wshngtn Av Ext -Albany 12203
(914) 237-5223 .. **Phelan,** John J '94 -151 Ludlow -Ynkrs 10705
(212) 315-3082 .. **Phelan,** John J III '66 JJ Phelan III,PC -1325 Av of Amer -NY 10019 **Fx:**315-3028
(518) 474-0388 .. **Phelan,** John T '74 %Ofc for the Aging -Bldg 2 ESP -Albany 12223 **Fx:**474-0608
(716) 845-9493 .. **Phelan,** Kimberly A '83 Sup Ct-8th Jud Dist -25 Delaware Av -Buffalo 14202
(845) 398-3273 .. **Phelan,** Patricia S '90 -Bx182 -Tappan 10983 **Fx:**398-3272
(518) 640-6900 .. **Phelan Phelan & Danek,LLP** -302 Wshngtn Av Ext -Albany 12203 **Fx:**640-6955
(518) 692-9645 .. **Phelan,** Robt '98 Cnsl Catalfimo Law Firm -18 Hill Bx184 -Greenwich 12834 **Fx:**692-2833
(212) 509-9400 .. **Phelan,** Robt W '01 (Cozen O) -45 Bway Atrium -NY 10006
(518) 640-6900 .. **Phelan,** Robin Bartlett '84 (Phelan P&D,LLP) -302 Wshngtn Av Ext -Albany 12203
(914) 769-2745 .. **Phelan,** Sarah E '77 -250 Sherman Av -Hawthorne 10532
(212) 345-1090 .. **Phelps,** Alexis T '99 %Marsh USA -1166 Av of Amer -NY 10036 **Fx:**345-4808
(716) 284-9901 .. **Phelps Gray & Hewitt** -345 3rd Bx816 -Niagara Fls 14303 **Fx:**284-7038
(212) 225-2000 .. **Phelps,** Jos T '08 %Cleary GS&H -1 Lbrty Plz -NY 10006
(518) 689-1427 .. **Phelps,** Whitney Magee '03 %Greenberg T,LLP -54 State -Albany 12207
(212) 713-9521 .. **Phelps,** Zachary A '05 UBS -1285 Av of Amer -NY 10019
(212) 962-1020 .. **Phemister,** Craig W '98 %M Lamonsoff -80 Maiden Ln -NY 10038 **Fx:**962-3078
(585) 546-5600 .. **Pheterson,** Irving '59 (Pheterson & P) -1 E Main -Rchstr 14614 **Fx:**546-7196
(585) 641-8000 .. **Pheterson,** Joshua S '05 %Fix SB&G,PC -295 Woodcliff Dr -Fairprt 14450
(585) 546-5600 .. **Pheterson Stern Calabrese Neilans & Spatorico, LLP** -1 E Main -Rchstr 14614 **Fx:**546-2474
(585) 546-5600 .. **Pheterson,** Steven J '78 (Pheterson SCN&S,LLP) -1 E Main -Rchstr 14614
(212) 773-3219 .. **Phethean,** Carol '86 %Ernst & Young,LLP -5 Times Sq -NY 10036
(718) 590-2000 .. **Philbert,** Jenetha G '08 %DA -198 E 161st -Bronx 10451 **Fx:**590-6477
(212) 801-6836 .. **Philbin,** Kenneth A '98 OfCnsl Greenberg T,LLP -200 Park Av -NY 10166
(212) 261-8000 .. **Philbin,** Kevin J '88 (Mendes & M,LLP) -750 7th Av -NY 10019
(716) 852-5200 .. **Philbin,** Prudence F '98 (Hamberger & W) -700 Main Pl Twr -Buffalo 14202
(716) 566-2800 .. **Philbin,** Scott M '98 SrCnsl Bond S&K,PLLC -40 Fountian Plz -Buffalo 14202
(518) 473-5671 .. **Philbrick,** Steven H '87 %Div of Parole -97 Central Av -Albany 12206 **Fx:**473-6037
(212) 318-6000 .. **Philion,** Danl M '09 %Paul HJ&W LLP -75 E 55th -NY 10022
(212) 440-3018 .. **Philip,** Betsy '05 CNA Ins -40 Wall -NY 10005
(518) 956-8010 .. **Philip,** George M '79 SUNY Albany -1400 Wshngtn Av -Albany 12222
(212) 596-9000 .. **Philip,** Jeril A '10 %Ropes & G LLP -1211 Av of Amer -NY 10036
(518) 474-8816 .. **Philip,** Michl Jr. '82 %Comm Prof Standrds -40 Steuben -Albany 12207 **Fx:**474-0389
(212) 335-9000 .. **Philippe,** Marcel J '78 %DA -1 Hogan Pl -NY 10013
(518) 455-7528 .. **Philippi,** Reed S '88 %Legis Bill Drftng Comm -310 The Cptl -Albany 12224 **Fx:**455-7598
(212) 909-6000 .. **Philippis,** Efstratios '07 %Debevoise & P LLP -919 3rd Av -NY 10022
(585) 325-7455 .. **Philippone,** Alex F '86 -31 E Main -Rchstr 14608 **Fx:**546-6565
(315) 379-1466 .. **Philippone,** David J '93 (Oot & Assoc,PLLC) -63 Main -Canton 13617 **Fx:**379-1433
(315) 471-6687 .. **Philippone,** David J '93 (Oot & Assoc,PLLC) -503 E Wshngtn -Syracuse 13202 **Fx:**476-7603
(585) 325-7455 .. **Philippone,** James V '54 -31 E Main -Rchstr 14608 **Fx:**546-6565
(585) 232-4810 .. **Philippone,** John E '66 -125 State -Rchstr 14614
(585) 325-7455 .. **Philippone,** Martin A '96 -31 E Main -Rchstr 14608 **Fx:**546-6565
(716) 633-3535 .. **Philipps,** John N Jr. '97 W Mattar,PC -6720 Main -Williamsvll 14221 **Fx:**631-9804
(631) 277-4300 .. **Philips,** Janet M '89 %Shlimbaum & S -265 Main Bx8 -Islip 11751 **Fx:**277-4350
(212) 714-3554 .. **Philips,** Jonathan '98 %Stargiving -292 5th Av -NY 10001
(718) 254-7000 .. **Philips,** Judith A '90 %US Atty -271 Cadman Plz E -Brklyn 11201 **Fx:**254-6479
(716) 847-2523 .. **Philips,** Kelly J '01 %Sugarman Law Firm,LLP -14 Lafayette Sq -Buffalo 14203
(212) 761-4000 .. **Philips,** Madhu V '96 Morgan Stanley -1585 Bway -NY 10036
(315) 379-2225 .. **Philips,** Rosemary R '92 DA -48 Court -Canton 13617 **Fx:**379-2301
(212) 908-0500 .. **Phillip,** Francis '94 Fitch,Inc -1 State Street Plz -NY 10004 **Fx:**480-4438
(518) 474-6740 .. **Phillip,** Natasha E '07 %Dept of State -41 State -Albany 12231 **Fx:**473-9211
(516) 248-9797 .. **Phillips,** Alexander D '01 -666 Old Cntry Rd -Gdn Cty 11530 **Fx:**248-9703
(518) 438-9907 .. **Phillips,** Allyson M '07 %Young SWRB&M,LLC -5 Palisades Dr -Albany 12205
(212) 468-8000 .. **Phillips,** Amy J '08 %Morrison & F LLP -1290 Av of Amer -NY 10104
(212) 277-6500 .. **Phillips,** Andrew A '09 %Dickstein S LLP -1633 Bway -NY 10019
(315) 788-6700 .. **Phillips,** Ann E '97 %Schwerzmann & W,PC -215 Wshngtn Bx704 -Watertwn 13601
(518) 474-5607 .. **Phillips,** Anne G '79 %Ofc Gnl Srvcs -Corning Twr ESP -Albany 12242 **Fx:**473-4973
(212) 735-3000 .. **Phillips,** Barnet IV '74 (Skadden ASM&F LLP) -4 Times Sq -NY 10036
(212) 720-5026 .. **Phillips,** Brett S '04 %Fed Reserve Bk -33 Lbrty -NY 10045 **Fx:**785-5748
(212) 841-1000 .. **Phillips,** C Wm '83 (Covington & B LLP) -620 8th Av -NY 10018
(212) 596-9000 .. **Phillips,** Carrie A '10 %Ropes & G LLP -1211 Av of Amer -NY 10036
(718) 590-2000 .. **Phillips,** Colleen M '10 %DA -198 E 161st -Bronx 10451 **Fx:**590-6477
(212) 450-4000 .. **Phillips,** Craig A '07 %Davis P&W LLP -450 Lex Av -NY 10017
(212) 696-6000 .. **Phillips,** Danny Eugene '06 %Curtis M-PC&M LLP -101 Park Av -NY 10178
(212) 225-9592 .. **Phillips,** David B '79 -1568 E 34th -Brklyn 11234
(973) 491-3530 .. **Phillips,** David W '86 (LeClairRyan,PC) -830 3rd Av -NY 10022 **Fx:**491-3555
(518) 664-2299 .. **Phillips,** Dawn M '98 -79 Smith Rd -Mechanicvll 12118
(518) 792-1174 .. **Phillips,** Dennis J '74 (McPhillips F&C,LLP) -288 Glen Bx299 -Glens Fls 12801
(516) 676-9568 .. **Phillips,** Diane '92 -5 Copperfld Ln -Glen Head 11545
(516) 571-2823 .. **Phillips,** Dorothy A '91 %Hon J Driscoll,Jr -100 Supreme Ct Dr -Mineola 11501
(718) 875-1300 .. **Phillips,** Dorothy A '91 %Hon E Hart -45 Monroe Pl -Brklyn 11201
(212) 782-4629 .. **Phillips,** Drew C '00 Bk of Tokyo-Mitsubishi -1251 Av of Amer -NY 10020 **Fx:**782-6420
(914) 946-4777 .. **Phillips,** Edw J '95 (Keane & B,PC) -445 Hmltn Av -White Plns 10601
(518) 891-4050 .. **Phillips,** Elizabeth A '01 %Adirondack Pk Agncy -Bx99 -Ray Brk 12977 **Fx:**891-3938
(516) 746-1144 .. **Phillips,** Elliot '70 (Kirschenbaum & P,PC) -3000 Hempstd Tpk -Levittwn 11756
(845) 291-2050 .. **Phillips,** Francis D II '75 (DA) -255-275 Main -Goshen 10924 **Fx:**291-2085
(845) 947-1100 .. **Phillips,** Frank J '91 (Phillips & M,LLP) -148 Route 9W -Stony Pnt 10980
(212) 735-3000 .. **Phillips,** Gary M '10 %Skadden ASM&F LLP -4 Times Sq -NY 10036
(585) 546-5530 .. **Phillips,** Gavin L '82 %Thomson West -50 E Broad -Rchstr 14694
(212) 446-4800 .. **Phillips,** Greer L '84 (Kirkland & E LLP) -153 E 53rd -NY 10022
(585) 475-1100 .. **Phillips,** Gregory T '85 Segar & S -400 Meridian Centre -Rchstr 14618
(845) 831-0670 .. **Phillips Heaney & Schofield** -33 Henry Bx430 -Beacon 12508 **Fx:**831-0744
(212) 747-9292 .. **Phillips,** James M '87 -40 Exchange PL -NY 10005
(516) 357-3634 .. **Phillips,** Janine Bender '84 OfCnsl Leventritt L&B -1010 Nrthrn Blvd -Gt Neck 11021
(212) 580-6500 .. **Phillips,** Jeffrey E '94 (Phillips K & Assoc,LLP) -204 W 84th -NY 10024
(212) 272-6101 .. **Phillips,** Jessica M '02 %JP Morgan Chase -383 Mad Av -NY 10179
(518) 357-2068 .. **Phillips,** Jill T '99 %DEC -1150 N Westcott Rd -Schnctdy 12306 **Fx:**357-2087
(212) 492-4149 .. **Phillips,** Kaare '85 %Deloitte LLP -1633 Bway -NY 10019 **Fx:**492-4380
(631) 853-4343 .. **Phillips,** Kathleen '92 %Leg Aid -400 Carleton Av Bx9082 -Central Islip 11722 **Fx:**853-7798
(518) 447-7324 .. **Phillips,** Kelly M '05 Cnty DCYF -112 State -Albany 12207 **Fx:**447-7386
(212) 343-1234 .. **Phillips,** Kirsa '98 Metropolitan College of NY -75 Varick -NY 10013
(212) 580-6500 .. **Phillips Krantz & Associates, LLP** -204 W 84th -NY 10024 **Fx:**580-7245
(518) 429-4200 .. **Phillips,** Lois R '88 OfCnsl Hiscock & B,LLP -50 Beaver -Albany 12207
(212) 762-7874 .. **Phillips,** Lyndelle T '87 Morgan Stanley -1221 Av of Amer -NY 10020

(631) 632-6110 .. **Phillips,** Lynette M '95 %SUNY Univ Cnsl -328 Admin Bldg -Stony Brk 11794
(716) 847-8400 .. **Phillips Lytle LLP** -3400 HSBC Ctr -Buffalo 14203 **Fx:**852-6100
(585) 238-2000 .. **Phillips Lytle LLP** -1400 First Fed Plz -Rchstr 14614 **Fx:**232-3141
(516) 742-5201 .. **Phillips Lytle LLP** -1100 Franklin Av -Gdn Cty 11530 **Fx:**742-3910
(518) 472-1224 .. **Phillips Lytle LLP** -30 S Pearl -Albany 12207 **Fx:**472-1227
(212) 759-4888 .. **Phillips Lytle LLP** -437 Mad Av -NY 10022 **Fx:**308-9079
(716) 664-3906 .. **Phillips Lytle LLP** -8 E 3rd Bx1279 -Jamestwn 14702 **Fx:**664-4230
(914) 798-5400 .. **Phillips,** M Regina '05 %Goldberg S LLP -11 Martine Av -White Plns 10606
(516) 482-4938 .. **Phillips,** Malcolm C '87 -1 Wht Pine Ln -Gt Neck 11023
(716) 645-7399 .. **Phillips,** Margaret L '93 Buffalo Schl of Law -709 O'Brian Hall -Buffalo 14260
(518) 402-0205 .. **Phillips,** Marybeth '92 %UIA Bd -Troy Atrium Bx15126 -Albany 12212 **Fx:**402-6208
(212) 259-8000 .. **Phillips,** Michl C '05 %Dewey & L LLP -1301 Av of Amer -NY 10019
(518) 385-0453 .. **Phillips,** Michl J '91 GE Intl -1 River Rd -Schnctdy 12345
(518) 297-6050 .. **Phillips,** Michl J '91 -88 Champlain -Rouses Pnt 12979 **Fx:**297-6049
(212) 785-4100 .. **Phillips,** Michl T '09 %Fensterstock & Prtnrs LLP -30 Wall -NY 10005
(914) 328-0404 .. **Phillips,** Michelle E '90 (Jackson L LLP) -1 N Bway -White Plns 10601
(518) 474-6530 .. **Phillips,** Michelle L '94 %Dept Pub Srvc -3 ESP -Albany 12223
(845) 947-1100 .. **Phillips & Millman,LLP** -148 Route 9W -Stony Pnt 10980 **Fx:**786-7207
(212) 977-9700 .. **Phillips Nizer LLP** -666 5th Av -NY 10103 **Fx:**262-5152
(516) 229-9400 .. **Phillips Nizer LLP** -600 Old Cntry Rd -Gdn Cty 11530 **Fx:**228-9612
(212) 888-6617 .. **Phillips,** Pamela A '85 -721 5th Av -NY 10022
(212) 661-8000 .. **Phillips,** Peter J '82 (Lucas & M,LLP) -475 Park Av S -NY 10016
(212) 506-5000 .. **Phillips,** Renee B '03 %Orrick H&S LLP -51 W 52nd -NY 10019
(845) 353-0100 .. **Phillips,** Ronald A '74 (McCormack & P) -51 N Bway #2 -Nyack 10960
(718) 520-4662 .. **Phillips,** Rosalyn B '82 %Hon D Lewis -125-01 Qns Blvd -Kew Gdns 11415
(212) 455-2000 .. **Phillips,** Sarah E '10 %Simpson T&B LLP -425 Lex Av -NY 10017
(212) 566-5000 .. **Phillips,** Sarah F '95 Dept of Bldgs -280 Bway -NY 10007
(212) 280-4005 .. **Phillips,** Sharon J '95 -825 W End Av -NY 10025 **Fx:**280-4245
(718) 999-2000 .. **Phillips,** Shawn E '01 NY Fire Dept -9 Metrotech Ctr -Brklyn 11201 **Fx:**999-1290
(585) 238-8522 .. **Phillips,** Spencer D '04 Div of Human Rights -259 Monroe Av -Rchstr 14607
(516) 484-2514 .. **Phillips,** Stanley '58 -4 Hrbr Ct W -Roslyn Harbor 11576
(212) 964-7400 .. **Phillips,** Steven D '99 Smith MDWY&Y,PC -111 John -NY 10038
(212) 605-6200 .. **Phillips,** Steven J '71 (Levy P&K,LLP) -800 3rd Av -NY 10022
(518) 437-6965 .. **Phillips,** Thos A '79 %State Ins Fund -15 Computer Dr W -Albany 12205 **Fx:**485-8761
(212) 225-2000 .. **Phillips,** Timothy A '10 %Cleary GS&H -1 Lbrty Plz -NY 10006
(212) 353-1160 .. **Phillips,** Todd R '84 %Lehr Construction -902 Bway -NY 10010 **Fx:**505-8169
(212) 593-1700 .. **Phillips,** Valerie A '02 %Kaplan L LLP -1065 Av of Amer -NY 10018
(212) 788-3300 .. **Phillips,** Valerie M '83 %Hlth & Hsptl Corp -125 Worth -NY 10013 **Fx:**267-6905
(718) 250-4274 .. **Phillips,** Vincent T '88 %Leg Aid -111 Lvngstn -Brklyn 11201 **Fx:**250-4243
(631) 226-2100 .. **Phillips Weiner Artura Cox & McDonaugh** -165 S Wellwood Av -Lindenhrst 11757 **Fx:**226-2160
(718) 923-4206 .. **Phillips,** Wendy G '91 %OTDA Fair Hearings -14 Boerum Pl -Brklyn 11201
(212) 450-4000 .. **Phillips,** Wendy M '08 %Davis P&W LLP -450 Lex Av -NY 10017
(718) 935-1954 .. **Phillips,** Wm R '87 -464 Sackett -Brklyn 11231
(718) 723-9440 .. **Phillips-Hantour,** Josephine '96 -1 Cross Isl Plz -Rosedale 11422
(212) 571-1255 .. **Phillipson,** Faun M '00 (Phillipson & U,LLP) -111 Bway -NY 10006 **Fx:**571-1167
(315) 424-1750 .. **Phillipson,** Scott R '05 Cnsl SEIU Local 200 United -1153 W Fayette Bx1540 -Syracuse 13201 **Fx:**479-9030
(212) 820-9338 .. **Philp,** Jeffrey C '05 %Hawkins D&W LLP -One Chase Manh Plz -NY 10005
(212) 966-6662 .. **Philwin,** Jed-Mathew D '93 -401 Bway -NY 10013
(631) 234-7900 .. **Phin,** Teresa D '91 (Lerner & P) -87 W Suffolk Av -Central Islip 11722 **Fx:**234-8026
(212) 637-3209 .. **Phinizy,** Coles H '71 %EPA -290 Bway -NY 10007 **Fx:**637-3096
(845) 365-9009 .. **Phinney,** Paul B III '77 -566 Route 303 S -Blauvelt 10913 **Fx:**365-9097
(716) 855-1111 .. **Photiadis,** Gregory P '78 (Duke HP&G LLP) -350 Main -Buffalo 14202
(212) 245-7500 .. **Phufas,** John M '78 -1270 Av of Amer -NY 10020 **Fx:**245-8296
(716) 693-0537 .. **Phufas,** Katherine C '86 -343 Christina -N Tonawanda 14120
(718) 899-1293 .. **Phulwani,** Michl '74 M Phulwani,PC -74-09 37th Av -Jcksn Hts 11372 **Fx:**899-1291
(212) 450-4000 .. **Phyfe,** James D '73 SrCnsl Davis P&W LLP -450 Lex Av -NY 10017
(212) 244-2999 .. **Piacentile,** Victor C Jr. '78 %Kopff N&D LLP -440 9th Av -NY 10001
(516) 944-7662 .. **Piacentini,** Anthony J '70 -31 S Bayles Av -Pt Wash 11050 **Fx:**944-7646
(516) 249-3450 .. **Piacentini,** Lauren M '09 %Carman C&I,LLP -266 Main -Farmngdl 11735
(585) 546-8161 .. **Piampiano,** James J '78 -30 W Broad -Rchstr 14614
(631) 853-4104 .. **Piana,** Jack R '09 %DA -400 Carleton Av Bx9082 -Central Islip 11722 **Fx:**853-7838
(914) 824-5732 .. **Pianforini,** Susan I '81 Hon JE Murphy -111 Dr Martin Luther King Jr Blvd -White Plns 10601 **Fx:**995-4010
(212) 218-5500 .. **Pianko,** Howard '69 (Seyfarth S LLP) -620 8th Av -NY 10018
(716) 633-1024 .. **Piasecki,** Brandon W '95 -18 The Spur -Williamsvll 14221 **Fx:**633-4069
(518) 483-2550 .. **Piasecki,** John A '74 -436 E Main Bx899 -Malone 12953 **Fx:**483-2054
(212) 756-2000 .. **Piasta,** Eric S '95 SpclCnsl Schulte R&Z LLP -919 3rd Av -NY 10022
(212) 278-1000 .. **Piazza,** Anna Maria '10 %Anderson K&O,PC -1251 Av of Amer -NY 10020
(585) 295-4400 .. **Piazza,** Anthony J '88 (Hiscock & B,LLP) -2000 HSBC Plz -Rchstr 14604
(716) 854-1300 .. **Piazza,** Barbara Ann '87 %Rosenthal S&M,LLP -300 Main -Buffalo 14202
(718) 389-0240 .. **Piazza D'Addario & Frumin** -824 Manh Av -Brklyn 11222 **Fx:**389-5542
(212) 661-3535 .. **Piazza,** Deborah J '97 (Hodgson R LLP) -60 E 42nd -NY 10165
(631) 499-2163 .. **Piazza,** Dominick '53 -16 Amalia Ln -Commack 11725
(718) 272-2025 .. **Piazza,** Franca B '89 -854 Shepherd Av -Brklyn 11208 **Fx:**272-6225
(212) 916-4258 .. **Piazza,** Harold D Jr. '77 %TIAA-CREF -730 3rd Av -NY 10017
(716) 483-0756 .. **Piazza,** Jeffrey A '93 (Hall & P) -600 Htl Jmstwn Ofc Bldg -Jamestwn 14702 **Fx:**484-7352
(914) 242-8481 .. **Piazza,** John S '94 -23 Carpenter Av -Mt Kisco 10549
(212) 825-5900 .. **Piazza,** Jos P '97 %Dept of Invstgtn -80 Maiden Ln -NY 10038 **Fx:**825-2860
(212) 916-4257 .. **Piazza,** Kathleen S '94 %TIAA-CREF -730 3rd Av -NY 10017
(718) 442-4600 .. **Piazza,** Mark S '89 (Jacobi SBP&F,PC) -235 Forest Av -Staten Isl 10301
(212) 264-3650 .. **Piazza Siegel,** Marla Jo '98 %SSA Ofc Genl Cnsl -26 Fed Plz -NY 10278 **Fx:**264-6372
(212) 589-4200 .. **Picard,** Irving H '82 (Baker & H LLP) -45 Rckfllr Plz -NY 10111
(516) 486-4640 .. **Picardi,** Alissa M '07 %Cherry E&K,LLP -1 Old Cntry Rd -Carle Pl 11514
(315) 637-9656 .. **Picardi,** Ferdinand L '56 -7 Wynnrdg Rd -Fayettevll 13066
(212) 662-9800 .. **Picariello,** Leonard S '69 -151 W 93rd -NY 10025 **Fx:**662-0421
(212) 935-3000 .. **Picca,** Dominic J '92 (Mintz LCFG&P,PC) -666 3rd Av -NY 10017
(212) 407-8245 .. **Picca,** Victoria R '95 NBA -645 5th Av -NY 10022
(516) 294-5200 .. **Picciano,** John F '71 (Picciano & S) -900 Merchants Cncrs -Westbury 11590
(516) 294-5200 .. **Picciano & Scahill** -900 Merchants Cncrs -Westbury 11590 **Fx:**873-6229
(631) 665-3400 .. **Picciano,** Wm P '54 -90 E Main -Bay Shr 11706 **Fx:**665-3557
(516) 623-1111 .. **Piccininni,** Dominick A '85 -2174 Hewlett Av Bx801 -Merrick 11566 **Fx:**623-0758
(212) 732-3320 .. **Piccininni,** Frank J '90 %Short & B,PC -217 Bway -NY 10007
(516) 328-2300 .. **Piccininni,** Patti '07 %Abrams FFEGF&E,LLP -1111 Marcus Av -Lk Success 11042
(212) 661-9100 .. **Piccione,** Anthony '79 (Otterbourg SH&R,PC) -230 Park Av -NY 10169
(585) 419-8800 .. **Picciotti,** Jos D III '88 (Harris B PLLC) -99 Garnsey Rd -Pittsfrd 14534
(212) 969-3000 .. **Piccirillo,** Antonio N '96 (Proskauer R LLP) -1585 Bway -NY 10036
(917) 991-7290 .. **Piccirillo,** Danielle '99 D Piccirillo,PC -100 Nevada Av -Staten Isl 10306
(516) 561-4100 .. **Piccirillo,** Joan L '86 (Piccirillo & P) -240 Rockaway Av -Vly Stream 11580 **Fx:**561-5258
(212) 655-5000 .. **Piccirillo,** John M '97 %Gannon R&M -120 Bway -NY 10271
(516) 561-4100 .. **Piccirillo,** Mark J '86 (Piccirillo & P) -240 Rockaway Av -Vly Stream 11580 **Fx:**561-5258
(914) 962-7400 .. **Picco,** Edw J '74 -1852 Commerce -Yorktwn Hts 10598 **Fx:**962-7310
(718) 886-7430 .. **Piccola,** Richd A '82 -163-10 Nrthrn Blvd -Flushng 11358 **Fx:**886-7432
(516) 759-4800 .. **Piccolo,** Michl A '92 -Bx818 -Locust Vly 11560 **Fx:**759-4818
(212) 873-6000 .. **Pichardo,** Edw '02 Transport Wkrs - Loc 100 -80 W End Av -NY 10023
(516) 921-3099 .. **Pichardo,** Julie A '84 %J Pichardo,PC -600 Old Cntry Rd -Gdn Cty 11530 **Fx:**832-7787
(212) 806-5400 .. **Pichardo,** Rodger '08 %Stroock &S&L LLP -180 Maiden Ln -NY 10038
(212) 238-2420 .. **Pichardo,** Wendy G '88 %UIA Bd -59 Maiden Ln -NY 10038 **Fx:**238-2451
(607) 273-1600 .. **Pichel,** Michl J '74 -320 N Aurora -Ithaca 14850 **Fx:**256-0852
(212) 819-8200 .. **Picherack,** John Roman '09 %White & C LLP -1155 Av of Amer -NY 10036
(212) 468-8000 .. **Pichler,** Rufus J '08 OfCnsl Morrison & F LLP -1290 Av of Amer -NY 10104
(212) 695-6000 .. **Pick,** Douglas J '81 (Pick & Z LLP) -369 Lex Av -NY 10017 **Fx:**695-6007
(914) 949-5485 .. **Pickard,** John A '87 -6 Roland Dr -White Plns 10605
(516) 921-4200 .. **Pickard,** Jos C '86 %David Lerner Assoc -Bx9006 -Syosset 11791
(315) 474-6448 .. **Pickard,** Terry R '71 (Byrne C&P PC) -100 Madison -Syracuse 13202
(212) 246-2400 .. **Pickard,** Todd S '75 (Balber PM&VDT,PC) -1370 Av of Amer -NY 10019
(212) 332-1200 .. **Pickel,** Robt G '85 %ISDA -360 Mad Av -NY 10017 **Fx:**332-1212
(212) 807-2835 .. **Pickelle,** Matthew G '99 %Thomson Reuters/RIA -195 Bway -NY 10007
(914) 946-2000 .. **Pickelle,** Paul W '66 -175 Main -White Plns 10601 **Fx:**946-2147
(212) 669-4410 .. **Picker,** Leonard I '90 Tax Commission -1 Centre -NY 10007 **Fx:**669-2003
(212) 715-1000 .. **Pickering,** Grace E '09 %Arnold & P LLP -399 Park Av -NY 10022
(212) 813-8800 .. **Pickett,** Georgia C '09 %Goodwin P LLP -620 8th Av -NY 10018
(212) 770-6887 .. **Pickett,** Kenneth '01 AIG -70 Pine -NY 10270
(212) 513-7788 .. **Pickett,** Patrick J '03 %Ahmuty D&M -123 William -NY 10038
(212) 849-7000 .. **Pickhardt,** Jonathan E '00 (Quinn EU&S,LLP) -51 Mad Av -NY 10010
(212) 692-1000 .. **Pickholz,** Jason R '95 (Duane M LLP) -1540 Bway -NY 10036
(516) 487-2020 .. **Pickholz,** Judith L '78 -111 Grt Nck Rd -Gt Neck 11021 **Fx:**829-1008
(212) 692-1000 .. **Pickholz,** Marvin G '67 (Duane M LLP) -1540 Bway -NY 10036
(212) 225-2000 .. **Picknally,** Nancy K '08 %Cleary GS&H -1 Lbrty Plz -NY 10006
(516) 565-5555 .. **Pickney,** Christian A '96 -190 Willis Av -Mineola 11501 **Fx:**485-1805
(914) 285-8434 .. **Pickup,** Jayne L '93 -75 S Bway -White Plns 10601 **Fx:**285-8436
(516) 379-9301 .. **Pickus,** Philip B '76 -848 Hayes -Baldwin 11510
(212) 969-3000 .. **Picon,** David A '87 (Proskauer R LLP) -1585 Bway -NY 10036
(212) 225-2000 .. **Picone,** Emily D '09 %Cleary GS&H -1 Lbrty Plz -NY 10006
(212) 867-4466 .. **Picone,** Noelle I '07 %Belkin BW&G,LLP -270 Mad Av -NY 10016

(914) 428-8300 .. **Picone-DeLarco,** Annmarie S '01 %Sacks,PC -707 Wstchstr Av -White Plns 10604 **Fx:**682-1707
(518) 449-3900 .. **Picotte,** Susan Carroll '80 (Cooper E&S,LLP) -39 N Pearl -Albany 12207
(631) 589-2888 .. **Picucci,** John J '69 -455 Greene Av -Sayvll 11782
(718) 721-7600 .. **Piddoubny,** Peter '86 -25-84 Steinway -Astoria 11103 **Fx:**721-9892
(212) 803-3100 .. **Pidedjian,** Antovk '96 %Empire State Dvlmnt Corp -633 3rd Av -NY 10017
(212) 318-6000 .. **Pidot,** Emily J '07 %Paul HJ&W LLP -75 E 55th -NY 10022
(718) 923-4206 .. **Piech,** Kenneth S '85 %OTDA Fair Hearings -14 Boerum Pl -Brklyn 11201
(212) 735-3000 .. **Pieciak,** Micheal S '10 %Skadden ASM&F LLP -4 Times Sq -NY 10036
(716) 834-9181 .. **Pieczynski,** Sandra L '98 %Blair & R,LLP -2645 Sheridan Dr -Tonawanda 14150
(518) 690-4200 .. **Piedmont,** Richd S '77 (Piedmont Law Firm) -4 British Amer Blvd -Latham 12110 **Fx:**690-4207
(518) 691-0351 .. **Piedmont,** Richd S '77 (Piedmont Law Firm) -376 Bway -Saratoga Spgs 12866 **Fx:**690-4206
(212) 735-8775 .. **Piedra,** David A '92 (Morrison C LLP) -909 3rd Av -NY 10022
(212) 683-1153 .. **Piegaro,** Cheryl Higley '94 -347 5th Av -NY 10016
(914) 328-0404 .. **Piekara,** Thos P '87 (Jackson L LLP) -1 N Bway -White Plns 10601
(718) 739-6400 .. **Piekarsky,** David G '87 %DHCR -92-31 Union Hall -Jamaica 11433 **Fx:**262-7938
(914) 274-8121 .. **Piekarz,** Victoria M '95 -248 E Grassy Sprain Rd -Ynkrs 10710 **Fx:**274-8121
(212) 423-0797 .. **Piel,** Eleanor Jackson '56 -2 E 93rd -NY 10128 **Fx:**423-0799
(518) 436-0751 .. **Piel,** Stephanie A '04 (Hinman S PC) -121 State -Albany 12207
(212) 776-5032 .. **Piela,** Caroline H '09 NYC Housing Auth -250 Bway -NY 10007 **Fx:**776-5039
(212) 746-1795 .. **Piels,** Louis I '02 NY Presbyterian Hsptl -525 E 68th Bx88 -NY 10065 **Fx:**746-8603
(212) 940-3000 .. **Piemont,** Jeffrey L '92 Cnsl Nixon P LLP -437 Mad Av -NY 10022
(315) 423-4444 .. **Piemonte,** Salvatore J '80 -Bx265 -Camillus 13031 **Fx:**672-8218
(845) 878-4191 .. **Pien,** Melanie H Fund '94 -801 Route 311 -Patterson 12563
(212) 339-8930 .. **Pieniek,** Tobias '65 (T Pieniek,PC) -1 Old Cntry Rd -Carle Pl 11514 **Fx:**(516) 280-3405
(631) 587-6500 .. **Pienkny,** Seymour '60 -51 John -Babylon 11702
(516) 747-4311 .. **Pieper,** Damian J '03 Pieper Bar Review -90 Willis Av -Mineola 11501 **Fx:**294-2614
(212) 707-6480 .. **Pieper,** Dawn '98 Jefferies & Co,Inc -520 Mad Av -NY 10022
(212) 384-1000 .. **Pieper,** Derek S '99 %FBI -26 Fed Plz -NY 10278
(516) 433-8050 .. **Pieper,** Erich A '99 (Stouges M&P LLC) -115 N Bway -Hicksvll 11801
(516) 747-9400 .. **Pieper Hoban & Royce** -92 Willis Av -Mineola 11501
(516) 747-9400 .. **Pieper,** J Gardiner '72 (Pieper H&R) -92 Willis Av -Mineola 11501
(212) 506-5000 .. **Pieper,** Kristina L '08 %Orrick H&S LLP -51 W 52nd -NY 10019
(212) 408-5100 .. **Pieper,** Thos N '01 Cnsl Chadbourne & P LLP -30 Rckfllr Plz -NY 10112
(516) 747-4311 .. **Pieper,** Troy G '98 Pieper NY Multistate Bar Review -90 Willis Av -Mineola 11501
(718) 896-1308 .. **Piepes,** Eric J '90 -24105A Oak Park Dr -Douglastn 11362
(212) 885-1500 .. **Piepul,** Jos M '73 %FCIA Mngmnt Co -125 Park Av -NY 10017 **Fx:**885-1535
(212) 787-0462 .. **Pier,** Nancy Glickenhaus '83 -110 Riverside Dr -NY 10024
(518) 388-2291 .. **Pieraccini,** Alisha M '06 MVP Health Care Inc -625 State -Schnctdy 12305
(914) 666-4321 .. **Pieragostini,** Anthony J '75 -126 Barker -Mt Kisco 10549 **Fx:**666-2325
(718) 487-2300 .. **Pieragostini,** David M '81 %Leg Srvcs Corp -256-260 Bway -Brklyn 11211 **Fx:**782-6790
(347) 678-7262 .. **Pierce,** Aaron H '10 -302 Bedford Av #165 -Brklyn 11211 **Fx:**422-0895
(315) 218-8000 .. **Pierce,** Aaron M '97 (Bond S&K,PLLC) -1 Lincoln Ctr -Syracuse 13202
(315) 471-3151 .. **Pierce,** Alan J '85 (Hancock & E,LLP) -1500 AXA Twr I Bx4976 -Syracuse 13221
(845) 291-0011 .. **Pierce,** Carol C '99 %Blustein SR&B,LLP -10 Matthews -Goshen 10924
(516) 802-0606 .. **Pierce,** Chas R Jr. '86 CR Pierce,PC -350 Lex Av -Oyster Bay 11771 **Fx:**802-0607
(212) 521-5400 .. **Pierce,** Clay J '96 (Reed S LLP) -599 Lex Av -NY 10022
(718) 250-2000 .. **Pierce,** Garey A '07 %DA -350 Jay -Brklyn 11201 **Fx:**250-2314
(212) 355-3627 .. **Pierce,** George A Jr. '82 %Toyota Tsusho Amer -805 3rd Av -NY 10022
(212) 596-9000 .. **Pierce,** Heather H '06 %Ropes & G LLP -1211 Av of Amer -NY 10036
(716) 856-4000 .. **Pierce,** Heather K '09 %Hodgson R LLP -140 Pearl -Buffalo 14202
(212) 230-8829 .. **Pierce,** John V H '97 (WilmerHale) -399 Park Av -NY 10022
(212) 506-2500 .. **Pierce,** Kenneth R '99 (Mayer B LLP) -1675 Bway -NY 10019
(212) 837-6813 .. **Pierce,** M Betsy '07 %Hughes H&R LLP -1 Bttry Pk Plz -NY 10004 **Fx:**299-6813
(212) 259-8000 .. **Pierce,** Morton A '75 (Dewey & L LLP) -1301 Av of Amer -NY 10019
(212) 761-4000 .. **Pierce,** Nathan M '08 %Morgan Stanley -1585 Bway -NY 10036
(212) 247-4844 .. **Pierce,** Philip '55 (Margolin & P,LLP) -111 W 57th -NY 10019
(716) 858-6537 .. **Pierce,** Robt J '69 %Dept Soc Srvcs -95 Franklin -Buffalo 14202 **Fx:**858-8072
(212) 421-4100 .. **Pierce,** Steven J '91 (Pryor C LLP) -7 Times Sq -NY 10036
(212) 385-0034 .. **Pierce,** Stuart M '91 %HL Fong -11E Bway -NY 10038 **Fx:**571-4807
(212) 468-8000 .. **Pierce,** Suhna N '10 %Morrison & F LLP -1290 Av of Amer -NY 10104
(518) 447-9664 .. **Pierce,** Veronica D '83 %MHLS -75 New Scotland Av -Albany 12208 **Fx:**447-9697
(516) 512-6590 .. **Pieret,** James R '68 Pieret & Assoc -400 Grdn City Plz -Gdn Cty 11530 **Fx:**742-4116
(516) 746-7371 .. **Pieret,** John T '75 %Burns RT&R,LLP -390 Old Cntry Rd -Gdn Cty 11530
(718) 822-0707 .. **Piergiovanni,** Peter J '95 -984 Morris Park Av -Bronx 10462 **Fx:**904-1030
(718) 515-6000 .. **Piergrossi,** Lawr A '67 (Corpina PK&P,LLP) -2344 Eastchstr Rd -Bronx 10469
(718) 590-2000 .. **Piergrossi,** Lawr D '99 %DA -198 E 161st -Bronx 10451 **Fx:**590-6477
(212) 967-8202 .. **Pierguidi,** David J '02 %Pagan Law Firm,PC -245 5th Av -NY 10016 **Fx:**967-8794
(716) 854-3207 .. **Pieri,** John P '73 -484 Delaware Av -Buffalo 14202 **Fx:**883-2163
(212) 956-9500 .. **Pieri,** Mark R '09 %Hand B&A LLP -8 W 40th -NY 10018 **Fx:**376-6080
(716) 845-6000 .. **Pieri,** Russell J '73 (Kavinoky C LLP) -726 Exchange -Buffalo 14210
(631) 853-6162 .. **Pierini,** Susan M '82 %Hon D Blydenburgh - Supreme Ct -400 Carleton Av -Central Islip 11722 **Fx:**853-6326
(212) 218-2100 .. **Pieroni,** Jos P '00 %Fitzpatrick CH&S -1290 Av of Amer -NY 10104
(212) 697-3750 .. **Pieroni,** Lisa A '91 %Kirschstein IS&P,PC -425 5th Av -NY 10016
(212) 326-3939 .. **Pierpont,** Scott N '97 (Jones D) -222 E 41st -NY 10017
(718) 797-3323 .. **Pierre,** Abel L '03 -31 Smith -Brklyn 11201 **Fx:**797-3324
(212) 227-1123 .. **Pierre,** Eddy Pierre '98 (Pierre Pierre & Assoc. LLP) -20 Vesey -NY 10007 **Fx:**227-8637
(718) 250-2000 .. **Pierre,** Luc R '03 %DA -350 Jay -Brklyn 11201 **Fx:**250-2314
(212) 323-2250 .. **Pierre,** Nicole '02 %HHC-OLA-Medical Litigation -346 Bway -NY 10013 **Fx:**323-2251
(516) 229-4200 .. **Pierre,** W Marilynn '01 %Mendolia & S -875 Merrick Av -Westbury 11590
(212) 335-4500 .. **Pierre,** Yvan-Claude J '97 (DLA Piper LLP) -1251 Av of Amer -NY 10020
(518) 257-3000 .. **Pierre-Louis,** Joel '95 %Dormitory Auth -515 Bway -Albany 12207 **Fx:**257-3101
(212) 245-1000 .. **Pierre-Louis,** Melissa E '09 %Outten & G LLP -3 Park Av -NY 10016
(718) 328-1064 .. **Pierre-Louis,** Rosemonde '90 %Banana Kelly Cmmnty Imprvmnt Assn -863 Prospect Av -Bronx 10459 **Fx:**991-3242
(212) 258-6000 .. **Pierre-Louis,** Stanley '03 Viacom -1515 Bway -NY 10036
(516) 424-2186 .. **Pierre-Outerbridge,** Altagracia B '07 -49 Gold -Vly Stream 11580
(914) 939-3300 .. **Pierro,** Dominick D '53 OfCnsl Pierro & K -327 Irving Av Bx471 -Pt Chester 10573
(914) 939-3300 .. **Pierro & Kamensky** -327 Irving Av Bx471 -Pt Chester 10573 **Fx:**939-0356
(315) 724-5147 .. **Pierro,** Louis W '84 (Compson E&P PLLC) -2621 Genesee -Utica 13501
(518) 459-2100 .. **Pierro,** Louis W '84 (Pierro Law Grp,LLC) -20 Corp Wds Blvd -Albany 12211 **Fx:**459-2200
(718) 463-0606 .. **Pierro,** Roger Jr. '89 -4240 Bell Blvd -Bayside 11361 **Fx:**463-0241
(718) 286-6000 .. **Pierse,** Heather R '05 %DA -125-01 Qns Blvd -Kew Gdns 11415
(212) 687-1980 .. **Pierson,** Aviah Cohen '06 %Kaplan F&K LLP -850 3rd Av -NY 10022
(212) 479-6000 .. **Pierson,** Benjamin D '97 (Cooley LLP) -1114 Av of Amer -NY 10036
(212) 238-3000 .. **Pierson,** Deirdre K '98 (Emmet M&M,LLP) -120 Bway -NY 10271
(212) 325-2000 .. **Pierson,** Douglas A '01 Credit Suisse -11 Mad Av -NY 10010
(212) 878-4043 .. **Pierson,** Eric F '02 %Mitsui & Co -200 Park Av -NY 10166 **Fx:**878-4800
(212) 465-5000 .. **Pierson,** George J '04 Parsons Brinckerhoff -1 Penn Plz -NY 10119
(212) 732-3200 .. **Pierson,** Richd G '92 (Carter L&M LLP) -2 Wall -NY 10005
(212) 218-2100 .. **Pierson,** Robt W '09 %Fitzpatrick CH&S -1290 Av of Amer -NY 10104
(212) 949-9022 .. **Pierson,** Theo J Jr. '04 %Abelman F&S -666 3rd Av -NY 10017
(212) 506-1700 .. **Piesco,** Jos A Jr. '98 (Kasowitz BT&F LLP) -1633 Bway -NY 10019
(212) 416-8102 .. **Piesman,** Marissa J '78 %Dept of Law -120 Bway -NY 10271
(718) 704-6482 .. **Pietanza,** Damian J '98 -16 Court -Brklyn 11241
(718) 250-2000 .. **Pieters,** Edwin E '04 DA -350 Jay -Brklyn 11201 **Fx:**250-2314
(585) 362-4700 .. **Pieterse,** David L '00 %Bond S&K,PLLC -350 Linden Oaks -Rchstr 14625
(516) 833-5081 .. **Pietra,** Benjamin B '04 -114 Old Cntry Rd -Mineola 11501 **Fx:**294-5348
(518) 218-0851 .. **Pietrafesa,** Anthony J '83 -210 Bell Ct -Schnctdy 12303
(212) 363-1380 .. **Pietrafesa,** Gianfranco A '96 (Herten BSCBL&H,LLC) -747 3rd Av -NY 10017
(516) 767-7200 .. **Pietrantonio,** Jacqueline '88 -334 Main -Pt Wash 11050 **Fx:**767-9809
(516) 944-6169 .. **Pietrantonio,** Thos '87 (T Pietrantonio,PC) -334 Main -Pt Wash 11050 **Fx:**944-6179
(716) 566-2800 .. **Pietraszewski,** Diane M '06 %Bond S&K,PLLC -40 Fountian Plz -Buffalo 14202
(212) 980-0120 .. **Pietri,** Tara '09 %Frankfurt KK&S,PC -488 Mad Av -NY 10022
(212) 558-4000 .. **Pietro,** D Andrew '06 %Sullivan & C LLP -125 Broad -NY 10004
(914) 666-8137 .. **Pietrobono,** Rex M '90 -2 Sarles -Mt Kisco 10549 **Fx:**666-5690
(585) 328-4250 .. **Pietropaoli,** Patrick J '63 -1411 Chili Av -Rchstr 14624
(212) 839-5537 .. **Pietrzak,** A Robt '75 (Sidley A LLP) -787 7th Av -NY 10019
(212) 415-9200 .. **Pietrzak,** Brooke E '98 (Dorsey & W LLP) -250 Park Av -NY 10177
(212) 925-6688 .. **Pietrzak,** Gregory B '98 %F Berger -335 Bway -NY 10013 **Fx:**925-6987
(716) 250-1800 .. **Piette,** Michl A '81 (Jaeckle F&M,LLP) -400 Essjay Rd -Amherst 14221
(631) 267-2677 .. **Piette,** Tina K '96 -Bx697 -Amagansett 11930
(212) 536-3900 .. **Pifko,** Marc A '03 %K&L Gates LLP -599 Lex Av -NY 10022
(212) 513-7788 .. **Pigeon,** Lisa M '04 %Ahmuty D&M -123 William -NY 10038
(212) 964-6611 .. **Pighi,** Alison J '92 %Lester SK&D -120 Bway -NY 10271
(908) 848-6300 .. **Pignataro,** Catherine '03 %Carroll M&K LLC -570 Lex Av -NY 10022 **Fx:**848-6310
(212) 408-5100 .. **Pignatelli,** Caroline M '08 %Chadbourne & P LLP -30 Rckfllr Plz -NY 10112
(315) 265-8680 .. **Pignone,** Nicholas '06 (Ingram & P) -63 Market -Potsdam 13676 **Fx:**265-8390
(914) 235-3200 .. **Pigott,** Gerald M '97 %Pelican Mgmt -524 North Av -New Rchll 10801
(718) 896-6500 .. **Pigott,** James Robt Jr. '87 Fidelis Care NY -95-25 Qns Blvd -Rego Pk 11374
(718) 768-4566 .. **Pigott,** Ruthanne '98 Brenton Realty -322 5th Av -Brklyn 11215
(212) 237-1000 .. **Piirimae,** Karl F '03 (Windels ML&M,LLP) -156 W 56th -NY 10019
(212) 888-5088 .. **Pike,** Mary Boresz '72 -245 E 63rd -NY 10065 **Fx:**888-6088
(631) 727-7204 .. **Pike,** Robt D '80 -138 Ostrander Av -Rvrhead 11901 **Fx:**727-7308

(516) 783-0062 .. **Pike,** Roberta C '87 (Pike & P,PC) -1921 Bellmore Av -Bellmore 11710 **Fx:**783-0082
(516) 938-2300 .. **Piken,** Kenneth M '81 K Piken & Assoc -333 Jericho Tpk -Jericho 11753 **Fx:**938-2303
(212) 760-9100 .. **Piken,** Marilyn D '72 -350 5th Av -NY 10118
(212) 682-5522 .. **Piken,** Robt W '72 (Piken & P) -630 3rd Av -NY 10017 **Fx:**682-5542
(212) 596-9000 .. **Piken,** Seth A '08 %Ropes & G LLP -1211 Av of Amer -NY 10036
(212) 318-3000 .. **Pikiel,** Michl E Jr. '03 %Fulbright & J LLP -666 5th Av -NY 10103
(212) 521-5400 .. **Pikser,** Meredith D '99 %Reed S LLP -599 Lex Av -NY 10022
(212) 425-9300 .. **Pikus,** David H '81 (Bressler A&R,PC) -17 State -NY 10004
(212) 225-2000 .. **Pilarski,** Danl A '06 %Cleary GS&H -1 Lbrty Plz -NY 10006
(716) 852-4351 .. **Pilarz,** Michl '79 -237 Main -Buffalo 14203 **Fx:**852-6457
(585) 753-4500 .. **Pilato,** Darren A '09 %DA -832 Watts Bldg -Rchstr 14614 **Fx:**753-4576
(914) 231-2700 .. **Pilato,** David C '07 %DA -104 S Bway -Ynkrs 10701 **Fx:**969-0574
(585) 235-0570 .. **Pilato,** John C III '05 JC Pilato,Inc -955 Buffalo Rd -Rchstr 14624 **Fx:**235-0460
(585) 325-6700 .. **Pilato,** Saml C '42 -510 Wilder Bldg -Rchstr 14614
(516) 921-2525 .. **Pilatsky,** Judith '86 %McHenry H&L,PC -6800 Jericho Tpk -Syosset 11791
(315) 379-2115 .. **Pilatzke,** Brian D '06 Pub Def -Cnty Cthse -Canton 13617 **Fx:**386-8241
(212) 661-9100 .. **Pilchik,** Evan A '00 %Otterbourg SH&R,PC -230 Park Av -NY 10169
(212) 715-1000 .. **Pildis,** Sara K '06 %Arnold & P LLP -399 Park Av -NY 10022
(315) 336-3900 .. **Pileckas,** Paul L '56 -220 W Court -Rome 13440
(212) 358-1500 .. **Pilecki,** Elizabeth M '99 (Kennedy J&M,PC) -113 Univ Pl -NY 10003
(212) 753-5000 .. **Pileggi,** Patricia A '80 (Schiff H LLP) -900 3rd Av -NY 10022
(516) 826-6500 .. **Pilevsky,** Jordan C '05 %LaMonica H&M LLP -3305 Jerusalem Av -Wantagh 11793
(718) 616-2000 .. **Pilevsky,** Seth I '00 -2555 Ocean Av -Brklyn 11229
(718) 643-7158 .. **Pilewski,** Steven A '95 %Hon G Mangano Jr -120 Schermerhorn -Brklyn 11201
(212) 806-5400 .. **Pilgrim,** Chauncey C '03 %Stroock &S&L LLP -180 Maiden Ln -NY 10038
(718) 261-6604 .. **Piliero,** Alfred S '63 (Casil P&Z) -118-21 Qns Blvd -Frst Hlls 11375 **Fx:**261-6609
(212) 818-1110 .. **Piliero,** Robt D '75 (Butzel L,PC) -380 Mad Av -NY 10017
(212) 218-5500 .. **Piliouras,** Sophia M '04 Seyfarth S LLP -620 8th Av -NY 10018
(914) 346-0226 .. **Pilipshen,** Kenneth S '71 -7 Mdlnd Gdns -Bronxvll 10708
(914) 946-6774 .. **Pilkington,** John J '76 (Pilkington & L,PC) -222 Bloomingdale Rd -White Plns 10605
(914) 946-6774 .. **Pilkington & Leggett,PC** -222 Bloomingdale Rd -White Plns 10605 **Fx:**946-6719
(716) 858-2424 .. **Pilkington,** Rachel E '07 %DA -25 Delaware Av -Buffalo 14202 **Fx:**858-7425
(914) 779-0053 .. **Pilla,** Alan C '87 -107 Lk Av -Tuckahoe 10707 **Fx:**793-2114
(315) 423-4400 .. **Pillari,** Suzanne Halloran '06 %Wolff G&G,LLP -217 Mntgmry -Syracuse 13202
(516) 873-8787 .. **Pillari,** Thos '89 (Pillari & V) -114 Old Cntry Rd -Mineola 11501
(516) 873-8787 .. **Pillari & Vella** -114 Old Cntry Rd -Mineola 11501 **Fx:**873-8790
(212) 318-6000 .. **Pillay,** Ravi P '09 %Paul HJ&W LLP -75 E 55th -NY 10022
(607) 723-5341 .. **Pille,** Richd H '62 OfCnsl Hinman H&K,LLP -80 Exchange Bx5250 -Bnghmtn 13902
(212) 596-9000 .. **Piller,** Alexander G '09 %Ropes & G LLP -1211 Av of Amer -NY 10036
(212) 558-2255 .. **Piller,** B Robt '70 Isee Communications LLC -275 7th Av -NY 10001 **Fx:**(419) 828-4160
(518) 561-1980 .. **Piller,** Jacob '92 (Niles P&B) -46-48 Cornelia Bx2729 -Plattsbrgh 12901
(518) 561-4400 .. **Piller,** Susanna Surface '93 Stafford OC&T,PLLC -1 Cumberland Av Bx2947 -Plattsbrgh 12901
(212) 406-4848 .. **Pillersdorf,** Andrew H '01 %G Pillersdorf & Assoc,PC -225 Bway -NY 10007 **Fx:**406-5884
(212) 406-4848 .. **Pillersdorf,** Gary B '72 G Pillersdorf & Assoc,PC -225 Bway -NY 10007 **Fx:**406-5884
(914) 703-6300 .. **Pillinger,** Marc H '79 (Pillinger MT,LLP) -570 Taxter Rd -Elmsfrd 10523
(914) 703-6300 .. **Pillinger Miller Tarallo, LLP** -570 Taxter Rd -Elmsfrd 10523 **Fx:**703-6688
(315) 295-3831 .. **Pillinger Miller Tarallo, LLP** -507 Plum -Syracuse 13204 **Fx:**295-2575
(212) 461-6115 .. **Pillinger Miller Tarallo, LLP** -17 State -NY 10004 **Fx:**461-6116
(631) 234-1500 .. **Pillischer,** Eric S '90 %Rubin & R LLC -1787 Vets Hwy -Islandia 11749
(716) 488-0758 .. **Pillittieri,** Peter A '93 (Bly SBP&M) -3 Lakevw Av Bx3327 -Jamestwn 14702
(212) 858-1000 .. **Pillsbury Winthrop Shaw Pittman LLP** -1540 Bway -NY 10036 **Fx:**858-1500
(212) 335-9000 .. **Pilnyak,** Steve '04 %DA -1 Hogan Pl -NY 10013
(631) 439-2450 .. **Pilo,** Michele '98 %Leg Aid -320 Carleton Av -Central Islip 11722 **Fx:**439-2453
(212) 450-4000 .. **Pilotti,** Carissa M '09 %Davis P&W LLP -450 Lex Av -NY 10017
(718) 992-8042 .. **Pilotti,** Eric '82 (Emmanuelli & P) -1188-A Grnd Cncrs -Bronx 10456 **Fx:**992-8419
(718) 579-6998 .. **Pilsner,** Toby J '79 Envrnmntl Cntrl Brd -3030 3rd Av -Bronx 10455
(212) 708-1800 .. **Pilson,** Allan S '70 (Ladas & P) -26 W 61st -NY 10023
(516) 304-5555 .. **Pilson,** Richd J '81 (Berliner & P) -80 Cuttermill Rd -Gt Neck 11021
(914) 997-2500 .. **Pilutik,** Scott '07 %Bodnar & M LLP -140 Grand -White Plns 10601 **Fx:**997-8155
(516) 216-5828 .. **Pimentel,** Alexis '05 %Martinez & Assoc LLP -91 N Franklin -Hempstd 11550
(212) 455-2000 .. **Pimentel,** Jodie B '06 %Simpson T&B LLP -425 Lex Av -NY 10017
(315) 724-5147 .. **Pimpinella,** Paul J '03 %Compson E&P PLLC -2621 Genesee -Utica 13501
(914) 640-7655 .. **Pina,** Jeannette N '00 %Starwood Hotels & Resorts -1111 Wstchstr Av -White Plns 10604 **Fx:**640-8250
(585) 724-6864 .. **Pincelli,** Frank '85 %Eastman Kodak -343 State -Rchstr 14650
(212) 576-4504 .. **Pinchiaroli,** Christopher '90 %NY Life Ins -51 Mad Av -NY 10010 **Fx:**447-0569
(716) 774-3202 .. **Pinchoff,** Allan M '75 Cannon Design -2170 Whitehaven Rd -Grand Isl 14072
(518) 869-9500 .. **Pinchuk,** Lianne S '01 %Ganz W&S,LLP -1 Columbia Cir -Albany 12203
(518) 449-0044 .. **Pinckney,** Matthew B '09 %Hoffman W&D LLC -75 State -Albany 12207 **Fx:**449-0047
(212) 521-5400 .. **Pincus,** Andrea J '92 (Reed S LLP) -599 Lex Av -NY 10022
(631) 673-5004 .. **Pincus,** David A '83 %Schoenfeld S&P,PC -999 Walt Whitman Rd -Melvll 11747 **Fx:**673-9031
(212) 360-1411 .. **Pincus,** David H '96 Dept Parks & Rec -1234 5th Av -NY 10029
(716) 858-2424 .. **Pincus,** Glenn '83 %DA -25 Delaware Av -Buffalo 14202 **Fx:**858-7425
(631) 755-0101 .. **Pincus,** Jeffrey M '90 (Lewis JAA,LLP) -425 Broad Hollow Rd -Melvll 11747
(585) 256-8000 .. **Pincus,** Jonathan D '88 -95 Allens Crk Rd -Rchstr 14618 **Fx:**256-8009
(212) 610-6300 .. **Pincus,** Lauren J '08 %Allen & O -1221 Av of Amer -NY 10020
(212) 701-3000 .. **Pincus,** Mark S '09 %Cahill G&R LLP -80 Pine -NY 10005 **Fx:**269-5420
(516) 222-7700 .. **Pincus,** Michele A '87 LI Power Auth -333 Earle Ovngton Blvd -Uniondale 11553 **Fx:**222-9137
(212) 935-0900 .. **Pincus,** Paul H '77 Cnsl Rubin & B,LLP -501 Mad Av -NY 10022
(914) 763-1111 .. **Pincus,** Robt '66 -12 Debbie Ln -Cross Rvr 10518 **Fx:**763-2479
(718) 891-8200 .. **Pinczewski,** Benjamin M '86 (Pinczewski & S,PC) -2753 Coney Isl Av -Brklyn 11235
(718) 891-8200 .. **Pinczewski & Shpelfogel, PC** -2753 Coney Isl Av -Brklyn 11235 **Fx:**891-5600
(212) 248-9100 .. **Pinczower,** Kenneth E '90 %Epstein M&M -1 Whitehall -NY 10004
(212) 278-1288 .. **Pine,** Bennett D '80 (Anderson K&O,PC) -1251 Av of Amer -NY 10020
(212) 500-3158 .. **Pine,** Danl H '99 Marathon Asset Mgt -1 Bryant Pk -NY 10036
(718) 646-2806 .. **Pine,** Jacob '50 -2435 Haring -Brklyn 11235
(845) 796-2100 .. **Pine,** Jordan R '93 Frontier Ins -195 Lk Louise Marie Rd -Rck Hll 12775
(914) 923-1231 .. **Pine,** Merle Susan '85 -1 Long Hill Rd E -Briarclff Mnr 10510
(212) 561-8470 .. **Pine,** Rachael N '84 %AVSC Intl -440 9th Av -NY 10001 **Fx:**779-9489
(585) 436-1242 .. **Pineau,** Maureen A '83 -1411 Chili Av Bx10687 -Rchstr 14610 **Fx:**436-9706
(212) 468-8000 .. **Pinedo,** Anna T '94 (Morrison & F LLP) -1290 Av of Amer -NY 10104
(212) 735-3000 .. **Pineiro,** Carlos R '06 %Skadden ASM&F LLP -4 Times Sq -NY 10036
(718) 286-2000 .. **Pineiro,** Michl A '83 %Leg Aid -120-46 Qns Blvd -Kew Gdns 11415 **Fx:**286-2286
(212) 373-3000 .. **Pinelli,** Michl A '98 Paul WRW&G LLP -1285 Av of Amer -NY 10019
(212) 751-4300 .. **Pinero,** Eric A '04 %Hodgson R LLP -1540 Bway -NY 10036
(914) 468-0829 .. **Pines,** Andrea '85 (Goldberg & P) -600 Mamaroneck Av -Harrison 10528 **Fx:**468-0870
(212) 788-0933 .. **Pines,** Jonathan L '82 %Law Dept -100 Church -NY 10007 **Fx:**788-0367
(212) 373-3000 .. **Pines,** Justin S '10 %Paul WRW&G LLP -1285 Av of Amer -NY 10019
(212) 310-8692 .. **Pines,** Lori L '93 (Weil G&M LLP) -767 5th Av -NY 10153
(212) 421-8495 .. **Pines,** Mitchell '75 (Pines & K) -110 E 59th -NY 10022 **Fx:**421-8492
(585) 546-5530 .. **Pingleton,** Donald C III '02 %Thomson West -50 E Broad -Rchstr 14694
(212) 483-9490 .. **Pini,** Joshua R '07 %McElroy DM&C,LLP -88 Pine -NY 10005
(212) 715-9100 .. **Pinilis,** Russell J '97 (Kramer LN&F,LLP) -1177 Av of Amer -NY 10036
(718) 268-3000 .. **Pinilla,** Alexandra F '95 %M Povman -108-18 Qns Blvd -Frst Hlls 11375 **Fx:**520-8175
(212) 855-3929 .. **Pinilla,** Costanza '98 %Depository Trust Co -55 Water -NY 10041
(212) 829-9090 .. **Pinkas,** Edan E '05 (Friedberg CC&P,LLP) -767 3rd Av -NY 10017
(212) 768-6700 .. **Pinkas,** Oscar A N '07 %Sonnenschein N&R LLP -1221 Av of Amer -NY 10020
(212) 458-2023 .. **Pinkerton,** David B '91 %AIG Global Invstmnt -175 Water -NY 10038
(914) 948-8466 .. **Pinkham,** Tara A '07 %Westchester Hispanic Coalition -46 Waller Av -White Plns 10605
(718) 459-2600 .. **Pinkhasov,** Nathan '00 (N Pinkhasov PLLC) -95-20 63rd Rd -Rego Pk 11374 **Fx:**459-2684
(212) 613-5000 .. **Pinkhasova,** Elvira '00 Leg Assist Grp -450 W 33rd -NY 10001 **Fx:**750-0820
(212) 957-0700 .. **Pinkins,** Gerome R '96 -250 W 57th -NY 10107
(631) 234-4400 .. **Pinks Arbeit & Nemeth** -140 Fell Ct -Hauppauge 11788 **Fx:**234-4445
(631) 234-4400 .. **Pinks,** Steven G '66 (Pinks A&N) -140 Fell Ct -Hauppauge 11788
(212) 770-2173 .. **Pinkston,** Dawn M '05 AIG -80 Pine -NY 10005
(212) 687-7400 .. **Pinkus,** Saml L '83 McIntosh & Otis,Inc -353 Lex Av -NY 10016 **Fx:**687-6894
(212) 819-8200 .. **Pinkusiewicz,** Tomer '99 (White & C LLP) -1155 Av of Amer -NY 10036
(212) 436-3917 .. **Pinnel,** Alison C '96 Deloitte & Touche LLP -2 World Fncl Ctr -NY 10281
(212) 455-9344 .. **Pinner,** Richd E '90 %LISC -501 Fashion Av -NY 10018 **Fx:**682-5929
(607) 257-8000 .. **Pinnisi & Anderson, LLP** -111 Tioga -Ithaca 14850 **Fx:**257-0990
(718) 243-2700 .. **Pinnisi,** Dawn M '00 %Talisman & D,PC -409 Fulton -Brklyn 11201 **Fx:**243-2707
(607) 257-8000 .. **Pinnisi,** Michl D '86 (Pinnisi & A,LLP) -111 Tioga -Ithaca 14850
(212) 266-1154 .. **Pinnock,** Nadene M '02 NYC Dept of Correction -60 Hudson -NY 10013 **Fx:**266-1596
(212) 593-6700 .. **Pinnock,** Tania N '94 %Aaronson RF&D,LLP -757 3rd Av -NY 10017
(631) 581-6592 .. **Pinnola,** Robt '84 -560 Main -Islip 11751 **Fx:**581-1974
(631) 864-5850 .. **Pino,** Richd A '84 -353 Vets Mem'l Hwy -Commack 11725 **Fx:**864-5843
(914) 946-0600 .. **Pino,** Rudolph V Jr. '78 (Pino & Assoc) -50 Main -White Plns 10606 **Fx:**946-0650
(212) 722-2000 .. **Pinott,** Mildred '87 %Leg Aid -230 E 106th -NY 10029 **Fx:**876-5365
(212) 666-1545 .. **Pinover,** Diana Elzey '74 -333 Cntrl Pk W -NY 10025

(212) 728-8000 .. **Pinover,** Eugene A '74 (Willkie F&G LLP) -787 7th Av -NY 10019
(212) 836-8000 .. **Pinskaya,** Mariya A '07 %Kaye S LLP -425 Park Av -NY 10022
(212) 309-6000 .. **Pinsker,** Darryl E '03 %Morgan L&B LLP -101 Park Av -NY 10178
(585) 325-5353 .. **Pinsky,** Albert H '62 -16 E Main -Rchstr 14614 **Fx:**262-4118
(315) 428-8344 .. **Pinsky,** Bradley M '96 (Scicchitano & P,PLLC) -5789 Widewaters Pkwy -Syracuse 13214
(212) 841-1000 .. **Pinsky,** David Z '06 %Covington & B LLP -620 8th Av -NY 10018
(845) 343-6227 .. **Pinsky,** Michl D '95 (Hayward PO&P) -225 Dolson Av Bx929 -Middletwn 10940 **Fx:**343-1927
(315) 446-2384 .. **Pinsky,** Philip C '61 (Pinsky & S) -5790 Widewaters Pkwy -Syracuse 13214
(315) 446-2384 .. **Pinsky,** Roy D '72 (Pinsky & S) -5790 Widewaters Pkwy -Syracuse 13214
(315) 446-2384 .. **Pinsky & Skandalis** -5790 Widewaters Pkwy -Syracuse 13214 **Fx:**446-3016
(212) 468-8000 .. **Pintarelli,** John A '07 %Morrison & F LLP -1290 Av of Amer -NY 10104
(516) 294-8844 .. **Pintauro,** Douglas L '81 (L'Abbate BC&C,LLP) -1001 Franklin Av -Gdn Cty 11530
(212) 972-5252 .. **Pintauro,** Frank S '01 (Donohue & Prtnrs,PC) -90 Broad -NY 10004 **Fx:**697-2737
(212) 490-5700 .. **Pintel,** Ira S '95 (Hecht KP&D) -19 W 44th -NY 10036
(212) 269-4900 .. **Pinter,** Edw M '90 (Ford MEW&G,LLP) -Wall Street Plz -NY 10005
(212) 655-5000 .. **Pinter,** Gregory S '99 %Gannon R&M -120 Bway -NY 10271
(212) 687-4900 .. **Pinter,** Keith M '75 (Wormser KG&J LLP) -825 3rd Av -NY 10022
(212) 730-7750 .. **Pinter,** Kevin F '91 (Nicoletti GS&O,LLP) -555 5th Av -NY 10017
(718) 780-7938 .. **Pinto,** Arthur R '73 %Bklyn Law Schl -250 Joralemon -Brklyn 11201 **Fx:**780-0393
(718) 286-6000 .. **Pinto,** Barry '86 %DA -125-01 Qns Blvd -Kew Gdns 11415
(516) 378-3737 .. **Pinto,** Felicia M '96 (Scanlon & P,PLLC) -450 Sunrise Hwy -Rockvll Ctr 11570
(718) 250-2000 .. **Pinto,** Gregg A '08 %DA -350 Jay -Brklyn 11201 **Fx:**250-2314
(518) 266-3036 .. **Pinto,** Jos W Jr. '81 %Tax Appls Tribunal -500 Fed -Troy 12180 **Fx:**271-0886
(716) 842-5690 .. **Pinto,** Lisa R '05 M&T Bank -1 M & T Plz -Buffalo 14203
(518) 457-2070 .. **Pinto,** Patricia Ahasic '84 %Dept of Tax & Fin -Bldg 9 State Campus -Albany 12227 **Fx:**457-6131
(212) 841-7500 .. **Pintoff,** Erika L '96 Cushman & Wakefield -1290 Av of Amer -NY 10104
(212) 968-2954 .. **Pintoff,** Scott E '97 Cnsl GFI Grp -55 Water -NY 10041
(516) 627-6601 .. **Pinzino,** Stephen C '99 (Pinzino & P) -160 Plandome Rd -Manhsst 11030 **Fx:**627-6602
(516) 627-6601 .. **Pinzino,** Stephen D '70 (Pinzino & P) -160 Plandome Rd -Manhsst 11030 **Fx:**627-6602
(716) 858-2093 .. **Pinzler,** Ann R '87 Erie Cnty Dept of Social Srvcs -95 Franklin -Buffalo 14202
(212) 486-9494 .. **Pinzler,** Wm M '72 -488 Mad Av -NY 10022 **Fx:**486-0701
(212) 883-4946 .. **Pinzon,** Albert J '90 (Cozen O) -277 Park Av -NY 10172
(516) 937-5900 .. **Pinzon,** Michelle R '05 %Moomjian WW&C LLP -100 Jericho Quad -Jericho 11753
(212) 768-6700 .. **Piontnica,** Abraham D '92 OfCnsl Sonnenschein N&R LLP -1221 Av of Amer -NY 10020
(212) 578-2502 .. **Piotrkowski,** Howard '09 MetLife -1095 Av of Amer -NY 10036
(516) 746-0707 .. **Piotroski,** Anton '80 %Hammill OCDP&K,PC -6851 Jericho Tpk -Syosset 11791
(914) 333-9624 .. **Piotrowski,** Danl J '97 Philips Electronics -345 Scarborough Rd -Briarclff Mnr 10510
(716) 712-0888 .. **Piotrowski,** Wallace C '87 -3881 Seneca -W Seneca 14224 **Fx:**712-0622
(718) 636-1155 .. **Piovia,** Sara '74 %Leg Srvcs -1368 Fulton -Brklyn 11216 **Fx:**398-6414
(212) 297-5800 .. **Piper,** Kristen Jasket '01 %Day P LLP -7 Times Sq -NY 10036
(585) 419-8800 .. **Piper,** Scott D '99 (Harris B PLLC) -99 Garnsey Rd -Pittsfrd 14534
(212) 973-0572 .. **Pipersburgh,** Denise J '04 %Wolff & S PC -140 Bway -NY 10005
(516) 489-5000 .. **Pipia,** Robt E '93 Town of Hempstead -1 Wshngtn -Hempstd 11550
(516) 433-7777 .. **Pipitone,** Frank P '09 %Blutter & B -497 S Oyster Bay Rd -Plainvw 11803 **Fx:**938-2915
(718) 286-6000 .. **Piplani,** Rajana C '89 %DA -125-01 Qns Blvd -Kew Gdns 11415
(212) 336-2000 .. **Pippert,** Thos W '76 OfCnsl Patterson BW&T LLP -1133 Av of Amer -NY 10036
(212) 309-6000 .. **Piracci,** Michl A '00 OfCnsl Morgan L&B LLP -101 Park Av -NY 10178
(315) 475-7777 .. **Piraino,** Andrew N '83 -117 S State -Syracuse 13202
(516) 741-4799 .. **Pirillo,** Melissa A '05 %Baker SBGFM&N,LLC -100 Grdn City Plz -Gdn Cty 11530
(212) 232-1300 .. **Pirk,** Wm R Jr. '90 (Lewis BB&S LLP) -77 Water -NY 10005
(914) 358-3274 .. **Piro,** Clare A '85 (Markowitz & P) -500 Mamaroneck Av -Harrison 10528
(212) 521-5400 .. **Piro,** Elisabeth J '08 %Reed S LLP -599 Lex Av -NY 10022
(516) 712-4000 .. **Pirog,** Jonathan P '01 %Milber MP&S LLP -1000 Woodbury Rd -Woodbury 11797
(212) 209-4800 .. **Piron,** Caleb B '08 %Brown R LLP -7 Times Sq -NY 10036
(914) 249-3719 .. **Pirone,** Renee M '99 MasterCard Worldwide -2000 Purchase -Purchase 10577
(212) 335-4500 .. **Pironti,** Michelle '08 %DLA Piper LLP -1251 Av of Amer -NY 10020
(516) 333-2553 .. **Pirotin,** Sanford L '86 (S Pirotin,PC) -323 Madison -Westbury 11590
(212) 407-4000 .. **Pirraglia,** Anthony '04 %Loeb & L,LLP -345 Park Av -NY 10154
(914) 684-0200 .. **Pirraglia,** Pat Edw '66 -200 Mamaroneck Av -White Plns 10601 **Fx:**684-9613
(718) 273-5950 .. **Pirraglia,** Raymond T '81 %Home Ins -74 Narrows Rd S -Staten Isl 10305 **Fx:**815-2987
(585) 544-7090 .. **Pirrello,** Mario J '58 (Pirrello MP&F) -2040 E Ridge Rd -Rchstr 14622
(585) 544-7090 .. **Pirrello Missal Personte & Feder** -2040 E Ridge Rd -Rchstr 14622 **Fx:**544-7093
(518) 393-7719 .. **Pirro,** Kendall R '60 -219 Putnam Rd -Schnctdy 12306
(516) 431-9500 .. **Pirrone,** Maria M '94 -42 W Park Av -Long Bch 11561
(516) 431-9500 .. **Pirrone,** Vincent A '64 -42 W Park Av -Long Bch 11561
(914) 723-4333 .. **Pirrotti,** Anthony Jr. '91 (Pirrotti Law Firm LLC) -2 Overhill Rd -Scarsdale 10583 **Fx:**723-4838
(914) 693-8000 .. **Pirrotti,** Anthony J '55 A Pirrotti,PC -501 Ashford Av -Ardsley 10502 **Fx:**693-8640
(212) 530-5000 .. **Pisa,** Albert A '97 (Milbank TH&M LLP) -1 Chase Manh Plz -NY 10005
(212) 980-0120 .. **Pisacane,** Antonia M '05 %Frankfurt KK&S,PC -488 Mad Av -NY 10022
(212) 370-1300 .. **Pisacane,** Christopher M '06 %Ellenoff G&S LLP -150 E 42nd -NY 10017
(212) 513-3200 .. **Pisacreta,** Edw A '84 (Holland & K LLP) -31 W 52nd -NY 10019
(914) 681-8700 .. **Pisanelli,** Andrew F '92 (Milber MP&S LLP) -3 Barker Av -White Plns 10601
(845) 463-4797 .. **Pisanelli,** David A '81 River City Abstract -2645 South Rd -Poughkeepsie 12601 **Fx:**463-4765
(845) 471-3330 .. **Pisanelli,** Gerard J '74 GJ Pisanelli -2 Cannon -Poughkeepsie 12601 **Fx:**471-3907
(631) 434-3311 .. **Pisani,** Amanda Jones '88 %Barron's Educ Series -250 Wireless Blvd -Hauppauge 11788
(516) 294-8844 .. **Pisani,** Dominic M '91 OfCnsl L'Abbate BC&C,LLP -1001 Franklin Av -Gdn Cty 11530
(845) 384-6932 .. **Pisani,** Jos R '54 -203 Burroughs Dr Bx159 -W Pk 12493 **Fx:**384-6747
(212) 318-6000 .. **Pisani,** Keith D '95 %Paul HJ&W LLP -75 E 55th -NY 10022
(516) 354-6500 .. **Pisani,** Michl J '69 Prudential -390 Franklin Av -Franklin Sq 11010
(315) 330-7686 .. **Pisano,** Carmen M '01 AFRL/IFOJ -26 Electronic Pkwy -Rome 13441
(212) 483-9490 .. **Pisano,** Carol A '80 (McElroy DM&C,LLP) -88 Pine -NY 10005
(914) 423-8912 .. **Pisano,** Joanne '89 J Pisano,PC -1250 Cntrl Pk Av -Ynkrs 10704 **Fx:**423-8964
(212) 536-3900 .. **Pisano,** Vincent J '79 (K&L Gates LLP) -599 Lex Av -NY 10022
(212) 341-6400 .. **Pisapia,** Michl F '90 %Liquidation Bur -123 William -NY 10038 **Fx:**608-3398
(212) 409-3689 .. **Pisapia,** Peter E '98 BlackRock -40 E 52nd -NY 10022
(631) 249-6600 .. **Pisarello,** Wm '78 (Rebore T&P PC) -500 Bi-Cnty Blvd -Farmngdl 11735 **Fx:**249-8190
(585) 352-8818 .. **Pisaturo,** John J '76 -380 S Union -Spencerprt 14559
(718) 222-2109 .. **Pischl,** Stephen P '08 %Law Dept -350 Jay -Brklyn 11201 **Fx:**222-2393
(914) 835-6900 .. **Piscionere,** Anthony G '81 (Piscionere & N,PC) -363 Bstn Post Rd -Rye 10580 **Fx:**835-6931
(212) 803-5100 .. **Pisciotta,** Christopher P '92 %NY Cnty Defender Srvcs -225 Bway -NY 10007 **Fx:**571-6035
(914) 287-7711 .. **Pisciotti,** Anthony M '94 (Pisciotti M&B,PC) -445 Hmltn Av -White Plns 10601 **Fx:**287-7715
(518) 449-8893 .. **Piscitelli,** Anthony P '89 (Wilson EME&D LLP) -677 Bway -Albany 12207
(212) 272-0094 .. **Piscitelli,** David A '99 %JP Morgan Chase -383 Mad Av -NY 10179
(718) 723-1616 .. **Piscitelli,** James F '94 %State Farm -23436 Merrick Blvd -Rosedale 11422
(518) 473-4596 .. **Piscitelli,** Ross M '98 %Gov Ofc Emply Rel -Agncy Bldg 2 ESP -Albany 12223
(631) 853-4547 .. **Piscitello,** Jos A '67 %District Ct Law Dept -400 Carleton Av Bx9075 -Central Islip 11722
(845) 561-0550 .. **Piscopo,** Lynn A '04 %Drake LHKGG&R PLLC -555 Hudson Valley Av -New Windsor 12553
(212) 858-1000 .. **Pisella,** Bart '90 (Pillsbury WSP LLP) -1540 Bway -NY 10036
(212) 903-8700 .. **Pisem,** Elliot '79 (Roberts & H,LLP) -825 8th Av -NY 10019
(212) 776-5212 .. **Pisem,** Rosanne R '88 %NYC Housing Auth -250 Bway -NY 10007 **Fx:**776-5039
(212) 248-8800 .. **Pisiewski,** Jon '07 %Callan KB&B LLP -1 Whitehall -NY 10004
(212) 407-4000 .. **Piskora,** John A '01 %Loeb & L,LLP -345 Park Av -NY 10154
(631) 232-2400 .. **Pismeny,** Miriam '83 %Nassau/Sfflk Law Srv -1757 Vets Hwy -Islandia 11749 **Fx:**232-2489
(212) 857-8533 .. **Pisnanont,** Judy '07 %US Ct of Appls -500 Pearl -NY 10007
(516) 873-2000 .. **Pistilli,** Lia M '02 %Moritt HH&H LLP -400 Grdn City Plz -Gdn Cty 11530
(212) 848-4000 .. **Pistillo,** Bernie J '85 (Shearman & S LLP) -599 Lex Av -NY 10022
(585) 753-4500 .. **Piston,** Matthew M '07 DA -832 Watts Bldg -Rchstr 14614 **Fx:**753-4576
(212) 584-0700 .. **Pi-Sunyer,** Andrea Mercedes '95 %Seeger W LLP -1 William -NY 10004
(718) 590-3928 .. **Pisupati,** Lavanya '02 %Law Dept -198 E 161st -Bronx 10451 **Fx:**590-2686
(917) 454-1100 .. **Piszczkiewicz,** Kristy L '02 Police Dept -2 Lafayette -NY 10007
(212) 666-0396 .. **Pita,** Henry M '91 -314 W 104th -NY 10025 **Fx:**663-9270
(718) 380-7100 .. **Pitaro,** Eugene D '82 (Pitaro & P) -77-11 164th -Flushng 11366 **Fx:**969-0721
(718) 380-7100 .. **Pitaro,** Vincent D '88 (Pitaro & P) -77-11 164th -Flushng 11366 **Fx:**969-0721
(646) 471-4000 .. **Pitch,** Michl J '03 PricewaterhouseCoopers LLP -300 Mad Av -NY 10017
(718) 478-9272 .. **Pitchayan,** Pat B '93 -72-30 Bway -Jcksn Hts 11372 **Fx:**478-9279
(212) 757-3343 .. **Pitchford,** David L '85 Pitchford Law Grp LLC -888 7th Av -NY 10106 **Fx:**757-2863
(212) 512-1000 .. **Pitcock,** Grace J '02 HBO -1100 Av of Amer -NY 10036 **Fx:**512-1986
(845) 215-9911 .. **Pitcock,** Jeremy S '99 -20 Old Nyack Tpke -Nanuet 10954
(212) 766-1888 .. **Pitcoff,** Kenneth E '97 (Morris DA&F) -2 Rector -NY 10006
(212) 533-1878 .. **Pitcoff,** Paul '91 -50 E 10th -NY 10003
(716) 780-4344 .. **Pitegoff,** Peter R '88 %SUNY Buffalo Lw Schl -O'Brian Hall -Buffalo 14260 **Fx:**645-2900
(914) 681-0100 .. **Pitegoff,** Thos M '77 Pitegoff Law Ofc,PLLC -445 Hmltn Av -White Plns 10601 **Fx:**206-6003
(917) 826-0017 .. **Pitkofsky,** Nancy S '95 -3818 Oceanside Rd E -Oceanside 11572
(212) 885-7700 .. **Pitkofsky,** Robt L '02 Anti-Defamation League -605 3rd Av -NY 10158
(516) 594-1944 .. **Pitkowsky,** Herbert G '85 -3232 Perry Av -Oceanside 11572 **Fx:**594-0989
(718) 780-7952 .. **Pitler,** Robt M '67 %Bklyn Law Schl -250 Joralemon -Brklyn 11201 **Fx:**780-0393
(212) 450-4000 .. **Pitluck,** David C '08 %Davis P&W LLP -450 Lex Av -NY 10017
(212) 847-7900 .. **Pitman,** Debora A '86 %Wechsler & C,LLP -17 State -NY 10004
(631) 853-4161 .. **Pitman,** Michelle A '04 %DA -N Cnty Cmplx Bldg 77 -Hauppauge 11788 **Fx:**853-4192

(212) 805-0036 .. **Pitman,** Nicole A '03 Hon A Peck -500 Pearl -NY 10007
(212) 504-6000 .. **Pitman,** Ryan G '10 %Cadwalader W&T LLP -1 World Fncl Ctr -NY 10281
(212) 455-2000 .. **Pitney,** Alexandra C '09 %Simpson T&B LLP -425 Lex Av -NY 10017
(212) 474-1000 .. **Pitney,** Thaddeus L '07 %Cravath S&M LLP -825 8th Av -NY 10019
(516) 921-3838 .. **Pitnick,** Irwin L '67 (Pitnick & M LLP) -6800 Jericho Tpk -Syosset 11791 **Fx:**921-3824
(516) 869-7600 .. **Pitnick,** Mitchell L '06 Town Atty -220 Plandome Rd -Manhsst 11030 **Fx:**869-7605
(212) 813-8800 .. **Pitofsky,** David B '92 (Goodwin P LLP) -620 8th Av -NY 10018
(212) 557-2900 .. **Pitofsky,** Donald A '83 (Schwartzman GW&T,PC) -355 Lex Av -NY 10017
(646) 943-8779 .. **Pitofsky,** Elizabeth R '98 After Schl Corp -1440 Bway -NY 10018
(212) 854-2195 .. **Pitruzzello,** Philip R '80 Columbia Univ -410 W 118th -NY 10027
(631) 374-8132 .. **Pitsiokos,** Peter '85 -1 Flowerfld -St James 11780
(718) 618-1200 .. **Pitt,** Bahaati E T '99 Supreme Ct -851 Grnd Cncrs -Bronx 10451
(518) 449-3320 .. **Pitta Bishop DelGiorno & Giblin LLP** -111 Wshngtn Av -Albany 12210 **Fx:**449-5812
(212) 652-3890 .. **Pitta & Giblin LLP** -120 Bway -NY 10271 **Fx:**652-3891
(212) 652-3890 .. **Pitta,** Vincent F '78 (Pitta & G LLP) -120 Bway -NY 10271
(212) 344-8888 .. **Pittaluga,** Elisabeth A '92 %Willis of NY,Inc -1 World Fncl Ctr -NY 10281
(212) 681-0117 .. **Pittard,** Jeffrey R '07 %Starr GD&R -530 5th Av -NY 10036
(914) 286-3400 .. **Pittari,** Stephen J '69 %Leg Aid -1 N Bway -White Plns 10601 **Fx:**682-4112
(718) 726-4184 .. **Pittas,** John E '83 -30-05 30th Av -Astoria 11102 **Fx:**726-4291
(516) 829-2299 .. **Pittell,** Jeffrey '88 (Maher & P,LLP) -299 E Shore Rd -Gt Neck 11023 **Fx:**977-3003
(631) 234-2222 .. **Pittelli,** Melissa B '05 %Siben & F -1455 Vets Mem'l Hwy -Hauppauge 11749
(212) 753-7500 .. **Pitter,** Anne E '79 (Hartman & C LLP) -488 Mad Av -NY 10022
(718) 325-2425 .. **Pitter,** Janet D '97 -4239 Byron Av -Bronx 10466 **Fx:**325-0606
(212) 684-1880 .. **Pitter,** Laura L '05 %Rheingold VRS&M LLP -113 E 37th -NY 10016
(212) 325-2343 .. **Pitters,** Caleb J A Jr. '05 Credit Suisse -11 Mad Av -NY 10010
(212) 313-3600 .. **Pitti,** Nicole L '09 %Barry M&M -2 Rector -NY 10006
(212) 286-6100 .. **Pittinsky,** Laurence D '91 (Rosenberg & P,LLP) -420 Lex Av -NY 10170
(212) 370-9600 .. **Pittleman,** Linda J '83 Pittleman & Assoc -336 E 43rd -NY 10017 **Fx:**370-9608
(631) 665-4477 .. **Pittman,** Barry V '77 -26 Saxon Av -Bay Shr 11706 **Fx:**665-6297
(212) 732-3200 .. **Pittman,** Dan S '03 %Carter L&M LLP -2 Wall -NY 10005
(212) 294-6700 .. **Pittman,** Jared M '07 %Winston & S -200 Park Av -NY 10166
(212) 975-5896 .. **Pittman,** Kimberly D '01 CBS Inc -51 W 52nd -NY 10019
(718) 444-8400 .. **Pitton,** Appolo '00 A Pitton,PC -5116 Av L -Brklyn 11234 **Fx:**444-5450
(212) 286-8585 .. **Pittoni,** Luke M '72 (Heidell PM&B,LLP) -99 Park Av -NY 10016
(516) 248-5400 .. **Pittoni,** M John '68 MJ Pittoni LLC -226 7th -Gdn Cty 11530 **Fx:**739-2010
(212) 474-1000 .. **Pitts,** Andrew J '95 (Cravath S&M LLP) -825 8th Av -NY 10019
(315) 479-3900 .. **Pitts,** Edw I '89 SSA-ODAR -300 S State -Syracuse 13202 **Fx:**479-3933
(212) 909-6000 .. **Pitts,** Jack N E Jr. '09 %Debevoise & P LLP -919 3rd Av -NY 10022
(212) 688-8555 .. **Pitts,** Jeffrey W '99 (Fragomen DB&L LLP) -7 Hanover Sq -NY 10004
(212) 455-2000 .. **Pitts,** John D '10 %Simpson T&B LLP -425 Lex Av -NY 10017
(718) 237-2000 .. **Pitts,** Lisa N '99 %Leg Aid -111 Lvngstn -Brklyn 11201 **Fx:**237-8737
(212) 554-1234 .. **Pitts,** Lydia M '80 %AXA Financial Inc -1290 Av of Amer -NY 10104 **Fx:**707-3963
(212) 559-8199 .. **Pitts,** Tammy E '99 Citigroup,Inc -425 Park Av -NY 10022
(212) 490-3000 .. **Pittsburg,** Adam D '06 %Wilson EME&D LLP -150 E 42nd -NY 10017
(518) 475-0837 .. **Pivar,** Jack J '74 -11 Stonewall Ln -Delmar 12054 **Fx:**475-0838
(716) 873-4619 .. **Piver,** Susan M '77 -315 Lincoln Pkwy -Buffalo 14216 **Fx:**871-3463
(212) 537-1187 .. **Pivnick,** Randi F '01 Morgan Stanley -1633 Bway -NY 10019 **Fx:**507-4765
(716) 856-0600 .. **Piwowarczyk,** Edw G '72 (Jaeckle F&M,LLP) -12 Fountain Plz -Buffalo 14202
(585) 244-5600 .. **Pixley,** Wm G '77 OfCnsl Wisner & W,LLP -1209 East Av -Rchstr 14607 **Fx:**244-5601
(212) 766-1001 .. **Piyatissa,** Pushpa L '01 %W Rita -291 Bway -NY 10007 **Fx:**608-6802
(347) 534-3727 .. **Pizarro,** Carol Sewell '95 US Probation Dept -75 Clinton -Brklyn 11201
(212) 833-6065 .. **Pizarro,** Marisa C '09 SONY Music -550 Mad Av -NY 10022
(718) 784-5080 .. **Pizarro,** Victor M '77 %Mision Hispana -42-15 Crescent -LIC 11101
(518) 828-1597 .. **Pizer,** Adam M '95 -117 Fairvw Av -Hudson 12534
(585) 232-5600 .. **Pizer,** Melvin H '69 (Blitman & K LLP) -16 W Main -Rchstr 14614
(516) 433-6677 .. **Pizza,** Anthony E '89 %Stewart GM&B -6800 Jericho Tpk -Syosset 11791
(718) 797-5700 .. **Pizzano,** John '81 %Wenig S LLP -26 Court -Brklyn 11242
(212) 715-9100 .. **Pizzarello,** Clara M '01 Kramer LN&F,LLP -1177 Av of Amer -NY 10036
(914) 750-5933 .. **Pizzey,** Julie L '10 %Kissel H&W LLP -580 Wht Plns Rd -Tarrytwn 10591
(212) 259-8000 .. **Pizzi,** Julia D '09 %Dewey & L LLP -1301 Av of Amer -NY 10019
(212) 262-2390 .. **Pizzi,** Peter J '79 (Connell F LLP) -888 7th Av -NY 10106
(914) 946-8100 .. **Pizzirusso,** Albert '05 %T Sundack & Assoc,LLC -19 Court -White Plns 10601 **Fx:**946-9585
(516) 352-2083 .. **Pizzo,** Anne F '96 -1613 Falmouth Av -New Hyde Pk 11040 **Fx:**355-5062
(631) 712-6335 .. **Pizzo,** Nicole M '03 US Probation Dept -Bx9012 -Central Islip 11722
(585) 231-1559 .. **Pizzo,** Robt F '79 -16 W Main -Rchstr 14614
(239) 225-7911 .. **Pizzolato,** Barbara M '88 (B Pizzolato,PC) -532 Broadhllw Rd -Melvll 11747 **Fx:**(801) 340-3656
(917) 378-7105 .. **Pizzulli,** Elizabeth '87 Corcoran Grp -36 E 12th -NY 10003 **Fx:**(212) 230-7449
(516) 296-7000 .. **Pizzulli,** Vincent J Jr. '83 (Certilman BA&H,LLP) -90 Merrick Av -E Meadow 11554
(212) 468-8000 .. **Pizzurro,** Eileen A '06 %Morrison & F LLP -1290 Av of Amer -NY 10104
(212) 696-6000 .. **Pizzurro,** Jos D '77 (Curtis M-PC&M LLP) -101 Park Av -NY 10178
(212) 804-4504 .. **Pizzuto,** Philip '97 SrCnsl Mound CW&G -One Bttry Pk Plz -NY 10004
(212) 931-7300 .. **Placa,** Alan J '84 %Giuliani Prtnrs -5 Times Sq -NY 10036
(585) 425-1060 .. **Place & Arnold** -27 Plsnt -Fairprt 14450 **Fx:**223-3252
(585) 425-1060 .. **Place,** Robt M '83 (Place & A) -27 Plsnt -Fairprt 14450
(518) 798-7981 .. **Place,** Rose T '93 (RT Place,PLLC) -93 Bay -Glens Fls 12801 **Fx:**798-2981
(212) 316-2373 .. **Placeres,** Alfred P '76 -2710 Bway -NY 10025
(716) 856-5500 .. **Plache,** Robt J '57 SpclCnsl Damon M LLP -200 Delaware Av -Buffalo 14202
(212) 788-1574 .. **Plache,** Wm S '99 %Law Dept -100 Church -NY 10007 **Fx:**788-0367
(212) 425-7200 .. **Plachy,** Robin M '10 %Kenyon & K,LLP -1 Bway -NY 10004
(212) 922-9700 .. **Plaia,** Vincent L '87 %1st Amer Title -633 3rd Av -NY 10017 **Fx:**922-0881
(718) 268-0279 .. **Plaine,** Mark I '88 MI Plaine,PC -80-02 Kew Grdns Rd -Kew Gdns 11415 **Fx:**268-2834
(212) 603-7523 .. **Plaine,** Moss J '94 %Burnham Securities -1325 Av of Amer -NY 10019 **Fx:**603-7537
(212) 259-8000 .. **Plaku,** Stela '08 %Dewey & L LLP -1301 Av of Amer -NY 10019
(212) 468-4800 .. **Plambeck,** Cheryl M '02 %Davis & G LLP -1740 Bway -NY 10019
(212) 250-3669 .. **Plana,** April N '04 Deutsche Bk Sec -60 Wall -NY 10005
(212) 697-3122 .. **Planas,** Carolyn M '05 %Martin C&B LLP -220 E 42nd -NY 10017
(212) 704-1355 .. **Planchard,** Steven C '96 Interpublic Grp -1114 Av of Amer -NY 10036 **Fx:**704-1201
(212) 698-3500 .. **Planell,** Michl E '04 %Dechert LLP -1095 Av of Amer -NY 10036
(914) 949-2700 .. **Planell,** Raymond M '76 (Bleakley P&S,LLP) -1 N Lex Av -White Plns 10601
(914) 636-2438 .. **Plank,** Michl E '88 -156 Centre Av -New Rchll 10805 **Fx:**636-2438
(212) 788-6783 .. **Plansky,** Richd M '93 Mayors Ofc-Crim Justice -1 Centre -NY 10007
(212) 425-9300 .. **Plant,** Matthew C '99 (Bressler A&R,PC) -17 State -NY 10004
(212) 506-1700 .. **Plante,** David J '10 Kasowitz BT&F LLP -1633 Bway -NY 10019
(212) 530-1800 .. **Plante,** Douglas R '05 %Richards K&O LLP -1 World Fncl Ctr -NY 10281
(516) 249-1342 .. **Plante,** Kevin M '93 (Grey & G,LLP) -360 Main -Farmngdl 11735
(716) 645-2093 .. **Plants,** Jennifer L '00 %SUNY Buffalo Lw Schl -O'Brian Hall -Buffalo 14260 **Fx:**645-5968
(631) 853-4161 .. **Planty,** Donna M '96 %DA -N Cnty Cmplx Bldg 77 -Hauppauge 11788 **Fx:**853-4192
(212) 336-2000 .. **Plasha,** Hope K '97 Cnsl Patterson BW&T LLP -1133 Av of Amer -NY 10036
(212) 318-6000 .. **Plaskon,** Leslie A '92 (Paul HJ&W LLP) -75 E 55th -NY 10022
(607) 776-1000 .. **Plaskov,** Robt H '79 -5 Gansvoort Bx551 -Bath 14810 **Fx:**776-3122
(212) 695-5811 .. **Plasse,** Andrew F '82 (A Plasse,PC) -352 7th Av -NY 10001 **Fx:**402-7737
(212) 907-0863 .. **Plasse,** Jonathan M '77 (Labaton S LLP) -140 Bway -NY 10005
(212) 512-1000 .. **Plasse,** Stephanie D '01 %HBO -1100 Av of Amer -NY 10036 **Fx:**512-1986
(516) 248-2002 .. **Plastaras,** Thos E '83 (Gallagher WB&P) -98 Willis Av -Mineola 11501
(845) 876-4057 .. **Platania,** Jade H '01 %S Melley -24 Closs Dr -Rhinebeck 12572 **Fx:**876-5745
(585) 546-2500 .. **Platania,** Jos A '68 OfCnsl McConville CC&M,PC -25 E Main -Rchstr 14614
(716) 845-9358 .. **Platek,** Fredk J '85 Supreme Ct -25 Delaware Av -Buffalo 14202 **Fx:**851-3293
(914) 686-1700 .. **Platek,** Jeremy '92 (O'Connor R,LLP) -200 Mamaroneck Av -White Plns 10601
(212) 757-2011 .. **Platek,** Todd L '87 -321 W 44th -NY 10036 **Fx:**757-2650
(315) 478-5820 .. **Platenik,** Nikki Rinaldi '96 %Rinaldi Law Firm -422 Univ Bldg -Syracuse 13202 **Fx:**478-5803
(718) 354-3200 .. **Platis,** Susan '89 Battiste A&S,Inc -60 Bay -Staten Isl 10301
(212) 367-7575 .. **Platkin,** Chas S '92 Diet Detective -17 E 17th -NY 10003
(212) 310-8000 .. **Platkov,** Margarita '01 %Weil G&M LLP -767 5th Av -NY 10153
(212) 245-7300 .. **Platnick,** Barry H '74 OfCnsl Serling R&F,LLP -119 5th Av -NY 10003
(212) 223-3900 .. **Platnick,** Jonathan D '79 OfCnsl Zwerling S&Z,LLP -41 Mad Av -NY 10010
(716) 433-5907 .. **Platt,** Abraham J '09 %Seaman JH&B,LLP -76 West Av -Lockprt 14094
(212) 230-8860 .. **Platt,** Chas C '80 (WilmerHale) -399 Park Av -NY 10022
(212) 455-2000 .. **Platt,** Chas R '07 %Simpson T&B LLP -425 Lex Av -NY 10017
(212) 576-2670 .. **Platt,** Christopher J '99 %J Osborn,PC -841 Bway -NY 10003 **Fx:**686-4023
(845) 471-4455 .. **Platt,** Clifford A '94 (Steinberg S&P,LLP) -27 Grdn -Poughkeepsie 12601
(518) 257-1620 .. **Platt,** Cynthia Ann '90 %Bankruptcy Ct -445 Bway -Albany 12207 **Fx:**431-0192
(212) 373-3000 .. **Platt,** Erica S '05 %Paul WRW&G LLP -1285 Av of Amer -NY 10019
(845) 638-9700 .. **Platt,** Frank D '69 (Feder & P) -151 N Main -New Cty 10956 **Fx:**638-0050
(631) 283-9365 .. **Platt,** Harold K '72 -99 Sanford Pl -Southampton 11968 **Fx:**283-0135
(212) 508-6700 .. **Platt,** Harvey J '61 OfCnsl Tannenbaum HS&H LLP -900 3rd Av -NY 10022
(212) 239-5731 .. **Platt,** Irene L '63 %Div Of Parole -314 W 40th -NY 10018 **Fx:**239-6160
(212) 332-3332 .. **Platt,** Jack M '78 -767 3rd Av -NY 10017 **Fx:**332-3315
(914) 478-8900 .. **Platt,** Jason J '96 (Hyman & P,PC) -145 Palisades -Dobbs Ferry 10522
(212) 610-6300 .. **Platt,** Jonah B '09 %Allen & O -1221 Av of Amer -NY 10020
(631) 283-0099 .. **Platt,** Jonathan J '77 -99 Sanford Pl -Southampton 11968 **Fx:**283-0135
(212) 607-2819 .. **Platt,** Jonathan W '01 FTC -1 Bowling Grn -NY 10004 **Fx:**607-2822
(212) 685-7474 .. **Platt,** Karen M '00 %Mayerson SA LLP -292 Mad Av -NY 10017
(212) 418-8600 .. **Platt,** Mark '83 Cnsl Kornstein VW&P,LLP -757 3rd Av -NY 10017
(518) 453-4500 .. **Platt,** Michl A '99 %Clough Harbour & Assoc LLP -3 Winners Cir -Albany 12205

(212) 332-3311 .. **Platt,** Myra '79 (Shwal & P) -767 3rd Av -NY 10017 **Fx:**332-3315
(212) 332-3311 .. **Platt,** Neal R '79 (Shwal & P) -767 3rd Av -NY 10017 **Fx:**332-3315
(516) 542-5900 .. **Platt,** Rona L '95 (Congdon FORDT&F) -333 Earle Ovngton Blvd -Uniondale 11553
(212) 344-0026 .. **Platt,** Sheldon '75 (S Platt,PC) -17 State -NY 10004 **Fx:**248-7380
(212) 483-0941 .. **Platt,** Stoddard D '64 -11 Bway -NY 10004
(631) 283-0572 .. **Platt,** Wm B III '79 -99 Sanford Pl -Southampton 11968 **Fx:**283-0135
(914) 967-8013 .. **Platt,** Wm I '67 (W Platt,PC) -73 Hewlett Av -Rye 10580 **Fx:**967-8643
(212) 514-5100 .. **Platta,** Slawek W '04 SW Platta,PLLC -42 Bway -NY 10004 **Fx:**514-9300
(212) 889-0707 .. **Platte,** Jeffrey '86 (Platte KL&L,LLP) -10 E 40th -NY 10016
(212) 889-0707 .. **Platte Klarsfeld Levine & Lachtman,LLP** -10 E 40th -NY 10016 **Fx:**889-9401
(212) 752-8000 .. **Platten,** Jaclyn C '08 %Cole SMF&L,PA -900 3rd Av -NY 10022
(518) 457-2070 .. **Plattner,** Robt D '78 %Dept of Tax & Fin -Bldg 9 State Campus -Albany 12227 **Fx:**457-6131
(212) 490-1700 .. **Platto,** Chas '70 (Wiggin & D) -450 Lex Av -NY 10017
(212) 935-3000 .. **Platton,** Brian J '83 (Mintz LCFG&P,PC) -666 3rd Av -NY 10017
(212) 336-2000 .. **Platton,** Claude S '08 %Patterson BW&T LLP -1133 Av of Amer -NY 10036
(718) 788-4911 .. **Plattus,** Rebecca L '85 -396 2nd -Brklyn 11215
(212) 891-2120 .. **Plattus,** Seth P '87 Cerberus Cptl Mgmt LP -299 Park Av -NY 10171 **Fx:**891-1541
(212) 925-6675 .. **Platt Zolov,** Leslie M '02 Fund For The City of NY -121 Av of Amer -NY 10013 **Fx:**925-5675
(516) 280-5516 .. **Platz,** Harlan A '88 (Fink & P) -1325 Franklin Av -Gdn Cty 11530
(212) 736-1940 .. **Platz,** Oliver '04 %Davidson D&K LLC -485 7th Av -NY 10018
(212) 697-4090 .. **Platzer,** Kenneth '71 (Platzer L&P LLP) -61 Bway -NY 10006
(212) 697-4090 .. **Platzer Luca & Pearl LLP** -61 Bway -NY 10006 **Fx:**972-4654
(516) 541-0021 .. **Platzer,** Philip '83 -544 Bway -Massapequa 11758 **Fx:**541-1964
(212) 593-3000 .. **Platzer Swergold Karlin Levine Goldberg & Jaslow,LLP** -1065 Av of Amer -NY 10018 **Fx:**593-0353
(212) 593-3000 .. **Platzer,** Sydney G '59 (Platzer SKLG&J,LLP) -1065 Av of Amer -NY 10018
(212) 609-6800 .. **Platzman-Diamant,** Stephanie '03 %McCarter & E,LLP -245 Park Av -NY 10167
(212) 906-1200 .. **Plaut,** Christopher R '89 (Latham & W) -885 3rd Av -NY 10022
(212) 999-5800 .. **Plaut,** Joshua A '04 %Wilson SG&R -1301 Av of Americas -NY 10019
(212) 704-1366 .. **Plaut,** Michl F '87 %Interpublic Grp -1114 Av of Amer -NY 10036 **Fx:**704-1201
(212) 682-5500 .. **Plautz,** Robt '76 -122 E 42nd -NY 10168
(212) 225-2000 .. **Plave,** Ruth Z '95 %Cleary GS&H -1 Lbrty Plz -NY 10006
(718) 542-9300 .. **Playter,** Savina P '04 %Rodriguez & F -644 Soundvw Av -Bronx 10473
(718) 302-2106 .. **Plaza,** Dagmar '96 -41 Schermerhorn -Brklyn 11201
(212) 643-2503 .. **Plaza,** Jeffrey W '95 (Levy E&P,PC) -555 5th Av -NY 10017
(212) 972-6161 .. **Pleasant,** Krishana '06 %Cassin & C LLP -711 3rd Av -NY 10017
(212) 583-4000 .. **Pleasant,** Robt A W '00 Perry Capital -767 5th Av -NY 10153
(212) 534-8570 .. **Pleasant,** Robt W '83 (RW Pleasant & Assoc) -1120 Park Av -NY 10128 **Fx:**534-8570
(518) 373-0333 .. **Pleat,** Tara Anne '03 (Jones W&P PLLC) -5 Emma Ln -Clifton Pk 12065
(212) 679-7007 .. **Pleban,** Brian T '06 %Brody B&B LLP -205 Lex Av -NY 10016
(516) 746-3500 .. **Pleiss,** Candice A '08 %Brand G&B,PC -600 Old Cntry Rd -Gdn Cty 11530
(212) 918-3000 .. **Plesent,** Stanley '53 OfCnsl Hogan L LLP -875 3rd Av -NY 10022
(716) 830-8486 .. **Pleshkewych,** Alexander M '03 US Cstms & Brdr Prot -726 Exchange -Buffalo 14210
(212) 801-9200 .. **Pleskow,** Alan H '86 (Greenberg T,LLP) -200 Park Av -NY 10166
(212) 804-4200 .. **Plessner,** Renee M '87 %Mound CW&G -One Bttry Pk Plz -NY 10004
(516) 931-0050 .. **Plesur,** Allison '90 (Lipman & P,LLP) -500 N Bway -Jericho 11753
(716) 362-1533 .. **Pletcher,** Jay C '96 (Goldstein A&P,LLP) -70 Niagara -Buffalo 14202
(212) 458-7023 .. **Pleva,** Eileen Biondi '98 %American Intl Co -175 Water -NY 10038
(212) 969-3000 .. **Plevan,** Bettina '71 (Proskauer R LLP) -1585 Bway -NY 10036
(212) 735-3000 .. **Plevan,** Kenneth A '70 (Skadden ASM&F LLP) -4 Times Sq -NY 10036
(718) 539-8448 .. **Plevretes,** George P '91 DMV-Traffic Violations -30-56 Whitestone Expy -Flushng 11354
(718) 631-0800 .. **Plevritis,** Peter '09 %Feinstein & N,PC -42-40 Bell Blvd -Bayside 11361
(518) 561-4400 .. **Plimpton,** Thos W '97 Stafford OC&T,PLLC -1 Cumberland Av Bx2947 -Plattsbrgh 12901
(516) 997-8080 .. **Pliskin,** Jeffrey L '85 %Irving Rlty & Tire -179 Westbury Av -Carle Pl 11514 **Fx:**997-8101
(718) 539-2100 .. **Pliskin Rubano & Baum** -137-11 Nrthrn Blvd -Flushng 11354 **Fx:**886-6432
(315) 425-1593 .. **Plochocki,** Richd P '73 -1 Lincoln Ctr -Syracuse 13202 **Fx:**478-1772
(716) 945-1360 .. **Ploetz,** Ronald D '83 (Peters & P) -680 Broad -Salamanca 14779 **Fx:**945-5674
(845) 658-3206 .. **Plonski,** Susan K '05 -33 Perrines Brdg Rd -Tillson 12486 **Fx:**658-3206
(631) 853-7916 .. **Plosky,** Jill R '94 %Family Ct -400 Carleton Av -Central Islip 11722
(212) 471-2300 .. **Plotka,** Richd F '59 -110 W 40th -NY 10018
(607) 273-3666 .. **Plotkin,** Alicia '81 %Leg Srvcs -215 N Cayuga -Ithaca 14850 **Fx:**273-5521
(718) 816-0005 .. **Plotkin,** Andrew '07 %Angiuli K&G,LLP -60 Bay -Staten Isl 10301
(212) 972-2300 .. **Plotkin,** Fred '65 (Plotkin & W) -551 5th Av -NY 10176 **Fx:**972-2303
(347) 350-6266 .. **Plotkin,** James M '98 -227 E 7th -Brklyn 11218
(212) 297-5800 .. **Plotkin,** Jeffrey '87 (Day P LLP) -7 Times Sq -NY 10036
(212) 490-3000 .. **Plotkin,** Jennifer C '04 %Wilson EME&D LLP -150 E 42nd -NY 10017
(212) 408-5100 .. **Plotkin,** Lawr R '91 (Chadbourne & P LLP) -30 Rckfllr Plz -NY 10112
(212) 245-6565 .. **Plotkin,** Loren H '66 (Levine P&M,LLP) -1740 Bway -NY 10019
(516) 488-3300 .. **Plotkin,** Mindy E '01 %Shaub AC&S,LLP -1983 Marcus Av -Lk Success 11042
(516) 364-7900 .. **Plotkin,** Russell M '89 Epstein F&G -45 Crsswys Park Dr W -Woodbury 11797
(212) 687-6262 .. **Plotkin,** Sherri L '89 (Barton B&P,LLP) -420 Lex Av -NY 10170
(212) 715-9100 .. **Plotko,** Gregory G '99 %Kramer LN&F,LLP -1177 Av of Amer -NY 10036
(718) 793-0101 .. **Plotner,** Jerome '53 J Plotner -108-18 Qns Blvd -Frst Hlls 11375
(212) 655-6000 .. **Plotner,** Todd R '07 (Chapman & C LLP) -330 Mad Av -NY 10017
(212) 536-3900 .. **Plotnick,** Lindsey N '09 %K&L Gates LLP -599 Lex Av -NY 10022
(212) 593-3255 .. **Plotnick,** Steven E '89 %IBE Trade Corp -950 3rd Av -NY 10022
(212) 687-1700 .. **Plotnicki,** Linda Sokoloff '80 (Kaufman FP&G,LLP) -300 E 42nd -NY 10017
(585) 586-7770 .. **Plotnik,** Joy Ryen '89 -3349 Monroe Av -Rchstr 14618
(718) 445-7658 .. **Plotnik,** Katya M '95 (Rodriguez & P) -39-15 Main -Flushng 11354 **Fx:**445-7169
(845) 856-4444 .. **Plotsky,** Glen A '88 (Bavoso P&O) -19 E Main Bx3139 -Pt Jervis 12771
(212) 586-2211 .. **Plotz,** Robt L '81 (Orans EL&B LLP) -875 3rd Av -NY 10022
(518) 443-5408 .. **Ploughman,** Penelope D '90 %SUNY Univ Cnsl -S333 SUNY Plz -Albany 12246 **Fx:**443-5409
(914) 681-8700 .. **Plousadis,** James '86 (Milber MP&S LLP) -3 Barker Av -White Plns 10601
(585) 232-2292 .. **Plovanich,** Chas '82 -171 State -Rchstr 14614
(516) 677-9660 .. **Pluchino,** Candice A '85 %Faber & T -180 Froehlich Farm Blvd -Woodbury 11797
(212) 210-9504 .. **Plucknett,** Leticia Brooke '05 %Alston & B LLP -90 Park Av -NY 10016
(212) 612-4200 .. **Pludwin,** Amy L '03 %Hoey KT&E -55 Water -NY 10041
(718) 246-5708 .. **Pludwin,** Howard '91 (Gonshorek & P) -50 Court -Brklyn 11201
(585) 546-5270 .. **Plukas,** Richd A '89 (Fitzsimmons NF&P,LLP) -16 E Main -Rchstr 14614
(212) 969-3000 .. **Plum,** Bernard M '80 (Proskauer R LLP) -1585 Bway -NY 10036
(716) 664-2346 .. **Plumb,** John K '70 OfCnsl Lundberg & G,LLP -202 W 4th -Jamestwn 14701
(212) 732-3200 .. **Plumb,** Michl K '09 %Carter L&M LLP -2 Wall -NY 10005
(212) 972-1000 .. **Plumer,** Alan J '10 %London F LLP -59 Maiden Ln -NY 10038
(631) 656-0188 .. **Plumer,** Debra L '92 -888 Vets Mem'l Hwy -Hauppauge 11788 **Fx:**656-9727
(315) 336-5450 .. **Plumley,** Judy L '93 (Rapke & P,LLP) -320 N George Bx928 -Rome 13440
(631) 231-3717 .. **Plummer,** Hubert G '91 (Plummer & P,LLP) -77 Arkay Dr -Hauppauge 11788 **Fx:**231-3896
(631) 231-3717 .. **Plummer,** W Hubert '57 (Plummer & P,LLP) -77 Arkay Dr -Hauppauge 11788 **Fx:**231-3896
(845) 331-5544 .. **Plunket,** Chas O '80 Plunket & P -611 Lucas Av -Hurley 12443 **Fx:**338-5544
(646) 471-6783 .. **Plunkett,** Andrew P '85 %PricewaterhouseCoopers LLP -300 Mad Av -NY 10017
(518) 393-0441 .. **Plunkett,** Barry C '71 -2202 Fairlawn Pkwy -Schnctdy 12309
(212) 277-6500 .. **Plunkett,** Denise Kosineski '02 (Dickstein S LLP) -1633 Bway -NY 10019
(212) 219-9866 .. **Plunkett & Donnard** -401 Bway -NY 10013 **Fx:**219-9868
(212) 922-1800 .. **Plunkett & Jaffe Group of McKenna Long & Aldridge** -230 Park Av -NY 10169 **Fx:**922-1819
(518) 462-1800 .. **Plunkett & Jaffe Group of McKenna Long & Aldridge** -111 Wshngtn Av -Albany 12210 **Fx:**462-4875
(212) 219-9866 .. **Plunkett,** Jos W '84 (Plunkett & D) -401 Bway -NY 10013
(212) 558-4000 .. **Plunkett,** Kathryn C '04 %Sullivan & C LLP -125 Broad -NY 10004
(914) 995-2909 .. **Plunkett,** Kevin J '76 %Cnty Executives Ofc -148 Martine Av -White Plns 10601
(518) 374-2222 .. **Plunkett,** Lorna Shaffer '92 Callanan Ind -Bx15097 -Albany 12212 **Fx:**381-6722
(212) 458-1519 .. **Plunkett,** Robt E '93 %AIG -175 Water -NY 10038 **Fx:**458-1476
(212) 922-1800 .. **Plunkett,** Timothy J '07 %Plunkett & J/ML&A -230 Park Av -NY 10169
(212) 922-1800 .. **Plunkett,** Wm F Jr. '66 (Plunkett & J/ML&A) -230 Park Av -NY 10169
(212) 506-2500 .. **Plush,** Lisa R '08 %Mayer B LLP -1675 Bway -NY 10019
(212) 588-0880 .. **Plush,** Mark D '77 %Michelstein & Assoc -485 Mad Av -NY 10022 **Fx:**588-0811
(212) 902-7109 .. **Plutzer,** David S '00 Goldman Sachs -1 NY Plz -NY 10004
(518) 873-3612 .. **Plymale,** Linda L '93 Hon J Dawson -100 Court Bx217 -Elizabethtwn 12932
(315) 475-1626 .. **Pobedinsky,** Alexander '92 (A Pobedinsky,LLC) -140 Crtland Av -Syracuse 13202
(203) 330-2134 .. **Pober,** Richd J '84 (Pullman & C,LLC) -50 Main -White Plns 10606
(212) 838-8686 .. **Pobereskin,** Stuart '74 -800 2nd Av -NY 10017 **Fx:**697-9249
(212) 227-5000 .. **Poblete,** Robt J '76 %Asher & Assoc,PC -111 John -NY 10038 **Fx:**227-7117
(718) 447-8311 .. **Pocchia,** Anthony J '83 -1001 Clove Rd -Staten Isl 10301
(718) 317-5001 .. **Pocchia,** James M '92 -114 Seguine Av -Staten Isl 10309
(718) 876-6300 .. **Pocchia,** Michl J '93 %DA -130 Styvsnt Pl -Staten Isl 10301
(212) 237-1000 .. **Pocchiari,** Danl A '85 SpclCnsl Windels ML&M,LLP -156 W 56th -NY 10019
(516) 358-5690 .. **Pocchiari,** Jaimee L '06 %V Toomey -3000 Marcus Av -Lk Success 11042 **Fx:**775-0237
(212) 344-4184 .. **Poch,** Howard '85 (H Poch,PC) -40 Exch Pl -NY 10005 **Fx:**482-6050
(716) 634-6204 .. **Poch,** Joel M '76 Cnsl AFSCME Cncl 66 AFL-CIO -160 Holtz Dr -Buffalo 14225 **Fx:**634-6207
(716) 856-7091 .. **Pochepan,** Paul M '90 %J Freedman -424 Main -Buffalo 14202 **Fx:**856-7097
(718) 651-4776 .. **Pochoday-Stelmach,** Donna '84 -43-09 56th -Woodside 11377 **Fx:**(973) 290-9614
(917) 846-1999 .. **Pochtar,** Deborah A '84 -150 E 69th -NY 10021 **Fx:**(646) 414-7602
(718) 493-0563 .. **Pocius,** Beth M '03 MHLS -681 Clarkson Av Bx62 -Brklyn 11203 **Fx:**953-0101
(914) 764-1282 .. **Pocker,** Beth Bird '93 -5 Patterson Rd Bx37 -Pound Rdg 10576 **Fx:**764-1281
(212) 787-3898 .. **Poda,** Phyllis Kaye '72 -1 Lincoln Plz -NY 10023
(212) 478-7200 .. **Podair,** Leonard L '86 (Hahn & H LLP) -488 Mad Av -NY 10022
(212) 481-6659 .. **Podell,** Albert '78 -275 Mad Av -NY 10016 **Fx:**370-4996
(212) 279-9600 .. **Podell,** Gary A '92 Vintage Grp LLC -15 W 39th -NY 10018

(212) 883-6500 .. **Podell**, Herbert Stanford '58 (Podell SS&B,LLP) -605 3rd Av -NY 10158
(212) 586-6165 .. **Podell**, Howard J '86 %N Liss,PC -200 W 57th -NY 10019 **Fx**:586-1194
(212) 728-8000 .. **Podell**, Margaret Ansell '94 %Willkie F&G LLP -787 7th Av -NY 10019
(212) 227-3333 .. **Podell**, Reed M '95 %Smith & L,LLP -291 Bway -NY 10007
(212) 883-6500 .. **Podell Schwartz Schechter & Banfield,LLP** -605 3rd Av -NY 10158 **Fx**:883-6518
(516) 248-5827 .. **Podell Schwartz Schechter & Banfield,LLP** -1205 Franklin Av -Gdn Cty 11530
(212) 879-9600 .. **Podell Schwartz Schechter & Banfield,LLP** -119 E 71st -NY 10021 **Fx**:879-9601
(718) 237-3100 .. **Podemski**, Lisa A '06 %Leg Aid -111 Lvngstn -Brklyn 11201 **Fx**:250-4243
(212) 909-6000 .. **Podesta**, Roger E '73 (Debevoise & P LLP) -919 3rd Av -NY 10022
(518) 474-7700 .. **Podgorski**, Patricia A '83 %NYS OPWDD -44 Holland Av -Albany 12229 **Fx**:474-7382
(718) 946-4140 .. **Podhaizer**, Alan '92 -601A Surf Av -Brklyn 11224 **Fx**:372-3295
(718) 208-5786 .. **Podhorzer**, Elliot R '86 -305 Bway -NY 10007 **Fx**:(212) 619-0714
(516) 571-3056 .. **Podlesak**, Gerald R '83 %Cnty Atty -1 West -Mineola 11501 **Fx**:571-6604
(516) 487-7300 .. **Podlofsky**, Ira C '80 (Podlofsky & O,LLP) -98 Cuttermill Rd -Gt Neck 11021
(516) 487-7300 .. **Podlofsky & Orange,LLP** -98 Cuttermill Rd -Gt Neck 11021 **Fx**:504-6390
(718) 248-7811 .. **Podobinski**, James R '79 %Citibank -1 Court Sq -LIC 11101
(212) 593-6700 .. **Podolnick**, Matthew S '05 %Aaronson RF&D,LLP -757 3rd Av -NY 10017
(212) 225-2000 .. **Podolsky**, Andrea '78 (Cleary GS&H) -1 Lbrty Plz -NY 10006
(212) 715-9100 .. **Podolsky**, Bonnie D '77 (Kramer LN&F,LLP) -1177 Av of Amer -NY 10036
(212) 450-4000 .. **Podolsky**, Matthew D '10 %Davis P&W LLP -450 Lex Av -NY 10017
(718) 449-5100 .. **Podolsky**, Steven V '98 (Cherny & P,PLLC) -8778 Bay Pkwy -Brklyn 11214 **Fx**:449-6661
(212) 770-7836 .. **Podrasky**, Sara E '95 %AIG -70 Pine -NY 10270
(718) 225-4546 .. **Podrid**, Albert '54 -15-50 212th -Bayside 11360 **Fx**:225-8598
(212) 432-7419 .. **Podvey Meanor Catenacci Hildner Cocoziello & Chattman** -400 Park Av -NY 10022 **Fx**:(973) 623-9131
(212) 521-5400 .. **Poe**, Alexandra '86 (Reed S LLP) -599 Lex Av -NY 10022
(212) 681-0117 .. **Poe**, Harvey R '85 OfCnsl Starr GD&R -530 5th Av -NY 10036
(516) 357-3000 .. **Poe**, Jos K '98 (Rivkin R LLP) -926 RXR Plz -Uniondale 11556
(631) 427-8100 .. **Poe**, Leslie E '00 %Margolin & M -52 Elm -Huntngtn 11743 **Fx**:427-8134
(212) 607-8600 .. **Poe**, Marisa A '08 Dept of Labor-EBSA -33 Whitehall -NY 10004
(718) 729-7400 .. **Poekel**, Chas A Jr. '90 Lcl 74 Leg Srvcs -24-09 38th Av -LIC 11101 **Fx**:361-5942
(212) 335-4500 .. **Poernig**, Claudia '05 %DLA Piper LLP -1251 Av of Amer -NY 10020
(212) 458-1097 .. **Poetzsch**, Douglas '91 %AIG -175 Water -NY 10038
(631) 913-4444 .. **Pogan**, Christopher J '09 %Dell LT&V LLP -5 Orvll Dr -Bohemia 11716
(212) 848-4000 .. **Poggi**, Christopher T '01 Cnsl Shearman & S LLP -599 Lex Av -NY 10022
(212) 325-9244 .. **Poggi**, Lisa '99 Credit Suisse -11 Mad Av -NY 10010
(212) 661-4600 .. **Poggi**, Paul T '93 %Dyson-Kissner-Moran -565 5th Av -NY 10017 **Fx**:599-5105
(845) 565-5252 .. **Poggioli**, John '84 -178 Grand -Newburgh 12550 **Fx**:565-1436
(718) 622-5540 .. **Poggioli**, Jos B '90 -32 7th Av -Brklyn 11217
(212) 574-1200 .. **Poglinco**, Patricia A '87 (Seward & K LLP) -1 Bttry Pk Plz -NY 10004
(212) 341-6400 .. **Pogoda**, Susan J '85 %Liquidation Bur -123 William -NY 10038 **Fx**:608-3398
(914) 235-3654 .. **Pogostin**, Jos M '64 (Pogostin & G) -305 North Av -New Rchll 10801 **Fx**:633-3894
(914) 654-1469 .. **Pogostin**, Marc D '93 -305 North Av -New Rchll 10801 **Fx**:633-3894
(212) 583-9600 .. **Pogrebin**, Bertrand B '59 (Littler M,PC) -900 3rd Av -NY 10022
(718) 875-0345 .. **Pogroszewski**, Stanley J '90 -155 Henry -Brklyn 11201
(914) 771-5575 .. **Pogrow**, Jeffrey O '74 -575 Wht Plns Rd -Eastchstr 10709
(607) 723-0446 .. **Pogson**, Christopher A '95 -34 Chenango -Bnghmtn 13901 **Fx**:723-0449
(585) 359-3344 .. **Pogue**, David L '76 -53 Rawhide Dr -W Henrietta 14586
(646) 315-7300 .. **Pogue**, Kevin E '89 %FINRA -14 Wall -NY 10005 **Fx**:315-7440
(845) 294-9123 .. **Pogue**, Robt '86 MHLS -5 Coates Dr -Goshen 10924 **Fx**:294-3506
(212) 903-9000 .. **Pogula**, Naveen '08 %Linklaters -1345 Av of Amer -NY 10105
(212) 836-8000 .. **Pogust**, Glenn J '81 (Kaye S LLP) -425 Park Av -NY 10022
(212) 931-8569 .. **Poh**, Philip R '07 (Byrne P LLP) -11 Bway -NY 10004 **Fx**:931-8521
(212) 373-3000 .. **Pohl**, Ian J D H '08 %Paul WRW&G LLP -1285 Av of Amer -NY 10019
(518) 486-7815 .. **Pohl**, Jeffrey J '00 %Insurance Dept -99 Wshngtn Av -Albany 12257 **Fx**:473-4600
(518) 257-3000 .. **Pohl**, Jeffrey M '77 %Dormitory Auth -515 Bway -Albany 12207 **Fx**:257-3101
(518) 745-0976 .. **Pohl**, John B '72 -33 Park Bx446 -Glens Fls 12801 **Fx**:745-7759
(212) 310-8000 .. **Pohl**, Joshua C '07 %Weil G&M LLP -767 5th Av -NY 10153
(315) 946-7541 .. **Pohl**, Kathleen Hanlon '86 Cnty Dept Socl Srvcs -77 Water Bx10 -Lyons 14489 **Fx**:946-7626
(212) 869-8100 .. **Pohl**, Ronald S '84 (Pohl Law Grp,LLC) -60 E 42nd -NY 10165 **Fx**:869-8270
(212) 813-8800 .. **Pohl**, Tanya C '09 %Goodwin P LLP -620 8th Av -NY 10018
(518) 474-8831 .. **Pohl**, Thos A '75 %Ofc Gnl Srvcs -Corning Twr ESP -Albany 12242 **Fx**:473-4973
(716) 825-2000 .. **Pohlman**, Jay A '81 -3990 McKinley Pkwy -Hambrg 14219 **Fx**:824-3920
(212) 903-9000 .. **Pohlman**, Jeffrey M '02 %Linklaters -1345 Av of Amer -NY 10105
(716) 646-5909 .. **Pohlman**, Richd C '69 -206 Lk -Hambrg 14075 **Fx**:649-4219
(631) 752-2590 .. **Pohly**, Lawr M '68 -532 Broadhllw Rd -Melvll 11747 **Fx**:752-2586
(516) 571-3800 .. **Pohmer**, Kristin M '08 %DA -262 Old Cntry Rd -Mineola 11501 **Fx**:248-9479
(212) 839-5300 .. **Pohulanik**, Hilel F '08 %Sidley A LLP -787 7th Av -NY 10019
(212) 815-1818 .. **Pointdujour**, Jacqueline '96 %DC 37 MELS -125 Barclay -NY 10007 **Fx**:815-1343
(212) 218-5500 .. **Pointer**, Kelly J '06 %Seyfarth S LLP -620 8th Av -NY 10018
(212) 326-3939 .. **Poissant**, Brian M '75 (Jones D) -222 E 41st -NY 10017
(212) 964-7400 .. **Poissant**, Catherine J '05 Smith MDWY&Y,PC -111 John -NY 10038
(518) 483-1440 .. **Poissant Nichols Grue & Vanier,PC** -367 W Main -Malone 12953 **Fx**:483-4984
(516) 921-8600 .. **Poisson**, Wm J '81 (McAndrew C&P) -95 Froehlich Farm Blvd -Woodbury 11797
(212) 326-3939 .. **Pojednic**, Leonard C '72 OfCnsl Jones D -222 E 41st -NY 10017
(516) 228-8484 .. **Pokalsky**, Ann R '94 OfCnsl Dilworth & B,LLP -1000 Woodbury Rd -Woodbury 11797
(212) 227-2305 .. **Pokalsky**, John S '87 -277 Bway -NY 10007
(212) 298-5226 .. **Pokart**, Stephen P '66 %Leg Aid -49 Thomas -NY 10013 **Fx**:349-8610
(212) 290-4700 .. **Pokempner**, Dinah Rebecca '92 %Human Rights Watch -350 5th Av -NY 10118 **Fx**:736-1300
(518) 581-9797 .. **Poklemba & Hobbs,LLC** -2715 State Route 9 -Malta 12020 **Fx**:581-9590
(518) 581-9797 .. **Poklemba**, John J '76 (Poklemba & H,LLC) -2715 State Route 9 -Malta 12020
(212) 506-1700 .. **Pokler**, Nancy '06 Kasowitz BT&F LLP -1633 Bway -NY 10019
(516) 773-2754 .. **Pokojny**, Nancy P '99 %Gould Investors -60 Cuttermill Rd -Gt Neck 11021 **Fx**:466-3132
(718) 254-7000 .. **Pokorny**, Carolyn '95 %US Atty -271 Cadman Plz E -Brklyn 11201 **Fx**:254-6479
(212) 969-3000 .. **Pokorny**, John F '03 %Proskauer R LLP -1585 Bway -NY 10036
(212) 806-5400 .. **Pokotilow**, Steven B '74 (Stroock &S&L LLP) -180 Maiden Ln -NY 10038
(315) 727-9627 .. **Pola**, Alberto A '95 -2194 W Lake Rd -Skaneateles 13152
(516) 922-6626 .. **Polacco**, Frank A '84 %J Shein & Assoc,PC -575 Underhill Blvd -Syosset 11791 **Fx**:922-2797
(212) 980-1900 .. **Polacek**, Alan C '84 (Donovan & G,LLP) -261 Mad Av -NY 10016
(646) 789-4272 .. **Polak**, Aaron J '94 -65 Bway -NY 10006 **Fx**:818-3956
(212) 480-7216 .. **Polak**, Alan G '78 %DHCR -25 Beaver -NY 10004 **Fx**:480-7416
(716) 675-2889 .. **Polak**, David W '01 -1370 Union Rd -W Seneca 14224
(212) 486-1455 .. **Polak**, Fredk B '80 (Post PGM&S,PA) -575 Mad Av -NY 10022
(212) 297-5800 .. **Polak**, Joshua A '01 %Day P LLP -7 Times Sq -NY 10036
(212) 816-6000 .. **Polak**, Karyn S W '95 Smith Barney -388 Greenwich -NY 10013
(212) 259-8000 .. **Polak**, Vivian L '78 (Dewey & L LLP) -1301 Av of Amer -NY 10019
(914) 332-5102 .. **Polak**, Werner L '63 -660 Wht Plns Rd -Tarrytwn 10591
(718) 875-1935 .. **Polakas**, John N '82 -52 Carroll -Brklyn 11231
(212) 735-3000 .. **Polan**, Lake C '09 %Skadden ASM&F LLP -4 Times Sq -NY 10036
(212) 790-4500 .. **Polan**, Steven M '77 (Manatt P&P,LLP) -7 Times Sq -NY 10036
(718) 779-0905 .. **Polanco**, Jose A '00 JA Polanco,PC -37-37 77th -Jcksn Hts 11372 **Fx**:779-2224
(718) 673-7772 .. **Polanco**, Jose C '05 Polanco & Assoc,PLLC -221-10 Jamaica Av -Qns Vllg 11428 **Fx**:673-7771
(718) 590-3722 .. **Polanco**, Lauvienska E '99 Supreme Ct -851 Grnd Cncrs -Bronx 10451
(607) 772-7013 .. **Poland**, Gregory J '98 (Law Dept) -City Hall 38 Hawley -Bnghmtn 13901 **Fx**:723-6164
(631) 264-1070 .. **Poland**, Jeremy M '02 Sobel Law Ofc,PC -121 W Oak -Amityvll 11701
(516) 741-9300 .. **Poland**, Melissa D '02 %Toscano & Assoc,PC -200 Old Cntry Rd -Mineola 11501 **Fx**:741-0345
(212) 609-6800 .. **Poland**, Todd M '75 (McCarter & E,LLP) -245 Park Av -NY 10167
(631) 940-4258 .. **Polani**, Leron '98 %CosmoCom Inc -121 Broadhllw Rd -Melvll 11747 **Fx**:940-4500
(516) 829-0363 .. **Polansky**, Evan J '92 %Israel I&P,LLP -11 Grace Av -Gt Neck 11021 **Fx**:829-0366
(212) 683-2210 .. **Polansky**, Jessica E '06 %Childrens Rts Inc -330 7th Av -NY 10001 **Fx**:683-4015
(516) 433-0598 .. **Polansky**, Michl D '65 -62 Sylvia Ln -Plainvw 11803 **Fx**:433-0919
(518) 272-2110 .. **Polansky**, Michl E '90 -64 2nd -Troy 12180
(212) 989-0404 .. **Polastri**, Pablo E '83 P Polastri,PC -63-56 Saunders Bx740155 -Rego Pk 11374 **Fx**:633-0190
(212) 509-0099 .. **Polat**, Mehmet F '03 %Haker & O,LLP -29 Bway -NY 10006 **Fx**:506-0488
(212) 509-3456 .. **Polchinski**, Peter D '81 %McGivney & K,PC -80 Broad -NY 10004
(315) 218-8000 .. **Pole**, Kevin M '02 (Bond S&K,PLLC) -1 Lincoln Ctr -Syracuse 13202
(212) 373-3000 .. **Polechronis**, Ralia E '07 %Paul WRW&G LLP -1285 Av of Amer -NY 10019
(718) 613-2430 .. **Polemeni**, Robt T '05 %Hon RJ Dearie -225 Cadman Plz E -Brklyn 11201 **Fx**:613-2437
(212) 277-6300 .. **Poler**, Emily A '01 %Schindler C&H LLP -100 Wall -NY 10005
(845) 471-4455 .. **Poles**, Carol M '91 (Steinberg S&P,LLP) -27 Grdn -Poughkeepsie 12601
(212) 943-0110 .. **Poles**, John G '54 (Poles TS&G, LLP) -46 Trinity Pl -NY 10006
(212) 943-0110 .. **Poles Tublin Stratakis & Gonzalez, LLP** -46 Trinity Pl -NY 10006 **Fx**:269-9875
(718) 995-4700 .. **Polese**, Marlo A '02 -165-25 147th Av -Jamaica 11434
(212) 986-6000 .. **Polevoy**, Jason T '99 (Kleinberg KW&C,PC) -551 5th Av -NY 10176
(212) 335-4500 .. **Polevoy**, Martin D '67 (DLA Piper LLP) -1251 Av of Amer -NY 10020
(212) 876-4049 .. **Polevoy**, Nancy T '87 -1155 Park Av -NY 10128
(718) 466-3000 .. **Poley**, Julie '01 %Civil Ct -1118 Grnd Cncrs -Bronx 10456 **Fx**:466-3006
(845) 877-6717 .. **Polhemus**, Richd V '77 -145 Craig Ln -Dover Plns 12522
(631) 262-9696 .. **Poli**, John G III '78 -Bx59 -Northprt 11768 **Fx**:470-2820
(718) 852-8300 .. **Polias**, Kathy A '04 %A Ofodile -498 Atl Av -Brklyn 11217 **Fx**:852-7361
(212) 490-3000 .. **Policano**, Emily S '07 %Wilson EME&D LLP -150 E 42nd -NY 10017
(845) 639-7800 .. **Policastro**, Kristen A '94 %Mandel K&B,LLP -210 Route 303 -Vly Cottage 10989
(631) 390-0010 .. **Polidore**, Alfred C '79 OfCnsl Bruno G&S,LLP -445 Broad Hollow Rd -Melvll 11747
(212) 479-5292 .. **Polidoro**, Michl A '05 Fortress Invstmt Grp LLC -1345 Av of Amer -NY 10105

(845) 306-1000 .. **Polidoro,** Paul D '82 %Watchtower -100 Watchtower Dr -Patterson 12563 **Fx:**306-0709
(718) 618-2500 .. **Polier,** A Nicole '03 Civil Ct -851 Grnd Cncrs -Bronx 10451 **Fx:**590-7294
(212) 759-3300 .. **Polifka,** Pearl '77 OfCnsl Dornbush SS&V,LLP -747 3rd Av -NY 10017
(212) 412-9500 .. **Polifka,** Robt '79 (Flemming ZWZ LLP) -1 Lbrty Plz -NY 10006
(845) 562-0203 .. **Polimeni,** Eleanor L '80 (Finkelstein & Prtnrs,LLP) -1279 Route 300 Bx1111 -Newburgh 12550
(585) 394-6600 .. **Polimeni,** John A '89 -540 S Main -Canandaigua 14424 **Fx:**394-6210
(516) 671-5300 .. **Polin,** Andrew D '74 (Polin P&V) -1 Schl -Glen Cove 11542
(914) 723-5771 .. **Polin,** Kenneth L '88 K Polin,PC -670 Wht Plns Rd -Scarsdale 10583 **Fx:**472-4316
(631) 232-0200 .. **Polin,** Lorraine Berlund '88 (Fumuso KDSS&F,LLP) -110 Marcus Blvd -Hauppauge 11788
(516) 671-5300 .. **Polin Prisco & Villafane** -1 Schl -Glen Cove 11542 **Fx:**671-3809
(212) 351-4500 .. **Polin,** Theo L '93 (Epstein B&G,PC) -250 Park Av -NY 10177
(212) 389-5000 .. **Poline,** David S '07 Sutherland A&B LLP -1114 Av of Amer -NY 10036
(212) 812-0528 .. **Polinsky,** Audrey L '91 Norhwestern Mtl Fincl Ntwrk -875 3rd Av -NY 10022 **Fx:**599-6268
(718) 237-9077 .. **Polinsky,** David A '97 %HG Polinsky -16 Court -Brklyn 11241 **Fx:**852-4147
(718) 237-9077 .. **Polinsky,** H Gilbert '57 -16 Court -Brklyn 11241 **Fx:**852-4147
(212) 431-1300 .. **Polinsky,** Harriet M '80 (Borah GAN&G PC) -377 Bway -NY 10013
(914) 681-0444 .. **Polinsky,** John '03 %Rende R&D,LLP -202 Mamaroneck Av -White Plns 10601
(516) 775-7007 .. **Polirer,** Russell '93 (Gutman MB&S,PC) -813 Jericho Tpk -New Hyde Pk 11040
(212) 667-1382 .. **Polirstok,** Scott M '06 Nomura Sec Intl Inc -2 WFC -NY 10281 **Fx:**(646) 587-1382
(917) 209-0768 .. **Polis,** Carol '80 -165 W 66th -NY 10023
(212) 735-3000 .. **Poliseno,** Stephanie U '05 %Skadden ASM&F LLP -4 Times Sq -NY 10036
(212) 416-8372 .. **Polishook,** Lewis A '96 %Dept of Law -120 Bway -NY 10271
(631) 754-3989 .. **Polisner,** Gae H '92 (G Polisner,PC) -7 Barbara Ct -Greenlawn 11740
(212) 635-6646 .. **Polissky,** Ellen '04 Bk of NY Mellon -1 Wall -NY 10286
(212) 265-6888 .. **Politan,** Mark J '02 Cnsl Porzio B&N,PC -156 W 56th -NY 10019
(212) 351-4000 .. **Politan,** Nicholas H Jr. '00 (Gibson D&C LLP) -200 Park Av -NY 10166
(212) 637-2412 .. **Polite,** Kenneth A Jr. '04 %US Atty -1 St Andrews Plz -NY 10007
(585) 262-8380 .. **Polito,** Jacqueline Phipps '94 Rochester City Schl Dist -131 W Broad -Rchstr 14614
(585) 428-1921 .. **Polito,** Thos W '91 Family Ct -99 Exchange Blvd -Rchstr 14614
(212) 880-3800 .. **Polivy,** Steven P '81 (Akerman S) -335 Mad Av -NY 10017
(646) 386-5700 .. **Polizano,** Christopher C '10 %Civil Ct -111 Centre -NY 10013
(646) 386-3238 .. **Polizano,** Frank '88 %Hon W Davis -60 Centre -NY 10007
(845) 338-0716 .. **Polizzi,** Anthony L '95 -72 Maiden Ln -Kingston 12401 **Fx:**338-6007
(212) 340-0400 .. **Polizzi,** Carol A '93 %Appllt Div 1st Dept -27 Mad Av -NY 10010 **Fx:**889-4412
(212) 526-7000 .. **Polizzi,** Elizabeth P '07 Barclays Capital -745 7th Av -NY 10019
(585) 426-8866 .. **Polizzi,** Norma A '02 -2117 Buffalo Rd -Rchstr 14624
(516) 592-6800 .. **Polizzi Kalenka,** Phyllisann '91 (Spellman RSGM&P,LLP) -229 Seventh -Gdn Cty 11530
(718) 232-1250 .. **Polizzotto,** Alfred J '90 (Polizzotto & P) -6911 18th Av -Brklyn 11204 **Fx:**256-0966
(212) 756-2000 .. **Polk,** Benjamin M '77 (Schulte R&Z LLP) -919 3rd Av -NY 10022
(518) 453-4600 .. **Polk,** Jill S '88 %Comm Judicial Cndct -ESP -Albany 12223 **Fx:**486-1850
(212) 720-5026 .. **Polk,** Jonathan I '87 %Fed Reserve Bk -33 Lbrty -NY 10045 **Fx:**785-5748
(212) 310-8000 .. **Polkes,** Jonathan D '85 (Weil G&M LLP) -767 5th Av -NY 10153
(212) 969-3000 .. **Polking,** Paul M '05 %Proskauer R LLP -1585 Bway -NY 10036
(973) 228-5700 .. **Polkowitz,** Stuart J '99 (Brach E LLC) -100 Park Av -NY 10017 **Fx:**228-7852
(845) 469-4900 .. **Poll,** Erno '86 %Greenwald Law Ofc -99 Brookside Av -Chester 10918 **Fx:**469-2022
(212) 619-5800 .. **Pollack,** Adam P '85 (Pollack & S,LLP) -15 Maiden Ln -NY 10038 **Fx:**267-2682
(973) 315-4439 .. **Pollack,** Alan H '87 (Budd L) -140 Bway -NY 10005
(908) 358-9738 .. **Pollack,** Alan J '99 -401 Bway -NY 10013
(212) 603-6300 .. **Pollack,** Alan M '75 (Robinson BLGG&G PC) -875 3rd Av -NY 10022
(516) 357-3700 .. **Pollack,** Bonnie L '90 OfCnsl Cullen and D LLP -100 Q Roosevelt Blvd -Gdn Cty 11530
(212) 839-5300 .. **Pollack,** Bracha '05 %Sidley A LLP -787 7th Av -NY 10019
(646) 878-0800 .. **Pollack,** Caleb J '98 (Pearl CZL,LLP) -1500 Bway -NY 10036
(212) 233-8100 .. **Pollack,** Conrad E '85 (Pollack PI&D) -225 Bway -NY 10007
(212) 609-6800 .. **Pollack,** Danl A '66 (McCarter & E,LLP) -245 Park Av -NY 10167
(212) 859-8000 .. **Pollack,** David Chas '06 %Fried FHS&J LLP -1 NY Plz -NY 10004
(212) 232-1300 .. **Pollack,** David M '81 (Lewis BB&S LLP) -77 Water -NY 10005
(212) 788-1894 .. **Pollack,** David M '89 %Law Dept -100 Church -NY 10007 **Fx:**788-0367
(516) 394-4200 .. **Pollack,** David S '81 Cnsl Duffy & D -1370 RXR Plz -Uniondale 11556
(212) 878-1034 .. **Pollack,** Debra Winthrop '81 %MTA -347 Mad Av -NY 10017
(212) 325-0509 .. **Pollack,** Dylan S '03 Credit Suisse Securities LLC -1 Mad Av -NY 10010
(516) 829-3843 .. **Pollack,** Eli '86 -924 Middle Nck Rd -Gt Neck 11024
(212) 326-0500 .. **Pollack,** Elisa B '93 %Sumitomo Trust -527 Mad Av -NY 10022 **Fx:**418-4866
(845) 473-2040 .. **Pollack,** Ellen G '90 %Levine H&F -316 Main -Poughkeepsie 12601
(516) 742-9220 .. **Pollack,** Fred L '78 -114 Old Cntry Rd -Mineola 11501
(212) 735-8600 .. **Pollack,** Gayle E '99 %Morrison C LLP -909 3rd Av -NY 10022
(914) 683-3990 .. **Pollack,** Gerald J '65 -707 Wstchstr Av -White Plns 10604
(212) 852-1308 .. **Pollack,** Gloria E '79 %US Trust Co,NA -114 W 47th -NY 10036 **Fx:**852-1310
(646) 265-1468 .. **Pollack,** Grant E '95 (Pollack,PC) -132 E 43rd -NY 10017 **Fx:**253-1276
(516) 228-0033 .. **Pollack,** Howard '86 (Pollack C&F,PC) -5372 Merrick Rd -Massapequa 11758 **Fx:**797-1227
(914) 592-2203 .. **Pollack,** I Miles '62 IM Pollack,PC -45 Knollwood Rd -Elmsfrd 10523
(917) 514-4669 .. **Pollack,** Ira B '78 I Pollack & Assoc PLLC -26 Austin Pl -Pt Chester 10573 **Fx:**(914) 937-1950
(212) 790-4500 .. **Pollack,** Jane G '02 %Manatt P&P,LLP -7 Times Sq -NY 10036
(212) 594-5300 .. **Pollack,** Janine Lee '90 (Milberg LLP) -1 Penn Plz -NY 10119
(914) 333-7420 .. **Pollack,** Jason M '00 %Akzo Nobel -120 Wht Plns Rd -Tarrytwn 10591
(212) 696-4848 .. **Pollack,** Jeffrey D '91 OfCnsl Mintz & G LLP -470 Park Av S -NY 10016
(914) 946-8100 .. **Pollack,** Jeffrey R '99 %T Sundack & Assoc,LLC -19 Court -White Plns 10601 **Fx:**946-9585
(212) 310-2231 .. **Pollack,** Jessica Glass '91 Colgate-Palmolive -300 Park Av -NY 10022 **Fx:**310-3230
(212) 756-2000 .. **Pollack,** John M '00 (Schulte R&Z LLP) -919 3rd Av -NY 10022
(212) 277-5817 .. **Pollack,** Jonathan K '92 (Beldock L&H LLP) -99 Park Av -NY 10016
(212) 772-8740 .. **Pollack,** Jonathan S '98 OfCnsl Barnes M&Y -129 E 82nd -NY 10028
(516) 742-8897 .. **Pollack,** Joshua D '91 (Kramer & P,LLP) -143 Willis Av -Mineola 11501
(212) 969-3000 .. **Pollack,** Joshua J '96 %Proskauer R LLP -1585 Bway -NY 10036
(914) 828-8000 .. **Pollack,** Julie B '93 %Swiss Re America -175 King -Armonk 10504 **Fx:**828-7000
(212) 758-7899 .. **Pollack,** Kevin A '97 Short Hills Capital LLC -251 E 51st -NY 10022
(212) 758-9700 .. **Pollack,** Lawr A '83 %KPMG LLP -345 Park Av -NY 10154
(212) 751-2700 .. **Pollack,** Lawr W '80 %JAMS -620 8th Av -NY 10018 **Fx:**751-4099
(212) 326-3939 .. **Pollack,** Lee M '07 %Jones D -222 E 41st -NY 10017
(516) 739-2229 .. **Pollack,** Lisa '89 -114 Old Cntry Rd -Mineola 11501
(516) 496-5822 .. **Pollack,** Lisa C '04 %T Spina -170 Froehlich Farm Blvd -Woodbury 11797 **Fx:**496-5420
(212) 310-8000 .. **Pollack,** Martin D '77 (Weil G&M LLP) -767 5th Av -NY 10153
(516) 739-2229 .. **Pollack,** Martin H '87 -114 Old Cntry Rd -Mineola 11501
(914) 332-0700 .. **Pollack,** Mitchell B '85 -150 Wht Plns Rd -Tarrytwn 10591 **Fx:**684-6069
(914) 524-2722 .. **Pollack,** Noam R '06 Siemens Healthcare Diagnostics,Inc -511 Benedict Av -Tarrytwn 10591
(718) 951-5277 .. **Pollack,** Pamela J '84 %Bklyn Cllg -2900 Bedford Av -Brklyn 11210
(212) 233-8100 .. **Pollack Pollack Isaac & DeCicco** -225 Bway -NY 10007 **Fx:**766-4380
(212) 558-4000 .. **Pollack,** Richd A '89 (Sullivan & C LLP) -125 Broad -NY 10004
(516) 938-3330 .. **Pollack,** Robt B '97 -350 Jericho Tpk -Jericho 11753 **Fx:**938-4981
(212) 490-2900 .. **Pollack,** Robt M '84 (Marcus & P LLP) -708 3rd Av -NY 10017 **Fx:**599-3167
(914) 238-1421 .. **Pollack,** Sharon Guss '87 -67 Cross Ridge Rd -Chappaqua 10514 **Fx:**238-1421
(212) 356-1441 .. **Pollack,** Stanley P '51 %Rosenthal & Rosenthal, Inc -1370 Bway -NY 10018 **Fx:**356-0900
(212) 661-9100 .. **Pollack,** Steven I '70 (Otterbourg SH&R,PC) -230 Park Av -NY 10169
(212) 335-4500 .. **Pollack,** Stuart E '99 (DLA Piper LLP) -1251 Av of Amer -NY 10020
(212) 696-6000 .. **Pollack,** Susan F '67 Cnsl Curtis M-PC&M LLP -101 Park Av -NY 10178
(212) 704-6000 .. **Pollack,** Todd D '99 %Troutman S LLP -405 Lex Av -NY 10174
(516) 296-7000 .. **Pollack,** Yale '07 %Certilman BA&H,LLP -90 Merrick Av -E Meadow 11554
(212) 903-9000 .. **Pollak,** Chas T '09 %Linklaters -1345 Av of Amer -NY 10105
(212) 697-1420 .. **Pollak,** Claudia R '00 %Jacobson M&S,LLP -52 Vndrblt Av -NY 10017 **Fx:**697-1427
(212) 309-6058 .. **Pollak,** David W '79 (Morgan L&B LLP) -101 Park Av -NY 10178
(212) 756-2000 .. **Pollak,** Justin R '10 %Schulte R&Z LLP -919 3rd Av -NY 10022
(212) 644-4420 .. **Pollak,** Kevin B '83 (Fabiani C&H,LLP) -570 Lex Av -NY 10022
(212) 326-3939 .. **Pollak,** Kristen E '08 %Jones D -222 E 41st -NY 10017
(718) 229-1904 .. **Pollak,** Martin A '77 (Pollak & S,LLP) -214-08 41st Av -Bayside 11361 **Fx:**423-2308
(212) 408-5100 .. **Pollak,** Noah B '06 %Chadbourne & P LLP -30 Rckfllr Plz -NY 10112
(212) 735-3000 .. **Pollak,** Robt M '08 %Skadden ASM&F LLP -4 Times Sq -NY 10036
(212) 503-0150 .. **Pollak,** Stephen P '71 Pentegra Srvcs,Inc -108 Corp Park Dr -White Plns 10604 **Fx:**503-0129
(917) 476-6712 .. **Pollak,** Stewart D '95 -100 Jericho Quadrangle -Jericho 11753 **Fx:**(516) 364-7107
(212) 450-4000 .. **Pollak,** Wm D '09 %Davis P&W LLP -450 Lex Av -NY 10017
(212) 682-0020 .. **Pollak,** Wm M '77 (Putney TH&H LLP) -521 5th Av -NY 10175
(212) 688-5900 .. **Pollan,** Stephen M '51 OfCnsl Shustak F & Prtnrs -400 Park Av -NY 10022 **Fx:**688-6151
(212) 338-0700 .. **Polland,** Elliot R '69 (Hoffman P&F PLLC) -220 E 42nd -NY 10017
(212) 259-8000 .. **Pollard,** Alicia S '09 %Dewey & L LLP -1301 Av of Amer -NY 10019
(718) 520-2381 .. **Pollard,** Angela McClammy '88 Supreme Ct -88-11 Stuphin Blvd -Jamaica 11435
(718) 624-0236 .. **Pollard,** Diane S '92 -125 Ashland Pl -Brklyn 11201
(212) 822-1439 .. **Pollard,** Mark H '88 (Pollard & K) -305 Bway -NY 10007 **Fx:**822-1441
(212) 664-5412 .. **Pollard,** Nadia J '01 %NBC -30 Rckfllr Plz -NY 10112
(212) 859-8000 .. **Pollard,** Tiffany A '99 (Fried FHS&J LLP) -1 NY Plz -NY 10004
(212) 418-8617 .. **Pollard,** Wm B III '75 (Kornstein VW&P,LLP) -757 3rd Av -NY 10017
(516) 877-2424 .. **Pollaro,** Anne C '81 OfCnsl Weinberg G&P LLP -400 Grdn City Plz -Gdn Cty 11530
(212) 504-6000 .. **Pollaro,** Robt M '01 SpclCnsl Cadwalader W&T LLP -1 World Fncl Ctr -NY 10281
(212) 421-4100 .. **Poller,** Judith L '84 (Pryor C LLP) -7 Times Sq -NY 10036
(212) 489-8888 .. **Pollet & Felleman,LLP** -1700 Bway -NY 10019 **Fx:**489-7975
(212) 489-8888 .. **Pollet,** Michl N '65 (Pollet & F,LLP) -1700 Bway -NY 10019
(212) 210-6960 .. **Pollet,** Richd '74 %J Walter Thompson -466 Lex Av -NY 10017
(212) 489-8888 .. **Pollet,** Sybil H '75 (Pollet & F,LLP) -1700 Bway -NY 10019
(718) 613-3505 .. **Polletta,** Leonard D '80 %UIA Bd -Bx29002 -Brklyn 11201 **Fx:**613-3507
(631) 537-8390 .. **Polley,** Alan S '93 AMS Tech/Aqous -Bx1478 -Sag Hbr 11963 **Fx:**537-8219
(212) 839-5300 .. **Pollin,** Myles C '85 (Sidley A LLP) -787 7th Av -NY 10019

(631) 979-9100 ..**Pollina,** Chas J '69 (Pollina & P) -180 E Main -Smithtwn 11787 **Fx:**979-9549
(631) 979-9500 ..**Pollina,** Robt B '63 (Pollina & P) -180 E Main -Smithtwn 11787 **Fx:**979-9549
(631) 406-7050 ..**Pollina,** Steven M '95 -235 Brooksite Dr -Hauppauge 11788
(516) 248-2500 ..**Pollio,** Benedict J '61 (Redmond P&C, LLP) -1461 Franklin Av -Gdn Cty 11530
(212) 506-1700 ..**Pollio,** Donald A '97 Kasowitz BT&F LLP -1633 Bway -NY 10019
(718) 980-6720 ..**Pollio,** Michl A '89 -41 Otis Av -Staten Isl 10306
(516) 248-2500 ..**Pollio,** Ronald A '93 (Redmond P&C, LLP) -1461 Franklin Av -Gdn Cty 11530
(212) 455-2000 ..**Pollitt,** Colette M '01 %Simpson T&B LLP -425 Lex Av -NY 10017
(212) 486-2100 ..**Pollitt,** Douglas B '74 -110 E 59th -NY 10022
(518) 234-4393 ..**Pollitzer,** David J '82 Fenimore Asset Mgmt -384 N Grand Bx310 -Cobleskill 12043 **Fx:**234-4473
(212) 351-4000 ..**Pollner,** Glenn R '92 (Gibson D&C LLP) -200 Park Av -NY 10166
(212) 407-4000 ..**Pollner,** Martin R '60 (Loeb & L,LLP) -345 Park Av -NY 10154
(212) 880-9487 ..**Pollock,** Adam L '07 %Morvillo AGIA&B,PC -565 5th Av -NY 10017
(518) 434-6111 ..**Pollock,** David J '85 -125 Wolf Rd -Albany 12205
(212) 506-1700 ..**Pollock,** Emily Senn '05 %Kasowitz BT&F LLP -1633 Bway -NY 10019
(607) 763-9200 ..**Pollock,** John J '83 (Levene G&T,LLP) -BxF-1706 -Bnghmtn 13902
(212) 756-2000 ..**Pollock,** Keith J '05 %Schulte R&Z LLP -919 3rd Av -NY 10022
(914) 251-1525 ..**Pollock,** Lee A '77 (Pollock & M,LLP) -106 Corp Park Dr -White Plns 10604
(914) 251-1525 ..**Pollock & Maguire,LLP** -106 Corp Park Dr -White Plns 10604 **Fx:**251-0662
(212) 362-7600 ..**Pollock,** Miriam L '00 Vivian Beaumont Theatre -150 W 65th -NY 10023
(212) 940-8800 ..**Pollock,** Paul J '86 (Katten MR LLP) -575 Mad Av -NY 10022
(212) 450-4000 ..**Pollock,** Sheldon L III '02 %Davis P&W LLP -450 Lex Av -NY 10017
(516) 883-8255 ..**Pollock,** Theo '56 -27 Seagull Ln -Pt Wash 11050 **Fx:**883-0433
(518) 325-4257 ..**Pollok,** John L '66 -64 Miller Brook Ln -Copake Fls 12517
(845) 758-3676 ..**Pollok,** Michl S '94 -Bx190 -Red Hook 12571 **Fx:**752-2253
(212) 422-0202 ..**Polloway,** Bridget M '01 %Sedgwick DM&A LLP -125 Broad -NY 10004
(914) 478-0079 ..**Polly,** Carole Travis '84 -12 Nichols Dr -Hastings-On-Hud 10706
(914) 681-8700 ..**Polner,** Richd B '99 %Milber MP&S LLP -3 Barker Av -White Plns 10601
(212) 596-9000 ..**Polniak,** Jos J Jr. '09 %Ropes & G LLP -1211 Av of Amer -NY 10036
(212) 642-0950 ..**Polo,** Adam D '95 %Newman & O,PC -8 W 38th -NY 10018
(212) 967-2262 ..**Polo,** David P '83 (Francisco & P) -421 7th Av -NY 10001
(212) 687-3000 ..**Polon,** Jamie P '02 %Jaffe & A,LLP -600 3rd Av -NY 10016
(631) 277-2062 ..**Polon,** Marion '84 (Polon & G) -Bx373 -Islip Terr 11752
(716) 858-8400 ..**Poloncarz,** Mark C '98 %Cnty Comptrollers Ofc -95 Franklin -Buffalo 14202
(212) 450-4000 ..**Poloner,** Seth H '05 %Davis P&W LLP -450 Lex Av -NY 10017
(212) 775-8700 ..**Polonsky,** Jonathan E '83 (Kilpatrick S,LLP) -31 W 52nd -NY 10019
(212) 735-3000 ..**Polonsky,** Max S '08 %Skadden ASM&F LLP -4 Times Sq -NY 10036
(212) 450-4000 ..**Polonsky,** Sasha E '07 %Davis P&W LLP -450 Lex Av -NY 10017
(212) 687-3747 ..**Polovetsky,** Jennifer '01 %Tuchman KWL&G,LLP -6 E 45th -NY 10017
(212) 848-4000 ..**Polovoy,** Brian H '93 (Shearman & S LLP) -599 Lex Av -NY 10022
(212) 696-0133 ..**Polovy,** Marian '80 M Polovy -192 Lex Av -NY 10016
(914) 235-7050 ..**Polow,** Ian L '68 -150 Woodlawn Av -New Rchll 10804 **Fx:**(212) 687-8865
(716) 852-0600 ..**Polowitz & Schwach, LLP** -43 Court -Buffalo 14202 **Fx:**852-3259
(716) 852-0600 ..**Polowitz,** Steven H '80 (Polowitz & S, LLP) -43 Court -Buffalo 14202
(716) 204-2400 ..**Polowy,** Amy E '04 %SJ Baum,PC -220 Nrthpnte Pkwy Bx1291 -Buffalo 14240 **Fx:**204-4600
(716) 753-4247 ..**Polowy,** Danl R '74 %Cnty Atty -3 N Erie -Mayvll 14757 **Fx:**753-4129
(716) 858-2200 ..**Polowy,** Martin A '04 %Cnty Atty -95 Franklin -Buffalo 14202 **Fx:**858-2281
(585) 385-4050 ..**Polozie,** Michl A '64 -349 W Cmmrcial -E Rchstr 14445 **Fx:**586-2023
(212) 490-2700 ..**Pols,** Donald J '84 (Beilis & P) -213 W 35th -NY 10001
(212) 477-1438 ..**Polshek,** Ellyn '86 -32 Wshngtn Sq W -NY 10011 **Fx:**473-9240
(212) 684-0199 ..**Polsinelli Shughart PC** -7 Penn Plz -NY 10001 **Fx:**684-0197
(518) 427-2650 ..**Polsinelli,** Vincent E '02 %Nixon P LLP -677 Bway -Albany 12207
(631) 589-6270 ..**Polsky,** Alan '78 -Bx170 -Bohemia 11716 **Fx:**589-6494
(212) 751-4989 ..**Polsky,** Leon B '56 -667 Madison -NY 10065 **Fx:**644-9587
(516) 594-0909 ..**Polsky,** Mark S '87 (Polsky S&R,PC) -500 Merrick Rd -Rockvll Ctr 11570
(718) 875-0909 ..**Polsky,** Mark S '87 (Polsky S&R,PC) -142 Joralemon -Brklyn 11201
(516) 594-0909 ..**Polsky Shouldice & Rosen,PC** -500 Merrick Rd -Rockvll Ctr 11570 **Fx:**594-0994
(718) 875-0909 ..**Polsky Shouldice & Rosen,PC** -142 Joralemon -Brklyn 11201
(212) 416-8961 ..**Polstein,** Janet L '86 %Dept of Law -120 Bway -NY 10271
(518) 374-2593 ..**Polster,** John R '78 -224 State -Schnctdy 12305 **Fx:**831-9038
(585) 641-0790 ..**Polster,** Morton A '56 Cnsl Brown & M,PC -1250 Pttsfrd Victor Rd -Pittsfrd 14534
(212) 223-0400 ..**Poltarak,** Wm J '70 OfCnsl Zeichner E&K LLP -575 Lex Av -NY 10022
(718) 943-8815 ..**Poltorak,** Elie C '07 (Poltorak,PC) -1650 Eastern Pkwy -Brklyn 11233 **Fx:**943-8816
(212) 450-4000 ..**Polubinski,** Edmund III '00 (Davis P&W LLP) -450 Lex Av -NY 10017
(212) 504-6000 ..**Polverino,** Frank '94 (Cadwalader W&T LLP) -1 World Fncl Ctr -NY 10281
(212) 610-6300 ..**Polydorou,** Desma '06 %Allen & O -1221 Av of Amer -NY 10020
(585) 338-6800 ..**Polyn,** Denis A '76 %Bausch & Lomb -One Bausch & Lomb Pl -Rchstr 14604 **Fx:**338-8706
(718) 441-8283 ..**Polywko,** Walentyn '64 -90-28 83rd Av -Glendale 11385 **Fx:**441-8551
(718) 250-2000 ..**Polyzos,** Helen M '98 %DA -350 Jay -Brklyn 11201 **Fx:**250-2314
(212) 909-6000 ..**Pomara,** Antonella M '09 %Debevoise & P LLP -919 3rd Av -NY 10022
(718) 461-6633 ..**Pomara,** Francesco Jr. '93 %Mallilo & G -163-09 Nrthrn Blvd -Flushng 11358
(516) 505-0044 ..**Pomares,** Luis A '08 %S Sands & Assoc,PLLC -250 Fulton Av -Hempstd 11550 **Fx:**505-0022
(212) 270-1023 ..**Pombo,** Danl E '97 %Chase Securities Inc -270 Park Av -NY 10017
(212) 922-9700 ..**Pombo,** Michelle M '01 %1st Amer Title -633 3rd Av -NY 10017 **Fx:**922-0881
(518) 561-8211 ..**Pombrio,** Emy L '90 E Pombrio,PC -Bx2924 -Plattsbrgh 12901
(212) 245-3940 ..**Pomerance,** Brenda '92 -310 W 52nd -NY 10019
(845) 368-4555 ..**Pomerance,** Ronald '62 -34 River Rd -Suffern 10901
(212) 506-5000 ..**Pomerantz,** Alan J '69 (Orrick H&S LLP) -51 W 52nd -NY 10019
(212) 889-2021 ..**Pomerantz,** Alyson B '02 %Rele & B LLC -1178 Bway -NY 10001 **Fx:**(646) 390-8000
(718) 596-9989 ..**Pomerantz,** Danl J '99 %Cohen HEP&T -25 Chapel -Brklyn 11201
(212) 794-2754 ..**Pomerantz,** David '73 -412 E 65th -NY 10065 **Fx:**794-2754
(646) 328-0850 ..**Pomerantz,** Devorah I '96 %Outside Cnsl Solutns LLP -1430 Bway -NY 10018 **Fx:**360-5000
(212) 490-3000 ..**Pomerantz,** Fredk J '80 (Wilson EME&D LLP) -150 E 42nd -NY 10017
(518) 479-3713 ..**Pomerantz,** Geri '88 -694 Columbia Tpk -E Greenbush 12061 **Fx:**479-3715
(212) 661-1100 ..**Pomerantz Haudek Grossman & Gross LLP** -100 Park Av -NY 10017 **Fx:**661-8665
(212) 267-6781 ..**Pomerantz,** Jeffrey S '76 -155 E 55th -NY 10022 **Fx:**267-6664
(212) 506-1700 ..**Pomerantz,** Jennifer L '05 %Kasowitz BT&F LLP -1633 Bway -NY 10019
(631) 727-0133 ..**Pomerantz,** Lance R '90 -140 Old Bway -Sayvll 11782 **Fx:**369-6127
(631) 567-1683 ..**Pomerantz,** Lisa R '88 -140 Old Bway Av -Sayvll 11782
(212) 373-3000 ..**Pomerantz,** Mark F '77 (Paul WRW&G LLP) -1285 Av of Amer -NY 10019 **Fx:**492-0010
(212) 696-4848 ..**Pomerantz,** Mark S '86 %Mintz & G LLP -470 Park Av S -NY 10016
(212) 836-8000 ..**Pomerantz,** Michl M '98 %Kaye S LLP -425 Park Av -NY 10022
(646) 428-3900 ..**Pomerantz,** Rachel D '95 %Dept of Educ -32 Old Slip -NY 10005 **Fx:**428-3890
(845) 708-0292 ..**Pomerantz,** Rhonda S '83 -5 Wayne Av -New Cty 10956 **Fx:**708-0293
(718) 465-6857 ..**Pomerantz,** Roy W '87 %Regent Baby Products -182-20 Lbrty Av -Jamaica 11412
(516) 676-3294 ..**Pomerantz,** Sanford A '69 -7 Jodi Ct -Glen Cove 11542 **Fx:**676-9581
(212) 357-7580 ..**Pomerantz,** Stewart A '84 Goldman Sachs -85 Broad -NY 10004
(212) 818-8800 ..**Pomeranz,** Edw H '86 (Graubard M) -405 Lex Av -NY 10174
(212) 508-6700 ..**Pomeranz,** James R '98 (Tannenbaum HS&H LLP) -900 3rd Av -NY 10022
(718) 923-4206 ..**Pomeranz,** Yvette H '83 %OTDA Fair Hearings -14 Boerum Pl -Brklyn 11201
(607) 756-7501 ..**Pomeroy Armstrong Casullo & Monty, LLP** -16 Tompkins Bx828 -Cortlnd 13045 **Fx:**753-8913
(212) 649-5808 ..**Pomeroy,** Ellen R C '80 -30 Rckfllr Plz -NY 10112 **Fx:**649-5939
(315) 474-7571 ..**Pomeroy,** Gay M '66 (Mackenzie H LLP) -101 S Salina Bx4967 -Syracuse 13221
(315) 492-9665 ..**Pomeroy,** Jeffrey G '95 %Greene & R,PLLC -173 Intrepid Ln -Syracuse 13205
(607) 753-3070 ..**Pomeroy,** Jeffrey G '95 %Greene & R,PLLC -39 Church -Cortlnd 13045
(607) 756-7501 ..**Pomeroy,** Wm J '72 (Pomeroy AC&M,LLP) -16 Tompkins Bx828 -Cortlnd 13045
(718) 286-6000 ..**Pomodore,** Debra L '86 %DA -125-01 Qns Blvd -Kew Gdns 11415
(212) 302-2400 ..**Pompei,** Diane M '03 (Lynch DE LLP) -264 W 40th -NY 10018
(212) 248-3140 ..**Pompeo,** Michl P '99 (Drinker B&R LLP) -140 Bway -NY 10005
(914) 995-2660 ..**Pompey,** Chevor O '04 %Cnty Atty -148 Martine Av -White Plns 10601 **Fx:**995-5858
(212) 587-9690 ..**Pomposello,** Michl G '96 %J Samel & Partners -150 Bway -NY 10038 **Fx:**587-9673
(516) 466-5769 ..**Pon,** Henry L '86 -160 Middle Nck Rd -Gt Neck 11021
(212) 455-2000 ..**Ponce,** Mario A '89 (Simpson T&B LLP) -425 Lex Av -NY 10017
(518) 429-4200 ..**Pond,** George M '94 (Hiscock & B,LLP) -50 Beaver -Albany 12207
(516) 296-7000 ..**Pond,** Gregory J '84 (Certilman BA&H,LLP) -90 Merrick Av -E Meadow 11554
(914) 686-4800 ..**Pondoff,** Kimberly A '99 (Harrington O&M,LLP) -81 Main -White Plns 10601
(607) 432-5785 ..**Pondolfino,** Jos T Jr. '66 -127 Commerce Rd Bx236 -Oneonta 13820 **Fx:**432-5789
(212) 963-2850 ..**Pongnon,** Miouly E '92 -2005 5th Av -NY 10035
(212) 530-5000 ..**Ponikvar,** Dale L '81 (Milbank TH&M LLP) -1 Chase Manh Plz -NY 10005
(212) 687-2770 ..**Pontani,** Thos C '83 (Cohen PL&P) -551 5th Av -NY 10176
(212) 698-3500 ..**Pontano,** Andrew P '04 %Dechert LLP -1095 Av of Amer -NY 10036
(212) 407-9149 ..**Pontano,** Kelly L '04 CKx,Inc -650 Mad Av -NY 10022
(212) 996-0630 ..**Pontell,** Steven '83 (Verde S&P,LLC) -276 5th Av -NY 10001
(212) 714-1200 ..**Ponterio,** John '92 (Schwartz & P,PLLC) -134 W 29th -NY 10001 **Fx:**714-1264
(716) 849-0701 ..**Ponterio,** Michl A '84 (Lipsitz & P LLC) -135 Delaware Av -Buffalo 14202
(585) 428-5210 ..**Ponticello,** Casie L '05 Pub Def -10 N Fitzhugh -Rchstr 14614 **Fx:**428-2234
(518) 792-2117 ..**Pontiff,** Paul E '59 (Bartlett PS&R,PC) -1 Wshngtn Bx2168 -Glens Fls 12801
(212) 506-1700 ..**Pontillo,** Charlotte A '04 %Kasowitz BT&F LLP -1633 Bway -NY 10019
(516) 795-0010 ..**Pontillo,** Salvatore B '84 -100 Clark Av -Massapequa 11758
(516) 627-5888 ..**Pontisakos,** John D '84 (Pontisakos & R,PC) -1025 Nrthrn Blvd -Roslyn 11576 **Fx:**627-5585
(315) 474-7571 ..**Pontius,** Nancy L '77 (Mackenzie H LLP) -101 S Salina Bx4967 -Syracuse 13221
(212) 640-1744 ..**Pontrelli,** Anne T '87 %Amer Exp -200 Vesey -NY 10285
(516) 538-7476 ..**Ponzini,** Jennifer '02 -220 Nassau Blvd S -Garden City South 11530
(914) 288-9595 ..**Ponzini,** Robt J '75 OfCnsl Gaines GP&N,LLP -1 N Bway -White Plns 10601

(646) 424-6236 .. **Ponzoa,** Nicole M '99 ING Fncl Svcs LLC -1325 Av of Amer -NY 10019
(607) 729-8105 .. **Pool,** Paul E '75 -246 Main -Johnson Cty 13790 **Fx:**729-8106
(315) 824-2575 .. **Pool,** Paul E '75 -10 Utica -Hamilton 13346 **Fx:**(607) 729-8106
(716) 852-3600 .. **Poole,** Christopher R '06 %Chelus HS&M,PC -438 Main -Buffalo 14202
(212) 335-9000 .. **Poole,** Dana R '01 %DA -1 Hogan Pl -NY 10013
(212) 820-9300 .. **Poole,** Ernest T '07 %Hawkins D&W LLP -One Chase Manh Plz -NY 10005
(845) 561-7770 .. **Poole,** Jacqueline M '86 -831 Little Britain Rd -New Windsor 12553
(516) 741-2585 .. **Poole,** Kelly Ann '92 (Rosicki R & Assoc,PC) -51 E Bethpage Rd -Plainvw 11803 **Fx:**741-4748
(212) 839-5300 .. **Poole,** Mark A '94 (Sidley A LLP) -787 7th Av -NY 10019
(315) 432-2774 .. **Pooler,** J Richd '83 %Bristol-Myers Squibb -Bx4755 -Syracuse 13221
(212) 735-3000 .. **Poon,** Cecilia '08 %Skadden ASM&F LLP -4 Times Sq -NY 10036
(212) 512-2000 .. **Poon,** Linda '83 %McGraw-Hill -1221 Av of Amer -NY 10020 **Fx:**512-4827
(212) 746-1795 .. **Poon,** Melinda '98 NY Presbyterian Hsptl -525 E 68th Bx88 -NY 10065 **Fx:**746-8603
(212) 385-4575 .. **Poon,** Yee Ling '90 -11 E Bway -NY 10038 **Fx:**385-4792
(212) 225-2000 .. **Poopoksakul,** Lertlar '09 %Cleary GS&H -1 Lbrty Plz -NY 10006
(914) 337-5014 .. **Poorman,** Anne Wilt '87 -54 Park Av -Bronxvll 10708
(646) 428-3829 .. **Poorten,** Wm J '05 US Dept Educ-Ofc Civil Rts -32 Old Slip -NY 10005
(212) 268-0900 .. **Pooyan,** Yasmin '04 %Miskin & T-Y -1350 Bway -NY 10018 **Fx:**268-0904
(212) 788-7018 .. **Popa,** Laura J '00 %NYC Council -250 Bway -NY 10007
(718) 855-9000 .. **Popadiuk,** Gregory J '07 %Cullen and D LLP -177 Montague -Brklyn 11201
(212) 335-4500 .. **Popalisky,** Wm M '87 OfCnsl DLA Piper LLP -1251 Av of Amer -NY 10020
(607) 584-4900 .. **Pope,** Alan J '80 (Pope & S,LLP) -2 Court Bx510 -Bnghmtn 13902
(718) 875-1300 .. **Pope,** Anne D '81 Appllt Div 2nd Dept -45 Monroe Pl -Brklyn 11201 **Fx:**858-2446
(212) 446-4800 .. **Pope,** Christine A '07 %Kirkland & E LLP -153 E 53rd -NY 10022
(646) 471-8473 .. **Pope,** David A '08 Price Waterhouse Coopers LLP -300 Mad Av -NY 10017
(914) 428-2100 .. **Pope,** Geoffrey S '86 OfCnsl Welby B&G,LLP -11 Martine Av -White Plns 10606
(716) 634-3320 .. **Pope,** Gregory A '81 (Pope Law Firm,PLLC) -6580 Main -Williamsvll 14221 **Fx:**204-2770
(716) 433-4881 .. **Pope,** Gregory A '81 (Pope Law Firm,PLLC) -247 East Av -Lockprt 14094 **Fx:**433-6327
(716) 285-7217 .. **Pope,** Gregory A '81 (Pope Law Firm,PLLC) -701 Pine Av -Niagara Fls 14301 **Fx:**433-6327
(716) 881-1202 .. **Pope,** Gregory A '81 (Pope Law Firm,PLLC) -329 Elmwood Av -Buffalo 14222 **Fx:**204-2770
(212) 351-4500 .. **Pope,** John Houston '88 (Epstein B&G,PC) -250 Park Av -NY 10177
(347) 489-8659 .. **Pope,** Marvin L '84 -Bx110773 -Cambria Hts 11411
(212) 333-0200 .. **Pope,** Peter B '88 Cnsl Arkin KR LLP -590 Mad Av -NY 10022
(607) 584-4900 .. **Pope & Schrader, LLP** -2 Court Bx510 -Bnghmtn 13902 **Fx:**584-4901
(212) 858-1000 .. **Pope,** Yuri M '05 %Pillsbury WSP LLP -1540 Bway -NY 10036
(212) 835-1514 .. **Popeil,** Derek A '92 %Dreifuss B&P,LLP -1 Penn Plz -NY 10019
(716) 847-8400 .. **Popek,** Thos E '03 %Phillips L LLP -3400 HSBC Ctr -Buffalo 14203
(212) 684-0317 .. **Popescu,** Andrei A '06 %A Spinnelll,LLC -286 Mad Av -NY 10017 **Fx:**696-2611
(212) 766-9696 .. **Popescu Iosepovici LLP** -225 Bway -NY 10007 **Fx:**766-2298
(212) 766-9696 .. **Popescu,** Robt S '02 (Popescu I LLP) -225 Bway -NY 10007
(212) 213-3676 .. **Popick,** Brad M '85 (Popick R&J,LLP) -41 Elizabeth -NY 10013
(212) 213-3676 .. **Popick Rutman & Jaw,LLP** -41 Elizabeth -NY 10013 **Fx:**213-3734
(716) 689-7700 .. **Popiel,** Mark P '03 (Malik & P,PC) -1404 Sweet Home Rd -Buffalo 14228
(516) 249-3450 .. **Popijakowska,** Ewelina '08 %Carman C&I,LLP -266 Main -Farmngdl 11735
(646) 562-2207 .. **Popik,** Roman V '88 (R Popik,PC) -1500 Bway -NY 10036 **Fx:**562-2208
(212) 692-1000 .. **Popin,** Jon C '02 %Duane M LLP -1540 Bway -NY 10036
(718) 222-9800 .. **Popish,** Abraham '55 -369 E 149th -Bronx 10455 **Fx:**742-5739
(315) 474-7571 .. **Popkess,** Alfred W '70 (Mackenzie H LLP) -101 S Salina Bx4967 -Syracuse 13221
(914) 286-3400 .. **Popkin,** Arlene R '75 %Leg Aid -1 N Bway -White Plns 10601 **Fx:**682-4112
(212) 600-0721 .. **Popkin,** Elizabeth Jackson '77 -7 W 96th -NY 10025 **Fx:**600-0722
(718) 703-6176 .. **Popkin,** Eric F '87 (Popkin & P,LLP) -276 Stratford Rd -Brklyn 11218 **Fx:**703-6177
(212) 346-2400 .. **Popkin,** Erica B '81 OfCnsl L Schoenbach -111 Bway -NY 10006 **Fx:**346-4665
(516) 746-2424 .. **Popkin,** Erwin '51 -500 N Bway -Jericho 11753 **Fx:**746-7691
(631) 281-0030 .. **Popkin,** Irwin '67 -445 Broad Hollow Rd -Melvll 11747 **Fx:**281-0174
(212) 343-9600 .. **Popkin,** Lucy S '07 %J Peikoff,PC -173 E Bway -NY 10002 **Fx:**343-3043
(212) 877-8464 .. **Popkin,** Michl S '93 -277 West End Av #15E -NY 10023 **Fx:**877-8465
(718) 703-6176 .. **Popkin,** Steven J '84 (Popkin & P,LLP) -276 Stratford Rd -Brklyn 11218 **Fx:**703-6177
(718) 383-0909 .. **Poplawski,** Zenon '07 (Dajka & P,PLLC) -596 Manh Av -Brklyn 11222 **Fx:**383-0350
(212) 489-1400 .. **Poplinger,** Andrew L '09 %Bickel & B -767 5th Av -NY 10153
(212) 545-4647 .. **Poplock,** Rachel S '06 %Wolf HAF&H LLP -270 Mad Av -NY 10016
(212) 626-4100 .. **Popoff,** Alexandra L '08 %Baker & M LLP -1114 Av of Amer -NY 10036
(212) 752-9700 .. **Popofsky,** Steven R '83 (Gersten S LLP) -600 Lex Av -NY 10022
(315) 673-2092 .. **Popov,** Richd '77 (Moss & P) -8 W Main Bx195 -Marcellus 13108 **Fx:**673-9247
(347) 404-9133 .. **Popova,** Elena A '07 Civil Ct -141 Lvngstn -Brklyn 11201 **Fx:**(718) 643-3733
(212) 909-6000 .. **Popova,** Ina C '08 %Debevoise & P LLP -919 3rd Av -NY 10022
(212) 373-3000 .. **Popova,** Irina V '07 %Paul WRW&G LLP -1285 Av of Amer -NY 10019
(212) 807-6337 .. **Popovic,** Elena '04 Media Dvlpmnt Loan Fund,Inc -37 W 20th -NY 10011
(718) 618-2325 .. **Popovic,** Martin L '95 %Surrogate's Ct -851 Grnd Cncrs -Bronx 10451 **Fx:**590-3575
(212) 592-1503 .. **Popovich,** Alexander M '00 Cnsl Herrick,F LLP -2 Park Av -NY 10016 **Fx:**545-2314
(718) 263-0180 .. **Popovitz,** Boris E '97 (BE Popovitz,PC) -Bx660037 -Flushng 11366 **Fx:**263-0190
(212) 425-7200 .. **Popovski,** Lupco '92 (Kenyon & K,LLP) -1 Bway -NY 10004
(973) 228-5700 .. **Popowitz,** Allen J '96 (Brach E LLC) -100 Park Av -NY 10017 **Fx:**228-7852
(212) 668-1900 .. **Popowsky,** Matthew F '07 %Brune & R LLP -80 Broad -NY 10004
(212) 532-3651 .. **Popp,** John R '05 Marwood Grp -733 3rd Av -NY 10017
(212) 695-1515 .. **Poppe & Bhouraskar,LLP** -350 5th Av -NY 10118 **Fx:**629-8691
(516) 520-0261 .. **Poppe,** Lynn '94 L Poppe,PC -42 Harness Ln -Levittwn 11756
(212) 695-1515 .. **Poppe,** Wm M '74 (Poppe & B,LLP) -350 5th Av -NY 10118
(212) 306-7166 .. **Poppell,** Beverly M '92 %Ofc Cllctv Brgn -40 Rector -NY 10006 **Fx:**306-7167
(718) 237-2000 .. **Popper,** Allen S '86 %Leg Aid -111 Lvngstn -Brklyn 11201 **Fx:**237-8737
(212) 290-2630 .. **Popper & Grafton** -225 W 34th -NY 10122 **Fx:**290-2633
(877) 222-1814 .. **Popper,** Kenneth F '86 %B Rothenberg -100 Duffy Av -Hicksvll 11801 **Fx:**(866) 894-2182
(718) 459-6000 .. **Popper,** Lauren K '89 (Pennisi D&N LLP) -97-77 Qns Blvd -Rego Pk 11374
(516) 431-1000 .. **Popper,** Philip '85 %Corp Cnsl -1 W Chester -Long Bch 11561 **Fx:**431-1016
(212) 986-6840 .. **Popper,** Robt D '90 %N Brickman -317 Mad Av -NY 10017 **Fx:**986-7691
(212) 969-3000 .. **Popper,** Seth '92 Cnsl Proskauer R LLP -1585 Bway -NY 10036
(516) 897-1205 .. **Popper,** Sharon K '84 %Long Bch Mem Hosp -455 E Bay Dr -Long Bch 11561 **Fx:**897-1214
(646) 386-4083 .. **Poppoly,** Janet '81 Hon J Cataldo -100 Centre -NY 10013
(212) 813-5900 .. **Popp-Rosenberg,** Laura E '01 (Fross ZL&Z,PC) -866 UN Plz -NY 10017
(212) 732-3355 .. **Pops,** Paul R '53 (Pops & Assoc) -225 Bway -NY 10007 **Fx:**732-8844
(212) 259-8000 .. **Por,** Andrew M '08 %Dewey & L LLP -1301 Av of Amer -NY 10019
(212) 284-6984 .. **Porath,** Rebecca '07 United Jewish Communities,Inc -25 Bway -NY 10004
(914) 377-6240 .. **Porcari,** Lawr A Jr. '86 %Law Dept -300 City Hall -Ynkrs 10701 **Fx:**964-0563
(914) 375-1100 .. **Porcari,** Lawr Anthony '58 -625 Palisade Av -Ynkrs 10703 **Fx:**423-3549
(212) 335-9000 .. **Porcaro,** Erik C '05 %DA -1 Hogan Pl -NY 10013
(212) 335-9000 .. **Porcaro,** Eugene J '69 %DA -1 Hogan Pl -NY 10013
(212) 366-6100 .. **Porcelli,** Joanne '02 %Weiss & R,PC -27 Union Sq W -NY 10003
(516) 742-3470 .. **Porcelli,** Leonard '90 (Kral CRRP&G,LLP) -538 Broadhllw Rd -Melvll 11747
(212) 458-3274 .. **Porcelli,** Margaret A '85 AIU Holdings,Inc -175 Water -NY 10038
(585) 454-0700 .. **Porcellio,** Sharon M '83 (Ward GH&R LLP) -300 State -Rchstr 14614
(212) 331-5058 .. **Porcello,** Michl A '95 NYC HRA -180 Water -NY 10038
(212) 846-4654 .. **Porch,** Antonious L K '00 %Nickelodeon -1515 Bway -NY 10036
(914) 417-3400 .. **Porch,** Brian D Jr. '05 %Littleton JUP&K LLP -1 Manhattanvll Rd -Purchase 10577
(585) 546-5530 .. **Porch,** Carl R '96 %Thomson West -50 E Broad -Rchstr 14694
(631) 669-3710 .. **Porchia,** John M III '04 %Lite & R,PLLC -212 Higbie Ln -W Islip 11795
(607) 272-2314 .. **Porciello,** Michl P '08 %Thaler & T -309 N Tioga Bx266 -Ithaca 14851 **Fx:**272-8466
(212) 790-9200 .. **Porcino,** Peter R '77 (Cowan L&L,PC) -1133 Av of Amer -NY 10036
(914) 725-6000 .. **Porco,** Domenick J '77 -108 Brook -Scarsdale 10583 **Fx:**725-8114
(212) 294-6700 .. **Porco,** Jamie A '08 %Winston & S -200 Park Av -NY 10166
(845) 225-8404 .. **Porco,** John A '62 (Daniels & P,LLP) -102 Gleneida Av -Carmel 10512
(646) 386-3363 .. **Porder,** Deborah A '81 Hon SW Kornreich-Supreme Ct -60 Centre -NY 10007
(212) 765-2100 .. **Pordy,** Hope A '95 %Spivak L LLP -1700 Bway -NY 10019
(518) 885-2263 .. **Poremba,** Alan M '00 %DA -25 W High -Ballston Spa 12020 **Fx:**884-8627
(212) 698-3500 .. **Poret,** Chas I '71 (Dechert LLP) -1095 Av of Amer -NY 10036
(212) 759-4433 .. **Poretsky,** Joel A '72 Alvarez & Marsal -600 Lex Av -NY 10022
(716) 649-0161 .. **Poretta,** Michl J '78 -Bx537 -Hambrg 14075
(212) 839-5300 .. **Poretz,** Alexi M '99 Cnsl Sidley A LLP -787 7th Av -NY 10019
(212) 370-1300 .. **Poretz,** Ted '80 (Ellenoff G&S LLP) -150 E 42nd -NY 10017
(212) 307-7060 .. **Porges,** Diana D'Alonzo '96 -1 Cntrl Pk W -NY 10023 **Fx:**262-5339
(914) 788-9522 .. **Porges,** Diane M '97 Guide Communications -22 N Division -Peekskill 10566
(212) 902-9918 .. **Porges,** Ellen R '85 %Goldman Sachs -1 NY Plz -NY 10004
(212) 843-8910 .. **Porges,** John A '95 Ascent Real Estate Advisors -1185 Av of Amer -NY 10036 **Fx:**843-6758
(718) 461-6633 .. **Porges,** Matthew S '05 %Mallilo & G -163-09 Nrthrn Blvd -Flushng 11358
(973) 596-4491 .. **Porio,** Megan Frese '06 %Gibbons PC -1 Penn Plz -NY 10119 **Fx:**639-8332
(646) 613-9633 .. **Poris,** Lisa K '02 LIFT -350 Bway -NY 10013
(212) 557-1818 .. **Poritz,** Rachel H '01 %Silverson P&L -192 Lex Av -NY 10016
(212) 284-1902 .. **Porosoff,** Marc '92 Oaktree Capital Mngt -1301 Av of Amer -NY 10019
(212) 270-5910 .. **Porosoff,** Tracy L '98 %JP Morgan Chase & Co -270 Park Av -NY 10017
(518) 487-7600 .. **Porpeglia,** Dorothy-Jane Goldsack '02 %Whiteman O&H LLP -1 Commerce Plz -Albany 12260
(718) 858-4366 .. **Porper,** Julia I '81 Fortunato & F,PLLC -26 Court -Brklyn 11242 **Fx:**852-6432
(212) 558-4000 .. **Porpora,** Matthew J '06 %Sullivan & C LLP -125 Broad -NY 10004
(718) 618-2543 .. **Porrata,** Magdalena '87 Civil Ct -851 Grnd Cncrs -Bronx 10451 **Fx:**590-7294
(347) 404-9400 .. **Porrazzo,** Romy M '79 %Criminal Ct -120 Schermerhorn -Brklyn 11201 **Fx:**(718) 643-3538

(585) 244-0140 .. **Porreca,** Chas G '57 -150 Edgemoor Rd -Rchstr 14618 **Fx:**442-1577
(212) 735-8600 .. **Porretta,** Paul L '96 (Morrison C LLP) -909 3rd Av -NY 10022
(212) 455-2000 .. **Porretti,** Alfredo '07 %Simpson T&B LLP -425 Lex Av -NY 10017
(631) 847-6333 .. **Porretto,** James '87 %Estee Lauder -7 Corp Ctr -Melvll 11747
(212) 812-8919 .. **Porrovecchio,** Jos J '04 %Lankler & C,LLP -845 3rd Av -NY 10022
(315) 539-1300 .. **Porsch,** Barry L '95 DA -48 W Williams -Waterloo 13165 **Fx:**539-0531
(212) 850-2800 .. **Porsch,** Cassandra L '06 %Andrews K LLP -450 Lex Av -NY 10017
(718) 739-6400 .. **Port,** Barry S '75 %DHCR -92-31 Union Hall -Jamaica 11433 **Fx:**262-7938
(212) 969-3000 .. **Port,** Gail Sherry '77 SrCnsl Proskauer R LLP -1585 Bway -NY 10036
(315) 449-1200 .. **Port,** Howard A '71 -5730 Cmmns Park -E Syracuse 13057 **Fx:**449-2650
(212) 909-6000 .. **Port,** Nicola C '02 Cnsl Debevoise & P LLP -919 3rd Av -NY 10022
(631) 247-0404 .. **Porta,** John J '04 %Jackson L LLP -58 S Srvc Rd -Melvll 11747
(212) 940-3008 .. **Portal,** David M '86 (Nixon P LLP) -437 Mad Av -NY 10022
(914) 772-3166 .. **Portale,** Richd A '99 -124 Walworth Av -White Plns 10606
(516) 746-3500 .. **Portale,** Susanne '00 %Brand G&B,PC -600 Old Cntry Rd -Gdn Cty 11530
(845) 469-5580 .. **Portararo,** Dennis P '83 -Bx276 -Chester 10918 **Fx:**469-5580
(212) 655-3500 .. **Portegello,** Robt S '85 SpclCnsl Meister S&F LLP -140 E 45th -NY 10017
(212) 801-6921 .. **Portela,** Jessica '07 %Greenberg T,LLP -200 Park Av -NY 10166
(212) 779-0900 .. **Portela,** Jos G '88 (Dragados USA,Inc) -500 5th Av -NY 10110 **Fx:**764-6020
(212) 965-9458 .. **Portela,** Manuel Jr. '93 (Portela Law Firm,PC) -177 Wadsworth Av -NY 10033 **Fx:**927-4690
(212) 878-8000 .. **Portella,** Joanna C '08 %Clifford C LLP -31 W 52nd -NY 10019
(212) 613-5000 .. **Portelli,** Christopher '87 Leg Assist Grp -450 W 33rd -NY 10001 **Fx:**750-0820
(212) 865-3368 .. **Porter,** Amy '89 -314 W 40th -NY 10018
(212) 545-1921 .. **Porter,** Arthur L Jr. '85 (Fischer PT&R,PC) -250 W 57th -NY 10107
(585) 737-0761 .. **Porter,** Bradley D '05 Mendon Forestry LLC -3115 Wesley Rd -Bloomfield 14469
(212) 486-6780 .. **Porter,** Carla V '84 %Renaissance Tech -800 3rd Av -NY 10022
(631) 471-5971 .. **Porter,** Charlene Anne '90 -3075 Vets Mem'l Hwy -Ronkonkoma 11779 **Fx:**580-3042
(518) 862-9292 .. **Porter,** Christina D '99 %Napierski V&N,LLP -296 Wshngtn Av Ext -Albany 12203
(212) 601-2425 .. **Porter,** Christina L '07 %J Miller & Assoc,PC -61 Bway -NY 10006 **Fx:**809-3660
(716) 631-3001 .. **Porter,** Christopher D '92 %Independent Hlth -511 Farber Lks Dr -Buffalo 14221 **Fx:**635-3838
(212) 735-3000 .. **Porter,** Claiborne W '02 %Skadden ASM&F LLP -4 Times Sq -NY 10036
(718) 590-2000 .. **Porter,** David S '06 DA -198 E 161st -Bronx 10451 **Fx:**590-6477
(212) 449-9853 .. **Porter,** Eileen M '95 %Merrill Lynch -4 Wrld Fncl Ctr -NY 10080
(212) 659-7300 .. **Porter,** Gilbert D '78 (Haynes & B,LLP) -1221 Av of Amer -NY 10020
(716) 853-5100 .. **Porter,** Henry M '60 (Lippes MWF LLP) -665 Main -Buffalo 14203
(315) 568-6136 .. **Porter,** J Scott '86 -78 Cayuga Bx365 -Seneca Fls 13148 **Fx:**568-6206
(212) 430-5400 .. **Porter,** Jason B '08 Diamond M LLP -620 8th Av -NY 10018
(973) 596-4615 .. **Porter,** Jennifer M '02 %Gibbons PC -1 Penn Plz -NY 10119 **Fx:**639-8324
(212) 309-6808 .. **Porter,** Jessica L '05 Morgan L&B LLP -101 Park Av -NY 10178
(315) 946-5050 .. **Porter,** John P '81 -12 Phelps -Lyons 14489 **Fx:**946-6462
(585) 243-1414 .. **Porter,** Jon H '66 J Porter,PC -131 Main Bx35 -Geneseo 14454 **Fx:**243-1438
(212) 326-8631 .. **Porter,** Jonathan D '94 %Julien Studley,Inc -300 Park Av -NY 10022
(518) 474-4393 .. **Porter,** Jos B '86 Dept of Ed -89 Wshngtn Av -Albany 12234
(212) 894-7200 .. **Porter,** Joshua K '03 %Entwistle & C LLP -280 Park Av -NY 10017
(646) 386-3500 .. **Porter,** Kay-Ann D '94 %OCA -25 Beaver -NY 10004 **Fx:**(212) 457-2669
(914) 448-0200 .. **Porter,** Kevin D '79 (Bartlett MB&M,LLP) -81 Main -White Plns 10601
(212) 636-2000 .. **Porter,** Marc B '89 Christie's -20 Rckfllr Plz -NY 10020
(212) 788-6818 .. **Porter,** Mary E '96 %Mayors Ofc of Crim Just Coordntr -1 Centre -NY 10007
(315) 785-3152 .. **Porter,** Matthew J '03 %Pub Def -175 Arsenal -Watertwn 13601 **Fx:**785-5060
(315) 477-9900 .. **Porter,** Michl Scott '98 (Porter NH LLP) -316 S Clinton -Syracuse 13202 **Fx:**477-9923
(212) 490-3000 .. **Porter,** Richd B '00 (Wilson EME&D LLP) -150 E 42nd -NY 10017
(315) 443-2524 .. **Porter,** Robt O '90 %Syracuse Univ Cllg of Law -Wht Hall -Syracuse 13244 **Fx:**443-4213
(212) 407-4000 .. **Porter,** Ronelle C '03 %Loeb & L,LLP -345 Park Av -NY 10154
(212) 698-3500 .. **Porter,** Sean H '97 (Dechert LLP) -1095 Av of Amer -NY 10036
(212) 310-4229 .. **Porter,** Sigele D '01 Instinet Grp,LLC -3 Times Sq -NY 10036
(518) 356-4445 .. **Porter,** Steven K '76 %Galesi Group -Bx98 -Guilderlnd Ctr 12085 **Fx:**356-5334
(917) 288-5899 .. **Porter,** Susan '69 -530 E 86th -NY 10028
(914) 714-4249 .. **Porter,** Susan I '83 -159 Waverly Rd -Scarsdale 10583
(212) 969-3000 .. **Porter,** Timothy L '75 SrCnsl Proskauer R LLP -1585 Bway -NY 10036
(212) 661-5600 .. **Porter,** Valerie '82 -51 E 42nd -NY 10017 **Fx:**681-4508
(631) 585-4050 .. **Porter,** Wm J '65 -1820 Middle Cntry Rd -Centereach 11720 **Fx:**585-5063
(212) 784-5800 .. **Portera,** Anthony N '97 (Hiscock & B,LLP) -7 Times Sq -NY 10036 **Fx:**784-5767
(914) 949-5300 .. **Portera,** Ginette M '97 (Brown & T,LLC) -1 N Bway -White Plns 10601
(716) 852-2223 .. **Porter-Goettel,** Noell J '05 Buyers & Kaczor Reprtng Srvcs -14 Lafayette Sq -Buffalo 14203
(212) 852-6000 .. **Portes,** Susan Lifsey '88 %WestLB AG -250 Greenwich -NY 10007 **Fx:**852-6148
(914) 271-2828 .. **Porteus,** Stephanie V '97 (McCarthy Law Firm,PC) -1 Croton Pnt Av -Croton-On-Hud 10520 **Fx:**271-2880
(212) 450-4000 .. **Portilla,** David L '07 %Davis P&W LLP -450 Lex Av -NY 10017
(212) 695-0060 .. **Portilla,** Julio E '07 %Wilens & B,PC -450 7th Av -NY 10123
(716) 856-5500 .. **Portin,** Robt J '81 (Damon M LLP) -200 Delaware Av -Buffalo 14202
(716) 845-7485 .. **Portis,** Brandon A '00 Family Ct -1 Niagara Plz -Buffalo 14202 **Fx:**858-7794
(914) 949-7830 .. **Portman,** Ellen B '93 -1 Water -White Plns 10601
(631) 475-4400 .. **Portman,** Elliott M '86 (Roe TT&P,LLP) -One Corp Dr -Bohemia 11716
(845) 486-6800 .. **Portman,** Lance N '88 (McCabe & M LLP) -63 Wshngtn Bx509 -Poughkeepsie 12602
(914) 288-8162 .. **Portney,** Dawn '00 Acadia Realty Trust -1311 Mamaroneck Av -White Plns 10605
(212) 836-8000 .. **Portnov,** Danl M '07 %Kaye S LLP -425 Park Av -NY 10022
(631) 427-6777 .. **Portnoy,** Henry B '55 (Portnoy & P,PLLC) -315 Walt Whitman Rd -Huntngtn Sta 11746 **Fx:**427-0229
(845) 567-0315 .. **Portnoy,** Irwin M '59 (I Portnoy & Assoc,PC) -542 Union Av -New Windsor 12553 **Fx:**567-1176
(212) 476-5343 .. **Portnoy,** Ksenia Y '06 Neuberger Berman,LLC -605 3rd Av -NY 10158 **Fx:**476-9862
(212) 450-4000 .. **Portnoy,** Lawr J '89 (Davis P&W LLP) -450 Lex Av -NY 10017
(212) 728-8000 .. **Portnoy,** Maor '07 %Willkie F&G LLP -787 7th Av -NY 10019
(212) 449-8413 .. **Portnoy,** Martin '65 %Merrill Lynch -220 Bway -NY 10038
(212) 704-6000 .. **Portnoy,** Mitchell P '84 (Troutman S LLP) -405 Lex Av -NY 10174
(212) 687-1101 .. **Portnoy,** Morton L '56 (Portnoy & G,PC) -260 Mad Av -NY 10016 **Fx:**949-9835
(631) 427-6777 .. **Portnoy,** Patricia E '89 (Portnoy & P,PLLC) -315 Walt Whitman Rd -Huntngtn Sta 11746 **Fx:**427-0229
(212) 450-4000 .. **Portnoy,** Saml I '07 %Davis P&W LLP -450 Lex Av -NY 10017
(917) 750-6678 .. **Portnoy,** Vlad '08 Cnsl Intway Corp -14 Wall -NY 10005
(212) 918-3000 .. **Porto,** Natalie M '07 %Hogan L LLP -875 3rd Av -NY 10022
(518) 943-3980 .. **Porto-Crossett,** Vicki M '95 F Porto Ins Agncy -332 Main -Catskill 12414
(212) 964-6611 .. **Portuguese,** Eric A '81 (Lester SK&D) -120 Bway -NY 10271
(212) 752-5258 .. **Portuondo,** Nuris E '05 (Schwartz SE&C LLC) -845 3rd Av -NY 10022
(516) 483-1500 .. **Portz,** Paul M Jr. '03 %Allen & A -100 Main -Hempstd 11550 **Fx:**483-1560
(914) 698-1736 .. **Porwick,** Morton '60 -951 Green Meadow Ln -Mamaroneck 10543
(212) 265-6888 .. **Porzio Bromberg & Newman,PC** -156 W 56th -NY 10019 **Fx:**957-3983
(212) 358-8234 .. **Porzio,** Christopher J '97 Phoenix Partners Grp,LP -315 Park Av -NY 10010
(718) 254-6668 .. **Posa,** Cristina M '01 US Atty - EDNY -271 Cadman Plz E -Brklyn 11201
(212) 808-7800 .. **Poscablo,** Christine Schessler '02 %Kelley D&W LLP -101 Park Av -NY 10178
(212) 637-2634 .. **Poscablo,** Ryan P '02 US Atty -1 St Andrews Plz -NY 10007
(845) 676-4034 .. **Posel,** Norman Sherab '97 -5468 Fall Clove Rd -DeLancey 13752
(585) 475-1100 .. **Poselovich,** Jason D '01 %Segar & S -400 Meridian Centre -Rchstr 14618
(914) 761-0381 .. **Posephney,** Jill A '06 %A Hazen -30 Glenn -White Plns 10603 **Fx:**948-3371
(212) 975-3968 .. **Poser,** Nicholas E '84 %CBS Inc -51 W 52nd -NY 10019 **Fx:**975-3930
(212) 214-9244 .. **Posilkin,** Mitchell L '80 %Rent Stblztn Assn -123 William -NY 10038 **Fx:**732-0617
(212) 775-9002 .. **Positan,** Wayne J '82 (Lum D&P,LLC) -325 Bway -NY 10007
(631) 451-7576 .. **Positano,** John A '87 (Positano & Assoc) -52 Beech Av -Farmngvll 11738
(518) 474-0571 .. **Posluszny,** Arthur K '97 %Ofc Gnl Srvcs -Corning Twr ESP -Albany 12242 **Fx:**473-4973
(212) 661-9191 .. **Posman,** Eva H '78 -570 Lex Av -NY 10022 **Fx:**(646) 380-0138
(212) 421-6492 .. **Posmyk,** Olga A '09 %Squitieri & F,LLP -32 E 57th -NY 10022 **Fx:**421-6553
(914) 271-4351 .. **Posner,** Agusta P '83 -22 Park Trl -Croton-On-Hud 10520
(212) 578-8909 .. **Posner,** Amy K '86 %MetLife -27-01 Qns Plz N -LIC 11101
(212) 909-9500 .. **Posner,** Avram E '96 (Wachtel & M,LLP) -885 2nd Av -NY 10017
(914) 460-1600 .. **Posner,** Barry A '89 %MIM Corp -100 Clearbrook Rd -Elmsfrd 10523
(845) 357-3536 .. **Posner,** Cindy Beth '89 -1 Exec Blvd -Suffern 10901 **Fx:**357-3828
(212) 259-8000 .. **Posner,** Courtney B '08 %Dewey & L LLP -1301 Av of Amer -NY 10019
(845) 486-6800 .. **Posner,** David L '74 (McCabe & M LLP) -63 Wshngtn Bx509 -Poughkeepsie 12602
(212) 661-9100 .. **Posner,** David M '89 OfCnsl Otterbourg SH&R,PC -230 Park Av -NY 10169
(212) 326-3939 .. **Posner,** Emily A '09 %Jones D -222 E 41st -NY 10017
(516) 489-6100 .. **Posner & Gaier** -215 Hilton Av Bx1200 -Hempstd 11551
(516) 248-1033 .. **Posner,** Jack N '70 -1100 Franklin Av -Gdn Cty 11530 **Fx:**248-2624
(212) 415-9200 .. **Posner,** Jesse A '09 %Dorsey & W LLP -250 Park Av -NY 10177
(718) 262-7100 .. **Posner,** Jill L '89 %Civil Ct -89-17 Sutphin Blvd -Jamaica 11435 **Fx:**262-7107
(914) 948-8044 .. **Posner,** Joy M '03 %Alimonti Law Ofcs,PC -200 Mamaroneck Av #304 -White Plns 10601 **Fx:**948-8058
(212) 490-9100 .. **Posner,** Katherine B '78 (Condon & F LLP) -7 Times Sq -NY 10036
(646) 315-7300 .. **Posner,** Lara M '98 %FINRA -14 Wall -NY 10005 **Fx:**315-7440
(845) 471-8848 .. **Posner,** Lawr R '77 Posner-Volper Co -4 Jffrsn Plz -Poughkeepsie 12601
(212) 686-4715 .. **Posner,** Marion F '85 -305 E 24th -NY 10010 **Fx:**686-4715
(718) 250-2000 .. **Posner,** Mark J '05 %DA -350 Jay -Brklyn 11201 **Fx:**250-2314
(212) 385-1772 .. **Posner,** Marshall '83 (Posner & P) -170 Bway -NY 10038 **Fx:**385-2061
(516) 571-2777 .. **Posner,** Mary Louise A '85 %Supreme Ct -100 Supreme Ct Dr -Mineola 11501
(646) 282-5951 .. **Posner,** Melanie E '06 Davidson Kempner Capital Mgmt LLC -65 E 55th -NY 10022
(212) 494-0035 .. **Posner,** Michl C '94 (Shaked & P) -255 W 36th -NY 10018 **Fx:**216-9049
(212) 440-9800 .. **Posner,** Rachel L '03 %Georgeson -199 Water -NY 10038
(212) 508-6100 .. **Posner,** Raphael A '06 %Bracewell & G,LLP -1251 Av of Amer -NY 10020
(212) 744-6899 .. **Posner,** Saml '59 -525 E 86th -NY 10028
(212) 687-6900 .. **Posner,** Simon B '73 %Connell & W -555 5th Av -NY 10017 **Fx:**687-6999

(212) 343-0303 .. **Posner,** Stacy L '92 -350 Bway -NY 10013 **Fx:**343-0712
(212) 425-1401 .. **Pospischil,** David '00 Cnsl O'Hare P LLP -82 Wall -NY 10005 **Fx:**425-1421
(212) 728-8000 .. **Poss,** Jeffrey R '92 (Willkie F&G LLP) -787 7th Av -NY 10019
(212) 450-4000 .. **Poss,** Lynn I '06 %Davis P&W LLP -450 Lex Av -NY 10017
(716) 566-5400 .. **Possenti,** Cheryl A '83 (Goldberg S LLP) -665 Main -Buffalo 14203
(646) 253-5400 .. **Possenti,** Cheryl A '83 (Goldberg S LLP) -1200 Av of Amer -NY 10036
(631) 842-7775 .. **Posser-Trink,** Jocelyn A '95 %Jaxson -145 Dixon Av -Amityvll 11701
(212) 558-4000 .. **Possick,** M David '05 %Sullivan & C LLP -125 Broad -NY 10004
(212) 307-5500 .. **Possidente,** Adam G '10 %Venable LLP -1270 Av of Amer -NY 10020
(212) 771-0763 .. **Post,** Barbara Lois '84 CCH -76 9th Av -NY 10011
(212) 752-1900 .. **Post,** Bernard G '68 (B Post,LLP) -950 3rd Av -NY 10022 **Fx:**752-1609
(212) 788-1498 .. **Post,** Carole Wallace '01 Mayors Ofc -225 W 60th -NY 10023
(914) 997-7707 .. **Post,** Craig A '85 (Barr P & Assoc PLLC) -11 Martine Av -White Plns 10606 **Fx:**(845) 352-6777
(845) 352-4080 .. **Post,** Craig A '85 (Barr P & Assoc PLLC) -664 Chestnut Rdg Rd Bx664 -Spg Vly 10977 **Fx:**352-6777
(212) 869-4080 .. **Post,** Craig A '85 (Barr P & Assoc PLLC) -419 Park Av S -NY 10016 **Fx:**(845) 352-6777
(212) 715-9100 .. **Post,** Dana '00 %Kramer LN&F,LLP -1177 Av of Amer -NY 10036
(718) 522-3333 .. **Post,** Dawn Jerusha '02 %Children's Law Ctr -44 Court -Brklyn 11201 **Fx:**522-7376
(212) 735-3000 .. **Post,** Debra A '92 %Skadden ASM&F LLP -4 Times Sq -NY 10036
(212) 808-7800 .. **Post,** Eric B '00 %Kelley D&W LLP -101 Park Av -NY 10178
(516) 681-3636 .. **Post Heymann & Koffler LLP** -2 Jericho Plz -Jericho 11753 **Fx:**433-2777
(516) 745-1331 .. **Post,** Joel G '79 -600 Old Cntry Rd -Gdn Cty 11530
(212) 321-8126 .. **Post,** Jos '81 Verizon -140 West -NY 10007
(718) 920-4096 .. **Post,** Linda Farber '96 %Montefiore Med Ctr-Einstein Cllg of Medicine -111 E 210th -Bronx 10467 **Fx:**920-4989
(212) 504-6000 .. **Post,** Lisa S '92 SpclCnsl Cadwalader W&T LLP -1 World Fncl Ctr -NY 10281
(212) 486-1455 .. **Post Polak Goodsell MacNeill & Strauchler,PA** -575 Mad Av -NY 10022 **Fx:**(973) 994-1705
(914) 949-6400 .. **Post,** Ruth F-L '93 %McCullough G&S,LLP -1311 Mamaroneck Av -White Plns 10605
(516) 681-3636 .. **Post,** Wm W '93 (Post H&K LLP) -2 Jericho Plz -Jericho 11753
(212) 279-9090 .. **Posta,** Jeffrey S '83 (Stark & S) -One Penn Plz -NY 10119 **Fx:**279-9113
(585) 232-5756 .. **Postel,** John J '81 %Comm Judicial Cndct -400 Andrews -Rchstr 14604 **Fx:**232-7834
(212) 425-3220 .. **Poster,** Harold S '72 (Gilmartin P&S LLP) -845 Third Av -NY 10022
(212) 763-6800 .. **Poster,** Michl Sollod '98 (Vandenberg & F,LLP) -60 E 42nd -NY 10165
(212) 425-3220 .. **Poster,** Robt L '65 (Gilmartin P&S LLP) -845 Third Av -NY 10022
(631) 673-6905 .. **Poster-Zimmerman,** Lynn D '84 -141 E Main -Huntngtn 11743 **Fx:**673-6947
(718) 694-4752 .. **Postiglione,** Leonard '79 MTA -130 Lvngstn -Brklyn 11201
(516) 750-8789 .. **Postiglione,** Michl G '05 (MG Postiglione,PC) -220 Old Cntry Rd -Mineola 11501
(516) 741-2585 .. **Postiglione,** Richd '07 %Rosicki R & Assoc,PC -51 E Bethpage Rd -Plainvw 11803 **Fx:**741-4748
(212) 836-8000 .. **Postman,** Rachel A '10 Kaye S LLP -425 Park Av -NY 10022
(718) 292-7073 .. **Potack,** Frederic B '62 -384 E 149th -Bronx 10455 **Fx:**993-4935
(718) 222-2016 .. **Potak,** Andrew J '04 %Law Dept -350 Jay -Brklyn 11201 **Fx:**222-2088
(212) 883-1700 .. **Potamianos,** Constantine S '98 (Duval & S LLP) -101 Park Av -NY 10178
(212) 770-2891 .. **Potamianos-Charas,** Elaina '91 %AIG -80 Pine -NY 10005 **Fx:**943-1125
(212) 373-3749 .. **Potamousis,** Ioannis D '99 Paul WRW&G LLP -1285 Av of Amer -NY 10019
(585) 232-6500 .. **Potash,** Christopher M '94 (Harter S&E LLP) -1600 Bausch & Lomb Pl -Rchstr 14604
(914) 665-0055 .. **Potash,** Eileen J '81 (Reback & P,LLP) -10 Fiske Pl -Mt Vernon 10550 **Fx:**665-0062
(212) 259-8000 .. **Potash,** Jeffrey A '94 (Dewey & L LLP) -1301 Av of Amer -NY 10019
(212) 487-9700 .. **Potash,** Patti Fern '83 (White F&F,LLP) -61 Bway -NY 10006
(212) 687-3000 .. **Potashner,** Marshall T '91 %Jaffe & A,LLP -600 3rd Av -NY 10016
(212) 335-9000 .. **Potashnick,** Beth F '04 %DA -1 Hogan Pl -NY 10013
(917) 744-8981 .. **Potashnick,** Hillary A '82 -286 Mad Av -NY 10017 **Fx:**(212) 686-8367
(516) 747-4001 .. **Potashnick,** Mark L '73 -200 Old Cntry Rd -Mineola 11501
(212) 609-6800 .. **Potdevin,** Kristin A '06 %McCarter & E,LLP -245 Park Av -NY 10167
(718) 430-2551 .. **Potel,** Mark J '91 %Yeshiva Univ -1300 Morris Park Av -Bronx 10461 **Fx:**430-8783
(212) 226-1965 .. **Potemkin,** Jan H '86 -7-8 Chatham Sq -NY 10038 **Fx:**226-3835
(845) 795-2488 .. **Potenza,** Betty J '96 -258 Milton Cross Rd -Highlnd 12528 **Fx:**795-2488
(516) 747-1990 .. **Potenza,** Jos A '06 %Cascone & K,LLP -1399 Franklin Av -Gdn Cty 11530
(716) 824-7200 .. **Potenza,** Mark S '87 -101 Slade Av -W Seneca 14224 **Fx:**824-8728
(716) 853-9555 .. **Potenza,** Matthew E '09 Leg Aid -237 Main -Buffalo 14203 **Fx:**853-3219
(212) 909-6000 .. **Potenza,** Michl R '97 Cnsl Debevoise & P LLP -919 3rd Av -NY 10022
(914) 697-5020 .. **Potenza,** Michl R '00 %Point & Click Inc -3000 Wstchstr Av -Purchase 10577
(212) 474-1000 .. **Potenza,** Stephen V '03 %Cravath S&M LLP -825 8th Av -NY 10019
(716) 849-8900 .. **Potenza,** V Christopher '03 %Hurwitz & F,PC -1300 Lbrty Bldg -Buffalo 14202
(212) 310-8680 .. **Potenzone,** Mary Jean M '81 (Weil G&M LLP) -767 5th Av -NY 10153
(212) 801-6509 .. **Potere,** Kevin P '09 %Greenberg T,LLP -200 Park Av -NY 10166
(212) 364-5340 .. **Potkin,** Vanessa C '01 %Innocence Project -100 5th Av -NY 10011 **Fx:**364-5341
(212) 265-6888 .. **Potoczak,** Spring C '06 %Porzio B&N,PC -156 W 56th -NY 10019
(516) 739-3737 .. **Potruch,** Alexander '70 (Alexander P,LLC) -666 Old Cntry Rd -Gdn Cty 11530
(518) 546-3391 .. **Potskowski,** Wm J '72 -56 Cllg -Pt Henry 12974 **Fx:**546-3426
(518) 374-7779 .. **Pott,** Carlton N II '65 -650 Franklin Bx957 -Schnctdy 12301 **Fx:**374-2180
(212) 758-9300 .. **Potter,** David E '87 (Lazare P&G LLP) -950 3rd Av -NY 10022
(585) 546-7830 .. **Potter,** Donald F '48 OfCnsl Culley MT&P,LLP -36 W Main -Rchstr 14614
(212) 336-2000 .. **Potter,** Geoffrey '89 (Patterson BW&T LLP) -1133 Av of Amer -NY 10036
(212) 593-5400 .. **Potter,** H David '59 (Baker N&W) -515 Mad Av -NY 10022
(518) 436-0751 .. **Potter,** James T '81 (Hinman S PC) -121 State -Albany 12207
(212) 490-3000 .. **Potter,** Jay A '05 %Wilson EME&D LLP -150 E 42nd -NY 10017
(212) 692-1000 .. **Potter,** Lee J '93 (Duane M LLP) -1540 Bway -NY 10036
(212) 909-6000 .. **Potter,** Nicholas F '89 (Debevoise & P LLP) -919 3rd Av -NY 10022
(212) 953-6633 .. **Potter,** Noah B '01 OfCnsl Cox PS&S LLP -630 3rd Av -NY 10017
(212) 450-4000 .. **Potter,** Philip C Jr. '52 SrCnsl Davis P&W LLP -450 Lex Av -NY 10017
(212) 598-8000 .. **Potter,** Richd T Jr. '80 %Guardian Life Ins -7 Hanover Sq -NY 10004 **Fx:**919-2693
(585) 546-5530 .. **Potter,** Robt L '01 %Thomson West -50 E Broad -Rchstr 14694
(212) 775-8700 .. **Potter,** Robt N '06 %Kilpatrick S,LLP -31 W 52nd -NY 10019
(315) 422-2763 .. **Potter,** Thos J '92 (DelDuchetto & P) -1 Lincoln Ctr -Syracuse 13202
(212) 355-8555 .. **Potters & Della Pietra LLP** -546 5th Av -NY 10036 **Fx:**(973) 575-4468
(716) 855-1118 .. **Pottle,** Willard M Jr. '65 -420 Main -Buffalo 14202
(212) 265-1826 .. **Pottratz Acosta,** Ana Catalina '05 Lutheran Family & Cmmnty Srvcs -308 W 46th -NY 10036
(716) 892-3290 .. **Potts,** Patricia Harbison '99 %Harbison Bros Inc -32 Appenheimer Av -Buffalo 14214
(212) 688-5151 .. **Potts,** Roderick A '09 %Gibney A&F,LLP -665 5th Av -NY 10022
(518) 436-0751 .. **Potvin-Hogan,** Cheryl E '94 (Hinman S PC) -121 State -Albany 12207
(716) 698-7406 .. **Potzler,** Melissa A '03 -181 Franklin -Buffalo 14202
(212) 858-3600 .. **Poulad,** S Emy '89 %Reliance Ins -75 Broad -NY 10004
(518) 863-8191 .. **Poulin,** Michl J '95 -111 N Main Bx1317 -Northvll 12134 **Fx:**863-2774
(631) 724-8833 .. **Poulis,** Andre N '96 Cnsl Devitt SB,LLP -50 Route 111 -Smithtwn 11787
(212) 473-0545 .. **Poulos,** Christopher G '83 -60 Gramercy Park N -NY 10010
(212) 335-9000 .. **Poulos,** Danl B '09 %DA -1 Hogan Pl -NY 10013
(631) 232-1130 .. **Poulos,** Deborah '89 (Lefkowitz & P) -1770 Motor Pkwy -Hauppauge 11788
(212) 619-5301 .. **Poulos,** Eric G '77 -30 Vesey -NY 10007
(718) 726-6993 .. **Poulos,** George '85 -29-16 23rd Av -Astoria 11105 **Fx:**721-7793
(518) 793-6611 .. **Poulos,** Jacquelyn E '09 %Miller MS&H,LLC -451 Glen Bx765 -Glens Fls 12801
(212) 326-3939 .. **Poulos,** Michelle M '07 %Jones D -222 E 41st -NY 10017
(212) 855-3200 .. **Poulos,** Nikki Mavrakakis '93 %Depository Trust -55 Water -NY 10041 **Fx:**855-3279
(631) 271-3737 .. **Poulos,** Stamatina P '96 %R Weiss,PC -734 Walt Whitman Rd -Melvll 11747 **Fx:**271-3784
(516) 876-0800 .. **Poulson,** Kiyam J '03 %Druckman Law Grp PLLC -242 Drexel Av -Westbury 11590 **Fx:**876-0888
(212) 248-1195 .. **Poulson,** Robt J Jr. '71 -67 Wall -NY 10005
(607) 547-1195 .. **Poulson,** Robt J Jr. '71 -29 Pioneer -Cooperstwn 13326
(212) 903-9000 .. **Poulter,** Matthew S '05 %Linklaters -1345 Av of Amer -NY 10105
(212) 294-6700 .. **Poumpouridis,** Evridiki '07 %Winston & S -200 Park Av -NY 10166
(212) 687-8181 .. **Pounian,** Steven R '81 (Kreindler & K) -750 3rd Av -NY 10017
(516) 829-1990 .. **Pour,** David E '98 (D Pour & Assoc,LLP) -10 Cuttermill Rd -Gt Neck 11021 **Fx:**466-7699
(516) 829-1990 .. **Pour,** Romina Kahen '97 (D Pour & Assoc,LLP) -10 Cuttermill Rd -Gt Neck 11021 **Fx:**466-7699
(212) 537-0409 .. **Pourakis,** Constantine D '01 (Stevens & L PC) -485 Mad Av -NY 10022 **Fx:**(610) 371-1237
(212) 619-8387 .. **Pourmohammadi,** Alireza '03 %J O'Malley,PC -299 Bway -NY 10007 **Fx:**406-2967
(917) 597-4766 .. **Pourtavoosi,** Babak '04 -320 E Shore Rd -Gt Neck 11023
(315) 474-2943 .. **Poushter,** Bruce M '77 (Sugarman Law Firm,LLP) -211 W Jffrsn -Syracuse 13202
(716) 852-6923 .. **Poveromo,** Richd S '05 %Taylor & Santacrose -300 Pearl -Buffalo 14202 **Fx:**856-7417
(845) 340-3280 .. **Povill,** Joshua H '04 DA -285 Wall -Kingston 12401 **Fx:**340-3185
(718) 268-3000 .. **Povman,** Bruce S '89 %M Povman -108-18 Qns Blvd -Frst Hlls 11375 **Fx:**520-8175
(718) 899-6848 .. **Povman,** Linda S '76 -12335 82nd Rd -Kew Gdns 11415
(212) 635-1077 .. **Povman,** Michl D '89 Bk of NY Mellon -1 Wall -NY 10286
(718) 268-3000 .. **Povman,** Morton '55 -108-18 Qns Blvd -Frst Hlls 11375 **Fx:**520-8175
(212) 957-7600 .. **Povolny,** Matthew V '08 %Cohen & G LLP -800 3rd Av -NY 10022
(718) 886-1958 .. **Powderly,** James A '02 C&L Contrctng Corp -14-20 128th -Cllg Pnt 11356 **Fx:**886-0620
(631) 786-6331 .. **Powell,** Andre '99 -Bx2568 -N Babylon 11703
(516) 560-6400 .. **Powell,** Catharine A '87 %Leg Aid -1 Helen Keller Way -Hempstd 11550 **Fx:**565-3694
(212) 636-7433 .. **Powell,** Catherine B '94 %Fordham Univ Sch of Law -140 W 62nd -NY 10023 **Fx:**636-6899
(212) 693-0085 .. **Powell,** Denice '85 %Appellate Advocates -2 Rector -NY 10006 **Fx:**693-0878
(716) 855-3200 .. **Powell,** Donald G '99 %Zdarsky S&A -298 Main -Buffalo 14202
(516) 921-0502 .. **Powell,** Fredric A '84 -2631 Merrick Rd -Bellmore 11710 **Fx:**921-7484
(718) 261-3047 .. **Powell,** Hettie V '93 %Queens Law Assoc -118-21 Qns Blvd -Frst Hlls 11375 **Fx:**261-0798
(212) 486-9494 .. **Powell,** James H '52 -488 Mad Av -NY 10022 **Fx:**486-0701
(631) 234-8585 .. **Powell,** Jeffrey D '85 Cnsl Bracken & M,LLP -1 Suffolk Sq -Islandia 11749

(212) 416-6396 .. **Powell**, Jeffrey K '98 %Dept of Law -120 Bway -NY 10271 **Fx**:416-8074
(315) 426-7403 .. **Powell**, Jennifer L '88 %DEC -615 Erie Blvd W -Syracuse 13204 **Fx**:426-7408
(212) 450-4000 .. **Powell**, Jeri E '08 %Davis P&W LLP -450 Lex Av -NY 10017
(212) 505-4087 .. **Powell**, Johan S '98 -65 Bway -NY 10006
(212) 742-0310 .. **Powell**, Jos M '93 (Powell & Assoc,LLC) -110 Wall -NY 10005
(516) 222-1111 .. **Powell**, Judith L '91 -250 Mineola Blvd -Mineola 11501 **Fx**:620-0250
(212) 909-6000 .. **Powell**, Julia S '08 %Debevoise & P LLP -919 3rd Av -NY 10022
(914) 967-3092 .. **Powell**, Kenneth E '75 -21 Hllcrst Ln -Rye 10580
(914) 253-3638 .. **Powell**, Krista A '08 Pepsi Co Inc -700 Andrsn Hill Rd -Purchase 10577
(585) 546-6448 .. **Powell**, Larry T '07 %Davidson F LLP -28 E Main -Rchstr 14614
(212) 264-1873 .. **Powell**, Marcella '00 US DOJ -26 Fed Plz -NY 10278 **Fx**:264-1916
(516) 931-4028 .. **Powell**, Norman E '68 -9 Chestnut Dr -Plainvw 11803
(212) 549-8587 .. **Powell**, Rhonda Edwards '94 Scripps Networks Inc -1180 Av of Amer -NY 10036
(212) 425-9300 .. **Powell**, Ronnie Ann '84 (Bressler A&R,PC) -17 State -NY 10004
(212) 285-3038 .. **Powell**, Roslyn I '94 %Better Balance -75 Maiden Ln -NY 10038 **Fx**:724-3535
(212) 435-3571 .. **Powell**, Stephen E '81 %Port Auth of NY/NJ -225 Park Av S -NY 10003 **Fx**:435-3555
(212) 509-2009 .. **Powell**, Todd J '06 %Maroney O LLP -11 Bway -NY 10004 **Fx**:504-2754
(212) 274-6705 .. **Powell**, Tyrone M '76 %Admin Children's Srvcs -220 Church -NY 10013
(212) 309-1000 .. **Powell**, Wesley R '95 (Hunton & W) -200 Park Av -NY 10166
(212) 267-1906 .. **Powell Monge**, Verena '88 Powell Law.PC -277 Bway -NY 10007 **Fx**:267-1893
(212) 478-7200 .. **Power**, Annie P '09 Hahn & H LLP -488 Mad Av -NY 10022
(631) 577-2400 .. **Power**, Christopher J '96 %Tromello M&K -25 Melvll Park Rd Bx9038 -Melvll 11747
(212) 878-0000 .. **Power**, Deirdre Waldron '92 %MTA -2 Penn Plz -NY 10121
(315) 483-6931 .. **Power**, Gregory J '83 (DeValk P&L,PC) -6 E Main -Sodus 14551
(212) 877-0100 .. **Power**, James A Jr. '83 (Power D LLP) -233 W 72nd -NY 10023 **Fx**:580-0325
(212) 513-3200 .. **Power**, James H '99 SrCnsl Holland & K LLP -31 W 52nd -NY 10019
(516) 576-0434 .. **Power**, James J '60 -88 Froehlich Farm Blvd -Woodbury 11797
(212) 715-9100 .. **Power**, James P '96 SpclCnsl Kramer LN&F,LLP -1177 Av of Amer -NY 10036
(800) 281-1515 .. **Power**, John M '65 (Power Law Firm LLP) -590 Mad Av -NY 10022 **Fx**:903-1993
(718) 520-3710 .. **Power**, Kevin J '97 Supreme Ct -88-11 Sutphin Blvd -Jamaica 11435
(212) 478-7200 .. **Power**, Mark T '89 (Hahn & H LLP) -488 Mad Av -NY 10022
(212) 227-3636 .. **Power**, Nancy Ann '94 %Spar & B,PC -225 Bway -NY 10007
(914) 834-7890 .. **Power**, Philip J '75 -36 Oak Av -Larchmnt 10538
(212) 735-3000 .. **Powers**, Albert T '03 %Skadden ASM&F LLP -4 Times Sq -NY 10036
(914) 422-4232 .. **Powers**, Ann '97 %Pace Law Schl -78 N Bway -White Plns 10603 **Fx**:422-4261
(718) 261-3000 .. **Powers**, Anne L '84 -118-21 Qns Blvd -Frst Hlls 11375 **Fx**:945-1071
(631) 787-6161 .. **Powers**, Arthur J '65 (Keenan P&A,PC) -2150 Joshuas Path -Hauppauge 11788
(914) 285-8500 .. **Powers**, Brian J '79 %TK Moore -701 Wstchstr Av -White Plns 10604 **Fx**:285-8510
(212) 318-6000 .. **Powers**, Brian J '06 %Paul HJ&W LLP -75 E 55th -NY 10022
(631) 462-3434 .. **Powers**, Chad M '97 (Wand P&G) -1776 E Jericho Tpk -Huntngtn 11743 **Fx**:462-3939
(631) 261-8834 .. **Powers**, Christopher M '86 (Ingerman S LLP) -150 Motor Pkwy -Hauppauge 11788
(212) 223-6700 .. **Powers**, Edw L '83 (Zukerman GB&C,LLP) -875 3rd Av -NY 10022
(631) 727-8250 .. **Powers**, Eileen A '92 (EA Powers,PLLC) -431 Griffing Av Bx1361 -Rvrhead 11901 **Fx**:727-7182
(212) 593-6111 .. **Powers**, Elizabeth A '09 %Greenberg & M -521 5th Av -NY 10175 **Fx**:(516) 887-1720
(212) 259-8000 .. **Powers**, Elizabeth W '79 (Dewey & L LLP) -1301 Av of Amer -NY 10019
(212) 735-3000 .. **Powers**, James R '07 %Skadden ASM&F LLP -4 Times Sq -NY 10036
(631) 231-7500 .. **Powers**, Jay Robt '81 (Zuckerman & P) -1622 Brentwood Rd -Bay Shr 11706 **Fx**:231-7561
(716) 250-1800 .. **Powers**, Jean C '80 (Jaeckle F&M,LLP) -400 Essjay Rd -Amherst 14221
(718) 222-2353 .. **Powers**, Jenna K '07 %Law Dept -350 Jay -Brklyn 11201 **Fx**:222-2373
(718) 945-4239 .. **Powers**, John C '91 -222 Beach 130th -Far Rckwy 11694
(315) 471-3151 .. **Powers**, John G '97 (Hancock & E,LLP) -1500 AXA Twr I Bx4976 -Syracuse 13221
(212) 483-2323 .. **Powers**, John J '88 %JP Morgan Chase -345 Park Av -NY 10154
(518) 465-5995 .. **Powers**, John K '73 (Powers & S,LLP) -39 N Pearl -Albany 12207
(315) 428-1380 .. **Powers**, John P '87 %Fager & A,LLP -2 Clinton Sq -Syracuse 13202
(631) 242-2020 .. **Powers**, John T Jr. '98 %JS Caramagno -1641 Deer Prk Av -Deer Pk 11729 **Fx**:242-2034
(212) 422-0202 .. **Powers**, Jos K '78 (Sedgwick DM&A LLP) -125 Broad -NY 10004
(518) 455-2225 .. **Powers**, Kate M '03 %Sen N Breslin -502 Cptl -Albany 12247
(631) 723-1032 .. **Powers**, Kerry L '01 -76 W Montauk Hwy -Hampton Bays 11946
(212) 464-1391 .. **Powers**, Laura J '92 JP Morgan Chase Bank NA -345 Park Av -NY 10154
(585) 244-2170 .. **Powers**, Lisa M '98 L Powers,PC -100 Allens Crk Rd -Rchstr 14618
(212) 589-4200 .. **Powers**, Marc D '81 (Baker & H LLP) -45 Rckfllr Plz -NY 10111
(716) 858-2424 .. **Powers**, Matthew B '06 %DA -25 Delaware Av -Buffalo 14202 **Fx**:858-7425
(212) 310-8000 .. **Powers**, Matthew D '99 (Weil G&M LLP) -767 5th Av -NY 10153
(516) 747-8641 .. **Powers**, Maura '91 -96 Moore -New Hyde Pk 11040
(716) 847-8400 .. **Powers**, Michl B '83 (Phillips L LLP) -3400 HSBC Ctr -Buffalo 14203
(585) 263-5812 .. **Powers**, Michl T '96 US Dist Ct WDNY -100 State -Rchstr 14614
(212) 404-8774 .. **Powers**, Paul J Jr. '67 (Satterlee SB&B LLP) -230 Park Av -NY 10169
(866) 348-5819 .. **Powers**, Peter L '90 SSA-ODAR -50 Fountain Plz -Buffalo 14202 **Fx**:(716) 551-4078
(914) 995-4752 .. **Powers**, Raymond '81 %Hon N Colabella -111 Martin Luther King Blvd -White Plns 10601
(212) 389-5000 .. **Powers**, Robin J '96 Cnsl Sutherland A&B LLP -1114 Av of Amer -NY 10036
(518) 465-5995 .. **Powers & Santola,LLP** -39 N Pearl -Albany 12207 **Fx**:426-4012
(518) 436-0344 .. **Powhida**, Alexander '00 Deily M&G,LLP -8 Thurlow Ter -Albany 12203
(518) 477-7951 .. **Powis**, Rodney C '97 (Maney M&L) -77 Troy Rd -E Greenbush 12061
(718) 802-2719 .. **Powlen**, Noah D '95 ACS -330 Jay -Brklyn 11201
(212) 226-5054 .. **Powley**, Robt L '92 (Powley & G,PC) -304 Hudson -NY 10013 **Fx**:266-5085
(718) 439-3600 .. **Poyau**, Frantz '88 -5615 5th Av -Brklyn 11220
(315) 471-3151 .. **Poyer**, Robt D '06 %Hancock & E,LLP -1500 AXA Twr I Bx4976 -Syracuse 13221
(718) 816-0005 .. **Poyerd**, Jeannette M '07 %Angiuli K&G,LLP -60 Bay -Staten Isl 10301
(315) 483-4995 .. **Poyzer**, Laura Jane '60 -Bx126 -Sodus Point 14555 **Fx**:483-2914
(516) 542-5059 .. **Pozdnyakov**, Alexandre '05 Cnsl Lukoil NA -1500 Hempstd Tpk -E Meadow 11554
(518) 434-2622 .. **Pozefsky Bramley & Murphy** -90 State -Albany 12207 **Fx**:434-0048
(518) 587-9400 .. **Pozefsky**, Martin W '85 -25 Walton -Saratoga Spgs 12866 **Fx**:587-0077
(518) 434-2622 .. **Pozefsky**, Wm '63 (Pozefsky B&M) -90 State -Albany 12207
(914) 997-0900 .. **Pozin**, Danl '88 (Wormser KG&J LLP) -399 Knollwood Rd -White Plns 10603
(212) 406-2000 .. **Poznanski**, Andrew V '03 (Irwin & P,LLP) -233 Bway -NY 10279
(718) 442-1550 .. **Poznansky**, Jonathan H '85 -1688 Victory Blvd -Staten Isl 10314 **Fx**:442-6560
(212) 483-0105 .. **Pozner**, Jason A '07 %Coughlin D LLP -88 Pine-Wall St Plz -NY 10005
(518) 463-4808 .. **Pozner**, Louis-Jack '72 L-J Pozner,PC -11 N Pearl -Albany 12207 **Fx**:463-6669
(212) 715-9100 .. **Pozon**, Sheila M '07 %Kramer LN&F,LLP -1177 Av of Amer -NY 10036
(212) 836-8000 .. **Pozzuoli**, Frank A '86 %Kaye S LLP -425 Park Av -NY 10022
(914) 684-2500 .. **Pozzuoli**, Jos A '79 %NorthEast Community Bk -325 Hmltn Av -White Plns 10601 **Fx**:684-0444
(212) 509-9400 .. **Pozzuto**, Vincent P '96 (Cozen O) -45 Bway Atrium -NY 10006
(718) 645-3111 .. **Prabhakar**, Ashwani '03 %Leg Aid Society Ofc for the Aging -111 Lvngstn -Brklyn 11201 **Fx**:260-4722
(212) 525-8685 .. **Prabhu**, Clifton M '99 HSBC Securities Inc -452 5th Av -NY 10018
(212) 393-1000 .. **Prabhu**, Jean M '82 %Burns & H -233 Bway -NY 10279
(212) 474-1000 .. **Prabhu**, Sarita S '08 %Cravath S&M LLP -825 8th Av -NY 10019
(212) 947-1079 .. **Pradhan**, Devendra P N '03 Chhetry & Assoc -363 7th Av -NY 10001
(212) 668-8888 .. **Prado**, Tomas N '85 (Prado & T,LLP) -305 Bway -NY 10007 **Fx**:668-8494
(212) 345-6658 .. **Praeger**, Andrea M '79 %Guy Carpenter & Co -1166 Av of Amer -NY 10036 **Fx**:345-3022
(718) 575-3288 .. **Praeger**, Helene Schechtman '71 -70-25 Yllwstn Blvd -Frst Hlls 11375
(914) 636-5588 .. **Praete**, Frank C Jr. '42 -271 North Av -New Rchll 10801
(914) 946-4777 .. **Praga**, Lawr '78 (Keane & B,PC) -445 Hmltn Av -White Plns 10601
(212) 906-1200 .. **Prager**, Bruce J '78 (Latham & W) -885 3rd Av -NY 10022
(646) 253-2300 .. **Prager**, David E '85 (Bond S&K,PLLC) -330 Mad Av -NY 10017
(212) 909-6000 .. **Prager**, Dietmar W '01 Cnsl Debevoise & P LLP -919 3rd Av -NY 10022
(718) 590-2000 .. **Prager**, Emily M '08 %DA -198 E 161st -Bronx 10451 **Fx**:590-6477
(212) 536-3900 .. **Prager**, Eric A '94 (K&L Gates LLP) -599 Lex Av -NY 10022
(212) 471-6200 .. **Prager**, Harvey '05 %Hinshaw & C LLP -780 3rd Av -NY 10017
(631) 289-1600 .. **Prager**, Ira C '87 (Davis & P,PC) -175 Oak -Patchogue 11772
(212) 396-8850 .. **Prager**, Joel B '92 %Avi Chai Fndtn -1015 Park Av -NY 10028
(212) 317-5400 .. **Prager**, Judith L '91 %Swiss Re New Markets -55 E 52nd -NY 10055
(516) 771-3280 .. **Prager**, Renee Jarubovic '91 -125 S Main -Freeprt 11520
(212) 363-2900 .. **Prager**, Steven D '81 (Krieger & P LLP) -39 Bway -NY 10006
(212) 554-0400 .. **Prager**, Stuart '80 (Grubman I&S,PC) -152 W 57th -NY 10019
(212) 446-4800 .. **Prager**, Wendy A '08 %Kirkland & E LLP -153 E 53rd -NY 10022
(212) 708-1800 .. **Prahl**, Dennis S '90 (Ladas & P) -26 W 61st -NY 10023
(914) 749-8200 .. **Prahl**, Roger '98 %Boies S&F LLP -333 Main -Armonk 10504
(212) 667-9300 .. **Prahofer**, Nancy '85 %Nomura Securities Intl -2 World Fncl Ctr -NY 10281
(718) 250-2000 .. **Prakash**, Reeta L '07 %DA -350 Jay -Brklyn 11201 **Fx**:250-2314
(718) 946-5099 .. **Prakhin**, Yuriy '02 -2174 86th -Brklyn 11214
(516) 764-2226 .. **Prandi**, Peter A '83 -430 Sunrise Hwy Bx1100 -Rockvll Ctr 11571 **Fx**:536-5389
(212) 682-3700 .. **Pranzo**, Gene M '61 -60 E 42nd -NY 10165 **Fx**:682-3704
(646) 386-5700 .. **Praport**, Karen M '05 %Civil Ct -111 Centre -NY 10013
(212) 557-4790 .. **Prashker**, Audrey E '84 Verizon Capital Grp -240 E 38th -NY 10016
(718) 852-3528 .. **Prashker**, Rochelle '05 %JA Simon,PC -356 Fulton -Brklyn 11201 **Fx**:875-5728
(607) 231-5900 .. **Praske**, Lauren A '09 %Leg Aid -30 Fayette -Bnghmtn 13901 **Fx**:724-7211
(646) 610-5560 .. **Prasso**, Thos M '85 NYPD -1 Police Plz -NY 10038 **Fx**:610-6399
(716) 541-8574 .. **Pratcher**, Daria L '04 -136 Bway -Buffalo 14203
(716) 838-4612 .. **Pratcher**, Franklin R '77 (Pratcher & Assoc,PC) -1133 Kensngtn Av -Buffalo 14215 **Fx**:838-4828
Prato, Saml F '55 -106 Cobblestone Ct Dr -Victor 14564
(585) 454-3377 .. **Prato**, Thos M '92 (Brown & T,LLC) -19 Prince -Rchstr 14607
(518) 792-2117 .. **Pratt**, Benjamin R Jr. '74 (Bartlett PS&R,PC) -1 Wshngtn Bx2168 -Glens Fls 12801
(212) 593-6700 .. **Pratt**, Christie J '03 %Aaronson RF&D,LLP -757 3rd Av -NY 10017
(585) 223-7430 .. **Pratt**, Christopher C '87 -6800 Pttsfrd Palmyra Rd -Fairprt 14450
(518) 445-2311 .. **Pratt**, David A '78 %Albany Law Schl -80 New Scotland Av -Albany 12208 **Fx**:445-2315
(212) 577-3500 .. **Pratt**, Frederic G '87 %Leg Aid -199 Water -NY 10038 **Fx**:809-1370

(631) 761-7000 .. **Pratt**, George C '53 %Touro Cllg Law Ctr -225 Eastvw Dr -Central Islip 11722
(516) 227-0700 .. **Pratt**, George C '53 SpclCnsl Farrell F,PC -1320 RXR Plz -Uniondale 11556
(212) 848-4000 .. **Pratt**, Jason Y '01 Cnsl Shearman & S LLP -599 Lex Av -NY 10022
(518) 438-9907 .. **Pratt**, Kristin M '06 %Young SWRB&M,LLC -5 Palisades Dr -Albany 12205
(718) 662-6464 .. **Pratt**, Louis A '87 -21 Freund Dr -Nanuet 10954
(212) 832-3086 .. **Pratt**, Mitchell C '87 %Scherman Foundation -16 E 52nd -NY 10022
(914) 245-4098 .. **Pratt**, Randal D '81 (Dineen & P,PC) -1335 Wht Hill Rd -Yorktwn Hts 10598
(845) 677-2600 .. **Pratt**, Shawn B '87 -3304 Franklin Av Bx1238 -Millbrook 12545 **Fx:**677-2603
(518) 449-3359 .. **Pratt**, Terrance N '06 Malkin & R -80 State -Albany 12207 **Fx:**449-5788
(212) 446-4862 .. **Pratt**, Wm H '90 (Kirkland & E LLP) -153 E 53rd -NY 10022
(518) 434-1022 .. **Pratt**, Zachary H '08 %Sullivan KO&V, LLP -152 Central Av -Albany 12206
(914) 723-9000 .. **Pravda**, David A '66 -14 Harwood Ct -Scarsdale 10583 **Fx:**723-2091
(212) 373-3000 .. **Pravda**, Douglas M '02 Cnsl Paul WRW&G LLP -1285 Av of Amer -NY 10019
(914) 712-2000 .. **Pravetz**, Carol M '82 (Meltzer & P,LLP) -145 Huguenot -New Rchll 10801
(718) 579-7900 .. **Pray**, Bethany S '05 Leg Aid -900 Sheridan Av -Bronx 10451 **Fx:**293-8744
(212) 598-5215 .. **Preble**, Judith '73 %Leg Aid -49 Thomas -NY 10013 **Fx:**298-5252
(646) 433-5620 .. **Predmore**, Dale D '96 AIG -180 Maiden Ln -NY 10038
(315) 422-1391 .. **Predmore**, Paul M '85 (Green & S,PLLC) -One Lincoln Ctr #900 -Syracuse 13202
(646) 733-3200 .. **Pree**, Cynthia J '00 %US Customs -1 Penn Plz -NY 10119
(212) 490-9524 .. **Preefer**, John J '74 -36 W 44th -NY 10036
(212) 735-3000 .. **Prehogan**, Michl '09 %Skadden ASM&F LLP -4 Times Sq -NY 10036
(212) 872-1000 .. **Preis**, Arik Y '01 -One Bryant Park -NY 10036 **Fx:**872-1002
(518) 433-0603 .. **Preiser**, Cynthia E '90 -100 State -Albany 12207 **Fx:**436-5793
(518) 445-2311 .. **Preiser**, Peter '57 Albany Law Schl -80 New Scotland Av -Albany 12208 **Fx:**445-2315
(212) 335-9000 .. **Preiss**, Richd T '81 %DA -1 Hogan Pl -NY 10013
(212) 909-6000 .. **Preissler**, Ann Marie '03 %Debevoise & P LLP -919 3rd Av -NY 10022
(212) 325-7617 .. **Preite**, Francis A '00 Credit Suisse -1 Mad Av -NY 10010
(212) 557-7200 .. **Preite**, Ralph E '90 (Davidoff M&H,LLP) -605 3rd Av -NY 10158
(212) 878-8890 .. **Preminger**, David S '73 (Keller R LLP) -275 Mad Av -NY 10016 **Fx:**878-8895
(212) 715-9100 .. **Preminger**, Eve '61 Cnsl Kramer LN&F,LLP -1177 Av of Amer -NY 10036
(212) 362-6223 .. **Preminger**, Katherine '67 -146 Cntrl Pk W -NY 10023
(212) 758-9300 .. **Premisler**, Andrew M '99 (Lazare P&G LLP) -950 3rd Av -NY 10022
(212) 878-8000 .. **Premisler**, Jennifer B '08 %Clifford C LLP -31 W 52nd -NY 10019
(516) 294-6260 .. **Premisler**, Michl M '71 -1 Old Cntry Rd -Carle Pl 11514 **Fx:**747-6384
(518) 436-8000 .. **Premo**, Brian D '86 (Premo Law Firm.PLLC) -20 Corp Wds Blvd -Albany 12211 **Fx:**436-0659
(585) 232-6500 .. **Premo**, Edw F II '83 (Harter S&E LLP) -1600 Bausch & Lomb Pl -Rchstr 14604
(315) 218-8000 .. **Premo**, Kseniya '05 %Bond S&K,PLLC -1 Lincoln Ctr -Syracuse 13202
(212) 513-3200 .. **Prempeh**, Nana B '08 %Holland & K LLP -31 W 52nd -NY 10019
(631) 777-6300 .. **Prendamano**, Jennifer Lynn '00 %True Ptnrs Consultng -145 Pinelawn Rd -Melvll 11747 **Fx:**777-6350
(212) 986-6000 .. **Prendergast**, Christopher S '98 Kleinberg KW&C,PC -551 5th Av -NY 10176 **Fx:**986-8866
(212) 530-3900 .. **Prendergast**, Sean M '88 (Hannum FP&M, LLC) -55 Bway -NY 10006
(718) 487-1300 .. **Prenoveau**, Nicole O '09 %Leg Srvcs Corp A -80 Jamaica Av -Brklyn 11207 **Fx:**342-1780
(212) 779-9910 .. **Prentice**, E Miles III '73 (Eaton & V LLP) -3 Park Av -NY 10016
(718) 923-4206 .. **Prentiss**, Paul R '88 %OTDA Fair Hearings -14 Boerum Pl -Brklyn 11201
(212) 839-5300 .. **Prepon**, Jocelyn N '03 %Sidley A LLP -787 7th Av -NY 10019
(212) 574-1200 .. **Preponis**, Evangellos '10 %Seward & K LLP -1 Bttry Pk Plz -NY 10004
(212) 867-4466 .. **Preponis**, Nikolaos '02 %Belkin BW&G,LLP -270 Mad Av -NY 10016
(718) 595-6607 .. **Prero**, Judah '97 %DEP -59-17 Junction Blvd -Flushng 11373 **Fx:**595-6543
(212) 557-7200 .. **Presant**, Howard B '62 (Davidoff M&H,LLP) -605 3rd Av -NY 10158
(212) 259-8000 .. **Presant**, Ivan J '95 (Dewey & L LLP) -1301 Av of Amer -NY 10019
(212) 335-9000 .. **Presant**, Molly E '00 %DA -1 Hogan Pl -NY 10013
(631) 232-4444 .. **Presberg**, Andrew D '80 -100 Corp Plz -Islandia 11749 **Fx:**232-2603
(718) 209-2099 .. **Prescod**, Marva A '84 -5121 Flatland Av -Brklyn 11234
(212) 963-6332 .. **Prescott**, Darlene '92 %UN -42nd & 1st Av -NY 10017 **Fx:**963-1963
(212) 626-4100 .. **Prescott**, Darrell '76 (Baker & M LLP) -1114 Av of Amer -NY 10036
(212) 794-5749 .. **Prescott**, Frank M '83 CUNY -535 E 80th -NY 10075 **Fx:**794-5426
(518) 473-4596 .. **Prescott**, Teresa A '98 Gov Ofc Emply Rel -ESP, Bldg 2 -Albany 12223
(212) 697-5631 .. **Present**, Harris L '40 -305 Mad Av -NY 10165 **Fx:**697-3052
(516) 747-4082 .. **Present**, Jeffrey D '88 (Montfort HM&S LLP) -1140 Franklin Av Bx7677 -Gdn Cty 11530
(917) 806-9060 .. **Present**, Lawr E '92 -340 E 64th -NY 10065
(212) 779-3207 .. **Present**, Michl '86 OfCnsl Vaslas LH&D LLP -630 3rd Av -NY 10017
(212) 857-8230 .. **Presnick**, John S '52 %Baker MM&M,PC -330 W 34th -NY 10001
(212) 988-7709 .. **Press**, Barbara H '86 -975 Park Av -NY 10028
(212) 357-3448 .. **Press**, Brandon T '00 %Goldman Sachs -1 NY Plz -NY 10004
(212) 416-8897 .. **Press**, Caroline S '92 Atty Gen -120 Bway -NY 10271
(212) 493-7023 .. **Press**, Donald '59 (D Press,PC) -80 Broad -NY 10004 **Fx:**797-3068
(212) 940-8800 .. **Press**, Elliot '98 (Katten MR LLP) -575 Mad Av -NY 10022
(718) 855-0200 .. **Press**, Elliot R '59 OfCnsl RD Herbert -26 Court -Brklyn 11242 **Fx:**855-3845
(212) 515-3243 .. **Press**, Eric L '93 Apollo Mgmt -9 W 57th -NY 10019
(914) 288-9595 .. **Press**, Eric P '84 OfCnsl Gaines GP&N,LLP -1 N Bway -White Plns 10601
(212) 371-6600 .. **Press**, Ira M '90 (Kirby M LLP) -825 3rd Av -NY 10022
(212) 455-2000 .. **Press**, Jacob '07 %Simpson T&B LLP -425 Lex Av -NY 10017
(631) 846-4460 .. **Press**, Jay A '82 J Press,PC -115 Broad Hollow Rd -Melvll 11747 **Fx:**846-8881
(212) 636-5400 .. **Press**, Joel C '95 %DC Comics -1700 Bway -NY 10019 **Fx:**636-5595
(718) 373-2413 .. **Press**, Jos R '75 -3000 Ocean Pkwy -Brklyn 11235
(914) 693-4017 .. **Press**, Mark L '74 -1055 Saw Mill Rvr Rd -Ardsley 10502 **Fx:**693-1603
(212) 715-0262 .. **Press**, Matthew J '99 Solow Realty & Dvlpmnt Co -9 W 57th -NY 10019
(212) 688-8555 .. **Press**, Sharon '01 %Fragomen DB&L LLP -7 Hanover Sq -NY 10004
(845) 294-7949 .. **Pressberg**, Harold M '75 (Norton & C) -60 Erie Bx308 -Goshen 10924
(212) 661-1010 .. **Presseau**, Matthew E '00 %Ogihara & Assoc,PLLC -122 E 42nd -NY 10168 **Fx:**661-6116
(212) 981-4500 .. **Presser**, Lee S '00 PeterSan Grp -1450 Bway -NY 10018 **Fx:**981-4560
(516) 742-4343 .. **Presser**, Leopold '62 (Scully SM&P PC) -400 Grdn City Plz -Gdn Cty 11530
(212) 379-7201 .. **Presser**, Mitchell S '90 Paine & Partners,LLC -461 5th Av -NY 10017
(516) 746-8000 .. **Presser**, Seth '08 %Jaspan S LLP -300 Grdn City Plz -Gdn Cty 11530
(212) 669-8400 .. **Presser**, Sheryl L '86 DCAS-DLS -1 Centre -NY 10007 **Fx:**669-2139
(212) 530-5000 .. **Pressler**, Kelly A '10 %Milbank TH&M LLP -1 Chase Manh Plz -NY 10005
(212) 935-6250 .. **Pressman**, Alan '66 -880 3rd Av -NY 10022 **Fx:**688-0066
(631) 234-3883 .. **Pressman**, Alan P '81 -1797-22 Vets Hwy -Islandia 11749 **Fx:**234-1716
(845) 383-3839 .. **Pressman**, Carol B '98 %MHLS -173 Boices Ln -Kingston 12401
(212) 529-0223 .. **Pressman**, David J '05 -119 W 23rd -NY 10011
(212) 756-2000 .. **Pressman**, Gregory P '70 (Schulte R&Z LLP) -919 3rd Av -NY 10022
(212) 421-4414 .. **Pressman**, Hayward R '67 -460 Park Av -NY 10022 **Fx:**421-4418
(212) 261-4388 .. **Pressman**, Joanna E '01 %Planned Parenthood -434 W 33rd -NY 10001 **Fx:**868-4677
(212) 230-8846 .. **Pressman**, Jonathan S '02 (WilmerHale) -399 Park Av -NY 10022
(212) 480-3030 .. **Pressman**, Michl E '77 -125 Maiden Ln -NY 10038 **Fx:**480-2590
(845) 358-2983 .. **Pressman**, Rebecca R '83 -80 Burd -Nyack 10960
(212) 659-7300 .. **Pressment**, Jonathan D '98 OfCnsl Haynes & B,LLP -1221 Av of Amer -NY 10020
(212) 588-0800 .. **Presson**, Thos F '99 (Frommer L&H LLP) -745 5th Av -NY 10151
(212) 697-6555 .. **Presta**, Anthony '07 %Biedermann RH&R -570 Lex Av -NY 10022
(585) 238-2000 .. **Prestegaard**, Linda T '89 (Phillips L LLP) -1400 First Fed Plz -Rchstr 14614
(212) 759-4888 .. **Prestegaard**, Linda T '89 (Phillips L LLP) -437 Mad Av -NY 10022
(518) 474-5016 .. **Prestemon**, David L '04 Consumer Protection Bd -5 ESP -Albany 12223 **Fx:**474-2474
(212) 506-1700 .. **Presti**, Vincent J III '98 %Kasowitz BT&F LLP -1633 Bway -NY 10019
(914) 633-5630 .. **Presti**, Wm S '93 %Sidney Frank Importing Co -20 Cedar -New Rchll 10801 **Fx:**633-5630
(212) 430-6313 .. **Prestia**, Paul V '99 -65 Bway -NY 10006 **Fx:**430-6314
(631) 499-6000 .. **Prestiano**, James A '91 -631 Commack Rd -Commack 11725 **Fx:**499-6001
(212) 841-1000 .. **Presto**, Jennifer G '04 %Covington & B LLP -620 8th Av -NY 10018
(718) 590-2000 .. **Preston**, Alyssa A '08 %DA -198 E 161st -Bronx 10451 **Fx:**590-6477
(518) 883-4816 .. **Preston**, Brett A '98 (Hoyt & P) -3734 State Hwy 30 Bx1119 -Broadalbin 12025
(212) 781-0681 .. **Preston**, Chet '83 -454 Ft Wshngtn Av -NY 10033 **Fx:**781-0444
(631) 451-6500 .. **Preston**, Christine J '92 %Brookhaven Law Dept -1 Indpndnc Hill -Farmngvll 11738 **Fx:**698-4489
(516) 248-1200 .. **Preston**, Dana M '90 %Mulholland M&R -374 Hillside Av -Williston Pk 11596
(646) 855-0873 .. **Preston**, Douglas G '90 Banc of America Securities LLC -1 Bryant Park -NY 10036
(212) 809-0000 .. **Preston**, Elsa Rodriguez '92 (Preston WM&E,PLLC) -65 Bway -NY 10006 **Fx:**809-4753
(212) 809-0000 .. **Preston**, Gregory R '92 (Preston WM&E,PLLC) -65 Bway -NY 10006 **Fx:**809-4753
(212) 237-0000 .. **Preston**, Hilary L '04 %Vinson & E LLP -666 5th Av -NY 10103
(631) 574-2221 .. **Preston**, James G '93 OfCnsl D Tetlak,PC -315 Walt Whitman Rd -Huntngtn Sta 11746 **Fx:**963-9020
(845) 343-3000 .. **Preston**, Kevin F '86 (MacVean LS&M,PC) -34 Grove Bx310 -Middletwn 10940
(212) 715-1000 .. **Preston**, Maxwell C '10 %Arnold & P LLP -399 Park Av -NY 10022
(212) 354-0808 .. **Preston**, Robt M '91 (Moses P&Z,LLP) -1065 Av of Amer -NY 10018
(585) 454-1130 .. **Preston**, Roger G Jr. '71 -1230 First Fed Plz -Rchstr 14614 **Fx:**454-6118
(518) 474-9155 .. **Preston**, Susan L '96 NYS Ofc Chldrn & Family Srvcs -52 Wshngtn Av -Rensselaer 12144 **Fx:**474-9218
(212) 756-2000 .. **Presutti**, Richd A '97 (Schulte R&Z LLP) -919 3rd Av -NY 10022
(585) 243-4320 .. **Presutti**, Robt A '81 Presutti Law Ofc,PC -32 Main Bx157 -Geneseo 14454 **Fx:**243-0420
(845) 339-7911 .. **Pretsch**, Wm D '67 -41 Pearl Bx4193 -Kingston 12402 **Fx:**331-2754
(212) 699-8400 .. **Pretsfelder**, Steven S '82 %Van Wagner Comm,LLC -800 3rd Av -NY 10022
(212) 980-9600 .. **Pretti**, Richd A '96 %Kaufman B&R -120 Bway -NY 10271
(212) 683-9199 .. **Pretto**, Ada Rachel '95 (AR Pretto,PC) -112 Mad Av -NY 10016 **Fx:**683-9268

(212) 558-4000 .. **Pretto-Sakmann**, Arianna '08 %Sullivan & C LLP -125 Broad -NY 10004
(917) 778-6500 .. **Prettypaul**, Tricia D '10 Cnsl K Dodson -485 Lex Av -NY 10017
(716) 853-9555 .. **Preve**, Kristin M '87 %Leg Aid -237 Main -Buffalo 14203 **Fx:**853-3219
(516) 248-7000 .. **Prevete**, Diana Centrella '82 (Albanese & A LLP) -1050 Franklin Av -Gdn Cty 11530
(212) 839-5300 .. **Prevete**, Kirsten E '07 %Sidley A LLP -787 7th Av -NY 10019
(315) 339-7670 .. **Previte**, Deana D '07 %Corp Cnsl -City Hall 198 N Wshngtn -Rome 13440 **Fx:**838-1166
(315) 361-8044 .. **Previte**, Jaime M '04 %Oneida Indian Nation Enterprises -5218 Patrick Rd -Verona 13478 **Fx:**361-8009
(516) 365-9802 .. **Previto**, Jos J '55 OfCnsl Collard & R,PC -1077 Nrthrn Blvd -Roslyn 11576
(631) 265-4494 .. **Previto**, Robt P '94 -33 Walt Whitman Rd -Huntngtn Sta 11746 **Fx:**265-4382
(212) 839-5300 .. **Prevost**, Ann Marie '91 Sidley A LLP -787 7th Av -NY 10019
(212) 325-7486 .. **Prevost**, Thos '96 CSFB -11 Mad Av -NY 10010
(212) 813-8800 .. **Prew**, Brian J '09 %Goodwin P LLP -620 8th Av -NY 10018
(607) 723-5341 .. **Prew**, Brian M '71 SpclCnsl Hinman H&K,LLP -80 Exchange Bx5250 -Bnghmtn 13902
(212) 756-2000 .. **Prewitt**, S Beverly '07 %Schulte R&Z LLP -919 3rd Av -NY 10022
(212) 425-7200 .. **Prey**, Kevin J '04 %Kenyon & K,LLP -1 Bway -NY 10004
(212) 696-6000 .. **Preziosi**, Benard V Jr. '83 (Curtis M-PC&M LLP) -101 Park Av -NY 10178
(914) 428-1100 .. **Preziosi**, Rick J '86 Westcor Land Title Ins Co -701 Wstchstr Av -White Plns 10604
(631) 853-5212 .. **Preziosi**, Stephen N '00 %Leg Aid -400 Carleton Av Bx9082 -Central Islip 11722 **Fx:**853-7798
(212) 504-6000 .. **Prezioso**, Danl V '09 %Cadwalader W&T LLP -1 World Fncl Ctr -NY 10281
(212) 308-0070 .. **Prezioso**, Patricia M '89 (McCusker AR&C,PC) -805 3rd Av -NY 10022
(212) 612-4200 .. **Prezioso**, Richd C '89 (Hoey KT&E) -55 Water -NY 10041
(212) 309-1000 .. **Prial**, Victor L '05 %Hunton & W -200 Park Av -NY 10166
(212) 885-5000 .. **Pribish**, John J '90 (Blank R LLP) -405 Lex Av -NY 10174
(212) 763-5680 .. **Pribor**, Jeffrey D '84 General Maritime Corp -299 Park Av -NY 10171
(212) 408-5100 .. **Price**, Adam H '00 %Chadbourne & P LLP -30 Rckfllr Plz -NY 10112
(212) 449-8111 .. **Price**, Barry S '90 Merrill Lynch & Co -4 World Fncl Ctr -NY 10080
(212) 403-1000 .. **Price**, Brandon C '07 %Wachtell LR&K -51 W 52nd -NY 10019
(212) 813-8800 .. **Price**, Christopher B '86 (Goodwin P LLP) -620 8th Av -NY 10018
(212) 867-4466 .. **Price**, Craig L '00 (Belkin BW&G,LLP) -270 Mad Av -NY 10016
(212) 655-6000 .. **Price**, Craig M '00 (Chapman & C LLP) -330 Mad Av -NY 10017
(212) 675-2052 .. **Price**, Dana A '83 -96 5th Av -NY 10011 **Fx:**229-6855
(716) 664-5210 .. **Price Flowers Malin & Westerberg** -400 Key Bk Bldg Bx1219 -Jamestwn 14702 **Fx:**664-1865
(315) 473-9414 .. **Price**, Francis D Jr. '75 SpclCnsl Hinman H&K,LLP -224 Harrison -Syracuse 13202
(315) 218-8000 .. **Price**, Fredk J M '04 %Bond S&K,PLLC -1 Lincoln Ctr -Syracuse 13202
(914) 251-1618 .. **Price**, Gail L '89 (Price MS&D,PC) -106 Corp Park Dr -White Plns 10604
(212) 578-3438 .. **Price**, Jennifer E '04 MetLife -1095 Av of Amer -NY 10036 **Fx:**578-3916
(212) 530-3900 .. **Price**, Jessica G '09 %Hannum FP&M, LLC -55 Bway -NY 10006
(212) 949-9022 .. **Price**, John S '06 %Abelman F&S -666 3rd Av -NY 10017
(212) 446-4800 .. **Price**, Jonah L '07 %Kirkland & E LLP -153 E 53rd -NY 10022
(212) 813-8800 .. **Price**, Jonathan I '81 (Goodwin P LLP) -620 8th Av -NY 10018
(718) 679-8800 .. **Price**, Jos A '97 -Bx106 -Fredonia 14063
(212) 446-4800 .. **Price**, Jos W '03 %Kirkland & E LLP -153 E 53rd -NY 10022
(212) 674-1111 .. **Price**, Joshua C '97 (Lipsig P,PLLC) -156 5th Av -NY 10010
(315) 443-1941 .. **Price**, Kimberly Wolf '04 Syracuse Univ -Wht Hall -Syracuse 13244
(212) 833-0702 .. **Price**, Lisa K '95 Pru -466 Lex Av -NY 10017
(212) 698-3500 .. **Price**, Lisa Rudikoff '06 %Dechert LLP -1095 Av of Amer -NY 10036
(516) 296-7000 .. **Price**, Marilyn '78 (Certilman BA&H,LLP) -90 Merrick Av -E Meadow 11554
(718) 643-1993 .. **Price**, Martin L '74 -26 Court -Brklyn 11242 **Fx:**858-3190
(212) 326-3939 .. **Price**, Maxim '09 %Jones D -222 E 41st -NY 10017
(914) 251-1618 .. **Price Meese Shulman & D'Arminio, PC** -106 Corp Park Dr -White Plns 10604
(315) 435-2470 .. **Price**, Michl A '78 %DA -505 S State -Syracuse 13202 **Fx:**435-3969
(212) 790-0402 .. **Price**, Monroe E '83 %Benj N Cardozo Schl of Law -55 5th Av -NY 10003 **Fx:**790-0345
(212) 790-9200 .. **Price**, Morton L '60 (Cowan L&L,PC) -1133 Av of Amer -NY 10036
(716) 851-4343 .. **Price**, Omar R '04 Law Dept -65 Niagara Sq -Buffalo 14202 **Fx:**851-4105
(607) 773-0711 .. **Price**, Paul M '85 -25 Main Bx1632 -Bnghmtn 13902 **Fx:**773-0708
(631) 288-3565 .. **Price**, Peter R '80 -24 Library Av Bx51 -Westhmptn Bch 11978 **Fx:**288-4810
(718) 834-6671 .. **Price**, Rebecca T '03 Safe Horizon -210 Joralemon -Brklyn 11201
(716) 664-5210 .. **Price**, Saml P Jr. '82 (Price FM&W) -400 Key Bk Bldg Bx1219 -Jamestwn 14702
(212) 446-4800 .. **Price**, Scott D '98 (Kirkland & E LLP) -153 E 53rd -NY 10022
(516) 791-7860 .. **Price**, Sidney '54 -729 Sherwood -Vly Stream 11581 **Fx:**791-7383
(716) 753-5000 .. **Price**, Thos A '81 Public Abstract -BxB -Mayvll 14757
(212) 907-7300 .. **Price**, Valerie A '91 OfCnsl Golenbock EAB&P -437 Mad Av -NY 10022
(718) 230-1370 .. **Price**, Vicki Gail '81 -111 Lvngstn -Brklyn 11201
(631) 477-1016 .. **Price**, Wm H Jr. '77 -828 Front Bx2065 -Greenprt 11944 **Fx:**477-0130
(212) 416-6276 .. **Prickett Morgan**, Elizabeth '01 %Dept of Law -120 Bway -NY 10271
(212) 788-0757 .. **Priddy**, David R '07 %Law Dept -100 Church -NY 10007 **Fx:**788-0367
(845) 353-0485 .. **Prier**, Robt J '84 -17 S Bway Bx205 -Nyack 10960 **Fx:**353-0487
(516) 248-3800 .. **Pries**, Wm E '72 -229 7th -Gdn Cty 11530
(315) 474-7401 .. **Priest**, Ellen C '80 %R Priest -333 E Onondaga -Syracuse 13202 **Fx:**474-4321
(315) 474-7401 .. **Priest**, Richd D '63 -333 E Onondaga -Syracuse 13202 **Fx:**474-4321
(212) 458-5896 .. **Prieto**, Andres G '97 %AIG -175 Water -NY 10038
(585) 325-2520 .. **Prieto**, Louis '77 %Leg Assistance -1 W Main -Rchstr 14614 **Fx:**325-2559
(631) 499-4000 .. **Prieto**, Oscar A '01 Vision Risk Srvc,LLC -6333 Jericho Tpk -Commack 11725 **Fx:**499-1792
(212) 344-0464 .. **Prieto**, Tulio R '75 (Cardillo & C) -29 Bway -NY 10006
(631) 617-5050 .. **Prignano**, Barbara M '01 Magnolia Abstract Srvcs -136 E Main -E Islip 11730
(718) 815-7800 .. **Prignoli**, Robt '89 -475 Bement Av -Staten Isl 10310 **Fx:**818-8430
(914) 766-2560 .. **Prill**, Danielle A '99 IBM Corp -294 Route 100 -Somers 10589
(646) 252-2732 .. **Primack**, Karen D '87 %Transit Auth -2 Bway -NY 10004 **Fx:**252-5559
(914) 961-4163 .. **Primack**, Russell D '99 -107 Lk Av -Tuckahoe 10707 **Fx:**793-2114
(212) 827-1518 .. **Primack**, Vanessa A '03 Screen Actors Guild -360 Mad Av -NY 10017 **Fx:**944-6774
(516) 742-3470 .. **Primavera**, Henry M '76 (Kral CRRP&G,LLP) -538 Broadhllw Rd -Melvll 11747
(212) 310-8000 .. **Primavera**, Wm E '00 Weil G&M LLP -767 5th Av -NY 10153
(516) 877-2055 .. **Prime**, Geoffrey N '02 (Prime & O,LLP) -1000 Franklin Av -Gdn Cty 11530 **Fx:**877-2894
(518) 793-3497 .. **Prime**, R Case '54 -100 Bay -Glens Fls 12801 **Fx:**793-0541
(716) 853-5100 .. **Primerano**, Lisa D '01 %Lippes MWF LLP -665 Main -Buffalo 14203
(718) 918-9090 .. **Primes**, Brian D '96 -3867 E Tremont Av -Bronx 10465 **Fx:**918-0300
(631) 761-0800 .. **Primis**, Tara M '01 %Lazer AR&Y,PC -225 Old Cntry Rd -Melvll 11747
(315) 452-2440 .. **Primo**, David M '84 (Primo P&K,LLP) -7075 Manlius Ctr Rd -E Syracuse 13057
(315) 474-1214 .. **Primo**, Mary Beth '90 %Syracuse Metro Abstract Co -6505A Basile Rowe -E Syracuse 13057
(315) 452-2440 .. **Primo Primo & Kirwan,LLP** -7075 Manlius Ctr Rd -E Syracuse 13057 **Fx:**671-1550
(315) 452-2440 .. **Primo**, Steven J '85 (Primo P&K,LLP) -7075 Manlius Ctr Rd -E Syracuse 13057
(212) 751-8899 .. **Primoff**, L Robt '53 (Alfieri F&P,LLP) -460 Park Av -NY 10022
(212) 836-8000 .. **Primoff**, Madlyn Gleich '88 (Kaye S LLP) -425 Park Av -NY 10022
(212) 336-0148 .. **Primoff**, Richd G '88 %SEC -3 World Fncl Ctr -NY 10281 **Fx:**336-1323
(518) 436-1850 .. **Primomo**, Gene V '98 %Fed Pub Def -39 N Pearl -Albany 12207 **Fx:**436-1780
(212) 259-8000 .. **Primps**, Wm G '75 (Dewey & L LLP) -1301 Av of Amer -NY 10019
(212) 878-4000 .. **Primrose**, Linda K '02 Mitsui & Co -200 Park Av -NY 10166
(347) 200-1908 .. **Primus**, Loris P '79 -18353 Camden Av -St Albans 11412
(718) 590-3556 .. **Primus**, Sharon K '90 %DA -198 E 161st -Bronx 10451 **Fx:**590-6477
(212) 259-8000 .. **Prince**, Aaron B K '09 %Dewey & L LLP -1301 Av of Amer -NY 10019
(212) 554-0400 .. **Prince**, Chas O IV '04 %Grubman I&S,PC -152 W 57th -NY 10019
(212) 309-6000 .. **Prince**, Jaime R '04 %Morgan L&B LLP -101 Park Av -NY 10178
(516) 767-5155 .. **Prince**, Jessica L '93 Ashley Legal Advertising -Bx851 -Pt Wash 11050
(212) 848-4000 .. **Prince**, Kenneth S '76 (Shearman & S LLP) -599 Lex Av -NY 10022
(718) 987-8700 .. **Prince**, Patricia A '98 -183 New Dorp Ln -Staten Isl 10306 **Fx:**351-4933
(212) 471-8458 .. **Prince**, Wendy L '86 (Herzfeld & R,PC) -125 Broad -NY 10004
(212) 468-8000 .. **Princi**, Anthony '83 (Morrison & F LLP) -1290 Av of Amer -NY 10104
(914) 627-3000 .. **Principal**, Quedel '99 Diversified Invstmnt Advsrs -440 Mamaroneck Av -Harrison 10528
(347) 273-1360 .. **Principato**, Susan A '98 -1110 South Av -Staten Isl 10314 **Fx:**273-1460
(716) 856-5500 .. **Principe**, David L '99 SpclCnsl Damon M LLP -200 Delaware Av -Buffalo 14202
(518) 770-1588 .. **Principe**, Jennifer D '09 %Schwartz Law Firm -191 Guy Park Av -Amsterdam 12010 **Fx:**770-6247
(516) 921-7120 .. **Principe**, John F '73 (Giorgio deP&P,LLP) -115 Eileen Way -Syosset 11791 **Fx:**921-4253
(917) 421-5355 .. **Principe**, Michl J '96 %SFX Entertainment -220 W 42nd -NY 10036
(212) 267-4177 .. **Principe**, Thos J '74 (Kramer DL&M) -217 Bway -NY 10007
(516) 684-9010 .. **Princivil**, Rony '98 (R Princivil PC) -1979 Marcus Av -Lk Success 11042 **Fx:**684-9011
(212) 404-5777 .. **Prindiville**, Michl J '07 %Littleton JUP&K LLP -39 Bway -NY 10006
(212) 504-6000 .. **Prindle**, Gregory M '05 %Cadwalader W&T LLP -1 World Fncl Ctr -NY 10281
(212) 613-2000 .. **Prindle**, Ryan Patrick '07 %Gibbons PC -1 Penn Plz -NY 10119
(212) 833-1124 .. **Pringle**, Katherine L '99 (Friedman KS&A LLP) -1633 Bway -NY 10019 **Fx:**373-7924
(607) 274-3836 .. **Pringle**, Nancy '89 %Ithaca Cllg -Job Hall -Ithaca 14850 **Fx:**274-1500
(212) 735-3000 .. **Prins**, Richd T '79 (Skadden ASM&F LLP) -4 Times Sq -NY 10036
(212) 468-8000 .. **Print**, Keith M '06 %Morrison & F LLP -1290 Av of Amer -NY 10104
(716) 648-3030 .. **Printup**, Scott C '98 %Chiacchia & F,LLP -5113 S Park Av -Hambrg 14075
(212) 308-6030 .. **Printz**, Carrie '99 David Carrie LLC -155 E 55th -NY 10022 **Fx:**308-6569
(516) 229-4200 .. **Printz**, Stacey E '92 %Mendolia & S -875 Merrick Av -Westbury 11590
(212) 492-4699 .. **Prinz**, Barrie Rosenberg '97 Deloitte LLP -1633 Bway -NY 10019 **Fx:**492-4201
(631) 360-0400 .. **Prinz**, Christal S '02 %Jakubowski RMG&T -969 Jericho Tpk -St James 11780 **Fx:**360-0408
(914) 244-3738 .. **Prinzivalli**, JoAnn J '79 Attys Title Ins Agncy -71 Smith Av -Mt Kisco 10549 **Fx:**244-3814
(212) 450-4000 .. **Prinzo**, Kristi T '00 %Davis P&W LLP -450 Lex Av -NY 10017
(914) 288-0400 .. **Priolet**, Claude P '80 (Priolet & Assoc,PC) -1025 Wstchstr Av -White Plns 10604 **Fx:**288-0404
(914) 813-7257 .. **Priolo**, Frank L '81 %DA -3010 Wstchstr Av -Purchase 10577 **Fx:**813-7211
(212) 742-8700 .. **Priolo**, Judith '05 %Garson D&C LLP -110 Wall -NY 10005

(212) 246-2400 .. **Prior,** Andrew W '04 %Balber PM&VDT,PC -1370 Av of Amer -NY 10019
(516) 829-6900 .. **Prior,** Christopher J '87 (Ackerman LCB&L,LLP) -1010 Nrthrn Blvd -Gt Neck 11021
(518) 862-1090 .. **Prior,** David J '91 %NYSERDA -17 Columbia Cir -Albany 12203 **Fx:**862-1091
(718) 445-1508 .. **Prior,** Michl J '75 -142-03 37th Av -Flushng 11354 **Fx:**358-9849
(516) 829-6900 .. **Prior,** Michelle Sheehan '87 SpclCnsl Ackerman LCB&L,LLP -1010 Nrthrn Blvd -Gt Neck 11021
(845) 586-2760 .. **Prior,** Nancy '84 (Prior & P) -1 Church St Station Bx506 -Arkvll 12406 **Fx:**586-4424
(845) 586-2760 .. **Prior,** Vincent W '85 (Prior & P) -1 Church St Station Bx506 -Arkvll 12406 **Fx:**586-4424
(716) 845-3650 .. **Priore,** Anne C '86 %MHLS -438 Main -Buffalo 14202 **Fx:**874-7794
(716) 853-9555 .. **Priore,** Jeffrey M D '92 Leg Aid -237 Main -Buffalo 14203 **Fx:**853-3219
(516) 625-1700 .. **Prisco,** Anthony '99 %Salamon GB&S,PC -97 Powerhse Rd -Roslyn Hts 11577
(516) 671-5300 .. **Prisco,** Armand J '74 (Polin P&V) -1 Schl -Glen Cove 11542
(914) 995-3419 .. **Prisco,** Jean L '01 %DA -111 Martin Luther King Blvd -White Plns 10601 **Fx:**995-3363
(631) 501-3100 .. **Prisco,** Jesse J '03 %J Humphreys -3 Huntngtn Quad Bx9028 -Melvll 11747 **Fx:**501-3085
(212) 661-7300 .. **Prisco,** Jos J '85 (Malapero & P LLP) -295 Mad Av -NY 10017
(212) 732-8700 .. **Prisco,** Matthew L '97 (McAloon & F,PC) -123 William -NY 10038
(516) 921-8600 .. **Prisco,** Peter '87 (McAndrew C&P) -95 Froehlich Farm Blvd -Woodbury 11797
(516) 676-4600 .. **Prisco,** Richd S '00 %Humes & W -147 Forest Av Bx546 -Locust Vly 11560
(914) 995-3338 .. **Prisco,** Robt J '87 %DA -111 Martin Luther King Blvd -White Plns 10601 **Fx:**995-3363
(518) 473-2057 .. **Priscott,** Ashley L '07 Dept Pub Srvc -3 ESP -Albany 12223
(212) 755-3333 .. **Prisk,** Simon H '93 (SC Ruchelman) -150 E 58th -NY 10155 **Fx:**755-5898
(212) 983-4141 .. **Pritchard,** David H '74 Cnsl D Rozenholc & Assoc -400 Mad Av -NY 10017 **Fx:**983-4356
(212) 858-1000 .. **Pritchard,** John F '70 (Pillsbury WSP LLP) -1540 Bway -NY 10036
(212) 513-3200 .. **Pritchard,** John F '77 (Holland & K LLP) -31 W 52nd -NY 10019
(212) 277-4000 .. **Pritchard,** Julian M '08 (Freshfields BD LLP) -520 Mad Av -NY 10022
(845) 485-5036 .. **Pritchard,** Kent A Jr. '89 -11 Market -Poughkeepsie 12601 **Fx:**485-3276
(212) 859-5027 .. **Pritchard,** Robt O '95 -110 Wall -NY 10005 **Fx:**202-7666
(212) 805-6189 .. **Pritchard,** Sally Spencer '05 Hon B Jones -40 Foley Sq -NY 10007
(212) 878-8000 .. **Pritz,** Richd D '85 (Clifford C LLP) -31 W 52nd -NY 10019
(716) 439-8098 .. **Privateer,** Christopher A '87 -272 East Av -Lockprt 14094
(732) 855-6093 .. **Prives,** Glenn P '10 %Wilentz G&S -110 William -NY 10038 **Fx:**726-6530
(732) 855-6074 .. **Prives,** Loretta Kirsch '83 %Wilentz G&S -110 William -NY 10038 **Fx:**726-4703
(518) 447-3200 .. **Privitera,** John J '78 (McNamee LT&W,PC) -677 Bway -Albany 12207
(212) 344-0900 .. **Priya,** Preeti '00 (N Dobshinsky,LLC) -61 Bway -NY 10006
(516) 741-0123 .. **Prizer,** Linda A '76 (Cohen & P) -130 Newbrdg Rd -Hicksvll 11801
(845) 340-3730 .. **Prizzia,** John W '81 Hon D Williams -285 Wall -Kingston 12401
(516) 229-4200 .. **Proano,** Cecilia '98 Mendolia & S -875 Merrick Av -Westbury 11590
(585) 428-1920 .. **Proano,** Galo M '79 Monroe Cnty Family Ct -99 Exchange Blvd -Rchstr 14614
(914) 390-4145 .. **Prober,** Bonnie J '04 %Hon C McMahon -300 Quarropas -White Plns 10601
(212) 715-9100 .. **Prober,** Melissa J '06 %Kramer LN&F,LLP -1177 Av of Amer -NY 10036
(914) 949-3250 .. **Probert,** Danl L '00 %Chicago Title/Ticor Title -245 Main -White Plns 10601 **Fx:**946-7698
(212) 265-6888 .. **Probst,** Eric L '95 (Porzio B&N,PC) -156 W 56th -NY 10019
(212) 504-6000 .. **Probst,** Tyler A '09 %Cadwalader W&T LLP -1 World Fncl Ctr -NY 10281
(212) 972-3250 .. **Probstein,** Jon Michl '77 -21 Turn lane -Levittwn 11756 **Fx:**202-6495
(914) 234-4095 .. **Procario,** Andrea S '86 -17 Brook Farm Ln -Bedfrd 10506
(212) 499-2186 .. **Procas,** Simone R '95 %Gruner & Jahr USA Publishing -375 Lex Av -NY 10017
(518) 473-8418 .. **Prochera,** Lee Dorrance '81 %OCFS -52 Wshngtn -Rensselaer 12144 **Fx:**486-6361
(212) 789-2000 .. **Prochnow,** Thos H '94 %NHL Enterprises,LP -1185 Av of Amer -NY 10036 **Fx:**789-2020
(212) 759-4888 .. **Prociv,** Justin G '07 %Phillips L LLP -437 Mad Av -NY 10022
(716) 847-8400 .. **Prociv,** Justin G '07 %Phillips L LLP -3400 HSBC Ctr -Buffalo 14203
(631) 952-6505 .. **Procopio,** Carol A '93 %UIA Bd -NYS Ofc Bldg -Hauppauge 11788 **Fx:**952-3385
(845) 634-7010 .. **Procopio,** Judith A '05 %Montalbano C&F,PC -67 N Main Bx1070 -New Cty 10956
(212) 250-0383 .. **Procopio,** Nikki E '87 Deutsche Bk Sec -60 Wall -NY 10005 **Fx:**797-5176
(718) 286-2000 .. **Procton,** Risa B '93 %Leg Aid -120-46 Qns Blvd -Kew Gdns 11415 **Fx:**286-2286
(212) 902-3309 .. **Proctor,** Mark E '04 %Goldman Sachs -1 NY Plz -NY 10004
(212) 351-4000 .. **Proctor,** Monika K '08 %Gibson D&C LLP -200 Park Av -NY 10166
(718) 470-0778 .. **Prodigalidad,** Anita O '86 -250-21 Elkmont Av -Bellerose 11426
(212) 354-7700 .. **Proefriedt,** Gerard '88 (Penn PS&S) -114 W 47th -NY 10036
(212) 298-5197 .. **Profaci,** Dominic J '65 %Leg Aid -49 Thomas -NY 10013 **Fx:**298-5252
(212) 577-6500 .. **Profeta,** Fred R Jr. '66 (Profeta & E) -14 Wall -NY 10005 **Fx:**577-6702
(212) 788-0954 .. **Profeta,** Lawr J '85 %Law Dept -100 Church -NY 10007 **Fx:**788-0367
(201) 227-1114 .. **Profita,** Michl '83 (Profita & Assoc,LLC) -11 Bway -NY 10004 **Fx:**227-1115
(212) 482-0001 .. **Profita,** Tina Altinel '06 %Russo K&T LLP -33 Whitehall -NY 10004
(212) 326-3939 .. **Profusek,** Robt A '94 (Jones D) -222 E 41st -NY 10017
(212) 596-9000 .. **Progoff,** Susan '80 (Ropes & G LLP) -1211 Av of Amer -NY 10036
(212) 458-6142 .. **Proia,** Andrea M '89 AIGTS -175 Water -NY 10038 **Fx:**458-1259
(516) 229-4400 .. **Proietto,** Wm D '91 %Kay & G -875 Merrick Av -Westbury 11590
(212) 279-8880 .. **Proios,** George N '91 (G Proios,PLLC) -65 W 36th -NY 10018 **Fx:**279-0670
(516) 565-4746 .. **Proios,** John J '62 -215 Uniondale Av -Uniondale 11553 **Fx:**505-5120
(212) 388-3600 .. **Projansky,** David M '86 %32B-J Leg Srvcs -101 Av of Amer -NY 10013 **Fx:**388-3061
(212) 969-3367 .. **Projansky,** Robt M '98 (Proskauer R LLP) -1585 Bway -NY 10036
(212) 640-2000 .. **Prokop,** Christopher J '04 %Amer Exp -200 Vesey -NY 10285
(631) 821-1314 .. **Prokop,** David B '90 -131 Route 25A -Rocky Pnt 11778
(212) 521-5400 .. **Prokop,** Edw L '10 %Reed S LLP -599 Lex Av -NY 10022
(212) 506-5000 .. **Prokop,** Jeffrey M '06 %Orrick H&S LLP -51 W 52nd -NY 10019
(212) 788-1038 .. **Prokop,** Natalie H '04 %Law Dept -100 Church -NY 10007 **Fx:**788-0367
(212) 408-5100 .. **Prokup,** Kevin L '05 %Chadbourne & P LLP -30 Rckfllr Plz -NY 10112
(212) 546-9255 .. **Prol,** Thos H '01 %Scarinci H -107 Grand -NY 10013
(518) 746-2525 .. **Proler,** Andrew J '09 %DA -383 Bway -Ft Edward 12828 **Fx:**746-2568
(212) 478-7200 .. **Proman,** Jonathan M '05 %Hahn & H LLP -488 Mad Av -NY 10022
(914) 245-3636 .. **Promisel,** Valorie Joy '91 -1860 Commerce -Yorktwn Hts 10598 **Fx:**245-5958
(516) 542-5900 .. **Prommersberger,** Lynne B '92 %Congdon FORDT&F -333 Earle Ovngton Blvd -Uniondale 11553
(718) 665-9825 .. **Promuto,** Vincent L '71 -920 E 132nd -Bronx 10454
(212) 986-3030 .. **Proner,** A Stanley '55 (Proner & P) -60 E 42nd -NY 10165 **Fx:**953-2079
(212) 986-3030 .. **Proner,** Mitchell '88 (Proner & P) -60 E 42nd -NY 10165 **Fx:**953-2079
(212) 574-1200 .. **Pront,** Peter E '78 Cnsl Seward & K LLP -1 Bttry Pk Plz -NY 10004
(585) 987-2800 .. **Pronti,** James P '01 (Woods OG LLP) -2 State -Rchstr 14614
(585) 232-6500 .. **Pronti,** Kelly A '01 (Harter S&E LLP) -1600 Bausch & Lomb Pl -Rchstr 14604
(518) 435-8092 .. **Pronti,** Thos J '73 %Finkelstein & Prtnrs,LLP -80 Wolf Rd -Albany 12205
(212) 773-6542 .. **Proper,** Donald V '81 Ernst & Young LLP -5 Times Sq -NY 10036
(212) 986-7714 .. **Propp Lapidus & Jaffe, LLP** -1500 Bway -NY 10036 **Fx:**687-0056
(914) 944-0618 .. **Propp,** Sharman T '87 -138 Sleepy Hllw Rd -Briarclff Mnr 10510
(212) 986-7714 .. **Propp,** Theo '49 OfCnsl Propp L&J,LLP -1500 Bway -NY 10036
(212) 232-1300 .. **Proscia,** Anthony '04 %Lewis BB&S LLP -77 Water -NY 10005
(212) 272-1735 .. **Proscia,** Frank P '99 %JP Morgan Chase -383 Mad Av -NY 10179
(212) 750-8585 .. **Proshan,** Alison Amsterdam '95 %WP Stewart & Co -527 Mad Av -NY 10022
(212) 350-5125 .. **Proshan,** David A '93 Libra Advsrs,LLC -909 3rd Av -NY 10022
(212) 788-1324 .. **Proshansky,** Eric '86 %Law Dept -100 Church -NY 10007 **Fx:**788-0367
(212) 969-3000 .. **Proskauer Rose LLP** -1585 Bway -NY 10036 **Fx:**969-2900
(716) 893-1088 .. **Proske,** Diana C '04 Special Funds -2875 Union Rd -Buffalo 14227
(518) 436-0775 .. **Proskin,** Arnold W '64 (Proskin,PC) -423 Loudon Rd -Albany 12211 **Fx:**436-0014
(518) 436-0776 .. **Proskin,** Lisa Anne '93 %Proskin,PC -423 Loudon Rd -Albany 12211 **Fx:**436-0014
(212) 695-0060 .. **Prosper,** Carla C J '06 %Wilens & B,PC -450 7th Av -NY 10123
(212) 416-8680 .. **Prosper,** Judy '98 %Dept of Law -120 Bway -NY 10271
(585) 753-4500 .. **Prosperi,** Timothy L '85 %DA -832 Watts Bldg -Rchstr 14614 **Fx:**753-4576
(518) 886-4000 .. **Prostick,** Arthur I '99 %AYCO -321 Bway Bx860 -Saratoga Spgs 12866
(516) 747-0300 .. **Proszak,** John P '81 (Meltzer LG&B,LLP) -190 Willis Av -Mineola 11501
(718) 741-8400 .. **Protano,** Thos S '91 Div of Human Rights -1 Fordham Plz -Bronx 10458
(212) 922-1080 .. **Protass,** Harlan J '96 (Clayman & R,LLP) -305 Mad Av -NY 10165
(914) 946-4808 .. **Proto,** Andrew J '00 (Riebling P&S,LLP) -1 N Bway -White Plns 10601 **Fx:**287-7578
(212) 532-4816 .. **Proto,** Rosemary '79 -40 Waterside Plz -NY 10010 **Fx:**686-9301
(973) 315-4435 .. **Proto,** Vincent J '97 (Budd L) -140 Bway -NY 10005
(845) 778-2121 .. **Protter,** Howard '81 (Jacobowitz & G,LLP) -158 Orange Av Bx367 -Walden 12586
(914) 872-8560 .. **Protzmann,** Laura J '05 %Dannon Co -100 Hillside Av -White Plns 10603
(607) 734-3400 .. **Proudfoot,** Stephen M '94 (Proudfoot Law Firm) -150 Lk -Elmira 14901 **Fx:**733-0439
(718) 260-2553 .. **Proujansky,** Joshua D '00 Hon M Go -225 Cadman Plz E -Brklyn 11201
(212) 883-4944 .. **Proulx,** Paul J '04 %Cozen O -277 Park Av -NY 10172 **Fx:**672-1144
(212) 596-9000 .. **Prounis,** Othon A '87 (Ropes & G LLP) -1211 Av of Amer -NY 10036
(516) 249-3450 .. **Proussalis,** Vassilios F '04 %Carman C&I,LLP -266 Main -Farmngdl 11735
(518) 272-6565 .. **Prout,** James E '90 (Martin SWD&J) -279 River Bx1530 -Troy 12181
(212) 984-7803 .. **Prouty,** Allison Simmons '81 OfCnsl Warshaw BCS&K,LLP -555 5th Av -NY 10017
(212) 265-7000 .. **Prouty,** David M '87 %UNITE HERE -275 7th Av -NY 10001 **Fx:**307-6904
(718) 934-6501 .. **Provda,** Bruce '73 -2509 Av U -Brklyn 11229
(212) 554-7800 .. **Provder,** Rebecca A '07 %Moses & S LLP -405 Lex Av -NY 10174
(315) 785-9333 .. **Proven,** Lisa A '86 (Proven & Q) -104 Court -Watertwn 13601 **Fx:**785-0973
(914) 937-2500 .. **Provenzano,** Anthony M '88 -320 Wstchstr Av -Pt Chester 10573 **Fx:**937-3629
(212) 506-2500 .. **Provenzano,** S Christopher '03 %Mayer B LLP -1675 Bway -NY 10019
(718) 370-7030 .. **Provenzano,** Vincent F '04 %Amabile & E,PC -1000 South Av -Staten Isl 10314
(914) 686-6100 .. **Provetto,** Joann '96 %Rosenblum & T LLC -50 Main -White Plns 10606
(631) 843-5500 .. **Providenti,** Anthony C '93 Henry Schein Inc -135 Duryea Rd -Melvll 11747 **Fx:**843-5660
(212) 326-1094 .. **Providenti,** David J '95 JJ Studley,Inc -300 Park Av -NY 10022

(585) 232-8080 .. **Provo,** Kelley A '04 -1 E Main -Rchstr 14614
(212) 430-5400 .. **Provost,** Christopher A '98 Diamond M LLP -620 8th Av -NY 10018
(718) 694-3885 .. **Provost,** Jennifer M '98 %Transit Auth -130 Lvngstn -Brklyn 11201 **Fx:**694-5726
(646) 442-3100 .. **Provost,** Jim E '85 %Legal Srvcs -90 John -NY 10038 **Fx:**(212) 227-9798
(212) 496-8658 .. **Prowda,** Judith B '87 -15 W 75th -NY 10023
(516) 439-5465 .. **Prox,** Donna K '02 %Timoshenko & S,LLP -175 E Shore Rd -Gt Neck 11023
(845) 292-0415 .. **Proyect,** Joel M '66 Conflict Leg Aid Bureau -Breezy Hill Rd Bx157 -Parksvll 12768 **Fx:**292-2601
(315) 781-6311 .. **Prozeller,** Bradley '81 -9 Genesee Park Pl -Geneva 14456 **Fx:**781-5476
(518) 465-3553 .. **Prudente,** Stephen C '77 (Maynard OS&C,LLP) -6 Twr Pl -Albany 12203
(631) 852-2166 .. **Prudenti,** Anita M '87 %Hon MF Mullen -210 Center Dr S -Rvrhead 11901 **Fx:**852-2729
(631) 852-2500 .. **Prudenti,** J Scott '86 %DA -200 Center Dr -Rvrhead 11901 **Fx:**852-1769
(631) 281-8724 .. **Prudenti,** John '62 -1235 Montauk High -Mastic 11950 **Fx:**281-2050
(212) 855-6177 .. **Pruess,** Kathryn A '05 Goldman Sachs -1 NY Plz -NY 10004
(518) 455-4311 .. **Prugh,** Cassie M '04 NYS Assembly -80 State -Albany 12248
(516) 676-4600 .. **Prugh,** Clayton A '83 Humes & W -147 Forest Av Bx546 -Locust Vly 11560
(212) 218-2100 .. **Prugo,** Filko '03 (Fitzpatrick CH&S) -1290 Av of Amer -NY 10104
(212) 396-0080 .. **Pruiti,** Graziella C '88 (G Pruiti,PC) -445 Park Av -NY 10022 **Fx:**396-0084
(212) 259-8000 .. **Pruitt,** John S '88 (Dewey & L LLP) -1301 Av of Amer -NY 10019
(212) 837-6705 .. **Pruitt,** Lindsay A-K '08 %Hughes H&R LLP -1 Bttry Pk Plz -NY 10004 **Fx:**299-6705
(718) 625-1721 .. **Pruitt,** Virginia Ann '84 -85 Hicks -Brklyn 11201
(212) 735-3000 .. **Pruneda Gonzalez Salas,** Jorge '07 %Skadden ASM&F LLP -4 Times Sq -NY 10036
(212) 238-3000 .. **Prunell,** Jessica M '03 %Emmet M&M,LLP -120 Bway -NY 10271
(212) 335-9000 .. **Prunty,** Ann P '85 %DA -1 Hogan Pl -NY 10013
(516) 747-6461 .. **Prusan,** Eric I '93 -200 Old Cntry Rd -Mineola 11501 **Fx:**739-3887
(718) 286-2308 .. **Pruser,** Elizabeth R '89 %Leg Aid -120-46 Qns Blvd -Kew Gdns 11415 **Fx:**286-2286
(585) 232-8314 .. **Prusik,** David D '88 (Buckner & K) -1 S Wshngtn -Rchstr 14614
(516) 222-2333 .. **Prusinowski,** Cindy A '82 %Barbara Law Firm -401 Franklin Av -Gdn Cty 11530 **Fx:**222-2935
(212) 922-6796 .. **Prusnofsky,** Jeff S '95 Dreyfus -200 Park Av -NY 10166
(212) 705-7000 .. **Pruss,** Seth J '09 %Bingham M LLP -399 Park Av -NY 10022
(212) 661-1100 .. **Prussin,** H Adam '75 (Pomerantz HG&G LLP) -100 Park Av -NY 10017
(646) 458-5622 .. **Pruszynski,** Stanley J '82 %Hlth & Hsptl Corp -160 Water -NY 10038
(212) 508-6700 .. **Prutzman,** L Donald '77 (Tannenbaum HS&H LLP) -900 3rd Av -NY 10022
(212) 468-8000 .. **Prutzman,** Sarah L '10 %Morrison & F LLP -1290 Av of Amer -NY 10104
(914) 231-1102 .. **Pruyne,** Justin D '02 Cnty Corrections Dept -10 Woods Rd Bx389 -Valhalla 10595
(212) 458-3893 .. **Pruzan,** Helaine A '02 -175 Water -NY 10038
(914) 378-1010 .. **Pruzan,** Mark S '89 Fitzgerald & F -538 Riverdale Av -Ynkrs 10705
(212) 967-3399 .. **Pruzan,** Peter J '76 -48 Wall -NY 10005 **Fx:**268-0287
(718) 875-1245 .. **Pruzan,** Thos B '85 (Pruzan Law Firm) -111 Lvngstn -Brklyn 11201 **Fx:**797-9087
(212) 997-4400 .. **Pruzan-Gaynor,** Lauren M '93 %Teitler & T,LLP -1114 Av of Amer -NY 10036 **Fx:**997-4949
(212) 310-8000 .. **Pruzansky,** Jason E '08 %Weil G&M LLP -767 5th Av -NY 10153
(631) 234-8585 .. **Pruzansky,** Joshua M '65 -1 Suffolk Sq -Islandia 11749 **Fx:**234-8702
(718) 742-0066 .. **Pruzansky,** Lawr M '81 -860 Grnd Cncrs -Bronx 10451 **Fx:**742-4994
(718) 742-0066 .. **Pruzansky,** Steven '82 -860 Grnd Cncrs -Bronx 10451
(718) 742-6066 .. **Pruzansky,** Wallace '61 -860 Grnd Cncrs -Bronx 10451 **Fx:**742-4994
(212) 669-0600 .. **Pruzinsky,** Anthony J '79 (Hill R LLP) -45 Bway -NY 10006
(212) 719-8364 .. **Pryba,** Bradley M '07 NYS SCPA -3 Park Av -NY 10016
(212) 816-6113 .. **Prybutok,** Mark D '02 Citigroup Invstmnts -388 Greenwich -NY 10013
(212) 809-7800 .. **Pryjma,** Jung F '03 %Jaffe & K,LLP -40 Wall -NY 10005
(718) 894-0297 .. **Pryor,** Barbara '83 -65-49 Grand Av -Maspeth 11378
(212) 421-4100 .. **Pryor Cashman LLP** -7 Times Sq -NY 10036 **Fx:**326-0806
(718) 829-0222 .. **Pryor,** Edmond J '90 -1925 Wllmsbrdg Rd -Bronx 10461 **Fx:**829-0032
(212) 819-8200 .. **Pryor,** Gregory '89 (White & C LLP) -1155 Av of Amer -NY 10036
(516) 741-8100 .. **Pryor,** Kenneth A '94 (K Pryor,LLC) -250 Mineola Blvd -Mineola 11501
(212) 872-1110 .. **Pryor,** Lindsey S '82 %Wm AM Burden & Co -10 E 53rd -NY 10022 **Fx:**872-1149
(516) 997-0999 .. **Pryor & Mandelup,LLP** -675 Old Cntry Rd -Westbury 11590 **Fx:**333-7333
(516) 997-0999 .. **Pryor,** Robt L '82 (Pryor & M,LLP) -675 Old Cntry Rd -Westbury 11590
(212) 450-4000 .. **Pryor,** Saml F III '58 SrCnsl Davis P&W LLP -450 Lex Av -NY 10017
(212) 396-3134 .. **Pryor,** Saml F IV '87 %BRP LLC -130 E 67th -NY 10065
(212) 227-7150 .. **Pryor,** Wm B '75 -277 Bway -NY 10007 **Fx:**385-4779
(212) 836-8000 .. **Prystowsky,** Margaret A '09 %Kaye S LLP -425 Park Av -NY 10022
(212) 964-6611 .. **Prystowsky,** Steven B '68 (Lester SK&D) -120 Bway -NY 10271
(516) 496-5822 .. **Przebowski,** Evan '02 %T Spina -170 Froehlich Farm Blvd -Woodbury 11797 **Fx:**496-5420
(212) 408-5100 .. **Przybylko,** Eric J '97 %Chadbourne & P LLP -30 Rckfllr Plz -NY 10112
(914) 777-1134 .. **Przybylo,** Carolyn J '06 %Ingerman S LLP -550 Mamaroneck Av -Harrison 10528
(212) 436-1140 .. **Przybylo,** Kim A '91 IRS -290 Bway -NY 10007
(212) 596-9000 .. **Przygoda,** David J '05 %Ropes & G LLP -1211 Av of Amer -NY 10036
(585) 755-1515 .. **Przysinda,** Richd S Jr. '09 -Bx425 -Mendon 14506
(718) 956-8968 .. **Psaros,** Michl '89 -29-15 Ditmars Blvd -Astoria 11105
(212) 859-8000 .. **Psathas,** Michl R '10 %Fried FHS&J LLP -1 NY Plz -NY 10004
(631) 435-0330 .. **Pshedesky,** Edw '77 -1363 Vets Hwy -Hauppauge 11788
(212) 225-2000 .. **Psiachos,** Panayiotis '06 %Cleary GS&H -1 Lbrty Plz -NY 10006
(516) 572-2376 .. **Psoinas,** Laura Ann '90 %Dist Ct -99 Main -Hempstd 11550
(518) 233-2444 .. **Psutka,** Stephen J '90 GE Advanced Materials -260 Hudson Rvr Rd -Waterfrd 12188
(845) 373-8453 .. **Psychoyos,** Wm S '89 -Bx464 -Wassaic 12592 **Fx:**373-8453
(718) 225-5416 .. **Psyllos,** Michl P '94 -213-35 40th Av -Bayside 11361
(212) 308-4411 .. **Ptak,** Saree R '83 Cnsl Edwards AP&D LLP -750 Lex Av -NY 10022
(212) 825-1565 .. **Ptashnik,** Neil B '87 (Ptashnik & Assoc) -45 Bway -NY 10006 **Fx:**825-1559
(914) 949-9075 .. **Ptasiewicz,** Seth '90 %Trivella & F LLP -1311 Mamaroneck Av -White Plns 10605 **Fx:**949-4752
(646) 386-5700 .. **Ptucha,** Paul W '76 %Civil Ct -111 Centre -NY 10013
(212) 632-6637 .. **Puccio,** Richd L '99 %Lazard Freres -30 Rckfllr Plz -NY 10112 **Fx:**632-6060
(516) 393-2200 .. **Puccio,** Salvatore '05 %Garfunkel W,PC -111 Grt Nck Rd -Gt Neck 11021
(212) 883-6383 .. **Puccio,** Thos P '69 -230 Park Av -NY 10169 **Fx:**883-6388
(212) 632-6000 .. **Puchala,** Alfred J Jr. '90 %Lazard Freres -30 Rckfllr Plz -NY 10112 **Fx:**632-6060
(212) 422-1200 .. **Puchalsky,** Gabrielle '06 %Abrams GF&J,PC -1 Bttry Pk Plz -NY 10004
(518) 487-7600 .. **Puchner,** Thos F '05 %Whiteman O&H LLP -1 Commerce Plz -Albany 12260
(845) 527-3432 .. **Pucino,** Lynn A '88 -45 Wellesley Pl -Fishkill 12524
(718) 250-2000 .. **Puckhaber,** Kerry J '95 %DA -350 Jay -Brklyn 11201 **Fx:**250-2314
(516) 796-4500 .. **Pudalov,** Grant S '89 (G Pudalov,PC) -3601 Hempstd Tpke -Levittwn 11756 **Fx:**796-4556
(212) 298-5082 .. **Pudberry,** Gene W '77 %Leg Aid -49 Thomas -NY 10013 **Fx:**298-5252
(631) 390-2055 .. **Pudell,** Stuart L '99 S Pudell,PC -Plainvw 11803 **Fx:**504-5490
(914) 666-2151 .. **Puder,** Susan '89 -20 Turner Dr -Chappaqua 10514
(516) 671-2577 .. **Puderbach,** John W '75 -Bx404 -Locust Vly 11560 **Fx:**671-4419
(516) 832-7547 .. **Puerta,** Edw A '09 %Nixon P LLP -50 Jericho Quadrangle -Jericho 11753
(914) 995-3000 .. **Puerto,** Amy S '01 %DA -111 Martin Luther King Blvd -White Plns 10601 **Fx:**995-3363
(516) 248-6960 .. **Pugach,** Jody C '84 -1055 Franklin Av -Gdn Cty 11530 **Fx:**742-8173
(212) 227-7465 .. **Pugacz,** Diane J '92 %HDC -110 William -NY 10038 **Fx:**227-6865
(516) 747-2440 .. **Pugatch,** Leonard J '77 (Pugatch & N) -1205 Franklin Av -Gdn Cty 11530
(516) 747-2440 .. **Pugatch & Nikolis** -1205 Franklin Av -Gdn Cty 11530 **Fx:**746-4733
Pugh, George E '69 -290 9th Av -NY 10001
(516) 572-2385 .. **Pugh,** Kathleen R '96 %Dist Ct -99 Main -Hempstd 11550
(212) 834-4525 .. **Puglia,** Karen A '04 JP Morgan Chase -270 Park Av -NY 10017
(845) 561-0550 .. **Puglielle,** Ralph L Jr. '99 Cnsl Drake LHKGG&R PLLC -555 Hudson Valley Av -New Windsor 12553
(516) 248-6777 .. **Pugliese,** Corey J '08 %Purcell & I,PC -204 Willis Av -Mineola 11501
(212) 318-6000 .. **Pugliese,** Domenick '86 (Paul HJ&W LLP) -75 E 55th -NY 10022
(212) 547-5400 .. **Pugliese,** Donald R '01 %McDermott W&E LLP -340 Mad Av -NY 10173
(718) 855-9000 .. **Pugliese,** Elisa M '79 %Cullen and D LLP -177 Montague -Brklyn 11201
(212) 589-4200 .. **Pugliese,** Frank A '92 (Baker & H LLP) -45 Rckfllr Plz -NY 10111
(516) 409-6565 .. **Pugliese,** Louis M '03 %J Bigler -1421 Wantagh Av -Wantagh 11793 **Fx:**409-6522
(518) 455-2015 .. **Pugliese,** Melissa H '96 NYS Sen J Alesi -905 LOB -Albany 12247 **Fx:**426-6968
(212) 596-9000 .. **Pugliese,** Rachel L '09 %Ropes & G LLP -1211 Av of Amer -NY 10036
(212) 514-5390 .. **Pugliese,** Steven F '74 -11 Bway -NY 10004 **Fx:**480-8560
(315) 798-5742 .. **Pugliese,** Tracy Lee '94 %Dept Soc Srvcs -800 Park Av -Utica 13501
(516) 496-5822 .. **Puglisi,** Andrew C '03 %T Spina -170 Froehlich Farm Blvd -Woodbury 11797 **Fx:**496-5420
(212) 268-2128 .. **Puglisi,** Concetta '90 (Fagenson & P) -450 7th Av -NY 10123
(212) 973-8000 .. **Puhala,** Kenneth R '89 (Schnader HS&L LLP) -140 Bway -NY 10005
(845) 242-3542 .. **Puig,** Kenneth '98 -Bx4796 -Poughkeepsie 12602
(718) 220-4892 .. **Pujara,** Munir '00 POTS -2763 Webster Av -Bronx 10458
(212) 259-8000 .. **Puk,** Peter T '09 %Dewey & L LLP -1301 Av of Amer -NY 10019
(516) 572-2000 .. **Pulaski,** Ania M '09 %DA -99 Main -Hempstd 11550 **Fx:**572-2606
(212) 373-3000 .. **Pulaski-Kelly,** Marta '00 %Paul WRW&G LLP -1285 Av of Amer -NY 10019
(631) 852-1761 .. **Pulcrano,** James J '83 %Supreme Ct -Center Dr S -Rvrhead 11901 **Fx:**852-2020
(212) 227-2555 .. **Puleo,** Andreea S '02 -321 Bway -NY 10007 **Fx:**571-4309
(716) 823-2558 .. **Puleo,** Dean S '03 -674 Ridge Rd -Lackawanna 14218 **Fx:**822-0009
(212) 732-3320 .. **Puleo,** Mark A '76 %Short & B,PC -217 Bway -NY 10007
(315) 724-6108 .. **Puleo,** Onofrio J '73 -329 Genesee -Utica 13501 **Fx:**724-6109
(631) 648-1358 .. **Puleo,** Peter M '87 (Puleo D,LLC) -444 Route 111 -Smithtwn 11787 **Fx:**648-1458
(716) 836-7111 .. **Puleo,** Saml G '84 S Puleo -3659 Harlem Rd -Cheektowaga 14215 **Fx:**836-0219
(716) 836-7111 .. **Puleo,** Saml P '04 S Puleo -3659 Harlem Rd -Cheektowaga 14215 **Fx:**836-0219
(518) 862-7300 .. **Puleo,** Theresa J '91 Cnsl T Puleo -900 Watervliet Shaker Rd Bx12699 -Albany 12212 **Fx:**862-7322
(315) 424-7209 .. **Puleo,** Theresa J '91 Cnsl T Puleo -441 S Salina -Syracuse 13202 **Fx:**424-5553
(845) 369-4580 .. **Puletz,** Matthew G '88 Dress Barn,Inc -30 Dunnigan Dr -Suffern 10901
(212) 225-2000 .. **Pulido,** Claudette A '07 %Cleary GS&H -1 Lbrty Plz -NY 10006
(914) 640-8118 .. **Pulito,** Tracy A '01 %Starwood Hotels & Resorts -1111 Wstchstr Av -White Plns 10604 **Fx:**640-8250

(914) 941-5668 .. **Pulitzer,** Douglas S '92 OfCnsl Collen IP -80 S Highland Av -Ossining 10562 **Fx:**941-6091
(718) 643-5425 .. **Pulizotto,** Michl J '98 Supreme Ct-Kings Cnty -120 Schermerhorn -Brklyn 11201 **Fx:**643-3813
(212) 476-5675 .. **Pullano,** Anthony A '87 %Neuberger Berman,LLC -605 3rd Av -NY 10158
(585) 232-6500 .. **Pullano,** Patrick '96 Cnsl Harter S&E LLP -1600 Bausch & Lomb Pl -Rchstr 14604
(585) 546-1090 .. **Pullano,** Peter J '87 -1 E Main -Rchstr 14614 **Fx:**262-2610
(585) 546-1090 .. **Pullano,** T Alexandra '89 -1 E Main -Rchstr 14614 **Fx:**262-2610
(631) 439-4200 .. **Pullara,** Salvatore V '88 %R Tusa -898 Vets Mem'l Hwy -Hauppauge 11788 **Fx:**439-4292
(585) 567-2222 .. **Pullen,** David T '76 (Richardson & P,PC) -21 Minard Bx182 -Fillmore 14735
(518) 761-6161 .. **Pullen,** Jane B '96 -58 Farr Ln -Queensbury 12804 **Fx:**761-6177
(914) 632-2262 .. **Pulley,** Arthur L '55 -381 5th Av -New Rchll 10801
(212) 408-5100 .. **Pulley,** J Carson '06 %Chadbourne & P LLP -30 Rckfllr Plz -NY 10112
(212) 450-4000 .. **Pulliam,** Joel A '09 %Davis P&W LLP -450 Lex Av -NY 10017
(516) 364-7500 .. **Pullin,** Allan L '74 (Weber & P,LLP) -7600 Jericho Tpk -Woodbury 11797
(718) 621-1446 .. **Pullini,** Lisa M '95 %Pullini Realty Corp -1406 W 3rd -Brklyn 11204
(212) 331-3015 .. **Pullio,** Robyn N '05 Dept of Invstgtn -180 Water -NY 10038 **Fx:**331-3060
(212) 536-3900 .. **Pullman,** Andrew B '83 (K&L Gates LLP) -599 Lex Av -NY 10022
(914) 682-6895 .. **Pullman & Comley, LLC** -50 Main -White Plns 10606 **Fx:**682-6894
(716) 856-5500 .. **Pullman,** Gust P '83 (Damon M LLP) -200 Delaware Av -Buffalo 14202
(212) 245-1000 .. **Pullman,** Sandra E '09 %Outten & G LLP -3 Park Av -NY 10016
(212) 839-9292 .. **Pullo,** Vincent '01 %Dept of Transportation -55 Water -NY 10041
(607) 324-7333 .. **Pulos,** Wm W '82 (Pulos & R,LLP) -70 Main Bx337 -Hornell 14843 **Fx:**324-1668
(518) 587-9105 .. **Pulsifer,** Robt W '92 -562 Maple Av Bx878 -Saratoga Spgs 12866 **Fx:**581-1003
(212) 610-6300 .. **Pultman,** Jacob S '91 (Allen & O) -1221 Av of Amer -NY 10020
(212) 763-5000 .. **Pulver,** Adam R '09 %Emery CB&A LLP -75 Rckfllr Plz -NY 10019
(914) 286-3400 .. **Pulver,** Sheralyn '85 %Leg Aid -1 N Bway -White Plns 10601 **Fx:**682-4112
(212) 689-6299 .. **Pulver,** Valerie '86 -120 E 34th -NY 10016
(212) 355-8000 .. **Pulvers,** Marvin '56 (Pulvers P&T,LLP) -110 E 59th -NY 10022
(212) 355-8000 .. **Pulvers,** Patrice M '86 (Pulvers P&T,LLP) -110 E 59th -NY 10022
(212) 355-8000 .. **Pulvers Pulvers & Thompson, LLP** -110 E 59th -NY 10022 **Fx:**355-9000
(212) 884-2149 .. **Pulvirenti,** Salvatore '02 %NY & CO -450 W 33rd -NY 10001 **Fx:**884-2965
(718) 597-3200 .. **Puma,** Anthony J '61 -2930 Wstchstr Av -Bronx 10461 **Fx:**931-7181
(516) 683-1717 .. **Puma,** Marie Elena R '92 (V Russo & Assoc,PC) -1600 Stewart Av -Westbury 11590 **Fx:**683-9393
(631) 582-1919 .. **Puma,** Marie Elena R '92 (V Russo & Assoc,PC) -3740 Expwy Dr S -Islandia 11749 **Fx:**582-8484
(212) 310-8000 .. **Pumputis,** Ausra O '09 %Weil G&M LLP -767 5th Av -NY 10153
(212) 966-6730 .. **Pun,** Siuling '02 S Pun,PC -55-59 Chrystie -NY 10002
(212) 761-6023 .. **Punnoose,** Joyce Babu '05 Morgan Stanley -1585 Bway -NY 10036
(212) 416-8211 .. **Punturo,** Jos J '92 %Dept of Law -120 Bway -NY 10271
(212) 702-5649 .. **Puntus,** Marc D '94 %Oresdner Kleinwort Wasserstein,Inc -1301 Av of Amer -NY 10019 **Fx:**969-2705
(212) 218-2100 .. **Puppa,** Thos J '95 %Fitzpatrick CH&S -1290 Av of Amer -NY 10104
(718) 250-2000 .. **Purce,** Edw J '99 %DA -350 Jay -Brklyn 11201 **Fx:**250-2314
(631) 751-5757 .. **Purcell,** A Craig '72 (Glynn M&P,LLP) -57 North Cntry Rd Bx712 -Stony Brk 11790
(212) 455-2000 .. **Purcell,** Andrew B '09 %Simpson T&B LLP -425 Lex Av -NY 10017
(212) 883-1300 .. **Purcell,** Arthur K '91 (Sandler T&R,PA) -551 5th Av -NY 10176
(212) 841-1000 .. **Purcell,** Charlotte Brooke '08 %Covington & B LLP -620 8th Av -NY 10018
(631) 231-1344 .. **Purcell,** Christopher J '92 (C Purcell,PC) -35 Arkay Dr -Hauppauge 11788
(585) 454-0700 .. **Purcell,** Danl P '94 (Ward GH&R LLP) -300 State -Rchstr 14614
(212) 431-2856 .. **Purcell,** Edw A Jr. '80 %NY Law Schl -185 W Bway -NY 10013 **Fx:**431-1864
(516) 248-6777 .. **Purcell & Ingrao,PC** -204 Willis Av -Mineola 11501 **Fx:**248-2897
(518) 434-4553 .. **Purcell,** Kevin '82 %Justice Dept -74 Chapel -Albany 12207 **Fx:**434-4459
(585) 295-5820 .. **Purcell,** Kevin M '06 Hon M Telesca -1 W Main -Rchstr 14614
(585) 419-8800 .. **Purcell,** Laura M '94 (Harris B PLLC) -99 Garnsey Rd -Pittsfrd 14534
(585) 232-6500 .. **Purcell,** Matthew D '09 %Harter S&E LLP -1600 Bausch & Lomb Pl -Rchstr 14604
(516) 248-6777 .. **Purcell,** Patrick J '56 (Purcell & I,PC) -204 Willis Av -Mineola 11501
(315) 671-0707 .. **Purcell,** Robt E '79 RE Purcell,PLLC -211 W Jffrsn -Syracuse 13202
(212) 318-2000 .. **Purcell,** Sharon N '04 Bloomberg LP -731 Lex Av -NY 10022
(212) 873-1701 .. **Purcell,** Thos R '60 -263 W 90th -NY 10024 **Fx:**385-0220
(212) 812-8910 .. **Purcell,** Wm O '71 OfCnsl Lankler & C,LLP -845 3rd Av -NY 10022
(718) 735-4747 .. **Purcell-Regis,** Debra Ann '95 -1169 Nostrand Av -Brklyn 11225
(631) 234-1600 .. **Purcell-Smith,** Carolyn J '91 -1737 Vets Hwy -Islandia 11749
(212) 964-9640 .. **Purcigliotti,** Robt A '66 (Cascione P&G,PC) -20 Vesey -NY 10007
(518) 743-0455 .. **Purdue,** Marsha K '89 (MK Purdue) -5 Sagamore -Glens Fls 12801 **Fx:**743-1827
(212) 489-8104 .. **Purdy,** James A '94 (Vittoria & P) -1 Rckfllr Plz -NY 10020
(212) 415-8600 .. **Purdy,** Steven M '06 %Locke LB&L LLP -3 World Fncl Ctr -NY 10281
(516) 829-0363 .. **Purdy,** Wm M '91 (Israel I&P,LLP) -11 Grace Av -Gt Neck 11021 **Fx:**829-0366
(914) 666-2328 .. **Pure,** Saml W '77 -23 Bretton Ridge Rd -Mt Kisco 10549
(212) 906-1200 .. **Puri,** Vanita Soni '06 %Latham & W -885 3rd Av -NY 10022
(516) 621-0222 .. **Purificato,** Vincenzo '08 GosmanLaw PC -55 Bryant Av -Roslyn 11576 **Fx:**621-3322
(212) 621-6000 .. **Purin,** Melissa '00 Cnsl ASCAP -1 Lincoln Plz -NY 10023 **Fx:**787-1381
(212) 479-6000 .. **Purintun,** Ann-Elizabeth '83 %Cooley LLP -1114 Av of Amer -NY 10036
(607) 287-2839 .. **Puritz,** Andrew M '79 -697 Winney Hill Rd -Oneonta 13820
(716) 883-0500 .. **Purizhansky,** Jon E '99 -420 Franklin -Buffalo 14202
(917) 778-6500 .. **Purohit,** Arvind '03 %K Dodson -485 Lex Av -NY 10017
(212) 251-5584 .. **Purohit,** Tara '87 %Towers Watson -875 3rd Av -NY 10022
(212) 616-4125 .. **Purow,** Jonathan M '09 Grand Army Entertainment,LLC -154 W 14th -NY 10011 **Fx:**242-8913
(212) 943-5757 .. **Purrington & McConnell** -82 Wall -NY 10005 **Fx:**(203) 762-8888
(212) 431-7129 .. **Purrington Moody Weil LLP** -320 W 13th -NY 10014 **Fx:**431-7124
(518) 447-5532 .. **Purrott,** Andrew M '04 %Cnty Alternate Pub Def -112 State -Albany 12207
(607) 753-0865 .. **Purser,** Edw R '63 -4 Lincoln Av Bx425 -Cortlnd 13045 **Fx:**753-0831
(516) 832-7542 .. **Pursley,** Denise D '89 (Nixon P LLP) -50 Jericho Quadrangle -Jericho 11753
(716) 858-2200 .. **Purtell,** Jeannine M '06 %Cnty Atty -95 Franklin -Buffalo 14202 **Fx:**858-2281
(212) 836-2600 .. **Purtell,** Lawr R '73 ALCOA,Inc -390 Park Av -NY 10022
(212) 725-4749 .. **Purup,** Signe B '07 Humanscale Corp -11 E 26th -NY 10010
(212) 455-2000 .. **Purushotham,** Ravi '10 %Simpson T&B LLP -425 Lex Av -NY 10017
(914) 834-0100 .. **Purves,** Edmund S '58 (Clifford & P) -1890 Palmer Av -Larchmnt 10538
(347) 406-1673 .. **Purvis,** Janice P '03 %Supreme Ct Law Dept -360 Adams -Brklyn 11201 **Fx:**643-6114
(212) 667-1477 .. **Purvis,** Kathryn A '99 Nomura Global Financial Products Inc -2 World Fncl Ctr -NY 10281
(516) 222-1188 .. **Purzak,** Robt '82 -600 Old Cntry Rd -Gdn Cty 11530 **Fx:**228-4278
(585) 987-2800 .. **Pusateri,** Christopher T '04 %Woods OG LLP -2 State -Rchstr 14614
(716) 434-9131 .. **Pusateri & Fitzgerald,LLP** -135 Main Bx850 -Lockprt 14095
(516) 248-1200 .. **Pusateri,** Jos F '89 Mulholland M&R -374 Hillside Av -Williston Pk 11596
(716) 434-9131 .. **Pusateri,** Robt M '70 (Pusateri & F,LLP) -135 Main Bx850 -Lockprt 14095
(716) 873-6765 .. **Pusatier Sherman & Abbott** -2464 Elmwood Av -Kenmore 14217 **Fx:**873-7709
(716) 873-6765 .. **Pusatier,** Stephen F '72 (Pusatier S&A) -2464 Elmwood Av -Kenmore 14217
(212) 980-0408 .. **Pusch,** Brian W '80 (Pusch & G) -31 W 31st -NY 10001 **Fx:**980-7055
(585) 263-6760 .. **Puscheck,** Bret A '89 US Atty -620 Fed Bldg -Rchstr 14614 **Fx:**263-6226
(212) 762-6367 .. **Pusey,** Kiernan W '02 Morgan Stanley -1221 Av of Amer -NY 10020
(212) 373-3000 .. **Pusey,** Nathan R '03 %Paul WRW&G LLP -1285 Av of Amer -NY 10019
(518) 486-2921 .. **Pushkarsh,** Christopher M '91 %OPRHP -Agncy Bldg 1 ESP -Albany 12238 **Fx:**474-5106
(212) 697-6555 .. **Pustel,** Helen B '08 %Biedermann RH&R -570 Lex Av -NY 10022
(212) 788-7015 .. **Pustilnik,** Alix S '95 %City Cncl Leg Div -250 Bway -NY 10007 **Fx:**341-0363
(212) 455-2000 .. **Putek,** Christine O'Grady '06 %Simpson T&B LLP -425 Lex Av -NY 10017
(212) 449-1000 .. **Putetti,** Michl A '97 Merrill Lynch -220 Bway -NY 10038
(212) 681-6500 .. **Puthiyamadam,** Allie '09 %Stempel BC&H,PC -675 3rd Av -NY 10017
(516) 933-1515 .. **Puthuparampil,** Janet J '98 (Santucci & W) -366 N Bway -Jericho 11753
(718) 875-1300 .. **Putignano,** Pasquale P '99 %Appllt Div 2nd Dept -45 Monroe Pl -Brklyn 11201 **Fx:**858-2446
(518) 234-7770 .. **Putnam,** Douglas V '86 -Bx300 -Warnerville 12187
(518) 471-4839 .. **Putnam,** Erica L '07 %Appllt Div 3rd Dept -Capitol Station Bx7288 -Albany 12224 **Fx:**471-4750
(212) 446-4914 .. **Putnam,** Jonathan F '94 (Kirkland & E LLP) -153 E 53rd -NY 10022
(212) 687-3000 .. **Putnam,** Jos R '09 %Jaffe & A,LLP -600 3rd Av -NY 10016
(212) 553-4736 .. **Putney,** Abraham B '05 %Moody's Invstr Srvc -250 Greenwich -NY 10007
(585) 658-2832 .. **Putney,** John C '82 -63 Main Bx307 -Mt Morris 14510 **Fx:**658-4098
(310) 277-7504 .. **Putney,** Laura Lea '97 SrCnsl Kauff M&M LLP -950 3rd Av -NY 10022 **Fx:**861-1385
(212) 682-0020 .. **Putney Twombly Hall & Hirson LLP** -521 5th Av -NY 10175 **Fx:**682-9380
(518) 402-9184 .. **Putnick,** Dena N '05 DEC -625 Bway -Albany 12233 **Fx:**402-9018
(518) 382-1044 .. **Putorti,** Frank M Jr. '77 -1338 Union -Schnctdy 12308 **Fx:**372-3686
(607) 754-1625 .. **Putrino,** Chas R '55 -3571 Smith Dr -Endwell 13760 **Fx:**754-1626
(716) 851-5333 .. **Putrino,** Christopher M '00 %Fire Dept -195 Court -Buffalo 14202
(212) 735-3000 .. **Putter,** Jason '07 %Skadden ASM&F LLP -4 Times Sq -NY 10036
(315) 337-8800 .. **Putter,** Michl G '76 -8703 Turin Rd Bx509 -Rome 13442 **Fx:**337-3334
(212) 319-0510 .. **Putterman,** Arnold L '64 (Putterman & P) -120 E 56th -NY 10022 **Fx:**750-1324
(201) 845-5400 .. **Putterman,** Bruce S '91 -6 Wooster -NY 10013 **Fx:**845-8084
(347) 592-2200 .. **Putterman,** Rachel A '95 %Leg Srvcs -89-00 Sutphin Blvd -Jamaica 11435 **Fx:**(718) 937-5350
(212) 661-0066 .. **Putzel,** Henry III '69 -565 5th Av -NY 10017 **Fx:**661-0415
(315) 458-3331 .. **Putzer,** Carl T '76 %Bertrand AW&P -107 S Main Bx277 -N Syracuse 13212
(212) 653-8700 .. **Puvalowski,** Kevin R '95 (Sheppard MR&H LLP) -30 Rckfllr Plz -NY 10112
(646) 701-4680 .. **Puygrenier,** Nicolas T O '07 (Puygrenier & L LLP) -1699 Lex Av -NY 10029 **Fx:**(800) 616-0253
(212) 335-9000 .. **Puzio,** Vanessa E '03 %DA -1 Hogan Pl -NY 10013
(631) 859-0300 .. **Puzo,** Jos M '92 (Zaklukiewicz P&M,LLP) -2701 Sunrise Hwy Bx389 -Islip Terr 11752
(212) 349-6009 .. **Pyati,** Archana P '03 %Sanctuary for Families -110 Wall -NY 10005 **Fx:**566-0344
(718) 692-2225 .. **Pye,** Loretta A '89 %Guardian Tax -1501 Av J -Brklyn 11230 **Fx:**377-6474
(212) 223-4000 .. **Pyenson,** Arlen E '10 %Crowell & M LLP -590 Mad Av -NY 10022
(212) 310-8000 .. **Pyle,** Bronwen R '09 %Weil G&M LLP -767 5th Av -NY 10153
(716) 841-2774 .. **Pyle,** Pamela J '88 %HSBC Bank -1 HSBC Ctr -Buffalo 14203 **Fx:**841-5087

(212) 486-1455 .. **Pyle,** Thos J Jr. '97 %Post PGM&S,PA -575 Mad Av -NY 10022
(315) 425-2700 .. **Pylman,** Jos P '09 %Hiscock & B,LLP -One Park Pl -Syracuse 13202
(212) 269-5500 .. **Pymm,** Jennifer '98 SrCnsl Gordon & R LLP -90 Broad -NY 10004
(716) 438-2636 .. **Pynn,** Matthew P '94 (M Pynn,PC) -272 East Av -Lockprt 14094 **Fx:**478-0070
(716) 873-2900 .. **Pyrak,** Theo J '56 -633-635 Hertel Av -Buffalo 14207 **Fx:**873-2431
(718) 626-7730 .. **Pyrros,** Michl C '99 (Pyrros & S LLP) -31-01 Bway -LIC 11106
(718) 626-7730 .. **Pyrros & Serres LLP** -31-01 Bway -LIC 11106 **Fx:**626-6506
(716) 649-6700 .. **Pysz,** Michl '83 (Abbott T&K,LLP) -44 Union -Hambrg 14075
(212) 858-1000 .. **Pyun,** Cynthia S Y '04 %Pillsbury WSP LLP -1540 Bway -NY 10036
(212) 709-8171 .. **Pyun,** David M '03 -110 Wall -NY 10005
(516) 742-7777 .. **Pyun,** James H '93 (Frazer & F,LLP) -1415 Kellum Pl -Gdn Cty 11530
(718) 250-3315 .. **Qamer,** Syed F '05 %DA -350 Jay -Brklyn 11201 **Fx:**250-2314
(212) 292-4978 .. **Qayyum,** Ayesha '00 -2 Penn Plz -NY 10121
(212) 259-8000 .. **Qi,** Fang '08 %Dewey & L LLP -1301 Av of Amer -NY 10019
(212) 661-1100 .. **Qian,** Fei-Lu '04 %Pomerantz HG&G LLP -100 Park Av -NY 10017
(212) 267-2555 .. **Qiu,** Huiyue '03 %Bretz & C,LLP -305 Bway -NY 10007
(212) 839-5300 .. **Qiu,** Xiaowen '01 (Sidley A LLP) -787 7th Av -NY 10019
(718) 984-5151 .. **Quaadman,** Thos '92 %NYC Council -3944 Richmond Av -Staten Isl 10312
(212) 909-6000 .. **Quach,** Anne-Lise '09 %Debevoise & P LLP -919 3rd Av -NY 10022
(212) 530-1800 .. **Quach,** Gianna Canh Ty '01 %Richards K&O LLP -1 World Fncl Ctr -NY 10281
(732) 855-5157 .. **Quackenbos,** Barbara G '90 (Wilentz G&S) -110 William -NY 10038 **Fx:**726-6544
(212) 735-3000 .. **Quackenbos,** Ellen Payne '92 Cnsl Skadden ASM&F LLP -4 Times Sq -NY 10036
(212) 309-1000 .. **Quackenboss,** Robt T Jr. '94 (Hunton & W) -200 Park Av -NY 10166
(609) 987-3994 .. **Quackenboss,** Wm E Jr. '04 %Smith SWH&B,LLP -100 Park Av -NY 10017
(716) 855-5710 .. **Quackenbush,** John J Jr. '73 -60 Lakefront Blvd -Buffalo 14202 **Fx:**855-5722
(516) 745-1122 .. **Quadrino,** Richd J '86 (Quadrino & S,PC) -666 Old Cntry Rd -Gdn Cty 11530
(516) 745-1122 .. **Quadrino & Schwartz,PC** -666 Old Cntry Rd -Gdn Cty 11530 **Fx:**745-0844
(212) 425-8235 .. **Quaglia,** Gayle F '86 -61 Bway -NY 10006 **Fx:**425-8244
(914) 736-9700 .. **Quagliato,** Fred C '85 -1831 Carhart Av -Peekskill 10566 **Fx:**737-2724
(516) 922-8242 .. **Quaid,** Rachel '87 OfCnsl Mulholland & K,LLP -28 Highwood Rd -E Norwich 11732 **Fx:**922-6325
(516) 822-1600 .. **Quaid,** Warren W '87 %Russo & P -16 E Old Cntry Rd -Hicksvll 11801
(212) 552-7814 .. **Quaife,** Nancy Jean '79 JP Morgan Chase -1 Chase Manh Plz -NY 10081
(212) 909-6000 .. **Quaintance,** Robt F Jr. '81 (Debevoise & P LLP) -919 3rd Av -NY 10022
(212) 839-5300 .. **Quale,** Andrew C Jr. '71 (Sidley A LLP) -787 7th Av -NY 10019
(212) 788-9475 .. **Qualliotine,** Tracey M '02 %City Cncl Leg Div -250 Bway -NY 10007 **Fx:**788-7034
(212) 940-3106 .. **Qually,** Elizabeth A '08 %Nixon P LLP -437 Mad Av -NY 10022
(212) 909-6000 .. **Quan,** Hongxia '10 %Debevoise & P LLP -919 3rd Av -NY 10022
(212) 608-4508 .. **Quan,** Peter L '08 -43 E Bway -NY 10002 **Fx:**608-4372
(718) 961-3236 .. **Quan,** Richd '82 -3370 Prince -Flushng 11354 **Fx:**(212) 219-8497
(718) 923-4236 .. **Quan,** Yuklan '91 %OTDA Fair Hearings -14 Boerum Pl -Brklyn 11201
(212) 688-8555 .. **Quane,** Patrick J '72 (Fragomen DB&L LLP) -7 Hanover Sq -NY 10004
(914) 995-4361 .. **Quaranta,** Christopher A '96 Hon O Bellantoni -111 Martin Luther King Blvd -White Plns 10601
(718) 402-4448 .. **Quaranta,** Kevin J '82 (Quaranta & Assoc) -888 Grnd Cncrs -Bronx 10451
(914) 244-0029 .. **Quaranta,** Kevin J '82 (Quaranta & Assoc) -121 Smith Av -Mt Kisco 10549 **Fx:**244-0031
(212) 490-3000 .. **Quaranta,** Philip '86 (Wilson EME&D LLP) -150 E 42nd -NY 10017
(914) 323-7000 .. **Quaranta,** Philip '86 (Wilson EME&D LLP) -3 Gannett Dr -White Plns 10604
(716) 285-3475 .. **Quarantillo,** Mark A '93 (Quarantillo & T) -625 6th -Niagara Fls 14301 **Fx:**285-8162
(212) 805-0200 .. **Quarcoo,** Stephen C '08 Hon D Chin -500 Pearl -NY 10007
(607) 778-2423 .. **Quaresimo,** Kristen M '10 DA -45 Hawley Bx1766 -Bnghmtn 13902 **Fx:**778-8870
(212) 455-2000 .. **Quarfordt,** Erik G '02 %Simpson T&B LLP -425 Lex Av -NY 10017
(917) 368-8230 .. **Quarles,** Denise L '91 (Quarles & Assoc,PC) -405 Lex Av -NY 10174 **Fx:**368-8234
(212) 849-7000 .. **Quarmby,** Benoit '05 %Quinn EU&S,LLP -51 Mad Av -NY 10010
(518) 473-3233 .. **Quarrier,** Jean Orzech '78 %Dept of Health -Corning Twr 24th Fl -Albany 12237 **Fx:**473-2019
(914) 470-0001 .. **Quart,** Dan '98 (Babchik & Y,LLP) -200 E Post Rd -White Plns 10601
(845) 471-4440 .. **Quartararo,** Anthony M '59 OfCnsl Quartararo & L PLLC -1399 Route 52 -Fishkill 12524 **Fx:**471-7318
(845) 471-4440 .. **Quartararo,** Jack M '58 OfCnsl Quartararo & L PLLC -1399 Route 52 -Fishkill 12524 **Fx:**471-7318
(631) 727-2180 .. **Quartararo,** Jay P '94 (Twomey LSKD&Q,LLP) -33 W 2nd Bx9398 -Rvrhead 11901
(845) 471-4440 .. **Quartararo,** Paul M '90 (Quartararo & L PLLC) -1399 Route 52 -Fishkill 12524 **Fx:**471-7318
(212) 922-2200 .. **Quartaro,** Neil A '03 %Watson F&W LLP -1133 Av of Amer -NY 10036
(212) 833-1126 .. **Quartner,** Andrew A '79 Cnsl Friedman KS&A LLP -1633 Bway -NY 10019 **Fx:**373-7926
(212) 557-0200 .. **Quarto,** Roslyn A '89 (Quarto L,LLP) -501 5th Av -NY 10017 **Fx:**557-0205
(914) 448-0200 .. **Quartucio,** John P '89 %Bartlett MB&M,LLP -81 Main -White Plns 10601
(212) 258-8000 .. **Quashie,** Derek M '02 MTV Network Inc -1515 Bway -NY 10036
(631) 231-1199 .. **Quatela,** Jos A '86 (Reynolds CGHL&Q,LLP) -35 Arkay Dr -Hauppauge 11788
(585) 724-3046 .. **Quatela,** Laura G '87 %Eastman Kodak -343 State -Rchstr 14650
(212) 431-1188 .. **Quatinetz,** Rebecca N '09 S Yutkin -401 Bway -NY 10013 **Fx:**294-1832
(646) 458-6949 .. **Quatrone,** Mary-Jo '01 ACE USA -140 Bway -NY 10005
(212) 504-6000 .. **Quattlebaum,** Poppy Bingham '77 Cadwalader W&T LLP -1 World Fncl Ctr -NY 10281
(716) 278-1880 .. **Quattrini,** Cathy S '81 %Family Ct -775 3rd -Niagara Fls 14301 **Fx:**278-1877
(212) 752-2670 .. **Quattrocchi,** Lisa Benenson '91 %Benenson Funding -20 W 55th -NY 10019 **Fx:**753-8734
(315) 474-3742 .. **Quattrocci,** Robt A '98 %Stanley Law Ofcs -500 S Salina -Syracuse 13202 **Fx:**471-1536
(716) 845-3630 .. **Quebral,** Roderick '86 %Atty Grievance Comm -438 Main -Buffalo 14202 **Fx:**856-2701
(516) 537-1130 .. **Queen,** Alan S '81 (Glinkenhouse F&Q) -116 Spruce -Cedarhrst 11516
(212) 558-4000 .. **Queen,** Eric H '77 SpclCnsl Sullivan & C LLP -125 Broad -NY 10004
(212) 735-3000 .. **Queen,** Juano R '09 %Skadden ASM&F LLP -4 Times Sq -NY 10036
(518) 462-3000 .. **Queenan,** John F '97 (Iseman CR&H,LLP) -9 Thurlow Ter -Albany 12203
(518) 445-2311 .. **Queenan,** Rosemary '95 Albany Law Schl -80 New Scotland Av -Albany 12208 **Fx:**445-2315
(212) 373-3000 .. **Quek,** Andrea M Y '08 %Paul WRW&G LLP -1285 Av of Amer -NY 10019
(212) 969-3000 .. **Queler,** Matthew S '97 (Proskauer R LLP) -1585 Bway -NY 10036
(212) 264-8843 .. **Queller,** Deborah '92 SpclCnsl ODAR-SSA -26 Fed Plz -NY 10278 **Fx:**264-8633
(212) 406-1700 .. **Queller Fisher Washor Fuchs & Kool LLP** -233 Bway -NY 10279 **Fx:**406-2313
(212) 406-1700 .. **Queller,** Fred '56 OfCnsl Queller FWF&K LLP -233 Bway -NY 10279
(212) 563-7242 .. **Queller,** Steve '77 -450 7th Av -NY 10123 **Fx:**563-6673
(315) 788-6700 .. **Quencer,** Catherine Burns '86 (Schwerzmann & W,PC) -215 Wshngtn Bx704 -Watertwn 13601
(315) 785-9333 .. **Quencer,** Kathy L '91 (Proven & Q) -104 Court -Watertwn 13601 **Fx:**785-0973
(212) 206-5200 .. **Quentzel,** Stephan J '97 %Phillips Family Practice -16 E 16th -NY 10003
(585) 269-5286 .. **Quercia,** Andrea Morano '84 %ITT Space Systems -1447 St Paul Bx60488 -Rchstr 14606
(718) 828-2866 .. **Quesada,** Jose A '78 -1424 Wllmsbrdg Rd -Bronx 10461 **Fx:**828-6658
(516) 486-7307 .. **Quesada,** Victoria '77 (Quesada & M,LLP) -128 Avon Pl -W Hempstead 11552
(518) 462-0300 .. **Quesnel,** Scott P '06 %Girvin & F,PC -20 Corp Wds Blvd -Albany 12211
(212) 918-3000 .. **Questembert,** Ilanit (Lani) '03 %Hogan L LLP -875 3rd Av -NY 10022
(212) 431-3322 .. **Questore,** Steven J '91 -350 Bway -NY 10013 **Fx:**965-9375
(917) 454-1100 .. **Quhshi,** Mohamed D '96 NYPD Civil Enforcement Unit -2 Lafayette -NY 10007
(212) 856-1214 .. **Quiat,** Michl E '82 (Uscher QU&R) -355 Lex Av -NY 10017
(716) 372-8293 .. **Quick,** Lynda M '93 %BOCES -1825 Windfall Rd -Olean 14760
(212) 446-4800 .. **Quient,** Jared M '08 %Kirkland & E LLP -153 E 53rd -NY 10022
(914) 745-4281 .. **Quier-Sheth,** Christine E '99 %Towers Watson -100 Summit Lk Dr -Valhalla 10595
(914) 633-5630 .. **Quigley,** Ann M '83 %Sidney Frank Importing Co -20 Cedar -New Rchll 10801
(212) 373-3000 .. **Quigley,** Brendan F '09 %Paul WRW&G LLP -1285 Av of Amer -NY 10019
(516) 479-6300 .. **Quigley,** Christine T '08 %Silverman A LLP -100 Jericho Quad -Jericho 11753
(516) 485-0014 .. **Quigley,** Edw J '99 -331 Charles -W Hempstead 11552
(212) 878-0000 .. **Quigley,** Francis D Jr. '73 MTA -2 Penn Plz -NY 10121
(607) 687-8253 .. **Quigley,** Judith M '81 Cnsl Cnty Atty -56 Main -Owego 13827 **Fx:**223-7003
(718) 784-4800 .. **Quigley,** Leonard M '95 Plaxall Inc -546 46th Av -LIC 11101
(212) 209-4800 .. **Quigley,** Maureen E '10 Brown R LLP -7 Times Sq -NY 10036
(631) 749-1115 .. **Quigley,** Patricia A '98 -Bx601 -Shelter Isl 11964
(585) 232-6500 .. **Quigley,** Patrick J Jr. '99 %Harter S&E LLP -1600 Bausch & Lomb Pl -Rchstr 14604
(212) 277-4000 .. **Quigley,** Paul J '05 Freshfields BD LLP -520 Mad Av -NY 10022
(315) 548-8434 .. **Quigley,** Robt M '49 -3 S Wayne -Phelps 14532 **Fx:**548-3819
(212) 382-0700 .. **Quigley,** Stephen J '82 OfCnsl Ostrolenk FG&S,LLP -1180 Av of Amer -NY 10036
(631) 537-3100 .. **Quigley,** Theresa K '83 Cnsl Farrell F,PC -2488 Montauk Hwy Bx1980 -Brdghmptn 11932
(212) 294-6700 .. **Quigley,** Thos J '84 (Winston & S) -200 Park Av -NY 10166
(212) 686-0666 .. **Quijano,** Peter E '75 (Quijano & E,PC) -381 Park Av S -NY 10016
(212) 205-7000 .. **Quill,** Patrick B '98 (Ashurst LLP) -7 Times Sq -NY 10036
(212) 479-6000 .. **Quill,** Timothy J Jr. '08 %Cooley LLP -1114 Av of Amer -NY 10036
(212) 415-1457 .. **Quillen,** Mary Humes '92 %McKinsey & Co -485 Mad Av -NY 10022 **Fx:**688-7375
(212) 223-0188 .. **Quillen,** Whitney Staples '94 Gravitas,LLC -145 E 57th -NY 10022
(212) 789-5308 .. **Quines,** Emilio P '01 JP Morgan Asset Mgmt -1211 Av of Amer -NY 10036
(212) 918-3000 .. **Quinio,** Dennis M '09 %Hogan L LLP -875 3rd Av -NY 10022
(914) 766-4021 .. **Quinlan,** Catherine M '89 IBM -294 Route 100 -Somers 10589
(607) 937-9585 .. **Quinlan,** Christopher G '90 -2 W Market -Corning 14830 **Fx:**654-7311
(212) 878-8219 .. **Quinlan,** Guy C '64 Cnsl Clifford C LLP -31 W 52nd -NY 10019
(914) 478-5129 .. **Quinlan,** Jeremiah '76 (Quinlan & F) -245 Saw Mill Rvr Rd -Hawthorne 10532 **Fx:**478-0817
(716) 852-5533 .. **Quinlan,** Lawlor F III '95 (Connors & V,LLP) -1000 Lbrty Bldg -Buffalo 14202
(518) 274-1861 .. **Quinlan,** Louis H '65 -Bx834 -Troy 12181
(631) 451-6500 .. **Quinlan,** Robt F '74 Brookhaven Law Dept -1 Indpndnc Hill -Farmngvll 11738 **Fx:**698-4489

(716) 852-1000 .. **Quinlan,** Russell T '63 %PW Beltz,PC -36 Church -Buffalo 14202 **Fx:**852-5887
(212) 349-5890 .. **Quinlan,** Tara Lai '05 NYS Trial Lawyers Assn -132 Nassau -NY 10038
(516) 222-2434 .. **Quinlan,** Terence M '74 (White Q&S) -377 Oak Bx9304 -Gdn Cty 11530
(516) 222-8500 .. **Quinlan,** Teri Ann M '06 %Martin C&B LLP -90 Merrick Av -E Meadow 11554
(716) 852-1000 .. **Quinlan,** Wm A '85 %PW Beltz,PC -36 Church -Buffalo 14202 **Fx:**852-5887
(716) 852-8222 .. **Quinlivan,** Patrick J '81 (Paladino C&Q) -295 Main -Buffalo 14203
(716) 853-4080 .. **Quinlivan,** Timothy J '92 %Colucci & G,PC -424 Main -Buffalo 14202
(518) 873-3326 .. **Quinn,** Amy N '96 Ct Atty -7559 Court Bx217 -Elizabethtwn 12932 **Fx:**873-3732
(914) 997-0555 .. **Quinn,** Andrew C '90 (Quinn & M,LLP) -399 Knollwood Rd -White Plns 10603
(212) 578-0262 .. **Quinn,** Andrew S '03 %MetLife -27-01 Qns Plz N -LIC 11101
(518) 449-3107 .. **Quinn,** Brendan G '87 %Buckley M&C,PC -29 Wards Ln -Albany 12204
(845) 634-7010 .. **Quinn,** Brian J '78 (Montalbano C&F,PC) -67 N Main Bx1070 -New Cty 10956
(518) 758-7885 .. **Quinn,** Brian Patrick '05 -3012 Main Bx254 -Valatie 12184
(212) 422-1200 .. **Quinn,** Bridget M '06 %Abrams GF&J,PC -1 Bttry Pk Plz -NY 10004
(212) 801-2164 .. **Quinn,** Candace L '83 (Greenberg T,LLP) -200 Park Av -NY 10166
(212) 297-5800 .. **Quinn,** Christopher J '00 %Day P LLP -7 Times Sq -NY 10036
(212) 506-5000 .. **Quinn,** Danielle M '10 %Orrick H&S LLP -51 W 52nd -NY 10019
(716) 633-2717 .. **Quinn,** David C '64 -4175 Oakwood Dr -Buffalo 14221
(518) 464-2437 .. **Quinn,** David M '79 %Ayco Corp -1 Wall -Albany 12205
(518) 457-2678 .. **Quinn,** David Pattison '83 %PERB -80 Wolf Rd -Albany 12205 **Fx:**457-2664
(845) 353-3500 .. **Quinn,** Deborah A '92 %Dorfman K&C LLP -51 N Bway -Nyack 10960
(516) 764-0007 .. **Quinn,** Denis J '85 -87 Riverside Dr -Rockvll Ctr 11570
(646) 386-5000 .. **Quinn,** Doreen Lerner '99 %Surrogates Ct -31 Chmbrs -NY 10007
(212) 849-7000 .. **Quinn Emanuel Urquhart & Sullivan, LLP** -51 Mad Av -NY 10010 **Fx:**849-7100
(212) 319-6898 .. **Quinn,** Francis F '95 (Lavin ORC&D) -420 Lex Av -NY 10170
(212) 237-1000 .. **Quinn,** Francis J '88 (Windels ML&M,LLP) -156 W 56th -NY 10019
(212) 597-0351 .. **Quinn,** Francis W III '02 Aspen Publishers -111 8th Av -NY 10011
(212) 310-8000 .. **Quinn,** Georgia D '08 %Weil G&M LLP -767 5th Av -NY 10153
(212) 313-1200 .. **Quinn,** Gerard J '80 %SIA -120 Bway -NY 10271 **Fx:**313-1301
(315) 822-4141 .. **Quinn,** Graceanne Snyder '96 %Cosentino S&Q -379 W Main Bx596 -W Winfld 13491
(315) 733-9900 .. **Quinn,** Graceanne Snyder '96 %Cosentino S&Q -605 French Rd -New Hartfrd 13413
(718) 286-6000 .. **Quinn,** James C '77 %DA -125-01 Qns Blvd -Kew Gdns 11415
(516) 357-3000 .. **Quinn,** James F '80 (Rivkin R LLP) -926 RXR Plz -Uniondale 11556
(518) 436-4850 .. **Quinn,** James F '90 -177 Cnty Rd 402 -Westerlo 12193 **Fx:**436-5759
(212) 697-0955 .. **Quinn,** James J '76 -300 Park Av -NY 10022
(585) 724-2479 .. **Quinn,** James M '76 Eastman Kodak -343 State -Rchstr 14650 **Fx:**724-6611
(212) 310-8000 .. **Quinn,** James W '72 (Weil G&M LLP) -767 5th Av -NY 10153
(914) 245-6060 .. **Quinn,** Jo-Ann Pepitone '92 OfCnsl Durante B&T,PLLC -2000 Maple Hill -Yorktwn Hts 10598
(845) 454-1200 .. **Quinn,** Joan E '99 %Lewis & G,PC -510 Haight Av Bx2990 -Poughkeepsie 12603
(516) 746-8000 .. **Quinn,** Joan M '82 (Jaspan S LLP) -300 Grdn City Plz -Gdn Cty 11530
(718) 575-8552 .. **Quinn,** John E '85 (Renfroe & Q) -118-35 Qns Blvd -Frst Hlls 11375
(716) 826-1878 .. **Quinn,** John F III '04 -3812 S Park Av -Blasdell 14219
(212) 872-1000 .. **Quinn,** John P '08 -One Bryant Park -NY 10036 **Fx:**872-1002
(516) 872-3256 .. **Quinn,** Jos A '96 -92 Cedarlawn Blvd -Vly Stream 11580
(212) 836-8000 .. **Quinn,** Justin R '09 %Kaye S LLP -425 Park Av -NY 10022
(212) 209-4800 .. **Quinn,** Kerry L '03 %Brown R LLP -7 Times Sq -NY 10036
(718) 258-1245 .. **Quinn,** Kevin '87 Cnsl Verrazano Closing Srvcs -1970 Flatbush Av -Brklyn 11234 **Fx:**692-3787
(212) 609-6800 .. **Quinn,** Kevin John '00 %McCarter & E,LLP -245 Park Av -NY 10167
(347) 296-1852 .. **Quinn,** Kevin P '84 %Hon V Del Guidice -320 Jay -Brklyn 11201
(518) 487-7600 .. **Quinn,** Kevin P '93 (Whiteman O&H LLP) -1 Commerce Plz -Albany 12260
(212) 376-6400 .. **Quinn,** Lori J '03 %Marshall DWC&G -88 Pine -NY 10005
(212) 594-5300 .. **Quinn,** M J '93 Milberg LLP -1 Penn Plz -NY 10119
(716) 634-8400 .. **Quinn,** Margaret J '70 -5500 Main -Williamsvll 14221
(212) 681-6681 .. **Quinn,** Mark D '86 -600 3rd Av -NY 10016 **Fx:**557-9610
(212) 447-5500 .. **Quinn,** Matthew S '91 (Quinn M LLP) -274 Mad Av -NY 10016 **Fx:**889-2981
(516) 746-0707 .. **Quinn,** Maureen '06 %Hammill OCDP&K,PC -6851 Jericho Tpk -Syosset 11791
(914) 997-0555 .. **Quinn & Mellea,LLP** -399 Knollwood Rd -White Plns 10603 **Fx:**997-0550
(212) 974-2400 .. **Quinn,** Michl C '92 %J Burstein -1790 Bway -NY 10019 **Fx:**974-2944
(716) 885-9700 .. **Quinn,** Michl P '09 Collins & B,LLP -267 North -Buffalo 14201
(212) 935-3131 .. **Quinn,** Michelle P '02 %Gallet D&B,LLP -845 3rd Av -NY 10022
(315) 435-2470 .. **Quinn,** Patrick J '83 %DA -505 S State -Syracuse 13202 **Fx:**435-3969
(516) 579-6500 .. **Quinn,** Patrick M '95 %A Clark & Assoc,LLC -650 Wantagh Av -Levittwn 11756 **Fx:**579-6604
(315) 822-4141 .. **Quinn,** Patrick M '97 %Cosentino S&Q -379 W Main Bx596 -W Winfld 13491
(315) 733-9900 .. **Quinn,** Patrick M '97 %Cosentino S&Q -605 French Rd -New Hartfrd 13413
(212) 504-6000 .. **Quinn,** Patrick T '89 (Cadwalader W&T LLP) -1 World Fncl Ctr -NY 10281
(516) 942-6110 .. **Quinn,** R Patrick '90 Roslyn Savings Bank -1 Jericho Plz -Jericho 11753
(716) 851-4343 .. **Quinn,** Robt E '09 Law Dept -65 Niagara Sq -Buffalo 14202 **Fx:**851-4105
(585) 232-6500 .. **Quinn,** Ryan S '10 %Harter S&E LLP -1600 Bausch & Lomb Pl -Rchstr 14604
(212) 541-9100 .. **Quinn,** Samantha E '95 (Schiavetti CDW&N,LLP) -575 8th Av -NY 10018
(212) 456-7777 .. **Quinn,** Sean T '90 %ABC -77 W 66th -NY 10023 **Fx:**456-6202
(212) 468-8000 .. **Quinn,** Susan E '01 Morrison & F LLP -1290 Av of Amer -NY 10104
(585) 454-1730 .. **Quinn,** Susan M '91 Closing USA Inc -250 Mile Xing -Rchstr 14624 **Fx:**454-5999
(631) 584-2020 .. **Quinn,** Terence M '87 -275 Lk Av -St James 11780 **Fx:**584-2023
(716) 856-3500 .. **Quinn,** Theresa E '02 %Magavern MG LLP -1100 Rand Bldg -Buffalo 14203
(212) 261-8000 .. **Quinn,** Thos J '77 (Mendes & M,LLP) -750 7th Av -NY 10019
(516) 229-6000 .. **Quinn,** Thos S Jr. '89 %R Lau & Assoc -300 Jericho Quad Bx9040 -Jericho 11753 **Fx:**229-6167
(516) 280-7700 .. **Quinn,** Timothy P '95 (Mirabella & Q,LLC) -400 Grdn City Plz -Gdn Cty 11530 **Fx:**280-7701
(716) 853-8100 .. **Quinn,** Vivian M '93 (Nixon P LLP) -40 Fountain Plz -Buffalo 14202
(212) 455-2000 .. **Quinn,** Wonda Jos '06 %Simpson T&B LLP -425 Lex Av -NY 10017
(212) 558-4000 .. **Quinn,** Yvonne S '78 (Sullivan & C LLP) -125 Broad -NY 10004
(212) 532-2100 .. **Quinones,** Aurelio C '89 %J Markman,PLLC -1775 Bway -NY 10019 **Fx:**532-2198
(718) 599-4490 .. **Quinones,** Elaine '85 -672 Grand -Brklyn 11211 **Fx:**388-7238
(646) 386-5700 .. **Quinones,** Joanne D '98 %Civil Ct -111 Centre -NY 10013
(646) 458-2436 .. **Quinones,** John '91 YMCA Retirement Fund -140 Bway -NY 10005
(212) 637-2487 .. **Quinones,** Pablo '96 US Atty -1 St Andrews Plz -NY 10007
(212) 374-7136 .. **Quinones,** Thos '90 %Family Ct-CSET -60 Lafayette -NY 10013
(212) 344-5680 .. **Quinones-Holmes,** Mildred '90 OfCnsl Thompson H LLP -335 Mad Av -NY 10017
(212) 306-7466 .. **Quinonez,** Judith Garcia '88 %Comm on Human Rights -40 Rector -NY 10006 **Fx:**306-7414
(212) 416-8407 .. **Quint,** Barbara L '88 %Dept of Law -120 Bway -NY 10271
(212) 804-4200 .. **Quint,** Jon '74 %Mound CW&G -One Bttry Pk Plz -NY 10004
(212) 768-3012 .. **Quintal,** Manuel B '89 -291 Bway -NY 10007
(631) 273-7187 .. **Quintana,** Arthur E '92 %A Quintana -1600 Islip Av -Brentwd 11717 **Fx:**273-7341
(631) 273-7187 .. **Quintana,** Arturo G '77 -1600 Islip Av -Brentwd 11717 **Fx:**273-7341
(212) 756-2000 .. **Quintana,** Beth M '07 %Schulte R&Z LLP -919 3rd Av -NY 10022
(718) 845-1886 .. **Quintana,** Frank '63 -179 Court -Brklyn 11201 **Fx:**845-0350
(212) 446-4800 .. **Quintana,** Jason M '06 %Kirkland & E LLP -153 E 53rd -NY 10022
(212) 573-1559 .. **Quintana,** Jose A '88 %Pfizer Inc -150 E 42nd -NY 10017 **Fx:**573-1445
(212) 343-2500 .. **Quintana,** Manuel H '75 Bravo Bravo -99 Hudson -NY 10013
(718) 797-1003 .. **Quintana,** Michl '90 -179 Court -Brklyn 11201 **Fx:**845-0350
(212) 446-4800 .. **Quintana,** Norberto E '04 %Kirkland & E LLP -153 E 53rd -NY 10022
(212) 282-7243 .. **Quintano,** Laura A '96 %Avon Products -1251 Av of Amer -NY 10020
(212) 698-3500 .. **Quintard-Morenas,** Francois '05 %Dechert LLP -1095 Av of Amer -NY 10036
(718) 694-3322 .. **Quintas,** Bettina '92 %Transit Auth -130 Lvngstn -Brklyn 11201 **Fx:**694-5726
(212) 835-1572 .. **Quintavalle,** Wm J '70 Lampf LP&P -5 Penn Plz 19th Fl -NY 10119
(212) 460-5200 .. **Quinterno,** Christopher J '85 1st Manhattan Abstract Corp -215 Park Av S -NY 10003 **Fx:**995-8184
(212) 455-2000 .. **Quintero,** Cristina '10 %Simpson T&B LLP -425 Lex Av -NY 10017
(212) 732-7378 .. **Quintero,** Leon J '93 -325 Bway -NY 10007 **Fx:**227-9692
(212) 637-3243 .. **Quintin,** Marie T '09 US EPA -290 Bway -NY 10007
(212) 223-1005 .. **Quinton,** James A '75 -551 5th Av -NY 10176 **Fx:**754-6262
(518) 388-4305 .. **Quirion,** Colleen M '84 Family Ct -620 State -Schnctdy 12305 **Fx:**388-4496
(212) 319-1000 .. **Quirk & Bakalor,PC** -845 3rd Av -NY 10022 **Fx:**319-1065
(212) 708-7293 .. **Quirk,** Elizabeth M '04 Intl Flavors & Fragrances -521 W 57th -NY 10019
(212) 688-8555 .. **Quirk,** Noreen '79 OfCnsl Fragomen DB&L LLP -7 Hanover Sq -NY 10004
(212) 319-1000 .. **Quirk,** Robt E '56 (Quirk & B,PC) -845 3rd Av -NY 10022
(718) 250-2000 .. **Quirk,** Susan '05 %DA -350 Jay -Brklyn 11201 **Fx:**250-2314
(518) 473-1403 .. **Quist,** David W '89 %Dept of Health -Corning Twr 24th Fl -Albany 12237 **Fx:**473-2019
(212) 935-7400 .. **Quitt,** Daniella '89 (Harwood F LLP) -488 Mad Av -NY 10022
(212) 799-6100 .. **Quittell,** Robin M '02 Fortress Invstmnt Grp LLC -1345 Av of Amer -NY 10105
(518) 257-8835 .. **Qulia,** Robt G '90 KeyBank Natl Assn -66 S Pearl -Albany 12207 **Fx:**257-8946
(212) 872-1000 .. **Qureshi,** Abid '95 -One Bryant Park -NY 10036 **Fx:**872-1002
(212) 521-5400 .. **Qureshi,** Rizwan A '08 %Reed S LLP -599 Lex Av -NY 10022
(212) 455-2000 .. **Qusba,** Sandeep '95 (Simpson T&B LLP) -425 Lex Av -NY 10017
(516) 489-5000 .. **Ra,** Jos John '75 %Town Atty -Town Hall -Hempstd 11550 **Fx:**489-5150
(718) 435-3053 .. **Raab,** Abraham D '04 -1217 48th -Brklyn 11219
(212) 906-1200 .. **Raab,** David S '99 (Latham & W) -885 3rd Av -NY 10022
(212) 369-0988 .. **Raab,** Edw L '95 -35 E 75th -NY 10021 **Fx:**289-5945
(516) 374-6500 .. **Raab,** Ira J '58 Natl Arbitration & Mediation -990 Stewart Av -Gdn Cty 11530 **Fx:**(561) 514-1347
(212) 669-7700 .. **Raab,** Jennifer J '86 %Landmarks Pres Comm -1 Centre -NY 10007
(914) 834-9461 .. **Raab,** Judith Deutsch '89 -7 Knollwood Dr -Larchmnt 10538
(212) 356-3820 .. **Raab,** Katie R '88 %NYC Dept Educ-OLS -52 Chmbrs -NY 10007 **Fx:**374-5596
(212) 527-8109 .. **Raab,** Mitchell '99 Seneca Capital -590 Mad Av -NY 10022
(914) 738-0280 .. **Raab,** Richd '84 %Frontier Kemper Constructors -415 5th Av -Pelham 10803
(212) 683-6699 .. **Raab,** Ronald P '70 (Raab SG&G,LLP) -317 Mad Av -NY 10017
(212) 859-8000 .. **Raab,** Sheldon '61 OfCnsl Fried FHS&J LLP -1 NY Plz -NY 10004
(212) 415-9200 .. **Raab,** Stephen M '06 %Dorsey & W LLP -250 Park Av -NY 10177
(212) 683-6699 .. **Raab Sturm Goldman & Ganchrow, LLP** -317 Mad Av -NY 10017 **Fx:**779-8596
(718) 748-0202 .. **Raab-Giamarino,** Linda B '86 -421 73rd -Brklyn 11209
(718) 613-2410 .. **Raalf,** Matthew S '06 %Hon C Amon -225 Cadman Plz E -Brklyn 11201
(347) 276-6506 .. **Rabah,** Mahmoud R '05 -118-35 Qns Blvd -Frst Hlls 11375

(212) 330-0291 .. **Rabar,** Maria Elyse '78 OfCnsl Kopff N&D LLP -440 9th Av -NY 10001 **Fx:**(718) 399-9509

(631) 751-0939 .. **Rabatin,** Richd P '98 -270 Rte 25-A -Setauket 11733

(212) 627-8100 .. **Rabb,** Alexander C '08 %Levy R,PC -80 8th Av -NY 10011

(212) 851-1996 .. **Rabb,** Katherine A '04 Columbia Univ-Resrch Compliance -535 W 116th -NY 10027

(631) 427-7888 .. **Rabbach,** Brett L '93 (Markowitz & R LLP) -290 Broadhllw Rd -Melvll 11747

(631) 427-7888 .. **Rabbach,** David J '64 OfCnsl Markowitz & R LLP -290 Broadhllw Rd -Melvll 11747

(212) 459-8850 .. **Rabbin,** Gille A '87 %Consumer Pritection Bd -1740 Bway -NY 10019 **Fx:**459-8855

(212) 818-1110 .. **Rabbino,** Anne A '81 (Butzel L,PC) -380 Mad Av -NY 10017

(212) 455-2000 .. **Rabe,** Drew C '08 %Simpson T&B LLP -425 Lex Av -NY 10017

(212) 841-1000 .. **Rabe,** Kyle D '10 %Covington & B LLP -620 8th Av -NY 10018

(212) 373-3000 .. **Rabe,** Scott R '06 %Paul WRW&G LLP -1285 Av of Amer -NY 10019

(212) 225-2000 .. **Raben,** Lillian E '02 %Cleary GS&H -1 Lbrty Plz -NY 10006

(212) 753-5000 .. **Raben,** Zev F '09 %Schiff H LLP -900 3rd Av -NY 10022

(212) 319-9800 .. **Raber,** Howard M '07 %Tashjian & P -729 7th Av -NY 10019

(212) 735-3000 .. **Rabia,** Vered '98 (Skadden ASM&F LLP) -4 Times Sq -NY 10036

(212) 504-6000 .. **Rabie,** Aseel M '98 %Cadwalader W&T LLP -1 World Fncl Ctr -NY 10281

(845) 291-3150 .. **Rabiet,** Michl '90 %Cnty Atty -255 Main -Goshen 10924 **Fx:**291-3167

(914) 332-4350 .. **Rabin,** Aaron '83 -220 Wht Plns Rd -Tarrytwn 10591

(518) 719-3590 .. **Rabin,** Ann-Marie '88 %DA -411 Main -Catskill 12414 **Fx:**719-3792

(315) 479-8660 .. **Rabin,** Benjamin C '94 %Alexander & C,LLC -115 E Jffrsn -Syracuse 13202

(212) 512-0812 .. **Rabin,** Bonnie E '85 (Cohen HB&R,PC) -11 W 42nd -NY 10036

(914) 948-2222 .. **Rabin,** Corey B '81 (Rabin P&H) -44 Church -White Plns 10601 **Fx:**948-2255

(212) 935-3555 .. **Rabin,** Corey B '81 (Rabin P&H) -675 3rd Av -NY 10017

(212) 536-3900 .. **Rabin,** David E '87 (K&L Gates LLP) -599 Lex Av -NY 10022

(516) 228-3505 .. **Rabin,** Howard '87 (H Rabin,PC) -585 Stewart Av -Gdn Cty 11530 **Fx:**228-8608

(212) 440-2745 .. **Rabin,** Howard R '88 Colliau EMCK&M -40 Wall -NY 10005

(212) 724-1050 .. **Rabin,** Jack '53 -10 W 66th -NY 10023 **Fx:**769-3311

(212) 318-3000 .. **Rabin,** Jaclyn L '09 %Fulbright & J LLP -666 5th Av -NY 10103

(212) 840-0008 .. **Rabin,** Jay H '90 Citigate Hudson Inc -62 W 45th -NY 10036 **Fx:**840-0707

(718) 625-2900 .. **Rabin,** Jeffrey A '71 -16 Court -Brklyn 11241 **Fx:**624-5626

(212) 442-1104 .. **Rabin,** Michl S '77 %Dept for Aging -2 Lafayette -NY 10007

(212) 872-1000 .. **Rabin,** Richd J '94 -One Bryant Park -NY 10036 **Fx:**872-1002

(631) 777-5720 .. **Rabin,** Walter D '85 %All Points Capital -275 Broadhllw Rd -Melvll 11747

(718) 931-6300 .. **Rabine,** Joel H '65 (Rabine & N) -993 Morris Park Av -Bronx 10462

(914) 949-2100 .. **Rabine,** Lawr S '73 -100 S Bedford Rd -Mt Kisco 10549 **Fx:**946-1813

(718) 931-6300 .. **Rabine & Nickelsberg** -993 Morris Park Av -Bronx 10462 **Fx:**792-4253

(212) 875-8030 .. **Rabiner,** Ellen '04 -316 W 75th -NY 10023

(212) 596-9000 .. **Rabin-Havt,** Raphael '09 %Ropes & G LLP -1211 Av of Amer -NY 10036

(212) 578-8190 .. **Rabinoff,** Ilana A '01 Legacy Heritage Fund Ltd -55 E 59th -NY 10022

(212) 679-5880 .. **Rabinoff & Rabinovich,PC** -275 Mad Av -NY 10016 **Fx:**679-7958

(212) 679-5880 .. **Rabinoff,** Regina '95 (Rabinoff & R,PC) -275 Mad Av -NY 10016

(212) 563-1710 .. **Rabinovich,** Laurence J '86 (Schindel FLG&R LLP) -14 Penn Plz -NY 10122

(212) 753-5000 .. **Rabinovich,** Marina '87 (Schiff H LLP) -900 3rd Av -NY 10022

(718) 338-6300 .. **Rabinovich,** Marina '03 -1115 Ocean Pkwy -Brklyn 11230 **Fx:**369-7570

(212) 619-2665 .. **Rabinovich,** Oleg '00 -77 Fulton -NY 10038 **Fx:**809-1218

(212) 679-5880 .. **Rabinovich,** Pyotr S '83 (Rabinoff & R,PC) -275 Mad Av -NY 10016

(212) 538-4521 .. **Rabinovich,** Richd M '01 Credit Suisse -1 Mad Av -NY 10010

(212) 285-0510 .. **Rabinovich,** Roman '04 %Wilkofsky FK&C -299 Bway -NY 10007

(212) 715-9100 .. **Rabinovich,** Russ '01 %Kramer LN&F,LLP -1177 Av of Amer -NY 10036

(212) 309-6000 .. **Rabinovici,** Sarah Sandok '06 %Morgan L&B LLP -101 Park Av -NY 10178

(212) 549-2500 .. **Rabinovitz,** Judy '86 %ACLU -125 Broad -NY 10004 **Fx:**549-2651

(845) 562-3125 .. **Rabinowe,** Fredric J '87 -13 San Giacomo Dr -New Windsor 12553 **Fx:**562-3125

(212) 848-4000 .. **Rabinowicz,** Jos D '05 %Shearman & S LLP -599 Lex Av -NY 10022

(718) 897-4433 .. **Rabinowitz,** Aaron E '02 (Burstein & R PC) -11325 Qns Blvd -Frst Hlls 11375

(212) 326-3939 .. **Rabinowitz,** Alan M '10 %Jones D -222 E 41st -NY 10017

(212) 997-4400 .. **Rabinowitz,** Alan S '98 Cnsl Teitler & T,LLP -1114 Av of Amer -NY 10036 **Fx:**997-4949

(212) 381-4461 .. **Rabinowitz,** Andrew H '01 Marathon Asset Mgmt LLC -461 5th Av -NY 10017 **Fx:**381-4446

(914) 241-3934 .. **Rabinowitz,** Audrey C '87 -14 Garey Dr -Chappaqua 10514

(718) 633-3290 .. **Rabinowitz,** Baruch '59 -1344 43rd -Brklyn 11219

(212) 254-1111 .. **Rabinowitz Boudin Standard Krinsky & Lieberman,PC** -111 Bway -NY 10006 **Fx:**674-4614

(212) 308-8505 .. **Rabinowitz,** Brad D '88 Akabas & S -488 Mad Av -NY 10022

(212) 558-4000 .. **Rabinowitz,** Danl A '95 SpclCnsl Sullivan & C LLP -125 Broad -NY 10004

(212) 259-0297 .. **Rabinowitz,** Danl L '76 Athena Grp -712 5th Av -NY 10019 **Fx:**459-2602

(212) 554-7815 .. **Rabinowitz,** David '77 (Moses & S LLP) -405 Lex Av -NY 10174

(212) 878-5134 .. **Rabinowitz,** David J '04 (Goulston & S,PC) -750 3rd Av -NY 10017 **Fx:**878-5534

(212) 632-3000 .. **Rabinowitz,** Denise G '80 Fiduciary Trust Co Intl -600 5th Av -NY 10020 **Fx:**632-3002

(845) 639-7800 .. **Rabinowitz,** Donna E '87 %Mandel K&B,LLP -210 Route 303 -Vly Cottage 10989

(845) 893-4809 .. **Rabinowitz,** Elizabeth N '09 -107-19 70th Av -Frst Hlls 11375 **Fx:**(347) 649-1133

(516) 739-8222 .. **Rabinowitz & Galina** -94 Willis Av -Mineola 11501 **Fx:**739-8225

(516) 931-5300 .. **Rabinowitz,** Hannah '76 %We're Associates -100 Jericho Quad -Jericho 11753

(212) 773-2223 .. **Rabinowitz,** Howard A '74 Ernst & Young LLP -5 Times Sq -NY 10036

(212) 619-2534 .. **Rabinowitz,** Jacob '51 -30 Vesey -NY 10007 **Fx:**233-0659

(914) 493-2101 .. **Rabinowitz,** Jordy '93 Westchester Medical Ctr -Taylor Care Ctr -Valhalla 10595

(585) 244-9514 .. **Rabinowitz,** Karen B '87 -65 Brandywine Ln -Rchstr 14618

(212) 883-1300 .. **Rabinowitz,** Laura Siegel '91 Cnsl Sandler T&R,PA -551 5th Av -NY 10176

(212) 969-3000 .. **Rabinowitz,** Lauren J '08 %Proskauer R LLP -1585 Bway -NY 10036

(212) 355-9615 .. **Rabinowitz,** Laurence P '79 Cohen Bros Rlty Corp -750 Lex Av -NY 10022

(516) 365-1400 .. **Rabinowitz,** Marci G '99 Cooperman LM LLP -1129 Nrthrn Blvd -Manhsst 11030

(212) 704-3840 .. **Rabinowitz,** Martin J '56 -111 8th Av -NY 10011

(718) 694-3900 .. **Rabinowitz,** Michl G '04 %Transit Auth -130 Lvngstn -Brklyn 11201 **Fx:**694-5726

(516) 739-8222 .. **Rabinowitz,** Michl M '85 (Rabinowitz & G) -94 Willis Av -Mineola 11501

(718) 403-3600 .. **Rabinowitz,** Peter '81 %Dept of Finance -345 Adams -Brklyn 11201 **Fx:**403-3650

(212) 566-5996 .. **Rabinowitz,** Rachel A '94 %Dept of Bldgs -280 Bway -NY 10007

(516) 571-3800 .. **Rabinowitz,** Sarah M '04 DA -262 Old Cntry Rd -Mineola 11501 **Fx:**248-9479

(212) 801-9295 .. **Rabinowitz,** Stephen L '87 (Greenberg T,LLP) -200 Park Av -NY 10166

(212) 859-8000 .. **Rabinowitz,** Stephen S '95 (Fried FHS&J LLP) -1 NY Plz -NY 10004

(212) 977-9700 .. **Rabinowitz,** Steven J '82 Cnsl Phillips N LLP -666 5th Av -NY 10103

(212) 421-4100 .. **Rabinowitz,** Steven M '84 (Pryor C LLP) -7 Times Sq -NY 10036

(914) 323-7000 .. **Rabinowitz,** Wayne I '76 (Wilson EME&D LLP) -3 Gannett Dr -White Plns 10604

(212) 806-5400 .. **Rabitz,** Steven W '96 (Stroock &S&L LLP) -180 Maiden Ln -NY 10038

(212) 635-6242 .. **Rabkin,** Ronald J '86 Bank of NY -1 Wall -NY 10005

(518) 689-1437 .. **Rabkin,** Saml S '72 OfCnsl Greenberg T,LLP -54 State -Albany 12207

(914) 273-7300 .. **Rabo,** Benedict A '90 %Schutz & M -6 Spruce Hill Rd -Armonk 10504

(212) 841-1000 .. **Raboy,** Amanda R '07 %Covington & B LLP -620 8th Av -NY 10018

(212) 682-1133 .. **Rabunski,** Alan E '75 -630 3rd Av -NY 10017 **Fx:**682-0508

(212) 513-7788 .. **Rabus,** Michl J '83 (Ahmuty D&M) -123 William -NY 10038

(631) 454-1010 .. **Racanelli,** Constance M '99 Racanelli Construction Co,Inc -1895 Walt Whitman Rd -Melvll 11747

(212) 483-2323 .. **Racanelli,** Janine A '88 %JP Morgan Chase -345 Park Av -NY 10154

(516) 227-0700 .. **Racanelli,** John '69 (Farrell F,PC) -1320 RXR Plz -Uniondale 11556

(516) 683-1717 .. **Racanelli,** Margherita '08 %V Russo & Assoc,PC -1600 Stewart Av -Westbury 11590 **Fx:**683-9393

(212) 326-2000 .. **Racanelli,** Mark A '95 (O'Melveny & M LLP) -7 Times Sq -NY 10036

(718) 740-7050 .. **Racano,** Frank A '86 F Racano,PC -Bx140131 -Howard Bch 11414 **Fx:**740-7051

(212) 532-8100 .. **Race,** Christina L '06 %Stern & M,LLP -115 Bway -NY 10006

(518) 483-4330 .. **Race,** Nathan N '01 (Hughes S&R,PC) -31 Elm Bx788 -Malone 12953

(718) 596-9855 .. **Race,** Robt R '75 -306 Atl Av -Brklyn 11201 **Fx:**596-9859

(518) 563-4022 .. **Racette,** Peter D '87 %Leg Aid -100 Court Bx989 -Plattsbrgh 12901 **Fx:**563-4058

(516) 294-5433 .. **Rach,** Michele D '05 %Ahmuty D&M -200 IU Willets Rd -Albertson 11507

(516) 409-6200 .. **Rach,** Stephen E II '03 %Furey KWM&C,PC -2174 Jackson Av -Seafrd 11783

(212) 563-4100 .. **Rachelson,** Jani K '79 (Cohen W&S LLP) -330 W 42nd -NY 10036

(212) 237-4000 .. **Rachleff,** Matthew G '01 Oglivy Intrctv -309 W 49th -NY 10019

(212) 480-5284 .. **Rachlin,** Alan S '76 %Insurance Dept -25 Beaver -NY 10004 **Fx:**480-5272

(212) 964-2552 .. **Rachlin,** Howard W '75 -11 Park Pl -NY 10007 **Fx:**227-2087

(716) 856-4000 .. **Rachlin,** Lauren D '52 (Hodgson R LLP) -140 Pearl -Buffalo 14202

(212) 819-8200 .. **Rachlin,** Leila '92 %White & C LLP -1155 Av of Amer -NY 10036

(516) 683-1717 .. **Rachlin,** Marvin '58 OfCnsl V Russo & Assoc,PC -1600 Stewart Av -Westbury 11590 **Fx:**683-9393

(212) 969-3000 .. **Rachlin,** Paul I '87 (Proskauer R LLP) -1585 Bway -NY 10036

(212) 450-4000 .. **Rachlis,** Adam B '09 %Davis P&W LLP -450 Lex Av -NY 10017

(845) 353-6930 .. **Rachlis,** Stephen P H '74 -99 Main -Nyack 10960 **Fx:**353-6932

(212) 468-4800 .. **Rachman,** Marc J '94 (Davis & G LLP) -1740 Bway -NY 10019

(212) 564-1900 .. **Rachmil,** Bruce E '95 %Cohen & K -450 7th Av -NY 10123

(212) 752-9700 .. **Rachmuth,** Paul A '96 (Gersten S LLP) -600 Lex Av -NY 10022

(212) 259-8000 .. **Rachofsky,** Robt S '86 (Dewey & L LLP) -1301 Av of Amer -NY 10019

(212) 681-8925 .. **Racht,** Theresa '86 (Racht & T,LLP) -7 Penn Plz -NY 10001 **Fx:**681-8928

(212) 506-5000 .. **Racic,** Mark M '03 %Orrick H&S LLP -51 W 52nd -NY 10019

(518) 761-6207 .. **Racino,** Bryan M '09 Warren Cnty Pub Def -1340 State Route 9 -Lk George 12845

(212) 277-4000 .. **Raciti-Knapp,** Melissa Y '94 (Freshfields BD LLP) -520 Mad Av -NY 10022

(718) 650-0900 .. **Rackett,** Kent R '01 -26 Court -Brklyn 11242

(212) 918-3000 .. **Rackman,** Jos R '73 (Hogan L LLP) -875 3rd Av -NY 10022

(212) 684-3900 .. **Rackman,** Michl I '65 (Gottlieb R&R,PC) -270 Mad Av -NY 10016

(914) 589-9321 .. **Rackman,** Shari B '89 -4 Disbrow Ln -New Rchll 10804 **Fx:**576-9425

(212) 506-5000 .. **Rackoff,** Sarah G '08 %Orrick H&S LLP -51 W 52nd -NY 10019

(212) 701-3000 .. **Rackow,** Lauren M '08 %Cahill G&R LLP -80 Pine -NY 10005 **Fx:**269-5420

(718) 625-1100 .. **Raclaw,** Adam F '97 %Hoberman & T,PC -2622 E Tremont Av -Bronx 10461

(212) 951-6563 .. **Racow,** Steven '81 %NYS Ed Dept-OLS -475 Park Av S -NY 10016 **Fx:**951-6573

(212) 834-3850 .. **Racy,** John A '83 %Chase Securities Inc -270 Park Av -NY 10017 **Fx:**834-6591
(212) 224-9520 .. **Racz,** Gregory N '99 Octavian Advisors,LP -650 Mad Av -NY 10022
(716) 894-2525 .. **Raczka,** Christine A '78 -2916 William -Cheektowaga 14227
(212) 464-1945 .. **Raczynski,** Michl C '02 JP Morgan -270 Park Av -NY 10017
(212) 351-4000 .. **Rada,** Jennifer L '08 Gibson D&C LLP -200 Park Av -NY 10166
(800) 416-5454 .. **Rada,** Milan '78 (Fusco B&R) -11 Penn Plz -NY 10001
(800) 416-5454 .. **Rada,** Milan '78 (Fusco B&R) -180 Froehlich Farm Blvd -Woodbury 11797
(800) 416-5454 .. **Rada,** Milan '78 (Fusco B&R) -626 RXR Plz -Uniondale 11553
(212) 947-1999 .. **Rada,** Wm J '81 %Methfessel & W,PC -450 7th Av -NY 10123
(914) 375-0100 .. **Radano,** Jos P '05 %Novick ELRW&L,PC -733 Ynkrs Av -Ynkrs 10704
(212) 389-5000 .. **Radchenko,** Tina '08 %Sutherland A&B LLP -1114 Av of Amer -NY 10036
(212) 421-4100 .. **Radcliff,** Jacob B '02 %Pryor C LLP -7 Times Sq -NY 10036
(212) 940-8800 .. **Radden,** Danl S '09 %Katten MR LLP -575 Mad Av -NY 10022
(212) 468-8000 .. **Radding,** Rory J '76 (Morrison & F LLP) -1290 Av of Amer -NY 10104
(212) 506-5282 .. **Radecki,** Alison J '96 (Orrick H&S LLP) -51 W 52nd -NY 10019
(315) 797-9261 .. **Radel,** Patrick G '03 %Getnick LA&P,LLP -258 Genesee -Utica 13502
(716) 883-4800 .. **Radel,** Robt R '91 -88 W Utica -Buffalo 14209
(212) 575-8500 .. **Radeljic,** Danielle L '02 Cnsl R Youdelman,PC -113 Univ Pl -NY 10003 **Fx:**937-2067
(212) 626-4100 .. **Rademacher,** April L '09 %Baker & M LLP -1114 Av of Amer -NY 10036
(212) 897-0234 .. **Rademacher,** John D '04 Intl Securities Exchng -60 Broad -NY 10004
(212) 554-7800 .. **Rademacher,** Kara L '10 %Moses & S LLP -405 Lex Av -NY 10174
(212) 309-6000 .. **Rademacher,** Kurt W '07 %Morgan L&B LLP -101 Park Av -NY 10178
(516) 571-1488 .. **Rademaker,** Thos A '97 Hon P Grella Cnty Ct -252 Old Cntry Rd -Mineola 11501
(212) 872-1500 .. **Rader,** Adam J '92 %Lacher & L-T -460 Park Av -NY 10022
(212) 855-6970 .. **Rader,** Benjamin J '00 %Goldman Sachs -1 NY Plz -NY 10004
(212) 813-8800 .. **Rader,** Bruce J '89 (Goodwin P LLP) -620 8th Av -NY 10018
(212) 791-5200 .. **Rader,** Lawr W '88 -225 Bway -NY 10007 **Fx:**791-5400
(646) 313-8268 .. **Radest,** Michl B '00 Bank of Amer Securities LLC -40 W 57th -NY 10019
(716) 882-8000 .. **Radetich,** Peter P '84 %Computer Task Grp -800 Delaware Av -Buffalo 14209 **Fx:**887-7370
(212) 310-8000 .. **Radetsky,** Alex '09 %Weil G&M LLP -767 5th Av -NY 10153
(212) 867-6000 .. **Radetsky,** Lisa R '83 (Rosenberg & E,PC) -733 3rd Av -NY 10017
(212) 325-2000 .. **Radey,** D Neil '88 Credit Suisse -1 Mad Av -NY 10010
(518) 828-3414 .. **Radez,** James J '06 %DA -325 Columbia -Hudson 12534 **Fx:**828-8491
(516) 334-4500 .. **Radi,** Mark A '09 %Sokoloff S LLP -355 Post Av -Westbury 11590 **Fx:**334-4501
(212) 446-2300 .. **Radic,** Ognjen Z '08 %Boies S&F LLP -575 Lex Av -NY 10022
(212) 468-8020 .. **Radice,** Anthony M '70 SrCnsl Morrison & F LLP -1290 Av of Amer -NY 10104
(212) 876-5500 .. **Radice,** Ellen J '03 Neighborhood Def Svc-Harlem -317 Malcolm X Blvd -NY 10027
(212) 687-1980 .. **Radice,** John D '05 %Kaplan F&K LLP -850 3rd Av -NY 10022
(315) 343-6363 .. **Radick,** Courtney S '06 %Amdursky PF&W,PC -26 E Oneida -Oswego 13126
(212) 856-9600 .. **Radick,** Robt M '98 (Morvillo AGIA&B,PC) -565 5th Av -NY 10017
(212) 450-4000 .. **Radigan,** Brian C '06 %Davis P&W LLP -450 Lex Av -NY 10017
(516) 663-6600 .. **Radigan,** C Raymond '62 Cnsl Ruskin MF,PC -1425 RXR Plz -Uniondale 11556
(518) 452-5600 .. **Radigan,** Kevin P '85 (Heslin RF&M PC) -5 Columbia Cir -Albany 12203
(212) 578-8226 .. **Radigan,** Michl G '86 %MetLife -1095 Av of Amer -NY 10036 **Fx:**252-7295
(212) 287-4457 .. **Radigan,** Raymond C '84 Bk of America -590 Mad Av -NY 10022
(973) 315-4430 .. **Radin,** Bruce D '90 (Budd L) -140 Bway -NY 10005
(845) 639-6728 .. **Radin,** Carl '57 -Bx856 -New Cty 10956 **Fx:**639-1002
(585) 232-3730 .. **Radin,** Edw C '78 (Chamberlain D LLP) -1600 Crssrds Bldg -Rchstr 14614
(212) 361-1237 .. **Radin,** Lee D '80 Dept of Finance -66 John -NY 10038
(631) 499-6499 .. **Radin,** Matthew E '83 -861 Larkfld Rd -Commack 11725 **Fx:**462-2857
(212) 858-7710 .. **Radin,** Michelle Just '90 %Nowell AKB,PA -140 Bway PMB 46028 -NY 10005
(212) 974-7474 .. **Radin,** Mitchell E '83 (Cowan DA&S LLP) -41 Mad Av -NY 10010
(212) 270-0938 .. **Radin,** Neila B '78 JP Morgan Chase -270 Park Av -NY 10017
(212) 277-4000 .. **Radin,** Olivia A '05 %Freshfields BD LLP -520 Mad Av -NY 10022
(212) 687-2800 .. **Radin,** Sam '78 %Natl Madison Grp -340 Mad Av -NY 10173 **Fx:**687-2990
(212) 310-8000 .. **Radin,** Stephen A '84 (Weil G&M LLP) -767 5th Av -NY 10153
(212) 351-4000 .. **Radine,** Michl J '10 Gibson D&C LLP -200 Park Av -NY 10166
(212) 428-6455 .. **Radisch,** Lois J '85 %Royal Bk of Canada -1 Lbrty Plz -NY 10006 **Fx:**968-1295
(212) 446-4800 .. **Radke,** Kirk A '91 (Kirkland & E LLP) -153 E 53rd -NY 10022
(585) 546-5530 .. **Radler,** Jean M '92 %Thomson West -50 E Broad -Rchstr 14694
(212) 687-7070 .. **Radley,** Philippe D '80 OfCnsl Rand RR&G LLP -800 3rd Av -NY 10022
(315) 894-8330 .. **Radley & Rheinhardt** -85 Otsego Bx360 -Ilion 13357 **Fx:**894-8421
(716) 688-1300 .. **Radlin,** Barry L '67 -2350 N Forest Rd -Getzvll 14068 **Fx:**636-0466
(212) 417-4357 .. **Radman,** Christine M '93 Dept of Health -90 Church -NY 10007 **Fx:**417-4392
(631) 261-8834 .. **Radman,** Frances A '87 %Ingerman S LLP -150 Motor Pkwy -Hauppauge 11788
(212) 977-7033 .. **Radna,** Rudolf B '02 %Perecman Firm PLLC -250 W 57th -NY 10107
(212) 742-0001 .. **Radna,** Sandra M '93 (Radna & A,LLP) -110 Wall -NY 10005 **Fx:**742-0005
(518) 793-6611 .. **Radner,** Cathi L '99 (Miller MS&H,LLC) -451 Glen Bx765 -Glens Fls 12801
(212) 594-5300 .. **Rado,** Andrei '00 (Milberg LLP) -1 Penn Plz -NY 10119
(212) 981-4500 .. **Rado,** Stephen F '95 PeterSan Grp -1450 Bway -NY 10018 **Fx:**981-4560
(212) 867-5800 .. **Radolinski,** Michl H '09 %Osler H&H LLP -620 8th Av -NY 10018
(212) 697-3122 .. **Radomisli,** Gregory J '93 (Martin C&B LLP) -220 E 42nd -NY 10017
(212) 496-2700 .. **Radon,** Jenik R '72 (Radon & I) -269 W 71st -NY 10023 **Fx:**724-3393
(212) 778-6082 .. **Radoncic,** Zejreme '02 Prudential Bache Commodities,LLC -1 NY Plz -NY 10292
(914) 761-1300 .. **Radow,** Elisabeth N '84 %Cuddy & F LLP -445 Hmltn Av -White Plns 10601
(516) 338-7800 .. **Radow,** Raymond D '93 (Radow Law Grp PC) -1010 Nrthrn Blvd -Gt Neck 11021 **Fx:**338-2549
(212) 436-1119 .. **Radow,** Tom A '90 %IRS -290 Bway -NY 10007
(212) 310-8000 .. **Radulescu,** David C '92 (Weil G&M LLP) -767 5th Av -NY 10153
(212) 670-0106 .. **Radulescu,** Robyn Fried '92 %Merrill Lynch -222 Bway -NY 10038 **Fx:**670-4527
(212) 636-6000 .. **Radvany,** Paul B '93 %Fordham Univ Sch of Law -140 W 62nd -NY 10023 **Fx:**636-6899
(212) 986-1000 .. **Radwan,** Jennifer E '05 %Goldberg C&G,LLP -331 Mad Av -NY 10017 **Fx:**986-8039
(212) 373-3000 .. **Radwaner,** Valerie E '89 (Paul WRW&G LLP) -1285 Av of Amer -NY 10019
(212) 376-6400 .. **Radzik,** Edw C '80 (Marshall DWC&G) -88 Pine -NY 10005
(212) 218-2100 .. **Radzik,** Margaret A '08 %Fitzpatrick CH&S -1290 Av of Amer -NY 10104
(212) 927-9652 .. **Radzivilover,** Elenor F '90 %Bd of Educ -650 Academy -NY 10034
(646) 227-3094 .. **Radzyner,** Mark H '86 %Memorial Sloan-Kettering Cancer Ctr -633 3rd Av -NY 10017
(212) 751-3596 .. **Rae,** Christopher D '04 Chilton Invstmnt Co -300 Park Av -NY 10022
(212) 384-1000 .. **Rae,** Courtland D '02 %FBI -26 Fed Plz -NY 10278
(646) 855-2556 .. **Rae,** Glen A '98 Bank of Amer -1 Bryant Pk -NY 10036
(212) 697-2700 .. **Rae,** James M '67 OfCnsl Stairs DF -200 Park Av S -NY 10003
(212) 806-5400 .. **Rae,** Mark N '96 (Stroock &S&L LLP) -180 Maiden Ln -NY 10038
(212) 714-1212 .. **Rae,** Robin S '09 %DL Rothberg & Assoc,PC -1065 Av of Amer -NY 10018 **Fx:**714-0969
(212) 770-6028 .. **Raebiger,** Marcelline E '96 %AIG -70 Pine -NY 10270
(212) 940-6830 .. **Raelson,** Douglas A '75 Fisher Bros -299 Park Av -NY 10171
(212) 878-8000 .. **Raetzer,** Jos J '07 %Clifford C LLP -31 W 52nd -NY 10019
(718) 618-2500 .. **Raez,** Evelyn '01 %Civil Ct -851 Grnd Cncrs -Bronx 10451 **Fx:**590-7294
(631) 962-2056 .. **Rafa,** Michl '04 OSI Pharmaceuticals Inc -41 Pinelawn Rd -Melvll 11747
(516) 741-4799 .. **Rafalko,** Malgorzata '05 %Baker SBGFM&N,LLC -100 Grdn City Plz -Gdn Cty 11530
(212) 554-1234 .. **Rafaloff,** Jill C '90 %AXA Financial Inc -1290 Av of Amer -NY 10104 **Fx:**707-3963
(914) 632-5250 .. **Rafalowicz,** Jos '79 -271 North Av -New Rchll 10801 **Fx:**654-1507
(718) 636-8000 .. **Rafalsky,** Thos R '69 (Wood R&W,LLP) -394-396 Waverly Av -Brklyn 11238 **Fx:**857-5628
(212) 661-9100 .. **Rafeek,** Ikhwan A '09 %Otterbourg SH&R,PC -230 Park Av -NY 10169
(212) 732-5400 .. **Raff & Becker,LLP** -470 Park Av S -NY 10016 **Fx:**732-0270
(212) 732-5400 .. **Raff,** David A '69 (Raff & B,LLP) -470 Park Av S -NY 10016
(212) 506-5000 .. **Raff,** Joshua E '89 (Orrick H&S LLP) -51 W 52nd -NY 10019
(718) 286-6000 .. **Raff,** Lois '79 %DA -125-01 Qns Blvd -Kew Gdns 11415
(212) 484-3900 .. **Raffa,** Connie A '77 (Arent F LLP) -1675 Bway -NY 10019
(516) 921-8320 .. **Raffa,** Sam J '54 -5 Northgate Dr -Syosset 11791
(212) 513-3200 .. **Raffaele,** Steve M '01 %Holland & K LLP -31 W 52nd -NY 10019
(718) 672-2605 .. **Raffaelli,** Rafael '92 -81-06 37th Av -Jcksn Hts 11372 **Fx:**672-3121
(516) 326-9462 .. **Raffalli,** Henri C '57 Nassau Comm College -Criminal Justice Dept -Gdn Cty 11530
(631) 727-3662 .. **Raffe,** Chas E '63 -727 Union Av -Rvrhead 11901 **Fx:**727-2761
(716) 878-3020 .. **Raffel,** Wm E '97 Buffalo State Cllg -1300 Elmwood Av -Buffalo 14222
(914) 696-0006 .. **Rafferty,** Robt G '91 (Rafferty & R) -800 Wstchstr Av -Rye Brook 10573 **Fx:**560-3333
(212) 474-1000 .. **Rafferty,** Thos G '89 (Cravath S&M LLP) -825 8th Av -NY 10019
(518) 402-0191 .. **Rafter,** Diane M '90 %UIA Bd -Troy Atrium Bx15126 -Albany 12212 **Fx:**402-6208
(212) 797-4362 .. **Rafter,** John T '79 (Rafter & Assoc,PLLC) -29 Bway -NY 10006 **Fx:**797-4363
(914) 967-7400 .. **Rafter,** Patricia Smithwick '79 -14 Elm Pl -Rye 10580 **Fx:**967-8090
(914) 939-3356 .. **Rafter,** Robt J '78 -18 Twr Hill Dr -Pt Chester 10573
(212) 592-1400 .. **Raftery,** Brian E '98 (Herrick,F LLP) -2 Park Av -NY 10016
(212) 504-6000 .. **Raftery,** Michelle '03 SpclCnsl Cadwalader W&T LLP -1 World Fncl Ctr -NY 10281
(212) 807-2980 .. **Raftery,** Ruth Ann Flynn '96 Thomson Reuters -395 Hudson -NY 10014
(212) 446-4800 .. **Raftery,** W Brian '98 (Kirkland & E LLP) -153 E 53rd -NY 10022
(212) 728-8000 .. **Ragan,** Colman B '04 %Willkie F&G LLP -787 7th Av -NY 10019
(212) 458-3245 .. **Ragan,** Ruth A '03 %AIG -175 Water -NY 10038
(212) 204-3505 .. **Ragan,** Thos C '71 (Ragan & F LLP) -11 E 44th -NY 10017 **Fx:**204-3515
(718) 843-7584 .. **Ragano,** John '74 (Ragano & R) -110-15 Lbrty Av -S Richmond Hll 11419
(212) 756-2000 .. **Ragauskaite,** Ausra '10 %Schulte R&Z LLP -919 3rd Av -NY 10022
(718) 590-2000 .. **Ragazzo,** Kimberly E '08 %DA -198 E 161st -Bronx 10451 **Fx:**590-6477
(212) 685-7474 .. **Raggio,** Grier H Jr. '69 OfCnsl Mayerson SA LLP -292 Mad Av -NY 10017
(518) 463-5400 .. **Raghavan,** Latha '90 (Goldberg S LLP) -8 Southwoods Blvd -Albany 12211
(718) 875-1300 .. **Raghavan,** Nisha D '00 %Appllt Div 2nd Dept -45 Monroe Pl -Brklyn 11201 **Fx:**858-2446
(212) 925-6635 .. **Raghu,** Maya '99 Legal Momentum -395 Hudson -NY 10014
(212) 209-3048 .. **Raghunathan,** Vaijayanthi '01 Cnsl Reitler K&R LLC -885 3rd Av -NY 10022
(212) 578-1083 .. **Ragin,** Ronald '02 %MetLife -1095 Av of Amer -NY 10036 **Fx:**578-3916
(212) 474-1000 .. **Raglan,** Christine '03 %Cravath S&M LLP -825 8th Av -NY 10019
(212) 880-6000 .. **Raglan,** Danl P '98 (Torys LLP) -237 Park Av -NY 10017

(212) 605-6200 .. **Ragland**, Graham Russell '02 %Levy P&K,LLP -800 3rd Av -NY 10022
(516) 535-4203 .. **Ragno**, Jos A '93 -820 Willis Av -Albertson 11507 **Fx**:535-4265
(631) 737-6040 .. **Rago**, Anne Marie '00 Dept of Law -2100 Middle Cntry Rd -Centereach 11720 **Fx**:737-6050
(718) 797-5700 .. **Ragone**, Hattie F '98 %Wenig S LLP -26 Court -Brklyn 11242
(212) 683-7100 .. **Ragone**, Heather C '01 %Gallo V&K,LLP -90 Broad -NY 10004
(646) 467-7557 .. **Ragone**, Mark A '92 City Lights Media Grp -6 E 39th -NY 10016
(212) 635-2244 .. **Ragone**, Peter A '84 (Rosner N&R LLP) -110 Wall -NY 10005
(212) 728-2200 .. **Ragosa**, Diane C '02 %Axinn V&H LLP -114 W 47th -NY 10036
(212) 794-5366 .. **Ragovin**, Marc '89 CUNY -535 E 80th -NY 10075 **Fx**:794-5667
(585) 530-3050 .. **Ragsdale**, Dana M '81 %MHLS -50 East Av -Rchstr 14604 **Fx**:530-3079
(845) 454-2200 .. **Ragucci**, Christopher P '08 %Wolfson G&E PC -11 Market -Poughkeepsie 12601
(212) 756-2000 .. **Ragucci**, Frederic L '83 (Schulte R&Z LLP) -919 3rd Av -NY 10022
(212) 766-1100 .. **Ragues & Min, LLP** -11 Bway -NY 10004
(212) 766-1100 .. **Ragues**, Raymond '86 (Ragues & M,LLP) -11 Bway -NY 10004
(212) 277-6500 .. **Ragusa**, Jos W '94 Cnsl Dickstein S LLP -1633 Bway -NY 10019
(212) 578-2873 .. **Ragusa**, Louis J '84 %MetLife -1095 Av of Amer -NY 10036
(631) 425-7700 .. **Ragusa**, Marc S '91 -25 High -Huntngtn 11743
(212) 408-2500 .. **Ragusa**, Paul A '94 (Baker B,LLP) -30 Rckfllr Plz -NY 10112
(212) 447-7373 .. **Rah**, Young '88 -450 7th AV -NY 10123 **Fx**:268-8529
(212) 574-1200 .. **Rahaghi**, Peter A '07 %Seward & K LLP -1 Bttry Pk Plz -NY 10004
(212) 649-2000 .. **Rahbar**, Peter P '00 %Hearst Corp -300 W 57th -NY 10019 **Fx**:649-2035
(212) 983-8120 .. **Rahbari**, Robt C '97 RAS Capital Mgmt LLC -111 Bway -NY 10006
(516) 829-0363 .. **Raheb**, Jennifer '05 %Israel I&P,LLP -11 Grace Av -Gt Neck 11021 **Fx**:829-0366
(845) 838-3335 .. **Rahemba**, Robt J '73 -Bx422 -Fishkill 12524 **Fx**:838-3338
(212) 277-4000 .. **Rahimi-Laridjani**, Eschrat '01 %Freshfields BD LLP -520 Mad Av -NY 10022
(212) 521-5400 .. **Rahl**, J Andrew Jr. '74 (Reed S LLP) -599 Lex Av -NY 10022
(212) 230-8800 .. **Rahm**, Catherine Marlantes '07 %WilmerHale -399 Park Av -NY 10022
(212) 836-8000 .. **Rahm**, Susan B '74 Kaye S LLP -425 Park Av -NY 10022
(917) 637-3600 .. **Rahman**, Anika '91 %Ctr for Reproductive Rts -120 Wall -NY 10005 **Fx**:637-3666
(212) 310-8000 .. **Rahman**, Faiza N '06 %Weil G&M LLP -767 5th Av -NY 10153
(212) 801-2198 .. **Rahman**, Hashim A '03 %Greenberg T,LLP -200 Park Av -NY 10166
Rahman, Kaisur '01 -85-64 113th -Richmnd Hll 11418
(212) 344-3800 .. **Rahman**, Meer M M '99 %Christophe & Assoc,PC -2 Wall -NY 10005 **Fx**:344-3212
(212) 506-2500 .. **Rahman**, Shaila S '08 %Mayer B LLP -1675 Bway -NY 10019
(718) 248-5738 .. **Rahman**, Sofia S '99 Citi Cards -1 Court Sq -LIC 11101
(212) 416-8000 .. **Rahman**, Tarek A '00 %Dept of Law -120 Bway -NY 10271
(212) 643-9190 .. **Rahmanan**, Anthony '88 Rahmanan & Assoc,LLC -1250 Bway -NY 10001 **Fx**:(646) 219-0714
(212) 909-6000 .. **Rahmanian**, Andra Nahal '05 %Debevoise & P LLP -919 3rd Av -NY 10022
(518) 447-7360 .. **Rahmas**, D Steve '68 Cnty DSS -162 Wshngtn Av -Albany 12210
(212) 448-9400 .. **Rahme**, Grace Ng '07 Triumph Prop Grp Ltd -12 W 23rd -NY 10010
(631) 777-3200 .. **Rahner**, Margaret B '04 %N Parsoff & Assoc,PC -425 Broad Hollow Rd -Melvll 11747 **Fx**:777-3204
(718) 767-0247 .. **Rahr**, Robt T '98 %Kinray Inc -152-35 10th Av -Whitestone 11357
(212) 836-8000 .. **Rai**, Dilpreet K '06 %Kaye S LLP -425 Park Av -NY 10022
(516) 826-6500 .. **Rai**, Holly '08 %LaMonica H&M LLP -3305 Jerusalem Av -Wantagh 11793
(212) 334-1300 .. **Rai**, Susan S '67 %Vera Inst of Justice -233 Bway -NY 10279 **Fx**:941-9407
(212) 681-3095 .. **Rai**, Yogesh Kumar '00 Fischer Francis Trees & Watts,Inc -200 Park Av -NY 10166
(516) 357-3000 .. **Raia**, Frank J '87 (Rivkin R LLP) -926 RXR Plz -Uniondale 11556
(212) 735-2404 .. **Raia**, Illana Post '94 %Skadden ASM&F LLP -4 Times Sq -NY 10036 **Fx**:(917) 777-2404
(845) 838-6600 .. **Raible**, James R '83 -33 Henry Bx910 -Beacon 12508 **Fx**:831-0744
(212) 421-4100 .. **Raice**, Pinchus D '87 (Pryor C LLP) -7 Times Sq -NY 10036
(845) 566-5345 .. **Raiche**, Raymond P '99 %Larkin AI&T,LLP -356 Meadow Av -Newburgh 12550
(212) 547-5400 .. **Raicht**, Geoffrey T '98 (McDermott W&E LLP) -340 Mad Av -NY 10173
(212) 765-9100 .. **Raicht**, Robt D '87 (Halperin BR,LLP) -555 Mad Av -NY 10022
(212) 221-5700 .. **Raider**, Eli D '03 %Goldberg WFG LLP -1501 Bway -NY 10036
(212) 508-6100 .. **Raifman**, Helena '02 %Bracewell & G,LLP -1251 Av of Amer -NY 10020
(212) 297-5800 .. **Raihofer**, Karen '94 %Day P LLP -7 Times Sq -NY 10036
(212) 506-1700 .. **Raikes**, Martin C '99 Kasowitz BT&F LLP -1633 Bway -NY 10019
(212) 735-3000 .. **Rail**, Brynn M '05 %Skadden ASM&F LLP -4 Times Sq -NY 10036
(631) 444-0260 .. **Rail**, Vernon G '00 %DEC -SUNY Campus 50 Circle Rd -Stony Brk 11790 **Fx**:444-0348
(212) 813-8800 .. **Railton**, Anne E '09 %Goodwin P LLP -620 8th Av -NY 10018
(718) 248-1548 .. **Raiman**, Ilyssa B '02 %Smith Barney -1 Court Sq -LIC 11101
(212) 860-3974 .. **Raimi**, Shepherd I '71 -1040 Park Av -NY 10028
(212) 788-0845 .. **Raimond**, Frank V '06 %Law Dept -100 Church -NY 10007 **Fx**:788-0367
(212) 603-6300 .. **Raimond**, Roger A '92 (Robinson BLGG&G PC) -875 3rd Av -NY 10022
(212) 709-8063 .. **Raimondi**, Guy C Jr. '90 -110 Wall -NY 10005
(914) 347-2600 .. **Raimondi**, Hillary Jacobs '94 %Traub LS&S LLP -7 Skyline Dr -Hawthorne 10532
(631) 852-2711 .. **Raimondi**, John E '93 %Family Ct -215 Griffing Av -Rvrhead 11901
(212) 384-1000 .. **Raimondi**, Paul F '95 %FBI -26 Fed Plz -NY 10278
(631) 471-1222 .. **Raimondo**, David J '90 D Raimondo & Assoc -2780 Middle Cntry Rd -Lk Grove 11755 **Fx**:471-1980
(914) 921-4820 .. **Raimondo**, John A '02 OfCnsl Bonnist & C,LLP -800 Wstchstr Av -Rye Brook 10573 **Fx**:921-4823
(212) 751-3001 .. **Rain**, John W '98 (Thompson & K LLP) -919 3rd Av -NY 10022
(315) 379-2115 .. **Rain**, Mary E '96 Pub Def -48 Court -Canton 13617
(212) 310-8000 .. **Raina**, Shrutee '10 %Weil G&M LLP -767 5th Av -NY 10153
(212) 442-4900 .. **Rainbow**, Martin M '85 %Ofc Admin Trials -40 Rector -NY 10006 **Fx**:442-4947
(718) 821-3407 .. **Rainer**, Flora '99 -72-34 73rd St -Glendale 11385
(212) 382-3300 .. **Rainer**, Randall R '99 (Wollmuth M&D LLP) -500 5th Av -NY 10110
(212) 508-6100 .. **Rainero**, Julian '99 (Bracewell & G,LLP) -1251 Av of Amer -NY 10020
(212) 953-9200 .. **Raines**, Alan P '80 -555 5th Av -NY 10017
(718) 643-5880 .. **Raines**, Elliott '86 %Hon A Cutrona -360 Adams -Brklyn 11201
(718) 237-2000 .. **Rainford**, Sharon M '99 %Leg Aid -111 Lvngstn -Brklyn 11201 **Fx**:237-8737
(631) 694-0033 .. **Rainis**, Matthew '86 (Lawrence WR&B,PC) -425 Broadhllw Rd -Melvll 11747
(718) 262-7100 .. **Rainone**, Susan Seidman '98 %Civil Ct -89-17 Sutphin Blvd -Jamaica 11435 **Fx**:262-7107
(212) 208-2186 .. **Raiola**, Christopher M '93 %Tullett & Tokyo Sec -80 Pine -NY 10005
(718) 816-1131 .. **Raisch**, Kenneth Lee '77 -1 Edgewtr Plz -Staten Isl 10305 **Fx**:816-1611
(516) 742-7600 .. **Raiser & Kenniff, PC** -1517 Franklin Av -Mineola 11501 **Fx**:742-7618
(212) 318-6000 .. **Raiser**, Rebecca E '10 %Paul HJ&W LLP -75 E 55th -NY 10022
(516) 742-7600 .. **Raiser**, Steven M '02 (Raiser & K,PC) -1517 Franklin Av -Mineola 11501
(516) 239-8514 .. **Raisfeld**, Lawr S '61 -40 Cayuga Av -Atlantic Bch 11509 **Fx**:239-7171
(914) 722-6006 .. **Raisfeld**, Ruth D '81 -47 Secor Rd -Scarsdale 10583
(212) 558-4000 .. **Raisler**, Kenneth M '77 (Sullivan & C LLP) -125 Broad -NY 10004
(631) 543-3000 .. **Raisman**, Myron S '60 (Raisman & Assoc,LLP) -996 W Jericho Tpk -Smithtwn 11787 **Fx**:543-7312
(631) 543-3000 .. **Raisman**, Nancy B '90 (Raisman & Assoc,LLP) -996 W Jericho Tpk -Smithtwn 11787 **Fx**:543-7312
(212) 245-1000 .. **Raisner**, Jack A '84 (Outten & G LLP) -3 Park Av -NY 10016
(212) 230-8800 .. **Raisner**, Sara N '10 %WilmerHale -399 Park Av -NY 10022
(212) 213-5575 .. **Raison**, Steven '69 -220 5th Av -NY 10001
(973) 315-4515 .. **Rait**, Mitchell '88 Cnsl Budd L -140 Bway -NY 10005
(212) 906-1200 .. **Raiten**, Gregory K '09 %Latham & W -885 3rd Av -NY 10022
(718) 763-7544 .. **Raiten**, Philip S '83 -2035 E 68th -Brklyn 11234
(212) 607-2818 .. **Raitt**, Susan E '97 FTC -1 Bowling Grn -NY 10004 **Fx**:607-2822
(212) 513-3200 .. **Raives**, Robt M '58 OfCnsl Holland & K LLP -31 W 52nd -NY 10019
(516) 221-8400 .. **Raizin**, Jamie W '94 -254 Pettit Av -Bellmore 11710
(212) 580-5070 .. **Raizner**, Bernard I '68 -23 W 82nd -NY 10024 **Fx**:579-9108
(212) 921-8399 .. **Rajan**, Deepa '97 %Lankler S&W LLP -500 5th Av -NY 10110
(212) 701-3000 .. **Rajan**, Neil S '09 %Cahill G&R LLP -80 Pine -NY 10005 **Fx**:269-5420
(212) 857-8230 .. **Rajan**, Nishi '03 %Baker MM&M,PC -330 W 34th -NY 10001
(646) 226-9185 .. **Rajan**, Viju P '09 -181 Brielle Av -Staten Isl 10314
(212) 506-1700 .. **Rajoo**, Shalini K '04 %Kasowitz BT&F LLP -1633 Bway -NY 10019
(212) 455-2000 .. **Raju**, Shruti V '09 %Simpson T&B LLP -425 Lex Av -NY 10017
(646) 746-7642 .. **Rak**, Andrew G '82 Reed Business Info -360 Park Av S -NY 10010
(212) 739-4063 .. **Rak**, Jos A '09 Allianz Global Investors of America -1345 Av of Amer -NY 10105
(212) 735-3000 .. **Rakhlin**, Serena G '09 %Skadden ASM&F LLP -4 Times Sq -NY 10036
(718) 372-7741 .. **Rakhmatkarieva**, Nodira '07 -1680 E 22nd -Brklyn 11229
(516) 576-5963 .. **Rakita**, Melana '03 Otis Elevator Co -65 Fairchild Av -Plainvw 11803
(212) 290-4700 .. **Rakita**, Sara E '01 Human Rghts Wtch -350 5th Av -NY 10118
(845) 339-3492 .. **Rakov**, Sarah E '98 -12 John -Kingston 12401
(212) 660-5550 .. **Rakower**, Michl C '00 -747 3rd Av -NY 10017 **Fx**:660-5551
(212) 238-3000 .. **Rakowicz**, Emilia '05 %Emmet M&M,LLP -120 Bway -NY 10271
(516) 484-6692 .. **Rakowski**, Edmund G '79 -78 Oak Rdg Ln -Albertson 11507
(212) 308-8505 .. **Rakowski**, Henry E '90 %Akabas & S -488 Mad Av -NY 10022
(212) 867-4466 .. **Rakowski**, Kara I '91 (Belkin BW&G,LLP) -270 Mad Av -NY 10016
(716) 564-4595 .. **Rakowski**, Michl S '02 -20 Nrthpnte Pkwy -Amherst 14228
(716) 631-0904 .. **Ralabate**, Frank T '70 -5792 Main -Williamsvll 14221
(716) 634-5525 .. **Ralabate & Galbo** -5792 Main -Buffalo 14221
(716) 634-2280 .. **Ralabate**, James J '59 -5792 Main -Williamsvll 14221
(716) 634-5525 .. **Ralabate**, Jos M '50 (Ralabate & G) -5792 Main -Buffalo 14221
(212) 532-2450 .. **Raldiris**, Hiram Anthony '87 %E Green -295 Mad Av -NY 10017 **Fx**:532-0117
(212) 509-9400 .. **Raleigh**, Christopher '81 (Cozen O) -45 Bway Atrium -NY 10006
(212) 768-6700 .. **Rall**, Lauris G L '78 (Sonnenschein N&R LLP) -2 World Fncl Ctr -NY 10281
(212) 660-3000 .. **Ralli**, Constantine P '74 (Sullivan & W LLP) -1290 Av of Amer -NY 10104
(917) 698-9537 .. **Rallo**, Christina A '92 -5 Brwstr #299 -Glen Cove 11542 **Fx**:(888) 267-5187
(212) 989-5500 .. **Ralls**, Robt Danl '00 Elsevier Inc -360 Park Av S -NY 10010
(718) 875-0260 .. **Ralph**, Arleen T '91 -26 Court -Brklyn 11242
(212) 889-7400 .. **Ralph**, Bethany A '77 %Lazarus & L,PC -240 Mad Av -NY 10016 **Fx**:684-0314
(607) 734-1647 .. **Ralph**, David E '75 (Leg Srvcs) -215 E Church -Elmira 14901 **Fx**:734-1018
(212) 440-3758 .. **Ralph**, Melissa J '00 CNA Global -40 Wall -NY 10005
(518) 810-0206 .. **Ralston**, Wm H '85 ReEnergy Holdings LLC -20 Century Hills Dr -Latham 12110
(212) 613-1900 .. **Ram**, Illana '01 Riese Org,Inc -560 5th Av -NY 10036
(212) 742-0500 .. **Ram**, Thos P '98 %Gucciardo Law Firm -99 Wall -NY 10005 **Fx**:742-0815
(212) 474-1000 .. **Ramachandran**, Manoj '08 %Cravath S&M LLP -825 8th Av -NY 10019
(212) 637-2546 .. **Ramachandran**, Seetha '01 %US Atty -1 St Andrews Plz -NY 10007
(212) 227-4747 .. **Ramadan**, Mahmoud '92 -299 Bway -NY 10007 **Fx**:732-6972
(212) 408-5100 .. **Ramadei**, Jos B '08 %Chadbourne & P LLP -30 Rckfllr Plz -NY 10112
(212) 474-1000 .. **Ramakrishnan**, Kavita B '10 %Cravath S&M LLP -825 8th Av -NY 10019
(212) 373-3000 .. **Raman**, Kripa A '00 Cnsl Paul WRW&G LLP -1285 Av of Amer -NY 10019
(212) 449-9954 .. **Raman**, Prabhu '03 Merrill Lynch -4 World Fncl Ctr -NY 10080

(516) 877-0800 .. **Ramasso,** Jeanne L '88 %Cartiglia C&R -1050 Franklin Av -Gdn Cty 11530
(917) 667-7535 .. **Rambadadt,** Robt M '03 -33 W 19th -NY 10011
(212) 515-7756 .. **Rambler,** Mark D '03 Fortress Invstmnt Grp LLC -1345 Av of Amer -NY 10105
(212) 513-3200 .. **Rambusch,** Lennard K '60 (Holland & K LLP) -31 W 52nd -NY 10019
(718) 441-1066 .. **Ramdass,** Parmanand '01 -97-13 101st Av -Ozone Pk 11416
(212) 790-4010 .. **Ramdhanie,** Ancris '05 Cmptrllr of Currency -340 Mad Av -NY 10017 **Fx:**790-4058
(718) 887-5536 .. **Rameau,** Amy '03 -61 Bway -NY 10006 **Fx:**(917) 551-0030
(212) 416-8000 .. **Rameau,** Cheryl M '94 %Dept of Law -120 Bway -NY 10271
(718) 739-6400 .. **Ramer,** Laurence A '80 %DHCR -92-31 Union Hall -Jamaica 11433 **Fx:**262-7938
(212) 836-8000 .. **Ramer,** Paula R '06 %Kaye S LLP -425 Park Av -NY 10022
(212) 403-1000 .. **Ramesh,** Sandeep C '09 %Wachtell LR&K -51 W 52nd -NY 10019
(845) 294-1464 .. **Rametta,** Michele '04 (Rametta & R,LLC) -15 Matthews -Goshen 10924 **Fx:**294-8072
(845) 294-1464 .. **Rametta,** Robt M '04 (Rametta & R,LLC) -15 Matthews -Goshen 10924 **Fx:**294-8072
(646) 964-5843 .. **Ramgopal,** Mahendra M '86 (Ramgopal & R) -Church St Station Bx1791 -NY 10008
(212) 909-6000 .. **Ramirez,** Anthony M '10 %Debevoise & P LLP -919 3rd Av -NY 10022
(212) 806-5400 .. **Ramirez,** Armando X '04 SpclCnsl Stroock &S&L LLP -180 Maiden Ln -NY 10038
(212) 554-7800 .. **Ramirez,** Carlos F '98 %Moses & S LLP -405 Lex Av -NY 10174
(718) 297-1000 .. **Ramirez,** Henry '77 -8000 Cooper Av -Glendale 11385
(718) 542-6629 .. **Ramirez,** Jaime '85 -751 Cmmnwlth Av -Bronx 10473 **Fx:**542-6630
(212) 558-4000 .. **Ramirez,** Jaime E '08 %Sullivan & C LLP -125 Broad -NY 10004
(212) 785-0900 .. **Ramirez,** John F '09 Winmill & Co Inc -11 Hanover Sq -NY 10005
(212) 935-3000 .. **Ramirez,** John J '09 %Mintz LCFG&P,PC -666 3rd Av -NY 10017
(718) 292-4176 .. **Ramirez,** Jos L '02 -762 Jackson Av -Bronx 10456
(718) 558-5550 .. **Ramirez,** Juan Antonio '03 -90-04 161st -Jamaica 11432
(212) 909-6000 .. **Ramirez,** Juan L '06 %Debevoise & P LLP -919 3rd Av -NY 10022
(718) 618-2500 .. **Ramirez,** Leticia M '00 %Civil Ct -851 Grnd Cncrs -Bronx 10451 **Fx:**590-7294
(212) 951-6400 .. **Ramirez,** Manuel E Jr. '09 Dept of Education -475 Park Av S -NY 10016 **Fx:**951-6465
(212) 210-9451 .. **Ramirez,** Porfirio F Jr. '78 (Alston & B LLP) -90 Park Av -NY 10016
(212) 505-6633 .. **Ramirez,** Roberto '97 Mirram Grp -895 Bway -NY 10003
(718) 268-8900 .. **Ramirez,** Ronald W '77 (Ribakove & R) -107-19 71st Av -Frst Hlls 11375 **Fx:**268-3045
(917) 639-4075 .. **Ramirez,** Sabrina C '05 -1230 Av of Amer -NY 10020
(212) 508-6700 .. **Ramirez,** Stefanie M '08 %Tannenbaum HS&H LLP -900 3rd Av -NY 10022
(212) 637-0378 .. **Ramirez-Fisher,** Leslie A '94 %US Atty -86 Chmbrs -NY 10007
(516) 623-9593 .. **Ramjeet,** Oscar D '88 -2315 Babylon Tpk -Merrick 11566
(631) 421-9051 .. **Ramme,** Roger D '78 OfCnsl Goldstein RG&D,PC -18 W Carver -Huntngtn 11743
(718) 454-3461 .. **Ramnarine-Jokhai,** Shearon '99 -8577 Chevy Chase -Jamaica 11432 **Fx:**454-0583
(718) 386-4345 .. **Ramo Nashak & Brown** -75-19 Myrtle Av -Glendale 11385 **Fx:**386-7873
(212) 545-7337 .. **Ramone,** Simon Q '06 %Greenberg & G,LLP -363 7th Av -NY 10001 **Fx:**545-7406
(212) 373-3000 .. **Ramos,** Carey R '82 (Paul WRW&G LLP) -1285 Av of Amer -NY 10019
(212) 297-5800 .. **Ramos,** Edgardo '88 (Day P LLP) -7 Times Sq -NY 10036
(718) 529-5900 .. **Ramos,** Efrain Jr. '98 -95-03 101st Av -Ozone Pk 11416 **Fx:**529-1419
(914) 995-3649 .. **Ramos,** Karen Ann '98 %Cnty Atty -148 Martine Av -White Plns 10601 **Fx:**995-5858
(212) 505-6633 .. **Ramos,** Kim '04 Mirran Grp LLC -895 Bway -NY 10003
(212) 468-8000 .. **Ramos,** Leah Andrea '05 %Morrison & F LLP -1290 Av of Amer -NY 10104
(718) 254-7000 .. **Ramos,** Michl J '99 %US Atty -271 Cadman Plz E -Brklyn 11201 **Fx:**254-6479
(516) 565-5377 .. **Ramos,** Rhina M '97 %Workplace Project -91 N Franklin -Hempstd 11550 **Fx:**565-5470
(212) 902-7530 .. **Ramos,** Saml '92 %Goldman Sachs -1 NY Plz -NY 10004
(845) 457-7501 .. **Ramos,** Sarah '05 (Fassnacht & R LLP) -201 Ward -Montgmry 12549 **Fx:**457-7503
(718) 993-1100 .. **Ramos,** Walter '88 -888 Grand Cncrs -Bronx 10451 **Fx:**993-2108
(845) 988-0915 .. **Ramos,** Wilbert '85 -4 Gordon Ter -Warwick 10990 **Fx:**988-0915
(212) 340-0400 .. **Ramos,** Wm '91 %Appllt Div 1st Dept -27 Mad Av -NY 10010 **Fx:**889-4412
(716) 854-2100 .. **Ramos-Caywood,** Dianna L '97 (Lewis & L,PC) -37 Franklin -Buffalo 14202 **Fx:**854-0433
(914) 798-5400 .. **Ramos-Herbert,** Yadira A '06 %Goldberg S LLP -11 Martine Av -White Plns 10606
(212) 599-3303 .. **Ramos-Persaud,** Maria D '99 %Helfand & H -350 5th Av -NY 10118 **Fx:**599-3029
(212) 874-7717 .. **Ramos-Quintana,** Juan M '91 -500 W End -NY 10024
(845) 735-1278 .. **Ramp,** Kenneth A '84 -371 Blauvelt Rd -Pearl Rvr 10965
(212) 962-2300 .. **Rampe,** Kevin M '92 Lower Manhattan Dvlpmnt Corp -1 Lbrty Plz -NY 10006
(212) 806-5400 .. **Rampersaud,** Sandra J '04 %Stroock &S&L LLP -180 Maiden Ln -NY 10038
(212) 566-4468 .. **Rampersaud,** Sharmila '01 NYC Dept of Bldg -1 Centre -NY 10007
(718) 761-3333 .. **Rampulla,** Lawr A '77 (Parisi R&L PC) -78 Martin Av -Staten Isl 10314
(718) 668-6800 .. **Rampulla,** Robt B '97 (Sak & R,LLP) -2675 Hylan Blvd -Staten Isl 10306 **Fx:**668-0051
(718) 761-3333 .. **Rampulla,** Valerie Lenza '78 (Parisi R&L PC) -78 Martin Av -Staten Isl 10314
(212) 425-0055 .. **Rampy,** Natouchka P '92 %Sharretts PC&B -75 Broad -NY 10004
(212) 264-3650 .. **Ramrup,** Sommattie '94 %SSA Ofc Genl Cnsl -26 Fed Plz -NY 10278 **Fx:**264-6372
(212) 891-1877 .. **Ramsay,** Christopher L '93 CDC Invstmnt -9 W 57th -NY 10019
(212) 450-4000 .. **Ramsay,** Jeffrey S '02 %Davis P&W LLP -450 Lex Av -NY 10017
(212) 816-8817 .. **Ramsay,** John M '01 Citigroup Global Mrkts -388 Greenwich -NY 10013
(845) 638-1956 .. **Ramsay,** Richd G '63 OfCnsl MP O'Connor -10 Esquire Rd -New Cty 10956 **Fx:**638-3916
(845) 359-0777 .. **Ramsay,** Richd G '63 OfCnsl K O'Malley -155 Washington Bx40 -Tappan 10983 **Fx:**359-0913
(212) 310-8000 .. **Ramsay,** Stanley E '07 (Weil G&M LLP) -767 5th Av -NY 10153
(585) 327-3233 .. **Ramsay,** Thos G '87 %Dept of Law -144 Exchange Blvd -Rchstr 14614 **Fx:**546-7514
(718) 250-2000 .. **Ramsay-Lowe,** Rachel A '10 %DA -350 Jay -Brklyn 11201 **Fx:**250-2314
(315) 655-4316 .. **Ramsdell,** Patricia P '80 -1409 Owahgena Rd -Cazenovia 13035 **Fx:**655-4360
(315) 686-5572 .. **Ramseier,** Wm F '94 (Carter R&H PLLC) -229 John -Clayton 13624
(516) 466-6680 .. **Ramsen,** John S '98 Jaclam Equities LLC -29 Barstow Rd -Gt Neck 11021 **Fx:**466-6684
(347) 404-9133 .. **Ramseur,** Dakota D '99 %Civil Ct -141 Lvngstn -Brklyn 11201 **Fx:**(718) 643-3733
(718) 262-7100 .. **Ramseur,** Jeanette '83 Civil Ct -89-17 Sutphin Blvd -Jamaica 11435 **Fx:**262-7107
(212) 964-1070 .. **Ramseur,** Kenneth E '76 -299 Bway -NY 10007 **Fx:**385-2742
(914) 391-3914 .. **Ramsey,** Charlotte R '95 -1 Lacey Ct -Wesley Hills 10977 **Fx:**(845) 664-9921
(718) 654-5252 .. **Ramsey,** Claude C III '98 SrCnsl Ramsey & Assoc -3935 Wht Plns Rd -Bronx 10466 **Fx:**(347) 341-5241
(716) 848-9000 .. **Ramsey,** Colin D '03 %Underberg & K LLP -1900 Main Pl Twr -Buffalo 14202
(315) 487-0074 .. **Ramsey,** Florence W '83 -210 Monte Vista Dr -Camillus 13031
(917) 749-8205 .. **Ramsey,** Harold B Jr. '89 -401 Bway -NY 10013
(212) 471-8517 .. **Ramsey,** Homer B '98 (Herzfeld & R,PC) -125 Broad -NY 10004
(212) 373-3000 .. **Ramsey,** Jana C '05 Paul WRW&G LLP -1285 Av of Amer -NY 10019
(518) 435-1919 .. **Ramsey,** Leith Carole '89 OfCnsl Stockton B&M,LLP -2 Twr Pl -Albany 12203
(315) 443-2529 .. **Ramsey,** Sarah H '88 %Syracuse Univ Cllg of Law -Wht Hall -Syracuse 13244 **Fx:**443-4213
(212) 744-8345 .. **Ramson,** Amy J '83 -300 E 71st -NY 10021 **Fx:**267-7187
(212) 962-0801 .. **Ramson,** Gamiel A '84 -277 Bway -NY 10007 **Fx:**267-7187
(212) 962-0801 .. **Ramson,** Murray '50 -277 Bway -NY 10007
(718) 657-6565 .. **Ramson,** Romeo A '81 -87-63 148th -Jamaica 11435 **Fx:**526-4763
(212) 318-2000 .. **Ramundo,** Paolo A '92 %Bloomberg LP -731 Lex Av -NY 10022
(212) 839-5300 .. **Ramzy,** Mark '10 %Sidley A LLP -787 7th Av -NY 10019
(518) 399-0696 .. **Rana,** Amardeep Singh '90 -58 Charlton Rd -Ballston Lk 12019
(212) 310-8000 .. **Rana,** Faraz A '09 %Weil G&M LLP -767 5th Av -NY 10153
(347) 857-6105 .. **Rana,** Harminderpal Singh '95 -102 Ward Av -Staten Isl 10304
(585) 454-3377 .. **Rana,** Sonal M '02 %Brown & T,LLC -19 Prince -Rchstr 14607
(212) 538-8105 .. **Rana,** Zainub '05 Credit Suisse -1 Mad Av -NY 10010
(212) 337-2096 .. **Ranada,** Vivien V '01 US Dept of Labor -201 Varick -NY 10014 **Fx:**337-2112
(212) 373-3000 .. **Ranade,** Samir K '07 %Paul WRW&G LLP -1285 Av of Amer -NY 10019
(516) 972-2205 .. **Ranaldo,** Jos C '03 -1295 Nrthrn Blvd -Manhsst 11030 **Fx:**365-2820
(518) 266-3000 .. **Ranalli,** Danl J '83 %Div Tax Appls -500 Fed -Troy 12180 **Fx:**272-5178
(631) 979-1291 .. **Ranalli,** Ernest E '90 -742 Vets Hwy -Hauppauge 11788 **Fx:**979-1461
(518) 452-5531 .. **Ranalli,** Michl D '92 -14 Debbie Marie Ct -Schnctdy 12309 **Fx:**452-5531
(212) 532-8100 .. **Ranallo,** Nicholas R '08 %Stern & M,LLP -115 Bway -NY 10006
(212) 277-4000 .. **Ranawake,** Jerome C '03 (Freshfields BD LLP) -520 Mad Av -NY 10022
(212) 277-4000 .. **Rance,** Brian D '86 (Freshfields BD LLP) -520 Mad Av -NY 10022
(914) 693-5255 .. **Rancic-DeNardo,** Sylvia '02 -83 Harriman Rd -Irvngtn 10533 **Fx:**693-5239
(212) 889-6565 .. **Rancier,** April M '09 %Schwartz & P LLP -295 Mad Av -NY 10017
(212) 863-6300 .. **Rand,** Deborah '75 %HPD -100 Gold -NY 10038 **Fx:**863-8201
(718) 553-1750 .. **Rand,** Deborah E '82 US Customs Srvc -Bldg 77 JFK Airport -Jamaica 11430
(212) 687-7070 .. **Rand,** E Cooke '66 (Rand RR&G LLP) -800 3rd Av -NY 10022
(212) 823-3582 .. **Rand,** Elizabeth '09 Alliance Bernstein LP -1345 Av of Amer -NY 10105 **Fx:**554-4639
(212) 493-8591 .. **Rand,** Elizabeth S '00 Brown Bros Harriman -140 Bway -NY 10005
(516) 379-2400 .. **Rand,** Howard '72 -50 Mill Rd -Freeprt 11520
(212) 618-6352 .. **Rand,** Jay S '88 (Sorin RC LLC) -1230 Av of Amer -NY 10020
(914) 946-8900 .. **Rand,** John S '90 (Clark G&M) -99 Court -White Plns 10601
(212) 698-3500 .. **Rand,** Jon S '84 (Dechert LLP) -1095 Av of Amer -NY 10036
(845) 770-1310 .. **Rand,** Jos W '93 Prudential Rand Rlty -268 S Main -New Cty 10956 **Fx:**634-0739
(212) 905-6095 .. **Rand,** Joshua D '02 Sapotek -41 E 11th -NY 10003
(212) 770-1737 .. **Rand,** Peter L '92 %AIG -80 Pine -NY 10005 **Fx:**344-2357
(212) 687-7070 .. **Rand Rosenzweig Radley & Gordon LLP** -800 3rd Av -NY 10022 **Fx:**557-1475
(914) 406-7000 .. **Rand Rosenzweig Radley & Gordon LLP** -50 Main -White Plns 10606 **Fx:**406-7010
(212) 849-7000 .. **Rand,** Sascha M '98 %Quinn EU&S,LLP -51 Mad Av -NY 10010
(212) 223-0400 .. **Rand,** Steven S '79 (Zeichner E&K LLP) -575 Lex Av -NY 10022
(212) 286-1425 .. **Rand,** Wm Coudert '93 -228 E 45th -NY 10017 **Fx:**599-7909
(716) 853-5100 .. **Randaccio,** Brad F '83 (Lippes MWF LLP) -665 Main -Buffalo 14203
(518) 402-0205 .. **Randall,** Cheryl L '91 %UIA Bd -Troy Atrium Bx15126 -Albany 12212 **Fx:**402-6208
(518) 869-1205 .. **Randall,** Denise McCarthy '77 (Randall Law Firm) -1777 Wstrn Av -Albany 12203 **Fx:**452-2145
(585) 753-4500 .. **Randall,** Douglas A '84 %DA -832 Watts Bldg -Rchstr 14614 **Fx:**753-4576
(518) 785-6314 .. **Randall,** Harvey '69 -887 Birchwood Ln -Niskayuna 12309
(516) 676-4900 .. **Randall,** John J IV '86 -222 Birch Hill Rd -Locust Vly 11560 **Fx:**674-3885
(212) 446-7000 .. **Randall,** Leigh J '96 %McKinsey & Co -55 E 52nd -NY 10055 **Fx:**688-9521

(516) 877-2720 .. **Randall,** Martin E '68 (Cohen & R) -1100 Franklin Av -Gdn Cty 11530 **Fx:**877-2736
(585) 458-2800 .. **Randall,** Mary W '90 (Moyer R&R,PC) -2300 W Ridge Rd -Rchstr 14626
(718) 263-3695 .. **Randall,** Percy A '83 -123-20 82nd Av -Kew Gdns 11415 **Fx:**263-3697
(518) 869-1205 .. **Randall,** Robt G Jr. '75 (Randall Law Firm) -1777 Wstrn Av -Albany 12203 **Fx:**452-2145
(212) 858-1000 .. **Randall,** Sharon Houle '08 Pillsbury WSP LLP -1540 Bway -NY 10036
(212) 225-2000 .. **Randazzo,** Anthony J '09 %Cleary GS&H -1 Lbrty Plz -NY 10006
(212) 903-9000 .. **Randazzo,** Danielle M '06 %Linklaters -1345 Av of Amer -NY 10105
(914) 946-0600 .. **Randazzo,** Frank C '93 %Pino & Assoc -50 Main -White Plns 10606 **Fx:**946-0650
(516) 496-3868 .. **Randazzo,** Gaspare J '98 %Keusey T&B,PC -20 Crsswys Park Dr N -Woodbury 11797
(914) 251-0603 .. **Randazzo,** James A '90 (Gelardi & R,LLP) -800 Wstchstr Av -Rye Brook 10573 **Fx:**253-0909
(914) 449-8357 .. **Randazzo,** John D '87 -450 Commerce -Hawthorne 10532 **Fx:**449-8364
(516) 542-1000 .. **Randazzo,** Jos '89 %Geisler & G,LLP -100 Q Roosevelt Blvd -Gdn Cty 11530
(516) 355-0780 .. **Randazzo,** Joyce D '88 (Randazzo & G PC) -3000 Marcus Av -Lk Success 11042
(631) 673-4998 .. **Randazzo,** Ralph M '94 (Randazzo & R,LLP) -464 NY Av -Huntngtn 11743 **Fx:**549-0826
(631) 673-4998 .. **Randazzo,** Sheryl L '94 (Randazzo & R,LLP) -464 NY Av -Huntngtn 11743 **Fx:**549-0826
(516) 791-3335 .. **Randell,** Robt J '54 -30 Amherst Rd -Vly Stream 11581 **Fx:**791-6721
(212) 752-3380 .. **Randell,** Robt J '54 -880 3rd Av 13th Fl -NY 10022 **Fx:**371-2988
(718) 522-1020 .. **Randesi,** Jera M '05 %Rubenstein & R -16 Court -Brklyn 11241
(585) 248-3800 .. **Randisi,** Andrew R '03 (WeinsteinMurphy) -290 Linden Oaks -Rchstr 14625 **Fx:**248-4961
(585) 248-3800 .. **Randisi,** Elizabeth K '05 %WeinsteinMurphy -290 Linden Oaks -Rchstr 14625 **Fx:**248-4961
(516) 799-9800 .. **Rando,** Robt J '90 (Rando Law Firm PC) -4940 Merrick Rd -Massapequa Pk 11762 **Fx:**799-9820
(212) 525-5551 .. **Randolph,** Kenneth V '02 HSBC Inc -452 5th Av -NY 10018
(212) 759-0097 .. **Randolph,** M Bradford '76 (MB Randolph,PLLC) -1230 Av of Amer -NY 10020
(718) 875-1245 .. **Randolph,** Sheila J '04 Pruzan Law Firm -111 Lvngstn -Brklyn 11201 **Fx:**797-9087
(212) 986-1200 .. **Randolph,** Wm B '79 (Gordon HR&C LLP) -355 Lex Av -NY 10017
(914) 761-4404 .. **Ranellone,** Steven N '98 -199 Main -White Plns 10601 **Fx:**761-4405
(914) 632-4700 .. **Raneri,** Michl J '00 %McDonough Law Firm, LLP -145 Huguenot -New Rchll 10801
(516) 560-6400 .. **Raney,** Barbara Ann '96 (Leg Aid) -1 Helen Keller Way -Hempstd 11550 **Fx:**565-3694
(212) 373-3000 .. **Ranga,** Rati '07 %Paul WRW&G LLP -1285 Av of Amer -NY 10019
(212) 384-3404 .. **Rangappa,** Renuka A '03 FBI -26 Fed Plz -NY 10278
(212) 530-5000 .. **Rangwala,** Tawfiq S '03 %Milbank TH&M LLP -1 Chase Manh Plz -NY 10005
(212) 402-9400 .. **Rangwala,** Yusuf A '06 %McKool S,PC -1 Bryant Park -NY 10036
(718) 590-2000 .. **Rani,** Reena '09 %DA -198 E 161st -Bronx 10451 **Fx:**590-6477
(516) 746-8000 .. **Raniere,** Michl D '04 %Jaspan S LLP -300 Grdn City Plz -Gdn City 11530
(212) 566-2240 .. **Ranieri,** Anthony '91 (Ranieri & N) -11 Park Pl -NY 10007 **Fx:**566-2249
(212) 269-7444 .. **Ranieri,** Jos N '04 Cilmi & Assoc PLLC -39 Bway -NY 10006 **Fx:**269-3958
(315) 422-8769 .. **Ranieri,** Michl J '07 -407 S Warren -Syracuse 13202 **Fx:**476-8002
(212) 952-0100 .. **Ranieri,** Wm F '91 US Aviation -199 Water -NY 10038
(914) 631-1999 .. **Raniolo,** Gary J '83 -150 Wht Plns Rd -Tarrytwn 10591 **Fx:**631-5827
(718) 618-2327 .. **Raniolo,** John '77 %Surrogate's Ct -851 Grnd Cncrs -Bronx 10451 **Fx:**590-3575
(212) 336-3620 .. **Ranis,** Michl B '89 %EEOC -33 Whitehall -NY 10004
(212) 319-9800 .. **Rank,** Bradley M '05 %Tashjian & P -729 7th Av -NY 10019
(212) 556-2100 .. **Rank Divine,** Jessica '07 %King & S -1185 Av of Amer -NY 10036
(516) 746-3500 .. **Rankin,** Carolyn Sicuranza '92 %Brand G&B,PC -600 Old Cntry Rd -Gdn Cty 11530
(212) 626-4100 .. **Rankin,** Clyde E III '76 (Baker & M LLP) -1114 Av of Amer -NY 10036
(212) 226-4507 .. **Rankin,** David B '06 (Rankin & T) -350 Bway -NY 10013
(212) 660-8110 .. **Rankin,** David P '94 MRSSI,Inc -350 7th Av -NY 10001
(718) 858-3000 .. **Rankin,** Douglas G '99 -26 Court -Brklyn 11242 **Fx:**858-9615
(718) 858-3000 .. **Rankin,** Fern Pruett '88 OfCnsl D Rankin & Assoc PC -26 Court -Brklyn 11242 **Fx:**858-9615
(212) 698-3500 .. **Rankin,** K Keely '09 %Dechert LLP -1095 Av of Amer -NY 10036
(718) 286-6236 .. **Rankin,** Karen H '90 %DA -125-01 Qns Blvd -Kew Gdns 11415
(212) 889-0320 .. **Rankow Cohen & Isaac** -220 E 42nd -NY 10017 **Fx:**545-8395
(315) 363-2382 .. **Rann,** Frederic N '59 -128 Main -Oneida 13421 **Fx:**361-4414
(212) 481-7007 .. **Rannells,** John M Jr. '87 (Baker & R) -1350 Bway -NY 10018
(845) 703-3101 .. **Ranni,** Jos J '87 %Bonacic KCM&B,LLP -90 Crystal Run Rd -Middletwn 10941
(716) 847-8400 .. **Ranni,** Sarah K '05 %Phillips L LLP -3400 HSBC Ctr -Buffalo 14203
(718) 222-8880 .. **Rannie,** Michele P '06 %Jones JO -45 Main -Brklyn 11201
(518) 471-4719 .. **Ranous,** James S '76 %Appllt Div 3rd Dept -Capitol Station Bx7288 -Albany 12224 **Fx:**471-4750
(212) 259-8000 .. **Ransom,** Linda E '79 (Dewey & L LLP) -1301 Av of Amer -NY 10019
(845) 565-5248 .. **Rant,** David R '79 -8 Cross -New Windsor 12553 **Fx:**565-9065
(607) 692-3300 .. **Rantanen,** Edw A '65 (E Rantanen,PC) -2638 Main Bx309 -Whitney Pnt 13862 **Fx:**692-2636
(212) 809-1111 .. **Rantas,** Thos G '02 %Morgan MA -39 Bway -NY 10006
(718) 933-8770 .. **Ranus,** Ronald N '73 ALJ -696 E Fordham Rd -Bronx 10458
(716) 542-5444 .. **Ranzenhofer,** Michl H '80 (Friedman & R,PC) -74 Main Bx31 -Akron 14001
(212) 455-9255 .. **Rao,** Anthony J '06 (Rao & T LLP) -90 Park Av -NY 10016 **Fx:**297-0005
(212) 335-9000 .. **Rao,** Archana '02 %DA -1 Hogan Pl -NY 10013
(646) 333-6051 .. **Rao,** Ashvin B '01 Lehman Bros -1271 Av of Amer -NY 10020
(914) 385-4100 .. **Rao,** Christopher E '97 (Hoffman W&R,LLP) -399 Knollwood Rd -White Plns 10603
(212) 848-4000 .. **Rao,** Dave N '06 %Shearman & S LLP -599 Lex Av -NY 10022
(212) 474-1000 .. **Rao,** Jayant D '09 %Cravath S&M LLP -825 8th Av -NY 10019
(718) 298-8900 .. **Rao,** Jess J '09 Leg Aid -153-01 Jamaica Av -Jamaica 11432 **Fx:**657-0537
(718) 838-7878 .. **Rao,** Kumar '07 %Bronx Defenders -860 Crtlandt Av -Bronx 10451 **Fx:**665-0100
(585) 428-4516 .. **Rao,** Michl G '90 Family Ct -99 Exchange Blvd -Rchstr 14614
(315) 432-7457 .. **Rao,** Patrick J '95 Carrier Corp -Carrier Pkwy Bldg TR4 Bx4800 -Syracuse 13221 **Fx:**432-7857
(212) 351-4000 .. **Rao,** Sandeep P '09 Gibson D&C LLP -200 Park Av -NY 10166
(212) 223-0400 .. **Rao,** Siddartha '09 %Zeichner E&K LLP -575 Lex Av -NY 10022
(212) 318-6000 .. **Rao,** Thos M '97 (Paul HJ&W LLP) -75 E 55th -NY 10022
(718) 250-2000 .. **Rao,** Vasantha Ramani '06 DA -350 Jay -Brklyn 11201 **Fx:**250-2314
(973) 503-5924 .. **Rao,** Vincent P II '06 %Kelley D&W LLP -101 Park Av -NY 10178 **Fx:**503-5950
(212) 909-6000 .. **Rao,** Y Rupa '06 %Debevoise & P LLP -919 3rd Av -NY 10022
(212) 770-1326 .. **Rapacioli,** David G '96 %AIG -70 Pine -NY 10270
(516) 295-7622 .. **Rapaport,** Aimee F '94 -1553 Bway -Hewlett 11557
(212) 259-8000 .. **Rapaport,** Andrea '99 Dewey & L LLP -1301 Av of Amer -NY 10019
(212) 355-4175 .. **Rapaport Brothers,PC** -18 E 48th -NY 10017 **Fx:**980-4890
(212) 355-4175 .. **Rapaport,** David A H '74 (Rapaport Bros,PC) -18 E 48th -NY 10017
(516) 295-2969 .. **Rapaport,** Heloisa Guimaraes '90 -112 Spruce -Cedarhrst 11516
(347) 296-1183 .. **Rapaport,** Jennifer R '96 %Hon K Rothenberg-Supreme Ct -360 Adams -Brklyn 11201
(212) 382-1600 .. **Rapaport,** Marc A '93 Rapaport Law Firm,PLLC -350 5th Av -NY 10118 **Fx:**382-0920
(212) 355-4175 .. **Rapaport,** Martin S '69 -18 E 48th -NY 10017 **Fx:**688-9374
(212) 355-4175 .. **Rapaport,** Michl S '64 (Rapaport Bros,PC) -18 E 48th -NY 10017
(315) 697-3105 .. **Rapasadi,** Kathleen A '93 (K Rapasadi,LLC) -201 S Peterboro Bx678 -Canastota 13032
(315) 366-2236 .. **Rapasadi,** Kathleen A '93 %DA -Cnty Cthse Bx578 -Wampsville 13163 **Fx:**366-2503
(212) 668-8400 .. **Rapawy,** John J '98 %L Grandelli,PC -90 Broad -NY 10004 **Fx:**483-0918
(212) 400-6900 .. **Rapfogel,** Scott E '83 %Gottbetter & Prtnrs -488 Mad Av -NY 10022 **Fx:**400-6901
(718) 590-2000 .. **Raphael,** Cassandra '09 %DA -198 E 161st -Bronx 10451 **Fx:**590-6477
Raphael, Felicia S '90 -Bx294 -Kerhonkson 12446
(212) 710-0030 .. **Raphael,** Gregory J '87 (Ryan & R,PC) -264 W 40th -NY 10018
(212) 264-3389 .. **Raphael,** Jason E '90 %DHS -26 Fed Plz -NY 10278
(212) 373-3000 .. **Raphael,** Justin P '10 %Paul WRW&G LLP -1285 Av of Amer -NY 10019
(212) 505-2880 .. **Raphael & Marks** -276 Park Av S -NY 10010 **Fx:**505-2881
(212) 759-4600 .. **Raphael,** Michele Fried '94 (Wolf P LLP) -845 3rd Av -NY 10022
(516) 764-0226 .. **Raphael,** Robt S '94 %Gilman Mgt -Bx222143 -Gt Neck 11022
(212) 505-2880 .. **Raphael,** Stephen M '67 (Raphael & M) -276 Park Av S -NY 10010
(212) 471-0007 .. **Raphael,** Steven M '90 -295 Mad Av -NY 10017 **Fx:**471-0009
(212) 268-3222 .. **Raphaelson,** Howard A '92 (Raphaelson & L,PC) -14 Penn Plz -NY 10122 **Fx:**268-3313
(212) 754-2233 .. **Raphaelson,** Ira H '06 Scientific Games -750 Lex Av -NY 10022
(212) 244-6255 .. **Raphan,** Bernard '52 -450 7th Av -NY 10123 **Fx:**244-6256
(212) 268-8200 .. **Raphan,** Brian A '89 (B Raphan,PC) -7 Penn Plz -NY 10001 **Fx:**244-3075
(212) 653-8700 .. **Raphan,** Eric D '02 %Sheppard MR&H LLP -30 Rckfllr Plz -NY 10112
(516) 488-3300 .. **Raphan,** Lori M '06 %Shaub AC&S,LLP -1983 Marcus Av -Lk Success 11042
(516) 536-7444 .. **Raphan,** Michl B '73 (Ackerman R&S) -2949 Lng Bch Rd -Oceanside 11572 **Fx:**536-8235
(212) 442-2220 .. **Rapisarda,** Diane '99 ACS -220 Church -NY 10013
(212) 629-8585 .. **Rapisarda,** Suzanne M '86 (Ellenberg & Prtnrs LLP) -575 8th Av -NY 10018
(212) 504-6000 .. **Rapisardi,** John J '83 (Cadwalader W&T LLP) -1 World Fncl Ctr -NY 10281
(315) 336-5450 .. **Rapke,** David J '82 (Rapke & P,LLP) -320 N George Bx928 -Rome 13440
(315) 336-5450 .. **Rapke & Plumley, LLP** -320 N George Bx928 -Rome 13440 **Fx:**336-3239
(718) 261-2224 .. **Rapoport,** Alla '03 A Rapoport,PC -118-21 Qns Blvd -Frst Hlls 11375 **Fx:**261-5356
(212) 486-7119 .. **Rapoport,** Bernard R '41 Lowenstein Fndtn -150 E 58th -NY 10155
(516) 922-1555 .. **Rapoport,** Robt Jay '58 -45 Foxhunt Cres -Oyster Bay Cove 11791 **Fx:**922-1529
(914) 241-1129 .. **Rapoport,** West Reid '90 -359 Cherry -Bedfrd Hlls 10507
(212) 596-9000 .. **Rapoport,** Yelena '09 %Ropes & G LLP -1211 Av of Amer -NY 10036
(212) 986-6000 .. **Rapp,** James I '99 OfCnsl Kleinberg KW&C,PC -551 5th Av -NY 10176
(516) 545-5027 .. **Rapp,** Richd A Jr. '84 KeySpan Corp -175 E Old Cntry Rd -Hicksvll 11801 **Fx:**545-5029
(914) 767-6000 .. **Rapp,** Steven M '84 %Pepsi Bottling Grp -1 Pepsi Way -Somers 10589
(212) 446-9166 .. **Rappa,** Salvatore '96 %Cohen & Steers Inc -280 Park Av -NY 10017
(212) 828-0727 .. **Rappaport,** Abe '85 -111 22nd -Brklyn 11232
(516) 742-6487 .. **Rappaport,** Brian C '65 (BC Rappaport,PC) -360 Merrick Rd -Lynbrk 11563 **Fx:**742-0974
(212) 921-5200 .. **Rappaport,** Chas J '64 (Rappaport GG&L LLP) -733 3rd Av -NY 10017
(212) 455-2000 .. **Rappaport,** Chas O '76 (Simpson T&B LLP) -425 Lex Av -NY 10017
(212) 259-5610 .. **Rappaport,** David R '85 %Investec USA Holdings Corp -666 5th Av -NY 10103
(212) 872-1000 .. **Rappaport,** Douglas A '92 -One Bryant Park -NY 10036 **Fx:**872-1002

(718) 237-1900 .. **Rappaport,** Edw M '58 OfCnsl Flamhaft LH&R -16 Court -Brklyn 11241
(212) 752-7474 .. **Rappaport,** Gary S '84 %Steinberg & Pokoik -575 Mad Av -NY 10022 **Fx:**421-6196
(631) 293-2300 .. **Rappaport Glass Greene & Levine LLP** -1355 Motor Pkwy -Hauppauge 11749 **Fx:**293-2918
(212) 921-5200 .. **Rappaport Glass Greene & Levine LLP** -733 3rd Av -NY 10017 **Fx:**921-5367
(718) 261-7700 .. **Rappaport Hertz Cherson & Rosenthal,PC** -118-35 Qns Blvd -Frst Hlls 11375 **Fx:**261-7336
(516) 997-0999 .. **Rappaport,** J Logan '07 %Pryor & M,LLP -675 Old Cntry Rd -Westbury 11590
(212) 715-9100 .. **Rappaport,** Jason S '09 %Kramer LN&F,LLP -1177 Av of Amer -NY 10036
(212) 593-6700 .. **Rappaport,** Jay A '74 (Aaronson RF&D,LLP) -757 3rd Av -NY 10017
(212) 848-7004 .. **Rappaport,** Linda E '78 (Shearman & S LLP) -599 Lex Av -NY 10022
(607) 723-9511 .. **Rappaport,** Mark L '69 OfCnsl Coughlin & G,LLP -19 Chenango Bx2039 -Bnghmtn 13902
(516) 364-3080 .. **Rappaport,** Melissa L '04 %R Lenowitz -7600 Jericho Tpk -Woodbury 11797
(800) 945-0848 .. **Rappaport,** Michl K '92 -530 E 20th -NY 10009 **Fx:**(212) 777-3135
(917) 778-6500 .. **Rappaport,** Michl L '74 %K Dodson -485 Lex Av -NY 10017
(212) 839-5300 .. **Rappaport,** Michl M '09 %Sidley A LLP -787 7th Av -NY 10019
(516) 222-8200 .. **Rappaport,** Richd V '79 RV Rappaport & Assoc -1900 Hempstd Tpk -E Meadow 11554 **Fx:**222-5262
(212) 530-5000 .. **Rappaport,** Stacey J '97 (Milbank TH&M LLP) -1 Chase Manh Plz -NY 10005
(212) 776-5000 .. **Rappaport,** Steven J '79 %NYC Housing Auth -250 Bway -NY 10007 **Fx:**776-5039
(212) 687-8700 .. **Rappaport,** Stuart J '81 Cnsl Malkin Hldngs,LLC -60 E 42nd -NY 10165 **Fx:**986-7679
(718) 261-7700 .. **Rappaport,** Wm J '79 (Rappaport HC&R,PC) -118-35 Qns Blvd -Frst Hlls 11375
(518) 384-3400 .. **Rappazzo,** Rachel A '04 %Harding Law Firm -1343 Balltown Rd -Niskayuna 12309 **Fx:**384-2293
(631) 673-6670 .. **Rappel,** Jacqueline A '93 %Speyer & P,LLP -115 Broadhllw Rd -Melvll 11747
(845) 454-1110 .. **Rappleyea,** Allan B '93 (Corbally G and R LLP) -35 Market -Poughkeepsie 12601
(845) 677-5539 .. **Rappleyea,** Allan B '93 (Corbally G and R LLP) -30 Front -Millbrook 12545
(845) 677-5539 .. **Rappleyea,** Allan E '53 (Corbally G and R LLP) -30 Front -Millbrook 12545
(845) 454-1110 .. **Rappleyea,** Allan E '53 (Corbally G and R LLP) -35 Market -Poughkeepsie 12601
(518) 758-8034 .. **Rappleyea,** Tal G '89 -Bx793 -Valatie 12184 **Fx:**758-8038
(212) 635-1466 .. **Rappold,** Chas II '78 %Bk of NY -1 Wall -NY 10286
(518) 474-1191 .. **Rappoport,** Lawr A '72 %Dept of Law -The Cptl -Albany 12224
(212) 476-9000 .. **Rappoport,** Margo '77 %Neuberger Berman Mgmt Inc -605 3rd Av -NY 10158 **Fx:**476-5781
(212) 558-4000 .. **Rappoport,** Steven T '10 %Sullivan & C LLP -125 Broad -NY 10004
(518) 828-9444 .. **Rapport,** Carmi '58 (Rapport MWS&R,LLP) -436 Union -Hudson 12534
(212) 833-1122 .. **Rapport,** Danl B '96 (Friedman KS&A LLP) -1633 Bway -NY 10019 **Fx:**373-7922
(212) 233-1515 .. **Rapport,** Jonathan A '99 %R Katz,LLP -80 Broad -NY 10004 **Fx:**571-3415
(518) 828-9444 .. **Rapport Meyers Whitbeck Shaw & Rodenhausen,LLP** -436 Union -Hudson 12534 **Fx:**828-9719
(845) 473-7766 .. **Rapport Meyers Whitbeck Shaw & Rodenhausen,LLP** -35 Main -Poughkeepsie 12601 **Fx:**473-7790
(518) 828-0185 .. **Rapport,** Seth L '90 %Valley Mortgage Co Inc -2 E Court -Hudson 12534 **Fx:**828-0459
(516) 739-5140 .. **Raptakis,** Harry '67 -88 2nd -Mineola 11501 **Fx:**747-2574
(212) 735-3000 .. **Raptis,** Maria A '03 %Skadden ASM&F LLP -4 Times Sq -NY 10036
(908) 221-1200 .. **Raptis,** Peggy C '88 OfCnsl Pinczewski & B,PC -2753 Coney Isl Av -Brklyn 11235 **Fx:**204-1350
(718) 250-2000 .. **Rapuano,** Marc W '05 DA -350 Jay -Brklyn 11201 **Fx:**250-2314
(212) 624-4300 .. **Rapuano,** Robt A '71 %BLDG Mgmt Co,Inc -417 5th Av -NY 10016 **Fx:**557-2531
(516) 783-6565 .. **Rapuzzi,** Patricia Anne '05 (Rapuzzi P&R,PC) -3361 Park Av -Wantagh 11793 **Fx:**783-6868
(585) 219-4900 .. **Rarick,** Fredk M '92 -Bx250 -Corfu 14036 **Fx:**219-4905
(914) 289-2909 .. **Ras,** Luis F '91 Ras Assoc,PLLC -10 Bank -White Plns 10606
(212) 354-4500 .. **Rasalingam,** Anusha '01 %Friedman & W -1500 Bway -NY 10036
(212) 574-1200 .. **Rasamny,** Kenneth B '09 %Seward & K LLP -1 Bttry Pk Plz -NY 10004
(914) 666-7770 .. **Rasamny,** Mary Kinnally '76 %Future Title -37 W Main -Mt Kisco 10549
(212) 450-4000 .. **Rasamny,** Robt R '09 %Davis P&W LLP -450 Lex Av -NY 10017
(212) 755-5510 .. **Rasch,** M Stephen '80 (Loeb B & Prtnrs) -505 Park Av -NY 10022
(518) 875-6063 .. **Rase,** D Jeremy '01 (DJ Rase,PLLC) -1646 State Hwy 30A -Esperance 12066
(212) 735-3000 .. **Rasenberger,** Mary E '90 Cnsl Skadden ASM&F LLP -4 Times Sq -NY 10036
(212) 687-6262 .. **Rasey,** Randall L '97 %Barton B&P,LLP -420 Lex Av -NY 10170
(315) 337-7492 .. **Rasheed,** Jawwaad A '82 %Family Ct -301 W Dominick -Rome 13440
Rasher, Howard Wm '57 -322 W 57th -NY 10019
(212) 661-7100 .. **Rashes,** Alan M '67 OfCnsl Salon MDN&B,LLP -292 Mad Av -NY 10017
(212) 964-0120 .. **Rashid,** Ayesha T '05 %Golden RSLB&G,PC -111 John -NY 10038
(212) 504-6000 .. **Rashid,** Ikhlas Sabreen '10 Cadwalader W&T LLP -1 World Fncl Ctr -NY 10281
(212) 849-7000 .. **Rashid,** Sami H '06 %Quinn EU&S,LLP -51 Mad Av -NY 10010
(212) 839-5300 .. **Rashid,** Suhaib '08 %Sidley A LLP -787 7th Av -NY 10019
(212) 839-5300 .. **Rashkover,** Barry W '87 (Sidley A LLP) -787 7th Av -NY 10019
(718) 725-1600 .. **Rashty,** Merav '03 -214-61 Jamaica Av -Qns Vllg 11428 **Fx:**725-1717
(212) 969-3000 .. **Rasin,** Gregory I '74 (Proskauer R LLP) -1585 Bway -NY 10036
(212) 564-5005 .. **Rasin,** Kim R '00 L Kucherovsky -212 W 35th -NY 10001 **Fx:**564-5121
(212) 813-8800 .. **Rasin,** Simon '06 %Goodwin P LLP -620 8th Av -NY 10018
(212) 381-7000 .. **Rask,** Pamela A '88 (Sabin B&G LLP) -4 Times Sq -NY 10036
(212) 587-3434 .. **Raskin,** Bruce J '85 (Raskin & K LLP) -160 Bway -NY 10038
(212) 637-2635 .. **Raskin,** David A '95 %US Atty -1 St Andrews Plz -NY 10007
(212) 403-7300 .. **Raskin,** Debra L '83 (Vladeck WE&E,PC) -1501 Bway -NY 10036
(631) 667-1023 .. **Raskin,** Edw S '66 -2137 Deer Prk Av -Deer Pk 11729
(212) 402-9400 .. **Raskin,** Elizabeth H '05 %McKool S,PC -1 Bryant Park -NY 10036
(914) 833-2598 .. **Raskin,** Ellen '82 -23 Kane Av -Larchmnt 10538 **Fx:**(212) 391-8370
(212) 391-1139 .. **Raskin,** Ellen '82 OfCnsl E Holzberg & Assoc -1700 Bway -NY 10019 **Fx:**391-8370
(212) 554-1400 .. **Raskin,** Joshua L '97 Cnsl Bernstein LB&G LLP -1285 Av of Amer -NY 10019
(516) 228-6522 .. **Raskin,** Judith B '87 (Raskin & M) -600 Old Cntry Rd -Gdn Cty 11530 **Fx:**228-6525
(212) 556-2162 .. **Raskin,** Kenneth A '85 (King & S) -1185 Av of Amer -NY 10036
(212) 587-3434 .. **Raskin & Kremins LLP** -160 Bway -NY 10038 **Fx:**608-1659
(212) 732-3053 .. **Raskin,** Lester '55 (Raskin & R,PC) -160 Bway -NY 10038
(212) 402-9400 .. **Raskin,** Mark S '01 SrCnsl McKool S,PC -1 Bryant Park -NY 10036
(212) 883-4908 .. **Raskin,** Martin G '73 (Cozen O) -277 Park Av -NY 10172 **Fx:**672-1108
(718) 293-2222 .. **Raskin,** Marvin Ray '73 -944 Gerard Av -Bronx 10452 **Fx:**293-0870
(718) 579-3000 .. **Raskin,** Michl '86 %Leg Aid -1020 Grnd Cncrs -Bronx 10451 **Fx:**588-2611
(718) 681-2680 .. **Raskin,** Michl A '92 Raskin & Assoc -903 Sheridan Av -Bronx 10451 **Fx:**588-9599
(212) 732-3053 .. **Raskin & Rappoport,PC** -160 Bway -NY 10038 **Fx:**608-1659
(718) 875-2060 .. **Raskin,** Raymond A '74 -26 Court -Brklyn 11242
(845) 354-4818 .. **Raskin,** Zvi N '88 -10 Kerri Ln -Spg Vly 10977
(516) 505-9866 .. **Raskind,** Steven L '74 -95 Front -Hempstd 11550
(518) 213-6000 .. **Raskin-Ortiz,** Marilyn S '81 %NYSUT -800 Troy-Schnctdy Rd -Latham 12110 **Fx:**213-6488
(631) 582-5151 .. **Raskin Rocco,** Cindy '09 %Haley W&C,LLP -1601 Vets Mem'l Hwy -Islandia 11749
(914) 271-5383 .. **Raskob,** Casey W III '90 (CW Raskob III,PC) -34 Lounsbury Rd -Croton-On-Hud 10520 **Fx:**271-4548
(212) 849-7000 .. **Raskopf,** Robt L '77 (Quinn EU&S,LLP) -51 Mad Av -NY 10010
(212) 677-6498 .. **Raskyn,** Terry '82 -651 E 14th -NY 10009
(212) 424-8024 .. **Rasmus,** Lauren G '00 -125 W 55th -NY 10019 **Fx:**424-8500
(607) 869-5111 .. **Rasmus,** Michl B '04 Dept Crrctnl Srvcs -6600 State Route 96 -Romulus 14541
(631) 288-2876 .. **Rasmussen,** Barbara A '99 %Kelly & H -323 Mill Rd -Westhmptn Bch 11978 **Fx:**288-1328
(914) 712-1100 .. **Rasmussen,** David J '86 %Murphy & H,LLP -1 Radisson Plz -New Rchll 10801
(585) 546-6448 .. **Rasmussen,** David L '86 (Davidson F LLP) -28 E Main -Rchstr 14614
(212) 336-2000 .. **Rasmussen,** Eric P '09 %Patterson BW&T LLP -1133 Av of Amer -NY 10036
(212) 848-8844 .. **Rasmussen,** Eva A '83 %Shearman & S LLP -599 Lex Av -NY 10022
(646) 825-3026 .. **Rasmussen,** Ian P '09 %MB Mitzner -405 Lex Av -NY 10174
(212) 755-0100 .. **Rasmussen,** Mark W '06 %Grais & E LLP -40 E 52nd -NY 10022
(212) 547-5400 .. **Rasmussen,** Matthew Paul '09 %McDermott W&E LLP -340 Mad Av -NY 10173
(212) 431-7200 .. **Rasmussen,** Raun J Jr. '85 Legal Srvcs NYC -350 Bway -NY 10013 **Fx:**966-9571
(212) 819-8200 .. **Rasmussen,** Rebecca A '08 %White & C LLP -1155 Av of Amer -NY 10036
(212) 351-4500 .. **Rasnick,** Lauri F '96 (Epstein B&G,PC) -250 Park Av -NY 10177
(845) 358-5115 .. **Raso,** Francis J '84 -3 Main -Nyack 10960 **Fx:**358-7092
(212) 962-6525 .. **Raso,** Matthew P '09 %Codispoti & Assoc,PC -111 John -NY 10038 **Fx:**962-6791
(212) 243-2424 .. **Raso,** Silvana '94 (Schepisi & M,PA) -200 Park Av S -NY 10003
(914) 798-5400 .. **Raso,** Suzin L '01 %Goldberg S LLP -11 Martine Av -White Plns 10606
(212) 735-3000 .. **Rasor,** Katherine E '09 %Skadden ASM&F LLP -4 Times Sq -NY 10036
(212) 903-9000 .. **Rasp,** Edw H III '08 %Linklaters -1345 Av of Amer -NY 10105
(845) 294-5755 .. **Raspa,** Ronald W '93 -Harriman Dr -Goshen 10924
(315) 798-5766 .. **Raspante,** John J '06 %DA -800 Park Av -Utica 13501 **Fx:**798-5582
(212) 336-2000 .. **Raspé,** Herman H '89 (Patterson BW&T LLP) -1133 Av of Amer -NY 10036
(212) 851-2862 .. **Rassas,** Lori B '98 %Columbia Univ Lbr Relatns -615 W 131st -NY 10027 **Fx:**234-1819
(516) 398-5476 .. **Rassiger,** Donald J '96 SrCnsl LiRo Grp -3 Aerial Way -Syosset 11791
(516) 626-2470 .. **Rassner,** Alan C '61 OfCnsl Rassner R&O -14 Twr Pl -Roslyn 11576
(516) 626-2470 .. **Rassner Rassner & Olman** -14 Twr Pl -Roslyn 11576 **Fx:**626-2472
(212) 613-2073 .. **Rastaetter,** Myriam P '06 %Gibbons PC -1 Penn Plz -NY 10119 **Fx:**554-9672
(212) 610-6300 .. **Rastegar,** Keyvan '06 %Allen & O -1221 Av of Amer -NY 10020
(212) 264-5916 .. **Rastegar,** Ramin '96 US DOJ INS -26 Fed Plz -NY 10278
(212) 230-8800 .. **Rastin,** Natalie Wray '09 %WilmerHale -399 Park Av -NY 10022
(212) 279-4403 .. **Rastogi,** Kamal K '97 Rastogi & Assoc -350 5th Av -NY 10118 **Fx:**563-4534
(212) 930-9700 .. **Rastogi,** Sameer '97 (Sichenzia RFF LLP) -61 Bway -NY 10006
(212) 747-9370 .. **Rasul,** Mohamed R '99 (Rasul & Assoc,LLC) -110 Wall -NY 10005
(585) 492-2532 .. **Raszeja,** Terry A '76 T Raszeja -26 West -Arcade 14009 **Fx:**(716) 496-5144
(716) 774-8507 .. **Ratajczak,** Robt M '97 (R Ratajczak Jr PC) -Bx914 -Grand Isl 14072 **Fx:**773-5708
(516) 692-8888 .. **Ratchford,** Richd D Jr. '02 %F Chau & Assoc,LLC -130 Woodbury Rd -Woodbury 11797 **Fx:**692-8889
(212) 226-6662 .. **Ratchik,** Jonathan R '98 %Kramer & D -350 Bway -NY 10013
(585) 546-5530 .. **Ratcliffe,** Scott M '99 %Thomson West -50 E Broad -Rchstr 14694

(631) 979-3000 .. **Rate,** Leigh E '01 %Certilman BA&H,LLP -1393 Vets Mem'l Hwy -Hauppauge 11788
(212) 599-8200 .. **Rath,** Gerard S '04 Shaub AC&S,LLP -655 3rd Av -NY 10017
(585) 244-8910 .. **Rath,** Timothy C '95 %Fiandach & F -100 Allens Crk Rd -Rchstr 14618 **Fx:**244-4863
(212) 408-1298 .. **Rathbun,** Peter F '03 American Bible Society -1865 Bway -NY 10023
(973) 596-4500 .. **Rathbun,** Roger M '66 Cnsl Gibbons PC -1 Penn Plz -NY 10119 **Fx:**596-0545
(212) 335-9000 .. **Rather,** Dan M '86 %DA -1 Hogan Pl -NY 10013
(212) 610-6300 .. **Rathi,** Rasika '09 %Allen & O -1221 Av of Amer -NY 10020
(516) 739-0400 .. **Rathje,** Colin '03 %Kelly R&K,LLP -330 Old Cntry Rd -Mineola 11501
(212) 681-8313 .. **Rathkopf,** Clifford A Jr. '71 OfCnsl Karaahmet L&G LLP -370 Lex Av -NY 10017 **Fx:**208-2917
(516) 671-5880 .. **Rathkopf,** Daren A '58 (Chase R&C,LLP) -48 Forest Av -Glen Cove 11542
(212) 592-1400 .. **Rathkopf,** Stephen M '69 (Herrick,F LLP) -2 Park Av -NY 10016
(631) 853-5761 .. **Ratje,** Randall J '91 %Cnty Atty -400 Carleton Av -Central Islip 11722 **Fx:**853-7788
(718) 768-0025 .. **Ratliff,** James R '88 -438 4th -Brklyn 11215
(718) 286-2476 .. **Ratliff,** Kyla L '02 %Leg Aid -120-46 Qns Blvd -Kew Gdns 11415 **Fx:**263-4234
(212) 318-6000 .. **Ratliff,** Preston K '00 (Paul HJ&W LLP) -75 E 55th -NY 10022
(516) 822-3102 .. **Ratner,** Adam J '05 -55 Flower Ln -Jericho 11753
(516) 294-8844 .. **Ratner,** Candice B '06 %L'Abbate BC&C,LLP -1001 Franklin Av -Gdn Cty 11530
(212) 627-8100 .. **Ratner,** Danl J '83 (Levy R,PC) -80 8th Av -NY 10011
(212) 286-8585 .. **Ratner,** Danl S '90 (Heidell PM&B,LLP) -99 Park Av -NY 10016
(212) 437-9110 .. **Ratner,** David R '78 (Hartman UR&R,LLP) -305 Bway -NY 10007
(212) 751-9800 .. **Ratner,** David S '74 (Morelli R PC) -950 3rd Av -NY 10022
(516) 803-3000 .. **Ratner,** Hank J '85 Rainbow Prog -1111 Stewart Av -Bethpage 11714
(212) 577-2523 .. **Ratner,** Jody G '99 %Ctr for Appllt Litigation -74 Trinity Pl -NY 10006 **Fx:**577-2535
(518) 473-2624 .. **Ratner,** Judith I '80 Dept of Civil Srvc -Alfred Smith Bldg -Albany 12239
(718) 920-7266 .. **Ratner,** Loren '98 Montefiore Med Ctr -111 E 210th -Bronx 10467 **Fx:**920-2637
(212) 614-6464 .. **Ratner,** Michl D '71 Ctr for Constitutional Rights -666 Bway -NY 10012
(516) 328-2300 .. **Ratner,** Michl E '03 %Abrams FFEGF&E,LLP -1111 Marcus Av -Lk Success 11042
(212) 779-8600 .. **Ratner,** Mikhail '02 %Silverman SS&B PLLC -381 Park Av S -NY 10016
(212) 355-9500 .. **Ratner,** Morris A '00 OfCnsl Lieff CH&B,LLP -250 Hudson -NY 10013
(212) 310-8000 .. **Ratner,** Philip S '08 %Weil G&M LLP -767 5th Av -NY 10153
(212) 401-4427 .. **Ratner,** Robt J '76 AFCO Credit Corp -14 Wall -NY 10005 **Fx:**401-4430
(212) 594-5000 .. **Ratner,** Scott E '88 %Togut S&S LLP -1 Penn Plz -NY 10119
(212) 969-3000 .. **Ratner,** Stephen L '75 (Proskauer R LLP) -1585 Bway -NY 10036
(607) 547-4209 .. **Ratner,** Steven E '86 %Cnty Atty -197 Main -Cooperstwn 13326 **Fx:**547-7572
(646) 290-9296 .. **Ratschko,** Imke '99 (Imke R,PLLC) -140 Bway -NY 10005 **Fx:**290-5965
(914) 381-7400 .. **Rattet Pasternak & Gordon-Oliver,LLP** -550 Mamaroneck Av -Harrison 10528 **Fx:**381-7406
(914) 381-7400 .. **Rattet,** Robt L '70 (Rattet P&G,LLP) -550 Mamaroneck Av -Harrison 10528
(212) 384-8480 .. **Rattigan,** Wilfred S '91 -175-20 Wexford Ter -Jamaica 11432
(212) 969-3000 .. **Rattner,** Andrea S '87 (Proskauer R LLP) -1585 Bway -NY 10036
(718) 853-8220 .. **Rattner,** Aron F '03 %Berman S&L -4607 Ft Hmltn Pkwy -Brklyn 11219
(845) 512-8700 .. **Rattner,** Brian M '90 (Rattner & Assoc) -2 Perlman Dr -Spg Vly 10977
(516) 872-4500 .. **Rattoballi,** Anthony J '80 -147 S Franklin Av -Vly Stream 11580 **Fx:**825-1318
(516) 825-7880 .. **Rattoballi,** Chas R '49 -147 S Franklin -Vly Stream 11580
(718) 286-2160 .. **Rattray-Gray,** Georgia YPE '89 %Leg Aid -120-46 Qns Blvd -Kew Gdns 11415 **Fx:**286-2286
(212) 344-0464 .. **Rau,** James P '81 (Cardillo & C) -29 Bway -NY 10006
(212) 715-9100 .. **Rau,** Kelly P '10 %Kramer LN&F,LLP -1177 Av of Amer -NY 10036
(212) 588-0800 .. **Raubicheck,** Chas J '76 (Frommer L&H LLP) -745 5th Av -NY 10151
(914) 253-8400 .. **Raucci,** Anthony L '92 %Professional Risk Managers,Inc -2500 Wstchstr Av -Purchase 10577
(212) 969-3000 .. **Rauch,** Brian S '02 %Proskauer R LLP -1585 Bway -NY 10036
(212) 836-8000 .. **Rauch,** Davina J '05 %Kaye S LLP -425 Park Av -NY 10022
(212) 484-3900 .. **Rauch,** Marc '76 (Arent F LLP) -1675 Bway -NY 10019
(212) 859-8000 .. **Rauch,** Michl H '64 OfCnsl Fried FHS&J LLP -1 NY Plz -NY 10004
(212) 298-5183 .. **Rauch,** Philip '85 %Leg Aid -49 Thomas -NY 10013 **Fx:**298-5252
(212) 788-0889 .. **Rauchberg,** Andrew J '07 %Law Dept -100 Church -NY 10007 **Fx:**788-0367
(212) 969-3000 .. **Rauchberg,** Ronald S '67 (Proskauer R LLP) -1585 Bway -NY 10036
(212) 971-9090 .. **Rauchberg,** Steven C '94 (S Rauchberg,PC) -350 5th Av -NY 10118 **Fx:**594-9829
(212) 277-4000 .. **Raudkivi,** Sarah Z '08 %Freshfields BD LLP -520 Mad Av -NY 10022
(212) 236-8252 .. **Rauen,** Gregory D '09 Merrill Lynch -2 World Fncl Ctr -NY 10281
(212) 358-2821 .. **Rauer,** Brian D '97 Better Bus Bur -257 Park Av S -NY 10010
(315) 426-0308 .. **Raus,** George M Jr. '76 -333 E Onondaga -Syracuse 13202
(518) 431-4761 .. **Rausch,** John F '65 %IRS -1 Clinton Av -Albany 12207
(718) 579-7910 .. **Rausch,** Kai-Lin '03 %Leg Aid -900 Sheridan Av -Bronx 10451 **Fx:**293-8744
(518) 465-3553 .. **Rausch,** Robt A '95 (Maynard OS&C,LLP) -6 Twr Pl -Albany 12203
(914) 421-2690 .. **Rauscher,** David G '98 Nextel Communications,Inc -1 N Bway -White Plns 10601
(718) 596-7333 .. **Rausher,** Danl E '84 -26 Court -Brklyn 11242 **Fx:**858-5455
(212) 471-8500 .. **Rauskolb,** Fred W III '71 (Herzfeld & R,PC) -125 Broad -NY 10004
(212) 637-3000 .. **Raut,** Leena A '05 US EPA-Region II -290 Bway -NY 10007
(212) 735-3000 .. **Rauterberg,** Gabriel V '10 %Skadden ASM&F LLP -4 Times Sq -NY 10036
(212) 615-9478 .. **Rauzzino,** Thos F '97 Citigroup,Inc -333 W 34th -NY 10001
(212) 644-4420 .. **Rava,** Jos J Jr. '90 (Fabiani C&H,LLP) -570 Lex Av -NY 10022
(212) 715-9100 .. **Ravago,** Ruben M III '06 %Kramer LN&F,LLP -1177 Av of Amer -NY 10036
(212) 530-5000 .. **Raval,** Abhilash M '03 %Milbank TH&M LLP -1 Chase Manh Plz -NY 10005
(212) 736-1940 .. **Raval,** Sunil G '05 %Davidson D&K LLC -485 7th Av -NY 10018
(518) 432-7511 .. **Ravalli,** Michl P '92 (Gleason DW&O) -40 Beaver -Albany 12207
(212) 735-3000 .. **Ravanides,** Christos '07 %Skadden ASM&F LLP -4 Times Sq -NY 10036
(212) 450-4000 .. **Ravat,** Abdurahman '10 %Davis P&W LLP -450 Lex Av -NY 10017
(516) 671-1295 .. **Rave,** Donald T '56 -11 The Plz -Locust Vly 11560 **Fx:**671-1294
(516) 671-1295 .. **Rave,** Donald T Jr. '79 -11 The Plz -Locust Vly 11560 **Fx:**671-1294
(212) 326-3939 .. **Rave,** Donald T III '07 %Jones D -222 E 41st -NY 10017
(212) 399-3600 .. **Raved,** James E '96 Tishman Construc Corp -666 5th Av -NY 10103
(212) 309-1000 .. **Ravelo,** Keila '92 (Hunton & W) -200 Park Av -NY 10166
(516) 463-7712 .. **Ravelo,** Mercedes '99 Hofstra Univ -117 Hofstra Univ -Hempstd 11549 **Fx:**564-0063
(212) 759-7466 .. **Raven,** Keith A '83 (Raven & K,LLP) -126 E 56th -NY 10022
(212) 759-7466 .. **Raven & Kolbe,LLP** -126 E 56th -NY 10022 **Fx:**759-0166
(212) 751-3001 .. **Raven,** Ricky A '08 (Thompson & K LLP) -919 3rd Av -NY 10022
(212) 715-9100 .. **Ravener,** Kimberly J '07 %Kramer LN&F,LLP -1177 Av of Amer -NY 10036
(315) 422-0496 .. **Ravera,** Robt L '93 -120 E Wshngtn -Syracuse 13202
(212) 733-7538 .. **Ravetti,** Alessandra '99 %Pfizer Inc -235 E 42nd -NY 10017
(212) 450-4000 .. **Ravi,** Sagar K '10 %Davis P&W LLP -450 Lex Av -NY 10017
(212) 210-9546 .. **Ravi,** Srilakshmi M '08 %Alston & B LLP -90 Park Av -NY 10016
(212) 808-7800 .. **Raviele,** Jennifer D '09 %Kelley D&W LLP -101 Park Av -NY 10178
(212) 906-1200 .. **Ravin,** Adam S '02 Cnsl Latham & W -885 3rd Av -NY 10022
(212) 973-0572 .. **Ravin,** David N '82 (Wolff & S PC) -140 Bway -NY 10005
(212) 687-8626 .. **Ravin,** Richd L '93 (Hartman & W,PC) -230 Park Av -NY 10169
(212) 335-4500 .. **Ravindranath,** Chandana T '09 %DLA Piper LLP -1251 Av of Amer -NY 10020
(718) 837-7747 .. **Ravitch,** Alexis '95 (A Ravitch,PC) -1920 86th -Brklyn 11214 **Fx:**837-4437
(212) 788-1040 .. **Ravitch,** Ellen S '91 %Law Dept -100 Church -NY 10007 **Fx:**788-0367
(212) 218-7880 .. **Ravitch,** Richd '59 (Ravitch Rice & Co) -610 5th Av -NY 10020
(212) 388-3203 .. **Ravitz Hogan,** Amie '98 32B-J Leg Srvcs -101 Av of Amer -NY 10013 **Fx:**388-3061
(212) 841-4100 .. **Raviv,** Gil A '98 Millennium Mgt LLC -666 5th Av -NY 10103 **Fx:**841-4141
(914) 366-0201 .. **Ravo,** Jules J '80 OfCnsl Reardon & S,PC -220 Wht Plns Rd -Tarrytwn 10591
(845) 434-4988 .. **Rawich,** Isabelle '77 -5208 Main Bx945 -S Fallsbrg 12779 **Fx:**434-2410
(212) 984-9201 .. **Rawitt,** Peggy D '80 %Guaranty Risk Srvcs -335 Mad Av -NY 10017
(212) 318-6000 .. **Rawitz,** Gary D '83 OfCnsl Paul HJ&W LLP -75 E 55th -NY 10022
(212) 323-7070 .. **Rawle & Henderson LLP** -14 Wall -NY 10005 **Fx:**323-7099
(212) 336-0149 .. **Rawlings,** Steven G '98 %SEC -3 World Fncl Ctr -NY 10281 **Fx:**336-1323
(212) 222-7005 .. **Rawlins,** Earl A '60 (Rawlins & G,LLP) -103 E 125th -NY 10035 **Fx:**222-7187
(212) 926-0050 .. **Rawlins,** Gary N '99 -80 Broad -NY 10004
(917) 517-2566 .. **Rawlins,** Katrina E '05 -Bx697 -Bronx 10460
(212) 747-1230 .. **Rawlinson,** Michl R '95 (McMahon M&G LLP) -55 Washington -Brklyn 11201
(212) 541-2000 .. **Rawn,** Robt J '91 (Bryan C LLP) -1290 Av of Amer -NY 10104
(212) 906-1200 .. **Rawner,** Danl S '10 %Latham & W -885 3rd Av -NY 10022
(212) 698-3500 .. **Rawson,** Joshua '89 (Dechert LLP) -1095 Av of Amer -NY 10036
(212) 335-9000 .. **Rawsthorne,** Christopher W '04 %DA -1 Hogan Pl -NY 10013
(516) 491-0565 .. **Raxenberg,** Jay D '01 JD Raxenberg,PC -600 Old Cntry Rd -Gdn Cty 11530 **Fx:**953-3235
(212) 504-6000 .. **Ray,** Amy W '04 %Cadwalader W&T LLP -1 World Fncl Ctr -NY 10281
(212) 909-6000 .. **Ray,** Christopher J '09 %Debevoise & P LLP -919 3rd Av -NY 10022
(212) 446-4800 .. **Ray,** Claudia E '93 (Kirkland & E LLP) -153 E 53rd -NY 10022
(718) 875-1300 .. **Ray,** Danl B '06 Appllt Div 2nd Dept -45 Monroe Pl -Brklyn 11201 **Fx:**858-2446
(212) 402-9400 .. **Ray,** Hugh M '92 (McKool S,PC) -1 Bryant Park -NY 10036
(212) 333-8763 .. **Ray,** James R III '08 -445 Park Av -NY 10022
(718) 888-8880 .. **Ray,** Joel Scott '01 %Dai & Assoc,PC -136-20 38th Av -Flushng 11354 **Fx:**888-9270
(631) 473-1000 .. **Ray,** John '83 (J Ray & Assoc) -122 N Cntry Rd Bx5440 -Miller Pl 11764
(631) 473-1000 .. **Ray,** John '83 (J Ray & Assoc) -640 Montauk Hwy -Shirley 11967
(516) 681-0100 .. **Ray,** John '83 (J Ray & Assoc) -2 Seaman Av at Bway -Bethpage 11714
(518) 668-3026 .. **Ray,** John J Jr. '86 -Bx646 -Lk George 12845 **Fx:**668-3027
(914) 422-3900 .. **Ray,** Kenneth G '76 %Oxman TKW&G LLP -120 Bloomingdale Rd -White Plns 10605
(212) 849-7000 .. **Ray,** Leah McCallister '07 %Quinn EU&S,LLP -51 Mad Av -NY 10010
(315) 253-0361 .. **Ray,** Randy J '96 -Bx731 -Baldwinsvll 13027 **Fx:**252-6493
(212) 421-4100 .. **Ray,** Robt W '86 (Pryor C LLP) -7 Times Sq -NY 10036
(212) 820-9427 .. **Ray,** Sarathi '04 %Hawkins D&W LLP -One Chase Manh Plz -NY 10005
(516) 536-2270 .. **Ray,** Stephanie '91 (S Ray,PC) -68 Andvr Rd -Rockvll Ctr 11570 **Fx:**536-3902
(631) 297-8360 .. **Rayano & Garabedian,PC** -267 Carleton Av -Central Islip 11722 **Fx:**297-8363
(631) 297-8360 .. **Rayano,** Janine M '86 (Rayano & G,PC) -267 Carleton Av -Central Islip 11722
(212) 732-8066 .. **Raybin,** Gregg A '96 Barrister Reporting Srvc,Inc -120 Bway -NY 10271 **Fx:**732-0126
(212) 348-9459 .. **Rayburn,** Mary D '87 -150 E 93rd -NY 10128
(212) 340-2538 .. **Raye,** Jesse A '79 %Metro-North -347 Mad Av -NY 10017 **Fx:**697-9079

(718) 343-5072 .. **Rayfield,** Jacqueline F '88 J Rayfield,PC -7930 256th -Floral Pk 11004 **Fx:**343-5076
(914) 347-6360 .. **Rayhill,** Brian J '88 Epstein & R -565 Taxter Rd -Elmsfrd 10523
(212) 895-1634 .. **Raykher,** Gregory '94 Dresdner Kleinwort Wasserstein -1301 Av od the Americas -NY 10019
(212) 209-2000 .. **Raykher,** Simon '96 Satellite Asset Mgmt -623 5th Av -NY 10022
(212) 408-5198 .. **Raylesberg,** Alan I '76 (Chadbourne & P LLP) -30 Rckfllr Plz -NY 10112
(212) 603-5014 .. **Rayman,** Danl J '00 %Lyra Capital LLC -1301 Av of Amer -NY 10019
(212) 687-6060 .. **Rayman,** S Eric '78 -317 Mad Av -NY 10017
(716) 856-4000 .. **Raymer,** Richd B '96 (Hodgson R LLP) -140 Pearl -Buffalo 14202
(516) 922-7848 .. **Raymon,** Gerald '64 -71 Highwood Rd -Oyster Bay 11771 **Fx:**922-7848
(212) 735-3000 .. **Raymond,** Amanda M '10 %Skadden ASM&F LLP -4 Times Sq -NY 10036
(646) 378-2192 .. **Raymond,** Catherine Olanich '85 (Christie PM&Y,PC) -5 Penn Plz -NY 10001
(212) 371-1492 .. **Raymond & Feldman** -110 E 59th -NY 10022 **Fx:**223-4911
(518) 745-6845 .. **Raymond,** Garfield P '79 -421 Bay Rd -Glens Fls 12804
(631) 424-6100 .. **Raymond,** Gary F '01 %Advantage Title -410 NY Av -Huntngtn 11743 **Fx:**424-6049
(315) 829-8455 .. **Raymond,** Gerald D '92 %Oneida Indian Nation -1256 Union Bx662 -Oneida 13421 **Fx:**829-8471
(212) 480-3300 .. **Raymond,** James Todd '94 Telx Grp Inc -1 State -NY 10004
(212) 794-5382 .. **Raymond,** Katherine M '84 %CUNY -535 E 80th -NY 10075 **Fx:**794-5426
(716) 856-5500 .. **Raymond,** Mary C '97 SpclCnsl Damon M LLP -200 Delaware Av -Buffalo 14202
(607) 723-2223 .. **Raymond,** Patrick J '65 -66 Hawley Bx607WVS -Bnghmtn 13905 **Fx:**723-3225
(212) 521-5400 .. **Raymond,** Peter D '80 (Reed S LLP) -599 Lex Av -NY 10022
(212) 225-2000 .. **Raymond,** Robt J '95 (Cleary GS&H) -1 Lbrty Plz -NY 10006
(212) 371-1492 .. **Raymond,** Steven P '67 (Raymond & F) -110 E 59th -NY 10022
(212) 474-1000 .. **Raymond,** Tashia '08 %Cravath S&M LLP -825 8th Av -NY 10019
(212) 497-8065 .. **Rayner,** Danl A '94 (Rayner R,LLP) -305 Bway -NY 10007 **Fx:**937-4680
(212) 940-8800 .. **Rayner,** Edw J '92 (Katten MR LLP) -575 Mad Av -NY 10022
(845) 356-4600 .. **Rayner,** Kim M '91 %D Goldstein -747 Chestnut Rdg Rd -Chestnut Rdg 10977
(212) 636-6000 .. **Rayner,** Martha G '87 %Fordham Univ Sch of Law -140 W 62nd -NY 10023 **Fx:**636-6899
(516) 942-0244 .. **Rayner,** Seymour '50 OHA-SSA -375 N Bway -Jericho 11753
(718) 222-2039 .. **Raynes,** Diana '07 %Law Dept -350 Jay -Brklyn 11201 **Fx:**222-2088
(516) 794-5310 .. **Raynor,** Deborah '00 %Abrams GMB,LLP -125 Jericho Tpk -Jericho 11753
(718) 858-0702 .. **Rayo,** Ingnazio Peter '60 -26 Court -Brklyn 11242 **Fx:**797-2288
(718) 834-0001 .. **Rayo,** Mark J '83 -26 Court -Brklyn 11242 **Fx:**834-0891
(718) 336-1090 .. **Raysin,** Alla '02 -1580 Dahill Rd -Brklyn 11204 **Fx:**336-1389
(212) 698-3500 .. **Rayski,** Thos A '00 %Dechert LLP -1095 Av of Amer -NY 10036
(212) 513-3200 .. **Raysman,** Richd '74 (Holland & K LLP) -31 W 52nd -NY 10019
(212) 946-2605 .. **Raysor,** Lauren P '89 -11 Penn Plz -NY 10001
(718) 714-1371 .. **Raytburg,** Leonid '94 -Bx67 -Brklyn 11214 **Fx:**714-1293
(212) 506-1700 .. **Raz,** Daniela '00 (Kasowitz BT&F LLP) -1633 Bway -NY 10019
(212) 319-3900 .. **Razgaitis,** Antanas V '01 %JE Bachelder LLP -437 Mad Av -NY 10022 **Fx:**319-3070
(212) 269-0927 .. **Razi,** Alexander M '04 %D'Amato & L,LLP -2 World Fncl Ctr -NY 10281
(914) 251-1618 .. **Razin,** Kathryn J '06 %Price MS&D,PC -106 Corp Park Dr -White Plns 10604
(718) 932-7500 .. **Razis,** Callie '00 %Razis & R,PC -23-09 31st -Astoria 11105
(718) 932-7500 .. **Razis,** Elena '01 %Razis & R,PC -23-09 31st -Astoria 11105
(718) 932-7500 .. **Razis,** George J '65 (Razis & R,PC) -23-09 31st -Astoria 11105
(718) 932-7500 .. **Razis & Ross,PC** -23-09 31st -Astoria 11105 **Fx:**956-0218
(518) 785-4141 .. **Razvi,** Kasim S '07 Northwestern Mutual Fncl Ntwrk -1201 Troy Schenectady Rd -Latham 12110 **Fx:**785-1353
(212) 558-4000 .. **Razza,** Jordan T '04 %Sullivan & C LLP -125 Broad -NY 10004
(212) 384-1000 .. **Razzagone,** Tracie A '01 %FBI -26 Fed Plz -NY 10278
(212) 504-6000 .. **Razzano,** Catherine L '03 %Cadwalader W&T LLP -1 World Fncl Ctr -NY 10281
(212) 218-2100 .. **Razzano,** Pasquale A '70 (Fitzpatrick CH&S) -1290 Av of Amer -NY 10104
(516) 512-8929 .. **Razzano,** Sandro '01 -1225 Franklin Av -Gdn Cty 11530
(212) 688-5151 .. **Razzolini,** J Claire '99 (Gibney A&F,LLP) -665 5th Av -NY 10022
(212) 752-7555 .. **Re,** Jennifer Parser '79 (Re P & Prtnrs) -445 Park Av -NY 10022
(212) 755-6000 .. **Re,** John C '88 (Aronauer R&Y,LLP) -444 Mad Av -NY 10022
(631) 425-4100 .. **Re,** Lawr C '74 (Ré NH&C,LLP) -36 N NY Av -Huntngtn 11743
(516) 873-2000 .. **Re,** Michl S '92 (Moritt HH&H LLP) -400 Grdn City Plz -Gdn Cty 11530
(631) 425-4100 .. **Ré Nielsen Huber & Coughlin, LLP** -36 N NY Av -Huntngtn 11743 **Fx:**425-4104
(212) 752-7555 .. **Re Parser & Partners** -445 Park Av -NY 10022 **Fx:**752-7675
(212) 335-9000 .. **Re,** Robt B '77 %DA -1 Hogan Pl -NY 10013
(718) 358-3997 .. **Re,** Robt V '74 -142-13 58th Rd -Flushng 11355
(212) 752-7555 .. **Re,** Thos C '77 (Re P & Prtnrs) -445 Park Av -NY 10022
(718) 474-1111 .. **Re,** Victor M '83 -257 Beach 116 -Far Rckwy 11694 **Fx:**474-2222
(212) 557-5050 .. **Rea,** Jeffrey J '87 (Rea & Assoc,LLC) -286 Mad Av -NY 10017 **Fx:**557-5051
(914) 288-9595 .. **Rea,** Kimberlea Shaw '92 OfCnsl Gaines GP&N,LLP -1 N Bway -White Plns 10601
(212) 577-3688 .. **Rea,** Natalie B '87 %Leg Aid -199 Water -NY 10038 **Fx:**509-8431
(212) 205-1800 .. **Reach,** Chas H III '81 %BT Amer -620 8th Av -NY 10018
(646) 471-1254 .. **Reach,** Diane Nicas '87 %PricewaterhouseCoopers LLP -300 Mad Av -NY 10017
(518) 583-2200 .. **Read,** Allen C '79 -1197 Route 9P Bx384 -Saratoga Spgs 12866
(631) 283-9696 .. **Read,** Carole L '97 %Bennett & R -212 Windmill Ln -Southampton 11968
(516) 227-6363 .. **Read,** Christopher M '99 OfCnsl Amato & Assoc,PC -666 Old Cntry Rd -Gdn Cty 11530 **Fx:**227-6367
(212) 506-2500 .. **Read,** Danl R '04 %Mayer B LLP -1675 Bway -NY 10019
(518) 465-9313 .. **Read,** Howard J '70 (Read and L,LLP) -25 Eagle -Albany 12207
(518) 465-9313 .. **Read and Laniado,LLP** -25 Eagle -Albany 12207 **Fx:**465-9315
(212) 957-7600 .. **Read,** Nathaniel P T '02 Cnsl Cohen & G LLP -800 3rd Av -NY 10022
(212) 527-1000 .. **Read,** Peter S '94 (Jones HC&B PC) -1 Bttry Pk Plz -NY 10004
(212) 749-4623 .. **Reader,** Barbara '84 -275 W 96th -NY 10025 **Fx:**749-6927
(212) 909-6000 .. **Reader,** Joshua D '07 %Debevoise & P LLP -919 3rd Av -NY 10022
(914) 834-9569 .. **Reader,** Marilyn S '76 -94 N Chatsworth Av -Larchmnt 10538 **Fx:**834-5921
(212) 859-8000 .. **Reader,** Rachel L '08 %Fried FHS&J LLP -1 NY Plz -NY 10004
(212) 696-6000 .. **Reader,** Shaun A '06 %Curtis M-PC&M LLP -101 Park Av -NY 10178
(212) 723-9587 .. **Reader,** Thos W '96 %Salomon Smith Barney -390 Greenwich -NY 10013
(212) 698-3500 .. **Reading,** Susan A '07 %Dechert LLP -1095 Av of Amer -NY 10036
(716) 693-2335 .. **Readling,** John A '04 Brick B&E,PC -91 Tremont Bx604 -N Tonawanda 14120
(212) 558-4000 .. **Readling,** Regina L '09 %Sullivan & C LLP -125 Broad -NY 10004
(212) 259-8000 .. **Readlinger,** April L '05 %Dewey & L LLP -1301 Av of Amer -NY 10019
(516) 741-6800 .. **Ready,** Kenneth J '84 (K Ready & Assoc) -1565 Franklin Av -Mineola 11501
(516) 746-5599 .. **Ready,** Richd P '88 (Bee RFH&D,LLP) -170 Old Cntry Rd -Mineola 11501
(315) 673-4864 .. **Reagan,** Bernard L '53 OfCnsl Reagan & D -18 E Main Bx196 -Marcellus 13108 **Fx:**673-3438
(315) 472-1175 .. **Reagan,** Brendan J '00 Knych & W,LLC -300 S State -Syracuse 13202
(212) 813-8800 .. **Reagan,** Danl B '10 %Goodwin P LLP -620 8th Av -NY 10018
(585) 613-4000 .. **Reagan,** Helen E '87 US Dist Ct WDNY -100 State -Rchstr 14614
(631) 777-2330 .. **Reagan,** Michl T '00 %O'Connor OH&D,LLP -1 Huntngtn Quad -Melvll 11747
(212) 964-8934 .. **Reagon,** Merble Harrington '96 -11 Bway -NY 10004
(315) 797-9261 .. **Reale,** Jeffrey M '08 %Getnick LA&P,LLP -258 Genesee -Utica 13502
(347) 296-1008 .. **Reale,** Louis M '88 Sup Ct -360 Adams -Brklyn 11201
(518) 474-0571 .. **Reale,** Michele M '96 Ofc Gnl Srvcs -Corning Twr ESP -Albany 12242 **Fx:**473-4973
(516) 681-0077 .. **Reali,** John P '61 -410 Jericho Tpk -Jericho 11753 **Fx:**681-0097
(212) 928-9471 .. **Realmuto,** Richd '84 -824 W 176th -NY 10033
(212) 594-2278 .. **Realuyo,** Pompeyo R '74 -350 5th Av -NY 10118
(212) 326-3939 .. **Ream,** Jonathan M '10 %Jones D -222 E 41st -NY 10017
(212) 685-2400 .. **Reamer,** Jodi B '94 Writers Hse LLC -21 W 26th -NY 10010 **Fx:**685-1781
(516) 571-9038 .. **Reany,** Kristen L '01 Family Ct -1200 Old Cntry Rd -Westbury 11590
(914) 761-7190 .. **Reap,** James B '57 ODAR-SSA -75 S Bway -White Plns 10601 **Fx:**682-7006
(646) 205-3116 .. **Reap,** Michl H '87 Landis & Gyr Holdings -500 Park Av -NY 10022
(516) 694-3000 .. **Reape,** Kelly A '95 %Guercio & G,LLP -77 Conklin -Farmngdl 11735 **Fx:**694-4738
(516) 822-8900 .. **Reape,** Thos J Jr. '93 Fiedelman & M -2 Jericho Plz -Jericho 11753
(516) 593-1964 .. **Rear,** Sherwin '58 -188 Surrey Cmmns -Lynbrk 11563
(212) 351-4000 .. **Rearden,** Jennifer Hutchison '97 (Gibson D&C LLP) -200 Park Av -NY 10166
(212) 940-3745 .. **Reardon,** Abigail T '82 Cnsl Nixon P LLP -437 Mad Av -NY 10022
(516) 746-7371 .. **Reardon,** Alan J '71 (Burns RT&R,LLP) -390 Old Cntry Rd -Gdn Cty 11530
(914) 273-1300 .. **Reardon,** Anastasia T '90 %Veneziano & Assoc -84 Business Park Dr -Armonk 10504 **Fx:**273-1303
(212) 728-8000 .. **Reardon,** Andrew T '06 %Willkie F&G LLP -787 7th Av -NY 10019
(585) 271-4470 .. **Reardon,** Carolyn A '93 %R Kroll -2425 Clover -Rchstr 14618 **Fx:**271-0847
(631) 273-7014 .. **Reardon,** Chas C '83 %Liberty Capital Group -255 Oser Av -Hauppauge 11788 **Fx:**273-7605
(718) 816-8880 .. **Reardon,** Edw P '66 -498 Ramoha Av -Staten Isl 10309
(212) 715-9100 .. **Reardon,** Eileen A '95 SpclCnsl Kramer LN&F,LLP -1177 Av of Amer -NY 10036
(212) 259-8000 .. **Reardon,** James J Jr. '06 %Dewey & L LLP -1301 Av of Amer -NY 10019
(516) 314-8433 .. **Reardon,** Jeanne '94 -8 Woodfld Ln -Old Brookvll 11545
(914) 666-5566 .. **Reardon,** Judith '82 -20 Woods Brdg Rd -Katonah 10536 **Fx:**666-4706
(585) 230-4881 .. **Reardon,** Kathleen P '88 -40 Humboldt -Rchstr 14609 **Fx:**292-5580
(516) 747-7400 .. **Reardon,** Lesley Radovich '94 (Rosenberg C&B LLP) -100 Grdn City Plz -Gdn Cty 11530
(845) 291-2050 .. **Reardon,** Meghan C '10 %DA -255-275 Main -Goshen 10924 **Fx:**291-2085
(212) 455-2000 .. **Reardon,** Roxane F '95 (Simpson T&B LLP) -425 Lex Av -NY 10017
(212) 455-2000 .. **Reardon,** Roy L '54 (Simpson T&B LLP) -425 Lex Av -NY 10017
(914) 366-0201 .. **Reardon & Sclafani,PC** -220 Wht Plns Rd -Tarrytwn 10591 **Fx:**366-0022
(212) 326-2000 .. **Rearick,** Janna K '10 %O'Melveny & M LLP -7 Times Sq -NY 10036
(516) 227-7900 .. **Rearick,** Joan M '05 Dept Soc Srvcs -60 Chas Lindbergh Blvd -Uniondale 11553
(718) 590-3309 .. **Reaves,** Kemp J '90 %Family Ct -900 Sheridan Av -Bronx 10451
(212) 763-4100 .. **Reavis,** Helen D '88 (Reavis PL LLP) -41 Mad Av -NY 10010
(212) 763-4100 .. **Reavis Parent Lehrer LLP** -41 Mad Av -NY 10010 **Fx:**763-4141
(646) 240-4872 .. **Reay,** D Brian '07 %Bortstein & I LLC -275 Mad Av -NY 10016 **Fx:**(866) 955-9403
(914) 665-0055 .. **Reback,** David C '65 (Reback & P,LLP) -10 Fiske Pl -Mt Vernon 10550 **Fx:**665-0062
(914) 723-5072 .. **Reback,** Miriam I '85 -270 Glendale Rd -Scarsdale 10583
(212) 582-9526 .. **Rebak,** Fred A '67 (Corbett & R) -250 W 57th -NY 10019
(212) 735-3000 .. **Rebek,** Arash A '08 %Skadden ASM&F LLP -4 Times Sq -NY 10036
(212) 859-8000 .. **Rebello,** Jos '03 %Fried FHS&J LLP -1 NY Plz -NY 10004
(716) 847-3004 .. **Rebhan,** Thos R '94 %OTDA -295 Main -Buffalo 14203 **Fx:**847-3699
(212) 909-6000 .. **Rebholz,** Shannon '09 %Debevoise & P LLP -919 3rd Av -NY 10022

(212) 730-5250 .. **Rebibo,** Michl '90 -15 W 44th -NY 10036 **Fx:**869-2303
(212) 425-9300 .. **Rebish,** Stuart T '92 Cnsl Bressler A&R,PC -17 State -NY 10004
(212) 644-4420 .. **Reboh,** Joelle Y '01 %Fabiani C&H,LLP -570 Lex Av -NY 10022
(212) 225-2000 .. **Rebollar,** Gina L R '07 %Cleary GS&H -1 Lbrty Plz -NY 10006
(631) 587-0938 .. **Rebore,** Deborah J '96 -500 Bl-Cntry Blvd -Farmngdl 11735
(212) 762-3337 .. **Reboredo,** Humberto M '01 Morgan Stanley -750 7th Av -NY 10019
(516) 357-3000 .. **Rebosa,** Sarah B '04 %Rivkin R LLP -926 RXR Plz -Uniondale 11556
(212) 596-9000 .. **Reboul,** John W '65 (Ropes & G LLP) -1211 Av of Amer -NY 10036
(914) 337-0703 .. **Recabo,** Jaime M '89 -34 Palmer Av -Bronxvll 10708 **Fx:**337-0706
(212) 877-6656 .. **Recanati-Capuano,** Joyce J '85 -315 W 70th -NY 10023 **Fx:**877-6656
(646) 688-6095 .. **Recant,** Donna G '82 OfCnsl Calabro & Assoc,PC -450 7th Av -NY 10123 **Fx:**688-6096
(212) 530-5000 .. **Recca,** Dennis J '06 %Milbank TH&M LLP -1 Chase Manh Plz -NY 10005
(718) 336-5550 .. **Recchia,** Domenic M '93 -172 Gravesend Neck Rd -Brklyn 11223 **Fx:**336-8466
(585) 362-4700 .. **Recchia,** Kevin V '87 %Bond S&K,PLLC -350 Linden Oaks -Rchstr 14625
(845) 357-2660 .. **Recchia,** Maurice J '94 %Kornfeld RN&S -46 Wshngtn Av Bx177 -Suffern 10901
(607) 231-5900 .. **Recchia,** Raymond O '96 %Leg Aid -30 Fayette -Bnghmtn 13901 **Fx:**724-7211
(212) 268-7222 .. **Rech,** Gustav P '81 (Soffer R&B LLP) -48 Wall -NY 10005
(631) 845-2600 .. **Rech,** Patricia K '89 %Morenus CG&B -58 S Srvc Rd -Melvll 11747
(212) 373-3000 .. **Recher,** Jeffrey J '10 %Paul WRW&G LLP -1285 Av of Amer -NY 10019
(212) 906-1200 .. **Recher,** Marianne M '08 %Latham & W -885 3rd Av -NY 10022
(716) 852-3540 .. **Recht,** David A '09 %Watson BCJ&S -12 Fountain Plz -Buffalo 14202
(917) 912-4300 .. **Rechtschaffen,** Alan N '94 -40 E 80th -NY 10075
(212) 554-1234 .. **Recine,** Anthony F '80 %AXA Financial Inc -1290 Av of Amer -NY 10104 **Fx:**707-3963
(212) 506-1700 .. **Recine,** Jennifer S '04 %Kasowitz BT&F LLP -1633 Bway -NY 10019
(914) 824-5500 .. **Recine,** Maria-Alana Salome '02 Hon K Davidson -111 Dr Martin Luther King Jr Blvd -White Plns 10601 **Fx:**995-4586
(516) 294-5555 .. **Recine,** Phyllis Agazarian '77 (Del Vecchio & R,LLP) -1100 Franklin Av -Gdn Cty 11530 **Fx:**873-5336
(914) 833-0202 .. **Recio,** Diane R '78 -11 Holly Pl -Larchmnt 10538
(212) 906-1200 .. **Reckler,** Wm O '03 %Latham & W -885 3rd Av -NY 10022
(212) 850-2800 .. **Reckmeyer,** Jeremy B '06 %Andrews K LLP -450 Lex Av -NY 10017
(212) 458-7018 .. **Reckseit,** Peter H '89 %AIG -175 Water -NY 10038
(716) 886-0211 .. **Recoon,** Eric L '91 %Benderson Dvlpmnt -570 Delaware Av -Buffalo 14202 **Fx:**886-2269
(516) 222-1350 .. **Record,** Emily Shaw '07 %Barrocas & R -100 Q Roosevelt Blvd -Gdn Cty 11530
(646) 496-6575 .. **Recto,** Edgar Ariel L '02 -308 W 94th -NY 10025 **Fx:**(212) 222-2991
(845) 638-5180 .. **Reda,** Antonio F '00 Cnty Atty -Cnty Ofc Bldg -New Cty 10956 **Fx:**638-5676
(845) 639-7722 .. **Reda,** Antonio F '00 (Reda S & Assoc,LLP) -20 S Main -New Cty 10956 **Fx:**639-7744
(212) 833-1157 .. **Reda,** Danya Shocair '05 %Friedman KS&A LLP -1633 Bway -NY 10019 **Fx:**373-7957
(516) 921-1873 .. **Reda,** Douglas M '81 -180 Froelich Farm Blvd -Woodbury 11797
(718) 597-3274 .. **Reda,** Jos A '85 -2710A E Tremont Av -Bronx 10461
(646) 610-5400 .. **Reda,** Jos A '99 %NYPD -1 Police Plz -NY 10038
(212) 351-4000 .. **Reda,** Justin J R '10 Gibson D&C LLP -200 Park Av -NY 10166
(914) 395-2646 .. **Reda,** Louis J '87 -107 Lk Av -Tuckahoe 10707
(716) 858-2424 .. **Reda,** Lynette M '94 %DA -25 Delaware Av -Buffalo 14202 **Fx:**858-7425
(914) 995-3101 .. **Reda,** Maryann C '99 %Cnty Atty -148 Martine Av -White Plns 10601
(516) 223-1900 .. **Reda,** Pietrina J '74 -294 W Merrick Rd Bx7416 -Freeprt 11520 **Fx:**223-1920
(914) 949-4200 .. **Reda,** Ralph R '86 -901 N Bway -White Plns 10603 **Fx:**949-6897
(845) 357-5555 .. **Reda,** Robt L '95 -1 Exec Blvd -Suffern 10901 **Fx:**357-3333
(212) 422-0202 .. **Redavid,** Frank V '10 %Sedgwick DM&A LLP -125 Broad -NY 10004
(914) 686-1700 .. **Redd,** Jos T '88 (O'Connor R,LLP) -200 Mamaroneck Av -White Plns 10601
(516) 294-2632 .. **Reddan,** James J '98 -151 Atl Av -New Hyde Pk 11040
(516) 255-5554 .. **Reddan,** Stephen G '83 -64 N Park Av -Rockvll Ctr 11570
(212) 468-8000 .. **Redden,** Jessie K '10 %Morrison & F LLP -1290 Av of Amer -NY 10104
(716) 856-4000 .. **Redder,** Bonnie A '85 (Hodgson R LLP) -140 Pearl -Buffalo 14202
(845) 331-1000 .. **Redder,** George W '84 -243 Wall Bx3100 -Kingston 12402 **Fx:**331-1009
(212) 385-1050 .. **Reddick,** Melvin L '05 -74 Trinity Pl -NY 10006 **Fx:**385-1017
(718) 357-5557 .. **Reddin Eliou,** Jennifer E '98 -5712 164th -Fresh Mdws 11365 **Fx:**357-7241
(518) 464-1300 .. **Redding,** Earl T '04 %Roemer WG&M LLP -13 Columbia Cir -Albany 12203
(716) 636-8660 .. **Redding,** Kenneth A '82 (K Redding & Assoc) -2420 Sweet Home Dr -Amherst 14228
(212) 826-0100 .. **Redding,** Martha Manson '96 %FSA -31 W 52nd -NY 10019 **Fx:**893-2710
(212) 988-4586 .. **Reddington,** Thos J '57 -401 E 74th -NY 10021
(212) 442-0396 .. **Reddington,** Tricia M '99 %Law Dept -100 Church -NY 10007 **Fx:**788-0367
(718) 613-2450 .. **Reddy,** Anitha '10 Hon J Gleeson -225 Cadman Plz E -Brklyn 11201
(212) 969-3000 .. **Reddy,** Anne C '06 %Proskauer R LLP -1585 Bway -NY 10036
(212) 326-3939 .. **Reddy,** Deepak '00 Cnsl Jones D -222 E 41st -NY 10017
(212) 858-1000 .. **Reddy,** Harsha 0 '98 %Pillsbury WSP LLP -1540 Bway -NY 10036
(212) 925-9100 .. **Reddy,** John J Jr. '80 (Reddy L&Z,PC) -85 Worth -NY 10013
(212) 446-2300 .. **Reddy,** Kavitha '05 %Boies S&F LLP -575 Lex Av -NY 10022
(212) 637-3106 .. **Reddy,** Kedari P '06 %US EPA -290 Bway -NY 10007 **Fx:**637-3096
(212) 637-2751 .. **Reddy,** Kirti V '01 US Atty -86 Chmbrs -NY 10007
(212) 925-9100 .. **Reddy Levy & Ziffer, PC** -85 Worth -NY 10013 **Fx:**925-8777
(212) 701-3000 .. **Reddy,** Michl '07 %Cahill G&R LLP -80 Pine -NY 10005 **Fx:**269-5420
(585) 342-4410 .. **Reddy,** Michl A '78 (Burke AH&R,LLP) -1800 Hudson Av -Rchstr 14617
(212) 788-0582 .. **Reddy,** Michl V Jr. '96 %Law Dept -100 Church -NY 10007 **Fx:**788-0367
(212) 446-2300 .. **Reddy,** Neena A '06 %Boies S&F LLP -575 Lex Av -NY 10022
(212) 626-4100 .. **Reddy,** Neil T '07 %Baker & M LLP -1114 Av of Amer -NY 10036
(212) 373-3000 .. **Reddy,** Nina A '97 Paul WRW&G LLP -1285 Av of Amer -NY 10019
(212) 629-9400 .. **Reddy,** Prashanthi '97 Intl Lgl & Trade Cnsltnts -315 5th Av -NY 10016
(212) 788-0903 .. **Reddy,** Prathyusha '05 %Law Dept -100 Church -NY 10007 **Fx:**788-0367
(212) 801-6920 .. **Reddy,** Sangeeta '06 %Greenberg T,LLP -200 Park Av -NY 10166
(212) 521-5400 .. **Reddy,** Saritha C '08 %Reed S LLP -599 Lex Av -NY 10022
(212) 574-1200 .. **Reddy,** Savitha '02 %Seward & K LLP -1 Bttry Pk Plz -NY 10004
(212) 837-6846 .. **Reddy,** Shashi R '10 %Hughes H&R LLP -1 Bttry Pk Plz -NY 10004 **Fx:**299-6846
(845) 638-1100 .. **Reddy,** Wm J '97 -216 Congers Rd -New Cty 10956 **Fx:**638-9313
(716) 852-3540 .. **Reddy-Price,** Prathima Chintala '06 %Watson BCJ&S -12 Fountain Plz -Buffalo 14202
(631) 271-6363 .. **Redeker,** June '89 %Cannon & A,LLP -1923 NY Av -Huntngtn Sta 11746 **Fx:**271-7128
(516) 935-0662 .. **Reden,** Carol L '91 -8 Rim Ln -Hicksvll 11801
(716) 856-0277 .. **Reden & O'Donnell LLP** -135 Delaware Av -Buffalo 14202 **Fx:**843-8698
(716) 856-0277 .. **Reden,** Robt J '85 (Reden & O LLP) -135 Delaware Av -Buffalo 14202
(212) 240-9465 .. **Redenburg,** Michl J '07 -150 Bway -NY 10038
(212) 974-7474 .. **Redente,** Gary E '00 OfCnsl Cowan DA&S LLP -41 Mad Av -NY 10010
(212) 530-5000 .. **Reder,** Robt S '79 (Milbank TH&M LLP) -1 Chase Manh Plz -NY 10005
(212) 935-5057 .. **Redfern,** Declan P '87 (Kayser & R,LLP) -515 Mad Av -NY 10022
(585) 428-3495 .. **Redfield,** Christine F '92 %Hon P Gallaher-Family Ct -99 Exchange Blvd -Rchstr 14614
(212) 776-5000 .. **Redican,** Laurence M '97 %NYC Housing Auth -250 Bway -NY 10007 **Fx:**776-5039
(315) 386-8576 .. **Rediehs,** Christopher R '99 St Lawrence Cnty Housing Cnsl,Inc -19 Main -Canton 13617
(718) 923-8406 .. **Rediker,** Robt J C '88 %Forest City Ratner -1 Metrotech Ctr N -Brklyn 11201 **Fx:**923-8706
(518) 434-9051 .. **Redington,** Philip E '78 -40 Steuben -Albany 12207
(914) 946-3700 .. **Redis,** Robt M '69 (McCarthy F LLP) -11 Martine Av -White Plns 10606
(212) 644-1710 .. **Redish,** Gary S '83 (Winne BH&B,PC) -286 Mad Av -NY 10017
(914) 909-0711 .. **Redlener,** David I '95 Sapphire Global -27 Division -New Rchll 10801
(212) 986-4030 .. **Redlich,** Catherine L '83 (Driscoll & R) -521 5th Av -NY 10175 **Fx:**986-4050
(518) 862-1877 .. **Redlich,** Heather J '95 %Redlich Law Firm -255 Washington Av Ext -Albany 12205 **Fx:**862-1551
(888) 733-5299 .. **Redlich,** Warren '95 Redlich Law Firm -255 Washington Av Ext -Albany 12205 **Fx:**(518) 862-1551
(914) 696-0006 .. **Redlisky,** Linda A '93 (Rafferty & R) -800 Wstchstr Av -Rye Brook 10573 **Fx:**560-3333
(518) 486-9854 .. **Redlo,** Richd S '77 %State Comptroller -110 State -Albany 12236 **Fx:**473-9104
(212) 859-8000 .. **Redman,** Alyson Leigh '02 SpclCnsl Fried FHS&J LLP -1 NY Plz -NY 10004
(347) 404-9133 .. **Redman,** Angela M '01 %Civil Ct -141 Lvngstn -Brklyn 11201 **Fx:**(718) 643-3733
(718) 250-2000 .. **Redman,** Courtney W '09 %DA -350 Jay -Brklyn 11201 **Fx:**250-2314
(212) 647-9878 .. **Redman,** Danl K '00 Thomson-West -530 5th Av -NY 10036
(212) 335-9000 .. **Redman,** Isabelle A '02 %DA -1 Hogan Pl -NY 10013
(212) 756-2000 .. **Redman,** Joshua A '10 %Schulte R&Z LLP -919 3rd Av -NY 10022
(212) 649-2000 .. **Redman,** Mark C '96 %Hearst Corp -300 W 57th -NY 10019 **Fx:**649-2035
(212) 918-3000 .. **Redmon,** John A '79 (Hogan L LLP) -875 3rd Av -NY 10022
(631) 582-3700 .. **Redmond,** Christopher M '85 (Turley RR&R,LLP) -3075 Vets Mem'l Hwy -Ronkonkoma 11779
(718) 694-5730 .. **Redmond,** Cornelius J '98 Transit Auth -130 Lvngstn -Brklyn 11201 **Fx:**694-5726
(212) 406-9710 .. **Redmond,** David P '82 (Kral CRRP&G,LLP) -170 Bway -NY 10038
(585) 544-3440 .. **Redmond,** Gregg H '94 %Pelkey & P -1134 Titus Av -Rchstr 14617 **Fx:**544-0132
(914) 682-8800 .. **Redmond,** Jeanette '98 Fed Bar Cncl -123 Main -White Plns 10601 **Fx:**682-4400
(212) 799-8989 .. **Redmond,** Jennifer A '98 -44 Wall -NY 10005
(914) 495-3515 .. **Redmond,** Kimberly K '87 (Ginsburg & R,PC) -245 Saw Mill Rvr Rd -Hawthorne 10532 **Fx:**495-3520
(212) 730-7700 .. **Redmond,** Kristyn M '08 %Michelman & R,LLP -114 W 47th -NY 10036
(212) 319-1000 .. **Redmond,** Loretta A '89 (Quirk & B,PC) -845 3rd Av -NY 10022
(518) 587-9105 .. **Redmond,** Mireille D '96 %R Pulsifer -562 Maple Av Bx878 -Saratoga Spgs 12866 **Fx:**581-1003
(518) 439-0375 .. **Redmond,** Nicole R '09 %Friedman & M,PC -2 Normanskill Blvd Bx69 -Delmar 12054
(585) 454-2321 .. **Redmond & Parrinello, LLP** -36 W Main -Rchstr 14614 **Fx:**454-6626
(800) 260-1710 .. **Redmond,** Peter M '67 P Redmond,PC -Bx610509 -Bayside 11361 **Fx:**(802) 319-0122
(516) 248-2500 .. **Redmond Pollio & Caso, LLP** -1461 Franklin Av -Gdn Cty 11530 **Fx:**248-2348
(518) 899-0035 .. **Redmond,** Robt W '72 -20 B Cass Ct -Ballston Lk 12019 **Fx:**899-5058
(315) 474-2943 .. **Redmond,** Shelby C '09 %Sugarman Law Firm,LLP -211 W Jffrsn -Syracuse 13202
(718) 694-3876 .. **Redmond-Smith,** Celeste R '87 %Transit Auth -130 Lvngstn -Brklyn 11201 **Fx:**694-5726
(718) 852-5769 .. **Redner,** Alan J '76 -26 Court -Brklyn 11242 **Fx:**858-4861

(914) 937-4620 .. **Rednick,** Jeffrey B '96 (Rednick & R,LLP) -125 N Main -Pt Chester 10573 **Fx:**937-9131
(914) 937-4620 .. **Rednick,** Robt I '58 (Rednick & R,LLP) -125 N Main -Pt Chester 10573 **Fx:**937-9131
(212) 334-9200 .. **Redniss,** Seth E '03 S Redniss LLC -79 5th Av -NY 10003
(212) 486-6000 .. **Redo,** Martha M '89 %Victor & B, PC -18 E 41st -NY 10017 **Fx:**486-8668
(212) 333-8374 .. **Redondo,** Roberto '95 %Equest Partners -825 8th Av -NY 10019
(716) 633-3200 .. **Redpath,** Ian J '86 -333 Intl Dr -Williamsvll 14221 **Fx:**633-0301
(646) 459-9642 .. **Redstone,** Allison Prescott '05 Man Invstmnts -1 Rckfllr Plz -NY 10020
(914) 472-7700 .. **Reduto,** James P '94 (Bertine HHZD&D,LLP) -700 Wht Plns Rd -Scarsdale 10583
(212) 230-8800 .. **Redwine,** Jonathan M '02 %WilmerHale -399 Park Av -NY 10022
(718) 774-0906 .. **Redwine,** Lesley E '04 Achievement First -790 E NY Av -Brklyn 11203
(518) 472-5839 .. **Redwood,** James D '99 Albany Law Schl -80 New Scotland Av -Albany 12208 **Fx:**445-2315
(212) 238-4800 .. **Ree,** Sophia Y '01 (Landman CB&F,PC) -120 Bway -NY 10271
(518) 402-7239 .. **Reeb,** Emily C '01 %OCFS -52 Wshngtn -Rensselaer 12144 **Fx:**486-6361
(716) 856-4000 .. **Reeb,** Kyle C '05 %Hodgson R LLP -140 Pearl -Buffalo 14202
(212) 962-1020 .. **Reece,** Ernest N '95 %M Lamonsoff -80 Maiden Ln -NY 10038 **Fx:**962-3078
(212) 820-4738 .. **Reed,** Adam C '00 %AIG -160 Water -NY 10038
(914) 579-2100 .. **Reed & Aibara, PLLC** -586 Commerce -Thornwd 10594 **Fx:**579-2112
(607) 776-9631 .. **Reed,** Alan P '90 %DA -3 E Pulteney Sq -Bath 14810 **Fx:**776-7052
(212) 506-5000 .. **Reed,** Amanda W '04 %Orrick H&S LLP -51 W 52nd -NY 10019
(212) 578-0145 .. **Reed,** Ann M '83 %MetLife -1095 Av of Amer -NY 10036
(914) 579-2100 .. **Reed,** Blake W '98 (Reed & A, PLLC) -586 Commerce -Thornwd 10594
(716) 551-5541 .. **Reed,** Christopher K '83 %US Trustee -42 Delaware Av -Buffalo 14202
(716) 856-4000 .. **Reed,** David G '00 (Hodgson R LLP) -140 Pearl -Buffalo 14202
(212) 643-2503 .. **Reed,** Derek D '05 %Levy E&P,PC -555 5th Av -NY 10017
(212) 318-3000 .. **Reed,** Erica A '06 %Fulbright & J LLP -666 5th Av -NY 10103
(914) 946-5000 .. **Reed,** George E Jr. '78 -222 Mamaroneck Av -White Plns 10605
(212) 701-3000 .. **Reed,** Ilana '08 %Cahill G&R LLP -80 Pine -NY 10005 **Fx:**269-5420
(607) 733-8866 .. **Reed,** James B '87 (Ziff Law Firm,LLP) -303 William -Elmira 14901 **Fx:**732-6062
(716) 373-4701 .. **Reed,** Jeffrey '92 %Leg Srvcs -103 S Barry -Olean 14760 **Fx:**373-7771
(212) 547-5400 .. **Reed,** Jeffrey S '06 %McDermott W&E LLP -340 Mad Av -NY 10173
(845) 454-4340 .. **Reed,** John M '59 -17 Cllgvw Av -Poughkeepsie 12603 **Fx:**454-7862
(914) 681-0444 .. **Reed,** Jonathan W '08 %Rende R&D,LLP -202 Mamaroneck Av -White Plns 10601
(212) 849-7000 .. **Reed,** Kevin S '94 (Quinn EU&S,LLP) -51 Mad Av -NY 10010
(516) 622-0606 .. **Reed,** Kristen N '97 %P Rizzuto,PC -1 Old Cntry Rd -Carle Pl 11514 **Fx:**622-2112
(212) 277-4000 .. **Reed,** Lucy F '85 (Freshfields BD LLP) -520 Mad Av -NY 10022
(518) 439-6001 .. **Reed,** Margaret Z '95 Reed & V,LLP -203 Delaware Av -Delmar 12054 **Fx:**439-6108
(585) 546-1980 .. **Reed,** Maria J '04 %Fulton F&G LLP -28 E Main -Rchstr 14614
(212) 506-5000 .. **Reed,** Marlene E Watts '86 %Orrick H&S LLP -51 W 52nd -NY 10019
(518) 272-5917 .. **Reed,** Milinda J '00 Unity House Law Project -504 Bway -Troy 12180
(212) 837-6000 .. **Reed,** Natasha N '01 %Hughes H&R LLP -1 Bttry Pk Plz -NY 10004
(212) 374-9300 .. **Reed,** Patrick C '82 OfCnsl Simons & W -45 Bway -NY 10006
(607) 273-4200 .. **Reed,** Randall L '75 OfCnsl Miller M,LLP -202 E State -Ithaca 14850
(518) 455-7700 .. **Reed,** Richd A '82 %Ct of Appls -20 Eagle -Albany 12207
(212) 578-2211 .. **Reed,** Rolon A III '95 %MetLife -27-01 Qns Plz N -LIC 11101
(212) 538-9685 .. **Reed,** Sally O '01 Credit Suisse -1 Mad Av -NY 10010
(212) 218-2100 .. **Reed,** Scott K '88 (Fitzpatrick CH&S) -1290 Av of Amer -NY 10104
(212) 521-5400 .. **Reed Smith LLP** -599 Lex Av -NY 10022 **Fx:**521-5450
(212) 608-2629 .. **Reed,** Steven J '89 (Gregory & R,PC) -111 Bway -NY 10006
(845) 454-7374 .. **Reed,** Thos A '66 -94 Market -Poughkeepsie 12601 **Fx:**454-7377
(212) 722-3610 .. **Reed,** Thos A '68 -1172 Park Av -NY 10128
(607) 937-5597 .. **Reed,** Thos W II '97 -88 Tioga Av -Corning 14830 **Fx:**937-6099
(914) 767-6000 .. **Reed,** Tracey D '02 %Pepsi Bottling Grp -1 Pepsi Way -Somers 10589
(518) 385-8458 .. **Reed,** Veronica L '05 GE Co -1 River Rd -Schnctdy 12345
(412) 288-3312 .. **Reed,** W Franklin '72 (Reed S LLP) -599 Lex Av -NY 10022 **Fx:**288-3063
(607) 569-2213 .. **Reed,** Wm Hunter '92 WH Reed PC -11 Water Bx396 -Hammondsprt 14840 **Fx:**569-2214
(201) 825-7575 .. **Reeder,** Donald W '71 -1 Exec Blvd -Suffern 10901 **Fx:**818-0427
(212) 558-4000 .. **Reeder,** Robt W III '85 (Sullivan & C LLP) -125 Broad -NY 10004
(212) 440-3773 .. **Reeder,** Shauna J '93 CNA Global -40 Wall -NY 10005 **Fx:**440-3710
(212) 735-3000 .. **Reeder,** Steven R '09 %Skadden ASM&F LLP -4 Times Sq -NY 10036
(518) 474-5714 .. **Reeder,** Wendy H '06 State Comptroller -110 State -Albany 12236 **Fx:**473-9104
(845) 343-3000 .. **Reed-McDermott,** Ferol L '94 %MacVean LS&M,PC -34 Grove Bx310 -Middletwn 10940
(212) 768-6700 .. **Reed Miles,** Jo Christine '04 (Sonnenschein N&R LLP) -1221 Av of Amer -NY 10020
(212) 732-3200 .. **Reeds,** Laura Anne '06 %Carter L&M LLP -2 Wall -NY 10005
(212) 974-7474 .. **Reedy,** M Kilburg '93 %Cowan DA&S LLP -41 Mad Av -NY 10010
(516) 746-1144 .. **Reel,** Scott R '04 %Kirschenbaum & P,PC -3000 Hempstd Tpk -Levittwn 11756
(212) 335-4500 .. **Reemer,** Ellis L '75 (DLA Piper LLP) -1251 Av of Amer -NY 10020
(212) 225-2000 .. **Reents,** Scott B '08 %Cleary GS&H -1 Lbrty Plz -NY 10006
(516) 742-3700 .. **Reers,** Richd L '80 (R Reers,PC) -436 Willis Av -Williston Pk 11596 **Fx:**742-6111
(212) 373-3000 .. **Rees,** Verity S '07 %Paul WRW&G LLP -1285 Av of Amer -NY 10019
(212) 530-5000 .. **Reese,** Blake E '08 %Milbank TH&M LLP -1 Chase Manh Plz -NY 10005
(518) 452-5600 .. **Reese,** Brian E '10 %Heslin RF&M PC -5 Columbia Cir -Albany 12203
(212) 572-4200 .. **Reese,** Chas E II '04 %Estee Lauder -767 5th Av -NY 10153 **Fx:**572-3989
(716) 656-1272 .. **Reese,** Melissa A '03 -3099 William -Buffalo 14227
(212) 579-4625 .. **Reese,** Michl R '97 (Reese R LLP) -875 6th Av 18th Fl -NY 10001 **Fx:**253-4272
(212) 858-1000 .. **Reese,** Michl T '02 %Pillsbury WSP LLP -1540 Bway -NY 10036
(716) 694-2800 .. **Reese,** Peter A '74 OfCnsl DM Heim -3060 Niagara Flls Blvd -N Tonawanda 14120 **Fx:**694-2801
(718) 286-6000 .. **Reese,** Peter T '83 %DA -125-01 Qns Blvd -Kew Gdns 11415
(315) 422-1152 .. **Reese,** Wendy S '03 %Costello C&F,PLLC -500 Plum -Syracuse 13204
(585) 287-5275 .. **Reeve,** C Allan '91 Reeve Law Firm,PLLC -2171 Monroe Av -Rchstr 14618 **Fx:**287-5272
(212) 619-4350 .. **Reeve,** David M '10 %Newman MKGH,PC -14 Wall -NY 10005
(585) 232-5300 .. **Reeves,** J Wm '56 (Boylan BCV&W,LLP) -2400 Chase Sq -Rchstr 14604
(718) 446-7474 .. **Reeves,** John W '94 -7032 Bway -Jcksn Hts 11372
(845) 225-5827 .. **Reeves,** Kevin J '93 %Berkman & H,PC -38 Gleneida Av -Carmel 10512
(718) 250-2000 .. **Reeves,** Kyle C '90 %DA -350 Jay -Brklyn 11201 **Fx:**250-2314
(212) 869-3000 .. **Reeves,** Lee B Jr. '03 %Centro US -420 Lex Av -NY 10170 **Fx:**302-4776
(212) 980-4500 .. **Reeves,** Natalie L '00 %Cohen L LLP -885 3rd Av -NY 10022
(212) 768-6700 .. **Reeves,** Ryan C '06 %Sonnenschein N&R LLP -2 World Fncl Ctr -NY 10281
(585) 454-5650 .. **Refermat,** John T '97 (Lacy K LLP) -130 E Main -Rchstr 14604
(718) 590-2000 .. **Refsal,** Carl C '09 %DA -198 E 161st -Bronx 10451 **Fx:**590-6477
(212) 788-1327 .. **Regal,** Bruce I '83 %Law Dept -100 Church -NY 10007 **Fx:**788-0367
(212) 689-8808 .. **Regal,** Dorothea W '79 (Hoguet NR&K,LLP) -10 E 40th -NY 10016
(212) 770-1789 .. **Regan,** Adeline M '93 %AIG -80 Pine -NY 10005 **Fx:**344-2357
(212) 848-4000 .. **Regan,** Andrew W '77 (Shearman & S LLP) -599 Lex Av -NY 10022
(718) 855-9000 .. **Regan,** Arlene B '04 %Cullen and D LLP -177 Montague -Brklyn 11201
(212) 299-2000 .. **Regan,** Brian J '99 %NYMEX -1 North End Av -NY 10282 **Fx:**301-4700
(631) 732-6614 .. **Regan,** Edw J '55 (Regan & R) -3 Timbercrest Ln -Centereach 11720
(212) 805-0260 .. **Regan,** Erin K '01 Hon RC Casey -500 Pearl -NY 10007
(718) 886-1100 .. **Regan,** Franklin F Jr. '56 -159-18 Nrthrn Blvd -Flushng 11358 **Fx:**461-5651
(212) 818-9200 .. **Regan,** James '03 %Satterlee SB&B LLP -230 Park Av -NY 10169
(212) 434-0100 .. **Regan,** James F '05 %Litchfield C LLP -420 Lex Av -NY 10170
(585) 546-8880 .. **Regan,** John M '59 -799 Oakrdg Dr -Rchstr 14617
(585) 325-5150 .. **Regan,** Jos A '73 (Faraci L,LLP) -28 E Main -Rchstr 14614
(718) 767-1746 .. **Regan,** Jos G '80 -8-07 149th -Whitestone 11357 **Fx:**747-1544
(212) 819-8200 .. **Regan,** Lauri '89 Cnsl White & C LLP -1155 Av of Amer -NY 10036
(716) 854-1652 .. **Regan,** Lawr J '85 Regan & R -438 Main -Buffalo 14202 **Fx:**854-1654
(516) 785-7094 .. **Regan,** Mary C '99 -2100 Pine -Wantagh 11793 **Fx:**785-7094
(631) 732-6614 .. **Regan,** Marylou B '78 (Regan & R) -3 Timbercrest Ln -Centereach 11720
(516) 394-4200 .. **Regan,** Michl J '94 Cnsl Duffy & D -1370 RXR Plz -Uniondale 11556
(212) 753-7500 .. **Regan,** Michl P '06 Hartman & C LLP -488 Mad Av -NY 10022
(315) 424-8944 .. **Regan,** Paul M '83 (Shulman CG&R,PC) -250 S Clinton -Syracuse 13202
(718) 596-9000 .. **Regan,** Paul R '94 (Cohen HEP&T) -25 Chapel -Brklyn 11201
(718) 694-3827 .. **Regan,** Regina K '85 %Transit Auth -130 Lvngstn -Brklyn 11201 **Fx:**694-5726
(585) 325-1230 .. **Regan,** Richd E '65 -30 W Broad -Rchstr 14614 **Fx:**546-3641
(518) 761-3804 .. **Regan,** Robt A '90 (Mayor Of Glens Falls) -42 Ridge -Glens Fls 12801
(516) 663-6600 .. **Regan,** Robt F '95 %Ruskin MF,PC -1425 RXR Plz -Uniondale 11556
(212) 768-6700 .. **Regan,** Robin M '04 %Sonnenschein N&R LLP -2 World Fncl Ctr -NY 10281
(212) 309-1000 .. **Regan,** Shawn P '97 (Hunton & W) -200 Park Av -NY 10166
(518) 292-5120 .. **Regan,** Thos P '96 %Dept Econ Dvlpmnt -30 S Pearl -Albany 12245 **Fx:**292-5807
(718) 286-6000 .. **Regan,** Timothy J '07 %DA -125-01 Qns Blvd -Kew Gdns 11415
(212) 438-3652 .. **Regan,** Tracy A '92 Standard & Poors -55 Water -NY 10041
(212) 297-6067 .. **Regan,** Tricia M '97 TMM -230 Park Av -NY 10169 **Fx:**297-6062
(716) 634-8400 .. **Regan,** Wm J '73 Regan & R -5500 Main -Buffalo 14221 **Fx:**634-6443
(212) 940-8800 .. **Regan,** Wm M '00 (Katten MR LLP) -575 Mad Av -NY 10022
(518) 877-5062 .. **Regan-Bianchini,** Patricia A '00 SrCnsl Bianchini Law,PLLC -2023 Route 9 -Round Lk 12151 **Fx:**877-5064
(914) 948-1450 .. **Regan-Henry,** Susan '84 (Henry & R) -44 Church -White Plns 10601 **Fx:**948-1439
(212) 530-5000 .. **Regante,** Mark L '79 (Milbank TH&M LLP) -1 Chase Manh Plz -NY 10005
(212) 683-3636 .. **Regel,** Walter W '86 (Krass S&S,PC) -419 Park Av S -NY 10016
(347) 296-1458 .. **Regelmann,** Carl F '07 %Hon C Demarest -360 Adams -Brklyn 11201
(212) 661-2720 .. **Regen,** Wm A '84 (Regen Benz & MacKenzie) -57 W 38th -NY 10018 **Fx:**681-6140
(845) 897-5199 .. **Regenbaum,** Andrew S '97 (Feldman K&C,LLP) -995 Main BxA -Fishkill 12524
(212) 474-1000 .. **Regenbaum,** Leslie W '08 %Cravath S&M LLP -825 8th Av -NY 10019
(516) 489-5000 .. **Regenbogen,** Brad E '87 %Town Atty -Town Hall -Hempstd 11550 **Fx:**489-5150
(212) 521-5400 .. **Regensburg,** Kenneth '97 (Reed S LLP) -599 Lex Av -NY 10022
(212) 567-8590 .. **Regenstreich,** Bruce N '76 (Burrell R LLC) -110 Wall -NY 10005 **Fx:**567-2630
(516) 294-6442 .. **Regenstreif,** Herbert '61 (Fried & R,PC) -358 Willis Av -Mineola 11501 **Fx:**294-6442
(518) 474-6777 .. **Reger,** C Michl '76 %Dept of Law -The Cptl -Albany 12224

(212) 944-0500 .. **Reger,** Ofer '08 %Hofheimer G&G,LLP -530 5th Av -NY 10036
(212) 309-6000 .. **Reger,** Robt J Jr. '74 (Morgan L&B LLP) -101 Park Av -NY 10178
(516) 472-0126 .. **Regev,** Eran '09 -10 Cuttermill Rd -Gt Neck 11021
(212) 227-7878 .. **Regina,** Giovanni '83 (Waters MM) -233 Bway -NY 10279
(516) 489-5000 .. **Regina,** Richd M '08 %Town Atty -Town Hall -Hempstd 11550 **Fx:**489-5150
(212) 903-9000 .. **Regis-Hallinan,** Linda M '01 %Linklaters -1345 Av of Amer -NY 10105
(718) 326-3434 .. **Reglis,** Marcela Sabani '04 (Sabani R&Z-M,PC) -65-17 Grand Av -Maspeth 11378
(212) 637-3164 .. **Regna,** Jean H '93 %EPA -290 Bway -NY 10007 **Fx:**637-3096
(212) 909-6000 .. **Regner,** Wm D '95 (Debevoise & P LLP) -919 3rd Av -NY 10022
(718) 858-7027 .. **Rego,** Susan M '01 -379 Henry -Brklyn 11201
(212) 450-4000 .. **Regojo,** Cristina Victoria '04 %Davis P&W LLP -450 Lex Av -NY 10017
(212) 335-4500 .. **Regojo Balboa,** Gabriela '09 %DLA Piper LLP -1251 Av of Amer -NY 10020
(212) 619-1910 .. **Regosin Edwards Stone & Feder** -225 Bway -NY 10007 **Fx:**964-9516
(585) 924-7420 .. **Reh,** Thos D '97 (Rose & R,LLC) -121 W Main -Victor 14564 **Fx:**924-0267
(718) 590-2000 .. **Rehak,** Jessica J '02 %DA -198 E 161st -Bronx 10451 **Fx:**590-6477
(212) 822-0200 .. **Rehany,** Alon '03 Artemis Grp Ltd -1430 Bway -NY 10018
(516) 827-9583 .. **Rehbock,** Richd A '74 -1 Maple Run Dr -Jericho 11753 **Fx:**827-9589
(914) 694-5900 .. **Rehbock,** Roy G '79 West World Mgmt Inc -4 Manhattanvll Rd -Purchase 10577 **Fx:**694-4642
(212) 878-8000 .. **Rehbock,** Timo '02 %Clifford C LLP -31 W 52nd -NY 10019
(518) 713-2144 .. **Rehfuss,** Stephen J '86 (Rehfuss L & Assoc,PC) -40 British Amer Blvd -Latham 12110 **Fx:**713-2148
(212) 268-9001 .. **Rehill,** Apolonia '97 %B Merkur,PC -225 W 35th -NY 10001
(585) 454-2000 .. **Rehkopf,** Donald G Jr. '89 %Brenna B&B,PLLC -31 E Main -Rchstr 14614
(518) 668-5968 .. **Rehm,** Mark C '01 -1557 State Route 9 Bx286 -Lk George 12845 **Fx:**668-5970
(212) 257-6960 .. **Rehman,** Asim '01 %Chaffetz L LLP -1350 Av of Amer -NY 10019
(212) 902-9124 .. **Rehman,** Omar R '01 Goldman Sachs -85 Broad -NY 10004
(212) 838-7797 .. **Rehns,** Danl B '06 %Cohen MS&T,PLLC -88 Pine -NY 10005
(212) 838-7797 .. **Rehns,** Kenneth M '09 %Cohen MS&T,PLLC -88 Pine -NY 10005
(914) 273-8325 .. **Reibeisen,** Mark '69 -7 Sterling Rd -Armonk 10504
(212) 697-9654 .. **Reiben,** Richd E '80 %West Group -551 5th Av -NY 10176 **Fx:**697-9655
(585) 427-7225 .. **Reiber,** George M '78 -3136 S Winton Rd -Rchstr 14623 **Fx:**427-7804
(212) 536-3900 .. **Reibman,** Andrew L '01 (K&L Gates LLP) -599 Lex Av -NY 10022
(718) 522-1743 .. **Reibman,** Marc '82 (Reibman & W) -26 Court -Brklyn 11242 **Fx:**643-9297
(718) 286-6000 .. **Reibstein,** Eugene '77 %DA -125-01 Qns Blvd -Kew Gdns 11415
(212) 808-2700 .. **Reibstein,** Richd J '76 (Pepper H LLP) -620 8th Av -NY 10018
(212) 450-4000 .. **Reibstein,** Susan F '83 Cnsl Davis P&W LLP -450 Lex Av -NY 10017
(718) 743-6000 .. **Reich,** Abraham '73 -2016 Av X -Brklyn 11235
(845) 639-7800 .. **Reich,** Allison N '99 (Mandel K&B,LLP) -210 Route 303 -Vly Cottage 10989
(212) 723-5781 .. **Reich,** Amy C '89 Citigroup Global Mrkts -390 Greenwich -NY 10013
(212) 589-4200 .. **Reich,** Andrew W '87 OfCnsl Baker & H LLP -45 Rckfllr Plz -NY 10111
(212) 770-2577 .. **Reich,** Arlene A '67 %AIG -80 Pine -NY 10005
(212) 755-4152 .. **Reich,** Arthur '53 -485 Mad Av -NY 10022 **Fx:**588-0471
(516) 679-8243 .. **Reich,** Barry '78 -2637 Marin Ln -E Meadow 11554
(212) 319-1000 .. **Reich,** Carter A '04 %Quirk & B,PC -845 3rd Av -NY 10022
(212) 761-7363 .. **Reich,** Christopher V '86 Morgan Stanley -1585 Bway -NY 10036
(212) 213-6996 .. **Reich,** Danl S '03 %Spears & I LLP -51 Mad Av -NY 10010
(917) 533-1621 .. **Reich,** David '91 -72-10 136th -Flushng 11367
(212) 768-6700 .. **Reich,** Edw J '92 (Sonnenschein N&R LLP) -1221 Av of Amer -NY 10020
(212) 818-8800 .. **Reich,** Elaine M '80 (Graubard M) -405 Lex Av -NY 10174
(518) 213-6000 .. **Reich,** Fredk K '81 %NYSUT -800 Troy-Schnctdy Rd -Latham 12110 **Fx:**213-6488
(212) 264-8819 .. **Reich,** Gitel '94 SSA-OHA -26 Fed Plz -NY 10278
(212) 344-3900 .. **Reich,** James B '60 %Belair & E LLP -61 Bway -NY 10006
(212) 294-6700 .. **Reich,** James David Jr. '88 (Winston & S) -200 Park Av -NY 10166
(914) 749-8200 .. **Reich,** Jarrod F '05 %Boies S&F LLP -333 Main -Armonk 10504
(914) 949-2126 .. **Reich,** Jeffrey A '00 %Reich R&R,PC -235 Main -White Plns 10601 **Fx:**949-1604
(212) 545-4620 .. **Reich,** Jeffrey S '94 (Wolf HAF&H LLP) -270 Mad Av -NY 10016
(212) 728-8000 .. **Reich,** Jonathan D '08 %Willkie F&G LLP -787 7th Av -NY 10019
(914) 304-4304 .. **Reich,** Jonathan S '88 %Michael Fox Intl -75 S Bway -White Plns 10601
(646) 471-4000 .. **Reich,** Julius S '80 %PricewaterhouseCoopers LLP -300 Mad Av -NY 10017
(212) 801-9327 .. **Reich,** Keith E '82 (Greenberg T,LLP) -200 Park Av -NY 10166
(212) 373-3000 .. **Reich,** Kevin R '07 %Paul WRW&G LLP -1285 Av of Amer -NY 10019
(914) 949-2126 .. **Reich,** Lawr R '65 (Reich R&R,PC) -235 Main -White Plns 10601 **Fx:**949-1604
(631) 757-7299 .. **Reich,** Lawr W '65 -73 Laurel Hill Rd -Centerprt 11721
(631) 367-7100 .. **Reich,** Mark S '01 %Coughlin SGR&R LLP -58 S Srvc Rd -Melvll 11747
(718) 459-9000 .. **Reich,** Michl H '80 (Sweeney GR&B,LLP) -95-25 Qns Blvd -Rego Pk 11374
(212) 714-0421 .. **Reich,** Michl W '01 %M Fuld,PC -38 W 32nd -NY 10001 **Fx:**714-0436
(212) 449-3050 .. **Reich,** Nancy E '82 Merrill Lynch -4 World Fncl Ctr -NY 10080
(585) 262-4700 .. **Reich,** Norman J '66 (Bilgore RLK&K) -950 Rynlds Arcd Bldg -Rchstr 14614
(212) 427-1909 .. **Reich,** Norman S '56 -401 E 86th -NY 10028
(646) 368-9096 .. **Reich,** Patricia N '98 -389 E 89th -NY 10128
(917) 836-6220 .. **Reich,** Paul S '05 -213-37 39th Av -Bayside 11361
(212) 332-8830 .. **Reich,** Richd I '80 (Lifflander & R LLP) -1221 Av of Amer -NY 10020
(212) 407-4000 .. **Reich,** Robt S '71 (Loeb & L,LLP) -345 Park Av -NY 10154
(914) 949-2126 .. **Reich,** Robin '92 %Reich R&R,PC -235 Main -White Plns 10601 **Fx:**949-1604
(212) 728-8000 .. **Reich,** Scott D '09 %Willkie F&G LLP -787 7th Av -NY 10019
(212) 223-4747 .. **Reich,** Seymour '53 -505 Park Av -NY 10022
(212) 935-3131 .. **Reich,** Seymour D '58 (Gallet D&B,LLP) -845 3rd Av -NY 10022
(716) 853-3801 .. **Reich,** Shari Jo '87 (Kenney SL&N,LLP) -14 Lafayette Sq -Buffalo 14203
(212) 737-0400 .. **Reich,** Sheryl E '79 %G Lefcourt,PC -148 E 78th -NY 10075 **Fx:**988-6192
(212) 935-6133 .. **Reich,** Stephen '64 -141 E 55th -NY 10022 **Fx:**750-6350
(212) 790-4500 .. **Reich,** Steven F '87 (Manatt P&P,LLP) -7 Times Sq -NY 10036
(212) 430-6582 .. **Reich,** Stuart J '05 -11 Bway -NY 10004 **Fx:**430-6583
(716) 854-7525 .. **Reich,** Wm Z '74 (Serotte R&W) -300 Delaware Av -Buffalo 14202
(212) 225-2000 .. **Reich,** Yaron Z '79 (Cleary GS&H) -1 Lbrty Plz -NY 10006
(212) 688-8555 .. **Reichard,** Elizabeth T '05 %Fragomen DB&L LLP -7 Hanover Sq -NY 10004
(212) 374-9101 .. **Reichardt,** Corey M '06 %Brill & Assoc,PC -111 John -NY 10038 **Fx:**374-9108
(718) 544-3333 .. **Reichel,** Aaron I '78 %L Hallock -77-42 164th -Fresh Mdws 11366 **Fx:**544-1341
(212) 930-9700 .. **Reichel,** Benjamin '92 (Sichenzia RFF LLP) -61 Bway -NY 10006
(631) 390-7713 .. **Reichel,** Harold I '56 -135 Pinelawn Rd -Melvll 11747
(646) 471-1861 .. **Reichel,** Heather D '04 PricewaterhouseCoopers LLP -300 Mad Av -NY 10017
(315) 218-8000 .. **Reichel,** Paul W '91 (Bond S&K,PLLC) -1 Lincoln Ctr -Syracuse 13202
(631) 969-7777 .. **Reichel,** Saml J '93 (Frenkel LWW&G,LLP) -20 W Main -Bay Shr 11706 **Fx:**206-0540
(718) 459-5870 .. **Reichelscheimer,** Glenn A '92 -98-87 Qns Blvd -Rego Pk 11374
(212) 880-3800 .. **Reichelscheimer,** Jerry D '93 (Akerman S) -335 Mad Av -NY 10017
(631) 499-3800 .. **Reichelscheimer,** Robt C '83 (Kalb & R,PC) -283 Commack Rd -Commack 11725
(518) 457-3177 .. **Reichenbach,** Brian S '90 Dept Civil Srvc -Harriman Campus Bldg 1 -Albany 12239 **Fx:**457-6654
(212) 259-8000 .. **Reichenbach,** Erin J '09 %Dewey & L LLP -1301 Av of Amer -NY 10019
(212) 999-5800 .. **Reichenberg,** David '07 %Wilson SG&R -1301 Av of Americas -NY 10019
(212) 310-8000 .. **Reicher,** Aliza R '08 %Weil G&M LLP -767 5th Av -NY 10153
(212) 984-8281 .. **Reicher,** Craig L '87 CB Richard Ellis -200 Park Av -NY 10166 **Fx:**984-8040
(212) 818-1110 .. **Reicher,** Irwin '51 Cnsl Butzel L,PC -380 Mad Av -NY 10017
(212) 701-3000 .. **Reicher,** Lawr A '09 %Cahill G&R LLP -80 Pine -NY 10005 **Fx:**269-5420
(212) 349-6006 .. **Reicher,** Lewis '71 -60 E 42nd -NY 10165
(212) 258-3770 .. **Reicher,** Robt J '81 -630 9th Av -NY 10036 **Fx:**258-3775
(716) 856-0600 .. **Reichert,** Raymond P '80 (Jaeckle F&M,LLP) -12 Fountain Plz -Buffalo 14202
(585) 546-8430 .. **Reichhart,** Amy L '05 %Knauf S LLP -2 State -Rchstr 14614
(212) 841-1000 .. **Reichl,** Nolan L '07 %Covington & B LLP -620 8th Av -NY 10018
(845) 255-0041 .. **Reichler,** Judith M '78 Justice Ct -23 Plattekill Av -New Paltz 12561
(516) 747-0300 .. **Reichler,** Richd '61 OfCnsl Meltzer LG&B,LLP -190 Willis Av -Mineola 11501
(212) 407-4000 .. **Reichman,** Danl L '06 %Loeb & L,LLP -345 Park Av -NY 10154
(718) 520-6737 .. **Reichman,** Ilene J '84 %Hon M Spires -125-01 Qns Blvd -Kew Gdns 11415
(914) 238-5740 .. **Reichman,** Jacqueline S '87 -1267 Hrdscrbble Rd -Chappaqua 10514
(212) 909-9500 .. **Reichman,** John H '78 (Wachtel & M,LLP) -885 2nd Av -NY 10017
(212) 425-7200 .. **Reichman,** Jonathan D '85 (Kenyon & K,LLP) -1 Bway -NY 10004
(212) 227-8448 .. **Reichman,** Maurice A '57 -33 Greenwich Av -NY 10014
(212) 449-1000 .. **Reichman,** Rebecca A '05 %Merrill Lynch -220 Bway -NY 10038
(212) 421-2233 .. **Reichman,** Robt P '75 (Wilk A LLP) -675 3rd Av -NY 10017
(914) 949-3250 .. **Reichner,** Donna Lynn '86 %Chicago Title/Ticor Title -245 Main -White Plns 10601 **Fx:**946-7698
(845) 735-8926 .. **Reichner,** Henry J '57 -18 Lenape Rd -Pearl Rvr 10965 **Fx:**735-8926
(212) 455-2000 .. **Reichstein,** Matthew H '10 %Simpson T&B LLP -425 Lex Av -NY 10017
(212) 806-5400 .. **Reichuber,** Courtney A '08 %Stroock &S&L LLP -180 Maiden Ln -NY 10038
(212) 880-6000 .. **Reicin,** Cheryl V '85 (Torys LLP) -237 Park Av -NY 10017
(212) 248-3140 .. **Reid,** Chas A III '74 (Drinker B&R LLP) -140 Bway -NY 10005
(585) 248-9620 .. **Reid,** David C '70 -65 Monroe Av -Pittsfrd 14534
(518) 381-7337 .. **Reid,** Deborah A '83 -1461 Garner Av -Schnctdy 12309
(212) 450-4000 .. **Reid,** Edw S '57 SrCnsl Davis P&W LLP -450 Lex Av -NY 10017
(646) 386-3250 .. **Reid,** Elenor C '98 Hon C Edmead -60 Centre -NY 10007
(212) 756-2000 .. **Reid,** F Barbara G '90 %Schulte R&Z LLP -919 3rd Av -NY 10022
(585) 546-6448 .. **Reid,** Fatimat O '06 %Davidson F LLP -28 E Main -Rchstr 14614
(212) 613-2019 .. **Reid,** Ghillaine A '96 (Gibbons PC) -1 Penn Plz -NY 10119 **Fx:**554-9645
(212) 728-8000 .. **Reid,** Gregory E '09 %Willkie F&G LLP -787 7th Av -NY 10019
(212) 626-6785 .. **Reid,** Gregory L '79 (Reid R&R,LLP) -1120 Av of Amer -NY 10036
(212) 935-5500 .. **Reid,** Heather J '02 %Franklin WR&V -488 Mad Av -NY 10022
(212) 626-4100 .. **Reid,** Ira A '88 (Baker & M LLP) -1114 Av of Amer -NY 10036
(315) 492-9665 .. **Reid,** James E '78 (Greene & R,PLLC) -173 Intrepid Ln -Syracuse 13205
(315) 331-5633 .. **Reid,** James E '78 (Greene & R,PLLC) -180 E Union -Newark 14513
(212) 818-9200 .. **Reid,** James W '72 (Satterlee SB&B LLP) -230 Park Av -NY 10169
(518) 581-8800 .. **Reid,** Jane R '84 Cnsl Lemery G LLC -60 Railroad Pl -Saratoga Spgs 12866
(212) 264-5916 .. **Reid,** Jessica Spear '98 DHS -26 Fed Plz -NY 10278
(212) 813-2010 .. **Reid,** Jos C '83 -230 Park Av -NY 10169
(212) 969-3000 .. **Reid,** Keri L '07 %Proskauer R LLP -1585 Bway -NY 10036
(516) 542-5900 .. **Reid,** Lawr H Jr. '72 (Congdon FORDT&F) -333 Earle Ovngton Blvd -Uniondale 11553
(866) 348-5819 .. **Reid,** Lori A '99 %SSA-ODAR -50 Fountain Plz -Buffalo 14202 **Fx:**(716) 551-4078
(516) 741-2148 .. **Reid,** Mark M '92 -336 1st -Mineola 11501
(607) 798-1521 .. **Reid,** Marylynn A '86 (Burr & R,LLP) -Bx2308 -Bnghmtn 13902
(212) 408-2500 .. **Reid,** Maureen P '05 %Baker B,LLP -30 Rckfllr Plz -NY 10112

(212) 909-6000 .. **Reid,** Natalie L '04 %Debevoise & P LLP -919 3rd Av -NY 10022
(212) 435-3571 .. **Reid,** Neil H '76 %Port Auth of NY/NJ -225 Park Av S -NY 10003 **Fx:**435-3555
(718) 464-6300 .. **Reid,** Neville A '82 -220-29 Jamaica Av -Qns Vllg 11428
(518) 581-8800 .. **Reid,** Patrick Scott '86 (Lemery G LLC) -60 Railroad Pl -Saratoga Spgs 12866
(716) 434-2885 .. **Reid,** Paul D '85 -100 W Genesee Bx987 -Lockprt 14095 **Fx:**434-3170
(212) 310-8000 .. **Reid,** Penny P '04 (Weil G&M LLP) -767 5th Av -NY 10153
(212) 980-0404 .. **Reid,** Robt J '76 %J Dearie & Assoc -515 Mad Av -NY 10022 **Fx:**980-0555
(212) 626-6785 .. **Reid Rodriguez & Rouse,LLP** -1120 Av of Amer -NY 10036
(516) 377-5613 .. **Reid,** Ronald D '96 -2425 Grand Av -Baldwin 11510 **Fx:**377-6105
(212) 653-8700 .. **Reid,** Russell L Jr. '05 (Sheppard MR&H LLP) -30 Rckfllr Plz -NY 10112
(212) 808-7800 .. **Reid,** Sarah L '78 (Kelley D&W LLP) -101 Park Av -NY 10178
(212) 930-9700 .. **Reid,** Sean F '08 %Sichenzia RFF LLP -61 Bway -NY 10006
(607) 656-7600 .. **Reid,** Steven R '78 -15 Genesee Bx561 -Greene 13778 **Fx:**656-7950
(212) 460-2635 .. **Reid,** Thos H '83 Con Ed -4 Irving Pl -NY 10003
(212) 450-4000 .. **Reid,** Thos J '89 %Davis P&W LLP -450 Lex Av -NY 10017
(718) 402-8127 .. **Reid,** Trevor A '79 T Reid,PC -391 E 149th -Bronx 10455 **Fx:**402-0371
(518) 402-1871 .. **Reid-Coleman,** Carleen M '07 %Dept of Health -Corning Twr 24th Fl -Albany 12237 **Fx:**473-4896
(212) 636-6000 .. **Reidenberg,** Joel R '86 %Fordham Univ Sch of Law -140 W 62nd -NY 10023 **Fx:**636-6899
(516) 296-7000 .. **Reid Gladston,** Candace '87 (Certilman BA&H,LLP) -90 Merrick Av -E Meadow 11554
(718) 694-3884 .. **Reid-Green,** Dawn '90 %Transit Auth -130 Lvngstn -Brklyn 11201 **Fx:**694-5726
(212) 687-8800 .. **Reidler,** Harry J '78 -108-20 68th Rd -Frst Hlls 11375
(516) 487-6585 .. **Reidman,** Fern '92 -185 Grt Nck Rd -Gt Neck 11021 **Fx:**487-6814
(212) 839-7000 .. **Reidy,** Christine A '88 Cnsl Hill B&N LLP -200 Lbrty -NY 10281
(212) 728-8000 .. **Reidy,** Owen D '10 %Willkie F&G LLP -787 7th Av -NY 10019
(212) 483-9600 .. **Reidy,** Patrick G '88 (Costello S&G LLP) -44 Wall -NY 10005
(718) 590-2000 .. **Reidy,** Seanan L '00 DA -198 E 161st -Bronx 10451 **Fx:**590-6477
(585) 454-0700 .. **Reidy,** Thos E Jr. '81 (Ward GH&R LLP) -300 State -Rchstr 14614
(212) 697-6555 .. **Reif,** Fredk W '87 (Biedermann RH&R) -570 Lex Av -NY 10022
(212) 228-7727 .. **Reif,** James '70 (Gladstein R&M,LLP) -817 Bway -NY 10003
(718) 222-2313 .. **Reife,** Luba '09 %Law Dept -350 Jay -Brklyn 11201 **Fx:**222-2373
(212) 538-9751 .. **Reifenberg,** Alan R '96 Credit Suisse -1 Mad Av -NY 10010
(212) 632-2660 .. **Reifenberg,** Marjorie L '92 Lazard Alternative Invstmnts LLC -30 Rckfllr Plz -NY 10020 **Fx:**332-1793
(585) 546-5510 .. **Reifenstein,** Michl '78 -263 Plymouth Av S -Rchstr 14608
(212) 801-9285 .. **Reifer,** Ira D '08 %Greenberg T,LLP -200 Park Av -NY 10166
(516) 249-3450 .. **Reifer,** Tracy S '00 %Carman C&I,LLP -266 Main -Farmngdl 11735
(212) 988-9000 .. **Reiff,** Devon '81 D Reiff,PC -55 Broad -NY 10004 **Fx:**(646) 225-6617
(212) 691-4128 .. **Reifler,** Margery Evans '73 -2 Grove -NY 10014
(212) 407-7700 .. **Reifler,** Stewart '92 (Vedder P,PC) -1633 Bway -NY 10019
(212) 859-8000 .. **Reifman,** Marli F '08 %Fried FHS&J LLP -1 NY Plz -NY 10004
(585) 546-7830 .. **Reifsteck,** Edw R '55 OfCnsl Culley MT&P,LLP -36 W Main -Rchstr 14614
(212) 265-6888 .. **Reig,** Linda Pissott '00 (Porzio B&N,PC) -156 W 56th -NY 10019
(914) 242-4800 .. **Reig,** Neil H '88 -15 Moore Av -Mt Kisco 10549 **Fx:**241-2402
(212) 705-7000 .. **Reig,** Shari C '88 OfCnsl Bingham M LLP -399 Park Av -NY 10022
(212) 468-8000 .. **Reigersman,** Remmelt A '07 %Morrison & F LLP -1290 Av of Amer -NY 10104
(212) 336-3620 .. **Reik,** Deborah '89 %EEOC -33 Whitehall -NY 10004
(212) 907-9411 .. **Reilly,** Andre T '97 A&E TV Ntwrk -235 E 45th -NY 10017
(631) 451-6500 .. **Reilly,** Beth Ann '05 %Brookhaven Law Dept -1 Indpndnc Hill -Farmngvll 11738 **Fx:**698-4489
(518) 486-5156 .. **Reilly,** Brenda M '03 %DHCR -38-40 State -Albany 12207
(212) 688-8555 .. **Reilly,** Brent P '99 %Fragomen DB&L LLP -7 Hanover Sq -NY 10004
(516) 409-6200 .. **Reilly,** Brian T '07 Furey KWM&C,PC -2174 Jackson Av -Seafrd 11783
(212) 403-1000 .. **Reilly,** Carrie M '06 %Wachtell LR&K -51 W 52nd -NY 10019
(212) 880-6000 .. **Reilly,** Cate F '06 Torys LLP -237 Park Av -NY 10017
(212) 264-0665 .. **Reilly,** Chas V '73 %US DOJ Antitrust Div -26 Fed Plz Ste 3630 -NY 10278
(518) 434-5050 .. **Reilly,** Danielle Neroni '02 %Law Dept -106 City Hall -Albany 12207 **Fx:**434-5070
(212) 697-1111 .. **Reilly,** David '91 %L-3 Cmmnctns Corp -600 3rd Av -NY 10016 **Fx:**682-7959
(212) 460-4786 .. **Reilly,** David J '73 Con Ed -4 Irving Pl -NY 10003
(631) 369-2270 .. **Reilly,** David M '93 %J Ryan & Assoc -633 Main Rd -Rvrhead 11901
(516) 248-2434 .. **Reilly,** David T '93 (Reilly & R,LLP) -170 Old Cntry Rd -Mineola 11501 **Fx:**248-2459
(212) 418-0500 .. **Reilly,** Edw A '69 (Morris & M LLP) -767 3rd Av -NY 10017
(212) 813-8800 .. **Reilly,** Edw A Jr. '04 (Goodwin P LLP) -620 8th Av -NY 10018
(212) 278-0400 .. **Reilly,** Elizabeth C '09 %Cooper & D LLP -30 Rckfllr Plz -NY 10112
(914) 761-0300 .. **Reilly,** Gerald D '76 (Stephens BR&L) -175 Main -White Plns 10601
(518) 455-4311 .. **Reilly,** Geraldine Anne '93 %NYS Assembly -80 State -Albany 12248 **Fx:**455-4128
(212) 583-9600 .. **Reilly,** Gregory B III '93 (Littler M,PC) -900 3rd Av -NY 10022
(516) 882-6666 .. **Reilly,** Ivy A '02 (I Reilly,PLLC) -100 Merrick Rd -Rockvll Ctr 11570 **Fx:**868-8666
(518) 487-7600 .. **Reilly,** J Stephen '79 (Whiteman O&H LLP) -1 Commerce Plz -Albany 12260
(516) 873-8636 .. **Reilly,** James A '69 -1 Old Cntry Rd -Carle Pl 11514 **Fx:**873-3956
(631) 232-0200 .. **Reilly,** James B '85 %Fumuso KDSS&F,LLP -110 Marcus Blvd -Hauppauge 11788
(518) 274-7252 .. **Reilly,** James J '58 -54 2nd -Troy 12180 **Fx:**274-0348
(212) 661-7777 .. **Reilly,** James J '87 %Condon O'Meara McGinty & Donnelly LLP -3 NY Plz -NY 10004
(518) 465-7581 .. **Reilly,** James M '75 (Herzog Law Firm,PC) -7 Southwoods Blvd -Albany 12211
(518) 266-1002 .. **Reilly,** James R '63 -Bx208 -Troy 12181
(212) 530-5000 .. **Reilly,** James T '10 %Milbank TH&M LLP -1 Chase Manh Plz -NY 10005
(631) 858-5800 .. **Reilly,** John E '83 (Reilly & M PLLC) -201 Moreland Rd -Hauppauge 11788
(631) 366-1919 .. **Reilly,** John F '73 -503 Main -Pt Jffrsn 11777 **Fx:**366-1983
(518) 443-5400 .. **Reilly,** John H '91 %SUNY Univ Cnsl -S333 SUNY Plz -Albany 12246 **Fx:**443-5409
(516) 248-2434 .. **Reilly,** John J '58 (Reilly & R,LLP) -170 Old Cntry Rd -Mineola 11501 **Fx:**248-2459
(212) 872-9800 .. **Reilly,** John J '68 (Squire S&D LLP) -30 Rckfllr Plz -NY 10112
(518) 434-5050 .. **Reilly,** John J '88 %Law Dept -106 City Hall -Albany 12207 **Fx:**434-5070
(212) 964-7400 .. **Reilly,** John K '83 Smith MDWY&Y,PC -111 John -NY 10038
(212) 323-7070 .. **Reilly,** John V III '98 %Rawle & H LLP -14 Wall -NY 10005
(516) 228-5100 .. **Reilly,** Justin M '00 %N Greenberg & Assoc -900 Merchants Cncrs -Westbury 11590 **Fx:**228-5106
(212) 313-3600 .. **Reilly,** Katherine M '09 %Barry M&M -2 Rector -NY 10006
(212) 715-1000 .. **Reilly,** Kathleen A '10 %Arnold & P LLP -399 Park Av -NY 10022
(716) 856-5500 .. **Reilly,** Kathleen M '92 (Damon M LLP) -200 Delaware Av -Buffalo 14202
(212) 558-4000 .. **Reilly,** Kathleen M '10 %Sullivan & C LLP -125 Broad -NY 10004
(212) 340-0400 .. **Reilly,** Kevin A '82 %Applt Div 1st Dept -27 Mad Av -NY 10010 **Fx:**889-4412
(718) 618-1406 .. **Reilly,** Kevin C '74 Supreme Ct -851 Grnd Cncrs -Bronx 10451
(631) 331-0900 .. **Reilly,** Kevin O '77 -1227 Main -Pt Jffrsn 11777 **Fx:**331-0998
(212) 421-2233 .. **Reilly,** Kimberly D '03 %Wilk A LLP -675 3rd Av -NY 10017
(631) 669-3000 .. **Reilly Like Tenety & Mescall** -179 Little East Neck Rd N -Babylon 11702 **Fx:**669-4122
(212) 805-3900 .. **Reilly,** Malcolm J '03 (Clausen M PC) -1 Chase Manh Plz -NY 10005
(212) 537-9000 .. **Reilly,** Mary Ellen '06 %Cohen G&S,LLP -850 3rd Av -NY 10022
(212) 839-7000 .. **Reilly,** Mary T '78 (Hill B&N LLP) -200 Lbrty -NY 10281
(631) 694-0033 .. **Reilly,** MaryBeth '89 %Lawrence WR&B,PC -425 Broadhllw Rd -Melvll 11747
(718) 390-5383 .. **Reilly,** Maureen A '94 %Supreme Ct Law Dept -18 Richmond Ter -Staten Isl 10301
(212) 473-7601 .. **Reilly,** Michl '83 -610 E 20th -NY 10009
(718) 575-9000 .. **Reilly,** Michl J '92 -123-40 83rd Av -Kew Gdns 11415 **Fx:**575-2880
(212) 705-7000 .. **Reilly,** Michl J '07 (Bingham M LLP) -399 Park Av -NY 10022
(631) 501-3100 .. **Reilly,** Michl T '88 %J Humphreys -3 Huntngtn Quad Bx9028 -Melvll 11747 **Fx:**501-3085
(212) 808-0700 .. **Reilly,** Michl T '02 %Norris M&M,PA -875 3rd Av -NY 10022
(212) 416-8860 .. **Reilly,** Nathan D '02 %Dept of Law -120 Bway -NY 10271
(914) 681-0200 .. **Reilly,** Patrick M '78 (DelBello DWW&W,LLP) -1 N Lex Av -White Plns 10601
(212) 408-2500 .. **Reilly,** Paul '95 SpclCnsl Baker B,LLP -30 Rckfllr Plz -NY 10112
(518) 371-8888 .. **Reilly,** Peter E '79 (Ianniello A&R,PC) -805 Route 146 -Clifton Pk 12065
(212) 354-8466 .. **Reilly,** Peter L '00 (P Reilly & Assoc,LLC) -1040 Av of Amer -NY 10018
(212) 259-8000 .. **Reilly,** Rebecca M '03 %Dewey & L LLP -1301 Av of Amer -NY 10019
(518) 432-7511 .. **Reilly,** Richd C '05 %Gleason DW&O -40 Beaver -Albany 12207
(315) 754-6214 .. **Reilly,** Richd G Jr. '81 (Kall & R) -6819 Main Bx189 -Red Crk 13143 **Fx:**754-6237
(315) 437-3321 .. **Reilly,** Richd G Jr. '81 (Kall & R) -3522 James -Syracuse 13206 **Fx:**437-0091
(212) 819-8200 .. **Reilly,** Richd J '93 (White & C LLP) -1155 Av of Amer -NY 10036
(212) 626-4100 .. **Reilly,** Richd R '80 (Baker & M LLP) -1114 Av of Amer -NY 10036
(212) 636-6807 .. **Reilly,** Robt J '76 Fordham Univ Sch of Law -140 W 62nd -NY 10023 **Fx:**636-6958
(212) 791-9730 .. **Reilly,** Robt J '99 %PF Adams,PC -30 Vesey -NY 10007
(718) 520-3805 .. **Reilly,** Robt M '77 %Supreme Ct -88-11 Sutphin Blvd -Jamaica 11435
(518) 213-6000 .. **Reilly,** Robt T Jr. '94 %NYSUT -800 Troy-Schnctdy Rd -Latham 12110 **Fx:**213-6488
(212) 667-9300 .. **Reilly,** Sean C '87 Nomura Securities Intl -2 World Fncl Ctr -NY 10281
(607) 734-1519 .. **Reilly,** Thos E '76 (Learned RL&H,LLP) -449 E Water -Elmira 14901
(518) 862-1386 .. **Reilly,** Thos J '03 %Burke SM&H,LLP -302 Wshngtn Av Ext Bx15085 -Albany 12212
(212) 696-6000 .. **Reilly,** Thos J Jr. '05 %Curtis M-PC&M LLP -101 Park Av -NY 10178
(516) 599-2020 .. **Reilly,** Thos P '02 %A Chianese & Assoc -100 Merrick Rd -Rockvll Ctr 11570 **Fx:**599-6476
(718) 876-6300 .. **Reilly,** Thos Patrick '97 %DA -130 Styvsnt Pl -Staten Isl 10301
(718) 428-1505 .. **Reilly,** Thos S '93 -36-19 202nd -Bayside 11361
(518) 785-3229 .. **Reilly,** Timothy J '94 -23 S Sparrowbush Rd -Latham 12110
(718) 590-3248 .. **Reilly,** Tracie L '07 %Law Dept -900 Sheridan Av -Bronx 10451 **Fx:**590-2699
(212) 986-6840 .. **Reilly,** Virginia Anne '82 %N Brickman -317 Mad Av -NY 10017 **Fx:**986-7691
(212) 909-6000 .. **Reilly,** Wendy B '02 %Debevoise & P LLP -919 3rd Av -NY 10022
(212) 637-3154 .. **Reilly,** Wm J '03 EPA -290 Bway -NY 10007 **Fx:**637-3096
(212) 210-1334 .. **Reilly-Brooks,** Margaret '88 A & E Network -235 E 45th -NY 10017 **Fx:**210-1308
(212) 264-8342 .. **Reiman,** Richd J '74 %SBA -26 Fed Plz -NY 10278
(212) 681-8313 .. **Reiman,** Ronnie Diane '81 %Karaahmet L&G LLP -370 Lex Av -NY 10017 **Fx:**208-2917
(212) 770-8768 .. **Reimann,** Christine L '96 %AIG Tech Srvcs -80 Pine -NY 10005
(914) 949-4600 .. **Reimann,** Tracy Christen '88 (Karlen S&R,LLP) -1 N Bway -White Plns 10601
(718) 590-2000 .. **Reimels,** Brian J '09 %DA -198 E 161st -Bronx 10451 **Fx:**590-6477
(212) 813-8800 .. **Reimer,** Eric R '04 %Goodwin P LLP -620 8th Av -NY 10018
(631) 499-3163 .. **Reimer,** Laura J '90 -49 E Deer Pk Rd -Dix Hlls 11746
(212) 576-7000 .. **Reimer,** Linda M '88 %NY Life Ins -51 Mad Av -NY 10010 **Fx:**447-0569
(202) 872-8600 .. **Reimer,** Norman L '78 NACDL -808 Bway -NY 10003 **Fx:**872-8690
(212) 621-6000 .. **Reimer,** Richd H '72 %ASCAP -1 Lincoln Plz -NY 10023 **Fx:**787-1381
(518) 455-7500 .. **Reimer,** Russell H '86 %Legis Bill Drftng Comm -310 The Cptl -Albany 12224 **Fx:**455-7598

(212) 558-4000 .. **Rein,** David M J '98 (Sullivan & C LLP) -125 Broad -NY 10004
(212) 813-8800 .. **Rein,** Fredk H '90 (Goodwin P LLP) -620 8th Av -NY 10018
(212) 357-4358 .. **Rein,** Jason S '96 Goldman Sachs & Co -1 NY Plz -NY 10004
(212) 424-7237 .. **Rein,** Linda S '78 %Lifetime TV -309 W 49th -NY 10019 **Fx:**957-4447
(212) 355-4141 .. **Rein,** Martin L '38 Stndrd Sec Life Ins -485 Mad Av -NY 10022 **Fx:**754-3346
(212) 921-5777 .. **Rein,** Saml '81 (Leicht & Rein) -570 7th Av -NY 10018 **Fx:**921-9756
(212) 735-3000 .. **Reina,** David C '08 %Skadden ASM&F LLP -4 Times Sq -NY 10036
(716) 849-1333 .. **Reina,** Jeffrey F '00 (Lipsitz GSC LLP) -42 Delaware Av -Buffalo 14202
(718) 370-7744 .. **Reina,** Kevin R '84 -900 South Av -Staten Isl 10314 **Fx:**370-1087
(212) 521-5400 .. **Reina,** Lawr J '91 Cnsl Reed S LLP -599 Lex Av -NY 10022
(973) 596-4655 .. **Reinartz,** Richd A '04 %Gibbons PC -1 Penn Plz -NY 10119 **Fx:**639-8357
(212) 335-4500 .. **Reinckens,** Melissa A '09 %DLA Piper LLP -1251 Av of Amer -NY 10020
(212) 833-1117 .. **Reindel,** Asaf '02 Cnsl Friedman KS&A LLP -1633 Bway -NY 10019 **Fx:**373-7917
(212) 859-8000 .. **Reindel,** F Wm '79 (Fried FHS&J LLP) -1 NY Plz -NY 10004
(607) 351-8350 .. **Reine,** Suzanne V '95 -Bx6646 -Ithaca 14851
(631) 348-9100 .. **Reinecke,** Mike G '96 Accretive Corp -105 Maxess Rd -Melvll 11747
(716) 937-9111 .. **Reinecke,** Susan P '05 %Cooke & S -13132 Main -Alden 14004
(845) 928-9444 .. **Reineke,** Stephen L '74 (Levinson R&O,PC) -Bx244 -Centrl Vly 10917
(212) 264-0300 .. **Reiner,** E Margit '86 %NLRB -26 Fed Plz -NY 10278 **Fx:**264-8427
(212) 269-2466 .. **Reiner,** Edw J '89 (Reiner R&R) -80 Wall -NY 10005 **Fx:**269-2467
(212) 447-5599 .. **Reiner,** Glenn A '84 (Agins SR&B,LLP) -386 Park Av S -NY 10016
(212) 925-1919 .. **Reiner,** Jan Allen '75 -291 Bway -NY 10007 **Fx:**941-5975
(646) 733-3200 .. **Reiner,** Jeanmarie Ressa '90 %US Customs -1 Penn Plz -NY 10119
(212) 460-3309 .. **Reiner,** Jeffrey A '75 Con Ed -4 Irving Pl -NY 10003
(212) 269-2466 .. **Reiner,** John Peter '59 (Reiner R&R) -80 Wall -NY 10005 **Fx:**269-2467
(718) 250-2000 .. **Reiner,** Jonathan S '09 %DA -350 Jay -Brklyn 11201 **Fx:**250-2314
(860) 275-6756 .. **Reiner,** Kevin L '99 %McCarter & E,LLP -245 Park Av -NY 10167 **Fx:**424-4765
(212) 415-9200 .. **Reiner,** Marc S '96 (Dorsey & W LLP) -250 Park Av -NY 10177
(516) 571-3800 .. **Reiner,** Michl '07 %DA -262 Old Cntry Rd -Mineola 11501 **Fx:**248-9479
(212) 832-1930 .. **Reiner,** Michl R '83 (Breslow & W,LLP) -767 3rd Av -NY 10017
(212) 349-6775 .. **Reiner,** Miles S '78 (Peltz & W) -222 Bway -NY 10038
(212) 925-4343 .. **Reiner,** Paul A '72 -350 Bway -NY 10013 **Fx:**965-0618
(914) 235-6065 .. **Reiner,** Richd C '57 -71 Disbrow Ln -New Rchll 10804 **Fx:**235-7823
(212) 877-6850 .. **Reiner,** Stephen R '64 -135 Cntrl Pk W -NY 10023
(718) 340-4200 .. **Reiner-Sotelo,** Lisa E '91 %CUNY Law Schl -65-21 Main -Flushng 11367 **Fx:**340-4482
(212) 790-0200 .. **Reinert,** Alexander A '00 %Benj N Cardozo Schl of Law -55 5th Av -NY 10003 **Fx:**790-0345
(212) 841-8609 .. **Reinert,** Michl L '83 %Universal Records -1755 Bway -NY 10019
(212) 966-9595 .. **Reiness,** Steven M '01 S Reiness,PLLC -401 Bway -NY 10013
(973) 992-4800 .. **Reinfeld,** Keith A '05 %Fox R LLP -100 Park Av -NY 10017 **Fx:**992-9125
(914) 245-7609 .. **Reing,** Gary M '78 -521 5th Av -NY 10175 **Fx:**245-7631
(718) 875-4805 .. **Reingold,** Abraham '60 (Reingold & T) -26 Court -Brklyn 11242
(718) 581-1000 .. **Reingold,** Danl A '82 %Hebrew Home For Aged -5901 Palisade Av -Bronx 10471 **Fx:**549-1269
(914) 833-0500 .. **Reingold,** Marvin D '61 Cnsl Eppinger R&K -131 Larchmnt Av Bx868 -Larchmnt 10538
(212) 683-3520 .. **Reingold,** Steven C '94 (Jager S,PC) -485 Mad Av -NY 10022
(718) 875-4805 .. **Reingold & Tucker** -26 Court -Brklyn 11242 **Fx:**875-4810
(518) 438-2000 .. **Reinhard,** Theo '58 (Lombardi WWHA&D PC) -III Winners Cir -Albany 12205
(212) 457-7701 .. **Reinhardt,** Edith '95 %American Lawyer Media -120 Bway -NY 10271
(845) 565-1100 .. **Reinhardt,** Holly L '09 %Tarshis CLM&M,PLLC -One Corwin Ct -Newburgh 12550
(516) 292-8100 .. **Reinhardt,** Jane C '81 %Nassau/Sfflk Law Srv -1 Helen Keller Way -Hempstd 11550 **Fx:**292-6529
(518) 235-0827 .. **Reinhardt,** Jean Mary '75 -130 Canvass -Cohoes 12047 **Fx:**235-2090
(518) 449-8893 .. **Reinhardt,** Jessica '07 %Wilson EME&D LLP -677 Bway -Albany 12207
(585) 396-4411 .. **Reinhardt,** Michl G '90 %Cnty Atty -27 N Main -Canandaigua 14424 **Fx:**396-4481
(718) 377-7798 .. **Reinhardt,** Michl S '87 M Reinhardt & Assoc -2990 Av U -Brklyn 11229 **Fx:**692-1012
(718) 377-8880 .. **Reinhardt,** Wm J Jr. '85 -2990 Av U -Brklyn 11229 **Fx:**258-3262
(212) 357-0151 .. **Reinhart,** Andrew J IV '03 %Goldman Sachs -1 NY Plz -NY 10004
(646) 333-9714 .. **Reinhart,** Scott M '04 Lehman Bros -1271 Av of Amer -NY 10020
(516) 868-5030 .. **Reinharz,** Alfred '50 -2152 Grand Av -Baldwin 11510 **Fx:**868-0456
(516) 267-6300 .. **Reinharz,** Mark N '85 (Bond S&K,PLLC) -1399 Franklin Av -Gdn Cty 11530
(516) 571-3056 .. **Reinharz,** Peter '81 %Cnty Atty -1 West -Mineola 11501 **Fx:**571-6604
(917) 545-5841 .. **Reinheimer,** Ariel '01 -519 E Market -Long Bch 11561
(212) 728-8000 .. **Reinhold,** Richd L '77 (Willkie F&G LLP) -787 7th Av -NY 10019
(718) 260-5767 .. **Reinig,** Timothy W '92 NYC Cllg of Tech -300 Jay -Brklyn 11201
(212) 972-5430 .. **Reiniger,** Anne '79 -801 2nd Av -NY 10017
(212) 972-5430 .. **Reiniger,** Douglas H '81 OfCnsl Rosin SM -801 2nd Av -NY 10017
(212) 982-2080 .. **Reininger,** Henry '74 -55 Av A -NY 10009
(914) 946-4777 .. **Reinke,** Jennifer L '07 %Keane & B,PC -445 Hmltn Av -White Plns 10601
(212) 859-3480 .. **Reinke,** John J '87 -110 Wall -NY 10005
(585) 288-4832 .. **Reinke,** Wayne F '93 (Heslin RF&M PC) -100 Meridian Centre -Rchstr 14618
(212) 736-3446 .. **Reinlieb,** Laurence '68 -350 5th Av -NY 10118
(716) 856-3500 .. **Reinoso,** Bruce D '95 (Magavern MG LLP) -1100 Rand Bldg -Buffalo 14203
(718) 250-2000 .. **Reinoso,** Yokasta '03 %DA -350 Jay -Brklyn 11201 **Fx:**250-2314
(212) 341-2752 .. **Reinstein,** Eric '84 %Admin Children's Srvcs -150 William -NY 10038 **Fx:**341-2700
(212) 617-6967 .. **Reinstein,** Marni Jill '02 Bloomberg LP -731 Lex Av -NY 10022
(585) 232-3730 .. **Reinstein,** Natalia '08 %Chamberlain D LLP -1600 Crssrds Bldg -Rchstr 14614
(212) 859-8000 .. **Reinstein,** Paul M '77 (Fried FHS&J LLP) -1 NY Plz -NY 10004
(212) 435-3571 .. **Reinstein,** Racquel H '07 Port Auth of NY/NJ -225 Park Av S -NY 10003 **Fx:**435-3555
(212) 857-8253 .. **Reinstein,** Richd A '93 -330 W 34th -NY 10001 **Fx:**857-8233
(212) 259-8000 .. **Reinthaler,** Richd W '74 (Dewey & L LLP) -1301 Av of Amer -NY 10019
(212) 785-5170 .. **Reis,** Brian H '92 (B Reis & Assoc) -80 Broad -NY 10004 **Fx:**785-5179
(212) 848-4000 .. **Reis,** Corey A '05 %Shearman & S LLP -599 Lex Av -NY 10022
(212) 788-3806 .. **Reis,** Evelyn H '74 %Dept of Sanitation -125 Worth -NY 10013 **Fx:**791-3824
(845) 291-2050 .. **Reis,** Tiffany N '07 %DA -255-275 Main -Goshen 10924 **Fx:**291-2085
(212) 633-4310 .. **Reisbaum,** Emily S '97 (Clarick GR LLP) -40 W 25th -NY 10010 **Fx:**(646) 478-9484
(212) 849-7000 .. **Reisberg,** Joshua S '07 %Quinn EU&S,LLP -51 Mad Av -NY 10010
(718) 237-3100 .. **Reisberg,** Sara H '07 Leg Aid -111 Lvngstn -Brklyn 11201 **Fx:**250-4243
(212) 728-8000 .. **Reisberg,** Steven H '82 (Willkie F&G LLP) -787 7th Av -NY 10019
(212) 563-3312 .. **Reisch,** Randy J '83 -350 5th Av -NY 10118 **Fx:**594-2944
(516) 742-4949 .. **Reisch,** Richd J '66 -1 Old Cntry Rd -Carle Pl 11514 **Fx:**742-1977
(212) 770-3075 .. **Reische,** John D '94 %AIG -70 Pine -NY 10270
(212) 531-6250 .. **Reischer,** David I '04 Nationwide Wholesale Mortgage Corp -2 Penn Plz -NY 10121
(212) 333-0200 .. **Reisen,** Alexander G '05 %Arkin KR LLP -590 Mad Av -NY 10022
(845) 227-7513 .. **Reisenauer,** Elyse '89 -4 Pray Ln -LaGrangevll 12540
(845) 352-9240 .. **Reisenman,** Debra J '95 %Finkelstein & Prtnrs,LLP -296 Main -Spg Vly 10977
(212) 370-0955 .. **Reiser,** Debra S '82 -100 Park Av -NY 10017 **Fx:**370-0944
(212) 775-8700 .. **Reiser,** Donald J '78 (Kilpatrick S,LLP) -31 W 52nd -NY 10019
(201) 498-0400 .. **Reiser,** Glenn R '91 (LoFaro & R,LLP) -100 Wall -NY 10005
(718) 849-0302 .. **Reiser,** James R '85 -109-19 Jamaica Av -Richmnd Hll 11418 **Fx:**849-9781
(516) 877-2900 .. **Reiser,** Kenneth R '79 (Bartlett MB&M,LLP) -300 Old Cntry Rd -Mineola 11501
(212) 752-1000 .. **Reiser,** Peter J '88 OfCnsl Eiseman LL&K,PC -805 3rd Av -NY 10022
(516) 938-8494 .. **Reiser,** Ralph G '81 -120 Old Cntry Rd Bx823 -Hicksvll 11802
(212) 867-6000 .. **Reiser,** Saml J '78 (Rosenberg & E,PC) -733 3rd Av -NY 10017
(212) 790-4500 .. **Reiser,** Stacey '05 %Manatt P&P,LLP -7 Times Sq -NY 10036
(212) 834-9364 .. **Reiser,** Walter Allen III '84 JP Morgan Chase & Co -270 Park Av -NY 10017
(914) 741-6100 .. **Reiser-Pertoso,** Tracey A '02 %Kaufman B&R -200 Summit Lk Dr -Valhalla 10595
(914) 666-2589 .. **Reiskind,** Andrew S '92 -53 Sarles -Armonk 10504
(212) 587-1960 .. **Reiskind,** Edwin M Jr. '63 (Friend & R PLLC) -100 William -NY 10038
(212) 454-1089 .. **Reiskind,** Jodi L '93 %Deutch Bank -280 Park Av -NY 10017
(212) 309-6000 .. **Reisler,** Kimberly M '93 (Morgan L&B LLP) -101 Park Av -NY 10178
(212) 513-3200 .. **Reisler,** Marc S '90 (Holland & K LLP) -31 W 52nd -NY 10019
(212) 461-6405 .. **Reisman,** David S '84 NIBC Credit Mgmt,Inc -1095 Av of Amer -NY 10036
(516) 466-2227 .. **Reisman,** Dennis M '77 -98 Cutter Mill Rd -Gt Neck 11021 **Fx:**829-6219
(914) 375-0100 .. **Reisman,** Eugene '77 (Novick ELRW&L,PC) -733 Ynkrs Av -Ynkrs 10704
(516) 393-2200 .. **Reisman,** Gregg D '97 (Garfunkel W,PC) -111 Grt Nck Rd -Gt Neck 11021
(212) 684-3900 .. **Reisman,** James '65 (Gottlieb R&R,PC) -270 Mad Av -NY 10016
(516) 746-7799 .. **Reisman,** Jerome '67 (Reisman P&R LLP) -1305 Franklin Av -Gdn Cty 11530
(212) 244-6600 .. **Reisman,** Lloyd F '08 %Schechter & B,PC -350 5th Av -NY 10118
(914) 495-3050 .. **Reisman,** Mark I '84 (Reisman R&M,LLP) -151 Bway -Hawthorne 10532 **Fx:**495-3051
(212) 696-5500 .. **Reisman,** Marvin '52 (Budin RK&B) -112 Mad Av -NY 10016
(212) 446-4800 .. **Reisman,** Michl D '06 %Kirkland & E LLP -153 E 53rd -NY 10022
(212) 902-5337 .. **Reisman,** Nicole Wilkes '01 Goldman Sachs -85 Broad -NY 10004
(212) 845-3111 .. **Reisman,** Paul P '89 %Fidelity Natl Title Ins -1 Park Av -NY 10016 **Fx:**(646) 424-9308
(516) 746-7799 .. **Reisman Peirez & Reisman LLP** -1305 Franklin Av -Gdn Cty 11530 **Fx:**742-4946
(518) 370-2500 .. **Reisman,** Richd A '77 (Antokol R&C) -514 State -Schnctdy 12305
(212) 723-9268 .. **Reisman,** Ronald H '69 Citigroup -388 Greenwich -NY 10013
(212) 969-3000 .. **Reisman,** Sarah '07 %Proskauer R LLP -1585 Bway -NY 10036
(212) 836-8000 .. **Reisman,** Sean P '08 %Kaye S LLP -425 Park Av -NY 10022
(516) 746-7799 .. **Reisman,** Seymour J '59 (Reisman P&R LLP) -1305 Franklin Av -Gdn Cty 11530
(212) 326-3939 .. **Reisman,** Sharyl A '98 (Jones D) -222 E 41st -NY 10017
(212) 696-6000 .. **Reisman,** Steven J '91 (Curtis M-PC&M LLP) -101 Park Av -NY 10178
(212) 756-2000 .. **Reisman,** Stuart M '01 %Schulte R&Z LLP -919 3rd Av -NY 10022
(718) 298-8953 .. **Reisner,** Alison D '06 %Leg Aid -153-01 Jamaica Av -Jamaica 11432 **Fx:**657-0537
(914) 271-9011 .. **Reisner,** Anna M '81 -8 Observatory Dr -Croton-On-Hud 10520
(212) 373-3000 .. **Reisner,** Carl L '79 (Paul WRW&G LLP) -1285 Av of Amer -NY 10019
(212) 836-8132 .. **Reisner,** Danl L '95 (Kaye S LLP) -425 Park Av -NY 10022
(718) 522-3902 .. **Reisner,** Edw M '86 -19 Cheever Pl -Brklyn 11231
(716) 375-4213 .. **Reisner,** Jeffrey P '04 JM Shane -188½ W Main -Allegany 14706 **Fx:**375-4214
(202) 551-4787 .. **Reisner,** Lorin L '87 SEC -3 World Fncl Ctr -NY 10281 **Fx:**(212) 336-1323
(212) 418-4700 .. **Reisner,** Michl A '97 ICON Capital Corp -100 5th Av -NY 10011
(212) 596-9000 .. **Reiss,** Adam J '07 %Ropes & G LLP -1211 Av of Amer -NY 10036
(212) 237-0000 .. **Reiss,** Allan D '88 (Vinson & E LLP) -666 5th Av -NY 10103
(212) 980-5244 .. **Reiss,** Amy '90 -110 E 59th -NY 10022 **Fx:**980-5245
(914) 693-4125 .. **Reiss,** Andrea P '81 -88 Ridge Rd -Ardsley 10502

(212) 832-0400 .. **Reiss,** Andrew W '99 %Berdon LLP -360 Mad Av -NY 10017 **Fx:**371-1159
(212) 849-6815 .. **Reiss,** Barry J '67 -5 Penn Plz -NY 10001 **Fx:**849-6816
(212) 535-0158 .. **Reiss,** Bonnie '70 -1001 Park Av -NY 10028
(516) 482-6442 .. **Reiss,** Brett M '79 -23 Schenck Av -Gt Neck 11021
(212) 464-2025 .. **Reiss,** Carl A '95 %JP Morgan Chase & Co -345 Park Av -NY 10154 **Fx:**504-6666
(718) 780-7994 .. **Reiss,** David J '97 Bklyn Law Schl -250 Joralemon -Brklyn 11201 **Fx:**780-0367
(718) 494-9441 .. **Reiss,** Deanna '92 -347 Watchogue Rd -Staten Isl 10314
(212) 272-7693 .. **Reiss,** Deborah Ann '96 %JP Morgan Chase -383 Mad Av -NY 10179
(631) 929-4711 .. **Reiss,** Dennis M '71 -67 Randall Rd Bx567 -Wading Rvr 11792 **Fx:**929-4632
(212) 753-2424 .. **Reiss Eisenpress LLP** -425 Mad Av -NY 10017 **Fx:**753-3829
(718) 720-0700 .. **Reiss,** Elaine D '81 -347 Watchogue Rd -Staten Isl 10314
(212) 545-4809 .. **Reiss,** Elaine S '65 %Weider Publications -1 Park Av -NY 10016 **Fx:**696-5391
(212) 753-2424 .. **Reiss,** Howard R '76 (Reiss E LLP) -425 Mad Av -NY 10017
(212) 885-5000 .. **Reiss,** Jeremy L '04 %Blank R LLP -405 Lex Av -NY 10174
(212) 848-4000 .. **Reiss,** John D '08 %Shearman & S LLP -599 Lex Av -NY 10022
(212) 819-8200 .. **Reiss,** John M '86 (White & C LLP) -1155 Av of Amer -NY 10036
(718) 548-4558 .. **Reiss,** Jonathan A '93 -640 W 238th -Bronx 10463
(718) 931-3300 .. **Reiss,** Kenneth '57 (Reiss & A LLP) -2590 Frisby Av -Bronx 10461 **Fx:**829-3626
(914) 592-4800 .. **Reiss,** Lawr J '85 %Mack-Cali Realty Corp -100 Clearbrook Rd -Elmsfrd 10523 **Fx:**592-2365
(212) 869-2300 .. **Reiss,** Leonard S '84 (Toback B&R,LLP) -15 W 44th -NY 10036
(718) 544-8760 .. **Reiss,** Lewis '75 -125-10 Qns Blvd -Kew Gdns 11415
(516) 571-3800 .. **Reiss,** Margaret Ann Gabrielle '94 %DA -262 Old Cntry Rd -Mineola 11501 **Fx:**248-9479
(516) 222-1300 .. **Reiss,** Mark R '92 (Abbott R&A,PC) -90 Merrick Av -E Meadow 11554
(631) 234-5558 .. **Reiss,** Maryann T '03 D Veraldi Jr -1601 Vets Hwy -Islandia 11749 **Fx:**234-5080
(212) 227-2222 .. **Reiss,** Melvyn M '71 -305 Bway -NY 10007 **Fx:**964-0643
(212) 323-2250 .. **Reiss,** Naomi L '92 %HHC-OLA-Medical Litigation -346 Bway -NY 10013 **Fx:**323-2251
(212) 643-6778 .. **Reiss,** Peter B '81 -350 5th Av -NY 10118
(212) 688-5900 .. **Reiss,** Peter L '77 OfCnsl Shustak F & Prtnrs -400 Park Av -NY 10022 **Fx:**688-6151
(212) 403-1000 .. **Reiss,** Sherri D '80 %Wachtell LR&K -51 W 52nd -NY 10019
(516) 599-1266 .. **Reiss,** Steven '79 -58 Reyam Rd -Lynbrk 11563
(212) 310-8000 .. **Reiss,** Steven A '87 (Weil G&M LLP) -767 5th Av -NY 10153
(212) 264-3650 .. **Reiss,** Susan J '87 %SSA Ofc Genl Cnsl -26 Fed Plz -NY 10278 **Fx:**264-6372
(212) 848-4337 .. **Reiss,** Susan R '82 Cnsl Shearman & S LLP -599 Lex Av -NY 10022
(845) 473-4440 .. **Reiss,** Warren P '83 %Scenic Hudson -1 Civic Ctr Plz -Poughkeepsie 12601
(212) 907-0858 .. **Reiss,** Wm V '02 %Labaton S LLP -140 Bway -NY 10005 **Fx:**883-7058
(845) 340-3315 .. **Reis Van Loan,** Katherine '00 %DA -285 Wall -Kingston 12401 **Fx:**340-3185
(718) 236-7600 .. **Reitano,** Anthony '98 (Reitano & S) -8817 3rd Av -Brklyn 11209
(212) 809-7600 .. **Reitano,** John P '95 %Cheven K&H -40 Wall -NY 10005
(718) 984-5085 .. **Reitano,** Jos J '94 -25 Ray -Staten Isl 10312
(212) 425-7200 .. **Reitboeck,** Georg C '01 %Kenyon & K,LLP -1 Bway -NY 10004
(212) 868-1330 .. **Reitelman,** Ruth Anne G '93 %B Siskin -225 W 34th -NY 10122
(212) 484-3900 .. **Reiter,** Allen G '76 (Arent F LLP) -1675 Bway -NY 10019
(845) 357-2215 .. **Reiter,** Arnold E '03 (Reiter & Z) -75 Montebello Rd -Suffern 10901 **Fx:**357-4437
(212) 448-9570 .. **Reiter,** Chas J '92 %Callahan & F,LLC -40 Exch Pl -NY 10005
(212) 455-2000 .. **Reiter,** Glenn M '79 (Simpson T&B LLP) -425 Lex Av -NY 10017
(212) 736-0979 .. **Reiter,** Jonathan C '76 -350 5th Av -NY 10118 **Fx:**268-5297
(845) 639-5800 .. **Reiter,** Jos '94 %Clarkstown Police Dept -20 Maple Av -New Cty 10956
(516) 931-1800 .. **Reiter,** June D '04 %Catalano G&P LLP -100 Jericho Quadrangle -Jericho 11753
(212) 222-0955 .. **Reiter,** Lorne M '96 L Reiter,LLC -14 Wall -NY 10005 **Fx:**202-4784
(516) 764-2800 .. **Reiter,** Mitchell '89 %Goldberg & C -66 N Vllg Av -Rockvll Ctr 11570
(212) 351-4500 .. **Reiter,** Nicholas M '09 %Epstein B&G,PC -250 Park Av -NY 10177
(212) 944-0500 .. **Reiter,** Peter I '69 (Hofheimer G&G,LLP) -530 5th Av -NY 10036 **Fx:**897-6934
(914) 323-7000 .. **Reiter,** Richd L '03 %Wilson EME&D LLP -3 Gannett Dr -White Plns 10604
(212) 754-3077 .. **Reiter,** Sheldon '67 -260 Mad Av -NY 10016 **Fx:**792-2699
(212) 486-2500 .. **Reitknecht,** Seymour '57 OfCnsl Mintz & F,PC -488 Mad Av -NY 10022
(212) 755-6106 .. **Reitknecht,** Seymour '57 -45 Chestnut Dr -Hastings-On-Hud 10706 **Fx:**(914) 478-1841
(585) 546-8955 .. **Reitkopp,** Richd I '62 (R Reitkopp,PC) -19 W Main -Rchstr 14614 **Fx:**546-1436
(212) 209-3010 .. **Reitler,** Edw G '91 (Reitler K&R LLC) -885 3rd Av -NY 10022
(212) 209-3050 .. **Reitler Kailas & Rosenblatt LLC** -885 3rd Av -NY 10022 **Fx:**371-5500
(212) 751-3001 .. **Reitman,** Glenn A '01 %Thompson & K LLP -919 3rd Av -NY 10022
(516) 599-4282 .. **Reitman,** Kathy Donna '79 -2 Howland Rd -E Rockaway 11518
(315) 868-6119 .. **Reittinger,** Robt R '92 -9772 Route 365 -Holland Patent 13354 **Fx:**266-1220
(716) 857-7991 .. **Reitz,** David W '79 %Natl Fuel Gas -6363 Main -Williamsvll 14221 **Fx:**857-7614
(315) 437-7600 .. **Reitz,** Marc H '78 (Ferrara FLB&R,PC) -5010 Campuswood Dr -E Syracuse 13057
(212) 687-3000 .. **Reitzas,** Joshua T '02 %Jaffe & A,LLP -600 3rd Av -NY 10016
(212) 872-9874 .. **Reitzel,** Christopher J '99 (Squire S&D LLP) -30 Rckfllr Plz -NY 10112
(212) 513-3400 .. **Reitzfeld,** Alan D '77 (Holland & K LLP) -31 W 52nd -NY 10019
(516) 374-0808 .. **Reiver,** Kenneth A '60 -123 Grove Av Bx89 -Cedarhrst 11516 **Fx:**295-4610
(718) 658-9800 .. **Reiver,** Mitchell D '87 %Melrose Crdt Union -139-30 Qns Blvd -Briarwd 11435 **Fx:**526-8530
(585) 987-2800 .. **Reixach,** Rene H Jr. '72 (Woods OG LLP) -2 State -Rchstr 14614
(914) 725-3922 .. **Rejan,** Jacquelyn B '88 -Bx2H -Scarsdale 10583
(212) 661-7300 .. **Rejan,** Jeffrey N '81 %Malapero & P LLP -295 Mad Av -NY 10017
(212) 398-3112 .. **Rekant,** Stuart B '76 Hidden Treasures,Inc -56 W 45th -NY 10036
(212) 851-1061 .. **Rekosh,** Edwin B '89 %Columbia Law Schl -435 W 116th -NY 10027 **Fx:**851-1064
(212) 490-1700 .. **Rele,** Niket Jeevan '96 (Wiggin & D) -450 Lex Av -NY 10017
(212) 906-1200 .. **Relea,** Veronica '05 %Latham & W -885 3rd Av -NY 10022
(315) 479-3900 .. **Religa,** Michl '85 %SSA-ODAR -300 S State -Syracuse 13202 **Fx:**479-3933
(585) 325-6202 .. **Relin Goldstein & Crane LLP** -28 E Main -Rchstr 14614 **Fx:**325-6201
(585) 454-4336 .. **Relin,** Leonard '63 -1 E Main -Rchstr 14614 **Fx:**232-6674
(212) 244-8722 .. **Relkin,** David H '87 -575 8th Av -NY 10018
(212) 558-5500 .. **Relkin,** Ellen '85 OfCnsl Weitz & L,PC -700 Bway -NY 10003
(914) 328-2810 .. **Rella,** Andrew J '98 (Ziccardi & R,PC) -237 Mamaroneck Av -White Plns 10605 **Fx:**328-2812
(212) 468-8000 .. **Rella,** Angela T '02 %Morrison & F LLP -1290 Av of Amer -NY 10104
(914) 835-3257 .. **Rella,** Anthony '63 -4 S Evarts Av -Elmsfrd 10523 **Fx:**835-3257
(212) 875-7921 .. **Rella,** Anthony J '95 (Lawlor & R LLP) -551 Fifth Av -NY 10176 **Fx:**712-8855
(718) 590-2000 .. **Rella,** Dawn M '08 %DA -198 E 161st -Bronx 10451 **Fx:**590-6477
(914) 747-7444 .. **Rella,** Gerarda M '87 (Rella & Assoc) -115 E Stevens Av -Valhalla 10595 **Fx:**747-7485
(212) 421-2233 .. **Rella,** Helen A '88 OfCnsl Wilk A LLP -675 3rd Av -NY 10017
(212) 237-0000 .. **Rella,** Michl V '05 %Vinson & E LLP -666 5th Av -NY 10103
(914) 328-0990 .. **Rella-Wagner,** Jennifer R '04 (Wagner Law Grp,PC) -30 Glenn -White Plns 10603 **Fx:**328-4663
(212) 756-2000 .. **Relles,** Eliot L '95 (Schulte R&Z LLP) -919 3rd Av -NY 10022
(518) 292-5700 .. **Relyea,** Michl J '01 Ofc Science Tech & Academy Resrch -30 S Pearl -Albany 12207
(914) 276-2920 .. **Rembar & Curtis** -Bx908 -Croton Fls 10519 **Fx:**931-3070
(914) 769-8090 .. **Remen,** Lynette '83 -980 Bway -Thornwd 10594
(212) 969-3000 .. **Remensperger,** D Eric '85 (Proskauer R LLP) -1585 Bway -NY 10036
(914) 944-4087 .. **Remer,** Danl V '97 (Castro & R,PC) -30 State -Ossining 10562 **Fx:**944-4103
(212) 564-1611 .. **Remer,** Gordon I '86 -1359 Bway -NY 10018 **Fx:**564-1886
(212) 720-5042 .. **Remer,** Jodi C '98 %Fed Reserve Bk -33 Lbrty -NY 10045 **Fx:**785-5748
(212) 974-7474 .. **Remer,** Michl D '58 OfCnsl Cowan DA&S LLP -41 Mad Av -NY 10010
(212) 698-7000 .. **Remes,** Emily R '83 %Simon & Schuster -1230 Av of Amer -NY 10020 **Fx:**698-7171
(845) 340-3441 .. **Remet,** Anna E '04 %Cnty Atty -244 Fiar Bx1800 -Kingston 12402 **Fx:**340-3691
(585) 232-5225 .. **Remington Gifford Williams & Colicchio,LLP** -183 E Main -Rchstr 14604 **Fx:**232-2557
(212) 207-2887 .. **Remis,** Jay L '93 Contifinancial Corp -277 Park Av -NY 10172
(718) 286-2217 .. **Remler,** Jane E '89 %Leg Aid -120-46 Qns Blvd -Kew Gdns 11415 **Fx:**286-2286
(212) 421-4100 .. **Remmel,** Lawr '80 (Pryor C LLP) -7 Times Sq -NY 10036
(631) 589-0628 .. **Remmer,** Richd H '91 -500 Shore Dr -Oakdale 11769 **Fx:**589-0572
(212) 596-9000 .. **Remmer,** Sharon '05 %Ropes & G LLP -1211 Av of Amer -NY 10036
(212) 326-3939 .. **Remmler,** Erik F '98 OfCnsl Jones D -222 E 41st -NY 10017
(518) 474-1697 .. **Remo,** Lorraine '83 %Dept of Law -The Cptl -Albany 12224
(212) 770-1746 .. **Remolina,** Victoria K '00 AIG Tech Srvcs -80 Pine -NY 10005
(631) 744-3636 .. **Remuzzi,** Stephen G Jr. '63 -5720 Route 25A -Wading Rvr 11792 **Fx:**744-3637
(516) 357-3700 .. **Remuzzi,** Suzanne '95 %Cullen and D LLP -100 Q Roosevelt Blvd -Gdn Cty 11530
(212) 335-9000 .. **Remy,** Jos D '09 %DA -1 Hogan Pl -NY 10013
(212) 506-2500 .. **Ren,** Yong '02 %Mayer B LLP -1675 Bway -NY 10019
(212) 818-1110 .. **Ren,** Yunling '97 Cnsl Butzel L,PC -380 Mad Av -NY 10017
(212) 903-9000 .. **Renas,** Stanford A '98 (Linklaters) -1345 Av of Amer -NY 10105
(646) 458-2436 .. **Renaud,** Brigette H '95 YMCA Retirement Fnd -140 Bway -NY 10005 **Fx:**458-2550
(212) 455-2000 .. **Renaud,** Kate '10 %Simpson T&B LLP -425 Lex Av -NY 10017
(212) 415-9200 .. **Renault,** Fanny '08 %Dorsey & W LLP -250 Park Av -NY 10177
(914) 997-1380 .. **Renauto,** Alfred T '84 -1 Barker Av -White Plns 10601 **Fx:**997-1096
(518) 373-8400 .. **Rench,** Fredk A '87 F Rench,PLLC -646 Plnk Rd -Clifton Pk 12065 **Fx:**383-6898
(212) 903-9000 .. **Rench,** Matthew D '08 %Linklaters -1345 Av of Amer -NY 10105
(716) 885-4335 .. **Renda,** James P '69 -69 Delaware Av -Buffalo 14202
(718) 921-3344 .. **Renda,** Sigismondo F '90 (Renda & Assoc,PC) -8118 13th Av -Brklyn 11228 **Fx:**921-3292
(516) 747-1136 .. **Renda,** Vincent '04 %Steinberg FB&F,PC -40 Crsswys Park Dr -Woodbury 11797
(914) 681-0444 .. **Rende,** Jos G '69 (Rende R&D,LLP) -202 Mamaroneck Av -White Plns 10601
(914) 681-0444 .. **Rende Ryan & Downes,LLP** -202 Mamaroneck Av -White Plns 10601 **Fx:**681-0875
(718) 237-1900 .. **Rendeiro,** Andrew S '91 (Flamhaft LH&R) -16 Court -Brklyn 11241
(914) 766-2350 .. **Rendeiro,** James C III '78 IBM -294 Route 100 -Somers 10589
(212) 701-3000 .. **Rendell,** Rebecca R '08 %Cahill G&R LLP -80 Pine -NY 10005 **Fx:**269-5420
(718) 250-2000 .. **Rendelman,** Julie B '93 %DA -350 Jay -Brklyn 11201 **Fx:**250-2314
(212) 416-8109 .. **Rendin,** Jeffrey R '05 %Dept of Law -120 Bway -NY 10271
(914) 242-9494 .. **Rendo,** Andrea Carapella '93 (Wallach & R,LLP) -239 Lex Av -Mt Kisco 10549
(212) 715-1000 .. **Rendon,** Veronica E '98 (Arnold & P LLP) -399 Park Av -NY 10022
(212) 455-2000 .. **Rendtorff,** Jakob '09 %Simpson T&B LLP -425 Lex Av -NY 10017
(718) 250-2000 .. **Rene,** Vladimir '06 %DA -350 Jay -Brklyn 11201 **Fx:**250-2314
(718) 390-5406 .. **Renehan,** Robt J '77 %Surrogates Ct -Cnty Cthse -Staten Isl 10301
(212) 484-3900 .. **Renert,** Jordana L '08 %Arent F LLP -1675 Bway -NY 10019
(212) 294-6700 .. **Renfrew,** Dwight H Jr. '94 Winston & S -200 Park Av -NY 10166
(518) 392-0552 .. **Renfro,** Jay B '01 -Bx112 -Ghent 12075
(212) 442-1104 .. **Renfro,** Sally J '86 Dept of Aging -2 Lafayette -NY 10007

(718) 575-8552 .. **Renfroe,** Christopher '85 (Renfroe & Q) -118-35 Qns Blvd -Frst Hlls 11375
(718) 575-8552 .. **Renfroe & Quinn** -118-35 Qns Blvd -Frst Hlls 11375 **Fx:**263-9465
(718) 397-8666 .. **Rengifo,** Ricardo '92 (R Rengifo,PC) -108-18 Qns Blvd -Frst Hlls 11375 **Fx:**520-8175
(518) 432-1200 .. **Renich,** Meghan E '03 %McGlinchey S PLLC -194 Wshngtn Av -Albany 12210
(212) 218-2100 .. **Renk,** Henry J '75 (Fitzpatrick CH&S) -1290 Av of Amer -NY 10104
(212) 674-3784 .. **Renkoff,** Franklin D '72 -40 5th Av -NY 10011
(516) 822-8900 .. **Renna,** Kristine A '98 Fiedelman & M -2 Jericho Plz -Jericho 11753
(914) 249-2000 .. **Renna,** Leonardo L '97 MasterCard Intl -2000 Purchase -Purchase 10577
(631) 283-4259 .. **Renna,** Michl J '94 -Bx2865 -Southampton 11969
(718) 422-1003 .. **Renna,** Robt J '93 R Renna,PC -26 Court -Brklyn 11242 **Fx:**422-1156
(914) 948-7000 .. **Renner,** Darren P '96 (Keidel W&C LLP) -925 Wstchstr Av -White Plns 10604
(212) 589-4200 .. **Renner,** Deborah H '93 (Baker & H LLP) -45 Rckfllr Plz -NY 10111
(212) 848-4000 .. **Renner,** Mark J '06 %Shearman & S LLP -599 Lex Av -NY 10022
(718) 707-3191 .. **Renner,** Paul J '82 Renner & Assoc -Bx323 -Mattituck 11952 **Fx:**707-2928
(716) 856-3500 .. **Rennie,** Aven '80 (Magavern MG LLP) -1100 Rand Bldg -Buffalo 14203
(212) 506-3900 .. **Rennock,** Michl J W '86 (Steptoe & J LLP) -750 7th Av -NY 10019
(631) 667-7366 .. **Reno,** John A '84 -1913 Deer Prk Av -Deer Pk 11729 **Fx:**667-7360
(845) 856-7377 .. **Reno,** Robt E '89 -39 Front -Pt Jervis 12771 **Fx:**856-7374
(315) 422-8191 .. **Renshaw,** Kara L '04 %Leg Aid -351 S Warren -Syracuse 13202 **Fx:**472-2819
(914) 948-8466 .. **Renteria Torres,** Ariadna '95 Westchester Hspnc Coalition -46 Waller Av -White Plns 10605
(315) 788-3360 .. **Renzi,** David A '95 (Brown D&R) -165 Mullin -Watertwn 13601
(315) 788-3360 .. **Renzi,** Eugene R '94 (Brown D&R) -165 Mullin -Watertwn 13601
(315) 788-3400 .. **Renzi,** Renée Louise '82 -1201 Wshngtn -Watertwn 13601 **Fx:**788-3466
(585) 586-8060 .. **Renzi,** Richd P '79 -359 N Wshngtn -Rchstr 14625 **Fx:**381-3559
(315) 782-3366 .. **Renzi,** Robt V '60 -120 Wshngtn -Watertwn 13601
(212) 223-0200 .. **Renzin,** Carolyn Barth '02 %Stillman F&S,PC -425 Park Av -NY 10022
(212) 637-2723 .. **Renzin,** Lee '00 %US Atty -1 St Andrews Plz -NY 10007
(914) 285-0700 .. **Renzulli,** Christopher '95 (Renzulli Law Firm,LLP) -81 Main -White Plns 10601 **Fx:**285-1213
(914) 285-0700 .. **Renzulli,** John F '84 (Renzulli Law Firm,LLP) -81 Main -White Plns 10601 **Fx:**285-1213
(718) 979-3300 .. **Renzulli,** Nora Drew '88 %MHLS -777 Seaview Av -Staten Isl 10305 **Fx:**667-2666
(718) 250-3121 .. **Renzulli,** Robt A M '97 %DA -350 Jay -Brklyn 11201 **Fx:**250-3092
(212) 788-0598 .. **Reo,** Christopher F '91 %Law Dept -100 Church -NY 10007 **Fx:**788-0367
(646) 386-5700 .. **Reo,** Denis M '04 %Civil Ct -111 Centre -NY 10013
(212) 449-8789 .. **Repaci,** Nicolette '94 Merrill Lynch -4 Wrld Fncl Ctr -NY 10080
(212) 310-8000 .. **Repash,** Philip F '04 %Weil G&M LLP -767 5th Av -NY 10153
(516) 248-1200 .. **Repetti,** George L '83 (Mulholland M&R) -374 Hillside Av -Williston Pk 11596
(212) 788-1200 .. **Rephen,** Paul T '74 %Law Dept -100 Church -NY 10007 **Fx:**788-0367
(212) 902-0324 .. **Repinsky,** Bradley P '05 %Goldman Sachs -1 NY Plz -NY 10004
(518) 398-5208 .. **Replansky,** Warren S '73 WS Replansky,PC -2990 Church Bx659 -Pine Plns 12567 **Fx:**398-5297
(845) 876-7979 .. **Replansky,** Warren S '73 -18-20 E Market Bx634 -Rhinebeck 12572
(212) 715-1100 .. **Replogle,** Ronald P '94 Solow Rlty & Dvlpmnt Co,LLC -9 W 57th -NY 10019
(212) 451-2300 .. **Replogle,** Ryan S '08 %Olshan GFR&W LLP -65 E 55th -NY 10022
(631) 366-0606 .. **Repole,** Michl E '86 -732 Smithtwn Bypass -Smithtwn 11787
(718) 329-7300 .. **Repole,** Palma S '97 Fieldston Middle Schl -3901 Fieldston Rd -Bronx 10471
(212) 813-8800 .. **Repose,** Lindsey Ann '05 %Goodwin P LLP -620 8th Av -NY 10018
(212) 557-4666 .. **Repp,** Paul H '83 -240 E 38th -NY 10016
(212) 258-8000 .. **Reppen,** Kyra Elena '91 %MTV Networks -1515 Bway -NY 10036 **Fx:**258-8358
(212) 539-4000 .. **Reppert,** Christine M '06 Focus Features Intl -65 Bleecker -NY 10012
(212) 490-0988 .. **Reppert,** J Vincent '89 (Reppert K,LLC) -570 Lex Av -NY 10022
(212) 490-0988 .. **Reppert Kelly,LLC** -570 Lex Av -NY 10022 **Fx:**490-0287
(212) 805-0200 .. **Requa,** Marny Anderson '05 Hon D Chin -500 Pearl -NY 10007
(646) 471-4000 .. **Requenez,** Arturo II '01 %PricewaterhouseCoopers LLP -300 Mad Av -NY 10017
(212) 735-3000 .. **Requenez,** Eric '08 %Skadden ASM&F LLP -4 Times Sq -NY 10036
(212) 495-0100 .. **Requets,** Susanna '08 %Gottesman WMF&W,PC -11 Hanover Sq -NY 10005
(716) 856-1300 .. **Rera,** Sarah P '10 %Barth SB -43 Court -Buffalo 14202
(516) 227-6363 .. **Reres,** Vincent '97 %Amato & Assoc,PC -666 Old Cntry Rd -Gdn Cty 11530 **Fx:**227-6367
(516) 939-0669 .. **Rerisi,** Gail A '89 -5 Bethpage Rd -Hicksvll 11801 **Fx:**939-9006
(201) 768-4184 .. **Res,** Barbara A '08 -217 Pickle Hill Rd -Ft Plain 13339
(516) 485-0040 .. **Resch,** Susan W '83 -474 Benito -E Meadow 11554
(718) 647-1200 .. **Resciniti,** S Edmund '59 Cnsl Miller M&S -99 Powerhse Rd -Roslyn Hts 11577 **Fx:**647-2391
(212) 425-7200 .. **Resek,** John F '01 %Kenyon & K,LLP -1 Bway -NY 10004
(212) 848-4000 .. **Resetarits,** Jeffrey J '00 %Shearman & S LLP -599 Lex Av -NY 10022
(212) 596-9000 .. **Reshtick,** Abraham A '03 %Ropes & G LLP -1211 Av of Amer -NY 10036
(518) 465-3484 .. **Resila,** James A '88 (Carter CCBM&L,PC) -20 Corp Wds Blvd -Albany 12211
(212) 687-1980 .. **Reska,** Jason P '06 %Kaplan F&K LLP -850 3rd Av -NY 10022
(212) 761-4551 .. **Reske,** James R '98 Morgan Stanley -1585 Bway -NY 10036
(212) 490-3010 .. **Resko,** Michl J '92 -711 3rd Av -NY 10017 **Fx:**338-9229
(212) 859-8000 .. **Resnick,** Alan N '73 OfCnsl Fried FHS&J LLP -1 NY Plz -NY 10004
(516) 463-5872 .. **Resnick,** Alan N '73 Hofstra Law Schl -121 Hofstra Univ -Hempstd 11549
(212) 240-9111 .. **Resnick,** Barbara J '95 -20 Vesey -NY 10007 **Fx:**766-5899
(212) 450-4000 .. **Resnick,** Brian M '04 %Davis P&W LLP -450 Lex Av -NY 10017
(212) 279-2000 .. **Resnick,** David A '96 (D Resnick & Assoc,PC) -450 7th Av -NY 10123
(845) 358-8900 .. **Resnick,** David J '97 -96 S Bway -Nyack 10960 **Fx:**358-8901
(646) 453-1272 .. **Resnick,** Debra Ivy '91 FTI Consulting -3 Times Square -NY 10036
(212) 684-8400 .. **Resnick,** Ellen B '91 %A Futerfas -260 Mad Av -NY 10016 **Fx:**684-5259
(212) 832-6825 .. **Resnick,** Gerald A '70 -420 E 64th -NY 10065
(212) 415-9200 .. **Resnick,** Hannah '04 %Dorsey & W LLP -250 Park Av -NY 10177
(212) 552-9507 .. **Resnick,** Harriette I '79 JP Morgan Chase -1 Chase Manh Plz -NY 10005
(212) 415-3727 .. **Resnick,** Jeffrey A '76 %Omnicom Group -437 Mad Av -NY 10022 **Fx:**415-3530
(718) 327-1808 .. **Resnick,** Judy '91 -2906 Bailey Ct -Far Rckwy 11691
(646) 213-5100 .. **Resnick,** Julia '09 WTAS LLC -452 5th Av -NY 10018
(212) 589-4200 .. **Resnick,** Lauren Jo '91 (Baker & H LLP) -45 Rckfllr Plz -NY 10111
(585) 263-6760 .. **Resnick,** Richd A '88 %US Atty -620 Fed Bldg -Rchstr 14614 **Fx:**263-6226
(212) 435-3571 .. **Resnick,** Risa A '97 %Port Auth of NY/NJ -225 Park Av S -NY 10003 **Fx:**435-3555
(212) 867-0200 .. **Resnick,** Ronald S '89 Counsel Works LLC -420 Lex Av -NY 10170
(212) 532-0222 .. **Resnick,** Steven E '77 -200 Mad Av -NY 10016 **Fx:**532-0224
(973) 315-4475 .. **Resnick,** Steven M '98 (Budd L) -140 Bway -NY 10005
(732) 855-6019 .. **Resnick-Parigian,** Abby '89 Cnsl Wilentz G&S -110 William -NY 10038 **Fx:**726-6568
(516) 829-2940 .. **Resnicoff,** Barton R '75 B Resnicoff -287 Nrthrn Blvd -Gt Neck 11021 **Fx:**829-0130
(212) 480-4800 .. **Resnicow,** Norman J '73 (Fox H&C LLP) -825 3rd Av -NY 10022
(212) 245-4580 .. **Resnik,** Elliot A '01 %Shukat AHW&H,LLP -111 W 57th -NY 10019
(212) 643-6900 .. **Resnik,** Herbert '55 -350 5th Av -NY 10118 **Fx:**279-8991
(516) 747-4082 .. **Resnik,** Joan E '87 %Montfort HM&S LLP -1140 Franklin Av Bx7677 -Gdn Cty 11530
(212) 218-5500 .. **Resnik,** Richd M '69 (Seyfarth S LLP) -620 8th Av -NY 10018
(212) 940-8800 .. **Resnik,** Scott A '97 (Katten MR LLP) -575 Mad Av -NY 10022
(212) 237-1000 .. **Resnikoff,** Michl H '92 %Windels ML&M,LLP -156 W 56th -NY 10019
(212) 704-6521 .. **Respass,** Helen L '02 Sojitz Corp of Amer -1211 Av of Amer -NY 10036
(516) 944-3000 .. **Ressa & Aitken** -33 Main -Pt Wash 11050 **Fx:**944-3017
(212) 455-2000 .. **Ressa,** Gregory J '88 (Simpson T&B LLP) -425 Lex Av -NY 10017
(516) 944-3000 .. **Ressa,** Stephen A '81 (Ressa & A) -33 Main -Pt Wash 11050
(212) 695-6446 .. **Ressler,** Bruce J '77 (Ressler & R) -48 Wall -NY 10005 **Fx:**268-0287
(212) 430-5400 .. **Ressler,** Howard D '74 (Diamond M LLP) -620 8th Av -NY 10018
(718) 780-7931 .. **Ressler,** Jayne S '98 %Bklyn Law Schl -250 Joralemon -Brklyn 11201 **Fx:**780-0393
(914) 761-9400 .. **Ressler,** Jessica H '03 %Farber P&C -200 E Post Rd -White Plns 10601
(212) 529-3054 .. **Ressler,** Jonathan '79 -442 E 20th -NY 10009 **Fx:**353-1061
(718) 263-6812 .. **Ressler,** Leonard I '76 -125-10 Qns Blvd -Kew Gdns 11415 **Fx:**263-6586
(212) 506-1700 .. **Ressler,** Mark P '89 (Kasowitz BT&F LLP) -1633 Bway -NY 10019
(212) 505-8330 .. **Ressler-Hochstat,** Stephanie J '84 -714 Bway -NY 10003 **Fx:**505-8360
(212) 350-3950 .. **Ressy,** Raymond '89 %Santander Invstmnt Securities -45 E 53rd -NY 10022
(212) 839-5300 .. **Restad,** Christopher J '01 Cnsl Sidley A LLP -787 7th Av -NY 10019
(212) 762-6374 .. **Restaino,** David P '03 Morgan Stanley -1221 Av of Amer -NY 10020
(518) 862-1200 .. **Resta-Tobin,** Denise M '07 %Martin H&M LLP -Bx15141 -Albany 12212
(212) 357-7718 .. **Restieri,** Lawr J Jr. '97 Goldman Sachs & Co -1 NY Plz -NY 10004
(212) 545-4702 .. **Restituyo,** Martin E '03 %Wolf HAF&H LLP -270 Mad Av -NY 10016
(718) 767-3798 .. **Restivo,** Carmen R '00 -299 Bway -NY 10007
(212) 809-7600 .. **Restivo,** Loretta A '01 %Cheven K&H -40 Wall -NY 10005
(516) 228-1501 .. **Restivo,** Nicole Brodsky '03 %Ivy Asset Mgmt -1 Jericho Plz -Jericho 11753
(516) 489-0800 .. **Restivo,** Todd A '98 -100 Q Roosevelt Blvd -Gdn Cty 11530 **Fx:**683-8732
(718) 590-2000 .. **Resto,** Jessica M '08 %DA -198 E 161st -Bronx 10451 **Fx:**590-6477
(914) 375-0100 .. **Restrepo,** Juan C '08 %Novick ELRW&L,PC -733 Ynkrs Av -Ynkrs 10704
(315) 462-2207 .. **Retchless,** David G '55 -Bx790 -Honeoye 14471 **Fx:**462-2289
(631) 744-6330 .. **Rethier,** Paul H '91 -Bx307 -Sound Bch 11789 **Fx:**744-6330
(212) 455-2000 .. **Rethy,** Isaac M '10 %Simpson T&B LLP -425 Lex Av -NY 10017
(212) 613-5000 .. **Retkin,** Randye S '79 %Leg Assist Grp -450 W 33rd -NY 10001 **Fx:**750-0820
(914) 779-1402 .. **Retta,** Robt J '85 -575 Wht Plns Rd -Eastchstr 10709
(631) 471-4200 .. **Rettaliata,** Donald A '66 -4250 Vets Mem'l Hwy -Holbrook 11741 **Fx:**588-2550
(631) 669-1000 .. **Rettaliata,** Donald A Jr. '95 %OPRHP -Belmont Lk State Park Bx247 -Babylon 11702
(212) 227-7727 .. **Retter,** Danl '69 (D Retter,PC) -2 Park Av -NY 10016 **Fx:**227-1199
(212) 808-7800 .. **Retter,** David E '81 (Kelley D&W LLP) -101 Park Av -NY 10178
(212) 592-6161 .. **Retter,** Margaret E '87 -2 Park Av -NY 10016 **Fx:**227-1199
(212) 335-9000 .. **Rettew,** Amyjane '79 %DA -1 Hogan Pl -NY 10013
(718) 595-5595 .. **Rettig,** Andrew S '00 Cnsl DEP -59-17 Junction Blvd -Flushng 11373 **Fx:**595-6543
(718) 596-4236 .. **Rettig,** David S '92 -174 Carroll -Brklyn 11231
(212) 233-2141 .. **Rettig,** George W '89 %B Bragg -11 Hanover Sq -NY 10005
(212) 474-1000 .. **Rettig,** Rebecca L '07 %Cravath S&M LLP -825 8th Av -NY 10019
(212) 335-9000 .. **Rettler,** Luke H '84 %DA -1 Hogan Pl -NY 10013
(212) 730-8133 .. **Reuben,** Adam S '06 %Gunderson DSVF&H,LLP -220 W 42nd -NY 10036
(212) 238-3000 .. **Reuben,** Eric M '75 (Emmet M&M,LLP) -120 Bway -NY 10271
(917) 407-7408 .. **Reuben,** Michl B '83 -70 E 77th -NY 10075 **Fx:**(212) 570-6686
(212) 735-3424 .. **Reuben,** Susan B '80 Cnsl Skadden ASM&F LLP -4 Times Sq -NY 10036 **Fx:**(917) 777-3424

(212) 449-8838 .. **Reubenstone,** Richd '84 Merrill Lynch & Co -2 World Fncl Ctr N -NY 10281
(518) 284-9733 .. **Reul,** Cheryl Parsons '87 -Bx155 -Sharon Spgs 13459
(212) 872-1000 .. **Reuss,** Alexandra I '09 -One Bryant Park -NY 10036 **Fx:**872-1002
(516) 358-1700 .. **Revellino,** Dominick P '76 %Cronin & B,LLP -1983 Marcus Av -Lk Success 11042
(212) 859-8000 .. **Revellino,** Jane B '83 %Fried FHS&J LLP -1 NY Plz -NY 10004
(212) 592-6700 .. **Revello,** Mark '96 %Bovis Lend Lease Hldngs -200 Park Av -NY 10166 **Fx:**592-6997
(212) 779-9910 .. **Reverdin,** Bernard J '55 OfCnsl Eaton & V LLP -3 Park Av -NY 10016
(212) 416-2000 .. **Revesz,** Deborah Torrisi '92 Dow Jones & Co -1155 Av of Amer -NY 10036 **Fx:**416-2524
(212) 998-6000 .. **Revesz,** Richd L '86 %NYU Law Schl -40 Wshngtn Sq S -NY 10012 **Fx:**995-3150
(914) 632-7275 .. **Reville & Cullen** -540 North Av -New Rchll 10801 **Fx:**632-7421
(716) 857-7991 .. **Reville,** Michl W '94 %Natl Fuel Gas -6363 Main -Williamsvll 14221 **Fx:**857-7614
(914) 632-7275 .. **Reville,** Patrick J '69 (Reville & C) -540 North Av -New Rchll 10801
(607) 334-1948 .. **Revoir,** Frank B Jr. '92 -10 Elm -Norwich 13815 **Fx:**334-1949
(516) 767-7100 .. **Revuelta,** Noreen M '88 %Wolfe & Y PLLC -14 Vanderventer Av -Pt Wash 11050
(212) 797-4362 .. **Rex,** Beth L '88 OfCnsl Rafter & Assoc,PLLC -29 Bway -NY 10006 **Fx:**797-4363
(212) 349-6009 .. **Rey,** Carmen M '07 %Sanctuary for Families -110 Wall -NY 10005 **Fx:**566-0344
(212) 984-1497 .. **Rey,** Jorge A '98 Radian Asset Assurance -335 Mad Av -NY 10017
(718) 424-2232 .. **Rey,** Jose A '75 -78-27 37th Av -Jcksn Hts 11372
(212) 349-6775 .. **Rey,** L Ruby '91 OfCnsl Peltz & W -222 Bway -NY 10038
(212) 819-8200 .. **Rey,** Nathalie '09 %White & C LLP -1155 Av of Amer -NY 10036
(212) 783-3990 .. **Reycraft,** Sheilah M '95 Citigroup Global Mkts -485 Lex Av -NY 10017
(716) 856-4000 .. **Reyen,** Michl E '10 %Hodgson R LLP -140 Pearl -Buffalo 14202
(516) 571-9180 .. **Reyer,** Arianne K '98 %Cnty Atty -1200 Old Cntry Rd -Westbury 11590 **Fx:**571-9189
(212) 480-6725 .. **Reyes,** Aida P '94 %DHCR -25 Beaver -NY 10004 **Fx:**480-7416
(212) 238-2420 .. **Reyes,** Benjamin H Jr. '97 %UIA Bd -59 Maiden Ln -NY 10038 **Fx:**238-2451
(212) 259-8000 .. **Reyes,** Beverly B '06 %Dewey & L LLP -1301 Av of Amer -NY 10019
(718) 538-6878 .. **Reyes,** Frank '87 -910 Grnd Cncrs -Bronx 10451
(212) 766-1888 .. **Reyes,** Joan A '00 %Morris DA&F -2 Rector -NY 10006
(212) 521-5400 .. **Reyes,** Juan De Dios '97 (Reed S LLP) -599 Lex Av -NY 10022
(718) 588-7877 .. **Reyes,** Lourdes '86 (L Reyes,PC) -901 Sheridan Av -Bronx 10451 **Fx:**588-8443
(585) 342-4600 .. **Reyes,** Miguel A '83 -1664 N Clinton Av -Rchstr 14621 **Fx:**342-9773
(212) 401-0800 .. **Reyes,** Orlando '05 %Disciplinary Comm -61 Bway -NY 10006 **Fx:**287-1045
(212) 530-5000 .. **Reyes,** Pedro '05 %Milbank TH&M LLP -1 Chase Manh Plz -NY 10005
(212) 966-3761 .. **Reyes,** Richd P '98 (Barnum & R,PC) -30 Vesey -NY 10007 **Fx:**651-9852
(718) 777-8887 .. **Reyes,** Therese M '04 OfCnsl Nanis & R,LLP -30-97 Steinway -Astoria 11103
(212) 221-6900 .. **Reyfman,** Yelena '08 %Winget S&S,LLP -45 Bway -NY 10006
(917) 523-4845 .. **Reyfman-Melamed,** Alla '05 IRS -110 W 44th -NY 10036
(212) 407-4000 .. **Reyhani,** Bryan I '00 (Loeb & L,LLP) -345 Park Av -NY 10154
(212) 558-4000 .. **Reynard,** Andrew H '06 %Sullivan & C LLP -125 Broad -NY 10004
(718) 248-5710 .. **Reynard,** Muriel J '84 %Citicorp -1 Court Sq -LIC 11101
(212) 859-8000 .. **Reyner,** Micah R '10 %Fried FHS&J LLP -1 NY Plz -NY 10004
(585) 419-8800 .. **Reyner,** Victoria A '00 %Harris B PLLC -99 Garnsey Rd -Pittsfrd 14534
(212) 909-6000 .. **Reynolds,** A David '85 Cnsl Debevoise & P LLP -919 3rd Av -NY 10022
(212) 538-7419 .. **Reynolds,** Amy P '02 Credit Suisse -11 Mad Av -NY 10010
(212) 588-4000 .. **Reynolds,** Benjamin A '05 ITG -380 Mad Av -NY 10017
(212) 336-2000 .. **Reynolds,** Carin Grant '93 Patterson BW&T LLP -1133 Av of Amer -NY 10036
(585) 454-5490 .. **Reynolds,** Carl R '75 -16 W Main -Rchstr 14614 **Fx:**454-5502
(716) 631-5767 .. **Reynolds,** Carla R '88 (Stamm R&S) -5555 Main -Williamsvll 14221
(631) 231-1199 .. **Reynolds Caronia Gianelli Hagney LaPinta & Quatela, LLP** -35 Arkay Dr -Hauppauge 11788 **Fx:**231-1344
(212) 506-5000 .. **Reynolds,** Clayton S '80 (Orrick H&S LLP) -51 W 52nd -NY 10019
(607) 723-5408 .. **Reynolds,** Danl O '97 %Shaw OC&R -55 Main -Bnghmtn 13905
(212) 921-8399 .. **Reynolds,** Danl E '93 (Lankler S&W LLP) -500 5th Av -NY 10110
(914) 862-4602 .. **Reynolds,** Donald L '97 -1 Croton Pnt Av -Croton-On-Hud 10520
(315) 536-3833 .. **Reynolds,** Douglas G '76 -3125 West Lk Rd -Penn Yan 14527 **Fx:**536-0732
(212) 267-7600 .. **Reynolds,** Edw B Jr. '84 OfCnsl Solomon PBH&S LLP -40 Wall -NY 10005
(718) 590-2000 .. **Reynolds,** Erin M '07 %DA -198 E 161st -Bronx 10451 **Fx:**590-6477
(585) 238-2000 .. **Reynolds,** Gavin G '09 %Phillips L LLP -1400 First Fed Plz -Rchstr 14614
(914) 723-7211 .. **Reynolds,** Harold J '56 -152 Bradley Rd -Scarsdale 10583
(516) 932-9500 .. **Reynolds,** Heather N '99 %Davis Vision Inc -159 Express -Plainvw 11803 **Fx:**932-9770
(585) 226-3311 .. **Reynolds,** J Thos '67 (Reynolds & H) -5579 Avon-Lima Rd Bx190 -Avon 14414 **Fx:**226-6740
(631) 231-1199 .. **Reynolds,** James T '72 (Reynolds CGHL&Q,LLP) -35 Arkay Dr -Hauppauge 11788
(585) 232-6500 .. **Reynolds,** Jodi A '07 %Harter S&E LLP -1600 Bausch & Lomb Pl -Rchstr 14604
(516) 564-8000 .. **Reynolds,** John A '01 %J Hiebler & Assoc -901 Franklin Av -Gdn Cty 11530 **Fx:**564-1714
(212) 670-0245 .. **Reynolds,** Jos E '00 Merrill Lynch -222 Bway -NY 10038
(516) 364-1095 .. **Reynolds,** Kenneth A '93 (McBreen & K) -500 N Bway -Jericho 11753
(212) 598-8000 .. **Reynolds,** Kevin T '86 %Guardian Life Ins -7 Hanover Sq -NY 10004 **Fx:**919-2693
(518) 853-4700 .. **Reynolds,** Leila '95 -Bx466 -Fultonvll 12072 **Fx:**853-4800
(212) 736-4500 .. **Reynolds,** Lori D '96 %Nesenoff & M,LLP -363 7th Av -NY 10001
(212) 848-4000 .. **Reynolds,** Matthew J '06 %Shearman & S LLP -599 Lex Av -NY 10022
(212) 609-6800 .. **Reynolds,** Michl J '02 %McCarter & E,LLP -245 Park Av -NY 10167
(516) 884-8002 .. **Reynolds,** Michl P '95 -30 Jericho Exec Plz -Jericho 11753
(212) 474-1000 .. **Reynolds,** Michl T '96 (Cravath S&M LLP) -825 8th Av -NY 10019
(212) 459-7827 .. **Reynolds,** Nicholas Y '00 Dept of Tax & Fin -1740 Bway -NY 10019
(718) 590-2000 .. **Reynolds,** Orville S C '09 %DA -198 E 161st -Bronx 10451 **Fx:**590-6477
(585) 203-3400 .. **Reynolds,** Pamela S '08 %Littler M,PC -400 Linden Oaks -Rchstr 14625
(845) 628-8080 .. **Reynolds,** Peter J '97 %J Tock -963 Route 6 -Mahopac 10541 **Fx:**628-5450
(607) 733-4635 .. **Reynolds,** Ransom P Jr. '70 (Davidson & O,PC) -243 Lk -Elmira 14901
(315) 448-0672 .. **Reynolds,** Ransom Pratt III '98 %US Atty -100 S Clinton Bx7198 -Syracuse 13261 **Fx:**448-0689
(518) 487-7600 .. **Reynolds,** Robt S '97 (Whiteman O&H LLP) -1 Commerce Plz -Albany 12260
(212) 351-4000 .. **Reynolds,** Ryan S '10 Gibson D&C LLP -200 Park Av -NY 10166
(518) 891-4050 .. **Reynolds,** Sarah H '06 Adirondack Pk Agncy -Bx99 -Ray Brk 12977 **Fx:**891-3938
(212) 918-3000 .. **Reynolds,** Scott W '96 (Hogan L LLP) -875 3rd Av -NY 10022
(914) 666-3086 .. **Reynolds,** Stacey S '96 -69 High Ridge Rd -Mt Kisco 10549 **Fx:**244-1149
(518) 457-0036 .. **Reynolds,** Stephen '61 %Ofc of Tax Enforcement -Harriman Campus Bldg 8 -Albany 12227 **Fx:**457-3836
(212) 878-8000 .. **Reynolds,** Stephen B '87 %Clifford C LLP -31 W 52nd -NY 10019
(914) 448-0200 .. **Reynolds,** Terence S '10 %Bartlett MB&M,LLP -81 Main -White Plns 10601
(315) 343-2451 .. **Reynolds,** Thos A '84 (Reynolds & M,PLLC) -138 W 4th -Oswego 13126 **Fx:**343-1125
(212) 735-3000 .. **Reynolds,** Timothy G '81 (Skadden ASM&F LLP) -4 Times Sq -NY 10036
(914) 995-3419 .. **Reynolds,** Toniann '07 %DA -111 Martin Luther King Blvd -White Plns 10601 **Fx:**995-3363
(518) 533-3000 .. **Reynolds,** Wm E '03 SrCnsl Bond S&K,PLLC -111 Wshngtn Av -Albany 12210
(518) 695-6857 .. **Reynolds,** Wm F '78 -Monument Dr Bx 74 -Schuylrvll 12871
(518) 786-3900 .. **Reynolds,** Wm H '92 OfCnsl Kelleher & Assoc -17 British Amer Blvd -Latham 12110 **Fx:**786-6446
(631) 853-4161 .. **Reynolds,** Wm J Jr. '98 %DA -N Cnty Cmplx Bldg 77 -Hauppauge 11788 **Fx:**853-4192
(716) 856-5012 .. **Reynolds,** Wm S '54 OfCnsl Anspach ME,LLP -2400 Main Pl Twr -Buffalo 14202
(315) 725-4848 .. **Reynolds-Amuso,** Jessica K '99 (Reynolds-Amuso & A) -1 Kirkland Av Bx191 -Clinton 13323
(212) 455-2000 .. **Reynoso,** Jennifer Goldberg '96 Cnsl Simpson T&B LLP -425 Lex Av -NY 10017
(212) 766-1888 .. **Reynoso,** Manuel R '00 %Morris DA&F -2 Rector -NY 10006
(212) 733-1376 .. **Reytblat,** Julia '99 %Pfizer Inc -235 E 42nd -NY 10017
(212) 331-4478 .. **Rezac,** Steven '99 %HRA/Ofc Leg Affrs -180 Water -NY 10038
(212) 918-8765 .. **Rezak,** Adam M '97 Guggenheim Prtnrs,LLC -135 E 57th -NY 10022
(212) 715-9100 .. **Reznick,** Allan E '82 (Kramer LN&F,LLP) -1177 Av of Amer -NY 10036
(718) 241-6460 .. **Reznick,** Bruce S '61 -958 E 81st -Brklyn 11236 **Fx:**241-2578
(212) 490-5900 .. **Reznick,** Felix B '99 -535 5th Av -NY 10017
(212) 250-8385 .. **Reznick,** Janice B '91 %Deutsche Bank -60 Wall -NY 10005
(212) 473-6279 .. **Reznick,** Nina J '75 -28 E 10th -NY 10003
(718) 241-6460 .. **Reznick,** Russell I '88 %B Reznick -958 E 81st -Brklyn 11236 **Fx:**241-2578
(212) 325-7973 .. **Reznik,** Edw J '88 Credit Suisse -11 Mad Av -NY 10010
(646) 386-4520 .. **Reznik,** Inna '00 %Criminal Ct -100 Centre -NY 10013
(212) 326-3939 .. **Reznik,** Miriam '09 %Jones D -222 E 41st -NY 10017
(212) 446-4800 .. **Reznik,** Victoria '00 (Kirkland & E LLP) -153 E 53rd -NY 10022
(212) 541-6222 .. **Reznik,** Yekaterina '09 %Kane K,PC -1350 Av of Amer -NY 10019
(212) 608-2100 .. **Rezvani,** Reza '02 -233 Bway -NY 10279
(212) 701-3000 .. **Rezzy,** Oleg '09 %Cahill G&R LLP -80 Pine -NY 10005 **Fx:**269-5420
(718) 321-9797 .. **Rha & Kim,LLP** -40-45 Utopia Pkwy -Flushng 11363
(718) 321-9797 .. **Rha,** Megan Jungmi '98 (Rha & K,LLP) -40-45 Utopia Pkwy -Flushng 11363
(212) 262-2390 .. **Rhatican,** James P '97 (Connell F LLP) -888 7th Av -NY 10106
(212) 483-9600 .. **Rhatigan,** Thos A '98 %Costello S&G LLP -44 Wall -NY 10005
(212) 553-3200 .. **Rhau,** Hernandez M '03 %Marulli LE&T,LLP -5 Hanover Sq -NY 10004
(212) 859-8000 .. **Rhee,** Michl J '99 SpclCnsl Fried FHS&J LLP -1 NY Plz -NY 10004
(212) 225-2000 .. **Rhee,** Sue '07 %Cleary GS&H -1 Lbrty Plz -NY 10006
(212) 979-1108 .. **Rheem,** Sue Hae-Suk '94 %Asian Amer for Equality -108-110 Norfolk -NY 10002 **Fx:**979-2219
(212) 239-4001 .. **Rheem,** Uel '90 (Rheem & B LLP) -302 5th Av -NY 10001 **Fx:**239-4125
(212) 213-5500 .. **Rheingold,** Arthur D '67 Cnsl Periconi,LLC -708 3rd Av -NY 10017 **Fx:**213-5030
(212) 684-1880 .. **Rheingold,** David B '94 (Rheingold VRS&M LLP) -113 E 37th -NY 10016
(212) 684-1880 .. **Rheingold,** Paul D '58 (Rheingold VRS&M LLP) -113 E 37th -NY 10016
(212) 684-1880 .. **Rheingold Valet Rheingold Shkolnik & McCartney LLP** -113 E 37th -NY 10016 **Fx:**689-8156
(315) 894-8330 .. **Rheinhardt,** Jeffrey N '82 (Radley & R) -85 Otsego Bx360 -Ilion 13357
(585) 262-1918 .. **Rheinstein,** Thos P '76 IRS -255 East Av -Rchstr 14604 **Fx:**263-5867
(917) 693-4689 .. **Rhew,** Kathleen Kyung-A '97 Axiom -75 Spring -NY 10012
(212) 509-0440 .. **Rhine,** Arthur '82 OfCnsl Goodfarb & S,LLP -112 Mad Av -NY 10016 **Fx:**689-9680
(212) 888-8200 .. **Rhine,** Howard I '63 (Feder K LLP) -845 3rd Av -NY 10022
(315) 435-2170 .. **Rhinehart,** Carol L '90 %Cnty Atty -421 Mntgmry -Syracuse 13202 **Fx:**435-5729

(716) 483-1289 .. **Rhinehart,** Randy E '82 -800 Fairmount Av -Jamestwn 14701 **Fx:**483-1920
(315) 422-4179 .. **Rhinehart,** Robt F '80 -224 Harrison -Syracuse 13202
(516) 742-8058 .. **Rho,** Theresa '92 %Abamont & Assoc -200 Grdn City Plz Bx9250 -Gdn Cty 11530 **Fx:**742-7308
(212) 250-3318 .. **Rho,** Usec N '04 Deutsche Bank -60 Wall -NY 10005
(518) 482-2500 .. **Rhoades,** Karen A '05 -428 Sand Crk Rd -Albany 12205 **Fx:**438-2304
(212) 715-9100 .. **Rhoads,** Donald L '90 (Kramer LN&F,LLP) -1177 Av of Amer -NY 10036
(516) 249-1342 .. **Rhoads,** Steven D '95 %Grey & G,LLP -360 Main -Farmngdl 11735
(212) 809-7074 .. **Rhoden,** Horace '99 (Armienti DG&R,LLP) -39 Bway -NY 10006
(518) 792-2117 .. **Rhodes,** Alan R '62 (Bartlett PS&R,PC) -1 Wshngtn Bx2168 -Glens Fls 12801
(212) 946-2816 .. **Rhodes,** Barry G '72 -11 Penn Plz -NY 10001
(212) 839-5300 .. **Rhodes,** Corban S '08 %Sidley A LLP -787 7th Av -NY 10019
(212) 208-1440 .. **Rhodes,** James M '71 -140 Bway -NY 10005
Rhodes, James M Jr. '75 -205 E 69th -NY 10021
(315) 785-3152 .. **Rhodes,** Jonathan D C '09 Pub Def -175 Arsenal -Watertwn 13601 **Fx:**785-5060
(212) 969-3000 .. **Rhodes,** Kate B '10 %Proskauer R LLP -1585 Bway -NY 10036
(212) 530-5000 .. **Rhodes,** Katherine E '10 %Milbank TH&M LLP -1 Chase Manh Plz -NY 10005
(212) 816-5822 .. **Rhodes,** Mark A '87 Citigroup Global Mrkts -388 Greenwich -NY 10013
(585) 248-8572 .. **Rhodes,** Mark S '84 -Bx25323 -Rchstr 14625
(516) 437-4385 .. **Rhodes,** Mary L '05 %Vishnick MM LLP -3000 Marcus Av -Lk Success 11042
(518) 452-1800 .. **Rhodes-Devey,** Michl '86 OfCnsl Towne R & Prtnrs,PC -450 New Karner Rd Bx15072 -Albany 12212
(585) 546-5530 .. **Rhoton,** Joanne W '81 %Thomson West -50 E Broad -Rchstr 14694
(718) 643-3191 .. **Rhudd,** Winsome N '92 %Hon Y Lewis -360 Adams -Brklyn 11201 **Fx:**643-4995
(845) 796-2100 .. **Rhulen,** Harry W '89 %Frontier Ins -Bx8000 -Rck Hll 12775
(212) 822-3255 .. **Riad,** Maged F '76 (Riad & Assoc,PC) -350 Theo Fremd Av -Rye 10580 **Fx:**(914) 315-0103
(212) 822-3266 .. **Riad,** Miriam '05 %Riad & Assoc,PC -350 Theo Fremd Av -Rye 10580 **Fx:**(914) 315-0103
(212) 906-1200 .. **Riahei,** Nazan K '08 %Latham & W -885 3rd Av -NY 10022
(212) 436-5809 .. **Rial,** Edw A '85 Deloitte & Touche,LLP -2 World Fncl Ctr -NY 10281
(516) 571-3800 .. **Riaz,** Hoorya '07 %DA -262 Old Cntry Rd -Mineola 11501 **Fx:**248-9479
(212) 460-6677 .. **Riback,** Jeffrey L '79 Con Ed -4 Irving Pl -NY 10003
(212) 421-2233 .. **Riback,** Stuart M '85 (Wilk A LLP) -675 3rd Av -NY 10017
(718) 263-7136 .. **Ribacoff,** Ralph N '93 -108-12 70th Av -Frst Hlls 11375
(718) 268-8900 .. **Ribakove,** Kevin D '77 (Ribakove & R) -107-19 71st Av -Frst Hlls 11375 **Fx:**268-3045
(212) 259-8000 .. **Ribando,** Monique L '99 %Dewey & L LLP -1301 Av of Amer -NY 10019
(315) 474-8800 .. **Ribarovski,** Robt B '00 -110 W Fayette -Syracuse 13202 **Fx:**476-0025
(212) 541-9100 .. **Ribaudo,** Angela M '03 %Schiavetti CDW&N,LLP -575 8th Av -NY 10018
(516) 822-4400 .. **Ribaudo,** Frank P '04 %Tunstead & S -500 N Bway -Jericho 11753
(212) 673-6669 .. **Ribeiro,** Agostinho J '91 (Ventura R&S) -280 Park Av S -NY 10010
(631) 300-2455 .. **Riber,** Arthur '66 -775 Park Av -Huntngtn 11743
(212) 261-8000 .. **Rible,** Stephen V '80 (Mendes & M,LLP) -750 7th Av -NY 10019
(212) 277-4000 .. **Riblett,** Phillip J '06 %Freshfields BD LLP -520 Mad Av -NY 10022
(315) 344-6642 .. **Ribley,** Michl P '88 -Bx396 -Canton 13617 **Fx:**344-6642
(516) 873-8000 .. **Ribnick,** Jacqueline S '94 %Kroll M&K,LLP -400 Grdn City Plz -Gdn Cty 11530
(718) 323-9100 .. **Ribowsky,** Elinor B '94 -109-12 Jamaica Av -Richmnd Hll 11418 **Fx:**835-2498
(718) 659-5333 .. **Ribowsky,** Michl '92 -109-12 Jamaica Av -Richmnd Hll 11418 **Fx:**835-2498
(914) 995-5102 .. **Ribreau,** Greg A '08 %Cnty Atty -148 Martine Av -White Plns 10601 **Fx:**995-5858
(718) 238-6500 .. **Ricaforte,** Terence J '07 %Connors & S,PC -7408 5th Av -Brklyn 11209
(212) 259-8000 .. **Ricardo,** Henry J '94 (Dewey & L LLP) -1301 Av of Amer -NY 10019
(212) 744-8982 .. **Ricardo,** Marta Galan '95 -129 E 82nd -NY 10028
(212) 907-7300 .. **Ricardo,** S Preston '02 (Golenbock EAB&P) -437 Mad Av -NY 10022
(516) 248-1700 .. **Ricca,** James C Jr. '88 (Forchelli CDSM&T,LLP) -333 Earle Ovngton Blvd -Uniondale 11553
(212) 715-9100 .. **Ricca,** John J '78 %Kramer LN&F,LLP -1177 Av of Amer -NY 10036
(516) 376-5746 .. **Ricca,** Mark A '92 -43 Rofay Dr -E Northprt 11731
(718) 625-8940 .. **Ricca,** Mindy R '92 %B Lawrence -15 Metrotech Ctr N -Brklyn 11201 **Fx:**624-5756
(716) 856-0600 .. **Ricca,** Steven J '88 (Jaeckle F&M,LLP) -12 Fountain Plz -Buffalo 14202
(212) 221-5700 .. **Riccardi,** Aubrey E '00 %Goldberg WFG LLP -1501 Bway -NY 10036
(212) 574-1200 .. **Riccardi,** Christopher C '01 (Seward & K LLP) -1 Bttry Pk Plz -NY 10004
(716) 895-4210 .. **Riccardi,** John J '96 D Jaworski -2988 William -Cheektowaga 14227 **Fx:**895-2516
(212) 530-1800 .. **Riccardi,** Matthew M '03 %Richards K&O LLP -1 World Fncl Ctr -NY 10281
(212) 825-5900 .. **Riccards,** Catherine M '02 %Dept of Invstgtn -80 Maiden Ln -NY 10038 **Fx:**825-2860
(212) 547-5430 .. **Riccardulli,** Meishin '03 %McDermott W&E LLP -340 Mad Av -NY 10173
(212) 547-5400 .. **Riccardulli,** Stephen J '01 (McDermott W&E LLP) -340 Mad Av -NY 10173
(212) 838-4840 .. **Ricchiuti,** James '92 Entreprenuer Growth Capital LLC -505 Park Av -NY 10022
(212) 839-5300 .. **Ricchiuto,** Edw D '85 (Sidley A LLP) -787 7th Av -NY 10019
(646) 386-5700 .. **Ricci,** Donna R '96 %Civil Ct -111 Centre -NY 10013
(516) 248-2824 .. **Ricci,** George P '80 -1000 Franklin Av -Gdn Cty 11530 **Fx:**742-4241
(585) 428-5755 .. **Ricci,** Lori Ann '86 %Cnty Atty -50 W Main -Rchstr 14614 **Fx:**428-2031
(315) 568-1345 .. **Ricci,** Stephen R '99 -141 Fall -Seneca Fls 13148
(212) 319-6898 .. **Ricci,** Wm J '93 (Lavin ORC&D) -420 Lex Av -NY 10170
(845) 791-7800 .. **Ricciani,** Jacqueline '95 (Ricciani & J,LLP) -17 St John -Monticello 12701 **Fx:**791-5923
(212) 735-3000 .. **Ricciardelli,** Chas M '07 %Skadden ASM&F LLP -4 Times Sq -NY 10036
(718) 258-1527 .. **Ricciardi,** Chas A '52 -2073 NY Av -Brklyn 11210
(212) 548-2100 .. **Ricciardi,** James P '93 (McGuire W LLP) -1345 Av of Amer -NY 10105
(212) 867-2700 .. **Ricciardi,** John J '95 %J Felice & Assoc,PC -11 E 44th -NY 10017 **Fx:**867-2783
(212) 683-7100 .. **Ricciardi,** Kimberly Leggio '95 %Gallo V&K,LLP -90 Broad -NY 10004
(516) 496-0062 .. **Ricciardi,** Mark S '89 -2 Roosevelt Av -Syosset 11791
(518) 487-7600 .. **Ricciardi,** Martin J '91 (Whiteman O&H LLP) -1 Commerce Plz -Albany 12260
(212) 578-2675 .. **Ricciardi,** Matthew M '93 MetLife Grp,Inc -1095 Av of Amer -NY 10036
(212) 455-2000 .. **Ricciardi,** Sara A '03 %Simpson T&B LLP -425 Lex Av -NY 10017
(212) 373-3000 .. **Ricciardi,** Walter G '85 (Paul WRW&G LLP) -1285 Av of Amer -NY 10019
(212) 530-5000 .. **Ricciardiello,** Joanne M '10 %Milbank TH&M LLP -1 Chase Manh Plz -NY 10005
(212) 483-0105 .. **Riccio,** Aurora N '02 %Coughlin D LLP -88 Pine-Wall St Plz -NY 10005
(212) 661-7300 .. **Riccio,** Christina D '10 %Malapero & P LLP -295 Mad Av -NY 10017
(518) 842-3742 .. **Riccio,** Michl J '52 -198 Market -Amsterdam 12010
(516) 571-2484 .. **Riccio,** Wm J '92 %Hon RB Cozzens -100 Supreme Ct Dr -Mineola 11501
(212) 569-5042 .. **Ricciuti,** Thos '95 -10 Park Ter E -NY 10034
(212) 791-3919 .. **Ricco,** Anthony L '82 -20 Vesey -NY 10007 **Fx:**791-3940
(631) 247-0404 .. **Ricco,** Jayne L '10 %Jackson L LLP -58 S Srvc Rd -Melvll 11747
(212) 587-1514 .. **Riccoboni,** Dana N '09 D Riccoboni,PLLC -20 Vesey -NY 10007 **Fx:**981-3259
(212) 438-4100 .. **Riccoboni,** Gene J '01 Standard & Poor's -55 Water -NY 10041
(516) 545-3411 .. **Riccobono,** Donna L '88 %Natl Grid -175 E Old Cntry Rd -Hicksvll 11801 **Fx:**545-5029
(212) 770-1708 .. **Riccobono,** Jos X '77 %AIG -80 Pine -NY 10005 **Fx:**344-2286
(212) 557-1818 .. **Riccobono,** Rocco R '02 %Silverson P&L -192 Lex Av -NY 10016
(212) 894-7050 .. **Rice,** Alan J '88 Vornado Realty Trust -888 7th Av -NY 10106
(212) 969-3000 .. **Rice,** Andrew E '07 %Proskauer R LLP -1585 Bway -NY 10036
(518) 473-6107 .. **Rice,** Bradley F '92 %Insurance Dept -99 Wshngtn Av -Albany 12257 **Fx:**473-4600
(212) 326-2000 .. **Rice,** Bradley L '09 %O'Melveny & M LLP -7 Times Sq -NY 10036
(212) 436-1081 .. **Rice,** Channa '92 IRS -Bx3100 -NY 10008
(212) 206-0444 .. **Rice,** Dan M '82 Rice Law Firm,PLLC -475 Park Av S -NY 10022 **Fx:**(646) 356-6940
(212) 775-3782 .. **Rice,** Devin A '02 NYS Industrial Bd of Appls -75 Varick -NY 10013
(212) 218-7880 .. **Rice,** Donald S '64 (Ravitch Rice & Co) -610 5th Av -NY 10020
(914) 633-9200 .. **Rice,** Gail B '77 (Rice & R) -270 North Av -New Rchll 10801 **Fx:**633-9291
(212) 455-2000 .. **Rice,** Gary '83 (Simpson T&B LLP) -425 Lex Av -NY 10017
(516) 592-6800 .. **Rice,** George F '70 (Spellman RSGM&P,LLP) -229 Seventh -Gdn Cty 11530
(212) 661-9100 .. **Rice,** Glenn B '72 (Otterbourg SH&R,PC) -230 Park Av -NY 10169
(914) 633-9200 .. **Rice,** J Roger '78 (Rice & R) -270 North Av -New Rchll 10801 **Fx:**633-9291
(914) 944-9384 .. **Rice,** James D '80 -Bx2525 -Briarclff Mnr 10510
(516) 869-8067 .. **Rice,** James P '57 -129 Plandome Rd Bx741 -Manhsst 11030 **Fx:**627-8755
(315) 637-5997 .. **Rice,** Jane E '86 -413 Lincoln Av -Fayettevll 13066
(914) 633-9200 .. **Rice,** Jared R '05 %Rice & R -270 North Av -New Rchll 10801 **Fx:**633-9291
(518) 434-8435 .. **Rice,** John C '60 (Rice & J) -111 Wshngtn Av -Albany 12210
(716) 753-7150 .. **Rice,** John P III '79 -Bx295 -Mayvll 14757 **Fx:**753-3566
(212) 465-1890 .. **Rice,** Jonathan C '85 -377 Ashford Av -Dobbs Ferry 10522 **Fx:**629-3055
(914) 633-9200 .. **Rice,** Jordan L '07 %Rice & R -270 North Av -New Rchll 10801 **Fx:**633-9291
(518) 434-8435 .. **Rice & Justice** -111 Wshngtn Av -Albany 12210 **Fx:**434-8462
(516) 571-3800 .. **Rice,** Kathleen M '92 (DA) -262 Old Cntry Rd -Mineola 11501 **Fx:**248-9479
(631) 231-1450 .. **Rice,** Kenneth D '09 %Feldman K&M,PC -330 Vndrbit Motor Pkwy -Hauppauge 11788
(516) 294-8844 .. **Rice,** Marian C '79 (L'Abbate BC&C,LLP) -1001 Franklin Av -Gdn Cty 11530
(212) 679-7007 .. **Rice,** Matthew F '04 %Brody B&B LLP -205 Lex Av -NY 10016
(518) 439-6065 .. **Rice,** Michl '86 -67 Nine Mile Ln -Delmar 12054
(212) 333-0200 .. **Rice,** Michelle A '87 (Arkin KR LLP) -590 Mad Av -NY 10022
(212) 351-4000 .. **Rice,** Mindy Foss '06 %Gibson D&C LLP -200 Park Av -NY 10166
(212) 741-2048 .. **Rice,** Nathan J '05 -55 Perry -NY 10014 **Fx:**507-5671
(212) 521-5400 .. **Rice,** Patrick F '98 Cnsl Reed S LLP -599 Lex Av -NY 10022
(716) 285-6953 .. **Rice Reid Broderick & Wattengel** -800 Main Bx219 -Niagara Fls 14302 **Fx:**285-6958
(518) 462-6765 .. **Rice,** Ricja D '06 Leg Aid -55 Colvin Av -Albany 12206 **Fx:**427-8352
(212) 250-7526 .. **Rice,** Robt E '88 %Deutsche Bank -60 Wall -NY 10005
(212) 687-0100 .. **Rice,** Steven J '78 (Harris B PLLC) -100 Wall -NY 10005
(845) 357-4000 .. **Rice,** Terry A '76 (Rice & A) -4 Exec Blvd -Suffern 10901 **Fx:**357-0765
(212) 309-1000 .. **Rice,** Thos A '05 (Hunton & W) -200 Park Av -NY 10166
(212) 455-2000 .. **Rice,** Thos C '82 (Simpson T&B LLP) -425 Lex Av -NY 10017
(212) 940-8800 .. **Rice,** Thos H '07 %Katten MR LLP -575 Mad Av -NY 10022
(212) 626-4100 .. **Rice,** Thos J '86 (Baker & M LLP) -1114 Av of Amer -NY 10036
(516) 248-7000 .. **Rice,** Thos O '69 (Albanese & A LLP) -1050 Franklin Av -Gdn Cty 11530
(212) 903-9000 .. **Rich,** A Hyun '02 %Linklaters -1345 Av of Amer -NY 10105
(212) 921-2244 .. **Rich,** Alan J '85 (A Rich,LLC) -26 Court -Brklyn 11242 **Fx:**921-5554

(585) 241-5999 .. **Rich,** Alison J '04 %Evans & F LLP -95 Allens Crk Rd -Rchstr 14618
(716) 847-8400 .. **Rich,** Brendan J '06 %Phillips L LLP -3400 HSBC Ctr -Buffalo 14203
(212) 732-3200 .. **Rich,** Bruce A '65 Cnsl Carter L&M LLP -2 Wall -NY 10005
(585) 232-5300 .. **Rich,** Cassandra Carter '05 %Boylan BCV&W,LLP -2400 Chase Sq -Rchstr 14604
(212) 907-7300 .. **Rich,** Chas B '98 OfCnsl Golenbock EAB&P -437 Mad Av -NY 10022
(212) 661-3080 .. **Rich,** Chas S '86 (Rottenberg LR,PC) -369 Lex Av -NY 10017
(914) 946-3737 .. **Rich,** David L '87 -175 Main -White Plns 10601
(212) 696-1999 .. **Rich,** David S '95 Lax & N LLP -1412 Bway -NY 10018
(212) 721-2570 .. **Rich,** Douglas S '73 -473 W End Av -NY 10024
(718) 681-5600 .. **Rich,** Franklin D '85 -881 Gerard Av -Bronx 10452
(212) 558-4000 .. **Rich,** Frederic C '82 (Sullivan & C LLP) -125 Broad -NY 10004
(718) 375-2003 .. **Rich,** Gail R '87 -14 Billings Pl -Brklyn 11223
(347) 875-7424 .. **Rich,** Jared M '05 -44 Court -Brklyn 11201
(212) 406-0440 .. **Rich,** Jeffrey M '86 (Rich & R,PC) -30 Vesey -NY 10007 **Fx:**233-3130
(212) 536-3900 .. **Rich,** Jeffrey N '70 (K&L Gates LLP) -599 Lex Av -NY 10022
(212) 566-7188 .. **Rich,** Jeffrey R '84 (Genova B&G) -115 Bway -NY 10006
(212) 262-2390 .. **Rich,** Joanna S '10 %Connell F LLP -888 7th Av -NY 10106
(212) 433-1480 .. **Rich,** John G '82 (Rich & I LLP) -111 Bway -NY 10006 **Fx:**433-1481
(212) 603-6300 .. **Rich,** Jonathan W '09 %Robinson BLGG&G PC -875 3rd Av -NY 10022
(212) 406-0440 .. **Rich,** Marc L '89 (Rich & R,PC) -30 Vesey -NY 10007 **Fx:**233-3130
(718) 380-0576 .. **Rich,** Marianne R '84 -184-52 Radnor Rd -Jamaica 11432
(585) 753-4500 .. **Rich,** Matthew J '04 %DA -832 Watts Bldg -Rchstr 14614 **Fx:**753-4576
(516) 742-7997 .. **Rich,** Michl A '75 -72 Jericho Tpk -Mineola 11501 **Fx:**294-0528
(516) 557-2325 .. **Rich,** Mitchell J '86 -3535 Jerusalem Av -Wantagh 11793 **Fx:**557-2324
(212) 310-8000 .. **Rich,** R Bruce '74 (Weil G&M LLP) -767 5th Av -NY 10153
(607) 737-5577 .. **Rich,** Richd W Jr. '95 Pub Advocate -219 Mad Av -Elmira 14901 **Fx:**737-2955
(845) 291-0011 .. **Rich,** Rita G '86 (Blustein SR&B,LLP) -10 Matthews -Goshen 10924
(845) 897-5199 .. **Rich,** Robt F Jr. '88 (Feldman K&C,LLP) -995 Main BxA -Fishkill 12524
(212) 686-0855 .. **Rich,** Robt P '81 (Zraick N&R) -303 5th Av -NY 10016
(516) 944-3417 .. **Rich,** Stephanie L '77 -3 Barkers Pnt Rd -Sands Pnt 11050
(212) 655-3500 .. **Rich,** Stuart I '92 (Meister S&F LLP) -140 E 45th -NY 10017
(212) 598-8000 .. **Rich,** Tracy '78 Guardian Life Ins -7 Hanover Sq -NY 10004 **Fx:**919-2693
(914) 682-8180 .. **Rich,** Walter L '73 (Kaminsky & R) -399 Knollwood Rd -White Plns 10603
(646) 435-9505 .. **Richan,** David S '93 (Baritz & C LLP) -233 Bway -NY 10279
(212) 668-1900 .. **Richard,** Hillary '89 (Brune & R LLP) -80 Broad -NY 10004
(212) 307-5500 .. **Richard,** Julie '02 (Venable LLP) -1270 Av of Amer -NY 10020
(212) 476-2429 .. **Richard,** Serena H '89 %Empire Blue Cross -1 Lbrty Plz -NY 10006
(212) 442-4900 .. **Richard,** Tynia D '95 %Ofc Admin Trials -40 Rector -NY 10006 **Fx:**442-4947
(212) 294-6700 .. **Richard,** Virginia R '69 (Winston & S) -200 Park Av -NY 10166
(718) 590-2000 .. **Richards,** Addisa Dafina '05 %DA -198 E 161st -Bronx 10451 **Fx:**590-6477
(516) 741-0515 .. **Richards,** Alan Z '63 -100 Ring Rd W -Gdn Cty 11530 **Fx:**741-0586
(631) 608-2828 .. **Richards,** Alia F '05 -25 Candee Av -Sayvll 11782 **Fx:**563-0737
(516) 681-1100 .. **Richards,** Andrew L '90 (Kaufman DV&G,LLP) -135 Crsswys Park Dr -Woodbury 11797
(212) 549-8400 .. **Richards,** Asha K '04 Hyperion Brookfield Asset Mgmt,Inc -200 Vesey -NY 10281
(212) 916-7308 .. **Richards,** Cynthia '76 %Atlantic Philanthropies -75 Varick -NY 10013
(212) 858-1000 .. **Richards,** Danl M '08 %Pillsbury WSP LLP -1540 Bway -NY 10036
(212) 609-6800 .. **Richards,** David A '73 (McCarter & E,LLP) -245 Park Av -NY 10167
(212) 998-6251 .. **Richards,** David A J '72 %NYU Law Schl -40 Wshngtn Sq S -NY 10012 **Fx:**995-4894
(518) 486-6398 .. **Richards,** Deborah D '84 %State Comptroller -110 State -Albany 12236 **Fx:**473-9104
(845) 371-4700 .. **Richards,** Donald A '82 OfCnsl Fein SK&S,PC -747 Chestnut Rdg Rd -Spg Vly 10977
(212) 468-8000 .. **Richards,** Erica J '07 %Morrison & F LLP -1290 Av of Amer -NY 10104
(212) 318-6000 .. **Richards,** Gillian E '07 %Paul HJ&W LLP -75 E 55th -NY 10022
(212) 838-7797 .. **Richards,** J Douglas '82 (Cohen MS&T,PLLC) -88 Pine -NY 10005
(800) 752-1821 .. **Richards,** Jacque A '05 -50 Clinton -Hempstd 11550 **Fx:**(516) 505-5309
(212) 450-4000 .. **Richards,** James P '09 %Davis P&W LLP -450 Lex Av -NY 10017
(516) 571-3800 .. **Richards,** Jason R '08 %DA -262 Old Cntry Rd -Mineola 11501 **Fx:**248-9479
(518) 482-6837 .. **Richards,** Jeffrey T '95 (J Richards,PC) -530 Morris -Albany 12208
(212) 458-2361 .. **Richards,** Jennifer M '02 AIG -175 Water -NY 10038
(212) 708-1800 .. **Richards,** John '81 (Ladas & P) -26 W 61st -NY 10023
(518) 745-5067 .. **Richards,** John H '77 -33 Park Bx389 -Glens Fls 12801
(212) 481-5858 .. **Richards,** Jonathan A '85 %Fidelity Natl Title Ins -1 Park Av -NY 10016 **Fx:**481-8747
(315) 464-4700 .. **Richards,** Karen M '96 Cnsl SUNY Univ Cnsl -60 Prsdntl Plz -Syracuse 13202 **Fx:**464-4706
(516) 538-7780 .. **Richards,** Katharine J '99 %N Pellegrini,LLC -320 Nassau Blvd -Garden City South 11530 **Fx:**564-0906
(212) 530-1800 .. **Richards Kibbe & Orbe LLP** -1 World Fncl Ctr -NY 10281 **Fx:**530-1801
(718) 720-1000 .. **Richards,** Kurt T '91 (K Richards,PC) -1200 South Av -Staten Isl 10314 **Fx:**720-1003
(212) 530-1800 .. **Richards,** Lee S III '76 (Richards K&O LLP) -1 World Fncl Ctr -NY 10281
(212) 885-5000 .. **Richards,** Marc E '78 (Blank R LLP) -405 Lex Av -NY 10174
(716) 843-5700 .. **Richards,** Monica J '97 %US Atty -138 Delaware Av -Buffalo 14202 **Fx:**551-3052
(212) 609-6800 .. **Richards,** R Andrew '96 (McCarter & E,LLP) -245 Park Av -NY 10167
(914) 237-2300 .. **Richards,** Randall '83 -1428 Mdlnd Av -Bronxvll 10708 **Fx:**237-0131
(212) 270-2353 .. **Richards,** Raymond R '99 JP Morgan Chase -270 Park Av -NY 10017
(212) 935-6502 .. **Richards,** Robt C '72 -531 Main -NY 10044
(607) 722-7573 .. **Richards,** Rodney A '59 -205 Richards Rd -Chenango Frks 13746 **Fx:**648-8297
(716) 847-8400 .. **Richards,** Rowland III '97 (Phillips L LLP) -3400 HSBC Ctr -Buffalo 14203
(518) 257-3000 .. **Richards,** Sara B '95 %Dormitory Auth -515 Bway -Albany 12207 **Fx:**257-3101
(212) 282-5521 .. **Richards,** Sarah C '00 %Avon Products -1345 Av of Amer -NY 10105
(718) 590-2000 .. **Richards,** Serena C '09 %DA -198 E 161st -Bronx 10451 **Fx:**590-6477
(212) 506-1700 .. **Richards,** Shela Omell '06 Kasowitz BT&F LLP -1633 Bway -NY 10019
(518) 580-9445 .. **Richards,** Steven L '98 -323 Daniels Rd -Saratoga Spgs 12866 **Fx:**587-1410
(212) 486-2400 .. **Richards,** Thos K '02 %Leader & B LLP -630 3rd Av -NY 10017
(585) 428-6986 .. **Richards,** Thos S '73 %Law Dept -30 Church -Rchstr 14614 **Fx:**428-6950
(212) 480-6792 .. **Richards,** Ursula M H '88 %DHCR -25 Beaver -NY 10004 **Fx:**480-7416
(212) 335-9000 .. **Richards,** Vanessa '04 DA -1 Hogan Pl -NY 10013
(516) 305-1047 .. **Richards-McKay,** Ayisha L N '09 -26 Court -Brklyn 11242
(914) 946-7902 .. **Richardson,** Althea F '89 -202 Mamaroneck Av -White Plns 10601 **Fx:**946-5090
(212) 530-4771 .. **Richardson,** Ambrose M III '71 (A Richardson,PC) -40 Wall -NY 10005 **Fx:**267-2030
(212) 659-7300 .. **Richardson,** Ann M '02 OfCnsl Haynes & B,LLP -1221 Av of Amer -NY 10020
(845) 565-9261 .. **Richardson,** Brian D '07 B Kulak -484 Temple Hill Rd -New Windsor 12553
(732) 380-0930 .. **Richardson,** Coulter K '00 -40 Wall -NY 10005 **Fx:**380-0931
(646) 471-4000 .. **Richardson,** David G '88 %PricewaterhouseCoopers LLP -300 Mad Av -NY 10017
(212) 732-3200 .. **Richardson,** Della '98 %Carter L&M LLP -2 Wall -NY 10005
(518) 463-1148 .. **Richardson,** Edw W '98 %NYS Auto Dealers Assn -37 Elk Bx7347 -Albany 12224
(518) 465-3444 .. **Richardson,** Florence M '84 (Kahn & R) -90 State Bx22006 -Albany 12201 **Fx:**465-3447
(212) 460-4121 .. **Richardson,** Gail L '91 Con Ed -4 Irving Pl -NY 10003
(212) 660-3000 .. **Richardson,** George O III '81 (Sullivan & W LLP) -1290 Av of Amer -NY 10104
(212) 661-7300 .. **Richardson,** Glenn E '80 %Malapero & P LLP -295 Mad Av -NY 10017
(212) 450-4000 .. **Richardson,** Ian C '10 %Davis P&W LLP -450 Lex Av -NY 10017
(518) 473-0620 .. **Richardson,** Jennifer '05 Governor's Ofc Reg Reform -ESP Bx2107 -Albany 12220 **Fx:**473-9962
(585) 454-6850 .. **Richardson,** Jennifer D '07 %J Iati,PC -1 Chase Sq -Rchstr 14604 **Fx:**325-6407
(212) 977-9700 .. **Richardson,** Jeremy D '95 (Phillips N LLP) -666 5th Av -NY 10103
(516) 305-4878 .. **Richardson,** John J '59 -60 Oaktree Ln -Manhsst 11030
(212) 277-0753 .. **Richardson,** John J '82 Hartford Fncl -2 Park Av -NY 10016
(212) 807-2910 .. **Richardson,** Judith M '88 %Thomson Reuters/RIA -195 Bway -NY 10007
(718) 298-1170 .. **Richardson,** Karen A '01 %Hon VB Nelson -88-11 Sutphin Blvd -Jamaica 11435
(716) 332-7870 .. **Richardson,** Karen E '98 %Hon HK Schroeder Jr -418 US Cthse -Buffalo 14202 **Fx:**332-7875
(212) 962-4277 .. **Richardson,** Kenneth W '83 -305 Bway -NY 10007
(212) 526-9583 .. **Richardson,** Keri A '06 Neuberger Berman LLC -399 Park Av -NY 10022
(718) 250-2000 .. **Richardson,** Kevin S '93 %DA -350 Jay -Brklyn 11201 **Fx:**250-2314
(212) 442-0832 .. **Richardson,** Lisa Marie '09 %Law Dept -100 Church -NY 10007 **Fx:**788-0367
(212) 440-4300 .. **Richardson,** Marie A '80 %Leg Aid -199 Water -NY 10038
(212) 756-2000 .. **Richardson,** Mark D '10 %Schulte R&Z LLP -919 3rd Av -NY 10022
(212) 715-9100 .. **Richardson,** Mary W '85 %Kramer LN&F,LLP -1177 Av of Amer -NY 10036
(516) 409-6200 .. **Richardson,** MaryAnne P '96 %Furey KWM&C,PC -2174 Jackson Av -Seafrd 11783
(212) 408-5100 .. **Richardson,** Morghan L '08 %Chadbourne & P LLP -30 Rckfllr Plz -NY 10112
(845) 454-3250 .. **Richardson,** Pamela E '00 %Gellert & K,PC -75 Wshngtn -Poughkeepsie 12601
(646) 755-7391 .. **Richardson & Patel, LLP** -750 3rd Av -NY 10017 **Fx:**(917) 591-6898
(585) 454-3616 .. **Richardson,** Paul E '79 %MA Bjork -2 State -Rchstr 14614 **Fx:**454-3664
(212) 573-7805 .. **Richardson,** Peter C '78 %Pfizer Inc -150 E 42nd -NY 10017 **Fx:**573-1445
(585) 567-2222 .. **Richardson & Pullen,PC** -21 Minard Bx182 -Fillmore 14735 **Fx:**567-2221
(716) 278-1816 .. **Richardson,** Robt N '05 Supreme Ct -775 3rd -Niagara Fls 14302
(718) 625-6777 .. **Richardson,** Sean K '92 (Jones R PC) -32 Court -Brklyn 11201 **Fx:**625-6977
(212) 504-6000 .. **Richardson,** Sharon J '88 SpclCnsl Cadwalader W&T LLP -1 World Fncl Ctr -NY 10281
(631) 929-3632 .. **Richardson,** Stephen M '74 -Bx958 -Wading Rvr 11792
(212) 371-3200 .. **Richardson,** Yolanda C '87 %Carnegie Corp -437 Mad Av -NY 10022 **Fx:**754-4073
(212) 975-4321 .. **Richburg,** Jos F '05 %CBS Inc -51 W 52nd -NY 10019 **Fx:**975-3930
(212) 267-1650 .. **Richemard,** Marjorie '99 %Fine O&A,LLP -39 Bway -NY 10006
(212) 637-2200 .. **Richenthal,** Danl C '06 %US Atty -1 St Andrews Plz -NY 10007
(631) 812-6570 .. **Richenthal,** Donald I '73 Leviton Manufacturing Co Inc -201 N Srvc Rd -Melvll 11747
(518) 435-8092 .. **Richer,** Marshall P '85 %Finkelstein & Prtnrs,LLP -80 Wolf Rd -Albany 12205

(716) 842-5762 .. **Richert,** Hedyanne '94 %M & T Bk -1 M & T Plz -Buffalo 14203
(212) 541-2000 .. **Richetti,** Jos J '99 (Bryan C LLP) -1290 Av of Amer -NY 10104
(315) 379-2217 .. **Richey,** John F '88 %Surrogates Ct -48 Court -Canton 13617 **Fx:**379-2372
(212) 326-3939 .. **Richey,** Kent R '87 (Jones D) -222 E 41st -NY 10017
(212) 596-9000 .. **Richheimer,** Jessica J '09 %Ropes & G LLP -1211 Av of Amer -NY 10036
(212) 265-6888 .. **Richheimer,** Todd C '09 %Porzio B&N,PC -156 W 56th -NY 10019
(212) 633-6967 .. **Richie,** Brooke J '05 Natl Ctr Law & Economic Justice -275 7th Av -NY 10001 **Fx:**633-6371
(212) 556-1995 .. **Richieri,** Kenneth '77 %The NY Times Co -620 8th Av -NY 10018 **Fx:**556-4634
(516) 678-7100 .. **Richland,** Danl H '08 G Lisi -55 Front -Rockvll Ctr 11570 **Fx:**536-9548
(212) 656-6204 .. **Richman,** Andrew D '93 NYSE EuroNext -11 Wall -NY 10005
(212) 854-2675 .. **Richman,** Danl C '86 %Columbia Law Schl -435 W 116th -NY 10027 **Fx:**854-7946
(914) 220-0038 .. **Richman,** David A '05 (Pattison & F) -1 N Lex Av -White Plns 10601
(516) 357-3000 .. **Richman,** David E '83 (Rivkin R LLP) -926 RXR Plz -Uniondale 11556
(212) 687-1425 .. **Richman,** David M '65 -360 Lex Av -NY 10017 **Fx:**682-6425
(315) 428-1380 .. **Richman,** Donnaline '78 %Fager & A,LLP -2 Clinton Sq -Syracuse 13202
(212) 701-3000 .. **Richman,** Elizabeth A '06 %Cahill G&R LLP -80 Pine -NY 10005 **Fx:**269-5420
(212) 468-8000 .. **Richman,** Emily S '04 %Morrison & F LLP -1290 Av of Amer -NY 10104
(212) 688-3965 .. **Richman,** Eric B '98 -188 E 64th -NY 10065 **Fx:**688-6007
(212) 487-9700 .. **Richman,** Evan A '99 (White F&F,LLP) -61 Bway -NY 10006
(516) 437-6443 .. **Richman,** Fredrick J '81 %Solomon R,PC -3000 Marcus Av -Lk Success 11042
(212) 695-3800 .. **Richman,** Gabriella F '94 %inMotion,Inc -70 W 36th -NY 10018 **Fx:**695-9519
(845) 271-4633 .. **Richman,** Howard S '78 (Grant R,PLLC) -Lbrty Bldg Route 9W -Stony Pnt 10980 **Fx:**(212) 202-3511
(212) 972-1100 .. **Richman,** Iris S '82 (Sylvor & R) -122 E 42nd -NY 10158 **Fx:**983-5271
(716) 634-0500 .. **Richman,** Jason A '97 %Ballow Law Firm -8226 Main -Williamsvll 14221 **Fx:**634-9075
(212) 683-7100 .. **Richman,** Jeffrey L '91 (Gallo V&K,LLP) -90 Broad -NY 10004
(212) 259-8000 .. **Richman,** Jonathan E '84 (Dewey & L LLP) -1301 Av of Amer -NY 10019
(212) 687-1425 .. **Richman,** Judith R '77 (Sonnenfeld & R) -360 Lex Av -NY 10017
(516) 228-9444 .. **Richman,** Keith H '78 (Richman & L,PC) -666 Old Cntry Rd -Gdn Cty 11530 **Fx:**228-9514
(212) 687-8291 .. **Richman,** Kim Eleazer '03 (Reese R LLP) -875 6th Av 18th Fl -NY 10001 **Fx:**253-4272
(212) 227-1914 .. **Richman,** Labe M '83 -305 Bway -NY 10007 **Fx:**267-2129
(917) 617-8811 .. **Richman,** Marla D '04 Priss & Empress Designs -888 8th Av -NY 10019
(212) 536-3900 .. **Richman,** Martin F '53 OfCnsl K&L Gates LLP -599 Lex Av -NY 10022
(212) 788-0738 .. **Richman,** Mary '89 %Law Dept -100 Church -NY 10007 **Fx:**788-0367
(914) 761-8084 .. **Richman,** Michl '70 -399 Knollwood Rd -White Plns 10603 **Fx:**761-8401
(212) 497-2977 .. **Richman,** Michl N '09 Fortress Invstmnt Grp LLC -1345 Av of Amer -NY 10105
(646) 557-5100 .. **Richman,** Michl P '79 (Patton B LLP) -1185 Av of Amer -NY 10036
(212) 668-0059 .. **Richman,** Michele A '07 %Zalman & S -61 Bway -NY 10006
(212) 768-6700 .. **Richman,** Monica B '02 (Sonnenschein N&R LLP) -1221 Av of Amer -NY 10020
(718) 892-8588 .. **Richman,** Murray '64 -2027 Wllmsbrdg Rd -Bronx 10461 **Fx:**518-0674
(212) 556-1760 .. **Richman,** Nancy E '89 %The NY Times Co -620 8th Av -NY 10018 **Fx:**556-4634
(212) 756-2000 .. **Richman,** Ronald E '82 (Schulte R&Z LLP) -919 3rd Av -NY 10022
(212) 885-0868 .. **Richman,** Scott A '95 %AJJDC -711 3rd Av -NY 10017
(718) 892-8588 .. **Richman,** Stacey '92 -2027 Wllmsbrdg Rd -Bronx 10461 **Fx:**518-0674
(212) 320-5715 .. **Richman,** Steven F '85 %East Side Capital -888 7th Av -NY 10106
(212) 487-5338 .. **Richman,** Steven H '84 Cnsl NYC Bd of Elections -32 Bway -NY 10004 **Fx:**487-5342
(609) 631-2426 .. **Richman,** Steven M '81 (Duane M LLP) -1540 Bway -NY 10036 **Fx:**631-2401
(516) 571-2797 .. **Richman,** Susan Katz '80 %Hon W Donnino -262 Old Cntry Rd -Mineola 11501
(516) 437-6443 .. **Richman,** Theo C '78 (Solomon R,PC) -3000 Marcus Av -Lk Success 11042
(212) 701-3000 .. **Richman,** Valery '10 %Cahill G&R LLP -80 Pine -NY 10005 **Fx:**269-5420
(718) 239-8000 .. **Richman-Epstein,** Risa '89 Cnsl Epstein & Assoc -Bx1278 -Bellmore 11710
(716) 881-6593 .. **Richmond,** Anna Marie '85 OfCnsl R Wyssling -375 Linwood Av -Buffalo 14209 **Fx:**883-7649
(212) 468-4800 .. **Richmond,** Brooke E '06 %Davis & G LLP -1740 Bway -NY 10019
(518) 463-5400 .. **Richmond,** Bryan D '04 %Goldberg S LLP -8 Southwoods Blvd -Albany 12211
(212) 878-7900 .. **Richmond,** Carolyn D '95 (Fox R LLP) -100 Park Av -NY 10017
(315) 342-4092 .. **Richmond,** Christopher R '90 SpclCnsl Hinman H&K,LLP -40 W Cayuga -Oswego 13126
(914) 682-7800 .. **Richmond,** Danl M '95 (Zarin & S) -81 Main -White Plns 10601
(212) 294-6700 .. **Richmond,** Harlee A '99 (Winston & S) -200 Park Av -NY 10166
(315) 797-9261 .. **Richmond,** Janet M '81 (Getnick LA&P,LLP) -258 Genesee -Utica 13502
(212) 558-5500 .. **Richmond,** John E '10 %Weitz & L,PC -700 Bway -NY 10003
(212) 909-6000 .. **Richmond,** Jonathan E '97 %Debevoise & P LLP -919 3rd Av -NY 10022
(914) 328-0340 .. **Richmond,** Paul S '74 -99 Court -White Plns 10601 **Fx:**761-7707
(914) 632-3399 .. **Richmond,** Sara M '90 -49 Overlook Cir -New Rchll 10804
(845) 357-0036 .. **Richmond,** Susan Mills '79 %Lexow B&A,PC -56 Park Av Bx239 -Suffern 10901
(631) 261-8834 .. **Richmond,** Warren H III '73 (Ingerman S LLP) -150 Motor Pkwy -Hauppauge 11788
(516) 569-4000 .. **Richner,** Clifford '79 %Richner Communications -2 Endo Blvd -Gdn Cty 11530 **Fx:**569-4942
(516) 569-4000 .. **Richner,** Stuart '82 %Richner Communications -2 Endo Blvd -Gdn Cty 11530 **Fx:**569-4942
(212) 725-7111 .. **Richter,** Aimee L '94 (Bender Rl&R LLP) -451 Park Av S -NY 10016
(212) 425-3100 .. **Richter,** Anne P '91 (McManus C&R,PC) -48 Wall -NY 10005
(212) 859-8000 .. **Richter,** Brad J '92 (Fried FHS&J LLP) -1 NY Plz -NY 10004
(212) 244-2999 .. **Richter,** Catherine R '88 (Kopff N&D LLP) -440 9th Av -NY 10001
(516) 365-9802 .. **Richter,** Elizabeth Collard '95 %Collard & R,PC -1077 Nrthrn Blvd -Roslyn 11576
(212) 460-4615 .. **Richter,** Marc '77 Con Ed -4 Irving Pl -NY 10003 **Fx:**677-5850
(212) 761-7869 .. **Richter,** Maria Del Carmen '84 Morgan Stanley -1585 Bway -NY 10036
(212) 788-0931 .. **Richter,** Marilyn '79 %Law Dept -100 Church -NY 10007 **Fx:**788-0367
(518) 462-5601 .. **Richter,** Mark G '95 (O'Connell & A) -54 State -Albany 12207
(212) 425-7200 .. **Richter,** Paul M Jr. '93 (Kenyon & K,LLP) -1 Bway -NY 10004
(212) 859-8000 .. **Richter,** Philip '95 (Fried FHS&J LLP) -1 NY Plz -NY 10004
(718) 848-6940 .. **Richter,** Roy T '99 (Bifulco & R,LLP) -160-36 91st -Howard Bch 11414 **Fx:**848-6664
(518) 387-4542 .. **Richter,** Stephanie L '04 Cnsl GE Co -1 Rsrch Cir -Niskayuna 12309
(212) 250-8193 .. **Richter,** Victoria Lee '95 %Deutsche Bank -60 Wall -NY 10005
(631) 470-3574 .. **Ricigliano,** Michl J '61 (Margiotta & R) -425 Broadhllw Rd -Melvll 11747
(631) 470-3574 .. **Ricigliano,** Michl T '99 (Margiotta & R) -425 Broadhllw Rd -Melvll 11747
(212) 637-2486 .. **Ricigliano,** Rebecca M '00 US Atty -1 St Andrews Plz -NY 10007
(212) 725-5755 .. **Ricigliano,** Wm '95 W Ricigliano,PC -232 Mad Av -NY 10016 **Fx:**532-4809
(212) 422-0488 .. **Rick,** Jay H '54 OfCnsl Rick SF&B,LLP -90 Broad -NY 10004
(212) 422-0488 .. **Rick Steiner Fell & Benowitz, LLP** -90 Broad -NY 10004 **Fx:**422-0158
(212) 735-3000 .. **Rickard,** Jill L '05 %Skadden ASM&F LLP -4 Times Sq -NY 10036
(212) 626-4100 .. **Rickards,** Clinton S II '10 %Baker & M LLP -1114 Av of Amer -NY 10036
(631) 821-8140 .. **Rickerby,** Vanessa '89 %Shoreham-Wdng Rvr High Schl -Route 25 A -Shoreham 11786
(716) 945-3060 .. **Rickert,** Thos W '81 (Congdon PD&R) -107 Main -Salamanca 14779
(718) 863-5071 .. **Ricketts,** Gail D '85 G Ricketts PC -Bx377 -Vly Cottage 10989
(716) 652-0828 .. **Ricketts,** Jay W '74 (Hall RM&G) -471 Main -E Aurora 14052
(212) 692-9666 .. **Rickles,** Frederic P '92 OfCnsl Gilbride TL&S LLC -708 3rd Av -NY 10017
(212) 687-3000 .. **Rickman,** Margaret A '00 %Jaffe & A,LLP -600 3rd Av -NY 10016
(718) 972-8484 .. **Rickman,** Steven S '80 -218 Foster Av -Brklyn 11230
(212) 753-5000 .. **Rickner,** Robt H III '06 %Schiff H LLP -900 3rd Av -NY 10022
(631) 852-8800 .. **Rickoff,** Tanya M '08 %DA -116 Hmptn Rd -Southampton 11968 **Fx:**852-8806
(212) 527-5624 .. **Ricks,** H Timothy '79 %Revlon -237 Park Av -NY 10017 **Fx:**527-5299
(845) 246-7600 .. **Ricks,** Wendy S '90 WS Ricks,PC -172 Main -Saugerties 12477 **Fx:**246-7660
(518) 436-0775 .. **Rico,** Salvatore J '66 %Proskin,PC -423 Loudon Rd -Albany 12211 **Fx:**436-0014
(516) 285-8867 .. **Riconda & Garnett,LLP** -753 W Merrick Rd -Vly Stream 11580 **Fx:**285-1210
(516) 285-8867 .. **Riconda,** John '83 (Riconda & G,LLP) -753 W Merrick Rd -Vly Stream 11580
(212) 878-8000 .. **Ricotta,** Alfred Q '00 %Clifford C LLP -31 W 52nd -NY 10019
(716) 854-6424 .. **Ricotta,** Kevin A '83 (K Ricotta) -350 Main -Buffalo 14202 **Fx:**854-6425
(212) 935-3000 .. **Ricotta,** Paul J '83 Mintz LCFG&P,PC -666 3rd Av -NY 10017
(716) 856-9533 .. **Ridall,** Barbara Roth '85 %Hartman & R PC -403 Main -Buffalo 14203
(212) 815-1818 .. **Riday,** Elizabeth B '89 %DC 37 MELS -125 Barclay -NY 10007 **Fx:**815-1343
(212) 841-1000 .. **Ridberg,** Maia A '08 %Covington & B LLP -620 8th Av -NY 10018
(212) 446-4800 .. **Ridder,** Allison Horsman '06 %Kirkland & E LLP -153 E 53rd -NY 10022
(518) 463-7784 .. **Riddett,** Kenneth E '76 -75 Columbia -Albany 12210 **Fx:**463-4039
(718) 833-0516 .. **Riddle,** John R '90 (Riddle Claims Cnsltng Inc) -7804 3rd Av -Brklyn 11209 **Fx:**833-0673
(718) 833-0516 .. **Riddle,** Leslie A '91 (Riddle Claims Cnsltng Inc) -7804 3rd Av -Brklyn 11209 **Fx:**833-0673
(716) 636-7600 .. **Riddle,** Tammy L '04 %HoganWillig -2410 N Forest Rd -Amherst 14068
(212) 223-4000 .. **Riddles,** Andrew M '85 (Crowell & M LLP) -590 Mad Av -NY 10022
(212) 859-8000 .. **Ridealgh,** Damian P '08 (Fried FHS&J LLP) -1 NY Plz -NY 10004
(212) 735-3000 .. **Rideout,** Patrick G '08 %Skadden ASM&F LLP -4 Times Sq -NY 10036
(845) 876-2703 .. **Rider,** Caroline V '76 (Wyner & R) -42 E Market -Red Hook 12571 **Fx:**876-2703
(212) 297-5800 .. **Rider,** Christopher M '00 Cnsl Day P LLP -7 Times Sq -NY 10036
(845) 562-9100 .. **Rider,** David L '66 (Rider W&F,PC) -655 Little Britain Rd -New Windsor 12553
(845) 562-9100 .. **Rider,** M Justin '96 %Rider W&F,PC -655 Little Britain Rd -New Windsor 12553
(518) 884-4770 .. **Rider,** Mark M '75 (Cnty Atty) -Cnty Mncpl Ctr -Ballston Spa 12020 **Fx:**884-4720
(845) 562-9100 .. **Rider Weiner & Frankel,PC** -655 Little Britain Rd -New Windsor 12553 **Fx:**562-9126
(607) 737-2944 .. **Rider-Ulacco,** Susan R '02 %DA -226 Lk Bx588 -Elmira 14902 **Fx:**737-2965
(718) 590-5400 .. **Ridge,** Michl T '75 -910 Grnd Cncrs -Bronx 10451 **Fx:**681-0285
(718) 590-5400 .. **Ridge,** Peter T '03 %M Ridge -910 Grnd Cncrs -Bronx 10451 **Fx:**681-0285
(718) 250-2000 .. **Ridges,** Thos C '00 %DA -350 Jay -Brklyn 11201 **Fx:**250-2314
(914) 725-2181 .. **Ridgway,** Catherine M '91 -700 Wht Plns Post Rd -Scarsdale 10583 **Fx:**725-6160

(718) 990-5803 .. **Ridha**, Jennifer R '05 St John's Law Schl -8000 Utopia Pkwy -Jamaica 11439 **Fx:**591-1855
(718) 390-0580 .. **Ridi**, Marisa C '98 %CC DeStefano -1082 Victory Blvd -Staten Isl 10301 **Fx:**442-3563
(631) 261-3939 .. **Ridini**, Christopher J '91 -4 Morahapa Rd -Centerprt 11721 **Fx:**261-4466
(516) 794-7500 .. **Ridini**, Leonard M Jr. '84 OfCnsl Westermann SKS&A,LLP -333 Earle Ovngton Blvd -Uniondale 11553
(212) 697-7383 .. **Ridley**, Donald T '85 %Mandel Law Firm -370 Lex Av -NY 10017 **Fx:**681-6157
(212) 538-2935 .. **Ridloff**, Jason B '02 CSFB -11 Mad Av -NY 10010
(212) 455-2000 .. **Rie**, Jennifer '00 %Simpson T&B LLP -425 Lex Av -NY 10017
(518) 371-0111 .. **Riebel**, David L '67 -521 Vischer Ferry Rd Bx405 -Clifton Pk 12065
(518) 373-4940 .. **Riebel**, Erika L '95 -521 Vischer Ferry Rd Bx405 -Clifton Pk 12065 **Fx:**371-4136
(845) 794-0363 .. **Rieber**, Nicole M '04 -390 Bway Bx1435 -Monticello 12701 **Fx:**(800) 530-7945
(914) 946-4808 .. **Riebling**, Stephen J '97 (Riebling P&S,LLP) -1 N Bway -White Plns 10601 **Fx:**287-7578
(212) 619-3730 .. **Rieck**, John J Jr. '72 (Doar RK&M) -217 Bway -NY 10007
(212) 903-9000 .. **Riecker**, Richd B '07 %Linklaters -1345 Av of Amer -NY 10105
(212) 728-8000 .. **Ried**, Wm M '83 OfCnsl Willkie F&G LLP -787 7th Av -NY 10019
(212) 450-4000 .. **Riedel**, Adam D '10 %Davis P&W LLP -450 Lex Av -NY 10017
(716) 849-1333 .. **Riedel**, George E Jr. '73 (Lipsitz GSC LLP) -42 Delaware Av -Buffalo 14202
(212) 541-2000 .. **Rieder**, Eric '87 (Bryan C LLP) -1290 Av of Amer -NY 10104
(718) 972-2002 .. **Rieder**, Stanley H '82 -1677 48th -Brklyn 11204 **Fx:**851-2686
(646) 471-6786 .. **Riedman**, Wm D '90 %PricewaterhouseCoopers LLP -300 Mad Av -NY 10017
(914) 827-2696 .. **Riedy**, Kathleen M '91 -Bx842 -Croton-On-Hud 10520 **Fx:**827-2698
(214) 466-4000 .. **Rief**, Carrie J '05 %Morgan L&B LLP -101 Park Av -NY 10178 **Fx:**466-4001
(646) 315-7300 .. **Riefberg**, Linda '85 %FINRA -14 Wall -NY 10005 **Fx:**315-7440
(516) 294-1700 .. **Rieff**, Saml E '78 -100 Grdn City Plz -Gdn Cty 11530 **Fx:**294-7203
(516) 295-3208 .. **Riegel**, Arthur A '95 -1 Willow Ln -Hewlett 11557 **Fx:**295-3208
(212) 867-6000 .. **Riegel**, Deborah E '94 (Rosenberg & E,PC) -733 3rd Av -NY 10017
(212) 450-4000 .. **Riegel**, Joerg P '06 %Davis P&W LLP -450 Lex Av -NY 10017
(212) 223-3900 .. **Riegel**, Stephen J '86 SrCnsl Zwerling S&Z,LLP -41 Mad Av -NY 10010
(212) 986-6000 .. **Rieger**, Alexis I '08 %Kleinberg KW&C,PC -551 5th Av -NY 10176
(212) 508-6700 .. **Rieger**, James '97 (Tannenbaum HS&H LLP) -900 3rd Av -NY 10022
(631) 261-6400 .. **Rieger**, John T '87 (Rieger & W,LLP) -199 Main -Northprt 11768
(516) 222-1350 .. **Rieger**, Kieth I '80 (Barrocas & R) -100 Q Roosevelt Blvd -Gdn Cty 11530
(845) 782-8333 .. **Rieger**, Steven E '78 -6 Old North Plnk Rd -Newburgh 12550
(518) 473-8418 .. **Rieger**, Steven E '85 OCFS -52 Wshngtn -Rensselaer 12144 **Fx:**486-6361
(631) 261-6400 .. **Rieger & Walsh,LLP** -199 Main -Northprt 11768 **Fx:**261-6431
(631) 874-2570 .. **Riegger**, Patricia S '93 -449 Uppr Mdlnd Pond Ct -Moriches 11955
(631) 608-4114 .. **Riegler**, Glenn S '94 (Riegler & B) -532 Broad Hollow Rd -Melvll 11747 **Fx:**396-1399
(516) 626-2900 .. **Riegler**, Jeffrey S '96 Glen Oaks Club -175 Post Rd Bx249 -Old Westbury 11568
(212) 909-6000 .. **Riehl**, Carl W '96 Cnsl Debevoise & P LLP -919 3rd Av -NY 10022
(716) 847-2523 .. **Riehler**, Michl A '92 (Sugarman Law Firm,LLP) -14 Lafayette Sq -Buffalo 14203
(315) 696-8918 .. **Riehlman Shafer & Shafer** -397 Route 281 Bx430 -Tully 13159 **Fx:**696-6019
(607) 756-4006 .. **Riehlman Shafer & Shafer** -39 Church -Cortlnd 13045 **Fx:**753-0182
(315) 696-8918 .. **Riehlman**, Timothy G '76 OfCnsl Riehlman S&S -397 Route 281 Bx430 -Tully 13159
(212) 221-6900 .. **Rieker**, Christina M '07 Winget S&S,LLP -45 Bway -NY 10006
(631) 756-4021 .. **Riekstins**, Janis M '80 %State Ins Fund -8 Corp Ctr Dr -Melvll 11747 **Fx:**756-4060
(212) 906-1200 .. **Riela**, Michl J '02 %Latham & W -885 3rd Av -NY 10022
(518) 474-3494 .. **Riell**, Dana '82 %State Comptroller -110 State -Albany 12236 **Fx:**473-9104
(212) 336-0535 .. **Riely**, Chas D '02 %SEC -3 World Fncl Ctr -NY 10281 **Fx:**336-1323
(212) 837-3643 .. **Rieman**, Barry D '86 JP Morgan Chase -530 5th Av -NY 10036
(716) 938-9111 .. **Rieman**, Lori Pettit '97 DA -303 Court -Little Vly 14755
(212) 373-3000 .. **Rieman**, Walter R '87 (Paul WRW&G LLP) -1285 Av of Amer -NY 10019
(212) 836-8000 .. **Riemer**, Danl S '09 %Kaye S LLP -425 Park Av -NY 10022
(516) 482-4118 .. **Riemer**, Ellen C '90 -42 Arrandale Av -Gt Neck 11024
(212) 509-3456 .. **Riemer**, Jason S '83 %McGivney & K,PC -80 Broad -NY 10004
(718) 261-7700 .. **Riemer**, Keith J '87 Rappaport HC&R,PC -118-35 Qns Blvd -Frst Hlls 11375
(212) 806-5400 .. **Riemer**, Keri E '04 %Stroock &S&L LLP -180 Maiden Ln -NY 10038
(212) 977-9700 .. **Riemer**, Sandra A '78 (Phillips N LLP) -666 5th Av -NY 10103
(212) 297-0700 .. **Riemer**, Scott '84 Riemer & Assoc,LLC -60 E 42nd -NY 10165
(212) 446-4800 .. **Riemer**, Yosef J '95 (Kirkland & E LLP) -153 E 53rd -NY 10022
(315) 379-2115 .. **Riendeau**, Bradford C '89 Pub Def -Cnty Cthse -Canton 13617 **Fx:**386-8241
(212) 512-1000 .. **Rienecker**, Peter R '86 %HBO -1100 Av of Amer -NY 10036 **Fx:**512-1986
(212) 335-9902 .. **Rienzi**, Peter M '06 %DA -1 Hogan Pl -NY 10013
(518) 783-4767 .. **Ries**, Chas B '65 (Wertime R&V,PC) -930 Albany Shaker Rd -Latham 12110
(518) 640-0270 .. **Ries**, Theresa Marinello '00 Marinello Ries LLC -142 Catherine -Albany 12202 **Fx:**640-6141
(212) 421-2150 .. **Riesel**, Danl '61 (Sive P&R,PC) -460 Park Av -NY 10022
(212) 885-5000 .. **Riesel**, Sheila Ginsberg '69 (Blank R LLP) -405 Lex Av -NY 10174
(212) 909-6000 .. **Riesenhuber**, Eva E '05 %Debevoise & P LLP -919 3rd Av -NY 10022
(212) 836-8000 .. **Rieser**, Ilene T '05 %Kaye S LLP -425 Park Av -NY 10022
(212) 279-4490 .. **Rieser**, Richd L '08 %D Bleckner,PC -350 5th Av -NY 10118 **Fx:**279-4495
(212) 586-5800 .. **Riess**, Yeu Ting '08 %Cohen TS&W PC -420 Lex Av -NY 10170
(518) 462-3000 .. **Riester**, Fredk C '68 SrCnsl Iseman CR&H,LLP -9 Thurlow Ter -Albany 12203
(212) 609-6800 .. **Riester**, Zane C '04 %McCarter & E,LLP -245 Park Av -NY 10167
(212) 225-2000 .. **Rietema**, Jamie L '10 %Cleary GS&H -1 Lbrty Plz -NY 10006
(585) 232-6520 .. **Rieth**, Wm C '85 -16 W Main -Rchstr 14614 **Fx:**325-5536
(716) 847-8400 .. **Rieth**, Wm L '48 OfCnsl Phillips L LLP -3400 HSBC Ctr -Buffalo 14203
(212) 790-9200 .. **Riether**, Robt A '07 %Cowan L&L,PC -1133 Av of Amer -NY 10036
(212) 735-3000 .. **Rievman**, David M '88 (Skadden ASM&F LLP) -4 Times Sq -NY 10036
(212) 689-8808 .. **Rievman**, Joshua D '91 (Hoguet NR&K,LLP) -10 E 40th -NY 10016
(631) 337-1977 .. **Riezenman**, Ryan A '06 %C Petroske,PC -4875 Sunrise Hwy -Bohemia 11716 **Fx:**337-1966
(212) 269-1600 .. **Riezman**, Joshua M '09 %Teigland-Hunt LLP -127 W 24th -NY 10011 **Fx:**269-1580
(917) 534-4943 .. **Rifai**, Ali E '86 Centre Grp Holdings -105 E 17th -NY 10003
(212) 953-2381 .. **Rifai**, Ronnie M '07 %Rubin F&F,LLP -292 Mad Av -NY 10017
(212) 863-6300 .. **Rifenburgh**, Mary Lynn E '86 %HPD -100 Gold -NY 10038
(212) 722-2000 .. **Riff**, Stephen F '90 %Leg Aid -230 E 106th -NY 10029 **Fx:**876-5365
(212) 556-3993 .. **Riffaterre**, Lee K '87 %The NY Times Co -620 8th Av -NY 10018 **Fx:**556-4634
(212) 250-7628 .. **Riffaud**, Marcelo L '92 %Deutsche Bank -60 Wall -NY 10005
(212) 510-0500 .. **Riffkin**, Linda A '86 %US Trustees Ofc -33 Whitehall -NY 10004 **Fx:**668-2255
(212) 723-7921 .. **Rifkin**, Alan M '91 Citigroup -390 Greenwich -NY 10013
(212) 349-3420 .. **Rifkin**, David B '91 %AM Cass -225 Bway -NY 10007 **Fx:**349-3462
(716) 510-5333 .. **Rifkin**, Hillary B '95 Eli Lilly & Co -118 Crosby Blvd -Amherst 14226
(212) 545-4762 .. **Rifkin**, Mark C '05 (Wolf HAF&H LLP) -270 Mad Av -NY 10016 **Fx:**545-4726
(518) 463-3200 .. **Rifkin**, Richd '66 NYS Bar Assn -1 Elk -Albany 12207 **Fx:**487-5544
(212) 770-8124 .. **Rifkin**, Ronnie A '89 AIG -70 Pine -NY 10270 **Fx:**943-4334
(212) 867-4466 .. **Rifkin**, Wm M '76 (Belkin BW&G,LLP) -270 Mad Av -NY 10016
(212) 756-2000 .. **Rifkind**, Neil C '99 %Schulte R&Z LLP -919 3rd Av -NY 10022
(212) 474-1000 .. **Rifkind**, Robt S '61 SrCnsl Cravath S&M LLP -825 8th Av -NY 10019
(631) 979-3000 .. **Rigano**, James P '82 (Certilman BA&H,LLP) -1393 Vets Mem'l Hwy -Hauppauge 11788
(212) 478-7200 .. **Rigano**, Nicholas C '09 %Hahn & H LLP -488 Mad Av -NY 10022
(631) 589-4774 .. **Rigas**, Dennis '80 -139 Homestead Rd -Oakdale 11769
(518) 486-2652 .. **Rigberg**, Saul '87 %Dept Pub Srvc -3 ESP -Albany 12223
(212) 293-8900 .. **Rigby**, Ellen November J '88 Emmes Asset Mgt Co LLC -420 Lex Av -NY 10170 **Fx:**293-8805
(212) 629-7575 .. **Rigby**, Kenneth A '85 -19 Fulton -NY 10038
(212) 715-9100 .. **Rigel**, Blake A '02 %Kramer LN&F,LLP -1177 Av of Amer -NY 10036
(212) 977-7033 .. **Rigelhaupt**, Peter D '89 Perecman Firm PLLC -250 W 57th -NY 10107
(212) 969-3000 .. **Riger**, Jody Sue '02 %Proskauer R LLP -1585 Bway -NY 10036
(212) 697-3122 .. **Riger**, Lee E '07 %Martin C&B LLP -220 E 42nd -NY 10017
(518) 474-6124 .. **Riggi**, Bonnie J '94 %Dept of Law -The Cptl -Albany 12224
(518) 377-8808 .. **Riggi**, Dean A '86 -101 Mohawk Av -Scotia 12302 **Fx:**346-3023
(212) 539-6703 .. **Riggio**, Karen M '83 -1562 1st Av -NY 10028 **Fx:**(203) 968-0349
(914) 948-1200 .. **Riggs**, Peter '96 (Cerussi & S,PC) -1 N Lex Av -White Plns 10601
(212) 594-5300 .. **Riggs**, Roland W IV '05 %Milberg LLP -1 Penn Plz -NY 10119
(212) 902-1426 .. **Riggs**, Thos S III '89 %Goldman Sachs -1 NY Plz -NY 10004
(914) 304-4082 .. **Rigie**, Lawr '80 -75 S Bway -White Plns 10601 **Fx:**304-4089
(212) 422-1200 .. **Rigney**, Alexandra E '06 %Abrams GF&J,PC -1 Bttry Pk Plz -NY 10004
(212) 574-1200 .. **Rigney**, John F '85 (Seward & K LLP) -1 Bttry Pk Plz -NY 10004
(212) 651-7500 .. **Rigolosi**, Robt R '01 %Segal MS&M -850 3rd Av -NY 10022
(845) 462-3390 .. **Rihn**, Jos A '77 -Bx1843 -Poughkeepsie 12601
(212) 403-1000 .. **Riina**, Andrea '96 %Wachtell LR&K -51 W 52nd -NY 10019
(518) 299-3333 .. **Rikard**, David A '89 -14602 Main Bx68 -Prattsville 12468 **Fx:**299-3339
(212) 302-6574 .. **Riker Danzig Scherer Hyland & Perretti LLP** -500 5th Av -NY 10110 **Fx:**302-6628
(315) 448-0672 .. **Riker**, Elizabeth S '86 %US Atty -100 S Clinton Bx7198 -Syracuse 13261 **Fx:**448-0689
(518) 452-0171 .. **Riker**, Katherine E '86 American Corp & Title Srvcs -678 Troy-Schnctdy Rd -Latham 12110 **Fx:**690-0760
(212) 661-6410 .. **Riker**, Steven M '95 -110 E 59th -NY 10022 **Fx:**994-2146
(212) 349-6775 .. **Rikhye**, Bhalinder L '79 (Peltz & W) -222 Bway -NY 10038
(212) 350-2700 .. **Rikkers**, Saml H '08 %Constantine C,PC -450 Lex Av -NY 10017
(212) 422-4000 .. **Rikon**, Joshua H '03 (Goldstein R&R) -80 Pine -NY 10005
(212) 422-4000 .. **Rikon**, Michl '70 (Goldstein R&R) -80 Pine -NY 10005
(914) 834-3500 .. **Rikoon**, Gary M '78 (McMillan CM&P LLP) -2180 Bstn Post Rd -Larchmnt 10538
(212) 909-6000 .. **Rikoon**, Jonathan J '80 (Debevoise & P LLP) -919 3rd Av -NY 10022
(212) 596-9000 .. **Rile**, Christopher W '97 (Ropes & G LLP) -1211 Av of Amer -NY 10036
(212) 530-5000 .. **Riley**, Brendan M '09 %Milbank TH&M LLP -1 Chase Manh Plz -NY 10005
(585) 987-2800 .. **Riley**, Brian P '10 %Woods OG LLP -2 State -Rchstr 14614
(212) 735-3000 .. **Riley**, Carl '89 Cnsl Skadden ASM&F LLP -4 Times Sq -NY 10036
(914) 428-4010 .. **Riley**, Christopher '83 -56 Greenrdg Av -White Plns 10605 **Fx:**948-4177
(212) 225-2000 .. **Riley**, Danl P '09 %Cleary GS&H -1 Lbrty Plz -NY 10006
(212) 383-2509 .. **Riley**, David '86 State Comptroller -59 Maiden Ln -NY 10038 **Fx:**383-3901
(585) 637-2310 .. **Riley**, Edw W '72 -21-25 Market -Brockprt 14420 **Fx:**637-2839
(585) 428-5210 .. **Riley**, Elizabeth Anne '99 %Pub Def -10 N Fitzhugh -Rchstr 14614 **Fx:**428-2234
(315) 462-3010 .. **Riley & Graff** -26 E Main Bx604 -Clifton Spgs 14432 **Fx:**462-5039
(845) 735-5050 .. **Riley**, James K '71 (O'Connell & R) -144 E Central Av Bx1050 -Pearl Rvr 10965
(518) 736-5511 .. **Riley**, James P '05 %DA -223 W Main -Johnstwn 12095 **Fx:**762-2042
(646) 284-6867 .. **Riley**, Jan Hudgins '93 -Bx708 -Parksvll 12768 **Fx:**(845) 292-1479
(212) 455-2000 .. **Riley**, John E '89 OfCnsl Simpson T&B LLP -425 Lex Av -NY 10017
(315) 462-3010 .. **Riley**, John F '66 OfCnsl Riley & G -26 E Main Bx604 -Clifton Spgs 14432
(212) 752-9700 .. **Riley**, John H '78 (Gersten S LLP) -600 Lex Av -NY 10022

(212) 728-8000 .. **Riley,** Jos A '06 (Willkie F&G LLP) -787 7th Av -NY 10019

(212) 625-2525 .. **Riley,** Julian D Jr. '97 -51 MacDougal -NY 10012 **Fx:**226-1775

(845) 291-2670 .. **Riley,** Karen A '96 %Childrens Rts Society -213 W Main Bx1002 -Goshen 10924 **Fx:**291-2679

(631) 287-3972 .. **Riley,** Linda '79 -235 Hmptn Rd -Southampton 11968

(518) 473-5115 .. **Riley,** Lori J '83 %Ofc for Technology -State Cptl ESP Bx2062 -Albany 12220

(212) 373-3000 .. **Riley,** Maureen A '98 Cnsl Paul WRW&G LLP -1285 Av of Amer -NY 10019

(212) 226-5054 .. **Riley,** Michelle K '09 %Powley & G,PC -304 Hudson -NY 10013 **Fx:**266-5085

(315) 254-4233 .. **Riley,** Robt L '86 -Bx938 -Syracuse 13201

(914) 750-5933 .. **Riley,** Samantha L '04 %Kissel H&W LLP -580 Wht Plns Rd -Tarrytwn 10591

(212) 408-5100 .. **Riley,** Thos E '80 (Chadbourne & P LLP) -30 Rckfllr Plz -NY 10112

(315) 942-4361 .. **Riley,** Wm J '76 Durr & R -322 Post Bx148 -Boonvll 13309 **Fx:**942-5671

(315) 422-1311 .. **Rill,** Thos A '71 OfCnsl Melvin & M,PLLC -217 S Salina -Syracuse 13202

(212) 536-3900 .. **Rim,** Eunice '08 %K&L Gates LLP -599 Lex Av -NY 10022

(212) 841-1204 .. **Rim,** James I '00 -620 8th Av -NY 10018 **Fx:**841-1010

(716) 631-3131 .. **Rimar,** Patrick G '71 -5467 Main -Williamsvll 14221

(212) 935-6020 .. **Rimas,** David C '05 %Klein ZR LLP -485 Mad Av -NY 10022

(212) 697-3250 .. **Rimberg,** Robt L '87 (Goldberg & R PLLC) -115 Bway -NY 10006 **Fx:**227-4533

(212) 326-3939 .. **Rimkunas,** Dennis '03 %Jones D -222 E 41st -NY 10017

(212) 374-0680 .. **Rimland,** Edw '82 (Rimland & Assoc) -225 Bway -NY 10007 **Fx:**374-0681

(212) 509-5050 .. **Rimland,** Jason M '00 SrCnsl Wuersch & G LLP -100 Wall -NY 10005

(212) 521-5400 .. **Rimm,** Harry H '96 Cnsl Reed S LLP -599 Lex Av -NY 10022

(516) 338-0793 .. **Rimmels,** Edw R '91 -22 Rugby Rd -Westbury 11590

(716) 852-1000 .. **Rimmler,** Anne Beltz '83 %PW Beltz,PC -36 Church -Buffalo 14202 **Fx:**852-5887

(716) 852-1000 .. **Rimmler,** Philipp L '83 %PW Beltz,PC -36 Church -Buffalo 14202 **Fx:**852-5887

(914) 761-1300 .. **Rimsky,** Neil T '78 (Cuddy & F LLP) -445 Hmltn Av -White Plns 10601

(315) 478-5820 .. **Rinaldi,** Angelo J '63 (Rinaldi Law Firm) -422 Univ Bldg -Syracuse 13202 **Fx:**478-5803

(212) 872-5934 .. **Rinaldi,** Benjamin M '02 KPMG LLP -345 Park Av -NY 10154

(718) 558-8352 .. **Rinaldi,** Catherine A '89 %LIRR -Jamaica Station -Jamaica 11435 **Fx:**558-8211

(914) 428-5730 .. **Rinaldi,** Edw '76 -175 Main -White Plns 10601 **Fx:**761-0995

(212) 340-2479 .. **Rinaldi,** Frank '92 Metro-North -347 Mad Av -NY 10017 **Fx:**697-9079

(212) 673-9723 .. **Rinaldi,** Frank R '51 -4 Peter Cooper Rd -NY 10010

(914) 750-5933 .. **Rinaldi,** Jennifer C '07 %Kissel H&W LLP -580 Wht Plns Rd -Tarrytwn 10591

(315) 475-2143 .. **Rinaldi,** John R '58 (J Rinaldi,PC) -125 Ross Park -Syracuse 13208 **Fx:**475-2031

(212) 450-4000 .. **Rinaldi,** Jos '85 (Davis P&W LLP) -450 Lex Av -NY 10017

(845) 471-3000 .. **Rinaldi,** Keith S '78 KS Rinaldi,PC -10 Arlngtn Av -Poughkeepsie 12603 **Fx:**471-3003

(212) 398-7900 .. **Rinaldi,** Lisa J '84 (Gerstein S&R LLP) -57 W 38th -NY 10018

(718) 777-8887 .. **Rinaldi,** Maximiliano '93 (Nanis & R,LLP) -30-97 Steinway -Astoria 11103

(718) 520-8722 .. **Rinaldo,** Paul P '73 (Grossman & R) -108-18 Qns Blvd -Frst Hlls 11375

(716) 884-6733 .. **Rinaldo,** Thos N '68 -305 Elmwood Av Bx1334 -Buffalo 14231 **Fx:**884-2899

(212) 661-2111 .. **Rinato,** Peter M '02 %S Mero -551 5th Av -NY 10176 **Fx:**573-9852

(518) 218-7100 .. **Rinckey,** Greg T '98 (Tully R,PLLC) -441 New Karner Rd -Albany 12205

(212) 885-5000 .. **Rinde,** Jeffrey A '92 (Blank R LLP) -405 Lex Av -NY 10174

(212) 589-6200 .. **Rindner,** Gary M '82 MF Global -712 5th Av -NY 10019

(845) 294-7990 .. **Rindner,** Howard C '91 (Stern & R) -15 Matthews Bx1028 -Goshen 10924 **Fx:**294-9233

(212) 626-4100 .. **Rindone,** Jos P Jr. '09 %Baker & M LLP -1114 Av of Amer -NY 10036

(212) 987-1238 .. **Rindsberg,** Danl '01 Rimon Ventures LLC -19 Oakvll -Staten Isl 10314

(631) 661-0001 .. **Rinear,** Robt T Jr. '76 -112 Route 109 -W Babylon 11704 **Fx:**661-0226

(212) 541-2000 .. **Rinearson,** Judith '82 (Bryan C LLP) -1290 Av of Amer -NY 10104

(212) 308-3999 .. **Rineer,** Courtney Tristen '05 %Akst & A -150 E 58th -NY 10155 **Fx:**317-2946

(212) 704-6000 .. **Rinehart,** Stephen G '83 (Troutman S LLP) -405 Lex Av -NY 10174

(212) 858-4314 .. **Rinehart Hogan,** Catherine '94 FINRA -1 Lbrty Plz -NY 10006

(518) 473-7470 .. **Rinella,** Austin J '78 %Insurance Dept -99 Wshngtn Av -Albany 12257 **Fx:**474-3397

(914) 793-7600 .. **Riner,** Sheldon M '04 S Riner,LLC -32 Lawrence Av -Tuckahoe 10707 **Fx:**793-7606

(585) 454-5930 .. **Rinere,** Jos C Jr. '67 (Rinere & R,LLP) -36 W Main -Rchstr 14614 **Fx:**454-5945

(585) 454-5930 .. **Rinere,** Jos D '92 (Rinere & R,LLP) -36 W Main -Rchstr 14614 **Fx:**454-5945

(212) 725-2727 .. **Rinesmith,** Joshua J '06 %S Lobel,PC -9 E 40th -NY 10016 **Fx:**725-3910

(212) 340-6173 .. **Rinesmith,** Lauren E '06 %Fortis Capital Corp -520 Mad Av -NY 10022

(212) 883-1300 .. **Ring,** Beth C '77 (Sandler T&R,PA) -551 5th Av -NY 10176

(631) 265-6600 .. **Ring,** Christopher P '97 -59 Lndng Av -Smithtwn 11787

(718) 268-0400 .. **Ring,** Gregory A '09 %Addabbo & G -118-21 Qns Blvd -Frst Hlls 11375

(716) 826-0770 .. **Ring,** John H III '87 -17 Vassar Dr -Getzvll 14068

(212) 578-2640 .. **Ring,** Timothy J '97 %MetLife -1095 Av of Amer -NY 10036

(914) 949-3250 .. **Ring,** Timothy P '93 %Chicago Title/Ticor Title -245 Main -White Plns 10601 **Fx:**946-7698

(212) 701-3000 .. **Ringel,** Dean '72 (Cahill G&R LLP) -80 Pine -NY 10005 **Fx:**269-5420

(212) 603-6300 .. **Ringel,** Fred B '86 (Robinson BLGG&G PC) -875 3rd Av -NY 10022

(212) 374-1100 .. **Ringel,** Jay B '81 -233 Bway -NY 10279 **Fx:**608-1072

(212) 980-3500 .. **Ringel,** Jordan E '62 (Pavia & H LLP) -600 Mad Av -NY 10022

(212) 340-0400 .. **Ringel,** Melissa B '98 %Appllt Div 1st Dept -27 Mad Av -NY 10010 **Fx:**889-4412

(212) 593-6700 .. **Ringel,** Peter C '06 %Aaronson RF&D,LLP -757 3rd Av -NY 10017

(212) 632-3000 .. **Ringel,** Ronnie '75 Fiduciary Trust Co Intl -600 5th Av -NY 10020 **Fx:**632-3198

(917) 778-6600 .. **Ringel,** Stephen G '75 %J Toomey -485 Lex Av -NY 10017 **Fx:**778-7048

(212) 213-5800 .. **Ringel,** Valerie D '86 %Margolis & T LLP -280 Mad Av -NY 10016

(212) 655-3500 .. **Ringer,** James M '68 (Meister S&F LLP) -140 E 45th -NY 10017

(718) 991-4758 .. **Ringer,** Katie M '07 Leg Aid -953 Southrn Blvd -Bronx 10459 **Fx:**842-2867

(516) 791-9176 .. **Ringer,** Marvin '71 -673 Colfax Pl -N Woodmere 11581 **Fx:**791-8504

(646) 746-9700 .. **Ringer,** Steven I '88 CFTC -140 Bway -NY 10005 **Fx:**746-9938

(914) 766-4325 .. **Ringes,** Mark J '96 IBM -294 Route 100 -Somers 10589 **Fx:**766-8444

(212) 261-9218 .. **Ringler,** Jeffrey '71 Hallmark Ent -1325 Av of Amer -NY 10019

(518) 899-2371 .. **Ringler,** Robyn D '87 -300 East Line Rd -Ballston Lk 12019

(585) 454-7145 .. **Ringrose,** Michl J '88 (Gallo & I,LLP) -39 State -Rchstr 14614

(518) 474-4899 .. **Rings,** Stephen L '86 %Insurance Dept -99 Wshngtn Av -Albany 12257 **Fx:**474-3397

(315) 474-2911 .. **Ringwood,** Michl P '80 (Smith SK&S,PC) -250 S Clinton -Syracuse 13202

(607) 723-5341 .. **Ringwood,** Richd S '57 SpclCnsl Hinman H&K,LLP -80 Exchange Bx5250 -Bnghmtn 13902

(212) 762-7297 .. **Rinker,** Hui-Chun '00 Morgan Stanley -1221 Av of Amer -NY 10020

(212) 909-6000 .. **Rinker,** Kevin A '01 (Debevoise & P LLP) -919 3rd Av -NY 10022

(212) 248-3140 .. **Rinschler,** Joshua D '10 %Drinker B&R LLP -140 Bway -NY 10005

(212) 815-1818 .. **Rinsler,** Steven H '75 DC 37 MELS -125 Barclay -NY 10007 **Fx:**815-1343

(212) 685-6500 .. **Rinzler,** James K '90 Dominion Servcing Corp -200 Mad Av -NY 10016

(212) 357-0390 .. **Rinzler,** Michl F '96 Goldman Sachs -85 Broad -NY 10004

(718) 258-2255 .. **Rio,** Christopher J '09 %F Rio -2011 Flatbush Av -Brklyn 11234

(718) 258-2255 .. **Rio,** Frank J '74 -2011 Flatbush Av -Brklyn 11234

(212) 545-9011 .. **Rio,** Richd R '84 R Rio PLLC -114 E 13th -NY 10003 **Fx:**545-9016

(914) 328-0404 .. **Riolo,** Greg A '94 (Jackson L LLP) -1 N Bway -White Plns 10601

(212) 935-4500 .. **Rionda,** Roberto A '98 %M Kennedy -419 Park Av S -NY 10016 **Fx:**980-6881

(212) 586-4900 .. **Riopelle,** Roland G '86 (Sercarz & R,LLP) -152 W 57th -NY 10019

(212) 479-7116 .. **Riordan,** Elizabeth E '09 Fortress Invesment Grp -1345 Av of Amer -NY 10105

(914) 237-2003 .. **Riordan,** Eugene J '99 -50 Main -White Plns 10606 **Fx:**682-2625

(212) 483-9490 .. **Riordan,** J Michl '95 (McElroy DM&C,LLP) -88 Pine -NY 10005

(716) 882-3333 .. **Riordan,** Kristy L '05 %PJ Fiorella -155 Summer -Buffalo 14222 **Fx:**882-4998

(212) 818-9200 .. **Riordan,** Marybeth N '87 Cnsl Satterlee SB&B LLP -230 Park Av -NY 10169

(212) 682-0020 .. **Riordan,** Matthew M '99 %Putney TH&H LLP -521 5th Av -NY 10175

(631) 537-0644 .. **Riordan,** P James '56 -Main Bx435 -Brdghmptn 11932 **Fx:**537-8314

(585) 428-2534 .. **Riordan,** Paul M '78 -Hall of Justice -Rchstr 14614

(716) 362-0470 .. **Riordan,** Scott F '99 (Riordan & K,LLC) -2982 Delaware Av -Kenmore 14217 **Fx:**362-0480

(631) 240-0811 .. **Riordan,** Sean P J '05 %Sherman FS&L LLP -8 E Main -Bay Shr 11706

(315) 735-5045 .. **Riordan,** Thos J '77 -180 Genesee -New Hartfrd 13413 **Fx:**734-2149

(212) 809-7600 .. **Rios,** Angelo '91 %Cheven K&H -40 Wall -NY 10005

(718) 250-2000 .. **Rios,** Gloria B '96 %DA -350 Jay -Brklyn 11201 **Fx:**250-2314

(718) 584-1916 .. **Rios,** Jose L '95 -2560 Matthews Av -Bronx 10467

(212) 340-2537 .. **Rios,** Jose R '85 %Metro-North -347 Mad Av -NY 10017 **Fx:**697-9079

(212) 474-1000 .. **Rios,** Lara M '07 %Cravath S&M LLP -825 8th Av -NY 10019

(212) 820-9325 .. **Rios,** Patrick '06 %Hawkins D&W LLP -One Chase Manh Plz -NY 10005

(718) 684-2530 .. **Rios,** Shane O '05 (Rios & L LLP) -3140 E Tremont Av -Bronx 10461 **Fx:**684-2531

(212) 344-5680 .. **Riozzi,** Thos P '00 %Thompson H LLP -335 Mad Av -NY 10017

(212) 732-5310 .. **Ripa,** Glenn '86 -225 Bway -NY 10007

(212) 867-5800 .. **Ripandelli,** Liliana '05 %Osler H&H LLP -620 8th Av -NY 10018

(914) 522-3500 .. **Ripepi,** Bruce F '88 -63 Amstrdm Av -Hawthorne 10532

(212) 557-7200 .. **Ripin,** Peter M '87 (Davidoff M&H,LLP) -605 3rd Av -NY 10158

(212) 918-3000 .. **Ripin,** Robt A '89 (Hogan L LLP) -875 3rd Av -NY 10022

(212) 267-3700 .. **Ripka,** Alan S '90 (Napoli BR LLP) -350 5th Av -NY 10118

(516) 933-8880 .. **Ripka,** Peter T '87 %Ripco Real Estate Corp -420 Jericho Tpk -Jericho 11753 **Fx:**933-2514

(631) 501-5700 .. **Ripley,** Justin J '06 %Carter DF&S LLP -445 Broadhallow Rd -Melvll 11747

(212) 294-6700 .. **Ripo,** Desiree M '08 %Winston & S -200 Park Av -NY 10166

(212) 867-9500 .. **Ripp,** Jared E '08 %Kurzman K&F,LLP -230 Park Av -NY 10169

(631) 385-1610 .. **Ripp,** Wm G '84 -775 Park Av -Huntngtn 11743 **Fx:**385-0279

(212) 732-7458 .. **Rippa,** Scott V '94 Salomon Smith Barney -390 Greenwich -NY 10013

(914) 696-1800 .. **Rippa,** Vincent R '63 -800 Wstchstr Av -Rye Brook 10573 **Fx:**696-1823

(845) 357-3100 .. **Ripps,** Jonathan B '95 -222 Route 59 -Suffern 10901 **Fx:**357-4574

(212) 245-6565 .. **Rippy,** Conrad M '94 (Levine P&M,LLP) -1740 Bway -NY 10019

(212) 735-3000 .. **Rips,** Anna '07 %Skadden ASM&F LLP -4 Times Sq -NY 10036

(212) 506-3900 .. **Rips,** Michl D '86 SpclCnsl Steptoe & J LLP -750 7th Av -NY 10019

(212) 435-3571 .. **Ripullone,** Shirley A '79 %Port Auth of NY/NJ -225 Park Av S -NY 10003 **Fx:**435-3555

(212) 756-2000 .. **Risdon,** Ronald B '78 (Schulte R&Z LLP) -919 3rd Av -NY 10022

(631) 232-0200 .. **Risebrow,** Albert E '89 %Fumuso KDSS&F,LLP -110 Marcus Blvd -Hauppauge 11788

(845) 338-6600 .. **Riseley & Ball** -111 Green Bx3296 -Kingston 12402 **Fx:**338-6421

(845) 338-6600 .. **Riseley & Moriello,PLLC** -111 Green Bx4465 -Kingston 12402 **Fx:**338-6421

(845) 338-6600 .. **Riseley,** Richd F '67 (Riseley & M,PLLC) -111 Green Bx4465 -Kingston 12402
(212) 909-6000 .. **Rishty,** Edw M '05 %Debevoise & P LLP -919 3rd Av -NY 10022
(212) 728-8000 .. **Rishty,** Elliot J '08 %Willkie F&G LLP -787 7th Av -NY 10019
(212) 801-6492 .. **Rishty,** Michl J '02 (Greenberg T,LLP) -200 Park Av -NY 10166
(914) 949-2700 .. **Risi,** John A '95 OfCnsl Bleakley P&S,LLP -1 N Lex Av -White Plns 10601
(718) 939-2020 .. **Risi,** John M '75 -192-08 Crocheron Av -Flushng 11358 **Fx:**939-1518
(718) 278-2600 .. **Risi,** Jos '83 (Risi & Assoc) -35-11 36th -Astoria 11106 **Fx:**956-4897
(516) 794-8519 .. **Risi,** Jos J '54 Natl Arbitration & Mediation -990 Stewart Av -Gdn Cty 11530 **Fx:**794-8518
(516) 839-9335 .. **Rising,** Christopher H '96 -66 Yale Pl -Rockvll Ctr 11570 **Fx:**594-0023
(212) 682-4100 .. **Risk,** Mark D '85 M Risk, PC -60 E 42nd -NY 10165 **Fx:**682-4775
(212) 859-8000 .. **Riskin,** Jonathan A '08 %Fried FHS&J LLP -1 NY Plz -NY 10004
(646) 264-3650 .. **Riskin,** Steven D '78 %US Dept of Labor -201 Varick -NY 10014 **Fx:**264-3660
(212) 839-5300 .. **Risko,** Paul K '83 (Sidley A LLP) -787 7th Av -NY 10019
(212) 233-6400 .. **Risman,** Maya '97 (M Risman,PC) -30 Vesey -NY 10007 **Fx:**233-6406
(716) 856-4000 .. **Risman,** Michl B '80 (Hodgson R LLP) -140 Pearl -Buffalo 14202
(315) 443-9543 .. **Risman,** Richd S '85 %Syracuse Univ Cllg of Law -Wht Hall -Syracuse 13244 **Fx:**443-4213
(212) 599-1515 .. **Riso,** Gerard A '83 (Stein RM,LLP) -405 Lex Av -NY 10174
(718) 667-8600 .. **Riso,** John L '91 (Borrell & R,LLP) -1500 Hylan Blvd -Staten Isl 10305 **Fx:**980-1745
(212) 771-9516 .. **Riso,** Salvatore V Jr. '98 CIT Group Inc -505 5th Av -NY 10017
(718) 238-6960 .. **Riso,** Valerie L '09 %Grimaldi & Y LLP -9201 4th Av -Brklyn 11209
(914) 793-9241 .. **Risoli,** Andrea '00 -484 Wht Plns Rd -Eastchstr 10709 **Fx:**793-9352
(914) 793-9241 .. **Risoli,** Andrew C '64 -484 Wht Plns Rd -Eastchstr 10709 **Fx:**793-9352
(914) 591-7722 .. **Risotto,** Christine L '93 (Roy ML&R) -56 Main Bx108 -Irvngtn 10533
(585) 426-4120 .. **Rissew,** Adam P '08 Lifetime Assistance,Inc -425 Paul Rd -Rchstr 14624
(212) 474-1000 .. **Rissmiller,** Joshua H '10 %Cravath S&M LLP -825 8th Av -NY 10019
(516) 742-9420 .. **Rissoff,** Stuart M '79 -300 Grdn City Plz -Gdn Cty 11530
(212) 940-3000 .. **Ristorucci,** Roberto J '04 %Nixon P LLP -437 Mad Av -NY 10022
(212) 766-1001 .. **Rita,** Wm J '84 -291 Bway -NY 10007 **Fx:**608-6802
(212) 335-9131 .. **Ritch,** Sarah J '03 DA -1 Hogan Pl -NY 10013
(212) 558-4000 .. **Ritchie,** Alexander R '10 %Sullivan & C LLP -125 Broad -NY 10004
(212) 815-1818 .. **Ritchie,** Carol Evadne '93 DC 37 MELS -125 Barclay -NY 10007 **Fx:**815-1343
(646) 386-4200 .. **Ritchie,** John W '80 OCA -25 Beaver -NY 10004
(212) 774-5819 .. **Ritchie,** Thos '04 Caxton Iseman Capital -500 Park Av -NY 10022
(212) 637-2503 .. **Ritchin,** Stephen J '81 %US Atty -1 St Andrews Plz -NY 10007
(877) 222-1814 .. **Ritchkin,** Michl E '05 %B Rothenberg -100 Duffy Av -Hicksvll 11801 **Fx:**(866) 894-2182
(212) 557-7700 .. **Ritger,** Mary Beth '77 OfCnsl Davidson D&C LLP -60 E 42nd -NY 10165
(212) 448-1800 .. **Ritholz,** Adam E '79 (Roberts RLSC&F LLP) -235 Park Av S -NY 10003
(212) 248-0800 .. **Ritorto,** Richd '87 (Martinez & R,PC) -67 Wall -NY 10005
(212) 458-7014 .. **Ritrivi,** Nicholas A '97 %AIG -175 Water -NY 10038
(518) 472-1224 .. **Ritschdorff,** Todd A '04 %Phillips L LLP -30 S Pearl -Albany 12207
(212) 532-1225 .. **Ritscher,** Andrea Katz '86 Katz & K -41 Mad Av -NY 10010 **Fx:**532-1195
(212) 363-1380 .. **Ritson,** Danl C '06 %Herten BSCBL&H,LLC -747 3rd Av -NY 10017
(347) 404-9920 .. **Rittberg,** Ellen Pober '91 %MHLS -120 Schermerhorn -Brklyn 11201 **Fx:**(718) 243-2410
(607) 763-9200 .. **Rittberg,** Howard M '76 (Levene G&T,LLP) -BxF-1706 -Bnghmtn 13902
(212) 458-6203 .. **Rittberg,** Jay J '03 AIG -175 Water -NY 10038
(212) 371-4050 .. **Ritter,** Ann L '71 -420 Mad Av -NY 10017 **Fx:**688-2386
(516) 681-7400 .. **Ritter,** Bruce E '90 (Larsson & S, PC) -575 Jericho Tpk -Jericho 11753 **Fx:**681-7444
(716) 855-1111 .. **Ritter,** Chas C Jr. '94 (Duke HP&G LLP) -350 Main -Buffalo 14202
(212) 272-3814 .. **Ritter,** Francine A '99 %JP Morgan Chase -320 Park Av -NY 10022
(212) 312-7837 .. **Ritter,** Jeffrey R '85 %State Ins Fund -199 Church -NY 10007 **Fx:**385-9199
(718) 237-2000 .. **Ritter,** Jennifer Lynn '94 %Leg Aid -111 Lvngstn -Brklyn 11201 **Fx:**237-8737
(718) 286-6000 .. **Ritter,** Joan I '86 %DA -125-01 Qns Blvd -Kew Gdns 11415
(914) 323-7000 .. **Ritter,** Jodi Gottesfeld '93 (Wilson EME&D LLP) -3 Gannett Dr -White Plns 10604
(516) 676-4600 .. **Ritter,** John Jr. '84 (Humes & W) -147 Forest Av Bx546 -Locust Vly 11560
(845) 471-7171 .. **Ritter,** Leo M '58 -303 Mill -Poughkeepsie 12601 **Fx:**471-7597
(212) 223-1700 .. **Ritter,** Neil P '83 %Classic Realty -400 Park Av -NY 10022 **Fx:**223-3867
(212) 715-9100 .. **Ritter,** Paul M '81 (Kramer LN&F,LLP) -1177 Av of Amer -NY 10036
(212) 486-9494 .. **Ritter,** Wm C '63 (Ritter & R) -488 Mad Av -NY 10022 **Fx:**468-0701
(914) 366-5700 .. **Ritterbusch,** Wm J '05 %MA Bjork -660 Wht Plns Rd -Tarrytwn 10591 **Fx:**366-5759
(212) 818-9200 .. **Rittinger,** James F '72 (Satterlee SB&B LLP) -230 Park Av -NY 10169
(607) 763-9200 .. **Rittinger,** John P '69 OfCnsl Levene G&T,LLP -BxF-1706 -Bnghmtn 13902
(516) 240-8900 .. **Rittmaster,** Steven H '94 (Torre LGG&R,LLP) -100 Jericho Quad -Jericho 11753
(585) 393-3055 .. **Ritts,** James B '97 %DA -27 N Main -Canandaigua 14424 **Fx:**396-4860
(315) 218-8000 .. **Ritts,** Katherine A '09 %Bond S&K,PLLC -1 Lincoln Ctr -Syracuse 13202
(212) 839-7000 .. **Rittweger,** Thos M '93 Hill B&N LLP -200 Lbrty -NY 10281
(212) 321-7075 .. **Ritz Clark & Ben-Asher LLP** -40 Exch Pl -NY 10005 **Fx:**321-7078
(212) 608-1445 .. **Ritz,** Leonard H '98 Ritz Law PLLC -22 Crtlandt -NY 10007 **Fx:**(866) 767-5550
(914) 667-1539 .. **Ritz,** Ronnie J '91 -Bx115 -Shrub Oak 10588 **Fx:**962-8903
(212) 321-7075 .. **Ritz,** Susan R '84 (Ritz C&B-A LLP) -40 Exch Pl -NY 10005
(518) 438-9907 .. **Ritzenberg,** Kenneth S '85 (Young SWRB&M,LLC) -5 Palisades Dr -Albany 12205
(516) 471-1900 .. **Ritzert,** Gail L '89 (Havkins RR&V,LLP) -114 Old Cntry Rd -Mineola 11501
(716) 847-8400 .. **Ritzert,** Jos '80 OfCnsl Phillips L LLP -3400 HSBC Ctr -Buffalo 14203
(212) 813-8800 .. **Ritzo,** Benjamin J '10 %Goodwin P LLP -620 8th Av -NY 10018
(212) 592-1400 .. **Riva,** Robt A '03 %Herrick,F LLP -2 Park Av -NY 10016
(212) 264-3435 .. **Rivas,** Alexandra '97 %DHS -26 Fed Plz -NY 10278
(212) 335-4500 .. **Rivas,** Carlos E '07 %DLA Piper LLP -1251 Av of Amer -NY 10020
(212) 836-8000 .. **Rivas,** Ursula P '08 %Kaye S LLP -425 Park Av -NY 10022
(518) 462-5601 .. **Rivchin,** Neil H '73 (O'Connell & A) -54 State -Albany 12207
(212) 557-3000 .. **Rivelis,** Lester E '78 (Rivelis P&B,LLP) -286 Mad Av -NY 10017
(212) 557-3000 .. **Rivelis Pawa & Blum,LLP** -286 Mad Av -NY 10017 **Fx:**557-5051
(212) 501-7899 .. **Rivellini,** Frank D '89 %FJ DeVito,PA -150 Bway -NY 10038
(212) 756-2000 .. **Rivera,** Adam J '09 %Schulte R&Z LLP -919 3rd Av -NY 10022
(212) 586-4333 .. **Rivera,** Alan L '88 Millbrook Capital Mgt -1370 Av of Amer -NY 10019 **Fx:**586-0340
(718) 579-3157 .. **Rivera,** Alfredo B '79 Leg Aid -1020 Grnd Cncrs -Bronx 10451 **Fx:**588-2611
(718) 562-7481 .. **Rivera,** Andrew A '89 -48 Adrian Av -Bronx 10463
(718) 590-2000 .. **Rivera,** Ben '94 %DA -198 E 161st -Bronx 10451 **Fx:**590-6477
(212) 484-3080 .. **Rivera,** Christine A '00 Optima Fund Mgmt LLC -10 E 53rd -NY 10022
(212) 408-5100 .. **Rivera,** Christy L '02 %Chadbourne & P LLP -30 Rckfllr Plz -NY 10112
(212) 230-8800 .. **Rivera,** Clara L '03 WilmerHale -399 Park Av -NY 10022
(917) 848-0362 .. **Rivera,** Daphne H '99 ACLA HS -1474 Gates Av -Brklyn 11237
(212) 619-3730 .. **Rivera,** David '89 Cnsl Doar RK&M -217 Bway -NY 10007
(212) 312-7766 .. **Rivera,** Edwin '95 %State Ins Fund -199 Church -NY 10007 **Fx:**385-9199
(212) 331-5051 .. **Rivera,** Frank '01 HRA-OLA -180 Water -NY 10038
(212) 648-0905 .. **Rivera,** Gerardo J '92 JP Morgan Chase -245 Park Av -NY 10167
(516) 747-0300 .. **Rivera,** Gisella '06 %Meltzer LG&B,LLP -190 Willis Av -Mineola 11501
(914) 734-1442 .. **Rivera,** Jason '97 -806 South -Peekskill 10566 **Fx:**736-1440
(212) 732-5800 .. **Rivera,** Jeannie I '00 %Friedman & M LLP -233 Bway -NY 10279
(718) 340-4304 .. **Rivera,** Jenny '86 %CUNY Law Schl -65-21 Main -Flushng 11367 **Fx:**340-4482
(914) 328-9529 .. **Rivera,** John '80 -175 Main -White Plns 10601 **Fx:**328-6384
(718) 492-4200 .. **Rivera,** Jonathan M '05 %M Romero,PC -5511 4th Av -Brklyn 11220 **Fx:**492-9494
(718) 871-7868 .. **Rivera,** Jose M '86 -913 52nd -Brklyn 11219
(212) 564-9800 .. **Rivera,** Jose M '99 (D'Agostino L&L,LLP) -345 7th Av -NY 10001
(718) 855-0071 .. **Rivera,** Juan '81 -26 Court -Brklyn 11242 **Fx:**596-7127
(212) 980-9600 .. **Rivera,** Julie A '05 %Kaufman B&R -120 Bway -NY 10271
(914) 734-1442 .. **Rivera,** Julius A '89 -806 South -Peekskill 10566 **Fx:**736-1440
(516) 385-8177 .. **Rivera,** Leonard R '97 -1225 Franklin Av -Gdn Cty 11530 **Fx:**338-2953
(212) 613-5000 .. **Rivera,** Lisa '03 Leg Assist Grp -450 W 33rd -NY 10001 **Fx:**750-0820
(914) 751-1280 .. **Rivera,** Luis A '01 -765 Brnx Rvr Rd -Bronxvll 10708
(718) 458-2929 .. **Rivera,** M Suzette '84 -84-30 Roosevelt Av -Jcksn Hts 11372
(212) 318-3000 .. **Rivera,** Manuel G R '97 SrCnsl Fulbright & J LLP -666 5th Av -NY 10103
(718) 515-6000 .. **Rivera,** Margie M '08 %Corpina PK&P,LLP -2344 Eastchstr Rd -Bronx 10469
(212) 335-9000 .. **Rivera,** Mayerling '98 %DA -1 Hogan Pl -NY 10013
(212) 239-6159 .. **Rivera,** Nilda E '03 Div Of Parole -314 W 40th -NY 10018 **Fx:**239-6160
(212) 685-0180 .. **Rivera,** Pedro A '05 -233 5th Av -NY 10016
(315) 474-7571 .. **Rivera,** Ramon E '95 (Mackenzie H LLP) -101 S Salina Bx4967 -Syracuse 13221
(212) 560-2040 .. **Rivera,** Ranfi '91 %EBC -450 W 33rd -NY 10001 **Fx:**560-6610
(518) 285-8600 .. **Rivera,** Richd '92 Family Ct -30 Clinton Av -Albany 12207
(212) 336-8330 .. **Rivera,** Robt '07 (Susman G LLP) -560 Lex Av -NY 10022
(518) 427-7350 .. **Rivera,** Sandra D '03 Brown & W PLLC -79 Columbia -Albany 12210
(212) 408-5100 .. **Rivera,** Seven R '01 (Chadbourne & P LLP) -30 Rckfllr Plz -NY 10112
(212) 416-8936 .. **Rivera,** Suzette C '02 %Dept of Law -120 Bway -NY 10271
(212) 730-7750 .. **Rivera,** Valerie '02 %Nicoletti GS&O,LLP -555 5th Av -NY 10017
(914) 630-2535 .. **Rivera,** Victor Jr. '89 -2042 Palmer Av -Larchmnt 10538 **Fx:**630-2534
(212) 269-2091 .. **Rivera,** Walter '80 (Espinosa & E,LLP) -61 Bway -NY 10006
(914) 833-3000 .. **Rivera,** Wanda '03 L&M Development Prtnrs -1865 Palmer Av -Larchmnt 10538
(212) 909-6000 .. **Rivera Jacobo,** Armando '08 %Debevoise & P LLP -919 3rd Av -NY 10022
(212) 909-6000 .. **Rivera-Lupu,** Maria C '07 %Debevoise & P LLP -919 3rd Av -NY 10022
(917) 551-1300 .. **Rivera-Sipes,** Yesenia '03 %Koehler & I LLP -61 Bway -NY 10006
(212) 294-6700 .. **Rivero,** Erick '08 %Winston & S -200 Park Av -NY 10166
(718) 590-2000 .. **Rivero,** Maria T '92 %DA -198 E 161st -Bronx 10451 **Fx:**590-6477
(212) 317-1200 .. **Rivero,** Yolanda '98 %M Faillace & Assoc,PC -110 E 59th -NY 10022
(212) 506-1700 .. **Rivers,** Ayana M '99 Kasowitz BT&F LLP -1633 Bway -NY 10019
(212) 722-4084 .. **Rivers,** Diane L '82 -185 E 85th -NY 10028 **Fx:**831-3218
(585) 343-3090 .. **Rivers,** Michl R '00 %Rybak M&G,LLP -104 Bank -Batavia 14020
(718) 451-9219 .. **Rivers,** Susie V '90 -26 Court -Brklyn 11242
(516) 357-3000 .. **Riverso,** Pia E '86 (Rivkin R LLP) -926 RXR Plz -Uniondale 11556
(914) 723-3474 .. **Riverso,** Vincent G '88 V Riverso,PE -1088 Central Av -Scarsdale 10583
(845) 359-1515 .. **Rivet,** Diana W '56 -35 Orangebrg Rd -Orangebrg 10962 **Fx:**359-4434
(315) 478-1122 .. **Rivette,** Francis R '78 (Rivette & R,PC) -224 Harrison -Syracuse 13202 **Fx:**461-1243
(212) 233-0318 .. **Rivieccio,** Rosemary '90 -299 Bway -NY 10007 **Fx:**233-5737
(212) 319-2787 .. **Riviere,** Juliette V '08 VLA -1 E 53rd -NY 10022 **Fx:**752-6575
(212) 715-4830 .. **Riviere,** Vanessa '03 Chanel -9 W 57th -NY 10019

(212) 571-7111 .. **Rivin,** Julia '96 (Goldin & R LLC) -225 Bway -NY 10007 **Fx:**571-3211
(212) 889-4100 .. **Rivituso,** Michl P '90 %Realty Advisory Bd -292 Mad Av -NY 10017 **Fx:**889-4105
(315) 442-0100 .. **Rivizzigno,** Anthony P '70 (Gilberti SH&S,PC) -555 E Genesee -Syracuse 13202
(212) 239-5190 .. **Rivkin,** Alexander '92 Div Of Parole -314 W 40th -NY 10018 **Fx:**239-6160
(212) 909-6000 .. **Rivkin,** David W '81 (Debevoise & P LLP) -919 3rd Av -NY 10022
(718) 286-6000 .. **Rivkin,** Eleonora B '02 %DA -125-01 Qns Blvd -Kew Gdns 11415
(516) 357-3269 .. **Rivkin,** John L '82 (Rivkin R LLP) -926 RXR Plz -Uniondale 11556
(212) 891-9100 .. **Rivkin,** Lawr '55 OfCnsl Goldfarb & F LLP -345 Park Av -NY 10154
(631) 844-7757 .. **Rivkin,** Natalya '98 Adecco USA,Inc -175 Broadhllw Rd -Melvll 11747
(212) 480-4800 .. **Rivkin,** Oleg '93 (Fox H&C LLP) -825 3rd Av -NY 10022
(516) 357-3000 .. **Rivkin Radler LLP** -926 RXR Plz -Uniondale 11556 **Fx:**357-3333
(718) 222-2322 .. **Rivkin,** Simcha B '09 %Law Dept -350 Jay -Brklyn 11201 **Fx:**222-2088
(212) 480-4800 .. **Rivkin,** V David '00 (Fox H&C LLP) -825 3rd Av -NY 10022
(212) 373-3000 .. **Rivkind,** Rachel M '06 %Paul WRW&G LLP -1285 Av of Amer -NY 10019
(212) 752-8626 .. **Rivkis,** Renee H '72 -531 Main -NY 10044
(212) 317-1717 .. **Rivlin,** Danl Z '02 %Chemtob MF&T LLP -3 E 54th -NY 10022
(212) 698-7000 .. **Rivlin,** Elisa M '80 %Simon & Schuster -1230 Av of Amer -NY 10020 **Fx:**698-7171
(212) 547-5400 .. **Rivlin,** Jay E '00 (McDermott W&E LLP) -340 Mad Av -NY 10173
(212) 610-6300 .. **Rivlin,** Kenneth S '97 (Allen & O) -1221 Av of Amer -NY 10020
(212) 248-8800 .. **Rivlin,** Keren Z '05 %Callan KB&B LLP -1 Whitehall -NY 10004
(212) 326-2000 .. **Rivner,** Asher Louis '05 Cnsl O'Melveny & M LLP -7 Times Sq -NY 10036
(212) 909-5000 .. **Rivner,** Randi B '99 KPMG LLP -757 3rd Av -NY 10017
(212) 474-1000 .. **Rivollier,** Bob A '07 %Cravath S&M LLP -825 8th Av -NY 10019
(212) 788-0591 .. **Rix,** Martha J '84 %Law Dept -100 Church -NY 10007 **Fx:**788-0367
(646) 746-9700 .. **Rix,** Philip D '96 CFTC -140 Bway -NY 10005 **Fx:**746-9938
(631) 727-7731 .. **Riyaz,** Zachary I '03 (Foster & V,LLP) -220 Roanoke Av -Rvrhead 11901
(212) 554-1400 .. **Rizio-Hamilton,** John J '05 %Bernstein LB&G LLP -1285 Av of Amer -NY 10019
(718) 286-6000 .. **Rizk,** Jacqueline '06 %DA -125-01 Qns Blvd -Kew Gdns 11415
(212) 425-7200 .. **Rizkalla,** Hany W '07 %Kenyon & K,LLP -1 Bway -NY 10004
(631) 853-4104 .. **Rizopoulos,** Dena C '08 %DA -400 Carleton Av Bx9082 -Central Islip 11722 **Fx:**853-7838
(718) 777-5750 .. **Rizos,** Susan E '98 -22-55 31st -Astoria 11105 **Fx:**777-5756
(212) 732-4336 .. **Rizvi,** Saleem S '90 -150 Bway -NY 10038 **Fx:**240-0365
(631) 957-3029 .. **Rizwan,** Afreen S '08 %Babylon Town Atty -200 E Sunrise Hwy -Lindenhrst 11757 **Fx:**957-3146
(212) 223-2100 .. **Rizzi,** Annette C '89 %Menz B&K LLP -444 Mad Av -NY 10022
(516) 832-7594 .. **Rizzi,** Danl A '82 (Nixon P LLP) -50 Jericho Quadrangle -Jericho 11753
(212) 682-7474 .. **Rizzi,** Steven J '93 (Foley & L LLP) -90 Park Av -NY 10016
(212) 679-5799 .. **Rizzo,** Albert '88 (A Rizzo,PC) -60 E 42nd -NY 10165 **Fx:**679-5766
(516) 741-4799 .. **Rizzo,** Angelo F '04 %Baker SBGFM&N,LLC -100 Grdn City Plz -Gdn Cty 11530
(516) 747-6300 .. **Rizzo,** Carol '92 %Koeppel M&L,LLP -155 First Bx863 -Mineola 11501
(516) 571-2878 .. **Rizzo,** Catherine '94 Supreme Ct -100 Supreme Ct Dr -Mineola 11501
(212) 732-3200 .. **Rizzo,** Christopher G '02 %Carter L&M LLP -2 Wall -NY 10005
(516) 877-2900 .. **Rizzo,** Craig V '96 (Bartlett MB&M,LLP) -300 Old Cntry Rd -Mineola 11501
(914) 325-6939 .. **Rizzo,** Danielle L '95 -61 Roosevelt Dr -Bedfrd Hlls 10507
(716) 633-9300 .. **Rizzo,** Danielle M '07 %J Eiss PLLC -19 Limestone Dr -Buffalo 14221 **Fx:**633-0492
(315) 463-7351 .. **Rizzo,** David C '68 -346 N Midler Av -Syracuse 13206 **Fx:**463-8242
(516) 822-8222 .. **Rizzo,** Dominic S '84 -1 Huntngtn Quad -Melvll 11747
(845) 452-6100 .. **Rizzo,** Eugene J '80 (Rizzo & K) -272 Mill -Poughkeepsie 12601 **Fx:**452-8459
(716) 439-7071 .. **Rizzo,** James A '88 %Pub Def -Cnty Cthse -Lockprt 14094 **Fx:**439-7076
(585) 546-4490 .. **Rizzo,** James J '76 -31 E Main -Rchstr 14614 **Fx:**546-3940
(315) 733-0419 .. **Rizzo,** James S '96 (Saunders K,LLP) -185 Genesee -Utica 13501
(718) 618-7509 .. **Rizzo,** Jeffrey W '04 -888 Grnd Cncrs -Bronx 10451 **Fx:**618-7515
(716) 853-5100 .. **Rizzo,** Jillian E '08 %Lippes MWF LLP -665 Main -Buffalo 14203
(585) 753-1380 .. **Rizzo,** John G '02 Cnty Atty -307 Cnty Ofc Bldg -Rchstr 14614 **Fx:**753-1331
(585) 768-2523 .. **Rizzo,** John L '75 -29 W Main Bx116 -Le Roy 14482 **Fx:**768-7840
(212) 981-3085 .. **Rizzo,** John M '89 Marcum & Kliegman LLP -655 3rd Av -NY 10017
(914) 747-4455 .. **Rizzo,** Jos '96 OfCnsl D'Agostino,PC -427 Bedford Rd -Plsntvll 10570 **Fx:**747-3626
(585) 454-7145 .. **Rizzo,** Jos B '90 (Gallo & I,LLP) -39 State -Rchstr 14614
(631) 734-9700 .. **Rizzo,** Jos N Jr. '75 (Rizzo Grp,LLP) -Bx986 -Cutchogue 11935 **Fx:**734-9702
(212) 768-4900 .. **Rizzo,** Laura-Michelle '03 %Gage S&F -410 Park Av -NY 10022
(914) 763-8881 .. **Rizzo,** Louis J '73 (Rizzo & R) -61 Scofld Rd -Pound Rdg 10576 **Fx:**763-8722
(212) 547-5400 .. **Rizzo,** Matthew J '02 (McDermott W&E LLP) -340 Mad Av -NY 10173
(518) 402-2684 .. **Rizzo,** Michl C '89 %Dept of Law -The Cptl -Albany 12224
(212) 996-0200 .. **Rizzo,** Rita M '85 Manhattan North Mgmt Co,Inc -107 E 126th -NY 10035
(212) 450-4000 .. **Rizzo,** Robt A '05 %Davis P&W LLP -450 Lex Av -NY 10017
(212) 819-8200 .. **Rizzo,** Sarah R '10 %White & C LLP -1155 Av of Amer -NY 10036
(585) 454-7145 .. **Rizzo,** Seema Ali '98 %Gallo & I,LLP -39 State -Rchstr 14614
(212) 695-5980 .. **Rizzo,** Stephen J '99 Cnsl Rizzo Grp LLP -11 Penn Plz -NY 10001
(914) 763-8881 .. **Rizzo,** Thos A '55 (Rizzo & R) -61 Scofld Rd -Pound Rdg 10576 **Fx:**763-8722
(716) 873-7559 .. **Rizzo,** Thos M '84 -3407 Delaware Av -Buffalo 14217
(212) 478-3544 .. **Rizzo,** Wm J '94 XL Capital Assurance -1221 Av of Amer -NY 10020
(718) 590-2000 .. **Rizzo-McClure,** Jena '00 %DA -198 E 161st -Bronx 10451 **Fx:**590-6477
(516) 622-0606 .. **Rizzuto,** Philip J '94 (P Rizzuto,PC) -1 Old Cntry Rd -Carle Pl 11514 **Fx:**622-2112
(607) 748-7351 .. **Rizzuto,** Thos P '84 (Leasure GM&R) -101 Jffrsn Av -Endicott 13760
(212) 732-3200 .. **Ro,** Jinsoo Justin '08 %Carter L&M LLP -2 Wall -NY 10005
(212) 259-8000 .. **Ro,** Paula Cho '06 %Dewey & L LLP -1301 Av of Amer -NY 10019
(716) 852-0400 .. **Roach Brown McCarthy & Gruber,PC** -424 Main -Buffalo 14202 **Fx:**852-2535
(716) 852-0400 .. **Roach,** Danl T '55 (Roach BM&G,PC) -424 Main -Buffalo 14202
(845) 331-2525 .. **Roach,** David A '76 OfCnsl Ryan R&R,LLP -115 Green Bx3153 -Kingston 12402
(716) 834-9181 .. **Roach,** David L '77 (Blair & R,LLP) -2645 Sheridan Dr -Tonawanda 14150
(585) 786-2110 .. **Roach,** David M '07 %DiMatteo Law Ofc -87 N Main Bx190 -Warsaw 14569 **Fx:**786-0126
(212) 513-7788 .. **Roach,** Erin D '04 %Ahmuty D&M -123 William -NY 10038
(716) 845-9355 .. **Roach,** Katherine B '92 %Supreme Ct -50 Delaware Av -Buffalo 14202
(347) 404-9920 .. **Roach,** Lanielle D '07 %MHLS -120 Schermerhorn -Brklyn 11201 **Fx:**(718) 243-2410
(716) 843-5700 .. **Roach,** Mary Keefe '84 %US Atty -138 Delaware Av -Buffalo 14202 **Fx:**551-3052
(518) 464-1300 .. **Roach,** Mary M '77 (Roemer WG&M LLP) -13 Columbia Cir -Albany 12203
(914) 962-8445 .. **Roach,** Matthew N L '98 -1929 Commerce -Yorktwn Hts 10598 **Fx:**962-4709
(716) 852-5533 .. **Roach,** Michl J '93 (Connors & V,LLP) -1000 Lbrty Bldg -Buffalo 14202
(516) 938-3100 .. **Roach,** Peter T '79 (P Roach & Assoc,PC) -125 Michl Dr -Syosset 11791 **Fx:**931-4403
(212) 998-2075 .. **Roach,** Robt F '88 %NYU Ofc Leg Cnsl -70 Wshngtn Sq S -NY 10012 **Fx:**995-3048
(212) 815-1450 .. **Roach,** Robin '91 %DC 37 Gen Cnsl -125 Barclay -NY 10007 **Fx:**815-1440
(212) 259-8000 .. **Roach,** Taliah Starr '06 %Dewey & L LLP -1301 Av of Amer -NY 10019
(914) 899-3100 .. **Roach,** Thos M Jr. '87 Mead HC&G -109 Spencer Pl -Mamaroneck 10543
(516) 568-7700 .. **Roach Bernard,** Seidia '02 (Roach Bernard,PLLC) -300 Merrick Rd -Lynbrk 11563 **Fx:**568-7699
(718) 923-6322 .. **Roaldsen,** Maureen F '91 Appltt Div 2nd Dept -335 Adams -Brklyn 11201 **Fx:**624-5603
(518) 624-2722 .. **Roalsvig,** Paul H '95 -8581 Newcomb Rd Bx735 -Long Lk 12847 **Fx:**624-2723
(914) 323-7000 .. **Roarke,** Robt F '82 (Wilson EME&D LLP) -3 Gannett Dr -White Plns 10604
(212) 490-3000 .. **Roarke,** Robt F '82 (Wilson EME&D LLP) -150 E 42nd -NY 10017
(212) 664-5165 .. **Roarty,** Allison B '01 %NBC Universal -30 Rckfllr Plz -NY 10112
(908) 334-3590 .. **Roat,** Rachel P '81 -275 7th Av -NY 10001 **Fx:**246-9856
(518) 457-4380 .. **Roback,** Louise G '85 %Dept of Labor -State Campus Bldg 12 -Albany 12240 **Fx:**457-1164
(212) 493-7587 .. **Robaina,** Alberto '91 NYC Investment Fund -1 Bttry Pk Plz -NY 10004
(718) 261-7700 .. **Robalino,** John D '96 %Rappaport HC&R,PC -118-35 Qns Blvd -Frst Hlls 11375
(212) 521-3500 .. **Robarge,** Karen L '87 (Aronson M&S, LLP) -485 Lex Av -NY 10017
(212) 687-7410 .. **Robb,** Arthur J '99 %Clifton B&D,LLP -420 Lex Av -NY 10170
(212) 697-3122 .. **Robb,** Brian T '06 %Martin C&B LLP -220 E 42nd -NY 10017
(212) 309-1000 .. **Robb,** Kathy E B '90 (Hunton & W) -200 Park Av -NY 10166
(585) 325-5150 .. **Robb,** Maggie Randall '01 %Faraci L,LLP -28 E Main -Rchstr 14614
(718) 888-9500 .. **Robb,** Michl D '06 %Kim & C,LLP -158-14 Nrthrn Blvd -Flushng 11358
(212) 301-1007 .. **Robb,** Timothy M '99 Natl Financial Prtnrs Corp -340 Mad Av -NY 10019 **Fx:**301-4001
(914) 741-4301 .. **Robb,** Wm J Jr. '97 -50 Bway -Hawthorne 10532 **Fx:**741-5850
(212) 808-7800 .. **Robben,** Philip D '99 (Kelley D&W LLP) -101 Park Av -NY 10178
(212) 636-6908 .. **Robbie,** Jorene Frenkl '80 %Fordham Univ Sch of Law -140 W 62nd -NY 10023 **Fx:**636-6899
(212) 223-0400 .. **Robbin,** Jonathan '07 %Zeichner E&K LLP -575 Lex Av -NY 10022
(212) 513-3200 .. **Robbin,** Robt S '67 (Holland & K LLP) -31 W 52nd -NY 10019
(212) 259-8000 .. **Robbins,** Andrew S '10 %Dewey & L LLP -1301 Av of Amer -NY 10019
(212) 455-2000 .. **Robbins,** Brian D '89 (Simpson T&B LLP) -425 Lex Av -NY 10017
(914) 793-8685 .. **Robbins,** Bruce J '66 -65 Hickory Hill Rd -Eastchstr 10709
(716) 488-3090 .. **Robbins,** Dale C '76 (Burgett & R) -15 E 5th Bx3090 -Jamestwn 14702
(212) 207-4125 .. **Robbins,** Danl R '90 -488 Mad Av -NY 10022 **Fx:**308-8582
(212) 755-3100 .. **Robbins,** David E '75 (Kaufmann GR&O LLP) -777 3rd Av -NY 10017
(212) 735-3000 .. **Robbins,** Edwin '58 OfCnsl Skadden ASM&F LLP -4 Times Sq -NY 10036
(516) 483-4642 .. **Robbins,** Gary J '97 -215 Uniondale Av -Uniondale 11553 **Fx:**505-5120
(212) 599-0307 .. **Robbins,** Glenn B '75 -250 E 40th -NY 10016 **Fx:**599-6030
(516) 677-0200 .. **Robbins,** Gregory A '92 Veeco Instruments Inc -1 Trmnl Dr -Plainvw 11803
(212) 848-4000 .. **Robbins,** Henry H '05 %Shearman & S LLP -599 Lex Av -NY 10022
(212) 969-3912 .. **Robbins,** Howard Z '95 (Proskauer R LLP) -1585 Bway -NY 10036
(212) 808-0444 .. **Robbins,** James A '79 (Robbins & Assoc,PC) -60 E 42nd -NY 10165 **Fx:**808-4150
(212) 872-7833 .. **Robbins,** James M '88 %KPMG LLP -757 3rd Av -NY 10017
(212) 857-8500 .. **Robbins,** Jeremy A '08 %US Ct of Appls -40 Foley Sq -NY 10007
(212) 249-1550 .. **Robbins,** Jerome '58 -40 E 69th -NY 10021 **Fx:**249-5451
(212) 448-1100 .. **Robbins,** Jon Paul '74 (McLaughlin & S,LLP) -260 Mad Av -NY 10016
(415) 693-6215 .. **Robbins,** Jonathan D '98 Morgan Stanley -2000 Wstchstr Av -Purchase 10577
(212) 416-8000 .. **Robbins,** Julia S '86 %Dept of Law -120 Bway -NY 10271
(212) 335-9000 .. **Robbins,** Kalyani '03 %DA -1 Hogan Pl -NY 10013
(212) 808-8008 .. **Robbins,** Lee J '52 -122 E 42nd -NY 10168

(607) 432-3611 .. **Robbins,** Michl P '10 %Harlem & J -493 Chestnut -Oneonta 13820 **Fx:**432-9761
(212) 344-1400 .. **Robbins,** Norman '51 OfCnsl Friedland L&R,LLP -62 William -NY 10005
(212) 836-7430 .. **Robbins,** Paul '00 Cnsl Kaye S LLP -425 Park Av -NY 10022 **Fx:**836-6778
(212) 957-1900 .. **Robbins,** Richd A '76 -305 Mad Av -NY 10165 **Fx:**957-1912
(212) 962-8020 .. **Robbins,** Richd A '81 %Julien & S,PC -1 Whitehall -NY 10004
(212) 344-1400 .. **Robbins,** Spencer B '81 (Friedland L&R,LLP) -62 William -NY 10005
(212) 943-8940 .. **Robbins,** Stephanie L '92 %Crisci W&H -17 State -NY 10004 **Fx:**425-3428
(212) 704-4400 .. **Robbins,** Susan I '87 %Miller CP&S,PLLC -500 5th Av -NY 10110
(315) 218-8000 .. **Robbins,** Virginia C '87 (Bond S&K,PLLC) -1 Lincoln Ctr -Syracuse 13202
(914) 682-2800 .. **Robbins,** Wm D '74 -6 Westway -White Plns 10605 **Fx:**682-7744
(212) 867-6000 .. **Robbins,** Wm J '77 (Rosenberg & E,PC) -733 3rd Av -NY 10017
(212) 504-6000 .. **Robbins,** Wm Z '10 %Cadwalader W&T LLP -1 World Fncl Ctr -NY 10281
(631) 476-5871 .. **Roben,** Christopher A '03 C Roben,PC -287 Mt Sinai Coram Rd Bx5 -Mt Sinai 11766 **Fx:**476-2351
(845) 626-4804 .. **Roberge,** Martha M '77 -39 Cliff Rd -Accord 12404 **Fx:**626-4804
(347) 296-1663 .. **Roberson,** Cynthia L '95 %Supreme Ct Law Dept -360 Adams -Brklyn 11201 **Fx:**643-6114
(212) 962-1450 .. **Roberson,** Joanna Martin '06 %Magovern & S -111 John -NY 10038
(212) 833-8000 .. **Roberson,** Michl J '89 Sony BMG Music Entrtnmnt -550 Mad Av -NY 10022 **Fx:**833-8406
(716) 433-5941 .. **Roberson,** Robt S '66 (Andrews PBS&R) -929 Lincoln Av -Lockprt 14094
(631) 271-3300 .. **Robert,** Clifford S '99 (Robert & R PLLC) -150 Broad Hollow Rd -Melvll 11747 **Fx:**271-1784
(212) 715-9100 .. **Robert,** Jay D '10 %Kramer LN&F,LLP -1177 Av of Amer -NY 10036
(516) 766-7700 .. **Robert,** Joan Lensky '91 (Kassoff R&L) -100 Merrick Rd -Rockvll Ctr 11570
(631) 271-3300 .. **Robert,** Seth P '92 -150 Broad Hollow Rd -Melvll 11747 **Fx:**271-1784
(516) 281-9800 .. **Roberto,** Joanna M '99 (Goldberg S LLP) -200 Old Cntry Rd -Mineola 11501
(212) 475-3300 .. **Roberts,** Abigail '02 Village Voice -36 Cooper Sq -NY 10003
(212) 385-1444 .. **Roberts,** Alan '88 Cnsl Silverstein & S,LLP -40 Fulton -NY 10038
(845) 298-2000 .. **Roberts,** Albert P '71 (Vergilis SRD&D,LLP) -1136 Route 9 -Wappingers Fls 12590
(212) 596-9000 .. **Roberts,** Alexandra J '09 %Ropes & G LLP -1211 Av of Amer -NY 10036
(212) 351-4500 .. **Roberts,** Allen B '75 (Epstein B&G,PC) -250 Park Av -NY 10177
(315) 682-4065 .. **Roberts,** Anita U '78 -8108 Cazenovia Rd -Manlius 13104
(212) 876-5500 .. **Roberts,** Anna '04 Neighborhood Def Srv -317 Lenox Av -NY 10027 **Fx:**876-5586
(212) 715-9100 .. **Roberts,** Ashley B '07 %Kramer LN&F,LLP -1177 Av of Amer -NY 10036
(914) 665-8375 .. **Roberts,** Avril D '01 -110 N 8th Av -Mt Vernon 10550 **Fx:**664-0102
(516) 227-0700 .. **Roberts,** Bruce N '82 Cnsl Farrell F,PC -1320 RXR Plz -Uniondale 11556
(212) 841-1000 .. **Roberts,** Carey S '06 (Covington & B LLP) -620 8th Av -NY 10018
(516) 379-1980 .. **Roberts,** Carol M '84 -527 S Ocean Av -Freeprt 11520
(315) 448-0672 .. **Roberts,** Chas E '77 US Atty -100 S Clinton Bx7198 -Syracuse 13261 **Fx:**488-0646
(518) 474-7330 .. **Roberts,** Christina L '02 %Dept of Law -The Cptl -Albany 12224
(212) 210-9538 .. **Roberts,** Colin W '09 %Alston & B LLP -90 Park Av -NY 10016
(631) 247-0404 .. **Roberts,** Craig S '98 (Jackson L LLP) -58 S Srvc Rd -Melvll 11747
(716) 858-5052 .. **Roberts,** D Chas Jr. '98 Delaware North -40 Fountain Plz -Buffalo 14202 Fx:858-5056
(718) 522-0666 .. **Roberts,** D Michl '98 %Sanders G&B,PC -26 Court -Brklyn 11242
(518) 408-2516 .. **Roberts,** David B '79 %Dept of Law -The Cptl -Albany 12224
(212) 808-0700 .. **Roberts,** Dean M '88 (Norris M&M,PA) -875 3rd Av -NY 10022
(716) 849-1333 .. **Roberts,** Diane M '91 SpclCnsl Lipsitz GSC LLP -42 Delaware Av -Buffalo 14202
(212) 686-7872 .. **Roberts,** Dianne I '91 -480 2nd Av -NY 10016 **Fx:**686-7867
(315) 422-0112 .. **Roberts,** Douglas G '74 -307 Hurlburt Rd -Syracuse 13224
(212) 724-9890 .. **Roberts,** Earl S '60 -670 West End Av -NY 10025
(718) 693-0800 .. **Roberts,** Earle C '78 -887 Flatbush Av -Brklyn 11226 **Fx:**284-0511
(718) 421-4300 .. **Roberts,** Edw A '85 -3009 Glenwood Rd -Brklyn 11210
(347) 592-2200 .. **Roberts,** Florence '79 %Leg Srvcs -89-00 Sutphin Blvd -Jamaica 11435 **Fx:**(718) 937-5350
(914) 232-5161 .. **Roberts,** George H '62 (Covey RC&C) -200 Katonah Av -Katonah 10536
(212) 768-6700 .. **Roberts,** Glen W II '97 (Sonnenschein N&R LLP) -2 World Fncl Ctr -NY 10281
(914) 946-1400 .. **Roberts,** Hal '95 %Vouté LM&C,LLP -170 Hmltn Av -White Plns 10601
(718) 923-4406 .. **Roberts,** Harold H '92 Div of Human Rights -55 Hanson Pl -Brklyn 11217 **Fx:**722-2869
(212) 903-8700 .. **Roberts & Holland,LLP** -825 8th Av -NY 10019 **Fx:**974-3059
(718) 250-2000 .. **Roberts,** Ilana '05 DA -350 Jay -Brklyn 11201 **Fx:**250-2314
(646) 386-5700 .. **Roberts,** Iris '08 %Civil Ct -111 Centre -NY 10013
(212) 448-1800 .. **Roberts,** Jaimison M '80 (Roberts RLSC&F LLP) -235 Park Av S -NY 10003
(212) 770-7876 .. **Roberts,** James B '00 AIG -70 Pine -NY 10270
(631) 863-2400 .. **Roberts,** Jeffrey M '81 J Roberts,PC -720 Smithtwn Bypass -Smithtwn 11787 **Fx:**863-2406
(516) 496-5822 .. **Roberts,** Joelle A '98 %T Spina -170 Froehlich Farm Blvd -Woodbury 11797 **Fx:**496-5420
(212) 696-4052 .. **Roberts,** John B '86 -250 W 57th -NY 10107 **Fx:**889-7791
(212) 474-1000 .. **Roberts,** John E '09 %Cravath S&M LLP -825 8th Av -NY 10019
(212) 773-7021 .. **Roberts,** Jonathan A '96 Ernst & Young LLP -5 Times Sq -NY 10036 **Fx:**773-2333
(212) 482-0007 .. **Roberts,** Jonathan E '93 (Talkin M&R,LLP) -40 Exch Pl -NY 10005 **Fx:**482-1303
(212) 680-8514 .. **Roberts,** Julia Belson '07 FEMA Region II -26 Fed Plz -NY 10278
(716) 854-2620 .. **Roberts,** Julia E '07 %Brown & K,LLP -1500 Lbrty Bldg -Buffalo 14202
(212) 225-2000 .. **Roberts,** Katherine J '02 %Cleary GS&H -1 Lbrty Plz -NY 10006
(212) 751-2700 .. **Roberts,** Kathleen A '79 %JAMS -620 8th Av -NY 10018 **Fx:**751-4099
(917) 441-8642 .. **Roberts,** Keith '04 Roberts Proprietaries -180 W 80th -NY 10024
(212) 820-9512 .. **Roberts,** Kenneth B '82 (Hawkins D&W LLP) -One Chase Manh Plz -NY 10005
(212) 883-4914 .. **Roberts,** Kenneth G '82 (Cozen O) -277 Park Av -NY 10172 **Fx:**672-1114
(212) 259-8000 .. **Roberts,** Kimberly L '03 %Dewey & L LLP -1301 Av of Amer -NY 10019
(845) 225-0176 .. **Roberts,** Laura Anne '05 %J Spofford Jr -20 Church -Carmel 10512 **Fx:**225-0274
(646) 616-8075 .. **Roberts,** Lauren A '09 Fairway Group Holdings Corp -2284 12th Av -NY 10027
(718) 579-3000 .. **Roberts,** Lauren Lee '94 %Leg Aid -1020 Grnd Cncrs -Bronx 10451 **Fx:**588-2611
(212) 879-6959 .. **Roberts,** Linda '80 -605 Park Av -NY 10065
(212) 553-9206 .. **Roberts,** Lloyd M '83 G Cannata -233 Bway -NY 10279 **Fx:**227-4141
(212) 259-8000 .. **Roberts,** Lynn W '91 Cnsl Dewey & L LLP -1301 Av of Amer -NY 10019
(516) 228-1298 .. **Roberts,** Marc W '78 -600 Old Cntry Rd -Gdn Cty 11530 **Fx:**228-4840
(212) 962-7083 .. **Roberts,** Mark J '76 -185 West End Av -NY 10023
(315) 781-1465 .. **Roberts,** Martha A '84 %Leg Assistance -361 S Main -Geneva 14456 **Fx:**781-2565
(212) 436-1090 .. **Roberts,** Marylee A '93 %IRS -290 Bway -NY 10007
(212) 487-8443 .. **Roberts,** Megan S '06 NYC Dept of Consumers Affairs -42 Bway -NY 10004
(212) 218-2100 .. **Roberts,** Melinda R '10 %Fitzpatrick CH&S -1290 Av of Amer -NY 10104
(212) 226-4925 .. **Roberts,** Michl J '80 -401 Bway -NY 10013 **Fx:**274-0109
(212) 373-3000 .. **Roberts,** Michl J '08 %Paul WRW&G LLP -1285 Av of Amer -NY 10019
(212) 558-5500 .. **Roberts,** Michl P '87 %Weitz & L,PC -700 Bway -NY 10003
(716) 818-1050 .. **Roberts,** Michl S L '05 -Bx91 -Buffalo 14205
(212) 336-3620 .. **Roberts,** Monique J '00 %EEOC -33 Whitehall -NY 10004
(716) 551-4931 .. **Roberts,** Nicole '01 %NLRB -130 S Elmwood Av -Buffalo 14202 **Fx:**551-4972
(212) 967-1800 .. **Roberts,** Paul C '97 (Bryant BJ&R LLP) -140 Bway -NY 10005
(212) 336-8486 .. **Roberts,** R Gregory '03 (Morrison & F LLP) -1290 Av of Amer -NY 10104
(716) 856-4000 .. **Roberts,** R Kent '00 (Hodgson R LLP) -140 Pearl -Buffalo 14202
(716) 753-4241 .. **Roberts,** Rachel E '02 %DA -Cnty Cthse -Mayvll 14757 **Fx:**753-4628
(631) 852-3579 .. **Roberts,** Renee J '96 Supreme Ct -235 Griffin Av -Rvrhead 11901
(914) 668-6622 .. **Roberts,** Richd A '84 -34 E 1st -Mt Vernon 10550 **Fx:**668-7763
(212) 448-1800 .. **Roberts Ritholz Levy Sanders Chidekel & Fields LLP** -235 Park Av S -NY 10003 **Fx:**448-0020
(212) 685-6500 .. **Roberts,** Robin B '04 Dominion Mgmt -200 Mad Av -NY 10016 **Fx:**(646) 447-2371
(585) 419-8800 .. **Roberts,** Russell W '84 Cnsl Harris B PLLC -99 Garnsey Rd -Pittsfrd 14534
(718) 250-2000 .. **Roberts,** Sandra D '05 DA -350 Jay -Brklyn 11201 **Fx:**250-2314
(212) 218-2100 .. **Roberts,** Simon D '95 %Fitzpatrick CH&S -1290 Av of Amer -NY 10104
(212) 558-4000 .. **Roberts,** Stanley Abbott '07 %Sullivan & C LLP -125 Broad -NY 10004
(212) 962-1590 .. **Roberts,** Stephen B '72 OfCnsl Tabak M&S -29 Bway -NY 10006
(212) 261-8000 .. **Roberts,** Stephen T '87 (Mendes & M,LLP) -750 7th Av -NY 10019
(585) 338-5979 .. **Roberts,** Susan '89 Bausch & Lomb -One Bausch & Lomb Pl -Rchstr 14604
(212) 310-8000 .. **Roberts,** Thos A '73 (Weil G&M LLP) -767 5th Av -NY 10153
(716) 856-1636 .. **Roberts,** Thos E '71 (Walsh R&G) -14 Lafayette Sq -Buffalo 14203
(212) 891-4150 .. **Roberts,** Thos R '78 -750 3rd Av -NY 10017 **Fx:**818-0038
(518) 785-5340 .. **Roberts,** Todd C '03 Shantz & B -26 Century Hill Dr -Latham 12110 **Fx:**785-5470
(212) 786-6321 .. **Roberts,** Todd M '88 Aegis Capital Grp -1325 Av of Amer -NY 10019
(212) 326-3939 .. **Roberts,** Valerie Pearsall '82 (Jones D) -222 E 41st -NY 10017
(518) 576-4286 .. **Roberts,** Wm B '08 W Roberts LLC -1019 Hurricane Rd Bx140 -Keene 12942 **Fx:**(866) 531-8907
(518) 453-0173 .. **Roberts,** Wm D '02 -668 Mad Av -Albany 12208 **Fx:**326-6470
(212) 902-1000 .. **Robertson,** Andrew '00 %Goldman Sachs -85 Broad -NY 10004
(212) 819-7503 .. **Robertson,** Andrew C '02 -1155 Av of Amer -NY 10036
(212) 530-5000 .. **Robertson,** Andrew W '05 %Milbank TH&M LLP -1 Chase Manh Plz -NY 10005
(212) 407-4000 .. **Robertson,** Ayana M '08 %Loeb & L,LLP -345 Park Av -NY 10154
(212) 560-8211 .. **Robertson,** Blanche Borzell '07 EBC -450 W 33rd -NY 10001 **Fx:**560-3191
(212) 506-5000 .. **Robertson,** Danl W '09 %Orrick H&S LLP -51 W 52nd -NY 10019
(518) 432-1200 .. **Robertson,** Deborah M '93 (McGlinchey S PLLC) -194 Wshngtn Av -Albany 12210
(631) 360-0400 .. **Robertson,** Edw A '77 (Jakubowski RMG&T) -969 Jericho Tpk -St James 11780 **Fx:**360-0408
(212) 504-6000 .. **Robertson,** Edwin D '72 (Cadwalader W&T LLP) -1 World Fncl Ctr -NY 10281
(212) 530-5000 .. **Robertson,** Elihu F '80 (Milbank TH&M LLP) -1 Chase Manh Plz -NY 10005
(718) 520-3772 .. **Robertson,** James D '62 %Hon P Flug -88-11 Sutphin Blvd -Jamaica 11435 **Fx:**520-1525
(914) 995-3641 .. **Robertson,** James M '83 %Cnty Atty -148 Martine Av -White Plns 10601 **Fx:**995-5858
(212) 756-2000 .. **Robertson,** Jeffrey F '96 SpclCnsl Schulte R&Z LLP -919 3rd Av -NY 10022
(212) 918-3000 .. **Robertson,** Jenny Rubin '05 %Hogan L LLP -875 3rd Av -NY 10022
(212) 559-1263 .. **Robertson,** Jill M '03 Citigroup Trust -153 E 53rd -NY 10022
(212) 225-2000 .. **Robertson,** Jos M '10 %Cleary GS&H -1 Lbrty Plz -NY 10006
(914) 323-7000 .. **Robertson,** Kurt D '01 %Wilson EME&D LLP -3 Gannett Dr -White Plns 10604
(212) 455-2000 .. **Robertson,** Lesley R '03 %Simpson T&B LLP -425 Lex Av -NY 10017

(518) 462-6765 .. **Robertson**, Lisa J '86 %Leg Aid -55 Colvin Av -Albany 12206 **Fx**:427-8352
(212) 318-3000 .. **Robertson**, Mark A '02 (Fulbright & J LLP) -666 5th Av -NY 10103
(212) 902-7407 .. **Robertson**, Mark T '05 %Goldman Sachs -1 NY Plz -NY 10004
(212) 326-2000 .. **Robertson**, Mark W '07 (O'Melveny & M LLP) -7 Times Sq -NY 10036
(212) 308-4411 .. **Robertson**, Pamela S '82 (Edwards AP&D LLP) -750 Lex Av -NY 10022
(516) 229-6000 .. **Robertson**, Paul '92 %R Lau & Assoc -300 Jericho Quad Bx9040 -Jericho 11753 **Fx**:229-6167
(212) 415-9200 .. **Robertson**, Sarah M '02 (Dorsey & W LLP) -250 Park Av -NY 10177
(212) 838-7797 .. **Robertson**, Sharon K '07 %Cohen MS&T,PLLC -88 Pine -NY 10005
(315) 426-1149 .. **Robertson**, Thos M '86 -333 E Onondaga -Syracuse 13202 **Fx**:422-1793
(212) 819-8200 .. **Robertson**, Wm C '08 %White & C LLP -1155 Av of Amer -NY 10036
(518) 627-0202 .. **Robeson**, John B '02 -4193 State Hwy 30 -Amsterdam 12010 **Fx**:627-0303
(585) 475-5607 .. **Robfogel**, Nathan J '59 %Roch Inst Tech -131 Lomb Mem'l Dr -Rchstr 14623 **Fx**:475-5533
(212) 940-3116 .. **Robfogel**, Susan S '67 (Nixon P LLP) -437 Mad Av -NY 10022
(518) 434-0446 .. **Robichaud**, Kathleen Leahey '90 -52 Green Bx299 -Rensselaer 12144 **Fx**:427-8229
(212) 363-9620 .. **Robichaud**, Todd D '95 Alacra Inc -100 Bway -NY 10005 **Fx**:363-9630
(518) 935-2881 .. **Robich-Wright**, Pamela M '92 Homefront Title -Bx5242 -Albany 12205 **Fx**:435-9143
(212) 610-6300 .. **Robilotti**, Mark G '98 Cnsl Allen & O -1221 Av of Amer -NY 10020
(212) 906-1200 .. **Robin**, Aviva F '10 %Latham & W -885 3rd Av -NY 10022
(212) 683-8000 .. **Robin**, Avrom '01 (London & R) -245 5th Av -NY 10016 **Fx**:683-9422
(212) 964-3400 .. **Robin**, Caitlin A '07 %Drabkin & M -120 Bway -NY 10271
(212) 487-9701 .. **Robin Harris King & Fodera** -1 Bttry Pk Plz -NY 10014 **Fx**:425-0472
(212) 286-4471 .. **Robin**, Marni R '94 SrCnsl McCormick & O,LLP -9 E 40th -NY 10016 **Fx**:504-9574
(607) 272-7124 .. **Robinow**, Lisa S '89 -104 Landmark Dr -Ithaca 14850
(914) 949-2826 .. **Robinowitz Cohlan Dubow & Doherty,LLP** -199 Main -White Plns 10601 **Fx**:949-2822
(212) 373-3000 .. **Robinowitz**, Stuart '53 OfCnsl Paul WRW&G LLP -1285 Av of Amer -NY 10019
(212) 599-0349 .. **Robins**, Bernard J '62 -551 5th Av -NY 10176 **Fx**:986-0943
(212) 888-8200 .. **Robins**, Bruce E '89 (Feder K LLP) -845 3rd Av -NY 10022
(516) 228-9800 .. **Robins**, Craig D '85 -180 Froehlich Farm Blvd -Woodbury 11797
(516) 931-0050 .. **Robins**, David A '93 (Lipman & P,LLP) -500 N Bway -Jericho 11753
(917) 406-5606 .. **Robins**, Elizabeth R '03 Modem Properties -530 1st Av -NY 10016
(212) 286-0747 .. **Robins**, Eric I '04 %D Brecher -99 Park Av -NY 10016 **Fx**:808-4155
(212) 309-6000 .. **Robins**, Harry T '97 (Morgan L&B LLP) -101 Park Av -NY 10178
(212) 408-5100 .. **Robins**, Jeffrey A '90 (Chadbourne & P LLP) -30 Rckfllr Plz -NY 10112
(212) 504-6000 .. **Robins**, Jeffrey L '03 SpclCnsl Cadwalader W&T LLP -1 World Fncl Ctr -NY 10281
(800) 553-9940 .. **Robins Kaplan Miller & Ciresi LLP** -499 Park Av -NY 10022
(212) 705-7000 .. **Robins**, Theo J '02 Cnsl Bingham M LLP -399 Park Av -NY 10022
(212) 839-5300 .. **Robinson**, A Francis Jr. '68 (Sidley A LLP) -787 7th Av -NY 10019
(212) 603-6300 .. **Robinson**, A Stanley '55 (Robinson BLGG&G PC) -875 3rd Av -NY 10022
(212) 715-7255 .. **Robinson**, Alexis L '09 Trump Org -725 5th Av -NY 10022
(518) 374-3399 .. **Robinson**, Amy Herter '88 (Higgins RB&C,PC) -1430 Balltown Rd -Niskayuna 12309
(718) 250-2000 .. **Robinson**, Andrea '96 %DA -350 Jay -Brklyn 11201 **Fx**:250-2314
(917) 488-2432 .. **Robinson**, Andrew J '84 -1550 York Av -NY 10028
(212) 455-2000 .. **Robinson**, Arthur D '89 (Simpson T&B LLP) -425 Lex Av -NY 10017
(212) 909-6000 .. **Robinson**, Barbara P '66 OfCnsl Debevoise & P LLP -919 3rd Av -NY 10022
(212) 213-0030 .. **Robinson**, Benjamin '69 (Ziegler & R) -25 W 43rd -NY 10036 **Fx**:696-9417
(212) 306-6051 .. **Robinson**, Billow W '74 %Housing Auth -250 Bway -NY 10007
(914) 769-5900 .. **Robinson Bradshaw & Hinson** -100 Summit Lk Dr -Valhalla 10595 **Fx**:769-5908
(212) 272-3056 .. **Robinson**, Brian D '03 JP Morgan Chase -383 Mad Av -NY 10179
(212) 425-7200 .. **Robinson**, Brian J '07 %Kenyon & K,LLP -1 Bway -NY 10004
(212) 456-2263 .. **Robinson**, Brian T '92 ESPN -47 W 66th -NY 10023
(212) 603-6300 .. **Robinson Brog Leinwand Greene Genovese & Gluck PC** -875 3rd Av -NY 10022 **Fx**:956-2164
(914) 642-4375 .. **Robinson**, Cari S '88 IBM -1133 Wstchstr Av -White Plns 10604
(212) 277-4000 .. **Robinson**, Chas A B '98 (Freshfields BD LLP) -520 Mad Av -NY 10022
(212) 878-8000 .. **Robinson**, Christopher C '10 %Clifford C LLP -31 W 52nd -NY 10019
(212) 489-8230 .. **Robinson**, Christopher J '02 %Davis WT LLP -1633 Bway -NY 10019
(212) 451-2900 .. **Robinson & Cole LLP** -885 3rd Av -NY 10022 **Fx**:451-2999
(212) 867-9140 .. **Robinson**, Cori A '07 %Lewis & G,PC -60 E 42nd -NY 10165 **Fx**:867-9143
(212) 431-7200 .. **Robinson**, David '90 %Legal Srvcs NYC -350 Bway -NY 10013 **Fx**:966-9571
(631) 501-3100 .. **Robinson**, David I '95 %J Humphreys -3 Huntngtn Quad Bx9028 -Melvll 11747 **Fx**:501-3086
(516) 364-6006 .. **Robinson**, David L '06 Cohen & S,LLP -199 Crsswys Park Dr Bx9004 -Woodbury 11797
(212) 324-5000 .. **Robinson**, David W '93 %Con Ed Communications -55 Broad -NY 10004
(516) 248-3302 .. **Robinson**, Derrick J '84 %Dept of Law -200 Old Cntry Rd -Mineola 11501 **Fx**:747-6432
(212) 983-9700 .. **Robinson**, Devin R '02 %Gallagher H&L LLP -380 Lex Av -NY 10168
(212) 506-5000 .. **Robinson**, Donald J '60 OfCnsl Orrick H&S LLP -51 W 52nd -NY 10019
(212) 692-0200 .. **Robinson**, Douglas E '99 Slater TF&H,PA -230 Park Av -NY 10169
(212) 759-4600 .. **Robinson**, E Elizabeth '05 %Wolf P LLP -845 3rd Av -NY 10022
(716) 879-6848 .. **Robinson**, Earl T III '78 %Outokumpu Amer Brass -Bx981 -Buffalo 14240 **Fx**:879-6735
(716) 849-8900 .. **Robinson**, Edw C '84 (Hurwitz & F,PC) -1300 Lbrty Bldg -Buffalo 14202
(631) 283-7100 .. **Robinson**, Elbert W Jr. '75 (Robinson & R PC) -61 Main -Southampton 11968 **Fx**:283-7101
(212) 294-6700 .. **Robinson**, Eric M '03 (Winston & S) -200 Park Av -NY 10166
(212) 337-0200 .. **Robinson**, Eric P '93 MLRC -520 8th Av -NY 10018 **Fx**:337-9893
(212) 403-1000 .. **Robinson**, Eric S '84 (Wachtell LR&K) -51 W 52nd -NY 10019
(718) 222-2001 .. **Robinson**, Gayonne N '09 %Law Dept -350 Jay -Brklyn 11201 **Fx**:222-2088
(585) 325-4953 .. **Robinson & Glavin** -16 E Main -Rchstr 14614 **Fx**:546-8129
(212) 412-1767 .. **Robinson**, Graham A '04 Barclays Capital Inc -745 7th Av -NY 10019
(718) 286-6000 .. **Robinson**, Gretchen K '03 %DA -125-01 Qns Blvd -Kew Gdns 11415
(516) 627-0163 .. **Robinson**, Irwin Z '62 -45 Clardg Cir -Manhsst 11030 **Fx**:627-0168
(212) 808-0033 .. **Robinson**, J Howland '78 -405 Lex Av -NY 10174 **Fx**:504-8174
(516) 470-1661 .. **Robinson**, James E '93 %J Myers,PC -267 Carleton Av -Central Islip 11722 **Fx**:470-1657
(212) 649-0623 .. **Robinson**, James M IV '08 Silvercrest Asst Mgmt Crp LLC -1330 Av of Amer -NY 10019 **Fx**:649-0625
(917) 778-6500 .. **Robinson**, Janice A '02 %K Dodson -485 Lex Av -NY 10017
(585) 374-8350 .. **Robinson**, Janice R '92 -102 N Main Bx728 -Naples 14512 **Fx**:374-8595
(212) 678-3732 .. **Robinson**, Janice S '83 Teachers College, Columbia Univ -525 W 120th Bx220 -NY 10027 **Fx**:678-3201
(212) 953-3400 .. **Robinson**, Jayne S '79 (Robinson & M) -61 Bway -NY 10006
(212) 554-1400 .. **Robinson**, Jeremy P '07 %Bernstein LB&G LLP -1285 Av of Amer -NY 10019
(212) 725-8566 .. **Robinson**, Joel Harris '95 (Robinson & Y,PC) -232 Mad Av -NY 10016
(212) 455-2000 .. **Robinson**, John A '10 %Simpson T&B LLP -425 Lex Av -NY 10017
(212) 484-3900 .. **Robinson**, John G '08 %Arent F LLP -1675 Bway -NY 10019
(212) 272-9649 .. **Robinson**, John K '95 %JP Morgan Chase -383 Mad Av -NY 10179
(212) 403-1000 .. **Robinson**, John L '10 %Wachtell LR&K -51 W 52nd -NY 10019
(212) 547-5400 .. **Robinson**, Jos R '89 (McDermott W&E LLP) -340 Mad Av -NY 10173
(212) 815-1875 .. **Robinson**, Karen A '91 %DC 37 MELS -125 Barclay -NY 10007 **Fx**:815-1343
(212) 808-0700 .. **Robinson**, Karol S '00 (Norris M&M,PA) -875 3rd Av -NY 10022
(212) 351-4000 .. **Robinson**, Kathryn A '06 %Gibson D&C LLP -200 Park Av -NY 10166
(516) 496-9044 .. **Robinson**, Kenneth L '79 (Robinson & Assoc,PC) -35 Roosevelt Av -Syosset 11791 **Fx**:496-9047
(718) 237-6282 .. **Robinson**, Kenneth M '78 %Family Ct -283 Adams -Brklyn 11201
(631) 385-3255 .. **Robinson**, Kenneth P '62 -Bx328 -Greenlawn 11740 **Fx**:757-2156
(716) 843-5700 .. **Robinson**, Kevin D '93 %US Atty -138 Delaware Av -Buffalo 14202 **Fx**:551-3052
(315) 393-3130 .. **Robinson**, Kirk T '91 %MHLS -804 Commerce Park Dr -Ogdensbrg 13669 **Fx**:393-9633
(212) 975-4380 .. **Robinson**, Laurie N '99 CBS Inc -51 W 52nd -NY 10019 **Fx**:975-3930
(212) 547-5400 .. **Robinson**, Leah Samit '06 (McDermott W&E LLP) -340 Mad Av -NY 10173
(212) 735-3000 .. **Robinson**, Limor '06 %Skadden ASM&F LLP -4 Times Sq -NY 10036
(212) 450-4000 .. **Robinson**, Lisa G '08 %Davis P&W LLP -450 Lex Av -NY 10017
(315) 413-5400 .. **Robinson**, Lisa M '05 %Goldberg S LLP -5789 Widewaters Pkwy -Syracuse 13214
(585) 591-1111 .. **Robinson**, Lucille D '05 (Dadd & R,PLLC) -17 Exchange Bx206 -Attica 14011 **Fx**:591-1116
(607) 753-3551 .. **Robinson**, Margaret M '95 -36 Main Bx866 -Cortlnd 13045 **Fx**:756-8768
(212) 353-8800 .. **Robinson**, Mark A '96 %Koch Entertainment -740 Bway -NY 10003 **Fx**:228-8886
(212) 788-5244 .. **Robinson**, Martha '84 %Dept Hlth -125 Worth CN-30 -NY 10013 **Fx**:788-4300
(212) 859-8000 .. **Robinson**, Martin E '03 SpclCnsl Fried FHS&J LLP -1 NY Plz -NY 10004
(212) 302-2900 .. **Robinson**, Marvin S '57 (Tannenbaum D&R) -1140 Av of Amer -NY 10036
(212) 953-3400 .. **Robinson & McDonald** -61 Bway -NY 10006 **Fx**:953-3690
(212) 297-5800 .. **Robinson**, Micala Campbell '06 %Day P LLP -7 Times Sq -NY 10036
(585) 374-5210 .. **Robinson**, Michl P '86 -118 N Main Bx417 -Naples 14512 **Fx**:374-9327
(716) 484-7196 .. **Robinson**, Neil M '77 (Fessenden L&D) -81 Forest Av Bx590 -Jamestwn 14702
(914) 422-4244 .. **Robinson**, Nicholas '71 %Pace Law Schl -78 N Bway -White Plns 10603 **Fx**:422-4039
(212) 530-5000 .. **Robinson**, Nicholas J '06 %Milbank TH&M LLP -1 Chase Manh Plz -NY 10005
(516) 741-2585 .. **Robinson**, Owen M '86 %Rosicki R & Assoc,PC -51 E Bethpage Rd -Plainvw 11803 **Fx**:741-4748
(212) 526-7000 .. **Robinson**, Paul A '97 %Barclays Capital Inc -745 7th Av -NY 10019
(212) 484-8000 .. **Robinson**, Paul M '84 %Warner Music Grp -75 Rckfllr Plz -NY 10019 **Fx**:489-3342
(516) 285-4565 .. **Robinson**, Ralph N '61 -682 Lorentz -Elmont 11003
(212) 909-6000 .. **Robinson**, Richd D Jr. '01 %Debevoise & P LLP -919 3rd Av -NY 10022
(716) 853-2251 .. **Robinson**, Richd O '58 -14 Lafayette Sq -Buffalo 14203 **Fx**:845-5669
(212) 382-0909 .. **Robinson**, Richd S '95 %Peckar & A,PC -41 Mad Av -NY 10154
(212) 839-5300 .. **Robinson**, Robt J '88 (Sidley A LLP) -787 7th Av -NY 10019
(518) 765-4470 .. **Robinson**, Roselyn '83 -57 Koonz Rd -Voorheesvll 12186 **Fx**:765-2316
(646) 333-8632 .. **Robinson**, Rosemarie D '02 Lehman Bros -1271 Av of Amer -NY 10020

(914) 272-3305 .. **Robinson**, Ruth '87 %Entergy Nuclear Operations -440 Hmltn Av -White Plns 10601 **Fx:**272-3304
(718) 655-4110 .. **Robinson**, Sonia V '87 -1301 Burke Av -Bronx 10469 **Fx:**515-7239
(516) 997-1699 .. **Robinson**, Stacy J '92 -734 Franklin Av -Gdn Cty 11530
(212) 735-3000 .. **Robinson**, Stephen C '85 (Skadden ASM&F LLP) -4 Times Sq -NY 10036
(212) 362-6760 .. **Robinson**, Steven H '83 -320 W 89th -NY 10024 **Fx:**595-3605
(347) 404-9133 .. **Robinson**, Tanya K '91 %Civil Ct -141 Lvngstn -Brklyn 11201 **Fx:**(718) 643-3733
(585) 263-1000 .. **Robinson**, Terence L Jr. '06 %Nixon P LLP -1100 Clinton Sq -Rchstr 14604
(518) 788-8510 .. **Robinson**, Theo P '95 OfCnsl M Kehoe & Assoc -Bx3975 -Albany 12203
(516) 248-6600 .. **Robinson**, Theo W '73 T Robinson,PC -26 St Pauls Pl -Hempstd 11550 **Fx:**248-5354
(845) 742-8053 .. **Robinson**, Todd N '90 -149 Grand -White Plns 10601
(212) 287-4402 .. **Robinson**, Virginia R '04 %US Trust Bk of Amer -590 Madison -NY 10022
(212) 286-0423 .. **Robinson**, W Chas '79 (Robinson T & Assoc) -820 2nd Av -NY 10017
(212) 725-8566 .. **Robinson & Yablon,PC** -232 Mad Av -NY 10016 **Fx:**725-8567
(212) 730-3499 .. **Robinson**, Yasmin Michelle '02 Hlth & Hosptl Corp -160 Water -NY 10038
(914) 668-5074 .. **Robinson-Kerr**, Sandra M '04 -11 E Prospect Av -Mt Vernon 10550
(212) 554-1234 .. **Robinson-McLymont**, Rekasha '89 %AXA Financial Inc -1290 Av of Amer -NY 10104 **Fx:**707-3963
(212) 309-6000 .. **Robison**, Robt G '78 (Morgan L&B LLP) -101 Park Av -NY 10178
(718) 250-2000 .. **Robitaille**, Jeanne M '00 %DA -350 Jay -Brklyn 11201 **Fx:**250-2314
(518) 674-0123 .. **Robitaille**, Marie B '92 -5 Glenwood Ter -Averill Pk 12018
(718) 250-2000 .. **Robitaille**, Theresa A '07 %DA -350 Jay -Brklyn 11201 **Fx:**250-2314
(718) 492-3600 .. **Robles**, Christopher J '99 -471 54th -Brklyn 11220 **Fx:**492-3008
(212) 788-1384 .. **Robles**, Danl G '05 Admin Children's Srvcs -220 Church -NY 10013
(718) 417-1414 .. **Robles**, Edna I '85 (E Robles,PC) -891 Cypress Av -Rdgwd 11385 **Fx:**417-4253
(212) 259-8000 .. **Robles**, Kristi M '07 %Dewey & L LLP -1301 Av of Amer -NY 10019
(718) 590-8589 .. **Robles**, Margaret '99 ACS-Family Ct -900 Sheridan Av -Bronx 10451
(212) 223-4000 .. **Robles**, Michl K '99 Cnsl Crowell & M LLP -590 Mad Av -NY 10022
(212) 213-8833 .. **Robles**, Victoria '95 El-Ad US Holding,Inc -575 Mad Av -NY 10022 **Fx:**213-8831
(212) 697-2700 .. **Robles-Madrigal**, Jorge '99 OfCnsl Stairs DF -200 Park Av S -NY 10003
(212) 788-3000 .. **Robles-Roman**, Carol A '90 Mayor's Ofc -City Hall -NY 10007 **Fx:**788-3229
(718) 797-2488 .. **Robley**, Fabien A '06 %Friedman K&S,LLP -16 Court -Brklyn 11241 **Fx:**797-4304
(212) 596-9000 .. **Robotti**, Michl P '09 %Ropes & G LLP -1211 Av of Amer -NY 10036
(212) 885-5000 .. **Robreno**, Kelly I '10 %Blank R LLP -405 Lex Av -NY 10174
(716) 633-4030 .. **Robshaw**, John P Jr. '63 (Robshaw & Assoc,PC) -5672 Main -Williamsvll 14221 **Fx:**633-8154
(716) 853-8400 .. **Robshaw**, Nora B '02 Dept of Law -350 Main Pl Twr -Buffalo 14202 **Fx:**853-8571
(212) 849-7000 .. **Robson**, Matthew D '09 %Quinn EU&S,LLP -51 Mad Av -NY 10010
(914) 288-0800 .. **Robustelli**, Dominick J '76 D Robustelli & Assoc,PLLC -200 Mamaroneck Av -White Plns 10601 **Fx:**328-5963
(845) 782-9571 .. **Robustelli**, Dominick J '76 -1 Freeland -Monroe 10950 **Fx:**(914) 328-5963
(212) 553-8300 .. **Robusto**, Leonard A '73 %Cohen K & Assoc -2 Park Av -NY 10016 **Fx:**553-8721
(212) 513-6300 .. **Roby**, Katherine S '86 %Dept Bus Srvcs -110 William -NY 10038
(212) 637-1081 .. **Rocah**, Miriam E '98 %US Atty -1 St Andrews Plz -NY 10007
(212) 608-1178 .. **Roccanova**, Jos T '89 (Yuen RS&S PC) -132 Nassau -NY 10038 **Fx:**608-2913
(212) 701-6820 .. **Rocchi**, Albino M '82 %Chase Manhattan Bk -270 Park Av -NY 10017
(212) 805-3900 .. **Rocco**, Chas J '94 (Clausen M PC) -1 Chase Manh Plz -NY 10005
(516) 731-5200 .. **Rocco**, Jos D '91 (Rocco & R,PC) -3601 Hempstd Tpk -Levittwn 11756 **Fx:**731-5202
(212) 474-1000 .. **Rocco**, Katherine A '10 %Cravath S&M LLP -825 8th Av -NY 10019
(718) 590-5977 .. **Rocco**, Mary J '03 ACS -900 Sheridan Av -Bronx 10451
(212) 239-4340 .. **Rocco**, Patrick L '89 (Shalov SB&R LLP) -485 7th Av -NY 10018
(516) 731-5200 .. **Rocco**, Richd J '62 (Rocco & R,PC) -3601 Hempstd Tpk -Levittwn 11756 **Fx:**731-5202
(212) 997-7595 .. **Rocco**, Victor J '72 (Hafetz N&R) -500 5th Av -NY 10110
(212) 506-5000 .. **Roch**, Christine L '06 %Orrick H&S LLP -51 W 52nd -NY 10019
(212) 336-2000 .. **Rocha**, Mary Tang '94 %Patterson BW&T LLP -1133 Av of Amer -NY 10036
(718) 522-1660 .. **Roche**, Christopher C '89 St Anns Schl -129 Pierrepont -Brklyn 11201
(212) 450-4000 .. **Roche**, Christopher J '07 %Davis P&W LLP -450 Lex Av -NY 10017
(212) 430-6380 .. **Roche**, David T '96 -160 Bway -NY 10038 **Fx:**566-4749
(518) 828-4149 .. **Roche**, Francis J '70 -538 Union Bx321 -Hudson 12534 **Fx:**828-8724
(212) 559-2720 .. **Roche**, John J '64 Citigroup -425 Park Av -NY 10022
(914) 761-9450 .. **Roche**, Kathryn Reyburn '92 %Mitsubishi Chem Amer -1 N Lex Av -White Plns 10601 **Fx:**761-0108
(212) 506-5000 .. **Roche**, Kevin M '02 %Orrick H&S LLP -51 W 52nd -NY 10019
(716) 853-5100 .. **Roche**, Mary Engler '78 (Lippes MWF LLP) -665 Main -Buffalo 14203
(718) 852-1879 .. **Roche**, Maureen '82 -322 5th Av -Brklyn 11215 **Fx:**852-4923
(607) 962-3194 .. **Roche**, Philip J '86 (Yorio & R) -145 W High -Painted Post 14870
(518) 436-9370 .. **Roche**, Robt P '61 -36 S Pearl -Albany 12207 **Fx:**436-8233
(212) 720-5026 .. **Roche**, Thos '71 %Fed Reserve Bk -33 Lbrty -NY 10045 **Fx:**785-5748
(631) 342-4528 .. **Rochelle**, Sheronda '04 CA,Inc -1 CA Plz -Islandia 11749 **Fx:**342-4866
(718) 875-1300 .. **Rochelson**, Myra Derkatch '84 %Applt Div 2nd Dept -45 Monroe Pl -Brklyn 11201 **Fx:**858-2446
(212) 872-1000 .. **Rochester**, Shaya '03 -One Bryant Park -NY 10036 **Fx:**872-1002
(516) 764-4019 .. **Rochford**, James T '63 -3 Thomas Rd -Rockvll Ctr 11570 **Fx:**208-6628
(212) 723-9644 .. **Rochford**, Nancy A '78 %Salomon Smith Barney -390 Greenwich -NY 10013
(585) 263-1000 .. **Rochford**, Richd D '82 (Nixon P LLP) -1100 Clinton Sq -Rchstr 14604
(212) 873-7063 .. **Rochkind**, Steven H '71 (Joelson & R) -149 W 72nd -NY 10023
(212) 373-3000 .. **Rochlin**, Mordecai '36 OfCnsl Paul WRW&G LLP -1285 Av of Amer -NY 10019
(212) 724-1116 .. **Rochlin**, Paul A '64 -11 Riverside Dr -NY 10023
(718) 653-4565 .. **Rochman**, Hyman '43 -2300 Olinvll Av -Bronx 10467
(212) 754-9000 .. **Rochman**, Irwin '63 (Tesser R&R LLP) -509 Mad Av -NY 10022
(212) 715-9100 .. **Rochon**, Jennifer L '98 (Kramer LN&F,LLP) -1177 Av of Amer -NY 10036
(212) 547-5400 .. **Rochwarger**, Jonathan P '97 (McDermott W&E LLP) -340 Mad Av -NY 10173
(631) 360-9300 .. **Rock**, Bradley E '79 -1 E Maim -Smithtwn 11787 **Fx:**360-9331
(845) 566-9200 .. **Rock**, Chas N '90 (C Rock,PLLC) -320 Robnsn Av -Newburgh 12550 **Fx:**566-7288
(518) 445-3393 .. **Rock**, Gerald J '98 %Albany Law Schl -80 New Scotland Av -Albany 12208 **Fx:**445-2315
(212) 906-1200 .. **Rock**, Kenneth M '10 %Latham & W -885 3rd Av -NY 10022
(518) 474-7731 .. **Rock**, Krista A '96 %Dept of Law -The Cptl -Albany 12224
(212) 676-0810 .. **Rock**, Marilyn H '83 %Business Integrity Comm -100 Church -NY 10007 **Fx:**676-6204
(212) 735-3000 .. **Rock**, Neil L '89 (Skadden ASM&F LLP) -4 Times Sq -NY 10036
(518) 463-5700 .. **Rock**, Robt J '82 -60 S Swan -Albany 12210
(212) 480-5284 .. **Rock**, Roger R '99 %Insurance Dept -25 Beaver -NY 10004 **Fx:**480-5272
(212) 735-3000 .. **Rockas**, Anastasia T '93 (Skadden ASM&F LLP) -4 Times Sq -NY 10036
(212) 727-2700 .. **Rockefeller**, Laurance '75 %NRDC -40 W 20th -NY 10011 **Fx:**727-1773
(646) 227-3544 .. **Rocker**, Nancy J '99 Mem Sloan-Kettering Cancer Ctr -633 3rd Av -NY 10017 **Fx:**227-3045
(212) 404-6804 .. **Rocker**, Sally Ann '89 JC Flowers & Co -717 5th Av -NY 10022
(914) 749-8200 .. **Rockett**, Courtney R '99 (Boies S&F LLP) -333 Main -Armonk 10504
(212) 841-1681 .. **Rockett**, Jeffrey P '98 %BBC Worldwide Americas -747 3rd Av -NY 10017 **Fx:**705-9338
(212) 292-4270 .. **Rockett**, Laurie R '71 (Rockett & S) -521 5th Av -NY 10175 **Fx:**573-6355
(516) 364-0600 .. **Rockitter**, Kevin E '83 KE Rockitter,PC -180 Froehlich Farm Blvd -Woodbury 11797
(212) 735-3000 .. **Rocklage**, Jeremy M '10 %Skadden ASM&F LLP -4 Times Sq -NY 10036
(212) 969-3000 .. **Rocklen**, Kathy H '78 (Proskauer R LLP) -1585 Bway -NY 10036
(212) 490-3000 .. **Rocklin**, Lauren J '00 OfCnsl Wilson EME&D LLP -150 E 42nd -NY 10017
(518) 393-7280 .. **Rockmacher**, Stephen L '91 -740 Union -Schnctdy 12305 **Fx:**723-9136
(845) 679-5745 .. **Rockman**, George '65 -Bx2 -Woodstock 12498 **Fx:**679-5745
(212) 504-6000 .. **Rockman**, Jason M '06 %Cadwalader W&T LLP -1 World Fncl Ctr -NY 10281
(516) 379-1323 .. **Rockmore**, Allison L '97 %Edwards & E -336 S Ocean Av Bx191 -Freeprt 11520 **Fx:**546-0384
(518) 392-6900 .. **Rockmuller**, Seth R '76 -29 Kinderhook -Chatham 12037 **Fx:**392-6900
(212) 836-8000 .. **Rockney**, Brant M '08 %Kaye S LLP -425 Park Av -NY 10022
(212) 735-8600 .. **Rockoff**, Steven N '00 (Morrison C LLP) -909 3rd Av -NY 10022
(516) 437-3100 .. **Rockower**, Ronald F '87 -3000 Marcus Av -Lk Success 11042 **Fx:**326-1576
(914) 725-2450 .. **Rockowitz**, Noah E '74 -149 Baraud Rd N -Scarsdale 10583 **Fx:**725-2450
(212) 225-2000 .. **Rocks**, Sandra M '81 Cnsl Cleary GS&H -1 Lbrty Plz -NY 10006
(212) 819-8200 .. **Rockwell**, Alan P '09 (White & C LLP) -1155 Av of Amer -NY 10036
(212) 330-8305 .. **Rockwell**, Alicia J '94 %KPMG LLP -345 Park Av -NY 10154
(315) 797-6660 .. **Rockwell**, Paul A R '91 %Midway IndstrlSupply -51 Wurz Av Bx303 -Utica 13503
(212) 891-8315 .. **Rockwell**, Peter C '88 %Mitsubishi UFJ -520 Mad Av -NY 10022 **Fx:**593-4691
(212) 906-1200 .. **Rod**, Jonathan R '88 (Latham & W) -885 3rd Av -NY 10022
(315) 342-7214 .. **Rodak**, Jos G '85 (Rodak & K) -55 W 2nd -Oswego 13126
(518) 474-1331 .. **Rodak**, Julie Anne '88 %Ofc Mntl Health -44 Holland Av -Albany 12229 **Fx:**473-7863
(212) 696-6000 .. **Rodas**, Remy A '82 (Curtis M-PC&M LLP) -101 Park Av -NY 10178
(212) 859-8000 .. **Rodburg**, Jennifer L '01 (Fried FHS&J LLP) -1 NY Plz -NY 10004
(845) 561-0550 .. **Rodd**, Adam L '88 (Drake LHKGG&R PLLC) -555 Hudson Valley Av -New Windsor 12553
(212) 867-9123 .. **Rodd**, Fellowes M '67 OfCnsl Berkman BN&R,LLP -521 5th Av -NY 10175
(212) 239-4999 .. **Rodd**, Linda E '84 OfCnsl Meyer SE&K,PC -1350 Bway Bx822 -NY 10018
(212) 889-3700 .. **Rodd**, Stephen T '76 (Abbey SR&A LLP) -212 E 39th -NY 10016
(718) 855-5670 .. **Rodda**, Donald T '77 -189 Montague -Brklyn 11201
(212) 267-3091 .. **Roddy**, Kevin P '04 (Wilentz G&S) -110 William -NY 10038 **Fx:**(732) 726-6686
(516) 747-4082 .. **Rode**, John Kenneth '61 OfCnsl Montfort HM&S LLP -1140 Franklin Av Bx7677 -Gdn Cty 11530
(212) 944-7333 .. **Rode**, John S '66 (Rode & Q) -55 W 39th -NY 10018
(212) 944-7333 .. **Rode & Qualey** -55 W 39th -NY 10018 **Fx:**719-1828
(516) 248-5378 .. **Rodecker**, Donna '01 Title Room -240 Old Cntry Rd -Mineola 11501
(212) 909-6000 .. **Rodel**, Paul M '97 (Debevoise & P LLP) -919 3rd Av -NY 10022
(585) 225-3446 .. **Rodeman**, Christopher K '98 Darweesh LK&V,LLP -1081 Long Pond Rd -Rchstr 14626
(845) 896-9750 .. **Roden**, Kenneth J '80 -851 Route 82 Bx281 -Hopewell Junct 12533 **Fx:**896-4330
(845) 473-7766 .. **Rodenhausen**, George A '70 (Rapport MWS&R,LLP) -35 Main -Poughkeepsie 12601

(646) 264-3650 .. **Rodenhausen,** Patricia M '72 US Dept of Labor -201 Varick -NY 10014 **Fx:**264-3660

(212) 850-0657 .. **Roder,** Natalya J '06 Cnsl 1st Amer Title -633 3rd Av -NY 10017 **Fx:**(646) 487-6947

(212) 554-7800 .. **Roder,** Paul M '00 (Moses & S LLP) -405 Lex Av -NY 10174

(212) 972-2929 .. **Rodes,** Leonard A '84 (Trachtenberg R&F LLP) -545 5th Av -NY 10017 **Fx:**972-7581

(212) 848-4000 .. **Rodgers,** Andrew J '10 Shearman & S LLP -599 Lex Av -NY 10022

(516) 803-3000 .. **Rodgers,** Anne E '00 Rainbow Media -200 Jericho Quadrangle -Jericho 11753

(212) 922-2200 .. **Rodgers,** Danl C '02 (Watson F&W LLP) -1133 Av of Amer -NY 10036

(631) 727-6966 .. **Rodgers,** Danl G '93 -214 Roanoke Av -Rvrhead 11901 **Fx:**369-2141

(212) 335-4500 .. **Rodgers,** Gail McLemore '03 %DLA Piper LLP -1251 Av of Amer -NY 10020

(212) 906-1200 .. **Rodgers,** Gregory P '08 (Latham & W) -885 3rd Av -NY 10022

(212) 527-1000 .. **Rodgers,** James H '89 (Jones HC&B PC) -1 Bttry Pk Plz -NY 10004

(212) 637-2513 .. **Rodgers,** Jennifer G '97 %US Atty -1 St Andrews Plz -NY 10007

(518) 436-0344 .. **Rodgers,** John D '81 OfCnsl Deily M&G,LLP -8 Thurlow Ter -Albany 12203

(212) 536-5609 .. **Rodgers,** John Salant '58 Salant Corp -1114 Av of Amer -NY 10036

(516) 393-2200 .. **Rodgers,** Karen L '00 %Garfunkel W,PC -111 Grt Nck Rd -Gt Neck 11021

(212) 925-6635 .. **Rodgers,** Kathryn J '74 %Legal Momentum -395 Hudson -NY 10014 **Fx:**226-1066

(718) 746-3440 .. **Rodgers,** Lamont K '03 %Sacco & F,LLP -141-07 20th Av -Whitestone 11357

(212) 834-0600 .. **Rodgers,** Laura E '06 %Gordon & S,PC -355 Lex Av -NY 10017

(212) 567-8590 .. **Rodgers,** Lindsey B '08 %Burrell R LLC -110 Wall -NY 10005 **Fx:**567-2630

(716) 853-1450 .. **Rodgers,** Mark C '78 -424 Main -Buffalo 14202 **Fx:**853-1305

(585) 454-5650 .. **Rodgers,** Peter T '77 (Lacy K LLP) -130 E Main -Rchstr 14604

(518) 402-2372 .. **Rodgers,** Richd L '83 %Dept of Law -The Cptl -Albany 12224

(212) 455-2000 .. **Rodgers,** Sean D '96 (Simpson T&B LLP) -425 Lex Av -NY 10017

(914) 253-2427 .. **Rodgers Pope,** Beth A '96 %Pepsico -700 Andrsn Hill Rd -Purchase 10577

(585) 987-2800 .. **Rodi,** Christopher R '09 %Woods OG LLP -2 State -Rchstr 14614

(212) 997-7634 .. **Rodi,** Maria E '03 %Kravet & V,LLP -1040 Av of Amer -NY 10018 **Fx:**997-7686

(212) 965-9351 .. **Rodi,** Michl A '88 -350 Bway -NY 10013 **Fx:**965-9375

(212) 270-5850 .. **Rodier,** Christopher P '74 JP Morgan Chase -245 Park Av -NY 10167

(212) 735-3000 .. **Rodin,** Rita A '94 (Skadden ASM&F LLP) -4 Times Sq -NY 10036

(212) 760-2222 .. **Rodin,** Stephanie J '00 %Kolenovsky & S,LLP -135 W 29th -NY 10001

(212) 225-2000 .. **Rodina,** Anastasiya S '10 %Cleary GS&H -1 Lbrty Plz -NY 10006

(212) 269-1400 .. **Roditi,** Robyn D '06 %Gusrae KB&N PLLC -120 Wall -NY 10005

(212) 541-2000 .. **Rodman,** Andrew S '02 %Bryan C LLP -1290 Av of Amer -NY 10104

(718) 882-2681 .. **Rodman & Campbell,PC** -1428 E Gun Hill Rd -Bronx 10469 **Fx:**654-3641

(914) 949-7210 .. **Rodman,** Chas B '75 (Rodman & R) -10 Stewart Pl -White Plns 10603

(347) 643-3612 .. **Rodman,** Jodi L '02 NYCERS -335 Adams -Brklyn 11201 **Fx:**643-3200

(212) 735-8787 .. **Rodman,** Lawr B '74 (Morrison C LLP) -909 3rd Av -NY 10022

(212) 837-6093 .. **Rodman,** Lindsay B '09 %Hughes H&R LLP -1 Bttry Pk Plz -NY 10004

(914) 949-7210 .. **Rodman,** Philip '68 (Rodman & R) -10 Stewart Pl -White Plns 10603

(212) 521-5400 .. **Rodman,** Richd B '61 Cnsl Reed S LLP -599 Lex Av -NY 10022

(845) 735-6335 .. **Rodman,** Rosemarie M '84 -1 Blue Hill Plz Bx1728 -Pearl Rvr 10965 **Fx:**425-0726

(718) 548-8811 .. **Rodman,** Wm B '64 -4617 Waldo Av -Bronx 10471 **Fx:**548-8811

(914) 644-8900 .. **Rodner,** Jeffrey S '69 Gellert & R -1 N Lex Av -White Plns 10601 **Fx:**644-8393

(212) 421-4100 .. **Rodner,** Stephen B '67 (Pryor C LLP) -7 Times Sq -NY 10036

(845) 895-9846 .. **Rodney,** Glenn '86 Cnsl G Rodney,PC -368 Birch Rd -Wallkill 12589 **Fx:**895-3992

(516) 498-1717 .. **Rodney,** Leonard '74 -80 Cuttermill Rd -Gt Neck 11021 **Fx:**829-8801

(212) 244-3810 .. **Rodney,** Michele S '90 -7 W 36th -NY 10018

(718) 625-1111 .. **Rodney,** Vladimir J '97 (Feder & R,PLLC) -105 Court -Brklyn 11201 **Fx:**875-1860

(212) 687-1980 .. **Rodon,** Melinda Dierre '05 %Kaplan F&K LLP -850 3rd Av -NY 10022

(212) 335-4500 .. **Rodrigues,** Airina L '08 %DLA Piper LLP -1251 Av of Amer -NY 10020

(516) 489-7070 .. **Rodrigues,** Albert J '81 Local 1298 Lgl Srvcs -3 Surrey Ln -Hempstd 11550

(516) 285-3795 .. **Rodrigues,** Maurice D '99 -360A W Merrick Rd -Vly Stream 11580 **Fx:**285-3721

(212) 698-3500 .. **Rodrigues,** Maximiliano G '05 Dechert LLP -1095 Av of Amer -NY 10036

(718) 250-2000 .. **Rodriguez,** Adriana '10 %DA -350 Jay -Brklyn 11201 **Fx:**250-2314

(718) 590-8555 .. **Rodriguez,** Albert M '94 Borough Pres -851 Grnd Cncrs -Bronx 10451 **Fx:**590-5280

(212) 589-4200 .. **Rodriguez,** Alberto '05 %Baker & H LLP -45 Rckfllr Plz -NY 10111

(516) 695-1799 .. **Rodriguez,** Andrea Del Pilar '06 SEIU 32BJ -101 Av of Amer -NY 10013

(212) 267-6364 .. **Rodriguez,** Anthony J Jr. '92 %Kossoff & U -217 Bway -NY 10007

(718) 286-6000 .. **Rodriguez,** Arsenio D '10 %DA -125-01 Qns Blvd -Kew Gdns 11415

(212) 417-5300 .. **Rodriguez,** Betty '98 %Medicaid Fraud Cntrl -120 Bway -NY 10271 **Fx:**417-5274

(585) 546-7430 .. **Rodriguez,** Carlos '77 %Dept of Law -144 Exchange Blvd -Rchstr 14614 **Fx:**546-7514

(212) 839-5300 .. **Rodriguez,** Carlos A '86 (Sidley A LLP) -787 7th Av -NY 10019

(212) 849-7000 .. **Rodriguez,** Carlos A '06 %Quinn EU&S,LLP -51 Mad Av -NY 10010

(631) 368-1303 .. **Rodriguez,** Carolyn '88 -249 4th -E Northprt 11731

(212) 577-3500 .. **Rodriguez,** Celena L '05 %Leg Aid -199 Water -NY 10038

(212) 747-0204 .. **Rodriguez,** Christine A '00 -26 Bway -NY 10004

(212) 992-8827 .. **Rodriguez,** Cristina M '01 %NYU Law Schl -40 Wshngtn Sq S -NY 10012 **Fx:**995-4341

(718) 720-6026 .. **Rodriguez,** Danielle M '07 ACS -51 Styvsnt Pl -Staten Isl 10301

(631) 247-0404 .. **Rodriguez,** Dariely '07 %Jackson L LLP -58 S Srvc Rd -Melvll 11747

(212) 906-1200 .. **Rodriguez,** Darlyn O '07 %Latham & W -885 3rd Av -NY 10022

(716) 851-4343 .. **Rodriguez,** David '97 Law Dept -65 Niagara Sq -Buffalo 14202 **Fx:**851-4105

(718) 250-2000 .. **Rodriguez,** Deanna M '86 %DA -350 Jay -Brklyn 11201 **Fx:**250-2314

(518) 581-8441 .. **Rodriguez & Doern,PLLC** -100 West Av -Saratoga Spgs 12866 **Fx:**583-9053

(518) 736-2408 .. **Rodriguez & Doern,PLLC** -122 W Main -Johnstwn 12095

(718) 518-8000 .. **Rodriguez,** Eliezer '01 Langsam Prop Serv Corp -1601 Brnxdale Av -Bronx 10462

(914) 472-9290 .. **Rodriguez,** Emilia '85 -334 Heathcote Rd -Scarsdale 10583

(716) 858-2424 .. **Rodriguez,** Emilia '88 %DA -25 Delaware Av -Buffalo 14202 **Fx:**858-7425

(914) 509-6738 .. **Rodriguez,** Emilio '05 -630 Gramatan Av -Mt Vernon 10552 **Fx:**931-5241

(585) 263-6760 .. **Rodriguez,** Everardo Andy '94 %US Atty -620 Fed Bldg -Rchstr 14614 **Fx:**263-6226

(212) 506-1700 .. **Rodriguez,** Fara K '02 %Kasowitz BT&F LLP -1633 Bway -NY 10019

(718) 542-9300 .. **Rodriguez,** Fiordaliza A '01 %Rodriguez & F -644 Soundvw Av -Bronx 10473

(212) 421-5500 .. **Rodriguez,** Francisco J '96 (Goldsmith C&R,LLP) -747 3rd Av -NY 10017

(973) 315-4460 .. **Rodriguez,** Frank D '95 (Budd L) -140 Bway -NY 10005

(718) 542-9300 .. **Rodriguez & Fuentes** -644 Soundvw Av -Bronx 10473 **Fx:**542-2244

(631) 756-2024 .. **Rodriguez,** Glen P '81 (Huenke & R) -1 Huntngtn Quad -Melvll 11747

(518) 464-6770 .. **Rodriguez,** Gregory J '94 (Thorn GT&B,LLP) -5 Wembley Ct Bx15054 -Albany 12212

(518) 393-8011 .. **Rodriguez,** Hazel R '76 (Grasso R&G) -751 State -Schnctdy 12307

(212) 962-2800 .. **Rodriguez,** Herbert Jr. '04 %Schwartz G&C,LLP -90 Broad -NY 10004

(718) 792-7100 .. **Rodriguez,** Heriberto J '97 -1378 Wht Plns Rd -Bronx 10462

(516) 538-2500 .. **Rodriguez,** Ingrid M '05 %Furey FLMW&D,PC -600 Front -Hempstd 11550

(212) 728-2200 .. **Rodriguez,** Irina C '07 %Axinn V&H LLP -114 W 47th -NY 10036

(212) 545-8611 .. **Rodriguez,** Isabel '87 (Solomon & B) -351 Bway -NY 10013

(212) 233-3305 .. **Rodriguez,** Ivan J '03 %L Rosenberg & Assoc,PLLC -11 Park Pl -NY 10007 **Fx:**233-3289

Rodriguez, Javier A '92 -63 Laurel -Floral Pk 11001

(212) 687-8500 .. **Rodriguez,** Jennifer '10 %Liddle & R,LLP -800 3rd Av -NY 10022

(212) 695-0060 .. **Rodriguez,** Jennifer J '02 %Wilens & B,PC -450 7th Av -NY 10123

(914) 798-9900 .. **Rodriguez,** Jorge '05 Grant McCarthy Grp -777 Wstchstr Av -White Plns 10604

(212) 385-1422 .. **Rodriguez,** Jorge A '05 %Mahoney & K,LLP -76 Beaver -NY 10005

(718) 542-9300 .. **Rodriguez,** Jose A '78 (Rodriguez & F) -644 Soundvw Av -Bronx 10473

(212) 442-4900 .. **Rodriguez,** Julio III '99 %Ofc Admin Trials -40 Rector -NY 10006 **Fx:**442-4947

(516) 227-6566 .. **Rodriguez,** Kelly '00 -90 Merrick Av -E Meadow 11554 **Fx:**345-1660

(212) 416-8000 .. **Rodriguez,** Leilani J '05 %Dept of Law -120 Bway -NY 10271

(718) 579-8945 .. **Rodriguez,** Lia A '04 %Leg Aid -1020 Grnd Cncrs -Bronx 10451 **Fx:**588-2611

(914) 995-3420 .. **Rodriguez,** Livia '96 %DA -111 Martin Luther King Blvd -White Plns 10601 **Fx:**995-3363

(212) 979-2040 .. **Rodriguez,** Luis '04 SEO -55 Exch Pl -NY 10005

(212) 250-5760 .. **Rodriguez,** Luis A '05 Deutsche Bank Securities,Inc -60 Wall -NY 10005

(212) 886-1892 .. **Rodriguez,** Luis Jr. '01 -305 Mad Av -NY 10165

(516) 483-4300 .. **Rodriguez,** Luis E '07 (Goldstein & R,LLP) -129 Hilton Av -Hempstd 11550 **Fx:**564-9363

(516) 571-3634 .. **Rodriguez,** Margalie '03 Comm on Human Rights -240 Old Cntry Rd -Mineola 11501

(212) 968-8600 .. **Rodriguez,** Marisel '02 %Manchanda Law Ofc,PLLC -80 Wall -NY 10005 **Fx:**968-8601

(212) 374-0380 .. **Rodriguez,** Mary McKenna '84 %NYC Dept Educ-OLS -52 Chmbrs -NY 10007 **Fx:**374-5596

(212) 406-9710 .. **Rodriguez,** Matthew J '07 %Kral CRRP&G,LLP -170 Bway -NY 10038

(212) 309-6000 .. **Rodriguez,** Melissa C '02 %Morgan L&B LLP -101 Park Av -NY 10178

(718) 445-7658 .. **Rodriguez,** Michelle '95 (Rodriguez & P) -39-15 Main -Flushng 11354 **Fx:**445-7169

(212) 626-6785 .. **Rodriguez,** Miguel A '80 (Reid R&R,LLP) -1120 Av of Amer -NY 10036

(212) 326-3939 .. **Rodriguez,** Nicholas E '95 Cnsl Jones D -222 E 41st -NY 10017

(212) 382-6600 .. **Rodriguez,** Nicole M '07 %NYC Bar -42 W 44th -NY 10036 **Fx:**398-6634

(718) 205-5003 .. **Rodriguez,** Olga J '01 -95-02 Roosevelt Av -Jcksn Hts 11372 **Fx:**205-0385

(518) 346-7275 .. **Rodriguez,** Phil A '67 -224 State -Schnctdy 12305 **Fx:**372-5071

(212) 827-1512 .. **Rodriguez,** Ray W '04 Screen Actors Guild -360 Mad Av -NY 10017 **Fx:**944-6774

(212) 695-0060 .. **Rodriguez,** Ricardo J '90 %Wilens & B,PC -450 7th Av -NY 10123

(212) 509-9400 .. **Rodriguez,** Richd A '10 %Cozen O -45 Bway Atrium -NY 10006

(718) 875-1800 .. **Rodriguez,** Richd R '02 R Rodriguez,PC -114 Court -Brklyn 11201 **Fx:**233-4177

(718) 293-4400 .. **Rodriguez,** Robt A '84 -954 Gerard Av -Bronx 10452

(212) 439-6456 .. **Rodriguez,** Robt W '88 -516 E 86th -NY 10028

(718) 222-2358 .. **Rodriguez,** Ruth E '09 %Law Dept -350 Jay -Brklyn 11201 **Fx:**222-2373

(212) 297-5800 .. **Rodriguez,** Sabino Rod III '79 (Day P LLP) -7 Times Sq -NY 10036

(212) 416-8250 .. **Rodriguez**, Sandra '03 %Dept of Law -120 Bway -NY 10271
(973) 503-5900 .. **Rodriguez**, Sandra M '05 %Kelley D&W LLP -101 Park Av -NY 10178 **Fx**:503-5950
(212) 351-4000 .. **Rodriguez**, Shawn D '10 Gibson D&C LLP -200 Park Av -NY 10166
(518) 581-8441 .. **Rodriguez**, Stephen T '83 (Rodriguez & D,PLLC) -100 West Av -Saratoga Spgs 12866
(212) 547-5400 .. **Rodriguez**, Taina Yendi '06 %McDermott W&E LLP -340 Mad Av -NY 10173
(212) 414-6109 .. **Rodriguez**, Teresita D '86 BarnesandNoble.com LLC -76 9th Av -NY 10011
(718) 741-8410 .. **Rodriguez**, Thelma J B '96 Div of Human Rights -1 Fordham Plz -Bronx 10458 **Fx**:741-8102
(718) 923-4206 .. **Rodriguez**, Tomas D '75 %OTDA Fair Hearings -14 Boerum Pl -Brklyn 11201
(212) 259-8000 .. **Rodriguez**, Veronica '06 %Dewey & L LLP -1301 Av of Amer -NY 10019
(212) 435-3413 .. **Rodriguez**, Veronica '09 Port Auth of NY/NJ -225 Park Av S -NY 10003 **Fx**:435-3555
(212) 558-4000 .. **Rodriguez**, Vincent A '47 SrCnsl Sullivan & C LLP -125 Broad -NY 10004
(212) 250-2500 .. **Rodriguez**, Yvette Marie G '02 %Deutsche Bank -60 Wall -NY 10005
(718) 439-6080 .. **Rodriguez-Arbelo**, Casto F '77 -5403 5th Av -Brklyn 11220 **Fx**:439-3602
(212) 374-2440 .. **Rodriguez-Betances**, Alba '02 Dept of Ed -51 Chmbrs -NY 10007
(646) 823-7208 .. **Rodriguez-Diaz**, Sandra M '05 -375 South End Av -NY 10280 **Fx**:(212) 945-6717
(212) 474-1000 .. **Rodriguez Garcia**, Sonia '08 %Cravath S&M LLP -825 8th Av -NY 10019
(212) 335-4500 .. **Rodriguez-Marin**, Fernando J '90 OfCnsl DLA Piper LLP -1251 Av of Amer -NY 10020
(914) 285-1400 .. **Rodriguez-McCloskey**, Yenisey '01 Cnsl Danzig F&D -1 N Bway -White Plns 10601
(212) 344-5680 .. **Rodriguez-Morick**, Jeanette '95 %Thompson H LLP -335 Mad Av -NY 10017
(212) 962-2605 .. **Rodriguez-Nunci**, Wilmer A '90 -225 Bway -NY 10007
(212) 513-6477 .. **Rodriguez-Reyes**, Michl E '91 Dept Business Srvcs -110 William -NY 10038 **Fx**:618-8989
(718) 822-6999 .. **Rodriguez-Soriano**, W Annette '96 A Rodriguez-Soriano,PC -1967 Turnbull Av -Bronx 10473 **Fx**:822-6995
(212) 732-5812 .. **Rodriques**, Lester C '86 (Kahn GT&R,PC) -20 Vesey -NY 10007
(716) 845-6000 .. **Rodwin**, Jonathan E '81 (Kavinoky C LLP) -726 Exchange -Buffalo 14210
(518) 427-8361 .. **Rody-Wright**, Anne L '92 Ctr for Law & Justice -Pine West Plz Bldg 2 Wshngtn Av Ext -Albany 12205 **Fx**:427-8362
(212) 588-5500 .. **Roe**, Bonnie J '83 (Davies WP&V LLP) -625 Mad Av -NY 10022
(212) 574-1200 .. **Roe**, Hadley S '65 (Seward & K LLP) -1 Bttry Pk Plz -NY 10004
(631) 475-4400 .. **Roe**, John J III '61 (Roe TT&P,LLP) -One Corp Dr -Bohemia 11716
(315) 442-0100 .. **Roe**, Kevin G '86 (Gilberti SH&S,PC) -555 E Genesee -Syracuse 13202
(212) 655-3520 .. **Roe & Kramer,LLP** -440 Park Av S -NY 10016
(917) 778-6600 .. **Roe**, Matthew J '88 %J Toomey -485 Lex Av -NY 10017 **Fx**:778-7048
(212) 425-7200 .. **Roe**, R Scott '07 %Kenyon & K,LLP -1 Bway -NY 10004
(315) 461-1400 .. **Roe**, Steven T '97 -103 Commerce Blvd -Liverpool 13088
(631) 475-4400 .. **Roe Taroff Taitz & Portman, LLP** -One Corp Dr -Bohemia 11716 **Fx**:475-9882
(607) 734-5004 .. **Roe**, Wesley A '03 (Hamm R&G) -523 W Church -Elmira 14905
(212) 536-3900 .. **Roeber**, Justin H '07 %K&L Gates LLP -599 Lex Av -NY 10022
(212) 872-1000 .. **Roebuck**, J Michl III '95 -One Bryant Park -NY 10036 **Fx**:872-1002
(914) 946-4777 .. **Roebuck**, Stephanie M '93 (Keane & B,PC) -445 Hmltn Av -White Plns 10601
(212) 326-2000 .. **Roeder**, Jacqueline V '08 %O'Melveny & M LLP -7 Times Sq -NY 10036
(212) 417-3700 .. **Roehl**, Amy L '07 MFY Legal Srvcs -299 Bway -NY 10007 **Fx**:417-3890
(716) 856-5500 .. **Roehl**, Meghann N '06 %Damon M LLP -200 Delaware Av -Buffalo 14202
(212) 848-4000 .. **Roehrig**, Christopher A '04 %Shearman & S LLP -599 Lex Av -NY 10022
(212) 770-7000 .. **Roehrs**, Christopher S '99 %AIG -70 Pine -NY 10270
(212) 779-8600 .. **Roemer**, David A '06 %Silverman SS&B PLLC -381 Park Av S -NY 10016
(518) 761-6547 .. **Roemer**, E Guy '73 Supreme Ct -1340 State Route 9 -Lk George 12845
(518) 464-1300 .. **Roemer**, James W Jr. '69 (Roemer WG&M LLP) -13 Columbia Cir -Albany 12203
(518) 464-1300 .. **Roemer Wallens Gold & Mineaux LLP** -13 Columbia Cir -Albany 12203 **Fx**:464-1010
(845) 457-5303 .. **Roepe**, David G '62 -201 Ward Bx 111 -Montgmry 12549 **Fx**:457-4417
(212) 490-3000 .. **Roer**, Ricki E '82 (Wilson EME&D LLP) -150 E 42nd -NY 10017
(585) 475-1100 .. **Roerden**, Thos P '87 Segar & S -400 Meridian Centre -Rchstr 14618
(315) 539-7682 .. **Roesch**, Barbara A '84 Cnty Ct -48 W Williams -Waterloo 13165 **Fx**:539-7850
(518) 457-2070 .. **Roesch**, Ellen S '86 %Dept of Tax & Fin -Bldg 9 State Campus -Albany 12227 **Fx**:457-6131
(516) 781-1719 .. **Roesch**, Kim M '01 %J Roesch -611 Newbrdg Rd -E Meadow 11554 **Fx**:221-4108
(516) 781-1719 .. **Roesch**, Scott T '03 %J Roesch -611 Newbrdg Rd -E Meadow 11554 **Fx**:221-4108
(631) 549-4677 .. **Roess**, Christopher J '02 Sobel K&S,PC -464 NY Av -Huntngtn 11743
(212) 218-5500 .. **Roesser**, John D '99 (Seyfarth S LLP) -620 8th Av -NY 10018
(212) 878-8335 .. **Roessner**, Karl A '93 (Clifford C LLP) -31 W 52nd -NY 10019
(607) 868-3500 .. **Roff**, Leslie A '85 -366 W Lake Rd -Branchport 14418
(718) 261-0181 .. **Roff**, Tamara J '05 %M Kule-Korgood -118-35 Qns Blvd -Frst Hlls 11375 **Fx**:268-2633
(212) 451-2900 .. **Roffe**, Andrew S '72 (Robinson & C LLP) -885 3rd Av -NY 10022
(516) 256-5636 .. **Roffe**, Brian '92 -540 Willow Av -Cedarhrst 11516
(212) 918-3000 .. **Roffe**, Michl P '06 %Hogan L LLP -875 3rd Av -NY 10022
(212) 279-9090 .. **Roffé**, Saul '88 (Stark & S) -One Penn Plz -NY 10119 **Fx**:279-9113
(212) 431-2150 .. **Roffer**, Michl H '84 NY Law Schl -185 W Bway -NY 10013 **Fx**:965-8839
(212) 506-5000 .. **Roffi**, Alison K '09 %Orrick H&S LLP -51 W 52nd -NY 10019
(718) 237-3100 .. **Roffman**, Elana E '06 Leg Aid -111 Lvngstn -Brklyn 11201 **Fx**:250-4243
(212) 435-3571 .. **Rogak**, Elizabeth '96 %Port Auth of NY/NJ -225 Park Av S -NY 10003 **Fx**:435-3555
(516) 620-6360 .. **Rogak & Gibbons,LLP** -50 Charles Lindburgh Blvd -Uniondale 11553 **Fx**:620-6361
(516) 620-6360 .. **Rogak**, Joyce Lipton '81 (Rogak & G,LLP) -50 Charles Lindburgh Blvd -Uniondale 11553
(516) 763-2996 .. **Rogak**, Lawr N '82 (L Rogak,LLC) -3355 Lawson Blvd -Oceanside 11572 **Fx**:763-2998
(718) 590-2000 .. **Rogal**, Erin '07 DA -198 E 161st -Bronx 10451 **Fx**:590-6477
(212) 909-6000 .. **Rogala**, Christopher H '10 %Debevoise & P LLP -919 3rd Av -NY 10022
(585) 346-1004 .. **Rogalskyj**, Peter '95 -63 Big Tree -Livonia 14487
(845) 735-5522 .. **Rogan**, Edw T '85 Rogan & Assoc,LLC -Bx219 -Blauvelt 10913
(914) 323-7000 .. **Rogan**, Kaitlin M '09 %Wilson EME&D LLP -3 Gannett Dr -White Plns 10604
(212) 335-4500 .. **Rogan**, Kristy M '07 %DLA Piper LLP -1251 Av of Amer -NY 10020
(518) 587-2845 .. **Rogan**, Paul D '99 -13 Azalea Dr -Saratoga Spgs 12866 **Fx**:226-0792
(212) 541-2000 .. **Rogatnick**, Howard Moss '88 Cnsl Bryan C LLP -1290 Av of Amer -NY 10104
(516) 682-3376 .. **Rogdakis**, Evan N '09 SpclCnsl Ctr for Wealth Preservation -6800 Jericho Tpk -Syosset 11791
(718) 941-0012 .. **Rogers**, Aubrey A '75 -2809 Church Av -Brklyn 11226
(914) 682-3390 .. **Rogers**, Beverley '99 -925 Wstchstr Av -White Plns 10604 **Fx**:(203) 431-6686
(212) 474-1000 .. **Rogers**, Brittain A IV '04 %Cravath S&M LLP -825 8th Av -NY 10019
(845) 359-5400 .. **Rogers**, Bruce A '65 Rogers M&H,PC -100 Dutch Hill Rd -Orangebrg 10962 **Fx**:359-5577
(585) 454-2338 .. **Rogers**, Chas W '59 -45 Exchange -Rchstr 14614 **Fx**:454-4066
(212) 715-1000 .. **Rogers**, Christine Duffy '81 (Arnold & P LLP) -399 Park Av -NY 10022
(202) 270-9330 .. **Rogers**, Christopher J '09 Rogers Law,Ltd -220 W 13th -NY 10011
(631) 777-2330 .. **Rogers**, Christopher M '91 (O'Connor OH&D,LLP) -1 Huntngtn Quad -Melvll 11747
(516) 931-1800 .. **Rogers**, Christopher T '07 %Catalano G&P LLP -100 Jericho Quadrangle -Jericho 11753
(631) 852-8800 .. **Rogers**, Cornelius S '76 %DA -116 Hmptn Rd -Southampton 11968 **Fx**:852-8806
(516) 393-2200 .. **Rogers**, Courtney A '06 %Garfunkel W,PC -111 Grt Nck Rd -Gt Neck 11021
(212) 506-5000 .. **Rogers**, Courtney M '07 %Orrick H&S LLP -51 W 52nd -NY 10019
(516) 759-6361 .. **Rogers**, Cynthia Shade '93 -26 Highfld Rd -Glen Cove 11542
(585) 345-1205 .. **Rogers**, Durin B '95 -211 Naramore Dr -Batavia 14020
(212) 835-1514 .. **Rogers**, Eli J '06 %Dreifuss B&P,LLP -1 Penn Plz -NY 10019
(718) 994-1640 .. **Rogers**, Evan D '82 Rogers & R -4419 Wht Plns Rd -Bronx 10470 **Fx**:325-7439
(518) 383-9440 .. **Rogers**, Geoffrey C '85 (Hudson C LLP) -636 Plnk Rd -Clifton Pk 12065
(585) 546-6448 .. **Rogers**, Heather C M '99 (Davidson F LLP) -28 E Main -Rchstr 14614
(212) 715-1000 .. **Rogers**, Jacob A '09 %Arnold & P LLP -399 Park Av -NY 10022
(212) 343-0708 .. **Rogers**, James A '91 Assoc of Leg Aid Attys -568 Bway -NY 10012
(914) 686-9010 .. **Rogers**, James A '00 %Wilson BCC&C,PC -2 William -White Plns 10601
(646) 207-7541 .. **Rogers**, James L '92 (Rogers IP Grp) -Church St Station Bx3115 -NY 10008 **Fx**:(866) 426-3525
(718) 250-0400 .. **Rogers**, James W '87 %R Tusa -1 MetroTech Ctr -Brklyn 11201 **Fx**:250-0591
(516) 571-3056 .. **Rogers**, Jennean R '99 %Cnty Atty -1 West -Mineola 11501 **Fx**:571-6604
(212) 592-1400 .. **Rogers**, John A Jr. '97 (Herrick,F LLP) -2 Park Av -NY 10016
(212) 309-1000 .. **Rogers**, John M '94 Cnsl Hunton & W -200 Park Av -NY 10166
(212) 820-9434 .. **Rogers**, Jos P Jr. '69 OfCnsl Hawkins D&W LLP -One Chase Manh Plz -NY 10005
(716) 883-3300 .. **Rogers**, Julie A '04 R Cercone -484 Delaware Av -Buffalo 14202 **Fx**:883-2163
(516) 248-2234 .. **Rogers**, Laurence D '99 %Sackstein S&L,LLP -1140 Franklin Av -Gdn Cty 11530
(212) 596-9000 .. **Rogers**, Laurence S '76 (Ropes & G LLP) -1211 Av of Amer -NY 10036
(212) 715-9100 .. **Rogers**, Mae R '02 %Kramer LN&F,LLP -1177 Av of Amer -NY 10036
(212) 318-3000 .. **Rogers**, Mara H '84 (Fulbright & J LLP) -666 5th Av -NY 10103
(518) 561-3700 .. **Rogers**, Mark J '80 (Lewis & R,PC) -53 Court -Plattsbrgh 12901
(212) 455-2000 .. **Rogers**, Matthew B '10 %Simpson T&B LLP -425 Lex Av -NY 10017
(917) 865-5204 .. **Rogers**, Matthew T '02 -26 Bergen -Brklyn 11201
(212) 907-0700 .. **Rogers**, Michl H '02 %Labaton S LLP -140 Bway -NY 10005
(212) 581-3320 .. **Rogers**, Michl T '87 (Wasserman G&R,LLP) -1700 Bway -NY 10019
(212) 763-6800 .. **Rogers**, Morlan Ty '92 Cnsl Vandenberg & F,LLP -60 E 42nd -NY 10165
(631) 852-3076 .. **Rogers**, Omar O '06 NYS Unified Ct Sys -210 Center Dr -Rvrhead 11901
(212) 916-0600 .. **Rogers**, Patricia A '93 Tweedy, Browne Co LLC -350 Park Av -NY 10022
(212) 307-1499 .. **Rogers**, Patrick S '03 %Lissner & L LLP -250 W 57th -NY 10107 **Fx**:757-1825
(212) 335-4500 .. **Rogers**, Philip Jr. '84 (DLA Piper LLP) -1251 Av of Amer -NY 10020
(212) 577-3544 .. **Rogers**, Raymond E '91 %Leg Aid -199 Water -NY 10038 **Fx**:577-3520
(914) 347-2600 .. **Rogers**, Richd J '96 (Traub LS&S LLP) -7 Skyline Dr -Hawthorne 10532
(212) 805-0179 .. **Rogers**, Robt W '94 %US Dist Ct -500 Pearl -NY 10007

(212) 906-1200 .. **Rogers,** Sarah B '09 %Latham & W -885 3rd Av -NY 10022
(716) 856-5500 .. **Rogers,** Sharyn G '78 (Damon M LLP) -200 Delaware Av -Buffalo 14202
(914) 420-3706 .. **Rogers,** Stephen J '79 -79 Brambach Rd Bx382 -Scarsdale 10583 **Fx:**472-1159
(516) 832-3200 .. **Rogers,** Steven G '92 %1st Amer Title -333 Earle Ovngton Blvd -Uniondale 11553 **Fx:**832-3299
(212) 325-4355 .. **Rogers,** Stuart C '94 CSFB -11 Mad Av -NY 10010
(212) 558-4000 .. **Rogers,** Theo O Jr. '80 (Sullivan & C LLP) -125 Broad -NY 10004
(212) 951-6451 .. **Rogers,** Thos M '97 NY Dept of Ed -475 Park Av S -NY 10016
(516) 594-0909 .. **Rogers,** Timothy J '90 %Polsky S&R,PC -500 Merrick Rd -Rockvll Ctr 11570
(212) 617-6321 .. **Rogers,** Tracey S '02 Bloomberg LP -731 Lex Av -NY 10022
(212) 845-7540 .. **Rogers,** Wm D '84 Thacher Assoc,LLC -330 W 42nd -NY 10036 **Fx:**845-7549
(212) 474-1000 .. **Rogers,** Wm P Jr. '80 (Cravath S&M LLP) -825 8th Av -NY 10019
(212) 839-6505 .. **Rogerson-Pondish,** Susan K '97 %Dept of Transportation -55 Water -NY 10041
(212) 596-9000 .. **Rogers-Seitz,** Lindsey T '10 %Ropes & G LLP -1211 Av of Amer -NY 10036
(212) 323-7070 .. **Rogers-Spang,** Christina M '97 %Rawle & H LLP -14 Wall -NY 10005
(212) 586-0700 .. **Rogge,** C Fredk III '69 (Fulton R&H,LLP) -1 Rckfllr Plz -NY 10020
(716) 485-6643 .. **Roggenbaum,** David R '02 -202 Main Bx209 -Hambrg 14075 **Fx:**649-4429
(212) 272-6301 .. **Roggenkamp,** Christoph J '00 %JP Morgan Chase -383 Mad Av -NY 10179
(212) 848-4000 .. **Roggow,** Kevin J '06 %Shearman & S LLP -599 Lex Av -NY 10022
(212) 839-5300 .. **Rogic,** Predrag '04 %Sidley A LLP -787 7th Av -NY 10019
(212) 319-1900 .. **Rogin,** Jonathan '95 (Berger & W,LLP) -1633 Bway -NY 10019
(212) 715-9100 .. **Rogoff,** Adam C '89 (Kramer LN&F,LLP) -1177 Av of Amer -NY 10036
(646) 264-3650 .. **Rogoff,** Jeffrey S '94 %US Dept of Labor -201 Varick -NY 10014 **Fx:**264-3660
(212) 903-9000 .. **Rogoff,** Lauren B '09 %Linklaters -1345 Av of Amer -NY 10105
(212) 836-8000 .. **Rogoff,** Michl A '88 (Kaye S LLP) -425 Park Av -NY 10022
(585) 295-4400 .. **Rogoff,** Scott P '98 (Hiscock & B,LLP) -2000 HSBC Plz -Rchstr 14604
(585) 327-5600 .. **Rogoff,** Stephen D '72 -1 E Main -Rchstr 14614 **Fx:**327-5609
(212) 820-7700 .. **Rogoski,** Alexis J '96 (Boundas SW&B,LLC) -1 Bttry Pk Plz -NY 10004
(212) 885-5000 .. **Rogove,** Adrienne C '95 (Blank R LLP) -405 Lex Av -NY 10174
(212) 859-8000 .. **Rogovin,** Marc A '06 %Fried FHS&J LLP -1 NY Plz -NY 10004
(212) 650-7298 .. **Rogovin,** Michl J '88 City College of NY -160 Convent Av -NY 10031 **Fx:**650-5785
(212) 686-4300 .. **Rogovin,** Stanley M '71 Rogovin & S LLP -10 E 40th -NY 10016 **Fx:**689-2079
(518) 462-5601 .. **Rogowski,** Jami Durante '97 (O'Connell & A) -54 State -Albany 12207
(716) 843-5700 .. **Rogowski,** John E '82 %US Atty -138 Delaware Av -Buffalo 14202 **Fx:**551-3052
(914) 939-1887 .. **Rogowsky,** Alan D '72 -125 N Main -Pt Chester 10573
(212) 732-3665 .. **Rogowsky,** Ira H '95 (Harmon L&R) -42 Bway -NY 10004
(914) 939-1887 .. **Rogowsky,** Martin L '74 (Rogowsky & R) -125 N Main -Pt Chester 10573
(914) 939-1887 .. **Rogowsky,** Stephen T '78 (Rogowsky & R) -125 N Main -Pt Chester 10573
(212) 849-7000 .. **Rogoyski,** Robt S '09 %Quinn EU&S,LLP -51 Mad Av -NY 10010
(914) 997-0500 .. **Rogozinski,** Deborah A '04 %Lowey DC&H,PC -1 N Bway -White Plns 10601
(646) 610-5400 .. **Rohack,** John T '96 NYPD -1 Police Plz -NY 10038
(212) 594-3330 .. **Rohan,** Audrey A '82 Haier Amer -1356 Bway -NY 10018
(518) 438-0010 .. **Rohan,** Brian P '91 (Rohan & Assoc.PC) -5 Computer Dr W -Albany 12205 **Fx:**438-0030
(212) 572-8600 .. **Rohan,** Patrick J '89 MacAndrews & Forbes -35 E 62nd -NY 10065
(914) 738-4418 .. **Rohan,** Thos E Jr. '90 -Bx108 -Pelham 10803
(212) 259-8000 .. **Rohback,** Thos G '79 (Dewey & L LLP) -1301 Av of Amer -NY 10019
(212) 935-3000 .. **Rohde,** Bridget M '00 (Mintz LCFG&P,PC) -666 3rd Av -NY 10017
(518) 449-3900 .. **Rohde,** Clifford C '06 %Cooper E&S,LLP -39 N Pearl -Albany 12207
(212) 953-3570 .. **Rohde,** David D '96 Baker Robbins & Co -195 Bway -NY 10007 **Fx:**953-0353
(212) 530-5862 .. **Rohde,** Michl A '94 -1 Chase Manh Plz -NY 10005
(212) 471-8454 .. **Roher,** Andrew M '98 %Herzfeld & R,PC -125 Broad -NY 10004
(516) 222-2828 .. **Roher,** Neal J '87 -600 Old Cntry Rd -Gdn Cty 11530 **Fx:**222-1499
(718) 590-2000 .. **Rohlfing,** Nicholas H '08 %DA -198 E 161st -Bronx 10451 **Fx:**590-6477
(212) 909-6000 .. **Rohlik,** Philip N '02 %Debevoise & P LLP -919 3rd Av -NY 10022
(516) 837-6115 .. **Rohling,** Valerie B '03 Progressive Closing & Escrow -515 Rockaway Av -Vly Stream 11581
(212) 692-1000 .. **Röhm,** Eberhard '75 (Duane M LLP) -1540 Bway -NY 10036
(212) 513-3200 .. **Rohn,** Fredk R '78 (Holland & K LLP) -31 W 52nd -NY 10019
(212) 558-4000 .. **Rohr,** Jonathan G '10 %Sullivan & C LLP -125 Broad -NY 10004
(212) 637-2531 .. **Rohr,** Rebecca '08 %US Atty -1 St Andrews Plz -NY 10007
(585) 663-7050 .. **Rohr,** Thos A '70 -109 Lk Av -Hilton 14468
(212) 515-3346 .. **Rohrbach,** Susan A '96 Area Property Partners LP -60 Columbus Cir -NY 10023
(212) 538-1021 .. **Rohrer,** Douglas S '03 Credit Suisse -11 Mad Av -NY 10010
(212) 659-7300 .. **Rohrer,** Eden L '90 (Haynes & B,LLP) -1221 Av of Amer -NY 10020
(212) 765-3040 .. **Rohrer,** Jennifer Gaylord '99 NS Bienstock Inc -250 W 57th -NY 10107 **Fx:**757-6411
(914) 793-7120 .. **Rohrig,** James L '84 -107 Lk Av -Tuckahoe 10707 **Fx:**793-2114
(585) 454-2020 .. **Rohring,** Scott K '97 (Cellino & B,PC) -16 W Main -Rchstr 14614
(212) 513-6478 .. **Rohrs,** Gale L '78 %Dept Business Srvcs -110 William -NY 10038 **Fx:**618-8989
(212) 561-7700 .. **Rohwer,** Gabrielle A '09 Pachulski SZ&J -780 3rd Av -NY 10017
(718) 206-4708 .. **Roif,** Susanna A '07 %Law Dept -89-17 Sutphin Blvd -Jamaica 11435 **Fx:**206-4702
(212) 335-9000 .. **Roig,** Alberto '78 %DA -1 Hogan Pl -NY 10013
(212) 431-2804 .. **Roiphe,** Rebecca '02 NY Law Schl -185 W Bway -NY 10013 **Fx:**431-8352
(212) 656-3000 .. **Roisman,** Elad L '07 NYSE EuroNext -11 Wall -NY 10005
(585) 454-7570 .. **Roisman,** Herbert '81 Roisman & Assoc,PC -36 W Main -Rchstr 14614
(212) 508-6700 .. **Roisman,** Roger M '81 (Tannenbaum HS&H LLP) -900 3rd Av -NY 10022
(212) 408-5100 .. **Roitman,** Marc B '10 Chadbourne & P LLP -30 Rckfllr Plz -NY 10112
(212) 686-3838 .. **Rojas,** Alexander G '89 (Barst M&K LLP) -2 Park Av -NY 10016
(631) 265-9191 .. **Rojas,** Helayne D '88 Epstein & G -1393 Vets Mem'l Hwy -Hauppauge 11788
(212) 736-1798 .. **Rojas,** Jose A '96 (JA Rojas,PC) -7 Penn Plz -NY 10001 **Fx:**279-7901
(212) 768-9005 .. **Rojas,** Stephen J '96 -500 5th Av -NY 10110 **Fx:**768-9030
(212) 340-0400 .. **Rojas,** Susanna Molina '96 %Appllt Div 1st Dept -27 Mad Av -NY 10010 **Fx:**889-4412
(212) 715-9100 .. **Rokeach,** Tzvi '99 %Kramer LN&F,LLP -1177 Av of Amer -NY 10036
(212) 451-2300 .. **Roket,** Nina '97 (Olshan GFR&W LLP) -65 E 55th -NY 10022
(212) 819-8200 .. **Rokoff,** Gerald '76 (White & C LLP) -1155 Av of Amer -NY 10036
(212) 643-0000 .. **Rokosz,** Shrage '99 (Fried & R,LLP) -247-249 W 36th -NY 10018 **Fx:**643-0035
(516) 783-6565 .. **Roland,** Constance F '91 Rapuzzi P&R,PC -3361 Park Av -Wantagh 11793 **Fx:**783-6868
(212) 688-6591 .. **Roland,** Joanne S '98 Gruss & Co,Inc -667 Mad Av -NY 10065
(518) 465-7581 .. **Roland,** Keith J '72 OfCnsl Herzog Law Firm,PC -7 Southwoods Blvd -Albany 12211
(716) 859-2540 .. **Roland,** M K Gaedeke '01 Kaleida Hlth -100 High -Buffalo 14203
(212) 486-1830 .. **Roland,** Stephen P '76 -14 E 60th -NY 10022 **Fx:**980-9863
(212) 455-2000 .. **Roland,** Whitney W '10 %Simpson T&B LLP -425 Lex Av -NY 10017
(212) 775-3615 .. **Rold,** Wm J '82 NYS Dept Labor -75 Varck -NY 10013
(212) 684-6900 .. **Roldan,** Kenneth '95 %Wesley Brown & Bartle Co -152 Mad Av -NY 10016 **Fx:**889-8597
(212) 335-4500 .. **Roldan,** Vincent J '99 %DLA Piper LLP -1251 Av of Amer -NY 10020
(212) 295-8190 .. **Rolfe,** Jennifer E '01 Integro Grp -1 State -NY 10004 **Fx:**295-8191
(212) 309-1000 .. **Rolfe,** Robt M '85 (Hunton & W) -200 Park Av -NY 10166
(212) 474-1000 .. **Rolfe,** Ronald S '69 (Cravath S&M LLP) -825 8th Av -NY 10019
(212) 261-8344 .. **Roll,** Heidi H '10 %Mendes & M,LLP -750 7th Av -NY 10019
(716) 886-0211 .. **Roll,** James M '97 %Benderson Dvlpmnt -570 Delaware Av -Buffalo 14202 **Fx:**886-2269
(212) 848-4000 .. **Roll,** Wm J F III '80 (Shearman & S LLP) -599 Lex Av -NY 10022
(914) 964-7063 .. **Rolla,** Adrienne M '84 (Ronayne H&R) -441 Saw Mill Rvr Rd -Ynkrs 10701
(914) 964-7063 .. **Rolla,** Peter M '83 %Ronayne H&R -441 Saw Mill Rvr Rd -Ynkrs 10701
(914) 347-2600 .. **Rolle,** Lisa M '95 (Traub LS&S LLP) -7 Skyline Dr -Hawthorne 10532
(716) 852-2000 .. **Roller,** Derek J '09 %B Fitzgerald,PC -509 Lbrty Bldg -Buffalo 14202 **Fx:**852-2002
(212) 688-1100 .. **Roller,** Irina '00 (I Roller,PLLC) -111 Bway -NY 10006
(718) 834-8514 .. **Roller,** Jonathan S '81 -26 Court -Brklyn 11242
(718) 222-2103 .. **Roller,** Mindy Kapner '94 %Law Dept -350 Jay -Brklyn 11201 **Fx:**222-2393
(914) 670-3830 .. **Rolleri,** Ronald J '94 Globe OP Financial Srvcs LLC -1 South Rd -Harrison 10528
(212) 277-5813 .. **Rollings,** Cynthia '74 (Beldock L&H LLP) -99 Park Av -NY 10016
(914) 699-5220 .. **Rollings,** Jacob '97 Immigration Law Ctr -57 Gramatan Av -Mt Vernon 10550 **Fx:**699-3740
(914) 723-4300 .. **Rollings,** Jeffrey M '00 %Lackenbach S LLP -1 Chase Rd -Scarsdale 10583
(212) 455-2000 .. **Rollins,** Pamela L '84 (Simpson T&B LLP) -425 Lex Av -NY 10017
(315) 478-9392 .. **Rollinson,** David C '75 Rollinson Law Firm -307 S Townsend -Syracuse 13202 **Fx:**478-9521
(212) 986-6000 .. **Rollo,** Rebekah '05 %Kleinberg KW&C,PC -551 5th Av -NY 10176
(516) 248-6080 .. **Rollock,** Donald T '99 (D Rollock,PC) -114 Old Cntry Rd -Mineola 11501 **Fx:**741-8243
(212) 490-9000 .. **Rollock,** Phillip T '88 %TIAA-CREF -730 3rd Av -NY 10017
(718) 243-6829 .. **Rolls,** Jacob B '05 %Leg Aid -111 Lvngstn -Brklyn 11201 **Fx:**237-8737
(716) 856-2700 .. **Rolls,** James E '70 (Rolls K,LLP) -438 Main -Buffalo 14202 **Fx:**856-2777
(212) 267-4000 .. **Rolnik,** Mark D '80 -325 Bway -NY 10007 **Fx:**267-5813
(845) 359-5400 .. **Rolo,** Derek J '09 %Rogers M&H,PC -100 Dutch Hill Rd -Orangebrg 10962 **Fx:**359-5577
(212) 855-0280 .. **Roloff,** Riva B '96 Goldman Sachs -85 Broad -NY 10004
(585) 394-5755 .. **Rolph,** Peter '04 %Hall & K -6 Gorham -Canandaigua 14424
(212) 416-3202 .. **Rolston,** Bradley P '95 Dow Jones & Co -200 Lbrty -NY 10281 **Fx:**416-2524
(212) 454-4543 .. **Rom,** Judith R '86 %Deutsche Bank -60 Wall -NY 10005
(718) 987-8444 .. **Romagnola,** Gregg S '94 Chelli & B -149 New Dorp Ln -Staten Isl 10306
(212) 880-6000 .. **Romagnoli,** Jos J '87 (Torys LLP) -237 Park Av -NY 10017
(212) 506-1700 .. **Romagnoli,** Natasha '00 (Kasowitz BT&F LLP) -1633 Bway -NY 10019
(718) 720-3300 .. **Romagnolo,** Jos A '96 (Romagnolo & M,LLP) -400 St Marks Pl -Staten Isl 10301 **Fx:**720-2995
(212) 912-7431 .. **Romain,** Patrick '93 Merrill Lynch -222 Bway -NY 10038
(518) 842-9466 .. **Romaker,** Robt R '09 %Leg Aid -1 Kimball -Amsterdam 12010 **Fx:**843-1792
(718) 875-4915 .. **Roman,** Bryant A '05 Roman & Assoc,PLLC -186 Montague -Brklyn 11201
(212) 878-8000 .. **Roman,** Christopher J '95 (Clifford C LLP) -31 W 52nd -NY 10019
(212) 318-6000 .. **Roman,** Edileno D '07 %Paul HJ&W LLP -75 E 55th -NY 10022
(212) 484-3900 .. **Roman,** Eric '97 %Arent F LLP -1675 Bway -NY 10019
(516) 739-5100 .. **Roman,** Heather M '02 %Farber B&Z LLP -51 Charles -Mineola 11501
(718) 533-8444 .. **Roman,** Hector M Jr. '95 (Roman & S,LLP) -37-18 73rd -Jcksn Hts 11372
(718) 347-4955 .. **Roman,** James F '85 -81-18 262nd -Floral Pk 11004 **Fx:**347-4955
(315) 687-6562 .. **Roman,** James P '85 -443 Genesee Bx277 -Chittenango 13037 **Fx:**687-6943
(718) 579-7927 .. **Roman,** Jonathan '96 %Leg Aid -900 Sheridan Av -Bronx 10451 **Fx:**293-8744

(212) 964-3855 .. **Roman**, Jorge T '09 %R Cardali & Assoc,LLP -39 Bway -NY 10006 **Fx:**634-4856
(212) 208-3408 .. **Roman**, Juan B '94 %Ambac Assurance -1 State Street Plz -NY 10004 **Fx:**785-1178
(718) 205-1010 .. **Roman**, Julio C '96 %E Ifraimoff & Assoc,PC -116-16 Qns Blvd -Frst Hlls 11375 **Fx:**205-2066
(718) 579-3000 .. **Roman**, Luis A '93 %Leg Aid -1020 Grnd Cncrs -Bronx 10451 **Fx:**588-2611
(518) 356-1296 .. **Roman**, Marc S '09 -1005 Palazini Dr -Schnctdy 12303
(212) 907-0600 .. **Roman**, Mindy S '96 OfCnsl Gardner W&R LLP -270 Mad Av -NY 10016
(516) 747-5566 .. **Roman**, Mindy S '96 OfCnsl Ezratty E&L -80 E Old Cntry Rd -Mineola 11501
(716) 856-4000 .. **Roman**, Paul J Jr. '08 %Hodgson R LLP -140 Pearl -Buffalo 14202
(516) 336-2020 .. **Roman**, Philip M '83 Landstar Title Agncy -170 Old Cntry Rd -Mineola 11501 **Fx:**336-2025
(718) 533-8444 .. **Roman & Singh,LLP** -37-18 73rd -Jcksn Hts 11372 **Fx:**533-8460
(718) 928-3700 .. **Roman**, Vito A '94 LSNYC-Bronx -579 Courtlandt Av -Bronx 10451 **Fx:**402-7586
(212) 558-5500 .. **Romanelli**, Christopher A '98 %Weitz & L,PC -700 Bway -NY 10003
(347) 296-1662 .. **Romanelli**, Marcello '02 Supreme Ct Law Dept -360 Adams -Brklyn 11201 **Fx:**643-6114
(212) 310-8000 .. **Romanello**, Salvatore A '98 (Weil G&M LLP) -767 5th Av -NY 10153
(607) 721-8771 .. **Romani**, Jos F '85 %Dept of Law -44 Hawley -Bnghmtn 13901 **Fx:**721-8789
(212) 239-5185 .. **Romanick**, Norman '62 %Div Of Parole -314 W 40th -NY 10018 **Fx:**239-6160
(212) 669-4904 .. **Romanick**, Raquel S '03 Manhattan Boro President Ofc -1 Centre -NY 10007 **Fx:**669-3840
(718) 624-2240 .. **Romanick**, Seth A '00 (Romanick & S,PLLC) -142 Joralemon -Brklyn 11201 **Fx:**624-1268
(914) 965-4221 .. **Romano**, Andrew M '83 -20 S Bway -Ynkrs 10701
(212) 262-2390 .. **Romano**, Anthony II '77 OfCnsl Connell F LLP -888 7th Av -NY 10106
(212) 277-4000 .. **Romano**, Benito '77 (Freshfields BD LLP) -520 Mad Av -NY 10022
(845) 291-2050 .. **Romano**, Christen M '10 %DA -255-275 Main -Goshen 10924 **Fx:**291-2085
(914) 779-7222 .. **Romano**, Christina Kendall '88 -2168 Cntrl Pk Av -Ynkrs 10710 **Fx:**779-7716
(631) 277-8080 .. **Romano**, Christopher M '00 (Cassidy R&L,PC) -70 W Main -E Islip 11730 **Fx:**277-4908
(585) 243-2920 .. **Romano**, Danl L '90 -131 Main Bx261 -Geneseo 14454 **Fx:**243-2925
(914) 779-7222 .. **Romano**, Danl P '87 -2168 Cntrl Pk Av -Ynkrs 10710 **Fx:**779-7716
(212) 865-9848 .. **Romano**, Domenic '93 D Romano,PLLC -1230 Av of Amer -NY 10020
(718) 222-9800 .. **Romano**, Edgar N '95 (Brecher FPWT&Z,PC) -369 E 149th -Bronx 10455
(212) 225-2000 .. **Romano**, Emily Bretas '09 %Cleary GS&H -1 Lbrty Plz -NY 10006
(518) 696-5068 .. **Romano**, Frank A '69 -HCR 17 Apple Crk Ln -Hadley 12835
(631) 656-1200 .. **Romano**, Frank J '93 (FJ Romano & Assoc) -51 E Main -Smithtwn 11787 **Fx:**656-1515
(212) 704-4784 .. **Romano**, Joanne M '97 Max Rave,LLC -1450 Bway -NY 10018
(914) 779-7222 .. **Romano**, John N '52 -2168 Cntrl Pk Av -Ynkrs 10710
(914) 965-1515 .. **Romano**, Jos A '86 -703 Ynkrs Av -Ynkrs 10704 **Fx:**965-0410
(516) 496-5822 .. **Romano**, Leonard M '00 %T Spina -170 Froehlich Farm Blvd -Woodbury 11797 **Fx:**496-5420
(315) 738-1223 .. **Romano**, Linda E '79 OfCnsl Bond S&K,PLLC -501 Main -Utica 13501
(718) 422-5050 .. **Romano**, Mara A '91 -9201 4th Av -Brklyn 11209 **Fx:**333-1246
(718) 238-1144 .. **Romano**, Mario '91 -8118 13th Av -Brklyn 11228 **Fx:**921-3292
(914) 946-6774 .. **Romano**, Michl N '97 (Pilkington & L,PC) -222 Bloomingdale Rd -White Plns 10605
(914) 946-1881 .. **Romano**, Michl P '81 M Romano,PC -2 William -White Plns 10601 **Fx:**328-8747
(718) 262-7100 .. **Romano**, Patricia Ann '95 %Civil Ct -89-17 Sutphin Blvd -Jamaica 11435 **Fx:**262-7107
(212) 415-8600 .. **Romano**, Robt A '79 (Locke LB&L LLP) -3 World Fncl Ctr -NY 10281
(212) 309-6000 .. **Romano**, Robt M '73 (Morgan L&B LLP) -101 Park Av -NY 10178
(212) 797-3544 .. **Romano**, Susan Anne '97 (French & C,LLP) -29 Bway -NY 10006
(212) 836-8000 .. **Romano**, Tracy A '08 %Kaye S LLP -425 Park Av -NY 10022
(718) 237-2000 .. **Romano**, Vincent J '77 %Leg Aid -111 Lvngstn -Brklyn 11201 **Fx:**237-8737
(718) 852-5200 .. **Romano**, Vincent J '91 -9201 4th Av -Brklyn 11209 **Fx:**333-1246
(212) 637-1037 .. **Romano**, Virginia Chavez '98 %US Atty -1 St Andrews Plz -NY 10007
(212) 274-0777 .. **Romano**, Wilfred Glenn '93 (Romano & K,PLLC) -100 Lafayette -NY 10013
(212) 859-8000 .. **Romanoff**, Marc R '06 %Fried FHS&J LLP -1 NY Plz -NY 10004
(914) 428-4200 .. **Romanoff**, Michl '59 -7-11 S Bway -White Plns 10601 **Fx:**428-1241
(315) 234-8570 .. **Romano-Schulman**, Melissa S '96 %Hon N Mordue USDC -100 S Clinton Bx7367 -Syracuse 13261 **Fx:**234-8571
(212) 225-2000 .. **Romanova**, Elena V '04 %Cleary GS&H -1 Lbrty Plz -NY 10006
(716) 853-1616 .. **Romanowski**, Marc A '00 %Harter S&E LLP -12 Fountain Plz -Buffalo 14202
(718) 633-5716 .. **Roman-Perez**, Henry '93 -7105 5th Av -Brklyn 11209
(212) 506-3900 .. **Romansic**, Lara E '00 OfCnsl Steptoe & J LLP -750 7th Av -NY 10019
(212) 265-6888 .. **Romanski**, Jennifer A '98 Cnsl Porzio B&N,PC -156 W 56th -NY 10019
(518) 783-5611 .. **Romanucci**, Demostene '91 -950 Loudon Rd Bx1035 -Latham 12110 **Fx:**783-5615
(607) 754-4545 .. **Romas**, Angelos Peter '59 -101 Wshngtn Av -Endicott 13760 **Fx:**754-4546
(212) 313-3600 .. **Rome**, Gary A '81 (Barry M&M) -2 Rector -NY 10006
(646) 373-4090 .. **Rome**, Thos '83 -1501 Bway -NY 10036 **Fx:**(212) 391-6743
(212) 679-2900 .. **Rome**, Wm A '87 (Hoffman & P LLP) -260 Mad Av -NY 10016
(315) 422-4163 .. **Romeo**, James N '89 (Romeo & R) -314 E Fayette -Syracuse 13202 **Fx:**476-4781
(516) 357-3000 .. **Romeo**, Jason M '04 %Rivkin R LLP -926 RXR Plz -Uniondale 11556
(718) 923-4206 .. **Romeo**, Lori Ann '81 %OTDA Fair Hearings -14 Boerum Pl -Brklyn 11201
(518) 796-8426 .. **Romeo**, Lucia '07 -149 Jffrsn Heights -Catskill 12414
(718) 802-9858 .. **Romeo**, Michl J '82 (Romeo & B) -411 Court -Brklyn 11231 **Fx:**802-9872
(631) 447-2606 .. **Romeo**, Patricia K '96 -124 Medford Av -Patchogue 11772 **Fx:**447-2609
(212) 640-3271 .. **Romeo**, Richd P '76 %Amer Exp -200 Vesey -NY 10285
(212) 661-7100 .. **Romeo**, Richd P '83 (Salon MDN&B,LLP) -292 Mad Av -NY 10017
(315) 422-4163 .. **Romeo**, Robt A '85 (Romeo & R) -314 E Fayette -Syracuse 13202 **Fx:**476-4781
(631) 853-4161 .. **Romeo**, Rosa M '99 %DA -N Cnty Cmplx Bldg 77 -Hauppauge 11788 **Fx:**853-4192
(585) 232-1770 .. **Romeo**, Stacey M '97 (Romeo & S LLP) -36 W Main -Rchstr 14614 **Fx:**546-6456
(914) 253-0601 .. **Romeo**, Tina '84 -800 Wstchstr Av -Rye Brook 10573
(212) 759-7466 .. **Romer**, Andrew B '05 %Raven & K,LLP -126 E 56th -NY 10022
(212) 661-7300 .. **Romer**, James E '98 %Malapero & P LLP -295 Mad Av -NY 10017
(212) 572-4231 .. **Romer**, Jennifer L '98 %Estee Lauder -767 5th Av -NY 10153 **Fx:**572-3989
(716) 753-4339 .. **Romer**, Lydia '81 %Surrogates Ct -Gerace Ofc Bldg BxC -Mayvll 14757 **Fx:**753-4600
(212) 599-3322 .. **Romer**, Michl J '00 (Becker P,LLP) -45 Bway -NY 10006
(212) 793-7583 .. **Romero**, Anita '84 Citigroup -399 Park Av -NY 10022
(646) 429-8058 .. **Romero**, Custodio A '08 -271 W 47th -NY 10036
(212) 455-2000 .. **Romero**, Javier '06 %Simpson T&B LLP -425 Lex Av -NY 10017
(212) 232-1300 .. **Romero**, Joanne J '01 %Lewis BB&S LLP -77 Water -NY 10005
(518) 474-7700 .. **Romero**, Kay C '99 %NYS OPWDD -44 Holland Av -Albany 12229 **Fx:**474-7382
(212) 661-3691 .. **Romero**, Luis Alfredo '84 (Lopez R&M,PC) -551 5th Av -NY 10176
(718) 492-4200 .. **Romero**, Manuel A '84 (M Romero,PC) -5511 4th Av -Brklyn 11220 **Fx:**492-9494
(212) 909-6000 .. **Romero**, Maria L '10 %Debevoise & P LLP -919 3rd Av -NY 10022
(516) 802-0630 .. **Romero**, Marvin N '03 %Simmons J,LLP -115 Eileen Way -Syosset 11791
(631) 756-0400 .. **Romero**, Peter A '03 %Frank & Assoc,PC -500 Bi-Cnty Blvd -Farmngdl 11735 **Fx:**756-0547
(212) 317-5400 .. **Romero**, Wilfred J '78 %Swiss Re New Markets -55 E 52nd -NY 10055
(212) 232-2500 .. **Romero-Bosch**, Ana Maria '10 %Torgan & C,PC -17 State -NY 10004
(212) 474-1000 .. **Romieu**, Solene A L '10 %Cravath S&M LLP -825 8th Av -NY 10019
(845) 297-1000 .. **Romig**, Fredk D '84 Romig Law Ofc -8 Barristers Row -Wappingers Fls 12590 **Fx:**297-1959
(914) 381-6500 .. **Romita**, Carla L '93 Castle Oil Corp -440 Mamaroneck Av -Harrison 10528 **Fx:**381-6501
(914) 381-6500 .. **Romita**, Mauro C '65 %Castle Oil Corp -440 Mamaroneck Av -Harrison 10528 **Fx:**381-6501
(914) 381-6500 .. **Romita**, Melissa J '00 Castle Oil Corp -440 Mamaroneck Av -Harrison 10528 **Fx:**381-6501
(914) 381-6500 .. **Romita**, Michl N '91 %Castle Oil Corp -440 Mamaroneck Av -Harrison 10528 **Fx:**381-6501
(212) 661-8700 .. **Rom-Jensen**, Stacy '86 %Mercury Capital -380 Lex Av -NY 10168
(212) 373-3000 .. **Romm**, Julie S '06 %Paul WRW&G LLP -1285 Av of Amer -NY 10019
(914) 238-3222 .. **Romney**, Richd B '73 -35 Deerfld Rd -Chappaqua 10514 **Fx:**238-2146
(212) 969-3000 .. **Romond**, Russell F '09 Proskauer R LLP -1585 Bway -NY 10036 **Fx:**969-2900
(212) 684-0300 .. **Romski**, Gerard J '87 OfCnsl Bauman K&G LLP -28 W 44th -NY 10036
(212) 542-3270 .. **Romulus**, Jos D '05 MBK Entertainment -240 W 35th -NY 10001
(914) 824-4777 .. **Ronai**, Holly Ostrov '96 (Ronai & R) -34 Adee -Pt Chester 10573 **Fx:**683-6568
(914) 824-4777 .. **Ronai**, Peter I '90 (Ronai & R) -34 Adee -Pt Chester 10573 **Fx:**683-6568
(516) 877-7000 .. **Ronan**, Christopher P '94 (McCoyd P&R,LLP) -1100 Franklin Av -Gdn Cty 11530
(914) 725-7218 .. **Ronan**, Danl S '83 -670 Wht Plns Rd -Scarsdale 10583 **Fx:**725-7724
(914) 834-1052 .. **Ronan**, Martin W Jr. '63 (Alger A&R) -17 Dante -Larchmnt 10538
(212) 780-0800 .. **Ronan**, Michele M '03 YMCA -344 E 14th -NY 10003
(716) 842-4200 .. **Ronan**, Sean D '02 Cnsl M&T Bk -1 M & T Plz -Buffalo 14203 **Fx:**842-5376
(914) 964-7063 .. **Ronayne Hackeling & Rolla** -441 Saw Mill Rvr Rd -Ynkrs 10701
(845) 735-4616 .. **Ronayne**, Mavis A '05 -65 Bogert Av -Pearl Rvr 10965
(212) 408-5100 .. **Roncalli**, Anthony M '90 (Chadbourne & P LLP) -30 Rckfllr Plz -NY 10112
(516) 624-6150 .. **Roncallo**, Jean M '88 %Town Atty -Town Hall -Oyster Bay 11771 **Fx:**624-6196
(914) 862-5140 .. **Ronco**, Stephen A '09 %DA -1940 Commerce -Yorktwn Hts 10598 **Fx:**862-5146
(518) 373-1500 .. **Ronda**, Scott M '96 %R Beebe LLC -514 Vischers Ferry Rd -Clifton Pk 12065 **Fx:**373-0030
(212) 422-9424 .. **Rondello**, John M '99 %Gogick B&O,LLP -11 Bway -NY 10004
(212) 735-3000 .. **Rondina**, Abraham '08 %Skadden ASM&F LLP -4 Times Sq -NY 10036
(212) 290-4700 .. **Rone**, Jemera '75 %Human Rights Watch -350 5th Av -NY 10118 **Fx:**736-1300
(212) 779-7070 .. **Ronemus**, Michl B '83 (Ronemus & V) -112 Mad Av -NY 10016
(212) 779-7070 .. **Ronemus & Vilensky** -112 Mad Av -NY 10016 **Fx:**889-3978
(845) 567-7776 .. **Rones**, Jos P '72 (Finkelstein & Prtnrs,LLP) -103 Exec Dr -New Windsor 12553
(845) 228-4200 .. **Rones**, Kenneth S '74 %W Sayegh,PC -65 Gleneida Av -Carmel 10512 **Fx:**228-4832
(212) 820-9405 .. **Roney**, Deirdre A '09 %Hawkins D&W LLP -One Chase Manh Plz -NY 10005
(716) 853-8100 .. **Roney**, Susan C '83 (Nixon P LLP) -40 Fountain Plz -Buffalo 14202
(315) 685-8525 .. **Roney**, Teresa M '93 T Roney PLLC -2-4 Fennell Bx789 -Skaneateles 13152 **Fx:**685-8526

(516) 542-5900 .. **Ronk,** Christopher S '00 %Congdon FORDT&F -333 Earle Ovngton Blvd -Uniondale 11553
(845) 602-2224 .. **Ronning,** Royal N Jr. '86 Pfizer,Inc -401 N Mddltwn Rd -Pearl Rvr 10965
(518) 644-2020 .. **Ronning,** Teresa J '89 -Lk Shr Dr Bx30 -Bolton Landing 12814 **Fx:**644-5555
(201) 393-0600 .. **Ronson,** Cindy Birnbaum '85 -119 E 84th -NY 10028 **Fx:**727-0327
(212) 732-8700 .. **Ronson,** Jos S '86 %McAloon & F,PC -123 William -NY 10038
(212) 455-2000 .. **Rontiris,** Nicholas E '08 %Simpson T&B LLP -425 Lex Av -NY 10017
(212) 408-2500 .. **Ronzio,** Rebecca R '10 %Baker B,LLP -30 Rckfllr Plz -NY 10112
(718) 520-3991 .. **Rood,** Amy Beth '80 %Family Ct -89-14 Parsons Blvd -Jamaica 11432
(718) 643-5084 .. **Rood,** Robt E '87 %Hon A Feldman -360 Adams -Brklyn 11201
(518) 439-4401 .. **Rood,** Thos M '94 -434 Delaware Av -Delmar 12054
(212) 450-4000 .. **Rooder,** Brian J '07 %Davis P&W LLP -450 Lex Av -NY 10017
(347) 404-9133 .. **Roofeh,** Audrey A '06 %Civil Ct -141 Lvngstn -Brklyn 11201 **Fx:**(718) 643-3733
(518) 449-0044 .. **Rook,** David E '95 %Hoffman W&D LLC -75 State -Albany 12207 **Fx:**449-0047
(585) 272-0540 .. **Rook,** Sara E '06 %Thomas & S LLP -693 East Av -Rchstr 14607
(212) 854-5918 .. **Rooker,** Melissa O '02 Columbia Univ -535 W 116th -NY 10027 **Fx:**854-1368
(212) 582-6810 .. **Rooks,** Wayne D '71 (Serling R&F,LLP) -119 5th Av -NY 10003
(212) 512-4064 .. **Roome,** Katherine D '78 %McGraw-Hill -1221 Av of Amer -NY 10020 **Fx:**512-4827
(212) 450-4000 .. **Roomer,** Jason '09 %Davis P&W LLP -450 Lex Av -NY 10017
(212) 671-1179 .. **Roonan,** Randall K '81 (Graham MNM&R,PC) -2350 Bway -NY 10024
(718) 596-4800 .. **Roond,** Estelle '85 -16 Court -Brklyn 11241 **Fx:**(888) 799-0966
(212) 450-4000 .. **Rooney,** Byron B '07 %Davis P&W LLP -450 Lex Av -NY 10017
(212) 692-1000 .. **Rooney,** Christopher J '03 %Duane M LLP -1540 Bway -NY 10036
(212) 584-2990 .. **Rooney,** Christopher S '76 (Lally M&R LLP) -36 W 44th -NY 10036
(631) 755-0101 .. **Rooney,** F Sean '87 (Lewis JAA,LLP) -425 Broad Hollow Rd -Melvll 11747
(516) 248-1200 .. **Rooney,** Garret P '99 %Mulholland M&R -374 Hillside Av -Williston Pk 11596
(212) 450-4000 .. **Rooney,** Ian R '04 %Davis P&W LLP -450 Lex Av -NY 10017
(718) 847-0090 .. **Rooney,** James F '77 -86-07 Jamaica Av -Woodhvn 11421 **Fx:**(888) 596-2410
(716) 566-2800 .. **Rooney,** James J '03 (Bond S&K,PLLC) -40 Fountian Plz -Buffalo 14202
(718) 250-2000 .. **Rooney,** Jessica Ann '05 DA -350 Jay -Brklyn 11201 **Fx:**250-2314
(914) 238-9705 .. **Rooney,** John P Jr. '61 -107 Campfire Rd -Chappaqua 10514
(718) 351-3552 .. **Rooney,** Kathryn K '77 -1475 Hylan Blvd -Staten Isl 10305 **Fx:**979-6940
(212) 670-0262 .. **Rooney,** Kevin J '97 Merrill Lynch -222 Bway -NY 10038 **Fx:**(917) 778-0848
(212) 397-3370 .. **Rooney,** Michl P '98 Harris CC&H LLP -111 Bway -NY 10006 **Fx:**202-6206
(212) 323-2272 .. **Rooney,** Patrick G '00 NYC Health & Hospital Corp -346 Bway -NY 10013
(212) 209-3943 .. **Rooney,** Paul K '63 (PK Rooney,PC) -708 3rd Av -NY 10017 **Fx:**209-7173
(212) 346-0579 .. **Rooney,** Paul P '99 (Fugazy & R LLP) -225 Bway -NY 10007 **Fx:**(484) 805-7022
(516) 656-5300 .. **Rooney,** Peter F '55 (Mullooly JR&F LLP) -6851 Jericho Tpk Bx9036 -Syosset 11791
(212) 547-5400 .. **Rooney,** Peter J '94 (McDermott W&E LLP) -340 Mad Av -NY 10173
(718) 243-2169 .. **Rooney,** Sean H '96 -189 Montague -Brklyn 11201
(212) 259-8000 .. **Rooney,** Stephen G '81 (Dewey & L LLP) -1301 Av of Amer -NY 10019
(516) 656-5300 .. **Rooney,** Timothy F '87 (Mullooly JR&F LLP) -6851 Jericho Tpk Bx9036 -Syosset 11791
(914) 378-8960 .. **Rooney,** Timothy J Jr. '95 %Cablevision -6 Exec Plz -Ynkrs 10701
(212) 728-8000 .. **Rooney,** Wm H '84 (Willkie F&G LLP) -787 7th Av -NY 10019
(212) 701-3000 .. **Roop,** Andrew R '08 %Cahill G&R LLP -80 Pine -NY 10005 **Fx:**269-5420
(914) 593-7918 .. **Roos,** Lloyd I '63 Robert Martin Co,LLC -100 Clearbrook Rd -Elmsfrd 10523 **Fx:**592-5486
(845) 831-0971 .. **Roosa,** Benjamin P Jr. '57 Roosa & R -398 Main Bx468 -Beacon 12508 **Fx:**831-0990
(845) 831-0971 .. **Roosa,** Elizabeth A '85 Roosa & R -398 Main Bx468 -Beacon 12508 **Fx:**831-0990
(212) 859-8000 .. **Roose,** Matthew '07 %Fried FHS&J LLP -1 NY Plz -NY 10004
(914) 666-8033 .. **Roosevelt,** Christopher duPont '70 Cnsl Banks SG&W,LLP -118 N Bedford Rd Bx320 -Mt Kisco 10549
(212) 788-0969 .. **Roosevelt,** Phoebe '99 %Law Dept -100 Church -NY 10007 **Fx:**788-0367
(212) 732-3482 .. **Roosevelt,** Ruth B '80 -165 William -NY 10038 **Fx:**732-3482
(607) 687-8640 .. **Root,** Christian J '92 %Cnty Atty -20 Court -Owego 13827 **Fx:**687-6160
(716) 542-5454 .. **Root,** Duane G '70 -14 Buffalo -Akron 14001 **Fx:**542-1600
(212) 864-4100 .. **Root,** Gregory S '90 -380 Lex Av -NY 10168 **Fx:**864-4040
(518) 465-1500 .. **Root,** Jeremy R '05 %Cannon H&W,LLP -54 State -Albany 12207
(212) 698-3500 .. **Root,** Matthew D '01 %Dechert LLP -1095 Av of Amer -NY 10036
(716) 270-2431 .. **Root,** Matthew I '87 %IRS -300 Pearl -Buffalo 14202
(212) 376-3106 .. **Root,** Oren '74 Vera Inst of Justice -233 Bway -NY 10279 **Fx:**941-9407
(212) 902-2203 .. **Root,** Pamela P '81 %Goldman Sachs -85 Broad -NY 10004
(212) 239-9669 .. **Root,** Stuart D '60 OfCnsl Catafago Law Firm -350 5th Av -NY 10118 **Fx:**239-9688
(212) 788-1049 .. **Rootenberg,** Sharyn M '95 %Law Dept -100 Church -NY 10007 **Fx:**788-0367
(212) 440-3752 .. **Rootenberg,** Shelby K '98 CNA Global -40 Wall -NY 10005
(716) 648-1360 .. **Rooth,** Walter L '67 -296 Buffalo -Hambrg 14075
(716) 648-1360 .. **Rooth,** Walter L III '95 -296 Buffalo -Hambrg 14075
(212) 416-8000 .. **Roots,** Linda L '81 %Dept of Law -120 Bway -NY 10271
(212) 326-3939 .. **Roovers,** Veerle '02 (Jones D) -222 E 41st -NY 10017
(212) 750-8700 .. **Rooz,** Efraim '91 -101 E 52nd 15th FL -NY 10022 **Fx:**223-8391
(518) 473-8411 .. **Ropelewski,** Irene K '82 OCFS -52 Wshngtn -Rensselaer 12144 **Fx:**486-6361
(212) 752-9700 .. **Roper,** Eric R '65 (Gersten S LLP) -600 Lex Av -NY 10022
(718) 858-4366 .. **Roper,** Milard K '73 Fortunato & F,PLLC -26 Court -Brklyn 11242 **Fx:**852-6432
(718) 208-6001 .. **Roper,** Sandra E '88 -1205 Atl Av Bx160132 -Brklyn 11216
(212) 668-5927 .. **Ropers Majeski Kohn & Bentley** -17 State -NY 10004 **Fx:**668-5929
(347) 529-4991 .. **Roper-Simpson,** Casilda E '96 -26 Court -Brklyn 11242 **Fx:**(646) 350-0010
(212) 596-9000 .. **Ropes & Gray LLP** -1211 Av of Amer -NY 10036 **Fx:**596-9090
(212) 277-6500 .. **Roque,** Danl K '06 %Dickstein S LLP -1633 Bway -NY 10019
(212) 878-8000 .. **Roque,** Jose A '09 %Clifford C LLP -31 W 52nd -NY 10019
(212) 335-9209 .. **Roque,** Susan C '91 %DA -1 Hogan Pl -NY 10013
(212) 670-0221 .. **Rosa,** Eneida '82 %Merrill Lynch -222 Bway -NY 10038
(845) 586-3022 .. **Rosa,** Gary A '86 -835 Main Bx839 -Margaretvll 12455 **Fx:**586-1033
(212) 506-2500 .. **Rosa,** Jennifer M '05 %Mayer B LLP -1675 Bway -NY 10019
(212) 674-1740 .. **Rosa,** Margarita '80 %Grand Street Settlement -80 Pitt -NY 10002
(845) 486-2532 .. **Rosa,** Maria G '88 Supreme Ct -10 Market -Poughkeepsie 12601 **Fx:**486-6497
(212) 269-7722 .. **Rosabianca,** Luigi '00 (Rosabianca & Assoc,PLLC) -14 Wall -NY 10005 **Fx:**269-7799
(212) 587-7570 .. **Rosa Di Sant,** Rudolph '81 %State Ins Fund -199 Church -NY 10007 **Fx:**385-9199
(718) 830-3200 .. **Rosado,** Alexander '97 (Rosado C&B,LLP) -31-00 47th Av -LIC 11101 **Fx:**830-3534
(516) 294-5301 .. **Rosado,** Christopher '89 -200 Old Cntry Rd -Mineola 11501 **Fx:**741-7758
(212) 848-4000 .. **Rosado,** Christopher P '08 %Shearman & S LLP -599 Lex Av -NY 10022
(845) 562-1515 .. **Rosado,** Gisele C '07 %T Murphy & Assoc -717 Bway -Newburgh 12550 **Fx:**562-1160
(716) 881-4109 .. **Rosado,** Louis '90 -215 Hmpshr -Buffalo 14213 **Fx:**881-2906
(212) 758-2104 .. **Rosado,** Mary V '83 -488 Mad Av -NY 10022 **Fx:**308-8582
(212) 781-4808 .. **Rosado,** Nestor '81 -55 Overlook Ter -NY 10033 **Fx:**781-5104
(212) 216-9029 .. **Rosado,** Zully A '07 -70 Bowery -NY 10013 **Fx:**216-9025
(718) 260-4750 .. **Rosahn,** Eve S '94 %Leg Aid -111 Lvngstn -Brklyn 11201 **Fx:**260-4744
(718) 762-2953 .. **Rosales,** Leo L '02 %S Gajo -39-01 Main -Flushng 11354
(212) 642-3400 .. **Rosales-Menzel,** Lorilyn M '03 Liberty Hlth Advntg Inc -1 Huntngtn Quad -Melvll 11747
(212) 854-0778 .. **Rosan,** Felice B '95 %Columbia Univ -535 W 116th 412 Low Mem'l Library -NY 10027
(212) 953-0335 .. **Rosan,** Robt J '58 (Rosan & R,PC) -50 E 42nd -NY 10017 **Fx:**953-0360
(401) 454-1038 .. **Rosan,** Shellie D '97 Cnsl Nixon P LLP -437 Mad Av -NY 10022 **Fx:**(866) 544-0494
(212) 816-7249 .. **Rosandich,** Steven J '88 Citigroup -388 Greenwich -NY 10013
(516) 681-3100 .. **Rosanes,** Erik Hunt '00 %Donohue MC&B -555 N Bway Bx350 -Jericho 11753
(718) 590-2000 .. **Rosario,** Alejandra '07 %DA -198 E 161st -Bronx 10451 **Fx:**590-6477
(718) 579-7900 .. **Rosario,** Angel C '06 Leg Aid -900 Sheridan Av -Bronx 10451 **Fx:**293-8744
(646) 533-4920 .. **Rosario,** Jackie Y '02 -19 Mplwd Blvd -Suffern 10901 **Fx:**638-0242
(718) 492-2626 .. **Rosario,** Jorge '03 -5417 4th Av -Brklyn 11220
(631) 853-4343 .. **Rosario,** Jorge L '02 %Leg Aid -400 Carleton Av Bx9082 -Central Islip 11722 **Fx:**853-7798
(718) 505-6650 .. **Rosario,** Olivia DaMaris '02 %Kaplan & M -75-20 Astoria Blvd -E Elmhrst 11370
(718) 694-0304 .. **Rosario,** Serena '98 -26 Court -Brklyn 11242 **Fx:**694-0305
(212) 479-4529 .. **Rosario-Griffin,** Lori '04 Coty Inc -2 Park Av -NY 10016
(212) 722-2000 .. **Rosa-Rios,** Magda '84 %Leg Aid -230 E 106th -NY 10029 **Fx:**876-5365
(212) 455-2000 .. **Rosas,** Ann Marie '08 %Simpson T&B LLP -425 Lex Av -NY 10017
(631) 761-0800 .. **Rosas,** Christina M '03 %Lazer AR&Y,PC -225 Old Cntry Rd -Melvll 11747
(631) 582-3700 .. **Rosasco,** Craig E '05 (Turley RR&R,LLP) -3075 Vets Mem'l Hwy -Ronkonkoma 11779
(631) 582-3700 .. **Rosasco,** Troy G '90 (Turley RR&R,LLP) -3075 Vets Mem'l Hwy -Ronkonkoma 11779
(212) 579-1172 .. **Rosati,** Michl W '68 %Bevan MG&Z,PC -200 Mad Av -NY 10016
(212) 425-7200 .. **Rosati,** Richd M '85 (Kenyon & K,LLP) -1 Bway -NY 10004
(212) 233-4700 .. **Rosato,** Jos S '93 (Rosato & L,PC) -233 Bway -NY 10279 **Fx:**233-6500
(914) 684-6800 .. **Rosato,** Peter P '59 OfCnsl Collier HNN&B,LLP -1 N Lex Av -White Plns 10601
(212) 626-4100 .. **Rosaya,** Lisa Weiss '06 (Baker & M LLP) -1114 Av of Amer -NY 10036
(212) 530-5000 .. **Rosberger,** Richd E '94 Cnsl Milbank TH&M LLP -1 Chase Manh Plz -NY 10005
(518) 455-7803 .. **Rosborough,** Robt S IV '09 Ct of Appeals -20 Eagle -Albany 12207
(315) 673-9390 .. **Rosbrook,** Wm B '68 -4080 S Street Rd -Marcellus 13108 **Fx:**673-0925
(716) 282-1242 .. **Roscetti,** Alan J '04 %Roscetti & D -730 Main -Niagara Fls 14301
(716) 282-1242 .. **Roscetti & DeCastro** -730 Main -Niagara Fls 14301 **Fx:**282-5090
(716) 282-1242 .. **Roscetti,** James C '74 (Roscetti & D) -730 Main -Niagara Fls 14301
(518) 885-5359 .. **Rosch & Conners,PLLC** -20 Church Av Bx463 -Ballston Spa 12020 **Fx:**885-8491
(631) 232-2400 .. **Rosch,** Darlene M '99 %Nassau/Sfflk Law Srv -1757 Vets Hwy -Islandia 11749 **Fx:**232-2489
(716) 741-9802 .. **Rosche,** Richd J '72 -6420 Thistle Ct -E Amherst 14051
(212) 620-2680 .. **Roschelle,** Andrea L '85 (Starr Assoc LLP) -245 5th Av -NY 10016 **Fx:**696-5013
(914) 592-5740 .. **Roscia,** Emily '02 %Barnes I&S,LLP -258 Saw Mill Rvr Rd -Elmsfrd 10523
(716) 645-2258 .. **Rosciglione,** Maria R '98 %SUNY Buffalo/Intl Students -Bx601604 -Buffalo 14260
(212) 418-8600 .. **Rosdeitcher,** Emily A '93 %Kornstein VW&P,LLP -757 3rd Av -NY 10017
(212) 373-3000 .. **Rosdeitcher,** Sidney S '61 OfCnsl Paul WRW&G LLP -1285 Av of Amer -NY 10019
(518) 427-2650 .. **Rose,** Andrew C '85 (Nixon P LLP) -677 Bway -Albany 12207

(585) 924-7420 .. **Rose,** Angelo A '94 (Rose & R,LLC) -121 W Main -Victor 14564 **Fx:**924-0267
(914) 273-5384 .. **Rose,** April L '89 -19 Thornewood Rd -Armonk 10504
(212) 981-9060 .. **Rose & Boxer** -1065 Av of Amer -NY 10018 **Fx:**981-9071
(212) 421-4100 .. **Rose,** Brad D '86 (Pryor C LLP) -7 Times Sq -NY 10036
(516) 918-7098 .. **Rose,** Bryon J '07 Deloitte Tax LLP -2 Jericho Plz -Jericho 11753
(718) 275-3660 .. **Rose,** Carolyn '95 Harris Law Grp,LLP -96-14 63rd Dr -Rego Pk 11374 **Fx:**275-3405
(631) 715-7900 .. **Rose,** Chas N '03 %US Atty -610 Fed Plz -Central Islip 11722
(212) 687-8181 .. **Rose,** Danl O '97 (Kreindler & K) -750 3rd Av -NY 10017
(212) 488-1200 .. **Rose,** Danielle L '02 %Kobre & K,LLP -800 3rd Av -NY 10022
(212) 421-4100 .. **Rose,** David C '95 (Pryor C LLP) -7 Times Sq -NY 10036
(212) 326-3939 .. **Rose,** Diane L '84 %Jones D -222 E 41st -NY 10017
(212) 909-5412 .. **Rose,** Donald W '83 KPMG LLP -757 3rd Av -NY 10017
(518) 218-7100 .. **Rose,** Douglas J '01 (Tully R,PLLC) -441 New Karner Rd -Albany 12205
(315) 823-0835 .. **Rose,** Edw J '64 OfCnsl E Rose -31 N Ann -Little Fls 13365 **Fx:**823-3826
(212) 895-3689 .. **Rose,** Edw L '92 Maxim Grp,LLC -405 Lex Av -NY 10174
(516) 326-2812 .. **Rose,** Elihu I '69 El Rose,PC -1983 Marcus Av -Lk Success 11042 **Fx:**326-2831
(212) 758-6620 .. **Rose,** Gerard A '99 Rubin & Katz LLP -135 W 50th -NY 10020
(212) 725-6100 .. **Rose,** Hal L '90 Amsterdam & L -9 E 40th -NY 10016
(516) 932-0846 .. **Rose,** Hedy P '95 Alliance Grp LLC -100 Jericho Quad -Jericho 11753
(914) 461-3520 .. **Rose,** Jack J '91 R&R Holdings Inc -Bx366 -Bronxvll 10708
(212) 259-8000 .. **Rose,** Jacqueline A '02 %Dewey & L LLP -1301 Av of Amer -NY 10019
(516) 296-7000 .. **Rose,** James A '97 (Certilman BA&H,LLP) -90 Merrick Av -E Meadow 11554
(914) 948-8100 .. **Rose,** James M '72 -595 W Hartsdale Av -White Plns 10607 **Fx:**682-7926
(212) 480-6780 .. **Rose,** Jan C '82 %DHCR -25 Beaver -NY 10004 **Fx:**480-7416
(212) 490-9100 .. **Rose,** Jean Cooper '98 %Condon & F LLP -7 Times Sq -NY 10036
(516) 203-7180 .. **Rose,** Jesse C '09 %Valli K&V,LLP -600 Old Cntry Rd -Gdn Cty 11530 **Fx:**706-0248
(718) 487-1300 .. **Rose,** Jessica A '02 Leg Srvcs Corp A -80 Jamaica Av -Brklyn 11207 **Fx:**342-1780
(212) 849-7000 .. **Rose,** Jessica A '04 %Quinn EU&S,LLP -51 Mad Av -NY 10010
(212) 962-2300 .. **Rose,** Joanna '02 LMDC -1 Lbrty Plz -NY 10006
(212) 438-6601 .. **Rose,** Joanne W '83 %Standard & Poor's -55 Water -NY 10041
(212) 374-6827 .. **Rose,** Joel E '99 Dept of Ed -52 Chmbrs -NY 10007
(315) 474-2644 .. **Rose & Jordan** -300 S State -Syracuse 13202 **Fx:**474-2703
(212) 307-5500 .. **Rose,** Jorian L '98 (Venable LLP) -1270 Av of Amer -NY 10020
(212) 578-1101 .. **Rose,** Joshua D '00 Metlife -1 Met Life Plz -LIC 11101
(646) 458-7006 .. **Rose,** Justin M '03 ACE USA -140 Bway -NY 10005
(212) 455-2000 .. **Rose,** Kate Weber '10 %Simpson T&B LLP -425 Lex Av -NY 10017
(212) 455-2000 .. **Rose,** Kathy L '84 Cnsl Simpson T&B LLP -425 Lex Av -NY 10017
(518) 869-9200 .. **Rose,** Keith B '86 (Rose Law Firm,PLLC) -501 New Karner Rd -Albany 12205 **Fx:**869-3334
(212) 838-1177 .. **Rose,** Kenneth S '84 (Morse ZR&L LLP) -405 Park Av -NY 10022
(516) 571-3800 .. **Rose,** Kyle I '89 %DA -262 Old Cntry Rd -Mineola 11501 **Fx:**248-9479
(212) 973-9100 .. **Rose,** Lawr G '82 (Rose & K LLP) -757 3rd Av -NY 10017 **Fx:**973-9101
(212) 308-0210 .. **Rose,** Maria S '77 OfCnsl C Kutner,LLP -110 E 59th -NY 10022 **Fx:**308-0213
(315) 823-0835 .. **Rose,** Mark R '91 -31 N Ann -Little Fls 13365 **Fx:**823-3826
(585) 924-7420 .. **Rose,** Michl A '62 (Rose & R,LLC) -121 W Main -Victor 14564 **Fx:**924-0267
(212) 779-0057 .. **Rose,** Michl A '97 (Hach & R,LLP) -185 Mad Av -NY 10016
(212) 832-1977 .. **Rose,** Nancy A '84 (Schreck RDA&H) -1790 Bway -NY 10019 **Fx:**832-2969
(315) 361-5200 .. **Rose,** Neal P '77 -60 E State Bx130 -Sherrill 13461 **Fx:**361-1102
(718) 261-0546 .. **Rose,** Nicholas '03 N Rose,PLLC -102-11 Metro Av -Frst Hlls 11375 **Fx:**575-1300
(212) 815-1818 .. **Rose,** Nora Ule '06 DC 37 MELS -125 Barclay -NY 10007 **Fx:**815-1343
(212) 349-3366 .. **Rose,** Peter '87 (Rose & R) -291 Bway -NY 10007 **Fx:**349-2292
(212) 336-3708 .. **Rose,** Robt D '95 %EEOC -33 Whitehall -NY 10004
(914) 366-7575 .. **Rose,** Scott B '96 Barrett Advisors LLC -520 Wht Plns Rd -Tarrytwn 10591 **Fx:**366-7556
(212) 728-8000 .. **Rose,** Scott S '98 (Willkie F&G LLP) -787 7th Av -NY 10019
(914) 668-6622 .. **Rose,** Sharon P '98 -34 E 1st -Mt Vernon 10550 **Fx:**668-7763
(212) 530-5000 .. **Rose,** Stephen F '09 %Milbank TH&M LLP -1 Chase Manh Plz -NY 10005
(212) 930-9700 .. **Rose,** Thos A '87 (Sichenzia RFF LLP) -61 Bway -NY 10006
(212) 349-3366 .. **Rose,** Todd A '91 (Rose & R) -291 Bway -NY 10007 **Fx:**349-2292
(315) 474-2644 .. **Rose,** Wm W '82 (Rose & J) -300 S State -Syracuse 13202
(212) 373-2577 .. **Roseborough,** Siheem A '04 Dept of Ed -1106 E 95th -Brklyn 11236
(315) 597-5337 .. **Rosekrans,** Bruce A '85 %Converse & M,LLP -224 E Main Bx215 -Palmyra 14522
(212) 909-6000 .. **Rosekrans,** Christopher S '03 %Debevoise & P LLP -919 3rd Av -NY 10022
(607) 723-5341 .. **Rosekrans,** John C '84 SpclCnsl Hinman H&K,LLP -80 Exchange Bx5250 -Bnghmtn 13902
(212) 756-2000 .. **Rosell,** Kurt F '86 (Schulte R&Z LLP) -919 3rd Av -NY 10022
(212) 458-1917 .. **Rosell,** Sarah C '03 Chartis -175 Water -NY 10038
(607) 324-7333 .. **Rosell,** Timothy J '96 (Pulos & R,LLP) -70 Main Bx337 -Hornell 14843 **Fx:**324-1668
(212) 318-6000 .. **Rosella,** Michl R '82 (Paul HJ&W LLP) -75 E 55th -NY 10022
(631) 761-0800 .. **Rosella,** Ralph A '84 (Lazer AR&Y,PC) -225 Old Cntry Rd -Melvll 11747
(212) 930-9481 .. **Roselle,** Mary-Beth C '01 Istar Fincl -1114 Av of Amer -NY 10036
(212) 375-2202 .. **Roseman,** Alan S '87 ACA Captl -140 Bway -NY 10005 **Fx:**375-2001
(516) 327-4600 .. **Roseman Beerman Beerman LLP** -3000 Marcus Av -Lk Success 11042 **Fx:**327-4608
(212) 538-4257 .. **Roseman,** Douglas '94 Credit Suisse -11 Mad Av -NY 10010
(212) 848-4000 .. **Roseman,** Elizabeth D '07 %Shearman & S LLP -599 Lex Av -NY 10022
(631) 845-7300 .. **Roseman,** Gilbert '57 Roseman & R,LLP -510 Broadhllw Rd -Melvll 11747 **Fx:**845-4925
(516) 357-3700 .. **Roseman,** Matthew G '89 (Cullen and D LLP) -100 Q Roosevelt Blvd -Gdn Cty 11530
(212) 425-6200 .. **Roseman,** Robt A '72 -42 Bway -NY 10004 **Fx:**809-6174
(516) 327-4600 .. **Roseman,** Stephen M '72 (Roseman BB LLP) -3000 Marcus Av -Lk Success 11042
(212) 921-8399 .. **Rosen,** Abigail E '06 %Lankler S&W LLP -500 5th Av -NY 10110
(212) 490-3000 .. **Rosen,** Adam B '94 (Wilson EME&D LLP) -150 E 42nd -NY 10017
(212) 541-2000 .. **Rosen,** Adam J '07 %Bryan C LLP -1290 Av of Amer -NY 10104
(516) 479-6300 .. **Rosen,** Adam L '90 (Silverman A LLP) -100 Jericho Quad -Jericho 11753
(516) 594-0909 .. **Rosen,** Adam L '96 (Polsky S&R,PC) -500 Merrick Rd -Rockvll Ctr 11570
(212) 801-6849 .. **Rosen,** Adam L '05 %Greenberg T,LLP -200 Park Av -NY 10166
(212) 775-8700 .. **Rosen,** Adrienne E '05 %Kilpatrick S,LLP -31 W 52nd -NY 10019
(845) 486-2280 .. **Rosen,** Alexander B '05 %Pub Def -22 Market -Poughkeepsie 12601 **Fx:**486-2266
(212) 863-2800 .. **Rosen,** Amy G '91 Telstra Inc -40 Wall -NY 10005
(718) 630-2900 .. **Rosen,** Arlene B '76 %VA -800 Poly Pl -Brklyn 11209 **Fx:**630-2917
(212) 547-5400 .. **Rosen,** Arthur R '75 (McDermott W&E LLP) -340 Mad Av -NY 10173
(631) 423-8527 .. **Rosen,** Avrum J '84 -38 New -Huntngtn 11743 **Fx:**423-4536
(212) 481-4801 .. **Rosen,** Barrie M '87 B Silberzweig -271 Mad Av -NY 10016 **Fx:**481-4971
(212) 686-7700 .. **Rosen,** Benjamin A '02 %Mazur CR&S PC -1250 Bway -NY 10001
(212) 849-7000 .. **Rosen,** Brad E '09 %Quinn EU&S,LLP -51 Mad Av -NY 10010
(212) 474-1000 .. **Rosen,** Bradley J '03 %Cravath S&M LLP -825 8th Av -NY 10019
(212) 310-8000 .. **Rosen,** Brian S '85 (Weil G&M LLP) -767 5th Av -NY 10153
(212) 308-0070 .. **Rosen,** Bruce S '06 (McCusker AR&C,PC) -805 3rd Av -NY 10022
(212) 909-6000 .. **Rosen,** Burt P '80 (Debevoise & P LLP) -919 3rd Av -NY 10022
(212) 921-2236 .. **Rosen,** Chas A '66 -60 E 42nd -NY 10165
(631) 231-1450 .. **Rosen,** Chas H '72 SrCnsl Feldman K&M,PC -330 Vndrblt Motor Pkwy -Hauppauge 11788
(212) 310-8000 .. **Rosen,** Chelsea M '10 %Weil G&M LLP -767 5th Av -NY 10153
(212) 490-3000 .. **Rosen,** Cori A '09 %Wilson EME&D LLP -150 E 42nd -NY 10017
(212) 366-2000 .. **Rosen,** Dana J '97 Penguin Group (USA)Inc -375 Hudson -NY 10014 **Fx:**366-2867
(212) 298-2060 .. **Rosen,** Danl A '97 %IRS Ofc Chief Cnsl -290 Bway -NY 10007
(646) 386-4060 .. **Rosen,** Danl E '82 %Hon B Soloff -100 Centre -NY 10013
(212) 873-6000 .. **Rosen,** David B '76 Transport Workers Union -80 West End Av -NY 10023
(212) 325-2000 .. **Rosen,** David C '02 Credit Suisse -1 Mad Av -NY 10010
(718) 520-3759 .. **Rosen,** David H '75 %Hon A Lonschein -88-11 Sutphin Blvd -Jamaica 11435
(973) 848-4700 .. **Rosen,** David I '78 (Littler M,PC) -900 3rd Av -NY 10022 **Fx:**643-5626
(212) 752-3348 .. **Rosen,** David J '73 Bluerock Media -575 Lex Av -NY 10022 **Fx:**752-4152
(718) 638-8700 .. **Rosen,** David M '88 -726 Argyle Rd -Brklyn 11230 **Fx:**638-6204
(212) 272-8845 .. **Rosen,** David S '84 %JP Morgan Chase -383 Mad Av -NY 10179
(212) 859-8000 .. **Rosen,** Dean J '00 Fried FHS&J LLP -1 NY Plz -NY 10004
(716) 853-8400 .. **Rosen,** Dennis C '72 %Dept of Law -350 Main Pl Twr -Buffalo 14202 **Fx:**853-8571
(631) 231-1450 .. **Rosen,** Donna '82 %Feldman K&M,PC -330 Vndrblt Motor Pkwy -Hauppauge 11788
(518) 257-3000 .. **Rosen,** Donna Avrach '96 %Dormitory Auth -515 Bway -Albany 12207 **Fx:**257-3101
(212) 225-2000 .. **Rosen,** Edw J '83 (Cleary GS&H) -1 Lbrty Plz -NY 10006
(516) 746-4373 .. **Rosen,** Felicia B '94 MHLS -170 Old Cntry Rd -Mineola 11501 **Fx:**746-0598
(212) 612-4000 .. **Rosen,** Felicia Lebewohl '86 %Chubb Grp -55 Water -NY 10041
(718) 706-3000 .. **Rosen,** Fred C '94 %UPS -46-05 56th Rd -Maspeth 11378
(212) 526-0618 .. **Rosen,** Gary M '91 Barclays Capital Inc -399 Park Av -NY 10022
(516) 437-3400 .. **Rosen,** Gary S '99 G Rosen,PC -1010 Nrthrn Blvd -Gt Neck 11021
(516) 739-8222 .. **Rosen,** Gayle A '96 %Rabinowitz & G -94 Willis Av -Mineola 11501
(516) 747-6700 .. **Rosen,** Gene W '07 %Kirschenbaum & K -200 Grdn City Plz -Gdn Cty 11530 **Fx:**747-6781
(212) 416-6356 .. **Rosen,** Harriet B '83 %Dept of Law -120 Bway -NY 10271
(212) 873-7098 .. **Rosen,** Harvey '68 -150 W 76th -NY 10023 **Fx:**875-8688
(212) 335-9000 .. **Rosen,** Harvey D '72 %DA -1 Hogan Pl -NY 10013
(212) 382-0909 .. **Rosen,** Howard M '77 (Peckar & A,PC) -41 Mad Av -NY 10154
(718) 618-2525 .. **Rosen,** Irving '59 Bronx Civil Ct -851 Grnd Cncrs -Bronx 10451 **Fx:**590-7292
(212) 310-8000 .. **Rosen,** J Philip '82 (Weil G&M LLP) -767 5th Av -NY 10153
(646) 354-0147 .. **Rosen,** Janet A '95 -26 Court -Brklyn 11242
(718) 495-2579 .. **Rosen,** Janice P '94 %M Doherty,PC -6900 Jericho Tpk -Syosset 11791 **Fx:**495-2738
(212) 436-3288 .. **Rosen,** Jay M '83 Deloitte & Touche,LLP -2 World Fncl Ctr -NY 10281
(212) 621-8216 .. **Rosen,** Jeffrey A '65 (Sargoy SR&S) -1790 Bway -NY 10019
(212) 909-6000 .. **Rosen,** Jeffrey J '87 (Debevoise & P LLP) -919 3rd Av -NY 10022
(212) 869-7000 .. **Rosen,** Jennifer L '01 SpclCnsl Feldman W&S LLP -420 Lex Av -NY 10170
(212) 259-3900 .. **Rosen,** Jeremy M '05 OfCnsl Selverne & Co,PLLC -485 Mad Av -NY 10022
(212) 730-0305 .. **Rosen,** Jerrold B '86 -1 Lbrty Plz -NY 10006 **Fx:**(646) 304-6306
(212) 756-2000 .. **Rosen,** Jessica L '09 %Schulte R&Z LLP -919 3rd Av -NY 10022
(212) 530-7336 .. **Rosen,** Jonathan '85 SrCnsl Home Ins -59 Maiden Ln -NY 10038
(516) 739-5200 .. **Rosen,** Jonathan M '85 -310 Old Cntry Rd -Gdn Cty 11530 **Fx:**739-5267
(212) 249-1550 .. **Rosen,** Jonathan P '71 (Bobrow & R) -40 E 69th -NY 10021 **Fx:**249-5451
(917) 414-2179 .. **Rosen,** Jonathan R '83 -10 Hadden Rd -Scarsdale 10583
(585) 258-4538 .. **Rosen,** Julie M '05 %UIA Bd -109 S Union -Rchstr 14607 **Fx:**258-4539
(212) 349-3366 .. **Rosen,** Kenneth E '84 Rose & R -291 Bway -NY 10007 **Fx:**349-2292
(212) 962-5858 .. **Rosen,** Kenneth J '85 -67 Wall -NY 10005 **Fx:**363-4436
(212) 907-0700 .. **Rosen,** Krista T '07 %Labaton S LLP -140 Bway -NY 10005

(518) 452-1772 .. **Rosen**, Larry J '74 -113 Great Oaks Ofc Pk -Albany 12203 **Fx**:459-3754
(212) 686-1060 .. **Rosen**, Laurence M '89 (Rosen Law Firm) -350 5th Av -NY 10118
(212) 530-4822 .. **Rosen**, Lawr S '89 (LaRocca HRG&B LLP) -40 Wall -NY 10005 **Fx**:530-4815
(518) 434-2519 .. **Rosen**, Lee J '86 -20 Corp Wds Blvd -Albany 12211 **Fx**:434-6157
(212) 403-1000 .. **Rosen**, Leonard M '55 OfCnsl Wachtell LR&K -51 W 52nd -NY 10019
(212) 318-6000 .. **Rosen**, Leslie A '08 %Paul HJ&W LLP -75 E 55th -NY 10022
(212) 687-7770 .. **Rosen Livingston & Cholst LLP** -275 Mad Av -NY 10016 **Fx**:687-8030
(516) 773-8300 .. **Rosen**, Lloyd C '94 %Wisselman H & Assoc,PC -1010 Nrthrn Blvd -Gt Neck 11021 **Fx**:773-8304
(914) 422-3900 .. **Rosen**, Lois N '80 %Oxman TKW&G LLP -120 Bloomingdale Rd -White Plns 10605
(212) 986-6000 .. **Rosen**, Marc R '99 (Kleinberg KW&C,PC) -551 5th Av -NY 10176
(212) 303-6575 .. **Rosen**, Maria '02 %Caxton Assoc LLC -500 Park Av -NY 10022
(212) 483-9490 .. **Rosen**, Mark A '82 (McElroy DM&C,LLP) -88 Pine -NY 10005
(646) 330-9642 .. **Rosen**, Mark B '75 (M Rosen,PC) -564 1st Av -NY 10016 **Fx**:607-1676
(212) 310-8000 .. **Rosen**, Mark B '08 %Weil G&M LLP -767 5th Av -NY 10153
(516) 349-7878 .. **Rosen**, Martin '50 -84 Radcliffe Rd -Plainvw 11803
(212) 768-6700 .. **Rosen**, Martin '52 (Sonnenschein N&R LLP) -1221 Av of Amer -NY 10020
(914) 761-6300 .. **Rosen**, Martin J '67 (MJ Rosen,PC) -175 Main -White Plns 10601 **Fx**:761-9322
(212) 735-3000 .. **Rosen**, Matthew A '80 (Skadden ASM&F LLP) -4 Times Sq -NY 10036
(212) 335-9000 .. **Rosen**, Matthew A '02 %DA -1 Hogan Pl -NY 10013
(914) 470-0001 .. **Rosen**, Matthew J '96 %Babchik & Y,LLP -200 E Post Rd -White Plns 10601
(212) 455-2000 .. **Rosen**, Meryl G '07 %Simpson T&B LLP -425 Lex Av -NY 10017
(212) 742-1717 .. **Rosen**, Michl '64 -61 Bway -NY 10006 **Fx**:248-4068
(518) 462-4715 .. **Rosen**, Michl E '79 (Pastel & R) -130 Wshngtn Av -Albany 12210 **Fx**:462-4756
(646) 557-7010 .. **Rosen**, Michl J '92 GM Planworks -1675 Bway -NY 10019
(212) 541-2000 .. **Rosen**, Michl N '66 (Bryan C LLP) -1290 Av of Amer -NY 10104
(212) 619-3485 .. **Rosen**, Michl W '78 -1 Penn Plz -NY 10119
(212) 848-4000 .. **Rosen**, Michelle L '04 %Shearman & S LLP -599 Lex Av -NY 10022
(212) 757-0909 .. **Rosen**, Mildred Pafundi '58 -860 UN Plz -NY 10017 **Fx**:956-3252
(212) 687-7770 .. **Rosen**, Morton H '62 (Rosen L&C LLP) -275 Mad Av -NY 10016
(212) 943-1200 .. **Rosen**, Myron S '64 (Edelman & E,PC) -61 Bway -NY 10006 **Fx**:943-0001
(212) 757-0909 .. **Rosen**, N Hilton '58 -860 UN Plz -NY 10017 **Fx**:757-0276
(212) 756-2000 .. **Rosen**, Naama '04 %Schulte R&Z LLP -919 3rd Av -NY 10022
(718) 237-5500 .. **Rosen**, Nadya E '05 %Leg Srvcs -105 Court -Brklyn 11201 **Fx**:855-0733
(212) 536-3900 .. **Rosen**, Omer '08 %K&L Gates LLP -599 Lex Av -NY 10022
(212) 231-1000 .. **Rosen**, Peter C '06 %MacQuarie Holdings Inc -125 W 55th -NY 10019 **Fx**:231-1010
(516) 535-1700 .. **Rosen**, Philip A '85 (Horing W&R,PC) -11 Hillside Av -Williston Pk 11596
(212) 545-4000 .. **Rosen**, Philip B '80 (Jackson L LLP) -666 3rd Av -NY 10017
(212) 223-0400 .. **Rosen**, Philip S '92 OfCnsl Zeichner E&K LLP -575 Lex Av -NY 10022
(914) 235-3626 .. **Rosen**, Reid A '81 -15 Wilputte Pl -New Rchll 10804 **Fx**:235-1369
(212) 323-2250 .. **Rosen**, Rhonda L '86 %HHC-OLA-Medical Litigation -346 Bway -NY 10013 **Fx**:323-2251
(212) 373-3000 .. **Rosen**, Richd A '80 (Paul WRW&G LLP) -1285 Av of Amer -NY 10019
(212) 345-5000 .. **Rosen**, Richd C '91 %Marsh & McLennan Cos -1166 Av of Amer -NY 10036
(212) 644-6644 .. **Rosen**, Richd L '68 (R Rosen,PLLC) -110 E 59th -NY 10022 **Fx**:644-3344
(845) 462-0001 .. **Rosen**, Richd T '61 OfCnsl Serino M&B,PLLC -12 Walker Rd -Poughkeepsie 12603
(516) 747-6300 .. **Rosen**, Rise E '91 %Koeppel M&L,LLP -155 First Bx863 -Mineola 11501
(516) 535-6666 .. **Rosen**, Robt D '85 -55 Bryant Av -Roslyn 11576 **Fx**:626-6696
(212) 935-3000 .. **Rosen**, Robt J '10 %Mintz LCFG&P,PC -666 3rd Av -NY 10017
(212) 903-9000 .. **Rosen**, Robt L '99 %Linklaters -1345 Av of Amer -NY 10105
(516) 203-7180 .. **Rosen**, Robt M '64 OfCnsl Valli K&V,LLP -600 Old Cntry Rd -Gdn Cty 11530 **Fx**:706-0248
(212) 643-2828 .. **Rosen**, Robin C '96 %GNYHCFA -360 W 31st -NY 10001 **Fx**:643-2956
(212) 647-8100 .. **Rosen**, Ross B '93 (Toorock & R) -20 W 20th -NY 10011
(212) 603-6321 .. **Rosen**, Russell W '68 (Robinson BLGG&G PC) -875 3rd Av -NY 10022
(914) 747-6776 .. **Rosen**, Sam S '00 (Rosen Law Grp PLLC) -Bx482 -White Plns 10603
(212) 935-7400 .. **Rosen**, Saml K '69 (Harwood F LLP) -488 Mad Av -NY 10022
(212) 803-5139 .. **Rosen**, Saml R '67 %NY Cnty Defender Srvcs -225 Bway -NY 10007 **Fx**:571-6035
(212) 223-1100 .. **Rosen**, Sanford P '79 (Rosen & Assoc,PC) -747 3rd Av -NY 10017 **Fx**:223-1102
(914) 946-7050 .. **Rosen**, Sara M '86 -35 Thompson Av -White Plns 10603 **Fx**:428-4881
(212) 474-1000 .. **Rosen**, Sarah F '07 %Cravath S&M LLP -825 8th Av -NY 10019
(212) 909-6000 .. **Rosen**, Seth L '81 (Debevoise & P LLP) -919 3rd Av -NY 10022
(212) 431-2169 .. **Rosen**, Seth Mitchell '00 %NY Law Schl -185 W Bway -NY 10013 **Fx**:406-0103
(212) 732-3200 .. **Rosen**, Sharon Ronit '06 %Carter L&M LLP -2 Wall -NY 10005
(718) 268-8200 .. **Rosen**, Sheldon Jay '78 -99-06 Metro Av -Frst Hlls 11375
(631) 439-1720 .. **Rosen**, Sheldon M '74 %MHLS -320 Carleton Av -Central Islip 11722 **Fx**:951-2562
(212) 581-4540 .. **Rosen**, Stephan C '76 US Realty Advisors,LLC -1370 Av of Amer -NY 10019
(212) 580-7200 .. **Rosen**, Stephen D '69 -247 W 87th -NY 10024
(212) 599-3970 .. **Rosen**, Steven A '82 -271 Mad Av -NY 10016
(212) 830-2562 .. **Rosen**, Stuart '85 %Broadcast Music Inc -250 Greenwich -NY 10007
(212) 688-1900 .. **Rosen**, Stuart B '99 %Greenberg T&H,LLP -767 3rd Av -NY 10017
(212) 451-3000 .. **Rosen**, Stuart I '85 %Trian Fund Mgmt,LP -280 Park Av -NY 10017 **Fx**:451-3216
(212) 310-8000 .. **Rosen**, Stuart M '65 (Weil G&M LLP) -767 5th Av -NY 10153
(212) 878-7900 .. **Rosen**, Ted D '85 (Fox R LLP) -100 Park Av -NY 10017
(516) 487-6988 .. **Rosen**, Ted M '72 -5 Longvw Pl -Gt Neck 11021 **Fx**:487-6956
(212) 848-4000 .. **Rosen**, Thos I '08 %Shearman & S LLP -599 Lex Av -NY 10022
(646) 386-5700 .. **Rosen**, Weslie Hope '83 %Civil Ct -111 Centre -NY 10013
(212) 415-9200 .. **Rosenau**, Brian R '06 %Dorsey & W LLP -250 Park Av -NY 10177
(212) 351-4000 .. **Rosenauer**, David B '93 (Gibson D&C LLP) -200 Park Av -NY 10166
(516) 795-7808 .. **Rosenbach**, Anne '79 A Rosenbach,PC -3 Delta Rd -Massapequa 11758 **Fx**:795-9584
(212) 558-5500 .. **Rosenband**, David L '01 %Weitz & L,PC -700 Bway -NY 10003
(212) 223-0400 .. **Rosenband**, Sandra F '99 %Zeichner E&K LLP -575 Lex Av -NY 10022
(718) 828-1400 .. **Rosenbaum**, Andrew H '91 -2622 E Tremont Av -Bronx 10461 **Fx**:828-9494
(212) 239-4999 .. **Rosenbaum**, Ary Dov '98 %Meyer SE&K,PC -1350 Bway Bx822 -NY 10018
(212) 788-0857 .. **Rosenbaum**, Bruce '90 %Law Dept -100 Church -NY 10007 **Fx**:788-0367
(914) 242-5487 .. **Rosenbaum**, Cindy Yost '82 Happy Kids Prdctns,Inc -247 Route 100 -Somers 10589 **Fx**:242-5941
(212) 514-5007 .. **Rosenbaum**, Craig D '96 (Rosenbaum & R,PC) -110 Wall -NY 10005 **Fx**:514-9178
(516) 571-9044 .. **Rosenbaum**, D J '89 %Cnty Atty -1200 Old Cntry Rd -Westbury 11590 **Fx**:571-9619
(212) 649-8000 .. **Rosenbaum**, Dan A '98 UBS Financial Srvcs Inc -1285 Av of Amer -NY 10019
(212) 891-5803 .. **Rosenbaum**, Dan L '89 Ixis Capital Mrkts -9 W 57th -NY 10019
(212) 915-6153 .. **Rosenbaum**, Dana E '05 XL Capital Invstmnt Prtnrs Inc -1540 Bway -NY 10036
(212) 319-1000 .. **Rosenbaum**, Dara L '01 %Quirk & B,PC -845 3rd Av -NY 10022
(212) 431-1300 .. **Rosenbaum**, David B '85 (Borah GAN&G PC) -377 Bway -NY 10013
(516) 561-2900 .. **Rosenbaum**, Elliott M '66 -265 E Merrick Rd -Vly Stream 11580 **Fx**:561-2525
(718) 286-6000 .. **Rosenbaum**, Eric C '92 %DA -125-01 Qns Blvd -Kew Gdns 11415
(212) 957-7600 .. **Rosenbaum**, Evan M '10 %Cohen & G LLP -800 3rd Av -NY 10022
(212) 514-5007 .. **Rosenbaum**, George D '59 (Rosenbaum & R,PC) -110 Wall -NY 10005 **Fx**:514-9178
(212) 593-3000 .. **Rosenbaum**, Janelle B '07 %Platzer SKLG&J,LLP -1065 Av of Amer -NY 10018
(212) 308-4411 .. **Rosenbaum**, Jay D '95 (Edwards AP&D LLP) -750 Lex Av -NY 10022
(518) 449-3166 .. **Rosenbaum**, Jeffrey M '82 (UHY Advisors) -66 State -Albany 12207 **Fx**:449-5832
(212) 808-4848 .. **Rosenbaum**, John E '97 OfCnsl Beckmann & Assoc LLC -90 Park Av -NY 10016 **Fx**:986-4939
(212) 806-5400 .. **Rosenbaum**, Jordan M '04 %Stroock &S&L LLP -180 Maiden Ln -NY 10038
(212) 521-5400 .. **Rosenbaum**, Jos I '78 (Reed S LLP) -599 Lex Av -NY 10022
(718) 547-6400 .. **Rosenbaum**, Joshua A '00 -2526 Wallace Av -Bronx 10467 **Fx**:547-9410
(516) 750-9375 .. **Rosenbaum**, Leonard S '94 Wright Risk Mgmt -333 Earle Ovngton Blvd -Uniondale 11553
(914) 962-4400 .. **Rosenbaum**, Lester '59 (Rosenbaum & R) -1884 Railroad Av Bx217 -Yorktwn Hts 10598 **Fx**:962-1567
(212) 214-1000 .. **Rosenbaum**, Lisa J '91 Fidelity Investments -200 Lbrty -NY 10281
(212) 596-9000 .. **Rosenbaum**, Lisa T '08 %Ropes & G LLP -1211 Av of Amer -NY 10036
(718) 852-0425 .. **Rosenbaum**, Marc H '76 %BNYDC -Bklyn Navy Yd Bldg 292 -Brklyn 11205 **Fx**:643-9296
(631) 366-3670 .. **Rosenbaum**, Marda A '94 -1363 Vets Mem'l Hwy -Hauppauge 11788 **Fx**:366-3902
(212) 806-5400 .. **Rosenbaum**, Mark '71 OfCnsl Stroock &S&L LLP -180 Maiden Ln -NY 10038
(518) 455-4313 .. **Rosenbaum**, Marty I '81 %NYS Assembly -Gov AE Smith State Ofc Bldg -Albany 12248
(212) 559-3627 .. **Rosenbaum**, Michl F '78 Citigroup Asset Mgmt -399 Park Av -NY 10022
(973) 315-4403 .. **Rosenbaum**, Michl M '88 (Budd L) -140 Bway -NY 10005
(212) 468-8000 .. **Rosenbaum**, Norman S '90 (Morrison & F LLP) -1290 Av of Amer -NY 10104
(212) 801-9320 .. **Rosenbaum**, Richd A '83 (Greenberg T,LLP) -200 Park Av -NY 10166
(585) 263-1000 .. **Rosenbaum**, Richd M '56 SrCnsl Nixon P LLP -1100 Clinton Sq -Rchstr 14604
(914) 962-4400 .. **Rosenbaum**, Sally '81 (Rosenbaum & R) -1884 Railroad Av Bx217 -Yorktwn Hts 10598 **Fx**:962-1567
(212) 966-6420 .. **Rosenbaum**, Serina M '89 %Lwyrs For Children -110 Lafayette -NY 10013 **Fx**:966-0531
(516) 829-0363 .. **Rosenbaum**, Spencer V '05 %Israel I&P,LLP -11 Grace Av -Gt Neck 11021 **Fx**:829-0366
(212) 972-0902 .. **Rosenbaum**, Stephan L '72 -261 Mad Av -NY 10016
(212) 808-0448 .. **Rosenbaum**, Steven E '98 (Brand BN&R,LLP) -286 Mad Av -NY 10017
(516) 466-3600 .. **Rosenbaum**, Sylvan '58 -98 Cutter Mill Rd -Gt Neck 11021
(845) 371-1705 .. **Rosenbaum**, Tara M '00 (Rosenbaum & Assoc) -2 Perlman Dr -Spg Vly 10977
(212) 877-7598 .. **Rosenbaum**, Thane N '89 -412 W 110th -NY 10025
(585) 987-2800 .. **Rosenbaum**, Warren B '73 (Woods OG LLP) -2 State -Rchstr 14614
(212) 204-8690 .. **Rosenbaum**, Zachary D '98 (Lowenstein S PC) -1251 Av of Amer -NY 10020 **Fx**:(973) 597-6351
(212) 973-9100 .. **Rosenbaum Kaplan**, Marcy C '99 %Rose & K LLP -757 3rd Av -NY 10017 **Fx**:973-9101
(518) 438-5010 .. **Rosenbaum-Weisz**, Diane H '79 -57 Mohawk Trl -Slingerlnds 12159
(212) 902-9679 .. **Rosenberg**, Adam C '94 %Goldman Sachs -85 Broad -NY 10004
(718) 254-0700 .. **Rosenberg**, Alan '79 %Bklyn Defender Srvcs -177 Lvngstn -Brklyn 11201 **Fx**:254-0897

(212) 506-3900 .. **Rosenberg,** Alejandro G '07 %Steptoe & J LLP -750 7th Av -NY 10019
(917) 767-4728 .. **Rosenberg,** Allison J '96 %UNITE -505 8th Av -NY 10018
(212) 318-6000 .. **Rosenberg,** Amy L '04 %Paul HJ&W LLP -75 E 55th -NY 10022
(212) 972-6161 .. **Rosenberg,** Andrew L '92 OfCnsl Cassin & C LLP -711 3rd Av -NY 10017
(212) 373-3000 .. **Rosenberg,** Andrew N '92 (Paul WRW&G LLP) -1285 Av of Amer -NY 10019
(212) 541-7272 .. **Rosenberg,** Armand J '51 -250 W 57th -NY 10107
(212) 513-3200 .. **Rosenberg,** Arthur E '84 (Holland & K LLP) -31 W 52nd -NY 10019
(631) 423-5600 .. **Rosenberg,** Arthur G '62 -10 Chichester Rd -Huntngtn Sta 11746
(516) 437-5400 .. **Rosenberg,** Arthur H '82 (Soberman & R) -2001 Marcus Av -Lk Success 11042
(212) 541-6222 .. **Rosenberg,** Arthur M '84 (Kane K,PC) -1350 Av of Amer -NY 10019
(585) 546-5960 .. **Rosenberg,** B Robt '50 OfCnsl Laverne & H -36 Main W -Rchstr 14614
(212) 848-4000 .. **Rosenberg,** Barbara E '91 Shearman & S LLP -599 Lex Av -NY 10022
(516) 884-6265 .. **Rosenberg,** Benjamin C '91 -859 Crestvw Av -Vly Stream 11581 **Fx:**706-6050
(212) 698-3500 .. **Rosenberg,** Benjamin E '87 (Dechert LLP) -1095 Av of Amer -NY 10036
(516) 221-1108 .. **Rosenberg,** Bruce S '88 (Rosenberg Law PC) -2631 Merrick Rd -Bellmore 11710
(516) 747-7400 .. **Rosenberg Calica & Birney LLP** -100 Grdn City Plz -Gdn Cty 11530 **Fx:**747-7480
(212) 679-6500 .. **Rosenberg,** Chas H '58 (Rosenberg & Z) -515 Mad Av -NY 10022 **Fx:**679-5888
(212) 902-8575 .. **Rosenberg,** Danl B '98 Goldman Sachs -1 NY Plz -NY 10004
(516) 569-4773 .. **Rosenberg,** Danl G '74 -116 Meadowvw Av -Hewlett 11557 **Fx:**569-4773
(212) 688-5055 .. **Rosenberg,** Danl H '94 Chanel Inc -9 W 57th -NY 10019 **Fx:**303-5979
(212) 755-7500 .. **Rosenberg,** David '72 (Marcus R&D LLP) -488 Mad Av -NY 10022
(646) 312-3582 .. **Rosenberg,** David '92 Baruch College -17 Lex Av Bx 316 -NY 10010
(212) 308-7400 .. **Rosenberg,** David B '96 (Todd & L,LLP) -444 Mad Av -NY 10022
(516) 747-7400 .. **Rosenberg,** David H '05 %Rosenberg C&B LLP -100 Grdn City Plz -Gdn Cty 11530
(516) 228-6666 .. **Rosenberg,** David I '77 (Rosenberg F&L,LLP) -666 Old Cntry Rd -Gdn Cty 11530
(212) 867-9595 .. **Rosenberg,** Donald B '59 (Vogel & R) -630 Third Av -NY 10017
(212) 447-7070 .. **Rosenberg,** Elizabeth '02 %Whatley D&K LLC -1540 Bway -NY 10036
(212) 455-2000 .. **Rosenberg,** Ellen D '06 %Simpson T&B LLP -425 Lex Av -NY 10017
(212) 349-6009 .. **Rosenberg,** Ellen V '95 %Sanctuary for Families -110 Wall -NY 10005 **Fx:**566-0344
(212) 670-0150 .. **Rosenberg,** Eric M '74 %Merrill Lynch -222 Bway -NY 10038
(212) 286-6100 .. **Rosenberg,** Eric S '89 (Rosenberg & P,LLP) -420 Lex Av -NY 10170
(212) 867-6000 .. **Rosenberg & Estis,PC** -733 3rd Av -NY 10017 **Fx:**551-8484
(212) 682-3454 .. **Rosenberg Feldman Smith LLP** -551 5th Av -NY 10176 **Fx:**867-9045
(516) 228-6666 .. **Rosenberg Fortuna & Laitman, LLP** -666 Old Cntry Rd -Gdn Cty 11530 **Fx:**228-6672
(212) 247-1851 .. **Rosenberg,** Fred C '80 -1776 Bway -NY 10019
(212) 856-9796 .. **Rosenberg,** Fred S '87 -230 E 44th -NY 10017
(516) 379-1397 .. **Rosenberg,** Frieda U '78 -2810 Lindenmere Dr -Merrick 11566 **Fx:**379-1399
(212) 450-4000 .. **Rosenberg,** Gabriel D '09 %Davis P&W LLP -450 Lex Av -NY 10017
(718) 520-8787 .. **Rosenberg,** Gary E '83 G Rosenberg, PC -109-01 72nd Rd Bx750070 -Frst Hlls 11375 **Fx:**520-2350
(212) 867-6000 .. **Rosenberg,** Gary M '75 (Rosenberg & E,PC) -733 3rd Av -NY 10017
(212) 869-3000 .. **Rosenberg,** Glen '97 Cnsl New Plan Excel Rlty Trust,Inc -420 Lex Av -NY 10170 **Fx:**869-6043
(631) 451-7900 .. **Rosenberg & Gluck,LLP** -1176 Portion Rd -Holtsvll 11742 **Fx:**451-7955
(914) 345-2800 .. **Rosenberg,** Helen K '75 Westhab -85 Exec Blvd -Elmsfrd 10523
(212) 335-9000 .. **Rosenberg,** Hillary '05 %DA -1 Hogan Pl -NY 10013
(516) 227-6500 .. **Rosenberg,** Howard S '91 (Kreinces & R,PC) -900 Merchants Cncrs -Westbury 11590 **Fx:**227-6594
(212) 456-0564 .. **Rosenberg,** Ian M '99 ABC -77 W 66th -NY 10023 **Fx:**456-6202
(631) 851-0600 .. **Rosenberg,** Ira S '87 -320 Carleton Av -Central Islip 11722
(212) 809-8551 .. **Rosenberg,** Jamie C '87 -116 John -NY 10038 **Fx:**248-5387
(212) 620-2680 .. **Rosenberg,** Jane '76 Cnsl Starr Assoc LLP -245 5th Av -NY 10016 **Fx:**696-5013
(212) 867-6000 .. **Rosenberg,** Janna '07 %Rosenberg & E,PC -733 3rd Av -NY 10017
(516) 921-3838 .. **Rosenberg,** Jeffrey B '87 %Pitnick & M LLP -6800 Jericho Tpk -Syosset 11791 **Fx:**921-3824
(212) 755-7700 .. **Rosenberg,** Jeffrey L '72 (J Rosenberg & Assoc,LLC) -425 Park Av -NY 10022 **Fx:**755-6060
(212) 661-9400 .. **Rosenberg,** Jeffrey M '01 %Klein & S LLP -275 Mad Av -NY 10016
(212) 425-2600 .. **Rosenberg,** Jeffrey T '09 %Harman Firm,PC -19 Fulton -NY 10038 **Fx:**202-3926
(212) 837-6000 .. **Rosenberg,** Jerome I '66 SrCnsl Hughes H&R LLP -1 Bttry Pk Plz -NY 10004
(212) 686-0002 .. **Rosenberg,** Jerome R '56 -50 Park Av -NY 10016 **Fx:**686-0003
(212) 506-1700 .. **Rosenberg,** Jessica A '06 %Kasowitz BT&F LLP -1633 Bway -NY 10019
(212) 973-0572 .. **Rosenberg,** Jill Daitch '93 (Wolff & S PC) -140 Bway -NY 10005
(212) 506-5000 .. **Rosenberg,** Jill L '87 (Orrick H&S LLP) -51 W 52nd -NY 10019
(212) 705-4824 .. **Rosenberg,** John J '05 (Rosenberg & G PC) -488 Mad Av -NY 10022 **Fx:**593-9175
(212) 326-2000 .. **Rosenberg,** Jonathan '85 (O'Melveny & M LLP) -7 Times Sq -NY 10036
(646) 695-2700 .. **Rosenberg,** Jonathan S '93 (Repair the World) -555 8th Av -NY 10018
(646) 746-9700 .. **Rosenberg,** Jos '81 CFTC -140 Bway -NY 10005 **Fx:**746-9938
(718) 340-4300 .. **Rosenberg,** Jos A '87 %CUNY Law Schl -65-21 Main -Flushng 11367 **Fx:**340-4482
(516) 745-0111 .. **Rosenberg,** Jos B '88 -666 Old Cntry Rd -Gdn Cty 11530 **Fx:**745-1686
(212) 722-0644 .. **Rosenberg,** Jos J '63 -1085 Park Av -NY 10128
(646) 352-5241 .. **Rosenberg,** Jos S '84 %HPD -100 Gold -NY 10038
(631) 265-8515 .. **Rosenberg,** Jules H '58 -64 Smithtwn Blvd -Smithtwn 11787 **Fx:**265-8577
(607) 778-2403 .. **Rosenberg,** Julie M '98 %Pub Def -45 Hawley Bx1766 -Bnghmtn 13902 **Fx:**778-2432
(212) 403-1000 .. **Rosenberg,** Justin S '08 %Wachtell LR&K -51 W 52nd -NY 10019
(212) 442-3249 .. **Rosenberg,** Keli Ann '00 %Law Dept -100 Church -NY 10007 **Fx:**788-0367
(973) 992-4800 .. **Rosenberg,** Kenneth A '96 (Fox R LLP) -100 Park Av -NY 10017 **Fx:**992-9125
(516) 837-6117 .. **Rosenberg,** Kevin D '02 Sutton Alliance -515 Rockaway Av -Vly Stream 11581
(212) 233-3305 .. **Rosenberg,** Laura '01 (L Rosenberg & Assoc,PLLC) -11 Park Pl -NY 10007 **Fx:**233-3289
(212) 408-5100 .. **Rosenberg,** Lawr '82 (Chadbourne & P LLP) -30 Rckfllr Plz -NY 10112
(516) 873-7200 .. **Rosenberg,** Lee '87 (Saltzman C&R,LLP) -300 Grdn City Plz -Gdn Cty 11530
(718) 248-9100 .. **Rosenberg,** Lee M '08 Citigroup,Inc -1 Court Sq -LIC 11120
(516) 393-2200 .. **Rosenberg,** Leonard M '80 (Garfunkel W,PC) -111 Grt Nck Rd -Gt Neck 11021
(212) 601-9700 .. **Rosenberg,** Lewis '63 OfCnsl Ginarte OGG&W,LLP -225 Bway -NY 10007
(914) 779-4500 .. **Rosenberg,** Lindsay J '79 -60 Morrow Av -Scarsdale 10583 **Fx:**779-0055
(212) 735-3000 .. **Rosenberg,** Lisa Koff '92 %Skadden ASM&F LLP -4 Times Sq -NY 10036
(212) 836-8000 .. **Rosenberg,** Marc D '89 (Kaye S LLP) -425 Park Av -NY 10022
(212) 448-1100 .. **Rosenberg,** Marc G '84 (McLaughlin & S,LLP) -260 Mad Av -NY 10016
(212) 474-1000 .. **Rosenberg,** Marc S '84 (Cravath S&M LLP) -825 8th Av -NY 10019
(718) 703-6568 .. **Rosenberg,** Marian J '88 Thomson Reuters -195 Bway -NY 10007
(212) 883-4900 .. **Rosenberg,** Marianne '81 (Cozen O) -277 Park Av -NY 10172
(631) 846-9459 .. **Rosenberg,** Mark '67 -45 Segatogue Ln -South Setauket 11720 **Fx:**846-9459
(212) 558-4000 .. **Rosenberg,** Mark F '81 (Sullivan & C LLP) -125 Broad -NY 10004
(212) 643-7000 .. **Rosenberg,** Mark J '90 OfCnsl Sills C&G PC -One Rckfllr Plz -NY 10020
(516) 487-3900 .. **Rosenberg,** Marvin J '59 -10 Cutter Mill Rd -Gt Neck 11021
(212) 840-3456 .. **Rosenberg,** Matthew R '68 %Anchin Block & Anchin -1375 Bway -NY 10018
(914) 273-3250 .. **Rosenberg,** Michl '63 -3 Spruce Hllw -Armonk 10504 **Fx:**273-3285
(212) 620-8080 .. **Rosenberg,** Michl '93 %klower Law Intl -233 Spring -NY 10013
(212) 972-3325 .. **Rosenberg,** Michl A '70 -122 E 42nd -NY 10168 **Fx:**972-3329
(212) 922-6000 .. **Rosenberg,** Michl A '91 Dreyfus -200 Park Av -NY 10166
(212) 972-6161 .. **Rosenberg,** Michl A '07 %Cassin & C LLP -711 3rd Av -NY 10017
(212) 701-3000 .. **Rosenberg,** Michl J '10 %Cahill G&R LLP -80 Pine -NY 10005 **Fx:**269-5420
(212) 584-0700 .. **Rosenberg,** Michl L '90 (Seeger W LLP) -1 William -NY 10004
(800) 656-9529 .. **Rosenberg,** Michl S '09 (Lynch Law Firm,PC) -222 Route 59 -Suffern 10901 **Fx:**(888) 271-9726
(718) 722-3100 .. **Rosenberg,** Mimi E '88 %Leg Aid -111 Lvngstn -Brklyn 11201 **Fx:**722-3093
(212) 697-9280 .. **Rosenberg Minc Falkoff & Wolff** -122 E 42nd -NY 10168 **Fx:**697-9284
(212) 233-3305 .. **Rosenberg,** Natalie '05 %L Rosenberg & Assoc,PLLC -11 Park Pl -NY 10007 **Fx:**233-3289
(212) 732-9450 .. **Rosenberg,** Neal H '75 -9 Murray -NY 10007 **Fx:**571-9893
(516) 496-1891 .. **Rosenberg,** Norman M '77 -175 Crsswys Park Dr W -Woodbury 11797
(212) 925-3456 .. **Rosenberg,** Paul D '97 OfCnsl Sedlmayr & Assoc -200 Park Av S -NY 10003 **Fx:**925-0554
(212) 425-9300 .. **Rosenberg,** Paul I '81 (Bressler A&R,PC) -17 State -NY 10004
(212) 697-9280 .. **Rosenberg,** Peter D '79 (Rosenberg MF&W) -122 E 42nd -NY 10168
(646) 654-8323 .. **Rosenberg,** Peter L '81 Nielsen Media Research -770 Bway -NY 10003
(518) 449-8893 .. **Rosenberg,** Philip E '87 (Wilson EME&D LLP) -677 Bway -Albany 12207
(212) 286-6100 .. **Rosenberg & Pittinsky,LLP** -420 Lex Av -NY 10170 **Fx:**286-6818
(585) 319-4848 .. **Rosenberg,** Priscilla Elliott '79 -49 Morrow Dr -Rchstr 14616
(516) 294-9292 .. **Rosenberg,** Rachel L '09 (Tabat CB&Y,LLP) -1205 Franklin Av -Gdn Cty 11530
(212) 238-2420 .. **Rosenberg,** Rachelle '86 %UIA Bd -59 Maiden Ln -NY 10038 **Fx:**238-2451
(212) 755-7500 .. **Rosenberg,** Rachelle '06 %Marcus R&D LLP -488 Mad Av -NY 10022
(212) 258-4000 .. **Rosenberg,** Randi I '89 %Siemens Corp -153 E 53rd -NY 10022 **Fx:**767-0580
(212) 586-3838 .. **Rosenberg,** Richd H '69 -217 Bway -NY 10007 **Fx:**962-5037
(212) 967-8500 .. **Rosenberg,** Richd H '75 (Ross LRZ&F,LLP) -450 7th Av -NY 10123
(212) 661-8900 .. **Rosenberg,** Richd M '67 (Rosenberg & W LLP) -100 Park Av -NY 10017
(516) 681-1000 .. **Rosenberg,** Richd W '86 (R Rosenberg,PC) -500 N Bway -Jericho 11753 **Fx:**681-6272
(212) 530-5000 .. **Rosenberg,** Risa M '84 OfCnsl Milbank TH&M LLP -1 Chase Manh Plz -NY 10005
(212) 476-0382 .. **Rosenberg,** Rita B '91 %Anvil Knitwear -228 E 45th -NY 10017
(212) 525-6641 .. **Rosenberg,** Robt '74 %HSBC Bank -452 5th Av -NY 10018
(212) 872-1000 .. **Rosenberg,** Robt '79 -One Bryant Park -NY 10036 **Fx:**872-1002
(212) 708-1345 .. **Rosenberg,** Robt A '97 %Showtime Networks Inc -1633 Bway -NY 10019 **Fx:**708-1391
(212) 645-2000 .. **Rosenberg,** Robt A '05 Marlboro Grp Intl -5 W 19th -NY 10011
(212) 689-7744 .. **Rosenberg,** Robt C '59 (Rosenberg Housing Grp) -3 Park Av -NY 10016 **Fx:**679-5576
(718) 624-8923 .. **Rosenberg,** Robt C '87 (Hill R&T LLC) -26 Court -Brklyn 11242 **Fx:**624-8335

(212) 906-1200 .. **Rosenberg,** Robt J '71 (Latham & W) -885 3rd Av -NY 10022

(845) 947-1155 .. **Rosenberg,** Robin E '83 Garnerville Holding Co -55 W Railroad Av -Garnervll 10923

(516) 747-7400 .. **Rosenberg,** Ronald J '79 (Rosenberg C&B LLP) -100 Grdn City Plz -Gdn Cty 11530

(212) 299-2000 .. **Rosenberg,** Ronney L '08 Cnsl NYMEX -1 North End Av -NY 10282 **Fx:**301-4700

(212) 996-0953 .. **Rosenberg,** Samantha '01 -1675 York Av -NY 10128

(718) 286-6000 .. **Rosenberg,** Samantha M '06 %DA -125-01 Qns Blvd -Kew Gdns 11415

(212) 759-3235 .. **Rosenberg,** Saml '51 -405 E 54th -NY 10022 **Fx:**759-3736

(212) 644-0500 .. **Rosenberg,** Saml '82 OfCnsl Jacobs R,LLC -777 3rd Av -NY 10017

(800) 811-7009 .. **Rosenberg,** Saml L '77 -394 Klemme Rd -Sprakers 12166

(212) 440-4300 .. **Rosenberg,** Scott A '83 %Leg Aid -199 Water -NY 10038

(516) 877-7205 .. **Rosenberg,** Scott A '85 S Rosenberg,PC -265 Post Av -Westbury 11590

(212) 538-4304 .. **Rosenberg,** Scott M '91 Credit Suisse -11 Mad Av -NY 10010

(212) 922-1080 .. **Rosenberg,** Seth L '75 (Clayman & R,LLP) -305 Mad Av -NY 10165

(212) 687-7410 .. **Rosenberg,** Seymour '55 SpclCnsl Clifton B&D,LLP -420 Lex Av -NY 10170

(212) 790-0200 .. **Rosenberg,** Sheri P '96 Benj N Cardozo Schl of Law -55 5th Av -NY 10003 **Fx:**790-0345

(212) 486-1455 .. **Rosenberg,** Stephen '68 Cnsl Post PGM&S,PA -575 Mad Av -NY 10022

(212) 682-3454 .. **Rosenberg,** Stephen M '72 (Rosenberg FS LLP) -551 5th Av -NY 10176

(631) 393-5069 .. **Rosenberg,** Steven '92 -200 Broad Hollow Rd -Melvll 11747

(845) 473-4440 .. **Rosenberg,** Steven E '91 %Scenic Hudson -1 Civic Ctr Plz -Poughkeepsie 12601

(845) 292-7422 .. **Rosenberg,** Stewart '72 -6 N Main Bx718 -Liberty 12754 **Fx:**292-7563

(212) 688-4100 .. **Rosenberg,** Susan R '79 -110 E 59th -NY 10022

(631) 451-7900 .. **Rosenberg,** Ted M '83 (Rosenberg & G,LLP) -1176 Portion Rd -Holtsvll 11742

(914) 946-9666 .. **Rosenberg,** Thos L '88 -11 Martine Av -White Plns 10606

(212) 661-8900 .. **Rosenberg & Williamson LLP** -100 Park Av -NY 10017 **Fx:**661-1533

(212) 806-5400 .. **Rosenberger,** Ernst H '58 OfCnsl Stroock &S&L LLP -180 Maiden Ln -NY 10038

(212) 916-0600 .. **Rosenberger,** M Gervase '85 %Tweedy Browne Co -350 Park Av -NY 10022

(516) 783-6565 .. **Rosenberger,** Michl Carl-Jude '05 (Rapuzzi P&R,PC) -3361 Park Av -Wantagh 11793 **Fx:**783-6868

(212) 556-2100 .. **Rosenblat,** Heath D '03 %King & S -1185 Av of Amer -NY 10036

(212) 403-1000 .. **Rosenblat,** Michl '05 %Wachtell LR&K -51 W 52nd -NY 10019

(845) 634-7010 .. **Rosenblatt,** Alan G '79 (Montalbano C&F,PC) -67 N Main Bx1070 -New Cty 10956

(845) 486-6800 .. **Rosenblatt,** Albert M '61 OfCnsl McCabe & M LLP -63 Wshngtn Bx509 -Poughkeepsie 12602

(212) 408-5100 .. **Rosenblatt,** Andrew R '98 (Chadbourne & P LLP) -30 Rckfllr Plz -NY 10112

(212) 237-0000 .. **Rosenblatt,** Brian J '09 %Vinson & E LLP -666 5th Av -NY 10103

(212) 544-8892 .. **Rosenblatt Frasciello & Knipping-Diaz,LLC** -4791 Bway -NY 10034 **Fx:**544-8173

(212) 566-7700 .. **Rosenblatt,** Harold J '70 (Kalman K&R) -30 Vesey -NY 10007 **Fx:**566-7743

(212) 872-1000 .. **Rosenblatt,** Ira L '99 -One Bryant Park -NY 10036 **Fx:**872-1002

(718) 286-6000 .. **Rosenblatt,** Jared R '04 %DA -125-01 Qns Blvd -Kew Gdns 11415

(646) 522-5527 .. **Rosenblatt,** Jesse S '01 -261 W 28th -NY 10001 **Fx:**652-9251

(631) 753-5252 .. **Rosenblatt,** John P '81 -100 Broadhllw Rd -Farmngdl 11735 **Fx:**753-2004

(973) 848-4700 .. **Rosenblatt,** Keith J '98 (Littler M,PC) -900 3rd Av -NY 10022 **Fx:**643-5626

(212) 544-8892 .. **Rosenblatt,** Lawr '97 (Rosenblatt F&K-D,LLC) -4791 Bway -NY 10034

(212) 593-6700 .. **Rosenblatt,** Lawr W '97 (Aaronson RF&D,LLP) -757 3rd Av -NY 10017

(718) 520-3710 .. **Rosenblatt,** Lois M '83 (Queens Cnty Pub Admin) -88-11 Sutphin Blvd -Jamaica 11435 **Fx:**526-5043

(914) 684-0200 .. **Rosenblatt & McGarrity LLP** -200 Mamaroneck Av -White Plns 10601 **Fx:**684-9613

(212) 833-1181 .. **Rosenblatt,** Meryl S '93 (Friedman KS&A LLP) -1633 Bway -NY 10019 **Fx:**373-7981

(718) 262-4713 .. **Rosenblatt,** Michl B '71 NYS DHCR -92-31 Union Hall -Jamaica 11433 **Fx:**262-7938

(718) 347-4113 .. **Rosenblatt,** Mitchell L '81 -8535 264th -Floral Pk 11001

(718) 585-2511 .. **Rosenblatt,** Randi B '79 (Gold & R) -840 Grnd Cncrs -Bronx 10451

(212) 308-4896 .. **Rosenblatt,** Robt G '81 -415 E 52nd -NY 10022

(914) 684-0200 .. **Rosenblatt,** Robt H '66 (Rosenblatt & M LLP) -200 Mamaroneck Av -White Plns 10601

(718) 858-7280 .. **Rosenblatt,** Robt T '86 (Balsamo & R,PC) -80 Lvngstn -Brklyn 11201 **Fx:**855-4173

(212) 209-3040 .. **Rosenblatt,** Scott H '93 (Reitler K&R LLC) -885 3rd Av -NY 10022

(212) 460-4786 .. **Rosenblatt,** Shira R '00 Con Ed NY Inc -4 Irving Pl -NY 10003

(212) 651-7500 .. **Rosenblatt,** Steven R '93 (Segal MS&M) -850 3rd Av -NY 10022

(212) 682-3366 .. **Rosenblatt,** Tzipporah R '84 Hill U&E,LLP -825 3rd Av -NY 10022

(845) 562-9020 .. **Rosenblatt-Dreyer,** Sarah E '94 %Silver FS&L -3250 Route 9W -New Windsor 12553

(845) 356-6778 .. **Rosenblith,** Robt M '68 -100 Red Schlhse Rd -Chestnut Rdg 10977 **Fx:**356-6795

(212) 768-6700 .. **Rosenbloom,** Allan M '69 (Sonnenschein N&R LLP) -1221 Av of Amer -NY 10020

(212) 366-6100 .. **Rosenbloom,** Amy '87 (Weiss & R,PC) -27 Union Sq W -NY 10003

(215) 461-1100 .. **Rosenbloom,** Andrew S '03 %Kaufman DV&G,LLP -135 Crsswys Park Dr -Woodbury 11797

(212) 806-5400 .. **Rosenbloom,** Anita S '81 (Stroock &S&L LLP) -180 Maiden Ln -NY 10038

(212) 227-6262 .. **Rosenbloom & Hofflich,LLP** -15 Maiden Ln -NY 10038 **Fx:**349-5779

(585) 724-8132 .. **Rosenbloom,** Jeffrey A '99 %Rochester Gas & Elec -89 East Av -Rchstr 14649 **Fx:**724-8967

(212) 227-6262 .. **Rosenbloom,** Jerald '60 (Rosenbloom & H,LLP) -15 Maiden Ln -NY 10038

(212) 370-1300 .. **Rosenbloom,** Lawr A '98 (Ellenoff G&S LLP) -150 E 42nd -NY 10017

(585) 325-1420 .. **Rosenbloom,** Michl A '75 -500 Times Sq Bldg -Rchstr 14614 **Fx:**325-6208

(212) 506-1700 .. **Rosenbloom,** Michl D '87 (Kasowitz BT&F LLP) -1633 Bway -NY 10019

(212) 577-3265 .. **Rosenbloom,** Nancy '88 %Leg Aid -199 Water -NY 10038 **Fx:**577-3520

(212) 221-5700 .. **Rosenbloom,** Neal M '77 (Goldberg WFG LLP) -1501 Bway -NY 10036

(585) 232-5300 .. **Rosenbloom,** Richd D '59 SpclCnsl Boylan BCV&W,LLP -2400 Chase Sq -Rchstr 14604

(212) 897-6000 .. **Rosenbloom,** Robt A '82 %NY Cnty Hlth Srvs Rvw Org -199 Water -NY 10038 **Fx:**897-6062

(212) 248-4720 .. **Rosenblueth,** Jeffrey '86 -225 Bway -NY 10007 **Fx:**344-8001

(518) 690-0445 .. **Rosenblum,** Adam H '05 (Rosenblum Law Firm) -111 Great Oaks Blvd -Albany 12203 **Fx:**533-2959

(347) 401-9260 .. **Rosenblum,** Alex S '83 %Civil Ct -141 Lvngstn -Brklyn 11201 **Fx:**401-9232

(212) 326-3939 .. **Rosenblum,** Benjamin '07 %Jones D -222 E 41st -NY 10017

(212) 446-7000 .. **Rosenblum,** Betsy D '90 %McKinsey & Co -55 E 52nd -NY 10055 **Fx:**688-9521

(516) 255-1800 .. **Rosenblum & Bianco, LLP** -100 Merrick Rd -Rockvll Ctr 11570 **Fx:**678-1885

(516) 868-0808 .. **Rosenblum,** Chas B '86 (Krohn R&R) -25 Merrick Av -Merrick 11566

(212) 267-7450 .. **Rosenblum,** Danl M '56 -305 Mad Av -NY 10165

(914) 422-4663 .. **Rosenblum,** Darren I '96 %Pace Law Schl -78 N Bway -White Plns 10603 **Fx:**422-4039

(212) 250-4295 .. **Rosenblum,** David H '02 %Deutsche Bank -60 Wall -NY 10005

(516) 741-6300 .. **Rosenblum,** David J '69 -1415 Kellum Pl -Gdn Cty 11530 **Fx:**741-5048

(516) 571-3518 .. **Rosenblum,** Elizabeth L '83 Supreme Ct -100 Supreme Ct Dr -Mineola 11501

(516) 731-7600 .. **Rosenblum,** Eric S '82 -2950 Hempstd Tpk -Levittwn 11756 **Fx:**731-4183

(516) 868-0808 .. **Rosenblum,** Everett A '50 OfCnsl Krohn R&R -25 Merrick Av -Merrick 11566

(212) 559-2697 .. **Rosenblum,** Garrett I '06 Citigroup Prop Investors -731 Lex Av -NY 10022

(212) 449-6309 .. **Rosenblum,** Gary M '86 Merrill Lynch -4 World Fncl Ctr -NY 10080

(631) 462-5888 .. **Rosenblum,** Gayle R '04 %Rubin & R, PLLC -6080 Jericho Tpk -Commack 11725

(631) 581-2900 .. **Rosenblum,** Gloria May '69 -134 4th Av -Bay Shr 11706

(212) 245-7300 .. **Rosenblum,** Harold '61 OfCnsl Serling R&F,LLP -119 5th Av -NY 10003

(631) 727-1010 .. **Rosenblum,** Helen J '84 -1287 E Main -Rvrhead 11901 **Fx:**727-5524

(516) 571-3800 .. **Rosenblum,** Jacqueline M '04 %DA -262 Old Cntry Rd -Mineola 11501 **Fx:**248-9479

(914) 686-6100 .. **Rosenblum,** James B '73 (Rosenblum & T LLC) -50 Main -White Plns 10606

(212) 888-8001 .. **Rosenblum,** James B '73 (Rosenblum & T LLC) -405 Lex Av -NY 10174

(212) 244-4422 .. **Rosenblum,** Jason H '04 %Feldman R -19 W 34th -NY 10001

(516) 829-4700 .. **Rosenblum,** Jeffrey M '74 (J Rosenblum,PC) -98 Cutter Mill Rd -Gt Neck 11021 **Fx:**829-4734

(516) 255-1800 .. **Rosenblum,** Josh B '89 (Rosenblum & B LLP) -100 Merrick Rd -Rockvll Ctr 11570

(631) 761-7000 .. **Rosenblum,** Kenneth A '67 %Touro Cllg Law Ctr -225 Eastvw Dr -Central Islip 11722

(212) 244-9000 .. **Rosenblum,** Kristin R '05 %Matalon SE -450 7th Av -NY 10123 **Fx:**244-4615

(845) 246-2888 .. **Rosenblum & Lamb** -41 Market Bx270 -Saugerties 12477 **Fx:**246-9060

(516) 803-2300 .. **Rosenblum,** Lisa '79 %Cablevision Sys -1111 Stewart Av -Bethpage 11714

(631) 972-5300 .. **Rosenblum,** Matthew Jay '85 -145 Rome -Farmngdl 11735

(212) 341-2711 .. **Rosenblum,** Michl D '98 Admin Childrens Srvcs -150 William -NY 10038

(212) 854-5709 .. **Rosenblum,** Peter J '09 Columbia Law Schl -435 W 116th -NY 10027 **Fx:**854-7946

(212) 907-0600 .. **Rosenblum,** Richd K '81 (Gardner W&R LLP) -270 Mad Av -NY 10016

(518) 464-1210 .. **Rosenblum,** Robin S '93 -111 Great Oaks Blvd -Albany 12203 **Fx:**464-0798

(518) 464-0444 .. **Rosenblum Ronan Kessler & Sarachan,LLP** -110 Great Oaks Blvd -Albany 12203 **Fx:**464-0798

(518) 464-0444 .. **Rosenblum,** Sanford '63 (Rosenblum RK&S,LLP) -110 Great Oaks Blvd -Albany 12203

(212) 715-9100 .. **Rosenblum,** Scott S '75 (Kramer LN&F,LLP) -1177 Av of Amer -NY 10036

(516) 803-2300 .. **Rosenblum,** Shari Lynn '96 %Cablevision Sys -1111 Stewart Av -Bethpage 11714

(516) 742-4274 .. **Rosenblum,** Sondra '86 -200 Old Cntry Rd -Mineola 11501 **Fx:**741-7758

(212) 403-1000 .. **Rosenblum,** Steven A '84 (Wachtell LR&K) -51 W 52nd -NY 10019

(212) 452-9400 .. **Rosenblum,** Tamir W '91 Mason Tenders Dist Cncl -520 8th Av -NY 10018 **Fx:**452-9419

(914) 686-6100 .. **Rosenblum & Tannenbaum LLC** -50 Main -White Plns 10606 **Fx:**686-6140

(212) 888-8001 .. **Rosenblum & Tannenbaum LLC** -405 Lex Av -NY 10174 **Fx:**888-3331

(914) 725-5313 .. **Rosenblum,** Wm F '61 -199 Highland Rd -Scarsdale 10583

(212) 723-7263 .. **Rosenbluth,** Adam S '03 Citigroup Global Mrkts -390 Greenwich -NY 10013

(212) 687-5154 .. **Rosenbluth,** Alan W '63 Atco Prop & Mgmt Inc -555 5th Av -NY 10017

(212) 751-7700 .. **Rosenbluth,** James E '87 Faust & O,LLP -488 Mad Av -NY 10022

(212) 697-3525 .. **Rosenbluth,** Lawr '69 (Rosenbluth & R) -122 E 42nd -NY 10168 **Fx:**697-3528
(212) 788-1276 .. **Rosencrantz,** Caryn A '97 %Law Dept -100 Church -NY 10007 **Fx:**788-0367
(212) 513-7918 .. **Rosencrantz,** Dawn Zuroff '98 %Law Dept -100 Church -NY 10007 **Fx:**788-0367
(212) 836-8000 .. **Rosendahl,** Roger W '73 (Kaye S LLP) -425 Park Av -NY 10022
(212) 827-7581 .. **Rosendale,** Jeanne M '90 TD Securities -31 W 52nd -NY 10019
(212) 808-2700 .. **Rosener,** James D '04 (Pepper H LLP) -620 8th Av -NY 10018
(212) 744-8869 .. **Rosenfarb,** Heidi Leigh '96 -315 E 72nd -NY 10021 **Fx:**(915) 773-8869
(212) 655-5000 .. **Rosenfarb,** Jason B '95 (Gannon R&M) -120 Bway -NY 10271
(716) 634-8330 .. **Rosenfeld,** Alan A '90 %Rosenfeld Dvlpmnt -5225 Sheridan Dr -Williamsvll 14221
(718) 459-1300 .. **Rosenfeld,** Alan M '73 -265-20 Hillside Av -Floral Pk 11004
(212) 858-4312 .. **Rosenfeld,** Avinoam Y '01 FINRA -1 Lbrty Plz -NY 10006 **Fx:**(301) 527-4778
(212) 417-8300 .. **Rosenfeld,** Carol R '92 %Research Fndtn CUNY -230 W 41st -NY 10036 **Fx:**417-8379
(212) 709-8286 .. **Rosenfeld,** Danl F '80 -110 Wall -NY 10005 **Fx:**(732) 775-6366
(212) 336-0153 .. **Rosenfeld,** David '91 %SEC -3 World Fncl Ctr -NY 10281 **Fx:**336-1323
(631) 367-7100 .. **Rosenfeld,** David A '00 (Coughlin SGR&R LLP) -58 S Srvc Rd -Melvll 11747
(516) 466-4422 .. **Rosenfeld,** Debby '87 %R Fatoullah & Assoc -425 Nrthrn Blvd -Gt Neck 11021 **Fx:**466-2219
(212) 223-1254 .. **Rosenfeld,** Eric D '65 -767 Bangall Amenia Rd -Amenia 12501
(212) 570-0514 .. **Rosenfeld,** Jack E '63 -176 E 70th -NY 10021 **Fx:**734-7029
(212) 489-8230 .. **Rosenfeld,** James E '97 (Davis WT LLP) -1633 Bway -NY 10019
(631) 424-4444 .. **Rosenfeld,** Jane B '93 -20 Broadhllw Rd -Melvll 11747
(212) 345-3389 .. **Rosenfeld,** Jordan H '05 Marsh & McLennan Co,Inc -1166 Av of Amer -NY 10036
(212) 682-1400 .. **Rosenfeld & Kaplan** -535 5th Av -NY 10017 **Fx:**682-1100
(212) 763-5000 .. **Rosenfeld,** Katherine R '02 OfCnsl Emery CB&A LLP -75 Rckfllr Plz -NY 10019
(212) 859-8000 .. **Rosenfeld,** Kenneth '07 %Fried FHS&J LLP -1 NY Plz -NY 10004
(212) 822-8300 .. **Rosenfeld,** Kenneth N '79 NMIC -76 Wadsworth Av -NY 10033 **Fx:**740-9645
(631) 661-5000 .. **Rosenfeld,** Larry '86 (Seidner R&G) -403 Deer Prk Av -Babylon 11702
(212) 627-4660 .. **Rosenfeld,** Madelon '87 -215 W 20th -NY 10011
(516) 569-8100 .. **Rosenfeld & Maidenbaum** -132 Spruce -Cedarhrst 11516 **Fx:**569-8105
(212) 538-1884 .. **Rosenfeld,** Marci A '00 %Credit Suisse First Boston -11 Mad Av -NY 10010
(212) 697-9011 .. **Rosenfeld,** Mark L '71 %A Winard,PC -60 E 42nd -NY 10165 **Fx:**682-7073
(516) 569-8100 .. **Rosenfeld,** Meir '87 OfCnsl Rosenfeld & M -132 Spruce -Cedarhrst 11516
(212) 790-0234 .. **Rosenfeld,** Michel '76 %Benj N Cardozo Schl of Law -55 5th Av -NY 10003 **Fx:**790-0345
(718) 590-2000 .. **Rosenfeld,** Paul C '81 %DA -198 E 161st -Bronx 10451 **Fx:**590-6477
(212) 790-0200 .. **Rosenfeld,** Rebecca B '97 %Benj N Cardozo Schl of Law -55 5th Av -NY 10003 **Fx:**790-0345
(631) 757-8080 .. **Rosenfeld,** Renee Pardo '97 -282 NY Av -Huntngtn 11743 **Fx:**757-8844
(631) 424-3888 .. **Rosenfeld,** Robt A '84 OfCnsl Finder & C LLP -150 Broadhllw Rd -Melvll 11747
(212) 792-0999 .. **Rosenfeld,** Shira Yael '00 (Manuel & R LLP) -1 Penn Plz -NY 10119
(718) 250-2000 .. **Rosenfeld,** Stephanie L '06 %DA -350 Jay -Brklyn 11201 **Fx:**250-2314
(212) 312-2260 .. **Rosenfeld,** Steven '09 Leg Aid -60 Lafayette -NY 10013 **Fx:**349-0874
(212) 373-3000 .. **Rosenfeld,** Steven B '67 OfCnsl Paul WRW&G LLP -1285 Av of Amer -NY 10019
(212) 953-1600 .. **Rosenfeld,** Steven E '82 (S Rosenfeld,PC) -777 3rd -NY 10017 **Fx:**953-1801
(212) 488-1598 .. **Rosenfeld,** Steven H '82 (Havkins RR&V,LLP) -11 Penn Plz -NY 10001
(212) 724-9395 .. **Rosenfeld,** Susan C '67 -585 West End Av -NY 10024
(212) 682-1400 .. **Rosenfeld,** Tab K '85 (Rosenfeld & K) -535 5th Av -NY 10017
(212) 344-5400 .. **Rosenfeld,** Vitali S '03 OfCnsl Schlam S&D LLP -26 Bway -NY 10004
(212) 250-5760 .. **Rosenfelt,** Ross B '03 Deutsche Bk Securities -60 Wall -NY 10005
(212) 592-1400 .. **Rosenfield,** David M '97 Cnsl Herrick,F LLP -2 Park Av -NY 10016
(212) 326-3939 .. **Rosenfield,** Karen '10 %Jones D -222 E 41st -NY 10017
(212) 790-4500 .. **Rosengart,** Mathew S '88 (Manatt P&P,LLP) -7 Times Sq -NY 10036
(718) 627-4460 .. **Rosengarten,** Avi '07 -1701 Av M -Brklyn 11230
(212) 533-2606 .. **Rosengarten,** Howard '67 (Guerrero & R) -363 7th Av -NY 10001 **Fx:**505-6681
(212) 546-0947 .. **Rosengarten,** Martin '73 -50 Sutton Pl S -NY 10022
(212) 338-0700 .. **Rosengarten,** Moses S '82 OfCnsl Hoffman P&F PLLC -220 E 42nd -NY 10017
(718) 627-4460 .. **Rosengarten,** Solomon '76 -1704 Av M -Brklyn 11230 **Fx:**627-4456
(212) 632-6000 .. **Rosengarten,** Steve '97 %Lazard Freres -30 Rckfllr Plz -NY 10112 **Fx:**632-6060
(212) 297-5800 .. **Rosenhaft,** Denise R '07 %Day P LLP -7 Times Sq -NY 10036
(212) 837-3686 .. **Rosenhaus,** Ruth H '80 JP Morgan Chase & Co -530 5th Av -NY 10036 **Fx:**837-3504
(516) 741-6266 .. **Rosenheck,** Doron '84 (McCabe CM&F,LLP) -346 Westbury Av Bx9000 -Carle Pl 11514
(716) 856-0600 .. **Rosenhoch,** Howard S '77 (Jaeckle F&M,LLP) -12 Fountain Plz -Buffalo 14202
(315) 425-2700 .. **Rosenholm,** R Stephen '06 Cnsl Hiscock & B,LLP -One Park Pl -Syracuse 13202
(585) 232-8500 .. **Rosenhouse,** Michl A '82 -16 W Main -Rchstr 14614 **Fx:**(866) 417-3420
(212) 381-7000 .. **Rosenhouse,** Neil M '00 %Sabin B&G LLP -4 Times Sq -NY 10036
(212) 406-0411 .. **Rosenkrantz,** Donald '63 -305 Bway -NY 10007
(212) 832-4913 .. **Rosenkrantz,** Edmund R '55 -355 Lex Av -NY 10017
(516) 877-1800 .. **Rosenkrantz,** Jennifer S '98 %Schlissel OK,PLLC -200 Grdn City Plz -Gdn Cty 11530
(212) 506-5000 .. **Rosenkranz,** E Joshua '88 (Orrick H&S LLP) -51 W 52nd -NY 10019
(718) 875-9440 .. **Rosenkranz,** Richd I '62 -32 Court -Brklyn 11201 **Fx:**625-6837
(845) 562-0203 .. **Rosenkranz,** Ronald '73 (Finkelstein & Prtnrs,LLP) -1279 Route 300 Bx1111 -Newburgh 12550
(516) 829-6863 .. **Rosenman,** Ellen '72 -3 Chestnut Dr -Gt Neck 11021
(212) 613-2029 .. **Rosenman,** Shira B '03 %Gibbons PC -1 Penn Plz -NY 10119 **Fx:**554-9656
(212) 715-9100 .. **Rosensaft,** Jodi '04 %Kramer LN&F,LLP -1177 Av of Amer -NY 10036
(212) 637-2366 .. **Rosensaft,** Michl M '04 %US Atty -1 St Andrews Plz -NY 10007
(212) 796-3912 .. **Rosenshine,** Jeremey S '05 Pattern Energy Grp -500 5th Av -NY 10110
(212) 588-0022 .. **Rosenstadt,** Wm S '96 (Sanders OV&R) -501 Mad Av -NY 10022
(212) 808-8300 .. **Rosensteel,** Edw M '85 SrCnsl Rosensteel Law -90 Park Av -NY 10016
(212) 310-8000 .. **Rosensteel,** Kimberly M '09 %Weil G&M LLP -767 5th Av -NY 10153
(518) 452-6979 .. **Rosenstein,** Chas B '90 -465 New Karner Rd -Albany 12205 **Fx:**452-6873
(212) 306-1554 .. **Rosenstein,** David E '89 %Amer Stock Exch -86 Trinity Pl -NY 10006
(845) 794-3000 .. **Rosenstein,** Glen H '90 %Div of Hlth & Fam Srvcs -Govt Center-100 North -Monticello 12701 **Fx:**807-0507
(914) 761-7190 .. **Rosenstein,** Herbert '58 %ODAR-SSA -75 S Bway -White Plns 10601 **Fx:**682-7006
(212) 506-5000 .. **Rosenstein,** Ira G '90 (Orrick H&S LLP) -51 W 52nd -NY 10019
(212) 294-6700 .. **Rosenstein,** Jeffrey P '93 (Winston & S) -200 Park Av -NY 10166
(516) 791-7572 .. **Rosenstein,** Leslie '94 -215 Adams Ln -Woodmere 11598
(718) 768-2932 .. **Rosenstein,** Michl C '92 -463 11th -Brklyn 11215
(212) 506-1700 .. **Rosenstein,** Michl P '98 SpclCnsl Kasowitz BT&F LLP -1633 Bway -NY 10019
(845) 692-8006 .. **Rosenstein,** Monte J '66 (M Rosenstein,PC) -250 Crystal Run Rd Bx2215 -Middletwn 10940 **Fx:**692-8404
(212) 458-3245 .. **Rosenstein,** Steven A '03 Chartis Claims -175 Water -NY 10038
(516) 766-7600 .. **Rosenstock,** E Michl '80 (EM Rosenstock,PC) -55 Maple Av -Rockvll Ctr 11570 **Fx:**766-6630
(212) 818-9200 .. **Rosenstock,** Joan '90 %Satterlee SB&B LLP -230 Park Av -NY 10169
(212) 542-3158 .. **Rosenstock,** Lawr M '68 (Markewich & R) -18 E 48th -NY 10017 **Fx:**308-7780
(914) 697-4870 .. **Rosenstock Lowe & Nichols** -800 Wstchstr Av -Rye Brook 10573 **Fx:**697-4888
(212) 819-8200 .. **Rosenstock,** Nicola '04 %White & C LLP -1155 Av of Amer -NY 10036
(914) 381-3534 .. **Rosenstrach & Beaver** -740 W Bstn Post Rd -Mamaroneck 10543 **Fx:**381-3531
(914) 381-3534 .. **Rosenstrach,** Joann C '86 (Rosenstrach & B) -740 W Bstn Post Rd -Mamaroneck 10543
(212) 284-9300 .. **Rosenstrock,** Jeffrey S '96 Piper Jaffray -245 Park Av -NY 10167
(212) 692-1000 .. **Rosensweig,** David Z '48 OfCnsl Duane M LLP -1540 Bway -NY 10036
(212) 351-4500 .. **Rosensweig,** Dorothy '76 (Epstein B&G,PC) -250 Park Av -NY 10177
(212) 506-1700 .. **Rosensweig,** Joshua D '08 %Kasowitz BT&F LLP -1633 Bway -NY 10019
(212) 508-6700 .. **Rosensweig,** Shelley J '99 (Tannenbaum HS&H LLP) -900 3rd Av -NY 10022
(315) 422-5638 .. **Rosenthal,** Alan '75 Cnsl Ctr for Cmmnty Alternatives -115 E Jffrsn -Syracuse 13202
(718) 992-1900 .. **Rosenthal,** Alina R '81 (Rosenthal & O) -909-C Sheridan Av -Bronx 10451 **Fx:**992-5296
(516) 938-0900 .. **Rosenthal,** Allen M '61 -550 W Old Cntry Rd -Hicksvll 11801 **Fx:**938-0989
(212) 695-5113 .. **Rosenthal,** Barbara R '92 %Royce Hosiery Mills -350 5th Av -NY 10118
(631) 595-7103 .. **Rosenthal,** Beth A '94 -1476 Deer Prk Av -N Babylon 11703 **Fx:**595-1072
(518) 584-0584 .. **Rosenthal,** Bruce R '87 -491 Bway -Saratoga Spgs 12866
(212) 859-8000 .. **Rosenthal,** Carol E '84 (Fried FHS&J LLP) -1 NY Plz -NY 10004
(716) 332-6114 .. **Rosenthal,** Carol R '92 -1207 Delaware Av -Buffalo 14209
(212) 788-6568 .. **Rosenthal,** Chad I '02 Dept of Info & Telecommunications -75 Park Pl -NY 10007
(212) 773-1613 .. **Rosenthal,** Corey L '89 Ernst & Young LLP -5 Times Sq -NY 10036
(516) 485-5577 .. **Rosenthal Curry & Kranz,LLP** -1600 Front -E Meadow 11554 **Fx:**485-5285
(516) 797-4953 .. **Rosenthal,** Danl P '88 -543 Bway -Massapequa 11758 **Fx:**541-1077
(212) 310-8000 .. **Rosenthal,** Danielle S '06 %Weil G&M LLP -767 5th Av -NY 10153
(212) 232-1300 .. **Rosenthal,** David L '05 %Lewis BB&S LLP -77 Water -NY 10005
(212) 698-3500 .. **Rosenthal,** David S '82 (Dechert LLP) -1095 Av of Amer -NY 10036
(516) 487-1612 .. **Rosenthal,** Deborah G '88 (Rosenthal,PC) -336 Nrthrn Blvd -Gt Neck 11021 **Fx:**487-1659
(212) 753-7500 .. **Rosenthal,** Donald L '86 (Hartman & C LLP) -488 Mad Av -NY 10022
(212) 625-8300 .. **Rosenthal,** Douglas U '95 Rosenthal Law Firm,PC -350 Bway -NY 10013
(718) 520-1100 .. **Rosenthal,** Edw '61 -125-10 Qns Blvd -Kew Gdns 11415 **Fx:**575-4062
(212) 980-0120 .. **Rosenthal,** Edw H '81 (Frankfurt KK&S,PC) -488 Mad Av -NY 10022
(516) 485-5577 .. **Rosenthal,** Edw M '87 (Rosenthal C&K,LLP) -1600 Front -E Meadow 11554
(516) 466-6500 .. **Rosenthal,** Fred R '75 Parker WA LLP -6 Hrbr Park Dr S -Pt Wash 11050
(212) 267-6700 .. **Rosenthal,** Fred R '75 Parker WA LLP -111 John -NY 10038
(631) 853-5761 .. **Rosenthal,** Gary '85 %Cnty Atty -400 Carleton Av -Central Islip 11722 **Fx:**853-7788

(212) 442-3217 .. **Rosenthal,** Gary P '66 %Law Dept -100 Church -NY 10007 **Fx:**788-0367
(631) 979-8500 .. **Rosenthal & Goldhaber,PC** -1393 Vets Mem'l Hwy -Hauppauge 11788 **Fx:**979-8555
(518) 473-4631 .. **Rosenthal,** Harold J '75 %Dept of Health -Corning Twr 24th Fl -Albany 12237 **Fx:**473-2802
(516) 535-1700 .. **Rosenthal,** Harold J '94 %Horing W&R,PC -11 Hillside Av -Williston Pk 11596
(212) 468-4800 .. **Rosenthal,** Heath J '04 %Davis & G LLP -1740 Bway -NY 10019
(212) 370-4900 .. **Rosenthal & Herman, PC** -420 Lex Av -NY 10170 **Fx:**370-7849
(212) 888-9200 .. **Rosenthal,** Irvin H '51 -708 3rd Av -NY 10017 **Fx:**888-9470
(516) 371-3500 .. **Rosenthal,** Jason O B '92 %Barnett Corp -77 Spruce -Cedarhrst 11516
(518) 473-0620 .. **Rosenthal,** Jeffrey '79 %Governor's Ofc Reg Reform -ESP Bx2107 -Albany 12220 **Fx:**473-9962
(212) 225-2086 .. **Rosenthal,** Jeffrey A '93 (Cleary GS&H) -1 Lbrty Plz -NY 10006
(518) 828-4447 .. **Rosenthal,** Jerald '65 -439 Union -Hudson 12534 **Fx:**828-6466
(516) 485-5577 .. **Rosenthal,** Jerrold P '57 (Rosenthal C&K,LLP) -1600 Front -E Meadow 11554
(914) 686-4800 .. **Rosenthal,** John T A '02 %Harrington O&M,LLP -81 Main -White Plns 10601
(631) 952-3500 .. **Rosenthal,** Jos M '64 (Rosenthal & M,LLP) -330 Vndrblt Motor Pkwy -Hauppauge 11788 **Fx:**952-5600
(212) 371-8008 .. **Rosenthal,** Jos S '58 OfCnsl Guzov O,LLC -600 Mad Av -NY 10022
(212) 532-4704 .. **Rosenthal,** Joy S '97 Rosenthal Law & Mediation -225 Bway -NY 10007 **Fx:**(646) 607-2277
(212) 725-7111 .. **Rosenthal,** Karen B '89 (Bender RI&R LLP) -451 Park Av S -NY 10016
(914) 347-1292 .. **Rosenthal,** Kathy N '78 (Rosenthal & M,LLP) -45 Knollwood Rd -Elmsfrd 10523
(212) 806-5400 .. **Rosenthal,** Lawr '64 (Stroock &S&L LLP) -180 Maiden Ln -NY 10038
(212) 504-6000 .. **Rosenthal,** Lawr S '08 %Cadwalader W&T LLP -1 World Fncl Ctr -NY 10281
(212) 875-5125 .. **Rosenthal,** Lesley Friedman '90 Lincoln Ctr for Performing Arts -70 Lincoln Ctr Plz -NY 10023
(518) 443-5400 .. **Rosenthal,** Lewis '76 %SUNY Univ Cnsl -S333 SUNY Plz -Albany 12246 **Fx:**443-5409
(212) 679-2900 .. **Rosenthal,** Lisa R '87 %Hoffman & P LLP -260 Mad Av -NY 10016
(914) 946-8900 .. **Rosenthal,** Lynn S '89 OfCnsl Clark G&M -99 Court -White Plns 10601
(212) 653-8700 .. **Rosenthal,** Maranda W '09 %Sheppard MR&H LLP -30 Rckfllr Plz -NY 10112
(516) 627-9325 .. **Rosenthal,** Marjorie L '77 (Ferrari & R) -100 Jericho Quad -Jericho 11753
(914) 347-1292 .. **Rosenthal & Markowitz,LLP** -45 Knollwood Rd -Elmsfrd 10523 **Fx:**347-1293
(631) 271-1725 .. **Rosenthal,** Marshall W '84 -5 Sycamore -Melvll 11747
(212) 335-9536 .. **Rosenthal,** Maxine B '96 %DA -1 Hogan Pl -NY 10013
(718) 424-3400 .. **Rosenthal,** Melvin '67 -33-29 85th -Jcksn Hts 11372 **Fx:**424-7223
(212) 351-4000 .. **Rosenthal,** Michl A '09 Gibson D&C LLP -200 Park Av -NY 10166
(718) 261-7700 .. **Rosenthal,** Michl C '82 (Rappaport HC&R,PC) -118-35 Qns Blvd -Frst Hlls 11375
(516) 764-2800 .. **Rosenthal,** Michl J '06 %Goldberg & C -66 N Vllg Av -Rockvll Ctr 11570
(212) 558-4000 .. **Rosenthal,** Michl J '08 %Sullivan & C LLP -125 Broad -NY 10004
(718) 665-2613 .. **Rosenthal,** Murray '57 -3 Knoll Ln -Smithtwn 11787
(516) 621-6859 .. **Rosenthal,** Norman L '56 -30 Fern Dr -Roslyn 11576
(212) 819-8200 .. **Rosenthal,** Patrick J '06 %White & C LLP -1155 Av of Amer -NY 10036
(212) 474-1000 .. **Rosenthal,** Paul E '01 %Cravath S&M LLP -825 8th Av -NY 10019
(212) 595-7421 .. **Rosenthal,** Peggy B '80 -161 W 86th -NY 10024
(212) 448-1800 .. **Rosenthal,** Peter D '96 Roberts RLSC&F LLP -235 Park Av S -NY 10003
(212) 356-1487 .. **Rosenthal,** Peter I '99 -1370 Bway -NY 10018
(212) 922-3238 .. **Rosenthal,** R Adina '03 Harry Fox Agncy,Inc -601 W 26th -NY 10001
(212) 267-2586 .. **Rosenthal,** Ralph '52 -225 Bway -NY 10007
(718) 261-0200 .. **Rosenthal,** Richd B '79 -120-82 Qns Blvd -Kew Gdns 11415 **Fx:**793-2791
(212) 595-1111 .. **Rosenthal,** Richd M '64 -2211 Bway -NY 10024
(212) 353-3752 .. **Rosenthal,** Robt '02 -Bx93 -NY 10009 **Fx:**995-9492
(516) 935-1200 .. **Rosenthal,** Robt D '75 %1st LI Invstrs,LLC -1 Jericho Plz -Jericho 11753 **Fx:**935-1274
(518) 402-2260 .. **Rosenthal,** Robt M '93 %Dept of Law -The Cptl -Albany 12224
(646) 557-5100 .. **Rosenthal,** Saml '99 (Patton B LLP) -1185 Av of Amer -NY 10036
(212) 697-3333 .. **Rosenthal,** Shawn M '98 Ackman Ziff RE Grp LLC -110 E 42nd -NY 10017 **Fx:**286-4033
(716) 854-1300 .. **Rosenthal Siegel & Muenkel, LLP** -300 Main -Buffalo 14202 **Fx:**842-6354
(516) 746-1144 .. **Rosenthal,** Steven L '87 %Kirschenbaum & P,PC -3000 Hempstd Tpk -Levittwn 11756
(718) 746-5900 .. **Rosenthal,** Stuart A '78 Greater NY Auto Dlrs Assn -18-10 Whitestone Expwy -Whitestone 11357 **Fx:**746-5557
(212) 813-8800 .. **Rosenthal,** Stuart L '05 (Goodwin P LLP) -620 8th Av -NY 10018
(212) 653-8700 .. **Rosenthal,** Susan G '75 (Sheppard MR&H LLP) -30 Rckfllr Plz -NY 10112
(212) 582-6651 .. **Rosenthal,** Thos S '83 -11 Bway -NY 10004 **Fx:**(646) 964-9698
(212) 701-3000 .. **Rosenthal,** Thorn '76 (Cahill G&R LLP) -80 Pine -NY 10005 **Fx:**269-5420
(212) 878-8000 .. **Rosenthal,** Wendy '98 %Clifford C LLP -31 W 52nd -NY 10019
(212) 477-8942 .. **Rosenwasser,** Arnold R '58 -201 E 17th -NY 10003
(845) 457-4646 .. **Rosenwasser,** Jason S '08 %Ostrer R,LLP -201 Ward Bx69 -Montgmry 12549
(212) 675-5097 .. **Rosenwasser,** Mark J '03 Jandale Rlty -Village Station Bx507 -NY 10014
(212) 237-0000 .. **Rosenwasser,** Michl '92 (Vinson & E LLP) -666 5th Av -NY 10103
(845) 469-7577 .. **Rosenwasser,** Stewart A '78 (Ostrer R,LLP) -111 Main Bx509 -Chester 10918
(212) 756-2000 .. **Rosenwasser,** Uriel '10 %Schulte R&Z LLP -919 3rd Av -NY 10022
(914) 420-5634 .. **Rosenzveig,** Ely J '88 -17 Wnchstr Oval -New Rchll 10805 **Fx:**813-2600
(212) 455-2000 .. **Rosenzweig,** Brian E '09 %Simpson T&B LLP -425 Lex Av -NY 10017
(212) 259-8000 .. **Rosenzweig,** Brian K '05 %Dewey & L LLP -1301 Av of Amer -NY 10019
(212) 687-7070 .. **Rosenzweig,** Chas L '78 (Rand RR&G LLP) -800 3rd Av -NY 10022
(845) 452-5900 .. **Rosenzweig,** Cynthia S '98 (Van DeWater & V,LLP) -85 Civic Ctr Plz Bx112 -Poughkeepsie 12602
(212) 318-3000 .. **Rosenzweig,** David A '88 (Fulbright & J LLP) -666 5th Av -NY 10103
(631) 444-0199 .. **Rosenzweig,** Dean T '91 -Bx1364 -Stony Brk 11790
(212) 797-3544 .. **Rosenzweig,** Douglas R '04 %French & C,LLP -29 Bway -NY 10006
(212) 481-4433 .. **Rosenzweig,** Ellen P '78 %Ctr On Aging -425 E 25th -NY 10010
(212) 513-3200 .. **Rosenzweig,** Henry A H '99 %Holland & K LLP -31 W 52nd -NY 10019
(212) 560-1749 .. **Rosenzweig,** James P '89 Riese Orgn -560 5th Av -NY 10036
(800) 446-9529 .. **Rosenzweig,** Jos A '60 -26 Court -Brklyn 11242 **Fx:**(888) 446-9529
(212) 285-4904 .. **Rosenzweig,** Jos I '83 -225 Bway -NY 10007 **Fx:**732-0198
(212) 391-8150 .. **Rosenzweig,** Kenneth '68 -55 W 47th -NY 10036 **Fx:**391-8186
(718) 643-3875 .. **Rosenzweig,** Lisa R '87 %Hon M Gary -360 Adams -Brklyn 11201
(212) 416-6382 .. **Rosenzweig,** Mark D '76 %Dept of Law -120 Bway -NY 10271
(212) 446-4800 .. **Rosenzweig,** Rebecca S '02 %Kirkland & E LLP -153 E 53rd -NY 10022
(718) 667-9090 .. **Rosenzweig,** Richd A '91 %Menicucci V & Assoc -2040 Victory Blvd -Staten Isl 10314 **Fx:**667-0700
(212) 728-8000 .. **Rosenzweig,** Steven '04 %Willkie F&G LLP -787 7th Av -NY 10019
(646) 392-9250 .. **Rosenzweig,** Steven Z '83 %M Klein & Assoc -200 Mad Av -NY 10016 **Fx:**(212) 779-1499
(212) 732-8700 .. **Rosenzweig,** Theo B '74 (McAloon & F,PC) -123 William -NY 10038
(212) 451-2300 .. **Rosenzweig,** Victor M '63 (Olshan GFR&W LLP) -65 E 55th -NY 10022
(718) 478-5502 .. **Rosero,** Karla P '09 Emerald Isle Immigration Ctr -59-26 Woodside Av -Woodside 11377 **Fx:**446-3727
(212) 756-2000 .. **Rosewater,** David E '96 (Schulte R&Z LLP) -919 3rd Av -NY 10022
(631) 232-0200 .. **Rosh,** Jos P '88 %Fumuso KDSS&F,LLP -110 Marcus Blvd -Hauppauge 11788
(212) 859-8000 .. **Rosh,** Kenneth I '89 (Fried FHS&J LLP) -1 NY Plz -NY 10004
(212) 697-7220 .. **Rosh,** Meyer '54 (Stein SC&R,LLP) -140 E 45th -NY 10017
(914) 946-3700 .. **Rosh,** Robt H '90 (McCarthy F LLP) -11 Martine Av -White Plns 10606
(212) 576-7000 .. **Rosh,** Robt M '92 %NY Life Ins -51 Mad Av -NY 10010 **Fx:**447-0569
(212) 869-6000 .. **Roshco,** Danl S '95 (Markowitz & R,LLP) -530 5th Av -NY 10036
(716) 856-5500 .. **Roshia,** Marylou K '90 (Damon M LLP) -200 Delaware Av -Buffalo 14202
(718) 788-6696 .. **Roshuk,** Alex T '98 -325 8th -Brklyn 11215 **Fx:**504-3995
(646) 885-4802 .. **Rosi,** Barbara A '85 %Dept of Sanitation -125 Worth -NY 10013 **Fx:**(212) 442-9090
(516) 741-2585 .. **Rosicki,** Cynthia G '87 (Rosicki R & Assoc,PC) -51 E Bethpage Rd -Plainvw 11803 **Fx:**741-4748
(516) 741-2585 .. **Rosicki,** Thos P '97 (Rosicki R & Assoc,PC) -51 E Bethpage Rd -Plainvw 11803 **Fx:**741-4748
(212) 506-2500 .. **Rosiecki,** Laura K '08 %Mayer B LLP -1675 Bway -NY 10019
(518) 929-3710 .. **Rosien,** Michelle I '94 -Bx908 -Philmont 12565 **Fx:**672-7658
(646) 471-4000 .. **Rosier,** Allison B '97 %PricewaterhouseCoopers LLP -300 Mad Av -NY 10017
(212) 345-3408 .. **Rosier,** Jeffrey P '97 Marsh & McLennan -1166 Av of Amer -NY 10036 **Fx:**345-5627
(212) 972-5430 .. **Rosin,** Benjamin J '66 (Rosin SM) -801 2nd Av -NY 10017
(212) 972-5430 .. **Rosin Steinhagen Mendel** -801 2nd Av -NY 10017 **Fx:**972-5835
(212) 451-2900 .. **Rosing,** Evan M '08 %Robinson & C LLP -885 3rd Av -NY 10022
(718) 391-1863 .. **Rosinger,** Cecilia B '83 NYC Dept of Design & Cnstrctn -3030 Thomson Av -LIC 11101
(212) 425-7200 .. **Rosini,** James E '79 (Kenyon & K,LLP) -1 Bway -NY 10004
(718) 250-2000 .. **Rosini,** Leila C '08 %DA -350 Jay -Brklyn 11201 **Fx:**250-2314
(212) 935-5500 .. **Rosini,** Neil J '76 (Franklin WR&V) -488 Mad Av -NY 10022
(516) 997-7330 .. **Rosinsky,** David L '98 %Baxter S&S,PC -99 N Bway -Hicksvll 11801
(212) 788-8316 .. **Rosinus,** D Alan Jr. '08 %Law Dept -100 Church -NY 10007 **Fx:**788-0367
(212) 841-1000 .. **Rosinus,** David A '79 (Covington & B LLP) -620 8th Av -NY 10018
(212) 349-8700 .. **Rosiny,** Allen P '70 (Rosiny & R) -345 W 58th -NY 10019
(212) 349-8700 .. **Rosiny,** Frank R '64 (Rosiny & R) -345 W 58th -NY 10019
(212) 584-4230 .. **Roske,** Henry '91 (Bagg R & Assoc,LLP) -500 5th Av -NY 10110 **Fx:**584-4233
(631) 379-9569 .. **Rosken,** Brad H '94 BH Rosken,PLLC -1772 E Jericho Tpk -Huntngtn 11743 **Fx:**270-4729
(516) 535-1700 .. **Roskoff,** Danl '96 %Horing W&R,PC -11 Hillside Av -Williston Pk 11596
(212) 998-6550 .. **Rosky,** Dianne L '95 %NYU Law Schl -245 Sullivan -NY 10012
(212) 688-4000 .. **Roslyn,** Barbara D '81 %NYS HFA -641 Lex Av -NY 10022 **Fx:**872-0362
(516) 803-2886 .. **Rosman,** Adam L '07 Cablevision Sys Corp -1111 Stewart Av -Bethpage 11714
(212) 942-2200 .. **Rosman,** Lawr '69 -4951 Bway -NY 10034 **Fx:**942-2354
(212) 244-4422 .. **Rosman,** Robt S '97 (Feldman R) -19 W 34th -NY 10001
(914) 683-5300 .. **Rosmarin,** Laura A '94 %Silverman B&S,LLP -81 Main -White Plns 10601
(914) 686-4000 .. **Rosmarin,** Sam '81 S Rosmarin,PLLC -11 Martine Av -White Plns 10606 **Fx:**686-0567
(516) 794-7500 .. **Rosmarin,** Seth D '03 %Westermann SKS&A,LLP -333 Earle Ovngton Blvd -Uniondale 11553
(585) 428-5210 .. **Rosmus,** Emily L '07 Pub Def -10 N Fitzhugh -Rchstr 14614 **Fx:**428-2234
(516) 228-1050 .. **Rosner,** Andrew '80 -600 Old Cntry Rd -Gdn Cty 11530 **Fx:**228-1055
(212) 940-3023 .. **Rosner,** Arthur J '77 (Nixon P LLP) -437 Mad Av -NY 10022
(212) 785-2577 .. **Rosner,** Brian '76 (Rosner & N) -26 Bway -NY 10004 **Fx:**785-5203

(845) 351-5100 .. **Rosner,** Cary G '88 LiveTechnology Holdings,Inc -16 Sterling Lk Rd -Tuxedo Pk 10987
(212) 506-1700 .. **Rosner,** David S '90 (Kasowitz BT&F LLP) -1633 Bway -NY 10019
(631) 475-9400 .. **Rosner,** Jamie G '99 (Keegan &KR&R,LLP) -147 N Ocean Av Bx918 -Patchogue 11772
(212) 541-2000 .. **Rosner,** Jeanette M '04 %Bryan C LLP -1290 Av of Amer -NY 10104
(212) 418-8600 .. **Rosner,** Joel H '05 Kornstein VW&P,LLP -757 3rd Av -NY 10017
(212) 348-7449 .. **Rosner,** Julia P '97 %Legal Srvcs -1 W 125th -NY 10027 **Fx:**348-4093
(585) 454-7145 .. **Rosner,** Leonard A '93 %Gallo & I,LLP -39 State -Rchstr 14614
(212) 474-1000 .. **Rosner,** Louis K '09 %Cravath S&M LLP -825 8th Av -NY 10019
(212) 759-4600 .. **Rosner,** Marian '74 (Wolf P LLP) -845 3rd Av -NY 10022
(718) 788-2606 .. **Rosner,** Martin B '59 -500 9th -Brklyn 11215
(212) 894-7200 .. **Rosner,** Michl H '01 %Entwistle & C LLP -280 Park Av -NY 10017
(212) 635-2244 .. **Rosner Nocera & Ragone LLP** -110 Wall -NY 10005 **Fx:**635-0533
(212) 669-4859 .. **Rosner,** Norman M '93 %Dept Fin-Pension Unt -1 Centre -NY 10007
(212) 635-2244 .. **Rosner,** Randy G '80 (Rosner N&R LLP) -110 Wall -NY 10005
(518) 587-4802 .. **Rosner,** Seth '55 -26 Saratoga Cir -Saratoga Spgs 12866 **Fx:**587-4802
(716) 849-3500 .. **Rosno,** Matthew J '10 Hagelin & K LLC -135 Delaware Av -Buffalo 14202 **Fx:**849-3501
(212) 436-1130 .. **Rosof,** Alan H '72 %IRS -290 Bway -NY 10007 **Fx:**436-1063
(212) 403-1000 .. **Rosof,** Eric M '98 (Wachtell LR&K) -51 W 52nd -NY 10019
(212) 806-5400 .. **Rosof,** Jeremy S '00 SpclCnsl Stroock &S&L LLP -180 Maiden Ln -NY 10038
(914) 949-6700 .. **Rosoff,** David M '80 (Carton & R,PC) -5 Waller Av -White Plns 10601 **Fx:**381-7158
(914) 949-6700 .. **Rosoff,** David M '80 (Carton & R,PC) -450 7th Av -NY 10123 **Fx:**381-7158
(212) 448-1100 .. **Rosoff,** Sidney D '53 (McLaughlin & S,LLP) -260 Mad Av -NY 10016
(212) 883-4903 .. **Rosoff,** Wm L '79 (Cozen O) -277 Park Av -NY 10172
(212) 969-3000 .. **Rosow,** Stuart L '76 (Proskauer R LLP) -1585 Bway -NY 10036
(516) 216-4024 .. **Rospars,** Wm G '97 -471 N Bway -Jericho 11753
(212) 309-6000 .. **Ross,** A Percy '08 %Morgan L&B LLP -101 Park Av -NY 10178
(212) 450-4000 .. **Ross,** Adam J '10 %Davis P&W LLP -450 Lex Av -NY 10017
(212) 701-9420 .. **Ross,** Adam S '03 United Fed of Teachers -52 Bway -NY 10004
(212) 728-8000 .. **Ross,** Adam S '06 %Willkie F&G LLP -787 7th Av -NY 10019
(516) 937-1700 .. **Ross,** Alan '71 -1772 E Jericho Tpke -Huntngtn 11743
(718) 554-3539 .. **Ross,** Alan '83 -125 Lvngstn -Brklyn 11201
(718) 646-8888 .. **Ross,** Alan '95 (A Ross & Assoc) -2649 Coney Isl Av -Brklyn 11223 **Fx:**646-7766
(585) 428-2757 .. **Ross,** Alan L '86 %Family Ct -333 Hall of Justice -Rchstr 14614 **Fx:**428-4068
(212) 661-1212 .. **Ross,** Alex K '02 %Levy S&S LLP -630 3rd Av -NY 10017
(631) 361-6900 .. **Ross,** Aleza '90 -320 Carleton Av -Central Islip 11722
(212) 423-9237 .. **Ross,** Alfred F '83 Inst for Democracy Studies -177 E 87th -NY 10128
(212) 692-1000 .. **Ross,** Allen J '64 (Duane M LLP) -1540 Bway -NY 10036
(212) 758-2222 .. **Ross,** Allen N '66 Genesis Captl Mgmt -590 Mad Av -NY 10022
(315) 473-9648 .. **Ross,** Amanda N '07 %McGivney & K,PC -110 W Fayette -Syracuse 13202
(212) 484-3900 .. **Ross,** Andrew '91 (Arent F LLP) -1675 Bway -NY 10019
(212) 407-4000 .. **Ross,** Andrew M '81 (Loeb & L,LLP) -345 Park Av -NY 10154
(845) 634-7010 .. **Ross,** Andrew P '93 %Montalbano C&F,PC -67 N Main Bx1070 -New Cty 10956
(212) 752-5202 .. **Ross,** Arnold J '63 -110 E 59th -NY 10022 **Fx:**752-5353
(212) 768-6766 .. **Ross,** Ayanna '99 Sonnenschein N&R LLP -1221 Av of Amer -NY 10020
(718) 923-2972 .. **Ross,** Barbara A '88 OTDA Fair Hearings -14 Boerum Pl -Brklyn 11201
(914) 668-4462 .. **Ross,** Barbara D '88 -27 Rockrdg Rd -Mt Vernon 10552 **Fx:**665-9201
(212) 541-2000 .. **Ross,** Barry C '76 (Bryan C LLP) -1290 Av of Amer -NY 10104
(516) 466-5180 .. **Ross,** Beth Ann '91 -1 Park Cir -Gt Neck 11024 **Fx:**466-6428
(212) 818-8800 .. **Ross,** Brian L '92 (Graubard M) -405 Lex Av -NY 10174
(212) 751-1700 .. **Ross,** Burton R '77 (Jaffe R&L LLP) -880 3rd Av -NY 10022
(856) 616-9747 .. **Ross,** C Randolph '94 Cnsl Breckenridge Pharm Inc -60 E 42nd -NY 10165 **Fx:**494-1647
(212) 364-1510 .. **Ross,** Carol Fein '76 %Hachette Book Grp -1271 Av of Amer -NY 10020
(914) 833-0776 .. **Ross,** Catherine J '88 -7 VA Pl -Larchmnt 10538
(212) 616-3030 .. **Ross,** Chas A '82 (C Ross & Assoc) -111 Bway -NY 10006 **Fx:**616-3031
(212) 848-4000 .. **Ross,** Christopher G '07 %Shearman & S LLP -599 Lex Av -NY 10022
(631) 654-5134 .. **Ross,** Christopher R '03 (Mayer R&H PC) -178 E Main -Patchogue 11772 **Fx:**654-5252
(631) 755-0101 .. **Ross,** CindyAnn '98 %Lewis JAA,LLP -425 Broad Hollow Rd -Melvll 11747
(212) 732-0843 .. **Ross,** Cye E '69 -30 Vesey -NY 10007 **Fx:**587-1039
(212) 806-5400 .. **Ross,** Danl A '76 (Stroock &S&L LLP) -180 Maiden Ln -NY 10038
(631) 298-1200 .. **Ross,** Danl C '82 (Keegan KR&R,LLP) -315 Westphalia Av Bx146 -Mattituck 11952
(631) 475-9400 .. **Ross,** Danl C '82 (Keegan &KR&R,LLP) -147 N Ocean Av Bx918 -Patchogue 11772
(212) 615-2002 .. **Ross,** Danl J '95 Coach,Inc -516 W 34th -NY 10001
(212) 750-3133 .. **Ross,** Danl M '76 -45 Main -Brklyn 11201 **Fx:**223-9174
(518) 827-6707 .. **Ross,** Danl S '80 -338 Main Bx990 -Middleburgh 12122 **Fx:**827-6750
(212) 218-5500 .. **Ross,** David B '91 (Seyfarth S LLP) -620 8th Av -NY 10018
(646) 429-1837 .. **Ross,** David C '08 MDC Partners Inc -950 3rd Av -NY 10022
(212) 506-1700 .. **Ross,** David E '81 (Kasowitz BT&F LLP) -1633 Bway -NY 10019
(212) 451-2900 .. **Ross,** David E '01 %Robinson & C LLP -885 3rd Av -NY 10022
(585) 325-6942 .. **Ross,** David G '77 (Ross & G-R) -16 E Main -Rchstr 14614 **Fx:**262-6486
(212) 578-3055 .. **Ross,** David M '87 %MetLife -27-01 Qns Plz N -LIC 11101
(518) 462-5601 .. **Ross,** David R '91 OfCnsl O'Connell & A -54 State -Albany 12207
(212) 751-2700 .. **Ross,** David S '90 %JAMS -620 8th Av -NY 10018 **Fx:**751-4099
(718) 520-3159 .. **Ross,** Debra '96 Supreme Ct -88-11 Sutphin Blvd -Jamaica 11435
(212) 867-5800 .. **Ross,** Donald C '03 (Osler H&H LLP) -620 8th Av -NY 10018
(845) 735-0088 .. **Ross,** Donald J '58 (Ross & G,PC) -275 N Mddltwn Rd -Pearl Rvr 10965
(518) 449-3359 .. **Ross,** Donald K '75 (Malkin & R) -80 State -Albany 12207 **Fx:**449-5788
(518) 476-2001 .. **Ross,** Donald T '99 %Gilberti SH&S,PC -111 Wshngtn Av -Albany 12210
(212) 627-3732 .. **Ross,** Donna '03 Nydick & R,PC -237 W 15th -NY 10011 **Fx:**(646) 607-6671
(518) 853-8107 .. **Ross,** Donna M '85 %Surrogates Ct -Bway Bx1500 -Fonda 12068 **Fx:**853-8230
(516) 747-7400 .. **Ross,** Edw M '92 (Rosenberg C&B LLP) -100 Grdn City Plz -Gdn Cty 11530
(518) 736-1146 .. **Ross,** Ellen S '83 -105 N Perry -Johnstwn 12095 **Fx:**684-9256
(212) 878-3500 .. **Ross,** Eric L '96 Avenue Capital Grp -535 Mad Av -NY 10022
(212) 967-8500 .. **Ross,** Evan N '04 (Ross LRZ&F,LLP) -450 7th Av -NY 10123
(212) 701-3000 .. **Ross,** Garrett M '09 %Cahill G&R LLP -80 Pine -NY 10005 **Fx:**269-5420
(212) 969-3000 .. **Ross,** Gary R '02 %Proskauer R LLP -1585 Bway -NY 10036
(212) 832-2000 .. **Ross,** George H '53 %Trump Orgn -725 5th Av -NY 10022 **Fx:**935-0141
(212) 286-0099 .. **Ross,** Gerald E '68 (Fryer & R LLP) -551 5th Av -NY 10176
(845) 735-0088 .. **Ross & Gess, PC** -275 N Mddltwn Rd -Pearl Rvr 10965 **Fx:**735-7660
(212) 451-2300 .. **Ross,** Herbert C '77 (Olshan GFR&W LLP) -65 E 55th -NY 10022
(718) 855-2324 .. **Ross & Hill** -16 Court -Brklyn 11241 **Fx:**855-4617
(212) 967-8500 .. **Ross,** Howard '69 (Ross LRZ&F,LLP) -450 7th Av -NY 10123
(212) 902-1000 .. **Ross,** Hugh M '93 %Goldman Sachs -1 NY Plz -NY 10004
(212) 530-5000 .. **Ross,** Ilya E '10 %Milbank TH&M LLP -1 Chase Manh Plz -NY 10005
(212) 349-6035 .. **Ross,** Irene S '51 -600 W 246th -Bronx 10471
(646) 654-5016 .. **Ross,** James A '83 %VNU USA -770 Bway -NY 10003
(212) 216-1251 .. **Ross,** James D '86 %Human Rights Watch -350 5th Av -NY 10118 **Fx:**736-1300
(718) 855-2324 .. **Ross,** James F '79 (Ross & H) -16 Court -Brklyn 11241
(212) 697-2310 .. **Ross,** James J '66 OfCnsl Becker R LLP -317 Mad Av -NY 10017
(716) 878-3353 .. **Ross,** James J '01 Buffalo State -Classroom Bldg C106 -Buffalo 14222 **Fx:**878-3240
(212) 425-1900 .. **Ross,** James L '73 (Freehill H&M LLP) -80 Pine -NY 10005
(212) 768-6700 .. **Ross,** Jason T '03 %Sonnenschein N&R LLP -2 World Fncl Ctr -NY 10281
(212) 816-7002 .. **Ross,** Jeffrey B '87 Citigroup -388 Greenwich -NY 10013
(212) 909-6000 .. **Ross,** Jeffrey E '00 (Debevoise & P LLP) -919 3rd Av -NY 10022
(212) 859-8000 .. **Ross,** Jeffrey W '02 (Fried FHS&J LLP) -1 NY Plz -NY 10004
(212) 455-2000 .. **Ross,** Jennifer A '09 %Simpson T&B LLP -425 Lex Av -NY 10017
(212) 969-3000 .. **Ross,** Jessica '08 %Proskauer R LLP -1585 Bway -NY 10036
(212) 735-3000 .. **Ross,** Jill A '91 Cnsl Skadden ASM&F LLP -4 Times Sq -NY 10036
(315) 696-8918 .. **Ross,** Joel I '86 (Riehlman S&S) -397 Route 281 Bx430 -Tully 13159
(212) 521-5400 .. **Ross,** Jonathan B '08 (Reed S LLP) -599 Lex Av -NY 10022
(212) 973-2376 .. **Ross,** Jonathan J '94 (Caplan & R,LLP) -270 Mad Av -NY 10016 **Fx:**661-4290
(212) 761-2035 .. **Ross,** Jonathan M '02 Morgan Stanley -1585 Bway -NY 10036
(212) 421-9630 .. **Ross,** Jonathan R '01 %Smythe Masterson & Judd -230 Park Av -NY 10169 **Fx:**421-9665
(212) 859-8000 .. **Ross,** Justin M '09 %Fried FHS&J LLP -1 NY Plz -NY 10004
(718) 286-6000 .. **Ross,** Karen L '98 %DA -125-01 Qns Blvd -Kew Gdns 11415
(212) 788-1147 .. **Ross,** Karen M '88 %Law Dept -100 Church -NY 10007 **Fx:**788-0367
(212) 492-5877 .. **Ross,** Karen P '80 Kaplan Inc -888 7th Av -NY 10106
(516) 560-6400 .. **Ross,** Kenneth L '70 %Leg Aid -1 Helen Keller Way -Hempstd 11550 **Fx:**565-3694
(212) 509-3456 .. **Ross,** Kenneth S '89 %McGivney & K,PC -80 Broad -NY 10004
(212) 915-8083 .. **Ross,** Kenneth W '88 Willis of NY -200 Lbrty -NY 10281
(212) 930-8959 .. **Ross,** Kevin G '75 %Lloyds TSB Bank -1251 Av of Amer -NY 10020
(718) 286-6865 .. **Ross,** Laura T '99 %DA -125-01 Qns Blvd -Kew Gdns 11415
(212) 742-0310 .. **Ross,** Laurie S '94 %Powell & Assoc,LLC -110 Wall -NY 10005
(212) 425-9300 .. **Ross,** Lawr D '65 (Bressler A&R,PC) -17 State -NY 10004
(716) 849-8900 .. **Ross,** Lawr M '80 (Hurwitz & F,PC) -1300 Lbrty Bldg -Buffalo 14202
(718) 250-2000 .. **Ross,** Leah E '06 DA -350 Jay -Brklyn 11201 **Fx:**250-2314
(212) 967-8500 .. **Ross Legan Rosenberg Zelen & Flaks,LLP** -450 7th Av -NY 10123 **Fx:**967-2218
(718) 321-1800 .. **Ross Legan Rosenberg Zelen & Flaks,LLP** -41-60 Main -Flushng 11355 **Fx:**321-9040
(516) 594-8150 .. **Ross,** Leonard M '80 (Ross & M) -265 Sunrise Hwy -Rockvll Ctr 11570 **Fx:**594-8108
(516) 571-3056 .. **Ross,** Lisa B '08 %Cnty Atty -1 West -Mineola 11501 **Fx:**571-6604
(631) 369-1700 .. **Ross,** Lisa J '03 %Esseks H&A,LLP -108 E Main Bx279 -Rvrhead 11901
(718) 590-3777 .. **Ross,** Lorraine '99 %Hon A Hunter -851 Grnd Cncrs -Bronx 10451
(718) 250-4523 .. **Ross,** Lydia A '09 Leg Aid -111 Lvngstn -Brklyn 11201 **Fx:**250-4243
(212) 277-6500 .. **Ross,** Malcolm I '76 (Dickstein S LLP) -1633 Bway -NY 10019
(212) 930-9700 .. **Ross,** Marc J '88 (Sichenzia RFF LLP) -61 Bway -NY 10006
(212) 250-3568 .. **Ross,** Margaret M '92 %Deutsche Bank -60 Wall -NY 10005
(212) 309-6000 .. **Ross,** Maria '88 Cnsl Morgan L&B LLP -101 Park Av -NY 10178
(212) 579-1172 .. **Ross,** Marisela S '82 %Bevan MG&Z,PC -200 Mad Av -NY 10016
(914) 699-8600 .. **Ross & Mark,LLP** -559 Gramatan Av -Mt Vernon 10552 **Fx:**699-8680
(212) 788-0847 .. **Ross,** Marta Soja '95 %Law Dept -100 Church -NY 10007 **Fx:**788-0367
(516) 746-8000 .. **Ross,** Marvin '51 OfCnsl Jaspan S LLP -300 Grdn City Plz -Gdn Cty 11530
(716) 853-1616 .. **Ross,** Mary E '83 (Harter S&E LLP) -12 Fountain Plz -Buffalo 14202
(585) 232-6500 .. **Ross,** Mary E '83 (Harter S&E LLP) -1600 Bausch & Lomb Pl -Rchstr 14604
(718) 286-2000 .. **Ross,** Mary R '99 %Leg Aid -120-46 Qns Blvd -Kew Gdns 11415 **Fx:**286-2286
(914) 323-7000 .. **Ross,** Mathew P '91 (Wilson EME&D LLP) -3 Gannett Dr -White Plns 10604

(212) 489-1600 .. **Ross,** Matthew '79 %Deloitte LLP -1633 Bway -NY 10019 **Fx:**492-4201
(718) 585-6551 .. **Ross,** Matthew J '94 %Pena & K,PLLC -1200 Waters Pl -Bronx 10461 **Fx:**585-6618
(212) 599-8200 .. **Ross,** Matthew J '96 (Shaub AC&S,LLP) -655 3rd Av -NY 10017
(212) 575-4874 .. **Ross,** Matthew N '98 -561 7th Av -NY 10018 **Fx:**504-2678
(212) 259-8000 .. **Ross,** Matthew W '08 %Dewey & L LLP -1301 Av of Amer -NY 10019
(212) 687-6262 .. **Ross,** Maurice N '81 (Barton B&P,LLP) -420 Lex Av -NY 10170
(646) 746-8088 .. **Ross,** Michl A '68 Blaqwell,Inc -845 3rd Av -NY 10022
(845) 794-3000 .. **Ross,** Michl C '86 %Div of Hlth & Fam Srvcs -Govt Center-100 North -Monticello 12701 **Fx:**807-0507
(212) 964-7400 .. **Ross,** Michl J '75 Smith MDWY&Y,PC -111 John -NY 10038
(212) 619-6000 .. **Ross,** Michl L '08 %Fay K&M,LLP -150 Bway -NY 10038 **Fx:**208-6879
(631) 421-1211 .. **Ross,** Michl P '00 %Martin F&M -100 E Carver -Huntngtn 11743
(212) 505-4060 .. **Ross,** Michl S '75 -60 E 42nd -NY 10165 **Fx:**505-4054
(631) 853-4104 .. **Ross,** Michl S '08 %DA -400 Carleton Av Bx9082 -Central Islip 11722 **Fx:**853-7838
(212) 238-3000 .. **Ross,** Michele D '86 (Emmet M&M,LLP) -120 Bway -NY 10271
(516) 745-1100 .. **Ross,** N Barry '57 (Kaplan BRB,LLP) -666 Old Cntry Rd -Gdn Cty 11530
(212) 824-1373 .. **Ross,** Neil '90 %Zomba Recording -137-139 W 25th -NY 10001
(212) 425-7774 .. **Ross,** Neil D '96 (MetroGroup) -61 Bway -NY 10006 **Fx:**425-8103
(914) 761-7190 .. **Ross,** Neil R '67 %ODAR-SSA -75 S Bway -White Plns 10601 **Fx:**682-7006
(212) 871-5770 .. **Ross,** Otho B '78 %Berry & Assoc PC -551 Mad Av -NY 10022 **Fx:**871-5774
(716) 856-4200 .. **Ross,** Paulette E '98 OfCnsl Gibson M&C,LLP -69 Delaware Av -Buffalo 14202
(212) 416-8000 .. **Ross,** Pauline L '04 %Dept of Law -120 Bway -NY 10271
(212) 421-4000 .. **Ross,** Philip S '74 (Hoffinger S&R,LLP) -150 E 58th -NY 10155
(516) 742-4400 .. **Ross,** Richd A '66 -100 Grdn City Plz -Gdn Cty 11530
(212) 403-1000 .. **Ross,** Richd M '70 %Wachtell LR&K -51 W 52nd -NY 10019
(212) 408-5100 .. **Ross,** Richd T '00 Cnsl Chadbourne & P LLP -30 Rckfllr Plz -NY 10112
(631) 673-8362 .. **Ross,** Robt A '75 -141 E Main -Huntngtn 11743 **Fx:**673-5690
(212) 986-8444 .. **Ross,** Robt B '57 (Katz & R) -60 E 42nd -NY 10165
(646) 386-5324 .. **Ross,** Robt F '83 %Family Ct -60 Lafayette -NY 10013
(315) 637-3149 .. **Ross,** Robt W III '93 -507 E Franklin -Fayettevll 13066 **Fx:**(405) 734-5884
(716) 849-8900 .. **Ross,** Roger L '80 (Hurwitz & F,PC) -1300 Lbrty Bldg -Buffalo 14202
(212) 553-3200 .. **Ross,** Roslyn Rosenwasser '93 %Marulli LE&T,LLP -5 Hanover Sq -NY 10004
(718) 250-2000 .. **Ross,** Ruth E '82 %DA -350 Jay -Brklyn 11201 **Fx:**250-2314
(212) 999-5800 .. **Ross,** Sacha D '07 %Wilson SG&R -1301 Av of Americas -NY 10019
(212) 451-2300 .. **Ross,** Saml P '73 (Olshan GFR&W LLP) -65 E 55th -NY 10022
(212) 756-2000 .. **Ross,** Sander B '74 SpclCnsl Schulte R&Z LLP -919 3rd Av -NY 10022
(516) 746-8000 .. **Ross,** Seth H '86 (Jaspan S LLP) -300 Grdn City Plz -Gdn Cty 11530
(212) 773-3800 .. **Ross,** Stacey B '04 Sterling Equities -111 Grt Nck Rd -Gt Neck 11021
(212) 736-4201 .. **Ross,** Steven B '93 (Ross & A LLC) -270 Mad Av -NY 10016 **Fx:**736-2873
(212) 819-8200 .. **Ross,** Steven K '82 Cnsl White & C LLP -1155 Av of Amer -NY 10036
(212) 351-4000 .. **Ross,** Stewart R '08 %Gibson D&C LLP -200 Park Av -NY 10166
(212) 318-3000 .. **Ross,** Susan Linda '86 SrCnsl Fulbright & J LLP -666 5th Av -NY 10103
(718) 250-2000 .. **Ross,** Thos M '90 %DA -350 Jay -Brklyn 11201 **Fx:**250-2314
(212) 532-8899 .. **Ross,** Todd M '97 (TMRIB) -183 Mad Av -NY 10016 **Fx:**687-2457
(716) 843-5700 .. **Ross,** Trini E '93 %US Atty -138 Delaware Av -Buffalo 14202 **Fx:**551-3052
(212) 450-4000 .. **Rossabi,** Amy '02 %Davis P&W LLP -450 Lex Av -NY 10017
(212) 947-3793 .. **Rossan,** Jennifer A '96 (Sadis & G LLP) -551 5th Av -NY 10176
(718) 340-4200 .. **Rossein,** Merrick T '76 %CUNY Law Schl -65-21 Main -Flushng 11367 **Fx:**340-4482
(212) 408-5100 .. **Rossell,** Marc M '84 (Chadbourne & P LLP) -30 Rckfllr Plz -NY 10112
(718) 250-2000 .. **Rossell,** Natasha Jaffe '07 %DA -350 Jay -Brklyn 11201 **Fx:**250-2314
(212) 450-4000 .. **Rosselli,** Matteo J '06 %Davis P&W LLP -450 Lex Av -NY 10017
(631) 501-5700 .. **Rosselli,** Thos M '04 %Carter DF&S LLP -445 Broadhallow Rd -Melvll 11747
(212) 326-3939 .. **Rosselot,** Julie A '09 %Jones D -222 E 41st -NY 10017
(212) 239-4999 .. **Rossen,** Jordan '98 OfCnsl Meyer SE&K,PC -1350 Bway Bx822 -NY 10018
(212) 596-9000 .. **Rossetti,** Adam D '08 %Ropes & G LLP -1211 Av of Amer -NY 10036
(518) 465-3808 .. **Rossetti,** Fernande '80 -Bx3085 -Albany 12203
(516) 877-5600 .. **Rossetti,** Frank III '85 %R Tusa -1225 Franklin Av -Gdn Cty 11530 **Fx:**877-5695
(212) 696-9100 .. **Rossetti,** Fredk A '59 -112 Mad Av -NY 10016 **Fx:**689-9680
(716) 852-3600 .. **Rossetti,** Victor A '50 OfCnsl Chelus HS&M,PC -438 Main -Buffalo 14202
(607) 936-3739 .. **Rossettie,** Gabriel V '09 %Rossettie R&M -269 W Pulteney -Corning 14830
(607) 936-3739 .. **Rossettie,** Richd P '78 (Rossettie R&M) -269 W Pulteney -Corning 14830
(607) 936-3739 .. **Rossettie Rossettie & Martino** -269 W Pulteney -Corning 14830 **Fx:**936-3008
(607) 936-3739 .. **Rossettie,** Stephen V '85 (Rossettie R&M) -269 W Pulteney -Corning 14830
(518) 238-4339 .. **Rossi,** Anthony C '02 %OCA -187 Wolf Rd -Albany 12205 **Fx:**438-3518
(212) 808-2700 .. **Rossi,** Christopher A '93 (Pepper H LLP) -620 8th Av -NY 10018
(718) 428-9180 .. **Rossi & Crowley,LLP** -42-24 235th -Douglastn 11363 **Fx:**279-8393
(518) 487-5460 .. **Rossi,** David M '99 %DA -6 Lodge -Albany 12207 **Fx:**487-5093
(212) 588-0800 .. **Rossi,** David V '97 OfCnsl Frommer L&H LLP -745 5th Av -NY 10151
(845) 279-2986 .. **Rossi,** Donald M '80 (Hogan & R) -1441 Route 22 -Brewstr 10509 **Fx:**279-6425
(315) 471-0126 .. **Rossi,** Emil M '73 -307 S Townsend -Syracuse 13202 **Fx:**234-4244
(212) 403-1000 .. **Rossi,** Emily Cohen '10 %Wachtell LR&K -51 W 52nd -NY 10019
(732) 227-7758 .. **Rossi,** Francis S '88 %Bristol-Myers Squibb Co -345 Park Av -NY 10154 **Fx:**227-3874
(212) 757-0007 .. **Rossi,** Frank S II '03 %Scarola E LLP -888 7th Av -NY 10106
(607) 721-8771 .. **Rossi,** Geoffrey B '94 %Dept of Law -44 Hawley -Bnghmtn 13901 **Fx:**721-8789
(914) 937-5525 .. **Rossi,** Indrani '84 -189 N Main -Pt Chester 10573 **Fx:**937-9407
(315) 252-9515 .. **Rossi,** John C '64 -198 W Genesee -Auburn 13021 **Fx:**253-4078
(315) 255-4176 .. **Rossi,** John C '64 Corp Cnsl -24 South -Auburn 13021 **Fx:**255-4735
(914) 723-4333 .. **Rossi,** Jos A Jr. '07 %Pirrotti Law Firm LLC -2 Overhill Rd -Scarsdale 10583 **Fx:**723-4838
(585) 753-4500 .. **Rossi,** Kyle P '07 DA -832 Watts Bldg -Rchstr 14614 **Fx:**753-4576
(516) 327-2700 .. **Rossi,** Leigh Ann '92 BWD Grp LLC -BWD Plz Bx9050 -Jericho 11753 **Fx:**327-2800
(516) 739-0000 .. **Rossi,** Lisa Mammone '90 %Martyn T&M -330 Old Cntry Rd -Mineola 11501
(516) 869-7163 .. **Rossi,** M Christina '96 %Kimco Realty Corp -3333 New Hyde Pk Rd -New Hyde Pk 11042 **Fx:**869-7199
(518) 429-4200 .. **Rossi,** Margaret Surowka '91 Cnsl Hiscock & B,LLP -50 Beaver -Albany 12207
(516) 627-5888 .. **Rossi,** Michl R '90 (Pontisakos & R,PC) -1025 Nrthrn Blvd -Roslyn 11576 **Fx:**627-5585
(315) 733-4671 .. **Rossi & Murnane** -587 Main -NY Mlls 13417 **Fx:**733-4609
(516) 357-3700 .. **Rossi,** Patricia Ann '91 %Cullen and D LLP -100 Q Roosevelt Blvd -Gdn Cty 11530
(212) 509-9400 .. **Rossi,** Peter G '97 (Cozen O) -45 Bway Atrium -NY 10006
(212) 812-8918 .. **Rossi,** Peter J '01 %Lankler & C,LLP -845 3rd Av -NY 10022
(518) 433-8277 .. **Rossi,** Ralph A II '93 Charter Schls Inst/SUNY -41 State -Albany 12207 **Fx:**427-6510
(212) 237-1000 .. **Rossi,** Robt A '89 (Windels ML&M,LLP) -156 W 56th -NY 10019
(347) 296-1536 .. **Rossi,** Ronald '84 %Supreme Ct -360 Adams -Brklyn 11201
(212) 506-1700 .. **Rossi,** Ronald R '97 (Kasowitz BT&F LLP) -1633 Bway -NY 10019
(718) 330-2860 .. **Rossi,** Rosalind Rowen '87 %NLRB -2 Metrotech Ctr -Brklyn 11201 **Fx:**330-7579
(914) 761-0358 .. **Rossi,** Rose A '89 -70 Soundvw Av -White Plns 10606 **Fx:**761-0358
(212) 762-7126 .. **Rossi,** Ruth A '87 Morgan Stanley Invsmnt Mgmt -1221 Av of Amer -NY 10020 **Fx:**762-7377
(212) 788-0483 .. **Rossi,** Sheila M '78 %Law Dept -100 Church -NY 10007 **Fx:**788-0367
(518) 383-1182 .. **Rossi,** Stephen W '04 %J Mahserjian,PC -1741 Route 9 -Clifton Pk 12065 **Fx:**375-9348
(518) 432-9220 .. **Rossi,** Teresa R '86 Patricia Lynch Assoc Inc -677 Bway -Albany 12207 **Fx:**432-9186
(718) 428-9180 .. **Rossi,** Thos J '86 (Rossi & C,LLP) -42-24 235th -Douglastn 11363
(315) 733-4671 .. **Rossi,** Vincent J Jr. '75 (Rossi & M) -587 Main -NY Mlls 13417
(516) 746-7780 .. **Rossillo,** John J '96 (Rossillo & L,PC) -355 Post Av -Westbury 11590
(516) 746-7780 .. **Rossillo & Licata,PC** -355 Post Av -Westbury 11590 **Fx:**746-7717
(212) 766-1888 .. **Rossillo,** Lina C '01 %Morris DA&F -2 Rector -NY 10006
(212) 267-1650 .. **Rossillo,** Vincent J '85 (Fine O&A,LLP) -39 Bway -NY 10006
(347) 401-9287 .. **Rossini,** Stephen A '05 Supreme Ct Law Dept -360 Adams -Brklyn 11201 **Fx:**643-6114
(914) 241-2060 .. **Rossi-Ortiz,** Laura E '94 -20 Laurelton Rd -Mt Kisco 10549 **Fx:**241-2060
(212) 849-7000 .. **Rossman,** Andrew J '93 (Quinn EU&S,LLP) -51 Mad Av -NY 10010
(212) 231-6590 .. **Rossman,** James E '94 MacQuarie Cptl Advsrs -125 W 55th -NY 10019
(212) 909-6000 .. **Rossman,** Jeremy A '06 %Debevoise & P LLP -919 3rd Av -NY 10022
(718) 250-2000 .. **Rossman,** Jordan W '00 %DA -350 Jay -Brklyn 11201 **Fx:**250-2314
(585) 546-5530 .. **Rossman,** Michl S '82 %Thomson West -50 E Broad -Rchstr 14694
(718) 588-2425 .. **Rossmer,** Andrew H '72 -189 E 163rd -Bronx 10451
(212) 695-1800 .. **Rossner,** Caryl B '80 -1350 Bway -NY 10018 **Fx:**643-1882
(212) 839-5300 .. **Rossner,** Danl M '79 (Sidley A LLP) -787 7th Av -NY 10019
(716) 874-0308 .. **Rosso,** Richd P '81 -722 Colvin Av -Kenmore 14217 **Fx:**873-5630
(212) 874-4722 .. **Rossoff,** Jeannette L '84 -101 Cntrl Pk W -NY 10023
(212) 725-8566 .. **Rossol,** Adam H '08 Robinson & Y,PC -232 Mad Av -NY 10016
(585) 899-1414 .. **Rossow,** Nicole A '05 %Harris COJW&L -300 Linden Oaks -Rchstr 14625
(212) 839-5300 .. **Rost,** Daniela '04 %Sidley A LLP -787 7th Av -NY 10019
(516) 248-1434 .. **Rost,** Wm L '73 (Braverman & R) -200 Old Cntry Rd -Mineola 11501
(718) 330-1200 .. **Rostal,** Jan A '91 %Fed Def of NY Inc -1 Pierrepont Plz -Brklyn 11201 **Fx:**855-0760
(212) 209-3962 .. **Rostami,** Florence '99 -708 3rd Av -NY 10017
(212) 406-0336 .. **Rostanski,** Bernard J '76 -305 Bway -NY 10007
(212) 376-5757 .. **Rostedt,** Kirsten A '01 %Agus & Prtnrs,PC -75 Maiden Ln -NY 10038 **Fx:**376-5752
(845) 621-1619 .. **Rosten,** Louis H '85 -38 Colton Rd -Mahopac 10541
(718) 668-2206 .. **Rostolder Peretz,** Michelle '02 -1 Rose Av -Staten Isl 10306 **Fx:**668-2241
(212) 953-1818 .. **Rosuck,** Craig M '94 C Rosuck,PC -275 Mad Av -NY 10016 **Fx:**953-0599
(631) 390-0010 .. **Rosvolos,** Paris T '01 %Bruno G&S,LLP -445 Broad Hollow Rd -Melvll 11747
(914) 422-2500 .. **Rotbard,** Eric J '94 -81 Main -White Plns 10601 **Fx:**683-1279
(914) 683-2500 .. **Rotbard,** Jerold C '94 Cnsl Harold SS&S -81 Main -White Plns 10601
(212) 486-7272 .. **Rotberg,** Tuvia '07 %Levisohn B,LLP -11 Bway -NY 10004
(212) 504-6000 .. **Rotblat,** Y Jeffrey '94 (Cadwalader W&T LLP) -1 World Fncl Ctr -NY 10281
(716) 282-1242 .. **Rotella,** Richd J '90 -730 Main -Niagara Fls 14301 **Fx:**282-5090
(518) 285-8301 .. **Rotello,** Catherine M '95 %Appllt Div 3rd Dept -Capitol Station Bx7288 -Albany 12224 **Fx:**471-4750

(518) 471-4777 .. **Rotello,** Jos C '95 Supreme Ct-Appellate Div -Bx7350 -Albany 12224
(212) 973-0572 .. **Rotenberg,** Beth J '06 %Wolff & S PC -140 Bway -NY 10005
(212) 728-8000 .. **Rotenberg,** Daniella T '10 %Willkie F&G LLP -787 7th Av -NY 10019
(212) 330-1000 .. **Rotenberg,** James C '69 %Buck Consultants -1 Penn Plz -NY 10119 **Fx:**695-4184
(212) 335-4500 .. **Rotenberg,** Jeffrey D '01 %DLA Piper LLP -1251 Av of Amer -NY 10020
(212) 940-8800 .. **Rotenberg,** Jonathan A '08 %Katten MR LLP -575 Mad Av -NY 10022
(585) 641-8000 .. **Rotenberg,** Roy Z '86 (Fix SB&G,PC) -295 Woodcliff Dr -Fairprt 14450
(212) 612-3270 .. **Rotenberg-Schwartz,** Elizabeth '04 %Mishcon de R NY LLP -200 Park Av -NY 10166
(212) 819-8200 .. **Rotenstein,** Jack '03 %White & C LLP -1155 Av of Amer -NY 10036
(212) 728-8000 .. **Rotgers,** Joanna R '02 %Willkie F&G LLP -787 7th Av -NY 10019
(516) 408-3170 .. **Rotgin,** Karen A '92 %Rotgin Law Firm -586 RXR Plz -Uniondale 11556 **Fx:**408-3169
(516) 408-3170 .. **Rotgin,** Philip N '67 (Rotgin Law Firm) -586 RXR Plz -Uniondale 11556 **Fx:**408-3169
(718) 403-3600 .. **Roth,** Alan S '66 Dept of Finance -345 Adams -Brklyn 11201 **Fx:**403-3650
(212) 935-3000 .. **Roth,** Andrew B '76 (Mintz LCFG&P,PC) -666 3rd Av -NY 10017
(212) 514-5007 .. **Roth,** Andrew B '09 %Rosenbaum & R,PC -110 Wall -NY 10005 **Fx:**514-9178
(914) 948-1556 .. **Roth,** Andrew E '82 (Danziger & M LLP) -123 Main -White Plns 10601
(516) 222-6200 .. **Roth,** Andrew M '93 %Berkman HPP&F,PC -100 Grdn City Plz -Gdn Cty 11530
(212) 272-9550 .. **Roth,** Anthony M '96 -383 Mad Av -NY 10179
(212) 940-7040 .. **Roth,** Arnold I '57 Cnsl Katten MR LLP -575 Mad Av -NY 10022
(212) 425-1020 .. **Roth,** Audra R '94 (Roth & R,LLP) -192 Lex Av -NY 10016 **Fx:**532-3801
(212) 918-3000 .. **Roth,** Barbara M '80 (Hogan L LLP) -875 3rd Av -NY 10022
(212) 408-5100 .. **Roth,** Benjamin B '07 %Chadbourne & P LLP -30 Rckfllr Plz -NY 10112
(212) 403-1000 .. **Roth,** Benjamin M '02 (Wachtell LR&K) -51 W 52nd -NY 10019
(212) 248-9100 .. **Roth,** Bruce '75 %Epstein H&M -1 Whitehall -NY 10004
(845) 398-5492 .. **Roth,** Carole K '76 Nathan Kline Inst -140 Old Orangebrg Rd -Orangebrg 10962
(914) 422-8700 .. **Roth,** Dana A '88 %OCTF -101 E Post Rd -White Plns 10601 **Fx:**422-8795
(212) 756-2000 .. **Roth,** Dana M '99 %Schulte R&Z LLP -919 3rd Av -NY 10022
(212) 261-8000 .. **Roth,** Danielle M '05 %Mendes & M,LLP -750 7th Av -NY 10019
(212) 425-1020 .. **Roth,** David A '92 (Roth & R,LLP) -192 Lex Av -NY 10016 **Fx:**532-3801
(516) 798-5363 .. **Roth,** David I '82 (Kressel RW&R,LLC) -684 Bway -Massapequa 11758
(212) 513-3200 .. **Roth,** Deborah C '04 %Holland & K LLP -31 W 52nd -NY 10019
(212) 762-7911 .. **Roth,** Debra A '81 Morgan Stanley -1221 Av of Amer -NY 10020
(212) 788-5014 .. **Roth,** Dennis '67 Dept Hlth -125 Worth CN-30 -NY 10013 **Fx:**788-4300
(212) 836-1163 .. **Roth,** Edw M '92 UJA-Federation of NY -130 E 59th -NY 10022 **Fx:**836-1779
(212) 813-8800 .. **Roth,** Eric D '96 SrCnsl Goodwin P LLP -620 8th Av -NY 10018
(212) 758-8575 .. **Roth,** Eric J '01 Goldsmith Agio Helms -11 W 42nd -NY 10036
(212) 403-1000 .. **Roth,** Eric M '78 (Wachtell LR&K) -51 W 52nd -NY 10019
(718) 858-4140 .. **Roth,** Erik M '97 (Singer BM&R) -189 Montague -Brklyn 11201
(212) 210-9441 .. **Roth,** Gary D '81 (Alston & B LLP) -90 Park Av -NY 10016
(212) 220-3000 .. **Roth,** Gary F '75 %Broadcast Music Inc -250 Greenwich -NY 10007
(718) 268-5170 .. **Roth,** George '77 -141-04 73rd Ter -Flushng 11367
(516) 742-1212 .. **Roth,** Gerald C '91 (Stein W&R) -1 Old Cntry Rd -Carle Pl 11514
(516) 571-9233 .. **Roth,** Gregg '94 Cnty Atty -1 West -Mineola 11501
(518) 869-6843 .. **Roth,** Howard W '63 -1 Columbia Cir -Albany 12203
(212) 307-1333 .. **Roth,** Irwin '56 -235 W 56th -NY 10019 **Fx:**246-2329
(518) 474-0571 .. **Roth,** Jaime I '03 Ofc Gnl Srvcs -Corning Twr ESP -Albany 12242 **Fx:**473-4973
(212) 964-1890 .. **Roth,** James A '82 (Hoffman & R,LLP) -505 8th Av -NY 10018
(212) 509-5999 .. **Roth,** James J '84 Americhoice -7 Hanover Sq -NY 10004
(212) 619-4240 .. **Roth,** James M '78 (Hurwitz S&R) -299 Bway -NY 10007
(212) 764-6800 .. **Roth,** Jarrett G '06 Cnsl Venio LLC -530 5th Av -NY 10036
(212) 728-8000 .. **Roth,** Jason A '09 %Willkie F&G LLP -787 7th Av -NY 10019
(585) 546-7830 .. **Roth,** Jason M '97 %Culley MT&P,LLP -36 W Main -Rchstr 14614
(212) 250-2500 .. **Roth,** Jeffrey A '01 Deutsche Bank AG -60 Wall -NY 10005
(212) 661-0500 .. **Roth,** Jeffrey H '84 -100 Park Av -NY 10017 **Fx:**661-0462
(212) 223-3562 .. **Roth,** Jeremy S '00 (Turek RM LLP) -377 5th Av -NY 10016
(212) 637-2347 .. **Roth,** Jessica A '98 %US Atty -1 St Andrews Plz -NY 10007
(212) 859-8000 .. **Roth,** Joshua D '07 %Fried FHS&J LLP -1 NY Plz -NY 10004
(212) 753-5000 .. **Roth,** Judith S '78 OfCnsl Schiff H LLP -900 3rd Av -NY 10022
(646) 746-9700 .. **Roth,** Karin N '97 CFTC -140 Bway -NY 10005 **Fx:**746-9938
(212) 290-4700 .. **Roth,** Kenneth T '81 %Human Rights Watch -350 5th Av -NY 10118 **Fx:**736-1300
(212) 962-2000 .. **Roth,** Kurt L '86 (Dickler & R,LLP) -19 Fulton -NY 10038 **Fx:**962-3222
(516) 877-5600 .. **Roth,** L Jeffrey '84 %R Tusa -1225 Franklin Av -Gdn Cty 11530 **Fx:**877-5695
(518) 793-8442 .. **Roth,** Lewis '75 -108 Bay -Glens Fls 12801
(212) 576-0681 .. **Roth,** Linda G '94 -2373 Bway -NY 10024 **Fx:**465-7410
(212) 216-8000 .. **Roth,** Linda Singer '85 Cnsl Tarter K&D LLP -1350 Bway -NY 10018
(212) 790-4500 .. **Roth,** Marc S '92 (Manatt P&P,LLP) -7 Times Sq -NY 10036
(718) 858-4140 .. **Roth,** Marcie G '97 Singer BM&R -189 Montague -Brklyn 11201
(516) 333-5557 .. **Roth,** Mark Bradley '74 -55 Post Av -Westbury 11590 **Fx:**334-2435
(718) 267-5170 .. **Roth,** Meir M '00 -141-04 73rd Ter -Flushng 11367
(516) 683-8400 .. **Roth,** Melvyn K '68 -666 Old Cntry Rd -Gdn Cty 11530 **Fx:**683-8410
(212) 940-8800 .. **Roth,** Michl '56 Cnsl Katten MR LLP -575 Mad Av -NY 10022
(718) 694-9673 .. **Roth,** Michl B '95 -425 Union -Brklyn 11231 **Fx:**694-9630
(212) 618-6352 .. **Roth,** Michl B '96 Cnsl Sorin RC LLC -1230 Av of Amer -NY 10020
(212) 556-2100 .. **Roth,** Monika '08 %King & S -1185 Av of Amer -NY 10036
(607) 255-2796 .. **Roth,** Nelson E '75 %Cornell Univ -300 CCC Bldg-Grdn Av -Ithaca 14853 **Fx:**255-2794
(212) 474-1000 .. **Roth,** Noah F '09 %Cravath S&M LLP -825 8th Av -NY 10019
(718) 802-9025 .. **Roth,** Pamela S '91 -9118 5th Av -Brklyn 11209
(607) 962-6162 .. **Roth,** Patrick J '00 -145 Chemung -Corning 14830 **Fx:**962-3713
(212) 756-2000 .. **Roth,** Paul N '66 (Schulte R&Z LLP) -919 3rd Av -NY 10022
(716) 204-9001 .. **Roth,** Rachel A '88 %DiNardo & M,PC -2813 Wehrle Dr -Williamsvll 14221
(212) 318-6000 .. **Roth,** Reagan T '07 %Paul HJ&W LLP -75 E 55th -NY 10022
(212) 593-6700 .. **Roth,** Rebecca L '07 Aaronson RF&D,LLP -757 3rd Av -NY 10017
(212) 448-1100 .. **Roth,** Renee R '69 OfCnsl McLaughlin & S,LLP -260 Mad Av -NY 10016
(212) 542-8882 .. **Roth,** Richd A '85 (Roth Law Firm,PLLC) -295 Mad Av -NY 10017 **Fx:**542-8883
(917) 507-1041 .. **Roth,** Richd M '80 -416 W 147th -NY 10031 **Fx:**(212) 202-7789
(718) 851-1416 .. **Roth,** Robt '80 -5115 15th Av -Brklyn 11219
(917) 751-5174 .. **Roth,** Robt M '98 Exclusive Capital Consultants,Inc -527 Townline Rd -Hauppauge 11788
(212) 608-3015 .. **Roth,** Ronald H '86 -233 Bway -NY 10279 **Fx:**608-2177
(914) 997-7201 .. **Roth,** Ronni J '82 -19 Dupont Av -White Plns 10605 **Fx:**997-7201
(914) 761-1300 .. **Roth,** Ruth E '59 (Cuddy & F LLP) -445 Hmltn Av -White Plns 10601
(914) 682-9100 .. **Roth,** Steven D '96 %NY Presbyterian Hsptl -21 Bloomingdale Rd -White Plns 10605
(212) 227-8111 .. **Roth,** Steven I '85 -217 Bway -NY 10007
(212) 207-2800 .. **Roth,** Todd H '95 %ContiFinancial Srvcs Corp -277 Park Av -NY 10172
(914) 448-0200 .. **Roth,** Warren J '91 OfCnsl Bartlett MB&M,LLP -81 Main -White Plns 10601
(212) 732-8700 .. **Roth,** Wayne M '74 (McAloon & F,PC) -123 William -NY 10038
(646) 454-1272 .. **Roth,** Wm H '78 -1 River Pl -NY 10036
(516) 747-3030 .. **Roth,** Wm M '85 (Cohn & R) -100 E Old Cntry Rd -Mineola 11501
(518) 402-2109 .. **Rothaupt,** Barbara A '03 DMV -6 ESP -Albany 12228
(718) 261-0600 .. **Rothbard,** Alan T '79 (Harrison & R PC) -105-15 Metro Av -Frst Hlls 11375
(212) 858-3600 .. **Rothbardt,** Patricia A '78 %Reliance Ins -75 Broad -NY 10004
(212) 812-0694 .. **Rothbart,** Lawr N '82 -115 Bway -NY 10006 **Fx:**227-4533
(212) 630-1059 .. **Rothbaum,** Alice C '89 Medical Assistance Program -330 W 34th -NY 10001 **Fx:**630-9897
(212) 267-6655 .. **Rothbaum,** Hugh L '88 -305 Bway -NY 10007
(631) 246-5904 .. **Rothbell,** Sheldon B '91 -6 Split Rail Ln -E Setauket 11733 **Fx:**751-0543
(718) 261-7579 .. **Rothberg,** Alan S '91 -292 Mad Av -NY 10017
(212) 455-2000 .. **Rothberg,** Allyson B '05 %Simpson T&B LLP -425 Lex Av -NY 10017
(212) 714-1212 .. **Rothberg,** Debra L '87 (DL Rothberg & Assoc,PC) -1065 Av of Amer -NY 10018 **Fx:**714-0969
(718) 624-2200 .. **Rothberg,** Jessica S '98 %W Rothberg -16 Court -Brklyn 11241
(212) 468-8000 .. **Rothberg,** Jonathan C '08 %Morrison & F LLP -1290 Av of Amer -NY 10104
(212) 509-6734 .. **Rothberg,** Mark A '92 -3 Hanover Sq -NY 10004
(212) 692-1000 .. **Rothberg,** Peter W '80 (Duane M LLP) -1540 Bway -NY 10036
(212) 397-6360 .. **Rothberg,** Randi M '04 (Thivierge & R,PC) -140 Bway -NY 10005 **Fx:**397-6361
(212) 479-6000 .. **Rothberg,** Richd S '71 (Cooley LLP) -1114 Av of Amer -NY 10036
(516) 792-9830 .. **Rothberg,** Russell '87 -65 Roosevelt Av -Vly Stream 11581 **Fx:**791-5283
(212) 348-6400 .. **Rothberg,** Steven S '71 -185 E 85th -NY 10028 **Fx:**876-7811
(718) 624-2200 .. **Rothberg,** Wm '68 W Rothberg -16 Court -Brklyn 11241
(212) 922-9250 .. **Rothberger-Zelefsky,** Daniella '01 %Ganfer & S LLP -360 Lex Av -NY 10017
(212) 480-5284 .. **Rothblatt,** Jon G '75 %Insurance Dept -25 Beaver -NY 10004 **Fx:**480-5272
(212) 735-3000 .. **Rothblatt,** Richd M '09 %Skadden ASM&F LLP -4 Times Sq -NY 10036
(212) 940-3187 .. **Rothchild,** Barry M '02 %Nixon P LLP -437 Mad Av -NY 10022
(212) 806-5400 .. **Rothchild,** Meryl L '10 %Stroock &S&L LLP -180 Maiden Ln -NY 10038
(212) 644-4420 .. **Rothchild,** Sander N '98 (Fabiani C&H,LLP) -570 Lex Av -NY 10022
(607) 723-8148 .. **Rothe,** James S '80 -5 Hawthorne Rd -Bnghmtn 13903
(518) 427-2650 .. **Rotheim,** Jena R '07 %Nixon P LLP -677 Bway -Albany 12207
(718) 793-6639 .. **Rotheim,** Marsha Weitz '92 -108-37 71st Av -Frst Hlls 11375 **Fx:**793-6507
(631) 543-2900 .. **Rothemich,** Christopher S '01 %Davis & H,LLP -1345 Motor Pkwy -Islandia 11749
(631) 979-2032 .. **Rothemich,** Kerry F '01 -198 Terry Rd -Smithtwn 11787
(212) 838-4511 .. **Rothenberg,** Alan M '66 -420 E 64th -NY 10065 **Fx:**838-4511
(212) 563-0100 .. **Rothenberg,** Allen L '81 (A Rothenberg) -450 7th Av -NY 10123 **Fx:**629-6813
(631) 363-8749 .. **Rothenberg,** Bruce A '89 (B Rothenberg,PC) -80 Orvll Dr -Bohemia 11716
(877) 222-1814 .. **Rothenberg,** Bryan '87 -100 Duffy Av -Hicksvll 11801 **Fx:**(866) 894-2182
(212) 975-4321 .. **Rothenberg,** Carla J '06 %CBS Inc -51 W 52nd -NY 10019 **Fx:**975-3930
(212) 238-4800 .. **Rothenberg,** Craig H '06 %Landman CB&F,PC -120 Bway -NY 10271
(585) 232-1946 .. **Rothenberg,** David '76 (Geiger & R,LLP) -45 Exchange -Rchstr 14614
(212) 357-2368 .. **Rothenberg,** David S '95 AYCO -1 NY Plz -NY 10004
(212) 326-2000 .. **Rothenberg,** Eric B '86 (O'Melveny & M LLP) -7 Times Sq -NY 10036
(212) 563-0100 .. **Rothenberg,** Harry '94 %A Rothenberg -450 7th Av -NY 10123 **Fx:**629-6813
(516) 569-8100 .. **Rothenberg,** Helene S '85 OfCnsl Rosenfeld & M -132 Spruce -Cedarhrst 11516
(518) 452-5600 .. **Rothenberg,** Jeff '76 (Heslin RF&M PC) -5 Columbia Cir -Albany 12203
(212) 940-1154 .. **Rothenberg,** Jennifer B '99 Bloomberg LP -499 Park Av -NY 10022
(212) 209-4800 .. **Rothenberg,** Jos B '09 Brown R LLP -7 Times Sq -NY 10036
(212) 850-2800 .. **Rothenberg,** Kenneth L '01 (Andrews K LLP) -450 Lex Av -NY 10017

(212) 751-4300 .. **Rothenberg,** Lance E '06 %Hodgson R LLP -1540 Bway -NY 10036
(212) 859-8000 .. **Rothenberg,** Laraine S '72 (Fried FHS&J LLP) -1 NY Plz -NY 10004
(212) 733-6316 .. **Rothenberg,** Laurie S '02 %Pfizer Inc -235 E 42nd -NY 10017
(212) 969-3000 .. **Rothenberg,** Lawr J '66 (Proskauer R LLP) -1585 Bway -NY 10036
(212) 407-4000 .. **Rothenberg,** Lloyd L '91 (Loeb & L,LLP) -345 Park Av -NY 10154
(212) 885-5000 .. **Rothenberg,** Marc '95 (Blank R LLP) -405 Lex Av -NY 10174
(212) 902-5098 .. **Rothenberg,** Marc A '91 Goldman Sachs -1 NY Plz -NY 10004
(212) 563-0100 .. **Rothenberg,** Marc J '98 %A Rothenberg -450 7th Av -NY 10123 **Fx:**629-6813
(212) 964-6611 .. **Rothenberg,** Michl '07 %Lester SK&D -120 Bway -NY 10271
(212) 244-4664 .. **Rothenberg,** Michl A '92 %NY Lawyers Pub Intrst -151 W 30th -NY 10001 **Fx:**244-4570
(212) 673-1360 .. **Rothenberg,** Paul H '99 -270 Lafayette -NY 10012 **Fx:**659-0095
(212) 880-0852 .. **Rothenberg,** Peter '65 -60 E 42nd -NY 10165
(212) 373-3000 .. **Rothenberg,** Peter J '65 (Paul WRW&G LLP) -1285 Av of Amer -NY 10019
(212) 563-0100 .. **Rothenberg,** Ross B '02 %A Rothenberg -450 7th Av -NY 10123 **Fx:**629-6813
(212) 563-0100 .. **Rothenberg,** Scott J '05 %A Rothenberg -450 7th Av -NY 10123 **Fx:**629-6813
(607) 563-2108 .. **Rothenberg,** Steven J '75 -23-25 Division Bx427 -Sidney 13838 **Fx:**563-2109
(914) 235-7234 .. **Rothenberg,** Todd '91 -271 North Av -New Rchll 10801
(516) 877-2141 .. **Rothenberg,** Wm L '38 -1 Old Cntry Rd -Carle Pl 11514 **Fx:**742-6595
(212) 563-0100 .. **Rothenberg-Kapustin,** Melissa L '08 %A Rothenberg -450 7th Av -NY 10123 **Fx:**629-6813
(212) 935-6020 .. **Rothermel,** Joan E '77 (Klein ZR LLP) -485 Mad Av -NY 10022
(607) 778-2403 .. **Rothermel,** Jonathan L '09 %Pub Def -45 Hawley Bx1766 -Bnghmtn 13902 **Fx:**778-2432
(607) 432-7410 .. **Rothermel,** Richd A '77 -48 Dietz -Oneonta 13820 **Fx:**433-2168
(212) 806-5400 .. **Rothery,** Brian M '91 (Stroock &S&L LLP) -180 Maiden Ln -NY 10038
(718) 282-5900 .. **Rothery,** Michele Bennett '88 (Bennett & R) -1970 Flatbush Av -Brklyn 11234 **Fx:**(516) 826-9581
(212) 706-0800 .. **Rothfeld,** Alan C '68 -275 Cntrl Pk W -NY 10024 **Fx:**706-0802
(212) 541-6222 .. **Rothfeld,** David R '81 (Kane K,PC) -1350 Av of Amer -NY 10019
(212) 409-9424 .. **Rothfeld,** Eric A '81 -667 Mad Av -NY 10065
(212) 663-6899 .. **Rothfeld,** Neil '79 -90 LaSalle -NY 10027
(212) 686-0070 .. **Rothfeld,** Norman '49 -276 5th Av -NY 10001
(516) 741-0166 .. **Rothkopf,** Douglas R '66 -666 Old Cntry Rd -Gdn Cty 11530 **Fx:**877-2100
(516) 571-3310 .. **Rothkopf,** Leslie K '86 Hon W LaMarca -100 Supreme Ct Dr -Mineola 11501 **Fx:**571-1316
(516) 487-2252 .. **Rothkrug,** Adam W '87 (Rothkrug R&S,LLP) -55 Watermill Ln -Gt Neck 11021
(516) 487-2252 .. **Rothkrug Rothkrug & Spector,LLP** -55 Watermill Ln -Gt Neck 11021 **Fx:**487-2439
(516) 487-2252 .. **Rothkrug,** Simon H '89 (Rothkrug R&S,LLP) -55 Watermill Ln -Gt Neck 11021
(516) 798-5363 .. **Rothlein,** Joel '53 (Kressel RW&R,LLC) -684 Bway -Massapequa 11758
(212) 859-8000 .. **Rothman,** Aaron S '09 %Fried FHS&J LLP -1 NY Plz -NY 10004
(212) 836-8000 .. **Rothman,** Alan E '94 %Kaye S LLP -425 Park Av -NY 10022 **Fx:**836-8689
(914) 216-5400 .. **Rothman,** Allan J '96 -798 Underhill Av -Yorktwn Hts 10598 **Fx:**243-0619
(212) 986-9700 .. **Rothman,** Allen J '82 Cnsl Eilenberg & K LLP -11 E 44th -NY 10017
(212) 689-1113 .. **Rothman,** Barry '81 %Garbarini & S,PC -432 Park Av S -NY 10016
(212) 931-8300 .. **Rothman,** Barry S '81 (Strongin R&A,LLP) -5 Hanover Sq -NY 10004
(212) 983-1999 .. **Rothman,** Bernard '59 -750 3rd Av -NY 10017 **Fx:**983-2253
(212) 530-4208 .. **Rothman,** Catherine E '94 %Risk Enterprise Mgmt -59 Maiden Ln -NY 10038
(212) 687-0100 .. **Rothman,** David M '00 %Harris B PLLC -100 Wall -NY 10005
(212) 964-6611 .. **Rothman,** Dennis M '78 (Lester SK&D) -120 Bway -NY 10271
(212) 408-5100 .. **Rothman,** Eric '08 %Chadbourne & P LLP -30 Rckfllr Plz -NY 10112
(212) 571-5500 .. **Rothman,** Frank A '85 (Rothman SS&S,LLP) -100 Lafayette -NY 10013
(212) 867-4000 .. **Rothman,** Fredk H '67 %Loeb & Troper -655 3rd Av -NY 10017 **Fx:**867-9810
(212) 571-7100 .. **Rothman,** Gary P '81 (O'Dwyer & B,LLP) -52 Duane -NY 10007
(516) 328-5122 .. **Rothman,** Helene M '94 %Canon USA -1 Canon Plz -Lk Success 11042
(212) 704-6000 .. **Rothman,** Henry I '67 (Troutman S LLP) -405 Lex Av -NY 10174
(212) 715-9100 .. **Rothman,** Howard J '72 (Kramer LN&F,LLP) -1177 Av of Amer -NY 10036
(516) 248-9880 .. **Rothman,** Jason L '97 (Agovino & A,LLP) -330 Old Cntry Rd -Mineola 11501
(212) 225-9200 .. **Rothman,** Jayne Leigh '98 EPIQ Systems Inc -90 Park Av -NY 10016
(212) 227-2980 .. **Rothman,** Jeffrey A '02 -315 Bway -NY 10007
(212) 966-5020 .. **Rothman,** Jeffrey E '81 %Seligson R&R -29 W 30th -NY 10001
(212) 374-5110 .. **Rothman,** Jerry N '78 %NYC Dept Educ -52 Chmbrs -NY 10007
(212) 907-9600 .. **Rothman,** Jessica L '01 %Ingram YGC&B,LLP -250 Park Av -NY 10177
(212) 218-2100 .. **Rothman,** Joshua I '99 (Fitzpatrick CH&S) -1290 Av of Amer -NY 10104
(845) 627-3200 .. **Rothman,** Kalman D '84 -55 Old Tpk Rd -Nanuet 10954 **Fx:**627-3220
(631) 234-1500 .. **Rothman,** Keith H '76 (Rubin & R LLC) -1787 Vets Hwy -Islandia 11749
(212) 640-5750 .. **Rothman,** Kevin F '04 Cnsl Amer Exp -200 Vesey -NY 10285
(607) 273-4200 .. **Rothman,** Kimberly N '06 %Miller M,LLP -202 E State -Ithaca 14850
(212) 966-5020 .. **Rothman,** Martin S '61 (Seligson R&R) -29 W 30th -NY 10001
(914) 253-2000 .. **Rothman,** Natalie S '04 %Pepsico -700 Andrsn Hill Rd -Purchase 10577
(914) 995-5428 .. **Rothman,** Noreen T '00 %Cnty Atty -148 Martine Av -White Plns 10601 **Fx:**995-5858
(212) 762-7085 .. **Rothman,** Philip A '96 Morgan Stanley -1221 Av of Amer -NY 10020
(212) 310-8000 .. **Rothman,** Richd A '78 (Weil G&M LLP) -767 5th Av -NY 10153
(631) 367-7100 .. **Rothman,** Robt M '94 (Coughlin SGR&R LLP) -58 S Srvc Rd -Melvll 11747
(315) 474-6077 .. **Rothman,** Robt P '72 (R Rothman PC) -120 E Wshngtn -Syracuse 13202 **Fx:**474-0126
(212) 872-1000 .. **Rothman,** Robt P '82 -One Bryant Park -NY 10036 **Fx:**872-1002
(631) 586-4004 .. **Rothman,** Roger B '78 -145 S 4th -Bay Shr 11706 **Fx:**586-2324
(212) 298-2139 .. **Rothman,** Ronald F '68 %IRS -290 Bway -NY 10007
(212) 571-5500 .. **Rothman Schneider Soloway & Stern,LLP** -100 Lafayette -NY 10013 **Fx:**571-5507
(212) 837-6000 .. **Rothman,** Seth D '91 (Hughes H&R LLP) -1 Bttry Pk Plz -NY 10004
(212) 966-5020 .. **Rothman,** Stewart E '85 (Seligson R&R) -29 W 30th -NY 10001
(212) 632-3373 .. **Rothner-Klein,** Sharon '90 Fiduciary Trust Co Intl -600 5th Av -NY 10020 **Fx:**632-3198
(914) 461-0280 .. **Rothschild,** Alan H '74 (Rothschild & P,LLP) -245 Main -White Plns 10601
(212) 788-1259 .. **Rothschild,** Amy Lee '01 %Law Dept -100 Church -NY 10007 **Fx:**788-0367
(212) 247-0848 .. **Rothschild,** Bradley S '08 %Bienstock & M,PC -250 W 57th -NY 10107
(315) 671-2793 .. **Rothschild,** David A '99 City Court Clerk -505 S State -Syracuse 13202
(212) 242-5868 .. **Rothschild,** Edmund L '75 -120 W 20th -NY 10011
(212) 816-1874 .. **Rothschild,** Gary A '91 %Citibank -388 Greenwich -NY 10013
(212) 554-7800 .. **Rothschild,** Gideon '81 (Moses & S LLP) -405 Lex Av -NY 10174
(212) 609-6800 .. **Rothschild,** Gita F '84 (McCarter & E,LLP) -245 Park Av -NY 10167
(212) 889-4100 .. **Rothschild,** Howard I '85 %Realty Advisory Bd -292 Mad Av -NY 10017 **Fx:**889-4105
(212) 370-9400 .. **Rothschild,** Ilissa '88 Lexolution,LLC -295 Mad Av -NY 10017 **Fx:**370-9401
(212) 819-8200 .. **Rothschild,** Jason M '01 Cnsl White & C LLP -1155 Av of Amer -NY 10036
(845) 855-5444 .. **Rothschild,** Jeffrey A '89 (Cappillino & R LLP) -7 Broad Bx390 -Pawling 12564
(845) 471-5535 .. **Rothschild,** Jeffrey A '89 (Cappillino & R LLP) -2 Cannon -Poughkeepsie 12601
(212) 547-5340 .. **Rothschild,** Jeffrey L '99 (McDermott W&E LLP) -340 Mad Av -NY 10173
(845) 359-0606 .. **Rothschild,** Laura '91 %MHLS -140 Old Orangebrg Rd -Orangebrg 10962 **Fx:**365-1773
(315) 449-9500 .. **Rothschild,** Martin J '79 Rothman Law Firm,PC -5781 Brdg -E Syracuse 13057 **Fx:**449-9804
(914) 461-0280 .. **Rothschild & Pearl,LLP** -245 Main -White Plns 10601 **Fx:**461-2369
(315) 422-8191 .. **Rothschild,** Philip '87 %Leg Aid -351 S Warren -Syracuse 13202 **Fx:**472-2819
(212) 449-0186 .. **Rothschild,** Randall S '98 Merrill Lynch -4 World Fncl Ctr -NY 10080
(845) 426-3117 .. **Rothschild,** Steven B '79 (S Rothschild,PC) -747 Chestnut Rdg Rd -Spg Vly 10977 **Fx:**426-6406
(718) 834-8877 .. **Rothschild,** Thos N '69 -16 Court -Brklyn 11241
(516) 869-2090 .. **Rothschild,** Valerie M '81 Kimco Rlty Corp -3333 New Hyde Pk Rd -New Hyde Pk 11042
(212) 225-2000 .. **Rothschild,** Walter S '53 OfCnsl Cleary GS&H -1 Lbrty Plz -NY 10006
(212) 382-6623 .. **Rothstein,** Alan J '79 %NYC Bar -42 W 44th -NY 10036 **Fx:**398-6634
(631) 543-2100 .. **Rothstein,** Alan S '78 (Rothstein & T,PC) -340 Vets Hwy -Commack 11725
(212) 619-3730 .. **Rothstein,** Amy '73 OfCnsl Doar RK&M -217 Bway -NY 10007
(212) 772-8580 .. **Rothstein,** Andrew G '90 -110 Wall -NY 10005 **Fx:**772-8580
(607) 732-2158 .. **Rothstein,** Andrew M '77 -420 Carroll -Elmira 14901 **Fx:**732-2158
(212) 373-3000 .. **Rothstein,** Benjamin D '10 %Paul WRW&G LLP -1285 Av of Amer -NY 10019
(212) 336-8000 .. **Rothstein,** Chester '91 (Amster R&E) -90 Park Av -NY 10016
(845) 369-8253 .. **Rothstein,** Danl G '95 %Provident Svngs Bk -400 Rella Blvd Bx600 -Suffern 10901
(718) 361-6100 .. **Rothstein,** David '85 %Dalow Industries -3100 47th Av -LIC 11101
(212) 986-1441 .. **Rothstein,** Ellen '83 -630 3rd Av -NY 10017
(212) 385-8015 .. **Rothstein,** Eric E '92 -11 Park Pl -NY 10007
(212) 309-6000 .. **Rothstein,** Gary S '94 (Morgan L&B LLP) -101 Park Av -NY 10178
(212) 888-8200 .. **Rothstein,** Irving '89 Cnsl Feder K LLP -845 3rd Av -NY 10022
(212) 813-8800 .. **Rothstein,** Jessica L '99 SrCnsl Goodwin P LLP -620 8th Av -NY 10018
(212) 373-3000 .. **Rothstein,** Joshua S '07 %Paul WRW&G LLP -1285 Av of Amer -NY 10019
(212) 227-5400 .. **Rothstein,** Laurence L '86 -225 Bway -NY 10007
(718) 643-3922 .. **Rothstein,** Marilyn '84 %Hon J Spodek -360 Adams -Brklyn 11201
(212) 686-3838 .. **Rothstein,** Martin L '68 (Barst M&K LLP) -2 Park Av -NY 10016
(212) 399-1600 .. **Rothstein,** Scott H '06 %Mutual of America -320 Park Av -NY 10022
(631) 543-2100 .. **Rothstein & Tufo,PC** -340 Vets Hwy -Commack 11725 **Fx:**543-5846
(212) 877-0798 .. **Rothstein,** Wendy A '89 -224 W 82nd -NY 10024
(212) 244-9000 .. **Rothstein,** Yosef '01 Cnsl Matalon SE -450 7th Av -NY 10123 **Fx:**244-4615
(212) 450-4000 .. **Rothwell,** James T '93 (Davis P&W LLP) -450 Lex Av -NY 10017
(212) 425-7200 .. **Rothwell,** Michl I '09 %Kenyon & K,LLP -1 Bway -NY 10004
(914) 995-3630 .. **Rotini,** Melissa-Jean '04 Cnty Atty -148 Martine Av -White Plns 10601 **Fx:**995-5858
(212) 806-5400 .. **Rotker,** Laurel S '85 SpclCnsl Stroock &S&L LLP -180 Maiden Ln -NY 10038
(347) 404-9929 .. **Rotkin,** Sara A '03 %MHLS -120 Schermerhorn -Brklyn 11201 **Fx:**(718) 243-2408
(212) 922-1080 .. **Rotko,** Thos C '96 (Clayman & R,LLP) -305 Mad Av -NY 10165
(212) 684-1422 .. **Rotlewicz,** Allan J '09 %Aboulafia Law Firm LLC -60 E 42nd -NY 10165 **Fx:**684-1428
(212) 879-7737 .. **Rotner,** Kenneth S '76 -330 E 71st -NY 10021

(212) 839-5300 .. **Rotner,** Stacy M '04 %Sidley A LLP -787 7th Av -NY 10019
(518) 447-9698 .. **Rotondi,** Anthony '97 %J Buttridge -20 Corp Wds Blvd Bx1690 -Albany 12201 **Fx:**426-7209
(212) 947-2233 .. **Rotondi,** Louis J '72 (Rontondi & Assoc,PC) -230 Park Av -NY 10169
(914) 694-5590 .. **Rotondo,** Kathi L '90 -25 W Red Oak Ln -White Plns 10604 **Fx:**694-5593
(315) 457-4211 .. **Rotondo,** Robt M '88 %Rotondo Trucking&Warehousing -Bx217 -Liverpool 13088
(631) 595-9418 .. **Rotondo,** Rosemarie N '96 -50 Gazza Blvd -Farmngdl 11735
(718) 398-1084 .. **Rotstein,** Andrew D '95 -535 Dean -Brklyn 11217 **Fx:**504-3754
(212) 506-2500 .. **Rotsztain,** Diego A '98 (Mayer B LLP) -1675 Bway -NY 10019
(718) 222-2361 .. **Rott,** Chas J '02 %Law Dept -350 Jay -Brklyn 11201 **Fx:**222-2373
(716) 858-2424 .. **Rott,** Lauren A '01 %DA -25 Delaware Av -Buffalo 14202 **Fx:**858-7425
(716) 284-8831 .. **Rottaris,** Albert '85 %Leg Aid -775 3rd Bx844 -Niagara Fls 14302 **Fx:**284-8040
(716) 854-4300 .. **Rottaris,** John K '90 (Gross SB&G,PC) -465 Main -Buffalo 14203
(718) 250-2000 .. **Rottenberg,** Ari '97 %DA -350 Jay -Brklyn 11201 **Fx:**250-2314
(212) 661-3080 .. **Rottenberg Lipman Rich,PC** -369 Lex Av -NY 10017 **Fx:**867-1914
(212) 661-3080 .. **Rottenberg,** Mark M '83 (Rottenberg LR,PC) -369 Lex Av -NY 10017
(212) 575-0055 .. **Rottenstreich,** Dan '98 (Rottenstreich & E LLP) -150 E 58th -NY 10155 **Fx:**575-0046
(212) 541-2000 .. **Rottenstreich,** Stacie '86 %Bryan C LLP -1290 Av of Amer -NY 10104
(212) 839-5300 .. **Rotter,** Irving L '82 (Sidley A LLP) -787 7th Av -NY 10019
(212) 225-2000 .. **Rotter,** Marc B '10 %Cleary GS&H -1 Lbrty Plz -NY 10006
(212) 455-2000 .. **Rotter,** Stephanie A '10 %Simpson T&B LLP -425 Lex Av -NY 10017
(516) 791-3500 .. **Rotto,** Howard F '80 -301 Mill Rd -Hewlett 11557 **Fx:**791-3676
(607) 722-9561 .. **Roueche,** Lori Ann '87 -34 Chenango Bx2504 -Bnghmtn 13902
(800) 636-5255 .. **Rougeux,** Debra C '84 %HoganWillig -705 Center -Lewiston 14092
(212) 450-4000 .. **Rouhandeh,** James P '88 (Davis P&W LLP) -450 Lex Av -NY 10017
(315) 789-8580 .. **Roulan,** Michl J '76 -407 S Main -Geneva 14456 **Fx:**789-4216
(315) 863-2745 .. **Roulan,** Timothy A '94 -Bx595 -Syracuse 13206 **Fx:**282-2882
(845) 331-1141 .. **Rounds,** Alexis Komarow '02 (Rounds & R) -2 Pearl -Kingston 12401 **Fx:**331-1141
(845) 331-1141 .. **Rounds,** Bryan E '95 (Rounds & R) -2 Pearl -Kingston 12401 **Fx:**331-1141
(212) 831-1607 .. **Rountree,** Cynthia W '73 -18 W 130th -NY 10037
(914) 235-8091 .. **Rountree,** Timothy '89 -140 Aviemore Dr -New Rchll 10804
(212) 245-1000 .. **Roupinian,** René S '03 (Outten & G LLP) -3 Park Av -NY 10016
(212) 227-6821 .. **Roura & Melamed** -233 Bway -NY 10279 **Fx:**385-2530
(212) 227-6821 .. **Roura,** Walter P '69 (Roura & M) -233 Bway -NY 10279
(845) 292-2000 .. **Rourke,** Brian P '99 (B Rourke,PC) -3 Maple Bx71 -Liberty 12754 **Fx:**292-0385
(518) 273-9346 .. **Rourke,** Michl E '75 -198 9th -Troy 12180 **Fx:**273-9346
(212) 326-2000 .. **Rousakis,** John '94 Cnsl O'Melveny & M LLP -7 Times Sq -NY 10036
(718) 789-4434 .. **Rouse,** Franklyn A '94 -217 St James Pl -Brklyn 11238
(212) 626-6785 .. **Rouse,** Holly E '99 (Reid R&R,LLP) -1120 Av of Amer -NY 10036
(631) 265-7200 .. **Rouse,** John H '88 -400 Townline Rd -Hauppauge 11788 **Fx:**265-7578
(631) 853-4049 .. **Rouse,** Patricia A '92 %Cnty Atty -Dennison Bldg Bx6100 -Hauppauge 11788 **Fx:**853-5169
(718) 588-7773 .. **Rouse,** Winston B '98 -901 Sheridan Av -Bronx 10451
(212) 425-7200 .. **Roush,** Bradley D '10 %Kenyon & K,LLP -1 Bway -NY 10004
(212) 504-6000 .. **Rouslin,** Lawr E '95 %Cadwalader W&T LLP -1 World Fncl Ctr -NY 10281
(212) 484-3900 .. **Rousseau,** Julius A III '93 (Arent F LLP) -1675 Bway -NY 10019
(914) 946-0600 .. **Rousseau,** Marc A '97 %Pino & Assoc -50 Main -White Plns 10606 **Fx:**946-0650
(212) 459-7197 .. **Rousseau,** Timothy J '09 %Goodwin P LLP -620 8th Av -NY 10018
(212) 221-6900 .. **Roussel,** Keith R M '06 %Winget S&S,LLP -45 Bway -NY 10006
(631) 366-6262 .. **Roussillon,** Paul W '74 -400 Town Line Rd -Hauppauge 11788
(212) 877-9746 .. **Roussin,** Lucille A '97 -37 Riverside Dr -NY 10023 **Fx:**501-9372
(212) 261-8000 .. **Routledge,** Linsey M '08 %Mendes & M,LLP -750 7th Av -NY 10019
(845) 634-0023 .. **Rouzard,** Reginald E '05 (Rouzard & R,LLP) -490 Route 304 -New Cty 10956 **Fx:**503-2224
(516) 876-9600 .. **Rovegno,** Robt P '73 (Rovegno & T,PC) -1010 Nrthrn Blvd -Gt Neck 11021
(516) 876-9600 .. **Rovegno & Taylor,PC** -1010 Nrthrn Blvd -Gt Neck 11021
(212) 318-2300 .. **Rovella,** David E '96 Bloomberg Business News -499 Park Av -NY 10022
(212) 262-3280 .. **Roven,** Janice G '86 -60 E 42nd -NY 10165 **Fx:**262-3282
(212) 819-8200 .. **Rover,** Edw F '64 OfCnsl White & C LLP -1155 Av of Amer -NY 10036
(212) 309-6000 .. **Rover,** Kevin T '81 (Morgan L&B LLP) -101 Park Av -NY 10178
(516) 496-5822 .. **Rovere,** John M '07 %T Spina -170 Froehlich Farm Blvd -Woodbury 11797 **Fx:**496-5420
(516) 822-8900 .. **Roveto,** Michl J '88 Fiedelman & M -2 Jericho Plz -Jericho 11753
(212) 891-3550 .. **Rovine,** Arthur W '85 -1114 Av of Amer -NY 10036 **Fx:**310-1750
(212) 583-5000 .. **Rovine,** Joshua B '91 Blackstone Grp -345 Park Av -NY 10154
(212) 839-5300 .. **Rovira,** Alex R '04 %Sidley A LLP -787 7th Av -NY 10019
(212) 635-1087 .. **Rovira-Paoli,** Alba J '76 Bk of NY Mellon -1 Wall -NY 10286 **Fx:**635-1665
(212) 836-8000 .. **Rovner,** Dina S '03 %Kaye S LLP -425 Park Av -NY 10022
(212) 403-1000 .. **Rovzar,** Leigh A '10 %Wachtell LR&K -51 W 52nd -NY 10019
(516) 222-2444 .. **Rowan,** Jeffrey D '95 -3601 Hempstd Tpk -Levittwn 11756
(631) 666-6200 .. **Rowan,** John '79 OfCnsl PF Adams,PC -49 5th Av Bx1089M -Bay Shr 11706 **Fx:**665-6739
(315) 868-3987 .. **Rowan,** Teresa M '09 Ayco Co LP -25 British Amer Blvd -Latham 12110
(212) 326-3939 .. **Rowan,** Thos G '89 (Jones D) -222 E 41st -NY 10017
(917) 542-3600 .. **Rowden,** Gwen A '80 %Jonathan Rose Cos -551 5th Av -NY 10176 **Fx:**542-3601
(718) 237-2000 .. **Rowe,** Andrew A '00 %Leg Aid -111 Lvngstn -Brklyn 11201 **Fx:**237-8737
(212) 578-6813 .. **Rowe,** Ashley B '01 %MetLife -27-01 Qns Plz N -LIC 11101
(212) 837-6000 .. **Rowe,** Damon G '02 %Hughes H&R LLP -1 Bttry Pk Plz -NY 10004
(315) 531-1889 .. **Rowe,** Douglas E '70 -1109 Anthony Beach Rd -Penn Yan 14527
(516) 296-7000 .. **Rowe,** Douglas E '81 (Certilman BA&H,LLP) -90 Merrick Av -E Meadow 11554
(212) 586-0700 .. **Rowe,** George Jr. '48 (Fulton R&H,LLP) -1 Rckfllr Plz -NY 10020
(212) 656-4655 .. **Rowe,** Gillian A '92 NYSE EuroNext -11 Wall -NY 10005
(212) 909-6000 .. **Rowe,** Katrina Szakal '02 %Debevoise & P LLP -919 3rd Av -NY 10022
(718) 250-2000 .. **Rowe,** Kerry '08 %DA -350 Jay -Brklyn 11201 **Fx:**250-2314
(212) 872-1000 .. **Rowe,** Kevin M '85 -One Bryant Park -NY 10036 **Fx:**872-1002
(518) 438-9907 .. **Rowe,** Kristin Carter '91 OfCnsl Young SWRB&M,LLC -5 Palisades Dr -Albany 12205
(646) 473-3955 .. **Rowe,** Leslie Labrousse '00 USPS Law Dept -380 W 33rd -NY 10199
(631) 755-0101 .. **Rowe,** Martin K '89 %Lewis JAA,LLP -425 Broad Hollow Rd -Melvll 11747
(212) 885-5000 .. **Rowe,** Michl A '99 (Blank R LLP) -405 Lex Av -NY 10174
(585) 530-3050 .. **Rowe,** Neil J '81 %MHLS -50 East Av -Rchstr 14604 **Fx:**530-3079
(212) 403-1000 .. **Rowe,** Paul K '80 (Wachtell LR&K) -51 W 52nd -NY 10019
(585) 350-7216 .. **Rowe,** Randolph W '96 Sagemark Consulting -200 Meridian Ctr -Rchstr 14618 **Fx:**271-4764
(212) 969-3000 .. **Rowe,** Richd H '80 (Proskauer R LLP) -1585 Bway -NY 10036
(631) 285-6500 .. **Rowe,** Richd R '94 -1919 Middle Cntry Rd -Centereach 11720
(212) 909-6000 .. **Rowe,** Samantha J M '09 %Debevoise & P LLP -919 3rd Av -NY 10022
(518) 486-9564 .. **Rowe,** Shane S '01 %Workers Comp Bd -20 Park -Albany 12207
(212) 932-1058 .. **Rowe,** Shirley A '85 Bd of Educ -209 W 125th -NY 10027
(212) 558-4000 .. **Rowen,** Andrew S '80 (Sullivan & C LLP) -125 Broad -NY 10004
(212) 388-3452 .. **Rowen,** Lyle D '04 Local 32BJ SEIU -101 Av of Amer -NY 10013
(212) 436-1144 .. **Rowen,** Mary '84 IRS -290 Bway -NY 10007
(212) 521-3500 .. **Rower,** Alyssa A '05 %Aronson M&S, LLP -485 Lex Av -NY 10017
(212) 417-5300 .. **Rowe-Smith,** Emily J '95 %Medicaid Fraud Cntrl -120 Bway -NY 10271 **Fx:**417-5274
(212) 682-4001 .. **Rowin,** Marc '73 (Lynch R LLP) -630 3rd Av -NY 10017
(212) 698-3500 .. **Rowland,** Adam B '84 Cnsl Dechert LLP -1095 Av of Amer -NY 10036
(212) 455-2000 .. **Rowland,** Amy E '04 %Simpson T&B LLP -425 Lex Av -NY 10017
(315) 342-7611 .. **Rowland,** Carole A '90 -85 Chase Rd -Fulton 13069 **Fx:**(866) 492-6758
(212) 685-5509 .. **Rowland,** David J '84 (Rowland & P) -2 Park Av -NY 10016
(212) 450-4000 .. **Rowland,** Gregory S '04 (Davis P&W LLP) -450 Lex Av -NY 10017
(212) 909-6000 .. **Rowland,** Hugh Jr. '68 OfCnsl Debevoise & P LLP -919 3rd Av -NY 10022
(212) 682-6800 .. **Rowland,** James H '97 (Zetlin & D LLP) -801 2nd Av -NY 10017
(212) 697-0734 .. **Rowland,** Joanne '88 -521 5th Av -NY 10175 **Fx:**697-7833
(516) 222-0676 .. **Rowland,** John C '08 %G Haggerty & Assoc,PC -500 N Bway -Jericho 11753 **Fx:**222-8011
(914) 967-6220 .. **Rowland,** John M '62 -2 Elm Pl -Rye 10580
(212) 450-4000 .. **Rowland,** Matthew B '06 %Davis P&W LLP -450 Lex Av -NY 10017
(212) 685-5509 .. **Rowland & Petroff** -2 Park Av -NY 10016 **Fx:**685-8862
(518) 486-7825 .. **Rowland,** Stacey B '97 %Insurance Dept -99 Wshngtn Av -Albany 12257 **Fx:**473-4600
(212) 704-2126 .. **Rowland,** Thos M '01 Musicnet Inc -845 3rd Av -NY 10022
(518) 462-0300 .. **Rowlands,** Richd E '74 OfCnsl Girvin & F,PC -20 Corp Wds Blvd -Albany 12211 **Fx:**874-5043
(518) 449-3900 .. **Rowley,** David C '88 (Cooper E&S,LLP) -39 N Pearl -Albany 12207
(518) 457-1059 .. **Rowley,** Edw S '77 %Agriculture & Mrkts -10B Airline Dr -Albany 12235 **Fx:**457-8842
(212) 825-2905 .. **Rowley,** John M '81 -130 Water -NY 10005
(315) 772-2892 .. **Rowley,** Leslie A '98 Ofc Staff Judge Advct -141 Lewis Av -Fort Drum 13602
(518) 474-3593 .. **Rowley,** Martin '74 %Dept of Law -The Cptl -Albany 12224
(212) 983-9330 .. **Rowley,** Shane T '90 %Faruqi & F,LLP -369 Lex Av -NY 10017 **Fx:**983-9331
(631) 853-4104 .. **Rowman,** Lois Sicignano '07 %DA -400 Carleton Av Bx9082 -Central Islip 11722 **Fx:**853-7838
(212) 408-5100 .. **Rowntree,** Laura C '10 %Chadbourne & P LLP -30 Rckfllr Plz -NY 10112
(516) 742-6546 .. **Rowsell,** Jamie A '04 %L Stober Jr,LLC -350 Old Cntry Rd -Gdn Cty 11530 **Fx:**742-8603
(212) 656-5284 .. **Rowsell,** Roy L '89 NYSE -20 Broad -NY 10005
(718) 588-4389 .. **Roxas,** Beverly A '08 %Law Dept -198 E 161st -Bronx 10451 **Fx:**590-2686
(631) 537-8887 .. **Roxbury,** Susanne M '89 (S Roxbury,PC) -360 Montauk Hwy Bx467 -Wainscott 11975 **Fx:**537-8889
(516) 873-3900 .. **Roxbury,** Susanne M '89 OfCnsl C Connick,PLLC -114 Old Cntry Rd -Mineola 11501 **Fx:**873-3904
(585) 753-1365 .. **Roxin,** Richd C '87 Dept of Law -39 W Main -Rchstr 14614
(212) 768-6700 .. **Roxland,** Ira I '67 (Sonnenschein N&R LLP) -2 World Fncl Ctr -NY 10281
(212) 980-4500 .. **Roy,** Howard P '69 (Cohen L LLP) -885 3rd Av -NY 10022
(212) 468-8000 .. **Roy,** Joshua A '10 Morrison & F LLP -1290 Av of Amer -NY 10104
(212) 735-8600 .. **Roy,** Kristin T '97 (Morrison C LLP) -909 3rd Av -NY 10022
(212) 841-1000 .. **Roy,** Meenakshi '09 %Covington & B LLP -620 8th Av -NY 10018
(914) 591-7722 .. **Roy Mondello LaRocca & Risotto** -56 Main Bx108 -Irvngtn 10533 **Fx:**591-5172
(212) 554-1234 .. **Roy,** Patricia A '86 AXA Financial Inc -1290 Av of Amer -NY 10104 **Fx:**707-3963
(617) 856-8241 .. **Roy,** Rahoul '07 %Brown R LLP -7 Times Sq -NY 10036 **Fx:**856-8201
(212) 422-9424 .. **Roy,** Sushmita '07 %Gogick B&O,LLP -11 Bway -NY 10004
(212) 701-3000 .. **Roy,** Tammy L '02 (Cahill G&R LLP) -80 Pine -NY 10005 **Fx:**269-5420
(516) 216-1675 .. **Roy,** Yana A '00 Y Roy & Assoc,PC -99 Tulip Av -Floral Pk 11001 **Fx:**775-0352
(516) 747-9400 .. **Royce,** Edgar J '77 (Pieper H&R) -92 Willis Av -Mineola 11501
(914) 633-3190 .. **Royce,** Kermit '51 -270 North Av -New Rchll 10801
(212) 258-4151 .. **Royer,** Kevin M '96 %Siemens Corp -153 E 53rd -NY 10022 **Fx:**767-0580
(212) 816-1680 .. **Royer,** Louis J '88 Citibank NA -388 Greenwich -NY 10013
(212) 554-7800 .. **Royer,** Marguerite E '81 (Moses & S LLP) -405 Lex Av -NY 10174

(718) 575-9479 .. **Roytberg,** Alla '92 -1 Station Sq -Frst Hlls 11375 **Fx:**575-8163
(718) 645-6030 .. **Royzman,** Elvira '01 E Royzman,PLLC -1101 Av U -Brklyn 11223 **Fx:**645-4347
(212) 336-2000 .. **Royzman,** Irena '04 Patterson BW&T LLP -1133 Av of Amer -NY 10036
(212) 687-1155 .. **Rozan,** Alain '85 (Rozan & N,LLP) -420 Lex Av -NY 10170 **Fx:**687-1118
(516) 742-3470 .. **Rozanski,** Thaddeus J '81 (Kral CRRP&G,LLP) -538 Broadhllw Rd -Melvll 11747
(718) 237-2000 .. **Rozansky,** Gail B '87 %Leg Aid -111 Lvngstn -Brklyn 11201 **Fx:**237-8737
(212) 848-4000 .. **Rozansky,** Gregg L '00 Cnsl Shearman & S LLP -599 Lex Av -NY 10022
(212) 525-8525 .. **Rozario,** Deborah J '00 HSBC -452 5th Av -NY 10018
(212) 832-4881 .. **Rozell,** Mark I '85 -950 3rd Av -NY 10022 **Fx:**750-4788
(212) 903-8700 .. **Rozen,** Mark David '83 (Roberts & H,LLP) -825 8th Av -NY 10019
(212) 527-9600 .. **Rozen,** Michl K '90 (Feinberg R,LLP) -780 3rd Av -NY 10017 **Fx:**527-9611
(516) 622-9200 .. **Rozenberg,** Barry S '91 Cnsl Westerman BEM&S,LLP -1201 RXR Plz -Uniondale 11553
(212) 225-2000 .. **Rozenberg,** Inna '01 %Cleary GS&H -1 Lbrty Plz -NY 10006
(212) 974-0044 .. **Rozenblatt,** Dan J '01 -221 W 38th -NY 10018
(212) 831-0995 .. **Rozencwaig,** Bryan L '91 -200 E 90th -NY 10128 **Fx:**831-0482
(212) 788-0789 .. **Rozenfeld,** Amy '05 Law Dept -100 Church -NY 10007 **Fx:**788-0367
(212) 588-0800 .. **Rozenfeld,** Magali Solange '04 %Frommer L&H LLP -745 5th Av -NY 10151
(212) 983-4141 .. **Rozenholc,** David '71 (D Rozenholc & Assoc) -400 Mad Av -NY 10017 **Fx:**983-4356
(212) 509-1616 .. **Rozger,** Jason J '98 %Beranbaum M LLP -80 Pine -NY 10005
(212) 969-3000 .. **Rozic,** Kristin S '02 %Proskauer R LLP -1585 Bway -NY 10036
(212) 558-4000 .. **Rozic,** Marc A '04 %Sullivan & C LLP -125 Broad -NY 10004
(212) 530-5000 .. **Rozic,** Scott S '04 %Milbank TH&M LLP -1 Chase Manh Plz -NY 10005
(212) 408-2500 .. **Rozier-Byrd,** Terence L '07 %Baker B,LLP -30 Rckfllr Plz -NY 10112
(212) 508-6100 .. **Rozin,** Anna '09 %Bracewell & G,LLP -1251 Av of Amer -NY 10020
(212) 415-9200 .. **Rozon,** Elizabeth '09 %Dorsey & W LLP -250 Park Av -NY 10177
(212) 941-1202 .. **Rozos,** Nicholas H '75 -350 Bway -NY 10013
(718) 725-3060 .. **Rozul,** Elaine O '04 ACS -15120 Jamaica Av -Jamaica 11432
(631) 360-2766 .. **Rozza,** Denise Furiano '88 -5 Grist Mill Dr -Kings Pk 11754 **Fx:**360-2766
(631) 271-0391 .. **Rozza,** Michl S '89 -155 W Carver -Huntngtn 11743 **Fx:**351-6064
(212) 872-1000 .. **Ru,** Meng '05 -One Bryant Park -NY 10036 **Fx:**872-1002
(716) 692-6119 .. **Rua,** S Michl '84 -535 Delaware -Tonawanda 14150 **Fx:**692-8728
(212) 825-0365 .. **Rualo,** Carolyn Z '03 %AL Bailey,PC -120 Bway -NY 10271 **Fx:**825-0999
(212) 343-9072 .. **Ruan,** J Jeffrey '92 -401 Bway -NY 10013 **Fx:**343-9817
(212) 245-1000 .. **Ruan,** Nantiya '01 OfCnsl Outten & G LLP -3 Park Av -NY 10016
(212) 808-8300 .. **Ruan,** Shaomei '04 %Rosensteel Law -90 Park Av -NY 10016
(315) 474-7447 .. **Ruark,** Jadi K '02 -333 E Onondaga -Syracuse 13202 **Fx:**474-0425
(212) 504-6000 .. **Ruaysamran,** Justin '05 %Cadwalader W&T LLP -1 World Fncl Ctr -NY 10281
(212) 969-3000 .. **Ruback,** Gregory D '00 (Proskauer R LLP) -1585 Bway -NY 10036
(718) 951-4128 .. **Rubain,** Jennifer S '95 Brooklyn Cllg Affirmative Actn Ofc -2900 Bedford Av -Brklyn 11210
(718) 539-2100 .. **Rubano,** Chas F Jr. '57 (Pliskin R&B) -137-11 Nrthrn Blvd -Flushng 11354
(212) 296-6993 .. **Rubano,** Debra I '01 Morgan Stanley -522 5th Av -NY 10036
(212) 969-3000 .. **Rubano,** Richd A '08 %Proskauer R LLP -1585 Bway -NY 10036
(315) 471-2181 .. **Rube,** Neil A '87 %Pioneer Dvlpmnt Co,LLC -250 S Clinton -Syracuse 13202 **Fx:**471-1154
(914) 312-2300 .. **Rube,** Patricia Schoor '93 Hoenig & Co Inc -4 Intl Dr -Rye Brook 10573
(212) 270-6000 .. **Rubecindo,** Marisol '04 JP Morgan Chase -245 Park Av -NY 10167
(212) 223-0400 .. **Rubel,** Danl P '04 %Zeichner E&K LLP -575 Lex Av -NY 10022
(212) 865-6658 .. **Rubel,** Hewitt L '57 (Maggin & S) -875 W End Av -NY 10025 **Fx:**865-6658
(516) 678-1800 .. **Rubel,** Steven '91 S Rubel,PC -371 Merrick Rd -Rockvll Ctr 11570 **Fx:**764-5540
(516) 747-0300 .. **Rubell,** Paul M '84 (Meltzer LG&B,LLP) -190 Willis Av -Mineola 11501
(212) 449-2370 .. **Rubel Lipsher,** Meredith '95 Merrill Lynch -225 Lbrty -NY 10080
(718) 722-3100 .. **Ruben,** Emily '86 %Leg Aid -111 Lvngstn -Brklyn 11201 **Fx:**722-3093
(212) 856-9600 .. **Ruben,** Eric M '08 %Morvillo AGIA&B,PC -565 5th Av -NY 10017
(212) 902-4881 .. **Ruben,** Gregory H '09 Goldman Sachs -85 Broad -NY 10004
(212) 980-0910 .. **Ruben,** Lawr '52 -600 Mad Av -NY 10022
(718) 579-3116 .. **Ruben,** Michl P '92 %Leg Aid -1020 Grnd Cncrs -Bronx 10451 **Fx:**588-2611
(212) 980-0910 .. **Ruben,** Richd G '81 -600 Mad Av -NY 10022
(212) 884-6200 .. **Rubenfeld,** Eric P '96 GSC Group -888 7th Av -NY 10019 **Fx:**884-6184
(845) 791-1670 .. **Rubenfeld,** Gail B '92 -34 North Bx281 -Monticello 12701 **Fx:**791-1670
(631) 777-7200 .. **Rubenfeld,** Herbert '60 (H Rubenfeld Law Ofc) -425 Broadhllw Rd -Melvll 11747
(631) 777-7200 .. **Rubenfeld,** Michl B '93 %H Rubenfeld Law Ofc -425 Broadhllw Rd -Melvll 11747
(212) 779-9910 .. **Rubenfeld,** Robt A '75 (Eaton & V LLP) -3 Park Av -NY 10016
(212) 596-9000 .. **Rubenfeld,** Sarah I '10 %Ropes & G LLP -1211 Av of Amer -NY 10036
(212) 805-0401 .. **Rubens,** Danl A '09 Hon J Rakoff -500 Pearl -NY 10007
(718) 257-9240 .. **Rubens,** Emily B '05 Lenkay Sani Products -473 Wortman Av -Brklyn 11208
(212) 372-2015 .. **Rubens,** Jesse L '92 %Newmark & Co -125 Park Av -NY 10017 **Fx:**372-2424
(212) 684-3900 .. **Rubenstein,** Allen I '75 (Gottlieb R&R,PC) -270 Mad Av -NY 10016
(212) 450-4000 .. **Rubenstein,** Arie M '07 %Davis P&W LLP -450 Lex Av -NY 10017
(212) 349-2000 .. **Rubenstein,** Arthur L '89 %Alpert & K, LLP -233 Bway -NY 10279
(914) 968-1246 .. **Rubenstein,** Benjamin '57 -1155 Warburton Av -Ynkrs 10701
(516) 869-9000 .. **Rubenstein,** Bruce M '85 %Kimco Realty Corp -3333 New Hyde Pk Rd -New Hyde Pk 11042 **Fx:**869-7199
(212) 801-3760 .. **Rubenstein,** David A '94 (Michael L&R LLP) -60 Columbus Cir -NY 10023
(212) 446-7000 .. **Rubenstein,** David A '99 %McKinsey & Co -55 E 52nd -NY 10055 **Fx:**688-9521
(212) 878-6900 .. **Rubenstein,** Eli '04 (Goulston & S,PC) -750 3rd Av -NY 10017
(516) 663-6600 .. **Rubenstein,** Eric C '82 (Ruskin MF,PC) -1425 RXR Plz -Uniondale 11556
(646) 654-5042 .. **Rubenstein,** Eric M '97 Nielsen Co -770 Bway -NY 10003
(212) 373-3000 .. **Rubenstein,** Ernest '54 OfCnsl Paul WRW&G LLP -1285 Av of Amer -NY 10019
(212) 489-6900 .. **Rubenstein,** Howard J '60 -1345 Av of Amer -NY 10105
(212) 940-7150 .. **Rubenstein,** Joshua S '80 (Katten MR LLP) -575 Mad Av -NY 10022
(718) 222-2014 .. **Rubenstein,** Julie B '08 %Law Dept -350 Jay -Brklyn 11201 **Fx:**222-2088
(212) 969-3000 .. **Rubenstein,** Kenneth '83 (Proskauer R LLP) -1585 Bway -NY 10036
(631) 622-2920 .. **Rubenstein,** Kenneth A '97 Amer Home Mortgage Corp -538 Broadhllw Rd -Melvll 11747
(212) 953-6814 .. **Rubenstein,** Lee A '86 -450 7th Av -NY 10123 **Fx:**953-9660
(845) 635-1870 .. **Rubenstein,** Lisa E '86 -15 Briar Patch Ln -Plsnt Vlly 12569 **Fx:**635-3642
(718) 698-7200 .. **Rubenstein,** Martin '74 -260 Christopher Ln -Staten Isl 10314 **Fx:**494-1776
(212) 490-3000 .. **Rubenstein,** Richd H '82 (Wilson EME&D LLP) -150 E 42nd -NY 10017
(718) 522-1020 .. **Rubenstein & Rynecki** -16 Court -Brklyn 11241 **Fx:**522-3804
(718) 522-1020 .. **Rubenstein,** Sanford A '72 (Rubenstein & R) -16 Court -Brklyn 11241
(718) 624-1084 .. **Rubenstein,** Seth '54 (S Rubenstein,PC) -26 Court -Brklyn 11242 **Fx:**624-1980
(516) 328-2300 .. **Rubenstein,** Todd C '93 %Abrams FFEGF&E,LLP -1111 Marcus Av -Lk Success 11042
(315) 218-8000 .. **Rubenstein,** Wm J '02 (Bond S&K,PLLC) -1 Lincoln Ctr -Syracuse 13202
(212) 735-3000 .. **Rubenstein,** Wm S '82 (Skadden ASM&F LLP) -4 Times Sq -NY 10036
(914) 591-7111 .. **Rubenzahl,** David J '89 -76 N Bway -Irvngtn 10533
(914) 495-3050 .. **Rubeo,** Mark A Jr. '97 (Reisman R&M,LLP) -151 Bway -Hawthorne 10532 **Fx:**495-3051
(914) 965-9555 .. **Rubeo,** Stephen V '93 -1 Exec Blvd -Ynkrs 10701 **Fx:**965-4618
(631) 369-1578 .. **Rubert,** Mary Catherine '84 -701 Bluffs Dr N -Baiting Hollow 11933 **Fx:**369-1578
(212) 608-3103 .. **Rubert,** Soledad '82 (Rubert & G,PC) -150 Bway -NY 10038
(518) 464-9500 .. **Ruberti,** E Michl '86 -499 Hurley Av -Hurley 12443 **Fx:**464-1237
(212) 739-1828 .. **Ruberti,** Wendy L '95 Clinton Grp Inc -9 W 57th -NY 10019
(516) 627-4850 .. **Rubertone,** Steven M '96 -136 Glen Cove Rd -East Hills 11577 **Fx:**627-4856
(315) 597-4471 .. **Rubery,** Paul T '56 -322 E Main Bx401 -Palmyra 14522 **Fx:**597-6156
(212) 506-5000 .. **Rubin,** Aaron G R '08 %Orrick H&S LLP -51 W 52nd -NY 10019
(212) 335-9000 .. **Rubin,** Aaron M '01 %DA -1 Hogan Pl -NY 10013
(914) 323-7000 .. **Rubin,** Abigail D '08 %Wilson EME&D LLP -3 Gannett Dr -White Plns 10604
(212) 964-3300 .. **Rubin Abramson LLP** -225 Bway -NY 10007 **Fx:**385-9119
(914) 682-6800 .. **Rubin,** Alan M '60 -50 Main -White Plns 10606
(212) 922-9700 .. **Rubin,** Alan M '78 %1st Amer Title -633 3rd Av -NY 10017 **Fx:**922-0881
(347) 756-4828 .. **Rubin,** Alix R '05 A Rubin Law,LLC -110 Wall -NY 10005 **Fx:**750-1235
(914) 333-0900 .. **Rubin,** Allan B '80 (Rubin & K) -660 Wht Plns Rd -Tarrytwn 10591 **Fx:**333-0495
(212) 264-9237 .. **Rubin,** Amy M '89 %US DOJ -26 Fed Plz -NY 10278 **Fx:**264-1916
(212) 310-8000 .. **Rubin,** Amy M '97 (Weil G&M LLP) -767 5th Av -NY 10153
(914) 761-9200 .. **Rubin,** Andrew A '74 (Mancuso R&F) -1 N Bway -White Plns 10601
(718) 250-2000 .. **Rubin,** Anna '07 %DA -350 Jay -Brklyn 11201 **Fx:**250-2314
(212) 735-3000 .. **Rubin,** Audrey Peltz '78 %Skadden ASM&F LLP -4 Times Sq -NY 10036
(212) 935-0900 .. **Rubin & Bailin,LLP** -501 Mad Av -NY 10022 **Fx:**826-9307
(516) 482-5020 .. **Rubin,** Barry '67 -5 The Hllws W -E Norwich 11732
(212) 302-6500 .. **Rubin,** Barry S '77 -500 5th Av -NY 10110
(914) 249-2000 .. **Rubin,** Bart H '00 %MasterCard Intl -2000 Purchase -Purchase 10577
(716) 635-1900 .. **Rubin,** Bethany A '00 %Kaplan HMAF&F -20 Lawrence Bell Dr -Buffalo 14214 **Fx:**634-0431
(212) 964-3300 .. **Rubin,** Brett E '06 %Rubin A LLP -225 Bway -NY 10007
(518) 270-9229 .. **Rubin,** Bruce B '85 -456 Bway -Troy 12180
(212) 768-6700 .. **Rubin,** Burton R '59 OfCnsl Sonnenschein N&R LLP -1221 Av of Amer -NY 10020
(212) 953-2381 .. **Rubin,** Chas T '74 (Rubin F&F,LLP) -292 Mad Av -NY 10017
(212) 449-7922 .. **Rubin,** Conrad P '95 %Merrill Lynch -4 Wrld Fncl Ctr -NY 10080
(516) 764-3335 .. **Rubin Cooper & Schwartz** -330 Sunrise Hwy -Rockvll Ctr 11570 **Fx:**536-5720
(212) 506-1700 .. **Rubin,** Craig E '06 Kasowitz BT&F LLP -1633 Bway -NY 10019
(917) 421-4655 .. **Rubin,** Curt M '86 IRS -33 Maiden Ln -NY 10038
(212) 412-9500 .. **Rubin,** Cynthia B '91 (Flemming ZWZ LLP) -1 Lbrty Plz -NY 10006
(212) 920-3072 .. **Rubin,** Dana B '00 %KamberEdelson,LLC -11 Bway -NY 10004 **Fx:**202-6364
(631) 393-5011 .. **Rubin,** Danl R '94 (Rubin & W,LLP) -200 Broadhllw Rd -Melvll 11747
(212) 554-7800 .. **Rubin,** Danl S '95 (Moses & S LLP) -405 Lex Av -NY 10174
(212) 907-7300 .. **Rubin,** David M '77 (Golenbock EAB&P) -437 Mad Av -NY 10022
(631) 952-5500 .. **Rubin,** David S J '65 -330 Vndrblt Motor Pkwy -Hauppauge 11788 **Fx:**952-5600
(631) 462-5888 .. **Rubin,** Debra L '91 (Rubin & R, PLLC) -6080 Jericho Tpk -Commack 11725
(212) 267-3700 .. **Rubin,** Denise A '91 %Napoli BR LLP -350 5th Av -NY 10118
(516) 773-8300 .. **Rubin,** Derrick A '85 %Wisselman H & Assoc,PC -1010 Nrthrn Blvd -Gt Neck 11021 **Fx:**773-8304
(212) 735-3000 .. **Rubin,** Diana R '05 %Skadden ASM&F LLP -4 Times Sq -NY 10036

(212) 759-4530 .. **Rubin DiPaola & DiPaola** -405 Park Av -NY 10022 **Fx:**319-0575
(212) 641-3200 .. **Rubin,** Edw '94 %NCH Advisors -712 5th Av -NY 10019 **Fx:**641-3201
(718) 871-1200 .. **Rubin,** Elliot M '83 -4915 12th Av -Brklyn 11219 **Fx:**972-0246
(212) 953-2381 .. **Rubin Fiorella & Friedman,LLP** -292 Mad Av -NY 10017 **Fx:**953-2462
(212) 586-2500 .. **Rubin,** Gabin B '95 Artists Rights Enfrcmnt Corp -1430 Bway -NY 10018 **Fx:**977-3110
(212) 788-0999 .. **Rubin,** Gail P '87 %Law Dept -100 Church -NY 10007 **Fx:**788-0367
(212) 686-7700 .. **Rubin,** Gary L '76 (Mazur CR&S PC) -1250 Bway -NY 10001
(718) 793-6400 .. **Rubin,** Harold J '96 -118-35 Qns Blvd -Frst Hlls 11375
(212) 596-9000 .. **Rubin,** Harry '96 (Ropes & G LLP) -1211 Av of Amer -NY 10036
(212) 471-8510 .. **Rubin,** Herbert '42 (Herzfeld & R,PC) -125 Broad -NY 10004
(212) 468-4800 .. **Rubin,** Howard J '73 (Davis & G LLP) -1740 Bway -NY 10019
(212) 695-8100 .. **Rubin,** Howard M '78 (Goetz F,LLP) -1 Penn Plz -NY 10119
(914) 948-1556 .. **Rubin,** Irwin N '75 OfCnsl Danziger & M LLP -123 Main -White Plns 10601
(212) 801-2226 .. **Rubin,** Israel '50 OfCnsl Greenberg T,LLP -200 Park Av -NY 10166
(212) 416-6046 .. **Rubin,** Ivan B '79 %Dept of Law -120 Bway -NY 10271
(212) 373-3000 .. **Rubin,** Jacqueline Pilar '01 (Paul WRW&G LLP) -1285 Av of Amer -NY 10019
(212) 988-0182 .. **Rubin,** Jane Gregory '76 -870 UN Plz -NY 10017
(973) 228-5700 .. **Rubin,** Jason A '07 %Brach E LLC -100 Park Av -NY 10017 **Fx:**228-7852
(212) 986-7353 .. **Rubin,** Jason M '94 %Wingate R&S -420 Lex Av -NY 10170
(212) 594-5000 .. **Rubin,** Jason P '05 Togut S&S LLP -1 Penn Plz -NY 10119
(914) 995-2508 .. **Rubin,** Jay '07 %Cnty Atty -148 Martine Av -White Plns 10601 **Fx:**995-5858
(212) 921-8399 .. **Rubin,** Jeannie Rose '07 %Lankler S&W LLP -500 5th Av -NY 10110
(212) 349-2844 .. **Rubin,** Jeffrey A '90 JA Rubin & Assoc,PC -225 Bway -NY 10007 **Fx:**732-6703
(212) 725-4600 .. **Rubin,** Jeffrey M '70 (Rubin & S) -9 E 40th -NY 10016
(212) 918-3000 .. **Rubin,** Jeffrey W '78 (Hogan L LLP) -875 3rd Av -NY 10022
(212) 856-8960 .. **Rubin,** Jennifer B '90 (Mintz LCFG&P,PC) -666 3rd Av -NY 10017
(212) 880-3800 .. **Rubin,** Jennifer L '04 %Akerman S -335 Mad Av -NY 10017
(212) 496-1865 .. **Rubin,** Jerilyn F '84 -303 W 66th -NY 10023
(212) 756-2000 .. **Rubin,** Jesse R '83 SpclCnsl Schulte R&Z LLP -919 3rd Av -NY 10022
(212) 964-3300 .. **Rubin,** Joel B '75 (Rubin A LLP) -225 Bway -NY 10007
(914) 923-7798 .. **Rubin,** John H '83 -2 Deer Tree Ln -Briarclff Mnr 10510 **Fx:**923-7793
(212) 980-9600 .. **Rubin,** Jonathan D '92 (Kaufman B&R) -120 Bway -NY 10271
(212) 935-0900 .. **Rubin,** Jos '65 (Rubin & B,LLP) -501 Mad Av -NY 10022
(347) 529-4676 .. **Rubin,** Joshua N '85 -30 Grafld Pl -Brklyn 11215
(212) 788-0995 .. **Rubin,** Joshua P '96 %Law Dept -100 Church -NY 10007 **Fx:**788-0367
(716) 856-1344 .. **Rubin,** Joshua P '03 %Bouvier Prtnrshp,LLP -350 Main -Buffalo 14202 **Fx:**856-1369
(212) 303-8049 .. **Rubin,** Julia '06 Hadassah Inc -50 W 58th -NY 10019
(212) 715-1000 .. **Rubin,** Karuna K '02 %Arnold & P LLP -399 Park Av -NY 10022
(212) 891-2116 .. **Rubin,** Kenneth L '89 Cerberus Capital Mgmt LP -299 Park Av -NY 10171
(212) 302-2900 .. **Rubin,** Laura Hoffberg '76 (Tannenbaum D&R) -1140 Av of Amer -NY 10036
(917) 992-6023 .. **Rubin,** Lauren P '08 US Dist Ct-SDNY -500 Pearl -NY 10007
(716) 845-6000 .. **Rubin,** Laurence K '78 Cnsl Kavinoky C LLP -726 Exchange -Buffalo 14210
(516) 357-3000 .. **Rubin,** Laurine M '97 (Rivkin R LLP) -926 RXR Plz -Uniondale 11556
(718) 613-2340 .. **Rubin,** Leslie A '92 %Hon R Levy -225 Cadman Plz E -Brklyn 11201
(516) 294-8229 .. **Rubin,** Leslie W '78 -1 E Cherry -Floral Pk 11001
(212) 468-4800 .. **Rubin,** Lewis A '85 (Davis & G LLP) -1740 Bway -NY 10019
(516) 227-2662 .. **Rubin & Licatesi,PC** -591 Stewart Av -Gdn Cty 11530 **Fx:**470-6498
(212) 882-6094 .. **Rubin,** Lina '01 %UBS -51 W 52nd -NY 10019
(212) 455-2000 .. **Rubin,** Lisa H '05 %Simpson T&B LLP -425 Lex Av -NY 10017
(646) 386-4031 .. **Rubin,** Lisa M '86 %Hon R Zweibel -100 Centre -NY 10013
(212) 310-8000 .. **Rubin,** Lois C '80 (Weil G&M LLP) -767 5th Av -NY 10153
(716) 634-6111 .. **Rubin,** Lois S '95 -3517 Genesee -Buffalo 14225 **Fx:**634-6222
(718) 282-4377 .. **Rubin,** Lowell M '77 -141 Argyle Rd -Brklyn 11218
(212) 308-9191 .. **Rubin,** Marc H '91 (Rubin & G) -488 Mad Av -NY 10022 **Fx:**308-1347
(518) 697-0393 .. **Rubin,** Margaret R '91 JP Morgan Chase -270 Park Av -NY 10017
(718) 231-1515 .. **Rubin,** Mark B '76 -3413 Wht Plns Rd -Bronx 10467 **Fx:**231-3003
(631) 723-0800 .. **Rubin,** Melinda A '93 -1 Jackson Av S -Hampton Bays 11946
(212) 804-4200 .. **Rubin,** Michl '01 %Mound CW&G -One Bttry Pk Plz -NY 10004
(914) 682-1600 .. **Rubin,** Michl A '71 -81 Main #118 -White Plns 10601
(212) 691-9393 .. **Rubin,** Michl F '87 (Kelly & R,LLP) -275 7th Av -NY 10001
(516) 248-0660 .. **Rubin,** Morton '61 -28 Martin Pl -Syosset 11791
(212) 455-2000 .. **Rubin,** Nicole B '10 %Simpson T&B LLP -425 Lex Av -NY 10017
(212) 679-5000 .. **Rubin,** Norman '51 -301 E 66th -NY 10065 **Fx:**628-1247
(212) 592-1400 .. **Rubin,** Paul A '92 (Herrick,F LLP) -2 Park Av -NY 10016
(212) 686-0100 .. **Rubin,** Peter G '94 %Frank FG&N,LLP -1430 Bway -NY 10018
(516) 764-3335 .. **Rubin,** Peter M '68 (Rubin C&S) -330 Sunrise Hwy -Rockvll Ctr 11570
(516) 829-6262 .. **Rubin,** Philip H '86 -175 Grt Nck Rd -Gt Neck 11021
(212) 487-9700 .. **Rubin,** Rebecca L '04 %White F&F,LLP -61 Bway -NY 10006
(212) 704-6000 .. **Rubin,** Richd A '67 (Troutman S LLP) -405 Lex Av -NY 10174
(212) 593-6700 .. **Rubin,** Richd E '74 %Aaronson RF&D,LLP -757 3rd Av -NY 10017
(516) 227-2662 .. **Rubin,** Richd H '76 (Rubin & L,PC) -591 Stewart Av -Gdn Cty 11530
(914) 381-7400 .. **Rubin,** Richd J '58 OfCnsl Rattet P&G,LLP -550 Mamaroneck Av -Harrison 10528
(212) 609-6800 .. **Rubin,** Robt A '64 SpclCnsl McCarter & E,LLP -245 Park Av -NY 10167
(914) 681-8700 .. **Rubin,** Robyn S '86 %Milber MP&S LLP -3 Barker Av -White Plns 10601
(212) 508-6700 .. **Rubin,** Ronald L '94 Cnsl Tannenbaum HS&H LLP -900 3rd Av -NY 10022
(631) 462-5888 .. **Rubin & Rosenblum, PLLC** -6080 Jericho Tpk -Commack 11725 **Fx:**462-5889
(631) 234-1500 .. **Rubin & Rothman LLC** -1787 Vets Hwy -Islandia 11749 **Fx:**234-1138
(212) 340-7300 .. **Rubin,** Saml J '01 Amber Capital -153 E 53rd -NY 10022
(516) 393-6116 .. **Rubin,** Saml K '89 -999 Stewart Av -Bethpage 11714 **Fx:**393-6150
(212) 483-2323 .. **Rubin,** Sarah Greenlee '93 %JP Morgan Chase -345 Park Av -NY 10154
(212) 849-7000 .. **Rubin,** Sarah L '08 %Quinn EU&S,LLP -51 Mad Av -NY 10010
(516) 248-7575 .. **Rubin,** Scott D '81 (Levine & G) -114 Old Cntry Rd -Mineola 11501
(516) 663-6600 .. **Rubin,** Seth I '95 %Ruskin MF,PC -1425 RXR Plz -Uniondale 11556
(212) 725-4600 .. **Rubin & Shang** -9 E 40th -NY 10016 **Fx:**725-4799
(718) 286-2416 .. **Rubin,** Stanley M '88 %Leg Aid -120-46 Qns Blvd -Kew Gdns 11415 **Fx:**286-2286
(212) 969-3000 .. **Rubin,** Stephen W '77 (Proskauer R LLP) -1585 Bway -NY 10036
(212) 643-5402 .. **Rubin,** Steven A '89 (SA Rubin & Assoc,PLLC) -350 5th Av -NY 10118 **Fx:**594-4082
(914) 220-0276 .. **Rubin,** Steven A '96 LCP Grp -711 Wstchstr Av -White Plns 10604
(516) 336-2684 .. **Rubin,** Steven G '72 -100 Jericho Quad -Jericho 11753 **Fx:**336-2688
(212) 742-8700 .. **Rubin,** Steven I '00 (Garson D&C LLP) -110 Wall -NY 10005
(718) 802-0778 .. **Rubin,** Stuart D '83 -26 Court -Brklyn 11242 **Fx:**802-0831
(516) 579-6200 .. **Rubin,** Susan A '99 %Solomon & H,PLLC -2950 Hempstd Tpk -Levittwn 11756 **Fx:**579-2409
(914) 428-9766 .. **Rubin,** Susan B '83 (Heilman & R) -399 Knollwood Rd -White Plns 10603 **Fx:**285-9769
(516) 433-3000 .. **Rubin,** Todd M '96 %Finz & F,PC -410 E Jericho Tpk -Mineola 11501 **Fx:**433-3001
(212) 983-1199 .. **Rubin,** Tyler R '05 %Cutler M&A,LLP -708 3rd Av -NY 10017
(212) 697-8590 .. **Rubin,** Victor R '69 (Rubin M Intl Law,PC) -303 5th Av -NY 10016 **Fx:**687-1407
(516) 741-5252 .. **Rubin,** Wayne M '79 Sanders SBWV&G,PC -100 Hrrcks Rd -Mineola 11501
(631) 393-5011 .. **Rubin & Weissman,LLP** -200 Broadhllw Rd -Melvll 11747 **Fx:**393-5047
(914) 481-5779 .. **Rubin,** Wm '57 Riad & Assoc,PC -350 Theo Fremd Av -Rye 10580 **Fx:**315-0103
(212) 309-1000 .. **Rubin,** Woodward L '08 %Hunton & W -200 Park Av -NY 10166
(212) 374-9333 .. **Rubin,** Yana '01 -11 Bway -NY 10004 **Fx:**374-9111
(212) 819-8200 .. **Rubin,** Yulia '05 %White & C LLP -1155 Av of Amer -NY 10036
(212) 465-6000 .. **Rubin-Carter,** Denise D '87 %Madison Sq Grdn,LP -2 Penn Plz -NY 10121 **Fx:**465-6011
(631) 224-2700 .. **Rubin-de-Cervens,** Andrea '84 -265 E Main -E Islip 11730 **Fx:**224-3760
(516) 739-0003 .. **Rubine,** Marilyn C '84 (Rubine & R) -114 Old Cntry Rd -Mineola 11501 **Fx:**739-1379
(516) 739-0003 .. **Rubine,** Robt S '72 (Rubine & R) -114 Old Cntry Rd -Mineola 11501 **Fx:**739-1379
(516) 801-9541 .. **Rubinfeld,** Edw '98 Pall Corp -25 Hrbr Park Dr -Pt Wash 11050
(212) 754-9400 .. **Rubinger,** Robt '49 -425 Park Av -NY 10022 **Fx:**754-6262
(914) 682-7800 .. **Rubin Goldstein,** Marsha '87 OfCnsl Zarin & S -81 Main -White Plns 10601
(518) 873-9242 .. **Rubino,** Carl J Jr. '74 -Court Bx817 -Elizabethtwn 12932
(212) 267-4177 .. **Rubino,** Carmine A '97 (Kramer DL&M) -217 Bway -NY 10007
(914) 683-1200 .. **Rubino,** Frank J '88 OfCnsl Harris B PLLC -445 Hmltn Av -White Plns 10601
(212) 983-8500 .. **Rubino,** Frank J Jr. '00 %Brown G&F LLP -355 Lex Av -NY 10017
(914) 995-3338 .. **Rubino,** Gary M '89 %DA -111 Martin Luther King Blvd -White Plns 10601 **Fx:**995-3363
(917) 399-1882 .. **Rubino,** JenniElena '07 -34 Olympus Rd -Highland Mills 10930
(212) 909-5604 .. **Rubino,** Mark D '09 KPMG LLP -757 3rd Av -NY 10017
(516) 747-1990 .. **Rubino,** Olympia '00 %Cascone & K,LLP -1399 Franklin Av -Gdn Cty 11530
(212) 458-1956 .. **Rubino,** Stephanie B '88 AIG -175 Water -NY 10038
(212) 824-5700 .. **Rubino,** Victor J '65 %Practising Law Inst -810 7th Av -NY 10019
(212) 425-7200 .. **Rubino,** Vincent J III '08 %Kenyon & K,LLP -1 Bway -NY 10004
(212) 848-4000 .. **Rubinov,** Elena V '04 %Shearman & S LLP -599 Lex Av -NY 10022
(212) 943-1090 .. **Rubinowitz,** Ben B '81 (Gair GCSMB&R) -80 Pine -NY 10005
(516) 741-5000 .. **Rubinowitz,** Michl '93 (Bass & R) -1 Old Cntry Rd -Carle Pl 11514
(212) 818-9200 .. **Rubins,** Joshua M '76 (Satterlee SB&B LLP) -230 Park Av -NY 10169
(212) 686-4401 .. **Rubinshteyn,** Steve A '98 %Abramson Law Grp PLLC -570 Lex Av -NY 10022 **Fx:**686-6515
(212) 728-8000 .. **Rubinsky,** David E '98 (Willkie F&G LLP) -787 7th Av -NY 10019
(212) 337-4204 .. **Rubinsky,** E H '85 %Thomson Reuters/RIA -195 Bway -NY 10007
(212) 298-5152 .. **Rubinsky,** Paulette A '83 %Leg Aid -49 Thomas -NY 10013 **Fx:**298-5252
(212) 857-8800 .. **Rubinson,** Eva S '03 US Ct Appls 2nd Circ -40 Foley Sq -NY 10007 **Fx:**857-8898
(212) 836-8000 .. **Rubinstein,** Aaron '76 (Kaye S LLP) -425 Park Av -NY 10022
(212) 802-1020 .. **Rubinstein,** Alan J '89 Berkshire Bk -4 E 39th -NY 10016
(212) 888-6600 .. **Rubinstein,** Asher '97 (Rubinstein & R,LLP) -18 E 48th -NY 10022 **Fx:**888-7443
(212) 408-5100 .. **Rubinstein,** Benjamin C '04 %Chadbourne & P LLP -30 Rckfllr Plz -NY 10112
(212) 806-5400 .. **Rubinstein,** Benjamin I '09 %Stroock &S&L LLP -180 Maiden Ln -NY 10038
(718) 438-8220 .. **Rubinstein,** Chas J '96 -1476A 54th -Brklyn 11219 **Fx:**438-0262
(212) 545-8777 .. **Rubinstein & Corozzo,PC** -260 Mad Av -NY 10016 **Fx:**679-1844
(212) 319-4000 .. **Rubinstein,** David P '90 %Weiss & H,PC -600 Mad Av -NY 10022
(212) 285-1200 .. **Rubinstein,** Eric W '95 %Mallin & Assoc,PC -132 Nassau -NY 10038 **Fx:**285-1202
(212) 808-7800 .. **Rubinstein,** Frederic A '55 (Kelley D&W LLP) -101 Park Av -NY 10178
(212) 279-1069 .. **Rubinstein,** H Jonathan '93 (Feinsilver Law Grp,PC) -26 Court -Brklyn 11242 **Fx:**(973) 376-4405
(315) 448-4800 .. **Rubinstein,** Heather R '98 %Dept of Law -615 Erie Blvd W -Syracuse 13204 **Fx:**448-4853
(212) 788-1571 .. **Rubinstein,** Heidi B '81 %Law Dept -100 Church -NY 10007 **Fx:**788-0367

(212) 848-4000 .. **Rubinstein,** Ivan S L '08 %Shearman & S LLP -599 Lex Av -NY 10022
(516) 741-6565 .. **Rubinstein,** Jack '79 (Meyer SE&K,PC) -990 Stewart Av Bx9194 -Gdn Cty 11530
(212) 833-1131 .. **Rubinstein,** Jason C '04 %Friedman KS&A LLP -1633 Bway -NY 10019 **Fx:**373-7931
(212) 547-5400 .. **Rubinstein,** Joel L '95 (McDermott W&E LLP) -340 Mad Av -NY 10173
(718) 590-5258 .. **Rubinstein,** Jonathan D '09 %Law Dept -198 E 161st -Bronx 10451 **Fx:**590-2686
(212) 354-3104 .. **Rubinstein,** Keith E '97 -2 Aspen Ln -Gt Neck 11021 **Fx:**768-3516
(516) 581-3334 .. **Rubinstein,** Kenneth '69 -1550 Bway -NY 10036
(212) 888-6600 .. **Rubinstein,** Kenneth '80 (Rubinstein & R,LLP) -18 E 48th -NY 10022 **Fx:**888-7443
(212) 659-7300 .. **Rubinstein,** Kenneth J '94 (Haynes & B,LLP) -1221 Av of Amer -NY 10020
(212) 455-2000 .. **Rubinstein,** Kevin L '08 %Simpson T&B LLP -425 Lex Av -NY 10017
(631) 761-7000 .. **Rubinstein,** Leif I '78 %Touro Cllg Law Ctr -225 Eastvw Dr -Central Islip 11722
(212) 533-6300 .. **Rubinstein,** Mitchell H '87 %NYSUT -52 Bway -NY 10004 **Fx:**995-2347
(212) 474-1000 .. **Rubinstein,** Nicole M '07 %Cravath S&M LLP -825 8th Av -NY 10019
(212) 683-9700 .. **Rubinstein,** Richd C '90 GNY Mutual Ins -200 Mad Av -NY 10016 **Fx:**843-1962
(718) 543-2600 .. **Rubinstein,** Robt J '59 -555 W 235th -Bronx 10463 **Fx:**543-2945
(212) 545-8777 .. **Rubinstein,** Ronald '64 (Rubinstein & C,PC) -260 Mad Av -NY 10016
(716) 856-5500 .. **Rubinstein,** Steven I '92 (Damon M LLP) -200 Delaware Av -Buffalo 14202
(212) 421-9630 .. **Rubinstein,** Suzette Simon '90 %Smythe Masterson & Judd -230 Park Av -NY 10169 **Fx:**421-9665
(212) 407-4000 .. **Rubinstein,** Vadim '98 (Loeb & L,LLP) -345 Park Av -NY 10154
(212) 522-4930 .. **Rubinstein Sternlicht,** Ilissa '93 Time Inc -1271 Av of Amer -NY 10020
(631) 421-9051 .. **Rubinton,** Peter D '61 OfCnsl Goldstein RG&D,PC -18 W Carver -Huntngtn 11743
(212) 530-5000 .. **Rubio,** Chas M '08 %Milbank TH&M LLP -1 Chase Manh Plz -NY 10005
(212) 810-5946 .. **Rublin,** Arthur S '97 SrCnsl BlackRock -40 E 52nd -NY 10022 **Fx:**810-5116
(212) 808-7800 .. **Rublin,** Joel S '81 (Kelley D&W LLP) -101 Park Av -NY 10178
(646) 784-1850 .. **Rubloff,** Rebecca S '98 %Admin Childrens Srvcs -150 William -NY 10038
(212) 245-1155 .. **Rublowsky,** Michl J '07 MJ Rublowsky LLC -180 Riverside Blvd -NY 10069
(212) 965-0010 .. **Rubman,** Scott A '75 -580 Bway -NY 10012 **Fx:**965-1301
(212) 553-4683 .. **Rubock,** Danl B '80 %Moody's Invstr Srvc -250 Greenwich -NY 10007
(518) 369-9717 .. **Rubtchinsky,** Ira Paul '68 -7 Hrdng -Albany 12208
(917) 617-6043 .. **Ruby,** Annette L '98 -241 86th -Brklyn 11209 **Fx:**(718) 491-1278
(646) 447-7833 .. **Ruby,** Joan '82 Emblem Health -55 Water -NY 10041
(516) 797-0991 .. **Rucci,** Frank J '90 -Bx455 -Massapequa 11758
(212) 238-4800 .. **Ruccia,** Diane J '05 (Landman CB&F,PC) -120 Bway -NY 10271
(716) 856-5500 .. **Ruchala,** Heidi Brauer '99 (Damon M LLP) -200 Delaware Av -Buffalo 14202
(516) 483-4848 .. **Ruchala,** Jos F '70 -230 Hilton Av -Hempstd 11550 **Fx:**292-3953
(212) 755-3333 .. **Ruchelman,** Stanley C '86 (SC Ruchelman) -150 E 58th -NY 10155 **Fx:**755-5898
(718) 821-6060 .. **Rucigay,** Emil J '53 (Rucigay & R) -69-03 Fresh Pond Rd -Rdgwd 11385 **Fx:**821-7470
(718) 821-6060 .. **Rucigay,** John D '86 (Rucigay & R) -69-03 Fresh Pond Rd -Rdgwd 11385 **Fx:**821-7470
(716) 857-7991 .. **Rucinski,** Randy C '92 Natl Fuel Gas -6363 Main -Williamsvll 14221 **Fx:**857-7614
(212) 349-5400 .. **Ruck,** David E '73 -120 Bway -NY 10271 **Fx:**349-5444
(212) 407-4000 .. **Ruckel,** Laurie S '83 (Loeb & L,LLP) -345 Park Av -NY 10154
(212) 285-3025 .. **Ruckelshaus,** Catherine Kiley '96 %NELP -75 Maiden Ln -NY 10038 **Fx:**285-3044
(718) 520-2215 .. **Rucker,** Elise Lara '95 Hon W Erlbaum -125-01 Qns Blvd -Kew Gdns 11415
(718) 590-2000 .. **Rucker,** Jeannette M '91 %DA -198 E 161st -Bronx 10451 **Fx:**590-6477
(212) 593-1000 .. **Rucker,** Steven M '76 (Kroll Assoc) -1166 Av of Amer -NY 10036 **Fx:**593-2631
(315) 326-0128 .. **Rucynski Coleman,** Lou Anne '00 -92 W 6th -Oswego 13126 **Fx:**326-0129
(212) 335-9000 .. **Ruda,** Gabrielle B '05 %DA -1 Hogan Pl -NY 10013
(212) 478-7265 .. **Ruda,** Howard '59 OfCnsl Hahn & H LLP -488 Mad Av -NY 10022
(631) 725-4778 .. **Rudansky,** Danl '82 -36 Woodvale -Sag Hbr 11963 **Fx:**725-8685
(516) 569-3231 .. **Rudansky,** Saml R '89 -212 Oakwood Av -Cedarhrst 11516
(212) 223-0400 .. **Rudd,** Kenneth C '97 OfCnsl Zeichner E&K LLP -575 Lex Av -NY 10022
(212) 888-2300 .. **Rudd,** Mark S '78 -149 Mad Av -NY 10016 **Fx:**888-7711
(212) 477-5125 .. **Rudden,** John P '78 -111 E 14th Bx 513 -NY 10003
(212) 826-9900 .. **Rudder,** Paul E '69 -110 E 59th -NY 10022 **Fx:**581-8958
(212) 626-4100 .. **Rudder,** Richd D '67 (Baker & M LLP) -1114 Av of Amer -NY 10036
(315) 472-7250 .. **Rudderow,** Michelle '05 %SR Williams,PLLC -250 Harrison -Syracuse 13202 **Fx:**476-5350
(212) 558-4000 .. **Ruddy,** Erica L '09 %Sullivan & C LLP -125 Broad -NY 10004
(718) 268-7740 .. **Ruddy,** Francis D '82 -12360 83rd Av -Kew Gdns 11415
(212) 376-6400 .. **Ruddy,** James J '76 OfCnsl Marshall DWC&G -88 Pine -NY 10005
(914) 517-5000 .. **Ruddy,** Joan M '94 Meiselman DPC&E,PC -1311 Mamaroneck Av -White Plns 10605
(516) 571-3800 .. **Ruddy,** Mary B '90 %DA -262 Old Cntry Rd -Mineola 11501 **Fx:**248-9479
(212) 789-4950 .. **Ruddy,** Roberta E '82 %Chase Manhattan Bk -1211 Av of Amer -NY 10036 **Fx:**944-0959
(212) 207-8400 .. **Rudell,** Joel M '69 (Kavanagh M&O LLP) -415 Mad Av -NY 10017
(212) 935-5500 .. **Rudell,** Michl I '67 (Franklin WR&V) -488 Mad Av -NY 10022
(212) 566-7188 .. **Ruden,** Eric W '09 %Genova B&G -115 Bway -NY 10006
(212) 790-0229 .. **Rudenstine,** David M '70 %Benj N Cardozo Schl of Law -55 5th Av -NY 10003 **Fx:**790-0345
(212) 689-1113 .. **Ruderman,** Barry M '65 %Garbarini & S,PC -432 Park Av S -NY 10016
(212) 661-6800 .. **Ruderman,** Jeffrey C '91 OfCnsl Cyruli SH&Z LLP -420 Lex Av -NY 10170
(914) 323-7000 .. **Ruderman,** Jerold R '67 OfCnsl Wilson EME&D LLP -3 Gannett Dr -White Plns 10604
(973) 992-4800 .. **Ruderman,** Suzanne J '96 %Fox R LLP -100 Park Av -NY 10017 **Fx:**992-9125
(212) 818-1975 .. **Rudes,** Saul '58 -276 5th Av -NY 10001
(212) 260-5650 .. **Rudgayzer,** Albert '97 -116 E 16th -NY 10003
(212) 859-8000 .. **Rudgayzer,** Steven '08 %Fried FHS&J LLP -1 NY Plz -NY 10004
(518) 585-6737 .. **Rudgers,** David E '88 (Viscardi H&R LLP) -15 Father Jogues Pl -Ticonderoga 12883 **Fx:**585-3572
(914) 934-9200 .. **Rudich,** Fran '87 %Klafter O&L LLP -2 Intl Dr -Rye Brook 10573 **Fx:**934-9220
(718) 876-6300 .. **Rudich,** Yolanda L '83 %DA -130 Styvsnt Pl -Staten Isl 10301 **Fx:**488-5784
(212) 233-3800 .. **Rudick,** Elliot M '67 E Rudick -225 Bway -NY 10007
(212) 319-4000 .. **Rudick,** Lauren A '05 %Weiss & H,PC -600 Mad Av -NY 10022
(845) 331-4520 .. **Rudikoff,** Dana L '01 -369 Wshngtn Av -Kingston 12401 **Fx:**331-4579
(718) 250-2000 .. **Rudikoff,** John L '07 %DA -350 Jay -Brklyn 11201 **Fx:**250-2314
(607) 274-5461 .. **Rudin,** Bradley L '92 %DA -320 N Tioga -Ithaca 14850 **Fx:**274-5429
(631) 462-9094 .. **Rudin,** Ellen S '88 -3 Durham Dr -Huntngtn Sta 11746
(516) 466-0033 .. **Rudin,** Fredk S '74 -475 Nrthrn Blvd -Gt Neck 11021 **Fx:**466-3867
(212) 752-7600 .. **Rudin,** Joel B '79 -200 W 57th -NY 10019 **Fx:**980-2968
(212) 506-2500 .. **Rudin,** Yuli '07 %Mayer B LLP -1675 Bway -NY 10019
(212) 849-7000 .. **Rudis,** Alexander '04 %Quinn EU&S,LLP -51 Mad Av -NY 10010
(212) 848-4000 .. **Rudloff Schoenmakers,** Christian E '09 %Shearman & S LLP -599 Lex Av -NY 10022
(516) 921-8888 .. **Rudman,** Alexis F '07 Natl Learning Corp -212 Michl Dr -Syosset 11791 **Fx:**921-8743
(516) 643-4006 .. **Rudman,** Leslie P '76 -47 Eagle Chase -Woodbury 11797 **Fx:**741-7485
(516) 921-8859 .. **Rudman,** Michl P '76 %NLC -212 Michl Dr -Syosset 11791
(631) 367-7100 .. **Rudman,** Saml H '93 (Coughlin SGR&R LLP) -58 S Srvc Rd -Melvll 11747
(631) 665-3400 .. **Rudner,** Mark A '91 (Siben & S,LLP) -90 E Main Bx149P -Bay Shr 11706
(212) 909-5396 .. **Rudnick,** Jill L '00 KPMG LLP -757 3rd Av -NY 10017
(315) 685-4551 .. **Rudnick,** M Jack '74 %Welch Allyn,Inc -4341 State Street Rd -Skaneateles Fls 13153 **Fx:**685-1769
(212) 687-1980 .. **Rudnick,** Nicholas J '09 %Kaplan F&K LLP -850 3rd Av -NY 10022
(212) 848-4000 .. **Rudnick,** Robt A '73 (Shearman & S LLP) -599 Lex Av -NY 10022
(973) 596-4727 .. **Rudnick,** Robt E '92 (Gibbons PC) -1 Penn Plz -NY 10119 **Fx:**639-8318
(718) 243-6446 .. **Rudnick,** Scott L '98 %Leg Aid -111 Lvngstn -Brklyn 11201 **Fx:**237-8737
(212) 983-8500 .. **Rudnicki,** Evan B '06 %Brown G&F LLP -355 Lex Av -NY 10017
(716) 823-5959 .. **Rudnicki,** Paul E '67 -2732 Seneca Bx527 -W Seneca 14224
(212) 977-9700 .. **Rudoff,** Sheldon '58 (Phillips N LLP) -666 5th Av -NY 10103
(212) 410-4993 .. **Rudoff,** Surie '80 -55 E 87th -NY 10128 **Fx:**860-0256
(718) 261-5235 .. **Rudofsky,** Barry S '85 %A Bronstein Real Est -108-18 Qns Blvd -Frst Hlls 11375 **Fx:**520-8907
(212) 245-2222 .. **Rudofsky,** Edw S '74 (Zane and R) -601 W 26th -NY 10001
(631) 673-1919 .. **Rudofsky,** Edw S '74 -5 Arrowwood Ln -Melvll 11747
(516) 294-4568 .. **Rudolf,** Karen J '93 (K Rudolf,PC) -200 Old Cntry Rd -Mineola 11501 **Fx:**294-4569
(212) 381-2921 .. **Rudolf,** Richd G '73 %Sulzer US Inc -245 Park Av -NY 10167
(516) 829-0363 .. **Rudolph,** Brian E '03 %Israel I&P,LLP -11 Grace Av -Gt Neck 11021 **Fx:**829-0366
(212) 869-5300 .. **Rudolph,** Helene S '92 %CPC -28 E 28th -NY 10016 **Fx:**683-2909
(212) 783-3722 .. **Rudolph,** James V '07 Citigroup Trust -485 Lex Av -NY 10017
(212) 382-3300 .. **Rudolph,** Jennifer L '03 %Wollmuth M&D LLP -500 5th Av -NY 10110
(212) 741-3344 .. **Rudolph,** L Michl '61 LM Rudolph,PC -100 Park Av -NY 10017 **Fx:**741-4666
(914) 949-2700 .. **Rudolph,** Nancy J '78 OfCnsl Bleakley P&S,LLP -1 N Lex Av -White Plns 10601
(212) 723-6088 .. **Rudolph,** Ronald M '92 %Citibank -388 Greenwich -NY 10013
(212) 685-9800 .. **Rudoltz,** Debra L '94 %Counsel Press,LLC -520 8th Av -NY 10018
(212) 290-2925 .. **Rudrakumaran,** Visuvanathan '93 -875 Av of Amer -NY 10001
(516) 334-2500 .. **Rudy,** Brian R '74 (Feldman RK&F,PC) -410 Jericho Tpk -Jericho 11753
(212) 969-3000 .. **Rudy,** Daniella M '07 %Proskauer R LLP -1585 Bway -NY 10036
(212) 506-2500 .. **Rudy,** George E '06 %Mayer B LLP -1675 Bway -NY 10019
(914) 637-5849 .. **Rudy,** Michl J '04 Sidney Frank Importing Co -20 Cedar -New Rchll 10801
(212) 629-6956 .. **Rudy,** Richd I '86 Stillwater Capital Prtnrs -41 Mad Av -NY 10010
(718) 340-7000 .. **Rudyk,** Andrew '85 %FDA-NE Region -158-15 Lbrty Av -Jamaica 11433
(718) 376-4766 .. **Rudyuk,** Ksenia '08 %Bukh & Assoc -1123 Av Z -Brklyn 11235 **Fx:**376-3033
(212) 326-2000 .. **Rudzin,** Abby F '03 (O'Melveny & M LLP) -7 Times Sq -NY 10036
(716) 848-9000 .. **Rudzinski,** Eugene A '80 (Underberg & K LLP) -1900 Main Pl Twr -Buffalo 14202
(212) 819-8200 .. **Rue,** John D '05 %White & C LLP -1155 Av of Amer -NY 10036
(914) 946-1400 .. **Rueckel,** Gail A '92 %Vouté LM&C,LLP -170 Hmltn Av -White Plns 10601
(212) 596-9000 .. **Rueckheim,** Michl R '09 %Ropes & G LLP -1211 Av of Amer -NY 10036
(646) 414-6869 .. **Rueda,** Andres '02 %Lowenstein S PC -1251 Av of Amer -NY 10020 **Fx:**(973) 422-6883
(212) 425-7200 .. **Ruedy,** Matthew C '10 %Kenyon & K,LLP -1 Bway -NY 10004
(212) 768-6700 .. **Ruegger,** Arthur H '78 (Sonnenschein N&R LLP) -1221 Av of Amer -NY 10020
(212) 455-2000 .. **Ruegger,** Philip T III '75 (Simpson T&B LLP) -425 Lex Av -NY 10017
(212) 335-4500 .. **Rueh,** Mark W '97 (DLA Piper LLP) -1251 Av of Amer -NY 10020
(212) 210-9588 .. **Ruehl,** Wm Bernard '01 %Alston & B LLP -90 Park Av -NY 10016

(585) 232-4090 .. **Ruehle,** Walter H '80 %Leg Aid -1 W Main -Rchstr 14614 **Fx:**232-2352
(212) 571-0550 .. **Ruesch,** Lisa L '03 %Allegaert B&V LLP -111 Bway -NY 10006
(212) 756-2000 .. **Ruesch,** Matthew J '10 %Schulte R&Z LLP -919 3rd Av -NY 10022
(212) 269-4900 .. **Ruesch,** Meghan E '09 %Ford MEW&G,LLP -Wall Street Plz -NY 10005
(516) 571-2766 .. **Ruescher,** Mary Lou A '81 %Supreme Ct -Supreme Ct Bldg -Mineola 11501
(718) 990-1831 .. **Ruescher,** Robt A '81 %St John's Law Schl -8000 Utopia Pkwy -Jamaica 11439 **Fx:**591-1855
(212) 326-3939 .. **Rue Wittstein,** Jane A '88 (Jones D) -222 E 41st -NY 10017
(212) 685-8515 .. **Ruf,** James A '71 (Ruf & B) -270 Mad Av -NY 10016 **Fx:**685-8516
(212) 685-8515 .. **Ruf,** Maureen Basquill '95 (Ruf & B) -270 Mad Av -NY 10016 **Fx:**685-8516
(212) 506-5000 .. **Ruff,** David M '09 %Orrick H&S LLP -51 W 52nd -NY 10019
(516) 292-8100 .. **Ruff,** Douglas R '78 %Nassau/Sfflk Law Srv -1 Helen Keller Way -Hempstd 11550 **Fx:**292-6529
(631) 390-8338 .. **Ruff,** Gary W '93 -200 Broadhllw Rd -Melvll 11747
(212) 909-5000 .. **Ruff,** Lauren D '02 %KPMG LLP -757 3rd Av -NY 10017
(212) 697-6555 .. **Ruff,** Leslie F '74 (Biedermann RH&R) -570 Lex Av -NY 10022
(585) 238-2000 .. **Ruff,** Raymond L '91 (Phillips L LLP) -1400 First Fed Plz -Rchstr 14614
(212) 759-4888 .. **Ruff,** Raymond L '91 (Phillips L LLP) -437 Mad Av -NY 10022
(212) 355-0606 .. **Ruffa,** Wm P Sr. '59 (Ruffa & R) -110 E 59th -NY 10022 **Fx:**759-7696
(212) 355-0606 .. **Ruffa,** Wm P Jr. '87 (Ruffa & R) -110 E 59th -NY 10022 **Fx:**759-7696
(315) 474-7571 .. **Ruffer,** Anne B '84 (Mackenzie H LLP) -101 S Salina Bx4967 -Syracuse 13221
(212) 481-8464 .. **Ruffer,** Wm C '85 -200 Mad Av -NY 10016 **Fx:**779-7295
(718) 876-6429 .. **Ruffini,** Anthony P '03 SpclCnsl US Supreme Ct -355 Front -Staten Isl 10304 **Fx:**876-6428
(212) 418-4700 .. **Ruffini,** Peter J '07 Icon Capital Corp -100 5th Av -NY 10011
(212) 841-1000 .. **Ruffino,** Andrew A '96 (Covington & B LLP) -620 8th Av -NY 10018
(914) 766-4234 .. **Ruffino,** Jos W '90 IBM -294 Route 100 -Somers 10589
(212) 688-5151 .. **Ruffino,** Stephen F '79 (Gibney A&F,LLP) -665 5th Av -NY 10022
(212) 323-5231 .. **Ruffle,** Adrienne M '03 Oppeheimer Funds -225 Lbrty -NY 10281
(518) 218-2088 .. **Ruffo,** David A '83 (Ruffo TM&M PC) -300 Great Oaks Blvd -Albany 12203
(212) 751-8000 .. **Ruffo,** Edw A '92 (Dankner & M,PC) -41 E 57th -NY 10022
(518) 218-2088 .. **Ruffo Tabora Mainello & McKay PC** -300 Great Oaks Blvd -Albany 12203 **Fx:**218-2086
(585) 388-5262 .. **Ruffo Tabora Mainello & McKay PC** -145 Sullys Trl -Pittsfrd 14534 **Fx:**586-4833
(516) 328-9201 .. **Ruffo Tabora Mainello & McKay PC** -3000 Marcus Av -Lk Success 11042 **Fx:**328-9203
(718) 703-1004 .. **Rugg,** Janet V '93 -1505 Albemarle Rd -Brklyn 11226
(845) 291-2050 .. **Ruggeri,** Richd E '83 %DA -255-275 Main -Goshen 10924 **Fx:**291-2085
(518) 443-5400 .. **Ruggeri,** Robt E '93 %SUNY Univ Cnsl -S333 SUNY Plz -Albany 12246 **Fx:**443-5409
(718) 680-1520 .. **Ruggieri,** Catherine J '99 -9437 Shore Rd -Brklyn 11209
(718) 824-3133 .. **Ruggieri,** John M '94 -1821 Pilgrim Av -Bronx 10461
(212) 446-2300 .. **Ruggieri,** Kate Tenney '02 %Boies S&F LLP -575 Lex Av -NY 10022
(212) 696-6000 .. **Ruggiero,** Carl A '83 (Curtis M-PC&M LLP) -101 Park Av -NY 10178
(212) 972-1000 .. **Ruggiero,** Christopher E '05 %London F LLP -59 Maiden Ln -NY 10038
(212) 715-1000 .. **Ruggiero,** Jeffrey R '91 (Arnold & P LLP) -399 Park Av -NY 10022
(716) 842-5261 .. **Ruggiero,** Jennifer C '99 M&T Bank Corp -1 M&T Plz -Buffalo 14203
(212) 264-9372 .. **Ruggiero,** JoAnn M '83 Merit Sys Prtctn Bd -26 Fed Plz -NY 10278 **Fx:**264-1417
(516) 294-4180 .. **Ruggiero,** John P '91 (Canfield M&R,LLP) -1461 Franklin Av -Gdn Cty 11530
(914) 476-6666 .. **Ruggiero,** Jos A '95 %Vido Restaurant Inc -351 Saw Mill Rvr Rd -Ynkrs 10701
(718) 745-8888 .. **Ruggiero,** Jos F Jr. '77 Ruggiero & R -26 Hilton Av -Gdn Cty 11530 **Fx:**(516) 561-0315
(212) 406-2910 .. **Ruggiero,** Lawr F '78 -167 E 61st -NY 10065
(212) 732-0002 .. **Ruggiero,** Louis J '86 (Cohen F&R,LLP) -20 Vesey -NY 10007
(718) 680-3293 .. **Ruggiero,** Margaret R '52 -7014 13th Av -Brklyn 11228
(718) 590-3942 .. **Ruggiero,** Richd R '75 %Hon G Esposito -851 Grnd Cncrs -Bronx 10451
(212) 218-2100 .. **Rugh,** Aaron J '09 %Fitzpatrick CH&S -1290 Av of Amer -NY 10104
(516) 741-2585 .. **Rugino,** Edw '96 %Rosicki R & Assoc,PC -51 E Bethpage Rd -Plainvw 11803 **Fx:**741-4748
(585) 724-4000 .. **Ruh,** Jos F Jr. '84 Eastman Kodak Co -343 State -Rchstr 14650
(516) 747-3200 .. **Ruh,** Olga '04 %Berwitz & D LLP -310 Old Cntry Rd -Gdn Cty 11530
(212) 530-5000 .. **Ruha,** Gabrielle L '08 %Milbank TH&M LLP -1 Chase Manh Plz -NY 10005
(212) 756-2000 .. **Ruhaak,** Martin Q '08 %Schulte R&Z LLP -919 3rd Av -NY 10022
(516) 522-2565 .. **Ruhl,** Chas T '92 (Greenfield & R) -626 RXR Plz -Uniondale 11556 **Fx:**522-2566
(718) 597-0808 .. **Ruhl,** Diana Cadeddu '95 -Bx3582 -New Hyde Pk 11040 **Fx:**597-0909
(914) 922-9450 .. **Ruhl,** Jos A '91 Hudson Valley Bk -399 Knollwood Rd -White Plns 10603 **Fx:**922-9455
(914) 993-9393 .. **Ruhlandt,** Henry R '78 %Stewart Title Ins -707 Wstchstr Av -White Plns 10604 **Fx:**997-1698
(212) 385-1050 .. **Ruhlin,** Robt C '07 %P Eikenberry -74 Trinity Pl -NY 10006 **Fx:**385-1017
(212) 458-1417 .. **Ruina,** Amy L '93 AIG,Inc -175 Water -NY 10038
(516) 433-6677 .. **Ruina,** Michl H '89 %Stewart GM&B -6800 Jericho Tpk -Syosset 11791
(212) 468-8000 .. **Ruiz,** Ariel F '10 %Morrison & F LLP -1290 Av of Amer -NY 10104
(212) 450-4000 .. **Ruiz,** Eric L '10 %Davis P&W LLP -450 Lex Av -NY 10017
(718) 505-3400 .. **Ruiz,** Frances Newman '96 Cnsl Ruiz Law Grp,PC -37-53 90th -Jcksn Hts 11372 **Fx:**228-6564
(212) 373-3000 .. **Ruiz,** Giulianna K '07 %Paul WRW&G LLP -1285 Av of Amer -NY 10019
(212) 262-2390 .. **Ruiz,** Hector D '02 %Connell F LLP -888 7th Av -NY 10106
(212) 691-5962 .. **Ruiz,** Lisa J '93 -420 W 24th -NY 10011 **Fx:**367-8991
(718) 585-5777 .. **Ruiz,** Michl A '96 -860 Grnd Cncrs -Bronx 10451 **Fx:**993-3543
(718) 286-6508 .. **Ruiz,** Oscar W '81 %DA -125-01 Qns Blvd -Kew Gdns 11415
(212) 351-4000 .. **Ruiz,** Vicente '09 Gibson D&C LLP -200 Park Av -NY 10166
(212) 751-9233 .. **Ruiz-Coloma,** Xavier '99 J&A Garrigues LLP -780 3rd Av -NY 10017
(212) 728-8000 .. **Ruiz DeLa Torre,** Jesenia M '06 %Willkie F&G LLP -787 7th Av -NY 10019
(516) 364-6444 .. **Ruiz-Lozado,** Diana '06 %Navaretta & H,LLP -567 Jericho Tpk -Syosset 11791 **Fx:**364-5005
(212) 998-5115 .. **Rukenstein,** Geraldine S '95 %Upward Bound -32 Wshngtn Pl -NY 10003
(631) 650-7112 .. **Ruland,** Eric C '05 -136 E Main -E Islip 11730 **Fx:**650-5171
(212) 450-4000 .. **Ruland,** Richd J '07 %Davis P&W LLP -450 Lex Av -NY 10017
(631) 928-1444 .. **Ruland,** Stephen A '89 %Tierney & T -409 Rt 112 Bx995 -Pt Jffrsn Sta 11776 **Fx:**928-5705
(212) 808-8100 .. **Rule,** Caroline '90 (Kostelanetz & F,LLP) -7 Wrld Trd Ctr -NY 10007
(212) 344-9022 .. **Rumack,** Darren P B '07 %Klein Law Grp,PC -11 Bway -NY 10004 **Fx:**344-0301
(646) 386-3635 .. **Rumberg,** Anna Y '87 %Supreme Ct-Law Dept -60 Centre -NY 10007
(914) 779-1050 .. **Rumbold,** Nina E '79 (Rumbold & S) -116 Kraft Av -Bronxvll 10708 **Fx:**931-1786
(212) 969-3000 .. **Rumeld,** Myron D '84 (Proskauer R LLP) -1585 Bway -NY 10036
(212) 627-8100 .. **Rumelt,** Owen M '85 (Levy R,PC) -80 8th Av -NY 10011
(585) 342-4600 .. **Rumi,** Fares A '04 %M Reyes -1664 N Clinton Av -Rchstr 14621 **Fx:**342-9773
(716) 852-1831 .. **Rumizen,** Arthur J '59 -69 Delaware Av -Buffalo 14202 **Fx:**856-6100
(212) 907-0700 .. **Rump,** Erin H '09 %Labaton S LLP -140 Bway -NY 10005
(631) 234-1500 .. **Rumph,** Scott H '90 %Rubin & R LLC -1787 Vets Hwy -Islandia 11749
(518) 473-7470 .. **Rumsey,** Colleen M '05 %Insurance Dept -99 Wshngtn Av -Albany 12257 **Fx:**473-4600
(212) 408-2500 .. **Rumsey,** Kathryn A '09 %Baker B,LLP -30 Rckfllr Plz -NY 10112
(516) 741-5050 .. **Rumsky,** Ross S '85 Fidelity Natl Title Ins -1415 Kellum Pl -Gdn Cty 11530 **Fx:**741-5363
(607) 843-2708 .. **Runcie,** Janet L '98 -Bx163 -Oxfrd 13830
(631) 321-7456 .. **Rund,** Thos G '82 -251 Tahlulah Ln -W Islip 11795 **Fx:**321-7605
(212) 788-1270 .. **Rundbaken,** Eric A '72 %Law Dept -100 Church -NY 10007 **Fx:**788-0367
(212) 682-7474 .. **Rundlof,** Dana C '05 %Foley & L LLP -90 Park Av -NY 10016
(800) 888-8300 .. **Runes,** Richd N '72 Amer Lawyer Media -120 Bway -NY 10271 **Fx:**(646) 822-5146
(716) 845-9448 .. **Runfola,** Jennifer Ann '97 %Supreme Ct -25 Delaware Av -Buffalo 14202 **Fx:**851-3293
(518) 464-2000 .. **Runfola,** Ross J '90 AYCO -1 Wall Bx15073 -Albany 12212
(716) 847-1900 .. **Runfola,** Ross L '51 -170 Franklin -Buffalo 14202
(212) 883-3800 .. **Rungta,** Ankur '09 Moelis & Co -399 Park Av -NY 10022 **Fx:**880-4260
(212) 859-8000 .. **Runje,** Kristina '05 %Fried FHS&J LLP -1 NY Plz -NY 10004
(585) 419-8800 .. **Runke,** Justin P '01 (Harris B PLLC) -99 Garnsey Rd -Pittsfrd 14534
(212) 848-4000 .. **Runkle,** Mary L '09 %Shearman & S LLP -599 Lex Av -NY 10022
(212) 909-6000 .. **Runtz,** David W '92 %Debevoise & P LLP -919 3rd Av -NY 10022
(212) 806-5400 .. **Runyan,** Nicole M '05 %Stroock &S&L LLP -180 Maiden Ln -NY 10038
(212) 850-2800 .. **Ruocco,** Antonette '03 %Andrews K LLP -450 Lex Av -NY 10017
(516) 542-1000 .. **Ruocco,** Valerie '05 %Geisler & G,LLP -100 Q Roosevelt Blvd -Gdn Cty 11530
(518) 449-0044 .. **Ruoff,** Carl '01 Cnsl Hoffman W&D LLC -75 State -Albany 12207 **Fx:**449-0047
(518) 455-7529 .. **Ruoso,** Yiselle '01 -The Cptl Rm 310 -Albany 12224
(516) 248-9595 .. **Ruotolo,** Rosanna '09 %Palmieri C & Assoc,PC -250 Mineola Blvd -Mineola 11501
(212) 556-2100 .. **Rupe,** Michl C '07 (King & S) -1185 Av of Amer -NY 10036
(315) 788-5100 .. **Rupert,** Krystal Ann '05 (Conboy MB&K,LLP) -407 Sherman -Watertwn 13601
(212) 446-4800 .. **Rupert,** Melanie R '02 (Kirkland & E LLP) -153 E 53rd -NY 10022
(718) 805-3500 .. **Rupnarain,** Trevor K '90 Rupnarain & Assoc -13110 Lbrty Av -S Richmond Hll 11419 **Fx:**805-2800
(716) 854-3400 .. **Rupp Baase Pfalzgraf Cunningham & Coppola LLC** -1600 Lbrty Bldg -Buffalo 14202 **Fx:**332-0336
(716) 362-0991 .. **Rupp Baase Pfalzgraf Cunningham & Coppola LLC** -2495 Kensngtn Av -Amherst 14226 **Fx:**362-0995
(585) 381-3400 .. **Rupp Baase Pfalzgraf Cunningham & Coppola LLC** -3300 Monroe Av -Rchstr 14618 **Fx:**381-6219
(212) 425-7200 .. **Rupp,** Mimi K '04 %Kenyon & K,LLP -1 Bway -NY 10004
(716) 854-3400 .. **Rupp,** R Anthony III '93 (Rupp BPC&C LLC) -1600 Lbrty Bldg -Buffalo 14202
(716) 855-1111 .. **Ruppar,** Peter G '74 (Duke HP&G LLP) -350 Main -Buffalo 14202
(212) 227-0347 .. **Rupwani,** Nicholas K '04 %Weiss W&W,PC -25 Park Pl -NY 10007
(212) 867-4100 .. **Rusanov,** Anna '08 %Furman K&B LLP -545 5th Av -NY 10017
(845) 855-0353 .. **Rusch Bellucci,** Patricia Ann '95 -Bx353 -Pawling 12564
(212) 403-1000 .. **Ruschell,** Jos M '09 %Wachtell LR&K -51 W 52nd -NY 10019
(212) 986-2340 .. **Ruschmann,** Herbert F '94 %Jordan & H -122 E 42nd -NY 10168
(212) 265-6888 .. **Ruscigno,** Anthony R '00 %Porzio B&N,PC -156 W 56th -NY 10019
(212) 480-3030 .. **Ruscito,** Jos L '89 %M Pressman -125 Maiden Ln -NY 10038 **Fx:**480-2590
(718) 658-0500 .. **Ruseskas,** Michl J '05 %Law Dept -151-20 Jamaica Av -Jamaica 11432 **Fx:**658-4025
(212) 482-0001 .. **Rush,** Claire F '84 (Russo K&T LLP) -33 Whitehall -NY 10004
(516) 608-7000 .. **Rush,** Curt S '85 Systemax Inc -11 Hrbr Park Dr -Pt Wash 11050
(212) 225-2000 .. **Rush,** David '02 %Cleary GS&H -1 Lbrty Plz -NY 10006
(718) 579-3000 .. **Rush,** Deborah F '90 %Leg Aid -1020 Grnd Cncrs -Bronx 10451 **Fx:**588-2611
(718) 537-9885 .. **Rush,** Kenneth R '96 (DiLorenzo & R) -944 Gerard Av -Bronx 10452
(516) 393-2200 .. **Rush,** Molly M '00 %Garfunkel W,PC -111 Grt Nck Rd -Gt Neck 11021

(212) 704-6000 .. **Rush,** Ralph Marios '07 %Troutman S LLP -405 Lex Av -NY 10174
(516) 829-8855 .. **Rush,** Richd E '92 -1 Barstow Rd -Gt Neck 11021 **Fx:**829-8951
(212) 661-1100 .. **Rushd,** Shaheen '82 (Pomerantz HG&G LLP) -100 Park Av -NY 10017
(212) 790-4010 .. **Rushdoony,** Jonathan '83 %Cmptrllr of Currency -340 Mad Av -NY 10017 **Fx:**790-4058
(845) 486-4200 .. **Rushfield,** Mark C '77 OfCnsl Shaw PM&L,LLP -21 Van Wagner Rd -Poughkeepsie 12603
(212) 854-0779 .. **Rushing,** Susan K '91 %Columbia Univ -535 W 116th 412 Low Mem'l Library -NY 10027
(607) 652-7327 .. **Rushmore Mason Marcus & Crocker** -11 Harper -Stamfrd 12167
(212) 773-2678 .. **Rushnak,** Mark A '07 Ernst & Y LLP -5 Times Sq -NY 10036
(716) 852-1111 .. **Rusin,** F David '84 %JM Hayes -69 Delaware Av -Buffalo 14202 **Fx:**852-0711
(914) 428-2505 .. **Rusinko,** Rosalie Kolb '91 %DEC -100 Hillside Av -White Plns 10603 **Fx:**428-0792
(845) 236-4411 .. **Rusk,** Danl J '95 %Rusk WH&M,LLP -1390 Route 9W Bx727 -Marlboro 12542
(845) 331-4100 .. **Rusk,** George Jr. '59 (Rusk WH&M,LLP) -255 Fair Bx3356 -Kingston 12402
(845) 236-4411 .. **Rusk,** George Jr. '59 (Rusk WH&M,LLP) -1390 Route 9W Bx727 -Marlboro 12542
(716) 684-8060 .. **Rusk,** George A '78 %Ecology & Envrnmnt -368 Plsntvw Dr -Lancaster 14086 **Fx:**684-0844
(845) 331-4100 .. **Rusk,** John G '89 (Rusk WH&M,LLP) -255 Fair Bx3356 -Kingston 12402
(845) 486-4200 .. **Rusk,** Lisa S '95 (Shaw PM&L,LLP) -21 Van Wagner Rd -Poughkeepsie 12603
(845) 236-4411 .. **Rusk,** Pamela D '92 %Rusk WH&M,LLP -1390 Route 9W Bx727 -Marlboro 12542
(845) 331-4100 .. **Rusk Wadlin Heppner & Martuscello,LLP** -255 Fair Bx3356 -Kingston 12402 **Fx:**331-6930
(845) 236-4411 .. **Rusk Wadlin Heppner & Martuscello,LLP** -1390 Route 9W Bx727 -Marlboro 12542 **Fx:**236-3190
(212) 715-9100 .. **Ruskay-Kidd,** Scott '99 %Kramer LN&F,LLP -1177 Av of Amer -NY 10036
(212) 596-9000 .. **Ruskin,** Barbara A '99 (Ropes & G LLP) -1211 Av of Amer -NY 10036
(212) 969-3000 .. **Ruskin,** Bradley I '82 (Proskauer R LLP) -1585 Bway -NY 10036
(516) 663-6600 .. **Ruskin,** Melvyn B '65 (Ruskin MF,PC) -1425 RXR Plz -Uniondale 11556
(516) 663-6600 .. **Ruskin Moscou Faltischek,PC** -1425 RXR Plz -Uniondale 11556 **Fx:**663-6601
(212) 225-2000 .. **Ruskin,** Nancy I '83 Cnsl Cleary GS&H -1 Lbrty Plz -NY 10006
(718) 237-1547 .. **Ruskin,** Neil S '72 -105 Court -Brklyn 11201 **Fx:**875-4011
(212) 967-1800 .. **Ruskin,** Steven A '68 (Bryant BJ&R LLP) -140 Bway -NY 10005
(212) 351-4500 .. **Ruskin,** Wm A '78 (Epstein B&G,PC) -250 Park Av -NY 10177
(518) 471-4826 .. **Ruslander,** Betsy R '87 %Appllt Div 3rd Dept -Capitol Station Bx7288 -Albany 12224 **Fx:**471-4750
(212) 858-1000 .. **Rusmisel,** Stephen R '72 (Pillsbury WSP LLP) -1540 Bway -NY 10036
(646) 386-4430 .. **Rusnak,** Nina '87 %Hon R Straus -111 Centre -NY 10013
(518) 457-2449 .. **Rusnica,** John F '90 %Agriculture & Mrkts -10B Airline Dr -Albany 12235 **Fx:**457-8842
(212) 902-4160 .. **Rusoff,** David T '01 %Goldman Sachs -1 NY Plz -NY 10004
(212) 430-6040 .. **Russ,** Adam H '97 (Wasser & R LLP) -80 Maiden Ln -NY 10038 **Fx:**430-6041
(716) 847-8400 .. **Russ,** Arthur A Jr. '67 (Phillips L LLP) -3400 HSBC Ctr -Buffalo 14203
(518) 408-3139 .. **Russ,** Caitlin D '10 %State Comptroller -110 State -Albany 12236 **Fx:**473-9104
(716) 856-4000 .. **Russ,** Hugh M III '88 (Hodgson R LLP) -140 Pearl -Buffalo 14202
(516) 541-1014 .. **Russ,** Jay E '75 (Russ & R,PC) -543 Bway Bx149 -Massapequa 11758 **Fx:**541-1077
(516) 750-9713 .. **Russ,** Jeffrey A '70 (JA Russ PLLC) -33 S Srvc Rd -Jericho 11753 **Fx:**334-5934
(516) 541-1014 .. **Russ,** Linda E '78 (Russ & R,PC) -543 Bway Bx149 -Massapequa 11758 **Fx:**541-1077
(516) 747-6300 .. **Russ,** Lisa LaValle '92 %Koeppel M&L,LLP -155 First Bx863 -Mineola 11501
(212) 455-2000 .. **Russ,** Philip R '09 %Simpson T&B LLP -425 Lex Av -NY 10017
(212) 609-2634 .. **Russ,** Sharon Portnof '96 SrCnsl Gibson & B,PC -14 Wall -NY 10005
(212) 450-4000 .. **Russano,** Michl Jos '02 %Davis P&W LLP -450 Lex Av -NY 10017
(914) 944-4087 .. **Russcol,** Fred C '75 F Russcol,PC -30 State -Ossining 10562
(516) 681-8200 .. **Russel,** John E '00 (Ambus R,PC) -380 N Bway -Jericho 11753 **Fx:**932-8353
(718) 403-2000 .. **Russell,** Aaron '08 National Grid US -1 Metrotech Ctr -Brklyn 11201
(212) 269-1400 .. **Russell,** Andrew G '94 %Gusrae KB&N PLLC -120 Wall -NY 10005
(518) 834-7700 .. **Russell,** Andrew J '09 %Russell & M -101 Clinton Bx549 -Keesevll 12944 **Fx:**834-9300
(212) 732-7800 .. **Russell,** Arthur D '88 -14 Wall -NY 10005 **Fx:**732-5778
(646) 386-4701 .. **Russell,** Beverly J '97 NYC Criminal Ct -100 Centre -NY 10013 **Fx:**(212) 374-3004
(212) 419-3771 .. **Russell,** C Mario '97 Catholic Charities -1011 1st Av -NY 10022
(516) 505-2300 .. **Russell,** Camille O '03 (Sharifov & R) -50 Main -Hempstd 11550 **Fx:**505-2379
(212) 593-6700 .. **Russell,** Carol E '89 (Aaronson RF&D,LLP) -757 3rd Av -NY 10017
(585) 419-8800 .. **Russell,** Chas W '96 (Harris B PLLC) -99 Garnsey Rd -Pittsfrd 14534
(212) 909-6000 .. **Russell,** Christopher M '10 %Debevoise & P LLP -919 3rd Av -NY 10022
(212) 416-8000 .. **Russell,** Clark P '97 %Dept of Law -120 Bway -NY 10271
(212) 593-9555 .. **Russell,** Cynthia J '84 -845 3rd Av -NY 10022 **Fx:**593-1318
(718) 389-8350 .. **Russell,** David B '77 -103 Kent -Brklyn 11222
(315) 668-2669 .. **Russell,** David E '99 (Russell R&G,PLLC) -3250 Fulton Av Bx503 -Centrl Sq 13036 **Fx:**668-3333
(845) 562-5550 .. **Russell,** David L '83 DL Russell,PC -52 N Plnk Rd -Newburgh 12550 **Fx:**562-6114
(212) 538-7596 .. **Russell,** David M '92 CSFB -11 Mad Av -NY 10010
(585) 546-7070 .. **Russell,** Dianne C '87 -16 W Main -Rchstr 14614 **Fx:**423-0890
(585) 258-2800 .. **Russell,** Edmund J III '00 %Underberg & K LLP -300 Bausch & Lomb Pl -Rchstr 14604
(212) 341-6400 .. **Russell,** Ellen Matowik '91 %Liquidation Bur -123 William -NY 10038 **Fx:**608-3398
(631) 669-3710 .. **Russell,** Frank S '82 (Lite & R,PLLC) -212 Higbie Ln -W Islip 11795
(212) 220-3830 .. **Russell,** Guerric S D L '01 (Nicoletti H&S) -88 Pine -NY 10005
(516) 829-6900 .. **Russell,** Hollis F '79 (Ackerman LCB&L,LLP) -1010 Nrthrn Blvd -Gt Neck 11021
(212) 449-2365 .. **Russell,** Jennifer A '01 Merrill Lynch -4 World Fncl Ctr -NY 10080
(212) 750-8585 .. **Russell,** John C '59 %WP Stewart & Co,Inc -527 Mad Av -NY 10022 **Fx:**980-8039
(212) 260-8690 .. **Russell,** John W '72 -60 E 12th -NY 10003 **Fx:**260-8692
(732) 855-6236 .. **Russell,** Jos J Jr. '05 %Wilentz G&S -110 William -NY 10038 **Fx:**726-6609
(315) 786-7950 .. **Russell,** Jos W '80 (Menter R&T,PC) -120 Wshngtn -Watertwn 13601
(718) 459-9000 .. **Russell,** Josh '06 %Sweeney GR&B,LLP -95-25 Qns Blvd -Rego Pk 11374
(718) 270-4736 .. **Russell,** Kathleen A '88 %HIV Ctr for Wmn & Chldrn -450 Clarkson Av -Brklyn 11203
(212) 908-0677 .. **Russell,** Kathryn Basile '91 Fitch Inc -1 State Street Plz -NY 10004
(212) 742-3390 .. **Russell,** Kevin J '91 (Lindabury ME&C,PC) -26 Bway -NY 10004
(585) 387-0500 .. **Russell,** Kimberly P '92 (Olver K LLP) -100 Ofc Park Way -Pittsfrd 14534
(718) 991-4600 .. **Russell,** Laura A '95 %Leg Aid -953 Southrn Blvd -Bronx 10459 **Fx:**842-2867
(212) 421-5500 .. **Russell,** Laura A '10 %Goldsmith C&R,LLP -747 3rd Av -NY 10017
(212) 210-9484 .. **Russell,** Lauren A '06 %Alston & B LLP -90 Park Av -NY 10016
(212) 659-7300 .. **Russell,** Matthew E '07 %Haynes & B,LLP -1221 Av of Amer -NY 10020
(212) 351-4500 .. **Russell,** Maura I '94 (Epstein B&G,PC) -250 Park Av -NY 10177
(631) 563-0555 .. **Russell,** Patricia J '86 %D O'Doherty Jr -25 Candee Av -Sayvll 11782 **Fx:**563-0737
(212) 593-3310 .. **Russell,** Paul K '99 %Dobis R&P,PC -7 Elk PMB 159 -NY 10007 **Fx:**(973) 740-2484
(917) 777-4200 .. **Russell,** Philip W '08 %Bingham M LLP -1 Bttry Pk Plz -NY 10004
(631) 543-7667 .. **Russell,** Regina G '89 OfCnsl Sarisohn Law Prtnrs LLP -350 Vets Mem'l Hwy -Commack 11725 **Fx:**543-7901
(845) 561-2889 .. **Russell,** Richd A '88 -189 N Plnk Rd -Newburgh 12550 **Fx:**562-1071
(212) 269-0927 .. **Russell,** Richd F '73 (D'Amato & L,LLP) -2 World Fncl Ctr -NY 10281
(212) 213-3549 .. **Russell,** Richd L '59 -404 Park Av S -NY 10016
(212) 877-7830 .. **Russell,** Robt A '75 -157 W 79th -NY 10024
(212) 538-2947 .. **Russell,** Robt W II '96 Credit Suisse -11 Mad Av -NY 10010
(212) 683-3995 .. **Russell,** Royce '93 (Emdin & R,LLP) -286 Mad Av -NY 10016 **Fx:**683-4032
(845) 794-0421 .. **Russell,** Scott A '04 -30 Glen Wild Rd Bx384 -Rck Hll 12775 **Fx:**796-0831
(631) 642-8903 .. **Russell,** Sean M '97 %Prudential Securities -414 Main -Pt Jffrsn 11777
(518) 383-4000 .. **Russell,** Stanley D '76 (Overton RD&D,LLP) -19 Halfmoon Exec Park Dr Bx437 -Clifton Pk 12065
(631) 419-6112 .. **Russell,** Steven T '93 -982 Montauk Hwy -Bayport 11705 **Fx:**363-6569
(212) 435-3571 .. **Russell,** Toby J '00 %Port Auth of NY/NJ -225 Park Av S -NY 10003 **Fx:**435-3555
(212) 848-4000 .. **Russell,** Walter Owen '07 Shearman & S LLP -599 Lex Av -NY 10022
(518) 834-7700 .. **Russell,** Wm E '73 (Russell & M) -101 Clinton Bx549 -Keesevll 12944 **Fx:**834-9300
(212) 455-2000 .. **Russell,** Wm T Jr. '91 (Simpson T&B LLP) -425 Lex Av -NY 10017
(212) 307-5500 .. **Russell,** Wm T '02 (Venable LLP) -1270 Av of Amer -NY 10020
(212) 728-8000 .. **Russello,** Alexandra Hines '99 %Willkie F&G LLP -787 7th Av -NY 10019
(212) 705-7000 .. **Russello,** Gerald J '97 OfCnsl Bingham M LLP -399 Park Av -NY 10022
(631) 367-7100 .. **Russello,** Jos F '02 %Coughlin SGR&R LLP -58 S Srvc Rd -Melvll 11747
(212) 281-5400 .. **Russi,** Louis S '86 -1524 Amstrdm Av -NY 10031
(585) 458-2800 .. **Russi,** Patrick K '91 (Moyer R&R,PC) -2300 W Ridge Rd -Rchstr 14626
(212) 349-6460 .. **Russianoff,** Gene '79 %NYPIRG -9 Murray -NY 10007 **Fx:**349-1366
(212) 279-3500 .. **Russin Vecchi Berg & Bernstein,LLP** -260 Mad Av -NY 10016 **Fx:**202-4930
(212) 482-0001 .. **Russo,** Alan '80 (Russo K&T LLP) -33 Whitehall -NY 10004
(212) 218-2100 .. **Russo,** Alicia A '01 %Fitzpatrick CH&S -1290 Av of Amer -NY 10104
(315) 498-2622 .. **Russo,** Amy M '99 %Onondaga Comm Cllg -4585 W Seneca Tpke -Syracuse 13215
(212) 506-1700 .. **Russo,** Angela M '05 Kasowitz BT&F LLP -1633 Bway -NY 10019
(631) 582-5753 .. **Russo,** Aniella '92 (Afran & R,PC) -300 Rabro Dr -Hauppauge 11788 **Fx:**582-5754
(718) 383-7800 .. **Russo,** Anne Marie D '88 -66-53 73rd Pl -Middl Vllg 11379
(516) 794-1100 .. **Russo,** Anthony F '84 (Russo D&L) -1975 Hempstd Tpk -E Meadow 11554
(516) 746-7371 .. **Russo,** Anthony W '91 (Burns RT&R,LLP) -390 Old Cntry Rd -Gdn Cty 11530
(516) 229-4501 .. **Russo Apoznanski & Tambasco** -875 Merrick Av -Westbury 11590 **Fx:**229-4503
(518) 266-3000 .. **Russo,** Barbara J '97 %Div Tax Appls -500 Fed -Troy 12180 **Fx:**272-5178
(212) 608-8840 .. **Russo,** Bartholomew T '88 (Bamundo Z&S,LLP) -111 John -NY 10038
(631) 567-4330 .. **Russo,** Benjamin D '56 -73 Benson Av -Sayvll 11782 **Fx:**776-8215
(212) 270-5918 .. **Russo,** Bianca '85 -270 Park Av -NY 10017
(212) 557-9600 .. **Russo & Burke** -600 3rd Av -NY 10016 **Fx:**557-9610
(212) 480-4200 .. **Russo,** Carmen A '68 Nausch Hogan & Murray -180 Maiden Ln -NY 10038
(631) 265-7200 .. **Russo,** Chas C '78 (Russo KW&C) -400 Townline Rd -Hauppauge 11788

(914) 347-2600 .. **Russo,** Christopher '02 %Traub LS&S LLP -7 Skyline Dr -Hawthorne 10532
(212) 861-8825 .. **Russo,** D Nicholas '72 -510 E 86th -NY 10028
(631) 447-1200 .. **Russo,** Danl A '99 (Russo & G) -31 W Main -Patchogue 11772
(212) 326-3939 .. **Russo,** Danl L Jr. '94 (Jones D) -222 E 41st -NY 10017
(516) 294-0300 .. **Russo,** Danl W '00 %Collins M&G -138 Mineola Blvd -Mineola 11501
(516) 794-1100 .. **Russo Darnell & Lodato** -1975 Hempstd Tpk -E Meadow 11554 **Fx:**794-5447
(718) 667-7777 .. **Russo,** Denise '92 -47 Hunt Ln -Staten Isl 10304 **Fx:**(973) 701-7171
(212) 592-1400 .. **Russo,** Dennis W '87 (Herrick,F LLP) -2 Park Av -NY 10016
(718) 667-7777 .. **Russo,** Donna M '96 -47 Hunt Ln -Staten Isl 10304 **Fx:**(973) 701-7171
(212) 735-3000 .. **Russo,** Elizabeth A '09 %Skadden ASM&F LLP -4 Times Sq -NY 10036
(631) 589-5000 .. **Russo,** Eric J '79 (Van Brunt J&R) -140 Main -Sayvll 11782
(516) 822-1600 .. **Russo,** Eugene O '77 (Russo & P) -16 E Old Cntry Rd -Hicksvll 11801
(917) 454-1100 .. **Russo,** Eva Marie E '98 %Police Dept -2 Lafayette -NY 10007
(212) 412-7543 .. **Russo,** Evan L '99 Barclays Capital -200 Park Av -NY 10166
(718) 390-5434 .. **Russo,** Frances '88 %Hon L Rienzi -18 Richmond Ter -Staten Isl 10301
(516) 333-9767 .. **Russo,** Fredk '68 -538 Woods Rd -Westbury 11590 **Fx:**997-8142
(718) 849-6900 .. **Russo,** George F '83 (G Russo & Assoc PC) -101-05 Lefferts Blvd -S Richmond Hll 11419 **Fx:**849-6930
(914) 428-9494 .. **Russo,** Giacchino J '84 -50 Main -White Plns 10606
(718) 855-9000 .. **Russo,** Graig A '08 %Cullen and D LLP -177 Montague -Brklyn 11201
(212) 294-6700 .. **Russo,** Jacqueline M '08 %Winston & S -200 Park Av -NY 10166
(607) 754-0500 .. **Russo,** Janet M '93 %Lachman & G -1500 E Main Bx89 -Endicott 13761 **Fx:**748-6978
(516) 522-2730 .. **Russo,** Jason L '99 -626 RXR Plz -Uniondale 11556
(212) 730-7750 .. **Russo,** John C '02 %Nicoletti GS&O,LLP -555 5th Av -NY 10017
(718) 777-1777 .. **Russo,** John L '90 -31-01 Bway -Astoria 11106
(631) 272-5225 .. **Russo,** John N '97 -320 Carleton Av -Central Islip 11722
(212) 858-1000 .. **Russo,** Jonathan J '90 (Pillsbury WSP LLP) -1540 Bway -NY 10036
(718) 875-1173 .. **Russo,** Jos '87 -16 Court -Brklyn 11241 **Fx:**875-5440
(914) 428-4420 .. **Russo,** Jos A Jr. '79 -50 Main -White Plns 10606 **Fx:**428-4988
(212) 856-1214 .. **Russo,** Jos A '89 (Uscher QU&R) -355 Lex Av -NY 10017
(718) 250-2000 .. **Russo,** Jos J '08 %DA -350 Jay -Brklyn 11201 **Fx:**250-2314
(516) 379-1851 .. **Russo,** Judith A '92 -2723 Cheshire Dr -Baldwin 11510 **Fx:**681-5456
(631) 265-7200 .. **Russo Karl Widmaier & Cordano** -400 Townline Rd -Hauppauge 11788 **Fx:**265-7578
(631) 247-0404 .. **Russo,** Kathryn J '89 OfCnsl Jackson L LLP -58 S Srvc Rd -Melvll 11747
(212) 482-0001 .. **Russo Keane & Toner LLP** -33 Whitehall -NY 10004 **Fx:**482-0002
(212) 406-7254 .. **Russo,** Kenneth B '92 -160 Bway -NY 10038 **Fx:**608-1659
(845) 786-0227 .. **Russo,** Kevin F '91 -8 Caruso Ct -Thiells 10984 **Fx:**947-2900
(212) 865-1189 .. **Russo,** Linda A '01 -392 Cntrl Pk W -NY 10025 **Fx:**(646) 349-2492
(212) 325-2000 .. **Russo,** Lori M '82 Credit Suisse -11 Mad Av -NY 10010
(212) 594-5300 .. **Russo,** Louis A '08 %Milberg LLP -1 Penn Plz -NY 10119
(718) 931-0468 .. **Russo,** Louis J III '02 (Russo & Assoc) -1200 Morris Pk Av -Bronx 10461 **Fx:**823-3533
(212) 440-2350 .. **Russo,** Marc S '80 %C Siegel -40 Wall -NY 10005 **Fx:**440-2385
(631) 249-8291 .. **Russo,** Maria '53 -255 Staples -Farmngdl 11735
(917) 509-1244 .. **Russo,** Maria E '83 -217 Bway -NY 10007
(631) 475-6390 .. **Russo,** Marian Haru '95 CHI Inc -55 Medford Av -Patchogue 11772 **Fx:**475-6393
(914) 793-0288 .. **Russo,** Marianne Manning '88 (Manning & R) -65 Pondfld Rd -Bronxvll 10708
(914) 249-5946 .. **Russo,** Marie V '91 Mastercard Worldwide -2000 Purchase -Purchase 10577
(212) 269-1400 .. **Russo,** Martin P '94 Gusrae KB&N PLLC -120 Wall -NY 10005
(716) 856-8200 .. **Russo,** Mary M '78 (Williams & W) -43 Court -Buffalo 14202 **Fx:**856-0559
(917) 454-1100 .. **Russo,** Matthew R '09 %Police Dept -2 Lafayette -NY 10007
(212) 693-1500 .. **Russo,** Michl '89 (Becker & R) -111 John -NY 10038
(914) 948-5719 .. **Russo,** Michl A '56 (M Russo) -56 Greenrdg Av -White Plns 10605 **Fx:**948-4177
(516) 229-4501 .. **Russo,** Michl C '79 %Russo A&T -875 Merrick Av -Westbury 11590
(716) 853-8479 .. **Russo,** Michl J '92 %Dept of Law -350 Main Pl Twr -Buffalo 14202 **Fx:**853-8571
(212) 779-8600 .. **Russo,** Michelle '84 %Silverman SS&B PLLC -381 Park Av S -NY 10016
(516) 767-2111 .. **Russo,** Michelle S '88 M Russo,PC -18 S Marylnd Av -Pt Wash 11050 **Fx:**767-2115
(516) 877-0800 .. **Russo,** Nicholas F '79 (Cartiglia C&R) -1050 Franklin Av -Gdn Cty 11530
(212) 697-3122 .. **Russo,** Olimpio A '97 (Martin C&B LLP) -220 E 42nd -NY 10017
(212) 732-2000 .. **Russo,** Patricia '03 %Cullen and D LLP -44 Wall -NY 10005
(516) 822-1600 .. **Russo & Pedranghelu** -16 E Old Cntry Rd -Hicksvll 11801 **Fx:**822-6160
(585) 232-5225 .. **Russo,** Peter M '65 (Remington GW&C,LLP) -183 E Main -Rchstr 14604
(631) 348-3636 .. **Russo,** Philip A '95 -1 Suffolk Sq -Islandia 11749
(212) 373-3309 .. **Russo,** Raphael M '96 (Paul WRW&G LLP) -1285 Av of Amer -NY 10019
(212) 344-5400 .. **Russo,** Ronald G '74 OfCnsl Schlam S&D LLP -26 Bway -NY 10004
(845) 452-9010 .. **Russo,** Rudolph P '57 -35 Market -Poughkeepsie 12601 **Fx:**473-8122
(845) 226-7002 .. **Russo,** Rudolph P '57 -Route 82 Bx189 -Hopewell Junct 12533 **Fx:**227-0880
(212) 788-3300 .. **Russo,** Salvatore J '82 %Hlth & Hsptl Corp -125 Worth -NY 10013 **Fx:**267-6905
(718) 442-0900 .. **Russo Scamardella & D'Amato,PC** -1010 Forest Av -Staten Isl 10310 **Fx:**816-8037
(212) 421-2150 .. **Russo,** Steven C '90 (Sive P&R,PC) -460 Park Av -NY 10022
(516) 393-2200 .. **Russo,** Terence A '99 SrCnsl Garfunkel W,PC -111 Grt Nck Rd -Gt Neck 11021
(518) 449-8893 .. **Russo,** Theresa M '99 (Wilson EME&D LLP) -677 Bway -Albany 12207
(212) 770-6200 .. **Russo,** Thos A '70 AIG -70 Pine -NY 10270
(718) 442-0900 .. **Russo,** Thos J '53 (Russo S&D,PC) -1010 Forest Av -Staten Isl 10310
(212) 425-1900 .. **Russo,** Thos M '76 (Freehill H&M LLP) -80 Pine -NY 10005
(516) 742-9200 .. **Russo,** Thos S '99 %Edelman K&J PLLC -1 Old Cntry Rd -Carle Pl 11514
(914) 761-7286 .. **Russo,** Thos W '91 (TW Russo,PC) -14 Mamaroneck Av -White Plns 10601
(718) 892-0070 .. **Russo,** Thos W '91 (TW Russo,PC) -2704 E Tremont Av -Bronx 10461 **Fx:**892-6966
(212) 858-1000 .. **Russo,** Timothy M '06 %Pillsbury WSP LLP -1540 Bway -NY 10036
(516) 897-7100 .. **Russo,** Vincent J '79 (V Russo & Assoc,PC) -250 Lido Blvd -Lido Bch 11561 **Fx:**897-7575
(516) 683-1717 .. **Russo,** Vincent J '79 (V Russo & Assoc,PC) -1600 Stewart Av -Westbury 11590 **Fx:**683-9393
(631) 582-1919 .. **Russo,** Vincent J '79 (V Russo & Assoc,PC) -3740 Expwy Dr S -Islandia 11749 **Fx:**582-8484
(518) 762-0011 .. **Russo Walsh & Walsh** -122 W Main -Johnstwn 12095 **Fx:**762-0013
(212) 557-9600 .. **Russo,** Wm J '76 (Russo & B) -600 3rd Av -NY 10016
(716) 853-9555 .. **Russo-McLaughlin,** Karen C '84 %Leg Aid -237 Main -Buffalo 14203 **Fx:**853-3219
(212) 735-3000 .. **Russotti,** Kelly A '09 %Skadden ASM&F LLP -4 Times Sq -NY 10036
(212) 986-7353 .. **Russotti,** Philip A '74 (Wingate R&S) -420 Lex Av -NY 10170
(718) 665-1700 .. **Rust,** Christopher W '09 %Gottlieb S&S,LLP -180 E 162nd -Bronx 10451
(516) 227-0700 .. **Rust,** Jeffrey P '00 Cnsl Farrell F,PC -1320 RXR Plz -Uniondale 11556
(212) 259-8000 .. **Rust,** Kai-Oliver '97 (Dewey & L LLP) -1301 Av of Amer -NY 10019
(716) 821-9001 .. **Rust,** Robt E Jr. '08 Cnsl World Wide Travel Staffing Ltd -2829 Sheridan Dr -Tonawanda 14150
(212) 351-4000 .. **Rustum,** Wm M '01 (Gibson D&C LLP) -200 Park Av -NY 10166
(607) 277-0110 .. **Ruswick,** Richd P '86 -401 E State -Ithaca 14850 **Fx:**272-1123
(716) 838-5550 .. **Ruszczyk,** Peter T '64 (Carey & R) -360 Crescent Av -Buffalo 14214
(212) 997-4500 .. **Ruta,** Jos A '93 (Ruta & S) -1500 Bway -NY 10036
(212) 997-4500 .. **Ruta & Soulios** -1500 Bway -NY 10036 **Fx:**768-0649
(212) 617-8422 .. **Rutan,** Kim Domilici '03 Bloomberg, LP -731 Lex Av -NY 10022
(845) 486-0300 .. **Rutberg,** Martin P '79 (Rutberg Pl Law) -3344 Route 9 N -Poughkeepsie 12601 **Fx:**486-0270
(212) 506-1700 .. **Rutcofsky,** Barry S '84 (Kasowitz BT&F LLP) -1633 Bway -NY 10019
(212) 839-5300 .. **Rutenberg,** Stephen A '02 (Sidley A LLP) -787 7th Av -NY 10019
(212) 906-1200 .. **Ruthberg,** Miles N '06 (Latham & W) -885 3rd Av -NY 10022
(212) 446-2300 .. **Rutherford,** Alanna C '01 (Boies S&F LLP) -575 Lex Av -NY 10022
(212) 909-6000 .. **Rutherford,** Christian D '06 %Debevoise & P LLP -919 3rd Av -NY 10022
(212) 599-5799 .. **Rutherford & Christie LLP** -369 Lex Av -NY 10017 **Fx:**599-5162
(212) 599-5799 .. **Rutherford,** David S '86 (Rutherford & C LLP) -369 Lex Av -NY 10017
(212) 297-5800 .. **Rutherford,** Randy K '99 (Day P LLP) -7 Times Sq -NY 10036
(212) 819-8200 .. **Rutherfurd,** Winthrop Jr. '69 (White & C LLP) -1155 Av of Amer -NY 10036
(607) 753-3551 .. **Ruthig,** Russell E '74 -36 Main Bx866 -Cortlnd 13045 **Fx:**756-8768
(212) 715-9100 .. **Ruthizer,** Theo '73 (Kramer LN&F,LLP) -1177 Av of Amer -NY 10036
(914) 241-4552 .. **Ruti,** John M '81 -100 S Bedford Rd -Mt Kisco 10549 **Fx:**241-2797
(718) 590-2000 .. **Ruti,** Jonathan D '09 %DA -198 E 161st -Bronx 10451 **Fx:**590-6477
(212) 576-4503 .. **Rutigliano,** Carla T '97 NY Life Ins Co -51 Mad Av -NY 10010
(718) 382-3560 .. **Rutigliano,** Emilia '96 (E Rutigliano,PC) -2503 65th -Brklyn 11204 **Fx:**382-6982
(845) 356-2570 .. **Rutishauser,** Reginald H '91 %Kantrowitz G&G,PC -747 Chestnut Rdg Rd -Chestnut Rdg 10977
(518) 399-5400 .. **Rutkey,** Jennifer S P '96 (Gordon T&D,LLP) -113 Saratoga Rd -Glenvll 12302
(516) 357-3000 .. **Rutkin,** Alan S '84 (Rivkin R LLP) -926 RXR Plz -Uniondale 11556
(212) 409-0470 .. **Rutkin,** David L '93 ING Financial Srvcs -1325 Av of Amer -NY 10019
(212) 272-1653 .. **Rutkoske,** Eric A '98 JP Morgan Chase -383 Mad Av -NY 10179
(212) 596-9000 .. **Rutkovsky,** Steven R '92 (Ropes & G LLP) -1211 Av of Amer -NY 10036
(631) 852-2500 .. **Rutkowski,** Anthony B '03 %DA -200 Center Dr -Rvrhead 11901 **Fx:**852-1769
(716) 853-9555 .. **Rutkowski,** Donna Alaimo '89 Leg Aid -237 Main -Buffalo 14203 **Fx:**853-3219
(212) 574-1200 .. **Rutkowski,** Lawr '79 (Seward & K LLP) -1 Bttry Pk Plz -NY 10004
(716) 851-3359 .. **Rutland,** Anne Solomon '89 Supreme Ct-Commercial Div -50 Delaware Av -Buffalo 14202
(212) 557-0517 .. **Rutledge,** Dane Keller '82 -150 E 39th -NY 10016
(212) 492-5800 .. **Rutledge-Parisi,** Allison K '97 %Kaplan Educ Ctrs,Inc -888 7th Av -NY 10106 **Fx:**489-2301
(631) 234-5110 .. **Rutman,** Hyman Lewis '54 -300 Rabro Dr -Hauppauge 11788 **Fx:**736-6180
(212) 213-3676 .. **Rutman,** Rick J '85 (Popick R&J,LLP) -41 Elizabeth -NY 10013
(518) 465-1451 .. **Rutnik,** Christopher P '77 C Rutnik -270 Mt Hope Dr -Albany 12202 **Fx:**465-1458
(518) 218-1218 .. **Rutnik,** Danl J '84 (Bender Lane Advisory,LLC) -Bx38016 -Albany 12203
(518) 436-9646 .. **Rutnik,** Douglas P '65 Rutnik Law Firm -80 State -Albany 12207 **Fx:**436-9648
(518) 436-9646 .. **Rutnik,** Gregory A '64 Rutnik Law Firm -80 State -Albany 12207 **Fx:**436-9648
(518) 447-7110 .. **Rutnik,** Gregory A '64 %Cnty Atty -112 State -Albany 12207
(518) 434-4544 .. **Rutnik,** Polly N '66 -2 Noonan Ln -Albany 12209 **Fx:**463-3417
(518) 474-7330 .. **Rutnik,** Tiffinay Mullane '02 %Dept of Law -The Cptl -Albany 12224
(212) 486-6060 .. **Rutsky,** Jordan K '05 %Trief & O -150 E 58th -NY 10155
(212) 969-3000 .. **Rutsky,** Scott K '91 (Proskauer R LLP) -1585 Bway -NY 10036
(212) 810-2331 .. **Rutstein,** Gregory E '06 FRM Americas Inc -888 7th Av -NY 10106

(212) 259-8000 .. **Rutta,** Michelle B '90 (Dewey & L LLP) -1301 Av of Amer -NY 10019
(646) 710-3777 .. **Ruttan,** Chas D '00 MD Rx Direct,Inc -488 Mad Av -NY 10022
(212) 545-4650 .. **Ruttenberg,** David A '62 (Wolf HAF&H LLP) -270 Mad Av -NY 10016
(516) 281-9800 .. **Rutter,** Jesse D '06 %Goldberg S LLP -200 Old Cntry Rd -Mineola 11501
(212) 683-2020 .. **Rutter,** Mitchell B '81 %Essex Capital Prtnrs -635 Mad Av -NY 10022 **Fx:**683-2373
(718) 694-3835 .. **Ruttman,** Danielle D '88 %Transit Auth -130 Lvngstn -Brklyn 11201 **Fx:**694-5726
(718) 324-0404 .. **Rutty,** Diron E '95 (D Rutty,PC) -3921 Dyre Av -Bronx 10466 **Fx:**324-2211
(914) 584-7641 .. **Rutty,** Sophia A '00 -12 Granada Cres -White Plns 10603 **Fx:**206-3783
(212) 259-8000 .. **Rutwind,** Victoria A '09 %Dewey & L LLP -1301 Av of Amer -NY 10019
(518) 786-9069 .. **Ruuska,** Ryan E '09 %Schiller & K LLP -950 New Loudon Rd -Latham 12110
(212) 751-4300 .. **Ruvoldt,** Harold J Jr. '81 (Hodgson R LLP) -1540 Bway -NY 10036
(845) 782-2155 .. **Ruyack,** Jos E III '92 -3 Twin Brooks Dr -Chester 10918
(212) 512-1000 .. **Ruza,** Kesari '00 %HBO -1100 Av of Amer -NY 10036 **Fx:**512-1986
(914) 640-8100 .. **Ruzi,** Seth H '89 %Starwood Hotels & Resorts -1111 Wstchstr Av -White Plns 10604 **Fx:**640-8250
(212) 326-3939 .. **Ruzow,** Benjamin A '09 %Jones D -222 E 41st -NY 10017
(518) 487-7600 .. **Ruzow,** Danl A '77 (Whiteman O&H LLP) -1 Commerce Plz -Albany 12260
(212) 335-9000 .. **Ruzow,** Elyse C '97 %DA -1 Hogan Pl -NY 10013
(212) 336-2000 .. **Ruzumna,** Danl S '05 (Patterson BW&T LLP) -1133 Av of Amer -NY 10036
(212) 891-0858 .. **Ruzzo,** Loreto J '82 FOJP Srvcs Corp -28 E 28th -NY 10016
(516) 334-4400 .. **Ryall,** Jeremiah J '97 %T Walker -260 Jericho Tpk -Westbury 11590 **Fx:**333-3017
(212) 458-1512 .. **Ryan,** Aileen Anne '91 %AIG -175 Water -NY 10038
(212) 688-5151 .. **Ryan,** Aisling M '08 %Gibney A&F,LLP -665 5th Av -NY 10022
(212) 596-9000 .. **Ryan,** Amanda S '09 %Ropes & G LLP -1211 Av of Amer -NY 10036
(212) 977-4660 .. **Ryan,** Andrew J '89 (Salisbury & R LLP) -1325 Av of Amer -NY 10019
(585) 987-2800 .. **Ryan,** Andrew J '95 (Woods OG LLP) -2 State -Rchstr 14614
(212) 724-7309 .. **Ryan,** Ann '85 -116 W 72nd -NY 10023
(212) 510-1400 .. **Ryan,** Ann E '85 %Spec Comm of Invstgtn -80 Maiden Ln -NY 10038 **Fx:**510-1550
(212) 953-6000 .. **Ryan,** Ann E '01 %Katsky K LLP -605 3rd Av -NY 10158
(212) 637-2213 .. **Ryan,** Anne C '81 %US Atty -1 St Andrews Plz -NY 10007
(212) 474-1000 .. **Ryan,** Antony L '97 (Cravath S&M LLP) -825 8th Av -NY 10019
(718) 590-2375 .. **Ryan,** Barbara A '74 %Supreme Ct Civil -851 Grand Cncrs -Bronx 10451
(212) 593-6700 .. **Ryan,** Barbara A '90 (Aaronson RF&D,LLP) -757 3rd Av -NY 10017
(845) 365-2500 .. **Ryan,** Barbara Leigh '97 Clarins USA,Inc -15 Olympic Dr -Orangebrg 10962
(516) 328-1100 .. **Ryan Brennan & Donnelly LLP** -131 Tulip Av -Floral Pk 11001 **Fx:**354-0814
(631) 715-7900 .. **Ryan,** Burton T Jr. '76 %US Atty -610 Fed Plz -Central Islip 11722
(585) 232-6500 .. **Ryan,** Cathy Kaman '81 (Harter S&E LLP) -1600 Bausch & Lomb Pl -Rchstr 14604
(212) 758-0050 .. **Ryan,** Chas E '81 %Title Assoc -825 3rd Av -NY 10022 **Fx:**758-8223
(631) 689-9036 .. **Ryan,** Chas S '94 %The Collaborative Group,Ltd -50 E Loop Rd -Stony Brk 11790 **Fx:**689-6880
(212) 416-8000 .. **Ryan,** Christine A '01 %Dept of Law -120 Bway -NY 10271
(212) 813-8800 .. **Ryan,** Christine E '10 Goodwin P LLP -620 8th Av -NY 10018
(212) 335-9000 .. **Ryan,** Christopher '99 %DA -1 Hogan Pl -NY 10013
(518) 452-1800 .. **Ryan,** Claudia A '80 (Towne R & Prtnrs,PC) -450 New Karner Rd Bx15072 -Albany 12212
(212) 977-9700 .. **Ryan,** Colleen M '04 %Phillips N LLP -666 5th Av -NY 10103
(518) 533-3000 .. **Ryan,** Colm P '09 %Bond S&K,PLLC -111 Wshngtn Av -Albany 12210
(212) 509-6009 .. **Ryan & Conlon LLP** -2 Wall -NY 10005 **Fx:**509-6119
(212) 446-2300 .. **Ryan,** Cristina Lucchetti '03 %Boies S&F LLP -575 Lex Av -NY 10022
(212) 431-5576 .. **Ryan,** Cynthia D '88 (Siskind SB) -430 W 14th -NY 10014
(315) 474-2911 .. **Ryan,** Danl R '00 %Smith SK&S,PC -250 S Clinton -Syracuse 13202
(315) 598-1700 .. **Ryan,** David T '76 (Ryan Law Ofc) -166 S 3rd -Fulton 13069 **Fx:**592-2199
(718) 237-2000 .. **Ryan,** Dawn C '81 %Leg Aid -111 Lvngstn -Brklyn 11201 **Fx:**237-8737
(212) 629-9690 .. **Ryan,** Dennis P '09 %P Merani -298 5th Av -NY 10001 **Fx:**629-9664
(212) 455-2000 .. **Ryan,** Devin F '06 %Simpson T&B LLP -425 Lex Av -NY 10017
(585) 325-7440 .. **Ryan,** Diana Deyo '95 (Kaman BMJ&G LLP) -135 Corp Woods -Rchstr 14623
(212) 948-2070 .. **Ryan,** Dorothy S '91 %Marsh,Inc -1166 Av of Amer -NY 10036
(516) 328-3500 .. **Ryan,** Edw M '94 (McDonnell & A,PC) -401 Franklin Av -Gdn Cty 11530
(518) 465-2488 .. **Ryan,** Edw P '78 -38 Eagle -Albany 12207 **Fx:**465-6612
(516) 496-3868 .. **Ryan,** Edw P '09 %Keusey T&B,PC -20 Crsswys Park Dr N -Woodbury 11797
(212) 325-2000 .. **Ryan,** Eileen E '90 Credit Suisse -11 Mad Av -NY 10010
(718) 722-6084 .. **Ryan,** Emmie Glynn '95 %Catholic Charities -191 Joralemon -Brklyn 11201
(518) 692-1200 .. **Ryan,** Erika Sellar '06 %Jordan & K LLC -4 Fisher -Greenwich 12834 **Fx:**692-1222
(212) 243-6005 .. **Ryan,** Faith Mei '96 %ATC Mgt -88 10th Av -NY 10011
(212) 335-4500 .. **Ryan,** Francis W IV '95 (DLA Piper LLP) -1251 Av of Amer -NY 10020
(212) 710-0030 .. **Ryan,** George L '65 (Ryan & R,PC) -264 W 40th -NY 10018
(516) 742-3470 .. **Ryan,** Gerald B '85 (Kral CRRP&G,LLP) -538 Broadhllw Rd -Melvll 11747
(212) 425-0700 .. **Ryan,** Gerard K Jr. '81 %Kelner & K -140 Bway -NY 10005
(631) 668-3818 .. **Ryan,** Gordon G '77 -33 The Plz -Montauk 11954 **Fx:**668-4618
(212) 754-9000 .. **Ryan,** Gregory J '85 (Tesser R&R LLP) -509 Mad Av -NY 10022
(845) 486-2300 .. **Ryan,** Heather A '06 %DA -236 Main -Poughkeepsie 12601 **Fx:**486-2324
(516) 747-9700 .. **Ryan & Henderson,PC** -1 Old Cntry Rd -Carle Pl 11514 **Fx:**747-9712
(718) 836-1797 .. **Ryan,** Herbert F '59 -1013 78th -Brklyn 11228
(914) 333-0300 .. **Ryan,** J Richd '56 (Ryan & S,LLP) -1 Neperan Rd -Tarrytwn 10591 **Fx:**333-0301
(212) 953-1855 .. **Ryan,** James B '00 (O'Halloran R LLP) -711 3rd Av -NY 10017
(212) 889-2300 .. **Ryan,** James E '75 (Dougherty RGZ&H) -131 E 38th -NY 10016
(845) 485-3900 .. **Ryan,** James G '78 %Dept of Law -235 Main -Poughkeepsie 12601 **Fx:**452-3303
(516) 357-3700 .. **Ryan,** James G '85 (Cullen and D LLP) -100 Q Roosevelt Blvd -Gdn Cty 11530
(914) 941-5500 .. **Ryan,** James J '51 OfCnsl Greene L&R -500 Exec Blvd -Ossining 10562
(518) 434-7400 .. **Ryan,** James J '66 -119 Wshngtn -Albany 12210 **Fx:**434-0558
(585) 338-6000 .. **Ryan,** James P '05 Bausch & Lomb,Inc -1 Bausch and Lomb Pl -Rchstr 14604
(518) 486-5479 .. **Ryan,** James W III '92 %OTDA -40 N Pearl -Albany 12243 **Fx:**474-9389
(212) 696-6000 .. **Ryan,** Jennifer L '10 %Curtis M-PC&M LLP -101 Park Av -NY 10178
(212) 310-8000 .. **Ryan,** Jessica S '07 %Weil G&M LLP -767 5th Av -NY 10153
(212) 859-8000 .. **Ryan,** Jocelyn Powers '10 %Fried FHS&J LLP -1 NY Plz -NY 10004
(585) 238-2000 .. **Ryan,** Jodie L '01 %Phillips L LLP -1400 First Fed Plz -Rchstr 14614
(212) 310-2184 .. **Ryan,** John C '82 %Colgate-Palmolive -300 Park Av -NY 10022
(516) 328-1100 .. **Ryan,** John E '81 (Ryan B&D LLP) -131 Tulip Av -Floral Pk 11001
(914) 286-3400 .. **Ryan,** John F '69 %Leg Aid -1 N Bway -White Plns 10601 **Fx:**682-4112
(607) 734-8161 .. **Ryan,** John J Jr. '77 (Buck DR&M) -100 Baldwin -Elmira 14901
(212) 681-1575 .. **Ryan,** John J '99 %Belluck & F LLP -546 5th Av -NY 10036
(516) 747-0393 .. **Ryan,** John L '65 -379 Marcellus Rd -Mineola 11501
(718) 286-6000 .. **Ryan,** John M '75 %DA -125-01 Qns Blvd -Kew Gdns 11415
(212) 238-3000 .. **Ryan,** John M '87 OfCnsl Emmet M&M,LLP -120 Bway -NY 10271
(607) 749-7296 .. **Ryan,** John T Jr. '64 OfCnsl NB Miner -25 S Main Bx310 -Homer 13077 **Fx:**749-4313
(631) 369-2270 .. **Ryan,** John T '78 %J Ryan & Assoc -633 Main Rd -Rvrhead 11901
(516) 759-2722 .. **Ryan,** Jos B '94 (Ryan M&L,LLP) -90 Forest Av -Locust Vly 11560
(212) 732-3200 .. **Ryan,** Jos M '63 (Carter L&M LLP) -2 Wall -NY 10005
(631) 629-4968 .. **Ryan,** Jos W Jr. '64 -225 Old Cntry Rd -Melvll 11747 **Fx:**629-4970
(212) 980-9600 .. **Ryan,** Julianna '84 (Kaufman B&R) -120 Bway -NY 10271
(212) 541-9100 .. **Ryan,** Karen P '92 (Schiavetti CDW&N,LLP) -575 8th Av -NY 10018
(516) 763-1042 .. **Ryan,** Karin Schult '88 -301 Morris Av -Rockvll Ctr 11570
(518) 474-4552 .. **Ryan,** Kathleen A '93 %Insurance Dept -99 Wshngtn Av -Albany 12257 **Fx:**486-2218
(518) 434-9807 .. **Ryan,** Kathleen M '87 (D'Agostino KM&C,PC) -16 Sage Estate -Menands 12204
(212) 626-4100 .. **Ryan,** Kathryn M '01 %Baker & M LLP -1114 Av of Amer -NY 10036
(518) 436-0751 .. **Ryan,** Kelly A '06 %Hinman S PC -121 State -Albany 12207
(914) 833-8378 .. **Ryan,** Kevin G '88 -10 Circle Av -Larchmnt 10538
(631) 754-3935 .. **Ryan,** Kevin J '83 -4 Linwood Ln -Ft Salonga 11768
(212) 761-4000 .. **Ryan,** Kevin J '97 Morgan Stanley -1585 Bway -NY 10036
(212) 527-1000 .. **Ryan,** Kevin M '86 (Jones HC&B PC) -1 Bttry Pk Plz -NY 10004
(212) 730-7750 .. **Ryan,** Kevin M '89 (Nicoletti GS&O,LLP) -555 5th Av -NY 10017
(585) 419-8800 .. **Ryan,** Kevin P '96 %Harris B PLLC -99 Garnsey Rd -Pittsfrd 14534
(718) 237-2000 .. **Ryan,** Kimberly A '97 %Leg Aid -111 Lvngstn -Brklyn 11201 **Fx:**237-8737
(718) 250-2000 .. **Ryan,** Kimberly S '98 %DA -350 Jay -Brklyn 11201 **Fx:**250-2314
(518) 747-0338 .. **Ryan,** Leslie W '85 -136 Bway -Ft Edward 12828 **Fx:**747-0771
(212) 688-8555 .. **Ryan,** Lisa '95 %Fragomen DB&L LLP -7 Hanover Sq -NY 10004
(212) 506-5416 .. **Ryan,** Lorraine M '91 Grtr NY Hsptl Assn -555 W 57th -NY 10019
(631) 712-5883 .. **Ryan,** Lynn M '97 %Hon M Cyganowski -290 Fed Plz Bx9013 -Central Islip 11722
(631) 329-0982 .. **Ryan,** Lynn N '97 -6 Bowling Grn Pl -E Hampton 11937 **Fx:**329-0982
(646) 610-5483 .. **Ryan,** Marie G '93 %NYPD -1 Police Plz -NY 10038
(212) 208-1216 .. **Ryan,** Mary E '91 %Standard & Poor's -55 Water -NY 10041 **Fx:**412-0242
(516) 759-2722 .. **Ryan Mason & Lewis, LLP** -90 Forest Av -Locust Vly 11560 **Fx:**759-9512
(212) 588-0800 .. **Ryan,** Matthew K '86 (Frommer L&H LLP) -745 5th Av -NY 10151
(518) 489-8424 .. **Ryan,** Matthew P '02 AFSCME Council 82 -63 Colvin Av -Albany 12206
(607) 772-7001 .. **Ryan,** Matthew T '91 Mayor -38 Hawley -Bnghmtn 13901
(516) 739-0000 .. **Ryan,** Megan C '06 Martyn T&M -330 Old Cntry Rd -Mineola 11501
(518) 455-2142 .. **Ryan,** Melissa Martin '94 %Leg Ethics Comm -Lgsltv Ofc Bldg -Albany 12247
(212) 504-6000 .. **Ryan,** Michl C '75 (Cadwalader W&T LLP) -1 World Fncl Ctr -NY 10281
(718) 250-2000 .. **Ryan,** Michl E '95 %DA -350 Jay -Brklyn 11201 **Fx:**250-2314
(914) 739-0002 .. **Ryan,** Michl F X '96 Ryan & R PC -3005 E Main -Cortlandt Manor 10567 **Fx:**739-3282
(212) 839-7000 .. **Ryan,** Michl J '63 Cnsl Hill B&N LLP -200 Lbrty -NY 10281
(716) 854-2211 .. **Ryan,** Michl J '70 %E Cosgrove -525 Delaware Av -Buffalo 14202 **Fx:**854-8122
(718) 351-1111 .. **Ryan,** Michl J '96 (Conigatti & R,LLP) -67 New Dorp Plz -Staten Isl 10306 **Fx:**351-8616
(212) 225-2000 .. **Ryan,** Michl L '79 (Cleary GS&H) -1 Lbrty Plz -NY 10006
(212) 834-0600 .. **Ryan,** Michl P '99 (Gordon & S,PC) -355 Lex Av -NY 10017
(716) 841-2293 .. **Ryan,** Michl T '83 %HSBC Bank -1 HSBC Ctr -Buffalo 14203 **Fx:**841-5087
(315) 413-5400 .. **Ryan,** Molly M '09 %Goldberg S LLP -5789 Widewaters Pkwy -Syracuse 13214
(212) 335-9000 .. **Ryan,** Nancy E '76 %DA -1 Hogan Pl -NY 10013
(212) 208-3203 .. **Ryan,** Nicola J '96 %Ambac Assurance -1 State Street Plz -NY 10004 **Fx:**785-1178
(914) 722-5208 .. **Ryan,** Padraic '80 %Merrill Lynch -670 Wht Plns Rd -Scarsdale 10583 **Fx:**722-5259

(914) 785-5300 .. **Ryan,** Patricia B '75 %A Lamer -555 Taxter Rd -Elmsfrd 10523 **Fx:**347-4269
(212) 455-2000 .. **Ryan,** Patrick J '90 (Simpson T&B LLP) -425 Lex Av -NY 10017
(212) 661-7300 .. **Ryan,** Patrick J '06 %Malapero & P LLP -295 Mad Av -NY 10017
(212) 635-3150 .. **Ryan,** Paul E '02 %Ofc Inspector Genl -61 Bway -NY 10006 **Fx:**809-6287
(914) 428-2100 .. **Ryan,** Paul G '96 %Welby B&G,LLP -11 Martine Av -White Plns 10606
(518) 393-4653 .. **Ryan,** Paul L '56 -Bx9062 -Schnctdy 12309
(212) 450-4000 .. **Ryan,** Paula A '87 (Davis P&W LLP) -450 Lex Av -NY 10017
(516) 248-8610 .. **Ryan Perrone & Hartlein,PC** -200 Old Cntry Rd -Mineola 11501
(518) 456-1187 .. **Ryan,** Peter J '72 -20 Hanes -Albany 12203
(518) 462-3000 .. **Ryan,** Rachel '06 %Iseman CR&H,LLP -9 Thurlow Ter -Albany 12203
(212) 710-0030 .. **Ryan & Raphael, PC** -264 W 40th -NY 10018 **Fx:**687-6953
(212) 848-4000 .. **Ryan,** Reade H Jr. '66 OfCnsl Shearman & S LLP -599 Lex Av -NY 10022
(845) 331-2525 .. **Ryan Roach & Ryan,LLP** -115 Green Bx3153 -Kingston 12402 **Fx:**331-2119
(212) 839-5300 .. **Ryan,** Robt A Jr. '03 %Sidley A LLP -787 7th Av -NY 10019
(914) 681-0444 .. **Ryan,** Robt D '73 (Rende R&D,LLP) -202 Mamaroneck Av -White Plns 10601
(518) 427-9700 .. **Ryan,** Robt J '98 OfCnsl Harris B PLLC -677 Bway -Albany 12207
(516) 747-9700 .. **Ryan,** Robt L Jr. '85 (Ryan & H,PC) -1 Old Cntry Rd -Carle Pl 11514
(212) 574-1200 .. **Ryan,** Saml John '89 (Seward & K LLP) -1 Bttry Pk Plz -NY 10004
(212) 714-1720 .. **Ryan,** Sarah A '06 %Tompkins MW&B LLP -140 Bway -NY 10005
(716) 858-2424 .. **Ryan,** Sarah E '08 %DA -25 Delaware Av -Buffalo 14202 **Fx:**858-7425
(212) 450-4000 .. **Ryan,** Sarah Murphy '07 %Davis P&W LLP -450 Lex Av -NY 10017
(212) 839-5300 .. **Ryan,** Sean C '05 %Sidley A LLP -787 7th Av -NY 10019
(212) 382-0909 .. **Ryan,** Sean P '95 %Peckar & A,PC -41 Mad Av -NY 10154
(212) 681-6500 .. **Ryan,** Sharon V '03 %Stempel BC&H,PC -675 3rd Av -NY 10017
(518) 499-1272 .. **Ryan Smith & Carbine,PC** -134 Main Bx75 -Whitehall 12887 **Fx:**499-1273
(212) 752-8000 .. **Ryan,** Tara Duggan '94 %Cole SMF&L,PA -900 3rd Av -NY 10022
(845) 357-7700 .. **Ryan,** Terrence '58 (Ryan & S LLP) -103 Wshngtn Av -Suffern 10901 **Fx:**357-7794
(212) 816-3302 .. **Ryan,** Thos F '93 Citigroup Global Mrkts Inc -388 Greenwich -NY 10013
(212) 640-5418 .. **Ryan,** Thos J '87 Amer Exp Travel Related Srvcs -200 Vesey -NY 10285
(212) 952-1111 .. **Ryan,** Thos P Jr. '94 %H Gladstein & Prtnrs LLC -110 Wall -NY 10005 **Fx:**943-7427
(315) 476-0781 .. **Ryan,** Thos W '72 -217 Mntgmry -Syracuse 13202 **Fx:**424-6826
(518) 465-9500 .. **Ryan,** Wm F Jr. '83 (Tabner R&K,LLP) -18 Corp Wds Blvd -Albany 12211
(212) 509-6009 .. **Ryan,** Wm F '89 (Ryan & C LLP) -2 Wall -NY 10005
(845) 331-2525 .. **Ryan,** Wm J '56 OfCnsl Ryan R&R,LLP -115 Green Bx3153 -Kingston 12402
(212) 685-7411 .. **Ryan,** Wm J '76 (Lurie IM&R,LLP) -475 Park Av S -NY 10016 **Fx:**685-9827
(845) 331-2525 .. **Ryan,** Wm J Jr. '79 (Ryan R&R,LLP) -115 Green Bx3153 -Kingston 12402
(516) 248-8610 .. **Ryan,** Wm T '60 (Ryan P&H,PC) -200 Old Cntry Rd -Mineola 11501
(631) 754-0600 .. **Ryan,** Winter Brook '94 -728 Ft Salonga Rd -Northprt 11768 **Fx:**754-3975
(212) 666-3500 .. **Ryan de Heredia,** Tomas L '93 (Ryan & R) -817 West End Av -NY 10025
(518) 463-1269 .. **Ryba,** Lauren E '02 %Walsh & H -18 Corp Wds Blvd -Albany 12211
(718) 852-8932 .. **Ryba,** Robt A '75 -142 Joralemon -Brklyn 11201
(212) 244-4111 .. **Rybak,** Chaim '06 %Shiboleth YR&Z,LLP -1 Penn Plz -NY 10119
(585) 343-3090 .. **Rybak Metzler & Grasso, LLP** -104 Bank -Batavia 14020 **Fx:**343-7919
(518) 457-2411 .. **Rybak,** Robt A '78 %DOT -50 Wolf Rd -Albany 12232 **Fx:**457-4021
(212) 766-4700 .. **Rychik,** Abe M '88 (Katz & R) -116 John -NY 10038 **Fx:**766-4705
(212) 225-2000 .. **Ryckaert,** Phillipe '08 %Cleary GS&H -1 Lbrty Plz -NY 10006
(212) 836-8000 .. **Rycroft,** Krista M '00 %Kaye S LLP -425 Park Av -NY 10022
(212) 489-1600 .. **Rydberg,** Darren K '02 %Deloitte LLP -1633 Bway -NY 10019 **Fx:**492-4201
(212) 297-5800 .. **Rydel,** Peter K '01 %Day P LLP -7 Times Sq -NY 10036
(315) 422-3466 .. **Ryder,** Aaron J '03 %Bottar L,PLLC -120 Madison -Syracuse 13202
(631) 848-1204 .. **Ryder,** Carol E '09 C Ryder,PC -10 Salonga Woods Rd -Northprt 11768
(585) 473-4122 .. **Ryder,** David C '05 -48 Eastland Av -Rchstr 14618
(212) 297-5800 .. **Ryder,** Herbert K '00 Cnsl Day P LLP -7 Times Sq -NY 10036
(315) 682-4000 .. **Ryder,** Jesse P '01 -121 E Water -Syracuse 13202 **Fx:**682-4700
(212) 330-5459 .. **Ryder,** Kathleen M '05 %USPS Law Dept -90 Church -NY 10007
(914) 422-6265 .. **Rydlun,** Darcy P '98 %DA -77 S Lex Av -White Plns 10601
(718) 739-6400 .. **Ryen,** Alice '80 %DHCR -92-31 Union Hall -Jamaica 11433 **Fx:**262-7938
(585) 454-5650 .. **Ryen,** Louis A '61 SrCnsl Lacy K LLP -130 E Main -Rchstr 14604
(585) 454-5650 .. **Ryen,** Matthew A '97 (Lacy K LLP) -130 E Main -Rchstr 14604
(212) 277-6500 .. **Ryerson,** James L '10 %Dickstein S LLP -1633 Bway -NY 10019
(631) 266-5854 .. **Ryesky,** Kenneth H '88 -Bx926 -E Northprt 11731
(212) 425-9300 .. **Ryfa,** Christina R '09 %Bressler A&R,PC -17 State -NY 10004
(917) 447-0552 .. **Ryklin,** Lolita '05 -303 E 57th -NY 10022
(212) 326-3939 .. **Ryland,** Erica M '92 (Jones D) -222 E 41st -NY 10017
(518) 257-1443 .. **Rylewicz,** Daren J '97 %CSEA,Inc -143 Wshngtn Av Bx7125 -Albany 12224 **Fx:**449-1525
(718) 260-4709 .. **Ryley,** Alexander H '09 Leg Aid -111 Lvngstn -Brklyn 11201
(212) 425-9300 .. **Ryman,** Shannon M '08 %Bressler A&R,PC -17 State -NY 10004
(212) 461-2323 .. **Rymer,** Agnes I '83 (Saiber LLC) -44 Wall -NY 10005
(212) 688-8555 .. **Rymer,** Justin A '06 %Fragomen DB&L LLP -7 Hanover Sq -NY 10004
(212) 735-3000 .. **Rymer,** Matthew I '08 %Skadden ASM&F LLP -4 Times Sq -NY 10036
(212) 925-1919 .. **Rymer,** Nataliya '06 %JA Reiner -291 Bway -NY 10007 **Fx:**941-5975
(607) 732-5367 .. **Rynders,** David B Jr. '85 -315 Lk -Elmira 14901
(718) 522-1020 .. **Rynecki,** Scott E '90 %Rubenstein & R -16 Court -Brklyn 11241
(315) 474-8735 .. **Ryniker,** Margaret R '79 -1917 W Colin -Syracuse 13207
(516) 294-5100 .. **Rynkar,** Robt D '70 OfCnsl Murphy B&O,LLP -22 Jericho Tpk -Mineola 11501
(516) 496-1903 .. **Rynsky,** Elena '04 (Fazio R & Assoc LLP) -175 Eileen Way -Syosset 11791 **Fx:**496-0912
(585) 657-6040 .. **Ryther,** Paul M '75 -97 Main Bx278 -E Bloomfld 14443
(212) 504-6000 .. **Rytter,** E Eric '04 %Cadwalader W&T LLP -1 World Fncl Ctr -NY 10281
(212) 643-8203 .. **Ryu,** Soomin Lisa '05 %Zhang & Assoc,PC -1350 Bway -NY 10018 **Fx:**643-5487
(212) 906-1200 .. **Ryu,** Young Hwan '10 %Latham & W -885 3rd Av -NY 10022
(212) 344-5680 .. **Rywkin,** Robt '79 (Thompson H LLP) -335 Mad Av -NY 10017
(585) 262-2120 .. **Rzepka,** Thos J '86 OfCnsl Bressler & K -16 W Main -Rchstr 14614 **Fx:**262-2625
(646) 861-5757 .. **Rzesniowiecki,** Linda '82 -11 Park Pl -NY 10007
(718) 275-3660 .. **Rzonca,** Tadeusz '08 (Harris Law Grp,LLP) -96-14 63rd Dr -Rego Pk 11374 **Fx:**275-3405
(718) 590-2000 .. **Saab-Dominguez,** Karen '04 %DA -198 E 161st -Bronx 10451 **Fx:**590-6477
(212) 848-4000 .. **Saad,** Peter A '09 %Shearman & S LLP -599 Lex Av -NY 10022
(516) 620-0814 .. **Saad,** Peter A Jr. '03 -114 Old Cntry Rd -Mineola 11501 **Fx:**294-4290
(212) 848-4000 .. **Saah,** Karen A '03 %Shearman & S LLP -599 Lex Av -NY 10022
(718) 286-2000 .. **Saal,** Theodora Mathilde '96 Leg Aid -120-46 Qns Blvd -Kew Gdns 11415 **Fx:**286-2286
(212) 735-3000 .. **Saarinen,** Michl D '04 %Skadden ASM&F LLP -4 Times Sq -NY 10036
(516) 822-1600 .. **Saasto,** Robt A '76 -16 E Old Cntry Rd -Hicksvll 11801 **Fx:**822-6160
(212) 310-8000 .. **Saavedra,** Andrea C '07 %Weil G&M LLP -767 5th Av -NY 10153
(315) 798-5766 .. **Saba,** Jos A Jr. '92 %DA -800 Park Av -Utica 13501 **Fx:**798-5582
(212) 909-6000 .. **Sabach,** Patrice McGuire '04 %Debevoise & P LLP -919 3rd Av -NY 10022
(914) 723-3567 .. **Sabadie,** Francisca A '76 -1 Walworth Av -Scarsdale 10583 **Fx:**723-6679
(212) 326-2000 .. **Sabado Green,** Nicole '02 Cnsl O'Melveny & M LLP -7 Times Sq -NY 10036
(212) 940-8800 .. **Sabados,** Bruce M '90 (Katten MR LLP) -575 Mad Av -NY 10022
(212) 318-6000 .. **Saban,** Cheryl R '86 (Paul HJ&W LLP) -75 E 55th -NY 10022
(718) 326-3434 .. **Sabani Reglis & Zero-Matuszewski, PC** -65-17 Grand Av -Maspeth 11378 **Fx:**326-3599
(212) 813-5900 .. **Sabarra,** Nancy E '98 (Fross ZL&Z,PC) -866 UN Plz -NY 10017
(212) 408-2500 .. **Sabat,** Jason B '06 %Baker B,LLP -30 Rckfllr Plz -NY 10112
(212) 902-1556 .. **Sabater,** Juan A '91 Goldman Sachs & Co -85 Broad -NY 10004
(914) 725-8048 .. **Sabatini,** Monica S '86 -2 Stonehouse Rd -Scarsdale 10583
(212) 239-5900 .. **Sabatini,** Richd J '80 (Sabatini & Assoc) -237 W 35th -NY 10001 **Fx:**279-1265
(631) 423-5222 .. **Sabatino,** Paul II '78 -1617 NY Av -Huntngtn Sta 11746
(718) 222-2301 .. **Sabatino,** Ralph M C '81 %Law Dept -350 Jay -Brklyn 11201 **Fx:**222-2373
(516) 437-4385 .. **Sabbagh,** Morris '94 (Vishnick MM LLP) -3000 Marcus Av -Lk Success 11042
(212) 403-1000 .. **Sabbah,** Michl '07 %Wachtell LR&K -51 W 52nd -NY 10019
(718) 590-3252 .. **Sabbah,** Tracy B '10 %Law Dept -900 Sheridan Av -Bronx 10451 **Fx:**590-2699
(212) 482-0001 .. **Sabbatino,** Francesca A '85 OfCnsl Russo K&T LLP -33 Whitehall -NY 10004
(212) 878-8000 .. **Sabel,** Allein '08 %Clifford C LLP -31 W 52nd -NY 10019
(212) 848-4000 .. **Sabel,** Bradley K '76 (Shearman & S LLP) -599 Lex Av -NY 10022
(212) 826-0880 .. **Sabel,** Chas R '81 -444 Mad Av -NY 10022 **Fx:**317-2331
(212) 298-5000 .. **Sabel,** Janet E '86 %Leg Aid -199 Water -NY 10038
(212) 918-3000 .. **Sabel,** Oleg R '01 %Hogan L LLP -875 3rd Av -NY 10022
(516) 432-6263 .. **Sabele,** Glenn L '79 %Elovich & A -164 W Park Av -Long Bch 11561
(212) 848-4000 .. **Sabella,** Christian R '05 %Shearman & S LLP -599 Lex Av -NY 10022
(631) 753-1056 .. **Sabella,** Christopher J '05 Proclaim America Inc -35 Pinelawn Rd -Melvll 11747
(646) 722-8500 .. **Sabella,** James J '77 (Grant & E,PA) -485 Lex Av -NY 10017
(718) 423-8886 .. **Sabella,** Robt P '90 -56-43 214th -Oakland Gdns 11364
(516) 741-6355 .. **Sabella,** Vince A '89 (Nicolini PF&S) -114 Old Cntry Rd Bx9006 -Mineola 11501
(516) 249-5800 .. **Sabellico,** Thos M '77 -1 West -Farmngdl 11735
(212) 490-7100 .. **Saber,** Bruce D '84 Monday Properties -230 Park Av -NY 10169
(212) 317-5043 .. **Saber,** Christina S '97 Swiss Re Fncl Products -55 E 52nd -NY 10055 **Fx:**317-5533
(212) 630-1059 .. **Saberski,** Lin Beth '85 %MAP - HRA -330 W 34th -NY 10001
(212) 577-7700 .. **Sabet,** Elizabeth W '04 %Safe Horizon -2 Lafayette -NY 10007 **Fx:**385-0331
(516) 466-9213 .. **Sabetfard,** Emil '96 -45 N Station Plz -Gt Neck 11021 **Fx:**482-5355
(516) 333-4030 .. **Sabeti,** Sean '96 (S Sabeti,PC) -22 Mike Ln -Smithtwn 11787 **Fx:**333-4032
(212) 218-5500 .. **Sabetta,** John C '67 (Seyfarth S LLP) -620 8th Av -NY 10018
(212) 956-9500 .. **Sabety,** Theo M '98 OfCnsl Hand B&A LLP -8 W 40th -NY 10018 **Fx:**376-6080
(212) 239-9009 .. **Sabharwal,** Rohit '90 Sabharwal & Assoc -350 5th Av -NY 10118 **Fx:**239-9229
(716) 592-4640 .. **Sabia,** Arthur V '65 -14079 Mill -Sprngvll 14141 **Fx:**592-4640
(718) 227-1800 .. **Sabian,** Andrea M '91 (DeMonaco & S) -114 Seguine Av -Staten Isl 10309 **Fx:**605-5156
(315) 785-3088 .. **Sabik,** John L '92 %Cnty Atty -175 Arsenal -Watertwn 13601 **Fx:**785-5178
(212) 619-4350 .. **Sabillon,** Luis G '04 %Newman MKGH,PC -14 Wall -NY 10005
(212) 381-7000 .. **Sabin Bermant & Gould LLP** -4 Times Sq -NY 10036 **Fx:**381-7201
(518) 457-0972 .. **Sabin,** Deborah A '79 %PERB -80 Wolf Rd -Albany 12205 **Fx:**457-2664
(212) 381-7000 .. **Sabin,** Elizabeth S '79 (Sabin B&G LLP) -4 Times Sq -NY 10036
(212) 705-7000 .. **Sabin,** Jeffrey S '78 (Bingham M LLP) -399 Park Av -NY 10022
(212) 455-2000 .. **Sabin,** Michl '08 %Simpson T&B LLP -425 Lex Av -NY 10017
(516) 294-3199 .. **Sabino,** Anthony M '84 (Sabino & S,PC) -92 Willis Av -Mineola 11501 **Fx:**747-9405

(516) 294-8844 ..**Sabino,** Elaine C '08 %L'Abbate BC&C,LLP -1001 Franklin Av -Gdn Cty 11530
(917) 939-0803 ..**Sabio,** Mirtha Camille '99 -105-74 Av N -Brklyn 11236 **Fx:**(973) 762-7394
(212) 351-4500 ..**Sable,** Alicia Hayes '07 %Epstein B&G,PC -250 Park Av -NY 10177
(212) 244-2740 ..**Sable,** Jesse C '57 -450 7th Av -NY 10123 **Fx:**244-2258
(212) 506-1700 ..**Sable,** Lauren E '07 %Kasowitz BT&F LLP -1633 Bway -NY 10019
(212) 223-6700 ..**Sabloff,** Matthew B '98 %Zukerman GB&C,LLP -875 3rd Av -NY 10022
(518) 458-8922 ..**Sabo,** Alvin O '69 (Donohue SV&H,LLP) -24 Aviation Rd -Albany 12205
(518) 286-9050 ..**Sabo,** Joshua A '97 -287 N Greenbush Rd -Troy 12180 **Fx:**286-9051
(212) 447-7070 ..**Sabo,** Lili R '03 %Whatley D&K LLC -1540 Bway -NY 10036
(212) 848-4000 ..**Sabo,** Martha C Hildebrand '08 %Shearman & S LLP -599 Lex Av -NY 10022
(518) 486-7470 ..**Sabo,** Mary F '97 %Insurance Dept -99 Wshngtn Av -Albany 12257 **Fx:**474-3397
(212) 613-1376 ..**Sabo,** Matthew J '00 HIAS -333 7th Av -NY 10001
(516) 622-8380 ..**Sabo,** Stacey '98 NeuLion Inc -1600 Old Cntry -Plainvw 11803
(212) 885-8000 ..**Sabol,** Catherine C '02 %BDO USA,LLP -330 Mad Av -NY 10017 **Fx:**697-1299
(718) 923-2956 ..**Sabol,** Lisbeth Jean '00 OTDA -14 Boerum Pl -Brklyn 11201
(212) 635-6654 ..**Sabot,** Jason '95 Bank of NY Mellon -1 Wall -NY 10005
(212) 761-1514 ..**Sabounghi,** Edgar '88 Morgan Stanley -1585 Bway -NY 10036
(518) 426-4600 ..**Sabourin,** Nathan R '09 %Couch W,LLP -540 Bway Bx22222 -Albany 12201
(315) 413-5400 ..**Sabourin,** Sandra J '93 SpclCnsl Goldberg S LLP -5789 Widewaters Pkwy -Syracuse 13214
(914) 390-4134 ..**Sabreen,** Susan Berger '93 %Hon LM Smith -300 Quarropas -White Plns 10601
(212) 872-9800 ..**Saburn,** Jos M '81 (Squire S&D LLP) -30 Rckfllr Plz -NY 10112
(716) 434-5518 ..**Sacca,** Gerald S '73 Sacca & S -781 Davison Rd -Lockprt 14094
(212) 735-3000 ..**Sacca,** Jos N '94 (Skadden ASM&F LLP) -4 Times Sq -NY 10036
(212) 576-4491 ..**Sacca,** Justin I '89 NYLIFE Securities -51 Mad Av -NY 10010
(518) 266-3000 ..**Sacca,** Thos C '81 %Div Tax Appls -500 Fed -Troy 12180 **Fx:**272-5178
(212) 688-5151 ..**Saccardi,** Meredith M '08 %Gibney A&F,LLP -665 5th Av -NY 10022
(914) 328-2969 ..**Saccente,** Trevor J '05 %Martin C&B LLP -245 Main -White Plns 10601
(518) 689-1433 ..**Sacco,** Elizabeth Corliss '00 %Greenberg T,LLP -54 State -Albany 12207
(718) 746-3440 ..**Sacco & Fillas, LLP** -141-07 20th Av -Whitestone 11357 **Fx:**746-4117
(718) 205-2441 ..**Sacco & Fillas, LLP** -78-05 Roosevelt Av -Jcksn Hts 11372 **Fx:**205-2442
(516) 248-6777 ..**Sacco,** George F '78 Cnsl Purcell & I,PC -204 Willis Av -Mineola 11501
(718) 727-2400 ..**Sacco,** George F '78 -811 Castleton Av -Staten Isl 10310 **Fx:**420-9030
(607) 724-6853 ..**Sacco,** James A '92 -53 Chenango -Bnghmtn 13901 **Fx:**723-3671
(518) 374-7411 ..**Sacco,** Mark J '99 -38 N Ferry -Schnctdy 12305 **Fx:**374-7475
(718) 746-3440 ..**Sacco,** Tonino '91 (Sacco & F,LLP) -141-07 20th Av -Whitestone 11357
(518) 782-0600 ..**Saccocio,** John R '89 School Admin Assn NYS -8 Airport Park Blvd -Latham 12110 **Fx:**782-9552
(518) 377-9096 ..**Saccocio,** Patrick J '89 (Parisi C&S,PLLC) -376 Bway Bx1087 -Schnctdy 12305 **Fx:**377-9108
(845) 331-1000 ..**Saccoman,** Chas J '40 OfCnsl G Redder -243 Wall Bx3100 -Kingston 12402 **Fx:**331-1009
(845) 331-1000 ..**Saccoman,** Jos D '51 -243 Wall -Kingston 12401 **Fx:**331-1009
(716) 856-5500 ..**Saccomando,** Vincent G '95 (Damon M LLP) -200 Delaware Av -Buffalo 14202
(914) 328-0404 ..**Saccomano,** Jos A Jr. '89 (Jackson L LLP) -1 N Bway -White Plns 10601
(516) 364-6006 ..**Saccone,** Dianne Miller '91 %Cohen & S,LLP -199 Crsswys Park Dr Bx9004 -Woodbury 11797
(212) 548-2100 ..**Saccone,** Girolamo M '80 (McGuire W LLP) -1345 Av of Amer -NY 10105
(212) 806-5400 ..**Sacerdoti,** Alessandro J '08 %Stroock &S&L LLP -180 Maiden Ln -NY 10038
(718) 984-2981 ..**Sach,** Mary Ellen '86 -124 Keegans Ln -Staten Isl 10308
(212) 752-6920 ..**Sachdev,** Rachna K '07 %Green & E -770 Lex Av -NY 10065
(212) 819-8200 ..**Sachdev,** Rohit '08 %White & C LLP -1155 Av of Amer -NY 10036
(212) 909-6000 ..**Sachdeva,** Raashi '06 %Debevoise & P LLP -919 3rd Av -NY 10022
(516) 741-4000 ..**Sachdeva,** Rompel '03 %Shanker Law Grp -101 Front -Mineola 11501 **Fx:**741-4665
(631) 629-4310 ..**Sachs,** Brian R '97 (The Sachs Firm,PC) -33 Walt Whitman Rd -Huntngtn Sta 11746 **Fx:**629-4311
(914) 946-4808 ..**Sachs,** David R '00 (Riebling P&S,LLP) -1 N Bway -White Plns 10601 **Fx:**287-7578
(516) 679-0400 ..**Sachs,** Eric '86 -254 Pettit Av -Bellmore 11710 **Fx:**679-7406
(516) 295-2894 ..**Sachs,** Ezekiel B '96 -821 W Bway -Woodmere 11598
(212) 201-6825 ..**Sachs,** Gary C '84 (Bolan JS&S) -One Lbrty Plz -NY 10006
(212) 619-5000 ..**Sachs,** Heidi N '07 %EDC -110 William -NY 10038 **Fx:**312-3912
(516) 221-0400 ..**Sachs,** Herbert '51 -254 Pettit Av -Bellmore 11710 **Fx:**221-0422
(212) 233-1400 ..**Sachs,** Jack '63 -111 John -NY 10038 **Fx:**233-1932
(914) 946-4777 ..**Sachs,** Joel H '66 (Keane & B,PC) -445 Hmltn Av -White Plns 10601
(917) 532-4385 ..**Sachs,** John R Jr. '89 -180 Cntrl Pk S -NY 10019
(212) 854-0691 ..**Sachs,** Lisa Ehrlich '09 Vale Columbia Center -435 W 116th -NY 10027
(212) 580-0210 ..**Sachs,** Michl C '97 %Mannes College of Music -150 W 85th -NY 10024
(845) 562-8890 ..**Sachs,** Michl S '73 -215 Quassaick Av Bx4277 -New Windsor 12553 **Fx:**562-8891
(212) 279-7300 ..**Sachs Spector & Glasser,PC** -450 7th Av -NY 10123 **Fx:**279-1456
(516) 248-7575 ..**Sachs,** Steven L '06 %Levine & G -114 Old Cntry Rd -Mineola 11501
(212) 597-8510 ..**Sachse,** Steffen D '04 WestLB AG -1211 Av of Amer -NY 10036
(212) 527-1000 ..**Sachs Feit,** Deborah '87 (Jones HC&B PC) -1 Bttry Pk Plz -NY 10004
(212) 415-8600 ..**Sack,** Alan M '84 OfCnsl Locke LB&L LLP -3 World Fncl Ctr -NY 10281
(212) 888-8200 ..**Sack,** David J '96 %Feder K LLP -845 3rd Av -NY 10022
(631) 543-2900 ..**Sack,** Ian M '03 %Davis & H,LLP -1345 Motor Pkwy -Islandia 11749
(212) 880-9410 ..**Sack,** Jonathan S '87 (Morvillo AGIA&B,PC) -565 5th Av -NY 10017
(212) 702-9000 ..**Sack,** Jonathan S '89 (Sack & S) -110 E 59th -NY 10022 **Fx:**702-9702
(914) 701-0806 ..**Sack,** Jos A '95 -2975 Wstchstr Av -Purchase 10577
(212) 431-6680 ..**Sack,** Jules '65 -401 Bway -NY 10013
(518) 533-1050 ..**Sack,** Kimberly M '89 %Conway & K LLP -9 Cornell Rd -Latham 12110
(212) 407-7700 ..**Sack,** Laura '92 Vedder P,PC -1633 Bway -NY 10019
(212) 267-1950 ..**Sack,** Robt '65 (Salenger SSK&B,LLP) -233 Bway -NY 10279
(212) 702-9000 ..**Sack,** Steven M '80 (Sack & S) -110 E 59th -NY 10022 **Fx:**702-9702
(212) 844-3534 ..**Sack,** Susan L '93 Robin Hood Fndtn -826 Bway -NY 10003
(716) 648-1300 ..**Sackel,** Roslyn Sireci '94 (Sawers & S,LLP) -81 Buffalo -Hambrg 14075 **Fx:**648-1700
(212) 801-2129 ..**Sackel,** Shelley C '09 %Greenberg T,LLP -200 Park Av -NY 10166
(518) 295-2272 ..**Sacket,** James '90 DA -Bx888 -Schoharie 12157 **Fx:**295-2273
(516) 294-8844 ..**Sacket,** Lee J '03 %L'Abbate BC&C,LLP -1001 Franklin Av -Gdn Cty 11530
(585) 263-1000 ..**Sackett,** Christine A '85 %Nixon P LLP -1100 Clinton Sq -Rchstr 14604
(315) 699-7345 ..**Sackett,** Michl A '90 -6202 Diffin Rd -Cicero 13039
(212) 839-5300 ..**Sackheim,** Michl S '75 (Sidley A LLP) -787 7th Av -NY 10019
(212) 626-4100 ..**Sackin,** Marc J '09 %Baker & M LLP -1114 Av of Amer -NY 10036
(212) 506-2500 ..**Sackmann,** Pamela J '92 Cnsl Mayer B LLP -1675 Bway -NY 10019
(516) 741-2585 ..**Sackoor,** Jason P '08 %Rosicki R & Assoc,PC -51 E Bethpage Rd -Plainvw 11803 **Fx:**741-4748
(212) 450-4000 ..**Sacks,** Aaron M '07 %Davis P&W LLP -450 Lex Av -NY 10017
(212) 832-1977 ..**Sacks,** Alan D '99 %Schreck RDA&H -1790 Bway -NY 10019 **Fx:**832-2969
(212) 231-8132 ..**Sacks,** Alan R '05 (Sacks & M LLC) -410 Park Av -NY 10022
(516) 357-3000 ..**Sacks,** Andrea C '03 %Rivkin R LLP -926 RXR Plz -Uniondale 11556
(914) 761-6552 ..**Sacks,** Brad R '81 (Sacks & Assoc) -99 Court -White Plns 10601 **Fx:**761-3042
(212) 349-6171 ..**Sacks,** Bradley A '78 -225 Bway -NY 10007 **Fx:**349-6240
(212) 481-4433 ..**Sacks,** Debra K '88 %Ctr On Aging -425 E 25th -NY 10010
(718) 237-2000 ..**Sacks,** Ellen S '86 %Leg Aid -111 Lvngstn -Brklyn 11201 **Fx:**237-8737
(212) 554-0400 ..**Sacks,** Eric D '94 (Grubman I&S,PC) -152 W 57th -NY 10019
(212) 964-5570 ..**Sacks,** Evan '89 (Sacks & S) -150 Bway -NY 10038 **Fx:**349-2141
(718) 643-5343 ..**Sacks,** Gillian '80 %Hon R Huttner -360 Adams -Brklyn 11201 **Fx:**643-6299
(212) 513-3200 ..**Sacks,** Harry P '60 OfCnsl Holland & K LLP -31 W 52nd -NY 10019
(212) 605-0355 ..**Sacks,** Ira S '75 -575 Mad Av -NY 10022
(212) 848-9800 ..**Sacks,** Ivan A '93 (Withers B LLP) -430 Park Av -NY 10022
(631) 853-4104 ..**Sacks,** Jennifer A '08 %DA -400 Carleton Av Bx9082 -Central Islip 11722 **Fx:**853-7838
(516) 569-8100 ..**Sacks,** Judy Bruckner '86 OfCnsl Rosenfeld & M -132 Spruce -Cedarhrst 11516
(212) 964-5570 ..**Sacks,** Kenneth '89 (Sacks & S) -150 Bway -NY 10038 **Fx:**349-2141
(212) 688-5151 ..**Sacks,** Kenneth N '79 (Gibney A&F,LLP) -665 5th Av -NY 10022
(212) 331-5045 ..**Sacks,** Lauren '90 HRA Ofc Lgl Affrs -180 Water -NY 10038
(212) 381-7000 ..**Sacks,** Lawr J '87 (Sabin B&G LLP) -4 Times Sq -NY 10036
(212) 451-2300 ..**Sacks,** Melanie J '05 %Olshan GFR&W LLP -65 E 55th -NY 10022
(212) 541-6222 ..**Sacks,** Robt L '74 Cnsl Kane K,PC -1350 Av of Amer -NY 10019
(212) 848-4000 ..**Sacks,** Russell D '01 (Shearman & S LLP) -599 Lex Av -NY 10022
(212) 815-0124 ..**Sacks,** Sarah M '01 DA Ofc Spcl Narcotics Pros -80 Centre -NY 10013
(212) 421-4100 ..**Sacks,** Selig D '75 (Pryor C LLP) -7 Times Sq -NY 10036
(516) 741-4799 ..**Sacks,** Shayna E '03 %Baker SBGFM&N,LLC -100 Grdn City Plz -Gdn Cty 11530
(212) 964-5570 ..**Sacks,** Stanley '49 %Sacks & S -150 Bway -NY 10038 **Fx:**349-2141
(212) 773-1815 ..**Sacks,** Stephen A '81 Ernst & Young LLP -5 Times Sq -NY 10036
(718) 618-3731 ..**Sacks,** Stuart '82 Supreme Ct Crim Div -265 E 161st -Bronx 10451
(914) 428-8300 ..**Sacks,** Warren S '89 (Sacks,PC) -707 Wstchstr Av -White Plns 10604 **Fx:**682-1707
(631) 495-8597 ..**Sackstein,** Eric A '72 -Bx436 -Pt Jffrsn 11777
(516) 248-2234 ..**Sackstein,** Harvey A '52 (Sackstein S&L,LLP) -1140 Franklin Av -Gdn Cty 11530
(516) 248-2234 ..**Sackstein,** Mark H '84 (Sackstein S&L,LLP) -1140 Franklin Av -Gdn Cty 11530
(516) 248-2234 ..**Sackstein Sackstein & Lee,LLP** -1140 Franklin Av -Gdn Cty 11530 **Fx:**248-7268
(212) 558-6668 ..**Sacoulas,** Peter '97 (Foley SO&W) -100 William -NY 10038
(212) 547-5400 ..**Sacripanti,** Peter J '85 (McDermott W&E LLP) -340 Mad Av -NY 10173
(212) 483-9490 ..**Sacro,** Mari Grace E '00 %McElroy DM&C,LLP -88 Pine -NY 10005
(845) 291-2050 ..**Sadaghiani,** Amir H '07 %DA -255-275 Main -Goshen 10924 **Fx:**291-2085
(212) 634-6451 ..**Sadaka,** Mark T '04 (Sadaka Assoc LLC) -641 Lex Av -NY 10022
(212) 446-8019 ..**Sadarangani,** Sapna '05 %McKinsey & Co -55 E 52nd -NY 10055 **Fx:**688-9521
(212) 792-7600 ..**Sade,** Dana '93 %Peak Cnsl Inc -25 W 31st -NY 10001
(973) 315-4404 ..**Sade,** Norman G '58 (Budd L) -140 Bway -NY 10005
(212) 701-3000 ..**Sadeghi,** Kayvan B '04 %Cahill G&R LLP -80 Pine -NY 10005 **Fx:**269-5420
(212) 705-8888 ..**Sadeghi-Nejad,** Fatemeh '96 QVT Financial LP -1177 Av of Amer -NY 10036
(212) 909-6000 ..**Sader,** Salim C '07 %Debevoise & P LLP -919 3rd Av -NY 10022
(212) 765-3040 ..**Sadicario,** Steven '76 %NS Bienstock,Inc -250 W 57th -NY 10107 **Fx:**757-6411
(212) 906-1200 ..**Sadik,** Noraan '06 %Latham & W -885 3rd Av -NY 10022

(585) 232-8340 .. **Sadinsky,** Lisa A '92 -19 W Main -Rchstr 14614
(716) 858-2424 .. **Sadinsky,** Susan H '83 DA -25 Delaware Av -Buffalo 14202 **Fx:**858-7425
(212) 947-3793 .. **Sadis & Goldberg LLP** -551 5th Av -NY 10176 **Fx:**947-3796
(212) 947-3793 .. **Sadis,** Jack M '58 (Sadis & G LLP) -551 5th Av -NY 10176
(516) 921-5026 .. **Sadis,** Jack M '58 -125 Hickman -Syosset 11791
(212) 629-2228 .. **Sadler,** Carole P '85 Coach -516 W 34th -NY 10001
(212) 506-5000 .. **Sadler,** Rodger A '99 (Orrick H&S LLP) -51 W 52nd -NY 10019
(212) 541-6000 .. **Sadlowski,** Dennis A '81 Renco Grp -1 Rckfllr Plz -NY 10020
(212) 225-2000 .. **Sado,** Stephanie D '09 %Cleary GS&H -1 Lbrty Plz -NY 10006
(212) 867-5800 .. **Sadofsky,** Matthew '07 %Osler H&H LLP -620 8th Av -NY 10018
(212) 676-6051 .. **Sadok,** Melanie V '03 %Law Dept -100 Church -NY 10007 **Fx:**788-0367
(212) 308-9800 .. **Sadow,** Jacqueline '88 -100 Wall -NY 10005 **Fx:**308-5068
(914) 235-5618 .. **Sadow,** Jos '56 -589 Wilmot Rd -New Rchll 10804
(315) 671-2785 .. **Sadowski,** David J '80 %City Ct -505 S State -Syracuse 13202 **Fx:**671-2740
(631) 261-8834 .. **Sadowski,** Mary Anne '91 (Ingerman S LLP) -150 Motor Pkwy -Hauppauge 11788
(212) 430-5400 .. **Sadowski,** Robt W '86 Diamond M LLP -620 8th Av -NY 10018
(212) 534-3465 .. **Sadowsky,** Edw '87 -303 E 90th -NY 10128 **Fx:**534-3465
(212) 335-4500 .. **Sadowsky,** Michelle W '01 %DLA Piper LLP -1251 Av of Amer -NY 10020
(212) 768-6700 .. **Sadowsky,** Richd L '81 (Sonnenschein N&R LLP) -2 World Fncl Ctr -NY 10281
(718) 250-2000 .. **Sadri,** Yas '00 %DA -350 Jay -Brklyn 11201 **Fx:**250-2314
(212) 788-0778 .. **Sadrieh,** Tahirih M '93 %Law Dept -100 Church -NY 10007 **Fx:**788-0367
(212) 446-4800 .. **Sadtler,** Edw H '00 (Kirkland & E LLP) -153 E 53rd -NY 10022
(212) 593-3000 .. **Sadutto-Carley,** Teresa G '03 %Platzer SKLG&J,LLP -1065 Av of Amer -NY 10018
(212) 980-9600 .. **Saechao,** Tyra R '08 %Kaufman B&R -120 Bway -NY 10271
(718) 590-5944 .. **Saed,** Jacquelin '92 %Admin Children's Srvcs -900 Sheridan Av -Bronx 10451
(516) 739-5403 .. **Saed,** Sherli S '98 -110 Old Cntry Rd -Mineola 11501 **Fx:**739-5405
(212) 425-7200 .. **Saed,** Shirley Othmana '00 -1 Bway -NY 10004 **Fx:**425-5288
(212) 474-1000 .. **Saeed,** Faiza J '92 (Cravath S&M LLP) -825 8th Av -NY 10019
(212) 684-0300 .. **Saeed,** Yasmin R '06 %Bauman K&G LLP -28 W 44th -NY 10036
(718) 250-2000 .. **Saeidi,** Mahsa '10 %DA -350 Jay -Brklyn 11201 **Fx:**250-2314
(212) 526-5443 .. **Saeki,** Runa '98 %Barclays Capital Inc -745 7th Av -NY 10019
(716) 839-6750 .. **Saeli,** Jos F Jr. '78 -4600 Main -Amherst 14226
(212) 735-8600 .. **Saenger,** Rebecca A '05 %Morrison C LLP -909 3rd Av -NY 10022
(212) 801-6930 .. **Saenz,** David J '05 (Greenberg T,LLP) -200 Park Av -NY 10166
(212) 489-8230 .. **Saer,** Kevin F '91 (Davis WT LLP) -1633 Bway -NY 10019
(212) 205-7000 .. **Safai,** Leila '05 %Ashurst LLP -7 Times Sq -NY 10036
(631) 650-1200 .. **Safar,** Jay '92 OfCnsl Sinnreich K&M LLP -267 Carleton Av -Central Islip 11722
(718) 637-3442 .. **Safarian,** Natalia '06 -Bx271 -Patchogue 11772 **Fx:**(631) 654-5561
(212) 907-0885 .. **Safar Lerner,** Kellie C '06 %Labaton S LLP -140 Bway -NY 10005 **Fx:**818-7085
(212) 336-3500 .. **Safer,** Adam J '95 (Miller & W,PC) -570 Lex Av -NY 10022
(212) 269-8628 .. **Safer,** David R '53 (Grubin S&T) -60 Broad -NY 10004 **Fx:**809-6185
(646) 613-4620 .. **Safer,** Ilana '03 Getty Images -75 Varick -NY 10013
(212) 415-8600 .. **Safer,** Jay G '72 (Locke LB&L LLP) -3 World Fncl Ctr -NY 10281
(516) 229-4300 .. **Safer,** Jesse A '81 J Bilello & Assoc -875 Merrick Av -Westbury 11590
(212) 670-0193 .. **Safer,** Phyllis '79 %Merrill Lynch -222 Bway -NY 10038
(212) 373-3000 .. **Saferstein,** Jeffrey D '90 (Paul WRW&G LLP) -1285 Av of Amer -NY 10019
(212) 209-4800 .. **Saffar,** Claudia J '05 %Brown R LLP -7 Times Sq -NY 10036
(212) 608-6968 .. **Saffer,** Jennifer L '96 (JL Saffer,PC) -20 Vesey -NY 10007
(212) 259-8000 .. **Saffi,** Alexander J '07 %Dewey & L LLP -1301 Av of Amer -NY 10019
(516) 432-9229 .. **Saffioti,** Gerald R Jr. '88 -265 E Beech -Long Bch 11561
(845) 562-3500 .. **Saffioti,** Jos M '85 (Saffioti & A) -5031 Route 9W -Newburgh 12550 **Fx:**562-3117
(212) 259-8000 .. **Saffitz,** Emily L '07 %Dewey & L LLP -1301 Av of Amer -NY 10019
(212) 619-6030 .. **Saffner,** Ronald '73 -110 Wall -NY 10005 **Fx:**943-2300
(212) 588-0800 .. **Safford,** A Thos S '62 OfCnsl Frommer L&H LLP -745 5th Av -NY 10151
(212) 906-1200 .. **Saffos,** Stelios G '07 %Latham & W -885 3rd Av -NY 10022
(212) 593-6700 .. **Saffra,** David N '97 %Aaronson RF&D,LLP -757 3rd Av -NY 10017
(516) 571-3966 .. **Saffran,** Dennis J '81 Cnty Atty -1 West -Mineola 11501 **Fx:**571-6604
(212) 872-5616 .. **Saffron,** Clifford R '85 KPMG LLP -345 Park Av -NY 10154 **Fx:**954-7656
(212) 450-4000 .. **Safi,** Jeannette '08 %Davis P&W LLP -450 Lex Av -NY 10017
(516) 248-3641 .. **Safian,** Norman T '62 -2 Birchwood Ct Bx207 -Mineola 11501 **Fx:**746-6053
(212) 408-5100 .. **Safier,** Isaac M '09 %Chadbourne & P LLP -30 Rckfllr Plz -NY 10112
(212) 267-1650 .. **Safier,** Jennifer H '96 %Fine O&A,LLP -39 Bway -NY 10006
(212) 817-6704 .. **Safir,** Adam G '98 Global Options Grp -415 Mad Av -NY 10017
(212) 594-5300 .. **Safirstein,** Peter G A '86 (Milberg LLP) -1 Penn Plz -NY 10119
(914) 323-7000 .. **Safko O'Meara,** Juliann '01 %Wilson EME&D LLP -3 Gannett Dr -White Plns 10604
(212) 906-1200 .. **Safran,** Lawr I '86 (Latham & W) -885 3rd Av -NY 10022
(516) 248-3302 .. **Safran,** Victoria L '85 %Dept of Law -200 Old Cntry Rd -Mineola 11501 **Fx:**747-6432
(914) 997-0072 .. **Safranek,** Michl L '93 -One Water -White Plns 10601 **Fx:**997-1182
(518) 462-5601 .. **Safranko,** Andrew R '99 (O'Connell & A) -54 State -Albany 12207
(518) 489-7661 .. **Safranko,** Stephen A '68 -40 Colvin Av -Albany 12206 **Fx:**689-5392
(212) 546-9255 .. **Safrin,** Allen '94 %Scarinci H -107 Grand -NY 10013
(646) 386-5393 .. **Safron,** Linda H '79 %Family Ct -60 Lafayette -NY 10013
(212) 336-2000 .. **Safron,** Robt M '69 (Patterson BW&T LLP) -1133 Av of Amer -NY 10036
(212) 559-3277 .. **Safron,** Terry A '87 -399 Park Av -NY 10022
(718) 254-0700 .. **Saft,** Laura '81 %Bklyn Defender Srvcs -177 Lvngstn -Brklyn 11201 **Fx:**254-0897
(212) 259-8000 .. **Saft,** Stuart M '72 (Dewey & L LLP) -1301 Av of Amer -NY 10019
(646) 865-0797 .. **Saftler,** Lawr B '78 Saftler Law Firm -275 Mad Av -NY 10016 **Fx:**865-0801
(212) 593-7979 .. **Sagal,** Lanny M '71 (Ziegler S&W,PC) -575 Lex Av -NY 10022
(212) 732-8700 .. **Sagalovich,** Alexandra '07 %McAloon & F,PC -123 William -NY 10038
(212) 770-6642 .. **Sagalow,** Ty R '84 %AIG -70 Pine -NY 10270
(212) 574-1200 .. **Sagalyn,** David H '02 %Seward & K LLP -1 Bttry Pk Plz -NY 10004
(212) 697-2800 .. **Sagar,** Janine M '97 %Sofer & H,LLP -317 Mad Av -NY 10017
(212) 672-1840 .. **Sagat,** Kenneth A '68 (Sagat B LLP) -245 Park Av -NY 10167 **Fx:**672-1842
(212) 255-8693 .. **Sage,** Andrea Levine '92 -145 W 27th -NY 10001
(212) 803-5100 .. **Sage,** Brad D '95 %NY Cnty Defender Srvcs -225 Bway -NY 10007 **Fx:**571-6035
(212) 986-0101 .. **Sage,** Malcolm '81 -45 Christopher -NY 10014 **Fx:**352-3344
(212) 632-5500 .. **Sage,** Marc L '02 Salans LLP -620 5th Av -NY 10020
(212) 698-3500 .. **Sage,** Michl J '95 (Dechert LLP) -1095 Av of Amer -NY 10036
(516) 944-8811 .. **Sage,** Paul '56 P Sage,PC -111 Grt Nck Rd -Gt Neck 11021 **Fx:**883-9537
(718) 261-2300 .. **Sager,** Audrey M '78 (Sager & G) -118-35 Qns Blvd -Frst Hlls 11375
(212) 297-5800 .. **Sager,** David S '96 (Day P LLP) -7 Times Sq -NY 10036
(718) 261-2300 .. **Sager & Gellerman** -118-35 Qns Blvd -Frst Hlls 11375 **Fx:**261-0821
(718) 645-6677 .. **Sager,** Karen Goldberg '88 (Goldberg S & Assoc) -1628 Kings Hwy -Brklyn 11229 **Fx:**339-7823
(212) 998-6442 .. **Sager,** Laura '73 %NYU Law Schl -245 Sullivan -NY 10012 **Fx:**995-4031
(212) 351-4000 .. **Sager,** Lauren M '09 %Gibson D&C LLP -200 Park Av -NY 10166
(718) 645-6677 .. **Sager,** Marcel A '87 (Goldberg S & Assoc) -1628 Kings Hwy -Brklyn 11229 **Fx:**339-7823
(212) 288-4247 .. **Sager,** Marilyn T '79 -200 E 78th -NY 10075 **Fx:**288-8211
(516) 488-3300 .. **Sagesser,** Regina M '00 %Shaub AC&S,LLP -1983 Marcus Av -Lk Success 11042
(201) 287-1500 .. **Saget,** Shara D '05 %J Samel & Partners -150 Bway -NY 10038 **Fx:**287-1555
(212) 728-8000 .. **Saggar,** Natasha A '09 %Willkie F&G LLP -787 7th Av -NY 10019
(212) 943-1090 .. **Saghir,** Peter J '05 %Gair GCSMB&R -80 Pine -NY 10005
(212) 448-1100 .. **Saginaw,** Aimee E '03 (McLaughlin & S,LLP) -260 Mad Av -NY 10016
(718) 923-0690 .. **Sagiv,** Paul J '01 %R Santoriella PC -335 Adams -Brklyn 11201 **Fx:**923-0683
(716) 372-4450 .. **Saglimben,** Michl J '95 (Carr S LLP) -235 N Union -Olean 14760 **Fx:**372-4011
(212) 408-2500 .. **Saglimbeni,** Saml '08 %Baker B,LLP -30 Rckfllr Plz -NY 10112
(212) 332-3238 .. **Sagona,** Marian N '06 -45 Rckfllr Ctr -NY 10111 **Fx:**(718) 841-7376
(212) 918-3000 .. **Sagor,** Elliot G '66 (Hogan L LLP) -875 3rd Av -NY 10022
(212) 310-8000 .. **Sagot,** Jonathan L '09 %Weil G&M LLP -767 5th Av -NY 10153
(212) 400-8250 .. **Sah,** Pamela Bailey '00 Fair Housing Justice Ctr Help USA -5 Hanover Sq -NY 10004
(212) 878-8000 .. **Saha,** Anand '06 %Clifford C LLP -31 W 52nd -NY 10019
(212) 949-7897 .. **Saha,** Matthew W '91 -80 Park Av -NY 10016 **Fx:**949-7897
(212) 330-8151 .. **Saha,** Milan '06 %Brinen & Assoc,LLC -7 Dey -NY 10007 **Fx:**202-5330
(212) 218-2100 .. **Saha,** Soma '09 %Fitzpatrick CH&S -1290 Av of Amer -NY 10104
(914) 777-3700 .. **Sahagian,** James A '99 -136 Palmer Av -Mamaroneck 10543 **Fx:**777-3707
(212) 350-2700 .. **Sahakian,** Taline '08 %Constantine C,PC -450 Lex Av -NY 10017
(212) 905-1700 .. **Sahgal,** Larissa U '05 Granada Ent -609 Greenwich -NY 10014
(646) 657-0486 .. **Sahid,** Jos R '73 -1065 Park Av -NY 10128 **Fx:**(212) 214-0998
(212) 549-2500 .. **Sahl,** Benjamin '06 ACLU -125 Broad -NY 10004 **Fx:**549-2651
(212) 296-0891 .. **Sahlman,** Wm W '96 %Morgan Stanley -522 5th Av -NY 10036
(516) 248-1700 .. **Sahn,** Brian R '84 (Forchelli CDSM&T,LLP) -333 Earle Ovngton Blvd -Uniondale 11553
(516) 228-1300 .. **Sahn,** Michl H '77 (Sahn WC&B,PLLC) -333 Earle Ovngton Blvd -Uniondale 11553
(516) 228-1300 .. **Sahn Ward Coschignano & Baker,PLLC** -333 Earle Ovngton Blvd -Uniondale 11553 **Fx:**228-0038
(212) 637-2491 .. **Sahni,** Anjan Singh '02 %US Atty -1 St Andrews Plz -NY 10007
(212) 363-9400 .. **Sahni,** Gurvinder S '91 -46 Trinity Pl -NY 10006 **Fx:**363-9444
(718) 636-1155 .. **Sahni,** Jasbrinder Singh '97 %Leg Srvcs -1368 Fulton -Brklyn 11216 **Fx:**398-6414
(516) 496-5822 .. **Sahni,** Rasleen K '05 %T Spina -170 Froehlich Farm Blvd -Woodbury 11797 **Fx:**496-5420
(212) 450-4000 .. **Sahni,** Reena Agrawal '03 Cnsl Davis P&W LLP -450 Lex Av -NY 10017
(914) 684-5800 .. **Sahota,** Saryadvinder S '97 %Brunschwig & Fils -75 VA Rd -N White Plns 10603
(718) 544-8665 .. **Sahr,** Seth '86 (Novitt S&S,LLP) -118-35 Qns Blvd -Frst Hlls 11375
(718) 250-2000 .. **Sahrawat,** Deepti P '07 %DA -350 Jay -Brklyn 11201 **Fx:**250-2314
(212) 902-2582 .. **Sahrbeck,** Heather M '98 Goldman Sachs -85 Broad -NY 10004
(518) 689-1430 .. **Saia,** Doreen U '94 (Greenberg T,LLP) -54 State -Albany 12207
(716) 832-1118 .. **Saia,** Nancy W '85 -1925 Kensngtn Av -Buffalo 14215 **Fx:**832-7074
(212) 695-0910 .. **Saia,** Suzanne M '01 (Sullivan Law Grp,LLP) -1350 Bway -NY 10018 **Fx:**695-0915
(212) 461-2323 .. **Saiber LLC** -44 Wall -NY 10005 **Fx:**461-2324
(212) 901-0999 .. **Saidel,** Eric M '02 %Easton Assoc,LLC -119 W 40th -NY 10018 **Fx:**901-2999
(914) 736-6500 .. **Saidel,** Marc L '72 (Saidel & S,PC) -Route 202 Bx308 -Yorktwn Hts 10598 **Fx:**736-6581
(914) 736-6500 .. **Saidel,** Sheryl M '91 (Saidel & S,PC) -Route 202 Bx308 -Yorktwn Hts 10598 **Fx:**736-6581
(212) 909-6000 .. **Saideman,** Seth L '03 %Debevoise & P LLP -919 3rd Av -NY 10022
(212) 319-3737 .. **Saidenberg,** Lynn R '83 (J Silberman Assoc,PC) -145 E 57th -NY 10022 **Fx:**319-8188
(212) 819-8200 .. **Saidi,** Pouria '09 %White & C LLP -1155 Av of Amer -NY 10036
(718) 291-9100 .. **Saidlower,** Emanuel '70 -90-50 Parsons Blvd -Jamaica 11432 **Fx:**206-9082
(212) 449-1000 .. **Saieva,** Frances M '87 %Merrill Lynch -220 Bway -NY 10038
(212) 715-9100 .. **Saifee,** Seema '05 %Kramer LN&F,LLP -1177 Av of Amer -NY 10036
(212) 239-8008 .. **Saigal,** Suishta '92 (Madan & S,LLC) -358 5th Av -NY 10001

(212) 446-4800 .. **Saijwani,** Angeli '07 %Kirkland & E LLP -153 E 53rd -NY 10022
(212) 682-1818 .. **Sailer,** Jacqueline '96 (Murray F&S LLP) -275 Mad Av -NY 10016
(212) 770-7789 .. **Sailer,** Rosemarie '89 Amer Intl Realty Corp -80 Pine -NY 10005 **Fx:**770-9331
(212) 455-2000 .. **Saily,** Michl D '07 %Simpson T&B LLP -425 Lex Av -NY 10017
(516) 739-0000 .. **Sain,** Nitin '09 Martyn T&M -330 Old Cntry Rd -Mineola 11501
(212) 578-6227 .. **Sainato,** Suzanne W '99 %MetLife -27-01 Qns Plz N -LIC 11101
(212) 612-2472 .. **Saine,** Jennifer Lee '98 Chubb Grp -55 Water -NY 10041
(212) 966-5932 .. **Saingchin,** Alexander W '07 AALDEF -99 Hudson -NY 10013 **Fx:**966-4303
(716) 852-3600 .. **Saini,** Manik J '09 %Chelus HS&M,PC -438 Main -Buffalo 14202
(516) 571-3800 .. **St Bernard,** Kenneth '00 %DA -262 Old Cntry Rd -Mineola 11501 **Fx:**248-9479
(212) 356-4791 .. **St Clair,** Elizabeth R '82 SVCMC -450 W 33rd -NY 10001
(718) 210-4802 .. **St Clair,** Jeffrey A '02 (St Clair & Assoc) -26 Court -Brklyn 11242
(212) 735-3000 .. **St Clair,** John Gregory '02 (Skadden ASM&F LLP) -4 Times Sq -NY 10036
(845) 623-3332 .. **St Clair,** Patricia L '98 -101 N Mddltwn Rd -Nanuet 10954
(585) 232-6500 .. **St Cyr,** Jesse A A '09 %Harter S&E LLP -1600 Bausch & Lomb Pl -Rchstr 14604
(212) 605-6200 .. **St George,** Carmen V '98 %Levy P&K,LLP -800 3rd Av -NY 10022
(212) 972-1000 .. **Saint-Hilaire,** Ericka '09 %London F LLP -59 Maiden Ln -NY 10038
(718) 771-4388 .. **St Hill Dodson,** Fitzpatrick N '95 -203 Utica -Brklyn 11213 **Fx:**771-3479
(718) 941-1212 .. **Saintiny,** Fritz R '88 -19305 Hillside Av -Hollis 11423 **Fx:**284-1082
(631) 853-5761 .. **St James,** Jayne M '97 %Cnty Atty -400 Carleton Av -Central Islip 11722 **Fx:**853-7788
(212) 728-8000 .. **St Jeanos,** Christopher J '97 (Willkie F&G LLP) -787 7th Av -NY 10019
(212) 592-1400 .. **St Jeanos,** John C '89 (Herrick,F LLP) -2 Park Av -NY 10016
(212) 836-8000 .. **St John,** Catherine Stayer '07 %Kaye S LLP -425 Park Av -NY 10022
(212) 749-3656 .. **St John,** Jacqueline A '95 %Harlem Dowling -2090 AC Powell Jr Blvd -NY 10027
(585) 454-7145 .. **St John,** Mindy A '99 (Gallo & I,LLP) -39 State -Rchstr 14614
(212) 286-8585 .. **St John,** Terrence P '89 (Heidell PM&B,LLP) -99 Park Av -NY 10016
(518) 455-2711 .. **St John,** Keith C '87 %NYS Senate -316 State Cptl -Albany 12247 **Fx:**426-6955
(212) 397-3370 .. **St Laurent,** Andrew M '99 Harris CC&H LLP -111 Bway -NY 10006 **Fx:**202-6206
(212) 225-2000 .. **St Ledger,** Megan M '08 %Cleary GS&H -1 Lbrty Plz -NY 10006
(716) 447-1380 .. **St Ledger-Roty,** Jill M '78 -560 Delaware Rd -Buffalo 14223 **Fx:**447-1380
(315) 363-4690 .. **St Leger,** Michl G '89 (Dunn B&S LLP) -1507 Uppr Lenox Av -Oneida 13421
(212) 581-4540 .. **St Lifer,** Elizabeth '87 US Realty Advisors,LLC -1370 Av of Amer -NY 10019 **Fx:**581-4950
(516) 354-0149 .. **St Louis,** Noyel '00 (Lubin & S) -229 Jericho Tpk -Floral Pk 11001
(212) 858-4036 .. **St Louis,** Wm A '95 FINRA -1 Lbrty Plz -NY 10006 **Fx:**858-4389
(718) 923-8225 .. **St Louis-McEachern,** Mirna '90 %Red Hook Comm Justice Ctr -88 Visitation Pl -Brklyn 11231
(212) 973-8000 .. **St Marie,** Scott D '78 (Schnader HS&L LLP) -140 Bway -NY 10005
(718) 520-0808 .. **Saint Martin,** Manuel L '90 -115-10 Qns Blvd -Frst Hlls 11375 **Fx:**544-0972
(716) 858-2424 .. **St Mary,** Kristin '04 %DA -25 Delaware Av -Buffalo 14202 **Fx:**858-7425
(212) 309-6000 .. **St Matthew-Daniel,** Eyitayo O '06 %Morgan L&B LLP -101 Park Av -NY 10178
(914) 472-1899 .. **St Onge,** Jos E '75 -670 Wht Plns Rd -Scarsdale 10583 **Fx:**472-2312
(212) 530-5000 .. **St Peter,** Jaime L '09 %Milbank TH&M LLP -1 Chase Manh Plz -NY 10005
(914) 997-0500 .. **St Phillip,** Peter D Jr. '04 (Lowey DC&H,PC) -1 N Bway -White Plns 10601
(212) 323-2250 .. **Saint-Pierre,** Edmire C '06 %HHC-OLA-Medical Litigation -346 Bway -NY 10013 **Fx:**323-2251
(212) 259-8000 .. **St Pierre,** Suzanne '93 (Dewey & L LLP) -1301 Av of Amer -NY 10019
(718) 250-2000 .. **Saint-Pre,** Mike E '05 DA -350 Jay -Brklyn 11201 **Fx:**250-2314
(315) 798-5870 .. **St Thomas,** Doreen M '04 %Pub Def -321 Main -Utica 13501 **Fx:**798-6419
(914) 225-5476 .. **Saint Victor,** Nicholas N '03 %Morgan Stanley -2000 Wstchstr Av -Purchase 10577
(212) 999-5800 .. **Saionz,** Jennifer R '10 %Wilson SG&R -1301 Av of Americas -NY 10019
(212) 648-1135 .. **Saito,** Lester Y '96 %JP Morgan Chase & Co -245 Park Av -NY 10167
(212) 732-3200 .. **Saito,** Yasuhiro '93 (Carter L&M LLP) -2 Wall -NY 10005
(607) 722-3495 .. **Saitta,** Thos A '81 (Aswad & I) -46 Front -Bnghmtn 13905
(212) 310-8000 .. **Saiz-Gonzalez,** Patricia '05 %Weil G&M LLP -767 5th Av -NY 10153
(716) 845-9451 .. **Sajda,** Kurt T '75 %Supreme Ct -92 Franklin -Buffalo 14202 **Fx:**851-3293
(212) 848-4000 .. **Sajous,** Isabelle '03 %Shearman & S LLP -599 Lex Av -NY 10022
(718) 668-6800 .. **Sak,** James E '77 (Sak & R,LLP) -2675 Hylan Blvd -Staten Isl 10306 **Fx:**668-0051
(212) 297-5800 .. **Sakai,** Hajime '06 Cnsl Day P LLP -7 Times Sq -NY 10036
(718) 601-6282 .. **Sakalis,** Elias N '93 -430 W 259th -Bronx 10471 **Fx:**601-9675
(646) 530-8412 .. **Sakany,** Ellen '93 -244 5th Av -NY 10001 **Fx:**(888) 230-5378
(212) 903-9000 .. **Saker,** John A '07 %Linklaters -1345 Av of Amer -NY 10105
(212) 649-2000 .. **Saketkoo,** Eva M '96 %Hearst Corp -300 W 57th -NY 10019 **Fx:**649-2035
(718) 204-0437 .. **Saketos,** John G '86 (Coritsidis S&S) -25-61 Steinway -LIC 11103 **Fx:**267-0330
(212) 693-1313 .. **Sakkas,** W Matthew '92 -150 Bway -NY 10038 **Fx:**693-1314
(516) 678-2500 .. **Sakofsky,** Richd K '78 (Sakofsky & Y,PC) -100 N Centre Av -Rockvll Ctr 11570
(516) 678-2500 .. **Sakofsky & Yegelwel,PC** -100 N Centre Av -Rockvll Ctr 11570 **Fx:**536-5230
(516) 294-9200 .. **Sakol,** Erica B '98 -114 Old Cntry Rd -Mineola 11501 **Fx:**746-1071
(212) 370-1300 .. **Sakosky,** Robt P '99 %Ellenoff G&S LLP -150 E 42nd -NY 10017
(914) 785-5300 .. **Sakow,** Gordon T '85 A Lamer -555 Taxter Rd -Elmsfrd 10523 **Fx:**347-4269
(212) 294-6700 .. **Sakowitz,** David A '95 (Winston & S) -200 Park Av -NY 10166
(716) 655-0102 .. **Sakowski,** Jos A '76 (Sakowski & M,LLP) -Bx399 -Elma 14059 **Fx:**655-1820
(845) 634-3500 .. **Sakowski,** Walter J '95 -10 Esquire Rd -New Cty 10956
(718) 998-1800 .. **Saks,** Boris '97 (Fridman S,LLP) -1795 Coney Isl Av -Brklyn 11230 **Fx:**998-1881
(516) 741-7575 .. **Saks,** Carl '63 Vecchione V&C LLP -147 Hrrcks Rd -Gdn Cty Pk 11040 **Fx:**294-4636
(212) 770-7004 .. **Saks,** David H '95 %AIG -70 Pine -NY 10270
(212) 455-2000 .. **Saks,** Jeremy R '05 %Simpson T&B LLP -425 Lex Av -NY 10017
(212) 578-8190 .. **Saks,** Mark '92 Legacy Heritage Fund -55 E 59th -NY 10022
(646) 386-3258 .. **Saks,** Michl '83 Hon E Lehner -60 Centre -NY 10007
(212) 318-6000 .. **Saks,** Scott R '96 %Paul HJ&W LLP -75 E 55th -NY 10022
(212) 363-3100 .. **Saks,** Shannon L '03 %Bivona & C,PC -88 Pine -NY 10005
(212) 566-7188 .. **Saks,** Shirin W '98 %Genova B&G -115 Bway -NY 10006
(212) 605-2115 .. **Sakuma,** Takayuki '09 Mitsubishi International Corp -655 3rd Av -NY 10017 **Fx:**605-2129
(212) 846-8941 .. **Salad,** Stephen M '03 MTV Networks -1515 Bway -NY 10036 **Fx:**258-8358
(518) 452-1000 .. **Salada,** James B Jr. '76 (Newkirk & S) -15 Corp Cir -Albany 12203
(212) 244-6600 .. **Saladin,** Jose A '00 %Schechter & B,PC -350 5th Av -NY 10118
(718) 497-4721 .. **Saladino,** Andrew J '62 -69-24 62nd Av -Middl Vllg 11379
(631) 727-6899 .. **Saladino & Hartill, LLP** -431 Griffing Av -Rvrhead 11901 **Fx:**727-7182
(631) 727-6899 .. **Saladino,** James A '91 (Saladino & H,LLP) -431 Griffing Av -Rvrhead 11901
(518) 474-2138 .. **Salage,** Gary '83 %Dept of Law -The Cptl -Albany 12224
(212) 556-2100 .. **Salah,** Isam '76 (King & S) -1185 Av of Amer -NY 10036
(585) 232-6500 .. **Salai,** Stephen B '75 (Harter S&E LLP) -1600 Bausch & Lomb Pl -Rchstr 14604
(212) 250-2500 .. **Salama,** Jos M '99 %Deutsche Bank -60 Wall -NY 10005
(212) 902-7689 .. **Salaman,** Ricardo '85 %Goldman Sachs -1 NY Plz -NY 10004
(212) 538-7094 .. **Salame,** Kamil M '96 Credit Suisse First Boston -11 Mad Av -NY 10010
(718) 298-6029 .. **Salami-Oyakhilome,** Sadatu '04 Salami-Oyakhilome,PC -147-26 Hillside Av -Jamaica 11435 **Fx:**298-6021
(516) 625-1700 .. **Salamon Gruber Blaymore & Strenger, PC** -97 Powerhse Rd -Roslyn Hts 11577 **Fx:**625-1795
(585) 248-2910 .. **Salamone,** Bernard L '92 -1000 Pttsfrd Victor Rd -Pittsfrd 14534
(631) 424-3597 .. **Salamone,** Bryan L '95 -8 Ford Pl -Dix Hlls 11746 **Fx:**424-5023
(845) 783-9193 .. **Salamone,** Carole T '98 Cnsl Atlantic Communication Srvcs -21 Pinehurst Cir -Monroe 10950 **Fx:**782-6337
(585) 248-2910 .. **Salamone,** Donald A '59 -1000 Pttsfrd Victor Rd -Pittsfrd 14534
(212) 573-1586 .. **Salamone,** Francine R '99 %Pfizer Inc -235 E 42nd -NY 10017 **Fx:**573-1445
(212) 593-3000 .. **Salan,** Evan J '96 %Platzer SKLG&J,LLP -1065 Av of Amer -NY 10018
(212) 312-7129 .. **Saland,** Jeremy M '01 (Crotty & S LLP) -52 Duane -NY 10007 **Fx:**918-9375
(845) 454-3250 .. **Saland,** Stephen M '69 OfCnsl Gellert & K,PC -75 Wshngtn -Poughkeepsie 12601
(646) 352-1239 .. **Salandra,** Mario V '93 Bank of Amer -1 Bryant Pk -NY 10036
(718) 231-1515 .. **Salanitro,** Fredk J '88 %M Rubin -3413 Wht Plns Rd -Bronx 10467 **Fx:**231-3003
(212) 632-5500 .. **Salans LLP** -620 5th Av -NY 10020 **Fx:**632-5555
(845) 357-9500 .. **Salant,** Eric '98 -55 Old Tpk Rd -Nanuet 10954 **Fx:**624-0288
(914) 683-2500 .. **Salant,** Gregory A '03 %Harold SS&S -81 Main -White Plns 10601
(914) 683-2500 .. **Salant,** Jeffrey R '76 (Harold SS&S) -81 Main -White Plns 10601
(914) 684-6800 .. **Salant,** Scott M '90 (Collier HNN&B,LLP) -1 N Lex Av -White Plns 10601
(212) 230-8800 .. **Salas Aguilar,** Claudio D '05 %WilmerHale -399 Park Av -NY 10022
(212) 667-2357 .. **Salatte,** Thos M '94 Nomura Global Finl -2 World Fncl Ctr -NY 10281
(631) 968-0500 .. **Salatto,** Gary A '85 (Urban & S) -130 Orinoco Dr -Brightwtrs 11718
(212) 366-9054 .. **Salaway,** Kenneth W '64 -10 W 15th -NY 10011
(212) 366-0355 .. **Salaway,** Mitchell '90 -10 W 15th -NY 10011
(212) 261-8000 .. **Salazar,** Carolina '08 %Mendes & M,LLP -750 7th Av -NY 10019
(518) 465-9500 .. **Salazar,** Dana L '06 %Tabner R&K,LLP -18 Corp Wds Blvd -Albany 12211
(718) 230-1234 .. **Salazar,** Hugo G '95 (H Salazar,PC) -261 4th Av -Brklyn 11215 **Fx:**230-1292
(718) 256-2000 .. **Salazar,** Paulino J '02 %M Zilberberg & Assoc,PC -6619 13th Av -Brklyn 11219 **Fx:**256-7900
(212) 732-5400 .. **Salazar,** Susan E '99 %Raff & B,LLP -470 Park Av S -NY 10016
(212) 278-1298 .. **Salberg,** Melvin '51 OfCnsl Anderson K&O,PC -1251 Av of Amer -NY 10020
(212) 490-2525 .. **Salberg,** Michl A '77 (ADL) -605 3rd Av -NY 10158 **Fx:**867-0779
(212) 218-5500 .. **Salcedo,** Eddy '00 %Seyfarth S LLP -620 8th Av -NY 10018
(212) 310-8000 .. **Salcedo,** Nadya L '09 %Weil G&M LLP -767 5th Av -NY 10153
(212) 765-2100 .. **Saldaña,** Adrienne L '95 (Spivak L LLP) -1700 Bway -NY 10019
(212) 545-4000 .. **Saldana,** Nicole Quick '04 %Jackson L LLP -666 3rd Av -NY 10017
(845) 794-4094 .. **Saldarelli,** David J '01 %Leg Aid -11 Bank -Monticello 12701 **Fx:**794-0119
(212) 798-6161 .. **Saldarelli,** Matthew D '06 Focus Invstmnt Grp -375 Park Av -NY 10152
(212) 682-4904 .. **Saldarriaga,** Victor H '98 -275 Mad Av -NY 10016 **Fx:**682-8978
(516) 486-8500 .. **Sale,** Robt '63 -64 Hilton Av -Hempstd 11550 **Fx:**486-8995
(212) 788-9580 .. **Saleem,** Afsaan '02 %Law Dept -100 Church -NY 10007 **Fx:**788-0367
(585) 343-6320 .. **Saleh,** David J '79 OfCnsl Oshlag S&E -216 E Main -Batavia 14020
(718) 250-0400 .. **Saleh,** Philip G '86 %R Tusa -1 MetroTech Ctr -Brklyn 11201 **Fx:**250-0591
(212) 705-7000 .. **Salehi,** Nader H '08 (Bingham M LLP) -399 Park Av -NY 10022
(212) 735-3000 .. **Salek,** Anna E '00 %Skadden ASM&F LLP -4 Times Sq -NY 10036
(212) 820-7700 .. **Salem,** Christina R '04 %Boundas SW&B,LLC -1 Bttry Pk Plz -NY 10004
(516) 472-7030 .. **Salem,** Dory '00 (Salem S&S,LLP) -3000 Marcus Av -Lk Success 11042

(718) 855-3627 .. **Salem,** Mark '09 C Berkman,LLC -111 Lvngstn -Brklyn 11201 **Fx:**855-4696
(516) 946-0385 .. **Salem,** Nancy '97 -69 Fifth Av -NY 10003
(516) 472-7030 .. **Salem Shor & Saperstein, LLP** -3000 Marcus Av -Lk Success 11042 **Fx:**472-7031
(212) 906-1200 .. **Salem,** Victoria B '09 %Latham & W -885 3rd Av -NY 10022
(718) 499-5477 .. **Salen,** Elizabeth J '82 -294 Windsor Pl -Brklyn 11218 **Fx:**499-5616
(212) 267-1950 .. **Salenger,** Marvin '66 (Salenger SSK&B,LLP) -233 Bway -NY 10279
(212) 267-1950 .. **Salenger Sack Schwartz Kimmel & Bavaro,LLP** -233 Bway -NY 10279 **Fx:**385-2170
(718) 590-3870 .. **Salensky,** Kathryn '98 Hon J Byrne -851 Grnd Cncrs -Bronx 10451
(212) 686-6650 .. **Saler,** Stephen L '06 (Langdon Title Agncy LLC) -232 Mad Av -NY 10016 **Fx:**(646) 330-5061
(718) 786-2321 .. **Salerni,** Robt '84 -10-11 49th Av -LIC 11101
(212) 277-4000 .. **Salerno,** Anthony J Jr. '09 %Freshfields BD LLP -520 Mad Av -NY 10022
(800) 358-2550 .. **Salerno,** George D '61 NAM -990 Stewart Av -Gdn Cty 11530
(212) 326-3939 .. **Salerno,** James J '93 (Jones D) -222 E 41st -NY 10017
(585) 399-6645 .. **Salerno,** Jill M '99 %Excellus Hlth Plan Inc -165 Court -Rchstr 14647 **Fx:**327-6570
(518) 371-0052 .. **Salerno,** Kimberly A '02 %Burgess & Assoc PC -646 Plnk Rd -Clifton Pk 12065 **Fx:**371-0053
(212) 619-8328 .. **Salerno,** Laure '88 (Lombardi & S PLLC) -52 Duane -NY 10007 **Fx:**732-6323
(212) 225-2000 .. **Salerno,** Matthew P '02 (Cleary GS&H) -1 Lbrty Plz -NY 10006
(914) 793-1222 .. **Salerno,** Rocco V Jr. '85 %A Colavita -575 Wht Plns Rd -Eastchstr 10709
(631) 501-5700 .. **Salerno,** Russell S '04 %Carter DF&S LLP -445 Broadhallow Rd -Melvll 11747
(212) 335-4500 .. **Salerno,** Victor E III '98 (DLA Piper LLP) -1251 Av of Amer -NY 10020
(718) 523-1111 .. **Sales,** Meredith L '07 %Gildin Z&S,PC -138-44 Qns Blvd -Briarwd 11435
(631) 577-7990 .. **Sales,** Raymond M '69 (Sales & S) -68 S Srvc Rd -Melvll 11747 **Fx:**577-7991
(845) 896-6758 .. **Salese,** Thos P '76 -145 Main BxH -Fishkill 12524 **Fx:**896-4018
(914) 323-7000 .. **Salese Tauber,** Danielle '02 %Wilson EME&D LLP -3 Gannett Dr -White Plns 10604
(914) 834-9140 .. **Saletsky,** Doria M '78 -78 N Chatsworth Av -Larchmnt 10538
(718) 291-7433 .. **Salfarlie,** Donald A '97 (Salfarlie S & Assoc PC) -88-18 Sutphin Blvd -Jamaica 11435 **Fx:**291-7424
(718) 291-7433 .. **Salfarlie,** Nazmeen '98 (Salfarlie S & Assoc PC) -88-18 Sutphin Blvd -Jamaica 11435 **Fx:**291-7424
(212) 735-8600 .. **Salfeld,** Chas B '65 (Morrison C LLP) -909 3rd Av -NY 10022
(914) 948-8466 .. **Salgado,** Danielle Paola '05 Westchester Hispanic Coalition -46 Waller Av -White Plns 10605
(718) 458-0047 .. **Salgado,** Wm H '85 -37-03 81st -Jcksn Hts 11372 **Fx:**899-6988
(516) 871-0221 .. **Salgo,** Michl '80 -500 N Bway -Jericho 11753 **Fx:**822-4462
(718) 489-5293 .. **Salholz,** Miriam '76 -61 Jane -NY 10014
(212) 478-0000 .. **Salhotra,** Ajay '05 DE Shaw & Co -120 W 45th -NY 10036 **Fx:**478-0100
(212) 230-8805 .. **Salhus,** Knute J '88 (WilmerHale) -399 Park Av -NY 10022
(516) 496-1215 .. **Salhus,** Victoria D '85 %Cablevision Sys -1111 Stewart Av -Bethpage 11714
(212) 642-0950 .. **Saliba,** Matthew W '99 %Newman & O,PC -8 W 38th -NY 10018
(212) 474-1000 .. **Saliba,** Michl '10 %Cravath S&M LLP -825 8th Av -NY 10019
(646) 721-1672 .. **Saliceti,** Brenda '06 -223 Emily Ln -Staten Isl 10312
(212) 755-5510 .. **Saliceti,** Diana M '02 %Loeb B & Prtnrs -505 Park Av -NY 10022
(212) 264-8819 .. **Salidar,** Jeanne E '93 %ODAR-SSA -26 Fed Plz -NY 10278
(718) 894-2778 .. **Salierno,** John V '72 -65-12 69th Pl -Middl Vllg 11379 **Fx:**326-3781
(914) 949-5623 .. **Salik,** Jacob P '75 -24 Oxford Rd -White Plns 10605
(212) 980-3500 .. **Saliman,** S Gerald '90 OfCnsl Pavia & H LLP -600 Mad Av -NY 10022
(631) 439-2960 .. **Salimando,** Scott J '81 (Cavalier & Assoc) -144-1 Remngtn Blvd -Ronkonkoma 11779 **Fx:**439-2961
(212) 973-0572 .. **Salimbene,** Melissa A '05 %Wolff & S PC -140 Bway -NY 10005
(212) 351-4500 .. **Salimi,** Parisa '08 %Epstein B&G,PC -250 Park Av -NY 10177
(212) 698-3500 .. **Salimi,** Sahba '04 Dechert LLP -1095 Av of Amer -NY 10036
(212) 948-2858 .. **Salimi,** Wasim B '79 %Marsh USA -1166 Av of Amer -NY 10036 **Fx:**345-4808
(212) 967-1800 .. **Salim-Williams,** Zakiyyah '02 OfCnsl Bryant BJ&R LLP -140 Bway -NY 10005
(212) 455-2000 .. **Salinas,** Danny H '09 %Simpson T&B LLP -425 Lex Av -NY 10017
(713) 651-5151 .. **Salinas,** Gabriel J '09 Fulbright & J LLP -666 5th Av -NY 10103 **Fx:**651-5246
(914) 681-9500 .. **Saline,** Anthony C '04 (Baker LS&B,LLP) -1 N Lex Av -White Plns 10601
(518) 474-4283 .. **Salinero,** Alvaro A '86 %Dept of Health -Corning Twr 24th Fl -Albany 12237 **Fx:**486-1858
(631) 853-8902 .. **Salinero,** Amelia R '91 Suffolk Cnty-Social Srvcs Dept -Bx18100 -Hauppauge 11788
(973) 848-4051 .. **Saling,** Alison T '89 Cnsl K&L Gates LLP -599 Lex Av -NY 10022 **Fx:**848-4001
(212) 848-4000 .. **Salinger,** Jeffrey L '01 Cnsl Shearman & S LLP -599 Lex Av -NY 10022
(516) 746-4747 .. **Salinger,** Joel R '98 -114 Old Cntry Rd -Mineola 11501 **Fx:**877-7161
(212) 558-4000 .. **Salinger,** Kevin M '10 %Sullivan & C LLP -125 Broad -NY 10004
(718) 987-9142 .. **Salinger,** Ronald D '74 -34 Whitaker Pl -Staten Isl 10304
(212) 735-3000 .. **Salins,** Risa Levine '02 Cnsl Skadden ASM&F LLP -4 Times Sq -NY 10036
(212) 407-7700 .. **Salins,** Roy P '02 %Vedder P,PC -1633 Bway -NY 10019
(212) 644-6644 .. **Salis,** Leonard S '96 (R Rosen,PLLC) -110 E 59th -NY 10022 **Fx:**644-3344
(212) 779-2900 .. **Salis,** Marc I '72 -200 Mad Av -NY 10016 **Fx:**(646) 442-2343
(212) 655-5749 .. **Salis,** Owolabi M '02 Salis & Assoc PC -42 Bway -NY 10004 **Fx:**742-0549
(212) 371-8008 .. **Salisbury,** Anne W '92 %Guzov O,LLC -600 Mad Av -NY 10022
(212) 775-8700 .. **Salisbury,** Carl A '90 (Kilpatrick S,LLP) -31 W 52nd -NY 10019
(716) 849-1333 .. **Salisbury,** Eugene W '60 OfCnsl Lipsitz GSC LLP -42 Delaware Av -Buffalo 14202
(607) 257-9455 .. **Salisbury,** Lance N '97 -408 N Tioga -Ithaca 14850 **Fx:**272-9877
(212) 977-4660 .. **Salisbury,** Patrick P '93 (Salisbury & R LLP) -1325 Av of Amer -NY 10019
(845) 452-8200 .. **Salisbury,** R Keith '69 (Walsh W&S) -75 Wshngtn BxQ -Poughkeepsie 12602
(212) 977-4660 .. **Salisbury & Ryan LLP** -1325 Av of Amer -NY 10019 **Fx:**977-4668
(212) 250-4655 .. **Salit,** Wayne S '93 Deutsche Bk -60 Wall -NY 10005
(607) 273-2202 .. **Salk,** James A '79 (Schlather SP&S) -200 E Buffalo Bx353 -Ithaca 14851
(718) 237-5500 .. **Salk,** Nicole E '97 %Leg Srvcs -105 Court -Brklyn 11201 **Fx:**855-0733
(212) 733-2122 .. **Salkeld,** Pamela G '94 Pfizer -150 E 42nd -NY 10017
(212) 451-2300 .. **Salkin,** Barry L '78 OfCnsl Olshan GFR&W LLP -65 E 55th -NY 10022
(518) 445-2329 .. **Salkin,** Patricia E '89 %Albany Law Schl -80 New Scotland Av -Albany 12208 **Fx:**445-2303
(914) 644-8300 .. **Sall,** Brandon R '86 (Schuman S&G) -1 N Lex Av -White Plns 10601
(845) 454-2569 .. **Sall Caltagirone & Coleman** -3 Cannon -Poughkeepsie 12601 **Fx:**454-8417
(212) 336-0130 .. **Sallah,** Danielle J '00 %SEC -3 World Fncl Ctr -NY 10281 **Fx:**336-1323
(631) 736-0500 .. **Sallah,** Dean J '97 (Sallah Law Firm PC) -110 Wshngtn Av -Holtsvll 11742 **Fx:**736-0179
(631) 736-0500 .. **Sallah,** Donald R '73 (Sallah Law Firm PC) -110 Wshngtn Av -Holtsvll 11742 **Fx:**736-0179
(212) 630-5627 .. **Sallata,** Peter T '00 Conde Nast -750 3rd Av -NY 10017
(315) 256-9240 .. **Sallaway,** George H '02 -7030 E Genesee -Fayettevll 13066 **Fx:**663-3013
(212) 943-1090 .. **Sallay,** Christopher L '97 (Gair GCSMB&R) -80 Pine -NY 10005
(917) 551-1300 .. **Salles,** Jessica A '01 OfCnsl Koehler & I LLP -61 Bway -NY 10006
(212) 267-9090 .. **Salles,** Stuart '67 -225 Bway -NY 10007 **Fx:**267-9175
(212) 558-4000 .. **Salley,** Stephen M '10 %Sullivan & C LLP -125 Broad -NY 10004
(716) 842-4200 .. **Salman,** Arthur H '88 %M&T Bk -1 M & T Plz -Buffalo 14203 **Fx:**842-5376
(212) 370-1600 .. **Salmen-Navarro,** Hedwin A '08 -501 5th Av -NY 10017 **Fx:**370-1606
(212) 751-9800 .. **Salmon,** Arthur L III '84 (Morelli R PC) -950 3rd Av -NY 10022
(518) 842-1650 .. **Salmon,** Del Benjamin '93 (Salmon & S,LLP) -179 Wallins Crnrs Rd -Amsterdam 12010 **Fx:**842-1390
(518) 842-1650 .. **Salmon,** James F '76 (Salmon & S,LLP) -179 Wallins Crnrs Rd -Amsterdam 12010 **Fx:**842-1390
(716) 871-9630 .. **Salmon,** Marlin B '54 -41 Ferndale Av -Kenmore 14217 **Fx:**871-9630
(212) 878-8000 .. **Salmon,** Michl G '04 %Clifford C LLP -31 W 52nd -NY 10019
(212) 704-6000 .. **Salmon,** Timothy M '05 %Troutman S LLP -405 Lex Av -NY 10174
(315) 821-6219 .. **Salmon-Conzola,** Cynthia M '01 -6676 Sanger Hill Rd -Oriskany Fls 13425
(212) 969-3000 .. **Saloman,** Mark A '97 %Proskauer R LLP -1585 Bway -NY 10036
(212) 776-5062 .. **Salome-Rodriguez,** Joan V '93 %NYC Housing Auth -250 Bway -NY 10007 **Fx:**776-5039
(212) 888-3033 .. **Salomon,** Chester B '68 OfCnsl Becker GM&M LLP -299 Park Av -NY 10171
(212) 335-4500 .. **Salomon,** Claudia T '05 (DLA Piper LLP) -1251 Av of Amer -NY 10020
(212) 732-6460 .. **Salomon,** Jos N '74 (Schwartz & S,PC) -225 Bway -NY 10007
(516) 485-3800 .. **Salomon,** Michl L '93 (Zemsky & S,PC) -95 Front -Hempstd 11550 **Fx:**485-3280
(212) 885-5000 .. **Salomon,** Philippe M '75 (Blank R LLP) -405 Lex Av -NY 10174
(212) 922-9700 .. **Salomon,** Phillip '86 %1st Amer Title -633 3rd Av -NY 10017 **Fx:**922-0881
(212) 883-4952 .. **Salomon,** Richd B '73 (Cozen O) -277 Park Av -NY 10172 **Fx:**672-1152
(212) 791-0890 .. **Salomon,** Ronald S '91 -325 Bway -NY 10007 **Fx:**964-1523
(212) 577-2523 .. **Salomon,** Susan Hofkin '74 %Ctr for Appllt Litigation -74 Trinity Pl -NY 10006 **Fx:**577-2535
(914) 273-1300 .. **Salomone,** Kory J '07 %Veneziano & Assoc -84 Business Park Dr -Armonk 10504 **Fx:**273-1303
(718) 990-6622 .. **Salomone,** Rosemary C '81 %St John's Law Schl -8000 Utopia Pkwy -Jamaica 11439 **Fx:**591-1855
(212) 661-7100 .. **Salon,** Joel '69 (Salon MDN&B,LLP) -292 Mad Av -NY 10017
(212) 661-7100 .. **Salon Marrow Dyckman Newman & Broudy,LLP** -292 Mad Av -NY 10017 **Fx:**661-3339
(212) 986-3030 .. **Salottolo,** Tobi R '79 %Proner & P -60 E 42nd -NY 10165 **Fx:**953-2079
(516) 781-1719 .. **Salowski,** Annemarie '93 %J Roesch -611 Newbrdg Rd -E Meadow 11554 **Fx:**221-4108
(212) 351-4500 .. **Salper,** Ana S '00 (Epstein B&G,PC) -250 Park Av -NY 10177
(646) 557-5100 .. **Salper,** Martha J '78 OfCnsl Patton B LLP -1185 Av of Amer -NY 10036
(212) 789-2000 .. **Salsberg,** Aaron E '07 %NHL Enterprises,LP -1185 Av of Amer -NY 10036 **Fx:**789-2020
(212) 446-7000 .. **Salsberg,** Brian S '99 %McKinsey & Co -55 E 52nd -NY 10055 **Fx:**688-9521
(516) 775-2236 .. **Salsberg,** Mark R '85 %Santangelo B&S -1800 Nrthrn Blvd -Roslyn 11576
(212) 987-1797 .. **Salsberg,** Steven P '92 %Promoceans Ltd -160 E 88th -NY 10128 **Fx:**831-5879
(212) 247-1400 .. **Salta,** Romeo J '81 -630 9th Av -NY 10036 **Fx:**247-1407
(212) 839-5300 .. **Saltarelli,** Gabriel '98 (Sidley A LLP) -787 7th Av -NY 10019
(212) 309-1000 .. **Saltarelli,** Jos J '87 Cnsl Hunton & W -200 Park Av -NY 10166
(716) 693-0070 .. **Saltarelli,** Mark E '80 (Saltarelli & Assoc,PC) -156 Delaware -Tonawanda 14150 **Fx:**693-5216
(212) 918-3000 .. **Salter,** George A '89 (Hogan L LLP) -875 3rd Av -NY 10022
(212) 201-6825 .. **Salter,** Kevin T '78 (Bolan JS&S) -One Lbrty Plz -NY 10006
(212) 598-9232 .. **Salter,** Maureen A '89 UFT -52 Bway -NY 10004
(212) 259-8000 .. **Salter,** Raya C '09 %Dewey & L LLP -1301 Av of Amer -NY 10019
(718) 802-9180 .. **Saltiel,** Jeffrey L '95 (Wenig S LLP) -26 Court -Brklyn 11242
(516) 803-4813 .. **Saltman,** Joshua D '96 Rainbow Media Holdings -200 Jericho Quadrangle -Jericho 11753
(607) 277-5476 .. **Salton,** Peter D '97 -309 N Tioga -Ithaca 14850 **Fx:**277-8742
(212) 451-2300 .. **Saltsberg,** Jason S '04 %Olshan GFR&W LLP -65 E 55th -NY 10022
(212) 735-3000 .. **Saltz,** Aaron J '06 %Skadden ASM&F LLP -4 Times Sq -NY 10036

(718) 558-8277 .. **Saltz,** Brian K '91 %LIRR -Jamaica Station -Jamaica 11435 **Fx:**558-8211
(212) 964-1882 .. **Saltz,** Leonard H '56 -401 Bway -NY 10013 **Fx:**966-1801
(631) 549-3131 .. **Saltz,** Susan '83 OfCnsl Moir & S,LLP -155 W Carver -Huntngtn 11743 **Fx:**549-3601
(585) 352-2658 .. **Saltzberg,** Jonathan P '07 %Bd Coop Ednl Srvcs -3599 Big Ridge Rd -Spencerprt 14559 **Fx:**352-2660
(212) 683-7999 .. **Saltzer,** Amanda Adams '00 Legal Srvcs for Children Inc -271 Mad Av -NY 10016
(212) 596-9000 .. **Saltzman,** Adam M '07 %Ropes & G LLP -1211 Av of Amer -NY 10036
(212) 691-6171 .. **Saltzman,** Amy '89 A Saltzman,PC -114 W 47th -NY 10036 **Fx:**921-2422
(212) 652-3890 .. **Saltzman,** Barry N '80 (Pitta & G LLP) -120 Bway -NY 10271
(516) 873-7200 .. **Saltzman Chetkof & Rosenberg,LLP** -300 Grdn City Plz -Gdn Cty 11530 **Fx:**873-0683
(212) 225-2000 .. **Saltzman,** David H '98 Cnsl Cleary GS&H -1 Lbrty Plz -NY 10006
(212) 204-5676 .. **Saltzman,** Jay P '95 -19 Fulton -NY 10038
(212) 632-5500 .. **Saltzman,** Jody E '05 %Salans LLP -620 5th Av -NY 10020
(914) 664-4616 .. **Saltzman,** Kenneth B '84 (Goodman & S) -22 W 1st -Mt Vernon 10550 **Fx:**664-4006
(718) 261-3047 .. **Saltzman,** Lisa A '92 %Queens Law Assoc -118-21 Qns Blvd -Frst Hlls 11375 **Fx:**261-0798
(914) 366-5700 .. **Saltzman,** Mark A '01 %MA Bjork -660 Wht Plns Rd -Tarrytwn 10591 **Fx:**366-5759
(914) 323-7000 .. **Saltzman,** Michl L '92 %Wilson EME&D LLP -3 Gannett Dr -White Plns 10604
(914) 829-7718 .. **Saltzman,** Nancy B '93 Westcon Grp Inc -520 Wht Plns Rd -Tarrytwn 10591
(212) 808-3065 .. **Saltzman,** Neil J '03 -230 Park Av -NY 10169
(212) 829-4711 .. **Saltzman,** Paul '86 espeed,Inc -110 E 59th -NY 10022 **Fx:**829-4708
(631) 293-6060 .. **Saltzman,** Stephen A '92 (Cellino & B,PC) -445 Broad Hollow Rd -Melvll 11747
(516) 873-7200 .. **Saltzman,** Wm B '57 (Saltzman C&R,LLP) -300 Grdn City Plz -Gdn Cty 11530
(212) 735-3000 .. **Saltzstein,** Susan L '92 (Skadden ASM&F LLP) -4 Times Sq -NY 10036
(212) 350-9909 .. **Salup,** Stephen '65 %Starrett Corp -70 E 55th -NY 10022
(212) 237-1000 .. **Salva,** Jorge R '02 %Windels ML&M,LLP -156 W 56th -NY 10019
(212) 816-0518 .. **Salva,** Laurence J '97 CitiGroup Global Mrkts Inc -388 Greenwich -NY 10013
(212) 661-8000 .. **Salvadori,** Silvia '06 %Lucas & M,LLP -475 Park Av S -NY 10016
(631) 231-1199 .. **Salvage,** James N Jr. '96 %Reynolds CGHL&Q,LLP -35 Arkay Dr -Hauppauge 11788
(718) 658-0500 .. **Salvaggio,** Meredith S '08 %Law Dept -151-20 Jamaica Av -Jamaica 11432 **Fx:**658-4025
(212) 752-2955 .. **Salvan,** Sherwood Allen '69 -526 E 83rd -NY 10028 **Fx:**861-6036
(212) 446-2300 .. **Salvati,** Lauren A '08 %Boies S&F LLP -575 Lex Av -NY 10022
(914) 242-0472 .. **Salvati,** Rodney L '73 -80 Grandvw Dr -Mt Kisco 10549
(212) 427-9616 .. **Salvato,** Lawr '87 -22 E 89th Bx6401 -NY 10128 **Fx:**427-9342
(845) 294-4462 .. **Salvato,** Ronald J '02 (R Salvato) -55 Main -Goshen 10924 **Fx:**294-6372
(718) 520-3741 .. **Salvatore,** David M '85 %Hon E Kassoff -88-11 Sutphin Blvd -Jamaica 11435
(212) 728-8000 .. **Salvatore,** Jeanine M '99 -787 7th Av -NY 10019 **Fx:**728-8111
(718) 261-3047 .. **Salvatore,** Lisa '92 %Queens Law Assoc -118-21 Qns Blvd -Frst Hlls 11375 **Fx:**261-0798
(212) 225-2000 .. **Salvatore,** Nora S '07 %Cleary GS&H -1 Lbrty Plz -NY 10006
(212) 969-3000 .. **Salvatore,** Paul '85 (Proskauer R LLP) -1585 Bway -NY 10036
(212) 714-1720 .. **Salvatoriello,** Shannon K '04 %Tompkins MW&B LLP -140 Bway -NY 10005
(212) 223-3900 .. **Salvetti,** Susan '80 (Zwerling S&Z,LLP) -41 Mad Av -NY 10010
(914) 428-1438 .. **Salvi,** Debra C '99 %T Bona,PC -123 Main -White Plns 10601 **Fx:**428-1413
(516) 739-5556 .. **Salvi,** Elisa K '90 (E Salvi,PC) -50 Chas Lindbergh Blvd -Uniondale 11553 **Fx:**739-2445
(914) 682-1993 .. **Salvi,** Frank J '95 (D'Agostino & S) -445 Hmltn Av -White Plns 10601
(631) 283-5100 .. **Salvi,** Jos A '93 -295 N Sea Rd -Southampton 11968 **Fx:**287-9273
(212) 653-8700 .. **Salvi,** Lucantonio N '96 (Sheppard MR&H LLP) -30 Rckfllr Plz -NY 10112
(914) 899-3100 .. **Salvi,** Sara Luca '93 %Mead HC&G -109 Spencer Pl -Mamaroneck 10543
(212) 998-2242 .. **Salvia,** Carolina '08 NYU Ofc Leg Cnsl -70 Wshngtn Sq S -NY 10012 **Fx:**995-3048
(518) 427-8361 .. **Salvin,** Danl F '01 %Ctr for Law & Justice -153 S Pearl -Albany 12202 **Fx:**427-8362
(518) 457-6137 .. **Salvino,** Paul M '98 %State Police -1220 Wshngtn Av -Albany 12226 **Fx:**485-1164
(914) 366-7466 .. **Salvo,** Cindy D '98 (Salvo Law Firm,PC) -303 S Bway -Tarrytwn 10591 **Fx:**(973) 228-6492
(212) 227-0347 .. **Salvo,** Donna M '93 %Weiss W&W,PC -25 Park Pl -NY 10007
(518) 377-1044 .. **Salvo,** Edw J Jr. '71 -115 Clinton -Schnctdy 12305 **Fx:**377-7928
(212) 269-5500 .. **Salvo,** Jos '05 %Gordon & R LLP -90 Broad -NY 10004
(718) 423-5500 .. **Salvo,** Jos A '62 -42-24 Douglstn Pkwy -Douglastn 11363 **Fx:**279-8393
(212) 513-7788 .. **Salvo,** Michl C '93 (Ahmuty D&M) -123 William -NY 10038
(212) 407-4000 .. **Salwen,** Estelita J '78 %Loeb & L,LLP -345 Park Av -NY 10154
(914) 723-0513 .. **Salwen,** Joan C '77 -15 Dickel Rd -Scarsdale 10583 **Fx:**723-3908
(212) 335-9000 .. **Salwen,** Judith '00 %DA -1 Hogan Pl -NY 10013
(212) 308-8200 .. **Salwen,** Robt J '78 -800 3rd Av -NY 10022 **Fx:**308-7952
(718) 643-8000 .. **Salyer,** John C '03 AAFSC -150 Court -Brklyn 11201
(212) 351-2000 .. **Salz,** Marlo D '97 Russell Reynolds Assoc -420 Lex Av -NY 10170
(212) 230-2967 .. **Salz,** Richd F '81 MSI Claims,Inc -560 Lex Av -NY 10022 **Fx:**319-7061
(631) 582-4990 .. **Salz,** Steven A '97 (LaCapra S&K,LLP) -320 Carleton Av -Central Islip 11722 **Fx:**582-4690
(212) 259-8000 .. **Salzano,** Frank C '03 %Dewey & L LLP -1301 Av of Amer -NY 10019
(212) 208-3323 .. **Salzano,** Jos V '82 %AMBAC -1 State Street Plz -NY 10004
(212) 492-4063 .. **Salzberg,** Barry '78 Deloitte & Touche LLP -1633 Bway -NY 10019
(212) 619-4949 .. **Salzberg,** Fredric E '87 Cnsl Record Press Inc -229 W 36th -NY 10018 **Fx:**608-3141
(212) 943-9000 .. **Salzberg,** Jenifer L '98 (Dewey P&K LLP) -220 E 42nd -NY 10017
(212) 682-0707 .. **Salzberg,** Lisa P '92 %S Krawitz,LLC -271 Mad Av -NY 10016 **Fx:**682-8821
(212) 336-0159 .. **Salzberg,** Mark D '98 %SEC -3 World Fncl Ctr -NY 10281 **Fx:**336-1323
(212) 558-4000 .. **Salzberger,** Jonathan E '09 %Sullivan & C LLP -125 Broad -NY 10004
(585) 454-2181 .. **Salzer,** Karl F '76 (Trevett CS&A,PC) -2 State -Rchstr 14614
(212) 975-1821 .. **Salzhauer,** Eliana R '98 Worldwide Pants -1697 Bway -NY 10019
(212) 233-6550 .. **Salzman,** Alan C '70 (Salzman & W LLP) -305 Bway -NY 10007
(212) 385-8000 .. **Salzman,** Barry A '89 (Barasch MS&P) -11 Park Pl -NY 10007
(631) 261-2969 .. **Salzman,** Claudia J '78 -34 Wren Ct -Northprt 11768
(212) 672-7013 .. **Salzman,** Glenn M '96 Viking Global -280 Park Av -NY 10017
(212) 907-0717 .. **Salzman,** Hollis L '96 (Labaton S LLP) -140 Bway -NY 10005
(212) 387-8400 .. **Salzman,** Ira '78 (Goldfarb AS&K LLP) -350 5th Av -NY 10118
(212) 309-6000 .. **Salzman,** James G '80 %Morgan L&B LLP -101 Park Av -NY 10178
(212) 277-0426 .. **Salzman,** Jeremy S '01 The Hartford -2 Park Av -NY 10016
(212) 442-4900 .. **Salzman,** Joan R '83 %Ofc Admin Trials -40 Rector -NY 10006 **Fx:**442-4947
(212) 489-1600 .. **Salzman,** Julie B '91 %Deloitte LLP -1633 Bway -NY 10019 **Fx:**492-4201
(718) 338-3183 .. **Salzman,** Leo '74 -2116 Av J -Brklyn 11210 **Fx:**252-5536
(212) 790-0243 .. **Salzman,** Leslie F '82 %Benj N Cardozo Schl of Law -55 5th Av -NY 10003 **Fx:**790-0345
(516) 487-1300 .. **Salzman,** Marilyn J '85 -11 Grace Av Bx400 -Gt Neck 11022 **Fx:**487-1320
(716) 645-7856 .. **Salzman,** Martha L '88 SUNY Buffalo-SOM -333 Jacobs Mgt Ctr -Buffalo 14260
(212) 837-6000 .. **Salzman,** Michl E '79 (Hughes H&R LLP) -1 Bttry Pk Plz -NY 10004
(516) 393-2200 .. **Salzman,** Michelle Lewis '95 %Garfunkel W,PC -111 Grt Nck Rd -Gt Neck 11021
(212) 819-8200 .. **Salzman,** Milana '05 %White & C LLP -1155 Av of Amer -NY 10036
(718) 624-2394 .. **Salzman,** Richd '67 (Salzman & S LLP) -26 Court -Brklyn 11201 **Fx:**875-7423
(718) 624-2394 .. **Salzman,** Robt M '78 (Salzman & S LLP) -26 Court -Brklyn 11201 **Fx:**875-7423
(516) 487-1300 .. **Salzman,** Stanley P '56 -1010 Nrthrn Blvd -Gt Neck 11021 **Fx:**487-1320
(212) 425-7775 .. **Salzman,** Steven L '86 -1350 Bway -NY 10018 **Fx:**643-1882
(212) 233-6550 .. **Salzman & Winer LLP** -305 Bway -NY 10007 **Fx:**233-6714
(212) 763-5000 .. **Salzman,** Zoe A '09 %Emery CB&A LLP -75 Rckfllr Plz -NY 10019
(212) 656-2616 .. **Salzman Kindler,** Elena E '95 NYSE -14 Wall -NY 10005
(212) 715-1000 .. **Salzmann,** Matthew T '05 %Arnold & P LLP -399 Park Av -NY 10022
(718) 279-4500 .. **Sam,** Doric V '03 -42-40 Bell Blvd -Bayside 11361
(212) 294-6700 .. **Sama,** Vincent A '83 (Winston & S) -200 Park Av -NY 10166
(718) 472-7577 .. **Samaan,** Lisa '00 MZ Berger & Co -2976 Nrthrn Blvd -LIC 11101
(516) 794-7500 .. **Samaan,** Peter S '91 (Westermann SKS&A,LLP) -333 Earle Ovngton Blvd -Uniondale 11553
(212) 906-1200 .. **Samalin,** Michl A '06 %Latham & W -885 3rd Av -NY 10022
(212) 816-7897 .. **Samanich,** Nancy M '99 Citigroup Global Mrkts -388 Grennwich -NY 10013
(516) 482-8500 .. **Samanowitz,** Ronald A '68 (Samanowitz & E) -98 Cutter Mill Rd -Gt Neck 11021 **Fx:**482-8655
(212) 614-6464 .. **Samant,** Anjana '04 Ctr Cnstnl Rights -666 Bway -NY 10012
(917) 637-3600 .. **Samanta,** Anamika '01 %Ctr for Reproductive Rts -120 Wall -NY 10005 **Fx:**637-3666
(212) 351-4000 .. **Samanta,** S Tina '03 %Gibson D&C LLP -200 Park Av -NY 10166
(845) 569-9110 .. **Samarel,** Jaime '96 %Leg Srvcs -123 Grand -Newburgh 12550 **Fx:**569-9120
(212) 848-4000 .. **Samarillo,** Adam P '07 %Shearman & S LLP -599 Lex Av -NY 10022
(212) 947-3333 .. **Samaroo,** Hari K '00 H Samaroo,PC -350 5th Av -NY 10118 **Fx:**947-4725
(212) 521-5400 .. **Samay,** Christian E '00 (Reed S LLP) -599 Lex Av -NY 10022
(212) 294-6700 .. **Samay,** Scott R '97 (Winston & S) -200 Park Av -NY 10166
(212) 935-3000 .. **Samberg,** Gilbert '77 (Mintz LCFG&P,PC) -666 3rd Av -NY 10017
(516) 693-0038 .. **Samberg,** Jeffrey M '70 (Koenig & S) -300 Old Cntry Rd -Mineola 11501 **Fx:**693-0042
(212) 558-5500 .. **Samberg,** Peter '79 Weitz & L,PC -700 Bway -NY 10003
(212) 805-0401 .. **Samberg-Champion,** Sasha Minh '05 Hon J Rakoff -500 Pearl -NY 10007
(845) 279-8354 .. **Sambora,** Martin D '94 -Drewvll Rd -Brewstr 10509
(914) 366-5700 .. **Sambrato,** Robt J '86 %MA Bjork -660 Wht Plns Rd -Tarrytwn 10591 **Fx:**366-5759
(914) 824-5808 .. **Sambuco,** Phyllis R '01 Judicial Institute -84 N Bway -White Plns 10603
(212) 530-1800 .. **Sambur,** Keith N '05 %Richards K&O LLP -1 World Fncl Ctr -NY 10281
(631) 665-0609 .. **Sambur,** Robin A '86 (Sherman FS&L LLP) -8 E Main -Bay Shr 11706
(212) 574-1200 .. **Sambur,** Scott M '08 %Seward & K LLP -1 Bttry Pk Plz -NY 10004
(212) 370-0877 .. **Sambursky,** Mark '92 -122 E 42nd -NY 10168
(516) 741-7676 .. **Sambursky,** Neil L '89 (Miranda SSSV LLP) -240 Mineola Blvd -Mineola 11501
(516) 742-1212 .. **Sambursky,** Robt C '01 %Stein W&R -1 Old Cntry Rd -Carle Pl 11514
(212) 587-9690 .. **Samel,** David '79 %J Samel & Partners -150 Bway -NY 10038 **Fx:**587-9673
(212) 587-9690 .. **Samel,** Dorothy T '83 (J Samel & Partners) -150 Bway -NY 10038 **Fx:**587-9673
(212) 587-9690 .. **Samel,** Jeffrey '77 (J Samel & Partners) -150 Bway -NY 10038 **Fx:**587-9673
(212) 446-4800 .. **Samenfeld,** Lisa A '94 (Kirkland & E LLP) -153 E 53rd -NY 10022
(212) 827-4437 .. **Samers,** Audrey '91 Ace Grp Holdings -1133 Av of Amer -NY 10036 **Fx:**642-7802
(212) 895-7944 .. **Samers,** Wm D '94 ACWIS -633 3rd Av -NY 10017 **Fx:**895-7999
(212) 490-4100 .. **Samet,** Avery D '04 %Storch A&M,PC -140 E 45th -NY 10017
(212) 626-4100 .. **Samet,** Jos '75 (Baker & M LLP) -1114 Av of Amer -NY 10036

(212) 450-4000 .. **Samet,** Lara M '09 %Davis P&W LLP -450 Lex Av -NY 10017
(212) 728-8898 .. **Samet,** Matthew R '05 -787 7th Av -NY 10019 **Fx:**728-9898
(212) 759-0700 .. **Samet,** Shai '02 ESRB -317 Mad Av -NY 10017
(212) 682-7500 .. **Sameth,** Marvin I '51 -330 Mad Av -NY 10017
(212) 558-4000 .. **Samida,** Dexter D J '06 %Sullivan & C LLP -125 Broad -NY 10004
(212) 696-4848 .. **Samide,** Steven A '95 %Mintz & G LLP -470 Park Av S -NY 10016
(212) 684-2200 .. **Samilow,** Gary B '78 -386 Park Av S -NY 10016 **Fx:**679-5875
(718) 222-9800 .. **Saminsky,** Robt L '76 (Brecher FPWT&Z,PC) -118-21 Qns Blvd -Frst Hlls 11375
(212) 308-6100 .. **Samios,** Gus D '86 (Levi L&F LLP) -1185 Av of Amer -NY 10036
(212) 344-2444 .. **Samit,** Audrey J '00 Frank Crystal & Co -32 Old Slip -NY 10005
(212) 909-6000 .. **Samit,** Joshua M '04 %Debevoise & P LLP -919 3rd Av -NY 10022
(585) 295-9500 .. **Samloff,** Harold '62 Buckingham Prop -1 Wshngtn S -Rchstr 14614
(212) 252-0300 .. **Samman,** Emil A '02 %Kagan LLLG&C,LLP -200 Mad Av -NY 10016
(716) 856-4829 .. **Sammarco,** Andrea Lee '93 (Sammarco M&S,LLP) -250 Delaware Av -Buffalo 14202
(212) 221-5999 .. **Sammarco,** Christine A '10 %Antin E&E,LLP -49 W 37th -NY 10018
(845) 986-2992 .. **Sammarco,** Diane Mall '99 -33 Old Ridge Rd -Warwick 10990 **Fx:**986-0971
(716) 856-4829 .. **Sammarco Mattacola & Sammarco, LLP** -250 Delaware Av -Buffalo 14202 **Fx:**856-0269
(315) 334-5050 .. **Sammarco Mattacola & Sammarco, LLP** -217 N Wshngtn Bx725 -Rome 13442 **Fx:**334-5060
(716) 856-4829 .. **Sammarco,** Tracy Dale '96 (Sammarco M&S,LLP) -250 Delaware Av -Buffalo 14202
(914) 682-4994 .. **Sammartano,** Anthony '68 -5 Waller Av -White Plns 10601 **Fx:**682-0123
(631) 656-0522 .. **Sammartino,** Marie A '94 -1300 Vets Mem'l Hwy -Hauppauge 11788 **Fx:**656-0524
(212) 735-3000 .. **Sammi,** Paramjeet S '99 (Skadden ASM&F LLP) -4 Times Sq -NY 10036
(212) 781-2111 .. **Sammis,** Wm R Jr. '89 %Fotopoulos R&G -4160 Bway -NY 10033
(516) 248-1700 .. **Sammon Burns,** Kathryn '09 %Forchelli CDSM&T,LLP -333 Earle Ovngton Blvd -Uniondale 11553
(845) 359-2500 .. **Sammons,** C David '89 Subaru Distributors Corp -6 Ramland Rd -Orangebrg 10962 **Fx:**359-4598
(315) 589-8132 .. **Sammons,** Elizabeth A '82 -6194 Lk Av Bx20 -Williamson 14589 **Fx:**589-8104
(516) 739-1735 .. **Sammut,** Norman A '83 -1205 Franklin Av -Gdn Cty 11530 **Fx:**739-1338
(212) 773-1465 .. **Samoc,** Agnieszka E '02 Ernst & Young LLP -5 Times Sq -NY 10036
(845) 331-4977 .. **Samoff & Benton,PLLC** -24 John Bx3870 -Kingston 12402 **Fx:**331-4726
(845) 331-4977 .. **Samoff,** Jay L '70 (Samoff & B,PLLC) -24 John Bx3870 -Kingston 12402
(212) 943-9000 .. **Samon,** Jonathan E '05 %Dewey P&K LLP -220 E 42nd -NY 10017
(646) 386-5325 .. **Samotin,** Nancy '85 %Family Ct -60 Lafayette -NY 10013
(212) 400-7177 .. **Samouilidis,** Paul A '09 %Garrity GMG&F -40 Wall -NY 10005
(212) 335-4500 .. **Samowitz,** Cary B '86 (DLA Piper LLP) -1251 Av of Amer -NY 10020
(516) 571-3056 .. **Samowitz,** Lee R '86 Cnty Atty -1 West -Mineola 11501 **Fx:**571-6604
(212) 509-3456 .. **Sampar,** Matthew D '06 %McGivney & K,PC -80 Broad -NY 10004
(212) 558-4000 .. **Sampas,** George J '92 (Sullivan & C LLP) -125 Broad -NY 10004
(718) 816-9060 .. **Sampel,** James J '81 (Sampel & N) -432 Forest Av -Staten Isl 10301 **Fx:**816-7669
(516) 463-5858 .. **Sample,** James J '04 %Hofstra Law Schl -121 Hofstra Univ -Hempstd 11549
(518) 465-1500 .. **Sample,** Kadan M '07 %Cannon H&W,LLP -54 State -Albany 12207
(716) 204-9483 .. **Samplin,** Caren L '84 %SJ Baum,PC -900 Merchants Cncrs -Westbury 11590 **Fx:**204-9683
(212) 564-9800 .. **Sampson,** Brian T '02 OfCnsl D'Agostino L&L,LLP -345 7th Av -NY 10001
(518) 402-9188 .. **Sampson,** David S '75 DEC -625 Bway -Albany 12233 **Fx:**402-9018
(716) 853-8400 .. **Sampson,** J David '83 %Dept of Law -350 Main Pl Twr -Buffalo 14202 **Fx:**853-8571
(631) 632-6110 .. **Sampson,** Jean A '83 SUNY Univ Cnsl -328 Admin Bldg -Stony Brk 11794
(212) 681-1575 .. **Sampson,** John L '92 OfCnsl Belluck & F LLP -546 5th Av -NY 10036
(212) 635-7429 .. **Sampson,** Patricia A '92 %Bk of NY -1 Wall -NY 10286
(212) 837-6746 .. **Sampson,** Robt '08 %Hughes H&R LLP -1 Bttry Pk Plz -NY 10004 **Fx:**299-6746
(718) 264-3340 .. **Sampson,** Ruben F '08 %MHLS -80-45 Wnchstr Blvd -Qns Vllg 11427 **Fx:**264-3559
(212) 856-5800 .. **Samson Fink & Dubow** -10 E 40th -NY 10016 **Fx:**856-5818
(212) 856-5800 .. **Samson,** James G '74 (Samson F&D) -10 E 40th -NY 10016
(914) 631-0600 .. **Samson,** Jeremy S '03 Hitachi America Ltd -50 Prospect Av -Tarrytwn 10591
(212) 557-7200 .. **Samson,** Martin H '82 (Davidoff M&H,LLP) -605 3rd Av -NY 10158
(212) 450-4000 .. **Samson,** Randall S '09 %Davis P&W LLP -450 Lex Av -NY 10017
(212) 877-2382 .. **Samson,** Richd S '90 -127 W 79th -NY 10024 **Fx:**874-6071
(631) 665-3400 .. **Samson,** Robt T '95 %Siben & S,LLP -90 E Main Bx149P -Bay Shr 11706
(212) 270-8863 .. **Samson,** Timothy H '95 JP Morgan Chase & Co -270 Park Av -NY 10017
(212) 557-3000 .. **Samter,** Jonathan A '06 -286 Mad Av -NY 10017
(212) 335-4500 .. **Samton,** Zachary E '95 OfCnsl DLA Piper LLP -1251 Av of Amer -NY 10020
(212) 310-2000 .. **Samuel,** Amanda C '98 %Colgate-Palmolive -300 Park Av -NY 10022 **Fx:**310-3406
(212) 249-6602 .. **Samuel,** Fred '86 -444 E 82nd -NY 10028
(516) 294-8844 .. **Samuel,** Ilene D '84 OfCnsl L'Abbate BC&C,LLP -1001 Franklin Av -Gdn Cty 11530
(212) 856-9101 .. **Samuel,** Mark A '00 -60 E 42nd -NY 10165
(212) 563-9884 .. **Samuel,** Michl S '93 (Samuel & S) -38 W 32nd -NY 10001 **Fx:**563-9870
(516) 488-1069 .. **Samuel,** Percy M '93 P Samuel,PC -591 Astor -Elmont 11003 **Fx:**488-0774
(212) 864-1350 .. **Samuel,** Raphael '72 -175 W 93rd -NY 10025 **Fx:**362-4183
(212) 596-0580 .. **Samuel,** Reuben '76 (Levine S,LLP) -130 W 42nd -NY 10036
(516) 326-2100 .. **Samuel,** Steven B '75 S Samuel,LLC -1979 Marcus Av -Lk Success 11042 **Fx:**326-2365
(718) 248-3999 .. **Samuel,** Victor T '05 CitiGroup -1 Court Sq -LIC 11101
(212) 448-1100 .. **Samuels,** Allan C '61 (McLaughlin & S,LLP) -260 Mad Av -NY 10016
(518) 993-2313 .. **Samuels,** Allen H '48 OfCnsl R Weinheimer -4 Canal Bx228 -Ft Plain 13339 **Fx:**993-2036
(718) 487-2300 .. **Samuels,** Barbara '86 %Leg Srvcs Corp -256-260 Bway -Brklyn 11211 **Fx:**782-6790
(212) 571-5971 .. **Samuels,** Colleen D '01 -233 Bway -NY 10279 **Fx:**571-5973
(212) 883-1700 .. **Samuels,** David G '79 (Duval & S LLP) -101 Park Av -NY 10178
(516) 873-1200 .. **Samuels,** Emil L '91 %Kelner & K -1 Old Cntry Rd -Carle Pl 11514
(212) 660-3000 .. **Samuels,** Emily A '04 %Sullivan & W LLP -1290 Av of Amer -NY 10104
(845) 364-3210 .. **Samuels,** Gary C '76 -Bx525 -Spg Vly 10977 **Fx:**364-3013
(845) 364-3210 .. **Samuels,** Gary C '76 %Dept of Social Srvcs -Sanatorium Rd Bldg L Bx307 -Pomona 10970 **Fx:**364-3013
(212) 648-0472 .. **Samuels,** Gregory S '07 %JP Morgan Chase -245 Park Av -NY 10167
(315) 733-8711 .. **Samuels,** Harris J '76 Samuels & S -239 Genesee -Utica 13501 **Fx:**733-8711
(631) 979-6262 .. **Samuels,** Howard J '74 -320 Carleton Av -Central Islip 11722 **Fx:**265-5952
(212) 298-5114 .. **Samuels,** Jacqueline '89 %Leg Aid -49 Thomas -NY 10013 **Fx:**298-5252
(718) 248-0346 .. **Samuels,** Jeanne '88 Citicorp Invstmnt Srvcs -1 Court Sq -LIC 11120
(212) 421-2233 .. **Samuels,** Jeffrey A '89 (Wilk A LLP) -675 3rd Av -NY 10017
(212) 373-3000 .. **Samuels,** Jeffrey B '82 (Paul WRW&G LLP) -1285 Av of Amer -NY 10019
(212) 879-9321 .. **Samuels,** Jody R '96 OfCnsl Richardson & P,LLP -750 3rd Av -NY 10017 **Fx:**993-6104
(212) 728-2200 .. **Samuels,** Joel R '09 %Axinn V&H LLP -114 W 47th -NY 10036
(718) 286-6000 .. **Samuels,** Kerona '08 %DA -125-01 Qns Blvd -Kew Gdns 11415
(212) 225-2000 .. **Samuels,** Leslie B '69 (Cleary GS&H) -1 Lbrty Plz -NY 10006
(212) 363-1200 .. **Samuels,** Lynn F '79 OfCnsl Baumeister & S -1 Exch Plz -NY 10006
(212) 819-1130 .. **Samuels,** Melanie B '79 OfCnsl Hirschen S&E -902 Bway -NY 10010
(212) 308-6100 .. **Samuels,** Michl A '93 %Levi L&F LLP -1185 Av of Amer -NY 10036
(212) 554-7800 .. **Samuels,** Michl N '03 OfCnsl Moses & S LLP -405 Lex Av -NY 10174
(212) 243-1313 .. **Samuels,** Paul N '80 %Leg Action Ctr -225 Varick -NY 10014 **Fx:**675-0286
(212) 969-3000 .. **Samuels,** Peter G '75 (Proskauer R LLP) -1585 Bway -NY 10036
(212) 735-3000 .. **Samuels,** Sarah E '10 %Skadden ASM&F LLP -4 Times Sq -NY 10036
(212) 500-5030 .. **Samuels,** Sheila Y '03 %Kehl K&S,LLP -317 Mad Av -NY 10017
(917) 335-8932 .. **Samuels,** Toure N '01 -120 Alcott Pl -Bronx 10475 **Fx:**(718) 379-5439
(718) 712-6464 .. **Samuels,** Violet E '00 Cnsl Samuels & Assoc,PC -135-13 Hook Crk Blvd -Rosedale 11422 **Fx:**977-4748
(718) 379-2110 .. **Samuels-Artis,** Donna M '92 -1447 E Gun Hill Rd -Bronx 10469
(212) 837-6000 .. **Samuelson,** Chas A '97 (Hughes H&R LLP) -1 Bttry Pk Plz -NY 10004
(718) 403-8505 .. **Samuelson,** Debra '90 %DOITT -11 Metrotech Ctr -Brklyn 11201
(516) 294-6666 .. **Samuelson,** Elliot D '60 (Samuelson H&S) -300 Grdn City Plz -Gdn Cty 11530
(516) 294-6666 .. **Samuelson Hause & Samuelson** -300 Grdn City Plz -Gdn Cty 11530 **Fx:**294-6622
(716) 484-7186 .. **Samuelson,** John R '73 -111 W 2nd Bx657 -Jamestwn 14702 **Fx:**484-2584
(212) 918-3000 .. **Samuelson,** Lee E '95 (Hogan L LLP) -875 3rd Av -NY 10022
(516) 294-6666 .. **Samuelson,** Wendy B '94 (Samuelson H&S) -300 Grdn City Plz -Gdn Cty 11530
(212) 736-2132 .. **Samuely,** Giselle M '93 -16 Penn Plz -NY 10001
(212) 922-7440 .. **Samulski,** Jos M '86 Bank of NY Mellon -200 Park Av -NY 10166 **Fx:**922-7451
(914) 682-2068 .. **Samurovich,** Gregory J '98 (Ansa A,LLP) -50 Main -White Plns 10606
(212) 587-8714 .. **Samus,** Natasha '91 Schimmel & S,PC -7 Dey -NY 10038 **Fx:**587-1334
(646) 442-3100 .. **Sanabria,** Diana '91 %Legal Srvcs -90 John -NY 10038 **Fx:**(212) 227-9798
(212) 878-8000 .. **Sanagavarapu,** Sapna '99 %Clifford C LLP -31 W 52nd -NY 10019
(212) 753-5000 .. **Sanakkayala,** Suma '04 %Schiff H LLP -900 3rd Av -NY 10022
(212) 450-4000 .. **Sanborn,** Nancy L '92 (Davis P&W LLP) -450 Lex Av -NY 10017
(914) 722-2529 .. **Sanchala,** Tejash V '97 (Villanueva & S,PLLC) -700 Wht Plns Rd -Scarsdale 10583 **Fx:**873-4827
(718) 665-0112 .. **Sanchez,** Alexander '82 -860 Grnd Cncrs -Bronx 10451
(718) 518-4329 .. **Sanchez,** Armando J '79 Hostos Lincoln Acdmy -475 Grnd Cncrs -Bronx 10451
(516) 741-1514 .. **Sanchez,** Carolyn '86 -734 Franklin Av -Gdn Cty 11530
(347) 651-1417 .. **Sanchez,** Cindy L '02 -26 Court -Brklyn 11242
(716) 854-4474 .. **Sanchez,** David V '99 %Stiller & V -300 Pearl -Buffalo 14202
(718) 797-2488 .. **Sanchez,** Emil J '94 (Friedman K&S,LLP) -16 Court -Brklyn 11241 **Fx:**797-4304
(718) 932-7711 .. **Sanchez,** Enedina Pilar '86 -22-07 Steinway -Astoria 11105 **Fx:**721-6846
(914) 378-9300 .. **Sanchez,** Felix '87 (Soto S&N,LLP) -281 S Bway -Ynkrs 10705
(212) 297-6128 .. **Sanchez,** Gregoria '90 -420 Lex Av -NY 10170
(716) 852-1300 .. **Sanchez,** Jack M '05 %Amigone S&M,LLP -350 Main -Buffalo 14202
(212) 763-4727 .. **Sanchez,** Jerald A '09 Ptnrs Grp (USA) Inc -450 Lex Av -NY 10017
(516) 997-4210 .. **Sanchez,** Jos R '00 %Grand Metro Bldrs -25 S Srvc Rd -Jericho 11753 **Fx:**997-0673
(212) 259-8000 .. **Sanchez,** Kaleb H '02 %Dewey & L LLP -1301 Av of Amer -NY 10019

(212) 336-2000 .. **Sanchez,** Karla G '96 (Patterson BW&T LLP) -1133 Av of Amer -NY 10036
(718) 590-2000 .. **Sanchez,** Kevin R '08 %DA -198 E 161st -Bronx 10451 **Fx:**590-6477
(212) 969-3000 .. **Sanchez,** Lucia A '04 %Proskauer R LLP -1585 Bway -NY 10036
(718) 892-4471 .. **Sanchez,** Manuel A Jr. '87 -2116 Wllmsbrdg Rd -Bronx 10461 **Fx:**792-7645
(845) 429-8411 .. **Sanchez,** Manuel R '75 -10 Sandusky Rd -New Cty 10956 **Fx:**429-8591
(718) 665-1170 .. **Sanchez,** Matilde B '88 -1180 Arnow Av -Bronx 10469 **Fx:**665-1484
(212) 523-1175 .. **Sanchez,** Michl F '97 %Do Something Inc -24 Union Sq E -NY 10003
(646) 214-0112 .. **Sanchez,** Peggy D '03 -350 5th Av -NY 10118 **Fx:**(212) 594-4082
(212) 422-4000 .. **Sanchez,** Philip A '99 (Goldstein R&R) -80 Pine -NY 10005
(212) 657-1351 .. **Sanchez,** Raul '96 Citigroup Global Mrkts -77 Water -NY 10005
(212) 999-5800 .. **Sanchez,** Robt D '92 (Wilson SG&R) -1301 Av of Americas -NY 10019
(646) 723-2286 .. **Sanchez,** Rodrigo A '04 Grace Point LLC -601 Lex Av -Brklyn 11211
(315) 788-9341 .. **Sánchez,** Ruthanne G '87 -215 Wshngtn -Watertwn 13601 **Fx:**788-9431
(212) 225-2000 .. **Sanchez,** Sara A '08 %Cleary GS&H -1 Lbrty Plz -NY 10006
(716) 852-1300 .. **Sanchez,** Vincent J '71 (Amigone S&M,LLP) -350 Main -Buffalo 14202
(212) 822-8300 .. **Sanchez-Camus,** Rodrigo '03 %NMIC -76 Wadsworth Av -NY 10033 **Fx:**740-9645
(718) 286-2450 .. **Sanchez Day,** Wanda I '04 %Leg Aid -120-46 Qns Blvd -Kew Gdns 11415 **Fx:**263-4234
(212) 696-6000 .. **Sanchez-Galindo,** Arianna M '08 %Curtis M-PC&M LLP -101 Park Av -NY 10178
(212) 225-2000 .. **Sanchez Herrera,** Ezequiel '07 %Cleary GS&H -1 Lbrty Plz -NY 10006
(212) 596-9000 .. **Sanchez Sandoval,** Rodrigo F '10 %Ropes & G LLP -1211 Av of Amer -NY 10036
(518) 463-5533 .. **Sancilio,** Gary '95 Affinity Grp -8 Southwoods Blvd -Albany 12211 **Fx:**463-7627
(718) 428-9180 .. **Sancimino,** Sally J '07 %Rossi & C,LLP -42-24 235th -Douglastn 11363
(718) 250-2000 .. **Sand,** Terry '02 %DA -350 Jay -Brklyn 11201 **Fx:**250-2314
(518) 745-1400 .. **Sanda,** Gregory J '06 FitzGerald MBF -16 Pearl Bx2017 -Glens Fls 12801
(212) 819-8200 .. **Sandak,** Heath A '09 %White & C LLP -1155 Av of Amer -NY 10036
(518) 248-8892 .. **Sandak,** Jeffrey W '07 %Insurance Dept -99 Wshngtn Av -Albany 12257 **Fx:**473-4600
(212) 969-3000 .. **Sandak,** Lawr R '79 (Proskauer R LLP) -1585 Bway -NY 10036
(212) 775-9002 .. **Sandars,** Paul A III '88 (Lum D&P,LLC) -325 Bway -NY 10007
(516) 248-8000 .. **Sandback Birnbaum & Michelen** -200 Old Cntry Rd -Mineola 11501 **Fx:**741-9398
(516) 248-8000 .. **Sandback,** Wm A '72 (Sandback B&M) -200 Old Cntry Rd -Mineola 11501
(914) 683-5300 .. **Sandberg,** Alicia K '95 (Silverman B&S,LLP) -81 Main -White Plns 10601
(212) 859-8000 .. **Sandberg,** Engla Caroline '07 %Fried FHS&J LLP -1 NY Plz -NY 10004
(212) 867-4100 .. **Sandberg,** Joshua B '05 %Furman K&B LLP -61 Bway -NY 10006
(212) 644-4420 .. **Sande,** Michl E '96 %Fabiani C&H,LLP -570 Lex Av -NY 10022
(212) 766-1888 .. **Sandel,** Carl S '95 %Morris DA&F -2 Rector -NY 10006
(212) 310-8000 .. **Sandel,** Peter C '04 %Weil G&M LLP -767 5th Av -NY 10153
(212) 714-1720 .. **Sandelands,** Wm C '00 (Tompkins MW&B LLP) -140 Bway -NY 10005
(212) 506-2500 .. **Sandell,** Sharon A '07 %Mayer B LLP -1675 Bway -NY 10019
(518) 436-2840 .. **Sandell,** Tracie M '05 %Thruway Auth -200 Southrn Blvd Bx189 -Albany 12201 **Fx:**471-4340
(212) 268-4477 .. **Sander,** Harvey S '75 -245 Fifth Av -NY 10016
(914) 763-3250 .. **Sander,** Ronni '81 (Bluestein & S,LLP) -333 Salem Rd -Pound Rdg 10576 **Fx:**763-3296
(212) 207-0458 .. **Sander,** Timothy E '92 %Sumitomo Corp of Amer -600 3rd Av -NY 10016
(212) 964-6611 .. **Sandercock,** John '80 OfCnsl Lester SK&D -120 Bway -NY 10271
(212) 509-0440 .. **Sandercock,** Margaret B '82 (Goodfarb & S,LLP) -112 Mad Av -NY 10016 **Fx:**689-9680
(315) 789-8480 .. **Sanders,** Aaron '07 Bond M&L,PC -91 Genesee -Geneva 14456
(212) 728-2000 .. **Sanders,** Alan '89 %SFX Sports Grp -220 W 42nd -NY 10036
(516) 742-6400 .. **Sanders,** Alan M '80 -1 Old Cntry Rd -Carle Pl 11514
(646) 509-8809 .. **Sanders,** Aleeshea '04 -511 Av of Amer -NY 10011
(607) 231-5900 .. **Sanders,** Arlene '89 %Leg Aid -30 Fayette -Bnghmtn 13901 **Fx:**724-7211
(212) 660-1050 .. **Sanders,** Arthur '82 -5 Hanover Sq -NY 10004 **Fx:**571-0965
(718) 515-4500 .. **Sanders,** Carl N '71 (Slingsby S&P) -3199 Bainbrdg Av -Bronx 10467
(212) 416-8594 .. **Sanders,** Chas F '83 %Dept of Law -120 Bway -NY 10271
(516) 741-5252 .. **Sanders,** Douglas H '01 (Sanders SBWV&G,PC) -100 Hrrcks Rd -Mineola 11501
(212) 354-4500 .. **Sanders,** Douglas L '07 %Friedman & W -1500 Bway -NY 10036
(212) 228-5546 .. **Sanders,** Eric '91 UBS Global Asset Mgt -51 W 2nd -NY 10019
(516) 775-9400 .. **Sanders,** Eric '04 %Jeffrey Goldberg,PC -2001 Marcus Av -Lk Success 11042 **Fx:**775-4477
(212) 586-5800 .. **Sanders,** Fredric M '65 (Cohen TS&W PC) -420 Lex Av -NY 10170
(212) 676-9220 .. **Sanders,** Gayle S '69 Law Dept -100 Church -NY 10007 **Fx:**788-0367
(718) 522-0666 .. **Sanders Gutman & Brodie,PC** -26 Court -Brklyn 11242 **Fx:**522-1121
(716) 839-1489 .. **Sanders,** Harvey P '90 (Sanders & S) -401 Maryvale Dr -Cheektowaga 14225 **Fx:**839-1512
(716) 839-1489 .. **Sanders,** Helaine E '94 (Sanders & S) -401 Maryvale Dr -Cheektowaga 14225 **Fx:**839-1512
(212) 983-5151 .. **Sanders,** Howard R '81 -60 E 42nd -NY 10165 **Fx:**983-1006
(212) 374-6888 .. **Sanders,** Ira S '76 %NYC Dept Educ-OLS -52 Chmbrs -NY 10007 **Fx:**374-5596
(212) 897-7660 .. **Sanders,** James M '86 Forex Cptl Mrkts LLC -32 Old Slip -NY 10005
(917) 836-8400 .. **Sanders,** Jason D '99 Oberon Media Inc -1 World Fncl Ctr -NY 10281
(212) 448-1800 .. **Sanders,** Jeff '95 (Roberts RLSC&F LLP) -235 Park Av S -NY 10003
(212) 735-3000 .. **Sanders,** Jeremy R '07 %Skadden ASM&F LLP -4 Times Sq -NY 10036
(212) 805-0177 .. **Sanders,** Kathleen H '98 USDC-SDNY -500 Pearl -NY 10007
(914) 997-1380 .. **Sanders,** Louis W '67 %Marino & C,PC -1 Barker Av -White Plns 10601
(212) 944-0600 .. **Sanders,** Marc H '96 %Hafif & Assoc,PLLC -275 Mad Av -NY 10016 **Fx:**944-7747
(212) 474-1000 .. **Sanders,** Nava S '09 %Cravath S&M LLP -825 8th Av -NY 10019
(212) 588-0022 .. **Sanders Ortoli Vaughn-Flam & Rosenstadt** -501 Mad Av -NY 10022 **Fx:**826-9307
(585) 295-4400 .. **Sanders,** Paul A '04 %Hiscock & B,LLP -2000 HSBC Plz -Rchstr 14604
(646) 227-3494 .. **Sanders,** Peter M '85 Memorial Sloan Kettering -633 3rd Av -NY 10017
(516) 625-4400 .. **Sanders,** Peter S '93 (Sanders Litgtn Assoc,PC) -69 Roslyn Rd -Roslyn Hts 11577 **Fx:**625-4410
(516) 741-5252 .. **Sanders,** Phyllis L '85 (Sanders SBWV&G,PC) -100 Hrrcks Rd -Mineola 11501
(212) 230-3300 .. **Sanders,** Ronald M '89 Colony Capital -660 Madison -NY 10065
(516) 741-5252 .. **Sanders Sanders Block Woycik Viener & Grossman, PC** -100 Hrrcks Rd -Mineola 11501 **Fx:**741-0799
(516) 746-5100 .. **Sanders,** Sheldon J '62 -500 Old Cntry Rd -Gdn Cty 11530 **Fx:**746-5225
(718) 531-7025 .. **Sanders,** Stanley A '78 -2030 Bergen Av -Brklyn 11234 **Fx:**531-7163
(516) 741-5252 .. **Sanders,** Stanley J '67 (Sanders SBWV&G,PC) -100 Hrrcks Rd -Mineola 11501
(212) 588-0022 .. **Sanders,** Steven A '72 (Sanders OV&R) -501 Mad Av -NY 10022
(212) 947-2900 .. **Sanders,** Stuart L '80 %Kazlow & K -237 W 35th -NY 10001
(212) 227-5220 .. **Sanders,** Susan '88 (Sanders & D LLP) -225 Bway -NY 10007 **Fx:**227-5221
(212) 455-2000 .. **Sanders,** Terry G '09 %Simpson T&B LLP -425 Lex Av -NY 10017
(212) 509-3456 .. **Sanders,** Wm D '83 (McGivney & K,PC) -80 Broad -NY 10004
(212) 219-3779 .. **Sanders,** Zachary J '02 Cnsl J Savastano -335 Bway -NY 10013
(718) 344-7161 .. **Sanderson,** Emily E '96 PS 246 -2641 Grnd Cncrs -Bronx 10468
(518) 388-4364 .. **Sanderson,** Wm J '00 %DA -612 State -Schnctdy 12305 **Fx:**388-4569
(914) 276-2012 .. **Sandford,** Irene W '81 -580A Heritage Hills -Somers 10589 **Fx:**276-2012
(914) 421-6700 .. **Sandford,** Jill E '93 Metromedia Fiber Ntwrk -360 Hmltn Av -White Plns 10601 **Fx:**421-6793
(212) 546-4000 .. **Sandgrund-Fisher,** Amy '98 %Bristol-Myers Squibb -345 Park Av -NY 10154 **Fx:**546-9562
(518) 449-8893 .. **Sandhaas,** Jill T '91 (Wilson EME&D LLP) -677 Bway -Albany 12207
(212) 490-3000 .. **Sandhaas,** Jill T '91 (Wilson EME&D LLP) -150 E 42nd -NY 10017
(212) 310-8000 .. **Sandhu,** Charan J '03 (Weil G&M LLP) -767 5th Av -NY 10153
(718) 672-8115 .. **Sandhu,** Munawar H '91 -74-09 37th Av -Jcksn Hts 11372 **Fx:**672-8117
(212) 756-2000 .. **Sandick,** Harry '96 SpclCnsl Schulte R&Z LLP -919 3rd Av -NY 10022
(212) 813-8800 .. **Sandidge,** Gregory T '06 %Goodwin P LLP -620 8th Av -NY 10018
(800) 732-3424 .. **Sandie,** Emily E '05 Independence Community Bank -195 Montague -Brklyn 11201
(716) 856-4000 .. **Sandison,** Patricia C '08 %Hodgson R LLP -140 Pearl -Buffalo 14202
(914) 949-7575 .. **Sandleitner,** Jennifer A '99 (Sandleitner & S) -50 Main -White Plns 10606 **Fx:**(718) 971-1033
(914) 949-7575 .. **Sandleitner,** John R '99 (Sandleitner & S) -50 Main -White Plns 10606 **Fx:**(718) 971-1033
(212) 796-8848 .. **Sandler,** Ebin N '04 %Klasko RS&S,LLP -317 Mad Av -NY 10017 **Fx:**297-1799
(212) 297-5800 .. **Sandler,** Erick M '03 Cnsl Day P LLP -7 Times Sq -NY 10036
(212) 878-8000 .. **Sandler,** Gregory T '01 %Clifford C LLP -31 W 52nd -NY 10019
(212) 259-8000 .. **Sandler,** Hugh D '09 %Dewey & L LLP -1301 Av of Amer -NY 10019
(718) 982-2921 .. **Sandler,** John B '03 Cllg of Staten Island -2900 Victory Blvd -Staten Isl 10314
(516) 938-4871 .. **Sandler,** Judy M '77 %NYSUT -1000 Woodbury Rd -Woodbury 11797
(212) 461-1908 .. **Sandler,** Karen M '02 Software Freedom Law Ctr -1995 Bway -NY 10023
(212) 489-1600 .. **Sandler,** Michl B '07 Deloitte LLP -1633 Bway -NY 10019 **Fx:**492-4201
(516) 876-9873 .. **Sandler,** Mitchell P '86 -380 N Bway -Jericho 11753 **Fx:**876-9869
(212) 450-4000 .. **Sandler,** Richd J '73 (Davis P&W LLP) -450 Lex Av -NY 10017
(516) 227-0700 .. **Sandler,** Robt E '88 (Farrell F,PC) -1320 RXR Plz -Uniondale 11556
(212) 431-2869 .. **Sandler,** Ross '65 %NY Law Schl -185 W Bway -NY 10013 **Fx:**431-1830
(212) 688-5055 .. **Sandler,** Stephanie H '03 Chanel Inc -9 W 57th -NY 10019 **Fx:**303-5979
(718) 260-4750 .. **Sandler,** Steven '68 %Leg Aid -111 Lvngstn -Brklyn 11201 **Fx:**260-4744
(212) 692-9666 .. **Sandler,** Theo L '93 %Gilbride TL&S LLC -708 3rd Av -NY 10017
(212) 883-1300 .. **Sandler Travis & Rosenberg,PA** -551 5th Av -NY 10176 **Fx:**883-0068
(212) 704-6000 .. **Sandler,** Will B '56 (Troutman S LLP) -405 Lex Av -NY 10174
(212) 867-4466 .. **Sandman,** Alyssa D '08 %Belkin BW&G,LLP -270 Mad Av -NY 10016
(718) 237-2000 .. **Sandman,** Jennifer R '01 %Leg Aid -111 Lvngstn -Brklyn 11201 **Fx:**237-8737
(631) 744-1900 .. **Sandmeier,** Pamela J '86 -135 Curtis Dr -Sound Bch 11789 **Fx:**744-1943
(212) 533-6300 .. **Sandner,** James R '68 %NYSUT -52 Bway -NY 10004 **Fx:**995-2347
(518) 213-6000 .. **Sandner,** James R '68 %NYSUT -800 Troy-Schnctdy Rd -Latham 12110 **Fx:**213-6488

(212) 820-7700 .. **Sandnes,** James T '87 Boundas SW&B,LLC -1 Bttry Pk Plz -NY 10004
(212) 969-3000 .. **Sandolo,** Joanna F '02 %Proskauer R LLP -1585 Bway -NY 10036
(585) 454-4161 .. **Sandonato,** Anthony G '95 %Davie Kaplan & Braverman -500 Rynlds Arcd -Rchstr 14614 **Fx:**454-2573
(914) 323-7000 .. **SanDonato,** Elizabeth J '02 %Wilson EME&D LLP -3 Gannett Dr -White Plns 10604
(212) 218-2100 .. **Sandonato,** Michl P '93 (Fitzpatrick CH&S) -1290 Av of Amer -NY 10104
(914) 276-2290 .. **Sandor,** Deanna Camac '02 -2 Route 100 -Somers 10589
(212) 530-5000 .. **Sandretto,** Steven P '03 %Milbank TH&M LLP -1 Chase Manh Plz -NY 10005
(212) 788-0961 .. **Sands,** Frances '88 %Law Dept -100 Church -NY 10007 **Fx:**788-0367
(845) 634-3627 .. **Sands,** Jacqueline '74 %Leg Aid -2 Congers Rd -New Cty 10956 **Fx:**634-8505
(914) 834-7510 .. **Sands,** Jonathan D '88 -1328 Bstn Post Rd -Larchmnt 10538 **Fx:**470-3682
(212) 564-6633 .. **Sands,** Jos W '89 %White & M,PC -875 Av of Amer -NY 10001
(212) 973-0572 .. **Sands,** Laurie J '00 %Wolff & S PC -140 Bway -NY 10005
(212) 701-3000 .. **Sands,** Marcus C '04 %Cahill G&R LLP -80 Pine -NY 10005 **Fx:**269-5420
(516) 739-3344 .. **Sands,** Philip '69 -301 Stewart Av -Gdn Cty 11530
(585) 678-7100 .. **Sands,** Robt S '85 %Constellation Brands -207 Hgh Pnt Dr -Victor 14564
(516) 505-0044 .. **Sands,** Sandra M '97 (S Sands & Assoc,PLLC) -250 Fulton Av -Hempstd 11550 **Fx:**505-0022
(212) 833-6764 .. **Sands,** Wendy S '84 %Sony Corp of America -555 Mad Av -NY 10022
(212) 733-0538 .. **Sandstedt,** John Erik '96 Pfizer -150 E 42nd -NY 10017
(212) 225-2000 .. **Sandstrom,** Brian T '08 %Cleary GS&H -1 Lbrty Plz -NY 10006
(718) 590-2000 .. **Sandusky,** Robt R III '97 %DA -198 E 161st -Bronx 10451 **Fx:**590-6477
(212) 888-4200 .. **Sanet,** Stephanie J '01 %Dembitzer & D LLP -100 Wall -NY 10005 **Fx:**230-1090
(585) 325-7127 .. **San Filipo,** Thos '53 -8 Exchange -Rchstr 14614
(585) 325-7127 .. **San Filipo,** Thos C '86 -600 Wilder Bldg -Rchstr 14614
(212) 943-0200 .. **San Filippo,** Augustin J '49 (A San Filippo,PC) -99 Wall -NY 10005
(212) 265-6888 .. **Sanfilippo,** Jennifer A '09 %Porzio B&N,PC -156 W 56th -NY 10019
(212) 474-1000 .. **Sanfilippo,** Michl A '10 %Cravath S&M LLP -825 8th Av -NY 10019
(716) 675-6111 .. **Sanfilippo,** Salvatore T '90 -3755 Seneca -Buffalo 14224
(212) 278-7002 .. **Sanford,** Eric '97 Societe Generale -1221 Av of Amer -NY 10020
(518) 487-5460 .. **Sanford,** Jarrod R '06 %DA -6 Lodge -Albany 12207 **Fx:**487-5093
(914) 730-3400 .. **Sanford,** Kimberly A '07 %Harriton & F,LLP -84 Business Park Dr -Armonk 10504 **Fx:**730-3405
(315) 422-2391 .. **Sanford,** Saml C '57 -717 Erie Blvd W -Syracuse 13204
(845) 471-8001 .. **Sanford,** Thos S '99 -224 Church -Poughkeepsie 12601
(646) 723-2947 .. **Sanford Wittels & Heisler,LLP** -1350 Av of Amer -NY 10019 **Fx:**723-2948
(212) 373-3000 .. **Sanft,** Andrea Levine '96 Cnsl Paul WRW&G LLP -1285 Av of Amer -NY 10019 **Fx:**373-2187
(516) 747-1990 .. **Sangalang,** Rendon P '03 %Cascone & K,LLP -1399 Franklin Av -Gdn Cty 11530
(212) 416-6542 .. **Sangeap,** Danl '01 NY Atty Gen -120 Bway -NY 10271
(718) 260-8700 .. **Sangenito,** Ian '00 Admin Childrens Srvcs-Div Lgl Srvcs -345 Adams -Brklyn 11201
(212) 969-3000 .. **Sanger,** Gail '68 (Proskauer R LLP) -1585 Bway -NY 10036
(212) 922-0711 .. **Sangerman,** Jay J '88 J Sangerman PLLC -60 E 42nd -NY 10165 **Fx:**922-0709
(212) 335-9000 .. **SanGermano,** Gregory M '04 %DA -1 Hogan Pl -NY 10013
(212) 218-5500 .. **Sangese,** August Jr. '09 %Seyfarth S LLP -620 8th Av -NY 10018
(212) 973-0572 .. **Sanghavi,** Maulik M '08 %Wolff & S PC -140 Bway -NY 10005
(516) 433-1415 .. **Sanghvi,** Alpa J '92 -15 E Carl -Hicksvll 11801
(646) 602-5600 .. **Sanghvi,** Ami T '06 %Urban Justice Ctr -123 William -NY 10038 **Fx:**(212) 533-4598
(212) 459-7766 .. **Sanghvi,** Rasik S '93 Dept of Tax & Fin -1740 Bway -NY 10019
(212) 248-3140 .. **San Giacomo,** Michl '03 (Drinker B&R LLP) -140 Bway -NY 10005
(212) 490-6600 .. **Sanginario,** Carol M '86 OfCnsl Beerman & D LLP -122 E 42nd -NY 10168
(212) 522-1212 .. **Sanhueza,** Rebecca '09 %Time Inc -1271 Av of Amer -NY 10020 **Fx:**522-0437
(718) 482-0700 .. **Sani,** Suresh L '89 1st Pioneer Prop -34-09 Qns Blvd -LIC 11101
(212) 906-1200 .. **Sanjana,** Jason B '07 %Latham & W -885 3rd Av -NY 10022
(212) 356-1408 .. **Sanjenis,** Michl '81 -1370 Bway -NY 10018 **Fx:**356-0900
(718) 250-0400 .. **Sanjour,** Claudia S '96 %R Tusa -1 MetroTech Ctr -Brklyn 11201 **Fx:**250-0591
(212) 593-6700 .. **San Julian,** Erik M '08 %Aaronson RF&D,LLP -757 3rd Av -NY 10017
(914) 682-2611 .. **Sank,** Mark A '85 (Trow & S,PC) -50 Main -White Plns 10606
(914) 668-8900 .. **Sankar,** Dion F '06 %Weisman & C LLP -6 Gramatan Av -Mt Vernon 10550
(212) 735-3000 .. **Sankar,** Shivram K '09 %Skadden ASM&F LLP -4 Times Sq -NY 10036
(212) 478-0000 .. **Sankari,** Andrea N '04 DE Shaw & Co -120 W 45th -NY 10036 **Fx:**478-0100
(212) 682-2288 .. **Sankel,** Joel S '60 (Sankel S&M,LLP) -750 3rd Av -NY 10017
(212) 682-2288 .. **Sankel Skurman & McCartin,LLP** -750 3rd Av -NY 10017 **Fx:**682-2474
(212) 336-2000 .. **Sankin,** Kenneth L '79 (Patterson BW&T LLP) -1133 Av of Amer -NY 10036
(212) 474-1000 .. **Sankoorikal,** Teena-Ann V '00 (Cravath S&M LLP) -825 8th Av -NY 10019
(212) 801-9200 .. **Sankus,** Mauri A '05 OfCnsl Greenberg T,LLP -200 Park Av -NY 10166
(212) 224-7242 .. **San Miguel,** Alejandro R '94 GLG Prtnrs,Inc -399 Park Av -NY 10022
(212) 297-5800 .. **Sanna,** Dina Kapur '97 (Day P LLP) -7 Times Sq -NY 10036
(315) 448-0672 .. **Sannes,** Brenda Kay '96 %US Atty -100 S Clinton Bx7198 -Syracuse 13261 **Fx:**448-0689
(646) 315-7401 .. **Sannicandro,** Ronald W '91 %FINRA -14 Wall -NY 10005 **Fx:**315-7440
(212) 962-1190 .. **Sanocki,** Edw J Jr. '78 (Sanocki N&T,LLP) -225 Bway -NY 10007
(212) 962-1190 .. **Sanocki Newman & Turret, LLP** -225 Bway -NY 10007 **Fx:**964-1573
(212) 265-3166 .. **Sanoff,** Jonathan S '84 -211 W 56th -NY 10019
(212) 640-2000 .. **Sanoubane,** Vyette S '04 Amer Exp -200 Vesey -NY 10285
(212) 233-9087 .. **Sanpedro & Jankowitz** -305 Bway -NY 10007 **Fx:**233-9144
(212) 233-9087 .. **Sanpedro,** Juan Jr. '86 (Sanpedro & J) -305 Bway -NY 10007
(212) 642-7861 .. **Sanpietro,** J Scott '98 Ace Finl Solutions -1133 Av of Amer -NY 10036
(212) 903-9000 .. **SanRoman,** Nicolas '05 %Linklaters -1345 Av of Amer -NY 10105
(212) 541-2000 .. **Sanscrainte,** Jos W '96 %Bryan C LLP -1290 Av of Amer -NY 10104
(212) 407-4000 .. **Sanseverino,** Raymond A '73 (Loeb & L,LLP) -345 Park Av -NY 10154
(212) 818-9200 .. **Sanson,** Olivia McMillan '05 %Satterlee SB&B LLP -230 Park Av -NY 10169
(516) 742-7200 .. **Sansone,** Alexander V '78 -245 Hillside Av -Williston Pk 11596
(716) 851-7190 .. **Sansone,** Annette M '82 %DEC -270 Mich Av -Buffalo 14203 **Fx:**851-7211
(212) 728-2200 .. **Sansone,** Gina M '08 Axinn V&H LLP -114 W 47th -NY 10036
(585) 590-4127 .. **Sansone,** John S '95 DA -13925 Route 31 -Albion 14411 **Fx:**590-4129
(716) 438-0488 .. **Sansone,** John S '95 (Ottaviano & S,LLP) -172 East Av Bx1230 -Lockprt 14095 **Fx:**438-0489
(212) 336-0517 .. **Sansone,** Jos G '02 %SEC -3 World Fncl Ctr -NY 10281 **Fx:**336-1323
(212) 822-9543 .. **Sansone,** Patricia Leigh '94 Advocates for Chldrn of NY -151 W 30th -NY 10001
(212) 267-5556 .. **Sansone,** Saml W '73 (O'Neill D&K) -15 Beekman -NY 10038
(212) 371-1011 .. **Sansted,** Douglas R '97 Archdiocese of NY -1011 1st Av -NY 10022
(212) 468-8000 .. **Sant,** Geoffrey R '09 %Morrison & F LLP -1290 Av of Amer -NY 10104
(585) 783-2603 .. **Sant,** Robt J '86 %Sugar Creek Corp -760 Brooks Av -Rchstr 14619
(212) 349-6009 .. **Sta Ana,** Andrew J '08 %Sanctuary for Families -110 Wall -NY 10005 **Fx:**566-0344
(212) 876-5500 .. **Santa Ana,** Wilfredo C '00 %Neighborhood Def Srv -317 Lenox Av -NY 10027 **Fx:**876-5586
(716) 852-6923 .. **Santacrose,** Destin C '03 -300 Pearl -Buffalo 14202 **Fx:**856-7417
(518) 456-6300 .. **Santacrose,** John J '89 -251 New Karner Rd -Albany 12205 **Fx:**456-7781
(212) 813-1600 .. **Santalone,** John J Jr. '86 %Kalow & S -488 Mad Av -NY 10022
(716) 856-5050 .. **Santa Lucia,** Thos '56 -69 Delaware Av -Buffalo 14202 **Fx:**856-1008
(201) 892-2230 .. **Santa-Maria,** Michl B '01 -9 Woodpointe Run -Williamsvll 14221
(631) 232-6130 .. **Santa Maria,** Noriel '00 %Weiner L LLP -888 Vets Mem'l Hwy -Hauppauge 11788
(212) 965-1678 .. **Santamarina,** Gil '93 Santamarina & Assoc -260 Mad Av -NY 10016 **Fx:**448-0066
(646) 386-5000 .. **Santamarina,** Mary Shein '95 %Surrogates Ct -31 Chmbrs -NY 10007
(718) 273-2092 .. **Santamauro,** Matthew J '96 -2550 Victory Blvd -Staten Isl 10314 **Fx:**816-0718
(718) 935-4481 .. **Santana,** Mecca E '01 NYC Dept Educ-OEO -52 Chmbrs -NY 10007
(212) 578-2127 .. **Santana,** Michl J '01 %MetLife -27-01 Qns Plz N -LIC 11101
(718) 590-2000 .. **Santana,** Penny '88 %DA -198 E 161st -Bronx 10451 **Fx:**590-6477
(212) 770-6633 .. **Santana Perez,** Rosemarie V '95 %AIG-NH Ins -70 Pine -NY 10270
(212) 355-3310 .. **Santander,** Robt S '91 American European Grp,Inc -444 Mad Av -NY 10022
(212) 530-5000 .. **Santanello,** Mary L '07 %Milbank TH&M LLP -1 Chase Manh Plz -NY 10005
(212) 566-6262 .. **Santangelo,** Anne Marie '77 %Wenger & A,LLP -20 Vesey -NY 10007
(516) 296-9284 .. **Santangelo,** Anthony A '63 %Lufthansa -1640 Hempstd Tpk -E Meadow 11554 **Fx:**296-9399
(516) 775-2236 .. **Santangelo Benvenuto & Slattery** -1800 Nrthrn Blvd -Roslyn 11576 **Fx:**684-2321
(212) 756-2000 .. **Santangelo,** Betty '75 (Schulte R&Z LLP) -919 3rd Av -NY 10022
(212) 408-5100 .. **Santangelo,** David M '02 %Chadbourne & P LLP -30 Rckfllr Plz -NY 10112
(212) 269-4488 .. **Santangelo,** George L '63 -111 Bway -NY 10006
(516) 248-4817 .. **Santangelo,** Jennifer P '01 %Comerford & D,LLP -1122 Franklin Av -Gdn Cty 11530
(718) 641-2300 .. **Santangelo,** Jos T '62 -110-22 Lbrty Av -S Richmond Hll 11419
(212) 657-1182 .. **Santangelo,** Louis G '93 Citigrp Glbl Mkts -77 Water -NY 10005
(914) 235-2790 .. **Santangelo,** Michl G '83 -75 S Bway -White Plns 10601 **Fx:**235-1397
(212) 325-2869 .. **Santangelo,** Robt A '97 Credit Suisse -11 Mad Av -NY 10010
(516) 775-2236 .. **Santangelo,** Vincent '83 (Santangelo B&S) -1800 Nrthrn Blvd -Roslyn 11576
(212) 973-0572 .. **Santarlas,** Rachel C '04 %Wolff & S PC -140 Bway -NY 10005
(212) 714-2744 .. **Santarpia,** Claudine M '96 -358 5th Av -NY 10001 **Fx:**695-4041
(718) 250-2000 .. **Santarpia,** Frank J '02 %DA -350 Jay -Brklyn 11201 **Fx:**250-2314
(716) 885-8855 .. **Santarpia,** Sabatino C '93 -568 Lafayette Av -Buffalo 14222 **Fx:**885-0208
(212) 775-9002 .. **Santarsiero,** Danl M '03 Cnsl Lum D&P,LLC -325 Bway -NY 10007
(212) 715-9170 .. **Sant'Elia,** Chas L '02 Kramer LN&F LLP -1177 Av of Amer -NY 10036
(212) 474-1000 .. **Sant'Elia,** Gillian Crenshaw '99 Cravath S&M LLP -825 8th Av -NY 10019
(212) 670-0404 .. **Santelli,** Jonathan N '97 Merrill Lynch -222 Bway -NY 10038
(585) 399-6648 .. **Santelli,** Lisa M '00 %Blue Cross/Blue Shield -165 Court -Rchstr 14647
(718) 855-8855 .. **Santelmo,** Deborah A '95 OfCnsl B Schulman -16 Court -Brklyn 11241 **Fx:**875-1768
(516) 496-8300 .. **Santemma,** Jon Noel '62 (Santemma & D,LLC) -575 Underhill Blvd -Syosset 11791 **Fx:**496-8303
(212) 819-8200 .. **Santens,** Ank A '00 (White & C LLP) -1155 Av of Amer -NY 10036
(516) 832-7500 .. **Santeramo,** Brooke A '10 %Nixon P LLP -50 Jericho Quadrangle -Jericho 11753
(516) 536-7792 .. **Santeramo,** Vera C '87 -159 Wright Rd -Rockvll Ctr 11570

(631) 582-3700 .. **Santeramo-Dewaele,** Janet D '06 %Turley RR&R,LLP -3075 Vets Mem'l Hwy -Ronkonkoma 11779

(585) 336-1000 .. **Santiago,** Arline L B '98 %ESL Fed Credit Union -225 Chestnut -Rchstr 14604 **Fx:**336-1014

(646) 386-5103 .. **Santiago,** Diego M '93 Family Ct -60 Lafayette -NY 10013

(585) 546-6448 .. **Santiago,** Fernando '97 (Davidson F LLP) -28 E Main -Rchstr 14614

(212) 974-1220 .. **Santiago,** Francisco '01 %Local 237-IBT -216 W 14th -NY 10011 **Fx:**647-9421

(518) 463-0380 .. **Santiago,** Fred '83 -817 Mad Av -Albany 12208

(718) 643-6555 .. **Santiago,** Guillermo J '03 %Marcus Attys -13 Greene Av -Brklyn 11238 **Fx:**643-9111

(718) 848-0008 .. **Santiago,** Hector L '84 -103-42 Lefferts Blvd -Richmnd Hll 11419 **Fx:**848-2365

(718) 254-0700 .. **Santiago,** Iliana T '06 %Bklyn Defender Srvcs -177 Lvngstn -Brklyn 11201 **Fx:**254-0897

(516) 573-6300 .. **Santiago,** Israel '91 Cnty Police Dept -1490 Franklin Av -Mineola 11501

(631) 324-8787 .. **Santiago,** Kathryn N '05 %Town Atty -159 Pantigo Rd -E Hampton 11937 **Fx:**329-5371

(212) 788-1573 .. **Santiago,** Leticia J '99 %Law Dept -100 Church -NY 10007 **Fx:**788-0367

(917) 553-3709 .. **Santiago,** Miguel A '83 -954 Gerard Av -Bronx 10452

(646) 610-5424 .. **Santiago,** Nilsa '83 %NYPD -1 Police Plz -NY 10038

(212) 336-0160 .. **Santiago-Acevedo,** Eduardo A '01 %SEC -3 World Fncl Ctr -NY 10281 **Fx:**336-1323

(212) 310-8000 .. **Santillan,** Aida Pilar '07 %Weil G&M LLP -767 5th Av -NY 10153

(917) 494-4245 .. **Santillo,** Keith R '94 -42 Bway -NY 10004

(212) 225-2000 .. **Santillo,** Kristen M '04 %Cleary GS&H -1 Lbrty Plz -NY 10006

(212) 282-5000 .. **Santini,** Anthony M '86 %Avon Products -1345 Av of Amer -NY 10105

(212) 360-2380 .. **Santin-Lerner,** Lynnette M '92 %Lincoln B LLP -110 E 59th -NY 10022 **Fx:**360-2381

(585) 232-6500 .. **Santmyer,** Wm A '97 %Harter S&E LLP -1600 Bausch & Lomb Pl -Rchstr 14604

(718) 727-7700 .. **Santner,** James M '88 (Minchew S&B,LLP) -1741 Victory Blvd -Staten Isl 10314

(718) 921-3286 .. **Santo,** Frank J '59 (F Santo,PC) -8118 13th Av -Brklyn 11228 **Fx:**921-3292

(212) 940-8800 .. **Santo,** Fred Michl '79 (Katten MR LLP) -575 Mad Av -NY 10022

(212) 225-2795 .. **Santo,** Giannina '05 %Cleary GS&H -1 Lbrty Plz -NY 10006

(914) 949-5018 .. **Santo,** Jos '89 -48 Grant Av -White Plns 10603 **Fx:**949-9543

(516) 394-4200 .. **Santo,** Michl A '83 %Duffy & D -1370 RXR Plz -Uniondale 11556

(212) 974-0940 .. **Santo,** Stephen S '83 -250 W 57th -NY 10107 **Fx:**586-8753

(718) 921-3286 .. **Santo,** Wm R '87 -8118 13th Av -Brklyn 11228 **Fx:**921-3292

(914) 846-7000 .. **Santoianni,** Kristy M '06 %NY Life Ins -1 Rockwood Rd -Sleepy Hollow 10591 **Fx:**846-4755

(212) 479-6000 .. **Santoiemma,** Nicholas M '09 %Cooley LLP -1114 Av of Amer -NY 10036

(518) 465-5995 .. **Santola,** Danl R '75 (Powers & S,LLP) -39 N Pearl -Albany 12207

(212) 237-0000 .. **Santoli,** Brett M '99 (Vinson & E LLP) -666 5th Av -NY 10103

(212) 571-2276 .. **Santoli,** Jos Ralph '89 -420 5th Av -NY 10018

(516) 829-6900 .. **Santoli,** Massimo A '97 %Ackerman LCB&L,LLP -1010 Nrthrn Blvd -Gt Neck 11021

(212) 768-6700 .. **Santoli,** Timothy J '02 %Sonnenschein N&R LLP -2 World Fncl Ctr -NY 10281

(212) 859-8000 .. **Santolli,** Justin J '09 %Fried FHS&J LLP -1 NY Plz -NY 10004

(631) 853-4104 .. **Santomartino,** Nicholas J '07 %DA -400 Carleton Av Bx9082 -Central Islip 11722 **Fx:**853-7838

(212) 972-0786 .. **Santomassimo,** Christopher M '93 (Nicoll D&S LLP) -250 Park Av -NY 10177 **Fx:**953-7201

(718) 250-2000 .. **Santomauro,** Allegra '04 %DA -350 Jay -Brklyn 11201 **Fx:**250-2314

(845) 735-1415 .. **Santomauro,** Cynthia D '89 (Cooke & S) -30 N William -Pearl Rvr 10965

(212) 645-2796 .. **Santoni,** Anthony '82 -250 W 19th -NY 10011 **Fx:**691-7116

(212) 559-2488 .. **Santonocito,** Patricia P '80 Citibank NA -425 Park Av -NY 10022 **Fx:**793-4400

(212) 883-6500 .. **Santopadre,** Ronald C '05 %Podell SS&B,LLP -605 3rd Av -NY 10158

(718) 778-5456 .. **Santora,** Anthony T '97 %Ornstein & O,PC -496 Clarkson Av -Brklyn 11203 **Fx:**756-0028

(516) 599-6999 .. **Santora,** John A '90 (Mandell & S) -29 Bway -Lynbrk 11563 **Fx:**599-2690

(718) 442-2272 .. **Santora,** Jos '81 (Lutfy & S) -1405 Clove Rd -Staten Isl 10301

(718) 243-2700 .. **Santora,** Nicholas R '97 %Talisman & D,PC -409 Fulton -Brklyn 11201

(212) 250-7506 .. **Santore,** David N '01 %Deutsche Bank -60 Wall -NY 10005

(718) 923-0690 .. **Santoriella,** Robt P '94 -335 Adams -Brklyn 11201 **Fx:**923-0683

(212) 788-0510 .. **Santoro,** David M '91 %Law Dept -100 Church -NY 10007 **Fx:**788-0367

(516) 803-6434 .. **Santoro,** Denyse J '96 Rainbow Media Holdings -200 Jericho Quadrangle -Jericho 11753

(631) 332-9034 .. **Santoro,** Dominic J '61 -15 Hmptn Ct -Coram 11727

(516) 676-4900 .. **Santoro,** Elisa M '02 %J Randall IV -222 Birch Hill Rd -Locust Vly 11560 **Fx:**674-3885

(585) 419-8060 .. **Santoro,** Ernest D '69 E Santoro PC -290 Linden Oaks -Rchstr 14625 **Fx:**419-8061

(516) 227-0700 .. **Santoro,** Frank T '02 %Farrell F,PC -1320 RXR Plz -Uniondale 11556

(212) 762-3305 .. **Santoro,** Janet T '82 Morgan Stanley -750 7th Av -NY 10019

(716) 361-8248 .. **Santoro,** Jeffrey P '91 -92 Richmond Av -Buffalo 14222

(914) 946-3700 .. **Santoro,** Michelle L '03 %McCarthy F LLP -11 Martine Av -White Plns 10606

(212) 318-6000 .. **Santoro,** Rachel '10 %Paul HJ&W LLP -75 E 55th -NY 10022

(718) 520-3595 .. **Santoro,** Rosemarie '88 %Criminal Ct -125-01 Qns Blvd -Kew Gdns 11415

(845) 228-4550 .. **Santoro,** Stephen M '87 (S Santoro Sr,PC) -105 Gleneida Av -Carmel 10512 **Fx:**225-4992

(516) 678-4505 .. **Santoro,** Susan E '87 -294 N Vllg Av -Rockvll Ctr 11570 **Fx:**678-5358

(212) 530-5000 .. **Santoro,** Thos H '09 %Milbank TH&M LLP -1 Chase Manh Plz -NY 10005

(516) 873-1777 .. **Santoro,** Wm '59 -100 Hilton Av -Gdn Cty 11530 **Fx:**294-7322

(516) 328-2300 .. **Santos,** Dorothy J '08 %Abrams FFEGF&E,LLP -1111 Marcus Av -Lk Success 11042

(845) 786-0500 .. **Santos,** Ivonne Suset '00 IS Santos,PC -11 Ramapo Rd -Garnervll 10923 **Fx:**786-0535

(631) 390-0010 .. **Santos,** Jeffrey M '08 %Bruno G&S,LLP -445 Broad Hollow Rd -Melvll 11747

(212) 664-4265 .. **Santos,** Jennifer M '05 %NBC Universal -30 Rckfllr Plz -NY 10112

(212) 822-1494 .. **Santos,** Jimmy M '96 J Santos,PLLC -305 Bway -NY 10007

(718) 263-4040 .. **Santos,** Jorge E '91 -118-35 Qns Blvd -Frst Hlls 11375

(212) 272-9211 .. **Santos,** Jose L '92 %JP Morgan Chase -383 Mad Av -NY 10179

(212) 967-5710 .. **Santos,** Miguel '07 %Weiss B&B -11 Park Pl -NY 10007

(212) 979-3000 .. **Santos,** Nuno M '00 %Natl Audubon Society -225 Varick -NY 10014

(631) 297-8360 .. **Santos,** Richd M '09 Rayano & G,PC -267 Carleton Av -Central Islip 11722

(212) 930-9203 .. **Santos,** Robt D '97 City College CUNY -160 Convent Av -NY 10031

(212) 321-5230 .. **Santos,** Teresa F '05 thestreet.com -14 Wall -NY 10005

(212) 513-3200 .. **Santos-Hernandez,** Rafael A '09 %Holland & K LLP -31 W 52nd -NY 10019

(212) 548-0340 .. **Santos Valentin,** Maria '88 Open Society Inst -400 W 59th -NY 10019

(718) 615-2100 .. **Santow,** Michl '84 -2920 Av R PMB 183 -Brklyn 11229

(212) 668-0340 .. **Santry,** Phyllis A '88 Ambac Indemnity Inc -1 State Street Plz -NY 10004

(718) 641-2000 .. **Santucci & Denkberg** -113-18A Lbrty Av -S Richmond Hll 11419

(718) 319-1400 .. **Santucci,** Fred T '96 (Klein C&S LLP) -1614 Wllmsbrdg Rd -Bronx 10461

(718) 641-2000 .. **Santucci,** John J '53 -113-18A Lbrty Av -S Richmond Hll 11419

(718) 886-7900 .. **Santucci,** Michl A '89 -42-40 Bell Blvd -Bayside 11361 **Fx:**358-3998

(518) 266-1000 .. **Santucci,** Michele A '82 OfCnsl Pattison SG&G,PC -22 1st Bx208 -Troy 12181

(212) 878-7900 .. **Santucci,** Nicole N '03 %Fox R LLP -100 Park Av -NY 10017

(212) 709-8357 .. **Santucci,** Robt A '78 -110 Wall -NY 10005 **Fx:**943-2300

(212) 588-0800 .. **Santucci,** Ronald R '79 (Frommer L&H LLP) -745 5th Av -NY 10151

(718) 448-4200 .. **Santucci,** Stephen '96 -1200 South Av -Staten Isl 10314

(516) 741-8989 .. **Santucci,** Thos '97 -1527 Franklin Av -Mineola 11501 **Fx:**741-8496

(718) 641-2000 .. **Santucci,** Thos J '84 (Santucci & D) -113-18A Lbrty Av -S Richmond Hll 11419

(516) 933-1515 .. **Santucci & Wasserstein** -366 N Bway -Jericho 11753 **Fx:**933-1666

(718) 677-7690 .. **Sanua,** David '92 -1486 E 26th -Brklyn 11210

(212) 684-3630 .. **Sanyer,** Wm J '08 %D Horowitz,PC -276 5th Av -NY 10001 **Fx:**685-8617

(518) 402-9205 .. **Sanza,** Mark D '92 Cnsl DEC -625 Bway -Albany 12233 **Fx:**402-9018

(212) 506-5000 .. **Sanzari,** Leah P '96 (Orrick H&S LLP) -51 W 52nd -NY 10019

(212) 857-8253 .. **Sanzo,** Edw J '84 %R Reinstein PC -330 W 34th -NY 10001 **Fx:**857-8233

(718) 298-8900 .. **Saoulis,** Ekaterini '06 Leg Aid -153-01 Jamaica Av -Jamaica 11432 **Fx:**657-0537

(914) 995-3496 .. **Sapakoff,** Laurie '86 %DA -111 Martin Luther King Blvd -White Plns 10601 **Fx:**995-3363

(212) 244-2999 .. **Sapanara,** Denise '90 (Kopff N&D LLP) -440 9th Av -NY 10001

(718) 286-6000 .. **Sapaskis,** Kristina '05 %DA -125-01 Qns Blvd -Kew Gdns 11415

(718) 253-3000 .. **Sapega,** Stephen S II '79 -2110 Flatbush Av -Brklyn 11234

(212) 310-8000 .. **Sapeika,** Tal S '03 %Weil G&M LLP -767 5th Av -NY 10153

(516) 873-2000 .. **Saperman,** Dylan '96 %Moritt HH&H LLP -400 Grdn City Plz -Gdn Cty 11530

(212) 909-6000 .. **Sapers,** Cristine Mesch '99 Cnsl Debevoise & P LLP -919 3rd Av -NY 10022

(718) 627-2200 .. **Saperstein,** Alan '85 -2925 W 5th -Brklyn 11224 **Fx:**627-2210

(718) 590-2162 .. **Saperstein,** Allen H '76 %DA -198 E 161st -Bronx 10451 **Fx:**590-6477

(212) 446-8705 .. **Saperstein,** Andrew M '96 %McKinsey & Co -55 E 52nd -NY 10055 **Fx:**688-9521

(212) 656-2355 .. **Saperstein,** Clare F '97 NYSE -20 Broad -NY 10005

(212) 321-7081 .. **Saperstein,** Ivan A '96 (Saperstein & C,LLP) -275 Mad Av -NY 10016 **Fx:**321-7082

(212) 335-5894 .. **Saperstein,** Karen L '79 Fidelity Invstmnts -200 Lbrty -NY 10281

(212) 610-6300 .. **Saperstein,** Lanier '98 %Allen & O -1221 Av of Amer -NY 10020

(212) 608-1917 .. **Saperstein,** Marc C '87 (Davis S&S,PC) -44 Wall -NY 10005

(516) 227-2100 .. **Saperstein,** Martin I '71 (Goodman & S) -100 Grdn City Plz -Gdn Cty 11530

(212) 303-6572 .. **Saperstein,** Robt A '89 Caxton Assoc -500 Park Av -NY 10022

(516) 472-7030 .. **Saperstein,** Tzvi '06 (Salem S&S,LLP) -3000 Marcus Av -Lk Success 11042

(212) 943-9000 .. **Saperstone,** Wendy J '05 %Dewey P&K LLP -220 E 42nd -NY 10017

(516) 294-8081 .. **Saperton,** Patricia Santemma '93 -300 Grdn City Plz -Gdn Cty 11530

(212) 455-2000 .. **Sapezhnikov,** Viktor '10 %Simpson T&B LLP -425 Lex Av -NY 10017

(212) 485-3784 .. **Sapherstein,** Michl B '98 MLB Advanced Media LP -75 9th Av -NY 10011

(212) 490-1700 .. **Saphia,** Jos V '01 (Wiggin & D) -450 Lex Av -NY 10017

(516) 731-6011 .. **Saphirstein,** Arnold '75 -155 Bellmore Rd -E Meadow 11554 **Fx:**731-5212

(914) 738-1182 .. **Sapienza,** Carmelina R '04 S Martin Johnson & Assoc,Ltd -11 5th Av -Pelham 10803 **Fx:**738-1266

(315) 597-4804 .. **Sapienza,** James L '58 -330 E Main Bx187 -Palmyra 14522 **Fx:**597-6637

(212) 836-8000 .. **Sapienza,** Michl '97 Cnsl Kaye S LLP -425 Park Av -NY 10022

(516) 798-1043 .. **Sapienza,** Salvatore A '76 (Sapienza & F) -5550 Merrick Rd -Massapequa 11758 **Fx:**798-3566

(212) 512-1000 .. **Sapienza,** Stephen L '80 %HBO -1100 Av of Amer -NY 10036 **Fx:**512-1986

(315) 585-6495 .. **Sapio,** Jos J '02 -2 South -Auburn 13021 **Fx:**585-6446

(212) 226-2376 .. **Sapir,** Brian J '09 %Oved & O LLP -101 Av of Amer -NY 10013 **Fx:**226-7555
(914) 328-0366 .. **Sapir,** Donald L '76 (Sapir & F LLP) -399 Knollwood Rd -White Plns 10603
(973) 642-1188 .. **Sapir,** Eric J '87 (Hawkins D&W LLP) -One Chase Manh Plz -NY 10005 **Fx:**642-6773
(914) 328-0366 .. **Sapir & Frumkin LLP** -399 Knollwood Rd -White Plns 10603 **Fx:**682-9128
(914) 328-7272 .. **Sapir,** Jeffrey L '67 -399 Knollwood Rd -White Plns 10603 **Fx:**328-8608
(212) 643-7000 .. **Sapir,** Lori K '03 %Sills C&G PC -One Rckfllr Plz -NY 10020
(631) 293-6061 .. **Sapir,** Robt E '69 (Cooper S&C,PC) -560 Broadhllw Rd -Melvll 11747
(516) 921-4400 .. **Sapodin,** Josh jfk '93 -333 Jericho Tpk -Jericho 11753 **Fx:**921-4948
(212) 363-3100 .. **Sapon,** Andrew '85 (Bivona & C,PC) -88 Pine -NY 10005
(212) 349-9000 .. **Sapone,** Edw V '00 -40 Fulton -NY 10038 **Fx:**349-9003
(212) 872-1000 .. **Sapone,** Monica I '00 -One Bryant Park -NY 10036 **Fx:**872-1002
(212) 637-3203 .. **Saporita,** Christopher '04 US EPA -290 Bway -NY 10007
(718) 833-3230 .. **Saporito,** Steven A '92 -449 77th -Brklyn 11209 **Fx:**833-3825
(516) 626-3547 .. **Saporta,** Jeffrey '75 -5 Copperfld Ln -Old Westbury 11568
(212) 539-5576 .. **Sapp,** David '90 Cnsl UNITE HERE Funds -333 Wstchstr Av -White Plns 10604 **Fx:**387-0710
(212) 484-3900 .. **Sapp,** Debra R '05 %Arent F LLP -1675 Bway -NY 10019
(631) 427-2900 .. **Sappé,** David F '83 -27 Fairvw -Huntngtn 11743
(845) 897-5199 .. **Sappe,** Robt R '86 (Feldman K&C,LLP) -995 Main BxA -Fishkill 12524
(212) 458-1621 .. **Sapru,** Tara '99 AIG Domestic Claims,Inc -175 Water -NY 10038
(585) 263-1000 .. **Saracene,** Katherine Ulrich '03 Cnsl Nixon P LLP -1100 Clinton Sq -Rchstr 14604
(518) 464-0444 .. **Sarachan,** George L '80 (Rosenblum RK&S,LLP) -110 Great Oaks Blvd -Albany 12203
(607) 277-5188 .. **Sarachan,** Robt A '89 -108 E Green -Ithaca 14850
(212) 980-3500 .. **Saracino,** Alessandro '92 (Pavia & H LLP) -600 Mad Av -NY 10022
(315) 331-0922 .. **Saracino,** David P '75 (De Staffan & S) -110 High -Newark 14513
(914) 681-8700 .. **Saracino,** Gregory R '06 %Milber MP&S LLP -3 Barker Av -White Plns 10601
(212) 335-4500 .. **Sarad,** Nicolai J '87 (DLA Piper LLP) -1251 Av of Amer -NY 10020
(716) 853-3801 .. **Saraf,** Richd T '88 (Kenney SL&N,LLP) -14 Lafayette Sq -Buffalo 14203
(212) 785-7575 .. **Sarafa,** Melinda M '00 Sarafa Law LLC -80 Pine -NY 10005 **Fx:**785-7577
(631) 271-8722 .. **Saraga,** Michl D '06 %JA Cirino -35 Pinelawn Rd -Melvll 11747 **Fx:**271-8699
(845) 634-7010 .. **Sarajian,** Richd H '77 (Montalbano C&F,PC) -67 N Main Bx1070 -New Cty 10956
(716) 645-6223 .. **Saran,** Melinda R '87 %SUNY Buffalo Lw Schl -O'Brian Hall -Buffalo 14260 **Fx:**645-5968
(212) 530-5000 .. **Saran,** Neema '10 %Milbank TH&M LLP -1 Chase Manh Plz -NY 10005
(516) 571-3056 .. **Sarandis,** Nicholas P '82 %Cnty Atty -1 West -Mineola 11501 **Fx:**571-6604
(516) 681-3453 .. **Sarandis,** Nicholas P '82 (Sarandis & T) -4 Tudor Rd -Hicksvll 11801 **Fx:**681-3453
(212) 836-8000 .. **Sarangi,** Nadia A '04 %Kaye S LLP -425 Park Av -NY 10022
(212) 341-4807 .. **Sarantopoulos,** Dorothy M '92 -36 Colfax Av -Staten Isl 10306
(212) 377-2093 .. **Sarantos,** Anastasia M '06 -555 5th Av -NY 10017 **Fx:**986-5316
(607) 749-2146 .. **Sarat,** Frank A '90 -Bx288 -Homer 13077
(212) 609-6800 .. **Saravay,** Adam N '91 (McCarter & E,LLP) -245 Park Av -NY 10167
(718) 217-9100 .. **Sarbofsky,** Sherry N '85 -Bx650309 -Fresh Mdws 11365 **Fx:**465-0450
(212) 340-2543 .. **Sarch,** Susan Holly '90 MTA Metro-North RR -347 Mad Av -NY 10017
(718) 286-2000 .. **Sarchiapone,** Eugene '88 %Leg Aid -120-46 Qns Blvd -Kew Gdns 11415 **Fx:**286-2286
(212) 408-5100 .. **Sarchio,** John J '80 (Chadbourne & P LLP) -30 Rckfllr Plz -NY 10112
(212) 756-2000 .. **Sarcinella,** Jos A '98 %Schulte R&Z LLP -919 3rd Av -NY 10022
(718) 608-2150 .. **Sarcona,** Paul A '02 P Sarcona,PC -5930 Amboy Rd -Staten Isl 10309 **Fx:**608-2149
(718) 481-7400 .. **Sarcona,** Richd J '79 %J & J Intl -150-18 132nd Av -Jamaica 11434
(914) 686-8200 .. **Sarcone,** John A III '97 (Sarcone Law Firm,PLLC) -222 Bloomingdale Rd -White Plns 10605 **Fx:**686-8988
(914) 734-9234 .. **Sarcone,** Richd N '01 -9 Oriole Ln -Cortlandt Manor 10567
(212) 335-9000 .. **Sard,** Bonnie '95 %DA -1 Hogan Pl -NY 10013
(315) 652-3758 .. **Sardano,** Richd J '73 (R Sardano,PC) -99 Ravenswood Rd -Liverpool 13090 **Fx:**652-2730
(212) 808-8100 .. **Sardar,** Michl '08 %Kostelanetz & F,LLP -7 Wrld Trd Ctr -NY 10007
(631) 838-0178 .. **Sardar,** Sheheryar T '09 -12 Desbrosses -NY 10013
(518) 456-7200 .. **Sardella,** Todd M '99 %Solomon & S,PC -5 Columbia Cir Bx15019 -Albany 12212
(315) 424-0513 .. **Sardella,** Wm J '97 %Carrols Corp -968 James -Syracuse 13203 **Fx:**475-9616
(315) 794-8866 .. **Sardelli,** Lawr A '69 -22 Prospect -Utica 13501
(212) 425-7200 .. **Sardesai,** Natasha G '10 %Kenyon & K,LLP -1 Bway -NY 10004
(315) 474-2911 .. **Sardino,** Patrick B '92 (Smith SK&S,PC) -250 S Clinton -Syracuse 13202
(631) 501-5700 .. **Sardone,** Francesco '00 (Carter DF&S LLP) -445 Broadhallow Rd -Melvll 11747
(212) 336-2000 .. **Sare,** John '91 (Patterson BW&T LLP) -1133 Av of Amer -NY 10036
(718) 244-4144 .. **Sareen,** Vikas '06 Port Auth of NY & NJ -JFK Airport-Bldg 14 S Srvc Rd -Jamaica 11430
(212) 312-7138 .. **Saren,** Melissa A '83 State Ins Fund -199 Church -NY 10007 **Fx:**385-9199
(212) 973-9797 .. **Saretsky,** Barry G '74 (Saretsky KD&G,LLP) -475 Park Av S -NY 10016
(212) 973-9797 .. **Saretsky Katz Dranoff & Glass,LLP** -475 Park Av S -NY 10016 **Fx:**973-0939
(845) 398-3030 .. **Saretsky Katz Dranoff & Glass,LLP** -450 Piermont Av -Piermont 10968 **Fx:**398-6019
(518) 465-0400 .. **Sarfoh,** Eugene N '95 (O'Connor OB&F,PC) -20 Corp Wds Blvd -Albany 12211
(518) 487-5460 .. **Sarfoh,** Shannon K '01 %DA -6 Lodge -Albany 12207 **Fx:**487-5093
(212) 578-9888 .. **Sarfoh,** Sheri N '02 %MetLife -1095 Av of Amer -NY 10036 **Fx:**578-3916
(315) 492-1666 .. **Sargent & Gilmore,LLP** -892 E Brighton Av -Syracuse 13205 **Fx:**492-0103
(212) 661-8895 .. **Sargent,** Hale C '81 (Sargent & S) -420 Lex Av -NY 10170
(716) 631-5700 .. **Sargent,** Nicholas J '72 (Sargent & C,LLP) -6245 Sheridan Dr -Williamsvll 14221 **Fx:**631-9120
(631) 427-6147 .. **Sargent,** Owen '05 -223 Wall -Huntngtn 11743
(315) 492-1666 .. **Sargent,** Richd H '67 (Sargent & G,LLP) -892 E Brighton Av -Syracuse 13205
(212) 661-8895 .. **Sargent,** Thos C C '76 (Sargent & S) -420 Lex Av -NY 10170
(212) 687-0100 .. **Sargente,** Alfred J '95 %Harris B PLLC -100 Wall -NY 10005
(718) 698-4884 .. **Sargente,** Christopher '90 (Sargente & M,LLC) -900 South Av -Staten Isl 10314
(718) 698-4884 .. **Sargente & McGinn, LLC** -900 South Av -Staten Isl 10314 **Fx:**698-0325
(718) 796-2210 .. **Sargiss,** Julia Ann '91 %Doyle & B,LLP -3152 Albany Crescent -Bronx 10463
(212) 581-2222 .. **Sargoy Stein Rosen & Shapiro** -1790 Bway -NY 10019 **Fx:**581-2755
(212) 980-0120 .. **Sarig,** Marisa L '06 %Frankfurt KK&S,PC -488 Mad Av -NY 10022
(718) 545-8866 .. **Sarikas,** Anastasios '84 -23-09 31st -Astoria 11105 **Fx:**956-0218
(845) 229-6300 .. **Saris,** Emanuel F '88 -4419 Albany Post Rd -Hyde Pk 12538
(212) 723-6194 .. **Sarisky,** Christopher E '95 %Solomon Smith Barney -390 Greenwich -NY 10013
(631) 543-7667 .. **Sarisohn,** Bernard '57 OfCnsl Sarisohn Law Prtnrs LLP -350 Vets Mem'l Hwy -Commack 11725 **Fx:**543-7901
(631) 543-7667 .. **Sarisohn,** Floyd '54 (Sarisohn Law Prtnrs LLP) -350 Vets Mem'l Hwy -Commack 11725 **Fx:**543-7901
(631) 543-7667 .. **Sarisohn,** Steven L '84 (Sarisohn Law Prtnrs LLP) -350 Vets Mem'l Hwy -Commack 11725 **Fx:**543-7901
(518) 487-7600 .. **Sarjeant,** Cheryl E '07 %Whiteman O&H LLP -1 Commerce Plz -Albany 12260
(718) 409-6606 .. **Sarkisova,** Zara K '02 -1937 Wllmsbrdg Rd -Bronx 10461
Sarkozi, Beverly S '86 -9 Walnut Pl -Briarclff Mnr 10510
(212) 508-6700 .. **Sarkozi,** Paul D '92 (Tannenbaum HS&H LLP) -900 3rd Av -NY 10022
(212) 836-8603 .. **Sarkozy,** Jamie M '05 Kaye S LLP -425 Park Av -NY 10022
(718) 276-0010 .. **Sarlis,** Jim D '88 -139-15 243rd -Rosedale 11422
(718) 410-0687 .. **Sarma,** Vadim Natrag '05 Leg Aid -1118 Grnd Cncrs -Bronx 10456
(212) 736-9119 .. **Sarmasti,** Vafa '03 (Sarmasti,PLLC) -729 7th Av -NY 10019 **Fx:**736-3820
(212) 880-6000 .. **Sarmazian,** Saro '03 %Torys LLP -237 Park Av -NY 10017
(212) 689-8131 .. **Sarna,** Dominic '90 -150 E 37th -NY 10016
(914) 734-1590 .. **Sarna,** Ira M '95 -31 Albany Post Rd -Montrose 10548 **Fx:**734-4486
(845) 348-9822 .. **Sarna,** James A '91 (Sarna & Assoc PC) -99 Main -Nyack 10960 **Fx:**818-9626
(718) 264-3340 .. **Sarner,** Michl D '84 %MHLS -80-45 Wnchstr Blvd -Qns Vllg 11427 **Fx:**264-3559
(800) 392-8550 .. **Sarner,** Richd A '82 -465 Park Av -NY 10022 **Fx:**(203) 967-8886
(212) 940-8800 .. **Sarney,** Michl F '91 SpclCnsl Katten MR LLP -575 Mad Av -NY 10022
(212) 401-4232 .. **Sarno & DeFelice LLC** -235 W 23rd -NY 10011 **Fx:**505-6444
(212) 455-2000 .. **Sarno,** Glenn R '93 (Simpson T&B LLP) -425 Lex Av -NY 10017
(212) 754-2233 .. **Sarno,** John B '00 %Scientific Games Corp -750 Lex Av -NY 10022 **Fx:**754-2372
(212) 231-2031 .. **Sarno,** L Lynette '96 MacQuarie Holdings (USA) Inc -125 W 55th -NY 10019 **Fx:**231-1010
(212) 401-4208 .. **Sarno,** Ronald A '92 (Sarno & D LLC) -235 W 23rd -NY 10011
(212) 786-6046 .. **Sarnoff,** David B '95 Morandi Taub & Sarnoff,LLC -1325 Av of Amer -NY 10019 **Fx:**786-6045
(516) 674-4666 .. **Sarnoff,** Norman '53 -32 Westland Dr -Glen Cove 11542 **Fx:**674-0649
(212) 850-7531 .. **Sarnoff,** Stuart M '85 Avenue Capital Mgmt -535 Mad Av -NY 10022
(315) 234-4229 .. **Sarofeen,** Michl J '81 (Sarofeen & A,PLLC) -1 Lincoln Ctr -Syracuse 13202 **Fx:**424-1011
(212) 664-4444 .. **Saroff,** John S '06 NBC-Universal -30 Rckfllr Plz -NY 10112
(212) 878-8000 .. **Sarok,** Louis '06 %Clifford C LLP -31 W 52nd -NY 10019
(212) 407-4000 .. **Sarowitz,** Jodi R '07 %Loeb & L,LLP -345 Park Av -NY 10154
(212) 968-8300 .. **Sarowitz,** Lawr S '79 (Mintzer SZL&M LLP) -39 Bway -NY 10006
(607) 778-6092 .. **Sarra,** Andrea B '01 %Hon J Tait-Supreme Ct -Broome Cnty Cthse -Bnghmtn 13901
(607) 723-5341 .. **Sarra,** Jon J '01 %Hinman H&K,LLP -80 Exchange Bx5250 -Bnghmtn 13902
(212) 852-3192 .. **Sarraf,** Niloo '03 US Trust Co of NY -114 W 47th -NY 10036 **Fx:**852-1310
(212) 868-3610 .. **Sarraf,** Ronen '01 (Sarraf G LLP) -116 John -NY 10038 **Fx:**918-7967
(518) 274-4800 .. **Sarratori,** Frank C '91 Pioneer Savings Bk -21 2nd -Troy 12180 **Fx:**274-7169
(718) 260-2450 .. **Sarratt,** Wm David '05 Hon J Gleeson -225 Cadman Plz E -Brklyn 11201
(212) 444-6162 .. **Sarrett,** Saul P '96 ITG Inc -380 Mad Av -NY 10017 **Fx:**444-6345
(518) 374-1200 .. **Sarris,** Chas A '76 OfCnsl Kouray & K -525 State -Schnctdy 12305 **Fx:**374-7414
(212) 753-7500 .. **Sarro,** Christine M '05 %Hartman & C LLP -488 Mad Av -NY 10022
(914) 245-4904 .. **Sarro,** Christopher A '83 -Bx34 -Yorktwn Hts 10598
(212) 373-3000 .. **Sarro,** Dale M '85 (Paul WRW&G LLP) -1285 Av of Amer -NY 10019
(914) 632-4700 .. **Sarro,** Mark J '84 (McDonough Law Firm, LLP) -145 Huguenot -New Rchll 10801
(646) 292-7733 .. **Sarro,** Paula M '85 Womens Prison Assn & Home -347 E 10th -NY 10009
(718) 520-3735 .. **Sarro,** Wm A '80 %Hon W Giaccio -88-11 Sutphin Blvd -Jamaica 11435
(212) 588-1400 .. **Sarshik,** Steven '71 -110 Wall -NY 10005

(631) 853-4343 .. **Sartain,** Thos R '79 %Leg Aid -400 Carleton Av Bx9082 -Central Islip 11722 **Fx:**853-7798
(914) 722-4400 .. **Sarter,** Alvin J '81 Treuhold Capital Grp LLC -670 Wht Plns Rd -Scarsdale 10583 **Fx:**722-4496
(347) 422-5320 .. **Sartori,** Louis S '89 %Leg Aid -60 Bay -Staten Isl 10301 **Fx:**(718) 981-6623
(607) 733-9187 .. **Sartori,** Paul A '86 -150 Lk -Elmira 14901
(585) 428-5210 .. **Sartori,** Seana L '94 %Pub Def -10 N Fitzhugh -Rchstr 14614 **Fx:**428-2234
(914) 669-8621 .. **Sartorio,** Lynda G '87 -8 Chestnut Dr -N Salem 10560 **Fx:**277-3114
(212) 451-2300 .. **Sartorius,** Peter M '08 %Olshan GFR&W LLP -65 E 55th -NY 10022
(914) 948-1839 .. **Sarubbi,** Janis W '86 -5 Waller Av -White Plns 10601 **Fx:**682-0123
(212) 421-4100 .. **Sarubbi,** Ronald T '99 (Pryor C LLP) -7 Times Sq -NY 10036
(212) 735-3000 .. **Sarumida,** Hiroshi '95 Cnsl Skadden ASM&F LLP -4 Times Sq -NY 10036
(718) 267-7779 .. **Sarver,** Eric M '99 -24-57 24th -Astoria 11102
(212) 361-4568 .. **Sarver,** Janet M '06 Dept Cnsmr Affrs -42 Bway -NY 10004 **Fx:**487-4197
(212) 344-6500 .. **Sarzin,** Evan '79 E Sarzin,PC -40 Exch Pl -NY 10005 **Fx:**344-0794
(716) 854-3400 .. **Sarzynski,** Danl E '00 (Rupp BPC&C LLC) -1600 Lbrty Bldg -Buffalo 14202
(607) 797-4839 .. **Sarzynski,** Edw J '71 (Hogan SLS&D,LLP) -Bx660 -Bnghmtn 13902
(212) 416-6393 .. **Sas,** Nina M '97 %Dept of Law -120 Bway -NY 10271
(516) 292-8100 .. **Sasala,** Andrea '98 %Nassau/Sfflk Law Srv -1 Helen Keller Way -Hempstd 11550 **Fx:**292-6529
(212) 788-1282 .. **Sasanow,** Terri Feinstein '79 %Law Dept -100 Church -NY 10007 **Fx:**788-0367
(212) 848-4000 .. **Sasanuma,** Joe M '08 %Shearman & S LLP -599 Lex Av -NY 10022
(212) 448-1100 .. **Sash,** Alan E '99 (McLaughlin & S,LLP) -260 Mad Av -NY 10016
(914) 251-0001 .. **Sash,** Sharon M '99 (Lane S&L LLP) -106 Corp Park Dr -White Plns 10604
(516) 742-7777 .. **Sasiadek,** Adam J '10 %Frazer & F,LLP -1415 Kellum Pl -Gdn Cty 11530
(718) 802-3965 .. **Sasitorn,** Narisa '05 Dept of Bldgs -210 Joralemon -Brklyn 11201
(718) 286-6000 .. **Saslaw,** Edw D '79 %DA -125-01 Qns Blvd -Kew Gdns 11415
(718) 739-6400 .. **Saslaw,** Susan R '86 DHCR -92-31 Union Hall -Jamaica 11433 **Fx:**262-7938
(212) 603-6300 .. **Sasloff,** Robt M '90 Cnsl Robinson BLGG&G PC -875 3rd Av -NY 10022
(212) 312-2260 .. **Saslovsky,** Heather J '06 %Leg Aid -60 Lafayette -NY 10013 **Fx:**349-0874
(914) 232-1748 .. **Saslow,** Susan A '83 -20 Lily Pond Ln -Katonah 10536
(212) 506-5000 .. **Saslow,** Susan Lee '97 OfCnsl Orrick H&S LLP -51 W 52nd -NY 10019
(212) 788-0511 .. **Sasmor,** Kenneth S '75 %Law Dept -100 Church -NY 10007 **Fx:**788-0367
(212) 613-2171 .. **Saso,** Paul A '02 %Gibbons PC -1 Penn Plz -NY 10119 **Fx:**554-9686
(212) 448-1100 .. **Sass,** David W '60 (McLaughlin & S,LLP) -260 Mad Av -NY 10016
(212) 267-6703 .. **Sass,** Laurence J '85 -170 Bway -NY 10038 **Fx:**267-6010
(718) 998-5898 .. **Sass,** Paul L '69 -1411 Av V -Brklyn 11229
(516) 627-7000 .. **Sass,** Russell I '08 %Weiss & Z,PC -3333 New Hyde Pk Rd -New Hyde Pk 11042
(315) 546-0068 .. **Sassani,** Kathleen C '86 (Sassani & S,PC) -7767 Oswego Rd -Liverpool 13090
(315) 546-0068 .. **Sassani & Schenck,PC** -7767 Oswego Rd -Liverpool 13090 **Fx:**546-0078
(585) 232-3240 .. **Sassenhausen,** Amy P '95 %V Criscuolo Jr -16 E Main -Rchstr 14614
(212) 450-4000 .. **Sasser,** Lauren E '10 %Davis P&W LLP -450 Lex Av -NY 10017
(516) 832-3274 .. **Sasso,** Michl P '89 Cnsl 1st Amer Title -333 Earle Ovngton Blvd -Uniondale 11553 **Fx:**(646) 487-1348
(212) 696-4822 .. **Sasson,** Ariel M '98 -10 E 40th -NY 10016 **Fx:**696-4854
(212) 960-0051 .. **Sasson,** Esther Kaufman '90 %Yeshiva Univ -500 W 185th -NY 10033 **Fx:**960-5346
(212) 806-5400 .. **Sasson,** Gabriel '10 %Stroock &S&L LLP -180 Maiden Ln -NY 10038
(516) 818-6600 .. **Sasson,** Jaclyn '98 -12 Holiday Pond Rd -Jericho 11753
(516) 487-9727 .. **Sasson,** Mojgan R '01 (Zaccaria & S) -175 E Shore Rd -Gt Neck 11023 **Fx:**487-4472
(212) 949-7501 .. **Sasson,** Moshe '95 (Sasson B LLP) -1350 Bway -NY 10018 **Fx:**949-7502
(646) 472-7971 .. **Sasson,** Sabra R '99 -315 Mad Av -NY 10017 **Fx:**(212) 937-4645
(315) 353-7398 .. **Sassone,** Robt J '77 (Sassone & M) -40 S Main -Norwd 13668 **Fx:**353-9957
(845) 639-4664 .. **Sassone,** Thos '93 (Mulgrew & S,PC) -22 S Main -New Cty 10956
(212) 333-1008 .. **Sassoon,** Danl P '94 %Polygram Holding Inc -825 8th Av -NY 10019 **Fx:**333-8296
(212) 897-7660 .. **Sassoon,** David S '97 Cnsl Forex Capital Markets LLC -32 Old Slip -NY 10005 **Fx:**897-7669
(212) 735-8620 .. **Sassoon,** Salomon R '77 (Morrison C LLP) -909 3rd Av -NY 10022
(212) 446-4800 .. **Sassower,** Edw O '00 (Kirkland & E LLP) -153 E 53rd -NY 10022
(212) 858-1000 .. **Sassower,** Herman '60 Cnsl Pillsbury WSP LLP -1540 Bway -NY 10036
(212) 732-4992 .. **Sassower,** Mitchell J '76 (Arye L&S,PC) -20 Vesey -NY 10007
(718) 250-2000 .. **Sastoque,** Jorge A '06 %DA -350 Jay -Brklyn 11201 **Fx:**250-2314
(917) 763-0855 .. **Sastow,** Gary S '92 G Sastow,PLLC -186 Drchstr Rd -Scarsdale 10583 **Fx:**(914) 722-7263
(516) 255-4160 .. **Sastow,** Sheryl-Anne '98 %Kardisch L & Assoc PC -80 E Old Cntry Rd -Mineola 11501 **Fx:**255-4163
(516) 663-6600 .. **Satin,** Richd G '81 OfCnsl Ruskin MF,PC -1425 RXR Plz -Uniondale 11556
(212) 326-3939 .. **Satine,** Barry R '76 (Jones D) -222 E 41st -NY 10017
(212) 858-7700 .. **Satine,** David I '07 %Budd L -140 Bway -NY 10005
(212) 962-0035 .. **Satine,** Roy A '72 -15 Maiden Ln -NY 10038 **Fx:**571-4613
(212) 681-1575 .. **Satisky,** David B '04 %Belluck & F LLP -546 5th Av -NY 10036
(212) 984-1871 .. **Satkiewicz,** Jeremy J '89 (J Satkiewicz,PC) -100 Park Av -NY 10017 **Fx:**937-3568
(212) 938-2337 .. **Satkin,** Stephen A '83 (Craner SS&S,PC) -60 E 42nd -NY 10165
(212) 319-6898 .. **Satkowski,** Susan E '00 (Lavin ORC&D) -420 Lex Av -NY 10170
(212) 223-2502 .. **Satloff,** Averell W '73 -130 W 42nd -NY 10036
(347) 853-2600 .. **Satloff,** Martin '66 -103 Park Dr N -Staten Isl 10314
(212) 407-4000 .. **Satnick,** David M '79 (Loeb & L,LLP) -345 Park Av -NY 10154
(212) 335-9000 .. **Sato,** Aaron I '06 %DA -1 Hogan Pl -NY 10013
(212) 735-3464 .. **Satorius,** Jos J '09 %Skadden ASM&F LLP -4 Times Sq -NY 10036 **Fx:**(917) 777-3464
(516) 496-5822 .. **Satran,** Edw S '65 %T Spina -170 Froehlich Farm Blvd -Woodbury 11797 **Fx:**496-5420
(914) 682-4100 .. **Satriale,** John T '60 -19 Court -White Plns 10601 **Fx:**682-4643
(212) 400-7422 .. **Satriale,** Louis R Jr. '87 (Gehring & S LLC) -370 Lex Av -NY 10017
(516) 267-6300 .. **Satriano,** Jessica C '07 %Bond S&K,PLLC -1399 Franklin Av -Gdn Cty 11530
(212) 458-3410 .. **Satriano,** Nicholas M '89 AIG Domestic Claims -175 Water -NY 10038
(212) 538-1780 .. **Satsky,** Jason M '00 Credit Suisse -11 Mad Av -NY 10010
(516) 741-2405 .. **Sattely,** Maris C '93 OfCnsl Geoghan C&B LLC -250 Mineola Blvd -Mineola 11501
(315) 471-0405 .. **Satter & Andrews,LLP** -217 S Salina -Syracuse 13202 **Fx:**471-7849
(315) 471-0405 .. **Satter,** Mimi C '81 (Satter & A,LLP) -217 S Salina -Syracuse 13202
(516) 292-2998 .. **Satterfield,** Kevin '96 -20520 Jamaica Av -Hollis 11423
(212) 818-9200 .. **Satterlee Stephens Burke & Burke LLP** -230 Park Av -NY 10169 **Fx:**818-9606
(516) 571-9041 .. **Satterthwaite,** Nadine J '02 %Cnty Atty -1200 Old Cntry Rd -Westbury 11590
(212) 609-6800 .. **Sattin,** Jerry P '84 Cnsl McCarter & E,LLP -245 Park Av -NY 10167
(212) 306-7100 .. **Sattinger,** Mark H '07 %Campaign Finance Bd -40 Rector -NY 10006 **Fx:**306-7143
(212) 766-4411 .. **Sattler,** Adam B '93 (Ebanks & S,LLP) -20 Vesey -NY 10007 **Fx:**766-5899
(212) 261-8000 .. **Sattler,** Allen E '08 %Mendes & M,LLP -750 7th Av -NY 10019
(212) 530-5000 .. **Sattler,** Dean W '08 %Milbank TH&M LLP -1 Chase Manh Plz -NY 10005
(212) 766-4411 .. **Sattler,** Erica B '94 OfCnsl Ebanks & S,LLP -20 Vesey -NY 10007 **Fx:**766-5899
(212) 715-9100 .. **Satto,** Jos A '99 %Kramer LN&F,LLP -1177 Av of Amer -NY 10036
(212) 408-5100 .. **Satty,** Andrea N '86 (Chadbourne & P LLP) -30 Rckfllr Plz -NY 10112
(716) 845-9489 .. **Saturnino,** Christine '87 Supreme Ct -25 Delaware Av -Buffalo 14202 **Fx:**851-3293
(516) 678-5800 .. **Saturno-Bonelli,** Teresa '88 %Diocese of Rockville Ctr -50 N Park Av -Rockvll Ctr 11570
(212) 336-0161 .. **Satwalekar,** Sandeep Mukund '05 %SEC -3 World Fncl Ctr -NY 10281 **Fx:**336-1323
(212) 456-7832 .. **Satyendra,** Indira S '99 ABC Inc -77 W 66th -NY 10023
(718) 787-9500 .. **Sauchik,** Alec '03 (Khenkin & S,PC) -9712 3rd Av -Brklyn 11209 **Fx:**787-9502
(212) 446-4800 .. **Saucier,** Evan J '08 %Kirkland & E LLP -153 E 53rd -NY 10022
(716) 891-5074 .. **Sauer,** Barbara Ann '94 -3620 Harlem Rd -Buffalo 14215 **Fx:**362-3142
(516) 747-1100 .. **Sauer,** Brian J '79 (Shayne DCS&D) -114 Old Cntry Rd -Mineola 11501
(212) 735-3000 .. **Sauer,** Jason T '09 %Skadden ASM&F LLP -4 Times Sq -NY 10036
(212) 308-4411 .. **Sauer,** Julie L '10 %Edwards AP&D LLP -750 Lex Av -NY 10022
(212) 688-4010 .. **Sauer,** Richd A '88 %First Springs Corp -499 Park Av -NY 10022 **Fx:**688-4236
(212) 297-6532 .. **Sauer,** Richd H '83 CBS Outdoor -405 Lex Av -NY 10174
(914) 995-4457 .. **Sauer,** Robt K '88 %DA -111 Martin Luther King Blvd -White Plns 10601 **Fx:**995-3363
(914) 765-4077 .. **Sauerborn,** Randa K '98 IBM -North Castle Dr -Armonk 10504
(212) 547-5400 .. **Sauermilch,** Thos '87 (McDermott W&E LLP) -340 Mad Av -NY 10173
(212) 867-9500 .. **Saufer,** Isaac A '79 (Kurzman K&F,LLP) -230 Park Av -NY 10169
(516) 794-1000 .. **Saul,** Gail B '95 -1103 Stewart Av -Gdn Cty 11530 **Fx:**794-0359
(201) 837-1090 .. **Saul,** Jos E '94 -431 W 261st -Bronx 10471 **Fx:**(718) 601-6931
(212) 578-5334 .. **Saul,** Myra L '78 %MetLife -27-01 Qns Plz N -LIC 11101
(631) 608-4100 .. **Saul,** Richd D '03 %K Mollins,PC -425 Broadhllw Rd -Melvll 11747 **Fx:**608-4107
(718) 233-6480 .. **Saul,** Susanna E '05 Leg Srvcs for NYC -36 Richmond Ter -Staten Isl 10301
(718) 615-7400 .. **Saulino,** Vincenzo '00 (Zwirn & S) -2606 E 15th -Brklyn 11235
(212) 459-0900 .. **Saulitis,** Andrew P '81 (A Saulitis,PC) -555 Mad Av -NY 10022 **Fx:**459-1826
(212) 969-6439 .. **Saulnier,** Jean-Paul '01 Alliance Bernstein LP -1345 Av of Amer -NY 10105 **Fx:**554-4639
(516) 572-0765 .. **Saumell,** Theresa Marie '96 %Nassau Case Mgt -175 Fulton Av -Hempstd 11550
(212) 415-0204 .. **Saunders,** Adrienne F '99 Babcock & Brown Ltd -101 E 52nd -NY 10022
(212) 805-3900 .. **Saunders,** Alexander X '05 %Clausen M PC -1 Chase Manh Plz -NY 10005
(212) 709-8014 .. **Saunders,** Calvin C '85 -110 Wall -NY 10005
(212) 755-0008 .. **Saunders,** Craig '89 Munzer & S LLP -18 E 48th -NY 10017 **Fx:**832-4092
(212) 472-3013 .. **Saunders,** D R '85 -326 E 74th -NY 10021
(718) 286-6000 .. **Saunders,** Danl A '82 %DA -125-01 Qns Blvd -Kew Gdns 11415
(212) 784-5800 .. **Saunders,** Darren W '89 (Hiscock & B,LLP) -7 Times Sq -NY 10036
(212) 788-1238 .. **Saunders,** Gail C '95 %Law Dept -100 Church -NY 10007 **Fx:**788-0367
(914) 273-4545 .. **Saunders,** Gary A '93 MBIA Ins Corp -113 King -Armonk 10504
(212) 799-3724 .. **Saunders,** James S '74 -255 W 84th -NY 10024 **Fx:**980-1521
(845) 267-4878 .. **Saunders,** Jeffrey B '90 (Birbrower & B,PC) -151 N Main -New Cty 10956
(315) 733-0419 .. **Saunders,** Jos E '81 (Saunders K,LLP) -185 Genesee -Utica 13501
(212) 290-4700 .. **Saunders,** Jos H '95 %Human Rights Watch -350 5th Av -NY 10118 **Fx:**736-1300
(917) 674-7753 .. **Saunders,** Judie A '99 -110 Wall -NY 10005
(315) 733-0419 .. **Saunders Kahler, LLP** -185 Genesee -Utica 13501 **Fx:**724-8522
(585) 263-1000 .. **Saunders,** Kevin T '98 %Nixon P LLP -1100 Clinton Sq -Rchstr 14604

(212) 209-3000 .. **Saunders,** Matthew '08 Brock Capital Grp LLC -622 3rd Av -NY 10017
(516) 674-8686 .. **Saunders,** Melvin A '57 %J Brady -333 Glen Head Rd -Old Brookvll 11545 **Fx:**674-8118
(212) 474-1000 .. **Saunders,** Paul C '66 (Cravath S&M LLP) -825 8th Av -NY 10019
(212) 751-3001 .. **Saunders,** Robt H '87 (Thompson & K LLP) -919 3rd Av -NY 10022
(917) 284-8202 .. **Saunders,** Saml W '09 -Bx485 -NY 10018
(212) 836-8000 .. **Saunders,** Sarah Welbourne '02 %Kaye S LLP -425 Park Av -NY 10022
(212) 239-6000 .. **Saunders,** Terry J '82 Div Of Parole -314 W 40th -NY 10018 **Fx:**239-6160
(212) 855-0746 .. **Saunders,** Timothy K Jr. '92 %Goldman Sachs -1 NY Plz -NY 10004
(631) 369-2270 .. **Saunderson,** Robt '73 %J Ryan & Assoc -633 Main Rd -Rvrhead 11901
(212) 335-4500 .. **Saur,** Anthony M '03 %DLA Piper LLP -1251 Av of Amer -NY 10020
(212) 818-9200 .. **Saurack,** Walter A '96 (Satterlee SB&B LLP) -230 Park Av -NY 10169
(212) 338-9100 .. **Saurborn,** Henry L Jr. '87 (Kaiser S&M,PC) -111 Bway -NY 10006
(607) 734-1519 .. **Sauro,** Shawn M '03 %Learned RL&H,LLP -449 E Water -Elmira 14901
(212) 836-8000 .. **Sausen,** David '02 %Kaye S LLP -425 Park Av -NY 10022
(518) 786-4541 .. **Sausville,** Paul J '88 %NYS DMNA -330 Old Niskayuna Rd -Latham 12110 **Fx:**786-4944
(212) 490-3000 .. **Sauter,** Eric J '89 (Wilson EME&D LLP) -150 E 42nd -NY 10017
(914) 323-7000 .. **Sauter,** Eric J '89 (Wilson EME&D LLP) -3 Gannett Dr -White Plns 10604
(212) 267-5556 .. **Sauter,** James P '87 (O'Neill D&K) -15 Beekman -NY 10038
(845) 283-6067 .. **Sautter,** Jason P '01 -20 Legion Dr Bx242 -Unionvll 10988 **Fx:**726-3239
(516) 352-2999 .. **Sava,** George S '97 -734 Franklin Av -Gdn Cty 11530
(212) 972-4900 .. **Sava,** Matthew J '95 (Shapiro FA&S LLP) -380 Mad Av -NY 10017
(845) 624-3820 .. **Savad,** Paul '66 (P Savad & Assoc) -55 Old Tpk Rd -Nanuet 10954 **Fx:**624-3821
(212) 867-8280 .. **Savage,** Arthur V '53 (Patton ELM&S) -420 Lex Av -NY 10170
(212) 521-5400 .. **Savage,** Edw T '76 (Reed S LLP) -599 Lex Av -NY 10022
(718) 286-2000 .. **Savage,** Gerard C '88 %Leg Aid -120-46 Qns Blvd -Kew Gdns 11415 **Fx:**286-2286
(315) 234-1864 .. **Savage,** J Wm '00 Barth SB -224 Harrison -Syracuse 13202
(212) 687-8500 .. **Savage,** Jessica H '08 %Liddle & R,LLP -800 3rd Av -NY 10022
(914) 668-4600 .. **Savage,** John S '85 %Bozeman Law Firm,LLP -6 Gramatan Av -Mt Vernon 10550 **Fx:**668-4721
(646) 452-2300 .. **Savage,** Kimberly A '09 %Crosby & H LLP -350 Bway -NY 10013 **Fx:**452-2301
(315) 427-7958 .. **Savage,** Leslie C '00 -8775 Rvr Watch -Baldwinsvll 13027
(212) 752-9700 .. **Savage,** Michl D '73 (Gersten S LLP) -600 Lex Av -NY 10022
(716) 851-4841 .. **Savage,** Peter J III '04 Ofc of Mayor B Brown -201 City Hall -Buffalo 14202
(518) 384-0216 .. **Savage,** Ralph M '78 Cnsl Savage Law Firm,PC -450 Schauber Rd Bx1160 -Ballston Lk 12019 **Fx:**(775) 254-8446
(631) 329-3356 .. **Savage,** Robt J '88 -Bx1012 -E Hampton 11937 **Fx:**329-3424
(212) 578-2211 .. **Savage,** Russell T '85 %MetLife -27-01 Qns Plz N -LIC 11101 **Fx:**578-3916
(877) 687-2889 .. **Savage,** Steven E '04 -14 Wall -NY 10005 **Fx:**471-2231
(212) 213-7077 .. **Savage,** Susan J '74 %DMB&B -79 Mad Av -NY 10016 **Fx:**213-7159
(585) 232-6500 .. **Savage,** Tyler J '00 %Harter S&E LLP -1600 Bausch & Lomb Pl -Rchstr 14604
(716) 822-9929 .. **Savaglio,** Antonio M '86 -609 Ridge Rd -Lackawanna 14218
(212) 209-4800 .. **Saval,** Danl J '07 (Brown R LLP) -7 Times Sq -NY 10036
(646) 386-4800 .. **Savanyu,** Jean M '80 %Comm Judicial Cndct -61 Bway -NY 10006 **Fx:**458-0037
(212) 403-1000 .. **Savarese,** John F '89 (Wachtell LR&K) -51 W 52nd -NY 10019
(718) 260-8700 .. **Savarese,** Paul J '91 %Admin Children's Srvcs -345 Adams -Brklyn 11201
(212) 566-2412 .. **Savaria,** Antonia I '02 InTrade LLC -2 Rector -NY 10006
(212) 788-2902 .. **Savasta,** Nancy B '92 %Law Dept -100 Church -NY 10007 **Fx:**788-0367
(212) 983-6000 .. **Savatta,** Don '97 -250 Park Av -NY 10177
(212) 452-9407 .. **Savci,** Haluk '92 Mason Tenders Dist Cncl -520 8th Av -NY 10018
(718) 515-0020 .. **Savedoff,** Laurence M '99 -3234 Wht Plns Rd -Bronx 10467
(212) 408-5100 .. **Savell,** Lawr E '83 Cnsl Chadbourne & P LLP -30 Rckfllr Plz -NY 10112
(917) 210-8340 .. **Savell,** Polly C '86 -410 Park Av -NY 10022
(212) 969-3000 .. **Savelson,** Donald W '67 (Proskauer R LLP) -1585 Bway -NY 10036
(212) 563-4100 .. **Savelson,** Robt S '64 (Cohen W&S LLP) -330 W 42nd -NY 10036
(212) 818-9200 .. **Saver,** J Gregory '75 (Satterlee SB&B LLP) -230 Park Av -NY 10169
(212) 345-6000 .. **Saveth,** Henry '76 %Marsh USA -1166 Av of Amer -NY 10036 **Fx:**345-4808
(631) 420-0300 .. **Savetz,** David H '94 UBS Financial Services Inc -225 Broadhllw Rd -Melvll 11747
(212) 532-7650 .. **Saviano,** Edw S '79 (Saviano,PC) -292 Mad Av -NY 10017 **Fx:**532-7651
(212) 969-3000 .. **Saviano,** Frank A '10 %Proskauer R LLP -1585 Bway -NY 10036
(212) 735-8600 .. **Saviano,** Joshua D '04 %Morrison C LLP -909 3rd Av -NY 10022
(212) 574-1200 .. **Savicki,** Kassandra L '04 %Seward & K LLP -1 Bttry Pk Plz -NY 10004
(212) 859-8000 .. **Savicki,** Michl F '04 %Fried FHS&J LLP -1 NY Plz -NY 10004
(516) 746-3500 .. **Savidge,** Edw John '97 (Brand G&B,PC) -600 Old Cntry Rd -Gdn Cty 11530
(212) 250-0753 .. **Savidis,** Irene '84 Deutsche Bk -60 Wall -NY 10005
(347) 401-9580 .. **Saviet,** Annette C '97 %Appllt Term -141 Lvngstn -Brklyn 11201 **Fx:**(718) 643-7889
(718) 464-1000 .. **Saville,** James A '63 -218-29 Jamaica Av -Qns Vllg 11428
(212) 669-0600 .. **Saville,** James A Jr. '98 (Hill R LLP) -45 Bway -NY 10006
(631) 369-7600 .. **Saville,** John B '00 %Lewis JAA,LLP -21 E 2nd -Rvrhead 11901
(914) 776-8000 .. **Saville,** Robt J '96 WDF Inc -30 N Macquesten Pkwy -Mt Vernon 10550
(631) 261-4555 .. **Savin,** Kenneth P '77 -54 Main Bx398 -Northprt 11768 **Fx:**261-0790
(914) 767-7613 .. **Savinelli,** Michl J '99 Pepsi Bottling Group,Inc -1 Pepsi Way -Somers 10589
(516) 572-6062 .. **Savinetti,** Louis G '97 %Nassau Health Care Corp -2201 Hempstd Tpk -E Meadow 11554
(718) 204-7878 .. **Savino,** Aldo '81 -32-26 Steinway -Astoria 11103
(212) 422-9424 .. **Savino,** Angela '04 %Gogick B&O,LLP -11 Bway -NY 10004
(212) 509-9400 .. **Savino,** Angelo G '82 (Cozen O) -45 Bway Atrium -NY 10006
(212) 732-8368 .. **Savino,** Danl J Jr. '91 (Caruso SLCU&S) -132 Nassau -NY 10038
(631) 755-0101 .. **Savino,** Ellen N '89 Cnsl Lewis JAA,LLP -425 Broad Hollow Rd -Melvll 11747
(631) 761-0800 .. **Savino,** Jos C '84 (Lazer AR&Y,PC) -225 Old Cntry Rd -Melvll 11747
(914) 592-0601 .. **Savino,** Jos J '01 (Faga S LLP) -399 Knollwood Rd -White Plns 10603
(212) 788-8681 .. **Savino,** Kimberly M '08 %Law Dept -100 Church -NY 10007 **Fx:**788-0367
(212) 526-7000 .. **Savino,** Matthew J '02 -745 7th Av -NY 10019
(914) 684-9100 .. **Savino,** Michl A '07 %Bailly & M,LLP -244 Wstchstr Av -White Plns 10604
(516) 334-1700 .. **Savino,** Thos V '01 %Inc Vlg of Westbury -235 Lincoln Pl -Westbury 11590
(516) 746-3500 .. **Savino,** Vincent J '92 (Brand G&B,PC) -600 Old Cntry Rd -Gdn Cty 11530
(716) 856-5500 .. **Savino,** Wm F '76 (Damon M LLP) -200 Delaware Av -Buffalo 14202
(516) 357-3000 .. **Savino,** Wm M '75 (Rivkin R LLP) -926 RXR Plz -Uniondale 11556
(212) 268-7900 .. **Savinon,** Francisco D Jr. '07 %Fischer & B,PC -888 7th Av -NY 10106
(212) 684-3900 .. **Savio,** Maria A '84 (Gottlieb R&R,PC) -270 Mad Av -NY 10016
(315) 448-8400 .. **Savion,** Jennifer E '06 Law Dept -233 E Wshngtn -Syracuse 13202 **Fx:**448-8381
(212) 820-9502 .. **Saviski,** Anna '02 %Hawkins D&W LLP -One Chase Manh Plz -NY 10005
(516) 292-4700 .. **Savit,** Joel B '76 (JB Savit,PC) -231 Mineola Blvd -Mineola 11501 **Fx:**292-5198
(212) 272-5633 .. **Savit,** Robt J '06 %JP Morgan Chase -383 Mad Av -NY 10179
(212) 247-1860 .. **Savitsky,** Arlene B '71 -353 W 56th -NY 10019
(631) 270-6038 .. **Savitsky,** Robt '89 -1670 Old Cntry Rd -Plainvw 11803 **Fx:**410-1966
(212) 583-1230 .. **Savitt,** Danl C '99 Panagea3 LLC -575 Mad Av -NY 10022
(212) 679-4470 .. **Savitt,** Ephraim '78 -260 Mad Av -NY 10016 **Fx:**679-6770
(631) 543-3750 .. **Savitt,** Harvey B '68 (Savitt K&S PC) -353 Vets Mem'l Hwy -Commack 11725
(631) 543-3750 .. **Savitt Krantz & Sellman PC** -353 Vets Mem'l Hwy -Commack 11725 **Fx:**543-3682
(212) 398-4300 .. **Savitt,** L Stephen '75 -1065 Av of Amer -NY 10018
(518) 475-9844 .. **Savitt,** Meredith H '86 M Savitt,PC -636 Delaware Av -Delmar 12054
(201) 954-0036 .. **Savitt,** Nancy L '85 -27-28 Thomson Av -LIC 11101
(917) 414-2523 .. **Savitt,** Richd P '96 (Savitt Law Firm,PLLC) -305 Bway -NY 10007
(914) 478-1480 .. **Savitt,** Susan Schenkel '68 Schenkel-Savitt Firm -16 Buena Vista Dr -Hastings-On-Hud 10706 **Fx:**478-4934
(212) 403-1000 .. **Savitt,** Wm '98 (Wachtell LR&K) -51 W 52nd -NY 10019
(516) 229-4432 .. **Savitz,** Burton D '80 Kay & G -875 Merrick Av -Westbury 11590
(212) 752-5258 .. **Savitz,** Joshua I '01 Cnsl Schwartz SE&C LLC -845 3rd Av -NY 10022
(212) 596-9000 .. **Savkar,** Sunil Wm '99 (Ropes & G LLP) -1211 Av of Amer -NY 10036
(212) 259-8000 .. **Savla,** Sandeep '01 %Dewey & L LLP -1301 Av of Amer -NY 10019
(315) 422-3626 .. **Savlov,** David B '85 -2 Clinton Sq -Syracuse 13202 **Fx:**478-3148
(212) 396-8484 .. **Savoca,** John P '87 Hudson Land Co -770 Lex Av -NY 10065
(516) 741-7676 .. **Savoiardo,** Maurizio III '93 OfCnsl Miranda SSSV LLP -240 Mineola Blvd -Mineola 11501
(212) 267-3320 .. **Savona D'Erasmo & Hyer LLC** -111 Bway -NY 10006 **Fx:**267-3372
(718) 966-2700 .. **Savona,** Frank V '97 -4459 Amboy Rd -Staten Isl 10312 **Fx:**317-5545
(212) 267-3320 .. **Savona,** Jos F X '70 (Savona D&H LLC) -111 Bway -NY 10006
(845) 344-5290 .. **Savona,** Keri E '03 Cnsl Cnty Soc Srvcs -1041 Development Ct -Kingston 12401 **Fx:**334-5284
(212) 384-1000 .. **Savona,** Meridith A '92 %FBI -26 Fed Plz -NY 10278
(914) 966-3333 .. **Savone,** Dino '94 -657 Ynkrs Av -Ynkrs 10704 **Fx:**966-3399
(516) 913-4400 .. **Savoy,** Marc E '91 -100 Ring Rd -Gdn Cty 11530 **Fx:**977-2822
(516) 739-7403 .. **Savran,** Edw A '82 (Savran Law,PLLC) -1 Old Cntry Rd -Carle Pl 11514 **Fx:**739-7408
(212) 564-8525 .. **Savrin,** Janet A '83 (Magier & S) -450 7th Av -NY 10123 **Fx:**967-0867
(212) 681-6195 .. **Savryn,** Karl '70 -630 3rd Av -NY 10017 **Fx:**486-3099
(212) 335-9000 .. **Savur,** Nitin S '01 %DA -1 Hogan Pl -NY 10013
(212) 918-3000 .. **Sawa,** Kyle M '10 %Hogan L LLP -875 3rd Av -NY 10022
(212) 682-5990 .. **Sawchuk,** Edw S '86 E Sawchuk,PC -381 Park Av S -NY 10016
(212) 969-3000 .. **Sawczyn,** Gerald W '04 %Proskauer R LLP -1585 Bway -NY 10036
(716) 648-1300 .. **Sawers,** Danl T '86 (Sawers & S,LLP) -81 Buffalo -Hambrg 14075 **Fx:**648-1700
(716) 856-4000 .. **Sawers,** Tim M '91 (Hodgson R LLP) -140 Pearl -Buffalo 14202
(212) 841-1000 .. **Sawhney,** Pamela '06 %Covington & B LLP -620 8th Av -NY 10018
(212) 553-8300 .. **Sawicki,** James V '87 %Cohen K & Assoc -2 Park Av -NY 10016 **Fx:**553-8721
(716) 855-3200 .. **Sawicki,** K Michl '74 (Zdarsky S&A) -298 Main -Buffalo 14202
(212) 698-9260 .. **Sawikin,** Harvey M '86 Firebird Mgmt LLC -152 W 57th -NY 10019
(516) 396-7700 .. **Sawits,** David A '05 Amer Home Mortgage -538 Broadhllw Rd -Melvll 11747
(212) 878-7900 .. **Sawwan,** Donia '02 %Fox R LLP -100 Park Av -NY 10017
(718) 222-2115 .. **Sawyer,** Elisabeth G '04 %Law Dept -350 Jay -Brklyn 11201 **Fx:**222-2393
(212) 761-8200 .. **Sawyer,** Ethan J '03 Morgan Stanley -1585 Bway -NY 10036
(516) 222-4567 .. **Sawyer Halpern & Demetri** -666 Old Cntry Rd -Gdn Cty 11530 **Fx:**222-4585
(516) 222-4567 .. **Sawyer,** James '70 (Sawyer H&D) -666 Old Cntry Rd -Gdn Cty 11530
(212) 279-9090 .. **Sawyer,** John Randy '99 (Stark & S) -One Penn Plz -NY 10119 **Fx:**279-9113
(212) 225-2000 .. **Sawyer,** Katherine A '98 %Cleary GS&H -1 Lbrty Plz -NY 10006

(212) 326-3939 .. **Sawyer,** Lauri W '00 %Jones D -222 E 41st -NY 10017
(212) 558-4000 .. **Sawyer,** Melissa '01 (Sullivan & C LLP) -125 Broad -NY 10004
(212) 848-4000 .. **Sawyer,** Nathan D '03 %Shearman & S LLP -599 Lex Av -NY 10022
(212) 345-3387 .. **Sawyer,** Stephen R '01 Marsh & McLennan -1166 Av of Amer -NY 10036
(212) 229-5432 .. **Sawyer,** Susan '96 New Schl Univ -80 5th Av -NY 10011
(212) 506-5000 .. **Sawyers,** Al B '95 (Orrick H&S LLP) -51 W 52nd -NY 10019
(631) 501-3100 .. **Sawyers,** Andrea G '92 %J Humphreys -3 Huntngtn Quad Bx9028 -Melvll 11747 **Fx:**501-3085
(212) 996-0788 .. **Sawyers,** John T '71 -120 E 90th -NY 10128 **Fx:**622-3554
(212) 513-3200 .. **Sawyier,** Stephen K '80 (Holland & K LLP) -31 W 52nd -NY 10019
(585) 419-8800 .. **Sawyko,** Leon T '70 (Harris B PLLC) -99 Garnsey Rd -Pittsfrd 14534
(516) 746-4313 .. **Sax,** Burton R '53 -174 Birch Dr -New Hyde Pk 11040
(845) 291-2650 .. **Sax,** Jonathan '74 %Cnty Atty -285 Main -Goshen 10924 **Fx:**291-3014
(212) 223-4000 .. **Saxe,** Ira M '89 (Crowell & M LLP) -590 Mad Av -NY 10022
(212) 988-9118 .. **Saxe,** Phyllis Krulik '83 -225 Bway -NY 10007 **Fx:**988-9113
(212) 549-2605 .. **Saxe,** Rose A '02 %ACLU -125 Broad -NY 10004 **Fx:**549-2651
(212) 373-3000 .. **Saxena,** Mayur P '07 %Paul WRW&G LLP -1285 Av of Amer -NY 10019
(212) 801-2184 .. **Saxl,** Stephen L '90 (Greenberg T,LLP) -200 Park Av -NY 10166
(646) 471-5728 .. **Saxman,** Michl B '81 %PricewaterhouseCoopers LLP -300 Mad Av -NY 10017
(516) 249-3450 .. **Saxon,** Jeffrey P '08 Carman C&I,LLP -266 Main -Farmngdl 11735
(718) 340-4242 .. **Saxon,** Jonathan K '94 %CUNY Law Schl -65-21 Main -Flushng 11367 **Fx:**340-4482
(212) 218-2100 .. **Saxon,** Peter '67 (Fitzpatrick CH&S) -1290 Av of Amer -NY 10104
(718) 339-3330 .. **Saxon,** Robt S '73 (Meyers S&C) -3620 Quentin Rd -Brklyn 11234
(716) 856-4000 .. **Saxon,** Victoria J '83 (Hodgson R LLP) -140 Pearl -Buffalo 14202
(585) 262-6390 .. **Saxum,** Gregory A '85 SpclCnsl Hamberger & W -1 S Wshngtn -Rchstr 14614
(212) 201-4829 .. **Sayago,** Andrea J S '03 Ramius HVB Prtnrs,LLC -599 Lex Av -NY 10022
(212) 640-8951 .. **Sayar,** Elizabeth A '99 American Express -200 Vesey -NY 10285
(212) 808-7800 .. **Saydah,** Gilbert R '09 %Kelley D&W LLP -101 Park Av -NY 10178
(212) 434-0100 .. **Saydak,** Beth A '01 Litchfield C LLP -420 Lex Av -NY 10170
(212) 596-9000 .. **Sayeed,** Hassen Amir '05 %Ropes & G LLP -1211 Av of Amer -NY 10036
(914) 963-4500 .. **Sayegh,** Andrew W '87 -984 N Bway -Ynkrs 10701 **Fx:**963-6200
(212) 556-2100 .. **Sayegh,** Elias '09 King & S -1185 Av of Amer -NY 10036
(914) 968-5800 .. **Sayegh,** Elias J '99 (Sayegh & S,PC) -615 Ynkrs Av -Ynkrs 10704 **Fx:**968-5950
(914) 968-5800 .. **Sayegh,** Emile P '89 (Sayegh & S,PC) -615 Ynkrs Av -Ynkrs 10704 **Fx:**968-5950
(845) 228-4200 .. **Sayegh,** Jos S '89 W Sayegh,PC -65 Gleneida Av -Carmel 10512 **Fx:**228-4832
(914) 423-0800 .. **Sayegh,** Nader J '91 -10 Palisade Av -Ynkrs 10701 **Fx:**423-7870
(212) 430-8020 .. **Sayegh,** Paul M '01 %LeClairRyan,PC -830 3rd Av -NY 10022
(914) 963-9487 .. **Sayegh,** Vincent '09 -984 N Bway -Ynkrs 10701
(845) 228-4200 .. **Sayegh,** Wm G '91 -65 Gleneida Av -Carmel 10512 **Fx:**228-4832
(585) 454-2320 .. **Sayers,** Sharon Kelly '79 -30 W Broad -Rchstr 14614 **Fx:**454-1612
(516) 921-0556 .. **Sayetta,** Howard E '79 -235 Southwood Cir -Syosset 11791
(212) 798-6106 .. **Sayetta,** Stacey L '98 %Fortress Invstmnts Grp -1345 Av of Amer -NY 10105
(516) 747-1136 .. **Sayevich-Horz,** Laurie '96 %Steinberg FB&F,PC -40 Crsswys Park Dr -Woodbury 11797
(212) 837-3208 .. **Sayko,** James P '06 JP Morgan Chase -530 5th Av -NY 10036
(212) 262-2390 .. **Sayles,** Andrew C '05 %Connell F LLP -888 7th Av -NY 10106
(607) 734-2271 .. **Sayles & Evans** -1 W Church -Elmira 14901 **Fx:**734-1754
(315) 425-2700 .. **Sayles,** Judith M '86 (Hiscock & B,LLP) -One Park Pl -Syracuse 13202
(212) 277-4000 .. **Sayles,** Perry M '93 (Freshfields BD LLP) -520 Mad Av -NY 10022
(212) 763-5000 .. **Saylor,** Elizabeth S '02 %Emery CB&A LLP -75 Rckfllr Plz -NY 10019
(212) 735-3000 .. **Saylor,** Sara M '09 %Skadden ASM&F LLP -4 Times Sq -NY 10036
(212) 278-0400 .. **Sayour,** Tonia '04 %Cooper & D LLP -30 Rckfllr Plz -NY 10112
(212) 209-0853 .. **Saypoff,** Jess M '87 New Oak Capital LLC -485 Lex Av -NY 10017
(585) 777-7270 .. **Sayre,** Gregg C '88 %Frontier & Citizens Communicatns -180 S Clinton Av -Rchstr 14646 **Fx:**263-9986
(212) 503-0900 .. **Saytanides,** Anthony M '68 %Meyers Parking Sys -441 Lex Av -NY 10017
(516) 470-2488 .. **Sazer,** Gary N '75 Sazer Cnsltng,Inc -200 Old Cntry Rd -Mineola 11501 **Fx:**742-1288
(718) 373-8376 .. **Sbano,** Gabrielle '00 -67 27th Av -Brklyn 11214
(516) 568-3045 .. **Sbano,** Vincent G '87 -34 Primrose Ln -Vly Stream 11580
(718) 463-0470 .. **Sbiroli,** Jos '87 %Ventura Land -149-45 Nrthrn Blvd -Flushng 11354
(212) 577-3394 .. **Sbrana,** Lisa B '94 Leg Aid -199 Water -NY 10038
(718) 590-2000 .. **Scaccia,** Christine '92 %DA -198 E 161st -Bronx 10451 **Fx:**590-6477
(315) 422-4000 .. **Scaccia,** Dante M '49 Scaccia Law Firm -109 S Warren -Syracuse 13202
(585) 414-0066 .. **Scaccia,** Donna M '95 -1900 Empire Blvd -Webster 14580
(212) 728-8000 .. **Scaduto,** Frank M '06 %Willkie F&G LLP -787 7th Av -NY 10019
(516) 781-1765 .. **Scaduto,** Karen Marie '85 -2467 Williams Ct -Bellmore 11710
(212) 593-2155 .. **Scaffidi,** Anthony J '10 %Scaffidi & Assoc -747 3rd Av -NY 10017 **Fx:**593-2257
(716) 849-1333 .. **Scaffidi,** Philip '96 (Lipsitz GSC LLP) -42 Delaware Av -Buffalo 14202
(212) 593-2155 .. **Scaffidi,** Roy F '79 (Scaffidi & Assoc) -747 3rd Av -NY 10017 **Fx:**593-2257
(518) 963-4510 .. **Scaglione,** David D '90 (Manning & S) -3665 Essex Rd Bx309 -Willsboro 12996 **Fx:**963-7557
(631) 265-9900 .. **Scagluso,** Frank S '85 (F Scagluso & Assoc) -191 Terry Rd -Smithtwn 11787 **Fx:**265-6273
(212) 546-9255 .. **Scagnelli,** John M '76 (Scarinci H) -107 Grand -NY 10013
(518) 463-0770 .. **Scagnelli,** Peter J '89 -48 Columbia -Albany 12207
(516) 294-5200 .. **Scahill,** Francis J '85 (Picciano & S) -900 Merchants Cncrs -Westbury 11590
(631) 421-2823 .. **Scal,** Carol L T '89 -27 W Neck Rd -Huntngtn 11743
(518) 583-4404 .. **Scala,** Jos C '87 (J Scala,LLP) -18 Division -Saratoga Spgs 12866
(917) 837-7141 .. **Scala,** Vincent D '84 -110 Wall -NY 10005
(914) 304-1783 .. **Scalard,** Joanne M '89 ITT Fluid Technology -1133 Wstchstr Av -White Plns 10604 **Fx:**696-2950
(212) 888-8200 .. **Scaldaferri,** Ezio '81 (Feder K LLP) -845 3rd Av -NY 10022
(845) 452-4100 .. **Scalera,** Erina R '98 Comp Risk Mngrs -2515 South Rd Bx1999 -Poughkeepsie 12601
(518) 473-5118 .. **Scales,** Benjamin A '03 Applt Div 3rd Dept -Bx7350 -Albany 12224 **Fx:**473-9920
(718) 624-4306 .. **Scales,** Claude M III '72 -57 Montague -Brklyn 11201
(716) 645-2093 .. **Scales-Trent,** Judy '86 %SUNY Buffalo Lw Schl -O'Brian Hall -Buffalo 14260 **Fx:**645-5968
(212) 832-5981 .. **Scali,** Anthony P '08 %Moulinos & Assoc LLC -445 Park Av -NY 10022 **Fx:**832-5982
(845) 344-3000 .. **Scali,** Jos G '74 (JG Scali & Assoc) -200 Midway Pk Dr -Middletwn 10940 **Fx:**344-3005
(212) 312-2329 .. **Scalia,** Ann Marie '94 %Leg Aid -60 Lafayette -NY 10013 **Fx:**349-0874
(585) 428-5210 .. **Scalia,** Donald M '02 Pub Def -10 N Fitzhugh -Rchstr 14614 **Fx:**428-2234
(631) 363-8600 .. **Scalia,** Jos '93 %Mazzei & B -9B Montauk Hwy -Blue Pnt 11715
(716) 854-2020 .. **Scalione,** Robt A '98 (Cellino & B,PC) -350 Main -Buffalo 14202
(315) 422-1311 .. **Scalione,** Robt S '70 (Melvin & M,PLLC) -217 S Salina -Syracuse 13202
(315) 866-3184 .. **Scalise,** Carl G '56 -264 Pinegrove Rd Bx209 -Herkimer 13350 **Fx:**866-3184
(914) 725-2801 .. **Scalise,** Deborah A '88 (Scalise & H LLP) -670 Wht Plns Rd -Scarsdale 10583 **Fx:**931-2112
(212) 374-7851 .. **Scalise,** Gabrielle Benadi '01 %NYC Dept Educ -52 Chmbrs -NY 10007
(914) 722-4100 .. **Scalise,** James T '88 (Lyder & S LLP) -670 Wht Plns Rd -Scarsdale 10583 **Fx:**722-6586
(212) 458-2644 .. **Scalise,** James W '02 AIG Domestic Claims -175 Water -NY 10038
(212) 909-6000 .. **Scalisi,** Jacqueline '88 %Debevoise & P LLP -919 3rd Av -NY 10022
(631) 261-2329 .. **Scalisi,** James M '92 -630 W 6th Av -E Northprt 11731
(718) 250-2000 .. **Scalley,** Kathleen L '06 DA -350 Jay -Brklyn 11201 **Fx:**250-2314
(212) 248-3140 .. **Scally,** John J Jr. '77 (Drinker B&R LLP) -140 Bway -NY 10005
(516) 872-7400 .. **Scalza,** Debra B '98 %Minerva & D -107 S Central Av -Vly Stream 11580
(631) 427-5050 .. **Scalzi & Nofi** -150 Broad Hollow Rd -Melvll 11747 **Fx:**427-5079
(315) 724-4694 .. **Scalzo,** Christine '83 -45 Arlngtn Ter -Utica 13501
(212) 728-8000 .. **Scalzo,** Danielle '07 %Willkie F&G LLP -787 7th Av -NY 10019
(212) 848-4000 .. **Scalzo,** John C '02 %Shearman & S LLP -599 Lex Av -NY 10022
(315) 266-6100 .. **Scalzo,** Maryangela '05 Pub Def -235 Elizabeth -Utica 13501 **Fx:**266-6105
(212) 788-0513 .. **Scalzo,** Victoria '83 %Law Dept -100 Church -NY 10007 **Fx:**788-0367
(718) 442-0900 .. **Scamardella,** Robt '76 (Russo S&D,PC) -1010 Forest Av -Staten Isl 10310
(212) 218-2100 .. **Scambia,** Diego '91 (Fitzpatrick CH&S) -1290 Av of Amer -NY 10104
(212) 237-0000 .. **Scamborova,** Petra '07 %Vinson & E LLP -666 5th Av -NY 10103
(212) 839-5300 .. **Scamparini,** Adriana R '04 %Sidley A LLP -787 7th Av -NY 10019
(914) 699-0600 .. **Scancarelli Jacobson & Uzzo,LLP** -22 W 1st -Mt Vernon 10550 **Fx:**664-2543
(212) 758-4040 .. **Scanga,** Frank A '89 -488 Mad Av -NY 10022 **Fx:**308-1347
(212) 698-3500 .. **Scanlan,** Kevin P '99 (Dechert LLP) -1095 Av of Amer -NY 10036
(914) 949-2560 .. **Scanlan,** Richd S '68 -245 Main -White Plns 10601
(845) 562-0203 .. **Scanlan,** Sharon A '88 Jacoby & M,LLP -1279 Route 300 Bx1111 -Newburgh 12550 **Fx:**562-3492
(718) 855-9000 .. **Scanlan,** Suzanne O '43 %Cullen and D LLP -177 Montague -Brklyn 11201
(212) 805-3900 .. **Scanlon,** Christopher T '97 %Clausen M PC -1 Chase Manh Plz -NY 10005
(212) 326-3939 .. **Scanlon,** Dulcie E '09 %Jones D -222 E 41st -NY 10017
(607) 722-7141 .. **Scanlon,** John M '83 -19 Chenango Bx2206 -Bnghmtn 13902 **Fx:**722-7142
(212) 267-7767 .. **Scanlon,** Jos K '94 (Gess G&S,PC) -30 Vesey -NY 10007
(315) 234-8565 .. **Scanlon,** Michl F '02 %Hon FJ Scullin Jr -100 S Clinton Bx7367 -Syracuse 13261
(212) 267-7767 .. **Scanlon,** Nancy E '91 OfCnsl Gess G&S,PC -30 Vesey -NY 10007
(212) 361-1742 .. **Scanlon,** Raymond C '89 Envrnmntl Cntrl Brd -66 John -NY 10038 **Fx:**361-1900
(585) 381-2050 .. **Scanlon,** Susan J '77 %Corp Legal Mgmt -18 Stonbrdg Ln -Pittsfrd 14534 **Fx:**248-4974
(516) 228-8600 .. **Scanlon,** Thos R '98 Interstate Natl Dealer Srvcs -333 Earle Ovngton Blvd -Uniondale 11553
(718) 262-7388 .. **Scanlon,** Tina Chan '90 %Civil Ct -89-17 Sutphin Blvd -Jamaica 11435 **Fx:**262-7107
(212) 277-5897 .. **Scanlon,** Vera M '96 (Beldock L&H LLP) -99 Park Av -NY 10016
(212) 806-5400 .. **Scanna,** Karen '96 (Stroock &S&L LLP) -180 Maiden Ln -NY 10038
(516) 938-5476 .. **Scannapieco,** Salvatore '99 The Liro Group -6 Aerial Way -Syosset 11791
(212) 723-6173 .. **Scannell,** John W '97 %Salomon Smith Barney -390 Greenwich -NY 10013
(516) 571-6205 .. **Scannell,** Jos K '90 County Legislator -1 West -Mineola 11501
(516) 572-2000 .. **Scannell,** Melissa A '09 %DA -99 Main -Hempstd 11550 **Fx:**572-2606
(212) 309-6000 .. **Scannell,** Robt M '06 %Morgan L&B LLP -101 Park Av -NY 10178
(718) 698-5400 .. **Scano,** Paul F '76 -1688 Victory Blvd -Staten Isl 10314 **Fx:**(347) 825-3038
(917) 532-3190 .. **Scantlebury,** Jos '94 -751 St Marks Av -Brklyn 11216
(212) 998-2240 .. **Scaraglino,** Pietrina V '87 %NYU Ofc Leg Cnsl -70 Wshngtn Sq S -NY 10012 **Fx:**995-3048
(315) 792-0171 .. **Scaramella,** Harry M '96 %Law Dept -1 Knndy Plz -Utica 13502 **Fx:**792-0175
(212) 485-3100 .. **Scaramucci,** Anthony '92 SkyBridge Capital LLC -527 Mad Av -NY 10022 **Fx:**485-3137
(845) 876-5568 .. **Scarano,** Annette M '86 -910 Route 308 -Rhinebeck 12572
(212) 943-0280 .. **Scarano,** Danielle '00 %McCanliss & E LLP -88 Pine -NY 10005
(212) 839-5300 .. **Scarantino,** Lauren A '08 %Sidley A LLP -787 7th Av -NY 10019

(607) 763-9200 .. **Scarantino,** Nicholas J '95 (Levene G&T,LLP) -BxF-1706 -Bnghmtn 13902
(212) 351-4000 .. **Scarazzo,** Eric M '06 %Gibson D&C LLP -200 Park Av -NY 10166
(914) 793-0561 .. **Scarborough,** Mary Ellen '88 -76 Dellwood Rd -Bronxvll 10708 **Fx:**779-4336
(212) 277-4000 .. **Scarborough,** Robt H '93 (Freshfields BD LLP) -520 Mad Av -NY 10022
(212) 815-1818 .. **Scarbrough,** Kaiesha Y '05 %DC 37 MELS -125 Barclay -NY 10007 **Fx:**815-1343
(914) 682-1400 .. **Scarcella,** Anthony J '90 -44 Church -White Plns 10601 **Fx:**948-2255
(718) 250-3851 .. **Scarcella,** Jacqueline M '01 %DA -350 Jay -Brklyn 11201 **Fx:**250-2314
(516) 227-0700 .. **Scarcella,** Louis A '78 (Farrell F,PC) -1320 RXR Plz -Uniondale 11556
(212) 448-2704 .. **Scarcella,** Russell B '95 LexisNexis -125 Park Av -NY 10017
(718) 261-5151 .. **Scardigno,** Luke '88 -123-60 83rd Av -Kew Gdns 11415
(212) 857-8760 .. **Scardilli,** Frank J '54 SrCnsl US Ct of Appls -40 Foley Sq -NY 10007 **Fx:**857-8765
(631) 439-2450 .. **Scardino,** Andrew J '97 %Leg Aid -320 Carleton Av -Central Islip 11722 **Fx:**439-2453
(646) 216-2400 .. **Scardino,** Anthony '99 OfCnsl Kranjac M&V LLP -40 Wall -NY 10005 **Fx:**216-2373
(718) 430-2551 .. **Scarfone,** John A '90 %Yeshiva Univ -1300 Morris Park Av -Bronx 10461 **Fx:**430-8783
(585) 295-4400 .. **Scarfone,** Nicholas A '98 Cnsl Hiscock & B,LLP -2000 HSBC Plz -Rchstr 14604
(631) 852-2500 .. **Scarglato,** John '97 %DA -200 Center Dr -Rvrhead 11901 **Fx:**852-1769
(212) 683-7100 .. **Scarglato,** Jos '89 %Gallo V&K,LLP -90 Broad -NY 10004
(914) 597-7800 .. **Scaria,** Susan A '02 %Lewis S&C,LLC -11 Martine Av -White Plns 10606 **Fx:**597-7801
(914) 468-0190 .. **Scariati,** Rosemary '92 %Corrigan & B,LLC -1311 Mamaroneck Av -White Plns 10605 **Fx:**468-0199
(212) 546-9255 .. **Scarinci,** Donald '91 (Scarinci H) -107 Grand -NY 10013
(212) 546-9255 .. **Scarinci Hollenbeck** -107 Grand -NY 10013 **Fx:**483-0876
(718) 875-1300 .. **Scarinci,** Michl J '07 %Appllt Div 2nd Dept -45 Monroe Pl -Brklyn 11201 **Fx:**858-2446
(516) 683-8500 .. **Scaring,** Stephen P '68 (Scaring & B,PLLC) -666 Old Cntry Rd -Gdn Cty 11530 **Fx:**683-8410
(518) 381-1998 .. **Scaringe,** Thos F '84 -13 Minuteman Ct -Clifton Pk 12065
(718) 522-6118 .. **Scarlato,** Angela E '83 (A Scarlato & Assoc) -26 Court -Brklyn 11242 **Fx:**596-2610
(631) 324-8787 .. **Scarlato,** Tiffany Sloane '00 %Town Atty -159 Pantigo Rd -E Hampton 11937 **Fx:**329-5371
(607) 777-4438 .. **Scarlett,** Barbara W '87 SUNY Binghamton Genl Cnsl -Bx6000 -Bnghmtn 13902 **Fx:**777-6453
(212) 757-0007 .. **Scarola Ellis LLP** -888 7th Av -NY 10106 **Fx:**757-0469
(212) 757-0007 .. **Scarola,** Richd J J '83 (Scarola E LLP) -888 7th Av -NY 10106
(718) 281-2311 .. **Scarpa,** John A Jr. '81 -47-03 Bell Blvd -Bayside 11361 **Fx:**423-2512
(516) 742-7430 .. **Scarpa,** Michl J Jr. '09 %Schroder & S LLP -114 Old Cntry Rd -Mineola 11501 **Fx:**742-7433
(212) 885-8000 .. **Scarpaci,** Alison M '97 %BDO USA,LLP -330 Mad Av -NY 10017 **Fx:**697-1299
(212) 551-4000 .. **Scarpaci,** Thos A '97 %Sanofi-Synthelabo Inc -90 Park Av -NY 10016
(718) 476-2411 .. **Scarpati,** Anthony J '94 A Scarpati -91-31 Qns Blvd -Elmhrst 11373 **Fx:**476-2318
(212) 596-9000 .. **Scarpati,** Jennifer N '07 %Ropes & G LLP -1211 Av of Amer -NY 10036
(631) 261-9533 .. **Scarpati,** Susan Jeanne '80 -30 Fresh Pond Rd -Ft Salonga 11768
(716) 878-9665 .. **Scarpello,** Robt J '09 Benderson Development Co,LLC -570 Delaware Av -Buffalo 14202
(716) 851-4343 .. **Scarpine,** Mary B '03 %Law Dept -65 Niagara Sq -Buffalo 14202 **Fx:**851-4105
(212) 682-1800 .. **Scarr-Konel,** Laurel B '89 (Grant HS&K LLP) -675 3rd Av -NY 10017
(585) 530-8465 .. **Scarsella,** Vincent L '80 Dept of Tax & Fin -340 E Main -Rchstr 14604 **Fx:**530-2017
(212) 619-3730 .. **Scarvalone,** Edw J '87 (Doar RK&M) -217 Bway -NY 10007
(607) 432-9341 .. **Scarzafava,** John '81 (Scarzafava & B) -48 Dietz -Oneonta 13820 **Fx:**432-1986
(607) 432-9341 .. **Scarzafava,** Nettie Jean '81 -48 Dietz -Oneonta 13820
(212) 972-7373 .. **Scatenato,** Amy '90 (Scatenato & A,PC) -276 5th Av -NY 10001 **Fx:**972-1311
(585) 458-0510 .. **Scatigno,** John M '92 -2038 Lk Av -Rchstr 14615
(518) 731-3002 .. **Scaturro,** Angelo F '94 -227 Mansion -Coxsackie 12051 **Fx:**731-6594
(516) 775-0300 .. **Scaturro,** Sharon P '83 %Kramer & Assoc,PC -99 Tulip Av -Floral Pk 11001 **Fx:**775-0352
(212) 233-6647 .. **Scavetta,** Marie J '89 -19 Fulton -NY 10038
(212) 819-8200 .. **Scavone,** Arthur A '86 (White & C LLP) -1155 Av of Amer -NY 10036
(212) 492-1248 .. **Scavuzzo,** Bruce D '89 EMI Music -75 9th Av -NY 10011
(212) 994-0260 .. **Scavuzzo,** Steven '89 -2 Wall -NY 10005
(516) 227-0700 .. **Scelfo,** Rachel Anne '03 Cnsl Farrell F,PC -1320 RXR Plz -Uniondale 11556
(212) 389-1529 .. **Scenna,** David P '09 Greenhill & Co -300 Park Av -NY 10022
(212) 344-5951 .. **Sceusa,** Peter P '87 -90 Broad -NY 10004 **Fx:**344-2133
(212) 421-4100 .. **Schaab,** Arnold J '67 (Pryor C LLP) -7 Times Sq -NY 10036
(716) 753-2128 .. **Schaack,** R Bard '66 (Schaack WCN PC) -31 S Erie Bx152 -Mayvll 14757
(716) 673-1361 .. **Schaack Whipple Clark Nelson PC** -2 W Main Bx109 -Fredonia 14063 **Fx:**673-1365
(716) 753-2128 .. **Schaack Whipple Clark Nelson PC** -31 S Erie Bx152 -Mayvll 14757 **Fx:**753-7141
(212) 888-3033 .. **Schaaf,** David W '74 (Becker GM&M LLP) -299 Park Av -NY 10171
(212) 637-3113 .. **Schaaf,** Eric '80 %EPA -290 Bway -NY 10007 **Fx:**637-3096
(518) 370-4645 .. **Schaaf,** Gregory E '99 %Englert CM&F,LLP -224 State Bx1092 -Schnctdy 12301
(212) 201-2533 .. **Schaaf,** Harold J Jr. '87 Aetos Capital LLC -875 3rd Av -NY 10022
(212) 839-5300 .. **Schaaf,** Homer D '66 (Sidley A LLP) -787 7th Av -NY 10019
(212) 468-8000 .. **Schaaf,** Kathleen E '78 SrCnsl Morrison & F LLP -1290 Av of Amer -NY 10104
(212) 504-6000 .. **Schaaf,** Wm S '01 %Cadwalader W&T LLP -1 World Fncl Ctr -NY 10281
(585) 244-1070 .. **Schaal,** Debora Kall '92 (Gordon & S,LLP) -1039 Monroe Av -Rchstr 14620 **Fx:**244-1085
(315) 363-6888 .. **Schaal,** Randy J '81 (DeBottis & S) -312 Broad -Oneida 13421 **Fx:**363-6801
(212) 995-2400 .. **Schaap,** Paula '81 -143 W 4th -NY 10012
(212) 995-2400 .. **Schaap,** Wm H '64 -143 W 4th -NY 10012
(631) 665-3400 .. **Schaber,** Andrew J '86 %Siben & S,LLP -90 E Main Bx149P -Bay Shr 11706
(516) 466-3177 .. **Schachar,** Henry S '78 -11 N Circle Dr -Gt Neck 11021
(212) 776-5000 .. **Schacher,** David B '88 %NYC Housing Auth -250 Bway -NY 10007 **Fx:**776-5039
(212) 370-1300 .. **Schachne,** Susan Donna '85 OfCnsl Ellenoff G&S LLP -150 E 42nd -NY 10017
(212) 872-7879 .. **Schachner,** Carol B '77 KPMG LLP -345 Park Av -NY 10154
(212) 730-7750 .. **Schachner,** Elana M '99 %Nicoletti GS&O,LLP -555 5th Av -NY 10017
(718) 254-7000 .. **Schachner,** Elliot M '85 %US Atty -271 Cadman Plz E -Brklyn 11201 **Fx:**254-6479
(845) 486-6494 .. **Schachner,** Jack E '73 Court Atty Referee -10 Market -Poughkeepsie 12601 **Fx:**473-5403
(518) 793-6611 .. **Schachner,** Mark '83 (Miller MS&H,LLC) -451 Glen Bx765 -Glens Fls 12801
(718) 448-7222 .. **Schachner,** Stewart B '85 S Schachner -390 St Marks Pl -Staten Isl 10301 **Fx:**448-2794
(212) 616-5540 .. **Schacht,** Alexei M '90 (Nalven & S) -350 5th Av -NY 10118 **Fx:**616-5543
(718) 268-9047 .. **Schacht,** Christa M '97 -190 Burns -Frst Hlls 11375
(212) 600-4912 .. **Schacht,** Nathan A '09 -229 E 79th -NY 10075
(718) 816-6767 .. **Schacht,** Robt G '01 (RG Schacht,PLLC) -1001 Clove Rd -Staten Isl 10301
(212) 755-7300 .. **Schachter,** Alexander '63 -445 Park Av -NY 10022 **Fx:**(413) 702-6268
(212) 819-8200 .. **Schachter,** Barry '07 %White & C LLP -1155 Av of Amer -NY 10036
(212) 685-4565 .. **Schachter,** Brian J '95 (Schachter & L,LLP) -419 Park Av -NY 10016 **Fx:**685-5980
(585) 419-8800 .. **Schachter,** Chas I '84 (Harris B PLLC) -99 Garnsey Rd -Pittsfrd 14534
(212) 264-8000 .. **Schachter,** Danl E '93 %HUD -26 Fed Plz -NY 10278 **Fx:**264-0246
(718) 639-0200 .. **Schachter,** David B S '00 -74-09 37th Av -Jcksn Hts 11372
(718) 520-3903 .. **Schachter,** Edw A '70 %Supreme Ct -25-10 Court Sq -LIC 11101
(646) 471-2900 .. **Schachter,** Ian S '88 PricewaterhouseCoopers LLP -300 Mad Av -NY 10017
(212) 643-7000 .. **Schachter,** Kenneth R '75 (Sills C&G PC) -One Rckfllr Plz -NY 10020
(516) 482-6166 .. **Schachter,** L Michl '76 (Kleiger & K) -80 Cuttermill Rd -Gt Neck 11021 **Fx:**482-6240
(212) 626-4100 .. **Schachter,** Madeleine '83 SpclCnsl Baker & M LLP -1114 Av of Amer -NY 10036
(212) 463-0900 .. **Schachter,** Marvin D '60 Hoberman Miller Goldstein & Lesser,PC -226 W 26th -NY 10001 **Fx:**691-6452
(212) 728-8000 .. **Schachter,** Michl S '00 (Willkie F&G LLP) -787 7th Av -NY 10019
(212) 627-8100 .. **Schachter,** Paul '75 SrCnsl Levy R,PC -80 8th Av -NY 10011
(212) 308-8505 .. **Schachter,** Robt A '75 Akabas & S -488 Mad Av -NY 10022
(212) 223-3900 .. **Schachter,** Robt S '72 (Zwerling S&Z,LLP) -41 Mad Av -NY 10010
(212) 989-6894 .. **Schachter,** Stuart S '60 -33 Greenwich Av -NY 10014
(646) 473-4115 .. **Schack,** Ira W '95 Selective Benefits Grp -1 Penn Plz -NY 10119
(516) 877-0926 .. **Schack,** Wendy G '86 -207 Derby -E Williston 11596
(718) 643-5873 .. **Schackett,** Patti Cohen '82 %Surrogates Ct -2 Johnson -Brklyn 11201
(212) 468-4800 .. **Schackman,** Walter M '50 OfCnsl Davis & G LLP -1740 Bway -NY 10019
(212) 504-6000 .. **Schacter,** Ira J '85 (Cadwalader W&T LLP) -1 World Fncl Ctr -NY 10281
(212) 705-7000 .. **Schacter,** Kenneth I '80 (Bingham M LLP) -399 Park Av -NY 10022
(716) 634-8906 .. **Schad,** Jerome D '72 -199 Meadowvw Ln -Williamsvll 14221 **Fx:**632-2048
(212) 408-5100 .. **Schad,** Maureen K '08 %Chadbourne & P LLP -30 Rckfllr Plz -NY 10112
(914) 834-4770 .. **Schade,** Malcolm R '75 -24 Beech Rd -New Rchll 10804 **Fx:**834-2808
(212) 770-5659 .. **Schader,** Chas R '72 %AIG -70 Pine -NY 10270
(315) 426-1466 .. **Schaeber,** Mark A '89 -300 Tulip -Liverpool 13088
(607) 974-3164 .. **Schaeberle,** Timothy M '91 %Corning Inc - Patent Dept -SP-TI-3-1 -Corning 14831
(212) 683-9700 .. **Schaechter,** N Jack '82 GNY Mutual Ins -200 Mad Av -NY 10016 **Fx:**843-1962
(631) 241-3200 .. **Schaedtler,** Stephen M '84 -409 Bay Av -Patchogue 11772
(716) 626-9999 .. **Schaefer,** Alan P '95 (Brady & S LLP) -4367 Harlem Rd -Buffalo 14226
(845) 695-6811 .. **Schaefer,** Amy L '06 %MA Bjork -100 Crystal Run Rd -Middletwn 10941 **Fx:**695-6818
(518) 943-6632 .. **Schaefer,** Chas H '77 (Deily & S) -1 Brdg Bx489 -Catskill 12414 **Fx:**943-1210
(518) 402-9184 .. **Schaefer,** Dana J '92 DEC -625 Bway -Albany 12233 **Fx:**402-9018
(212) 407-4000 .. **Schaefer,** David S '82 (Loeb & L,LLP) -345 Park Av -NY 10154
(914) 740-4000 .. **Schaefer,** Elizabeth '95 RAS Grp,Inc -438 5th Av -Pelham 10803 **Fx:**740-4031
(212) 309-6000 .. **Schaefer,** Georgette A '88 (Morgan L&B LLP) -101 Park Av -NY 10178
(212) 969-3000 .. **Schaefer,** Ian Carleton '05 %Proskauer R LLP -1585 Bway -NY 10036
(212) 918-3000 .. **Schaefer,** Ira J '74 (Hogan L LLP) -875 3rd Av -NY 10022
(516) 248-7000 .. **Schaefer,** John E Jr. '72 OfCnsl Albanese & A LLP -1050 Franklin Av -Gdn Cty 11530
(585) 582-3025 .. **Schaefer,** John P '59 -1136 Pttsfrd Mendon Ctr Rd -Honeoye Fls 14472
(585) 454-5650 .. **Schaefer,** Karen '80 (Lacy K LLP) -130 E Main -Rchstr 14604

(212) 693-0085 .. **Schaefer**, Katherine R '89 %Appellate Advocates -2 Rector -NY 10006 **Fx**:693-0878
(518) 462-0110 .. **Schaefer**, Lawr H '92 %Sheehan GCG&J LLP -54 State -Albany 12207
(716) 854-2620 .. **Schaefer**, Mark J '94 %Brown & K,LLP -1500 Lbrty Bldg -Buffalo 14202
(212) 964-5000 .. **Schaefer**, Matthew E '03 (Peisner GS&S) -225 Bway -NY 10007
(718) 488-7500 .. **Schaefer**, Patrick K '93 (Doyaga & S) -26 Court -Brklyn 11242 **Fx**:488-7505
(315) 478-0525 .. **Schaefer**, Peter C '84 -313 E Willow -Syracuse 13203 **Fx**:478-0106
(516) 479-6300 .. **Schaefer**, Randy J '92 OfCnsl Silverman A LLP -100 Jericho Quad -Jericho 11753
(212) 687-0100 .. **Schaefer**, Robt A Jr. '99 %Harris B PLLC -100 Wall -NY 10005
(516) 432-9400 .. **Schaefer**, Sean W '97 (Peknic P&S LLC) -1005 W Beech -Long Bch 11561 **Fx**:432-5396
(212) 236-6039 .. **Schaefer**, Stanley '77 %Merrill Lynch -225 Lbrty WFC -NY 10080
(631) 382-4800 .. **Schaefer**, Wayne J '87 (W Schaefer,LLC) -199 E Main -Smithtwn 11787 **Fx**:382-4801
(212) 621-6000 .. **Schaeffer**, Andrew J '88 %ASCAP -1 Lincoln Plz -NY 10023 **Fx**:787-1381
(212) 689-0400 .. **Schaeffer**, Bruce S '76 -404 Park Av S -NY 10016 **Fx**:689-3315
(716) 856-0600 .. **Schaeffer**, Dennis K '00 (Jaeckle F&M,LLP) -12 Fountain Plz -Buffalo 14202
(212) 279-3467 .. **Schaeffer**, Elliot L '74 (Schaeffer & K LLP) -450 7th Av -NY 10123
(212) 326-3939 .. **Schaeffer**, Fiona A '01 (Jones D) -222 E 41st -NY 10017
(845) 454-1190 .. **Schaeffer**, Fred W '69 -12 Raymnd Av -Poughkeepsie 12603 **Fx**:454-2319
(212) 489-1600 .. **Schaeffer**, Glen '74 %Deloitte LLP -1633 Bway -NY 10019 **Fx**:492-4201
(718) 250-2000 .. **Schaeffer**, Hillary E '00 %DA -350 Jay -Brklyn 11201 **Fx**:250-2314
(518) 459-2100 .. **Schaeffer**, Jane-Marie '94 Pierro Law Grp,LLC -20 Corp Wds Blvd -Albany 12211 **Fx**:459-2200
(212) 310-8000 .. **Schaeffer**, Jenna E '09 %Weil G&M LLP -767 5th Av -NY 10153
(212) 279-3467 .. **Schaeffer & Krongold LLP** -450 7th Av -NY 10123 **Fx**:695-3575
(516) 571-1488 .. **Schaeffer**, Lawr '84 Hon D Sullivan -262 Old Cntry Rd -Mineola 11501
(212) 632-5500 .. **Schaeffer**, Liza V '05 %Salans LLP -620 5th Av -NY 10020
(212) 210-1275 .. **Schaeffer**, Maritza C '10 %Alston & B LLP -90 Park Av -NY 10016
(212) 336-2000 .. **Schaeffer**, Peter J '92 (Patterson BW&T LLP) -1133 Av of Amer -NY 10036
(212) 819-8200 .. **Schaeffer**, Philip H '60 (White & C LLP) -1155 Av of Amer -NY 10036
(718) 286-6000 .. **Schaeffer**, Richd B '82 %DA -125-01 Qns Blvd -Kew Gdns 11415
(212) 759-3300 .. **Schaeffer**, Richd J '69 (Dornbush SS&V,LLP) -747 3rd Av -NY 10017
(585) 263-6417 .. **Schaeffer**, Stephanie L '96 %Hon M Telesca -100 State -Rchstr 14614
(718) 254-6059 .. **Schaeffer**, Wm E '94 %US Atty -271 Cadman Plz E -Brklyn 11201 **Fx**:254-6479
(212) 421-1011 .. **Schaeffer Grossberg**, Marjorie R '96 (Major Lindsey & Africa) -551 5th Av -NY 10176 **Fx**:421-1042
(212) 548-2100 .. **Schaeffer-Roth**, Sarah H E '04 %McGuire W LLP -1345 Av of Amer -NY 10105
(631) 232-2400 .. **Schaefler**, Margaret '83 %Nassau/Sfflk Law Srv -1757 Vets Hwy -Islandia 11749 **Fx**:232-2489
(212) 787-0370 .. **Schaenman**, Leslie D '88 -2350 Bway -NY 10024
(212) 983-6900 .. **Schaer**, Eric S '09 OfCnsl Kaplan & L PC -630 3rd Av -NY 10017
(212) 973-8000 .. **Schaerf**, Carl J '92 (Schnader HS&L LLP) -140 Bway -NY 10005
(212) 838-8686 .. **Schaerf**, Howard '66 (Schaerf & S) -232 Mad Av -NY 10016 **Fx**:725-8567
(212) 524-5000 .. **Schaevitz**, Barry '88 (Jacob M&F) -1270 Av of Amer -NY 10020
(212) 867-4100 .. **Schaevitz**, Jennifer G '97 %Furman K&B LLP -61 Bway -NY 10006
(518) 563-4022 .. **Schafer**, Gerry A '91 %Leg Aid -100 Court Bx989 -Plattsbrgh 12901 **Fx**:563-4058
(518) 371-8888 .. **Schafer**, Michl W '90 -805 Route 146 -Clifton Pk 12065 **Fx**:371-4349
(212) 610-6300 .. **Schafer**, Reginald B '09 %Allen & O -1221 Av of Amer -NY 10020
(716) 685-4636 .. **Schaff**, Gary M '77 -33 Central Av -Lancaster 14086 **Fx**:683-3341
(732) 855-6047 .. **Schaff**, Michl F '83 (Wilentz G&S) -110 William -NY 10038 **Fx**:726-6552
(732) 726-7474 .. **Schaffer**, Alyson M '04 %Wilentz G&S -110 William -NY 10038 **Fx**:726-6679
(646) 429-7500 .. **Schaffer**, Amanda J '05 %Macys,Inc -11 Penn Plz -NY 10001 **Fx**:429-7521
(212) 349-0900 .. **Schaffer**, Barbara J '86 (Lansner KS&Z) -325 Bway -NY 10007
(212) 300-0375 .. **Schaffer**, Brian S '04 (Fitapelli & S,LLP) -1250 Bway -NY 10001 **Fx**:564-5468
(718) 875-1300 .. **Schaffer**, Bruce R '81 %Appllt Div 2nd Dept -45 Monroe Pl -Brklyn 11201 **Fx**:858-2446
(516) 747-0300 .. **Schaffer**, David I '60 (Meltzer LG&B,LLP) -190 Willis Av -Mineola 11501
(212) 791-0285 .. **Schaffer**, David P '88 (Malaby & B,LLC) -150 Bway -NY 10038 **Fx**:791-0286
(845) 225-1884 .. **Schaffer**, Edw M '80 -104 Gleneida Av -Carmel 10512 **Fx**:225-3526
(631) 351-3042 .. **Schaffer**, Ellen C '89 %Town Atty -100 Main -Huntngtn 11743 **Fx**:351-3032
(412) 288-4202 .. **Schaffer**, Eric A '03 (Reed S LLP) -599 Lex Av -NY 10022
(516) 379-1311 .. **Schaffer**, Eugene '60 (Mintz & S) -30 S Ocean Av -Freeprt 11520
(212) 794-5382 .. **Schaffer**, Fredk P '79 %CUNY -535 E 80th -NY 10075 **Fx**:794-5426
(716) 854-2020 .. **Schaffer**, Gerald W Jr. '92 (Cellino & B,PC) -350 Main -Buffalo 14202
(212) 692-1000 .. **Schaffer**, Hyman L '80 (Duane M LLP) -1540 Bway -NY 10036
(914) 949-7755 .. **Schaffer**, Joanna Makarczyk '95 -445 Hmltn Av -White Plns 10601 **Fx**:(866) 833-9130
(212) 267-7342 .. **Schaffer**, Karl R '01 OfCnsl Neiger LLP -317 Mad Av -NY 10017 **Fx**:406-3677
(212) 224-5621 .. **Schaffer**, Laura Ann '93 Praedium Grp LLC -825 3rd Av -NY 10022
(516) 571-3511 .. **Schaffer**, Lawr M '80 %Supreme Ct -Supreme Ct Bldg -Mineola 11501
(845) 783-4178 .. **Schaffer**, Martin B '74 -8 Lex Hills Rd -Harriman 10926
(516) 747-0300 .. **Schaffer**, Michl J '92 (Meltzer LG&B,LLP) -190 Willis Av -Mineola 11501
(718) 875-3191 .. **Schaffer**, Milton B '49 -32 Court -Brklyn 11201
(718) 585-4444 .. **Schaffer**, Peter J '87 -184 E 161st -Bronx 10451
(631) 422-2900 .. **Schaffer**, Richd H '92 -816 Deer Prk Av -N Babylon 11703 **Fx**:422-0987
(212) 547-5400 .. **Schaffer**, Robt '85 (McDermott W&E LLP) -340 Mad Av -NY 10173
(646) 878-0800 .. **Schaffer**, Robt D '89 Cnsl Pearl CZL,LLP -1500 Bway -NY 10036
(646) 610-8423 .. **Schaffer**, S Andrew '70 NYPD -1 Police Plz -NY 10038 **Fx**:610-8422
(212) 490-3000 .. **Schaffer**, Scott R '86 (Wilson EME&D LLP) -150 E 42nd -NY 10017
(718) 969-0549 .. **Schaffer**, Sylvan J '82 -138-44 Jewel Av -Flushng 11367
(718) 403-9696 .. **Schaffer**, Toby M '79 %Shapiro & S -90 Meadow Woods Rd -Gt Neck 11020
(212) 326-3939 .. **Schaffer**, Tracy V '01 (Jones D) -222 E 41st -NY 10017
(716) 434-2825 .. **Schaffner**, Clark F '91 %Ticor Title -122 Niagara -Lockprt 14094
(212) 309-6000 .. **Schaffran**, Andrew J '80 (Morgan L&B LLP) -101 Park Av -NY 10178
(212) 969-2303 .. **Schaffran**, Chas B '76 %Alliance Capital Mgmt Corp -1345 Av of Amer -NY 10105 **Fx**:969-2302
(212) 757-0007 .. **Schaffzin**, Edmund A '64 (Scarola E LLP) -888 7th Av -NY 10106
(212) 701-3000 .. **Schaffzin**, Jonathan A '86 (Cahill G&R LLP) -80 Pine -NY 10005 **Fx**:269-5420
(212) 592-1400 .. **Schafhauser**, Paul H '94 (Herrick,F LLP) -2 Park Av -NY 10016
(212) 969-3000 .. **Schafler**, Seth B '84 (Proskauer R LLP) -1585 Bway -NY 10036
(212) 772-9215 .. **Schafman**, Limor '94 -60 East End Av -NY 10028
(212) 925-6635 .. **Schafran**, Lynn Hecht '75 %Legal Momentum -395 Hudson -NY 10014 **Fx**:226-1066
(212) 902-0694 .. **Schafrann**, Richd A '79 %Goldman Sachs -1 NY Plz -NY 10004
(212) 566-4047 .. **Schager**, Richd J Jr. '79 (Stamell & S,LLP) -1 Lbrty Plz -NY 10006
(212) 450-4000 .. **Schaible**, Damian S '02 (Davis P&W LLP) -450 Lex Av -NY 10017
(516) 746-7799 .. **Schaich**, Gabrielle R '04 %Reisman P&R LLP -1305 Franklin Av -Gdn Cty 11530
(212) 788-0432 .. **Schaier**, Neil E '94 %Law Dept -100 Church -NY 10007 **Fx**:788-0367
(212) 689-4244 .. **Schaier**, Susan P '76 (Schaier T&S) -275 Mad Av -NY 10016
(212) 689-4244 .. **Schaier Tribbitt & Schaier** -275 Mad Av -NY 10016 **Fx**:545-1537
(347) 404-9133 .. **Schain**, Douglas S '83 %Civil Ct -141 Lvngstn -Brklyn 11201 **Fx**:(718) 643-3733
(718) 330-0242 .. **Schain**, Howard J '83 -370 Atl Av -Brklyn 11217
(212) 907-9600 .. **Schain**, Jennifer B '05 %Ingram YGC&B,LLP -250 Park Av -NY 10177
(718) 522-3333 .. **Schair**, Fern '70 Children's Law Ctr -44 Court -Brklyn 11201 **Fx**:522-7376
(914) 681-8700 .. **Schair**, Robin A '86 OfCnsl Milber MP&S LLP -3 Barker Av -White Plns 10601
(212) 341-7900 .. **Schaktman**, Elliot M '82 (Brecher FPWT&Z,PC) -233 Bway -NY 10279
(212) 922-6640 .. **Schalda**, Wm C '91 Dreyfus -200 Park Av -NY 10166
(718) 237-2000 .. **Schaldach**, Jeannie '99 %Leg Aid -111 Lvngstn -Brklyn 11201 **Fx**:237-8737
(212) 661-0085 .. **Schalet**, Lizabeth S '89 (Lipman & P,LLP) -1350 Bway -NY 10018
(212) 878-8000 .. **Schalit**, Jonathan M '08 %Clifford C LLP -31 W 52nd -NY 10019
(212) 974-2400 .. **Schalk**, Peter B '96 %J Burstein -1790 Bway -NY 10019 **Fx**:974-2944
(516) 294-0300 .. **Schalk**, Robt F '06 %Collins M&G -138 Mineola Blvd -Mineola 11501
(718) 546-4004 .. **Schall**, Burton F '86 Dept of Hlth & Mntl Hygiene -225 Bway -NY 10007
(212) 998-7420 .. **Schall**, Ellen '73 %NYU Wagner School -40 W 4th -NY 10012 **Fx**:995-4162
(212) 703-8484 .. **Schall**, Jeffrey '81 (Wang & S) -305 Mad Av -NY 10165 **Fx**:768-2766
(631) 231-2424 .. **Schall**, Todd A '90 %Dept of Law -300 Motor Pkwy -Hauppauge 11788 **Fx**:435-4757
(718) 852-0251 .. **Schaller**, John F '91 -344 Degraw -Brklyn 11231
(716) 856-4000 .. **Schaller**, Pamela S '10 %Hodgson R LLP -140 Pearl -Buffalo 14202
(212) 909-6295 .. **Schallert**, Edwin G '84 (Debevoise & P LLP) -919 3rd Av -NY 10022
(518) 486-4555 .. **Schallop**, Amy D '85 %Dept of Law -The Cptl -Albany 12224
(212) 682-0020 .. **Schallop**, Shaina J '09 %Putney TH&H LLP -521 5th Av -NY 10175
(212) 519-2561 .. **Schanback**, Jeffrey E '75 Neighborhood Housing Srvcs NYC -307 W 36th -NY 10018 **Fx**:(646) 383-9330
(516) 663-6280 .. **Schancupp**, Peter J '98 Private Cap Grp -2 Jericho Plz -Jericho 11753 **Fx**:663-6299
(212) 728-8000 .. **Schanes**, Jennifer R '09 %Willkie F&G LLP -787 7th Av -NY 10019
(585) 248-5162 .. **Schank**, Martin J '81 -1595 Elmwood Av -Rchstr 14620
(631) 424-5400 .. **Schanker**, Andrea B '04 %Schanker & H -27 West Neck Rd Bx1905 -Huntngtn 11743
(631) 424-5400 .. **Schanker & Hochberg** -27 West Neck Rd Bx1905 -Huntngtn 11743 **Fx**:424-0048
(631) 424-5400 .. **Schanker**, Steven '75 (Schanker & H) -27 West Neck Rd Bx1905 -Huntngtn 11743
(516) 791-0044 .. **Schantz**, Jeffrey A '84 -1257 Veeder Dr -Hewlett 11557
(718) 254-7035 .. **Schantz**, Jennifer E '96 %US Atty -271 Cadman Plz E -Brklyn 11201 **Fx**:254-6479
(646) 315-7300 .. **Schanz**, Danielle I '87 %FINRA -14 Wall -NY 10005 **Fx**:315-7440
(607) 723-7913 .. **Schanz**, Gary W '75 (Sukloff & S) -19 Chenango -Bnghmtn 13901
(518) 402-6757 .. **Schanz**, Kevin L '96 %Workers Comp Bd -20 Park -Albany 12207
(914) 235-5000 .. **Schanzer**, Ayall Simon '94 %Utilisave LLC -1 Ramada Plz -New Rchll 10801
(212) 449-3640 .. **Schanzer**, Bruce J '94 Merrill Lynch & Co -250 Vesey -NY 10080
(516) 681-1100 .. **Schanzer**, Robt M '62 OfCnsl Kaufman DV&G,LLP -135 Crsswys Park Dr -Woodbury 11797
(212) 909-6000 .. **Schaper**, Michl '02 %Debevoise & P LLP -919 3rd Av -NY 10022
(718) 707-3174 .. **Schapira**, Gill S '00 (G Schapira & Assoc,PLLC) -4 Court Sq -LIC 11101
(212) 506-2500 .. **Schapiro**, Andrew H '96 (Mayer B LLP) -1675 Bway -NY 10019
(212) 408-5100 .. **Schapiro**, Donald '49 (Chadbourne & P LLP) -30 Rckfllr Plz -NY 10112

(607) 723-5341 .. **Schapiro,** Lori Grumet '86 SpclCnsl Hinman H&K,LLP -80 Exchange Bx5250 -Bnghmtn 13902
(212) 572-3749 .. **Schapiro,** Louis A '74 %Estee Lauder -767 5th Av -NY 10153 **Fx:**572-3989
(716) 856-0600 .. **Schapiro,** Wm I '57 SrCnsl Jaeckle F&M,LLP -12 Fountain Plz -Buffalo 14202
(716) 856-4022 .. **Schapp,** Jonathan '90 %Mattar D&G,LLP -17 Court -Buffalo 14202
(212) 488-1598 .. **Scharaga,** Gregg S '03 %Havkins RR&V,LLP -11 Penn Plz -NY 10001
(718) 852-9444 .. **Scharaga,** Ira '80 (I Scharaga,PC) -16 Court -Brklyn 11241 **Fx:**855-2765
(212) 416-8111 .. **Scharbach,** Susan M '95 %Dept of Law -120 Bway -NY 10271
(212) 506-5000 .. **Schare,** Brian F '94 Orrick H&S LLP -51 W 52nd -NY 10019
(914) 682-9777 .. **Scharf,** Adam L '05 %J Scharf -1025 Wstchstr Av -White Plns 10604
(212) 867-8200 .. **Scharf,** Frank D '54 -275 Mad Av -NY 10016 **Fx:**867-8294
(212) 561-7700 .. **Scharf,** Ilan D '02 (Pachulski SZ&J) -780 3rd Av -NY 10017
(845) 893-7500 .. **Scharf,** Irwin L '57 -55 Old Tpk Way -Nanuet 10954 **Fx:**624-0288
(914) 682-9777 .. **Scharf,** Jared J '74 -1025 Wstchstr Av -White Plns 10604
(516) 223-7177 .. **Scharf,** Jay E '90 -27 St Johns Pl -Freeprt 11520
(716) 852-5533 .. **Scharf,** Jennifer R '06 %Connors & V,LLP -1000 Lbrty Bldg -Buffalo 14202
(718) 286-6000 .. **Scharf,** Jonathan D '06 %DA -125-01 Qns Blvd -Kew Gdns 11415
(718) 643-7156 .. **Scharf,** Marvin K '67 %Hon A Marrus -120 Schermerhorn -Brklyn 11201
(212) 835-7845 .. **Scharf,** Nathalie Chetrite '96 %Dept Soc Srvcs Fair Hearings -109 E 16th -NY 10003
(914) 995-3359 .. **Scharf,** Paul S '71 %DA -111 Martin Luther King Blvd -White Plns 10601 **Fx:**995-3363
(607) 547-8960 .. **Scharf,** Randel A '89 -29 Pioneer -Cooperstwn 13326 **Fx:**547-8304
(212) 806-5400 .. **Scharf,** Sondra R '10 %Stroock &S&L LLP -180 Maiden Ln -NY 10038
(212) 440-3092 .. **Scharf,** Susan D '85 CNA -40 Wall -NY 10005
(212) 735-8600 .. **Scharf,** Y David '92 (Morrison C LLP) -909 3rd Av -NY 10022
(631) 472-3779 .. **Scharfenberg,** Theo M '89 -3330 Vets Mem'l Hwy -Bohemia 11716 **Fx:**472-8244
(845) 986-5608 .. **Scharfenberger,** James D '87 -6 Henry Close -Warwick 10990
(212) 906-1200 .. **Scharfman,** Emily B '08 %Latham & W -885 3rd Av -NY 10022
(914) 997-2435 .. **Scharfman,** Sheila Buchholtz '83 %Scharfman Orgn -280 N Central Av -Hartsdale 10530
(212) 836-8000 .. **Scharfstein,** David A '09 %Kaye S LLP -425 Park Av -NY 10022
(212) 859-8000 .. **Scharfstein,** Joel '78 (Fried FHS&J LLP) -1 NY Plz -NY 10004
(212) 227-4071 .. **Scharfstein,** Susan P '87 %Law Dept -100 Church -NY 10007 **Fx:**788-0367
(212) 218-5500 .. **Scharlat,** Richd I '01 (Seyfarth S LLP) -620 8th Av -NY 10018
(516) 294-7227 .. **Scharoff,** Jerome A '99 -100 Grdn City Plz -Gdn Cty 11530 **Fx:**294-7203
(212) 446-4800 .. **Schartz,** Brian E '08 %Kirkland & E LLP -153 E 53rd -NY 10022
(212) 351-4000 .. **Schary,** Alison B '09 %Gibson D&C LLP -200 Park Av -NY 10166
(516) 932-8120 .. **Schatkin,** Andrew J '77 -350 Jericho Tpk -Jericho 11753 **Fx:**465-7068
(212) 998-6272 .. **Schatman Manny,** Jill '83 %NYU Law Schl -40 Wshngtn Sq S -NY 10012 **Fx:**995-3149
(518) 438-6566 .. **Schatsky,** Gary H '90 %IFC -105 Wolf Rd -Albany 12205
(212) 587-7565 .. **Schatten,** David J '81 %State Ins Fund -199 Church -NY 10007 **Fx:**385-9199
(631) 232-0200 .. **Schattner,** Ann D '87 %Fumuso KDSS&F,LLP -110 Marcus Blvd -Hauppauge 11788
(631) 421-3505 .. **Schattner,** Glenn '80 (Schattner & S) -20 Norma Ln -Dix Hlls 11746
(631) 421-3505 .. **Schattner,** Rochelle D '81 (Schattner & S) -20 Norma Ln -Dix Hlls 11746
(212) 854-3867 .. **Schatz,** Barbara A '74 %Columbia Law Schl -435 W 116th -NY 10027 **Fx:**854-7946
(212) 701-3000 .. **Schatz,** Ben A '09 %Cahill G&R LLP -80 Pine -NY 10005 **Fx:**269-5420
(212) 941-1888 .. **Schatz,** Brett M '08 (Mann M&S,PC) -153 Centre -NY 10013 **Fx:**941-0554
(212) 354-6800 .. **Schatz,** Howard R '89 (Silbowitz GSS&F,LLP) -25 W 43rd -NY 10036
(914) 478-2801 .. **Schatz,** Julie Pearlman '96 %R Greenspan,PC -220 Heatherdell Rd -Ardsley 10502 **Fx:**478-2913
(212) 554-0400 .. **Schatz,** Larry H '70 OfCnsl Grubman I&S,PC -152 W 57th -NY 10019
(516) 794-7340 .. **Schatz,** Marilyn B '82 %Fager & A,LLP -90 Merrick Av -E Meadow 11554
(212) 889-6565 .. **Schatz,** Matthew T '05 %Schwartz & P LLP -295 Mad Av -NY 10017
(212) 421-8100 .. **Schatz,** Philip R '87 (Wrobel & S LLP) -1040 Av of Amer -NY 10018
(212) 999-5800 .. **Schatz,** Steven M '73 (Wilson SG&R) -1301 Av of Americas -NY 10019
(212) 735-3000 .. **Schatzberg,** Lindsey D '08 %Skadden ASM&F LLP -4 Times Sq -NY 10036
(212) 841-1007 .. **Schau,** Andrew D '84 OfCnsl Covington & B LLP -620 8th Av -NY 10018 **Fx:**(646) 441-9007
(631) 727-9140 .. **Schaub,** Heather L '02 (Schaub & D,LLP) -131 W Main -Rvrhead 11901
(212) 858-1000 .. **Schaub,** Karl C '08 Pillsbury WSP LLP -1540 Bway -NY 10036
(516) 949-3935 .. **Schaub,** Kristin '95 American Home Mortgage Corp -538 Broadhllw Rd -Melvll 11747 **Fx:**(866) 307-4965
(631) 271-3300 .. **Schaub,** Kurt A '00 %Robert & R PLLC -150 Broad Hollow Rd -Melvll 11747 **Fx:**271-1784
(516) 465-2336 .. **Schaubeck,** Patricia M '95 State Bank of Long Island -2 Jericho Plz -Jericho 11753 **Fx:**465-6700
(212) 659-7300 .. **Schauder,** Edw H '88 OfCnsl Haynes & B,LLP -1221 Av of Amer -NY 10020
(212) 806-5400 .. **Schauder,** Stephen M '08 %Stroock &S&L LLP -180 Maiden Ln -NY 10038
(914) 824-5510 .. **Schauer,** Michelle I '85 Family Ct -111 Martin Luther King Blvd -White Plns 10601 **Fx:**995-8648
(718) 821-2800 .. **Schauer,** Wm A '52 -66-61 Forest Av -Rdgwd 11385
(718) 821-2800 .. **Schauer,** Wm J '91 -66-61 Forest Av -Rdgwd 11385
(516) 487-9507 .. **Schaufeld,** Robt M '82 -85 Grace Av -Gt Neck 11021
(516) 228-8766 .. **Schaum,** Craig A '99 %Schaum -600 Old Cntry Rd -Gdn Cty 11530 **Fx:**228-3559
(516) 228-8766 .. **Schaum,** Martin '58 (Schaum) -600 Old Cntry Rd -Gdn Cty 11530 **Fx:**228-3559
(212) 698-3500 .. **Schaum,** Meredith '01 %Dechert LLP -1095 Av of Amer -NY 10036
(212) 836-8000 .. **Schaumberger,** Debra R '93 Cnsl Kaye S LLP -425 Park Av -NY 10022
(845) 359-1844 .. **Schaumberger,** Norman H '60 -126 Newport Av -Tappan 10983 **Fx:**359-1849
(212) 513-3200 .. **Schaupp,** Lissa D '06 %Holland & K LLP -31 W 52nd -NY 10019
(716) 838-5095 .. **Schaus,** Barbara A '91 (Schaus & S) -1925 Kensngtn Av -Buffalo 14215
(716) 838-5095 .. **Schaus,** Richd M '86 (Schaus & S) -1925 Kensngtn Av -Buffalo 14215
(212) 702-5400 .. **Schauwecker,** Paula J '03 (Beveridge & D,PC) -477 Mad Av -NY 10022
(607) 273-4200 .. **Schaye,** Adam R '00 (Miller M,LLP) -202 E State -Ithaca 14850
(212) 474-1000 .. **Schaye,** Benjamin P '09 %Cravath S&M LLP -825 8th Av -NY 10019
(631) 420-1414 .. **Schear,** Andrea Seychett '91 -425 Broadhllw Rd -Melvll 11747 **Fx:**454-6910
(607) 432-1400 .. **Schebaum,** Wm H '76 -93 Main -Oneonta 13820
(212) 421-4100 .. **Schechner,** Danielle '02 %Pryor C LLP -7 Times Sq -NY 10036
(212) 715-9100 .. **Schechner,** Laura S '10 %Kramer LN&F,LLP -1177 Av of Amer -NY 10036
(212) 526-5639 .. **Schechner,** P Sheridan '85 %Barclays Capital Inc -745 7th Av -NY 10019
(718) 366-0464 .. **Schechner,** Richd A '84 (Abbott B&S,LLP) -70-11 Fresh Pond Rd -Rdgwd 11385
(516) 739-3435 .. **Schechter,** Arlene H '91 Media Referral -294 Elm Pl -Mineola 11501
(212) 994-9955 .. **Schechter,** Brian '02 -NY 10016
(516) 747-1136 .. **Schechter,** Brian P '91 %Steinberg FB&F,PC -40 Crsswys Park Dr -Woodbury 11797
(212) 244-6600 .. **Schechter & Brucker,PC** -350 5th Av -NY 10118 **Fx:**244-6784
(212) 374-7973 .. **Schechter,** Carol '80 Dept of Ed -4951 Chmbrs -NY 10007
(212) 697-3122 .. **Schechter,** Chas S '97 (Martin C&B LLP) -220 E 42nd -NY 10017
(631) 249-1134 .. **Schechter,** Danl R '97 %Parkell -300 Exec Dr -Edgewood 11717 **Fx:**249-1242
(516) 829-4867 .. **Schechter,** Donald L '70 -10 Cuttermill Rd -Gt Neck 11021
(718) 263-4450 .. **Schechter,** Donald R '72 (D Schechter,PC) -80-02 Kew Grdns Rd -Kew Gdns 11415 **Fx:**520-0921
(212) 816-3836 .. **Schechter,** Dov S '78 Citigroup -388 Greenwich -NY 10013
(516) 466-8005 .. **Schechter,** Hillel S '00 (Tashlik KG&C PC) -40 Cuttermill Rd -Gt Neck 11021
(212) 244-6600 .. **Schechter,** Howard '76 (Schechter & B,PC) -350 5th Av -NY 10118
(212) 755-5511 .. **Schechter,** Israel '75 I Schechter,PLLC -570 Lex Av -NY 10022 **Fx:**755-5554
(646) 674-1185 .. **Schechter,** Jeffrey E '92 Liquid Knits Inc -237 W 35th -NY 10001
(716) 852-3540 .. **Schechter,** Joel B '79 (Watson BCJ&S) -12 Fountain Plz -Buffalo 14202
(212) 819-8200 .. **Schechter,** Jonathan A '99 (White & C LLP) -1155 Av of Amer -NY 10036
(716) 854-4300 .. **Schechter,** Jonathan D '93 (Gross SB&G,PC) -465 Main -Buffalo 14203
(716) 551-3341 .. **Schechter,** Kimberly A '88 %Fed Pub Def -300 Pearl -Buffalo 14202 **Fx:**551-3346
(631) 547-0300 .. **Schechter,** Kimberly A '07 %Novick & Assoc,PC -202 E Main -Huntngtn 11743 **Fx:**547-0212
(914) 722-6255 .. **Schechter,** Linda S '86 -59 Brite Av -Scarsdale 10583 **Fx:**722-0977
(212) 692-1000 .. **Schechter,** Loren '68 (Duane M LLP) -1540 Bway -NY 10036
(516) 822-4400 .. **Schechter,** Marvin '61 (Tunstead & S) -500 N Bway -Jericho 11753
(212) 307-1405 .. **Schechter,** Marvin E '73 -1790 Bway -NY 10019 **Fx:**307-1431
(212) 517-2572 .. **Schechter,** Pamela Anne '89 -420 E 72nd -NY 10021
(212) 308-4411 .. **Schechter,** Peter C '85 (Edwards AP&D LLP) -750 Lex Av -NY 10022
(212) 265-6888 .. **Schechter,** Robt M '07 %Porzio B&N,PC -156 W 56th -NY 10019
(212) 980-9600 .. **Schechter,** Scott A '94 (Kaufman B&R) -120 Bway -NY 10271
(212) 980-0120 .. **Schechter,** Wendy Jo '98 %Frankfurt KK&S,PC -488 Mad Av -NY 10022
(516) 791-8010 .. **Schechter,** Wendy Z '89 -711 Emerson -Woodmere 11598 **Fx:**569-4815
(212) 335-4500 .. **Schechtman,** Caryn Mazin '98 (DLA Piper LLP) -1251 Av of Amer -NY 10020
(646) 658-7352 .. **Schechtman,** David B '01 Eastern Consolidated -355 Lex Av -NY 10017 **Fx:**(212) 499-7718
(212) 698-3500 .. **Schechtman,** Seth C '07 Dechert LLP -1095 Av of Amer -NY 10036
(212) 364-5340 .. **Scheck,** Barry C '75 Innocence Project -100 5th Av -NY 10011 **Fx:**364-5341
(212) 790-0200 .. **Scheck,** Barry C '75 Benj N Cardozo Schl of Law -55 5th Av -NY 10003 **Fx:**790-0345
(646) 386-4800 .. **Scheckman,** Steven R '86 Comm Judicial Cndct -61 Bway -NY 10006 **Fx:**458-0037
(516) 698-9509 .. **Scheckner,** Donna R '80 -875 Cliffside Av -Vly Stream 11581
(516) 747-6910 .. **Schecter,** Alvin J '52 -114 Old Cntry Rd -Mineola 11501 **Fx:**747-1580
(212) 310-8000 .. **Schecter,** Eric A '05 %Weil G&M LLP -767 5th Av -NY 10153
(516) 222-2299 .. **Schecter,** Jeffrey S '85 (J Schecter & Assoc) -595 Stewart Av -Gdn Cty 11530 **Fx:**222-2303
(212) 286-0040 .. **Schecter,** Mardi J '87 (Younkins & S LLP) -420 Lex Av -NY 10170 **Fx:**949-1920
(212) 530-5000 .. **Schecter,** Mikhel C '08 %Milbank TH&M LLP -1 Chase Manh Plz -NY 10005
(845) 356-1101 .. **Schecter,** Mitchell P '77 M Schecter -250 Route 59 -Spg Vly 10977 **Fx:**356-0190
(845) 359-0606 .. **Schecter,** Pamela J '80 %MHLS -140 Old Orangebrg Rd -Orangebrg 10962 **Fx:**365-1773
(718) 279-7097 .. **Schecter,** Stanley A '70 -38-16 208th -Bayside 11361 **Fx:**225-2813
(212) 227-6645 .. **Schecter,** Stephen M '65 -42 Bway -NY 10004 **Fx:**766-9736

(212) 969-3003 .. **Schectman**, Bart '85 OfCnsl Proskauer R LLP -1585 Bway -NY 10036
(212) 849-7000 .. **Scheef**, Robt W '03 %Quinn EU&S,LLP -51 Mad Av -NY 10010
(212) 284-2069 .. **Scheehle**, Stacy F '99 Jeffries & Co -520 Mad Av -NY 10022
(212) 407-7700 .. **Scheer**, Chas A '05 %Vedder P,PC -1633 Bway -NY 10019
(315) 331-7171 .. **Scheer**, David A '90 -1444 Hydesvll Rd -Newark 14513
(212) 456-3473 .. **Scheer**, Heather L '09 ESPN Inc -77 W 66th -NY 10023
(315) 471-8111 .. **Scheer**, Jeffrey B '97 (Scolaro SCF&B,PC) -507 Plum -Syracuse 13204
(212) 440-6804 .. **Scheer**, Lawr J P '02 Mediant Comm LLC -17 State -NY 10004
(212) 938-2337 .. **Scheer**, M Richd '89 (Craner SS&S,PC) -60 E 42nd -NY 10165
(310) 772-8364 .. **Scheer**, Michl J '92 (Dickstein S LLP) -1633 Bway -NY 10019 **Fx:**772-8301
(516) 741-2590 .. **Scheer**, Pamela Peninah '90 %J Schwitzer -1 Old Cntry Rd -Carle Pl 11514
(718) 286-6000 .. **Scheer**, Raymond E '87 %DA -125-01 Qns Blvd -Kew Gdns 11415
(212) 799-4160 .. **Scheer**, Richd A '59 -370 Riverside Dr -NY 10025 **Fx:**799-8221
(212) 755-5551 .. **Scheff**, Robt '58 %L Constantin & Co -575 Mad Av -NY 10022
(212) 415-9200 .. **Scheffel**, David A '97 (Dorsey & W LLP) -250 Park Av -NY 10177
(631) 580-6240 .. **Scheffel**, Jennifer L '98 Cnsl PFM Asset Mgmt LLC -One Corp Dr -Bohemia 11716 **Fx:**580-8803
(716) 434-6883 .. **Scheffer**, Robt P '75 -80 Park Av -Lockprt 14094
(212) 448-1100 .. **Scheffer**, Wm E '03 %McLaughlin & S,LLP -260 Mad Av -NY 10016
(516) 572-2000 .. **Schefflein**, Elan J '10 DA -99 Main -Hempstd 11550 **Fx:**572-2606
(888) 261-6234 .. **Scheffler**, Eric R '95 Madison Realty Cptl -825 3rd Av -NY 10022 **Fx:**(646) 219-5643
(212) 885-5000 .. **Scheffler**, Michl A '80 (Blank R LLP) -405 Lex Av -NY 10174
(212) 245-6565 .. **Schefler**, Kim S '83 (Levine P&M,LLP) -1740 Bway -NY 10019
(212) 689-8999 .. **Scheib**, Paul M '58 -295 Mad Av -NY 10017 **Fx:**599-6272
(212) 547-5400 .. **Scheibe**, Alexandra C '01 (McDermott W&E LLP) -340 Mad Av -NY 10173
(212) 446-4800 .. **Scheibe**, Robt H '71 OfCnsl Kirkland & E LLP -153 E 53rd -NY 10022
(212) 819-8200 .. **Scheibeler**, John P '95 Cnsl White & C LLP -1155 Av of Amer -NY 10036
(518) 463-1311 .. **Scheiberling Rogan & Maney** -100 State -Albany 12207 **Fx:**426-0127
(718) 843-7200 .. **Scheich & Goldsmith,PC** -103-42 Lefferts Blvd -S Richmond Hll 11419 **Fx:**845-0275
(516) 433-3300 .. **Scheich & Goldsmith,PC** -109 Newbrdg Rd -Hicksvll 11801 **Fx:**822-2178
(516) 433-3300 .. **Scheich**, John F '67 (Scheich & G,PC) -109 Newbrdg Rd -Hicksvll 11801
(718) 843-7200 .. **Scheich**, John F '67 (Scheich & G,PC) -103-42 Lefferts Blvd -S Richmond Hll 11419
(212) 688-3200 .. **Scheichet**, David I '66 (Scheichet & D,PC) -767 3rd Av -NY 10017
(212) 688-3200 .. **Scheichet & Davis,PC** -767 3rd Av -NY 10017 **Fx:**371-7634
(212) 414-3003 .. **Scheid**, Susan '79 -150 W 28th -NY 10001
(212) 362-9271 .. **Scheidt**, Chas '68 -20 W 86th -NY 10024
(718) 264-3340 .. **Scheidt**, Peter J '02 %MHLS -80-45 Wnchstr Blvd -Qns Vllg 11427 **Fx:**264-3559
(718) 243-6221 .. **Scheier**, Joshua F '93 Leg Aid -111 Lvngstn -Brklyn 11201
(201) 334-9876 .. **Scheier**, Justin H '06 Scheier Law Firm,LLC -1710 1st Av -NY 10128 **Fx:**426-2347
(212) 484-3900 .. **Scheiman**, Eugene R '70 (Arent F LLP) -1675 Bway -NY 10019
(212) 935-1400 .. **Schein**, Alvin S '77 (Seiden & S,PC) -570 Lex Av -NY 10022
(212) 679-6605 .. **Schein**, Bettina '87 -260 Mad Av -NY 10016
(212) 300-1372 .. **Schein**, Mark D '92 York Capital Mgmt -767 5th Av -NY 10153 **Fx:**300-1301
(212) 407-7700 .. **Schein**, Michl L '94 (Vedder P,PC) -1633 Bway -NY 10019
(917) 406-9846 .. **Scheinbach**, Adam W '97 -2500 Johnson Av -Bronx 10463 **Fx:**677-8848
(212) 408-2500 .. **Scheinberg**, Danielle R '05 %Baker B,LLP -30 Rckfllr Plz -NY 10112
(718) 855-2335 .. **Scheinberg Finno & Schwartz, PC** -16 Court -Brklyn 11241 **Fx:**875-4859
(212) 240-5184 .. **Scheinberg**, Jonathan J '05 Cnsl Capstone Equities -14 Wall -NY 10005
(212) 407-7700 .. **Scheinberg**, Ronald '84 (Vedder P,PC) -1633 Bway -NY 10019
(631) 951-4300 .. **Scheine**, Edw R '76 -200 Motor Pkwy -Hauppauge 11788 **Fx:**273-2505
(212) 836-8000 .. **Scheine**, Jeffrey D '86 (Kaye S LLP) -425 Park Av -NY 10022
(212) 308-6100 .. **Scheiner**, Alan H '95 Cnsl Levi L&F LLP -1185 Av of Amer -NY 10036
(917) 657-2826 .. **Scheiner**, Allen V '89 -115 Central Av -Lawrence 11559
(212) 742-8700 .. **Scheiner**, Amy H '08 Garson D&C LLP -110 Wall -NY 10005
(212) 692-1000 .. **Scheiner**, Barbara J '85 (Duane M LLP) -1540 Bway -NY 10036
(718) 596-9000 .. **Scheiner**, Bruce M '81 %Cohen HEP&T -25 Chapel -Brklyn 11201
(212) 593-6700 .. **Scheiner**, Cori '05 %Aaronson RF&D,LLP -757 3rd Av -NY 10017
(845) 364-0700 .. **Scheiner**, Isaac S '93 -441 Route 306 -Monsey 10952 **Fx:**364-0707
(516) 482-8282 .. **Scheiner**, Jay L '86 -14 N Gate Rd -Gt Neck 11023 **Fx:**482-8323
(516) 944-4046 .. **Scheiner**, Terry E '97 -14 Vanderventer Av -Pt Wash 11050 **Fx:**944-2486
(845) 623-0883 .. **Scheinert**, Joel L '61 (Scheinert & K) -404 E Route 59 Bx220 -Nanuet 10954
(845) 623-0883 .. **Scheinert & Kobb** -404 E Route 59 Bx220 -Nanuet 10954 **Fx:**623-0966
(516) 248-6800 .. **Scheinfeld**, Fredric '62 -1565 Franklin Av -Mineola 11501 **Fx:**248-6921
(212) 408-2500 .. **Scheinfeld**, Robt C '85 (Baker B,LLP) -30 Rckfllr Plz -NY 10112
(212) 859-8000 .. **Scheinfeld**, Steven G '86 (Fried FHS&J LLP) -1 NY Plz -NY 10004
(212) 839-5300 .. **Scheininger**, S Robt '05 %Sidley A LLP -787 7th Av -NY 10019
(212) 450-4000 .. **Scheinkman**, Michl '07 %Davis P&W LLP -450 Lex Av -NY 10017
(516) 823-0500 .. **Scheinman**, Douglas M '89 -104 S Central Av -Vly Stream 11580 **Fx:**823-0105
(516) 944-1700 .. **Scheinman**, Martin F '80 -38 Arden Ln -Sands Pnt 11050 **Fx:**944-1771
(914) 924-3483 .. **Scheir**, Caitlin G '08 (Ciaramella & S,LLP) -1 Renaissance Sq -White Plns 10601
(212) 969-3085 .. **Schelberg**, Neal S '80 (Proskauer R LLP) -1585 Bway -NY 10036
(718) 828-8270 .. **Scheld**, Chas J '82 (Seedorf & S) -3453 E Tremont Av -Bronx 10461
(212) 859-8000 .. **Scheler**, Brad Eric '78 (Fried FHS&J LLP) -1 NY Plz -NY 10004
(212) 388-3600 .. **Schelin**, Carol L '88 %32B-J Leg Srvcs -101 Av of Amer -NY 10013 **Fx:**388-3061
(212) 450-4000 .. **Schell**, Christopher S '99 (Davis P&W LLP) -450 Lex Av -NY 10017
(212) 963-8924 .. **Schell**, Deirdre A '99 UN Ofc of Leg Affrs -318 Mad Av -NY 10017 **Fx:**963-6430
(518) 435-1770 .. **Schell**, Ellen C '94 Legal Project -1475 Wstrn Av -Albany 12203
(585) 377-2682 .. **Schell**, George A '70 (Schell & S,PC) -200 Perinton Hills Ofc Park -Fairprt 14450 **Fx:**377-2999
(585) 377-2682 .. **Schell**, George A Jr. '94 (Schell & S,PC) -200 Perinton Hills Ofc Park -Fairprt 14450 **Fx:**377-2999
(212) 816-0444 .. **Schell**, J Michl '78 Citigroup -388 Greenwich -NY 10013
(212) 735-3000 .. **Schell**, James Michl '77 (Skadden ASM&F LLP) -4 Times Sq -NY 10036
(631) 283-0092 .. **Schell**, Renee E '83 -284 Seven Ponds Towd Rd -Water Mill 11976 **Fx:**283-0265
(212) 541-2000 .. **Schell**, Thos J '99 Cnsl Bryan C LLP -1290 Av of Amer -NY 10104
(516) 688-1700 .. **Schellas**, Rosemarie '86 %IRS -1600 Stewart Av -Westbury 11590 **Fx:**688-1750
(631) 232-7888 .. **Scheller**, Anthony '90 -320 Carleton Av -Central Islip 11722 **Fx:**234-1635
(212) 935-3000 .. **Scheller**, Brad M '05 %Mintz LCFG&P,PC -666 3rd Av -NY 10017
(518) 485-2312 .. **Schell-Guy**, Trisha R '95 %OASAS -1450 Wstrn Av -Albany 12203 **Fx:**485-2335
(212) 416-8931 .. **Schellhammer**, Thos A '99 Atty Gen -120 Bway -NY 10271
(518) 565-4770 .. **Schember**, Chantelle '07 %DA -137 Margaret -Plattsbrgh 12901 **Fx:**565-4777
(212) 282-5069 .. **Schembri**, Cara A '04 Avon Products Inc -1345 Av of Amer -NY 10105
(914) 681-8700 .. **Schembri**, Nancy R '04 %Milber MP&S LLP -3 Barker Av -White Plns 10601
(212) 875-7106 .. **Schenck**, Eleanore M '06 -545 8th Av -NY 10018 **Fx:**(732) 492-8385
(631) 465-0058 .. **Schenck**, Susan '03 %S Schwaber & Assoc -6 Corp Ctr Dr -Melvll 11747 **Fx:**465-0057
(716) 857-7991 .. **Schenk**, Christopher A '03 Natl Fuel Gas -6363 Main -Williamsvll 14221 **Fx:**857-7614
(212) 998-6163 .. **Schenk**, Deborah H '73 %NYU Law Schl -40 Wshngtn Sq S -NY 10012 **Fx:**995-4894
(516) 571-5315 .. **Schenk**, Edw J '81 Cnsl Nassau Cnty Prob Dept -400 Cnty Seat Dr -Mineola 11501 **Fx:**571-5611
(716) 684-0621 .. **Schenk**, Kevin G '82 -Bx240 -Buffalo 14225 **Fx:**684-1382
(716) 686-3457 .. **Schenk**, Kevin G '82 %Town Atty -Town Hall -Cheektowaga 14227
(914) 286-3400 .. **Schenk**, Rebecca A '77 %Leg Aid -1 N Bway -White Plns 10601 **Fx:**682-4112
(212) 523-2162 .. **Schenkel**, Louis I '85 %Beth Israel Med Ctr -555 W 57th -NY 10019
(212) 294-6700 .. **Schenker**, Michl D '10 %Winston & S -200 Park Av -NY 10166
(845) 679-2038 .. **Schenker**, Rebecca K '76 -4 Hervey White Rd -Woodstock 12498
(212) 363-6900 .. **Schenker**, Robt G '85 (Faust GS&B LLP) -2 Rector -NY 10006
(716) 856-5500 .. **Schenkler**, Bernard '74 SpclCnsl Damon M LLP -200 Delaware Av -Buffalo 14202
(516) 826-8938 .. **Scheno**, Jos J '10 %R Young & Assoc -1321 Bellmore Av -Bellmore 11710 **Fx:**826-8932
(718) 222-2072 .. **Schepanski**, Liza '08 %Law Dept -350 Jay -Brklyn 11201 **Fx:**222-2088
(516) 463-5890 .. **Schepard**, Andrew '80 %Hofstra Law Schl -121 Hofstra Univ -Hempstd 11549
(718) 590-2000 .. **Schepis**, Anthony J '75 %DA -198 E 161st -Bronx 10451 **Fx:**590-6477
(212) 538-1057 .. **Schepis**, Michl '09 Credit Suisse -1 Mad Av -NY 10010
(718) 792-1888 .. **Schepis**, Steven C '89 -1635 Crosby Av -Bronx 10461
(212) 243-2424 .. **Schepisi**, John A '83 (Schepisi & M,PA) -200 Park Av S -NY 10003
(212) 243-2424 .. **Schepisi & McLaughlin,PA** -200 Park Av S -NY 10003 **Fx:**243-9888
(212) 295-6302 .. **Schepp**, Carol Robinson '75 SpclCnsl WilmerHale -399 Park Av -NY 10022
(914) 232-9373 .. **Schepps**, Solomon J '83 -4 David Dr -N Salem 10560
(914) 328-5600 .. **Scher**, Andrea D '88 OfCnsl Wood & S -222 Bloomingdale Rd -White Plns 10605
(212) 460-6209 .. **Scher**, Andrew W '85 Con Ed -4 Irving Pl -NY 10003 **Fx:**677-5849
(917) 628-8926 .. **Scher**, Ann K '95 -609 Columbus Av -NY 10024
(914) 328-5600 .. **Scher**, Anthony Z '76 (Wood & S) -222 Bloomingdale Rd -White Plns 10605
(914) 737-3344 .. **Scher**, Bob N '99 -8 N Division -Peekskill 10566 **Fx:**737-3357
(516) 681-1100 .. **Scher**, Brett A '97 (Kaufman DV&G,LLP) -135 Crsswys Park Dr -Woodbury 11797
(516) 747-2424 .. **Scher**, Bruce M '75 (BM Scher,PC) -200 Willis Av -Mineola 11501 **Fx:**747-2448
(516) 482-1777 .. **Scher**, Danl J '87 (Scher & S,PC) -55 Water Mill LN Bx376 -Gt Neck 11021 **Fx:**829-3198
(212) 736-5300 .. **Scher**, David L '04 %Block O&M LLP -1 Penn Plz -NY 10119
(212) 759-9770 .. **Scher**, Davida S '86 (Meier F&S,LLP) -570 Lex Av -NY 10022
(518) 474-7339 .. **Scher**, Edw M '73 %Dept of Law -The Cptl -Albany 12224
(212) 480-8800 .. **Scher**, Eric D '95 (Furnari L LLP) -11 Bway -NY 10004 **Fx:**480-4208
(212) 468-4800 .. **Scher**, Ina B '93 (Davis & G LLP) -1740 Bway -NY 10019
(212) 801-9321 .. **Scher**, Irving '63 SrCnsl Greenberg T,LLP -200 Park Av -NY 10166
(516) 746-5040 .. **Scher**, Jonathan L '95 %Scher Law Firm,LLP -1 Old Cntry Rd -Carle Pl 11514 **Fx:**747-9100
(212) 272-7195 .. **Scher**, Lori E '03 %JP Morgan Chase -383 Mad Av -NY 10179
(516) 746-5040 .. **Scher**, Martin H '61 (Scher Law Firm,LLP) -1 Old Cntry Rd -Carle Pl 11514 **Fx:**747-9100
(212) 755-6000 .. **Scher**, Michl S '78 OfCnsl Aronauer R&Y,LLP -444 Mad Av -NY 10022
(516) 482-1777 .. **Scher**, Robt A '58 (Scher & S,PC) -55 Water Mill LN Bx376 -Gt Neck 11021 **Fx:**829-3198
(212) 682-7474 .. **Scher**, Robt A '87 (Foley & L LLP) -90 Park Av -NY 10016
(718) 222-2318 .. **Scher**, Sharon N '07 %Law Dept -350 Jay -Brklyn 11201 **Fx:**222-2373
(212) 689-1113 .. **Scher**, Wm G '86 (Garbarini & S,PC) -432 Park Av S -NY 10016

(212) 431-7200 .. **Scherer,** Andrew A '79 %Legal Srvcs NYC -350 Bway -NY 10013 **Fx:**966-9571
(212) 837-6000 .. **Scherer,** Chas H '71 (Hughes H&R LLP) -1 Bttry Pk Plz -NY 10004
(212) 839-5300 .. **Scherer,** Elizabeth M '04 %Sidley A LLP -787 7th Av -NY 10019
(212) 421-7140 .. **Scherer,** Jack F '64 -99 Park Av -NY 10016 **Fx:**421-7148
(518) 729-4555 .. **Scherer,** Lawr E '93 State & Broadway,Inc -21 Elk -Albany 12207 **Fx:**729-5175
(516) 747-7007 .. **Scherer,** Lawr J '90 (Scherer & Assoc,PLLC) -600 Old Cntry Rd -Gdn Cty 11530 **Fx:**747-7008
(212) 421-2233 .. **Scherer,** M Wm '75 (Wilk A LLP) -675 3rd Av -NY 10017
(212) 357-9975 .. **Scherer,** Pedro E '95 %Goldman Sachs -1 NY Plz -NY 10004
(212) 504-6000 .. **Scherer,** Robt C '98 %Cadwalader W&T LLP -1 World Fncl Ctr -NY 10281
(212) 317-5362 .. **Scherer,** Thos J '92 Swiss Re New Markets -55 E 52nd -NY 10055
(631) 265-4787 .. **Scheriff,** Kenneth M '78 -39 Maple Glen Ln -Nesconset 11767
(212) 735-8716 .. **Scherl,** David A '87 (Morrison C LLP) -909 3rd Av -NY 10022
(212) 849-7000 .. **Scherling,** Katherine A '10 %Quinn EU&S,LLP -51 Mad Av -NY 10010
(212) 490-3000 .. **Scherling,** Matthew E '09 %Wilson EME&D LLP -150 E 42nd -NY 10017
(315) 676-7314 .. **Schermer,** Patience E '02 %Sheats & Assoc,PC -9650 Brewertn Rd Bx820 -Brewertn 13029 **Fx:**676-7189
(212) 608-8840 .. **Schermerhorn,** James R '86 (Bamundo Z&S,LLP) -111 John -NY 10038
(212) 309-6000 .. **Schernecke,** Matthew E '03 %Morgan L&B LLP -101 Park Av -NY 10178
(212) 902-1000 .. **Scherr,** Stephen M '91 %Goldman Sachs -1 NY Plz -NY 10004
(212) 301-4051 .. **Scherr Olson,** Stephanie '96 Natl Financial Prtnrs Corp -340 Mad Av -NY 10173
(212) 907-0700 .. **Schervish,** Wm H '08 Labaton S LLP -140 Bway -NY 10005
(212) 966-6420 .. **Scherz,** Michl D '87 Lwyrs For Children -110 Lafayette -NY 10013 **Fx:**966-0531
(212) 401-0800 .. **Scherzer,** Ann Celia '88 %Disciplinary Comm -61 Bway -NY 10006 **Fx:**287-1045
(212) 451-2300 .. **Scherzer,** Dov H '90 (Olshan GFR&W LLP) -65 E 55th -NY 10022
(212) 813-8800 .. **Scherzer,** Erin Russ '09 %Goodwin P LLP -620 8th Av -NY 10018
(212) 406-9606 .. **Scherzer,** Mark '79 -7 Dey -NY 10007 **Fx:**964-6903
(212) 935-6020 .. **Schess,** Nancy B '86 (Klein ZR LLP) -485 Mad Av -NY 10022
(212) 504-6000 .. **Schetman,** Richd M '84 (Cadwalader W&T LLP) -1 World Fncl Ctr -NY 10281
(516) 825-4466 .. **Schettino,** Jos V '81 -437 Rockaway Av -Vly Stream 11581
(518) 388-4364 .. **Schettino,** Michele '03 DA -612 State -Schnctdy 12305 **Fx:**388-4569
(718) 796-1300 .. **Scheuer,** Elizabeth H '82 -4730 Fieldston Rd -Bronx 10471
(212) 207-0468 .. **Scheuer,** Jill C '80 %Sumitomo Corp -600 3rd Av -NY 10016
(718) 250-2000 .. **Scheuerer,** Susan K '08 %DA -350 Jay -Brklyn 11201 **Fx:**250-2314
(212) 509-3456 .. **Scheuerman,** Amy R '09 McGivney & K,PC -80 Broad -NY 10004
(212) 924-7111 .. **Scheuerman,** Karl E '93 (Warner & S) -6 W 18th -NY 10011
(585) 325-1944 .. **Scheuerman,** Mark C '88 %Empire State Devpt Corp -400 Andrews -Rchstr 14604
(516) 393-6447 .. **Scheuerman,** Theresa A '92 Robert Plan Corp -999 Stewart Av -Bethpage 11714
(518) 782-0600 .. **Scheuermann,** Arthur P '87 SrCnsl School Admin Assn NYS -8 Airport Park Blvd -Latham 12110 **Fx:**782-9552
(847) 275-7413 .. **Scheunemann,** Richd N '10 -354 New Scotland Av -Albany 12208
(516) 535-1500 .. **Scheurer,** Terence C '94 TC Scheuer,PC -1 Old Cntry Rd -Carle Pl 11514
(631) 289-8244 .. **Scheurer,** Wm H '00 -129 Fairfld Dr -Holbrook 11741
(516) 294-2978 .. **Scheuring-Elbert,** Maria C '00 (Elbert & E,LLP) -221 Mineola Blvd -Mineola 11501 **Fx:**294-2979
(516) 883-9029 .. **Scheyer,** Danl '50 -7 Tibbits Ln -Sands Pnt 11050 **Fx:**883-9042
(631) 265-8500 .. **Scheyer & Jellenik** -110 Lk Av S -Nesconset 11767 **Fx:**265-8558
(212) 420-1945 .. **Scheyer,** Lawr W '81 -6 Styvsnt Oval -NY 10009 **Fx:**358-1788
(631) 265-8500 .. **Scheyer,** Richd I '62 (Scheyer & J) -110 Lk Av S -Nesconset 11767
(585) 546-7150 .. **Schiano,** Chas A Jr. '87 -1 E Main -Rchstr 14614 **Fx:**546-5314
(585) 546-7150 .. **Schiano,** Christopher A '91 %Schiano,PC -1 E Main -Rchstr 14614 **Fx:**546-5314
(718) 595-6539 .. **Schiano,** Francis S '79 %DEP -59-17 Junction Blvd -Flushng 11373 **Fx:**595-6543
(631) 232-2400 .. **Schiano,** Jane M '87 %Nassau/Sfflk Law Srv -1757 Vets Hwy -Islandia 11749 **Fx:**232-2489
(585) 235-6611 .. **Schiano,** Margaret A '91 %Panzarella & C -1411 Chili Av -Rchstr 14624 **Fx:**436-9706
(585) 546-7150 .. **Schiano,** Michl P '89 %Schiano,PC -1 E Main -Rchstr 14614 **Fx:**546-5314
(212) 603-8378 .. **Schiano,** Patrice '95 Protiviti Inc -1290 Av of Amer -NY 10104
(212) 541-6222 .. **Schiano-Strain,** Gerard '03 Kane K,PC -1350 Av of Amer -NY 10019
(212) 425-5005 .. **Schiappa,** Matthew A '97 %Clemente M&T,PA -14 Wall -NY 10005
(914) 712-1100 .. **Schiavetta,** Danl M Jr. '93 %Murphy & H,LLP -1 Radisson Plz -New Rchll 10801
(212) 541-9100 .. **Schiavetti Corgan DiEdwards Weinberg & Nicholson,LLP** -575 8th Av -NY 10018 **Fx:**262-0824
(914) 946-0400 .. **Schiavetti Corgan DiEdwards Weinberg & Nicholson,LLP** -709 Wstchstr Av -White Plns 10604 **Fx:**946-2327
(631) 969-3100 .. **Schiavo,** Nicole E '07 %Frenkel LWW&G,LLP -20 W Main -Bay Shr 11706
(914) 323-7000 .. **Schiavone,** Heather A '09 %Wilson EME&D LLP -3 Gannett Dr -White Plns 10604
(973) 315-4407 .. **Schiavone,** Jos J '81 (Budd L) -140 Bway -NY 10005
(716) 849-1333 .. **Schiavone,** Michl '82 (Lipsitz GSC LLP) -42 Delaware Av -Buffalo 14202
(212) 848-4000 .. **Schiavone,** Michl J '90 (Shearman & S LLP) -599 Lex Av -NY 10022
(212) 458-1212 .. **Schiavone,** Polly '88 %AIG -175 Water -NY 10038 **Fx:**458-1259
(631) 871-2250 .. **Schiavoni,** Andrea Harum '04 -Bx3025 -Sag Hbr 11963
(212) 326-2000 .. **Schiavoni,** Tancred V III '89 (O'Melveny & M LLP) -7 Times Sq -NY 10036
(516) 794-7340 .. **Schiazzano,** Robt C '09 %Fager & A,LLP -90 Merrick Av -E Meadow 11554
(631) 289-4600 .. **Schibani,** Christine M '01 %Jacoby & J -1737 N Ocean Av -Medfrd 11763 **Fx:**654-5095
(212) 768-6700 .. **Schick,** Avi David '95 (Sonnenschein N&R LLP) -1221 Av of Amer -NY 10020
(631) 852-1650 .. **Schick,** John R '81 %Leg Aid -300 Center Dr -Rvrhead 11901 **Fx:**852-1655
(212) 685-7600 .. **Schick,** Jos S '98 %Heller H&F,PC -292 Mad Av -NY 10017
(212) 619-1498 .. **Schick,** Nance L '02 -310 E 46th -NY 10017 **Fx:**608-2088
(212) 407-4000 .. **Schick,** Stefan G '00 %Loeb & L,LLP -345 Park Av -NY 10154
(845) 794-4094 .. **Schick,** Stephan '78 %Leg Aid -11 Bank -Monticello 12701 **Fx:**794-0119
(607) 844-4994 .. **Schicker,** Cathleen Donovan '79 -1564 Slatervll Rd -Ithaca 14850
(212) 262-6400 .. **Schickler,** Arnold S '59 (Schickler & S,LLP) -1700 Bway -NY 10019 **Fx:**262-6298
(212) 259-8000 .. **Schickler,** Howard M '93 (Dewey & L LLP) -1301 Av of Amer -NY 10019
(212) 262-6400 .. **Schickler,** Sloan '89 (Schickler & S,LLP) -1700 Bway -NY 10019 **Fx:**262-6298
(212) 620-2680 .. **Schieber,** Evan R '93 %Starr Assoc LLP -245 5th Av -NY 10016 **Fx:**696-5013
(516) 294-0080 .. **Schieck,** Jeanne Schilling '90 -200 Old Cntry Rd -Mineola 11501 **Fx:**741-7758
(212) 297-5800 .. **Schiefelbein,** David I '09 %Day P LLP -7 Times Sq -NY 10036
(718) 590-2000 .. **Schieffer,** Matthew K '09 %DA -198 E 161st -Bronx 10451 **Fx:**590-6477
(212) 474-1000 .. **Schiele,** Eric L '01 (Cravath S&M LLP) -825 8th Av -NY 10019
(212) 732-3200 .. **Schiele,** Karen T '01 Cnsl Carter L&M LLP -2 Wall -NY 10005
(212) 460-2629 .. **Schieler,** Jean M '90 Con Ed -4 Irving Pl -NY 10003
(212) 335-9000 .. **Schiels,** Thos B '80 %DA -1 Hogan Pl -NY 10013
(585) 243-7020 .. **Schiener,** Eric R '98 DA -2 Court -Geneseo 14454 **Fx:**243-7199
(917) 777-4200 .. **Schiera,** Thos M '08 %Bingham M LLP -1 Bttry Pk Plz -NY 10004
(212) 351-4000 .. **Schieren,** George A '75 (Gibson D&C LLP) -200 Park Av -NY 10166
(212) 286-0225 .. **Schierloh,** Christopher '06 %Casey & B LLC -65 W 36th -NY 10018 **Fx:**286-0261
(212) 728-8000 .. **Schiesel,** Julia R '10 %Willkie F&G LLP -787 7th Av -NY 10019
(212) 344-5053 .. **Schiesel,** Steven G '93 (Pecoraro & S) -41 Mad Av -NY 10010 **Fx:**743-8120
(212) 714-2100 .. **Schietroma,** Paul H '76 -237 W 35th -NY 10001
(212) 557-1818 .. **Schietzelt,** Jeffrey J '03 %Silverson P&L -192 Lex Av -NY 10016
(716) 856-5500 .. **Schifeling,** Barbara L '85 (Damon M LLP) -200 Delaware Av -Buffalo 14202
(716) 631-3001 .. **Schifeling,** Iris B '83 %Independent Hlth -511 Farber Lks Dr -Buffalo 14221 **Fx:**635-3838
(718) 590-2000 .. **Schiferle Goldfarb,** Brooke K '10 %DA -198 E 161st -Bronx 10451 **Fx:**590-6477
(516) 791-1282 .. **Schiff,** Alisa Tannenbaum '93 (Schiff & S PLLC) -112 Spruce -Cedarhrst 11516 **Fx:**791-2087
(212) 753-0300 .. **Schiff,** Andrew J '73 (Dahan & N LLP) -1700 Bway -NY 10019
(212) 706-2918 .. **Schiff,** Arthur L '65 -488 Mad Av -NY 10022 **Fx:**308-8582
(212) 547-5400 .. **Schiff,** Carolyn Traister '95 (McDermott W&E LLP) -340 Mad Av -NY 10173
(212) 549-2588 .. **Schiff,** Corinne '00 %ACLU -125 Broad -NY 10004 **Fx:**549-2651
(212) 753-7500 .. **Schiff,** Edw L '52 Cnsl Hartman & C LLP -488 Mad Av -NY 10022
(212) 753-5000 .. **Schiff Hardin LLP** -900 3rd Av -NY 10022 **Fx:**753-5044
(212) 238-3000 .. **Schiff,** Howard '93 OfCnsl Emmet M&M,LLP -120 Bway -NY 10271
(212) 335-9000 .. **Schiff,** James A '03 %DA -1 Hogan Pl -NY 10013
(718) 934-6460 .. **Schiff,** Jeffrey R '74 -2727 Ocean Pkwy -Brklyn 11235
(212) 631-7436 .. **Schiff,** Jordan E '88 (Bronfeld & S) -352 7th Av -NY 10001 **Fx:**379-8311
(718) 743-8610 .. **Schiff,** Marcia '84 Sen C Kruger -2201 Av U -Brklyn 11229 **Fx:**743-5958
(914) 421-1800 .. **Schiff,** Marshall S '78 Cnsl Hocherman T&W LLP -1 N Bway -White Plns 10601
(718) 526-6757 .. **Schiff,** Martin '80 Parking Violations Bureau -210 Joralemon -Brklyn 11201
(516) 742-2266 .. **Schiff,** Marvin Evan '66 ME Schiff,PC -1 Old Cntry Rd -Carle Pl 11514 **Fx:**742-8040
(212) 634-6322 .. **Schiff,** Michl '86 Madison Title -641 Lex Av -NY 10022
(518) 473-0330 .. **Schiff,** Peter H '71 %Dept of Law -The Cptl -Albany 12224
(212) 607-8635 .. **Schiffer,** Danl J '04 US Dept of Labor -33 Whitehall -NY 10004
(212) 571-0550 .. **Schiffer,** James R '04 %Allegaert B&V LLP -111 Bway -NY 10006
(212) 259-8000 .. **Schiffer,** Larry P '80 (Dewey & L LLP) -1301 Av of Amer -NY 10019
(212) 310-8000 .. **Schiffer,** Lori M '03 %Weil G&M LLP -767 5th Av -NY 10153
(212) 980-0120 .. **Schiffer,** Michl B '05 %Frankfurt KK&S,PC -488 Mad Av -NY 10022
(212) 806-5400 .. **Schiffer,** Stefanie A '10 %Stroock &S&L LLP -180 Maiden Ln -NY 10038
(212) 751-3001 .. **Schiffer,** Vivienne R '06 (Thompson & K LLP) -919 3rd Av -NY 10022
(914) 741-6100 .. **Schiffhauer,** Matthew I '10 %Kaufman B&R -200 Summit Lk Dr -Valhalla 10595
(716) 856-8200 .. **Schiffhauer,** Wayne D '98 %Williams & W -43 Court -Buffalo 14202 **Fx:**856-0559
(716) 854-6800 .. **Schiffler,** Geralyn A '86 -300 Pearl -Buffalo 14202 **Fx:**854-3020
(716) 632-8328 .. **Schiffmacher,** Jennifer Volhard '99 Epstein & H -2350 N Forest Rd -Getzvll 14068
(716) 633-3535 .. **Schiffmacher,** Todd M '99 %W Mattar,PC -6720 Main -Williamsvll 14221 **Fx:**631-9804
(212) 972-1000 .. **Schiffman,** Benjamin L '07 %London F LLP -59 Maiden Ln -NY 10038
(212) 450-4000 .. **Schiffman,** Carole '89 (Davis P&W LLP) -450 Lex Av -NY 10017
(212) 628-6433 .. **Schiffman,** Danl '62 -903 Park Av -NY 10075
(212) 762-4000 .. **Schiffman,** Ethan J '98 Morgan Stanley -1633 Bway -NY 10019
(212) 756-2000 .. **Schiffman,** Howard '78 (Schulte R&Z LLP) -919 3rd Av -NY 10022
(718) 643-6550 .. **Schiffman,** Lawr M '91 -26 Court -Brklyn 11242
(516) 227-2323 .. **Schiffman,** Ronald M '77 -666 Old Cntry Rd -Gdn Cty 11530 **Fx:**227-2328
(845) 356-2570 .. **Schiffman,** Wm T '75 %Kantrowitz G&G,PC -747 Chestnut Rdg Rd -Chestnut Rdg 10977
(212) 697-3750 .. **Schiffmiller,** Martin W '80 (Kirschstein IS&P,PC) -425 5th Av -NY 10016
(718) 248-5708 .. **Schiffres,** Michl E '79 %Citicorp -1 Court Sq -LIC 11101 **Fx:**248-5092
(212) 300-1326 .. **Schiffrin,** Andrew '03 York Capital Mgmt -767 5th Av -NY 10153

(347) 401-9183 .. **Schiffrin**, Kenneth H '72 %Supreme Ct Law Dept -360 Adams -Brklyn 11201 **Fx**:643-6114
(212) 490-9100 .. **Schifini**, Allison Harris '97 %Condon & F LLP -7 Times Sq -NY 10036
(212) 277-6500 .. **Schifrin**, Andrew D '90 (Dickstein S LLP) -1633 Bway -NY 10019
(212) 431-2100 .. **Schikler**, Peter A '09 %NY Law Schl -185 W Bway -NY 10013 **Fx**:406-0103
(585) 223-2650 .. **Schild**, Robt M '75 -500 Perinton Hills Ofc Pk -Fairprt 14450
(212) 506-2500 .. **Schildcrout**, Jeremy D '09 %Mayer B LLP -1675 Bway -NY 10019
(212) 682-4940 .. **Schildkraut**, Lance A '98 OfCnsl DiConza Law,PC -630 3rd Av -NY 10017
(716) 849-8900 .. **Schillaci**, Andrea '83 (Hurwitz & F,PC) -1300 Lbrty Bldg -Buffalo 14202
(212) 617-2000 .. **Schillaci**, Jacques L '04 Bloomberg LP -731 Lex Av -NY 10022
(518) 408-3976 .. **Schillaci**, Theresa A '90 %NYS Comm Pub Integrity -540 Bway -Albany 12207
(917) 606-4731 .. **Schillan**, Monica F '01 AOL,LLC -770 Bway -NY 10003
(212) 768-8700 .. **Schiller**, Allan '85 A Schiller,PC -130 W 42nd -NY 10036
(518) 452-5600 .. **Schiller**, Blanche E '90 (Heslin RF&M PC) -5 Columbia Cir -Albany 12203
(914) 245-3776 .. **Schiller**, Chas P '69 -3600 Curry -Yorktwn Hts 10598 **Fx**:962-5070
(212) 688-4100 .. **Schiller**, Craig '76 (Schiller & Assoc,PC) -110 E 59th -NY 10022 **Fx**:688-6551
(212) 262-2390 .. **Schiller**, Francis E '87 OfCnsl Connell F LLP -888 7th Av -NY 10106
(212) 446-2300 .. **Schiller**, Joshua I '09 %Boies S&F LLP -575 Lex Av -NY 10022
(914) 358-1400 .. **Schiller**, Karyn S '90 K Schiller LLC -151 E Post Rd -White Plns 10601
(518) 786-9069 .. **Schiller & Knapp LLP** -950 New Loudon Rd -Latham 12110 **Fx**:786-1246
(212) 977-9700 .. **Schiller**, Laura B '08 %Phillips N LLP -666 5th Av -NY 10103
(716) 484-7196 .. **Schiller**, Mary B '88 (Fessenden L&D) -81 Forest Av Bx590 -Jamestwn 14702
(212) 310-8000 .. **Schiller**, Miranda S '89 (Weil G&M LLP) -767 5th Av -NY 10153
(516) 393-2200 .. **Schiller**, Robt E '93 (Garfunkel W,PC) -111 Grt Nck Rd -Gt Neck 11021
(516) 476-5542 .. **Schiller**, Ross L '05 -474 Lakevll Ln -E Meadow 11554
(212) 878-8000 .. **Schiller**, Teresa B '97 %Clifford C LLP -31 W 52nd -NY 10019
(518) 786-9069 .. **Schiller**, Wm B '88 (Schiller & K LLP) -950 New Loudon Rd -Latham 12110
(212) 637-2695 .. **Schilling**, Andrew W '93 %US Atty -86 Chmbrs -NY 10007
(518) 238-4339 .. **Schilling**, Diane Lufkin '91 %OCA -187 Wolf Rd -Albany 12205 **Fx**:438-3518
(212) 964-2469 .. **Schilling**, Richd R Jr. '49 (Burns KS&O,PC) -120 Bway -NY 10271
(516) 921-7375 .. **Schilling**, Sue Belevich '80 -67 Mdwbrk Rd -Syosset 11791 **Fx**:921-7468
(518) 438-9907 .. **Schillinger**, Lawr R '84 OfCnsl Young SWRB&M,LLC -5 Palisades Dr -Albany 12205
(914) 949-7800 .. **Schillinger**, Peter '84 (Schillinger & F,LLP) -81 Main -White Plns 10601 **Fx**:206-3870
(212) 461-2323 .. **Schillinger**, Randi '84 (Saiber LLC) -44 Wall -NY 10005
(212) 969-3000 .. **Schilowitz**, Elias L '06 %Proskauer R LLP -1585 Bway -NY 10036
(646) 434-1661 .. **Schimek**, Michl D '06 Cnsl Cahill/Wink LLP -5 Penn Plz -NY 10001
(212) 373-3000 .. **Schimek**, Terry E '82 (Paul WRW&G LLP) -1285 Av of Amer -NY 10019
(516) 877-7000 .. **Schimel**, Michl M '09 %McCoyd P&R,LLP -1100 Franklin Av -Gdn Cty 11530
(212) 808-7800 .. **Schimmel**, Danl '95 (Kelley D&W LLP) -101 Park Av -NY 10178
(212) 681-2584 .. **Schimmel**, Lawr M '05 %State Comptroller -633 3rd Av -NY 10017
(212) 509-0918 .. **Schimmel**, Wm G '05 Cnsl Weissman & M LLC -80 Pine -NY 10005
(607) 746-2193 .. **Schimmerling**, Thos E '77 Schimmerling Law Ofc -98 Main Bx168 -Delhi 13753 **Fx**:746-6057
(716) 873-2540 .. **Schimminger**, Robin '74 %NYS Assembly -3514 Delaware Av -Kenmore 14217
(212) 969-3000 .. **Schindel**, Aaron J '79 (Proskauer R LLP) -1585 Bway -NY 10036
(212) 909-6000 .. **Schindel**, Carolyn K '93 %Debevoise & P LLP -919 3rd Av -NY 10022
(914) 698-3313 .. **Schindel**, Donald '73 (Lichtenstein & S) -158 W Bstn Post Rd -Mamaroneck 10543
(212) 563-1710 .. **Schindel Farman Lipsius Gardner & Rabinovich LLP** -14 Penn Plz -NY 10122 **Fx**:695-1618
(914) 694-4102 .. **Schindel**, Miriam '82 SpclCnsl Hinman H&K,LLP -106 Corp Park Dr -White Plns 10604
(212) 521-3500 .. **Schindel**, Ronnie M '94 (Aronson M&S, LLP) -485 Lex Av -NY 10017
(631) 952-4955 .. **Schindelheim**, Lawr A '93 %Ct of Claims -NYS Ofc Bldg Vets Mem'l Hwy -Hauppauge 11788 **Fx**:952-6727
(914) 846-7000 .. **Schindelheim**, Marc S '77 %NY Life Ins -1 Rockwood Rd -Sleepy Hollow 10591 **Fx**:846-4755
(212) 480-7120 .. **Schindelman**, Dawn I '96 %DHCR -25 Beaver -NY 10004 **Fx**:480-7416
(718) 286-6000 .. **Schindhelm**, Michl C '07 %DA -125-01 Qns Blvd -Kew Gdns 11415
(212) 720-5026 .. **Schindler**, Barry M '99 %Fed Reserve Bk -33 Lbrty -NY 10045 **Fx**:785-5748
(212) 578-2903 .. **Schindler**, Bruce H '00 %MetLife -27-01 Qns Plz N -LIC 11101
(212) 277-6300 .. **Schindler Cohen & Hochman LLP** -100 Wall -NY 10005
(631) 474-5373 .. **Schindler**, Edwin D '85 -5 Hirsch Av Bx966 -Coram 11727 **Fx**:474-5374
(518) 279-1900 .. **Schindler**, George Albee '59 -908 Hoosick -Troy 12180 **Fx**:279-9516
(718) 382-8700 .. **Schindler**, Joel '95 %M Geller & Assoc,PC -1639 E 13th -Brklyn 11229 **Fx**:377-3624
(516) 571-1181 .. **Schindler**, Loren B '90 %Cnty Atty -1 West -Mineola 11501 **Fx**:571-1692
(212) 361-7770 .. **Schindler**, Nancy J '89 %Dept Consumer Affrs -66 John -NY 10038
(212) 801-6785 .. **Schindler**, Paul D '72 (Greenberg T,LLP) -200 Park Av -NY 10166
(845) 331-4496 .. **Schindler**, Russell A '85 -245 Wall -Kingston 12401 **Fx**:331-0501
(212) 277-6300 .. **Schindler**, Steven R '86 (Schindler C&H LLP) -100 Wall -NY 10005
(631) 444-0345 .. **Schindler**, Susan H '86 DEC -SUNY Campus 50 Circle Rd -Stony Brk 11790 **Fx**:444-0348
(212) 715-9100 .. **Schindler-Williams**, Sarah K '08 %Kramer LN&F,LLP -1177 Av of Amer -NY 10036
(212) 964-6611 .. **Schiner**, Curt J '96 (Lester SK&D) -120 Bway -NY 10271
(212) 715-9100 .. **Schinfeld**, Seth F '07 %Kramer LN&F,LLP -1177 Av of Amer -NY 10036
(718) 263-7800 .. **Schioppi**, Jos C '74 -123-35 82nd Rd -Kew Gdns 11415
(212) 345-6492 .. **Schioppo**, Craig A '01 Marsh,Inc -1166 Av of Amer -NY 10036 **Fx**:345-3706
(212) 643-0393 .. **Schioppo**, Richd A '93 Greener & S,PC -450 7th Av -NY 10123 **Fx**:268-7439
(212) 267-6557 .. **Schiowitz**, Jeremy J '04 %Isaacson S&K -150 Bway -NY 10038
(212) 267-6557 .. **Schiowitz**, Martin '73 (Isaacson S&K) -150 Bway -NY 10038
(212) 848-4000 .. **Schipper**, Rachel Minden '08 %Shearman & S LLP -599 Lex Av -NY 10022
(631) 361-9494 .. **Schiralli**, Frank Jr. '92 %A Vardaro,PC -732 Smithtwn Bypass -Smithtwn 11787 **Fx**:361-8752
(212) 403-1000 .. **Schireson**, Benjamin D '09 %Wachtell LR&K -51 W 52nd -NY 10019
(212) 880-9428 .. **Schirick**, E Scott '04 %Morvillo AGIA&B,PC -565 5th Av -NY 10017
(212) 506-5000 .. **Schirick**, Elizabeth A '04 %Orrick H&S LLP -51 W 52nd -NY 10019
(631) 853-4049 .. **Schirmer**, Drew W '91 Cnty Atty -Dennison Bldg Bx6100 -Hauppauge 11788 **Fx**:853-5169
(845) 246-9596 .. **Schirmer Hrdlicka & Strohsahl** -110 Market Bx240 -Saugerties 12477 **Fx**:246-5460
(516) 263-6446 .. **Schirmer**, Richd E '96 -805 Avalon Pines Dr -Coram 11727
(212) 570-3715 .. **Schirmer**, Robt W '05 Metropolitan Museum -1000 5th Av -NY 10028
(914) 741-9870 .. **Schiro**, Jeffrey J '98 %Shaw PM&L,LLP -115 Stevens Av -Valhalla 10595
(212) 264-3650 .. **Schiro**, Kimberly Luana '00 %SSA Ofc Genl Cnsl -26 Fed Plz -NY 10278 **Fx**:264-6372
(914) 375-0100 .. **Schiro**, Lawr '83 (Novick ELRW&L,PC) -733 Ynkrs Av -Ynkrs 10704
(212) 986-4500 .. **Schirripa**, Frank R '03 %Horwitz H&P -405 Lex Av -NY 10174
(212) 964-6611 .. **Schirripa**, Kimberly A '03 %Lester SK&D -120 Bway -NY 10271
(718) 247-7294 .. **Schirtzer**, Robt '01 (Nassiripour & S,PC) -4027 74th -Elmhrst 11373
(845) 562-9020 .. **Schisano**, Richd '80 (Silver FS&L) -3250 Route 9W -New Windsor 12553
(212) 278-5656 .. **Schisgall**, Laura J '92 %Societe Generale -1221 Av of Amer -NY 10020
(845) 486-2211 .. **Schisler**, Richd C '75 Supreme Ct -10 Market -Poughkeepsie 12601 **Fx**:473-5403
(212) 966-6420 .. **Schissel**, Anna V '02 Lwyrs For Children -110 Lafayette -NY 10013 **Fx**:966-0531
(212) 715-1000 .. **Schissel**, Michl D '85 (Arnold & P LLP) -399 Park Av -NY 10022
(212) 848-4000 .. **Schiwek**, Heiko '97 Cnsl Shearman & S LLP -599 Lex Av -NY 10022
(212) 854-2599 .. **Schizer**, David M '96 %Columbia Law Schl -435 W 116th -NY 10027 **Fx**:854-7946
(212) 422-0488 .. **Schizer**, Hazel G '60 Rick SF&B,LLP -90 Broad -NY 10004 **Fx**:422-0158
(212) 510-1400 .. **Schlachet**, Danl I '00 %Spec Comm of Invstgtn -80 Maiden Ln -NY 10038 **Fx**:510-1550
(631) 543-0300 .. **Schlachter**, David '74 -626 RXR Plz -Uniondale 11556
(212) 695-2000 .. **Schlacter**, Jed R '78 -450 7th Av -NY 10123 **Fx**:629-5825
(212) 922-1920 .. **Schlaff**, Abigail Zucker '05 %West Group -530 5th Av -NY 10036 **Fx**:867-2404
(212) 292-4510 .. **Schlafly**, Andrew L '92 -521 5th Av -NY 10175
(914) 962-3700 .. **Schlageter**, Mary O'Neill '00 Measter & S -1961 Commerce -Yorktwn Hts 10598 **Fx**:962-5515
(212) 512-6530 .. **Schlain**, Barbara E '74 %McGraw-Hill -1221 Av of Amer -NY 10020 **Fx**:512-4827
(212) 741-8290 .. **Schlakman**, Stephen '67 %Bruno Scheidt Inc -71 W 23rd -NY 10010 **Fx**:206-0530
(212) 344-5400 .. **Schlam Stone & Dolan LLP** -26 Bway -NY 10004 **Fx**:344-7677
(212) 535-5227 .. **Schlang**, David '35 -737 Park Av -NY 10021 **Fx**:650-0270
(212) 947-6600 .. **Schlanger**, Arnold G '68 %Peak Cnsl Inc -25 W 31st -NY 10001 **Fx**:947-6780
(315) 422-1122 .. **Schlanger**, Craig P '78 -120 E Wshngtn -Syracuse 13202 **Fx**:410-1723
(914) 946-1981 .. **Schlanger**, Danl A '06 (Schlanger & S,LLP) -1025 Wstchstr Av -White Plns 10604 **Fx**:946-2930
(212) 424-0350 .. **Schlanger**, Darren L '02 Gilder Gagnon Howe & Co -1775 Bway -NY 10019
(646) 315-7403 .. **Schlanger**, Eugene A '82 FINRA -14 Wall -NY 10005 **Fx**:(202) 689-3468
(845) 562-0203 .. **Schlanger**, Gail F '96 %Finkelstein & Prtnrs,LLP -1279 Route 300 Bx1111 -Newburgh 12550
(845) 294-7949 .. **Schlanger**, Ian L '06 %Norton & C -60 Erie Bx308 -Goshen 10924
(212) 593-1000 .. **Schlanger**, Jeffrey '79 %Kroll Assoc -1166 Av of Amer -NY 10036 **Fx**:593-2631
(212) 608-1445 .. **Schlanger**, Mark '07 %DJ Feit,PLLC -22 Crtlandt -NY 10007 **Fx**:608-1803
(914) 946-1981 .. **Schlanger**, Michl '63 (Schlanger & S,LLP) -1025 Wstchstr Av -White Plns 10604 **Fx**:946-2930
(845) 359-7747 .. **Schlanger**, Robt M '71 -33 Dutchess Dr -Orangebrg 10962
(518) 372-8534 .. **Schlansker**, Robt A '79 -1389 Myron -Schnctdy 12309
(518) 689-0966 .. **Schlansker**, Robt A '79 OfCnsl Hite & B,PC -20 Corp Wds Blvd -Albany 12211
(631) 269-1055 .. **Schlansky**, Bennett I '00 Sportime -Bx326 -Kings Pk 11754 **Fx**:269-1270
(716) 855-3200 .. **Schlant**, Mark J '87 %Zdarsky S&A -298 Main -Buffalo 14202
(212) 450-4000 .. **Schlaphoff**, Aaron J '05 %Davis P&W LLP -450 Lex Av -NY 10017
(607) 273-2202 .. **Schlather**, Raymond M '77 (Schlather SP&S) -200 E Buffalo Bx353 -Ithaca 14851
(607) 547-5253 .. **Schlather**, Robt B '72 (Schlather & B) -192 Main Bx391 -Cooperstwn 13326 **Fx**:547-2420
(607) 273-2202 .. **Schlather Stumbar Parks & Salk** -200 E Buffalo Bx353 -Ithaca 14851 **Fx**:273-4436
(212) 294-6700 .. **Schlatner**, Adam J '94 (Winston & S) -200 Park Av -NY 10166

(315) 253-1391 .. **Schlecht,** Christopher W '99 %DA -95 Genesee -Auburn 13021 **Fx:**253-1521
(607) 776-9631 .. **Schlechter,** Mark A '92 %Hon P Bradstreet -3 E Pulteney Sq -Bath 14810 **Fx:**776-9631
(212) 521-5400 .. **Schlecker,** David M '83 (Reed S LLP) -599 Lex Av -NY 10022
(212) 980-8000 .. **Schlegel,** Beth J '87 %Sherwood Equities -745 5th Av -NY 10151 **Fx:**980-8109
(212) 909-6000 .. **Schlegel,** Mark E '06 %Debevoise & P LLP -919 3rd Av -NY 10022
(315) 474-7571 .. **Schlegel,** Mark R '00 (Mackenzie H LLP) -101 S Salina Bx4967 -Syracuse 13221
(212) 972-1000 .. **Schlegel,** Portia L '09 %London F LLP -59 Maiden Ln -NY 10038
(718) 694-8208 .. **Schlehr,** Sarah B '04 Legal Outreach -141 Macon -Brklyn 11216
(212) 848-7293 .. **Schleider,** Andrew R '90 (Shearman & S LLP) -599 Lex Av -NY 10022
(315) 471-1664 .. **Schleider,** Edwina C '79 (Meggesto C&V,LLP) -313 E Willow -Syracuse 13203
(631) 549-4677 .. **Schleier,** Robt E Jr. '00 (Sobel K&S,PC) -464 NY Av -Huntngtn 11743
(716) 853-8500 .. **Schleif,** Thos N '98 %Medicaid Fraud Cntrl -350 Main Pl Twr -Buffalo 14202 **Fx:**853-8525
(212) 403-1000 .. **Schleifer,** Adam P '07 %Wachtell LR&K -51 W 52nd -NY 10019
(914) 347-7039 .. **Schleifer,** Harriet P '85 Student Advocacy,Inc -3 W Main -Elmsfrd 10523 **Fx:**347-6382
(516) 357-2000 .. **Schleifer,** Nicholas P '00 Robert Half Intl -522 RXR Plz -Uniondale 11556
(212) 388-3274 .. **Schleifer,** Rebecca A '02 Local 32B-32J SEIU -101 Av of the Americas -NY 10013 **Fx:**388-2180
(212) 973-3366 .. **Schleiff,** Henry S '74 Court TV -600 3rd Av -NY 10016 **Fx:**973-3355
(212) 521-5400 .. **Schleifstein,** Danl A '09 %Reed S LLP -599 Lex Av -NY 10022
(212) 801-2112 .. **Schleifstein,** Ellen B '97 %Greenberg T,LLP -200 Park Av -NY 10166
(212) 986-8282 .. **Schleifstein,** Scott A '94 %Cohen & S -360 Lex Av -NY 10017
(212) 541-9330 .. **Schleimer,** Karen Beth '77 -250 W 57th -NY 10107 **Fx:**(914) 244-1139
(212) 659-7300 .. **Schleimer,** Walter F '83 (Haynes & B,LLP) -1221 Av of Amer -NY 10020
(212) 319-6600 .. **Schlein,** Danl '94 -145 E 48th -NY 10017 **Fx:**981-2525
(212) 248-5060 .. **Schlemmer,** Paul N '98 (Schlemmer & M LLP) -111 Bway -NY 10006 **Fx:**389-9793
(518) 463-4473 .. **Schlenker,** Dennis '69 -174 Wshngtn Av -Albany 12210 **Fx:**463-7926
(212) 474-1000 .. **Schler,** Michl L '74 (Cravath S&M LLP) -825 8th Av -NY 10019
(212) 382-0909 .. **Schlesinger,** Aaron C '97 (Peckar & A,PC) -41 Mad Av -NY 10154
(212) 962-8020 .. **Schlesinger,** Adam L '92 %Julien & S,PC -1 Whitehall -NY 10004
(516) 536-1625 .. **Schlesinger,** Adriane Wolfsohn '86 -345 Dennis -Oceanside 11572
(212) 788-0952 .. **Schlesinger,** Alan M '82 %Law Dept -100 Church -NY 10007 **Fx:**788-0367
(914) 312-6384 .. **Schlesinger,** Alexandra W '99 %MCI -2 Intl Dr -Rye Brook 10573
(212) 944-0500 .. **Schlesinger,** Edw S '62 (Hofheimer G&G,LLP) -530 5th Av -NY 10036 **Fx:**869-4930
(212) 964-0120 .. **Schlesinger,** Eric S '98 (Golden RSLB&G,PC) -111 John -NY 10038
(212) 652-3800 .. **Schlesinger Gannon & Lazetera LLP** -535 Mad Av -NY 10022 **Fx:**652-3789
(212) 226-4200 .. **Schlesinger,** Glenn N '85 (Suckle S&L PLLC) -224 W 35th -NY 10001
(212) 270-6000 .. **Schlesinger,** Jarrod S '95 JP Morgan Chase & Co -270 Park Av -NY 10017
(212) 451-2300 .. **Schlesinger,** Kenneth A '88 (Olshan GFR&W LLP) -65 E 55th -NY 10022
(845) 639-9200 .. **Schlesinger,** Leslye M '83 (L Schlesinger,PC) -151 S Main -New Cty 10956 **Fx:**639-9261
(212) 704-6000 .. **Schlesinger,** Mark I '75 OfCnsl Troutman S LLP -405 Lex Av -NY 10174
(212) 568-4245 .. **Schlesinger,** Marni F '08 %Apicella & S -1454 St Nicholas Av -NY 10033
(212) 980-9622 .. **Schlesinger,** Michl '70 -167 N Grand Av -Poughkeepsie 12603 **Fx:**725-0622
(212) 962-8020 .. **Schlesinger,** Michl S '96 %Julien & S,PC -1 Whitehall -NY 10004
(212) 568-4245 .. **Schlesinger,** Philip '71 (Apicella & S) -1454 St Nicholas Av -NY 10033
(212) 652-3777 .. **Schlesinger,** Sanford J '66 (Schlesinger G&L LLP) -535 Mad Av -NY 10022
(516) 746-8000 .. **Schlesinger,** Steven R '77 (Jaspan S LLP) -300 Grdn City Plz -Gdn Cty 11530
(212) 962-8020 .. **Schlesinger,** Stuart A '65 (Julien & S,PC) -1 Whitehall -NY 10004
(212) 506-5000 .. **Schlessel,** Jason S '03 %Orrick H&S LLP -51 W 52nd -NY 10019
(212) 558-4000 .. **Schleyer,** Glen T '99 (Sullivan & C LLP) -125 Broad -NY 10004
(585) 753-4500 .. **Schlia,** Robin E '06 DA -832 Watts Bldg -Rchstr 14614 **Fx:**753-4576
(212) 450-4000 .. **Schlichter,** Andrew D '06 %Davis P&W LLP -450 Lex Av -NY 10017
(212) 822-8300 .. **Schlick,** Daphne R '06 NMIC -76 Wadsworth Av -NY 10033 **Fx:**740-9645
(212) 249-3571 .. **Schliesser,** Peter C O '60 -315 E 68th -NY 10065 **Fx:**525-2263
(315) 422-8191 .. **Schliffer,** Stacey M '08 %Leg Aid -351 S Warren -Syracuse 13202 **Fx:**472-2819
(212) 841-5200 .. **Schlinger,** Tamara L '01 Natl Ctr Addctn & Substnc Abuse -633 3rd Av -NY 10017
(516) 932-0534 .. **Schlingheyde,** John '85 -550 W Old Cntry Rd -Hicksvll 11801 **Fx:**932-0538
(516) 741-2100 .. **Schlissel,** Alan M '97 Alacqua & B -265 Post Av -Westbury 11590
(516) 561-6645 .. **Schlissel,** Elliot S '77 -479 Merrick Rd -Lynbrk 11563 **Fx:**561-6716
(516) 741-6565 .. **Schlissel,** Lois Carter '76 (Meyer SE&K,PC) -990 Stewart Av Bx9194 -Gdn Cty 11530
(516) 877-1800 .. **Schlissel Ostrow Karabatos, PLLC** -200 Grdn City Plz -Gdn Cty 11530 **Fx:**294-3188
(516) 877-1800 .. **Schlissel,** Stephen W '62 (Schlissel OK,PLLC) -200 Grdn City Plz -Gdn Cty 11530
(800) 660-1466 .. **Schlitt,** Carol L '87 -223 Wall -Huntngtn 11743
(914) 693-3739 .. **Schlitt,** Irving '49 -10 Darwood Pl -Hartsdale 10530 **Fx:**693-4214
(914) 834-5010 .. **Schloat,** Janet Kneubuhl '92 Cnsl B Lerman -5 Waller Av -White Plns 10601 **Fx:**834-5024
(212) 728-8000 .. **Schloendorn,** Danl '74 (Willkie F&G LLP) -787 7th Av -NY 10019
(212) 310-8000 .. **Schloss,** Adam M '04 %Weil G&M LLP -767 5th Av -NY 10153
(646) 386-3627 .. **Schloss,** Barbara A '83 %Supreme Ct-Law Dept -60 Centre -NY 10007
(212) 541-6222 .. **Schloss,** Bruce M '81 Cnsl Kane K,PC -1350 Av of Amer -NY 10019
(212) 801-2256 .. **Schloss,** Danl I '98 OfCnsl Greenberg T,LLP -200 Park Av -NY 10166
(845) 425-4200 .. **Schloss,** Jack '76 (Schloss & S) -420 Route 59 -Airmont 10952 **Fx:**425-4404
(845) 425-4200 .. **Schloss,** Jonathan B '99 (Schloss & S) -420 Route 59 -Airmont 10952 **Fx:**425-4404
(212) 922-9250 .. **Schloss,** Martin E '72 OfCnsl Ganfer & S LLP -360 Lex Av -NY 10017
(212) 581-0990 .. **Schloss,** Stephanie H '05 %M O'Neill -30 Vesey -NY 10007 **Fx:**581-5897
(212) 488-1598 .. **Schlossberg,** Aaron M '03 %Havkins RR&V,LLP -11 Penn Plz -NY 10001
(516) 745-1122 .. **Schlossberg,** Brad A '97 Cnsl Quadrino & S,PC -666 Old Cntry Rd -Gdn Cty 11530
(516) 663-6600 .. **Schlossberg,** Jeffrey M '85 (Ruskin MF,PC) -1425 RXR Plz -Uniondale 11556
(212) 335-9000 .. **Schlossberg,** Karen S '99 %DA -1 Hogan Pl -NY 10013
(914) 701-0008 .. **Schlossberg,** Morton J '55 %Imperial Sterling Ltd -287 Bowman Av -Purchase 10577
(212) 735-3000 .. **Schlossberg,** Resa K '05 %Skadden ASM&F LLP -4 Times Sq -NY 10036
(516) 357-3000 .. **Schlosser,** Brian S '01 (Rivkin R LLP) -926 RXR Plz -Uniondale 11556
(212) 226-2703 .. **Schlosser,** Eric '78 -350 Bway -NY 10013
(212) 806-5400 .. **Schlosser,** Jared E '03 %Stroock &S&L LLP -180 Maiden Ln -NY 10038
(607) 733-9706 .. **Schlosser,** Karin A '87 -391 Harris Hill Rd -Elmira 14903 **Fx:**733-9877
(516) 741-6565 .. **Schlosser,** Kevin '85 (Meyer SE&K,PC) -990 Stewart Av Bx9194 -Gdn Cty 11530
(212) 662-6662 .. **Schlosser,** Robt H '88 -275 Mad Av -NY 10016 **Fx:**662-0966
(718) 522-5000 .. **Schlossman,** Beth J '81 -26 Court -Brklyn 11242 **Fx:**522-5082
(518) 474-5745 .. **Schlosstein,** Mark F '02 %State Comptroller -110 State -Albany 12236 **Fx:**473-9104
(212) 267-8600 .. **Schlusberg,** Seth '91 %Bridge Svc Corp -277 Bway -NY 10007 **Fx:**267-8687
(212) 478-7200 .. **Schlussel,** Lauren S '10 %Hahn & H LLP -488 Mad Av -NY 10022
(212) 223-0400 .. **Schlussel,** Mark W '79 (Zeichner E&K LLP) -575 Lex Av -NY 10022
(516) 487-1235 .. **Schlussel,** Steven M '71 -80 Cutter Mill Rd -Gt Neck 11021
(212) 972-1000 .. **Schlusselberg,** Adam '10 %London F LLP -59 Maiden Ln -NY 10038
(516) 487-3012 .. **Schlusselberg,** Irving '52 -14 Cypress Av -Gt Neck 11024 **Fx:**487-3012
(212) 450-4000 .. **Schmale,** Eric C '10 %Davis P&W LLP -450 Lex Av -NY 10017
(212) 688-5000 .. **Schmalz,** Richd L '65 %Westvaco -299 Park Av -NY 10171
(212) 619-4350 .. **Schmedake,** Richd E '98 %Newman MKGH,PC -14 Wall -NY 10005
(212) 336-2000 .. **Schmedlin,** Wm F '10 %Patterson BW&T LLP -1133 Av of Amer -NY 10036
(212) 885-5000 .. **Schmeidler,** Ephraim '06 %Blank R LLP -405 Lex Av -NY 10174
(518) 220-1850 .. **Schmeiser Olsen & Watts** -22 Century Hill Dr -Latham 12110 **Fx:**220-1857
(914) 664-8610 .. **Schmelkin,** Chas L '48 -54 W Broad -Mt Vernon 10552 **Fx:**664-8949
(212) 227-8865 .. **Schmelkin,** Joel '84 (Breadbar G&S) -11 Park Pl -NY 10007
(914) 664-8610 .. **Schmelkin,** Kenneth L '75 -54 W Broad -Mt Vernon 10552
(212) 902-0866 .. **Schmelkin,** Martin L '95 %Goldman Sachs -1 NY Plz -NY 10004
(212) 227-8865 .. **Schmelkin,** Steven H '98 OfCnsl Breadbar G&S -11 Park Pl -NY 10007
(212) 568-4267 .. **Schmell,** Herbert L '58 -1454 St Nicholas Av -NY 10033
(212) 336-2000 .. **Schmeltzer,** John E III '74 OfCnsl Patterson BW&T LLP -1133 Av of Amer -NY 10036
(212) 788-3160 .. **Schmelzer,** Leah S '06 %Law Dept -100 Church -NY 10007 **Fx:**788-0367
(585) 899-1414 .. **Schmergel,** George '70 (Harris COJW&L) -300 Linden Oaks -Rchstr 14625
(212) 318-3000 .. **Schmerler,** Chas D '85 (Fulbright & J LLP) -666 5th Av -NY 10103
(212) 407-4000 .. **Schmerler,** David '92 SrCnsl Loeb & L,LLP -345 Park Av -NY 10154
(212) 687-8200 .. **Schmertz,** Eric J '55 OfCnsl Dweck Law Firm,LLP -75 Rckfllr Plz -NY 10019 **Fx:**697-2521
(212) 309-1312 .. **Schmicker,** Robt D '78 SrCnsl Hunton & W -200 Park Av -NY 10166
(212) 609-6800 .. **Schmid,** Christina M '07 %McCarter & E,LLP -245 Park Av -NY 10167
(212) 221-6900 .. **Schmid,** Elizabeth A '06 %Winget S&S,LLP -45 Bway -NY 10006
(212) 903-9000 .. **Schmid,** Heidi J '02 %Linklaters -1345 Av of Amer -NY 10105
(212) 545-4723 .. **Schmidt,** Alexander H '86 (Wolf HAF&H LLP) -270 Mad Av -NY 10016
(631) 665-8100 .. **Schmidt,** Anthony J '85 -1 E Main -Bay Shr 11706 **Fx:**665-8639
(212) 998-6095 .. **Schmidt,** Astrid '03 NYU Law Schl -245 Sullivan -NY 10012
(212) 940-8800 .. **Schmidt,** Brian A '08 %Katten MR LLP -575 Mad Av -NY 10022
(914) 384-2997 .. **Schmidt,** Brian T '01 -100 S Bedford Rd -Mt Kisco 10549
(716) 837-1515 .. **Schmidt,** Bruce R '66 %Kustell Law Grp,LLP -1660 Kensngtn Av -Buffalo 14215 **Fx:**837-0090
(212) 336-2000 .. **Schmidt,** Catherine Grevers '94 (Patterson BW&T LLP) -1133 Av of Amer -NY 10036
(212) 430-0800 .. **Schmidt,** Chas E '76 (Kennedy LS&E) -75 Maiden Ln -NY 10038
(516) 408-1600 .. **Schmidt,** Corey E '90 %Heidell PM&B,LLP -1050 Franklin Av -Gdn Cty 11530
(212) 480-1900 .. **Schmidt,** Danl E IV '76 %Sorema -199 Water -NY 10038 **Fx:**480-1328
(212) 227-4100 .. **Schmidt,** David W '79 (Lubiner & S) -111 Bway -NY 10006 **Fx:**406-3244

(212) 336-0150 ..**Schmidt**, Eric M '83 %SEC -3 World Fncl Ctr -NY 10281 **Fx**:336-1323
(917) 778-6600 ..**Schmidt**, Fredk D Jr. '86 %J Toomey -485 Lex Av -NY 10017 **Fx**:778-7048
(212) 592-1400 ..**Schmidt**, Fredk Erik '95 %Herrick,F LLP -2 Park Av -NY 10016
(212) 370-4000 ..**Schmidt**, Gary B '77 (Sweeney L LLC) -708 3rd Av -NY 10017
(716) 433-0143 ..**Schmidt**, Henry W '76 -8 W Main -Lockprt 14094 **Fx**:433-4526
(716) 439-7085 ..**Schmidt**, Henry W '76 %DA -175 Hawley -Lockprt 14094 **Fx**:439-7102
(631) 665-8100 ..**Schmidt**, J Lorraine '85 -1 E Main -Bay Shr 11706 **Fx**:665-8639
(716) 753-4241 ..**Schmidt**, Jason L '97 DA -Cnty Cthse -Mayvll 14757 **Fx**:753-4628
(212) 583-9600 ..**Schmidt**, Jean L '83 (Littler M,PC) -900 3rd Av -NY 10022
(212) 556-2100 ..**Schmidt**, Jennifer J '07 %King & S -1185 Av of Amer -NY 10036
(212) 790-9244 ..**Schmidt**, Joel '97 (Cowan L&L,PC) -1133 Av of Amer -NY 10036
(716) 847-8400 ..**Schmidt**, John G Jr. '96 (Phillips L LLP) -3400 HSBC Ctr -Buffalo 14203
(212) 759-4888 ..**Schmidt**, John G Jr. '96 (Phillips L LLP) -437 Mad Av -NY 10022
(718) 590-6173 ..**Schmidt**, John R '93 %Law Dept -198 E 161st -Bronx 10451 **Fx**:590-2686
(718) 441-4343 ..**Schmidt**, Jos T '59 -95-31 Jamaica Av -Woodhvn 11421 **Fx**:441-4346
(212) 922-1640 ..**Schmidt**, Jos W '76 Dover Corp -280 Park Av -NY 10017
(631) 501-5700 ..**Schmidt**, Jos W '91 (Carter DF&S LLP) -445 Broadhallow Rd -Melvll 11747
(212) 490-9100 ..**Schmidt**, Justin M '09 %Condon & F LLP -7 Times Sq -NY 10036
(516) 408-1600 ..**Schmidt**, Karen '07 %Heidell PM&B,LLP -1050 Franklin Av -Gdn Cty 11530
(646) 386-4652 ..**Schmidt**, Keith E '06 Criminal Ct -100 Centre -NY 10013
(212) 909-6000 ..**Schmidt**, Kevin M '95 (Debevoise & P LLP) -919 3rd Av -NY 10022
(718) 921-6601 ..**Schmidt**, Leah A '09 %T Beinert -155 Bay Ridge Av -Brklyn 11220 **Fx**:921-6609
(631) 277-7300 ..**Schmidt**, Leslie M '97 %Steinberg & B,LLP -136 E Main -E Islip 11730
(212) 701-3000 ..**Schmidt**, Lynn R '10 %Cahill G&R LLP -80 Pine -NY 10005 **Fx**:269-5420
(718) 667-9421 ..**Schmidt**, Martina I '96 (Woitkowski & S) -159 Sand Ln -Staten Isl 10305 **Fx**:667-9422
(212) 756-2000 ..**Schmidt**, Matthew W '10 %Schulte R&Z LLP -919 3rd Av -NY 10022
(212) 701-3000 ..**Schmidt**, Merrill T '10 %Cahill G&R LLP -80 Pine -NY 10005 **Fx**:269-5420
(212) 883-4900 ..**Schmidt**, Michl C '94 (Cozen O) -277 Park Av -NY 10172
(212) 386-7050 ..**Schmidt**, Nicole A '92 -600 W End Av -NY 10024
(212) 756-2000 ..**Schmidt**, Owen M '09 %Schulte R&Z LLP -919 3rd Av -NY 10022
(212) 534-7759 ..**Schmidt**, Peter W '74 -1755 York Av -NY 10128
(718) 250-2000 ..**Schmidt**, Rachel G '97 %DA -350 Jay -Brklyn 11201 **Fx**:250-2314
(914) 377-6240 ..**Schmidt**, Raymond P '02 Law Dept -300 City Hall -Ynkrs 10701 **Fx**:964-0563
(718) 863-5553 ..**Schmidt**, Richd R '83 -1446 Wllmsbrdg Rd -Bronx 10461 **Fx**:863-5554
(212) 715-9100 ..**Schmidt**, Robt T '90 (Kramer LN&F,LLP) -1177 Av of Amer -NY 10036
(212) 346-4666 ..**Schmidt**, Sam A '76 -111 Bway -NY 10006 **Fx**:346-4665
(212) 310-8000 ..**Schmidt**, Stefanie K '08 %Weil G&M LLP -767 5th Av -NY 10153
(212) 545-4096 ..**Schmidt**, Thorsten '01 -59 Maiden Ln -NY 10038
(212) 465-6795 ..**Schmidt**, Timothy B '96 MSG Entertainment -2 Penn Plz -NY 10121
(212) 261-8000 ..**Schmidt**, Valerie J '09 %Mendes & M,LLP -750 7th Av -NY 10019
(212) 903-9000 ..**Schmidt**, W Jeffrey '09 (Linklaters) -1345 Av of Amer -NY 10105
(212) 813-1600 ..**Schmidt**, Wm D '94 %Kalow & S -488 Mad Av -NY 10022
(212) 839-5300 ..**Schmidtberger**, Michl J '86 (Sidley A LLP) -787 7th Av -NY 10019
(212) 330-1205 ..**Schmieder**, Deborah '87 %Buck Consultants -1 Penn Plz -NY 10119 **Fx**:695-4184
(585) 786-8160 ..**Schmieder**, Jane A C '93 -140 N Main -Warsaw 14569 **Fx**:786-2208
(212) 732-7184 ..**Schmierer**, Rachael A '03 %Leser HT&T -17 State -NY 10004
(716) 856-5500 ..**Schmit**, James N '67 SpclCnsl Damon M LLP -200 Delaware Av -Buffalo 14202
(212) 903-9000 ..**Schmit**, Jos B '98 Cnsl Linklaters -1345 Av of Amer -NY 10105
(914) 949-1305 ..**Schmits**, Geoffrey B '95 %Leg Srvcs -90 Maple Av -White Plns 10601 **Fx**:949-6213
(518) 356-5357 ..**Schmitt**, Deborah Cowie '83 (Robinson & S) -411 Meghan Blvd -Schnctdy 12306 **Fx**:356-7269
(914) 366-0201 ..**Schmitt**, Edw D '92 %Reardon & S,PC -220 Wht Plns Rd -Tarrytwn 10591
(212) 446-4800 ..**Schmitt**, Johanna '00 (Kirkland & E LLP) -153 E 53rd -NY 10022
(212) 336-2000 ..**Schmitt**, John P '81 (Patterson BW&T LLP) -1133 Av of Amer -NY 10036
(212) 768-6700 ..**Schmitt**, Jos H '90 OfCnsl Sonnenschein N&R LLP -2 World Fncl Ctr -NY 10281
(516) 794-0774 ..**Schmitt**, Kevin E '07 K Schmitt & Assoc,PC -990 Stewart Av -Gdn Cty 11530 **Fx**:977-8477
(607) 272-2314 ..**Schmitt**, Lorraine Moynihan '99 (Thaler & T) -309 N Tioga Bx266 -Ithaca 14851 **Fx**:272-8466
(585) 232-1770 ..**Schmitt**, Michl D '99 (Romeo & S LLP) -36 W Main -Rchstr 14614 **Fx**:546-6456
(212) 337-4170 ..**Schmitt**, Suzanne B '80 %Thomson Reuters/RIA -195 Bway -NY 10007
(315) 724-2147 ..**Schmitt**, Wm P '82 (Gorman WG&S) -1508 Genesee -Utica 13502
(212) 635-1085 ..**Schmitter**, Patrick C '97 Bk of NY Mellon -1 Wall -NY 10286
(212) 309-6000 ..**Schmitz**, Emily D '08 %Morgan L&B LLP -101 Park Av -NY 10178
(212) 834-9377 ..**Schmitz**, Stefan '98 JP Morgan Chase & Co -270 Park Av -NY 10017
(315) 434-1360 ..**Schmitz**, Tom '80 %Salvation Army -200 Twin Oaks Dr Bx148 -Syracuse 13206
(607) 778-2423 ..**Schmitz**, Torrance Lane '00 %DA -45 Hawley Bx1766 -Bnghmtn 13902 **Fx**:778-8870
(212) 310-8000 ..**Schmolka**, Leo L '64 Cnsl Weil G&M LLP -767 5th Av -NY 10153
(212) 719-6004 ..**Schmuck**, Reinhard H '98 %IRS -110 W 44th -NY 10036
(212) 636-6000 ..**Schmudde**, David A '73 %Fordham Univ Sch of Law -140 W 62nd -NY 10023 **Fx**:636-6899
(212) 213-9400 ..**Schmukler**, Martin L '68 M Schmukler,PC -41 Mad Av -NY 10010 **Fx**:684-0620
(718) 834-1144 ..**Schmukler**, Nelson W '69 -288 Atl Av -Brklyn 11201
(516) 594-0830 ..**Schmutter**, David '84 -563 Links Dr S -Oceanside 11572
(212) 351-4000 ..**Schmutter**, Rebecca '08 %Gibson D&C LLP -200 Park Av -NY 10166
(212) 683-3636 ..**Schmutter**, Steven '79 (Krass S&S,PC) -419 Park Av S -NY 10016
(212) 236-4350 ..**Schnaars**, Keith L '97 Merrill Lynch -225 Lbrty - World Fncl Ctr -NY 10281
(212) 909-6000 ..**Schnabel**, David H '96 (Debevoise & P LLP) -919 3rd Av -NY 10022
(718) 694-3901 ..**Schnabel**, Martin B '76 %Transit Auth -130 Lvngstn -Brklyn 11201 **Fx**:694-5726
(845) 469-2023 ..**Schnabel**, Philip H '95 Schnabel Law Ofcs -33 Schnabel Ln -Chester 10918 **Fx**:469-2023
(212) 735-3000 ..**Schnabl**, Marc E '82 (Skadden ASM&F LLP) -4 Times Sq -NY 10036
(212) 973-8000 ..**Schnader Harrison Segal & Lewis LLP** -140 Bway -NY 10005 **Fx**:972-8798
(212) 448-1100 ..**Schnaier**, Stuart J '82 (McLaughlin & S,LLP) -260 Mad Av -NY 10016
(212) 371-2407 ..**Schnall**, David '92 -404 E 55th -NY 10022 **Fx**:980-4962
(212) 759-6469 ..**Schnall**, Flora '60 (FS Assoc) -303 E 57th -NY 10022 **Fx**:750-7177
(212) 770-1751 ..**Schnall**, Nancy E '95 %AIG Tech Srvcs -80 Pine -NY 10005
(212) 878-7900 ..**Schnapp**, Danl A '01 %Fox R LLP -100 Park Av -NY 10017
(212) 837-6000 ..**Schnapp**, Danl E '95 (Hughes H&R LLP) -1 Bttry Pk Plz -NY 10004
(212) 829-1991 ..**Schnapp**, Douglas S '84 -488 Mad Av -NY 10022 **Fx**:813-9600
(212) 355-3200 ..**Schnapp**, Elliot '74 (Gordon G&S,PC) -437 Mad Av -NY 10022 **Fx**:355-3292
(212) 697-5582 ..**Schnapp**, Robt '69 -60 E 42nd -NY 10165 **Fx**:697-6458
(914) 288-9700 ..**Schnaufer**, John C '63 (Schnaufer & M,LLP) -280 N Central Av -Hartsdale 10530 **Fx**:288-9717
(212) 554-7800 ..**Schneck**, Arthur M '50 OfCnsl Moses & S LLP -405 Lex Av -NY 10174
(212) 278-1000 ..**Schneck**, Eric E '90 (Anderson K&O,PC) -1251 Av of Amer -NY 10020
(212) 596-9000 ..**Schneck**, Ezra S '10 %Ropes & G LLP -1211 Av of Amer -NY 10036
(212) 697-3250 ..**Schneck**, Joel S '99 %Goldberg & R PLLC -115 Bway -NY 10006 **Fx**:227-4533
(212) 921-5107 ..**Schneck**, Michl M '83 -15 Maiden Ln -NY 10038 **Fx**:921-4575
(212) 857-1521 ..**Schneck**, Wm C '84 Financial Info Srvcs Agncy -450 W 33rd -NY 10001
(718) 403-3673 ..**Schneebalg**, Connie G '81 %Dept of Finance -345 Adams -Brklyn 11201 **Fx**:403-3650
(212) 337-4148 ..**Schneebalg**, Simon '82 %Thomson Reuters/RIA -195 Bway -NY 10007
(212) 486-9494 ..**Schneer**, Stephen B '55 -488 Mad Av -NY 10022
(212) 969-3000 ..**Schneid**, Adam W '07 %Proskauer R LLP -1585 Bway -NY 10036
(347) 401-9580 ..**Schneidau**, Gretchen O '06 %Applt Term -141 Lvngstn -Brklyn 11201 **Fx**:(718) 643-7889
(518) 474-8211 ..**Schneider**, Amy M '78 %Law Reporting Bur -1 Commerce Plz -Albany 12210 **Fx**:463-6869
(212) 972-1000 ..**Schneider**, Aryeh B '10 %London F LLP -59 Maiden Ln -NY 10038
(212) 596-9000 ..**Schneider**, Benjamin L '09 %Ropes & G LLP -1211 Av of Amer -NY 10036
(212) 269-5500 ..**Schneider**, Brooke A '05 %Gordon & R LLP -90 Broad -NY 10004
(212) 806-5400 ..**Schneider**, Bruce H '75 (Stroock &S&L LLP) -180 Maiden Ln -NY 10038
(845) 452-0200 ..**Schneider**, Bryan G '99 %Basso & Assoc,PC -1171 Route 55 -LaGrangevll 12540 **Fx**:452-0261
(212) 878-6659 ..**Schneider**, Cliff S '04 (Cohen S LLP) -275 Mad Av -NY 10016 **Fx**:878-6661
(212) 446-4800 ..**Schneider**, Courtney '07 %Kirkland & E LLP -153 E 53rd -NY 10022
(212) 629-7744 ..**Schneider**, Danl H '83 (Schneider P&R LLP) -2 Park Av -NY 10016
(845) 471-0058 ..**Schneider**, Danl J '92 %Leg Srvcs -29 N Hmltn -Poughkeepsie 12601 **Fx**:471-0244
(212) 481-9600 ..**Schneider**, Danl J '06 %Wagner D,PC -99 Mad Av -NY 10016
(914) 725-5374 ..**Schneider**, Danl L '81 -49 Walworth Av -Scarsdale 10583
(212) 455-2000 ..**Schneider**, David E '10 %Simpson T&B LLP -425 Lex Av -NY 10017
(315) 536-2100 ..**Schneider**, Donald A '63 -307 Lbrty -Penn Yan 14527 **Fx**:536-0391
(212) 265-2266 ..**Schneider**, Donald F '77 (Schneider GB LLP) -90 Broad -NY 10004
(212) 406-4448 ..**Schneider**, Edw A '93 -110 Wall -NY 10005 **Fx**:406-6048
(718) 250-2000 ..**Schneider**, Eileen F '09 %DA -350 Jay -Brklyn 11201 **Fx**:250-2314
(718) 780-7988 ..**Schneider**, Elizabeth M '74 %Bklyn Law Schl -250 Joralemon -Brklyn 11201 **Fx**:780-0393
(845) 339-6733 ..**Schneider**, Eric '91 -41 Pearl Bx3936 -Kingston 12402 **Fx**:331-2754
(212) 351-8022 ..**Schneider**, Eric S '09 WCS Lending -660 Mad Av -NY 10065
(212) 756-2000 ..**Schneider**, Erik '10 %Schulte R&Z LLP -919 3rd Av -NY 10022
(646) 512-5730 ..**Schneider**, Frederic P '77 (Gilman & S) -40 Wall -NY 10005 **Fx**:512-5733
(212) 426-0648 ..**Schneider**, George A '73 -61 E 93rd -NY 10128
(212) 265-2266 ..**Schneider Goldstein Bloomfield LLP** -90 Broad -NY 10004 **Fx**:265-2442
(212) 962-5352 ..**Schneider**, Graham M '52 Schneider & H -111 John -NY 10038 **Fx**:(646) 378-4410
(212) 682-0020 ..**Schneider**, Harvey I '58 (Putney TH&H LLP) -521 5th Av -NY 10175
(212) 728-8000 ..**Schneider**, Heather M '07 %Willkie F&G LLP -787 7th Av -NY 10019
(212) 269-4310 ..**Schneider**, Herbert A '60 (Frankenthaler KS&K) -420 Lex Av -NY 10170
(212) 589-6266 ..**Schneider**, Howard '60 Man Financial,Inc -717 5th Av -NY 10022
(212) 878-4167 ..**Schneider**, Iris '86 %Mitsui & Co -200 Park Av -NY 10166 **Fx**:878-6718
(516) 496-0618 ..**Schneider**, Isabel A '95 -6 Convent Ct -Syosset 11791
(212) 553-9215 ..**Schneider**, Ivan S '54 IS Schneider PC -233 Bway -NY 10279 **Fx**:227-8763
(518) 434-5267 ..**Schneider**, Jane B '73 %Albany Comm Dvlpmnt Agency -200 Henry Johnson Blvd -Albany 12210
(212) 593-4683 ..**Schneider**, Jeffrey G '88 Schneider Legal Srch -1230 Av of Amer -NY 10020 **Fx**:(917) 639-4370

(212) 918-3000 .. **Schneider,** Jeffrey G '99 (Hogan L LLP) -875 3rd Av -NY 10022
(212) 818-9600 .. **Schneider,** Jeffrey H '70 (Greenfield S&S,LLP) -600 3rd Av -NY 10016
(212) 571-5500 .. **Schneider,** Jeremy '78 (Rothman SS&S,LLP) -100 Lafayette -NY 10013
(212) 468-4800 .. **Schneider,** Jesse B '99 Cnsl Davis & G LLP -1740 Bway -NY 10019
(631) 753-2823 .. **Schneider,** Jill '95 PricewaterhouseCoopers LLP -401 Broadhllw Rd -Melvll 11747
(212) 756-2000 .. **Schneider,** Jos D '05 %Schulte R&Z LLP -919 3rd Av -NY 10022
(516) 921-2525 .. **Schneider,** Joy Woda '92 %McHenry H&L,PC -6800 Jericho Tpk -Syosset 11791
(212) 703-7157 .. **Schneider,** Kathryn E '92 ACE Grp Holdings,Inc -1133 Av of Amer -NY 10036
(212) 964-4717 .. **Schneider Kaufman & Sherman** -233 Bway -NY 10279
(212) 373-3000 .. **Schneider,** Kenneth M '85 (Paul WRW&G LLP) -1285 Av of Amer -NY 10019
(212) 734-2297 .. **Schneider,** Kenneth P '79 -500 E 77th -NY 10162 **Fx:**734-2297
(212) 468-7767 .. **Schneider,** Lee A '92 %BNY ConvergEx -1633 Bway -NY 10019
(212) 770-1943 .. **Schneider,** Leslie R '88 %AIG -80 Pine -NY 10005 **Fx:**809-2452
(212) 859-8000 .. **Schneider,** Lisa Mandell '03 %Fried FHS&J LLP -1 NY Plz -NY 10004
(516) 662-9723 .. **Schneider,** Lisa S '89 -3601 Hempstd Tpk -Levittwn 11756
(212) 878-3500 .. **Schneider,** Marc E '90 Avenue Capital Grp -535 Mad Av -NY 10022
(516) 393-5555 .. **Schneider,** Marc H '94 (Schneider M LLP) -666 Old Cntry Rd -Gdn Cty 11530 **Fx:**393-5556
(212) 661-6800 .. **Schneider,** Marc J '86 OfCnsl Cyruli SH&Z LLP -420 Lex Av -NY 10170
(518) 566-6666 .. **Schneider,** Mark A '99 -57 Court -Plattsbrgh 12901 **Fx:**566-6667
(212) 480-6783 .. **Schneider,** Martin B '83 %DHCR -25 Beaver -NY 10004 **Fx:**480-7416
(212) 935-8808 .. **Schneider,** Martin H '49 -110 E 59th -NY 10022 **Fx:**753-2750
(212) 468-4800 .. **Schneider,** Matthew B '00 (Davis & G LLP) -1740 Bway -NY 10019
(212) 756-2000 .. **Schneider,** Matthew D '09 %Schulte R&Z LLP -919 3rd Av -NY 10022
(212) 566-2113 .. **Schneider,** Matthew S '09 %Linowes Law Firm -150 Bway -NY 10038 **Fx:**566-2114
(212) 969-3000 .. **Schneider,** Matthew S '09 %Proskauer R LLP -1585 Bway -NY 10036
(212) 857-0100 .. **Schneider,** Michl B '03 Blesso Properties -320 W 13th -NY 10014 **Fx:**857-0110
(718) 330-1200 .. **Schneider,** Michl K '93 %Fed Def of NY Inc -1 Pierrepont Plz -Brklyn 11201 **Fx:**855-0760
(212) 252-0004 .. **Schneider,** Michl R '99 %Carroll M&K LLC -570 Lex Av -NY 10022
(212) 888-2100 .. **Schneider,** Michl S '86 -444 Mad Av -NY 10022 **Fx:**888-7306
(212) 859-8000 .. **Schneider,** Michl T '07 %Fried FHS&J LLP -1 NY Plz -NY 10004
(315) 682-9731 .. **Schneider,** Michelle C '98 -300 S State -Syracuse 13202
(845) 496-0355 .. **Schneider,** Nancy J '83 -22 North -Washingtnvll 10992 **Fx:**496-7580
(914) 366-6445 .. **Schneider,** Nathaniel '83 Select Fincl Srvcs -303 S Bway -Tarrytwn 10591 **Fx:**366-6444
(518) 622-2123 .. **Schneider,** Patricia G '96 (Schneider & Assoc,PLLC) -130 Main -Cairo 12413 **Fx:**622-2594
(631) 777-3519 .. **Schneider,** Paul B '94 P Schneider,PC -445 Broad Hollow Rd -Melvll 11747 **Fx:**536-2239
(516) 747-0300 .. **Schneider,** Peter A '75 (Meltzer LG&B,LLP) -190 Willis Av -Mineola 11501
(212) 629-7744 .. **Schneider Pfahl & Rahmé LLP** -2 Park Av -NY 10016 **Fx:**(646) 514-0297
(212) 883-6500 .. **Schneider,** Reed G '78 SpclCnsl Podell SS&B,LLP -605 3rd Av -NY 10158
(516) 832-7701 .. **Schneider,** Robt '60 -1600 Stewart -Westbury 11590 **Fx:**832-9091
(212) 751-3709 .. **Schneider,** Robt A '80 -301 E 48th -NY 10017 **Fx:**755-3176
(914) 761-1300 .. **Schneider,** Robt C '80 %Cuddy & F LLP -445 Hmltn Av -White Plns 10601
(914) 946-2828 .. **Schneider,** Robt G '74 -576 Kimball Av -Ynkrs 10704
(212) 986-6000 .. **Schneider,** Robt S '67 (Kleinberg KW&C,PC) -551 5th Av -NY 10176
(212) 878-8000 .. **Schneider,** Robyn J '01 %Clifford C LLP -31 W 52nd -NY 10019
(212) 486-9494 .. **Schneider,** Ronald G '70 -488 Mad Av -NY 10022
(212) 581-3320 .. **Schneider,** Ronald R '00 %Wasserman G&R,LLP -1700 Bway -NY 10019
(212) 969-3000 .. **Schneider,** Sally L '84 %Proskauer R LLP -1585 Bway -NY 10036
(518) 589-7700 .. **Schneider,** Sarah M '07 (Simon & S,PLLC) -6193 Main Bx908 -Tannersvll 12485 **Fx:**589-4076
(718) 361-3363 .. **Schneider,** Saul C '91 -1375 Coney Isl Av -Brklyn 11230
(212) 705-7000 .. **Schneider,** Scott A '05 %Bingham M LLP -399 Park Av -NY 10022
(212) 407-4000 .. **Schneider,** Scott I '88 (Loeb & L,LLP) -345 Park Av -NY 10154
(516) 433-1555 .. **Schneider,** Scott R '91 -117 Bway -Hicksvll 11801 **Fx:**433-1511
(212) 259-8000 .. **Schneider,** Spencer H '99 %Dewey & L LLP -1301 Av of Amer -NY 10019
(212) 233-7400 .. **Schneider,** Spencer L '86 -70 Lafayette -NY 10013 **Fx:**233-9713
(212) 298-5000 .. **Schneider,** Stacy M '00 Leg Aid -199 Water -NY 10038
(212) 631-5851 .. **Schneider,** Stanley H '73 -535 5th Av -NY 10017
(212) 564-5332 .. **Schneider,** Stephen B '68 -350 5th Av -NY 10118 **Fx:**967-5809
(516) 569-2525 .. **Schneider,** Steven A '89 -124 Cedarhrst Av -Cedarhrst 11516 **Fx:**374-7697
(718) 248-2503 .. **Schneider,** Susan J '07 Citi Ethics Ofc -1 Court Sq -LIC 11101
(718) 447-5540 .. **Schneider,** Susan R '89 (Behrins & B,PC) -1 Edgewtr Plz -Staten Isl 10305 **Fx:**816-5483
(212) 697-0808 .. **Schneider,** Warren A '57 (Vail & S,PC) -275 Mad Av -NY 10016
(518) 447-2722 .. **Schneider,** Wayne '72 Tchrs Rtrmnt Sys -10 Corp Woods Dr -Albany 12211 **Fx:**447-2679
(516) 248-7000 .. **Schneider,** Wm Scott '88 (Albanese & A LLP) -1050 Franklin Av -Gdn Cty 11530
(718) 513-3620 .. **Schneider,** Wm Z '02 (W Schneider & Assoc,PC) -1400 Av Z -Brklyn 11235
(212) 836-8000 .. **Schneider,** Willys H '78 (Kaye S LLP) -425 Park Av -NY 10022
(917) 320-2500 .. **Schneider-Levy,** Carol R '81 %FDIC -350 5th Av -NY 10118 **Fx:**320-2917
(315) 425-9000 .. **Schneiderman,** Anne M '01 OfCnsl Marjama MB&S LLP -250 S Clinton -Syracuse 13202
(607) 227-7263 .. **Schneiderman,** Anne M '01 -102 E State Bx422 -Ithaca 14851 **Fx:**(815) 361-9050
(718) 268-1500 .. **Schneiderman,** Jos '74 J Schneiderman & Assoc -125-10 Qns Blvd -Kew Gdns 11415 **Fx:**268-5179
(718) 522-3333 .. **Schneiderman,** Martha '91 Childrens Law Ctr -44 Court -Brklyn 11201
(212) 954-3767 .. **Schneiderman,** Paul N '89 %KPMG -757 3rd Av -NY 10017
(212) 574-1200 .. **Schneidman,** Douglas P '99 %Seward & K LLP -1 Bttry Pk Plz -NY 10004
(212) 526-7304 .. **Schneidman,** Jon B '01 Lehman Brothers -399 Park Av -NY 10022
(718) 286-6000 .. **Schneidmill,** Naomi K '06 %DA -125-01 Qns Blvd -Kew Gdns 11415
(212) 878-8000 .. **Schneier,** Adrienne N '05 %Clifford C LLP -31 W 52nd -NY 10019
(516) 561-7766 .. **Schneier,** Alan N '77 (McKenna & S) -Bx250 -Vly Stream 11582 **Fx:**561-7793
(212) 492-4555 .. **Schneier,** Alan S '75 %Deloitte & Touche LLP -1633 Bway -NY 10019
(212) 752-1000 .. **Schneier,** Murray D '91 (Eiseman LL&K,PC) -805 3rd Av -NY 10022
(212) 417-5776 .. **Schneier,** Roger '75 %Dept of State Ofc of Admin Hearings -123 William -NY 10038 **Fx:**417-4678
(212) 489-8230 .. **Schneier,** Sharon '86 (Davis WT LLP) -1633 Bway -NY 10019
(212) 735-3000 .. **Schneirov,** Allison R '92 (Skadden ASM&F LLP) -4 Times Sq -NY 10036
(716) 693-0070 .. **Schnell,** David R '85 Schnell & S,PC -156 Delaware -Tonawanda 14150 **Fx:**693-5216
(212) 735-3000 .. **Schnell,** Douglas K '06 %Skadden ASM&F LLP -4 Times Sq -NY 10036
(646) 394-7352 .. **Schnell,** Erica K '06 PricewaterhouseCoopers LLP -300 Mad Av -NY 10017
(212) 350-2700 .. **Schnell,** Gordon '92 (Constantine C,PC) -450 Lex Av -NY 10017
(212) 966-8900 .. **Schnell,** Laura S '85 (Eisenberg & S,LLP) -233 Bway -NY 10279
(716) 373-1176 .. **Schnell,** Linda M '03 -201 N Union -Olean 14760
(212) 735-3000 .. **Schnell,** Paul T '81 (Skadden ASM&F LLP) -4 Times Sq -NY 10036
(518) 562-0600 .. **Schneller,** Dean C '08 O'Connell & A -206 W Bay Plz -Plattsbrgh 12901
(212) 858-1000 .. **Schneller,** Douglas J '93 (Pillsbury WSP LLP) -1540 Bway -NY 10036
(914) 328-0074 .. **Schnelwar,** Philip G '71 -5 Waller Av -White Plns 10601 **Fx:**949-0672
(518) 329-4520 .. **Schnepf,** George J '97 -2877 Cnty Route 7 Bx470 -Copake 12516
(516) 542-5900 .. **Schnepp,** Chas M Jr. '84 (Congdon FORDT&F) -333 Earle Ovngton Blvd -Uniondale 11553
(516) 357-3000 .. **Schnepper,** Michl B '08 %Rivkin R LLP -926 RXR Plz -Uniondale 11556
(718) 961-7442 .. **Schneps,** Barry C '84 -4160 Main -Flushng 11355
(212) 581-3320 .. **Schneps,** Jonathan M '86 OfCnsl Wasserman G&R,LLP -1700 Bway -NY 10019
(631) 722-5100 .. **Schneps,** Murray B '62 -5 Lyn Ln -Baiting Hollow 11933 **Fx:**722-5093
(516) 365-3000 .. **Schneps,** Robt L '83 (Levy & S,PC) -1615 Nrthrn Blvd -Manhsst 11030
(646) 502-7191 .. **Schneur,** Eugene '99 (Omni NY LLC) -885 2nd Av -NY 10017
(212) 508-6745 .. **Schneyer,** Richd E '72 (Tannenbaum HS&H LLP) -900 3rd Av -NY 10022 **Fx:**937-4613
(212) 986-7150 .. **Schnier,** Andrew M '73 -250 Park Av -NY 10177 **Fx:**661-8368
(212) 850-1802 .. **Schnier,** David J '02 J&W Seligman -100 Park Av -NY 10017
(212) 986-7150 .. **Schnier,** Krystyna '86 %A Schnier -250 Park Av -NY 10177 **Fx:**661-8368
(212) 816-3158 .. **Schnipper,** Danl R '98 Citigroup -388 Greenwich -NY 10013
(516) 832-7518 .. **Schnipper,** Michl I '05 %Nixon P LLP -50 Jericho Quadrangle -Jericho 11753
(212) 309-8100 .. **Schnipper,** Rhonda Ebert '97 %Lexis/Nexis -125 Park Av -NY 10017 **Fx:**309-8187
(716) 854-2620 .. **Schnitter,** Jos M '80 (Brown & K,LLP) -1500 Lbrty Bldg -Buffalo 14202
(631) 423-0893 .. **Schnittman,** Barry '76 (Schnittman & S) -56 Melrose Rd -Dix Hlls 11746
(718) 625-8940 .. **Schnittman,** Eric A '83 %B Lawrence -15 Metrotech Ctr N -Brklyn 11201 **Fx:**624-5756
(585) 324-5704 .. **Schnittman,** Michl S '70 (Lacy K LLP) -130 E Main -Rchstr 14604 **Fx:**269-3065
(631) 423-0893 .. **Schnittman,** Steven N '76 (Schnittman & S) -56 Melrose Rd -Dix Hlls 11746
(212) 687-2961 .. **Schnitzer,** Alan D '92 Travelers Cos -485 Lex Av -NY 10017
(212) 478-7200 .. **Schnitzer,** Edw L '98 (Hahn & H LLP) -488 Mad Av -NY 10022
(718) 319-8902 .. **Schnitzer,** Howard B '82 (Kafko S) -7 Hugh Grant Cir -Bronx 10462 **Fx:**319-8915
(631) 694-2300 .. **Schnitzer,** Lauren R '08 %Lamb & B,LLP -534 Broadhllw Rd Bx9034 -Melvll 11747
(516) 621-0600 .. **Schnitzer,** Michl S '91 -69 Roslyn Rd -Roslyn Hts 11577
(716) 487-3332 .. **Schnizler,** Robt W '88 -Bx792 -Jamestwn 14702
(718) 722-5300 .. **Schnock,** John K '85 %Independence Svngs Bk -195 Montague -Brklyn 11201 **Fx:**722-5381
(212) 816-9359 .. **Schnoll,** Melanie Caren '95 Citigroup -388 Greenwich -NY 10013
(212) 788-3980 .. **Schnuer,** Jessica A '03 Admin Children's Srvcs -220 Church -NY 10013
(516) 932-4400 .. **Schnur,** Bradley D '98 (B Schnur,PC) -380 N Bway -Jericho 11753 **Fx:**932-9195
(212) 250-0689 .. **Schnur,** Margo E '95 %Deutsche Bank -60 Wall -NY 10005
(212) 885-5000 .. **Schnur,** Peter '94 (Blank R LLP) -405 Lex Av -NY 10174
(212) 668-0059 .. **Schnurman,** Alan J '72 (Zalman & S) -61 Bway -NY 10006
(212) 668-0059 .. **Schnurman,** David A '07 %Zalman & S -61 Bway -NY 10006
(716) 856-6086 .. **Schnurr,** Jeremy M '82 (Tiernan K&S) -110 Pearl -Buffalo 14202
(516) 877-5600 .. **Schnurr,** Jos T '78 Cnsl R Tusa -1225 Franklin Av -Gdn Cty 11530 **Fx:**877-5779
(212) 382-6600 .. **Schnurr,** Julia E '96 %NYC Bar -42 W 44th -NY 10036 **Fx:**398-6634
(212) 306-7160 .. **Schnurr,** Rory G '99 %Ofc Cllctv Brgn -40 Rector -NY 10006 **Fx:**306-7167
(212) 474-1000 .. **Schobel,** Michl J '10 %Cravath S&M LLP -825 8th Av -NY 10019
(716) 856-4000 .. **Schober,** Gary M '80 (Hodgson R LLP) -140 Pearl -Buffalo 14202

(716) 366-3075 .. **Schober,** John J '83 (Schober & S) -625 Central Av -Dunkirk 14048 **Fx:**366-3072
(716) 366-3075 .. **Schober,** Wm F '83 (Schober & S) -625 Central Av -Dunkirk 14048 **Fx:**366-3072
(212) 766-1427 .. **Schochat,** Harry '83 -325 Bway -NY 10007 **Fx:**571-7004
(212) 736-3250 .. **Schochet,** Brian '81 (Toberoff T&S,LLP) -330 7th Av -NY 10001
(212) 801-6833 .. **Schochet,** Howard S '97 (Greenberg T,LLP) -200 Park Av -NY 10166
(212) 907-0864 .. **Schochet,** Ira A '83 (Labaton S LLP) -140 Bway -NY 10005
(313) 496-7636 .. **Schochet,** P Rivka '89 (Miller CP&S,PLLC) -500 5th Av -NY 10110 **Fx:**496-8454
(212) 344-8000 .. **Schochet,** Schneur Zalman '00 (Altman & S LLP) -225 Bway -NY 10007
(518) 435-9360 .. **Schockmel,** Keith F '84 -4 Atrium Dr -Albany 12205
(212) 848-4000 .. **Schodek,** Ned S '03 %Shearman & S LLP -599 Lex Av -NY 10022
(212) 577-3688 .. **Schoeffel,** John C '97 %Leg Aid -199 Water -NY 10038 **Fx:**509-8431
(716) 853-8400 .. **Schoellkopf,** Thos J '91 %Dept of Law -350 Main Pl Twr -Buffalo 14202 **Fx:**853-8571
(716) 551-4221 .. **Schoellkopf,** Wm C '88 Hon JT Curtin -68 Court -Buffalo 14202
(212) 661-5030 .. **Schoeman,** Michl E '62 (Schoeman U&K,LLP) -60 E 42nd -NY 10165
(212) 715-9100 .. **Schoeman,** Paul H '96 (Kramer LN&F,LLP) -1177 Av of Amer -NY 10036
(212) 661-5030 .. **Schoeman, Updike & Kaufman,LLP** -60 E 42nd -NY 10165 **Fx:**687-2123
(716) 858-2424 .. **Schoemick,** John G '94 %DA -25 Delaware Av -Buffalo 14202 **Fx:**858-7425
(212) 859-3954 .. **Schoen,** Cristina M '01 US Aviation -199 Water -NY 10038
(631) 421-0700 .. **Schoen,** David I '80 (Schoen & S,LLP) -52 Elm -Huntngtn 11743
(516) 561-4230 .. **Schoen,** David M '97 -246 Rockaway Av -Vly Stream 11580
(631) 907-3500 .. **Schoen,** Denise R '98 (Tarbet L&S) -524 Montauk Hwy Bx2635 -Amagansett 11930 **Fx:**907-3501
(212) 534-4000 .. **Schoen,** Douglas E '81 (Penn Schoen & Berland Assoc, Inc) -245 E 92nd -NY 10128
(212) 534-4000 .. **Schoen,** Douglas E '02 Penn Schoen & Berland Assoc, Inc -245 E 92nd -NY 10128 **Fx:**360-7423
(718) 625-2200 .. **Schoen,** Estella J '00 Bklyn Law Schl -250 Joralemon -Brklyn 11201 **Fx:**780-0393
(646) 366-5500 .. **Schoen,** Frank X '06 1st Solar,Inc -620 8th Av -NY 10018
(212) 474-1000 .. **Schoen,** George F '99 (Cravath S&M LLP) -825 8th Av -NY 10019
(212) 742-9280 .. **Schoen,** Jeffrey R '00 Waterfront Comm -39 Bway -NY 10006 **Fx:**480-0587
(212) 902-3070 .. **Schoen,** Karen A '03 Goldman Sachs & Co -85 Broad -NY 10004
(212) 268-7535 .. **Schoen,** Kenneth A '89 (Bonner KT&C,LLP) -350 5th Av -NY 10118
(212) 790-4500 .. **Schoen,** Lindsay M '99 %Manatt P&P,LLP -7 Times Sq -NY 10036
(212) 566-7500 .. **Schoen,** Matthew S '09 Douglas & L -111 John -NY 10038
(518) 474-0871 .. **Schoen,** Neal W '77 %DMV -6 ESP -Albany 12228 **Fx:**486-4485
(631) 421-0700 .. **Schoen & Strassman,LLP** -52 Elm -Huntngtn 11743 **Fx:**421-0324
(516) 766-7007 .. **Schoen & Strassman,LLP** -11 Clinton Av -Rockvll Ctr 11570 **Fx:**(631) 421-0324
(212) 355-6182 .. **Schoen,** Wendy L '92 %EP Dine Inc -115 E 57th -NY 10022 **Fx:**755-8486
(212) 346-2400 .. **Schoenbach,** Lawr H '81 -111 Bway -NY 10006 **Fx:**346-4665
(212) 986-4888 .. **Schoenberg,** Bruce A '89 (Schrader & S,LLP) -711 3rd Av -NY 10017
(212) 506-2500 .. **Schoenberg,** Clifford H '76 (Mayer B LLP) -1675 Bway -NY 10019
(212) 545-4785 .. **Schoenberg,** Debra M '02 %Wolf HAF&H LLP -270 Mad Av -NY 10016
(718) 876-6300 .. **Schoenberg,** Karen '81 %DA -130 Styvsnt Pl -Staten Isl 10301
(516) 227-0700 .. **Schoenberg,** Michl A H '04 %Farrell F,PC -1320 RXR Plz -Uniondale 11556
(845) 695-6811 .. **Schoenberg,** Richd B '93 %MA Bjork -100 Crystal Run Rd -Middletwn 10941 **Fx:**695-6818
(516) 693-0222 .. **Schoenberg,** Ronald L '71 -200 Willis -Mineola 11501
(845) 638-5240 .. **Schoenberger,** Arielle N '06 %Hon C Apotheker -1 S Main -New Cty 10956
(845) 356-6700 .. **Schoenberger,** Ilan '72 (Schoenberger & S) -272 Route 59 -Spg Vly 10977 **Fx:**356-6704
(845) 356-6700 .. **Schoenberger,** Rhoda F '80 (Schoenberger & S) -272 Route 59 -Spg Vly 10977 **Fx:**356-6704
(718) 459-7710 .. **Schoenberger,** Stuart J '83 Panache Enterprises,LLC -63-84 Saunders -Rego Pk 11374 **Fx:**459-4946
(716) 856-0024 .. **Schoenborn,** Danl L '73 (DeMarie & S,PC) -800 Convntn Twr -Buffalo 14202
(716) 854-3455 .. **Schoenborn,** Holly L '03 %Gielowski F&C,LLP -135 Delaware Av -Buffalo 14202 **Fx:**854-2797
(716) 853-8500 .. **Schoenborn,** Margot Penfold '01 %Medicaid Fraud Cntrl -350 Main Pl Twr -Buffalo 14202 **Fx:**853-8525
(716) 856-0024 .. **Schoenborn,** Sean D '02 (DeMarie & S,PC) -800 Convntn Twr -Buffalo 14202
(212) 431-2339 .. **Schoenbrod,** David '71 %NY Law Schl -185 W Bway -NY 10013 **Fx:**431-9205
(212) 277-6500 .. **Schoenbrun,** Gary L '84 (Dickstein S LLP) -1633 Bway -NY 10019
(914) 946-1400 .. **Schoene,** Ralph F '79 (Vouté LM&C,LLP) -170 Hmltn Av -White Plns 10601
(585) 396-4411 .. **Schoeneman,** Andrea J '00 %Cnty Atty -27 N Main -Canandaigua 14424 **Fx:**396-4481
(212) 397-5584 .. **Schoenfarber,** Jay A '97 Soros Fund Mgmt LLC -888 7th Av -NY 10106
(212) 230-8800 .. **Schoenfeld,** Alan E '07 %WilmerHale -399 Park Av -NY 10022
(718) 875-1300 .. **Schoenfeld,** Bradley S '03 %Appllt Div 2nd Dept -45 Monroe Pl -Brklyn 11201 **Fx:**858-2446
(212) 509-0500 .. **Schoenfeld,** Eric B '73 (Schoenfeld M,PC) -61 Bway -NY 10006
(212) 508-6700 .. **Schoenfeld,** Eric S '91 (Tannenbaum HS&H LLP) -900 3rd Av -NY 10022
(212) 754-7000 .. **Schoenfeld,** Glenn E '98 Cnsl Danziger D&M -405 Park Av -NY 10022 **Fx:**758-0143
(631) 673-5004 .. **Schoenfeld,** Harris '58 (Schoenfeld S&P,PC) -999 Walt Whitman Rd -Melvll 11747 **Fx:**673-9031
(212) 542-7207 .. **Schoenfeld,** Henry '74 Cnsl HUD -26 Fed Plz -NY 10278
(718) 262-0300 .. **Schoenfeld,** Howard K '72 -85-66 159th -Jamaica Hll 11432
(212) 509-3900 .. **Schoenfeld,** Joel M '77 (Mitchell S&K LLP) -12 E 49th -NY 10017
(212) 964-5313 .. **Schoenfeld,** Lawr R '74 -305 Bway -NY 10007 **Fx:**732-5486
(516) 877-1800 .. **Schoenfeld,** Lisa R '03 (Schlissel OK,PLLC) -200 Grdn City Plz -Gdn Cty 11530
(212) 465-6000 .. **Schoenfeld,** Marc J '90 %Madison Sq Grdn,LP -2 Penn Plz -NY 10121 **Fx:**465-6011
(631) 673-5004 .. **Schoenfeld,** Michl P '58 (Schoenfeld S&P,PC) -999 Walt Whitman Rd -Melvll 11747 **Fx:**673-9031
(212) 509-0500 .. **Schoenfeld Moreland,PC** -61 Bway -NY 10006 **Fx:**363-2909
(212) 381-5963 .. **Schoenfeld,** Pamela '91 Doubleclick Inc -111 8th Av -NY 10011
(516) 621-1517 .. **Schoenfeld,** Richd B '96 -1500 Old Nrthrn Blvd -Roslyn 11576
(631) 673-5004 .. **Schoenfeld,** Robin B '88 %Schoenfeld S&P,PC -999 Walt Whitman Rd -Melvll 11747 **Fx:**673-9031
(212) 884-9074 .. **Schoenfeld,** Sage L '92 SCOR Re -1 Seaport Plz -NY 10038
(212) 415-9200 .. **Schoenfeld,** Steven R '91 (Dorsey & W LLP) -250 Park Av -NY 10177
(516) 931-8100 .. **Schoenfeld,** Stuart H '86 (Capell BM&S,LLP) -100 Jericho Quadrangle -Jericho 11753
(914) 725-5161 .. **Schoenfeld,** Susan R '85 -106 Highland Rd -Scarsdale 10583
(212) 351-4000 .. **Schoenfeldt,** Brad L '09 Gibson D&C LLP -200 Park Av -NY 10166
(212) 964-0046 .. **Schoengold & Sporn,PC** -19 Fulton -NY 10038 **Fx:**267-8137
(516) 663-6600 .. **Schoenhaar,** David R '08 %Ruskin MF,PC -1425 RXR Plz -Uniondale 11556
(212) 557-4000 .. **Schoenig,** John A '03 %Grunfeld DLS&K LLP -399 Park Av -NY 10022
(212) 349-6775 .. **Schoenman,** Edw M '78 (Peltz & W) -222 Bway -NY 10038
(212) 728-8000 .. **Schoenmann,** Derek M '04 %Willkie F&G LLP -787 7th Av -NY 10019
(212) 421-4100 .. **Schoenstein,** Richd C '91 (Pryor C LLP) -7 Times Sq -NY 10036
(212) 918-3000 .. **Schoenthal,** Allison J '01 (Hogan L LLP) -875 3rd Av -NY 10022
(631) 423-7373 .. **Schoenwald,** David J '80 (Schoenwald & S,PC) -150 Broadhllw Rd -Melvll 11747 **Fx:**423-7393
(315) 474-2943 .. **Schoenwald,** Donald L '56 OfCnsl Sugarman Law Firm,LLP -211 W Jffrsn -Syracuse 13202
(212) 460-3143 .. **Schoenwetter,** Sara '79 Con Ed -4 Irving Pl -NY 10003 **Fx:**677-5850
(518) 474-6623 .. **Schoep,** Nancy E '88 %Insurance Dept -99 Wshngtn Av -Albany 12257 **Fx:**474-5473
(716) 882-5868 .. **Schoepperle,** Susan Westbrook '89 -760 Potomac Av -Buffalo 14209
(845) 624-1041 .. **Schoeps,** Ira '91 (Schoeps & S) -334 S Mddltwn Rd -Nanuet 10954 **Fx:**624-1049
(516) 496-3500 .. **Schoer,** Gary '76 -6800 Jericho Tpk -Syosset 11791 **Fx:**496-3530
(716) 856-8111 .. **Schoetz,** Kenneth A '85 Empire State Dvlpmnt Corp -95 Perry -Buffalo 14203
(718) 852-0900 .. **Schoffman,** Michl D '74 -26 Court -Brklyn 11242 **Fx:**852-1895
(845) 638-3240 .. **Schofield,** Eileen M '83 (Schofield S&C,LLP) -9 Elyse Dr -New Cty 10956
(845) 638-3240 .. **Schofield,** John P '58 (Schofield S&C,LLP) -9 Elyse Dr -New Cty 10956
(212) 909-6000 .. **Schofield,** Lorna '82 (Debevoise & P LLP) -919 3rd Av -NY 10022
(845) 638-3240 .. **Schofield,** Paul K '88 (Schofield S&C,LLP) -9 Elyse Dr -New Cty 10956
(518) 487-7600 .. **Schofield,** Robt T IV '97 (Whiteman O&H LLP) -1 Commerce Plz -Albany 12260
(607) 622-5099 .. **Schofield,** Sarah Falk '00 -Bx829 -Bath 14810
(845) 638-3240 .. **Schofield Schofield & Cosgrove,LLP** -9 Elyse Dr -New Cty 10956
(716) 856-3500 .. **Schofield,** Thos E '76 (Magavern MG LLP) -1100 Rand Bldg -Buffalo 14203
(585) 325-7455 .. **Schofield,** Timothy J '81 OfCnsl Philippone Law Ofc,PC -31 E Main -Rchstr 14608 **Fx:**546-6565
(212) 402-9400 .. **Schofield Baker,** Ann '98 (McKool S,PC) -1 Bryant Park -NY 10036
(212) 264-8062 .. **Schofield-Lake,** Jennifer '93 US HUD -26 Fed Plz -NY 10278
(212) 735-3000 .. **Schohn,** Erica F '04 %Skadden ASM&F LLP -4 Times Sq -NY 10036
(212) 370-1300 .. **Schole,** Allen '87 (Ellenoff G&S LLP) -150 E 42nd -NY 10017
(212) 532-1934 .. **Scholem,** Jeremy D '09 J Kousouros -260 Mad Av -NY 10016 **Fx:**532-1939
(315) 435-2470 .. **Scholl,** Bridget A '00 %DA -505 S State -Syracuse 13202 **Fx:**435-3969
(718) 667-0626 .. **Scholl,** Gerola Aloisi '93 -139 Riedel Av -Staten Isl 10306 **Fx:**667-1089
(718) 884-7654 .. **Scholl,** Judith T '76 -2575 Palisade Av -Bronx 10463 **Fx:**(347) 964-6388
(212) 335-9324 .. **Scholl,** Marc F '79 %DA -1 Hogan Pl -NY 10013
(646) 594-0298 .. **Scholtz,** Otto R '98 (Rearden Cptl Mgmt LLC) -171 E 77th -NY 10075
(212) 412-9500 .. **Scholz,** Andrew J '02 %Flemming ZWZ LLP -1 Lbrty Plz -NY 10006
(212) 609-6800 .. **Scholz,** Jos R '93 (McCarter & E,LLP) -245 Park Av -NY 10167
(212) 788-7001 .. **Schomburg,** Aysha E '09 NY City Council -250 Bway -NY 10007
(212) 619-5400 .. **Schomer,** Jesse Danl '09 %Newman F LLP -1250 Bway -NY 10001
(212) 547-5400 .. **Schonback,** Danielle K '03 (McDermott W&E LLP) -340 Mad Av -NY 10173
(845) 928-3030 .. **Schonberg,** Bruce A '85 -219 Route 32 Bx194 -Centrl Vly 10917
(212) 751-3001 .. **Schonberg,** Michl E '06 (Thompson & K LLP) -919 3rd Av -NY 10022
(212) 318-6000 .. **Schonberger,** Mark '80 (Paul HJ&W LLP) -75 E 55th -NY 10022
Schonbrun, David I '90 -180 Beverly Rd -White Plns 10605
(914) 428-2155 .. **Schonbrun,** Helene R '94 -180 Beverly Rd -White Plns 10605
(845) 634-3245 .. **Schonbrun,** Jeffrey '98 -14 S Main -New Cty 10956 **Fx:**634-3247
(631) 580-3400 .. **Schondebare,** James A '74 (Schondebare & K) -3555 Vets Mem'l Hwy -Ronkonkoma 11779 **Fx:**581-3030
(718) 896-9600 .. **Schonfeld,** Bennet L '95 %Algin Mgmt Co,LLC -64-35 Yllwstn Blvd -Frst Hlls 11375 **Fx:**997-8084
(516) 569-5001 .. **Schonfeld,** Esther M '00 (Schonfeld & G,LLP) -112 Spruce -Cedarhrst 11516
(516) 569-5001 .. **Schonfeld & Goldring, LLP** -112 Spruce -Cedarhrst 11516 **Fx:**569-3360
(845) 222-7134 .. **Schonfeld,** Jerry Y '84 -430 Route 306 -Monsey 10952
(212) 344-1600 .. **Schonfeld,** Joel '59 (Schonfeld & W) -80 Wall -NY 10005 **Fx:**480-0717

(212) 233-1433 .. **Schonfeld,** Kenneth M '92 (Schonfeld & U) -299 Bway -NY 10007 **Fx:**571-5340
(212) 351-4000 .. **Schonfeld,** Mark K '89 (Gibson D&C LLP) -200 Park Av -NY 10166
(516) 873-2000 .. **Schonfeld,** Robt L '78 OfCnsl Moritt HH&H LLP -400 Grdn City Plz -Gdn Cty 11530
(212) 290-4000 .. **Schonfeld,** Samantha Fisherman '01 OfCnsl Ebert & Assoc,LLC -110 E 30th -NY 10016 **Fx:**290-1717
(212) 796-8914 .. **Schonfeld,** Simcha D '04 (Koss & S,LLP) -500 5th Av -NY 10110 **Fx:**(801) 650-8733
(212) 728-8000 .. **Schonholtz,** Margot B '80 (Willkie F&G LLP) -787 7th Av -NY 10019
(212) 209-3090 .. **Schonwald,** Gary A '67 Cnsl Reitler K&R LLC -885 3rd Av -NY 10022
(718) 694-4667 .. **Schoolman,** Richd '72 %Transit Auth -130 Lvngstn -Brklyn 11201 **Fx:**694-5726
(716) 856-5800 .. **Schoonmaker,** Duane D '86 %J Greco & Assoc,PLLC -14 Lafayette Sq -Buffalo 14203 **Fx:**856-5801
(212) 773-6014 .. **Schoonmaker,** Michl T '00 Ernst & Young LLP -5 Times Sq -NY 10036 **Fx:**773-1888
(212) 446-7147 .. **Schoor,** Asher '04 McKinsey & Co -55 E 52nd -NY 10055 **Fx:**688-9521
(212) 407-8080 .. **Schoor-Rube,** Danl A '92 NBA -645 5th Av -NY 10022
(716) 200-5050 .. **Schop,** Stephen J '86 (Harris B PLLC) -726 Exchange -Buffalo 14210
(518) 266-1000 .. **Schopf,** Jonathan G '05 %Pattison SG&G,PC -22 1st Bx208 -Troy 12181
(845) 454-2540 .. **Schopfer,** Jana M '07 %Brooke & B,LLP -31 Cllgvw Av -Poughkeepsie 12603 **Fx:**454-2542
(716) 687-3465 .. **Schopp,** Carolyn C '02 %Fisher-Price,Inc -636 Girard Av -E Aurora 14052
(716) 853-9555 .. **Schopp,** David C '83 %Leg Aid -237 Main -Buffalo 14203 **Fx:**853-3219
(516) 294-5432 .. **Schoppmann,** Michl J '94 (Kern AC&S,PC) -1325 Franklin Av -Gdn Cty 11530
(516) 921-2525 .. **Schor,** Alise B '92 %McHenry H&L,PC -6800 Jericho Tpk -Syosset 11791
(516) 837-8000 .. **Schor,** C Glenn '73 -200 Grdn City Plz -Gdn Cty 11530
(516) 746-5599 .. **Schor,** Danl J '10 %Bee RFH&D,LLP -170 Old Cntry Rd -Mineola 11501
(212) 999-5800 .. **Schor,** Gideon A '90 (Wilson SG&R) -1301 Av of Americas -NY 10019
(516) 837-8010 .. **Schor,** Michl I '96 The Treeline Cos -200 Grdn City Plz -Gdn Cty 11530 **Fx:**837-8500
(718) 590-2000 .. **Schordine,** Michl J '09 %DA -198 E 161st -Bronx 10451 **Fx:**590-6477
(212) 228-7851 .. **Schore,** Roger E '88 -545 E 14th -NY 10009
(212) 643-8811 .. **Schorr,** Andrew W '90 Cnsl W Midtown Mgmt Grp -505 8th Av -NY 10018 **Fx:**643-9440
(212) 451-3000 .. **Schorr,** Brian L '83 Trian Fund Mgmt,LP -280 Park Av -NY 10017 **Fx:**451-3216
(212) 949-4430 .. **Schorr,** David E '00 Schorr Assoc -171 Mad Av -NY 10016
(212) 918-3000 .. **Schorr,** Edw T '86 (Hogan L LLP) -875 3rd Av -NY 10022
(212) 456-6608 .. **Schorr,** Elizabeth L '88 %ABC -77 W 66th -NY 10023 **Fx:**456-6202
(212) 670-0155 .. **Schorr,** Jonathan A '84 %Merrill Lynch -222 Bway -NY 10038
(212) 525-5096 .. **Schorr,** Jonathan M '89 %HSBC -452 5th Av -NY 10018
(212) 801-2121 .. **Schorr,** Katherine S '09 %Greenberg T,LLP -200 Park Av -NY 10166
(607) 763-9200 .. **Schorr,** Lawr J '82 SpclCnsl Levene G&T,LLP -BxF-1706 -Bnghmtn 13902
(718) 928-3700 .. **Schorr,** Nanette H '83 %LSNYC-Bronx -579 Courtlandt Av -Bronx 10451 **Fx:**402-7586
(212) 715-9100 .. **Schorr,** Naomi '84 SpclCnsl Kramer LN&F,LLP -1177 Av of Amer -NY 10036
(212) 768-3878 .. **Schorr,** Thos E '89 (Smith SWH&B,LLP) -100 Park Av -NY 10017
(914) 328-8610 .. **Schorsch,** Walter B '63 -6 Chester Av -White Plns 10601 **Fx:**428-2647
(212) 921-2200 .. **Schott,** Joshua H '94 %Update Staffing -1140 Av of Amer -NY 10036
(212) 806-5400 .. **Schott,** Michelle H '03 %Stroock &S&L LLP -180 Maiden Ln -NY 10038
(212) 362-0553 .. **Schottenstein,** Diane Steinberg '82 -165 W End Av -NY 10023
(212) 924-1220 .. **Schotzinger,** Kristianne '05 Local 237 -216 W 14th -NY 10011
(212) 508-6100 .. **Schoulder,** Andrew J '03 %Bracewell & G,LLP -1251 Av of Amer -NY 10020
(212) 806-5400 .. **Schouten,** Anthony '00 (Stroock &S&L LLP) -180 Maiden Ln -NY 10038
(212) 450-4000 .. **Schouten,** Schuyler J '08 %Davis P&W LLP -450 Lex Av -NY 10017
(212) 980-0120 .. **Schowengerdt,** John S '08 %Frankfurt KK&S,PC -488 Mad Av -NY 10022
(212) 792-6070 .. **Schpoont,** Sandra L '83 (Schpoont & C,LLP) -50 Bway -NY 10004 **Fx:**792-6071
(212) 986-4888 .. **Schrader,** David A '89 (Schrader & S,LLP) -711 3rd Av -NY 10017
(212) 468-4800 .. **Schrader,** Holly A '06 %Davis & G LLP -1740 Bway -NY 10019
(212) 827-4491 .. **Schrader,** Howard S '85 ACE Ltd -1133 Av of Amer -NY 10036
(607) 584-4900 .. **Schrader,** Kurt D '79 (Pope & S,LLP) -2 Court Bx510 -Bnghmtn 13902
(212) 801-2204 .. **Schrader,** Michl J '08 %Greenberg T,LLP -200 Park Av -NY 10166
(212) 986-4888 .. **Schrader & Schoenberg,LLP** -711 3rd Av -NY 10017 **Fx:**986-4228
(718) 286-6000 .. **Schraeter,** Paul E '84 %DA -125-01 Qns Blvd -Kew Gdns 11415
(212) 478-7200 .. **Schrag,** Alison Moore '07 %Hahn & H LLP -488 Mad Av -NY 10022
(917) 281-4826 .. **Schrag,** Benjamin P D '07 Kurtzman Carson Consultants -599 Lex Av -NY 10022
(212) 854-8123 .. **Schrag,** Naomi J '96 Columbia Univ -535 W 116th -NY 10027 **Fx:**854-1680
(212) 704-0505 .. **Schrag,** Raymond V J '74 -36 W 44th -NY 10036
(212) 692-1000 .. **Schrag,** Wm H '79 (Duane M LLP) -1540 Bway -NY 10036
(718) 858-0751 .. **Schrage,** Leon '93 -26 Court -Brklyn 11242
(212) 506-1700 .. **Schrage,** Mitchell R '76 (Kasowitz BT&F LLP) -1633 Bway -NY 10019
(212) 336-0163 .. **Schrage,** Patricia H '95 %SEC -3 World Fncl Ctr -NY 10281 **Fx:**336-1323
(212) 244-1737 .. **Schrager,** Amy H '91 -372 5th Av -NY 10018
(212) 213-0657 .. **Schrager,** Carol A '80 -404 Park Av S -NY 10016 **Fx:**689-3315
(212) 770-2459 .. **Schrager,** David '85 %AIG -80 Pine -NY 10005 **Fx:**344-2357
(212) 883-4900 .. **Schrager,** Gerald N '65 OfCnsl Cozen O -277 Park Av -NY 10172
(212) 230-2883 .. **Schrager,** Jenny S '03 %Fragomen DB&L LLP -7 Hanover Sq -NY 10004 **Fx:**223-8757
(516) 746-0707 .. **Schrager,** Merle '85 %Hammill OCDP&K,PC -6851 Jericho Tpk -Syosset 11791
(212) 661-3535 .. **Schrager,** S Robt '77 (Hodgson R LLP) -60 E 42nd -NY 10165
(718) 634-6350 .. **Schrager,** Wm G '70 -154 Beach 141st -Belle Hbr 11694
(212) 351-4500 .. **Schragin,** Howard T '98 %Epstein B&G,PC -250 Park Av -NY 10177
(212) 896-3310 .. **Schram,** Peter S '77 (PS Schram,PC) -350 Bway -NY 10013 **Fx:**896-3316
(212) 279-9090 .. **Schrama,** Martin P '98 (Stark & S) -One Penn Plz -NY 10119 **Fx:**279-9113
(212) 326-3939 .. **Schramm,** Jennifer B '09 %Jones D -222 E 41st -NY 10017
(212) 421-9630 .. **Schramm Peluso,** Amy '00 Smythe Masterson & Judd -230 Park Av -NY 10169 **Fx:**421-9665
(585) 263-1000 .. **Schraver,** David M '71 (Nixon P LLP) -1100 Clinton Sq -Rchstr 14604
(212) 574-1200 .. **Schreck,** Adam '05 %Seward & K LLP -1 Bttry Pk Plz -NY 10004
(212) 867-3838 .. **Schreck,** Danl F '05 %GO Koppell & Assoc -99 Park Av -NY 10016 **Fx:**681-0810
(212) 836-8000 .. **Schreck,** Debra E '07 %Kaye S LLP -425 Park Av -NY 10022
(212) 832-1977 .. **Schreck,** Ira '81 (Schreck RDA&H) -1790 Bway -NY 10019 **Fx:**832-2969
(212) 590-6837 .. **Schreck,** Jamie A '99 (JA Schreck,PC) -520 8th Av -NY 10018 **Fx:**643-2843
(917) 579-2613 .. **Schreck,** Mark I '95 -33 Meadow Ln -Lawrence 11559
(716) 854-2020 .. **Schreck,** Robt J '82 (Cellino & B,PC) -350 Main -Buffalo 14202
(212) 762-4000 .. **Schreck,** Sheri L '00 Morgan Stanley -1221 Av of Amer -NY 10020
(212) 422-9424 .. **Schreckinger,** Stephen P '96 %Gogick B&O,LLP -11 Bway -NY 10004
(718) 761-9300 .. **Schreffler,** Neil F '74 Vaslas LH&D LLP -201 Edward Curry Av -Staten Isl 10314
(212) 407-4000 .. **Schreger,** Ira A '76 (Loeb & L,LLP) -345 Park Av -NY 10154
(914) 640-1889 .. **Schreiber,** Ainslee A '98 %Starwood Hotels & Resorts -1111 Wstchstr Av -White Plns 10604 **Fx:**640-8250
(212) 425-7670 .. **Schreiber,** Avram H '69 -40 Exch Pl -NY 10005 **Fx:**425-9237
(516) 561-8800 .. **Schreiber,** B David '84 -366 Pearsall Av -Cedarhrst 11516 **Fx:**561-1003
(212) 593-6700 .. **Schreiber,** Barry M '72 (Aaronson RF&D,LLP) -757 3rd Av -NY 10017
(585) 546-6368 .. **Schreiber,** Burton S '54 -320 Exec Ofc Bldg -Rchstr 14614
(212) 294-6700 .. **Schreiber,** Carey D '97 (Winston & S) -200 Park Av -NY 10166
(212) 969-3000 .. **Schreiber,** Dale A '65 (Proskauer R LLP) -1585 Bway -NY 10036
(212) 559-0970 .. **Schreiber,** David L '91 -825 3rd Av -NY 10022
(212) 826-0100 .. **Schreiber,** Elliot J '83 %FSA -31 W 52nd -NY 10019 **Fx:**893-2710
(212) 425-7200 .. **Schreiber,** Eric T '07 %Kenyon & K,LLP -1 Bway -NY 10004
(212) 953-2381 .. **Schreiber,** Harlan R '01 (Rubin F&F,LLP) -292 Mad Av -NY 10017
(212) 717-2614 .. **Schreiber,** James '68 -815 Park Av -NY 10021 **Fx:**717-2072
(212) 340-0400 .. **Schreiber,** Jane R '82 %Applt Div 1st Dept -27 Mad Av -NY 10010 **Fx:**889-4412
(212) 655-3500 .. **Schreiber,** Jeffrey '91 (Meister S&F LLP) -140 E 45th -NY 10017
(212) 259-8000 .. **Schreiber,** John E '01 (Dewey & L LLP) -1301 Av of Amer -NY 10019
(718) 261-4040 .. **Schreiber,** Kenneth J '66 (Sparrow S&S) -125-10 Qns Blvd -Kew Gdns 11415
(212) 750-3100 .. **Schreiber,** Mayo Jr. '90 %Kaplan & K -767 3rd Av -NY 10017
(518) 664-2951 .. **Schreiber,** Oscar L '84 -215 Park Av -Mechanicvll 12118 **Fx:**664-1150
(212) 863-8354 .. **Schreiber,** Paul J '77 %HPD -100 Gold -NY 10038 **Fx:**863-8377
(212) 848-4000 .. **Schreiber,** Paul S '66 (Shearman & S LLP) -599 Lex Av -NY 10022
(212) 884-2122 .. **Schreiber,** Ryan A '95 New York & Co -450 W 33rd -NY 10001 **Fx:**884-2965
(212) 762-7294 .. **Schreiber,** Samantha L '00 %Morgan Stanley -1221 Av of Amer -NY 10020
(212) 786-8896 .. **Schreiber,** Scott M '06 EMI Music NA -150 5th Av -NY 10011
(212) 594-5300 .. **Schreiber,** Sol '55 OfCnsl Milberg LLP -1 Penn Plz -NY 10119
(212) 687-4900 .. **Schreiber,** Wm B '62 (Wormser KG&J LLP) -825 3rd Av -NY 10022
(718) 254-0700 .. **Schreibersdorf,** Lisa '85 %Bklyn Defender Srvcs -177 Lvngstn -Brklyn 11201 **Fx:**254-0897
(914) 949-4878 .. **Schreier,** Arthur M '56 -8 Chester Av -White Plns 10601
(212) 889-0686 .. **Schreier,** David M '83 (Schreier & W,LLP) -240 Mad Av -NY 10016 **Fx:**889-0279
(212) 769-8959 .. **Schreier,** Jean E '79 -585 West End Av -NY 10024
(212) 635-1856 .. **Schreier,** Jeffrey B '79 %Bk of NY -1 Wall -NY 10286 **Fx:**635-1867
(718) 336-1413 .. **Schreier,** Lawr W '89 -1838 Coney Isl Av -Brklyn 11230
(212) 885-4035 .. **Schreier,** Wm S '82 BMO Capital Markets Corp -3 Times Sq -NY 10036
(212) 735-3000 .. **Schreiner,** Benjamin M '09 %Skadden ASM&F LLP -4 Times Sq -NY 10036
(516) 922-8400 .. **Schreiner,** Gary B '78 -19 W Main -Oyster Bay 11771
(518) 474-1718 .. **Schrempf,** Thos J '92 %Dept of Law -The Cptl -Albany 12224
(212) 218-5500 .. **Schrero,** Elizabeth D '81 (Seyfarth S LLP) -620 8th Av -NY 10018
(212) 309-6000 .. **Schretzman,** Nicholas '09 %Morgan L&B LLP -101 Park Av -NY 10178
(518) 783-4767 .. **Schreyer,** Fredk J '79 %Wertime R&V,PC -930 Albany Shaker Rd -Latham 12110
(212) 408-5100 .. **Schreyer,** Leslie J '71 (Chadbourne & P LLP) -30 Rckfllr Plz -NY 10112
(212) 969-3000 .. **Schriber,** Wendy J '79 (Proskauer R LLP) -1585 Bway -NY 10036
(516) 739-8000 .. **Schrier Fiscella & Sussman** -825 E Gate Blvd -Gdn Cty 11530 **Fx:**739-8004
(516) 739-8000 .. **Schrier,** Richd E '78 (Schrier F&S) -825 E Gate Blvd -Gdn Cty 11530
(631) 451-4113 .. **Schrier,** Steven F '76 %Sfflk Cnty Comm Cllg -533 Cllg Rd -Selden 11784 **Fx:**451-4681

(914) 761-1300 .. **Schriever,** Andrew P '99 (Cuddy & F LLP) -445 Hmltn Av -White Plns 10601
(212) 770-7406 .. **Schrift,** Karen J '96 %AIG - Envir Claims -80 Pine -NY 10005
(315) 516-2283 .. **Schrimpf,** Joshua R '09 -892 E Brighton Av -Syracuse 13205 **Fx:**399-4880
(212) 264-3650 .. **Schriver,** Robt R '04 %SSA Ofc Genl Cnsl -26 Fed Plz -NY 10278 **Fx:**264-6372
(518) 429-0404 .. **Schrock Seeley,** Cynthia L '00 -Bx138 -Glens Fls 12801 **Fx:**338-3103
(716) 881-4900 .. **Schröder,** Ginger D '91 (Schröder J & Assoc) -766 Ellicott -Buffalo 14203
(585) 546-5530 .. **Schroder,** Kevin J '00 %Thomson West -50 E Broad -Rchstr 14694
(516) 742-7430 .. **Schroder,** Michl T '80 (Schroder & S LLP) -114 Old Cntry Rd -Mineola 11501 **Fx:**742-7433
(212) 264-3391 .. **Schroeck,** Bonnie Ann '90 %DHS -26 Fed Plz -NY 10278
(631) 580-0505 .. **Schroeder,** Edw P '51 -Bx933 -Remsenbrg 11960
(914) 725-4164 .. **Schroeder,** Elaine D '55 -169 Brite Av -Scarsdale 10583
(516) 542-5900 .. **Schroeder,** Francis Xavier '90 (Congdon FORDT&F) -333 Earle Ovngton Blvd -Uniondale 11553
(212) 774-1122 .. **Schroeder,** Jack B '87 -500 E 77th -NY 10162
(212) 790-0211 .. **Schroeder,** Jeanne L '79 %Benj N Cardozo Schl of Law -55 5th Av -NY 10003 **Fx:**790-0345
(516) 746-3500 .. **Schroeder,** Mary C '92 %Brand G&B,PC -600 Old Cntry Rd -Gdn Cty 11530
(212) 532-1200 .. **Schroeder,** Matthew A '08 %A Bernstone -292 Mad Av -NY 10017 **Fx:**532-6330
(212) 665-5937 .. **Schroeder,** Regina A '99 JD Searchlight -364 W 117th -NY 10026 **Fx:**655-5940
(516) 822-3550 .. **Schroeder,** Robt Glenn '91 (Hoffmann & B LLP) -6900 Jericho Tpk -Syosset 11791 **Fx:**822-3582
(212) 224-1569 .. **Schroeder,** Scott N '91 %Mutual of America -320 Park Av -NY 10022
(212) 230-8837 .. **Schroeder,** Susan M '02 (WilmerHale) -399 Park Av -NY 10022
(212) 558-4000 .. **Schroeder,** Wm E '86 SpclCnsl Sullivan & C LLP -125 Broad -NY 10004
(914) 725-5813 .. **Schroeger,** Robt '68 -20 Sherwood Pl -Scarsdale 10583
(212) 944-0600 .. **Schroer,** Monica N '03 %Hafif & Assoc,PLLC -275 Mad Av -NY 10016 **Fx:**944-7747
(845) 602-5186 .. **Schroeter,** Melissa A '09 Pfizer,Inc -401 N Mddltwn Rd -Pearl Rvr 10965
(212) 752-8000 .. **Schroth,** Kevin R '98 SpclCnsl Cole SMF&L,PA -900 3rd Av -NY 10022
(718) 928-3700 .. **Schryver,** Erik '93 %LSNYC-Bronx -579 Courtlandt Av -Bronx 10451 **Fx:**402-7586
(212) 506-1700 .. **Schryver,** Gavin D '08 %Kasowitz BT&F LLP -1633 Bway -NY 10019
(607) 324-5711 .. **Schu,** Brian C '84 -226 Main -Hornell 14843 **Fx:**324-5383
(914) 997-7100 .. **Schub,** Benjamin E '92 (Berman BF&G pc) -123 Main -White Plns 10601
(212) 506-1700 .. **Schub,** Howard W '91 (Kasowitz BT&F LLP) -1633 Bway -NY 10019
(585) 798-2250 .. **Schubel,** David C '74 (Webster S&M,LLP) -343 Main Bx606 -Medina 14103 **Fx:**798-0776
(212) 756-5391 .. **Schubert,** Aba R '01 Eton Park Capital Mgmt -825 3rd Av -NY 10022
(212) 450-4000 .. **Schubert,** Danl F '03 %Davis P&W LLP -450 Lex Av -NY 10017
(212) 402-9400 .. **Schubert,** Kevin R '10 %McKool S,PC -1 Bryant Park -NY 10036
(607) 273-2301 .. **Schubert,** Mary Jane '03 (True W&S,LLP) -950 Danby Rd -Ithaca 14850
(718) 377-4938 .. **Schubin,** Jos A '81 -1262 E 38th -Brklyn 11210 **Fx:**692-4737
(212) 762-5413 .. **Schuch,** John W '03 Morgan Stanley -1221 Av of Amer -NY 10020
(212) 240-9100 .. **Schuchman,** Roy S '79 (Schuchman S&Z-L,LLP) -225 Bway -NY 10007 **Fx:**732-4580
(631) 821-6163 .. **Schuchmann,** Maria G '88 (M Schuchmann,PC) -2 Union -Miller Pl 11764
(212) 421-4100 .. **Schuck,** Donald Lockhart '81 (Pryor C LLP) -7 Times Sq -NY 10036
(718) 250-2000 .. **Schuck,** Zachary G '07 %DA -350 Jay -Brklyn 11201 **Fx:**250-2314
(212) 545-4000 .. **Schudroff,** Danl D '09 %Jackson L LLP -666 3rd Av -NY 10017
(212) 455-2000 .. **Schueller,** John D '00 Cnsl Simpson T&B LLP -425 Lex Av -NY 10017
(212) 837-6000 .. **Schueller,** Thos G '63 SrCnsl Hughes H&R LLP -1 Bttry Pk Plz -NY 10004
(212) 756-2000 .. **Schuerman,** Katherine L '09 %Schulte R&Z LLP -919 3rd Av -NY 10022
(212) 935-2179 .. **Schuessler,** Dana L '05 -301 E 63rd -NY 10065
(212) 770-6333 .. **Schuette,** Elizabeth L '02 Amer Intl Realty Corp -72 Wall -NY 10005
(212) 460-2496 .. **Schuette,** Mary Kathryn '75 Con Ed -4 Irving Pl -NY 10003
(716) 833-9752 .. **Schuetze,** Mark M '80 -117 Findlay Av -Tonawanda 14150 **Fx:**833-0662
(845) 565-1100 .. **Schuh,** Mark L '01 %Tarshis CLM&M,PLLC -One Corwin Ct -Newburgh 12550
(212) 450-4000 .. **Schuh,** Steven D '09 %Davis P&W LLP -450 Lex Av -NY 10017
(212) 508-6700 .. **Schulder,** David '71 (Tannenbaum HS&H LLP) -900 3rd Av -NY 10022
(212) 244-1200 .. **Schulder,** Howard A '71 %Summa Capital -350 5th Av -NY 10118
(212) 588-5605 .. **Schulder Abrams,** Diane '65 Brown Harris Stevens -1926 Bway -NY 10023
(212) 272-4938 .. **Schuldiner,** Rachel A '97 %JP Morgan Chase -383 Mad Av -NY 10179
(716) 853-3801 .. **Schule,** Nelson E Jr. '90 (Kenney SL&N,LLP) -14 Lafayette Sq -Buffalo 14203
(631) 360-0011 .. **Schule,** Ronald C '75 -1 Glamore Ct -Smithtwn 11787 **Fx:**360-1477
(716) 632-5919 .. **Schulefand,** Keith B '89 -1301 N Forest Rd -Buffalo 14221
(212) 504-6000 .. **Schuler,** Gary E '94 %Cadwalader W&T LLP -1 World Fncl Ctr -NY 10281
(718) 268-4155 .. **Schuley,** Marc B '02 %Barrett L,LLC -109-01 72nd Rd -Frst Hlls 11375
(718) 998-1755 .. **Schulgasser,** David S '58 -1457 E 8th -Brklyn 11230
(718) 853-5449 .. **Schulgasser,** Leon I '56 -733 E 4th -Brklyn 11218
(212) 941-5757 .. **Schulhof,** David K '97 Evergreen Copyright Acquisitions,LLC -11 Beach -NY 10013
(212) 685-0751 .. **Schulhof,** Thos B '73 -30 E 33rd -NY 10016
(212) 943-1200 .. **Schuller,** David M '78 (Edelman & E,PC) -61 Bway -NY 10006 **Fx:**943-0001
(212) 883-6500 .. **Schuller,** Gary '79 (Podell SS&B,LLP) -605 3rd Av -NY 10158
(212) 554-7800 .. **Schulman,** Alvin H '58 (Moses & S LLP) -405 Lex Av -NY 10174
(212) 733-1144 .. **Schulman,** Amy Weinfeld '90 Cnsl Pfizer Inc -235 E 42nd -NY 10017
(914) 736-1800 .. **Schulman,** Bari J '77 -5 William Puckey Dr -Cortlandt Manor 10567 **Fx:**736-6030
(718) 855-8855 .. **Schulman,** Barry E '76 -16 Court -Brklyn 11241 **Fx:**875-1768
(212) 832-4000 .. **Schulman,** Bernard '59 (Eisen & S,LLP) -18 E 48th -NY 10017
(212) 715-9100 .. **Schulman,** Brendan M '01 %Kramer LN&F,LLP -1177 Av of Amer -NY 10036
(212) 632-5500 .. **Schulman,** Dan J '86 OfCnsl Salans LLP -620 5th Av -NY 10020
(516) 484-1956 .. **Schulman,** Danl M '78 -98 Crows Nest -Manhsst 11030
(732) 636-8800 .. **Schulman,** David M '80 (Greenberg & S) -1600 Stewart Av -Westbury 11590
(212) 688-5640 .. **Schulman,** Denise A '09 %Joseph & H LLP -757 3rd Av -NY 10017
(212) 288-5616 .. **Schulman,** Douglas H '88 %Manhtn Shade & Glass -1299 3rd Av -NY 10021
(718) 793-7153 .. **Schulman,** Edwin Ira '72 -123-60 83rd Av -Kew Gdns 11415
(585) 424-1330 .. **Schulman,** Edwin R '66 -3445 Winton Pl -Rchstr 14623
(212) 805-0234 .. **Schulman,** Eli C '98 %Hon M Mukasey -500 Pearl -NY 10007
(718) 590-3910 .. **Schulman,** Eylan '05 %Law Dept -198 E 161st -Bronx 10451 **Fx:**590-2686
(212) 686-1515 .. **Schulman,** Fredk '78 East Coast Venture Capital -30 E 29th -NY 10016
(212) 871-1300 .. **Schulman,** Fredrick A '99 (Schulman B&W,LLP) -980 Av of Amer -NY 10018 **Fx:**(646) 599-9320
(212) 686-7700 .. **Schulman,** Ira M '80 (Mazur CR&S PC) -1250 Bway -NY 10001
(212) 506-1700 .. **Schulman,** Jack N '87 (Kasowitz BT&F LLP) -1633 Bway -NY 10019
(315) 295-3831 .. **Schulman,** Jeffrey D '94 %Pillinger MT,LLP -507 Plum -Syracuse 13204
(212) 599-1515 .. **Schulman,** Jeffrey I '04 %Stein RM,LLP -405 Lex Av -NY 10174
(212) 277-6500 .. **Schulman,** Jeffrey L '00 %Dickstein S LLP -1633 Bway -NY 10019
(212) 481-1312 .. **Schulman,** Jeffrey S '94 %Gulotta Law Grp PLLC -271 Mad Av -NY 10016 **Fx:**481-1316
(718) 853-8220 .. **Schulman,** Jonathan S '00 (Berman S&L) -4607 Ft Hmltn Pkwy -Brklyn 11219
(212) 509-4222 .. **Schulman,** Joshua A '94 -80 Wall -NY 10005 **Fx:**509-4522
(845) 368-0104 .. **Schulman,** Julian Alan '79 (Schulman K&K,PC) -1 Exec Blvd #202 -Suffern 10901
(212) 421-4100 .. **Schulman,** Kenneth A '78 (Pryor C LLP) -7 Times Sq -NY 10036
(845) 368-0104 .. **Schulman Kissel & Keene,PC** -1 Exec Blvd #202 -Suffern 10901 **Fx:**368-0168
(845) 794-2424 .. **Schulman,** Mark L '77 -372 E Bway Bx945 -Monticello 12701 **Fx:**794-2599
(315) 463-4032 .. **Schulman,** Mark N '95 %Koldin Law Ctr -6661 Kirkvll Rd Bx279 -E Syracuse 13057 **Fx:**463-6512
(718) 426-2800 .. **Schulman,** Martin '79 (Schulman & S) -57-00 Bway -Woodside 11377 **Fx:**426-1137
(631) 622-2080 .. **Schulman,** Michl B '78 (M Schulman & Assoc,PC) -145 Pinelawn Rd -Melvll 11747 **Fx:**622-2084
(212) 724-8000 .. **Schulman,** Mortimer '51 -115 Cntrl Pk W -NY 10023
(718) 426-2800 .. **Schulman,** Myron '86 (Schulman & S) -57-00 Bway -Woodside 11377 **Fx:**426-1137
(518) 242-3703 .. **Schulman,** Nancy L '93 %Ct of Claims -Justice Bldg ESP Bx7344 -Albany 12224 **Fx:**242-3704
(212) 883-1700 .. **Schulman,** Richd J '71 (Duval & S LLP) -101 Park Av -NY 10178
(212) 682-3377 .. **Schulman,** Stephanie F '95 %Oaktree Capital Mngt -1301 Av of Amer -NY 10019
(212) 688-6363 .. **Schulman,** Stephen B '70 SB Schulman,PC -137 E 36th -NY 10016
(718) 853-8220 .. **Schulman,** Steven G '67 (Berman S&L) -4607 Ft Hmltn Pkwy -Brklyn 11219
(212) 754-9400 .. **Schulman,** Todd A '04 %Todtman NS&J,PC -425 Park Av -NY 10022
(212) 613-5000 .. **Schulman,** Yisroel Y '88 %Leg Assist Grp -450 W 33rd -NY 10001 **Fx:**750-0820
(212) 837-6849 .. **Schulman-Marcus,** Seth '10 %Hughes H&R LLP -1 Bttry Pk Plz -NY 10004 **Fx:**299-6849
(212) 788-1198 .. **Schulsohn,** Richd A '88 %Law Dept -100 Church -NY 10007 **Fx:**788-0367
(212) 648-0967 .. **Schulsohn,** Robbin D '91 JP Morgan Chase -245 Park Av -NY 10167
(516) 393-2200 .. **Schulson,** Andrew J '98 (Garfunkel W,PC) -111 Grt Nck Rd -Gt Neck 11021
(212) 951-6559 .. **Schulte,** Gregory C '86 %NYS Ed Dept-OLS -475 Park Av S -NY 10016 **Fx:**951-6573
(212) 225-2000 .. **Schulte,** Katherine F '09 %Cleary GS&H -1 Lbrty Plz -NY 10006
(315) 471-3151 .. **Schulte,** Mark J '85 (Hancock & E,LLP) -1500 AXA Twr I Bx4976 -Syracuse 13221
(212) 756-2000 .. **Schulte Roth & Zabel LLP** -919 3rd Av -NY 10022 **Fx:**593-5955
(212) 756-2000 .. **Schulte,** Stephen J '64 OfCnsl Schulte R&Z LLP -919 3rd Av -NY 10022
(212) 878-8403 .. **Schulte,** Thos K '89 (Clifford C LLP) -31 W 52nd -NY 10019
(212) 872-1000 .. **Schulten,** Christopher T '02 -One Bryant Park -NY 10036 **Fx:**872-1002
(212) 939-7514 .. **Schultis,** Lawr A '08 Schultis & V Law Grp -295 Mad Av -NY 10017
(315) 442-0100 .. **Schultz,** Adam J '91 OfCnsl Gilberti SH&S,PC -555 E Genesee -Syracuse 13202
(516) 482-5100 .. **Schultz,** Andrew B '69 -500 N Bway -Jericho 11753 **Fx:**605-0385
(212) 909-6000 .. **Schultz,** Andrew E '85 Cnsl Debevoise & P LLP -919 3rd Av -NY 10022
(212) 506-2355 .. **Schultz,** Beth Ann '00 %Mayer B LLP -1675 Bway -NY 10019 **Fx:**849-5855
(212) 610-6300 .. **Schultz,** Brian A '07 %Allen & O -1221 Av of Amer -NY 10020
(212) 265-6888 .. **Schultz,** Christopher F '78 (Porzio B&N,PC) -156 W 56th -NY 10019
(212) 313-3600 .. **Schultz,** David H '96 %Barry M&M -2 Rector -NY 10006
(212) 326-2000 .. **Schultz,** David Ian '02 Cnsl O'Melveny & M LLP -7 Times Sq -NY 10036

(212) 878-8000 .. **Schultz,** Elizabeth E '10 %Clifford C LLP -31 W 52nd -NY 10019
(516) 482-0857 .. **Schultz,** Enid Hochstein '75 -1 Rutland Rd -Gt Neck 11020
(516) 280-5021 .. **Schultz,** Eric B '80 -1 Scott Pl -Plainvw 11803 **Fx:**280-5022
(716) 566-1300 .. **Schultz,** Eric W '96 OfCnsl Hiscock & B,LLP -1100 M&T Ctr -Buffalo 14203
(518) 434-2622 .. **Schultz,** Erika J '91 %Pozefsky B&M -90 State -Albany 12207
(212) 267-6655 .. **Schultz,** Gary '79 -305 Bway -NY 10007 **Fx:**732-2191
(607) 778-2686 .. **Schultz,** Howard '81 %Dept Soc Srvcs -36-42 Main -Bnghmtn 13905 **Fx:**778-2710
(212) 436-1102 .. **Schultz,** Ira H '88 IRS -290 Bway -NY 10007
(315) 446-3557 .. **Schultz,** Jack '54 -48 Ely Dr -Fayettevll 13066
(631) 285-1073 .. **Schultz,** James C '67 -12 South Dr -Lk Ronkonkoma 11779 **Fx:**285-1706
(716) 847-0680 .. **Schultz,** James D Jr. '79 %W Pacer Jr -298 Main -Buffalo 14202
(518) 465-3553 .. **Schultz,** James R '82 (Maynard OS&C,LLP) -6 Twr Pl -Albany 12203
(212) 537-1079 .. **Schultz,** Jami '01 Morgan Stanley -1633 Bway -NY 10019
(212) 762-7296 .. **Schultz,** Jarett H '05 Morgan Stanley -1221 Av of Amer -NY 10020 **Fx:**507-6547
(212) 841-4100 .. **Schultz,** Jeffrey L '95 Millenium Prtnrs -666 Fifth Av -NY 10103
(212) 935-3000 .. **Schultz,** Jeffrey P '97 (Mintz LCFG&P,PC) -666 3rd Av -NY 10017
(212) 878-0243 .. **Schultz,** Jennifer L '92 MTA -347 Mad Av -NY 10017
(212) 573-4954 .. **Schultz,** Jessica L '01 %Ford Fndtn -320 E 43rd -NY 10017
(585) 672-2600 .. **Schultz,** Jill K '88 (Burns & S LLP) -28 E Main -Rchstr 14614 **Fx:**(866) 825-7217
(212) 818-9200 .. **Schultz,** Kenneth A '77 (Satterlee SB&B LLP) -230 Park Av -NY 10169
(518) 474-6908 .. **Schultz,** Kenneth J '86 Ofc for Technology -State Cptl ESP Bx2062 -Albany 12220
(516) 357-3000 .. **Schultz,** Kenneth R '03 %Rivkin R LLP -926 RXR Plz -Uniondale 11556
(315) 798-5766 .. **Schultz,** Kurt D '06 DA -800 Park Av -Utica 13501 **Fx:**798-5582
(212) 964-1800 .. **Schultz,** Leonard Jay '74 -135 William -NY 10038 **Fx:**732-4539
(718) 855-7882 .. **Schultz,** Leslie Griesbach '84 BRIC,Inc -647 Fulton -Brklyn 11217
(516) 536-0900 .. **Schultz,** Marc G '73 %Jacobson & S -510 Merrick Rd Bx46 -Rockvll Ctr 11571
(212) 710-3900 .. **Schultz,** Matthew S '03 %Clyde & Co US LLP -405 Lex Av -NY 10174 **Fx:**710-3950
(315) 734-2000 .. **Schultz,** Michl J '86 %Utica Natl Ins -180 Genesee Bx530 -Utica 13502 **Fx:**734-2662
(212) 820-7700 .. **Schultz,** Polina Shklyanoy '06 %Boundas SW&B,LLC -1 Bttry Pk Plz -NY 10004
(631) 501-3069 .. **Schultz,** Robt A '80 %J Humphreys -3 Huntngtn Quad Bx9028 -Melvll 11747 **Fx:**501-3085
(585) 641-8000 .. **Schultz,** Robt D '80 (Fix SB&G,PC) -295 Woodcliff Dr -Fairprt 14450
(212) 986-6000 .. **Schultz,** Stephen M '75 (Kleinberg KW&C,PC) -551 5th Av -NY 10176
(516) 621-0167 .. **Schultz,** Steven B '94 -57 Wagon Rd -Roslyn Hts 11577
(212) 922-9300 .. **Schultz,** Steven L '81 Silversmith & V,LLP -30 Broad -NY 10004
(516) 465-8090 .. **Schulz,** Andrew J '81 %North Shore-LIJ Hlth Systm -145 Community Dr -Gt Neck 11021 **Fx:**465-8013
(212) 902-0028 .. **Schulz,** Christina Ann '93 Goldman Sachs -1 NY Plz -NY 10004
(212) 850-6100 .. **Schulz,** David A '79 (Levine SK&S,LLP) -321 W 44th -NY 10036
(212) 735-3000 .. **Schulz,** Kelly G '08 %Skadden ASM&F LLP -4 Times Sq -NY 10036
(716) 662-5431 .. **Schulz,** Lawr A '70 -Bx1050 -Orchard Pk 14127 **Fx:**662-9587
(716) 853-5100 .. **Schulz,** Paul J '82 (Lippes MWF LLP) -665 Main -Buffalo 14203
(631) 753-9000 .. **Schulz,** Thos P '85 (Schulz & Assoc,PC) -225 Broadhllw Rd -Melvll 11747 **Fx:**753-0950
(716) 855-1111 .. **Schulz,** Wm D '62 (Duke HP&G LLP) -350 Main -Buffalo 14202
(212) 416-6557 .. **Schulze,** Danl A '94 %Dept of Law -120 Bway -NY 10271
(516) 542-5900 .. **Schulze,** Kathy A '90 (Congdon FORDT&F) -333 Earle Ovngton Blvd -Uniondale 11553
(212) 975-4321 .. **Schulzinger,** Leon '79 %CBS -51 W 52nd -NY 10019
(585) 352-0700 .. **Schum,** Danl G '73 (Kennedy & S) -43 Nichols Bx102 -Spencerprt 14559 **Fx:**352-0701
(607) 687-1350 .. **Schumacher,** Adam R '92 (Dixson S,PC) -212 Front Bx236 -Owego 13827 **Fx:**785-2355
(212) 294-6700 .. **Schumacher,** Catherine B '02 %Winston & S -200 Park Av -NY 10166
(212) 340-0400 .. **Schumacher,** Eric B '85 %Appllt Div 1st Dept -27 Mad Av -NY 10010 **Fx:**889-4412
(585) 249-0142 .. **Schumacher,** Janet Haviland '93 (Schumacher Law Ofc) -17 Harwood Ln -E Rchstr 14445 **Fx:**249-0361
(917) 912-2945 .. **Schumacher,** Robt W II '01 -82 S Cntry Rd Bx90 -Remsenbrg 11960
(212) 858-1000 .. **Schumaecker,** Michl P '73 (Pillsbury WSP LLP) -1540 Bway -NY 10036
(212) 512-4882 .. **Schuman,** Adam H '92 %McGraw-Hill -1221 Av of Amer -NY 10020 **Fx:**512-4827
(212) 247-0848 .. **Schuman,** Danl S '04 %Bienstock & M,PC -250 W 57th -NY 10107
(646) 755-3304 .. **Schuman,** Danl S '07 %Shanker & S,PC -420 Lex Av -NY 10170
(212) 334-0090 .. **Schuman,** Dennis A '76 -350 Bway -NY 10013 **Fx:**274-1060
(914) 644-8300 .. **Schuman,** Eliot M '80 (Schuman S&G) -1 N Lex Av -White Plns 10601
(212) 803-5136 .. **Schuman,** H Mitchell '84 SrCnsl NY Cnty Defender Srvcs -225 Bway -NY 10007 **Fx:**571-6035
(212) 906-1200 .. **Schuman,** Ian D '01 (Latham & W) -885 3rd Av -NY 10022
(212) 859-8000 .. **Schuman,** Jason A '08 %Fried FHS&J LLP -1 NY Plz -NY 10004
(212) 335-9017 .. **Schuman,** Jennifer H '96 %DA -1 Hogan Pl -NY 10013
(212) 770-6879 .. **Schuman,** Jonathan D '00 %AIG, Inc -70 Pine -NY 10270
(516) 889-7900 .. **Schuman,** Jos '62 (Schuman & S,PC) -3000-39 Stevens -Oceanside 11572
(212) 490-0100 .. **Schuman,** Keith A '84 (Schuman & Assoc) -1536 3rd Av -NY 10028 **Fx:**490-0156
(212) 701-8684 .. **Schuman,** Marc A '87 Bisys Grp -199 Water -NY 10038
(718) 392-6650 .. **Schuman,** Marian Maura '79 %Propper Mfg Co -36-04 Skillman -LIC 11101
(516) 889-7900 .. **Schuman,** Mark '96 (Schuman & S,PC) -3000-39 Stevens -Oceanside 11572
(212) 578-9043 .. **Schuman,** Mark A '92 %MetLife -27-01 Qns Plz N -LIC 11101 **Fx:**578-3916
(914) 644-8300 .. **Schuman Sall & Geist** -1 N Lex Av -White Plns 10601 **Fx:**644-8393
(518) 474-4552 .. **Schumann,** Alexa M '99 %Insurance Dept -99 Wshngtn Av -Albany 12257 **Fx:**473-4600
(212) 512-0814 .. **Schumann,** Gretchen Beall '02 %Cohen HB&R,PC -11 W 42nd -NY 10036
(646) 425-8089 .. **Schumann,** Roger N '92 -433 E 56th -NY 10022
(518) 843-4228 .. **Schumann-McGhee,** Bethany '06 -164 Guy Park Av -Amsterdam 12010 **Fx:**(888) 842-1286
(212) 956-9500 .. **Schumeister,** David N '99 OfCnsl Hand B&A LLP -8 W 40th -NY 10018 **Fx:**376-6080
(516) 803-2300 .. **Schumer,** Lee S '93 %Cablevision Sys -1111 Stewart Av -Bethpage 11714
(212) 373-3000 .. **Schumer,** Robt B '83 (Paul WRW&G LLP) -1285 Av of Amer -NY 10019
(518) 459-2667 .. **Schunk,** Catherine M '84 (Welt G&S LLP) -4 Exec Park Dr Bx3716 -Albany 12203
(845) 883-7423 .. **Schunk,** Philip W '57 P Schunk,PC -500 S Ohiovll Rd Bx460 -New Paltz 12561 **Fx:**883-6443
(212) 582-4210 .. **Schupak,** Donald C '67 Schupak Grp,Inc -595 Mad Av -NY 10022 **Fx:**262-1031
(516) 742-0888 .. **Schupbach,** Arthur C '74 (Schupbach W&P LLP) -1010 Franklin Av -Gdn Cty 11530
(516) 742-0888 .. **Schupbach Williams & Pavone LLP** -1010 Franklin Av -Gdn Cty 11530 **Fx:**742-4211
(518) 447-7150 .. **Schupp,** Edmund J '91 Pub Def -60 S Pearl -Albany 12207
(585) 394-0570 .. **Schuppenhauer,** John A '77 -35 S Main -Canandaigua 14424 **Fx:**394-5136
(212) 509-9400 .. **Schur,** Jordan W '09 Cozen O -45 Bway Atrium -NY 10006
(518) 661-5001 .. **Schur,** Ronald R Jr. '89 -2431 State Hwy 30 BxXX -Mayfield 12117 **Fx:**661-4664
(516) 592-6800 .. **Schure,** Richd J '65 (Spellman RSGM&P,LLP) -229 Seventh -Gdn Cty 11530
(212) 634-6375 .. **Schurgin,** Michelle S '03 Festival Co -641 Lex Av -NY 10022
(516) 294-5200 .. **Schurin,** Marilyn C '91 %Picciano & S -900 Merchants Cncrs -Westbury 11590
(212) 684-3900 .. **Schurin,** Richd S '95 (Gottlieb R&R,PC) -270 Mad Av -NY 10016
(914) 946-4777 .. **Schurkman,** Steven A '81 (Keane & B,PC) -445 Hmltn Av -White Plns 10601
(914) 738-9421 .. **Schurr,** Victor '78 -188 E Post Rd -White Plns 10601 **Fx:**738-9426
(718) 681-1111 .. **Schurr,** Victor '78 -910 Sheridan Av -Bronx 10451 **Fx:**681-2890
(212) 503-3500 .. **Schurr Levin,** Carolyn '88 %Ziff-Davis Media -28 E 28th -NY 10016
(212) 210-9490 .. **Schurtman,** Wm '58 SrCnsl Alston & B LLP -90 Park Av -NY 10016
(212) 720-2813 .. **Schussler,** Michl '84 %Fed Reserve Bk -33 Lbrty -NY 10045
(718) 238-1400 .. **Schustal,** Randy C '89 (Cantor C&S,LLP) -8778 Bay Pkwy -Brklyn 11214 **Fx:**238-7642
(518) 213-6000 .. **Schuster,** Elizabeth R '90 %NYSUT -800 Troy-Schnctdy Rd -Latham 12110 **Fx:**213-6488
(845) 778-2121 .. **Schuster,** Gary M '89 %Jacobowitz & G,LLP -158 Orange Av Bx367 -Walden 12586
(212) 373-3000 .. **Schuster,** Jane C '08 %Paul WRW&G LLP -1285 Av of Amer -NY 10019
(212) 701-3000 .. **Schuster,** John '78 (Cahill G&R LLP) -80 Pine -NY 10005 **Fx:**269-5420
(212) 698-3500 .. **Schuster,** Jos M '07 %Dechert LLP -1095 Av of Amer -NY 10036
(646) 392-9250 .. **Schuster,** Michele '84 %M Klein & Assoc -200 Mad Av -NY 10016 **Fx:**(212) 779-1499
(212) 655-3500 .. **Schuster,** Mitchell '90 %Meister S&F LLP -140 E 45th -NY 10017
(212) 697-6900 .. **Schuster,** Randi A '86 (Holtz Rubenstein Reminick LLP) -1430 Bway -NY 10018
(212) 448-1100 .. **Schuster,** Steven W '81 (McLaughlin & S,LLP) -260 Mad Av -NY 10016
(716) 852-8222 .. **Schuster,** Wendy K '01 %Paladino C&Q -295 Main -Buffalo 14203
(212) 836-4796 .. **Schutty,** John F III '84 -445 Park Av -NY 10022
(914) 995-3547 .. **Schutz,** Donald E '84 Dept of Probation -112 E Post Rd -White Plns 10601
(646) 386-4033 .. **Schutz,** Ellen L '80 %Hon M Wiley -111 Centre -NY 10013
(914) 273-7300 .. **Schutz & Markin** -6 Spruce Hill Rd -Armonk 10504 **Fx:**273-8619
(914) 472-8562 .. **Schutzer,** Eric P '94 -8 Whig Rd -Scarsdale 10583
(516) 536-4411 .. **Schutzman,** Andrew M '86 %AMS Risk Mgmt -Bx170 -Rockvll Ctr 11571
(914) 964-3990 .. **Schutzman,** Keith E '86 AVR Realty Co -1 Exec Blvd -Ynkrs 10701
(212) 557-4000 .. **Schutzman,** Max F '73 (Grunfeld DLS&K LLP) -399 Park Av -NY 10022
(845) 471-7177 .. **Schutzman,** Stanley A '78 (Hanig & S,LLP) -22 IBM Rd -Poughkeepsie 12601 **Fx:**790-1212
(518) 357-8684 .. **Schutzman,** Steven J '84 -2402 Loudon Pl -Niskayuna 12309
(212) 909-6000 .. **Schuur,** Peter F G '93 (Debevoise & P LLP) -919 3rd Av -NY 10022
(212) 373-3000 .. **Schuwerk,** Robt C '06 %Paul WRW&G LLP -1285 Av of Amer -NY 10019
(914) 347-2600 .. **Schuyler,** Roseann Kitson '01 %Traub LS&S LLP -7 Skyline Dr -Hawthorne 10532
(212) 636-6862 .. **Schvey,** Aram A '02 Fordham Law Schl -33 W 60th -NY 10023
(315) 471-1318 .. **Schwab,** Andrew J '92 %Lynch Law Ofc -2700 Bellevue Av -Syracuse 13219 **Fx:**471-1409
(212) 454-4544 .. **Schwab,** Anne T '79 %Deutsche Bank -60 Wall -NY 10005
(212) 790-9200 .. **Schwab,** David E II '55 OfCnsl Cowan L&L,PC -1133 Av of Amer -NY 10036
(212) 621-0302 .. **Schwab,** George B '87 Salisbury & R LLP -1325 Av of Amer -NY 10019
(212) 372-2000 .. **Schwab,** George L IV '03 %Newmark Knight Frank -125 Park Av -NY 10017 **Fx:**372-2386
(212) 341-4234 .. **Schwab,** Harold Lee '57 (Lester SK&D) -120 Bway -NY 10271
(212) 373-3000 .. **Schwab,** James H '88 (Paul WRW&G LLP) -1285 Av of Amer -NY 10019
(212) 949-9022 .. **Schwab,** Jeffrey A '64 (Abelman F&S) -666 3rd Av -NY 10017
(212) 697-7500 .. **Schwab,** Madelaine L '77 Schwab & Assoc LLC -122 E 42nd -NY 10168 **Fx:**697-7501
(212) 735-3000 .. **Schwab,** Mairead J '09 %Skadden ASM&F LLP -4 Times Sq -NY 10036

(845) 294-2544 .. **Schwab,** Mark A '08 %Zeccola & S -45 Webster Av -Goshen 10924
(315) 218-8000 .. **Schwab,** Martin A '91 (Bond S&K,PLLC) -1 Lincoln Ctr -Syracuse 13202
(212) 949-9022 .. **Schwab,** Michl J '95 (Abelman F&S) -666 3rd Av -NY 10017
(607) 254-8431 .. **Schwab,** Norma Weatherly '84 Cornell Univ -300 CCC Bldg-Grdn Av -Ithaca 14853 **Fx:**255-2794
(212) 237-1000 .. **Schwabacher,** Christopher C '67 (Windels ML&M,LLP) -156 W 56th -NY 10019
(212) 382-6600 .. **Schwabe,** Clara G '74 %NYC Bar -42 W 44th -NY 10036 **Fx:**398-6634
(212) 643-9140 .. **Schwaber,** Fern H '82 (Schwaber & K) -350 7th Av -NY 10001 **Fx:**643-9151
(631) 465-0058 .. **Schwaber,** Scott E '98 (S Schwaber & Assoc) -6 Corp Ctr Dr -Melvll 11747 **Fx:**465-0057
(716) 551-5755 .. **Schwach,** Diane Musarra '74 %HUD -465 Main -Buffalo 14203 **Fx:**551-5752
(716) 852-0600 .. **Schwach,** Lawr R '84 (Polowitz & S, LLP) -43 Court -Buffalo 14202
(716) 881-3010 .. **Schwach,** Michelle M F '09 %Cohen & L,PC -343 Elmwood Av Bx5204 -Buffalo 14213
(212) 867-6000 .. **Schwadel,** Blaine Z '81 (Rosenberg & E,PC) -733 3rd Av -NY 10017
(917) 669-9654 .. **Schwadron,** Joshua S '07 Schwadron Law PLLC -250 E 34th -NY 10016 **Fx:**591-3351
(516) 931-3100 .. **Schwaeber,** Henry T '59 %David Berdon & Co -1 Jericho Plz -Jericho 11753
(516) 465-4700 .. **Schwaeber,** Lois '92 Coalition Against Dom Violence -15 Grumman Rd W -Bethpage 11714
(631) 234-2813 .. **Schwager,** Danielle Ivy '00 -320 Carleton Av -Central Islip 11722
(201) 337-5166 .. **Schwager,** Linda H '97 -75 Montebello Rd -Suffern 10901 **Fx:**337-6100
(212) 458-1765 .. **Schwager,** Pamela H '92 %AIG -175 Water -NY 10038
(212) 687-1980 .. **Schwaiger,** Susan Rogers '93 OfCnsl Kaplan F&K LLP -850 3rd Av -NY 10022
(212) 836-8000 .. **Schwalb,** Efrem T '96 %Kaye S LLP -425 Park Av -NY 10022
(212) 751-5884 .. **Schwalbe,** James E '94 (J Schwalbe,PC) -185 Mad Av -NY 10016 **Fx:**684-0600
(212) 504-6000 .. **Schwalbe,** Laura K '10 %Cadwalader W&T LLP -1 World Fncl Ctr -NY 10281
(845) 928-2122 .. **Schwall,** Leonard '53 -Bx481 -Highland Mills 10930
(585) 530-3128 .. **Schwallie,** Sheila '07 %Appllt Div 4th Dept -50 East Av Ste 200 -Rchstr 14604 **Fx:**530-3247
(914) 666-2161 .. **Schwam,** Barbara Banks '79 (Banks CS&S,LLP) -61 Smith Av -Mt Kisco 10549
(212) 825-5900 .. **Schwam,** Keith A '79 %Dept of Invstgtn -80 Maiden Ln -NY 10038 **Fx:**825-2860
(212) 692-1000 .. **Schwamm,** Michl D '84 (Duane M LLP) -1540 Bway -NY 10036
(845) 639-7722 .. **Schwan,** David S '94 (Reda S & Assoc,LLP) -20 S Main -New Cty 10956 **Fx:**639-7744
(716) 845-5205 .. **Schwan,** W James II '73 -295 Main -Buffalo 14203 **Fx:**854-2228
(716) 845-9330 .. **Schwanekamp,** Sheila W '86 %Family Ct -1 Niagara Plz -Buffalo 14202 **Fx:**858-4739
(212) 850-2800 .. **Schwarcz,** Jeffrey B '06 %Andrews K LLP -450 Lex Av -NY 10017
(718) 544-7701 .. **Schwarsin,** Andrew W '01 -118-35 Qns Blvd -Frst Hlls 11375 **Fx:**520-1213
(212) 940-8800 .. **Schwartsman,** Marianna '08 Katten MR LLP -575 Mad Av -NY 10022
(212) 483-9490 .. **Schwartz,** Adam R '93 (McElroy DM&C,LLP) -88 Pine -NY 10005
(212) 237-8402 .. **Schwartz,** Adina '86 %John Jay Cllg -899 10th Av -NY 10019 **Fx:**237-8901
(212) 756-2000 .. **Schwartz,** Adriana F '06 %Schulte R&Z LLP -919 3rd Av -NY 10022
(212) 350-2700 .. **Schwartz,** Alan H '95 %Constantine C,PC -450 Lex Av -NY 10017
(516) 248-6311 .. **Schwartz,** Alan J '81 AJ Schwartz,PC -1010 Franklin Av -Gdn Cty 11530 **Fx:**294-2954
(212) 547-5400 .. **Schwartz,** Alan J '01 (McDermott W&E LLP) -340 Mad Av -NY 10173
(212) 878-7237 .. **Schwartz,** Alan R '79 %MTA -347 Mad Av -NY 10017
(212) 975-2935 .. **Schwartz,** Alison J '99 CBS News -524 W 57th -NY 10019
(212) 879-9600 .. **Schwartz,** Allan C '74 SrCnsl Podell SS&B,LLP -119 E 71st -NY 10021
(585) 442-5111 .. **Schwartz,** Allan L '67 -179 Ashbourne Rd -Rchstr 14618 **Fx:**442-8483
(917) 454-1100 .. **Schwartz,** Allen F '94 %Police Dept -2 Lafayette -NY 10007
(212) 643-8250 .. **Schwartz,** Allen M '56 -350 5th Av -NY 10118 **Fx:**643-8256
(212) 878-8000 .. **Schwartz,** Allison M '08 %Clifford C LLP -31 W 52nd -NY 10019
(585) 454-4060 .. **Schwartz,** Amy E '00 %Empire Justice Ctr -1 W Main -Rchstr 14614 **Fx:**454-4019
(212) 759-3100 .. **Schwartz,** Amy I '92 -300 E 52nd -NY 10022
(212) 335-9000 .. **Schwartz,** Amy L '86 %DA -1 Hogan Pl -NY 10013
(212) 510-0500 .. **Schwartz,** Andrea B '97 US Trustees Ofc -33 Whitehall -NY 10004 **Fx:**668-2255
(212) 728-8000 .. **Schwartz,** Andrew E '10 %Willkie F&G LLP -787 7th Av -NY 10019
(212) 513-6428 .. **Schwartz,** Andrew I '85 %Dept Business Srvcs -110 William -NY 10038 **Fx:**618-8989
(212) 455-2000 .. **Schwartz,** Anna B '08 %Simpson T&B LLP -425 Lex Av -NY 10017
(212) 742-8700 .. **Schwartz,** Anna R '97 (Garson D&C LLP) -110 Wall -NY 10005
(212) 335-4038 .. **Schwartz,** Anne L '97 %DA -1 Hogan Pl -NY 10013
(212) 228-6320 .. **Schwartz,** Arthur Z '79 (Schwartz L&B,PC) -275 7th Av -NY 10001
(516) 542-1000 .. **Schwartz,** Avraham Z '98 %Geisler & G,LLP -100 Q Roosevelt Blvd -Gdn Cty 11530
(718) 520-2615 .. **Schwartz,** Barry A '73 -25-10 Court Sq -LIC 11101
(212) 572-8600 .. **Schwartz,** Barry F '92 %MacAndrews & Forbes -35 E 62nd -NY 10065
(718) 595-6534 .. **Schwartz,** Barry L '67 %DEP -59-17 Junction Blvd -Flushng 11373 **Fx:**595-6543
(212) 788-1073 .. **Schwartz,** Barry P '76 %Law Dept -100 Church -NY 10007 **Fx:**788-0367
(212) 397-6661 .. **Schwartz,** Barry S '76 -119 W 57th -NY 10019 **Fx:**307-5197
(212) 817-6733 .. **Schwartz,** Bart M '72 -415 Mad Av -NY 10017 **Fx:**817-6729
(212) 859-7000 .. **Schwartz,** Bart R '79 Assurant,Inc -1 Chase Manh Plz -NY 10005
(212) 592-1400 .. **Schwartz,** Belinda G '84 (Herrick,F LLP) -2 Park Av -NY 10016
(212) 636-6821 .. **Schwartz,** Beth '79 %Fordham Univ Sch of Law -140 W 62nd -NY 10023 **Fx:**636-6899
(718) 254-7000 .. **Schwartz,** Beth P '84 %US Atty -271 Cadman Plz E -Brklyn 11201 **Fx:**254-6479
(716) 853-5100 .. **Schwartz,** Blaine S '84 %Lippes MWF LLP -665 Main -Buffalo 14203
(914) 682-7800 .. **Schwartz,** Brad K '02 (Zarin & S) -81 Main -White Plns 10601
(212) 594-2030 .. **Schwartz,** Brett R '98 %Lebensfeld BS&S LLP -31 South -Mt Vernon 10550
(212) 406-1700 .. **Schwartz,** Brian S '93 %Queller FWF&K LLP -233 Bway -NY 10279
(914) 328-0404 .. **Schwartz,** Bruce H '82 (Jackson L LLP) -1 N Bway -White Plns 10601
(212) 232-1300 .. **Schwartz,** Bryan T '00 (Lewis BB&S LLP) -77 Water -NY 10005
(212) 592-1400 .. **Schwartz,** Carl F '80 (Herrick,F LLP) -2 Park Av -NY 10016
(212) 594-8818 .. **Schwartz,** Carl I '79 -354 W 30th -NY 10001
(315) 536-4223 .. **Schwartz,** Carl J Jr. '93 Finger Lks Law Grp -131 Main Bx681 -Penn Yan 14527 **Fx:**536-3603
(212) 640-5714 .. **Schwartz,** Carol V '78 %Amer Exp -200 Vesey -NY 10285
(212) 361-1729 .. **Schwartz,** Chana H '82 Envrnmntl Cntrl Brd -66 John -NY 10038 **Fx:**361-1900
(518) 770-1588 .. **Schwartz,** Chas R '01 (Schwartz Law Firm) -191 Guy Park Av -Amsterdam 12010 **Fx:**770-6247
(212) 417-3700 .. **Schwartz,** Christopher M '02 %MFY Legal Srvcs -299 Bway -NY 10007 **Fx:**417-3890
(646) 230-1010 .. **Schwartz,** Clifford E '77 (Schwartz & B) -250 W 57th -NY 10107 **Fx:**(212) 582-2670
(212) 867-6000 .. **Schwartz,** Dani L '04 %Rosenberg & E,PC -733 3rd Av -NY 10017
(212) 973-0572 .. **Schwartz,** Danl A '78 (Wolff & S PC) -140 Bway -NY 10005
(860) 424-4359 .. **Schwartz,** Danl A '97 (Pullman & C,LLC) -50 Main -White Plns 10606
(845) 356-2570 .. **Schwartz,** Danl B '95 %Kantrowitz G&G,PC -747 Chestnut Rdg Rd -Chestnut Rdg 10977
(212) 450-4000 .. **Schwartz,** Danl J '03 %Davis P&W LLP -450 Lex Av -NY 10017
(212) 297-5800 .. **Schwartz,** Danl L '92 (Day P LLP) -7 Times Sq -NY 10036
(212) 730-7700 .. **Schwartz,** David A '89 (Michelman & R,LLP) -114 W 47th -NY 10036
(212) 221-8096 .. **Schwartz,** David A '95 (Gruber S&P,LLP) -350 5th Av #4022 -NY 10118
(212) 403-1000 .. **Schwartz,** David A '96 (Wachtell LR&K) -51 W 52nd -NY 10019
(212) 735-3000 .. **Schwartz,** David E '95 (Skadden ASM&F LLP) -4 Times Sq -NY 10036
(212) 353-9049 .. **Schwartz,** David F '07 (Feldshon & S,LLP) -505 Grand -NY 10002
(212) 909-6000 .. **Schwartz,** David J '80 (Debevoise & P LLP) -919 3rd Av -NY 10022
(212) 310-8000 .. **Schwartz,** David J '09 %Weil G&M LLP -767 5th Av -NY 10153
(718) 852-9226 .. **Schwartz,** David M '50 -26 Court -Brklyn 11242 **Fx:**858-8472
(516) 880-8170 .. **Schwartz,** David M '93 (Gerstman S LLP) -1044 Nrthrn Blvd -Roslyn 11576 **Fx:**880-8171
(718) 343-4711 .. **Schwartz,** David S '83 -79-04 261st -Floral Pk 11004 **Fx:**470-6621
(212) 530-5000 .. **Schwartz,** David S '01 %Milbank TH&M LLP -1 Chase Manh Plz -NY 10005
(212) 582-0200 .. **Schwartz,** Deborah A '77 -152 W 57th -NY 10019
(516) 229-4802 .. **Schwartz,** Donald C '84 (Schwartz & S) -900 Merchants Cncrs -Westbury 11590
(607) 432-0911 .. **Schwartz,** Donald J '80 -189 Main -Oneonta 13820 **Fx:**431-9201
(516) 248-1700 .. **Schwartz,** Donald Jay '74 (Forchelli CDSM&T,LLP) -333 Earle Ovngton Blvd -Uniondale 11553
(212) 537-6269 .. **Schwartz,** Douglas R '04 (Schwartz & C LLP) -350 5th Av -NY 10118 **Fx:**(917) 591-5184
(212) 577-3500 .. **Schwartz,** Edna '72 %Leg Aid -199 Water -NY 10038 **Fx:**809-1370
(516) 487-0175 .. **Schwartz,** Elias C '80 -343 Grt Nck Rd -Gt Neck 11021 **Fx:**773-7706
(212) 416-8329 .. **Schwartz,** Ellen K '77 %Dept of Law -120 Bway -NY 10271
(800) 742-9696 .. **Schwartz,** Ellen T '88 %Binder & B,PC -33-00 Nrthrn Blvd -LIC 11101 **Fx:**(718) 512-2424
(516) 229-4802 .. **Schwartz,** Elliot G '86 (Schwartz & S) -900 Merchants Cncrs -Westbury 11590
(718) 224-8750 .. **Schwartz,** Emily A '99 -153-01 Jamaica Av -Jamaica 11432
(212) 553-5637 .. **Schwartz,** Emily J '00 Zurich NA -1 Lbrty Plz -NY 10006
(212) 693-5806 .. **Schwartz,** Eric A '94 (E Schwartz,PC) -111 John -NY 10038
(212) 250-4542 .. **Schwartz,** Eric M '89 Deutsche Bk Sec -60 Wall -NY 10005
(212) 818-8800 .. **Schwartz,** Eric T '07 %Graubard M -405 Lex Av -NY 10174
(212) 385-0503 .. **Schwartz,** Esther E '04 %Stein F&S LLP -16 E 34th -NY 10016
(212) 685-6200 .. **Schwartz,** Eugene A '77 %Walter & Samuels Inc -419 Park Av S -NY 10016 **Fx:**685-6429
(212) 489-1600 .. **Schwartz,** Evan R '05 %Deloitte LLP -1633 Bway -NY 10019 **Fx:**492-4201
(516) 745-1122 .. **Schwartz,** Evan S '91 (Quadrino & S,PC) -666 Old Cntry Rd -Gdn Cty 11530
(718) 624-0075 .. **Schwartz,** Franklin R '49 -26 Court -Brklyn 11242 **Fx:**237-1393
(631) 724-2300 .. **Schwartz,** Fred M '72 -317 Middle Cntry Rd -Smithtwn 11787
(917) 620-1020 .. **Schwartz,** Garrison S '83 -Planetarium Station Bx897 -NY 10024 **Fx:**(212) 799-4362
(212) 770-2050 .. **Schwartz,** Gary A '86 %Transatlantic Hldngs -80 Pine -NY 10005 **Fx:**785-7230
(516) 536-0900 .. **Schwartz,** Gary R '80 (Jacobson & S) -510 Merrick Rd Bx46 -Rockvll Ctr 11571
(212) 468-4800 .. **Schwartz,** Gerald B '66 (Davis & G LLP) -1740 Bway -NY 10019
(212) 608-1516 .. **Schwartz,** Gideon S '97 -277 Bway -NY 10007
(718) 250-0400 .. **Schwartz,** Glenn D '93 %R Tusa -1 MetroTech Ctr -Brklyn 11201 **Fx:**250-0591
(516) 229-4300 .. **Schwartz,** Glenn R '79 %J Bilello & Assoc -875 Merrick Av -Westbury 11590
(212) 962-2800 .. **Schwartz Goldstone & Campisi,LLP** -90 Broad -NY 10004 **Fx:**385-2308
(212) 267-4455 .. **Schwartz & Greenberg** -520 8th Av -NY 10018 **Fx:**(561) 447-9923
(212) 335-4500 .. **Schwartz,** H Jeffrey '07 (DLA Piper LLP) -1251 Av of Amer -NY 10020
(718) 851-1900 .. **Schwartz,** Harold '81 -4920 15th Av -Brklyn 11219 **Fx:**851-4530
(212) 640-2000 .. **Schwartz,** Harold E '90 Amer Exp -200 Vesey -NY 10285
(212) 935-3131 .. **Schwartz,** Harvey '67 OfCnsl Gallet D&B,LLP -845 3rd Av -NY 10022
(212) 439-9678 .. **Schwartz,** Henry R '91 -219 E 69th -NY 10021 **Fx:**439-6728

(212) 596-9000 .. **Schwartz,** Herbert F '64 (Ropes & G LLP) -1211 Av of Amer -NY 10036
(212) 818-1660 .. **Schwartz,** Howard '86 -820 2nd Av -NY 10017
(718) 643-9333 .. **Schwartz,** Howard A '88 -50 Court -Brklyn 11201 **Fx:**522-5644
(212) 973-0572 .. **Schwartz,** Howard J '73 (Wolff & S PC) -140 Bway -NY 10005
(212) 687-3747 .. **Schwartz,** Howard L '49 OfCnsl Tuchman KWL&G,LLP -6 E 45th -NY 10017
(212) 446-4800 .. **Schwartz,** Ian M '03 (Kirkland & E LLP) -153 E 53rd -NY 10022
(212) 971-0416 .. **Schwartz,** Jackie J '93 (J Schwartz & Assoc,PLLC) -245 5th Av -NY 10016 **Fx:**971-0417
(516) 536-0900 .. **Schwartz,** Jacob N '60 (Jacobson & S) -510 Merrick Rd Bx46 -Rockvll Ctr 11571
(212) 649-9713 .. **Schwartz,** Jaimee B '05 %Greystone & Co -152 W 57th -NY 10019
(917) 546-7711 .. **Schwartz,** James E '82 (Mitchell S&K LLP) -12 E 49th -NY 10017 **Fx:**546-7768
(914) 241-1769 .. **Schwartz,** James E '88 -21 Mdwbrk Ln -Mt Kisco 10549
(212) 756-2000 .. **Schwartz,** Jamie Powell '09 %Schulte R&Z LLP -919 3rd Av -NY 10022
(212) 504-6000 .. **Schwartz,** Jason D '10 %Cadwalader W&T LLP -1 World Fncl Ctr -NY 10281
(212) 805-0262 .. **Schwartz,** Jed '07 %Hon PK Castel -500 Pearl -NY 10007
(718) 728-4544 .. **Schwartz,** Jeffrey '78 -21-36 33rd Rd -LIC 11106
(212) 661-6800 .. **Schwartz,** Jeffrey A '06 Cyruli SH&Z LLP -420 Lex Av -NY 10170
(518) 472-1224 .. **Schwartz,** Jeffrey B '96 (Phillips L LLP) -30 S Pearl -Albany 12207
(212) 964-2160 .. **Schwartz,** Jeffrey H '84 -160 Bway -NY 10038
(516) 873-8700 .. **Schwartz,** Jeffrey H '91 (Jones & S,PC) -1 Old Cntry Rd -Carle Pl 11514 **Fx:**873-8711
(212) 538-9069 .. **Schwartz,** Jeffrey I '99 Credit Suisse -1 Mad Av -NY 10010
(516) 833-5630 .. **Schwartz,** Jeffrey L '74 (Beekman SK&L,LLP) -1050 Franklin Av -Gdn Cty 11530
(212) 478-7200 .. **Schwartz,** Jeffrey L '77 (Hahn & H LLP) -488 Mad Av -NY 10022
(516) 487-6550 .. **Schwartz,** Jeffrey M '78 -98 Cuttermill Rd -Gt Neck 11021 **Fx:**829-3946
(212) 545-4678 .. **Schwartz,** Jeffrey M '87 (Wolf HAF&H LLP) -270 Mad Av -NY 10016
(212) 385-0503 .. **Schwartz,** Jeffrey M '95 (Stein F&S LLP) -16 E 34th -NY 10016
(914) 637-8730 .. **Schwartz,** Jeffrey Mark '87 -271 North Av -New Rchll 10801
(212) 450-4000 .. **Schwartz,** Jeffrey N '92 (Davis P&W LLP) -450 Lex Av -NY 10017
(516) 938-3888 .. **Schwartz,** Jeffrey S '03 -410 E Jericho Tpk -Mineola 11501 **Fx:**938-3887
(212) 766-8020 .. **Schwartz,** Jeffrey T '88 -225 Bway -NY 10007 **Fx:**766-8039
(212) 661-2900 .. **Schwartz,** Jennifer A '00 %Kriss & F LLP -360 Lex Av -NY 10017
(212) 907-9600 .. **Schwartz,** Jennifer E '94 %Ingram YGC&B,LLP -250 Park Av -NY 10177
(716) 885-2889 .. **Schwartz,** Jeremy D '05 %Eoannou L&D -484 Delaware Av -Buffalo 14202
(212) 450-4000 .. **Schwartz,** Jeremy M '07 %Davis P&W LLP -450 Lex Av -NY 10017
(212) 252-0300 .. **Schwartz,** Jesse P '06 %Kagan LLLG&C,LLP -200 Mad Av -NY 10016
(212) 403-1000 .. **Schwartz,** Jodi J '85 (Wachtell LR&K) -51 W 52nd -NY 10019
(718) 343-2371 .. **Schwartz,** Joel M '75 -246-16 Union Tpk -Bellerose 11426
(631) 424-0524 .. **Schwartz,** Joel R '93 -3 Hilton Ct -Huntngtn 11743 **Fx:**424-0524
(212) 416-8559 .. **Schwartz,** John M '64 Dept of Law -120 Bway -NY 10271 **Fx:**416-6075
(516) 803-1125 .. **Schwartz,** Jonathan D '87 Cablevision Sys -1111 Stewart Av -Bethpage 11714
(212) 836-8000 .. **Schwartz,** Jordan B '03 %Kaye S LLP -425 Park Av -NY 10022
(212) 326-3939 .. **Schwartz,** Jordan L '10 %Jones D -222 E 41st -NY 10017
(212) 504-6000 .. **Schwartz,** Jordan M '88 (Cadwalader W&T LLP) -1 World Fncl Ctr -NY 10281
(212) 570-3002 .. **Schwartz,** Jordana G '92 NY Blood Ctr,Inc -310 E 67th -NY 10065 **Fx:**879-3158
(212) 813-8800 .. **Schwartz,** Jos A '07 %Goodwin P LLP -620 8th Av -NY 10018
(212) 889-6565 .. **Schwartz,** Joshua N '88 East Wind Advisors LLC -295 Mad Av -NY 10017
(212) 453-3676 .. **Schwartz,** Joshua R '00 ACE INA -1325 Av of Amer -NY 10019
(212) 788-9541 .. **Schwartz,** Joy S '92 Mayor's Ofc -City Hall -NY 10007
(212) 289-7478 .. **Schwartz,** Judith A '75 -160 E 88th -NY 10128
(646) 610-5400 .. **Schwartz,** Julie L '90 NYPD -1 Police Plz -NY 10038
(646) 386-3190 .. **Schwartz,** Karen S '87 %Hon J Madden -60 Centre -NY 10007
(631) 287-2800 .. **Schwartz,** Kathleen F '85 (Schwartz & S,PC) -149 Hmptn Rd -Southampton 11969 **Fx:**287-4842
(212) 880-3800 .. **Schwartz,** Kathlyn M '09 %Akerman S -335 Mad Av -NY 10017
(516) 333-7020 .. **Schwartz,** Kenneth B '84 -555 Westbury Av -Carle Pl 11514
(212) 735-3000 .. **Schwartz,** Kenneth B '01 Cnsl Skadden ASM&F LLP -4 Times Sq -NY 10036
(212) 938-0600 .. **Schwartz,** Kenneth L '92 (Schwartz LLC) -90 Broad -NY 10004 **Fx:**938-0601
(518) 785-1111 .. **Schwartz,** Kenneth M '85 (Farer & S,PC) -12 Century Hill Dr -Latham 12110 **Fx:**785-4325
(212) 403-1000 .. **Schwartz,** Kevin S '08 %Wachtell LR&K -51 W 52nd -NY 10019
(212) 224-6991 .. **Schwartz,** Kira Malyarov '99 %Forest Labs -909 3rd Av -NY 10022
(212) 839-5300 .. **Schwartz,** Kristina S '09 %Sidley A LLP -787 7th Av -NY 10019
(212) 450-4000 .. **Schwartz,** Lanny A '84 (Davis P&W LLP) -450 Lex Av -NY 10017
(845) 638-9400 .. **Schwartz,** Larry J '81 (Schwartz & S) -254 S Main -New Cty 10956
(212) 370-9600 .. **Schwartz,** Laura B '91 Pittleman & Assoc -336 E 43rd -NY 10017 **Fx:**370-9608
(212) 228-2614 .. **Schwartz,** Laurens R '82 -5 E 22nd -NY 10010
(212) 820-9531 .. **Schwartz,** Laurie Lawlor '09 %Hawkins D&W LLP -One Chase Manh Plz -NY 10005
(212) 922-3300 .. **Schwartz,** Lawr '80 Exec Monetary Mgmt -220 E 42nd -NY 10017
(212) 969-0183 .. **Schwartz,** Lawr J '89 -305 W Bway -NY 10013
(212) 626-4100 .. **Schwartz,** Lea K '04 %Baker & M LLP -1114 Av of Amer -NY 10036
(917) 841-7810 .. **Schwartz,** Leana '96 -401 E 80th -NY 10075 **Fx:**(212) 734-7461
(212) 297-5800 .. **Schwartz,** Leaor D '08 %Day P LLP -7 Times Sq -NY 10036
(516) 677-9551 .. **Schwartz,** Lee A '93 -425 Broadhllw Rd -Melvll 11747 **Fx:**(631) 777-2402
(212) 485-9804 .. **Schwartz Levine & Kaplan,PLLC** -60 E 42nd -NY 10165 **Fx:**813-1454
(716) 634-3320 .. **Schwartz,** Lewis L '96 %Pope Law Firm,PLLC -6580 Main -Williamsvll 14221 **Fx:**204-2770
(716) 881-1202 .. **Schwartz,** Lewis L '96 %Pope Law Firm,PLLC -329 Elmwood Av -Buffalo 14222 **Fx:**204-2770
(212) 935-1330 .. **Schwartz,** Lewis M '77 Mall Properties,Inc -654 Mad Av -NY 10065
(212) 228-6320 .. **Schwartz Lichten & Bright, PC** -275 7th Av -NY 10001 **Fx:**358-1353
(212) 389-7818 .. **Schwartz,Lichtenberg LLP** -420 Lex Av -NY 10170 **Fx:**682-6511
(914) 696-5144 .. **Schwartz,Lichtenberg LLP** -2900 Wstchstr Av -Purchase 10577 **Fx:**696-5918
(212) 801-2255 .. **Schwartz,** Lisa A '07 %Greenberg T,LLP -200 Park Av -NY 10166
(212) 403-1000 .. **Schwartz,** Lisa Beth '09 %Wachtell LR&K -51 W 52nd -NY 10019
(212) 649-9700 .. **Schwartz,** Lisa R '90 %Greystone & Co -152 W 57th -NY 10019 **Fx:**649-9701
(516) 364-7659 .. **Schwartz,** Lonny M '88 -203 Brookvll Rd -Glen Head 11545
(212) 603-6300 .. **Schwartz,** Lori A '98 (Robinson BLGG&G PC) -875 3rd Av -NY 10022
(518) 581-8800 .. **Schwartz,** Lynn E '01 %Lemery G LLC -60 Railroad Pl -Saratoga Spgs 12866
(212) 813-1900 .. **Schwartz,** Marc A '89 -230 Park Av -NY 10169
(646) 471-1101 .. **Schwartz,** Marc A '01 PricewaterhouseCoopers LLP -300 Mad Av -NY 10017
(718) 855-2335 .. **Schwartz,** Marc S '75 (Scheinberg F&S,PC) -16 Court -Brklyn 11241
(516) 735-8100 .. **Schwartz,** Margaret L '02 M Schwartz,PLLC -25 Sherwood Rd -Levittwn 11756 **Fx:**735-8188
(516) 294-4433 .. **Schwartz,** Maria M '96 -666 Old Cntry Rd -Gdn Cty 11530
(914) 367-5000 .. **Schwartz,** Mark '78 Amalgamated Life -333 Wstchstr Av -White Plns 10604 **Fx:**367-5792
(914) 696-5144 .. **Schwartz,** Mark H '86 (Schwartz L LLP) -2900 Wstchstr Av -Purchase 10577
(914) 693-8911 .. **Schwartz,** Mark J '84 -18 Sage Ter -Scarsdale 10583
(212) 669-4501 .. **Schwartz,** Marlene F '78 %Tax Appls Tribunal -1 Centre -NY 10007 **Fx:**669-4503
(718) 729-5440 .. **Schwartz,** Marni '92 %Intl Newspaper Printing Co -13-05 44th Av -LIC 11101
(631) 761-7000 .. **Schwartz,** Martin A '68 %Touro Cllg Law Ctr -225 Eastvw Dr -Central Islip 11722
(516) 432-0302 .. **Schwartz,** Martin E '57 (Schwartz & W) -1839 Wilson Av -N Merrick 11566
(212) 768-6700 .. **Schwartz,** Martin J '75 OfCnsl Sonnenschein N&R LLP -1221 Av of Amer -NY 10020
(212) 475-2464 .. **Schwartz,** Martin J '91 -300 Mercer -NY 10003
(212) 759-4888 .. **Schwartz,** Martin V '76 SpclCnsl Phillips L LLP -437 Mad Av -NY 10022
(845) 356-3644 .. **Schwartz,** Martin W '71 -119 Rockland Ctr -Nanuet 10954
(212) 841-4100 .. **Schwartz,** Martin Z '99 Millennium Prtnrs -666 5th Av -NY 10103
(212) 558-4000 .. **Schwartz,** Marvin '52 SrCnsl Sullivan & C LLP -125 Broad -NY 10004
(914) 834-0808 .. **Schwartz,** Marvin L '48 -16 Bayard -Larchmnt 10538
(845) 425-1832 .. **Schwartz,** Marvin L '84 -9 Balanchine Ct -Monsey 10952 **Fx:**425-0606
(585) 753-4500 .. **Schwartz,** Matthew '02 %DA -832 Watts Bldg -Rchstr 14614 **Fx:**753-4576
(212) 806-5400 .. **Schwartz,** Matthew A '00 (Stroock &S&L LLP) -180 Maiden Ln -NY 10038
(212) 558-4000 .. **Schwartz,** Matthew A '04 %Sullivan & C LLP -125 Broad -NY 10004
(212) 714-1200 .. **Schwartz,** Matthew F '92 (Schwartz & P,PLLC) -134 W 29th -NY 10001 **Fx:**714-1264
(212) 637-1945 .. **Schwartz,** Matthew L '03 US Atty -86 Chmbrs -NY 10007
(212) 558-4000 .. **Schwartz,** Max J '75 (Sullivan & C LLP) -125 Broad -NY 10004
(212) 836-8000 .. **Schwartz,** Max R '07 %Kaye S LLP -425 Park Av -NY 10022
(212) 376-3159 .. **Schwartz,** Meryl B '88 Vera Inst of Justice -233 Bway -NY 10279
(212) 736-0979 .. **Schwartz,** Meryl I '91 %J Reiter -350 5th Av -NY 10118 **Fx:**268-5297
(212) 728-8000 .. **Schwartz,** Michl A '83 (Willkie F&G LLP) -787 7th Av -NY 10019
(212) 986-4500 .. **Schwartz,** Michl A '93 (Horwitz H&P) -405 Lex Av -NY 10174
(212) 354-7700 .. **Schwartz,** Michl F '76 (Penn PS&S) -114 W 47th -NY 10036
(212) 267-1950 .. **Schwartz,** Michl F '87 (Salenger SSK&B,LLP) -233 Bway -NY 10279
(914) 997-0071 .. **Schwartz,** Michl H '83 M Schwartz & Assoc,PC -1 Water -White Plns 10601 **Fx:**997-0536
(212) 209-3149 .. **Schwartz,** Michl I '00 Taconic Capital Advisors LLC -450 Park Av -NY 10022
(212) 735-3000 .. **Schwartz,** Michl J '02 Cnsl Skadden ASM&F LLP -4 Times Sq -NY 10036
(212) 479-6000 .. **Schwartz,** Michl S '08 %Cooley LLP -1114 Av of Amer -NY 10036
(212) 403-1000 .. **Schwartz,** Michl W '68 OfCnsl Wachtell LR&K -51 W 52nd -NY 10019
(212) 318-3000 .. **Schwartz,** Michelle '07 %Fulbright & J LLP -666 5th Av -NY 10103
(212) 682-1800 .. **Schwartz,** Milton '56 (Grant HS&K LLP) -675 3rd Av -NY 10017
(212) 306-7434 .. **Schwartz,** Mindi I '88 NYC Deferred Comp -40 Rector -NY 10006
(212) 812-0057 .. **Schwartz,** Mitchell B '98 Clear Channel Outdoor -110 E 42nd -NY 10017
(212) 485-3444 .. **Schwartz,** Mitchell P '04 MLB Advncd Media -75 9th Av -NY 10011 **Fx:**485-3456
(212) 962-2800 .. **Schwartz,** Mordecai T '84 (Schwartz G&C,LLP) -90 Broad -NY 10004
(212) 889-6565 .. **Schwartz,** Murray '49 (Schwartz & P LLP) -295 Mad Av -NY 10017
(212) 592-1400 .. **Schwartz,** Murray D '73 Cnsl Herrick,F LLP -2 Park Av -NY 10016
(212) 223-6700 .. **Schwartz,** Nancy '91 %Zukerman GB&C,LLP -875 3rd Av -NY 10022
(212) 446-4800 .. **Schwartz,** Nicholas M '09 %Kirkland & E LLP -153 E 53rd -NY 10022
(212) 889-6565 .. **Schwartz & Perry LLP** -295 Mad Av -NY 10017 **Fx:**779-8208
(212) 818-8800 .. **Schwartz,** Peter A '82 (Graubard M) -405 Lex Av -NY 10174
(212) 841-1000 .. **Schwartz,** Peter A '99 (Covington & B LLP) -620 8th Av -NY 10018
(212) 756-2000 .. **Schwartz,** Phyllis A '84 (Schulte R&Z LLP) -919 3rd Av -NY 10022
(212) 318-6000 .. **Schwartz,** Rachael L '08 %Paul HJ&W LLP -75 E 55th -NY 10022
(212) 227-4300 .. **Schwartz,** Rachel '95 (Schwartz & T LLP) -15 Maiden Ln -NY 10038 **Fx:**227-4311
(516) 798-2712 .. **Schwartz,** Rand P '67 -1000 Park Blvd -Massapequa Pk 11762 **Fx:**798-7732

(516) 357-3000 .. **Schwartz,** Randi B '07 %Rivkin R LLP -926 RXR Plz -Uniondale 11556
(718) 613-3500 .. **Schwartz,** Rebecca S '91 %UIA Bd -Bx29002 -Brklyn 11201 **Fx:**613-3566
(212) 479-6000 .. **Schwartz,** Renee '56 (Cooley LLP) -1114 Av of Amer -NY 10036
(212) 487-9700 .. **Schwartz,** Renee S P '80 OfCnsl White F&F,LLP -61 Bway -NY 10006
(631) 752-8600 .. **Schwartz,** Revan R '82 -110 Schmitt Blvd -Farmngdl 11735
(516) 558-7672 .. **Schwartz,** Richd B '53 (RB Schwartz & Assoc,PC) -6800 Jericho Tpk -Syosset 11791 **Fx:**558-7673
(212) 983-9330 .. **Schwartz,** Richd D '05 %Faruqi & F,LLP -369 Lex Av -NY 10017 **Fx:**983-9331
(212) 218-5500 .. **Schwartz,** Richd G '87 (Seyfarth S LLP) -620 8th Av -NY 10018
(212) 416-8284 .. **Schwartz,** Richd L '82 %Dept of Law -120 Bway -NY 10271
(607) 687-8888 .. **Schwartz,** Richd M '72 -442 Front -Owego 13827 **Fx:**687-5448
(212) 859-8000 .. **Schwartz,** Richd M '78 (Fried FHS&J LLP) -1 NY Plz -NY 10004
(212) 363-3939 .. **Schwartz,** Richd S '79 Lawrence Grp -45 Bway -NY 10006
(718) 897-9400 .. **Schwartz,** Robt '73 -85-20 68th Av -Rego Pk 11374
(212) 593-2628 .. **Schwartz,** Robt '04 JL Advisors,LLC -400 Mad Av -NY 10017
(718) 948-6100 .. **Schwartz,** Robt A '73 -201 Keegans Ln -Staten Isl 10308
(585) 334-4270 .. **Schwartz,** Robt A '79 -2468 E Henrietta Rd -Rchstr 14623 **Fx:**334-4275
(516) 571-3800 .. **Schwartz,** Robt A '87 %DA -262 Old Cntry Rd -Mineola 11501 **Fx:**248-9479
(212) 237-1000 .. **Schwartz,** Robt A '89 (Windels ML&M,LLP) -156 W 56th -NY 10019
(914) 262-2292 .. **Schwartz,** Robt C '01 -19 Roble Rd -Suffern 10901 **Fx:**(845) 362-1583
(914) 698-7579 .. **Schwartz,** Robt E '63 -315 Claflin Av -Mamaroneck 10543 **Fx:**698-6569
(212) 308-7300 .. **Schwartz,** Robt Hill '58 -950 3rd Av -NY 10022 **Fx:**826-3273
(845) 896-9651 .. **Schwartz,** Robt M '77 (Lazar & S) -280 Route 82 -Hopewell Junct 12533
(212) 473-3275 .. **Schwartz,** Robt M '86 -16 Bayard -Larchmnt 10538
(212) 644-0900 .. **Schwartz,** Robt R '55 -300 E 52nd -NY 10022
(516) 832-2525 .. **Schwartz,** Robt S '67 (Holmes S&G) -320 Endo Blvd -Gdn Cty 11530
(212) 742-3390 .. **Schwartz,** Robt S '86 Lindabury ME&C,PC -26 Bway -NY 10004
(212) 218-2100 .. **Schwartz,** Robt S '04 %Fitzpatrick CH&S -1290 Av of Amer -NY 10104
(973) 274-3230 .. **Schwartz,** Robt S '04 %Proskauer R LLP -1585 Bway -NY 10036 **Fx:**274-3299
(212) 906-1200 .. **Schwartz,** Roger G '97 (Latham & W) -885 3rd Av -NY 10022
(646) 392-9250 .. **Schwartz,** Ronald A '75 %M Klein & Assoc -200 Mad Av -NY 10016 **Fx:**(212) 779-1499
(718) 347-6100 .. **Schwartz,** Ronald J '64 RJ Schwartz,PC -246-16 Union Tpk -Bellerose 11426 **Fx:**347-2012
(718) 692-2984 .. **Schwartz,** Ronald L '89 -809 Av M -Brklyn 11230
(212) 935-5500 .. **Schwartz,** Rose Hilary '81 (Franklin WR&V) -488 Mad Av -NY 10022
(212) 644-9236 .. **Schwartz,** Rose-Ellen '79 -235 E 49th -NY 10017
(212) 686-1666 .. **Schwartz,** Roy J '56 -112 Mad Av -NY 10016 **Fx:**689-9680
(212) 732-6460 .. **Schwartz & Salomon,PC** -225 Bway -NY 10007 **Fx:**608-3785
(212) 752-1000 .. **Schwartz,** Sam '80 (Eiseman LL&K,PC) -805 3rd Av -NY 10022
(914) 750-5933 .. **Schwartz,** Samantha J '10 %Kissel H&W LLP -580 Wht Plns Rd -Tarrytwn 10591
(212) 485-9804 .. **Schwartz,** Sandy T '04 (Schwartz L&K,PLLC) -60 E 42nd -NY 10165
(212) 779-0057 .. **Schwartz,** Scott B '00 Hach & R,LLP -185 Mad Av -NY 10016
(516) 663-6600 .. **Schwartz,** Scott D '00 %Ruskin MF,PC -1425 RXR Plz -Uniondale 11556
(716) 849-1333 .. **Schwartz,** Scott M '75 SpclCnsl Lipsitz GSC LLP -42 Delaware Av -Buffalo 14202 **Fx:**849-1314
(917) 655-4598 .. **Schwartz,** Scott M '95 -110 Wall -NY 10005
(516) 542-9000 .. **Schwartz,** Scott R '93 %R Marnell,PC -90 Merrick Av -E Meadow 11554 **Fx:**542-2039
(212) 735-3000 .. **Schwartz,** Seth M '83 (Skadden ASM&F LLP) -4 Times Sq -NY 10036
(212) 751-2700 .. **Schwartz,** Seymour '51 %JAMS -620 8th Av -NY 10018 **Fx:**751-4099
(516) 621-0900 .. **Schwartz,** Shalom A '05 %Natiss & G,PC -277 Willis Av -Roslyn Hts 11577
(718) 390-5422 .. **Schwartz,** Sharon D '85 %Civil Ct -927 Castleton Av -Staten Isl 10310 **Fx:**390-8108
(716) 200-5050 .. **Schwartz,** Sharon J '93 (Harris B PLLC) -726 Exchange -Buffalo 14210
(212) 685-9660 .. **Schwartz,** Sheldon '63 (Schwartz & B) -295 Mad Av -NY 10017 **Fx:**599-6272
(212) 709-8342 .. **Schwartz,** Shelley G '79 %JK Hargrove -110 Wall -NY 10005 **Fx:**(973) 580-1740
(212) 398-4300 .. **Schwartz,** Shoshana Miller '96 OfCnsl LS Savitt -1065 Av of Amer -NY 10018 **Fx:**398-4309
(845) 638-9400 .. **Schwartz & Silverstein** -254 S Main -New Cty 10956 **Fx:**638-9090
(212) 752-5258 .. **Schwartz Simon Edelstein & Celso LLC** -845 3rd Av -NY 10022
(914) 828-8193 .. **Schwartz,** Stacey L '09 Swiss RE Life & Health America Inc -175 King -Armonk 10504
(212) 788-7993 .. **Schwartz,** Stephanie '00 ACS-Legal -220 Church -NY 10013
(718) 390-5337 .. **Schwartz,** Stephanie A '03 %Law Dept -60 Bay -Staten Isl 10301 **Fx:**390-5338
(516) 620-8585 .. **Schwartz,** Stephen J '68 (Schwartz & F,PC) -3000 Marcus Av -Lk Success 11042 **Fx:**488-1238
(914) 793-1400 .. **Schwartz,** Stephen J '70 (Veneruso CS&C,LLP) -35 E Grassy Sprain Rd -Ynkrs 10710 **Fx:**793-1867
(212) 964-3290 .. **Schwartz,** Steven A '92 %Levidow L&O -299 Bway -NY 10007
(212) 415-8600 .. **Schwartz,** Steven C '85 (Locke LB&L LLP) -3 World Fncl Ctr -NY 10281
(631) 424-5100 .. **Schwartz,** Steven D '88 -410 NY Av -Huntngtn 11743
(518) 473-8047 .. **Schwartz,** Steven H '82 %Dept of Law -The Cptl -Albany 12224
(516) 572-2000 .. **Schwartz,** Steven L '81 %DA -99 Main -Hempstd 11550 **Fx:**572-2606
(212) 294-6700 .. **Schwartz,** Steven M '88 (Winston & S) -200 Park Av -NY 10166
(631) 329-2330 .. **Schwartz,** Steven P '74 -Bx1895 -E Hampton 11937
(212) 481-2200 .. **Schwartz,** Steven T '97 -1901 Emmons Av -Brklyn 11235 **Fx:**481-2290
(718) 665-1700 .. **Schwartz,** Stuart D '83 (Gottlieb S&S,LLP) -180 E 162nd -Bronx 10451
(518) 426-3409 .. **Schwartz,** Stuart M '86 Transatlantic Global,LLC -302 Loudon Rd -Loudonvll 12211
(212) 682-7474 .. **Schwartz,** Susan J '80 (Foley & L LLP) -90 Park Av -NY 10016
(646) 386-5129 .. **Schwartz,** Tamara Lee '99 Family Ct -60 Lafayette -NY 10013
(212) 776-5000 .. **Schwartz,** Terence B '90 %NYC Housing Auth -250 Bway -NY 10007 **Fx:**776-5039
(212) 977-9700 .. **Schwartz,** Tiberio '77 (Phillips N LLP) -666 5th Av -NY 10103
(212) 841-7500 .. **Schwartz,** Todd A '97 Cushman & Wakefield -1290 Av of Amer -NY 10104
(516) 432-0302 .. **Schwartz & Waldman** -1839 Wilson Av -N Merrick 11566 **Fx:**(212) 295-2233
(212) 735-3000 .. **Schwartz,** Wallace L '78 (Skadden ASM&F LLP) -4 Times Sq -NY 10036
(914) 478-3667 .. **Schwartz,** Walter M '63 -56 Main Bx104 -Irvngtn 10533 **Fx:**591-5172
(718) 630-4589 .. **Schwartz,** Warren M '00 %US Army -117 Gen Lee Av -Brklyn 11252 **Fx:**630-4303
(516) 739-8111 .. **Schwartz,** Wendy B '95 %D Lavelle -38 Willis Av -Mineola 11501 **Fx:**739-3917
(212) 521-5400 .. **Schwartz,** Wendy H '91 (Reed S LLP) -599 Lex Av -NY 10022
(212) 790-0200 .. **Schwartz,** Wm '89 Benj N Cardozo Schl of Law -55 5th Av -NY 10003 **Fx:**790-0345
(212) 504-6000 .. **Schwartz,** Wm '89 Cnsl Cadwalader W&T LLP -1 World Fncl Ctr -NY 10281
(212) 479-6000 .. **Schwartz,** Wm J '79 (Cooley LLP) -1114 Av of Amer -NY 10036
(718) 509-9453 .. **Schwartz,** Yisroel S '08 (Augenstein & S,PC) -1244 49th -Brklyn 11219 **Fx:**504-7755
(516) 342-2200 .. **Schwartzapfel Partners** -300 Jericho Quad -Jericho 11753 **Fx:**342-2400
(631) 271-7200 .. **Schwartzapfel Partners** -202 E Main -Huntngtn 11743 **Fx:**547-0212
(516) 342-2200 .. **Schwartzapfel,** Steven J '81 (Schwartzapfel Prtnrs) -300 Jericho Quad -Jericho 11753
(212) 801-6544 .. **Schwartzbaum,** David M '88 (Greenberg T,LLP) -200 Park Av -NY 10166
(212) 468-4800 .. **Schwartzberg,** Brad J '90 (Davis & G LLP) -1740 Bway -NY 10019
(212) 857-8230 .. **Schwartzberg,** David A '92 %Baker MM&M,PC -330 W 34th -NY 10001
(212) 687-1736 .. **Schwartzberg,** Hilary M '09 R Schwartzberg & Assoc,PLLC -60 E 42nd -NY 10165
(212) 267-1950 .. **Schwartzberg,** Jack '63 -233 Bway -NY 10279
(516) 294-8844 .. **Schwartzberg,** Martin A '89 (L'Abbate BC&C,LLP) -1001 Franklin Av -Gdn Cty 11530
(212) 221-6900 .. **Schwartzberg,** Michl '90 (Winget S&S,LLP) -45 Bway -NY 10006
(212) 510-0500 .. **Schwartzberg,** Paul K '93 %US Trustees Ofc -33 Whitehall -NY 10004 **Fx:**668-2255
(212) 687-1736 .. **Schwartzberg,** Raymond B '67 (R Schwartzberg & Assoc,PLLC) -60 E 42nd -NY 10165
(631) 666-3300 .. **Schwartzer,** Richd D '73 Askinas & M -1991 Union Blvd -Bay Shr 11706 **Fx:**666-3392
(212) 906-1200 .. **Schwartzman,** Andrea J '97 (Latham & W) -885 3rd Av -NY 10022
(212) 206-6101 .. **Schwartzman,** Danl A '83 Time Equities Inc -55 5th Av -NY 10003 **Fx:**675-1489
(212) 906-1200 .. **Schwartzman,** Eric J '96 (Latham & W) -885 3rd Av -NY 10022
(212) 583-6000 .. **Schwartzman,** Eric S '94 Geller & Co LLC -800 3rd Av -NY 10022
(585) 546-7686 .. **Schwartzman,** Frank A '70 (Claus CS&S) -19 W Main -Rchstr 14614
(212) 581-0031 .. **Schwartzman,** Fredk '61 -420 Lex Av -NY 10170 **Fx:**582-0176
(212) 557-2900 .. **Schwartzman Garelik Walker & Troy,PC** -355 Lex Av -NY 10017 **Fx:**983-4193
(212) 557-2900 .. **Schwartzman,** Herman '55 (Schwartzman GW&T,PC) -355 Lex Av -NY 10017
(212) 867-4488 .. **Schwartzman,** James '86 %Moss & K -122 E 42nd -NY 10168
(516) 741-0070 .. **Schwartzman,** Jonathan B '96 (Cordova & S,LLP) -666 Old Cntry Rd -Gdn Cty 11530 **Fx:**741-4225
(212) 245-1000 .. **Schwartzreich,** Lauren E '05 %Outten & G LLP -3 Park Av -NY 10016
(516) 569-9539 .. **Schwartz-Sidrane,** Karen L '86 (Sidrane & S-S) -1427 Sturl Av -Hewlett 11557
(212) 264-8819 .. **Schwartz Simins,** Lyllian '93 %SSA-ODAR -26 Fed Plz -NY 10278 **Fx:**264-8633
(212) 232-1300 .. **Schwartzstein,** Adam N '95 (Lewis BB&S LLP) -77 Water -NY 10005
(212) 337-5767 .. **Schwartz-Weinstock,** Nancy '90 Village Care of NY -154 Christopher -NY 10014
(212) 218-2100 .. **Schwarz,** Christina A L '09 %Fitzpatrick CH&S -1290 Av of Amer -NY 10104
(212) 688-8555 .. **Schwarz,** Danl D '08 %Fragomen DB&L LLP -7 Hanover Sq -NY 10004
(631) 491-5660 .. **Schwarz,** David M '73 (D Schwarz,PC) -15 Gorham Ln -Dix Hlls 11746 **Fx:**491-3318
(212) 967-1800 .. **Schwarz,** David M '00 (Bryant BJ&R LLP) -140 Bway -NY 10005
(212) 705-7000 .. **Schwarz,** Douglas T '04 (Bingham M LLP) -399 Park Av -NY 10022
(212) 557-1400 .. **Schwarz,** Edw J '75 %Marx Rlty -708 3rd Av -NY 10017 **Fx:**983-4532
(908) 654-1761 .. **Schwarz,** Elan S '96 -96 West Shore Dr -Putnam Vly 10579
(212) 566-5500 .. **Schwarz,** Elise '03 -225 Bway -NY 10007 **Fx:**566-5924
(212) 732-9000 .. **Schwarz,** Eric K '01 %Sullivan PBM&C PC -120 Bway -NY 10271
(212) 474-1000 .. **Schwarz,** Fredk A O Jr. '61 SrCnsl Cravath S&M LLP -825 8th Av -NY 10019
(212) 219-3360 .. **Schwarz,** Ghita '00 %Latino Justice PRLDEF -99 Hudson -NY 10013 **Fx:**431-4276
(718) 250-2000 .. **Schwarz,** Gregory R '09 %DA -350 Jay -Brklyn 11201 **Fx:**250-2314
(212) 530-5000 .. **Schwarz,** Helfried J '89 (Milbank TH&M LLP) -1 Chase Manh Plz -NY 10005
(516) 390-1020 .. **Schwarz,** Jean-Paul '97 Marcum & Kliegman LLC -10 Melvll Park Rd -Melvll 11747
(212) 506-1700 .. **Schwarz,** Jennifer Blumenfeld '03 %Kasowitz BT&F LLP -1633 Bway -NY 10019

(845) 357-7700 .. **Schwarz**, John M Jr. '89 (Ryan & S LLP) -103 Wshngtn Av -Suffern 10901 **Fx**:357-7794
(212) 272-9120 .. **Schwarz**, John M '94 %JP Morgan Chase -383 Mad Av -NY 10179
(212) 240-9100 .. **Schwarz**, Jos K '83 (Schuchman S&Z-L,LLP) -225 Bway -NY 10007 **Fx**:732-4580
(212) 207-6650 .. **Schwarz**, Julius Randolph '96 Bayrock Grp, LLC -725 5th Av -NY 10022 **Fx**:(646) 536-8929
(212) 509-9400 .. **Schwarz**, Kenneth G '67 (Cozen O) -45 Bway Atrium -NY 10006
(212) 577-3688 .. **Schwarz**, Kristina '89 %Leg Aid -199 Water -NY 10038 **Fx**:509-8431
(212) 682-6800 .. **Schwarz**, Lori Samet '83 (Zetlin & D LLP) -801 2nd Av -NY 10017
(212) 838-2828 .. **Schwarz**, Mark '70 -485 Mad Av -NY 10022 **Fx**:826-1046
(914) 948-2222 .. **Schwarz**, Matthew D '99 %Rabin P&H -44 Church -White Plns 10601 **Fx**:948-2255
(914) 681-0200 .. **Schwarz**, Michl J '06 %DelBello DWW&W,LLP -1 N Lex Av -White Plns 10601
(845) 291-2650 .. **Schwarz**, Peter R '83 %Cnty Atty -285 Main -Goshen 10924 **Fx**:291-3014
(212) 980-4500 .. **Schwarz**, Raimonde L '86 Cnsl Cohen L LLP -885 3rd Av -NY 10022
(646) 386-4789 .. **Schwarz**, Roger J '77 %Comm Judicial Cndct -61 Bway -NY 10006 **Fx**:458-0037
(212) 447-0950 .. **Schwarz**, S Bernard '75 -305 Bway -NY 10007 **Fx**:447-0804
(212) 825-5974 .. **Schwarz**, Sandra F '95 %Dept of Invstgtn -80 Maiden Ln -NY 10038 **Fx**:825-2860
(212) 439-6330 .. **Schwarz**, Simon '98 -954 Lex Av -NY 10021
(585) 325-5150 .. **Schwarz**, Stephen G '82 (Faraci L,LLP) -28 E Main -Rchstr 14614
(718) 681-6711 .. **Schwarz**, Steven G '83 -895 Sheridan Av -Bronx 10451 **Fx**:538-5101
(914) 251-6010 .. **Schwarz**, Thos J '69 Purchase Cllg -735 Andrsn Hill Rd -Purchase 10577 **Fx**:251-6014
(845) 592-2301 .. **Schwarz**, Wm K '97 -97 Spy Glass Hl -Hopewell Junct 12533
(516) 328-3500 .. **Schwarzenberg**, Jos A '97 %McDonnell & A,PC -401 Franklin Av -Gdn Cty 11530
(212) 354-7700 .. **Schwarzfeld**, Neal '72 (Penn PS&S) -114 W 47th -NY 10036
(212) 204-7979 .. **Schwarzman**, Edw '07 Cinetic Media -555 W 25th -NY 10001 **Fx**:204-7980
(716) 633-5050 .. **Schwarzmueller**, Kristopher A '00 %Gelber & O,LLC -6512 Main -Amherst 14221 **Fx**:633-9052
(212) 785-9100 .. **Schweber**, Matthew S '95 %Paduano & W LLP -1251 Av of Amer -NY 10020
(212) 245-4871 .. **Schweber**, Scott '92 S Schweber,PC -250 W 57th -NY 10107 **Fx**:956-4374
(718) 590-2000 .. **Schwechter**, Melissa P '07 %DA -198 E 161st -Bronx 10451 **Fx**:590-6477
(917) 796-3459 .. **Schwecke**, Carmena B '87 -2027 Wllmsbrdg Rd -Bronx 10461
(212) 657-1394 .. **Schwed**, Alejandro '85 Citigroup Global Mrkts -77 Water -NY 10005
(212) 664-4444 .. **Schwed**, Mariano '98 NBC -30 Rckfllr Plz -NY 10112
(212) 310-8000 .. **Schwed**, Mark '06 %Weil G&M LLP -767 5th Av -NY 10153
(718) 263-7676 .. **Schwed**, Michl J '72 (Schwed & Z) -125-10 Qns Blvd -Kew Gdns 11415
(212) 223-0400 .. **Schwed**, Nathan '82 (Zeichner E&K LLP) -575 Lex Av -NY 10022
(212) 407-4000 .. **Schwed**, P Gregory '77 (Loeb & L,LLP) -345 Park Av -NY 10154
(212) 848-5445 .. **Schwed**, Richd F '94 (Shearman & S LLP) -599 Lex Av -NY 10022
(212) 937-7276 .. **Schwed**, Robt A '75 (WilmerHale) -399 Park Av -NY 10022
(646) 346-7000 .. **Schwed**, Roger E '87 %Maxcor Fncl Grp Inc -1 Seaport Plz -NY 10038
(631) 962-2033 .. **Schwedes**, Janine M '09 OSI Pharmaceuticals Inc -41 Pinelawn Rd -Melvll 11747
(315) 461-0091 .. **Schwedes**, Sheila Finn '93 %Epstein & H -110 Elwood-Davis Rd -N Syracuse 13212
(716) 858-2424 .. **Schwegler**, James C '09 %DA -25 Delaware Av -Buffalo 14202 **Fx**:858-7425
(716) 858-2424 .. **Schwegler**, Lawr M '87 %DA -25 Delaware Av -Buffalo 14202 **Fx**:858-7425
(845) 684-5143 .. **Schweidel**, Joel R '72 -150 Purdy Hllw Rd -Woodstock 12498
(212) 471-8492 .. **Schweidel**, Sharon '87 %Herzfeld & R,PC -125 Broad -NY 10004
(914) 833-0922 .. **Schweig**, Emery McClennen '86 -26 Stone Cabin Rd -New Rchll 10801
(516) 877-2157 .. **Schweiger**, Harvey A '66 -1 Old Cntry Rd -Carle Pl 11514
(516) 622-0324 .. **Schweiger**, Sandor C '62 (S Schweiger,PC) -8 Locust Dr -Gt Neck 11021 **Fx**:622-0328
(212) 789-3100 .. **Schweiger**, Stephen G '97 %Riemer & B LLP -7 Times Sq -NY 10036 **Fx**:719-0140
(646) 386-5700 .. **Schweiloch**, Danielle A '00 %Civil Ct -111 Centre -NY 10013
(212) 335-9000 .. **Schweiloch**, Harrison C '05 DA -1 Hogan Pl -NY 10013
(212) 225-2000 .. **Schweitzer**, Lisa M '97 (Cleary GS&H) -1 Lbrty Plz -NY 10006
(347) 334-4584 .. **Schweitzer**, Mark A '09 %Hurwitz S&R -299 Bway -NY 10007
(718) 435-4318 .. **Schweitzer**, Robt L '75 -1754 52nd -Brklyn 11204
(212) 715-0300 .. **Schweitzer**, Theo U '95 %Tishman Speyer Prop -45 Rckfllr Plz -NY 10111 **Fx**:332-6603
(212) 465-8840 .. **Schweitzer**, Timothy F '00 (Hofmann & S) -360 W 31st -NY 10001 **Fx**:465-8849
(212) 471-8522 .. **Schweizer**, C Thos '77 (Herzfeld & R,PC) -125 Broad -NY 10004
(212) 885-2870 .. **Schweizer**, Ricki J '87 %Interpublic Grp -100 W 33rd -NY 10001 **Fx**:885-2823
(646) 328-0850 .. **Schwell**, Dov '92 %Outside Cnsl Solutns LLP -1430 Bway -NY 10018 **Fx**:360-5000
(516) 281-9800 .. **Schwendemann**, Edw V '86 (Goldberg S LLP) -200 Old Cntry Rd -Mineola 11501
(716) 854-7690 .. **Schwendler**, Edw J Jr. '51 -515 Brisbane Bldg -Buffalo 14203 **Fx**:854-7692
(716) 853-1887 .. **Schwendler**, Edw J III '82 %E Tenney -5 Niagara Sq -Buffalo 14202 **Fx**:853-1893
(716) 688-6994 .. **Schwendler**, Judith A '83 -11 Spicebush Ln -Williamsvll 14221
(914) 690-2103 .. **Schwenk**, Michl R '97 %Oak Hill Platinum Prtnrs,LLC -1100 King -Rye Brook 10573 **Fx**:690-2118
(212) 859-8000 .. **Schwenkel**, Robt C '83 (Fried FHS&J LLP) -1 NY Plz -NY 10004
(518) 793-3424 .. **Schwenker**, Eric C '06 %Brennan & W LLP -163 Haviland Rd -Queensbury 12804 **Fx**:793-3422
(607) 737-2969 .. **Schwenkler**, John E '01 %Pub Def -163 Lk Bx588 -Elmira 14902 **Fx**:737-2853
(212) 455-2000 .. **Schwerd**, Moshe '86 SrCnsl Simpson T&B LLP -425 Lex Av -NY 10017
(212) 416-8000 .. **Schwerdt**, Robt J '87 %Dept of Law -120 Bway -NY 10271
(914) 734-4180 .. **Schwerman**, Paul E '84 Cnsl Law Dept -840 Main -Peekskill 10566 **Fx**:734-4183
(315) 788-6700 .. **Schwerzmann & Wise,PC** -215 Wshngtn Bx704 -Watertwn 13601 **Fx**:788-2813
(212) 728-8000 .. **Schwesinger**, S Kathrin '10 %Willkie F&G LLP -787 7th Av -NY 10019
(212) 344-6700 .. **Schwimmer**, Jeffrey I '80 -50 Broad -NY 10004 **Fx**:344-5163
(212) 504-6000 .. **Schwimmer**, Jodi E '02 %Cadwalader W&T LLP -1 World Fncl Ctr -NY 10281
(212) 554-7800 .. **Schwimmer**, Martin B '89 (Moses & S LLP) -405 Lex Av -NY 10174
(212) 980-9600 .. **Schwimmer**, Stacey L '10 %Kaufman B&R -120 Bway -NY 10271
(212) 951-6557 .. **Schwind**, Donald J '75 %NYS Ed Dept-OLS -475 Park Av S -NY 10016 **Fx**:951-6573
(585) 225-2470 .. **Schwind**, Lawr J '83 (Lacy K LLP) -1101-C English Rd -Rchstr 14616
(585) 454-5650 .. **Schwind**, Lawr J '83 (Lacy K LLP) -130 E Main -Rchstr 14604
(585) 225-2470 .. **Schwind**, Lawr J '83 (Lacy K LLP) -20 Main -Hilton 14468
(716) 881-1800 .. **Schwind**, Richd G '59 (Fiorella & S,LLP) -155 Summer -Buffalo 14222 **Fx**:881-1897
(716) 626-2547 .. **Schwinge**, Kimberly J '98 AXA Advsrs -325 Essjay Rd -Buffalo 14221
(212) 408-5100 .. **Schwinger**, Robt A '85 (Chadbourne & P LLP) -30 Rckfllr Plz -NY 10112
(212) 610-6300 .. **Schwisow**, Adrienne B '09 %Allen & O -1221 Av of Amer -NY 10020
(212) 318-6000 .. **Schwitter**, Wm F Jr. '84 (Paul HJ&W LLP) -75 E 55th -NY 10022
(212) 318-6000 .. **Schwitzer**, Eric '10 %Paul HJ&W LLP -75 E 55th -NY 10022
(718) 258-9511 .. **Schwitzer**, Ilana R '80 -1435 Coney Isl Av -Brklyn 11230
(516) 741-2590 .. **Schwitzer**, Joel S '75 -1 Old Cntry Rd -Carle Pl 11514
(212) 683-3800 .. **Schwitzer**, Wm '85 (Dinkes & S,PC) -112 Mad Av -NY 10016
(718) 797-1000 .. **Schwitzman**, Jay H '87 -26 Court -Brklyn 11242 **Fx**:643-5800
(212) 259-8000 .. **Schwolsky**, John M '86 (Dewey & L LLP) -1301 Av of Amer -NY 10019
(516) 944-6058 .. **Sciacca**, Jos J '80 -33 Main -Pt Wash 11050 **Fx**:944-2751
(212) 891-2100 .. **Sciacca**, Jos P '97 Blackacre Cptl Mgmt,LLC -299 Park Av -NY 10171
(212) 495-0317 .. **Sciacca**, Thos '04 (Caraway & S,LLP) -44 Wall -NY 10005 **Fx**:(646) 786-4888
(914) 517-5000 .. **Scialabba**, Donald J '81 (Meiselman DPC&E,PC) -1311 Mamaroneck Av -White Plns 10605
(914) 997-0332 .. **Scialdone**, Gregory P '85 -405 Tarrytown Rd -White Plns 10607
(212) 450-4000 .. **Scialla**, Crystal M '10 %Davis P&W LLP -450 Lex Av -NY 10017
(845) 892-0872 .. **Sciallo**, Lisa A '04 IBM -2070 Route 52 -Hopewell Junct 12533
(631) 543-2953 .. **Sciandra**, Kathleen Daniels '76 -5 Wesleyan Ct -Smithtwn 11787 **Fx**:543-1526
(716) 855-6711 .. **Sciandra**, Russell J '76 Housing Auth -300 Perry -Buffalo 14204 **Fx**:855-6761
(212) 228-2528 .. **Sciangula**, Salvatore J '04 D Katz & Assoc,LLP -116 E 16th -NY 10003 **Fx**:228-4744
(212) 626-4100 .. **Sciarra**, Anthony T '08 %Baker & M LLP -1114 Av of Amer -NY 10036
(585) 245-5361 .. **Sciarrino**, Alfred J '77 SUNY Geneseo Schl of Business -Fraser 214 -Geneseo 14454
(718) 428-4949 .. **Sciarrino**, Nicholas J '87 (Kim P&S,PC) -42-40 Bell Blvd -Bayside 11361 **Fx**:428-1316
(585) 658-2844 .. **Sciarrino**, Raymond L '63 RL Sciarrino,PC -106 Main -Mt Morris 14510 **Fx**:658-4355
(585) 237-4120 .. **Sciarrino**, Raymond P '96 Sciarrino & S,PC -59 Leicester -Perry 14530 **Fx**:237-0056
(212) 907-0990 .. **Sciascia**, Joel M '98 Pavarini McGovern LLC -352 Park Av S -NY 10010 **Fx**:991-0373
(212) 848-4000 .. **Scibetta**, Brian P '09 %Shearman & S LLP -599 Lex Av -NY 10022
(212) 257-6960 .. **Scibetta**, Chas J Jr. '96 (Chaffetz L LLP) -1350 Av of Amer -NY 10019
(585) 232-2770 .. **Scibetta**, Michl P '93 (Scibetta Law Ofc) -30 W Broad -Rchstr 14614 **Fx**:232-2803
(315) 472-5856 .. **Scibilia**, Frank B '91 -307 S Clinton -Syracuse 13202 **Fx**:479-8847
(212) 421-4100 .. **Scibilia**, Frank P '96 (Pryor C LLP) -7 Times Sq -NY 10036
(516) 766-6200 .. **Scibilia**, Jos C '63 -100 N Centre Av -Rockvll Ctr 11570
(315) 428-8344 .. **Scicchitano**, Gregory A '93 (Scicchitano & P,PLLC) -5789 Widewaters Pkwy -Syracuse 13214
(315) 428-8344 .. **Scicchitano & Pinsky,PLLC** -5789 Widewaters Pkwy -Syracuse 13214 **Fx**:475-8230
(212) 782-4837 .. **Scifo**, Francis Hugh '83 Bank of Tokyo-Mitsubishi UFJ,Ltd -1251 Av of Amer -NY 10020
(845) 228-4550 .. **Scigliano**, Sarah R '06 %S Santoro Sr,PC -105 Gleneida Av -Carmel 10512 **Fx**:225-4992
(631) 853-4161 .. **Scileppi**, Jeremy J '91 %DA -N Cnty Cmplx Bldg 77 -Hauppauge 11788 **Fx**:853-4192
(212) 332-8300 .. **Scileppi**, Laura J '08 %Dunnegan LLC -350 5th Av -NY 10118 **Fx**:332-8301
(716) 853-1887 .. **Scime**, Courtney C '94 %E Tenney -5 Niagara Sq -Buffalo 14202 **Fx**:853-1893
(716) 849-1333 .. **Scime**, James T '77 (Lipsitz GSC LLP) -42 Delaware Av -Buffalo 14202
(212) 245-1000 .. **Scimone**, Michl J '10 %Outten & G LLP -3 Park Av -NY 10016
(716) 877-8889 .. **Scinta**, Deborah J '95 -9 Westgate Rd -Kenmore 14217 **Fx**:877-4818
(716) 565-1200 .. **Scinta**, Denis A '70 SpclCnsl Lipsitz GSC LLP -35 Maple Rd -Williamsvll 14221
(716) 877-8889 .. **Scinta**, Jos J Jr. '95 -9 Westgate Rd -Kenmore 14217 **Fx**:877-4818
(716) 681-7190 .. **Scinta**, Michl Christopher '96 %Brown C LLP -5775 Bway -Lancaster 14086
(212) 218-2100 .. **Scinto**, Lawr F '57 OfCnsl Fitzpatrick CH&S -1290 Av of Amer -NY 10104
(518) 462-5601 .. **Sciocchetti**, Nancy '87 (O'Connell & A) -54 State -Albany 12207
(518) 867-3001 .. **Sciocchetti**, Paul V '87 (Sciocchetti & Assoc,PLLC) -12 Century Hill Dr -Latham 12110 **Fx**:867-3017
(585) 475-1100 .. **Sciortino**, John '87 (Segar & S) -400 Meridian Centre -Rchstr 14618

(212) 487-7350 .. **Sciortino,** Maria C '03 %CCPC -17 Battery Pl -NY 10004
(585) 232-3730 .. **Sciortino,** Michl A '01 (Chamberlain D LLP) -1600 Crssrds Bldg -Rchstr 14614
(845) 294-3139 .. **Sciortino,** Sandra B '87 -1 Railroad Av Bx1003 -Goshen 10924 **Fx:**294-7448
(585) 295-4400 .. **Sciortino,** Tara J '01 %Hiscock & B,LLP -2000 HSBC Plz -Rchstr 14604
(315) 471-3151 .. **Sciotti,** Michl J '92 (Hancock & E,LLP) -1500 AXA Twr I Bx4976 -Syracuse 13221
(718) 797-9405 .. **Scipio-Brim,** Patricia '83 -285 Wyckoff -Brklyn 11217
(718) 783-4545 .. **Sciretta,** Antonia '85 (Sciretta & V, LLP) -753 Carroll -Brklyn 11215
(718) 783-4545 .. **Sciretta,** Antonia '85 (Sciretta & V, LLP) -26 Park Ct -Staten Isl 10301
(718) 783-4545 .. **Sciretta & Venterina, LLP** -26 Park Ct -Staten Isl 10301
(718) 783-4545 .. **Sciretta & Venterina, LLP** -753 Carroll -Brklyn 11215
(315) 255-3158 .. **Sciria,** Patricia A '86 -144 Genesee -Auburn 13021 **Fx:**258-0005
(716) 433-0013 .. **Scirto,** Thos W '87 -7 Main Bx1227 -Lockprt 14095 **Fx:**433-0014
(716) 439-7606 .. **Scirto,** Thos W '87 Niagara Cnty DSS -100 Davison Rd Bx506 -Lockprt 14095 **Fx:**439-7609
(516) 301-8617 .. **Sciscente,** Marybeth Pascale '94 -168 Kensngtn Rd -Gdn Cty 11530 **Fx:**747-6792
(718) 234-3232 .. **Scissura,** Carlo A '00 -8024 13th Av -Brklyn 11228
(917) 441-2859 .. **Sciurba,** Dennis V '74 -2130 Bway -NY 10023
(212) 259-8000 .. **Sciuto,** Linda Ann '93 (Dewey & L LLP) -1301 Av of Amer -NY 10019
(212) 422-1200 .. **Sckolnick,** Shari D '09 %Abrams GF&J,PC -1 Bttry Pk Plz -NY 10004
(212) 983-3443 .. **Sclafani,** Accursio P '77 -80 Park Av -NY 10016
(631) 584-9167 .. **Sclafani,** Chas J '59 -Bx805 -St James 11780 **Fx:**584-6846
(631) 390-5000 .. **Sclafani,** Elisabeth A '09 %Genser DG&C,LLP -445 Broad Hollow Rd -Melvll 11747
(212) 696-9880 .. **Sclafani,** Leonard '76 L Sclafani,PC -2 Wall -NY 10005
(212) 962-1450 .. **Sclafani,** Mary Jane '80 (Magovern & S) -111 John -NY 10038
(914) 366-0201 .. **Sclafani,** Michl V '86 (Reardon & S,PC) -220 Wht Plns Rd -Tarrytwn 10591
(914) 366-0201 .. **Sclafani,** Vincent M '53 (Reardon & S,PC) -220 Wht Plns Rd -Tarrytwn 10591
(212) 779-8600 .. **Sclar,** Alan '92 (Silverman SS&B PLLC) -381 Park Av S -NY 10016
(212) 596-9000 .. **Sclar,** David I '09 %Ropes & G LLP -1211 Av of Amer -NY 10036
(212) 736-2121 .. **Sclar,** Jennifer '96 %Drubner & H,LLC -1540 Bway -NY 10036
(212) 760-2554 .. **Sclater,** Alison L '03 Pro Bono Net -151 W 30th -NY 10001
(315) 474-5533 .. **Scofield,** Christine A '79 -506 E Wshngtn -Syracuse 13202
(212) 480-8800 .. **Scofield,** Edw A '99 %Furnari L LLP -11 Bway -NY 10004 **Fx:**480-4208
(607) 936-3739 .. **Scofield,** Teresa B '92 %Rossettie R&M -269 W Pulteney -Corning 14830
(914) 761-0444 .. **Scofield,** Wm '92 (W Scofield,LLC) -800 Wstchstr Av -Rye Brook 10573 **Fx:**761-8788
(212) 521-5400 .. **Scogin,** Hugh T Jr. '83 (Reed S LLP) -599 Lex Av -NY 10022
(212) 369-6436 .. **Scognamiglio,** Marcia Ruskin '85 -235 E 95th -NY 10128 **Fx:**369-7794
(212) 259-8000 .. **Scognamiglio,** Patrick J '70 SpclCnsl Dewey & L LLP -1301 Av of Amer -NY 10019
(516) 877-2225 .. **Scognamillo,** Lisa A '92 %Badiak & W,LLP -106 3rd -Mineola 11501
(516) 877-2900 .. **Scognamillo,** Tina '90 %Bartlett MB&M,LLP -300 Old Cntry Rd -Mineola 11501
(518) 862-1386 .. **Scolamiero,** Peter M '89 (Burke SM&H,LLP) -302 Wshngtn Av Ext Bx15085 -Albany 12212
(212) 889-4440 .. **Scolari Goldsmith & Weiss** -475 Park Av S -NY 10016
(212) 227-8899 .. **Scolari,** Lisa '82 -20 Vesey -NY 10007 **Fx:**964-2926
(315) 471-8111 .. **Scolaro,** Richd S '62 OfCnsl Scolaro SCF&B,PC -507 Plum -Syracuse 13204
(315) 471-8111 .. **Scolaro,** Robt D '01 (Scolaro SCF&B,PC) -507 Plum -Syracuse 13204 **Fx:**425-3636
(315) 471-8111 .. **Scolaro Shulman Cohen Fetter & Burstein,PC** -507 Plum -Syracuse 13204 **Fx:**471-1355
(585) 232-6460 .. **Scolaro Shulman Cohen Fetter & Burstein,PC** -16 W Main -Rchstr 14614 **Fx:**232-6475
(212) 489-1600 .. **Scoles,** Antony J '00 %Deloitte LLP -1633 Bway -NY 10019 **Fx:**492-4201
(315) 252-8704 .. **Scollan,** Jos C '67 -119 N Seward Av -Auburn 13021
(516) 545-5160 .. **Scollan,** Paul F '83 SrCnsl Natl Grid -175 E Old Cntry Rd -Hicksvll 11801 **Fx:**545-5029
(212) 254-1444 .. **Scollar,** Allison '91 (Gold SM PLLC) -134 Spring -NY 10012 **Fx:**966-2322
(718) 448-7028 .. **Scollar,** Marc E '90 (Scollar & S) -1031 Victory Blvd -Staten Isl 10301
(718) 448-7028 .. **Scollar,** Saml L '58 (Scollar & S) -1031 Victory Blvd -Staten Isl 10301
(212) 223-6444 .. **Scolnick,** Judith S '81 Scott +S,LLP -500 5th Av -NY 10110 **Fx:**223-6334
(845) 354-9339 .. **Scolnick,** Michl R '68 -420 Route 59 -Airmont 10952
(716) 488-1178 .. **Scolton,** Bruce S '77 (Erickson WS&H) -414 E Fairmount Av Bx414 -Lakewd 14750
(716) 693-2771 .. **Sconiers,** Lester G '74 -8711 Buffalo Av -Niagara Fls 14304
(516) 248-4771 .. **Sconzo,** Lisa M '02 %Laurino & L -229 7th -Gdn Cty 11530 **Fx:**248-4785
(718) 618-2329 .. **Scooler,** Kate E '69 %Surrogate's Ct -851 Grnd Cncrs -Bronx 10451 **Fx:**590-3575
(718) 618-2330 .. **Scooler,** Matthew J '01 %Surrogate's Ct -851 Grnd Cncrs -Bronx 10451 **Fx:**590-3575
(212) 818-8800 .. **Scooler,** Noah '69 (Graubard M) -405 Lex Av -NY 10174
(212) 701-3000 .. **Scoolidge,** Peter J '09 %Cahill G&R LLP -80 Pine -NY 10005 **Fx:**269-5420
(718) 437-6155 .. **Scop,** David '99 -4522 18th Av -Brklyn 11204
(212) 336-2000 .. **Scopino,** Gregory A '06 %Patterson BW&T LLP -1133 Av of Amer -NY 10036
(212) 598-1710 .. **Scopp,** Kathleen H '77 %Time Warner NYC Cable Grp -120 E 23rd -NY 10010 **Fx:**420-4812
(212) 340-0400 .. **Scopp,** Leland S '71 %Appllt Div 1st Dept -27 Mad Av -NY 10010 **Fx:**889-4412
(212) 341-0903 .. **Scoppetta,** Nicholas '62 %Admin Children's Srvcs -150 William -NY 10038 **Fx:**266-2250
(212) 809-5500 .. **Scorcia,** Henry J '83 -Bx1084 -NY 10274
(212) 949-9022 .. **Scordato,** Caridad Piñeiro '86 (Abelman F&S) -666 3rd Av -NY 10017
(212) 632-1594 .. **Scordato,** Jos P '81 Lazard Freres & Co -30 Rckfllr Plz -NY 10112
(212) 446-4800 .. **Scordino,** Ellen Agnes '02 (Kirkland & E LLP) -153 E 53rd -NY 10022
(845) 440-2426 .. **Scordino Ludwig,** Annette '90 %IRS -153 Sawkill Rd -Kingston 12401
(212) 297-5800 .. **Scordo,** John P '89 (Day P LLP) -7 Times Sq -NY 10036
(212) 268-5136 .. **Scorese,** Jos P '90 (Harwood L) -350 5th Av -NY 10118
(631) 421-1995 .. **Scorzari,** Wm A Jr. '89 Scorzari & S,PC -141 E Main -Huntngtn 11743 **Fx:**421-0940
(212) 705-7000 .. **Scotch-Marmo,** Stephen '08 %Bingham M LLP -399 Park Av -NY 10022
(516) 280-2060 .. **Scotman,** Beverly M '83 -357 Hempstd Tpk -W Hempstead 11552 **Fx:**706-2874
(518) 465-2333 .. **Scott,** A Jos III '84 (Hodgson R LLP) -677 Bway -Albany 12207
(212) 599-6260 .. **Scott,** Alan '84 -485 Mad Av -NY 10022 **Fx:**588-0471
(212) 350-2700 .. **Scott,** Alee N '08 %Constantine C,PC -450 Lex Av -NY 10017
(212) 225-2000 .. **Scott,** Andrew M Jr. '03 Cleary GS&H -1 Lbrty Plz -NY 10006
(212) 449-1000 .. **Scott,** Andrew P '03 Merrill Lynch -4 World Fncl Ctr -NY 10281
(718) 852-7000 .. **Scott,** Armani B '99 -802 Kent Av -Brklyn 11205 **Fx:**852-3302
(212) 558-4000 .. **Scott,** Ashley C '09 %Sullivan & C LLP -125 Broad -NY 10004
(845) 452-5900 .. **Scott,** Audrey Friedrichsen '05 %Van DeWater & V,LLP -85 Civic Ctr Plz Bx112 -Poughkeepsie 12602
(212) 972-3000 .. **Scott,** Brendan M '03 %Klestadt & W,LLP -292 Mad Av -NY 10017
(718) 744-0340 .. **Scott,** Carolyn '99 C Scott,LLC -40 Macon -Brklyn 11216 **Fx:**744-0351
(315) 469-3246 .. **Scott,** Catherine A '84 (Scott & W) -4110 S Salina -Syracuse 13205 **Fx:**469-3249
(914) 824-5646 .. **Scott,** Chas T '80 %Surrogates Ct -111 Dr MLK Jr Blvd -White Plns 10601 **Fx:**995-3728
(212) 425-7200 .. **Scott,** Christopher M '06 %Kenyon & K,LLP -1 Bway -NY 10004
(646) 833-0900 .. **Scott,** Courtney E '94 (Tressler LLP) -One Penn Plz -NY 10119
(516) 364-6006 .. **Scott,** Crystal S A '05 %Cohen & S,LLP -199 Crsswys Park Dr Bx9004 -Woodbury 11797
(212) 558-4000 .. **Scott,** Damien G '10 %Sullivan & C LLP -125 Broad -NY 10004
(212) 408-5100 .. **Scott,** Danl J '03 %Chadbourne & P LLP -30 Rckfllr Plz -NY 10112
(716) 845-7497 .. **Scott,** Danl U '94 Family Ct -1 Niagara Plz -Buffalo 14202 **Fx:**858-7788
(212) 233-9716 .. **Scott,** Danl W '83 -70 Lafayette -NY 10013
(212) 661-0001 .. **Scott,** David A '85 -60 E 42nd -NY 10165 **Fx:**661-8042
(631) 474-5051 .. **Scott,** David A '92 -24 Mdlnd Av -Pt Jffrsn 11777
(800) 742-9696 .. **Scott,** David C '02 %Binder & B,PC -33-00 Nrthrn Blvd -LIC 11101 **Fx:**(718) 512-2424
(718) 590-2000 .. **Scott,** Donna L '99 %DA -198 E 161st -Bronx 10451 **Fx:**590-6477
(212) 571-6788 .. **Scott,** Earl L '78 -170 Bway -NY 10038 **Fx:**571-7475
(212) 351-3869 .. **Scott,** Edw S '95 -30 Broad -NY 10004
(646) 840-1832 .. **Scott,** Edwin D '72 -425 Mad Av -NY 10017
(212) 460-2488 .. **Scott,** Edwin W '73 Con Ed -4 Irving Pl -NY 10003
(631) 474-5555 .. **Scott,** Elisa J '96 -24 Mdlnd Av -Pt Jffrsn 11777
(212) 318-6000 .. **Scott,** Eliza Hamilton '07 %Paul HJ&W LLP -75 E 55th -NY 10022
(585) 394-7970 .. **Scott & Gilbert,LLP** -28 S Main -Canandaigua 14424 **Fx:**396-9859
(212) 450-4000 .. **Scott,** Gregory C '10 %Davis P&W LLP -450 Lex Av -NY 10017
(845) 561-5100 .. **Scott,** H Morton '52 -600 Bway -Newburgh 12550
(212) 998-6206 .. **Scott,** Helen S '78 %NYU Law Schl -40 Wshngtn Sq S -NY 10012 **Fx:**995-4692
(212) 692-1000 .. **Scott,** Ian '97 (Duane M LLP) -1540 Bway -NY 10036
(646) 855-0904 .. **Scott,** James E '00 B of A Merrill Lynch -1 Bryant Park -NY 10036
(516) 571-3056 .. **Scott,** James R '75 Cnty Atty -1 West -Mineola 11501 **Fx:**571-6604
(212) 848-7702 .. **Scott,** James S Sr. '89 (Shearman & S LLP) -599 Lex Av -NY 10022
(518) 402-0205 .. **Scott,** Jane E '80 %UIA Bd -Troy Atrium Bx15126 -Albany 12212 **Fx:**402-6208
(718) 990-2308 .. **Scott,** Jane E '85 St John's Law Schl -8000 Utopia Pkwy -Jamaica 11439 **Fx:**591-1855
(212) 505-2100 .. **Scott,** Janea A '01 %Envrnmntl Def -257 Park Av S -NY 10010
(516) 393-2200 .. **Scott,** Jason C '09 %Garfunkel W,PC -111 Grt Nck Rd -Gt Neck 11021
(518) 452-8574 .. **Scott,** Jeffrey B '92 -860 Greenthorne Blvd -Schnctdy 12303
(212) 558-4000 .. **Scott,** Jeffrey T '98 (Sullivan & C LLP) -125 Broad -NY 10004
(518) 438-7985 .. **Scott,** John C '87 JC Scott Law Firm PC -19 Av B -Albany 12208 **Fx:**438-7985
(212) 521-5400 .. **Scott,** John L '03 (Reed S LLP) -599 Lex Av -NY 10022
(212) 326-2000 .. **Scott,** John M '88 (O'Melveny & M LLP) -7 Times Sq -NY 10036
(518) 402-6337 .. **Scott,** John W '82 Workers Comp Bd -20 Park -Albany 12207
(631) 265-4884 .. **Scott,** Jonathan C '87 -50 Karl Av -Smithtwn 11787
(716) 627-3300 .. **Scott,** Karen Gaughan '93 -5020 Lk Shr Rd -Hambrg 14075 **Fx:**627-7279
(212) 715-1000 .. **Scott,** Kathleen A '91 Cnsl Arnold & P LLP -399 Park Av -NY 10022
(518) 218-7100 .. **Scott,** Kiley D '04 %Tully R,PLLC -441 New Karner Rd -Albany 12205
(212) 822-1435 .. **Scott,** Kofi D '79 (Scott & L) -305 Bway -NY 10007
(212) 627-3388 .. **Scott,** Lael French '83 -136 W 11th -NY 10011 **Fx:**929-1930
(212) 707-2520 .. **Scott,** Margo '89 %Atlantic Recording Corp -1290 Av of Amer -NY 10104 **Fx:**405-5620
(516) 944-9745 .. **Scott,** Mary Anne '84 -113 Main -Pt Wash 11050
(212) 843-7660 .. **Scott,** Michelle P '82 East-West Mgt Inst Inc -575 Mad Av -NY 10022 **Fx:**843-1485
(718) 250-2000 .. **Scott,** Nicholas M '08 %DA -350 Jay -Brklyn 11201 **Fx:**250-2314
(914) 745-4000 .. **Scott,** Pamela C '86 %Towers Watson -100 Summit Lk Dr -Valhalla 10595
(718) 403-3068 .. **Scott,** Phillip R '91 %National Grid -1 MetroTech Ctr -Brklyn 11201
(516) 745-4502 .. **Scott,** Raymond C '96 %JP Morgan Chase & Co -900 Stewart Av -Gdn Cty 11530 **Fx:**745-4528
(716) 852-2025 .. **Scott,** Richd B '67 -80 W Huron -Buffalo 14202 **Fx:**852-8013
(716) 856-4200 .. **Scott,** Robt E '78 OfCnsl Gibson M&C,LLP -69 Delaware Av -Buffalo 14202

(212) 956-9500 .. **Scott**, Robt G '02 OfCnsl Hand B&A LLP -8 W 40th -NY 10018 **Fx:**376-6080
(716) 551-4946 .. **Scott**, Ronald H '88 %NLRB -130 S Elmwood Av -Buffalo 14202 **Fx:**551-4972
(713) 221-1125 .. **Scott**, Ronald R '05 (Bracewell & G,LLP) -1251 Av of Amer -NY 10020 **Fx:**221-2143
(212) 512-1000 .. **Scott**, Sandra Lee '91 %HBO -1100 Av of Amer -NY 10036 **Fx:**512-1986
(718) 701-2896 .. **Scott**, Shane D '03 -40 Wall -NY 10005
(516) 826-6500 .. **Scott**, Shannon A '05 %LaMonica H&M LLP -3305 Jerusalem Av -Wantagh 11793
(212) 227-6080 .. **Scott**, Stephen R '96 -305 Bway -NY 10007 **Fx:**233-9144
(516) 739-0400 .. **Scott**, Steve K F '95 %Kelly R&K,LLP -330 Old Cntry Rd -Mineola 11501
(212) 612-6266 .. **Scott**, Stewart M III '90 Daiwa Securities Amer -32 Old Slip -NY 10005 **Fx:**612-7155
(631) 501-3100 .. **Scott**, Thos E '77 %J Humphreys -3 Huntngtn Quad Bx9028 -Melvll 11747 **Fx:**501-3085
(607) 478-8000 .. **Scott**, W Ross '97 -1759 Hawks Rd -Andover 14806 **Fx:**478-5138
(212) 210-9518 .. **Scott**, Walter '85 Cnsl Alston & B LLP -90 Park Av -NY 10016
(646) 471-4000 .. **Scott**, Walter Keating '99 %PricewaterhouseCoopers LLP -300 Mad Av -NY 10017
(716) 853-3801 .. **Scott**, Wendy A '94 %Kenney SL&N,LLP -14 Lafayette Sq -Buffalo 14203
(518) 745-1400 .. **Scott**, Wm A '04 %FitzGerald MBF -16 Pearl Bx2017 -Glens Fls 12801
(716) 854-8850 .. **Scott**, Wm D '65 -410 Main -Buffalo 14202
(718) 762-6944 .. **Scott**, Wm H '96 -109-10 Park Ln S -Richmnd Hll 11418
(518) 427-2650 .. **Scott**, Wm P III '01 (Nixon P LLP) -677 Bway -Albany 12207
(212) 445-1076 .. **Scott**, Wm P '02 Asset Control Syst,Inc -1450 Bway -NY 10018 **Fx:**445-1079
(718) 286-6000 .. **Scott Brooking**, Sharon Y '84 %DA -125-01 Qns Blvd -Kew Gdns 11415
(212) 481-6000 .. **Scotti**, Gavin W '85 -260 Mad Av -NY 10016
(212) 880-6000 .. **Scotti**, Gavin W Jr. '06 %Torys LLP -237 Park Av -NY 10017
(914) 968-1266 .. **Scotti**, James P '84 -37 Vredenburgh Av -Ynkrs 10704 **Fx:**968-4110
(212) 331-5145 .. **Scotti**, Patricia Hurley '86 HRA -180 Water -NY 10038
(212) 460-3528 .. **Scotti**, Steven M '86 Con Ed -4 Irving Pl -NY 10003
(718) 424-5850 .. **Scotti**, Tammy '91 (Marino & S) -104-14 Roosevelt Av -Corona 11368
(646) 386-5700 .. **Scott-McLaughlin**, Malaika N '10 Civil Ct -111 Centre -NY 10013
(516) 222-2080 .. **Scotto**, Anthony T '76 -1225 Franklin Av -Gdn Cty 11530 **Fx:**222-0265
(718) 403-0570 .. **Scotto**, Debra '98 -389 Court -Brklyn 11231
(516) 439-5465 .. **Scotto**, Francine '92 (Timoshenko & S,LLP) -175 E Shore Rd -Gt Neck 11023
(212) 335-9000 .. **Scotto**, Michl A '89 %DA -1 Hogan Pl -NY 10013
(212) 791-0285 .. **Scotto**, Michl J '09 %Malaby & B,LLC -150 Bway -NY 10038 **Fx:**791-0286
(212) 425-7814 .. **Scotto**, Michele F '80 -17 Battery Pl -NY 10004 **Fx:**422-5360
(212) 425-7814 .. **Scotto**, Raphael '72 -17 Battery Pl -NY 10004 **Fx:**422-5171
(212) 233-7195 .. **Scotto-Lavino**, Theresa E '00 %Lewis JAA,LLP -61 Bway -NY 10006
(516) 741-4875 .. **Scourby**, Nicholas '56 -111 Cherry Vlly Av -Gdn Cty 11530
(212) 423-3530 .. **Scovell**, Gail Aidonoff '89 %Guggenheim Msm -1071 5th Av -NY 10128 **Fx:**423-3641
(212) 940-8800 .. **Scoville**, Matthew A '08 %Katten MR LLP -575 Mad Av -NY 10022
(212) 594-5300 .. **Scoville**, Wm B Jr. '93 %Milberg LLP -1 Penn Plz -NY 10119
(212) 771-9501 .. **Scowcroft**, Karen '85 CIT Grp Inc -505 5th Av -NY 10017
(516) 873-6200 .. **Scozzari**, James F '09 %R Macchia & Assoc -98 Front -Mineola 11501 **Fx:**873-1611
(718) 920-2857 .. **Scranton**, Mary F '93 %Montefiore Med Ctr -111 E 210th -Bronx 10467 **Fx:**920-2637
(718) 725-2121 .. **Screen**, Crystal L '93 -89-31 161st -Jamaica 11432
(212) 848-4000 .. **Scribner**, Curtis D '08 %Shearman & S LLP -599 Lex Av -NY 10022
(212) 578-2211 .. **Scribner**, J Joshua Jr. '93 %MetLife -27-01 Qns Plz N -LIC 11101
(585) 261-6461 .. **Scribner**, Peter R '87 -1110 Park Av -Rchstr 14610
(917) 592-2203 .. **Scribner**, Robt J '60 -180 E 79th -NY 10075
(631) 261-8834 .. **Scricca**, Anna M '83 (Ingerman S LLP) -150 Motor Pkwy -Hauppauge 11788
(315) 471-8111 .. **Scrimale**, Richd E '94 (Scolaro SCF&B,PC) -507 Plum -Syracuse 13204 **Fx:**425-3627
(212) 735-3000 .. **Scrivani**, Brian P '08 %Skadden ASM&F LLP -4 Times Sq -NY 10036
(212) 326-2000 .. **Scrivano**, Paul S '97 (O'Melveny & M LLP) -7 Times Sq -NY 10036
(631) 753-4600 .. **Scro**, David A '86 (Scro & S) -68 S Srvc Rd -Melvll 11747 **Fx:**753-4094
(631) 753-4600 .. **Scro**, Lisa Fortunato '85 (Scro & S) -68 S Srvc Rd -Melvll 11747 **Fx:**753-4094
(518) 443-5400 .. **Scrodanus**, Rose Marie S '73 %SUNY Univ Cnsl -S333 SUNY Plz -Albany 12246 **Fx:**443-5409
(212) 753-5000 .. **Scrudato**, Paul A '87 (Schiff H LLP) -900 3rd Av -NY 10022
(914) 333-7420 .. **Scudder**, Chas '76 %Akzo Nobel -120 Wht Plns Rd -Tarrytwn 10591
(212) 239-4340 .. **Scuder**, Amanda C '04 %Shalov SB&R LLP -485 7th Av -NY 10018
(315) 785-3343 .. **Scuderi**, Michelle M '99 Dept of Social Srvcs -250 Arsenal -Watertwn 13601 **Fx:**785-3109
(212) 262-2390 .. **Scuderi**, Thos M '94 Cnsl Connell F LLP -888 7th Av -NY 10106
(212) 921-1600 .. **Scudieri**, David G '09 (Goldberg SL&B,PC) -45 W 45th -NY 10036
(845) 562-9100 .. **Sculley**, Jeffrey S E '03 %Rider W&F,PC -655 Little Britain Rd -New Windsor 12553
(718) 499-6481 .. **Sculley**, Lynn '81 -563 8th -Brklyn 11215
(631) 273-7171 .. **Sculley**, Michl P '95 %Vaccaro & P -325 Wireless Blvd -Hauppauge 11788
(212) 969-3000 .. **Scullion**, Jennifer R '00 (Proskauer R LLP) -1585 Bway -NY 10036
(212) 574-1200 .. **Scully**, Christopher J '10 %Seward & K LLP -1 Bttry Pk Plz -NY 10004
(212) 940-8800 .. **Scully**, Craig '82 (Katten MR LLP) -575 Mad Av -NY 10022
(716) 856-1200 .. **Scully**, Danl J '89 %Buffalo Medical Grp -85 High -Buffalo 14203
(516) 338-7520 .. **Scully**, James P '05 (Daniels & N,PC) -900 Merchants Cncrs -Westbury 11590
(917) 778-6600 .. **Scully**, Janet Vagt '82 %J Toomey -485 Lex Av -NY 10017 **Fx:**778-7048
(914) 699-1919 .. **Scully**, Karl A '02 (Gross S&S LLP) -9 W Prospect Av -Mt Vernon 10550 **Fx:**699-6106
(315) 798-5766 .. **Scully**, Patrick F '05 %DA -800 Park Av -Utica 13501 **Fx:**798-5582
(516) 742-4343 .. **Scully Scott Murphy & Presser PC** -400 Grdn City Plz -Gdn Cty 11530 **Fx:**742-4366
(631) 941-3434 .. **Scully**, Tara A '05 %Burner S & Assoc LLP -46 Route 25A -Setauket 11733 **Fx:**941-3443
(646) 674-2000 .. **Scully**, Thos P '00 Liquidnet Hldngs Inc -498 7th Av -NY 10018 **Fx:**674-2003
(212) 599-1515 .. **Sculnick**, David H '74 Cnsl Stein RM,LLP -405 Lex Av -NY 10174
(716) 856-4200 .. **Scumaci**, Robt G '93 (Gibson M&C,LLP) -69 Delaware Av -Buffalo 14202
(212) 308-4411 .. **Scungio**, Maria A '94 (Edwards AP&D LLP) -750 Lex Av -NY 10022
(718) 491-3396 .. **Scunziano**, Nicholas P '90 -8304 13th Av -Brklyn 11228 **Fx:**921-9381
(516) 683-1990 .. **Scupp**, Chas H '83 (Scupp & B LLP) -220 Old Cntry Rd -Mineola 11501 **Fx:**683-1992
(212) 350-2700 .. **Scupp**, David A '06 %Constantine C,PC -450 Lex Av -NY 10017
(585) 335-5610 .. **Scura**, John R '68 -131 Main Bx468 -Dansvll 14437 **Fx:**335-7994
(585) 335-5610 .. **Scura Lickliter**, Rachel '02 %Scura Law Ofc -131 Main Bx468 -Dansvll 14437 **Fx:**335-7994
(212) 801-2153 .. **Scurti**, Jason A '97 OfCnsl Greenberg T,LLP -200 Park Av -NY 10166
(585) 419-8800 .. **Scutt**, Robt C '77 (Harris B PLLC) -99 Garnsey Rd -Pittsfrd 14534
(212) 837-6097 .. **Sczesnik**, Julie S '09 %Hughes H&R LLP -1 Bttry Pk Plz -NY 10004
(212) 297-5800 .. **Sea**, Nexus U '10 %Day P LLP -7 Times Sq -NY 10036
(518) 439-8311 .. **Seaburg**, Tania Fay '00 NYSARC,Inc -393 Delaware Av -Delmar 12054 **Fx:**439-1893
(585) 258-4538 .. **Seaburg-Brackett**, Marcella '89 %UIA Bd -109 S Union -Rchstr 14607 **Fx:**258-4539
(212) 984-4000 .. **Seabury**, Elizabeth '01 Cnsl L'Oreal USA,Inc -575 5th Av -NY 10017
(607) 772-7013 .. **Seachrist**, Brian M '01 %Law Dept -City Hall 38 Hawley -Bnghmtn 13901 **Fx:**723-6164
(716) 326-2700 .. **Seachrist**, Joel H '00 Seachrist Law Ofc,PC -31 E Main -Westfld 14787 **Fx:**326-2102
(212) 788-0866 .. **Seacord**, Christopher A '05 %Law Dept -100 Church -NY 10007 **Fx:**788-0367
(212) 571-6002 .. **Seadie**, Keshab Raj '97 -146 W 29th -NY 10001 **Fx:**571-7302
(315) 426-2148 .. **Seagriff**, Michl '79 OCFS -333 E Wshngtn -Syracuse 13202
(212) 906-1200 .. **Seale**, Danl C '96 (Latham & W) -885 3rd Av -NY 10022
(212) 310-8000 .. **Seales**, Jannelle M '09 %Weil G&M LLP -767 5th Av -NY 10153
(212) 838-8686 .. **Sealove**, Morton '71 (Schaerf & S) -232 Mad Av -NY 10016 **Fx:**725-8567
(212) 431-1300 .. **Seals**, Carla M '86 (Borah GAN&G PC) -377 Bway -NY 10013
(516) 572-2375 .. **Sealy**, Melissa G '96 %Dist Ct -99 Main -Hempstd 11550 **Fx:**572-2260
(212) 709-8330 .. **Sealy**, Patrick C '82 (Sealy & Assoc) -110 Wall -NY 10005 **Fx:**(718) 421-5946
(212) 413-7580 .. **Sealy**, Raven S '09 Legal Momentum -395 Hudson -NY 10014 **Fx:**226-1066
(716) 433-5907 .. **Seaman**, Danl E '72 (Seaman JH&B,LLP) -76 West Av -Lockprt 14094
(914) 666-8033 .. **Seaman**, David P '54 -118 N Bedford Rd -Mt Kisco 10549 **Fx:**666-4459
(518) 486-6561 .. **Seaman**, James J '89 %Dept of Law -The Cptl -Albany 12224
(716) 433-5907 .. **Seaman Jones Hogan & Brooks,LLP** -76 West Av -Lockprt 14094 **Fx:**433-0032
(516) 822-2980 .. **Seaman**, Kathleen O'Rourke '97 (O'Rourke S LLP) -6800 Jericho Tpk -Syosset 11791
(631) 751-3700 .. **Seaman**, Kevin A '74 -300 Rhododendron Rd Bx580 -Stony Brk 11790
(212) 935-5300 .. **Seaman**, Robt L '68 (Seaman & W,LLP) -160 E 38th -NY 10016 **Fx:**935-5301
(716) 856-0875 .. **Seaman**, Thos D '08 %D Archilla -170 Franklin -Buffalo 14202 **Fx:**853-1897
(212) 798-7279 .. **Seaman**, Thos G '87 Golden Source Corp -22 Crtlandt -NY 10007 **Fx:**798-7116
(212) 705-7000 .. **Seamon**, Scott K '02 Cnsl Bingham M LLP -399 Park Av -NY 10022
(518) 785-1900 .. **Seamon**, Wm P '84 %PEF -1168-70 Troy-Schnctdy Rd Bx12414 -Albany 12212 **Fx:**785-1323
(212) 370-1300 .. **Seamster**, Christopher D '06 %Ellenoff G&S LLP -150 E 42nd -NY 10017
(607) 274-3944 .. **Seaquist**, Gwen E '78 Ithaca Cllg -Bus Schl-Smiddy 409 -Ithaca 14850
(212) 326-3939 .. **Sear**, Thos H '73 (Jones D) -222 E 41st -NY 10017
(212) 969-3000 .. **Searfoorce**, Ryan D '09 %Proskauer R LLP -1585 Bway -NY 10036
(212) 526-0464 .. **Searl**, Christine P '96 Cnsl Lehman Bros -1271 Av of Amer -NY 10020
(212) 758-0447 .. **Searle**, S Elizabeth '81 %All Saints Episcopal Church -230 E 60th -NY 10022
(212) 751-4300 .. **Searles**, Jillian M '07 %Hodgson R LLP -1540 Bway -NY 10036
(845) 483-7327 .. **Sears**, David A '89 -1 Civic Ctr Plz -Poughkeepsie 12601 **Fx:**483-0723
(212) 252-8560 .. **Sears**, Eric M '75 EM Sears,PC -61 Bway -NY 10006 **Fx:**267-3024
(212) 854-5176 .. **Sears**, Jeffrey M '06 %Columbia Univ -535 W 116th 412 Low Mem'l Library -NY 10027 **Fx:**854-7607
(646) 386-5000 .. **Sears**, Juliette C '03 %Surrogates Ct -31 Chmbrs -NY 10007
(212) 969-3000 .. **Sears**, Marvin '53 (Proskauer R LLP) -1585 Bway -NY 10036
(718) 291-3400 .. **Sears**, Stuart L '92 %Shaevitz & S -148-55 Hillside Av -Jamaica 11435 **Fx:**739-5654
(585) 454-0700 .. **Sears**, Tony R '04 %Ward GH&R LLP -300 State -Rchstr 14614
(212) 878-8000 .. **Seaton**, Michl T '05 %Clifford C LLP -31 W 52nd -NY 10019
(646) 623-5135 .. **Seaver**, Christopher B '87 %JP Morgan Chase -60 Wall -NY 10260
(212) 532-0333 .. **Seavey**, Avery B '83 %Seavey Org -3 Park Av -NY 10016 **Fx:**481-3390
(212) 532-0333 .. **Seavey**, Nealle B '85 %Seavey Org -3 Park Av -NY 10016 **Fx:**481-3390

(212) 532-0333 .. **Seavey,** Robt W '52 %Seavey Org -3 Park Av -NY 10016 **Fx:**481-3390
(516) 877-7300 .. **Seavey Vogel & Associates, LLP** -500 N Bway -Jericho 11753 **Fx:**877-2340
(212) 532-0333 .. **Seavey-Seltzer,** Nealle B '85 -3 Park Av -NY 10016 **Fx:**481-3390
(212) 932-4281 .. **Seawell,** Petra D '06 -5141 Bway -NY 10034
(212) 494-0718 .. **Seay,** J David '82 %United Hospital Fund -350 5th Av -NY 10118 **Fx:**494-0800
(212) 310-8000 .. **Seay,** Kerrick E '02 %Weil G&M LLP -767 5th Av -NY 10153
(718) 729-1753 .. **Sebag,** Jacob '83 (Ochoa & S) -21-50 44th Dr -LIC 11101
(716) 579-3516 .. **Sebekos,** Peter J '90 -3909 Witmer Rd -Niagara Fls 14305
(212) 237-0000 .. **Seber,** Robt '87 (Vinson & E LLP) -666 5th Av -NY 10103
(212) 790-0200 .. **Sebok,** Anthony J '95 Benj N Cardozo Schl of Law -55 5th Av -NY 10003 **Fx:**790-0345
(212) 772-9064 .. **Sebolao,** Brenda L '94 -338 E 70th -NY 10021 **Fx:**249-3958
(347) 404-9133 .. **Secaira-Cotto,** Damian '97 %Civil Ct -141 Lvngstn -Brklyn 11201 **Fx:**(718) 643-3733
(631) 424-3597 .. **Secas,** Donny O '06 %B Salamone & Assoc,PC -8 Ford Pl -Dix Hlls 11746 **Fx:**424-5023
(718) 222-8880 .. **Secemski,** David S '02 %Jones JO -45 Main -Brklyn 11201
(607) 255-5124 .. **Sechler,** Stephanie A '01 %Cornell Univ -300 CCC Bldg-Grdn Av -Ithaca 14853 **Fx:**255-2794
(212) 869-0070 .. **Sechrest,** Marisa A '04 Araca Grp -545 W 45th -NY 10036
(212) 298-5230 .. **Seckler,** Marcia '88 %Leg Aid -49 Thomas -NY 10013 **Fx:**298-5252
(212) 430-5400 .. **Secofsky,** Joan '74 SrCnsl Diamond M LLP -620 8th Av -NY 10018
(212) 872-1000 .. **Secol,** Geoffrey E '99 -One Bryant Park -NY 10036 **Fx:**872-1002
(212) 563-4100 .. **Secular,** Keith E '76 (Cohen W&S LLP) -330 W 42nd -NY 10036
(212) 374-3444 .. **Secular,** Lisa S '84 %NYC Dept Educ-OLS -52 Chmbrs -NY 10007 **Fx:**374-5596
(718) 694-3989 .. **Seda,** Antonio '89 %Transit Auth -130 Lvngstn -Brklyn 11201
(718) 286-2000 .. **Seda,** Samantha C '95 %Leg Aid -120-46 Qns Blvd -Kew Gdns 11415 **Fx:**286-2286
(212) 344-3440 .. **Sedaghati,** Natalie '99 (Ogen & S,PC) -202 E 35th -NY 10016
(516) 466-7370 .. **Sedaghat-Pour,** Farhid '05 -8 Sycamore Dr -Gt Neck 11021 **Fx:**466-7849
(718) 272-6040 .. **Seddio,** Frank R '91 -9306 Flatlands Av -Brklyn 11236 **Fx:**(347) 750-8344
(212) 205-7000 .. **Seddon,** Patricia A '91 Cnsl Ashurst LLP -7 Times Sq -NY 10036
(212) 227-1735 .. **Sedereas,** Christian C '05 %Bates & B -60 E 42nd -NY 10165 **Fx:**(201) 518-2552
(212) 558-5500 .. **Sedgh,** Jonathan M '08 Weitz & L,PC -700 Bway -NY 10003
(516) 683-6200 .. **Sedgh,** Shahriar '05 %Betesh & Assoc PLLC -585 Stewart Av -Gdn Cty 11530
(212) 422-0202 .. **Sedgwick Detert Moran & Arnold LLP** -125 Broad -NY 10004 **Fx:**422-0925
(212) 735-8633 .. **Sedgwick,** Robt M '86 (Morrison C LLP) -909 3rd Av -NY 10022
(212) 330-1208 .. **Sedhom,** Rania V '98 Buck Consultants -1 Penn Plz -NY 10119 **Fx:**330-1225
(716) 858-2424 .. **Sedita,** Frank A III '87 %DA -25 Delaware Av -Buffalo 14202 **Fx:**858-7425
(716) 856-4000 .. **Sedita,** Jos V '70 (Hodgson R LLP) -140 Pearl -Buffalo 14202
(646) 225-6549 .. **Sediva,** Alexander '06 (Marzano & S) -65 Bway -NY 10006 **Fx:**349-2053
(212) 558-4000 .. **Sedlak,** Jonathan M '05 %Sullivan & C LLP -125 Broad -NY 10004
(212) 661-9100 .. **Sedlander,** Mark S '09 %Otterbourg SH&R,PC -230 Park Av -NY 10169
(914) 642-4837 .. **Sedlarcik,** Frank P '04 IBM -1133 Wstchstr Av -White Plns 10604
(212) 925-3456 .. **Sedlmayr,** Theodor K '94 (Sedlmayr & Assoc) -200 Park Av S -NY 10003 **Fx:**925-0554
(315) 255-1195 .. **Sedor,** Dennis P '82 -108 Genesee -Auburn 13021 **Fx:**255-0623
(212) 408-5100 .. **Sedor,** Sumantha Rani '06 %Chadbourne & P LLP -30 Rckfllr Plz -NY 10112
(212) 626-4100 .. **Sedore,** F Roy '81 (Baker & M LLP) -1114 Av of Amer -NY 10036
(212) 772-7600 .. **Sedransk,** Dori '96 %David Frankel Rlty -160 E 65th -NY 10065 **Fx:**772-8163
(212) 686-0010 .. **Sedreddine,** Amarah K '05 NY Community Trust -909 3rd Av -NY 10022
(212) 728-8000 .. **Sedrish,** Melissa P '10 %Willkie F&G LLP -787 7th Av -NY 10019
(212) 596-9000 .. **See,** Beverly '09 %Ropes & G LLP -1211 Av of Amer -NY 10036
(518) 374-1800 .. **Seebold,** John R '91 (Capasso & M LLP) -215 State Bx1088 -Schnctdy 12301
(212) 357-6337 .. **Seecharan,** Beesham A '99 Goldman Sachs -1 NY Plz -NY 10004
(718) 828-8270 .. **Seedorf,** Marc A '82 (Seedorf & S) -3453 E Tremont Av -Bronx 10461
(718) 828-8270 .. **Seedorf & Scheld** -3453 E Tremont Av -Bronx 10461
(212) 584-0700 .. **Seeger,** Christopher A '91 (Seeger W LLP) -1 William -NY 10004
(716) 856-1536 .. **Seeger,** David J '81 -69 Delaware Av -Buffalo 14202 **Fx:**856-1408
(212) 584-0700 .. **Seeger Weiss LLP** -1 William -NY 10004 **Fx:**584-0799
(914) 681-9300 .. **Seeger,** Wm E '73 Seeger & S -81 Main -White Plns 10601 **Fx:**948-9214
(212) 583-7300 .. **Seegers,** Lori C '83 PPM America Inc -750 Lex Av -NY 10022 **Fx:**583-7311
(631) 501-3100 .. **Seegers,** Patricia H '96 %J Humphreys -3 Huntngtn Quad Bx9028 -Melvll 11747 **Fx:**501-3085
(716) 854-1002 .. **Seegert,** Walter P '74 (Miserendino CS&E,PC) -295 Main -Buffalo 14203
(518) 455-4371 .. **Seehase,** Jennifer M '97 NYS Assembly -522 State Cptl -Albany 12248 **Fx:**455-4693
(212) 223-4000 .. **Seeler,** Evelyn H '87 (Crowell & M LLP) -590 Mad Av -NY 10022
(716) 849-8900 .. **Seeley,** Audrey A '02 (Hurwitz & F,PC) -1300 Lbrty Bldg -Buffalo 14202
(518) 357-3761 .. **Seeley,** James F '75 -7 Southside Dr -Clifton Pk 12065 **Fx:**357-3763
(315) 218-8000 .. **Seeley,** James N '80 (Bond S&K,PLLC) -1 Lincoln Ctr -Syracuse 13202
(212) 962-4266 .. **Seeley,** Louise V '99 Citywide Task Force on Housing Ct -125 Maiden Ln -NY 10038 **Fx:**962-4799
(845) 294-2325 .. **Seeley,** Terrence P '88 %P Botti -14 Scotchtown Av Bx388 -Goshen 10924 **Fx:**294-2088
(315) 685-3416 .. **Seeley,** Thos W '04 %Milford L&S -2-4 Fennell Bx47 -Skaneateles 13152
(212) 655-3500 .. **Seelig,** Mark J '92 (Meister S&F LLP) -140 E 45th -NY 10017
(212) 766-0600 .. **Seelig,** Philip H '92 -299 Bway -NY 10007 **Fx:**766-2616
(212) 766-0600 .. **Seelig,** Richd B '10 %Seelig Law Ofc,LLC -299 Bway -NY 10007 **Fx:**766-2616
(212) 265-1826 .. **Seelinger,** Kim T '03 Lutheran Family & Cmmnty Srvcs -308 W 46th -NY 10036
(718) 250-2000 .. **Seely,** Anne W '85 %DA -350 Jay -Brklyn 11201 **Fx:**250-2314
(518) 783-3843 .. **Seely,** Patrick L Jr. '93 %Hacker & M,LLP -7 Airport Park Blvd -Latham 12110
(212) 557-4000 .. **Seely,** Robt F '76 OfCnsl Grunfeld DLS&K LLP -399 Park Av -NY 10022
(212) 608-5000 .. **Seeman,** Fred L '84 -170 Bway -NY 10038 **Fx:**385-8161
(917) 763-3913 .. **Seeman,** Jay W '61 -5 W 86th -NY 10024
(516) 482-2570 .. **Seeman,** Murray '37 -6 Grace Av -Gt Neck 11021
(718) 823-2000 .. **Seeman,** Robt A '08 J DeGuardia -991 Morris Park Av -Bronx 10462
(914) 422-8755 .. **Seeman,** Russell T '78 %Dept of Law -101 E Post Rd -White Plns 10601 **Fx:**422-8706
(518) 455-3630 .. **Seemann,** Lisa J '89 NYS Assembly -Empire Plz Agncy Bldg 4 -Albany 12248
(718) 222-2306 .. **Seemen,** Karen J '94 %Law Dept -350 Jay -Brklyn 11201 **Fx:**222-2373
(212) 541-6050 .. **Seemer,** Karl H '01 Broadway West -234 W 56th -NY 10019
(212) 766-2050 .. **Seener,** Michelle S '82 (Seener & S) -11 Park Pl -NY 10007 **Fx:**766-2051
(212) 766-2050 .. **Seener,** Steven '82 (Seener & S) -11 Park Pl -NY 10007 **Fx:**766-2051
(212) 885-5000 .. **Seer,** Ethan M '80 (Blank R LLP) -405 Lex Av -NY 10174
(718) 849-2800 .. **Seeram,** Gail S '00 -101-05 Lefferts Blvd -Jamaica 11419 **Fx:**849-2880
(212) 839-5300 .. **Seery,** James P Jr. '91 (Sidley A LLP) -787 7th Av -NY 10019
(212) 430-8020 .. **Seery,** James T '91 (LeClairRyan,PC) -830 3rd Av -NY 10022
(212) 225-2000 .. **Seery,** Justin W '09 %Cleary GS&H -1 Lbrty Plz -NY 10006
(212) 559-1855 .. **Seery,** Trudi Ann '93 %Citibank -399 Park Av -NY 10022
(516) 746-4373 .. **Seevers,** Rachael E '07 %MHLS -170 Old Cntry Rd -Mineola 11501 **Fx:**746-0598
(212) 335-9000 .. **Seewald,** Andrew E '97 %DA -1 Hogan Pl -NY 10013
(212) 384-1000 .. **Seewald,** Jeffrey '00 %FBI -26 Fed Plz -NY 10278
(212) 980-0120 .. **Seewann,** Amelia K '03 %Frankfurt KK&S,PC -488 Mad Av -NY 10022
(917) 777-4200 .. **Seferi,** Edmond '99 (Bingham M LLP) -1 Bttry Pk Plz -NY 10004
(845) 371-4700 .. **Seffer,** Shari '85 OfCnsl Fein SK&S,PC -747 Chestnut Rdg Rd -Spg Vly 10977
(212) 250-8176 .. **Seffinger,** Mark L '93 %Deutsche Bank -60 Wall -NY 10005
(212) 202-0342 .. **Segal,** Alexander J '02 (Grinberg & S,PLLC) -111 Bway -NY 10006 **Fx:**(718) 228-9601
(212) 574-1200 .. **Segal,** Alexandra K '09 %Seward & K LLP -1 Bttry Pk Plz -NY 10004
(212) 530-1800 .. **Segal,** Amanda J '05 %Richards K&O LLP -1 World Fncl Ctr -NY 10281
(212) 640-5730 .. **Segal,** Anne L '78 %Amer Exp -200 Vesey -NY 10285
(845) 297-5218 .. **Segal,** Aviv '96 -12 Plz Rd -Wappingers Fls 12590 **Fx:**297-0424
(631) 758-6500 .. **Segal,** Barry B '71 -629 Rte 112 -Patchogue 11772 **Fx:**758-6383
Segal, Benjamin H '57 -12 Grdn Ct -Far Rckwy 11691
(914) 699-0000 .. **Segal,** Bernard '62 -53 Trenor Dr -New Rchll 10804 **Fx:**699-6308
(212) 290-1841 .. **Segal,** Betsy J '92 OTDA Fair Hearings -330 W 34th -NY 10001 **Fx:**290-1926
(212) 513-0665 .. **Segal,** Chas David '80 -225 Bway -NY 10007 **Fx:**608-4647
(516) 746-8000 .. **Segal,** Chas W '74 (Jaspan S LLP) -300 Grdn City Plz -Gdn Cty 11530
(212) 848-4000 .. **Segal,** Danl M '03 %Shearman & S LLP -599 Lex Av -NY 10022
(212) 406-9200 .. **Segal,** David '74 -30 Vesey -NY 10007 **Fx:**571-0938
(212) 725-9300 .. **Segal,** David C '65 (Sukenik S&G,PC) -404 5th Av -NY 10018
(212) 643-7000 .. **Segal,** David F '76 (Sills C&G PC) -One Rckfllr Plz -NY 10020
(518) 473-4863 .. **Segal,** Donald P '81 %Dept of Law -The Cptl -Albany 12224
(212) 961-8254 .. **Segal,** Elizabeth Grant '98 OTDA -317 Lenox Av -NY 10027
(212) 376-3032 .. **Segal,** Heidi J '94 Vera Inst of Justice -233 Bway -NY 10279
(212) 223-3880 .. **Segal,** Howard W '68 (HW Segal,PC) -845 3rd Av -NY 10022 **Fx:**223-4858
(718) 633-9100 .. **Segal,** Jack '86 (J Segal,LLP) -1428 36th -Brklyn 11218 **Fx:**633-9199
(212) 801-9265 .. **Segal,** Jay A '76 (Greenberg T,LLP) -200 Park Av -NY 10166
(212) 323-7070 .. **Segal,** Jeffrey A '95 (Rawle & H LLP) -14 Wall -NY 10005
(845) 486-2300 .. **Segal,** Jessica Z '00 %DA -236 Main -Poughkeepsie 12601 **Fx:**486-2324
(212) 237-8000 .. **Segal,** Lydia G '89 %John Jay Cllg -899 10th Av -NY 10019
(212) 922-0891 .. **Segal,** Mark S '85 (Segal & L) -501 5th Av -NY 10017
(212) 972-1000 .. **Segal,** Marvin B '62 -59 Maiden Ln -NY 10038 **Fx:**972-1030
(212) 651-7500 .. **Segal McCambridge Singer & Mahoney** -850 3rd Av -NY 10022 **Fx:**651-7499
(212) 403-1000 .. **Segal,** Michl J '86 (Wachtell LR&K) -51 W 52nd -NY 10019
(646) 386-5273 .. **Segal,** Moshe J '81 %Family Ct -60 Lafayette -NY 10013
(212) 756-2000 .. **Segal,** Nathaniel '06 %Schulte R&Z LLP -919 3rd Av -NY 10022
(212) 573-0970 .. **Segal,** Philip '07 GPW & Co -330 Mad Av -NY 10017 **Fx:**573-0971
(212) 297-0503 .. **Segal,** Philip C '74 (Segal & G LLP) -179 Franklin -NY 10013 **Fx:**297-0572
(212) 688-3200 .. **Segal,** Robt E '67 Cnsl Scheichet & D,PC -767 3rd Av -NY 10017
(212) 297-6231 .. **Segal,** Samantha L '04 -420 Lex Av -NY 10170
(212) 447-6660 .. **Segal,** Scott I '86 -10 E 40th -NY 10016
(518) 477-7951 .. **Segal,** Stanley B '78 OfCnsl Maney M&L -77 Troy Rd -E Greenbush 12061
(212) 715-9100 .. **Segal,** Steven J '10 %Kramer LN&F,LLP -1177 Av of Amer -NY 10036
(212) 906-1200 .. **Segal,** Theo Z '10 %Latham & W -885 3rd Av -NY 10022
(212) 805-6309 .. **Segal,** Yitzchok '09 US Courthouse -500 Pearl -NY 10007
(212) 244-2805 .. **Segal-Gebski,** Marius '06 -989 Av of Amer -NY 10018 **Fx:**378-2054
(212) 309-1000 .. **Segalis,** Boris '04 %Hunton & W -200 Park Av -NY 10166
(212) 627-9898 .. **Segall,** Karen M '06 %Sloss Law Ofc,PC -555 W 25th -NY 10001 **Fx:**627-9498
(212) 682-7474 .. **Segall,** Karin Fromson '93 (Foley & L LLP) -90 Park Av -NY 10016
(212) 474-1000 .. **Segall,** Margaret T '09 %Cravath S&M LLP -825 8th Av -NY 10019

(212) 752-4404 .. **Segall**, Mark B '88 Kidron Corp Advsrs -555 5th Av -NY 10017
(212) 552-3042 .. **Segall**, Mark E '79 JP Morgan Chase -1 Chase Manh Plz -NY 10081
(914) 328-0674 .. **Segall**, Maurice K '89 Pro Bono Prtnrshp,Inc -237 Mamaroneck Av -White Plns 10605 **Fx:**328-0538
(212) 450-4000 .. **Segall**, Michl H '07 %Davis P&W LLP -450 Lex Av -NY 10017
(212) 536-8716 .. **Segall**, Robt J '92 St George Financial Prtnrs -530 5th Av -NY 10036
(516) 767-2200 .. **Segall**, Sidney M '76 -150 Main -Pt Wash 11050
(914) 358-9595 .. **Segall**, Stephen L '86 S Segall,PC -202 Mamaroneck Av -White Plns 10601
(212) 416-6138 .. **Segall**, Steven A '80 %Dept of Law -120 Bway -NY 10271
(716) 566-5400 .. **Segalla**, Thos F '73 (Goldberg S LLP) -665 Main -Buffalo 14203
(212) 541-7800 .. **Segal-Reichlin**, Zoe L '07 %Planned Parenthood -434 W 33rd -NY 10001 **Fx:**868-4677
(212) 696-9100 .. **Segan**, Lawr M '89 -112 Mad Av -NY 10016 **Fx:**689-9680
(212) 696-9100 .. **Segan**, Leon '54 (Segan N&S PC) -112 Mad Av -NY 10016
(212) 696-9100 .. **Segan Nemerov & Singer PC** -112 Mad Av -NY 10016 **Fx:**689-9680
(212) 859-8000 .. **Segan**, Seth D '07 %Fried FHS&J LLP -1 NY Plz -NY 10004
(585) 475-1100 .. **Segar & Sciortino** -400 Meridian Centre -Rchstr 14618 **Fx:**475-1490
(585) 475-1100 .. **Segar**, Stephen A '87 (Segar & S) -400 Meridian Centre -Rchstr 14618
(347) 410-5332 .. **Segarra**, Angelique I '05 (Segarra & F) -540 Prsdnt -Brklyn 11215 **Fx:**(562) 286-5202
(212) 657-0441 .. **Segarra**, Carmen M '05 Citigroup -77 Water -NY 10005
(518) 364-0873 .. **Segarra**, Herbert P '82 -159 Prnctn Dr -Hartsdale 10530
(718) 466-3000 .. **Segarra**, Marlin '91 %Civil Ct -1118 Grnd Cncrs -Bronx 10456 **Fx:**466-3006
(212) 480-3100 .. **Segarra**, Ninfa '83 NYC Police Museum -100 Old Slip -NY 10005
(212) 619-4350 .. **Segear**, Robt C '08 %Newman MKGH,PC -14 Wall -NY 10005
(518) 452-0941 .. **Segel Goldman Mazzotta & Siegel,PC** -9 Wshngtn Sq -Albany 12205 **Fx:**452-0417
(518) 452-0941 .. **Segel**, Kenneth B '77 OfCnsl Segel GM&S,PC -9 Wshngtn Sq -Albany 12205
(212) 506-1784 .. **Segel**, Scott J '88 Peak Cnsl Inc -25 W 31st -NY 10001
(631) 650-1200 .. **Segelke**, Shauna L '09 %Sinnreich K&M LLP -267 Carleton Av -Central Islip 11722
(212) 889-0972 .. **Segen**, Leon S '80 -10 E 40th -NY 10016
(631) 543-3585 .. **Seger**, Bruce H '92 -102 New Hwy -Commack 11725 **Fx:**543-5834
(212) 557-7700 .. **Seget**, Alan D '75 (Davidson D&C LLP) -60 E 42nd -NY 10165
(212) 278-5436 .. **Segev**, Lior '99 SG Asset Mgmt,Inc -1221 Av of Amer -NY 10020
(917) 509-1598 .. **Segler**, Florence Hagan '01 -Morningside Station Bx1394 -NY 10026
(212) 596-9000 .. **Segovia**, TerriAnn Ge-heh '09 %Ropes & G LLP -1211 Av of Amer -NY 10036
(212) 418-0513 .. **Segreti**, Judith D '72 (Morris & M LLP) -767 3rd Av -NY 10017 **Fx:**980-5273
(212) 617-8734 .. **Segreti**, Margaret Byrnes '03 Bloomberg LP -731 Lex Av -NY 10022
(212) 222-3882 .. **Segun**, Olubunmi B '09 African Srvcs Committee -429 W 127th -NY 10027
(718) 767-1177 .. **Segura**, Venecia Maria '04 %Coran O,PC -25-02 F Lewis Blvd -Flushng 11358
(212) 374-2990 .. **Segure**, Celeste Thos '97 %NYC Dept Educ-OLS -52 Chmbrs -NY 10007 **Fx:**374-5939
(212) 785-1989 .. **Segure**, Dorian V '96 %Constitution Works -26 Wall -NY 10005
(212) 695-5281 .. **Seguritan**, Reuben S '75 -450 7th Av -NY 10123 **Fx:**563-2664
(914) 997-1346 .. **Seham**, Lee R A '88 (Seham SM&P,LLP) -445 Hmltn Av -White Plns 10601
(914) 997-1346 .. **Seham Seham Meltz & Petersen,LLP** -445 Hmltn Av -White Plns 10601
(212) 644-3707 .. **Seham Seham Meltz & Petersen,LLP** -145 E 48th -NY 10017
(718) 736-8460 .. **Sehati**, Tali B '99 -197-01 Hillside Av -Hollis 11423 **Fx:**736-1493
(212) 798-5490 .. **Sehgal**, Alpna Cassidy '99 Registry Pro -575 8th Av -NY 10018
(212) 566-3353 .. **Sehgal**, Mona '91 %Dept of Bldgs -280 Bway -NY 10007
(212) 878-8000 .. **Sehgal**, Zarrar '98 (Clifford C LLP) -31 W 52nd -NY 10019
(212) 336-2000 .. **Seib**, Karl E Jr. '71 OfCnsl Patterson BW&T LLP -1133 Av of Amer -NY 10036
(212) 248-3140 .. **Seib**, Katherine D '07 %Drinker B&R LLP -140 Bway -NY 10005
(212) 351-4000 .. **Seibald**, Marc Jonathan '08 %Gibson D&C LLP -200 Park Av -NY 10166
(212) 983-9200 .. **Seibel**, Robt A '72 Seibel & R -560 3rd Av -NY 10016 **Fx:**983-9201
(516) 466-1401 .. **Seibel**, Robt F '89 (Bai & S) -505 Nrthrn Blvd -Gt Neck 11021
(212) 635-7944 .. **Seibel**, Susan J '77 Bk of NY Mellon -1 Wall -NY 10286
(516) 867-7778 .. **Seibert**, Joel M '76 -2389 Kowal Ct -Merrick 11566
(716) 823-2558 .. **Seibert**, Michl '03 %F Bybel -674 Ridge Rd -Lackawanna 14218 **Fx:**822-0009
(212) 335-4500 .. **Seibert**, R Brian '05 %DLA Piper LLP -1251 Av of Amer -NY 10020
(716) 652-9560 .. **Seibold**, Maura C '08 %Bennett D&K,LLP -681 Main -E Aurora 14052
(716) 204-2400 .. **Seibold**, Timothy P '06 %SJ Baum,PC -220 Nrthpnte Pkwy Bx1291 -Buffalo 14240 **Fx:**204-4600
(516) 746-2300 .. **Seid**, Danielle J '04 %A Capetola -2C Hillside Av -Williston Pk 11596 **Fx:**746-2318
(516) 759-0801 .. **Seid**, Leonora C '90 -92 Dosoris Ln -Glen Cove 11542 **Fx:**656-0518
(315) 218-0250 .. **Seidberg**, Danl R '94 (D Seidberg,LLC) -5789 Widewaters Pkwy -Syracuse 13214 **Fx:**218-0253
(212) 818-1110 .. **Seidel**, Barry N '79 (Butzel L,PC) -380 Mad Av -NY 10017
(718) 793-1133 .. **Seidel**, Barry S '82 (B Seidel & Assoc) -88-03 69th Av -Frst Hlls 11375 **Fx:**263-8811
(914) 682-3131 .. **Seidel**, Danl R '82 (D Seidel,PC) -29 Hotel Dr -White Plns 10605 **Fx:**946-2773
(212) 335-9000 .. **Seidel**, Eric S '79 %DA -1 Hogan Pl -NY 10013
(917) 720-4104 .. **Seidel**, Erik Jordan '09 Art of Charm,LLC -80 Nassau -NY 10038
(212) 521-5400 .. **Seidel**, Jacqueline K '04 %Reed S LLP -599 Lex Av -NY 10022
(212) 807-2987 .. **Seidel**, James A '82 Thomson Reuters -195 Bway -NY 10007
(212) 504-6000 .. **Seidel**, Martin L '91 (Cadwalader W&T LLP) -1 World Fncl Ctr -NY 10281
(518) 473-1416 .. **Seidel**, Maureen '88 %Gvrnr's Ofc Employee Rel -Agncy Bldg 2 ESP -Albany 12223
(718) 590-2000 .. **Seidel**, Patrick R '09 %DA -198 E 161st -Bronx 10451 **Fx:**590-6477
(631) 724-8833 .. **Seidell**, Kenneth M '85 Cnsl Devitt SB,LLP -50 Route 111 -Smithtwn 11787
(914) 779-1050 .. **Seidelman**, Denise '80 (Rumbold & S) -116 Kraft Av -Bronxvll 10708 **Fx:**931-1786
(914) 249-2885 .. **Seideman**, Michelle J '94 Mastercard Intl -2000 Purchase -Purchase 10577
(631) 224-4040 .. **Seideman**, Peter '71 P Seideman,LLC -136 E Main -E Islip 11730 **Fx:**224-4044
(718) 692-1013 .. **Seidemann**, David J '90 (Seidemann & M) -974 E 27th -Brklyn 11210
(212) 335-9000 .. **Seidemann**, Joel J '80 %DA -1 Hogan Pl -NY 10013
(718) 692-1013 .. **Seidemann & Mermelstein** -974 E 27th -Brklyn 11210 **Fx:**692-1166
(914) 699-6287 .. **Seiden**, Adam '76 -9 W Prospect Av -Mt Vernon 10550 **Fx:**699-6398
(516) 606-7626 .. **Seiden**, Alyssa N '02 -55 Nrthrn Blvd -Gt Neck 11021
(212) 696-6000 .. **Seiden**, Andrew H '93 (Curtis M-PC&M LLP) -101 Park Av -NY 10178
(718) 590-2000 .. **Seiden**, Carrie B '04 %DA -198 E 161st -Bronx 10451 **Fx:**590-6477
(607) 754-0410 .. **Seiden**, Danl L '91 %Thomas C&M -1201 Monroe Bx329 -Endicott 13761
(212) 456-7026 .. **Seiden**, David T '96 %ABC -77 W 66th -NY 10023 **Fx:**456-6202
(212) 935-1400 .. **Seiden**, Jay G '68 (Seiden & S,PC) -570 Lex Av -NY 10022
(212) 431-1300 .. **Seiden**, Jeffrey H '05 %Borah GAN&G PC -377 Bway -NY 10013
(212) 407-9199 .. **Seiden**, Jonathan M '02 CKX Inc -650 Mad Av -NY 10022
(914) 636-7079 .. **Seiden**, Katherine H '89 -46 Aspen Rd -New Rchll 10804
(516) 747-2433 .. **Seiden & Kaufman** -1 Old Cntry Rd -Carle Pl 11514 **Fx:**294-4339
(914) 681-8700 .. **Seiden**, Mark '86 (Milber MP&S LLP) -3 Barker Av -White Plns 10601
(212) 326-3939 .. **Seiden**, Mark R '93 (Jones D) -222 E 41st -NY 10017
(516) 712-4000 .. **Seiden**, Peter '92 (Milber MP&S LLP) -1000 Woodbury Rd -Woodbury 11797
(212) 430-8020 .. **Seiden**, Peter G '77 (LeClairRyan,PC) -830 3rd Av -NY 10022
(212) 935-1400 .. **Seiden & Schein,PC** -570 Lex Av -NY 10022 **Fx:**593-4545
(212) 430-6324 .. **Seiden**, Steven E '94 -1515 Bway -NY 10036 **Fx:**(646) 219-4287
(516) 747-2433 .. **Seiden**, Steven J '85 (Seiden & K) -1 Old Cntry Rd -Carle Pl 11514
(845) 294-3105 .. **Seidenberg**, Harold A '57 -One South -Goshen 10924
(212) 284-5826 .. **Seidenberg**, Marc D '95 Merrill Lynch -153 E 53rd -NY 10022
(914) 961-9783 .. **Seidenberg**, Robt A '61 -10 Scenic Ln -Ynkrs 10710 **Fx:**961-9783
(212) 732-8900 .. **Seidenfeld**, Mark S '80 Seidenfeld Assoc LLC -225 Bway -NY 10007 **Fx:**732-8983
(212) 572-6228 .. **Seidenfeld**, Norman '79 -5807 12th Av -Brklyn 11219 **Fx:**(718) 436-2405
(212) 969-3000 .. **Seidenfeld**, Steven J '09 %Proskauer R LLP -1585 Bway -NY 10036
(718) 960-5813 .. **Seiden-Schneider**, Deborah '93 St Barnabas Hospital -4422 3rd Av -Bronx 10457
(212) 226-2376 .. **Seidenstein**, Danl M '06 %Oved & O LLP -101 Av of Amer -NY 10013 **Fx:**226-7555
(518) 719-3700 .. **Seidenstock**, Amy B '01 Greene Cnty DSS -411 Main Bx528 -Catskill 12414 **Fx:**719-3694
(718) 875-1300 .. **Seidenstock**, Paul H '87 %Applt Div 2nd Dept -45 Monroe Pl -Brklyn 11201 **Fx:**858-2446
(718) 263-3800 .. **Seidenwar**, Michl F '77 %Muss & M -118-35 Qns Blvd -Frst Hlls 11375
(212) 906-1200 .. **Seider**, Mitchell A '05 (Latham & W) -885 3rd Av -NY 10022
(212) 334-3131 .. **Seidler**, B Alan '73 -580 Bway -NY 10012 **Fx:**334-2211
(212) 557-7700 .. **Seidler**, Chas J Jr. '60 OfCnsl Davidson D&C LLP -60 E 42nd -NY 10165
(631) 853-4104 .. **Seidler**, Karen E '09 %DA -400 Carleton Av Bx9082 -Central Islip 11722 **Fx:**853-7838
(212) 373-3000 .. **Seidlin-Bernstein**, Elizabeth '10 %Paul WRW&G LLP -1285 Av of Amer -NY 10019
(212) 619-4444 .. **Seidman**, Allison J '08 %Marshall CW&B,PC -116 John -NY 10038
(212) 326-1018 .. **Seidman**, Andrew P '70 SrCnsl Studley,Inc -300 Park Av -NY 10022 **Fx:**326-1057
(212) 563-5666 .. **Seidman**, Bernard H '55 (Seidman & M) -330 7th Av -NY 10001
(212) 922-1900 .. **Seidman**, Brian W '89 (Seidman & S) -405 Lex Av -NY 10174 **Fx:**922-1912
(212) 319-1000 .. **Seidman**, Debra E '90 (Quirk & B,PC) -845 3rd Av -NY 10022
(212) 440-4300 .. **Seidman**, Douglass J '76 %Leg Aid -199 Water -NY 10038
(212) 922-1900 .. **Seidman**, Irving P '59 (Seidman & S) -405 Lex Av -NY 10174 **Fx:**922-1912
(516) 747-1010 .. **Seidman**, Jessica M '86 %Dollinger G&G -1 Old Cntry Rd -Carle Pl 11514
(212) 563-5666 .. **Seidman**, Jos M '97 OfCnsl Seidman & M -330 7th Av -NY 10001
(212) 779-1414 .. **Seidman**, Jos R '98 %Bernstein L LLP -10 E 40th -NY 10016
(212) 480-6784 .. **Seidman**, Kurt W '81 %DHCR -25 Beaver -NY 10004 **Fx:**480-7416
(212) 769-4343 .. **Seidman**, Leon B '83 -142 W End Av -NY 10023 **Fx:**769-4986
(212) 709-8223 .. **Seidman**, Lester A '93 Seidman & M -110 Wall -NY 10005 **Fx:**(718) 657-8601
(516) 479-6300 .. **Seidman**, Lon J '95 (Silverman A LLP) -100 Jericho Quad -Jericho 11753
(914) 472-8455 .. **Seidman**, Marco '93 (Bernstein & S) -670 Wht Plns Rd -Scarsdale 10583 **Fx:**472-8755
(212) 563-5666 .. **Seidman & Morenstein** -330 7th Av -NY 10001 **Fx:**563-6864
(212) 345-8891 .. **Seidman**, Paula-Jane '76 Marsh USA Inc -1166 Av of Amer -NY 10036 **Fx:**345-9467
(212) 594-5300 .. **Seidman**, Peter E '95 (Milberg LLP) -1 Penn Plz -NY 10119
(631) 853-4049 .. **Seidman**, Phyllis '90 %Cnty Atty -Dennison Bldg Bx6100 -Hauppauge 11788 **Fx:**853-5169
(212) 770-7000 .. **Seidman**, Sharon R '93 %AIG -80 Pine -NY 10005 **Fx:**344-2286
(212) 728-8000 .. **Seidman**, Steven Alan '91 (Willkie F&G LLP) -787 7th Av -NY 10019
(212) 286-8585 .. **Seidman**, Steven F '03 %Heidell PM&B,LLP -99 Park Av -NY 10016
(646) 386-3632 .. **Seidner**, Catalina '90 %Supreme Ct-Law Dept -60 Centre -NY 10007
(516) 570-3875 .. **Seidner**, Matthew S '03 (Seidner V LLP) -19 Park -Manhsst 11030 **Fx:**546-6880

(631) 661-5000 .. **Seidner Rosenfeld & Guttentag** -403 Deer Prk Av -Babylon 11702 **Fx:**661-5005
(631) 661-5000 .. **Seidner,** Stephen '64 (Seidner R&G) -403 Deer Prk Av -Babylon 11702
(212) 478-7200 .. **Seif,** Steven J '79 (Hahn & H LLP) -488 Mad Av -NY 10022
(718) 254-6008 .. **Seifan,** Marisa Megur '02 %US Atty -271 Cadman Plz E -Brklyn 11201 **Fx:**254-6479
(914) 946-0150 .. **Seife,** Alan '83 (Coleman & S) -41 Winslow Rd -White Plns 10606 **Fx:**997-0375
(212) 408-5100 .. **Seife,** Howard '79 (Chadbourne & P LLP) -30 Rckfllr Plz -NY 10112
(410) 992-1382 .. **Seiferas,** Gershon '01 %Outside Cnsl Solutns LLP -1430 Bway -NY 10018 **Fx:**(646) 360-5000
(518) 457-2070 .. **Seifert,** Christina L '93 %Dept of Tax & Fin -Bldg 9 State Campus -Albany 12227 **Fx:**457-6131
(212) 735-3000 .. **Seifert,** Joshua L '08 %Skadden ASM&F LLP -4 Times Sq -NY 10036
(631) 385-4450 .. **Seifert,** Randolph W '76 -5 Emil Ct -Huntngtn 11743
(212) 371-4500 .. **Seiff,** Eric A '58 (Seiff K&A) -444 Mad Av -NY 10022
(212) 371-4500 .. **Seiff Kretz & Abercrombie** -444 Mad Av -NY 10022 **Fx:**371-6883
(516) 766-7965 .. **Seiffert,** Robt W '83 -2787 Lng Bch Rd -Oceanside 11572 **Fx:**766-4922
(212) 735-3000 .. **Seifried,** Kyle T '06 %Skadden ASM&F LLP -4 Times Sq -NY 10036
(315) 422-1391 .. **Seifter,** Lowell A '78 (Green & S,PLLC) -One Lincoln Ctr #900 -Syracuse 13202
(212) 450-4000 .. **Seifu,** Rahael '08 %Davis P&W LLP -450 Lex Av -NY 10017
(212) 252-0004 .. **Seigal,** Robt '05 %Carroll M&K LLC -570 Lex Av -NY 10022
(212) 728-8000 .. **Seigal,** Teri M '10 %Willkie F&G LLP -787 7th Av -NY 10019
(212) 883-8833 .. **Seigel,** Chad D '98 %Tacopina & A -275 Mad Av -NY 10016
(212) 227-8877 .. **Seigel,** Chad D '98 (Tacopina S&T,PC) -275 Mad Av -NY 10016
(212) 564-1250 .. **Seigel,** Chas J '81 %Karp & K -370 7th Av -NY 10001
(516) 292-8100 .. **Seigel,** Jeffrey A '81 %Nassau/Sfflk Law Srv -1 Helen Keller Way -Hempstd 11550 **Fx:**292-6529
(516) 393-2200 .. **Seigel,** Randi E '07 %Garfunkel W,PC -111 Grt Nck Rd -Gt Neck 11021
(212) 974-7474 .. **Seigel,** Robt L '88 (Cowan DA&S LLP) -41 Mad Av -NY 10010
(718) 254-7000 .. **Seigel,** Thos J '95 %US Atty -271 Cadman Plz E -Brklyn 11201 **Fx:**254-6479
(212) 688-3200 .. **Seigerman,** Stacia A '94 %Scheichet & D,PC -767 3rd Av -NY 10017
(631) 853-4507 .. **Seigneuray,** Catherine A '84 Supreme Ct -400 Carleton Av -Central Islip 11722
(315) 435-2170 .. **Seikaly,** Maggie '92 %Cnty Atty -421 Mntgmry -Syracuse 13202 **Fx:**435-5729
(212) 642-0950 .. **Seilback,** Darren R '05 %Newman & O,PC -8 W 38th -NY 10018
(212) 833-1103 .. **Seiler,** Eric J '83 (Friedman KS&A LLP) -1633 Bway -NY 10019 **Fx:**373-7903
(212) 259-8000 .. **Seiler,** Jos L III '81 (Dewey & L LLP) -1301 Av of Amer -NY 10019
(212) 918-3000 .. **Sein,** Andrew J '09 %Hogan L LLP -875 3rd Av -NY 10022
(212) 848-4000 .. **Sein,** Robt J '04 %Shearman & S LLP -599 Lex Av -NY 10022
(718) 261-9460 .. **Seinfeld,** Martin M '79 (Pearlman AFS&S,LLP) -80-02 Kew Grdns Rd -Kew Gdns 11415
(212) 756-2000 .. **Seinsheimer,** Eric '07 %Schulte R&Z LLP -919 3rd Av -NY 10022
(518) 445-2311 .. **Seita,** Alex Y '80 Albany Law Schl -80 New Scotland Av -Albany 12208 **Fx:**445-2315
(212) 226-6620 .. **Seitel,** Stanley '55 -401 Bway -NY 10013 **Fx:**966-4057
(212) 962-2626 .. **Seitelman,** Mark E '80 -111 Bway -NY 10006 **Fx:**962-5050
(315) 963-7333 .. **Seiter,** Graham B '05 -Bx120 -Mexico 13114
(315) 423-7100 .. **Seiter,** Lauren Hornish '05 %Harris B PLLC -300 S State -Syracuse 13202
(716) 833-2284 .. **Seitz,** Donald F '60 -54 Hyledge Dr -Amherst 14226
(212) 818-9200 .. **Seitz,** Howard G '66 OfCnsl Satterlee SB&B LLP -230 Park Av -NY 10169
(845) 691-6244 .. **Seitz,** Julie R '90 -221 Pancake Hllw Rd -Highlnd 12528
(716) 847-8400 .. **Seitz,** Raymond H '72 (Phillips L LLP) -3400 HSBC Ctr -Buffalo 14203
(212) 722-1224 .. **Sekaloff,** Dennis K '72 -115 E 87th -NY 10128
(212) 695-7577 .. **Sekas,** Nicholas G '87 (Sekas & Assoc,LLC) -515 Mad Av -NY 10022 **Fx:**695-0152
(212) 682-7474 .. **Sekel,** Anne B '06 %Foley & L LLP -90 Park Av -NY 10016
(212) 587-0760 .. **Sekendiz,** Ismail Sinan '05 %Akin & S,LLC -30 Broad -NY 10004 **Fx:**587-4169
(585) 272-7007 .. **Sekharan,** Raja Narayanswami '95 Sekharan Law Ofc -2540 Brghtn-Henrietta Townline Rd -Rchstr 14623 **Fx:**272-7011
(212) 530-5000 .. **Sekino,** Renee H '03 %Milbank TH&M LLP -1 Chase Manh Plz -NY 10005
(212) 833-7821 .. **Seklir,** David P '95 Sony BMG Music Entrtnmnt -550 Mad Av -NY 10022 **Fx:**833-8406
(212) 505-4040 .. **Seklir,** Steven A '71 -386 Park Av S -NY 10016 **Fx:**505-4008
(631) 853-5761 .. **Sekora-Edmunds,** Stephanie '86 %Cnty Atty -400 Carleton Av -Central Islip 11722 **Fx:**853-7788
(212) 446-2300 .. **Sekowski,** Michelle M '05 %Boies S&F LLP -575 Lex Av -NY 10022
(315) 793-7000 .. **Sekreta,** Ellen '07 %Leg Aid -255 Genesee -Utica 13501 **Fx:**732-3202
(631) 424-2345 .. **Sekuler,** Amy I '89 -21 Norma Ln -Dix Hlls 11746 **Fx:**424-2345
(212) 804-4200 .. **Sekulic,** Olga '00 %Mound CW&G -One Bttry Pk Plz -NY 10004
(718) 286-6000 .. **Sela,** Ayelet '05 %DA -125-01 Qns Blvd -Kew Gdns 11415
(646) 266-8124 .. **Sela,** Candace '03 (Sela & Assoc,PC) -5355 H Hdsn Pkwy -Bronx 10471 **Fx:**(347) 427-6494
(212) 278-5723 .. **Selassie,** Sengal M G '97 SG Capital Prtnrs LLC -1221 Av of Amer -NY 10020
(315) 471-6611 .. **Selbach,** James F '80 J Selbach,PC -5858 E Molloy Rd -Syracuse 13211
(718) 543-2200 .. **Selber,** Marilyn G '69 %Coyle & Assoc,LLP -5911 Riverdale Av -Bronx 10471 **Fx:**543-2156
(212) 355-9500 .. **Selbin,** Jonathan D '02 (Lieff CH&B,LLP) -250 Hudson -NY 10013
(212) 592-1400 .. **Selbst,** Stephen B '84 (Herrick,F LLP) -2 Park Av -NY 10016
(212) 351-4500 .. **Selby,** Jackie '99 SrCnsl Epstein B&G,PC -250 Park Av -NY 10177
(585) 385-8810 .. **Selby,** Jon S '87 -19 Circle Wood Rd -Rchstr 14625
(718) 941-2621 .. **Selby,** Ruth K '91 -400 Argyke Rd -Brklyn 11218 **Fx:**941-2621
(212) 750-6776 .. **Selby,** Steven J '89 Cnsl Morgenstern & B,LLC -885 3rd Av -NY 10022
(212) 210-9494 .. **Selby,** Timothy P '93 (Alston & B LLP) -90 Park Av -NY 10016
(518) 783-0016 .. **Selchick,** Jeffrey M '76 -Bx11280 -Albany 12211
(845) 471-0058 .. **Selcov,** Robt '78 %Leg Srvcs -29 N Hmltn -Poughkeepsie 12601 **Fx:**471-0244
(212) 906-6453 .. **Selde,** Lynda M '89 %UNIFEM -304 E 45th -NY 10017
(212) 859-8000 .. **Selden,** David W '02 (Fried FHS&J LLP) -1 NY Plz -NY 10004
(212) 685-8456 .. **Selden,** Marc E '94 (Eagle & S) -303 5th Av -NY 10016
(212) 909-6000 .. **Selden,** Shannon R '02 %Debevoise & P LLP -919 3rd Av -NY 10022
(212) 816-7077 .. **Seledee,** Craig A '76 %Citibank NA -250 West -NY 10013
(212) 446-4800 .. **Selendy,** Jennifer M '96 (Kirkland & E LLP) -153 E 53rd -NY 10022
(212) 849-7000 .. **Selendy,** Philippe Z '94 (Quinn EU&S,LLP) -51 Mad Av -NY 10010
(212) 370-1300 .. **Selengut,** Chaim David '82 (Ellenoff G&S LLP) -150 E 42nd -NY 10017
(212) 839-5300 .. **Selengut,** Shira A '09 %Sidley A LLP -787 7th Av -NY 10019
(212) 588-9600 .. **Selfon Puma,** Lysa '00 %Wise Counsel LLC -767 3rd Av -NY 10017 **Fx:**355-5983
(845) 942-2222 .. **Selig,** Benjamin E '67 -65 S Lbrty Dr -Stony Pnt 10980 **Fx:**942-0378
(212) 788-0462 .. **Selig,** Edwin '72 %Law Dept -100 Church -NY 10007 **Fx:**788-0367
(718) 449-9200 .. **Selig,** Krista F '01 Grant Abstract -1908 Bath Av -Brklyn 11214
(914) 686-0108 .. **Selig,** Marjory M '08 %Glassman & B -99 Court -White Plns 10601
(212) 909-6000 .. **Selig,** P Scott '07 %Debevoise & P LLP -919 3rd Av -NY 10022
(212) 855-0224 .. **Selig,** Stacey D '00 Goldman Sachs & Co -180 Maiden Ln -NY 10038
(212) 873-7131 .. **Selig,** Stephen F '57 -115 Cntrl Pk W -NY 10023 **Fx:**873-7131
(516) 742-7301 .. **Seliger,** Irwin '56 -129 Marcellus Rd -Mineola 11501 **Fx:**385-6521
(212) 316-3159 .. **Seliger,** Jonathan N '99 Axiom -75 Spring -NY 10012
(845) 338-4100 .. **Seligman,** Delice '72 Seligman & S -70 Main -Kingston 12401
(631) 666-5766 .. **Seligman,** Harold '72 (Long TBSWJ&S) -120 4th Av Bx5591 -Bay Shr 11706
(212) 468-4800 .. **Seligman,** John P '73 (Davis & G LLP) -1740 Bway -NY 10019
(212) 953-2400 .. **Seligman,** Michl L '81 -708 3rd Av -NY 10017
(212) 833-4838 .. **Seligman,** Nicole K '93 Sony Corp of Amer -550 Mad Av -NY 10022
(212) 788-0784 .. **Seligman,** Rachel A '01 %Law Dept -100 Church -NY 10007 **Fx:**788-0367
(518) 374-3373 .. **Seligman,** Raymond J '77 (Silverman S&S) -527 State -Schnctdy 12305
(212) 403-1000 .. **Seligman,** Stephanie J '86 (Wachtell LR&K) -51 W 52nd -NY 10019
(212) 980-0120 .. **Seligman,** Terri J '86 (Frankfurt KK&S,PC) -488 Mad Av -NY 10022
(212) 966-5020 .. **Seligson,** Aaron '53 (Seligson R&R) -29 W 30th -NY 10001
(212) 966-5020 .. **Seligson,** Alexander W '93 %Seligson R&R -29 W 30th -NY 10001
(516) 222-6200 .. **Seligson,** Jessica E '10 %Berkman HPP&F,PC -100 Grdn City Plz -Gdn Cty 11530
(212) 966-5020 .. **Seligson Rothman & Rothman** -29 W 30th -NY 10001 **Fx:**(646) 514-9980
(914) 633-3147 .. **Selin,** M Christina '77 -114 Sutton Mnr Rd -New Rchll 10801
(212) 474-1000 .. **Selinger,** David L '10 %Cravath S&M LLP -825 8th Av -NY 10019
(845) 294-2544 .. **Selinger,** John S '95 (Zeccola & S) -45 Webster Av -Goshen 10924
(212) 547-5400 .. **Selinger,** Mark S '85 (McDermott W&E LLP) -340 Mad Av -NY 10173
(914) 997-0500 .. **Selinger,** Neil L '79 Cnsl Lowey DC&H,PC -1 N Bway -White Plns 10601
(212) 909-6000 .. **Selinger,** Scott B '07 %Debevoise & P LLP -919 3rd Av -NY 10022
(516) 465-9100 .. **Selinger,** Stephen J '06 %W McDermott -499 Jericho Tpk -Mineola 11501 **Fx:**465-9105
(516) 771-8999 .. **Selinger,** Wanda L '98 -190 Lena Av -Freeprt 11520 **Fx:**771-9599
(516) 535-8599 .. **Selip,** Melissa A '93 Astoria Fed Savings & Loan -211 Station Rd -Mineola 11501 **Fx:**535-8103
(516) 364-6006 .. **Selip,** Mitchell '92 OfCnsl Cohen & S,LLP -199 Crsswys Park Dr Bx9004 -Woodbury 11797
(212) 506-5000 .. **Selipanov,** Aleksey L '04 %Orrick H&S LLP -51 W 52nd -NY 10019
(718) 336-5643 .. **Selit,** Max '61 -1773 E 12th -Brklyn 11229
(631) 375-9990 .. **Selkin,** Pamela L '99 -6 Tuxedo Dr -Melvll 11747 **Fx:**367-3261
(718) 286-6000 .. **Selkowe,** Jonathan '10 %DA -125-01 Qns Blvd -Kew Gdns 11415
(212) 450-4000 .. **Sellers,** Britton M '10 %Davis P&W LLP -450 Lex Av -NY 10017
(212) 455-2000 .. **Sellers,** Gary L '79 (Simpson T&B LLP) -425 Lex Av -NY 10017
(716) 854-6495 .. **Sellers,** Jeffrey A '68 (Silverberg YS&M) -515 Brisbane Bldg -Buffalo 14203
(716) 627-5400 .. **Sellers,** Kathleen M '98 %CJ Sellers & Co Inc -4300 Camp Rd Bx14010 -Athol Spgs 14010 **Fx:**627-5440
(212) 446-8066 .. **Sellers,** Robin Stone '79 %McKinsey & Co -55 E 52nd -NY 10055 **Fx:**688-9521
(212) 558-4000 .. **Sellers,** Saml B '09 %Sullivan & C LLP -125 Broad -NY 10004
(212) 788-1146 .. **Sellers,** Terryl Ann '89 %Law Dept -100 Church -NY 10007 **Fx:**788-0367
(716) 627-5400 .. **Sellers,** Thos G '72 -4300 Camp Rd Bx 460 -Athol Spgs 14010 **Fx:**627-5923
(212) 969-3000 .. **Sellier,** Bertrand C '82 (Proskauer R LLP) -1585 Bway -NY 10036
(212) 277-4000 .. **Sellman,** Angela R '03 %Freshfields BD LLP -520 Mad Av -NY 10022
(631) 543-3750 .. **Sellman,** Wm F '88 (Savitt K&S PC) -353 Vets Mem'l Hwy -Commack 11725
(212) 340-0400 .. **Sells,** Cecil J '80 %Appllt Div 1st Dept -27 Mad Av -NY 10010 **Fx:**889-4412
(212) 553-9215 .. **Sells,** Derek S '89 (Cochran Firm) -233 Bway -NY 10279
(212) 854-0314 .. **Sells,** Marcia L '86 Columbia Univ -535 W 116th -NY 10027
(716) 484-7191 .. **Sellstrom,** John L '64 (Sellstrom LLP) -9-11 E 4th Bx50 -Jamestwn 14702 **Fx:**484-2133
(716) 484-7191 .. **Sellstrom,** Stephen E '94 (Sellstrom LLP) -9-11 E 4th Bx50 -Jamestwn 14702 **Fx:**484-2133
(212) 937-6955 .. **Sellwood,** Scott M '09 Rightsflow, Inc -29 W 17th -NY 10011
(212) 735-3000 .. **Selman,** Ari M '10 %Skadden ASM&F LLP -4 Times Sq -NY 10036
(212) 490-3000 .. **Selmeci,** Judy '06 %Wilson EME&D LLP -150 E 42nd -NY 10017
(212) 245-3700 .. **Selmon,** Eric H '02 Longbow Cptl Prtnrs -598 Mad Av -NY 10022
(716) 847-0650 .. **Selmonsky,** Penny B '96 %Leg Srvcs -237 Main -Buffalo 14203 **Fx:**847-0227
(917) 693-0247 .. **Selsky,** Ira B '68 -1 Columbus Pl -NY 10019

(212) 355-9500 .. **Seltz,** Danl E '04 (Lieff CH&B,LLP) -250 Hudson -NY 10013
(212) 661-1873 .. **Seltzer,** Adolph D '60 -501 5th Av -NY 10017 **Fx:**661-7952
(516) 741-6565 .. **Seltzer,** Brian Michl '64 (Meyer SE&K,PC) -990 Stewart Av Bx9194 -Gdn Cty 11530
(212) 481-0077 .. **Seltzer,** Danl L '73 -280 Mad Av -NY 10016
(212) 692-9666 .. **Seltzer,** Eric H '85 (Gilbride TL&S LLC) -708 3rd Av -NY 10017
(631) 421-3850 .. **Seltzer,** Jay S '79 -3 Mechanic Ct -Huntngtn 11743
(212) 839-5300 .. **Seltzer,** Joanne '00 %Sidley A LLP -787 7th Av -NY 10019
(212) 655-4000 .. **Seltzer,** Joshua L '04 %M Gershweir -120 Bway -NY 10271 **Fx:**655-5039
(212) 289-8798 .. **Seltzer,** Marion A '69 -1725 York Av -NY 10128 **Fx:**410-9443
(212) 943-8940 .. **Seltzer,** Michl I '82 %Crisci W&H -17 State -NY 10004 **Fx:**425-3428
(516) 922-9100 .. **Seltzer,** Michl S '73 %V McNamara -1045 Oyster Bay Rd -E Norwich 11732 **Fx:**922-9208
(631) 286-8849 .. **Seltzer,** Regina '84 -30 S Brwstr Ln -Bellprt 11713
(212) 836-8000 .. **Seltzer,** Richd C '68 (Kaye S LLP) -425 Park Av -NY 10022
(212) 563-4100 .. **Seltzer,** Richd M '76 (Cohen W&S LLP) -330 W 42nd -NY 10036
(516) 935-3600 .. **Seltzer,** Stephen '63 (Seltzer SH&H LLP) -100 Jericho Quad -Jericho 11753
(212) 608-1178 .. **Seltzer,** Steven '00 (Yuen RS&S PC) -132 Nassau -NY 10038 **Fx:**608-2913
(212) 578-0394 .. **Seltzer,** Steven P '85 %MetLife -27-01 Qns Plz N -LIC 11101 **Fx:**578-3916
(516) 935-3600 .. **Seltzer Sussman Habermann & Heitner LLP** -100 Jericho Quad -Jericho 11753 **Fx:**933-3030
(212) 796-8848 .. **Seltzer,** Suzanne B '94 (Klasko RS&S,LLP) -317 Mad Av -NY 10017 **Fx:**297-1799
(212) 980-3500 .. **Selva,** Jonathan '02 %Pavia & H LLP -600 Mad Av -NY 10022
(585) 263-1000 .. **Selvaggio,** Anthony T '95 Cnsl Nixon P LLP -1100 Clinton Sq -Rchstr 14604
(631) 427-0100 .. **Selvaggio,** Raymond A '91 (Pezold SH&S,LLC) -120 Main -Huntngtn 11743
(212) 450-4000 .. **Selvam,** Vijay S V '09 %Davis P&W LLP -450 Lex Av -NY 10017
(212) 715-9100 .. **Selver,** Paul '73 (Kramer LN&F,LLP) -1177 Av of Amer -NY 10036
(212) 259-3900 .. **Selverne,** Michl '85 (Selverne & Co,PLLC) -485 Mad Av -NY 10022
(212) 267-3091 .. **Selvers,** Robt L '03 %Wilentz G&S -110 William -NY 10038 **Fx:**(732) 726-6642
(212) 806-5400 .. **Selvidio,** Jos R '05 %Stroock &S&L LLP -180 Maiden Ln -NY 10038
(516) 992-0805 .. **Selvin,** Jared M '98 (Selvin Law Firm PLLC) -1225 Franklin Av -Gdn Cty 11530 **Fx:**678-3090
(212) 442-0588 .. **Selvin,** Karen B '96 %Law Dept -100 Church -NY 10007 **Fx:**788-0367
(212) 315-3755 .. **Selwanes,** Wendy '02 %C Juntikka & Assoc,LLP -350 5th Av -NY 10118 **Fx:**315-9032
(212) 837-6207 .. **Selwyn,** Madeleine C '10 %Hughes H&R LLP -1 Bttry Pk Plz -NY 10004 **Fx:**299-6207
(212) 799-7320 .. **Selya,** Robt '64 -180 Riverside Dr -NY 10024
(212) 980-0120 .. **Selz,** Thos D '72 (Frankfurt KK&S,PC) -488 Mad Av -NY 10022
(212) 755-5510 .. **Selzer,** Herbert M '72 (Loeb B & Prtnrs) -505 Park Av -NY 10022
(212) 458-1078 .. **Selzer,** Steven '94 %AIG -175 Water -NY 10038 **Fx:**458-1048
(914) 946-4000 .. **Selznick,** David R '84 -145 Bedford Rd -Armonk 10504 **Fx:**946-4006
(914) 276-2727 .. **Selznick,** Helene M '83 -293 Route 100 -Somers 10589 **Fx:**276-0795
(212) 867-1475 .. **Selznick,** Loren F '84 (Dailey & S) -405 Lex Av -NY 10174
(212) 267-7600 .. **Semack,** Michl J '97 OfCnsl Solomon PBH&S LLP -40 Wall -NY 10005
(212) 698-3500 .. **Semah,** Victor '07 %Dechert LLP -1095 Av of Amer -NY 10036
(718) 618-2500 .. **Semaj,** Naita A '06 %Civil Ct -851 Grnd Cncrs -Bronx 10451 **Fx:**590-7294
(212) 323-7070 .. **Seman,** Dean C '09 %Rawle & H LLP -14 Wall -NY 10005
(516) 248-8889 .. **Seman,** Karl C '84 (Grunwald & S,PC) -100 Grdn City Plz -Gdn Cty 11530
(212) 878-7248 .. **Semancik,** Anthony P Jr. '84 %MTA -347 Mad Av -NY 10017
(212) 272-2440 .. **Semaya,** Arlene N '78 %JP Morgan Chase -383 Mad Av -NY 10179
(212) 233-0130 .. **Semaya,** Francine L '83 (Nelson Ld&H) -120 Bway -NY 10271
(212) 554-7800 .. **Semaya,** Robt J '85 (Moses & S LLP) -405 Lex Av -NY 10174
(212) 561-3615 .. **Semaya,** Ted G '81 (Eaton & V LLP) -3 Park Av -NY 10016
(631) 853-5212 .. **Semble,** Monroe A '79 %Leg Aid -400 Carleton Av Bx9082 -Central Islip 11722 **Fx:**853-7798
(212) 750-4483 .. **Sembler,** Fredk M '89 -501 Mad Av -NY 10022 **Fx:**750-4491
(212) 628-5613 .. **Semel,** Benjamin K '99 -245 E 80th -NY 10075
(212) 628-5613 .. **Semel,** Danl M '60 -245 E 80th -NY 10075
(212) 419-1550 .. **Semel,** Gabrielle '87 CWA Legal Dept -350 7th Av -NY 10001 **Fx:**419-1555
(212) 508-6700 .. **Semel,** Hilary '99 %Tannenbaum HS&H LLP -900 3rd Av -NY 10022
(631) 234-1699 .. **Semel,** Martin '63 -87 W Suffolk Av -Central Islip 11722
(631) 761-0847 .. **Semel,** Martin I '59 OfCnsl Lazer AR&Y,PC -225 Old Cntry Rd -Melvll 11747
(212) 758-5894 .. **Semel,** Martin J '59 -340 E 64th -NY 10065 **Fx:**223-0427
(914) 997-9556 .. **Semel,** Randie L '91 (R Semel PC) -399 Knollwood Rd -White Plns 10603 **Fx:**997-9558
(212) 964-6611 .. **Semel-Weinstein,** Barry A '08 %Lester SK&D -120 Bway -NY 10271
(516) 767-3600 .. **Semenoro,** Timothy '02 %Chalos O&D -366 Main -Pt Wash 11050
(212) 688-8555 .. **Semenova,** Marina V '08 Fragomen DB&L LLP -7 Hanover Sq -NY 10004
(212) 728-8000 .. **Semensohn,** Jaime L '09 %Willkie F&G LLP -787 7th Av -NY 10019
(516) 745-1000 .. **Semensohn,** Robt E '78 -585 Stewart Av -Gdn Cty 11530 **Fx:**227-2741
(212) 588-5500 .. **Semer,** Scott L '98 (Davies WP&V LLP) -625 Mad Av -NY 10022
(212) 407-4000 .. **Semerdjian,** Steve A '98 (Loeb & L,LLP) -345 Park Av -NY 10154
(212) 557-5055 .. **Semetis,** Arthur J '82 (Semetis Law Firm) -286 Mad Av -NY 10017 **Fx:**557-5051
(212) 984-7764 .. **Semian,** Stephen W '98 (Warshaw BCS&K,LLP) -555 5th Av -NY 10017
(212) 563-0499 .. **Semidei-Otero,** Maria E '83 %Women's Venture Fund -318 W 39th -NY 10018
(716) 847-8400 .. **Semidey,** Melissa A '09 %Phillips L LLP -3400 HSBC Ctr -Buffalo 14203
(845) 344-2524 .. **Semidey,** Pascual R '02 %C Curcio -1 Edgewtr Dr -Middletwn 10940 **Fx:**344-2528
(212) 657-1397 .. **Seminara,** Alisa K '90 Citigroup Global Mrkts -77 Water -NY 10005
(212) 867-9500 .. **Seminara,** Joanne '86 (Kurzman K&F,LLP) -230 Park Av -NY 10169
(212) 867-9500 .. **Seminara,** Jos F '56 OfCnsl Kurzman K&F,LLP -230 Park Av -NY 10169
(212) 688-5151 .. **Seminara,** Matthew S '09 %Gibney A&F,LLP -665 5th Av -NY 10022
(315) 785-3053 .. **Seminerio,** Frank A '09 DA -175 Arsenal -Watertwn 13601 **Fx:**785-3371
(718) 664-1805 .. **Semino,** Lauren '05 %ACS -900 Sheridan Av -Bronx 10451
(212) 277-4000 .. **Semino,** Matthew J '06 %Freshfields BD LLP -520 Mad Av -NY 10022
(212) 490-3000 .. **Semlies,** Lori R '95 (Wilson EME&D LLP) -150 E 42nd -NY 10017
(914) 323-7000 .. **Semlies,** Lori R '95 (Wilson EME&D LLP) -3 Gannett Dr -White Plns 10604
(212) 810-4007 .. **Semmel,** Jason P '98 Broadway Prtnrs Fund Mngr LLC -1 Penn Plz -NY 10119
(718) 838-7878 .. **Semmel,** Jenny '97 %Bronx Defenders -860 Crtlandt Av -Bronx 10451 **Fx:**665-0100
(212) 406-6000 .. **Semmel,** Nathan M '99 (Semmel & L,LLP) -20 Vesey -NY 10007 **Fx:**406-6001
(212) 696-6000 .. **Semmelman,** Jacques '84 (Curtis M-PC&M LLP) -101 Park Av -NY 10178
(516) 542-1000 .. **Semmig,** Heidelind M '03 %Geisler & G,LLP -100 Q Roosevelt Blvd -Gdn Cty 11530
(516) 747-0300 .. **Semon,** Sigmund S '62 Cnsl Meltzer LG&B,LLP -190 Willis Av -Mineola 11501
(212) 818-9200 .. **Semonite,** Sally R '92 %Satterlee SB&B LLP -230 Park Av -NY 10169
(646) 392-9250 .. **Semos,** George W '75 %M Klein & Assoc -200 Mad Av -NY 10016 **Fx:**(212) 779-1499
(212) 819-8200 .. **Sempertegui,** Ana C '10 %White & C LLP -1155 Av of Amer -NY 10036
(716) 204-9001 .. **Semple,** E Michl '73 OfCnsl DiNardo & M,PC -2813 Wehrle Dr -Williamsvll 14221
(212) 697-6555 .. **Semprevivo,** Philip C Jr. '95 (Biedermann RH&R) -570 Lex Av -NY 10022
(212) 450-4000 .. **Sen,** Apratim '09 %Davis P&W LLP -450 Lex Av -NY 10017
(212) 259-8000 .. **Sen,** Dev R '90 (Dewey & L LLP) -1301 Av of Amer -NY 10019
(212) 219-3360 .. **Sen,** Diana S '01 %Latino Justice PRLDEF -99 Hudson -NY 10013 **Fx:**431-4276
(212) 617-2000 .. **Sen,** Pia M '07 Bloomberg LP -731 Lex Av -NY 10022
(716) 847-8400 .. **Sen,** Taylan K '09 %Phillips L LLP -3400 HSBC Ctr -Buffalo 14203
(585) 238-2000 .. **Sen,** Taylan K '09 %Phillips L LLP -1400 First Fed Plz -Rchstr 14614
(212) 259-8000 .. **Sen,** Urvashi '05 %Dewey & L LLP -1301 Av of Amer -NY 10019
(212) 538-5879 .. **Sena,** Francesca M '98 Credit Suisse -11 Mad Av -NY 10010
(516) 877-5600 .. **Sena,** Frank '60 %R Tusa -1225 Franklin Av -Gdn Cty 11530 **Fx:**877-5695
(516) 739-1584 .. **Sena,** Jeffrey L '79 -106 Grdn -Gdn Cty 11530
(914) 287-0888 .. **Sena,** Jos A Jr. '80 -55 Church -White Plns 10601 **Fx:**997-1204
(212) 468-4800 .. **Sena,** Jos A Jr. '05 %Davis & G LLP -1740 Bway -NY 10019
(212) 471-8527 .. **Sena,** Michl B '81 (Herzfeld & R,PC) -125 Broad -NY 10004
(718) 478-7755 .. **Sena,** Wm L '85 -37-32 75th -Jcksn Hts 11372
(212) 670-0318 .. **Senatore,** Chas V '82 %Merrill Lynch -222 Bway -NY 10038
(212) 446-2300 .. **Senatore,** Matthew J '08 %Boies S&F LLP -575 Lex Av -NY 10022
(212) 566-3330 .. **Senatus,** Chantal N '98 NYC Dept Bldgs-Ofc of Gen Cnsl -280 Bway -NY 10007
(646) 282-5907 .. **Senbanjo,** Olaitan B '01 Davidson Kampren Capital Mgmt LLC -65 E 55th -NY 10022
(516) 739-1546 .. **Sencer,** Myra G '88 -250 Old Cntry Rd -Mineola 11501 **Fx:**739-5341
(212) 335-9000 .. **Sender,** Amy R '01 %DA -1 Hogan Pl -NY 10013
(212) 225-2000 .. **Sender,** Elisabeth '08 %Cleary GS&H -1 Lbrty Plz -NY 10006
(212) 732-5000 .. **Sender,** Julie A '98 %Leg Aid -49 Thomas -NY 10013 **Fx:**298-5252
(973) 315-4462 .. **Sender,** Stuart D '81 (Budd L) -140 Bway -NY 10005
(212) 878-8000 .. **Senderowicz,** Jeremy I '01 %Clifford C LLP -31 W 52nd -NY 10019
(718) 286-6000 .. **Sendlein,** Kirk A '09 DA -125-01 Qns Blvd -Kew Gdns 11415
(631) 287-3065 .. **Sendlenski,** Michl P '04 %Town Atty -116 Hmptn Rd -Southampton 11968 **Fx:**287-3662
(212) 576-7000 .. **Sendor,** Jennifer '99 NY Life Ins -51 Mad Av -NY 10010 **Fx:**447-0569
(212) 840-6400 .. **Sendroff,** Mark D '76 (Sendroff & B,LLP) -1500 Bway -NY 10036 **Fx:**840-6401
(516) 498-9100 .. **Sendrovic,** Barry D '96 %Benedict Properties LLC -150 Grt Nck Rd -Gt Neck 11021
(212) 903-1328 .. **Sendrow,** Becky A '06 William Morris Agency -1325 Av of Amer -NY 10019
(212) 818-8030 .. **Sendyk,** Karen B '88 Itochu Intl -335 Mad Av -NY 10017 **Fx:**818-8493
(716) 854-2020 .. **Sendziak,** Jeffrey C '90 (Cellino & B,PC) -350 Main -Buffalo 14202
(212) 715-9100 .. **Senecal,** Guilaine '05 %Kramer LN&F,LLP -1177 Av of Amer -NY 10036
(212) 578-2984 .. **Senezhak,** Diana M '78 %MetLife -27-01 Qns Plz N -LIC 11101
(212) 218-5500 .. **Senff,** Caitlin A '09 %Seyfarth S LLP -620 8th Av -NY 10018
(631) 277-9000 .. **Senft,** Anthony S Jr. '93 A Senft Jr,PC -21 Carleton Av -E Islip 11730 **Fx:**277-6860
(914) 667-6517 .. **Senft,** Mitchell F '84 -7 Elena Dr -Cortlandt Manor 10567 **Fx:**455-4288
(212) 545-3781 .. **Sengers,** Maarten W '97 %Marubik -244 5th Av -NY 10001
(212) 640-2000 .. **Senghore,** Medina N J '02 Amer Exp -200 Vesey -NY 10285
(585) 232-6500 .. **Senglaub,** Leslie M '93 (Harter S&E LLP) -1600 Bausch & Lomb Pl -Rchstr 14604
(716) 853-1616 .. **Senglaub,** Leslie M '93 (Harter S&E LLP) -12 Fountain Plz -Buffalo 14202
(212) 335-4500 .. **Seniawski,** Barbara L '02 %DLA Piper LLP -1251 Av of Amer -NY 10020

(212) 698-3500 .. **Senich,** George A '97 Cnsl Dechert LLP -1095 Av of Amer -NY 10036
(212) 715-9100 .. **Senie,** Stephen R '68 Cnsl Kramer LN&F,LLP -1177 Av of Amer -NY 10036
(212) 435-3571 .. **Senio,** Ronald M '70 %Port Auth of NY/NJ -225 Park Av S -NY 10003 **Fx:**435-3555
(212) 839-5300 .. **Senior,** Jaime M '08 %Sidley A LLP -787 7th Av -NY 10019
(212) 818-9600 .. **Senior,** Norman A '70 (Greenfield S&S,LLP) -600 3rd Av -NY 10016
(518) 429-4200 .. **Senlet,** Ekin '09 %Hiscock & B,LLP -50 Beaver -Albany 12207
(315) 435-2470 .. **Senn,** Jessica '07 %DA -505 S State -Syracuse 13202 **Fx:**435-3969
(845) 383-1202 .. **Sennett,** Jonathan R '94 JR Sennett,PC -2 Main -Kingston 12401 **Fx:**383-1853
(631) 348-7500 .. **Sensale,** Jos F '01 (Chase S Law Grp,LLP) -64 Smithtwn Blvd -Smithtwn 11787 **Fx:**348-7501
(212) 559-1085 .. **Sensale,** Paul M '88 Citigroup -909 3rd Av -NY 10022 **Fx:**559-3445
(212) 670-0266 .. **Sensale,** Robt B '85 %Merrill Lynch -222 Bway -NY 10038
(516) 742-4343 .. **Sensny,** John S '78 (Scully SM&P PC) -400 Grdn City Plz -Gdn Cty 11530
(646) 602-5600 .. **Senter,** Jeffrey R '09 %Urban Justice Ctr -123 William -NY 10038 **Fx:**(212) 533-4598
(973) 228-5700 .. **Senthil,** Isai '06 %Brach E LLC -100 Park Av -NY 10017 **Fx:**228-7852
(212) 940-3114 .. **Sentner,** Robt C '85 (Nixon P LLP) -437 Mad Av -NY 10022
(212) 351-4000 .. **Sentome,** Vladimir W '08 %Gibson D&C LLP -200 Park Av -NY 10166
(917) 322-2151 .. **Senturk,** Sekip S '01 EPE Inc -445 Park Av -NY 10022
(212) 574-1200 .. **Senzel,** Bruce D '68 Cnsl Seward & K LLP -1 Bttry Pk Plz -NY 10004
(516) 294-2626 .. **Senzer,** Paul H '81 -224 7th -Gdn Cty 11530 **Fx:**248-8670
(631) 757-0935 .. **Senzer,** Paul H '81 (Village Justice) -224 Main -Northprt 11768
(631) 470-5161 .. **Senzer,** Richd A '88 The Garden City Grp,Inc -105 Maxess Rd -Melvll 11747 **Fx:**940-6547
(212) 935-3000 .. **Senzer,** Robt O '88 OfCnsl Mintz LCFG&P,PC -666 3rd Av -NY 10017
(516) 222-0888 .. **Senzer,** Stephanie G '89 %Lehman & E LLP -50 Chas Lindbergh Blvd -Uniondale 11553
(212) 728-8000 .. **Seo,** Hilary S '99 %Willkie F&G LLP -787 7th Av -NY 10019
(516) 766-0477 .. **Sepe,** Michl J '96 M Sepe,PC -11 Clinton Av -Rockvll Ctr 11570
(845) 877-7240 .. **Seperac,** Jos J '06 -211 Main -Goshen 10924 **Fx:**230-6284
(212) 218-2100 .. **Sephton,** Gregory B '95 (Fitzpatrick CH&S) -1290 Av of Amer -NY 10104
(718) 318-8100 .. **Seplow,** Ira F '78 -181 Beach 116th -Rckwy Pk 11694 **Fx:**318-8111
(718) 779-8910 .. **Seplowe,** Jonathan B '93 %MA Cervini -Bx800018 -Elmhrst 11380 **Fx:**205-5830
(631) 761-7000 .. **Seplowitz,** Rena C '76 %Touro Cllg Law Ctr -225 Eastvw Dr -Central Islip 11722
(212) 267-1278 .. **Seplowitz,** Terry F '83 %Bailin & S -299 Bway -NY 10007 **Fx:**285-0531
(212) 267-1278 .. **Seplowitz,** Wm S '83 (Bailin & S) -299 Bway -NY 10007 **Fx:**285-0531
(212) 558-4000 .. **Septimus,** Jos '03 %Sullivan & C LLP -125 Broad -NY 10004
(718) 232-6787 .. **Septimus,** Judah '82 -5417 18th Av -Brklyn 11204 **Fx:**232-8510
(718) 361-9191 .. **Sepulveda,** Doris L '99 Hereford Ins -36-01 43rd Av -LIC 11101 **Fx:**361-9651
(347) 582-8173 .. **Sepulveda,** Luis R '92 -Hub Station Bx834 -Bronx 10455
(845) 628-1818 .. **Sequeira,** Manuel A Jr. '57 -58 Maple Hill Dr Bx563 -Mahopac 10541 **Fx:**628-1861
(212) 744-5022 .. **Serafi,** Kinda '00 Lenox Hill Neighborhood House -331 E 70th -NY 10021
(212) 208-2836 .. **Serafini,** Barbara C '05 Liberty Intl Underwriters -55 Water -NY 10041
(212) 685-3650 .. **Serafinn,** Patricia A M '03 -120 E 37th -NY 10016 **Fx:**685-3317
(212) 867-5800 .. **Seraganian,** Paul V '01 (Osler H&H LLP) -620 8th Av -NY 10018
(212) 926-7200 .. **Seraile,** Janette '75 -740 St Nicholas Av -NY 10031 **Fx:**281-9723
(212) 735-3000 .. **Serating,** Peter D '03 %Skadden ASM&F LLP -4 Times Sq -NY 10036
(212) 593-2112 .. **Serbagi,** Christopher O '96 -488 Mad Av -NY 10022 **Fx:**308-8582
(518) 664-7342 .. **Serbalik,** Val M '77 City Atty -100 N Main -Mechanicvll 12118 **Fx:**664-2315
(212) 801-2212 .. **Serbaroli,** Francis J '78 (Greenberg T,LLP) -200 Park Av -NY 10166
(212) 428-2100 .. **Serber,** Marcie A '88 OCA -25 Beaver -NY 10004
(212) 918-3000 .. **Serbin,** Gary '99 OfCnsl Hogan L LLP -875 3rd Av -NY 10022
(516) 432-4022 .. **Serby,** Anne M '86 -165 W Olive -Long Bch 11561
(516) 374-2455 .. **Serby,** Victor M '98 -255 Hewlet Neck Rd -Woodmere 11598 **Fx:**(267) 841-0009
(212) 586-4900 .. **Sercarz,** Maurice H '77 (Sercarz & R,LLP) -152 W 57th -NY 10019
(212) 586-4900 .. **Sercarz & Riopelle,LLP** -152 W 57th -NY 10019 **Fx:**586-1234
(212) 754-9400 .. **Serchuk,** Ivan '61 (Todtman NS&J,PC) -425 Park Av -NY 10022
(212) 225-2000 .. **Sercombe,** Meghan M '09 %Cleary GS&H -1 Lbrty Plz -NY 10006
(585) 385-2510 .. **Sercu,** Marilee Green '99 (Sercu & S LLP) -31 N Main -Pittsfrd 14534
(585) 385-2510 .. **Sercu,** Stephen J '93 (Sercu & S LLP) -31 N Main -Pittsfrd 14534
(212) 909-6000 .. **Serebransky,** Elizabeth Pagel '85 (Debevoise & P LLP) -919 3rd Av -NY 10022
(212) 768-2221 .. **Serebro,** Boris '99 Serebro Law PLLC -33 Miles Av -White Plns 10605
(914) 698-2251 .. **Serenbetz,** Clay R '95 Radcliff Grp Inc -695 West -Harrison 10528
(518) 462-5040 .. **Serenka,** Robt L Jr. '91 R Serenka,PLLC -61 Columbia -Albany 12210 **Fx:**462-5049
(212) 596-9000 .. **Sereny,** Carla E '06 %Ropes & G LLP -1211 Av of Amer -NY 10036
(516) 747-5500 .. **Seres,** Paul S '91 -146 Old Cntry Rd -Mineola 11501 **Fx:**747-5515
(212) 265-1790 .. **Serfaty,** Armand '85 -130 W 57th -NY 10019 **Fx:**265-1876
(516) 747-7400 .. **Serfaty,** Judah '94 %Rosenberg C&B LLP -100 Grdn City Plz -Gdn Cty 11530
(914) 995-3481 .. **Sergi,** John J '78 %DA -111 Martin Luther King Blvd -White Plns 10601 **Fx:**995-3363
(516) 294-5433 .. **Sergiacomi,** Danl G '84 (Ahmuty D&M) -200 IU Willets Rd -Albertson 11507
(914) 417-3400 .. **Sergiou,** Ioana J '10 %Littleton JUP&K LLP -1 Manhattanvll Rd -Purchase 10577
(212) 864-0724 .. **Seri,** Gnoleba R '02 OfCnsl Stevens H&W,PC -116 W 111th -NY 10026
(212) 327-0011 .. **Seril,** Barbara S '97 Longfellow Properties -30 E 76th -NY 10021
(212) 335-9000 .. **Serino,** Bryan F '09 %DA -1 Hogan Pl -NY 10013
(212) 446-4800 .. **Serino,** Jos Jr. '91 (Kirkland & E LLP) -153 E 53rd -NY 10022
(845) 462-0001 .. **Serino MacKay & Berube, PLLC** -12 Walker Rd -Poughkeepsie 12603 **Fx:**462-0002
(845) 462-0001 .. **Serino,** Mark H '90 (Serino M&B,PLLC) -12 Walker Rd -Poughkeepsie 12603
(212) 883-5608 .. **Serio,** Gregory V '87 Park Strategies -101 Park Av -NY 10178 **Fx:**883-5643
(516) 248-5317 .. **Serio,** John T '90 (Grandinette & S,LLP) -114 Old Cntry Rd -Mineola 11501 **Fx:**294-5348
(212) 351-4000 .. **Serio,** Robt F '86 (Gibson D&C LLP) -200 Park Av -NY 10166
(631) 854-9680 .. **Serkes,** Colin '86 %District Ct Law Dept -400 Carleton Av Bx9075 -Central Islip 11722
(718) 625-2200 .. **Serkin,** Christopher '00 %Bklyn Law Schl -250 Joralemon -Brklyn 11201 **Fx:**780-0393
(212) 382-0909 .. **Serkin,** Denis '05 %Peckar & A,PC -41 Mad Av -NY 10154
(212) 705-7000 .. **Serkin,** Melanie S '08 %Bingham M LLP -399 Park Av -NY 10022
(516) 626-3069 .. **Serle,** Alayne F '84 -30 Percheron Ln -Roslyn Hts 11577
(212) 909-6000 .. **Serle,** Mordechai '09 %Debevoise & P LLP -919 3rd Av -NY 10022
(212) 318-6000 .. **Serle,** Phara A '07 %Paul HJ&W LLP -75 E 55th -NY 10022
(212) 687-1425 .. **Serlen,** Brad Evan '99 %Sonnenfeld & R -360 Lex Av -NY 10017
(718) 250-4265 .. **Serlin,** Amy B '91 %Leg Aid -111 Lvngstn -Brklyn 11201 **Fx:**250-4243
(516) 334-2211 .. **Serlin,** Ethan J '96 %Serlin & S -55 Post Av -Westbury 11590 **Fx:**334-2435
(516) 334-2211 .. **Serlin,** Gerald M '67 (Serlin & S) -55 Post Av -Westbury 11590 **Fx:**334-2435
(315) 474-7447 .. **Serlin,** Gerard D '99 (Hemmerlein & S,PC) -333 E Onondaga -Syracuse 13202 **Fx:**474-0425
(718) 972-2727 .. **Serlin,** Myla '01 (Titone & S,LLP) -4719 13th Av -Brklyn 11219
(212) 683-8100 .. **Serlin,** Rachel M '07 PR Consulting Grp -45 Bway -NY 10006
(516) 292-8100 .. **Serlin,** Regan S '09 %Nassau/Sfflk Law Srv -1 Helen Keller Way -Hempstd 11550 **Fx:**292-6529
(315) 446-5238 .. **Serlin,** Richd S '59 -125 Stonerdg Dr -DeWitt 13214
(516) 334-2211 .. **Serlin,** Susan C '88 (Serlin & S) -55 Post Av -Westbury 11590 **Fx:**334-2435
(315) 568-5825 .. **Serling,** Bertram C '56 Serling & S -18-20 State Bx418 -Seneca Fls 13148 **Fx:**568-6122
(212) 245-7300 .. **Serling,** Jos L '69 (Serling R&F,LLP) -119 5th Av -NY 10003
(212) 245-7300 .. **Serling Rooks & Ferrara, LLP** -119 5th Av -NY 10003 **Fx:**586-5175
(212) 969-3000 .. **Sernau,** Ronald D '87 (Proskauer R LLP) -1585 Bway -NY 10036
(718) 780-1333 .. **Sernick,** Tina H '89 LI College Hospital -339 Hicks -Brklyn 11201
(212) 371-8008 .. **Seroklinov,** Pavel '05 Guzov O,LLC -600 Mad Av -NY 10022
(716) 204-1062 .. **Serota,** Damon H '91 B Canty,PA -5780 Main -Buffalo 14221
(212) 558-4000 .. **Serota,** Danl L '02 %Sullivan & C LLP -125 Broad -NY 10004
(212) 732-6366 .. **Serota,** Irving '54 (Kaufman & S,PC) -225 Bway -NY 10007
(516) 791-8888 .. **Serota,** Irving '54 (Kaufman & S,PC) -896 Longvw Av -N Woodmere 11581
(516) 248-1482 .. **Serota,** Irving '60 -576 Pontiac Rd -E Meadow 11554 **Fx:**248-1492
(212) 224-4000 .. **Serota,** Jack N '87 %Sumitomo Mitsui -277 Park Av -NY 10172 **Fx:**593-9522
(212) 801-2277 .. **Serota,** James I '81 (Greenberg T,LLP) -200 Park Av -NY 10166
(212) 732-6366 .. **Serota,** Stuart D '97 (Kaufman & S,PC) -225 Bway -NY 10007
(516) 763-2211 .. **Serota,** Stuart G '72 (Kaufman & S) -119 N Park Av -Rockvll Ctr 11570
(212) 858-1000 .. **Serota,** Susan P '81 (Pillsbury WSP LLP) -1540 Bway -NY 10036
(516) 364-8864 .. **Serotta,** Meryl D '89 Learning Enhncmnt for Students of Law,Inc -500 Old Cntry Rd -Gdn Cty 11530
(716) 854-2620 .. **Serotte,** Karen Cook '92 Cnsl Brown & K,LLP -1500 Lbrty Bldg -Buffalo 14202
(716) 881-2600 .. **Serotte,** Michl I '86 (Serotte S & Assoc) -300 Delaware Av -Buffalo 14202 **Fx:**886-9061
(716) 854-7525 .. **Serotte Reich & Wilson** -300 Delaware Av -Buffalo 14202 **Fx:**854-0294
(631) 421-4488 .. **Serpe Andree & Kaufman** -149 Main Bx165 -Huntngtn 11743 **Fx:**421-4483
(212) 725-3600 .. **Serpe,** Sean C '01 Serpe & Assoc,PC -450 7th Av -NY 10123 **Fx:**385-4600
(212) 213-8053 .. **Serpe,** Silvia L '96 S Serpe,LLC -800 3rd Av -NY 10022 **Fx:**981-2720
Serper, Barry H '60 -101 Hmltn Av -Atlantic Bch 11509
(718) 875-4003 .. **Serpico,** John G '90 (Serpico S&S,PC) -105 Court -Brklyn 11201 **Fx:**875-4011
(212) 770-7415 .. **Serpico,** Vincent '97 AIG -70 Pine -NY 10270
(585) 268-7603 .. **Serra,** Wesley J '48 (Serra & F,PC) -25 Schuyler -Belmont 14813 **Fx:**268-5750
(718) 665-0220 .. **Serra,** Wesley M '77 (Irom WFB&S,PC) -349 E 149th -Bronx 10451
(718) 892-8588 .. **Serrano,** Danl '03 -2027 Wllmsbrdg Rd -Bronx 10461 **Fx:**518-0674
(718) 439-3377 .. **Serrano,** Diana '93 -5613 5th Av -Brklyn 11220 **Fx:**439-6226
(718) 261-9460 .. **Serrano,** Gilbert J '99 %Pearlman AFS&S,LLP -80-02 Kew Grdns Rd -Kew Gdns 11415
(212) 770-3649 .. **Serrano,** Glenn M '81 AIGTS -80 Pine -NY 10005
(917) 551-1300 .. **Serrano,** Luis A '01 %Koehler & I LLP -61 Bway -NY 10006
(212) 589-4200 .. **Serrano,** Marco Gabriel '07 %Baker & H LLP -45 Rckfllr Plz -NY 10111
(212) 756-2000 .. **Serranzana,** Pamela C '04 %Schulte R&Z LLP -919 3rd Av -NY 10022
(212) 695-0060 .. **Serras,** Spiro '88 %Wilens & B,PC -450 7th Av -NY 10123
(212) 701-3000 .. **Serratore,** Nicole M '06 %Cahill G&R LLP -80 Pine -NY 10005 **Fx:**269-5420
(718) 626-7730 .. **Serres,** Michl '90 (Pyrros & S LLP) -31-01 Bway -LIC 11106
(212) 384-0202 .. **Serrins,** Alan '75 (Serrins & Assoc,LLC) -233 Bway -NY 10279 **Fx:**406-2313
(212) 278-1000 .. **Serritella,** James R '08 %Anderson K&O,PC -1251 Av of Amer -NY 10020
(212) 906-1200 .. **Serritella,** Paul A '06 %Latham & W -885 3rd Av -NY 10022
(212) 682-7474 .. **Sertich,** Manda M '05 %Foley & L LLP -90 Park Av -NY 10016
(212) 728-8000 .. **Serure,** Mal E '01 %Willkie F&G LLP -787 7th Av -NY 10019

(516) 471-1900 .. **Serva**, Jessica M '04 %Havkins RR&V,LLP -114 Old Cntry Rd -Mineola 11501
(212) 554-7800 .. **Servello**, Saml J '95 %Moses & S LLP -405 Lex Av -NY 10174
(212) 227-5500 .. **Serviansky**, Danl S '07 HDC -110 William -NY 10038 **Fx**:227-6865
(718) 894-6300 .. **Servider**, John A '88 -65-12 69th Pl -Middl Vllg 11379 **Fx**:894-4417
(585) 720-0570 .. **Servis**, Terry '80 -1379 Long Pond Rd -Rchstr 14626 **Fx**:720-0575
(212) 891-1600 .. **Servodidio**, Gianni P '94 (Jenner & B LLP) -919 3rd Av -NY 10022
(914) 337-0696 .. **Servodidio**, Michl P '98 -279 Main -Eastchstr 10709 **Fx**:779-0383
(914) 682-2001 .. **Sese**, Nathaniel T '96 -50 Main -White Plns 10606
(212) 450-4000 .. **Seshens**, Dana M '03 %Davis P&W LLP -450 Lex Av -NY 10017
Seskin, Scott H '89 -110 E 59th -NY 10022
(718) 591-2000 .. **Sessa**, Christina Ann '95 Cnsl Jt Ind Bd of Elctrcl Indstry -158-11 Harry Van Arsdale Jr Av -Flushng 11365 **Fx**:591-1102
(212) 732-3200 .. **Sesser**, Gary D '77 (Carter L&M LLP) -2 Wall -NY 10005
(585) 285-5931 .. **Session**, Jerry A '86 -16 W Main -Rchstr 14614
(212) 682-0660 .. **Sessler**, Ira L '00 -228 E 45th -NY 10017 **Fx**:682-0767
(212) 682-0660 .. **Sessler**, Jennifer R '93 (Sessler & S,LLP) -228 E 45th -NY 10017 **Fx**:682-0767
(212) 448-1800 .. **Sessler**, Joshua B '98 Cnsl Roberts RLSC&F LLP -235 Park Av S -NY 10003
(212) 682-0660 .. **Sessler**, Paul G '64 (Sessler & S,LLP) -228 E 45th -NY 10017 **Fx**:682-0767
(585) 243-1340 .. **Sessler**, Steven D '95 -131 Main Bx313 -Geneseo 14454 **Fx**:243-9157
(718) 286-6000 .. **Sessoms**, Kelly E '94 %DA -125-01 Qns Blvd -Kew Gdns 11415
(212) 490-3000 .. **Sestack**, Ryan J '06 %Wilson EME&D LLP -150 E 42nd -NY 10017
(212) 888-5361 .. **Sesti**, Robt A '86 Sesti & Assoc,PC -747 3rd Av -NY 10017
(914) 285-8500 .. **Sestito**, Maria '88 %TK Moore -701 Wstchstr Av -White Plns 10604 **Fx**:285-8510
(914) 747-5570 .. **Setareh**, Benjamin E '95 -29 Marble -Plsntvll 10570 **Fx**:747-5576
(716) 854-5200 .. **Setel**, Eugene M '55 (Borins SS&B) -403 Main -Buffalo 14203
(212) 715-1000 .. **Seth**, Rashmi '97 Cnsl Arnold & P LLP -399 Park Av -NY 10022
(212) 310-8000 .. **Sethi**, Nicholas '10 %Weil G&M LLP -767 5th Av -NY 10153
(718) 583-9715 .. **Sethi**, Subhash C '88 -208 E 179th -Bronx 10457
(718) 237-2507 .. **Seto**, Stephanie Blum '95 -120 S Elliot Pl -Brklyn 11217
(212) 259-8000 .. **Setrakian**, Berge '83 (Dewey & L LLP) -1301 Av of Amer -NY 10019
(315) 682-3187 .. **Setright**, John C '50 -5024 Fayettevll Manlius Rd -Manlius 13104
(718) 254-0700 .. **Sette**, Laura P '05 %Bklyn Defender Srvcs -177 Lvngstn -Brklyn 11201 **Fx**:254-0897
(212) 848-4000 .. **Setteducati**, Christopher A '08 %Shearman & S LLP -599 Lex Av -NY 10022
(212) 244-3823 .. **Settenbrino**, Susan D '94 -225 W 34th -NY 10122
(212) 407-4000 .. **Settineri**, John F '83 (Loeb & L,LLP) -345 Park Av -NY 10154
(212) 836-8399 .. **Settle**, Marci G '91 Cnsl Kaye S LLP -425 Park Av -NY 10022
(212) 818-1500 .. **Settle**, Nancy E '85 %Cosmair -575 5th Av -NY 10017
(212) 455-2000 .. **Settle**, W Sydnor '58 OfCnsl Simpson T&B LLP -425 Lex Av -NY 10017
(212) 504-6000 .. **Setton**, Ronit '93 (Cadwalader W&T LLP) -1 World Fncl Ctr -NY 10281
(212) 974-0500 .. **Setty**, Sumana '08 %Stone Twr Captl -152 W 57th -NY 10019
(631) 744-8550 .. **Setzer**, Wilfried A '67 -Polk Bx1224 -Rocky Pnt 11778
(212) 425-3220 .. **Seuffert**, Andreas '01 %Gilmartin P&S LLP -845 Third Av -NY 10022
(212) 732-0030 .. **Seung**, Stephen K '81 -2 Mott -NY 10013 **Fx**:227-5097
(212) 436-2953 .. **Sevak**, Praveer Nitin '01 Deloitte & Touche LLP -2 World Fncl Ctr -NY 10281
(845) 358-5115 .. **Sevastian**, Walter R '88 -3 Main -Nyack 10960 **Fx**:358-7092
(212) 754-5948 .. **Sevcik**, Lea Z '04 Catholic Family & Human Rights Inst -866 UN Plz -NY 10017
(212) 708-1600 .. **Sevener**, Kent L '93 %Showtime Networks Inc -1633 Bway -NY 10019 **Fx**:708-1391
(718) 625-2300 .. **Severance Burko & Spalter,PC** -16 Court -Brklyn 11241 **Fx**:522-3766
(845) 679-8596 .. **Severing**, Raymond '84 -151 Tinker -Woodstock 12498 **Fx**:679-0729
(718) 243-2168 .. **Severino**, Ronald M '88 -189 Montague -Brklyn 11201
(718) 667-6167 .. **Severinsen**, Robt '84 -2040 Victory Blvd -Staten Isl 10314
(212) 848-4000 .. **Sevilla**, Jean Paul '08 Shearman & S LLP -599 Lex Av -NY 10022
(212) 506-2500 .. **Sevilla**, Nathan H '02 %Mayer B LLP -1675 Bway -NY 10019
(212) 715-1000 .. **Sevilla-Sharon**, Maia '05 %Arnold & P LLP -399 Park Av -NY 10022
(518) 385-8080 .. **Sevinsky**, James A '74 GE Co -1 River Rd -Schnctdy 12345
(212) 398-9366 .. **Sevush**, Ralph '92 %Dramatists Guild of America,Inc -1501 Bway -NY 10036 **Fx**:944-0420
(518) 725-0653 .. **Seward**, David R '75 (Wood & S,LLP) -8 Fremont -Gloversvll 12078
(212) 574-1200 .. **Seward**, George C '37 SrCnsl Seward & K LLP -1 Bttry Pk Plz -NY 10004
(212) 574-1200 .. **Seward & Kissel LLP** -1 Bttry Pk Plz -NY 10004 **Fx**:480-8421
(914) 286-3400 .. **Seward**, Netikka Dahmeen '00 %Leg Aid -1 N Bway -White Plns 10601 **Fx**:682-4112
(516) 766-1415 .. **Seward**, Robt S '74 (Seward & S) -51 Front -Rockvll Ctr 11570 **Fx**:766-1592
(516) 766-1415 .. **Seward**, Wm A '86 (Seward & S) -51 Front -Rockvll Ctr 11570 **Fx**:766-1592
(212) 727-2700 .. **Sewell**, Bradford H '93 %NRDC -40 W 20th -NY 10011 **Fx**:727-1773
(212) 720-5344 .. **Sewell**, David G '06 %Fed Reserve Bk -33 Lbrty -NY 10045 **Fx**:785-5748
(212) 788-7000 .. **Sewell**, Jamin R '99 City Cncl Leg Div -250 Bway -NY 10007 **Fx**:788-7034
(516) 997-0400 .. **Sewell**, Steven H '80 (S Sewell,PC) -675 Old Cntry Rd -Westbury 11590 **Fx**:997-0029
(212) 474-1000 .. **Sewell**, Tyler J '09 %Cravath S&M LLP -825 8th Av -NY 10019
(585) 232-6500 .. **Sewruck**, Julia Green '07 %Harter S&E LLP -1600 Bausch & Lomb Pl -Rchstr 14604
(212) 577-2800 .. **Sexter**, Allan S '63 (Sexter & W) -115 Bway -NY 10006
(212) 577-2800 .. **Sexter & Warmflash** -115 Bway -NY 10006 **Fx**:577-2865
(212) 319-1000 .. **Sexton**, Brian P '93 (Quirk & B,PC) -845 3rd Av -NY 10022
(212) 735-3000 .. **Sexton**, Brittain W '09 %Skadden ASM&F LLP -4 Times Sq -NY 10036
(845) 708-9100 .. **Sexton**, James J '01 (J Sexton,PC) -130 N Main -New Cty 10956 **Fx**:708-0027
(212) 998-2345 .. **Sexton**, John E '81 NYU-President -70 Wshngtn Sq S -NY 10012 **Fx**:995-4790
(212) 880-9441 .. **Sexton**, Maryanne '05 %Morvillo AGIA&B,PC -565 5th Av -NY 10017
(716) 845-8717 .. **Sexton**, Michl B '84 %Roswell Park Cancer Inst -Elm & Carlton -Buffalo 14263 **Fx**:845-8057
(212) 829-8681 .. **Sexton**, Richd J '59 -488 Mad Av -NY 10022 **Fx**:813-9600
(212) 848-4000 .. **Sexton**, Ryan T '08 %Shearman & S LLP -599 Lex Av -NY 10022
(212) 422-0202 .. **Seybert**, John T '00 %Sedgwick DM&A LLP -125 Broad -NY 10004
(212) 889-2121 .. **Seyedian Choubi**, Elnaz '05 %Kellner HG&F -470 Park Av S -NY 10016
(212) 218-5500 .. **Seyfarth Shaw LLP** -620 8th Av -NY 10018 **Fx**:218-5526
(212) 345-3482 .. **Seyfried**, Eric G '96 Marsh USA Inc -1166 Av of Amer -NY 10036
(212) 949-9022 .. **Seyler**, Julie B '90 (Abelman F&S) -666 3rd Av -NY 10017
(212) 403-1000 .. **Seymon**, Pamela S '83 (Wachtell LR&K) -51 W 52nd -NY 10019
(646) 610-5400 .. **Seymore**, Javier R '05 %NYPD -1 Police Plz -NY 10038
(212) 269-0927 .. **Seymour**, Barbara R '84 (D'Amato & L,LLP) -2 World Fncl Ctr -NY 10281
(914) 761-9111 .. **Seymour**, Danl A '85 (Bank SS&H) -399 Knollwood Rd -White Plns 10603
(212) 270-2444 .. **Seymour**, Everett H Jr. '88 JP Morgan Chase & Co -270 Park Av -NY 10017
(212) 558-4000 .. **Seymour**, Karen Patton '88 (Sullivan & C LLP) -125 Broad -NY 10004
(646) 840-5708 .. **Seymour**, Leah D '02 RCA Music Grp -745 5th Av -NY 10151
(212) 558-4000 .. **Seymour**, Saml W '83 (Sullivan & C LLP) -125 Broad -NY 10004
(212) 455-7640 .. **Seymour**, Whitney North Jr. '50 -425 Lex Av -NY 10017 **Fx**:455-2502
(212) 806-5400 .. **Seymour**, Wm J '10 %Stroock &S&L LLP -180 Maiden Ln -NY 10038
(212) 421-4100 .. **Sfakianaki**, Melina '00 %Pryor C LLP -7 Times Sq -NY 10036
(718) 631-2811 .. **Sfantos**, Marios C '95 -42-40 Bell Blvd -Bayside 11361 **Fx**:631-8804
(212) 475-8137 .. **Sfarti**, Miriam '78 -20 E 9th -NY 10003
(631) 753-4400 .. **Sferrazza**, Jos '86 (Sferrazza & K,PLLC) -532 Broad Hollow Rd -Melvll 11747
(631) 753-4400 .. **Sferrazza & Keenan,PLLC** -532 Broad Hollow Rd -Melvll 11747 **Fx**:753-4065
(212) 964-5000 .. **Sfouggatakis**, Andrew G '00 (Peisner GS&S) -225 Bway -NY 10007
(212) 576-7908 .. **Sfraga Panza**, Georgene A '99 NY Life Ins -51 Mad Av -NY 10010
(718) 204-0700 .. **Sfyroeras**, Stamatios '90 -25-25 31st Av -Astoria 11106 **Fx**:278-8570
(212) 553-3301 .. **Sgaglione**, Lucille T '84 %Zurich NA -1 Lbrty Plz -NY 10006
(518) 877-7600 .. **Sgambettera**, Matthew J '01 (M Sgambettera) -Bx1550 -Clifton Pk 12065 **Fx**:877-7611
(212) 761-6653 .. **Sgaraglino**, Marc A '97 Morgan Stanley -1585 Bway -NY 10036
(518) 370-1443 .. **Sgarlata**, Anthony B '59 -170 Lafayette -Schnctdy 12305 **Fx**:370-1443
(718) 788-6646 .. **Sgarlato**, Emily C '89 -332A 9th -Brklyn 11215 **Fx**:788-7966
(718) 273-7900 .. **Sgarlato**, Gina M '91 (Sgarlato & S,PLLC) -1444 Clove Rd -Staten Isl 10301 **Fx**:273-9629
(718) 273-7900 .. **Sgarlato**, Richd J '69 (Sgarlato & S,PLLC) -1444 Clove Rd -Staten Isl 10301 **Fx**:273-9629
(718) 448-6400 .. **Sgarlato**, Robt A '72 (Slater S&C,PC) -1298 Victory Blvd -Staten Isl 10301
(718) 788-6646 .. **Sgarlato**, Santo D '55 -332A 9th -Brklyn 11215 **Fx**:788-7966
(718) 668-2716 .. **Sgarlato**, Santo R Jr. '55 OfCnsl Sgarlato & S,PLLC -1444 Clove Rd -Staten Isl 10301 **Fx**:273-9629
(631) 727-2180 .. **Sguazzin**, Laura I '98 (Twomey LSKD&Q,LLP) -33 W 2nd Bx9398 -Rvrhead 11901
(212) 272-4764 .. **Sha**, Jeannie '00 %JP Morgan Chase -383 Mad Av -NY 10179
(212) 761-4000 .. **Shabaka**, Nubiaa K '04 Morgan Stanley -1633 Bway -NY 10019
(718) 250-2000 .. **Shaban**, Ephraim W '88 %DA -350 Jay -Brklyn 11201 **Fx**:250-2314
(212) 724-1452 .. **Shabason**, Helen T '85 Helen Shabason Talent LLC -412 West End Av -NY 10024
(718) 658-3975 .. **Shabbir**, Muhammad '04 -159-11 Hillside Av -Jamaica 11432
(646) 562-3405 .. **Shaber**, Steven J '97 Cnsl PLC -747 3rd Av -NY 10017
(212) 403-1000 .. **Shabot**, Joey '07 %Wachtell LR&K -51 W 52nd -NY 10019
(212) 966-5005 .. **Shabsels**, Chas '71 -Empire State Bldg -NY 10118 **Fx**:239-6900
(212) 450-4000 .. **Shachar**, Avishai '84 (Davis P&W LLP) -450 Lex Av -NY 10017
(212) 310-8000 .. **Shachar**, Sharon '04 %Weil G&M LLP -767 5th Av -NY 10153
(212) 592-1400 .. **Shachnow**, Barbara J '88 Cnsl Herrick,F LLP -2 Park Av -NY 10016
(212) 885-5000 .. **Shack**, Donald D '51 SrCnsl Blank R LLP -405 Lex Av -NY 10174
(800) 595-5520 .. **Shackleton & Hazeltine** -104 W 40th -NY 10018 **Fx**:(212) 202-3888
(800) 595-5520 .. **Shackleton**, Richd J '82 (Shackleton & H) -104 W 40th -NY 10018
(212) 362-7275 .. **Shackman**, Beverly Sisskind '82 -36 W 76th -NY 10023 **Fx**:362-7230
(212) 370-4040 .. **Shackman**, Steven B '94 (Lambert & S,PLLC) -274 Mad Av -NY 10016 **Fx**:697-7919
(212) 341-2755 .. **Shacknai**, Danl A '95 %Admin Children's Srvcs -150 William -NY 10038 **Fx**:341-2700
(212) 477-4785 .. **Shactman**, Murray '85 -68 W 10th -NY 10011
(212) 431-2100 .. **Shadab**, Houman B '09 %NY Law Schl -185 W Bway -NY 10013 **Fx**:406-0103
(585) 295-4400 .. **Shaddock**, Robt M '79 (Hiscock & B,LLP) -2000 HSBC Plz -Rchstr 14604
(212) 309-6000 .. **Shade**, Jonathan T '06 %Morgan L&B LLP -101 Park Av -NY 10178
(212) 819-8200 .. **Shadek**, Caitlin Thistle '09 %White & C LLP -1155 Av of Amer -NY 10036
(212) 841-7295 .. **Shadley**, Kay L '79 Nautica Enterprises -40 N 57th -NY 10019 **Fx**:841-7193
(518) 432-3310 .. **Shadlock**, Nadine Feiden '90 -12 Van Rensselaer Blvd -Albany 12204 **Fx**:432-9440
(631) 470-6861 .. **Shaer**, Karen B '85 Garden City Grp Inc -105 Maxess Rd -Melvll 11747 **Fx**:470-5100
(212) 239-3800 .. **Shaev**, David B '74 -350 5th Av -NY 10118 **Fx**:695-3008
(718) 291-3400 .. **Shaevitz**, Eric G '94 (Shaevitz & S) -148-55 Hillside Av -Jamaica 11435 **Fx**:739-5654

(718) 291-3400 .. **Shaevitz,** Mark '89 (Shaevitz & S) -148-55 Hillside Av -Jamaica 11435 **Fx:**739-5654
(718) 291-3400 .. **Shaevitz,** Oliver '55 (Shaevitz & S) -148-55 Hillside Av -Jamaica 11435 **Fx:**739-5654
(516) 249-1342 .. **Shafeek,** Sasha S '05 %Grey & G,LLP -360 Main -Farmngdl 11735
(315) 696-8918 .. **Shafer,** Chas E '78 OfCnsl Riehlman S&S -397 Route 281 Bx430 -Tully 13159
(516) 877-2000 .. **Shafer,** Danl A '02 %Ketover & Assoc,LLC -1225 Franklin Av -Gdn Cty 11530 **Fx:**877-2586
(212) 222-5703 .. **Shafer,** Elizabeth J '97 -285 Riverside Dr -NY 10025
(212) 267-0011 .. **Shafer Glazer,LLP** -90 John -NY 10038 **Fx:**(646) 435-9434
(212) 267-0011 .. **Shafer,** Howard S '89 (Shafer G,LLP) -90 John -NY 10038
(315) 696-8918 .. **Shafer,** Robt M '80 (Riehlman S&S) -397 Route 281 Bx430 -Tully 13159
(607) 756-4006 .. **Shafer,** Robt M '80 (Riehlman S&S) -39 Church -Cortlnd 13045
(212) 506-2500 .. **Shaffer,** Andrew D '01 %Mayer B LLP -1675 Bway -NY 10019
(315) 568-9479 .. **Shaffer,** Chas E '72 -47 W Bayard Bx648 -Seneca Fls 13148 **Fx:**568-6370
(585) 987-2800 .. **Shaffer,** David P '08 %Woods OG LLP -2 State -Rchstr 14614
(212) 549-2612 .. **Shaffer,** Donald '92 NY Civil Liberties Union -125 Broad -NY 10004 **Fx:**344-3318
(212) 566-5000 .. **Shaffer,** Gary P '80 %Dept of Bldgs -280 Bway -NY 10007
(315) 724-1123 .. **Shaffer,** George A '50 -4-6 N Park Row -Clinton 13323 **Fx:**724-3805
(732) 855-6152 .. **Shaffer,** Greg D '00 %Wilentz G&S -110 William -NY 10038 **Fx:**726-6590
(212) 455-2000 .. **Shaffer,** Heather L '07 %Simpson T&B LLP -425 Lex Av -NY 10017
(585) 383-3754 .. **Shaffer,** Kim M '99 Cnsl Paychex,Inc -911 Panorama Trl S -Rchstr 14625 **Fx:**383-3441
(315) 798-4282 .. **Shaffer,** Lloyd C '89 %Blue Cross/Blue Shield -12 Rhoads Dr -Utica 13502 **Fx:**797-4298
(212) 788-1041 .. **Shaffer,** Ryan G '10 %Law Dept -100 Church -NY 10007 **Fx:**788-0367
(212) 683-9180 .. **Shaffer,** Scott A '97 (Lustigman Firm,PC) -149 Mad Av -NY 10016 **Fx:**683-9181
(212) 455-4502 .. **Shaffer,** Stefan L '83 %SPP Hambrow & Co -330 Mad Av -NY 10017
(212) 509-1802 .. **Shafferman,** Joel M '86 -350 5th Av -NY 10118 **Fx:**509-1831
(212) 757-4500 .. **Shafferman,** Victor N '74 -22 W 48th -NY 10036
(212) 684-7308 .. **Shaffir,** Melvyn L '63 -251 E 32nd -NY 10016
(212) 863-6300 .. **Shafit,** Matthew E '85 %HPD -100 Gold -NY 10038
(212) 679-4666 .. **Shafran,** Bernard A '78 (Frenkel H&S LLP) -16 E 34th -NY 10016
(212) 984-7840 .. **Shafran,** Chaya R '89 Cnsl Warshaw BCS&K,LLP -555 5th Av -NY 10017
(212) 631-7000 .. **Shafran,** Howard E '85 (Shafran & M,PC) -350 5th Av -NY 10118
(212) 755-4100 .. **Shafran,** Irving '69 -650 Mad Av -NY 10022 **Fx:**755-4177
(212) 631-7000 .. **Shafran & Mosley,PC** -350 5th Av -NY 10118 **Fx:**239-6900
(845) 638-3925 .. **Shafran,** Peter W '85 -155 N Main -New Cty 10956 **Fx:**(203) 327-7468
(718) 382-1010 .. **Shafran,** Robt M '98 -1555 Bay Ridge Av -Brklyn 11219
(917) 514-6684 .. **Shafranov,** Alina '99 -51 MacDougal -NY 10012
(212) 363-1380 .. **Shafron,** Jason T '97 OfCnsl Herten BSCBL&H,LLC -747 3rd Av -NY 10017
(212) 962-0800 .. **Shaftan,** Kevin D '97 %Estrin B&L -225 Bway -NY 10007 **Fx:**732-1408
(718) 786-2995 .. **Shaftel,** Eve '84 -39-15 45th -LIC 11104
(212) 504-6000 .. **Shaftel,** Harold S '90 (Cadwalader W&T LLP) -1 World Fncl Ctr -NY 10281
(516) 944-1741 .. **Shafter,** Allan D '64 Shafter & S -921 Port Wshngtn Blvd -Pt Wash 11050 **Fx:**944-0938
(212) 425-3220 .. **Shafto,** Donald B '67 (Gilmartin P&S LLP) -845 Third Av -NY 10022
(631) 422-5511 .. **Shagam,** Jerome I '70 Coldwell Banker Cmmrcl -136 W Main -Babylon 11702
(212) 373-8097 .. **Shagan,** Jillian L '99 Ctr for Ct Innovation -520 8th Av -NY 10018 **Fx:**397-0985
(718) 748-4848 .. **Shagenov,** Michelle J '08 %FT Strafaci -569 Bay Ridge Pkwy -Brklyn 11209 **Fx:**748-6399
(212) 819-8200 .. **Shaghaf,** Sheikh M '09 %White & C LLP -1155 Av of Amer -NY 10036
(516) 393-2200 .. **Shah,** Afsheen '99 %Garfunkel W,PC -111 Grt Nck Rd -Gt Neck 11021
(914) 686-1700 .. **Shah,** Alak '08 %O'Connor R,LLP -200 Mamaroneck Av -White Plns 10601
(212) 309-6000 .. **Shah,** Anand S '08 %Morgan L&B LLP -101 Park Av -NY 10178
(212) 728-8000 .. **Shah,** Avani M '07 %Willkie F&G LLP -787 7th Av -NY 10019
(212) 298-2049 .. **Shah,** Bejal J '03 %Leg Aid -49 Thomas -NY 10013 **Fx:**298-5252
(718) 261-8803 .. **Shah,** Devang C '99 -116-55 Qns Blvd -Frst Hlls 11375 **Fx:**268-3894
(212) 233-5531 .. **Shah,** Gaurav I '02 Cnsl NYC PBA -40 Fulton -NY 10038
(212) 345-6000 .. **Shah,** Hiral N '98 Marsh USA -1166 Av of Amer -NY 10036 **Fx:**345-4808
(212) 848-4000 .. **Shah,** Jeena D '09 %Shearman & S LLP -599 Lex Av -NY 10022
(516) 357-3000 .. **Shah,** Krishna J '06 %Rivkin R LLP -926 RXR Plz -Uniondale 11556
(516) 496-5822 .. **Shah,** Malav M '09 T Spina -170 Froehlich Farm Blvd -Woodbury 11797 **Fx:**496-5420
(212) 704-6000 .. **Shah,** Mamta K '02 %Troutman S LLP -405 Lex Av -NY 10174
(212) 310-8000 .. **Shah,** Mamta L '06 %Weil G&M LLP -767 5th Av -NY 10153
(212) 326-3939 .. **Shah,** Manan D '02 (Jones D) -222 E 41st -NY 10017
(212) 532-3651 .. **Shah,** Manish I '04 Marwood Grp & Co -733 3rd Av -NY 10017
(212) 530-5000 .. **Shah,** Megha D '10 %Milbank TH&M LLP -1 Chase Manh Plz -NY 10005
(212) 233-7473 .. **Shah,** Mona '97 (M Shah & S) -299 Bway -NY 10007 **Fx:**233-4877
(212) 506-5000 .. **Shah,** Neel B '09 %Orrick H&S LLP -51 W 52nd -NY 10019
(212) 878-8000 .. **Shah,** Neha D '10 %Clifford C LLP -31 W 52nd -NY 10019
(212) 262-2390 .. **Shah,** Neil V '10 %Connell F LLP -888 7th Av -NY 10106
(212) 698-3500 .. **Shah,** Nirali R '06 %Dechert LLP -1095 Av of Amer -NY 10036
(212) 446-4800 .. **Shah,** Nirav S '08 %Kirkland & E LLP -153 E 53rd -NY 10022
(212) 869-3200 .. **Shah,** Nirav Y '01 %Molod S&D,PC -104 W 40th -NY 10018
(212) 487-4444 .. **Shah,** Niyati K '06 %Dept Cnsmr Affrs -42 Bway -NY 10004 **Fx:**487-4197
(212) 238-3000 .. **Shah,** Nutan Christine '97 %Emmet M&M,LLP -120 Bway -NY 10271
(212) 259-8000 .. **Shah,** Prachi D '09 %Dewey & L LLP -1301 Av of Amer -NY 10019
(212) 450-4000 .. **Shah,** Pritesh P '09 %Davis P&W LLP -450 Lex Av -NY 10017
(212) 812-4700 .. **Shah,** Purvi H '03 Glenview Cptl Mgmt -767 5th Av -NY 10153
(315) 422-8191 .. **Shah,** Rupak R '08 %Leg Aid -351 S Warren -Syracuse 13202 **Fx:**472-2819
(212) 596-9000 .. **Shah,** Sachin B '09 %Ropes & G LLP -1211 Av of Amer -NY 10036
(212) 207-5834 .. **Shah,** Samir M '93 %Conti Fncl Srvcs -277 Park Av -NY 10172
(212) 474-1000 .. **Shah,** Samira '99 Cravath S&M LLP -825 8th Av -NY 10019
(212) 804-4200 .. **Shah,** Sanjit S '92 %Mound CW&G -One Bttry Pk Plz -NY 10004
(212) 236-8039 .. **Shah,** Saurabh K '97 %Merrill Lynch -2 Wrld Fncl Ctr -NY 10281
(212) 739-1013 .. **Shah,** Shefali A '04 %Comverse Tech -810 7th Av -NY 10019
(212) 223-3900 .. **Shah,** Sona Ramesh '98 %Zwerling S&Z,LLP -41 Mad Av -NY 10010
(212) 479-6000 .. **Shah,** Tejal '06 %Cooley LLP -1114 Av of Amer -NY 10036
(212) 712-2722 .. **Shah,** Tejal Navin '06 CitiHabitats -222 W 72nd -NY 10023
(212) 883-1700 .. **Shah,** Vidhi R '09 %Duval & S LLP -101 Park Av -NY 10178
(315) 422-6666 .. **Shahan,** Steven C '92 (Taddeo & S,LLP) -472 S Salina -Syracuse 13202
(212) 225-2000 .. **Shaheen,** Fadi '07 %Cleary GS&H -1 Lbrty Plz -NY 10006
(845) 626-2244 .. **Shaheen,** Paul D '86 -623 Granite Rd -Kerhonkson 12446
(212) 474-1000 .. **Shahgoli,** Elnaz '09 %Cravath S&M LLP -825 8th Av -NY 10019
(718) 243-6895 .. **Shahid,** Shekera '01 %Leg Aid -111 Lvngstn -Brklyn 11201 **Fx:**237-8737
(718) 919-8704 .. **Shahied,** Edw K '91 -550 Putnam Av -Brklyn 11221
(631) 271-4543 .. **Shahin-Elbaba,** Lina '94 -877 Stewart Av -Gdn Cty 11530 **Fx:**549-2726
(212) 973-0572 .. **Shahinian,** Armen '80 (Wolff & S PC) -140 Bway -NY 10005
(212) 559-9151 .. **Shahmanesh,** Jane '86 Citigroup Private Bank -153 E 53rd -NY 10022
(716) 565-1299 .. **Shahram,** Nadia N '08 -5500 Main -Buffalo 14221
(212) 225-2000 .. **Shahrooz,** Kaveh '07 %Cleary GS&H -1 Lbrty Plz -NY 10006
(212) 582-7579 .. **Shai,** Maggie '86 -853 7th Av -NY 10019 **Fx:**582-4718
(718) 398-7560 .. **Shaievitz,** Sidney '88 -886 Union -Brklyn 11215
(718) 398-7560 .. **Shaievitz,** Sondra A '93 -886 Union -Brklyn 11215
(914) 829-7564 .. **Shaifer,** Seth I '07 Westcon Grp LLC -520 Wht Plns Rd -Tarrytwn 10591
(212) 344-5680 .. **Shaikh,** Amir '07 %Thompson H LLP -335 Mad Av -NY 10017
(212) 858-1000 .. **Shaikh,** Ayaz R '93 (Pillsbury WSP LLP) -1540 Bway -NY 10036
(718) 238-6960 .. **Shaikh,** Heena '05 Grimaldi & Y LLP -9201 4th Av -Brklyn 11209
(212) 693-1660 .. **Shaikh,** Inayat Ilahi '93 -139 Fulton -NY 10038
(212) 698-3500 .. **Shaikh,** Nilufer R '03 %Dechert LLP -1095 Av of Amer -NY 10036
(631) 499-4407 .. **Shaiman,** Milton '83 -1 Rural Pl -Commack 11725
(718) 627-8151 .. **Shainberg,** Abe M '78 -1749 E 24th -Brklyn 11229
(718) 382-1010 .. **Shainberg,** Abe M '78 -2080 Coney Isl Av -Brklyn 11223 **Fx:**382-1515
(716) 854-3400 .. **Shainbrown,** Danielle E '06 %Rupp BPC&C LLC -1600 Lbrty Bldg -Buffalo 14202
(212) 425-5566 .. **Shainwald,** Sybil '77 (S Shainwald,PC) -200 W 57th -NY 10019 **Fx:**608-5863
(212) 756-2000 .. **Shaitanau,** Pavel '10 %Schulte R&Z LLP -919 3rd Av -NY 10022
(212) 250-1043 .. **Shajnfeld,** Saul M '80 Deutsche Bk -60 Wall -NY 10005
(212) 953-6633 .. **Shakarchy,** Jacob S '81 (Cox PS&S LLP) -630 3rd Av -NY 10017
(212) 494-0035 .. **Shaked,** Dan '91 (Shaked & P) -255 W 36th -NY 10018 **Fx:**216-9049
(516) 746-0232 .. **Shakh,** Roman J '09 %Farley G&H,LLP -200 Old Cntry Rd -Mineola 11501
(212) 587-3777 .. **Shakhnevich,** Steven '07 %S Sherman & Assoc,PC -233 Bway -NY 10279 **Fx:**732-5431
(516) 933-1933 .. **Shakin,** Debra '86 -821 Franklin Av -Gdn Cty 11530 **Fx:**877-0095
(212) 940-8800 .. **Shakir,** Hassan Abbas '03 %Katten MR LLP -575 Mad Av -NY 10022
(212) 294-6700 .. **Shaknes,** Alexander '96 (Winston & S) -200 Park Av -NY 10166
(914) 474-0200 .. **Shalek,** Donna E '90 AMEX Fincl Advsrs -100 Summit Lk Dr -Valhalla 10595
(212) 969-3000 .. **Shalek,** James H '97 (Proskauer R LLP) -1585 Bway -NY 10036
(212) 225-2000 .. **Shalen,** Stephen '75 (Cleary GS&H) -1 Lbrty Plz -NY 10006
(212) 756-2000 .. **Shalet,** Leonora M '08 %Schulte R&Z LLP -919 3rd Av -NY 10022
(212) 605-2000 .. **Shalette,** Erika A '02 %Mitsubishi Intl -655 3rd Av -NY 10017 **Fx:**605-2129
(914) 798-5400 .. **Shalhoub,** Michl D '83 (Goldberg S LLP) -11 Martine Av -White Plns 10606
(212) 728-8000 .. **Shalhoub,** Paul V '92 (Willkie F&G LLP) -787 7th Av -NY 10019
(212) 262-2390 .. **Shalit,** Brad D '98 (Connell F LLP) -888 7th Av -NY 10106
(212) 408-5100 .. **Shalit,** Joel R '01 %Chadbourne & P LLP -30 Rckfllr Plz -NY 10112
(212) 697-6262 .. **Shallenburger,** Joe H '98 %Ward & O -380 Mad Av -NY 10017
(718) 268-2171 .. **Shalley,** James M '90 (Shalley & M) -118-35 Qns Blvd -Frst Hlls 11375 **Fx:**520-8544
(212) 566-6212 .. **Shalley,** Margaret M '84 (Fasulo S&D) -225 Bway -NY 10007
(518) 828-5400 .. **Shallo,** Scott D '93 (Guterman S&A,PLLC) -21 N 7th -Hudson 12534
(212) 848-4000 .. **Shally,** Joanna '80 Cnsl Shearman & S LLP -599 Lex Av -NY 10022
(212) 695-0700 .. **Shalo,** Abraham '52 -370 7th Av -NY 10001 **Fx:**629-7996
(212) 239-4340 .. **Shalov,** Lee S '85 (Shalov SB&R LLP) -485 7th Av -NY 10018
(212) 239-4340 .. **Shalov Stone Bonner & Rocco LLP** -485 7th Av -NY 10018 **Fx:**239-4310
(631) 852-8600 .. **Shalvey,** Kimberly A '08 %DA -Feather Hill Shopping Ctr Main Rd -Southold 11971
(917) 498-9009 .. **Sham,** Alexus P '03 (Sham & S LLP) -353 W 48th -NY 10036
(212) 326-2000 .. **Shamah,** Danl S '07 %O'Melveny & M LLP -7 Times Sq -NY 10036
(718) 643-3839 .. **Shamahs,** Elizabeth Y '92 Family Ct -283 Adams -Brklyn 11201
(212) 858-1000 .. **Shamash,** Rachel A '07 %Pillsbury WSP LLP -1540 Bway -NY 10036
(914) 666-5600 .. **Shamberg Marwell Davis & Hollis,PC** -55 Smith Av -Mt Kisco 10549 **Fx:**666-6267
(914) 666-5600 .. **Shamberg,** Stuart R '54 (Shamberg MD&H,PC) -55 Smith Av -Mt Kisco 10549
(518) 265-0716 .. **Shambo,** Christopher C '09 -Bx464 -Saratoga Spgs 12866 **Fx:**885-8706
(917) 742-3104 .. **Shames,** Eric J '93 -301 E 79th -NY 10075

(212) 957-9751 .. **Shames,** Harry '62 -305 Bway -NY 10007 **Fx:**822-1493
(212) 551-8541 .. **Shames,** Jason K '00 Israel Discount Bk of NY -511 5th Av -NY 10017
(212) 446-4800 .. **Shames,** Joshua S '05 %Kirkland & E LLP -153 E 53rd -NY 10022
(516) 889-9200 .. **Shamis,** Leslie Martin '82 -64 W Park Av Bx570 -Long Bch 11561 **Fx:**889-9105
(315) 234-8590 .. **Shamlian,** Catherine A '04 Hon N McCurn -100 S Clinton -Syracuse 13261
(212) 788-1570 .. **Shammas,** Cheryl L '01 %Law Dept -100 Church -NY 10007 **Fx:**788-0367
(212) 265-6888 .. **Shammas,** Damian Christian '00 Cnsl Porzio B&N,PC -156 W 56th -NY 10019
(718) 725-3030 .. **Shammas,** Dawn M '00 Admin Children's Srvcs -151-20 Jamaica Av -Jamaica 11432
(315) 255-4303 .. **Shamon,** George J '71 (Hearing Examiner) -Cnty Cthse -Auburn 13021
(315) 252-7536 .. **Shamon,** Thos J '73 (Shamon & S) -33 William -Auburn 13021
(718) 595-6546 .. **Shamoon,** Chas H '87 %DEP -59-17 Junction Blvd -Flushng 11373 **Fx:**595-6543
(212) 735-2833 .. **Shamoon,** Rona G '94 %Skadden ASM&F LLP -4 Times Sq -NY 10036
(212) 878-8000 .. **Shamos,** Richd L '10 %Clifford C LLP -31 W 52nd -NY 10019
(212) 952-1111 .. **Shamoun,** Simon '07 %H Gladstein & Prtnrs LLC -110 Wall -NY 10005 **Fx:**943-7427
(212) 490-0100 .. **Shampan,** Michl J '10 %Schuman & Assoc -1536 3rd Av -NY 10028 **Fx:**490-0156
(914) 824-5416 .. **Shampanier,** Judith M '94 Hon L Jamieson -111 Martin Luther King Blvd -White Plns 10601
(212) 490-4100 .. **Shampnoi,** Elizabeth J '04 %Storch A&M,PC -140 E 45th -NY 10017
(212) 371-9400 .. **Shamroth,** Tara M '09 %Newman & N,PC -460 Park Av -NY 10022 **Fx:**371-8022
(212) 538-2963 .. **Shams,** Howard N '91 CSFB -11 Mad Av -NY 10010
(212) 701-3000 .. **Shamshovich,** David '08 %Cahill G&R LLP -80 Pine -NY 10005 **Fx:**269-5420
(212) 845-5200 .. **Shamsi,** Hina '99 Human Rights First -333 7th Av -NY 10001
(212) 728-8000 .. **Shams-Molkara,** Leah '08 %Willkie F&G LLP -787 7th Av -NY 10019
(212) 608-1009 .. **Shamuil,** Morris '02 -132 Nassau -NY 10038 **Fx:**608-1433
(212) 566-8080 .. **Shan,** Huichen '09 %Wong W & Assoc,PC -150 Bway -NY 10038 **Fx:**566-8960
(917) 328-7118 .. **Shanabrook,** Michl D '95 -135 W 16th -NY 10011 **Fx:**(212) 691-7252
(212) 308-0070 .. **Shanahan,** Alice M '02 (McCusker AR&C,PC) -805 3rd Av -NY 10022
(212) 723-9754 .. **Shanahan,** Eamon J '05 Citigroup -390 Greenwich -NY 10013
(212) 637-3171 .. **Shanahan,** George A '75 %EPA -290 Bway -NY 10007 **Fx:**637-3096
(212) 547-5400 .. **Shanahan,** Michl E '01 (McDermott W&E LLP) -340 Mad Av -NY 10173
(212) 752-8000 .. **Shanahan,** Nolan E '00 %Cole SMF&L,PA -900 3rd Av -NY 10022
(716) 858-2424 .. **Shanahan,** Patrick B '05 %DA -25 Delaware Av -Buffalo 14202 **Fx:**858-7425
(315) 475-8461 .. **Shanahan,** Paul F '83 OfCnsl Coulter V&M,LLP -636 Old Liverpool Rd -Liverpool 13088
(516) 799-5100 .. **Shanahan,** Robt J '82 -686 Bway -Massapequa 11758 **Fx:**799-5145
(516) 535-2500 .. **Shanahan,** Wm D '90 -224 7th -Gdn Cty 11530
(212) 419-3935 .. **Shanahan,** Wm P '08 RNK Capital LLC -527 Mad Av -NY 10022
(716) 856-8200 .. **Shanahan Becker,** Ellen J '94 %Williams & W -43 Court -Buffalo 14202 **Fx:**856-0559
(718) 250-2000 .. **Shanahan-Good,** Theresa M '91 %DA -350 Jay -Brklyn 11201 **Fx:**250-2314
(212) 735-3000 .. **Shanan,** Tamir U '09 %Skadden ASM&F LLP -4 Times Sq -NY 10036
(248) 884-2182 .. **Shanbaum,** Jason B '08 -1014 Av J -Brklyn 11230
(212) 849-7000 .. **Shandel,** Jeffrey G '92 %Quinn EU&S,LLP -51 Mad Av -NY 10010
(845) 429-5371 .. **Shandler,** Phyllis W '87 (Miller M&S,PC) -90 New Main Bx360 -Haverstraw 10927
(212) 855-9191 .. **Shandling,** Judith L '87 Goldman Sachs -32 Old Slip -NY 10005 **Fx:**428-1859
(212) 508-6167 .. **Shane,** Adam B '10 %Bracewell & G,LLP -1251 Av of Amer -NY 10020 **Fx:**938-3822
(212) 617-3733 .. **Shane,** Andrew L '03 Bloomberg LP -731 Lex Av -NY 10022
(212) 907-7300 .. **Shane,** David Ian '97 OfCnsl Golenbock EAB&P -437 Mad Av -NY 10022
(716) 375-4213 .. **Shane,** J Michl '59 -188½ W Main -Allegany 14706 **Fx:**375-4214
(212) 558-4000 .. **Shane,** Penny '89 (Sullivan & C LLP) -125 Broad -NY 10004
(212) 533-6300 .. **Shane,** Richd A '74 %NYSUT -52 Bway -NY 10004 **Fx:**995-2347
(516) 299-4063 .. **Shane,** Suzanne Voss '89 Long Island Univ -Univ Ctr Bush Brown Hall -Brookvll 11548 **Fx:**299-2072
(212) 609-6800 .. **Shanes,** Jacqueline P '86 (McCarter & E,LLP) -245 Park Av -NY 10167
(212) 725-4600 .. **Shang,** Carmen '68 (Rubin & S) -9 E 40th -NY 10016
(503) 608-2524 .. **Shang,** Doudou '09 -100 Marymount Av -Tarrytwn 10591
(516) 883-3258 .. **Shang,** Robt Tachau '88 -1 Fenimore Rd -Pt Wash 11050 **Fx:**883-3258
(212) 906-1200 .. **Shanghavi,** Manasi P '10 %Latham & W -885 3rd Av -NY 10022
(212) 837-6457 .. **Shanies,** David B '07 %Hughes H&R LLP -1 Bttry Pk Plz -NY 10004 **Fx:**299-6457
(732) 855-6145 .. **Shank,** C Kenneth '70 (Wilentz G&S) -110 William -NY 10038 **Fx:**726-6575
(212) 506-1700 .. **Shank,** Ross G '00 %Kasowitz BT&F LLP -1633 Bway -NY 10019
(212) 841-1000 .. **Shankar,** Vishnu V '09 %Covington & B LLP -620 8th Av -NY 10018
(212) 309-6000 .. **Shanker,** Marc J '03 %Morgan L&B LLP -101 Park Av -NY 10178
(516) 741-4000 .. **Shanker,** Michl L '92 (Shanker Law Grp) -101 Front -Mineola 11501 **Fx:**741-4665
(212) 964-3300 .. **Shanker,** Nadine S '95 %Rubin A LLP -225 Bway -NY 10007
(646) 755-3304 .. **Shanker,** Steven J '98 (Shanker & S,PC) -420 Lex Av -NY 10170
(212) 632-5500 .. **Shanklin,** Susan '91 OfCnsl Salans LLP -620 5th Av -NY 10020
(212) 450-4000 .. **Shankman,** Zachary D '07 %Davis P&W LLP -450 Lex Av -NY 10017
(518) 445-2311 .. **Shanks,** Laurie F '89 %Law Clinic & Justice Ctr -80 New Scotland Av -Albany 12208
(518) 434-1493 .. **Shanks,** Laurie F '89 (Kindlon & S,PC) -74 Chapel -Albany 12207
(212) 661-6800 .. **Shanks,** Russell J '84 (Cyruli SH&Z LLP) -420 Lex Av -NY 10170
(845) 426-6544 .. **Shanks,** Ruthanne Brain '90 -112 Union Rd -Spg Vly 10977
(212) 578-2211 .. **Shanler,** Dana E '89 %MetLife -27-01 Qns Plz N -LIC 11101
(646) 315-7300 .. **Shanley,** Chas J Jr. '86 %FINRA -14 Wall -NY 10005 **Fx:**315-7440
(518) 266-1029 .. **Shanley,** Donald J '54 %Pattison SG&G,PC -22 1st Bx208 -Troy 12181
(315) 343-2610 .. **Shanley,** Kristin A '03 %Shanley Law Ofc -100 W Utica -Oswego 13126 **Fx:**342-1563
(518) 266-1039 .. **Shanley,** Michl W '10 -22 First Bx208 -Troy 12181
(315) 963-8288 .. **Shanley,** P Michl '70 Shanley Law Ofc -Main Bx359 -Mexico 13114 **Fx:**963-3909
(315) 343-2610 .. **Shanley,** P Michl '70 Shanley Law Ofc -100 W Utica -Oswego 13126 **Fx:**342-1563
(718) 789-2003 .. **Shanley,** Richd J '85 -123 7th Av -Brklyn 11215
(518) 266-1000 .. **Shanley,** Terence E '68 Cnsl Pattison SG&G,PC -22 1st Bx208 -Troy 12181
(518) 474-7668 .. **Shanley,** W Jos III '82 %Insurance Dept -99 Wshngtn Av -Albany 12257 **Fx:**486-2218
(203) 353-6825 .. **Shanman,** James A '67 (Edwards AP&D LLP) -750 Lex Av -NY 10022 **Fx:**975-7180
(212) 687-0100 .. **Shanmugham,** Devi '03 %Harris B PLLC -100 Wall -NY 10005
(212) 688-8555 .. **Shannon,** Careen B '90 %Fragomen DB&L LLP -7 Hanover Sq -NY 10004
(518) 449-8893 .. **Shannon,** James A '98 OfCnsl Wilson EME&D LLP -677 Bway -Albany 12207
(212) 449-1962 .. **Shannon,** John K Jr. '85 %Merrill Lynch -220 Bway -NY 10038
(718) 442-5184 .. **Shannon,** Jos J '84 -14 Glenwood Pl -Staten Isl 10310
(212) 770-7000 .. **Shannon,** Kathleen E '75 %AIG -70 Pine -NY 10270
(315) 477-0100 .. **Shannon,** Michl E '03 %Baldwin & S,LLP -126 N Salina -Syracuse 13202
(212) 344-5680 .. **Shannon,** Michl G '75 (Thompson H LLP) -335 Mad Av -NY 10017
(716) 852-0202 .. **Shannon,** Michl R '81 OfCnsl Farner & F -808 Main Seneca Bldg -Buffalo 14203 **Fx:**852-0271
(716) 852-0202 .. **Shannon,** Michl R '81 -808 Main Seneca Bldg -Buffalo 14203 **Fx:**852-0271
(315) 369-6114 .. **Shannon,** Peter A '80 -Main Bx1169 -Old Forge 13420
(212) 308-4411 .. **Shannon,** Philip T '66 Cnsl Edwards AP&D LLP -750 Lex Av -NY 10022
(718) 855-9000 .. **Shannon,** Richd A '87 %Cullen and D LLP -177 Montague -Brklyn 11201
(212) 227-6821 .. **Shannon,** Robt J '86 (Roura & M) -233 Bway -NY 10279
(212) 885-2780 .. **Shannon,** Robt V Jr. '98 (IQPC) -535 5th Av -NY 10017 **Fx:**973-1042
(212) 916-3469 .. **Shannon,** Sean J '98 %Lexis Publishing Co -125 Park Av -NY 10017 **Fx:**309-8187
(315) 474-1267 .. **Shannon,** Thos F '83 (Lynn Law Firm,LLP) -101 S Salina -Syracuse 13202 **Fx:**474-4514
(516) 227-2300 .. **Shannon,** Thos J '94 Wright Risk Mgmt -333 Earle Ovngton Blvd -Uniondale 11553 **Fx:**227-2352
(212) 309-6000 .. **Shanon,** Etienne Dovalier '02 %Morgan L&B LLP -101 Park Av -NY 10178
(212) 326-3939 .. **Shansky,** Robt J '72 OfCnsl Jones D -222 E 41st -NY 10017
(518) 785-5340 .. **Shantz,** Fredk F '83 Shantz & B -26 Century Hill Dr -Latham 12110 **Fx:**785-5470
(914) 253-6500 .. **Shanus,** Corey R '83 Sobert Rlty Corp -2700 Wstchstr Av -Purchase 10577
(914) 253-6500 .. **Shanus,** Sarene P '88 Harlorn,LLC -2700 Wstchstr Av -Purchase 10577 **Fx:**253-8058
(516) 487-4461 .. **Shapero,** Lori H '85 -41 Amherst Rd -Gt Neck 11021 **Fx:**482-5594
(212) 285-3300 .. **Shapey,** Alan M '80 (Lipsig SM&M,PC) -40 Fulton -NY 10038
(212) 286-8585 .. **Shapiro,** Aaron '09 %Heidell PM&B,LLP -99 Park Av -NY 10016
(917) 829-3305 .. **Shapiro,** Aaron D P '09 Cnsl Shapiro Law Firm,LLC -11 Bway -NY 10004 **Fx:**(212) 981-2726
(631) 543-3700 .. **Shapiro,** Abbe C '99 %A Firestone,PC -612 Vets Mem'l Hwy -Hauppauge 11788 **Fx:**543-3737
(212) 878-7900 .. **Shapiro,** Abbe G '88 (Fox R LLP) -100 Park Av -NY 10017
(914) 428-3313 .. **Shapiro,** Adam A '03 %Curan AF&N,LLP -14 Mamaroneck Av -White Plns 10601 **Fx:**949-5800
(212) 455-2000 .. **Shapiro,** Adam D '08 %Simpson T&B LLP -425 Lex Av -NY 10017
(212) 403-1000 .. **Shapiro,** Adam J '97 (Wachtell LR&K) -51 W 52nd -NY 10019
(516) 749-1626 .. **Shapiro,** Adam L '98 (A Shapiro & Assoc,PC) -1 Radnor Rd -Plainvw 11803 **Fx:**908-3825
(718) 250-0400 .. **Shapiro,** Adam P '91 %R Tusa -1 MetroTech Ctr -Brklyn 11201 **Fx:**250-0591
(212) 351-4000 .. **Shapiro,** Akiva '09 Gibson D&C LLP -200 Park Av -NY 10166
(212) 977-9700 .. **Shapiro,** Alan '74 (Phillips N LLP) -666 5th Av -NY 10103
(212) 753-7500 .. **Shapiro,** Aleena R '82 Cnsl Hartman & C LLP -488 Mad Av -NY 10022
(212) 336-2000 .. **Shapiro,** Alexander '96 (Patterson BW&T LLP) -1133 Av of Amer -NY 10036
(212) 635-1596 .. **Shapiro,** Alexander H '92 Bk of NY Mellon -1 Wall -NY 10286
(212) 479-6724 .. **Shapiro,** Alexandra A E '00 (Macht SA&I LLP) -1114 Av of Amer -NY 10036 **Fx:**202-6417
(212) 708-1800 .. **Shapiro,** Alissa N '05 %Ladas & P -26 W 61st -NY 10023
(607) 723-5341 .. **Shapiro,** Amy '89 SpclCnsl Hinman H&K,LLP -80 Exchange Bx5250 -Bnghmtn 13902
(914) 328-2969 .. **Shapiro,** Amy M '05 %Martin C&B LLP -245 Main -White Plns 10601
(212) 225-2000 .. **Shapiro,** Amy R '04 %Cleary GS&H -1 Lbrty Plz -NY 10006
(212) 258-8000 .. **Shapiro,** Andra '86 %MTV Networks -1515 Bway -NY 10036 **Fx:**258-8358
(212) 965-8300 .. **Shapiro,** Andrea F '90 -42 Bway -NY 10004 **Fx:**483-2404
(212) 596-9000 .. **Shapiro,** Andrew E '09 %Ropes & G LLP -1211 Av of Amer -NY 10036
(212) 938-5000 .. **Shapiro,** Andrew M '98 Cantor Fitzgerald -110 E 59th -NY 10022
(212) 969-3000 .. **Shapiro,** Andrew R '08 %Proskauer R LLP -1585 Bway -NY 10036
(212) 824-5700 .. **Shapiro,** Anita Carr '91 Practising Law Inst -810 7th Av -NY 10019
(845) 291-0011 .. **Shapiro,** Arthur '58 OfCnsl Blustein SR&B,LLP -10 Matthews -Goshen 10924
(212) 924-9015 .. **Shapiro,** Barbara A '80 -3 Sheridan Sq -NY 10014

(516) 741-6565 .. **Shapiro,** Barry R '73 (Meyer SE&K,PC) -990 Stewart Av Bx9194 -Gdn Cty 11530
(212) 267-9020 .. **Shapiro Beilly & Aronowitz LLP** -225 Bway -NY 10007 **Fx:**608-2072
(718) 403-9696 .. **Shapiro,** Bernard L '76 (Shapiro & S) -90 Meadow Woods Rd -Gt Neck 11020
(212) 267-9020 .. **Shapiro,** Beth '80 (Shapiro B&A LLP) -225 Bway -NY 10007
(718) 653-0835 .. **Shapiro,** Caren A '89 %Public Schl 89 -980 Mace Av -Bronx 10469
(212) 986-7353 .. **Shapiro,** Clifford H '86 (Wingate R&S) -420 Lex Av -NY 10170
(516) 798-7800 .. **Shapiro & Coleman,PC** -727 N Bway -N Massapequa 11758
(212) 233-0314 .. **Shapiro,** Corey M '02 (Wolfson & C) -233 Bway -NY 10279 **Fx:**349-4911
(212) 308-6163 .. **Shapiro,** Danl '79 -201 E 42nd -NY 10017
(212) 832-0400 .. **Shapiro,** Danl A '94 Berdon LLP -360 Mad Av -NY 10017
(518) 474-6740 .. **Shapiro,** Danl E '86 %Dept of State -41 State -Albany 12231 **Fx:**473-9211
(516) 746-8000 .. **Shapiro,** Danl E '09 %Jaspan S LLP -300 Grdn City Plz -Gdn Cty 11530
(516) 625-9850 .. **Shapiro,** Danl M '78 (Shapiro U&M,PC) -Expwy Plz 1-#120 -Roslyn Hts 11577
(212) 756-2000 .. **Shapiro,** Danl S '64 (Schulte R&Z LLP) -919 3rd Av -NY 10022
(212) 223-0200 .. **Shapiro,** Danl V '06 %Stillman F&S,PC -425 Park Av -NY 10022
(718) 523-1111 .. **Shapiro,** David A '96 (Gildin Z&S,PC) -138-44 Qns Blvd -Briarwd 11435
(212) 403-1000 .. **Shapiro,** David E '00 (Wachtell LR&K) -51 W 52nd -NY 10019
(212) 859-8000 .. **Shapiro,** David I '93 (Fried FHS&J LLP) -1 NY Plz -NY 10004
(212) 506-1700 .. **Shapiro,** David J '91 SpclCnsl Kasowitz BT&F LLP -1633 Bway -NY 10019
(212) 455-2000 .. **Shapiro,** David S '10 %Simpson T&B LLP -425 Lex Av -NY 10017
(212) 593-6700 .. **Shapiro,** Dawn C '93 (Aaronson RF&D,LLP) -757 3rd Av -NY 10017
(212) 248-2085 .. **Shapiro,** Deborah A '96 (DA Shapiro,LLC) -270 Mad Av -NY 10016 **Fx:**658-9536
(516) 478-4100 .. **Shapiro,** Deborah B '99 Cnsl Hlth Care Comp Strategies -30 Jericho Exec Plz -Jericho 11753 **Fx:**478-6773
(212) 849-7000 .. **Shapiro,** Deborah L '01 %Quinn EU&S,LLP -51 Mad Av -NY 10010
(631) 844-9611 .. **Shapiro DiCaro & Barak,LLP** -105 Maxness Rd -Melvll 11747 **Fx:**844-9525
(585) 247-9000 .. **Shapiro DiCaro & Barak,LLP** -250 Mile Xing Blvd -Rchstr 14624 **Fx:**247-7380
(212) 361-8112 .. **Shapiro,** Edw G '00 %Ct of Claims -26 Bway -NY 10004 **Fx:**361-8103
(212) 554-0400 .. **Shapiro,** Edw H '92 %Grubman I&S,PC -152 W 57th -NY 10019
(212) 962-7267 .. **Shapiro,** Edw M '90 -225 Bway -NY 10007 **Fx:**504-8052
(914) 941-2606 .. **Shapiro,** Edwin S '56 -29 Quinn Rd -Briarcliff Mnr 10510 **Fx:**944-0891
(718) 643-8003 .. **Shapiro,** Ellen J '78 %Hon T Carroll -120 Schermerhorn -Brklyn 11201
(212) 872-9800 .. **Shapiro,** Ellen L '92 (Squire S&D LLP) -30 Rckfllr Plz -NY 10112
(212) 820-7700 .. **Shapiro,** Evan '88 (Boundas SW&B,LLC) -1 Bttry Pk Plz -NY 10004
(212) 725-4650 .. **Shapiro,** Felice K '86 %Old Republic Natl Title Ins Co -192 Lex Av -NY 10016 **Fx:**725-4655
(212) 972-4900 .. **Shapiro Forman Allen & Sava LLP** -380 Mad Av -NY 10017 **Fx:**557-1275
(914) 997-7600 .. **Shapiro,** Fred L '74 OfCnsl Penichet Firm,PC -140 Grand -White Plns 10601 **Fx:**997-8155
(212) 583-9600 .. **Shapiro,** Gary D '07 %Littler M,PC -900 3rd Av -NY 10022
(516) 367-4697 .. **Shapiro,** Gary E '72 -6 Livengood Ct -Woodbury 11797 **Fx:**367-1545
(212) 901-2667 .. **Shapiro,** Gary E '94 -27 W 44th -NY 10036
(212) 736-0500 .. **Shapiro,** Gerald '75 (Mitofsky SN&H LLP) -152 Mad Av -NY 10016
(212) 213-1220 .. **Shapiro,** Gregory M '05 %Weiner MM&B,LLC -220 5th Av -NY 10001
(212) 264-5958 .. **Shapiro,** Hannah R '02 NY Immigration Ct -26 Fed Plz -NY 10278
(631) 761-0094 .. **Shapiro,** Harold A '62 H Shapiro,PC -320 Carleton Av -Central Islip 11722
(212) 685-6400 .. **Shapiro,** Harry '77 (Smith & S) -116 E 27th -NY 10016
(212) 621-8224 .. **Shapiro,** Harvey '76 (Sargoy SR&S) -1790 Bway -NY 10019
(212) 355-5240 .. **Shapiro,** Harvey '78 -250 W 57th -NY 10107
(212) 801-6490 .. **Shapiro,** Howard R '76 (Greenberg T,LLP) -200 Park Av -NY 10166
(212) 479-6000 .. **Shapiro,** Ian R '01 (Cooley LLP) -1114 Av of Amer -NY 10036
(212) 306-7062 .. **Shapiro,** Irene C '82 %Housing Auth -250 Bway -NY 10007
(212) 735-3000 .. **Shapiro,** Isaac '57 OfCnsl Skadden ASM&F LLP -4 Times Sq -NY 10036
(607) 762-6278 .. **Shapiro,** J Jay '94 %NYSEG -4425 Old Vestal Rd -Bnghmtn 13902 **Fx:**762-6296
(631) 661-0006 .. **Shapiro,** Jason S '98 OfCnsl E Young & Assoc -112 Route 109 -W Babylon 11704 **Fx:**661-0226
(212) 940-8800 .. **Shapiro,** Jay '81 (Katten MR LLP) -575 Mad Av -NY 10022
(212) 331-5066 .. **Shapiro,** Jeffrey A '87 HRA-OLA -180 Water -NY 10038
(518) 457-4380 .. **Shapiro,** Jeffrey G '86 %Dept of Labor -State Campus Bldg 12 -Albany 12240 **Fx:**485-1819
(212) 779-9100 .. **Shapiro,** Jeffrey J '79 J Shapiro & Assoc LLC -201 E 42nd -NY 10017 **Fx:**684-4923
(212) 558-4000 .. **Shapiro,** Jonathan C '07 %Sullivan & C LLP -125 Broad -NY 10004
(212) 558-4000 .. **Shapiro,** Jonathan L '09 %Sullivan & C LLP -125 Broad -NY 10004
(212) 297-5800 .. **Shapiro,** Jonathan M '03 %Day P LLP -7 Times Sq -NY 10036
(212) 391-6464 .. **Shapiro,** Jonathan S '95 (Shapiro Firm,LLP) -500 5th Av -NY 10110 **Fx:**719-1616
(518) 439-2197 .. **Shapiro,** Jos C '58 -106 Marsdale Ct -Selkirk 12158
(212) 504-6000 .. **Shapiro,** Joshua L '07 %Cadwalader W&T LLP -1 World Fncl Ctr -NY 10281
(631) 852-8800 .. **Shapiro,** Joshua S '07 %DA -116 Hmptn Rd -Southampton 11968 **Fx:**852-8806
(212) 953-6633 .. **Shapiro,** Judah S '86 -630 3rd Av -NY 10017 **Fx:**949-6943
(212) 490-3000 .. **Shapiro,** Kenneth L '61 (Wilson EME&D LLP) -150 E 42nd -NY 10017
(518) 449-8893 .. **Shapiro,** Kenneth L '61 (Wilson EME&D LLP) -677 Bway -Albany 12207
(516) 622-0606 .. **Shapiro,** Kenneth R '81 SrCnsl P Rizzuto,PC -1 Old Cntry Rd -Carle Pl 11514 **Fx:**622-2112
(212) 732-8700 .. **Shapiro,** Laura R '82 (McAloon & F,PC) -123 William -NY 10038
(212) 883-4954 .. **Shapiro,** Laurance D '07 %Cozen O -277 Park Av -NY 10172
(347) 592-2500 .. **Shapiro,** Lauren Anne '87 %Bklyn Fam Def Proj -177 Lvngstn -Brklyn 11201 **Fx:**(718) 596-4704
(212) 812-4256 .. **Shapiro,** Lawr G '87 Rockefeller Family Fund -437 Mad Av -NY 10022
(212) 730-8133 .. **Shapiro,** Lee Matthew '02 %Gunderson DSVF&H,LLP -220 W 42nd -NY 10036
(718) 846-7100 .. **Shapiro,** Leesa '88 -106-05 Lbrty Av -Ozone Pk 11417 **Fx:**846-8866
(212) 391-6464 .. **Shapiro,** Leonard N '61 (Shapiro Firm,LLP) -500 5th Av -NY 10110 **Fx:**719-1616
(631) 952-6505 .. **Shapiro,** Leonard R '74 %UIA Bd -NYS Ofc Bldg -Hauppauge 11788 **Fx:**952-3385
(718) 838-7878 .. **Shapiro,** Lily J '04 %Bronx Defenders -860 Crtlandt Av -Bronx 10451 **Fx:**665-0100
(212) 233-0403 .. **Shapiro,** Lori A '84 -10 West -NY 10004 **Fx:**233-4441
(212) 506-5000 .. **Shapiro,** Marc S '84 (Orrick H&S LLP) -51 W 52nd -NY 10019
(718) 923-4206 .. **Shapiro,** Marilyn Mosberg '65 %OTDA Fair Hearings -14 Boerum Pl -Brklyn 11201
(212) 526-5937 .. **Shapiro,** Mark J '87 Barclays Capital Inc -745 7th Av -NY 10019
(347) 462-9900 .. **Shapiro,** Marla S '02 %Shapiro & S,LLP -3145 Coney Isl Av -Brklyn 11235
(607) 273-4044 .. **Shapiro,** Martin A '73 (Shapiro & K-S) -120 W State -Ithaca 14850 **Fx:**697-0113
(212) 506-1700 .. **Shapiro,** Maxine R '81 %Kasowitz BT&F LLP -1633 Bway -NY 10019
(212) 312-2361 .. **Shapiro,** Melanie D '05 Leg Aid -60 Lafayette -NY 10013 **Fx:**349-0874
(212) 213-9252 .. **Shapiro,** Meryl '79 -305 E 24th -NY 10010
(212) 732-3200 .. **Shapiro,** Michl '74 (Carter L&M LLP) -2 Wall -NY 10005
(631) 777-5115 .. **Shapiro,** Michl A '81 -31 Apricot Ct -Melvll 11747
(718) 520-1600 .. **Shapiro,** Michl A '82 (Kramer & S) -80-02 Kew Grdns Rd -Kew Gdns 11415
(212) 888-6600 .. **Shapiro,** Michl B '09 %Rubinstein & R,LLP -18 E 48th -NY 10022 **Fx:**888-7443
(212) 417-9191 .. **Shapiro,** Michl J '79 (M Shapiro,PLLC) -270 Mad Av -NY 10016 **Fx:**417-9190
(212) 499-6644 .. **Shapiro,** Michl S '95 %M Cohen & Assoc,PC -7 Penn Plz -NY 10001 **Fx:**818-0625
(212) 999-5800 .. **Shapiro,** Michelle J '99 %Wilson SG&R -1301 Av of Americas -NY 10019
(845) 371-2100 .. **Shapiro,** Milton B '53 (MB&SH Shapiro) -21 Perlman Dr -Spg Vly 10977 **Fx:**371-3721
(212) 233-6550 .. **Shapiro,** Mitchell G '80 %Salzman & W LLP -305 Bway -NY 10007
(914) 666-8033 .. **Shapiro,** Mona D '75 (Banks SG&W,LLP) -118 N Bedford Rd Bx320 -Mt Kisco 10549
(212) 637-3000 .. **Shapiro,** Naomi P '93 US EPA -290 Bway -NY 10007
(718) 252-2800 .. **Shapiro,** Nathaniel '98 %Hirsch Wolf & Co -1505 Coney Isl Av -Brklyn 11230 **Fx:**338-0024
(212) 592-1400 .. **Shapiro,** Neil R '88 (Herrick,F LLP) -2 Park Av -NY 10016
(212) 659-7300 .. **Shapiro,** Noah D '02 OfCnsl Haynes & B,LLP -1221 Av of Amer -NY 10020
(845) 341-1673 .. **Shapiro,** Norman '53 -Bx696 -Goshen 10924
(914) 345-1700 .. **Shapiro,** Oren A '02 Mrs Blooms Direct Inc -175 Clearbrook Rd -Elmsfrd 10523
(212) 867-4466 .. **Shapiro,** Orie C '83 (Belkin BW&G,LLP) -270 Mad Av -NY 10016
(631) 543-5800 .. **Shapiro,** Paul L '77 OfCnsl LJ Shore -366 Vets Mem'l Hwy -Commack 11725 **Fx:**543-5899
(212) 218-2100 .. **Shapiro,** Peter D '00 (Fitzpatrick CH&S) -1290 Av of Amer -NY 10104
(718) 643-5094 .. **Shapiro,** Peter R '83 Appellate Div -45 Monroe Pl -Brklyn 11201
(212) 232-1300 .. **Shapiro,** Peter T '82 (Lewis BB&S LLP) -77 Water -NY 10005
(516) 488-8800 .. **Shapiro,** Philip J '79 Liberty Maritime Corp -1979 Marcus Av -Lk Success 11042 **Fx:**488-8806
(212) 445-4713 .. **Shapiro,** Randy L '90 %Newsweek -395 Hudson -NY 10014
(212) 885-5000 .. **Shapiro,** Raymond L '03 (Blank R LLP) -405 Lex Av -NY 10174
(914) 683-1386 .. **Shapiro,** Richd A '64 -6 Roland Dr -White Plns 10605 **Fx:**946-8883
(212) 687-8700 .. **Shapiro,** Richd A '70 Cnsl Malkin Hldngs,LLC -60 E 42nd -NY 10165 **Fx:**986-7679
(212) 768-0300 .. **Shapiro,** Richd I '83 -220 W 42nd -NY 10036
(845) 291-0011 .. **Shapiro,** Richd J '91 (Blustein SR&B,LLP) -10 Matthews -Goshen 10924
(914) 997-1405 .. **Shapiro,** Richd L '77 -8 Ria Dr -White Plns 10605
(718) 579-7902 .. **Shapiro,** Rita '87 %Leg Aid -900 Sheridan Av -Bronx 10451 **Fx:**293-8744
(585) 546-6170 .. **Shapiro,** Robt A '69 -36 W Main -Rchstr 14614
(212) 391-6464 .. **Shapiro,** Robt J '94 (Shapiro Firm,LLP) -500 5th Av -NY 10110 **Fx:**719-1616
(347) 462-9900 .. **Shapiro,** Saadia M '87 (Shapiro & S,LLP) -3145 Coney Isl Av -Brklyn 11235
(212) 593-6700 .. **Shapiro,** Saml J '95 (Aaronson RF&D,LLP) -757 3rd Av -NY 10017
(716) 845-6000 .. **Shapiro,** Saml L '65 (Kavinoky C LLP) -726 Exchange -Buffalo 14210
(585) 232-5300 .. **Shapiro,** Sanford R '61 OfCnsl Boylan BCV&W,LLP -2400 Chase Sq -Rchstr 14604
(212) 336-2000 .. **Shapiro,** Saul B '87 (Patterson BW&T LLP) -1133 Av of Amer -NY 10036
(212) 972-1000 .. **Shapiro,** Scott M '04 %London F LLP -59 Maiden Ln -NY 10038
(914) 684-1055 .. **Shapiro,** Sim R '94 (Baxter S&S,PC) -200 Mamaroneck Av -White Plns 10601
(718) 665-0050 .. **Shapiro,** Sophia M '88 -865B Walton Av -Bronx 10451
(212) 693-1076 .. **Shapiro,** Stanley K '81 -225 Bway -NY 10007 **Fx:**406-3677
(212) 513-3200 .. **Shapiro,** Stephen B '03 (Holland & K LLP) -31 W 52nd -NY 10019
(212) 246-2025 .. **Shapiro,** Stephen J '82 -101 W 57th -NY 10019
(212) 619-4350 .. **Shapiro,** Stephen N '73 (Newman MKGH,PC) -14 Wall -NY 10005
(212) 571-0068 .. **Shapiro,** Steven '87 (Ullman S&U,LLP) -299 Bway -NY 10007
(212) 801-9317 .. **Shapiro,** Steven '88 (Greenberg T,LLP) -200 Park Av -NY 10166
(212) 315-0518 .. **Shapiro,** Steven B '84 -340 W 57th -NY 10019 **Fx:**956-4767
(212) 230-5500 .. **Shapiro,** Steven G '84 (Davis SLM&H LLP) -689 5th Av -NY 10022
(212) 549-2500 .. **Shapiro,** Steven R '76 %ACLU -125 Broad -NY 10004 **Fx:**549-2651

(716) 881-3010 .. **Shapiro,** Stuart B '83 (Cohen & L,PC) -343 Elmwood Av Bx5204 -Buffalo 14213
(516) 488-7808 .. **Shapiro,** Stuart B '86 -828 Hempstd Tpk -Franklin Sq 11010 **Fx:**488-7808
(212) 972-4900 .. **Shapiro,** Stuart L '72 (Shapiro FA&S LLP) -380 Mad Av -NY 10017
(845) 371-2100 .. **Shapiro,** Susan H '84 (MB&SH Shapiro) -21 Perlman Dr -Spg Vly 10977 **Fx:**371-3721
(212) 788-1141 .. **Shapiro,** Susan M '79 %Law Dept -100 Church -NY 10007 **Fx:**788-0367
(212) 777-7128 .. **Shapiro,** Sylvia L '79 -63 E 9th -NY 10003
(516) 741-2585 .. **Shapiro,** Tammy J '03 %Rosicki R & Assoc,PC -51 E Bethpage Rd -Plainvw 11803 **Fx:**741-4748
(631) 951-3150 .. **Shapiro,** Ted S '80 -150 Motor Pkwy -Hauppauge 11788
(646) 336-4409 .. **Shapiro,** Tod L '86 %PC Learn -71 W 23rd -NY 10010
(516) 625-9850 .. **Shapiro Uchman & Myers,PC** -Expwy Plz 1-#120 -Roslyn Hts 11577 **Fx:**625-9851
(212) 374-3407 .. **Shapiro,** Zvia A '98 %NYC Dept Educ-OLS -52 Chmbrs -NY 10007 **Fx:**374-5939
(212) 259-8000 .. **Shapland,** Michl D '06 %Dewey & L LLP -1301 Av of Amer -NY 10019
(212) 450-4000 .. **Shapleigh,** Kerry McIntyre '10 %Davis P&W LLP -450 Lex Av -NY 10017
(212) 336-8000 .. **Shapley,** Stuart D '05 %Amster R&E -90 Park Av -NY 10016
(212) 592-1400 .. **Shapses,** Paul M '84 (Herrick,F LLP) -2 Park Av -NY 10016
(845) 368-3449 .. **Shapss,** Ronald I '71 -75 Montebello Rd -Suffern 10901
(212) 476-9000 .. **Sharaby,** Linda '04 %Neuberger Berman,LLC -605 3rd Av -NY 10158 **Fx:**476-9862
(212) 872-1000 .. **Sharaf,** Cleo F '96 -One Bryant Park -NY 10036 **Fx:**872-1002
(212) 619-5800 .. **Sharan,** Richd S '90 (Pollack & S,LLP) -15 Maiden Ln -NY 10038 **Fx:**267-2682
(212) 819-8200 .. **Sharapan,** Boris '09 %White & C LLP -1155 Av of Amer -NY 10036
(516) 829-4879 .. **Sharara,** Elana '98 -20 Gilchrest Rd -Gt Neck 11021 **Fx:**829-3572
(212) 446-4800 .. **Share,** Ashley '07 %Kirkland & E LLP -153 E 53rd -NY 10022
(212) 643-0700 .. **Share,** Paul A '74 -236 W 30th -NY 10001 **Fx:**643-0701
(212) 367-6300 .. **Shareef,** Saleem A '01 -395 Hudson -NY 10014
(212) 768-6700 .. **Sharetta,** Andrea '01 (Sonnenschein N&R LLP) -2 World Fncl Ctr -NY 10281
(516) 625-9120 .. **Sharf,** Erica G '93 -34 Valley Rd -Old Westbury 11568 **Fx:**625-9121
(212) 548-7947 .. **Sharf,** Jennifer F '05 %West Group -530 5th Av -NY 10036 **Fx:**548-7401
(646) 386-4071 .. **Sharf,** Lawr H '72 Hon C Berkman -100 Centre -NY 10013
(212) 758-9700 .. **Sharf,** Michl L '01 %KPMG LLP -345 Park Av -NY 10154
(914) 741-9870 .. **Sharff,** Marc E '84 (Shaw PM&L,LLP) -115 Stevens Av -Valhalla 10595
(212) 806-5400 .. **Sharfman,** Richd M '66 (Stroock &S&L LLP) -180 Maiden Ln -NY 10038
(646) 386-5700 .. **Sharfman,** Ruth S '84 %Civil Ct -111 Centre -NY 10013
(212) 756-2000 .. **Sharfstein,** Howard F '71 (Schulte R&Z LLP) -919 3rd Av -NY 10022
(516) 622-9200 .. **Sharfstein,** Philip L '85 (Westerman BEM&S,LLP) -1201 RXR Plz -Uniondale 11553
(212) 508-6100 .. **Shargel,** David A '06 %Bracewell & G,LLP -1251 Av of Amer -NY 10020
(212) 446-2323 .. **Shargel,** Gerald L '69 -570 Lex Av -NY 10022 **Fx:**446-2330
(212) 846-4059 .. **Sharif-Drinkard,** Khadijah Fatinah '98 %Nickelodeon -1515 Bway -NY 10036
(212) 878-8000 .. **Shariff,** Viqar M '96 (Clifford C LLP) -31 W 52nd -NY 10019
(212) 530-1800 .. **Sharifi,** Jahangier '96 %Richards K&O LLP -1 World Fncl Ctr -NY 10281
(212) 294-6700 .. **Sharifi,** Pejman F '00 (Winston & S) -200 Park Av -NY 10166
(212) 872-1000 .. **Sharifi-Azad,** Sheila '06 -One Bryant Park -NY 10036 **Fx:**872-1002
(516) 505-2300 .. **Sharifov,** Rovshan C '03 (Sharifov & R) -50 Main -Hempstd 11550 **Fx:**505-2379
(516) 873-6600 .. **Sharinn,** Harvey '63 (Sharinn & L) -333 Earle Ovngton Blvd -Uniondale 11553
(516) 873-6600 .. **Sharinn & Lipshie** -333 Earle Ovngton Blvd -Uniondale 11553 **Fx:**873-7808
(212) 687-0100 .. **Sharinn,** Todd S '01 (Harris B PLLC) -100 Wall -NY 10005
(516) 248-3510 .. **Sharit & Deliyannis** -1 Old Cntry Rd -Carle Pl 11514
(516) 248-3510 .. **Sharit,** Martin C '85 (Sharit & D) -1 Old Cntry Rd -Carle Pl 11514
(212) 265-6888 .. **Sharkey,** Brian P '01 Cnsl Porzio B&N,PC -156 W 56th -NY 10019
(212) 998-6729 .. **Sharkey,** Catherine Moira '00 NYU Law Schl -40 Wshngtn Sq S -NY 10012 **Fx:**995-4590
(716) 938-9111 .. **Sharkey,** Edw M '78 (DA) -303 Court -Little Vly 14755
(212) 902-1000 .. **Sharkey,** James R '04 %Goldman Sachs -85 Broad -NY 10004
(516) 414-4995 .. **Sharkey,** Jeffrey P '82 -2564 Aster Pl S -Westbury 11590 **Fx:**279-4965
(518) 423-3464 .. **Sharkey,** John K '78 -1908 Baker Av -Niskayuna 12309 **Fx:**377-6110
(718) 858-8843 .. **Sharkey,** Kelley J '84 -26 Court -Brklyn 11242
(716) 566-2800 .. **Sharkey,** Stephen A '99 SrCnsl Bond S&K,PLLC -40 Fountian Plz -Buffalo 14202
(212) 277-6500 .. **Sharkin,** Keith E '83 (Dickstein S LLP) -1633 Bway -NY 10019
(212) 657-0351 .. **Sharko,** Emily Copland '01 Citigroup Global Mrkts -77 Water -NY 10005
(212) 521-5400 .. **Sharlach,** Darren M '97 (Reed S LLP) -599 Lex Av -NY 10022
(315) 442-0100 .. **Sharlow,** Paul T '04 %Gilberti SH&S,PC -555 E Genesee -Syracuse 13202
(212) 310-8000 .. **Sharma,** Aabha '07 %Weil G&M LLP -767 5th Av -NY 10153
(212) 849-4511 .. **Sharma,** Ambika '00 %Dover Corp -280 Park Av -NY 10017
(212) 237-4424 .. **Sharma,** Ami Nayak '96 Ogilry & Mather -309 W 49th -NY 10019
(212) 728-8000 .. **Sharma,** Devon S '10 %Willkie F&G LLP -787 7th Av -NY 10019
(718) 322-1717 .. **Sharma,** Jageshwar '03 (Sharma Law Grp PLLC) -10914 Lbrty Av -S Richmond Hll 11419 **Fx:**322-8360
(212) 373-3000 .. **Sharma,** Jyoti '06 %Paul WRW&G LLP -1285 Av of Amer -NY 10019
(212) 455-2000 .. **Sharma,** Parijat '09 %Simpson T&B LLP -425 Lex Av -NY 10017
(212) 481-4900 .. **Sharma,** Parkash C '94 P Sharma & Assoc,PLLC -38 W 32nd -NY 10001 **Fx:**481-9227
(212) 733-6879 .. **Sharma,** Piyush '02 Pfizer,Inc -150 E 42nd -NY 10017
(212) 310-8000 .. **Sharma,** Rahul K '09 %Weil G&M LLP -767 5th Av -NY 10153
(212) 537-5957 .. **Sharma,** Ravi Ivan '91 -200 Park Av S -NY 10003 **Fx:**537-5956
(212) 351-3000 .. **Sharma,** Rick K '99 Plural Investments LLC -909 3rd Av -NY 10022
(646) 205-7880 .. **Sharma,** Sahil '08 %Cruz & G & Assoc -110 William -NY 10038 **Fx:**(212) 233-9848
(212) 521-3500 .. **Sharma,** Sherri '04 %Aronson M&S, LLP -485 Lex Av -NY 10017
(516) 783-3104 .. **Sharma,** Vandana P '97 -3087 Susan Rd -Bellmore 11710
(212) 318-3000 .. **Sharoky,** Meredith A '08 %Fulbright & J LLP -666 5th Av -NY 10103
(315) 435-2170 .. **Sharon,** John W '92 %Cnty Atty -421 Mntgmry -Syracuse 13202 **Fx:**435-5729
(212) 681-1555 .. **Sharon,** Robt '62 (R Sharon,PC) -240 Mad Av -NY 10016 **Fx:**681-1556
(518) 563-4022 .. **Sharp,** Brenna K '08 %Leg Aid -100 Court Bx989 -Plattsbrgh 12901 **Fx:**563-4058
(212) 370-9400 .. **Sharp,** Deborah C '82 Lexolution LLC -295 Mad Av -NY 10017
(212) 297-5800 .. **Sharp,** Erek M '03 %Day P LLP -7 Times Sq -NY 10036
(212) 506-5000 .. **Sharp,** Gaelyn E '02 (Orrick H&S LLP) -51 W 52nd -NY 10019
(212) 230-5319 .. **Sharp,** Karen L '85 %Tiffany & Co -600 Mad Av -NY 10022 **Fx:**230-5323
(212) 284-2300 .. **Sharp,** Michl J '93 Jefferies Grp,Inc -520 Mad Av -NY 10022
(718) 369-0189 .. **Sharp,** Michl S '99 %NY Methodist Hospital -506 6th -Brklyn 11201
(212) 335-4500 .. **Sharp,** Peter D '00 %DLA Piper LLP -1251 Av of Amer -NY 10020
(212) 530-5000 .. **Sharp,** Richd T '84 (Milbank TH&M LLP) -1 Chase Manh Plz -NY 10005
(212) 272-0838 .. **Sharp,** Simon M '04 JP Morgan Chase -383 Mad Av -NY 10179
(315) 479-3900 .. **Sharp,** Steven K '90 %SSA-ODAR -300 S State -Syracuse 13202 **Fx:**479-3933
(518) 474-6740 .. **Sharp,** Wm L '83 %Dept of State -41 State -Albany 12231 **Fx:**473-9211
(212) 335-9000 .. **Sharpe,** Amy Abrons '09 %DA -1 Hogan Pl -NY 10013
(518) 377-6700 .. **Sharpe,** Ann M '95 OfCnsl Cioffi SW PC -2310 Nott E -Niskayuna 12309
(718) 618-3697 .. **Sharpe,** Carol '85 OCA -265 E 161st -Bronx 10451
(716) 856-4000 .. **Sharpe,** Danl R '76 (Hodgson R LLP) -140 Pearl -Buffalo 14202
(212) 636-6000 .. **Sharpe,** Donald L '68 %Fordham Univ Sch of Law -140 W 62nd -NY 10023 **Fx:**636-6899
(347) 404-9133 .. **Sharpe,** Larry S '95 %Civil Ct -141 Lvngstn -Brklyn 11201 **Fx:**(718) 643-3733
(518) 474-1620 .. **Sharpe,** Michl A '96 %OCTF -The Cptl -Albany 12224 **Fx:**474-7258
(212) 351-4000 .. **Sharpe,** Nicole Phillips '08 %Gibson D&C LLP -200 Park Av -NY 10166
(518) 431-0247 .. **Sharpe,** Robt A '95 %US Atty -445 Bway -Albany 12207 **Fx:**431-0249
(212) 576-1600 .. **Sharpe,** Ronald E '86 Premier Technology -232 Mad Av -NY 10016
(315) 422-6154 .. **Sharpe,** Ronald V '60 (Greene H&S) -1 Lincoln Ctr -Syracuse 13202
(718) 325-5055 .. **Sharpe,** Ryan R '04 -3539 Tiemann Av -Bronx 10469
(212) 969-3000 .. **Sharpe,** Simon '09 %Proskauer R LLP -1585 Bway -NY 10036
(212) 891-6191 .. **Sharpe,** Thos G '93 CDC Ixis NA -9 W 57th -NY 10019 **Fx:**891-1922
(718) 250-2000 .. **Sharpe,** Wynton O '04 %DA -350 Jay -Brklyn 11201 **Fx:**250-2314
(631) 727-2226 .. **Sharpelletti,** Darrell J '83 (D Sharpelletti,PC) -Bx1183 -Rvrhead 11901 **Fx:**727-2298
(631) 231-3775 .. **Sharpelletti,** Stacey J '93 %Atty Grievance Comm -150 Motor Pkwy -Hauppauge 11788
(718) 250-2000 .. **Sharples,** John W '03 %DA -350 Jay -Brklyn 11201 **Fx:**250-2314
(718) 286-6000 .. **Sharples,** Nicole D '05 %DA -125-01 Qns Blvd -Kew Gdns 11415
(212) 688-8555 .. **Sharp Ziegler,** Nancy A '94 %Fragomen DB&L LLP -7 Hanover Sq -NY 10004
(212) 715-9100 .. **Sharret,** Jennifer R '08 %Kramer LN&F,LLP -1177 Av of Amer -NY 10036
(212) 425-0055 .. **Sharretts Paley Carter & Blauvelt** -75 Broad -NY 10004 **Fx:**425-1797
(212) 227-5550 .. **Sharron,** Robt P '93 (RP Sharron & Assoc,PC) -110 Wall -NY 10005 **Fx:**267-0402
(212) 218-2100 .. **Sharrott,** Douglas '95 (Fitzpatrick CH&S) -1290 Av of Amer -NY 10104
(212) 554-7800 .. **Sharrow,** Joel D '72 OfCnsl Moses & S LLP -405 Lex Av -NY 10174
(518) 786-3900 .. **Shartrand,** Douglas A '85 (Shartrand & S) -17 British Amer Blvd -Latham 12110 **Fx:**786-6446
(518) 786-3900 .. **Shartrand,** JoAnn '86 (Shartrand & S) -17 British Amer Blvd -Latham 12110 **Fx:**786-6446
(212) 691-6200 .. **Sharugrudsky,** Irving '95 -330 W 28th -NY 10001
(212) 259-8000 .. **Shasanmi,** John O '06 %Dewey & L LLP -1301 Av of Amer -NY 10019
(212) 733-8609 .. **Shastri,** Umang G '05 Pfizer Inc -235 E 42nd -NY 10017
(212) 521-5400 .. **Shatan,** Gregory S '87 (Reed S LLP) -599 Lex Av -NY 10022
(716) 842-0550 .. **Shatkin,** Marc S '95 (Shatkin & S) -434 Delaware Av -Buffalo 14202 **Fx:**853-6506
(716) 842-0550 .. **Shatkin,** Paul '57 (Shatkin & S) -434 Delaware Av -Buffalo 14202 **Fx:**853-6506
(212) 751-9800 .. **Shatynski,** Jennie L '97 %Morelli R PC -950 3rd Av -NY 10022
(212) 361-1890 .. **Shatz,** Harry '74 NYC Envrnmntl Cntrl Bd -66 John -NY 10038
(518) 270-3735 .. **Shatz,** Jennifer C '03 %Hon P McGrath -80 2nd -Troy 12180
(212) 607-3300 .. **Shatz,** Naomi Rivkind '09 %NYCLU -125 Broad -NY 10004
(845) 486-6800 .. **Shatz,** Phillip '54 OfCnsl McCabe & M LLP -63 Wshngtn Bx509 -Poughkeepsie 12602
(516) 883-7000 .. **Shatzkamer,** Ronnie '83 Village of Manorhaven -33 Manorhaven Blvd -Pt Wash 11050 **Fx:**883-4535
(212) 684-3000 .. **Shatzkin,** Karen '78 (Shatzkin & M,PC) -1776 Bway -NY 10019 **Fx:**684-5333
(212) 406-2545 .. **Shatzkin,** Peter J '77 (P Shatzkin,PC) -363 Greenwich -NY 10013 **Fx:**233-4002
(212) 349-6775 .. **Shatzky,** Benjamin A '99 %Peltz & W -222 Bway -NY 10038
(516) 488-3300 .. **Shaub Ahmuty Citrin & Spratt,LLP** -1983 Marcus Av -Lk Success 11042 **Fx:**488-2324
(212) 599-8200 .. **Shaub Ahmuty Citrin & Spratt,LLP** -655 3rd Av -NY 10017 **Fx:**599-7765
(516) 767-2100 .. **Shaub,** Gregory G '96 -125 Mineola Av -Roslyn Hts 11577 **Fx:**767-2104
(516) 488-3300 .. **Shaub,** Henry Z '81 (Shaub AC&S,LLP) -1983 Marcus Av -Lk Success 11042

(212) 506-1700 ..**Shaughnessy,** Brian F '07 %Kasowitz BT&F LLP -1633 Bway -NY 10019
(212) 594-5300 ..**Shaughnessy,** James M '70 (Milberg LLP) -1 Penn Plz -NY 10119
(212) 309-6000 ..**Shaulson,** Saml S '94 (Morgan L&B LLP) -101 Park Av -NY 10178
(212) 773-7491 ..**Shaver,** Chas Rhett '00 Ernst & Young LLP -5 Times Sq -NY 10036
(212) 446-7000 ..**Shavers,** Timothy B '94 %McKinsey & Co -55 E 52nd -NY 10055 **Fx:**688-9521
(212) 954-2871 ..**Shaw,** Adam M '92 KPMG LLP -345 Park Av -NY 10154
(518) 434-0600 ..**Shaw,** Adam R '94 (Boies S&F LLP) -10 N Pearl -Albany 12207
(718) 229-9192 ..**Shaw,** Alan J '82 -64-30 214th -Oakland Gdns 11364
(315) 696-8918 ..**Shaw,** Amanda C '95 (Riehlman S&S) -397 Route 281 Bx430 -Tully 13159
(212) 360-0209 ..**Shaw,** Amy K '00 Spence-Chapin -410 E 92nd -NY 10128
(516) 222-1995 ..**Shaw,** Arthur I '71 -600 Old Cntry Rd -Gdn Cty 11530 **Fx:**357-9281
(518) 457-4380 ..**Shaw,** Benjamin A '99 Dept of Labor -State Campus Bldg 12 -Albany 12240 **Fx:**485-1819
(212) 481-9011 ..**Shaw & Binder** -9 E 40th -NY 10016 **Fx:**764-0900
(212) 822-1477 ..**Shaw,** Bradley D '92 BD Shaw,PC -305 Bway -NY 10007 **Fx:**822-1461
(585) 232-6500 ..**Shaw,** Brian B '91 (Harter S&E LLP) -1600 Bausch & Lomb Pl -Rchstr 14604
(212) 344-9300 ..**Shaw,** Brian W '06 %S Golino -46 Trinity Pl -NY 10006 **Fx:**363-9444
(845) 369-1890 ..**Shaw,** Chester '91 -1 Exec Blvd -Suffern 10901 **Fx:**369-1890
(212) 417-5339 ..**Shaw,** Christopher M '90 %Medicaid Fraud Cntrl -120 Bway -NY 10271 **Fx:**417-5274
(212) 277-6300 ..**Shaw,** Danl E '04 %Schindler C&H LLP -100 Wall -NY 10005
(800) 477-4252 ..**Shaw,** Darren K G '03 NY Central Mutual Ins Co -Bx737 -Sherburne 13460
(212) 859-8000 ..**Shaw,** David L '99 (Fried FHS&J LLP) -1 NY Plz -NY 10004
(845) 486-4200 ..**Shaw,** David S '77 (Shaw PM&L,LLP) -21 Van Wagner Rd -Poughkeepsie 12603
(315) 946-5905 ..**Shaw,** David V '76 %DA -54 Broad -Lyons 14489 **Fx:**946-5911
(212) 727-0007 ..**Shaw,** Donald H '56 Shaw & M -310 W 19th -NY 10011 **Fx:**727-0008
(914) 833-2620 ..**Shaw,** Doris Kobrin '73 -18 Cntry Clb Dr -Larchmnt 10538 **Fx:**833-2606
(212) 593-6700 ..**Shaw,** Douglas R '06 %Aaronson RF&D,LLP -757 3rd Av -NY 10017
(212) 885-5000 ..**Shaw,** Ekaterini Pergantis '86 (Blank R LLP) -405 Lex Av -NY 10174
(718) 694-3802 ..**Shaw,** Emily M '86 %Transit Auth -130 Lvngstn -Brklyn 11201 **Fx:**694-5726
(212) 318-6000 ..**Shaw,** Eric W '71 SrCnsl Paul HJ&W LLP -75 E 55th -NY 10022
(607) 723-5408 ..**Shaw,** Frank C '46 (Shaw OC&R) -55 Main -Bnghmtn 13905
(212) 474-1000 ..**Shaw,** Gregory M '82 (Cravath S&M LLP) -825 8th Av -NY 10019
(718) 472-8232 ..**Shaw,** Gregory P '84 %Schl Cnstrctn Auth -30-30 Thomson Av -LIC 11101 **Fx:**472-8088
(212) 788-0120 ..**Shaw,** Heather M '91 %Mayor's Ofc -100 Gold -NY 10038 **Fx:**788-0070
(212) 298-5174 ..**Shaw,** Irwin '69 %Leg Aid -49 Thomas -NY 10013 **Fx:**298-5252
(716) 648-3020 ..**Shaw,** James M '74 Shaw & S -4819 S Park Av -Hambrg 14075 **Fx:**648-3730
(518) 828-9444 ..**Shaw,** Jason L '81 (Rapport MWS&R,LLP) -436 Union -Hudson 12534
(212) 349-5506 ..**Shaw,** Jeffrey '79 -15 Maiden Ln -NY 10038 **Fx:**385-4661
(718) 590-2000 ..**Shaw,** Jennifer L '05 %DA -198 E 161st -Bronx 10451 **Fx:**590-6477
(212) 267-9222 ..**Shaw,** John M '91 (Gorayeb & Assoc,PC) -100 William -NY 10038 **Fx:**962-5418
(716) 648-3020 ..**Shaw,** Jos H '76 (Shaw & S) -4819 S Park Av -Hambrg 14075 **Fx:**648-3730
(845) 486-4200 ..**Shaw,** Julie M '08 %Shaw PM&L,LLP -21 Van Wagner Rd -Poughkeepsie 12603
(845) 463-1220 ..**Shaw,** Kayan S '92 -234 Wilbur Blvd -Poughkeepsie 12603
(718) 284-6737 ..**Shaw,** Kenneth R '81 -25 Parade Pl -Brklyn 11226
(607) 273-0300 ..**Shaw,** Kristine M '02 -122 S Cayuga -Ithaca 14850
(914) 428-8288 ..**Shaw,** Laurence '92 -75 S Bway -White Plns 10601 **Fx:**428-8181
(212) 837-3612 ..**Shaw,** Lin J '96 JP Morgan Chase -530 5th Av -NY 10036
(585) 546-8430 ..**Shaw,** Linda R '92 (Knauf S LLP) -2 State -Rchstr 14614
(212) 751-2700 ..**Shaw,** Margaret L '73 %JAMS -620 8th Av -NY 10018 **Fx:**751-4099
(212) 279-4490 ..**Shaw,** Martin '80 -350 5th Av -NY 10118
(212) 635-2730 ..**Shaw,** Matthew G '85 Neville P LLP -17 State -NY 10004
(518) 439-7415 ..**Shaw,** Melanie '83 Policy Research -345 Delaware Av -Delmar 12054
(212) 272-7488 ..**Shaw,** Melissa S '04 %JP Morgan Chase -383 Mad Av -NY 10179
(212) 849-7000 ..**Shaw,** Meredith M '07 %Quinn EU&S,LLP -51 Mad Av -NY 10010
(718) 250-2000 ..**Shaw,** Michl E '08 %DA -350 Jay -Brklyn 11201 **Fx:**250-2314
(212) 546-4000 ..**Shaw,** Michl H '96 Bristol-Myers Squibb -345 Park Av -NY 10154 **Fx:**546-9562
(212) 448-1100 ..**Shaw,** Norman '59 (McLaughlin & S,LLP) -260 Mad Av -NY 10016
(607) 723-5408 ..**Shaw O'Brien Crowley & Reynolds** -55 Main -Bnghmtn 13905 **Fx:**723-6745
(212) 751-5959 ..**Shaw,** Patrick J C '99 (Ehrenkranz & E,LLP) -375 Park Av -NY 10152 **Fx:**754-1905
(845) 486-4200 ..**Shaw Perelson May & Lambert, LLP** -21 Van Wagner Rd -Poughkeepsie 12603 **Fx:**486-4268
(914) 741-9870 ..**Shaw Perelson May & Lambert, LLP** -115 Stevens Av -Valhalla 10595 **Fx:**741-9875
(212) 788-0583 ..**Shaw,** Peter J '83 %Law Dept -100 Church -NY 10007 **Fx:**788-0367
(212) 545-4000 ..**Shaw,** Ravindra K '07 %Jackson L LLP -666 3rd Av -NY 10017
(607) 723-3551 ..**Shaw,** Richd H '79 Security Mtl Life -Bx1625 -Bnghmtn 13902 **Fx:**772-2114
(716) 656-1272 ..**Shaw,** Richd R '00 -3099 William -Buffalo 14227
(212) 513-7788 ..**Shaw,** Robt A '73 (Ahmuty D&M) -123 William -NY 10038
(212) 768-6700 ..**Shaw,** Robt B '07 %Sonnenschein N&R LLP -2 World Fncl Ctr -NY 10281
(914) 328-1222 ..**Shaw,** Robt W '77 -146 Davis Av -White Plns 10605 **Fx:**686-3820
(518) 346-4249 ..**Shaw,** Ronald R '68 (McGivern S&O) -207 Mohawk Av -Scotia 12302
(212) 699-8427 ..**Shaw,** Stefanie P '98 %Van Wagner Comm,LLC -800 3rd Av -NY 10022
(212) 348-9009 ..**Shaw,** Steven A '95 -106 W 69th -NY 10023
(315) 471-3151 ..**Shaw,** Steven R '83 (Hancock & E,LLP) -1500 AXA Twr I Bx4976 -Syracuse 13221
(212) 481-9011 ..**Shaw,** Stuart F '73 (Shaw & B) -9 E 40th -NY 10016
(212) 661-6750 ..**Shaw,** Stuart R '69 -30 W 95th -NY 10025 **Fx:**661-6594
(845) 340-3248 ..**Shaw,** Susan '79 Ulster Cnty Cthse -285 Wall -Kingston 12401
(212) 318-3000 ..**Shaw,** Theo M '80 OfCnsl Fulbright & J LLP -666 5th Av -NY 10103
(315) 445-9894 ..**Shaw,** Thos Elmer '73 -6315 Fly Rd -E Syracuse 13057
(212) 701-3000 ..**Shaw,** Vernicka L '10 %Cahill G&R LLP -80 Pine -NY 10005 **Fx:**269-5420
(212) 788-1154 ..**Shaw,** Warren W '84 %Law Dept -100 Church -NY 10007 **Fx:**788-0367
(607) 273-2900 ..**Shaw,** Wm R '74 (Shaw Law Firm) -109 E Seneca -Ithaca 14850 **Fx:**273-2933
(518) 457-2411 ..**Shawhan,** Peter B '79 %DOT -50 Wolf Rd -Albany 12232 **Fx:**457-4021
(212) 841-1000 ..**Shaw-Lorello,** Loretta '95 (Covington & B LLP) -620 8th Av -NY 10018
(516) 562-5000 ..**Shaw-Lorenzo,** Karen M '96 %CMP Media LLC -600 Community Dr -Manhsst 11030 **Fx:**562-7123
(212) 403-1000 ..**Shawn,** Brett K '10 %Wachtell LR&K -51 W 52nd -NY 10019
(212) 605-6200 ..**Shawn,** Erik L '96 %Levy P&K,LLP -800 3rd Av -NY 10022
(845) 791-7676 ..**Shawn,** Henri '73 -30 North Bx1320 -Monticello 12701 **Fx:**791-4660
(212) 880-1475 ..**Shay,** Carrie A '96 Chicago Title Ins Co -711 3rd Av -NY 10017
(212) 403-1000 ..**Shay,** Christina T '09 %Wachtell LR&K -51 W 52nd -NY 10019
(516) 285-1000 ..**Shay,** Denise M '92 (Barry & S) -700 Elmont Rd -Elmont 11003
(914) 533-2633 ..**Shay,** John J Jr. '73 -94G Tribrook Dr -S Salem 10590
(914) 772-6435 ..**Shay,** Lori A '91 -38 Eastvw Av -Plsntvll 10570 **Fx:**747-6798
(516) 228-8400 ..**Shay & Maguire LLP** -1900 Hempstd Tpk -E Meadow 11554 **Fx:**228-8415
(516) 228-8400 ..**Shay,** Michl E '75 (Shay & M LLP) -1900 Hempstd Tpk -E Meadow 11554
(516) 747-1100 ..**Shayne Dachs Corker Sauer & Dachs** -114 Old Cntry Rd -Mineola 11501 **Fx:**747-1185
(212) 341-7900 ..**Shayne,** Douglas E '01 Brecher FPWT&Z,PC -233 Bway -NY 10279
(212) 566-4949 ..**Shayne,** Wm C '82 (Shayne Law Grp,PC) -64 Fulton -NY 10038 **Fx:**202-5423
(914) 390-8035 ..**Shea,** Allison '90 %NYPA -123 Main -White Plns 10601 **Fx:**390-8038
(212) 237-1000 ..**Shea,** Edw E '61 (Windels ML&M,LLP) -156 W 56th -NY 10019
(516) 229-6000 ..**Shea,** Elizabeth M '94 %R Lau & Assoc -300 Jericho Quad Bx9040 -Jericho 11753 **Fx:**229-6167
(516) 766-7966 ..**Shea,** Gerald B '80 -78 Yale Pl -Rockvll Ctr 11570
(212) 572-6269 ..**Shea,** Gerald C '91 Shea & S -300 Park Av -NY 10022 **Fx:**935-1377
(631) 979-3000 ..**Shea,** J Timothy Jr. '93 %Certilman BA&H,LLP -1393 Vets Mem'l Hwy -Hauppauge 11788
(212) 558-4000 ..**Shea,** James M '10 %Sullivan & C LLP -125 Broad -NY 10004
(914) 969-2300 ..**Shea,** James P '63 J Shea -116 Hllywd Av -Ynkrs 10707
(716) 885-3500 ..**Shea,** James P '63 (Flaherty & S) -329 Elmwood Av -Buffalo 14222 **Fx:**885-3505
(212) 309-1000 ..**Shea,** James W '62 SrCnsl Hunton & W -200 Park Av -NY 10166
(516) 741-6565 ..**Shea,** Janice Whelan '92 %Meyer SE&K,PC -990 Stewart Av Bx9194 -Gdn Cty 11530
(631) 727-2180 ..**Shea,** John F III '73 (Twomey LSKD&Q,LLP) -33 W 2nd Bx9398 -Rvrhead 11901
(518) 693-6839 ..**Shea,** John L '80 -445 Bway -Saratoga Spgs 12866 **Fx:**693-6840
(631) 271-4319 ..**Shea,** John M '92 -42 Woodbury Rd -Huntngtn 11743 **Fx:**271-5873
(212) 929-8628 ..**Shea,** Kevin C '97 Municipal Expediting -15 Maiden Ln -NY 10038
(646) 943-8382 ..**Shea,** Michl J '09 Linkshare Corp -215 Park Av -NY 10003
(315) 476-3101 ..**Shea,** Noreen A '90 %VNA of CNY -1050 W Genesee -Syracuse 13204
(212) 318-6000 ..**Shea,** Patrick W '08 (Paul HJ&W LLP) -75 E 55th -NY 10022
(212) 940-8800 ..**Shea,** Peter J '08 (Katten MR LLP) -575 Mad Av -NY 10022
(212) 754-5579 ..**Shea,** Richd M '86 %BlackRock -40 E 52nd -NY 10022
(212) 336-2000 ..**Shea,** Robt B '55 OfCnsl Patterson BW&T LLP -1133 Av of Amer -NY 10036
(518) 486-5152 ..**Shea,** Sean P '81 %DHCR -38-40 State -Albany 12207
(518) 474-4453 ..**Shea,** Sheila E '87 %MHLS -40 Steuben -Albany 12207 **Fx:**473-5849
(607) 257-5165 ..**Shea Stokes, ALC** -1405 Hanshaw Rd -Ithaca 14850 **Fx:**257-6293
(631) 821-6500 ..**Shea,** Thos C '72 -27 Valley Dr -Sound Bch 11789
(718) 990-6625 ..**Shea,** Thos F '61 %St John's Law Schl -8000 Utopia Pkwy -Jamaica 11439 **Fx:**591-1855
(845) 294-3765 ..**Shea,** Veronica A '79 -11 Webster Av Bx244 -Goshen 10924 **Fx:**294-6852
(212) 869-2147 ..**Shea,** Virginia T '89 %Carlet GK&Z -645 5th Av -NY 10022
(917) 301-0980 ..**Shea,** Wm A '96 Hilltop Private Equity Prtnrs -240 Milton Rd -Rye 10580
(212) 420-9160 ..**Sheaffer,** Jennifer A '02 Artists Rights Society -536 Bway -NY 10012
(212) 756-2000 ..**Sheaffer,** Valerie L '98 %Schulte R&Z LLP -919 3rd Av -NY 10022
(516) 694-3000 ..**Sheahan,** John P '95 (Guercio & G,LLP) -77 Conklin -Farmngdl 11735 **Fx:**694-4738
(516) 487-1602 ..**Sheahan,** Timothy P '05 Zaccaria & S -175 E Shore Rd -Gt Neck 11023
(212) 335-4500 ..**Shea Harwick,** Megan '01 %DLA Piper LLP -1251 Av of Amer -NY 10020
(212) 848-4000 ..**Shearer,** Anna '08 %Shearman & S LLP -599 Lex Av -NY 10022
(518) 533-3000 ..**Shearer,** Carolyn '80 SrCnsl Bond S&K,PLLC -111 Wshngtn Av -Albany 12210
(212) 750-4949 ..**Shearer,** David M '88 (Shearer & E,LLP) -50 Bway -NY 10004
(212) 661-4200 ..**Shearer,** Douglas A '92 (McKeegan & S,PC) -192 Lex Av -NY 10016
(212) 750-4949 ..**Shearer & Essner,LLP** -50 Bway -NY 10004 **Fx:**324-9292
(212) 574-1200 ..**Shearer,** Justin L '08 %Seward & K LLP -1 Bttry Pk Plz -NY 10004
(212) 848-4000 ..**Shearman & Sterling LLP** -599 Lex Av -NY 10022 **Fx:**848-7179
(212) 848-4000 ..**Shearn,** Catherine C '10 Shearman & S LLP -599 Lex Av -NY 10022

(212) 756-2000 .. **Sheats,** Brett D '10 %Schulte R&Z LLP -919 3rd Av -NY 10022
(315) 676-7314 .. **Sheats,** Edw J Jr. '84 SrCnsl Sheats & Assoc,PC -9650 Brewertn Rd Bx820 -Brewertn 13029 **Fx:**676-7189
(516) 785-6300 .. **Shebar,** Jonathan '93 -3296 Waterbury Dr -Wantagh 11793 **Fx:**785-6333
(212) 996-7715 .. **Shebar,** Mathew J '83 -178 E 88th -NY 10128
(212) 331-2564 .. **Shebar,** Steven M '92 Universal Music Grp -1755 Bway -NY 10019 **Fx:**331-2582
(212) 832-2797 .. **Shebitz Berman & Cohen,PC** -1325 Av of Amer -NY 10019 **Fx:**832-2782
(212) 267-3091 .. **Shechter,** Amanda F '92 Cnsl Wilentz G&S -110 William -NY 10038 **Fx:**(732) 726-4765
(212) 930-9700 .. **Shechter,** Jonathan R '07 %Sichenzia RFF LLP -61 Bway -NY 10006
(212) 270-7689 .. **Shechter,** Judah Aryeh '90 JP Morgan Chase -277 Park Av -NY 10172
(212) 223-0200 .. **Shechtman,** Paul '89 (Stillman F&S,PC) -425 Park Av -NY 10022
(212) 421-4100 .. **Shechtman,** Ronald H '73 (Pryor C LLP) -7 Times Sq -NY 10036
(215) 241-5471 .. **Shecter,** Howard L '96 (Reed S LLP) -599 Lex Av -NY 10022 **Fx:**(212) 521-5471
(212) 819-8200 .. **Shecter,** Sean P '09 %White & C LLP -1155 Av of Amer -NY 10036
(212) 736-4500 .. **Shectman,** Alan M '95 (Nesenoff & M,LLP) -363 7th Av -NY 10001
(212) 545-7373 .. **Shectman,** Rory M '98 %K Wilhelm -445 Park Av -NY 10022 **Fx:**545-9093
(212) 779-1779 .. **Shed,** James T '81 Comm on Character & Fitness -41 Mad Av -NY 10010
(212) 248-3140 .. **Shedd,** Adam M '04 %Drinker B&R LLP -140 Bway -NY 10005
(718) 544-8881 .. **Shedlo,** Leah Zahava '01 (Kleinman & S) -14415 Melbourne Av -Flushng 11367 **Fx:**544-7281
(212) 225-2000 .. **Shedlosky,** Eric C '09 %Cleary GS&H -1 Lbrty Plz -NY 10006
(212) 679-0505 .. **Shedrinsky,** Mikhail A '00 (Bekker Law Group PC) -233 5th Av -NY 10016 **Fx:**679-0502
(212) 620-2680 .. **Sheeber,** Samantha '94 (Starr Assoc LLP) -245 5th Av -NY 10016 **Fx:**696-5013
(516) 513-1016 .. **Sheeckutz,** Wm A '86 -898 N Bway -Massapequa 11758 **Fx:**977-9655
(212) 790-4500 .. **Sheehan,** Amy T '05 %Manatt P&P,LLP -7 Times Sq -NY 10036
(212) 220-3830 .. **Sheehan,** Barbara A '85 (Nicoletti H&S) -88 Pine -NY 10005
(212) 839-8652 .. **Sheehan,** Bartholomew A III '96 (Sidley A LLP) -787 7th Av -NY 10019
(631) 844-7800 .. **Sheehan,** Brendan R '93 %Olsten Corp -175 Broadhllw Rd -Melvll 11747 **Fx:**844-7414
(518) 474-7330 .. **Sheehan,** Cathy Y '07 %Dept of Law -The Cptl -Albany 12224
(212) 850-8500 .. **Sheehan,** Danl J '02 %Bruckmann & V,LLP -420 Lex Av -NY 10170
(516) 877-5600 .. **Sheehan,** Darren E '01 %R Tusa -1225 Franklin Av -Gdn Cty 11530 **Fx:**877-5695
(212) 589-4200 .. **Sheehan,** David J '02 (Baker & H LLP) -45 Rckfllr Plz -NY 10111
(646) 386-3032 .. **Sheehan,** David L III '76 Supreme Ct Motions Support Ofc -60 Centre -NY 10007
(845) 358-4460 .. **Sheehan,** Deborah A '87 Sheehan & S -1 Piermont Av -Nyack 10960 **Fx:**358-6623
(518) 456-5644 .. **Sheehan,** Deborah Hardick '87 -20 W Meadow Dr -Albany 12203 **Fx:**456-4512
(212) 720-3700 .. **Sheehan,** Dennis E '80 %Foot Locker,Inc -112 W 34th -NY 10120 **Fx:**720-4116
(607) 723-1990 .. **Sheehan,** Dennis P '77 (Hickey S&G) -160 Hawley Bx2124 -Bnghmtn 13902
(516) 735-1100 .. **Sheehan,** Dennis P '93 -216 Wantage Av -Levittwn 11756
(718) 248-9095 .. **Sheehan,** Diane Marie '75 Citibank -1 Court Sq -LIC 11101
(212) 751-3001 .. **Sheehan,** E Michl '06 (Thompson & K LLP) -919 3rd Av -NY 10022
(518) 462-0110 .. **Sheehan Greene Carraway Golderman & Jacques LLP** -54 State -Albany 12207 **Fx:**462-5260
(845) 338-4993 .. **Sheehan,** Heather K '94 OfCnsl Wilkie & G LLC -78 Main Bx4148 -Kingston 12402
(518) 436-0751 .. **Sheehan,** Jennifer Bassett '08 (Hinman S PC) -121 State -Albany 12207
(212) 790-4500 .. **Sheehan,** Jeremiah P '76 (Manatt P&P,LLP) -7 Times Sq -NY 10036
(212) 351-0000 .. **Sheehan,** Jeremiah P '99 Sithe Golbal Power,LLC -245 Park Av -NY 10167 **Fx:**351-0880
(716) 854-2020 .. **Sheehan,** John A '90 (Cellino & B,PC) -350 Main -Buffalo 14202
(646) 557-5100 .. **Sheehan,** John D '05 %Patton B LLP -1185 Av of Amer -NY 10036
(212) 859-7189 .. **Sheehan,** John F '84 %Fortis,Inc -1 Chase Manh Plz -NY 10005 **Fx:**859-7202
(718) 278-5000 .. **Sheehan,** John J '63 -45-02 Bway -LIC 11103 **Fx:**274-5670
(212) 384-1000 .. **Sheehan,** John L '89 %FBI -26 Fed Plz -NY 10278
(518) 664-7311 .. **Sheehan,** Jos W '79 Sheehan & S -706 Grand Bx9 -Mechanicvll 12118 **Fx:**664-4852
(516) 741-2585 .. **Sheehan,** Karen M '92 %Rosicki R & Assoc,PC -51 E Bethpage Rd -Plainvw 11803 **Fx:**741-4748
(518) 782-1122 .. **Sheehan,** Katherine Moran '95 Intermagnetics Genrl -450 Old Niskayuna Rd Bx461 -Latham 12110 **Fx:**783-2602
(516) 741-2585 .. **Sheehan,** Kenneth M '94 %Rosicki R & Assoc,PC -51 E Bethpage Rd -Plainvw 11803 **Fx:**741-4748
(914) 428-1438 .. **Sheehan,** Kimberly C '85 %T Bona,PC -123 Main -White Plns 10601 **Fx:**428-1413
(718) 401-7724 .. **Sheehan,** Lawr J '84 -840 Grnd Cncrs -Bronx 10451
(212) 649-2000 .. **Sheehan,** Maureen Walsh '90 %Hearst Corp -300 W 57th -NY 10019 **Fx:**649-2035
(607) 326-3206 .. **Sheehan,** Michl H '76 -Brdg Bx121 -Roxbury 12474 **Fx:**326-4611
(718) 243-6825 .. **Sheehan,** Monica F '86 %Leg Aid -111 Lvngstn -Brklyn 11201 **Fx:**237-8737
(716) 886-8200 .. **Sheehan,** Nancy J '95 %Brylin Hospitals, Inc -1263 Delaware Av -Buffalo 14209 **Fx:**886-1986
(212) 447-7070 .. **Sheehan,** Patrick J '00 %Whatley D&K LLC -1540 Bway -NY 10036
(212) 460-2195 .. **Sheehan,** Philip H Jr. '93 ConEd -4 Irving Pl -NY 10003
(718) 747-2137 .. **Sheehan,** Rebecca A '94 Cnsl Cncl T Avella -38-50 Bell Blvd -Bayside 11361
(212) 735-3000 .. **Sheehan,** Robt C '70 (Skadden ASM&F LLP) -4 Times Sq -NY 10036
(212) 696-6000 .. **Sheehan,** Robt W '75 (Curtis M-PC&M LLP) -101 Park Av -NY 10178
(212) 425-7200 .. **Sheehan,** Ryan J '08 %Kenyon & K,LLP -1 Bway -NY 10004
(212) 416-8000 .. **Sheehan,** Stephanie Alpert '06 %Dept of Law -120 Bway -NY 10271
(212) 417-4357 .. **Sheehan,** Terrence J '76 %Dept of Health -90 Church -NY 10007 **Fx:**417-4392
(212) 489-1600 .. **Sheehan,** Thos C '97 %Deloitte LLP -1633 Bway -NY 10019 **Fx:**492-4201
(716) 847-8400 .. **Sheehan,** Thos J '01 (Phillips L LLP) -3400 HSBC Ctr -Buffalo 14203
(212) 490-3000 .. **Sheehan,** Timothy J '85 (Wilson EME&D LLP) -150 E 42nd -NY 10017
(914) 323-7000 .. **Sheehan,** Timothy J '85 (Wilson EME&D LLP) -3 Gannett Dr -White Plns 10604
(914) 681-6200 .. **Sheehan,** Timothy P '80 NYPA -123 Main -White Plns 10601 **Fx:**390-8038
(585) 377-2810 .. **Sheehan,** Timothy P '93 Midwest Inc -200 Cross Keys Ofc Pk -Fairprt 14450
(516) 694-3000 .. **Sheehan,** Vanessa M '77 (Guercio & G,LLP) -77 Conklin -Farmngdl 11735 **Fx:**694-4738
(212) 455-2000 .. **Sheehan,** Wm B '97 (Simpson T&B LLP) -425 Lex Av -NY 10017
(518) 462-0110 .. **Sheehan,** Wm F '75 (Sheehan GCG&J LLP) -54 State -Albany 12207
(212) 525-4701 .. **Sheehan,** Wm J '89 Wealth & Tax Advsr Srvcs -452 5th Av -NY 10018
(212) 819-8200 .. **Sheehan,** Zita M '03 %White & C LLP -1155 Av of Amer -NY 10036
(212) 732-3200 .. **Sheehy,** Catherine B '07 %Carter L&M LLP -2 Wall -NY 10005
(516) 794-7500 .. **Sheehy,** Christopher J '91 (Westermann SKS&A,LLP) -333 Earle Ovngton Blvd -Uniondale 11553
(212) 384-1000 .. **Sheehy,** Gregory J '97 FBI -26 Fed Plz -NY 10278
(212) 422-0700 .. **Sheeley,** Andrew T '04 %Gerspach S LLP -59 Maiden Ln -NY 10038 **Fx:**545-4095
(212) 513-3200 .. **Sheely,** Sean C '94 (Holland & K LLP) -31 W 52nd -NY 10019
(315) 426-7435 .. **Sheen,** Margaret Ann '97 %DEC -615 Erie Blvd W -Syracuse 13204 **Fx:**426-7408
(516) 338-7800 .. **Sheena,** Michl S '06 (Radow Law Grp PC) -1010 Nrthrn Blvd -Gt Neck 11021 **Fx:**338-2549
(631) 694-2300 .. **Sheena,** Rita F '81 Cnsl Lamb & B,LLP -534 Broadhllw Rd Bx9034 -Melvll 11747
(914) 761-9111 .. **Sheer,** Norman '68 (Bank SS&H) -399 Knollwood Rd -White Plns 10603
(914) 698-3313 .. **Sheer,** Seth A '75 %Lichtenstein & S -158 W Bstn Post Rd -Mamaroneck 10543
(607) 721-8623 .. **Sheerin,** Denise M '92 %Ct of Claims -44 Hawley -Bnghmtn 13901 **Fx:**721-8590
(516) 656-5300 .. **Sheerin,** John J '93 (Mullooly JR&F LLP) -6851 Jericho Tpk Bx9036 -Syosset 11791
(516) 248-3494 .. **Sheerin,** Kevin P '94 -323 Willis Av -Mineola 11501 **Fx:**248-2808
(212) 272-7458 .. **Sheers,** Alexander M '84 %JP Morgan Chase -383 Mad Av -NY 10179
(212) 818-9600 .. **Sheetz,** Jeffrey H '77 %Greenfield S&S,LLP -600 3rd Av -NY 10016
(718) 780-7963 .. **Sheetz,** Megan L '99 Brooklyn Law Schl -250 Joralemon -Brklyn 11201
(212) 704-6000 .. **Shef,** Michl J '66 (Troutman S LLP) -405 Lex Av -NY 10174
(212) 201-8242 .. **Sheff,** Gary I '91 SHL Invstmt Grp USA Inc -11 W 42nd -NY 10036
(718) 990-5504 .. **Sheff,** Jeremy N '03 St John's Law Schl -8000 Utopia Pkwy -Jamaica 11439 **Fx:**591-1855
(917) 434-4343 .. **Sheff,** Jesse J K '07 Apartmenities LLC -405 Lex Av -NY 10174
(516) 482-5423 .. **Sheffer,** Abner '64 -7 Piccadilly Rd -Gt Neck 11023
(716) 634-6750 .. **Sheffer,** John B II '74 (Sheffer M&W) -6461 Main -Williamsvll 14221
(716) 634-6750 .. **Sheffer Murphy & White** -6461 Main -Williamsvll 14221 **Fx:**634-5642
(716) 759-1500 .. **Sheffer Murphy & White** -10535 Main -Clarence 14031
(212) 813-3700 .. **Sheffi-Coussin,** Halit '01 Pershing Sq Cptl Mgmt,LP -888 7th Av -NY 10106
(716) 488-0758 .. **Sheffield,** Lanny R '77 (Bly SBP&M) -3 Lakevw Av Bx3327 -Jamestwn 14702
(212) 446-4800 .. **Sheffield-Whitehead,** Kristin I '09 %Kirkland & E LLP -153 E 53rd -NY 10022
(212) 408-5100 .. **Sheffler,** Bruce G '83 (Chadbourne & P LLP) -30 Rckfllr Plz -NY 10112
(516) 379-3593 .. **Sheffler,** Steven P '80 -1286 Grand Av -Baldwin 11510 **Fx:**379-3594
(212) 804-4200 .. **Sheft,** Leonard A '56 OfCnsl Mound CW&G -One Bttry Pk Plz -NY 10004
(631) 284-2461 .. **Sheh,** Tomson S '63 Chicago Title Ins -901 E Main -Rvrhead 11901
(212) 839-5300 .. **Shehan,** Mark T '75 Cnsl Sidley A LLP -787 7th Av -NY 10019
(212) 825-1565 .. **Shehi,** Christina M '99 %Ptashnik & Assoc -45 Bway -NY 10006 **Fx:**825-1559
(518) 486-4504 .. **Shehigian,** Donald E '77 %Dept of Law -The Cptl -Albany 12224 **Fx:**474-0862
(212) 412-9500 .. **Shehigian,** Grant A '08 %Flemming ZWZ LLP -1 Lbrty Plz -NY 10006
(516) 296-1000 .. **Sheidlower,** Donna F '85 %Miller & M,PC -100 Q Roosevelt Blvd -Gdn Cty 11530
(718) 459-9000 .. **Sheidlower,** Eric '87 Sweeney GR&B,LLP -95-25 Qns Blvd -Rego Pk 11374
(212) 490-3000 .. **Sheiffer,** David S '88 (Wilson EME&D LLP) -150 E 42nd -NY 10017
(212) 849-8888 .. **Sheikh,** Kashif Zahid '98 Westbrook Prtnrs -645 Mad Av -NY 10022
(212) 696-6000 .. **Sheikh,** Kemal A '87 Cnsl Curtis M-PC&M LLP -101 Park Av -NY 10178
(212) 594-5000 .. **Sheikh,** Lara R '02 %Togut S&S LLP -1 Penn Plz -NY 10119
(212) 735-3000 .. **Sheikh,** Naved '10 %Skadden ASM&F LLP -4 Times Sq -NY 10036
(914) 767-6673 .. **Sheikh,** Rabia Q '04 %Pepsi Bottling Grp -1 Pepsi Way -Somers 10589
(212) 564-1619 .. **Sheikh,** Salim '93 -875 Av of Amer -NY 10001 **Fx:**564-3158
(212) 609-6800 .. **Sheil,** James C '01 %McCarter & E,LLP -245 Park Av -NY 10167
(212) 753-0300 .. **Sheils,** J Stephen '67 Cnsl Dahan & N LLP -1700 Bway -NY 10019
(516) 922-6626 .. **Shein,** Jeffrey S '84 (J Shein & Assoc,PC) -575 Underhill Blvd -Syosset 11791 **Fx:**922-2797
(212) 687-1600 .. **Sheinbaum,** James B '80 (Borstein & S) -420 Lex Av -NY 10170
(718) 852-8282 .. **Sheinberg,** George '61 -50 Court -Brklyn 11201 **Fx:**852-6086

(718) 852-8270 .. **Sheinberg**, Joy A '91 -50 Court -Brklyn 11201
(718) 852-0079 .. **Sheinberg**, Michl A '91 -50 Court -Brklyn 11201 **Fx**:852-8270
(646) 471-2596 .. **Sheinberg**, Rebecca A '04 PricewaterhouseCoopers LLP -300 Mad Av -NY 10017 **Fx**:(813) 990-1572
(631) 234-3030 .. **Sheinberg**, Wendy H '92 (Davidow DS&S,LLP) -1601 Vets Mem'l Hwy -Islandia 11749
(212) 625-8030 .. **Sheindlin**, Gregory E '90 (Sheindlin & S LLP) -350 Bway -NY 10013 **Fx**:202-4378
(212) 595-3782 .. **Sheiner**, Naomi F '79 -127 W 79th -NY 10024
(212) 918-3000 .. **Sheinfeld**, Ira S '85 (Hogan L LLP) -875 3rd Av -NY 10022
(212) 558-4000 .. **Sheinfeld**, Jennifer M '05 %Sullivan & C LLP -125 Broad -NY 10004
(212) 294-6700 .. **Sheinfeld**, Stephen L '84 (Winston & S) -200 Park Av -NY 10166
(212) 610-6300 .. **Sheinfeld**, Yaakov Y '07 %Allen & O -1221 Av of Amer -NY 10020
(518) 474-8890 .. **Sheingold**, Kathryn J '95 %Dept of Law -The Cptl -Albany 12224 **Fx**:486-3176
(518) 474-1010 .. **Sheingold**, Nelson R '95 %Ofc Inspector Genl -ESP Agncy Bldg 2 -Albany 12223 **Fx**:486-3745
(212) 806-5400 .. **Sheinkin**, Adam H '03 %Stroock &S&L LLP -180 Maiden Ln -NY 10038
(212) 583-9600 .. **Sheinkin**, Sara D '06 %Littler M,PC -900 3rd Av -NY 10022
(212) 357-4282 .. **Sheinman**, Kenneth R '97 Goldman Sachs & Co -180 Maiden Ln -NY 10038
(212) 612-4619 .. **Sheinmel**, Courtney L '03 Chubb Grp -55 Water -NY 10041
(516) 747-6700 .. **Sheinwald**, Steven B '83 (Kirschenbaum & K) -200 Grdn City Plz -Gdn Cty 11530 **Fx**:747-6781
(516) 496-5822 .. **Sheinwald**, Warren M '07 %T Spina -170 Froehlich Farm Blvd -Woodbury 11797 **Fx**:496-5420
(631) 755-0101 .. **Sheinwold**, Marcy D '88 (Lewis JAA,LLP) -425 Broad Hollow Rd -Melvll 11747
(718) 654-1400 .. **Sheiowitz**, Gerald L '69 -1067 Allerton Av -Bronx 10469 **Fx**:405-9819
(845) 362-1092 .. **Sheivachman**, Mark '75 -9 Emerald Dr -Pomona 10970
(212) 997-7595 .. **Shelanski**, Noah E '07 %Hafetz N&R -500 5th Av -NY 10110
(212) 751-2700 .. **Shelanski**, Vivien B '85 %JAMS -620 8th Av -NY 10018 **Fx**:751-4099
(716) 839-4622 .. **Shelby**, Kevin P '88 (Shelby B&W) -5662 Main -Williamsvll 14221 **Fx**:631-7546
(716) 626-3534 .. **Sheldon**, Donald P '60 -300 Intl Dr -Williamsvll 14221 **Fx**:626-3001
(716) 847-0650 .. **Sheldon**, James R Jr. '79 %Leg Srvcs -237 Main -Buffalo 14203 **Fx**:847-0227
(212) 687-2777 .. **Sheldon**, Kimberly L '06 %Levine & S -60 E 42nd -NY 10165
(212) 657-5273 .. **Sheldon**, Marcia D '81 %Citigroup -111 Wall -NY 10005
(212) 715-9100 .. **Sheldon**, Marjorie E '94 SpclCnsl Kramer LN&F,LLP -1177 Av of Amer -NY 10036
(212) 804-4200 .. **Sheldon**, Scott J '09 OfCnsl Mound CW&G -One Bttry Pk Plz -NY 10004
(212) 572-6238 .. **Sheldrick**, Andrew W '81 Sheldrick Intl -300 Park Av -NY 10022
(718) 260-2513 .. **Sheley**, Karen Ann '05 Hon D Trager -225 Cadman Plz E -Brklyn 11201
(212) 732-3200 .. **Shelinsky**, Pamela S '06 %Carter L&M LLP -2 Wall -NY 10005
(212) 264-7500 .. **Shelkin**, Scott P '83 (Baron & S,PC) -291 Bway -NY 10007
(212) 548-2100 .. **Shelko**, Loree J '97 %McGuire W LLP -1345 Av of Amer -NY 10105
(585) 781-5822 .. **Sheller**, Patrick M '87 %Eastman Kodak -343 State -Rchstr 14650
(646) 282-3382 .. **Shelley**, Anne-Marie '93 Accretive Technology Prtnrs -51 Mad Av -NY 10010
(212) 732-3200 .. **Shelley**, Heywood '50 Cnsl Carter L&M LLP -2 Wall -NY 10005
(212) 755-3100 .. **Shelley**, Kevin M '93 (Kaufmann GR&O LLP) -777 3rd Av -NY 10017
(516) 409-6200 .. **Shelley**, Patrick J '03 %Furey KWM&C,PC -2174 Jackson Av -Seafrd 11783
(212) 849-7000 .. **Shelley**, Scott C '94 %Quinn EU&S,LLP -51 Mad Av -NY 10010
(212) 792-4911 .. **Shellow**, Jill R '00 -111 Bway -NY 10006 **Fx**:792-4946
(212) 808-7800 .. **Shelly**, Jason E '09 %Kelley D&W LLP -101 Park Av -NY 10178
(518) 434-0600 .. **Shelly**, Jeffrey S '92 Cnsl Boies S&F LLP -10 N Pearl -Albany 12207
(631) 476-7577 .. **Shelmidine**, Jody Alton '03 %Geisler & G,LLP -417 E Main -Pt Jffrsn 11777
(212) 655-9384 .. **Shelowitz**, Mitchell C '92 Shelowitz & Assoc,PLLC -450 7th Av -NY 10123
(718) 341-8293 .. **Shelton**, Angela A '99 -168-34 127th Av -Jamaica 11434
(718) 250-2000 .. **Shelton**, Dennis R '08 %DA -350 Jay -Brklyn 11201 **Fx**:250-2314
(716) 992-9300 .. **Shelton**, Eric M '85 (Campbell & S,LLP) -8274 N Main -Eden 14057
(716) 853-3801 .. **Shelton**, Judith Treger '85 (Kenney SL&N,LLP) -14 Lafayette Sq -Buffalo 14203
(516) 463-6150 .. **Shelton**, Kevin B '92 Hofstra Univ Law Schl -121 Hofstra Univ -Hempstd 11549
(845) 338-6496 .. **Shelton**, Lawr R '78 -261 Fair -Kingston 12401 **Fx**:338-3126
(212) 425-7200 .. **Shelton**, Lee B '97 %Kenyon & K,LLP -1 Bway -NY 10004
(212) 878-3423 .. **Shelton**, Steven T '94 Cnsl Clifford C LLP -31 W 52nd -NY 10019
(212) 887-6861 .. **Shelton**, Susan C '00 Heast-Argyle -300 W 57th -NY 10019
(716) 676-2510 .. **Shemeld**, Gregory E '92 -13 Plymouth Av -Franklinvll 14737
(212) 607-3815 .. **Shemie**, Lisa A '97 Banca Intesa SPA -1 William -NY 10004 **Fx**:607-3732
Shemtob, Jack A '83 -195 Nelson Rd -Scarsdale 10583
(212) 244-4187 .. **Shemtob**, Penny '83 (Weingrad & W) -350 5th Av -NY 10118 **Fx**:594-2944
(212) 554-7800 .. **Shem-Tov**, Inbal '03 %Moses & S LLP -405 Lex Av -NY 10174
(212) 455-2000 .. **Shen**, Edw '06 %Simpson T&B LLP -425 Lex Av -NY 10017
(212) 941-2621 .. **Shen**, I C Judy '99 Corcoran Grp Real Estate -490 Bway -NY 10012
(212) 225-2000 .. **Shen**, Jane J '08 %Cleary GS&H -1 Lbrty Plz -NY 10006
(201) 227-8700 .. **Shen**, Jenny J '08 -1133 Bway -NY 10010 **Fx**:227-8701
(718) 888-1006 .. **Shen**, Jianming '02 Shenlaw,LLC -142 North Ct -Roslyn Hts 11577
(212) 425-7200 .. **Shen**, Karen C '08 %Kenyon & K,LLP -1 Bway -NY 10004
(212) 595-5500 .. **Shen**, Michl '80 -55 W End -NY 10023
(212) 230-8895 .. **Shen**, Peter J '04 Cnsl WilmerHale -399 Park Av -NY 10022
(212) 310-8000 .. **Shen**, Shu-Ping '09 %Weil G&M LLP -767 5th Av -NY 10153
(212) 715-9100 .. **Shen**, Terrence L '96 (Kramer LN&F,LLP) -1177 Av of Amer -NY 10036
(718) 237-5500 .. **Shen**, Yanfei '10 Leg Srvcs -105 Court -Brklyn 11201 **Fx**:855-0733
(212) 819-8200 .. **Shenberg**, Michl S '86 (White & C LLP) -1155 Av of Amer -NY 10036
(315) 446-1484 .. **Shende**, Suzanne L '91 -5197 Pnte East Dr -Jamesvll 13078
(718) 222-2032 .. **Shender**, Michl '04 %Law Dept -350 Jay -Brklyn 11201 **Fx**:222-2088
(212) 446-4800 .. **Sheng**, Yi Claire '03 (Kirkland & E LLP) -153 E 53rd -NY 10022
(212) 233-8300 .. **Shenghit**, Clifford R '68 (Epstein & C) -7 Dey -NY 10007
(518) 449-8893 .. **Shenker**, Cynthia D '82 (Wilson EME&D LLP) -677 Bway -Albany 12207
(212) 558-4000 .. **Shenker**, Jos C '81 (Sullivan & C LLP) -125 Broad -NY 10004
(212) 980-2110 .. **Shenker**, Judith J '75 -2 Lincoln Sq -NY 10023
(212) 564-5200 .. **Shenker**, Leon '01 -45 W 34th Bx20155 -NY 10001 **Fx**:504-2797
(516) 683-5687 .. **Shenker**, Michl D '83 %Dept of Treasury -107 Chas Lindbergh Blvd -Gdn Cty 11530
(212) 837-1376 .. **Shenker**, Nina O '83 %JP Morgan Fleming Asset Mgmt -1211 Av of Amer -NY 10036
(212) 608-1870 .. **Shenker**, Robt H '63 -160 Bway -NY 10038 **Fx**:962-7228
(212) 578-2863 .. **Shenkin**, Todd S '96 %MetLife -27-01 Qns Plz N -LIC 11101 **Fx**:251-1673
(212) 374-6765 .. **Shenkman**, Jordana '05 Cnsl NYC Educ Dept -49 Chmbrs -NY 10007
(212) 661-3129 .. **Shenkman**, Martin M '86 -275 Mad Av -NY 10016 **Fx**:(201) 845-8433
(212) 686-4401 .. **Shenkman**, Mitchell B '78 %Abramson Law Grp PLLC -570 Lex Av -NY 10022 **Fx**:686-6515
(212) 661-6000 .. **Shenkman**, Robt J '63 -333 E 38th -NY 10016 **Fx**:481-8209
(212) 667-5652 .. **Shenman**, Rodney L '00 CIBC -300 Mad Av -NY 10017 **Fx**:667-5656
(631) 694-2300 .. **Shenn**, Patrice Dowd '77 (Lamb & B,LLP) -534 Broadhllw Rd Bx9034 -Melvll 11747
(212) 455-2000 .. **Shenoi**, Hema V '10 %Simpson T&B LLP -425 Lex Av -NY 10017
(212) 326-3939 .. **Shentov**, Ognjan V '98 (Jones D) -222 E 41st -NY 10017
(212) 541-6224 .. **Shenwick**, James H '83 Shenwick & Assoc -655 3rd Av -NY 10017 **Fx**:(646) 218-4600
(212) 856-9444 .. **Shepard**, Allyn C '87 -555 5th Av -NY 10017 **Fx**:856-7219
(718) 224-9278 .. **Shepard**, Danl J '87 -67-29 215th -Oakland Gdns 11364
(585) 429-5422 .. **Shepard**, John '80 %Upstate Leg Ctr -Bx60886 -Rchstr 14606
(212) 421-4100 .. **Shepard**, Jonathan T '02 (Pryor C LLP) -7 Times Sq -NY 10036
(516) 229-4200 .. **Shepard**, Martha D '80 Mendolia & S -875 Merrick Av -Westbury 11590
(718) 248-1936 .. **Shepard**, Natasha L '99 Citibank -1 Court Sq -LIC 11120
(212) 575-7900 .. **Shepard**, Robt M '64 (Ballon SB&N,PC) -729 7th Av -NY 10019
(212) 848-4000 .. **Shepard**, Rodrick E '08 %Shearman & S LLP -599 Lex Av -NY 10022
(212) 483-9490 .. **Shepard**, Scott M '79 OfCnsl McElroy DM&C,LLP -88 Pine -NY 10005
(212) 506-2500 .. **Shepard**, Shari A '99 %Mayer B LLP -1675 Bway -NY 10019
(718) 403-3365 .. **Shepard**, Stephanie A '86 KeySpan Corp -1 MetroTech Ctr -Brklyn 11201
(212) 815-1818 .. **Shepard**, Stephen III '89 %DC 37 MELS -125 Barclay -NY 10007 **Fx**:815-1343
(212) 222-1205 .. **Shepard**, Timothy C '88 -685 West End Av -NY 10025
(212) 681-6863 .. **Shepard**, Wm T '94 W Shepard,PC -192 Lex Av -NY 10016 **Fx**:681-4091
(585) 753-4500 .. **Shepard**, Zuleika Z '08 DA -832 Watts Bldg -Rchstr 14614 **Fx**:753-4576
(212) 344-3900 .. **Shepardson**, Marshall J '06 %Belair & E LLP -61 Bway -NY 10006
(631) 351-3291 .. **Shepardson**, Rhonda T '88 Huntington Womens Advsry Cncl -423 Park Av -Huntngtn 11743 **Fx**:351-3221
(518) 487-7600 .. **Shepardson**, Thos A '89 (Whiteman O&H LLP) -1 Commerce Plz -Albany 12260
(914) 747-5907 .. **Shepetuk**, Raymond T '81 -415 Bedford Rd -Plsntvll 10570 **Fx**:747-5905
(315) 433-0100 .. **Shephard**, Thos M '92 Dairylea Cooperative Inc -Bx4844 -Syracuse 13221 **Fx**:433-2345
(212) 588-5500 .. **Shepherd**, Gerald D '90 (Davies WP&V LLP) -625 Mad Av -NY 10022
(212) 336-2000 .. **Shepherd**, Matthew J '04 %Patterson BW&T LLP -1133 Av of Amer -NY 10036
(212) 530-5000 .. **Shepherd**, Michl T '07 %Milbank TH&M LLP -1 Chase Manh Plz -NY 10005
(716) 885-3500 .. **Shepherd**, Robt A '84 -329 Elmwood Av -Buffalo 14222
(914) 592-5740 .. **Shepherd**, Wendell V '81 (Barnes I&S,LLP) -258 Saw Mill Rvr Rd -Elmsfrd 10523
(516) 358-7599 .. **Sheppard**, Brian S '80 -516 N 9th Pl -New Hyde Pk 11040
(212) 974-7474 .. **Sheppard**, J Stephen '69 (Cowan DA&S LLP) -41 Mad Av -NY 10010
(212) 653-8700 .. **Sheppard Mullin Richter & Hampton LLP** -30 Rckfllr Plz -NY 10112 **Fx**:653-8701
(518) 486-1336 .. **Sheppard**, Patricia B '00 %Dept of Health -Corning Twr 24th Fl -Albany 12237 **Fx**:486-4834
(607) 723-5341 .. **Sheppard**, Paul T '88 (Hinman H&K,LLP) -80 Exchange Bx5250 -Bnghmtn 13902
(212) 949-7120 .. **Sheppard**, Ralph H '82 (Meeks & S) -330 Mad Av -NY 10017
(315) 428-8420 .. **Sheppard**, Robt O '86 %Lincoln Life & Annuity -100 Madison -Syracuse 13202
(212) 424-7135 .. **Sheppard**, Susan R '89 %Lifetime TV -309 W 49th -NY 10019 **Fx**:957-4447
(212) 753-2424 .. **Sheppe**, Matthew H '96 (Reiss E LLP) -425 Mad Av -NY 10017
(212) 575-7900 .. **Sheppeard**, Michl J '05 %Ballon SB&N,PC -729 7th Av -NY 10019
(212) 909-9500 .. **Shepps**, Lawr T '99 %Wachtel & M,LLP -885 2nd Av -NY 10017
(212) 404-5777 .. **Shepps**, Wendy B '98 OfCnsl Littleton JUP&K LLP -39 Bway -NY 10006
(212) 575-2683 .. **Shepro**, Jeffrey '07 J Shepro,PC -42 W 38th -NY 10018 **Fx**:575-2684
(212) 986-2260 .. **Sheps**, Elaine R '68 -305 Mad Av -NY 10165
(631) 249-5600 .. **Sheps**, Robt C '96 (Sheps Law Grp,PC) -35 Pinelawn Rd -Melvll 11747 **Fx**:249-5613
(845) 486-4300 .. **Shequine**, Elizabeth K '75 -17 Cllgvw Av -Poughkeepsie 12603 **Fx**:486-4080
(212) 318-6000 .. **Sher**, Barry G '90 (Paul HJ&W LLP) -75 E 55th -NY 10022
(212) 980-9600 .. **Sher**, Brian M '03 %Kaufman B&R -120 Bway -NY 10271
(212) 297-5800 .. **Sher**, Elizabeth J '84 (Day P LLP) -7 Times Sq -NY 10036

(212) 732-8579 .. **Sher Herman Bellone & Tipograph,PC** -277 Bway -NY 10007 **Fx:**349-5910
(212) 336-3500 .. **Sher,** Jeremy M '05 %Miller & W,PC -570 Lex Av -NY 10022
(212) 628-0560 .. **Sher,** Jo Ann G '68 %Merit Operating Corp -351 E 83rd -NY 10028
(212) 202-2600 .. **Sher,** Justin M '01 (Sher LLP) -41 Mad Av -NY 10010 **Fx:**202-4156
(212) 267-9020 .. **Sher,** Laura E '97 %Shapiro B&A LLP -225 Bway -NY 10007
(212) 925-0017 .. **Sher,** Olga '04 %RMTS LLC -6 Harrison -NY 10013 **Fx:**925-8760
(914) 682-0040 .. **Sher,** Ronald A '74 (Himmelfarb & S,LLP) -1 N Bway -White Plns 10601
(212) 732-8579 .. **Sher,** Stanley '59 (Sher HB&T,PC) -277 Bway -NY 10007
(518) 438-1642 .. **Sheraw,** Donald M '69 -215 S Main Av -Albany 12208
(212) 860-8840 .. **Sherbell,** Suzanne '83 -322 E 90th -NY 10128
(518) 843-2800 .. **Sherbunt,** Norbert J '67 -4722 State Hwy 30 -Amsterdam 12010 **Fx:**843-2801
(631) 755-2020 .. **Sherer,** Jos P '75 Marchon Eyewear,Inc -35 Hub Dr -Melvll 11747 **Fx:**755-3689
(718) 595-6613 .. **Sherer,** Melinda S '75 %DEP -59-17 Junction Blvd -Flushng 11373 **Fx:**595-6543
(212) 578-3102 .. **Sherer,** Tomasita L '00 %MetLife -27-01 Qns Plz N -LIC 11101
(212) 973-9797 .. **Sheridan,** Allen L '85 (Saretsky KD&G,LLP) -475 Park Av S -NY 10016
(212) 428-2892 .. **Sheridan,** Amy M '06 OCA -25 Beaver -NY 10004
(914) 921-1200 .. **Sheridan,** Barbara Ann '98 %Maloof B&E LLC -411 Theo Fremd Av -Rye 10580 **Fx:**921-1023
(631) 854-1996 .. **Sheridan,** Catherine A '94 Appllt Div 2nd Dept -30 E Hoffman Av -Lindenhrst 11757
(212) 408-5100 .. **Sheridan,** Danl C '07 %Chadbourne & P LLP -30 Rckfllr Plz -NY 10112
(518) 475-1378 .. **Sheridan,** David R '78 -33 Grantwood Rd -Delmar 12054 **Fx:**475-1378
(212) 661-5030 .. **Sheridan,** Deirdre J '01 Schoeman U&K,LLP -60 E 42nd -NY 10165
(212) 988-6524 .. **Sheridan,** Dennis J '81 -415 E 80th -NY 10075
(212) 450-8034 .. **Sheridan,** Eric J '98 Intrepid Capital Mgmt -360 Mad Av -NY 10017
(212) 592-1400 .. **Sheridan,** John P '83 Cnsl Herrick,F LLP -2 Park Av -NY 10016
(212) 425-3240 .. **Sheridan,** John P '01 %Marrinan & MM,PC -26 Bway -NY 10004
(518) 486-5355 .. **Sheridan,** Julie M '87 %Dept of Law -The Cptl -Albany 12224
(212) 442-1400 .. **Sheridan,** Karrie Ann '02 Conflicts of Int Bd -2 Lafayette -NY 10007 **Fx:**442-1407
(845) 340-3315 .. **Sheridan,** Kathleen E '04 %DA -285 Wall -Kingston 12401 **Fx:**340-3185
(212) 274-1555 .. **Sheridan,** Kevin M '85 Ponte Equities -268 West -NY 10013
(212) 813-8800 .. **Sheridan,** L Kevin Jr. '89 (Goodwin P LLP) -620 8th Av -NY 10018
(212) 937-7235 .. **Sheridan,** Laura A '06 Cnsl WilmerHale -399 Park Av -NY 10022
(212) 532-8100 .. **Sheridan,** Lee T '04 AIG -175 Water -NY 10038
(914) 232-6689 .. **Sheridan,** Loretta A '79 -35 High -Katonah 10536 **Fx:**232-6689
(914) 241-6300 .. **Sheridan,** Marc O '00 (Markus & S,LLP) -116 Radio Cir -Mt Kisco 10549 **Fx:**241-6308
(212) 924-1220 .. **Sheridan,** Mary E '90 %Local 237-IBT -216 W 14th -NY 10011
(718) 694-5714 .. **Sheridan,** Michele L '00 %Transit Auth -130 Lvngstn -Brklyn 11201 **Fx:**694-5726
(914) 969-2300 .. **Sheridan,** Patricia M '90 %J Shea -116 Hllywd Av -Ynkrs 10707
(845) 620-0047 .. **Sheridan,** Peter T '85 -Bx743 -Pearl Rvr 10965 **Fx:**735-5057
(212) 458-1137 .. **Sheridan,** Richd J '90 %AIG Tech Srvcs -175 Water -NY 10038 **Fx:**458-1153
(631) 547-5900 .. **Sheridan,** Richd M '01 (Kelly & S,LLP) -150 Broadhllw Rd -Melvll 11747 **Fx:**547-9125
(516) 496-5822 .. **Sheridan,** Robt P '06 %T Spina -170 Froehlich Farm Blvd -Woodbury 11797 **Fx:**496-5420
(212) 848-4000 .. **Sheridan,** Tanya '05 %Shearman & S LLP -599 Lex Av -NY 10022
(212) 784-6400 .. **Sheridan,** Thos I III '77 (Hanly CBSF&H LLP) -112 Mad Av -NY 10016
(212) 668-8000 .. **Sheridan-Cona,** Ellen M '00 Oppenheimer & Co -125 Broad -NY 10004
(516) 398-4315 .. **Sheridan-Levine,** Caroline '88 -2301 Kings Hwy -Brklyn 11229
(212) 506-5000 .. **Sherinsky,** Jos A '07 %Orrick H&S LLP -51 W 52nd -NY 10019
(212) 326-3939 .. **Sherique,** Elie J '08 %Jones D -222 E 41st -NY 10017
(646) 264-3650 .. **Sheris,** Marc G '90 %US Dept of Labor -201 Varick -NY 10014 **Fx:**264-3660
(716) 645-5591 .. **Sherk,** Barbara A '03 %SUNY Buffalo Lw Schl -O'Brian Hall -Buffalo 14260 **Fx:**645-5968
(914) 241-1747 .. **Sherlock,** John J '48 -100 Woodcrst Ln -Mt Kisco 10549
(845) 703-1111 .. **Sherlock,** Steven J '98 -1012 Route 211 E -Middletwn 10941 **Fx:**703-1112
(516) 472-7030 .. **Sherman,** Alexander M '08 %Salem S&S,LLP -3000 Marcus Av -Lk Success 11042
(212) 949-8700 .. **Sherman,** Aliza S '07 %Eisner LLP -750 3rd Av -NY 10017 **Fx:**891-4100
(212) 808-2513 .. **Sherman,** Andrew L '93 %Rabobank -245 Park Av -NY 10167
(212) 903-9000 .. **Sherman,** Antonia Birgitta '98 %Linklaters -1345 Av of Amer -NY 10105
(212) 401-3547 .. **Sherman,** Barbara D '81 Royal Bk of Scotland -101 Park Av -NY 10178
(631) 665-0609 .. **Sherman,** Benson '52 (Sherman FS&L LLP) -8 E Main -Bay Shr 11706
(518) 487-5460 .. **Sherman,** Bradley A '94 %DA -6 Lodge -Albany 12207 **Fx:**487-5093
(212) 762-4901 .. **Sherman,** Brett D '99 Morgan Stanley -1221 Av of Amer -NY 10020 **Fx:**762-8950
(212) 626-4892 .. **Sherman,** Burton S '51 -1114 Av of Amer -NY 10036
(212) 808-7800 .. **Sherman,** Carol Weiss '89 SpclCnsl Kelley D&W LLP -101 Park Av -NY 10178
(516) 742-7400 .. **Sherman,** Chas S '75 -666 Old Cntry Rd -Gdn Cty 11530 **Fx:**742-7402
(212) 455-0450 .. **Sherman Citron & Karasik,PC** -605 3rd Av -NY 10158 **Fx:**986-1455
(212) 486-2500 .. **Sherman,** Collin R '05 Mintz & F,PC -488 Mad Av -NY 10022
(631) 543-6360 .. **Sherman,** David '83 -205 Commack Rd -Commack 11725
(212) 940-8800 .. **Sherman,** David B '08 %Katten MR LLP -575 Mad Av -NY 10022
(212) 735-3000 .. **Sherman,** David B '10 %Skadden ASM&F LLP -4 Times Sq -NY 10036
(914) 683-3523 .. **Sherman,** Deborah '82 %Kramer K,LLP -445 Hmltn Av -White Plns 10601
(212) 551-6520 .. **Sherman,** Deborah E '92 %Booz Allen & Hamilton Inc -101 Park Av -NY 10178 **Fx:**551-6562
(646) 264-3650 .. **Sherman,** Diane C '80 US Dept of Labor -201 Varick -NY 10014 **Fx:**264-3660
(212) 878-6900 .. **Sherman,** Dominique H '04 %Goulston & S,PC -750 3rd Av -NY 10017
(212) 486-1455 .. **Sherman,** Douglas J '94 (Post PGM&S,PA) -575 Mad Av -NY 10022
(212) 421-4100 .. **Sherman,** Eric D '97 (Pryor C LLP) -7 Times Sq -NY 10036
(914) 684-0090 .. **Sherman,** Eric R '05 %Diserio MO&C LLP -50 Main -White Plns 10606
(631) 665-0609 .. **Sherman Federman Sambur & Levine LLP** -8 E Main -Bay Shr 11706 **Fx:**665-7409
(516) 564-7791 .. **Sherman Federman Sambur & Levine LLP** -175 Fulton Av -Hempstd 11550
(585) 263-6760 .. **Sherman,** Frank H '86 %US Atty -620 Fed Bldg -Rchstr 14614 **Fx:**263-6226
(212) 326-3939 .. **Sherman,** Fredrick E '69 (Jones D) -222 E 41st -NY 10017
(212) 302-3600 .. **Sherman & Gordon,PC** -494 8th Av -NY 10001 **Fx:**575-9308
(315) 445-9405 .. **Sherman,** Honor A '03 Spcl Funds Conservation Comm -5789 Widewaters Pkwy -Syracuse 13214
(212) 964-4717 .. **Sherman,** Howard B '65 (Schneider K&S) -233 Bway -NY 10279
(212) 836-8000 .. **Sherman,** Howard I '06 %Kaye S LLP -425 Park Av -NY 10022
(914) 941-4000 .. **Sherman,** Howard L '74 -15 Croton Av -Ossining 10562
(212) 302-3600 .. **Sherman,** Isaac '58 (Sherman & G,PC) -494 8th Av -NY 10001
(212) 572-0779 .. **Sherman,** Jacob B '95 -575 Lex Av -NY 10022 **Fx:**572-8304
(212) 788-7015 .. **Sherman,** Jacqueline D '96 %City Cncl Leg Div -250 Bway -NY 10007 **Fx:**788-7034
(718) 631-2500 .. **Sherman,** Jeffrey M '84 (Bailey & S,PC) -42-21 Douglstn Pkwy -Douglastn 11363
(212) 239-1946 .. **Sherman,** Jill '93 J Sherman,PC -37 W 20th -NY 10011 **Fx:**239-1967
(212) 371-5400 .. **Sherman,** John B '72 %Weisman CS&M PC -445 Park Av -NY 10022
(518) 285-8748 .. **Sherman,** John S '82 %Ofc of Admin Judge 3rd Jud Dist -40 Steuben -Albany 12207
(212) 302-3600 .. **Sherman,** Jonathan L '89 (Sherman & G,PC) -494 8th Av -NY 10001
(212) 698-3500 .. **Sherman,** Joshua I '05 %Dechert LLP -1095 Av of Amer -NY 10036
(315) 671-2022 .. **Sherman,** Kurt R '85 %Hon MW Hood -401 Mntgmry -Syracuse 13202
(212) 264-2685 .. **Sherman,** Lloyd A '69 %DHS -26 Fed Plz -NY 10278
(212) 403-1000 .. **Sherman,** Lori S '91 %Wachtell LR&K -51 W 52nd -NY 10019
(212) 944-0500 .. **Sherman,** Louis '79 (Hofheimer G&G,LLP) -530 5th Av -NY 10036 **Fx:**897-4992
(212) 815-1818 .. **Sherman,** Malikah '06 DC 37 MELS -125 Barclay -NY 10007 **Fx:**815-1343
(718) 590-2000 .. **Sherman,** Marc A '07 %DA -198 E 161st -Bronx 10451 **Fx:**590-6477
(718) 997-9240 .. **Sherman,** Marc C '83 -Bx750622 -Frst Hlls 11375 **Fx:**997-9242
(212) 323-2250 .. **Sherman,** Margaret Anne '93 %HHC-OLA-Medical Litigation -346 Bway -NY 10013 **Fx:**323-2251
(845) 794-4094 .. **Sherman,** Mark J '98 %Leg Aid -11 Bank -Monticello 12701 **Fx:**794-0119
(212) 701-3000 .. **Sherman,** Michl A '98 (Cahill G&R LLP) -80 Pine -NY 10005 **Fx:**269-5420
(212) 301-8400 .. **Sherman,** Michl D '04 Dune Real Estate Prtnrs -623 5th Av -NY 10022
(212) 421-4000 .. **Sherman,** Michl J '78 %Hoffinger S&R,LLP -150 E 58th -NY 10155
(718) 739-6400 .. **Sherman,** Michl L '86 %DHCR -92-31 Union Hall -Jamaica 11433 **Fx:**262-7938
(212) 836-8000 .. **Sherman,** Milton '68 (Kaye S LLP) -425 Park Av -NY 10022
(516) 270-1698 .. **Sherman,** Nancy T '83 N Sherman,PC -3000 Marcus Av -Lk Success 11042 **Fx:**270-1685
(212) 622-2094 .. **Sherman,** Neil H '84 %JP Morgan Chase -277 Park Av -NY 10172
(914) 253-2000 .. **Sherman,** Olga Gutman '08 Pepsico -700 Andrsn Hill Rd -Purchase 10577
(212) 893-3516 .. **Sherman,** Peter F '92 %Bloomberg LP -499 Park Av -NY 10022 **Fx:**(917) 369-6046
(516) 572-7543 .. **Sherman,** Phylis D '90 Nassau Cmmnty College -1 Educ Dr -Gdn Cty 11530
(212) 310-8000 .. **Sherman,** Rachel B '09 %Weil G&M LLP -767 5th Av -NY 10153
(518) 833-6690 .. **Sherman,** Rachel Sutel '05 -287 N Greenbush Rd -Troy 12180 **Fx:**283-8060
(212) 836-8000 .. **Sherman,** Randolph S '70 (Kaye S LLP) -425 Park Av -NY 10022
(518) 402-1859 .. **Sherman,** Richd A '97 %DEC -625 Bway -Albany 12233 **Fx:**402-9018
(212) 580-0084 .. **Sherman,** Richd B '65 -1650 Bway -NY 10019
(212) 318-6000 .. **Sherman,** Robt L '72 (Paul HJ&W LLP) -75 E 55th -NY 10022
(212) 625-5700 .. **Sherman,** Sara R '04 Two Sigma Invstmts -379 W Bway -NY 10012
(212) 697-3122 .. **Sherman,** Sara V '10 %Martin C&B LLP -220 E 42nd -NY 10017
(631) 537-5841 .. **Sherman,** Saul L '49 -Bx820 -Water Mill 11976
(212) 587-3777 .. **Sherman,** Scott L '83 (S Sherman & Assoc,PC) -233 Bway -NY 10279 **Fx:**732-5431
(914) 481-8311 .. **Sherman,** Scott M '78 -800 Wstchstr Av -Rye Brook 10573 **Fx:**697-4923
(212) 583-5218 .. **Sherman,** Scott M '01 Blackstone Grp -345 Park Av -NY 10154
(212) 848-4000 .. **Sherman,** Steven E '76 (Shearman & S LLP) -599 Lex Av -NY 10022
(212) 545-1993 .. **Sherman,** Todd B '94 %R Batra,PC -142 Lex Av -NY 10016 **Fx:**545-0967
(212) 336-0124 .. **Sherman,** Vincent P '99 %SEC -3 World Fncl Ctr -NY 10281 **Fx:**336-1323
(212) 909-6000 .. **Sherno,** Tricia Bozyk '08 %Debevoise & P LLP -919 3rd Av -NY 10022
(973) 376-4087 .. **Shernoff,** Frank L '82 -140 53rd -Brklyn 11232 **Fx:**564-5152
(212) 619-3530 .. **Shernoff,** Jeffrey L '69 (Greenberg & S) -9 Murray -NY 10007 **Fx:**732-4443
(845) 471-4386 .. **Sherow,** Gary W '90 -11 Market -Poughkeepsie 12601 **Fx:**454-6612
(866) 706-8814 .. **Sherr,** Paul B '98 -4 Josephine Ln -Castleton On Hudson 12033

(212) 687-6920 .. **Sherrell,** George W '90 %L Tempelsman & Son -19 W 44th -NY 10036 **Fx:**986-0654
(212) 446-4800 .. **Sherrill,** Rebecca M '09 %Kirkland & E LLP -153 E 53rd -NY 10022
(518) 462-5601 .. **Sherrin,** Jeffrey J '76 (O'Connell & A) -54 State -Albany 12207
(516) 248-6550 .. **Sherris,** Theo P '52 -400 Post Av -Westbury 11590
(212) 696-6000 .. **Sherrod,** Sara D R '10 %Curtis M-PC&M LLP -101 Park Av -NY 10178
(212) 944-1377 .. **Sherrod,** Tonia '99 %M Kassimir & Assoc,PC -1065 Av of Amer -NY 10018 **Fx:**790-5868
(518) 402-2227 .. **Sherry,** James M '92 NYS Ofc Homeland Security -Bldg 7A State Campus -Albany 12226 **Fx:**402-2052
(212) 474-1000 .. **Sherry,** Jason B '09 %Cravath S&M LLP -825 8th Av -NY 10019
(212) 697-3050 .. **Sherry,** John E '61 (Sherry & O) -305 Mad Av -NY 10165
(212) 697-3050 .. **Sherry & O'Neill** -305 Mad Av -NY 10165 **Fx:**697-3052
(516) 681-1100 .. **Sherven,** Jennifer E '02 %Kaufman DV&G,LLP -135 Crsswys Park Dr -Woodbury 11797
(212) 808-7800 .. **Sherwin,** Alison P '05 %Kelley D&W LLP -101 Park Av -NY 10178
(212) 449-4385 .. **Sherwin,** Benjamin E '98 Mewrrill Lynch -4 World Fncl Ctr -NY 10080
(516) 357-3700 .. **Sherwin,** David L '10 %Cullen and D LLP -100 Q Roosevelt Blvd -Gdn Cty 11530
(212) 450-4000 .. **Sherwin,** Edw D '06 %Davis P&W LLP -450 Lex Av -NY 10017
(212) 506-1700 .. **Sherwin,** Elizabeth '85 (Kasowitz BT&F LLP) -1633 Bway -NY 10019
(212) 607-3300 .. **Sherwin,** Galen L '04 NYCLU -125 Broad -NY 10004
(845) 634-3627 .. **Sherwin,** Howard D '85 %Leg Aid -2 Congers Rd -New Cty 10956 **Fx:**634-8505
(845) 343-3000 .. **Sherwin,** Jeffrey D '74 (MacVean LS&M,PC) -34 Grove Bx310 -Middletwn 10940
(212) 735-3000 .. **Sherwin,** Jonathan R '10 %Skadden ASM&F LLP -4 Times Sq -NY 10036
(845) 343-3000 .. **Sherwin,** Louis H '41 OfCnsl MacVean LS&M,PC -34 Grove Bx310 -Middletwn 10940
(212) 969-3000 .. **Sherwin,** Peter J W '94 (Proskauer R LLP) -1585 Bway -NY 10036
(212) 431-2868 .. **Sherwin,** Richd K '83 %NY Law Schl -185 W Bway -NY 10013 **Fx:**343-2039
(518) 285-8381 .. **Sherwin,** Stephen P '03 Ct of Appeals -20 Eagle -Albany 12207
(718) 590-2000 .. **Sherwood,** Andrew P '07 %DA -198 E 161st -Bronx 10451 **Fx:**590-6477
(716) 847-8400 .. **Sherwood,** Arthur M '67 OfCnsl Phillips L LLP -3400 HSBC Ctr -Buffalo 14203
(315) 473-9985 .. **Sherwood,** Eric W '99 -307 S Clinton -Syracuse 13202 **Fx:**479-8847
(212) 344-5400 .. **Sherwood,** James C '78 (Schlam S&D LLP) -26 Bway -NY 10004
(914) 378-3900 .. **Sherwood,** Julie M '99 %Kaplan & M -1 Exec Blvd -Ynkrs 10701
(212) 980-3500 .. **Sherwood,** Meryl P '82 OfCnsl Pavia & H LLP -600 Mad Av -NY 10022
(607) 754-6260 .. **Sherwood,** Michl D '76 (Sherwood & S,PC) -158 Front Bx426 -Vestal 13851 **Fx:**754-3186
(716) 881-3010 .. **Sherwood,** Neil R '94 (Cohen & L,PC) -343 Elmwood Av Bx5204 -Buffalo 14213
(716) 684-5123 .. **Sherwood,** Richd J '74 -25 Central Av -Lancaster 14086
(518) 452-0941 .. **Sherwood,** Richd J '88 OfCnsl Segel GM&S,PC -9 Wshngtn Sq -Albany 12205
(212) 644-1429 .. **Sherwood,** Stanley G '72 (Sherwood Law Assoc) -445 Park Av -NY 10022
(516) 408-7030 .. **Sherwood,** Thos G '79 (T Sherwood,LLC) -300 Grdn City Plz -Gdn Cty 11530 **Fx:**408-7032
(607) 255-1711 .. **Sherwyn,** David S '95 %Cornell Univ -541 Statler Hall -Ithaca 14853
(212) 671-6459 .. **Sherwyn,** Steven M '87 Hypo Real Estate Capital Corp -622 3rd Av -NY 10017
(212) 766-1200 .. **Shestack,** Stuart G '65 (Shestack & Y,LLP) -233 Bway -NY 10279
(212) 766-1200 .. **Shestack & Young,LLP** -233 Bway -NY 10279 **Fx:**349-4911
(212) 688-1669 .. **Shestakov,** Vadim '00 %Granger & Assoc LLC -40 Fulton -NY 10038 **Fx:**346-9319
(212) 849-7000 .. **Sheth,** Manisha M '99 OfCnsl Quinn EU&S,LLP -51 Mad Av -NY 10010
(646) 723-2947 .. **Sheth,** Tushar J '02 Sanford W&H,LLP -1350 Av of Amer -NY 10019
(516) 877-7000 .. **Shetrit,** Kseniya '06 %McCoyd P&R,LLP -1100 Franklin Av -Gdn Cty 11530
(631) 853-4104 .. **Shetty,** Sheetal '07 %DA -400 Carleton Av Bx9082 -Central Islip 11722 **Fx:**853-7838
(516) 949-4237 .. **Shetty,** Vaishali S '00 %FINRA -2 Jericho Plz -Jericho 11753 **Fx:**949-4201
(212) 735-3000 .. **Shetty,** Varun S '08 %Skadden ASM&F LLP -4 Times Sq -NY 10036
(212) 909-6000 .. **Sheu,** Ann E '06 %Debevoise & P LLP -919 3rd Av -NY 10022
(212) 297-5800 .. **Shevade,** Renu A '97 SrCnsl Day P LLP -7 Times Sq -NY 10036
(212) 373-3000 .. **Shevell,** Adam L '08 %Paul WRW&G LLP -1285 Av of Amer -NY 10019
(914) 747-0828 .. **Shevell,** Jamie B '98 %Nrthrn Westchester Shelter Inc -Bx203 -Plsntvll 10570 **Fx:**747-3825
(914) 763-2122 .. **Shevitz,** Vivian '78 -46 Truesdale Lk Dr -S Salem 10590 **Fx:**763-2322
(212) 455-2000 .. **Shevlin,** David A '93 SrCnsl Simpson T&B LLP -425 Lex Av -NY 10017
(212) 416-8561 .. **Shevlin,** Neil S '00 %Dept of Law -120 Bway -NY 10271
(718) 261-3075 .. **Shevrin,** Mark A '91 -123-60 83rd Av -Kew Gdns 11415
(518) 456-6705 .. **Shevy,** Patricia J '98 (Shevy Law Firm,LLC) -7 Exec Centre Dr -Albany 12203 **Fx:**456-6709
(518) 833-6000 .. **Shevy,** Timothy R '09 %Dept Soc Srvcs -127 Bloomingrove Dr -Troy 12180 **Fx:**833-6121
(212) 661-1200 .. **Shey,** Andrew M '88 (Newhouse & S LLP) -3 W 35th -NY 10001
(631) 491-9190 .. **Shey,** Audrey '83 -134 Burrs Ln -Dix Hlls 11746
(212) 450-4000 .. **Shi,** Chaoyuan '09 %Davis P&W LLP -450 Lex Av -NY 10017
(212) 450-4000 .. **Shi,** Hong Henry '09 %Davis P&W LLP -450 Lex Av -NY 10017
(718) 353-8890 .. **Shi,** Liping '03 -3609 Main -Flushng 11354
(212) 906-1200 .. **Shi,** Min '10 %Latham & W -885 3rd Av -NY 10022
(718) 321-7000 .. **Shiau,** Cindy '09 %Shih & F -136-20 38th Av -Flushng 11354 **Fx:**762-7679
(212) 819-8200 .. **Shiba,** Michl J '09 %White & C LLP -1155 Av of Amer -NY 10036
(212) 244-4111 .. **Shiboleth,** Amnon '68 (Shiboleth YR&Z,LLP) -1 Penn Plz -NY 10119
(212) 244-4111 .. **Shiboleth Yisraeli Roberts & Zisman,LLP** -1 Penn Plz -NY 10119 **Fx:**563-7108
(516) 671-6388 .. **Shichman,** Michl A '83 -109 High Farms Rd -Old Brookvll 11545 **Fx:**671-6384
(516) 741-5222 .. **Shichtman,** Marshal D '01 (M Shichtman & Assoc PC) -1 Old Cntry Rd -Carle Pl 11514 **Fx:**741-5212
(212) 326-2000 .. **Shick,** Jerri Eden '01 Cnsl O'Melveny & M LLP -7 Times Sq -NY 10036
(631) 543-7667 .. **Shiebler,** Christine R '94 (Sarisohn Law Prtnrs LLP) -350 Vets Mem'l Hwy -Commack 11725 **Fx:**543-7901
(718) 237-5500 .. **Shield,** Sonja E '06 %Leg Srvcs -105 Court -Brklyn 11201 **Fx:**855-0733
(212) 593-6700 .. **Shields,** Alison R '90 (Aaronson RF&D,LLP) -757 3rd Av -NY 10017
(631) 247-0404 .. **Shields,** Ana C '04 %Jackson L LLP -58 S Srvc Rd -Melvll 11747
(631) 712-5640 .. **Shields,** Anne Y '85 %Hon L Wexler -100 Fed Plz -Central Islip 11722
(631) 874-0079 .. **Shields,** Christine M '89 -2 Florence Dr -Manorvll 11949
(212) 876-4234 .. **Shields,** Craig M '67 -103 E 86th -NY 10028 **Fx:**348-3119
(212) 401-0800 .. **Shields,** Eileen J '90 %Disciplinary Comm -61 Bway -NY 10006 **Fx:**287-1045
(212) 849-7000 .. **Shields,** Jake M '04 %Quinn EU&S,LLP -51 Mad Av -NY 10010
(631) 231-2171 .. **Shields,** John M '94 %Dept of Law -300 Motor Pkwy -Hauppauge 11788 **Fx:**435-4757
(315) 437-7600 .. **Shields,** Jos G '92 (Ferrara FLB&R,PC) -5010 Campuswood Dr -E Syracuse 13057
(914) 961-1300 .. **Shields,** Kathleen A '08 %Griffin CB&S,PC -51 Pondfld Rd -Bronxvll 10708
(646) 610-5400 .. **Shields,** Margaret L '89 %NYPD -1 Police Plz -NY 10038
(212) 859-8000 .. **Shields,** Nkosi Diallo '03 Fried FHS&J LLP -1 NY Plz -NY 10004
(212) 580-1370 .. **Shields,** Rosalie B '88 -145 W 67th -NY 10023
(212) 633-8100 .. **Shiels,** A Lawr Jr. '88 Donovan Data Systems -115 W 18th -NY 10011
(212) 848-4000 .. **Shiels,** Ellen M '10 Shearman & S LLP -599 Lex Av -NY 10022
(212) 969-3000 .. **Shiels,** Matthew T '08 %Proskauer R LLP -1585 Bway -NY 10036
(716) 434-3300 .. **Shierling,** Stephen P '79 -221 Bewley Bldg Bx1003 -Lockprt 14095 **Fx:**434-1706
(212) 980-0120 .. **Shiers,** Barbara E '81 (Frankfurt KK&S,PC) -488 Mad Av -NY 10022
(212) 715-9100 .. **Shifer,** Jos A '10 %Kramer LN&F,LLP -1177 Av of Amer -NY 10036
(212) 964-6611 .. **Shiferman,** Julie '03 %Lester SK&D -120 Bway -NY 10271
(212) 506-1700 .. **Shiff,** Adam L '93 (Kasowitz BT&F LLP) -1633 Bway -NY 10019
(212) 532-0222 .. **Shiff,** Harvey I '76 -200 Mad Av -NY 10016 **Fx:**532-0224
(212) 354-6920 .. **Shiff,** Laurence P '66 L Shiff PC -275 Mad Av -NY 10016 **Fx:**354-6923
(716) 845-2560 .. **Shifflett,** Jos A '75 Surrogates Ct -92 Franklin -Buffalo 14202 **Fx:**853-3741
(212) 770-1791 .. **Shiffman,** Andrea Brahms '00 %AIG -80 Pine -NY 10005
(212) 885-5000 .. **Shiffman,** Brad '91 (Blank R LLP) -405 Lex Av -NY 10174
(212) 310-8000 .. **Shiffman,** Jonathan A '00 %Weil G&M LLP -767 5th Av -NY 10153
(212) 451-2900 .. **Shiffman,** Melissa F '01 Cnsl Robinson & C LLP -885 3rd Av -NY 10022
(315) 737-5191 .. **Shiffman,** Sidney J '51 -17 Court Knolle -New Hartfrd 13413
(212) 940-8800 .. **Shiffman,** Steven '92 (Katten MR LLP) -575 Mad Av -NY 10022
(212) 697-2310 .. **Shiffman,** Theo R '69 (Becker R LLP) -317 Mad Av -NY 10017
(585) 423-8290 .. **Shiffrin,** Brian '78 (Easton TKS,LLP) -16 W Main -Rchstr 14614 **Fx:**423-0890
(212) 326-7198 .. **Shifman,** Pamela G '99 UNICEF -3 UN Plz -NY 10017
(516) 759-2722 .. **Shifren,** David E '07 %Ryan M&L,LLP -90 Forest Av -Locust Vly 11560
(914) 472-7713 .. **Shifren,** Nancy Zena '94 -127 Edgemont Rd -Scarsdale 10583
(516) 571-2848 .. **Shifrin,** Eugene H '69 Supreme Ct -100 Supreme Ct Dr -Mineola 11501 **Fx:**571-5098
(212) 676-2020 .. **Shifrin,** Ilene '85 %DOH-Admin Tribunal -2 Lafayette -NY 10007
(212) 228-1900 .. **Shifrin,** Robin M '97 -1230 Av of Amer -NY 10020
(212) 998-5471 .. **Shigaki,** Irene Shikibu '95 %NYU -239 Greene-East Bldg -NY 10003
(718) 321-7000 .. **Shih,** Christine '87 (Shih & F) -136-20 38th Av -Flushng 11354 **Fx:**762-7679
(212) 326-3939 .. **Shih,** Evangeline L '02 %Jones D -222 E 41st -NY 10017
(212) 268-4422 .. **Shih,** George C '86 -4211 Parsons Blvd -Flushng 11355 **Fx:**564-9639
(212) 558-4000 .. **Shih,** Gregory C '08 %Sullivan & C LLP -125 Broad -NY 10004
(212) 848-4000 .. **Shih,** Irene Hsuan-I '06 %Shearman & S LLP -599 Lex Av -NY 10022
(212) 790-9200 .. **Shih,** Jane '03 %Cowan L&L,PC -1133 Av of Amer -NY 10036
(718) 613-2600 .. **Shih,** Jonathan L '07 US Dist Ct -225 Cadman Plz E -Brklyn 11201
(212) 474-1000 .. **Shih,** Timothy Y '09 %Cravath S&M LLP -825 8th Av -NY 10019
(212) 267-3091 .. **Shih,** Willard C '97 (Wilentz G&S) -110 William -NY 10038 **Fx:**(732) 726-6682
(914) 682-2068 .. **Shikhovets,** Katerina '09 %Ansa A,LLP -50 Main -White Plns 10606
(516) 625-1234 .. **Shilensky,** Wendy A '98 -332 Willis Av -Roslyn Hts 11577 **Fx:**625-4321
(914) 741-0452 .. **Shilinski,** Michl T '05 OfCnsl S Gullotta -390 Bedford Rd -Plsntvll 10570 **Fx:**741-2736
(212) 351-4000 .. **Shill,** Gregory H '09 Gibson D&C LLP -200 Park Av -NY 10166
(845) 291-2454 .. **Shiller,** Eric S '02 %Leg Aid -2 Court Ln Bx328 -Goshen 10924 **Fx:**294-2638
(212) 949-8700 .. **Shillet,** Dayna M '04 %Eisner LLP -750 3rd Av -NY 10017 **Fx:**891-4100
(718) 618-2500 .. **Shillin,** Beth I '92 %Civil Ct -851 Grnd Cncrs -Bronx 10451 **Fx:**590-7294
(212) 557-2800 .. **Shilling,** Alison J '05 Barger & W LLP -10 E 40th -NY 10016
(212) 455-2000 .. **Shilling,** Patrick T '03 %Simpson T&B LLP -425 Lex Av -NY 10017
(212) 330-6380 .. **Shilling,** Susan '97 Ofc of Mental Hlth -330 5th Av -NY 10001
(845) 225-7500 .. **Shilling,** Wm A Jr. '82 W Shilling,PC -105 Gleneida Av -Carmel 10512 **Fx:**225-5692
(631) 749-2616 .. **Shillingburg,** J Edw '70 -4 West Neck Rd Bx3032 -Shelter Isl Hts 11965 **Fx:**749-3031

(212) 471-6208 .. **Shillingford,** Khardeen I '07 %Hinshaw & C LLP -780 3rd Av -NY 10017
(607) 974-8164 .. **Shillinglaw,** Thos L '85 %Corning -1 Rvrfrnt Plz -Corning 14831 **Fx:**974-6135
(718) 275-6700 .. **Shillito,** Nils C '07 %S Hans & Assoc PC -45-18 Court Sq -LIC 11101 **Fx:**275-6704
(646) 878-0800 .. **Shiloh,** Dekel '98 (Pearl CZL,LLP) -1500 Bway -NY 10036
(212) 269-5500 .. **Shiloh,** Elior D '08 %Gordon & R LLP -90 Broad -NY 10004
(212) 885-5000 .. **Shim,** Danl J '10 %Blank R LLP -405 Lex Av -NY 10174
(212) 972-1000 .. **Shim,** Hae J '05 %London F LLP -59 Maiden Ln -NY 10038
(516) 222-1030 .. **Shim,** Jonathan H '94 %S Friedman,PC -666 Old Cntry Rd -Gdn Cty 11530 **Fx:**222-1053
(212) 225-2000 .. **Shim,** Paul J '83 (Cleary GS&H) -1 Lbrty Plz -NY 10006
(212) 310-8000 .. **Shim,** Soo-Jin '98 (Weil G&M LLP) -767 5th Av -NY 10153
(212) 310-8000 .. **Shim,** Suhan '10 %Weil G&M LLP -767 5th Av -NY 10153
(212) 450-4000 .. **Shima,** Mary E '08 %Davis P&W LLP -450 Lex Av -NY 10017
(212) 839-5300 .. **Shimada,** Yoshiki '86 (Sidley A LLP) -787 7th Av -NY 10019
(212) 790-9200 .. **Shimanoff,** Eric J '03 %Cowan L&L,PC -1133 Av of Amer -NY 10036
(845) 534-3229 .. **Shimek,** Danl W '83 -Angola Rd -Cornwall 12518
(585) 258-2800 .. **Shimick,** Scott D '02 %Underberg & K LLP -300 Bausch & Lomb Pl -Rchstr 14604
(212) 801-9291 .. **Shimkin,** Barry E '74 (Greenberg T,LLP) -200 Park Av -NY 10166
(212) 509-9400 .. **Shimkin,** David A '98 (Cozen O) -45 Bway Atrium -NY 10006
(718) 855-3627 .. **Shimko,** Danl S '09 C Berkman,LLC -111 Lvngstn -Brklyn 11201 **Fx:**855-4696
(585) 232-6500 .. **Shimomura,** Kimberly I '02 %Harter S&E LLP -1600 Bausch & Lomb Pl -Rchstr 14604
(212) 935-7400 .. **Shimon,** Roy '07 %Harwood F LLP -488 Mad Av -NY 10022
(212) 819-8200 .. **Shimotake,** Jean E '92 (White & C LLP) -1155 Av of Amer -NY 10036
(212) 373-3000 .. **Shimshak,** Stephen J '83 (Paul WRW&G LLP) -1285 Av of Amer -NY 10019
(212) 612-4000 .. **Shimshidian,** Laura '90 %Chubb Grp -55 Water -NY 10041
(212) 381-7000 .. **Shin,** Benjamin J '00 %Sabin B&G LLP -4 Times Sq -NY 10036
(212) 953-6633 .. **Shin,** D B David '88 (Cox PS&S LLP) -630 3rd Av -NY 10017
(212) 335-9000 .. **Shin,** Danl K '09 %DA -1 Hogan Pl -NY 10013
(212) 455-2000 .. **Shin,** Danl Y '10 %Simpson T&B LLP -425 Lex Av -NY 10017
(212) 268-5000 .. **Shin,** Dong K '86 -120 W 31st -NY 10001 **Fx:**268-5125
(212) 723-7349 .. **Shin,** E Julia '97 Citigroup -390 Greenwich -NY 10013
(718) 463-3131 .. **Shin,** E Peter '97 -158-14 Nrthrn Blvd -Flushng 11358 **Fx:**463-6789
(914) 640-5908 .. **Shin,** Helen '91 %Nine West Group Inc -1129 Wstchstr Av -White Plns 10604 **Fx:**640-1676
(212) 735-3000 .. **Shin,** Helen '09 %Skadden ASM&F LLP -4 Times Sq -NY 10036
(212) 872-1000 .. **Shin,** Henry E '01 -One Bryant Park -NY 10036 **Fx:**872-1002
(212) 294-6700 .. **Shin,** Howard I '01 %Winston & S -200 Park Av -NY 10166
(212) 732-8700 .. **Shin,** Hyejung '07 %McAloon & F,PC -123 William -NY 10038
(212) 735-3000 .. **Shin,** Hyun Young '00 Cnsl Skadden ASM&F LLP -4 Times Sq -NY 10036
(212) 536-4242 .. **Shin,** Jee-Young '02 Ann Taylor Stores Corp -7 Times Sq -NY 10036
(212) 309-6000 .. **Shin,** John '05 %Morgan L&B LLP -101 Park Av -NY 10178
(212) 655-5000 .. **Shin,** John H '92 %Gannon R&M -120 Bway -NY 10271
(212) 779-8600 .. **Shin,** John H '94 (Silverman SS&B PLLC) -381 Park Av S -NY 10016
(212) 272-2000 .. **Shin,** Juliet Joo Hyon '98 %JP Morgan Chase -383 Mad Av -NY 10179
(212) 450-4000 .. **Shin,** Lucie E M '07 %Davis P&W LLP -450 Lex Av -NY 10017
(718) 224-7535 .. **Shin,** Richd W '97 -208-24 30th Av -Bayside 11360 **Fx:**224-4322
(212) 536-3900 .. **Shin,** Robt D '07 %K&L Gates LLP -599 Lex Av -NY 10022
(212) 715-1000 .. **Shin,** Susan L '02 %Arnold & P LLP -399 Park Av -NY 10022
(212) 735-3000 .. **Shin,** Victoria Soo-Kyeong '05 %Skadden ASM&F LLP -4 Times Sq -NY 10036
(212) 403-1000 .. **Shin,** Won S '07 %Wachtell LR&K -51 W 52nd -NY 10019
(212) 225-2000 .. **Shin,** You Jung '10 %Cleary GS&H -1 Lbrty Plz -NY 10006
(585) 758-7609 .. **Shinaman,** M Aileen '89 %Univ of Rochester Med Ctr -Bx278979 -Rchstr 14627 **Fx:**272-9311
(585) 263-1000 .. **Shinaman,** Todd R '89 Cnsl Nixon P LLP -1100 Clinton Sq -Rchstr 14604
(631) 265-2550 .. **Shindel,** Doreen J '97 -199 E Main -Smithtwn 11787
(516) 683-6000 .. **Shindel,** Sara A '00 Lifetime Brands,Inc -1000 Stewart Av -Gdn Cty 11530
(212) 350-2709 .. **Shinder,** Jeffrey I '94 (Constantine C,PC) -450 Lex Av -NY 10017
(585) 244-2340 .. **Shinder & Newman** -95 Allens Crk Rd -Rchstr 14618 **Fx:**244-2354
(585) 244-2340 .. **Shinder,** Solomon '54 (Shinder & N) -95 Allens Crk Rd -Rchstr 14618
(212) 233-6686 .. **Shindler,** Alexander '10 %Novo Law Firm,PC -299 Bway -NY 10007 **Fx:**233-6687
(516) 733-7600 .. **Shindler,** Douglas B '94 -51 Alpha Plz -Hicksvll 11801
(212) 521-2434 .. **Shindler,** Martin L '96 Loews Corp -655 Mad Av -NY 10065
(212) 788-7302 .. **Shine,** Carol J '84 %City Cncl Land Use -250 Bway -NY 10007 **Fx:**788-7337
(212) 969-1420 .. **Shine,** Cathleen '89 Alliance Bernstein LP -1345 Av of Amer -NY 10105 **Fx:**554-4639
(212) 859-8000 .. **Shine,** David N '87 (Fried FHS&J LLP) -1 NY Plz -NY 10004
(888) 201-6643 .. **Shine,** Kevin Z '92 KZ Shine,PLLC -8203 Main -Williamsvll 14221 **Fx:**(716) 204-8995
(212) 819-8200 .. **Shiner,** Andrew F '01 %White & C LLP -1155 Av of Amer -NY 10036
(716) 854-3455 .. **Shiner,** Danl R '04 %Gielowski F&C,LLP -135 Delaware Av -Buffalo 14202 **Fx:**854-2797
(212) 878-8000 .. **Shingler,** Angelique M '04 %Clifford C LLP -31 W 52nd -NY 10019
(646) 386-3611 .. **Shinn,** David S '91 %Supreme Ct-Law Dept -60 Centre -NY 10007
(212) 450-4000 .. **Shioleno,** Lewis C '10 %Davis P&W LLP -450 Lex Av -NY 10017
(212) 563-2100 .. **Shipkevich,** Felix '04 Capital Market Srvcs,LLC -350 5th Av -NY 10118
(212) 318-6000 .. **Shipley,** Ann '66 (Paul HJ&W LLP) -75 E 55th -NY 10022
(212) 340-0400 .. **Shipley,** Kim Marlowe '07 %Appllt Div 1st Dept -27 Mad Av -NY 10010 **Fx:**889-4412
(718) 931-2575 .. **Shipman,** Peter R '77 %Codelia & S PC -1967 Turnbull Av -Bronx 10473
(212) 504-6000 .. **Shipp,** Bryan T '09 %Cadwalader W&T LLP -1 World Fncl Ctr -NY 10281
(212) 455-2000 .. **Shipp,** Samantha A '08 %Simpson T&B LLP -425 Lex Av -NY 10017
(212) 599-5600 .. **Shipper,** Andrew M '94 (Shipper & S) -380 Lex Av -NY 10168 **Fx:**389-7808
(212) 599-5600 .. **Shipper,** David W '83 (Shipper & S) -380 Lex Av -NY 10168 **Fx:**389-7808
(212) 425-0055 .. **Shira,** Donna L '84 %Sharretts PC&B -75 Broad -NY 10004
(212) 504-6000 .. **Shirazi,** Ray I '94 (Cadwalader W&T LLP) -1 World Fncl Ctr -NY 10281
(516) 812-4500 .. **Shirazi,** Sahar H '06 %Stagg TC&W LLP -401 Franklin Av -Gdn Cty 11530
(212) 425-7200 .. **Shire,** Howard J '80 (Kenyon & K,LLP) -1 Bway -NY 10004
(212) 554-0400 .. **Shire,** Lawr '83 (Grubman I&S,PC) -152 W 57th -NY 10019
(718) 330-7861 .. **Shire,** Miriam Lisa '84 %ODAR-SSA -111 Lvngstn -Brklyn 11201 **Fx:**330-2009
(718) 997-9800 .. **Shiryak,** Alexander '01 (A Shiryak,PC) -125-10 Qns Blvd -Kew Gdns 11415 **Fx:**261-3470
(212) 962-1590 .. **Shisha,** Jacob '89 (Tabak M&S) -29 Bway -NY 10006
(212) 336-2000 .. **Shissler,** Janine E '02 %Patterson BW&T LLP -1133 Av of Amer -NY 10036
(212) 576-7000 .. **Shively,** George S '87 %NYLIM -51 Mad Av -NY 10010
(212) 480-4000 .. **Shivers,** Yvonne P '89 SrCnsl Levitt & K -40 Fulton -NY 10038 **Fx:**480-4444
(212) 735-3000 .. **Shivnarain,** Dwayne A '01 %Skadden ASM&F LLP -4 Times Sq -NY 10036
(212) 909-6000 .. **Shivpuri,** Shubhra '09 %Debevoise & P LLP -919 3rd Av -NY 10022
(212) 530-5000 .. **Shkolnik,** Ariella '10 %Milbank TH&M LLP -1 Chase Manh Plz -NY 10005
(212) 684-1880 .. **Shkolnik,** Hunter J '86 (Rheingold VRS&M LLP) -113 E 37th -NY 10016
(212) 613-5000 .. **Shkolnik,** Maria '09 %Leg Assist Grp -450 W 33rd -NY 10001 **Fx:**750-0820
(212) 421-2233 .. **Shkolnik,** Natalie '00 %Wilk A LLP -675 3rd Av -NY 10017
(518) 402-2227 .. **Shkreli,** Linda '05 NYS Ofc Homeland Security -1220 Wshngtn Av -Albany 12242
(585) 253-0123 .. **Shkurko,** Eugene I '93 Eastman Kodak Co -343 State -Rchstr 14650
(212) 417-5638 .. **Shlahet,** Adam D '03 %Medicaid Fraud Cntrl -120 Bway -NY 10271 **Fx:**417-5274
(212) 388-3600 .. **Shlevin,** Loran '85 %32B-J Leg Srvcs -101 Av of Amer -NY 10013 **Fx:**388-3061
(631) 277-4300 .. **Shlimbaum,** C Donald '74 (Shlimbaum & S) -265 Main Bx8 -Islip 11751 **Fx:**277-4350
(631) 277-4300 .. **Shlimbaum,** Lark J '75 (Shlimbaum & S) -265 Main Bx8 -Islip 11751 **Fx:**277-4350
(212) 610-6300 .. **Shlimovich,** Eugenia '09 %Allen & O -1221 Av of Amer -NY 10020
(212) 872-3145 .. **Shlivko,** Alex '00 %KPMG -345 Park Av -NY 10154
(212) 532-6682 .. **Shlom & Littman** -370 Lex Av -NY 10017 **Fx:**889-7725
(917) 575-6977 .. **Shlufman,** Danl M '89 -32 Irene Ln E -Plainvw 11803 **Fx:**(973) 574-0999
(516) 681-7979 .. **Shlufman,** Martin A '63 -32 Irene Ln E -Plainvw 11803 **Fx:**681-7979
(718) 265-7770 .. **Shlyamkovich,** Yelena '08 -220 Av U -Brklyn 11223
(212) 310-8000 .. **Shmalo,** Robt C '04 %Weil G&M LLP -767 5th Av -NY 10153
(516) 747-0300 .. **Shmuely,** Jamie E '06 %Meltzer LG&B,LLP -190 Willis Av -Mineola 11501
(212) 867-4466 .. **Shmulewitz,** Aaron '83 (Belkin BW&G,LLP) -270 Mad Av -NY 10016
(914) 640-6423 .. **Shmulewitz,** Jennifer M '00 Jones Apparel Grp -1129 Wstchstr Av -White Plns 10604
(718) 590-2000 .. **Shmulewitz,** Jos E '09 %DA -198 E 161st -Bronx 10451 **Fx:**590-6477
(212) 595-7575 .. **Shneyer,** Paul A '80 (Shneyer & Assoc Ltd) -1790 Bway -NY 10019 **Fx:**(646) 390-7000
(212) 225-2000 .. **Shnitser,** Natalya '10 %Cleary GS&H -1 Lbrty Plz -NY 10006
(212) 302-2400 .. **Shoai-Naini,** Golriz '09 %Lynch DE LLP -264 W 40th -NY 10018
(718) 522-1786 .. **Shochet,** Erin J '09 %Bonina & B,PC -16 Court -Brklyn 11241 **Fx:**243-0414
(718) 590-2000 .. **Shockett,** Jeremy B '95 %DA -198 E 161st -Bronx 10451 **Fx:**590-6477
(212) 806-5400 .. **Shockey,** George R Jr. '77 (Stroock &S&L LLP) -180 Maiden Ln -NY 10038
(516) 357-3000 .. **Shockley,** Laura L '02 (Rivkin R LLP) -926 RXR Plz -Uniondale 11556
(315) 536-5532 .. **Shoemaker,** Alice '84 Cnty Ct -415 Lbrty -Penn Yan 14527 **Fx:**536-5197
(212) 902-7952 .. **Shoemaker,** Connie J '97 %Goldman Sachs -1 NY Plz -NY 10004
(716) 433-5941 .. **Shoemaker,** Edwin J '62 (Andrews PBS&R) -929 Lincoln Av -Lockprt 14094
(607) 721-8774 .. **Shoemaker,** James E '87 %Dept of Law -44 Hawley -Bnghmtn 13901 **Fx:**721-8789
(212) 818-9600 .. **Shoemaker,** Paul T '79 (Greenfield S&S,LLP) -600 3rd Av -NY 10016
(212) 351-4000 .. **Shoemate,** Steven R '89 (Gibson D&C LLP) -200 Park Av -NY 10166
(845) 354-0479 .. **Shoenthal,** Lawr E '68 -6 Dorothy Dr -Spg Vly 10977
(212) 848-4000 .. **Shoenthal,** Matthew '10 Shearman & S LLP -599 Lex Av -NY 10022
(718) 590-8147 .. **Shoffner,** Gail '89 Div of Leg Srvcs -900 Sheridan Av -Bronx 10451
(212) 336-2000 .. **Shofner,** Elizabeth Hardeman '99 %Patterson BW&T LLP -1133 Av of Amer -NY 10036
(212) 568-4680 .. **Shogan,** Amelia Ford '99 %CUNY Citizenshp & Immig Prjct -560 W 181st -NY 10033
(212) 697-8500 .. **Shogan,** Steven J '07 %Konner T&G -462 7th Av -NY 10018
(212) 403-1000 .. **Shohet,** Tegan S '08 %Wachtell LR&K -51 W 52nd -NY 10019
(212) 446-7716 .. **Shohet,** Zion Moshe '97 %McKinsey & Co -55 E 52nd -NY 10055 **Fx:**688-9521
(212) 944-6611 .. **Shoichet,** Louis S '76 (Tompkins & D,LLP) -5 Hanover Sq -NY 10004

(212) 261-8000 .. **Shoikhetman,** Eric '07 %Mendes & M,LLP -750 7th Av -NY 10019
(212) 373-3000 .. **Sholder,** Scott J '08 %Paul WRW&G LLP -1285 Av of Amer -NY 10019
(845) 454-5909 .. **Sholes & Miller,LLP** -327 Mill -Poughkeepsie 12601 **Fx:**454-5971
(845) 454-5909 .. **Sholes,** Sarah E '79 (Sholes & M,LLP) -327 Mill -Poughkeepsie 12601
(212) 351-4500 .. **Sholinsky,** Susan Gross '01 (Epstein B&G,PC) -250 Park Av -NY 10177
(212) 373-3000 .. **Sholl,** Hannah S '05 %Paul WRW&G LLP -1285 Av of Amer -NY 10019
(212) 732-5050 .. **Sholla,** Gentian '07 %Kuba Law Firm -321 Bway -NY 10007 **Fx:**766-0049
(347) 592-2200 .. **Shollenberger,** Elizabeth '82 %Leg Srvcs -42-15 Crescent -LIC 11101 **Fx:**(718) 937-5350
(212) 455-2000 .. **Sholly,** Katherine A '09 %Simpson T&B LLP -425 Lex Av -NY 10017
(914) 949-4300 .. **Sholz,** Robt T '66 -77 W Post Rd -White Plns 10606
(212) 756-2000 .. **Shon,** Dong Hoon '02 %Schulte R&Z LLP -919 3rd Av -NY 10022
(212) 805-3900 .. **Shon,** Jennifer W '01 %Clausen M PC -1 Chase Manh Plz -NY 10005
(212) 859-8000 .. **Shong,** Dave S '07 %Fried FHS&J LLP -1 NY Plz -NY 10004
(716) 882-2300 .. **Shonn,** Danl D Jr. '76 OfCnsl McCready & T -6 N Pearl -Buffalo 14202
(212) 909-5305 .. **Shontz,** David B '88 %KPMG LLP -757 3rd Av -NY 10017
(718) 250-2000 .. **Shoock,** Corey S '09 %DA -350 Jay -Brklyn 11201 **Fx:**250-2314
(845) 986-7400 .. **Shoock,** Paul S '77 (PS Shoock,PC) -5 1st -Warwick 10990 **Fx:**986-7407
(516) 280-4106 .. **Shook,** James C '97 J Shook,PC -666 Old Cntry Rd -Gdn Cty 11530
(212) 808-7800 .. **Shook,** Jessica K '08 %Kelley D&W LLP -101 Park Av -NY 10178
(212) 732-9000 .. **Shoot,** Brian J '80 (Sullivan PBM&C PC) -120 Bway -NY 10271
(212) 969-3000 .. **Shophet,** Judith '08 Proskauer R LLP -1585 Bway -NY 10036 **Fx:**969-2900
(516) 472-7030 .. **Shor,** David S '05 (Salem S&S,LLP) -3000 Marcus Av -Lk Success 11042
(212) 697-3122 .. **Shor,** Jeffrey A '77 (Martin C&B LLP) -220 E 42nd -NY 10017
(212) 885-5000 .. **Shor,** Lloyd '64 (Blank R LLP) -405 Lex Av -NY 10174
(516) 829-5206 .. **Shor,** Stephen A '75 -4 Grassfld Rd -Gt Neck 11024
(212) 819-8200 .. **Shoranick,** Tammy M '09 %White & C LLP -1155 Av of Amer -NY 10036
(212) 374-9494 .. **Shore,** Glenn '86 G Shore,PC -100 William -NY 10038 **Fx:**346-9437
(212) 819-8200 .. **Shore,** J Christopher '93 (White & C LLP) -1155 Av of Amer -NY 10036
(212) 977-9700 .. **Shore,** Jeffrey L '91 Cnsl Phillips N LLP -666 5th Av -NY 10103
(212) 351-4000 .. **Shore,** Laurence '08 (Gibson D&C LLP) -200 Park Av -NY 10166
(631) 543-5800 .. **Shore,** Leonard J '77 -366 Vets Mem'l Hwy -Commack 11725 **Fx:**543-5899
(518) 473-9200 .. **Shore,** Paul B '82 Workers Comp Bd -100 Bway -Albany 12204
(212) 922-9250 .. **Shore,** Richd J '08 %Ganfer & S LLP -360 Lex Av -NY 10017
(516) 869-4942 .. **Shore,** Sam Z '92 -445 Central Av -Cedarhrst 11516
(212) 687-8500 .. **Shore,** Sherry M '08 %Liddle & R,LLP -800 3rd Av -NY 10022
(212) 891-9100 .. **Shore,** Steven B '73 (Goldfarb & F LLP) -345 Park Av -NY 10154
(212) 922-9250 .. **Shore,** Steven J '72 (Ganfer & S LLP) -360 Lex Av -NY 10017
(212) 573-7486 .. **Shore,** Timothy P '86 %Pfizer Inc -235 E 42nd -NY 10017
(718) 454-9673 .. **Shore,** Wm I '42 -186-19 Radnor Rd -Jamaica 11432
(212) 883-4923 .. **Shorenstein,** Stuart A '72 (Cozen O) -277 Park Av -NY 10172 **Fx:**672-1123
(631) 715-4160 .. **Shores,** Nancy Gottheimer '85 %Sbarro -401 Broad Hollow Rd -Melvll 11747
(914) 723-4300 .. **Shore-Sirotin,** Cathy E '91 %Lackenbach S LLP -1 Chase Rd -Scarsdale 10583
(212) 909-6000 .. **Shoretz,** Rochelle Lee '97 %Debevoise & P LLP -919 3rd Av -NY 10022
(212) 582-0598 .. **Shorin,** Iris W '86 -27 W 55th -NY 10019 **Fx:**489-3303
(212) 788-1089 .. **Shorr,** Scott N '96 %Law Dept -100 Church -NY 10007 **Fx:**788-0367
(212) 882-5142 .. **Shors,** Thos E '98 UBS Asset Mgmt -51 W 52nd -NY 10019
(212) 318-6000 .. **Short,** Andrew M '86 (Paul HJ&W LLP) -75 E 55th -NY 10022
(212) 732-3320 .. **Short & Billy, PC** -217 Bway -NY 10007 **Fx:**732-3326
(212) 850-6220 .. **Short,** Bridget A '99 (Lathrop & G LC) -230 Park Av -NY 10169
(212) 382-0909 .. **Short,** Doris D '07 %Peckar & A,PC -41 Mad Av -NY 10154
(212) 262-2390 .. **Short,** Douglas J '01 %Connell F LLP -888 7th Av -NY 10106
(315) 671-1108 .. **Short,** John E '89 Supreme Ct -401 Mntgmry -Syracuse 13202
(212) 556-5807 .. **Short,** Randall K '84 %The NY Times Co -620 8th Av -NY 10018
(212) 732-3320 .. **Short,** Skip '76 (Short & B,PC) -217 Bway -NY 10007
(212) 735-3000 .. **Short,** Spencer R '08 %Skadden ASM&F LLP -4 Times Sq -NY 10036
(212) 267-5606 .. **Short,** Stephen '84 -40 Harrison -NY 10013
(607) 974-0412 .. **Short,** Svetlana Zonis '95 Corning Inc -SP-TI-3-1 -Corning 14831 **Fx:**974-3848
(914) 948-4500 .. **Shorte,** Aaliyah C '04 %O'Connor MCD&O -1 Barker Av -White Plns 10601
(718) 337-4900 .. **Shortell,** Jane K '97 %Leg Aid -1600 Central Av -Far Rckwy 11691 **Fx:**327-3415
(212) 709-8148 .. **Shortell-McSweeney,** Jacqueline '97 -110 Wall -NY 10005 **Fx:**943-2300
(212) 307-0023 .. **Shorter,** C Toby '95 %DeSimone AS&O LLP -145 Hudson -NY 10013
(917) 459-3697 .. **Shorter,** James R Jr. '76 -345 E 80th -NY 10075
(585) 255-1429 .. **Shortley,** Michl J '80 %Global Crossing -225 Kenneth Dr -Rchstr 14623 **Fx:**(877) 769-9844
(212) 407-4000 .. **Shortnacy,** Michl B '04 %Loeb & L,LLP -345 Park Av -NY 10154
(212) 768-6700 .. **Shortt,** Brian J '07 %Sonnenschein N&R LLP -2 World Fncl Ctr -NY 10281
(516) 877-5600 .. **Shortt,** James J '71 %R Tusa -1225 Franklin Av -Gdn Cty 11530 **Fx:**877-5695
(718) 286-6000 .. **Shortt,** Timothy J '10 %DA -125-01 Qns Blvd -Kew Gdns 11415
(212) 259-8000 .. **Shoss,** Cynthia R '90 (Dewey & L LLP) -1301 Av of Amer -NY 10019
(845) 566-9200 .. **Shost,** Elizabeth M '93 OfCnsl C Rock,PLLC -320 Robnsn Av -Newburgh 12550 **Fx:**566-7288
(212) 619-5000 .. **Shostak,** Scott E '85 %EDC -110 William -NY 10038 **Fx:**312-3912
(631) 234-0893 .. **Shotten,** David S '91 (D Shotten,PC) -1707-26 Vets Mem'l Hwy -Islandia 11749 **Fx:**234-0894
(516) 594-0909 .. **Shouldice,** Donald T '92 (Polsky S&R,PC) -500 Merrick Rd -Rockvll Ctr 11570
(718) 875-0909 .. **Shouldice,** Donald T '92 (Polsky S&R,PC) -142 Joralemon -Brklyn 11201
(718) 278-2224 .. **Shoulson,** Jay C '87 -31-51 Crescent -LIC 11106 **Fx:**726-8722
(212) 504-6000 .. **Shouse,** Sara N '10 %Cadwalader W&T LLP -1 World Fncl Ctr -NY 10281
(212) 747-1230 .. **Showers,** Andrew D '04 %McMahon M&G LLP -55 Washington -Brklyn 11201
(917) 553-1426 .. **Showman,** Wallace A '89 -200 Cabrini Blvd -NY 10033
(718) 646-5709 .. **Shpak,** Rimma '96 -1517 Voorhies Av -Brklyn 11235 **Fx:**646-8300
(718) 891-8200 .. **Shpelfogel,** Mitchell B '06 (Pinczewski & S,PC) -2753 Coney Isl Av -Brklyn 11235
(212) 526-1472 .. **Shpetner,** Thos D '99 %Barclays Capital Inc -745 7th Av -NY 10019
(718) 222-2330 .. **Shrader,** Brittany L '10 %Law Dept -350 Jay -Brklyn 11201 **Fx:**222-2373
(516) 333-2800 .. **Shrader,** J Carl '86 %E Schloss & Co -1400 Old Cntry Rd -Westbury 11590
(212) 827-7622 .. **Shrago,** Alvin H '88 %TD Securities -31 W 52nd -NY 10019
(585) 752-7523 .. **Shramek,** Wm J '04 -250 Mill -Rchstr 14614 **Fx:**672-5252
(212) 749-3121 .. **Shramko,** Jonathan D '81 -145 W 96th -NY 10025
(212) 610-6300 .. **Shrank,** Ian '79 (Allen & O) -1221 Av of Amer -NY 10020
(212) 415-9200 .. **Shravah,** Aasheesh V '03 %Dorsey & W LLP -250 Park Av -NY 10177
(516) 741-2585 .. **Shravah,** Aashmita V '00 %Rosicki R & Assoc,PC -51 E Bethpage Rd -Plainvw 11803 **Fx:**741-4748
(212) 733-7902 .. **Shrayer,** Lisa A '02 Pfizer -150 E 42nd -NY 10017
(212) 504-6000 .. **Shreeves,** Kathryn Fleury '01 %Cadwalader W&T LLP -1 World Fncl Ctr -NY 10281
(212) 440-2745 .. **Shreiber,** Lisa S '98 Colliau EMCK&M -40 Wall -NY 10005
(516) 571-2323 .. **Shrenkel,** Jane '84 %Hon T Adams -100 Supreme Ct Dr -Mineola 11501
(212) 855-9067 .. **Shrestha,** Pankauz Narayan '99 Goldman Sachs -1 NY Plz -NY 10004
(212) 218-2100 .. **Shreve,** Nina '78 (Fitzpatrick CH&S) -1290 Av of Amer -NY 10104
(914) 347-2600 .. **Shrewsberry,** Lisa L '89 (Traub LS&S LLP) -7 Skyline Dr -Hawthorne 10532
(917) 777-4200 .. **Shrier,** Allison L '04 %Bingham M LLP -1 Bttry Pk Plz -NY 10004
(718) 832-6500 .. **Shrier,** Leonard A '80 OfCnsl Belson & S -1310 8th Av -Brklyn 11215
(212) 223-4000 .. **Shrimanker,** Amisha '08 %Crowell & M LLP -590 Mad Av -NY 10022
(212) 687-8838 .. **Shrivastava,** Kaveri '04 Rosy Blue Inc -529 5th Av -NY 10017
(212) 808-3778 .. **Shrock,** Gregory J '86 Arklow Advisors,LLC -237 Park Av -NY 10017
(212) 417-8700 .. **Shroff,** Sabrina '92 %Fed Def of NY Inc -52 Duane -NY 10007 **Fx:**571-0392
(212) 759-3300 .. **Shroff,** Vijay J '05 %Dornbush SS&V,LLP -747 3rd Av -NY 10017
(212) 969-3000 .. **Shron,** Bradley S '06 %Proskauer R LLP -1585 Bway -NY 10036
(212) 682-8811 .. **Shroyer,** John W '59 (Dunnington B&M LLP) -1359 Bway -NY 10018
(212) 449-2572 .. **Shryoc,** K Kirk Jr. '05 Merrill Lynch -4 World Fncl Ctr -NY 10080
(212) 821-3678 .. **Shryock,** Kristine M '06 UBS Investment Bk -299 Park Av -NY 10171
(718) 338-6300 .. **Shtaynberg,** Arthur '02 -1115 Ocean Pkwy -Brklyn 11230
(631) 724-8833 .. **Shteierman,** Joshua S '09 %Devitt SB,LLP -50 Route 111 -Smithtwn 11787
(718) 370-7080 .. **Shteiman,** Victoria '02 -37 Josephine -Staten Isl 10314
(718) 853-7807 .. **Shtern,** Herman '97 Shtern Construction & Remodeling -5521 11th Av -Brklyn 11219
(212) 819-8200 .. **Shterngel,** Max '10 %White & C LLP -1155 Av of Amer -NY 10036
(516) 992-8082 .. **Shteyman,** Zory '08 %H Davoli Jr -342 N Lng Bch Rd -Rockvll Ctr 11570 **Fx:**543-4190
(212) 698-4550 .. **Shteynberg,** Irina '03 %Thieffry & Assoc -150 E 58th -NY 10155 **Fx:**698-4551
(212) 259-8000 .. **Shtilerman,** Mark D '08 %Dewey & L LLP -1301 Av of Amer -NY 10019
(718) 351-9500 .. **Shtindler,** Yana '01 (Y Shtindler,PC) -380 Sand Ln -Staten Isl 10305 **Fx:**351-6945
(212) 698-3500 .. **Shtob,** Danl A '05 %Dechert LLP -1095 Av of Amer -NY 10036
(212) 278-0400 .. **Shu,** Cindy S '08 %Cooper & D LLP -30 Rckfllr Plz -NY 10112
(212) 610-6300 .. **Shube,** Eric S '85 (Allen & O) -1221 Av of Amer -NY 10020
(212) 274-8638 .. **Shube,** Noah '93 -434 Bway -NY 10013
(716) 847-8400 .. **Shubert,** Ronald S '79 (Phillips L LLP) -3400 HSBC Ctr -Buffalo 14203
(212) 966-0466 .. **Shubert,** Virginia G '80 %Housing Works,Inc -594 Bway -NY 10012 **Fx:**966-0866
(212) 867-5800 .. **Shubitz,** Mark J '05 %Osler H&H LLP -620 8th Av -NY 10018
(212) 489-1600 .. **Shubrick,** Adreme M '99 %Deloitte LLP -1633 Bway -NY 10019 **Fx:**492-4201
(212) 446-2300 .. **Shuchart,** Scott L '05 %Boies S&F LLP -575 Lex Av -NY 10022
(212) 940-8800 .. **Shuchat,** Jeffrey L '79 (Katten MR LLP) -575 Mad Av -NY 10022
(212) 687-1736 .. **Shuchatowitz,** Alan J '95 %R Schwartzberg & Assoc,PLLC -60 E 42nd -NY 10165
(212) 682-0580 .. **Shuck,** Maria Tufvesson '93 (Mannheimer S) -101 Park Av -NY 10178
(212) 664-3795 .. **Shudofsky,** Alisa D '84 %NBC -30 Rckfllr Plz -NY 10112 **Fx:**664-6572
(212) 213-6996 .. **Shudofsky,** Sara L '87 OfCnsl Spears & I LLP -51 Mad Av -NY 10010
(518) 272-6565 .. **Shudt,** Edwyn L '55 OfCnsl Martin SWD&J -279 River Bx1530 -Troy 12181
(718) 694-5719 .. **Shufer,** Jane '06 Transit Auth -130 Lvngstn -Brklyn 11201 **Fx:**694-5726
(212) 755-0006 .. **Shuffman,** David K '73 -16 W 46th -NY 10036 **Fx:**755-0007
(212) 756-2000 .. **Shufro,** Jennifer W '01 %Schulte R&Z LLP -919 3rd Av -NY 10022
(212) 245-4580 .. **Shukat Arrow Hafer Weber & Herbsman,LLP** -111 W 57th -NY 10019 **Fx:**956-6471
(212) 245-4580 .. **Shukat,** Peter S '70 (Shukat AHW&H,LLP) -111 W 57th -NY 10019
(212) 848-4000 .. **Shukrie,** Itzhak '10 Shearman & S LLP -599 Lex Av -NY 10022

(516) 873-6200 .. **Shukry,** Jamila '07 %R Macchia & Assoc -98 Front -Mineola 11501 **Fx:**873-1611
(914) 949-1305 .. **Shula,** Sharon Lee '93 %Leg Srvcs -90 Maple Av -White Plns 10601 **Fx:**949-6213
(212) 336-0166 .. **Shuler,** Stephanie D '04 %SEC -3 World Fncl Ctr -NY 10281 **Fx:**336-1323
(518) 792-1174 .. **Shuler,** Timothy S '89 %McPhillips F&C,LLP -288 Glen Bx299 -Glens Fls 12801
(212) 666-3938 .. **Shulklapper,** Gregg B '93 -306 W 105th -NY 10025
(518) 449-8893 .. **Shulklapper,** Lester M '58 OfCnsl Wilson EME&D LLP -677 Bway -Albany 12207
(212) 788-0457 .. **Shull,** Hugh H III '91 %Law Dept -100 Church -NY 10007 **Fx:**788-0367
(212) 335-9000 .. **Shull,** Robt D '02 %DA -1 Hogan Pl -NY 10013
(212) 906-1200 .. **Shullman,** Julia M '08 %Latham & W -885 3rd Av -NY 10022
(212) 798-8136 .. **Shulman,** Adam M '06 Globe Specialty Metals Inc -250 W 34th -NY 10119 **Fx:**798-8138
(212) 758-2020 .. **Shulman,** Alan L '58 OfCnsl N Silverman -200 Park Av S -NY 10003 **Fx:**758-2025
(718) 522-6725 .. **Shulman,** Alex '67 -26 Court -Brklyn 11242
(718) 275-3660 .. **Shulman,** Alexander '08 (Harris Law Grp,LLP) -96-14 63rd Dr -Rego Pk 11374 **Fx:**275-3405
(212) 268-1000 .. **Shulman,** Amy F '97 (Broach & S,LLP) -1 Penn Plz -NY 10119
(631) 582-9400 .. **Shulman,** Arthur E '74 -1601 Vets Mem'l Hwy -Islandia 11749 **Fx:**582-9408
(212) 734-7965 .. **Shulman,** Barbara J '84 -850 Park Av -NY 10075
(315) 471-8111 .. **Shulman,** Barry M '66 (Scolaro SCF&B,PC) -507 Plum -Syracuse 13204
(585) 454-4750 .. **Shulman,** Brian J '89 -1 E Main -Rchstr 14614
(315) 424-8944 .. **Shulman,** C Danl '65 (Shulman CG&R,PC) -250 S Clinton -Syracuse 13202
(212) 653-8700 .. **Shulman,** Carren '92 (Sheppard MR&H LLP) -30 Rckfllr Plz -NY 10112
(315) 424-8944 .. **Shulman Curtin Grundner & Regan,PC** -250 S Clinton -Syracuse 13202 **Fx:**424-8205
(212) 705-4874 .. **Shulman,** Danl M '05 %Tavel & Assoc,PC -488 Mad Av -NY 10022 **Fx:**537-4724
(212) 735-3000 .. **Shulman,** Dean S '92 (Skadden ASM&F LLP) -4 Times Sq -NY 10036
(718) 205-1010 .. **Shulman,** Dmitriy '03 %E Ifraimoff & Assoc,PC -116-16 Qns Blvd -Frst Hlls 11375 **Fx:**205-2066
(914) 251-1618 .. **Shulman,** Frederic M '79 (Price MS&D,PC) -106 Corp Park Dr -White Plns 10604
(212) 566-2900 .. **Shulman,** Harry G '94 -1 North End Av -NY 10282
(212) 733-4329 .. **Shulman,** Ilana Meredith '96 %Pfizer Inc -235 E 42nd -NY 10017 **Fx:**573-1445
(212) 878-8000 .. **Shulman,** Ilya N '08 %Clifford C LLP -31 W 52nd -NY 10019
(212) 759-1333 .. **Shulman,** Jason M '53 -122 E 42nd -NY 10168 **Fx:**972-3329
(516) 365-3173 .. **Shulman,** Jay M '95 -1 Cherrywood Ln -Manhsst 11030
(631) 499-9100 .. **Shulman Kessler,LLP** -510 Broadhllw Rd -Melvll 11747 **Fx:**499-9120
(845) 338-7970 .. **Shulman,** Laura G '98 (L Shulman,PC) -231 Clinton Av Bx4082 -Kingston 12402 **Fx:**338-7270
(212) 330-1222 .. **Shulman,** Laurence J '81 %Buck Consultants -1 Penn Plz -NY 10119 **Fx:**695-4184
(516) 942-5100 .. **Shulman,** Madelyn Spatt '80 (MS Shulman PC) -3000 Marcus Av -Lk Success 11042 **Fx:**437-6434
(212) 277-0451 .. **Shulman,** Matthew A '05 Hartford Fncl Grp -2 Park Av -NY 10016
(212) 474-1000 .. **Shulman,** Max R '72 (Cravath S&M LLP) -825 8th Av -NY 10019
(212) 335-4254 .. **Shulman,** Michele Dara '95 %DA -1 Hogan Pl -NY 10013
(718) 590-5978 .. **Shulman,** Monica D '97 %Admin Children's Srvcs -900 Sheridan Av -Bronx 10451
(718) 899-1102 .. **Shulman,** Monica L '05 %News Realty -3736 75th -Jcksn Hts 11372
(516) 486-4640 .. **Shulman,** Morgan E '94 (Cherry E&K,LLP) -1 Old Cntry Rd -Carle Pl 11514
(518) 674-3805 .. **Shulman,** Morton D '57 -Bx1000 -Averill Pk 12018 **Fx:**674-3964
(914) 749-8200 .. **Shulman,** Motty '01 (Boies S&F LLP) -333 Main -Armonk 10504
(212) 806-5400 .. **Shulman,** Regan A '89 SpclCnsl Stroock &S&L LLP -180 Maiden Ln -NY 10038
(212) 964-4686 .. **Shulman,** Robt A '87 %Mutual Abstract -132 Nassau -NY 10038 **Fx:**385-0758
(646) 252-6653 .. **Shulman,** Sanford M '99 NYC Transit Auth -2 Bway -NY 10004
(718) 997-5709 .. **Shulman,** Sharon Sendyk '84 %Queens Cllg Paralgl Studies -65-30 Kissena Blvd -Flushng 11367 **Fx:**997-5723
(212) 431-1300 .. **Shulman,** Stephen C '87 (Borah GAN&G PC) -377 Bway -NY 10013
(631) 499-9100 .. **Shulman,** Steven '90 (Shulman K,LLP) -510 Broadhllw Rd -Melvll 11747
(212) 578-6199 .. **Shulman,** Steven R '94 MetLife -27-01 Qns Plz N -LIC 11101
(914) 632-0787 .. **Shulman,** Sydelle '58 -46 Longue Vue Av -New Rchll 10804 **Fx:**632-7745
(607) 255-3012 .. **Shulman,** Zachary J '91 %Cornell Univ -142D Sage Hall -Ithaca 14853
(516) 505-2300 .. **Shulov,** Victor L '10 %Sharifov & R -50 Main -Hempstd 11550 **Fx:**505-2379
(518) 234-2317 .. **Shultes,** Michl J '03 -523 W Main -Cobleskill 12043 **Fx:**234-3848
(607) 324-1104 .. **Shults,** David A '69 (Shults & S) -9 Seneca -Hornell 14843 **Fx:**324-7983
(607) 324-1104 .. **Shults,** Eric '72 (Shults & S) -9 Seneca -Hornell 14843 **Fx:**324-7983
(212) 788-0081 .. **Shultz,** Harold M '75 %Mayors Ofc of Contracts -253 Bway -NY 10007 **Fx:**788-0049
(518) 435-8092 .. **Shultz,** Steven P '86 %Finkelstein & Prtnrs,LLP -80 Wolf Rd -Albany 12205
(212) 310-8000 .. **Shulzhenko,** Oleksandr '01 %Weil G&M LLP -767 5th Av -NY 10153
(212) 455-2000 .. **Shum,** Chi H '02 %Simpson T&B LLP -425 Lex Av -NY 10017
(718) 888-7930 .. **Shum,** Wilson '01 -37-01 Main -Flushng 11354 **Fx:**888-7851
(646) 878-0800 .. **Shuman,** Clyde A '98 %Pearl CZL,LLP -1500 Bway -NY 10036
(212) 578-2211 .. **Shuman,** Ira H '76 %MetLife -27-01 Qns Plz N -LIC 11101
(716) 854-4300 .. **Shuman,** Irving M '56 (Gross SB&G,PC) -465 Main -Buffalo 14203
(212) 832-8000 .. **Shuman,** Stanley S '91 Allen & Co -711 5th Av -NY 10022 **Fx:**339-2305
(914) 631-4800 .. **Shumejda,** Jeffrey S '75 -47 Beekman Av -Sleepy Hollow 10591 **Fx:**631-5388
(212) 373-3000 .. **Shumejda,** Lauren E '08 %Paul WRW&G LLP -1285 Av of Amer -NY 10019
(516) 228-1050 .. **Shumer,** David M '01 %A Rosner -600 Old Cntry Rd -Gdn Cty 11530 **Fx:**228-1055
(516) 747-1136 .. **Shumer,** Steven E '92 %Steinberg FB&F,PC -40 Crsswys Park Dr -Woodbury 11797
(631) 224-5260 .. **Shumicky,** Alex '91 -254 Islip Av -Islip 11751 **Fx:**224-5168
(212) 338-9700 .. **Shupack & Hardy, LLP** -450 7th Av -NY 10123
(212) 338-9700 .. **Shupack,** Jeffrey S '95 (Shupack & H,LLP) -450 7th Av -NY 10123
(212) 790-0249 .. **Shupack,** Paul M '71 %Benj N Cardozo Schl of Law -55 5th Av -NY 10003 **Fx:**790-0345
(585) 325-6202 .. **Shur,** Jos M '90 (Relin G&C LLP) -28 E Main -Rchstr 14614
(718) 692-1294 .. **Shur,** Paul D '75 -1149 Ocean Pkwy -Brklyn 11230
(212) 643-7000 .. **Shur,** Paul H '89 (Sills C&G PC) -One Rckfllr Plz -NY 10020
(212) 789-8183 .. **Shurdut,** Jennifer H '96 Patina Restaurant Grp -120 W 45th -NY 10036
(212) 326-2000 .. **Shure,** Jared E '08 %O'Melveny & M LLP -7 Times Sq -NY 10036
(718) 250-2834 .. **Shurka,** Nancy R '01 DA -350 Jay -Brklyn 11201
(516) 485-4221 .. **Shurman,** Paul S '85 (Foley SO&W) -175 Fulton Av -Hempstd 11550
(877) 222-1814 .. **Shushan,** Alan M '93 %B Rothenberg -100 Duffy Av -Hicksvll 11801 **Fx:**(866) 894-2182
(845) 294-8112 .. **Shust,** Christopher M '94 -210 Main -Goshen 10924
(212) 688-5900 .. **Shustak,** Erwin J '77 (Shustak F & Prtnrs) -400 Park Av -NY 10022 **Fx:**688-6151
(516) 336-2436 .. **Shuster,** David A '93 Grassi & Co CPAS -50 Jericho Quad -Jericho 11753 **Fx:**256-3510
(631) 969-7777 .. **Shuster,** Dina L '91 %Frenkel LWW&G,LLP -20 W Main -Bay Shr 11706 **Fx:**206-0540
(212) 230-8800 .. **Shuster,** George W Jr. '10 (WilmerHale) -399 Park Av -NY 10022
(212) 506-1700 .. **Shuster,** Michl '87 (Kasowitz BT&F LLP) -1633 Bway -NY 10019
(516) 584-2743 .. **Shusterhoff,** Jay '78 -2 Bay Club Dr -Bayside 11360
(212) 210-9558 .. **Shusterman,** Anna R '06 %Alston & B LLP -90 Park Av -NY 10016
(212) 685-7600 .. **Shusterman,** Evan R '05 %Heller H&F,PC -292 Mad Av -NY 10017
(215) 864-6217 .. **Shusterman,** Richd M '96 (White and W LLP) -1 Penn Plz -NY 10119 **Fx:**864-7517
(212) 940-8800 .. **Shusterman,** Victoria '07 (Katten MR LLP) -575 Mad Av -NY 10022
(212) 530-5000 .. **Shutkin,** Anne V '09 %Milbank TH&M LLP -1 Chase Manh Plz -NY 10005
(212) 909-5008 .. **Shutkin,** John A '75 KPMG Intl -345 Park Av -NY 10154
(212) 259-8000 .. **Shutran,** Richd '79 (Dewey & L LLP) -1301 Av of Amer -NY 10019
(845) 562-0203 .. **Shuttleworth,** James W III '89 (Finkelstein & Prtnrs,LLP) -1279 Route 300 Bx1111 -Newburgh 12550
(212) 697-5551 .. **Shuzman,** Wm I '77 %Allied Bldg Mtls Ind -211 E 43rd -NY 10017
(212) 909-6000 .. **Shvets,** Yeugenia '08 %Debevoise & P LLP -919 3rd Av -NY 10022
(212) 909-6000 .. **Shwartz,** Robt N '76 (Debevoise & P LLP) -919 3rd Av -NY 10022
(212) 856-9600 .. **Shweder,** Jeremy W '09 %Morvillo AGIA&B,PC -565 5th Av -NY 10017
(718) 254-6092 .. **Shweder,** Sylvia Shaz '06 US Atty-EDNY -271 Cadman Plz E -Brklyn 11201
(212) 244-9000 .. **Shweky,** Barbara R '86 Matalon SE -450 7th Av -NY 10123 **Fx:**244-4615
(646) 596-5258 .. **Shweky,** Evan Y '92 %Royal Bank of Canada -666 E 43rd -NY 10017
(631) 755-0101 .. **Shwom,** Matthew D '99 %Lewis JAA,LLP -425 Broad Hollow Rd -Melvll 11747
(212) 688-8555 .. **Shy,** Lauren B '00 %Fragomen DB&L LLP -7 Hanover Sq -NY 10004
(212) 538-9354 .. **Shy,** Randall E '97 Credit Suisse -11 Mad Av -NY 10010
(212) 998-2266 .. **Shy,** Yael L A '08 NYU Ctr on Violence & Recovery -194 Mercer -NY 10012
(516) 223-3115 .. **Shyab,** Suzanne '78 -562 Burger Pl -Baldwin 11510
(212) 687-3000 .. **Shyer,** David R '05 %Jaffe & A,LLP -600 3rd Av -NY 10016
(212) 906-1200 .. **Shyer,** John D '82 (Latham & W) -885 3rd Av -NY 10022
(516) 393-2200 .. **Siachos,** Peter G '06 %Garfunkel W,PC -111 Grt Nck Rd -Gt Neck 11021
(914) 997-0100 .. **Siano,** Anthony J '72 -333 Wstchstr Av -White Plns 10604 **Fx:**997-4179
(516) 868-1791 .. **Siano,** Lisa '79 -2872 Merrick Rd -Bellmore 11710 **Fx:**868-0805
(212) 625-5712 .. **Siano,** Matthew B '99 Two Sigma Invstmnts -379 W Bway -NY 10012
(212) 723-3596 .. **Siano,** Michele '98 Citigroup Global Mrkts -250 West -NY 10013
(914) 681-9065 .. **Siano,** Robt D '04 (Libous & S) -399 Knollwood Rd -White Plns 10603
(212) 878-8000 .. **Sibbett,** Benjamin K '00 (Clifford C LLP) -31 W 52nd -NY 10019
(516) 333-5000 .. **Sibell,** Stanley J '69 (Gordon S&I PC) -400 Grdn City Plz -Gdn Cty 11530 **Fx:**333-3260
(631) 665-3400 .. **Siben,** Andrew B '85 (Siben & S,LLP) -90 E Main Bx149P -Bay Shr 11706
(631) 234-2222 .. **Siben & Ferber** -1455 Vets Mem'l Hwy -Hauppauge 11749 **Fx:**234-2460
(631) 234-2222 .. **Siben,** Gary L '75 Cnsl Siben & F -1455 Vets Mem'l Hwy -Hauppauge 11749
(631) 665-3400 .. **Siben,** Jacqueline '94 (Siben & S,LLP) -90 E Main Bx149P -Bay Shr 11706
(631) 665-3400 .. **Siben & Siben,LLP** -90 E Main Bx149P -Bay Shr 11706 **Fx:**665-3236
(631) 665-3400 .. **Siben,** Stephen G '65 (Siben & S,LLP) -90 E Main Bx149P -Bay Shr 11706
(631) 360-7800 .. **Sibener,** Paul S '73 (Spada A&S,PLLC) -64 Smithtwn Blvd -Smithtwn 11787
(212) 589-4200 .. **Siber,** Victor '71 (Baker & H LLP) -45 Rckfllr Plz -NY 10111
(212) 773-6274 .. **Sibery,** Richd A II '99 Ernst & Young LLP -5 Times Sq -NY 10036
(845) 256-9096 .. **Sibley,** Charlotte C '92 %Farmworker Law Proj -52 S Manheim Blvd -New Paltz 12561 **Fx:**256-0494
(212) 421-4100 .. **Sibley,** Patrick '08 %Pryor C LLP -7 Times Sq -NY 10036

(212) 759-6767 ..**Sibony**, Oren L '05 %R Kornfeld -570 Lex Av -NY 10022 **Fx:**759-6766
(718) 590-2000 ..**Sibovits**, Danit L '09 %DA -198 E 161st -Bronx 10451 **Fx:**590-6477
(212) 406-0552 ..**Sica**, Alfred F '51 Cnsl A Sica,PC -321 Bway -NY 10007 **Fx:**349-4037
(212) 525-4729 ..**Sica**, Gary P '99 Advisory Srvcs -452 5th Av -NY 10018
(212) 642-7847 ..**Sica**, Richd M '91 %Ace Financial Solutions -1133 Av of Amer -NY 10036
(212) 351-4000 ..**Sica**, Theo C '03 %Gibson D&C LLP -200 Park Av -NY 10166
(516) 877-5600 ..**Sica**, Thos '93 %R Tusa -1225 Franklin Av -Gdn Cty 11530 **Fx:**877-5695
(518) 465-1100 ..**Sica**, Thos A '88 %Boeggeman G&C,PC -46 Columbia -Albany 12207
(718) 261-7660 ..**Siccardi**, Vincent F '86 -125-10 Qns Blvd -Kew Gdns 11415 **Fx:**261-3482
(212) 272-9889 ..**Sichel**, Robt L '02 %JP Morgan Chase -383 Mad Av -NY 10179
(718) 745-3080 ..**Sichenze**, Andrew L '59 -7703 5th Av -Brklyn 11209
(718) 237-2000 ..**Sichenze**, Cynthia K '88 %Leg Aid -111 Lvngstn -Brklyn 11201 **Fx:**237-8737
(718) 680-0400 ..**Sichenze**, Sylvester J '90 -7703 5th Av -Brklyn 11209
(516) 739-1937 ..**Sichenzia**, Dominic J '72 -1 Old Cntry Rd -Carle Pl 11514 **Fx:**739-1938
(212) 930-9700 ..**Sichenzia**, Gregory '88 (Sichenzia RFF LLP) -61 Bway -NY 10006
(212) 930-9700 ..**Sichenzia Ross Friedman Ference LLP** -61 Bway -NY 10006 **Fx:**930-9725
(212) 448-9570 ..**Sicheri**, Wm A '04 %Callahan & F,LLC -40 Exch Pl -NY 10005
(845) 357-4422 ..**Sichol**, Brian A '71 (Sichol & H) -139 Lafayette Av Bx359 -Suffern 10901
(845) 357-4422 ..**Sichol & Hicks** -139 Lafayette Av Bx359 -Suffern 10901 **Fx:**357-0998
(845) 357-4422 ..**Sichol**, Wm R Jr. '66 (Sichol & H) -139 Lafayette Av Bx359 -Suffern 10901
(212) 446-8699 ..**Sicignano**, Karen A '93 %McKinsey & Co -55 E 52nd -NY 10055 **Fx:**688-9521
(212) 508-6700 ..**Siciliano**, Ralph A '76 (Tannenbaum HS&H LLP) -900 3rd Av -NY 10022
(212) 238-3361 ..**Siciliano**, Thos G '80 %Mncpl Crdt Union -22 Crtlandt -NY 10007 **Fx:**479-2975
(585) 546-3820 ..**Sickelco**, James H '79 -19 Main W -Rchstr 14614 **Fx:**232-6595
(212) 801-6569 ..**Sickelka**, Elizabeth J '09 %Greenberg T,LLP -200 Park Av -NY 10166
(585) 338-6800 ..**Sickinger**, Gina M '00 Bausch & Lomb -One Bausch & Lomb Pl -Rchstr 14604 **Fx:**338-8706
(212) 418-6100 ..**Sickinger**, Peter X '64 %GM -767 5th Av -NY 10153 **Fx:**418-6123
(212) 728-8000 ..**Sicklick**, Kenneth A '04 %Willkie F&G LLP -787 7th Av -NY 10019
(973) 315-4482 ..**Siclari**, Laura A '05 %Budd L -140 Bway -NY 10005
(914) 828-8812 ..**Siconolfi**, Rocco J '99 %Swiss Re America -175 King -Armonk 10504 **Fx:**828-7000
(212) 373-3000 ..**Sicular**, David R '84 (Paul WRW&G LLP) -1285 Av of Amer -NY 10019
(212) 872-1500 ..**Sidamon-Eristoff**, Constantine '58 OfCnsl Lacher & L-T -460 Park Av -NY 10022 **Fx:**872-1630
(631) 447-8799 ..**Sidaras**, Erin A '99 -35 Patchogue Yaphank Rd -Patchogue 11772
(315) 474-7541 ..**Sidd**, John P '92 %Menter R&T,PC -308 Maltbie -Syracuse 13204
(212) 651-5868 ..**Sidd**, Susan E '91 %Jane Street Captl -1 NY Plz -NY 10004
(212) 446-4000 ..**Siddiky**, Rinku Rumana '03 Davidson Kempner Cptl Mgmt LLC -65 E 55th -NY 10022
(212) 449-3507 ..**Siddiq**, Nizam M '98 Merrill Lynch -4 World Fncl Ctr -NY 10080
(212) 574-1200 ..**Siddiqi**, Sehar N '09 %Seward & K LLP -1 Bttry Pk Plz -NY 10004
(212) 514-5900 ..**Siddiqi**, Zafar A '91 -11 Bway -NY 10004 **Fx:**514-5005
(212) 715-9100 ..**Siddique**, Nakeeb '08 %Kramer LN&F,LLP -1177 Av of Amer -NY 10036
(516) 877-5600 ..**Siddiqui**, Hamid M '97 %R Tusa -1225 Franklin Av -Gdn Cty 11530 **Fx:**877-5695
(212) 608-1900 ..**Siddiqui**, Imtiaz A '04 %Lovell SH LLP -61 Bway -NY 10006
(516) 683-3786 ..**Siddiqui**, Maqsood H '90 -600 Old Cntry Rd -Gdn Cty 11530 **Fx:**683-6115
(212) 318-6000 ..**Siddiqui**, Mohammad S R '10 %Paul HJ&W LLP -75 E 55th -NY 10022
(212) 530-5000 ..**Siddiqui**, Nehal M '10 %Milbank TH&M LLP -1 Chase Manh Plz -NY 10005
(718) 875-4003 ..**Siddiqui**, Rashidah Sakeenah '03 (Serpico S&S,PC) -105 Court -Brklyn 11201 **Fx:**875-4011
(212) 735-3000 ..**Siddiqui**, Shahram M '07 %Skadden ASM&F LLP -4 Times Sq -NY 10036
(212) 918-3000 ..**Siddiqui**, Waajid '08 (Hogan L LLP) -875 3rd Av -NY 10022
(914) 834-3500 ..**Siddons**, Chas L '93 OfCnsl McMillan CM&P LLP -2180 Bstn Post Rd -Larchmnt 10538
(845) 794-8811 ..**Side**, Matthew P '00 Appellate Div 3rd Dept -414 Bway -Monticello 12701
(212) 267-4710 ..**Sidelle**, Ronald A '56 (Erstein & S) -7 Dey -NY 10007
(212) 553-5541 ..**Sider**, Gail Robin '84 Zurich Amer Ins -165 Bway -NY 10006
(212) 559-5328 ..**Sider**, Richd D '84 Citigroup -425 Park Av -NY 10022 **Fx:**793-4400
(516) 746-8000 ..**Sideris**, Maria '01 %Jaspan S LLP -300 Grdn City Plz -Gdn Cty 11530
(212) 715-9100 ..**Siderman**, Cynthia Lovinger '02 %Kramer LN&F,LLP -1177 Av of Amer -NY 10036
(212) 446-8242 ..**Siderow**, Stephen M '92 %McKinsey & Co -55 E 52nd -NY 10055 **Fx:**688-9521
(212) 506-2500 ..**Sidhu**, Vikram '02 Cnsl Mayer B LLP -1675 Bway -NY 10019
(212) 941-4700 ..**Sidi**, Robt J '85 -377 Bway -NY 10013 **Fx:**431-4460
(212) 839-5300 ..**Sidley Austin LLP** -787 7th Av -NY 10019 **Fx:**839-5599
(212) 425-9300 ..**Sidman**, Andrew W '78 (Bressler A&R,PC) -17 State -NY 10004
(212) 521-4870 ..**Sidman**, Hope '00 %Kerst & Co -437 Mad Av -NY 10022
(212) 326-3939 ..**Sidman**, Howard F '01 (Jones D) -222 E 41st -NY 10017
(212) 310-8000 ..**Sidman**, Lisa D '05 %Weil G&M LLP -767 5th Av -NY 10153
(212) 653-8700 ..**Sidney**, Ethel B '88 SpclCnsl Sheppard MR&H LLP -30 Rckfllr Plz -NY 10112
(718) 250-2000 ..**Sidney**, Lowell J '05 %DA -350 Jay -Brklyn 11201 **Fx:**250-2314
(516) 294-5433 ..**Sidney**, Steven L '73 (Ahmuty D&M) -200 IU Willets Rd -Albertson 11507
(212) 818-1110 ..**Sidorsky**, Robt '83 (Butzel L,PC) -380 Mad Av -NY 10017
(212) 558-5500 ..**Sidoti**, Francis Thos '08 %Weitz & L,PC -700 Bway -NY 10003
(585) 454-7545 ..**Sidoti**, Frank V '55 (Dutcher & S) -183 E Main -Rchstr 14604
(516) 868-3233 ..**Sidoti**, Gregg M '93 -1 North Dr -Baldwin 11510
(212) 613-2007 ..**Sidoti**, Mark S '89 (Gibbons PC) -1 Penn Plz -NY 10119 **Fx:**554-9660
(516) 569-9539 ..**Sidrane & Schwartz-Sidrane** -1427 Sturl Av -Hewlett 11557 **Fx:**569-9560
(516) 569-9539 ..**Sidrane**, Steven D '95 (Sidrane & S-S) -1427 Sturl Av -Hewlett 11557
(516) 208-3679 ..**Sieban**, Edw T Jr. '95 -74 N Vllg Av -Rockvll Ctr 11570 **Fx:**764-1446
(718) 923-6362 ..**Sieber**, Stephen B '72 Appllt Div 2nd Dept -335 Adams -Brklyn 11201
(212) 455-2000 ..**Siebert**, Amiekole R '08 %Simpson T&B LLP -425 Lex Av -NY 10017
(914) 946-4777 ..**Siebert**, Judson K '86 (Keane & B,PC) -445 Hmltn Av -White Plns 10601
(212) 779-1414 ..**Siebott**, Christian P '02 (Bernstein L LLP) -10 E 40th -NY 10016
(212) 581-6556 ..**Sieck**, John C '76 -250 W 57th -NY 10107 **Fx:**581-6557
(212) 571-1866 ..**Siegal**, Allen H '89 -299 Bway -NY 10007
(518) 431-1000 ..**Siegal**, David M '77 -16 Corp Wds Blvd -Albany 12211 **Fx:**465-7200
(212) 659-7300 ..**Siegal**, David M '93 (Haynes & B,LLP) -1221 Av of Amer -NY 10020
(845) 639-7800 ..**Siegal**, Helen L '89 %Mandel K&B,LLP -210 Route 303 -Vly Cottage 10989
(212) 589-4200 ..**Siegal**, John '87 (Baker & H LLP) -45 Rckfllr Plz -NY 10111
(212) 400-6900 ..**Siegal**, Laura B '91 OfCnsl Gottbetter & Prtnrs -488 Mad Av -NY 10022 **Fx:**400-6901
(212) 806-5400 ..**Siegal**, Matthew W '88 (Stroock &S&L LLP) -180 Maiden Ln -NY 10038
(212) 969-3000 ..**Siegartel**, Adam D '02 %Proskauer R LLP -1585 Bway -NY 10036
(212) 277-4000 ..**Siegel**, Adam B '96 (Freshfields BD LLP) -520 Mad Av -NY 10022
(212) 661-1212 ..**Siegel**, Alan M '73 (Levy S&S LLP) -630 3rd Av -NY 10017
(212) 397-3050 ..**Siegel**, Alfred '76 %Ctr for Ct Innovation -520 8th Av -NY 10018 **Fx:**397-0985
(212) 840-3737 ..**Siegel**, Andrew B '87 (Goidel & SL LLP) -122 E 42nd -NY 10168 **Fx:**840-3793
(212) 975-4480 ..**Siegel**, Andrew J '85 %CBS Inc -51 W 52nd -NY 10019
(212) 762-8592 ..**Siegel**, Andrew N '95 %Morgan Stanley -1221 Av of Amer -NY 10020
(914) 421-0080 ..**Siegel**, Andrew R '91 (Cohen & S LLP) -14 Mamaroneck Av -White Plns 10601 **Fx:**421-0035
(212) 532-0532 ..**Siegel**, Andrew W '89 (Geller & S,LLP) -419 Park Av S -NY 10016 **Fx:**532-1871
(516) 741-6100 ..**Siegel**, Angela '89 -1205 Franklin Av -Gdn Cty 11530 **Fx:**741-3133
(518) 533-3000 ..**Siegel**, Arthur J '85 (Bond S&K,PLLC) -111 Wshngtn Av -Albany 12210
(877) 324-7549 ..**Siegel**, Barry I '74 -3000 Marcus Av -Lk Success 11042 **Fx:**(201) 816-1522
(212) 489-1600 ..**Siegel**, Benjamin L '98 %Deloitte LLP -1633 Bway -NY 10019 **Fx:**492-4201
(315) 295-1485 ..**Siegel**, Birgitta K '05 Pearl Law -214 N State -Syracuse 13203
(212) 345-7000 ..**Siegel**, Blaine J '95 Mercer HR Cnsltng -1166 Av of Amer -NY 10036
(516) 935-1200 ..**Siegel**, Bruce A '75 %1st LI Invstrs,LLC -1 Jericho Plz -Jericho 11753 **Fx:**935-1274
(718) 354-3200 ..**Siegel**, Carol '82 %Battiste A&S,Inc -60 Bay -Staten Isl 10301
(212) 465-5000 ..**Siegel**, Cary M '83 %Parsons Brinckerhoff -1 Penn Plz -NY 10119
(212) 440-2350 ..**Siegel**, Chas J '82 -40 Wall -NY 10005 **Fx:**440-2385
(347) 296-1498 ..**Siegel**, Chas S '85 %Hon A Cutrona -360 Adams -Brklyn 11201
(212) 715-9100 ..**Siegel**, Craig L '99 %Kramer LN&F,LLP -1177 Av of Amer -NY 10036
(914) 422-0810 ..**Siegel**, Dale R '87 Circle Mortgage Grp -500 Mamaroneck Av -Harrison 10528 **Fx:**422-2994
(212) 737-9506 ..**Siegel**, Danl '50 -444 E 82nd -NY 10028
(212) 956-5770 ..**Siegel**, Dara R '01 Red Apple Grp -823 11th Av -NY 10019
(716) 854-1300 ..**Siegel**, David Alan '64 (Rosenthal S&M,LLP) -300 Main -Buffalo 14202
(518) 445-2318 ..**Siegel**, David D '58 Albany Law Schl -80 New Scotland Av -Albany 12208 **Fx:**445-2315
(914) 576-1006 ..**Siegel**, David Lincoln '62 %Blimpie Intl,Inc -145 Hugenot -New Rchll 10801
(518) 388-4466 ..**Siegel**, Deanna L '85 Dept Soc Srvcs -106 Erie Blvd -Schnctdy 12307 **Fx:**382-1256
(718) 286-2000 ..**Siegel**, Debra L '88 %Leg Aid -120-46 Qns Blvd -Kew Gdns 11415 **Fx:**286-2286
(516) 487-6920 ..**Siegel**, Donald R '53 -150 Grt Nck Rd -Gt Neck 11021 **Fx:**482-3226
(212) 312-7893 ..**Siegel**, Edw D '81 %State Ins Fund -199 Church -NY 10007 **Fx:**385-9199
(212) 737-7153 ..**Siegel**, Edw M '61 -1036 Park Av -NY 10028 **Fx:**737-3878
(212) 297-5800 ..**Siegel**, Elizabeth Baker '09 %Day P LLP -7 Times Sq -NY 10036
(646) 252-2979 ..**Siegel**, Erica R '01 NYC Transit Auth -2 Bway -NY 10004
(212) 406-0700 ..**Siegel**, Franklin D R '77 Ctr for Constitutional Rights -666 Bway -NY 10012 **Fx:**614-6499
(203) 326-3333 ..**Siegel**, Frederic J '83 (Siegel R&C,LLC) -158 Scarborough Rd -Briarcliff Mnr 10510 **Fx:**965-0509
(516) 574-6140 ..**Siegel**, Gail '76 %JP Morgan Chase -1985 Marcus Av -New Hyde Pk 11040
(212) 698-3500 ..**Siegel**, Glenn E '83 (Dechert LLP) -1095 Av of Amer -NY 10036
(718) 442-1700 ..**Siegel**, Harold J '63 %Connors & C,PC -766 Castleton Av -Staten Isl 10310 **Fx:**442-1717
(716) 883-4800 ..**Siegel**, Harvey F '97 -88 W Utica -Buffalo 14209
(718) 596-9000 ..**Siegel**, Hayward H '68 (Cohen HEP&T) -25 Chapel -Brklyn 11201
(212) 244-2999 ..**Siegel**, Heather S '99 %Kopff N&D LLP -440 9th Av -NY 10001
(716) 881-5800 ..**Siegel**, Herbert M '69 Siegel K&K -426 Franklin -Buffalo 14202
(212) 421-4100 ..**Siegel**, Howard '71 (Pryor C LLP) -7 Times Sq -NY 10036
(212) 972-7900 ..**Siegel**, Howard F '91 -260 Mad Av -NY 10016 **Fx:**972-7903
(212) 462-4000 ..**Siegel**, Howard J '94 %Natl Flag & Display Co -22 W 21st -NY 10010
(212) 554-7800 ..**Siegel**, Howard L '93 (Moses & S LLP) -405 Lex Av -NY 10174
(212) 447-5599 ..**Siegel**, Irwin '75 (Agins SR&B,LLP) -386 Park Av S -NY 10016
(212) 716-3690 ..**Siegel**, Jack M '75 SrCnsl 1sr Srvc Williams LLC -380 Mad Av -NY 10017 **Fx:**716-3531

(646) 227-8224 .. **Siegel**, James D '97 NY Life Ins Co -420 Lex Av -NY 10170
(718) 544-3635 .. **Siegel**, James E '84 (J Siegel & Assoc,PLLC) -108-18 Qns Blvd -Frst Hlls 11375 **Fx**:544-7812
(212) 895-3500 .. **Siegel**, James E '94 Maxim Grp -405 Lex Av -NY 10174
(516) 482-4436 .. **Siegel**, Jane Cohen '85 (Gleich S&F) -36 S Station Plz -Gt Neck 11021
(212) 790-0375 .. **Siegel**, Jane L '96 Innocence Project -55 5th Av -NY 10003
(212) 858-7374 .. **Siegel**, Jason S '99 RBC Dominion Securities -165 Bway -NY 10006
(212) 478-7200 .. **Siegel**, Jeanne Ferris '85 SpclCnsl Hahn & H LLP -488 Mad Av -NY 10022
(518) 452-0941 .. **Siegel**, Jeffrey A '87 (Segel GM&S,PC) -9 Wshngtn Sq -Albany 12205
(212) 848-4000 .. **Siegel**, Jeffrey D '06 %Shearman & S LLP -599 Lex Av -NY 10022
(212) 885-5000 .. **Siegel**, Jeffrey N '68 (Blank R LLP) -405 Lex Av -NY 10174
(631) 390-0010 .. **Siegel**, Jeffrey S '91 (Bruno G&S,LLP) -445 Broad Hollow Rd -Melvll 11747
(212) 724-3355 .. **Siegel**, Jerome A '69 -473 West End Av -NY 10024
(516) 741-6266 .. **Siegel**, Jesse L '09 %McCabe CM&F,LLP -346 Westbury Av Bx9000 -Carle Pl 11514
(212) 207-9009 .. **Siegel**, Jesse M '87 -233 Bway -NY 10007
(718) 928-3700 .. **Siegel**, Jill A '82 %LSNYC-Bronx -579 Courtlandt Av -Bronx 10451 **Fx**:402-7586
(212) 341-2743 .. **Siegel**, Joan A '96 %Admin Children's Srvcs -150 William -NY 10038 **Fx**:341-2700
(212) 909-9500 .. **Siegel**, Jodi R '07 %Wachtel & M,LLP -885 2nd Av -NY 10017
(212) 233-6900 .. **Siegel**, Joel A '85 -70 Lafayette -NY 10013
(718) 403-9696 .. **Siegel**, John J '67 (Shapiro & S) -90 Meadow Woods Rd -Gt Neck 11020
(718) 665-1700 .. **Siegel**, Jonathan D '83 (Gottlieb S&S,LLP) -180 E 162nd -Bronx 10451
(212) 637-3208 .. **Siegel**, Jos A '84 %EPA -290 Bway -NY 10007 **Fx**:637-3096
(516) 931-2380 .. **Siegel**, Jos W '75 -20 Plsnt Av -Plainvw 11803
(212) 506-1700 .. **Siegel**, Joshua A '02 %Kasowitz BT&F LLP -1633 Bway -NY 10019
(914) 332-8000 .. **Siegel**, Judith L '92 %Kittay & G,PC -100 Wht Plns Rd -Tarrytwn 10591
(212) 768-9500 .. **Siegel**, Judith L '92 %Kittay & G,PC -1 Exch Plz 55 Bway -NY 10016
(646) 562-4501 .. **Siegel**, Julie '92 %OZ Mgt LLC -9 W 57th -NY 10019
(212) 940-8800 .. **Siegel**, Julie A '07 %Katten MR LLP -575 Mad Av -NY 10022
(212) 943-9000 .. **Siegel**, Kara D '07 %Dewey P&K LLP -220 E 42nd -NY 10017
(716) 881-5800 .. **Siegel Kelleher & Kahn** -426 Franklin -Buffalo 14202 **Fx**:881-5779
(716) 631-3600 .. **Siegel Kelleher & Kahn** -22 Evans -Williamsvll 14221
(716) 834-5800 .. **Siegel Kelleher & Kahn** -4249 Maple Rd -Amherst 14226 **Fx**:834-5814
(716) 681-1500 .. **Siegel Kelleher & Kahn** -43 Central Av -Lancaster 14086 **Fx**:681-2541
(914) 640-8235 .. **Siegel**, Kenneth S '81 Starwood Hotels & Resorts -1111 Wstchstr Av -White Plns 10604 **Fx**:640-8260
(631) 234-3030 .. **Siegel**, Lawr A '81 (Davidow DS&S,LLP) -1601 Vets Mem'l Hwy -Islandia 11749
(212) 697-2700 .. **Siegel**, Lewis W '75 OfCnsl Stairs DF -200 Park Av S -NY 10003
(212) 468-4800 .. **Siegel**, Linda J '97 %Davis & G LLP -1740 Bway -NY 10019
(212) 891-9100 .. **Siegel**, Lisa '84 (Goldfarb & F LLP) -345 Park Av -NY 10154
(716) 854-2626 .. **Siegel**, Louis H '64 -17 Beresford Ct -Buffalo 14221 **Fx**:854-2629
(518) 928-4048 .. **Siegel**, Lowell R '88 -1450 Wstrn Av -Albany 12203
(212) 370-0103 .. **Siegel**, Marjorie J '82 -60 E 42nd -NY 10165 **Fx**:370-0250
(914) 864-0575 .. **Siegel**, Mark A '79 -344 E Main -Mt Kisco 10549
(845) 486-4200 .. **Siegel**, Marla B '08 %Shaw PM&L,LLP -21 Van Wagner Rd -Poughkeepsie 12603
(212) 349-9190 .. **Siegel**, Martin Jay '67 -170 Bway -NY 10038 **Fx**:349-1451
(212) 209-4800 .. **Siegel**, Martin S '68 (Brown R LLP) -7 Times Sq -NY 10036
(212) 909-6000 .. **Siegel**, Matthew D '04 %Debevoise & P LLP -919 3rd Av -NY 10022
(917) 757-5574 .. **Siegel**, Melanie B '01 (Keil & S,LLP) -1983 Marcus Av -Lk Success 11042
(718) 651-9500 .. **Siegel**, Michl '87 -82-18 Roosevelt Av -Jcksn Hts 11372
(212) 721-5300 .. **Siegel**, Michl D '90 (Siegel & S,PC) -1 Penn Plz -NY 10119 **Fx**:947-9967
(845) 647-5150 .. **Siegel**, Michl R '00 MR Siegel & Assoc -77 N Main -Ellenvll 12428 **Fx**:647-9089
(914) 925-0000 .. **Siegel**, Michl S '91 Elias Grp -411 Theo Fremd Av -Rye 10580
(631) 952-6725 .. **Siegel**, Morton J '67 %DMV Safety Hearing -3B49 State Ofc Bldg -Hauppauge 11788 **Fx**:952-6314
(716) 874-2111 .. **Siegel**, Myron M '54 (Hawthorne & S PLLC) -3080 Delaware Av -Buffalo 14217
(212) 752-8000 .. **Siegel**, Neil Y '99 %Cole SMF&L,PA -900 3rd Av -NY 10022
(212) 532-7586 .. **Siegel**, Norman H '80 -260 Mad Av -NY 10016
(631) 247-0404 .. **Siegel**, Paul J '85 (Jackson L LLP) -58 S Srvc Rd -Melvll 11747
(631) 727-4100 .. **Siegel**, Philip J '99 %Smith FLI&Y -456 Griffing Av Bx389 -Rvrhead 11901
(516) 482-1823 .. **Siegel**, Randi B '95 -1010 Nrthrn Blvd -Gt Neck 11021 **Fx**:504-1224
(516) 746-5858 .. **Siegel**, Richd A '69 -15 Roslyn Rd -Mineola 11501
(914) 244-1450 .. **Siegel**, Richd S '80 TransUnion Interactive -27 Radio Circle Dr -Mt Kisco 10549
(212) 750-1000 .. **Siegel**, Robt A '87 -205 E 60th -NY 10022
(631) 324-6258 .. **Siegel**, Robt H '55 -Bx2292 -E Hampton 11937 **Fx**:324-6494
(212) 964-7400 .. **Siegel**, Robt P '82 Smith MDWY&Y,PC -111 John -NY 10038
(914) 347-2600 .. **Siegel**, Robt P '82 (Traub LS&S LLP) -7 Skyline Dr -Hawthorne 10532
(718) 852-3113 .. **Siegel**, Roger E '79 (Siegel & E) -16 Court -Brklyn 11241 **Fx**:852-0285
(212) 421-6060 .. **Siegel**, Seth M '79 (Beanstalk Grp) -220 E 42nd -NY 10017 **Fx**:421-6388
(631) 342-5224 .. **Siegel**, Shari '90 Computer Assocs Intl,Inc -1 Computer Associates Plz -Islandia 11749
(518) 862-1386 .. **Siegel**, Sharon '88 %Burke SM&H,LLP -302 Wshngtn Av Ext Bx15085 -Albany 12212
(212) 721-5300 .. **Siegel**, Sharon M '94 (Siegel & S,PC) -1 Penn Plz -NY 10119 **Fx**:947-9967
(212) 998-6106 .. **Siegel**, Stanley '63 %NYU Law Schl -40 Wshngtn Sq S -NY 10012 **Fx**:995-4692
(718) 575-3900 .. **Siegel**, Stephan J '77 -109-01 72nd Rd -Frst Hlls 11375
(718) 520-0413 .. **Siegel**, Steven '72 -123-12 82nd Av -Kew Gdns 11415 **Fx**:544-7044
(212) 869-3000 .. **Siegel**, Steven F '86 %Centro US -420 Lex Av -NY 10170 **Fx**:302-4776
(212) 661-8400 .. **Siegel**, Steven S '84 -60 E 42nd -NY 10165
(631) 435-6688 .. **Siegel**, Walter '85 Cnsl Standard Microsystems -80 Arkay Dr -Hauppauge 11788 **Fx**:434-1348
(516) 747-6300 .. **Siegel**, Wm D '63 OfCnsl Koeppel M&L,LLP -155 First Bx863 -Mineola 11501
(212) 813-8800 .. **Siegelbaum**, Jos R '80 (Goodwin P LLP) -620 8th Av -NY 10018
(212) 883-4902 .. **Siegel-Baum**, Judith E '79 (Cozen O) -277 Park Av -NY 10172 **Fx**:986-0604
(212) 986-1512 .. **Siegelbaum**, Stanley J '75 -275 Mad Av -NY 10016 **Fx**:687-8030
(212) 265-6888 .. **Siegelheim**, Heather B '10 %Porzio B&N,PC -156 W 56th -NY 10019
(212) 221-8538 .. **Siegelman**, Heather M '94 H Siegelman,LLC -546 5th Av -NY 10036
(914) 725-6472 .. **Siegel-Puhala**, Laura '89 -1 Mt Joy Av -Scarsdale 10583
(212) 870-2003 .. **Sieger**, Carol E '95 Ctr to Advance Palliative Care -1255 5th Av -NY 10029
(631) 424-2525 .. **Sieger**, Hal E '85 (Mandler & S,LLP) -1609 NY Av -Huntngtn Sta 11746
(718) 254-0700 .. **Sieger**, Jos P '85 %Bklyn Defender Srvcs -177 Lvngstn -Brklyn 11201 **Fx**:254-0897
(516) 663-6600 .. **Sieger**, Stuart M '68 OfCnsl Ruskin MF,PC -1425 RXR Plz -Uniondale 11556
(212) 564-8181 .. **Siegert**, Paul W '74 -15 E 32nd -NY 10016 **Fx**:564-4414
(518) 869-9500 .. **Siegfeld**, David E '96 (Ganz W&S,LLP) -1 Columbia Cir -Albany 12203
(212) 645-3444 .. **Siegfried**, Heidi J '88 Prtnrshp for the Homeless -305 7th Av -NY 10001 **Fx**:477-4663
(212) 259-8000 .. **Siegfried**, Jonathan D '76 (Dewey & L LLP) -1301 Av of Amer -NY 10019
(212) 907-7395 .. **Siegfried**, Paul D '73 -437 Mad Av -NY 10022 **Fx**:754-0330
(914) 696-9060 .. **Siegfried**, Peter C '68 %Centrl Natl-Gottesman -3 Manhattanvll Rd -Purchase 10577 **Fx**:696-1066
(518) 473-5097 .. **Siegfried**, Robt A '83 %Dept of Law -The Cptl -Albany 12224
(718) 442-4600 .. **Sieghardt**, George A '69 (Jacobi SBP&F,PC) -235 Forest Av -Staten Isl 10301
(212) 438-1164 .. **Sieghart**, Andrew J '05 Standard & Poor's -55 Water -NY 10041
(212) 406-0110 .. **Siegle**, Eric W '94 (Siegle & S LLP) -217 Bway -NY 10007 **Fx**:406-5259
(212) 752-5000 .. **Siegler**, James J '98 %Fisher Brothers -299 Park Av -NY 10171
(212) 806-5400 .. **Siegler**, Richd '65 (Stroock &S&L LLP) -180 Maiden Ln -NY 10038
(212) 683-5372 .. **Siegler**, Scott M '93 -122 E 42nd -NY 10168
(212) 560-1313 .. **Siegmeister**, Richd I '04 EBC -450 W 33rd -NY 10001 **Fx**:560-3191
(212) 684-7240 .. **Siegmund**, Fredk '54 -270 Mad Av -NY 10016 **Fx**:684-7175
(212) 335-9000 .. **Siegmund**, Joanne H '79 %DA -1 Hogan Pl -NY 10013
(212) 859-8000 .. **Siegmund**, Mark '09 %Fried FHS&J LLP -1 NY Plz -NY 10004
(212) 765-5070 .. **Siem**, Michl A '01 OfCnsl Fish & R,PC -153 E 53rd -NY 10022
(212) 929-0021 .. **Siemann**, Catherine Ann '89 -421 W 21st -NY 10011
(212) 258-4287 .. **Siemens**, Mark A '92 %Siemens Corp -153 E 53rd -NY 10022 **Fx**:767-0580
(212) 649-2000 .. **Siemer**, Calvin '94 %Hearst Corp -300 W 57th -NY 10019 **Fx**:649-2035
(212) 446-4800 .. **Siems**, Molly M '08 %Kirkland & E LLP -153 E 53rd -NY 10022
(212) 458-3197 .. **Sieni**, Francesca M '97 AIG -175 Water -NY 10038
(607) 637-5400 .. **Sienko**, Leonard E Jr. '78 -12 E Main Bx579 -Hancock 13783
(212) 909-6000 .. **Siepker**, Brita M '07 %Debevoise & P LLP -919 3rd Av -NY 10022
(631) 727-3904 .. **Siepmann**, Paul K '97 %H Arnoff -206 Roanoke Av -Rvrhead 11901 **Fx**:727-3940
(212) 949-5555 .. **Sier**, Lisa B '91 L Sier,PC -600 Mad Av -NY 10022 **Fx**:949-5550
(212) 791-3159 .. **Sieradzki**, Maurice '67 -225 Bway -NY 10007 **Fx**:227-5090
(212) 471-9525 .. **Sieratzki**, Steven S '80 -40 Exch Pl -NY 10005 **Fx**:482-1303
(212) 246-3030 .. **Sierchio Greco & Greco,LLP** -110 E 59th -NY 10022
(212) 246-3030 .. **Sierchio**, Jos '75 (Sierchio G&G,LLP) -110 E 59th -NY 10022
(212) 355-7900 .. **Sierchio**, Lauren P '05 Hadassah -50 W 58th -NY 10019
(212) 609-1517 .. **Sierchio**, Mara Brooke '05 %VNSNY -107 E 70th -NY 10021 **Fx**:794-6357
(914) 761-7633 .. **Siesel**, Mark A '87 -200 Mamaroneck Av -White Plns 10601 **Fx**:761-2446
(914) 381-2728 .. **Siesel**, Nikki A '94 OfCnsl J Messina -424 Mamaroneck Av -Mamaroneck 10543 **Fx**:381-0907
(212) 204-8688 .. **Siesser**, Steven E '06 (Lowenstein S PC) -1251 Av of Amer -NY 10020 **Fx**:(973) 597-2507
(212) 521-5400 .. **Siev**, Jordan W '89 (Reed S LLP) -599 Lex Av -NY 10022
(718) 852-0451 .. **Siev**, Kenneth A '98 -41 Schermerhorn -Brklyn 11201
(212) 267-0800 .. **Sieven**, Howard A '56 -30 Vesey -NY 10007 **Fx**:(917) 441-1734
(518) 436-0751 .. **Sievers**, Lori A '03 (Hinman S PC) -121 State -Albany 12207
(212) 735-3000 .. **Sievertsen**, Eric D '09 %Skadden ASM&F LLP -4 Times Sq -NY 10036
(212) 245-8970 .. **Siff**, Andrew P '55 -122 E 42nd -NY 10168 **Fx**:661-0413
(212) 277-6500 .. **Siff**, Brian D '91 (Dickstein S LLP) -1633 Bway -NY 10019
(212) 447-1111 .. **Siff**, Danl E '65 (Ledy-Gurren B&S) -475 Park Av S -NY 10016
(718) 544-7600 .. **Siff**, Michl D '89 (M Siff,PC) -125-01 Qns Blvd -Kew Gdns 11415 **Fx**:263-1705
(212) 351-4000 .. **Siffert**, David A '10 Gibson D&C LLP -200 Park Av -NY 10166
(212) 921-8399 .. **Siffert**, John S '73 (Lankler S&W LLP) -500 5th Av -NY 10110
(212) 806-5400 .. **Sifre**, David A '94 SpclCnsl Stroock &S&L LLP -180 Maiden Ln -NY 10038
(212) 290-4700 .. **Sifton**, John '02 %Human Rights Watch -350 5th Av -NY 10118 **Fx**:736-1300
(212) 532-0800 .. **Sigal**, Laura R '89 %Amer Fed TV & Radio -260 Mad Av -NY 10016 **Fx**:545-1238
(212) 336-0209 .. **Sigal**, Michele S '91 SpencerStuart -277 Park Av -NY 10172 **Fx**:336-0296
(212) 288-1474 .. **Sigal**, R Ellen '92 -299 Bway -NY 10007 **Fx**:517-0050
(212) 820-9404 .. **Sigal**, Richd L '64 (Hawkins D&W LLP) -One Chase Manh Plz -NY 10005
(212) 527-8114 .. **Sigal**, Tracy M '05 Seneca Capital -590 Mad Av -NY 10022

(212) 335-9000 .. **Sigall,** Jennifer '99 %DA -1 Hogan Pl -NY 10013
(212) 446-4800 .. **Sigall,** Jeremy K '09 %Kirkland & E LLP -153 E 53rd -NY 10022
(212) 244-6611 .. **Sigall,** Michl W '78 -347 5th Av -NY 10016
(718) 739-6400 .. **Sigalow,** Alan M '81 %DHCR -92-31 Union Hall -Jamaica 11433 **Fx:**262-7938
(212) 801-9386 .. **Sigda,** Eric B '92 (Greenberg T,LLP) -200 Park Av -NY 10166
(212) 490-9100 .. **Sigda,** Jane M '00 %Condon & F LLP -7 Times Sq -NY 10036
(212) 606-7072 .. **Sigda,** Stacey B '93 %Sotheby's,Inc -1334 York Av -NY 10021 **Fx:**606-7574
(212) 765-2100 .. **Sigelakis,** Lydia A '04 %Spivak L LLP -1700 Bway -NY 10019
(212) 780-2050 .. **Sigelbaum,** Harvey C '63 %Multiplan Inc -115 5th Av -NY 10003
(212) 953-6000 .. **Siger,** Jeffrey M '70 SrCnsl Katsky K LLP -605 3rd Av -NY 10158
(215) 918-3554 .. **Sigety,** Elizabeth Donnem '90 (Fox R LLP) -100 Park Av -NY 10017 **Fx:**345-7507
(585) 546-5530 .. **Sigillo,** Wendy S '97 %Thomson West -50 E Broad -Rchstr 14694
(212) 401-1344 .. **Sigismonti,** Thos A '90 Royal Bank of Scotland -101 Park Av -NY 10178
(607) 737-2944 .. **Siglin,** Robt D '06 %DA -226 Lk Bx588 -Elmira 14902 **Fx:**737-2965
(212) 220-3830 .. **Sigmon,** David E '10 %Nicoletti H&S -88 Pine -NY 10005
(212) 682-8811 .. **Sigmond,** Carol A '90 (Dunnington B&M LLP) -1359 Bway -NY 10018
(518) 346-8090 .. **Signore,** Stephen M '91 -1528 Union -Schnctdy 12309 **Fx:**346-8103
(518) 388-4276 .. **Signore,** Stephen M '91 %Cnty Atty -620 State -Schnctdy 12305 **Fx:**388-4493
(212) 254-4218 .. **Signorelli,** Richd E '88 -799 Bway -NY 10003 **Fx:**254-1396
(212) 574-1200 .. **Signoriello,** Meagan R '10 %Seward & K LLP -1 Bttry Pk Plz -NY 10004
(646) 367-5204 .. **Sigoura,** Victor H '02 El-Ad Properties NY LLC -575 Mad Av -NY 10022
(585) 753-4500 .. **Siguenza,** Teodoro '07 DA -832 Watts Bldg -Rchstr 14614 **Fx:**753-4576
(914) 946-0992 .. **Siino,** Ben Paul '58 -115 Lk -White Plns 10604 **Fx:**946-1708
(718) 286-6000 .. **Sikes,** Richd B '09 DA -125-01 Qns Blvd -Kew Gdns 11415
(716) 445-7782 .. **Sikka,** Linda S '97 -Bx508 -Buffalo 14226
(716) 672-4371 .. **Sikora,** Paul '79 %Fredonia BOCES -9520 Fredonia-Stockton -Fredonia 14063
(516) 747-2473 .. **Sikorski,** Laura Paglia '90 -11 Euston Rd -Gdn Cty 11530
(716) 668-8888 .. **Sikorski,** Robt J '78 %NFRRS -Bx575 -Buffalo 14225
(212) 532-7191 .. **Sikorski,** Robt S '73 (Busson & S) -381 Park Av S -NY 10016 **Fx:**532-7184
(716) 631-5767 .. **Sikorski-Petritz,** Darlene A '04 -5555 Main -Williamsvll 14221 **Fx:**631-5354
(212) 422-0700 .. **Sikoscow,** Alexander '05 (Gerspach S LLP) -59 Maiden Ln -NY 10038 **Fx:**545-4095
(631) 669-3080 .. **Sikowitz,** Joel '61 -179 Little East Neck Rd -Babylon 11704
(212) 949-7300 .. **Silagy,** Yoram '90 (Vernon & G,LLP) -261 Mad Av -NY 10016
(718) 810-0932 .. **Silas,** Rudolph N '77 -20 E 46th -NY 10017
(516) 623-1430 .. **Silber,** Harvey B '67 -30 S Ocean Av Bx718 -Freeprt 11520 **Fx:**623-1910
(914) 312-2101 .. **Silber,** Jerome S '84 %MCI -2 Intl Dr -Rye Brook 10573
(212) 532-7575 .. **Silber,** Joshua '97 (Abend & S,PLLC) -440 Park Av S -NY 10016 **Fx:**532-8180
(212) 373-3000 .. **Silber,** Lindsay N '05 %Paul WRW&G LLP -1285 Av of Amer -NY 10019
(212) 834-0600 .. **Silber,** Marian E '69 OfCnsl Gordon & S,PC -355 Lex Av -NY 10017
(212) 486-6780 .. **Silber,** Mendel M '84 %Renaissance Tech -800 3rd Av -NY 10022 **Fx:**758-7136
(212) 765-4567 .. **Silber,** Meyer Y '97 -233 Bway -NY 10279 **Fx:**504-8165
(516) 463-5866 .. **Silber,** Norman '87 %Hofstra Law Schl -121 Hofstra Univ -Hempstd 11549
(212) 474-1000 .. **Silber,** Rebecca R '07 %Cravath S&M LLP -825 8th Av -NY 10019
(518) 439-0027 .. **Silber,** Richd J '67 -4 Brightonwood Rd -Glenmont 12077 **Fx:**783-5207
(212) 813-8800 .. **Silberberg,** Justin E '07 %Goodwin P LLP -620 8th Av -NY 10018
(212) 310-8261 .. **Silberberg,** Marc L '80 (Weil G&M LLP) -767 5th Av -NY 10153
(212) 953-9595 .. **Silberberg,** Michl '91 (Silberberg & K LLP) -360 Lex Av -NY 10017 **Fx:**953-7755
(845) 371-6600 .. **Silberberg,** Morton N '83 -95 New Clarkstown Rd -Nanuet 10954 **Fx:**371-6611
(212) 735-3000 .. **Silberberg,** Rebecca C '09 %Skadden ASM&F LLP -4 Times Sq -NY 10036
(212) 415-9200 .. **Silberberg,** Richd H '76 (Dorsey & W LLP) -250 Park Av -NY 10177
(212) 682-8089 .. **Silberblatt,** Mark I '72 %Bisceglie & D,LLC -711 3rd Av -NY 10017
(718) 286-2000 .. **Silberblatt,** Steven W '74 %Leg Aid -120-46 Qns Blvd -Kew Gdns 11415 **Fx:**286-2286
(212) 326-3939 .. **Silberfarb,** Michl D '05 %Jones D -222 E 41st -NY 10017
(800) 614-0700 .. **Silberfarb,** Paul '91 -26 W 85th -NY 10024
(212) 554-7800 .. **Silberfein,** Scott E '00 OfCnsl Moses & S LLP -405 Lex Av -NY 10174
(212) 755-3200 .. **Silberfein,** Stephen I '71 -1212 Av of Amer -NY 10036 **Fx:**944-6600
(917) 661-8740 .. **Silberfeld,** Laurie '86 Hudson River Park Trust -Pier 40 at W Houston -NY 10014
(212) 335-9000 .. **Silberg,** Stuart R '87 %DA -1 Hogan Pl -NY 10013
(212) 889-9338 .. **Silberglied,** Robt '64 -10 E 40th -NY 10016 **Fx:**889-1203
(877) 222-1814 .. **Silberglitt,** Mark S '74 %B Rothenberg -100 Duffy Av -Hicksvll 11801 **Fx:**(866) 894-2182
(212) 661-7510 .. **Silbering,** Robt H '75 %Forensic Investigative Assoc -230 Park Av -NY 10169 **Fx:**661-7516
(631) 348-0800 .. **Silberling,** Stephen P '85 Silberling & S -300 Rabro Dr -Hauppauge 11788 **Fx:**348-0827
(646) 386-5000 .. **Silberman,** Ann Wendlandt '96 %Surrogates Ct -31 Chmbrs -NY 10007
(212) 480-7401 .. **Silberman,** Arnold L '90 %DHCR -25 Beaver -NY 10004 **Fx:**480-7416
(718) 834-9377 .. **Silberman,** Claire M '90 -70 Willow -Brklyn 11201 **Fx:**522-3119
(212) 456-6422 .. **Silberman,** David J '94 ABC -77 W 66th -NY 10023 **Fx:**456-6202
(718) 579-3000 .. **Silberman,** Elana '90 %Leg Aid -1020 Grnd Cncrs -Bronx 10451 **Fx:**588-2611
(212) 836-8000 .. **Silberman,** Gregory P '01 (Kaye S LLP) -425 Park Av -NY 10022
(516) 781-5810 .. **Silberman,** Jeffrey '76 -2749 Patricia Ln -Bellmore 11710
(212) 319-3737 .. **Silberman,** John A '77 (J Silberman Assoc,PC) -145 E 57th -NY 10022 **Fx:**319-8188
(212) 679-0968 .. **Silberman,** Lawr J '91 L Silberman,PC -146 E 37th -NY 10016
(212) 669-7700 .. **Silberman,** Mark A '91 %Landmarks Pres Comm -1 Centre -NY 10007
(212) 219-2100 .. **Silberman,** Martin N '78 Silberman Law -110 William -NY 10038 **Fx:**226-7554
(212) 408-5100 .. **Silberman,** Patricia '07 %Chadbourne & P LLP -30 Rckfllr Plz -NY 10112
(212) 885-5000 .. **Silbermann,** Jacqueline W '73 OfCnsl Blank R LLP -405 Lex Av -NY 10174
(718) 556-7110 .. **Silbermann,** Jonathan J '74 %DA -130 Styvsnt Pl -Staten Isl 10301 **Fx:**556-7054
(212) 415-8600 .. **Silbersher,** Zachary D '03 %Locke LB&L LLP -3 World Fncl Ctr -NY 10281
(646) 840-5847 .. **Silberstein,** Allen G '01 Visium Asset Mgmt -950 3rd Av -NY 10022
(212) 859-8000 .. **Silberstein,** Andrew G '98 SpclCnsl Fried FHS&J LLP -1 NY Plz -NY 10004
(516) 832-7777 .. **Silberstein Awad & Miklos,PC** -600 Old Cntry Rd -Gdn Cty 11530 **Fx:**832-7877
(212) 297-1276 .. **Silberstein,** Beth N '92 %CTI Legal Staffing -331 Mad Av -NY 10017 **Fx:**697-1244
(212) 361-1758 .. **Silberstein,** Debra J '83 Envrnmntl Cntrl Brd -66 John -NY 10038
(212) 813-5900 .. **Silberstein,** James D '90 Cnsl Fross ZL&Z,PC -866 UN Plz -NY 10017
(212) 669-3163 .. **Silberstein,** Janice '91 NYC Comptrollers Ofc -1 Centre -NY 10007
(212) 385-2896 .. **Silberstein,** Michl R '62 -7 Dey -NY 10007 **Fx:**(732) 972-7988
(212) 385-0066 .. **Silberstein,** Milo S '97 (Dealy & S,LLP) -225 Bway -NY 10007
(212) 909-6000 .. **Silberstein,** Rebecca Fishman '94 (Debevoise & P LLP) -919 3rd Av -NY 10022
(212) 669-8400 .. **Silberstein,** Robt S '83 %DCAS-DLS -1 Centre -NY 10007 **Fx:**669-2139
(212) 325-2000 .. **Silbert,** Benjamin A '99 Credit Suisse -11 Mad Av -NY 10010
(718) 875-1300 .. **Silbert,** Claudia E '88 Applt Div 2nd Dept -45 Monroe Pl -Brklyn 11201 **Fx:**858-2446
(212) 310-8000 .. **Silbert,** Gregory S '04 %Weil G&M LLP -767 5th Av -NY 10153
(212) 245-0808 .. **Silbert & Hiller,LLP** -1500 Bway -NY 10036 **Fx:**245-2630
(212) 245-0808 .. **Silbert,** James D '70 (Silbert & H,LLP) -1500 Bway -NY 10036
(212) 351-4000 .. **Silbert,** Jennifer Goldman '99 %Gibson D&C LLP -200 Park Av -NY 10166
(212) 481-4801 .. **Silberzweig,** Barry S '87 -271 Mad Av -NY 10016 **Fx:**481-4971
(718) 783-6800 .. **Silberzweig,** David '61 -267 Flatbush Av -Brklyn 11217
(212) 246-2400 .. **Silberzweig,** Robin T '97 (Balber PM&VDT,PC) -1370 Av of Amer -NY 10019
(646) 840-6666 .. **Silbiger,** Thos '63 (Cameron & H) -230 Park Av -NY 10169
(212) 354-6800 .. **Silbowitz Garafola Silbowitz Schatz & Frederick, LLP** -25 W 43rd -NY 10036 **Fx:**354-3737
(212) 354-6800 .. **Silbowitz,** Irwin M '61 OfCnsl Silbowitz GSS&F,LLP -25 W 43rd -NY 10036
(212) 354-6800 .. **Silbowitz,** Mitchell E '89 (Silbowitz GSS&F,LLP) -25 W 43rd -NY 10036
(516) 873-0505 .. **Sileo,** Michl G Jr. '77 -229 7th -Gdn Cty 11530 **Fx:**742-7088
(718) 250-2000 .. **Siler,** Denise S '04 %DA -350 Jay -Brklyn 11201 **Fx:**250-2314
(516) 294-2666 .. **Siler & Ingber,LLP** -301 Mineola Blvd -Mineola 11501 **Fx:**294-0870
(516) 294-2666 .. **Siler,** Jeffrey B '92 (Siler & I,LLP) -301 Mineola Blvd -Mineola 11501
(212) 436-1106 .. **Siler,** Patricia '92 %IRS -290 Bway -NY 10007
(212) 298-5085 .. **Siletti,** Jennifer A '88 %Leg Aid -49 Thomas -NY 10013 **Fx:**298-5252
(212) 484-3900 .. **Silfen,** Andrew I '87 (Arent F LLP) -1675 Bway -NY 10019
(212) 756-2000 .. **Silfen,** George M '95 (Schulte R&Z LLP) -919 3rd Av -NY 10022
(212) 237-1000 .. **Silfen,** Nina P '82 SpclCnsl Windels ML&M,LLP -156 W 56th -NY 10019
(212) 826-5548 .. **Silfen,** Stuart '62 OfCnsl Frankfurt KK&S,PC -488 Mad Av -NY 10022
(212) 207-7000 .. **Silfin,** Beth Neelman '88 %HarperCollins Pub -10 E 53rd -NY 10022 **Fx:**207-7552
(212) 336-8000 .. **Silfin,** Ira E '89 (Amster R&E) -90 Park Av -NY 10016
(212) 351-4500 .. **Silie,** Catherine Flores '05 %Epstein B&G,PC -250 Park Av -NY 10177
(212) 957-7600 .. **Silikovitz,** Harvey B '96 %Cohen & G LLP -800 3rd Av -NY 10022
(212) 232-1300 .. **Silk,** Andrea '01 OfCnsl Lewis BB&S LLP -77 Water -NY 10005
(212) 788-1152 .. **Silk,** Caroline T '87 %Law Dept -100 Church -NY 10007 **Fx:**788-0367
(212) 403-1000 .. **Silk,** David M '89 (Wachtell LR&K) -51 W 52nd -NY 10019
(212) 554-1400 .. **Silk,** Gerald H '96 (Bernstein LB&G LLP) -1285 Av of Amer -NY 10019
(212) 610-6300 .. **Silk,** Mitchell A '90 (Allen & O) -1221 Av of Amer -NY 10020
(212) 684-3888 .. **Silk,** Robt '64 -112 Mad Av -NY 10016 **Fx:**889-3978
(212) 941-5964 .. **Silk,** Robt H '52 -201 W 85th -NY 10024
(212) 660-3000 .. **Silkenat,** James R '73 (Sullivan & W LLP) -1290 Av of Amer -NY 10104
(315) 474-7541 .. **Silkey,** Robt F '72 (Menter R&T,PC) -308 Maltbie -Syracuse 13204
(212) 307-6655 .. **Sill,** Sara '79 %Young Concert Artist -250 W 57th -NY 10107
(212) 232-1300 .. **Sill,** Tyler E '03 %Lewis BB&S LLP -77 Water -NY 10005
(212) 833-5707 .. **Silla,** David '82 -550 Mad Av -NY 10022
(718) 809-3834 .. **Silla-Miller,** Julia '95 -131 Burke Av -Staten Isl 10314
(716) 759-6807 .. **Sillars,** Robt G '75 -10560 Main -Clarence 14031 **Fx:**759-6265
(585) 590-4127 .. **Silleman,** Susan M '04 %DA -13925 Route 31 -Albion 14411 **Fx:**590-4129
(212) 825-5900 .. **Siller,** Michl B '90 Dept of Invstgtn -80 Maiden Ln -NY 10038 **Fx:**825-2505
(516) 621-9688 .. **Siller,** Scott H '88 -55 Nrthrn Blvd -Greenvale 11548 **Fx:**621-9690
(212) 766-4030 .. **Siller,** Sidney '52 -30 Vesey -NY 10007 **Fx:**233-3130
(212) 430-8020 .. **Siller,** Stephen I '74 (LeClairRyan,PC) -830 3rd Av -NY 10022
(212) 715-9100 .. **Sillerman,** Michl T '77 (Kramer LN&F,LLP) -1177 Av of Amer -NY 10036
(212) 474-1000 .. **Sillers,** David Y '10 %Cravath S&M LLP -825 8th Av -NY 10019
(516) 248-9700 .. **Silliman,** Catherine B '03 %S Levitt & Assoc,PC -2 Hillside Av -Williston Pk 11596 **Fx:**741-9224

(212) 643-7000 .. **Sills Cummis & Gross PC** -One Rckfllr Plz -NY 10020 **Fx:**643-6500
(518) 456-6456 .. **Sills,** Eric H '93 (Gerstenzang OH&G) -210 Great Oaks Blvd -Albany 12203
(212) 986-5524 .. **Sills,** John L '70 -230 Park Av -NY 10169 **Fx:**599-5085
(585) 546-5530 .. **Sills,** Kenneth B '91 %Thomson West -50 E Broad -Rchstr 14694
(212) 818-8800 .. **Sills,** Nancy R '80 SpclCnsl Graubard M -405 Lex Av -NY 10174
(212) 506-5000 .. **Sills,** Robt L '77 (Orrick H&S LLP) -51 W 52nd -NY 10019
(212) 537-9000 .. **Silpe,** Steven M '81 (Cohen G&S,LLP) -850 3rd Av -NY 10022
(518) 445-2277 .. **Silva,** Chas J Jr. '90 %Albany Intl Corp -1373 Bway Bx1907 -Albany 12201 **Fx:**447-6575
(212) 804-4200 .. **Silva,** David A '86 (Mound CW&G) -One Bttry Pk Plz -NY 10004
(718) 643-7450 .. **Silva,** Fernando H '89 %Family Ct -283 Adams -Brklyn 11201
(718) 745-0880 .. **Silva,** George '97 %Bisogno & M -7018 Ft Hmltn Pkwy -Brklyn 11228 **Fx:**680-3891
(518) 377-3408 .. **Silva,** Laura L '98 -670 Franklin -Schnctdy 12305 **Fx:**374-0791
(516) 294-5614 .. **Silva,** Marco D '99 (Martins & S) -221 Mineola Blvd -Mineola 11501
(212) 720-8193 .. **Silva,** Michl F '93 %Fed Reserve Bk -33 Lbrty -NY 10045 **Fx:**785-5748
(212) 977-9700 .. **Silva,** Michele A '92 (Phillips N LLP) -666 5th Av -NY 10103
(212) 885-5000 .. **Silva,** Victoria D '10 %Blank R LLP -405 Lex Av -NY 10174
(212) 822-8300 .. **Silva,** Wendy '00 Nrthrn Manhattan Imprvmnt Corp -76 Wadsworth Av -NY 10033
(718) 238-6500 .. **Silvagni,** Giovanni P '00 %Connors & S,PC -7408 5th Av -Brklyn 11209
(845) 486-4200 .. **Silveira,** Garret L '85 %Shaw PM&L,LLP -21 Van Wagner Rd -Poughkeepsie 12603
(212) 407-8060 .. **Silver,** Adam '89 NBA -645 5th Av -NY 10022
(212) 294-6700 .. **Silver,** Adam R '06 %Winston & S -200 Park Av -NY 10166
(212) 857-0100 .. **Silver,** Alan M '03 Blesso Properties -320 W 13th -NY 10014 **Fx:**857-0110
(212) 490-3000 .. **Silver,** Alicia '02 %Wilson EME&D LLP -150 E 42nd -NY 10017
(516) 328-2300 .. **Silver,** Allan E '83 (Abrams FFEGF&E,LLP) -1111 Marcus Av -Lk Success 11042
(212) 907-7300 .. **Silver,** Amy L '98 (Golenbock EAB&P) -437 Mad Av -NY 10022
(315) 386-8506 .. **Silver,** Andrew W '93 (Silver & C) -44 Court -Canton 13617 **Fx:**386-8507
(718) 376-5122 .. **Silver,** Ann B '93 -2312 Quentin Rd -Brklyn 11229
(845) 562-9020 .. **Silver,** Barry B '65 (Silver FS&L) -3250 Route 9W -New Windsor 12553
(516) 498-8500 .. **Silver,** Barry E '98 -14 Bond -Gt Neck 11021 **Fx:**482-5428
(516) 433-4220 .. **Silver,** Beverly David '89 OfCnsl Farley & K,PC -55 Jericho Tpk -Jericho 11753
(212) 446-4800 .. **Silver,** Blair A '09 %Kirkland & E LLP -153 E 53rd -NY 10022
(212) 484-8000 .. **Silver,** Bradley '02 Time Warner -1 Time Warner Ctr -NY 10019
(212) 761-4000 .. **Silver,** Brian M '95 Morgan Stanley -1585 Bway -NY 10036
(212) 744-5022 .. **Silver,** Carolyn D '99 Lenox Hill Neighborhood House -331 E 70th -NY 10021 **Fx:**288-0722
(212) 697-6201 .. **Silver,** Chad M '06 BlueOcean Worldwide -227 E 45th -NY 10017
(718) 254-7000 .. **Silver,** Danl S '03 %US Atty -271 Cadman Plz E -Brklyn 11201 **Fx:**254-6479
(212) 701-3000 .. **Silver,** Darren S '99 (Cahill G&R LLP) -80 Pine -NY 10005 **Fx:**269-5420
(212) 854-0776 .. **Silver,** Edw A '85 %Columbia Univ -535 W 116th 412 Low Mem'l Library -NY 10027
(212) 735-3000 .. **Silver,** Elliot A '08 %Skadden ASM&F LLP -4 Times Sq -NY 10036
(212) 732-3200 .. **Silver,** Ethan L '05 %Carter L&M LLP -2 Wall -NY 10005
(585) 424-4760 .. **Silver & Feldman** -3445 Winton Pl -Rchstr 14623 **Fx:**424-6915
(845) 562-9020 .. **Silver Forrester Schisano & Lesser** -3250 Route 9W -New Windsor 12553 **Fx:**562-9025
(845) 794-4300 .. **Silver,** Gary D '84 (Stoloff & S,LLP) -26 Hmltn Av Bx1129 -Monticello 12701
(315) 375-8836 .. **Silver,** George E '70 Silver & C -316 Main Bx218 -Morristwn 13664 **Fx:**375-4021
(212) 408-5100 .. **Silver,** Gerald D '91 (Chadbourne & P LLP) -30 Rckfllr Plz -NY 10112
(914) 939-0805 .. **Silver,** Gerald J '52 -5 Arrowwood Cir -Rye Brook 10573
(212) 660-3000 .. **Silver,** Gretchen S '06 %Sullivan & W LLP -1290 Av of Amer -NY 10104
(732) 246-3336 .. **Silver,** Herbert J '59 (Silver & S LLP) -500 5th Av -NY 10110
(212) 407-4000 .. **Silver,** Ian H '00 %Loeb & L,LLP -345 Park Av -NY 10154
(718) 855-3834 .. **Silver,** Jacob '94 -26 Court -Brklyn 11242 **Fx:**797-4141
(518) 436-0751 .. **Silver,** Janet M '04 (Hinman S PC) -121 State -Albany 12207
(212) 619-4350 .. **Silver,** Janine '84 %Newman MKGH,PC -14 Wall -NY 10005
(212) 471-6201 .. **Silver,** Jasmine H '08 %Advocate & L,LLP -780 3rd Av -NY 10017 **Fx:**935-1166
(212) 969-1639 .. **Silver,** Jeff W '95 %Alliance Bernstein LP -1345 Av of Amer -NY 10105 **Fx:**554-4639
(518) 486-9785 .. **Silver,** Jeffrey I '71 %DMV -6 ESP -Albany 12228 **Fx:**473-3490
(212) 846-5253 .. **Silver,** Jennifer R '99 %TV Land -345 Hudson -NY 10014
(718) 780-0198 .. **Silver,** Joanna L '98 (Cullen and D LLP) -177 Montague -Brklyn 11201 **Fx:**935-1304
(212) 717-9578 .. **Silver,** Joel J '60 -203 E 72nd -NY 10021 **Fx:**717-9581
(718) 261-1100 .. **Silver,** Jonathan '79 -80-02 Kew Grdns Rd -Kew Gdns 11415 **Fx:**575-9842
(212) 762-4000 .. **Silver,** Jonathan A '04 Morgan Stanley -1633 Bway -NY 10019
(212) 488-1598 .. **Silver,** Jos '07 %Havkins RR&V,LLP -11 Penn Plz -NY 10001
(212) 848-4000 .. **Silver,** Kerri N '09 %Shearman & S LLP -599 Lex Av -NY 10022
(718) 250-2000 .. **Silver,** Lauren F '09 %DA -350 Jay -Brklyn 11201 **Fx:**250-2314
(718) 694-3852 .. **Silver,** Lawr A '78 %Transit Auth -130 Lvngstn -Brklyn 11201 **Fx:**694-5726
(212) 335-9000 .. **Silver,** Leah H '09 %DA -1 Hogan Pl -NY 10013
(212) 735-3000 .. **Silver,** Levi Y '06 %Skadden ASM&F LLP -4 Times Sq -NY 10036
(212) 312-7016 .. **Silver,** Marc H '83 %State Ins Fund -199 Church -NY 10007 **Fx:**385-9199
(631) 761-7000 .. **Silver,** Marjorie A '81 %Touro Cllg Law Ctr -225 Eastvw Dr -Central Islip 11722
(212) 373-3000 .. **Silver,** Mark S '10 %Paul WRW&G LLP -1285 Av of Amer -NY 10019
(631) 435-0700 .. **Silver,** Martin '79 (M Silver,PC) -330 Motor Pkwy -Hauppauge 11788 **Fx:**435-8253
(212) 952-1111 .. **Silver,** Miriam Joels '83 %H Gladstein & Prtnrs LLC -110 Wall -NY 10005 **Fx:**943-7427
(212) 777-4850 .. **Silver,** Morton F '59 -225 Park Av S -NY 10003
(212) 480-3400 .. **Silver,** Moshe K '09 %Tamir Law Grp -55 Broad -NY 10004
(732) 246-3336 .. **Silver,** Nancy J '88 Silver & S LLP -500 5th Av -NY 10110
(518) 431-0247 .. **Silver,** Paul D '83 %US Atty -445 Bway -Albany 12207 **Fx:**431-0249
(212) 661-8400 .. **Silver,** Perry D '80 -60 E 42nd -NY 10165 **Fx:**661-1242
(585) 424-4760 .. **Silver,** Philip M '61 (Silver & F) -3445 Winton Pl -Rchstr 14623
(212) 309-6000 .. **Silver,** Rebecca A '08 %Morgan L&B LLP -101 Park Av -NY 10178
(212) 508-6700 .. **Silver,** Renee J '84 SrCnsl Tannenbaum HS&H LLP -900 3rd Av -NY 10022
(315) 853-5243 .. **Silver,** Richd I '08 -109 Pheasants Run -Clinton 13323
(212) 554-1234 .. **Silver,** Richd V '82 %AXA Financial Inc -1290 Av of Amer -NY 10104 **Fx:**707-3963
(914) 749-8200 .. **Silver,** Robt B '85 (Boies S&F LLP) -333 Main -Armonk 10504
(212) 859-8000 .. **Silver,** Ross Z '88 (Fried FHS&J LLP) -1 NY Plz -NY 10004
(212) 903-9000 .. **Silver,** Sabrena A '96 (Linklaters) -1345 Av of Amer -NY 10105
(212) 922-1616 .. **Silver,** Scott E '86 Sherman Finl Grp -335 Mad Av -NY 10017
(631) 467-0700 .. **Silver,** Sharon L '88 -405 Ft Salonga Rd -Northprt 11768 **Fx:**651-2774
(212) 558-5500 .. **Silver,** Sheldon '69 OfCnsl Weitz & L,PC -700 Bway -NY 10003
(732) 246-3336 .. **Silver & Silver LLP** -500 5th Av -NY 10110 **Fx:**214-1649
(516) 354-0200 .. **Silver,** Vickie R '85 (Horowitz T&S,PC) -2001 Marcus Av -Lk Success 11042
(212) 640-4751 .. **Silver,** Wendy L '04 %Amer Exp -200 Vesey -NY 10285
(212) 346-0045 .. **Silvera,** Adam '02 %P Weitz & Assoc,PC -233 Bway -NY 10279 **Fx:**346-0876
(212) 859-8000 .. **Silvera,** Harry R '96 (Fried FHS&J LLP) -1 NY Plz -NY 10004
(212) 335-4500 .. **Silverberg,** Bennett S '01 OfCnsl DLA Piper LLP -1251 Av of Amer -NY 10020
(718) 694-3872 .. **Silverberg,** David J '80 %Transit Auth -130 Lvngstn -Brklyn 11201 **Fx:**694-5726
(716) 854-6495 .. **Silverberg,** David K '87 (Silverberg YS&M) -515 Brisbane Bldg -Buffalo 14203
(212) 351-4500 .. **Silverberg,** Dean L '78 (Epstein B&G,PC) -250 Park Av -NY 10177
(716) 634-5038 .. **Silverberg,** Donald M '60 -84 Lord Byron Ln -Williamsvll 14221
(516) 294-8585 .. **Silverberg,** Ian B '94 -100 Ring Rd W -Gdn Cty 11530
(212) 788-8119 .. **Silverberg,** Janice Casey '05 %Law Dept -100 Church -NY 10007 **Fx:**788-0367
(212) 643-7000 .. **Silverberg,** Jay L '87 (Sills C&G PC) -One Rckfllr Plz -NY 10020
(718) 923-4206 .. **Silverberg,** John E '54 %OTDA Fair Hearings -14 Boerum Pl -Brklyn 11201
(718) 896-6554 .. **Silverberg,** Karl J '04 (King & K LLP) -27-12 37th Av -LIC 11101
(212) 732-0030 .. **Silverberg,** Lawr E '95 %S Seung -2 Mott -NY 10013 **Fx:**227-5097
(212) 438-2000 .. **Silverberg,** Michl '99 Standard & Poor's -55 Water -NY 10041
(212) 804-4200 .. **Silverberg,** Philip C '85 (Mound CW&G) -One Bttry Pk Plz -NY 10004
(212) 403-1000 .. **Silverberg,** Rachelle '94 (Wachtell LR&K) -51 W 52nd -NY 10019
(718) 627-0800 .. **Silverberg,** Robt E '97 -1829 E 19th -Brklyn 11229
(212) 949-5800 .. **Silverberg,** Ronnie L '91 %Brady K&W,LLP -501 5th Av -NY 10017
(212) 258-8000 .. **Silverberg,** Sabrina E '90 %MTV Networks -1515 Bway -NY 10036 **Fx:**258-8358
(716) 854-6495 .. **Silverberg,** Sanford M '57 (Silverberg YS&M) -515 Brisbane Bldg -Buffalo 14203
(516) 522-2575 .. **Silverberg,** Stephen C '71 -165 EAB Plz -Uniondale 11556 **Fx:**522-2809
(516) 229-2366 .. **Silverberg,** Stephen J '77 -50 Chas Lindbergh Blvd -Uniondale 11553 **Fx:**908-9601
(914) 682-0707 .. **Silverberg,** Steven M '73 (Silverberg Z LLP) -220 Wht Plns Rd -Tarrytwn 10591
(716) 854-6495 .. **Silverberg Yood Sellers & McGorry** -515 Brisbane Bldg -Buffalo 14203 **Fx:**854-5080
(914) 682-0707 .. **Silverberg Zalantis LLP** -220 Wht Plns Rd -Tarrytwn 10591 **Fx:**682-0708
(212) 977-9700 .. **Silverblatt,** Jonathan E '95 (Phillips N LLP) -666 5th Av -NY 10103
(212) 794-5568 .. **Silverblatt,** Pamela Sue '88 CUNY -535 E 80th -NY 10075 **Fx:**794-5530
(212) 232-0708 .. **Silverblatt,** Sheri A '93 %Dept Probation -33 Beaver -NY 10004 **Fx:**232-0718
(212) 683-7999 .. **Silverblatt,** Todd '79 Partnrshp for Childrens Rts -271 Mad Av -NY 10016 **Fx:**683-5544
(212) 819-8200 .. **Silverbrand,** Ian J '09 %White & C LLP -1155 Av of Amer -NY 10036
(315) 383-0247 .. **Silverbush,** Bnai R '05 -959 Westcott -Syracuse 13210 **Fx:**474-3229
(212) 867-6000 .. **Silverbush,** Bradley S '82 (Rosenberg & E,PC) -733 3rd Av -NY 10017
(718) 618-2500 .. **Silverbush,** Jeffrey S '90 %Civil Ct -851 Grnd Cncrs -Bronx 10451 **Fx:**590-7294
(212) 416-8107 .. **Silverglad,** Donna R '91 Atty Gen -120 W Bway -NY 10013
(212) 674-0066 .. **Silverglad,** Hyman '66 -170 E 3rd -NY 10009
(212) 940-8800 .. **Silverglad,** James A '02 %Katten MR LLP -575 Mad Av -NY 10022
(212) 513-7788 .. **Silvergleid,** Diane R '83 (Ahmuty D&M) -123 William -NY 10038
(845) 222-8393 .. **Silveri,** Jon M '82 -11 Gardner Hllw Ext -Poughquag 12570
(516) 479-6300 .. **Silverman Acampora LLP** -100 Jericho Quad -Jericho 11753 **Fx:**479-6301
(516) 561-5300 .. **Silverman,** Adam '88 (Silverman & D) -41B W Merrick Rd -Vly Stream 11580 **Fx:**561-5379
(518) 473-6045 .. **Silverman,** Adam W '09 %Dept of Law -The Cptl -Albany 12224
(516) 739-6001 .. **Silverman,** Alan '67 -1 Old Cntry Rd -Carle Pl 11514 **Fx:**873-3956
(845) 425-1642 .. **Silverman,** Allyson J '97 -166 E Central Av -Spg Vly 10977
(212) 687-8700 .. **Silverman,** Alvin '50 Cnsl Malkin Hldngs,LLC -60 E 42nd -NY 10165 **Fx:**986-7679
(212) 969-1000 .. **Silverman,** Andrew J '03 AllianceBernstein LP -1345 Av of Amer -NY 10105
(212) 504-6000 .. **Silverman,** Ari J '08 %Cadwalader W&T LLP -1 World Fncl Ctr -NY 10281
(212) 692-1096 .. **Silverman,** Arthur C '65 (Duane M LLP) -1540 Bway -NY 10036 **Fx:**401-4729
(914) 478-0177 .. **Silverman,** Bennet H '63 (Katz WL&S) -10 Old Jackson Av -Hastings-On-Hud 10706
(631) 666-0228 .. **Silverman,** Bernard S '60 -1365 Bstn Av -Bay Shr 11706

(914) 683-5300 .. **Silverman Bikkal & Sandberg,LLP** -81 Main -White Plns 10601 **Fx:**683-6240
(516) 479-6300 .. **Silverman**, Brett S '01 %Silverman A LLP -100 Jericho Quad -Jericho 11753
(212) 585-1131 .. **Silverman**, Bruce H '87 -435 E 65th -NY 10065
(212) 345-7000 .. **Silverman**, Carol S '90 %Mercer HR Cnsltng -1166 Av of Amer -NY 10036
(212) 422-0202 .. **Silverman**, Caryn M '93 (Sedgwick DM&A LLP) -125 Broad -NY 10004
(212) 735-3000 .. **Silverman**, Chad E '06 %Skadden ASM&F LLP -4 Times Sq -NY 10036
(718) 237-8693 .. **Silverman**, Danl '66 (Silverman & S,LLP) -52 3rd -Brklyn 11231 **Fx:**855-2933
(212) 504-6000 .. **Silverman**, David I '08 %Cadwalader W&T LLP -1 World Fncl Ctr -NY 10281
(516) 466-5900 .. **Silverman**, David L '90 -2001 Marcus Av -New Hyde Pk 11042
(516) 393-2200 .. **Silverman**, Debra A '86 SrCnsl Garfunkel W,PC -111 Grt Nck Rd -Gt Neck 11021
(212) 806-5400 .. **Silverman**, Derek I A '08 %Stroock &S&L LLP -180 Maiden Ln -NY 10038
(631) 852-1650 .. **Silverman**, Donald H '72 %Leg Aid -300 Center Dr -Rvrhead 11901 **Fx:**852-1655
(516) 759-0488 .. **Silverman**, Donna Zausmer '94 -1 Beatrice Ln -Glen Cove 11542 **Fx:**759-0488
(212) 695-0060 .. **Silverman**, Dorea H '10 %Wilens & B,PC -450 7th Av -NY 10123
(212) 962-1133 .. **Silverman**, Ellie A '09 %S Wolinetz,PC -233 Bway -NY 10279 **Fx:**962-1144
(212) 530-5000 .. **Silverman**, Eric F '83 (Milbank TH&M LLP) -1 Chase Manh Plz -NY 10005
(516) 662-2230 .. **Silverman**, Eric G '00 -760 Bethynn Ct -E Meadow 11554 **Fx:**(251) 252-1622
(212) 571-7100 .. **Silverman**, Gary '82 (O'Dwyer & B,LLP) -52 Duane -NY 10007
(212) 836-8000 .. **Silverman**, Gary R '94 (Kaye S LLP) -425 Park Av -NY 10022
(212) 966-6420 .. **Silverman**, Hal '85 %Lwyrs For Children -110 Lafayette -NY 10013 **Fx:**966-0531
(315) 422-7281 .. **Silverman**, Harold I '41 -601 Univ Bldg -Syracuse 13202 **Fx:**422-2755
(212) 208-9522 .. **Silverman**, Israel A '82 Liberty Intl Underwriters -55 Water -NY 10041
(212) 484-8000 .. **Silverman**, Janet A '94 Time Warner -1 Time Warner Ctr -NY 10019
(516) 663-6600 .. **Silverman**, Jay B '89 (Ruskin MF,PC) -1425 RXR Plz -Uniondale 11556
(631) 784-7711 .. **Silverman**, Jeffrey R '87 -775 Park Av -Huntngtn 11743
(212) 370-1300 .. **Silverman**, Jennifer D '97 (Ellenoff G&S LLP) -150 E 42nd -NY 10017
(631) 261-1847 .. **Silverman**, Joan P '77 -139 Burr Av -Northprt 11768
(914) 948-2210 .. **Silverman**, Joan S '75 -81 Main -White Plns 10601 **Fx:**686-4824
(631) 738-5901 .. **Silverman**, Joel A '76 Cnsl Symbol Technologies,Inc -1 Symbol Plz -Holtsvll 11742 **Fx:**438-4110
(212) 249-1550 .. **Silverman**, John E '95 %Bobrow & R -40 E 69th -NY 10021 **Fx:**249-5451
(212) 616-7713 .. **Silverman**, Jonathan R '99 Seaport Grp LLC -360 Mad Av -NY 10017
(212) 986-8282 .. **Silverman**, Jos E '58 (Cohen & S) -360 Lex Av -NY 10017
(212) 576-4097 .. **Silverman**, Joshua M '03 Marvel Enterprises,Inc -417 5th Av -NY 10016
(212) 686-3100 .. **Silverman**, Karen F '82 (Haftel & S,PC) -260 Mad Av -NY 10016
(631) 385-8600 .. **Silverman**, Karen Grasberger '88 -83 Prospect -Huntngtn 11743 **Fx:**385-8601
(212) 922-8900 .. **Silverman**, Kenneth D '05 Dreyfus Corp -200 Park Av -NY 10166
(212) 451-2300 .. **Silverman**, Kenneth M '96 (Olshan GFR&W LLP) -65 E 55th -NY 10022
(516) 479-6300 .. **Silverman**, Kenneth P '81 (Silverman A LLP) -100 Jericho Quad -Jericho 11753
(212) 425-1616 .. **Silverman**, Larry J '69 -26 Bway -NY 10004 **Fx:**425-9375
(631) 499-3333 .. **Silverman**, Laurence A '76 -1776 E Jericho Tpk -Huntngtn 11743 **Fx:**462-7548
(212) 841-1000 .. **Silverman**, Laurence A '78 (Covington & B LLP) -620 8th Av -NY 10018
(516) 486-7475 .. **Silverman**, Lawr '97 Risk Mgmt Planning Grp -211 Station Rd -Mineola 11501
(631) 543-5434 .. **Silverman**, Lawr H '78 OfCnsl Sarisohn Law Prtnrs LLP -350 Vets Mem'l Hwy -Commack 11725 **Fx:**543-7901
(212) 599-5414 .. **Silverman**, Lawr H '78 OfCnsl Helfand & H -350 5th Av -NY 10118 **Fx:**599-3029
(212) 940-8800 .. **Silverman**, Leah V '99 %Katten MR LLP -575 Mad Av -NY 10022
(212) 859-8000 .. **Silverman**, Leon '49 OfCnsl Fried FHS&J LLP -1 NY Plz -NY 10004
(646) 375-2432 .. **Silverman**, Leonard C '74 -116 W 23rd -NY 10011
(212) 774-5680 .. **Silverman**, Leonard S '93 Cong Kehilath Jeshurun -125 E 85th -NY 10028 **Fx:**534-4120
(212) 619-4444 .. **Silverman**, Leonard Steven '92 %Marshall CW&B,PC -116 John -NY 10038
(212) 225-2000 .. **Silverman**, Leslie N '75 (Cleary GS&H) -1 Lbrty Plz -NY 10006
(631) 853-4377 .. **Silverman**, Lewis A '77 %Family Ct -Bx9077 -Central Islip 11722
(914) 328-0404 .. **Silverman**, Lewis H '74 (Jackson L LLP) -1 N Bway -White Plns 10601
(212) 599-5799 .. **Silverman**, Lewis R '93 (Rutherford & C LLP) -369 Lex Av -NY 10017
(516) 746-2300 .. **Silverman**, Lisa J '02 %A Capetola -2C Hillside Av -Williston Pk 11596 **Fx:**746-2318
(212) 832-9170 .. **Silverman**, Lorin '78 %Natl Enterprises -830 3rd Av -NY 10022 **Fx:**755-1410
(212) 813-8800 .. **Silverman**, Mandee R '03 %Goodwin P LLP -620 8th Av -NY 10018
(516) 562-7284 .. **Silverman**, Marc D '89 %CMP Media LLC -600 Community Dr -Manhsst 11030
(212) 753-5000 .. **Silverman**, Marc L '73 (Schiff H LLP) -900 3rd Av -NY 10022
(212) 636-7703 .. **Silverman**, Marcella B '83 %Fordham Univ Sch of Law -140 W 62nd -NY 10023 **Fx:**636-6899
(516) 379-5200 .. **Silverman**, Mark D '85 (Silverman & T) -33 Guy Lombardo Av -Freeprt 11520 **Fx:**771-9650
(914) 312-6450 .. **Silverman**, Martin J '84 Verizon Business -1 Intl Dr -Rye Brook 10573
(212) 263-6702 .. **Silverman**, Matthew D '05 %NYU Med Schl -550 1st Av -NY 10016
(718) 993-9999 .. **Silverman**, Maxine S '93 %J Oresky & Assoc,PLLC -155 E 149th -Bronx 10451 **Fx:**993-0142
(646) 862-9396 .. **Silverman**, Michl D '95 TLDEF -151 W 19th -NY 10011
(718) 237-8693 .. **Silverman**, Michl L '05 (Silverman & S,LLP) -52 3rd -Brklyn 11231 **Fx:**855-2933
(212) 373-3000 .. **Silverman**, Moses '74 (Paul WRW&G LLP) -1285 Av of Amer -NY 10019
(631) 369-1700 .. **Silverman**, Nancy '01 %Esseks H&A,LLP -108 E Main Bx279 -Rvrhead 11901
(212) 398-0055 .. **Silverman**, Noah '91 (Garwin G&F,LLP) -1501 Bway -NY 10036
(212) 889-6371 .. **Silverman**, Noel A '03 -192 Lex Av -NY 10016
(212) 758-2020 .. **Silverman**, Noel L '56 -200 Park Av S -NY 10003 **Fx:**758-2025
(212) 448-1100 .. **Silverman**, Paul H '72 (McLaughlin & S,LLP) -260 Mad Av -NY 10016
(212) 836-8000 .. **Silverman**, Peter B '07 %Kaye S LLP -425 Park Av -NY 10022
(212) 813-5900 .. **Silverman**, Peter J '81 (Fross ZL&Z,PC) -866 UN Plz -NY 10017
(212) 779-8600 .. **Silverman**, Peter R '71 (Silverman SS&B PLLC) -381 Park Av S -NY 10016
(212) 988-7100 .. **Silverman**, Philip E '88 -350 E 79th -NY 10075
(718) 319-1400 .. **Silverman**, Ralph W '92 Klein C&S LLP -1614 Wllmsbrdg Rd -Bronx 10461
(518) 463-3615 .. **Silverman**, Randi Fraiman '98 -105 Mosher Rd -Glenmont 12077
(516) 466-6500 .. **Silverman**, Raymond C '00 %Parker WA LLP -6 Hrbr Park Dr S -Pt Wash 11050
(212) 331-9305 .. **Silverman**, Rhona A '96 (R Silverman,PLLC) -40 Fulton -NY 10038 **Fx:**331-9305
(212) 557-4000 .. **Silverman**, Robt B '73 (Grunfeld DLS&K LLP) -399 Park Av -NY 10022
(315) 435-2585 .. **Silverman**, Robt M '61 %Dept Social Srvcs -421 Mntgmry -Syracuse 13202
(718) 698-8740 .. **Silverman**, Robin A '87 %MHLS -1150 Forest Hll Rd -Staten Isl 10314 **Fx:**370-1972
(212) 907-7300 .. **Silverman**, Robin E '85 (Golenbock EAB&P) -437 Mad Av -NY 10022
(212) 986-7180 .. **Silverman**, Robyn B '81 -501 5th Av -NY 10017 **Fx:**986-3752
(516) 463-5892 .. **Silverman**, Ronald H '81 %Hofstra Law Schl -121 Hofstra Univ -Hempstd 11549
(212) 705-7000 .. **Silverman**, Ronald J '01 (Bingham M LLP) -399 Park Av -NY 10022
(212) 506-1700 .. **Silverman**, Sari A '06 %Kasowitz BT&F LLP -1633 Bway -NY 10019
(212) 779-8600 .. **Silverman Sclar Shin & Byrne PLLC** -381 Park Av S -NY 10016 **Fx:**779-8858
(917) 343-2357 .. **Silverman**, Scott D '84 Goldman Sachs -1 NY Plz -NY 10004
(212) 872-1000 .. **Silverman**, Shari L '06 -One Bryant Park -NY 10036 **Fx:**872-1002
(212) 644-1010 .. **Silverman**, Shelby A '07 %Kauff M&M LLP -950 3rd Av -NY 10022
(212) 331-5046 .. **Silverman**, Sheri P '91 HRA -180 Water -NY 10038
(646) 672-0054 .. **Silverman**, Sidney B '57 -3½ E 93rd -NY 10128
(518) 374-3373 .. **Silverman Silverman & Seligman** -527 State -Schnctdy 12305 **Fx:**344-4338
(718) 224-1659 .. **Silverman**, Stephen B '68 OfCnsl Taylor,C&S,LLP -26910 Grnd Cntrl Pkwy -Floral Pk 11005
(212) 793-0321 .. **Silverman**, Stephen B '89 Citigroup -601 Lex Av -NY 10022
(212) 349-6775 .. **Silverman**, Steven M '86 OfCnsl Peltz & W -222 Bway -NY 10038
(516) 536-6116 .. **Silverman**, Stuart J '68 -100 Merrick Rd -Rockvll Ctr 11570 **Fx:**536-2189
(212) 451-2900 .. **Silverman**, Sue E '07 %Robinson & C LLP -885 3rd Av -NY 10022
(718) 225-4740 .. **Silverman**, Susan M '88 -38-15 Bell Blvd -Bayside 11361
(718) 281-2311 .. **Silverman**, Warren M '81 -4703 Bell Blvd -Bayside 11361 **Fx:**423-2512
(212) 682-2800 .. **Silverman & Weinraub** -50 E 42nd -NY 10017 **Fx:**682-4309
(212) 801-3148 .. **Silverman**, Wm C '93 (Greenberg T,LLP) -200 Park Av -NY 10166
(212) 661-9100 .. **Silverman**, Wm M '66 (Otterbourg SH&R,PC) -230 Park Av -NY 10169
(212) 839-5300 .. **Silverman**, Zachary P '07 %Sidley A LLP -787 7th Av -NY 10019
(212) 308-4411 .. **Silverman**, Zachary W '08 %Edwards AP&D LLP -750 Lex Av -NY 10022
(212) 891-9100 .. **Silverman Leibow**, Pamela '96 (Goldfarb & F LLP) -345 Park Av -NY 10154
(212) 557-3000 .. **Silvermintz**, Michl B '90 %Rivelis P&B,LLP -286 Mad Av -NY 10017
(212) 221-6900 .. **Silvermintz**, Robyn L '05 %Winget S&S,LLP -45 Bway -NY 10006
(607) 432-7222 .. **Silvernell**, George R '58 -21 Walnut Bx1365 -Oneonta 13820 **Fx:**432-7506
(516) 663-6600 .. **Silvers**, Adam P '94 (Ruskin MF,PC) -1425 RXR Plz -Uniondale 11556
(718) 883-8134 .. **Silvers**, Carolyn J '88 %Leg Aid -153-01 Jamaica Av -Jamaica 11432 **Fx:**657-0537
(212) 302-7890 .. **Silvers**, Dean A '80 -1560 Bway -NY 10036
(212) 436-4733 .. **Silvers**, Eileen S '77 Deloitte & Touche LLP -2 World Fncl Ctr -NY 10281
(718) 876-6300 .. **Silvers**, Janet '88 %DA -130 Styvsnt Pl -Staten Isl 10301
(917) 237-2900 .. **Silvers**, Laura R '91 Axiom -75 Spring -NY 10012
(212) 854-7941 .. **Silvers**, Teri D '92 Columbia Law Schl -435 W 116th -NY 10027
(212) 521-5400 .. **Silverschotz**, Mark D '84 (Reed S LLP) -599 Lex Av -NY 10022
(212) 387-7880 .. **Silvershein**, Danl M '93 -262 W 38th -NY 10018 **Fx:**260-8930
(718) 859-0638 .. **Silversmith**, Lyle F '74 -761 Wstmnstr Rd -Brklyn 11230 **Fx:**434-1324
(212) 619-5000 .. **Silversmith**, Mark Lee '77 %EDC -110 William -NY 10038 **Fx:**312-3912
(212) 922-9300 .. **Silversmith**, Robt G '82 (Silversmith & V,LLP) -30 Broad -NY 10004
(518) 473-4725 .. **Silversmith**, Sharon G '75 %OTDA-Fair Hearings -40 N Pearl -Albany 12243 **Fx:**473-6735
(212) 922-9300 .. **Silversmith & Veraja,LLP** -30 Broad -NY 10004 **Fx:**681-1904
(212) 557-1818 .. **Silverson Pareres & Lombardi** -192 Lex Av -NY 10016 **Fx:**557-1336
(212) 557-1818 .. **Silverson**, Robt M Jr. '70 (Silverson P&L) -192 Lex Av -NY 10016
(212) 233-4995 .. **Silverstein**, Adam '96 -15 Maiden Ln -NY 10038 **Fx:**385-4661

(212) 907-7300 .. **Silverstein,** Adam C '93 (Golenbock EAB&P) -437 Mad Av -NY 10022
(212) 868-1010 .. **Silverstein,** Alisa L '98 %Kudman TA LLP -350 5th Av -NY 10118
(516) 466-6500 .. **Silverstein,** Allan M '86 %Parker WA LLP -6 Hrbr Park Dr S -Pt Wash 11050
(212) 267-6700 .. **Silverstein,** Allan M '86 %Parker WA LLP -111 John -NY 10038
(718) 590-2000 .. **Silverstein,** Amanda B '08 %DA -198 E 161st -Bronx 10451 **Fx:**590-6477
(212) 574-1200 .. **Silverstein,** Andrew L '91 (Seward & K LLP) -1 Bttry Pk Plz -NY 10004
(646) 264-3650 .. **Silverstein,** Barnett '75 %US Dept of Labor -201 Varick -NY 10014 **Fx:**264-3660
(212) 315-5575 .. **Silverstein,** Barry W '81 Cnsl Muchnick G&G,PC -200 Park Av S -NY 10003
(212) 608-4040 .. **Silverstein & Bast** -217 Bway -NY 10007
(212) 267-6456 .. **Silverstein,** Bennett I '98 Fischer Bros -217 Bway -NY 10007 **Fx:**267-6468
(845) 794-6572 .. **Silverstein,** Carl J '58 -Bx854 -Monticello 12701 **Fx:**794-6572
(212) 608-4040 .. **Silverstein,** Chas '85 (Silverstein & B) -217 Bway -NY 10007
(212) 425-7200 .. **Silverstein,** David H '04 %Kenyon & K,LLP -1 Bway -NY 10004
(212) 230-3926 .. **Silverstein,** Edw J '96 Mackay-Shields Financial Corp -9 W 57th -NY 10019
(347) 545-1112 .. **Silverstein,** Francine J '98 -26 Court -Brklyn 11242
(212) 697-9280 .. **Silverstein,** Gary '89 %Rosenberg MF&W -122 E 42nd -NY 10168
(212) 504-6000 .. **Silverstein,** Gary T '97 (Cadwalader W&T LLP) -1 World Fncl Ctr -NY 10281
(212) 486-2400 .. **Silverstein,** Glen A '91 (Leader & B LLP) -630 3rd Av -NY 10017
(212) 644-1010 .. **Silverstein,** Harlan J '86 (Kauff M&M LLP) -950 3rd Av -NY 10022
(518) 473-4290 .. **Silverstein,** Harvey C '81 %State Comptroller -110 State -Albany 12236 **Fx:**473-9104
(212) 299-2000 .. **Silverstein,** Jason S '02 NYMEX -1 North End Av -NY 10282 **Fx:**301-4700
(212) 885-5000 .. **Silverstein,** Jay D '71 (Blank R LLP) -405 Lex Av -NY 10174
(212) 574-1200 .. **Silverstein,** Jeffrey D '90 (Seward & K LLP) -1 Bttry Pk Plz -NY 10004
(516) 746-3500 .. **Silverstein,** Jonathan D '01 %Brand G&B,PC -600 Old Cntry Rd -Gdn Cty 11530
(718) 544-2856 .. **Silverstein,** Judi L '86 -35 Bow -Frst Hlls 11375 **Fx:**544-2956
(212) 385-1444 .. **Silverstein,** Keith D '87 (Silverstein & S,LLP) -40 Fulton -NY 10038
(212) 302-5101 .. **Silverstein Langer Newburgh & McElyea,LLP** -500 5th Av -NY 10110 **Fx:**302-5788
(631) 424-6850 .. **Silverstein,** Larry '86 (Silverstein & K) -1160 E Jericho Tpk -Huntngtn 11743 **Fx:**424-0636
(212) 490-0666 .. **Silverstein,** Larry A '56 (Silvestein Properties) -250 Greenwich -NY 10007
(914) 946-1400 .. **Silverstein,** Laura K '06 %Vouté LM&C,LLP -170 Hmltn Av -White Plns 10601
(212) 209-3005 .. **Silverstein,** Leo '54 SrCnsl Reitler K&R LLC -885 3rd Av -NY 10022
(718) 633-8900 .. **Silverstein,** Linda A '03 -127 Beverley Rd -Brklyn 11218 **Fx:**633-8912
(718) 250-1100 .. **Silverstein,** Marc '85 %E Garfinkel -12 Metrotech Ctr -Brklyn 11201 **Fx:**250-1168
(212) 545-4780 .. **Silverstein,** Mark C '84 (Wolf HAF&H LLP) -270 Mad Av -NY 10016
(212) 474-1000 .. **Silverstein,** Mark L '08 %Cravath S&M LLP -825 8th Av -NY 10019
(212) 801-6900 .. **Silverstein,** Martin J '05 SrCnsl Greenberg T,LLP -200 Park Av -NY 10166
(914) 428-2100 .. **Silverstein,** Michl I '84 %Welby B&G,LLP -11 Martine Av -White Plns 10606
(212) 850-2800 .. **Silverstein,** Paul N '82 (Andrews K LLP) -450 Lex Av -NY 10017
(718) 824-6500 .. **Silverstein,** Robt M '81 (Coiro WC&S) -1206 Castle Hill Av -Bronx 10462
(718) 686-0200 .. **Silverstein,** Rosilyn '85 -132 Ocean Pkwy -Brklyn 11218 **Fx:**686-1800
(212) 376-0440 .. **Silverstein,** Scott A '89 %The Topps Co,Inc -1 Whitehall -NY 10004
(212) 489-1600 .. **Silverstein,** Scott Evan '98 %Deloitte LLP -1633 Bway -NY 10019 **Fx:**492-4201
(212) 370-8455 .. **Silverstein,** Stanley P '78 %Warnaco Inc -501 7th Av -NY 10018
(716) 881-5800 .. **Silverstein,** Stephen R '81 %Siegel K&K -426 Franklin -Buffalo 14202
(212) 385-1444 .. **Silverstein & Stern,LLP** -40 Fulton -NY 10038 **Fx:**385-7933
(845) 638-9400 .. **Silverstein,** Steven M '85 (Schwartz & S) -254 S Main -New Cty 10956
(718) 633-8900 .. **Silverstein,** Walter C '59 -127 Beverley Rd -Brklyn 11218 **Fx:**633-8912
(212) 766-1888 .. **Silverstine,** Betsy K '07 %Morris DA&F -2 Rector -NY 10006
(631) 755-0101 .. **Silverstone,** Adam H '93 %Lewis JAA,LLP -425 Broad Hollow Rd -Melvll 11747
(914) 997-1346 .. **Silverstone,** Stanley J '91 %Seham SM&P,LLP -445 Hmltn Av -White Plns 10601
(212) 698-3500 .. **Silverthorn,** Danl J '09 %Dechert LLP -1095 Av of Amer -NY 10036
(212) 906-1200 .. **Silverthorn,** Michelle A '09 %Latham & W -885 3rd Av -NY 10022
(212) 301-3075 .. **Silvestri,** Christopher J '99 %Fox News Ntwrk,LLC -1211 Av of Amer -NY 10036 **Fx:**301-5785
(518) 494-3404 .. **Silvestri,** John M '82 JM Silvestri -6348 State Route 9 Bx715 -Chestertwn 12817 **Fx:**494-7571
(212) 733-5382 .. **Silvestri,** Louis S '99 Pfizer Inc -150 E 42nd -NY 10017
(718) 447-8300 .. **Silvestri,** Lynette '92 %W Frew -791 Jewett Av Bx179 -Staten Isl 10314 **Fx:**727-8985
(631) 761-0800 .. **Silvestro,** Jennifer L '99 %Lazer AR&Y,PC -225 Old Cntry Rd -Melvll 11747
(212) 804-4200 .. **Silvestro,** Michl V '09 %Mound CW&G -One Bttry Pk Plz -NY 10004
(914) 937-4844 .. **Silvestro,** Tracie J '01 TJ Silvestro,PLLC -17 King -Pt Chester 10573 **Fx:**934-2942
(212) 932-1980 .. **Silvia,** Andrea Jo '96 %Sts Hilda & Hughes Schl -619 W 114th -NY 10025
(518) 457-2070 .. **Sim,** Jennifer J '02 %Dept of Tax & Fin -Bldg 9 State Campus -Albany 12227 **Fx:**457-6131
(212) 326-3939 .. **Sim,** Joan M '09 %Jones D -222 E 41st -NY 10017
(212) 728-8000 .. **Sim,** John T '09 %Willkie F&G LLP -787 7th Av -NY 10019
(212) 239-3680 .. **Sim,** Sang Joon '97 (Sim & P,LLP) -450 7th Av -NY 10123 **Fx:**239-3683
(212) 608-1009 .. **Siman,** Farzad '93 (Levine & S,PC) -132 Nassau -NY 10038
(212) 723-3373 .. **Siman,** Haley B '01 Citigroup -250 West -NY 10013
(212) 867-4466 .. **Simanca-Proctor,** Christina '05 %Belkin BW&G,LLP -270 Mad Av -NY 10016
(212) 730-8860 .. **Simantov,** A Z '95 (Simantov & Assoc,PC) -132 Spruce -Cedarhrst 11516 **Fx:**730-8861
(718) 239-6777 .. **Simantov,** Jos '04 -2747 Coney Isl Av -Brklyn 11235 **Fx:**339-6969
(212) 609-6800 .. **Simao,** Salvador P '98 (McCarter & E,LLP) -245 Park Av -NY 10167
(914) 476-0600 .. **Simari,** Anthony T '98 (Smith B&J,LLP) -733 Ynkrs Av -Ynkrs 10704
(212) 758-0050 .. **Simat,** Kristen M '05 %Title Assoc -825 3rd Av -NY 10022 **Fx:**758-8223
(518) 487-7600 .. **Simcoe,** Thos W '06 %Whiteman O&H LLP -1 Commerce Plz -Albany 12260
(516) 826-0400 .. **Simendinger,** Donna L '87 %Goldstein & G PC -1800 Bellmore Av -Bellmore 11710
(212) 848-9800 .. **Simensky,** Brenda T '76 OfCnsl Withers B LLP -430 Park Av -NY 10022
(212) 962-2244 .. **Simensky,** Melvin R '51 -30 Vesey -NY 10007 **Fx:**732-4923
(914) 232-2326 .. **Simensky,** Robt A '96 Convergent Capital -51 Katonah Woods Rd -Katonah 10536
(212) 836-8000 .. **Simeon,** Jean '10 Kaye S LLP -425 Park Av -NY 10022
(631) 737-8200 .. **Simeone,** Ettore A '82 T Campagna -4949 Express Dr N -Ronkonkoma 11779 **Fx:**737-8687
(845) 357-2660 .. **Simeone,** Frank T '73 (Kornfeld RN&S) -46 Wshngtn Av Bx177 -Suffern 10901
(212) 317-6000 .. **Simeone,** Jill '95 Cemex -590 Mad Av -NY 10022 **Fx:**317-6048
(212) 691-7070 .. **Simermeyer,** James F '78 -148 Mad Av -NY 10016 **Fx:**691-7097
(212) 813-8800 .. **Simes,** Jeffrey A '97 (Goodwin P LLP) -620 8th Av -NY 10018
(212) 506-2500 .. **Simes,** Michl L '01 %Mayer B LLP -1675 Bway -NY 10019
(212) 735-3000 .. **Simes,** Nicole Mulle '01 %Skadden ASM&F LLP -4 Times Sq -NY 10036
(716) 856-4000 .. **Simet,** Anne Smith '79 (Hodgson R LLP) -140 Pearl -Buffalo 14202
(845) 627-7900 .. **Simeti,** Thos '89 -Bx2 -Nanuet 10954 **Fx:**627-7932
(845) 638-5180 .. **Simeti,** Thos '89 %Cnty Atty -Cnty Ofc Bldg -New Cty 10956 **Fx:**638-5676
(516) 486-4640 .. **Siminerio,** Paul R '80 (Cherry E&K,LLP) -1 Old Cntry Rd -Carle Pl 11514
(973) 992-4800 .. **Siminoff,** Ian W '98 %Fox R LLP -100 Park Av -NY 10017 **Fx:**992-9125
(212) 683-8400 .. **Siminou,** Stephen S '95 (Siminou & Assoc,PC) -950 3rd Av -NY 10022 **Fx:**683-8422
(212) 880-1200 .. **Simins,** Robt A '87 %Chicago Title/Ticor -711 3rd Av -NY 10017 **Fx:**880-1400
(212) 455-2000 .. **Simkin,** Alexander '07 %Simpson T&B LLP -425 Lex Av -NY 10017
(212) 348-5627 .. **Simkin,** Carol F '74 Arts Mediation Grp -1185 Park Av -NY 10128 **Fx:**348-5628
(212) 373-3000 .. **Simkin,** Steven '74 (Paul WRW&G LLP) -1285 Av of Amer -NY 10019
(718) 739-2020 .. **Simkovic,** Neal A '96 -118-21 Qns Blvd -Frst Hlls 11375
(212) 244-4187 .. **Simmon,** G Michl '80 (Weingrad & W) -350 5th Av -NY 10118 **Fx:**594-2944
(212) 269-0927 .. **Simmonds,** Andrew R '75 (D'Amato & L,LLP) -2 World Fncl Ctr -NY 10281
(212) 848-4000 .. **Simmonds,** Kim A '07 %Shearman & S LLP -599 Lex Av -NY 10022
(914) 993-1939 .. **Simmons,** Alicia M '07 US Atty -300 Quarropas -White Plns 10601 **Fx:**993-9036
(212) 617-5718 .. **Simmons,** Amy L '02 Bloomberg LP -731 Lex Av -NY 10022
(212) 335-4500 .. **Simmons,** Camisha L '08 %DLA Piper LLP -1251 Av of Amer -NY 10020
(212) 801-9311 .. **Simmons,** Chas A '63 (Greenberg T,LLP) -200 Park Av -NY 10166
(212) 546-3103 .. **Simmons,** Chas H '96 Bristol-Myers Squibb Co -345 Park Av -NY 10154
(718) 588-8400 .. **Simmons,** Deirdre '94 HW Wilson Co -950 Univ Av -Bronx 10452 **Fx:**992-4712
(315) 471-3151 .. **Simmons,** Doreen A '75 (Hancock & E,LLP) -1500 AXA Twr I Bx4976 -Syracuse 13221
(212) 732-0400 .. **Simmons,** Douglas '79 OfCnsl Grad & W,LLP -305 Bway -NY 10007 **Fx:**571-0831
(212) 294-6700 .. **Simmons,** Erin A '10 %Winston & S -200 Park Av -NY 10166
(718) 804-8893 .. **Simmons,** Esmeralda I '78 %Ctr Law & Social Jus -1150 Carroll -Brklyn 11225 **Fx:**804-8833
(212) 852-1000 .. **Simmons,** Gwendolyn D '00 %US Trust Co,NA -114 W 47th -NY 10036 **Fx:**852-1310
(212) 233-1486 .. **Simmons,** Howard D '90 (H Simmons,PC) -217 Bway -NY 10007
(631) 582-3700 .. **Simmons,** Jaclyn '05 %Turley RR&R,LLP -3075 Vets Mem'l Hwy -Ronkonkoma 11779
(716) 632-7702 .. **Simmons,** James C '92 -11 Falmouth Ln -Williamsvll 14221 **Fx:**632-2570
(914) 631-3248 .. **Simmons,** James H '94 -47 Beekman Av Bx722 -Sleepy Hollow 10591 **Fx:**631-5388
(516) 802-0630 .. **Simmons Jannace,LLP** -115 Eileen Way -Syosset 11791 **Fx:**802-0631
(518) 860-1444 .. **Simmons,** Jennifer E '10 %Persing & O,LLP -10 Century Hill Dr -Latham 12110 **Fx:**860-1448
(718) 522-3333 .. **Simmons,** Karen P '95 %Children's Law Ctr -44 Court -Brklyn 11201 **Fx:**522-7376
(516) 802-0630 .. **Simmons,** Kevin P '80 (Simmons J,LLP) -115 Eileen Way -Syosset 11791
(212) 947-3800 .. **Simmons,** Linda '88 -350 5th Av -NY 10118 **Fx:**947-9374
(516) 538-2500 .. **Simmons,** Mario E '98 %Furey FLMW&D,PC -600 Front -Hempstd 11550
(718) 998-2227 .. **Simmons,** Melvin '99 -3017 Quentin Rd -Brklyn 11234
(212) 791-8400 .. **Simmons,** Michl C '81 (Mait W&S) -110 Wall -NY 10005
(718) 250-0400 .. **Simmons,** Nicole J '92 %R Tusa -1 MetroTech Ctr -Brklyn 11201 **Fx:**250-0591
(212) 859-8000 .. **Simmons,** Peter L '87 (Fried FHS&J LLP) -1 NY Plz -NY 10004

(212) 558-4000 .. **Simmons,** Rebecca J '92 (Sullivan & C LLP) -125 Broad -NY 10004
(631) 665-3400 .. **Simmons,** Richd F '85 %Siben & S,LLP -90 E Main Bx149P -Bay Shr 11706
(212) 225-2000 .. **Simmons,** Shana A '10 %Cleary GS&H -1 Lbrty Plz -NY 10006
(212) 751-3001 .. **Simmons,** Terry L '06 (Thompson & K LLP) -919 3rd Av -NY 10022
(718) 286-6000 .. **Simmons-McGhee,** Josette L '98 %DA -125-01 Qns Blvd -Kew Gdns 11415
(516) 741-5252 .. **Simms,** Cindy S '92 Sanders SBWV&G,PC -100 Hrrcks Rd -Mineola 11501
(212) 655-5802 .. **Simms,** Howard M '81 -295 Greenwich -NY 10007
(212) 931-7968 .. **Simms,** Jennifer R '90 %MLB Properties -245 Park Av -NY 10167 **Fx:**949-5697
(212) 254-4430 .. **Simms,** Kervin A '85 (K Simms,PC) -636 Bway -NY 10012 **Fx:**254-3861
(212) 310-8000 .. **Simms,** Marsha E '78 (Weil G&M LLP) -767 5th Av -NY 10153
(516) 466-6050 .. **Simms,** Marvin '60 Guardian Land Abstrct -1010 Nrthrn Blvd Bx385 -Gt Neck 11022 **Fx:**466-6011
(212) 376-8900 .. **Simms,** Stephen R '69 (Jacobs & S) -757 3rd Av -NY 10017 **Fx:**376-8989
(212) 244-9500 .. **Simnowitz,** Danl H '06 %White and W LLP -1 Penn Plz -NY 10119
(718) 590-2000 .. **Simoes,** Remi E '06 DA -198 E 161st -Bronx 10451 **Fx:**590-6477
(845) 356-8700 .. **Simon,** Alan M '68 -664 Chestnut Rdg Rd -Spg Vly 10977 **Fx:**356-0755
(347) 401-9184 .. **Simon,** Alexander '90 Supreme Ct Law Dept -360 Adams -Brklyn 11201 **Fx:**643-6114
(212) 789-2703 .. **Simon,** Alexandre G '02 NHL Enterprises,LP -1185 Av of Amer -NY 10036
(212) 674-3948 .. **Simon,** Amy Edelstein '77 -242 E 19th -NY 10003 **Fx:**835-2408
(212) 708-1600 .. **Simon,** Andrea G '85 %Showtime Networks Inc -1633 Bway -NY 10019 **Fx:**708-1391
(212) 848-4000 .. **Simon,** Ansgar A '00 Cnsl Shearman & S LLP -599 Lex Av -NY 10022
(516) 495-7373 .. **Simon,** Arnold '62 -88 Froehlich Farm Blvd -Woodbury 11797 **Fx:**495-7371
(718) 497-2552 .. **Simon,** Arthur Jay '58 (A Simon & Assoc) -228 Montrose Av -Brklyn 11206 **Fx:**497-1146
(585) 546-5530 .. **Simon,** Audrey M '05 Thomson West -50 E Broad -Rchstr 14694
(212) 867-3456 .. **Simon,** Barbara '79 (Delafield H&L) -311 E 38th -NY 10016
(212) 579-2918 .. **Simon,** Barbara Ann '98 -165 W End Av -NY 10023
(718) 459-6200 .. **Simon,** Barry '77 (Simon & G) -91-31 Qns Blvd -Elmhrst 11373
(212) 541-2000 .. **Simon,** Beth D '09 %Bryan C LLP -1290 Av of Amer -NY 10104
(212) 332-8900 .. **Simon,** Bradley D '83 (Simon & Prtnrs LLP) -551 5th Av -NY 10176 **Fx:**332-8909
(212) 850-1864 .. **Simon,** Brian D '93 %J&W Seligman & Co -100 Park Av -NY 10017 **Fx:**922-5731
(212) 563-4100 .. **Simon,** Bruce H '61 (Cohen W&S LLP) -330 W 42nd -NY 10036
(914) 362-0134 .. **Simon,** Carole '85 -5 Michl -Spg Vly 10977
(212) 785-2929 .. **Simon,** Caroline H '04 %Conway FC&K,PC -48 Wall -NY 10005
(212) 551-2729 .. **Simon,** Carrie A '02 Intl Rescue Comm -122 E 42nd -NY 10168 **Fx:**551-3184
(212) 267-3091 .. **Simon,** Chad B '06 %Wilentz G&S -110 William -NY 10038 **Fx:**(732) 726-4723
(212) 310-8000 .. **Simon,** Cinthia J '04 %Weil G&M LLP -767 5th Av -NY 10153
(212) 683-9300 .. **Simon,** Claude A C '82 %Veratex Inc -160 Mad Av -NY 10016
(845) 928-7604 .. **Simon,** Craig F '83 -11 Van Buren Ct -Highland Mills 10930
(212) 536-3900 .. **Simon,** David '52 OfCnsl K&L Gates LLP -599 Lex Av -NY 10022
(845) 279-2986 .. **Simon,** David '95 OfCnsl Hogan & R -1441 Route 22 -Brewstr 10509
(718) 248-5995 .. **Simon,** David S '93 Citibank -1 Court Sq -LIC 11120
(646) 442-3100 .. **Simon,** Edw N '81 %Legal Srvcs -90 John -NY 10038 **Fx:**(212) 227-9798
(914) 249-6229 .. **Simon,** Eileen S '91 MasterCard Intl -2000 Purchase -Purchase 10577
(212) 545-4000 .. **Simon,** Eric P '80 (Jackson L LLP) -666 3rd Av -NY 10017
(212) 361-7724 .. **Simon,** Esther M '90 Dept Consumer Affrs -66 John -NY 10038
(914) 428-1438 .. **Simon,** Ezra '78 %T Bona,PC -123 Main -White Plns 10601 **Fx:**428-1413
(718) 680-8400 .. **Simon,** Fredk J '94 (Simon M&S,LLC) -7504 5th Av -Brklyn 11209
(212) 837-6000 .. **Simon,** Gary J '84 (Hughes H&R LLP) -1 Bttry Pk Plz -NY 10004
(212) 935-0300 .. **Simon,** Gary R '75 Martexport,Inc -155 E 55th -NY 10022
(718) 459-6200 .. **Simon & Gilman** -91-31 Qns Blvd -Elmhrst 11373 **Fx:**459-6270
(212) 775-0055 .. **Simon Gluck & Kane LLP** -1700 Bway -NY 10019 **Fx:**839-9103
(212) 382-0080 .. **Simon,** Harvey J '00 -410 Park Av -NY 10022
(516) 561-6622 .. **Simon,** Herbert A '51 (Simon & M) -99 W Hawthorne Av -Vly Stream 11580
(212) 575-1292 .. **Simon,** Herman '61 -114 W 47th -NY 10036 **Fx:**768-4469
(212) 237-1000 .. **Simon,** Howard L '77 (Windels ML&M,LLP) -156 W 56th -NY 10019
(212) 481-5644 .. **Simon,** Irwin F '64 -320 E 46th -NY 10017
(212) 906-9077 .. **Simon,** Jacques G '89 -488 Mad Av -NY 10022
(212) 431-2352 .. **Simon,** James F '92 %NY Law Schl -185 W Bway -NY 10013 **Fx:**431-3295
(212) 779-8111 .. **Simon,** Jamil '87 APC Funding Grp -60 Mad Av -NY 10010 **Fx:**779-8220
(718) 852-3528 .. **Simon,** Jo Anne '91 (JA Simon,PC) -356 Fulton -Brklyn 11201 **Fx:**875-5728
(212) 775-0055 .. **Simon,** Joel K '68 (Simon G&K LLP) -1700 Bway -NY 10019
(212) 964-7400 .. **Simon,** Joel M '86 Smith MDWY&Y,PC -111 John -NY 10038
(212) 293-2029 .. **Simon,** Jonathan R '00 Van Eck Assoc Corp -335 Mad Av -NY 10017
(516) 357-3700 .. **Simon,** Jos D '87 (Cullen and D LLP) -100 Q Roosevelt Blvd -Gdn Cty 11530
(212) 446-4800 .. **Simon,** Joshua B '03 (Kirkland & E LLP) -153 E 53rd -NY 10022
(917) 757-9911 .. **Simon,** Joy R '84 -500 E 77th -NY 10162
(212) 319-0990 .. **Simon,** Judith F '87 %Toby Spitz Assoc -110 E 59th -NY 10022 **Fx:**319-1555
(212) 906-1200 .. **Simon,** Keith A '08 (Latham & W) -885 3rd Av -NY 10022
(914) 935-2974 .. **Simon,** Kenneth J '81 %Avon Products Inc -Mdlnd & Peck Av -Rye 10580
(212) 319-5240 .. **Simon,** Kenneth M '95 %Flicker G & Assoc,LLP -45 Bway -NY 10006
(212) 308-6560 .. **Simon,** Kimberly D '04 D Carrie LLC -155 E 55th -NY 10022
(516) 746-2300 .. **Simon,** Lance D '08 %A Capetola -2C Hillside Av -Williston Pk 11596 **Fx:**746-2318
(212) 599-0900 .. **Simon,** Lauren C '09 %Bower & L,PC -261 Mad Av -NY 10016
(212) 735-8600 .. **Simon,** Lawr B '85 (Morrison C LLP) -909 3rd Av -NY 10022
(800) 784-5140 .. **Simon,** Lawr M '90 -1997 Route 17 M -Goshen 10924 **Fx:**(201) 445-3033
(212) 450-4000 .. **Simon,** Leslie Anne '79 %Davis P&W LLP -450 Lex Av -NY 10017
(914) 763-5892 .. **Simon,** Leslie N '94 -787 Route 35 Bx273 -Cross Rvr 10518 **Fx:**763-8693
(518) 402-2724 .. **Simon,** Loretta '87 %Dept of Law -The Cptl -Albany 12224 **Fx:**473-2534
(315) 732-3059 .. **Simon,** Lyn '77 -201 Gilbert Rd -New Hartfrd 13413
(212) 267-1900 .. **Simon,** M Mendel '08 %Wade CM -111 Bway -NY 10006
(212) 974-7474 .. **Simon,** Marc H '02 (Cowan DA&S LLP) -41 Mad Av -NY 10010
(718) 643-6462 .. **Simon,** Marc W '78 -522 Rugby Rd -Brklyn 11226
(718) 923-5120 .. **Simon,** Margareth Garnier '03 Dept of Ed -335 Adams -Brklyn 11201
(212) 759-7909 .. **Simon,** Marilyn '71 (M Simon & Assoc) -110 E 59th -NY 10022 **Fx:**759-7690
(631) 751-5757 .. **Simon,** Martin F '01 %Glynn M&P,LLP -57 North Cntry Rd Bx712 -Stony Brk 11790
(212) 353-8700 .. **Simon,** Matthew J '96 (Simon E&B LLP) -24 Union Sq E -NY 10003 **Fx:**353-1708
(212) 686-3300 .. **Simon Meyrowitz & Meyrowitz,PC** -470 Park Av S -NY 10016 **Fx:**686-3822
(212) 897-0230 .. **Simon,** Michl J '84 %International Securities Exchange -60 Broad -NY 10004 **Fx:**635-0210
(212) 681-1000 .. **Simon,** Michl J '85 -100 Park Av -NY 10017 **Fx:**818-9148
(212) 880-3800 .. **Simon,** Michl S '80 (Akerman S) -335 Mad Av -NY 10017
(716) 674-4443 .. **Simon,** Michl S '84 -5266 Seneca -W Seneca 14224 **Fx:**674-4214
(718) 680-8400 .. **Simon,** Michl S '96 (Simon M&S,LLC) -7504 5th Av -Brklyn 11209
(914) 422-4407 .. **Simon,** Michelle S '82 %Pace Law Schl -78 N Bway -White Plns 10603 **Fx:**422-4039
(845) 634-2286 .. **Simon,** Morton S '68 -3 Roseland Ct -New Cty 10956
(212) 752-5258 .. **Simon,** Nathanya G '84 (Schwartz SE&C LLC) -845 3rd Av -NY 10022
(212) 266-8240 .. **Simon,** Neil A '85 %FBE Ltd -111 Bway -NY 10006 **Fx:**732-1824
(212) 715-9100 .. **Simon,** Norman C '98 (Kramer LN&F,LLP) -1177 Av of Amer -NY 10036
(212) 637-3172 .. **Simon,** Paul F '94 %EPA -290 Bway -NY 10007 **Fx:**637-3096
(212) 361-8160 .. **Simon,** Priva H '83 %Ct of Claims -26 Bway -NY 10004 **Fx:**361-8103
(212) 820-7700 .. **Simon,** Rachel L '97 (Boundas SW&B,LLC) -1 Bttry Pk Plz -NY 10004
(212) 819-8200 .. **Simon,** Raymond J '86 (White & C LLP) -1155 Av of Amer -NY 10036
(646) 277-8800 .. **Simon,** Richd A '99 Huron Consulting Grp -1120 Av of Amer -NY 10036 **Fx:**(212) 785-1313
(718) 680-8400 .. **Simon,** Richd D '67 (Simon M&S,LLC) -7504 5th Av -Brklyn 11209
(718) 263-6928 .. **Simon,** Richd S '84 -110-45 71st Rd -Frst Hlls 11375
(518) 494-3171 .. **Simon,** Robt B '82 (Smith & S,LLC) -38 Art Tennyson Rd -Chestertwn 12817 **Fx:**494-7869
(914) 738-4638 .. **Simon,** Robt G '51 -2 Grdn Pl -Pelham 10803 **Fx:**738-5210
(716) 372-4164 .. **Simon,** Robt J '74 (Backhaus & S,PC) -Community Bk Bldg -Olean 14760
(716) 856-4200 .. **Simon,** Roger B '64 (Gibson M&C,LLP) -69 Delaware Av -Buffalo 14202
(516) 932-0400 .. **Simon,** Roger L '86 (Friedman & S) -333 Jericho Tpk -Jericho 11753 **Fx:**932-0455
(516) 463-5289 .. **Simon,** Roy D Jr. '92 %Hofstra Law Schl -121 Hofstra Univ -Hempstd 11549
(212) 461-5519 .. **Simon,** Ruth '85 SrCnsl CIT Grp,Inc -11 W 42nd -NY 10036
(212) 805-3900 .. **Simon,** Ruth V '83 %Clausen M PC -1 Chase Manh Plz -NY 10005
(212) 989-6617 .. **Simon,** Scot E '91 -253 W 15th -NY 10011
(914) 417-3400 .. **Simon,** Scott D '06 %Littleton JUP&K LLP -1 Manhattanvll Rd -Purchase 10577
(631) 247-1224 .. **Simon,** Sharon D '81 %Steinberg FB&F,PC -401 Broadhllw Rd -Melvll 11747
(212) 753-3468 .. **Simon,** Stacey A '99 %Wildes & W,PC -515 Mad Av -NY 10022
(212) 353-0040 .. **Simon,** Stanley R '86 (Allen MT&S) -112 E 19th -NY 10003
(518) 482-5114 .. **Simon,** Steven J '71 -2 Twr Pl -Albany 12203 **Fx:**435-1939
(516) 357-9030 .. **Simon,** Stuart '54 (Simon & S) -3601 Hempstd Tpk -Levittwn 11756
(646) 472-3868 .. **Simon,** Stuart H '73 CNET Ntwrks -28 E 28th -NY 10016
(914) 763-8831 .. **Simon,** Susan C '94 -787 Route 35 Bx273 -Cross Rvr 10518 **Fx:**763-8693
(212) 500-5030 .. **Simon,** Terri E '77 OfCnsl Kehl K&S,LLP -317 Mad Av -NY 10017
(212) 330-6073 .. **Simon,** Victor '62 -2 Penn Plz -NY 10121
(212) 867-0100 .. **Simon,** Wm A '76 (McGarry & S) -317 Mad Av -NY 10017 **Fx:**867-3243
(518) 589-7700 .. **Simon,** Wm M '72 (Simon & S,PLLC) -6193 Main Bx908 -Tannersvll 12485 **Fx:**589-4076
(201) 321-7448 .. **Simon,** Zoltan '04 Z Simon,PC -110 Wall -NY 10005 **Fx:**(206) 350-4388
(516) 248-1700 .. **Simoncic,** Judy Lynn '93 (Forchelli CDSM&T,LLP) -333 Earle Ovngton Blvd -Uniondale 11553
(212) 768-6700 .. **Simonds,** Richd D Jr. '94 (Sonnenschein N&R LLP) -2 World Fncl Ctr -NY 10281
(516) 488-3300 .. **Simone,** Christopher '95 %Shaub AC&S,LLP -1983 Marcus Av -Lk Success 11042
(646) 708-8088 .. **Simone,** Danielle '05 Fidelity Natl Law Grp -350 5th Av -NY 10118 **Fx:**(212) 594-8378
(212) 768-6700 .. **Simone,** Donald F '82 (Sonnenschein N&R LLP) -2 World Fncl Ctr -NY 10281
(212) 813-0620 .. **Simone,** Emilie '07 (Brodegaard & S,LLC) -110 E 59th -NY 10022 **Fx:**(646) 355-1920
(212) 297-5800 .. **Simone,** Jos R '75 (Day P LLP) -7 Times Sq -NY 10036
(516) 832-7524 .. **Simone,** Rebecca L '07 %Nixon P LLP -50 Jericho Quadrangle -Jericho 11753
(631) 423-7755 .. **Simonelli,** Gina M '09 %Bragoli & Assoc,PC -999 Walt Whitman Rd -Melvll 11747 **Fx:**423-5299
(866) 331-3271 .. **Simonet-Bertino,** Conny '01 %SSA-ODAR -100 State -Rchstr 14614 **Fx:**(585) 263-5792

(315) 472-3328 .. **Simonetta,** Russell S '99 (Simonetta & Assoc,PC) -109 S Warren -Syracuse 13202 **Fx:**472-4321
(212) 794-5729 .. **Simonette,** Danl R '92 CUNY -535 E 80th -NY 10075 **Fx:**794-5426
(212) 872-1000 .. **Simonetti,** Bruce E '95 -One Bryant Park -NY 10036 **Fx:**872-1002
(212) 767-8863 .. **Simonetti,** Danl J '04 %Spike -345 Hudson Av -NY 10014
(212) 372-1388 .. **Simonetti,** David P '89 Amer Exp -1185 Av of Amer -NY 10036 **Fx:**(646) 885-1388
(516) 248-5600 .. **Simonetti,** Louis F '88 (Simonetti & Assoc) -400 Jericho Tpk -Jericho 11753 **Fx:**470-9019
(212) 389-5000 .. **Simonetti,** Marc '01 %Sutherland A&B LLP -1114 Av of Amer -NY 10036
(914) 422-4069 .. **Simonetti-Anderson,** Cara E '06 %Pace Law Schl -78 N Bway -White Plns 10603 **Fx:**422-4039
(212) 695-8100 .. **Simoni,** John B Jr. '88 (Goetz F,LLP) -1 Penn Plz -NY 10119
(516) 944-8252 .. **Simoni,** Marianne A '89 -34 Bar Beach Rd -Pt Wash 11050
(212) 421-4100 .. **Simonian,** Maryaneh Mona '04 %Pryor C LLP -7 Times Sq -NY 10036
(212) 909-6000 .. **Simonoff,** Jessica R '06 %Debevoise & P LLP -919 3rd Av -NY 10022
(212) 506-5000 .. **Simons,** Albert III '78 (Orrick H&S LLP) -51 W 52nd -NY 10019
(718) 990-6098 .. **Simons,** Andrew J '65 St John's Law Schl -8000 Utopia Pkwy -Jamaica 11439 **Fx:**591-1855
(718) 467-1526 .. **Simons,** Calvin J Jr. '87 -616 Eastern Pkwy -Brklyn 11225 **Fx:**773-1528
(212) 310-8000 .. **Simons,** Caroline T '09 %Weil G&M LLP -767 5th Av -NY 10153
(212) 537-2270 .. **Simons,** Diane Gelch '95 Morgan Stanley -1633 Bway -NY 10019
(212) 858-1000 .. **Simons,** John C '87 Cnsl Pillsbury WSP LLP -1540 Bway -NY 10036
(518) 463-0380 .. **Simons,** Karen B '94 -817 Mad Av -Albany 12208 **Fx:**427-6720
(718) 990-6600 .. **Simons,** Michl A '91 %St John's Law Schl -8000 Utopia Pkwy -Jamaica 11439 **Fx:**591-1855
(212) 374-9300 .. **Simons,** Philip Y '77 (Simons & W) -45 Bway -NY 10006
(315) 336-4700 .. **Simons,** Richd D '52 OfCnsl McMahon & G -301 N Wshngtn Bx4350 -Rome 13442
(212) 374-9300 .. **Simons & Wiskin** -45 Bway -NY 10006 **Fx:**684-5716
(718) 948-2100 .. **Simonson & Cohen,PC** -4060 Amboy Rd -Staten Isl 10308 **Fx:**356-2379
(212) 233-5000 .. **Simonson Hess Leibowitz & Goodman, PC** -15 Maiden Ln -NY 10038 **Fx:**233-6257
(845) 255-4600 .. **Simonson,** Jon A '80 (Blatchly & S,PC) -3 Academy Bx280 -New Paltz 12561
(212) 233-5000 .. **Simonson,** Paul A '74 (Simonson HL&G,PC) -15 Maiden Ln -NY 10038
(212) 969-3000 .. **Simonyuk,** Yelena '03 %Proskauer R LLP -1585 Bway -NY 10036
(914) 253-2000 .. **Simoson,** Wm E '77 %Pepsico -700 Andrsn Hill Rd -Purchase 10577
(212) 489-1400 .. **Simotas,** Aravella '03 %Bickel & B -767 5th Av -NY 10153
(212) 351-4000 .. **Simowitz,** Aaron '09 %Gibson D&C LLP -200 Park Av -NY 10166
(914) 949-1070 .. **Simpkins,** Gilbert A '55 OfCnsl van N&M,LLP -199 Main -White Plns 10601
(212) 309-1000 .. **Simpson,** Aaron P '03 (Hunton & W) -200 Park Av -NY 10166
(212) 380-1059 .. **Simpson,** Alexander G '94 A Simpson PLLC -330 West End Av -NY 10023 **Fx:**(916) 404-7328
(212) 344-3800 .. **Simpson,** Alicia T '02 %Christophe & Assoc,PC -2 Wall -NY 10005 **Fx:**344-3212
(212) 644-1710 .. **Simpson,** Arthur J Jr. '52 OfCnsl Winne BH&B,PC -286 Mad Av -NY 10017
(212) 237-1000 .. **Simpson,** Chas E '78 (Windels ML&M,LLP) -156 W 56th -NY 10019
(607) 648-5339 .. **Simpson,** David B '85 -718 River Rd -Bnghmtn 13901
(212) 909-6000 .. **Simpson,** Elizabeth Lauren '09 %Debevoise & P LLP -919 3rd Av -NY 10022
(716) 759-2952 .. **Simpson,** Elizabeth Mallory '01 %Campbell & Assoc,LLP -10535 Main -Clarence 14031 **Fx:**759-8609
(716) 626-1564 .. **Simpson,** Ellen Swartz '91 (Simpson & S PLLC) -5555 Main -Williamsvll 14221 **Fx:**626-0366
(212) 836-8000 .. **Simpson,** Franklin L '01 %Kaye S LLP -425 Park Av -NY 10022
(718) 345-8213 .. **Simpson,** Gaymon Wesley '90 -1016 Ralph Av -Brklyn 11236 **Fx:**345-3995
(914) 824-5070 .. **Simpson,** Glenn E '88 %Atty Grievance Comm -399 Knollwood Rd -White Plns 10603 **Fx:**949-0997
(845) 565-1100 .. **Simpson,** Hobart J '01 (Tarshis CLM&M,PLLC) -One Corwin Ct -Newburgh 12550
(212) 883-4900 .. **Simpson,** James L '07 %Cozen O -277 Park Av -NY 10172
(585) 232-6500 .. **Simpson,** Jos E '02 Cnsl Harter S&E LLP -1600 Bausch & Lomb Pl -Rchstr 14604
(212) 450-4000 .. **Simpson,** Linda A '80 (Davis P&W LLP) -450 Lex Av -NY 10017
(212) 506-5000 .. **Simpson,** Lisa '95 (Orrick H&S LLP) -51 W 52nd -NY 10019
(212) 669-2073 .. **Simpson,** Marla G '79 %Borough Pres -19 Fl S Mncpl Bldg -NY 10007 **Fx:**669-3380
(212) 209-4800 .. **Simpson,** Mason C '03 %Brown R LLP -7 Times Sq -NY 10036
(212) 858-1000 .. **Simpson,** Michl P '06 %Pillsbury WSP LLP -1540 Bway -NY 10036
(212) 575-6206 .. **Simpson,** Nancy S '67 (Stein S&R,PA) -1285 Av of Amer -NY 10019
(585) 203-3400 .. **Simpson,** Patrick J '01 %Littler M,PC -400 Linden Oaks -Rchstr 14625
(718) 488-5501 .. **Simpson,** Paula M '84 -26 Court -Brklyn 11242 **Fx:**855-4885
(212) 603-6300 .. **Simpson,** Philip T '85 (Robinson BLGG&G PC) -875 3rd Av -NY 10022
(716) 626-1564 .. **Simpson,** Robt P '88 (Simpson & S PLLC) -5555 Main -Williamsvll 14221 **Fx:**626-0366
(212) 489-1600 .. **Simpson,** Sarah B '96 %Deloitte LLP -1633 Bway -NY 10019 **Fx:**492-4201
(718) 838-7878 .. **Simpson,** Scott E '09 Bronx Defenders -860 Crtlandt Av -Bronx 10451 **Fx:**665-0100
(585) 232-6002 .. **Simpson,** Scott R '06 %Abrams FFEGF&E,LLP -45 Exchange Blvd -Rchstr 14614
(212) 980-4500 .. **Simpson,** Shannon R '03 %Cohen L LLP -885 3rd Av -NY 10022
(212) 808-7800 .. **Simpson,** Shoshana R '09 %Kelley D&W LLP -101 Park Av -NY 10178
(212) 455-2000 .. **Simpson Thacher & Bartlett LLP** -425 Lex Av -NY 10017 **Fx:**455-2502
(212) 771-9506 .. **Simpson,** Thos M '98 CIT Grp -505 5th Av -NY 10017
(212) 596-9000 .. **Simpson,** Todd M '07 %Ropes & G LLP -1211 Av of Amer -NY 10036
(212) 636-6000 .. **Sims,** Andrew '74 %Fordham Univ Sch of Law -140 W 62nd -NY 10023 **Fx:**636-6899
(845) 486-4200 .. **Sims,** Beth L '01 (Shaw PM&L,LLP) -21 Van Wagner Rd -Poughkeepsie 12603
(212) 969-3000 .. **Sims,** Chas S '78 (Proskauer R LLP) -1585 Bway -NY 10036
(718) 250-2000 .. **Sims,** Damani C '08 %DA -350 Jay -Brklyn 11201 **Fx:**250-2314
(212) 504-6000 .. **Sims,** David A '05 %Cadwalader W&T LLP -1 World Fncl Ctr -NY 10281
(212) 610-6300 .. **Sims,** Douglass D '03 %Allen & O -1221 Av of Amer -NY 10020
(212) 521-5400 .. **Sims,** Elizabeth P '09 %Reed S LLP -599 Lex Av -NY 10022
(212) 635-1688 .. **Sims,** Garland D '79 Bk of NY Mellon -1 Wall -NY 10286
(212) 406-0110 .. **Sims,** Jonathan D '94 (Siegle & S LLP) -217 Bway -NY 10007 **Fx:**406-5259
(516) 872-7400 .. **Sims,** Melinda Bloom '82 -107 S Central Av -Vly Stream 11580
(518) 402-6582 .. **Sims,** Michl A '81 Dept of Law -The Cptl -Albany 12224
(212) 223-0400 .. **Sims,** Michl E '05 %Zeichner E&K LLP -575 Lex Av -NY 10022
(516) 739-9009 .. **Sims Moss Kline & Davis LLP** -129 3rd -Mineola 11501 **Fx:**739-9011
(212) 323-8255 .. **Sims Moss Kline & Davis LLP** -67 Wall -NY 10005 **Fx:**422-0537
(212) 932-7995 .. **Sims,** Peter '75 -700 West End Av -NY 10025
(212) 801-2110 .. **Sims,** Rachel '02 %Greenberg T,LLP -200 Park Av -NY 10166
(212) 213-3030 .. **Sims,** Randall T '75 -1370 Av of Amer -NY 10019 **Fx:**213-3232
(212) 864-1600 .. **Sims,** Robt L Jr. '79 OfCnsl Stevens H&W,PC -116 W 111th -NY 10026
(607) 753-5008 .. **Simser,** Christopher I '01 %DA -46 Greenbush -Cortlnd 13045 **Fx:**756-3477
(212) 532-0835 .. **Simson,** Jean Birdsall '88 -36 E 36th -NY 10016
(212) 310-8000 .. **Simson,** Sylvia E '10 %Weil G&M LLP -767 5th Av -NY 10153
(212) 422-0488 .. **Simulcik,** Garrett P Jr. '05 %Rick SF&B,LLP -90 Broad -NY 10004
(212) 588-0800 .. **Simunovich,** Ami E '08 %Frommer L&H LLP -745 5th Av -NY 10151
(516) 747-4082 .. **Simuro,** Arthur '87 %Montfort HM&S LLP -1140 Franklin Av Bx7677 -Gdn Cty 11530
(212) 756-2000 .. **Simyar,** Tannaz '06 %Schulte R&Z LLP -919 3rd Av -NY 10022
(718) 701-3914 .. **Sin,** Jessica '07 -163-10 Nrthrn Blvd -Flushng 11358 **Fx:**799-5522
(631) 454-6092 .. **Sin,** Vivian K '98 Cnsl World Alliance Fncl Corp -3 Huntngtn Quad -Melvll 11747 **Fx:**663-4431
(212) 880-3800 .. **Sinacori,** Steven M '97 (Akerman S) -335 Mad Av -NY 10017
(212) 269-1600 .. **Sinai,** Karen C '05 %Teigland-Hunt LLP -127 W 24th -NY 10011 **Fx:**269-1580
(212) 715-9100 .. **Sinaiko,** Stephen M '93 (Kramer LN&F,LLP) -1177 Av of Amer -NY 10036
(212) 801-9235 .. **Sinanian,** Shahe '80 (Greenberg T,LLP) -200 Park Av -NY 10166
(516) 714-7283 .. **Sinatra,** AnnaElena '94 %T Spina -170 Froehlich Farm Blvd -Woodbury 11797 **Fx:**496-5420
(212) 513-3200 .. **Sinatra,** Frank G '85 SrCnsl Holland & K LLP -31 W 52nd -NY 10019
(716) 856-4000 .. **Sinatra,** John L Jr. '97 (Hodgson R LLP) -140 Pearl -Buffalo 14202
(716) 285-2533 .. **Sinatra,** Randall P '95 -1024 Cayuga Dr -Niagara Fls 14304 **Fx:**282-6945
(212) 801-6847 .. **Sinatra,** Steven '90 (Greenberg T,LLP) -200 Park Av -NY 10166
(516) 971-7783 .. **Sinawski,** Gary '75 -180 Montague -Brklyn 11201
(212) 483-9490 .. **Sinclair,** Cristina Zampetti '99 (McElroy DM&C,LLP) -88 Pine -NY 10005
(212) 487-9700 .. **Sinclair,** Dionne G '93 %White F&F,LLP -61 Bway -NY 10006
(212) 880-6000 .. **Sinclair,** Gavin '03 %Torys LLP -237 Park Av -NY 10017
(585) 381-0233 .. **Sinclair,** Judith '91 -7 State -Pittsfrd 14534 **Fx:**381-9819
(212) 685-4565 .. **Sinclair,** Nicole N '01 %Schachter & L,LLP -419 Park Av -NY 10016 **Fx:**685-5980
(718) 254-7000 .. **Sinclair,** Patrick S '01 %US Atty -271 Cadman Plz E -Brklyn 11201 **Fx:**254-6479
(646) 471-4000 .. **Sincoff,** Gregg M '89 %PricewaterhouseCoopers LLP -300 Mad Av -NY 10017
(212) 652-3735 .. **Sindel,** Sandra B '84 %Schlesinger G&L LLP -535 Mad Av -NY 10022
(212) 459-3800 .. **Sindell,** David S '94 (Sindell,PC) -7 W 36th -NY 10018
(212) 425-7200 .. **Sinder,** Stuart J '69 (Kenyon & K,LLP) -1 Bway -NY 10004
(212) 554-1400 .. **Sinderson,** Katherine McCracken '07 %Bernstein LB&G LLP -1285 Av of Amer -NY 10019
(212) 727-2700 .. **Sinding,** Katherine Anne '98 %NRDC -40 W 20th -NY 10011 **Fx:**727-1773
(212) 879-0527 .. **Sindle,** Harvey B '57 -300 E 71st -NY 10021 **Fx:**879-0527
(315) 425-2700 .. **Sindoni,** John P '71 (Hiscock & B,LLP) -One Park Pl -Syracuse 13202
(212) 821-6161 .. **Sine,** Jeffrey A '83 UBS -299 Park Av -NY 10171
(212) 268-2665 .. **Sinel,** Elliot B '91 (Sinel & Assoc,PLLC) -7 Penn Plz -NY 10001 **Fx:**268-6250
(845) 638-3012 .. **Sinensky,** Morris '79 %R Neimark & Assoc,LLP -37 Congers Rd -New Cty 10956 **Fx:**638-3093
(212) 670-0116 .. **Sinensky,** Yosef '01 %Merrill Lynch -222 Bway -NY 10038
(315) 476-7248 .. **Sinesi,** Robt M '94 -103 E Water -Syracuse 13202 **Fx:**474-8867
(212) 771-0626 .. **Sinesio,** Ronald V '82 Aspen Publishers -111 8th Av -NY 10011
(212) 373-3000 .. **Singapore,** Aun A '03 %Paul WRW&G LLP -1285 Av of Amer -NY 10019
(516) 571-3800 .. **Singas,** Madeline '92 %DA -262 Old Cntry Rd -Mineola 11501 **Fx:**248-9479
(212) 705-7000 .. **Singer,** Aaron J '05 %Bingham M LLP -399 Park Av -NY 10022
(212) 906-1200 .. **Singer,** Aaron M '08 %Latham & W -885 3rd Av -NY 10022
(914) 428-2100 .. **Singer,** Alan D '68 (Welby B&G,LLP) -11 Martine Av -White Plns 10606
(718) 625-3204 .. **Singer,** Alexander T '71 -26 Court -Brklyn 11242
(212) 924-8600 .. **Singer,** Andrew N '76 -18 E 16th -NY 10003
(212) 508-6700 .. **Singer,** Andrew W '92 (Tannenbaum HS&H LLP) -900 3rd Av -NY 10022
(212) 416-8616 .. **Singer,** Arielle B '09 %Dept of Law -120 Bway -NY 10271
(718) 745-1797 .. **Singer,** Barbara Conroy '95 %S Harrison -544 Bay Ridge Pkwy -Brklyn 11209 **Fx:**745-2786
(212) 949-7600 .. **Singer,** Barry '68 (Weinberger S PC) -230 Park Av -NY 10169
(212) 446-4800 .. **Singer,** Benjamin C '09 %Kirkland & E LLP -153 E 53rd -NY 10022
(212) 269-1400 .. **Singer,** Bill T '85 Gusrae KB&N PLLC -120 Wall -NY 10005

(718) 858-4140 .. **Singer Block Matles & Roth** -189 Montague -Brklyn 11201 **Fx**:858-5144
(212) 794-5537 .. **Singer**, Bonnie P '68 %CUNY -535 E 80th -NY 10075 **Fx**:794-5530
(516) 482-0666 .. **Singer**, Chas A '75 -11 Middle Nck Rd -Gt Neck 11021 **Fx**:482-0644
(914) 666-2003 .. **Singer**, Craig '73 Westminster Fncl Grp -148 Meeting House Rd -Bedford Corners 10549 **Fx**:666-2003
(212) 569-7853 .. **Singer**, Danl A '04 -234 5th Av -NY 10001
(212) 415-9200 .. **Singer**, David C '81 (Dorsey & W LLP) -250 Park Av -NY 10177
(845) 304-0931 .. **Singer**, David E '86 -860 Grnd Cncrs -Bronx 10451 **Fx**:(718) 732-0049
(212) 233-8800 .. **Singer**, David H '70 DH Singer & Assoc,LLP -233 Bway -NY 10279 **Fx**:385-4870
(914) 345-5700 .. **Singer**, David I '88 %Original Oil -500 Exec Blvd -Elmsfrd 10523
(631) 673-6670 .. **Singer**, David L '08 %Speyer & P,LLP -115 Broadhllw Rd -Melvll 11747
(914) 739-1164 .. **Singer**, Donald L '86 -74 Cordwood Rd -Cortlandt Manor 10567 **Fx**:293-7714
(914) 739-1164 .. **Singer**, Donald L Jr. '91 -74 Corwood Rd -Cortlandt Manor 10567
(914) 723-3919 .. **Singer**, Douglas E '78 (Falcon & S PC) -14 Harwood Ct -Scarsdale 10583
(212) 610-6300 .. **Singer**, Erika L '08 %Allen & O -1221 Av of Amer -NY 10020
(212) 559-2912 .. **Singer**, Eugenia McGinness '93 %Citibank -399 Park Av -NY 10022 **Fx**:793-4031
(914) 242-8646 .. **Singer**, Garry C '00 (Singer & F) -40 W Main -Mt Kisco 10549 **Fx**:242-1672
(212) 769-5590 .. **Singer**, Gerald R '98 %Amer Museum Natural Hist -79th & Cntrl Pk W -NY 10024
(212) 227-6655 .. **Singer**, Gino Josh '81 -299 Bway -NY 10007 **Fx**:732-6972
(718) 250-2000 .. **Singer**, Glenn E '00 %DA -350 Jay -Brklyn 11201 **Fx**:250-2314
(212) 532-3590 .. **Singer**, Howard A '58 -295 Mad Av -NY 10017 **Fx**:(914) 967-2391
(718) 222-2085 .. **Singer**, Howard L '89 %Law Dept -350 Jay -Brklyn 11201 **Fx**:222-2088
(516) 485-6480 .. **Singer**, Irving '65 (I Singer,PC) -223 Fulton Av -Hempstd 11550 **Fx**:489-5067
(631) 544-6331 .. **Singer**, Janet C '77 -Bx114 -Kings Pk 11754 **Fx**:544-6221
(212) 696-9100 .. **Singer**, Jeffrey '80 (Segan N&S PC) -112 Mad Av -NY 10016
(212) 267-6456 .. **Singer**, Jill B '02 %Fischer Bros -217 Bway -NY 10007 **Fx**:267-6468
(212) 323-7070 .. **Singer**, Jocelin F '08 %Rawle & H LLP -14 Wall -NY 10005
(518) 371-5977 .. **Singer**, Judith Hastings '90 -514 Vischers Ferry Rd -Clifton Pk 12065 **Fx**:383-7988
(800) 910-0529 .. **Singer**, Julian '83 OfCnsl Blau B&L,LLC -224 W 30th -NY 10001 **Fx**:(212) 488-4848
(212) 592-1400 .. **Singer**, Justin B '10 %Herrick,F LLP -2 Park Av -NY 10016
(516) 328-2300 .. **Singer**, Keith J '89 (Abrams FFEGF&E,LLP) -1111 Marcus Av -Lk Success 11042
(718) 330-7694 .. **Singer**, Larry '85 %NLRB -2 Metrotech Ctr -Brklyn 11201 **Fx**:330-7579
(845) 786-3141 .. **Singer**, Larry D '83 -Bx420 -Thiells 10984 **Fx**:786-3142
(212) 481-2350 .. **Singer**, Lawr H '76 -112 Mad Av -NY 10016 **Fx**:659-9680
(212) 473-0523 .. **Singer**, Lea S '42 -575 Grand -NY 10002
(212) 675-6181 .. **Singer**, Leigh S '01 Youth Advocacy Ctr -281 6th Av -NY 10014
(518) 426-4600 .. **Singer**, Leonard H '84 (Couch W,LLP) -540 Bway Bx22222 -Albany 12201
(718) 332-4130 .. **Singer**, Lina E '85 -3041 Av U -Brklyn 11229 **Fx**:332-5565
(516) 741-2585 .. **Singer**, Lisa B '94 %Rosicki R & Assoc,PC -51 E Bethpage Rd -Plainvw 11803 **Fx**:741-4748
(212) 661-9100 .. **Singer**, Lon M '87 OfCnsl Otterbourg SH&R,PC -230 Park Av -NY 10169
(718) 604-6900 .. **Singer**, Lori Sue '90 %Transit Auth -505 Fulton -Brklyn 11201 **Fx**:694-5726
(212) 309-6000 .. **Singer**, Louis H '80 (Morgan L&B LLP) -101 Park Av -NY 10178
(212) 461-2323 .. **Singer**, Marc C '01 (Saiber LLC) -44 Wall -NY 10005
(212) 553-6332 .. **Singer**, Marjorie '78 Cases,Inc -346 Bway -NY 10013
(718) 528-5400 .. **Singer**, Marvin '62 -132-10 Hook Crk Blvd -Rosedale 11422 **Fx**:528-1107
(914) 946-2500 .. **Singer**, Melinda L '95 OfCnsl Greenspan & G -150 Grand -White Plns 10601 **Fx**:946-1432
(212) 986-5900 .. **Singer**, Michl '86 (Myers S&G) -299 Bway -NY 10007 **Fx**:986-6250
(212) 662-6606 .. **Singer**, Michl '96 -300 W 108th -NY 10025
(516) 228-1518 .. **Singer**, Michl E '95 Ivy Asset Mgmt -1 Jericho Plz -Jericho 11753
(516) 877-2000 .. **Singer**, Michl H '69 (M Singer PC) -1225 Franklin Av -Gdn Cty 11530
(914) 304-1179 .. **Singer**, Michl H '79 -1311 Mamaroneck Av -White Plns 10605 **Fx**:(646) 349-4400
(914) 682-2010 .. **Singer Netter Dowd & Berman PLLC** -50 Main -White Plns 10606 **Fx**:682-2133
(718) 590-2000 .. **Singer**, Rachel S '00 %DA -198 E 161st -Bronx 10451 **Fx**:590-6477
(212) 310-8000 .. **Singer**, Randi W '99 (Weil G&M LLP) -767 5th Av -NY 10153
(718) 631-5437 .. **Singer**, Renee Feldman '84 -211-53 18th Av -Bayside 11360
(212) 819-1130 .. **Singer**, Richd C '75 (Hirschen S&E) -902 Bway -NY 10010
(212) 650-0004 .. **Singer**, Rickie L J '77 -45 E 82nd -NY 10028
(212) 906-1200 .. **Singer**, Rifka M '08 %Latham & W -885 3rd Av -NY 10022
(212) 922-4508 .. **Singer**, Rita Ann '95 Mellon Fncl Corp -200 Park Av -NY 10166
(212) 878-3288 .. **Singer**, Roger D '97 (Clifford C LLP) -31 W 52nd -NY 10019
(718) 575-1414 .. **Singer**, Ronald '63 -80-02 Kew Grdns Rd -Kew Gdns 11415 **Fx**:261-0316
(212) 788-0010 .. **Singer**, Sandi Allyn '95 NYC Mayors Ofc of Contracts -253 Bway -NY 10007
(212) 944-8800 .. **Singer**, Sandra F '76 -145 E 92nd -NY 10128
(516) 877-2900 .. **Singer**, Scott A '88 (Bartlett MB&M,LLP) -300 Old Cntry Rd -Mineola 11501
(212) 468-4800 .. **Singer**, Scott M '04 %Davis & G LLP -1740 Bway -NY 10019
(212) 964-5570 .. **Singer**, Scott N '78 %Sacks & S -150 Bway -NY 10038 **Fx**:349-2141
(212) 940-3182 .. **Singer**, Scott R '85 (Nixon P LLP) -437 Mad Av -NY 10022
(212) 643-0748 .. **Singer**, Sherry L '74 -1430 Bway -NY 10018
(718) 338-7733 .. **Singer**, Simon '05 E&S Mgmt LLC -1493 E 31st -Brklyn 11234
(212) 595-9349 .. **Singer**, Stanford M '76 -1 W 85th -NY 10024 **Fx**:874-5138
(212) 686-3838 .. **Singer**, Stephen '71 (Barst M&K LLP) -2 Park Av -NY 10016
(718) 261-4040 .. **Singer**, Stephen J '67 (Sparrow S&S) -125-10 Qns Blvd -Kew Gdns 11415
(212) 289-0564 .. **Singer**, Stephen Sayre '64 -200 East End Av -NY 10128 **Fx**:987-9737
(212) 554-1400 .. **Singer**, Steven B '92 (Bernstein LB&G LLP) -1285 Av of Amer -NY 10019
(212) 937-6307 .. **Singer**, Steven D '08 (WilmerHale) -399 Park Av -NY 10022
(212) 822-1453 .. **Singer**, Stuart R '85 -305 Bway -NY 10007
(518) 587-4407 .. **Singer**, Suzanne B '96 -16 Beacon Hill Dr -Saratoga Spgs 12866 **Fx**:587-2961
(212) 850-2800 .. **Singer**, Taryn A '08 %Andrews K LLP -450 Lex Av -NY 10017
(718) 222-2415 .. **Singer**, Zev '08 %Law Dept -350 Jay -Brklyn 11201 **Fx**:222-2088
(716) 634-7132 .. **Singer-Blumberg**, Tara '90 %NYSUT -270 Essjay Rd -Williamsvll 14221
(212) 626-4100 .. **Singer-Freeman**, Jose S '04 %Baker & M LLP -1114 Av of Amer -NY 10036
(212) 912-2926 .. **Singh**, Allison J '03 %Edwards AP&D LLP -750 Lex Av -NY 10022
(212) 549-2500 .. **Singh**, Amrit '02 %ACLU -125 Broad -NY 10004 **Fx**:549-2651
(212) 340-0400 .. **Singh**, Anil Sugrim '06 Appllt Div 1st Dept -27 Mad Av -NY 10010 **Fx**:889-4412
(212) 225-2000 .. **Singh**, Ashika '06 %Cleary GS&H -1 Lbrty Plz -NY 10006
(212) 687-2770 .. **Singh**, Atul R '01 %Cohen PL&P -551 5th Av -NY 10176
(718) 239-3141 .. **Singh**, Balwan R '93 -1654 Castle Hill Av -Bronx 10462 **Fx**:239-7650
(516) 572-2000 .. **Singh**, Christina H '09 %DA -99 Main -Hempstd 11550 **Fx**:572-2606
(212) 310-8000 .. **Singh**, David R '04 %Weil G&M LLP -767 5th Av -NY 10153
(516) 358-3767 .. **Singh**, Dervinder '96 AXA Advisors,LLC -1111 Marcus Av -Lk Success 11042
(718) 237-5500 .. **Singh**, Ermela '07 %Leg Srvcs -105 Court -Brklyn 11201 **Fx**:855-0733
(646) 386-5000 .. **Singh**, Gunwanti '01 Surrogates Ct -31 Chmbrs -NY 10007
(212) 446-7000 .. **Singh**, Himanshu Pratap '05 %McKinsey & Co -55 E 52nd -NY 10055 **Fx**:688-9521
(718) 533-8444 .. **Singh**, Jaspreet '97 (Roman & S,LLP) -37-18 73rd -Jcksn Hts 11372
(212) 692-1000 .. **Singh**, Jessica Y '02 %Duane M LLP -1540 Bway -NY 10036
(718) 843-2200 .. **Singh**, Keith R '91 -107-29 Lbrty Av -Ozone Pk 11417 **Fx**:843-4406
(518) 736-5533 .. **Singh**, Krishna K '96 Hon R Aulisi -223 W Main -Johnstwn 12095 **Fx**:762-1158
(718) 478-4000 .. **Singh**, Mahipal '93 -37-11 74th -Jcksn Hts 11372 **Fx**:478-6579
(516) 741-2585 .. **Singh**, Mitra '08 %Rosicki R & Assoc,PC -51 E Bethpage Rd -Plainvw 11803 **Fx**:741-4748
(212) 826-3800 .. **Singh**, Narendra V '05 C Castro & Assoc,PLLC -355 Lex Av -NY 10017 **Fx**:486-6583
(212) 871-5711 .. **Singh**, Neelam K '06 %Nissenbaum Law Grp,LLC -140 Bway -NY 10005 **Fx**:871-5712
(212) 290-4700 .. **Singh**, Param-Preet K '01 Cnsl Human Rights Watch -350 5th Av -NY 10118 **Fx**:736-1300
(212) 556-2100 .. **Singh**, Preetma '09 King & S -1185 Av of Amer -NY 10036
(212) 326-2000 .. **Singh**, Rajanpreet '09 %O'Melveny & M LLP -7 Times Sq -NY 10036
(212) 373-3000 .. **Singh**, Romica '06 %Paul WRW&G LLP -1285 Av of Amer -NY 10019
(212) 626-4100 .. **Singh**, Sapna '10 %Baker & M LLP -1114 Av of Amer -NY 10036
(917) 777-4200 .. **Singh**, Seema '03 %Bingham M LLP -1 Bttry Pk Plz -NY 10004
(212) 698-3500 .. **Singh**, Shimona Pratap '04 %Dechert LLP -1095 Av of Amer -NY 10036
(212) 506-1700 .. **Singh**, Simarjeet '09 %Kasowitz BT&F LLP -1633 Bway -NY 10019
(212) 310-8000 .. **Singh**, Sunny '07 %Weil G&M LLP -767 5th Av -NY 10153
(212) 446-4800 .. **Singh**, Vanessa C '07 %Kirkland & E LLP -153 E 53rd -NY 10022
(516) 997-6000 .. **Singh-Castillo**, Kalpana M '05 %Marshall & M -30 Jericho Exec Plz -Jericho 11753 **Fx**:997-0860
(718) 935-4400 .. **Singh-Mergeche**, Lakshmi '07 NYC Dept Education -335 Adams -Brklyn 11201
(718) 590-5979 .. **Singh Walia**, Simrata '05 -900 Sheridan Av -Bronx 10451
(212) 571-3800 .. **Singla**, Pradeep '01 -511 Av of Amer -NY 10011
(631) 589-6300 .. **Single**, Robt C '78 %Dayton T Brown Inc -555 Church -Bohemia 11716
(212) 788-0760 .. **Singleton**, Gerald E '77 Law Dept -100 Church -NY 10007 **Fx**:788-0367
(212) 841-7500 .. **Singleton**, Kenneth P '88 %Cushman & Wakefield -1290 Av of Amer -NY 10104
(212) 885-5000 .. **Singleton**, Richd V II '83 (Blank R LLP) -405 Lex Av -NY 10174
(212) 457-9593 .. **Singleton**, Ruth '92 Natl Law Journal -120 Bway -NY 10271
(914) 666-4400 .. **Singleton**, Thos J '59 (Singleton & S) -50 Main -Mt Kisco 10549 **Fx**:666-6442
(516) 248-3302 .. **Singleton**, Valerie '91 %Dept of Law -200 Old Cntry Rd -Mineola 11501 **Fx**:747-6432
(914) 666-4400 .. **Singleton**, Whitney W '95 (Singleton & S) -50 Main -Mt Kisco 10549 **Fx**:666-6442
(212) 373-3000 .. **Sinha**, Priyamvada '04 %Paul WRW&G LLP -1285 Av of Amer -NY 10019
(212) 226-2800 .. **Sinha**, S Tito '98 %Alterman & B LLP -35 Worth -NY 10013
(212) 735-3000 .. **Sinha**, Seema A '07 %Skadden ASM&F LLP -4 Times Sq -NY 10036
(212) 903-9000 .. **Sinha**, Sumeet '09 %Linklaters -1345 Av of Amer -NY 10105
(718) 351-8111 .. **Sini**, Andrew J '97 -123 Buffalo -Staten Isl 10306
(212) 586-2211 .. **Sini**, Timothy D '06 %Orans EL&B LLP -875 3rd Av -NY 10022
(212) 474-1000 .. **Siniawer**, Paul D '68 Cravath S&M LLP -825 8th Av -NY 10019
(212) 872-9835 .. **Sinick**, Edw S '83 (Squire S&D LLP) -30 Rckfllr Plz -NY 10112
(607) 723-5341 .. **Sinicki**, Michl S '93 (Hinman H&K,LLP) -80 Exchange Bx5250 -Bnghmtn 13902
(212) 758-5777 .. **Sinisi**, Ann Marie T '00 (Pereira & S,LLP) -150 E 58th -NY 10155 **Fx**:751-6950
(716) 893-4900 .. **Sinkewicz**, Jos F Jr. '91 -808 Fillmore Av -Buffalo 14212
(315) 539-1300 .. **Sinkiewicz**, Mark S '02 DA -48 W Williams -Waterloo 13165 **Fx**:539-0531
(718) 590-2000 .. **Sinkler**, Randy C '08 %DA -198 E 161st -Bronx 10451 **Fx**:590-6477
(212) 373-3000 .. **Sinkman**, David H '09 %Paul WRW&G LLP -1285 Av of Amer -NY 10019
(631) 874-3344 .. **Sinnickson**, Thos J '82 -43 Montauk Hwy -Ctr Moriches 11934

(212) 723-6364 .. **Sinniger,** Jean-Luc H '90 Citigroup Global Mrkts -390 Greenwich -NY 10013
(718) 546-0950 .. **Sinnott,** Alexis '01 %Dept of Correction -75-20 Astoria Blvd -E Elmhrst 11370
(518) 668-3538 .. **Sinnott,** Robt W '90 -24 Brereton Rd -Diamond Pt 12824
(631) 650-1200 .. **Sinnreich,** Jonathan H '75 (Sinnreich K&M LLP) -267 Carleton Av -Central Islip 11722
(631) 650-1200 .. **Sinnreich Kosakoff & Messina LLP** -267 Carleton Av -Central Islip 11722 **Fx:**650-1207
(212) 410-1466 .. **Sinnreich,** Naomi W '82 -161 E 91st -NY 10128 **Fx:**410-9394
(914) 730-3025 .. **Sinon,** Gina M '93 -48 Banksvll Rd -Armonk 10504 **Fx:**730-3026
(516) 248-0990 .. **Sinon,** John W '65 -397 Titus Way -E Williston 11596
(212) 558-4000 .. **Sinopole,** Angelica M '10 %Sullivan & C LLP -125 Broad -NY 10004
(914) 631-3131 .. **Sinreich,** Ellen J '82 %DLC Management Corp -580 Wht Plns Rd -Tarrytwn 10591
(212) 706-1880 .. **Sinrich,** Norman '52 -1330 Av of Amer -NY 10019
(518) 371-2075 .. **Sinrod,** Amanda L '06 Wilhelm Law Firm,PLLC -Park Nine Plz Bx869 -Clifton Pk 12065 **Fx:**371-2440
(212) 909-6000 .. **Sinrod,** Danl Z '08 %Debevoise & P LLP -919 3rd Av -NY 10022
(212) 859-8000 .. **Sinrod,** Laura Israel '08 %Fried FHS&J LLP -1 NY Plz -NY 10004
(845) 677-3678 .. **Sinrod,** Richd T '66 -693 Twr Hill Rd -Millbrook 12545 **Fx:**677-3678
(212) 558-4000 .. **Sinsheimer,** Alan J '82 (Sullivan & C LLP) -125 Broad -NY 10004
(212) 683-7999 .. **Sinsheimer,** Warren J '50 Prtnrshp for Childrens Rts -271 Mad Av -NY 10016 **Fx:**683-5544
(631) 287-2800 .. **Sinski,** Douglas C '87 (Schwartz & S,PC) -149 Hmptn Rd -Southampton 11969 **Fx:**287-4842
(718) 237-5500 .. **Sinton,** Jennifer '99 %Leg Srvcs -105 Court -Brklyn 11201 **Fx:**855-0733
(212) 398-9701 .. **Siolas,** George P '98 Madinia Rlty Corp -55 W 45th -NY 10036
(212) 872-6758 .. **Sion,** Jeffrey S '87 KPMG LLP -345 Park Av -NY 10154
(212) 909-5216 .. **Sion,** L Gilles '81 KPMG LLP -757 3rd Av -NY 10017
(212) 840-2644 .. **Sioris,** Gregory A '86 (Sioris & M) -350 5th Av -NY 10118 **Fx:**921-0163
(212) 339-0870 .. **Siper,** Brian M '98 %FSA -31 W 52nd -NY 10019 **Fx:**893-2710
(845) 457-4737 .. **Siper,** Randy I '00 -159 Ward -Montgmry 12549 **Fx:**457-1378
(212) 341-6795 .. **Siponen,** Gail Pierce '85 %Liquidation Bur -123 William -NY 10038 **Fx:**608-3398
(212) 839-5300 .. **Sipos,** Adam C '09 %Sidley A LLP -787 7th Av -NY 10019
(518) 402-2251 .. **Sipos,** John J '88 %Dept of Law -The Cptl -Albany 12224
(315) 568-5221 .. **Sipos,** John M '67 OfCnsl Morrell & S -102 Fall -Seneca Fls 13148
(516) 822-3550 .. **Sipos,** Susan A '98 %Hoffmann & B LLP -6900 Jericho Tpk -Syosset 11791 **Fx:**822-3582
(718) 273-6000 .. **Sipp,** John P Jr. '97 (Sipp Law Firm) -801 Castleton Av -Staten Isl 10310 **Fx:**273-6009
(718) 273-6000 .. **Sipp,** John Peter '71 (Sipp Law Firm) -801 Castleton Av -Staten Isl 10310 **Fx:**273-6009
(718) 273-6000 .. **Sipp,** Thos A '99 (Sipp Law Firm) -801 Castleton Av -Staten Isl 10310 **Fx:**273-6009
(212) 210-9581 .. **Sippel,** Matthew C '08 %Alston & B LLP -90 Park Av -NY 10016
(631) 751-1332 .. **Sipperly,** David P '50 OfCnsl K Jacoppi -194 Main -E Setauket 11733 **Fx:**751-1205
(518) 583-7200 .. **Sipperly,** Peter C '83 -Bx477 -Saratoga Spgs 12866
(212) 670-1834 .. **Sippy,** Anita '91 Merrill Lynch -222 Bway -NY 10038
(718) 250-2418 .. **Sipress,** Jennifer L '01 %DA -350 Jay -Brklyn 11201 **Fx:**250-2314
(718) 935-1010 .. **Sipress,** Mannie '61 OfCnsl Lonuzzi & W,LLP -60 Sackett -Brklyn 11231 **Fx:**935-1935
(718) 759-9777 .. **Sipsas,** Ioannis P '04 %Nazrisho & Assoc,PC -8023 7th Av -Brklyn 11228 **Fx:**759-9700
(212) 766-9100 .. **Sipser,** Wm J '86 (Tuckner SW&S) -120 Bway -NY 10271
(518) 736-5511 .. **Sira,** Louise K '94 (DA) -223 W Main -Johnstwn 12095 **Fx:**762-2042
(315) 432-5452 .. **Siracusa,** Jos '60 -2001 James -Syracuse 13206 **Fx:**432-5457
(212) 619-5703 .. **Siracusa,** Richd A '75 -299 Bway -NY 10007 **Fx:**349-1782
(516) 599-2020 .. **Siracusano,** Louis V '76 OfCnsl A Chianese & Assoc -100 Merrick Rd -Rockvll Ctr 11570 **Fx:**599-6476
(585) 232-3730 .. **Siracuse,** Andrew V '59 OfCnsl Chamberlain D LLP -1600 Crssrds Bldg -Rchstr 14614
(718) 442-9000 .. **Siracuse,** George J '48 OfCnsl Ameduri G&F -471 Bement Av -Staten Isl 10310
(631) 234-1500 .. **Siragusa,** Angelo L '99 %Rubin & R LLC -1787 Vets Hwy -Islandia 11749
(516) 342-2200 .. **Siragusa,** Christian '93 %Schwartzapfel Prtnrs -300 Jericho Quad -Jericho 11753
(585) 454-3377 .. **Siragusa,** Lisa Serio '95 (Brown & T,LLC) -19 Prince -Rchstr 14607
(716) 853-8485 .. **Siragusa,** Michl A '94 %Dept of Law -350 Main Pl Twr -Buffalo 14202 **Fx:**853-8571
(516) 741-7676 .. **Siravo,** Michl P '98 %Miranda SSSV LLP -240 Mineola Blvd -Mineola 11501
(212) 309-1000 .. **Sirgado,** Jo Anne E '91 (Hunton & W) -200 Park Av -NY 10166
(718) 248-0395 .. **Sirgado,** Michl A '98 %Citigroup -1 Court Sq -LIC 11101
(212) 906-1200 .. **Siri,** Aaron '05 %Latham & W -885 3rd Av -NY 10022
(212) 841-7554 .. **Sirianni,** Anthony F '77 %Cushman & Wakefield -51 W 52nd -NY 10019 **Fx:**841-7715
(212) 336-2000 .. **Sirianni,** Ryan '09 %Patterson BW&T LLP -1133 Av of Amer -NY 10036
Sirianni, Thos A '99 -5020 Sunrise Hwy -Massapequa Pk 11762
(716) 753-4339 .. **Sirianno,** Marlene '91 %Surrogates Ct -Gerace Ofc Bldg BxC -Mayvll 14757
(914) 941-2800 .. **Siriano,** Anthony F '86 (Siriano & B,PC) -515 N State Rd -Briarcliff 10510
(718) 823-2600 .. **Siriano,** Anthony F '86 (Siriano & B,PC) -2027 Wllmsbrdg Rd -Bronx 10461
(718) 823-2600 .. **Siriano & Bernstein,PC** -2027 Wllmsbrdg Rd -Bronx 10461 **Fx:**823-3488
(914) 941-2800 .. **Siriano & Bernstein,PC** -515 N State Rd -Briarcliff 10510
(914) 948-1500 .. **Sirignano,** George A Jr. '72 (Enea S&S LLP) -245 Main -White Plns 10601
(516) 357-3000 .. **Sirignano,** Michl A '89 (Rivkin R LLP) -926 RXR Plz -Uniondale 11556
(914) 763-5500 .. **Sirignano,** Michl F '80 -892 Route 35 Bx784 -Cross Rvr 10518 **Fx:**763-9589
(914) 684-6800 .. **Sirignano,** Paul D '82 (Collier HNN&B,LLP) -1 N Lex Av -White Plns 10601
(212) 668-0340 .. **Siris,** John P '02 Ambac Assurance Corp -1 State Plz -NY 10004
(516) 228-9350 .. **Siris,** Michl J '71 Cnsl Solomon & S -50 Chas Lindbergh Blvd -Uniondale 11553
(516) 228-9350 .. **Siris,** Stuart '80 (Solomon & S) -50 Chas Lindbergh Blvd -Uniondale 11553
(212) 728-8000 .. **Sirkin,** Danl E '09 %Willkie F&G LLP -787 7th Av -NY 10019
(212) 969-3000 .. **Sirkin,** Michl S '73 (Proskauer R LLP) -1585 Bway -NY 10036
(212) 455-2000 .. **Sirkis,** Danl '08 %Simpson T&B LLP -425 Lex Av -NY 10017
(212) 455-2000 .. **Sirkis,** Paul J '06 %Simpson T&B LLP -425 Lex Av -NY 10017
(516) 285-4373 .. **Sirlin,** Alan R '77 -178 Fir -Vly Stream 11580 **Fx:**285-4779
(914) 698-3930 .. **Sirlin,** Roger H '66 (R Sirlin & Assoc) -500 Mamaroneck Av -Harrison 10528 **Fx:**698-3727
(212) 705-7000 .. **Siroka,** Martin I '79 (Bingham M LLP) -399 Park Av -NY 10022
(212) 859-8000 .. **Siroka,** Peter B '07 %Fried FHS&J LLP -1 NY Plz -NY 10004
(212) 909-6000 .. **Sirota,** Benjamin D V '06 %Debevoise & P LLP -919 3rd Av -NY 10022
(212) 275-4897 .. **Sirota,** Jeremy P '05 WEA Corp -75 Rckfllr Plz -NY 10019
(212) 373-9352 .. **Sirota,** Jonathan '99 Smart Money -1755 Bway -NY 10019
(914) 238-1000 .. **Sirota,** Mark A '86 Reader's Digest -Readers Digest Rd -Plsntvll 10570 **Fx:**241-5644
(212) 408-2500 .. **Sirota,** Neil P '93 (Baker B,LLP) -30 Rckfllr Plz -NY 10112
(212) 340-0400 .. **Sirota,** Rachell Roffe '79 Appllt Div 1st Dept -27 Mad Av -NY 10010 **Fx:**889-4412
(212) 545-4000 .. **Sirota,** Steven A '10 %Jackson L LLP -666 3rd Av -NY 10017
(718) 265-5900 .. **Sirota,** Vladislav '05 -1661 Sheepshead Bay Rd -Brklyn 11235
(718) 261-9460 .. **Sirotkin,** Lynn L '83 (Pearlman AFS&S,LLP) -80-02 Kew Grdns Rd -Kew Gdns 11415
(716) 487-1142 .. **Sirwatka,** Kevin J '93 (Spoto S&S) -112 Htl Jmstwn Ofc Bldg -Jamestwn 14701
(914) 937-3000 .. **Sisca,** Francis J '57 (Sisca & S,PC) -461 Wstchstr Av -Pt Chester 10573 **Fx:**937-8019
(845) 279-6111 .. **Sisca,** Jos J III '04 Sisca NE Inc -1944 Route 22 -Brewstr 10509
(914) 937-3000 .. **Sisca,** Peter F '85 (Sisca & S,PC) -461 Wstchstr Av -Pt Chester 10573 **Fx:**937-8019
(203) 629-3831 .. **Sisca,** Robt Vincent '98 R Sisca & Assoc,LLC -25 Rosemere -Rye 10580 **Fx:**629-9869
(718) 286-6000 .. **Siscaretti,** Christine M '05 %DA -125-01 Qns Blvd -Kew Gdns 11415
(518) 783-2315 .. **Sise,** John R '80 Siena College -515 Loudon Rd -Albany 12211
(518) 843-5522 .. **Sise,** Thos E '82 (Sise & S) -120 Genesee Ln -Amsterdam 12010 **Fx:**843-8259
(212) 326-3939 .. **Sisitsky,** Mark K '71 (Jones D) -222 E 41st -NY 10017
(631) 589-2501 .. **Siska,** Gary R '79 -1587 Montauk Hwy -Oakdale 11769
(631) 472-5354 .. **Siska,** Warren R '86 -566 Middle Rd -Bayport 11705
(212) 696-6000 .. **Siskin,** Jerrold A '76 %Curtis M-PC&M LLP -101 Park Av -NY 10178
(212) 852-7000 .. **Siskind,** Arthur M '62 %News Corp -1211 Av of Amer -NY 10036 **Fx:**852-7147
(212) 940-8610 .. **Siskind,** Donald H '63 Cnsl Katten MR LLP -575 Mad Av -NY 10022
(212) 964-7400 .. **Siskind,** Lesley C '92 (Smith MDWY&Y,PC) -111 John -NY 10038
(914) 765-1900 .. **Siskind,** Marcy A '91 IBM -1 New Orchrd Rd -Armonk 10504 **Fx:**765-7533
(718) 863-4878 .. **Siskind,** Neil M '87 -2024 Wllmsbrdg Rd -Bronx 10461
(212) 840-0880 .. **Siskind,** Neil S '97 -1385 Bway -NY 10018
(212) 922-9300 .. **Siskind,** Rachel A '03 %Silversmith & V,LLP -30 Broad -NY 10004
(516) 222-1100 .. **Siskind,** Steven L '64 -1103 Stewart Av -Gdn Cty 11530 **Fx:**222-1106
(212) 431-5576 .. **Siskind Susser Bland** -430 W 14th -NY 10014 **Fx:**431-6468
(212) 744-5022 .. **Sismondo,** Lauren J '09 Lenox Hill Neighborhood Hse -331 E 70th -NY 10021
(212) 788-0752 .. **Sisolak,** Ilyse E '07 %Law Dept -100 Church -NY 10007 **Fx:**788-0367
(212) 594-8292 .. **Sison,** Victor G '93 OfCnsl Vinluan & T -224 W 35th -NY 10001 **Fx:**594-8296
(212) 693-1671 .. **Sisser,** Arthur R '71 H Kulefsky -111 John -NY 10038 **Fx:**385-4846
(914) 366-5700 .. **Sisser,** Roger P '87 %MA Bjork -660 Wht Plns Rd -Tarrytwn 10591 **Fx:**366-5759
(212) 541-9100 .. **Sisskind,** David W '87 (Schiavetti CDW&N,LLP) -575 8th Av -NY 10018
(315) 946-5445 .. **Sisson,** Jacqueline '86 %Hon S Sirkin -54 Broad -Lyons 14489
(212) 723-9629 .. **Sisson,** Kevin M '97 Citigroup Global Mrkts -390 Greenwich -NY 10013
(585) 704-0109 .. **Sisson,** Wendy S '98 -131 Main Bx242 -Geneseo 14454
(845) 255-9100 .. **Sisti,** John G '74 -207 Main Bx185 -New Paltz 12561 **Fx:**255-9134
(212) 878-7176 .. **Sistrom,** Peter A '87 %MTA -347 Mad Av -NY 10017
(212) 732-3200 .. **Sisun,** Scott M '02 %Carter L&M LLP -2 Wall -NY 10005
(212) 450-4000 .. **Sit,** Po '89 (Davis P&W LLP) -450 Lex Av -NY 10017
(212) 788-0879 .. **Sitaras,** Basil C '05 %Law Dept -100 Church -NY 10007 **Fx:**788-0367
(212) 986-7353 .. **Sitinas,** Stavros E '97 (Wingate R&S) -420 Lex Av -NY 10170
(516) 484-2017 .. **Sitkoff,** Saml '66 -64 Highland Av -Roslyn 11576 **Fx:**484-2017
(212) 859-8000 .. **Sitman,** Robt J '09 %Fried FHS&J LLP -1 NY Plz -NY 10004
(212) 554-7800 .. **Sitnick,** Irving '70 (Moses & S LLP) -405 Lex Av -NY 10174
(212) 683-3636 .. **Sitomer,** Alvin Lester '45 OfCnsl Krass S&S,PC -419 Park Av S -NY 10016
(914) 661-7700 .. **Sitomer,** Danl J '78 -445 Hmltn Av -White Plns 10601
(212) 626-4100 .. **Sitrick,** James B '61 OfCnsl Baker & M LLP -1114 Av of Amer -NY 10036
(212) 458-7042 .. **Sitrin,** Sherman A '76 %AIG -175 Water -NY 10038
(607) 547-6233 .. **Sittler,** Lester A '79 -187 Cemetery Rd Bx235 -Fly Crk 13337 **Fx:**547-5996
(516) 747-4343 .. **Sittner,** Christina L '07 %JP DiMascio & Assoc,LLP -300 Grdn City Plz -Gdn Cty 11530 **Fx:**747-0204
(212) 335-9000 .. **Sittnick,** Cynthia M '81 %DA -1 Hogan Pl -NY 10013
(212) 768-6700 .. **Sitton,** Ron B '99 (Sonnenschein N&R LLP) -2 World Fncl Ctr -NY 10281
(212) 649-2000 .. **Sitwala,** Ravi Viren '05 %Hearst Corp -300 W 57th -NY 10019 **Fx:**649-2035
(516) 338-7520 .. **Sitzer,** Ira R '78 %Daniels & N,PC -900 Merchants Cncrs -Westbury 11590

(212) 996-5336 ..**Siu,** Chi-Yim '83 -Knckrbckr Sta Bx893 -NY 10002
(315) 448-4800 ..**Siuda,** Senta B '95 %Dept of Law -615 Erie Blvd W -Syracuse 13204 **Fx:**448-4853
(212) 416-8552 ..**Siudzinski,** Michl J '09 %Dept of Law -120 Bway -NY 10271
(212) 421-2150 ..**Sive Paget & Riesel,PC** -460 Park Av -NY 10022 **Fx:**421-2035
(212) 331-5062 ..**Sively,** Susan Kirkpatrick '93 Cnsl HRA-OLA -180 Water -NY 10038 **Fx:**331-4448
(914) 366-7877 ..**Siviglia,** Peter '65 -200 Wht Plns Rd -Tarrytwn 10591
(212) 349-0300 ..**Sivin,** Edw '82 (Sivin & M LLP) -170 Bway -NY 10038
(212) 248-2220 ..**Sivin,** Joshua M '03 %Kennedy JG LLC -99 Wall -NY 10005 **Fx:**248-0170
(212) 349-0300 ..**Sivin & Miller LLP** -170 Bway -NY 10038 **Fx:**406-9462
(212) 730-2000 ..**Sivin,** Philip M '97 %MD Sass Investor Srvcs -1185 Av of Amer -NY 10036
(212) 997-7595 ..**Sivitz,** Tracy E '05 %Hafetz N&R -500 5th Av -NY 10110
(212) 730-8133 ..**Sivolella,** John J '98 %Gunderson DSVF&H,LLP -220 W 42nd -NY 10036
(212) 683-7841 ..**Siwulec,** Cynthia A '79 -292 5th Av -NY 10001
(315) 393-1807 ..**Sizeland-Ross,** Lisa A '90 -615 Ford -Ogdensbrg 13669
(212) 819-8200 ..**Sizemore,** Laura M '97 (White & C LLP) -1155 Av of Amer -NY 10036
(212) 969-3000 ..**Sjoblom,** Thos V '03 (Proskauer R LLP) -1585 Bway -NY 10036
(212) 670-0224 ..**Sjogren,** Michl P '86 -222 Bway -NY 10038
(212) 683-7100 ..**Sjoquist,** Chad E '00 %Gallo V&K,LLP -90 Broad -NY 10004
(718) 260-4702 ..**Skadan,** Kimberly M '08 Leg Aid -111 Lvngstn -Brklyn 11201 **Fx:**260-4722
(212) 735-3000 ..**Skadden Arps Slate Meagher & Flom LLP** -4 Times Sq -NY 10036 **Fx:**735-2000
(516) 829-0363 ..**Skaferowsky,** Justin P '04 %Israel I&P,LLP -11 Grace Av -Gt Neck 11021 **Fx:**829-0366
(212) 998-6730 ..**Skaggs,** John Adam '04 Brennan Ctr for Justice -161 Av of Amer -NY 10013 **Fx:**995-4550
(518) 581-8800 ..**Skaine,** Theresa M '94 (Lemery G LLC) -60 Railroad Pl -Saratoga Spgs 12866
(212) 474-1000 ..**Skaistis,** Rachel G '98 (Cravath S&M LLP) -825 8th Av -NY 10019
(212) 277-6500 ..**Skakel,** Deborah A '84 (Dickstein S LLP) -1633 Bway -NY 10019
(212) 888-8200 ..**Skala,** Murray L '72 (Feder K LLP) -845 3rd Av -NY 10022
(914) 271-4245 ..**Skalak,** Diane R '87 -190 Cleveland Dr -Croton-On-Hud 10520
(718) 579-3059 ..**Skaletsky,** Shana E '02 %Leg Aid -1020 Grnd Cncrs -Bronx 10451 **Fx:**588-2611
(212) 205-7000 ..**Skalla,** Nicole M '08 %Ashurst LLP -7 Times Sq -NY 10036
(212) 867-4466 ..**Skaller,** David M '87 (Belkin BW&G,LLP) -270 Mad Av -NY 10016
(315) 768-1896 ..**Skanadore Reisdorph,** Deborah S '02 Skanadore Reisdorph Law Ofcs -Bx536 -Whitesboro 13492 **Fx:**(866) 820-5436
(315) 446-2384 ..**Skandalis,** George '81 (Pinsky & S) -5790 Widewaters Pkwy -Syracuse 13214
(518) 869-9200 ..**Skanes,** Mark W '09 %Rose Law Firm,PLLC -501 New Karner Rd -Albany 12205 **Fx:**869-3334
(718) 298-8900 ..**Skariah,** Sherine E '08 Leg Aid -153-01 Jamaica Av -Jamaica 11432 **Fx:**657-0537
(212) 808-8100 ..**Skarlatos,** Bryan C '86 (Kostelanetz & F,LLP) -7 Wrld Trd Ctr -NY 10007
(631) 424-3888 ..**Skartsiaris,** Vangeles N '01 %Finder & C LLP -150 Broadhllw Rd -Melvll 11747
(212) 548-2100 ..**Skartvedt,** Brooke M '08 %McGuire W LLP -1345 Av of Amer -NY 10105
(212) 906-1200 ..**Skarvelis,** Constantine N '03 %Latham & W -885 3rd Av -NY 10022
(212) 820-7700 ..**Skarzynski,** James A '95 (Boundas SW&B,LLC) -1 Bttry Pk Plz -NY 10004
(315) 336-1410 ..**Skavina,** Paul '80 -301 N Wshngtn -Rome 13440 **Fx:**336-1434
(718) 767-6800 ..**Skedelsky,** Marvin D '70 (Birnbaum & S) -149-40 14th Av Bx156 -Whitestone 11357 **Fx:**746-8715
(212) 513-3200 ..**Skeele,** Katherine A '09 %Holland & K LLP -31 W 52nd -NY 10019
(212) 310-8000 ..**Skeete,** Hannah '08 %Weil G&M LLP -767 5th Av -NY 10153
(212) 259-8000 ..**Skellet,** Alexandra K '03 %Dewey & L LLP -1301 Av of Amer -NY 10019
(518) 402-6729 ..**Skelly,** Diana E '99 %Workers Comp Bd -20 Park -Albany 12207
(914) 345-3701 ..**Skelly,** James M '89 (Marks OO&C,PC) -530 Saw Mill Rvr Rd -Elmsfrd 10523
(212) 297-5800 ..**Skelly,** Kevin J '10 %Day P LLP -7 Times Sq -NY 10036
(212) 594-5000 ..**Skelly,** Stephanie A '08 %Togut S&S LLP -1 Penn Plz -NY 10119
(516) 663-6600 ..**Skelos,** Dean G '76 OfCnsl Ruskin MF,PC -1425 RXR Plz -Uniondale 11556
(212) 258-4000 ..**Skelskie,** Arthur N '85 %Siemens Corp -153 E 53rd -NY 10022 **Fx:**767-0580
(212) 964-8038 ..**Skelton,** James J Jr. '86 %Worth L&L,LLP -111 John -NY 10038
(914) 997-0500 ..**Skelton,** Thos M '92 (Lowey DC&H,PC) -1 N Bway -White Plns 10601
(718) 730-6333 ..**Skenderis,** S Stavros '07 (Skenderis & C PC) -45-07 Davis -LIC 11101 **Fx:**730-6334
(212) 450-4000 ..**Skene,** Gavin R '07 %Davis P&W LLP -450 Lex Av -NY 10017
(212) 889-4220 ..**Skene,** Robt D '95 -10 E 40th -NY 10016 **Fx:**889-4221
(718) 875-1300 ..**Skenyon,** Mary-Ellen '78 %Appllt Div 2nd Dept -45 Monroe Pl -Brklyn 11201 **Fx:**858-2446
(516) 535-1700 ..**Skiadas,** Peter H '93 %Horing W&R,PC -11 Hillside Av -Williston Pk 11596
(212) 833-1133 ..**Skibell,** Lindsey Rudd '05 %Friedman KS&A LLP -1633 Bway -NY 10019 **Fx:**373-7933
(631) 853-4104 ..**Skiber,** Mary F '07 %DA -400 Carleton Av Bx9082 -Central Islip 11722 **Fx:**853-7838
(518) 486-1283 ..**Skibinski,** Laura M '04 %State Comptroller -110 State -Albany 12236 **Fx:**474-5119
(212) 440-7331 ..**Skidds,** Jan Michl '03 CNA Global -40 Wall -NY 10005
(212) 832-4800 ..**Skidelsky,** Barry '83 -185 E 85th -NY 10028
(212) 973-8000 ..**Skidmore,** Martha M '02 %Schnader HS&L LLP -140 Bway -NY 10005
(212) 262-2390 ..**Skidmore,** Nancy A '99 OfCnsl Connell F LLP -888 7th Av -NY 10106
(212) 201-1170 ..**Skiena,** Alan N '82 -237 W 35th -NY 10001 **Fx:**202-6012
(315) 425-2700 ..**Skiff,** Matthew J '07 %Hiscock & B,LLP -One Park Pl -Syracuse 13202
(212) 770-8805 ..**Skigen,** Patricia S '68 AIG Inc -70 Pine -NY 10270
(212) 836-8000 ..**Skiles,** Seth A '08 %Kaye S LLP -425 Park Av -NY 10022
(212) 376-5666 ..**Skillen,** Lesley A '94 (Getnick & G) -620 5th Av -NY 10020 **Fx:**292-3942
(212) 785-0808 ..**Skillman,** Joshua W '01 -100 William -NY 10038 **Fx:**785-0177
(212) 225-2000 ..**Skinner,** Helen A '09 %Cleary GS&H -1 Lbrty Plz -NY 10006
(212) 730-7700 ..**Skinner,** John J Jr. '96 (Michelman & R,LLP) -114 W 47th -NY 10036
(212) 637-2601 ..**Skinner,** Peter M '01 %US Atty -1 St Andrews Plz -NY 10007
(212) 373-3000 ..**Skinner,** Suzanne K '09 %Paul WRW&G LLP -1285 Av of Amer -NY 10019
(718) 590-3251 ..**Skinner-Cifuentes,** Melinda L '09 %Law Dept -900 Sheridan Av -Bronx 10451 **Fx:**590-2699
(718) 904-4957 ..**Skipper,** John N '93 %ConEd -1615 Brnxdale Av -Bronx 10462
(212) 287-3104 ..**Skirnick,** Gabriella N '09 Perella Weinberg Partners LP -767 5th Av -NY 10153
(212) 240-0020 ..**Skirnick,** Robt A '82 (Meredith CG&S) -1 Lbrty Plz -NY 10006
(212) 689-8808 ..**Skirrow,** Juan A '04 %Hoguet NR&K,LLP -10 E 40th -NY 10016
(718) 797-9039 ..**Skittone,** Philip '85 -26 Court -Brklyn 11242
(585) 724-2453 ..**Skivington,** Dale E '80 %Eastman Kodak -343 State -Rchstr 14650
(585) 243-0313 ..**Skivington,** Peter K '80 (Jones & S) -31 Main -Geneseo 14454 **Fx:**243-3625
(845) 892-5366 ..**Skladony,** Wm P '99 IBM Inc -N Castle Dr -Armonk 10504
(212) 962-6435 ..**Sklamberg,** Marvin S '57 -56-03 E Hmptn Blvd -Oakland Gdns 11364
(212) 757-5178 ..**Sklar,** Adam B '06 (Sklar Law Firm LLC) -250 W 57th -NY 10107 **Fx:**(732) 289-6253
(718) 658-0500 ..**Sklar,** Aimee L '05 %Law Dept -151-20 Jamaica Av -Jamaica 11432 **Fx:**658-4025
(516) 222-2333 ..**Sklar,** Amy '81 %Barbara Law Firm -401 Franklin Av -Gdn Cty 11530 **Fx:**222-2935
(212) 580-8055 ..**Sklar,** Amy F '84 -239 Cntrl Pk W -NY 10024
(212) 836-8000 ..**Sklar,** Brandon N '86 Cnsl Kaye S LLP -425 Park Av -NY 10022
(212) 574-1200 ..**Sklar,** Craig A '96 (Seward & K LLP) -1 Bttry Pk Plz -NY 10004
(516) 739-3535 ..**Sklar,** Howard M '90 -1 Old Cntry Rd -Carle Pl 11514 **Fx:**739-3539
(212) 640-2008 ..**Sklar,** Howard M '95 Amer Express -200 Vesey -NY 10285
(212) 244-6222 ..**Sklar,** Jeffrey H '93 (Melucci C&S,LLP) -26 Bway -NY 10004 **Fx:**244-7165
(914) 470-0001 ..**Sklar,** Jordan M '88 (Babchik & Y,LLP) -200 E Post Rd -White Plns 10601
(212) 931-5500 ..**Sklar,** Keith G '06 McCue S&Z,PC -521 5th Av -NY 10175
(212) 801-9305 ..**Sklar,** Kenneth M '96 (Greenberg T,LLP) -200 Park Av -NY 10166
(212) 986-6000 ..**Sklar,** Martin D '85 (Kleinberg KW&C,PC) -551 5th Av -NY 10176
(212) 836-8000 ..**Sklar,** Matthew A '09 Kaye S LLP -425 Park Av -NY 10022
(212) 672-1500 ..**Sklar,** Paul R '79 -551 5th Av -NY 10176
(212) 530-5000 ..**Sklar,** Stephanie '07 %Milbank TH&M LLP -1 Chase Manh Plz -NY 10005
(212) 757-5178 ..**Sklar,** Steven I '69 OfCnsl Sklar Law Firm LLC -250 W 57th -NY 10107 **Fx:**(732) 289-6253
(631) 369-1700 ..**Sklar,** Theo D '82 (Esseks H&A,LLP) -108 E Main Bx279 -Rvrhead 11901
(212) 471-8468 ..**Sklaren,** Cary Stewart '69 (Herzfeld & R,PC) -125 Broad -NY 10004
(212) 984-7832 ..**Sklaren,** Linda Genero '85 (Warshaw BCS&K,LLP) -555 5th Av -NY 10017
(212) 742-3390 ..**Sklarin,** Joshua S '09 %Lindabury ME&C,PC -26 Bway -NY 10004
(914) 345-6510 ..**Sklarin,** Richd S '92 (Miranda SSSV LLP) -570 Taxter Rd -Elmsfrd 10523
(845) 368-4999 ..**Sklar Israel,** Chana '80 -2 Perlman Dr -Spg Vly 10977 **Fx:**230-8672
(212) 801-9227 ..**Sklaroff,** Jeffrey B '81 (Greenberg T,LLP) -200 Park Av -NY 10166
(718) 792-0444 ..**Sklaroff,** Susan R '83 %MHLS -1500 Waters Pl -Bronx 10461 **Fx:**597-7385
(212) 833-6800 ..**Sklar-Romano,** Jennifer L '01 %Sony Corp of America -555 Mad Av -NY 10022
(914) 788-1300 ..**Sklaver,** Alfred '62 -2117 Crompond Rd -Cortlandt Manor 10567 **Fx:**788-5741
(516) 248-4000 ..**Sklavos,** Alexander E '97 A Sklavos PC -265 Post Av -Westbury 11590 **Fx:**877-8010
(212) 685-6100 ..**Sklaw,** Laurence M '89 (Berger & S LLP) -295 Mad Av -NY 10017 **Fx:**685-6862
(845) 639-5071 ..**Sklerov,** Leonard J '75 Sklerov Law Ofc,PC -17H Heritage Dr -New Cty 10956 **Fx:**639-6087
(212) 269-3444 ..**Skliar,** Michl H '86 (Capriano L&F,LLP) -80 Wall -NY 10005
(315) 471-3151 ..**Skloda,** James S '03 (Hancock & E,LLP) -1500 AXA Twr I Bx4976 -Syracuse 13221
(212) 757-5000 ..**Sklover,** Alan L '83 (Sklover D&F,LLC) -10 Rckfllr Plz -NY 10020 **Fx:**757-5002
(212) 756-2000 ..**Sklute,** Jessica '98 SpclCnsl Schulte R&Z LLP -919 3rd Av -NY 10022
(212) 244-7676 ..**Sklyar,** Adelina M '99 (Ferro KMS,PC) -424 W 33rd -NY 10001
(212) 943-2296 ..**Skoblow,** David V '78 CLS Bank Intl -39 Bway -NY 10006
(212) 425-3100 ..**Skoczen,** Christopher D '00 OfCnsl McManus C&R,PC -48 Wall -NY 10005
(212) 554-7800 ..**Skoff,** Abraham Y '76 (Moses & S LLP) -405 Lex Av -NY 10174
(212) 846-4153 ..**Skog,** Kiersten M '00 MTV Ntwrks -1515 Bway -NY 10036 **Fx:**846-1774
(845) 486-3048 ..**Skojec,** Laura G '92 %Cnty Atty -60 Market -Poughkeepsie 12601 **Fx:**486-2796
(212) 664-6562 ..**Skokowski,** Catherine '04 %NBC Universal -30 Rckfllr Plz -NY 10112
(212) 258-8000 ..**Skoler,** Elizabeth F '94 %MTV Networks -1515 Bway -NY 10036 **Fx:**258-8358
(212) 768-0404 ..**Skoler,** Ronald L '81 -226 W 47th -NY 10036 **Fx:**768-1044
(212) 401-3636 ..**Skoller,** Richd M '85 Royal Bk of Scotland -101 Park Av -NY 10178 **Fx:**401-3612
(212) 230-2424 ..**Skoller,** Shana Madoff '97 %B Madoff Invstmnt Sec -885 3rd Av -NY 10022 **Fx:**271-0473
(212) 902-1000 ..**Skolnick,** Fred J '03 Goldman Sachs & Co -85 Broad -NY 10004
(212) 416-8556 ..**Skolnick,** Joanne '98 %Dept of Law -120 Bway -NY 10271
(718) 624-2240 ..**Skolnick,** Jonathan C '03 %Romanick & S,PLLC -142 Joralemon -Brklyn 11201 **Fx:**624-1268
(212) 593-3000 ..**Skolnick,** Mark '66 (Platzer SKLG&J,LLP) -1065 Av of Amer -NY 10018

(212) 888-8240 .. **Skolnick,** Martin P '99 -400 Park Av -NY 10022 **Fx:**688-6151
(718) 273-7900 .. **Skolnik,** Brooke T '07 %Sgarlato & S,PLLC -1444 Clove Rd -Staten Isl 10301 **Fx:**273-9629
(212) 526-8534 .. **Skolnik,** Deborah R '97 Barclays Capital Inc -745 7th Av -NY 10019
(914) 421-1086 .. **Skolnik,** Edw L '60 -5 Waller Av -White Plns 10601 **Fx:**421-1087
(516) 296-7000 .. **Skolnik,** Fred '80 (Certilman BA&H,LLP) -90 Merrick Av -E Meadow 11554
(212) 471-8457 .. **Skolnik,** Miriam '80 (Herzfeld & R,PC) -125 Broad -NY 10004
(212) 953-6633 .. **Skolnik,** Steven D '76 (Cox PS&S LLP) -630 3rd Av -NY 10017
Skolozdra, Gregory P '87 -930 2nd Av -NY 10022
(212) 369-2324 .. **Skomorowsky,** Peter '92 -25 E 86th -NY 10028 **Fx:**410-4123
(212) 836-8000 .. **Skonberg,** Kurt E '94 (Kaye S LLP) -425 Park Av -NY 10022
(716) 285-9555 .. **Skoney,** Michl J '85 (Viola C&L) -770 Main Bx948 -Niagara Fls 14302
(212) 698-3500 .. **Skonieczny,** Stephen W '85 (Dechert LLP) -1095 Av of Amer -NY 10036
(516) 741-6565 .. **Skop,** Chas '83 (Meyer SE&K,PC) -990 Stewart Av Bx9194 -Gdn Cty 11530
(718) 645-5500 .. **Skopp,** Arnold S '56 -1101 Av U -Brklyn 11223 **Fx:**645-5530
(718) 850-6990 .. **Skor,** Stephen A '93 -114-08 101st Av -Richmnd Hll 11419 **Fx:**850-6999
(212) 335-4500 .. **Skornicki,** Leon C '10 %DLA Piper LLP -1251 Av of Amer -NY 10020
(631) 852-2500 .. **Skorupa,** Stacy A '06 %DA -200 Center Dr -Rvrhead 11901 **Fx:**852-1769
(212) 983-8500 .. **Skoufalos,** Peter '83 %Brown G&F LLP -355 Lex Av -NY 10017
(646) 756-2661 .. **Skoufalos,** Stephan '85 (Skoufalos LLC) -1230 Av of Amer -NY 10020 **Fx:**756-2999
(917) 343-7356 .. **Skouloudi,** Gavriela Antoniou '06 Goldman Sachs & Co -1 NY Plz -NY 10004
(212) 233-2505 .. **Skountzos,** Magdalene P '05 %Brody O&O -111 John -NY 10038
(212) 682-9898 .. **Skovgaard,** Barry C '81 -800 Av of Amer -NY 10001
(212) 279-5050 .. **Skovron,** Ximena R '04 %Abraham F&T LLP -1 Penn Plz -NY 10119
(718) 336-8886 .. **Skovronsky,** Harold '75 -1810 Av N -Brklyn 11230 **Fx:**336-8104
(212) 259-4378 .. **Skowronski,** Stephanie S '05 LongAcre Fund Mgmt LLC -810 7th Av -NY 10019
(516) 379-7600 .. **Skoy,** Robt I '66 (R Skoy,PC) -328 Bedell -Freeprt 11520 **Fx:**379-7151
(716) 843-8489 .. **Skretny,** Jill M '02 US Cstms & Brdr Prot -726 Exchange -Buffalo 14210
(212) 808-0800 .. **Skrilow,** David C '78 -551 5th Av -NY 10176 **Fx:**808-0807
(347) 296-1659 .. **Skrzypczak,** Steven J '94 %Supreme Ct Law Dept -360 Adams -Brklyn 11201 **Fx:**643-6114
(631) 543-3030 .. **Skubik,** Jacqueline M '86 (Miller & S,LLP) -356 Vets Mem'l Hwy -Commack 11725 **Fx:**543-2888
(518) 785-1410 .. **Skubis,** Stanley J '84 S Skubis,PC -1147 Troy Schenectady Rd -Latham 12110 **Fx:**785-1262
(212) 556-2100 .. **Skucas,** Alexas Donatas '95 (King & S) -1185 Av of Amer -NY 10036
(315) 471-0524 .. **Skuce,** Erin K '07 %Kenny & K PLLC -W 315 Fayette -Syracuse 13202 **Fx:**471-4238
(212) 225-2000 .. **Skulan,** Catherine A '07 %Cleary GS&H -1 Lbrty Plz -NY 10006
(718) 939-4444 .. **Skulikidis,** Pantelis '04 %GJ Dmoch & Assoc -171-22 Nrthrn Blvd -Flushng 11358 **Fx:**445-2520
(212) 872-9800 .. **Skulnik,** Steven '84 OfCnsl Squire S&D LLP -30 Rckfllr Plz -NY 10112
(212) 474-1000 .. **Skumpija,** Johnny G '06 %Cravath S&M LLP -825 8th Av -NY 10019
(212) 683-3800 .. **Skura,** Naomi J '07 %Dinkes & S,PC -112 Mad Av -NY 10016
(212) 682-2288 .. **Skurman,** Paul S '80 (Sankel S&M,LLP) -750 3rd Av -NY 10017
(516) 791-1282 .. **Skurnik,** Linda H '96 (Schiff & S PLLC) -112 Spruce -Cedarhrst 11516 **Fx:**791-2087
(718) 676-9061 .. **Skvortsova,** Natalia '06 N Skvortsova,PLLC -336 Kings Hwy -Brklyn 11223
(914) 824-5430 .. **Skwiersky,** Barry J '75 Hon W Giacomo -111 Martin Luther King Blvd -White Plns 10601 **Fx:**995-4182
(914) 450-4394 .. **Skydel,** Elliot '73 -43 Gladstone Rd -New Rchll 10804 **Fx:**813-2478
(212) 585-3031 .. **Skydell,** Norman B '68 (N Skydell,PC) -140 E 80th -NY 10075 **Fx:**585-3038
(518) 402-6757 .. **Skyer,** Marc V '96 %Workers Comp Bd -20 Park -Albany 12207
(212) 532-9736 .. **Skyer,** Regina '92 (R Skyer & Assoc,LLP) -276 5th Av -NY 10001 **Fx:**532-9846
(718) 466-3000 .. **Skylakos,** Effie A '91 %Civil Ct -1118 Grnd Cncrs -Bronx 10456 **Fx:**466-3006
(212) 793-2183 .. **Skyler,** Edw G '04 Citigroup -499 Park Av -NY 10022
(212) 225-2000 .. **Slack,** Catharine G '08 %Cleary GS&H -1 Lbrty Plz -NY 10006
(212) 326-3939 .. **Slack,** Charmaine L '02 (Jones D) -222 E 41st -NY 10017
(212) 310-8017 .. **Slack,** Richd W '87 (Weil G&M LLP) -767 5th Av -NY 10153
(518) 386-2266 .. **Slack-Bean,** Deborah '02 %Pub Def -519 State -Schnctdy 12305 **Fx:**386-2814
(212) 610-6300 .. **Slade,** David '81 (Allen & O) -1221 Av of Amer -NY 10020
(212) 530-5000 .. **Slade,** Georgiana '86 (Milbank TH&M LLP) -1 Chase Manh Plz -NY 10005
(212) 684-1000 .. **Slade,** Ira L '65 (Slade & N LLP) -245 5th Av -NY 10016 **Fx:**684-0646
(516) 869-7014 .. **Slade,** Jodi B '94 %Apple Bank -1395 Nrthrn Blvd -Manhsst 11030
(914) 499-6490 .. **Sladek,** Maureen '95 IBM -1 New Orchrd Rd -Armonk 10504 **Fx:**765-7533
(212) 754-9400 .. **Sladkus,** Harvey I '62 OfCnsl Todtman NS&J,PC -425 Park Av -NY 10022
(212) 893-8181 .. **Sladkus,** Jeffrey B '05 J Sladkus,LLC -400 E 56th -NY 10022 **Fx:**583-1919
(212) 545-4700 .. **Sladkus,** Steven D '95 (Wolf HAF&H LLP) -270 Mad Av -NY 10016
(212) 871-6797 .. **Slakas,** Kevin D '73 -12 E 33rd -NY 10016 **Fx:**871-6799
(212) 237-1000 .. **Slama,** Mark A '87 (Windels ML&M,LLP) -156 W 56th -NY 10019
(646) 356-8612 .. **Slamowitz,** Greg '91 Ambrose Employer Grp -199 Water -NY 10038
(516) 364-6006 .. **Slamowitz,** Mitchell G '85 (Cohen & S,LLP) -199 Crsswys Park Dr Bx9004 -Woodbury 11797
(914) 328-8844 .. **Slane,** Bruce W '08 %Meagher & M -175 Main -White Plns 10601 **Fx:**328-8570
(914) 773-7700 .. **Slaney,** Paul H '92 Geo A Fuller Co -115 E Stevens Av -Valhalla 10595
(212) 918-3000 .. **Slanover,** Russell C '84 Cnsl Hogan L LLP -875 3rd Av -NY 10022
(212) 878-7900 .. **Slapo,** Michl I '98 (Fox R LLP) -100 Park Av -NY 10017
(212) 336-2000 .. **Slarskey,** David N '06 %Patterson BW&T LLP -1133 Av of Amer -NY 10036
(845) 471-4141 .. **Slate,** Jerold S '67 -303 Mill -Poughkeepsie 12601 **Fx:**471-7597
(631) 420-9300 .. **Slater,** Adam P '05 (Obasanjo & S LLP) -445 Broadhllw Rd -Melvll 11747 **Fx:**465-7052
(212) 326-2000 .. **Slater,** Alexander E '08 %O'Melveny & M LLP -7 Times Sq -NY 10036
(212) 726-9161 .. **Slater,** Alice J '85 %GRACE -215 Lex Av -NY 10016 **Fx:**726-9160
(212) 966-6420 .. **Slater,** Amanda Post '03 Lwyrs For Children -110 Lafayette -NY 10013 **Fx:**966-0531
(212) 218-2100 .. **Slater,** Brian V '91 (Fitzpatrick CH&S) -1290 Av of Amer -NY 10104
(212) 391-8045 .. **Slater,** Carole S '81 (Slater & B LLP) -61 Bway -NY 10006 **Fx:**391-8047
(914) 423-8880 .. **Slater,** Cheryl E '05 (Farrauto B&S) -1250 Cntrl Pk Av -Ynkrs 10704
(716) 853-1616 .. **Slater,** Craig A '82 (Harter S&E LLP) -12 Fountain Plz -Buffalo 14202
(212) 489-6500 .. **Slater,** David M '88 -240 W 73rd -NY 10023 **Fx:**489-5315
(212) 909-6000 .. **Slater,** Emily O'Neill '02 %Debevoise & P LLP -919 3rd Av -NY 10022
(718) 253-9190 .. **Slater,** Harvey L '81 -1761 E 21st -Brklyn 11229
(212) 757-5412 .. **Slater,** Ilene J '67 -30 W 60th -NY 10023
(212) 906-5273 .. **Slater,** Jeffrey A '98 %UN Devlpmnt Programme -1 UN Plz -NY 10017
(631) 420-9300 .. **Slater,** Jos M '77 J Slater,PC -445 Broad Hollow Rd -Melvll 11747 **Fx:**293-2060
(212) 589-4200 .. **Slater,** Lourdes M '93 Cnsl Baker & H LLP -45 Rckfllr Plz -NY 10111
(212) 848-9800 .. **Slater,** Peter J '98 %Withers B LLP -430 Park Av -NY 10022
(212) 964-3855 .. **Slater,** Richd N '75 %R Cardali & Assoc,LLP -39 Bway -NY 10006 **Fx:**634-4856
(716) 487-1142 .. **Slater,** Richd V '64 (Spoto S&S) -112 Htl Jmstwn Ofc Bldg -Jamestwn 14701
(212) 425-3158 .. **Slater,** Robt L Jr. '75 Slater & C,PC -11 Bway -NY 10004 **Fx:**422-1283
(845) 306-1000 .. **Slater,** Ronald L '08 %Watchtower -100 Watchtower Dr -Patterson 12563 **Fx:**306-0709
(718) 448-6400 .. **Slater Sgarlato & Cappello, PC** -1298 Victory Blvd -Staten Isl 10301 **Fx:**448-0617
(212) 940-3119 .. **Slater,** Stacey B '96 (Nixon P LLP) -437 Mad Av -NY 10022
(914) 385-6000 .. **Slater,** Stephen '87 (Hodges W&S LLP) -55 Church -White Plns 10601 **Fx:**385-6060
(914) 285-9800 .. **Slater-Jansen,** Susan B '81 (Kurzman EC&L,LLP) -1 N Bway -White Plns 10601
(212) 309-6000 .. **Slatin,** Amanda N '05 %Morgan L&B LLP -101 Park Av -NY 10178
(716) 753-4376 .. **Slaton,** Janice D '02 Pub Def -7 N Erie -Mayvll 14757 **Fx:**753-4751
(718) 590-2000 .. **Slattery,** Catherine A '06 DA -198 E 161st -Bronx 10451 **Fx:**590-6477
(212) 664-5165 .. **Slattery,** James F '86 %NBC Universal -30 Rckfllr Plz -NY 10112
(212) 909-6000 .. **Slattery,** Keith J '09 Cnsl Debevoise & P LLP -919 3rd Av -NY 10022
(914) 824-5886 .. **Slattery,** Kevan T '78 Hon D Angiolillo -140 Grand -White Plns 10601
(631) 577-2400 .. **Slattery,** Kevin P '87 %Tromello M&K -25 Melvll Park Rd Bx9038 -Melvll 11747
(212) 247-1010 .. **Slattery,** Michl J Jr. '97 FTI Consulting -3 Times Sq -NY 10036 **Fx:**841-8350
(212) 277-6500 .. **Slattery,** Michl J '99 %Dickstein S LLP -1633 Bway -NY 10019
(212) 225-7700 .. **Slattery,** Raymond F '80 (Cartafalsa ST&L) -165 Bway -NY 10006
(516) 775-2236 .. **Slattery,** Timothy J '87 (Santangelo B&S) -1800 Nrthrn Blvd -Roslyn 11576
(914) 834-3322 .. **Slattery,** Wm H '69 %Atlantic Lgl Fndtn -2039 Palmer Av -Larchmnt 10538 **Fx:**833-1022
(212) 465-0537 .. **Slatus,** Robt E '73 -225 W 34th -NY 10122 **Fx:**465-0635
(212) 704-6000 .. **Slatz,** Danl J '81 (Troutman S LLP) -405 Lex Av -NY 10174
(212) 906-1200 .. **Slavens,** Aaron T '06 %Latham & W -885 3rd Av -NY 10022
(516) 775-1414 .. **Slavin,** Barton L '83 Monsour WK&W,LLP -3000 Marcus Av -Lk Success 11042
(516) 766-1621 .. **Slavin,** David A '79 -182 Morris Av -Rockvll Ctr 11570
(914) 277-7176 .. **Slavin,** Irma '85 -Bx320 -Somers 10589 **Fx:**(203) 431-7785
(212) 750-1333 .. **Slavin,** Jane R '84 %I Garr,PC -777 3rd Av -NY 10017 **Fx:**486-2978
(516) 432-0030 .. **Slavin,** Janet D '78 -58 W Park Av -Long Bch 11561
(516) 437-2754 .. **Slavin,** John J '64 -214 Bellmore -Floral Pk 11001
(212) 233-1010 .. **Slavin,** Jos '52 -170 Morris Av -Rockvll Ctr 11570
(631) 293-4525 .. **Slavin,** Loretta Susan '88 SpclCnsl Littler M,PC -290 Broadhllw Rd -Melvll 11747
(212) 297-5800 .. **Slavin,** Lorraine '86 (Day P LLP) -7 Times Sq -NY 10036
(585) 546-2500 .. **Slavin,** Shannon L '07 %McConville CC&M,PC -25 E Main -Rchstr 14614
(914) 323-7000 .. **Slavina,** Jana A '04 %Wilson EME&D LLP -3 Gannett Dr -White Plns 10604
(631) 716-1600 .. **Slavis,** Mark G '78 -3237 Route 112 -Medfrd 11763
(212) 687-2777 .. **Slavit,** Ira S '84 (Levine & S) -60 E 42nd -NY 10165
(212) 687-2777 .. **Slavit,** Leonard S '57 (Levine & S) -60 E 42nd -NY 10165
(212) 594-5300 .. **Sleater,** Jessica J '08 %Milberg LLP -1 Penn Plz -NY 10119
(631) 727-1515 .. **Sledjeski,** Thos C II '89 (TC Sledjeski II & Assoc,PLLC) -18 1st Bx479 -Rvrhead 11901 **Fx:**727-7693
(914) 472-2300 .. **Sledzik,** Steven T '93 (Jones G,LLP) -670 Wht Plns Rd -Scarsdale 10583
(212) 885-8818 .. **Sleeper,** Eric W '87 (Barton B&P,LLP) -420 Lex Av -NY 10170 **Fx:**687-3667
(212) 224-5649 .. **Sleeper,** Mason C '90 Praedium Grp -825 3rd Av -NY 10022 **Fx:**224-5698
(212) 479-6000 .. **Sleeper,** Maxine G '04 %Cooley LLP -1114 Av of Amer -NY 10036
(518) 279-1781 .. **Sleicher,** Richd E '94 %Troy City Garage Inc -810 Hoosick Rd -Troy 12180

(716) 858-2200 .. **Sleight**, David J '89 Cnty Atty -95 Franklin -Buffalo 14202 **Fx:**858-2281
(518) 427-9700 .. **Sleight**, Karl Jay '90 (Harris B PLLC) -677 Bway -Albany 12207
(518) 792-5992 .. **Sleight**, Virginia M '64 -369 Aviation Rd -Queensbury 12804 **Fx:**792-5992
(860) 275-6708 .. **Sleman**, Peter D '09 (McCarter & E,LLP) -245 Park Av -NY 10167 **Fx:**724-3397
(585) 593-7810 .. **Slep**, Keith A '89 -168½ N Main Bx1237 -Wellsvll 14895 **Fx:**593-2345
(212) 264-9271 .. **Slepak**, Yelena '96 %US Customs -26 Fed Plz -NY 10278
(718) 229-1904 .. **Slepian**, Jack I '77 (Pollak & S,LLP) -214-08 41st Av -Bayside 11361 **Fx:**423-2308
(212) 532-4000 .. **Slepowitz**, Samantha H '08 %Dobrish ZG LLP -757 3rd Av -NY 10017
(212) 674-5151 .. **Sleven**, Paul J '82 %Macmillan -175 5th Av -NY 10010 **Fx:**529-0594
(212) 683-4832 .. **Slevin**, James M '01 Uniformed Firefighters Assn -204 E 23rd -NY 10010 **Fx:**683-0710
(718) 250-2000 .. **Slevin**, Joyce Bresnick '85 %DA -350 Jay -Brklyn 11201 **Fx:**250-2314
(516) 248-6000 .. **Slevin**, Maribeth '89 OfCnsl Kaufman B&R -1205 Franklin Av -Gdn Cty 11530
(518) 449-3125 .. **Slevin**, Mary Elizabeth '88 (Stockli GS&P,LLP) -90 State -Albany 12207
(516) 357-3000 .. **Slevin**, Michl J '86 %Rivkin R LLP -926 RXR Plz -Uniondale 11556
(212) 788-3300 .. **Slevinski**, Danette L '06 %Hlth & Hsptl Corp -125 Worth -NY 10013 **Fx:**267-6905
(516) 822-1371 .. **Slewett**, Franklyn R '64 -8 Wayland Rd -Plainvw 11803
(518) 377-6700 .. **Slezak**, Deborah A '95 (Cioffi SW PC) -2310 Nott E -Niskayuna 12309
(646) 452-1851 .. **Slezak**, Edw M '94 Aeropostale,Inc -112 W 34th -NY 10120
(516) 248-7000 .. **Slezak**, Erica M '95 %Albanese & A LLP -1050 Franklin Av -Gdn Cty 11530
(518) 853-8130 .. **Slezak**, Rebecca A '97 Family Ct -58 Bway Bx1500 -Fonda 12068 **Fx:**853-8148
(212) 594-5300 .. **Slidders**, Chas '09 %Milberg LLP -1 Penn Plz -NY 10119
(212) 474-1000 .. **Slifkin**, Danl '91 (Cravath S&M LLP) -825 8th Av -NY 10019
(585) 419-8800 .. **Slifkin**, Neal L '95 (Harris B PLLC) -99 Garnsey Rd -Pittsfrd 14534
(212) 530-5000 .. **Sligar**, James S '75 (Milbank TH&M LLP) -1 Chase Manh Plz -NY 10005
(718) 286-6000 .. **Sligh**, Jesse J '83 %DA -125-01 Qns Blvd -Kew Gdns 11415
(212) 805-3900 .. **Slim**, Susan K '05 %Clausen M PC -1 Chase Manh Plz -NY 10005
(718) 590-2000 .. **Slimak**, Katherin M '06 DA -198 E 161st -Bronx 10451 **Fx:**590-6477
(315) 471-1664 .. **Slimbaugh**, Kimberly A '92 (Meggesto C&V,LLP) -313 E Willow -Syracuse 13203
(516) 679-3277 .. **Sliney**, Benedict L '79 -3991 Eve Dr -Seafrd 11783
(518) 782-9500 .. **Slingerland**, George R '03 (Kerr S PC) -12 Cornell Rd -Latham 12110 **Fx:**782-9700
(718) 515-4500 .. **Slingsby**, Robt D '83 (Slingsby S&P) -3199 Bainbrdg Av -Bronx 10467
(718) 515-4500 .. **Slingsby Sanders & Pagano** -3199 Bainbrdg Av -Bronx 10467 **Fx:**515-4968
(212) 657-1402 .. **Slipp**, Ellen '90 Citigroup -77 Water -NY 10005
(212) 647-8100 .. **Slippen**, Jeffrey N '93 %Toorock & R -20 W 20th -NY 10011
(716) 855-3761 .. **Slisz**, Mary L '84 (LoTempio & B,PC) -181 Franklin -Buffalo 14202 **Fx:**855-3437
(716) 854-4400 .. **Slisz**, Richd C '89 -14 Lafayette Sq -Buffalo 14203 **Fx:**856-5801
(212) 859-8000 .. **Slivinski**, Richd J '02 %Fried FHS&J LLP -1 NY Plz -NY 10004
(212) 447-5599 .. **Slivka**, Wm '55 OfCnsl Agins SR&B,LLP -386 Park Av S -NY 10016
(716) 881-5400 .. **Sliwa**, Flora Miller '78 %NEANY -271 Porter Av -Buffalo 14201 **Fx:**881-6678
(716) 853-2050 .. **Sliwa & Lane** -237 Main -Buffalo 14203 **Fx:**853-2057
(716) 853-2050 .. **Sliwa**, Stanley J '80 (Sliwa & L) -237 Main -Buffalo 14203
(518) 285-8600 .. **Sliwinski**, Catherine Ann '95 Family Ct -30 Clinton Av -Albany 12207
(212) 448-1100 .. **Sloan**, Barbara A '99 (McLaughlin & S,LLP) -260 Mad Av -NY 10016
(212) 525-8228 .. **Sloan**, Bryan K '97 %HSBC Bank -452 5th Av -NY 10018
(212) 545-4600 .. **Sloan**, Carl R '67 OfCnsl Wolf HAF&H LLP -270 Mad Av -NY 10016
(716) 821-7410 .. **Sloan**, Colleen Ann '91 %Erie 1 BOCES -355 Harlem Rd -W Seneca 14224
(718) 265-1500 .. **Sloan**, David H '95 %Aini & L,PLLC -2615 Coney Isl Av -Brklyn 11223 **Fx:**265-1515
(516) 333-2300 .. **Sloan**, David N '79 -321 Newbrdg Rd -Hicksvll 11801 **Fx:**333-4264
(212) 969-3000 .. **Sloan**, David W '62 (Proskauer R LLP) -1585 Bway -NY 10036
(845) 621-8640 .. **Sloan & Feller** -880 S Lk Blvd -Mahopac 10541 **Fx:**621-8639
(212) 902-6323 .. **Sloan**, Jeffrey S '93 Goldman Sachs & Co -85 Broad -NY 10004
(845) 621-8640 .. **Sloan**, Leslie J '90 (Sloan & F) -880 S Lk Blvd -Mahopac 10541
(212) 407-1200 .. **Sloan**, Michl B '06 %Joseph Law Ofcs LLC -485 Lex Av -NY 10017 **Fx:**407-1299
(212) 521-3500 .. **Sloan**, Pamela M '81 (Aronson M&S, LLP) -485 Lex Av -NY 10017
(212) 687-6900 .. **Sloan**, Phillip E '81 %Connell & W -555 5th Av -NY 10017 **Fx:**687-6999
(585) 327-7581 .. **Sloan**, Stephen R '83 Excellus Hlth Plan -165 Court -Rchstr 14647 **Fx:**327-7585
(212) 221-5200 .. **Sloan**, Stevan E '76 OTB -1501 Bway -NY 10036 **Fx:**221-8025
(212) 351-4500 .. **Sloan**, Victoria M '06 %Epstein B&G,PC -250 Park Av -NY 10177
(212) 788-3300 .. **Sloane**, Catherine L '99 %Hlth & Hsptl Corp -125 Worth -NY 10013 **Fx:**267-6905
(516) 512-8971 .. **Sloane**, Chas E '79 C Sloane PC -1225 Franklin Av -Gdn Cty 11530 **Fx:**(347) 235-0477
(631) 979-3000 .. **Sloane**, David A '63 (Certilman BA&H,LLP) -1393 Vets Mem'l Hwy -Hauppauge 11788
(212) 295-6458 .. **Sloane**, Erin G H '04 Cnsl WilmerHale -399 Park Av -NY 10022
(212) 701-3000 .. **Sloane**, Howard Peter '77 (Cahill G&R LLP) -80 Pine -NY 10005 **Fx:**269-5420
(212) 327-3068 .. **Sloane**, Jaar-Mel Sevin '79 Sloane Sq -115 E 72nd -NY 10021
(516) 939-9200 .. **Sloane**, Marc D '89 %Mintzer SZL&M LLP -17 W John -Hicksvll 11801
(212) 758-0050 .. **Sloane**, Norman J '74 %Title Assoc -825 3rd Av -NY 10022 **Fx:**758-8223
(914) 288-0022 .. **Sloane**, Peter S '95 (Leason E LLP) -81 Main -White Plns 10601
(212) 841-9386 .. **Sloane**, Raymond T '85 FTI Consulting -3 Times Sq -NY 10036
(212) 805-0432 .. **Sloane**, Robt D '01 %Hon G Lynch USDC -40 Foley Sq -NY 10007
(212) 349-2000 .. **Slobin**, Gary '97 %Alpert & K, LLP -233 Bway -NY 10279
(718) 590-2000 .. **Slobin**, Irene A '09 %DA -198 E 161st -Bronx 10451 **Fx:**590-6477
(914) 332-0222 .. **Slobod**, Jack D '75 %Philips Electronics -345 Scarborough Rd Bx3001 -Briarclff Mnr 10510 **Fx:**332-0615
(718) 625-0987 .. **Slochowsky**, Israel '50 (Slochowsky & S) -26 Court -Brklyn 11242 **Fx:**625-5628
(718) 625-0987 .. **Slochowsky**, Wm '84 (Slochowsky & S) -26 Court -Brklyn 11242 **Fx:**625-5628
(518) 392-7064 .. **Slocum**, Garth J '96 -Bx472 -Ghent 12075 **Fx:**392-7064
(914) 941-5668 .. **Slocum**, Jenny T '06 %Collen IP -80 S Highland Av -Ossining 10562 **Fx:**941-6091
(212) 349-6009 .. **Slocum**, Kathleen M '99 %Sanctuary for Families -110 Wall -NY 10005 **Fx:**566-0344
(646) 230-8266 .. **Sloezen**, Raul J '94 -137 5th Av -NY 10010
(716) 439-7085 .. **Sloma**, Holly E '99 %DA -175 Hawley -Lockprt 14094 **Fx:**439-7102
(718) 789-9252 .. **Sloman**, Gary '76 -42 Sterling Pl -Brklyn 11217
(607) 432-0879 .. **Sloman**, Richd D '95 -26 Hudson -Oneonta 13820 **Fx:**432-0879
(516) 741-6565 .. **Slome**, Thos R '84 (Meyer SE&K,PC) -990 Stewart Av Bx9194 -Gdn Cty 11530
(212) 468-8000 .. **Slomka**, Irwin M '80 SrCnsl Morrison & F LLP -1290 Av of Amer -NY 10104
(212) 819-8000 .. **Slomovic**, Ephraim J '90 %Hecht & Co -622 3rd Av -NY 10017 **Fx:**302-0973
(631) 447-0520 .. **Slomovitz-Glaser**, Penny S '88 -755 Waverly Av -Holtsvll 11742 **Fx:**447-0518
(212) 839-5300 .. **Slonaker**, Norman D '66 (Sidley A LLP) -787 7th Av -NY 10019
(516) 741-7676 .. **Slone**, Ondine C '90 (Miranda SSSV LLP) -240 Mineola Blvd -Mineola 11501
(607) 734-7286 .. **Sloniger**, Thos E '64 -361 Diven Av -Elmira 14901
(212) 836-8000 .. **Slonim**, Bert L '77 OfCnsl Kaye S LLP -425 Park Av -NY 10022
(212) 692-9538 .. **Slonim**, Howard R '64 H Slonim,PC -270 Mad Av -NY 10016 **Fx:**697-4432
(212) 217-4030 .. **Slonim**, Jeffrey I '76 FIT Gen Cnsl Ofc -7th Av and 27th -NY 10001 **Fx:**217-4031
(212) 415-5355 .. **Slonim**, Jonathan B '05 McKinsey & Co -55 E 52nd -NY 10055
(212) 935-3000 .. **Slonim**, Timur E '00 (Mintz LCFG&P,PC) -666 3rd Av -NY 10017
(212) 227-7456 .. **Slosberg**, Laurie J '95 -25 N Moore -NY 10013
(212) 627-9898 .. **Sloss**, John M '82 -555 W 25th -NY 10001 **Fx:**627-9498
(212) 504-6000 .. **Slosson**, John R '10 %Cadwalader W&T LLP -1 World Fncl Ctr -NY 10281
(212) 878-8000 .. **Sloszar**, Jennifer N '09 %Clifford C LLP -31 W 52nd -NY 10019
(212) 312-7256 .. **Slotkin**, Mark H '74 %State Ins Fund -199 Church -NY 10007 **Fx:**385-9199
(212) 806-5400 .. **Slotkin**, Seth D '96 (Stroock &S&L LLP) -180 Maiden Ln -NY 10038
(212) 319-4000 .. **Slotnick**, Amy P '96 Weiss & H,PC -600 Mad Av -NY 10022
(212) 440-4400 .. **Slotnick**, Barry I '61 (Buchanan I&R PC) -620 8th Av -NY 10018
(212) 407-4000 .. **Slotnick**, Barry I '72 (Loeb & L,LLP) -345 Park Av -NY 10154
(914) 949-9500 .. **Slotnick**, Howard J '77 -399 Knollwood Rd -White Plns 10603 **Fx:**949-2366
(212) 701-3000 .. **Slotnick**, Josiah M '07 %Cahill G&R LLP -80 Pine -NY 10005 **Fx:**269-5420
(212) 903-1348 .. **Slotnick**, Kenneth J '96 Wm Morris Agency -1325 Av of Amer -NY 10019
(516) 568-1850 .. **Slotnick**, Steven J '77 (Werner ZSS&A) -360 Merrick Rd -Lynbrk 11563
(212) 440-4400 .. **Slotnick**, Stuart P '95 (Buchanan I&R PC) -620 8th Av -NY 10018
(718) 339-3330 .. **Slotnik**, Gerald '77 %Meyers S&C -3620 Quentin Rd -Brklyn 11234
(212) 687-1222 .. **Slotnik**, Sol V '69 (S Slotnik,PC) -11 E 44th -NY 10017 **Fx:**986-2399
(212) 903-9000 .. **Slotsky**, Karen L '08 %Linklaters -1345 Av of Amer -NY 10105
(718) 590-2000 .. **Slott**, David A '09 %DA -198 E 161st -Bronx 10451 **Fx:**590-6477
(631) 782-1100 .. **Slott**, Kenneth A '85 -300 E Main -Smithtwn 11787 **Fx:**782-1202
(212) 695-9112 .. **Slott**, Robt W '59 (Sunshine S&S,PC) -150 W 25th -NY 10001
(212) 756-2000 .. **Slovacek**, Caitlyn A '10 %Schulte R&Z LLP -919 3rd Av -NY 10022
(516) 997-2700 .. **Slover**, Bradley T '09 %A Core,PC -173 Schl -Westbury 11590 **Fx:**997-7334
(212) 274-6739 .. **Slovin**, Randy '98 %Admin Children's Srvcs -220 Church -NY 10013
(212) 925-0101 .. **Slovinsky**, Claudia '81 -401 Bway -NY 10013 **Fx:**219-9412
(718) 993-3888 .. **Slovis**, Harvey J '74 -831 Gerard Av -Bronx 10451 **Fx:**993-3971
(212) 858-7706 .. **Slowinski Atkins,LLP** -140 Bway PMB 46039 -NY 10005 **Fx:**858-7750
(212) 318-9508 .. **Sloyer**, Michl '91 Ruane Cunniff & Goldfarb Inc -767 5th Av -NY 10153
(212) 481-1900 .. **Sluka**, Michl J '85 (Del Valle & Assoc) -445 Park Av -NY 10022 **Fx:**481-4853
(212) 326-2000 .. **Slutsky**, Adam '07 %O'Melveny & M LLP -7 Times Sq -NY 10036
(845) 647-6000 .. **Slutsky**, David A '74 %Nevele Hotel -Nevele Rd -Ellenvll 12428
(212) 627-8100 .. **Slutsky**, David M '99 (Levy R,PC) -80 8th Av -NY 10011
(516) 678-4165 .. **Slutsky**, J Bernard '55 -1 Behnke Ct -Rockvll Ctr 11570 **Fx:**766-4705
(212) 969-3000 .. **Slutsky**, Jason W '10 %Proskauer R LLP -1585 Bway -NY 10036
(212) 349-7020 .. **Slutsky**, Michl A '80 (Slutsky M&M, LLP) -100 Park Av -NY 10017 **Fx:**(203) 762-9864
(718) 263-9292 .. **Slutsky**, Wm A '82 (W Slutsky,PC) -118-21 Qns Blvd -Frst Hlls 11375 **Fx:**263-4817
(212) 909-6000 .. **Slutzky**, Steven J '94 (Debevoise & P LLP) -919 3rd Av -NY 10022
(607) 778-2117 .. **Sluzar**, Jos J '77 Cnsl Cnty Atty -Cnty Ofc Bldg Bx1766 -Bnghmtn 13902 **Fx:**778-6122
(315) 786-0266 .. **Slye & Burrows** -104 Wshngtn -Watertwn 13601 **Fx:**786-3488
(212) 382-0909 .. **Slye**, Kathryn A '08 %Peckar & A,PC -41 Mad Av -NY 10154
(315) 786-0266 .. **Slye**, Robt J '85 (Slye & B) -104 Wshngtn -Watertwn 13601
(212) 687-7230 .. **Slyne**, Patrick K '89 Stull S&B -6 E 45th -NY 10017
(212) 761-8289 .. **Slyz**, Yurij '97 Morgan Stanley -1585 Bway -NY 10036
(212) 474-1000 .. **Smadja**, Clement J '10 %Cravath S&M LLP -825 8th Av -NY 10019
(212) 370-1999 .. **Smagula**, David '00 Choice Logistics Inc -1 Whitehall -NY 10004
(716) 838-3754 .. **Smaldone**, Paul J '70 -20 Depew Av -Buffalo 14214

(516) 413-6831 .. **Small,** Adam E '99 -25 Merrick Av Bx494 -Merrick 11566 **Fx:**867-4060
(212) 983-0921 .. **Small,** Andrew B '87 -230 Park Av -NY 10169
(212) 230-8869 .. **Small,** Anne K '05 (WilmerHale) -399 Park Av -NY 10022
(716) 858-2424 .. **Small,** Ashley R '10 %DA -25 Delaware Av -Buffalo 14202 **Fx:**858-7425
(518) 402-6757 .. **Small,** B Casey '98 %Workers Comp Bd -20 Park -Albany 12207
(212) 259-8000 .. **Small,** Carla C '08 %Dewey & L LLP -1301 Av of Amer -NY 10019
(716) 847-2600 .. **Small,** Craig Z '98 -1725 Lbrty Bldg -Buffalo 14202
(212) 670-0250 .. **Small,** Elizabeth '98 Merrill Lynch -222 Bway -NY 10038
(516) 809-0502 .. **Small,** Elliot S '94 -5020 Sunrise Hwy -Massapequa Pk 11762 **Fx:**795-2619
(212) 613-2087 .. **Small,** Eugene L '83 (Gibbons PC) -1 Penn Plz -NY 10119 **Fx:**554-9694
(631) 271-6363 .. **Small,** Gary R '80 Cannon & A,LLP -1923 NY Av -Huntngtn Sta 11746 **Fx:**271-7128
(212) 225-2000 .. **Small,** James D III '99 Cnsl Cleary GS&H -1 Lbrty Plz -NY 10006
(212) 759-2300 .. **Small,** Janine S '92 Carroll G&G,LLP -1790 Bway -NY 10019
(212) 450-4000 .. **Small,** Jeffrey '67 (Davis P&W LLP) -450 Lex Av -NY 10017
(212) 909-6461 .. **Small,** Jonathan A '67 SrCnsl Debevoise & P LLP -919 3rd Av -NY 10022
(716) 856-1600 .. **Small,** Karen Hurwitz '98 Hurwitz & D -424 Main -Buffalo 14202
(212) 867-5422 .. **Small,** Kenneth L '80 -317 Mad Av -NY 10017 **Fx:**867-5424
(516) 688-1700 .. **Small,** Marie E '99 IRS -1600 Stewart Av -Westbury 11590 **Fx:**688-1750
(212) 810-5300 .. **Small,** Martin S '01 BlackRock,Inc -40 E 52nd -NY 10022
(212) 977-9700 .. **Small,** Rachel E '01 Cnsl Phillips N LLP -666 5th Av -NY 10103
(914) 633-4022 .. **Small,** Sheila E '87 -Station Plz 2nd Fl -New Rchll 10801 **Fx:**633-4202
(718) 928-3700 .. **Small,** Shervon M '08 %LSNYC-Bronx -579 Courtlandt Av -Bronx 10451 **Fx:**402-7586
(845) 708-7152 .. **Small,** Stephanie A '96 %Hon V Alfieri Jr -1 S Main -New Cty 10956
(315) 393-3840 .. **Small,** Wm R '75 WR Small,PC -314 Ford -Ogdensbrg 13669 **Fx:**393-1641
(518) 671-6004 .. **Smallacombe,** Melissa J '85 (Burke SM&H,LLP) -437 E Allen -Hudson 12534
(585) 546-5530 .. **Smalley,** Eric S '98 %Thomson West -50 E Broad -Rchstr 14694
(585) 419-8800 .. **Smalley,** Laura W '98 (Harris B PLLC) -99 Garnsey Rd -Pittsfrd 14534
(212) 969-3000 .. **Smallheer,** Randi-Lynn '02 %Proskauer R LLP -1585 Bway -NY 10036
(518) 426-7750 .. **Smalline and Harri** -100 State -Albany 12207 **Fx:**426-7965
(518) 766-4071 .. **Smalline and Harri** -Bx80 -N Chatham 12132 **Fx:**766-4071
(518) 426-7750 .. **Smalline,** Martin D '87 (Smalline and H) -100 State -Albany 12207
(518) 766-4071 .. **Smalline,** Martin D '87 (Smalline and H) -Bx80 -N Chatham 12132
(212) 226-6696 .. **Smallman,** David B '90 (Smallman Law PLLC) -276 5th Av -NY 10001 **Fx:**(917) 720-9921
(718) 222-3073 .. **Smallman,** Philip J '84 -32 Court -Brklyn 11201
(212) 762-5427 .. **Smallman,** Thos E '95 Morgan Stanley -1221 Av of Amer -NY 10020
(631) 360-0600 .. **Small-Mazzara,** Kathy '88 (Mazzara & S,PC) -800 Vets Mem'l Hwy -Hauppauge 11788 **Fx:**360-0669
(518) 455-2870 .. **Smalls,** Matthew R '06 NYS Senate -516 Cptl Bldg -Albany 12247
(518) 455-3635 .. **Smalls,** Samantha E '01 NYS Assembly -80 S Swan -Albany 12210
(516) 292-5180 .. **Smalls-Toogood,** Nina M '91 -678 Fulton AV -Hempstd 11550
(212) 530-5000 .. **Smallwood,** Nicholas J '09 %Milbank TH&M LLP -1 Chase Manh Plz -NY 10005
(585) 786-2274 .. **Smallwood-Cook,** Charlotte '47 C Smallwood-Cook -140 N Main -Warsaw 14569 **Fx:**786-2138
(516) 355-9600 .. **Smar,** Heather L '01 %Friedman HK&P -3000 Marcus Av -Lk Success 11042
(516) 741-6266 .. **Smar,** Michl L '01 %McCabe CM&F,LLP -346 Westbury Av Bx9000 -Carle Pl 11514
(212) 625-9156 .. **Smargiassi,** John '95 (Joseph & S,LLC) -2 Rector -NY 10006
(212) 259-8000 .. **Smarsh,** Brian M '03 %Dewey & L LLP -1301 Av of Amer -NY 10019
(646) 638-8210 .. **Smarsh,** Brooke A '01 IN DEMAND,LLC -345 Hudson -NY 10014
(212) 588-5500 .. **Smart,** Gawain S E '03 (Davies WP&V LLP) -625 Mad Av -NY 10022
(212) 458-2670 .. **Smart,** Gilda M '99 AIGTS -175 Water -NY 10038
(212) 836-8000 .. **Smart,** Thos A '76 (Kaye S LLP) -425 Park Av -NY 10022
(212) 506-5000 .. **Smaylovsky,** Philipp '06 %Orrick H&S LLP -51 W 52nd -NY 10019
(716) 834-9181 .. **Smeader,** Michl A '04 %Blair & R,LLP -2645 Sheridan Dr -Tonawanda 14150
(212) 909-6000 .. **Smeall,** Christopher '82 (Debevoise & P LLP) -919 3rd Av -NY 10022
(212) 655-2143 .. **Smedes,** Bronwyn J '97 %Tower Insurance -120 Bway -NY 10271
(212) 698-3500 .. **Smedley,** Donald Scott '06 %Dechert LLP -1095 Av of Amer -NY 10036
(646) 557-5100 .. **Smedresman,** Peter S '75 (Patton B LLP) -1185 Av of Amer -NY 10036
(212) 490-3000 .. **Smedresman,** Scott M '08 %Wilson EME&D LLP -150 E 42nd -NY 10017
(212) 571-5022 .. **Smedresman,** Steven '81 S Smedresman,PC -41 Mad Av -NY 10010 **Fx:**619-3002
(212) 272-6682 .. **Smek,** Dagmar J '00 %JP Morgan Chase -383 Mad Av -NY 10179
(212) 813-1600 .. **Smeland,** Tor Einar '98 %Kalow & S -488 Mad Av -NY 10022
(212) 294-6700 .. **Smetana,** Brian S '05 %Winston & S -200 Park Av -NY 10166
(631) 390-4200 .. **Smetana,** Steven J '76 -201 Old Cntry Rd -Melvll 11747 **Fx:**385-5833
(212) 422-0202 .. **Smick,** Jos M '01 (Sedgwick DM&A LLP) -125 Broad -NY 10004
(212) 508-6700 .. **Smigel,** Beth B '01 (Tannenbaum HS&H LLP) -900 3rd Av -NY 10022
(631) 232-2400 .. **Smigelski,** Thos H '93 %Nassau/Sfflk Law Srv -1757 Vets Hwy -Islandia 11749 **Fx:**232-2489
(212) 935-3131 .. **Smiler,** Scott M '99 %Gallet D&B,LLP -845 3rd Av -NY 10022
(212) 986-2022 .. **Smiley,** Andrew J '97 (Smiley & S LLP) -60 E 42nd -NY 10165
(516) 229-6000 .. **Smiley,** Bruce R '84 %R Lau & Assoc -300 Jericho Quad Bx9040 -Jericho 11753 **Fx:**229-6167
(212) 455-2000 .. **Smiley,** Ellen B '04 %Simpson T&B LLP -425 Lex Av -NY 10017
(212) 986-2022 .. **Smiley,** Guy I '64 (Smiley & S LLP) -60 E 42nd -NY 10165
(212) 986-2022 .. **Smiley & Smiley LLP** -60 E 42nd -NY 10165 **Fx:**697-4689
(516) 571-3386 .. **Smiley,** Tammy J '87 %DA -262 Old Cntry Rd -Mineola 11501 **Fx:**248-9479
(631) 853-4049 .. **Smiloff,** Justin '07 %Cnty Atty -Dennison Bldg Bx6100 -Hauppauge 11788 **Fx:**853-5169
(212) 682-3025 .. **Smilow,** Mark D '94 %Weiss & L -551 5th Av -NY 10176
(212) 382-0909 .. **Smilow,** Michl E '08 %Peckar & A,PC -41 Mad Av -NY 10154
(516) 565-9573 .. **Smilowitz,** Alan '77 -676 Knollwood Dr -W Hempstead 11552 **Fx:**565-1306
(516) 565-9573 .. **Smilowitz,** Karen M '94 -676 Knollwood Dr -W Hempstead 11552 **Fx:**565-1306
(518) 457-2070 .. **Smirlock,** Danl '84 %Dept of Tax & Fin -Bldg 9 State Campus -Albany 12227 **Fx:**457-6131
(516) 357-3000 .. **Smirti,** Stephen J Jr. '77 (Rivkin R LLP) -926 RXR Plz -Uniondale 11556
(516) 572-2000 .. **Smit,** George J '09 %DA -99 Main -Hempstd 11550 **Fx:**572-2606
(212) 455-2000 .. **Smit,** Robt '86 (Simpson T&B LLP) -425 Lex Av -NY 10017
(516) 763-6700 .. **Smitelli,** Janet L H '87 Davidson & C,PC -265 Sunrise Hwy -Rockvll Ctr 11570
(212) 412-4000 .. **Smith,** A MacKenzie '06 Barclays Capital -200 Park Av -NY 10166 **Fx:**412-7300
(212) 454-7358 .. **Smith,** A Thos III '90 %Deutsche Bank -60 Wall -NY 10005
(212) 981-4501 .. **Smith Abbot,LLP** -90 Broad -NY 10004 **Fx:**981-4502
(212) 483-0105 .. **Smith,** Adam M '96 (Coughlin D LLP) -88 Pine-Wall St Plz -NY 10005
(212) 909-6000 .. **Smith,** Adam M '08 %Debevoise & P LLP -919 3rd Av -NY 10022
(212) 723-3124 .. **Smith,** Adrienne Y '01 Citigroup -250 West -NY 10013
(845) 634-7265 .. **Smith,** Alden B '84 -216 Congers Rd -New Cty 10956 **Fx:**638-9313
(845) 344-4322 .. **Smith,** Alex '78 -6 North -Middletwn 10940 **Fx:**341-1760
(212) 986-2251 .. **Smith,** Alfred E '91 -60 E 42nd -NY 10165 **Fx:**986-2238
(212) 850-6100 .. **Smith,** Alia Lyerly '01 %Levine SK&S,LLP -321 W 44th -NY 10036
(212) 416-8190 .. **Smith,** Alisha C '03 %Dept of Law -120 Bway -NY 10271
(212) 891-1600 .. **Smith,** Alixandra E '06 %Jenner & B LLP -919 3rd Av -NY 10022
(631) 727-3947 .. **Smith,** Allen M '67 -737 Roanoke Av -Rvrhead 11901 **Fx:**727-3950
(212) 450-4000 .. **Smith,** Alvey B '10 %Davis P&W LLP -450 Lex Av -NY 10017
(212) 819-8200 .. **Smith,** Alyna C '10 %White & C LLP -1155 Av of Amer -NY 10036
(212) 309-6000 .. **Smith,** Amanda D '99 (Morgan L&B LLP) -101 Park Av -NY 10178
(212) 461-2323 .. **Smith,** Amy K '07 %Saiber LLC -44 Wall -NY 10005
(518) 523-4580 .. **Smith,** Amy L '97 -282 Old Military Rd Bx687 -Lk Placid 12946 **Fx:**523-4380
(914) 798-5400 .. **Smith,** Andrea J '95 SpclCnsl Goldberg S LLP -11 Martine Av -White Plns 10606
(212) 425-5005 .. **Smith,** Andrea Kitzis '96 %Clemente M&T,PA -14 Wall -NY 10005
(212) 450-4000 .. **Smith,** Andrew A '04 %Davis P&W LLP -450 Lex Av -NY 10017
(212) 858-1000 .. **Smith,** Andrew C '03 %Pillsbury WSP LLP -1540 Bway -NY 10036
(212) 657-1229 .. **Smith,** Andrew H '94 Citigroup -111 Wall -NY 10005
(212) 930-9700 .. **Smith,** Andrew M '82 Cnsl Sichenzia RFF LLP -61 Bway -NY 10006
(212) 696-6000 .. **Smith,** Andrew M '08 %Curtis M-PC&M LLP -101 Park Av -NY 10178
(212) 455-2000 .. **Smith,** Andrew W '97 (Simpson T&B LLP) -425 Lex Av -NY 10017
(212) 318-3000 .. **Smith,** Anita Tucker '99 SrCnsl Fulbright & J LLP -666 5th Av -NY 10103
(845) 486-2280 .. **Smith,** Anne Marie '92 %Pub Def -22 Market -Poughkeepsie 12601 **Fx:**486-2266
(212) 269-0927 .. **Smith,** Annemarie M '96 (D'Amato & L,LLP) -2 World Fncl Ctr -NY 10281
(607) 721-8440 .. **Smith,** April J '92 %MHLS -44 Hawley -Bnghmtn 13901 **Fx:**721-8447
(212) 732-9800 .. **Smith,** Arthur J '90 (Baxter S&S,PC) -505 8th Av -NY 10018
(516) 997-7330 .. **Smith,** Arthur J '90 (Baxter S&S,PC) -99 N Bway -Hicksvll 11801
(716) 488-0758 .. **Smith,** Ashley E '09 %Bly SBP&M -3 Lakevw Av Bx3327 -Jamestwn 14702
(212) 735-3000 .. **Smith,** Aubry D '01 Cnsl Skadden ASM&F LLP -4 Times Sq -NY 10036
(212) 435-3571 .. **Smith,** Barbara C '02 %Port Auth of NY/NJ -225 Park Av S -NY 10003 **Fx:**435-3555
(212) 856-9060 .. **Smith,** Barry M '67 -331 Mad Av -NY 10017 **Fx:**983-0859
(212) 809-3154 .. **Smith,** Bernadette A '92 -65 Bway -NY 10006 **Fx:**809-4753
(914) 636-8138 .. **Smith,** Bernice W '83 -300 Pelham Rd -New Rchll 10805
(718) 520-3985 .. **Smith,** Beth P '84 Family Ct -89-14 Parsons Blvd -Jamaica 11432
(212) 599-1717 .. **Smith,** Beverly A '81 %Barnett EGK&L,PC -122 E 42nd -NY 10168
(212) 450-4000 .. **Smith,** Blake A '10 %Davis P&W LLP -450 Lex Av -NY 10017
(212) 446-2300 .. **Smith,** Brad G '05 %Boies S&F LLP -575 Lex Av -NY 10022
(212) 558-4000 .. **Smith,** Bradley P '98 SpclCnsl Sullivan & C LLP -125 Broad -NY 10004
(212) 450-4000 .. **Smith,** Bradley Y '75 (Davis P&W LLP) -450 Lex Av -NY 10017
(718) 250-2000 .. **Smith,** Brandon C '09 %DA -350 Jay -Brklyn 11201 **Fx:**250-2314
(212) 972-1355 .. **Smith,** Brandy A '03 %T Fleishell & Assoc PC -561 7th Av -NY 10018 **Fx:**972-1356
(718) 590-2000 .. **Smith,** Breanne M '08 %DA -198 E 161st -Bronx 10451 **Fx:**590-6477
(585) 394-7199 .. **Smith,** Brenda J '87 -493 S Main -Canandaigua 14424 **Fx:**394-6559
(212) 355-5575 .. **Smith,** Brian A '95 (Smith & N,LLP) -363 7th Av -NY 10001 **Fx:**486-3150
(212) 435-3571 .. **Smith,** Brian F '88 %Port Auth of NY/NJ -225 Park Av S -NY 10003 **Fx:**435-3555
(212) 732-3200 .. **Smith,** Brian G '09 %Carter L&M LLP -2 Wall -NY 10005
(518) 474-7330 .. **Smith,** Brian J '79 %Dept of Law -The Cptl -Albany 12224
(315) 437-7600 .. **Smith,** Brian J '01 %Ferrara FLB&R,PC -5010 Campuswood Dr -E Syracuse 13057
(516) 739-0000 .. **Smith,** Brian L '82 Martyn T&M -330 Old Cntry Rd -Mineola 11501
(914) 834-3322 .. **Smith,** Briscoe R '64 %Atlantic Lgl Fndtn -2039 Palmer Av -Larchmnt 10538 **Fx:**833-1022
(315) 218-8000 .. **Smith,** Brody D '04 %Bond S&K,PLLC -1 Lincoln Ctr -Syracuse 13202
(718) 402-1990 .. **Smith,** Bruce '64 (Dubow & S) -860 Grnd Cncrs -Bronx 10451
(315) 423-0400 .. **Smith,** Bruce A '89 (Wood & S,PC) -110 W Fayette -Syracuse 13202 **Fx:**424-1011
(212) 683-3520 .. **Smith,** Bruce F '70 (Jager S,PC) -485 Mad Av -NY 10022
(914) 476-0600 .. **Smith Buss & Jacobs,LLP** -733 Ynkrs Av -Ynkrs 10704 **Fx:**476-0614
(212) 688-2400 .. **Smith Buss & Jacobs,LLP** -500 5th Av -NY 10110 **Fx:**688-3058

(212) 906-1200 ..**Smith,** Cameron '07 %Latham & W -885 3rd Av -NY 10022
(212) 344-1500 ..**Smith Campbell,LLP** -110 Wall -NY 10005 **Fx:**344-5585
(212) 906-1200 ..**Smith,** Carla J '08 %Latham & W -885 3rd Av -NY 10022
(212) 790-0200 ..**Smith,** Carlton M '82 Benj N Cardozo Schl of Law -55 5th Av -NY 10003 **Fx:**790-0345
(716) 855-3611 ..**Smith,** Carrie L '90 (Smith MO&S,LLP) -69 Delaware Av -Buffalo 14202
(631) 499-5400 ..**Smith Carroad Levy PC** -5036 Jericho Tpk Bx49 -Commack 11725 **Fx:**493-0189
(585) 428-5755 ..**Smith,** Cary C '91 %Cnty Atty -50 W Main -Rchstr 14614 **Fx:**428-2031
(212) 239-4001 ..**Smith,** Casey J '08 %Rheem & B LLP -302 5th Av -NY 10001 **Fx:**239-4125
(212) 336-0170 ..**Smith,** Catherine M '97 %SEC -3 World Fncl Ctr -NY 10281 **Fx:**336-1323
(716) 836-7111 ..**Smith,** Cathleen W '85 %S Puleo -3659 Harlem Rd -Cheektowaga 14215 **Fx:**836-0219
(212) 460-6699 ..**Smith,** Celeste '81 Con Ed -4 Irving Pl -NY 10003
(212) 458-7024 ..**Smith,** Chas H III '00 AIG -175 Water -NY 10038
(212) 688-8555 ..**Smith,** Charlotte W '07 Fragomen DB&L LLP -7 Hanover Sq -NY 10004
(212) 374-6700 ..**Smith,** Cheryl A '02 %NYC Dept Educ -52 Chmbrs -NY 10007
(212) 848-4000 ..**Smith,** Chris M '77 (Shearman & S LLP) -599 Lex Av -NY 10022
(914) 949-9075 ..**Smith,** Christopher A '90 OfCnsl Trivella & F LLP -1311 Mamaroneck Av -White Plns 10605 **Fx:**949-4752
(607) 231-5900 ..**Smith,** Christopher A '06 %Leg Aid -30 Fayette -Bnghmtn 13901 **Fx:**724-7211
(716) 648-1400 ..**Smith,** Christopher D '03 -42 Lake -Hambrg 14075
(212) 458-1066 ..**Smith,** Christopher F '92 %AIG -175 Water -NY 10038
(212) 768-6700 ..**Smith,** Christopher G '05 %Sonnenschein N&R LLP -2 World Fncl Ctr -NY 10281
(516) 764-2800 ..**Smith,** Christopher K '07 %Goldberg & C -66 N Vllg Av -Rockvll Ctr 11570
(315) 471-3151 ..**Smith,** Christopher R '09 %Hancock & E,LLP -1500 AXA Twr I Bx4976 -Syracuse 13221
(212) 608-3200 ..**Smith,** Clarence Jr. '89 -305 Bway -NY 10007
(212) 819-8200 ..**Smith,** Claudia A '87 Cnsl White & C LLP -1155 Av of Amer -NY 10036
(914) 997-0900 ..**Smith,** Clinton B '79 (Wormser KG&J LLP) -399 Knollwood Rd -White Plns 10603
(212) 512-5029 ..**Smith,** Colette G '90 %HBO -1100 Av of Amer -NY 10036 **Fx:**512-5572
(212) 759-0304 ..**Smith,** Craig L '89 %Tiedermann Trust Co -535 Mad Av -NY 10022 **Fx:**759-0109
(631) 360-7570 ..**Smith,** Craig L '00 %Town Atty -99 W Main -Smithtwn 11787 **Fx:**360-7719
(212) 526-7000 ..**Smith,** Craig M '07 Barclays PLC -745 7th Av -NY 10019
(212) 219-1000 ..**Smith,** Dale Lionel '89 -99 Park Av -NY 10016
(212) 980-9600 ..**Smith,** Damien '05 %Kaufman B&R -120 Bway -NY 10271
(212) 779-1414 ..**Smith,** Dana Statsky '06 %Bernstein L LLP -10 E 40th -NY 10016
(516) 328-2300 ..**Smith,** Danl H '05 %Abrams FFEGF&E,LLP -1111 Marcus Av -Lk Success 11042
(516) 294-7301 ..**Smith,** Danl J '07 %D Smith -500 Old Cntry Rd -Gdn Cty 11530 **Fx:**393-7594
(518) 494-3171 ..**Smith,** Danl T '68 (Smith & S,LLC) -38 Art Tennyson Rd -Chestertwn 12817 **Fx:**494-7869
(315) 453-9426 ..**Smith,** Danl T '90 (Nicholas PSW&S) -219 1st Bx720 -Liverpool 13088
(516) 294-7301 ..**Smith,** David A '79 -500 Old Cntry Rd -Gdn Cty 11530 **Fx:**393-7594
(716) 856-9704 ..**Smith,** David B '94 (Feuerstein & S,LLP) -17 St Louis Pl -Buffalo 14202 **Fx:**856-9707
(516) 739-0000 ..**Smith,** David C '97 %Martyn T&M -330 Old Cntry Rd -Mineola 11501
(716) 857-7991 ..**Smith,** David F '79 %Natl Fuel Gas -6363 Main -Williamsvll 14221 **Fx:**857-7614
(212) 221-5700 ..**Smith,** David L '80 (Smith & N PLLC) -1501 Bway -NY 10036 **Fx:**221-6350
(212) 594-5000 ..**Smith,** David M '07 %Togut S&S LLP -1 Penn Plz -NY 10119
(212) 335-9000 ..**Smith,** David R '07 %DA -1 Hogan Pl -NY 10013
(212) 968-1001 ..**Smith,** David S '82 (Gwertzman LBS&M) -80 Broad -NY 10004
(212) 344-1500 ..**Smith,** David S '83 (Smith C,LLP) -110 Wall -NY 10005
(212) 559-3431 ..**Smith,** David S '86 Citigroup Invstmnts -731 Lex Av -NY 10022 **Fx:**793-4400
(212) 681-2800 ..**Smith,** David Scott '95 DS Smith,LLC -626 RXR Plz -Uniondale 11556 **Fx:**(917) 591-3244
(212) 681-2800 ..**Smith,** David Scott '95 DS Smith,LLC -275 Mad Av -NY 10016 **Fx:**(917) 591-3244
(212) 770-2162 ..**Smith,** David W '77 %Transatlantic Hldngs -80 Pine -NY 10005 **Fx:**785-7230
(212) 574-1200 ..**Smith,** David W '03 %Seward & K LLP -1 Bttry Pk Plz -NY 10004
(718) 990-2337 ..**Smith,** Dawne M '87 %St John's Law Schl -8000 Utopia Pkwy -Jamaica 11439 **Fx:**591-1855
(716) 633-3535 ..**Smith,** Dean P '90 %W Mattar,PC -6720 Main -Williamsvll 14221 **Fx:**631-9804
(917) 777-4200 ..**Smith,** Deanna M '07 %Bingham M LLP -1 Bttry Pk Plz -NY 10004
(585) 454-3377 ..**Smith,** Deborah Caruso '91 (Brown & T,LLC) -19 Prince -Rchstr 14607
(212) 587-0760 ..**Smith,** Derek T '95 (Akin & S,LLC) -30 Broad -NY 10004 **Fx:**587-4169
(718) 590-3219 ..**Smith,** Deven A '07 %Law Dept -198 E 161st -Bronx 10451 **Fx:**590-2686
(518) 457-6468 ..**Smith,** Diane B '85 %Agriculture & Mrkts -10B Airline Dr -Albany 12235 **Fx:**457-8842
(212) 389-5000 ..**Smith,** Diann L '95 Cnsl Sutherland A&B LLP -1114 Av of Amer -NY 10036
(585) 381-3866 ..**Smith,** Donald A W '80 (DAW Smith,PC) -125 Sullys Trl -Pittsfrd 14534 **Fx:**381-6907
(631) 231-2121 ..**Smith,** Donald B '83 DB Smith,PLLC -77 Arkay Dr -Hauppauge 11788 **Fx:**231-2120
(914) 967-7478 ..**Smith,** Donna Scovotti '82 -6 Platt Ln -Rye 10580 **Fx:**967-4536
(914) 745-4000 ..**Smith,** Dorian Z '99 %Towers Watson -100 Summit Lk Dr -Valhalla 10595
(914) 288-0400 ..**Smith,** Douglas J '02 %Priolet & Assoc,PC -1025 Wstchstr Av -White Plns 10604 **Fx:**288-0404
(631) 755-0100 ..**Smith & Downey,PA** -145 Pinelawn Rd -Melvll 11747 **Fx:**755-0110
(516) 794-4700 ..**Smith,** Drummond C '02 %T Liotti -600 Old Cntry Rd -Gdn Cty 11530 **Fx:**794-2816
(212) 682-0020 ..**Smith,** Dustan T '80 OfCnsl Putney TH&H LLP -521 5th Av -NY 10175
(212) 837-6126 ..**Smith,** Dustin P '09 %Hughes H&R LLP -1 Bttry Pk Plz -NY 10004
(212) 661-7010 ..**Smith,** E David '01 (Smith & Assoc) -570 Lex Av -NY 10022 **Fx:**661-8285
(212) 768-6700 ..**Smith,** E Lee '86 (Sonnenschein N&R LLP) -2 World Fncl Ctr -NY 10281
(212) 307-5500 ..**Smith,** Edw A '84 (Venable LLP) -1270 Av of Amer -NY 10020
(315) 474-2911 ..**Smith,** Edw J III '91 (Smith SK&S,PC) -250 S Clinton -Syracuse 13202
(516) 228-8484 ..**Smith,** Edw J '04 %Dilworth & B,LLP -1000 Woodbury Rd -Woodbury 11797
(212) 292-4270 ..**Smith,** Edw L '62 (Rockett & S) -521 5th Av -NY 10175 **Fx:**573-6355
(716) 852-1888 ..**Smith,** Edw L III '91 (Cantor LD&P,PC) -350 Main -Buffalo 14202
(212) 408-5100 ..**Smith,** Edw P '64 (Chadbourne & P LLP) -30 Rckfllr Plz -NY 10112
(212) 261-8000 ..**Smith,** Edw T '98 (Mendes & M,LLP) -750 7th Av -NY 10019
(212) 705-7000 ..**Smith,** Edwin E '05 (Bingham M LLP) -399 Park Av -NY 10022
(212) 227-3333 ..**Smith,** Edwin L '68 (Smith & L,LLP) -291 Bway -NY 10007
(716) 847-7632 ..**Smith,** Elaine A '87 %Div of Human Rights -65 Court -Buffalo 14202 **Fx:**847-7625
(212) 419-1500 ..**Smith,** Elaine L '98 (Lewis C&N,PC) -350 7th Av -NY 10001
(212) 221-5700 ..**Smith,** Elizabeth '96 (Goldberg WFG LLP) -1501 Bway -NY 10036
(212) 589-4200 ..**Smith,** Elizabeth A '83 (Baker & H LLP) -45 Rckfllr Plz -NY 10111
(212) 373-3000 ..**Smith,** Elizabeth L '07 %Paul WRW&G LLP -1285 Av of Amer -NY 10019
(212) 259-8000 ..**Smith,** Elizabeth Page '87 SpclCnsl Dewey & L LLP -1301 Av of Amer -NY 10019
(914) 377-6349 ..**Smith,** Elizabeth W '04 %Law Dept -100 S Bway -Ynkrs 10701
(718) 874-5999 ..**Smith,** Eon R '04 Smith & Co,PLLC -50 Court -Brklyn 11201
(315) 453-9426 ..**Smith,** Eric P '97 (Nicholas PSW&S) -219 1st Bx720 -Liverpool 13088
(212) 318-6000 ..**Smith,** Eric S '02 %Paul HJ&W LLP -75 E 55th -NY 10022
(212) 318-2000 ..**Smith,** Erica L '04 Bloomberg LP -731 Lex Av -NY 10022
(212) 632-3257 ..**Smith,** Erin Gilmore '06 Fiduciary Trust Co Intl -600 5th Av -NY 10020
(585) 987-2800 ..**Smith,** Erin W '07 %Woods OG LLP -2 State -Rchstr 14614
(212) 239-9669 ..**Smith,** Evan '95 %Catafago Law Firm -350 5th Av -NY 10118 **Fx:**239-9688
(518) 946-8223 ..**Smith,** Favor J '97 (F Smith,PC) -5964 NYS Route 86 -Wilmngtn 12997 **Fx:**946-8224
(631) 727-4100 ..**Smith Finkelstein Lundberg Isler & Yakaboski** -456 Griffing Av Bx389 -Rvrhead 11901 **Fx:**727-4130
(518) 447-3200 ..**Smith,** Francis J Jr. '81 (McNamee LT&W,PC) -677 Bway -Albany 12207
(516) 739-3443 ..**Smith,** Frank J Jr. '70 -229 7th -Gdn Cty 11530
(212) 440-2350 ..**Smith,** Fredk B '84 %C Siegel -40 Wall -NY 10005 **Fx:**440-2385
(212) 907-9700 ..**Smith Gambrell & Russell, LLP** -250 Park Av -NY 10177 **Fx:**907-9800
(212) 940-3000 ..**Smith,** Garrett K '76 Cnsl Nixon P LLP -437 Mad Av -NY 10022
(212) 416-8575 ..**Smith,** Garvin V '77 %Dept of Law -120 Bway -NY 10271
(631) 952-5555 ..**Smith,** Gary F '74 -330 Vndrblt Motor Pkwy -Hauppauge 11788 **Fx:**952-5600
(212) 944-0500 ..**Smith,** Gary N '05 %Hofheimer G&G,LLP -530 5th Av -NY 10036 **Fx:**897-7901
(914) 907-3329 ..**Smith,** Geoffrey D '78 Cnsl Hyatt S Assoc -20A Mdlnd Av -White Plns 10606 **Fx:**686-3460
(212) 250-0502 ..**Smith,** Geoffrey R '91 Deutsche Bank -60 Wall -NY 10005
(845) 291-7100 ..**Smith,** George A '88 (Murphy & L) -1997 State Route 17M -Goshen 10924
(212) 260-9588 ..**Smith,** George A '93 -23 Lex Av -NY 10010
(212) 408-5100 ..**Smith,** George Bundy '63 (Chadbourne & P LLP) -30 Rckfllr Plz -NY 10112
(315) 554-6858 ..**Smith,** George S II '91 Hand Held Products -Bx208 -Skaneateles Fls 13153
(212) 513-7927 ..**Smith,** Gerald S '01 %Law Dept -100 Church -NY 10007 **Fx:**788-0367
(212) 969-3000 ..**Smith,** Gershom R '04 %Proskauer R LLP -1585 Bway -NY 10036
(646) 810-6597 ..**Smith,** Glen P '99 Magnetar Capital LLC -500 Park Av -NY 10022
(585) 338-6800 ..**Smith,** Glenn D '01 %Bausch & Lomb -One Bausch & Lomb Pl -Rchstr 14604 **Fx:**338-8706
(973) 848-4700 ..**Smith,** Glenn J '98 (Littler M,PC) -900 3rd Av -NY 10022 **Fx:**643-5626
(516) 357-3700 ..**Smith,** Grace A '09 %Cullen and D LLP -100 Q Roosevelt Blvd -Gdn Cty 11530
(212) 489-1600 ..**Smith,** Gregg D '94 %Deloitte LLP -1633 Bway -NY 10019 **Fx:**492-4201
(212) 267-2042 ..**Smith,** Gregory G '90 -225 Bway -NY 10007 **Fx:**267-2048
(718) 210-3641 ..**Smith,** Gregory L '93 -155 Water -Brklyn 11201 **Fx:**872-9688
(516) 393-2200 ..**Smith,** Gregory R '00 %Garfunkel W,PC -111 Grt Nck Rd -Gt Neck 11021
(212) 805-3900 ..**Smith,** Gregory S '90 (Clausen M PC) -1 Chase Manh Plz -NY 10005
(718) 261-7700 ..**Smith,** Gregory T '95 %Rappaport HC&R,PC -118-35 Qns Blvd -Frst Hlls 11375
(516) 676-4600 ..**Smith,** H Brooks '81 %Humes & W -147 Forest Av Bx546 -Locust Vly 11560
(518) 489-1098 ..**Smith,** Hannelore F '08 %D Vincelette,PC -21 Everett Rd Ext -Albany 12205 **Fx:**489-3304
(212) 302-1113 ..**Smith,** Harold J '67 %Carpet Resources -37 W 39th -NY 10018
(212) 450-4000 ..**Smith,** Hayward H '02 %Davis P&W LLP -450 Lex Av -NY 10017
(212) 298-5240 ..**Smith,** Heather A '03 %Leg Aid -49 Thomas -NY 10013 **Fx:**298-5252
(212) 969-3000 ..**Smith,** Henry O III '78 SrCnsl Proskauer R LLP -1585 Bway -NY 10036
(212) 450-4000 ..**Smith,** Henry Oliver '05 %Davis P&W LLP -450 Lex Av -NY 10017
(212) 381-5251 ..**Smith,** Hillary B '97 %Doubleclick Inc -111 8th Av -NY 10011

(212) 489-1600 .. **Smith,** Howard A '80 %Deloitte LLP -1633 Bway -NY 10019 **Fx:**492-4201
(212) 451-2300 .. **Smith,** Howard J III '00 %Olshan GFR&W LLP -65 E 55th -NY 10022
(516) 626-1212 .. **Smith,** Howard M '79 -5 Deepwood Ct -Old Westbury 11568 **Fx:**626-1273
(718) 466-3000 .. **Smith,** Ilene '76 %Civil Ct -1118 Grnd Cncrs -Bronx 10456 **Fx:**466-3006
(212) 232-1300 .. **Smith,** Ivan D '89 (Lewis BB&S LLP) -77 Water -NY 10005
(212) 763-8610 .. **Smith,** J Ryan '00 Zuber & T LLP -1325 Av of Amer -NY 10019 **Fx:**763-8611
(212) 417-5822 .. **Smith,** Jacqueline A '89 Welfare Inspector Genl -22 Crtlandt -NY 10007 **Fx:**417-5849
(212) 373-3739 .. **Smith,** James C '80 Paul WRW&G LLP -1285 Av of Amer -NY 10019
(212) 216-8000 .. **Smith,** James G '95 (Tarter K&D LLP) -1350 Bway -NY 10018
(212) 402-9400 .. **Smith,** James H '08 %McKool S,PC -1 Bryant Park -NY 10036
(212) 259-8000 .. **Smith,** James P III '94 (Dewey & L LLP) -1301 Av of Amer -NY 10019
(315) 423-4400 .. **Smith,** James W '72 %Wolff G&G,LLP -217 Mntgmry -Syracuse 13202
(212) 981-4501 .. **Smith,** James W '83 (Smith A,LLP) -90 Broad -NY 10004
(716) 204-1055 .. **Smith,** Jamie M '04 %Pfalzgraf B&M LLP -455 Cayuga Rd -Buffalo 14225 **Fx:**204-1080
(845) 724-3415 .. **Smith,** Jane Simkin '81 -Bx1277 -Millbrook 12545 **Fx:**724-3417
(646) 862-8569 .. **Smith,** Janeen M '93 %Global Crossing -80 Pine -NY 10005
(212) 953-4100 .. **Smith,** Janice Keely '91 Overseas Shipholding Grp -666 3rd Av -NY 10017
(315) 277-5370 .. **Smith,** Jarrod W '04 -11 S Main Bx173 -Jordan 13080 **Fx:**277-5395
(212) 310-8000 .. **Smith,** Jason A B '98 (Weil G&M LLP) -767 5th Av -NY 10153
(212) 637-1026 .. **Smith,** Jason B '04 US Atty -1 St Andrews Plz -NY 10007
(518) 786-1800 .. **Smith,** Jay A '86 (Flink S LLC) -23 British Amer Blvd -Latham 12110 **Fx:**786-1969
(212) 361-8045 .. **Smith,** Jeannette R '96 DHS-Legal Affairs Div -33 Beaver -NY 10004
(212) 474-1000 .. **Smith,** Jeffrey A '94 (Cravath S&M LLP) -825 8th Av -NY 10019
(212) 545-4740 .. **Smith,** Jeffrey G '79 (Wolf HAF&H LLP) -270 Mad Av -NY 10016
(212) 424-7000 .. **Smith,** Jeffrey L '80 %Lifetime TV -309 W 49th -NY 10019 **Fx:**957-4447
(212) 705-7000 .. **Smith,** Jeffrey Q '78 (Bingham M LLP) -399 Park Av -NY 10022
(315) 424-1105 .. **Smith,** Jennifer Gale '86 (McMahon K&S,PC) -500 S Salina -Syracuse 13202
(212) 603-6300 .. **Smith,** Jennifer S '06 %Robinson BLGG&G PC -875 3rd Av -NY 10022
(315) 455-2000 .. **Smith,** Jennifer T '02 C&S -499 Col Eileen Collins Blvd -Syracuse 13212
(212) 909-6000 .. **Smith,** Jeremy B '07 %Debevoise & P LLP -919 3rd Av -NY 10022
(518) 426-4600 .. **Smith,** Jeremy M '01 (Couch W,LLP) -540 Bway Bx22222 -Albany 12201
(212) 761-4000 .. **Smith,** Jerry L '00 Morgan Stanley -1585 Bway -NY 10036
(212) 833-1155 .. **Smith,** Jessica Richman '06 %Friedman KS&A LLP -1633 Bway -NY 10019 **Fx:**373-7955
(518) 370-4793 .. **Smith,** Jill Novak '02 Cnsl MVP Health Care -625 State -Schnctdy 12305
(212) 806-5400 .. **Smith,** Joanna S '10 %Stroock &S&L LLP -180 Maiden Ln -NY 10038
(315) 376-3028 .. **Smith,** Joanne Kohler '75 -5393 Bostwick -Lowvll 13367
(212) 815-1818 .. **Smith,** Jocelyn A '01 %DC 37 MELS -125 Barclay -NY 10007 **Fx:**815-1343
(718) 579-3065 .. **Smith,** Jodi R '05 %Leg Aid -1020 Grnd Cncrs -Bronx 10451 **Fx:**588-2611
(585) 546-5530 .. **Smith,** Joel E '77 %Thomson West -50 E Broad -Rchstr 14694
(646) 386-5700 .. **Smith,** John '82 %Civil Ct -111 Centre -NY 10013
(212) 859-8000 .. **Smith,** Johnathan J '08 %Fried FHS&J LLP -1 NY Plz -NY 10004
(212) 827-7000 .. **Smith,** Jonathan B '05 TD Securities -31 W 52nd -NY 10019
(212) 450-4000 .. **Smith,** Jordan Leigh '04 %Davis P&W LLP -450 Lex Av -NY 10017
(212) 880-3800 .. **Smith,** Jordan M '04 %Akerman S -335 Mad Av -NY 10017
(212) 259-8000 .. **Smith,** Jos A '90 (Dewey & L LLP) -1301 Av of Amer -NY 10019
(212) 869-7000 .. **Smith,** Jos A '93 (Feldman W&S LLP) -420 Lex Av -NY 10170
(212) 685-6400 .. **Smith,** Joshua M '03 %Smith & S -116 E 27th -NY 10016
(585) 395-5835 .. **Smith,** Josie Neal '96 %SUNY Brockport -222 Holmes Hall -Brockprt 14420
(518) 587-5188 .. **Smith,** Joy M '03 %Leg Aid -112 Spring -Saratoga Spgs 12866 **Fx:**587-0959
(718) 286-6000 .. **Smith,** Joyce A '97 DA -125-01 Qns Blvd -Kew Gdns 11415
(585) 232-5600 .. **Smith,** Jules L '72 (Blitman & K LLP) -16 W Main -Rchstr 14614
(212) 223-4000 .. **Smith,** Julia K '05 Cnsl Crowell & M LLP -590 Mad Av -NY 10022
(212) 770-6647 .. **Smith,** Juliette S '98 %AIG -70 Pine -NY 10270
(212) 909-6000 .. **Smith,** Justin P '00 %Debevoise & P LLP -919 3rd Av -NY 10022
(212) 594-5300 .. **Smith,** K Leigh '00 (Milberg LLP) -1 Penn Plz -NY 10119
(212) 237-0000 .. **Smith,** Karen A '88 (Vinson & E LLP) -666 5th Av -NY 10103
(212) 417-8300 .. **Smith,** Karl H '99 %Research Fndtn CUNY -230 W 41st -NY 10036 **Fx:**417-8379
(212) 909-6000 .. **Smith,** Kate Kochendorfer '08 %Debevoise & P LLP -919 3rd Av -NY 10022
(212) 513-0462 .. **Smith,** Katherine E '08 %Law Dept -100 Church -NY 10007 **Fx:**788-0367
(585) 263-6760 .. **Smith,** Kathryn L '99 US Atty -620 Fed Bldg -Rchstr 14614 **Fx:**263-6226
(518) 548-2771 .. **Smith,** Katie M '05 (Lawrence & S PLLC) -2917 State Route 30 Bx156 -Speculator 12164 **Fx:**548-2447
(518) 499-1272 .. **Smith,** Kelly A '09 %Ryan S&C,PC -134 Main Bx75 -Whitehall 12887
(718) 250-2000 .. **Smith,** Kenneth F '07 %DA -350 Jay -Brklyn 11201 **Fx:**250-2314
(212) 245-4580 .. **Smith,** Kerry L '01 OfCnsl Shukat AHW&H,LLP -111 W 57th -NY 10019
(718) 260-2304 .. **Smith,** Kevin A '05 Hon C Sifton -225 Cadman Plz E -Brklyn 11201
(212) 408-5100 .. **Smith,** Kevin C '93 (Chadbourne & P LLP) -30 Rckfllr Plz -NY 10112
(212) 808-7800 .. **Smith,** Kevin J '98 %Kelley D&W LLP -101 Park Av -NY 10178
(212) 806-5400 .. **Smith,** Kevin L '73 (Stroock &S&L LLP) -180 Maiden Ln -NY 10038
(212) 364-8507 .. **Smith,** Kevin M '93 Time Warner Cable -60 Columbus Av -NY 10023 **Fx:**364-8460
(212) 306-3339 .. **Smith,** Kevin R '81 %Housing Auth -250 Bway -NY 10007
(212) 701-3000 .. **Smith,** Kim A '04 %Cahill G&R LLP -80 Pine -NY 10005 **Fx:**269-5420
(631) 941-3434 .. **Smith,** Kim M '03 (Burner S & Assoc LLP) -46 Route 25A -Setauket 11733 **Fx:**941-3443
(212) 612-3270 .. **Smith,** Kimberly K '09 %Mishcon de R NY LLP -200 Park Av -NY 10166
(212) 661-0279 .. **Smith & Krantz,LLP** -122 E 42nd -NY 10168
(315) 218-8000 .. **Smith,** Kristen E '06 %Bond S&K,PLLC -1 Lincoln Ctr -Syracuse 13202
(212) 728-8000 .. **Smith,** Kristen E '09 %Willkie F&G LLP -787 7th Av -NY 10019
(212) 578-2211 .. **Smith,** Kristin H '96 %MetLife -27-01 Qns Plz N -LIC 11101
(212) 878-8000 .. **Smith,** Kristin S '08 %Clifford C LLP -31 W 52nd -NY 10019
(718) 330-7861 .. **Smith,** Kyle B '10 SSA-ODAR -111 Lvngstn -Brklyn 11201
(516) 741-6565 .. **Smith,** Lainie E '09 %Meyer SE&K,PC -990 Stewart Av Bx9194 -Gdn Cty 11530
(516) 564-8000 .. **Smith,** Lance I '02 %J Hiebler & Assoc -901 Franklin Av -Gdn Cty 11530 **Fx:**564-1714
(212) 227-3333 .. **Smith & Laquercia, LLP** -291 Bway -NY 10007 **Fx:**732-5590
(212) 813-1600 .. **Smith,** Laura E '90 %Kalow & S -488 Mad Av -NY 10022
(212) 428-2504 .. **Smith,** Laura Lee '00 %OCA -25 Beaver -NY 10004
(718) 222-2304 .. **Smith,** Laurie T '95 %Law Dept -350 Jay -Brklyn 11201 **Fx:**222-2373
(607) 334-6800 .. **Smith,** Leonard W '76 -1 S Broad -Norwich 13815 **Fx:**336-7230
(914) 762-7478 .. **Smith,** Linda Kohl '91 -103 Old Briarcliff Rd -Briarclff Mnr 10510
(212) 474-1000 .. **Smith,** Lindsay J '10 %Cravath S&M LLP -825 8th Av -NY 10019
(212) 545-4603 .. **Smith,** Lisa Anne '96 (Wolf HAF&H LLP) -270 Mad Av -NY 10016
(718) 780-0337 .. **Smith,** Lisa C '79 %Bklyn Law Schl -250 Joralemon -Brklyn 11201 **Fx:**780-0393
(607) 772-7013 .. **Smith,** Lisa Daniels '02 Law Dept -City Hall 38 Hawley -Bnghmtn 13901 **Fx:**723-6164
(914) 682-7800 .. **Smith,** Lisa Fishman '90 OfCnsl Zarin & S -81 Main -White Plns 10601
(716) 847-8400 .. **Smith,** Lisa L '90 (Phillips L LLP) -3400 HSBC Ctr -Buffalo 14203
(212) 962-2910 .. **Smith,** Lisa R '86 %D Gold,PC -800 2nd Av -NY 10017 **Fx:**962-2919
(212) 977-9700 .. **Smith,** Lonica L '03 %Phillips N LLP -666 5th Av -NY 10103
(212) 533-6300 .. **Smith,** Lori M '91 NYSUT -52 Bway -NY 10004 **Fx:**995-2347
(212) 422-0202 .. **Smith,** Lori S '85 (Sedgwick DM&A LLP) -125 Broad -NY 10004
(212) 576-7000 .. **Smith,** Lorne M '94 %NYLIM -51 Mad Av -NY 10010
(315) 442-0100 .. **Smith,** Lynn H '60 (Gilberti SH&S,PC) -555 E Genesee -Syracuse 13202
(718) 525-6725 .. **Smith,** Lynn H '89 -120-23 171st -Jamaica 11434 **Fx:**712-7028
(212) 506-5000 .. **Smith,** M Brendan '07 %Orrick H&S LLP -51 W 52nd -NY 10019
(716) 938-9111 .. **Smith,** M Kathryn '81 %Surrogates Ct -303 Court -Little Vly 14755 **Fx:**938-6983
(518) 462-3000 .. **Smith,** Marcia B '97 (Iseman CR&H,LLP) -9 Thurlow Ter -Albany 12203
(845) 657-8140 .. **Smith,** Margaret R '84 -94 Glenford Wttnbrg Rd -Glenford 12433
(845) 639-3445 .. **Smith,** Margaret R '04 OfCnsl C Bilotta -14 S Main -New Cty 10956 **Fx:**639-3442
(631) 369-0157 .. **Smith,** Marguerite A '75 -Bx959 -Southampton 11969
(845) 486-2300 .. **Smith,** Marjorie J '81 %DA -236 Main -Poughkeepsie 12601 **Fx:**486-2324
(845) 365-6335 .. **Smith,** Marjorie M '71 -102 Paradise Av Bx234 -Piermont 10968 **Fx:**365-2358
(914) 747-8184 .. **Smith,** Mark A '87 -Bx2690 -Briarclff Mnr 10510 **Fx:**747-1094
(212) 735-3000 .. **Smith,** Mark C '84 (Skadden ASM&F LLP) -4 Times Sq -NY 10036
(585) 232-6500 .. **Smith,** Mark C '09 %Harter S&E LLP -1600 Bausch & Lomb Pl -Rchstr 14604
(607) 734-1315 .. **Smith,** Mark H '98 (Barton S&B,LLP) -304 E Church -Elmira 14901 **Fx:**734-1326
(212) 755-5200 .. **Smith,** Mark W '96 (Smith V PLLC) -509 Mad Av -NY 10022 **Fx:**755-5203
(716) 200-5050 .. **Smith,** Marnie E '10 %Harris B PLLC -726 Exchange -Buffalo 14210
(914) 328-0404 .. **Smith,** Mary A '91 OfCnsl Jackson L LLP -1 N Bway -White Plns 10601
(212) 468-4800 .. **Smith,** Matthew E '04 %Davis & G LLP -1740 Bway -NY 10019
(212) 474-1000 .. **Smith,** Matthew E '06 %Cravath S&M LLP -825 8th Av -NY 10019
(518) 474-4623 .. **Smith,** Matthew J '92 Lt Gov's Ofc -The Cptl -Albany 12224
(212) 509-6300 .. **Smith,** Matthew J '94 (Melli GW&M) -17 Battery Pl -NY 10004
(914) 476-0600 .. **Smith,** Matthew J '04 %Smith B&J,LLP -733 Ynkrs Av -Ynkrs 10704
(212) 474-1000 .. **Smith,** Maura Caffrey '06 %Cravath S&M LLP -825 8th Av -NY 10019
(212) 664-4444 .. **Smith,** Maureen N '02 %NBC -30 Rckfllr Plz -NY 10112
(212) 832-0400 .. **Smith,** Maurice L '02 Berdon LLP -360 Mad Av -NY 10017 **Fx:**371-1159
(212) 964-7400 .. **Smith Mazure Director Wilkins Young & Yagerman, PC** -111 John -NY 10038 **Fx:**374-1935
(212) 768-4900 .. **Smith,** Megan S '09 %Gage S&F -410 Park Av -NY 10022
(212) 415-7587 .. **Smith,** Melanie '91 Merrill Lynch -717 5th Av -NY 10022 **Fx:**415-7905
(585) 753-1380 .. **Smith,** Merideth H '88 %Cnty Atty -307 Cnty Ofc Bldg -Rchstr 14614 **Fx:**753-1331
(212) 213-8585 .. **Smith,** Miatta Haj '84 NY Beacon -237 W 37th -NY 10018 **Fx:**213-6291
(212) 521-5400 .. **Smith,** Michl A '00 (Reed S LLP) -599 Lex Av -NY 10022
(212) 248-3140 .. **Smith,** Michl A '09 %Drinker B&R LLP -140 Bway -NY 10005
(650) 849-5338 .. **Smith,** Michl B '01 %Gibson D&C LLP -200 Park Av -NY 10166 **Fx:**849-5038
(212) 795-6630 .. **Smith,** Michl F '87 Smith & S,PC -600 W 161st -NY 10032 **Fx:**740-1498
(212) 270-0942 .. **Smith,** Michl H '73 JP Morgan Chase -270 Park Av -NY 10017
(212) 682-3454 .. **Smith,** Michl H '80 (Rosenberg FS LLP) -551 5th Av -NY 10176
(518) 429-4200 .. **Smith,** Michl J '76 (Hiscock & B,LLP) -50 Beaver -Albany 12207
(212) 310-2201 .. **Smith,** Michl J '06 %Colgate-Palmolive -300 Park Av -NY 10022 **Fx:**310-3406
(716) 753-4241 .. **Smith,** Michl P '92 %DA -Cnty Cthse -Mayvll 14757 **Fx:**753-4628
(212) 885-5000 .. **Smith,** Michl P '02 %Blank R LLP -405 Lex Av -NY 10174
(212) 732-8705 .. **Smith,** Michl S '77 (MS Smith & Assoc) -30 Vesey -NY 10007

(212) 770-5197 .. **Smith,** Michl S '02 AIG -70 Pine -NY 10270
(212) 819-8200 .. **Smith,** Michl W '81 (White & C LLP) -1155 Av of Amer -NY 10036
(585) 613-1999 .. **Smith,** Michele Owdienko '98 City Corp Cnsl -2 N Main -Canandaigua 14424 **Fx:**396-5016
(646) 386-3864 .. **Smith,** Michelle Morcos '99 Sup Ct -100 Centre -NY 10013
(716) 855-3611 .. **Smith Miner O'Shea & Smith, LLP** -69 Delaware Av -Buffalo 14202 **Fx:**855-3250
(716) 852-1544 .. **Smith Murphy & Schoepperle, LLC** -786 Ellicott Sq Bldg -Buffalo 14203 **Fx:**852-3559
(914) 333-6844 .. **Smith,** Mylyn Alexander '01 Cnsl Bayer Health Care LLC -555 Wht Plns Rd -Tarrytwn 10591 **Fx:**366-1880
(718) 243-6293 .. **Smith,** Natalie L '03 %Leg Aid -111 Lvngstn -Brklyn 11201 **Fx:**237-8737
(212) 227-7062 .. **Smith,** Nathaniel B '88 -111 Bway -NY 10006 **Fx:**346-4665
(315) 474-7571 .. **Smith,** Neil J '06 %Mackenzie H LLP -101 S Salina Bx4967 -Syracuse 13221
(212) 530-5000 .. **Smith,** Nicholas A '03 %Milbank TH&M LLP -1 Chase Manh Plz -NY 10005
(718) 340-4541 .. **Smith,** Nicole L '05 %CUNY Law Schl -65-21 Main -Flushng 11367 **Fx:**340-4482
(212) 558-4000 .. **Smith,** Nicole R '10 %Sullivan & C LLP -125 Broad -NY 10004
(212) 406-6783 .. **Smith,** Oliver A '87 -225 Bway -NY 10007
(212) 839-5300 .. **Smith,** Owen H '06 %Sidley A LLP -787 7th Av -NY 10019
(516) 712-4000 .. **Smith,** Pamela A '98 %Milber MP&S LLP -1000 Woodbury Rd -Woodbury 11797
(212) 335-4500 .. **Smith,** Patrick J '91 DLA Piper LLP -1251 Av of Amer -NY 10020
(631) 577-2400 .. **Smith,** Peter D '99 %Tromello M&K -25 Melvll Park Rd Bx9038 -Melvll 11747
(315) 361-4001 .. **Smith,** Peter E '82 -Bx543 -Wampsville 13163
(212) 715-9100 .. **Smith,** Peter G '79 (Kramer LN&F,LLP) -1177 Av of Amer -NY 10036
(212) 262-2390 .. **Smith,** Peter J '88 (Connell F LLP) -888 7th Av -NY 10106
(518) 725-7195 .. **Smith,** Peter K '74 (Maider & S) -37 E Fulton -Gloversvll 12078
(212) 632-6000 .. **Smith,** Peter L '69 %Lazard Freres -30 Rckfllr Plz -NY 10112 **Fx:**632-6060
(212) 344-5680 .. **Smith,** Peter W '91 (Thompson H LLP) -335 Mad Av -NY 10017
(212) 766-1888 .. **Smith,** Philip J '81 %Morris DA&F -2 Rector -NY 10006
(212) 685-5509 .. **Smith,** Philip J '92 OfCnsl Rowland & P -2 Park Av -NY 10016
(646) 557-5100 .. **Smith,** Philip M '90 (Patton B LLP) -1185 Av of Amer -NY 10036
(212) 309-6206 .. **Smith,** Philippa J '95 HBO -1100 Av of Amer -NY 10036
(917) 637-3600 .. **Smith,** Priscilla J '03 Ctr for Reproductive Rts -120 Wall -NY 10005 **Fx:**637-3666
(718) 876-6300 .. **Smith,** Quentin F '91 %DA -130 Styvsnt Pl -Staten Isl 10301
(212) 478-3673 .. **Smith,** R Sharon '98 Syncora Guarantee Inc -825 8th Av -NY 10019
(212) 687-3860 .. **Smith,** Ralph K Jr. '52 (Snow BK,PC) -605 3rd Av -NY 10158
(631) 470-9525 .. **Smith,** Randall B '76 R Smith,PC -20 Broadhllw Rd -Melvll 11747 **Fx:**470-9528
(212) 474-1000 .. **Smith,** Raneshia L '07 %Cravath S&M LLP -825 8th Av -NY 10019
(914) 946-8800 .. **Smith Ranscht Connors & Mutino, PC** -235 Main -White Plns 10601 **Fx:**946-8861
(631) 941-4411 .. **Smith,** Raymond F '87 -290 Main -E Setauket 11733
(212) 479-6000 .. **Smith,** Reed A '99 %Cooley LLP -1114 Av of Amer -NY 10036
(212) 412-2478 .. **Smith,** Richd D '94 Barclays Capital -200 Park Av -NY 10166
(518) 533-3000 .. **Smith,** Richd L '72 (Bond S&K,PLLC) -111 Wshngtn Av -Albany 12210
(585) 258-5403 .. **Smith,** Richd L '80 (JP Morgan Chase) -1 Chase Sq -Rchstr 14643 **Fx:**258-6458
(315) 433-0100 .. **Smith,** Richd P '80 %Dairylea Cooperative Inc -Bx4844 -Syracuse 13221 **Fx:**433-2345
(212) 762-7497 .. **Smith,** Richd P '98 Morgan Stanley -1221 Av of Amer -NY 10020
(516) 431-3777 .. **Smith,** Robt A '62 -68 W Park Av Bx58 -Long Bch 11561
(518) 761-7696 .. **Smith,** Robt A '97 Cnty Ct -1340 State Route 9 -Lk George 12845
(212) 949-9022 .. **Smith,** Robt B '77 OfCnsl Abelman F&S -666 3rd Av -NY 10017
(212) 648-6015 .. **Smith,** Robt C '84 %JP Morgan Chase & Co -60 Wall -NY 10260
(212) 940-8850 .. **Smith,** Robt E '60 Cnsl Katten MR LLP -575 Mad Av -NY 10022
(212) 499-0940 .. **Smith,** Robt G '74 -261 Mad Av -NY 10016
(585) 263-6201 .. **Smith,** Robt G '78 %Fed Pub Def -28 E Main -Rchstr 14614 **Fx:**263-5871
(315) 422-1311 .. **Smith,** Robt G '89 %Melvin & M,PLLC -217 S Salina -Syracuse 13202
(315) 422-1152 .. **Smith,** Robt J '84 (Costello C&F,PLLC) -500 Plum -Syracuse 13204
(212) 922-0394 .. **Smith,** Robt J '84 -370 Lex Av -NY 10017 **Fx:**214-0819
(516) 229-6000 .. **Smith,** Robt M '96 %R Lau & Assoc -300 Jericho Quad Bx9040 -Jericho 11753 **Fx:**229-6167
(212) 820-9662 .. **Smith,** Robt P '90 (Hawkins D&W LLP) -One Chase Manh Plz -NY 10005
(212) 878-8000 .. **Smith,** Robt Thornton '70 (Clifford C LLP) -31 W 52nd -NY 10019
(718) 403-9599 .. **Smith,** Robin C '92 -44 Court -Brklyn 11201
(212) 350-1459 .. **Smith,** Robin M '00 JP Morgan Chase -909 3rd Av -NY 10022
(607) 962-4641 .. **Smith,** Roger W III '88 (Welch & Z) -19 E Market -Corning 14830
(212) 368-7191 .. **Smith,** Ronald M '84 -720 Lenox Av -NY 10039
(516) 393-6116 .. **Smith,** Rory A '93 %S Rubin -999 Stewart Av -Bethpage 11714 **Fx:**393-6150
(718) 276-7512 .. **Smith,** Rudolph D Jr. '72 -179-51 Andrsn Rd -Jamaica 11434
(212) 370-1843 .. **Smith,** Russell A '86 (SmithDehn LLP) -381 Park Av S -NY 10016
(914) 997-0555 .. **Smith,** Russell B '90 Quinn & M,LLP -399 Knollwood Rd -White Plns 10603
(212) 492-4067 .. **Smith,** Russell F III '00 Deloitte Touche Tohmatsu -1633 Bway -NY 10019
(914) 948-8432 .. **Smith,** Russell M '72 -333 Ridgeway Av -White Plns 10605 **Fx:**948-8432
(716) 842-2800 .. **Smith,** Ryan G '08 %Webster S LLP -1400 Lbrty Bldg -Buffalo 14202
(212) 629-5590 .. **Smith,** S Jean '87 (SJ Smith,PC) -45 W 34th -NY 10001 **Fx:**629-5591
(212) 867-4466 .. **Smith,** S Stewart '88 %Belkin BW&G,LLP -270 Mad Av -NY 10016
(212) 460-4502 .. **Smith,** Saddie L '79 Con Ed -4 Irving Pl -NY 10003
(585) 387-0500 .. **Smith,** Sally A '77 (Olver K LLP) -100 Ofc Park Way -Pittsfrd 14534
(212) 931-7300 .. **Smith,** Saml B V '04 %Ernst & Young LLP -5 Times Sq -NY 10036
(518) 449-8893 .. **Smith,** Sandra McDermott '90 (Wilson EME&D LLP) -677 Bway -Albany 12207
(585) 428-6990 .. **Smith,** Scott C '79 Law Dept -30 Church -Rchstr 14614 **Fx:**428-6950
(212) 401-0800 .. **Smith,** Scott D '08 %Disciplinary Comm -61 Bway -NY 10006 **Fx:**287-1045
(212) 841-1000 .. **Smith,** Scott F '81 (Covington & B LLP) -620 8th Av -NY 10018
(585) 546-6312 .. **Smith,** Scott H '72 -197 S Fitzhugh -Rchstr 14608 **Fx:**546-2793
(212) 885-5000 .. **Smith,** Scott R '87 (Blank R LLP) -405 Lex Av -NY 10174
(973) 228-5700 .. **Smith,** Sean A '02 %Brach E LLC -100 Park Av -NY 10017 **Fx:**228-7852
(518) 432-1100 .. **Smith,** Sean E '99 %NYPTI -107 Columbia -Albany 12210 **Fx:**432-1180
(212) 733-1112 .. **Smith,** Seana H '00 %Pfizer Inc -150 E 42nd -NY 10017
(914) 762-7478 .. **Smith,** Seth S '85 -103 Old Briarcliff Rd -Briarclff Mnr 10510
(212) 318-3000 .. **Smith,** Shani S '07 %Fulbright & J LLP -666 5th Av -NY 10103
(212) 506-2500 .. **Smith,** Shannon L '06 Westwood One,Inc -1114 Av of Amer -NY 10036
(212) 685-6400 .. **Smith & Shapiro** -116 E 27th -NY 10016 **Fx:**779-7881
(646) 227-3441 .. **Smith,** Shaun E '03 Memorial Sloan Kettering -633 3rd Av -NY 10017
(716) 853-8100 .. **Smith,** Sheldon K '02 %Nixon P LLP -40 Fountain Plz -Buffalo 14202
(315) 474-2911 .. **Smith Sovik Kendrick & Sugnet,PC** -250 S Clinton -Syracuse 13202 **Fx:**474-6015
(716) 433-5921 .. **Smith Speranza Foltz & May** -131 East Av Bx540 -Lockprt 14095 **Fx:**439-5941
(212) 228-5597 .. **Smith,** Stanley V '92 -249 E 7th -NY 10009 **Fx:**780-0065
(718) 767-3333 .. **Smith,** Stephen J '95 %Borchert GL&L,PC -19-02 Whitestone Expy -Whitestone 11357
(718) 743-5800 .. **Smith,** Steven '05 -2402 Gerritsen Av -Brklyn 11229
(315) 724-1530 .. **Smith,** Steven A '84 (McLane S and L,LLP) -20 Elizabeth Bx524 -Utica 13503 **Fx:**724-1852
(631) 577-7990 .. **Smith,** Steven A '89 (Sales & S) -68 S Srvc Rd -Melvll 11747 **Fx:**577-7991
(212) 698-3500 .. **Smith,** Steven B '01 Cnsl Dechert LLP -1095 Av of Amer -NY 10036
(212) 335-4500 .. **Smith,** Steven L '06 %DLA Piper LLP -1251 Av of Amer -NY 10020
(516) 741-5454 .. **Smith,** Steven R '88 -1050 Franklin Av -Gdn Cty 11530 **Fx:**741-5557
(212) 768-3878 .. **Smith Stratton Wise Heher & Brennan,LLP** -100 Park Av -NY 10017 **Fx:**768-3978
(212) 759-8285 .. **Smith,** Stuart A '64 -460 Park Av -NY 10022 **Fx:**223-0072
(212) 788-1100 .. **Smith,** Stuart D '87 %Law Dept -100 Church -NY 10007 **Fx:**788-0367
(845) 623-3332 .. **Smith,** Susan M '92 -101 N Mddltwn Rd -Nanuet 10954 **Fx:**623-1051
(718) 254-9300 .. **Smith,** Susan M '98 -26 Court -Brklyn 11242 **Fx:**(347) 493-3555
(518) 862-3334 .. **Smith,** Suzanne D '96 %Newkirk Products -15 Corp Cir -Albany 12203 **Fx:**862-3371
(212) 953-2381 .. **Smith,** Suzanne L '97 %Rubin F&F,LLP -292 Mad Av -NY 10017
(212) 907-7300 .. **Smith,** Sydney R '98 %Golenbock EAB&P -437 Mad Av -NY 10022
(914) 242-7821 .. **Smith,** Tara E '00 Prof Indemnity Agency -37 Radio Circle Dr Bx5000 -Mt Kisco 10549 **Fx:**241-8098
(716) 855-3611 .. **Smith,** Terry D '66 (Smith MO&S,LLP) -69 Delaware Av -Buffalo 14202
(718) 286-6000 .. **Smith,** Theresa E '92 %DA -125-01 Qns Blvd -Kew Gdns 11415
(518) 474-4755 .. **Smith,** Thos D '83 %Ofc of Cyber Security -30 S Pearl -Albany 12207
(646) 857-1129 .. **Smith,** Thos E '02 AIG -32 Old Slip -NY 10005
(585) 232-6500 .. **Smith,** Thos G '75 (Harter S&E LLP) -1600 Bausch & Lomb Pl -Rchstr 14604
(315) 234-8500 .. **Smith,** Thos G '90 US Courts -100 S Clinton Bx7367 -Syracuse 13261 **Fx:**234-8501
(914) 949-2909 .. **Smith,** Thos M '83 (Eckert SC&M,LLC) -10 Bank -White Plns 10606
(212) 336-0171 .. **Smith,** Thos P Jr. '08 %SEC -3 World Fncl Ctr -NY 10281 **Fx:**336-1323
(315) 218-8000 .. **Smith,** Thos R '79 (Bond S&K,PLLC) -1 Lincoln Ctr -Syracuse 13202
(716) 845-7476 .. **Smith,** Thos R '90 %Family Ct -1 Niagara Plz -Buffalo 14202 **Fx:**858-7789
(914) 476-0600 .. **Smith,** Thos W '84 (Smith B&J,LLP) -733 Ynkrs Av -Ynkrs 10704
(646) 447-6178 .. **Smith,** Timothy F '79 Emblem Hlth Srvcs Co LLC -55 Water -NY 10041
(212) 335-9000 .. **Smith,** Timothy J '05 %DA -1 Hogan Pl -NY 10013
(914) 328-2969 .. **Smith,** Timothy M '96 (Martin C&B LLP) -245 Main -White Plns 10601
(518) 523-3300 .. **Smith,** Timothy R '74 -2296 Saranac Av -Lk Placid 12946 **Fx:**523-2480
(646) 733-3200 .. **Smith,** Todd F '96 %US Customs -1 Penn Plz -NY 10119 **Fx:**733-3243
(315) 473-0899 .. **Smith,** Todd M '02 %Anelli X,PC -441 S Salina -Syracuse 13202 **Fx:**473-0530
(718) 250-4297 .. **Smith,** Todd P '01 %Leg Aid -111 Lvngstn -Brklyn 11201 **Fx:**250-4243
(585) 396-7189 .. **Smith,** Tracey Quick '87 Constellation Wines US Inc -235 N Blmfld Rd -Canandaigua 14424
(212) 425-9300 .. **Smith,** Tracey Salmon '91 Cnsl Bressler A&R,PC -17 State -NY 10004
(518) 283-4100 .. **Smith,** Trey YC '87 (Smith H LLC) -105 Jordan Rd -Troy 12180
(212) 216-8000 .. **Smith,** Trisha L '00 Cnsl Tarter K&D LLP -1350 Bway -NY 10018
(718) 590-2000 .. **Smith,** Troy A '93 %DA -198 E 161st -Bronx 10451 **Fx:**590-6477
(212) 696-6000 .. **Smith,** Turner P '80 (Curtis M-PC&M LLP) -101 Park Av -NY 10178
(718) 254-7000 .. **Smith,** Tyler J '05 %US Atty -271 Cadman Plz E -Brklyn 11201 **Fx:**254-6479
(212) 903-9000 .. **Smith,** Ulysses S IV '08 %Linklaters -1345 Av of Amer -NY 10105
(631) 351-3042 .. **Smith,** Valerie E '94 Town Atty -100 Main -Huntngtn 11743 **Fx:**351-3032
(315) 298-5217 .. **Smith,** Walter W '60 -4836 N Jffrsn Bx211 -Pulaski 13142
(518) 489-5600 .. **Smith,** Wayne A Jr. '04 (Smith P,PLLC) -Bx128 -Slingerlnds 12159 **Fx:**489-0550
(518) 393-1371 .. **Smith,** Wayne P '68 -157 Barrett -Schnctdy 12305 **Fx:**393-6030
(212) 661-0279 .. **Smith,** Wayne R '84 (Smith & K,LLP) -122 E 42nd -NY 10168
(212) 536-3900 .. **Smith,** Whitney J '95 (K&L Gates LLP) -599 Lex Av -NY 10022

(212) 701-3000 .. **Smith,** Whitney M '07 %Cahill G&R LLP -80 Pine -NY 10005 **Fx:**269-5420
(718) 351-5814 .. **Smith,** Wm A Jr. '60 -65 Mplwd Av -Staten Isl 10306
(716) 501-2007 .. **Smith,** Wm A Jr. '85 Seneca Gaming Corp -310 4th -Niagara Fls 14303 **Fx:**501-2898
(212) 395-6495 .. **Smith,** Wm D '83 %Verizon -140 West -NY 10007
(845) 634-2221 .. **Smith,** Wm F '85 -317 Little Tor Rd S -New Cty 10956 **Fx:**634-6538
(212) 363-6900 .. **Smith,** Wm J '95 (Faust GS&B LLP) -2 Rector -NY 10006
(585) 987-2800 .. **Smith,** Wm P Jr. '92 (Woods OG LLP) -2 State -Rchstr 14614
(212) 504-6000 .. **Smith,** Zachary H '04 %Cadwalader W&T LLP -1 World Fncl Ctr -NY 10281
(212) 474-1000 .. **Smith,** Zachary R '09 %Cravath S&M LLP -825 8th Av -NY 10019
(212) 425-9300 .. **Smitham,** David G '04 %Bressler A&R,PC -17 State -NY 10004
(212) 428-2150 .. **Smithberg,** Ellen '81 %OCA -25 Beaver -NY 10004 **Fx:**428-2155
(212) 479-6000 .. **Smithberg,** Nicholas E '95 %Cooley LLP -1114 Av of Amer -NY 10036
(212) 370-1843 .. **SmithDehn LLP** -381 Park Av S -NY 10016 **Fx:**(646) 417-7974
(212) 297-0200 .. **Smithers,** Barbara L '78 Cnsl ABM Indstrs Inc -551 5th Av -NY 10176 **Fx:**297-0375
(212) 965-2200 .. **Smith-Evans,** Leticia V '06 %NAACP/LDF -99 Hudson -NY 10013 **Fx:**226-7592
(516) 546-2046 .. **Smith-Hill,** Norma P A '91 -3517 Milburn Av -Baldwin 11510 **Fx:**546-4352
(212) 261-7000 .. **Smith Howard,** Christine M '94 %Calyon -1301 Av of Amer -NY 10019
(212) 779-9910 .. **Smithline,** Fredk E '56 Cnsl Eaton & V LLP -3 Park Av -NY 10016
(646) 758-6752 .. **Smithline,** Richd '85 Centrecourt Asset Mgmt -350 Mad Av -NY 10017
(212) 468-8000 .. **Smithline,** Ruti '03 %Morrison & F LLP -1290 Av of Amer -NY 10104
(631) 269-3119 .. **Smith-Mines,** Lita '82 -24 Oak Meadow Rd -Commack 11725
(212) 588-9080 .. **Smithsimon,** Molly '04 Conover Law Ofc -75 Rckfllr Pl -NY 10019 **Fx:**763-5001
(607) 273-0075 .. **Smithson,** Frank '77 -102 E State -Ithaca 14850
(631) 283-6400 .. **Smith-Stahl,** Marianne Crossley '97 %JM Hazelton,PC -176 N Sea Rd Bx5041 -Southampton 11969 **Fx:**283-5385
(212) 788-1580 .. **Smith-Williams,** Qiana C '05 %Law Dept -100 Church -NY 10007 **Fx:**788-0367
(212) 632-5500 .. **Smits,** Robt K '90 (Salans LLP) -620 5th Av -NY 10020
(212) 557-2800 .. **Smoak,** Evan L '93 (Barger & W LLP) -10 E 40th -NY 10016
(212) 809-7074 .. **Smodish,** Susan D '79 %Armienti DG&R,LLP -39 Bway -NY 10006
(212) 877-3846 .. **Smoke,** Gary S '84 -666 W End Av -NY 10025
(212) 530-5000 .. **Smokowski,** Krista A '07 %Milbank TH&M LLP -1 Chase Manh Plz -NY 10005
(315) 253-3293 .. **Smolak,** Jan M '87 (Michaels & S,PC) -71 South -Auburn 13021
(718) 499-5633 .. **Smolansky,** Innes '96 -761 Carroll -Brklyn 11215 **Fx:**499-5632
(212) 701-3000 .. **Smolansky,** Jennifer E '06 %Cahill G&R LLP -80 Pine -NY 10005 **Fx:**269-5420
(212) 373-3000 .. **Smolansky,** Nicholas J '02 %Paul WRW&G LLP -1285 Av of Amer -NY 10019
(718) 838-7878 .. **Smolar,** Karen G '93 %Bronx Defenders -860 Crtlandt Av -Bronx 10451 **Fx:**665-0100
(212) 551-0464 .. **Smolarchik,** Yaara T '05 Israel Ministry of Def -800 2nd Av -NY 10017
(716) 685-2400 .. **Smolarek,** Danl L '93 -2998 Union Rd -Cheektowaga 14227 **Fx:**685-6500
(716) 685-2400 .. **Smolarek,** Lisa Anne '95 -2998 Union Rd -Cheektowaga 14227
(917) 324-1948 .. **Smolarz,** Roy B '91 Dominick & Dominick LLC -150 E 52nd -NY 10022
(718) 896-5131 .. **Smolek,** Norman C '81 -105-05 69th Av -Frst Hlls 11375
(516) 482-0033 .. **Smolen,** Howard '79 (Smolen & S) -360 Grt Nck Rd -Gt Neck 11021 **Fx:**773-9858
(516) 482-0033 .. **Smolen,** Jack '49 (Smolen & S) -360 Grt Nck Rd -Gt Neck 11021 **Fx:**773-9858
(212) 436-6499 .. **Smolens,** Robt M '85 Deloitte & Touche,LLP -2 World Fncl Ctr -NY 10281
(631) 665-3400 .. **Smolenski,** Raymond M '84 %Siben & S,LLP -90 E Main Bx149P -Bay Shr 11706
(212) 416-8000 .. **Smoler,** Arlene R '89 %Dept of Law -120 Bway -NY 10271
(212) 836-8000 .. **Smolev,** Richd G '03 (Kaye S LLP) -425 Park Av -NY 10022
(516) 248-1700 .. **Smolev,** Terence E '70 (Forchelli CDSM&T,LLP) -333 Earle Ovngton Blvd -Uniondale 11553
(516) 746-8000 .. **Smolevitz,** Mindy K '88 (Jaspan S LLP) -300 Grdn City Plz -Gdn Cty 11530
(212) 557-7200 .. **Smoley,** Lewis M '69 OfCnsl Davidoff M&H,LLP -605 3rd Av -NY 10158
(315) 488-1881 .. **Smolinski,** Wm A '91 -2010 W Genesee -Syracuse 13219
(212) 310-8000 .. **Smolinsky,** Jos H '89 (Weil G&M LLP) -767 5th Av -NY 10153
(716) 849-1333 .. **Smolka,** Christopher J '87 SpclCnsl Lipsitz GSC LLP -42 Delaware Av -Buffalo 14202
(212) 689-6060 .. **Smolka,** Edw R '77 (Smolka & S) -274 Mad Av -NY 10016 **Fx:**545-0715
(716) 694-5934 .. **Smolka,** Eugene J '63 -683 Shad -N Tonawanda 14120 **Fx:**694-5934
(212) 732-8368 .. **Smollar,** Jason '00 %Caruso SLCU&S -132 Nassau -NY 10038
(212) 619-7787 .. **Smollens,** Steven W '76 -225 Bway -NY 10007 **Fx:**619-7765
(212) 788-1263 .. **Smollens,** Susan '05 %Law Dept -100 Church -NY 10007 **Fx:**788-0367
(631) 544-0759 .. **Smolowitz,** Barry M '87 -7 Marilyn Dr -Kings Pk 11754
(212) 859-8000 .. **Smolyanskiy,** Julia V '02 %Fried FHS&J LLP -1 NY Plz -NY 10004
(516) 496-9525 .. **Smook,** Naomi '85 %Jewish Theological Seminary -575 Underhill Blvd -Syosset 11791
(212) 209-3059 .. **Smookler,** Louis '03 %Reitler K&R LLC -885 3rd Av -NY 10022
(212) 761-7923 .. **Smoot,** David M IV '97 Morgan Stanley -1585 Bway -NY 10036
(212) 336-2000 .. **Smoot,** Edw H '00 %Patterson BW&T LLP -1133 Av of Amer -NY 10036
(718) 225-6700 .. **Smoren,** David '05 -254-10 Nrthrn Blvd -Little Neck 11362
(212) 714-4192 .. **Smothers,** Alice J '02 Cisco Systms -1 Penn Plz -NY 10119
(914) 288-8102 .. **Smrek,** Carol Anne '92 Acadia Realty Trust -1311 Mamaroneck Av -White Plns 10605
(518) 843-3180 .. **Smrtic,** John S '05 Greater Amsterdam Schl Dist -11 Lbrty -Amsterdam 12010
(518) 773-8225 .. **Smrtic,** Michl W '92 -289 N Main -Gloversvll 12078
(716) 838-5515 .. **Smukler,** Oscar '80 -1438 Hertel Av -Buffalo 14216
(212) 527-7927 .. **Smul,** Spencer G '89 %Estee Lauder -767 5th Av -NY 10153 **Fx:**572-3989
(718) 625-2200 .. **Smulian,** Dan R '97 %Bklyn Law Schl -250 Joralemon -Brklyn 11201 **Fx:**780-0393
(212) 801-3156 .. **Smulian,** Danl '08 %Greenberg T,LLP -200 Park Av -NY 10166
(212) 556-5802 .. **Smurl,** Paul F '94 NY Times Co -620 8th Av -NY 10018
(212) 682-8222 .. **Smyth,** Christina A '04 (Tolman S LLP) -355 Lex Av -NY 10017
(631) 271-7500 .. **Smyth,** Edmund J M '97 (Smyth N LLP) -143 Main -Huntngtn 11743
(212) 906-1200 .. **Smyth,** Graeme P '05 %Latham & W -885 3rd Av -NY 10022
(718) 838-7878 .. **Smyth,** J McGregor Jr. '00 %Bronx Defenders -860 Crtlandt Av -Bronx 10451 **Fx:**665-0100
(516) 248-9880 .. **Smyth,** Jean M '97 %Agovino & A,LLP -330 Old Cntry Rd -Mineola 11501
(212) 788-9089 .. **Smyth,** John P '00 City Cncl Leg Div -250 Bway -NY 10007 **Fx:**788-7034
(631) 271-7500 .. **Smyth Nora LLP** -143 Main -Huntngtn 11743 **Fx:**271-7504
(716) 819-0891 .. **Smyth,** Theresa A '97 -14 Lafayette -Buffalo 14203
(631) 321-8500 .. **Smyth,** Thos A '94 %R Passarelli & Assoc -One John -Babylon 11702 **Fx:**321-8591
(631) 271-7500 .. **Smyth,** Vincent A '75 Cnsl Smyth N LLP -143 Main -Huntngtn 11743
(212) 969-3000 .. **Smythe,** Lauren C '08 %Proskauer R LLP -1585 Bway -NY 10036
(716) 847-8400 .. **Smyton,** James W '72 (Phillips L LLP) -3400 HSBC Ctr -Buffalo 14203
(718) 424-0122 .. **Snape,** Jacqueline L '93 -82-10 Qns Blvd -Elmhrst 11373
(212) 446-4800 .. **Snare,** Ellen M '04 %Kirkland & E LLP -153 E 53rd -NY 10022
(212) 735-8831 .. **Snarr,** Brian B '83 (Morrison C LLP) -909 3rd Av -NY 10022
(212) 788-0587 .. **Snashall,** James G '91 %Law Dept -100 Church -NY 10007 **Fx:**788-0367
Snashall, Robt R III '79 -6 Audubon Dr -Cazenovia 13035
(631) 286-0488 .. **Snead,** J Lee '93 -155-C S Cnty Rd Bx489 -Bellprt 11713
(631) 727-2180 .. **Snead,** Janice L '92 (Twomey LSKD&Q,LLP) -33 W 2nd Bx9398 -Rvrhead 11901
(212) 653-8874 .. **Snedeker,** Wm A '84 (Liebman & S LLC) -330 Mad Av -NY 10017 **Fx:**(646) 495-5006
(212) 318-6000 .. **Snediker,** David E '76 (Paul HJ&W LLP) -75 E 55th -NY 10022
(585) 724-4404 .. **Snee,** Chas E III '98 %Eastman Kodak -343 State -Rchstr 14650
(212) 547-5400 .. **Sneed,** Saml C '09 %McDermott W&E LLP -340 Mad Av -NY 10173
(718) 664-1958 .. **Sneed,** Stephanie M '05 ACS -900 Sheridan Av -Bronx 10451
(518) 434-0127 .. **Sneeringer,** Eugene M '51 (Sneeringer MPR) -50 Chapel -Albany 12207
(518) 434-0127 .. **Sneeringer,** Eugene M Jr. '80 (Sneeringer MPR) -50 Chapel -Albany 12207
(518) 434-0127 .. **Sneeringer Monahan Provost Redgrave** -50 Chapel -Albany 12207 **Fx:**434-9997
(518) 885-8700 .. **Sneeringer Monahan Provost Redgrave** -36 Remsen -Ballston Spa 12020 **Fx:**884-2564
(518) 828-4351 .. **Sneeringer Monahan Provost Redgrave** -420 Warren -Hudson 12534 **Fx:**828-7494
(518) 434-0127 .. **Sneeringer Monahan Provost Redgrave** -52 2nd -Troy 12180 **Fx:**434-9997
(518) 434-0127 .. **Sneeringer,** Robt J '89 (Sneeringer MPR) -50 Chapel -Albany 12207
(212) 474-1000 .. **Sneider,** Jaime '09 %Cravath S&M LLP -825 8th Av -NY 10019
(518) 561-7190 .. **Snell,** Brian A '98 -201 W Bay Plz -Plattsbrgh 12901 **Fx:**562-3446
(518) 762-3067 .. **Snell,** Calvin J '02 -804 Cnty Hwy 107 -Johnstwn 12095
(212) 747-9560 .. **Snell,** Darlene Y '02 (Hemmings & S LLP) -39 Bway -NY 10006 **Fx:**747-9564
(212) 969-3000 .. **Snell,** Dietrich '84 (Proskauer R LLP) -1585 Bway -NY 10036
(212) 448-1100 .. **Snell,** George B '53 (McLaughlin & S,LLP) -260 Mad Av -NY 10016
(212) 695-2442 .. **Snell,** Harrison J '73 -2 Penn Plz -NY 10121 **Fx:**868-0713
(212) 935-3000 .. **Snell,** Peter F '07 %Mintz LCFG&P,PC -666 3rd Av -NY 10017
(212) 878-8000 .. **Snell,** Tamara M '09 %Clifford C LLP -31 W 52nd -NY 10019
(716) 852-2330 .. **Snell,** Timothy J '84 -268 Main -Buffalo 14202 **Fx:**853-2892
(212) 334-1300 .. **Snelson,** Andrea N '01 %Vera Inst of Justice -233 Bway -NY 10279 **Fx:**941-9407
(212) 977-7033 .. **Sniarowski,** Mariusz J '04 %Perecman Firm PLLC -250 W 57th -NY 10107
(914) 472-1956 .. **Snider,** Alan '85 -800 Cntrl Pk Av -Scarsdale 10583
(716) 856-5500 .. **Snider,** Carol Guck '84 (Damon M LLP) -200 Delaware Av -Buffalo 14202
(212) 309-6000 .. **Snider,** David A '09 %Morgan L&B LLP -101 Park Av -NY 10178
(914) 644-7300 .. **Snider,** Donald S '69 -932 Lester Av -Mamaroneck 10543 **Fx:**644-7301
(212) 732-3665 .. **Snider,** Jennifer R '05 %Harmon L&R -42 Bway -NY 10004
(212) 450-4000 .. **Snider,** Jerome G '76 Cnsl Davis P&W LLP -450 Lex Av -NY 10017
(315) 764-0513 .. **Snider,** Mark F '78 (Snider & S) -252 Main -Massena 13662 **Fx:**764-9230
(315) 764-0513 .. **Snider,** Thos J '79 (Snider & S) -252 Main -Massena 13662 **Fx:**764-9230
(212) 351-4000 .. **Snider,** Virginia Creary '10 Gibson D&C LLP -200 Park Av -NY 10166
(212) 340-0400 .. **Snigur,** Gregg G '89 %Applt Div 1st Dept -27 Mad Av -NY 10010 **Fx:**889-4412
(212) 558-4000 .. **Snipes,** Wm J '87 (Sullivan & C LLP) -125 Broad -NY 10004
(914) 948-4500 .. **Snitily,** Monica G '04 %O'Connor MCD&O -1 Barker Av -White Plns 10601
(212) 885-5000 .. **Snitman,** Shaun '08 %Blank R LLP -405 Lex Av -NY 10174
(212) 317-8500 .. **Snitow,** Franklyn H '71 (Snitow KH&M,LLP) -575 Lex Av -NY 10022
(212) 594-5300 .. **Snitow,** Gary S '06 %Milberg LLP -1 Penn Plz -NY 10119
(212) 317-8500 .. **Snitow Kanfer Holtzer & Millus,LLP** -575 Lex Av -NY 10022 **Fx:**317-1308
(716) 854-5200 .. **Snitzer,** Isadore '47 (Borins SS&B) -403 Main -Buffalo 14203
(212) 762-5103 .. **Snodgrass,** Brendan N '03 Morgan Stanley -1221 Av of Amer -NY 10020
(585) 292-5750 .. **Snodgrass,** Cynthia L '93 (Morris and M) -120 Corp Woods -Rchstr 14623 **Fx:**292-5793
(631) 422-2900 .. **Snover,** Kevin G '90 -816 Deer Prk Av -N Babylon 11703
(212) 818-9200 .. **Snow,** Abigail E '02 %Satterlee SB&B LLP -230 Park Av -NY 10169

(212) 687-3860 ..**Snow Becker Krauss,PC** -605 3rd Av -NY 10158 **Fx:**949-7052
(845) 446-5082 ..**Snow,** Bonnie J '98 -41 Ft Putnam -Highlnd Fls 10928 **Fx:**446-5082
(212) 687-3860 ..**Snow,** Chas '59 OfCnsl Snow BK,PC -605 3rd Av -NY 10158
(212) 373-3000 ..**Snow,** Elanit A '09 %Paul WRW&G LLP -1285 Av of Amer -NY 10019
(516) 496-5822 ..**Snow,** Ellen M '93 %T Spina -170 Froehlich Farm Blvd -Woodbury 11797 **Fx:**496-5420
(212) 788-0581 ..**Snow,** Keith M '01 %Law Dept -100 Church -NY 10007 **Fx:**788-0367
(516) 571-9283 ..**Snow,** Kimberly L '96 %Cnty Atty -1200 Old Cntry Rd -Westbury 11590 **Fx:**571-9189
(212) 683-3636 ..**Snow,** Lee A '82 (Krass S&S,PC) -419 Park Av S -NY 10016
(212) 407-8000 ..**Snow,** Sloan W '01 NBA Properties -645 5th Av -NY 10022
(718) 544-8665 ..**Snow,** Tara Ash '01 (Novitt S&S,LLP) -118-35 Qns Blvd -Frst Hlls 11375
(212) 697-7004 ..**Snow,** Zachary '76 Primus Finl Products,LLC -360 Mad Av -NY 10017
(516) 935-1144 ..**Snowe,** Alan M '62 (Snowe & G) -382 S Oyster Bay Rd -Hicksvll 11801 **Fx:**935-8193
(212) 521-5400 ..**Snukal,** Adam W '00 %Reed S LLP -599 Lex Av -NY 10022
(716) 851-7000 ..**Snyder,** Abby M '88 %DEC -270 Mich Av -Buffalo 14203 **Fx:**851-7211
(212) 388-3600 ..**Snyder,** Alan M '73 %32B-J Leg Srvcs -101 Av of Amer -NY 10013 **Fx:**388-3061
(212) 713-5883 ..**Snyder,** Allen T Jr. '85 -1562 1st Av -NY 10028
(212) 973-8000 ..**Snyder,** Allison A '96 %Schnader HS&L LLP -140 Bway -NY 10005
(212) 902-4251 ..**Snyder,** Andrew M '97 Goldman Sachs & Co -85 Broad -NY 10004
(212) 398-6628 ..**Snyder,** Beryl L '83 HBJ Invstmnts LLC -592 5th Av -NY 10036
(212) 442-9892 ..**Snyder,** Brad M '03 %Law Dept -100 Church -NY 10007 **Fx:**788-0367
(212) 450-4000 ..**Snyder,** Brian J '09 %Davis P&W LLP -450 Lex Av -NY 10017
(212) 819-3139 ..**Snyder,** Christopher T '03 King St Capital Mgmt -65 E 55th -NY 10022
(212) 474-1000 ..**Snyder,** Courtney A '10 %Cravath S&M LLP -825 8th Av -NY 10019
(212) 826-3800 ..**Snyder,** Craig H '96 (S Karten & Assoc,LLP) -355 Lex Av -NY 10017 **Fx:**486-6583
(607) 776-9631 ..**Snyder,** Craig R '82 %Hon J Latham -3 E Pulteney Sq -Bath 14810
(315) 425-1100 ..**Snyder,** David B '03 %Keidel W&C LLP -4625 Onondaga Blvd -Syracuse 13219
(914) 333-0700 ..**Snyder,** David L '81 (Snyder & S) -94 Wht Plns Rd -Tarrytwn 10591 **Fx:**333-0743
(607) 749-7081 ..**Snyder,** David L '86 -102 S Main -Homer 13077
(585) 262-6390 ..**Snyder,** David L '89 (Hamberger & W) -1 S Wshngtn -Rchstr 14614
(845) 639-3172 ..**Snyder,** Diane Prestia '00 -107 N Main -New Cty 10956
(585) 919-0009 ..**Snyder,** Donald E Jr. '83 SrCnsl Underberg & K LLP -23 Sly -Canandaigua 14424
(315) 822-4141 ..**Snyder,** Donald J '66 OfCnsl Cosentino S&Q -379 W Main Bx596 -W Winfld 13491
(315) 733-9900 ..**Snyder,** Donald J '66 OfCnsl Cosentino S&Q -605 French Rd -New Hartfrd 13413
(716) 675-1066 ..**Snyder,** Edw J '75 -3976 Seneca -W Seneca 14224 **Fx:**674-4772
(716) 853-1616 ..**Snyder,** Edw J '07 %Harter S&E LLP -12 Fountain Plz -Buffalo 14202
(212) 421-2233 ..**Snyder,** Eric J '88 (Wilk A LLP) -675 3rd Av -NY 10017
(212) 637-2534 ..**Snyder,** Eric J '96 %US Atty -1 St Andrews Plz -NY 10007
(718) 339-5491 ..**Snyder,** Gay H '81 -2920 Av R -Brklyn 11229 **Fx:**339-5417
(212) 704-6000 ..**Snyder,** George B '76 (Troutman S LLP) -405 Lex Av -NY 10174
(716) 856-4000 ..**Snyder,** George L Jr. '93 (Hodgson R LLP) -140 Pearl -Buffalo 14202
(315) 429-3127 ..**Snyder,** Gerard J '82 Sullivan & S -8 S Main Bx146 -Dolgevll 13329
(518) 584-1500 ..**Snyder,** Harry D Jr. '55 (Snyder KTC&C,LLP) -160 West Av Bx4367 -Saratoga Spgs 12866
(212) 969-1000 ..**Snyder,** Henry K '97 Alliance Bernstein LP -1345 Av of Amer -NY 10105 **Fx:**554-4639
(212) 964-7400 ..**Snyder,** Howard J '97 Smith MDWY&Y,PC -111 John -NY 10038
(631) 232-0200 ..**Snyder,** Howard R '75 (Fumuso KDSS&F,LLP) -110 Marcus Blvd -Hauppauge 11788
(518) 584-1500 ..**Snyder,** James G '88 (Snyder KTC&C,LLP) -160 West Av Bx4367 -Saratoga Spgs 12866
(315) 492-9665 ..**Snyder,** James T '84 %Greene & R,PLLC -173 Intrepid Ln -Syracuse 13205
(212) 785-9100 ..**Snyder,** Jason J '99 %Paduano & W LLP -1251 Av of Amer -NY 10020
(212) 953-6000 ..**Snyder,** Jeffrey R '82 OfCnsl Katsky K LLP -605 3rd Av -NY 10158
(212) 545-4000 ..**Snyder,** John A II '94 (Jackson L LLP) -666 3rd Av -NY 10017
(607) 723-0600 ..**Snyder,** John H '99 (Gitto & N,LLP) -71 State -Bnghmtn 13901 **Fx:**723-0634
(212) 969-3000 ..**Snyder,** John H '04 %Proskauer R LLP -1585 Bway -NY 10036
(212) 323-7070 ..**Snyder,** John J '01 (Rawle & H LLP) -14 Wall -NY 10005
(315) 445-8550 ..**Snyder,** Jos M '87 %Widewaters Grp -5786 Widewaters Pkwy Bx3 -DeWitt 13214 **Fx:**445-8570
(518) 584-1500 ..**Snyder Kiley Toohey Corbett & Cox,LLP** -160 West Av Bx4367 -Saratoga Spgs 12866 **Fx:**584-1503
(607) 753-5046 ..**Snyder,** Kristin M '07 %Pub Def -60 Central Av -Cortlnd 13045 **Fx:**753-0781
(212) 506-1700 ..**Snyder,** Leslie Crocker '67 (Kasowitz BT&F LLP) -1633 Bway -NY 10019
(914) 333-0700 ..**Snyder,** Leslie J '86 (Snyder & S) -94 Wht Plns Rd -Tarrytwn 10591 **Fx:**333-0743
(718) 590-3870 ..**Snyder,** Mark H '80 %Supreme Ct -851 Grnd Cncrs -Bronx 10451 **Fx:**590-8914
(315) 218-8000 ..**Snyder,** Mary L '03 %Bond S&K,PLLC -1 Lincoln Ctr -Syracuse 13202
(716) 972-2397 ..**Snyder,** Michele K '89 Tara Cares -3690 Southwestern Blvd -Orchard Pk 14127
(518) 474-4096 ..**Snyder,** Nancy D '84 %Dept of Law -The Cptl -Albany 12224
(212) 458-5684 ..**Snyder,** Nicole M '01 AIG -175 Water -NY 10038
(212) 351-4000 ..**Snyder,** Orin S '87 (Gibson D&C LLP) -200 Park Av -NY 10166
(607) 753-8050 ..**Snyder,** Patrick M '87 -70 Port Watson -Cortlnd 13045 **Fx:**753-6540
(212) 318-6000 ..**Snyder,** Rachel L '09 %Paul HJ&W LLP -75 E 55th -NY 10022
(845) 225-3224 ..**Snyder,** Reynold J '81 Hon SB Hickman -40 Gleneida Av -Carmel 10512 **Fx:**228-0656
(607) 974-3054 ..**Snyder,** Ronald J '05 Corning Inc -SP-TI-3-1 -Corning 14831 **Fx:**974-3848
(718) 250-2000 ..**Snyder,** Ronald J '06 %DA -350 Jay -Brklyn 11201 **Fx:**250-2314
(631) 467-6337 ..**Snyder,** Ronald S '93 (Anes L&S PLLC) -266 Smithtown Blvd -Nesconset 11767
(212) 619-4444 ..**Snyder,** Stacey H '90 %Marshall CW&B,PC -116 John -NY 10038
(212) 292-6372 ..**Snyder,** Steven J '09 Ziff Bros Inv -350 Park Av -NY 10022
(212) 556-2100 ..**Snyder,** Steven T '04 %King & S -1185 Av of Amer -NY 10036
(315) 706-0042 ..**Snyder,** Steven W '82 Fitzpatrick & S,PC -7641 Henry Clay Blvd -Liverpool 13088 **Fx:**706-0015
(212) 752-5200 ..**Snyder,** Susan Kurz '86 Greene Levin Snyder LLC -150 E 58th -NY 10155
(212) 825-9811 ..**Snyder,** Theo R '89 (Krebsbach & S,PC) -55 Bway -NY 10006
(315) 822-4141 ..**Snyder,** Theresa H '66 (Cosentino S&Q) -379 W Main Bx596 -W Winfld 13491
(315) 733-9900 ..**Snyder,** Theresa H '66 (Cosentino S&Q) -605 French Rd -New Hartfrd 13413
(518) 464-0640 ..**Snyder,** Thos A '90 (Devine M&S LLP) -52 Corp Cir -Albany 12203
(212) 506-1700 ..**Snyder,** Tobias G '10 Kasowitz BT&F LLP -1633 Bway -NY 10019
(585) 428-2091 ..**Snyder-Haas,** Jennifer J '01 %Hon H Galloway -545 Hall of Justice -Rchstr 14614
(212) 286-2234 ..**Snyderman,** Marc I '98 Insight Communications -810 7th Av -NY 10019 **Fx:**935-2575
(212) 558-4000 ..**Snypes,** J Michl Jr. '07 %Sullivan & C LLP -125 Broad -NY 10004
(212) 351-4500 ..**So,** Adam D '04 %Epstein B&G,PC -250 Park Av -NY 10177
(212) 872-1000 ..**So,** Austin Kyongwon '03 -One Bryant Park -NY 10036 **Fx:**872-1002
(212) 909-6000 ..**So,** Jaeyong '96 Cnsl Debevoise & P LLP -919 3rd Av -NY 10022
(212) 292-4288 ..**So,** Lord Chester '97 -521 5th Av -NY 10175 **Fx:**(718) 701-1279
(646) 552-9375 ..**So,** Suyin '05 DGenerate Films,Inc -2 E Bway -NY 10038
(914) 472-5500 ..**Soares,** Angela Pilla '03 -670 Wht Plns Rd -Scarsdale 10583 **Fx:**725-7724
(718) 575-2225 ..**Soares,** Joan A '98 J Soares,PLLC -118-35 Qns Blvd -Frst Hlls 11375 **Fx:**575-2228
(212) 422-1200 ..**Soares,** Maria M '97 %Abrams GF&J,PC -1 Bttry Pk Plz -NY 10004
(518) 487-5460 ..**Soares,** Paul David '00 (DA) -6 Lodge -Albany 12207 **Fx:**487-5093
(212) 980-4002 ..**Sobal,** Barbara Bevando '89 -300 E 64th -NY 10065 **Fx:**980-4001
(212) 805-0177 ..**Sobchak,** Natalie J '90 %USDC -500 Pearl -NY 10007
(212) 889-7546 ..**Sobel,** Alvin N '54 King & S -401 2nd Av -NY 10010 **Fx:**889-7546
(212) 670-0368 ..**Sobel,** Arthur H '62 %Merrill Lynch -222 Bway -NY 10038
(516) 487-0700 ..**Sobel,** Barton '88 (Behren & S) -55 Water Mill Ln -Gt Neck 11021 **Fx:**829-3198
(631) 549-4677 ..**Sobel,** Curtis '86 (Sobel K&S,PC) -464 NY Av -Huntngtn 11743
(631) 265-9575 ..**Sobel,** David J '87 D Sobel,PC -811 W Jericho Tpk -Smithtwn 11787 **Fx:**265-4895
(646) 432-4170 ..**Sobel,** David M '98 Abel Noser Corp -1 Bttry Pk Plz -NY 10004
(845) 353-1818 ..**Sobel,** Donna Corby '98 %Furgang & A,LLP -2 Crosfld Av -W Nyack 10994 **Fx:**353-1996
(212) 836-8000 ..**Sobel,** Gerald '63 (Kaye S LLP) -425 Park Av -NY 10022
(516) 621-9600 ..**Sobel,** Glenn J '76 -27 Powerhse Rd -Roslyn Hts 11577 **Fx:**621-7249
(212) 223-3900 ..**Sobel,** Hillary '89 SrCnsl Zwerling S&Z,LLP -41 Mad Av -NY 10010
(212) 906-1200 ..**Sobel,** Howard A '79 (Latham & W) -885 3rd Av -NY 10022
(212) 806-5400 ..**Sobel,** Jason '04 %Stroock &S&L LLP -180 Maiden Ln -NY 10038
(212) 566-7188 ..**Sobel,** Jason L '98 %Genova B&G -115 Bway -NY 10006
(212) 246-2233 ..**Sobel,** Jonathan A '86 Livingston Asset Mgmt -Bx2535 -Amagansett 11930
(212) 308-0600 ..**Sobel,** Jonathan M '95 (Sobel & F LLP) -444 Mad Av -NY 10022 **Fx:**308-0611
(631) 549-4677 ..**Sobel Kelly & Schleier, PC** -464 NY Av -Huntngtn 11743 **Fx:**549-0826
(212) 428-6216 ..**Sobel,** Leslie J '01 RBC -1 Lbrty Plz -NY 10006
(212) 373-3000 ..**Sobel,** Marilyn '79 (Paul WRW&G LLP) -1285 Av of Amer -NY 10019
(718) 237-8849 ..**Sobel,** Martin R '80 -26 Court -Brklyn 11242
(212) 522-4869 ..**Sobel,** Melissa P '97 %Time Inc -1271 Av of Amer -NY 10020 **Fx:**522-0437
(212) 421-2233 ..**Sobel,** Michl '03 %Wilk A LLP -675 3rd Av -NY 10017
(212) 345-5880 ..**Sobel,** Richd G '85 %Marsh USA -1166 Av of Amer -NY 10036 **Fx:**345-4808
(212) 233-0350 ..**Sobel Ross Fliegel & Suss,LLP** -150 Bway -NY 10038 **Fx:**233-2977
(212) 965-4661 ..**Sobel,** Sarah B '99 Weinstein Co -345 Hudson -NY 10014
(212) 840-2196 ..**Sobel,** Sol N '55 -36 W 44th -NY 10036 **Fx:**764-6795
(973) 239-7606 ..**Sobel,** Stephen B '56 %LIU-Schl of Business -Univ Plz -Brklyn 11201 **Fx:**239-7606
(631) 264-1070 ..**Sobel,** Svetlana '02 Sobel Law Ofcs,PC -121 W Oak -Amityvll 11701
(646) 386-4062 ..**Sobell,** Paul A '70 %Hon R White -100 Centre -NY 10013
(973) 642-5143 ..**Sobel-Shapiro,** Lauren B '90 (Anderson K&O,PC) -1251 Av of Amer -NY 10020 **Fx:**642-6361
(212) 554-7800 ..**Sobelsohn,** Richd J '98 %Moses & S LLP -405 Lex Av -NY 10174
(518) 274-5490 ..**Sober,** Frederic E Jr. '98 -403 19th -Watervliet 12189
(518) 436-5794 ..**Sober,** Jennifer G '99 -100 State -Albany 12207 **Fx:**436-5793
(212) 732-3320 ..**Soberano,** Patrice M '97 %Short & B,PC -217 Bway -NY 10007
(516) 437-5400 ..**Soberman,** Alan R '73 (Soberman & R) -2001 Marcus Av -Lk Success 11042
(212) 587-9690 ..**Soberman,** Richd A '77 (J Samel & Partners) -150 Bway -NY 10038 **Fx:**587-9673
(516) 437-5400 ..**Soberman & Rosenberg** -2001 Marcus Av -Lk Success 11042 **Fx:**437-7292
(212) 813-8800 ..**Sobey,** Jordana F '08 %Goodwin P LLP -620 8th Av -NY 10018
(718) 925-8930 ..**Sobhai,** Loaknauth Rajesh '99 -110-10 Jamaica Av -Richmnd Hll 11418 **Fx:**925-8931
(914) 422-4251 ..**Sobie,** Merril '65 Pace Law Schl -78 N Bway -White Plns 10603 **Fx:**422-4168
(212) 751-9800 ..**Sobiloff,** David L '82 (Tai & S) -950 3rd Av -NY 10022 **Fx:**751-0046
(212) 460-3331 ..**Sobin,** Carole '75 Con Ed -4 Irving Pl -NY 10003
(212) 408-5100 ..**Sobin,** Melinda A '10 %Chadbourne & P LLP -30 Rckfllr Plz -NY 10112

(716) 847-7679 .. **Sobkowski**, Erin M '05 Div of Human Rights -65 Court -Buffalo 14202
(845) 343-7626 .. **Sobo**, Gary M '70 (Sobo & S) -1 Dolson Av -Middletwn 10940 **Fx**:343-0929
(845) 343-7626 .. **Sobo**, Gregory M '00 (Sobo & S) -1 Dolson Av -Middletwn 10940 **Fx**:343-0929
(212) 872-1000 .. **Sobol**, David T '05 -One Bryant Park -NY 10036 **Fx**:872-1002
(212) 351-7589 .. **Sobol**, Jennifer F '00 TMP Directional Mrktng,LLC -317 Mad Av -NY 10017
(212) 637-2201 .. **Sobol**, Peter B '67 US Atty -1 St Andrews Plz -NY 10007 **Fx**:637-2429
(212) 822-1426 .. **Sobolevsky**, Andre R '85 -305 Bway -NY 10007
(212) 474-1000 .. **Sobolewski**, John R '09 %Cravath S&M LLP -825 8th Av -NY 10019
(212) 592-1400 .. **Sobolewski**, Matthew D '05 %Herrick,F LLP -2 Park Av -NY 10016
(315) 437-7600 .. **Sobota**, Henry F '78 (Ferrara FLB&R,PC) -5010 Campuswood Dr -E Syracuse 13057
(516) 739-0000 .. **Sobotta**, Jacqueline R '99 %Martyn T&M -330 Old Cntry Rd -Mineola 11501
(212) 949-5800 .. **Socarides**, Richd C '80 OfCnsl Brady K&W,LLP -501 5th Av -NY 10017
(212) 264-8819 .. **Sochaczewsky**, Mark S '84 %ODAR-SSA -26 Fed Plz -NY 10278
(212) 489-1400 .. **Sochar**, Betsy H '09 %Bickel & B -767 5th Av -NY 10153
(212) 682-4426 .. **Sockol**, Andrew J '04 %O'Shea Prtnrs LLP -521 5th Av -NY 10175 **Fx**:682-4437
(212) 407-4000 .. **Socolow**, Brian R '91 %Loeb & L,LLP -345 Park Av -NY 10154
(914) 946-0600 .. **Socolow**, John M '87 Pino & Assoc -50 Main -White Plns 10606 **Fx**:946-0650
(212) 592-1632 .. **So-Conrad**, Yuri '04 -2 Park Av -NY 10016
(718) 931-2575 .. **Socorro**, Myrna M '04 (Codelia & S PC) -1967 Turnbull Av -Bronx 10473
(516) 295-0707 .. **Sod**, Paul M '86 -337R Central Av -Lawrence 11559 **Fx**:295-0722
(212) 779-8600 .. **Sodafsky**, Jill E '05 %Silverman SS&B PLLC -381 Park Av S -NY 10016
(716) 887-6900 .. **Sodaro**, Kenneth J '93 %Healthnow NY -257 W Genesee -Buffalo 14202 **Fx**:887-8548
(315) 422-6154 .. **Soden**, Bruce G '63 OfCnsl Greene H&S -1 Lincoln Ctr -Syracuse 13202 **Fx**:475-2672
(516) 746-8000 .. **Soderberg**, Jessica L '08 %Jaspan S LLP -300 Grdn City Plz -Gdn Cty 11530
(631) 751-6458 .. **Soderberg**, John V '88 -207 Hallock Rd -Stony Brk 11790 **Fx**:751-6434
(315) 685-4685 .. **Soderberg**, Jon A '95 Welch Allyn,Inc -4341 State Street Rd -Skaneateles Fls 13153
(212) 735-3000 .. **Soderstrom**, Nathan G '09 %Skadden ASM&F LLP -4 Times Sq -NY 10036
(516) 545-5160 .. **Soebke**, Bernard M '88 SrCnsl Natl Grid -175 E Old Cntry Rd -Hicksvll 11801 **Fx**:545-5029
(716) 854-2100 .. **Soeder**, Arnold H '78 (Lewis & L,PC) -37 Franklin -Buffalo 14202 **Fx**:854-0433
(518) 465-5995 .. **Soehl**, Margie A '09 %Powers & S,LLP -39 N Pearl -Albany 12207
(212) 924-2825 .. **Soeiro**, David V '63 -511 6th Av PMB 186 -NY 10011 **Fx**:675-6726
(212) 415-9200 .. **Soekawa**, Sumiko '04 %Dorsey & W LLP -250 Park Av -NY 10177
(718) 923-4233 .. **Soetan**, Oluseye Olayemi '95 NYS OTDA -111 Lvngstn -Brklyn 11201
(212) 221-6900 .. **Sofair-Fisch**, Adam L '09 %Winget S&S,LLP -45 Bway -NY 10006
(212) 558-4000 .. **Sofen**, Adam A '09 %Sullivan & C LLP -125 Broad -NY 10004
(212) 697-2800 .. **Sofer & Haroun,LLP** -317 Mad Av -NY 10017 **Fx**:697-3004
(212) 697-2800 .. **Sofer**, Jos '90 (Sofer & H,LLP) -317 Mad Av -NY 10017
(646) 495-7385 .. **Sofer**, Meredith Young '05 H&M LP -909 3rd Av -NY 10022
(212) 346-2000 .. **Sofer**, Tzadok '93 -115 Bway -NY 10006
(212) 244-7770 .. **Soffer**, Jos '88 -7 Penn Plz -NY 10001 **Fx**:244-1947
(516) 571-3800 .. **Soffer**, Michl E '05 DA -262 Old Cntry Rd -Mineola 11501 **Fx**:248-9479
(212) 268-7222 .. **Soffer Rech & Borg LLP** -48 Wall -NY 10005 **Fx**:268-0287
Soffer, Sanford '51 -87 S Manning Blvd -Albany 12203
(212) 268-7222 .. **Soffer**, Victor K '78 (Soffer R&B LLP) -48 Wall -NY 10005
(716) 854-2620 .. **Sofferin**, Lisa T '90 (Brown & K,LLP) -1500 Lbrty Bldg -Buffalo 14202
(212) 343-4681 .. **Sofferman**, Perry F '00 Scholastic,Inc -557 Bway -NY 10012
(516) 294-1996 .. **Soffey**, Douglas M '91 (Soffey & S) -226 7th -Gdn Cty 11530 **Fx**:294-1085
(516) 294-1996 .. **Soffey**, Jos Emmett '50 (Soffey & S) -226 7th -Gdn Cty 11530 **Fx**:294-1085
(516) 437-5354 .. **Soffientini**, Raymond J '72 -1032 Hancock Av -Franklin Sq 11010
(212) 553-8300 .. **Soffientini**, Robt J '75 %Cohen K & Assoc -2 Park Av -NY 10016 **Fx**:553-8721
(212) 873-3600 .. **Sofia**, Frank J '63 %Sofia Bros -475 Amstrdm Av -NY 10024
(347) 643-5805 .. **Sofield**, Raymond J '85 Transit Auth-Adjudication Bureau -505 Fulton -Brklyn 11201
(516) 766-6200 .. **Sofield**, Thos R '93 (Crafa & S PC) -100 N Centre Av -Rockvll Ctr 11570
(212) 294-6700 .. **Sofio**, Lisa M '08 %Winston & S -200 Park Av -NY 10166
(718) 596-4877 .. **Sofola**, Olatokunbo '97 -26 Court -Brklyn 11242 **Fx**:596-5009
(212) 818-8028 .. **Sogabe**, Masahiro '02 Itochu Intl -335 Mad Av -NY 10017 **Fx**:818-8493
(315) 734-8493 .. **Soggs**, Randolph B '94 %Soggs Development -5 Oxford Rd Bx684 -New Hartfrd 13413
(212) 808-7800 .. **Sogi**, Francis Y '52 (Kelley D&W LLP) -101 Park Av -NY 10178
(914) 749-8200 .. **Soh**, Andy Y L '08 %Boies S&F LLP -333 Main -Armonk 10504
(212) 287-3200 .. **Soh**, Suzanna J L '95 Perella Weinberg Ptnrs LP -767 5th Av -NY 10153 **Fx**:287-3201
(212) 788-0435 .. **Sohigian**, Walter '80 %Law Dept -100 Church -NY 10007 **Fx**:788-0367
(212) 335-4323 .. **Sohmer**, Olivia '87 %DA -1 Hogan Pl -NY 10013
(212) 686-4345 .. **Sohn**, Chang M '74 -445 5th Av -NY 10016 **Fx**:686-4347
(516) 239-1396 .. **Sohn**, David '84 -9 Regent Dr -Lawrence 11559 **Fx**:239-1396
(718) 999-0337 .. **Sohn**, Eugene B '99 %Fire Dept -9 Metrotech Ctr -Brklyn 11201
(516) 379-2500 .. **Sohn**, Garry D '78 (Malone T&S) -147 W Merrick Rd Bx589 -Freeprt 11520
(212) 455-2000 .. **Sohn**, Jiyoung '08 %Simpson T&B LLP -425 Lex Av -NY 10017
(212) 335-4500 .. **Sohn**, Joshua S '98 (DLA Piper LLP) -1251 Av of Amer -NY 10020
(718) 556-7458 .. **Sohn**, Liza J K '10 %Law Dept -60 Bay -Staten Isl 10301 **Fx**:981-4459
(212) 684-2277 .. **Sohn**, Sangwon D '03 -315 5th Av -NY 10016 **Fx**:684-2272
(718) 295-5598 .. **Sohn**, Sarah H '05 Bronx AIDS Srvcs -540 E Fordham Rd -Bronx 10458 **Fx**:733-3429
(212) 312-3568 .. **Sohn**, Susie C '05 EDC -110 William -NY 10038 **Fx**:312-3912
(212) 964-7400 .. **Sohnen**, Danl Y '08 Smith MDWY&Y,PC -111 John -NY 10038
(212) 355-2777 .. **Sohns**, Gregory E '76 -260 Mad Av -NY 10016 **Fx**:355-0529
(212) 891-1600 .. **Sohoni**, Sharmila '06 %Jenner & B LLP -919 3rd Av -NY 10022
(914) 946-3700 .. **Sohr**, Katherine M '08 %McCarthy F LLP -11 Martine Av -White Plns 10606
(516) 228-8560 .. **Soicher**, Harvey E '60 -666 Old Cntry Rd -Gdn Cty 11530 **Fx**:393-5556
(212) 883-8000 .. **Soicher**, Lawr G '65 -110 E 59th -NY 10022 **Fx**:355-6900
(212) 578-2211 .. **Soiefer**, Alan J '76 %MetLife -27-01 Qns Plz N -LIC 11101
(914) 736-7368 .. **Soja**, Mark S '94 Marathon Dvlpmnt Grp Ltd -901 Main -Peekskill 10566
(315) 624-5050 .. **Soja**, Thos S '79 %Faxton-St Lukes Hlthcr -Bx479 -Utica 13503 **Fx**:624-5052
(212) 789-5789 .. **Sojka**, Sandra '95 %Chase Asset Mgt -1211 Av of Amer -NY 10036 **Fx**:596-3871
(516) 739-0400 .. **Sokel**, Sol Zalman '00 %Kelly R&K,LLP -330 Old Cntry Rd -Mineola 11501
(212) 715-1000 .. **Sokenu**, Claudius O T '97 (Arnold & P LLP) -399 Park Av -NY 10022
(212) 818-9191 .. **Sokol**, Andrew L '80 -420 Lex Av -NY 10170 **Fx**:818-0121
(718) 781-8565 .. **Sokol**, Eric M '89 -122 Plainfld Av -Floral Pk 11001 **Fx**:(516) 437-6197
(212) 513-3200 .. **Sokol**, Howard '01 %Holland & K LLP -31 W 52nd -NY 10019
(718) 389-5115 .. **Sokol**, Jerzy '97 -861 Manh Av -Brklyn 11222 **Fx**:389-0478
(646) 783-6040 .. **Sokol**, Jessica M '03 -1430 Bway -NY 10018
(917) 856-1653 .. **Sokol**, Jodi A '96 -711 West End Av -NY 10025
(516) 294-8844 .. **Sokol**, Monte E '80 (L'Abbate BC&C,LLP) -1001 Franklin Av -Gdn Cty 11530
(518) 783-0200 .. **Sokol**, Pilar '88 %NYS Schl Bds Assn -24 Century Hill Dr -Latham 12110
(212) 385-4410 .. **Sokol**, Stacey T '00 %Gersowitz L&K,PC -111 Bway -NY 10006
(718) 487-2300 .. **Sokol**, Susan J '86 %Leg Srvcs Corp -256-260 Bway -Brklyn 11211 **Fx**:782-6790
(718) 293-1669 .. **Sokoler**, Corey A '84 -881 Gerard Av -Bronx 10452
(516) 222-0572 .. **Sokolich**, Patricia A '94 -595 Stewart Av -Gdn Cty 11530 **Fx**:222-2971
(212) 607-2013 .. **Sokolin-Maimon**, Anna '00 Metropolitan Telecom -44 Wall -NY 10005
(212) 521-5400 .. **Sokoloff**, Alexander '88 %Reed S LLP -599 Lex Av -NY 10022
(516) 334-4500 .. **Sokoloff**, Brian S '87 (Sokoloff S LLP) -355 Post Av -Westbury 11590 **Fx**:334-4501
(516) 883-8621 .. **Sokoloff**, Harold L '51 -218 Miro Pl -Pt Wash 11050 **Fx**:883-6994
(212) 643-7000 .. **Sokoloff**, Lisa A '84 %Sills C&G PC -One Rckfllr Plz -NY 10020
(212) 341-7900 .. **Sokoloff**, Mark G '79 %Brecher FPWT&Z,PC -233 Bway -NY 10279
(631) 696-8545 .. **Sokoloff**, Richd '86 -3245 Route 112 -Medfrd 11763 **Fx**:696-8794
(212) 585-3425 .. **Sokolov**, Brooke M '05 %B Kishner & Assoc -420 Lex Av -NY 10170 **Fx**:752-1810
(212) 768-6700 .. **Sokolow**, Mark I '83 (Sonnenschein N&R LLP) -2 World Fncl Ctr -NY 10281
(718) 390-5433 .. **Sokolow**, Nechama '87 %Hon L Rienzi -18 Richmond Ter -Staten Isl 10301
(716) 851-2711 .. **Sokolowski**, Mark R '85 %UIA Bd -290 Main -Buffalo 14202 **Fx**:851-2795
(212) 571-4080 .. **Sokolski**, Robt E '97 (Sokolski & Z,PC) -305 Bway -NY 10007 **Fx**:571-4079
(212) 259-8000 .. **Sokoly**, Benjamin '99 Cnsl Dewey & L LLP -1301 Av of Amer -NY 10019
(607) 274-6504 .. **Sokoni**, Khandikile P M '99 %City Atty -108 E Green -Ithaca 14850 **Fx**:274-6507
(212) 758-9300 .. **Sokop**, Jeremy M '03 %Lazare P&G LLP -950 3rd Av -NY 10022
(212) 310-8000 .. **Sokotch**, Jonathan E '05 %Weil G&M LLP -767 5th Av -NY 10153
(212) 697-3122 .. **Sola**, Anthony M '78 (Martin C&B LLP) -220 E 42nd -NY 10017
(631) 366-5700 .. **Solages**, Philippe '01 -1300 Vets Hwy -Hauppauge 11788
(212) 310-8000 .. **Solaimani**, Farbod '08 %Weil G&M LLP -767 5th Av -NY 10153
(718) 780-0357 .. **Solan**, Lawr M '84 %Bklyn Law Schl -250 Joralemon -Brklyn 11201 **Fx**:780-0393
(212) 218-2100 .. **Solander**, Wm E '96 (Fitzpatrick CH&S) -1290 Av of Amer -NY 10104
(212) 715-6600 .. **Solano**, Javier A '97 -350 5th Av -NY 10118 **Fx**:629-8969
(212) 833-1121 .. **Solano**, Ricardo Jr. '00 (Friedman KS&A LLP) -1633 Bway -NY 10019 **Fx**:373-7921
(914) 725-7070 .. **Solarsh**, Marna E '81 -670 Post Rd -Scarsdale 10583
(212) 541-2000 .. **Solarz**, Alan H '84 (Bryan C LLP) -1290 Av of Amer -NY 10104
(212) 333-0200 .. **Solbakken**, Lisa C '99 (Arkin KR LLP) -590 Mad Av -NY 10022
(212) 297-5800 .. **Solberg**, Jennifer L '06 %Day P LLP -7 Times Sq -NY 10036
(212) 407-4000 .. **Sold**, Kenneth W '82 (Loeb & L,LLP) -345 Park Av -NY 10154
(914) 946-6774 .. **Sold**, Steven M '78 (Pilkington & L,PC) -222 Bloomingdale Rd -White Plns 10605
(212) 967-3393 .. **Solda**, Paul J '89 -350 5th Av -NY 10118
(518) 477-5766 .. **Soldini**, David J '92 -1 Kristen Ct -E Greenbush 12061
(212) 478-0000 .. **Sole**, Marc S '97 DE Shaw & Co -120 W 45th -NY 10036
(212) 813-8800 .. **Solecki**, Albert J Jr. '91 (Goodwin P LLP) -620 8th Av -NY 10018
(212) 458-6705 .. **Soleimani**, Elana '06 AIG Domestic Claims -175 Water -NY 10038
(516) 482-9100 .. **Soleiman-Tehrani**, Michl '99 (Amirian S& Assoc LLP) -40 Cuttermill Rd -Gt Neck 11021
(716) 858-2424 .. **Solek**, Bethany A '05 %DA -25 Delaware Av -Buffalo 14202 **Fx**:858-7425
(212) 773-3000 .. **Solender**, Michl S '90 (Ernst & Young,LLP) -5 Times Sq -NY 10036
(212) 504-6000 .. **Soler**, Albert J '04 %Cadwalader W&T LLP -1 World Fncl Ctr -NY 10281
(212) 736-1798 .. **Soler**, Fermin C '93 -370 7th Av -NY 10001
(212) 804-4200 .. **Soler**, John R '08 %Mound CW&G -One Bttry Pk Plz -NY 10004
(212) 310-8000 .. **Soler**, Jonathan G '99 (Weil G&M LLP) -767 5th Av -NY 10153
(212) 735-8600 .. **Soleymani**, Stephen '92 (Morrison C LLP) -909 3rd Av -NY 10022
(516) 538-8007 .. **Soleymanzadeh**, Richd J '01 -320 Nassau Blvd -Gdn Cty 11530

(212) 756-2000 ..**Solfanelli,** Sara E '08 %Schulte R&Z LLP -919 3rd Av -NY 10022
(516) 873-1711 ..**Solferino,** Carol Ann '91 (Solferino & S,LLP) -15 Roslyn Rd -Mineola 11501 **Fx:**873-1721
(516) 873-1711 ..**Solferino,** Thos P '88 (Solferino & S,LLP) -15 Roslyn Rd -Mineola 11501 **Fx:**873-1721
(212) 801-3196 ..**Soli,** Toby S '98 (Greenberg T,LLP) -200 Park Av -NY 10166
(516) 328-2300 ..**Soliman,** Ayman '05 %Abrams FFEGF&E,LLP -1111 Marcus Av -Lk Success 11042
(212) 272-6852 ..**Soliman,** Meriem '03 %JP Morgan Chase -383 Mad Av -NY 10179
(718) 892-0400 ..**Solimano,** Louis G '77 -1180 Morris Park Av -Bronx 10461
(212) 636-6000 ..**Solimene,** Gemma '88 %Fordham Univ Sch of Law -140 W 62nd -NY 10023 **Fx:**636-6899
(718) 250-2000 ..**Solimeo,** Connie '08 %DA -350 Jay -Brklyn 11201 **Fx:**250-2314
(212) 906-1200 ..**Solimine,** Peter A '07 %Latham & W -885 3rd Av -NY 10022
(212) 526-0456 ..**Solinger,** Martha E '81 Lehman Bros -1271 Av of Amer -NY 10020
(914) 250-2400 ..**Solinski,** Robt W '67 Cnsl Benchmark Title -222 Bloomingdale Rd -White Plns 10605 **Fx:**422-1500
(718) 618-3096 ..**Solinsky,** Danl J '03 Supreme Ct -265 E 161st -Bronx 10451
(212) 553-3200 ..**Solis,** Claudia E '99 %Marulli LE&T,LLP -5 Hanover Sq -NY 10004
(212) 529-5055 ..**Solis,** Lino A II '00 Thor Equities,LLC -25 W 39th -NY 10018 **Fx:**460-9243
(646) 386-3637 ..**Solitar,** Susan Parker '89 %Supreme Ct-Law Dept -60 Centre -NY 10007
(212) 661-9100 ..**Soll,** Steven B '81 (Otterbourg SH&R,PC) -230 Park Av -NY 10169
(212) 753-6407 ..**Sollar,** Arnold R '55 -805 3rd Av -NY 10022
(973) 743-2708 ..**Sollecito,** Danl V '72 -1590 Paulding Av -Bronx 10462
(212) 790-9200 ..**Soller,** Carl R '72 (Cowan L&L,PC) -1133 Av of Amer -NY 10036
(518) 465-2333 ..**Soller,** Christian J '99 (Hodgson R LLP) -677 Bway -Albany 12207
(212) 626-4100 ..**Soller,** Derek A '09 Baker & M LLP -1114 Av of Amer -NY 10036
(212) 859-8000 ..**Sollie,** Erica '09 %Fried FHS&J LLP -1 NY Plz -NY 10004
(212) 688-1256 ..**Sollis,** Todd B '73 -330 Mad Av -NY 10017 **Fx:**688-8386
(212) 558-4000 ..**Sollors,** David M '06 %Sullivan & C LLP -125 Broad -NY 10004
(212) 476-5674 ..**Solmonson,** Leslie '83 %Neuberger Berman,LLC -605 3rd Av -NY 10158 **Fx:**476-9862
(347) 533-7990 ..**Solny,** Sanford '82 -150 Bway -NY 10038 **Fx:**533-7995
(347) 533-7990 ..**Solny,** Sanford '82 -3813 13th Av -Brklyn 11218
(212) 806-5400 ..**Solo,** Alexander '08 %Stroock &S&L LLP -180 Maiden Ln -NY 10038
(212) 843-0050 ..**Solodchikova,** Alina Nikolaevna '05 %S Kass,PC -225 Bway -NY 10007 **Fx:**571-0640
(212) 848-9800 ..**Soloff,** Sharon Beth '88 OfCnsl Withers B LLP -430 Park Av -NY 10022
(212) 336-8000 ..**Solomita,** Michl V '98 (Amster R&E) -90 Park Av -NY 10016
(646) 386-3618 ..**Solomkin,** David L '90 %Supreme Ct-Law Dept -60 Centre -NY 10007
(212) 226-2376 ..**Solomon,** Aaron J '06 %Oved & O LLP -101 Av of Amer -NY 10013 **Fx:**226-7555
(718) 432-0500 ..**Solomon,** Aaron N '10 %Krieger W&H -5602 Bway -Bronx 10463
(212) 683-9180 ..**Solomon,** Adam Z '01 (Lustigman Firm,PC) -149 Mad Av -NY 10016 **Fx:**683-9181
(212) 310-8000 ..**Solomon,** Alex M '10 %Weil G&M LLP -767 5th Av -NY 10153
(718) 254-7000 ..**Solomon,** Alexander A '05 %US Atty -271 Cadman Plz E -Brklyn 11201 **Fx:**254-6479
(212) 450-4000 ..**Solomon,** Aman D '09 %Davis P&W LLP -450 Lex Av -NY 10017
(718) 263-8580 ..**Solomon,** Andrew D '85 (Orbit II Prtnrs) -67-38 108th -Frst Hlls 11375 **Fx:**(212) 374-7869
(845) 627-7629 ..**Solomon,** Andrew H '87 -105 Brookhill Dr -W Nyack 10994
(212) 558-4000 ..**Solomon,** Andrew P '85 (Sullivan & C LLP) -125 Broad -NY 10004
(212) 660-3000 ..**Solomon,** Andrew T '96 (Sullivan & W LLP) -1290 Av of Amer -NY 10104
(212) 813-5900 ..**Solomon,** Barbara A '85 (Fross ZL&Z,PC) -866 UN Plz -NY 10017
(516) 572-2383 ..**Solomon,** Barbara C '02 Dist Ct Law Dept -99 Main -Hempstd 11550 **Fx:**572-2260
(212) 545-8611 ..**Solomon & Bernstein** -351 Bway -NY 10013 **Fx:**545-0238
(718) 698-1287 ..**Solomon,** Brian D '90 -193 Merrymount -Staten Isl 10314 **Fx:**698-1287
(212) 808-0700 ..**Solomon,** Burt A '69 (Norris M&M,PA) -875 3rd Av -NY 10022
(718) 855-4805 ..**Solomon,** Cheryl S '84 -26 Court -Brklyn 11242 **Fx:**855-2057
(914) 289-0800 ..**Solomon,** Clifford M '78 (Solomon & T,PC) -707 Wstchstr Av -White Plns 10604
(212) 605-1000 ..**Solomon,** Craig H '83 Square Mile Captl -450 Park Av -NY 10022
(212) 224-6715 ..**Solomon,** David F '93 %Forest Labs -909 3rd Av -NY 10022
(212) 357-1570 ..**Solomon,** David Z '98 %Goldman Sachs & Co -One NY Plz -NY 10004 **Fx:**493-0188
(212) 680-5150 ..**Solomon,** Dean M '02 %Friedman Law Grp LLP -270 Lafayette -NY 10012
(212) 566-7188 ..**Solomon,** Douglas E '96 (Genova B&G) -115 Bway -NY 10006
(212) 424-7112 ..**Solomon,** Elise S '73 %Lifetime TV -309 W 49th -NY 10019 **Fx:**957-4447
(212) 993-2274 ..**Solomon,** Eric R '02 Update,Inc -1140 Av of Amer -NY 10036
(516) 327-2866 ..**Solomon,** Frederic S '95 BWD Grp LLC -BWD Plz Bx9050 -Jericho 11753 **Fx:**327-2800
(212) 577-3510 ..**Solomon,** Gary S '77 %Leg Aid -199 Water -NY 10038 **Fx:**577-3520
(516) 764-2226 ..**Solomon,** Harold '62 (Solomon & D) -430 Sunrise Hwy Bx1100 -Rockvll Ctr 11570 **Fx:**536-5389
(518) 456-7200 ..**Solomon,** Harold L '63 (Solomon & S,PC) -5 Columbia Cir Bx15019 -Albany 12212
(516) 747-0300 ..**Solomon,** Herbert W '60 OfCnsl Meltzer LG&B,LLP -190 Willis Av -Mineola 11501
(212) 421-7850 ..**Solomon,** Howard '52 %Forest Labs Inc -909 3rd Av -NY 10022 **Fx:**224-6740
(212) 752-2800 ..**Solomon,** Howard B '67 (Markfield & S LLP) -805 3rd Av -NY 10022
(212) 756-2000 ..**Solomon,** Jaime L '04 Schulte R&Z LLP -919 3rd Av -NY 10022
(212) 437-8672 ..**Solomon,** Jason Scott '04 Ameriprise Fincl -250 Greenwich -NY 10007
(212) 661-9400 ..**Solomon,** Jay B '86 (Klein & S LLP) -275 Mad Av -NY 10016
(212) 964-1860 ..**Solomon,** Jay M '77 %Wertheimer Assoc,PC -225 Bway -NY 10007 **Fx:**349-2439
(212) 808-7800 ..**Solomon,** Jeanne R '93 %Kelley D&W LLP -101 Park Av -NY 10178
(212) 223-0400 ..**Solomon,** Jerome S '71 OfCnsl Zeichner E&K LLP -575 Lex Av -NY 10022
(585) 262-2860 ..**Solomon,** Jerry M '74 %Medicaid Fraud Cntrl -144 Exchange Blvd -Rchstr 14614 **Fx:**262-2866
(212) 474-1000 ..**Solomon,** Jonathan P '08 %Cravath S&M LLP -825 8th Av -NY 10019
(212) 225-2000 ..**Solomon,** Jordan '07 %Cleary GS&H -1 Lbrty Plz -NY 10006
(973) 596-4659 ..**Solomon,** Jordan S '94 Cnsl Gibbons PC -1 Penn Plz -NY 10119 **Fx:**639-6243
(518) 456-7200 ..**Solomon,** Julie B '98 %Solomon & S,PC -5 Columbia Cir Bx15019 -Albany 12212
(516) 487-5800 ..**Solomon,** Katherine Herr '96 (Mauro G&L LLP) -60 Cuttermill Rd -Gt Neck 11021
(516) 228-9350 ..**Solomon,** Lewis J '52 (Solomon & S) -50 Chas Lindbergh Blvd -Uniondale 11553
(914) 674-8573 ..**Solomon,** Lisa '94 -67 Beacon Hill Rd -Ardsley 10502 **Fx:**(815) 346-3468
(212) 471-0067 ..**Solomon,** Lisa M '85 -305 Mad Av -NY 10165 **Fx:**980-6965
(212) 504-6000 ..**Solomon,** Louis M '80 (Cadwalader W&T LLP) -1 World Fncl Ctr -NY 10281
(212) 698-3500 ..**Solomon,** Louis M '90 (Dechert LLP) -1095 Av of Amer -NY 10036
(212) 475-6386 ..**Solomon,** M Bruce '57 -60 Gramercy Park N -NY 10010 **Fx:**475-6386
(212) 444-6201 ..**Solomon,** Mark B '04 Investment Technology Grp,Inc -380 Mad Av -NY 10017
(212) 264-8819 ..**Solomon,** Mark D '77 %ODAR-SSA -26 Fed Plz -NY 10278
(607) 273-2202 ..**Solomon,** Mark J '85 -200 E Buffalo Bx353 -Ithaca 14851 **Fx:**273-4436
(914) 470-0001 ..**Solomon,** Matthew P '04 %Babchik & Y,LLP -200 E Post Rd -White Plns 10601
(631) 427-3333 ..**Solomon,** Michl B '60 (Sanders & S) -510 Broadhllw Rd -Melvll 11747 **Fx:**427-3342
(212) 794-5322 ..**Solomon,** Michl D '70 %CUNY -535 E 80th -NY 10075 **Fx:**794-5426
(516) 579-6200 ..**Solomon,** Michl D '77 (Solomon & H,PLLC) -2950 Hempstd Tpk -Levittwn 11756 **Fx:**579-2409
(516) 378-4700 ..**Solomon,** Michl I '64 -30 S Ocean Av Bx428 -Freeprt 11520 **Fx:**868-4315
(212) 736-4536 ..**Solomon,** Michelle L '05 Manhttn Cmmnty Bd #4 -330 W 42nd -NY 10036
(212) 735-3000 ..**Solomon,** Mitchell J '80 (Skadden ASM&F LLP) -4 Times Sq -NY 10036
(212) 594-7070 ..**Solomon,** Moshie '02 -450 7th Av -NY 10123 **Fx:**268-8529
(212) 969-3000 ..**Solomon,** Oriel '99 (Proskauer R LLP) -1585 Bway -NY 10036
(585) 272-0540 ..**Solomon,** Patrick J '96 (Thomas & S LLP) -693 East Av -Rchstr 14607
(516) 239-7052 ..**Solomon,** Paul D '91 (P Solomon,LLP) -290 Central Av -Lawrence 11559
(212) 267-7600 ..**Solomon Pearl Blum Heymann & Stich LLP** -40 Wall -NY 10005 **Fx:**267-2030
(212) 752-8910 ..**Solomon,** Phyllis C '87 -488 Mad Av -NY 10022 **Fx:**(877) 700-8879
(585) 753-3487 ..**Solomon,** R Adrian '90 %Conflict Def -30 W Broad -Rchstr 14614 **Fx:**753-3489
(516) 371-4924 ..**Solomon,** Richd A '86 (R Solomon,LLP) -290 Central Av -Lawrence 11559
(212) 808-7800 ..**Solomon,** Richd B '88 %Kelley D&W LLP -101 Park Av -NY 10178
(212) 977-9700 ..**Solomon,** Richd I '70 Cnsl Phillips N LLP -666 5th Av -NY 10103
(516) 437-6443 ..**Solomon Richman, PC** -3000 Marcus Av -Lk Success 11042 **Fx:**437-6434
(718) 984-2626 ..**Solomon,** Robt A '80 (Solomon & Assoc,PC) -3309 Richmond Av -Staten Isl 10312 **Fx:**984-5820
(212) 267-7600 ..**Solomon,** Robt A '95 (Solomon PBH&S LLP) -40 Wall -NY 10005
(516) 432-1622 ..**Solomon,** Robt H '83 (R Solomon,PC) -24 E Park Av -Long Bch 11561 **Fx:**432-1713
(212) 768-9500 ..**Solomon,** Robt N '69 -1212 Av of Amer -NY 10036 **Fx:**944-6600
(212) 685-7228 ..**Solomon,** Robt R '58 (R Solomon,PC) -475 5th Av -NY 10017 **Fx:**725-1293
(845) 564-6115 ..**Solomon,** Ross '81 -843 Union Av -New Windsor 12553 **Fx:**564-8069
(212) 837-4800 ..**Solomon,** Scott E '89 -18 E 50th -NY 10022 **Fx:**837-4939
(212) 415-8600 ..**Solomon,** Shelley R '06 %Locke LB&L LLP -3 World Fncl Ctr -NY 10281
(516) 437-6443 ..**Solomon,** Sidney N '60 (Solomon R,PC) -3000 Marcus Av -Lk Success 11042
(516) 228-9350 ..**Solomon & Siris** -50 Chas Lindbergh Blvd -Uniondale 11553 **Fx:**228-4305
(518) 456-7200 ..**Solomon & Solomon,PC** -5 Columbia Cir Bx15019 -Albany 12212 **Fx:**456-0651
(212) 867-0652 ..**Solomon,** Stanley N '61 -25 Smith -Nanuet 10954 **Fx:**683-0104
(212) 788-9172 ..**Solomon,** Stephen J '92 NYC Council Finance Div -250 Bway -NY 10007
(212) 682-5702 ..**Solomon,** Stephen L '64 (Hutton & S) -475 5th Av -NY 10017
(212) 768-6700 ..**Solomon,** Stephen L '67 (Sonnenschein N&R LLP) -1221 Av of Amer -NY 10020
(212) 541-9100 ..**Solomon,** Steven N '01 %Schiavetti CDW&N,LLP -575 8th Av -NY 10018
(585) 454-3030 ..**Solomon,** Steven Y '99 %Merzbach,PC -73 State -Rchstr 14614 **Fx:**454-3044
(212) 969-3000 ..**Solomon,** Suzanne E '10 %Proskauer R LLP -1585 Bway -NY 10036
(914) 289-0800 ..**Solomon & Tanenbaum,PC** -707 Wstchstr Av -White Plns 10604 **Fx:**289-1800
(212) 327-7598 ..**Solomon,** Teresa L '91 Rockefeller Univ -1230 York Av -NY 10065
(212) 583-9600 ..**Solomon,** Terri M '80 (Littler M,PC) -900 3rd Av -NY 10022
(585) 292-5130 ..**Solomon,** Thos J '68 -400 W Metro Park -Rchstr 14623 **Fx:**292-0491
(718) 531-9700 ..**Solomon,** Thos J '91 %Lazarowitz & M,LLP -2004 Ralph Av -Brklyn 11234
(518) 456-7200 ..**Solomon,** Valerie Nelson '71 (Solomon & S,PC) -5 Columbia Cir Bx15019 -Albany 12212
(212) 733-6706 ..**Solomon Weiss,** Nancy I '94 %Pfizer Inc -235 E 42nd -NY 10017 **Fx:**573-1445

(212) 489-1600 .. **Solomons**, Ella K '81 %Deloitte LLP -1633 Bway -NY 10019 **Fx**:492-4201
(718) 278-5900 .. **Solomos**, Jimmy C '01 -33-08 Bway -Astoria 11106 **Fx**:278-6969
(212) 735-3000 .. **Solorzano**, Jonathan S '09 %Skadden ASM&F LLP -4 Times Sq -NY 10036
(914) 828-8262 .. **Solorzano**, R Alexandra '04 Swiss Reinsurance -175 King -Armonk 10504 **Fx**:828-7262
(212) 403-1000 .. **Solotar**, Gavin D '93 (Wachtell LR&K) -51 W 52nd -NY 10019
(212) 847-8315 .. **Solotaroff**, Jason L '91 (Giskan S&A) -11 Bway -NY 10004 **Fx**:(646) 520-3235
(516) 466-5522 .. **Solotoff**, Cheryl '88 (Solotoff & S) -Bx4686 -Gt Neck 11023 **Fx**:466-5562
(516) 432-6263 .. **Solotoff**, Darryn G '05 %Elovich & A -164 W Park Av -Long Bch 11561
(516) 466-5522 .. **Solotoff**, Lawr '74 (Solotoff & S) -Bx4686 -Gt Neck 11023 **Fx**:466-5562
(212) 801-6529 .. **Solovay**, Michl B '86 (Greenberg T,LLP) -200 Park Av -NY 10166
(212) 448-1100 .. **Solovay**, Norman '58 (McLaughlin & S,LLP) -260 Mad Av -NY 10016
(718) 254-7000 .. **Soloveichik**, Layaliza Klein '98 %US Atty -271 Cadman Plz E -Brklyn 11201 **Fx**:254-6479
(212) 373-3000 .. **Soloveichik**, Yitzchak E '09 %Paul WRW&G LLP -1285 Av of Amer -NY 10019
(212) 289-4928 .. **Solow**, Allan W '95 -1825 Park Av -NY 10035
(212) 350-2700 .. **Solow**, Alysia Dashef '96 (Constantine C,PC) -450 Lex Av -NY 10017
(212) 836-8000 .. **Solow**, Andrew K '00 %Kaye S LLP -425 Park Av -NY 10022
(212) 478-7200 .. **Solow**, Graig B '06 %Hahn & H LLP -488 Mad Av -NY 10022
(212) 310-8000 .. **Solow**, Heather R '04 %Weil G&M LLP -767 5th Av -NY 10153
(914) 286-3400 .. **Solow**, Jay '76 %Leg Aid -1 N Bway -White Plns 10601 **Fx**:682-4112
(631) 231-1450 .. **Solow**, Jos A '79 OfCnsl Feldman K&M,PC -330 Vndrblt Motor Pkwy -Hauppauge 11788
(212) 836-7240 .. **Solow**, Michl B '03 (Kaye S LLP) -425 Park Av -NY 10022
(516) 229-4200 .. **Solowan**, Richd A '92 %Mendolia & S -875 Merrick Av -Westbury 11590
(212) 373-3000 .. **Soloway**, Audra J '03 %Paul WRW&G LLP -1285 Av of Amer -NY 10019
(212) 661-0945 .. **Soloway**, Herman J '61 -275 Mad Av -NY 10016
(212) 270-8216 .. **Soloway**, Jay N '73 JP Morgan Chase -270 Park Av -NY 10017
(212) 227-9390 .. **Soloway**, Lavi S '92 (Masliah & S,PC) -225 Bway -NY 10007 **Fx**:227-9564
(516) 296-7000 .. **Soloway**, Louis '56 (Certilman BA&H,LLP) -90 Merrick Av -E Meadow 11554
(917) 554-2332 .. **Soloway**, Michl E '05 Rudius Media,LLC -319 Lafayette -NY 10012
(212) 571-5500 .. **Soloway**, Robt A '84 (Rothman SS&S,LLP) -100 Lafayette -NY 10013
(914) 949-3411 .. **Soloway**, Shari L '96 K Cohen,PC -30 Glenn -White Plns 10603 **Fx**:949-3444
(212) 878-8000 .. **Soloway**, Shari L '07 %Clifford C LLP -31 W 52nd -NY 10019
(212) 421-4100 .. **Soloway**, Todd E '92 (Pryor C LLP) -7 Times Sq -NY 10036
(212) 918-3000 .. **Solowsky**, Adam D '99 OfCnsl Hogan L LLP -875 3rd Av -NY 10022
(212) 408-2500 .. **Solsky**, Stuart T '83 (Baker B,LLP) -30 Rckfllr Plz -NY 10112
(718) 250-1100 .. **Solstein**, Lawr '93 %E Garfinkel -12 Metrotech Ctr -Brklyn 11201 **Fx**:250-1168
(212) 421-2233 .. **Soltani**, Hamid R '04 Wilk A LLP -675 3rd Av -NY 10017
(212) 735-3000 .. **Soltani**, Nooshin '07 %Skadden ASM&F LLP -4 Times Sq -NY 10036
(212) 344-1744 .. **Solton**, Michl Y '96 (Solton R&B LLP) -110 Wall -NY 10005 **Fx**:344-1734
(212) 374-9840 .. **Soltys**, Christopher J '94 %Wenig & W -150 Bway -NY 10038 **Fx**:374-9844
(917) 701-9008 .. **Soltys**, Rostyslav M '04 -425 Neptune Av -Brklyn 11224 **Fx**:(212) 507-9164
(718) 286-6000 .. **Soltys**, Veronica C '87 %DA -125-01 Qns Blvd -Kew Gdns 11415
(212) 446-4800 .. **Solum**, Matthew O '00 (Kirkland & E LLP) -153 E 53rd -NY 10022
(212) 307-5500 .. **Som**, Sumit '08 %Venable LLP -1270 Av of Amer -NY 10020
(212) 973-0572 .. **Somashekara**, Kiran V '07 %Wolff & S PC -140 Bway -NY 10005
(631) 439-2450 .. **Somberg**, Diane M '04 %Leg Aid -320 Carleton Av -Central Islip 11722 **Fx**:439-2453
(914) 767-7587 .. **Sombra**, Valeria P '06 %Pepsi Bottling Grp -1 Pepsi Way -Somers 10589
(718) 740-3300 .. **Somekh**, Lori R '95 Somekh & Assoc -240-19 Jamaica Av -Bellerose 11426 **Fx**:343-3343
(212) 701-3000 .. **Somekh**, Sogol D '08 %Cahill G&R LLP -80 Pine -NY 10005 **Fx**:269-5420
(212) 218-7170 .. **Somelofske**, Paul J '90 Special Cnsl Inc -600 5th Av -NY 10020
(516) 248-8962 .. **Somer**, Harold M '84 (H Somer,PC) -1025 Old Cntry Rd -Westbury 11590 **Fx**:333-0654
(212) 629-7001 .. **Somer**, Lloyd '77 -330 7th Av -NY 10001 **Fx**:629-7026
(631) 462-2323 .. **Somer**, Stanley J '70 (Somer & H LLP) -2171 Jericho Tpk -Commack 11725 **Fx**:462-2338
(212) 310-8000 .. **Somerman**, Caitlin I '09 %Weil G&M LLP -767 5th Av -NY 10153
(212) 610-6300 .. **Somers**, Angela J '87 SrCnsl Allen & O -1221 Av of Amer -NY 10020
(212) 481-5858 .. **Somers**, Avis A '05 %Fidelity Natl Title Ins -1 Park Av -NY 10016 **Fx**:481-8747
(585) 262-6390 .. **Somers**, Mark C '96 (Hamberger & W) -1 S Wshngtn -Rchstr 14614
(212) 857-2100 .. **Somers**, Patrick J '08 Hon W Feinberg -40 Foley Sq -NY 10007
(718) 466-3000 .. **Somerset**, E Patricia '76 %Civil Ct -1118 Grnd Cncrs -Bronx 10456 **Fx**:466-3006
(585) 919-0009 .. **Somerset**, Margaret E '90 (Underberg & K LLP) -23 Sly -Canandaigua 14424
(516) 484-0254 .. **Somerstein**, Bruce '83 (B Somerstein & Assoc,PC) -203 Glen Cove Av -Sea Cliff 11579
(212) 268-1188 .. **Somerstein**, Bruce '83 (B Somerstein & Assoc,PC) -370 7th Av -NY 10001 **Fx**:268-2688
(516) 596-9300 .. **Somerstein**, Jonathan J '93 -59 Rockaway Av -Vly Stream 11580 **Fx**:208-4880
(212) 596-9000 .. **Somerstein**, Mark R '91 (Ropes & G LLP) -1211 Av of Amer -NY 10036
(516) 873-3000 .. **Somerstein**, Stephen A '72 Bellavia G & Assoc,LLP -200 Old Cntry Rd -Mineola 11501 **Fx**:873-9032
(212) 425-7200 .. **Somerville**, Deborah A '85 (Kenyon & K,LLP) -1 Bway -NY 10004
(845) 649-2909 .. **Somerville**, Gary R '04 -30 Matthews Bx241 -Goshen 10924 **Fx**:294-3619
(585) 428-5210 .. **Somes**, Janet C '85 %Pub Def -10 N Fitzhugh -Rchstr 14614 **Fx**:428-2234
(212) 362-5966 .. **Somlyo**, David M '86 Museum Music Inc -98 Riverside Dr -NY 10024 **Fx**:362-5977
(631) 957-3029 .. **Somma**, Donna Marie '99 %Babylon Town Atty -200 E Sunrise Hwy -Lindenhrst 11757 **Fx**:957-3146
(212) 586-2774 .. **Somma**, Louis A '57 -250 W 57th -NY 10107
(212) 596-9000 .. **Somma**, Louis T '03 %Ropes & G LLP -1211 Av of Amer -NY 10036
(607) 770-8870 .. **Somma**, Michl A '89 (Somma & S) -400 Plz Dr -Vestal 13850
(718) 692-3921 .. **Somma**, Michl S Jr. '88 -2430 E 74th -Brklyn 11234
(631) 587-1699 .. **Somma**, Ralph A '93 -175 W Main -Babylon 11702 **Fx**:587-1760
(607) 770-8870 .. **Somma & Sullivan** -400 Plz Dr -Vestal 13850 **Fx**:770-9059
(914) 686-8200 .. **Sommella**, Pasquale '98 %Sarcone Law Firm,PLLC -222 Bloomingdale Rd -White Plns 10605 **Fx**:686-8988
(716) 434-5170 .. **Sommer**, Amelia M '59 -112 Levan Av -Lockprt 14094 **Fx**:434-4213
(212) 909-6000 .. **Sommer**, Andrew L '84 (Debevoise & P LLP) -919 3rd Av -NY 10022
(212) 232-1300 .. **Sommer**, Christopher H '96 (Lewis BB&S LLP) -77 Water -NY 10005
(518) 438-9907 .. **Sommer**, Dean S '79 (Young SWRB&M,LLC) -5 Palisades Dr -Albany 12205
(212) 476-9000 .. **Sommer**, Elizabeth M '85 %Neuberger Berman Trust Co -605 3rd Av -NY 10158 **Fx**:476-9090
(212) 527-2657 .. **Sommer**, Evelyn M '56 -570 Lex Av -NY 10022 **Fx**:681-0300
(315) 476-4482 .. **Sommer**, Gary M '74 (Sommer & S,PC) -103 E Water -Syracuse 13202 **Fx**:474-8867
(516) 228-8181 .. **Sommer**, Herbert H '83 -595 Stewart Av -Gdn Cty 11530
(315) 476-4482 .. **Sommer**, Irene R '79 (Sommer & S,PC) -103 E Water -Syracuse 13202 **Fx**:474-8867
(212) 705-7000 .. **Sommer**, James R '03 Cnsl Bingham M LLP -399 Park Av -NY 10022
(212) 720-5026 .. **Sommer**, Jos H '89 %Fed Reserve Bk -33 Lbrty -NY 10045 **Fx**:785-5748
(212) 967-5383 .. **Sommer**, Kenneth A '79 -350 5th Av -NY 10118
(212) 530-5000 .. **Sommer**, Leonard '49 -1 Chase Manh Plz -NY 10005 **Fx**:530-5219
(212) 308-0070 .. **Sommer**, Maura W '01 %McCusker AR&C,PC -805 3rd Av -NY 10022
(212) 999-5800 .. **Sommer**, Michl S '88 (Wilson SG&R) -1301 Av of Americas -NY 10019
(516) 432-6263 .. **Sommer**, Mitchel '79 %Elovich & A -164 W Park Av -Long Bch 11561
(212) 949-7600 .. **Sommer**, Paul S '85 (Weinberger S PC) -230 Park Av -NY 10169
(716) 847-8400 .. **Sommer**, Peter K '73 OfCnsl Phillips L LLP -3400 HSBC Ctr -Buffalo 14203
(212) 529-2580 .. **Sommer**, Scott M '87 UAW -113 Univ Pl -NY 10003
(212) 809-8585 .. **Sommer**, Susan L '88 Lambda Leg Def -120 Wall -NY 10005 **Fx**:809-0055
(212) 603-7503 .. **Sommerfeld**, George '59 %Burnham Securities -1325 Av of Amer -NY 10019 **Fx**:603-7537
(914) 472-4434 .. **Sommerfield**, Robt D '67 -24 Downer Av -Scarsdale 10583 **Fx**:725-2242
(212) 751-5959 .. **Sommers**, Andrew '95 (Ehrenkranz & E,LLP) -375 Park Av -NY 10152 **Fx**:754-1905
(518) 465-2426 .. **Sommers**, Andrew C '83 (Sommers & S LLP) -7 Thurlow Ter -Albany 12203 **Fx**:455-8907
(732) 214-0303 .. **Sommers**, Bruce W '66 -25 Clara -Brklyn 11218 **Fx**:214-0299
(518) 465-2426 .. **Sommers**, Donald H '50 (Sommers & S LLP) -7 Thurlow Ter -Albany 12203 **Fx**:455-8907
(518) 432-3476 .. **Sommers**, Elizabeth B '82 %Ct of Claims -Justice Bldg ESP Bx7344 -Albany 12224 **Fx**:432-3450
(212) 709-8389 .. **Sommers**, George R '88 -110 Wall -NY 10005
(212) 486-4300 .. **Sommers**, Harold S '62 (Forbes & S) -150 E 58th -NY 10155
(212) 755-6000 .. **Sommers**, Howard M '78 OfCnsl Aronauer R&Y,LLP -444 Mad Av -NY 10022
(631) 231-7725 .. **Sommers**, John G '91 %JS Beige -200 Motor Pkwy -Hauppauge 11788
(212) 450-4000 .. **Sommers**, Justin G '08 %Davis P&W LLP -450 Lex Av -NY 10017
(716) 849-8900 .. **Sommers**, Kirstin Lowry '00 OfCnsl Hurwitz & F,PC -1300 Lbrty Bldg -Buffalo 14202
(212) 752-9200 .. **Sommers**, Louise '77 (Miller KS LLP) -488 Mad Av -NY 10022 **Fx**:688-3996
(718) 490-2164 .. **Sommers**, Susan J '95 -88-10 161st Av -Howard Bch 11414 **Fx**:843-1508
(716) 725-0185 .. **Sommerstein**, Robt B '70 -69 Delaware Av -Buffalo 14202 **Fx**:725-0190
(718) 836-8900 .. **Somos**, Ted '95 -120 Bay Ridge Av -Brklyn 11220 **Fx**:836-8981
(516) 484-3800 .. **Somosi**, Anette M '01 Luxottica Grp -44 Hrbr Park Dr -Pt Wash 11050
(212) 238-8900 .. **Somoza**, John H '80 (Melito & A,PC) -233 Bway -NY 10279
(212) 705-7000 .. **Son**, John P '07 %Bingham M LLP -399 Park Av -NY 10022
(718) 260-4703 .. **Son**, Lea '08 Leg Aid Society Ofc for the Aging -111 Lvngstn -Brklyn 11201 **Fx**:260-4722
(718) 389-2427 .. **Son**, Soh-Yung Erica '05 %Agostino & Assoc,PC -500 Kngslnd Av -Brklyn 11222
(516) 739-1100 .. **Sonageri & Fallon,LLC** -1461 Franklin Av -Gdn Cty 11530 **Fx**:739-1103
(516) 739-1100 .. **Sonageri**, James L '81 (Sonageri & F,LLC) -1461 Franklin Av -Gdn Cty 11530
(212) 451-2300 .. **Soncini**, Jason W '08 %Olshan GFR&W LLP -65 E 55th -NY 10022
(315) 451-2387 .. **Sondej**, Thad F '77 (Granito & S) -890 7th N -Liverpool 13088 **Fx**:451-3981
(716) 694-9841 .. **Sondel**, Robt '86 -318 Wheatfld -N Tonawanda 14120
(212) 732-3200 .. **Sondericker**, Wm F '53 (Carter L&M LLP) -2 Wall -NY 10005
(718) 643-4546 .. **Sonderlich**, Marlene '72 %Hon M Martinez-Perez -283 Adams -Brklyn 11201

(518) 783-3843 ..**Sonders**, Mark R '73 %Hacker & M,LLP -7 Airport Park Blvd -Latham 12110
(212) 238-4800 ..**Sondhi**, Amit '08 %Landman CB&F,PC -120 Bway -NY 10271
(516) 294-8844 ..**Sondhi**, Sumeet '04 %L'Abbate BC&C,LLP -1001 Franklin Av -Gdn Cty 11530
(516) 572-6818 ..**Sondon**, Lillian '89 %MHLS -2201 Hempstd Tpk -E Meadow 11554 **Fx**:572-4926
(212) 969-3000 ..**Sonenshein**, Jessica L '05 %Proskauer R LLP -1585 Bway -NY 10036
(212) 503-6306 ..**Sonet**, Richd H '84 %Marks Paneth & Shron LLP -622 3rd Av -NY 10017
(212) 661-1212 ..**Sonet**, Steven G '82 (Levy S&S LLP) -630 3rd Av -NY 10017
(212) 637-0244 ..**Sonfield**, Brian J '95 %Hon L Sand -500 Pearl -NY 10007
(212) 735-3000 ..**Song**, Albert '08 %Skadden ASM&F LLP -4 Times Sq -NY 10036
(212) 465-6331 ..**Song**, Christina Y '02 MGS Media -2 Penn Plz -NY 10121
(212) 599-0700 ..**Song**, David Sungyup '97 (Mazzeo S&B LLP) -708 3rd Av -NY 10017 **Fx**:599-8400
(212) 403-1000 ..**Song**, Dong Ju '05 %Wachtell LR&K -51 W 52nd -NY 10019
(212) 735-3000 ..**Song**, Giyoung '03 %Skadden ASM&F LLP -4 Times Sq -NY 10036
(201) 461-0031 ..**Song**, Gyu-Churl '05 %Song Law Firm -1261 Bway #204 -NY 10001 **Fx**:461-0032
(212) 848-4000 ..**Song**, Hae-Ran '02 %Shearman & S LLP -599 Lex Av -NY 10022
(212) 319-6888 ..**Song**, Jimmy J '08 Kim & B PC -110 E 59th -NY 10022
(212) 878-8000 ..**Song**, John J H '07 %Clifford C LLP -31 W 52nd -NY 10019
(718) 888-9500 ..**Song**, Ju-Youn '05 %Kim & C,LLP -158-14 Nrthrn Blvd -Flushng 11358
(917) 301-7545 ..**Song**, Kristina M '97 BBC America -747 3rd Av -NY 10017
(646) 839-2616 ..**Song**, Michl '96 -43 W 33rd -NY 10001 **Fx**:(201) 592-1084
(212) 538-5295 ..**Song**, Peter '96 Credit Suisse -11 Mad Av -NY 10010
(212) 402-9400 ..**Song**, Peter Hyungsup '06 %McKool S,PC -1 Bryant Park -NY 10036
(212) 928-5100 ..**Song**, Simone Yen '77 Simone Song Properties,LLC -241 Cabrini Blvd -NY 10033 **Fx**:928-5770
(212) 574-1200 ..**Song**, Stacey C E '09 %Seward & K LLP -1 Bttry Pk Plz -NY 10004
(718) 224-0888 ..**Song**, Tae Stephen '00 (Choi & S,PLLC) -38-39 Bell Blvd -Bayside 11361 **Fx**:224-0868
(973) 596-4817 ..**Songonuga**, Natasha M '04 %Gibbons PC -1 Penn Plz -NY 10119 **Fx**:639-6208
(212) 261-8000 ..**Soni**, Aarti '02 %Mendes & M,LLP -750 7th Av -NY 10019
(212) 896-6500 ..**Soni**, Gazeena Kaur '06 %Howrey LLP -601 Lex Av -NY 10022
(212) 400-4930 ..**Soniker**, Hilton '79 (Kamerman & S PC) -708 3rd Av -NY 10017
(212) 400-4930 ..**Soniker**, Robt H '08 %Kamerman & S PC -708 3rd Av -NY 10017
(718) 561-4444 ..**Sonin**, Sherri '83 (Sonin & G) -1 Fordham Plz -Bronx 10458 **Fx**:561-2162
(212) 594-9190 ..**Sonkin & Fifer** -1350 Bway -NY 10018 **Fx**:643-1882
(212) 594-9190 ..**Sonkin**, Mark A '78 (Sonkin & F) -1350 Bway -NY 10018
(212) 697-3122 ..**Sonkin**, Michl A '94 (Martin C&B LLP) -220 E 42nd -NY 10017
(914) 765-3640 ..**Sonkin**, Mitchell I '78 MBIA Ins Corp -113 King -Armonk 10504
(212) 408-5100 ..**Sonkin**, Richd '75 (Chadbourne & P LLP) -30 Rckfllr Plz -NY 10112
(212) 619-4444 ..**Sonkin**, Steven L '87 %Marshall CW&B,PC -116 John -NY 10038
(315) 691-4818 ..**Sonn**, David E '74 Pub Def -2 E Main Bx408 -Earlville 13332
(212) 481-0091 ..**Sonn**, Karen S '91 (Sonn & Assoc,PC) -207 W 25th -NY 10001 **Fx**:481-0112
(212) 998-6730 ..**Sonn**, Paul K '95 %Brennan Ctr for Justice -161 Av of Amer -NY 10013
(315) 422-1391 ..**Sonneborn**, James L '73 (Green & S,PLLC) -One Lincoln Ctr #900 -Syracuse 13202
(212) 869-3200 ..**Sonneborn**, Marcy '79 OfCnsl Molod S&D,PC -104 W 40th -NY 10018
(212) 508-6100 ..**Sonnenberg**, Jay T '05 (Bracewell & G,LLP) -1251 Av of Amer -NY 10020
(212) 318-6000 ..**Sonnenberg**, Stephen P '06 (Paul HJ&W LLP) -75 E 55th -NY 10022
(212) 903-9000 ..**Sonnenblick**, Scott I '98 (Linklaters) -1345 Av of Amer -NY 10105
(212) 468-4800 ..**Sonnenborn**, Donald E '71 (Davis & G LLP) -1740 Bway -NY 10019
(212) 556-2100 ..**Sonnenfeld**, Kenneth H '91 (King & S) -1185 Av of Amer -NY 10036
(212) 687-1425 ..**Sonnenfeld & Richman** -360 Lex Av -NY 10017 **Fx**:682-6425
(516) 775-7007 ..**Sonnenfeldt**, Neil D '82 (Gutman MB&S,PC) -813 Jericho Tpk -New Hyde Pk 11040
(516) 627-7000 ..**Sonnenklar**, Alan H '94 (Weiss & Z,PC) -3333 New Hyde Pk Rd -New Hyde Pk 11042
(212) 906-1200 ..**Sonnenschein**, Edw Jr. '07 (Latham & W) -885 3rd Av -NY 10022
(718) 250-2000 ..**Sonnenschein**, Eric A '85 %DA -350 Jay -Brklyn 11201 **Fx**:250-2314
(212) 245-6754 ..**Sonnenschein**, Irving '41 (Sonnenschein S&D,LLP) -7 Penn Plz -NY 10001
(212) 768-6700 ..**Sonnenschein Nath & Rosenthal LLP** -1221 Av of Amer -NY 10020 **Fx**:768-6800
(212) 768-6700 ..**Sonnenschein Nath & Rosenthal LLP** -2 World Fncl Ctr -NY 10281 **Fx**:768-6800
(212) 245-6754 ..**Sonnenschein Sherman & Deutsch,LLP** -7 Penn Plz -NY 10001 **Fx**:956-7549
(212) 788-1067 ..**Sonnenshein**, Larry A '74 %Law Dept -100 Church -NY 10007 **Fx**:788-0367
(212) 326-3939 ..**Sonnie**, Marilyn Weaver '03 (Jones D) -222 E 41st -NY 10017
(212) 475-3519 ..**Sonnino**, Edw A '79 -44 Gramercy Pk -NY 10010
(845) 473-0936 ..**Sonoda**, Diane Yukiko '94 %Hudson/Green Assoc -248 Church -Poughkeepsie 12601
(212) 833-1144 ..**Sonpal**, Rickie M '05 %Friedman KS&A LLP -1633 Bway -NY 10019 **Fx**:373-7964
(607) 733-8866 ..**Sonsire**, Christina M '05 %Ziff Law Firm,LLP -303 William -Elmira 14901 **Fx**:732-6062
(607) 737-2944 ..**Sonsire**, Damian M '01 %DA -226 Lk Bx588 -Elmira 14902 **Fx**:737-2965
(516) 621-0600 ..**Sontag**, Bruce '89 (Sontag & H) -69 Roslyn Rd -Roslyn Hts 11577
(516) 621-0600 ..**Sontag & Hyman** -69 Roslyn Rd -Roslyn Hts 11577
(212) 310-8000 ..**Sontag**, Scott M '98 (Weil G&M LLP) -767 5th Av -NY 10153
(718) 654-4673 ..**Sontag**, Steven P '97 (Hampton & S,LLC) -4215 Katonah Av -Bronx 10470 **Fx**:654-4675
(212) 416-6383 ..**Sontupe**, Felice A '94 %Dept of Law -120 Bway -NY 10271
(212) 836-8000 ..**Soofian**, David '10 Kaye S LLP -425 Park Av -NY 10022
(212) 854-0706 ..**Soohoo**, Cynthia '93 Columbia Law School -435 W 116th -NY 10027
(212) 331-5130 ..**Soohoo**, Patrick S '05 HRA -180 Water -NY 10038
(718) 330-7861 ..**Soo-Hoo**, Wm C '93 %ODAR-SSA -111 Lvngstn -Brklyn 11201 **Fx**:330-2009
(212) 373-3000 ..**Soojian**, Jessica D '07 %Paul WRW&G LLP -1285 Av of Amer -NY 10019
(212) 608-3700 ..**Soong**, Arthur J '78 (Soong & L) -305 Bway -NY 10007
(585) 423-4292 ..**Soong**, Zosan Sam '87 %Xerox -100 Clinton Av S -Rchstr 14644
(718) 667-3077 ..**Soos**, Robt W '88 -1491 Richmond Rd -Staten Isl 10304 **Fx**:983-5088
(212) 455-2000 ..**Soots**, Christopher R '08 %Simpson T&B LLP -425 Lex Av -NY 10017
(212) 351-4000 ..**Sopher**, Edw D '86 (Gibson D&C LLP) -200 Park Av -NY 10166
(212) 577-7965 ..**Sopher**, Meredith Felise '96 %Leg Aid -199 Water -NY 10038 **Fx**:577-3520
(212) 825-1212 ..**Sophocleous**, Demetra '99 (Morrison M LLP) -17 State -NY 10004
(718) 250-0400 ..**Sophocleous**, Steve M '01 %R Tusa -1 MetroTech Ctr -Brklyn 11201 **Fx**:250-0591
(212) 710-3900 ..**Sorabella**, Eileen C '01 %Clyde & Co US LLP -405 Lex Av -NY 10174 **Fx**:710-3950
(212) 446-4800 ..**Sorabella**, Wm B '01 (Kirkland & E LLP) -153 E 53rd -NY 10022
(212) 326-2000 ..**Soran**, Matthew V '06 %O'Melveny & M LLP -7 Times Sq -NY 10036
(212) 237-1000 ..**Sorbera**, Christina J '07 %Windels ML&M,LLP -156 W 56th -NY 10019
(212) 635-6604 ..**Sorce**, C Becket '99 Bk of NY Mellon -1 Wall -NY 10286
(585) 678-7100 ..**Sorce**, David S '81 %Constellation Brands -207 Hgh Pnt Dr -Victor 14564
(631) 287-3065 ..**Sordi**, Michl C '84 Town Atty -116 Hmptn Rd -Southampton 11968 **Fx**:287-3662
Sordi, Nicholas A '50 -Bx398 -Nesconset 11767
(212) 483-9490 ..**Sordillo**, Jos V '05 %McElroy DM&C,LLP -88 Pine -NY 10005
(212) 294-6700 ..**Sordina**, Micol O '08 %Winston & S -200 Park Av -NY 10166
(631) 421-8780 ..**Sorel**, Scott P '02 (Sorel G,LLP) -196 E Main -Huntngtn 11743 **Fx**:421-8786
(212) 813-8800 ..**Sorell**, Louis S '87 (Goodwin P LLP) -620 8th Av -NY 10018
(516) 228-8484 ..**Sorell**, Peter B '98 Dilworth & B,LLP -1000 Woodbury Rd -Woodbury 11797
(516) 294-1949 ..**Sorell**, Timothy V '05 OfCnsl Mangi & G LLP -1400 Old Cntry Rd -Westbury 11590
(718) 815-4500 ..**Soren**, Karen B '96 (Soren & S) -57 Beach -Staten Isl 10304 **Fx**:815-5562
(718) 815-4500 ..**Soren**, Steven J '97 (Soren & S) -57 Beach -Staten Isl 10304 **Fx**:815-5562
(212) 483-9490 ..**Sorensen**, Brian J '09 %McElroy DM&C,LLP -88 Pine -NY 10005
(585) 987-3000 ..**Sorensen**, Sarah Ayer '86 %ACC Telecom -400 West Av -Rchstr 14611 **Fx**:987-3335
(212) 373-3000 ..**Sorensen**, Theo C '66 OfCnsl Paul WRW&G LLP -1285 Av of Amer -NY 10019
(212) 735-3000 ..**Sorenson**, Bjorn C '09 %Skadden ASM&F LLP -4 Times Sq -NY 10036
(212) 626-4100 ..**Sorenson**, Sigurd Ansgar '95 (Baker & M LLP) -1114 Av of Amer -NY 10036
(212) 564-0088 ..**Soressa**, Shifa D '02 -1 W 34th -NY 10001
(212) 552-2869 ..**Sorge**, Anthony R '67 JP Morgan Chase & Co -1 Chase Manh Plz -NY 10005
(516) 560-6400 ..**Sorge**, G Jeffrey '70 %Leg Aid -1 Helen Keller Way -Hempstd 11550 **Fx**:565-3694
(718) 855-9000 ..**Sorge**, Robt J '84 (Cullen and D LLP) -177 Montague -Brklyn 11201
(212) 489-1600 ..**Sorgen**, David L '93 %Deloitte LLP -1633 Bway -NY 10019 **Fx**:492-4201
(516) 520-8350 ..**Sorgen**, Melissa L '02 Division Av High Schl -120 Division Av -Levittwn 11756
(315) 536-4223 ..**Sorgen**, Tiffany M '05 %Finger Lks Law Grp -131 Main Bx681 -Penn Yan 14527 **Fx**:536-3603
(716) 614-8801 ..**Sorgi**, Peter J '03 (Hopkins & S,PLLC) -5500 Main -Williamsvll 14221
(212) 832-2000 ..**Sorial**, George A '97 Trump Orgn -725 5th Av -NY 10022 **Fx**:935-0141
(631) 390-0010 ..**Soriano**, Michl A '90 (Bruno G&S,LLP) -445 Broad Hollow Rd -Melvll 11747
(914) 949-3393 ..**Soriano**, Nicholas M '67 -175 Main -White Plns 10601 **Fx**:761-0995
(914) 747-0677 ..**Soriano**, Nicholas M '67 -8 Munson Rd -Plsntvll 10570
(212) 541-6222 ..**Soric**, Alexander '01 %Kane K,PC -1350 Av of Amer -NY 10019
(631) 393-5186 ..**Soricelli**, Gary P '84 -200 Broadhllw Rd -Melvll 11747
(516) 223-8000 ..**Sorid**, Harvey '70 -358 RXR Plz -Uniondale 11556 **Fx**:378-8412
(516) 889-8000 ..**Sorid**, Jay C '97 -192 EAB Plz -Uniondale 11556 **Fx**:378-8412
(212) 742-3390 ..**Soriero**, Kenneth J '06 %Lindabury ME&C,PC -26 Bway -NY 10004
(212) 972-1100 ..**Sorin**, Boris '03 %Sylvor & R -122 E 42nd -NY 10158 **Fx**:983-5271
(212) 859-8000 ..**Sorin**, Robt J '83 (Fried FHS&J LLP) -1 NY Plz -NY 10004
(914) 241-7073 ..**Sorio**, Ashley B '01 -11 Caren Ct -Mt Kisco 10549 **Fx**:241-7073
(212) 728-8000 ..**Sorkin**, Andrew D '08 %Willkie F&G LLP -787 7th Av -NY 10019
(212) 750-8300 ..**Sorkin**, David J '85 Kohlberg Kravis Roberts -9 W 57th -NY 10019
(212) 277-6500 ..**Sorkin**, Ira L '70 (Dickstein S LLP) -1633 Bway -NY 10019
(212) 458-1575 ..**Sorkin**, Jeffrey A '94 %AIG -175 Water -NY 10038
(212) 859-8000 ..**Sorkin**, John E '95 (Fried FHS&J LLP) -1 NY Plz -NY 10004
(212) 872-1000 ..**Sorkin**, Jos L '08 -One Bryant Park -NY 10036 **Fx**:872-1002
(212) 701-3000 ..**Sorkin**, Laurence T '68 SrCnsl Cahill G&R LLP -80 Pine -NY 10005 **Fx**:269-5420
(212) 373-3000 ..**Sorkin**, Sharon A '09 Paul WRW&G LLP -1285 Av of Amer -NY 10019
(212) 450-4000 ..**Sorkin**, Steve '10 %Davis P&W LLP -450 Lex Av -NY 10017
(212) 839-5300 ..**Sorkowitz**, Alan J '81 Cnsl Sidley A LLP -787 7th Av -NY 10019
(212) 227-8140 ..**Soroka**, Mark S '77 (Taubman K&S LLP) -30 Vesey -NY 10007
(516) 742-2002 ..**Soroka**, Michl H '74 -300 Old Cntry Rd -Mineola 11501 **Fx**:742-0953
(646) 865-1590 ..**Sorokanich**, Tamara '07 %Carlucci & G,LLP -11 E 44th -NY 10017

(516) 829-2570 .. **Sorokoff,** Caroline '98 Great Neck Arts Ctr -113 Middle Nck Rd -Gt Neck 11021
(914) 478-0211 .. **Sorokoff,** David H '86 -1 Southgate Av -Hastings-On-Hud 10706
(212) 490-3000 .. **Soronen,** Christian D '09 %Wilson EME&D LLP -150 E 42nd -NY 10017
(518) 242-3720 .. **Soronen,** Laurence '86 %Ct of Claims -Justice Bldg ESP Bx7344 -Albany 12224 **Fx:**432-3450
(212) 262-6300 .. **Soros,** Jonathan T A '01 SPFM -888 7th Av -NY 10106
(212) 506-1700 .. **Sorota,** Alexandra J '04 %Kasowitz BT&F LLP -1633 Bway -NY 10019
(212) 804-5703 .. **Sorote,** Jorge '85 -110 Wall -NY 10005
(716) 852-5875 .. **Sorrels,** Stephen M '96 (Feldman K LLP) -110 Pearl -Buffalo 14202
(914) 592-6648 .. **Sorrentino,** Dominick '55 (Sorrentino T&S) -12 Armand Pl -Valhalla 10595
(914) 592-6648 .. **Sorrentino,** Frances A '90 (Sorrentino T&S) -12 Armand Pl -Valhalla 10595
(914) 747-8676 .. **Sorrentino,** John R '84 USI Holdings Corp -555 Plsntvll Rd -Briarclff Mnr 10510
(718) 875-1300 .. **Sorrentino,** Jos M '06 Appllt Div 2nd Dept -45 Monroe Pl -Brklyn 11201 **Fx:**858-2446
(718) 720-4943 .. **Sorrentino,** Jos V '85 -404 Manor Rd -Staten Isl 10314 **Fx:**720-5009
(914) 592-6648 .. **Sorrentino Thomas & Sorrentino** -12 Armand Pl -Valhalla 10595 **Fx:**592-4252
(716) 856-3646 .. **Sorrentino,** Vincent J '64 (Cole SHH&G,PC) -37 Franklin -Buffalo 14202
(516) 496-5822 .. **Sorrese,** Joyce D '01 %T Spina -170 Froehlich Farm Blvd -Woodbury 11797 **Fx:**496-5420
(212) 335-9000 .. **Sorrett,** Ayanna McLean '05 %DA -1 Hogan Pl -NY 10013
(516) 536-6067 .. **Sorscher,** Randall A '95 %M Hassin -330 Sunrise Hwy -Rockvll Ctr 11570 **Fx:**536-3122
(585) 454-7145 .. **Sortino,** Anthony M '61 OfCnsl Gallo & I,LLP -39 State -Rchstr 14614
(212) 232-1300 .. **Sorvino,** Heidi J '90 (Lewis BB&S LLP) -77 Water -NY 10005
(646) 672-3004 .. **Sosa,** Jeannith M G '99 NYC H&HC Metropolitan Hospital -1901 1st Av -NY 10029
(212) 594-5300 .. **Sosa,** Jennifer J '06 %Milberg LLP -1 Penn Plz -NY 10119
(718) 235-8791 .. **Sosa,** Jose A '82 -171 Sunnyside Av -Brklyn 11207
(718) 579-7900 .. **Sosa,** Maria A '09 %Leg Aid -900 Sheridan Av -Bronx 10451 **Fx:**293-8744
(718) 892-0400 .. **Sosa,** Pablo A '96 %W Gallina -1180 Morris Park Av -Bronx 10461 **Fx:**892-0033
(914) 457-2300 .. **Soscia,** Anthony M Jr. '74 (Kanterman & S,LLP) -50 Main -White Plns 10606
(516) 482-1415 .. **Soshnick,** Harold F '76 -37 Merrivale Rd -Gt Neck 11020
(516) 294-1111 .. **Soshnick,** Michl L '79 -190 Willis Av -Mineola 11501 **Fx:**294-5465
(718) 263-8565 .. **Soshnick,** Robt A '76 Rubenfeld & S -125-10 Qns Blvd -Kew Gdns 11415 **Fx:**263-2233
(516) 488-3300 .. **Sosin,** Joan S '85 %Shaub AC&S,LLP -1983 Marcus Av -Lk Success 11042
(516) 822-3913 .. **Sosinsky,** Bernard '70 -18 Netto Ln -Plainvw 11803
(212) 285-2270 .. **Sosinsky,** Fredk L '87 -225 Bway -NY 10007
(646) 638-8600 .. **Sosinsky,** Joel '75 Cnsl Teamsters Pub Srvc Div -216 W 14th -NY 10011 **Fx:**(212) 741-8615
(914) 632-5151 .. **Sosis,** Richd A '67 (Bobrow & S) -271 North Av -New Rchll 10801
(212) 456-2847 .. **Soskin,** David G '09 ESPN -77 W 66th -NY 10023
(518) 462-3000 .. **Sosler,** Karen E '98 (Iseman CR&H,LLP) -9 Thurlow Ter -Albany 12203
(718) 875-1300 .. **Sosna,** Donna M '81 %Appllt Div 2nd Dept -45 Monroe Pl -Brklyn 11201 **Fx:**858-2446
(631) 537-9000 .. **Sosne,** Alan I '94 -2316 Main Bx102 -Brdghmptn 11932 **Fx:**537-5744
(718) 875-1300 .. **Sosne,** Ben L '10 %Appllt Div 2nd Dept -45 Monroe Pl -Brklyn 11201 **Fx:**858-2446
(917) 778-6600 .. **Sosnick,** Chas J '95 %J Toomey -485 Lex Av -NY 10017 **Fx:**778-7048
(212) 848-4000 .. **Sosnick,** Fredric '92 (Shearman & S LLP) -599 Lex Av -NY 10022
(516) 745-0066 .. **Sosnik,** Howard L '87 (Karol H&S,PC) -600 Old Cntry Rd -Gdn Cty 11530
(212) 744-9577 .. **Sosnik,** Matthew A '90 -125-10 Qns Blvd -Kew Gdns 11415 **Fx:**706-9093
(212) 859-8000 .. **Sosnow,** Phillip S '09 %Fried FHS&J LLP -1 NY Plz -NY 10004
(718) 724-2222 .. **Sosnow,** Sherman F '53 -20 Wellngtn Ct -Brklyn 11230 **Fx:**421-6301
(212) 698-4570 .. **Sosnowitz,** Linda J '74 (Stapper & V) -10 Rckfllr Plz -NY 10020
(718) 875-6651 .. **Soss,** Harvey P '80 -26 Court -Brklyn 11242
(315) 733-2208 .. **Sossen,** R Robt Jr. '75 -10 Steuben Park -Utica 13501 **Fx:**793-8743
(518) 463-3600 .. **Sossner,** Edw M '93 -350 Nrthrn Blvd -Albany 12204 **Fx:**463-6223
(212) 751-3001 .. **Sostek,** Bruce S '06 (Thompson & K LLP) -919 3rd Av -NY 10022
(212) 779-1414 .. **Sosunova,** Sabina '03 %Bernstein L LLP -10 E 40th -NY 10016
(212) 446-4800 .. **Soszynski,** Joshua F '08 %Kirkland & E LLP -153 E 53rd -NY 10022
(718) 767-1177 .. **Soterakis,** Alexis '04 %Coran O,PC -25-02 F Lewis Blvd -Flushng 11358
(212) 294-6700 .. **Soterakis,** George T '04 %Winston & S -200 Park Av -NY 10166
(718) 767-1177 .. **Soterakis,** Simeon '70 (Coran O,PC) -25-02 F Lewis Blvd -Flushng 11358
(716) 487-0106 .. **Sotir,** Richd L Jr. '74 -8 E 4th -Jamestwn 14701 **Fx:**487-0694
(718) 204-0437 .. **Sotirakis,** John A '75 (Coritsidis S&S) -25-61 Steinway -LIC 11103 **Fx:**267-0330
(718) 590-2000 .. **Sotirhos,** Matthew P '07 %DA -198 E 161st -Bronx 10451 **Fx:**590-6477
(212) 980-0120 .. **Sotis,** Mary J '89 (Frankfurt KK&S,PC) -488 Mad Av -NY 10022
(212) 298-5102 .. **Soto,** Angel '97 %Leg Aid -49 Thomas -NY 10013 **Fx:**298-5252
(212) 225-2000 .. **Soto,** Carlos M '10 %Cleary GS&H -1 Lbrty Plz -NY 10006
(718) 590-2000 .. **Soto,** Juan D '00 %DA -198 E 161st -Bronx 10451 **Fx:**590-6477
(212) 859-8000 .. **Soto,** Marissa '07 %Fried FHS&J LLP -1 NY Plz -NY 10004
(646) 710-8611 .. **Soto,** Myriam '00 Bk of NY -1633 Bway -NY 10019
(718) 267-0032 .. **Soto,** Nestor '88 -31-26 Steinway -Astoria 11103
(212) 687-8080 .. **Soto,** Renee '03 %Citigate Sard Verbinnen -630 3rd Av -NY 10017
(914) 378-9000 .. **Soto Sanchez & Negron,LLP** -281 S Bway -Ynkrs 10705 **Fx:**378-1188
(914) 378-9000 .. **Soto,** Wilson '99 (Soto S&N,LLP) -281 S Bway -Ynkrs 10705
(516) 921-8600 .. **Soto,** Yasmin D '04 %McAndrew C&P -95 Froehlich Farm Blvd -Woodbury 11797
(716) 853-3087 .. **Sotolongo,** Maria A '95 %Leg Srvcs -237 Main -Buffalo 14203 **Fx:**856-5317
(718) 618-2331 .. **Soto-Maldonado,** Evette '97 Surrogate's Ct -851 Grnd Cncrs -Bronx 10451 **Fx:**590-3575
(212) 553-0300 .. **Sotomayor,** Felix '94 %Moody's Invstr Srvc -250 Greenwich -NY 10007
(914) 297-8123 .. **Sotomayor,** James A '96 -Bx352 -Tuckahoe 10707
(212) 819-8200 .. **Sotomayor,** Marisa A '08 %White & C LLP -1155 Av of Amer -NY 10036
(212) 245-4125 .. **Sotos,** Peter G '97 The Music Law Grp LLC -250 W 57th -NY 10107 **Fx:**245-6293
(718) 391-1720 .. **Sottile,** Robt J '79 %Dept Design & Cnstrctn -30-30 Thomson Av -LIC 11101 **Fx:**391-1894
(212) 309-1000 .. **Sotto,** Lisa J '88 (Hunton & W) -200 Park Av -NY 10166
(914) 766-1900 .. **Soucar,** Steven J '98 IBM -294 Route 100 -Somers 10589
(518) 481-1624 .. **Soucia,** Thos G '97 Pub Def -355 W Main -Malone 12953 **Fx:**483-4690
(212) 805-0177 .. **Souffrant,** Emmanuella '96 %USDC -500 Pearl -NY 10007
(212) 858-7710 .. **Soukas,** Wm C '95 (Nowell AKB,PA) -140 Bway PMB 46028 -NY 10005
(212) 852-2913 .. **Soukavanitch Axel,** Marlene '02 US Trust Bk of Amer Private Wlth Mgmt -114 W 47th -NY 10036
(718) 896-6550 .. **Soukeras,** Robt '98 ATF -9745 Qns Blvd -Rego Pk 11374
(516) 679-5400 .. **Soukup,** Jeffrey E '81 Automotive Law Ctr of LI -3350 Sunrise Hwy -Wantagh 11793 **Fx:**679-0065
(212) 957-7600 .. **Soule,** Chas D '01 %Cohen & G LLP -800 3rd Av -NY 10022
(212) 997-4500 .. **Soulios,** Steven A '90 (Ruta & S) -1500 Bway -NY 10036
(212) 431-1300 .. **Soumas,** Gregory C '91 (Borah GAN&G PC) -377 Bway -NY 10013
(212) 903-9000 .. **Souris,** Constantin '10 %Linklaters -1345 Av of Amer -NY 10105
(212) 468-4800 .. **Soussa,** Jennifer B '02 %Davis & G LLP -1740 Bway -NY 10019
(212) 558-4000 .. **Soussloff,** Andrew D '80 (Sullivan & C LLP) -125 Broad -NY 10004
(607) 734-8433 .. **Soutar,** Sarah K '03 -200 William -Elmira 14901
(212) 440-2350 .. **South,** Christopher A '80 %C Siegel -40 Wall -NY 10005 **Fx:**440-2385
(212) 335-4500 .. **South,** George B III '92 (DLA Piper LLP) -1251 Av of Amer -NY 10020
(518) 783-8366 .. **Southard,** Cynthia J '97 -19 Knadler Dr -Latham 12110
(212) 385-8600 .. **Southard,** Richd C '97 -401 Bway -NY 10013 **Fx:**566-1068
(212) 972-3000 .. **Southard,** Sean C '01 (Klestadt & W,LLP) -292 Mad Av -NY 10017
(212) 574-1200 .. **Souther,** Eugene P '59 SrCnsl Seward & K LLP -1 Bttry Pk Plz -NY 10004
(212) 896-6512 .. **Souther,** Thos M '85 (Freeh S&S LLP) -601 Lex Av -NY 10022
(518) 431-4761 .. **Southgate,** James C '72 %IRS -1 Clinton Av -Albany 12207
(212) 351-4000 .. **Southwell,** Alexander H '98 (Gibson D&C LLP) -200 Park Av -NY 10166
(212) 504-6000 .. **Southwick,** Michl J '89 SpclCnsl Cadwalader W&T LLP -1 World Fncl Ctr -NY 10281
(315) 448-0672 .. **Southwick,** Richd R '85 %US Atty -100 S Clinton Bx7198 -Syracuse 13261 **Fx:**448-0689
(845) 294-6155 .. **Souto,** Edw P '88 (Grogan & S,PC) -14 Scotchtown Av Bx330 -Goshen 10924
(914) 524-5600 .. **Souto,** Silvia C '90 %L Fishman -303 S Bway -Tarrytwn 10591 **Fx:**524-5742
(212) 937-7224 .. **Souto,** Victor F '89 SpclCnsl WilmerHale -399 Park Av -NY 10022
(516) 681-1000 .. **Souza-Tortorella,** Tagiana S '07 %R Rosenberg,PC -500 N Bway -Jericho 11753 **Fx:**681-6272
(212) 307-5500 .. **Sova,** Kristine A '03 %Venable LLP -1270 Av of Amer -NY 10020
(212) 949-4700 .. **Sovak,** Christopher J '94 (Bushell SO&G LLP) -60 E 42nd -NY 10165 **Fx:**286-0513
(518) 373-1482 .. **Sovern,** Cheryl L '07 %DuCharme H&C,LLP -10 Maxwell Dr -Clifton Pk 12065
(212) 264-3650 .. **Sovern,** Ellen E '88 %SSA Ofc Genl Cnsl -26 Fed Plz -NY 10278 **Fx:**264-6372
(212) 794-5382 .. **Sovern,** Jane M '87 %CUNY -535 E 80th -NY 10075 **Fx:**794-5426
(718) 990-6429 .. **Sovern,** Jeff '82 (St John's Law Schl) -8000 Utopia Pkwy -Jamaica 11439 **Fx:**591-1855
(315) 836-1546 .. **Sovie,** Susan Anne '95 -200 Wshngtn -Watertwn 13601
(315) 474-2911 .. **Sovik,** Laurence F '57 (Smith SK&S,PC) -250 S Clinton -Syracuse 13202
(631) 265-2077 .. **Sovronsky,** Ruth '79 OfCnsl Castrovinci & M -1 Edgewood Av -Smithtwn 11787 **Fx:**265-0627
(212) 340-0400 .. **Sowah,** Margaret O '86 %Appllt Div 1st Dept -27 Mad Av -NY 10010 **Fx:**889-4412
(212) 709-8302 .. **Sowande,** Beverly Folasade '86 (Sowande & Assoc,PC) -110 Wall -NY 10005
(212) 573-6852 .. **Sowder,** Donald S '95 %Pfizer Inc -235 E 42nd -NY 10017
(212) 909-6000 .. **Sowder,** Zahra J '09 %Debevoise & P LLP -919 3rd Av -NY 10022
(212) 907-9700 .. **Sowell,** Paul J '96 %Smith G&R,LLP -250 Park Av -NY 10177
(718) 636-6100 .. **Sowers,** Christopher K '79 (CK Sowers,PC) -907 Fulton -Brklyn 11238 **Fx:**636-5744
(212) 840-6543 .. **Soybel,** Arthur '55 (Weinstein S&K) -36 W 44th -NY 10036
(212) 805-3900 .. **Soyka,** Edw L '02 %Clausen M PC -1 Chase Manh Plz -NY 10005
(212) 848-4000 .. **Soysa,** Shihani '07 %Shearman & S LLP -599 Lex Av -NY 10022
(212) 878-8479 .. **Soyster,** Margaret B '77 (Clifford C LLP) -31 W 52nd -NY 10019
(212) 735-3000 .. **Sozzani,** Jos R '08 %Skadden ASM&F LLP -4 Times Sq -NY 10036
(212) 849-7000 .. **Spaccarotella,** John C '05 %Quinn EU&S,LLP -51 Mad Av -NY 10010
(914) 750-5933 .. **Spacek,** Edw G '78 (Kissel H&W LLP) -580 Wht Plns Rd -Tarrytwn 10591
(631) 360-7800 .. **Spada Ardam & Sibener, PLLC** -64 Smithtwn Blvd -Smithtwn 11787 **Fx:**360-8835
(212) 921-8399 .. **Spada,** Chas T '91 (Lankler S&W LLP) -500 5th Av -NY 10110
(845) 338-8884 .. **Spada,** Derek J '03 %Basch & K,LLP -307 Clinton Av Bx4235 -Kingston 12402
(518) 459-7000 .. **Spada,** Eugene R '67 (Spada) -107 Everett Rd -Albany 12205 **Fx:**459-7025
(518) 459-7000 .. **Spada,** Justine L '94 (Spada) -107 Everett Rd -Albany 12205 **Fx:**459-7025
(631) 360-7800 .. **Spada,** Lawr J '76 (Spada A&S,PLLC) -64 Smithtwn Blvd -Smithtwn 11787

(917) 509-6714 .. **Spadaccini,** Robt L '04 -330 Wyona Av -Lindenhrst 11757 **Fx:**(631) 225-7386
(212) 770-1530 .. **Spadacenta,** Marco L '91 %AIG -80 Pine -NY 10005
(716) 854-1111 .. **Spadafora,** John E '72 (Spadafora & V) -2 Symphony Cir -Buffalo 14201
(212) 794-1645 .. **Spadafora,** Jo-Una '76 -201 E 83rd -NY 10028
(212) 221-6900 .. **Spadafora,** Luigi '89 (Winget S&S,LLP) -45 Bway -NY 10006
(718) 556-7083 .. **Spadafora,** Nina D '07 %DA -130 Styvsnt Pl -Staten Isl 10301
(716) 886-0211 .. **Spadafora,** Peggy W '98 %Benderson Dvlpmnt -570 Delaware Av -Buffalo 14202 **Fx:**886-2269
(716) 854-1111 .. **Spadafora & Verrastro** -2 Symphony Cir -Buffalo 14201 **Fx:**854-3460
(718) 948-1140 .. **Spadaro,** Alice M '99 (Ajello & S) -3974 Amboy Rd -Staten Isl 10308 **Fx:**948-1160
(518) 862-1200 .. **Spadaro,** Gina M '02 %Martin H&M LLP -Bx15141 -Albany 12212
(212) 580-6406 .. **Spadaro,** Keith M '05 NYPD 20th Pct -120 W 82nd -NY 10024
(212) 635-0577 .. **Spadaro,** Robt M '72 -17 Battery Pl -NY 10004 **Fx:**635-0733
(212) 732-6577 .. **Spadaro,** Stephanie J '84 -20 Vesey -NY 10007 **Fx:**732-5091
(212) 373-3000 .. **Spader,** John P '06 Paul WRW&G LLP -1285 Av of Amer -NY 10019
(646) 728-3684 .. **Spadone,** Melina '96 Intl Cncl of Shopping Ctrs -1221 Av of Amer -NY 10020 **Fx:**(212) 589-5575
(212) 973-0572 .. **Spadoro,** George A Jr. '73 (Wolff & S PC) -140 Bway -NY 10005 **Fx:**(973) 530-2313
(212) 705-0117 .. **Spaeth,** Phyllis B '73 Chldrns Advrtsng Review Unit -70 W 36th -NY 10018
(516) 931-1800 .. **Spaeth,** Wayne E '83 OfCnsl Catalano G&P LLP -100 Jericho Quadrangle -Jericho 11753
(212) 570-1240 .. **Spagna,** Susan L '76 -45 East End Av -NY 10028
(212) 450-4000 .. **Spagnoletti,** Paul M '99 (Davis P&W LLP) -450 Lex Av -NY 10017
(212) 554-1234 .. **Spagnoli,** Chas C '95 AXA Financial Inc -1290 Av of Amer -NY 10104 **Fx:**707-3963
(914) 681-8700 .. **Spagnoli,** Kevin L '01 %Milber MP&S LLP -3 Barker Av -White Plns 10601
(631) 853-4161 .. **Spagnolo,** Jodi Franzese '97 %DA -N Cnty Cmplx Bldg 77 -Hauppauge 11788 **Fx:**853-4192
(914) 234-6363 .. **Spagnuolo,** Mario L '89 (Kuntz S&M,PC) -444 Old Post Rd -Bedfrd 10506 **Fx:**234-6249
(585) 641-8000 .. **Spahn,** Philip F Jr. '75 (Fix SB&G,PC) -295 Woodcliff Dr -Fairprt 14450
(718) 558-3322 .. **Spahr,** Laurence C '94 %LIRR Police Dept -93-59 183rd -Hollis 11423
(631) 853-4049 .. **Spahr,** Linda A '80 %Cnty Atty -Dennison Bldg Bx6100 -Hauppauge 11788 **Fx:**853-5169
(212) 261-8000 .. **Spain,** Anthony P '84 (Mendes & M,LLP) -750 7th Av -NY 10019
(845) 628-5900 .. **Spain,** C Compton '82 (Spain & S) -671 Route 6 -Mahopac 10541 **Fx:**628-0694
(212) 909-6000 .. **Spain,** Jennifer E '05 %Debevoise & P LLP -919 3rd Av -NY 10022
(718) 738-7405 .. **Spain,** Melvyn N '57 -238 St Johns Pl -Brklyn 11217
(212) 676-0985 .. **Spain,** Nicole A '04 %Law Dept -60 Lafayette -NY 10013 **Fx:**442-6865
(518) 279-1212 .. **Spain,** Thos D '95 (Doyle D&S) -317 Brick Church Rd -Troy 12180
(845) 628-5900 .. **Spain,** Wm D Jr. '76 (Spain & S) -671 Route 6 -Mahopac 10541 **Fx:**628-0694
(212) 310-8000 .. **Spake,** Robt V Jr. '09 %Weil G&M LLP -767 5th Av -NY 10153
(212) 262-2390 .. **Spalding,** Karin I '97 Cnsl Connell F LLP -888 7th Av -NY 10106
(212) 617-8341 .. **Spampata,** Nicholas R '01 Bloomberg LP -731 Lex Av -NY 10022
(716) 200-5050 .. **Spampata,** Robt G Jr. '05 SrCnsl Harris B PLLC -726 Exchange -Buffalo 14210
(518) 325-4142 .. **Spampinato,** Wm J '73 -287 Lakevw Rd -Craryville 12521
(718) 875-4073 .. **Spanakos,** Alexandria Cira '00 -50 Lvngstn -Brklyn 11201
(718) 875-1100 .. **Spanakos,** Andrea G '99 -50 Lvngstn -Brklyn 11201
(718) 875-1100 .. **Spanakos,** George M '65 -50 Lvngstn -Brklyn 11201 **Fx:**596-4434
(718) 833-6900 .. **Spanakos,** John M '60 (Spanakos & S) -7207 Ft Hmltn Pkwy -Brklyn 11228 **Fx:**680-6732
(718) 250-2000 .. **Spanakos,** Michel P '96 %DA -350 Jay -Brklyn 11201 **Fx:**250-2314
(718) 833-6900 .. **Spanakos,** Wm M '55 (Spanakos & S) -7207 Ft Hmltn Pkwy -Brklyn 11228 **Fx:**680-6732
(718) 286-6000 .. **Spanakos-Orfan,** Anastasia '98 %DA -125-01 Qns Blvd -Kew Gdns 11415
(212) 986-6000 .. **Spanbock,** Maurice S '50 OfCnsl Kleinberg KW&C,PC -551 5th Av -NY 10176
(212) 836-8000 .. **Spangler,** Timothy A '95 (Kaye S LLP) -425 Park Av -NY 10022
(917) 439-8645 .. **Spanier,** David B '76 Dextra Baldwin McGonagle Fndtn -Bx709 -S Salem 10590
(212) 889-3700 .. **Spanier,** Judith L '79 (Abbey SR&A LLP) -212 E 39th -NY 10016
(716) 366-2010 .. **Spann,** Anthony J '54 OfCnsl Spann & C,PC -643 Central Av Bx262 -Dunkirk 14048
(716) 366-2010 .. **Spann & Civilette,PC** -643 Central Av Bx262 -Dunkirk 14048 **Fx:**366-5387
(716) 366-2010 .. **Spann,** James J Jr. '85 (Spann & C,PC) -643 Central Av Bx262 -Dunkirk 14048
(607) 692-3300 .. **Spann,** Kathleen M '74 E Rantanen,PC -2638 Main Bx309 -Whitney Pnt 13862 **Fx:**692-2636
(914) 664-2741 .. **Spann,** Ronald G '93 -33 Vernon Av -Mt Vernon 10553
(585) 428-5861 .. **Spano,** Alecia J '94 %Cnty Atty -50 W Main -Rchstr 14614 **Fx:**428-4160
(212) 918-3000 .. **Spano,** Frank T '89 (Hogan L LLP) -875 3rd Av -NY 10022
(516) 571-3779 .. **Spano,** Gregory F '76 %Hon S Bucaria -100 Supreme Ct Dr -Mineola 11501
(631) 385-1423 .. **Spano,** John J '00 -1940 Deer Prk Av #267 -Deer Pk 11729 **Fx:**385-1424
(845) 343-5050 .. **Spano,** Jos A '69 (Spano & S) -44 W Main -Middletwn 10940
(845) 856-1000 .. **Spano,** Jos A '69 (Spano & S) -6-8 Hammond Bx3136 -Pt Jervis 12771
(516) 742-9200 .. **Spano,** Sal A '90 Cnsl Edelman K&J PLLC -1 Old Cntry Rd -Carle Pl 11514
(516) 746-7915 .. **Spano,** Salvatore '61 -370 Old Cntry Rd -Gdn Cty 11530
(212) 753-1800 .. **Spanos,** Dimitrios '03 (Vaneria & S) -52 Vndrblt Av -NY 10017
(212) 815-1160 .. **Spanos,** Karen M '88 %DC 37 MELS -125 Barclay -NY 10007 **Fx:**815-1343
(718) 274-6300 .. **Spanos,** Vasilios '04 %B Vasiliadis -32-07 Bway -Astoria 11106 **Fx:**274-9500
(516) 877-0600 .. **Spanos,** Wm G '88 -300 Old Cntry Rd -Mineola 11501 **Fx:**742-2221
(631) 777-3200 .. **Spanton & Dehan,LLP** -425 Broad Hollow Rd -Melvll 11747 **Fx:**777-3204
(631) 777-3200 .. **Spanton,** Donald M '60 (Spanton & D,LLP) -425 Broad Hollow Rd -Melvll 11747
(212) 227-3636 .. **Spar & Bernstein, PC** -225 Bway -NY 10007 **Fx:**227-3030
(516) 714-7028 .. **Sparacino,** Frank J Jr. '02 %T Spina -170 Froehlich Farm Blvd -Woodbury 11797 **Fx:**496-5420
(516) 483-6480 .. **Sparacio,** Anthony B '66 -500 Front -Hempstd 11550
(718) 966-0055 .. **Sparacio,** Jos '83 -2555 Richmond Av -Staten Isl 10314 **Fx:**227-5920
(631) 549-0492 .. **Sparaco,** Robt J '87 -8 Basswood Pl -Melvll 11747
(518) 474-8625 .. **Sparagna,** Peter A '78 %Dept of Law -The Cptl -Albany 12224
(631) 501-3100 .. **Sparago,** Lorraine '86 %J Humphreys -3 Huntngtn Quad Bx9028 -Melvll 11747 **Fx:**501-3085
(212) 318-3000 .. **Sparber,** Neil G '84 (Fulbright & J LLP) -666 5th Av -NY 10103
(212) 635-4100 .. **Sparber,** Roy M '70 RM Sparber,LLC -299 Bway -NY 10007 **Fx:**269-0255
(631) 661-6500 .. **Sparer,** Alan B '66 %Pace & P,LLP -400 Montauk Hwy -W Islip 11795 **Fx:**661-6678
(212) 687-7410 .. **Sparer,** Robt A '87 %Clifton B&D,LLP -420 Lex Av -NY 10170
(212) 213-3111 .. **Spark,** Edw V '02 %Weiser & Assoc -150 E 58th -NY 10155 **Fx:**213-5939
(315) 474-2943 .. **Sparkes,** James E '77 (Sugarman Law Firm,LLP) -211 W Jffrsn -Syracuse 13202
(212) 621-6000 .. **Sparkler,** Andrew P '06 %ASCAP -1 Lincoln Plz -NY 10023 **Fx:**787-1381
(212) 856-9600 .. **Sparkler,** Erica K '06 %Morvillo AGIA&B,PC -565 5th Av -NY 10017
(212) 773-4299 .. **Sparks,** Benjamin A '03 Ernst & Young LLP -5 Times Sq -NY 10036
(212) 698-3500 .. **Sparks,** Robt W '64 (Dechert LLP) -1095 Av of Amer -NY 10036
(516) 292-8100 .. **Sparks,** Robin '85 %Nassau/Sfflk Law Srv -1 Helen Keller Way -Hempstd 11550 **Fx:**292-6529
(516) 240-8077 .. **Sparks,** Wm J A '74 -1225 Franklin Av -Gdn Cty 11530 **Fx:**873-8881
(212) 972-1000 .. **Sparling,** John E '88 (London F LLP) -59 Maiden Ln -NY 10038
(516) 237-4965 .. **Sparling,** Michl S '94 1-800-Flowers.com -One Old Cntry Rd -Carle Pl 11514
(212) 715-9100 .. **Sparling,** Steven S '99 (Kramer LN&F,LLP) -1177 Av of Amer -NY 10036
(212) 640-8265 .. **Sparrow,** Andrea L '98 Amer Express -3 World Fncl Ctr -NY 10281
(516) 564-8000 .. **Sparrow,** David W '98 %J Hiebler & Assoc -901 Franklin Av -Gdn Cty 11530 **Fx:**564-1714
(212) 906-1200 .. **Sparrow,** David W '08 %Latham & W -885 3rd Av -NY 10022
(212) 570-3009 .. **Sparrow,** Miriam '81 %NY Blood Ctr -310 E 67th -NY 10065 **Fx:**879-3158
(718) 261-4040 .. **Sparrow,** Robt E '57 (Sparrow S&S) -125-10 Qns Blvd -Kew Gdns 11415
(718) 261-4040 .. **Sparrow Singer & Schreiber** -125-10 Qns Blvd -Kew Gdns 11415 **Fx:**261-2129
(718) 236-7600 .. **Spata,** Vincent F '01 (Reitano & S) -8817 3rd Av -Brklyn 11209
(315) 457-0506 .. **Spatari,** Richd J '82 -201 2nd -Liverpool 13088 **Fx:**457-3306
(917) 778-6600 .. **Spataro,** John C '98 %J Toomey -485 Lex Av -NY 10017 **Fx:**778-7048
(212) 859-8000 .. **Spataro,** Michl C '07 %Fried FHS&J LLP -1 NY Plz -NY 10004
(516) 229-6000 .. **Spataro,** Paul T '91 %R Lau & Assoc -300 Jericho Quad Bx9040 -Jericho 11753 **Fx:**229-6167
(212) 210-9465 .. **Spataro,** Victoria E '07 %Alston & B LLP -90 Park Av -NY 10016
(212) 925-2020 .. **Spates,** Dennis P '83 (Pelosi WE&S LLP) -233 Bway -NY 10279 **Fx:**965-1488
(518) 783-2704 .. **Spath,** John A '99 Colonie Town Atty -Mem'l Town Hall Bx508 -Newtonville 12128 **Fx:**786-7324
(212) 949-9022 .. **Spath,** Thos E '70 OfCnsl Abelman F&S -666 3rd Av -NY 10017
(212) 436-4383 .. **Spatoliatore,** Luciano V '94 Deloitte & Touche,LLP -2 World Fncl Ctr -NY 10281
(585) 546-5600 .. **Spatorico,** Derrick A '96 (Pheterson SCN&S,LLP) -1 E Main -Rchstr 14614
(212) 455-2000 .. **Spatt,** Robt E '81 (Simpson T&B LLP) -425 Lex Av -NY 10017
(914) 777-0593 .. **Spatz,** Andrew M '00 -650 Halstead Av -Mamaroneck 10543
(718) 298-0500 .. **Spatz,** Bilha '88 %Surrogate's Ct -88-11 Sutphin Blvd -Jamaica 11435 **Fx:**520-5048
(212) 836-8000 .. **Spatz,** Mark D '03 %Kaye S LLP -425 Park Av -NY 10022
(646) 386-3500 .. **Spatz,** Sherrill R '86 %OCA -25 Beaver -NY 10004 **Fx:**(212) 514-0158
(212) 715-9100 .. **Spatz,** Wm J '80 (Kramer LN&F,LLP) -1177 Av of Amer -NY 10036
(212) 373-3000 .. **Spatzer,** Barry J '08 %Paul WRW&G LLP -1285 Av of Amer -NY 10019
(716) 887-4466 .. **Spaulding,** Alyson E '93 %Millard Fillmore Hlth Sys -3 Gates Cir -Buffalo 14209
(914) 286-3400 .. **Spaulding,** Lynette V '80 Leg Aid -1 N Bway -White Plns 10601 **Fx:**682-4112
(914) 824-5387 .. **Spaulding,** N Lee '93 NYS Unified Ct Sys -111 Martin Luther King Blvd -White Plns 10601
(518) 486-5258 .. **Spaulding,** Ralph D '82 %Insurance Dept -99 Wshngtn Av -Albany 12257 **Fx:**486-2218
(914) 428-2100 .. **Spaun,** Gregory J '01 %Welby B&G,LLP -11 Martine Av -White Plns 10606
(212) 258-6000 .. **Spavin,** Shana Ledah '03 %Viacom -1515 Bway -NY 10036
(212) 768-6700 .. **Spaziani,** Rosemary '08 %Sonnenschein N&R LLP -2 World Fncl Ctr -NY 10281
(631) 669-1730 .. **Speal,** Gerald K '81 (Speal & S) -42 Fire Isl Av -Babylon 11702 **Fx:**669-6115
(631) 669-1730 .. **Speal,** Sherry Lee '90 (Speal & S) -42 Fire Isl Av -Babylon 11702 **Fx:**669-6115
(718) 692-4127 .. **Speal,** Shoshana Samantha '95 -957 E 10th -Brklyn 11230
(212) 858-1000 .. **Spear,** Robin L '81 (Pillsbury WSP LLP) -1540 Bway -NY 10036
(716) 373-3363 .. **Spears,** Alan L '84 (Mountain & S) -70 W Main Bx99 -Allegany 14706 **Fx:**372-3251
(212) 786-8942 .. **Spears,** Darrelle M '01 EMI Music NA -150 5th Av -NY 10011
(212) 213-6996 .. **Spears,** David W '78 (Spears & I LLP) -51 Mad Av -NY 10010
(212) 213-6996 .. **Spears & Imes LLP** -51 Mad Av -NY 10010 **Fx:**213-0849
(212) 210-9562 .. **Spears,** John W '09 %Alston & B LLP -90 Park Av -NY 10016
(212) 252-3809 .. **Spears,** Vanessa J '97 -401 Bway -NY 10013

(516) 383-2939 .. **Specht,** Anne M '85 -8 Elks Ct -Huntngtn 11743
(845) 624-1041 .. **Specht,** Michl B '90 (Schoeps & S) -334 S Mddltwn Rd -Nanuet 10954 **Fx:**624-1049
(212) 819-8200 .. **Specht,** W Alexander '09 %White & C LLP -1155 Av of Amer -NY 10036
(212) 969-3000 .. **Speciale,** Benjamin B '07 Proskauer R LLP -1585 Bway -NY 10036 **Fx:**969-2900
(518) 402-0205 .. **Speciale,** Victoria E '96 %UIA Bd -Troy Atrium Bx15126 -Albany 12212 **Fx:**402-6208
(212) 210-9495 .. **Speciner,** David P '91 Cnsl Alston & B LLP -90 Park Av -NY 10016
(845) 344-1918 .. **Specthrie,** Mark '86 -225 Dolson Av -Middletwn 10940 **Fx:**342-2425
(516) 295-1484 .. **Spector,** Abraham '51 -979 East End -Woodmere 11598 **Fx:**(718) 852-3200
(718) 875-3900 .. **Spector,** Abraham '51 -185 Montague -Brklyn 11201 **Fx:**852-3200
(315) 687-6516 .. **Spector,** Ann F '90 -1559 Route 173 -Chittenango 13037 **Fx:**687-5427
(212) 683-5912 .. **Spector,** Carl S '87 -110 Wall -NY 10005
(212) 382-0909 .. **Spector,** Craig D '87 (Peckar & A,PC) -41 Mad Av -NY 10154
(718) 254-6345 .. **Spector,** Danl A '02 US Atty-EDNY -271 Cadman Plz E -Brklyn 11201
(212) 670-0148 .. **Spector,** Danl R '70 %Merrill Lynch -222 Bway -NY 10038
(646) 602-5600 .. **Spector,** Danielle J '03 %Urban Justice Ctr -123 William -NY 10038 **Fx:**(212) 533-4598
(516) 487-2252 .. **Spector,** Douglas M '85 (Rothkrug R&S,LLP) -55 Watermill Ln -Gt Neck 11021
(716) 876-4564 .. **Spector,** Edw S '51 -123 Irving Ter -Buffalo 14223 **Fx:**876-4564
(516) 812-6045 .. **Spector & Feldman,LLP** -360 Merrick Rd -Lynbrk 11563 **Fx:**812-6046
(212) 331-3030 .. **Spector,** Inna '01 %Dept of Invstgtn -180 Water -NY 10038 **Fx:**331-3060
(914) 993-0427 .. **Spector,** James M '63 -400 Hgh Pnt Dr -Hartsdale 10530
(201) 998-9244 .. **Spector,** Jay Steven '84 -12 Waverly Pl -Lawrence 11559 **Fx:**998-3349
(212) 935-3000 .. **Spector,** Jeremy A '83 (Mintz LCFG&P,PC) -666 3rd Av -NY 10017
(516) 812-6045 .. **Spector,** Joel J '60 (Spector & F,LLP) -360 Merrick Rd -Lynbrk 11563
(212) 878-8126 .. **Spector,** Joshua S '00 GFK US Holdings,Inc -75 9th Av -NY 10011
(212) 421-4100 .. **Spector,** Lawr A '85 (Pryor C LLP) -7 Times Sq -NY 10036
(718) 875-3900 .. **Spector,** Leonard C '83 -185 Montigue -Brklyn 11201 **Fx:**852-3200
(718) 993-3788 .. **Spector,** Malcolm B '95 Envrnmntl Cntrl Bd -3030 3rd Av -Bronx 10455 **Fx:**993-3022
(631) 752-8580 .. **Spector,** Michl A '05 Odierno Law Firm,PC -560 Broadhllw Rd -Melvll 11747 **Fx:**752-7476
(212) 310-8000 .. **Spector,** Mindy J '81 (Weil G&M LLP) -767 5th Av -NY 10153
(516) 873-8989 .. **Spector,** Neal S '84 N Spector,PC -300 Old Cntry Rd -Mineola 11501 **Fx:**873-8992
(914) 682-2055 .. **Spector,** Neil L '94 %H Adler -50 Main -White Plns 10606 **Fx:**682-2093
(212) 704-6000 .. **Spector,** Philip H '82 (Troutman S LLP) -405 Lex Av -NY 10174
(516) 513-1300 .. **Spector,** Sandra M '02 -Bx711 -Bethpage 11714 **Fx:**495-4608
(516) 747-6700 .. **Spector,** Stacy R '04 %Kirschenbaum & K -200 Grdn City Plz -Gdn Cty 11530 **Fx:**747-6781
(212) 556-1234 .. **Spector,** Suzanne A '84 %The NY Times Co -620 8th Av -NY 10018
(518) 668-5412 .. **Spector,** Suzanne Lee '95 %Stafford C&M,PC -175 Ottawa -Lk George 12845
(914) 428-0505 .. **Spector,** Wayne H '85 (Cohn & S) -200 E Post Rd -White Plns 10601
(914) 683-5900 .. **Spedaliere,** Stephen M '00 Statewide Abstract -202 Mamaroneck Av -White Plns 10601
(212) 344-3339 .. **Speed,** Mark D '79 -325 W 38th -NY 10018 **Fx:**(646) 349-2511
(212) 557-7260 .. **Speer,** Doris L '91 ALSTOM Trans -353 Lex Av -NY 10016 **Fx:**972-4404
(914) 329-3333 .. **Speer,** Edw I '69 -27 Barker Av -White Plns 10601 **Fx:**831-7660
(212) 417-5300 .. **Speers,** Jay S '91 %Medicaid Fraud Cntrl -120 Bway -NY 10271 **Fx:**417-5274
(212) 614-6431 .. **Spees,** Pamela C '01 Ctr for Constitutional Rights -666 Bway -NY 10012
(212) 506-2500 .. **Spehr,** Richd A '87 (Mayer B LLP) -1675 Bway -NY 10019
(518) 447-3200 .. **Speich,** Jeremy H '03 (McNamee LT&W,PC) -677 Bway -Albany 12207
(518) 271-6960 .. **Speidel,** Robt B '97 -65 2nd -Troy 12180 **Fx:**271-6726
(212) 728-8000 .. **Speier,** Erica J '07 %Willkie F&G LLP -787 7th Av -NY 10019
(212) 595-5480 .. **Speier,** Leonard M '52 -190 Riverside Dr -NY 10024 **Fx:**595-5482
(212) 848-4000 .. **Speigel,** Allison J '09 %Shearman & S LLP -599 Lex Av -NY 10022
(212) 223-3900 .. **Speirs,** Richd A '86 (Zwerling S&Z,LLP) -41 Mad Av -NY 10010
(212) 421-5333 .. **Speiser,** David S '02 Related,LP -60 Columbus Cir -NY 10023
(914) 965-1963 .. **Speiser,** James '75 -6 Exec Plz -Ynkrs 10701
(212) 661-0011 .. **Speiser Krause Nolan & Granito** -140 E 45th -NY 10017 **Fx:**953-6483
(212) 806-5400 .. **Speiser,** Mark A '79 (Stroock &S&L LLP) -180 Maiden Ln -NY 10038
(212) 310-8000 .. **Speiser,** Matthew M '09 %Weil G&M LLP -767 5th Av -NY 10153
(914) 686-5300 .. **Speiser,** Tina L '88 (Speiser & H) -50 Main Bx58 -White Plns 10602 **Fx:**(203) 894-1508
(212) 728-8000 .. **Spekman,** Marit R '10 %Willkie F&G LLP -787 7th Av -NY 10019
(212) 336-0562 .. **Spekman,** Nell A '05 SEC -3 World Fncl Ctr -NY 10281
(718) 554-3630 .. **Spektor,** Yakov '07 (Smotritsky & S,PLLC) -1928 Kings Hwy -Brklyn 11229
(212) 779-8600 .. **Spektor,** Zena L '08 %Silverman SS&B PLLC -381 Park Av S -NY 10016
(212) 682-7474 .. **Spelfogel,** Douglas '89 (Foley & L LLP) -90 Park Av -NY 10016
(212) 351-4500 .. **Spelfogel,** Evan J '59 (Epstein B&G,PC) -250 Park Av -NY 10177
(212) 592-1400 .. **Spell,** Michelle Bergeron '01 %Herrick,F LLP -2 Park Av -NY 10016
(585) 419-8800 .. **Spellane,** Philip G '82 (Harris B PLLC) -99 Garnsey Rd -Pittsfrd 14534
(212) 692-9666 .. **Spellane,** Thos P '76 (Gilbride TL&S LLC) -708 3rd Av -NY 10017
(716) 636-8364 .. **Speller,** Dennis J '61 (D Speller,PC) -6161 Transit Rd -E Amherst 14051 **Fx:**636-8392
(716) 636-8364 .. **Speller,** Glenn J '88 (D Speller,PC) -6161 Transit Rd -E Amherst 14051 **Fx:**636-8392
(212) 513-3200 .. **Spelliscy,** M J M '95 (Holland & K LLP) -31 W 52nd -NY 10019
(718) 579-3000 .. **Spellman,** Christopher J Jr. '77 %Leg Aid -1020 Grnd Cncrs -Bronx 10451 **Fx:**588-2611
(518) 348-1000 .. **Spellman,** Debra A '91 (Block CS&P,LLP) -9 Exec Park Dr -Clifton Pk 12065
(212) 918-3000 .. **Spellman,** Denise '07 %Hogan L LLP -875 3rd Av -NY 10022
(516) 592-6800 .. **Spellman,** John M '77 (Spellman RSGM&P,LLP) -229 Seventh -Gdn Cty 11530
(631) 724-8833 .. **Spellman,** Kevin M '92 (Devitt SB,LLP) -50 Route 111 -Smithtwn 11787
(516) 592-6800 .. **Spellman Rice Schure Gibbons McDonough & Polizzi,LLP** -229 Seventh -Gdn Cty 11530 **Fx:**742-1305
(631) 724-8833 .. **Spellman,** Thos J Jr. '66 (Devitt SB,LLP) -50 Route 111 -Smithtwn 11787
(631) 325-8030 .. **Spellman-Frey,** Cecilia Anne '97 -6 Strathmore Ct Bx650 -Remsenbrg 11960 **Fx:**325-8030
(212) 209-1530 .. **Spellun,** Arnold '58 Cnsl McLaughlin & S,LLP -260 Mad Av -NY 10016
(716) 886-0211 .. **Spelman,** Mark G '77 %Benderson Dvlpmnt -570 Delaware Av -Buffalo 14202 **Fx:**886-2269
(914) 245-6525 .. **Spelman,** Mary Ann G '83 -2340 Broad -Yorktwn Hts 10598 **Fx:**245-6595
(212) 381-9700 .. **Spelman,** Wm M '80 (Lambos Firm,LLP) -303 S Bway -Tarrytwn 10591 **Fx:**797-9213
(914) 245-6525 .. **Spelman,** Wm V '59 -2340 Broad -Yorktwn Hts 10598 **Fx:**245-6595
(607) 336-2327 .. **Spence,** Adam J '07 -Bx208 -Norwich 13815 **Fx:**(877) 316-2327
(914) 261-5254 .. **Spence,** Andrew L '98 Pilates Inc -75 Lafayette Av -Suffern 10901
(212) 416-8817 .. **Spence,** Lakisha M '09 %Dept of Law -120 Bway -NY 10271
(718) 286-6000 .. **Spence,** Michael-Sean '09 %DA -125-01 Qns Blvd -Kew Gdns 11415
(516) 364-1095 .. **Spence,** Robt J '95 (McBreen & K) -500 N Bway -Jericho 11753
(212) 674-3664 .. **Spencer,** Albert E '98 -195 Chrystie -NY 10002 **Fx:**674-1690
(917) 639-4265 .. **Spencer,** Anatoly '99 Schneider Legal Search -1230 Av of Amer -NY 10020
(212) 473-0255 .. **Spencer,** Aruna Chandra '97 Seedco -915 Bway -NY 10010 **Fx:**473-0357
(585) 753-4500 .. **Spencer,** Casey F '05 DA -832 Watts Bldg -Rchstr 14614 **Fx:**753-4576
(212) 592-1400 .. **Spencer,** Dana M '07 %Herrick,F LLP -2 Park Av -NY 10016
(914) 422-1241 .. **Spencer,** Danl K '83 %Law Dept -255 Main -White Plns 10601 **Fx:**422-1231
(212) 310-8000 .. **Spencer,** Danitra T '06 %Weil G&M LLP -767 5th Av -NY 10153
(212) 751-3864 .. **Spencer,** David E '68 -866 UN Plz -NY 10017
(212) 506-3900 .. **Spencer,** David H '81 SrCnsl Steptoe & J LLP -750 7th Av -NY 10019
(212) 332-5105 .. **Spencer,** Donald P '81 %Suguler Guff & Co -825 3rd Av -NY 10022
(516) 694-3000 .. **Spencer,** Douglas A '02 %Guercio & G,LLP -77 Conklin -Farmngdl 11735 **Fx:**694-4738
(315) 474-7571 .. **Spencer,** Edw J III '81 (Mackenzie H LLP) -101 S Salina Bx4967 -Syracuse 13221
(716) 856-3500 .. **Spencer,** Ellen Grimm '08 %Magavern MG LLP -1100 Rand Bldg -Buffalo 14203
(212) 326-3939 .. **Spencer,** George E '08 %Jones D -222 E 41st -NY 10017
(631) 427-2099 .. **Spencer,** Gilbert G Jr. '79 (Spencer M&M,LLP) -Bx128 -Huntngtn Sta 11746 **Fx:**427-2996
(212) 831-0421 .. **Spencer,** Janet M '65 -1112 Park Av -NY 10128
(716) 845-9332 .. **Spencer,** Jeffrey A '74 %Supreme Ct -92 Franklin -Buffalo 14202 **Fx:**856-4670
(607) 756-4970 .. **Spencer,** Jeffrey W '97 %McNeil & Co -20 Church Bx5670 -Cortlnd 13045 **Fx:**756-5051
(718) 262-4077 .. **Spencer,** Jennifer L '05 DHCR -92-31 Union Hall -Jamaica 11433 **Fx:**262-7938
(518) 487-5460 .. **Spencer,** John D '02 %DA -6 Lodge -Albany 12207 **Fx:**487-5093
(212) 848-4223 .. **Spencer,** John M '87 Shearman & Sterling LLP -599 Lex Av -NY 10022
(212) 735-3000 .. **Spencer,** Jonathan P '10 %Skadden ASM&F LLP -4 Times Sq -NY 10036
(914) 337-7375 .. **Spencer,** Jos F '58 -40 Brnxvll Ln -Bronxvll 10708
(716) 655-5631 .. **Spencer,** Karen L '88 -4249 Reiter Rd -E Aurora 14052
(212) 306-7176 .. **Spencer,** Karine C M '99 Ofc Cllctv Brgn -40 Rector -NY 10006 **Fx:**306-7167
(917) 778-6600 .. **Spencer,** Kevin J '87 %J Toomey -485 Lex Av -NY 10017 **Fx:**778-7048
(212) 596-9000 .. **Spencer,** Leslie M F '01 %Ropes & G LLP -1211 Av of Amer -NY 10036
(212) 505-2100 .. **Spencer,** Louisa Clark '89 %Envrnmntl Def Fund -257 Park Av S -NY 10010 **Fx:**505-2375
(212) 596-9000 .. **Spencer,** Magdalena Hale '10 %Ropes & G LLP -1211 Av of Amer -NY 10036
(212) 768-4900 .. **Spencer,** Margaret Marrin '94 (Gage S&F) -410 Park Av -NY 10022
(212) 417-4989 .. **Spencer,** Marie D '97 %Medicaid Fraud Cntrl -120 Bway -NY 10271 **Fx:**417-5274
(914) 238-2860 .. **Spencer,** Matthew S '92 (Meyer & S LLP) -27 S Greeley Av -Chappaqua 10514 **Fx:**238-2833
(212) 407-1200 .. **Spencer,** Meredith McGrady '04 %Joseph Law Ofcs LLC -485 Lex Av -NY 10017 **Fx:**407-1299
(212) 594-5300 .. **Spencer,** Michl C '78 (Milberg LLP) -1 Penn Plz -NY 10119
(315) 422-8191 .. **Spencer,** Robt J '07 %Leg Aid -351 S Warren -Syracuse 13202 **Fx:**472-2819
(914) 472-2300 .. **Spencer,** Robt W '63 OfCnsl Jones G,LLP -670 Wht Plns Rd -Scarsdale 10583
(212) 732-3200 .. **Spencer,** Ronald D '66 Cnsl Carter L&M LLP -2 Wall -NY 10005
(212) 504-6000 .. **Spencer,** Scott A '09 %Cadwalader W&T LLP -1 World Fncl Ctr -NY 10281
(716) 849-3500 .. **Spencer,** Sean M '08 Hagelin & K LLC -135 Delaware Av -Buffalo 14202 **Fx:**849-3501
(212) 269-4900 .. **Spencer,** Shayne W '06 %Ford MEW&G,LLP -Wall Street Plz -NY 10005
(212) 773-1486 .. **Spencer-James,** Angela E '91 Ernst & Young LLP -5 Times Sq -NY 10036
(212) 878-8000 .. **Spenner,** Craig W Jr. '00 %Clifford C LLP -31 W 52nd -NY 10019
(212) 839-5300 .. **Spenner,** Dorothy J '00 %Sidley A LLP -787 7th Av -NY 10019

(212) 819-8200 .. **Spenner**, Katherine A '09 %White & C LLP -1155 Av of Amer -NY 10036
(315) 218-8000 .. **Speno**, Rebecca M '03 %Bond S&K,PLLC -1 Lincoln Ctr -Syracuse 13202
Speno, Sarah Rose A '78 -1775 York Av -NY 10128
(212) 848-7636 .. **Spera**, George T Jr. '82 Cnsl Shearman & S LLP -599 Lex Av -NY 10022
(585) 454-1500 .. **Speranza**, John F '72 -28 E Main -Rchstr 14614
(914) 286-3400 .. **Speranza**, Nicholas A '05 %Leg Aid -1 N Bway -White Plns 10601 **Fx**:682-4112
(585) 328-2550 .. **Speranza**, Paul S Jr. '72 %Wegmans Food Mrkts -1500 Brooks Av Bx30844 -Rchstr 14603 **Fx**:464-4636
(917) 351-1335 .. **Sperber Denenberg & Kahan,PC** -48 W 37th -NY 10018 **Fx**:351-1303
(212) 686-4300 .. **Sperber**, Jeffrey M '93 Rogovin & S LLP -10 E 40th -NY 10016 **Fx**:689-2079
(516) 739-3979 .. **Sperber**, Leonard R '89 -100 Grdn City Plz -Gdn Cty 11530 **Fx**:294-7203
(212) 592-1400 .. **Sperber**, Lisa '09 %Herrick,F LLP -2 Park Av -NY 10016
(917) 351-1335 .. **Sperber**, Steven B '81 (Sperber D&K,PC) -48 W 37th -NY 10018
(716) 204-9480 .. **Speregen**, Adam B '95 %SJ Baum,PC -900 Merchants Cncrs -Westbury 11590 **Fx**:204-9680
(516) 742-3777 .. **Sperendi**, Michl F '68 (Limoncelli & S) -229 7th -Gdn Cty 11530
(914) 741-6100 .. **Spergel**, Matthew B '04 %Kaufman B&R -200 Summit Lk Dr -Valhalla 10595
(845) 371-8465 .. **Sperka**, Stacy F '94 -5 Langeries Dr -Monsey 10952
(212) 225-2000 .. **Sperling**, Allan G '69 (Cleary GS&H) -1 Lbrty Plz -NY 10006
(212) 762-4000 .. **Sperling**, Andrew N '89 Morgan Stanley -1221 Av of Amer -NY 10020
(631) 427-1158 .. **Sperling**, David M '95 -1355 NY Av -Huntngtn Sta 11746 **Fx**:427-6551
(914) 828-8573 .. **Sperling**, Erika L '98 Swiss Re America Holding Corp -175 King -Armonk 10504 **Fx**:828-7573
(516) 482-7695 .. **Sperling**, Gery Wm '58 -27 Rose Av -Gt Neck 11021
(212) 448-6224 .. **Sperling**, Harvey J '95 %D Fish,LLC -260 Mad Av -NY 10016 **Fx**:448-6227
(718) 402-1990 .. **Sperling**, Henry I '67 -860 Grnd Cncrs -Bronx 10451 **Fx**:993-3543
(212) 841-1000 .. **Sperling**, Jonathan M '96 (Covington & B LLP) -620 8th Av -NY 10018
(718) 537-4958 .. **Spern**, David J '88 OHA -226 E 161st -Bronx 10451
(212) 407-4000 .. **Spero**, C Michl '61 (Loeb & L,LLP) -345 Park Av -NY 10154
(718) 448-8400 .. **Spero**, Maria D '96 (O'Leary & S) -25 Manor Rd -Staten Isl 10310
(516) 357-3000 .. **Spero**, Matthew V '02 %Rivkin R LLP -926 RXR Plz -Uniondale 11556
(716) 881-3010 .. **Sperrazza**, Danl J '84 (Cohen & L,PC) -343 Elmwood Av Bx5204 -Buffalo 14213
(212) 697-3122 .. **Sperry**, Jana B '01 %Martin C&B LLP -220 E 42nd -NY 10017
(516) 546-9115 .. **Sperry Weinberg & Cohen** -62 Lena Av -Freeprt 11520
(212) 770-1006 .. **Spessard**, Callahan A '81 %AIG -70 Pine -NY 10270 **Fx**:428-6027
(646) 461-6122 .. **Spett**, Peter M '94 -235 W 56th -NY 10019
Spevack, Michl J '93 -320 7th Av -Brklyn 11215
(212) 587-9663 .. **Spevack**, Robt G '82 -150 Bway -NY 10038 **Fx**:587-9673
(212) 225-2000 .. **Speyer**, Alex J '10 %Cleary GS&H -1 Lbrty Plz -NY 10006
(716) 636-7600 .. **Speyer**, Carly Wilsman '02 %HoganWillig -2410 N Forest Rd -Amherst 14068
(212) 735-8600 .. **Speyer**, Jay R '00 %Morrison C LLP -909 3rd Av -NY 10022
(212) 943-1550 .. **Speyer**, John M '56 SrCnsl Speyer & P,LLP -26 Bway -NY 10004
(631) 673-6670 .. **Speyer & Perlberg,LLP** -115 Broadhllw Rd -Melvll 11747 **Fx**:673-7073
(212) 943-1550 .. **Speyer & Perlberg,LLP** -26 Bway -NY 10004 **Fx**:943-1896
(716) 852-3600 .. **Speyer**, Thos J '86 (Chelus HS&M,PC) -438 Main -Buffalo 14202
(845) 359-7700 .. **Spezio**, Salvatore P '06 %Notaro M&Z PC -100 Dutch Hill Rd -Orangebrg 10962
(212) 964-8580 .. **Spicer**, Gary S '87 %TMCA -217 Bway -NY 10007
(914) 995-3616 .. **Spicer**, Gregory S '05 %Cnty Atty -148 Martine Av -White Plns 10601 **Fx**:995-5858
(212) 652-3720 .. **Spickler**, Beth E '86 %Schlesinger G&L LLP -535 Mad Av -NY 10022
(212) 687-5225 .. **Spiegel**, Arnold '74 Spiegel & S -50 E 42nd -NY 10017 **Fx**:972-4037
(718) 828-8200 .. **Spiegel & Barbato,LLP** -2622 E Tremont Av -Bronx 10461 **Fx**:823-1180
(845) 452-7400 .. **Spiegel Brown Fichera & Coté,LLP** -272 Mill -Poughkeepsie 12601 **Fx**:452-4731
(845) 831-8840 .. **Spiegel Brown Fichera & Coté,LLP** -1203 North Av -Beacon 12508 **Fx**:452-4731
(718) 828-8200 .. **Spiegel**, Chas H '65 (Spiegel & B,LLP) -2622 E Tremont Av -Bronx 10461
(914) 337-6910 .. **Spiegel**, Chas J Jr. '66 -33 Ft Hill Rd -Ynkrs 10710 **Fx**:337-6839
(718) 846-4465 .. **Spiegel**, Edw H '87 -87-16 Woodhvn Blvd -Woodhvn 11421
(212) 619-5400 .. **Spiegel**, Glenn H '98 (Newman F LLP) -1250 Bway -NY 10001
(212) 373-3000 .. **Spiegel**, Jennifer A '98 Cnsl Paul WRW&G LLP -1285 Av of Amer -NY 10019
(212) 599-5799 .. **Spiegel**, Jeremy P '03 %Rutherford & C LLP -369 Lex Av -NY 10017
(212) 980-0120 .. **Spiegel**, Jerrold B '74 (Frankfurt KK&S,PC) -488 Mad Av -NY 10022
(212) 806-5400 .. **Spiegel**, Jessica M '09 %Stroock &S&L LLP -180 Maiden Ln -NY 10038
(646) 285-7344 .. **Spiegel**, Jonathan M '05 -500 5th Av -NY 10110
(845) 452-7400 .. **Spiegel**, Jos L '60 OfCnsl Spiegel BF&C,LLP -272 Mill -Poughkeepsie 12601
(212) 756-2000 .. **Spiegel**, Karen '06 %Schulte R&Z LLP -919 3rd Av -NY 10022
(212) 735-3000 .. **Spiegel**, Lawr S '92 (Skadden ASM&F LLP) -4 Times Sq -NY 10036
(212) 587-8558 .. **Spiegel**, Michl L '85 -111 Bway -NY 10006 **Fx**:571-7767
(845) 362-6410 .. **Spiegel**, Mordecai J '98 Cnsl Imperial Abstract Corp -367 Route 306 -Monsey 10952 **Fx**:362-6415
(518) 474-7168 .. **Spiegel**, Nancy A '77 %Dept of Law -The Cptl -Albany 12224
(212) 416-8454 .. **Spiegel**, Norman '74 %Dept of Law -120 Bway -NY 10271
(212) 227-0347 .. **Spiegel**, Sara R '08 %Weiss W&W,PC -25 Park Pl -NY 10007
(212) 282-3639 .. **Spiegel**, Scott B '87 %Industrial Bk of Japan -1251 Av of Amer -NY 10020 **Fx**:354-7434
(212) 720-4155 .. **Spiegel**, Steven I '87 Foot Locker,Inc -112 W 34th -NY 10120 **Fx**:720-4116
(845) 651-5000 .. **Spiegel**, Steven J '86 Spiegel L,LLC -148 N Main -Florida 10921 **Fx**:651-5111
(212) 760-2222 .. **Spiegel**, Wm S '99 (Kolenovsky & S,LLP) -135 W 29th -NY 10001
(718) 725-1600 .. **Spiegelman**, David '00 -214-61 Jamaica Av -Qns Vllg 11428 **Fx**:725-1717
(212) 446-4800 .. **Spiegelman**, Gina S '07 %Kirkland & E LLP -153 E 53rd -NY 10022
(212) 559-8066 .. **Spiegelman**, Isabelle B '84 %Citibank -909 3rd Av -NY 10022
(212) 947-4575 .. **Spiegelman**, Robt A '76 %Jordache -1400 Bway -NY 10018 **Fx**:(646) 383-8289
(212) 909-9500 .. **Spiegelman**, Sara G '08 %Wachtel & M,LLP -885 2nd Av -NY 10017
(212) 878-8000 .. **Spiegelman**, Todd A '06 %Clifford C LLP -31 W 52nd -NY 10019
(212) 816-0441 .. **Spiegler**, Bruce A '92 Citigroup -388 Greenwich -NY 10013
(212) 592-1400 .. **Spiegler**, Howard N '75 (Herrick,F LLP) -2 Park Av -NY 10016
(212) 868-3434 .. **Spiegler**, Stanley M '58 -450 7th Av -NY 10123 **Fx**:695-3575
(914) 683-2500 .. **Spielberg**, Jill F '06 %Harold SS&S -81 Main -White Plns 10601
(212) 788-1311 .. **Spielberg**, Lawr B '84 %Law Dept -100 Church -NY 10007 **Fx**:788-0367
(914) 683-2500 .. **Spielberg**, Leonard '73 (Harold SS&S) -81 Main -White Plns 10601
(212) 670-0337 .. **Spielfogel**, Kenneth '77 -222 Bway -NY 10038
(305) 347-6567 .. **Spielman**, Joshua E '07 %McDermott W&E LLP -340 Mad Av -NY 10173 **Fx**:675-8190
(212) 695-5670 .. **Spielman**, Robt A '78 Goldfinger & L LLP -750 3rd Av -NY 10017
(212) 250-6895 .. **Spielman**, Robt M '77 %Deutsche Bank -60 Wall -NY 10005
(212) 637-3222 .. **Spielmann**, Lee A '87 %EPA -290 Bway -NY 10007 **Fx**:637-3096
(212) 710-5160 .. **Spielvogel**, Steven '94 (Gallion & S) -75 Rckfllr Plz -NY 10019 **Fx**:428-6777
(914) 998-8170 .. **Spier**, Ian P '71 -550 Mamaroneck Av -Harrison 10528 **Fx**:328-7243
(212) 566-4681 .. **Spier**, Thos P '89 (Tumelty & S,LLP) -160 Bway -NY 10038 **Fx**:566-4749
(212) 931-5500 .. **Spierer**, Craig M '05 %McCue S&Z,PC -521 5th Av -NY 10175
(908) 221-4858 .. **Spierer**, Howard '89 AT&T -32 Av of Amer -NY 10013
(212) 225-2000 .. **Spiering**, Kimberly C '05 %Cleary GS&H -1 Lbrty Plz -NY 10006
(212) 265-6888 .. **Spiesman**, Thos '86 (Porzio B&N,PC) -156 W 56th -NY 10019
(914) 684-0090 .. **Spiess**, Chas J '98 %Diserio MO&C LLP -50 Main -White Plns 10606
(631) 727-8200 .. **Spiess**, James '82 (McNulty-Spiess,PC) -214 Roanoke Av Bx757 -Rvrhead 11901
(518) 279-1143 .. **Spiess**, Susan M '00 -1011 Hoosick Rd -Troy 12180 **Fx**:279-4320
(212) 586-5800 .. **Spievack**, Jay B '88 (Cohen TS&W PC) -420 Lex Av -NY 10170
(212) 210-9489 .. **Spiewak**, Danielle G '07 %Alston & B LLP -90 Park Av -NY 10016
(212) 771-0784 .. **Spiezia**, Gina A '00 Aspen Publishers -76 9th Av -NY 10011 **Fx**:771-0688
(212) 952-1111 .. **Spiga**, Anthony J '92 (H Gladstein & Prtnrs LLC) -110 Wall -NY 10005 **Fx**:943-7427
(212) 728-8000 .. **Spigel**, Robin L '98 %Willkie F&G LLP -787 7th Av -NY 10019
(212) 446-4800 .. **Spigelman**, Rebecca M '09 %Kirkland & E LLP -153 E 53rd -NY 10022
(212) 815-1818 .. **Spiker**, Andreas '99 %DC 37 MELS -125 Barclay -NY 10007 **Fx**:815-1343
(718) 852-1899 .. **Spikes**, Kevin H '94 (Thomas & S) -111 Court -Brklyn 11201
(845) 485-2529 .. **Spilbor**, Jonna M '02 (J Spilbor,LLC) -35 Main -Poughkeepsie 12601
(212) 969-2326 .. **Spilka**, Adam R '88 %Alliance Bernstein LP -1345 Av of Amer -NY 10105 **Fx**:554-4639
(212) 715-9100 .. **Spilko**, Howard T '93 (Kramer LN&F,LLP) -1177 Av of Amer -NY 10036
(212) 558-4000 .. **Spillane**, Christine A '97 (Sullivan & C LLP) -125 Broad -NY 10004
(212) 407-8000 .. **Spillane**, Danl J '01 NBA -645 5th Av -NY 10022 **Fx**:888-7931
(212) 951-6400 .. **Spillane**, Dennis K '79 %Dept of Education -475 Park Av S -NY 10016 **Fx**:951-6465
(212) 813-8800 .. **Spillane**, Meghan K '09 %Goodwin P LLP -620 8th Av -NY 10018
(212) 210-9540 .. **Spiller**, Christina '08 %Alston & B LLP -90 Park Av -NY 10016
(845) 782-7795 .. **Spillers**, Bonnie E '85 -31 Old Cntry Rd -Monroe 10950 **Fx**:782-3137
(212) 309-8100 .. **Spina**, Allison M '91 %Lexis/Nexis -125 Park Av -NY 10017 **Fx**:309-8187
(212) 732-9000 .. **Spina**, Christopher P '06 %Sullivan PBM&C PC -120 Bway -NY 10271
(631) 342-8388 .. **Spina**, Frank G '94 (Spina & K) -300 Rabro Dr -Hauppauge 11788
(516) 832-7777 .. **Spina**, Jennifer M '05 %Silberstein A&M,PC -600 Old Cntry Rd -Gdn Cty 11530
(631) 342-8388 .. **Spina & Kreitzman** -300 Rabro Dr -Hauppauge 11788 **Fx**:342-8366
(516) 593-1810 .. **Spina**, Robt R '61 -21 Hempstd Av -Lynbrk 11563
(516) 496-5822 .. **Spina**, Teresa M '83 -170 Froehlich Farm Blvd -Woodbury 11797 **Fx**:496-5420
(518) 431-0247 .. **Spina**, Thos Jr. '86 %US Atty -445 Bway -Albany 12207 **Fx**:431-0249
(845) 331-5777 .. **Spinac**, Mitchell H '80 -325 Wall Bx3748 -Kingston 12402 **Fx**:331-0108
(212) 854-3123 .. **Spinak**, Jane M '80 %Columbia Law Schl -435 W 116th -NY 10027 **Fx**:854-7946
(585) 641-8000 .. **Spindelman**, Norman M '53 (Fix SB&G,PC) -295 Woodcliff Dr -Fairprt 14450
(718) 941-5000 .. **Spindler**, David S '92 -1431 Nostrand Av -Brklyn 11226
(212) 964-6611 .. **Spindler**, Ellen M '83 (Lester SK&D) -120 Bway -NY 10271
(718) 357-4333 .. **Spindler**, Gail E '78 (Trop & S) -19-02 Whitestone Expy -Whitestone 11357
(212) 451-2300 .. **Spindler**, Jeffrey S '89 (Olshan GFR&W LLP) -65 E 55th -NY 10022
(212) 446-4800 .. **Spindler**, Kester L '04 (Kirkland & E LLP) -153 E 53rd -NY 10022
(212) 417-5703 .. **Spindola**, Hugo B '98 NYS Athletic Commssn -123 William -NY 10038 **Fx**:417-4987
(212) 972-0786 .. **Spinella**, Jack T '97 (Nicoll D&S LLP) -250 Park Av -NY 10177 **Fx**:953-7201
(212) 980-3500 .. **Spinelli**, Giovanni E '96 %Pavia & H LLP -600 Mad Av -NY 10022
(212) 471-8503 .. **Spinelli**, Kate D '05 %Herzfeld & R,PC -125 Broad -NY 10004

(585) 419-8800 .. **Spinelli**, Peter J '72 (Harris B PLLC) -99 Garnsey Rd -Pittsfrd 14534
(631) 367-0037 .. **Spinelli**, Salvatore '70 -204 Montecito Cres -Melvll 11747 **Fx**:367-2772
(718) 256-3333 .. **Spinelli**, Stephen A '83 (S Spinelli & Assoc) -1861 86th -Brklyn 11214 **Fx**:256-1399
(516) 742-4343 .. **Spinelli**, Thos '96 (Scully SM&P PC) -400 Grdn City Plz -Gdn Cty 11530
(716) 204-9480 .. **Spinelli**, Victor '98 %SJ Baum,PC -900 Merchants Cncrs -Westbury 11590 **Fx**:204-9680
(516) 747-4343 .. **Spinillo-Beck**, Theresa A '02 %JP DiMascio & Assoc,LLP -300 Grdn City Plz -Gdn Cty 11530 **Fx**:747-0204
(212) 551-4000 .. **Spinnato**, John M '84 %Sanofi-Synthelabo -90 Park Av -NY 10016 **Fx**:551-4919
(212) 754-6700 .. **Spinnato**, Jos E '65 %Hotel Assn of NYC -320 Park Av -NY 10022 **Fx**:754-0243
(212) 684-0317 .. **Spinnell**, Andrew J '83 -286 Mad Av -NY 10017 **Fx**:696-2611
(212) 219-0223 .. **Spinner**, Chas P '80 -1725 York Av -NY 10128
(716) 648-0853 .. **Spinner**, Chas S '68 -6194 S Park Av -Hambrg 14075 **Fx**:648-0880
(631) 451-7900 .. **Spinner**, Diane '96 OfCnsl Rosenberg & G,LLP -1176 Portion Rd -Holtsvll 11742
(718) 250-2000 .. **Spinner**, Ileane J '80 %DA -350 Jay -Brklyn 11201 **Fx**:250-2314
(212) 730-7750 .. **Spinner**, Marina A '95 (Nicoletti GS&O,LLP) -555 5th Av -NY 10017
(607) 798-1521 .. **Spinner**, Mark D '99 (Burr & R,LLP) -Bx2308 -Bnghmtn 13902
(516) 837-6109 .. **Spinner**, Scott '85 Sutton Land Srvcs LLC -515 Rockaway Av -Vly Stream 11581
(607) 652-3443 .. **Spinney**, Richd B '72 -74 Main -Stamfrd 12167
(212) 969-3000 .. **Spinogatti**, Richd L '72 SrCnsl Proskauer R LLP -1585 Bway -NY 10036
(516) 222-0688 .. **Spinola**, Jos P '85 Resolute Systems,LLC -825 E Gate Blvd -Gdn Cty 11530
(212) 728-8000 .. **Spinola**, Patrick J Jr. '01 %Willkie F&G LLP -787 7th Av -NY 10019
(212) 735-3000 .. **Spira**, Avi Abraham '07 Telman Grp,Inc -470 Park Av S -NY 10016
(212) 679-3124 .. **Spira**, Shirley J '86 %T McCauley LLC -274 Mad Av -NY 10016 **Fx**:679-3105
(585) 288-1881 .. **Spires**, Edw J '62 -108 Fairhvn Rd -Rchstr 14610 **Fx**:288-1881
(212) 265-6888 .. **Spires**, Genevieve M '06 %Porzio B&N,PC -156 W 56th -NY 10019
(212) 768-8088 .. **Spiridakis**, John '85 -350 Bway -NY 10013
(718) 298-8900 .. **Spiridigliozzi**, Ian Z '09 Leg Aid -153-01 Jamaica Av -Jamaica 11432 **Fx**:657-0537
(631) 277-8844 .. **Spirio**, Concetta G '87 -173 N Main PMB#320 -Sayvll 11782 **Fx**:277-5547
(212) 868-8100 .. **Spiritis**, Jenni B '03 Nimkoff Firm -1 Penn Plz -NY 10119 **Fx**:868-0227
(516) 538-5222 .. **Spirn**, Arthur L '65 A Spirn,PC -600 Old Cntry Rd -Gdn Cty 11530 **Fx**:292-3556
(631) 787-8560 .. **Spirn**, Jennifer '03 (Spirn & S) -150 Motor Pkwy -Hauppauge 11788 **Fx**:787-8564
(631) 787-8560 .. **Spirn**, Lawr F '70 (Spirn & S) -150 Motor Pkwy -Hauppauge 11788 **Fx**:787-8564
(516) 596-8670 .. **Spirn**, Ronald A '93 R Spirn,PC -540B Willow Av -Cedarhrst 11516 **Fx**:596-8676
(646) 392-9250 .. **Spiro**, A Jeffrey '73 %M Klein & Assoc -200 Mad Av -NY 10016 **Fx**:(212) 779-1499
(718) 222-2364 .. **Spiro**, Bryan S '04 %Law Dept -350 Jay -Brklyn 11201 **Fx**:222-2373
(212) 880-9460 .. **Spiro**, Edw M '77 (Morvillo AGIA&B,PC) -565 5th Av -NY 10017
(212) 529-5440 .. **Spiro**, Miriam R '96 -26 W 9th -NY 10011
(212) 326-3939 .. **Spiro**, Vanessa Green '90 (Jones D) -222 E 41st -NY 10017
(212) 608-4140 .. **Spirollari**, Adrian '03 %I Marku,PC -299 Bway -NY 10007 **Fx**:608-6256
(914) 763-9614 .. **Spiros**, Andrew G '82 -288 Todd Rd -Katonah 10536 **Fx**:763-9618
(914) 323-7000 .. **Spisek**, Milan P '88 %Wilson EME&D LLP -3 Gannett Dr -White Plns 10604
(718) 390-5422 .. **Spisso**, Jennifer G '03 %Civil Ct -927 Castleton Av -Staten Isl 10310 **Fx**:390-8108
(516) 938-4660 .. **Spisto**, Phyllis E '89 (P Spisto,PC) -15 Bay Av -Hicksvll 11801 **Fx**:938-5907
(212) 728-8000 .. **Spital**, Andrew '07 %Willkie F&G LLP -787 7th Av -NY 10019
(212) 872-9800 .. **Spital**, Saml '05 %Squire S&D LLP -30 Rckfllr Plz -NY 10112
(212) 705-7000 .. **Spitaleri**, Richd Jr. '05 %Bingham M LLP -399 Park Av -NY 10022
(516) 439-4001 .. **Spitalnic**, Danl F '03 -6 Grace Av -Gt Neck 11021
(212) 326-2000 .. **Spitalnick**, Jared '06 %O'Melveny & M LLP -7 Times Sq -NY 10036
(212) 450-4000 .. **Spitalnick**, Jason M '08 %Davis P&W LLP -450 Lex Av -NY 10017
(212) 788-1230 .. **Spitalnick**, Leslie '07 %Law Dept -100 Church -NY 10007 **Fx**:788-0367
(516) 482-5844 .. **Spitalnick**, Robt E '79 -17 Barstow Rd -Gt Neck 11021 **Fx**:487-7185
(516) 746-3000 .. **Spitalnik**, Joshua D '06 %M Kalish -114 Old Cntry Rd -Mineola 11501 **Fx**:746-3079
(917) 778-6500 .. **Spiteri**, Gina M '03 %K Dodson -485 Lex Av -NY 10017
(516) 747-1010 .. **Spithogiannis**, Michl J '85 (Dollinger G&G) -1 Old Cntry Rd -Carle Pl 11514
(716) 877-2251 .. **Spitler**, Kevin W '81 -560 Delaware Rd -Buffalo 14223 **Fx**:873-8168
(716) 856-4200 .. **Spitler**, Mark '83 (Gibson M&C,LLP) -69 Delaware Av -Buffalo 14202
(212) 841-1000 .. **Spitser**, Brian P '07 %Covington & B LLP -620 8th Av -NY 10018
(212) 869-3200 .. **Spitz**, Alice '83 (Molod S&D,PC) -104 W 40th -NY 10018
(845) 562-0203 .. **Spitz**, Andrew L '79 (Finkelstein & Prtnrs,LLP) -1279 Route 300 Bx1111 -Newburgh 12550
(917) 417-8394 .. **Spitz**, Arnold '71 -35 Sutton Pl -NY 10022
(718) 347-7918 .. **Spitz**, Gary F '91 -69-10 261st -Glen Oaks 11004 **Fx**:347-7918
(914) 683-8484 .. **Spitz**, Howard '54 OfCnsl Goodrich & B -5 Old Rd -Elmsfrd 10523
(585) 419-8800 .. **Spitz**, James A Jr. '76 (Harris B PLLC) -99 Garnsey Rd -Pittsfrd 14534
(718) 643-2884 .. **Spitz**, Leslie N '84 -53 3rd -Brklyn 11231 **Fx**:643-0488
(845) 639-1900 .. **Spitzer**, Alvin L '65 -275 N Mddltwn Rd -Pearl Rvr 10965 **Fx**:638-8048
(716) 856-4000 .. **Spitzer**, Danl A '94 (Hodgson R LLP) -140 Pearl -Buffalo 14202
(212) 450-4000 .. **Spitzer**, Danl A '10 %Davis P&W LLP -450 Lex Av -NY 10017
(212) 558-4000 .. **Spitzer**, David C '96 (Sullivan & C LLP) -125 Broad -NY 10004
(212) 969-3000 .. **Spitzer**, Delia B '83 (Proskauer R LLP) -1585 Bway -NY 10036
(212) 650-7000 .. **Spitzer**, Eliot L '85 CCNY -160 Convent Av -NY 10031
(212) 513-3200 .. **Spitzer**, M James Jr. '69 (Holland & K LLP) -31 W 52nd -NY 10019
(646) 328-0850 .. **Spitzer**, Melinda H '98 %Outside Cnsl Solutns LLP -1430 Bway -NY 10018 **Fx**:360-5000
(212) 259-8000 .. **Spitzer**, Richd B '02 (Dewey & L LLP) -1301 Av of Amer -NY 10019
(718) 553-3285 .. **Spitzer**, Robt D '08 FAA -1 Aviation Plz -Jamaica 11434 **Fx**:995-5699
(212) 486-1455 .. **Spitzer**, Robt E '07 %Post PGM&S,PA -575 Mad Av -NY 10022
(212) 973-8000 .. **Spitzer**, Seth E '05 %Schnader HS&L LLP -140 Bway -NY 10005
(516) 379-2500 .. **Spitzer**, Stuart T '78 %Malone T&S -147 W Merrick Rd Bx589 -Freeprt 11520
(716) 847-8400 .. **Spitzmiller**, John C '73 (Phillips L LLP) -3400 HSBC Ctr -Buffalo 14203
(212) 737-0343 .. **Spitz-Perry**, Allison '89 (Perry & S) -75 East End Av -NY 10028 **Fx**:737-0172
(212) 545-4000 .. **Spivack**, Allison Cohen '07 %Jackson L LLP -666 3rd Av -NY 10017
(212) 758-5400 .. **Spivack**, Byron H '98 %MacKayShields LLC -9 W 57th -NY 10019
(212) 574-1200 .. **Spivack**, Julia C '04 %Seward & K LLP -1 Bttry Pk Plz -NY 10004
(914) 934-5200 .. **Spivack**, Lisa M '95 Universal Amer Fncl Corp -6 Intl Dr -Rye Brook 10573
(718) 544-1000 .. **Spivack**, Richd C '78 -118-21 Qns Blvd -Frst Hlls 11375 **Fx**:261-8255
(212) 264-3650 .. **Spivak**, Barbara L '73 %SSA Ofc Genl Cnsl -26 Fed Plz -NY 10278 **Fx**:264-6372
(212) 504-6000 .. **Spivak**, Burton '90 Cnsl Cadwalader W&T LLP -1 World Fncl Ctr -NY 10281
(212) 779-9910 .. **Spivak**, David B '75 (Eaton & V LLP) -3 Park Av -NY 10016
(516) 829-3939 .. **Spivak**, Joel '72 -98 Cutter Mill Rd -Gt Neck 11021 **Fx**:829-3946
(718) 971-5339 .. **Spivak**, Lawr G '88 -7232 Bway -Jcksn Hts 11372
(212) 765-2100 .. **Spivak Lipton LLP** -1700 Bway -NY 10019 **Fx**:765-8954
(845) 473-2450 .. **Spivak**, Melvin P '78 -47 S Hmltn -Poughkeepsie 12601
(718) 471-6350 .. **Spivak**, Milton '55 -1473 Granada Pl -Far Rckwy 11691
(212) 754-9400 .. **Spizz**, Alex '74 (Todtman NS&J,PC) -425 Park Av -NY 10022
(516) 747-8877 .. **Spizz & Cooper,LLP** -114 Old Cntry Rd -Mineola 11501 **Fx**:747-8741
(516) 747-8877 .. **Spizz**, Harvey W '68 (Spizz & C,LLP) -114 Old Cntry Rd -Mineola 11501
(212) 649-2000 .. **Spizz**, Jack B '00 %Hearst Corp -300 W 57th -NY 10019 **Fx**:649-2035
(212) 450-4000 .. **Spizzirri**, Richd D '59 SrCnsl Davis P&W LLP -450 Lex Av -NY 10017
(914) 963-2200 .. **Spizzirro**, Louis M '89 Precise Mortgage -165 Brnx Rvr Rd -Ynkrs 10704
(212) 883-1700 .. **Spletzer**, Christine A '89 (Duval & S LLP) -101 Park Av -NY 10178
(212) 344-7778 .. **Splittgerber**, Scott J '99 %Bachner & Assoc -26 Bway -NY 10004
(212) 545-4711 .. **Spodek**, Israel '06 %Wolf HAF&H LLP -270 Mad Av -NY 10016
(212) 349-6505 .. **Spodek**, Lance Roger '76 (LR Spodek,PC) -330 W 58th -NY 10019 **Fx**:267-3766
(212) 232-1300 .. **Spodick**, Stacy C '04 (Lewis BB&S LLP) -77 Water -NY 10005
(718) 250-2000 .. **Spoerel**, Kristen L '08 %DA -350 Jay -Brklyn 11201 **Fx**:250-2314
(212) 225-2000 .. **Spoerri**, Kimberly R '09 %Cleary GS&H -1 Lbrty Plz -NY 10006
(845) 225-0176 .. **Spofford**, Jos J Jr. '87 J Spofford Jr -20 Church -Carmel 10512 **Fx**:225-0274
(212) 340-0400 .. **Spokony**, David '76 %Appllt Div 1st Dept -27 Mad Av -NY 10010 **Fx**:889-4412
(631) 231-1450 .. **Spole**, Kenneth M '97 Feldman K&M,PC -330 Vndrblt Motor Pkwy -Hauppauge 11788
(212) 455-2000 .. **Spollen**, John W '74 OfCnsl Simpson T&B LLP -425 Lex Av -NY 10017
(914) 285-9800 .. **Spollen**, Moira A '00 Kurzman EC&L,LLP -1 N Bway -White Plns 10601
(917) 232-6872 .. **Spollen**, Thos P '81 -585 N Railroad Av -Staten Isl 10304
(718) 298-0242 .. **Spolzino**, Richd P '99 Family Ct -151-20 Jamaica Av -Jamaica 11432
(914) 323-7000 .. **Spolzino**, Robt A '84 (Wilson EME&D LLP) -3 Gannett Dr -White Plns 10604
(212) 697-1900 .. **Sponholz**, Jos C '98 %Booz Allen Hamilton -101 Park Av -NY 10178
(212) 872-6660 .. **Sponzilli**, Jennifer A '98 KPMG,LLP -345 Park Av -NY 10154
(212) 969-3000 .. **Spooner**, A Nicole '06 %Proskauer R LLP -1585 Bway -NY 10036
(212) 442-4922 .. **Spooner**, John B '84 %Ofc Admin Trials -40 Rector -NY 10006 **Fx**:442-4947
(516) 240-8030 .. **Spooner**, Kristen M '06 (Vasselman & S) -1225 Franklin Av -Gdn Cty 11530
(347) 296-1751 .. **Sporn**, Chas M '78 %Supreme Ct Law Dept -360 Adams -Brklyn 11201 **Fx**:643-6114
(212) 791-1200 .. **Sporn**, Michl H '73 -299 Bway -NY 10007 **Fx**:791-3047
(212) 986-0411 .. **Sporn**, Richd A '78 -521 5th Av -NY 10175
(212) 817-4218 .. **Sporn**, Robt A '96 Weightwatchers.com -11 Mad Av -NY 10010
(212) 964-0046 .. **Sporn**, Saml P '53 (Schoengold & S,PC) -19 Fulton -NY 10038
(212) 773-5417 .. **Sportelli**, Anthony J '97 Ernst & Young LLP -5 Times Sq -NY 10036
(646) 386-3638 .. **Sposito**, Loretta Anne '87 %Supreme Ct-Law Dept -60 Centre -NY 10007
(212) 815-0975 .. **Spota**, Kathryn M '05 DA - Special Narcotics -80 Centre -NY 10013
(631) 853-4161 .. **Spota**, Thos J III '67 (DA) -N Cnty Cmplx Bldg 77 -Hauppauge 11788 **Fx**:853-4192
(585) 454-7145 .. **Spoto**, David D '93 (Gallo & I,LLP) -39 State -Rchstr 14614
(716) 487-1142 .. **Spoto**, Douglas A '68 (Spoto S&S) -112 Htl Jmstwn Ofc Bldg -Jamestwn 14701
(518) 455-2788 .. **Spotts**, Timothy P '00 %Sen J Sampson -506 LOB -Albany 12247
(212) 523-0932 .. **Sprafkin**, David C '77 -36 E 20th -NY 10003 **Fx**:(646) 390-8197
(212) 687-8181 .. **Spragg**, Robt J '92 (Kreindler & K) -750 3rd Av -NY 10017
(718) 520-8300 .. **Sprague**, John P '72 -80-02 Kew Grdns Rd -Kew Gdns 11415 **Fx**:520-8751
(212) 259-8000 .. **Sprague**, Joshua S '08 %Dewey & L LLP -1301 Av of Amer -NY 10019
(518) 873-3335 .. **Sprague**, Kristy L '99 %DA -Cthse -Elizabethtwn 12932 **Fx**:873-3788
(518) 473-3303 .. **Sprague**, Laura A '01 %Dept of Health -Corning Twr 24th Fl -Albany 12237 **Fx**:473-2019

(212) 667-9300 .. **Sprague**, Sarah H '09 Nomura Securities Intl -2 World Fncl Ctr -NY 10281
(212) 733-1443 .. **Spraguer**, Patricia Ann '94 %Pfizer Inc -235 E 42nd -NY 10017
(315) 422-5557 .. **Sprancmanis**, Arnis V '96 -6315 Fly Rd Bx5119 -Syracuse 13220 **Fx:**701-1283
(212) 557-4000 .. **Spraragen**, Jos M '97 %Grunfeld DLS&K LLP -399 Park Av -NY 10022
(718) 254-7000 .. **Spratt**, Jacqueline L '87 %US Atty -271 Cadman Plz E -Brklyn 11201 **Fx:**254-6479
(516) 488-3300 .. **Spratt**, Wm G '78 (Shaub AC&S,LLP) -1983 Marcus Av -Lk Success 11042
(212) 849-7000 .. **Spray**, Judd R '03 %Quinn EU&S,LLP -51 Mad Av -NY 10010
(212) 464-1383 .. **Sprechman**, Jordan A '87 JP Morgan Chase -270 Park Av -NY 10017 **Fx:**464-1303
(631) 587-0004 .. **Spreer**, Thos H '94 -100 Fire Isl Av -Babylon 11702 **Fx:**587-0100
(718) 431-2900 .. **Sprei**, Michl '03 -1370 60th -Brklyn 11219 **Fx:**972-7612
(518) 402-9223 .. **Spreitzer**, Carin E '05 %DEC -625 Bway -Albany 12233 **Fx:**402-9018
(212) 715-1000 .. **Sprie**, Ingo W Jr. '87 (Arnold & P LLP) -399 Park Av -NY 10022
(716) 842-4611 .. **Spriegel**, David D '97 M&T Bk -1 M & T Plz -Buffalo 14203 **Fx:**842-5376
(518) 762-4503 .. **Spring**, Arthur C '73 -10 S Market -Johnstwn 12095 **Fx:**762-4504
(212) 419-3638 .. **Spring**, Julia C '77 NY Academy of Medicine -1216 5th Av -NY 10029
(315) 474-2943 .. **Spring**, Laura Lee '87 (Sugarman Law Firm,LLP) -211 W Jffrsn -Syracuse 13202
(212) 440-3447 .. **Spring**, Lisa Carol '82 %CNA Ins Co -40 Wall -NY 10005 **Fx:**440-7050
(631) 242-3555 .. **Spring**, Robt B '66 (R Spring,PC) -Bx280 -Commack 11725
(212) 916-7464 .. **Spring**, Robt E '78 Gracie Sq Captl LLC -420 Lex Av -NY 10170
(518) 449-9680 .. **Spring**, Stephen R '71 -Bx98 -Woodgate 13494 **Fx:**439-9681
(212) 259-8000 .. **Springel**, Bartholomew W '04 %Dewey & L LLP -1301 Av of Amer -NY 10019
(212) 264-1609 .. **Springer**, Adrian R '98 %ODAR-SSA -26 Fed Plz -NY 10278 **Fx:**264-8633
(718) 624-0054 .. **Springer**, Allen D '82 A Springer,PLLC -155 W 68th -NY 10023
(212) 803-3612 .. **Springer**, Jonathan D '00 Empire State Dvlmpmnt Corp -633 3rd Av -NY 10017
(212) 577-2523 .. **Springer**, Lauren J '06 Ctr for Applt Litigation -74 Trinity Pl -NY 10006 **Fx:**577-2535
(212) 326-2000 .. **Springer**, Rachel Burke '08 %O'Melveny & M LLP -7 Times Sq -NY 10036
(212) 478-7200 .. **Springer**, Tracy '92 %Hahn & H LLP -488 Mad Av -NY 10022
(212) 326-2000 .. **Springer**, Wm R B '07 %O'Melveny & M LLP -7 Times Sq -NY 10036
(718) 462-3690 .. **Springle**, Stephen V M '00 -2196 Pitkin Av -Brklyn 11207
(212) 436-2229 .. **Springs**, Christanna R '03 Deloitte & Touche LLP -2 World Fncl Ctr -NY 10281
(212) 813-1600 .. **Springut**, Milton '77 (Kalow & S) -488 Mad Av -NY 10022
(212) 310-8000 .. **Spritz**, Matthew M '09 %Weil G&M LLP -767 5th Av -NY 10153
(315) 477-0100 .. **Sprock**, Chas M Jr. '90 (Baldwin & S,LLP) -126 N Salina -Syracuse 13202
(212) 850-8500 .. **Sprock**, Richd J '99 %Bruckmann & V,LLP -420 Lex Av -NY 10170
(607) 272-8500 .. **Sprole**, Robt R III '89 %Therm, Inc -Bx220 -Ithaca 14851
(212) 521-4430 .. **Sprong**, David J '01 (Becker M LLC) -590 Mad Av -NY 10022
(518) 474-7330 .. **Sprotbery**, Kent B '94 %Dept of Law -The Cptl -Albany 12224
(212) 850-6100 .. **Sproul**, Gayle '91 (Levine SK&S,LLP) -321 W 44th -NY 10036
(516) 804-5598 .. **Sproule**, Clare M '98 -3056 Riverside Dr -Wantagh 11793
(212) 308-8505 .. **Sproule**, Michl H '93 (Akabas & S) -488 Mad Av -NY 10022
(212) 578-0678 .. **Sproule**, Robt C '98 %MetLife -27-01 Qns Plz N -LIC 11101
(212) 225-2000 .. **Spruce**, Craig M '01 %Cleary GS&H -1 Lbrty Plz -NY 10006
(212) 449-0383 .. **Sprung**, John B '71 %Merrill Lynch -220 Bway -NY 10038 **Fx:**449-9858
(315) 435-2470 .. **Spuches**, Melanie C '09 DA -505 S State -Syracuse 13202 **Fx:**435-3969
(516) 248-6400 .. **Spund**, Mark E '75 (Davidoff M&H,LLP) -200 Grdn City Plz -Gdn Cty 11530
(518) 565-4693 .. **Spurgeon**, Jani L '85 -137 Margaret -Plattsbrgh 12901 **Fx:**565-4887
(212) 902-0041 .. **Spurr**, David R '99 Goldman Sachs & Co -85 Broad -NY 10004
(212) 676-0982 .. **Sputz**, Alan W '95 %Law Dept -60 Lafayette -NY 10013 **Fx:**442-6865
(212) 719-5640 .. **Squadron**, Anne Strickland '75 %Theater Unlimited,Inc -211 Cntrl Pk W -NY 10024 **Fx:**719-5668
(718) 537-4958 .. **Squarcia**, Suzanne M '98 %ODAR-SSA -226 E 161st -Bronx 10451 **Fx:**590-1673
(212) 922-8327 .. **Squasoni**, Douglas W '02 Bank of NY -200 Park Av -NY 10166
(201) 315-4712 .. **Squasoni**, Patricia A '96 -2686 Claredon Av -Bellmore 11710 **Fx:**327-5159
(718) 579-7900 .. **Squatriglia**, Heather P '09 %Leg Aid -900 Sheridan Av -Bronx 10451 **Fx:**293-8744
(212) 262-2390 .. **Squeo**, Eugene P '87 OfCnsl Connell F LLP -888 7th Av -NY 10106
(631) 853-4049 .. **Squicciarini**, James A '04 %Cnty Atty -Dennison Bldg Bx6100 -Hauppauge 11788 **Fx:**853-5169
(212) 790-9200 .. **Squiers**, Deborah K '95 (Cowan L&L,PC) -1133 Av of Amer -NY 10036
(718) 776-0001 .. **Squillace**, JoAnn '02 %Drummond & C PC -221-10 Jamaica Av -Qns Vllg 11428
(212) 815-1818 .. **Squillance**, Marianna '90 %DC 37 MELS -125 Barclay -NY 10007 **Fx:**815-1343
(212) 686-2466 .. **Squillante**, Neil J '94 Peerviews Inc -825 3rd Av -NY 10022
(718) 771-2221 .. **Squire**, Andrew '82 -379 Decatur -Brklyn 11233 **Fx:**771-2243
(212) 308-5858 .. **Squire**, Jeffrey H '77 (Bragar WE&S,PC) -885 3rd Av -NY 10022
(212) 636-6000 .. **Squire**, Richd C '03 %Fordham Univ Sch of Law -140 W 62nd -NY 10023 **Fx:**636-6899
(212) 872-9800 .. **Squire Sanders & Dempsey LLP** -30 Rckfllr Plz -NY 10112 **Fx:**872-9815
(212) 697-1420 .. **Squire**, Walter C '71 (Jacobson M&S,LLP) -52 Vndrblt Av -NY 10017 **Fx:**697-1427
(607) 776-2158 .. **Squires**, Jeffrey E '80 -14 E Pulteney Sq Bx113 -Bath 14810 **Fx:**776-5806
(212) 408-5100 .. **Squires**, John A '93 (Chadbourne & P LLP) -30 Rckfllr Plz -NY 10112
(212) 471-8494 .. **Squires**, Lawton W '84 (Herzfeld & R,PC) -125 Broad -NY 10004
(212) 530-5000 .. **Squires**, Matthew L '09 %Milbank TH&M LLP -1 Chase Manh Plz -NY 10005
(914) 666-2161 .. **Squirrell**, David J '91 (Banks CS&S,LLP) -61 Smith Av -Mt Kisco 10549
(917) 981-8282 .. **Squitieri**, Jeffrey P '97 -245 E 63rd -NY 10065
(212) 421-6492 .. **Squitieri**, Lee '84 (Squitieri & F,LLP) -32 E 57th -NY 10022 **Fx:**421-6553
(212) 490-3000 .. **Squitieri**, Virginia P '06 %Wilson EME&D LLP -150 E 42nd -NY 10017
(212) 506-2500 .. **Sramek**, Megan A '09 %Mayer B LLP -1675 Bway -NY 10019
(212) 530-5000 .. **Sreepada**, Sunila '10 %Milbank TH&M LLP -1 Chase Manh Plz -NY 10005
(212) 351-4000 .. **Sreeprakash**, Netra '07 %Gibson D&C LLP -200 Park Av -NY 10166
(212) 773-5848 .. **Sreter**, David J '00 Ernst & Young LLP -5 Times Sq -NY 10036
(212) 416-8680 .. **Srinivasan**, Sudarsana '08 %Dept of Law -120 Bway -NY 10271
(212) 835-1572 .. **Srivastav**, Divya H '90 %Lampf LP&P -5 Penn Plz 19th Fl -NY 10119
(212) 779-1208 .. **Srivastava**, Lina P '96 -300 E 33rd -NY 10016
(212) 318-6000 .. **Srivastava**, Ritu '08 %Paul HJ&W LLP -75 E 55th -NY 10022
(631) 331-7228 .. **Srivastava**, Usha '81 -Bx72 -Pt Jffrsn Sta 11776 **Fx:**828-1122
(516) 931-8900 .. **Sroka**, Louis S '89 -366 N Bway -Jericho 11753 **Fx:**931-2034
(212) 558-5500 .. **Srolovic**, Lemuel M '90 Weitz & L,PC -700 Bway -NY 10003
(212) 953-6633 .. **Srour**, Deborah Renata '93 (Cox PS&S LLP) -630 3rd Av -NY 10017
(212) 909-6000 .. **Srulowitz**, Mark '07 %Debevoise & P LLP -919 3rd Av -NY 10022
(212) 686-1224 .. **Srulowitz**, Marvin '73 -16 E 34th -NY 10016 **Fx:**532-3206
(212) 245-6754 .. **Srulowitz**, Sander '77 (Sonnenschein S&D,LLP) -7 Penn Plz -NY 10001
(212) 310-8000 .. **Srulowitz**, Stephanie E '06 %Weil G&M LLP -767 5th Av -NY 10153
(212) 618-1322 .. **Ssemogerere**, Karoli L '00 -14 Wall -NY 10005 **Fx:**618-1705
(914) 220-0030 .. **Staab**, Gary G '85 -2 William -White Plns 10601
(212) 756-2000 .. **Staba**, Katherine A '10 %Schulte R&Z LLP -919 3rd Av -NY 10022
(212) 425-9300 .. **Stabbert**, Gerd W '01 %Bressler A&R,PC -17 State -NY 10004
(516) 249-3450 .. **Stabenau**, Craig M '02 %Carman C&I,LLP -266 Main -Farmngdl 11735
(212) 756-4659 .. **Stabholz-Navot**, Karin '07 Alliance Bernstein LP -1345 Av of Amer -NY 10105 **Fx:**554-4639
(212) 259-8000 .. **Stabile**, Danl T '09 %Dewey & L LLP -1301 Av of Amer -NY 10019
(914) 699-1919 .. **Stabile**, Joanne '97 (Gross S&S LLP) -9 W Prospect Av -Mt Vernon 10550 **Fx:**699-6106
(917) 421-4672 .. **Stabile**, Maria Treglia '90 IRS -33 Maiden Ln -NY 10038
(212) 344-3100 .. **Stabile**, Matthew C '07 %Frenkel LWW&G,LLP -1 Whitehall -NY 10004
(212) 737-0400 .. **Stabile**, Renato C '98 %G Lefcourt,PC -148 E 78th -NY 10075 **Fx:**988-6192
(518) 465-3553 .. **Stabinski**, Alexander L '04 %Maynard OS&C,LLP -6 Twr Pl -Albany 12203
(914) 273-6637 .. **Stabinsky**, Harvey '71 -15 Boulder Trl -Armonk 10504
(212) 592-1400 .. **Stabler**, Eric A '96 Cnsl Herrick,F LLP -2 Park Av -NY 10016
(516) 472-7300 .. **Stacchini**, Jennifer Tomeny '97 %AS Cannatella -53 Orchrd -Manhsst 11030
(516) 437-4385 .. **Stacchini**, Michl J '97 %Vishnick MM LLP -3000 Marcus Av -Lk Success 11042
(212) 883-1700 .. **Stachenfeld**, Bruce M '84 (Duval & S LLP) -101 Park Av -NY 10178
(716) 856-1010 .. **Stachowiak**, Franklin A '65 -69 Delaware Av -Buffalo 14202 **Fx:**856-1008
(716) 824-5353 .. **Stachowski**, Michl J '74 -2025 Clinton -Buffalo 14206 **Fx:**824-6674
(212) 627-9810 .. **Stachtiaris**, Theo J '96 (Kline & S LLP) -440 W 15th -NY 10011 **Fx:**727-2144
(716) 204-2400 .. **Stachura**, Michelle C '04 %SJ Baum,PC -220 Nrthpnte Pkwy Bx1291 -Buffalo 14240 **Fx:**204-4600
(716) 285-9696 .. **Stack**, Bernard E '55 -631 Main -Niagara Fls 14301
(845) 357-3149 .. **Stack**, Danl '56 -8 Linda Dr -Suffern 10901 **Fx:**357-4253
(845) 677-5700 .. **Stack**, David R '85 (McLaughlin & S,LLP) -3304 Franklin Av Bx1369 -Millbrook 12545
(212) 448-1100 .. **Stack**, David R '85 (McLaughlin & S,LLP) -260 Mad Av -NY 10016
(518) 473-1949 .. **Stack**, Eileen M '90 %OTDA -40 N Pearl -Albany 12243 **Fx:**474-9389
(516) 463-5858 .. **Stack**, Elaine Jackson '80 %Hofstra Law Schl -121 Hofstra Univ -Hempstd 11549
(315) 425-2700 .. **Stack**, Gerald F '80 (Hiscock & B,LLP) -One Park Pl -Syracuse 13202
(718) 741-3225 .. **Stack**, Jane M '84 %Div of Human Rights -1 Fordham Plz -Bronx 10458 **Fx:**741-8102
(315) 478-6016 .. **Stack**, Joshua R '04 NE Natural Homes -5110 Velasko Rd -Syracuse 13215
(212) 944-6611 .. **Stack**, Robt T '84 (Tompkins & D,LLP) -5 Hanover Sq -NY 10004
(315) 673-0948 .. **Stack**, Rosemary '86 -3517 Ambler Rd -Syracuse 13215
(212) 490-5688 .. **Stack**, Tamara L '93 -261 Mad Av -NY 10016 **Fx:**808-9808
(516) 741-3300 .. **Stackel**, Stephen '65 (Borden SF&S) -666 Old Cntry Rd -Gdn Cty 11530
(212) 458-1258 .. **Stackell**, Esther I '81 AIG -175 Water -NY 10038
(718) 492-7777 .. **Staco**, Michelle E '95 -189 Montague -Brklyn 11201 **Fx:**222-0122
(585) 339-9539 .. **Stacy**, Michl P '94 -125 State -Rchstr 14614 **Fx:**232-4251
(212) 455-2000 .. **Stacy**, Neera Rellan '98 Cnsl Simpson T&B LLP -425 Lex Av -NY 10017
(716) 852-1380 .. **Stadelmaier**, Kevin M '02 %Abbarno M&K -314 Brisbane Bldg -Buffalo 14203
(212) 455-2000 .. **Stadler**, Brian M '91 (Simpson T&B LLP) -425 Lex Av -NY 10017
(516) 663-6600 .. **Stadler**, Jeffrey L '64 OfCnsl Ruskin MF,PC -1425 RXR Plz -Uniondale 11556
(716) 856-4400 .. **Stadler**, Jos W '96 (Gibbons SG&K,PC) -181 Franklin -Buffalo 14202
(845) 855-5808 .. **Stadler**, Lewis B '80 -12 E Main -Pawling 12564 **Fx:**855-5809
(212) 351-3400 .. **Stadnick**, Michl P '01 (Desmarais LLP) -230 Park Av -NY 10169 **Fx:**351-3401
(631) 219-6209 .. **Stadtman**, Scott D '71 -258 15th -W Babylon 11704
(212) 442-5980 .. **Stadtmauer**, Catherine S '85 %Dept Youth & Comm Dvlpmnt -156 William -NY 10038 **Fx:**442-5997

(212) 880-3800 .. **Stadtmauer,** David I '61 (Akerman S) -335 Mad Av -NY 10017
(212) 986-6200 .. **Stadtmauer,** Marc A '94 -230 Park Av -NY 10169 **Fx:**661-2153
(973) 778-1771 .. **Stadtmauer,** Steven '95 -50 Murray -NY 10007 **Fx:**778-4136
(212) 687-0100 .. **Stadtmauer,** Steven A '95 (Harris B PLLC) -100 Wall -NY 10005
(716) 631-7250 .. **Staehr,** Jonathan E '02 (Hemming & S PC) -336 Harris Hill Rd -Williamsvll 14221 **Fx:**929-3333
(212) 733-9153 .. **Staff,** Karen L '87 Pfizer Inc -150 E 42nd -NY 10017
(212) 553-4667 .. **Staffa,** Jos '83 %Moody's Invstr Srvc -250 Greenwich -NY 10007
(212) 909-6000 .. **Staffaroni,** Robt J '78 (Debevoise & P LLP) -919 3rd Av -NY 10022
(518) 668-5412 .. **Stafford Carr & McNally,PC** -175 Ottawa -Lk George 12845 **Fx:**668-3629
(212) 310-8000 .. **Stafford,** Caryn R '89 %Weil G&M LLP -767 5th Av -NY 10153
(212) 512-3914 .. **Stafford,** David B '88 McGraw-Hill -1221 Av of Amer -NY 10020
(516) 938-3100 .. **Stafford,** Kathleen M '01 %P Roach & Assoc,PC -125 Michl Dr -Syosset 11791 **Fx:**931-4403
(518) 668-5412 .. **Stafford,** Michl E '76 (Stafford C&M,PC) -175 Ottawa -Lk George 12845
(516) 227-0700 .. **Stafford,** Michl P '74 Cnsl Farrell F,PC -1320 RXR Plz -Uniondale 11556
(518) 561-4400 .. **Stafford Owens Curtin & Trombley, PLLC** -1 Cumberland Av Bx2947 -Plattsbrgh 12901 **Fx:**561-4848
(631) 422-4000 .. **Stafford,** Richd B '02 -4875 Sunrise Hwy -Bohemia 11716
(631) 728-5151 .. **Stafford,** Robt E '67 -188 W Montauk Hwy Bx1014 -Hampton Bays 11946 **Fx:**728-5152
(212) 728-8604 .. **Stafford,** Shernette A L '99 -787 7th Av -NY 10019 **Fx:**728-9604
(212) 698-3500 .. **Stafford,** Timothy A '84 (Dechert LLP) -1095 Av of Amer -NY 10036
(212) 689-3858 .. **Stafford,** Ying '04 -276 5th Av -NY 10001
(845) 291-2650 .. **Stage,** Christine Foy '82 %Cnty Atty -285 Main -Goshen 10924 **Fx:**291-3014
(845) 986-1136 .. **Stage,** Douglas R '82 (Stage N&Z,LLP) -23 West -Warwick 10990
(845) 986-1136 .. **Stage Nathans & Ziobro,LLP** -23 West -Warwick 10990 **Fx:**986-8478
(845) 291-3037 .. **Stage,** Rebecca E '77 %Family Ct -255-275 Main -Goshen 10924 **Fx:**291-3051
(212) 526-1012 .. **Stagg,** David J '97 Barclays Capital -745 7th Av -NY 10019
(212) 870-7479 .. **Stagg,** Nancy '62 Metropolitan Opera -30 Lincoln Ctr Plz -NY 10023
(516) 812-4500 .. **Stagg Terenzi Confusione & Wabnik LLP** -401 Franklin Av -Gdn Cty 11530 **Fx:**812-4600
(516) 812-4500 .. **Stagg,** Thos E '91 (Stagg TC&W LLP) -401 Franklin Av -Gdn Cty 11530
(212) 267-1900 .. **Stagias,** Georgia G '10 %Wade CM -111 Bway -NY 10006
(718) 330-7861 .. **Stagno,** Linda A '83 SSA-OHA -111 Lvngstn -Brklyn 11201 **Fx:**330-2009
(212) 903-8700 .. **Stahl,** Danl W '09 %Roberts & H,LLP -825 8th Av -NY 10019
(212) 826-6422 .. **Stahl,** Douglas '78 (Stahl & Z) -747 3rd Av -NY 10017 **Fx:**826-6402
(631) 841-3088 .. **Stahl,** Eliza D '96 -21 Dixon Av -Copiague 11726 **Fx:**841-3089
(646) 386-5700 .. **Stahl,** Frances C '83 %Civil Ct -111 Centre -NY 10013
(212) 223-4000 .. **Stahl,** Gary A '82 Cnsl Crowell & M LLP -590 Mad Av -NY 10022
(212) 909-6000 .. **Stahl,** Jacob W '06 %Debevoise & P LLP -919 3rd Av -NY 10022
(212) 318-3000 .. **Stahl,** James E '81 SrCnsl Fulbright & J LLP -666 5th Av -NY 10103
(212) 839-5300 .. **Stahl,** Stuart Z '04 %Sidley A LLP -787 7th Av -NY 10019
(716) 847-0650 .. **Stahl,** Tara J '09 %Leg Srvcs -237 Main -Buffalo 14203 **Fx:**847-0227
(212) 557-7285 .. **Stahlmann,** Peter '76 %ALSTOM Trans -353 Lex Av -NY 10016
(607) 776-3371 .. **Stahr,** Thos J '79 -7 W Morris Bx386 -Bath 14810 **Fx:**776-9796
(646) 458-6807 .. **Staiano,** Frank K '03 ACE USA -140 Bway -NY 10005 **Fx:**(866) 635-5687
(212) 615-3441 .. **Staikos,** John '99 LS Power -1700 Bway -NY 10019
(212) 964-6611 .. **Staines,** Timothy J '05 %Lester SK&D -120 Bway -NY 10271
(212) 697-2700 .. **Stairs Dillenbeck Finley** -200 Park Av S -NY 10003 **Fx:**687-3523
(212) 697-2700 .. **Stairs,** Stanley T '72 (Stairs DF) -200 Park Av S -NY 10003
(914) 245-2440 .. **Staker,** John R '83 -2074 Crompond Rd -Yorktwn Hts 10598
(718) 222-2268 .. **Staker,** Keegan K '08 %Law Dept -350 Jay -Brklyn 11201 **Fx:**222-2088
(212) 541-7676 .. **Stakias,** G Michl '93 %Liberty Partners -1370 Av of Amer -NY 10019
(212) 504-6000 .. **Staler,** Jessica R '10 %Cadwalader W&T LLP -1 World Fncl Ctr -NY 10281
(516) 222-2434 .. **Staley,** Regis E Jr. '83 (White Q&S) -377 Oak Bx9304 -Gdn Cty 11530
(212) 513-1075 .. **Stalker Vogrin Bracken & Frimet, LLP** -80 Broad -NY 10004 **Fx:**346-9063
(631) 234-7711 .. **Staller,** Cary F '81 -1455 Vets Hwy -Hauppauge 11749
(718) 243-6207 .. **Stallings,** Shannon J '05 Leg Aid -111 Lvngstn -Brklyn 11201 **Fx:**237-8737
(212) 382-0909 .. **Stallings,** Stephen A '90 (Peckar & A,PC) -41 Mad Av -NY 10154
(631) 249-6644 .. **Stallone,** Jos A '62 (Garcia & S) -2076 Deer Prk Av -Deer Pk 11729
(212) 508-6700 .. **Stallone,** Maryann C '08 %Tannenbaum HS&H LLP -900 3rd Av -NY 10022
(212) 770-6328 .. **Stallone,** Patricia M '91 %AIG -70 Pine -NY 10270
(212) 820-9317 .. **Stallworth,** Nicole A '04 %Hawkins D&W LLP -One Chase Manh Plz -NY 10005
(212) 468-4800 .. **Stalman,** Martin '06 %Davis & G LLP -1740 Bway -NY 10019
(212) 619-2501 .. **Stalonas,** Michl D '71 Warner Fnd,Inc -2 Rector -NY 10006 **Fx:**587-0075
(718) 590-2000 .. **Stalzer,** Michelle R '03 %DA -198 E 161st -Bronx 10451 **Fx:**590-6477
(516) 739-3739 .. **Stamas,** Theo A '85 -1 Old Cntry Rd -Carle Pl 11514 **Fx:**739-5432
(212) 816-9048 .. **Stamas,** Theo S '88 Citibank NA -388 Greenwich -NY 10013
(212) 637-3000 .. **Stamataky,** Evans J '83 EPA -290 Bway -NY 10007 **Fx:**637-3096
(212) 506-1700 .. **Stamatelos,** Paulina A '05 %Kasowitz BT&F LLP -1633 Bway -NY 10019
(917) 856-2534 .. **Stamatin,** Ioana F '06 (Sham & S LLP) -353 W 48th -NY 10036
(607) 778-2684 .. **Stamato,** Philomena M '83 %Dept Soc Srvcs -36-42 Main -Bnghmtn 13905 **Fx:**778-2710
(212) 450-4000 .. **Stamatovic,** Nino '10 %Davis P&W LLP -450 Lex Av -NY 10017
(212) 521-3500 .. **Stambleck,** Peter R '04 %Aronson M&S, LLP -485 Lex Av -NY 10017
(212) 589-4211 .. **Stamboulidis,** George A '86 (Baker & H LLP) -45 Rckfllr Plz -NY 10111 **Fx:**589-4201
(212) 566-4047 .. **Stamell,** Jared B '73 (Stamell & S,LLP) -1 Lbrty Plz -NY 10006
(212) 566-4047 .. **Stamell & Schager,LLP** -1 Lbrty Plz -NY 10006 **Fx:**566-4061
(518) 383-4943 .. **Stamer,** Jeffrey C '82 -20 Solar Dr -Clifton Pk 12065
(212) 872-1000 .. **Stamer,** Michl S '90 -One Bryant Park -NY 10036 **Fx:**872-1002
(315) 448-8400 .. **Stamey,** Robt P '89 %Law Dept -233 E Wshngtn -Syracuse 13202 **Fx:**448-8381
(718) 875-1300 .. **Stamey,** Vija Kemanis '82 %Applt Div 2nd Dept -45 Monroe Pl -Brklyn 11201 **Fx:**858-2446
(914) 523-1365 .. **Stamler,** Jeffrey S '89 -Bx1589 -Pt Chester 10573 **Fx:**(802) 251-1044
(716) 631-5767 .. **Stamm,** Bradley J '96 (Stamm R&S) -5555 Main -Williamsvll 14221
(716) 631-5767 .. **Stamm,** Brian G '98 Stamm R&S -5555 Main -Williamsvll 14221
(716) 631-5767 .. **Stamm,** Gregory '72 (Stamm R&S) -5555 Main -Williamsvll 14221
(212) 750-8585 .. **Stamm,** Michl W '77 WP Stewart & Co -527 Mad Av -NY 10022
(212) 416-6544 .. **Stamm,** Monica J '02 %Dept of Law -120 Bway -NY 10271
(212) 587-2400 .. **Stamm,** Olive K '86 OfCnsl Collins D&M,LLP -277 Bway -NY 10007
(212) 267-7900 .. **Stamm & Olivo, LLP** -295 Mad Av -NY 10017 **Fx:**267-8006
(212) 267-7900 .. **Stamm,** Philip M '85 (Stamm & O,LLP) -295 Mad Av -NY 10017
(716) 631-5767 .. **Stamm Reynolds & Stamm** -5555 Main -Williamsvll 14221 **Fx:**631-5354
(607) 652-7511 .. **Stammel,** Andrew D '09 %Jacobs & J -31 Lake Bx159 -Stamfrd 12167 **Fx:**652-7262
(716) 434-8733 .. **Stamm-Philipps,** Angela '98 -415 Bewley Bldg -Lockprt 14094 **Fx:**434-9105
(718) 250-2000 .. **Stamos,** Colleen D '08 %DA -350 Jay -Brklyn 11201 **Fx:**250-2314
(845) 519-4273 .. **Stamos-Salotto,** Theoni '97 -677 Dutchess Tpk -Poughkeepsie 12603 **Fx:**440-3351
(516) 355-9600 .. **Stamper,** Erin S '08 Friedman HK&P -3000 Marcus Av -Lk Success 11042
(212) 417-3700 .. **Stamper,** Scott Carpenter '07 MFY Legal Srvcs -299 Bway -NY 10007 **Fx:**417-3890
(212) 232-1300 .. **Stampp,** Maureen M '93 (Lewis BB&S LLP) -77 Water -NY 10005
(212) 619-4240 .. **Stampur,** Wm J '73 (Hurwitz S&R) -299 Bway -NY 10007
(212) 450-4000 .. **Stan,** Andreea '08 %Davis P&W LLP -450 Lex Av -NY 10017
(585) 232-6500 .. **Stanat,** Erika N D '98 (Harter S&E LLP) -1600 Bausch & Lomb Pl -Rchstr 14604
(212) 515-1126 .. **Stancati,** Lisa A '93 ESPN Inc -19 E 34th -NY 10016
(718) 984-1662 .. **Stancato,** Gerardette Chionchio '85 -23 Eugene Pl -Staten Isl 10312
(718) 643-5427 .. **Stancato,** Vincent J '83 Criminal Ct -120 Schermerhorn -Brklyn 11201
(212) 766-1888 .. **Stanchfield,** Tara L '04 %Morris DA&F -2 Rector -NY 10006
(518) 745-4343 .. **Stanclift,** Tucker C '98 (Stanclift L&M,PC) -3 Warren Bx358 -Glens Fls 12801 **Fx:**745-4344
(212) 596-9000 .. **Stanco,** Danl L '06 %Ropes & G LLP -1211 Av of Amer -NY 10036
(631) 853-5212 .. **Stanco,** Robin S '04 %Leg Aid -400 Carleton Av Bx9082 -Central Islip 11722 **Fx:**853-7798
(315) 442-0100 .. **Stanczyk,** Michl T '08 %Gilberti SH&S,PC -555 E Genesee -Syracuse 13202
(212) 757-5000 .. **Stand,** David M '89 %Sklover D&F,LLC -10 Rckfllr Plz -NY 10020 **Fx:**757-5002
(518) 433-4335 .. **Standage,** Rodney H '96 %GE -12 Corp Wds Blvd -Albany 12211 **Fx:**433-4378
(212) 351-4500 .. **Standard,** Kenneth G '62 Epstein B&G,PC -250 Park Av -NY 10177
(718) 725-4416 .. **Standel,** David G '90 -90-50 Parsons Blvd -Jamaica 11432
(212) 210-1316 .. **Stander,** Stephen F '68 A & E Network -235 E 45th -NY 10017 **Fx:**210-1308
(646) 386-5700 .. **Standish,** Alexandra '02 %Civil Ct -111 Centre -NY 10013
(212) 310-8000 .. **Standish,** Peter D '67 (Weil G&M LLP) -767 5th Av -NY 10153
(212) 549-6000 .. **Stanford,** Colette H '00 Tommy Hilfiger Inc -601 W 26th -NY 10001 **Fx:**549-6743
(212) 262-1000 .. **Stanford,** Natalie '04 %Levinsohn & A LLP -1790 Bway -NY 10019
(212) 758-9700 .. **Stang,** Robt D '85 %KPMG LLP -345 Park Av -NY 10154
(212) 589-4200 .. **Stanganelli,** Maryanne '05 %Baker & H LLP -45 Rckfllr Plz -NY 10111
(212) 403-1000 .. **Stange,** Tjark Eiko '97 (Wachtell LR&K) -51 W 52nd -NY 10019
(212) 608-2629 .. **St Angelo,** Tara Ann '10 %Gregory & R,PC -111 Bway -NY 10006
(212) 370-1300 .. **Stanger,** Jeffrey D '83 OfCnsl Ellenoff G&S LLP -150 E 42nd -NY 10017
(212) 310-8000 .. **Stangland,** Elaine H '91 (Weil G&M LLP) -767 5th Av -NY 10153
(516) 742-9200 .. **Stangler,** Harold J '54 SrCnsl Edelman K&J PLLC -1 Old Cntry Rd -Carle Pl 11514
(516) 742-9200 .. **Stangler,** Shelley L '82 -1 Old Cntry Rd -Carle Pl 11514
(212) 314-7312 .. **Stanich,** Tanya M '98 SrCnsl IAC -555 W 18th -NY 10011
(212) 504-6000 .. **Stanisci,** Jared '09 %Cadwalader W&T LLP -1 World Fncl Ctr -NY 10281
(212) 878-4669 .. **Stanisich,** Michl A '05 %MTA -347 Mad Av -NY 10017
(315) 853-4436 .. **Stanislaus-Fung,** Karen '99 %Felt E,LLP -4-6 N Park Row -Clinton 13323
(212) 880-9431 .. **Stankiewicz,** David J '07 %Morvillo AGIA&B,PC -565 5th Av -NY 10017
(212) 834-0600 .. **Stanleigh,** Shadrach A '99 %Gordon & S,PC -355 Lex Av -NY 10017
(914) 779-8466 .. **Stanley,** Anne Elizabeth '77 -3 Sussex Av -Bronxvll 10708
(212) 228-1331 .. **Stanley,** Christopher L '94 %Kuharski L&G -176 Hart Blvd -Staten Isl 10301
(315) 312-2211 .. **Stanley,** Deborah Flemma '78 SUNY Oswego -706 Culkin Hall -Oswego 13126 **Fx:**312-5438
(518) 873-3335 .. **Stanley,** Hilary D '07 %DA -Cthse -Elizabethtwn 12932 **Fx:**873-3788
(315) 474-3742 .. **Stanley,** Jos P '82 -500 S Salina -Syracuse 13202 **Fx:**471-1536
(718) 694-3830 .. **Stanley,** Marie A '92 %Transit Auth -130 Lvngstn -Brklyn 11201 **Fx:**694-5726
(315) 343-9631 .. **Stanley,** Michl J '78 (M Stanley) -44 E Brdg -Oswego 13126 **Fx:**343-9644
(212) 972-1355 .. **Stanley,** Susan C '85 %T Fleishell & Assoc PC -561 7th Av -NY 10018 **Fx:**972-1356
(973) 315-4470 .. **Stanley,** Tremain L '00 (Budd L) -140 Bway -NY 10005
(518) 447-7736 .. **Stano,** Edw W '04 Cnsl Cnty Dept Socl Srvcs -162 Wshngtn Av -Albany 12210
(212) 637-2641 .. **Stansbury,** Shane T '04 US Atty -1 St Andrews Plz -NY 10007

(718) 920-6624 .. **Stansel**, Lynn A '86 %Montefiore Med Ctr -111 E 210th -Bronx 10467 **Fx:**920-2637
(631) 421-6161 .. **Stansky**, Jos '75 -2 Melrose Ct -Dix Hlls 11746 **Fx:**421-5144
(212) 803-3738 .. **Stanton**, Alexandra '03 Empire State Dvlpmnt Corp -633 3rd Av -NY 10017
(516) 742-3636 .. **Stanton**, Catherine M '90 (Brecher FPWT&Z,PC) -1325 Franklin Av -Gdn Cty 11530
(212) 849-7000 .. **Stanton**, Christopher A '07 %Quinn EU&S,LLP -51 Mad Av -NY 10010
(212) 558-4000 .. **Stanton**, Clea M '04 %Sullivan & C LLP -125 Broad -NY 10004
(315) 478-1411 .. **Stanton**, David M '92 -Bx11068 -Syracuse 13218
(516) 222-0099 .. **Stanton**, Jack '90 (Stanton & G,LLP) -585 Stewart Av -Gdn Cty 11530 **Fx:**222-0079
(212) 765-5070 .. **Stanton**, Joy M '05 %Fish & R,PC -153 E 53rd -NY 10022
(718) 520-3989 .. **Stanton**, Julie '96 %Family Ct -89-14 Parsons Blvd -Jamaica 11432
(914) 249-1436 .. **Stanton**, Kevin J '97 %MasterCard Intl -2000 Purchase -Purchase 10577
(718) 833-9433 .. **Stanton**, Margaret M '81 (Stanton & P) -457 77th -Brklyn 11209 **Fx:**680-8572
(914) 333-0300 .. **Stanton**, Mark K '84 (Ryan & S,LLP) -1 Neperan Rd -Tarrytwn 10591 **Fx:**333-0301
(516) 294-7301 .. **Stanton**, Michl J '09 %D Smith -500 Old Cntry Rd -Gdn Cty 11530 **Fx:**393-7594
(914) 472-2300 .. **Stanton**, Michl K Jr. '87 (Jones G,LLP) -670 Wht Plns Rd -Scarsdale 10583
(212) 872-9830 .. **Stanton**, R Thos '83 (Squire S&D LLP) -30 Rckfllr Plz -NY 10112
(631) 439-2450 .. **Stanton**, Regina Proscia '97 %Leg Aid -320 Carleton Av -Central Islip 11722 **Fx:**439-2453
(315) 331-6222 .. **Stanton**, Robt J '65 %Refractron Tech Corp -5750 Stuart Av -Newark 14513
(212) 435-3571 .. **Stanton**, Sam M '02 Port Auth of NY/NJ -225 Park Av S -NY 10003 **Fx:**435-3555
(212) 987-9058 .. **Stanton**, Sean E '87 -203 E 116th -NY 10029 **Fx:**426-3237
(518) 431-5000 .. **Stanton**, Victoria M '88 %Farm Family Ins -Bx656 -Albany 12201 **Fx:**431-5979
(212) 779-8600 .. **Stanton**, Wayne S '85 %Silverman SS&B PLLC -381 Park Av S -NY 10016
(845) 868-7514 .. **Stanton**, Wm E '73 -1958 Bulls Head Rd -Stanfrdvll 12581
(516) 746-6054 .. **Stanziale**, Henry '69 -72 Jericho Tpk -Mineola 11501 **Fx:**746-6321
(212) 688-1900 .. **Stanziale**, Laurie A '98 %Greenberg T&H,LLP -767 3rd Av -NY 10017
(518) 943-6667 .. **Stanzione**, Jos '84 (Lewis & S) -287 Main Bx383 -Catskill 12414
(212) 714-1184 .. **Stapel**, Sharon L '99 %Anti-Violence Proj -240 W 35th -NY 10001
(716) 200-5050 .. **Stapell**, Raymond J '76 (Harris B PLLC) -726 Exchange -Buffalo 14210
(212) 859-8000 .. **Stapen**, Carl I '09 %Fried FHS&J LLP -1 NY Plz -NY 10004
(212) 237-8188 .. **Staple**, Dina S '00 %John Jay Cllg -899 10th Av -NY 10019
(914) 632-5920 .. **Staple**, Irwin '52 -Bx705 -New Rchll 10802 **Fx:**632-5937
(516) 739-1462 .. **Staples**, Christian P '03 %Brosnan & H -1325 Franklin Av -Gdn Cty 11530
(518) 251-2215 .. **Staples**, Scott D '91 (Staples & D,PC) -280 Main Bx66 -N Creek 12853 **Fx:**251-5038
(518) 281-0385 .. **Stapleton**, Anne '85 -Bx685 -Newtonville 12128 **Fx:**782-4430
(212) 558-4000 .. **Stapleton**, Benjamin F III '72 (Sullivan & C LLP) -125 Broad -NY 10004
(914) 798-5400 .. **Stapleton**, Brian T '90 (Goldberg S LLP) -11 Martine Av -White Plns 10606
(716) 483-3017 .. **Stapleton**, David R '79 -306 Spring Bx3206 -Jamestwn 14702
(516) 735-6053 .. **Stapleton**, Eileen T '95 -26 Family Ln -Levittwn 11756
(212) 626-4100 .. **Stapleton**, Jonathan C '74 (Baker & M LLP) -1114 Av of Amer -NY 10036
(516) 248-5270 .. **Stapleton**, Robt J '55 -229 7th -Gdn Cty 11530 **Fx:**248-5293
(315) 253-6219 .. **Stapleton**, T David '67 (Karpinski SG&T) -110 Genesee -Auburn 13021
(631) 979-6666 .. **Stapleton**, Tracy J '96 %PA Miller,PC -308 W Main -Smithtwn 11787 **Fx:**979-6701
(212) 935-2476 .. **Stapor**, Marcella A '62 -1040 1st Av -NY 10022
(212) 698-4570 .. **Stapper**, Erik J '61 (Stapper & V) -10 Rckfllr Plz -NY 10020
(212) 698-4570 .. **Stapper & VanDoren** -10 Rckfllr Plz -NY 10020 **Fx:**698-4567
(718) 255-1552 .. **Star**, Gregg N '93 SrCnsl Star Law Firm -87-02 Qns Blvd -Elmhrst 11373 **Fx:**228-9839
(718) 498-3333 .. **Star**, Scott L '98 (Blank & S) -387 New Lots Av -Brklyn 11207 **Fx:**498-4715
(212) 239-4999 .. **Star**, Steven E '98 (Meyer SE&K,PC) -1350 Bway Bx822 -NY 10018
(212) 533-6300 .. **Star**, Wendy M '00 %NYSUT -52 Bway -NY 10004 **Fx:**995-2347
(718) 876-6433 .. **Starace**, Kenneth P '79 %Hon G Rosenberg -355 Front -Staten Isl 10304 **Fx:**876-6434
(212) 509-2805 .. **Starczewski**, Gregg A '04 G Starczewski,PC -160 Bway -NY 10038
(914) 722-4008 .. **Starer**, Ann R '88 -15 Horseguard Ln -Scarsdale 10583 **Fx:**722-4009
(212) 872-9800 .. **Starer**, Brian D '73 (Squire S&D LLP) -30 Rckfllr Plz -NY 10112
(212) 364-5361 .. **Starger**, Colin P '03 Innocence Project -100 5th Av -NY 10011 **Fx:**364-5341
(914) 747-7410 .. **Stargiotti**, Jos A '88 (Stargiotti & B,PC) -48 Wheeler Av -Plsntvll 10570 **Fx:**747-7590
(718) 590-6339 .. **Starishevsky**, Jill S '98 %DA -198 E 161st -Bronx 10451 **Fx:**992-8244
(212) 487-9700 .. **Stark**, Adam P '99 %White F&F,LLP -61 Bway -NY 10006
(212) 354-0600 .. **Stark Amron & Liner,LLP** -7 Penn Plz -NY 10001 **Fx:**719-5961
(212) 442-8599 .. **Stark**, April B '04 %Law Dept -100 Church -NY 10007 **Fx:**788-0367
(516) 463-5994 .. **Stark**, Barbara J '83 Hofstra Law Schl -121 Hofstra Univ -Hempstd 11549
(718) 792-1200 .. **Stark**, Brian A '96 (Cohen & S,LLP) -1325 Castle Hill Av -Bronx 10462
(212) 581-0990 .. **Stark**, Corey S '02 %M O'Neill -30 Vesey -NY 10007 **Fx:**581-5897
(716) 856-4000 .. **Stark**, David M '84 (Hodgson R LLP) -140 Pearl -Buffalo 14202
(585) 753-1380 .. **Stark**, Howard A '77 %Cnty Atty -307 Cnty Ofc Bldg -Rchstr 14614 **Fx:**753-1331
(212) 964-7521 .. **Stark**, James H '78 -366 Bway -NY 10013
(212) 326-2000 .. **Stark**, Jason G '10 %O'Melveny & M LLP -7 Times Sq -NY 10036
(212) 836-8000 .. **Stark**, Javier F '10 Kaye S LLP -425 Park Av -NY 10022
(516) 741-6565 .. **Stark**, Jeffrey G '68 (Meyer SE&K,PC) -990 Stewart Av Bx9194 -Gdn Cty 11530
(212) 813-9148 .. **Stark**, Linda A '82 -245 E 54th -NY 10022 **Fx:**308-9114
(716) 845-2560 .. **Stark**, Linda Lalli '85 %Surrogates Ct -92 Franklin -Buffalo 14202 **Fx:**853-3741
(718) 998-3600 .. **Stark**, Lubov '96 (Stark & Assoc) -807 Kings Hwy -Brklyn 11223 **Fx:**998-0622
(631) 474-9544 .. **Stark**, Lynn M '99 -1 Seaside Dr -Pt Jffrsn 11777
(212) 669-8155 .. **Stark**, Martha E '87 Dept of Finance -1 Centre -NY 10007 **Fx:**267-5328
(212) 259-8000 .. **Stark**, Matthew A '10 %Dewey & L LLP -1301 Av of Amer -NY 10019
(212) 848-4000 .. **Stark**, Molly O '08 %Shearman & S LLP -599 Lex Av -NY 10022
(212) 335-9000 .. **Stark**, Paula-Rose '02 %DA -1 Hogan Pl -NY 10013
(212) 279-9090 .. **Stark**, Rachel Lilienthal '96 (Stark & S) -One Penn Plz -NY 10119 **Fx:**279-9113
(212) 474-1000 .. **Stark**, Richd J '92 (Cravath S&M LLP) -825 8th Av -NY 10019
(716) 838-4300 .. **Stark**, Richd L '99 %Bulan CH&I -1320 Millersport Hwy -Williamsvll 14221 **Fx:**204-9728
(212) 209-4800 .. **Stark**, Robt J '96 (Brown R LLP) -7 Times Sq -NY 10036
(212) 312-9917 .. **Stark**, Shirley '78 %State Ins Fund -199 Church -NY 10007 **Fx:**385-9199
(212) 799-7200 .. **Stark**, Tina L '81 %In-House Lgl Educ -325 West End Av -NY 10023 **Fx:**799-1222
(212) 349-1600 .. **Stark**, Vivien I '86 V Stark,PC -370 Lex Av -NY 10017 **Fx:**349-1601
(718) 260-8700 .. **Starker**, Susan '90 %Admin Children's Srvcs -345 Adams -Brklyn 11201
(716) 434-6641 .. **Starkey**, David J '85 %P George -37 East Av Bx456 -Lockprt 14095 **Fx:**434-1443
(212) 465-8840 .. **Starkey**, Elizabeth B '77 %Hofmann & S -360 W 31st -NY 10001 **Fx:**465-8849
(212) 449-7024 .. **Starkins**, Gregory C '93 Merrill Lynch -4 World Fncl Ctr -NY 10080
(518) 464-4100 .. **Starkman**, Andrew Michl '91 -Bx14261 -Albany 12212
(845) 778-2121 .. **Starkman**, Mark T '95 %Jacobowitz & G,LLP -158 Orange Av Bx367 -Walden 12586
(212) 753-5000 .. **Starkman**, Natalie '08 %Schiff H LLP -900 3rd Av -NY 10022
(518) 474-1331 .. **Stark-Riemer**, Steven '83 %Ofc Mntl Health -44 Holland Av -Albany 12229 **Fx:**473-7863
(212) 333-0200 .. **Starks**, Brent T '05 %Arkin KR LLP -590 Mad Av -NY 10022
(518) 862-1200 .. **Starlin**, Keith J '99 %Martin H&M LLP -Bx15141 -Albany 12212
(212) 819-8200 .. **Starner**, Gregory M '03 %White & C LLP -1155 Av of Amer -NY 10036
(914) 833-5297 .. **Staropoli**, Catherine M '95 %Hyman & G -1843 Palmer Av -Larchmnt 10538
(914) 946-7108 .. **Staropoli**, Jos J Jr. '96 -925 Wstchstr Av -White Plns 10604 **Fx:**946-3708
(866) 348-5819 .. **Starosielec**, Mark A '04 %SSA-ODAR -50 Fountain Plz -Buffalo 14202 **Fx:**(716) 551-4078
(212) 232-0292 .. **Starosolsky**, Wolodymyr M '72 (WM Starosolsky & Assoc) -116 John -NY 10038 **Fx:**571-6201
(212) 620-2680 .. **Starr**, Allan '74 (Starr Assoc LLP) -245 5th Av -NY 10016 **Fx:**696-5013
(212) 450-4000 .. **Starr**, Amelia T R '95 (Davis P&W LLP) -450 Lex Av -NY 10017
(516) 797-0662 .. **Starr**, Angela Heres '96 -4940 Merrick Rd -Massapequa Pk 11762
(212) 681-0117 .. **Starr Gern Davison & Rubin** -530 5th Av -NY 10036 **Fx:**(973) 226-0031
(914) 666-9601 .. **Starr**, Janice '99 (Starr & S) -91 Smith Av -Mt Kisco 10549
(631) 844-1000 .. **Starr**, Jeffrey '89 %North Fork Bk -275 Broad Hollow Rd -Melvll 11747 **Fx:**694-1536
(212) 986-2340 .. **Starr**, John B Jr. '98 %Jordan & H -122 E 42nd -NY 10168
(212) 759-6556 .. **Starr**, Kenneth I '67 (Starr & Co,LLC) -850 3rd Av -NY 10022
(212) 790-4010 .. **Starr**, Madonna Kissel '82 %Cmptrllr of Currency -340 Mad Av -NY 10017 **Fx:**790-4058
(718) 631-5206 .. **Starr**, Mary Burke '79 -315 Kenmore Rd -Douglastn 11363
(212) 513-3200 .. **Starr**, Michl G '80 (Holland & K LLP) -31 W 52nd -NY 10019
(212) 640-5785 .. **Starr**, Richd M '83 %Amer Exp -200 Vesey -NY 10285
(914) 831-7001 .. **Starr**, Robt S '52 R Starr PC -369 Rosedale Av -White Plns 10605 **Fx:**358-5331
(212) 759-6556 .. **Starr**, Ronald M '95 %Starr & Co,LLC -850 3rd Av -NY 10022 **Fx:**759-6694
(914) 666-9601 .. **Starr & Sandor** -91 Smith Av -Mt Kisco 10549 **Fx:**666-9202
(212) 867-8165 .. **Starr**, Stephen Z '95 (Starr & S,PLLC) -260 Mad Av -NY 10016 **Fx:**867-8139
(718) 292-4100 .. **Starr**, Susan K '70 -840 Grnd Cncrs -Bronx 10451 **Fx:**292-8073
(212) 867-8165 .. **Starr**, Vildan Erturk '98 (Starr & S,PLLC) -260 Mad Av -NY 10016 **Fx:**867-8139
(516) 883-0303 .. **Starr**, Warren D '66 (Starr & S) -111 Grt Nck Rd -Gt Neck 11021
(516) 883-0303 .. **Starr**, Wendy B '89 (Starr & S) -111 Grt Nck Rd -Gt Neck 11021
(718) 250-4210 .. **Starritt**, Adam T '07 Leg Aid -111 Lvngstn -Brklyn 11201 **Fx:**250-4243
(518) 474-6530 .. **Starrs**, John P '70 %Dept Pub Srvc -3 ESP -Albany 12223
(845) 398-7711 .. **Starvaggi**, Michl A '95 (M Starvaggi,PC) -80 Red Schl Hse Rd -Chestnut Rdg 10977 **Fx:**215-0122
(518) 283-1020 .. **Stasack**, Stephen A '76 -203 Menemsha Ln -Wynantskill 12198 **Fx:**283-1020
(201) 407-3888 .. **Stasiuk**, George P '01 (Transmodal Corp) -10905 Route 23A Bx341 -Lexington 12452 **Fx:**995-9980
(212) 909-9500 .. **Stasiuk**, Walter P '76 OfCnsl Wachtel & M,LLP -885 2nd Av -NY 10017
(631) 425-4155 .. **Stasko**, Paul A '92 (Mielo & S,LLP) -61 Chichester Rd -Huntngtn 11743
(212) 554-1234 .. **Stassa**, Eileen '90 %AXA Financial Inc -1290 Av of Amer -NY 10104 **Fx:**707-3963
(212) 325-2095 .. **Stastney**, Shadron Lee '95 %Credit Suisse First Boston -11 Mad Av -NY 10010
(315) 539-0524 .. **Stasz**, Thos E '95 %FMS Foundation Inc -877 Marshall Rd -Waterloo 13165 **Fx:**539-0953
(716) 853-8400 .. **State**, David J '92 %Dept of Law -350 Main Pl Twr -Buffalo 14202 **Fx:**853-8571
(518) 465-2333 .. **State**, John F '90 (Hodgson R LLP) -677 Bway -Albany 12207
(212) 788-0852 .. **Stateman**, Janet S '05 ACS -220 Church -NY 10013
(212) 849-7000 .. **Statfeld**, Courtney B '08 %Quinn EU&S,LLP -51 Mad Av -NY 10010

(212) 947-9166 .. **Statfeld**, George '62 -3 W 35th -NY 10001 **Fx**:594-0019
(212) 599-8200 .. **Stathatos**, Gerasimia '95 %Shaub AC&S,LLP -655 3rd Av -NY 10017
(718) 707-2915 .. **Stathopoulos**, Dimitrios C '97 -33-43 Vernon Blvd -LIC 11106 **Fx**:707-2921
(718) 833-3903 .. **Stathoudakis**, Nick M '97 -9214 3rd Av -Brklyn 11209
(212) 605-6200 .. **Statman**, Bracha Y '06 %Levy P&K,LLP -800 3rd Av -NY 10022
(212) 918-3000 .. **Statman**, Eric D '82 Cnsl Hogan L LLP -875 3rd Av -NY 10022
(212) 528-8629 .. **Statman**, Russell K '87 -334 Cornelia -Plattsbrgh 12901
(212) 417-8700 .. **Statsinger**, Steven M '88 %Fed Def of NY Inc -52 Duane -NY 10007 **Fx**:571-0392
(212) 765-4715 .. **Statz**, Olga '88 -108 E 38th -NY 10016 **Fx**:707-8468
(646) 205-7880 .. **Staub**, Andrew J '05 %Cruz & G & Assoc -110 William -NY 10038 **Fx**:(212) 233-9848
(516) 239-6202 .. **Stauber**, Aaron D '91 -34 Meadow Ln -Lawrence 11559 **Fx**:239-6202
(518) 435-8092 .. **Stauber**, David A '91 (Fine O&A,LLP) -80 Wolf Rd -Albany 12205
(212) 728-8000 .. **Stauber**, David Y '09 %Willkie F&G LLP -787 7th Av -NY 10019
(212) 460-4494 .. **Stauber**, Donald J '84 Con Ed -4 Irving Pl -NY 10003
(212) 698-3500 .. **Staubitz**, David P '06 %Dechert LLP -1095 Av of Amer -NY 10036
(914) 944-4087 .. **Stauch**, Nancie '89 -30 State -Ossining 10562
(212) 909-6000 .. **Stauder**, Stefan P '00 Cnsl Debevoise & P LLP -919 3rd Av -NY 10022
(631) 271-6363 .. **Staudigel**, Sharon D '93 OfCnsl Cannon & A,LLP -1923 NY Av -Huntngtn Sta 11746 **Fx**:271-7128
(914) 949-6400 .. **Staudt**, James '78 (McCullough G&S,LLP) -1311 Mamaroneck Av -White Plns 10605
(914) 834-6397 .. **Staudt**, Kathleen K '81 -184 Larchmnt Av -Larchmnt 10538
(212) 318-2000 .. **Stauffer**, Clinton M '02 Bloomberg LP -731 Lex Av -NY 10022
(212) 820-6717 .. **Stauffer**, Kent T '75 AIG -160 Water -NY 10038
(212) 652-3844 .. **Stauffer**, Ruth Ann '77 %Schlesinger G&L LLP -535 Mad Av -NY 10022
(516) 627-6300 .. **Stave**, Howard D '55 -473 Old Cthse Rd -Manhsst Hlls 11040 **Fx**:627-4568
(212) 455-2000 .. **Stavenas**, Marisa D '00 (Simpson T&B LLP) -425 Lex Av -NY 10017
(212) 259-8000 .. **Stavile**, Patrice D '88 Cnsl Dewey & L LLP -1301 Av of Amer -NY 10019
(212) 953-6000 .. **Stavis**, George N '02 %Katsky K LLP -605 3rd Av -NY 10158
(212) 935-3131 .. **Stavis**, Roger L '83 (Gallet D&B,LLP) -845 3rd Av -NY 10022
(646) 595-7005 .. **Stavitsky**, Bruce J '90 (Stavitsky & Assoc LLC) -5 Penn Plz -NY 10001
(516) 625-6382 .. **Stavola**, Stephen '05 Roslyn Schl Dist -Round Hill Rd Bx367 -Roslyn 11576
(631) 424-3597 .. **Stavrakis**, Maria G '08 %B Salamone & Assoc,PC -8 Ford Pl -Dix Hlls 11746 **Fx**:424-5023
(631) 853-4161 .. **Stavrides**, Thalia M '87 %DA -N Cnty Cmplx Bldg 77 -Hauppauge 11788 **Fx**:853-4192
(212) 788-8698 .. **Stavridis**, Steve '99 %Law Dept -100 Church -NY 10007 **Fx**:788-0367
(718) 748-7196 .. **Stavropoulos**, George '91 -120 Bay Ridge Av -Brklyn 11220 **Fx**:680-6404
(518) 789-3636 .. **Stavropoulos**, Peter G '97 %Davis & T -Millerton Plz Bx481 -Millerton 12546 **Fx**:789-6654
(212) 233-4949 .. **Stavros**, Joan A '78 (Adler & S) -110 Wall -NY 10005 **Fx**:(732) 748-2079
(212) 455-2000 .. **Stavsky**, Ari D '05 %Simpson T&B LLP -425 Lex Av -NY 10017
(718) 205-1010 .. **Stea**, Michl A '01 %E Ifraimoff & Assoc,PC -116-16 Qns Blvd -Frst Hlls 11375 **Fx**:205-2066
(212) 837-6000 .. **Stead**, Meredith M '07 %Hughes H&R LLP -1 Bttry Pk Plz -NY 10004
(518) 449-3107 .. **Steadman**, Christopher A H '00 Buckley M&C,PC -29 Wards Ln -Albany 12204
(212) 880-3800 .. **Steamer**, Julie Bible '00 OfCnsl Akerman S -335 Mad Av -NY 10017
(516) 576-3200 .. **Stearn**, Alan J '67 -50 Fairchild Ct -Plainvw 11803 **Fx**:576-3221
(212) 506-5000 .. **Stearns**, Craig E '86 OfCnsl Orrick H&S LLP -51 W 52nd -NY 10019
(212) 422-6111 .. **Stearns**, Jos T '65 (Kenny S&Z) -26 Bway -NY 10004
(315) 366-2321 .. **Stearns**, Melissa Countryman '94 Hon D Cerio -N Court -Wampsville 13163
(646) 386-3663 .. **Stearns**, Nancy '67 %Supreme Ct-Law Dept -60 Centre -NY 10007
(212) 756-3300 .. **Stearns**, Neal K '83 %First Manhattan Co -437 Mad Av -NY 10022 **Fx**:751-0497
(315) 724-6175 .. **Steates**, Alison Leslie '80 %Steates RS&D -408 Lomond Pl -Utica 13502
(315) 724-6175 .. **Steates**, F Paul '80 (Steates RS&D) -408 Lomond Pl -Utica 13502
(315) 724-6175 .. **Steates Remmell Steates & Dziekan** -408 Lomond Pl -Utica 13502 **Fx**:724-2931
(212) 938-0600 .. **Stebbings**, Robt Y '69 SrCnsl Schwartz LLC -90 Broad -NY 10004 **Fx**:938-0601
(212) 735-3000 .. **Stebbins**, Ann Beth '95 (Skadden ASM&F LLP) -4 Times Sq -NY 10036
(212) 599-0900 .. **Stebbins**, Douglas B '92 (Bower & L,PC) -261 Mad Av -NY 10016
(212) 728-8000 .. **Stebbins**, Robt B '94 (Willkie F&G LLP) -787 7th Av -NY 10019
(718) 490-7130 .. **Stebe**, John P '00 %RV Archibald,PC -26 Court -Brklyn 11242 **Fx**:237-1425
(212) 490-3000 .. **Steccato**, Carl L '87 (Wilson EME&D LLP) -150 E 42nd -NY 10017
(914) 323-7000 .. **Steccato**, Carl L '87 (Wilson EME&D LLP) -3 Gannett Dr -White Plns 10604
(212) 687-4900 .. **Stechel**, Ira B '73 (Wormser KG&J LLP) -825 3rd Av -NY 10022
(212) 902-3490 .. **Stecher**, Esta Eiger '83 %Goldman Sachs -1 NY Plz -NY 10004
(212) 508-6700 .. **Stecher**, Jamie B W '78 (Tannenbaum HS&H LLP) -900 3rd Av -NY 10022
(516) 222-0888 .. **Stechman**, Scott D '86 %Lehman & E LLP -50 Chas Lindbergh Blvd -Uniondale 11553
(914) 674-4100 .. **Stecich**, Marianne '79 (Stecich M&L,LLP) -828 S Bway -Tarrytwn 10591
(914) 674-4100 .. **Stecich Murphy & Lammers, LLP** -828 S Bway -Tarrytwn 10591 **Fx**:674-2987
(212) 558-4000 .. **Steciuk**, Peter A '08 %Sullivan & C LLP -125 Broad -NY 10004
(516) 281-9800 .. **Steck**, Paul C '03 %Goldberg S LLP -200 Old Cntry Rd -Mineola 11501
(518) 449-3900 .. **Steck**, Phillip G '85 (Cooper E&S,LLP) -39 N Pearl -Albany 12207
(212) 530-5000 .. **Steckel**, Jeremy S '09 %Milbank TH&M LLP -1 Chase Manh Plz -NY 10005
(212) 331-5135 .. **Steckelman**, Rachel B '95 %HRA -180 Water -NY 10038 **Fx**:331-4462
(716) 847-8400 .. **Stecker**, Paul K '77 (Phillips L LLP) -3400 HSBC Ctr -Buffalo 14203
(516) 393-2200 .. **Steckler**, David E '76 OfCnsl Garfunkel W,PC -111 Grt Nck Rd -Gt Neck 11021
(718) 243-1915 .. **Steckler**, Jonathan S '97 -44 Court -Brklyn 11201 **Fx**:243-1916
(917) 741-8784 .. **Steckler**, Monty '05 1st Dominion Properties -215 W 95th -NY 10025
(212) 577-3502 .. **Steckler**, Tamara A '87 %Leg Aid -199 Water -NY 10038 **Fx**:577-3520
(516) 222-6200 .. **Steckler**, Todd C '84 (Berkman HPP&F,PC) -100 Grdn City Plz -Gdn Cty 11530
(212) 341-4218 .. **Stecklow**, David S '01 OfCnsl Lester SK&D -120 Bway -NY 10271
(212) 566-8000 .. **Stecklow**, Wylie M '91 Wylie Law -10 Spring -NY 10012 **Fx**:202-4952
(212) 964-6611 .. **Steckman**, Lawr A '89 (Lester SK&D) -120 Bway -NY 10271
(212) 313-9898 .. **Steckman**, Robt M '99 R Steckman,PC -111 John -NY 10038 **Fx**:313-9899
(212) 571-3702 .. **Stecopoulos**, Nicholas '56 -116 John -NY 10038 **Fx**:406-4225
(212) 837-6000 .. **Stecura**, Christine M '06 %Hughes H&R LLP -1 Bttry Pk Plz -NY 10004
(845) 225-9578 .. **Stedina**, Aloysius P '67 -1 Ridge Ct -Carmel 10512 **Fx**:225-9578
(212) 876-5500 .. **Steed**, Seth A '09 %Neighborhood Def Srv -317 Lenox Av -NY 10027 **Fx**:876-5586
(212) 474-1000 .. **Steefel**, Kimberly L '08 %Cravath S&M LLP -825 8th Av -NY 10019
(212) 816-2949 .. **Steel**, Brian W '92 Citigroup -388 Greenwich -NY 10013
(212) 209-4800 .. **Steel**, Howard S '05 %Brown R LLP -7 Times Sq -NY 10036
(212) 416-8704 .. **Steel**, Iris '64 %Dept of Law -120 Bway -NY 10271
(212) 245-1000 .. **Steel**, Lewis M '63 OfCnsl Outten & G LLP -3 Park Av -NY 10016
(212) 609-6800 .. **Steel**, Marisa J '05 %McCarter & E,LLP -245 Park Av -NY 10167
(212) 446-4800 .. **Steele**, Benjamin J '09 %Kirkland & E LLP -153 E 53rd -NY 10022
(516) 745-6644 .. **Steele**, Christopher J '96 Ranieri & Co -50 Chas Lindbergh Blvd -Uniondale 11553 **Fx**:745-6787
(585) 419-8800 .. **Steele**, Joshua D '07 %Harris B PLLC -99 Garnsey Rd -Pittsfrd 14534
(315) 216-4721 .. **Steele**, Kimberly A '01 -949 Cnty Route 53 -Oswego 13126
(718) 286-6000 .. **Steele**, Lauren D '06 %DA -125-01 Qns Blvd -Kew Gdns 11415
(212) 421-4100 .. **Steele**, Lloyd N '02 %Pryor C LLP -7 Times Sq -NY 10036
(516) 466-6030 .. **Steele**, Matthew A '04 %Mirkin & G,PC -98 Cuttermill Rd -Gt Neck 11021
(212) 770-1081 .. **Steele**, Monica I '94 %AIG -70 Pine -NY 10270
(212) 545-4760 .. **Steele**, Robt D '82 (Wolf HAF&H LLP) -270 Mad Av -NY 10016
(516) 328-2300 .. **Steele-Baird**, Svetlana '06 %Abrams FFEGF&E,LLP -1111 Marcus Av -Lk Success 11042
(212) 735-3000 .. **Steelman**, Donald J '00 Cnsl Skadden ASM&F LLP -4 Times Sq -NY 10036
(212) 309-6000 .. **Steelman**, Elliot H '04 %Morgan L&B LLP -101 Park Av -NY 10178
(212) 790-0250 .. **Steelman**, Eun-Shil Selene '03 Cardozo Schl of Law -55 5th Av -NY 10003
(631) 501-5700 .. **Steen**, Jeffrey S '87 (Carter DF&S LLP) -445 Broadhallow Rd -Melvll 11747
(518) 873-3267 .. **Steenburg**, Thos N '05 IM Solutions -Bx768 -Elizabethtwn 12932
(212) 216-8000 .. **Steer**, Richd L '75 (Tarter K&D LLP) -1350 Bway -NY 10018
(845) 340-3315 .. **Steeves**, Tracy E '03 DA -285 Wall -Kingston 12401 **Fx**:340-3185
(917) 777-4200 .. **Stefanak**, Curtis '02 Cnsl Bingham M LLP -1 Bttry Pk Plz -NY 10004
(212) 605-0425 .. **Stefanakis**, Michl '00 M Stefanakis,PC -575 Mad Av -NY 10022 **Fx**:656-1022
(212) 528-5946 .. **Stefanelli**, Valorie J '92 -277 Bway -NY 10007
(518) 473-1707 .. **Stefani**, John N '76 %Dept of Health -Corning Twr 24th Fl -Albany 12237 **Fx**:486-1858
(212) 698-3500 .. **Stefanick**, James G '00 %Dechert LLP -1095 Av of Amer -NY 10036
(718) 545-5518 .. **Stefanidis**, Chris N '90 (Stefanidis & M LLP) -31-10 37th Av -LIC 11101 **Fx**:545-5087
(212) 483-0105 .. **Stefanitsis**, Dennis '09 %Coughlin D LLP -88 Pine-Wall St Plz -NY 10005
(212) 610-6300 .. **Stefano**, Jos M '96 (Allen & O) -1221 Av of Amer -NY 10020
(973) 520-2302 .. **Stefanowicz**, Lydia C '80 (Edwards AP&D LLP) -750 Lex Av -NY 10022 **Fx**:520-2600
(516) 692-2744 .. **Stefans**, Donna M '00 (Stefans Law Grp,PC) -137 Woodbury Rd -Woodbury 11797 **Fx**:692-2746
(716) 845-9463 .. **Stefanski**, Donald S '84 %Supreme Ct -50 Delaware Av -Buffalo 14202
(518) 402-9184 .. **Stefanucci**, Michele M '96 DEC -625 Bway -Albany 12233 **Fx**:402-9018
(212) 820-7700 .. **Stefas**, Eleftherios '02 %Boundas SW&B,LLC -1 Bttry Pk Plz -NY 10004
(212) 803-5100 .. **Stefel**, Shari B '08 %NY Cnty Defender Srvcs -225 Bway -NY 10007 **Fx**:571-6035
(212) 762-7183 .. **Steffan**, Jos C '95 %Morgan Stanley -1221 Av of Amer -NY 10020
(716) 937-9111 .. **Steffan**, Thos A '86 (Cooke & S) -13132 Main -Alden 14004
(516) 694-3000 .. **Steffanetta**, Gary L '84 (Guercio & G,LLP) -77 Conklin -Farmngdl 11735 **Fx**:694-4738
(212) 525-8119 .. **Steffensen**, Mark A '99 HSBC Bank -452 5th Av -NY 10018
(212) 346-1274 .. **Steffire**, Karen Leta '87 Pace Univ -156 William -NY 10038
(212) 749-0726 .. **Steffy**, John M '05 A&E TV Networks -235 E 45th -NY 10017
(718) 250-2000 .. **Steffy**, John R '08 %DA -350 Jay -Brklyn 11201 **Fx**:250-2314
(212) 698-3500 .. **Stefko**, Wm C '07 (Dechert LLP) -1095 Av of Amer -NY 10036
(607) 723-9511 .. **Steflik**, Jos J Jr. '72 (Coughlin & G,LLP) -19 Chenango Bx2039 -Bnghmtn 13902
(716) 965-2065 .. **Steger**, Betsy Sue '83 -11274 Walnut Rd -Forestvll 14062
(212) 655-3500 .. **Stegich**, Debora L '95 %Meister S&F LLP -140 E 45th -NY 10017
(212) 490-9100 .. **Stegich**, Stephen R III '73 (Condon & F LLP) -7 Times Sq -NY 10036
(212) 308-9700 .. **Steginsky**, Eileen L '84 -405 E 56th -NY 10022 **Fx**:308-9706
(718) 579-7900 .. **Stegman**, Rebecca L '06 Leg Aid -900 Sheridan Av -Bronx 10451 **Fx**:293-8744
(212) 661-9100 .. **Stehl**, Richd L '93 (Otterbourg SH&R,PC) -230 Park Av -NY 10169

(516) 229-4300 .. **Stehn,** Eric P '08 J Bilello & Assoc -875 Merrick Av -Westbury 11590

(212) 665-3348 .. **Steier,** Susan F '89 SF Steier LLC -233 Bway -NY 10279 **Fx:**665-3550

(212) 994-9963 .. **Steifman,** Seth P '97 (Federman S LLP) -220 E 42nd -NY 10017 **Fx:**685-5199

(718) 646-8888 .. **Steigbigel,** David S '92 %A Ross & Assoc -2649 Coney Isl Av -Brklyn 11223 **Fx:**646-7766

(516) 764-2800 .. **Steiger,** Norman A '60 OfCnsl Goldberg & C -66 N Vllg Av -Rockvll Ctr 11570

(212) 880-0865 .. **Steiger,** Susan J '82 -60 E 42nd -NY 10165 **Fx:**983-0415

(518) 436-6202 .. **Steigerwald,** Barbara L '02 Ostroff Hiffa & Assoc -12 Sheridan Av -Albany 12207 **Fx:**436-1956

(631) 501-3100 .. **Steigerwald,** Steven A '83 %J Humphreys -3 Huntngtn Quad Bx9028 -Melvll 11747 **Fx:**501-3085

(718) 459-9000 .. **Steigler,** John W '89 %Sweeney GR&B,LLP -95-25 Qns Blvd -Rego Pk 11374

(212) 277-0721 .. **Steigman,** Elizabeth C '85 %Hartford Fncl Products -2 Park Av -NY 10016

(212) 943-1090 .. **Steigman,** Ernest R '65 (Gair GCSMB&R) -80 Pine -NY 10005

(212) 880-9591 .. **Steigman,** Jerrold L '05 %Morvillo AGIA&B,PC -565 5th Av -NY 10017

(212) 943-1090 .. **Steigman,** Richd M '98 (Gair GCSMB&R) -80 Pine -NY 10005

(845) 229-6300 .. **Steiman,** Mickey A '73 -4419 Albany Post Rd Bx665 -Hyde Pk 12538 **Fx:**229-6338

(718) 645-5600 .. **Stein,** Aaron M '84 (Stein F&S LLP) -1639 E 13th -Brklyn 11229

(212) 592-1400 .. **Stein,** Adam '09 %Herrick,F LLP -2 Park Av -NY 10016

(212) 596-9000 .. **Stein,** Adam I '85 (Ropes & G LLP) -1211 Av of Amer -NY 10036

(212) 586-5800 .. **Stein,** Adam J '84 (Cohen TS&W PC) -420 Lex Av -NY 10170

(212) 465-1110 .. **Stein,** Adam J '06 %Bader Y&N LLP -350 5th Av -NY 10118 **Fx:**279-8991

(516) 932-1800 .. **Stein,** Alan C '95 (AC Stein,PC) -479 S Oyster Bay Rd -Plainvw 11803 **Fx:**932-0220

(212) 282-2018 .. **Stein,** Alan L '74 %Rckflr Grp Development Corp -1221 Av of Amer -NY 10020 **Fx:**282-2142

(516) 741-4600 .. **Stein,** Alan M '71 -1050 Franklin Av -Gdn Cty 11530 **Fx:**746-4932

(845) 429-3900 .. **Stein,** Alisa '94 (Stein & S) -1 Railroad Sq -Haverstraw 10927 **Fx:**429-4392

(212) 704-6000 .. **Stein,** Alvin M '48 SrCnsl Troutman S LLP -405 Lex Av -NY 10174

(212) 986-4500 .. **Stein,** Amanda K '10 %Horwitz H&P -405 Lex Av -NY 10174

(516) 463-5858 .. **Stein,** Amy R '89 %Hofstra Law Schl -121 Hofstra Univ -Hempstd 11549

(212) 813-8800 .. **Stein,** Andrew N '07 %Goodwin P LLP -620 8th Av -NY 10018

(845) 429-3900 .. **Stein,** Ari J '03 %Stein & S -1 Railroad Sq -Haverstraw 10927 **Fx:**429-4392

(212) 490-3000 .. **Stein,** Aviva '06 %Wilson EME&D LLP -150 E 42nd -NY 10017

(518) 269-4306 .. **Stein,** Barbara E '56 -40 Autumn Dr -Slingerlnds 12159 **Fx:**269-4306

(914) 834-2302 .. **Stein & Battalia** -2001 Palmer Av -Larchmnt 10538 **Fx:**833-1350

(212) 417-5263 .. **Stein,** Bonnie H '78 %Medicaid Fraud Cntrl -120 Bway -NY 10271 **Fx:**417-5274

(718) 665-0711 .. **Stein,** Carl '82 -860 Grnd Cncrs -Bronx 10451

(212) 629-8585 .. **Stein,** Cheryl '06 %Ellenberg & Prtnrs LLP -575 8th Av -NY 10018

(716) 855-1777 .. **Stein,** Cheryl L '89 -4043 Main -Buffalo 14226 **Fx:**855-1317

(212) 237-1000 .. **Stein,** Clifford H '81 SpclCnsl Windels ML&M,LLP -156 W 56th -NY 10019

(718) 222-2343 .. **Stein,** Courtney B '06 %Law Dept -350 Jay -Brklyn 11201 **Fx:**222-2373

(212) 756-2000 .. **Stein,** Craig '93 (Schulte R&Z LLP) -919 3rd Av -NY 10022

(212) 637-2407 .. **Stein,** Danl L '00 %US Atty -1 St Andrews Plz -NY 10007

(212) 563-9884 .. **Stein,** David '00 (Samuel & S) -38 W 32nd -NY 10001 **Fx:**563-9870

(212) 779-9800 .. **Stein,** David A '83 (Luboja & T,LLP) -10 E 40th -NY 10016

(212) 848-9800 .. **Stein,** David A '99 (Withers B LLP) -430 Park Av -NY 10022

(845) 634-4637 .. **Stein,** David J '77 -20 S Main -New Cty 10956

(212) 529-5500 .. **Stein,** David J '91 -5 Great Jones -NY 10012 **Fx:**529-3117

(212) 981-1777 .. **Stein,** David L '92 %SLRDC -Bx599 -Armonk 10504 **Fx:**981-1761

(516) 877-0944 .. **Stein,** David M '85 -585 Stewart Av -Gdn Cty 11530

(212) 440-3669 .. **Stein,** Deborah L '95 CNA Ins -40 Wall -NY 10005

(212) 385-8279 .. **Stein,** Debra Schiraldi '85 %HRA -60 Lafayette -NY 10013

(212) 599-1515 .. **Stein,** Dennis L '81 (Stein RM,LLP) -405 Lex Av -NY 10174

(212) 907-9700 .. **Stein,** Douglas W '98 (Smith G&R,LLP) -250 Park Av -NY 10177

(212) 628-1600 .. **Stein,** Dustin A '07 Cnsl David Benrimon Fine Art LLC -21 E 65th -NY 10065

(845) 634-0499 .. **Stein,** Edw A '81 -169 S Main -New Cty 10956

(212) 790-0200 .. **Stein,** Edw D '01 Benj N Cardozo Schl of Law -55 5th Av -NY 10003 **Fx:**790-0345

(212) 278-1745 .. **Stein,** Edw J '01 (Anderson K&O,PC) -1251 Av of Amer -NY 10020

(212) 804-1108 .. **Stein,** Elaine Francine '94 %TBWA -488 Mad Av -NY 10022

(518) 474-6530 .. **Stein,** Eleanor '87 Dept Pub Srvc -3 ESP -Albany 12223

(212) 616-1327 .. **Stein,** Elizabeth B '04 Environmental Defense Fund -257 Park Av S -NY 10010

(914) 238-5719 .. **Stein,** Ellen J '83 -7 Whippoorwill Rd -Chappaqua 10514

(212) 319-8500 .. **Stein,** Elliott J '95 (Stevens & L PC) -485 Mad Av -NY 10022

(212) 403-1000 .. **Stein,** Elliott V '84 OfCnsl Wachtell LR&K -51 W 52nd -NY 10019

(212) 277-6500 .. **Stein,** Elliott Z '06 %Dickstein S LLP -1633 Bway -NY 10019

(212) 613-2041 .. **Stein,** Ethan D '05 Cnsl Gibbons PC -1 Penn Plz -NY 10119 **Fx:**554-9677

(212) 819-8795 .. **Stein,** Eugene P '95 -1155 Av of Amer -NY 10036 **Fx:**354-8113

(212) 421-4100 .. **Stein,** F Robt '72 OfCnsl Pryor C LLP -7 Times Sq -NY 10036

(718) 645-5600 .. **Stein Farkas & Schwartz LLP** -1639 E 13th -Brklyn 11229 **Fx:**645-3767

(212) 385-0503 .. **Stein Farkas & Schwartz LLP** -16 E 34th -NY 10016 **Fx:**385-0506

(212) 756-2000 .. **Stein,** Gary '87 (Schulte R&Z LLP) -919 3rd Av -NY 10022

(212) 683-5320 .. **Stein,** George N '77 -270 Mad Av -NY 10016 **Fx:**686-2182

(212) 607-2834 .. **Stein,** Gerald A '94 FTC -1 Bowling Grn -NY 10004 **Fx:**607-2822

(212) 592-1400 .. **Stein,** Glenn L '04 %Herrick,F LLP -2 Park Av -NY 10016

(212) 788-0788 .. **Stein,** Haley H '06 %Law Dept -100 Church -NY 10007 **Fx:**788-0367

(212) 861-9365 .. **Stein,** Harriet S '74 -235 E 78th -NY 10075

(212) 583-5114 .. **Stein,** Hayley A '03 Blackstone Grp -345 Park Av -NY 10154

(516) 742-1212 .. **Stein,** Howard H '71 (Stein W&R) -1 Old Cntry Rd -Carle Pl 11514

(516) 296-7000 .. **Stein,** Howard M '79 (Certilman BA&H,LLP) -90 Merrick Av -E Meadow 11554

(718) 375-3300 .. **Stein,** Irene '00 -2899 Ocean Av -Brklyn 11235 **Fx:**769-8810

(212) 442-4113 .. **Stein,** Jacqueline B '87 SrCnsl Hlth & Hsptl Corp -346 Bway -NY 10013

(212) 648-1063 .. **Stein,** Jacqueline F '80 JP Morgan Chase -245 Park Av -NY 10167

(212) 858-1000 .. **Stein,** Jane Wallison '75 (Pillsbury WSP LLP) -1540 Bway -NY 10036

(518) 346-2618 .. **Stein,** Janet M '85 -30 Union Av -Schnctdy 12308 **Fx:**346-5120

(212) 947-9779 .. **Stein,** Jared S '06 %Advocates for Chldrn -151 W 30th -NY 10001 **Fx:**947-9790

(646) 473-6037 .. **Stein,** Jeffrey G '83 1199 Natl Benefit Fund -330 W 42nd -NY 10036 **Fx:**473-6049

(631) 470-5000 .. **Stein,** Jeffrey S '82 Garden City Grp,Inc -105 Maxess Rd -Melvll 11747 **Fx:**940-6554

(212) 481-6698 .. **Stein,** Jerald M '91 -470 Park Av S -NY 10016 **Fx:**481-6803

(212) 373-3000 .. **Stein,** Jeremy B '07 %Paul WRW&G LLP -1285 Av of Amer -NY 10019

(914) 323-7000 .. **Stein,** Jeremy I '04 %Wilson EME&D LLP -3 Gannett Dr -White Plns 10604

(212) 397-6360 .. **Stein,** Jessica '10 %Thivierge & R,PC -140 Bway -NY 10005 **Fx:**397-6361

(212) 344-8008 .. **Stein,** Joel M '71 -39 Bway -NY 10006 **Fx:**571-0860

(646) 878-0800 .. **Stein,** Joel M '88 (Pearl CZL,LLP) -1500 Bway -NY 10036

(845) 358-6000 .. **Stein,** John E '97 %General Bearing Corp -44 High -W Nyack 10994 **Fx:**358-3619

(516) 569-8100 .. **Stein,** Jonathan A '82 OfCnsl Rosenfeld & M -132 Spruce -Cedarhrst 11516

(516) 328-3500 .. **Stein,** Jonathan M '06 %McDonnell & A,PC -401 Franklin Av -Gdn Cty 11530

(212) 538-6323 .. **Stein,** Jonathan W '02 Credit Suisse Securities -11 Mad Av -NY 10010

(212) 688-3300 .. **Stein,** Joshua '85 -59 E 54th -NY 10022

(917) 509-1801 .. **Stein,** Joshua '97 -1251 E 32nd -Brklyn 11210

(212) 969-3000 .. **Stein,** Joshua A '01 %Proskauer R LLP -1585 Bway -NY 10036

(212) 681-2535 .. **Stein,** Joshua N '95 (Greenberg & S,PC) -275 Mad Av -NY 10016

(212) 233-3348 .. **Stein,** Judith E '88 -139 Fulton -NY 10038

(631) 360-1433 .. **Stein,** Kathryn E '92 (Stein & S,PC) -195 E Main -Smithtwn 11787 **Fx:**360-8323

(212) 527-9903 .. **Stein,** Keith B '87 %Pembroke Co -70 E 55th -NY 10022

(212) 818-9600 .. **Stein,** Kenneth L '63 (Greenfield S&S,LLP) -600 3rd Av -NY 10016

(212) 806-5400 .. **Stein,** Kenneth L '94 (Stroock &S&L LLP) -180 Maiden Ln -NY 10038

(212) 848-4859 .. **Stein,** Laurie K '01 Shearman & S LLP -599 Lex Av -NY 10022

(212) 809-7800 .. **Stein,** Leslie A '06 %Jaffe & K,LLP -40 Wall -NY 10005

(212) 431-5557 .. **Stein,** Linda S '86 -122 Spring -NY 10012 **Fx:**226-8116

(212) 756-2000 .. **Stein,** Lyle P '99 %Schulte R&Z LLP -919 3rd Av -NY 10022

(516) 997-0999 .. **Stein,** Marc A '03 %Pryor & M,LLP -675 Old Cntry Rd -Westbury 11590

(631) 424-3597 .. **Stein,** Marc H '04 %B Salamone & Assoc,PC -8 Ford Pl -Dix Hlls 11746 **Fx:**424-5023

(585) 454-5650 .. **Stein,** Mark H '89 (Lacy K LLP) -130 E Main -Rchstr 14604

(212) 455-2000 .. **Stein,** Mark J '85 (Simpson T&B LLP) -425 Lex Av -NY 10017

(914) 826-2032 .. **Stein,** Mark J '95 IAC -555 W 18th -NY 10011

(917) 836-1754 .. **Stein,** Marla L '88 -1385 York Av -NY 10021 **Fx:**(212) 772-6111

(212) 685-7600 .. **Stein,** Martin '73 OfCnsl Heller H&F,PC -292 Mad Av -NY 10017

(212) 302-6300 .. **Stein,** Martin '87 %Joel Isaacson Co Inc -546 5th Av -NY 10036 **Fx:**302-6390

(212) 363-6900 .. **Stein,** Matthew B '98 %Faust GS&B LLP -2 Rector -NY 10006

(212) 506-1700 .. **Stein,** Matthew B '04 %Kasowitz BT&F LLP -1633 Bway -NY 10019

(212) 908-0500 .. **Stein,** Melanie Hadar '91 Fitch Ratings Srvcs -1 State Street Plz -NY 10004

(212) 513-3200 .. **Stein,** Melvin '58 (Holland & K LLP) -31 W 52nd -NY 10019

(516) 739-1200 .. **Stein,** Melvyn I '71 (Stein & S,PC) -666 Old Cntry Rd -Gdn Cty 11530 **Fx:**873-9108

(631) 757-8400 .. **Stein,** Mitchell A '84 (Stein Law,PC) -24 Woodbine Av -Northprt 11768 **Fx:**757-8404

(212) 660-3000 .. **Stein,** Mitchell C '89 (Sullivan & W LLP) -1290 Av of Amer -NY 10104

(631) 467-7788 .. **Stein,** Mitchell R '89 -34 Av A -Holbrook 11741

(212) 753-6900 .. **Stein,** Myron '61 %Sugar Foods Corp -950 3rd Av -NY 10022

(212) 223-0400 .. **Stein,** Norman H '86 (Stein & H) -575 Lex Av -NY 10022

(914) 231-2700 .. **Stein,** Paul D '89 %DA -104 S Bway -Ynkrs 10701 **Fx:**969-0574

(631) 360-1433 .. **Stein,** Peter C '97 (Stein & S,PC) -195 E Main -Smithtwn 11787 **Fx:**360-8323

(516) 248-8899 .. **Stein,** Randy M '85 -170 Old Cntry Rd -Mineola 11501

(718) 847-4000 .. **Stein,** Richd H '82 (Stein & Z) -86-52 Woodhvn Blvd -Woodhvn 11421

(718) 645-5688 .. **Stein,** Rick '81 -1609 Kings Hwy -Brklyn 11229

(212) 599-1515 .. **Stein Riso Mantel,LLP** -405 Lex Av -NY 10174 **Fx:**599-6155

(516) 294-0288 .. **Stein,** Rita '79 -200 Old Cntry Rd -Mineola 11501 **Fx:**741-7758

(646) 405-9622 .. **Stein,** Robt '77 (Caesar & N) -350 Bway -NY 10013 **Fx:**405-9635

(212) 885-5000 .. **Stein,** Robt '79 (Blank R LLP) -405 Lex Av -NY 10174

(212) 578-2211 .. **Stein,** Robt B '71 %MetLife -27-01 Qns Plz N -LIC 11101

(212) 474-1000 .. **Stein,** Robt J '10 %Cravath S&M LLP -825 8th Av -NY 10019

(585) 546-4900 .. **Stein,** Robin L '95 %Home Properties of NY -850 Clinton Sq -Rchstr 14604 **Fx:**546-5433

(212) 806-5400 .. **Stein,** Ronald J '59 OfCnsl Stroock &S&L LLP -180 Maiden Ln -NY 10038

(646) 345-7244 .. **Stein,** Ronald J '86 -325 W 45th -NY 10036

(585) 586-2525 .. **Stein,** Roy J '82 %Nazareth College -4245 East Av -Rchstr 14618

(646) 386-5700 .. **Stein,** Saul '06 %Civil Ct -111 Centre -NY 10013

(212) 697-7220 .. **Stein Schwartz Chesir & Rosh, LLP** -140 E 45th -NY 10017 **Fx:**697-7164

(516) 873-2000 .. **Stein,** Seth P '73 (Moritt HH&H LLP) -400 Grdn City Plz -Gdn Cty 11530

(212) 532-5533 .. **Stein,** Seth W '00 -370 Lex Av -NY 10017 **Fx:**532-5501

(212) 697-4500 .. **Stein,** Sharon '81 (S Stein,PC) -551 5th Av -NY 10176 **Fx:**972-0620

(212) 751-7326 .. **Stein,** Sheldon '64 (Bragin S&P,PC) -320 E 58th -NY 10022

(212) 575-6206 .. **Stein Simpson & Rosen,PA** -1285 Av of Amer -NY 10019 **Fx:**(201) 944-4438
(212) 891-9100 .. **Stein,** Spencer K '94 (Goldfarb & F LLP) -345 Park Av -NY 10154
(212) 808-7794 .. **Stein,** Stephen W '62 (Kelley D&W LLP) -101 Park Av -NY 10178
(212) 310-8000 .. **Stein,** Steven B '08 %Weil G&M LLP -767 5th Av -NY 10153
(212) 768-6700 .. **Stein,** Steven J '64 Cnsl Sonnenschein N&R LLP -2 World Fncl Ctr -NY 10281
(914) 428-5100 .. **Stein,** Stuart M '79 -30 Glenn -White Plns 10603
(212) 746-1795 .. **Stein,** Tara N '01 NY Presbyterian Hsptl -525 E 68th Bx88 -NY 10065 **Fx:**746-8603
(518) 442-5303 .. **Stein,** Theo J '96 SUNY Schl of Social Welfare -135 Wstrn Av -Albany 12203
(212) 613-2049 .. **Stein,** Wendy R '03 %Gibbons PC -1 Penn Plz -NY 10119 **Fx:**554-9647
(516) 742-1212 .. **Stein Wiener & Roth** -1 Old Cntry Rd -Carle Pl 11514 **Fx:**742-6595
(845) 429-3900 .. **Stein,** Wm M '76 (Stein & S) -1 Railroad Sq -Haverstraw 10927 **Fx:**429-4392
(845) 429-2200 .. **Stein,** Wm M '76 Haverstraw Town Atty -1 Rosman Rd -Garnervll 10923 **Fx:**429-4701
(718) 847-4000 .. **Stein & Zadek** -86-52 Woodhvn Blvd -Woodhvn 11421 **Fx:**847-6276
(212) 421-2233 .. **Steinau,** Leslie '68 OfCnsl Wilk A LLP -675 3rd Av -NY 10017
(212) 586-1515 .. **Steinbach,** Harold I '82 (Steinbach & Assoc,PC) -420 Lex Av -NY 10170 **Fx:**656-1701
(212) 526-7000 .. **Steinbauer,** Adam '07 Barclays Capital -745 7th Av -NY 10019
(212) 363-3100 .. **Steinbauer,** Patrick T '94 (Bivona & C,PC) -88 Pine -NY 10005
(212) 637-5000 .. **Steinberg,** Alan J '90 EPA -290 Bway -NY 10007 **Fx:**637-5024
(212) 846-6866 .. **Steinberg,** Andrew B '09 MTV Networks -1515 Bway -NY 10036
(212) 789-8709 .. **Steinberg,** Arthur '98 %Maalouf Law Firm,LLC -500 5th Av -NY 10110 **Fx:**789-8718
(212) 556-2100 .. **Steinberg,** Arthur J '80 (King & S) -1185 Av of Amer -NY 10036
(914) 375-7174 .. **Steinberg,** Avery '82 -50 Leighton Av -Ynkrs 10705 **Fx:**840-1212
(212) 752-3575 .. **Steinberg Barness Glasgow & Foster,LLP** -767 3rd Av -NY 10017 **Fx:**752-3471
(212) 887-7777 .. **Steinberg,** Bennet '95 Keefe Bruyette & Woods Inc -787 7th Av -NY 10019
(631) 277-7300 .. **Steinberg & Boyle,LLP** -136 E Main -E Islip 11730 **Fx:**277-7641
(212) 398-7900 .. **Steinberg,** Brad Lee '85 OfCnsl Gerstein S&R LLP -57 W 38th -NY 10018
(212) 863-6300 .. **Steinberg,** Carol J '83 %HPD -100 Gold -NY 10038
(914) 761-4200 .. **Steinberg & Cavaliere,LLP** -50 Main -White Plns 10606 **Fx:**761-4256
(212) 867-7779 .. **Steinberg & Cavaliere,LLP** -60 E 42nd -NY 10165
(212) 349-6775 .. **Steinberg,** Dana L '08 %Peltz & W -222 Bway -NY 10038
(212) 751-4300 .. **Steinberg,** Danl S '91 (Hodgson R LLP) -1540 Bway -NY 10036
(212) 236-6534 .. **Steinberg,** Darryl R '90 %Merrill Lynch -225 Lbrty WFC -NY 10080
(845) 229-6300 .. **Steinberg,** David L '75 -4419 Albany Post Rd -Hyde Pk 12538 **Fx:**229-6338
(212) 504-6000 .. **Steinberg,** Debra Brown '80 (Cadwalader W&T LLP) -1 World Fncl Ctr -NY 10281
(516) 333-7799 .. **Steinberg & Early-Hubelbank PLLC** -1400 Old Cntry Rd -Westbury 11590 **Fx:**333-3113
(212) 766-5222 .. **Steinberg,** Edw A '97 (Leav & S LLP) -120 Bway -NY 10271 **Fx:**693-2377
(212) 355-5240 .. **Steinberg,** Edwin A '59 E Steinberg,PC -250 W 57th -NY 10107 **Fx:**935-6857
(516) 747-1136 .. **Steinberg Fineo Berger & Fischoff, PC** -40 Crsswys Park Dr -Woodbury 11797 **Fx:**747-0382
(631) 247-1224 .. **Steinberg Fineo Berger & Fischoff, PC** -401 Broadhllw Rd -Melvll 11747 **Fx:**715-4186
(585) 255-1435 .. **Steinberg,** Gary P '83 Global Crossing -225 Kenneth Dr -Rchstr 14623
(516) 248-7000 .. **Steinberg,** Gary R '77 (Albanese & A LLP) -1050 Franklin Av -Gdn Cty 11530
(212) 490-3000 .. **Steinberg,** Greg M '10 %Wilson EME&D LLP -150 E 42nd -NY 10017
(516) 663-0999 .. **Steinberg & Gruber, PC** -300 Grdn City Plz -Gdn Cty 11530 **Fx:**663-0990
(516) 333-7799 .. **Steinberg,** Harriette M '82 (Steinberg & E-H PLLC) -1400 Old Cntry Rd -Westbury 11590
(212) 964-6611 .. **Steinberg,** Harry '86 (Lester SK&D) -120 Bway -NY 10271
(718) 263-2922 .. **Steinberg,** Herbert N '81 (Steinberg & Assoc) -80-02 Kew Grdns Rd -Kew Gdns 11415 **Fx:**575-4070
(212) 732-4992 .. **Steinberg,** Herman S '75 %Arye L&S,PC -20 Vesey -NY 10007
(212) 547-5400 .. **Steinberg,** Howard E '70 (McDermott W&E LLP) -340 Mad Av -NY 10173
(212) 225-6522 .. **Steinberg,** Howard M '88 Bank of Nova Scotia -1 Lbrty Plz -NY 10006
(212) 848-4000 .. **Steinberg,** Howard M '90 (Shearman & S LLP) -599 Lex Av -NY 10022
(845) 471-4455 .. **Steinberg,** James A '75 (Steinberg S&P,LLP) -27 Grdn -Poughkeepsie 12601
(914) 478-4293 .. **Steinberg,** James M '95 (Brady M&S,PC) -603 Warburton Av -Hastings-On-Hud 10706
(516) 455-2852 .. **Steinberg,** Jason B '05 -67-30 Dartmth -Frst Hlls 11375
(212) 487-9700 .. **Steinberg,** Jason S '04 %White F&F,LLP -61 Bway -NY 10006
(718) 436-7373 .. **Steinberg,** Jeffrey A '02 Nachas Healthnet -1310 48th -Brklyn 11219
(914) 761-4200 .. **Steinberg,** Jeffrey G '77 (Steinberg & C,LLP) -50 Main -White Plns 10606
(212) 465-9300 .. **Steinberg,** Jeffrey M '77 Tiger J,LLC -1430 Bway -NY 10018 **Fx:**(646) 435-7409
(212) 421-2150 .. **Steinberg,** Jessica A '08 %Sive P&R,PC -460 Park Av -NY 10022
(212) 484-3900 .. **Steinberg,** Jill A '93 (Arent F LLP) -1675 Bway -NY 10019
(212) 344-4745 .. **Steinberg,** Joel M '82 -5 Hanover Sq -NY 10004 **Fx:**509-5088
(718) 291-0282 .. **Steinberg,** John H '77 %Greater Jamaica Devl -90-04 161st -Jamaica 11432 **Fx:**658-1405
(212) 481-8484 .. **Steinberg,** Karen D '90 -31 E 32nd -NY 10016
(212) 450-4000 .. **Steinberg,** Kenneth J '06 %Davis P&W LLP -450 Lex Av -NY 10017
(212) 446-7656 .. **Steinberg,** Kevin P '97 %McKinsey & Co -55 E 52nd -NY 10055 **Fx:**838-9130
(212) 821-5656 .. **Steinberg,** Lewis R '85 UBS Securities LLC -299 Park Av -NY 10171
(516) 466-8005 .. **Steinberg,** Lynn '81 %Tashlik KG&C PC -40 Cuttermill Rd -Gt Neck 11021
(718) 390-5422 .. **Steinberg,** Marjorie R '94 %Civil Ct -927 Castleton Av -Staten Isl 10310 **Fx:**390-8108
(212) 545-4000 .. **Steinberg,** Matthew A '01 (Jackson L LLP) -666 3rd Av -NY 10017
(212) 752-7474 .. **Steinberg,** Matthew L '03 Steinberg & Pokoik -575 Mad Av -NY 10022 **Fx:**421-6196
(212) 768-9500 .. **Steinberg,** Melissa L '09 %Kittay & G,PC -1 Exch Plz 55 Bway -NY 10016
(212) 996-0630 .. **Steinberg,** Merrick D '82 (Verde S&P,LLC) -276 5th Av -NY 10001
(212) 245-0900 .. **Steinberg,** Merryl E '07 %R Michaels,PC -150 E 52nd -NY 10022 **Fx:**245-5459
(212) 450-4000 .. **Steinberg,** Michl '06 %Davis P&W LLP -450 Lex Av -NY 10017
(212) 830-2535 .. **Steinberg,** Michl G '90 %Broadcast Music Inc -250 Greenwich -NY 10007
(212) 848-4000 .. **Steinberg,** Michl J '03 %Shearman & S LLP -599 Lex Av -NY 10022
(212) 752-7474 .. **Steinberg,** Michl L '71 (Steinberg & Pokoik) -575 Mad Av -NY 10022 **Fx:**421-6196
(212) 334-8448 .. **Steinberg,** Michl R '78 -401 Bway -NY 10013 **Fx:**334-8449
(212) 335-4500 .. **Steinberg,** Morton M '03 (DLA Piper LLP) -1251 Av of Amer -NY 10020
(212) 236-5530 .. **Steinberg,** Nathan '04 Merrill Lynch -225 Lbrty -NY 10080
(212) 529-5400 .. **Steinberg,** Paul '03 -14 E 4th -NY 10012
(212) 859-8221 .. **Steinberg,** Paul I '88 -1 NY Plz -NY 10004 **Fx:**859-4000
(212) 563-2200 .. **Steinberg,** Richd A '74 (Brandt S&L LLP) -386 Park Av S -NY 10016
(212) 858-7710 .. **Steinberg,** Rick A '00 Cnsl Nowell AKB,PA -140 Bway PMB 46028 -NY 10005
(516) 663-0999 .. **Steinberg,** Robt B '84 (Steinberg & G,PC) -300 Grdn City Plz -Gdn Cty 11530
(631) 277-7300 .. **Steinberg,** Robt G '88 (Steinberg & B,LLP) -136 E Main -E Islip 11730
(718) 838-7878 .. **Steinberg,** Robin G '83 %Bronx Defenders -860 Crtlandt Av -Bronx 10451 **Fx:**665-0100
(914) 263-1244 .. **Steinberg,** Ronald F '95 -53 Phillips Hill Rd -New Cty 10956 **Fx:**(845) 639-7574
(212) 442-7532 .. **Steinberg,** Russell A '04 %Juvenile Justice -110 William -NY 10038 **Fx:**442-8517
(914) 381-7400 .. **Steinberg,** Scott A '83 %Rattet P&G,LLP -550 Mamaroneck Av -Harrison 10528
(212) 681-2535 .. **Steinberg,** Scott A '02 %Greenberg & S,PC -275 Mad Av -NY 10016
(516) 227-0808 .. **Steinberg,** Scott L '87 (Lasky & S,PC) -595 Stewart Av -Gdn Cty 11530 **Fx:**745-0769
(631) 537-8460 .. **Steinberg,** Stephen R '62 -Bx2158 -Brdghmptn 11932 **Fx:**537-8461
(516) 747-1136 .. **Steinberg,** Stuart M '83 (Steinberg FB&F,PC) -40 Crsswys Park Dr -Woodbury 11797
(845) 471-4455 .. **Steinberg Symer & Platt, LLP** -27 Grdn -Poughkeepsie 12601 **Fx:**471-8065
(212) 530-5000 .. **Steinberg,** Tara '10 %Milbank TH&M LLP -1 Chase Manh Plz -NY 10005
(646) 772-6464 .. **Steinberg & Wolff** -95 Joralemon -Brklyn 11201 **Fx:**(718) 797-0519
(212) 964-6100 .. **Steinberger,** Chaim '95 C Steinberger,PC -331 Mad Av -NY 10017 **Fx:**500-7559
(212) 532-8100 .. **Steinberger,** Dayna R '04 %Stern & M,LLP -115 Bway -NY 10006
(212) 575-0985 .. **Steinbock,** Sigal '96 Limor TB -580 5th Av -NY 10036
(212) 541-6222 .. **Steinbrecher,** Stephen '58 SrCnsl Kane K,PC -1350 Av of Amer -NY 10019
(212) 421-7807 .. **Steincolor,** Deborah '85 -845 3rd Av -NY 10022
(212) 355-2700 .. **Steindl,** Ethel J '81 -400 Park Av -NY 10022
(914) 428-1438 .. **Steindorf,** Robt H '75 %T Bona,PC -123 Main -White Plns 10601 **Fx:**428-1413
(585) 753-4500 .. **Steinebach,** Kyle R '06 DA -832 Watts Bldg -Rchstr 14614 **Fx:**753-4576
(212) 782-9861 .. **Steinecke,** Anke E '99 Random House -1745 Bway -NY 10019 **Fx:**782-8879
(212) 474-1000 .. **Steineker,** Clyde Witt '09 %Cravath S&M LLP -825 8th Av -NY 10019
(914) 739-9191 .. **Steiner,** Alan '73 -12 N Division -Peekskill 10566 **Fx:**739-9195
(518) 432-8000 .. **Steiner,** Alan E '64 OfCnsl Crane & P -48 Howard -Albany 12207
(212) 468-8000 .. **Steiner,** Alfred F '02 Morrison & F LLP -1290 Av of Amer -NY 10104
(212) 381-7000 .. **Steiner,** Barry N '65 (Sabin B&G LLP) -4 Times Sq -NY 10036
(716) 847-6500 .. **Steiner & Blotnik** -300 Delaware Av -Buffalo 14202 **Fx:**847-0705
(212) 986-6000 .. **Steiner,** Bruce D '76 OfCnsl Kleinberg KW&C,PC -551 5th Av -NY 10176
(212) 656-2132 .. **Steiner,** David H '78 NYSE -20 Broad -NY 10005
(212) 521-3500 .. **Steiner,** Diane B '90 (Aronson M&S, LLP) -485 Lex Av -NY 10017
(212) 761-1207 .. **Steiner,** Fatima I '99 Morgan Stanley -1585 Bway -NY 10036
(212) 909-6000 .. **Steiner,** Gail D '05 %Debevoise & P LLP -919 3rd Av -NY 10022
(212) 863-8346 .. **Steiner,** H Benjamin '98 HPD -100 Gold -NY 10038
(212) 744-4276 .. **Steiner,** Henry H '50 -274 First Av -NY 10009 **Fx:**744-0552
(212) 872-1000 .. **Steiner,** Irene A '82 -One Bryant Park -NY 10036 **Fx:**872-1002
(212) 422-0488 .. **Steiner,** Jacob '81 (Rick SF&B,LLP) -90 Broad -NY 10004
(212) 335-4500 .. **Steiner,** Jeffrey B '81 (DLA Piper LLP) -1251 Av of Amer -NY 10020
(914) 285-9800 .. **Steiner,** Katherine R '83 (Kurzman EC&L,LLP) -1 N Bway -White Plns 10601
(716) 852-1888 .. **Steiner,** Mark F '93 OfCnsl Cantor LD&P,PC -350 Main -Buffalo 14202
(718) 261-7700 .. **Steiner,** Michl A '79 (Rappaport HC&R,PC) -118-35 Qns Blvd -Frst Hlls 11375
(718) 209-9707 .. **Steiner,** Michl E '83 -9526 Av L -Brklyn 11236 **Fx:**209-2241
(212) 446-4800 .. **Steiner,** Michele R '08 %Kirkland & E LLP -153 E 53rd -NY 10022
(212) 698-3500 .. **Steiner,** Neil A '98 (Dechert LLP) -1095 Av of Amer -NY 10036
(914) 378-1010 .. **Steiner,** Norman M '97 Fitzgerald & F -538 Riverdale Av -Ynkrs 10705
(716) 847-6500 .. **Steiner,** Richd J '73 (Steiner & B) -300 Delaware Av -Buffalo 14202

(212) 808-7800 .. **Steiner,** Robt I '97 (Kelley D&W LLP) -101 Park Av -NY 10178
(914) 328-4734 .. **Steiner,** Scott J '83 (S Steiner,PC) -2 William -White Plns 10601 **Fx:**328-8648
(212) 788-1051 .. **Steiner-Korn,** Julie R '97 %Law Dept -100 Church -NY 10007 **Fx:**788-0367
(516) 796-1400 .. **Steinert,** Robt M '72 -187 William Rd -N Massapequa 11758
(212) 479-6000 .. **Steines,** John P '81 OfCnsl Cooley LLP -1114 Av of Amer -NY 10036
(212) 998-6167 .. **Steines,** John P '81 %NYU Law Schl -40 Wshngtn Sq S -NY 10012 **Fx:**995-4075
(718) 370-7030 .. **Steinfeld,** Shari D '00 %Amabile & E,PC -1000 South Av -Staten Isl 10314
(914) 273-8383 .. **Steinfink,** Barry '68 -1 Byram Brook Pl -Armonk 10504
(212) 837-6000 .. **Steinfink,** Jaime S '94 Cnsl Hughes H&R LLP -1 Bttry Pk Plz -NY 10004
(212) 859-8000 .. **Steingart,** Bonnie '80 (Fried FHS&J LLP) -1 NY Plz -NY 10004
(212) 406-7700 .. **Steinglass,** Henry J '67 -299 Bway -NY 10007 **Fx:**406-7702
(212) 335-9000 .. **Steinglass,** Joshua A '99 %DA -1 Hogan Pl -NY 10013
(212) 580-4070 .. **Steingut,** Robt '82 -344 W 72nd -NY 10023
(212) 422-0010 .. **Steingut,** Theo S '74 -150 E 58th -NY 10155 **Fx:**422-0030
(212) 972-5430 .. **Steinhagen,** Gail '77 (Rosin SM) -801 2nd Av -NY 10017
(212) 455-2000 .. **Steinhardt,** Brian M '99 (Simpson T&B LLP) -425 Lex Av -NY 10017
(518) 449-3300 .. **Steinhardt,** Steven B '72 SpclCnsl Nolan & H,LLP -39 N Pearl -Albany 12207
(212) 308-0888 .. **Steinhart,** Barry N '85 (Widowski & S LLP) -425 Mad Av -NY 10017
(212) 267-6364 .. **Steinhart,** Steven Y '94 %Kossoff & U -217 Bway -NY 10007
(212) 381-7000 .. **Steinhauer,** Arthur J '78 (Sabin B&G LLP) -4 Times Sq -NY 10036
(716) 881-5800 .. **Steinhaus,** Robt D '87 Siegel K&K -426 Franklin -Buffalo 14202
(212) 373-3000 .. **Steinherr,** Franz P '06 %Paul WRW&G LLP -1285 Av of Amer -NY 10019
(716) 632-6677 .. **Steinhilber,** David C '82 -Bx412 -Williamsvll 14231
(718) 261-7700 .. **Steinitz,** Jeffrey M '73 -118-35 Qns Blvd -Frst Hlls 11375 **Fx:**261-7336
(212) 854-1908 .. **Steinitz,** Maya '04 %Columbia Law Schl -435 W 116th -NY 10027 **Fx:**854-7946
(718) 319-0337 .. **Steinke,** Andre '92 -2704 Tremont Av -Bronx 10461
(212) 269-4900 .. **Steinke,** Douglas J '06 %Ford MEW&G,LLP -Wall Street Plz -NY 10005
(212) 735-3000 .. **Steinman,** Andrew K '09 %Skadden ASM&F LLP -4 Times Sq -NY 10036
(212) 277-9000 .. **Steinman,** Danl M '00 Creative Artists Agency -162 5th Av -NY 10010 **Fx:**277-9099
(212) 885-5000 .. **Steinman,** Leonard D '85 (Blank R LLP) -405 Lex Av -NY 10174
(914) 997-0900 .. **Steinman,** Lester D '75 OfCnsl Wormser KG&J LLP -399 Knollwood Rd -White Plns 10603
(212) 489-8230 .. **Steinman,** Linda '87 (Davis WT LLP) -1633 Bway -NY 10019
(914) 524-9000 .. **Steinman,** Marshall L '56 -660 Wht Plns Rd -Tarrytwn 10591 **Fx:**524-9185
(212) 259-8000 .. **Steinman,** Martha N '90 (Dewey & L LLP) -1301 Av of Amer -NY 10019
(212) 701-3000 .. **Steinman,** Mayer J '10 %Cahill G&R LLP -80 Pine -NY 10005 **Fx:**269-5420
(212) 265-6600 .. **Steinman,** Robt C '98 RD Mgmt Corp -810 7th Av -NY 10019
(212) 326-2000 .. **Steinman,** Ryan C '10 %O'Melveny & M LLP -7 Times Sq -NY 10036
(212) 521-5400 .. **Steinman,** Sandra K '00 %Reed S LLP -599 Lex Av -NY 10022
(212) 859-8000 .. **Steinman,** Steven J '94 (Fried FHS&J LLP) -1 NY Plz -NY 10004
(212) 860-4825 .. **Steinmann,** David P '67 -1185 Park Av -NY 10128
(914) 995-2660 .. **Steinmann,** Wanda '01 %Cnty Atty -148 Martine Av -White Plns 10601 **Fx:**995-5858
(914) 328-0674 .. **Steinmetz,** Cynthia '94 Pro Bono Prtnrshp,Inc -237 Mamaroneck Av -White Plns 10605 **Fx:**328-0538
(914) 682-7800 .. **Steinmetz,** David S '86 (Zarin & S) -81 Main -White Plns 10601
(212) 475-4958 .. **Steinmetz,** Debra '82 -300 Mercer -NY 10003
(212) 218-5500 .. **Steinmetz,** Victoria L '04 Seyfarth S LLP -620 8th Av -NY 10018
(212) 728-2200 .. **Steinthal,** Russell M '03 %Axinn V&H LLP -114 W 47th -NY 10036
(914) 288-0103 .. **Steinvurzel,** Ronald E '00 -34 S Bway -White Plns 10601
(212) 681-1575 .. **Steinwolf,** Bonnie M '99 %Belluck & F LLP -546 5th Av -NY 10036
(212) 210-7216 .. **Stelboum,** Barry S '91 %J Walter Thompson -466 Lex Av -NY 10017 **Fx:**210-6852
(212) 558-4000 .. **Stelcen,** Lindsey B '10 %Sullivan & C LLP -125 Broad -NY 10004
(212) 596-9000 .. **Stella,** Adam E '09 %Ropes & G LLP -1211 Av of Amer -NY 10036
(973) 228-5700 .. **Stella,** Frances B '92 (Brach E LLC) -100 Park Av -NY 10017 **Fx:**228-7852
(516) 294-6800 .. **Stella,** George E '76 -100 Grdn City Plz -Gdn Cty 11530 **Fx:**294-5682
(212) 474-1000 .. **Stella,** Rose R '08 %Cravath S&M LLP -825 8th Av -NY 10019
(212) 969-3000 .. **Stellabotte,** John C '94 SrCnsl Proskauer R LLP -1585 Bway -NY 10036
(212) 480-6778 .. **Stellar,** John '80 %DHCR -25 Beaver -NY 10004 **Fx:**480-7416
(212) 357-9895 .. **Stellato,** Elizabeth M '05 Goldman Sachs -85 Broad -NY 10004
(212) 839-5300 .. **Stellato,** Gary F '01 %Sidley A LLP -787 7th Av -NY 10019
(845) 486-2300 .. **Steller,** Bridget Rahilly '75 %DA -236 Main -Poughkeepsie 12601 **Fx:**486-2324
(212) 664-4444 .. **Stellings,** Brande M '94 %NBC -30 Rckfllr Plz -NY 10112
(212) 355-9500 .. **Stellings,** David S '94 (Lieff CH&B,LLP) -250 Hudson -NY 10013
(212) 637-2101 .. **Stellmach,** Wm J '99 %US Atty -1 St Andrews Plz -NY 10007
(212) 706-7160 .. **Stello,** Jos R '89 -110 Wall -NY 10005
(212) 964-6430 .. **Stelnik,** Richd G '78 -225 Bway -NY 10007
(212) 318-3000 .. **Stelwagon,** Wm M '97 SrCnsl Fulbright & J LLP -666 5th Av -NY 10103
(917) 534-4834 .. **Stelzer,** Edw A '94 Zurich Capital Mrkts -105 E 17th -NY 10003
(212) 504-6000 .. **Stemmer,** Andrew I '04 %Cadwalader W&T LLP -1 World Fncl Ctr -NY 10281
(212) 278-7169 .. **Stempel,** Andrea H '91 %Societe Generale -1221 Av of Amer -NY 10020
(212) 681-6500 .. **Stempel Bennett Claman & Hochberg,PC** -675 3rd Av -NY 10017 **Fx:**681-4041
(212) 225-2000 .. **Stempel,** Ivy B '82 Cleary GS&H -1 Lbrty Plz -NY 10006
(646) 223-6000 .. **Stempel,** Jonathan E '93 Reuters America -3 Times Sq -NY 10036
(212) 268-4400 .. **Stempel,** Lee A '83 -310 5th Av -NY 10001
(212) 681-6500 .. **Stempel,** Richd C '68 (Stempel BC&H,PC) -675 3rd Av -NY 10017
(516) 742-8620 .. **Stempel,** Vincent F '83 -1205 Franklin Av -Gdn Cty 11530 **Fx:**742-6859
(212) 547-5400 .. **Stempel,** Wm E '02 (McDermott W&E LLP) -340 Mad Av -NY 10173
(212) 728-8000 .. **Stempler,** Laurie N '10 %Willkie F&G LLP -787 7th Av -NY 10019
(212) 836-8000 .. **Stempler,** Randall I '83 Cnsl Kaye S LLP -425 Park Av -NY 10022
(212) 221-5700 .. **Stempler,** Randi K '99 %Goldberg WFG LLP -1501 Bway -NY 10036
(212) 693-0085 .. **Stendig,** Barry S '76 %Appellate Advocates -2 Rector -NY 10006 **Fx:**693-0878
(212) 564-3222 .. **Stengel,** Adam M '96 -358 5th Av -NY 10001 **Fx:**967-0749
(212) 506-5000 .. **Stengel,** James L '81 (Orrick H&S LLP) -51 W 52nd -NY 10019
(914) 421-5656 .. **Stengel,** Stuart S '66 -1 Barker Av -White Plns 10601
(845) 298-2000 .. **Stenger,** Kenneth M '77 (Vergilis SRD&D,LLP) -1136 Route 9 -Wappingers Fls 12590
(716) 853-1111 .. **Stenger,** Mitchell M '87 (Kloss S&L) -69 Delaware Av -Buffalo 14202 **Fx:**847-2924
(212) 434-0100 .. **Stenroos,** Angela M '95 %Litchfield C LLP -420 Lex Av -NY 10170
(212) 682-1555 .. **Stenseth,** Mark D '09 %MacLean Law Firm,LLC -100 Park Av -NY 10017 **Fx:**682-6999
(212) 696-6000 .. **Stenshoel,** Eric J '81 Cnsl Curtis M-PC&M LLP -101 Park Av -NY 10178
(212) 578-2211 .. **Stenson,** Lisa M '91 %MetLife -27-01 Qns Plz N -LIC 11101
(212) 309-5410 .. **Stenson,** Thos G '94 %Lexis/Nexis -125 Park Av -NY 10017 **Fx:**309-8187
(212) 250-8993 .. **Stenstrom,** Kelli J '01 %Deutsche Bank -60 Wall -NY 10005
(315) 656-8743 .. **Stenuf,** Theo W '81 -141 N Main -Minoa 13116 **Fx:**656-4244
(516) 229-4200 .. **Stenz,** Robt D '84 (Mendolia & S) -875 Merrick Av -Westbury 11590
(212) 242-4665 .. **Stenzel,** Robt D '66 -27 W 11th -NY 10011
(212) 336-0173 .. **Stepaniuk,** George N '87 %SEC -3 World Fncl Ctr -NY 10281 **Fx:**336-1323
(212) 309-1000 .. **Stephan,** Paul B '09 %Hunton & W -200 Park Av -NY 10166
(212) 474-1000 .. **Stephanakis,** George A '98 (Cravath S&M LLP) -825 8th Av -NY 10019
(212) 659-1977 .. **Stephanopoulos,** George E '09 Classic Media Inc -85 5th Av -NY 10003
(212) 504-6000 .. **Stephansen,** Nicole M '09 %Cadwalader W&T LLP -1 World Fncl Ctr -NY 10281
(212) 878-8410 .. **Stephanz,** Rita McCloy '87 Cnsl Clifford C LLP -31 W 52nd -NY 10019
(212) 854-6182 .. **Stephen,** Jomysha '00 Barnard Cllg Ofc Gen Cnsl -3009 Bway -NY 10027
(212) 761-4000 .. **Stephen,** Jos V '04 Morgan Stanley -1585 Bway -NY 10036
(516) 463-5871 .. **Stephen,** Tamara '97 Hofstra Univ Schl of Law -108 Hofstra Univ -Hempstd 11549 **Fx:**463-7351
(212) 848-4000 .. **Stephens,** Andrew B '08 %Shearman & S LLP -599 Lex Av -NY 10022
(914) 761-0300 .. **Stephens Baroni Reilly & Lewis** -175 Main -White Plns 10601 **Fx:**761-0995
(212) 425-7200 .. **Stephens,** Carmella L '99 Cnsl Kenyon & K,LLP -1 Bway -NY 10004
(212) 416-6040 .. **Stephens,** Carol Dancy '84 %Dept of Law -120 Bway -NY 10271
(212) 806-5400 .. **Stephens,** David '85 (Stroock &S&L LLP) -180 Maiden Ln -NY 10038
(212) 326-3939 .. **Stephens,** Eric P '09 %Jones D -222 E 41st -NY 10017
(315) 478-0969 .. **Stephens,** George H III '50 Stephens Law Firm -118 Clyde Av -Syracuse 13207 **Fx:**478-0969
(212) 822-1446 .. **Stephens,** Glendoval J '94 -305 Bway -NY 10007
(212) 318-3000 .. **Stephens,** Jarret '07 %Fulbright & J LLP -666 5th Av -NY 10103
(718) 852-1919 .. **Stephens,** Jeremy E '96 %RBA Inc -45 Main -Brklyn 11201 **Fx:**852-3022
(315) 797-8300 .. **Stephens,** Michl H '70 (Kernan and K,PC) -258 Genesee -Utica 13502 **Fx:**797-6467
(212) 918-3000 .. **Stephens,** Oscar '07 %Hogan L LLP -875 3rd Av -NY 10022
(716) 852-7587 .. **Stephens,** R Wm '65 (Stephens & S,LLP) -410 Main -Buffalo 14202 **Fx:**852-7599
(716) 852-7587 .. **Stephens,** Robt Hugh '96 (Stephens & S,LLP) -410 Main -Buffalo 14202 **Fx:**852-7599
(212) 238-8900 .. **Stephens,** S Dwight '86 (Melito & A,PC) -233 Bway -NY 10279
(212) 335-4500 .. **Stephens,** Shand S '09 DLA Piper LLP -1251 Av of Amer -NY 10020
(212) 705-7000 .. **Stephens,** Timothy J '95 (Bingham M LLP) -399 Park Av -NY 10022
(845) 279-4226 .. **Stephens,** Willis H Jr. '81 -328 Clock Twr Cmmns -Brewstr 10509 **Fx:**279-7154
(212) 402-4100 .. **Stephens-Davidowitz,** Lauren P '10 Ofc Appllt Def -11 Park Pl -NY 10007 **Fx:**402-4199
(518) 213-6000 .. **Stephenson,** A Kathya '07 NYSUT -800 Troy-Schnctdy Rd -Latham 12110 **Fx:**213-6488
(212) 883-1700 .. **Stephenson,** J Andrew '92 (Duval & S LLP) -101 Park Av -NY 10178
(212) 552-4408 .. **Stephenson,** Lisa Olive '95 JP Morgan Chase -1 Chase Manh Plz -NY 10081
(212) 552-0948 .. **Stephenson,** Robt T '77 JP Morgan Chase -1 Chase Manh Plz -NY 10081
(212) 460-2183 .. **Stepien,** Walter P Jr. '82 Con Ed -4 Irving Pl -NY 10003
(718) 250-2000 .. **Stepner,** Caryn J '89 %DA -350 Jay -Brklyn 11201 **Fx:**250-2314
(212) 752-5200 .. **Steppe,** Jolie M '01 Greene-Levin-Snyder LLP -150 E 58th -NY 10155
(212) 593-6700 .. **Steproe,** Nancy A '88 (Aaronson RF&D,LLP) -757 3rd Av -NY 10017
(212) 506-3900 .. **Steptoe & Johnson LLP** -750 7th Av -NY 10019 **Fx:**506-3950
(212) 924-2196 .. **Sterba,** M John Jr. '72 -489 W 22nd -NY 10011
(212) 728-8000 .. **Steren,** Yael '07 %Willkie F&G LLP -787 7th Av -NY 10019
(212) 609-6800 .. **Stergios,** Peter D '73 (McCarter & E,LLP) -245 Park Av -NY 10167
(212) 964-8038 .. **Sterinbach,** Howard B '91 %Worth L&L,LLP -111 John -NY 10038
(212) 790-0230 .. **Sterk,** Stewart E '77 %Benj N Cardozo Schl of Law -55 5th Av -NY 10003 **Fx:**790-0345
(212) 506-2500 .. **Sterken,** Sarah J '04 %Mayer B LLP -1675 Bway -NY 10019
(718) 477-3700 .. **Sterlacci,** Michl J '85 %Reuben Warner Assoc -1655 Richmond Av -Staten Isl 10314
(212) 337-1327 .. **Sterlacci,** Mona L '98 %DOT-OIG -201 Varick -NY 10014

(607) 273-2283 .. **Sterling,** Betsy C '84 %Prisoners' Leg Srvcs -114 Prospect -Ithaca 14850 **Fx:**272-9122

(212) 839-5300 .. **Sterling,** Carol A '06 %Sidley A LLP -787 7th Av -NY 10019

(212) 412-2783 .. **Sterling,** Ian W '98 Barclays Capital -200 Park Av -NY 10166

(212) 683-1988 .. **Sterman,** Cara G '05 Greenkey Resources -475 Park Av S -NY 10016 **Fx:**213-1871

(716) 882-7330 .. **Sterman,** Gary M '89 -100 Robie -Buffalo 14214

(585) 343-5450 .. **Stermole,** Mary C '09 %Leg Srvcs -5073 Clinton St Rd -Batavia 14020 **Fx:**343-5503

(212) 407-4000 .. **Stern,** Akiba '81 (Loeb & L,LLP) -345 Park Av -NY 10154

(516) 294-2664 .. **Stern,** Alan J '83 (A Stern,PC) -300 Grdn City Plz -Gdn Cty 11530 **Fx:**294-5830

(516) 747-6223 .. **Stern,** Allan M '74 -Bx823 -Glenwd Landing 11547 **Fx:**747-6225

(518) 452-1800 .. **Stern,** Amanda R '03 %Towne R & Prtnrs,PC -450 New Karner Rd Bx15072 -Albany 12212

(518) 473-8197 .. **Stern,** Amelia F '82 %Governor's Ofc Reg Reform -ESP Bx2107 -Albany 12220 **Fx:**473-9962

(212) 312-3813 .. **Stern,** Andrew M '92 %EDC -110 William -NY 10038

(212) 839-5300 .. **Stern,** Andrew W '92 (Sidley A LLP) -787 7th Av -NY 10019

(212) 431-4030 .. **Stern,** Anna '83 -351 Bway -NY 10013 **Fx:**941-0980

(212) 728-8000 .. **Stern,** Anna P '09 %Willkie F&G LLP -787 7th Av -NY 10019

(212) 906-1200 .. **Stern,** Benjamin D '05 Latham & W -885 3rd Av -NY 10022

(212) 826-0100 .. **Stern,** Bruce E '80 %FSA -31 W 52nd -NY 10019 **Fx:**893-2710

(845) 561-8435 .. **Stern,** Bruce M '88 -825 Bway -Newburgh 12550 **Fx:**(800) 615-9015

(718) 625-5430 .. **Stern Bryk & Hoffman, PC** -26 Court -Brklyn 11242 **Fx:**858-0748

(914) 285-9477 .. **Stern,** Carol Meyer '83 -235 Mamaroneck Av -White Plns 10605

(212) 902-4087 .. **Stern,** Chaim '01 Goldman Sachs -180 Maiden Ln -NY 10038

(212) 474-1000 .. **Stern,** Chas '09 %Cravath S&M LLP -825 8th Av -NY 10019

(212) 951-6400 .. **Stern,** Claudia J '80 %Dept of Education -475 Park Av S -NY 10016 **Fx:**951-6465

(212) 385-1444 .. **Stern,** Clifford J '88 (Silverstein & S,LLP) -40 Fulton -NY 10038

(212) 425-9300 .. **Stern,** Coren Harris '01 %Bressler A&R,PC -17 State -NY 10004

(212) 298-5000 .. **Stern,** Danl D '06 Leg Aid -49 Thomas -NY 10013 **Fx:**298-5252

(212) 571-5500 .. **Stern,** David '83 (Rothman SS&S,LLP) -100 Lafayette -NY 10013

(973) 455-1812 .. **Stern,** David A '92 (Davis & S,PC) -422 2nd Av -NY 10010 **Fx:**455-1056

(212) 407-8300 .. **Stern,** David J '66 NBA -645 5th Av -NY 10022

(212) 242-5800 .. **Stern,** David J '09 Gusto Grilled Organics,Inc -519 6th Av -NY 10011

(718) 935-9458 .. **Stern,** David L '87 (Stern & S) -50 Court -Brklyn 11201 **Fx:**797-3226

(914) 428-8800 .. **Stern,** David M '74 (Stern KP&W,LLP) -1025 Wstchstr Av -White Plns 10604

(212) 440-4300 .. **Stern,** David M '93 %Leg Aid -199 Water -NY 10038

(585) 546-5600 .. **Stern,** David S '90 (Pheterson SCN&S,LLP) -1 E Main -Rchstr 14614

(585) 232-4724 .. **Stern,** David S '90 %Elliott S&C,LLP -1 E Main -Rchstr 14614

(212) 225-2000 .. **Stern,** Donald A '81 (Cleary GS&H) -1 Lbrty Plz -NY 10006

(516) 328-2300 .. **Stern,** Douglas K '94 (Abrams FFEGF&E,LLP) -1111 Marcus Av -Lk Success 11042

(212) 969-3000 .. **Stern,** Emily '95 SrCnsl Proskauer R LLP -1585 Bway -NY 10036

(516) 569-3030 .. **Stern,** Fay Taub '83 (Novak J&S) -483 Chestnut -Cedarhrst 11516

(212) 779-1414 .. **Stern,** Felecia B '93 (Bernstein L LLP) -10 E 40th -NY 10016

(631) 650-9260 .. **Stern,** Fredrick P '87 -2163 Sunrise Hwy -Islip 11751 **Fx:**650-9259

(212) 389-6591 .. **Stern,** Gabriel E '06 Salesforce.com -140 E 45th -NY 10017

(914) 949-8888 .. **Stern,** Gerald '63 Judicial Inst -84 N Bway -White Plns 10603

(516) 747-2290 .. **Stern,** H Michl '86 -Bx710 -Merrick 11566 **Fx:**747-2293

(212) 360-1313 .. **Stern,** Henry J '58 %Dept of Parks & Rec -The Arsenal Cntrl Pk -NY 10065 **Fx:**360-1373

(212) 506-1700 .. **Stern,** Hershy '09 %Kasowitz BT&F LLP -1633 Bway -NY 10019

(914) 683-0505 .. **Stern,** Howard '78 H Stern -3 Barker Av -White Plns 10601 **Fx:**683-0508

(516) 568-1850 .. **Stern,** Howard J '83 (Werner ZSS&A) -360 Merrick Rd -Lynbrk 11563

(516) 747-2290 .. **Stern,** Howard M '86 -1 Old Cntry Rd -Carle Pl 11514

(914) 285-9800 .. **Stern,** Ilene Blair '87 (Kurzman EC&L,LLP) -1 N Bway -White Plns 10601

(718) 448-6767 .. **Stern,** Jack '77 J Stern -1189 Forest Av -Staten Isl 10310 **Fx:**448-4509

(212) 446-2300 .. **Stern,** Jack G '86 (Boies S&F LLP) -575 Lex Av -NY 10022

(315) 475-4010 .. **Stern,** James E '94 -103 E Water -Syracuse 13202 **Fx:**474-8867

(631) 427-3533 .. **Stern,** James K '86 (Widlitz & S,PC) -700 NY Av -Huntngtn 11743

(212) 309-1712 .. **Stern,** Jamie Ellen '77 ING Ins Amer -230 Park Av -NY 10169

(212) 686-0010 .. **Stern,** Jane R '59 %NY Community Trst -909 3rd Av -NY 10022 **Fx:**532-8528

(516) 280-6900 .. **Stern,** Janet S '89 (Stern & D,LLP) -1 Old Cntry Rd -Carle Pl 11514 **Fx:**294-0094

(212) 326-8654 .. **Stern,** Jarod M '01 Studley,Inc -300 Park Av -NY 10022

(212) 344-3600 .. **Stern,** Jason A '99 (Anderson & O,LLP) -61 Bway -NY 10006 **Fx:**344-0970

(212) 702-9090 .. **Stern,** Jeff H '87 -250 W 57th -NY 10107 **Fx:**977-7035

(516) 742-7030 .. **Stern,** Jeffrey '78 J Stern -128 Front -Mineola 11501 **Fx:**742-5108

(212) 806-5400 .. **Stern,** Jeffrey '92 (Stroock &S&L LLP) -180 Maiden Ln -NY 10038

(718) 927-0100 .. **Stern,** Jeffrey '03 -1219 Av J -Brklyn 11230

(212) 489-6801 .. **Stern,** Jeffrey R '95 Morgan Stanley -1633 Bway -NY 10019

(212) 207-3825 .. **Stern,** Joel S '59 (Stern & Z LLP) -110 E 59th -NY 10022 **Fx:**583-7464

(585) 454-6124 .. **Stern,** Jon M '01 Wilder Bldg -1 E Main -Rchstr 14614 **Fx:**262-2610

(212) 455-2000 .. **Stern,** Jonathan '09 %Simpson T&B LLP -425 Lex Av -NY 10017

(516) 634-0345 .. **Stern,** Jordan A '92 (Stern & S) -49 W Merrick Rd -Freeprt 11520 **Fx:**634-0348

(212) 888-3033 .. **Stern,** Jordan E '99 %Becker GM&M LLP -299 Park Av -NY 10171

(212) 373-3000 .. **Stern,** Joshua L '09 %Paul WRW&G LLP -1285 Av of Amer -NY 10019

(516) 227-6300 .. **Stern,** Joshua S '09 %Ettelman & H,PC -100 Q Roosevelt Blvd -Gdn Cty 11530

(212) 577-3617 .. **Stern,** Judith S '91 %Leg Aid -199 Water -NY 10038 **Fx:**577-3520

(914) 428-8800 .. **Stern Keiser Panken & Wohl,LLP** -1025 Wstchstr Av -White Plns 10604 **Fx:**428-3199

(212) 370-5970 .. **Stern Keiser Panken & Wohl,LLP** -675 3rd Av -NY 10017 **Fx:**(914) 428-3199

(516) 771-0710 .. **Stern,** Kenneth D '92 (Stern & S,PC) -3002 Merrick Av -Bellmore 11710 **Fx:**771-0723

(631) 421-4200 .. **Stern,** Kenneth J '63 (Levenbron & S) -Bx2229 -Huntngtn 11743

(212) 891-1444 .. **Stern,** Kenneth S '86 %Amer Jewish Comm -165 E 56th -NY 10022 **Fx:**891-1495

(212) 525-6616 .. **Stern,** Laurence R '65 %HSBC Bank -452 5th Av -NY 10018

(718) 935-9458 .. **Stern,** Lawr M '82 (Stern & S) -50 Court -Brklyn 11201 **Fx:**797-3226

(212) 925-6863 .. **Stern,** Lawr Mark '69 -100 Hudson -NY 10013 **Fx:**925-6863

(718) 784-0505 .. **Stern,** Leslie F '84 Natl Envelope Corp -29-10 Hunts Pnt Av -LIC 11101

(212) 362-1200 .. **Stern,** Lilian S '85 Stern Investor -19 W 87th -NY 10024

(212) 787-7282 .. **Stern,** Lisa E '95 -5 W 86th -NY 10024

(212) 969-3000 .. **Stern,** Lisa M '99 %Proskauer R LLP -1585 Bway -NY 10036

(212) 891-1480 .. **Stern,** Marc D '77 Amer Jewish Comm -165 E 56th -NY 10022 **Fx:**891-1495

(212) 660-3000 .. **Stern,** Marc L '83 (Sullivan & W LLP) -1290 Av of Amer -NY 10104

(845) 294-7990 .. **Stern,** Mark D '74 (Stern & R) -15 Matthews Bx1028 -Goshen 10924 **Fx:**294-9233

(631) 427-0101 .. **Stern,** Marshall M '75 M Stern,PC -17 Cardiff Ct -Huntngtn Sta 11746 **Fx:**427-0196

(212) 259-8000 .. **Stern,** Matthew B '07 %Dewey & L LLP -1301 Av of Amer -NY 10019

(212) 968-8300 .. **Stern,** Michl E '72 SrCnsl Mintzer SZL&M LLP -39 Bway -NY 10006

(212) 953-2381 .. **Stern,** Michl E '92 %Rubin F&F,LLP -292 Mad Av -NY 10017

(212) 909-6000 .. **Stern,** Michl G '10 %Debevoise & P LLP -919 3rd Av -NY 10022

(518) 746-2525 .. **Stern,** Michl R '92 %DA -383 Bway -Ft Edward 12828 **Fx:**746-2568

(212) 669-2320 .. **Stern,** Michl W '85 %NYC Comptrollers Ofc -1 Centre -NY 10007

(212) 661-5030 .. **Stern,** Mindy H '84 (Schoeman U&K,LLP) -60 E 42nd -NY 10165

(212) 794-1289 .. **Stern,** Miriam '89 -303 E 83rd -NY 10028

(212) 451-2300 .. **Stern,** Mitchell B '87 (Olshan GFR&W LLP) -65 E 55th -NY 10022

(212) 532-8100 .. **Stern & Montana,LLP** -115 Bway -NY 10006 **Fx:**532-7271

(212) 988-1794 .. **Stern,** Nancy Ann '71 -180 E 79th -NY 10075

(212) 223-8330 .. **Stern,** Nelson M '93 -630 3rd Av -NY 10017 **Fx:**949-1857

(212) 455-2000 .. **Stern,** Noah F '10 %Simpson T&B LLP -425 Lex Av -NY 10017

(212) 857-8800 .. **Stern,** Noelle B '01 US Ct Appls 2nd Circ -40 Foley Sq -NY 10007 **Fx:**857-8898

(631) 650-9260 .. **Stern,** Patricia A '99 %F Stern & Assoc -2163 Sunrise Hwy -Islip 11751 **Fx:**650-9259

(212) 947-2111 .. **Stern,** Peter Marc '63 -37 W 39th -NY 10018 **Fx:**947-2602

(212) 448-1100 .. **Stern,** Peter R '73 OfCnsl McLaughlin & S,LLP -260 Mad Av -NY 10016

(212) 841-9342 .. **Stern,** Philip H '72 FTI Consulting -3 Times Sq -NY 10036 **Fx:**841-9350

(646) 429-7500 .. **Stern,** Rachelle '78 %Macys,Inc -11 Penn Plz -NY 10001 **Fx:**429-7521

(212) 837-6000 .. **Stern,** Richd '80 (Hughes H&R LLP) -1 Bttry Pk Plz -NY 10004

(646) 642-1019 .. **Stern,** Richd I '90 -11 Riverside Dr -NY 10023

(631) 549-7900 .. **Stern,** Richd L '77 (Macco & S,LLP) -135 Pinelawn Rd -Melvll 11747

(212) 773-2183 .. **Stern,** Richd W '90 Ernst & Young LLP -5 Times Sq -NY 10036

(212) 532-8100 .. **Stern,** Robt A '89 (Stern & M,LLP) -115 Bway -NY 10006

(212) 805-3900 .. **Stern,** Robt A '91 (Clausen M PC) -1 Chase Manh Plz -NY 10005

(516) 634-0345 .. **Stern,** Robt T '63 (Stern & S) -49 W Merrick Rd -Freeprt 11520 **Fx:**634-0348

(516) 296-7000 .. **Stern,** Russell H '99 (Certilman BA&H,LLP) -90 Merrick Av -E Meadow 11554

(212) 869-1090 .. **Stern,** Saml A '75 (Angell & B) -36 W 44th -NY 10036 **Fx:**869-1091

(212) 207-8150 .. **Stern,** Sandra '74 Nordquist & S PLLC -909 3rd Av -NY 10022 **Fx:**317-1030

(212) 435-7000 .. **Stern,** Sarah K '08 Port Auth of NY/NJ -225 Park Av S -NY 10003 **Fx:**435-3555

(212) 705-7000 .. **Stern,** Scott L '97 (Bingham M LLP) -399 Park Av -NY 10022

(212) 704-6000 .. **Stern,** Sharon H '87 OfCnsl Troutman S LLP -405 Lex Av -NY 10174

(212) 640-0944 .. **Stern,** Stephanie J '09 AmEx -200 Vesey -NY 10285

(212) 421-4000 .. **Stern,** Stephen R '73 (Hoffinger S&R,LLP) -150 E 58th -NY 10155

(212) 684-3900 .. **Stern,** Steven '01 (Gottlieb R&R,PC) -270 Mad Av -NY 10016

(516) 334-4500 .. **Stern,** Steven C '96 (Sokoloff S LLP) -355 Post Av -Westbury 11590 **Fx:**334-4501

(631) 234-3030 .. **Stern,** Steven H '94 (Davidow DS&S,LLP) -1601 Vets Mem'l Hwy -Islandia 11749

(212) 819-8091 .. **Stern,** Steven S '76 %Hecht & Co,PC -622 3rd Av -NY 10017

(212) 792-8484 .. **Stern,** Stewart J '86 (Stern T&B LLP) -380 Lex Av -NY 10168

(718) 755-9637 .. **Stern,** Sy '99 -1556 E 29th -Brklyn 11229

(212) 792-8484 .. **Stern Tannenbaum & Bell LLP** -380 Lex Av -NY 10168 **Fx:**792-8489

(212) 373-3000 .. **Stern,** Tobias J '05 %Paul WRW&G LLP -1285 Av of Amer -NY 10019

(718) 625-5430 .. **Stern,** Trudy H '86 (Stern B&H,PC) -26 Court -Brklyn 11242

(212) 403-1000 .. **Stern,** Warren R '80 (Wachtell LR&K) -51 W 52nd -NY 10019

(212) 813-8800 .. **Stern,** Wm E '06 (Goodwin P LLP) -620 8th Av -NY 10018

(212) 762-5394 .. **Stern,** Zachary D '98 Morgan Stanley -1221 Av of Amer -NY 10020

(212) 210-1400 .. **Sternbach,** David G '97 %A&E TV Network -235 E 45th -NY 10017

(212) 661-4040 .. **Sternbach,** Robt A '84 -274 Mad Av -NY 10016 **Fx:**679-6302

(718) 748-8080 .. **Sternback,** Cary R '93 (Heitner & B) -26 Court -Brklyn 11242

(212) 947-1999 .. **Sternback,** Lori Brown '94 Cnsl Methfessel & W,PC -450 7th Av -NY 10123

(716) 839-2700 .. **Sternberg,** Barry H '87 -4245 Union Rd -Buffalo 14225 **Fx:**839-2977

(212) 225-2000 .. **Sternberg,** Danl S '80 (Cleary GS&H) -1 Lbrty Plz -NY 10006

(212) 490-3000 .. **Sternberg,** Dov G '03 %Wilson EME&D LLP -150 E 42nd -NY 10017

(718) 250-2000 .. **Sternberg,** Efrat '09 %DA -350 Jay -Brklyn 11201 **Fx:**250-2314

(212) 776-5000 .. **Sternberg,** Gerald C '77 %NYC Housing Auth -250 Bway -NY 10007 **Fx:**776-5039

(516) 569-8100 .. **Sternberg,** Ilyse Gellar '88 (Rosenfeld & M) -132 Spruce -Cedarhrst 11516

(212) 907-0851 .. **Sternberg,** Jos V '67 (Labaton S LLP) -140 Bway -NY 10005

(516) 571-3800 .. **Sternberg,** Judith R '74 %DA -262 Old Cntry Rd -Mineola 11501 **Fx:**248-9479

(212) 319-0560 .. **Sternberg,** Kenneth S '84 -270 Mad Av -NY 10016 **Fx:**980-7660

(212) 836-8000 .. **Sternberg,** Laurie J '98 Cnsl Kaye S LLP -425 Park Av -NY 10022

(212) 909-6000 .. **Sternberg**, Luke T '04 %Debevoise & P LLP -919 3rd Av -NY 10022
(646) 313-6524 .. **Sternberg**, Marc J '09 Blackstone Grp LP -345 Park Av -NY 10154
(646) 471-4000 .. **Sternberg**, Mark A '09 %PricewaterhouseCoopers LLP -300 Mad Av -NY 10017
(212) 506-5000 .. **Sternberg**, Peter R '86 (Orrick H&S LLP) -51 W 52nd -NY 10019
(518) 686-4331 .. **Sternberg**, Rolf M '74 (Sternberg & G,LLP) -5 Main Bx68 -Hoosick Fls 12090 **Fx:**686-7596
(212) 788-1070 .. **Sternberg**, Ronald E '74 %Law Dept -100 Church -NY 10007 **Fx:**788-0367
(718) 263-8205 .. **Sternberg**, Steven '83 -118-21 Qns Blvd -Frst Hlls 11375
(718) 722-3100 .. **Sternberg**, Susan R '82 %Leg Aid -111 Lvngstn -Brklyn 11201 **Fx:**722-3093
(212) 701-3000 .. **Sterner**, Amy K '07 %Cahill G&R LLP -80 Pine -NY 10005 **Fx:**269-5420
(718) 875-1892 .. **Sterner**, Anders R '70 -546 Rugby Rd -Brklyn 11230 **Fx:**875-2033
(518) 436-0344 .. **Sternheimer**, Joann '96 (Deily M&G,LLP) -8 Thurlow Ter -Albany 12203
(212) 715-9100 .. **Sternhell**, Michl J '03 %Kramer LN&F,LLP -1177 Av of Amer -NY 10036
(212) 849-7000 .. **Sternhell**, Philip C '07 %Quinn EU&S,LLP -51 Mad Av -NY 10010
(718) 261-9300 .. **Sternick**, Mark C '81 -105-14 Metro Av -Frst Hlls 11375 **Fx:**261-0800
(212) 702-9580 .. **Sternin**, Erica L '98 TSG Reporting Inc -747 3rd Av -NY 10017
(212) 619-0099 .. **Sternklar**, Cindy '91 -156 William -NY 10038 **Fx:**619-2683
(212) 440-4400 .. **Sternklar**, Theo '58 (Buchanan I&R PC) -620 8th Av -NY 10018
(917) 825-1740 .. **Sternlicht**, David G '92 -2628 Bway -NY 10025
(212) 664-4444 .. **Sternlicht**, David N '83 %NBC -30 Rckfllr Plz -NY 10112 **Fx:**262-4955
(631) 277-3900 .. **Sternlicht**, Steven A '67 -1000 Main -Pt Jffrsn 11777 **Fx:**277-3928
(212) 916-7300 .. **Sternlieb**, David F '89 %Atlantic Philanthropies -75 Varick -NY 10013
(212) 687-6262 .. **Sternlieb**, Joanne R '88 Cnsl Barton B&P,LLP -420 Lex Av -NY 10170
(212) 996-2971 .. **Sternlieb**, Joanne R '88 -250 E 87th -NY 10128 **Fx:**427-5645
(212) 940-7060 .. **Sternman**, Joel W '70 (Katten MR LLP) -575 Mad Av -NY 10022
(212) 318-6000 .. **Sternoff**, Joshua H '96 (Paul HJ&W LLP) -75 E 55th -NY 10022
(845) 634-3696 .. **Sterns**, James E '59 OfCnsl I Becker,LLC -49 Maple Av Bx796 -New Cty 10956 **Fx:**634-3019
(212) 210-9530 .. **Sterns**, Wm S III '78 (Alston & B LLP) -90 Park Av -NY 10016
(212) 653-8700 .. **Sternstein**, Malani Jan '03 (Sheppard MR&H LLP) -30 Rckfllr Plz -NY 10112
(212) 325-0957 .. **Sternthal**, Robt J '96 Credit Suisse -11 Mad Av -NY 10010
(518) 383-9440 .. **Sterrett**, Grace '75 (Hudson C LLP) -636 Plnk Rd -Clifton Pk 12065
(212) 351-4000 .. **Sterrett**, Kelli E '05 %Gibson D&C LLP -200 Park Av -NY 10166
(518) 487-7600 .. **Sterthous**, Michl G '92 (Whiteman O&H LLP) -1 Commerce Plz -Albany 12260
(212) 553-0300 .. **Stesney**, Linda A '84 %Moody's Invstr Srvc -250 Greenwich -NY 10007
(718) 788-2100 .. **Stetch**, Jack '62 -244 Prospect Park W -Brklyn 11215
(347) 404-9400 .. **Stetson**, Fredric W '90 %Criminal Ct -120 Schermerhorn -Brklyn 11201 **Fx:**(718) 643-3538
(631) 234-4848 .. **Stettine**, Richd A '71 R Stettine,PC -320 Carleton Av -Central Islip 11722 **Fx:**415-4809
(212) 407-6152 .. **Stetz**, Carl E '89 HSH Nordbnk AG -230 Park -NY 10169
(212) 506-2500 .. **Steuer**, Richd M '74 (Mayer B LLP) -1675 Bway -NY 10019
(631) 451-6500 .. **Steuerwald**, Harold A '88 %Brookhaven Law Dept -1 Indpndnc Hill -Farmngvll 11738 **Fx:**698-4489
(518) 445-2311 .. **Steuerwald**, Holly E '98 Albany Law Schl -80 New Scotland Av -Albany 12208
(716) 683-0343 .. **Stevanovic**, D Danl '89 -3729 Union -Buffalo 14225
(518) 457-0036 .. **Steve**, Paul A '80 %Tax Dept -Bldg 8 State Ofc Campus -Albany 12227
(212) 431-2197 .. **Stevelman**, Faith '90 %NY Law Schl -185 W Bway -NY 10013 **Fx:**431-1830
(914) 763-6114 .. **Stevelman**, Paul D '89 -Peaceable -S Salem 10590
(212) 421-4100 .. **Stevens**, Amanda C '09 %Pryor C LLP -7 Times Sq -NY 10036
(212) 486-6060 .. **Stevens**, Arlene '09 %Trief & O -150 E 58th -NY 10155
(518) 719-3540 .. **Stevens**, Carol D '80 Greene Cnty Atty -411 Main -Catskill 12414 **Fx:**719-3790
(212) 735-3000 .. **Stevens**, Catherine Brand '04 Cnsl Skadden ASM&F LLP -4 Times Sq -NY 10036
(518) 485-9489 .. **Stevens**, Christine B '98 %Dept Tax & Fin -WA Harriman Campus Bldg 8 -Albany 12227 **Fx:**457-3836
(718) 389-8841 .. **Stevens**, Damon T '87 (Stevens & M) -835 Manh Av -Brklyn 11222
(607) 565-2775 .. **Stevens**, Dorothy K '97 -438 Park Av -Waverly 14892
(516) 484-2271 .. **Stevens**, Elaine M '05 -23 Milburn Ln -East Hills 11577
(212) 883-1700 .. **Stevens**, Erica L '08 %Duval & S LLP -101 Park Av -NY 10178
(212) 474-1000 .. **Stevens**, Felicia S '86 Cravath S&M LLP -825 8th Av -NY 10019
(212) 878-7900 .. **Stevens**, Fred N '00 (Fox R LLP) -100 Park Av -NY 10017
(212) 421-6492 .. **Stevens**, Garry T Jr. '09 %Squitieri & F,LLP -32 E 57th -NY 10022 **Fx:**421-6553
(212) 864-4445 .. **Stevens Hinds & White,PC** -116 W 111th -NY 10026 **Fx:**222-2680
(212) 873-0389 .. **Stevens**, Howard L '63 -320 Cntrl Pk W -NY 10025
(718) 838-7878 .. **Stevens**, Jacob L '94 %Bronx Defenders -860 Crtlandt Av -Bronx 10451 **Fx:**665-0100
(315) 474-2943 .. **Stevens**, James G Jr. '77 (Sugarman Law Firm,LLP) -211 W Jffrsn -Syracuse 13202
(212) 509-3900 .. **Stevens**, Jane G '78 (Mitchell S&K LLP) -12 E 49th -NY 10017
(212) 613-5031 .. **Stevens**, Jane Greengold '76 %Leg Assist Grp -450 W 33rd -NY 10001 **Fx:**750-0820
(516) 747-2075 .. **Stevens**, Joanne Ellen '86 (JE Stevens,PC) -1225 Franklin Av -Gdn Cty 11530 **Fx:**747-1019
(607) 273-3339 .. **Stevens**, John Alden '81 (Williamson C&S) -317 N Tioga Bx126 -Ithaca 14850
(212) 626-4100 .. **Stevens**, Jonathan A '98 (Baker & M LLP) -1114 Av of Amer -NY 10036
(718) 855-9000 .. **Stevens**, Jos P '69 Cnsl Cullen and D LLP -177 Montague -Brklyn 11201
(516) 294-8844 .. **Stevens**, Keith J '01 %L'Abbate BC&C,LLP -1001 Franklin Av -Gdn Cty 11530
(914) 428-1826 .. **Stevens**, Kerry B '84 -15 Stewart Pl -White Plns 10603 **Fx:**428-1827
(845) 357-9144 .. **Stevens**, Kevin A '89 -98 Lafayette Av -Suffern 10901 **Fx:**357-4848
(212) 319-8500 .. **Stevens & Lee PC** -485 Mad Av -NY 10022 **Fx:**319-8505
(518) 402-4437 .. **Stevens**, Mark R '08 State Comptroller -110 State -Albany 12236 **Fx:**473-9104
(212) 504-6000 .. **Stevens**, Michl A '10 %Cadwalader W&T LLP -1 World Fncl Ctr -NY 10281
(212) 490-3000 .. **Stevens**, Michl N '75 (Wilson EME&D LLP) -150 E 42nd -NY 10017
(718) 389-8841 .. **Stevens & Moszczynski** -835 Manh Av -Brklyn 11222 **Fx:**349-3482
(212) 431-4638 .. **Stevens**, Neal R '99 -150 Franklin -NY 10013
(212) 335-4500 .. **Stevens**, Rachel V '05 (DLA Piper LLP) -1251 Av of Amer -NY 10020
(585) 227-8600 .. **Stevens**, Robt E '77 -2450 Ridge Rd W -Rchstr 14626 **Fx:**227-1075
(718) 694-4350 .. **Stevens**, Robin C '82 %Transit Auth -130 Lvngstn -Brklyn 11201 **Fx:**488-6458
(914) 633-7500 .. **Stevens**, Roger R '80 PMS Construction Mgmt -92 North Av -New Rchll 10801 **Fx:**633-0407
(212) 228-7273 .. **Stevens**, Sanford S '86 S Stevens,PC -244 Mad Av -NY 10016 **Fx:**228-7273
(212) 994-0621 .. **Stevens**, Shannon G '10 Vantage Prtnrs,LLC -767 3rd Av -NY 10017 **Fx:**994-0622
(212) 536-3900 .. **Stevens**, Terrell T '06 %K&L Gates LLP -599 Lex Av -NY 10022
(212) 374-7645 .. **Stevens**, Terri A '01 NYC Dept Educ-OLS -52 Chmbrs -NY 10007
(718) 357-7075 .. **Stevens**, Thos Robt '82 -331 Willis Av -Mineola 11501 **Fx:**(516) 248-4405
(860) 275-6701 .. **Stevens**, Tiffany L '07 %McCarter & E,LLP -245 Park Av -NY 10167 **Fx:**724-3397
(315) 336-4500 .. **Stevens**, Wm R '65 (O'Shea M&S,LLP) -107 W Lbrty Bx4310 -Rome 13442
(212) 909-9604 .. **Stevens-Haynes**, Mia A '04 %Wachtel & M,LLP -885 2nd Av -NY 10017 **Fx:**909-9415
(631) 852-2500 .. **Stevens-Messina**, Leslie A '06 %DA -200 Center Dr -Rvrhead 11901 **Fx:**852-1769
(212) 349-9090 .. **Stevenson**, Douglas B '82 %Seaman's Church Inst -241 Water -NY 10038 **Fx:**349-8342
(212) 592-1400 .. **Stevenson**, Edw B '09 (Herrick,F LLP) -2 Park Av -NY 10016
(585) 530-3283 .. **Stevenson**, James D '83 Hon N Smith -50 East Av -Rchstr 14604
(212) 344-8700 .. **Stevenson**, John M '88 Country-Wide Ins -40 Wall -NY 10005 **Fx:**514-7291
(315) 437-6655 .. **Stevenson**, Kathleen A '85 UAW Lgl Srvcs Plan -6712 Brooklawn Pkwy -Syracuse 13211 **Fx:**432-9341
(914) 686-1700 .. **Stevenson**, Kimberly '07 %O'Connor R,LLP -200 Mamaroneck Av -White Plns 10601
(516) 572-2000 .. **Stevenson**, Kimberly D '08 %DA -99 Main -Hempstd 11550 **Fx:**572-2606
(212) 446-4800 .. **Stevenson**, Lee Ann '99 (Kirkland & E LLP) -153 E 53rd -NY 10022
(212) 219-1800 .. **Stevenson**, Neil '83 %Lawyers Alliance NY -171 Mad Av -NY 10016 **Fx:**941-7458
(212) 326-3939 .. **Stevenson**, Pantea Farhi '09 %Jones D -222 E 41st -NY 10017
(518) 445-2371 .. **Stevenson**, Sandra M '72 %Albany Law Schl -80 New Scotland Av -Albany 12208 **Fx:**445-2315
(315) 788-5100 .. **Stever**, Arthur C III '77 (Conboy MB&K,LLP) -407 Sherman -Watertwn 13601
(716) 851-7190 .. **Stever**, David F '77 %DEC -270 Mich Av -Buffalo 14203 **Fx:**851-7211
(212) 536-3900 .. **Stever**, Donald W Jr. '83 (K&L Gates LLP) -599 Lex Av -NY 10022
(212) 292-8300 .. **Stever**, Tara Constance '99 Cnsl Spring Mtn Cptl,LP -65 E 55th -NY 10022
(845) 562-0203 .. **Steves**, Edw M '79 %Finkelstein & Prtnrs,LLP -1279 Route 300 Bx1111 -Newburgh 12550
(212) 237-1000 .. **Stevinson**, Douglas A '99 (Windels ML&M,LLP) -156 W 56th -NY 10019
(716) 626-1330 .. **Steward**, Annemarie E '01 -2801 Wehrle Dr -Buffalo 14221
(646) 708-8098 .. **Steward**, Ethan J '04 Fidelity National Law Grp -350 5th Av -NY 10118
(212) 308-2210 .. **Steward**, Nicole S '08 %Eviction Intrvntn Srvcs -1233 2nd Av -NY 10065 **Fx:**888-7140
(212) 416-8000 .. **Steward**, Priscilla I '99 %Dept of Law -120 Bway -NY 10271
(212) 270-1025 .. **Stewart**, Adrian R '02 JP Morgan Chase -270 Park Av -NY 10017
(212) 506-1700 .. **Stewart**, Anna L '07 %Kasowitz BT&F LLP -1633 Bway -NY 10019
(212) 450-4000 .. **Stewart**, Arthur Brendan '05 %Davis P&W LLP -450 Lex Av -NY 10017
(212) 625-9696 .. **Stewart**, Brenna L '95 LegalEase -350 Bway -NY 10013 **Fx:**625-3939
(518) 483-4330 .. **Stewart**, Brian S '83 (Hughes S&R,PC) -31 Elm Bx788 -Malone 12953
(212) 450-4000 .. **Stewart**, Carson T '08 %Davis P&W LLP -450 Lex Av -NY 10017
(212) 239-5500 .. **Stewart**, Chas A III '88 (Stewart O,LLP) -65 W 36th -NY 10018
(845) 855-5900 .. **Stewart**, Chas E III '83 OfCnsl Daniels & P,LLP -517 Route 22 -Pawling 12564
(212) 704-9600 .. **Stewart**, Chas Evan '78 (Zuckerman S,LLP) -1540 Bway -NY 10036
(718) 527-9862 .. **Stewart**, Charmaine M '92 (Stewart Law Firm,LLP) -133-40 Hook Crk Blvd -Rosedale 11422 **Fx:**527-7624
(212) 941-9090 .. **Stewart**, Christa M '97 %The Door -121 Av of Amer -NY 10013 **Fx:**941-0714
(315) 363-7777 .. **Stewart**, Christine L '89 %Suttmeier Law Firm -233 Cedar -Oneida 13421 **Fx:**363-9401
(212) 715-1000 .. **Stewart**, Craig A '84 (Arnold & P LLP) -399 Park Av -NY 10022
(516) 742-3636 .. **Stewart**, Crystal T '06 %Brecher FPWT&Z,PC -1325 Franklin Av -Gdn Cty 11530
(518) 793-3424 .. **Stewart**, Danl J '89 %Brennan & W LLP -163 Haviland Rd -Queensbury 12804 **Fx:**793-3422
(212) 487-9700 .. **Stewart**, Danl M '97 (White F&F,LLP) -61 Bway -NY 10006
(212) 847-8315 .. **Stewart**, Darnley D '93 Giskan S&A -11 Bway -NY 10004 **Fx:**(646) 520-3235
(212) 906-1200 .. **Stewart**, David M '88 (Latham & W) -885 3rd Av -NY 10022
(315) 474-6448 .. **Stewart**, David M '02 %Byrne C&P PC -100 Madison -Syracuse 13202

(516) 433-6677 .. **Stewart,** Donald R '77 (Stewart GM&B) -6800 Jericho Tpk -Syosset 11791
(212) 864-4445 .. **Stewart,** Gareth Winston '88 Stevens H&W,PC -116 W 111th -NY 10026
(212) 625-9696 .. **Stewart,** Geoffrey S '90 -350 Bway -NY 10013 **Fx:**625-3939
(516) 433-6677 .. **Stewart Greenblatt Manning & Baez** -6800 Jericho Tpk -Syosset 11791 **Fx:**433-4342
(716) 847-0662 .. **Stewart,** Gregory J '87 SrCnsl Volunteer Lwyrs Prjt -237 Main -Buffalo 14203 **Fx:**847-0307
(914) 347-5522 .. **Stewart,** H Malcolm III '77 %D Frum -565 Taxter Rd -Elmsfrd 10523 **Fx:**347-8760
(718) 312-4245 .. **Stewart,** Hazel L '92 Empire Blue Cross/Blue Shield -15 MetroTech Ctr -Brklyn 11201
(585) 227-1812 .. **Stewart,** Henry Scovel '82 -42 Interlaken Rd -Rchstr 14612 **Fx:**227-1812
(585) 271-7918 .. **Stewart,** James C '68 -354 Wstmnstr Rd -Rchstr 14607 **Fx:**271-8936
(516) 512-6333 .. **Stewart,** James F '92 (Gold SKB LLP) -1025 Old Cntry Rd -Westbury 11590
(212) 456-7777 .. **Stewart,** Jane B '86 %ABC -77 W 66th -NY 10023 **Fx:**456-6202
(212) 259-8000 .. **Stewart,** Jennifer M '09 %Dewey & L LLP -1301 Av of Amer -NY 10019
(516) 739-0400 .. **Stewart,** John J Jr. '67 %Kelly R&K,LLP -330 Old Cntry Rd -Mineola 11501
(518) 455-7500 .. **Stewart,** Kelly Ann '94 NYS Legislature -310 Cptl -Albany 12210
(212) 848-4000 .. **Stewart,** Kyla J '09 %Shearman & S LLP -599 Lex Av -NY 10022
(212) 351-4000 .. **Stewart,** Ladan F '05 %Gibson D&C LLP -200 Park Av -NY 10166
(718) 483-3000 .. **Stewart,** Leonard W '91 %Miracle Makers,Inc -510 Gates Av -Brklyn 11216
(718) 250-2000 .. **Stewart,** Matthew S '99 %DA -350 Jay -Brklyn 11201 **Fx:**250-2314
(212) 605-6200 .. **Stewart,** Melissa L '04 Levy P&K,LLP -800 3rd Av -NY 10022
(718) 823-0217 .. **Stewart,** Mildred L '86 -1966 Newbold Av -Bronx 10472
(718) 238-6500 .. **Stewart,** Miles J M '09 Connors & S,PC -7408 5th Av -Brklyn 11209
(718) 527-9862 .. **Stewart,** Nadira S '03 %Stewart Law Firm,LLP -133-40 Hook Crk Blvd -Rosedale 11422 **Fx:**527-7624
(631) 286-0858 .. **Stewart,** Nina Greenfield '93 -Bx463 -Bellprt 11713 **Fx:**776-0609
(212) 239-5500 .. **Stewart Occhipinti,LLP** -65 W 36th -NY 10018 **Fx:**239-7030
(631) 293-4992 .. **Stewart,** Paul P '83 Advanced CleanUp Tech -960 S Bway -Hicksvll 11801
(718) 720-1514 .. **Stewart,** Quentin M '72 -12 Coughlan Av -Staten Isl 10310
(315) 422-7000 .. **Stewart,** Robt J III '98 Pyramid Mgmt Grp,Inc -4 Clinton Sq -Syracuse 13202 **Fx:**472-4035
(212) 331-5149 .. **Stewart,** Samantha L '02 HRA-OLA -180 Water -NY 10038 **Fx:**331-5023
(212) 384-1000 .. **Stewart,** Sharon M '96 FBI -26 Fed Plz -NY 10278
(585) 273-5824 .. **Stewart,** Sue Stern '67 %Univ of Rochester Med Ctr -Bx278979 -Rchstr 14627 **Fx:**272-9311
(212) 270-2166 .. **Stewart,** Tab T '97 %JP Morgan Chase & Co -270 Park Av -NY 10017 **Fx:**270-7467
(212) 373-3000 .. **Stewart,** Tarun M '97 (Paul WRW&G LLP) -1285 Av of Amer -NY 10019
(914) 323-7000 .. **Stewart,** Tracey A '08 %Wilson EME&D LLP -3 Gannett Dr -White Plns 10604
(212) 608-1900 .. **Stewart,** Victor E '80 (Lovell SH LLP) -61 Bway -NY 10006
(631) 351-3042 .. **Stewart-Suchow,** Johanna M '00 %Town Atty -100 Main -Huntngtn 11743 **Fx:**351-3032
(212) 574-1200 .. **Steyer,** Hume R '79 (Seward & K LLP) -1 Bttry Pk Plz -NY 10004
(212) 297-5800 .. **Stiber,** Cecilia Zhang '06 %Day P LLP -7 Times Sq -NY 10036
(212) 267-7600 .. **Stich,** David P '91 (Solomon PBH&S LLP) -40 Wall -NY 10005
(347) 296-1658 .. **Stichinsky,** Jeffrey S '69 %Supreme Ct Law Dept -360 Adams -Brklyn 11201 **Fx:**643-6114
(212) 751-3488 .. **Stichter,** John A '61 -9 E 40th -NY 10016 **Fx:**486-1600
(212) 435-3571 .. **Stickelman,** Timothy G '91 %Port Auth of NY/NJ -225 Park Av S -NY 10003 **Fx:**435-3555
(631) 501-5700 .. **Stickler,** Ira '08 %Carter DF&S LLP -445 Broadhallow Rd -Melvll 11747
(212) 907-6442 .. **Stickler,** Margaret E '04 (Conaway & S,PC) -4045 Lex Av -NY 10174
(212) 455-2000 .. **Stickler,** Steven C '90 SrCnsl Simpson T&B LLP -425 Lex Av -NY 10017
(718) 263-6430 .. **Stidolph,** Robt A '74 -103-08 Metro Av -Frst Hlls 11375 **Fx:**544-2763
(914) 949-1305 .. **Stiebel,** Robin L '80 %Leg Srvcs -90 Maple Av -White Plns 10601 **Fx:**949-6213
(212) 836-8000 .. **Stiefel,** Aaron '82 (Kaye S LLP) -425 Park Av -NY 10022
(212) 809-2663 .. **Stiefel,** Bryna J '02 Bondholder Comm Grp -30 Broad -NY 10004
(212) 755-2800 .. **Stiefel & Cohen** -770 Lex Av -NY 10065 **Fx:**755-4199
(212) 755-2800 .. **Stiefel,** George '72 (Stiefel & C) -770 Lex Av -NY 10065
(716) 854-2100 .. **Stiefel,** Jack G '75 (Lewis & L,PC) -37 Franklin -Buffalo 14202 **Fx:**854-0433
(212) 335-4500 .. **Stiefel,** Spencer '07 %DLA Piper LLP -1251 Av of Amer -NY 10020
(518) 943-4330 .. **Stiefel & Winans** -331 Main -Catskill 12414 **Fx:**943-2123
(212) 506-1700 .. **Stieglitz,** Eric J '08 %Kasowitz BT&F LLP -1633 Bway -NY 10019
(212) 233-0350 .. **Stieglitz,** Michl P '73 (Sobel RF&S,LLP) -150 Bway -NY 10038
(212) 701-3000 .. **Stieglitz,** Richd A Jr. '04 %Cahill G&R LLP -80 Pine -NY 10005 **Fx:**269-5420
(631) 935-1616 .. **Stiene,** Chas G '86 Stiene & Assoc,PC -187 E Main -Huntngtn 11743 **Fx:**935-1223
(212) 450-4000 .. **Stier,** David A '04 %Davis P&W LLP -450 Lex Av -NY 10017
(516) 829-9595 .. **Stier,** Eileen D '85 (Busell & S PLLC) -98 Cuttermill Rd -Gt Neck 11021
(212) 362-7044 .. **Stier,** Jeff A '97 %Amer Cncl on Sci & Hlth -1995 Bway -NY 10023
(845) 292-6544 .. **Stier,** Lawr '52 -65 Willey Av Bx70 -Liberty 12754
(914) 934-5200 .. **Stier,** Mitchell J '87 Universal American Fncl Corp -6 Intl Dr -Rye Brook 10573
(212) 318-6000 .. **Stiffle,** Dean A '71 (Paul HJ&W LLP) -75 E 55th -NY 10022
(212) 640-5704 .. **Stigliani,** Linda A '82 %Amer Exp -200 Vesey -NY 10285 **Fx:**619-8755
(518) 436-3404 .. **Stiglmeier,** Carol R '94 (Bixby C&S,PLLC) -19 Dove -Albany 12210
(518) 463-3385 .. **Stiglmeier,** Eileen M '03 -600 Bway -Albany 12207 **Fx:**463-3440
(212) 371-8855 .. **Stikeman Elliott LLP** -445 Park Av -NY 10022 **Fx:**371-7087
(845) 496-2946 .. **Stiles,** David J '89 -4 Shea Knolls Ct -Campbell Hall 10916 **Fx:**496-8046
(212) 854-0490 .. **Stiles,** Deborah F '75 Columbia Univ -535 W 116th MC 4310 -NY 10027
(631) 727-2180 .. **Stiles,** Lauren E '07 %Twomey LSKD&Q,LLP -33 W 2nd Bx9398 -Rvrhead 11901
(212) 259-8000 .. **Stiles,** Mae A '08 %Dewey & L LLP -1301 Av of Amer -NY 10019
(585) 394-3400 .. **Still,** Ann Hollingsworth '95 Finger Lakes Comm Cllg -4355 Lakeshr Dr -Canandaigua 14424
(914) 824-5070 .. **Still,** Eddie '82 %Atty Grievance Comm -399 Knollwood Rd -White Plns 10603 **Fx:**949-0997
(516) 222-7929 .. **Stiller,** Craig S '95 %Pressler & P LLP -305 Bway -NY 10007 **Fx:**(973) 753-5353
(716) 854-4474 .. **Stiller,** David G '64 (Stiller & V) -300 Pearl -Buffalo 14202
(716) 856-4400 .. **Stiller,** Douglas P '92 -181 Franklin -Buffalo 14202
(585) 232-5300 .. **Stiller,** Sharon P '76 (Boylan BCV&W,LLP) -2400 Chase Sq -Rchstr 14604
(716) 854-4474 .. **Stiller & Vance** -300 Pearl -Buffalo 14202
(716) 204-9480 .. **Stillman,** Alicia S '97 %SJ Baum,PC -900 Merchants Cncrs -Westbury 11590 **Fx:**204-9680
(914) 461-3222 .. **Stillman,** Amy S '92 OfCnsl Kipness & Assoc -460 Old Post Rd -Bedfrd 10506 **Fx:**(800) 414-2044
(212) 223-0200 .. **Stillman,** Chas A '62 (Stillman F&S,PC) -425 Park Av -NY 10022
(914) 723-0443 .. **Stillman,** Dianne B '77 -194 Nelson Rd -Scarsdale 10583
(212) 223-0200 .. **Stillman Friedman & Shechtman,PC** -425 Park Av -NY 10022 **Fx:**223-1942
(212) 686-2400 .. **Stillman,** Irwin '57 %Stillman Organization Ltd -505 Park Av -NY 10022 **Fx:**686-5650
(718) 828-1400 .. **Stillman,** Jeffrey S '89 (Stillman & S,PC) -2622 E Tremont Av -Bronx 10461
(845) 534-3439 .. **Stillman,** Mark C '87 -9 Stillwood Rd -Cornwall-On-Hud 12520
(718) 828-1400 .. **Stillman,** Marvin '65 OfCnsl Stillman & S,PC -2622 E Tremont Av -Bronx 10461
(718) 250-2000 .. **Stillman,** Nancy '06 DA -350 Jay -Brklyn 11201 **Fx:**250-2314
(914) 961-9400 .. **Stillman,** Roy A '74 -1101 Mdlnd Av -Bronxvll 10708
(212) 686-2400 .. **Stillman,** Roy A '89 Stillman Dvlpmnt Intl -505 Park Av -NY 10022
(718) 828-1400 .. **Stillman & Stillman,PC** -2622 E Tremont Av -Bronx 10461 **Fx:**828-9494
(518) 473-2181 .. **Stillman,** W Bartlett '75 %OCFS -52 Wshngtn -Rensselaer 12144
(914) 935-5300 .. **Stillo,** Maria T '01 %Compass Grp USA -3 Intl Dr -Rye Brook 10573
(212) 836-7366 .. **Stillufsen,** Andrew Davin '04 %Kaye S LLP -425 Park Av -NY 10022 **Fx:**836-6304
(212) 819-8200 .. **Stillwaggon,** James '75 OfCnsl White & C LLP -1155 Av of Amer -NY 10036
(716) 856-5012 .. **Stillwell,** David M '88 (Anspach ME,LLP) -2400 Main Pl Twr -Buffalo 14202
(212) 705-7000 .. **Stillwell,** Robt C '08 %Bingham M LLP -399 Park Av -NY 10022
(914) 472-7669 .. **Stilo,** Teresa '90 -41 Tewkesbury Rd -Scarsdale 10583
(716) 634-8307 .. **Stilwell,** Raymond C '85 -17 Beresford Ct -Buffalo 14221
(718) 442-1182 .. **Stilwell,** Rodney '83 (Tracy & S,PC) -1688 Victory Blvd -Staten Isl 10314 **Fx:**442-0552
(212) 977-7950 .. **Stim,** Stephen G '81 Stim Multimedia -Bx792 -Hicksvll 11802
(212) 541-2000 .. **Stimell,** Steven M '88 (Bryan C LLP) -1290 Av of Amer -NY 10104
(718) 229-3507 .. **Stimler,** Bernard '75 -53-16 244th -Douglastn 11362 **Fx:**423-9339
(212) 688-0800 .. **Stimmel,** Todd R '80 -570 Lex Av -NY 10022
(516) 357-3000 .. **Stimpfl,** Wendy A '96 %Rivkin R LLP -926 RXR Plz -Uniondale 11556
(212) 643-7000 .. **Stimpson,** Scott D '90 (Sills C&G PC) -One Rckfllr Plz -NY 10020
(212) 619-8387 .. **Stinaroff,** Diana '08 %J O'Malley,PC -299 Bway -NY 10007 **Fx:**406-2967
(718) 721-3240 .. **Stincone,** Diego R '55 -31-16 30th Av -LIC 11102 **Fx:**728-2069
(212) 759-4600 .. **Stine,** Carl L '90 (Wolf P LLP) -845 3rd Av -NY 10022
(212) 512-0810 .. **Stine,** Martha Cohen '80 (Cohen HB&R,PC) -11 W 42nd -NY 10036
(914) 591-5044 .. **Stine,** Michele Porto '82 -783 Sleepy Hllw Rd -Briarcliff Mnr 10510
(212) 382-6600 .. **Stine Poles,** Laura A '92 %NYC Bar -42 W 44th -NY 10036 **Fx:**398-6634
(718) 657-8951 .. **Stingone,** Pascal W '64 -85-44 148th -Jamaica 11435 **Fx:**657-1850
(518) 285-8987 .. **Stinson,** Jos D '98 %Hon W McCarthy Applt Div -16 Eagle -Albany 12207
(518) 640-5148 .. **Stinton,** Keith J '94 AYCO -25 British Amer Blvd -Latham 12110
(315) 442-0100 .. **Stinziano,** Francis D '61 (Gilberti SH&S,PC) -555 E Genesee -Syracuse 13202
(315) 442-0100 .. **Stinziano,** Francis D Jr. '98 (Gilberti SH&S,PC) -555 E Genesee -Syracuse 13202
(716) 854-6600 .. **Stirling,** Howard J '78 -135 Delaware Av -Buffalo 14202 **Fx:**856-1008
(212) 735-3000 .. **Stirling,** Kelann Brook '05 %Skadden ASM&F LLP -4 Times Sq -NY 10036
(845) 358-7772 .. **Stiskin,** Ronald E '96 Summit Childrens Residence Ctr -339 N Bway -Upper Nyack 10960
(212) 412-9500 .. **Stitelman,** Emily K '06 %Flemming ZWZ LLP -1 Lbrty Plz -NY 10006
(212) 902-1000 .. **Stites,** Stephen W '02 %Goldman Sachs -200 West -NY 10282
(212) 480-3030 .. **Stith,** Gene M '97 %M Pressman -125 Maiden Ln -NY 10038 **Fx:**480-2590
(585) 576-8010 .. **Stivers,** Michl W '02 -Bx204 -Leicester 14481
(914) 750-5933 .. **Stivrins,** Jennifer R '07 %Kissel H&W LLP -580 Wht Plns Rd -Tarrytwn 10591
(914) 285-1820 .. **Stix,** Wayne P '75 -333 Wstchstr Av -White Plns 10604 **Fx:**285-1822
(516) 742-6546 .. **Stober,** Louis D Jr. '84 (L Stober Jr,LLC) -350 Old Cntry Rd -Gdn Cty 11530 **Fx:**742-8603
(973) 778-0130 .. **Stober,** Robt L '75 -974 Putnam Av -Merrick 11566 **Fx:**779-0996
(646) 414-6886 .. **Stock,** Alice B '87 (Lowenstein S PC) -1251 Av of Amer -NY 10020 **Fx:**(973) 422-6891
(718) 579-7944 .. **Stock,** Barbara '89 %Leg Aid -900 Sheridan Av -Bronx 10451 **Fx:**293-8744
(914) 997-7100 .. **Stock,** Danl H '85 (Berman BF&G pc) -123 Main -White Plns 10601
(212) 918-3000 .. **Stock,** Eric J '99 (Hogan L LLP) -875 3rd Av -NY 10022
(518) 438-0752 .. **Stock,** Roy H '83 -9 Gadsen Ct -Albany 12205 **Fx:**453-9552

(516) 747-2478 ..**Stock,** Thos J '79 TJ Stock & Assoc -88 2nd -Mineola 11501 **Fx:**747-2574
(212) 809-7600 ..**Stock,** Wm B '84 %Cheven K&H -40 Wall -NY 10005
(585) 697-5100 ..**Stockdale,** Chas B '81 Fibertech Ntwks LLC -300 Meridian Centre -Rchstr 14618
(212) 765-5070 ..**Stockell,** Catherine H '86 OfCnsl Fish & R,PC -153 E 53rd -NY 10022
(516) 676-2715 ..**Stockell,** Mercer L '49 -7 Pine Low -Glen Cove 11542
(716) 505-2700 ..**Stocker,** Kevin T '91 (Felle S&M,LLC) -6024 Main -Williamsvll 14221 **Fx:**506-2727
(212) 907-0700 ..**Stocker,** Michl W '06 OfCnsl Labaton S LLP -140 Bway -NY 10005
(212) 355-9500 ..**Stocking,** Alison '08 %Lieff CH&B,LLP -250 Hudson -NY 10013
(212) 909-6000 ..**Stockley,** Molly '88 %Debevoise & P LLP -919 3rd Av -NY 10022
(518) 449-3125 ..**Stockli Greene Slevin & Peters, LLP** -90 State -Albany 12207 **Fx:**449-4798
(518) 449-3125 ..**Stockli,** John P Jr. '89 (Stockli GS&P,LLP) -90 State -Albany 12207
(518) 463-3200 ..**Stockli,** Patricia Betz '90 %NYS Bar Assn -1 Elk -Albany 12207 **Fx:**487-5544
(212) 788-1177 ..**Stockman,** Benjamin '07 %Law Dept -100 Church -NY 10007 **Fx:**788-0367
(516) 240-8900 ..**Stockman,** Lewis '60 OfCnsl Torre LGG&R,LLP -100 Jericho Quad -Jericho 11753
(212) 655-3500 ..**Stocks,** Remy J '10 %Meister S&F LLP -140 E 45th -NY 10017
(212) 608-1911 ..**Stockschlaeder McDonald & Sules,PC** -110 William -NY 10038 **Fx:**608-2121
(212) 233-6097 ..**Stockschlaeder,** Paul F '70 -111 Bway -NY 10006 **Fx:**566-4795
(518) 435-1919 ..**Stockton Barker & Mead, LLP** -2 Twr Pl -Albany 12203 **Fx:**435-1939
(212) 735-3000 ..**Stockton,** Jamie E '09 %Skadden ASM&F LLP -4 Times Sq -NY 10036
(518) 435-1919 ..**Stockton,** Robt S '73 (Stockton B&M,LLP) -2 Twr Pl -Albany 12203
(212) 448-9570 ..**Stockwell,** Matthew D '06 %Callahan & F,LLC -40 Exch Pl -NY 10005
(518) 474-4453 ..**Stockwell,** Shannon L '01 %MHLS -40 Steuben -Albany 12207 **Fx:**473-5849
(212) 732-9500 ..**Stoddard,** Larry O III '05 %Avelino N LLP -225 Bway -NY 10007 **Fx:**732-4580
(518) 377-1138 ..**Stoddard,** Robt J '89 -670 Franklin -Schnctdy 12305 **Fx:**377-0507
(212) 538-8217 ..**Stoddard,** Thos D '93 Credit Suisse First Boston -11 Mad Av -NY 10010
(212) 468-8000 ..**Stodola,** Damion K L '02 %Morrison & F LLP -1290 Av of Amer -NY 10104
(212) 819-8200 ..**Stodola,** Eric K '08 %White & C LLP -1155 Av of Amer -NY 10036
(212) 986-7353 ..**Stoduto,** Jos P '04 %Wingate R&S -420 Lex Av -NY 10170
(914) 750-5933 ..**Stoeberl,** Amy K '01 (Kissel H&W LLP) -580 Wht Plns Rd -Tarrytwn 10591
(212) 318-6000 ..**Stoeckel,** Sarah E '06 %Paul HJ&W LLP -75 E 55th -NY 10022
(212) 818-0080 ..**Stoecker,** Karl J '88 -425 5th Av -NY 10016 **Fx:**818-9055
(716) 856-9090 ..**Stoeckl,** Jos A '71 (Kennedy S&M) -1100 Lbrty Bldg -Buffalo 14202
(212) 336-0174 ..**Stoelting,** David P '92 %SEC -3 World Fncl Ctr -NY 10281 **Fx:**336-1323
(718) 254-7000 ..**Stoer,** Michl F '03 %US Atty -271 Cadman Plz E -Brklyn 11201 **Fx:**254-6479
(212) 969-6291 ..**Stoeterau,** Ross K '03 Alliance Bernstein LP -1345 Av of Amer -NY 10105 **Fx:**554-4639
(718) 601-5368 ..**Stoeth,** Teresa M Grant '81 -3336 Giles Pl -Bronx 10463 **Fx:**601-5368
(212) 661-8000 ..**Stoffel,** Klaus P '85 (Lucas & M,LLP) -475 Park Av S -NY 10016
(857) 212-1165 ..**Stofsky,** Adam T '05 New Media Advocacy Project -4 W 22nd -NY 10010
(718) 624-7544 ..**Stofsky,** Mark H '73 -189 Montague -Brklyn 11201 **Fx:**858-0284
(516) 222-7700 ..**Stohner,** Wm '09 %LI Power Auth -333 Earle Ovngton Blvd -Uniondale 11553 **Fx:**222-9137
(212) 265-6888 ..**Stoia,** Chas J '89 (Porzio B&N,PC) -156 W 56th -NY 10019
(212) 574-1200 ..**Stoian,** Jonathan D '09 %Seward & K LLP -1 Bttry Pk Plz -NY 10004
(516) 296-7000 ..**Stoiber,** Elke M '03 %Certilman BA&H,LLP -90 Merrick Av -E Meadow 11554
(718) 965-4025 ..**Stoil Fernandez,** Julie M '93 J Stoil Fernandez,PLLC -21 Webster Pl -Brklyn 11215 **Fx:**965-3185
(212) 489-1600 ..**Stojanow,** Victor K '01 %Deloitte LLP -1633 Bway -NY 10019 **Fx:**492-4201
(212) 489-1600 ..**Stok,** Avery I '83 %Deloitte & Touche LLP -1633 Bway -NY 10019
(212) 436-4496 ..**Stok,** Dena '08 Deloitte Tax LLP -2 World Fncl Ctr -NY 10281
(212) 925-7881 ..**Stokamer,** Michl P '66 -225 Bway -NY 10007 **Fx:**966-8253
(212) 277-4000 ..**Stokes,** Danl E '07 %Freshfields BD LLP -520 Mad Av -NY 10022
(315) 431-4000 ..**Stokes,** Francis C '86 Knudsen Leg Srvcs -2711 James -Syracuse 13206 **Fx:**431-4363
(914) 248-7759 ..**Stokes,** Harry M '91 -49 Raemont Rd Bx192 -Granite Spgs 10527 **Fx:**248-4015
(315) 655-3463 ..**Stokes,** James T '84 (Mitchell G&S,LLC) -5 Mill Bx312 -Cazenovia 13035
(212) 558-4000 ..**Stokes,** Jessica P '09 %Sullivan & C LLP -125 Broad -NY 10004
(607) 275-3152 ..**Stokes,** Jillian E '94 %Fleet Invstmnt Srvcs -202 The Cmmns -Ithaca 14850 **Fx:**275-3159
(718) 461-6633 ..**Stokes,** Kelly '03 %Mallilo & G -163-09 Nrthrn Blvd -Flushng 11358
(914) 245-5769 ..**Stokes,** Ron '77 -3224 S Shelley -Mohegan Lk 10547
(212) 701-3000 ..**Stokinger,** Mary Anne '87 %Cahill G&R LLP -80 Pine -NY 10005 **Fx:**269-5420
(718) 590-2000 ..**Stokman,** Stephanie M '08 %DA -198 E 161st -Bronx 10451 **Fx:**590-6477
(631) 393-6220 ..**Stolar,** Brian S '94 Cnsl Harras B&A LLP -445 Broad Hollow Rd -Melvll 11747
(914) 641-2067 ..**Stolar,** Kathleen S '98 %ITT Corp -1133 Wstchstr Av -White Plns 10604
(212) 219-1919 ..**Stolar,** Martin R '68 -351 Bway -NY 10013 **Fx:**941-0980
(516) 741-2585 ..**Stolar,** Sandy Jo '93 Rosicki R & Assoc,PC -51 E Bethpage Rd -Plainvw 11803 **Fx:**741-4748
(212) 386-7342 ..**Stolarik,** Debbra '98 American Greetings Corp -12 W 31st -NY 10001
(718) 237-2000 ..**Stolarz,** Brian W '02 %Leg Aid -111 Lvngstn -Brklyn 11201 **Fx:**237-8737
(631) 361-7050 ..**Stolba,** James '99 %Mullen & I,PC -300 E Main -Smithtwn 11787
(212) 508-6700 ..**Stolberg,** Juan C '07 %Tannenbaum HS&H LLP -900 3rd Av -NY 10022
(212) 836-8000 ..**Stoldt,** Derek M '95 (Kaye S LLP) -425 Park Av -NY 10022
(212) 653-8700 ..**Stoler,** Jonathan H '96 (Sheppard MR&H LLP) -30 Rckfllr Plz -NY 10112
(212) 335-9000 ..**Stolfi,** Patricia '02 %DA -1 Hogan Pl -NY 10013
(718) 852-3710 ..**Stoll,** Andrew B '98 (Stoll G&B) -71 Nevins -Brklyn 11217 **Fx:**852-3586
(718) 857-1840 ..**Stoll,** Carl B Sr. '99 -130 8th Av -Brklyn 11215
(212) 530-5000 ..**Stoll,** David J '92 (Milbank TH&M LLP) -1 Chase Manh Plz -NY 10005
(212) 608-1900 ..**Stoll,** Ian T '98 %Lovell SH LLP -61 Bway -NY 10006
(212) 506-2500 ..**Stoll,** J Robt '89 (Mayer B LLP) -1675 Bway -NY 10019
(212) 541-6222 ..**Stoll,** Judith A '84 (Kane K,PC) -1350 Av of Amer -NY 10019
(212) 682-3488 ..**Stoll,** Martin A '63 -60 E 42nd -NY 10165
(212) 735-3000 ..**Stoll,** Neal R '74 (Skadden ASM&F LLP) -4 Times Sq -NY 10036
(212) 736-0290 ..**Stoll,** Robt S '66 (Stoll S&H) -1350 Bway -NY 10018
(212) 736-0290 ..**Stoll Stoll & Hoffman** -1350 Bway -NY 10018 **Fx:**564-5131
(212) 735-3000 ..**Stoller,** Danl E '69 (Skadden ASM&F LLP) -4 Times Sq -NY 10036
(212) 373-3000 ..**Stoller,** Eric J '06 %Paul WRW&G LLP -1285 Av of Amer -NY 10019
(212) 458-5745 ..**Stoller,** Evan H '89 AIGTS -175 Water -NY 10038
(212) 407-4000 ..**Stoller,** Fran M '84 (Loeb & L,LLP) -345 Park Av -NY 10154
(516) 328-2300 ..**Stoller,** Greg H '04 %Abrams FFEGF&E,LLP -1111 Marcus Av -Lk Success 11042
(914) 666-7917 ..**Stoller,** Helen B '66 -19 Fox Den Rd -Mt Kisco 10549
(212) 696-6000 ..**Stoller,** Herbert '53 Cnsl Curtis M-PC&M LLP -101 Park Av -NY 10178
(212) 788-0743 ..**Stoller,** Jack '95 %Law Dept -100 Church -NY 10007 **Fx:**788-0367
(212) 558-4000 ..**Stoller,** Katherine J '07 %Sullivan & C LLP -125 Broad -NY 10004
(212) 836-1138 ..**Stoller,** Michl A '77 Human Srvcs Cncl of NYC -130 E 59th -NY 10022
(212) 676-0960 ..**Stoller,** Philip D '78 %Law Dept -52 Duane -NY 10007 **Fx:**442-6868
(212) 558-4000 ..**Stoller,** Sarah E '10 %Sullivan & C LLP -125 Broad -NY 10004
(212) 309-6000 ..**Stolley,** Martha B '99 %Morgan L&B LLP -101 Park Av -NY 10178
(212) 779-3510 ..**Stollow,** Aury Bennett '82 (AB Stollow,PC) -475 Park Av S -NY 10016 **Fx:**679-9064
(845) 794-4300 ..**Stoloff,** Richd A '74 (Stoloff & S,LLP) -26 Hmltn Av Bx1129 -Monticello 12701
(845) 794-4300 ..**Stoloff & Silver,LLP** -26 Hmltn Av Bx1129 -Monticello 12701 **Fx:**794-1371
(212) 788-1579 ..**Stolorow,** Adam M '09 %Law Dept -100 Church -NY 10007 **Fx:**788-0367
(212) 762-7969 ..**Stolow,** David M '82 Morgan Stanley -1221 Av of Amer -NY 10020
(631) 342-0066 ..**Stolowitz,** Joel P '65 -140 Fell Ct -Hauppauge 11788 **Fx:**234-4445
(607) 273-7070 ..**Stolp,** Robt W '73 -320 N Aurora -Ithaca 14850 **Fx:**273-0822
(212) 848-4000 ..**Stolper,** Antonia E '89 (Shearman & S LLP) -599 Lex Av -NY 10022
(212) 620-0500 ..**Stolper,** Michl T '94 Stolper Grp LLP -155 Av of Amer -NY 10013
(212) 238-4800 ..**Stoltz,** Patrick '07 %Landman CB&F,PC -120 Bway -NY 10271
(212) 220-3830 ..**Stoltz,** Terry L '76 (Nicoletti H&S) -88 Pine -NY 10005
(718) 938-5220 ..**Stolyar,** Larissa '00 -Dix Hlls 11746
(516) 741-8020 ..**Stolz,** Noreen E '82 -1539 Franklin Av -Mineola 11501 **Fx:**741-5429
(917) 637-3616 ..**Stolz,** Suzanne L '04 Ctr for Reproductive Rts -120 Wall -NY 10005
(914) 949-4600 ..**Stolzar,** Michl I '73 (Karlen S&R,LLP) -1 N Bway -White Plns 10601
(518) 885-1904 ..**Stolzar,** Peter H '70 -161 White Rd -Ballston Spa 12020
(914) 390-4300 ..**Stolzberg,** Maxwell '67 -44 S Bway -White Plns 10601
(914) 288-9191 ..**Stolzenberg,** Howard B '90 (Lever & S,LLP) -303 Old Tarrytown Rd -White Plns 10603
(718) 423-1145 ..**Stolzenberg,** Marc A '87 ACS -150 William -NY 10038
(646) 253-2300 ..**Stolzer,** Ernest R '80 (Bond S&K,PLLC) -330 Mad Av -NY 10017
(212) 733-1385 ..**Stolzer,** Susan C '88 %Pfizer Inc -235 E 42nd -NY 10017
(212) 681-1575 ..**Stolzman,** Kardon A '08 %Belluck & F LLP -546 5th Av -NY 10036
(212) 809-1111 ..**Stoma,** Meredith Kaplan '92 (Morgan MA) -39 Bway -NY 10006
(212) 672-4770 ..**Stomber,** James F Jr. '82 (Witkoff Group LLC) -220 E 42nd -NY 10017 **Fx:**672-3434
(212) 504-6000 ..**Stombock,** Megan A '07 %Cadwalader W&T LLP -1 World Fncl Ctr -NY 10281
(212) 980-1031 ..**Stompor,** John F '97 No Peace without Justice -866 UN Plz -NY 10017
(631) 582-5588 ..**Stona,** Jane B '93 -320 Carleton Av -Central Islip 11722
(212) 577-3530 ..**Stonbely,** Jonathan L '09 Leg Aid -199 Water -NY 10038 **Fx:**425-2465
(716) 853-3801 ..**Stonberg,** Michl L '91 (Kenney SL&N,LLP) -14 Lafayette Sq -Buffalo 14203
(212) 619-1910 ..**Stone,** Adam H '97 (Regosin ES&F) -225 Bway -NY 10007
(212) 530-5000 ..**Stone,** Alan J '88 (Milbank TH&M LLP) -1 Chase Manh Plz -NY 10005
(212) 957-7600 ..**Stone,** Alexis G '07 %Cohen & G LLP -800 3rd Av -NY 10022
(212) 255-2934 ..**Stone,** Alicia '93 -Bx 82 -NY 10014
(607) 239-6165 ..**Stone,** Allen '81 (Stone & S) -Bx118 -Vestal 13851 **Fx:**239-6169
(212) 506-2500 ..**Stone,** Amanda L '10 %Mayer B LLP -1675 Bway -NY 10019
(914) 738-2288 ..**Stone,** Andrew D '73 -261 Eastland Av -Pelham 10803 **Fx:**738-2288
(646) 610-5400 ..**Stone,** Anne E '00 %NYPD -1 Police Plz -NY 10038
(914) 995-3000 ..**Stone,** Audrey '92 %DA -111 Martin Luther King Blvd -White Plns 10601 **Fx:**995-3363
(212) 506-5000 ..**Stone,** Benjamin D '05 %Orrick H&S LLP -51 W 52nd -NY 10019
(914) 422-3900 ..**Stone,** Brian J '72 %Oxman TKW&G LLP -120 Bloomingdale Rd -White Plns 10605
(212) 268-2510 ..**Stone,** Carol Garofalo '84 -350 5th Av -NY 10118
(315) 786-0266 ..**Stone,** Christina E '93 %Slye & B -104 Wshngtn -Watertwn 13601
(914) 235-8900 ..**Stone,** David '93 (D Stone & Assoc) -Bx224 -New Rchll 10804 **Fx:**633-4008
(212) 310-8000 ..**Stone,** David P '71 (Weil G&M LLP) -767 5th Av -NY 10153
(917) 534-4900 ..**Stone,** Debra F '83 Zurich Capital Mrkts -105 E 17th -NY 10003
(212) 259-8000 ..**Stone,** Deidrie A '10 %Dewey & L LLP -1301 Av of Amer -NY 10019
(914) 636-2648 ..**Stone,** Douglas F '03 (Moise & S,PC) -30 Church -New Rchll 10801 **Fx:**626-2528
(212) 446-4800 ..**Stone,** Edw M '08 %Kirkland & E LLP -153 E 53rd -NY 10022

(212) 373-3000 .. **Stone,** Eric A '99 (Paul WRW&G LLP) -1285 Av of Amer -NY 10019
(212) 841-4124 .. **Stone,** Fred M '68 Millennium Partners,LP -666 5th Av -NY 10103 **Fx:**841-4141
(718) 237-5500 .. **Stone,** Gary S '82 Leg Srvcs -105 Court -Brklyn 11201 **Fx:**855-0733
(212) 935-7800 .. **Stone,** George M '93 %Babcock & Brown -600 Lex Av -NY 10022
(212) 697-6200 .. **Stone,** George S '71 (Burke S&A,LLP) -370 Lex Av -NY 10017
(212) 715-9100 .. **Stone,** Gordon P III '98 %Kramer LN&F,LLP -1177 Av of Amer -NY 10036
(212) 344-5400 .. **Stone,** Harvey M '80 (Schlam S&D LLP) -26 Bway -NY 10004
(631) 427-4020 .. **Stone,** Herbert '51 -33 E Carver -Huntngtn 11743 **Fx:**427-4041
(212) 349-5150 .. **Stone,** Jane L '87 OfCnsl Galvano & X,PC -150 Bway -NY 10038
(212) 227-7450 .. **Stone,** Jeffrey B '67 HDC -110 William -NY 10038 **Fx:**227-6865
(585) 475-1440 .. **Stone,** Jeffrey P '89 Stabtec Cnsltng -2060 Brghtn-Henrietta Townline Rd -Rchstr 14623 **Fx:**272-1814
(716) 856-4000 .. **Stone,** Jeffrey W '84 (Hodgson R LLP) -140 Pearl -Buffalo 14202
(914) 725-2080 .. **Stone,** Jennifer Drew '89 -1 Sheldrake Rd -Scarsdale 10583 **Fx:**725-5904
(718) 268-0400 .. **Stone,** Jill C '87 OfCnsl Addabbo & G -118-21 Qns Blvd -Frst Hlls 11375
(516) 679-4300 .. **Stone,** Jill C '87 (J Stone,PC) -2872 Merrick Rd -Bellmore 11710
(315) 671-1137 .. **Stone,** John G '88 Hon J Murphy -401 Mntgmry -Syracuse 13202 **Fx:**671-1186
(212) 732-2270 .. **Stone,** Jos I '59 -277 Bway -NY 10007
(516) 623-0897 .. **Stone,** Judith Ellen '91 -2819 Hrbr Rd -Merrick 11566 **Fx:**867-7936
(631) 738-8157 .. **Stone,** Kerie P '94 -258 Hawkins Av -Ronkonkoma 11779
(718) 875-1300 .. **Stone,** Lisa M '04 %Appllt Div 2nd Dept -45 Monroe Pl -Brklyn 11201 **Fx:**858-2446
(585) 232-6500 .. **Stone,** Lori J '02 Cnsl Harter S&E LLP -1600 Bausch & Lomb Pl -Rchstr 14604
(212) 513-3200 .. **Stone,** Mark '72 (Holland & K LLP) -31 W 52nd -NY 10019
(212) 808-7800 .. **Stone,** Merrill B '77 (Kelley D&W LLP) -101 Park Av -NY 10178
(212) 984-8133 .. **Stone,** Michl M '97 CB Richard Ellis -200 Park Av -NY 10166
(518) 473-3303 .. **Stone,** Michl M '04 Dept of Health -Corning Twr 24th Fl -Albany 12237 **Fx:**473-2019
(212) 421-6060 .. **Stone,** Michl S '78 (Beanstalk Grp) -220 E 42nd -NY 10017 **Fx:**421-6388
(212) 962-1020 .. **Stone,** Michele '89 %M Lamonsoff -80 Maiden Ln -NY 10038 **Fx:**962-3078
(607) 239-6165 .. **Stone,** Michelle E '80 (Stone & S) -Bx118 -Vestal 13851 **Fx:**239-6169
(212) 779-9910 .. **Stone,** Nancy R '91 (Eaton & V LLP) -3 Park Av -NY 10016
(212) 672-1635 .. **Stone,** Nina E '98 -245 Park Av -NY 10167 **Fx:**372-8798
(212) 867-6000 .. **Stone,** Patti Ann '93 (Rosenberg & E,PC) -733 3rd Av -NY 10017
(914) 366-9680 .. **Stone,** Paul D '87 (P Stone,PC) -303 S Bway -Tarrytwn 10591 **Fx:**366-9682
(212) 937-8470 .. **Stone,** Philip B '77 -575 Mad Av -NY 10022 **Fx:**605-0222
(212) 753-5000 .. **Stone,** Phoebe A '10 %Schiff H LLP -900 3rd Av -NY 10022
(212) 239-4340 .. **Stone,** Ralph M '91 (Shalov SB&R LLP) -485 7th Av -NY 10018
(212) 371-6600 .. **Stone,** Richd L '84 OfCnsl Kirby M LLP -825 3rd Av -NY 10022
(212) 564-8220 .. **Stone,** Richd Paul '88 -225 W 34th -NY 10122
(212) 227-3550 .. **Stone,** Richd W II '78 (Waesche S&O,PC) -111 Bway -NY 10006
(212) 878-8144 .. **Stone,** Robt A '93 %Clifford C LLP -31 W 52nd -NY 10019
(212) 619-1910 .. **Stone,** Robt M '64 (Regosin ES&F) -225 Bway -NY 10007
(914) 381-7600 .. **Stone,** Robt S '63 OfCnsl Dorf Law Firm,LLP -740 W Bstn Post Rd -Mamaroneck 10543 **Fx:**381-7608
(716) 886-1242 .. **Stone,** Roger E '73 %Mental Hlth Assn -999 Delaware Av -Buffalo 14209 **Fx:**881-6428
(516) 593-0202 .. **Stone,** Scott A '93 -340 Atl Av -E Rockaway 11518 **Fx:**593-0297
(914) 682-1400 .. **Stone,** Scott H '95 OfCnsl Scarcella Law Ofc -44 Church -White Plns 10601 **Fx:**948-2255
(518) 886-4130 .. **Stone,** Shelly L '98 AYCO -321 Bway Bx860 -Saratoga Spgs 12866
(212) 839-5300 .. **Stone,** Susan A '09 (Sidley A LLP) -787 7th Av -NY 10019
(212) 790-0332 .. **Stone,** Suzanne L '80 %Benj N Cardozo Schl of Law -55 5th Av -NY 10003 **Fx:**790-0345
(212) 960-0051 .. **Stone,** Toby E '83 %Yeshiva Univ -500 W 185th -NY 10033 **Fx:**960-5346
(212) 838-1032 .. **Stone,** Warren N '84 -10 Mitchell Pl -NY 10017 **Fx:**838-0540
(212) 878-8000 .. **Stonecash,** Aaron C '05 %Clifford C LLP -31 W 52nd -NY 10019
(212) 790-0187 .. **Stonehill,** David A '98 Och-Ziff Cptl Mgmt -9 W 57th -NY 10019
(516) 378-7627 .. **Stonehill,** David H '84 (D Stonehill,PC) -43 Central Blvd -Merrick 11566 **Fx:**378-7356
(585) 419-8800 .. **Stonehill,** Eric '74 (Harris B PLLC) -99 Garnsey Rd -Pittsfrd 14534
(212) 480-5284 .. **Stonehill,** Jeffrey A '78 %Insurance Dept -25 Beaver -NY 10004 **Fx:**480-5272
(212) 643-7000 .. **Stonehill,** Robt '67 OfCnsl Sills C&G PC -One Rckfllr Plz -NY 10020
(585) 272-7007 .. **Stoner,** Max T '68 (Stoner & Assoc,PC) -2540 Brighton Henrietta Town Line Rd -Rchstr 14623 **Fx:**272-7011
(718) 447-8841 .. **Stonick,** Serena M '00 %Lahr DMK&P -33 Decker Av -Staten Isl 10302
(914) 249-2000 .. **Stonier,** Joann C '94 %MasterCard Intl -2000 Purchase -Purchase 10577
(518) 798-1938 .. **Stonner,** John P '91 -10 Lawrence Bx2546 -Glens Fls 12801 **Fx:**798-2200
(212) 696-6000 .. **Stookey,** Maria E '09 %Curtis M-PC&M LLP -101 Park Av -NY 10178
(212) 715-9100 .. **Stoopack,** Helayne O '82 SpclCnsl Kramer LN&F,LLP -1177 Av of Amer -NY 10036
(212) 309-3738 .. **Stoopler,** Eric '79 %Towers Watson -335 Mad Av -NY 10017
(716) 439-4444 .. **Stopa,** Scott R '06 (Douglas & S) -260 East Av -Lockprt 14094 **Fx:**439-4452
(212) 349-0522 .. **Stopek,** Alan J '69 -217 Bway -NY 10007
(914) 828-8279 .. **Stopler,** Barry S '89 Swiss Re -175 King -Armonk 10504 **Fx:**828-7279
(212) 490-3000 .. **Stopnik,** Scott H '96 (Wilson EME&D LLP) -150 E 42nd -NY 10017
(516) 802-7007 .. **Stopol,** Larry N '79 (Levy S&C,LLP) -1425 RXR Plz -Uniondale 11556
(845) 225-2397 .. **Stoppel,** Kirsten A '99 -45 Gleneida Av Bx1653 -Carmel 10512 **Fx:**225-2398
(315) 336-4162 .. **Stopper,** Larry R Jr. '83 -Bx377 -Westmoreland 13490
(212) 326-3939 .. **Stops,** Eric '02 (Jones D) -222 E 41st -NY 10017
(516) 433-7394 .. **Stopsky,** David C '52 -7 Eva Ln -Plainvw 11803 **Fx:**932-6944
(315) 255-2731 .. **Stopyra,** Thos P '64 -5 N Park -Auburn 13021
(518) 438-5439 .. **Storace,** A Thos '58 -1 Stonehenge Ln -Albany 12203
(212) 506-1700 .. **Storch,** Adina G '00 (Kasowitz BT&F LLP) -1633 Bway -NY 10019
(212) 490-4100 .. **Storch Amini & Munves,PC** -140 E 45th -NY 10017 **Fx:**490-4208
(516) 334-1714 .. **Storch,** Irving R '41 -342 Post Av -Westbury 11590 **Fx:**338-6745
(646) 434-1661 .. **Storch,** Jeffrey E '00 Cnsl Cahill/Wink LLP -5 Penn Plz -NY 10001
(212) 551-1755 .. **Storch,** Kym H '97 Lombard & G LLP -230 Park Av -NY 10169 **Fx:**(646) 349-5567
(518) 402-0748 .. **Storch,** Larry G '84 %Dept of Health -433 River -Troy 12180 **Fx:**402-0751
(212) 572-8600 .. **Storch,** Monica L '04 MacAndrews & Forbes Inc -35 E 62nd -NY 10065
(212) 587-2383 .. **Storch,** Oliver S '92 -305 Bway -NY 10007 **Fx:**732-7080
(518) 431-0247 .. **Storch,** Robt P '94 %US Atty -445 Bway -Albany 12207 **Fx:**431-0249
(212) 490-4100 .. **Storch,** Steven G '78 (Storch A&M,PC) -140 E 45th -NY 10017
(716) 853-5100 .. **Storck,** Michl E '88 (Lippes MWF LLP) -665 Main -Buffalo 14203
(914) 202-9808 .. **Storette,** Monique B '80 -949 Palmer Rd -Bronxvll 10708 **Fx:**202-9808
(212) 512-4476 .. **Storey,** Jason M H '07 McGraw-Hill -1221 Av of Amer -NY 10020 **Fx:**512-4827
(585) 256-0090 .. **Storey,** Jeffrey M '09 %Dutcher & Z -1399 Monroe Av -Rchstr 14618
(212) 545-6138 .. **Storey,** Walter J '02 IncisiveMedia /NYLJ -120 Bway -NY 10271
(914) 497-8943 .. **Storino,** Stacey A '00 -Bx158 -LaGrangevll 12540 **Fx:**(845) 849-0113
(212) 599-1300 .. **Stork,** Aloysius P '85 %Lex Terrae Ltd -331 Mad Av -NY 10017 **Fx:**983-2791
(212) 728-2200 .. **Storm,** Evan S '09 %Axinn V&H LLP -114 W 47th -NY 10036
(518) 462-6765 .. **Storm,** Jennifer L '07 %Leg Aid -55 Colvin Av -Albany 12206 **Fx:**427-8352
(212) 742-8700 .. **Storm,** Samantha '02 Garson D&C LLP -110 Wall -NY 10005
(716) 855-2800 .. **Storm,** Scott D '98 (Mura & S,PLLC) -14 Lafayette Sq #930 -Buffalo 14203
(212) 336-2000 .. **Storm,** Vivian R M '08 %Patterson BW&T LLP -1133 Av of Amer -NY 10036
(315) 724-6528 .. **Stormer,** Nancy R '83 (N Stormer,PC) -1314 Rutger -Utica 13501
(212) 903-9000 .. **Storms,** Justin S '06 %Linklaters -1345 Av of Amer -NY 10105
(718) 256-2792 .. **Storobin,** David '04 Aimco Corp -2911 W 36th -Brklyn 11224
(716) 856-5500 .. **Storr,** Amber E '07 %Damon M LLP -200 Delaware Av -Buffalo 14202
(518) 474-5464 .. **Storrs,** Wm E '81 %Dept of Law -The Cptl -Albany 12224
(518) 762-4010 .. **Stortecky,** Fredk R '72 -34 S Market -Johnstwn 12095 **Fx:**762-7425
(516) 877-8836 .. **Storti,** Robt J '94 US Trust Co of NY -1581 Franklin Av -Gdn Cty 11530
(315) 422-1311 .. **Storto,** Richd M '75 (Melvin & M,PLLC) -217 S Salina -Syracuse 13202
(315) 733-4764 .. **Story,** John H Jr. '76 -233 Bleecker -Utica 13501 **Fx:**733-1024
(212) 209-4800 .. **Storz,** John F '97 (Brown R LLP) -7 Times Sq -NY 10036
(212) 297-5800 .. **Stosser,** Michl A '04 OfCnsl Day P LLP -7 Times Sq -NY 10036
(845) 340-3685 .. **Stote,** Valerie Paul '94 %Cnty Atty -244 Fair Bx1800 -Kingston 12402 **Fx:**340-3691
(212) 408-5100 .. **Stothers,** H Hedley Jr. '73 (Chadbourne & P LLP) -30 Rckfllr Plz -NY 10112
(212) 941-9090 .. **Stotland,** Eve A '03 The Door -121 Av of Amer -NY 10013 **Fx:**941-0714
(718) 261-0133 .. **Stotland,** Nelly '00 (Stotland & Assoc,PC) -118-21 Qns Blvd -Frst Hlls 11375 **Fx:**261-0340
(973) 520-2326 .. **Stotter,** Chas W '78 Cnsl Edwards AP&D LLP -750 Lex Av -NY 10022 **Fx:**520-2600
(516) 433-8050 .. **Stouges Morgan & Pieper LLC** -115 N Bway -Hicksvll 11801 **Fx:**433-8066
(516) 433-8050 .. **Stouges,** Wm A '91 (Stouges M&P LLC) -115 N Bway -Hicksvll 11801
(212) 607-3300 .. **Stoughton,** Corey L '03 %NYCLU -125 Broad -NY 10004
(212) 918-3000 .. **Stout,** Arthur D III '74 (Hogan L LLP) -875 3rd Av -NY 10022
(585) 786-8822 .. **Stout,** Gerald L '73 (DA) -147 N Main -Warsaw 14569 **Fx:**786-8842
(212) 909-6000 .. **Stout,** Joan M '91 Cnsl Debevoise & P LLP -919 3rd Av -NY 10022
(212) 859-8000 .. **Stout,** Kelly L '10 %Fried FHS&J LLP -1 NY Plz -NY 10004
(212) 754-6120 .. **Stout,** Michl W '70 (Stout & T) -477 Mad Av -NY 10022 **Fx:**754-6809
(212) 701-3000 .. **Stout,** Michl W '09 %Cahill G&R LLP -80 Pine -NY 10005 **Fx:**269-5420
(518) 487-7600 .. **Stout,** Robt A Jr. '09 %Whiteman O&H LLP -1 Commerce Plz -Albany 12260
(212) 803-3819 .. **Stout,** Robin J '82 Empire State Dvlmnt Corp -633 3rd Av -NY 10017 **Fx:**803-3838
(212) 613-2027 .. **Stoutenburg,** Mark W '97 (Gibbons PC) -1 Penn Plz -NY 10119 **Fx:**554-9648
(212) 350-2700 .. **Stovall,** Amianna '95 (Constantine C,PC) -450 Lex Av -NY 10017
(212) 880-9582 .. **Stovall,** James R '03 %Morvillo AGIA&B,PC -565 5th Av -NY 10017
(718) 590-2000 .. **Stover,** Christiana C '01 %DA -198 E 161st -Bronx 10451 **Fx:**590-6477
(518) 274-3510 .. **Stover,** Jessica E '03 %Bartle MD&J,LLP -251 River Bx448 -Troy 12181
(212) 941-8695 .. **Stover,** Susan A '89 -209 Mulberry -NY 10012
(212) 866-2877 .. **Stover-Stitts,** Jacqueline '85 -130-36 W 124th -NY 10027
(585) 753-4500 .. **Stowe,** Eric W '07 DA -832 Watts Bldg -Rchstr 14614 **Fx:**753-4576
(585) 262-6390 .. **Stowe,** Neha S '07 %Hamberger & W -1 S Wshngtn -Rchstr 14614
(585) 352-1831 .. **Stowe,** Richd E '79 -52 Nichols Bx116 -Spencerprt 14559
(212) 506-1700 .. **Stoyanov,** Stefan R '04 %Kasowitz BT&F LLP -1633 Bway -NY 10019
(212) 757-5000 .. **Strachan,** David D Jr. '93 Sklover D&F,LLC -10 Rckfllr Plz -NY 10020 **Fx:**757-5002
(607) 776-3306 .. **Strache,** Vivian C '93 OfCnsl Cole & V,PC -7 E Steuben Bx232 -Bath 14810 **Fx:**776-4189
(516) 437-5900 .. **Stracher,** Richd L '62 -3000 Marcus Av -Lk Success 11042 **Fx:**354-4731

(212) 943-0880 .. **Straci,** Ronald A '60 -17 Battery Pl -NY 10004 **Fx:**809-6908
(516) 938-1633 .. **Strack,** Robt R '60 -410 Jericho Tpke -Jericho 11753 **Fx:**942-3758
(845) 561-8000 .. **Stradar,** Elizabeth A '91 %Northrop & S,PC -1 Corwin Ct Bx2395 -Newburgh 12550
(845) 561-8000 .. **Stradar,** George F Jr. '62 (Northrop & S,PC) -1 Corwin Ct Bx2395 -Newburgh 12550
(718) 748-4848 .. **Strafaci,** Frank T '75 -569 Bay Ridge Pkwy -Brklyn 11209 **Fx:**748-6399
(718) 748-4848 .. **Strafaci,** Irene F '82 -569 Bay Ridge Pkwy -Brklyn 11209 **Fx:**748-6399
(516) 294-8844 .. **Strafford,** Katie L '02 %L'Abbate BC&C,LLP -1001 Franklin Av -Gdn Cty 11530
(212) 593-1000 .. **Straight,** R Jason '01 %Kroll Assoc -1166 Av of Amer -NY 10036 **Fx:**593-2631
(516) 227-0700 .. **Strain,** Chas M '78 (Farrell F,PC) -1320 RXR Plz -Uniondale 11556
(212) 768-6700 .. **Strain,** Daniele B '99 Sonnenschein N&R LLP -1221 Av of Amer -NY 10020
(585) 232-4090 .. **Strait,** Brian '76 %Leg Aid -1 W Main -Rchstr 14614 **Fx:**232-2352
(646) 722-8500 .. **Straite,** David A '00 %Grant & E,PA -485 Lex Av -NY 10017
(212) 975-5889 .. **Straka,** Angeline C '99 %CBS Inc -51 W 52nd -NY 10019 **Fx:**975-3930
(212) 918-3000 .. **Straley,** Jessica C '08 %Hogan L LLP -875 3rd Av -NY 10022
(212) 373-3000 .. **Stramiello,** Warren A '08 %Paul WRW&G LLP -1285 Av of Amer -NY 10019
(212) 918-3000 .. **Strand,** Brian G '09 %Hogan L LLP -875 3rd Av -NY 10022
(631) 265-6300 .. **Strang,** Jos K '82 (Birzon S&B) -222 E Main -Smithtwn 11787
(212) 637-2627 .. **Strang,** Robt '92 US Atty -1 St Andrews Plz -NY 10007
(718) 262-4110 .. **Strangeways,** Erik '82 %DHCR -92-31 Union Hall -Jamaica 11433 **Fx:**262-7938
(718) 966-2424 .. **Straniere,** Robt A '66 -885 Annadale Rd -Staten Isl 10312
(516) 484-4010 .. **Strano,** David M '94 (Miller M&S) -99 Powerhse Rd -Roslyn Hts 11577
(212) 867-4466 .. **Strasburg,** Diana R '09 %Belkin BW&G,LLP -270 Mad Av -NY 10016
(212) 214-9222 .. **Strasburg,** Jos '90 %Rent Stblztn Assn -123 William -NY 10038 **Fx:**732-0617
(212) 683-6699 .. **Strasfeld,** Nancy B '05 %Raab SG&G,LLP -317 Mad Av -NY 10017
(212) 906-1200 .. **Strasler Vitkowsky,** Pandora D '97 Cnsl Latham & W -885 3rd Av -NY 10022
(845) 623-5163 .. **Strassberg,** Carolyn J '96 CJ Strassberg,LLC -104 E Route 59 -Nanuet 10954 **Fx:**623-5164
(212) 863-6300 .. **Strassberg,** Jaclyn '06 %HPD -100 Gold -NY 10038 **Fx:**863-8201
(212) 736-9500 .. **Strassberg,** Milton '61 -57 W 38th -NY 10018
(212) 813-8800 .. **Strassberg,** Richd M '89 (Goodwin P LLP) -620 8th Av -NY 10018
(212) 736-9500 .. **Strassberg,** Robt L '90 (Strassberg & S,PC) -57 W 38th -NY 10018 **Fx:**629-8729
(212) 736-9500 .. **Strassberg,** Todd A '89 (Strassberg & S,PC) -57 W 38th -NY 10018 **Fx:**629-8729
(718) 838-7878 .. **Strassburger,** Gertrude '08 Bronx Defenders -860 Crtlandt Av -Bronx 10451 **Fx:**665-0100
(212) 351-4500 .. **Strasser,** Fredk W '03 SrCnsl Epstein B&G,PC -250 Park Av -NY 10177
(718) 692-0608 .. **Strassfeld,** Abraham B '78 -1293 Ocean Pkwy -Brklyn 11230 **Fx:**692-0608
(914) 683-2500 .. **Strassfield,** Richd J '79 (Harold SS&S) -81 Main -White Plns 10601
(631) 421-0700 .. **Strassman,** Jos B '82 (Schoen & S,LLP) -52 Elm -Huntngtn 11743
(212) 935-3000 .. **Strassner,** Anne L '82 OfCnsl Mintz LCFG&P,PC -666 3rd Av -NY 10017
(347) 404-9133 .. **Strassner,** Meryl L '84 %Civil Ct -141 Lvngstn -Brklyn 11201 **Fx:**(718) 643-3733
(212) 943-0110 .. **Stratakis,** Christ '56 (Poles TS&G, LLP) -46 Trinity Pl -NY 10006
(212) 943-0110 .. **Stratakis,** John C '90 (Poles TS&G, LLP) -46 Trinity Pl -NY 10006
(212) 966-6700 .. **Stratford,** Ian M '04 %Gray K LLP -207 W 25th -NY 10001 **Fx:**966-6051
(212) 425-9300 .. **Stratton,** Matthew D '06 %Bressler A&R,PC -17 State -NY 10004
(212) 909-6000 .. **Stratton,** Matthew P '07 %Debevoise & P LLP -919 3rd Av -NY 10022
(315) 449-4306 .. **Stratton,** Peter C '83 (Oot & S) -4983 Brittonfld Pkwy -E Syracuse 13057 **Fx:**449-4358
(212) 264-9230 .. **Stratvert,** Bruce N '85 %US DOJ -26 Fed Plz -NY 10278 **Fx:**264-1916
(212) 403-1000 .. **Straub,** Amanda L '06 %Wachtell LR&K -51 W 52nd -NY 10019
(212) 849-7000 .. **Straub,** Stephen T '00 %Quinn EU&S,LLP -51 Mad Av -NY 10010
(866) 348-5819 .. **Straub,** Wm E '64 SSA-ODAR -50 Fountain Plz -Buffalo 14202 **Fx:**(716) 551-4078
(716) 847-0650 .. **Straube,** Diana M '88 %Leg Srvcs -237 Main -Buffalo 14203 **Fx:**847-0227
(212) 408-5100 .. **Strauber,** Donald I '61 (Chadbourne & P LLP) -30 Rckfllr Plz -NY 10112
(212) 637-1034 .. **Strauber,** Jocelyn E '00 %US Atty -1 St Andrews Plz -NY 10007
(718) 478-6744 .. **Strauch,** George J '67 (Strauch & K) -34-21 87th -Jcksn Hts 11372 **Fx:**478-2381
(212) 486-1455 .. **Strauchler,** Paul D '79 (Post PGM&S,PA) -575 Mad Av -NY 10022
(212) 506-5000 .. **Strauch Weiss,** Laurie '93 (Orrick H&S LLP) -51 W 52nd -NY 10019
(212) 968-9797 .. **Straus,** Alan Jay '77 (AJ Straus,PC) -42 Bway -NY 10004 **Fx:**968-1833
(212) 696-6000 .. **Straus,** Dora '00 %Curtis M-PC&M LLP -101 Park Av -NY 10178
(212) 728-8000 .. **Straus,** Jay B '99 SpclCnsl Willkie F&G LLP -787 7th Av -NY 10019
(212) 791-0285 .. **Straus,** Matthew R '00 %Malaby & B,LLC -150 Bway -NY 10038 **Fx:**791-0286
(212) 966-4400 .. **Straus,** Oscar S III '86 VOLS -54 Greene -NY 10013 **Fx:**219-8943
(212) 556-2100 .. **Straus,** Paul A '93 (King & S) -1185 Av of Amer -NY 10036
(914) 347-2600 .. **Straus,** Stephen D '87 (Traub LS&S LLP) -7 Skyline Dr -Hawthorne 10532
(718) 318-8805 .. **Straus,** Zahava B '81 %L Brickman -224 Beach 147th -Rckwy Pk 11694 **Fx:**318-8806
(718) 624-2200 .. **Straus-Figueroa,** Sylvie '05 %W Rothberg -16 Court -Brklyn 11241
(212) 598-7211 .. **Strauss,** Abby F '82 %Time Warner NYC Cable Grp -120 E 23rd -NY 10010 **Fx:**420-4812
(212) 471-8472 .. **Strauss,** Arthur M '69 (Herzfeld & R,PC) -125 Broad -NY 10004
(212) 859-8000 .. **Strauss,** Audrey '72 (Fried FHS&J LLP) -1 NY Plz -NY 10004
(845) 294-2616 .. **Strauss,** Barbara J '80 -60 Erie -Goshen 10924 **Fx:**294-3861
(212) 779-4700 .. **Strauss,** Barry M '68 -307 5th Av -NY 10016
(516) 365-1015 .. **Strauss,** Elise I '77 %Sullivan & Strauss Agency -1 Hllw Ln -Lk Success 11042
(914) 824-5070 .. **Strauss,** Forrest '89 %Atty Grievance Comm -399 Knollwood Rd -White Plns 10603 **Fx:**949-0997
(212) 935-5057 .. **Strauss,** G Kayser '09 %Kayser & R,LLP -515 Mad Av -NY 10022
(212) 398-7900 .. **Strauss,** Gary J '78 (Gerstein S&R LLP) -57 W 38th -NY 10018
(716) 648-5061 .. **Strauss,** Gerard A '84 -180 Main -Hambrg 14075 **Fx:**649-6746
(212) 277-4000 .. **Strauss,** Gil J '00 (Freshfields BD LLP) -520 Mad Av -NY 10022
(212) 682-0020 .. **Strauss,** James M '91 (Putney TH&H LLP) -521 5th Av -NY 10175
(646) 885-5004 .. **Strauss,** James S '73 %Dept of Sanitation -125 Worth -NY 10013 **Fx:**(212) 442-9090
(914) 323-7000 .. **Strauss,** Jason C '09 %Wilson EME&D LLP -3 Gannett Dr -White Plns 10604
(212) 250-0937 .. **Strauss,** Jay F '93 Deutsche Bank -60 Wall -NY 10005
(845) 623-0090 .. **Strauss,** Jeffrey E '04 (Weiner & S) -119 Rockland Ctr -Nanuet 10954
(212) 909-9500 .. **Strauss,** Jeffrey T '81 (Wachtel & M,LLP) -885 2nd Av -NY 10017
(516) 484-2514 .. **Strauss,** Jeffrey T '81 -4 Hrbr Ct W -Roslyn Harbor 11576
(212) 907-0700 .. **Strauss,** Jesse '04 %Labaton S LLP -140 Bway -NY 10005
(212) 687-1980 .. **Strauss,** Joel B '93 (Kaplan F&K LLP) -850 3rd Av -NY 10022
(212) 792-7948 .. **Strauss,** Jonathan B '90 -233 Bway -NY 10279
(212) 407-4000 .. **Strauss,** Jonathan N '03 %Loeb & L,LLP -345 Park Av -NY 10154
(212) 806-5400 .. **Strauss,** Jos E '98 SpclCnsl Stroock &S&L LLP -180 Maiden Ln -NY 10038
(585) 815-0288 .. **Strauss,** Laura M '07 %Rosicki R & Assoc,PC -26 Harvester Av -Batavia 14020 **Fx:**815-0299
(212) 483-0105 .. **Strauss,** Linda S '03 %Coughlin D LLP -88 Pine-Wall St Plz -NY 10005
(718) 626-7730 .. **Strauss,** Marc A '92 (Pyrros & S LLP) -31-01 Bway -LIC 11106
(212) 403-3500 .. **Strauss,** Marc A '01 Rothschild Inc -1251 Av of Amer -NY 10020
(718) 725-0022 .. **Strauss,** Marc E '91 -153-01 Jamaica Av -Jamaica 11432
(212) 371-6600 .. **Strauss,** Mark A '94 (Kirby M LLP) -825 3rd Av -NY 10022
(212) 986-2233 .. **Strauss,** Mark G '90 (Early & S LLC) -360 Lex Av Bx3601 -NY 10163
(212) 806-5400 .. **Strauss,** Meredith L '01 %Stroock &S&L LLP -180 Maiden Ln -NY 10038
(631) 331-5300 .. **Strauss,** Michl '85 -1303 Main -Pt Jffrsn 11777 **Fx:**331-5341
(516) 498-1000 .. **Strauss,** Michl R '85 (Hollander & S,LLP) -40 Cuttermill Rd -Gt Neck 11021
(212) 319-1500 .. **Strauss,** Michl R '91 %Strauss & S -275 7th Av -NY 10001 **Fx:**691-1485
(518) 374-4951 .. **Strauss,** Morris D '73 -265 Mohawk Av -Scotia 12302 **Fx:**377-7320
(917) 637-3600 .. **Strauss,** Nan E '03 Ctr for Reproductive Rts -120 Wall -NY 10005 **Fx:**637-3666
(212) 848-4000 .. **Strauss,** Peter A '88 Cnsl Shearman & S LLP -599 Lex Av -NY 10022
(212) 351-4500 .. **Strauss,** Peter J '63 SrCnsl Epstein B&G,PC -250 Park Av -NY 10177
(212) 431-2196 .. **Strauss,** Peter J '63 %NY Law Schl -185 W Bway -NY 10013 **Fx:**406-0103
(212) 554-7800 .. **Strauss,** Richd E '68 (Moses & S LLP) -405 Lex Av -NY 10174
(516) 764-2285 .. **Strauss,** Richd L '91 -2492 Oceanside Rd -Oceanside 11572
(212) 659-8105 .. **Strauss,** Sara H '87 %Mt Sinai Med Ctr -1 Gustave L Levy Pl Bx 1099 -NY 10029 **Fx:**348-2230
(516) 228-8383 .. **Strauss,** Scott J '91 (Beck & S,PLLC) -50 Chas Lindbergh Blvd -Uniondale 11553
(718) 767-6100 .. **Strauss,** Stephen A '99 -1244 A Clintonvll -Whitestone 11357 **Fx:**767-6101
(631) 267-6499 .. **Strauss,** Steven D '91 -Bx154 -Amagansett 11930
(212) 698-3500 .. **Strauss,** Stuart M '79 (Dechert LLP) -1095 Av of Amer -NY 10036
(585) 383-1300 .. **Strauss,** Wayne C '84 %OppenheimerFunds,Inc -350 Linden Oaks -Rchstr 14625
(716) 633-9922 .. **Stravalaci-Mikienis,** Mariella '00 (Mikienis & M PC) -5838 Main -Williamsvll 14221
(631) 845-1200 .. **Stravato,** John M '90 -Bx298 -Bethpage 11714 **Fx:**845-8183
(716) 856-4000 .. **Stravino,** Jeffrey C '98 (Hodgson R LLP) -140 Pearl -Buffalo 14202
(716) 856-8200 .. **Straw,** Stephanie A '07 %Williams & W -43 Court -Buffalo 14202 **Fx:**856-0559
(212) 649-5600 .. **Strawbridge,** David A '68 %Rockefeller & Co,Inc -30 Rckfllr Plz -NY 10112 **Fx:**649-5977
(212) 801-2176 .. **Strawbridge,** Jill E '88 OfCnsl Greenberg T,LLP -200 Park Av -NY 10166
(914) 923-3654 .. **Strawgate,** Susan L '84 %Houlihan/LawrenceInc -18 Hungerford Rd -Briarclff Mnr 10510 **Fx:**923-3558
(607) 778-2685 .. **Strawn,** Tamarra L '04 %Dept Soc Srvcs -36-42 Main -Bnghmtn 13905 **Fx:**778-2710
(718) 823-6622 .. **Strazza,** Anthony '04 -2027 Wllmsbrdg Rd -Bronx 10461 **Fx:**239-2141
(646) 828-1408 .. **Strazza,** Gloria A '85 %Signature Bnk -29 W 38th -NY 10018
(212) 326-3939 .. **Strazzeri,** Jos A '04 %Jones D -222 E 41st -NY 10017
(716) 856-0600 .. **Strazzulla,** Jenna Slavet '09 %Jaeckle F&M,LLP -12 Fountain Plz -Buffalo 14202
(718) 259-4600 .. **Strazzullo,** Salvatore E '02 (Strazzullo Law Firm PC) -7101 18th Av -Brklyn 11204 **Fx:**259-4494
(516) 746-7371 .. **Stream,** Arnold '81 %Burns RT&R,LLP -390 Old Cntry Rd -Gdn Cty 11530
(716) 874-8295 .. **Streb,** John R '81 -2953 Elmwood Av -Kenmore 14217 **Fx:**871-1216
(716) 875-5662 .. **Strebel,** Milton J '56 -3080 Delaware Av -Buffalo 14217 **Fx:**874-0680
(212) 489-1600 .. **Streck,** Eric T '99 %Deloitte LLP -1633 Bway -NY 10019 **Fx:**492-4201
(631) 929-6060 .. **Strecker,** Robt F '96 Meadowcrest Corp -Bx846 -Quogue 11959
(212) 867-4466 .. **Streekmann,** Corina '02 %Belkin BW&G,LLP -270 Mad Av -NY 10016
(516) 605-1666 .. **Streelman,** Elizabeth '10 %Yanover & Y -300 Grdn City Plz -Gdn Cty 11530 **Fx:**605-1667
(516) 248-4011 .. **Streich,** Chas R '92 -128 Front -Mineola 11501 **Fx:**742-5345
(212) 599-0971 .. **Streich,** Eric '86 (E Streich,PC) -51 E 42nd -NY 10017 **Fx:**599-0972

(212) 408-2908 ..**Streicker,** John Harrison '67 -108 E 73rd -NY 10021
(212) 307-4827 ..**Streicker,** Richd D '94 -454 W 46th -NY 10036
(212) 610-6300 ..**Streiff,** Kimberlee R '03 %Allen & O -1221 Av of Amer -NY 10020
(516) 801-4990 ..**Streiner,** David M '03 (Irwin & S LLC) -1180 Nrthrn Blvd -Manhsst 11030
(914) 686-0558 ..**Streisfeld,** Arnold R '80 (A Streisfeld,PC) -301 Old Tarrytown Rd -White Plns 10603 **Fx:**686-2516
(845) 225-6600 ..**Streisfeld,** Arnold R '80 (A Streisfeld,PC) -1849 Route 6 -Carmel 10512 **Fx:**(914) 686-2516
(516) 354-4600 ..**Streisfeld,** Jeffrey D '73 (King & S) -3000 Marcus Av -Lk Success 11042 **Fx:**352-7966
(212) 448-1100 ..**Streisfeld-Leitner,** Karen M '91 OfCnsl McLaughlin & S,LLP -260 Mad Av -NY 10016
(212) 532-3255 ..**Streit,** Martin S '56 -240 Mad Av -NY 10016 **Fx:**532-6855
(212) 836-1314 ..**Streit,** Meredith A '87 UJA-Federation -130 E 59th -NY 10022 **Fx:**888-7538
(212) 732-3200 ..**Strell,** Ethan I '02 %Carter L&M LLP -2 Wall -NY 10005
(212) 980-0120 ..**Strelov,** Jerome J '77 OfCnsl Frankfurt KK&S,PC -488 Mad Av -NY 10022
(212) 704-6000 ..**Stremba,** Lee W '76 (Troutman S LLP) -405 Lex Av -NY 10174
(914) 946-3700 ..**Streng,** Frank W '83 (McCarthy F LLP) -11 Martine Av -White Plns 10606
(212) 319-9404 ..**Strenger,** Laurence N '69 %Ampton Invstmnts -885 3rd Av -NY 10022 **Fx:**593-0140
(516) 625-1700 ..**Strenger,** Sanford '85 (Salamon GB&S,PC) -97 Powerhse Rd -Roslyn Hts 11577
(845) 294-3361 ..**Strenger,** Saul W '63 -42 Park Pl -Goshen 10924
(631) 499-3833 ..**Strenk,** Michl J '72 -6080 Jericho Tpk -Commack 11725 **Fx:**499-3862
(212) 554-0400 ..**Strent,** Robt A '00 (Grubman I&S,PC) -152 W 57th -NY 10019
(585) 419-8800 ..**Streppa,** Alfred L '65 (Harris B PLLC) -99 Garnsey Rd -Pittsfrd 14534
(631) 543-3663 ..**Streppone,** Wm A '96 OfCnsl Migliore & I,PC -353 Vets Mem'l Hwy -Commack 11725
(518) 641-5571 ..**Streznewski,** Alexandra Jane '94 %Cptl Dist Physicians Hlth Plan,Inc -500 Patroon Crk Blvd -Albany 12206 **Fx:**641-5505
(212) 541-2000 ..**Strianese,** Christoper R '05 %Bryan C LLP -1290 Av of Amer -NY 10104
(914) 313-5280 ..**Striar,** James G '96 -2500 Wstchstr Av -Purchase 10577 **Fx:**313-5281
(212) 506-1700 ..**Stricker,** James J '91 (Kasowitz BT&F LLP) -1633 Bway -NY 10019
(516) 364-1200 ..**Stricker,** Jed M '85 CLK/Houlihan Parnes LLC -7600 Jericho Tpke -Woodbury 11797
(315) 474-7571 ..**Strickland,** Carter H '65 (Mackenzie H LLP) -101 S Salina Bx4967 -Syracuse 13221
(212) 813-5900 ..**Strickland,** J Allison '94 (Fross ZL&Z,PC) -866 UN Plz -NY 10017
(212) 458-3154 ..**Strickland,** Jos I III '02 AIG -175 Water -NY 10038
(212) 728-8000 ..**Strickland,** Rachel C '99 (Willkie F&G LLP) -787 7th Av -NY 10019
(518) 584-2200 ..**Strickland,** Wm E Jr. '04 %King A&A -2911 Route 9 Bx4580 -Saratoga Spgs 12866
(845) 485-3900 ..**Strickland-Smith,** Jeane L '91 Dept of Law -235 Main -Poughkeepsie 12601 **Fx:**452-3303
(718) 248-5103 ..**Strickler,** Susan A '82 Citibank NA -1 Court Sq -LIC 11120
(212) 318-6000 ..**Strickon,** Harvey A '72 OfCnsl Paul HJ&W LLP -75 E 55th -NY 10022
(212) 425-0700 ..**Strier,** Todd J '96 %Kelner & K -140 Bway -NY 10005
(516) 873-1200 ..**Strier,** Todd J '96 %Kelner & K -1 Old Cntry Rd -Carle Pl 11514
(917) 509-4200 ..**Striggles,** Theo W '69 -230 Park Av -NY 10169 **Fx:**(212) 661-2153
(212) 973-8000 ..**Strikowsky,** Bruce M '95 (Schnader HS&L LLP) -140 Bway -NY 10005
(212) 225-2000 ..**Stringer,** Dana W '07 %Cleary GS&H -1 Lbrty Plz -NY 10006
(212) 735-3000 ..**Stringfellow,** James S '88 (Skadden ASM&F LLP) -4 Times Sq -NY 10036
(212) 661-8000 ..**Strino,** Paolo A '07 %Lucas & M,LLP -475 Park Av S -NY 10016
(518) 869-9094 ..**Strippoli,** Nicole '06 %Wein & F -951 Albany Shaker Rd -Latham 12110
(516) 357-3000 ..**Strober,** Eric S '96 (Rivkin R LLP) -926 RXR Plz -Uniondale 11556
(631) 754-7274 ..**Strober,** Shari Lynn '93 %Commack School Dist -Bx150 -Commack 11725
(631) 363-5533 ..**Stroble,** Jos C '85 -Bx596 -Sayvll 11782
(212) 264-6373 ..**Strobos,** Judy C Wong '98 %HHS -26 Fed Plz -NY 10278 **Fx:**264-6364
(212) 833-7380 ..**Strobos,** Katharine L '97 Sony Corp of America -550 Mad Av -NY 10022
(212) 730-8133 ..**Strobridge,** Scott R '03 %Gunderson DSVF&H,LLP -220 W 42nd -NY 10036
(212) 351-4000 ..**Strochlic,** Jerry J '73 (Gibson D&C LLP) -200 Park Av -NY 10166
(212) 715-9100 ..**Strock,** Lee C '10 %Kramer LN&F,LLP -1177 Av of Amer -NY 10036
(212) 909-6000 ..**Strock,** Marcus H '72 OfCnsl Debevoise & P LLP -919 3rd Av -NY 10022
(516) 488-3300 ..**Strockyj,** Sean R '03 %Shaub AC&S,LLP -1983 Marcus Av -Lk Success 11042
(631) 727-2322 ..**Strode,** John D '75 -214 Roanoke Av -Rvrhead 11901 **Fx:**727-8262
(315) 473-9495 ..**Strodel,** Kathryn A '02 %MHLS -224 Harrison -Syracuse 13202 **Fx:**473-9646
(315) 252-8290 ..**Strods,** Jonis J '90 -33 William -Auburn 13021 **Fx:**282-0337
(718) 875-1300 ..**Stroh,** Todd L B '97 %Appllt Div 2nd Dept -45 Monroe Pl -Brklyn 11201 **Fx:**858-2446
(212) 335-9000 ..**Strohbehn,** Maria D '09 %DA -1 Hogan Pl -NY 10013
(212) 326-3939 ..**Strohbehn,** Xochitl S '10 %Jones D -222 E 41st -NY 10017
(518) 383-4000 ..**Strohl,** Brian S '02 (Overton RD&D,LLP) -19 Halfmoon Exec Park Dr Bx437 -Clifton Pk 12065
(718) 279-2700 ..**Strohl,** Robt J '07 -214-11 Nrthrn Blvd -Bayside 11361 **Fx:**279-2707
(212) 417-4357 ..**Strohmeyer,** Nancy H '90 %Dept of Health -90 Church -NY 10007 **Fx:**417-4392
(212) 269-0927 ..**Stroili,** Peter A '90 (D'Amato & L,LLP) -2 World Fncl Ctr -NY 10281
(607) 255-4196 ..**Strom,** Barry '75 %Leg Aid -Myron Taylor Hall -Ithaca 14853 **Fx:**255-3269
(212) 688-4572 ..**Strom,** Dennis '54 -225 Bway -NY 10007 **Fx:**661-3622
(646) 386-3622 ..**Strom,** Frank I '70 %Supreme Ct-Law Dept -60 Centre -NY 10007
(212) 455-2000 ..**Strom,** Jonathan B '08 %Simpson T&B LLP -425 Lex Av -NY 10017
(516) 742-7430 ..**Strom,** Karen '89 (Schroder & S LLP) -114 Old Cntry Rd -Mineola 11501 **Fx:**742-7433
(212) 596-9000 ..**Strom,** Kevin E '09 %Ropes & G LLP -1211 Av of Amer -NY 10036
(212) 735-3000 ..**Strom,** Milton G '68 OfCnsl Skadden ASM&F LLP -4 Times Sq -NY 10036
(212) 724-6148 ..**Strom,** Neva Dayton '92 -190 Riverside Dr -NY 10024
(212) 918-3000 ..**Strom,** Rachel Fan Stern '07 %Hogan L LLP -875 3rd Av -NY 10022
(716) 856-0875 ..**Strom,** Shauna L '06 D Archilla -170 Franklin -Buffalo 14202 **Fx:**853-1897
(315) 472-4431 ..**Stroman,** Kurt M '02 Camex Mgmt Grp,LLC -605 W Genesee -Syracuse 13204 **Fx:**472-3140
(716) 636-7600 ..**Stromberg,** Amy Valk '84 OfCnsl HoganWillig -2410 N Forest Rd -Amherst 14068
(212) 850-1864 ..**Stromberg,** Edw G III '03 J&W Seligman & Co,Inc -100 Park Av -NY 10017
(516) 248-1700 ..**Stromberg,** Michl S '89 Cnsl Forchelli CDSM&T,LLP -333 Earle Ovngton Blvd -Uniondale 11553
(516) 712-4000 ..**Stromberg,** Susan J '91 (Milber MP&S LLP) -1000 Woodbury Rd -Woodbury 11797
(518) 402-6995 ..**Strome,** Tana Thompson '91 %OCFS -52 Wshngtn -Rensselaer 12144 **Fx:**486-6361
(716) 845-2102 ..**Stromecki,** Kristie Haslinger '03 %Hon E Pigott-Applt Div -50 Delaware Av -Buffalo 14202
(212) 335-9000 ..**Stromes,** David P '09 %DA -1 Hogan Pl -NY 10013
(212) 504-6000 ..**Stromfeld,** Lary '82 (Cadwalader W&T LLP) -1 World Fncl Ctr -NY 10281
(212) 401-0283 ..**Strong,** Alison B '08 Talk WW Production,Inc -433 W 53rd -NY 10019
(914) 948-1200 ..**Strong,** David H '09 %Cerussi & S,PC -1 N Lex Av -White Plns 10601
(914) 723-7180 ..**Strong,** Edw J '88 -11 Olmstead Rd -Scarsdale 10583
(212) 226-1900 ..**Strong,** Gary '02 %Tesser & C -591 Bway -NY 10012
(212) 407-4000 ..**Strong,** Jennifer B '07 %Loeb & L,LLP -345 Park Av -NY 10154
(716) 937-3353 ..**Strong,** Jennifer L '98 (Neill & S,PLLC) -13166 Main Bx395 -Alden 14004 **Fx:**937-7222
(212) 652-3785 ..**Strong,** Jonnie '83 (Schlesinger G&L LLP) -535 Mad Av -NY 10022
(212) 619-4444 ..**Strong,** Linda Sue '04 %Marshall CW&B,PC -116 John -NY 10038
(212) 998-6716 ..**Strongarone,** Stacey M '04 NYU Problem Solving Ctr -245 Sullivan -NY 10012
(212) 931-8300 ..**Strongin,** Howard F '82 (Strongin R&A,LLP) -5 Hanover Sq -NY 10004
(914) 995-4172 ..**Strongin,** Jonathan S '01 %DA -111 Martin Luther King Blvd -White Plns 10601 **Fx:**995-3363
(212) 759-3300 ..**Strongin,** Landey '70 (Dornbush SS&V,LLP) -747 3rd Av -NY 10017
(914) 763-5614 ..**Strongin,** Robt H '86 Greenwald & S PC -6 Adams Hills Rd -Cross Rvr 10518
(212) 931-8300 ..**Strongin Rothman & Abrams,LLP** -5 Hanover Sq -NY 10004 **Fx:**931-8319
(212) 335-4500 ..**Strongosky,** Christopher M '01 (DLA Piper LLP) -1251 Av of Amer -NY 10020
(212) 588-0800 ..**Stronski,** James K '89 (Frommer L&H LLP) -745 5th Av -NY 10151
(212) 735-3000 ..**Stronski,** Neil P '96 (Skadden ASM&F LLP) -4 Times Sq -NY 10036
(212) 806-5400 ..**Stroock & Stroock & Lavan LLP** -180 Maiden Ln -NY 10038 **Fx:**806-6006
(212) 431-2375 ..**Strossen,** Nadine '80 %NY Law Schl -185 W Bway -NY 10013 **Fx:**431-1992
(646) 386-5700 ..**Stroth,** Leslie Ann '88 %Civil Ct -111 Centre -NY 10013
(646) 225-4274 ..**Strott,** Elizabeth S '06 MSN Money -1290 Av of Amer -NY 10104
(212) 250-1193 ..**Stroud,** Marcus A '04 Deutsche Bank Securities,Inc -60 Wall -NY 10005
(518) 782-4900 ..**Stroud,** Nancy E '96 (LaFave L&S,LLP) -951 Albany Shaker Rd -Latham 12110 **Fx:**785-9705
(212) 504-6000 ..**Stroud,** Shane J '02 SpclCnsl Cadwalader W&T LLP -1 World Fncl Ctr -NY 10281
(212) 779-0991 ..**Strougo,** Robt I '71 -286 Mad Av -NY 10017 **Fx:**779-7884
(212) 627-8100 ..**Stroup,** Robt H '97 (Levy R,PC) -80 8th Av -NY 10011
(914) 376-3757 ..**Strout,** Jessica C '08 %Leg Srvcs -30 S Bway -Ynkrs 10701 **Fx:**376-8739
(212) 596-9000 ..**Stroy,** Brandon H '07 %Ropes & G LLP -1211 Av of Amer -NY 10036
(212) 272-2266 ..**Stroz,** Eugene J Jr. '02 %JP Morgan Chase -383 Mad Av -NY 10179
(212) 373-3000 ..**Struck,** Christian A '98 Cnsl Paul WRW&G LLP -1285 Av of Amer -NY 10019
(212) 326-3939 ..**Strudler,** Randi L '88 (Jones D) -222 E 41st -NY 10017
(914) 785-5300 ..**Strudwick,** Donna M '95 %A Lamer -555 Taxter Rd -Elmsfrd 10523 **Fx:**347-4269
(212) 622-2259 ..**Strug,** Lowell A '99 %JP Morgan Chase -60 Wall -NY 10260
(631) 749-1456 ..**Strugats,** Robt '50 -Bx273 -Shelter Isl Hts 11965
(516) 922-6626 ..**Strugatz,** Chas R '78 %J Shein & Assoc,PC -575 Underhill Blvd -Syosset 11791 **Fx:**922-2797
(212) 505-6233 ..**Strugatz,** Donna L '84 -250 Mercer -NY 10012 **Fx:**979-5506
(518) 464-3199 ..**Struhs,** Ronald E '97 AIG Claim Srvcs -1 Park Pl -Albany 12205
(212) 836-8000 ..**Strum,** Jay G '63 (Kaye S LLP) -425 Park Av -NY 10022
(516) 496-5822 ..**Strum,** Stacey A '05 %T Spina -170 Froehlich Farm Blvd -Woodbury 11797 **Fx:**496-5420
(212) 566-6800 ..**Strumpf,** Linda '76 -2 West Rd -S Salem 10590 **Fx:**566-6808
(516) 799-6773 ..**Strumpfler,** Robt L '58 -251 N Beech -Massapequa 11758
(914) 683-1002 ..**Strumwasser,** David A '77 (Whippoorwill Assoc,Inc) -11 Martine Av -White Plns 10606 **Fx:**683-1242
(631) 369-1700 ..**Strunk,** Nica B '97 (Esseks H&A,LLP) -108 E Main Bx279 -Rvrhead 11901
(212) 622-3333 ..**Strupp,** Cory N '78 JP Morgan Chase & Co -270 Park Av -NY 10017
(518) 465-3524 ..**Strutin,** Kennard R '86 %NYS Defenders Assn -194 Wshngtn Av -Albany 12210 **Fx:**465-3249
(212) 370-0447 ..**Strutinskiy,** Andrey '04 -286 Mad Av -NY 10017 **Fx:**370-0465

(914) 683-1100 .. **Strutt,** Barry R '89 (Keegan KK&S,LLP) -81 Main -White Plns 10601
(212) 403-1000 .. **Strutt,** Holly M '98 Cnsl Wachtell LR&K -51 W 52nd -NY 10019
(212) 450-4000 .. **Struve,** Guy Miller '67 (Davis P&W LLP) -450 Lex Av -NY 10017
(518) 431-4761 .. **Struzzi,** Judith Ann '88 %IRS -1 Clinton Av -Albany 12207
(212) 432-9180 .. **Stryker Tams & Dill LLP** -2 Penn Plz -NY 10121
(212) 980-0120 .. **Stryker,** Wendy E '97 %Frankfurt KK&S,PC -488 Mad Av -NY 10022
(716) 855-1111 .. **Strzemski-Haase,** Barbara B '98 %Duke HP&G LLP -350 Main -Buffalo 14202
(212) 259-8000 .. **Stuart,** Alice M '81 %Dewey & L LLP -1301 Av of Amer -NY 10019
(845) 486-2300 .. **Stuart,** Allison J '05 %DA -236 Main -Poughkeepsie 12601 **Fx:**486-2324
(518) 434-8441 .. **Stuart,** Bruce H '75 -172 Jay -Albany 12210
(212) 735-3000 .. **Stuart,** Chase A '09 %Skadden ASM&F LLP -4 Times Sq -NY 10036
(212) 335-9000 .. **Stuart,** David A '08 DA -1 Hogan Pl -NY 10013
(212) 474-1000 .. **Stuart,** David M '96 Cravath S&M LLP -825 8th Av -NY 10019
(212) 725-7260 .. **Stuart,** Enid Nagler '81 HQ Inc -377 Park Av S -NY 10016
(212) 660-5550 .. **Stuart,** Harvey '65 OfCnsl MC Rakower,PC -747 3rd Av -NY 10017 **Fx:**660-5551
(212) 888-3033 .. **Stuart,** Kenneth J '65 OfCnsl Becker GM&M LLP -299 Park Av -NY 10171
(716) 282-0267 .. **Stuart,** Lawr G '85 -770 Main Bx693 -Niagara Fls 14302 **Fx:**282-0287
(518) 395-5400 .. **Stuart,** Mark A '99 %Racing & Wagering Bd -1 Bway Ctr -Schnctdy 12305 **Fx:**347-1292
(212) 687-2770 .. **Stuart,** Michl C '82 (Cohen PL&P) -551 5th Av -NY 10176
(212) 332-8915 .. **Stuart,** Pamela Bruce '74 Cnsl Simon & Prtnrs LLP -551 5th Av -NY 10176 **Fx:**332-8918
(315) 422-8191 .. **Stuart,** Patricia L '08 Leg Aid -351 S Warren -Syracuse 13202 **Fx:**472-2819
(212) 481-1411 .. **Stuart,** Scott Y '88 Donlin Recano & Comp,Inc -419 Park Av S -NY 10016 **Fx:**481-1416
(631) 724-5800 .. **Stuart,** Susan D '80 -50 Route 111 -Smithtwn 11787 **Fx:**656-0081
(212) 277-4000 .. **Stuart,** Walter B '80 (Freshfields BD LLP) -520 Mad Av -NY 10022
(585) 428-5210 .. **Stubbe,** Joshua F '01 Pub Def -10 N Fitzhugh -Rchstr 14614 **Fx:**428-2234
(607) 776-9631 .. **Stubblefield,** Bonita J '95 DA -3 E Pulteney Sq -Bath 14810 **Fx:**776-7052
(212) 626-4100 .. **Stubblefield,** Carol B '93 (Baker & M LLP) -1114 Av of Amer -NY 10036
(212) 833-1193 .. **Stubbs,** Emily A '99 (Friedman KS&A LLP) -1633 Bway -NY 10019 **Fx:**373-7993
(212) 732-8700 .. **Stucchio,** Caryn '07 %McAloon & F,PC -123 William -NY 10038
(212) 876-4424 .. **Stuchiner,** Theresa B '48 -1148 5th Av -NY 10128
(607) 798-1074 .. **Stuckart,** Catherine E '85 -156 Crary Av -Bnghmtn 13905
(212) 878-8000 .. **Stucke,** Pia Z '02 %Clifford C LLP -31 W 52nd -NY 10019
(212) 681-2004 .. **Stuckey,** Darla Chaddick '89 Society of Corp Secretaries & Governance Prof -521 5th Av -NY 10175
(212) 371-6600 .. **Studebaker,** Christopher S '06 %Kirby M LLP -825 3rd Av -NY 10022
(518) 464-2000 .. **Studebaker,** Donna L '97 AYCO -1 Wall Bx15073 -Albany 12212
(914) 949-1305 .. **Studebaker,** Judith B '77 %Leg Srvcs -90 Maple Av -White Plns 10601 **Fx:**949-6213
(212) 660-3000 .. **Student,** Michl J '82 Cnsl Sullivan & W LLP -1290 Av of Amer -NY 10104
(516) 679-4300 .. **Studin,** Melissa S '09 J Stone,PC -2872 Merrick Rd -Bellmore 11710
(718) 658-3000 .. **Studley,** Mitchell J '80 (Debrosse & S,LLP) -182-38 Hillside Av -Jamaica 11432 **Fx:**658-3187
(212) 837-6000 .. **Studness,** Jessica S '02 %Hughes H&R LLP -1 Bttry Pk Plz -NY 10004
(212) 254-3550 .. **Studnicky,** Lawr J III '85 (Winslett SM&B LLP) -6 E 39th -NY 10016 **Fx:**937-3393
(585) 758-7602 .. **Studwell,** Spencer L '83 Univ of Rochester Med Ctr -Bx278979 -Rchstr 14627 **Fx:**272-9311
(212) 362-7123 .. **Studwell,** Thos W '97 -320 W 89th -NY 10024
(716) 849-1333 .. **Stuermer,** Michl P '98 (Lipsitz GSC LLP) -42 Delaware Av -Buffalo 14202
(212) 827-5518 .. **Stuhl,** Seth A '98 Disney Theatrical Productions -214 W 42nd -NY 10036
(716) 887-7225 .. **Stuhlmiller,** Mark J '99 %Computer Task Grp -800 Delaware Av -Buffalo 14209 **Fx:**887-7370
(212) 455-2000 .. **Stujenske,** Danl J '08 %Simpson T&B LLP -425 Lex Av -NY 10017
(212) 332-7300 .. **Stulberg,** Jonathen E '95 Millburn Corp -1270 Av of Amer -NY 10020
(212) 268-1000 .. **Stulberg,** Robt B '81 (Broach & S,LLP) -1 Penn Plz -NY 10119
(516) 877-5600 .. **Stulgaitis,** Karen A '84 %R Tusa -1225 Franklin Av -Gdn Cty 11530 **Fx:**877-5695
(212) 791-0285 .. **Stull,** P Tobias '08 %Malaby & B,LLC -150 Bway -NY 10038 **Fx:**791-0286
(212) 687-7230 .. **Stull Stull & Brody** -6 E 45th -NY 10017 **Fx:**490-2022
(716) 849-1333 .. **Stulmaker,** Mark L '82 (Lipsitz GSC LLP) -42 Delaware Av -Buffalo 14202
(212) 637-4919 .. **Stulman,** Amanda B '96 %EPA -290 Bway -NY 10007 **Fx:**637-3096
(914) 249-6225 .. **Stumacher,** Jenya E '00 MasterCard Worldwide -2000 Purchase -Purchase 10577
(212) 684-0300 .. **Stumacher,** Lee '97 %Bauman K&G LLP -28 W 44th -NY 10036
(718) 979-1800 .. **Stumacher,** Mark D '76 Eger Health Care & Rehab Ctr -140 Meisner Av -Staten Isl 10306 **Fx:**979-6930
(607) 273-2202 .. **Stumbar,** L Richd '75 (Schlather SP&S) -200 E Buffalo Bx353 -Ithaca 14851
(212) 351-4500 .. **Stumbo,** Anthony B '01 %Epstein B&G,PC -250 Park Av -NY 10177
(212) 633-2225 .. **Stumer,** Mark B '95 (M Stumer & Assoc,PC) -306 5th Av -NY 10001 **Fx:**691-3642
(212) 314-3924 .. **Stumpf,** Richd H '73 %AXA Financial Inc -1290 Av of Amer -NY 10104 **Fx:**707-7134
(212) 406-2300 .. **Stumpp & Bond,LLP** -One Lbrty Plz -NY 10006 **Fx:**406-2332
(212) 406-2300 .. **Stumpp,** Gary D '78 (Stumpp & B,LLP) -One Lbrty Plz -NY 10006
(212) 593-6700 .. **Stupak,** Jeffrey W '04 %Aaronson RF&D,LLP -757 3rd Av -NY 10017
(212) 878-8000 .. **Stupart,** Miranda J '04 Clifford C LLP -31 W 52nd -NY 10019
(518) 473-8418 .. **Stupp,** John E '78 %OCFS -52 Wshngtn -Rensselaer 12144 **Fx:**486-6361
(718) 595-6568 .. **Sturcken,** Chas G Jr. '83 DEP-Ofc Pub Affrs -59-17 Junction Blvd -Flushng 11373
(212) 825-6855 .. **Sturcken,** Kyle '84 %Dept of Invstgtn -80 Maiden Ln -NY 10038 **Fx:**825-2860
(212) 582-9873 .. **Sturges,** Leatha J '94 -600 W 57th -NY 10019 **Fx:**582-4813
(347) 295-2730 .. **Sturges,** Philip P '89 -144 Marlboro Rd -Brklyn 11226
(212) 336-0404 .. **Sturges,** Zachary B '03 %SEC -3 World Fncl Ctr -NY 10281 **Fx:**336-1323
(585) 419-8800 .. **Sturgess,** Kyle W '08 %Harris B PLLC -99 Garnsey Rd -Pittsfrd 14534
(718) 263-2411 .. **Sturim,** Allan '55 -125-10 Qns Blvd -Kew Gdns 11415 **Fx:**263-2911
(516) 571-3833 .. **Sturim,** Howard E '92 %Hon A Honorof -252 Old Cntry Rd -Mineola 11501 **Fx:**571-2137
(917) 454-1040 .. **Sturla,** Mario J '07 Cnsl Exec Ofc for Immigration Review -26 Fed Plz -NY 10278
(212) 530-5000 .. **Sturm,** Brian J '10 %Milbank TH&M LLP -1 Chase Manh Plz -NY 10005
(212) 623-3391 .. **Sturm,** David C '80 JP Morgan Chase -4 NY Plz -NY 10004
(516) 326-2400 .. **Sturm,** Deborah C '01 %Ivone D&J,LLP -2001 Marcus Av -Lk Success 11042
(716) 854-2020 .. **Sturm,** Ellen B '02 (Cellino & B,PC) -350 Main -Buffalo 14202
(212) 683-6699 .. **Sturm,** Ira A '76 (Raab SG&G,LLP) -317 Mad Av -NY 10017
(212) 872-1000 .. **Sturm,** Joshua '07 -One Bryant Park -NY 10036 **Fx:**872-1002
(718) 590-2000 .. **Sturm,** Leslie '07 %DA -198 E 161st -Bronx 10451 **Fx:**590-6477
(718) 579-3000 .. **Sturman,** Stephen G '77 %Leg Aid -1020 Grnd Cncrs -Bronx 10451 **Fx:**588-2611
(716) 645-3381 .. **Sturman,** Steven J '99 %SUNY Buffalo -664 Baldy Hall -Buffalo 14260
(212) 872-1000 .. **Sturman,** Wm L Jr. '99 -One Bryant Park -NY 10036 **Fx:**872-1002
(212) 922-1177 .. **Stursberg,** C Walter Jr. '78 (Stursberg & V) -1500 Bway -NY 10036
(212) 922-1177 .. **Stursberg & Veith** -1500 Bway -NY 10036 **Fx:**922-0995
(845) 369-3000 .. **Sturtz,** Barry A '76 (B Sturtz,PC) -134 Route 59 -Suffern 10901 **Fx:**369-1618
(212) 735-8600 .. **Stutius,** Amy L '07 %Morrison C LLP -909 3rd Av -NY 10022
(718) 875-3452 .. **Stutman,** Alan I '69 -50 Court -Brklyn 11201 **Fx:**875-3947
(212) 685-7474 .. **Stutman,** Dana M '96 (Mayerson SA LLP) -292 Mad Av -NY 10017
(212) 685-7474 .. **Stutman,** Michl D '85 (Mayerson SA LLP) -292 Mad Av -NY 10017
(212) 791-1222 .. **Stutman,** Robt A '99 -225 Bway -NY 10007 **Fx:**791-0891
(516) 408-7320 .. **Stutman,** Steven W '74 -2938 Hemstead Tpk -Levittwn 11756 **Fx:**248-1350
(518) 242-2222 .. **Stuto,** Peter F '86 %Airport Auth -200 Admin Bldg -Albany 12211
(914) 948-8392 .. **Stuttman,** Joel S '91 (J Stuttman,PC) -44 S Bway -White Plns 10601 **Fx:**948-6973
(212) 440-2874 .. **Stuttman,** Karen L '92 CNA Ins -40 Wall -NY 10005
(212) 536-3900 .. **Stutz,** Laura A '01 %K&L Gates LLP -599 Lex Av -NY 10022
(718) 526-7976 .. **Stutz,** Toba Beth '85 -90-50 Parsons Blvd -Jamaica 11432 **Fx:**725-0567
(914) 764-8669 .. **Stutz,** Toba Beth '85 -5 Donbrook Rd -Pound Rdg 10576 **Fx:**764-8669
(212) 574-1200 .. **Stutzman,** David E '90 Cnsl Seward & K LLP -1 Bttry Pk Plz -NY 10004
(585) 271-4440 .. **Stutzman,** Gary L '83 %Sagemark Consulting -200 Meridian Ctr -Rchstr 14618
(212) 902-1000 .. **Stuzin,** Randolph A '92 %Goldman Sachs -1 NY Plz -NY 10004
(516) 222-0980 .. **Stuzin,** Theo D '58 (Stuzin & S) -585 Stewart Av -Gdn Cty 11530 **Fx:**935-0606
(212) 662-9218 .. **Styers,** Randall G '85 Union Theological Seminary -3041 Bway -NY 10027
(516) 889-6335 .. **Stykes,** Donna M '85 -115 Bay -Long Bch 11561
(718) 855-9000 .. **Styles,** Paula J '89 %Cullen and D LLP -177 Montague -Brklyn 11201
(212) 436-1098 .. **Stylianou,** Theresa L '85 IRS -290 Bway -NY 10007
(718) 875-1300 .. **Stynes,** Wendy Ann '94 %Appllt Div 2nd Dept -45 Monroe Pl -Brklyn 11201 **Fx:**858-2446
(212) 431-2366 .. **Su,** Lynn B '86 %NY Law Schl -185 W Bway -NY 10013 **Fx:**343-1860
(631) 738-4154 .. **Su,** Wang '00 Symbol Technologies Inc -1 Symbol Plz -Holtsvll 11742
(718) 206-4689 .. **Suares-Douglas,** Nicole K '01 %Law Dept -89-17 Sutphin Blvd -Jamaica 11435 **Fx:**206-4702
(631) 239-5100 .. **Suarez,** Glen A '00 (G Suarez,PC) -50 Elm -Huntngtn 11743 **Fx:**421-2110
(212) 764-7220 .. **Suarez,** Jennifer C '05 Jantex Mrkting -159 W 53rd -NY 10019
(212) 595-8393 .. **Suarez,** Jos A '66 -332 W 83rd -NY 10024
(845) 425-3108 .. **Suarez,** Jos E '80 Village of Chestnut Ridge -277 Old Nyack Tpk -Chestnut Rdg 10977 **Fx:**352-6277
(212) 553-5535 .. **Suarez,** Katharine M '02 Zurich NA -1 Lbrty Plz -NY 10006
(718) 286-6000 .. **Suarez,** Lucinda C '85 %DA -125-01 Qns Blvd -Kew Gdns 11415
(212) 344-5680 .. **Suarez,** Mario J '82 (Thompson H LLP) -335 Mad Av -NY 10017
(212) 822-1452 .. **Suarez,** Melissa '01 -305 Bway -NY 10007 **Fx:**822-1449
(914) 798-5400 .. **Suarez,** Michl A '07 %Goldberg S LLP -11 Martine Av -White Plns 10606
(212) 278-1000 .. **Suarez,** Patricio A '03 %Anderson K&O,PC -1251 Av of Amer -NY 10020
(516) 248-5757 .. **Suarez,** Stephanie M '99 (Colleran O&M,LLP) -1225 Franklin Av -Gdn Cty 11530
(212) 947-0010 .. **Suba,** Ferdinand G '89 -450 7th Av -NY 10123 **Fx:**947-0042
(212) 220-3830 .. **Suba,** Vincent A '96 (Nicoletti H&S) -88 Pine -NY 10005
(212) 468-4800 .. **Subar,** Jos N '03 %Davis & G LLP -1740 Bway -NY 10019
(914) 347-2600 .. **Suben,** Eric D '96 %Traub LS&S LLP -7 Skyline Dr -Hawthorne 10532
(607) 753-5008 .. **Suben,** Mark D '83 DA -46 Greenbush -Cortlnd 13045 **Fx:**756-3477
(212) 735-3000 .. **Suber,** Karen M '07 %Skadden ASM&F LLP -4 Times Sq -NY 10036
(516) 229-4400 .. **Subhan,** Soraya '02 %Kay & G -875 Merrick Av -Westbury 11590
(518) 762-8268 .. **Subik,** Robt M '79 -26 N Perry -Johnstwn 12095 **Fx:**762-4908
(212) 285-3800 .. **Subin,** Herbert '89 (Subin Assoc LLP) -150 Bway -NY 10007

(212) 854-7424 .. **Subotnik,** Eva E '04 Columbia Law Schl -435 W 116th -NY 10027 **Fx:**854-7946
(212) 336-8330 .. **Subramanian,** Arun S '08 %Susman G LLP -560 Lex Av -NY 10022
(212) 909-6000 .. **Subramanian,** Lila C '09 %Debevoise & P LLP -919 3rd Av -NY 10022
(212) 251-2500 .. **Subramanian,** Sunita '99 United Way of NYC -2 Park Av -NY 10016
(212) 782-2000 .. **Subryan,** Jennifer D '96 %Bk Hapoalim -1177 Av of Amer -NY 10036 **Fx:**782-2141
(516) 364-0519 .. **Subudhi,** Saroj Kumar '95 -2206 Route 106 -Syosset 11791
(845) 371-4700 .. **Such,** Alan F '76 (Fein SK&S,PC) -747 Chestnut Rdg Rd -Spg Vly 10977
(212) 759-8373 .. **Such,** Shannon K '89 -600 Mad Av -NY 10022 **Fx:**319-6913
(516) 369-2093 .. **Suchadola,** Jason W '04 -3771 Jerusalem Av -Seafrd 11783 **Fx:**740-2812
(716) 847-8400 .. **Suchan,** Donna Hoelscher '86 %Phillips L LLP -3400 HSBC Ctr -Buffalo 14203
(212) 907-0860 .. **Sucharow,** Lawr A '76 (Labaton S LLP) -140 Bway -NY 10005
(212) 635-1095 .. **Suchdev,** Vijay Kailash '95 Bk of NY Mellon -1 Wall -NY 10286
(718) 682-2661 .. **Sucher,** Danielle E '06 -26 Court -Brklyn 11242
(718) 522-1995 .. **Sucher,** Michl T '80 -26 Court -Brklyn 11242 **Fx:**797-3174
(914) 949-3788 .. **Suchin,** Miles Bertram '52 -499 N Bway -White Plns 10603
(212) 806-5400 .. **Suchman,** E Gail '86 SpclCnsl Stroock &S&L LLP -180 Maiden Ln -NY 10038
(518) 487-5552 .. **Suchocki,** Katherine '03 NYS Bar Assn -1 Elk -Albany 12207 **Fx:**463-8844
(212) 304-3994 .. **Suchoff,** Brian K '88 (Ross & S,LLC) -60 E 42nd -NY 10165 **Fx:**(973) 564-5120
(718) 354-3200 .. **Suchow,** Arthur D '76 (Battiste A&S,Inc) -60 Bay -Staten Isl 10301
(585) 722-9844 .. **Suchy,** Donna P '03 Eastman Kodak -343 State -Rchstr 14650
(212) 944-1030 .. **Sucke,** John H III '74 %Screen Actors Guild -360 Mad Av -NY 10017 **Fx:**944-6774
(212) 883-4900 .. **Suckewer,** Benjamin '75 (Cozen O) -277 Park Av -NY 10172
(212) 226-4200 .. **Suckle,** Howard A '87 (Suckle S&L PLLC) -224 W 35th -NY 10001
(212) 226-4200 .. **Suckle Schlesinger & Leifert PLLC** -224 W 35th -NY 10001 **Fx:**226-4226
(718) 579-7900 .. **Suckoo,** Stacy-Ann E '05 Leg Aid -900 Sheridan Av -Bronx 10451 **Fx:**293-8744
(212) 848-4000 .. **Sud,** Gaurav '08 %Shearman & S LLP -599 Lex Av -NY 10022
(212) 788-1096 .. **Sud,** Sumit '07 %Law Dept -100 Church -NY 10007 **Fx:**788-0367
(212) 259-8000 .. **Sud,** Uma '08 %Dewey & L LLP -1301 Av of Amer -NY 10019
(585) 436-7720 .. **Suda,** John A III '79 %UAW Leg Srvcs Plan -1200C Scottsvll Rd -Rchstr 14624 **Fx:**436-7741
(212) 277-4000 .. **Suda,** Ryan W '07 %Freshfields BD LLP -520 Mad Av -NY 10022
(212) 839-5300 .. **Sudduth,** Brandon K '08 %Sidley A LLP -787 7th Av -NY 10019
(212) 808-7800 .. **Suden,** Damon W '03 %Kelley D&W LLP -101 Park Av -NY 10178
(212) 407-4000 .. **Sudentas,** Paul B '09 %Loeb & L,LLP -345 Park Av -NY 10154
(212) 692-1000 .. **Sudnik,** Alexander K '98 (Duane M LLP) -1540 Bway -NY 10036
(212) 819-8200 .. **Sudo,** Amiko '03 %White & C LLP -1155 Av of Amer -NY 10036
(914) 559-3100 .. **Sudol,** Aneta '06 %Heidell PM&B,LLP -81 Main -White Plns 10601
(212) 967-1001 .. **Sue,** Jonathan Y '99 -1220 Bway -NY 10001 **Fx:**967-1112
(718) 340-4233 .. **Sue,** Sam '87 %CUNY Law Schl -65-21 Main -Flushng 11367 **Fx:**340-4482
(212) 841-1123 .. **Suedkamp,** Ashley D '04 -620 8th Av -NY 10018 **Fx:**841-1010
(212) 841-2000 .. **Sueiro,** Hugo F '02 BNP Paribas -787 7th Av -NY 10019
(212) 335-5102 .. **Suellentrop,** Jennifer S R '03 Fidelity Investments -200 Lbrty -NY 10281
(212) 421-4100 .. **Sues,** Christopher J '79 (Pryor C LLP) -7 Times Sq -NY 10036
(212) 986-4888 .. **Suess,** Benjamin '00 %Schrader & S,LLP -711 3rd Av -NY 10017
(212) 922-1640 .. **Suesser,** Alfred '70 %Dover Corp -280 Park Av -NY 10017 **Fx:**922-1656
(845) 355-2889 .. **Suffern,** Marc W II '76 -2579 Route 6 Bx300 -Slate Hll 10973 **Fx:**355-4103
(516) 887-8200 .. **Sufott,** Michl M '96 %D Lubin & Assoc,PLLC -5 N Vllg Av -Rockvll Ctr 11570 **Fx:**887-8250
(718) 590-6179 .. **Sugar,** Eric P '04 %Law Dept -198 E 161st -Bronx 10451 **Fx:**590-2686
(315) 593-9999 .. **Sugar,** Samuel J '84 -189 S 1st -Fulton 13069 **Fx:**593-9997
(212) 873-6982 .. **Sugarman,** Alan D '72 -17 W 70th -NY 10023
(212) 816-0275 .. **Sugarman,** Ian K '96 Citigroup -388 Greenwich -NY 10013
(718) 237-2000 .. **Sugarman,** Jeffrey S '99 %Leg Aid -111 Lvngstn -Brklyn 11201 **Fx:**237-8737
(716) 835-1835 .. **Sugarman,** Julian J '57 -124 St Johns Pl -Kenmore 14223
(212) 777-4827 .. **Sugarman,** Kenneth '76 -652 Bway -NY 10012 **Fx:**460-9818
(315) 474-2943 .. **Sugarman Law Firm,LLP** -211 W Jffrsn -Syracuse 13202 **Fx:**474-0235
(716) 847-2523 .. **Sugarman Law Firm,LLP** -14 Lafayette Sq -Buffalo 14203 **Fx:**847-2589
(646) 386-3247 .. **Sugarman,** Marilyn Trautfield '85 %Hon J Lobis -60 Centre -NY 10007
(212) 541-2000 .. **Sugarman,** Mark J '80 (Bryan C LLP) -1290 Av of Amer -NY 10104
(845) 485-3900 .. **Sugarman,** Risa S '78 %Dept of Law -235 Main -Poughkeepsie 12601 **Fx:**452-3303
(212) 310-8000 .. **Sugarman,** Robt G '63 SrCnsl Weil G&M LLP -767 5th Av -NY 10153
(516) 390-4748 .. **Sugarman,** Robt P '76 -50 Chas Lindbergh Blvd -Uniondale 11553 **Fx:**390-4749
(631) 406-7600 .. **Sugarman,** Shari Lee '98 SL Sugarman PC -900 Wheeler Rd -Hauppauge 11788 **Fx:**361-9601
(716) 873-6765 .. **Sugarman,** Steven R '85 %Pusatier S&A -2464 Elmwood Av -Kenmore 14217
(212) 725-4423 .. **Sugarman,** Stuart '78 (Paykin K&A LLP) -185 Mad Av -NY 10016
(212) 225-2000 .. **Sugerman,** David L '81 (Cleary GS&H) -1 Lbrty Plz -NY 10006
(212) 819-8200 .. **Suggs,** David H '06 %White & C LLP -1155 Av of Amer -NY 10036
(212) 733-9239 .. **Suggs,** Michele E '02 Pfizer -235 E 42nd -NY 10017
(212) 592-1400 .. **Sughrue,** Dennis M '93 (Herrick,F LLP) -2 Park Av -NY 10016
(212) 388-3208 .. **Sugimori,** Amy C '00 La Fuente -101 Av of Amer -NY 10013
(212) 636-6000 .. **Sugin,** Linda F '89 %Fordham Univ Sch of Law -140 W 62nd -NY 10023 **Fx:**636-6899
(212) 596-9000 .. **Sugino,** Mark M '83 Cnsl Ropes & G LLP -1211 Av of Amer -NY 10036
(212) 425-3100 .. **Suglia,** Peter D '96 OfCnsl McManus C&R,PC -48 Wall -NY 10005
(212) 785-7520 .. **Sugrue,** Stephen R '79 (Coti & S) -17 State -NY 10004
(716) 856-0277 .. **Sugrue,** Terry M '02 %Reden & O LLP -135 Delaware Av -Buffalo 14202
(212) 225-2000 .. **Suh,** David D '02 %Cleary GS&H -1 Lbrty Plz -NY 10006
(212) 848-4000 .. **Suh,** Dong C '03 %Shearman & S LLP -599 Lex Av -NY 10022
(718) 505-6650 .. **Suh,** Edw B '01 %Kaplan & M -75-20 Astoria Blvd -E Elmhrst 11370
(718) 286-6000 .. **Suh,** Edw K '07 %DA -125-01 Qns Blvd -Kew Gdns 11415
(631) 390-0080 .. **Suh,** Eugene M '02 Triboro Settlement -1121 Old Walt Whitman Rd -Melvll 11747
(212) 836-8000 .. **Suh,** Howard S '96 Cnsl Kaye S LLP -425 Park Av -NY 10022
(212) 859-8000 .. **Suh,** Hyorim '09 %Fried FHS&J LLP -1 NY Plz -NY 10004
(212) 839-5300 .. **Suh,** James '06 %Sidley A LLP -787 7th Av -NY 10019
(212) 558-4000 .. **Suh,** Jason Junghun '09 %Sullivan & C LLP -125 Broad -NY 10004
(212) 756-2000 .. **Suh,** Jos '95 (Schulte R&Z LLP) -919 3rd Av -NY 10022
(212) 909-6000 .. **Suh,** Julie S '07 %Debevoise & P LLP -919 3rd Av -NY 10022
(212) 819-8200 .. **Suh,** Kenneth '98 (White & C LLP) -1155 Av of Amer -NY 10036
(212) 891-6151 .. **Suh,** Michelle '03 Ixis Cptl Mrkts -9 W 57th -NY 10019
(212) 808-8300 .. **Suh,** Minjung '09 %Rosensteel Law -90 Park Av -NY 10016
(212) 664-2743 .. **Suh,** Patricia M '94 %NBC -30 Rckfllr Plz -NY 10112 **Fx:**664-2147
(212) 808-7800 .. **Suh,** Seulgey '07 %Kelley D&W LLP -101 Park Av -NY 10178
(212) 903-9000 .. **Suh,** Suin '09 %Linklaters -1345 Av of Amer -NY 10105
(212) 756-2000 .. **Suh,** Sung-Hee '91 (Schulte R&Z LLP) -919 3rd Av -NY 10022
(212) 701-3000 .. **Suh,** Susanna M '95 (Cahill G&R LLP) -80 Pine -NY 10005 **Fx:**269-5420
(212) 594-0796 .. **Suh,** Yoon S '94 -350 Fifth Av -NY 10118
(585) 546-4900 .. **Suher,** Kathleen K '94 %Home Properties of NY -850 Clinton Sq -Rchstr 14604 **Fx:**546-5433
(212) 216-1249 .. **Suhr,** Brigitte Helgard '97 %Human Rights Watch -350 5th Av -NY 10118 **Fx:**736-1300
(646) 672-4350 .. **Suhr,** J Nicholas '67 -6 E 87th -NY 10128 **Fx:**672-4353
(212) 238-4800 .. **Suhrada,** Melanie K '95 (Landman CB&F,PC) -120 Bway -NY 10271
(212) 628-1940 .. **Suisman,** Elsa D '76 -33 E 70th -NY 10021 **Fx:**628-1043
(212) 381-1540 .. **Suite,** Andre Martin '99 %Bad Boy Ent -1710 Bway -NY 10019
(212) 318-6000 .. **Suk,** Jonathan M '09 %Paul HJ&W LLP -75 E 55th -NY 10022
(518) 455-2484 .. **Sukatos,** Kristen M '98 %Senator J Bruno -The Cptl -Albany 12247
(212) 455-2000 .. **Sukenick,** Scott '07 %Simpson T&B LLP -425 Lex Av -NY 10017
(212) 725-9300 .. **Sukenik,** Martin C '61 (Sukenik S&G,PC) -404 5th Av -NY 10018
(212) 725-9300 .. **Sukenik Segal & Graff,PC** -404 5th Av -NY 10018 **Fx:**481-5520
(716) 551-4931 .. **Sukert,** Aaron B '01 %NLRB -130 S Elmwood Av -Buffalo 14202 **Fx:**551-4972
(212) 336-0136 .. **Sukhatme,** Liora '08 SEC -3 World Fncl Ctr -NY 10281 **Fx:**336-1323
(718) 787-0500 .. **Sukherman,** Leonard B '02 -3171 Coney Isl Av -Brklyn 11235
(718) 206-4685 .. **Sukhu,** Anita '02 %Law Dept -89-17 Sutphin Blvd -Jamaica 11435 **Fx:**206-4702
(718) 243-6224 .. **Sukhu,** Taramanie '97 %Leg Aid -111 Lvngstn -Brklyn 11201 **Fx:**237-8737
(212) 302-5800 .. **Sukin,** Michl F '68 Sukin Law Grp -1501 Bway -NY 10036
(607) 723-7913 .. **Sukloff,** Donald M '51 (Sukloff & S) -19 Chenango -Bnghmtn 13901
(607) 723-7913 .. **Sukloff & Schanz** -19 Chenango -Bnghmtn 13901 **Fx:**723-7916
(212) 735-3000 .. **Suksomnil,** Benjamin '03 %Skadden ASM&F LLP -4 Times Sq -NY 10036
(212) 801-6882 .. **Sulds,** Jonathan L '75 (Greenberg T,LLP) -200 Park Av -NY 10166
(212) 907-7300 .. **Sulem,** Laura A '00 %Golenbock EAB&P -437 Mad Av -NY 10022
(212) 909-6000 .. **Suleman,** Binish Hasan '10 %Debevoise & P LLP -919 3rd Av -NY 10022
(212) 909-6000 .. **Suleman,** M Arsalan '08 %Debevoise & P LLP -919 3rd Av -NY 10022
(212) 608-1911 .. **Sules,** Richd T '87 (Stockschlaeder M&S,PC) -110 William -NY 10038
(718) 232-7670 .. **Sulfaro,** Carl A '84 OfCnsl Friedland L&R -245 Bay 10th -Brklyn 11228 **Fx:**236-5199
(212) 430-8020 .. **Sulieman,** Afaf S '01 Cnsl LeClairRyan,PC -830 3rd Av -NY 10022
(718) 544-5404 .. **Sulik,** Jos G '72 -125-10 Qns Blvd -Jamaica 11415
(607) 256-0727 .. **Sulimowicz,** Sharon M '96 -118 N Tioga -Ithaca 14850 **Fx:**256-0729
(516) 803-2300 .. **Suljic,** Lucia M '05 %Cablevision Sys -1111 Stewart Av -Bethpage 11714
(212) 345-6941 .. **Sulkes,** Jill '05 Marsh Inc -1166 Av of Amer -NY 10036
(212) 902-1000 .. **Sulkes,** Joel M '01 %Goldman Sachs -85 Broad -NY 10004
(212) 559-9436 .. **Sulkowski,** Erica E '01 %Citigrp -485 Lex Av -NY 10017
(518) 474-5790 .. **Sullivan,** Alicia M '00 %OTDA -40 N Pearl -Albany 12243 **Fx:**474-9389
(917) 714-8894 .. **Sullivan,** Allen F '67 -225 Bway -NY 10007
(212) 530-5000 .. **Sullivan,** Andrew P '08 %Milbank TH&M LLP -1 Chase Manh Plz -NY 10005
(518) 885-2263 .. **Sullivan,** Ann C '88 DA -25 W High -Ballston Spa 12020 **Fx:**884-8627
(212) 699-8400 .. **Sullivan,** Brian A '04 Van Wagner Communications LLC -800 3rd Av -NY 10022 **Fx:**986-0927
(212) 530-1800 .. **Sullivan,** Brian C '05 Richards K&O LLP -1 World Fncl Ctr -NY 10281
(516) 746-6446 .. **Sullivan,** Brian P '03 (Sullivan and S,LLP) -200 Grdn City Plz -Gdn Cty 11530 **Fx:**746-6448
(516) 248-6000 .. **Sullivan,** Caroline A '10 %Kaufman B&R -1205 Franklin Av -Gdn Cty 11530
(212) 480-7449 .. **Sullivan,** Caroline M '81 %DHCR -25 Beaver -NY 10004 **Fx:**480-7416
(212) 659-7300 .. **Sullivan,** Carolyn '93 (Haynes & B,LLP) -1221 Av of Amer -NY 10020
(315) 638-3113 .. **Sullivan,** Catherine M '93 -Bx524 -Baldwinsvll 13027
(315) 218-8000 .. **Sullivan,** Chas J '93 (Bond S&K,PLLC) -1 Lincoln Ctr -Syracuse 13202
(212) 551-6134 .. **Sullivan,** Chas S '87 Booz & Co Inc -101 Park Av -NY 10178
(607) 778-2117 .. **Sullivan,** Cheryl D '89 %Cnty Atty -Cnty Ofc Bldg Bx1766 -Bnghmtn 13902 **Fx:**778-6122
(212) 867-4100 .. **Sullivan,** Christina H '07 %Furman K&B LLP -61 Bway -NY 10006
(631) 242-1888 .. **Sullivan,** Christine Lobasso '99 %N Campasano -2000 Deer Prk Av -Deer Pk 11729
(212) 592-1400 .. **Sullivan,** Christopher J '82 (Herrick,F LLP) -2 Park Av -NY 10016

(845) 794-1303 .. **Sullivan,** Claire I '89 (Ferrara & S) -34 North Bx785 -Monticello 12701 **Fx:**794-1305
(212) 683-7050 .. **Sullivan,** Claudia H '96 %JM Abramson -375 5th Av -NY 10016 **Fx:**683-7076
(212) 558-4000 .. **Sullivan & Cromwell LLP** -125 Broad -NY 10004 **Fx:**558-3588
(845) 565-1100 .. **Sullivan,** Danl F '91 %Tarshis CLM&M,PLLC -One Corwin Ct -Newburgh 12550
(718) 286-6000 .. **Sullivan,** Danl M '79 %DA -125-01 Qns Blvd -Kew Gdns 11415
(518) 474-1010 .. **Sullivan,** Danl M '99 %Ofc Inspector Genl -ESP Agncy Bldg 2 -Albany 12223 **Fx:**486-3745
(212) 736-1940 .. **Sullivan,** Danielle C '07 %Davidson D&K LLC -485 7th Av -NY 10018
(516) 877-1485 .. **Sullivan,** Daria M '91 -19 Franklin -Williston Pk 11596
(718) 250-2000 .. **Sullivan,** Darren B '10 %DA -350 Jay -Brklyn 11201 **Fx:**250-2314
(212) 878-8000 .. **Sullivan,** David A '98 %Clifford C LLP -31 W 52nd -NY 10019
(212) 484-8955 .. **Sullivan,** David P '09 Time Warner -1 Time Warner Ctr -NY 10019
(315) 471-3151 .. **Sullivan,** Debra Chini '91 (Hancock & E,LLP) -1500 AXA Twr I Bx4976 -Syracuse 13221
(212) 232-0400 .. **Sullivan,** Deirdre Ann '89 BCG Atty Srch -1560 Bway -NY 10036
(212) 556-1760 .. **Sullivan,** Deirdre C '00 The NY Times Co -620 8th Av -NY 10018
(315) 425-9000 .. **Sullivan,** Denis J '03 (Marjama MB&S LLP) -250 S Clinton -Syracuse 13202
(845) 735-5050 .. **Sullivan,** Denise A '01 %O'Connell & R -144 E Central Av Bx1050 -Pearl Rvr 10965
(212) 541-2000 .. **Sullivan,** Dermot J '99 (Bryan C LLP) -1290 Av of Amer -NY 10104
(914) 949-2700 .. **Sullivan,** Donald J '55 OfCnsl Bleakley P&S,LLP -1 N Lex Av -White Plns 10601
(631) 654-4900 .. **Sullivan,** Donald S '76 OfCnsl Cartier BA&D,PC -100 Austin -Patchogue 11772
(718) 358-6400 .. **Sullivan,** Donna M '90 (Hammock & S,LLC) -130-30 31st Av -Flushng 11354 **Fx:**358-6424
(212) 340-0400 .. **Sullivan,** Douglas C '95 %Appllt Div 1st Dept -27 Mad Av -NY 10010 **Fx:**889-4412
(718) 286-6000 .. **Sullivan,** Eileen Mary '76 %DA -125-01 Qns Blvd -Kew Gdns 11415
(212) 559-0528 .. **Sullivan,** Ellen Manion '93 Citibank NA -425 Park Av -NY 10022
(516) 764-2278 .. **Sullivan,** Eric P '63 -23 Dogwood Ln -Rockvll Ctr 11570
(212) 714-1720 .. **Sullivan,** Eugene J '73 (Tompkins MW&B LLP) -140 Bway -NY 10005
(212) 408-5100 .. **Sullivan,** Eugene R Jr. '65 OfCnsl Chadbourne & P LLP -30 Rckfllr Plz -NY 10112
(914) 995-4269 .. **Sullivan,** Fredk M '00 %Cnty Atty -148 Martine Av -White Plns 10601 **Fx:**995-5858
(516) 285-1575 .. **Sullivan,** Garnett H '82 -245-02 Jericho Tpke -Floral Pk 11001 **Fx:**285-1608
(718) 248-0727 .. **Sullivan,** Gary J '82 %Citibank -1 Court Sq -LIC 11101
(212) 801-6541 .. **Sullivan,** George D '83 (Greenberg T,LLP) -200 Park Av -NY 10166
(917) 454-1100 .. **Sullivan,** Gregory '03 %Police Dept -2 Lafayette -NY 10007
(212) 725-0200 .. **Sullivan,** Helena D '98 %Barnes R&C -475 Park Av S -NY 10016
(212) 238-2420 .. **Sullivan,** Henry A '72 %UIA Bd -59 Maiden Ln -NY 10038 **Fx:**238-2451
(518) 438-5364 .. **Sullivan Hess & Youngblood,PC** -4 Exec Park Dr -Albany 12203 **Fx:**438-0348
(212) 858-7158 .. **Sullivan,** Howard E III '91 RBC Capital Mrkts -165 Bway -NY 10006
(646) 213-5100 .. **Sullivan,** James D '09 WTAS,LLC -452 5th Av -NY 10018
(212) 374-0009 .. **Sullivan,** James F III '97 -52 Duane -NY 10007 **Fx:**374-9931
(646) 286-9930 .. **Sullivan,** James F X '83 FX Alliance,LLC -900 3rd Av -NY 10022
(212) 210-9522 .. **Sullivan,** James H '09 (Alston & B LLP) -90 Park Av -NY 10016
(914) 949-2700 .. **Sullivan,** James J '73 (Bleakley P&S,LLP) -1 N Lex Av -White Plns 10601
(212) 484-3900 .. **Sullivan,** James M '96 (Arent F LLP) -1675 Bway -NY 10019
(212) 408-2500 .. **Sullivan,** Jamie Ellis '08 %Baker B,LLP -30 Rckfllr Plz -NY 10112
(212) 334-7192 .. **Sullivan,** Janet A '89 (Sullivan & L,PC) -401 Bway -NY 10013 **Fx:**431-9444
(516) 294-8844 .. **Sullivan,** Jared T '06 %L'Abbate BC&C,LLP -1001 Franklin Av -Gdn Cty 11530
(516) 742-0820 .. **Sullivan,** Jean E '80 -1140 Franklin Av -Gdn Cty 11530
(212) 408-2500 .. **Sullivan,** Jeffrey D '97 (Baker B,LLP) -30 Rckfllr Plz -NY 10112
(518) 438-5364 .. **Sullivan,** Jeffrey G '90 (Sullivan H&Y,PC) -4 Exec Park Dr -Albany 12203
(631) 342-5602 .. **Sullivan,** Jennifer P '01 CA Inc -1 CA Plz -Islandia 11749
(518) 427-9700 .. **Sullivan,** Joan P '87 OfCnsl Harris B PLLC -677 Bway -Albany 12207
(315) 379-2410 .. **Sullivan,** Johanne L '03 %Family Ct -48 Court -Canton 13617 **Fx:**386-3197
(212) 252-5855 .. **Sullivan,** John A '90 %Exec/Comm -28 W 44th -NY 10036 **Fx:**684-2688
(212) 709-1648 .. **Sullivan,** John B '69 %Banking Dept -1 State -NY 10004 **Fx:**709-1655
(631) 789-4000 .. **Sullivan,** John C '49 OfCnsl Blumberg CF&B -330 Bway -Amityvll 11701
(914) 592-7300 .. **Sullivan,** John C '89 (J Sullivan,PC) -22 Saw Mill Rvr Rd -Hawthorne 10532 **Fx:**592-8152
(516) 877-1485 .. **Sullivan,** John J '63 -19 Franklin -Williston Pk 11596
(212) 547-5400 .. **Sullivan,** John J '78 (McDermott W&E LLP) -340 Mad Av -NY 10173
(212) 918-3000 .. **Sullivan,** John J '81 (Hogan L LLP) -875 3rd Av -NY 10022
(518) 474-7469 .. **Sullivan,** John J '89 %OCA -Agncy Bldg 4 ESP -Albany 12223 **Fx:**473-5514
(212) 669-0600 .. **Sullivan,** John J '95 (Hill R LLP) -45 Bway -NY 10006
(585) 238-2000 .. **Sullivan,** John T Jr. '67 OfCnsl Phillips L LLP -1400 First Fed Plz -Rchstr 14614
(315) 785-2444 .. **Sullivan,** John T Jr. '76 Atty Gen -317 Wshngtn -Watertwn 13601 **Fx:**785-2294
(212) 490-3000 .. **Sullivan,** John W '74 (Wilson EME&D LLP) -150 E 42nd -NY 10017
(516) 663-6600 .. **Sullivan,** Jonathan C '02 %Ruskin MF,PC -1425 RXR Plz -Uniondale 11556
(516) 248-7777 .. **Sullivan,** Jos D '92 (Sullivan & S) -1305 Franklin Av -Gdn Cty 11530 **Fx:**746-6170
(212) 566-1000 .. **Sullivan,** Jos F '95 (Sullivan & B LLP) -115 Bway -NY 10006 **Fx:**566-1068
(212) 625-8030 .. **Sullivan,** Jos J III '90 (Sheindlin & S LLP) -350 Bway -NY 10013 **Fx:**202-4378
(212) 820-9513 .. **Sullivan,** Jos L '01 (Hawkins D&W LLP) -One Chase Manh Plz -NY 10005
(212) 513-3200 .. **Sullivan,** Jos P '57 OfCnsl Holland & K LLP -31 W 52nd -NY 10019
(212) 787-3202 .. **Sullivan,** Jos P '61 (McCarthy & S) -2095 Bway -NY 10023
(212) 730-7700 .. **Sullivan,** Judith J '94 (Michelman & R,LLP) -114 W 47th -NY 10036
(914) 725-1787 .. **Sullivan,** Kathleen E '91 -28 Rodney Rd -Scarsdale 10583 **Fx:**725-5495
(212) 864-0433 .. **Sullivan,** Kathleen F '83 %DMV -159 E 125th -NY 10035
(212) 849-7000 .. **Sullivan,** Kathleen M '82 (Quinn EU&S,LLP) -51 Mad Av -NY 10010
(518) 434-1022 .. **Sullivan Keenan Oliver & Violando, LLP** -152 Central Av -Albany 12206 **Fx:**434-2304
(631) 269-1515 .. **Sullivan & Kehoe,LLP** -44 Main -Kings Pk 11754 **Fx:**269-1521
(718) 326-6200 .. **Sullivan,** Keith M '99 (Sullivan & G) -73-42 68th Av -Middl Vllg 11379 **Fx:**228-7010
(914) 592-7300 .. **Sullivan,** Kevin C '93 %J Sullivan,PC -22 Saw Mill Rvr Rd -Hawthorne 10532 **Fx:**592-8152
(212) 357-5690 .. **Sullivan,** Kevin F '03 Goldman Sachs -1 NY Plz -NY 10004
(716) 852-1000 .. **Sullivan,** Kevin J '78 %PW Beltz,PC -36 Church -Buffalo 14202 **Fx:**852-5887
(631) 979-8366 .. **Sullivan,** Kevin M '97 -45 Columbine Ln -Kings Pk 11754 **Fx:**979-8366
(646) 471-4000 .. **Sullivan,** Kevin P '09 %PricewaterhouseCoopers LLP -300 Mad Av -NY 10017
(914) 428-2323 .. **Sullivan,** Kiernan J '94 -399 Knollwood Rd -White Plns 10603 **Fx:**428-3298
(516) 545-5160 .. **Sullivan,** Linda D '00 SrCnsl Natl Grid -175 E Old Cntry Rd -Hicksvll 11801 **Fx:**545-5029
(914) 287-2000 .. **Sullivan,** Lori A '88 -470 Mamaroneck Av -White Plns 10605
(516) 571-2042 .. **Sullivan,** Lori A '90 %Surrogate's Ct -262 Old Cntry Rd -Mineola 11501 **Fx:**571-3864
(212) 566-4547 .. **Sullivan,** M Virginia '86 %Dept of Bldgs -280 Bway -NY 10007
(631) 853-4161 .. **Sullivan,** Mallory Osgood '05 %DA -N Cnty Cmplx Bldg 77 -Hauppauge 11788 **Fx:**853-4192
(914) 846-7000 .. **Sullivan,** Maria '88 %NY Life Ins -1 Rockwood Rd -Sleepy Hollow 10591 **Fx:**846-4755
(212) 340-0400 .. **Sullivan,** Mariann '81 %Appllt Div 1st Dept -27 Mad Av -NY 10010 **Fx:**889-4412
(212) 323-2290 .. **Sullivan,** Mark P '96 Hlth & Hsptl Corp -346 Bway -NY 10013
(212) 415-9200 .. **Sullivan,** Mark S '85 (Dorsey & W LLP) -250 Park Av -NY 10177
(716) 372-4220 .. **Sullivan,** Mary M '82 -406 King -Olean 14760 **Fx:**372-4220
(516) 616-0422 .. **Sullivan,** Maryellen C '82 -99 Tulip Av -Floral Pk 11001 **Fx:**616-0280
(212) 337-2228 .. **Sullivan,** Matthew M '03 US Dept Labor -201 Varick -NY 10014
(716) 842-5705 .. **Sullivan,** Maureen Wellman '82 %M&T Bk -1 M & T Plz -Buffalo 14203 **Fx:**842-5376
(212) 416-8000 .. **Sullivan,** Michl A '98 %Dept of Law -120 Bway -NY 10271
(716) 673-9595 .. **Sullivan,** Michl J '85 -7 E Main Bx182 -Fredonia 14063 **Fx:**673-9596
(607) 770-8870 .. **Sullivan,** Michl J '89 (Somma & S) -400 Plz Dr -Vestal 13850
(212) 483-0105 .. **Sullivan,** Michl J '89 (Coughlin D LLP) -88 Pine-Wall St Plz -NY 10005
(631) 547-0300 .. **Sullivan,** Michl J '90 %Novick & Assoc,PC -202 E Main -Huntngtn 11743 **Fx:**547-0212
(716) 856-4200 .. **Sullivan,** Michl P '08 %Gibson M&C,LLP -69 Delaware Av -Buffalo 14202
(716) 856-4091 .. **Sullivan,** Michl T Jr. '56 (Gannon G&S,LLP) -618 Brisbane Bldg -Buffalo 14203
(631) 269-1515 .. **Sullivan,** Michl T '76 (Sullivan & K,LLP) -44 Main -Kings Pk 11754
(212) 660-3000 .. **Sullivan,** Michl T '81 (Sullivan & W LLP) -1290 Av of Amer -NY 10104
(212) 450-4000 .. **Sullivan,** Monica N '09 %Davis P&W LLP -450 Lex Av -NY 10017
(716) 667-7800 .. **Sullivan,** Mortimer A Jr. '64 -3623 Eggert Rd Bx1003 -Orchard Pk 14127 **Fx:**662-0238
(212) 319-3862 .. **Sullivan,** Natalie A '09 -425 Mad Av -NY 10017
(212) 697-6555 .. **Sullivan,** Nicole A '02 %Biedermann RH&R -570 Lex Av -NY 10022
(212) 732-9000 .. **Sullivan Papain Block McGrath & Cannavo PC** -120 Bway -NY 10271 **Fx:**571-3903
(516) 742-0707 .. **Sullivan Papain Block McGrath & Cannavo PC** -55 Mineola Blvd -Mineola 11501 **Fx:**742-7350
(212) 313-3600 .. **Sullivan,** Patricia A '81 (Barry M&M) -2 Rector -NY 10006
(516) 342-1248 .. **Sullivan,** Patrick J '90 (PJ Sullivan,PLLC) -92 Willis Av -Mineola 11501 **Fx:**747-9405
(718) 875-7428 .. **Sullivan,** Patrick J '92 Envrnmntl Cntrl Brd -233 Schermerhorn -Brklyn 11201
(212) 715-9100 .. **Sullivan,** Patrick L '03 %Kramer LN&F,LLP -1177 Av of Amer -NY 10036
(212) 323-1998 .. **Sullivan,** Patrick R '94 Guy Carpenter & Co -1166 Av of Amer -NY 10036
(800) 878-1432 .. **Sullivan,** Paul C '05 (Fields SS PLLC) -65 E 55th -NY 10022 **Fx:**(866) 529-3291
(845) 454-1110 .. **Sullivan,** Paul O '76 (Corbally G and R LLP) -35 Market -Poughkeepsie 12601
(212) 486-0124 .. **Sullivan,** Paul T '70 (Trowbridge & S) -515 Mad Av -NY 10022
(212) 351-4000 .. **Sullivan,** Peter '78 (Gibson D&C LLP) -200 Park Av -NY 10166
(516) 222-6200 .. **Sullivan,** Peter '79 (Berkman HPP&F,PC) -100 Grdn City Plz -Gdn Cty 11530
(212) 370-4900 .. **Sullivan,** Peter '88 OfCnsl Rosenthal & H,PC -420 Lex Av -NY 10170
(212) 837-6000 .. **Sullivan,** Peter A '93 (Hughes H&R LLP) -1 Bttry Pk Plz -NY 10004
(212) 687-5900 .. **Sullivan,** Peter R '82 (Sullivan & G,LLP) -475 Park Av S -NY 10016 **Fx:**687-4060
(516) 229-4522 .. **Sullivan,** Richd B '99 Russo A&T -875 Merrick Av -Westbury 11590
(631) 265-7507 .. **Sullivan,** Richd J '81 -400 Town Line Rd -Hauppauge 11788
(212) 335-9000 .. **Sullivan,** Richd L '05 %DA -1 Hogan Pl -NY 10013
(212) 286-8585 .. **Sullivan,** Richd Michl Jr. '96 (Heidell PM&B,LLP) -99 Park Av -NY 10016
(716) 200-5050 .. **Sullivan,** Richd T '70 (Harris B PLLC) -726 Exchange -Buffalo 14210
(914) 238-8355 .. **Sullivan,** Robt C '64 -3 Grdn Ridge Rd -Chappaqua 10514

(212) 765-5070 .. **Sullivan,** Robt C Jr. '88 OfCnsl Fish & R,PC -153 E 53rd -NY 10022

(914) 323-7000 .. **Sullivan,** Robt D Jr. '04 %Wilson EME&D LLP -3 Gannett Dr -White Plns 10604

(315) 825-0000 .. **Sullivan,** Robt F '89 -67 Hmltn -Hamilton 13346 **Fx:**825-0000

(516) 742-0707 .. **Sullivan,** Robt G '74 (Sullivan PBM&C PC) -55 Mineola Blvd -Mineola 11501

(212) 732-9000 .. **Sullivan,** Robt G '74 -120 Bway -NY 10271 **Fx:**571-3903

(516) 746-6446 .. **Sullivan,** Robt G '99 (Sullivan and S,LLP) -200 Grdn City Plz -Gdn Cty 11530 **Fx:**746-6448

(212) 735-3000 .. **Sullivan,** Robt J '75 (Skadden ASM&F LLP) -4 Times Sq -NY 10036

(212) 905-9151 .. **Sullivan,** Robt J '89 (Alston & B LLP) -90 Park Av -NY 10016

(212) 695-0910 .. **Sullivan,** Robt M '82 (Sullivan Law Grp,LLP) -1350 Bway -NY 10018 **Fx:**695-0915

(914) 287-2000 .. **Sullivan,** Scott G '99 -470 Mamaroneck Av -White Plns 10605

(212) 335-9000 .. **Sullivan,** Sean J '04 %DA -1 Hogan Pl -NY 10013

(212) 334-7192 .. **Sullivan,** Sean P '89 (Sullivan & L,PC) -401 Bway -NY 10013 **Fx:**431-9444

(212) 374-0009 .. **Sullivan,** Shannon R '07 %J Sullivan,PC -52 Duane -NY 10007 **Fx:**374-9931

(315) 429-3127 .. **Sullivan & Snyder** -8 S Main Bx146 -Dolgevll 13329 **Fx:**429-8873

(631) 852-2500 .. **Sullivan,** Sona M '01 %DA -200 Center Dr -Rvrhead 11901 **Fx:**852-1769

(212) 218-2100 .. **Sullivan,** Stephen K '03 %Fitzpatrick CH&S -1290 Av of Amer -NY 10104

(631) 232-2600 .. **Sullivan,** Susan Riley '99 Roux Assoc Inc -209 Shafter -Islandia 11749

(518) 473-1403 .. **Sullivan,** Suzanne Aldridge '92 %Dept of Health -Corning Twr 24th Fl -Albany 12237 **Fx:**473-2019

(718) 286-6000 .. **Sullivan,** Suzanne H '00 %DA -125-01 Qns Blvd -Kew Gdns 11415

(212) 264-0300 .. **Sullivan,** Suzanne K '90 %NLRB -26 Fed Plz -NY 10278 **Fx:**264-8427

(212) 506-1700 .. **Sullivan,** Teresa A '84 Kasowitz BT&F LLP -1633 Bway -NY 10019

(718) 590-7800 .. **Sullivan,** Thos J '03 -930 Grnd Cncrs -Bronx 10451

(631) 715-7900 .. **Sullivan,** Thos M '97 US Atty -610 Fed Plz -Central Islip 11722

(518) 668-2435 .. **Sullivan,** Thos Michl '99 %Life Ins Specialists -77 Philip -Lk George 12845

(718) 442-1182 .. **Sullivan,** Thos R '52 OfCnsl Tracy & S,PC -1688 Victory Blvd -Staten Isl 10314 **Fx:**442-0552

(212) 566-8860 .. **Sullivan,** Timothy M '99 (Sullivan Law Firm) -217 Bway -NY 10007 **Fx:**233-1060

(212) 816-6381 .. **Sullivan,** Timothy Patrick '99 Citigroup Global Mrkts -388 Greenwich -NY 10013

(516) 248-7777 .. **Sullivan,** Timothy W '61 (Sullivan & S) -1305 Franklin Av -Gdn Cty 11530 **Fx:**746-6170

(646) 471-4000 .. **Sullivan,** Ulric R '71 %PricewaterhouseCoopers LLP -300 Mad Av -NY 10017

(914) 967-1019 .. **Sullivan,** Wm A '73 -2 Elm Pl Bx157 -Rye 10580 **Fx:**921-2499

(315) 476-8144 .. **Sullivan,** Wm C '96 -120 E Wshngtn -Syracuse 13202 **Fx:**476-8147

(631) 666-5766 .. **Sullivan,** Wm M '92 (Long TBSWJ&S) -120 4th Av Bx5591 -Bay Shr 11706

(212) 660-3000 .. **Sullivan & Worcester LLP** -1290 Av of Amer -NY 10104 **Fx:**660-3001

(845) 432-2510 .. **Sullivan-Bisceglia,** Susan M '98 %IBM -2455 South Rd -Poughkeepsie 12601

(212) 323-0200 .. **Sullivan-Melgar,** Deborah A '98 OppenheimerFunds,Inc -225 Lbrty -NY 10281

(914) 366-5700 .. **Sullivan-Reed,** Deborah '90 %MA Bjork -660 Wht Plns Rd -Tarrytwn 10591 **Fx:**366-5759

(718) 748-8257 .. **Sully,** Danl E '97 -241 86th -Brklyn 11209 **Fx:**491-1278

(212) 364-8514 .. **Sully,** Sarah E '95 Time Warner Cable -60 Columbus Av -NY 10023 **Fx:**364-8460

(212) 888-8181 .. **Sulner,** Andrew '77 -220 E 57th -NY 10022 **Fx:**888-6006

(516) 296-7000 .. **Sulsky,** Steven '84 %Certilman BA&H,LLP -90 Merrick Av -E Meadow 11554

(646) 746-9761 .. **Sultan,** Manal M '96 CFTC -140 Bway -NY 10005 **Fx:**746-9938

(212) 683-8960 .. **Sultan,** Stephen '59 Dramatists Play Srvc,Inc -440 Park Av S -NY 10016 **Fx:**213-1539

(212) 837-6000 .. **Sultanik,** Saml '79 (Hughes H&R LLP) -1 Bttry Pk Plz -NY 10004

(917) 656-8446 .. **Sultan-Mizrahi,** Sheryl '97 -2401 Av T -Brklyn 11229

(914) 417-3400 .. **Sultzer,** Jason P '98 (Littleton JUP&K LLP) -1 Manhattanvll Rd -Purchase 10577

(516) 536-7444 .. **Sultzer,** Neal H '77 (Ackerman R&S) -2949 Lng Bch Rd -Oceanside 11572 **Fx:**536-8235

(914) 961-1300 .. **Sulzer,** Wm E '98 (Griffin CB&S,PC) -51 Pondfld Rd -Bronxvll 10708

(917) 923-1134 .. **Sulzman,** Richd A '89 -110 Wall -NY 10005

(914) 997-6000 .. **Sumber,** Edw I '69 -399 Knollwood Rd -White Plns 10603 **Fx:**(845) 225-1187

(845) 225-1100 .. **Sumber,** Edw I '69 -18 Fair -Carmel 10512 **Fx:**225-1187

(212) 836-8000 .. **Sumer,** Jacquelyn L '04 %Kaye S LLP -425 Park Av -NY 10022

(718) 590-2000 .. **Suminski,** George M '98 %DA -198 E 161st -Bronx 10451 **Fx:**590-6477

(347) 418-3830 .. **Summa,** Matthew '03 %L Miles -36-01 43rd Av -LIC 11101 **Fx:**418-3838

(212) 901-6000 .. **Summe,** Kimberly Anne '97 ISDA -360 Mad Av -NY 10017

(212) 755-7500 .. **Summer,** Erica J '02 %Marcus R&D LLP -488 Mad Av -NY 10022

(516) 829-8100 .. **Summer,** Fern '86 %1st Rehab Life Ins -600 Nrthrn Blvd -Gt Neck 11021 **Fx:**829-8210

(718) 325-5000 .. **Summer,** Robt S '91 %M Pfeifer -714 E 241st -Bronx 10470 **Fx:**324-0333

(212) 363-2500 .. **Summerfield,** Jason N '09 %Finkelstein & V PC -90 Broad -NY 10004

(212) 701-3000 .. **Summers,** Adam D '07 %Cahill G&R LLP -80 Pine -NY 10005 **Fx:**269-5420

(516) 354-6400 .. **Summers,** Allan D '73 -15 Friendly Ln -Jericho 11753 **Fx:**938-7566

(914) 597-7800 .. **Summers,** Deborah A '02 %Lewis S&C,LLC -11 Martine Av -White Plns 10606 **Fx:**597-7801

(212) 526-7000 .. **Summers,** Elisabeth Stuart '04 Barclays Capital -745 7th Av -NY 10019

(212) 906-1200 .. **Summers,** Jane '85 (Latham & W) -885 3rd Av -NY 10022

(518) 459-2495 .. **Summers,** Jonathan B '87 (Summers Law Firm,PC) -125 Wolf Rd -Albany 12205 **Fx:**459-2571

(516) 873-2000 .. **Summers,** Joshua B '05 %Moritt HH&H LLP -400 Grdn City Plz -Gdn Cty 11530

(607) 286-7575 .. **Summers,** Linden D III '85 -Bx602 -Milford 13807

(585) 265-3990 .. **Summers,** Reed N '83 -20 W Main -Webster 14580 **Fx:**265-2805

(212) 689-6060 .. **Summers,** Robt I '96 (Smolka & S) -274 Mad Av -NY 10016 **Fx:**545-0715

(212) 489-8230 .. **Summerscales,** Joanna E '09 %Davis WT LLP -1633 Bway -NY 10019

(212) 977-9700 .. **Summit,** Stuart A '61 (Phillips N LLP) -666 5th Av -NY 10103

(315) 592-4241 .. **Sumner & Auser** -226 Oneida Bx549 -Fulton 13069 **Fx:**598-8557

(315) 592-4241 .. **Sumner,** Fred I '58 (Sumner & A) -226 Oneida Bx549 -Fulton 13069

(212) 938-1930 .. **Sumner,** Neil '94 -115 W 29th -NY 10001

(212) 596-9000 .. **Sum Ping,** Joan K '09 %Ropes & G LLP -1211 Av of Amer -NY 10036

(212) 841-1000 .. **Sum-Ping,** Joanne '07 %Covington & B LLP -620 8th Av -NY 10018

(212) 751-3001 .. **Sumrow,** Shad E '05 (Thompson & K LLP) -919 3rd Av -NY 10022

(212) 406-5551 .. **Sun,** Able Man-Hoi '92 -70 Lafayette -NY 10013

(212) 425-7200 .. **Sun,** Caroline '09 %Kenyon & K,LLP -1 Bway -NY 10004

(212) 318-6000 .. **Sun,** Charlene C '09 %Paul HJ&W LLP -75 E 55th -NY 10022

(212) 947-3330 .. **Sun,** Jianlong '98 %Tuan & C,LLP -225 Bway -NY 10007

(212) 425-7854 .. **Sun,** Joyce J '94 %Georgoulis & Assoc PLLC -45 Bway -NY 10006 **Fx:**422-5360

(212) 310-8000 .. **Sun,** Qiong '08 %Weil G&M LLP -767 5th Av -NY 10153

(212) 966-2116 .. **Sun,** Thos '95 -401 Bway -NY 10013

(212) 973-0572 .. **Sun,** Xiaolei '09 %Wolff & S PC -140 Bway -NY 10005

(347) 592-2200 .. **Sun,** Xiyuan '08 %Leg Srvcs -89-00 Sutphin Blvd -Jamaica 11435 **Fx:**(718) 937-5350

(212) 264-3511 .. **Suna,** David B '99 US Homeland Sec-ICE -26 Fed Plz -NY 10278 **Fx:**264-4534

(914) 946-8100 .. **Sundack,** Tracie A '90 (T Sundack & Assoc,LLC) -19 Court -White Plns 10601 **Fx:**946-9585

(212) 298-5157 .. **Sundaram,** Kannan '91 %Leg Aid -49 Thomas -NY 10013 **Fx:**298-5252

(212) 788-0467 .. **Sundaran,** Raju '03 %Law Dept -100 Church -NY 10007 **Fx:**788-0367

(212) 223-4000 .. **Sundaresh,** Neeti '06 %Crowell & M LLP -590 Mad Av -NY 10022

(212) 599-6868 .. **Sundarraj,** Shivaprasad B '92 1st Commercial Bk -750 3rd Av -NY 10017

(718) 241-7239 .. **Sundel,** Arnold H '58 -49 Barlow Dr N -Brklyn 11234

(212) 566-7403 .. **Sundel,** Mitchel S '86 -225 Bway -NY 10007 **Fx:**766-4380

(212) 907-0700 .. **Sundel,** Stefanie J '05 %Labaton S LLP -140 Bway -NY 10005

(212) 925-4848 .. **Sunden,** Gary R '66 -299 Bway -NY 10007 **Fx:**(646) 613-8512

(212) 373-3000 .. **Sunderji,** Alykhan A '10 %Paul WRW&G LLP -1285 Av of Amer -NY 10019

(212) 728-8000 .. **Sunderji,** Fara S '07 %Willkie F&G LLP -787 7th Av -NY 10019

(914) 472-2300 .. **Sundheim,** Steven R '85 (Jones G,LLP) -670 Wht Plns Rd -Scarsdale 10583

(518) 445-2311 .. **Sundquist,** Christian B '03 Albany Law Schl -80 New Scotland Av -Albany 12208 **Fx:**445-2315

(518) 527-1918 .. **Sundram,** Clarence J '72 -28 Tierney Dr -Delmar 12054 **Fx:**439-9740

(716) 845-6000 .. **Suneson,** Steve V '01 %Kavinoky C LLP -726 Exchange -Buffalo 14210

(212) 455-2000 .. **Sung,** Andrea H '10 %Simpson T&B LLP -425 Lex Av -NY 10017

(212) 925-8818 .. **Sung,** April C '77 (Sung & H) -350 Bway -NY 10013 **Fx:**925-8897

(212) 903-9000 .. **Sung,** Brian Y '01 %Linklaters -1345 Av of Amer -NY 10105

(212) 335-9000 .. **Sung,** Chanterelle '05 %DA -1 Hogan Pl -NY 10013

(212) 218-2100 .. **Sung,** Christine '10 %Fitzpatrick CH&S -1290 Av of Amer -NY 10104

(212) 250-2500 .. **Sung,** Donald D '93 %Deutsche Bank -60 Wall -NY 10005

(718) 939-0200 .. **Sung,** Jeremy D '05 (Sung & C,PC) -38-12 150th -Flushng 11354 **Fx:**939-2179

(212) 285-4770 .. **Sung,** Jill '94 Abacus FSB -6 Bowery -NY 10013 **Fx:**285-4773

(212) 668-1900 .. **Sung,** MaryAnn J '04 %Brune & R LLP -80 Broad -NY 10004

(212) 964-8366 .. **Sung,** Thos C C '64 (Sung & Company,PC) -6-8 Bowery -NY 10013 **Fx:**964-8582

(212) 964-8366 .. **Sung,** Vera '91 %Sung & Company,PC -6-8 Bowery -NY 10013 **Fx:**964-8582

(212) 294-6700 .. **Sunkel,** Wm M '89 %Winston & S -200 Park Av -NY 10166

(518) 402-6722 .. **Sunkes,** Craig R '00 %OCFS -52 Wshngtn -Rensselaer 12144 **Fx:**486-6378

(315) 425-2700 .. **Sunser,** Heather L '02 %Hiscock & B,LLP -One Park Pl -Syracuse 13202

(315) 472-0919 .. **Sunser-King,** Kristin M '87 -239 E Water -Syracuse 13202

(212) 839-5300 .. **Sunshine,** Amy R '96 Cnsl Sidley A LLP -787 7th Av -NY 10019

(212) 883-4900 .. **Sunshine,** David B '01 (Cozen O) -277 Park Av -NY 10172

(212) 695-9112 .. **Sunshine,** Donald M '60 OfCnsl Sunshine S&S,PC -150 W 25th -NY 10001

(516) 294-3186 .. **Sunshine,** Gary M '91 (Taddonio & S,PC) -114 Old Cntry Rd -Mineola 11501 **Fx:**294-7861

(212) 504-6000 .. **Sunshine,** Jared S '09 %Cadwalader W&T LLP -1 World Fncl Ctr -NY 10281

(212) 872-1000 .. **Sunshine,** Jason W '06 -One Bryant Park -NY 10036 **Fx:**872-1002

(516) 352-2100 .. **Sunshine,** Jeffrey A '87 (J Sunshine,PC) -3000 Marcus Av -Lk Success 11042 **Fx:**354-4731

(516) 742-6444 .. **Sunshine,** Joel M '95 (Sunshine & F,LLP) -666 Old Cntry Rd -Gdn Cty 11530 **Fx:**794-0463

(347) 401-9259 .. **Sunshine,** Miriam P '81 Supreme Ct Law Dept -360 Adams -Brklyn 11201 **Fx:**643-6114

(347) 404-9750 .. **Sunshine,** Nancy T '82 %Cnty Clerk -360 Adams -Brklyn 11201 **Fx:**(718) 643-8187

(845) 735-1300 .. **Sunshine,** Robt S '91 (RS Sunshine,PC) -One Blue Hill Plz Bx1647 -Pearl Rvr 10965 **Fx:**735-2826

(212) 695-9112 .. **Sunshine Slott & Sunshine,PC** -150 W 25th -NY 10001 **Fx:**695-9110

(516) 294-5555 .. **Sunshine,** Stacey Pena '96 OfCnsl Del Vecchio & R,LLP -1100 Franklin Av -Gdn Cty 11530 **Fx:**873-5336

(518) 238-4339 .. **Sunukjian,** Nancy M '91 %OCA -187 Wolf Rd -Albany 12205 **Fx:**438-3518

(914) 253-2000 .. **Sunwoo,** Michl S '01 %Pepsico -700 Andrsn Hill Rd -Purchase 10577
(212) 326-3939 .. **Sunwoo,** Monica Cha '08 %Jones D -222 E 41st -NY 10017
(516) 741-6565 .. **Suozzi,** Jos A '48 (Meyer SE&K,PC) -990 Stewart Av Bx9194 -Gdn Cty 11530
(716) 849-8900 .. **Suozzi,** Paul J '80 (Hurwitz & F,PC) -1300 Lbrty Bldg -Buffalo 14202
(518) 581-3166 .. **Suozzi,** Theresa M '96 -480 Bway -Saratoga Spgs 12866 **Fx:**587-0575
(516) 880-8484 .. **Suozzi,** Thos R '90 OfCnsl Harris B PLLC -333 Earle Ovngton Blvd -Uniondale 11553
(646) 278-9975 .. **Supcoff,** Marc H '93 -1375 Bway -NY 10018
(212) 557-7200 .. **Super,** Steven Ira '98 Davidoff M&H,LLP -605 3rd Av -NY 10158
(212) 210-9400 .. **Supernaw,** Jessica L '09 %Alston & B LLP -90 Park Av -NY 10016
(212) 336-2000 .. **Suplina,** Nicholas O '06 %Patterson BW&T LLP -1133 Av of Amer -NY 10036
(518) 424-5521 .. **Supovitz,** Ruth H '86 -Bx421 -Latham 12110
(212) 525-8920 .. **Suppa,** Dana A '99 HSBC -452 5th Av -NY 10018
(845) 297-0600 .. **Supple,** Gregory D '78 (Lyons & S) -92 E Main Bx 46 -Wappingers Fls 12590
(212) 471-6210 .. **Supple,** J Richd '90 (Hinshaw & C LLP) -780 3rd Av -NY 10017
(845) 297-0600 .. **Supple,** John L '56 (Lyons & S) -92 E Main Bx 46 -Wappingers Fls 12590
(845) 831-1234 .. **Supple,** John L '56 (Lyons & S) -5 Cliff Bx510 -Beacon 12508
(845) 297-0600 .. **Supple,** Paul B '89 (Lyons & S) -92 E Main Bx 46 -Wappingers Fls 12590
(845) 831-1234 .. **Supple,** Paul B '89 (Lyons & S) -5 Cliff Bx510 -Beacon 12508
(518) 374-3399 .. **Suprunowicz,** Michl R '82 (Higgins RB&C,PC) -1430 Balltown Rd -Niskayuna 12309
(212) 966-6420 .. **Suquet,** Stephanie A '02 Lwyrs For Children -110 Lafayette -NY 10013 **Fx:**966-0531
(212) 668-8955 .. **Sur,** Diana H '09 Cnsl Oppenheimer & Co,Inc -125 Broad -NY 10004
(212) 839-5300 .. **Sur,** Joanne M '09 %Sidley A LLP -787 7th Av -NY 10019
(212) 558-4000 .. **Surapaneni,** Pavan C '10 %Sullivan & C LLP -125 Broad -NY 10004
(212) 490-9100 .. **Surcouf,** Allison '07 %Condon & F LLP -7 Times Sq -NY 10036
(607) 274-5461 .. **Surdell,** Gary U '88 %DA -320 N Tioga -Ithaca 14850 **Fx:**274-5429
(718) 482-1555 .. **Surdez,** Silvia M '93 (S Surdez,PC) -23-24 Steinway -Astoria 11105 **Fx:**482-1566
(917) 778-6542 .. **Suresh,** Pavithra C '04 K Dodson -485 Lex Av -NY 10017
(718) 487-2300 .. **Surette,** Gibb '87 %Leg Srvcs Corp -256-260 Bway -Brklyn 11211 **Fx:**782-6790
(716) 856-2626 .. **Surgalla,** John B '85 (Tronolone & S,PC) -298 Main -Buffalo 14202
(518) 474-6400 .. **Surgalla,** Kathleen E '80 %Dept of Ed -89 Wshngtn Av -Albany 12234 **Fx:**473-2925
(212) 816-1608 .. **Surgan,** Andrew N '95 %Salomon Smith Barney -388 Greenwich -NY 10013 **Fx:**816-6336
(212) 765-8888 .. **Surgent,** George F '80 -350 5th Av -NY 10118 **Fx:**765-1460
(212) 537-6936 .. **Suri,** Vivek S '99 -401 Bway -NY 10013 **Fx:**(646) 356-6914
(212) 804-4200 .. **Suriano,** Costantino P '81 (Mound CW&G) -One Bttry Pk Plz -NY 10004
(718) 279-2000 .. **Surico,** Vincent '78 (DeRose & S) -213-44 38th Av -Bayside 11361
(631) 423-9700 .. **Suris,** Raymond J '99 (Suris & Assoc,PC) -999 Walt Whitman Rd -Melvll 11747 **Fx:**423-9765
(212) 966-5932 .. **Suriyopas,** Ivy O '06 AALDEF -99 Hudson -NY 10013 **Fx:**966-4303
(212) 303-1887 .. **Surkin,** Dean L '77 %Rosen Seymour Shapss Martin & Co -757 3rd Av -NY 10017 **Fx:**(914) 206-3711
(212) 819-8200 .. **Surmacz,** Nicholas E '08 %White & C LLP -1155 Av of Amer -NY 10036
(607) 797-4839 .. **Surowka,** Michl G '90 (Hogan SLS&D,LLP) -Bx660 -Bnghmtn 13902
(212) 474-1000 .. **Surprenant,** Jennifer A '10 %Cravath S&M LLP -825 8th Av -NY 10019
(212) 499-2196 .. **Surprenant,** Katherine A '93 %Gruner & Jahr USA Publishing -375 Lex Av -NY 10017 **Fx:**499-2199
(212) 326-2000 .. **Surrick,** Maryann P '02 Cnsl O'Melveny & M LLP -7 Times Sq -NY 10036
(212) 408-5100 .. **Susalka,** Richd J '09 %Chadbourne & P LLP -30 Rckfllr Plz -NY 10112
(212) 310-8000 .. **Susanin,** Audrey K '08 %Weil G&M LLP -767 5th Av -NY 10153
(631) 501-9615 .. **Susca,** Nancy E '88 Stewart Title -125 Baylis Rd -Melvll 11747 **Fx:**501-9623
(212) 326-2000 .. **Sushon,** Wm J '96 (O'Melveny & M LLP) -7 Times Sq -NY 10036
(212) 906-1200 .. **Suskin,** Marc R '06 %Latham & W -885 3rd Av -NY 10022
(212) 225-2000 .. **Susko,** A Richd '74 (Cleary GS&H) -1 Lbrty Plz -NY 10006
(212) 929-7333 .. **Suslensky,** Alexander '99 (A Suslensky,PC) -120 E 37th -NY 10016 **Fx:**929-7102
(718) 266-1555 .. **Suslova,** Olga '01 O Suslova,PC -8622 Bay Pkwy -Brklyn 11214 **Fx:**333-1223
(718) 382-5700 .. **Suslovich,** Jacob F '74 (Suslovich & K) -1507 Av M -Brklyn 11230 **Fx:**375-3677
(212) 541-6222 .. **Susman,** Dana M '95 (Kane K,PC) -1350 Av of Amer -NY 10019
(212) 336-8330 .. **Susman Godfrey LLP** -560 Lex Av -NY 10022 **Fx:**336-8340
(212) 336-8330 .. **Susman,** Stephen D '00 (Susman G LLP) -560 Lex Av -NY 10022
(212) 578-5595 .. **Susnick,** Ruth '86 %MetLife -27-01 Qns Plz N -LIC 11101 **Fx:**578-3916
(718) 336-2540 .. **Susnow,** Arthur '57 -1314 Kings Hwy -Brklyn 11229 **Fx:**382-4677
(212) 233-0350 .. **Suss,** Sherwin A '83 (Sobel RF&S,LLP) -150 Bway -NY 10038
(212) 446-4800 .. **Sussberg,** Joshua A '04 %Kirkland & E LLP -153 E 53rd -NY 10022
(914) 686-0044 .. **Susseles,** Maxine J '89 M Susseles,PLLC -Bx720 -Hartsdale 10530 **Fx:**948-1750
(212) 613-5000 .. **Susser,** Kim '90 %Leg Assist Grp -450 W 33rd -NY 10001 **Fx:**750-0820
(212) 808-0298 .. **Susser,** Robt C '93 (R Susser,PC) -270 Mad Av -NY 10016 **Fx:**949-0966
(212) 666-4371 .. **Susser,** Robt J '93 -200 Riverside Dr -NY 10025
(718) 836-6312 .. **Sussillo,** Jos M '63 -435 77th -Brklyn 11209
(212) 859-8000 .. **Sussman,** Alexander R '73 OfCnsl Fried FHS&J LLP -1 NY Plz -NY 10004
(516) 739-8000 .. **Sussman,** Amy R '86 (Schrier F&S) -825 E Gate Blvd -Gdn Cty 11530
(212) 245-1000 .. **Sussman,** Dana G '09 %Outten & G LLP -3 Park Av -NY 10016
(516) 822-8671 .. **Sussman,** Danl L '71 -100 Jericho Quad -Jericho 11753
(212) 773-7365 .. **Sussman,** David '07 Ernst & Young LLP -5 Times Sq -NY 10036
(212) 735-3000 .. **Sussman,** David W '81 OfCnsl Skadden ASM&F LLP -4 Times Sq -NY 10036
(212) 338-0922 .. **Sussman,** Edw '71 -122 E 42nd -NY 10168 **Fx:**338-0924
(516) 763-9500 .. **Sussman,** Eric J '88 -2303 Grand Av -Baldwin 11510
(212) 421-8100 .. **Sussman,** Howard S '64 OfCnsl Wrobel & S LLP -1040 Av of Amer -NY 10018
(718) 596-9000 .. **Sussman,** Ilene M '95 %Cohen HEP&T -25 Chapel -Brklyn 11201
(212) 450-4000 .. **Sussman,** Jason R '06 %Davis P&W LLP -450 Lex Av -NY 10017
(212) 213-3903 .. **Sussman,** Jeremy D '70 -236 5th Av -NY 10001
(212) 530-5000 .. **Sussman,** Jeremy S '07 %Milbank TH&M LLP -1 Chase Manh Plz -NY 10005
(718) 855-9622 .. **Sussman,** Jerome '59 -186 Joralemon -Brklyn 11201
(718) 465-7132 .. **Sussman,** Jill H '74 -900 Willis Av -Albertson 11507 **Fx:**465-6829
(212) 457-8590 .. **Sussman,** Jos '02 (J Sussman,PC) -132 W 31st -NY 10001 **Fx:**947-4967
(212) 906-1200 .. **Sussman,** Joshua M '08 %Latham & W -885 3rd Av -NY 10022
(212) 314-7300 .. **Sussman,** Joshua W '01 IAC/InterActive -555 W 18th -NY 10011
(212) 373-3000 .. **Sussman,** Joshua W '10 %Paul WRW&G LLP -1285 Av of Amer -NY 10019
(212) 906-1200 .. **Sussman,** Kelli Greer '09 %Latham & W -885 3rd Av -NY 10022
(914) 683-0090 .. **Sussman,** Marianne L '80 (Marcus G&S,LLP) -222 Bloomingdale Rd -White Plns 10605
(631) 247-0404 .. **Sussman,** Mark L '76 (Jackson L LLP) -58 S Srvc Rd -Melvll 11747
(516) 935-3600 .. **Sussman,** Martin S '60 (Seltzer SH&H LLP) -100 Jericho Quad -Jericho 11753
(212) 655-3550 .. **Sussman,** Marvin '51 OfCnsl Freiman F PC -140 E 45th -NY 10017 **Fx:**655-3529
(845) 294-3991 .. **Sussman,** Michl H '86 (Sussman & W) -40 Park Pl Bx1028 -Goshen 10924 **Fx:**294-1623
(212) 688-8895 .. **Sussman,** Neil A '87 (Sussman & F,LLP) -805 3rd Av -NY 10022 **Fx:**688-4252
(516) 466-1146 .. **Sussman,** Neil Z '68 -8 Barstow Rd -Gt Neck 11021
(212) 402-4227 .. **Sussman,** Pierre '00 P Sussman,PC -75 Maiden Ln -NY 10038 **Fx:**402-4226
(718) 338-3302 .. **Sussman,** Raymond S '67 -4523 Av H -Brklyn 11234 **Fx:**(347) 438-3338
(212) 756-8602 .. **Sussman,** Richd '86 -380 Lex Av -NY 10168 **Fx:**756-8603
(212) 867-6000 .. **Sussman,** Richd L '85 (Rosenberg & E,PC) -733 3rd Av -NY 10017
(212) 635-1089 .. **Sussman,** Robt J '73 Bk of NY Mellon -1 Wall -NY 10286 **Fx:**635-1999
(212) 479-6000 .. **Sussman,** Ronald R '79 (Cooley LLP) -1114 Av of Amer -NY 10036
(212) 594-2030 .. **Sussman,** Stephen '71 (Lebensfeld BS&S LLP) -31 South -Mt Vernon 10550
(716) 278-8604 .. **Sussman,** Susan M '95 Cnty Dept Soc Srvcs -301 10th -Niagara Fls 14303
(516) 678-1510 .. **Sussman,** Warren '00 -100 Merrick Rd -Rockvll Ctr 11570
(212) 596-9000 .. **Sussman,** Wm I '79 (Ropes & G LLP) -1211 Av of Amer -NY 10036
(212) 931-5500 .. **Sussmane,** Kenneth S '81 (McCue S&Z,PC) -521 5th Av -NY 10175
(212) 683-5304 .. **Sussna,** Stephen '55 Baruch Cllg CUNY -111 E 30th -NY 10016 **Fx:**684-5679
(212) 735-3000 .. **Sussner,** Danl M '08 %Skadden ASM&F LLP -4 Times Sq -NY 10036
(212) 592-1400 .. **Sussner,** Jaimee Katz '98 (Herrick,F LLP) -2 Park Av -NY 10016
(212) 344-5210 .. **Susswein,** David M '96 Wolfson Grp -1 State -NY 10004
(718) 403-3600 .. **Susswein,** Linda K '91 Dept of Finance -345 Adams -Brklyn 11201 **Fx:**403-3650
(212) 687-8500 .. **Susswein,** Marc A '93 (Liddle & R,LLP) -800 3rd Av -NY 10022
(212) 969-3000 .. **Susswein,** Philip M '82 (Proskauer R LLP) -1585 Bway -NY 10036
(212) 725-3131 .. **Sutak,** Kenneth C '75 OfCnsl Franklin G&C,PC -150 E 58th -NY 10155
(212) 551-0600 .. **Sutcliffe,** George '01 Mutual Marine Ofc,Inc -919 3rd Av -NY 10022
(212) 984-2500 .. **Sutcliffe,** Kirstin L '03 Tiger Mgmt,LLC -101 Park Av -NY 10178
(212) 479-6000 .. **Sutcliffe,** Ralph J '69 SrCnsl Cooley LLP -1114 Av of Amer -NY 10036
(646) 386-3678 .. **Suter,** Jack D '79 %Supreme Ct-Law Dept -60 Centre -NY 10007
(212) 788-1339 .. **Suter,** Marion P '82 %Law Dept -100 Church -NY 10007 **Fx:**788-0367
(518) 473-4350 .. **Suter,** Patricia G '97 State Comptroller -110 State -Albany 12236 **Fx:**473-9104
(718) 698-7300 .. **Sutera,** Emanuele J '62 -2153 Richmond Av -Staten Isl 10314 **Fx:**698-7928
(516) 747-2204 .. **Sutfin,** Timothy W '97 %New Beginnings -87 Mineola Blvd -Mineola 11501 **Fx:**747-2505
(212) 701-3000 .. **Suthammanont,** Victor E '06 %Cahill G&R LLP -80 Pine -NY 10005 **Fx:**269-5420
(212) 389-5000 .. **Sutherland Asbill & Brennan LLP** -1114 Av of Amer -NY 10036 **Fx:**389-5099
(212) 230-8800 .. **Sutherland,** Brian A '09 %WilmerHale -399 Park Av -NY 10022
(212) 670-0185 .. **Sutherland,** Howard R '94 %Merrill Lynch -222 Bway -NY 10038
(631) 853-7709 .. **Sutherland,** Janet M '93 Supreme Ct -400 Carleton Av -Central Islip 11722
(212) 735-3000 .. **Sutherland,** Susan J '83 (Skadden ASM&F LLP) -4 Times Sq -NY 10036
(718) 237-2556 .. **Sutherland,** Tanisha K '03 New Start,LLC -32 Court -Brklyn 11201
(212) 801-9286 .. **Sutin,** Alan N '85 (Greenberg T,LLP) -200 Park Av -NY 10166
(518) 583-7110 .. **Sutin,** Nancy C '85 -530 Maple Av -Saratoga Spgs 12866 **Fx:**583-7219
(212) 506-1700 .. **Sutliff,** Jessica C '96 Kasowitz BT&F LLP -1633 Bway -NY 10019
(212) 414-4330 .. **Sutnick,** Laura C '93 (Sutnick & S,LLC) -172 E 161st -Bronx 10451 **Fx:**(201) 342-7557
(212) 414-4330 .. **Sutnick,** Warren S '92 (Sutnick & S,LLC) -172 E 161st -Bronx 10451 **Fx:**(201) 342-7557
(315) 477-0100 .. **Sutphen,** Jamie L '86 (Baldwin & S,LLP) -126 N Salina -Syracuse 13202
(315) 437-6100 .. **Sutphen,** John F '85 %O'Brien & G Ltd -5000 Brittonfld Pkwy Bx4873 -Syracuse 13221 **Fx:**463-7554
(518) 464-0444 .. **Sutphin,** Bruce A '85 Cnsl Rosenblum RK&S,LLP -110 Great Oaks Blvd -Albany 12203

(212) 791-9620 .. **Suttenberg,** Robin J '75 -111 John -NY 10038 **Fx:**406-3677
(716) 847-2523 .. **Sutter,** Brian '87 (Sugarman Law Firm,LLP) -14 Lafayette Sq -Buffalo 14203
(585) 265-3990 .. **Sutter,** James D '55 %Sutter S&L PC -20 W Main -Webster 14580
(212) 702-6000 .. **Sutter,** Laurence B '77 Penthouse Media/Friend Finder Ntwrks Inc -20 Broad -NY 10005 **Fx:**702-6274
(315) 623-7133 .. **Sutter,** Sharon A '91 (Buchan & S) -21 Lakeshr Dr -Constantia 13044 **Fx:**623-7130
(607) 723-5417 .. **Sutter,** Stephen A '73 -57 Front -Bnghmtn 13905 **Fx:**723-4765
(585) 265-3990 .. **Sutter Summers & Lydon PC** -20 W Main -Webster 14580 **Fx:**265-2805
(212) 635-1183 .. **Suttlehan,** Kevin J '88 Bk of NY Mellon -1 Wall -NY 10286
(315) 361-3636 .. **Suttmeier,** Catherine H '83 %Oneida Ltd -Kenwood Av -Oneida 13421 **Fx:**361-3700
(315) 363-7777 .. **Suttmeier,** Robt G '84 (Suttmeier Law Firm) -233 Cedar -Oneida 13421 **Fx:**363-9401
(212) 354-3600 .. **Sutton,** Abraham M '91 -291 Bway -NY 10007
(212) 980-1999 .. **Sutton,** Adam I '01 -160 High Pond Dr -Jericho 11753 **Fx:**(917) 522-9596
(212) 246-2400 .. **Sutton,** Anna Nicolas '09 %Balber PM&VDT,PC -1370 Av of Amer -NY 10019
(516) 294-8797 .. **Sutton,** David J '82 (D Sutton PC) -1205 Franklin Av -Gdn Cty 11530 **Fx:**294-2758
(315) 448-4800 .. **Sutton,** December E '99 %Dept of Law -615 Erie Blvd W -Syracuse 13204 **Fx:**448-4853
(585) 586-8060 .. **Sutton DeLeeuw Clark & Darcy,PLLC** -359 N Wshngtn -Rchstr 14625 **Fx:**586-9895
(212) 849-7000 .. **Sutton,** Elinor C '08 %Quinn EU&S,LLP -51 Mad Av -NY 10010
(212) 801-2259 .. **Sutton,** Holly J '98 %Greenberg T,LLP -200 Park Av -NY 10166
(212) 538-3372 .. **Sutton,** John T '94 Credit Suisse -11 Mad Av -NY 10010
(518) 882-9630 .. **Sutton,** John W '79 -5212 South Bx97 -Galway 12074 **Fx:**882-1587
(516) 466-6500 .. **Sutton,** Lauren B '07 %Parker WA LLP -6 Hrbr Park Dr S -Pt Wash 11050
(212) 766-1888 .. **Sutton,** Leigh Harris '07 %Morris DA&F -2 Rector -NY 10006
(716) 845-3650 .. **Sutton,** Margaret F '93 %MHLS -438 Main -Buffalo 14202 **Fx:**874-7794
(518) 465-1862 .. **Sutton,** Michl E '05 Sutton Law Firm,PLLC -323 Hmltn Bx2057 -Albany 12220 **Fx:**465-1864
(516) 223-3841 .. **Sutton,** Michl R '81 (Eckhardt & S) -2020 Grand Av -Baldwin 11510
(212) 289-2100 .. **Sutton,** Morris '84 -985 3rd Av -NY 10022
(212) 974-7474 .. **Sutton,** Ralph J '01 (Cowan DA&S LLP) -41 Mad Av -NY 10010
(212) 867-2700 .. **Sutton,** Richd W '06 %J Felice & Assoc,PC -11 E 44th -NY 10017 **Fx:**867-2783
(212) 446-4800 .. **Sutton,** Robt H '99 (Kirkland & E LLP) -153 E 53rd -NY 10022
(716) 439-7130 .. **Sutton,** Ronald A '85 Cnty Surrogates Ct -Bx1023 -Lockprt 14095 **Fx:**439-7319
(516) 901-1212 .. **Sutton,** Shane Henty '94 -590 Mad Av -NY 10022
(212) 696-0090 .. **Sutton,** Steven R '77 -630 3rd Av -NY 10017 **Fx:**297-1853
(585) 203-3400 .. **Sutton,** Trent M '07 %Littler M,PC -400 Linden Oaks -Rchstr 14625
(212) 701-3000 .. **Suvari,** Catherine '07 %Cahill G&R LLP -80 Pine -NY 10005 **Fx:**269-5420
(212) 537-3237 .. **Suydam,** John J '86 Apollo Mgmt -9 W 57th -NY 10019
(716) 856-4000 .. **Suzan,** Kenneth D '97 (Hodgson R LLP) -140 Pearl -Buffalo 14202
(212) 588-0800 .. **Suzuki,** Chiemi D '05 %Frommer L&H LLP -745 5th Av -NY 10151
(212) 859-8000 .. **Suzuki,** David A '08 %Fried FHS&J LLP -1 NY Plz -NY 10004
(212) 808-7800 .. **Suzuki,** Yutaka '07 %Kelley D&W LLP -101 Park Av -NY 10178
(212) 318-3000 .. **Suzzan,** Steven I '90 (Fulbright & J LLP) -666 5th Av -NY 10103
(518) 792-2117 .. **Svare,** John D '05 %Bartlett PS&R,PC -1 Wshngtn Bx2168 -Glens Fls 12801
(212) 916-4229 .. **Svarre,** Andrew C '93 %TIAA-CREF -730 3rd Av -NY 10017
(631) 598-0337 .. **Svendsen,** Karen S '92 (Ansanelli K&S,LLP) -92 Bway -Amityvll 11701 **Fx:**598-0352
(212) 848-4000 .. **Svenson,** Tait O '08 %Shearman & S LLP -599 Lex Av -NY 10022
(914) 385-6000 .. **Svensson,** Paul E '03 (Hodges W&S LLP) -55 Church -White Plns 10601 **Fx:**385-6060
(212) 608-1178 .. **Sverd,** Peter E '03 (Yuen RS&S PC) -132 Nassau -NY 10038 **Fx:**608-2913
(516) 678-9797 .. **Sverdloff,** Julia '09 %Civardi O&B,LLP -23 S Main -Freeprt 11520 **Fx:**678-2266
(718) 780-0603 .. **Svetiev,** Yane '06 %Bklyn Law Schl -250 Joralemon -Brklyn 11201 **Fx:**780-0393
(212) 679-8999 .. **Svetkey,** Jonathan '85 (Watters & S,LLP) -286 Mad Av -NY 10017 **Fx:**679-9791
(212) 326-2000 .. **Svirsky,** Gary '98 (O'Melveny & M LLP) -7 Times Sq -NY 10036
(716) 856-3500 .. **Svisco,** Rosa S '86 SpclCnsl Magavern MG LLP -1100 Rand Bldg -Buffalo 14203
(631) 886-2036 .. **Svoboda,** Jane Robbins '84 -27 Farm Rd N -Wading Rvr 11792
(718) 227-3100 .. **Swaaley,** Michl '80 -4459 Amboy Av -Staten Isl 10312 **Fx:**966-0667
(716) 847-8400 .. **Swados,** Robt O '42 SpclCnsl Phillips L LLP -3400 HSBC Ctr -Buffalo 14203
(212) 554-7800 .. **Swagert,** Dean R Jr. '88 (Moses & S LLP) -405 Lex Av -NY 10174
(212) 351-4000 .. **Swain,** Timothy D '06 %Gibson D&C LLP -200 Park Av -NY 10166
(212) 846-4728 .. **Swalsky,** Stephen J '96 VH-1 -1515 Bway -NY 10036
(212) 403-7300 .. **Swaminathan,** Anand '07 %Vladeck WE&E,PC -1501 Bway -NY 10036
(212) 696-6000 .. **Swaminathan,** Priya '07 %Curtis M-PC&M LLP -101 Park Av -NY 10178
(914) 949-1305 .. **Swan,** Eileen F '00 %Leg Srvcs -90 Maple Av -White Plns 10601 **Fx:**949-6213
(212) 450-4000 .. **Swan,** Katherine '09 %Davis P&W LLP -450 Lex Av -NY 10017
(845) 340-3315 .. **Swan,** Lauren E '04 DA -285 Wall -Kingston 12401 **Fx:**340-3185
(212) 579-9120 .. **Swan,** Michl W '95 IP Finl Mgmt -1 W 64th -NY 10023
(914) 666-4400 .. **Swander,** George J '76 -50 Main -Mt Kisco 10549
(716) 856-0600 .. **Swanekamp,** Chas C '80 (Jaeckle F&M,LLP) -12 Fountain Plz -Buffalo 14202
(212) 294-6700 .. **Swaney,** Devin M '09 %Winston & S -200 Park Av -NY 10166
(212) 415-9200 .. **Swanick,** Christine L '05 (Dorsey & W LLP) -250 Park Av -NY 10177
(716) 204-2400 .. **Swann,** Brian M '06 %SJ Baum,PC -220 Nrthpnte Pkwy Bx1291 -Buffalo 14240 **Fx:**204-4600
(212) 848-4000 .. **Swann,** Eliza W '99 (Shearman & S LLP) -599 Lex Av -NY 10022
(914) 725-3317 .. **Swann,** Linda G '00 -717 Wht Plns Rd -Scarsdale 10583 **Fx:**725-6377
(516) 624-6150 .. **Swanson,** Donna B '92 %Town Atty -Town Hall -Oyster Bay 11771 **Fx:**624-6196
(518) 877-6670 .. **Swanson,** Edw W '88 -232 Round Lk Rd -Ballston Lk 12019 **Fx:**877-0510
(212) 701-3000 .. **Swanson,** Erica Lynn '02 %Cahill G&R LLP -80 Pine -NY 10005 **Fx:**269-5420
(212) 530-5000 .. **Swanson,** Jay W '79 OfCnsl Milbank TH&M LLP -1 Chase Manh Plz -NY 10005
(212) 438-6534 .. **Swanson,** Kevin D '03 %Standard & Poor's -55 Water -NY 10041
(212) 506-5000 .. **Swanson,** Lisa '99 Orrick H&S LLP -51 W 52nd -NY 10019
(212) 969-3000 .. **Swanson,** Praveena N '09 %Proskauer R LLP -1585 Bway -NY 10036
(212) 715-1000 .. **Swanson,** Richd P '81 (Arnold & P LLP) -399 Park Av -NY 10022
(716) 488-0700 .. **Swanson,** Sandra Fisher '91 -111 W 2nd -Jamestwn 14701
(212) 530-5000 .. **Swanson,** Stephanie E '09 %Milbank TH&M LLP -1 Chase Manh Plz -NY 10005
(212) 559-9124 .. **Swanson,** Stephen W '94 Citigroup Private Bk -153 E 53rd -NY 10022
(718) 468-6975 .. **Swarbrick,** Eileen F '85 -80-46 213th -Qns Vllg 11427
(212) 965-2200 .. **Swarns,** Christina A '94 %NAACP/LDF -99 Hudson -NY 10013 **Fx:**226-7592
(631) 232-0200 .. **Swart,** Douglas J '80 (Fumuso KDSS&F,LLP) -110 Marcus Blvd -Hauppauge 11788
(212) 742-8700 .. **Swart,** Joe B '97 %Garson D&C LLP -110 Wall -NY 10005
(212) 538-2346 .. **Swart,** Martina '03 CSFB LLC -1 Mad Av -NY 10010
(716) 481-4790 .. **Swart,** Michl '67 %HSBC Bk USA -Main & Seneca -Buffalo 14203
(585) 394-4260 .. **Swartout,** Steven H '84 Canandaigua Natl Bk -72 S Main -Canandaigua 14424
(212) 558-4000 .. **Swarts,** David E '03 %Sullivan & C LLP -125 Broad -NY 10004
(212) 310-8000 .. **Swartz,** Alexander J '08 %Weil G&M LLP -767 5th Av -NY 10153
(716) 873-2167 .. **Swartz,** Ava S '90 -61 LaSalle Av -Kenmore 14217
(212) 474-1000 .. **Swartz,** Denise M '78 %Cravath S&M LLP -825 8th Av -NY 10019
(315) 836-1540 .. **Swartz,** Eric T '94 Swartz Law Firm,PC -200 Wshngtn -Watertwn 13601 **Fx:**836-1543
(212) 527-5618 .. **Swartz,** Erica J '08 Cnsl Revlon -237 Park Av -NY 10017 **Fx:**527-5299
(212) 725-7070 .. **Swartz,** Gerald Neal '76 -475 Park Av S -NY 10016
(212) 272-3028 .. **Swartz,** Heidi L '03 %JP Morgan Chase -383 Mad Av -NY 10179
(212) 245-1000 .. **Swartz,** Justin M '02 (Outten & G LLP) -3 Park Av -NY 10016
(212) 762-6605 .. **Swartz,** Kevin A '95 Morgan Stanley -1221 Av of Amer -NY 10020
(518) 457-5608 .. **Swartz,** Larry A '77 %Agriculture & Mrkts -10B Airline Dr -Albany 12235 **Fx:**457-8842
(212) 504-6000 .. **Swartz,** Linda Z '88 (Cadwalader W&T LLP) -1 World Fncl Ctr -NY 10281
(845) 634-4673 .. **Swartz,** Mark S '86 -20 Squadron Blvd Bx825 -New Cty 10956 **Fx:**634-4670
(212) 756-2000 .. **Swartz,** Michl E '92 (Schulte R&Z LLP) -919 3rd Av -NY 10022
(212) 558-4000 .. **Swartz,** Rhiana L '07 %Sullivan & C LLP -125 Broad -NY 10004
(516) 466-6100 .. **Swartz,** Ronald J '83 (Swartz & S) -80 Cutter Mill Rd -Gt Neck 11021 **Fx:**466-6104
(914) 684-7000 .. **Swartz,** Sheldon M '86 -149 Grand -White Plns 10601 **Fx:**761-5444
(516) 466-6100 .. **Swartz,** Steven I '86 (Swartz & S) -80 Cutter Mill Rd -Gt Neck 11021 **Fx:**466-6104
(212) 735-3000 .. **Swayne,** Jennifer L '10 %Skadden ASM&F LLP -4 Times Sq -NY 10036
(212) 449-2612 .. **Swearengin,** Julian C '99 Cnsl Merrill Lynch -4 World Fncl Ctr -NY 10080
(212) 308-6100 .. **Swearingen,** Walter E '95 %Levi L&F LLP -1185 Av of Amer -NY 10036
(212) 506-1700 .. **Sweberg,** Lisa A '04 %Kasowitz BT&F LLP -1633 Bway -NY 10019
(212) 455-2000 .. **Swedenburg,** Eric M '00 (Simpson T&B LLP) -425 Lex Av -NY 10017
(518) 765-0300 .. **Swedick,** Matthew J '98 -Bx33 -Voorheesvll 12186 **Fx:**765-2129
(914) 288-0022 .. **Sweedler,** Michl J '61 OfCnsl Leason E LLP -81 Main -White Plns 10601
(914) 763-0205 .. **Sweeney,** Barry M '80 -892 Route 35 Bx814 -Cross Rvr 10518 **Fx:**763-9589
(516) 484-3800 .. **Sweeney,** Brendan M '01 Luxottica Grp -44 Hrbr Park Dr -Pt Wash 11050
(914) 358-1220 .. **Sweeney,** Danl J '87 (D Sweeney & Assoc PLLC) -941 N Bway -White Plns 10603 **Fx:**358-1219
(212) 943-0280 .. **Sweeney,** Deidre A '79 OfCnsl McCanliss & E LLP -88 Pine -NY 10005
(516) 877-5600 .. **Sweeney,** Donald W '92 %R Tusa -1225 Franklin Av -Gdn Cty 11530 **Fx:**877-5695
(631) 253-0286 .. **Sweeney,** Edw J '62 -70 Bagatelle Rd -Melvll 11747
(516) 247-4070 .. **Sweeney,** Erin King '99 Swiss Intl Airlines -776 RXR Plz -Uniondale 11556
(516) 535-2888 .. **Sweeney,** Francis J Jr. '80 TDK USA Corp -525 RXR Plz -Uniondale 11556
(718) 459-9000 .. **Sweeney Gallo Reich & Bolz,LLP** -95-25 Qns Blvd -Rego Pk 11374 **Fx:**459-0999
(212) 370-4000 .. **Sweeney,** Gerald B '72 (Sweeney L LLC) -708 3rd Av -NY 10017
(718) 459-9000 .. **Sweeney,** Gerard J '79 (Sweeney GR&B,LLP) -95-25 Qns Blvd -Rego Pk 11374
(212) 220-3830 .. **Sweeney,** James F III '80 (Nicoletti H&S) -88 Pine -NY 10005
(845) 291-1100 .. **Sweeney,** James G '67 -1 Harriman Sq Bx806 -Goshen 10924 **Fx:**294-3994
(518) 487-7600 .. **Sweeney,** James H '09 %Whiteman O&H LLP -1 Commerce Plz -Albany 12260
(914) 921-1200 .. **Sweeney,** Jean M '83 %Maloof B&E LLC -411 Theo Fremd Av -Rye 10580 **Fx:**921-1023
(718) 222-2101 .. **Sweeney,** John '89 %Law Dept -350 Jay -Brklyn 11201 **Fx:**222-2393
(212) 415-8600 .. **Sweeney,** John F '74 (Locke LB&L LLP) -3 World Fncl Ctr -NY 10281
(518) 274-4391 .. **Sweeney,** John J Jr. '66 Sweeney Law Firm -11 1st Bx356 -Troy 12181 **Fx:**273-9205
(212) 636-6000 .. **Sweeney,** Jos '57 %Fordham Univ Sch of Law -140 W 62nd -NY 10023 **Fx:**636-6899

(212) 747-1230 .. **Sweeney,** Kathleen M '91 McMahon M&G LLP -55 Washington -Brklyn 11201
(718) 761-9300 .. **Sweeney,** Kathryn Mary '02 %Vaslas LH&D LLP -201 Edward Curry Av -Staten Isl 10314
(212) 370-4000 .. **Sweeney Lev LLC** -708 3rd Av -NY 10017 **Fx:**370-7336
(212) 373-3000 .. **Sweeney,** Margaret M '02 Paul WRW&G LLP -1285 Av of Amer -NY 10019
(518) 487-7600 .. **Sweeney,** Mark T '96 (Whiteman O&H LLP) -1 Commerce Plz -Albany 12260
(212) 593-1700 .. **Sweeney,** Mary Cecilia '04 %Kaplan L LLP -1065 Av of Amer -NY 10018
(212) 929-7298 .. **Sweeney,** Mary Ellen '69 -319 W 21st -NY 10011 **Fx:**929-7298
(518) 783-2714 .. **Sweeney,** Mary Sutton '81 Colonie Town Justice -312 Wolf Rd -Latham 12110
(631) 360-7333 .. **Sweeney,** Maureen Doran '89 -1383 Vets Mem'l Hwy -Hauppauge 11788 **Fx:**360-3763
(718) 459-9000 .. **Sweeney,** Melanie A '06 %Sweeney GR&B,LLP -95-25 Qns Blvd -Rego Pk 11374
(212) 482-0001 .. **Sweeney,** Michl J '92 %Russo K&T LLP -33 Whitehall -NY 10004
(845) 294-2004 .. **Sweeney,** Michl J '94 -1 Harriman Sq Bx362 -Goshen 10924 **Fx:**294-3994
(212) 592-1400 .. **Sweeney,** Patrick D '82 (Herrick,F LLP) -2 Park Av -NY 10016
(212) 770-1732 .. **Sweeney,** Patrick J '95 AIG -82 Pine -NY 10005
(212) 513-3200 .. **Sweeney,** Patrick J '08 %Holland & K LLP -31 W 52nd -NY 10019
(516) 296-7000 .. **Sweeney,** Paul B '93 (Certilman BA&H,LLP) -90 Merrick Av -E Meadow 11554
(607) 273-3339 .. **Sweeney,** Paul D '94 %Williamson C&S -317 N Tioga Bx126 -Ithaca 14850
(607) 723-9511 .. **Sweeney,** Paul J '88 (Coughlin & G,LLP) -19 Chenango Bx2039 -Bnghmtn 13902
(212) 709-8070 .. **Sweeney,** Peter J '92 -110 Wall -NY 10005
(914) 686-0108 .. **Sweeney,** Robbin E '88 %Glassman & B -99 Court -White Plns 10601
(718) 466-3000 .. **Sweeney,** Robt J '97 %Civil Ct -1118 Grnd Cncrs -Bronx 10456 **Fx:**466-3006
(518) 487-7600 .. **Sweeney,** Robt L '81 (Whiteman O&H LLP) -1 Commerce Plz -Albany 12260
(914) 238-8924 .. **Sweeney,** Robt L '86 -100 Valley Vw Rd -Chappaqua 10514
(631) 360-7333 .. **Sweeney,** Robt P '85 (De Sena & S) -1383 Vets Mem'l Hwy -Hauppauge 11788
(212) 727-0721 .. **Sweeney,** Terence J '88 -225 Bway -NY 10007 **Fx:**(908) 598-1961
(212) 918-3000 .. **Sweeney,** Thos J III '75 (Hogan L LLP) -875 3rd Av -NY 10022
(631) 361-6401 .. **Sweeney,** Wm H Jr. '94 (Sweeney & O) -742 Vets Mem'l Hwy -Hauppauge 11788 **Fx:**361-6404
(516) 248-7900 .. **Sweeny,** Dennis J '74 (Sweeny & S) -510 Broad Hollow Rd -Melvll 11747 **Fx:**248-8730
(718) 312-4244 .. **Sweeny,** Paul '74 -15 Metrotech Ctr -Brklyn 11201
(212) 278-6124 .. **Sweeny,** Robt H '91 %SG Capital Prtnrs LLC -1221 Av of Amer -NY 10020
(212) 836-8000 .. **Sweet,** Brian M '09 %Kaye S LLP -425 Park Av -NY 10022
(212) 448-1100 .. **Sweet,** David J '62 (McLaughlin & S,LLP) -260 Mad Av -NY 10016
(716) 854-5960 .. **Sweet,** David L '56 (Heffernan & S) -237 Main -Buffalo 14203
(212) 788-1171 .. **Sweet,** Emily '00 %Law Dept -100 Church -NY 10007 **Fx:**788-0367
(212) 556-2100 .. **Sweet,** John K '00 (King & S) -1185 Av of Amer -NY 10036
(917) 452-4400 .. **Sweet,** Julie Spellman '93 Accenture -1345 Av of Amer -NY 10105 **Fx:**527-9915
(716) 856-4200 .. **Sweet,** Kathleen M '91 (Gibson M&C,LLP) -69 Delaware Av -Buffalo 14202
(646) 610-5400 .. **Sweet,** Kerry R '92 %NYPD -1 Police Plz -NY 10038
(212) 244-4664 .. **Sweet,** Kimberly B '93 %NY Lawyers Pub Intrst -151 W 30th -NY 10001 **Fx:**244-4570
(718) 286-6000 .. **Sweet,** Matthew J '07 DA -125-01 Qns Blvd -Kew Gdns 11415
(516) 352-1922 .. **Sweetbaum,** Joel A '80 (Sweetbaum & S) -3000 Marcus Av -Lk Success 11042 **Fx:**354-6923
(516) 352-1922 .. **Sweetbaum,** Marshall D '51 (Sweetbaum & S) -3000 Marcus Av -Lk Success 11042 **Fx:**354-6923
(212) 458-1154 .. **Sweetgall,** Roy L '82 %AIGTS,Inc -175 Water -NY 10038
(718) 875-1300 .. **Sweeting,** J Machelle '98 %Appllt Div 2nd Dept -45 Monroe Pl -Brklyn 11201 **Fx:**858-2446
(212) 406-1919 .. **Sweetman,** Donald G '01 (Gennet KA&R,PC) -140 Bway -NY 10005
(516) 873-0028 .. **Swendsen-Dowd,** Beth A '90 -165 William -Williston Pk 11596
(212) 577-7957 .. **Swenson,** Amy B '09 Leg Aid -199 Water -NY 10038
(516) 677-5811 .. **Swenson,** Eric D '87 %Oyster Bay DPW -150 Miller Pl -Syosset 11791
(212) 450-4000 .. **Swenson,** Marc D '09 %Davis P&W LLP -450 Lex Av -NY 10017
(716) 945-2000 .. **Swenson,** Matthew R '02 (Brady & S) -41 Main -Salamanca 14779
(718) 505-6660 .. **Swenton,** Stephanie J '98 (S Swenton & Assoc) -75-20 Astoria Blvd -E Elmhrst 11370
(212) 756-4515 .. **Swerdloff,** Alan M '94 Bernstein Invstmnt Rsrch & Mgmt -1345 Av of Amer -NY 10105
(212) 264-3650 .. **Swerdloff,** Arthur '88 %SSA Ofc Genl Cnsl -26 Fed Plz -NY 10278 **Fx:**264-6372
(212) 837-6000 .. **Swerdloff,** Jonathan E '01 %Hughes H&R LLP -1 Bttry Pk Plz -NY 10004
(718) 339-1400 .. **Swerdloff,** Leonard '88 (Michael & S,LLC) -2226 Ocean Av -Brklyn 11229
(212) 768-6700 .. **Swerdloff,** Scott J '98 (Sonnenschein N&R LLP) -2 World Fncl Ctr -NY 10281
(212) 237-1000 .. **Swerdlow,** David F '94 (Windels ML&M,LLP) -156 W 56th -NY 10019
(212) 984-8222 .. **Swerdlow,** Steven A '76 CB Richard Ellis -200 Park Av -NY 10166
(646) 746-7633 .. **Sweren,** Marci E '94 Reed Business Info -360 Park Av S -NY 10010
(212) 593-3000 .. **Swergold,** Henry G '77 (Platzer SKLG&J,LLP) -1065 Av of Amer -NY 10018
(516) 569-2266 .. **Swergold,** Nathaniel M '61 -124 Cedarhrst Av -Cedarhrst 11516 **Fx:**374-7697
(212) 226-6662 .. **Swerling,** Bryan J '04 -310 Greenwich -NY 10013 **Fx:**226-8089
(718) 250-2000 .. **Swern,** Anne J '81 %DA -350 Jay -Brklyn 11201 **Fx:**250-2314
(212) 487-7219 .. **Swersey,** Julie L '04 Dept Cnsmr Affrs -42 Bway -NY 10004 **Fx:**487-4197
(315) 478-7869 .. **Swete,** Donald R '85 -1632 W Genesee -Syracuse 13204 **Fx:**478-8582
(212) 779-9910 .. **Swetnick,** Robt N '75 (Eaton & V LLP) -3 Park Av -NY 10016
(716) 634-2497 .. **Swetz,** Darren M '97 (Kelly & S) -5678 Main -Williamsvll 14221
(212) 974-7474 .. **Swezey,** Kenneth N '89 (Cowan DA&S LLP) -41 Mad Av -NY 10010
(212) 250-9031 .. **Swiader,** Michl C '02 %Deutsche Bk -60 Wall -NY 10005
(716) 856-4000 .. **Swiatek,** Jeffrey F '94 (Hodgson R LLP) -140 Pearl -Buffalo 14202
(212) 953-6000 .. **Swiatkiewicz,** Stephen '82 (Katsky K LLP) -605 3rd Av -NY 10158
(212) 553-3200 .. **Swicicki,** Patricia A '04 %Marulli LE&T,LLP -5 Hanover Sq -NY 10004
(716) 282-5334 .. **Swick,** Wilbur K '93 -558 5th -Niagara Fls 14301
(716) 830-6102 .. **Swick,** Wm D '01 -416 Pearl -Buffalo 14202
(718) 383-6604 .. **Swidler,** Barry J '81 -301 Norman Av -Brklyn 11222
(914) 824-5320 .. **Swidler,** Carol S '90 %Supreme Ct -111 Martin Luther King Blvd -White Plns 10601 **Fx:**995-4215
(212) 449-0418 .. **Swidler,** Gary M '96 Merrill Lynch & Co -250 Vesey -NY 10281
(646) 840-5730 .. **Swidler,** Julie Greifer '83 %RCA Music Grp -745 5th Av -NY 10151
(518) 408-0469 .. **Swidler,** Kim S '84 Workers Comp Bd -20 Park -Albany 12207
(212) 237-0000 .. **Swidler,** Michl J '83 (Vinson & E LLP) -666 5th Av -NY 10103
(212) 715-9100 .. **Swidler,** Pamela R '09 %Kramer LN&F,LLP -1177 Av of Amer -NY 10036
(518) 271-5027 .. **Swidler,** Robt N '83 %Northeast Health -2212 Burdett Av -Troy 12180
(212) 398-2900 .. **Swidler,** Steven A '77 (Swidler & M LLP) -57 W 38th -NY 10018 **Fx:**398-0405
(212) 832-0745 .. **Swiedler,** Alan M '78 (A Swiedler,PC) -60 E 8th -NY 10003 **Fx:**202-3771
(518) 462-6765 .. **Swierczewski,** Judy '06 Leg Aid -55 Colvin Av -Albany 12206 **Fx:**427-8352
(212) 909-6000 .. **Swiergula,** Jennae R '09 %Debevoise & P LLP -919 3rd Av -NY 10022
(516) 482-3737 .. **Swift,** Albert M '59 -45 N Station Plz -Gt Neck 11021
(845) 634-7010 .. **Swift,** Charlotte G '95 %Montalbano C&F,PC -67 N Main Bx1070 -New Cty 10956
(845) 294-8572 .. **Swift,** John B III '88 -6 Corral Ln -Goshen 10924 **Fx:**294-1257
(212) 704-6000 .. **Swift,** Lawr D '78 (Troutman S LLP) -405 Lex Av -NY 10174
(585) 753-4500 .. **Swift,** Leslie E '01 %DA -832 Watts Bldg -Rchstr 14614 **Fx:**753-4576
(212) 250-2965 .. **Swift,** Nancy L '93 %Deutsche Bank -60 Wall -NY 10005
(516) 482-3737 .. **Swift,** Phyllis '92 %A Swift -45 N Station Plz -Gt Neck 11021
(716) 856-5500 .. **Swift,** Sharon A '95 %Damon M LLP -200 Delaware Av -Buffalo 14202
(212) 325-2000 .. **Swift,** Thos F Jr. '89 Credit Suisse -1 Mad Av -NY 10010
(516) 677-9660 .. **Swift,** Wm M '03 %Faber & T -180 Froehlich Farm Blvd -Woodbury 11797
(718) 590-2000 .. **Swiger,** Karen P '86 %DA -198 E 161st -Bronx 10451 **Fx:**590-6477
(516) 684-3442 .. **Swiger Kelley Harragan & Schott** -14 Shore Dr -Plandome 11030
(212) 294-6700 .. **Swihart,** Laura '00 (Winston & S) -200 Park Av -NY 10166
(315) 471-1499 .. **Swimelar,** Mark W '87 -250 S Clinton -Syracuse 13202
(212) 344-3900 .. **Swimmer,** Michl A '90 %Belair & E LLP -61 Bway -NY 10006
(315) 539-1300 .. **Swinehart,** Richd E '89 %DA -48 W Williams -Waterloo 13165 **Fx:**539-0531
(212) 395-6138 .. **Swingle,** Loren Carl '91 %Verizon -140 West -NY 10007
(518) 242-3710 .. **Swingruber-Sprotbery,** Jill P '95 %Ct of Claims -Justice Bldg ESP Bx7344 -Albany 12224 **Fx:**432-3450
Swinton, Stephanie A '96 -2433 Bstn Rd -Bronx 10467
(518) 449-0044 .. **Swinton,** Stephen F '04 Hoffman W&D LLC -75 State -Albany 12207 **Fx:**449-0047
(212) 715-1000 .. **Swire,** James Bennett '67 (Arnold & P LLP) -399 Park Av -NY 10022
(877) 786-7552 .. **Swire Falker,** Elizabeth E '94 (E Swire Falker,PC) -42 Lovell Ln -New Rchll 10804 **Fx:**(914) 738-5654
(212) 698-3500 .. **Swirnoff,** Alexander H '04 %Dechert LLP -1095 Av of Amer -NY 10036
(718) 741-8408 .. **Swirsky,** Michl K '85 %Div of Human Rights -1 Fordham Plz -Bronx 10458 **Fx:**741-8102
(212) 351-4500 .. **Swirsky,** Steven M '79 (Epstein B&G,PC) -250 Park Av -NY 10177
(212) 574-1200 .. **Swiss,** Bryan D '08 %Seward & K LLP -1 Bttry Pk Plz -NY 10004
(212) 571-2777 .. **Switnicki,** George '80 -30 Vesey -NY 10007 **Fx:**571-5285
(212) 788-0956 .. **Switzer,** Cindy '00 %Law Dept -100 Church -NY 10007 **Fx:**788-0367
(585) 263-6201 .. **Switzer,** Elizabeth J '95 %Fed Pub Def -28 E Main -Rchstr 14614 **Fx:**263-5871
(212) 574-1200 .. **Switzer,** Kristin H '09 %Seward & K LLP -1 Bttry Pk Plz -NY 10004
(518) 473-5534 .. **Swolak,** Patricia L '95 %Insurance Dept -99 Wshngtn Av -Albany 12257 **Fx:**473-5311
(718) 556-3823 .. **Sword,** Laura A '98 (Sword Law LLC) -692 Jewett Av -Staten Isl 10314
(518) 463-7857 .. **Swyer,** David H '77 -237 S Pearl -Albany 12202 **Fx:**463-7863
(212) 813-8800 .. **Swyers,** Joanna Lea '06 %Goodwin P LLP -620 8th Av -NY 10018
(518) 785-5702 .. **Swyers,** Thos A '89 -949 Birchwood Ln -Schnctdy 12309
(585) 325-7515 .. **Sydelnik,** Scott A '05 %Forsyth HOK&M,PC -1 Chase Sq -Rchstr 14604
(212) 986-8671 .. **Sydney Amster & Green,PLLC** -122 E 42nd -NY 10168 **Fx:**883-8947
(212) 986-8671 .. **Sydney,** Herbert P '56 (Sydney A&G,PLLC) -122 E 42nd -NY 10168
(212) 869-3200 .. **Syed,** Ayesha T '09 %Molod S&D,PC -104 W 40th -NY 10018
(212) 267-2324 .. **Syed,** Imtiaz S '91 -305 Bway -NY 10007
(212) 594-6657 .. **Syed,** Simin H '90 (S Syed,PC) -875 6th Av -NY 10001 **Fx:**594-6780
(212) 688-5151 .. **Syed,** Zarina H '10 %Gibney A&F,LLP -665 5th Av -NY 10022
(212) 679-7007 .. **Syken,** Matthew E '06 %Brody B&B LLP -205 Lex Av -NY 10016
(212) 848-4000 .. **Sykes,** John M III '82 (Shearman & S LLP) -599 Lex Av -NY 10022
(212) 628-8708 .. **Sykes,** Judith L '81 -370 E 76th -NY 10021
(914) 423-7075 .. **Sykes,** Lawr R '75 -4 Delavan Ter -Ynkrs 10703 **Fx:**423-5059
(716) 853-3801 .. **Sykes,** Maurice L '76 Kenney SL&N,LLP -14 Lafayette Sq -Buffalo 14203
(212) 815-1450 .. **Sykes,** Steven E '05 %DC 37 Gen Cnsl -125 Barclay -NY 10007 **Fx:**815-1440
(212) 839-5300 .. **Sylofski,** David D '05 %Sidley A LLP -787 7th Av -NY 10019

(212) 513-3200 .. **Sylva,** Summer L H '08 %Holland & K LLP -31 W 52nd -NY 10019
(718) 380-3708 .. **Sylvan,** Robt T '81 (Colin & S) -164-16 73rd Av -Fresh Mdws 11366 **Fx:**591-8535
(716) 566-2800 .. **Sylvester,** Erin E '08 %Bond S&K,PLLC -40 Fountian Plz -Buffalo 14202
(585) 243-7300 .. **Sylvester,** John T '79 Dept Soc Srvcs -1 Murray Hill Dr -Mt Morris 14510 **Fx:**243-7497
(212) 261-8000 .. **Sylvester,** Lorraine C '08 %Mendes & M,LLP -750 7th Av -NY 10019
(212) 770-5197 .. **Sylvester,** Suzanne R '03 AIG -70 Pine -NY 10270
(212) 863-8311 .. **Sylvester,** Symone E '00 HPD -100 Gold -NY 10038
(212) 225-2000 .. **Sylvester,** Thos K '07 %Cleary GS&H -1 Lbrty Plz -NY 10006
(718) 403-0325 .. **Sylvestre-Johnson,** Andree '92 -26 Court -Brklyn 11242
(585) 232-6500 .. **Sylvestri,** Paul D '91 (Harter S&E LLP) -1600 Bausch & Lomb Pl -Rchstr 14604
(212) 972-1100 .. **Sylvor,** Robt '61 (Sylvor & R) -122 E 42nd -NY 10158 **Fx:**983-5271
(212) 819-8200 .. **Sym,** Agnes L '03 %White & C LLP -1155 Av of Amer -NY 10036
(518) 273-7005 .. **Symansky,** Richd D '71 (RD Symansky,PC) -Bx479 -Troy 12181 **Fx:**273-7218
(212) 336-2000 .. **Syme,** Carrie A '01 %Patterson BW&T LLP -1133 Av of Amer -NY 10036
(845) 471-4455 .. **Symer,** Jonathan E '85 (Steinberg S&P,LLP) -27 Grdn -Poughkeepsie 12601
(212) 446-4800 .. **Symon,** M Scott '01 (Kirkland & E LLP) -153 E 53rd -NY 10022
(315) 437-7600 .. **Symons,** Chas E '02 %Ferrara FLB&R,PC -5010 Campuswood Dr -E Syracuse 13057
(212) 446-4800 .. **Symons,** Jeffrey D '99 (Kirkland & E LLP) -153 E 53rd -NY 10022
(516) 832-2445 .. **Symons,** Leonard B '69 -2 Hillside Av -Williston Pk 11596 **Fx:**408-3833
(585) 593-3170 .. **Synakowski,** Danl G '76 -95 N Main Bx643 -Wellsvll 14895
(212) 669-8171 .. **Synmoie,** Patrick L '87 City Clerks Ofc -1 Centre -NY 10007
(212) 373-3000 .. **Synnott,** Aidan '89 (Paul WRW&G LLP) -1285 Av of Amer -NY 10019
(212) 909-6000 .. **Sypek,** Lauren E '07 %Debevoise & P LLP -919 3rd Av -NY 10022
(518) 388-4364 .. **Sypniewski,** Matthew J '02 DA -612 State -Schnctdy 12305 **Fx:**388-4569
(585) 415-7960 .. **Sypniewski,** Michl A '96 -44 Rosemount -Rchstr 14620 **Fx:**454-6755
(212) 753-7500 .. **Syracuse,** Dana V '05 %Hartman & C LLP -488 Mad Av -NY 10022
(212) 508-6700 .. **Syracuse,** Vincent J '69 (Tannenbaum HS&H LLP) -900 3rd Av -NY 10022
(866) 348-5819 .. **Syraski,** Tina L '94 %SSA-ODAR -50 Fountain Plz -Buffalo 14202 **Fx:**(716) 551-4078
(212) 837-6046 .. **Syrkin,** Matthew J '06 %Hughes H&R LLP -1 Bttry Pk Plz -NY 10004 **Fx:**299-6046
(212) 859-8000 .. **Sysel,** Jan '06 %Fried FHS&J LLP -1 NY Plz -NY 10004
(518) 220-1850 .. **Syta,** James M '97 %Schmeiser O&W -22 Century Hill Dr -Latham 12110
(212) 451-2300 .. **Syvertsen,** Erik D '09 %Olshan GFR&W LLP -65 E 55th -NY 10022
(518) 474-0388 .. **Syzdek,** Stephen A '98 Ofc for the Aging -Bldg 2 ESP -Albany 12223 **Fx:**474-0608
(212) 431-4913 .. **Szabo,** Elizabeth M '91 -Bx1245 -NY 10013 **Fx:**343-0938
(212) 442-8711 .. **Szabo,** Mary Anne E '83 %Admin Children's Srvcs -220 Church -NY 10013
(212) 541-6222 .. **Szabo,** Paul E '08 OfCnsl Kane K,PC -1350 Av of Amer -NY 10019
(718) 990-6161 .. **Szabo,** Paul S Jr. '75 %St Vincent's Cllg -St John's Univ -Jamaica 11439
(718) 403-8235 .. **Szafran,** Marc E '98 %DOITT -11 Metrotech Ctr -Brklyn 11201
(212) 297-5800 .. **Szafranski,** Susan M '01 (Day P LLP) -7 Times Sq -NY 10036
(212) 308-4411 .. **Szalai,** Marcella D '08 %Edwards AP&D LLP -750 Lex Av -NY 10022
(212) 261-8000 .. **Szalai,** Michelle '04 %Mendes & M,LLP -750 7th Av -NY 10019
(716) 842-2800 .. **Szanyi,** Kevin A '86 (Webster S LLP) -1400 Lbrty Bldg -Buffalo 14202
(212) 530-5000 .. **Szanzer,** Steven Z '01 %Milbank TH&M LLP -1 Chase Manh Plz -NY 10005
(718) 466-3000 .. **Szap,** Tara M '05 %Civil Ct -1118 Grnd Cncrs -Bronx 10456 **Fx:**466-3006
(845) 344-2524 .. **Szarka,** Louis K '87 %C Curcio -1 Edgewtr Dr -Middletwn 10940 **Fx:**344-2528
(518) 462-5300 .. **Szary,** George J '91 (DeGraff F&K LLP) -90 State -Albany 12207
(212) 336-0175 .. **Szczepanik,** Valerie Ann '02 %SEC -3 World Fncl Ctr -NY 10281 **Fx:**336-1323
(516) 228-3553 .. **Szczepanowski,** Lidia D '91 %Thaler & G,LLP -90 Merrick Av -E Meadow 11554
(716) 856-4000 .. **Szczepanski,** Kevin D '96 (Hodgson R LLP) -140 Pearl -Buffalo 14202
(212) 403-1000 .. **Szczerban,** S Christopher '08 %Wachtell LR&K -51 W 52nd -NY 10019
(914) 682-9282 .. **Szczesniak,** Andrew W '79 -222 Mamaroneck Av -White Plns 10605 **Fx:**682-0631
(716) 645-2167 .. **Szczygiel,** Anthony H '77 %SUNY Buffalo Lw Schl -O'Brian Hall -Buffalo 14260 **Fx:**645-5968
(607) 330-4000 .. **Szecsy,** Alek P '94 OfCnsl Bond S&K,PLLC -10 Brown Rd -Ithaca 14850
(212) 506-5000 .. **Szego,** Diana M '08 %Orrick H&S LLP -666 5th Av -NY 10103
(716) 204-2400 .. **Szeliga,** Megan B '04 %SJ Baum,PC -220 Nrthpnte Pkwy Bx1291 -Buffalo 14240 **Fx:**204-4600
(212) 683-7100 .. **Szemer,** Alana J '98 %Gallo V&K,LLP -90 Broad -NY 10004
(212) 558-4000 .. **Szenberg,** Avi '94 SpclCnsl Sullivan & C LLP -125 Broad -NY 10004
(212) 269-4900 .. **Szendel,** Adrian M '04 %Ford MEW&G,LLP -Wall Street Plz -NY 10005
(516) 935-1100 .. **Szenicer,** Harry L '83 Spiegel Assoc -375 N Bway -Jericho 11753 **Fx:**932-0302
(212) 218-2100 .. **Szeto,** Kenneth J-H '08 %Fitzpatrick CH&S -1290 Av of Amer -NY 10104
(212) 902-6147 .. **Szeto,** Lester '01 Goldman Sachs -1 NY Plz -NY 10004
(212) 918-3000 .. **Szeto,** Stella '09 %Hogan L LLP -875 3rd Av -NY 10022
(212) 619-4444 .. **Szewczuk,** John C '80 OfCnsl Marshall CW&B,PC -116 John -NY 10038
(212) 455-2000 .. **Szewczyk,** Gregory P '10 %Simpson T&B LLP -425 Lex Av -NY 10017
(631) 499-2555 .. **Szilveszter Lipari,** E Emma '02 %A Gallo,PC -6080 Jericho Tpk -Commack 11725 **Fx:**499-4318
(212) 330-1259 .. **Szip,** Natalia E '04 Mellon Consultants -1 Penn Plz -NY 10119
(914) 632-8247 .. **Szklarski,** Thea K '81 -200 Rodgers Dr -Scarsdale 10583
(212) 310-8000 .. **Szlamkowicz,** Michl '09 %Weil G&M LLP -767 5th Av -NY 10153
(212) 827-7590 .. **Szmukler,** David I '98 %TD Securities -31 W 52nd -NY 10019
(516) 466-6520 .. **Sznay,** Jack '86 %Tusco Dev Corp -98 Cuttermill Rd -Gt Neck 11021
(718) 783-6800 .. **Sznitken,** Neil '73 -267 Flatbush Av -Brklyn 11217
(212) 742-9280 .. **Szober,** Jason M '06 Waterfront Comm -39 Bway -NY 10006 **Fx:**480-0587
(914) 271-1044 .. **Szoboszlai,** Tomas T '84 -1 Eklof Ct -Croton-On-Hud 10520 **Fx:**271-5468
(718) 923-6300 .. **Szochet,** Diana J '86 %Atty Grievance Comm -335 Adams -Brklyn 11201 **Fx:**624-2978
(212) 408-4010 .. **Szokol,** Judith D '84 Bk of NY -1290 Av of Amer -NY 10104
(212) 557-3233 .. **Szold,** Martin '51 -317 Mad Av -NY 10017 **Fx:**557-3235
(716) 366-2124 .. **Szot,** Ronald A '87 -130 E Green Bx12 -Dunkirk 14048
(718) 383-5929 .. **Szpara,** Janusz '03 Szpara & Assoc -861 Manh Av -Brklyn 11222 **Fx:**383-2693
(212) 541-5800 .. **Szpilzinger,** Isaac D '86 Laurus Cptl Mgmt,LLC -335 Mad Av -NY 10017 **Fx:**541-4434
(315) 435-2470 .. **Sztechmiler,** Christine A '83 %DA -505 S State -Syracuse 13202 **Fx:**435-3969
(212) 351-4000 .. **Szteinbok,** Marina C '92 Gibson D&C LLP -200 Park Av -NY 10166
(212) 232-2394 .. **Sztulwark,** Lynne Naavah '06 %M Caracta,PC -80 Wall -NY 10005 **Fx:**344-5437
(315) 738-0600 .. **Szuba,** Theresa '96 Cnsl PAR Technology Corp -8383 Seneca Tpk -New Hartfrd 13413
(212) 335-9000 .. **Szuchman,** David M '98 %DA -1 Hogan Pl -NY 10013
(718) 832-6500 .. **Szuflita,** Gene M J '80 (Belson & S) -1310 8th Av -Brklyn 11215
(212) 677-4422 .. **Szul,** Andrij V R '90 (Szul & Assocs) -Bx1008 -Bellmore 11710 **Fx:**898-9040
(212) 514-5577 .. **Szulman,** Douglas E '92 (Szulman & Assoc) -110 Wall -NY 10005 **Fx:**635-0533
(646) 722-8500 .. **Szydlo,** Brenda F '89 SrCnsl Grant & E,PA -485 Lex Av -NY 10017
(212) 806-5400 .. **Szyfer,** Claude G '96 (Stroock &S&L LLP) -180 Maiden Ln -NY 10038
(212) 643-6400 .. **Szyffer,** Alicia '82 %Garganigo G&W -14 Penn Plz -NY 10122
(718) 482-9292 .. **Szymanik,** Teresa K '00 -896 Manh Av -Brklyn 11222
(212) 545-7373 .. **Szymanska,** Jolanta '01 %K Wilhelm -445 Park Av -NY 10022 **Fx:**545-9093
(212) 297-5800 .. **Szymanski,** James G '69 (Day P LLP) -7 Times Sq -NY 10036
(212) 408-5100 .. **Szymanski,** Monika B '05 %Chadbourne & P LLP -30 Rckfllr Plz -NY 10112
(718) 331-7700 .. **Szymanski,** Pawel '07 %Frekhtman & Assoc -60 Bay 26th -Brklyn 11214
(212) 489-8230 .. **Szymanski,** Wendy K '04 %Davis WT LLP -1633 Bway -NY 10019
(716) 856-0600 .. **Szymczak,** Heath J '99 (Jaeckle F&M,LLP) -12 Fountain Plz -Buffalo 14202
(718) 780-7975 .. **Szymczak,** Victoria J '95 %Bklyn Law Schl -250 Joralemon -Brklyn 11201 **Fx:**780-0393
(716) 632-2546 .. **Szymoniak,** Amy Klein '90 -5672 Main -Williamsvll 14221 **Fx:**633-8154
(646) 722-8500 .. **Ta,** Hung Gia '01 %Grant & E,PA -485 Lex Av -NY 10017
(212) 474-1000 .. **Tabacco,** Ria A '09 %Cravath S&M LLP -825 8th Av -NY 10019
(212) 736-1898 .. **Tabachnick,** Kenneth E '97 -450 7th Av -NY 10123 **Fx:**736-1884
(212) 661-5123 .. **Tabachnick,** Lauren R '00 Audrey Golden Assoc -633 3rd Av -NY 10017 **Fx:**867-8068
(212) 682-4002 .. **Tabachnik,** Douglas T '81 Novack BC LLP -300 E 42nd -NY 10017
(212) 922-9250 .. **Taback,** Anne Deborah '98 %Ganfer & S LLP -360 Lex Av -NY 10017
(212) 679-5400 .. **Taback,** David L '73 (D Taback,PC) -470 Park Av S -NY 10016 **Fx:**679-1033
(212) 969-3000 .. **Taback,** Ivan '94 (Proskauer R LLP) -1585 Bway -NY 10036
(212) 312-2260 .. **Tabacznik,** Sharona M '07 Leg Aid -60 Lafayette -NY 10013 **Fx:**349-0874
(212) 435-3571 .. **Tabafunda,** Faith '05 Port Auth of NY/NJ -225 Park Av S -NY 10003 **Fx:**435-3555
(212) 957-7600 .. **Tabak,** Danl H '96 Cnsl Cohen & G LLP -800 3rd Av -NY 10022
(212) 735-8600 .. **Tabak,** Eitan '98 SrCnsl Morrison C LLP -909 3rd Av -NY 10022
(212) 455-2000 .. **Tabak,** Emily N '05 %Simpson T&B LLP -425 Lex Av -NY 10017
(212) 962-1914 .. **Tabak,** Jeffrey A '84 %Tabak Real Estate -137 Reade -NY 10013
(212) 310-8343 .. **Tabak,** Jeffrey E '83 (Weil G&M LLP) -767 5th Av -NY 10153
(518) 464-4095 .. **Tabak,** Margaret C '88 -100 Great Oaks Blvd -Albany 12203 **Fx:**464-4096
(212) 962-1590 .. **Tabak Mellusi & Shisha** -29 Bway -NY 10006 **Fx:**385-0920
(212) 735-3000 .. **Tabak,** Ronald J '75 SpclCnsl Skadden ASM&F LLP -4 Times Sq -NY 10036
(845) 371-4700 .. **Tabakin,** Gregg P '88 (Fein SK&S,PC) -747 Chestnut Rdg Rd -Spg Vly 10977
(845) 638-1400 .. **Tabakman,** Alan '68 (Freedman WT&W) -130 N Main -New Cty 10956
(212) 506-1700 .. **Tabaksblat,** Lauren '09 %Kasowitz BT&F LLP -1633 Bway -NY 10019
(914) 920-4019 .. **Tabankin,** Jennifer M '06 (Tabankin & T,PLLC) -268 Babbitt Rd -Bedfrd Hlls 10507
(914) 920-4019 .. **Tabankin,** Shawn L '08 (Tabankin & T,PLLC) -268 Babbitt Rd -Bedfrd Hlls 10507
(212) 384-0250 .. **Tabar,** Jonathan '97 J Tabar,PC -233 Bway -NY 10279 **Fx:**406-2313
(516) 822-3550 .. **Tabarovsky,** Julie '06 %Hoffmann & B LLP -6900 Jericho Tpk -Syosset 11791 **Fx:**822-3582
(631) 587-5100 .. **Tabat Cohen Blum & Yovino, LLP** -500 Montauk Hwy -W Islip 11795 **Fx:**587-5064
(516) 294-9292 .. **Tabat Cohen Blum & Yovino, LLP** -1205 Franklin Av -Gdn Cty 11530 **Fx:**294-5533
(631) 587-5100 .. **Tabat,** Gary H '72 (Tabat CB&Y,LLP) -500 Montauk Hwy -W Islip 11795
(212) 837-6296 .. **Tabatabai Asl,** Faranak S '07 %Hughes H&R LLP -1 Bttry Pk Plz -NY 10004 **Fx:**422-4726
(716) 664-3906 .. **Taber,** Jonathan P '00 (Phillips L LLP) -8 E 3rd Bx1279 -Jamestwn 14702

(716) 847-8400 .. **Taber,** Jonathan P '00 (Phillips L LLP) -3400 HSBC Ctr -Buffalo 14203
(212) 858-1000 .. **Taber,** Kenneth W '81 (Pillsbury WSP LLP) -1540 Bway -NY 10036
(212) 918-3000 .. **Taber-Kewene,** Christina M '03 %Hogan L LLP -875 3rd Av -NY 10022
(212) 577-3001 .. **Tabi,** Yasmin '09 %HIV Law Proj -15 Maiden Ln -NY 10038 **Fx:**577-3192
(212) 355-5200 .. **Tabin,** Stewart E '83 %Mason Cptl Mgt -110 E 59th -NY 10022 **Fx:**355-5336
(718) 515-0165 .. **Tabiv,** Batia '82 %ODAR-SSA -226 E 161st -Bronx 10451 **Fx:**547-7420
(516) 328-7181 .. **Tablante,** Albert S Jr. '74 (Alvy & T,LLP) -1979 Marcus Av -Lk Success 11042
(212) 506-5000 .. **Tabler,** Wm B III '00 %Orrick H&S LLP -51 W 52nd -NY 10019
(518) 465-9500 .. **Tabner,** John W '51 (Tabner R&K,LLP) -18 Corp Wds Blvd -Albany 12211
(518) 465-9500 .. **Tabner Ryan & Keniry, LLP** -18 Corp Wds Blvd -Albany 12211 **Fx:**465-5112
(212) 341-6612 .. **Tabone,** Vincent J '99 Liquidation Bur -123 William -NY 10038 **Fx:**341-6861
(518) 218-2088 .. **Tabora,** Raul A Jr. '87 (Ruffo TM&M PC) -300 Great Oaks Blvd -Albany 12203
(212) 335-9000 .. **Taborga,** Alan R '05 %DA -1 Hogan Pl -NY 10013
(212) 952-0100 .. **Taccetta,** Jos P '89 US Aviation -199 Water -NY 10038
(718) 236-8891 .. **Taccetta,** Nanette C '85 %Big Apple Car Inc -169 Bay 17th -Brklyn 11214 **Fx:**256-7253
(845) 454-5909 .. **Tackach,** John J '76 %Sholes & M,LLP -327 Mill -Poughkeepsie 12601
(914) 997-0905 .. **Tackel,** Martin S '86 (Tackel & V,LLP) -445 Hmltn Av -White Plns 10601 **Fx:**997-2021
(212) 906-1200 .. **Tackenberg,** Annemarie V '10 %Latham & W -885 3rd Av -NY 10022
(516) 796-7142 .. **Tackenberg,** Victoria A '84 -94 Diamond Av -E Meadow 11554
(718) 590-2000 .. **Tacoma,** Linda R '84 %DA -198 E 161st -Bronx 10451 **Fx:**590-6477
(212) 883-8833 .. **Tacopina & Arnold** -275 Mad Av -NY 10016 **Fx:**619-1028
(212) 883-8833 .. **Tacopina,** Jos '92 (Tacopina & A) -275 Mad Av -NY 10016
(212) 227-8877 .. **Tacopina,** Jos '92 (Tacopina S&T,PC) -275 Mad Av -NY 10016
(212) 227-8877 .. **Tacopina Seigel & Turano, PC** -275 Mad Av -NY 10016 **Fx:**619-1028
(212) 872-1000 .. **Tadajweski,** Ann E '95 -One Bryant Park -NY 10036 **Fx:**872-1002
(212) 363-8400 .. **Taddeo,** Frank A Jr. '76 -100 Wall -NY 10005
(585) 325-2124 .. **Taddeo,** Jos A Sr. '53 -45 Exchange Blvd -Rchstr 14614
(585) 325-2124 .. **Taddeo,** Jos A Jr. '82 -45 Exchange Blvd -Rchstr 14614
(315) 422-6666 .. **Taddeo,** Karen M '91 (Taddeo & S,LLP) -472 S Salina -Syracuse 13202
(212) 384-1000 .. **Taddeo,** Leo '95 %FBI -26 Fed Plz -NY 10278
(315) 422-6666 .. **Taddeo & Shahan,LLP** -472 S Salina -Syracuse 13202 **Fx:**422-5050
(516) 294-3186 .. **Taddonio,** Robt S '76 (Taddonio & S,PC) -114 Old Cntry Rd -Mineola 11501 **Fx:**294-7861
(212) 878-3577 .. **Tadelis,** Jamie H '02 Avenue Capital Grp -535 Mad Av -NY 10022
(212) 594-5300 .. **Tadler,** Ariana J '93 (Milberg LLP) -1 Penn Plz -NY 10119
(315) 472-5281 .. **Tadros,** Shadia '07 -103 E Water -Syracuse 13202 **Fx:**472-5002
(718) 855-9000 .. **Tafe,** Justin M '06 %Cullen and D LLP -177 Montague -Brklyn 11201
(212) 681-8925 .. **Taffae,** Alfred M '79 (Racht & T,LLP) -7 Penn Plz -NY 10001 **Fx:**681-8928
(518) 785-4900 .. **Taffany,** David J '85 (Anderson M&T,PLLC) -26 Century Hill Dr -Latham 12110
(585) 428-5755 .. **Taffe,** Elizabeth Deutsch '90 %Cnty Atty -50 W Main -Rchstr 14614 **Fx:**428-2031
(914) 763-5353 .. **Taffera,** Louis R '72 -Spring Bx420 -S Salem 10590
(212) 883-1700 .. **Taffet,** Allan N '85 (Duval & S LLP) -101 Park Av -NY 10178
(516) 883-7134 .. **Taffet,** Bertram L '61 -32 Lewis Ln -Pt Wash 11050
(212) 329-2001 .. **Taffet,** Edw D '82 TransitCenter Inc -1065 Av of Amer -NY 10018 **Fx:**(646) 839-1515
(212) 872-6561 .. **Taffet,** Mark S '85 %KPMG Peat Marwick, LLP -345 Park Av -NY 10154
(212) 705-7000 .. **Taffet,** Richd S '81 (Bingham M LLP) -399 Park Av -NY 10022
(914) 949-6996 .. **Taffet,** Scott D '08 %Penino & M,LLP -180 E Post Rd -White Plns 10601
(718) 260-8700 .. **Taffuri,** Rosina '96 Admin Children's Srvcs -345 Adams -Brklyn 11201
(718) 963-5774 .. **Taffy,** Amanda '00 %MHLS -760 Bway -Brklyn 11206 **Fx:**384-2702
(212) 318-6000 .. **Tafone,** Christopher J '01 %Paul HJ&W LLP -75 E 55th -NY 10022
(914) 934-8792 .. **Taft,** Cathey A '89 %Klein & F -219 Wstchstr Av -Pt Chester 10573 **Fx:**934-8793
(914) 683-8792 .. **Taft,** Cathey A '89 %Klein & F -1849 Route 6 -Carmel 10512 **Fx:**683-8790
(212) 909-5000 .. **Taft,** Claudia L '79 %KPMG LLP -280 Park Av -NY 10017
(609) 758-8810 .. **Taft,** Ronald S '70 R Taft,PC -45 Gramercy Pk N -NY 10010 **Fx:**758-8831
(212) 909-6000 .. **Taft,** Wm H V '05 %Debevoise & P LLP -919 3rd Av -NY 10022
(914) 422-4141 .. **Tafur,** Victor M '02 Pace Energy Project -78 N Bway -White Plns 10603
(212) 269-5900 .. **Tafuri,** Peter T '90 (Tafuri & T) -90 Broad -NY 10004 **Fx:**269-5922
(212) 269-5900 .. **Tafuri,** Thos P '89 (Tafuri & T) -90 Broad -NY 10004 **Fx:**269-5922
(212) 596-9000 .. **Tagaban,** Marvin B '06 %Ropes & G LLP -1211 Av of Amer -NY 10036
(212) 256-8000 .. **Tagami,** Kevin M '02 Atticus Capital LP -767 5th Av -NY 10153
(212) 944-1377 .. **Tager,** Cheryl B '83 OfCnsl M Kassimir & Assoc,PC -1065 Av of Amer -NY 10018 **Fx:**790-5868
(212) 643-8904 .. **Tagg,** Michl L '91 %Assadi & M,LLP -200 W 57th -NY 10019 **Fx:**643-9192
(631) 727-4900 .. **Taggart,** John P '94 %P Danowski Jr -616 Roanoke Av Bx779 -Rvrhead 11901
(646) 471-4000 .. **Taggart,** Wm Jr. '87 %PricewaterhouseCoopers LLP -300 Mad Av -NY 10017
(914) 993-1546 .. **Taglia,** Margaret M '89 Town Atty -177 Hillside Av -Greenburgh 10607 **Fx:**993-1656
(914) 937-9009 .. **Taglia,** Mark J '05 Parsons & Whittemore -4 Intl Dr -Rye Brook 10573
(212) 227-6000 .. **Taglia,** Peter R '81 (Dwyer & T) -111 John -NY 10038
(716) 853-8400 .. **Tagliafierro,** Letizia P '00 %Dept of Law -350 Main Pl Twr -Buffalo 14202 **Fx:**853-8571
(914) 946-4777 .. **Tagliafierro,** Nancy A '00 %Keane & B,PC -445 Hmltn Av -White Plns 10601
(212) 972-1000 .. **Tagliagambe,** Anthony F '79 (London F LLP) -59 Maiden Ln -NY 10038
(914) 846-3899 .. **Tagliamonte,** Anthony D Jr. '02 %NY Life Ins -1 Rockwood Rd -Sleepy Hollow 10591 **Fx:**846-5497
(212) 294-6700 .. **Tagliamonti,** Beth A '01 %Winston & S -200 Park Av -NY 10166
(212) 848-4000 .. **Tagliavia,** Keith '04 %Shearman & S LLP -599 Lex Av -NY 10022
(212) 577-3688 .. **Taglieri,** Michl '91 %Leg Aid -199 Water -NY 10038 **Fx:**509-8431
(914) 961-3375 .. **Tague,** Cynthia V '87 (Tague & V,LLP) -116 Kraft Av -Bronxvll 10708 **Fx:**961-3944
(914) 961-3375 .. **Tague,** John F III '87 (Tague & V,LLP) -116 Kraft Av -Bronxvll 10708 **Fx:**961-3944
(212) 506-5000 .. **Tague,** Matthew R '06 %Orrick H&S LLP -51 W 52nd -NY 10019
(212) 909-6000 .. **Tahbaz,** Christopher K '91 (Debevoise & P LLP) -919 3rd Av -NY 10022
(212) 407-4000 .. **Taheri,** Lili '06 %Loeb & L,LLP -345 Park Av -NY 10154
(716) 633-0374 .. **Taheri,** Michl S '88 (Taheri & T,PC) -388 Evans -Buffalo 14221
(212) 841-1000 .. **Taheri,** Ramin J '06 %Covington & B LLP -620 8th Av -NY 10018
(716) 633-0374 .. **Taheri & Todoro,PC** -388 Evans -Buffalo 14221 **Fx:**634-4957
(718) 332-5751 .. **Tahir,** Muhammad S '04 -2637 Coney Isl Av -Brklyn 11223
(212) 459-1706 .. **Tahl,** Jos A '88 %The Thena Group -712 5th Av -NY 10019 **Fx:**459-2602
(518) 474-6400 .. **Tahoe,** Shannon L '02 %Dept of Ed -89 Wshngtn Av -Albany 12234 **Fx:**473-2925
(212) 450-4000 .. **Tahyar,** Margaret E '96 (Davis P&W LLP) -450 Lex Av -NY 10017
(212) 751-9800 .. **Tai,** Allan Y '85 (Tai & S) -950 3rd Av -NY 10022 **Fx:**751-0046
(646) 602-5600 .. **Tai,** Amy '09 Urban Justice Ctr -123 William -NY 10038 **Fx:**(212) 533-4598
(212) 460-1008 .. **Tai,** Luther '86 -4 Irving Pl -NY 10003
(718) 547-0477 .. **Taibi,** Chas F '88 -770 Allerton Av -Bronx 10467 **Fx:**504-4851
(212) 572-8600 .. **Taibi,** Edw P '99 MacAndrews & Forbes -35 E 62nd -NY 10065
(212) 576-4490 .. **Taigue,** Richd J '82 NY Life Ins -51 Mad Av -NY 10010 **Fx:**576-7101
(518) 719-3590 .. **Tailleur,** Chas M '93 %DA -411 Main -Catskill 12414 **Fx:**719-3792
(518) 731-8677 .. **Tailleur,** Joan P '86 -10 Mansion Bx28 -Coxsackie 12051 **Fx:**731-1037
(212) 610-6300 .. **Taing,** Susan '06 %Allen & O -1221 Av of Amer -NY 10020
(212) 513-3200 .. **Taisey,** Robt D '53 (Holland & K LLP) -31 W 52nd -NY 10019
(212) 448-1100 .. **Taishoff,** Aaron P '10 %McLaughlin & S,LLP -260 Mad Av -NY 10016
(516) 482-4455 .. **Taishoff,** Howard A '72 -105 Oxford Blvd -Gt Neck 11023
(212) 259-8000 .. **Tait,** Jennifer A '09 %Dewey & L LLP -1301 Av of Amer -NY 10019
(914) 285-0700 .. **Tait,** John V '00 %Renzulli Law Firm,LLP -81 Main -White Plns 10601 **Fx:**285-1213
(212) 722-8522 .. **Taitt,** Edwin '52 -16 W 123rd -NY 10027
(212) 275-4826 .. **Taitz,** Ariel B '97 %Warner Music Grp -75 Rckfllr Plz -NY 10019 **Fx:**489-3342
(212) 455-5200 .. **Taitz,** Danl M '87 Univision Communications -605 3rd Av -NY 10158
(631) 475-4400 .. **Taitz,** Steven C '89 (Roe TT&P,LLP) -One Corp Dr -Bohemia 11716
(212) 225-2000 .. **Taiwo,** Ebunoluwa A '09 %Cleary GS&H -1 Lbrty Plz -NY 10006
(212) 815-0907 .. **Taiwo,** Hafeez A '10 DA -1 Hogan Pl -NY 10013
(212) 735-3000 .. **Taj,** Allam '10 %Skadden ASM&F LLP -4 Times Sq -NY 10036
(212) 309-6000 .. **Tajcher,** Eric '03 %Morgan L&B LLP -101 Park Av -NY 10178
(516) 292-8028 .. **Tajerstein,** David A '98 -408 Lopez Dr -W Hempstead 11552
(212) 907-9600 .. **Tajika,** Mioko C '05 %Ingram YGC&B,LLP -250 Park Av -NY 10177
(212) 819-8200 .. **Tajo,** Yara M '08 %White & C LLP -1155 Av of Amer -NY 10036
(212) 415-9200 .. **Tak,** Charisa S '06 %Dorsey & W LLP -250 Park Av -NY 10177
(212) 788-0740 .. **Tak,** Esther S '05 %Law Dept -100 Church -NY 10007 **Fx:**788-0367
(212) 897-5840 .. **Takach,** Karen A '85 %Fishman & N -305 Bway -NY 10007 **Fx:**897-5841
(212) 230-5500 .. **Takacs,** Louis Jr. '05 Davis SLM&H LLP -689 5th Av -NY 10022
(212) 557-4000 .. **Takacs,** Nikolas E '10 %Grunfeld DLS&K LLP -399 Park Av -NY 10022
(718) 298-8927 .. **Takahashi,** Meredith L '05 %Leg Aid -153-01 Jamaica Av -Jamaica 11432 **Fx:**657-0537
(212) 667-9396 .. **Takahashi,** Yoko '09 Nomura Securities Intl,Inc -2 World Fncl Ctr -NY 10281
(212) 785-2929 .. **Takakjian,** Debra '91 %Conway FC&K,PC -48 Wall -NY 10005
(718) 590-2000 .. **Takantzas,** Cleopatra L '98 %DA -198 E 161st -Bronx 10451 **Fx:**590-6477
(917) 741-0249 .. **Takayama,** Tamayu '02 Copetin -305 W 50th -NY 10019
(212) 798-9100 .. **Takeuchi,** Yukiko '99 Register.com -575 8th Av -NY 10018
(212) 425-7200 .. **Takhistova,** Ksenia '10 %Kenyon & K,LLP -1 Bway -NY 10004
(212) 878-7900 .. **Takikawa,** Reiko '99 (Fox R LLP) -100 Park Av -NY 10017
(212) 838-3324 .. **Takvorian,** Richd C '01 (Takvorian & Assoc,LLC) -415 E 80th -NY 10021 **Fx:**(201) 489-4509
(212) 838-3324 .. **Takvorian,** S Theo '82 (Takvorian & Assoc,LLC) -415 E 80th -NY 10021 **Fx:**(201) 489-4509
(718) 579-3000 .. **Talaber,** Stephen J '89 %Leg Aid -1020 Grnd Cncrs -Bronx 10451 **Fx:**588-2611
(973) 992-4800 .. **Talan,** Lauren J '01 %Fox R LLP -100 Park Av -NY 10017 **Fx:**992-9125
(516) 741-6729 .. **Talan,** Steven R '92 -11 Carling Dr -Gdn Cty Pk 11040
(212) 455-2000 .. **Talansky,** Jonathan R '07 %Simpson T&B LLP -425 Lex Av -NY 10017
(212) 735-3000 .. **Talarek,** Marta '05 %Skadden ASM&F LLP -4 Times Sq -NY 10036
(212) 815-1140 .. **Talarico,** Belkis '99 %DC 37 MELS -125 Barclay -NY 10007 **Fx:**815-1343
(516) 794-7500 .. **Talarico,** Fabiana Ida '06 %Westermann SKS&A,LLP -333 Earle Ovngton Blvd -Uniondale 11553
(973) 520-2389 .. **Talarico,** George R '89 (Edwards AP&D LLP) -750 Lex Av -NY 10022 **Fx:**(888) 325-9122
(315) 410-9200 .. **Talarico,** Jos R II '94 -356 N Midler Av -Syracuse 13206 **Fx:**410-9292
(516) 773-8300 .. **Talassazan,** Eyal '05 %Wisselman H & Assoc,PC -1010 Nrthrn Blvd -Gt Neck 11021 **Fx:**773-8304
(212) 922-1640 .. **Talbert,** Chelley E '02 %Dover Corp -280 Park Av -NY 10017 **Fx:**922-1656

(212) 317-1717 .. **Talbert**, Paul M '96 (Chemtob MF&T LLP) -3 E 54th -NY 10022
(212) 447-7220 .. **Talbot**, J Tiffani Choe '98 -15 E 32nd -NY 10016
(212) 735-3000 .. **Talbot**, James S '99 Cnsl Skadden ASM&F LLP -4 Times Sq -NY 10036
(716) 856-4000 .. **Talbot**, Kevin R '07 %Hodgson R LLP -140 Pearl -Buffalo 14202
(917) 494-1957 .. **Talbot**, Marianne Merritt '02 -210 Berkeley Pl -Brklyn 11217
(212) 806-5400 .. **Talel**, Eva '74 (Stroock &S&L LLP) -180 Maiden Ln -NY 10038
(212) 610-6300 .. **Talenti**, Livia '04 %Allen & O -1221 Av of Amer -NY 10020
(718) 261-6780 .. **Talero**, Albert '85 -71-50 Austin -Frst Hlls 11375 **Fx**:261-6478
(212) 238-3000 .. **Talesnick**, Richd S '82 (Emmet M&M,LLP) -120 Bway -NY 10271
(212) 832-2000 .. **Talesnik**, Sonja '81 Trump Orgn -725 5th Av -NY 10022 **Fx**:935-0141
(315) 457-0506 .. **Talev**, Peter N '79 -201 2nd -Liverpool 13088 **Fx**:457-3306
(585) 454-0700 .. **Talia**, Elizabeth Anne '94 Cnsl Ward GH&R LLP -300 State -Rchstr 14614
(585) 272-0540 .. **Talia**, Guy A '97 %Thomas & S LLP -693 East Av -Rchstr 14607
(718) 243-2700 .. **Talisman & DeLorenz,PC** -409 Fulton -Brklyn 11201
(212) 626-4100 .. **Talke**, Julia R '07 %Baker & M LLP -1114 Av of Amer -NY 10036
(212) 482-0007 .. **Talkin**, Sanford N '93 (Talkin M&R,LLP) -40 Exch Pl -NY 10005 **Fx**:482-1303
(908) 687-4494 .. **Talkow**, Andrew M '93 -44 W 62nd -NY 10023 **Fx**:668-6684
(518) 851-7212 .. **Tallackson**, Christine J '78 -1060 New Forge Rd II -Ancram 12502
(212) 292-4978 .. **Tallackson**, Jeffrey S '68 -2 Penn Plz -NY 10121 **Fx**:292-4972
(212) 818-9200 .. **Tallan**, Martin B '88 Cnsl Satterlee SB&B LLP -230 Park Av -NY 10169
(212) 336-2000 .. **Tallbe**, Alicia A '07 %Patterson BW&T LLP -1133 Av of Amer -NY 10036
(212) 490-3000 .. **Tallbe**, Keith S J '06 %Wilson EME&D LLP -150 E 42nd -NY 10017
(518) 673-5656 .. **Tallent**, Chas J '75 (MacKenzie & T) -42 Church Bx330 -Canajoharie 13317 **Fx**:673-3501
(212) 885-5000 .. **Tallentire**, Heidi A '06 %Blank R LLP -405 Lex Av -NY 10174
(718) 896-2000 .. **Taller & Wizman, PC** -118-35 Qns Blvd -Frst Hlls 11375 **Fx**:896-2850
(718) 896-2000 .. **Taller**, Yehuda D '96 (Taller & W,PC) -118-35 Qns Blvd -Frst Hlls 11375
(631) 267-5253 .. **Talley**, Thos N '71 -19 Bell Pl Bx1991 -Amagansett 11930
(212) 822-8536 .. **Talleyrand**, Isabelle '01 -20 W 20th -NY 10011 **Fx**:822-8505
(516) 352-2867 .. **Tallini**, Muzzio '00 -1311 Hempstd Tpk -Elmont 11003
(212) 331-5951 .. **Tallis**, Andrew '95 Cnsl NYC HRA -180 Water -NY 10038
(518) 464-2186 .. **Tallon**, Barbara D '99 AYCO -1 Wall Bx15073 -Albany 12212
(212) 848-4000 .. **Tallon**, James P '81 (Shearman & S LLP) -599 Lex Av -NY 10022
(212) 252-5152 .. **Tally**, Lou '03 -160 Wadsworth Av -NY 10033 **Fx**:591-6777
(212) 246-9600 .. **Talmadge**, Richd E '69 -22 Bisbee Ln -Bedfrd Hlls 10507
(212) 836-8000 .. **Talmadge**, Scott D '90 (Kaye S LLP) -425 Park Av -NY 10022
(716) 580-3360 .. **Talmud**, Rebecca J '05 -5550 Main -Williamsvll 14221 **Fx**:580-3361
(212) 225-2000 .. **Talsma**, Alexander J '10 %Cleary GS&H -1 Lbrty Plz -NY 10006
(718) 590-2232 .. **Talty**, Edw J '81 %DA -198 E 161st -Bronx 10451 **Fx**:590-6477
(516) 488-6100 .. **Talty**, Matthew T '98 %Medical Society -865 Merrick Av Bx9007 -Westbury 11590 **Fx**:488-8389
(212) 419-1550 .. **Talwar**, Atul '03 CWA Legal Dept -350 7th Av -NY 10001 **Fx**:419-1555
(212) 259-8000 .. **Tam**, Allison J '98 (Dewey & L LLP) -1301 Av of Amer -NY 10019
(212) 373-3000 .. **Tam**, Eric S '10 Paul WRW&G LLP -1285 Av of Amer -NY 10019
(212) 735-3000 .. **Tam**, Jonathan S '09 %Skadden ASM&F LLP -4 Times Sq -NY 10036
(212) 238-4800 .. **Tam**, Kevin B '08 %Landman CB&F,PC -120 Bway -NY 10271
(212) 227-0347 .. **Tam**, Maggie L '94 %Weiss W&W,PC -25 Park Pl -NY 10007
(212) 513-3200 .. **Tam**, Philip C '02 %Holland & K LLP -31 W 52nd -NY 10019
(212) 701-3000 .. **Tama**, Anthony K '03 %Cahill G&R LLP -80 Pine -NY 10005 **Fx**:269-5420
(212) 697-6555 .. **Tama**, Debra A '89 (Biedermann RH&R) -570 Lex Av -NY 10022
(516) 739-5900 .. **Tama**, Michl A '90 -1551 Kellum Pl -Mineola 11501 **Fx**:739-0892
(212) 986-0947 .. **Tamai**, Julianne Sumiyo '04 -122 E 42nd -NY 10168
(212) 808-7800 .. **Tamamoto**, Craig A '07 %Kelley D&W LLP -101 Park Av -NY 10178
(646) 610-5400 .. **Tamari**, Doram '97 %NYPD -1 Police Plz -NY 10038
(212) 616-1500 .. **Tamarin**, Jeffrey M '84 Sweetface Fashion Co,LLC -1071 Av of Amer -NY 10018
(212) 973-8000 .. **Tamasco**, Matthew S '02 (Schnader HS&L LLP) -140 Bway -NY 10005
(212) 972-6161 .. **Tambaro**, Jos L '96 (Cassin & C LLP) -711 3rd Av -NY 10017
(516) 229-4501 .. **Tambasco**, Danl J '89 (Russo A&T) -875 Merrick Av -Westbury 11590
(212) 326-3939 .. **Tambe**, Jayant W '98 (Jones D) -222 E 41st -NY 10017
(315) 422-8131 .. **Tamber**, David S '97 %Alderman & A -472 S Salina -Syracuse 13202 **Fx**:474-7507
(212) 643-5454 .. **Tamber**, Stephen I '68 (Paskoff & T) -225 W 34th -NY 10122
(212) 558-5500 .. **Tambini**, Peter '99 Weitz & L,PC -700 Bway -NY 10003
(315) 468-2595 .. **Tamburo**, Saml M '68 -4914 W Genesee -Camillus 13031 **Fx**:468-0054
(315) 253-0326 .. **Tamburrino**, Stacy L '03 %Boyle & A,PC -110 Genesee -Auburn 13021
(212) 461-2323 .. **Tamburro**, Rina G '05 %Saiber LLC -44 Wall -NY 10005
(212) 431-1777 .. **Tamen**, Jack '61 -342 Bway -NY 10013
(516) 746-7371 .. **Tamigi**, Peter F '89 (Burns RT&R,LLP) -390 Old Cntry Rd -Gdn Cty 11530
(914) 674-4144 .. **Tamir**, Adilia '91 H Lawrence Inc -726 Saw Mill Rvr Rd -Ardsley 10502
(212) 506-2500 .. **Tamir**, Sagi '05 %Mayer B LLP -1675 Bway -NY 10019
(212) 480-3400 .. **Tamir**, Zaki Isaac B '05 (Tamir Law Grp) -55 Broad -NY 10004
(718) 442-4506 .. **Tamis**, Catalina '03 -28 Carroll Pl -Staten Isl 10301
(212) 541-2000 .. **Tamkin**, Danl S '85 OfCnsl Bryan C LLP -1290 Av of Amer -NY 10104
(212) 983-0900 .. **Tamlyn**, Thos T Jr. '82 (Yeskoo H&T LLP) -909 3rd Av -NY 10022
(585) 703-2163 .. **Tamm**, Linda Ratnik '96 Compendium Rsrch -20 Partrdg Hill -Honeoye Fls 14472
(914) 476-0600 .. **Tammaro**, Domenick J '89 (Smith B&J,LLP) -733 Ynkrs Av -Ynkrs 10704
(914) 332-0222 .. **Tamoshunas**, Algy '75 %Philips Electronics -345 Scarborough Rd Bx3001 -Briarclff Mnr 10510 **Fx**:332-0615
(212) 398-0055 .. **Tamoshunas**, Archana '00 %Garwin G&F,LLP -1501 Bway -NY 10036
(212) 421-4100 .. **Tamoshunas**, Mark A '00 OfCnsl Pryor C LLP -7 Times Sq -NY 10036
(212) 940-8800 .. **Tampellini**, James '02 %Katten MR LLP -575 Mad Av -NY 10022
(718) 523-6868 .. **Tampey**, Elisabeth J '02 %Comm Mediation Svcs -89-64 163rd -Jamaica 11432
(516) 683-4085 .. **Tamres**, Herbert J '64 NY Community Bk -615 Merrick Av -Westbury 11590 **Fx**:683-8371
(516) 771-0710 .. **Tamsen**, Elaine S '84 %Stern & S,PC -3002 Merrick Av -Bellmore 11710 **Fx**:771-0723
(631) 666-6929 .. **Tamsen**, Peter D '84 -260 Montauk Hwy -Bay Shr 11706 **Fx**:666-6907
(607) 336-2216 .. **Tamsett**, Clifton M Jr. '67 -306 Aurora Dr -Norwich 13815
(212) 940-8800 .. **Tamulewicz**, Jan '97 (Katten MR LLP) -575 Mad Av -NY 10022
(914) 428-2505 .. **Tamuno**, Alali M '95 %DEC -100 Hillside Av -White Plns 10603 **Fx**:428-0792
(212) 841-1000 .. **Tamussino**, Philipp '91 (Covington & B LLP) -620 8th Av -NY 10018
(212) 930-9700 .. **Tan**, Benjamin A '02 OfCnsl Sichenzia RFF LLP -61 Bway -NY 10006
(212) 412-4000 .. **Tan**, Bin '03 Barclays Captl -200 Park Av -NY 10166
(212) 947-9779 .. **Tan**, Christopher J '05 Advocates for Children -151 W 30th -NY 10001
(212) 906-1200 .. **Tan**, Danl S '05 Latham & W -885 3rd Av -NY 10022
(212) 848-4000 .. **Tan**, Gregory '00 (Shearman & S LLP) -599 Lex Av -NY 10022
(718) 590-2000 .. **Tan**, Justin C '09 %DA -198 E 161st -Bronx 10451 **Fx**:590-6477
(212) 225-2000 .. **Tan**, Kuang '10 %Cleary GS&H -1 Lbrty Plz -NY 10006
(212) 836-8000 .. **Tan**, Madeleine M L '98 (Kaye S LLP) -425 Park Av -NY 10022
(212) 610-6300 .. **Tan**, Oscar F B '09 %Allen & O -1221 Av of Amer -NY 10020
(212) 859-8000 .. **Tan**, Shuya '10 %Fried FHS&J LLP -1 NY Plz -NY 10004
(718) 939-8887 .. **Tan**, Tien H '86 -13608 38th Av -Flushng 11354
(212) 878-8000 .. **Tan**, Yi Tyng '09 %Clifford C LLP -31 W 52nd -NY 10019
(212) 969-3000 .. **Tanaka**, James A '03 %Proskauer R LLP -1585 Bway -NY 10036
(212) 703-3502 .. **Tananbaum**, Andrew H '73 %Century Bus Crdt -119 W 40th -NY 10018
(212) 806-5400 .. **Tanase**, Iuliana '09 %Stroock &S&L LLP -180 Maiden Ln -NY 10038
(212) 696-9100 .. **Tancer**, Joan S '84 %Segan N&S PC -112 Mad Av -NY 10016
(212) 599-0777 .. **Tanchum**, Letty M '74 OfCnsl Eisenberg T&L -675 3rd Av -NY 10017
(914) 725-2007 .. **Tanchum**, Letty M '74 -21 Chedworth Rd -Scarsdale 10583 **Fx**:725-2027
(212) 756-2000 .. **Tanchum**, Meredith J '08 %Schulte R&Z LLP -919 3rd Av -NY 10022
(212) 599-0777 .. **Tanchum**, Michl L '73 (Eisenberg T&L) -675 3rd Av -NY 10017
(516) 870-0335 .. **Tanck**, Henry C '95 (Vollmer & T) -500 N Bway -Jericho 11753 **Fx**:342-1551
(212) 408-5100 .. **Tanck**, Paul J '05 %Chadbourne & P LLP -30 Rckfllr Plz -NY 10112
(212) 261-8000 .. **Tancona**, David L '07 %Mendes & M,LLP -750 7th Av -NY 10019
(212) 225-2000 .. **Tancredi**, Jennifer G '09 %Cleary GS&H -1 Lbrty Plz -NY 10006
(212) 724-6217 .. **Tancredi**, Laurence R '82 -22 Riverside Dr -NY 10023 **Fx**:877-6755
(516) 364-7900 .. **Tand**, Jonathan A '08 Epstein F&G -45 Crsswys Park Dr W -Woodbury 11797
(212) 521-5400 .. **Tandler**, James R '94 (Reed S LLP) -599 Lex Av -NY 10022
(212) 791-7163 .. **Tandon**, Aarti '02 Tandon Law -276 5th Av -NY 10001 **Fx**:(646) 219-7785
(212) 297-6218 .. **Tandon**, Amit '97 Emissary Captl Grp,LLC -420 Lex Av -NY 10170
(212) 766-4000 .. **Tane**, David A '84 (Deutsch TW&W,PC) -120 Bway -NY 10271
(914) 944-9003 .. **Tane**, Lisa Fishman '87 -6 Fox Run Rd -Briarclff Mnr 10510
(646) 335-3256 .. **Taneja**, Anil '03 -244 5th Av -NY 10001
(516) 877-7100 .. **Tanen**, Jeffrey S '88 (Bank T&B,PC) -400 Post Av -Westbury 11590
(212) 218-5500 .. **Tanen**, Lauren R '02 %Seyfarth S LLP -620 8th Av -NY 10018
(516) 829-4620 .. **Tanenbaum**, Danl M '83 -1 Channel Dr -Pt Wash 11050 **Fx**:829-1008
(212) 833-1189 .. **Tanenbaum**, David I '96 (Friedman KS&A LLP) -1633 Bway -NY 10019 **Fx**:373-7989
(212) 210-9425 .. **Tanenbaum**, Edw '75 (Alston & B LLP) -90 Park Av -NY 10016
(212) 772-2230 .. **Tanenbaum**, Ellen L '78 -301 E 78th -NY 10021
(631) 979-1027 .. **Tanenbaum**, Evan S '91 (Berler & T,PC) -503 Main -Pt Jffrsn 11777 **Fx**:360-2175
(212) 701-3000 .. **Tanenbaum**, Gerald S '71 SrCnsl Cahill G&R LLP -80 Pine -NY 10005 **Fx**:269-5420
(212) 468-8000 .. **Tanenbaum**, James R '77 (Morrison & F LLP) -1290 Av of Amer -NY 10104
(212) 422-1765 .. **Tanenbaum**, Jay H '59 -110 Wall -NY 10005 **Fx**:425-7492
(212) 310-8000 .. **Tanenbaum**, Jeffrey L '77 (Weil G&M LLP) -767 5th Av -NY 10153
(212) 725-4423 .. **Tanenbaum**, John M '92 OfCnsl Paykin K&A LLP -185 Mad Av -NY 10016
(718) 224-6300 .. **Tanenbaum**, Jos '49 OfCnsl Tanenbaum Assoc,LLP -43-29 Bell Blvd -Bayside 11361 **Fx**:224-7646
(718) 224-6300 .. **Tanenbaum**, Mark J '84 (Tanenbaum Assoc,LLP) -43-29 Bell Blvd -Bayside 11361 **Fx**:224-7646
(212) 422-0202 .. **Tanenbaum**, Michl A '89 (Sedgwick DM&A LLP) -125 Broad -NY 10004
(718) 224-6300 .. **Tanenbaum**, Richd E '86 (Tanenbaum Assoc,LLP) -43-29 Bell Blvd -Bayside 11361 **Fx**:224-7646
(347) 291-1776 .. **Tanenbaum**, Richd N '98 -172 5th Av -Brklyn 11217
(914) 289-0800 .. **Tanenbaum**, Steven R '78 (Solomon & T,PC) -707 Wstchstr Av -White Plns 10604
(516) 741-6565 .. **Tanenbaum**, Ted J '75 (Meyer SE&K,PC) -990 Stewart Av Bx9194 -Gdn Cty 11530
(212) 836-8000 .. **Tanenbaum**, Wm A '80 (Kaye S LLP) -425 Park Av -NY 10022
(212) 575-7700 .. **Tanenhaus**, Edw D '71 (E Tanenhaus,PC) -250 Greenwich -NY 10007 **Fx**:575-8771
(607) 722-5429 .. **Tanenhaus**, Marvin S '42 -Bx1824 -Bnghmtn 13902
(607) 763-9200 .. **Tanenhaus**, Sanford P '53 OfCnsl Levene G&T,LLP -BxF-1706 -Bnghmtn 13902
(212) 885-8000 .. **Tang**, Catherine K '04 BDO Seidman LLP -135 W 50th -NY 10020
(585) 419-8800 .. **Tang**, David M '06 %Harris B PLLC -99 Garnsey Rd -Pittsfrd 14534
(212) 418-1775 .. **Tang**, David W '04 Quadrangle Grp LLC -375 Park Av -NY 10152
(212) 474-1000 .. **Tang**, Derek J '07 %Cravath S&M LLP -825 8th Av -NY 10019
(212) 455-2000 .. **Tang**, Douglas L '09 %Simpson T&B LLP -425 Lex Av -NY 10017
(347) 404-9133 .. **Tang**, Eric '07 Civil Ct -141 Lvngstn -Brklyn 11201 **Fx**:(718) 643-3733

(212) 310-8000 ..**Tang,** Huimin '08 %Weil G&M LLP -767 5th Av -NY 10153

(212) 267-6633 ..**Tang,** James C '94 -198 Canal -NY 10013 **Fx:**267-3383

(631) 852-2500 ..**Tang,** Marion M '95 %DA -200 Center Dr -Rvrhead 11901 **Fx:**852-1769

(212) 521-4872 ..**Tang,** Micheline S '97 Kekst & Co -437 Mad Av -NY 10022

(516) 560-6400 ..**Tang,** Michelle Yan Qiu '06 Leg Aid -1 Helen Keller Way -Hempstd 11550 **Fx:**565-3694

(212) 450-4000 ..**Tang,** Niya '09 %Davis P&W LLP -450 Lex Av -NY 10017

(212) 221-0010 ..**Tang,** Paul C '81 Burlington Coat Factory -263 W 38th -NY 10018 **Fx:**391-0074

(212) 848-4000 ..**Tang,** Shirin Li-Wen '05 %Shearman & S LLP -599 Lex Av -NY 10022

(212) 586-5800 ..**Tang,** Shirley '93 Cnsl Cohen TS&W PC -420 Lex Av -NY 10170

(212) 878-3490 ..**Tang,** Wenchen '04 %Clifford C LLP -31 W 52nd -NY 10019

(718) 939-3088 ..**Tang,** Xuewu Michl '04 -39-01 Main -Flushng 11354 **Fx:**228-8996

(516) 921-1200 ..**Tangel,** John M '94 %Zavatsky M&L,LLP -33 Qns Bx510 -Syosset 11791

(518) 433-7395 ..**Tangredi,** Christina L '81 -79 N Pearl -Albany 12207 **Fx:**433-7398

(914) 328-6900 ..**Tangredi,** Elizabeth L '95 %P Tangredi & Assoc -202 Mamaroneck Av -White Plns 10601 **Fx:**328-7639

(914) 428-5981 ..**Tangredi,** John A '81 -14 Mamaroneck Av -White Plns 10601 **Fx:**428-3780

(914) 328-6900 ..**Tangredi,** Peter E '73 (P Tangredi & Assoc) -202 Mamaroneck Av -White Plns 10601 **Fx:**328-7639

(845) 639-6900 ..**Tanguay-McGuane,** Rachel '99 -20 Squadron Blvd -New Cty 10956 **Fx:**639-3801

(212) 318-3000 ..**Tani,** Stefania '09 %Fulbright & J LLP -666 5th Av -NY 10103

(212) 808-3750 ..**Tanico,** Paul P '81 %Castlerock Prtnrs -237 Park Av -NY 10017

(212) 705-7000 ..**Tanikella,** Sujata M '05 %Bingham M LLP -399 Park Av -NY 10022

(212) 344-9244 ..**Tanksley,** Sonia M '93 -330 Mad Av -NY 10017 **Fx:**410-6953

(212) 859-8000 ..**Tanlamai,** Tanna Van '10 %Fried FHS&J LLP -1 NY Plz -NY 10004

(212) 232-1300 ..**Tann,** Sabrina M '02 %Lewis BB&S LLP -77 Water -NY 10005

(212) 446-4831 ..**Tanne,** Fredk '87 (Kirkland & E LLP) -153 E 53rd -NY 10022

(718) 694-3900 ..**Tanne,** Mariel A '09 %Transit Auth -130 Lvngstn -Brklyn 11201 **Fx:**694-5726

(212) 326-3939 ..**Tannen,** Ilene B '87 (Jones D) -222 E 41st -NY 10017

(516) 248-8115 ..**Tannen,** Leonard N '57 %NY Abstract Co -66 Old Cntry Rd -Mineola 11501

(212) 883-7700 ..**Tannenbaum,** Calvin M '74 Morgan Stanley -330 Mad Av -NY 10017

(212) 792-8484 ..**Tannenbaum,** David S '84 (Stern T&B LLP) -380 Lex Av -NY 10168

(212) 302-2900 ..**Tannenbaum Dubin & Robinson** -1140 Av of Amer -NY 10036 **Fx:**302-2906

(718) 528-3700 ..**Tannenbaum,** Eliot B '83 (Naimark & T) -169-95 137th Av -Jamaica 11434 **Fx:**528-3809

(631) 694-2300 ..**Tannenbaum,** Erica B '09 %Lamb & B,LLP -534 Broadhllw Rd Bx9034 -Melvll 11747

(718) 312-4100 ..**Tannenbaum,** Gary K '79 %Empire Blue Cross -15 MetroTech Ctr -Brklyn 11201 **Fx:**312-6010

(212) 508-6700 ..**Tannenbaum Helpern Syracuse & Hirschtritt LLP** -900 3rd Av -NY 10022 **Fx:**371-1084

(718) 590-8340 ..**Tannenbaum,** Joan B '85 %Admin Children's Srvcs -900 Sheridan Av -Bronx 10451

(212) 596-9000 ..**Tannenbaum,** Mark J '79 (Ropes & G LLP) -1211 Av of Amer -NY 10036

(516) 683-1200 ..**Tannenbaum,** Matthew K '90 (Janus & T PC) -825 E Gate Blvd -Gdn Cty 11530 **Fx:**222-5510

(212) 508-6700 ..**Tannenbaum,** Michl G '71 (Tannenbaum HS&H LLP) -900 3rd Av -NY 10022

(516) 228-9181 ..**Tannenbaum,** Richd N '77 (Gassman BB&T,PC) -666 Old Cntry Rd -Gdn Cty 11530

(516) 354-0200 ..**Tannenbaum,** Steven B '79 (Horowitz T&S,PC) -2001 Marcus Av -Lk Success 11042

(212) 949-9022 ..**Tannenbaum,** Victor M '75 (Abelman F&S) -666 3rd Av -NY 10017

(212) 264-8819 ..**Tannenbaum,** Wallace '51 %ODAR-SSA -26 Fed Plz -NY 10278

(212) 799-6165 ..**Tannenhauser,** Robt F '71 (Rosenfeld B&T) -50 W 72nd -NY 10023

(212) 679-3124 ..**Tanner,** Brooke A '09 %T McCauley LLC -274 Mad Av -NY 10016 **Fx:**679-3105

(212) 418-1720 ..**Tanner,** David A '88 Quadrangle Group LLC -375 Park Av -NY 10152

(212) 530-5000 ..**Tanner,** Douglas A '87 (Milbank TH&M LLP) -1 Chase Manh Plz -NY 10005

(212) 962-1333 ..**Tanner,** Howard E '90 (Tanner & O) -30 Vesey -NY 10007 **Fx:**962-1778

(914) 385-0244 ..**Tanner,** Lester J '49 -145 Huguenot -New Rchll 10801

(212) 756-2000 ..**Tanner,** Lynn S '97 SpclCnsl Schulte R&Z LLP -919 3rd Av -NY 10022

(646) 315-7300 ..**Tanner,** Steven M '89 FINRA -14 Wall -NY 10005 **Fx:**315-7440

(518) 487-5460 ..**Tanner-Richter,** Mary C '99 %DA -6 Lodge -Albany 12207 **Fx:**487-5093

(718) 261-1200 ..**Tannuzzo,** Angelo J '90 -123-60 83rd Av -Kew Gdns 11415

(718) 835-4525 ..**Tanon,** Danl '95 -96-11 101st Av -Ozone Pk 11416 **Fx:**738-6103

(212) 557-7700 ..**Tansey,** Andrew L '91 (Davidson D&C LLP) -60 E 42nd -NY 10165

(718) 233-3785 ..**Tansey Tracy & Convery** -221 Jffrsn Av -Staten Isl 10306 **Fx:**233-3805

(716) 857-7991 ..**Tanski,** Ronald J '79 %Natl Fuel Gas -6363 Main -Williamsvll 14221 **Fx:**857-7614

(212) 262-2390 ..**Tantalla,** Michele T '04 %Connell F LLP -888 7th Av -NY 10106

(716) 566-5400 ..**Tantillo,** Anthony J '02 %Goldberg S LLP -665 Main -Buffalo 14203

(585) 396-4010 ..**Tantillo,** R Michl '78 (DA) -27 N Main -Canandaigua 14424 **Fx:**396-4860

(718) 522-4604 ..**Tantleff Cohen & Tantleff,PC** -188 Montague -Brklyn 11201 **Fx:**596-1766

(718) 522-4604 ..**Tantleff,** Edw D '92 (Tantleff C&T,PC) -188 Montague -Brklyn 11201

(718) 522-4604 ..**Tantleff,** Ivan L '65 %Tantleff C&T,PC -188 Montague -Brklyn 11201

(718) 522-4604 ..**Tantleff,** Susan D '92 -188 Montague -Brklyn 11201

(631) 285-7000 ..**Tantone,** Frank A '86 (Tantone & G) -2459 Ocean Av -Ronkonkoma 11779 **Fx:**285-7006

(212) 207-8400 ..**Tanzer,** Kenneth M '07 %Kavanagh M&O LLP -415 Mad Av -NY 10017

(212) 975-5886 ..**Tanzi,** Lisa Maria '02 %CBS Corp -51 W 52nd -NY 10019

(914) 468-1990 ..**Tanzman,** Cary M '79 -399 Knollwood Rd -White Plns 10603

(212) 317-9200 ..**Tanzman,** Mitchell A '85 Central Park Grp,LLC -12 E 49th -NY 10017 **Fx:**813-1543

(212) 559-2363 ..**Tao,** Curtis K '00 Citigroup -425 Park Av -NY 10022

(212) 335-4500 ..**Tao,** Peng '01 OfCnsl DLA Piper LLP -1251 Av of Amer -NY 10020

(212) 986-6330 ..**Taormina,** Louis C '01 Frederic W Cook & Co,Inc -90 Park Av -NY 10016

(646) 823-5800 ..**Tapalaga,** Gabriel '99 -44 Wall -NY 10005

(914) 948-1556 ..**Tapfar,** Gregory R '82 (Danziger & M LLP) -123 Main -White Plns 10601

(845) 462-3262 ..**Taphorn,** Jos B '52 -8 Scenic Dr; Hagan Farms -Poughkeepsie 12603 **Fx:**462-3262

(212) 373-3000 ..**Tapia,** Edwin J '01 Paul WRW&G LLP -1285 Av of Amer -NY 10019

(585) 987-2800 ..**Tapia,** Javier R '10 %Woods OG LLP -2 State -Rchstr 14614

(718) 590-6212 ..**Tapia,** Ricardo '08 %Law Dept -198 E 161st -Bronx 10451 **Fx:**590-2686

(212) 878-8569 ..**Tapineski,** Sara M '02 %Clifford C LLP -31 W 52nd -NY 10019

(212) 254-3471 ..**Taplitz,** David A '95 OfCnsl Taplitz & T -25 Grove -NY 10014 **Fx:**228-0121

(212) 254-3471 ..**Taplitz,** Wm Chester '49 (Taplitz & T) -25 Grove -NY 10014 **Fx:**228-0121

(518) 767-9766 ..**Tapp,** Lillian Kearsley '78 -Bx606 -Glenmont 12077 **Fx:**767-2766

(212) 474-1000 ..**Tapp,** Richd Elliott '09 %Cravath S&M LLP -825 8th Av -NY 10019

(212) 275-2045 ..**Tappe,** Trent N '97 %Warner Music Grp -75 Rckfllr Plz -NY 10019 **Fx:**489-3342

(631) 484-9597 ..**Tapper,** Una R '86 -20 Goldenwood Cir -Central Islip 11722 **Fx:**232-3418

(646) 694-9921 ..**Taqi,** Irum '02 PRCH -55 W 39th -NY 10018 **Fx:**366-1897

(516) 741-2585 ..**Tarab,** Margaret Burke '96 %Rosicki R & Assoc,PC -51 E Bethpage Rd -Plainvw 11803 **Fx:**741-4748

(212) 835-1572 ..**Tarabour,** Sheila W '83 (Lampf LP&P) -5 Penn Plz 19th Fl -NY 10119

(212) 243-2212 ..**Taracido,** M D Lita '73 Dixie Foam Ltd -107 W 25th -NY 10001

(914) 703-6300 ..**Tarallo,** Nicholas '80 (Pillinger MT,LLP) -570 Taxter Rd -Elmsfrd 10523

(212) 816-2847 ..**Taran,** Jesse D '98 Citigrp Glbl Mkts -388 Greenwich -NY 10013

(212) 421-2233 ..**Taran,** Jessica Y '05 %Wilk A LLP -675 3rd Av -NY 10017

(607) 739-3836 ..**Tarantelli,** Louis E '66 -205 John Bx244 -Horseheads 14845 **Fx:**739-3025

(607) 739-3836 ..**Tarantelli,** Mary M '01 %Tarantelli -205 John Bx244 -Horseheads 14845 **Fx:**739-3025

(518) 486-1336 ..**Tarantino,** Danl J '85 %Dept of Health -Corning Twr 24th Fl -Albany 12237 **Fx:**486-4834

(518) 792-6516 ..**Tarantino,** Dennis J '75 (Kenneally & T) -470 Glen Bx379 -Glens Fls 12801

(518) 783-2720 ..**Tarantino,** Joyce Clements '86 %Town of Colonie -Mem'l Town Hall Bx508 -Newtonville 12128 **Fx:**786-7324

(518) 462-6831 ..**Tarantino,** Louise M '78 %Empire Justice Ctr -119 Wshngtn Av -Albany 12210 **Fx:**462-6687

(212) 272-6458 ..**Tarantino,** Thos E '79 -383 Mad Av -NY 10179 **Fx:**272-7382

(518) 445-2311 ..**Taranto,** Jenean M '89 Albany Law Schl -80 New Scotland Av -Albany 12208 **Fx:**445-2315

(718) 495-2579 ..**Taranto,** Lisa M '01 %M Doherty,PC -6900 Jericho Tpk -Syosset 11791 **Fx:**495-2738

(516) 759-1111 ..**Taranto,** Vincent K '03 %V Taranto,PC -3 Schl -Glen Cove 11542 **Fx:**676-3969

(516) 759-1111 ..**Taranto,** Vincent P '72 (V Taranto,PC) -3 Schl -Glen Cove 11542 **Fx:**676-3969

(718) 625-2020 ..**Taras,** Bert '65 (B Taras PC) -Bx149 -Old Westbury 11568 **Fx:**243-1440

(716) 204-9480 ..**Taras,** Estee M '98 %SJ Baum,PC -900 Merchants Cncrs -Westbury 11590 **Fx:**204-9680

(212) 947-3793 ..**Taras,** Mitchell B '97 OfCnsl Sadis & G LLP -551 5th Av -NY 10176

(718) 579-7735 ..**Tarasuk,** Ian B '06 %Leg Aid -900 Sheridan Av -Bronx 10451 **Fx:**293-8744

(212) 735-3000 ..**Tarazi,** Monica E '10 %Skadden ASM&F LLP -4 Times Sq -NY 10036

(631) 907-3500 ..**Tarbet,** Jonathan G '98 (Tarbet L&S) -524 Montauk Hwy Bx2635 -Amagansett 11930 **Fx:**907-3501

(516) 571-2797 ..**Tarbutton,** Michl D '01 %Hon W Donnino -262 Old Cntry Rd -Mineola 11501

(914) 738-4575 ..**Tarcher,** Herbert P '70 (Conforti & T) -14 Clifford Av -Pelham 10803 **Fx:**738-4684

(212) 373-3000 ..**Tarczynska,** Dominika N '06 %Paul WRW&G LLP -1285 Av of Amer -NY 10019

(718) 876-6300 ..**Tardanico,** Guy R '09 %DA -130 Styvsnt Pl -Staten Isl 10301

(212) 768-6700 ..**Tardif,** Nicholas J '09 %Sonnenschein N&R LLP -1221 Av of Amer -NY 10020

(212) 684-0300 ..**Tare,** Joshua M '01 %Bauman K&G LLP -28 W 44th -NY 10036

(212) 284-2587 ..**Targoff,** Joshua L '97 Jefferies & Co Inc -520 Mad Av -NY 10022

(212) 697-5381 ..**Targoff,** Michl B '69 -600 3rd Av -NY 10016

(212) 512-0585 ..**Targownik,** Israel Murrey '00 -1040 Av of Amer -NY 10018

(212) 349-2727 ..**Targum,** Andrew S '91 (Targum B&T,LLP) -233 Bway -NY 10279 **Fx:**672-0094

(212) 756-2000 ..**Tarkan,** Adam J '09 %Schulte R&Z LLP -919 3rd Av -NY 10022

(646) 386-5891 ..**Tarkow,** Amanda A '03 MHLS -41 Mad Av -NY 10010

(315) 435-2470 ..**Tarkowski,** Andrew J '05 %DA -505 S State -Syracuse 13202 **Fx:**435-3969

(315) 337-6102 ..**Tarkowski,** Raymond A '71 -806 Hickory -Rome 13440

(607) 255-2796 ..**Tarlow,** Wendy E '93 %Cornell Univ -300 CCC Bldg-Grdn Av -Ithaca 14853 **Fx:**255-2794

(212) 637-2330 ..**Tarlowe,** Richd C '03 %US Atty -1 St Andrews Plz -NY 10007

(212) 553-0300 ..**Tarlowe,** Rochelle M '98 %Moody's Invstr Srvc -250 Greenwich -NY 10007

(212) 574-1200 ..**Tarn,** Dewen '06 %Seward & K LLP -1 Bttry Pk Plz -NY 10004

(212) 715-9100 ..**Tarnoff,** Gary '75 (Kramer LN&F,LLP) -1177 Av of Amer -NY 10036

(212) 735-8632 ..**Tarnoff,** Jerome '57 (Morrison C LLP) -909 3rd Av -NY 10022

(212) 972-1355 ..**Tarnofsky,** Madeline '88 -360 Cntrl Pk W -NY 10025 **Fx:**972-1356

(212) 373-3000 .. **Tarnofsky,** Robyn F '96 (Paul WRW&G LLP) -1285 Av of Amer -NY 10019

(212) 599-5550 .. **Tarnok,** Christopher M '09 %Omrani & T,PC -909 3rd Av -NY 10022

(212) 701-3000 .. **Tarnopol,** Danl J '10 %Cahill G&R LLP -80 Pine -NY 10005 **Fx:**269-5420

(718) 787-1811 .. **Tarnovsky,** Rada '99 (Lubarsky & T) -2699 Coney Isl Av -Brklyn 11223 **Fx:**787-1511

(212) 964-6611 .. **Tarnowski,** John L '00 %Lester SK&D -120 Bway -NY 10271

(631) 475-4400 .. **Taroff,** Lester P '72 (Roe TT&P,LLP) -One Corp Dr -Bohemia 11716

(315) 488-1975 .. **Tarolli,** Eugene D '58 -4914 W Genesee -Camillus 13031 **Fx:**468-0054

(315) 488-1975 .. **Tarolli,** James R '84 %E Tarolli -4914 W Genesee -Camillus 13031 **Fx:**468-0054

(315) 435-2170 .. **Tarolli,** Lori Honey '84 %Cnty Atty -421 Mntgmry -Syracuse 13202 **Fx:**435-5729

(212) 564-1400 .. **Tarowsky,** Laurence C '88 -352 7th Av -NY 10001

(516) 393-2200 .. **Tarpey,** Colleen M '01 %Garfunkel W,PC -111 Grt Nck Rd -Gt Neck 11021

(518) 438-8055 .. **Tarpinian,** Anne S '94 -21 Melrose Av -Albany 12203

(631) 847-5453 .. **Tarpinian,** Gregory P '90 %Arrow Electronics -50 Marcus Dr -Melvll 11747

(212) 559-9583 .. **Tarpley,** Michl J '83 Citibank NA -425 Park Av -NY 10022 **Fx:**793-4400

(212) 407-4000 .. **Tarr,** Alan J '80 (Loeb & L,LLP) -345 Park Av -NY 10154

(516) 513-0815 .. **Tarr,** Leonard N '60 L Tarr,PC -333 Earle Ovngton Blvd -Uniondale 11553 **Fx:**832-3233

(212) 416-8785 .. **Tarr,** Paul M '92 Atty Gen -120 Bway -NY 10271

(212) 335-4500 .. **Tarr,** Robin Cottrell '98 OfCnsl DLA Piper LLP -1251 Av of Amer -NY 10020

(718) 997-0836 .. **Tarrab,** Robt H '01 -66-36 Yllwstn Blvd -Frst Hlls 11375 **Fx:**897-1985

(845) 565-1100 .. **Tarshis Catania Liberth Mahon & Milligram, PLLC** -One Corwin Ct -Newburgh 12550 **Fx:**565-1999

(845) 426-7799 .. **Tarshis Catania Liberth Mahon & Milligram, PLLC** -100 Red Schlhse Rd -Chestnut Rdg 10977

(718) 793-5000 .. **Tarshis & Hammerman,LLP** -118-35 Qns Blvd -Frst Hlls 11375 **Fx:**793-5008

(212) 223-3900 .. **Tarshis,** Justin M '03 %Zwerling S&Z,LLP -41 Mad Av -NY 10010

(718) 793-5000 .. **Tarshis,** Roberta E '79 OfCnsl Tarshis & H,LLP -118-35 Qns Blvd -Frst Hlls 11375

(845) 565-1100 .. **Tarshis,** Steven L '72 (Tarshis CLM&M,PLLC) -One Corwin Ct -Newburgh 12550

(718) 793-5000 .. **Tarshis,** Stuart M '73 (Tarshis & H,LLP) -118-35 Qns Blvd -Frst Hlls 11375

(845) 634-3627 .. **Tarson,** Derek S '05 Leg Aid -2 Congers Rd -New Cty 10956 **Fx:**634-8505

(516) 812-4500 .. **Tarson,** Michelle E '99 %Stagg TC&W LLP -401 Franklin Av -Gdn Cty 11530

(718) 590-3784 .. **Tartaglia,** Alfred C '81 %Hon G Friedman -851 Grnd Cncrs -Bronx 10451

(631) 360-0400 .. **Tartaglia,** Bridget J '96 (Jakubowski RMG&T) -969 Jericho Tpk -St James 11780 **Fx:**360-0408

(914) 285-0700 .. **Tartaglia,** John A III '08 %Renzulli Law Firm,LLP -81 Main -White Plns 10601 **Fx:**285-1213

(718) 792-1364 .. **Tartaglia,** Maria A '87 -1953 Wallace Av -Bronx 10462 **Fx:**792-1364

(646) 386-5699 .. **Tartaglia,** Rita Jean '96 %Civil Ct -111 Centre -NY 10013

(518) 640-6900 .. **Tartaglia,** Stanley J Jr. '07 %Phelan P&D,LLP -302 Wshngtn Av Ext -Albany 12203

(718) 250-2000 .. **Tartak,** Nicole A '07 %DA -350 Jay -Brklyn 11201 **Fx:**250-2314

(212) 909-6000 .. **Tartakovskiy,** Dmitriy A '02 %Debevoise & P LLP -919 3rd Av -NY 10022

(212) 848-4000 .. **Tartakovsky,** Adam F '10 Shearman & S LLP -599 Lex Av -NY 10022

(631) 366-2300 .. **Tartamella,** Leonard J '78 (Tartamella T&F) -235 Brooksite Dr -Hauppauge 11788

(631) 366-2300 .. **Tartamella,** Michl R '95 %Tartamella T&F -235 Brooksite Dr -Hauppauge 11788

(631) 366-2300 .. **Tartamella,** Natale '68 (Tartamella T&F) -235 Brooksite Dr -Hauppauge 11788

(516) 775-6800 .. **Tartamella,** Stefani Lynn '00 %CK Verkowitz -561 Lakevll Rd -New Hyde Pk 11040 **Fx:**775-0641

(631) 366-2300 .. **Tartamella Tartamella & Fresolone** -235 Brooksite Dr -Hauppauge 11788 **Fx:**366-2575

(914) 682-3390 .. **Tartaro,** Angelo D '95 (A Tartaro,PC) -925 Wstchstr Av -White Plns 10604 **Fx:**287-0874

(212) 216-8000 .. **Tarter,** Alan M '90 (Tarter K&D LLP) -1350 Bway -NY 10018

(212) 216-8000 .. **Tarter Krinsky & Drogin LLP** -1350 Bway -NY 10018 **Fx:**216-8001

(212) 269-5500 .. **Tarter,** Mitchel '04 %Gordon & R LLP -90 Broad -NY 10004

(212) 998-2240 .. **Taruschio,** Anna Marta '01 %NYU Ofc Leg Cnsl -70 Wshngtn Sq S -NY 10012 **Fx:**995-3048

(212) 732-9000 .. **Tarver,** Terrence L '08 %Sullivan PBM&C PC -120 Bway -NY 10271

(212) 966-6420 .. **Tarvin,** Margaret A '88 %Lwyrs For Children -110 Lafayette -NY 10013 **Fx:**966-0531

(718) 575-1244 .. **Taryan,** Peter J '83 (Furst & T) -71-21 Austin -Frst Hlls 11375 **Fx:**575-1544

(212) 436-5518 .. **Tarzia,** Dale '95 Deloitte & Touche LLP -2 World Fncl Ctr -NY 10281

(212) 885-5000 .. **Tarzik,** Corey E '03 %Blank R LLP -405 Lex Av -NY 10174

(212) 370-9000 .. **Tarzy,** Alan A '79 -275 Mad Av -NY 10016 **Fx:**370-1566

(718) 434-8300 .. **Tasevich,** Marina '05 %A Bespechny -1122 Coney Isl Av -Brklyn 11230 **Fx:**434-6112

(212) 633-6967 .. **Tasheff,** Petra T '94 Natl Ctr Law & Economic Justice -275 7th Av -NY 10001 **Fx:**633-6371

(212) 513-3200 .. **Tasher,** Lindsay H '06 %Holland & K LLP -31 W 52nd -NY 10019

(212) 319-9800 .. **Tashjian & Padian** -729 7th Av -NY 10019 **Fx:**319-9883

(212) 319-9800 .. **Tashjian,** Richd G '83 (Tashjian & P) -729 7th Av -NY 10019

(516) 357-3700 .. **Tashjian,** Roxanne L '09 %Cullen and D LLP -100 Q Roosevelt Blvd -Gdn Cty 11530

(212) 821-3387 .. **Tashkovich,** Mark A '96 UBS -299 Park Av -NY 10171

(516) 466-8005 .. **Tashlik Kreutzer Goldwyn & Crandell PC** -40 Cuttermill Rd -Gt Neck 11021 **Fx:**829-6509

(516) 466-8005 .. **Tashlik,** Theo W '65 (Tashlik KG&C PC) -40 Cuttermill Rd -Gt Neck 11021

(212) 784-5800 .. **Tashman,** Monika A '00 (Hiscock & B,LLP) -7 Times Sq -NY 10036

(212) 947-6555 .. **Tashman,** Sheldon J '69 -3 W 35th -NY 10001 **Fx:**594-0019

(718) 263-4017 .. **Tasker,** Arthur M '92 Tasker Law Ofcs -110-11 Qns Blvd Bx750799 -Frst Hlls 11375

(516) 682-8220 .. **Tasolides,** John N '82 -6800 Jericho Tpk -Syosset 11791 **Fx:**921-1223

(516) 712-4000 .. **Tassan,** Louis S '86 (Milber MP&S LLP) -1000 Woodbury Rd -Woodbury 11797

(718) 361-9200 .. **Tasso,** Lorenzo '89 (L Tasso,PC) -29-27 41st Av -LIC 11101 **Fx:**361-2758

(914) 323-7000 .. **Tatarka,** Gregg A '06 %Wilson EME&D LLP -3 Gannett Dr -White Plns 10604

(212) 705-7000 .. **Tatarowicz,** Christopher P '09 %Bingham M LLP -399 Park Av -NY 10022

(518) 402-0205 .. **Tate,** Christopher M '92 %UIA Bd -Troy Atrium Bx15126 -Albany 12212 **Fx:**402-6208

(518) 686-7324 .. **Tate,** Donald J Jr. '95 (Holbrook J&T) -12 Main Bx146 -Hoosick Fls 12090

(212) 859-8000 .. **Tate,** Elizabeth Greene '09 %Fried FHS&J LLP -1 NY Plz -NY 10004

(315) 472-4313 .. **Tate,** Jonathan O '86 %Ventre Law Ofc -5112 W Taft Rd -Liverpool 13088 **Fx:**472-4314

(518) 869-3466 .. **Tate,** Michl E '84 %Malone & Tate Bldrs -2217 Central Av -Schnctdy 12304

(212) 514-8888 .. **Tate,** Princess M '03 %Fisher & F -New Dorp Station Bx61060 -Staten Isl 10306 **Fx:**514-9016

(212) 779-1734 .. **Tate-Brown,** Kimberly J '06 MHLS -41 Mad Av -NY 10010

(718) 286-2000 .. **Tate-Cousins,** Sonia C '87 %Leg Aid -120-46 Qns Blvd -Kew Gdns 11415 **Fx:**286-2286

(917) 778-6600 .. **Tatham,** Beverly S '02 %J Toomey -485 Lex Av -NY 10017 **Fx:**778-7048

(212) 259-8000 .. **Tato,** Jos A '79 (Dewey & L LLP) -1301 Av of Amer -NY 10019

(718) 487-2300 .. **Tatro,** Marie A '94 %Leg Srvcs Corp -256-260 Bway -Brklyn 11211 **Fx:**782-6790

(212) 530-1800 .. **Tatsch,** Simone C '08 Richards K&O LLP -1 World Fncl Ctr -NY 10281

(212) 839-5300 .. **Tattan,** Shane M '09 %Sidley A LLP -787 7th Av -NY 10019

(212) 836-8000 .. **Tattenbaum,** Ian S '98 Cnsl Kaye S LLP -425 Park Av -NY 10022

(212) 237-1000 .. **Tattoni,** Julie Riley '87 SpclCnsl Windels ML&M,LLP -156 W 56th -NY 10019

(631) 897-1717 .. **Tatun,** Jonathan M '04 -197 Schoenfeld Blvd -Patchogue 11772

(212) 824-5700 .. **Taub,** Amy Rosenthal '85 Practising Law Inst -810 7th Av -NY 10019

(718) 891-1200 .. **Taub,** Asher Erwin '96 (Alatsas & T,PC) -2115 Av U -Brklyn 11229

(212) 423-2404 .. **Taub,** Barry '74 North General Hospital -1879 Mad Av -NY 10035

(212) 672-7000 .. **Taub,** Danl P '05 Viking Global Investors LP -280 Park Av -NY 10017

(212) 272-2543 .. **Taub,** Danl S '77 %JP Morgan Chase -383 Mad Av -NY 10179

(212) 547-5400 .. **Taub,** David L '85 (McDermott W&E LLP) -340 Mad Av -NY 10173

(914) 948-3354 .. **Taub,** Douglas H '02 (Britt & T,PLLC) -149 Grand -White Plns 10601 **Fx:**(845) 496-1112

(518) 664-5440 .. **Taub,** Eli I '64 -7 Camden Ct -Mechanicvll 12118 **Fx:**664-5278

(646) 484-5020 .. **Taub,** Elliot H '78 (Taub Law Firm,PC) -14 Penn Plz -NY 10122 **Fx:**429-9806

(516) 877-0777 .. **Taub Hametz & Waldman, PLLC** -190 Willis Av -Mineola 11501 **Fx:**747-2956

(212) 349-0200 .. **Taub,** Herman '61 -225 Bway -NY 10007 **Fx:**349-5110

(212) 286-7700 .. **Taub,** Iven R '79 -355 Lex Av -NY 10017 **Fx:**481-2488

(212) 557-2655 .. **Taub,** Jeffrey D '86 J Taub,PC -570 Lex Av -NY 10022 **Fx:**(646) 380-0102

(212) 681-6500 .. **Taub,** Joelle B '93 (Stempel BC&H,PC) -675 3rd Av -NY 10017

(212) 786-6046 .. **Taub,** Jonathan A '92 Morandi Taub & Sarnoff,LLC -1325 Av of Amer -NY 10019 **Fx:**786-6045

(718) 250-2000 .. **Taub,** Kenneth M '81 %DA -350 Jay -Brklyn 11201 **Fx:**250-2314

(212) 504-6000 .. **Taub,** Loren R '97 SpclCnsl Cadwalader W&T LLP -1 World Fncl Ctr -NY 10281

(212) 265-8600 .. **Taub,** Malcolm S '74 (MS Taub LLP) -110 E 59th -NY 10022 **Fx:**581-8958

(212) 267-7342 .. **Taub,** Mark '02 OfCnsl Neiger LLP -317 Mad Av -NY 10017 **Fx:**406-3677

(646) 484-5020 .. **Taub,** Matthew A '09 %Taub Law Firm,PC -14 Penn Plz -NY 10122 **Fx:**429-9806

(212) 599-5550 .. **Taub,** Michl A '98 (Omrani & T,PC) -909 3rd Av -NY 10022

(212) 962-8020 .. **Taub,** Michl J '85 %Julien & S,PC -1 Whitehall -NY 10004

(914) 686-3700 .. **Taub,** Michl L '84 (Worby GE LLP) -11 Martine Av -White Plns 10606

(212) 425-5191 .. **Taub,** Naomi M '09 %Mischel & H,PC -1 Whitehall -NY 10004

(212) 345-6558 .. **Taub,** Peter S '94 Marsh & McLennan Cos -1166 Avnus of the Americas -NY 10036

(516) 745-6830 .. **Taub,** Randi E '86 %Golden W&B PC -900 Merchants Cncrs -Westbury 11590

(212) 693-1000 .. **Taub,** Randi S '07 Golub & G,LLP -225 Bway -NY 10007 **Fx:**693-0090

(212) 801-3197 .. **Taub,** Roy '05 %Greenberg T,LLP -200 Park Av -NY 10166

(516) 992-0805 .. **Taub,** Sabrina E '04 (Selvin Law Firm PLLC) -1225 Franklin Av -Gdn Cty 11530 **Fx:**678-3090

(718) 633-5378 .. **Taub,** Shmuel D '90 (S Taub,PC) -1466 60th -Brklyn 11219 **Fx:**633-3144

(516) 877-0777 .. **Taub,** Stephen R '69 (Taub H&W,PLLC) -190 Willis Av -Mineola 11501

(212) 408-2500 .. **Taube,** Seth T '80 (Baker B,LLP) -30 Rckfllr Plz -NY 10112

(718) 692-3131 .. **Taubenblat,** Michl J '89 -113 Av I -Brklyn 11230 **Fx:**692-3133

(212) 964-4664 .. **Taubenblatt,** Leonard '50 -217 Bway -NY 10007 **Fx:**385-2707

(516) 374-3133 .. **Taubenfeld,** Harry S '55 (Zuckerbrod & T) -575 Chestnut Bx488 -Cedarhrst 11516

(347) 404-9133 .. **Tauber,** Aaron Evan '84 %Civil Ct -141 Lvngstn -Brklyn 11201 **Fx:**(718) 643-3733

(212) 570-1118 .. **Tauber,** Adele S '77 -885 Park Av -NY 10075

(212) 595-8470 .. **Tauber,** Alan L '95 (A Tauber,PC) -26 W 85th -NY 10024 **Fx:**769-9335
(212) 586-5800 .. **Tauber,** Laurence S '81 (Cohen TS&W PC) -420 Lex Av -NY 10170
(212) 735-3000 .. **Tauber,** Miriam '07 %Skadden ASM&F LLP -4 Times Sq -NY 10036
(516) 832-7521 .. **Taubin,** Michl J '76 (Nixon P LLP) -50 Jericho Quadrangle -Jericho 11753
(518) 869-0901 .. **Taubkin,** Peter M '91 %Time Warner Cable -130 Wshngtn Av Ext -Albany 12203 **Fx:**869-1007
(716) 838-6430 .. **Taublieb,** Edw J '73 -187 Norwalk Av -Buffalo 14216
(212) 715-9100 .. **Taubman,** Adam B '09 %Kramer LN&F,LLP -1177 Av of Amer -NY 10036
(212) 227-8140 .. **Taubman Kimelman & Soroka LLP** -30 Vesey -NY 10007 **Fx:**385-0662
(212) 732-7184 .. **Taubman,** Louis E '94 (Leser HT&T) -17 State -NY 10004
(212) 227-8140 .. **Taubman,** Philip '75 (Taubman K&S LLP) -30 Vesey -NY 10007
(212) 285-3038 .. **Taubman,** Phoebe E '05 Better Balance -75 Maiden Ln -NY 10038 **Fx:**724-3535
(718) 987-3380 .. **Taubman,** Robt S '92 -74 Lincoln Av -Staten Isl 10306
(212) 770-2533 .. **Taubner,** Corinna M '01 AIG -80 Pine -NY 10005
(914) 997-1212 .. **Taubner,** Frank K '05 %Jasne & F,LLP -30 Glenn -White Plns 10603
(516) 327-4050 .. **Tauches,** Frank A Jr. '71 %Water Auth -58 S Tyson Av -Floral Pk 11001
(718) 595-4717 .. **Taule,** Chas '95 %DEP-BWT -96-05 Horace Hrdng Expy -Corona 11368 **Fx:**595-6950
(212) 446-4800 .. **Taurassi,** Vincent E '08 %Kirkland & E LLP -153 E 53rd -NY 10022
(518) 474-1331 .. **Tauriello,** John V '81 %Ofc Mntl Health -44 Holland Av -Albany 12229 **Fx:**473-7863
(800) 598-3325 .. **Taurisano,** Jon M '08 Allegretto Ltd -5786 Widewaters Pkwy -Syracuse 13214
(212) 398-0055 .. **Taus,** Barry S '90 (Garwin G&F,LLP) -1501 Bway -NY 10036
(212) 398-0055 .. **Taus,** David M '86 (DM Taus,LLC) -1501 Bway -NY 10036 **Fx:**(646) 291-4753
(212) 221-5700 .. **Taus,** Douglas C '93 (Goldberg WFG LLP) -1501 Bway -NY 10036
(212) 233-2122 .. **Taus,** Marla Wolfe '87 %Ferrara TH&G -711 3rd Av -NY 10017
(212) 907-7300 .. **Tausner,** Eric R '08 OfCnsl Golenbock EAB&P -437 Mad Av -NY 10022
(212) 325-2326 .. **Taussig,** Andrew R '79 Credit Suisse -11 Mad Av -NY 10010
(212) 788-0813 .. **Taussig,** Gabriel '75 %Law Dept -100 Church -NY 10007 **Fx:**788-0367
(212) 964-7400 .. **Taustine,** Mark A '00 Smith MDWY&Y,PC -111 John -NY 10038
(518) 455-4964 .. **Tauzin,** Dominique Y '03 NYS Assembly -508 Cptl Bldg -Albany 12248
(646) 386-3178 .. **Tavarez,** Manuel J '01 Hon M Tingling -60 Centre -NY 10007
(212) 705-4874 .. **Tavel,** Andrew G '83 (Tavel & Assoc,PC) -488 Mad Av -NY 10022 **Fx:**537-4724
(212) 964-7400 .. **Tavel,** Corey A '91 Smith MDWY&Y,PC -111 John -NY 10038
(718) 459-6000 .. **Tavel,** Eric T '97 (Pennisi D&N LLP) -97-77 Qns Blvd -Rego Pk 11374
(631) 853-5761 .. **Tavel,** Jeffrey P '86 %Cnty Atty -400 Carleton Av -Central Islip 11722 **Fx:**853-7788
(212) 267-1900 .. **Tavella,** David F '93 (Wade CM) -111 Bway -NY 10006
(607) 273-3900 .. **Tavelli,** Paul N '67 -405 N Tioga Bx695 -Ithaca 14851 **Fx:**273-3802
(718) 476-2300 .. **Taveras,** Manuel A '97 -10622 Nrthrn Blvd -Corona 11368 **Fx:**476-2304
(212) 779-1414 .. **Taveras,** Tania T '05 %Bernstein L LLP -10 E 40th -NY 10016
(212) 397-3050 .. **Taveras-Perez,** Luisa H '94 Ctr for Court Innovation -520 8th Av -NY 10018 **Fx:**397-0985
(585) 352-2658 .. **Taverna,** Diahn B '97 %Labor Relations -3599 Big Ridge Rd -Spencerprt 14559
(212) 613-5000 .. **Tavi,** Sabrina '00 %Leg Assist Grp -450 W 33rd -NY 10001 **Fx:**750-0820
(718) 351-0621 .. **Tavolacci,** Carl E '36 -93 Cromwell Cir -Staten Isl 10304 **Fx:**351-0621
(212) 574-1200 .. **Tavss,** John E '80 (Seward & K LLP) -1 Bttry Pk Plz -NY 10004
(212) 474-1000 .. **Tavzel,** Erik R '99 (Cravath S&M LLP) -825 8th Av -NY 10019
(212) 538-5028 .. **Tawil,** David D '00 Credit Suisse -11 Mad Av -NY 10010
(212) 964-3400 .. **Tawil,** Michl L '92 %Drabkin & M -120 Bway -NY 10271
(212) 545-4707 .. **Tawil,** Raphael A '00 %Wolf HAF&H LLP -270 Mad Av -NY 10016
(212) 474-1000 .. **Tawil,** Sophia D '07 %Cravath S&M LLP -825 8th Av -NY 10019
(212) 753-0300 .. **Taxin,** David R '78 (Dahan & N LLP) -1700 Bway -NY 10019
(212) 599-3700 .. **Taxin,** Michl F '06 Cnsl Robt K Futterman & Assoc,LLC -521 5th Av -NY 10175
(212) 530-1800 .. **Tay,** Selina Wanmei '00 %Richards K&O LLP -1 World Fncl Ctr -NY 10281
(212) 373-3000 .. **Tayar,** David J '03 %Paul WRW&G LLP -1285 Av of Amer -NY 10019
(212) 468-4800 .. **Taylor,** Aaron K '05 %Davis & G LLP -1740 Bway -NY 10019
(212) 643-9668 .. **Taylor,** Amelia T '90 %Wong F,PC -350 5th Av -NY 10118
(212) 431-7200 .. **Taylor,** Amy S '07 Legal Srvcs NYC -350 Bway -NY 10013 **Fx:**966-9571
(646) 826-5747 .. **Taylor,** Anthony J '04 %Och-Ziff -9 W 57th -NY 10019
(212) 885-8000 .. **Taylor,** Barbara Anne '89 %BDO USA,LLP -330 Mad Av -NY 10017 **Fx:**697-1299
(212) 613-5000 .. **Taylor,** Benjamin W '05 Leg Assist Grp -450 W 33rd -NY 10001 **Fx:**750-0820
(212) 298-5067 .. **Taylor,** Bret J '05 Leg Aid -49 Thomas -NY 10013 **Fx:**298-5252
(212) 259-8000 .. **Taylor,** Brian L '82 Cnsl Dewey & L LLP -1301 Av of Amer -NY 10019
(516) 742-0101 .. **Taylor,** Carol Needham '83 (Pasta N&T) -436 Willis Av -Williston Pk 11596
(212) 841-1000 .. **Taylor,** Carolyn Eaton '86 (Covington & B LLP) -620 8th Av -NY 10018
(212) 477-0134 .. **Taylor,** Cathy D '03 -702 E 5th -NY 10009
(518) 383-6110 .. **Taylor,** Chas A '91 -87 Valencia Ln -Clifton Pk 12065 **Fx:**383-6110
(212) 878-8000 .. **Taylor,** Christopher D '07 %Clifford C LLP -31 W 52nd -NY 10019
(212) 820-9374 .. **Taylor,** Christopher M '06 %Hawkins D&W LLP -One Chase Manh Plz -NY 10005
(718) 224-1659 .. **Taylor,Colicchio & Silverman,LLP** -26910 Grnd Cntrl Pkwy -Floral Pk 11005
(212) 969-3000 .. **Taylor,** Courtney D '09 %Proskauer R LLP -1585 Bway -NY 10036
(212) 318-3000 .. **Taylor,** Cybil E '09 %Fulbright & J LLP -666 5th Av -NY 10103
(516) 379-5200 .. **Taylor,** Daivery G '94 (Silverman & T) -33 Guy Lombardo Av -Freeprt 11520 **Fx:**771-9650
(212) 262-6300 .. **Taylor,** David G '05 Soros Fund Mgmt LLC -888 7th Av -NY 10106
(607) 293-8460 .. **Taylor,** David K '90 -3095 Cnty Hwy 11 Bx188 -Hartwick 13348
(518) 452-0802 .. **Taylor,** David R '75 OfCnsl Taylor & Assoc -1 Columbia Cir -Albany 12203 **Fx:**452-1863
(914) 681-8700 .. **Taylor,** David S '03 %Milber MP&S LLP -3 Barker Av -White Plns 10601
(212) 474-1000 .. **Taylor,** Delceta B '10 %Cravath S&M LLP -825 8th Av -NY 10019
(212) 701-3000 .. **Taylor,** Devin L '09 %Cahill G&R LLP -80 Pine -NY 10005 **Fx:**269-5420
(914) 564-9700 .. **Taylor,** Diane F '86 -24 Whitman -Hastings-On-Hud 10706
(315) 673-2053 .. **Taylor,** Douglas W '82 D Taylor -17 North -Marcellus 13108 **Fx:**673-2023
(914) 273-7471 .. **Taylor,** Edw '84 Hiscox Inc -357 Main -Armonk 10504 **Fx:**273-4716
(631) 265-5550 .. **Taylor,** Edw M '92 -811 W Jericho Tpke -Smithtwn 11787 **Fx:**265-5590
(212) 909-2523 .. **Taylor,** Elena L '05 Unison Site Mgt -340 Mad Av -NY 10173
(212) 980-3549 .. **Taylor,** Elizabeth M '70 -25 Sutton Pl S -NY 10022
(212) 687-0100 .. **Taylor,** Eric P '89 (Harris B PLLC) -100 Wall -NY 10005
(212) 530-5000 .. **Taylor,** Errol B '88 (Milbank TH&M LLP) -1 Chase Manh Plz -NY 10005
(718) 624-1288 .. **Taylor,** George E '81 -136 Hicks -Brklyn 11201
(315) 697-2288 .. **Taylor,** Gerald H '85 (Taylor & M LLP) -133 S Peterboro -Canastota 13032 **Fx:**697-8428
(212) 687-6200 .. **Taylor,** Gideon '94 %JDC -711 3rd Av -NY 10017 **Fx:**370-5467
(212) 341-2640 .. **Taylor,** Gilbert A '95 NYC Admin for Children's Srvcs -150 William -NY 10038
(212) 794-5394 .. **Taylor,** Gordon C '99 CUNY -535 E 80th -NY 10075
(212) 837-6822 .. **Taylor,** Hannah E '08 %Hughes H&R LLP -1 Bttry Pk Plz -NY 10004 **Fx:**299-6822
(212) 609-6800 .. **Taylor,** Heather V '96 (McCarter & E,LLP) -245 Park Av -NY 10167
(212) 407-4000 .. **Taylor,** James D '88 (Loeb & L,LLP) -345 Park Av -NY 10154
(607) 674-2191 .. **Taylor,** James F '69 (Taylor & M) -5 N Main Bx713 -Sherburne 13460 **Fx:**674-4744
(212) 703-7116 .. **Taylor,** Jamie L '04 ACE USA Ins -1133 Av of Amer -NY 10036
(212) 416-8439 .. **Taylor,** Janice B '90 %Dept of Law -120 Bway -NY 10271
(914) 824-5780 .. **Taylor,** Janice E '73 Hon T Jones -140 Grand -White Plns 10601
(212) 335-4500 .. **Taylor,** Jay L Jr. '96 SpclCnsl DLA Piper LLP -1251 Av of Amer -NY 10020
(585) 396-4011 .. **Taylor,** Jeffrey L '82 %DA -27 N Main -Canandaigua 14424 **Fx:**396-4860
(212) 715-9100 .. **Taylor,** Jeffrey L '01 %Kramer LN&F,LLP -1177 Av of Amer -NY 10036
(518) 218-1053 .. **Taylor,** Jennifer L '94 %Ianniello A&R,PC -8 Airline Dr -Albany 12205
(212) 931-8300 .. **Taylor,** Jill S '02 %Strongin R&A,LLP -5 Hanover Sq -NY 10004
(914) 366-5700 .. **Taylor,** Jo Ann '84 %MA Bjork -660 Wht Plns Rd -Tarrytwn 10591 **Fx:**366-5759
(212) 906-1200 .. **Taylor,** Job III '72 (Latham & W) -885 3rd Av -NY 10022
(212) 715-9100 .. **Taylor,** Joel M '01 %Kramer LN&F,LLP -1177 Av of Amer -NY 10036
(212) 373-3000 .. **Taylor,** John C 3rd '50 OfCnsl Paul WRW&G LLP -1285 Av of Amer -NY 10019
(212) 588-0800 .. **Taylor,** John G '95 (Frommer L&H LLP) -745 5th Av -NY 10151
(212) 455-2000 .. **Taylor,** Jordan K '10 %Simpson T&B LLP -425 Lex Av -NY 10017
(212) 837-6000 .. **Taylor,** Kathryn A '99 %Hughes H&R LLP -1 Bttry Pk Plz -NY 10004
(212) 580-5858 .. **Taylor,** Keith A '76 -1 Sherman Sq -NY 10023
(212) 683-0010 .. **Taylor,** Kevin C '94 (Taylor & M,LLP) -305 Mad Av -NY 10165
(347) 726-8136 .. **Taylor,** Khalilah '02 -30 Bradhurst Av -NY 10030
(212) 318-3000 .. **Taylor,** Kiki L '10 %Fulbright & J LLP -666 5th Av -NY 10103
(212) 446-4800 .. **Taylor,** Kimberly P '94 (Kirkland & E LLP) -153 E 53rd -NY 10022
(212) 730-8133 .. **Taylor,** Kirsten J '05 %Gunderson DSVF&H,LLP -220 W 42nd -NY 10036
(212) 984-7797 .. **Taylor,** Kyle A '02 %Warshaw BCS&K,LLP -555 5th Av -NY 10017
(212) 849-7000 .. **Taylor,** Kyle R '09 %Quinn EU&S,LLP -51 Mad Av -NY 10010
(585) 458-0190 .. **Taylor,** Laura J '87 -Bx67183 -Rchstr 14617 **Fx:**458-0191
(212) 848-4000 .. **Taylor,** Lawr B W '06 %Shearman & S LLP -599 Lex Av -NY 10022
(212) 998-2240 .. **Taylor,** Lee E '99 NYU Ofc Leg Cnsl -70 Wshngtn Sq S -NY 10012 **Fx:**995-3048
(212) 345-2268 .. **Taylor,** Lynn Jennings '84 %Marsh USA -1166 Av of Amer -NY 10036 **Fx:**345-4808
(212) 969-3000 .. **Taylor,** Mara L '99 %Proskauer R LLP -1585 Bway -NY 10036
(516) 997-6994 .. **Taylor,** Marc D '96 (Taylor N & Assoc,PC) -323 Post Av -Westbury 11590 **Fx:**334-8992
(212) 916-4263 .. **Taylor,** Margaret E '81 %TIAA-CREF -730 3rd Av -NY 10017
(845) 562-9100 .. **Taylor,** Mark C '88 (Rider W&F,PC) -655 Little Britain Rd -New Windsor 12553
(212) 226-4507 .. **Taylor,** Mark C '09 (Rankin & T) -350 Bway -NY 10013
(718) 657-7640 .. **Taylor,** Martha '93 -175-14 Mayfld Rd -Jamaica 11432 **Fx:**657-7641
(212) 820-7700 .. **Taylor,** Maryann '92 (Boundas SW&B,LLC) -1 Bttry Pk Plz -NY 10004
(716) 204-2400 .. **Taylor,** Morgan K '07 %SJ Baum,PC -220 Nrthpnte Pkwy Bx1291 -Buffalo 14240 **Fx:**204-4600
(212) 925-7434 .. **Taylor,** Nina '87 -2 Prince -NY 10012 **Fx:**925-7434
(212) 505-4087 .. **Taylor,** Octavia Trinette '02 %JS Powell -65 Bway -NY 10006
(212) 801-6972 .. **Taylor,** Parker F '05 %Greenberg T,LLP -200 Park Av -NY 10166
(347) 404-9133 .. **Taylor,** Patricia A '88 %Civil Ct -141 Lvngstn -Brklyn 11201 **Fx:**(718) 643-3733
(877) 373-8218 .. **Taylor,** Paulette '84 -382 Cntrl Pk W -NY 10025
(212) 609-6800 .. **Taylor,** Penelope M '88 (McCarter & E,LLP) -245 Park Av -NY 10167
(212) 669-2048 .. **Taylor,** Phyllis D '84 %Comptroller -1 Centre -NY 10007 **Fx:**669-2884
(516) 876-9600 .. **Taylor,** Robt B '71 (Rovegno & T,PC) -1010 Nrthrn Blvd -Gt Neck 11021
(516) 935-5911 .. **Taylor,** Robt J '78 -160 W Old Cntry Rd -Hicksvll 11801 **Fx:**935-5930
(212) 233-0677 .. **Taylor,** Robt W '61 -160 Bway -NY 10038
(212) 310-8000 .. **Taylor,** Ryan C '09 %Weil G&M LLP -767 5th Av -NY 10153

(212) 490-8511 .. **Taylor,** Scott '88 (Taylor & Taylor) -16 E 40th -NY 10016
(212) 319-1000 .. **Taylor,** Scott P '83 (Quirk & B,PC) -845 3rd Av -NY 10022
(631) 331-1205 .. **Taylor,** Sean C '89 -655-9 Belle Terre Rd -Pt Jffrsn 11777
(914) 995-3357 .. **Taylor,** Shameika M '07 %DA -111 Martin Luther King Blvd -White Plns 10601 **Fx:**995-3363
(347) 404-9400 .. **Taylor,** Shannon Zachary '80 %Criminal Ct -120 Schermerhorn -Brklyn 11201 **Fx:**(718) 643-3538
(718) 459-6000 .. **Taylor,** Sherrie A '88 OfCnsl Pennisi D&N LLP -97-77 Qns Blvd -Rego Pk 11374
(516) 569-9539 .. **Taylor,** Sherrie A '88 OfCnsl Sidrane & S-S -1427 Sturl Av -Hewlett 11557
(518) 474-8096 .. **Taylor,** Susan L '94 %Dept of Law -The Cptl -Albany 12224
(716) 855-2030 .. **Taylor,** Suzanne K '93 -27 Hrbr Pnte Cmmn -Buffalo 14202 **Fx:**855-0018
(718) 222-2324 .. **Taylor,** Terrica M '07 %Law Dept -350 Jay -Brklyn 11201 **Fx:**222-2373
(315) 422-1391 .. **Taylor,** Thos E '87 OfCnsl Green & S,PLLC -One Lincoln Ctr #900 -Syracuse 13202
(518) 213-6000 .. **Taylor,** Timothy S '88 %NYSUT -800 Troy-Schnctdy Rd -Latham 12110 **Fx:**213-6488
(718) 286-7309 .. **Taylor,** Tina M '97 %FBI -80-02 Kew Grdns Rd -Kew Gdns 11415
(516) 767-1200 .. **Taylor,** Valerie L '93 %B Clark & Assoc,PC -22 S Bayles Av -Pt Wash 11050 **Fx:**767-1702
(718) 237-2000 .. **Taylor,** W Brett '91 %Leg Aid -111 Lvngstn -Brklyn 11201 **Fx:**237-8737
(212) 558-4000 .. **Taylor,** Willard B '66 OfCnsl Sullivan & C LLP -125 Broad -NY 10004
(212) 373-3000 .. **Taylor,** Wm J Jr. '01 %Paul WRW&G LLP -1285 Av of Amer -NY 10019
(585) 753-1380 .. **Taylor,** Wm K '02 Cnty Atty -307 Cnty Ofc Bldg -Rchstr 14614 **Fx:**753-1331
(212) 450-4000 .. **Taylor,** Wm L '91 (Davis P&W LLP) -450 Lex Av -NY 10017
(718) 780-0644 .. **Taylor,** Winnie F '76 %Bklyn Law Schl -250 Joralemon -Brklyn 11201 **Fx:**780-0393
(212) 351-4000 .. **Taylor,** Zachary S '04 Gibson D&C LLP -200 Park Av -NY 10166
(718) 268-1300 .. **Taylor,** Zenith T '93 -118-35 Qns Blvd -Frst Hlls 11375 **Fx:**268-3343
(212) 504-6000 .. **Taylor Enis,** Alison '02 -1 World Fncl Ctr -NY 10281 **Fx:**504-6666
(212) 435-3571 .. **Taylor-Finucane,** Margaret M '98 %Port Auth of NY/NJ -225 Park Av S -NY 10003 **Fx:**435-3555
(518) 473-8328 .. **Taylor-Scott,** Adele '85 Dept of Law -The Cptl -Albany 12224
(631) 470-8204 .. **Tayne,** Leslie H '97 -150 Broadhllw Rd -Melvll 11747
(212) 588-5500 .. **Tayne,** Scott M '77 (Davies WP&V LLP) -625 Mad Av -NY 10022
(914) 242-3222 .. **Tayts,** Dmitry '08 -37 W Main -Mt Kisco 10549 **Fx:**242-6082
(212) 277-0469 .. **Tazzi,** Jennifer A '03 Hartford Ins Co -2 Park Av -NY 10016
(212) 293-5100 .. **Teadore,** Edwin F '63 Matthews & Co -270 Mad Av -NY 10016
(646) 386-5000 .. **Teague,** Del Elaine '87 %Surrogates Ct -31 Chmbrs -NY 10007
(718) 882-5792 .. **Teague,** Eamon '93 -75 E 236th -Bronx 10470
(212) 504-6000 .. **Teague,** Mary M '07 %Cadwalader W&T LLP -1 World Fncl Ctr -NY 10281
(845) 452-1834 .. **Teahan & Constantino** -2780 South Rd Bx1969 -Poughkeepsie 12601 **Fx:**452-1421
(845) 677-2101 .. **Teahan & Constantino** -41 Front Bx1181 -Millbrook 12545 **Fx:**677-1054
(845) 677-2101 .. **Teahan,** Vincent L '75 (Teahan & C) -41 Front Bx1181 -Millbrook 12545
(518) 626-0959 .. **Teal,** Kathryn Lamont '99 -36 Willett Bx10457 -Albany 12201 **Fx:**465-1160
(212) 816-8591 .. **Teano,** Christopher A '85 Citigroup -250 West -NY 10013
(212) 248-3140 .. **Tears,** Gregory M '07 %Drinker B&R LLP -140 Bway -NY 10005
(212) 770-2461 .. **Teas,** Kerry A '95 %AIG -80 Pine -NY 10005
(585) 428-5755 .. **Teator,** Mary E '95 %Cnty Atty -50 W Main -Rchstr 14614 **Fx:**428-2031
(212) 698-3500 .. **Tebaldi Castelli,** Alessandra '06 %Dechert LLP -1095 Av of Amer -NY 10036
(518) 218-7100 .. **Tebano,** Maria C '94 (Tully R,PLLC) -441 New Karner Rd -Albany 12205
(212) 468-8000 .. **Tebbe,** Chas E III '94 OfCnsl Morrison & F LLP -1290 Av of Amer -NY 10104
(718) 625-2200 .. **Tebbe,** Nelson W '00 Bklyn Law Schl -250 Joralemon -Brklyn 11201 **Fx:**780-0393
(516) 571-3800 .. **Tebbett,** Theresa A '00 %DA -262 Old Cntry Rd -Mineola 11501 **Fx:**248-9479
(914) 846-3606 .. **Tebeau,** Christopher J '95 NY Life Ins -1 Rockwood Rd -Sleepy Hollow 10591
(212) 596-9000 .. **Tebelekian,** Nicholas '08 %Ropes & G LLP -1211 Av of Amer -NY 10036
(212) 456-6076 .. **Tebid,** Muriel A '83 %Walt Disney -77 W 66th -NY 10023 **Fx:**456-6565
(518) 474-6740 .. **Tebo,** Matthew W '04 %Dept of State -41 State -Albany 12231 **Fx:**473-9211
(585) 419-8800 .. **Tebor,** Sue Schmutter '83 (Harris B PLLC) -99 Garnsey Rd -Pittsfrd 14534
(212) 849-7000 .. **Tecce,** James C '98 %Quinn EU&S,LLP -51 Mad Av -NY 10010
(718) 856-3001 .. **Techeira,** Adrian D '95 -559 Marlboro Rd -Brklyn 11226
(212) 685-9460 .. **Tecklin,** David L '58 -292 Mad Av -NY 10017 **Fx:**685-9462
(212) 279-7300 .. **Tedeschi,** Elizabeth Anne '00 Sachs S&G,PC -450 7th Av -NY 10123
(315) 464-8309 .. **Tedeschi,** Francis J '74 %Dept of Law -750 E Adams -Syracuse 13210 **Fx:**464-8327
(518) 377-6839 .. **Tedeschi,** Frank '75 -518 Rankin Av -Schnctdy 12308
(631) 765-3524 .. **Tedeschi,** Fredk J '43 -2555 Youngs Av -Southold 11971 **Fx:**765-4172
(212) 816-3879 .. **Tedeschi,** Jos C '95 Citigroup -388 Greenwich -NY 10013
(914) 946-0400 .. **Tedeschi,** Marco Q '01 %Schiavetti CDW&N,LLP -709 Wstchstr Av -White Plns 10604
(516) 794-1428 .. **Tedeschi,** Thos P '77 -1975 Hempstd Tpk -E Meadow 11554 **Fx:**794-1359
(212) 237-0000 .. **Tedesco,** Patrick F '03 %Vinson & E LLP -666 5th Av -NY 10103
(212) 472-9733 .. **Tedlis,** Bernard '53 -500 E 85th -NY 10028
(516) 294-3555 .. **Tedone,** Matthew A '77 Tedone & T -983 Willis Av -Albertson 11507 **Fx:**742-3943
(585) 546-5530 .. **Teegarden,** Henry D '00 %Thomson West -50 E Broad -Rchstr 14694
(212) 909-6000 .. **Teehan,** Jill S '09 %Debevoise & P LLP -919 3rd Av -NY 10022
(212) 697-3122 .. **Teekah,** Anita S '09 %Martin C&B LLP -220 E 42nd -NY 10017
(212) 425-9300 .. **Teer,** Richd J '97 OfCnsl Bressler A&R,PC -17 State -NY 10004
(516) 542-2000 .. **Teeter,** David W '92 %JP Joseph & Assoc -666 Old Cntry Rd -Gdn Cty 11530 **Fx:**542-2001
(518) 438-3585 .. **Teff,** Justin S '02 Special Funds -2 Twr Pl -Albany 12203
(212) 373-3000 .. **Tegelman,** John K '02 Paul WRW&G LLP -1285 Av of Amer -NY 10019
(212) 906-1200 .. **Teh,** David C T '05 (Latham & W) -885 3rd Av -NY 10022
(917) 778-6846 .. **Tehan,** Aaron J '00 Travelers Cos, Inc -485 Lex Av -NY 10017
(315) 253-6219 .. **Tehan,** David G '97 (Karpinski SG&T) -110 Genesee -Auburn 13021
(212) 455-2000 .. **Tehan,** John B '74 (Simpson T&B LLP) -425 Lex Av -NY 10017
(212) 891-1600 .. **Tehrani,** Danl B '06 %Jenner & B LLP -919 3rd Av -NY 10022
(212) 250-5711 .. **Tehrani,** Patty P '93 %Deutsche Bk -60 Wall -NY 10005
(212) 667-9505 .. **Tehrani,** Penny P '02 %Nomura Securities Intl -2 World Fncl Ctr -NY 10281
(516) 682-0022 .. **Tehranian,** Lisa M '97 -180 Froehlich Farm Blvd -Woodbury 11797 **Fx:**682-0024
(212) 233-2141 .. **Teich,** Genise W '81 %B Bragg -11 Hanover Sq -NY 10005
(212) 696-4004 .. **Teich,** Howard B '71 -260 Mad Av -NY 10016 **Fx:**696-1837
(718) 243-1700 .. **Teich,** Jason M '05 Allen School -188 Montague -Brklyn 11201
(845) 634-4999 .. **Teich,** Stanley J '95 -14 S Main -New Cty 10956 **Fx:**634-3999
(212) 725-8544 .. **Teichberg,** Arthur J '59 (A Teichberg,PC) -216 E 45th -NY 10017 **Fx:**370-6935
(212) 553-0300 .. **Teicher,** David L '86 %Moody's Invstr Srvc -250 Greenwich -NY 10007
(212) 506-1700 .. **Teicher,** Marissa E '09 %Kasowitz BT&F LLP -1633 Bway -NY 10019
(212) 586-0541 .. **Teicher,** Milton S '40 -75 Rckfllr Plz -NY 10019
(212) 735-3000 .. **Teicher,** Stephanie L '97 (Skadden ASM&F LLP) -4 Times Sq -NY 10036
(732) 986-7003 .. **Teicher,** Stuart I '94 -6 W 28th -NY 10001 **Fx:**343-6868
(516) 571-3800 .. **Teichman,** Albert J '74 %DA -262 Old Cntry Rd -Mineola 11501 **Fx:**248-9479
(212) 819-8200 .. **Teichman,** Steven J '93 (White & C LLP) -1155 Av of Amer -NY 10036
(718) 222-2037 .. **Teichman,** Tzipora E '07 %Law Dept -350 Jay -Brklyn 11201 **Fx:**222-2088
(516) 393-5840 .. **Teichner,** Howard R '81 (Kelton & T) -6800 Jericho Tpk -Syosset 11791 **Fx:**393-5839
(585) 428-5210 .. **Teifke,** Erik R '93 %Pub Def -10 N Fitzhugh -Rchstr 14614 **Fx:**428-2234
(212) 421-4100 .. **Teig,** Benjamin J '03 %Pryor C LLP -7 Times Sq -NY 10036
(212) 521-5400 .. **Teig,** Jos B '08 %Reed S LLP -599 Lex Av -NY 10022
(212) 269-1600 .. **Teigland-Hunt,** Lauren '97 (Teigland-Hunt LLP) -127 W 24th -NY 10011 **Fx:**269-1580
(212) 558-4000 .. **Teigman,** David B '05 %Sullivan & C LLP -125 Broad -NY 10004
(212) 756-2000 .. **Teigman,** Wayne '99 %Schulte R&Z LLP -919 3rd Av -NY 10022
(212) 964-6611 .. **Teiling,** Annabel V '00 %Lester SK&D -120 Bway -NY 10271
(212) 294-6700 .. **Teiman,** Richd B '63 (Winston & S) -200 Park Av -NY 10166
(646) 452-9645 .. **Teira,** Elizabeth '03 Man Invstmnts -1 Rckfllr Plz -NY 10020
(718) 780-7513 .. **Teitcher,** Carrie W '82 %Bklyn Law Schl -250 Joralemon -Brklyn 11201 **Fx:**780-0393
(212) 267-7600 .. **Teitel,** Jill H '96 %Solomon PBH&S LLP -40 Wall -NY 10005
(212) 682-8811 .. **Teitel,** Louis E '74 (Dunnington B&M LLP) -1359 Bway -NY 10018
(212) 374-6031 .. **Teitel,** Rachael L '09 NYC Dept Educ -52 Chmbrs -NY 10007
(212) 431-2322 .. **Teitel,** Ruti G '81 %NY Law Schl -185 W Bway -NY 10013 **Fx:**431-1804
(212) 704-6000 .. **Teitelbaum,** Bruce J '99 OfCnsl Troutman S LLP -405 Lex Av -NY 10174
(212) 447-7676 .. **Teitelbaum,** Edw M '90 -245 E 30th -NY 10016 **Fx:**213-0581
(646) 252-2980 .. **Teitelbaum,** Iris J '99 %Transit Auth -2 Bway -NY 10004 **Fx:**252-5559
(914) 437-7670 .. **Teitelbaum,** Jay '86 (Teitelbaum & B LLP) -3 Barker Av -White Plns 10601 **Fx:**437-7672
(212) 768-6700 .. **Teitelbaum,** Marc D '78 (Sonnenschein N&R LLP) -2 World Fncl Ctr -NY 10281
(631) 360-1640 .. **Teitelbaum,** Martin J '76 -195 E Main Bx514 -Smithtwn 11787 **Fx:**360-2132
(516) 747-4301 .. **Teitelbaum,** Mitchell '91 %Torino & B,PC -200 Old Cntry Rd -Mineola 11501
(212) 227-8515 .. **Teitelbaum,** Noah E '98 -225 Bway -NY 10007
(718) 633-4545 .. **Teitelbaum,** Robt '89 R Teitelbaum & Assoc,PC -1310 52nd -Brklyn 11219 **Fx:**871-1685
(212) 697-8500 .. **Teitelbaum,** Robt J '89 (Konner T&G) -462 7th Av -NY 10018
(212) 277-4000 .. **Teitelbaum,** Ruth M '09 %Freshfields BD LLP -520 Mad Av -NY 10022
(212) 473-7080 .. **Teitelbaum,** Shelley '79 -28 E 11th -NY 10003
(718) 250-2000 .. **Teitelman,** Caryn G '98 DA -350 Jay -Brklyn 11201 **Fx:**250-2314
(718) 250-2000 .. **Teitgen,** Katherine E '05 %DA -350 Jay -Brklyn 11201 **Fx:**250-2314
(718) 474-2813 .. **Teitler,** Allison B '02 -152 Beach 136th -Rckwy Pk 11694
(516) 571-3010 .. **Teitler,** Ilene Lark '94 %Cnty Atty -1 West -Mineola 11501 **Fx:**571-6604
(212) 997-4400 .. **Teitler,** John M '91 (Teitler & T,LLP) -1114 Av of Amer -NY 10036 **Fx:**997-4949
(212) 997-4400 .. **Teitler,** Michl F '55 (Teitler & T,LLP) -1114 Av of Amer -NY 10036 **Fx:**997-4949
(212) 808-7800 .. **Teitz,** Elisheva '80 (Kelley D&W LLP) -101 Park Av -NY 10178
(212) 415-7773 .. **Teixeira,** C Steven '87 Merrill Lynch -717 5th Av -NY 10022 **Fx:**415-7905
(718) 777-8887 .. **Teixeira,** Chas D '09 Nanis & R,LLP -30-97 Steinway -Astoria 11103
(212) 595-3500 .. **Teixeira,** Ian G S '09 Fine Creative Media,Inc -322 8th Av -NY 10001
(212) 536-3900 .. **Tejeda,** Adam J '06 %K&L Gates LLP -599 Lex Av -NY 10022
(212) 715-1000 .. **Tejeda,** Laura W '06 %Arnold & P LLP -399 Park Av -NY 10022
(914) 285-8500 .. **Tejeiro,** Jos V '85 %TK Moore -701 Wstchstr Av -White Plns 10604 **Fx:**285-8510
(212) 455-2000 .. **Tejtel,** David F E '09 %Simpson T&B LLP -425 Lex Av -NY 10017

(212) 547-5400 .. **Tejwani,** Shruti Kumar '10 %McDermott W&E LLP -340 Mad Av -NY 10173
(516) 683-1700 .. **Tekiel,** Leo '83 -623 Stewart Av -Gdn Cty 11530 **Fx:**228-0230
(631) 324-5164 .. **Tekulsky,** Steven '78 -113 Cedar -E Hampton 11937 **Fx:**329-2654
(646) 366-0730 .. **Tela,** Donald A '79 -213-37 39th Av -Bayside 11361 **Fx:**365-3214
(516) 485-2162 .. **Teleisha,** Wm C '87 -64 St Pauls Rd N -Hempstd 11550
(347) 448-4522 .. **Telemaque,** Yves-Merry '95 Y-M Telemaque,PC -400 Park Av -NY 10022 **Fx:**521-1376
(516) 663-6600 .. **Telesca,** Thos A '04 %Ruskin MF,PC -1425 RXR Plz -Uniondale 11556
(212) 682-6800 .. **Telese,** Lina G '93 (Zetlin & D LLP) -801 2nd Av -NY 10017
(716) 856-5500 .. **Telford,** Chas E III '87 (Damon M LLP) -200 Delaware Av -Buffalo 14202
(212) 530-5000 .. **Telford,** Matthew P '10 %Milbank TH&M LLP -1 Chase Manh Plz -NY 10005
(212) 701-3000 .. **Telfort,** Mirlande '10 %Cahill G&R LLP -80 Pine -NY 10005 **Fx:**269-5420
(518) 283-4520 .. **Teliska,** John J Jr. '72 -225 N Greenbush Rd -Troy 12180
(516) 535-1550 .. **Tell Cheser & Breitbart** -320 Old Cntry Rd -Gdn Cty 11530 **Fx:**535-1552
(516) 826-5525 .. **Tell,** M David '61 -1846 Vllg Ln N -Wantagh 11793
(718) 527-3140 .. **Tella,** Augustin D A '95 -189-19 Linden Blvd -St Albans 11412
(212) 793-3825 .. **Tellam,** Leza S '02 Citigroup -425 Park Av -NY 10022
(212) 268-4848 .. **Teller,** Jonathan C '80 -39 W 32nd -NY 10001
(212) 243-4949 .. **Teller,** Philip '80 -22 W 16th -NY 10011 **Fx:**243-8877
(212) 661-7755 .. **Telleysh,** Gail H '79 -300 E 42nd -NY 10017 **Fx:**661-8016
(212) 412-2743 .. **Tellgmann,** Bonnie S '07 Barclays Capital Inc -1301 6th Av -NY 10019
(212) 770-7000 .. **Tellie,** Cara A '06 %AIG -70 Pine -NY 10270
(212) 757-8438 .. **Tello,** Renee J '07 %Levitt & N,PC -250 W 57th -NY 10107
(718) 556-7605 .. **Tello,** Victor M '09 %Law Dept -60 Bay -Staten Isl 10301 **Fx:**981-4459
(212) 753-5000 .. **Tellock,** Don M '97 (Schiff H LLP) -900 3rd Av -NY 10022
(212) 326-3939 .. **Telpner,** Joel S '84 (Jones D) -222 E 41st -NY 10017
(212) 512-2000 .. **Telsey,** Suzanne L '85 %McGraw-Hill -1221 Av of Amer -NY 10020 **Fx:**512-4827
(914) 313-5290 .. **Tembeck,** Gregory J '99 -2500 Wstchstr Av -Purchase 10577
(646) 386-4800 .. **Tembeckjian,** Robt H '83 %Comm Judicial Cndct -61 Bway -NY 10006 **Fx:**458-0037
(212) 458-3765 .. **Temech,** Mia S '02 AIG -175 Water -NY 10038
(315) 422-1391 .. **Temes,** David C '06 %Green & S,PLLC -One Lincoln Ctr #900 -Syracuse 13202
(315) 218-8000 .. **Temes,** Sara C '05 %Bond S&K,PLLC -1 Lincoln Ctr -Syracuse 13202
(212) 804-4221 .. **Temkin,** Barry R '83 OfCnsl Mound CW&G -One Bttry Pk Plz -NY 10004
(646) 386-5891 .. **Temkin,** Diane Goldstein '90 %MHLS -41 Mad Av -NY 10010
(212) 880-9470 .. **Temkin,** Jeremy H '88 (Morvillo AGIA&B,PC) -565 5th Av -NY 10017
(718) 286-6000 .. **Temkin,** Marc '79 %DA -125-01 Qns Blvd -Kew Gdns 11415
(212) 715-9100 .. **Temkin,** Matthew C '09 %Kramer LN&F,LLP -1177 Av of Amer -NY 10036
(212) 698-3500 .. **Tempest,** Drake S '80 (Dechert LLP) -1095 Av of Amer -NY 10036
(914) 345-3701 .. **Tempesta,** Carol M '03 %Marks OO&C,PC -530 Saw Mill Rvr Rd -Elmsfrd 10523
(212) 336-2000 .. **Tempesta,** Edw R '06 %Patterson BW&T LLP -1133 Av of Amer -NY 10036
(212) 408-2500 .. **Tempesta,** Jennifer '06 %Baker B,LLP -30 Rckfllr Plz -NY 10112
(212) 530-5000 .. **Tempesta,** Marceline B '06 %Milbank TH&M LLP -1 Chase Manh Plz -NY 10005
(212) 742-3800 .. **Tempesta,** Michl P '86 -39 Bway -NY 10006 **Fx:**571-0860
(516) 745-8310 .. **Temple,** Alex M '09 %Perez & V -333 Earle Ovngton Blvd Bx9372 -Uniondale 11553
(212) 772-1654 .. **Temple,** Iris '88 -440 E 79th -NY 10075
(212) 468-8000 .. **Temple,** Jeffrey J '85 (Morrison & F LLP) -1290 Av of Amer -NY 10104
(212) 335-9000 .. **Temple,** John F III '04 %DA -1 Hogan Pl -NY 10013
(646) 264-3650 .. **Temple,** Margaret A '95 %US Dept of Labor -201 Varick -NY 10014 **Fx:**264-3660
(315) 437-2684 .. **Temple,** Marisa Vesnaver '89 (Temple & T) -211 N Center -E Syracuse 13057 **Fx:**437-3430
(914) 946-3700 .. **Temple,** Philip T '57 (McCarthy F LLP) -11 Martine Av -White Plns 10606
(315) 437-2684 .. **Temple,** Robt S '88 (Temple & T) -211 N Center -E Syracuse 13057 **Fx:**437-3430
(212) 735-3000 .. **Temple,** Vanessa '09 %Skadden ASM&F LLP -4 Times Sq -NY 10036
(212) 653-8700 .. **Templeman,** Blaine E '95 (Sheppard MR&H LLP) -30 Rckfllr Plz -NY 10112
(212) 859-8000 .. **Templeton,** Andrea Webster '09 %Fried FHS&J LLP -1 NY Plz -NY 10004
(212) 326-3939 .. **Templeton,** Michl J '95 (Jones D) -222 E 41st -NY 10017
(212) 668-8888 .. **Templo,** Michl E D Jr. '03 %Prado & T,LLP -305 Bway -NY 10007 **Fx:**668-8494
(212) 246-7100 .. **Tena-Nelson,** Roxanne G '99 Grtr NY Hsptl Assn -555 W 57th -NY 10019
(212) 909-6000 .. **Tencza,** Darius D '77 (Debevoise & P LLP) -919 3rd Av -NY 10022
(212) 488-1200 .. **Tendler,** Carrie A '06 %Kobre & K,LLP -800 3rd Av -NY 10022
(212) 994-0260 .. **Tendler,** David B '92 (Cornicello T&B-C,LLP) -2 Wall -NY 10005
(718) 694-5127 .. **Tendler,** Lois H '82 %Transit Auth-Govt Relations -130 Lvngstn -Brklyn 11201
(212) 819-8200 .. **Tendler,** Y Isaac '08 %White & C LLP -1155 Av of Amer -NY 10036
(845) 297-7777 .. **Tendy & Cantor** -62 E Main -Wappingers Fls 12590 **Fx:**297-5555
(845) 297-7777 .. **Tendy,** Robt V '90 Tendy & C -62 E Main -Wappingers Fls 12590
(845) 297-7777 .. **Tendy,** Wm M Jr. '80 (Tendy & C) -62 E Main -Wappingers Fls 12590
(516) 248-9700 .. **Tenedios,** Irene '04 %S Levitt & Assoc,PC -2 Hillside Av -Williston Pk 11596 **Fx:**741-9224
(212) 458-1378 .. **Tenem,** Samantha J '04 AIG -175 Water -NY 10038
(212) 687-2770 .. **Tenenbaum,** Alan '89 %Cohen PL&P -551 5th Av -NY 10176
(718) 596-9000 .. **Tenenbaum,** Alan S '72 (Cohen HEP&T) -25 Chapel -Brklyn 11201
(718) 596-3800 .. **Tenenbaum & Berger LLP** -26 Court -Brklyn 11242 **Fx:**596-4433
(212) 732-8700 .. **Tenenbaum,** Dana A '05 %McAloon & F,PC -123 William -NY 10038
(518) 445-2311 .. **Tenenbaum,** Evelyn M '77 %Albany Law Schl -80 New Scotland Av -Albany 12208 **Fx:**445-2315
(516) 294-5200 .. **Tenenbaum,** Jason '03 %Picciano & S -900 Merchants Cncrs -Westbury 11590
(212) 620-0935 .. **Tenenbaum,** Jerald M '99 %Fridman Law Grp PLLC -287 Spring -NY 10013 **Fx:**(646) 304-1030
(914) 949-1305 .. **Tenenbaum,** Karen B '08 %Leg Srvcs -90 Maple Av -White Plns 10601 **Fx:**949-6213
(631) 465-5000 .. **Tenenbaum,** Karen J '84 (K Tenenbaum,PC) -225 Old Cntry Rd -Melvll 11747 **Fx:**465-5003
(212) 733-5482 .. **Tenenbaum,** Keren '07 Pfizer -235 E 42nd -NY 10017
(516) 746-8000 .. **Tenenbaum,** Lawr J '91 (Jaspan S LLP) -300 Grdn City Plz -Gdn Cty 11530
(212) 943-9080 .. **Tenenbaum,** Marc A '07 OfCnsl Virginia & A -111 Bway -NY 10006
(718) 596-3800 .. **Tenenbaum,** Martin '85 (Tenenbaum & B LLP) -26 Court -Brklyn 11242
(212) 221-6900 .. **Tenenbaum,** Scott B '06 %Winget S&S,LLP -45 Bway -NY 10006
(914) 253-2537 .. **Tenenzapf,** Russell J '88 %Pepsico -700 Andrsn Hill Rd -Purchase 10577
(212) 812-5832 .. **Tener,** Alexis M '09 Jones Lang LaSalle -601 Lex Av -NY 10022
(347) 401-9403 .. **Tener,** Christina M '07 Supreme Ct Law Dept -360 Adams -Brklyn 11201 **Fx:**643-6114
(631) 669-3000 .. **Tenety,** Vincent C '83 (Reilly LT&M) -179 Little East Neck Rd N -Babylon 11702
(212) 564-6633 .. **Tenety,** Vincent C '83 OfCnsl White & M,PC -875 Av of Amer -NY 10001
(212) 513-3200 .. **Tenev,** Jovi '85 (Holland & K LLP) -31 W 52nd -NY 10019
(212) 278-0400 .. **Teng,** Paul '95 (Cooper & D LLP) -30 Rckfllr Plz -NY 10112
(518) 429-4200 .. **Tengeler,** Robt G '75 OfCnsl Hiscock & B,LLP -50 Beaver -Albany 12207
(516) 229-4200 .. **Tenke,** Timothy J '91 %Mendolia & S -875 Merrick Av -Westbury 11590
(212) 999-5800 .. **Tenley,** Scott D '09 %Wilson SG&R -1301 Av of Americas -NY 10019
(212) 450-4000 .. **Tennant,** Catherine P '08 %Davis P&W LLP -450 Lex Av -NY 10017
(585) 263-1000 .. **Tennant,** David H '93 (Nixon P LLP) -1100 Clinton Sq -Rchstr 14604
(212) 676-0910 .. **Tennell,** Sonya R '89 %Hlth & Hsptl Corp -346 Bway -NY 10013
(212) 872-1000 .. **Tennenbaum,** Robt J '09 -One Bryant Park -NY 10036 **Fx:**872-1002
(212) 229-5376 .. **Tennent,** Keila C '98 New Schl Univ -66 W 12th -NY 10011
(212) 457-7723 .. **Tenner,** Morris P '58 NY Law Publishing -120 Bway -NY 10271
(315) 853-3023 .. **Tenney,** Claudia L '89 -28 Robnsn Rd -Clinton 13323
(716) 853-1887 .. **Tenney,** Eugene C '54 -5 Niagara Sq -Buffalo 14202 **Fx:**853-1893
(212) 269-7308 .. **Tenney,** James P '90 (Leahey & J PC) -120 Wall -NY 10005
(212) 264-0652 .. **Tenney,** Julie A '04 US DOJ Antitrust Div -26 Fed Plz Ste 3630 -NY 10278
(212) 573-4740 .. **Tenny,** Barron M '70 Ford Fndtn -320 E 43rd -NY 10017
(212) 506-1700 .. **Tenorio,** Charlotte P '06 Kasowitz BT&F LLP -1633 Bway -NY 10019
(212) 225-2000 .. **Tenreiro,** Jorge G '07 %Cleary GS&H -1 Lbrty Plz -NY 10006
(212) 906-1200 .. **Tent,** Virginia Foster '04 %Latham & W -885 3rd Av -NY 10022
(212) 848-4000 .. **Tenzer,** Andrew V '91 (Shearman & S LLP) -599 Lex Av -NY 10022
(212) 373-3000 .. **Tenzer,** Gabrielle E '07 %Paul WRW&G LLP -1285 Av of Amer -NY 10019
(212) 262-6699 .. **Tenzer,** Joshua M '06 %Tenzer & L LLP -1775 Bway -NY 10019
(631) 586-6464 .. **Tenzer,** Leslie '57 -1125 Deer Prk Av Bx2002 -Babylon 11703
(212) 262-6699 .. **Tenzer and Lunin LLP** -1775 Bway -NY 10019 **Fx:**262-6959
(212) 262-6699 .. **Tenzer,** Marvin L '68 (Tenzer & L LLP) -1775 Bway -NY 10019
(212) 839-5300 .. **Teodoro,** Carla G '04 %Sidley A LLP -787 7th Av -NY 10019
(212) 225-2000 .. **Teofan,** Yvette P '89 (Cleary GS&H) -1 Lbrty Plz -NY 10006
(212) 735-3000 .. **Tepe,** Sean M '05 %Skadden ASM&F LLP -4 Times Sq -NY 10036
(718) 259-4500 .. **Tepedino,** Anna M '92 (Vanchieri & F) -1724 86th -Brklyn 11214
(212) 909-6000 .. **Tepedino,** John J '05 %Debevoise & P LLP -919 3rd Av -NY 10022
(718) 250-1100 .. **Teper,** Helene '81 -12 Metrotech Ctr -Brklyn 11201 **Fx:**250-1168
(212) 725-2313 .. **Teperman,** Bruce R '85 Teperman & T,LLC -15 E 40th -NY 10016 **Fx:**725-2319
(845) 566-5345 .. **Tepermayster,** Milana '09 %Larkin AI&T,LLP -356 Meadow Av -Newburgh 12550
(718) 854-7200 .. **Tepfer,** Herbert '76 (Tepfer & T,PC) -4429 18th Av -Brklyn 11204 **Fx:**438-4947
(718) 854-7200 .. **Tepfer,** Jos '80 (Tepfer & T,PC) -4429 18th Av -Brklyn 11204 **Fx:**438-4947
(212) 401-4040 .. **Teplen,** Philip H '83 (Teplen & Assoc,PLLC) -350 5th Av -NY 10118 **Fx:**401-4041
(212) 277-6500 .. **Tepper,** Chad E '04 %Dickstein S LLP -1633 Bway -NY 10019
(212) 490-3232 .. **Tepper,** Danl '02 %Hecht & Assoc,PC -275 Mad Av -NY 10016 **Fx:**490-3263
(845) 639-6105 .. **Tepper,** David B '77 -6 Fieldstone Ct -New Cty 10956
(518) 399-5400 .. **Tepper,** Eric A '83 (Gordon T&D,LLP) -113 Saratoga Rd -Glenvll 12302
(212) 878-8000 .. **Tepper,** Jonathan '02 %Clifford C LLP -31 W 52nd -NY 10019
(212) 487-4444 .. **Tepper,** Marla '82 %Dept Cnsmr Affrs -42 Bway -NY 10004 **Fx:**487-4197
(516) 994-8605 .. **Tepper,** Marvin B '58 %Sterling Equities -24 Barkers Pnt Rd -Pt Wash 11050 **Fx:**883-4649
(516) 334-4433 .. **Tepper,** Melvin W '55 -120 Bethpage Rd -Hicksvll 11801
(917) 270-1935 .. **Tepper,** Michelle R '03 (Tepper & T LLP) -1641 3rd Av -NY 10128 **Fx:**(973) 731-1829
(845) 452-5010 .. **Tepper,** Noel '61 -143 Academy -Poughkeepsie 12601 **Fx:**471-9599
(516) 572-0123 .. **Tepper,** Robt S '00 Cnsl Nassau Hlth Care Corp -2201 Hempstd Tpk -E Meadow 11554 **Fx:**572-4831
(212) 750-5030 .. **Tepper,** Steven G '79 (Arnold & P LLP) -399 Park Av -NY 10022
(212) 434-9512 .. **Tepperman,** Jonathan D '99 %Foreign Affairs Magazine -58 E 68th -NY 10065
(212) 557-3000 .. **Tepperman,** Lynda L '86 OfCnsl Rivelis P&B,LLP -286 Mad Av -NY 10017
(212) 920-3072 .. **Teppler,** Steven W '81 SrCnsl KamberEdelson,LLC -11 Bway -NY 10004 **Fx:**202-6364

(212) 279-2262 .. **Terai,** Mami '02 -1230 Av of Amer -NY 10020 **Fx:**279-1909
(212) 225-2000 .. **Terai,** Tsunemasa '82 (Cleary GS&H) -1 Lbrty Plz -NY 10006
(212) 455-2000 .. **Terbell,** Thos G III '06 %Simpson T&B LLP -425 Lex Av -NY 10017
(212) 330-8090 .. **Terc,** Miguel A Jr. '04 -192 Lex Av -NY 10016
(212) 225-2000 .. **Terceño,** Joaquin P '08 %Cleary GS&H -1 Lbrty Plz -NY 10006
(631) 653-6322 .. **Terchunian,** Kent T '82 -19 The Registry -E Quogue 11942 **Fx:**653-6340
(516) 812-4500 .. **Terenzi,** Ronald M '87 (Stagg TC&W LLP) -401 Franklin Av -Gdn Cty 11530
(585) 238-8242 .. **Terepka,** John H '81 %Dept of Health -259 Monroe Av -Rchstr 14607 **Fx:**238-8244
(518) 233-2114 .. **Teresi,** Gregory J '05 Corp Cnsl -97 Mohawk -Cohoes 12047 **Fx:**233-2160
(631) 634-0025 .. **Teresky,** Thos G '96 -8 Bartel Pl -Huntngtn Sta 11746
(516) 742-3838 .. **Terezakis,** George A '86 -170 Old Cntry Rd -Mineola 11501
(845) 778-2121 .. **Terhune,** Alyse D '07 %Jacobowitz & G,LLP -158 Orange Av Bx367 -Walden 12586
(914) 962-3152 .. **Terhune,** Stella C '88 -1992 Commerce -Yorktwn Hts 10598 **Fx:**962-4503
(212) 962-6454 .. **Terilli,** Giancarlo '00 (Terilli & T,PLLC) -225 Bway -NY 10007 **Fx:**962-6045
(516) 742-9090 .. **Terino,** Jos M '96 (Terino K&F) -Bx1185 -Syosset 11791
(516) 742-9090 .. **Terino Kephart & Favale** -Bx1185 -Syosset 11791 **Fx:**742-9080
(914) 684-2800 .. **Ter-Jung,** Susanna Karin '96 Bunge Ltd -50 Main -White Plns 10606
(212) 571-4080 .. **Terk,** Michl B '07 Cnsl Sokolski & Z,PC -305 Bway -NY 10007 **Fx:**571-4079
(845) 517-0670 .. **Terkell,** Jos I '81 SrCnsl Terkell Law Firm -19 Bender Rd Bx764 -New Cty 10956 **Fx:**517-0671
(516) 343-3274 .. **Termini,** Chas A '83 -82 Fairvw Av -Oceanside 11572
(631) 853-4049 .. **Termini,** Chris P '74 %Cnty Atty -Dennison Bldg Bx6100 -Hauppauge 11788 **Fx:**853-5169
(845) 473-8100 .. **Terner,** Linda J '81 %Iseman CR&H,LLP -2649 South Rd -Poughkeepsie 12601
(516) 746-1230 .. **Terpening,** Armand T '49 -229 7th -Gdn Cty 11530
(516) 496-0202 .. **Terracciano,** Peter J '92 (Joseph & T,LLP) -2 Roosevelt Av -Syosset 11791 **Fx:**921-7785
(212) 474-1000 .. **Terraciano,** Annmarie M '99 %Cravath S&M LLP -825 8th Av -NY 10019
(212) 701-3000 .. **Terrana,** Jason H '05 %Cahill G&R LLP -80 Pine -NY 10005 **Fx:**269-5420
(516) 248-1700 .. **Terrana,** John V '85 (Forchelli CDSM&T,LLP) -333 Earle Ovngton Blvd -Uniondale 11553
(212) 949-9022 .. **Terranella,** Frank '84 %Abelman F&S -666 3rd Av -NY 10017
(718) 464-7674 .. **Terrano,** Susan L '91 -75-08 Bell Blvd -Bayside 11364 **Fx:**464-7674
(212) 232-1300 .. **Terranova,** Anthony P '05 %Lewis BB&S LLP -77 Water -NY 10005
(718) 291-4503 .. **Terranova,** Arthur N '75 -14-37 140th -Whitestone 11357
(212) 373-3000 .. **Terranova,** Christopher '10 %Paul WRW&G LLP -1285 Av of Amer -NY 10019
(716) 683-0717 .. **Terranova,** Dominic J '52 -5647 Bway -Lancaster 14086 **Fx:**683-7473
(718) 250-1100 .. **Terranova,** Paul '73 %E Garfinkel -12 Metrotech Ctr -Brklyn 11201 **Fx:**250-1168
(718) 613-2510 .. **Terranova,** Robt A '08 %Hon D Trager -225 Cadman Plz E -Brklyn 11201
(212) 564-6633 .. **Terrasi,** Vincent F '99 %White & M,PC -875 Av of Amer -NY 10001
(212) 217-6432 .. **Terrazas,** Norberto S '04 Consulate Genl of Mexico -27 E 39th -NY 10016
(212) 953-1922 .. **Terrell,** Francis D '74 -50 Main -White Plns 10606 **Fx:**(518) 966-8606
(212) 259-8000 .. **Terrell,** J Anthony '70 (Dewey & L LLP) -1301 Av of Amer -NY 10019
(212) 839-5300 .. **Terrero,** Kenny S '07 %Sidley A LLP -787 7th Av -NY 10019
(212) 696-1999 .. **Terrigno,** Raquel '07 Lax & N LLP -1412 Bway -NY 10018
(212) 683-6383 .. **Terrill,** Jerry A '69 %Gersen B&A LLP -270 Mad Av -NY 10016
(212) 340-2883 .. **Terrillion,** Andrea M B '91 %Cornell Univ-ILR -16 E 34th -NY 10016 **Fx:**340-2822
(585) 325-3920 .. **Terrillion,** Scott M '91 %Preferred Care -259 Monroe Av -Rchstr 14607
(716) 362-1206 .. **Terrizzi,** Thos D '76 -651 Delaware Av -Buffalo 14202 **Fx:**362-1205
(718) 923-4206 .. **Terrusa,** Benny F '00 %OTDA Fair Hearings -14 Boerum Pl -Brklyn 11201
(518) 457-2327 .. **Terry,** Berthlynn J '77 %Affrmtv Action DOCS -Bldg 2 State Ofc Campus -Albany 12226 **Fx:**457-7113
(212) 986-6000 .. **Terry,** Christopher M '09 %Kleinberg KW&C,PC -551 5th Av -NY 10176
(516) 741-4799 .. **Terry,** Colleen M '03 %Baker SBGFM&N,LLC -100 Grdn City Plz -Gdn Cty 11530
(718) 298-8900 .. **Terry,** Dodd R '98 Leg Aid -153-01 Jamaica Av -Jamaica 11432 **Fx:**657-0537
(212) 558-4000 .. **Terry,** Fredk A Jr. '57 SrCnsl Sullivan & C LLP -125 Broad -NY 10004
(212) 682-6800 .. **Terry,** James Jos Jr. '78 (Zetlin & D LLP) -801 2nd Av -NY 10017
(315) 253-1097 .. **Terry,** Jill L '95 %Cnty Atty -160 Genesee -Auburn 13021 **Fx:**253-1098
(646) 252-7000 .. **Terry,** M Margaret '81 %TBTA -2 Bway -NY 10004
(631) 694-2300 .. **Terry,** Margaret Kayhoe '02 %Lamb & B,LLP -534 Broadhllw Rd Bx9034 -Melvll 11747
(212) 782-7325 .. **Terry,** Marshall MacLeod '96 %Moore Capital Mgmt,Inc -1251 Av of the Ameicas -NY 10020
(212) 308-4411 .. **Terry,** Mohana P '04 %Edwards AP&D LLP -750 Lex Av -NY 10022
(518) 891-4050 .. **Terry,** Richd R '75 %Adirondack Pk Agncy -Bx99 -Ray Brk 12977 **Fx:**891-3938
(718) 237-2000 .. **Terry,** Stephen B '90 Leg Aid -111 Lvngstn -Brklyn 11201 **Fx:**237-8737
(212) 484-8000 .. **Terry,** Tai C '82 %Time Warner -1 Time Warner Ctr -NY 10019
(607) 432-1521 .. **Terry,** Walter L III '66 -22 Dietz Bx945 -Oneonta 13820 **Fx:**432-1527
(518) 474-3494 .. **Tersago,** Tanya G '96 %State Comptroller -110 State -Albany 12236 **Fx:**473-9104
(212) 422-1500 .. **Tersigni,** Andrea '05 %Meyers TF&G LLP -14 Wall -NY 10005
(212) 422-1500 .. **Tersigni,** Anthony L '63 (Meyers TF&G LLP) -14 Wall -NY 10005
(914) 448-0200 .. **Terzian,** Christopher A '88 (Bartlett MB&M,LLP) -81 Main -White Plns 10601
(212) 872-6756 .. **Terzian,** Lincoln A '95 %KPMG LLP -345 Park Av -NY 10154
(716) 852-5200 .. **Terzulli,** John A '06 %Hamberger & W -700 Main Pl Twr -Buffalo 14202
(212) 983-6000 .. **Tesar,** Ann-Marie '07 %M Berger -250 Park Av -NY 10177 **Fx:**983-6008
(212) 697-3122 .. **Tesauro,** Graziella P '10 %Martin C&B LLP -220 E 42nd -NY 10017
(212) 475-3673 .. **Tese & Milner** -1 Minetta Ln -NY 10012 **Fx:**598-5864
(212) 475-3673 .. **Tese-Milner,** Angela '83 (Tese & M) -1 Minetta Ln -NY 10012
(212) 918-3000 .. **Teshome,** Hewan E '09 %Hogan L LLP -875 3rd Av -NY 10022
(607) 273-6841 .. **Tesi,** Virginia A '03 %Barney GDM&O,LLP -119 E Seneca -Ithaca 14850
(212) 314-5377 .. **Tesler,** Merril A '96 %AXA Financial Inc -1290 Av of Amer -NY 10104 **Fx:**707-3963
(212) 362-6961 .. **Tesler,** Richd E '83 -41 W 72nd -NY 10023 **Fx:**362-6810
(212) 468-8477 .. **Tesler,** Wm '96 BNY Securities Grp -1633 Bway -NY 10019
(718) 447-2340 .. **Tesnakis,** Costa N '52 -482 Manor Rd -Staten Isl 10314 **Fx:**447-0626
(718) 447-2340 .. **Tesnakis,** Jon P '98 -482 Manor Rd -Staten Isl 10314 **Fx:**447-0626
(212) 335-9000 .. **Tesoriero,** Jos J '82 %DA -1 Hogan Pl -NY 10013
(212) 966-6420 .. **Tesoro,** Carla Scotti '05 %Lwyrs For Children -110 Lafayette -NY 10013 **Fx:**966-0531
(212) 943-8940 .. **Tesoro,** Fe D '82 %Crisci W&H -17 State -NY 10004 **Fx:**425-3428
(212) 226-1900 .. **Tesser & Cohen** -591 Bway -NY 10012 **Fx:**(201) 343-0885
(212) 804-4200 .. **Tesser,** Jodi S '02 %Mound CW&G -One Bttry Pk Plz -NY 10004
(212) 754-9000 .. **Tesser,** Lewis F '71 (Tesser R&R LLP) -509 Mad Av -NY 10022
(212) 754-9000 .. **Tesser Ryan & Rochman LLP** -509 Mad Av -NY 10022 **Fx:**754-5906
(212) 417-2190 .. **Tessler,** Akiva '83 Liquor Auth -105 W 125th -NY 10027
(212) 366-6100 .. **Tessler,** Andrea Krugman '98 %Weiss & R,PC -27 Union Sq W -NY 10003
(212) 294-6700 .. **Tessler,** Corey A '87 (Winston & S) -200 Park Av -NY 10166
(212) 929-1888 .. **Tessler,** Craig L '78 -345 W 21st -NY 10011
(212) 587-0941 .. **Tessler,** Danl '88 -277 Bway -NY 10007 **Fx:**766-8012
(212) 736-3250 .. **Tessler,** David A '93 %Toberoff T&S,LLP -330 7th Av -NY 10001
(212) 277-6500 .. **Tessler,** Edw '80 (Dickstein S LLP) -1633 Bway -NY 10019
(718) 377-7731 .. **Tessler,** Isaac '83 -1425 E 21st -Brklyn 11210 **Fx:**377-7095
(212) 736-3250 .. **Tessler,** Robt L '82 (Toberoff T&S,LLP) -330 7th Av -NY 10001
(212) 566-3451 .. **Tessler,** Rose C '83 Dept Hlth Emplymnt Law -291 Bway -NY 10007
(315) 253-1304 .. **Testa,** Danl A '04 Cnty Atty -160 Genesee -Auburn 13021
(646) 386-3617 .. **Testa,** Gregory F '06 Supreme Ct-Law Dept -60 Centre -NY 10007
(607) 778-2156 .. **Testa,** Jacinta M '05 Broome Cnty Family Ct -65 Hawley -Bnghmtn 13901
(914) 779-5388 .. **Testa,** John A '98 (Mizzone & T,PA) -520 Wht Plns Rd -Tarrytwn 10591 **Fx:**(973) 785-0950
(718) 653-3290 .. **Testa,** Thos N '92 -2525 Paulding Av -Bronx 10469 **Fx:**653-0425
(718) 286-6000 .. **Testagrossa,** Chas A '77 %DA -125-01 Qns Blvd -Kew Gdns 11415
(516) 571-3800 .. **Testagrossa,** Maria Beltram '91 %DA -262 Old Cntry Rd -Mineola 11501 **Fx:**248-9479
(516) 771-3500 .. **Testaiuti,** John A '93 -172 Merrick Rd -Merrick 11566 **Fx:**771-7555
(516) 921-2525 .. **Testani,** Jacqueline P '86 %McHenry H&L,PC -6800 Jericho Tpk -Syosset 11791
(212) 872-1000 .. **Testani,** Rosa A '89 -One Bryant Park -NY 10036 **Fx:**872-1002
(914) 750-5933 .. **Testaverde,** Christine J '89 OfCnsl Kissel H&W LLP -580 Wht Plns Rd -Tarrytwn 10591
(718) 779-8282 .. **Testaverde,** Paul '83 -4042 Natl -Corona 11368 **Fx:**779-3306
(585) 243-7028 .. **Tetamore,** Marcea Clark '93 %Pub Def -6 Court -Geneseo 14454 **Fx:**243-7193
(212) 991-9590 .. **Tetelman,** Larry '86 (Lustrin T,LLP) -28 W 44th -NY 10036 **Fx:**991-9595
(845) 562-3366 .. **Tetenbaum,** Elliot S '74 OfCnsl Larkin Al&T,LLP -34 Route 17K -Newburgh 12550
(212) 474-1000 .. **Teti,** Jos L II '06 %Cravath S&M LLP -825 8th Av -NY 10019
(631) 574-2221 .. **Tetlak,** David J '96 -315 Walt Whitman Rd -Huntngtn Sta 11746 **Fx:**963-9020
(516) 326-9608 .. **Tetmeyer,** Robt G '67 (Connolly FE&L) -250-A Jericho Tpk -Floral Pk 11001
(212) 655-5000 .. **Teubner,** Gary A '95 %Gannon R&M -120 Bway -NY 10271
(212) 903-9000 .. **Teuscher,** Carlos M '09 %Linklaters -1345 Av of Amer -NY 10105
(914) 747-1622 .. **Tevelowitz,** Harold B '76 -3 Valley Rd -Thornwd 10594 **Fx:**741-1192
(212) 302-2400 .. **Tevis,** Mark D '09 %Lynch DE LLP -264 W 40th -NY 10018
(212) 901-6031 .. **Tew,** Katherine Elizabeth '98 ISDA -360 Mad Av -NY 10017
(212) 294-6700 .. **Tewarie,** Shanta A '09 %Winston & S -200 Park Av -NY 10166
(716) 853-9555 .. **Texido,** Nicholas T '07 %Leg Aid -237 Main -Buffalo 14203 **Fx:**853-3219
(212) 344-7042 .. **Textor,** James M '81 (Cichanowicz CKV&T,LLP) -61 Bway -NY 10006
(212) 943-0280 .. **Textor,** Melinda Rose '84 (McCanliss & E LLP) -88 Pine -NY 10005
(914) 949-2909 .. **Thabet,** Mark E '04 %Eckert SC&M,LLC -10 Bank -White Plns 10606
(718) 748-6861 .. **Thabit,** Robt W '52 -259-86th -Brklyn 11209 **Fx:**748-7041
(212) 845-7525 .. **Thacher,** Thos D II '75 (Thacher Assoc,LLC) -330 W 42nd -NY 10036 **Fx:**845-7549
(212) 373-3000 .. **Thacker,** Danl B '05 %Paul WRW&G LLP -1285 Av of Amer -NY 10019
(212) 735-3000 .. **Thadani,** Kavin S '10 %Skadden ASM&F LLP -4 Times Sq -NY 10036
(585) 262-6390 .. **Thai,** Van M '04 %Hamberger & W -1 S Wshngtn -Rchstr 14614
(518) 474-4552 .. **Thaisz,** Peter M '05 %Insurance Dept -99 Wshngtn Av -Albany 12257 **Fx:**473-4600
(212) 513-1713 .. **Thaker,** Ruchi '03 (Thaker B LLP) -225 Bway -NY 10007 **Fx:**513-7737
(212) 476-9000 .. **Thakkar,** Pinakini '93 %Neuberger Berman,LLC -605 3rd Av -NY 10158 **Fx:**476-9862
(212) 819-8200 .. **Thakore,** Amit Hasit '06 %White & C LLP -1155 Av of Amer -NY 10036
(212) 878-8000 .. **Thakur,** Neeta '02 %Clifford C LLP -31 W 52nd -NY 10019
(212) 977-9700 .. **Thal,** Steven H '68 Cnsl Phillips N LLP -666 5th Av -NY 10103

(212) 848-7085 .. **Thalacker,** Arbie R '61 OfCnsl Shearman & S LLP -599 Lex Av -NY 10022
(212) 980-7852 .. **Thalasinos,** Jonathan N '80 -Peck Slip Sta Bx919 -NY 10272
(917) 723-2474 .. **Thalasinos,** Nicholas '79 -43 Valentine Av -Glen Cove 11542
(845) 291-1900 .. **Thalblum,** Stuart '90 OfCnsl Cohen E & Assoc,LLP -40 Matthews -Goshen 10924 **Fx:**291-8601
(516) 295-1809 .. **Thalen,** Stanley '55 -649 Derby Av -Woodmere 11598 **Fx:**295-1809
(516) 228-3553 .. **Thaler,** Andrew M '84 (Thaler & G,LLP) -90 Merrick Av -E Meadow 11554
(516) 228-3553 .. **Thaler & Gertler,LLP** -90 Merrick Av -E Meadow 11554 **Fx:**228-3396
(607) 272-2314 .. **Thaler,** Richd B '58 (Thaler & T) -309 N Tioga Bx266 -Ithaca 14851 **Fx:**272-8466
(914) 941-1891 .. **Thaler,** Robt '75 -11 Tappan Ter -Briarclff Mnr 10510 **Fx:**941-1925
(516) 463-6314 .. **Thaler,** Robt S '90 %Hofstra Law Schl -121 Hofstra Univ -Hempstd 11549 **Fx:**463-5937
(516) 228-3553 .. **Thaler,** Stanley '49 OfCnsl Thaler & G,LLP -90 Merrick Av -E Meadow 11554
(212) 463-0401 .. **Thaler,** Steven '68 -545 Hudson -NY 10014
(212) 903-9000 .. **Thalhammer,** Christopher L '09 %Linklaters -1345 Av of Amer -NY 10105
(212) 245-6221 .. **Thall,** Peter M '68 -10 W End Av -NY 10023
(212) 521-5400 .. **Thanasoulis,** Alicia C '01 %Reed S LLP -599 Lex Av -NY 10022
(718) 545-4300 .. **Thanasoulis,** Triantafyllos '65 -23-09 31st -Astoria 11105 **Fx:**956-0218
(212) 922-9700 .. **Thanasules,** Demetri '96 %1st Amer Title -633 3rd Av -NY 10017 **Fx:**922-0881
(718) 250-2000 .. **Thanse,** Sabrina '08 %DA -350 Jay -Brklyn 11201 **Fx:**250-2314
(212) 756-2000 .. **Thapar,** Sanjay '98 %Schulte R&Z LLP -919 3rd Av -NY 10022
(212) 819-8200 .. **Tharamangalam,** Melanie M '08 %White & C LLP -1155 Av of Amer -NY 10036
(212) 609-6800 .. **Tharney,** Matthew J '00 (McCarter & E,LLP) -245 Park Av -NY 10167
(518) 798-1785 .. **Tharp,** Russell C Jr. '72 -1 Southwestern Plz Bx705 -Glens Fls 12801 **Fx:**798-3108
(212) 819-8200 .. **Thatch,** David W '98 (White & C LLP) -1155 Av of Amer -NY 10036
(212) 874-2774 .. **Thatcher,** Judith A '71 -320 Cntrl Pk W -NY 10025
(845) 462-6500 .. **Thatcher,** Wayne '93 (O'Neill & T LLP) -15 Davis Av -Poughkeepsie 12603
(718) 268-1726 .. **Thau,** Alan F '69 -125-10 Qns Blvd -Kew Gdns 11415
(212) 735-3000 .. **Thau,** Andrew M '04 %Skadden ASM&F LLP -4 Times Sq -NY 10036
(212) 237-0000 .. **Thau,** Clifford L '82 (Vinson & E LLP) -666 5th Av -NY 10103
(212) 458-1833 .. **Thau,** Debra McCabe '99 %AIG -175 Water -NY 10038
(212) 779-9800 .. **Thau,** Jonathan C '80 (Luboja & T,LLP) -10 E 40th -NY 10016
(212) 417-8700 .. **Thau,** Roland '63 %Fed Def of NY Inc -52 Duane -NY 10007 **Fx:**571-0392
(212) 885-5000 .. **Thau,** Suzanne L '06 %Blank R LLP -405 Lex Av -NY 10174
(631) 752-1760 .. **Thaw,** Bruce R '78 -45 Banfi Plz -Farmngdl 11735 **Fx:**752-2710
(212) 909-6000 .. **Thaw,** Tulani E '10 %Debevoise & P LLP -919 3rd Av -NY 10022
(212) 730-8133 .. **Thaxter,** Chelsea V '10 %Gunderson DSVF&H,LLP -220 W 42nd -NY 10036
(631) 249-6565 .. **Thayer,** Gary A '01 %Archer BG&L,LLP -425 Broadhllw Rd -Melvll 11747
(212) 355-3200 .. **Thayer,** James M '98 %Gordon G&S,PC -437 Mad Av -NY 10022 **Fx:**355-3292
(518) 690-0096 .. **Thayer,** Janet M '89 OfCnsl Murphy BB&M,LLP -226 Great Oaks Blvd -Albany 12203
(518) 473-6107 .. **Thayer,** Jon P '07 %Insurance Dept -99 Wshngtn Av -Albany 12257 **Fx:**473-4600
(212) 326-3939 .. **Thayer,** Michl O '10 %Jones D -222 E 41st -NY 10017
(607) 724-8529 .. **Thayne,** Timothy E '04 (Battisti G&T) -19 Chenango -Bnghmtn 13901
(212) 762-8137 .. **Theard,** Kara Isabelle '01 Morgan Stanley -1221 Av of Amer -NY 10020
(212) 728-8000 .. **Theil,** C Philip '08 %Willkie F&G LLP -787 7th Av -NY 10019
(212) 806-5400 .. **Theil,** Kenneth H '82 %Stroock &S&L LLP -180 Maiden Ln -NY 10038
(212) 867-6000 .. **Theis,** Brett B '04 %Rosenberg & E,PC -733 3rd Av -NY 10017
(212) 577-2523 .. **Theis,** Peter F '02 %Ctr for Appllt Litigation -74 Trinity Pl -NY 10006 **Fx:**577-2535
(315) 682-8311 .. **Theiss,** Mary Anne '84 -7828 Rolling Ridge Dr -Manlius 13104 **Fx:**682-4995
(212) 871-1025 .. **Thelander,** Lauren Crandall '05 Cnsl Spa Chakra Acquisition Corp -663 5th Av -NY 10022 **Fx:**871-3250
(914) 468-8021 .. **Theleen,** Ronald J '93 Endurance Relnsurance Corp of America -333 Wstchstr Av -White Plns 10604
(718) 590-3468 .. **Theodore,** Christine A '01 ACS -900 Sheridan Av -Bronx 10451
(315) 474-6896 .. **Theodore,** Eleanor '52 -504 Hills Bldg -Syracuse 13202 **Fx:**422-7675
(212) 969-3000 .. **Theodore,** Mark '91 (Proskauer R LLP) -1585 Bway -NY 10036
(212) 577-2000 .. **Theodorellis,** John C '94 %A Kriss -123 William -NY 10038 **Fx:**577-2138
(516) 496-5822 .. **Theodorou,** Michl S '98 %T Spina -170 Froehlich Farm Blvd -Woodbury 11797 **Fx:**496-5420
(718) 286-6000 .. **Theodorou,** Patricia Ann '94 %DA -125-01 Qns Blvd -Kew Gdns 11415
(212) 682-2900 .. **Theodosiou,** Andreas E '95 (Braverman & Assoc,PC) -331 Mad Av -NY 10017 **Fx:**682-7718
(212) 837-6868 .. **Theodosiou-Pisanelli,** Eleni D '10 %Hughes H&R LLP -1 Bttry Pk Plz -NY 10004 **Fx:**299-6868
(516) 538-7100 .. **Theofan,** Chas T '79 Hempstead Planning Dept -200 N Franklin -Hempstd 11550
(914) 285-8500 .. **Theofanis,** Roula '87 %TK Moore -701 Wstchstr Av -White Plns 10604 **Fx:**285-8510
(212) 902-2172 .. **Theriault,** Rene J III '03 Goldman Sachs & Co -85 Broad -NY 10004
(718) 777-9070 .. **Thermos,** Kimon C '91 -26-20 23rd Av -Astoria 11105 **Fx:**777-9069
(716) 855-5229 .. **Therolf,** Wanda M '89 %L Ogden -60 Lakefront Blvd -Buffalo 14202 **Fx:**855-5078
(212) 735-3000 .. **Thetford,** Blair T '09 %Skadden ASM&F LLP -4 Times Sq -NY 10036
(585) 419-8800 .. **Thiagarajan,** Vivek J '10 %Harris B PLLC -99 Garnsey Rd -Pittsfrd 14534
(973) 596-4839 .. **Thibodaux,** Jennifer Marino '06 %Gibbons PC -1 Penn Plz -NY 10119 **Fx:**639-6254
(212) 698-4550 .. **Thieffry,** Patrick '83 (Thieffry & Assoc) -150 E 58th -NY 10155 **Fx:**698-4551
(716) 434-0562 .. **Thiel,** Edw R '72 -131 East Av -Lockprt 14094 **Fx:**434-0563
(212) 530-5000 .. **Thiel,** Matthew A '09 %Milbank TH&M LLP -1 Chase Manh Plz -NY 10005
(631) 537-2583 .. **Thiele,** Fred W Jr. '80 %NYS Assembly -Bx3062 -Brdghmptn 11932 **Fx:**537-2836
(518) 487-7600 .. **Thiele,** Leslie K L '90 (Whiteman O&H LLP) -1 Commerce Plz -Albany 12260
(716) 853-4123 .. **Thielman,** Phillip A '62 -1156 E Lovejoy -Buffalo 14206
(212) 447-7070 .. **Thielmann,** Ilze C '95 %Whatley D&K LLC -1540 Bway -NY 10036
(518) 828-5554 .. **Thiemann,** Kevin B '84 %R Gagen -424 Warren -Hudson 12534 **Fx:**828-2685
(212) 701-3000 .. **Thier,** Jonathan D '84 (Cahill G&R LLP) -80 Pine -NY 10005 **Fx:**269-5420
(212) 698-3500 .. **Thierfelder,** Mark E '94 (Dechert LLP) -1095 Av of Amer -NY 10036
(718) 243-6810 .. **Thiesenhusen,** Kathryn H '03 %Leg Aid -111 Lvngstn -Brklyn 11201 **Fx:**237-8737
(718) 349-3800 .. **Thifault,** Ernest G '75 -150 Java -Brklyn 11222 **Fx:**389-0297
(718) 590-2000 .. **Thill,** Cheryl A '08 %DA -198 E 161st -Bronx 10451 **Fx:**590-6477
(585) 263-1000 .. **Thisse,** Megan L '09 %Nixon P LLP -1100 Clinton Sq -Rchstr 14604
(315) 781-1465 .. **Thistlethwaite,** Dale A '81 %Leg Assistance -361 S Main -Geneva 14456 **Fx:**781-2565
(212) 688-8555 .. **Thistlethwaite,** Hugh W III '06 %Fragomen DB&L LLP -7 Hanover Sq -NY 10004
(212) 397-6360 .. **Thivierge,** Christina D '01 (Thivierge & R,PC) -140 Bway -NY 10005 **Fx:**397-6361
(516) 571-2683 .. **Thoden,** Lauren E '10 Hon L Austin -100 Supreme Ct Dr -Mineola 11501
(585) 546-5530 .. **Thody,** Lora C '81 -50 E Broad -Rchstr 14694
(212) 682-0580 .. **Thofte,** Carl H '09 %Mannheimer S -101 Park Av -NY 10178
(212) 770-1956 .. **Thom,** Cathryn A '95 %AIG -80 Pine -NY 10005
(315) 474-7541 .. **Thoman,** James C '03 %Menter R&T,PC -308 Maltbie -Syracuse 13204
(518) 899-1518 .. **Thomas,** Alison C '99 (Peterson & T,PC) -49 Burlngtn Av Bx578 -Round Lk 12151
(212) 733-1622 .. **Thomas,** Alvin J '01 %FW Mettrick,Inc -150 E 42nd -NY 10017
(212) 431-2328 .. **Thomas,** Ann F '77 %NY Law Schl -185 W Bway -NY 10013 **Fx:**343-2039
(866) 434-2993 .. **Thomas,** Anne M '05 (Thomas Law Ofcs,PLLC) -7 Skyline Dr -Hawthorne 10532 **Fx:**(914) 345-0117
(718) 276-2729 .. **Thomas,** Audrey A '02 -245-07 F Lewis Blvd -Rosedale 11422
(212) 278-7121 .. **Thomas,** Caroline F '99 Societe Generale -1221 Av of Amer -NY 10020
(212) 636-6959 .. **Thomas,** Chantal J M '96 %Fordham Univ Sch of Law -140 W 62nd -NY 10023 **Fx:**636-6899
(315) 282-7963 .. **Thomas,** Chas M '93 -2 South -Auburn 13021 **Fx:**515-3152
(518) 271-0359 .. **Thomas,** Chas W '85 -105 Jordan Rd -Troy 12180
(212) 541-5800 .. **Thomas,** Christian R '00 Laurus Captl Mgmt -335 Mad Av -NY 10017 **Fx:**541-4434
(212) 725-4423 .. **Thomas,** Christina M '99 -185 Mad Av -NY 10016 **Fx:**684-9022
(585) 263-1000 .. **Thomas,** Christopher D '92 (Nixon P LLP) -1100 Clinton Sq -Rchstr 14604
(607) 754-0410 .. **Thomas Collison & Meagher** -1201 Monroe Bx329 -Endicott 13761 **Fx:**754-6293
(212) 530-1800 .. **Thomas,** Courtney B '04 %Richards K&O LLP -1 World Fncl Ctr -NY 10281
(718) 250-2000 .. **Thomas,** Cyril J '07 %DA -350 Jay -Brklyn 11201 **Fx:**250-2314
(212) 307-0200 .. **Thomas,** Danl A '94 (D Thomas,PC) -888 7th Av 45th Fl -NY 10106 **Fx:**307-0925
(212) 326-3939 .. **Thomas,** Danl F '08 %Jones D -222 E 41st -NY 10017
(212) 609-6800 .. **Thomas,** David A '91 %McCarter & E,LLP -245 Park Av -NY 10167
(212) 369-7031 .. **Thomas,** David E '80 -103 E 125th -NY 10035
(212) 902-5587 .. **Thomas,** David S '00 Goldman Sachs -1 NY Plz -NY 10004
(631) 727-3200 .. **Thomas,** Dawn C '90 (Town Atty) -200 Howell Av -Rvrhead 11901
(718) 584-2330 .. **Thomas,** Demond Kamuti '05 NYC Bd of Ed -577 E 179th -Bronx 10457
(212) 839-5300 .. **Thomas,** DeNae M '10 %Sidley A LLP -787 7th Av -NY 10019
(212) 661-7300 .. **Thomas,** Denise L '81 %Malapero & P LLP -295 Mad Av -NY 10017
(212) 715-1000 .. **Thomas,** Dermond E '02 %Arnold & P LLP -399 Park Av -NY 10022
(315) 361-8687 .. **Thomas,** Derrek T '03 Oneida Indian Nation Enterprises -5218 Patrick Rd -Verona 13478 **Fx:**361-8009
(212) 250-1602 .. **Thomas,** Dionne A '05 Deutsche Bk -60 Wall -NY 10005
(718) 852-0865 .. **Thomas,** Donald A '87 -188 Montague -Brklyn 11201
(516) 486-0980 .. **Thomas,** Douglas L '72 -120A Ingraham Blvd -Hempstd 11550 **Fx:**485-1229
(212) 535-2110 .. **Thomas,** Ellen Fluhr '83 -2 East End Av -NY 10075
(914) 592-6648 .. **Thomas,** Elvira Sorrentino '84 (Sorrentino T&S) -12 Armand Pl -Valhalla 10595
(212) 610-6300 .. **Thomas,** Erin T '08 %Allen & O -1221 Av of Amer -NY 10020
(212) 962-5535 .. **Thomas,** Galen C '77 -11 Park Pl -NY 10007
(212) 286-8585 .. **Thomas,** Gillian C '02 %Heidell PM&B,LLP -99 Park Av -NY 10016
(516) 502-2620 .. **Thomas & Graham LLP** -1983 Marcus Av -Lk Success 11042 **Fx:**465-9350
(607) 273-3666 .. **Thomas,** Gregg A '76 %Leg Srvcs -215 N Cayuga -Ithaca 14850 **Fx:**273-5521
(212) 699-8582 .. **Thomas,** Hillary B '06 Highland Development Grp -800 3rd Av -NY 10022
(516) 791-7230 .. **Thomas,** Ira M '91 -445 Central Av -Cedarhrst 11516
(718) 493-9287 .. **Thomas,** Irene Donna '98 (Thomas & Assoc) -977 St Johns Pl -Brklyn 11213
(585) 272-0540 .. **Thomas,** J Nelson '94 (Thomas & S LLP) -693 East Av -Rchstr 14607
(212) 223-4000 .. **Thomas,** Jack(John) N '97 (Crowell & M LLP) -590 Mad Av -NY 10022

(212) 593-3000 .. **Thomas,** Jaclyn E '06 %Platzer SKLG&J,LLP -1065 Av of Amer -NY 10018
(585) 454-5650 .. **Thomas,** Jacqueline M '92 (Lacy K LLP) -130 E Main -Rchstr 14604
(518) 786-9069 .. **Thomas,** Jaime B '89 %Schiller & K LLP -950 New Loudon Rd -Latham 12110
(718) 852-1899 .. **Thomas,** James '84 (Thomas & S) -111 Court -Brklyn 11201
(212) 436-2176 .. **Thomas,** James E '99 Deloitte Tax LLP -2 World Fncl Ctr -NY 10281
(212) 237-1000 .. **Thomas,** James J '86 (Windels ML&M,LLP) -156 W 56th -NY 10019
(212) 509-0500 .. **Thomas,** Jeff R '03 %Schoenfeld M,PC -61 Bway -NY 10006
(212) 455-2000 .. **Thomas,** Jeremiah L III '73 OfCnsl Simpson T&B LLP -425 Lex Av -NY 10017
(212) 312-2260 .. **Thomas,** Jessica D '09 Leg Aid -60 Lafayette -NY 10013 **Fx:**349-0874
(212) 255-8747 .. **Thomas,** Jettie K '91 -247 W 15th -NY 10011
(212) 972-6161 .. **Thomas,** John B '96 (Cassin & C LLP) -711 3rd Av -NY 10017
(212) 754-6120 .. **Thomas,** John C '85 (Stout & T) -477 Mad Av -NY 10022 **Fx:**754-6809
(914) 995-4172 .. **Thomas,** John C '02 %DA -111 Martin Luther King Blvd -White Plns 10601 **Fx:**995-3363
(845) 778-2121 .. **Thomas,** John H Jr. '69 (Jacobowitz & G,LLP) -158 Orange Av Bx367 -Walden 12586
(607) 723-9511 .. **Thomas,** John M '58 OfCnsl Coughlin & G,LLP -19 Chenango Bx2039 -Bnghmtn 13902
(607) 687-0567 .. **Thomas,** John M '58 OfCnsl Coughlin & G,LLP -27-29 Lk Bx250 -Owego 13827
(914) 965-1515 .. **Thomas,** Joju J '03 %J Romano -703 Ynkrs Av -Ynkrs 10704 **Fx:**965-0410
(516) 292-2438 .. **Thomas,** Jomo G '01 Nighe Lab -628 Clinton Av -Uniondale 11553
(212) 889-7990 .. **Thomas,** Kenneth '76 (Thomas & W) -104 W 27th -NY 10001
(914) 725-7893 .. **Thomas,** Lawr W '78 (Donoghue TA&D LLP) -700 Wht Plns Rd -Scarsdale 10583
(212) 385-4840 .. **Thomas,** Leslie Jones '85 -299 Bway -NY 10007 **Fx:**385-4844
(518) 459-6422 .. **Thomas,** Lincy M '08 Cptl Dist Ctr for Independence -875 Central Av -Albany 12206 **Fx:**459-7847
(347) 529-1136 .. **Thomas,** Linden E '96 -1431 Nostrand Av -Brklyn 11226
(518) 456-3415 .. **Thomas,** Margot Lucy '77 -100 Trillium Ln -Albany 12203 **Fx:**456-3465
(518) 449-8893 .. **Thomas,** Mark W '79 (Wilson EME&D LLP) -677 Bway -Albany 12207
(718) 298-8900 .. **Thomas,** Megan L '08 Leg Aid -153-01 Jamaica Av -Jamaica 11432 **Fx:**657-0537
(718) 802-2790 .. **Thomas,** Meredith R '08 ACS -330 Jay -Brklyn 11201
(212) 521-5400 .. **Thomas,** Michl J '07 %Reed S LLP -599 Lex Av -NY 10022
(518) 462-6765 .. **Thomas,** Monique N '08 %Leg Aid -55 Colvin Av -Albany 12206 **Fx:**427-8352
(212) 848-4000 .. **Thomas,** Naveen '10 Shearman & S LLP -599 Lex Av -NY 10022
(212) 446-4800 .. **Thomas,** Nikki R '09 %Kirkland & E LLP -153 E 53rd -NY 10022
(212) 267-1650 .. **Thomas,** Pamela '90 (Fine O&A,LLP) -39 Bway -NY 10006
(212) 762-7780 .. **Thomas,** Paul G '87 Morgan Stanley -1221 Av of Amer -NY 10020
(212) 345-6586 .. **Thomas,** Pauline R '97 %Marsh & McLennan Cos -1166 Av of Amer -NY 10036
(718) 896-7200 .. **Thomas,** Peter S '93 (P Thomas,PC) -108-18 Qns Blvd -Frst Hlls 11375 **Fx:**275-5793
(212) 603-6300 .. **Thomas,** Philip H '85 (Robinson BLGG&G PC) -875 3rd Av -NY 10022
(212) 832-0900 .. **Thomas,** Philip K '05 SB Schonfeld Inc -460 Park Av -NY 10022
(212) 551-0956 .. **Thomas,** Philip T '02 Intl Rescue Comm -122 E 42nd -NY 10168
(607) 754-0410 .. **Thomas,** Robt B '51 (Thomas C&M) -1201 Monroe Bx329 -Endicott 13761
(212) 558-4000 .. **Thomas,** Robt M Jr. '70 OfCnsl Sullivan & C LLP -125 Broad -NY 10004
(212) 225-2000 .. **Thomas,** Roger W '64 SrCnsl Cleary GS&H -1 Lbrty Plz -NY 10006
(212) 521-5400 .. **Thomas,** Ruth M '10 %Reed S LLP -599 Lex Av -NY 10022
(212) 425-9300 .. **Thomas,** Saml J '99 (Bressler A&R,PC) -17 State -NY 10004
(516) 538-1360 .. **Thomas,** Sandrea S '00 NYS Div Human Rights -175 Fulton Av -Hempstd 11550
(212) 909-6000 .. **Thomas,** Sarah J '08 %Debevoise & P LLP -919 3rd Av -NY 10022
(212) 858-1000 .. **Thomas,** Shawn P '09 %Pillsbury WSP LLP -1540 Bway -NY 10036
(585) 272-0540 .. **Thomas & Solomon LLP** -693 East Av -Rchstr 14607 **Fx:**272-0574
(914) 946-4656 .. **Thomas,** Sophy Sajan '96 (Ahmad & T) -199 Main -White Plns 10601 **Fx:**946-7828
(631) 727-0600 .. **Thomas,** Spencer L '80 %Fidelity Natl Title Ins -20 Commerce Dr -Rvrhead 11901 **Fx:**727-0606
(718) 852-1899 .. **Thomas & Spikes** -111 Court -Brklyn 11201 **Fx:**852-8093
(518) 869-6227 .. **Thomas,** Steven G '96 %Lavelle & F,LLP -29 British Amer Blvd -Latham 12110
(607) 777-4712 .. **Thomas,** Susan Decker '88 %Binghamton Univ Fndtn -Vestal Pkwy Ext Bx6005 -Bnghmtn 13902 **Fx:**777-2945
(212) 632-3000 .. **Thomas,** Suzan Barnes '73 Fiduciary Trust Co Intl -600 5th Av -NY 10020 **Fx:**632-3002
(212) 455-2000 .. **Thomas,** Tashia A '10 %Simpson T&B LLP -425 Lex Av -NY 10017
(716) 664-4535 .. **Thomas,** Todd M '05 Leg Srvcs -110 W 3rd -Jamestwn 14701
(212) 728-8000 .. **Thomas,** Tracy J '04 %Willkie F&G LLP -787 7th Av -NY 10019
(212) 878-8000 .. **Thomas,** Tulani A '07 %Clifford C LLP -31 W 52nd -NY 10019
(516) 465-8090 .. **Thomas,** Vanessa M '04 %North Shore-LIJ Hlth Systm -145 Community Dr -Gt Neck 11021 **Fx:**465-8013
(516) 496-5822 .. **Thomas,** Victoria Williams '98 %T Spina -170 Froehlich Farm Blvd -Woodbury 11797 **Fx:**496-5420
(212) 735-3000 .. **Thomas,** Vikram '08 %Skadden ASM&F LLP -4 Times Sq -NY 10036
(212) 889-7990 .. **Thomas & White** -104 W 27th -NY 10001 **Fx:**689-2864
(518) 695-3958 .. **Thomas,** Wm A '81 -27 Church Bx116 -Schuylrvll 12871
(212) 741-8900 .. **Thomas,** Wm A '92 -89 5th Av -NY 10003 **Fx:**937-4687
(516) 502-2620 .. **Thomas,** Wm M Jr. '68 OfCnsl Thomas & G LLP -1983 Marcus Av -Lk Success 11042
(607) 722-3495 .. **Thomas,** Wm M '91 (Aswad & I) -46 Front -Bnghmtn 13905
(718) 856-9285 .. **Thomas-Ahyase,** Gemma Y '89 -385 E 18th -Brklyn 11226
(212) 506-5000 .. **Thomasch,** Danl J '82 (Orrick H&S LLP) -51 W 52nd -NY 10019
(212) 227-4300 .. **Thomashower,** Wm J '74 (Schwartz & T LLP) -15 Maiden Ln -NY 10038 **Fx:**227-4311
(212) 512-4858 .. **Thomas-Yuille,** Erika K '95 McGraw-Hill Co,Inc -1221 Av of Amer -NY 10020
(212) 609-6800 .. **Thomen,** Jeffrey M '99 (McCarter & E,LLP) -245 Park Av -NY 10167
(212) 318-6000 .. **Thomma,** Friedemann '04 %Paul HJ&W LLP -75 E 55th -NY 10022
(212) 267-2424 .. **Thompson,** Adam M '89 -111 John -NY 10038 **Fx:**267-9177
(212) 474-1000 .. **Thompson,** Andrew R '00 (Cravath S&M LLP) -825 8th Av -NY 10019
(212) 998-6430 .. **Thompson,** Anthony C '97 %NYU Law Schl -245 Sullivan -NY 10012 **Fx:**995-4031
(631) 853-4104 .. **Thompson,** Avemaria '01 %DA -400 Carleton Av Bx9082 -Central Islip 11722 **Fx:**853-7838
(212) 728-8000 .. **Thompson,** Benjamin G '06 %Willkie F&G LLP -787 7th Av -NY 10019
(212) 837-6298 .. **Thompson,** Benjamin S '10 Hughes H&R LLP -1 Bttry Pk Plz -NY 10004 **Fx:**299-6298
(212) 984-3813 .. **Thompson,** Carlton E '94 Fore Advisors -280 Park Av -NY 10017
(212) 268-3560 .. **Thompson,** Charlene R '95 %Mondo Publishing -980 Av of Amer -NY 10018 **Fx:**268-3561
(212) 408-6027 .. **Thompson,** Chas D '03 Assured Guaranty Corp -1325 Av of Amer -NY 10019
(212) 460-4418 .. **Thompson,** Christine A '98 Con Ed -4 Irving Pl -NY 10003
(516) 448-6169 .. **Thompson,** Christopher A '05 -1 Dupont -Plainvw 11803
(631) 249-9500 .. **Thompson,** Christopher H '89 -Bx824 -Melvll 11747
(212) 986-6700 .. **Thompson,** Craig S '81 %Thompson Pension -420 Lex Av -NY 10170
(716) 847-8400 .. **Thompson,** Cynthia L '08 %Phillips L LLP -3400 HSBC Ctr -Buffalo 14203
(212) 506-1700 .. **Thompson,** David A '09 %Kasowitz BT&F LLP -1633 Bway -NY 10019
(631) 424-6100 .. **Thompson,** Debra R '92 Cnsl Advantage Title -410 NY Av -Huntngtn 11743 **Fx:**424-6049
(718) 262-7100 .. **Thompson,** Denetra M '07 %Civil Ct -89-17 Sutphin Blvd -Jamaica 11435 **Fx:**262-7107
(212) 648-3409 .. **Thompson,** Don '85 Morgan Guaranty Trust -60 Wall -NY 10260
(585) 423-8290 .. **Thompson,** Donald M '87 (Easton TKS,LLP) -16 W Main -Rchstr 14614 **Fx:**423-0890
(646) 264-3650 .. **Thompson,** Donyell M '01 %US Dept of Labor -201 Varick -NY 10014 **Fx:**264-3660
(315) 448-4800 .. **Thompson,** Ed J '86 %Dept of Law -615 Erie Blvd W -Syracuse 13204 **Fx:**448-4853
(212) 363-1380 .. **Thompson,** Eimi S '06 %Herten BSCBL&H,LLC -747 3rd Av -NY 10017
(212) 232-1300 .. **Thompson,** Frank D II '04 %Lewis BB&S LLP -77 Water -NY 10005
(212) 854-4411 .. **Thompson,** George C '50 %Columbia Univ -514 Uris Bldg -NY 10027
(518) 383-1500 .. **Thompson,** Gerald A Jr. '96 G Thompson Jr,PLLC -440 Route 146 -Clifton Pk 12065 **Fx:**383-3838
(607) 723-9511 .. **Thompson,** Gordon E '76 (Coughlin & G,LLP) -19 Chenango Bx2039 -Bnghmtn 13902
(607) 687-0567 .. **Thompson,** Gordon E '76 (Coughlin & G,LLP) -27-29 Lk Bx250 -Owego 13827
(914) 305-9053 .. **Thompson,** Gregory J '83 Sagemark Cnsltng -800 Wstchstr Av -Rye Brook 10573
(212) 355-8000 .. **Thompson,** Harlan '07 %Pulvers P&T,LLP -110 E 59th -NY 10022
(212) 326-3939 .. **Thompson,** Heather '07 %Jones D -222 E 41st -NY 10017
(212) 536-3900 .. **Thompson,** Heather L '09 %K&L Gates LLP -599 Lex Av -NY 10022
(631) 928-9271 .. **Thompson,** Helen M '82 -2 High Ct -Mt Sinai 11766
(212) 344-5680 .. **Thompson Hine LLP** -335 Mad Av -NY 10017 **Fx:**344-6101
(212) 558-5500 .. **Thompson,** James S '96 %Weitz & L,PC -700 Bway -NY 10003
(212) 455-2000 .. **Thompson,** James S '07 %Simpson T&B LLP -425 Lex Av -NY 10017
(212) 286-0423 .. **Thompson,** Janese N '99 %Robinson T & Assoc -820 2nd Av -NY 10017
(631) 581-2444 .. **Thompson,** Janet K '62 -361 Great Rvr Rd Bx273 -Great Rvr 11739
(914) 766-1757 .. **Thompson,** Jeffrey C '93 IBM -294 Route 100 -Somers 10589
(212) 442-8833 .. **Thompson,** Joan M '00 %CCRB -40 Rector -NY 10006 **Fx:**442-8800
(716) 832-9447 .. **Thompson,** John C '83 -69 Grayton Rd -Tonawanda 14150 **Fx:**832-9392
(212) 504-6000 .. **Thompson,** John Henry '02 %Cadwalader W&T LLP -1 World Fncl Ctr -NY 10281
(516) 431-6092 .. **Thompson,** Jordan III '04 %J Petrilli -370 W Park Av -Long Bch 11561 **Fx:**889-8904
(212) 355-8000 .. **Thompson,** Jordan R '09 %Pulvers P&T,LLP -110 E 59th -NY 10022
(212) 980-9600 .. **Thompson,** Karen A '08 %Kaufman B&R -120 Bway -NY 10271
(718) 935-5958 .. **Thompson,** Karyn R '01 NYC Dept Educ -131 Lvngstn -Brklyn 11201
(212) 277-5840 .. **Thompson,** Katherine G '71 (Beldock L&H LLP) -99 Park Av -NY 10016
(516) 465-8090 .. **Thompson,** Keith C '66 %North Shore-LIJ Hlth Systm -145 Community Dr -Gt Neck 11021 **Fx:**465-8013
(212) 257-6800 .. **Thompson,** Kenneth P '93 (Thompson W&G LLP) -85 5th Av -NY 10003
(212) 969-3000 .. **Thompson,** Kimberly M '08 %Proskauer R LLP -1585 Bway -NY 10036
(212) 751-3001 .. **Thompson & Knight LLP** -919 3rd Av -NY 10022 **Fx:**751-3113
(212) 855-3200 .. **Thompson,** Larry E '77 %Depository Trust -55 Water -NY 10041 **Fx:**855-3279
(212) 735-8600 .. **Thompson,** Latisha V '04 %Morrison C LLP -909 3rd Av -NY 10022
(212) 238-3000 .. **Thompson,** Lawr B '63 SrCnsl Emmet M&M,LLP -120 Bway -NY 10271
(212) 819-8200 .. **Thompson,** Lisa A '97 %White & C LLP -1155 Av of Amer -NY 10036
(212) 838-5122 .. **Thompson,** Livia D '85 %Central Synagogue -123 E 55th -NY 10022 **Fx:**644-2168

(718) 447-3600 ..**Thompson,** Lloyd D '90 -2110D Clove Rd -Staten Isl 10305 **Fx:**447-7250

(212) 969-3000 ..**Thompson,** Lois Devore '70 (Proskauer R LLP) -1585 Bway -NY 10036

(212) 294-6700 ..**Thompson,** Loran T '77 (Winston & S) -200 Park Av -NY 10166

(212) 355-8000 ..**Thompson,** Marc R '74 (Pulvers P&T,LLP) -110 E 59th -NY 10022

(212) 770-2602 ..**Thompson,** Marjorie J '96 %AIG -80 Pine -NY 10005

(212) 455-2000 ..**Thompson,** Mark J '85 (Simpson T&B LLP) -425 Lex Av -NY 10017

(631) 852-2500 ..**Thompson,** Martin J '82 %DA -200 Center Dr -Rvrhead 11901 **Fx:**852-1769

(716) 824-7200 ..**Thompson,** Mary Beth '93 %R Lorigo -101 Slade Av -W Seneca 14224 **Fx:**824-8728

(914) 312-2277 ..**Thompson,** Maureen F '82 Verizon Business Inc -1 Intl Dr -Rye Brook 10573

(518) 563-4884 ..**Thompson,** Michl C '77 (Clute C&T) -121 Brdg Bx2885 -Plattsbrgh 12901 **Fx:**563-5845

(212) 483-0105 ..**Thompson,** Michl T '98 %Coughlin D LLP -88 Pine-Wall St Plz -NY 10005

(212) 277-6500 ..**Thompson,** Nikol Gruning '00 %Dickstein S LLP -1633 Bway -NY 10019

(718) 264-1677 ..**Thompson,** Otis A '99 -209-09 Jamaica Av -Qns Vllg 11428 **Fx:**217-7441

(315) 475-0000 ..**Thompson,** Peter J '98 %Hill & F,PC -1117 E Genesee -Syracuse 13210 **Fx:**475-8498

(212) 670-0425 ..**Thompson,** Pia K '00 Merrill Lynch & Co Inc -222 Bway -NY 10038

(631) 669-4350 ..**Thompson,** Richd N '96 -73 W Main -Babylon 11702 **Fx:**661-3902

(631) 427-1212 ..**Thompson,** Robt H '65 -425 NY Av Bx666 -Huntngtn 11743

(212) 307-1122 ..**Thompson,** Robt L Jr. '84 %Sandoz Corp -608 5th Av -NY 10020

(212) 687-2770 ..**Thompson,** Roger S '79 %Cohen PL&P -551 5th Av -NY 10176

(845) 225-3641 ..**Thompson,** Rosa Cabanillas '98 Family Ct -40 Gleneida Av -Carmel 10512

(914) 670-4335 ..**Thompson,** Russell A '96 Mariner Inv Grp -500 Mamaroneck Av -Harrison 10528

(718) 422-7417 ..**Thompson,** Ryan '05 Brooklyn Daily Eagle -30 Henry -Brklyn 11201

(845) 486-2300 ..**Thompson,** Sara J '99 %DA -236 Main -Poughkeepsie 12601 **Fx:**486-2324

(212) 530-5000 ..**Thompson,** Sara R '08 %Milbank TH&M LLP -1 Chase Manh Plz -NY 10005

(212) 859-8000 ..**Thompson,** Scott A '09 %Fried FHS&J LLP -1 NY Plz -NY 10004

(212) 801-6581 ..**Thompson,** Scott E '84 (Greenberg T,LLP) -200 Park Av -NY 10166

(212) 474-1000 ..**Thompson,** Sean K '06 %Cravath S&M LLP -825 8th Av -NY 10019

(212) 951-6401 ..**Thompson,** Sherrie B '81 %Dept of Education -475 Park Av S -NY 10016 **Fx:**951-6465

(845) 357-1189 ..**Thompson,** Sidney H '61 -12 Brookside Av -Suffern 10901 **Fx:**623-4434

(212) 355-8000 ..**Thompson,** Stacy L '07 %Pulvers P&T,LLP -110 E 59th -NY 10022

(212) 943-0280 ..**Thompson,** Timothy L '75 (McCanliss & E LLP) -88 Pine -NY 10005

(718) 590-2865 ..**Thompson,** Tionnei M '07 Criminal Ct -265 E 161st -Bronx 10451

(718) 993-4066 ..**Thompson,** Walker T Jr. '69 -199 Lincoln Av -Bronx 10454

(212) 257-6800 ..**Thompson Wigdor & Gilly LLP** -85 5th Av -NY 10003 **Fx:**257-6845

(718) 855-2324 ..**Thompson,** Wm C '55 OfCnsl Ross & H -16 Court -Brklyn 11241

(212) 406-9710 ..**Thompson-Lester,** Rhonda '94 (Kral CRRP&G,LLP) -170 Bway -NY 10038

(718) 399-3025 ..**Thompson-Shand,** Harriet L '86 -890 Atl Av -Brklyn 11238

(845) 454-5909 ..**Thompson-Tinsley,** Angela S '95 %Sholes & M,LLP -327 Mill -Poughkeepsie 12601

(212) 468-8000 ..**Thomsen,** Gerd D '03 %Morrison & F LLP -1290 Av of Amer -NY 10104

(212) 554-1234 ..**Thomsen,** Jordan K '05 AXA Financial Inc -1290 Av of Amer -NY 10104 **Fx:**707-3963

(914) 329-7823 ..**Thomsen,** Kimberly S '98 -72 W 82nd -NY 10024

(212) 450-4000 ..**Thomsen,** Linda Chatman '80 (Davis P&W LLP) -450 Lex Av -NY 10017

(212) 335-4500 ..**Thomson,** Christopher R '04 %DLA Piper LLP -1251 Av of Amer -NY 10020

(585) 292-5627 ..**Thomson,** Derek A '03 Bryant & Stratton Cllg -1225 Jffrsn Rd -Rchstr 14623

(607) 733-4635 ..**Thomson,** Donald S '92 (Davidson & O,PC) -243 Lk -Elmira 14901

(917) 408-6495 ..**Thomson,** Gregory A '04 -233 Bway -NY 10279

(212) 735-3000 ..**Thomson,** Karolina E '08 %Skadden ASM&F LLP -4 Times Sq -NY 10036

(718) 590-5438 ..**Thomson,** Nancy '82 %Admin Children's Srvcs -900 Sheridan Av -Bronx 10451

(518) 463-1269 ..**Thomson,** R Scott '84 (Walsh & H) -18 Corp Wds Blvd -Albany 12211

(212) 957-7600 ..**Thomson,** Scott D '98 %Cohen & G LLP -800 3rd Av -NY 10022

(315) 448-0672 ..**Thomson,** Tamara B '03 US Atty -100 S Clinton Bx7198 -Syracuse 13261 **Fx:**448-0689

(212) 640-2000 ..**Thomson,** Wayne H '83 SrCnsl Amer Exp -200 Vesey -NY 10285

(516) 766-7007 ..**Thon,** Rhonda Eve '82 OfCnsl Schoen & S,LLP -11 Clinton Av -Rockvll Ctr 11570

(212) 290-4700 ..**Thonden,** Yodon '94 %Human Rights Watch -350 5th Av -NY 10118 **Fx:**736-1300

(212) 558-4035 ..**Thonfeld,** Ina C '05 Settle One -125 Broad -NY 10004

(716) 854-1002 ..**Thore,** Melissa Hardy '02 %Miserendino CS&E,PC -295 Main -Buffalo 14203

(212) 247-6400 ..**Thoren,** Peter L '83 Access Industries -730 5th Av -NY 10019

(518) 464-6770 ..**Thorn,** Arthur H '69 (Thorn GT&B,LLP) -5 Wembley Ct Bx15054 -Albany 12212

(212) 849-7000 ..**Thorn,** Benjamin W '04 %Quinn EU&S,LLP -51 Mad Av -NY 10010

(212) 487-9700 ..**Thorn,** Brian M '00 (White F&F,LLP) -61 Bway -NY 10006

(518) 464-6770 ..**Thorn Gershon Tymann and Bonanni,LLP** -5 Wembley Ct Bx15054 -Albany 12212 **Fx:**464-6778

(518) 580-0234 ..**Thorn Gershon Tymann and Bonanni,LLP** -229 Wshngtn -Saratoga Spgs 12866 **Fx:**464-6778

(212) 848-4000 ..**Thorn,** Jeffrey G '07 %Shearman & S LLP -599 Lex Av -NY 10022

(212) 998-6100 ..**Thorn,** Sandra Dilorio '77 %NYU Law Schl -40 Wshngtn Sq S -NY 10012 **Fx:**995-3156

(212) 450-4000 ..**Thorn,** Tyler W '07 %Davis P&W LLP -450 Lex Av -NY 10017

(212) 446-4800 ..**Thorn,** Vincent P '09 %Kirkland & E LLP -153 E 53rd -NY 10022

(212) 514-9190 ..**Thorn,** Wm J '09 %Downing & P,PC -17 Battery Pl -NY 10004

(212) 402-9400 ..**Thornburgh,** Katherine B '06 %McKool S,PC -1 Bryant Park -NY 10036

(518) 487-5460 ..**Thorne,** Alison M '06 %DA -6 Lodge -Albany 12207 **Fx:**487-5093

(631) 665-5139 ..**Thorne,** Gregory L '96 (Thorne & H,LLP) -111 W Main -Bay Shr 11706

(212) 319-6060 ..**Thorne,** Michl S '04 Fairfield Greenwich Advsrs -919 3rd Av -NY 10022

(914) 288-0022 ..**Thornewell,** Wm R II '07 %Leason E LLP -81 Main -White Plns 10601

(718) 797-1003 ..**Thornhill,** Holden E '93 -179 Court -Brklyn 11201

(212) 997-7595 ..**Thornhill,** Thos E '03 %Hafetz N&R -500 5th Av -NY 10110

(212) 891-9100 ..**Thornquist,** S Britta '05 %Goldfarb & F LLP -345 Park Av -NY 10154

(914) 793-0760 ..**Thornton,** Edna Lawson '55 -55 Prescott Av -Bronxvll 10708

(315) 422-6900 ..**Thornton,** Gregory R '74 1st Amer Title -351 S Warren -Syracuse 13202 **Fx:**422-7400

(914) 965-4288 ..**Thornton,** Jock '60 OfCnsl L Ecker,PLLC -1250 Cntrl Pk Av -Ynkrs 10704 **Fx:**968-0918

(212) 286-8585 ..**Thornton,** Patricia A '07 %Heidell PM&B,LLP -99 Park Av -NY 10016

(518) 943-4320 ..**Thornton,** Thos B '64 T Thornton Inc -143 Wshngtn Av -Saugerties 12477 **Fx:**943-6319

(518) 447-3200 ..**Thornton,** Timothy B '71 (McNamee LT&W,PC) -677 Bway -Albany 12207

(845) 298-1600 ..**Thorpe,** B Faye '04 %Genova & M -1136 Route 9 -Wappingers Fls 12590 **Fx:**298-1265

(212) 548-7404 ..**Thorpe,** Carey O '99 WestLaw -530 5th Av -NY 10036

(315) 637-7233 ..**Thorpe,** Christopher D '08 Cnsl WorkRite Safety -7211 E Genesse -Fayettevll 13066 **Fx:**637-0708

(212) 674-8642 ..**Thorpe,** David J '96 -477 FDR Dr -NY 10002

(212) 980-4500 ..**Thorpe,** Mara Traylor '67 (Cohen L LLP) -885 3rd Av -NY 10022

(631) 249-6600 ..**Thorpe,** Paul Jr. '67 (Rebore T&P PC) -500 Bi-Cnty Blvd -Farmngdl 11735 **Fx:**249-8190

(845) 638-2726 ..**Thorsen,** Eric Ole '77 -5 S Little Tor Rd -New Cty 10956 **Fx:**638-1125

(845) 638-2726 ..**Thorsen,** Kathryn Berit '02 %Thorsen Law Ofc -5 S Little Tor Rd -New Cty 10956 **Fx:**638-1125

(845) 942-4200 ..**Thorsen,** Rolf M '87 -11 Ramapo Rd -Garnervll 10923 **Fx:**942-4211

(212) 701-3000 ..**Thorsen,** Sean S '09 %Cahill G&R LLP -80 Pine -NY 10005 **Fx:**269-5420

(585) 396-4411 ..**Thorsness,** Kristen J '03 %Cnty Atty -27 N Main -Canandaigua 14424 **Fx:**396-4481

(516) 739-5044 ..**Thorstenn,** Magnus G '85 (Thorstenn & T) -1461 Franklin Av -Gdn Cty 11530 **Fx:**739-5048

(516) 739-5044 ..**Thorstenn,** Susan E '83 (Thorstenn & T) -1461 Franklin Av -Gdn Cty 11530 **Fx:**739-5048

(212) 373-3000 ..**Thoyer,** Judith R '66 (Paul WRW&G LLP) -1285 Av of Amer -NY 10019

(212) 530-5000 ..**Thrasher,** Laurice B '08 %Milbank TH&M LLP -1 Chase Manh Plz -NY 10005

(212) 214-6277 ..**Threadgill,** Wm A '90 Wachovia -375 Park Av -NY 10152

(518) 427-2650 ..**Threatte,** Leah R '05 %Nixon P LLP -677 Bway -Albany 12207

(212) 245-6754 ..**Throne,** Sara R '78 (Sonnenschein S&D,LLP) -7 Penn Plz -NY 10001

(212) 931-9108 ..**Thrope,** Irwin M '51 -440 Park Av S -NY 10016 **Fx:**931-9109

(212) 682-7474 ..**Thrope,** Jeffrey C '81 (Foley & L LLP) -90 Park Av -NY 10016

(212) 790-0360 ..**Thrope,** Leslie DeMontis '95 Cardozo Sch of Law -55 5th Av -NY 10003

(212) 576-7000 ..**Thrope,** Susan '82 %NY Life Ins -51 Mad Av -NY 10010 **Fx:**447-0569

(212) 330-8151 ..**Thrush,** Martha S '00 %Brinen & Assoc,LLC -7 Dey -NY 10007 **Fx:**202-5330

(518) 455-9952 ..**Thuillez,** Dale M '73 OfCnsl Thuillez FGB&Y,LLP -20 Corp Wds Blvd -Albany 12211

(518) 455-9952 ..**Thuillez Ford Gold Butler & Young, LLP** -20 Corp Wds Blvd -Albany 12211 **Fx:**462-4031

(646) 602-5690 ..**Thukral,** Juhu '00 %Urban Justice Ctr -123 William -NY 10038 **Fx:**(212) 533-4598

(212) 859-8000 ..**Thum,** Wm C '09 (Fried FHS&J LLP) -1 NY Plz -NY 10004

(212) 903-9000 ..**Thummala,** Pramod '08 %Linklaters -1345 Av of Amer -NY 10105

(845) 534-2742 ..**Thurau,** Talitha C '92 -348 Angola Rd Bx15 -Cornwall 12518 **Fx:**534-2743

(516) 571-3800 ..**Thurer,** Warren N '90 %DA -262 Old Cntry Rd -Mineola 11501 **Fx:**248-9479

(315) 696-8918 ..**Thurlow,** Louise M '88 %Riehlman S&S -397 Route 281 Bx430 -Tully 13159

(212) 326-3939 ..**Thurlow,** Peter G '97 %Jones D -222 E 41st -NY 10017

(315) 464-4700 ..**Thurlow,** Winthrop H '88 SUNY Univ Cnsl -60 Prsdntl Plz -Syracuse 13202 **Fx:**464-4706

(212) 556-1714 ..**Thurm,** David A '79 %The NY Times -620 8th Av -NY 10018

(800) 285-3000 ..**Thurm,** Kevin L '90 Citigroup -399 Park Av -NY 10043

(212) 326-2000 ..**Thurmond,** Monica K '97 (O'Melveny & M LLP) -7 Times Sq -NY 10036

(518) 464-5302 ..**Thurnau,** Elizabeth M '92 %SEFCU -Bx12189 -Albany 12212 **Fx:**464-5213

(631) 271-2020 ..**Thurneau,** Christopher D '91 -275 Wolf Hill Rd -Huntngtn Sta 11747

(315) 252-5840 ..**Thurston,** David B '05 Thurston Law Ofc,PC -100 Genesee -Auburn 13021 **Fx:**252-1754

(718) 624-8923 ..**Thurston,** Donna T '84 (Hill R&T LLC) -26 Court -Brklyn 11242 **Fx:**624-8335

(315) 626-2138 ..**Thurston,** Earle E '75 -Bx218 -Cato 13033 **Fx:**626-3282

(315) 252-5840 ..**Thurston,** Earle E '75 -100 Genesee -Auburn 13021 **Fx:**252-1754

(315) 701-0379 ..**Thurston,** Morgan R '94 (Moen & T) -5100 W Genesee -Camillus 13031

(212) 735-3000 ..**Thurston,** Sally Ann '87 (Skadden ASM&F LLP) -4 Times Sq -NY 10036

(914) 789-5020 ..**Thwaites,** Danl J '00 (Thwaites & L) -3 W Main -Elmsfrd 10523 **Fx:**789-5022

(607) 737-2944 .. **Thweatt**, John R '90 %DA -226 Lk Bx588 -Elmira 14902 **Fx**:737-2965
(212) 858-4000 .. **Thyagarajan**, Lara C '07 %FINRA -1 Lbrty Plz -NY 10006 **Fx**:858-4389
(212) 514-7800 .. **Thymius**, Wm '86 %C DiGiulio,PC -111 John -NY 10038 **Fx**:514-7838
(212) 490-3285 .. **Tiajoloff**, Andrew L '84 (Tiajoloff & K) -405 Lex Av -NY 10174 **Fx**:490-3295
(212) 530-5000 .. **Tian**, Shujun '10 %Milbank TH&M LLP -1 Chase Manh Plz -NY 10005
(212) 916-7800 .. **Tian**, Ye '04 Rabobank Intl -245 Park Av -NY 10167
(914) 725-9600 .. **Tiangco**, Kenneth T '97 (Filannino & T,LLP) -188 Summerfld -Scarsdale 10583 **Fx**:725-9604
(212) 735-3000 .. **Tiarks**, Melissa M '09 %Skadden ASM&F LLP -4 Times Sq -NY 10036
(646) 471-5566 .. **Tibaldi**, Mark J '00 PricewaterhouseCoopers -300 Mad Av -NY 10017
(914) 472-3600 .. **Tibaldi**, Thos J '83 (Tibaldi & B) -1075 Cntrl Pk Av -Scarsdale 10583 **Fx**:472-8943
(718) 545-3614 .. **Tibas**, Maria '93 %Pappas & P -33-20 Bway -Astoria 11106 **Fx**:726-6545
(212) 318-3000 .. **Tibberts**, Mark S '02 (Fulbright & J LLP) -666 5th Av -NY 10103
(212) 526-0471 .. **Tibbetts**, Pamela J '01 Lehman Bros -1271 Av of Amer -NY 10020
(212) 336-2000 .. **Tiberio**, Matthew S '09 %Patterson BW&T LLP -1133 Av of Amer -NY 10036
(212) 728-8000 .. **Tichacek**, Kyra K '09 %Willkie F&G LLP -787 7th Av -NY 10019
(212) 688-4000 .. **Ticker**, Jay M '82 %NYS HFA -641 Lex Av -NY 10022 **Fx**:872-0362
(212) 603-6300 .. **Ticktin**, Richd M '52 (Robinson BLGG&G PC) -875 3rd Av -NY 10022
(212) 801-2203 .. **Ticoll**, Gary D '00 (Greenberg T,LLP) -200 Park Av -NY 10166
(518) 427-2650 .. **Tidgewell**, Todd M '03 (Nixon P LLP) -677 Bway -Albany 12207
(212) 656-2680 .. **Tidona**, George J '81 NYSE-Div of Enfrcmnt -14 Wall -NY 10005
(716) 884-2558 .. **Tiede**, Danl P '85 -Bx192 -Buffalo 14202 **Fx**:884-6459
(212) 819-8200 .. **Tiedemann**, Robt E III '94 Cnsl White & C LLP -1155 Av of Amer -NY 10036
(212) 450-0122 .. **Tiegel**, Howard '94 Marubeni America -375 Lex Av -NY 10017 **Fx**:450-0706
(212) 557-1854 .. **Tierman**, Robt D '80 (Litwin & T,PA) -292 Mad Av -NY 10016 **Fx**:557-1856
(631) 673-3200 .. **Tiernan**, Bradford J '01 -150 Motor Pkwy -Hauppauge 11788
(347) 401-9116 .. **Tiernan**, Carol Stark '87 Ct Atty-Referee -360 Adams -Brklyn 11201 **Fx**:401-9131
(212) 548-7926 .. **Tiernan**, Erin T '05 Thomson West -530 5th Av -NY 10036
(716) 856-6086 .. **Tiernan Krug & Schnurr** -110 Pearl -Buffalo 14202 **Fx**:852-0706
(585) 232-7510 .. **Tiernan**, Mark H '73 (Duffy & T) -45 Exchange -Rchstr 14614 **Fx**:232-9110
(212) 504-6000 .. **Tierney**, Danl E '10 %Cadwalader W&T LLP -1 World Fncl Ctr -NY 10281
(631) 724-8833 .. **Tierney**, Francis J '80 (Devitt SB,LLP) -50 Route 111 -Smithtwn 11787
(212) 509-9400 .. **Tierney**, J Donald '65 OfCnsl Cozen O -45 Bway Atrium -NY 10006
(516) 822-4100 .. **Tierney**, James E '03 %R List -109 Newbrdg Rd -Hicksvll 11801 **Fx**:822-2178
(518) 402-2794 .. **Tierney**, James M '89 %DEC -625 Bway -Albany 12233 **Fx**:402-9018
(631) 928-1444 .. **Tierney**, John A '08 %Tierney & T -409 Rt 112 Bx995 -Pt Jffrsn Sta 11776 **Fx**:928-5705
(631) 928-1444 .. **Tierney**, John J '69 (Tierney & T) -409 Rt 112 Bx995 -Pt Jffrsn Sta 11776 **Fx**:928-5705
(516) 394-4200 .. **Tierney**, Mary D '83 %Duffy & D -1370 RXR Plz -Uniondale 11556
(518) 402-0205 .. **Tierney**, Matthew J '84 %UIA Bd -Troy Atrium Bx15126 -Albany 12212 **Fx**:402-6208
(631) 928-1444 .. **Tierney**, Michl E '69 (Tierney & T) -409 Rt 112 Bx995 -Pt Jffrsn Sta 11776 **Fx**:928-5705
(845) 398-0361 .. **Tierney**, Michelle L '04 %K Mulhearn,PC -60 Dutch Hill Rd -Orangebrg 10962 **Fx**:398-3836
(212) 732-8700 .. **Tierney**, Patricia A '03 %McAloon & F,PC -123 William -NY 10038
(516) 747-2478 .. **Tierney**, Peter T '61 TJ Stock & Assoc -88 2nd -Mineola 11501 **Fx**:747-2574
(718) 254-7000 .. **Tierney**, Raymond A '93 %US Atty -271 Cadman Plz E -Brklyn 11201 **Fx**:254-6479
(212) 701-3000 .. **Tierney**, Sean R '06 %Cahill G&R LLP -80 Pine -NY 10005 **Fx**:269-5420
(585) 987-2800 .. **Tierney**, W Stephen '83 (Woods OG LLP) -2 State -Rchstr 14614
(914) 835-0229 .. **Tiesi**, Michl A '05 -260 Harrison Av -Harrison 10528 **Fx**:835-1752
(914) 478-5129 .. **Tietjen**, Deana '96 OfCnsl Quinlan & F -245 Saw Mill Rvr Rd -Hawthorne 10532 **Fx**:478-0817
(845) 876-7066 .. **Tietjen**, Herman H '63 -60 E Market Bx201 -Rhinebeck 12572 **Fx**:876-2513
(518) 434-0600 .. **Tietjen**, Robt C '03 %Boies S&F LLP -10 N Pearl -Albany 12207
(212) 460-1090 .. **Tietjen**, Wm F '93 Con Ed -4 Irving Pl -NY 10003
(212) 578-6475 .. **Tietz**, Michl F '79 %MetLife -200 Park Av -NY 10166
(212) 710-3900 .. **Tiffany**, Kristin L '06 %Clyde & Co US LLP -405 Lex Av -NY 10174 **Fx**:710-3950
(212) 486-2400 .. **Tiffany**, Michl J '03 %Leader & B LLP -630 3rd Av -NY 10017
(518) 388-4364 .. **Tiffany**, Michl W '06 %DA -612 State -Schnctdy 12305 **Fx**:388-4569
(212) 246-4300 .. **Tiffenberg**, Filip L '80 -1775 Bway -NY 10019
(212) 259-8000 .. **Tigar**, Andrea R '88 %Dewey & L LLP -1301 Av of Amer -NY 10019
(212) 837-6000 .. **Tiger**, Michl D '02 %Hughes H&R LLP -1 Bttry Pk Plz -NY 10004
(631) 853-1000 .. **Tiger**, Neil H '79 Suffolk Regional OTB Corp -5 Davids Dr -Hauppauge 11788 **Fx**:853-1080
(212) 225-2000 .. **Tiger**, Paul M '07 %Cleary GS&H -1 Lbrty Plz -NY 10006
(212) 279-3355 .. **Tiger**, Stephen B '95 (Tiger & D,LLP) -31 E 32nd -NY 10016 **Fx**:643-8083
(212) 797-3544 .. **Tiggs**, Bryan F '01 %French & C,LLP -29 Bway -NY 10006
(212) 785-1844 .. **Tighe**, Maureen Ann '89 -11 Hanover Sq -NY 10005 **Fx**:248-2848
(518) 862-1200 .. **Tighe**, Maureen N '91 %Martin H&M LLP -Bx15141 -Albany 12212
(518) 370-5151 .. **Tighe**, Michl J '73 %Off-Track Betting Corp -510 Smith -Schnctdy 12305
(518) 462-6765 .. **Tighe**, Paul A '09 %Leg Aid -55 Colvin Av -Albany 12206 **Fx**:427-8352
(516) 357-3700 .. **Tighe**, Rodger W '74 (Cullen and D LLP) -100 Q Roosevelt Blvd -Gdn Cty 11530
(518) 464-2284 .. **Tighe**, Tina M '99 AYCO -1 Wall Bx15073 -Albany 12212
(212) 728-8000 .. **Tihin**, Maria T '09 %Willkie F&G LLP -787 7th Av -NY 10019
(212) 997-4400 .. **Tilahun**, Beth-El '99 %Teitler & T,LLP -1114 Av of Amer -NY 10036 **Fx**:997-4949
(212) 697-3250 .. **Tilajef**, Yael '00 %Goldberg & R PLLC -115 Bway -NY 10006 **Fx**:227-4533
(718) 497-2552 .. **Tilem**, Andrew M '94 %A Simon & Assoc -228 Montrose Av -Brklyn 11206 **Fx**:497-1146
(914) 833-9785 .. **Tilem**, Peter H '92 (Tilem & C,LLP) -188 E Post Rd -White Plns 10601 **Fx**:833-9788
(718) 854-1099 .. **Tilevitz**, Orrin E '80 -507 Beverley -Brklyn 11218
(212) 455-9255 .. **Tiliakos**, Michl '97 (Rao & T LLP) -90 Park Av -NY 10016 **Fx**:297-0005
(631) 244-1615 .. **Tilis**, Harry F '90 Tilis & L -80 Orvll Dr -Bohemia 11716 **Fx**:244-1699
(516) 742-3773 .. **Tilker**, Barbara D '78 (Brecher FPWT&Z,PC) -1325 Franklin Av -Gdn Cty 11530
(607) 547-7004 .. **Tillapaugh**, Martin H '77 -30½ Pioneer -Cooperstwn 13326 **Fx**:547-2572
(914) 323-7000 .. **Tillem**, David L '80 (Wilson EME&D LLP) -3 Gannett Dr -White Plns 10604
(516) 822-7162 .. **Tillem**, Jack D '58 -20 W Marie -Hicksvll 11801 **Fx**:822-6049
(212) 977-9700 .. **Tillem**, Jonathan R '78 (Phillips N LLP) -666 5th Av -NY 10103
(917) 421-4620 .. **Tillem**, Steven D '93 IRS -33 Maiden Ln -NY 10038
(212) 909-6000 .. **Tiller**, Ramya S '06 %Debevoise & P LLP -919 3rd Av -NY 10022
(212) 344-9022 .. **Tilles**, Leslie Grobman '91 %Klein Law Grp,PC -11 Bway -NY 10004 **Fx**:344-0301
(516) 364-2533 .. **Tilles**, Roger B '90 -98 Myrtle Dr -Gt Neck 11021 **Fx**:364-1973
(212) 626-4100 .. **Tillinghast**, David R '55 (Baker & M LLP) -1114 Av of Amer -NY 10036
(212) 653-8700 .. **Tillinghast**, Edw H III '85 (Sheppard MR&H LLP) -30 Rckfllr Plz -NY 10112
(212) 721-3026 .. **Tillinghast**, Elizabeth '87 -262 Cntrl Pk W -NY 10024
(718) 403-3600 .. **Tillman**, H Gregory '76 %Dept of Finance -345 Adams -Brklyn 11201 **Fx**:403-3650
(718) 442-4424 .. **Tillman**, Pamela I '92 %Corash & H,PC -1200 South Av -Staten Isl 10314
(914) 846-3631 .. **Tillotson**, Sandra Grandison '02 NY Life Ins -1 Rockwood Rd -Sleepy Hollow 10591 **Fx**:846-4755
(716) 649-6700 .. **Tills**, Robt W '60 OfCnsl Abbott T&K,LLP -44 Union -Hambrg 14075
(212) 838-1177 .. **Tillyard**, H Virginia '98 %Morse ZR&L LLP -405 Park Av -NY 10022
(716) 434-6000 .. **Tilney**, Leonard G Jr. '72 -80 Park Av -Lockprt 14094 **Fx**:434-6298
(516) 873-2000 .. **Tils**, Robt M '86 (Moritt HH&H LLP) -400 Grdn City Plz -Gdn Cty 11530
(631) 427-1299 .. **Tilschner**, George R '97 (G Tilschner,PC) -141 E Main -Huntngtn 11743 **Fx**:427-1631
(646) 822-1801 .. **Tilton**, Isaac D '09 %Itkowitz & H -305 Bway -NY 10007
(212) 697-5550 .. **Tilton**, Lois '85 (G & L Blumberg,LLP) -521 5th Av -NY 10175 **Fx**:697-9570
(212) 455-2000 .. **Tilton**, Maina A '04 %Simpson T&B LLP -425 Lex Av -NY 10017
(212) 716-5790 .. **Tilton**, Richd N '75 Cnsl Cohen Lgl Grp,LLC -230 Park Av -NY 10169
(585) 987-2800 .. **Tilton**, Saml O '70 (Woods OG LLP) -2 State -Rchstr 14614
(518) 505-4244 .. **Timber**, Christine J '76 -12 Austain Av -Albany 12205
(718) 222-2363 .. **Timbers**, Edw T '08 %Law Dept -350 Jay -Brklyn 11201 **Fx**:222-2088
(646) 315-7413 .. **Timbers**, Meredith M '98 %FINRA -14 Wall -NY 10005 **Fx**:315-7440
(315) 466-7151 .. **Timian**, Richd F '76 %Ct of Claims -205 S Salina -Syracuse 13202 **Fx**:466-7154
(585) 453-5630 .. **Timian**, Susan J '89 Johnson & Johnson -100 Indigo Crk Dr -Rchstr 14626 **Fx**:899-2931
(718) 262-7100 .. **Timken**, Nelson E '88 %Civil Ct -89-17 Sutphin Blvd -Jamaica 11435 **Fx**:262-7107
(914) 993-0600 .. **Timko**, James M '84 (Keogh T&M) -1 N Bway -White Plns 10601 **Fx**:993-0251
(212) 340-3322 .. **Timko**, Karen L '84 %Metro-North -347 Mad Av -NY 10017 **Fx**:697-9079
(914) 249-2000 .. **Timko**, Michl J '77 %MasterCard Intl -2000 Purchase -Purchase 10577
(212) 233-2040 .. **Timko**, Nicholas I '83 (Kahn GT&R,PC) -20 Vesey -NY 10007
(212) 848-4000 .. **Timlin**, Edw G '10 Shearman & S LLP -599 Lex Av -NY 10022
(845) 462-5444 .. **Timm**, Michl E '68 -7 Volino Dr -Poughkeepsie 12603
(212) 813-8800 .. **Timmer**, Edw '01 %Goodwin P LLP -620 8th Av -NY 10018
(212) 530-5000 .. **Timmermann**, John C '07 %Milbank TH&M LLP -1 Chase Manh Plz -NY 10005
(631) 853-4161 .. **Timmons**, Peter W '86 %DA -N Cnty Cmplx Bldg 77 -Hauppauge 11788 **Fx**:853-4192
(212) 919-3083 .. **Timon**, Kimon P '86 Park Ave Securities -7 Hanover Sq -NY 10004 **Fx**:919-3781
(914) 669-0900 .. **Timone**, Denis J '71 -293 Route 100 -Somers 10589 **Fx**:669-0902
(212) 909-6000 .. **Timoney**, Liam F '07 %Debevoise & P LLP -919 3rd Av -NY 10022
(516) 439-5465 .. **Timoshenko & Scotto,LLP** -175 E Shore Rd -Gt Neck 11023 **Fx**:439-5464
(516) 439-5465 .. **Timoshenko**, Victor '92 (Timoshenko & S,LLP) -175 E Shore Rd -Gt Neck 11023
(212) 574-1200 .. **Timpone**, Michl S '01 %Seward & K LLP -1 Bttry Pk Plz -NY 10004
(212) 483-9490 .. **Timpone**, Walter F '80 (McElroy DM&C,LLP) -88 Pine -NY 10005
(718) 740-1234 .. **Tinagero**, James D '91 -214-47 Jamaica Av -Qns Vllg 11428
(631) 342-8070 .. **Tinari**, Frank A '81 (Tinari OO&K,LLP) -320 Carleton Av -Central Islip 11722
(631) 342-8070 .. **Tinari O'Connell Osborn & Kaufman,LLP** -320 Carleton Av -Central Islip 11722 **Fx**:342-8350
(212) 308-4411 .. **Tindall**, Alphonso E Jr. '87 (Edwards AP&D LLP) -750 Lex Av -NY 10022
(212) 385-3030 .. **Tindall-O'Brien**, Pamela '78 ICL -40 Rector -NY 10006
(631) 969-3100 .. **Tindell**, Edw J '90 %Frenkel LWW&G,LLP -20 W Main -Bay Shr 11706

(212) 735-3000 .. **Tindell,** Jeffrey W '75 (Skadden ASM&F LLP) -4 Times Sq -NY 10036
(718) 966-6155 .. **Tineo,** Licet '01 DMV Traffic Violations Bur -696 E Fordham Rd -Bronx 10458
(212) 480-6779 .. **Ting,** Eu '08 DHCR -25 Beaver -NY 10004 **Fx:**480-7416
(212) 922-1800 .. **Tingey,** Rebecca '07 %McKenna L&A -230 Park Av -NY 10169
(212) 416-8715 .. **Tinghino,** Frank J '73 %Dept of Law -120 Bway -NY 10271
(212) 918-3000 .. **Tingir,** Roxanne A '09 %Hogan L LLP -875 3rd Av -NY 10022
(518) 463-3990 .. **Tingley,** Jonathon B '07 %Tuczinski CG&C,PC -54 State -Albany 12207
(212) 232-1300 .. **Tingling,** Aija M '06 %Lewis BB&S LLP -77 Water -NY 10005
(516) 759-1212 .. **Tini,** Edw A '99 %Mohen & T LLP -186 Birch Hill Rd -Locust Vly 11560
(212) 336-8330 .. **Tinio,** Rebecca S '09 %Susman G LLP -560 Lex Av -NY 10022
(212) 906-1200 .. **Tinkelman,** Joshua A '99 %Latham & W -885 3rd Av -NY 10022
(212) 387-8400 .. **Tinker,** Catherine J '88 %Goldfarb AS&K LLP -350 5th Av -NY 10118
(315) 785-4331 .. **Tinker,** David E '81 %Samaritan Med Ctr -830 Wshngtn -Watertwn 13601
(212) 451-2900 .. **Tinnerello,** Christopher D '03 %Robinson & C LLP -885 3rd Av -NY 10022
(585) 728-2041 .. **Tinney,** Carolyn L '93 Cnsl Catholic Charities Livingston Cnty -7633 Thunder Mtn Trl -Wayland 14572 **Fx:**658-2513
(631) 439-1720 .. **Tinnie,** Elynda Hickson '81 %MHLS -320 Carleton Av -Central Islip 11722 **Fx:**951-2562
(914) 696-0600 .. **Tino,** Rita J '91 -2 Gannett Dr -White Plns 10604 **Fx:**206-9608
(585) 377-2810 .. **Tinsley,** Dusty R '06 Midwest,Inc -6894 Pttsfrd Palmyra Rd -Fairprt 14450
(212) 903-9000 .. **Tinsley,** Edw R '10 %Linklaters -1345 Av of Amer -NY 10105
(631) 586-1316 .. **Tinsley-Colbert,** Janice E '93 -323 W 20th -Deer Pk 11729 **Fx:**586-3426
(212) 962-6454 .. **Tintle,** Myles L III '95 (Terilli & T,PLLC) -225 Bway -NY 10007 **Fx:**962-6045
(718) 337-4317 .. **Tinubu,** Babatunde Gbadebo '92 -12-03 Norton Dr -Far Rckwy 11691 **Fx:**337-9846
(212) 613-5000 .. **Tinubu,** Norma Avril '00 Leg Assist Grp -450 W 33rd -NY 10001 **Fx:**750-0820
(212) 416-8000 .. **Tipaldo,** Jos F '96 %Dept of Law -120 Bway -NY 10271
(212) 326-3939 .. **Tipi,** Stela C '05 %Jones D -222 E 41st -NY 10017
(212) 732-8580 .. **Tipograph,** Peter S '81 (Sher HB&T,PC) -277 Bway -NY 10007
(212) 999-5800 .. **Tippett,** Elizabeth C '09 %Wilson SG&R -1301 Av of Americas -NY 10019
(518) 477-5127 .. **Tippins,** Cynthia J '89 -Bx580 -E Greenbush 12061
(518) 686-1905 .. **Tippins,** Timothy M '75 Matlaw Systems -138 Lebarron Rd -Hoosick Fls 12090 **Fx:**(802) 753-2003
(212) 735-3000 .. **Tippy,** Michl E '09 %Skadden ASM&F LLP -4 Times Sq -NY 10036
(212) 278-6974 .. **Tipton,** Governor '76 %Societe Generale -1221 Av of Amer -NY 10020
(212) 402-1321 .. **Tiranno,** Paul G '00 Pioneer Alt Invstmnts -535 5th Av -NY 10017
(718) 725-1200 .. **Tirgary,** Sarah Ann '93 -90-50 Parsons Blvd -Jamaica 11432
(718) 286-6000 .. **Tirino,** Denise '88 %DA -125-01 Qns Blvd -Kew Gdns 11415
(516) 766-1619 .. **Tirino,** Jessica C '03 Dergarabedian D & Assoc -11 Clinton Av -Rockvll Ctr 11570 **Fx:**766-6121
(914) 686-7007 .. **Tirone,** Anthony R '91 A Tirone,PC -10 Bank -White Plns 10606 **Fx:**686-7019
(585) 248-0170 .. **Tirone,** Gregg M '87 -130 D Linden Oaks -Rchstr 14625
(716) 645-5500 .. **Tirpak,** Edw T '93 STOR -1576 Sweet Home Rd -Buffalo 14228
(631) 582-3700 .. **Tirrell,** Scott R '95 %Turley RR&R,LLP -3075 Vets Mem'l Hwy -Ronkonkoma 11779
(212) 458-1371 .. **Tirro,** Christopher '96 %AIG -175 Water -NY 10038
(845) 634-4687 .. **Tirschwell,** Donald '60 -108 New Hempstd Rd -New Cty 10956 **Fx:**634-6962
(212) 715-9100 .. **Tirschwell,** Eric A '93 (Kramer LN&F,LLP) -1177 Av of Amer -NY 10036
(212) 480-5288 .. **Tisch,** Alexander M '97 %Insurance Dept -25 Beaver -NY 10004 **Fx:**480-5272
(212) 558-4000 .. **Tisch,** Michl J '10 %Sullivan & C LLP -125 Broad -NY 10004
(914) 764-4236 .. **Tisch,** Wendy J '88 -Uppr Shad Rd RR1 Bx7 -Pound Rdg 10576
(518) 250-4444 .. **Tischler,** Dorothy R '87 -1202 Troy Schenectady Rd -Latham 12110
(516) 357-3000 .. **Tischler,** Douglas G '92 (Rivkin R LLP) -926 RXR Plz -Uniondale 11556
(212) 293-8900 .. **Tischler,** Gary M '88 %EMMES Asset Mgt -420 Lex Av -NY 10170 **Fx:**293-8805
(212) 583-9500 .. **Tischler,** Jessica N '08 %Berke-Weiss & P LLP -488 Mad Av -NY 10022 **Fx:**308-8582
(718) 229-5390 .. **Tischler,** Perry I '91 -38-39 Bell Blvd -Bayside 11361 **Fx:**229-5759
(845) 657-9820 .. **Tischler,** Robt G '58 -323 Mtn Rd -Shokan 12481 **Fx:**657-7067
(212) 777-4850 .. **Tischler,** Robt G '58 -225 Park Av S -NY 10003 **Fx:**353-0876
(585) 263-1000 .. **Tischner,** Tate L '04 %Nixon P LLP -1100 Clinton Sq -Rchstr 14604
(716) 856-4200 .. **Tisci,** Kristin A '06 %Gibson M&C,LLP -69 Delaware Av -Buffalo 14202
(516) 357-3000 .. **Tiscione,** Frank P '08 %Rivkin R LLP -926 RXR Plz -Uniondale 11556
(718) 260-2475 .. **Tiscione,** Steven L '03 %Hon E Korman -225 Cadman Plz E -Brklyn 11201
(716) 285-3525 .. **Tisdale,** Melanie Collins '89 (Tisdale C&W) -800 Main -Niagara Fls 14302 **Fx:**285-8574
(212) 859-8000 .. **Tisdale,** Richd C '05 %Fried FHS&J LLP -1 NY Plz -NY 10004
(212) 354-0025 .. **Tisdale,** Thos L '82 -60 E 42nd -NY 10165 **Fx:**869-0067
(315) 423-4400 .. **Tisdell,** Alicia M '05 %Wolff G&G,LLP -217 Mntgmry -Syracuse 13202
(212) 632-6000 .. **Tisdell,** Benjamin A '05 %Lazard Freres -30 Rckfllr Plz -NY 10112 **Fx:**632-6060
(315) 474-2981 .. **Tisdell Moore & Walter** -120 E Wshngtn -Syracuse 13202 **Fx:**474-5574
(315) 474-2981 .. **Tisdell,** Robt L '75 (Tisdell M&W) -120 E Wshngtn -Syracuse 13202
(212) 478-7200 .. **Tishco,** Sharon Selter '05 %Hahn & H LLP -488 Mad Av -NY 10022
(212) 788-1161 .. **Tishco,** Steven '05 Law Dept -100 Church -NY 10007 **Fx:**788-0367
(212) 388-3600 .. **Tishler,** Leslie G '83 %32B-J Leg Srvcs -101 Av of Amer -NY 10013 **Fx:**388-3061
(518) 372-1357 .. **Tishler,** Nicholas E '81 -1917 Mayfair Rd -Niskayuna 12309 **Fx:**382-8934
(718) 694-9768 .. **Tishman,** Allen J '77 -16 Court -Brklyn 11241 **Fx:**875-1768
(212) 388-3614 .. **Tishman,** Lonnie G '74 (32B-J Leg Srvcs) -101 Av of Amer -NY 10013 **Fx:**388-3061
(212) 878-0000 .. **Tishman,** Pamela B '87 %MTA -2 Penn Plz -NY 10121
(212) 697-9280 .. **Tisi,** Arthur O '96 %Rosenberg MF&W -122 E 42nd -NY 10168
(212) 918-3000 .. **Tiska,** Tracey A '96 (Hogan L LLP) -875 3rd Av -NY 10022
(516) 248-1700 .. **Tisman,** Russell G '78 (Forchelli CDSM&T,LLP) -333 Earle Ovngton Blvd -Uniondale 11553
(212) 213-5800 .. **Tisman,** Stephen E '73 (Margolis & T LLP) -280 Mad Av -NY 10016
(212) 238-3000 .. **Tisne,** Peter B '68 (Emmet M&M,LLP) -120 Bway -NY 10271
(212) 857-8500 .. **Tisne,** Philip V '08 %Hon R Raggi -225 Cadman Plz E -Brklyn 11201
(914) 777-2591 .. **Tisnovsky,** Elena A '05 -416 Florence -Mamaroneck 10543
(212) 570-3000 .. **Tiso,** Bernadette J '08 NY Blood Ctr -310 E 67th -NY 10065
(212) 746-1337 .. **Title,** Fredk S '00 %NY Presbyterian Hsptl -525 E 68th Bx88 -NY 10065 **Fx:**746-8603
(212) 456-6665 .. **Title,** Heidi S '87 %ABC -77 W 66th -NY 10023
(718) 972-2727 .. **Titone,** Lucy Frances '96 (Titone & S,LLP) -4719 13th Av -Brklyn 11219
(718) 390-0555 .. **Titone,** Matthew J '92 OfCnsl Gabor & M LLC -1878 Victory Blvd -Staten Isl 10314
(212) 766-1888 .. **Titowsky,** Michl B '82 (Morris DA&F) -2 Rector -NY 10006
(518) 388-2270 .. **Titsworth,** Emily H '05 MVP Hlthcare -675 State -Schnctdy 12305
(518) 453-4583 .. **Titsworth,** Thos D Jr. '05 Cnsl CHA,Inc -3 Winners Cir -Albany 12205 **Fx:**453-2873
(845) 296-3084 .. **Tittle,** Patrick S '95 -1207 Route 9 -Wappingers Fls 12590
(212) 922-9550 .. **Titus,** Andrew D K '96 Clutch Grp -370 Lex Av -NY 10017
(212) 236-1781 .. **Titus,** Christina M '78 %Merrill Lynch -225 Lbrty WFC -NY 10080
(212) 663-3869 .. **Titus,** M J F '93 -255 W 108th -NY 10025 **Fx:**663-3877
(212) 374-6888 .. **Titus,** Michele R '94 %NYC Dept Educ-OLS -52 Chmbrs -NY 10007 **Fx:**374-5596
(347) 374-4599 .. **Titus,** Raye C R '79 -5316 Av I -Brklyn 11234 **Fx:**(718) 444-1340
(212) 449-2084 .. **Tiu,** Ernie T '04 Merrill Lynch -1 World Fncl Ctr -NY 10080
(212) 805-6186 .. **Tiven,** Rachel B '04 Hon B Jones -40 Centre -NY 10007
(716) 636-7600 .. **Tiveron,** Diane R '90 (HoganWillig) -2410 N Forest Rd -Amherst 14068
(212) 872-1000 .. **Tizravesh,** Roxanne '09 -One Bryant Park -NY 10036 **Fx:**872-1002
(631) 622-5340 .. **Tizzano,** Christopher R '01 Amer Home Mortgage -538 Broadhllw Rd -Melvll 11747
(585) 530-3143 .. **Tkachyk,** Danl G '06 %Applt Div 4th Dept -50 East Av Ste 200 -Rchstr 14604 **Fx:**530-3247
(212) 297-5800 .. **Tlusty,** Megan K '10 %Day P LLP -7 Times Sq -NY 10036
(212) 909-6000 .. **To,** My Chi '99 (Debevoise & P LLP) -919 3rd Av -NY 10022
(518) 346-0134 .. **Toal,** Brian J '94 -34 Jay -Schnctdy 12305 **Fx:**381-8957
(845) 351-5453 .. **Toal,** Chas A '77 -216 Route 17 Bx778 -Tuxedo Pk 10987 **Fx:**351-5037
(212) 373-3000 .. **Toal,** Danl J '97 (Paul WRW&G LLP) -1285 Av of Amer -NY 10019
(212) 788-5533 .. **Toan,** Vivian I '74 Div of Hlth Care Access & Imprvmnt -161 William -NY 10038
(518) 434-7045 .. **Toas,** Joshua B '97 Research Fndtn SUNY -Bx9 -Albany 12201 **Fx:**935-6707
(212) 889-6800 .. **Toback,** Ann Beth '01 Workmens Circle -45 E 33rd -NY 10016 **Fx:**532-7518
(212) 869-2300 .. **Toback,** Arthur M '69 (Toback B&R,LLP) -15 W 44th -NY 10036
(212) 869-2300 .. **Toback Bernstein & Reiss,LLP** -15 W 44th -NY 10036 **Fx:**869-2303
(516) 644-1558 .. **Toback,** Jeffrey W '85 -314 VA Av -Oceanside 11572 **Fx:**608-4329
(212) 455-2000 .. **Toback,** Lia S '08 %Simpson T&B LLP -425 Lex Av -NY 10017
(212) 450-4000 .. **Tobak,** Marc J '09 %Davis P&W LLP -450 Lex Av -NY 10017
(914) 967-6500 .. **Tobak,** Mark '80 %St Vincents Hsptl -275 North -Harrison 10528
(212) 756-2000 .. **Tobar,** Nathalie A '09 %Schulte R&Z LLP -919 3rd Av -NY 10022
(716) 858-6716 .. **Tobe,** Richd M '75 %Envrnmt & Planning -95 Franklin -Buffalo 14202 **Fx:**858-7248
(716) 829-3777 .. **Tobe,** Susan Bring '75 SUNY at Buffalo -3435 Main -Buffalo 14214 **Fx:**829-3776
(212) 736-3250 .. **Toberoff,** Max '48 OfCnsl Toberoff T&S,LLP -330 7th Av -NY 10001
(212) 736-3250 .. **Toberoff Tessler & Schochet,LLP** -330 7th Av -NY 10001 **Fx:**971-9067
(631) 852-2881 .. **Tobey,** Susan S '78 %Hon E Burke -235 Griffing Av -Rvrhead 11901 **Fx:**852-2884
(718) 838-7878 .. **Tobia,** Maria S '88 %Bronx Defenders -860 Crtlandt Av -Bronx 10451 **Fx:**665-0100
(631) 582-3700 .. **Tobias,** David E '92 (Turley RR&R,LLP) -3075 Vets Mem'l Hwy -Ronkonkoma 11779
(212) 661-5460 .. **Tobias,** David G '81 (Tobias Law Firm,PC) -600 3rd Av -NY 10016 **Fx:**557-9610
(212) 759-4200 .. **Tobias,** Donald J '72 -445 Park Av -NY 10022 **Fx:**207-8727
(845) 634-2450 .. **Tobias,** Jennifer P '90 -353 Plsnt Hill Rd -New Cty 10956 **Fx:**634-2342
(845) 876-3300 .. **Tobias,** Karen '92 %M Haggerty -37 W Market -Rhinebeck 12572 **Fx:**876-3195
(212) 922-9250 .. **Tobias,** Matthew N '02 %Ganfer & S LLP -360 Lex Av -NY 10017
(631) 756-6275 .. **Tobias,** Ted M '81 -1 Huntngtn Quadrangle Bx9099 -Melvll 11747 **Fx:**756-6288
(718) 855-9000 .. **Tobias,** Wendy M '02 %Cullen and D LLP -177 Montague -Brklyn 11201
(212) 436-5479 .. **Tobin,** Allen F '99 Deloitte & Touche,LLP -2 World Fncl Ctr -NY 10281
(518) 452-2552 .. **Tobin,** Chas J III '69 OfCnsl Tobin & G,PC -678 Troy Schenectady Rd -Latham 12110
(631) 577-7770 .. **Tobin,** Deirdre J '98 %K Dodson -100 Baylis Rd -Melvll 11747 **Fx:**577-7199
(518) 463-1177 .. **Tobin & Dempf, LLP** -33 Elk -Albany 12207 **Fx:**463-7489
(212) 589-4200 .. **Tobin,** Donna Ann '87 (Baker & H LLP) -45 Rckfllr Plz -NY 10111
(212) 805-3900 .. **Tobin,** Edw M '00 %Clausen M PC -1 Chase Manh Plz -NY 10005
(518) 465-7581 .. **Tobin,** Edwin J '62 OfCnsl Herzog Law Firm,PC -7 Southwoods Blvd -Albany 12211

(518) 465-3553 .. **Tobin,** Edwin J Jr. '89 (Maynard OS&C,LLP) -6 Twr Pl -Albany 12203
(516) 542-2000 .. **Tobin,** Elsa Ann '94 %JP Joseph & Assoc -666 Old Cntry Rd -Gdn Cty 11530 **Fx:**542-2001
(212) 205-7000 .. **Tobin,** Erin K '08 %Ashurst LLP -7 Times Sq -NY 10036
(518) 452-2552 .. **Tobin & Grifferty,PC** -678 Troy Schenectady Rd -Latham 12110 **Fx:**452-0175
(212) 538-2542 .. **Tobin,** John E '96 CSFB -1 Mad Av -NY 10010
(845) 340-3315 .. **Tobin,** John F '83 %DA -285 Wall -Kingston 12401 **Fx:**340-3185
(585) 624-3311 .. **Tobin,** Michl J '66 -29 W Main -Honeoye Fls 14472 **Fx:**624-4167
(212) 576-4625 .. **Tobin,** Michl J '97 NY Life Ins -51 Mad Av -NY 10010
(212) 644-4420 .. **Tobin,** Michl P '00 %Fabiani C&H,LLP -570 Lex Av -NY 10022
(212) 319-7125 .. **Tobin,** Rita C '91 %Caplin & D -375 Park Av -NY 10152
(212) 556-7029 .. **Tobin,** Robt S '75 %The NY Times Co -620 8th Av -NY 10018
(716) 633-1807 .. **Tobin,** Thos F '85 -207 Cindy Dr Bx1793 -Williamsvll 14231
(212) 490-3000 .. **Tobin,** Thos W '81 (Wilson EME&D LLP) -150 E 42nd -NY 10017
(914) 323-7000 .. **Tobin,** Thos W '81 (Wilson EME&D LLP) -3 Gannett Dr -White Plns 10604
(212) 593-6700 .. **Tobman,** Andrew C '01 %Aaronson RF&D,LLP -757 3rd Av -NY 10017
(212) 989-6000 .. **Tobman,** Michl D '99 (Tobman Strategies) -22 W 23rd -NY 10010
(914) 948-6206 .. **Tobol,** Amy Ruth '84 %SUNY Empire State College -200 N Central Av -Hartsdale 10530
(716) 938-9111 .. **Tobolski,** Dennis V '78 (Cnty Atty) -303 Court -Little Vly 14755 **Fx:**938-2763
(212) 682-1800 .. **Tobon,** David '02 %Grant HS&K LLP -675 3rd Av -NY 10017
(212) 319-5873 .. **Toboroff,** Leonard '59 -780 3rd Av -NY 10017 **Fx:**755-5457
(212) 250-2500 .. **Toborowsky,** Brad M '99 Deutsche Bank -60 Wall -NY 10005
(631) 447-8100 .. **Tocci,** Justine E '02 %Egan & G,LLP -96 S Ocean Av -Patchogue 11772 **Fx:**447-8181
(212) 317-1717 .. **Tocci,** Valerie H '04 %Chemtob MF&T LLP -3 E 54th -NY 10022
(212) 906-1200 .. **Tochner,** Jeffrey A '94 (Latham & W) -885 3rd Av -NY 10022
(845) 628-8080 .. **Tock,** Jos J '84 -963 Route 6 -Mahopac 10541 **Fx:**628-5450
(516) 812-4500 .. **Tock,** Shawn L '08 %Stagg TC&W LLP -401 Franklin Av -Gdn Cty 11530
(518) 372-5821 .. **Tocker,** Paul H '66 -18 Jay -Schnctdy 12305 **Fx:**372-5821
(516) 433-1400 .. **Tockman,** Michl E '69 -130 Newbrdg Rd -Hicksvll 11801 **Fx:**433-6324
(716) 882-2300 .. **Todaro,** David P '88 (McCready & T) -6 N Pearl -Buffalo 14202
(516) 997-3893 .. **Todaro,** Jacquelyn '97 -11 Mellow Ln -Westbury 11590 **Fx:**908-4823
(315) 422-1152 .. **Todd,** Christopher G '03 %Costello C&F,PLLC -500 Plum -Syracuse 13204
(718) 353-5500 .. **Todd,** Christopher J '89 (Mattone MMMMM&T) -134-01 20th Av -Cllg Pnt 11356
(315) 349-3200 .. **Todd,** Donald E '83 %DA -Pub Safety Ctr -Oswego 13126 **Fx:**349-3212
(718) 463-2100 .. **Todd,** George D '94 %ABC -151-23 34th Av -Flushng 11354
(646) 855-0928 .. **Todd,** Gregory A '03 Bk of America -1 Bryant Pk -NY 10036
(212) 808-5151 .. **Todd,** Gregory F W '89 -101 Park Av -NY 10178 **Fx:**808-5155
(212) 460-3055 .. **Todd,** Guillermo E Jr. '98 Con Ed -4 Irving Pl -NY 10003
(212) 308-7400 .. **Todd,** John F '80 (Todd & L,LLP) -444 Mad Av -NY 10022
(212) 902-0857 .. **Todd,** Jos K '96 %Goldman Sachs -85 Broad -NY 10004
(646) 536-2869 .. **Todd,** Katherine M '06 Take Two Interactive -622 Bway -NY 10012
(212) 308-7400 .. **Todd & Levi,LLP** -444 Mad Av -NY 10022 **Fx:**308-8450
(718) 797-3055 .. **Todd,** Natali J H '01 NJH Todd,PC -188 Montague -Brklyn 11201 **Fx:**504-3900
(212) 922-9700 .. **Todd,** Ronald G '73 1st Amer Title -633 3rd Av -NY 10017 **Fx:**922-0881
(212) 402-9400 .. **Todd,** Wm G '77 (McKool S,PC) -1 Bryant Park -NY 10036
(212) 309-6000 .. **Toder,** Richd S '65 (Morgan L&B LLP) -101 Park Av -NY 10178
(212) 554-7800 .. **Todman,** Myka W '06 %Moses & S LLP -405 Lex Av -NY 10174
(212) 496-1969 .. **Todman,** Terence A Jr. '79 -171 W 71st -NY 10023 **Fx:**496-1969
(716) 854-1111 .. **Todoro,** Jos C '09 %Spadafora & V -2 Symphony Cir -Buffalo 14201
(716) 633-0374 .. **Todoro,** Peter J Jr. '93 (Taheri & T,PC) -388 Evans -Buffalo 14221
(716) 649-4623 .. **Todoro,** Phyllis M '93 %Attea & A -7202 Bstn State Rd Bx120 -N Boston 14110 **Fx:**649-2951
(212) 599-7900 .. **Todorovich,** John B '79 -60 E 42nd -NY 10165 **Fx:**599-7902
(212) 855-0480 .. **Todorovich,** Serge '03 Goldman Sachs -1 NY Plz -NY 10004
(212) 819-8200 .. **Todres,** Debra L '95 White & C LLP -1155 Av of Amer -NY 10036
(718) 990-6627 .. **Todres,** Jacob L '73 %St John's Law Schl -8000 Utopia Pkwy -Jamaica 11439 **Fx:**591-1855
(212) 998-6550 .. **Todres,** Jonathan '01 %NYU Law Schl -245 Sullivan -NY 10012
(212) 455-2000 .. **Todrys,** Steven C '80 (Simpson T&B LLP) -425 Lex Av -NY 10017
(212) 754-9400 .. **Todtman,** Martin '68 (Todtman NS&J,PC) -425 Park Av -NY 10022
(212) 754-9400 .. **Todtman Nachamie Spizz & Johns,PC** -425 Park Av -NY 10022 **Fx:**754-6262
(516) 204-4775 .. **Toell,** Damin J '04 (DJ Toell,PC) -Bx245112 -Brklyn 11224 **Fx:**394-0855
(212) 216-8000 .. **Toevs,** Tara T '05 %Tarter K&D LLP -1350 Bway -NY 10018
(212) 788-0928 .. **Toews,** Mark G '07 %Law Dept -350 Jay -Brklyn 11201 **Fx:**(718) 222-2088
(914) 723-4300 .. **Tofano,** Rosemarie '91 (Lackenbach S LLP) -1 Chase Rd -Scarsdale 10583
(212) 752-0007 .. **Tofel,** Lawr E '85 (Tofel & Prtnrs,LLP) -730 3rd Av -NY 10017 **Fx:**752-8881
(917) 512-0250 .. **Tofel,** Richd J '84 ProPublica -55 Bway -NY 10006
(212) 752-0007 .. **Tofel,** Robt L '57 (Tofel & Prtnrs,LLP) -730 3rd Av -NY 10017 **Fx:**752-8881
(212) 258-8780 .. **Toffler,** Van E '85 %MTV Networks -1515 Bway -NY 10036 **Fx:**258-8358
(212) 553-7436 .. **Toft,** Adam B '90 %Moody's Invstr Srvc -250 Greenwich -NY 10007
(631) 444-5605 .. **Toga,** Linda M '99 LM Toga,PC -175 Main -E Setauket 11733 **Fx:**444-5607
(845) 429-5607 .. **Tognino,** Michl A '97 (Tognino & G,LLP) -50 Route 9W -Stony Pnt 10980 **Fx:**429-2576
(212) 594-5000 .. **Togut,** Albert '75 (Togut S&S LLP) -1 Penn Plz -NY 10119
(212) 594-5000 .. **Togut Segal & Segal LLP** -1 Penn Plz -NY 10119 **Fx:**967-4258
(516) 739-0000 .. **Toher,** Frank P '82 (Martyn T&M) -330 Old Cntry Rd -Mineola 11501
(631) 727-8383 .. **Tohill,** Anthony B '71 AB Tohill,PC -12 1st Bx1330 -Rvrhead 11901 **Fx:**727-6336
(315) 342-2191 .. **Tohtz,** James E '94 %Leg Srvcs -108 W Brdg -Oswego 13126 **Fx:**342-1891
(516) 681-3453 .. **Tokarski,** Susan M '86 (Sarandis & T) -4 Tudor Rd -Hicksvll 11801 **Fx:**681-3453
(516) 571-3001 .. **Tokarski,** Susan M '86 %Cnty Atty -1 West -Mineola 11501 **Fx:**571-6684
(845) 463-0416 .. **Tokarz,** Mary R '91 -20 Winnie Ln -Poughkeepsie 12603
(212) 695-5250 .. **Tokayer,** Ira D '85 -405 Lex Av -NY 10174 **Fx:**695-5450
(212) 849-7000 .. **Toker,** Anne S '92 OfCnsl Quinn EU&S,LLP -51 Mad Av -NY 10010
(212) 612-4200 .. **Toker,** H Leonard '77 (Hoey KT&E) -55 Water -NY 10041
(212) 450-0100 .. **Toki,** Kaoru '01 Marubeni America -375 Lex Av -NY 10017 **Fx:**450-0706
(585) 383-8521 .. **Tokoli,** John F '81 -27 Winding Rd -Rchstr 14618
(718) 913-6890 .. **Toksoy,** Meryem '05 (Toksoy & T PC) -15801 Crossbay Blvd -Howard Bch 11414
(631) 539-0375 .. **Tola,** Keith V '04 %Cruser M&N,LLP -175 Pinelawn Rd -Melvll 11747
(212) 698-3500 .. **Tolan,** James E '62 OfCnsl Dechert LLP -1095 Av of Amer -NY 10036
(212) 269-0927 .. **Tolan,** James E '94 (D'Amato & L,LLP) -2 World Fncl Ctr -NY 10281
(212) 906-1200 .. **Tolan,** Laura E '09 %Latham & W -885 3rd Av -NY 10022
(212) 227-2780 .. **Tolchin,** David W '99 %Jaroslawicz & J -225 Bway -NY 10007
(212) 504-6000 .. **Tolchin,** Marc A '96 %Cadwalader W&T LLP -1 World Fncl Ctr -NY 10281
(914) 725-7770 .. **Tolchin,** Richd '56 -75 Hmptn Rd -Scarsdale 10583
(212) 227-2181 .. **Tolchin,** Robt J '93 -225 Bway -NY 10007
(212) 721-1093 .. **Tolchinsky,** Gary S '89 -185 West End Av -NY 10023
(718) 858-5915 .. **Tolciss,** A Neil '80 -230 Jay -Brklyn 11201 **Fx:**403-9668
(718) 260-4592 .. **Toledo,** Amelia E '03 Hon L Bloom -225 Cadman Plz E -Brklyn 11201
(516) 741-2585 .. **Toleno,** Jessica A '09 Rosicki R & Assoc,PC -51 E Bethpage Rd -Plainvw 11803 **Fx:**741-4748
(631) 269-1508 .. **Tolentino,** Francis N '91 -9 Blackgum Ln -Kings Pk 11754
(212) 391-9090 .. **Tolentino,** Manolo E '80 -43 W 46th -NY 10036
(212) 617-3357 .. **Tolentino,** Tina V '06 Bloomberg LP -731 Lex Av -NY 10022
(212) 857-8230 .. **Toler,** Edw '80 %Baker MM&M,PC -330 W 34th -NY 10001
(631) 588-5000 .. **Toler,** Sara A '84 %AN Guzzone & Assoc,PC -2450 Middle Cntry Rd -Centereach 11720 **Fx:**588-5001
(212) 918-3000 .. **Tolin,** Jeffrey J '97 (Hogan L LLP) -875 3rd Av -NY 10022
(212) 421-1965 .. **Tolins & Lowenfels** -747 3rd Av -NY 10017 **Fx:**888-7706
(212) 421-1965 .. **Tolins,** Roger A '59 (Tolins & L) -747 3rd Av -NY 10017
(631) 845-8000 .. **Tolkin,** Jeffrey D '82 %Travel Impressions -465 Smith -Farmngdl 11735 **Fx:**845-4745
(212) 951-6564 .. **Tolkoff,** Andrew B '77 %NYS Ed Dept-OLS -475 Park Av S -NY 10016 **Fx:**951-6573
(516) 364-6489 .. **Tolkoff,** Rochelle D '78 -179 The Vale -Syosset 11791
(212) 490-4100 .. **Toll,** Elizabeth M '74 Cnsl Storch A&M,PC -140 E 45th -NY 10017
(212) 250-8181 .. **Toll,** Michelle L '96 %Deutsche Bank -60 Wall -NY 10005
(914) 323-7000 .. **Tolle,** Leanne S '90 OfCnsl Wilson EME&D LLP -3 Gannett Dr -White Plns 10604
(516) 357-3000 .. **Tolle,** Norman L '73 (Rivkin R LLP) -926 RXR Plz -Uniondale 11556
(718) 263-0522 .. **Tolle,** Robt M '78 -118-21 Qns Blvd -Frst Hlls 11375
(212) 720-4267 .. **Tolles,** Denise D '79 Foot Locker Inc -112 W 34th -NY 10120
(212) 309-1000 .. **Tolley,** B Cary III '88 (Hunton & W) -200 Park Av -NY 10166
(212) 455-2000 .. **Tolley,** Edw P III '91 (Simpson T&B LLP) -425 Lex Av -NY 10017
(212) 963-8783 .. **Tolley,** Joyce L '83 UN -1 UN Plz -NY 10017
(212) 455-2000 .. **Tollin,** Bryan A '07 %Simpson T&B LLP -425 Lex Av -NY 10017
(516) 569-2550 .. **Tollin,** Howard M '89 Breitstone & Co Ltd -534 Willow Av -Cedarhrst 11516 **Fx:**569-2016
(212) 846-6758 .. **Tollinche,** Evelyn M '05 %MTV Networks -1515 Bway -NY 10036 **Fx:**258-8358
(212) 458-7051 .. **Tollis,** Salvatore '01 American Intl Co -175 Water -NY 10038
(212) 403-6700 .. **Tollis,** Vanessa E '01 %Gide LN LLP -120 W 45th -NY 10036
(518) 664-2951 .. **Tollisen,** Kevin J '98 (Carola B&T,PLLC) -215 Park Av -Mechanicvll 12118 **Fx:**664-1150
(212) 252-9050 .. **Tolmach,** David M '64 OfCnsl Kreitzman M&B -100 Wall -NY 10005
(212) 964-1390 .. **Tolmage Peskin Harris & Falick** -20 Vesey -NY 10007 **Fx:**608-4959
(212) 682-8222 .. **Tolman,** Jordan D '05 (Tolman S LLP) -355 Lex Av -NY 10017
(212) 949-8770 .. **Tolman,** Steven I '77 (Levy T&C,LLP) -630 3rd Av -NY 10017
(212) 350-2646 .. **Tolpin,** Jonathan S '93 M&T Bank -350 Park Av -NY 10022 **Fx:**350-2065
(212) 373-3000 .. **Tolston,** Alex J '10 %Paul WRW&G LLP -1285 Av of Amer -NY 10019
(212) 349-2727 .. **Tolud,** John E '98 (Targum B&T,LLP) -233 Bway -NY 10279 **Fx:**672-0094
(212) 754-9400 .. **Tolz,** Robt D '76 (Todtman NS&J,PC) -425 Park Av -NY 10022
(212) 765-5070 .. **Tom,** Christopher D '08 Fish & R,PC -153 E 53rd -NY 10022
(212) 962-2877 .. **Tom,** Jason M '03 %M Friedlander -15 Maiden Ln -NY 10038 **Fx:**571-4613
(212) 336-2000 .. **Tom,** Jean L '03 %Patterson BW&T LLP -1133 Av of Amer -NY 10036
(212) 867-6000 .. **Tom,** Jean S '04 %Rosenberg & E,PC -733 3rd Av -NY 10017
(212) 735-3000 .. **Tom,** Joshua F '09 %Skadden ASM&F LLP -4 Times Sq -NY 10036
(212) 626-4100 .. **Tom,** Roslyn '91 (Baker & M LLP) -1114 Av of Amer -NY 10036
(585) 530-3180 .. **Tomaino,** Andrea E '89 %Atty Grievance Comm -50 East Av -Rchstr 14604 **Fx:**530-3191
(585) 325-8000 .. **Tomaino,** Michl T '62 SrCnsl Wolford Law LLP -16 E Main -Rchstr 14614 **Fx:**325-8009
(212) 558-4000 .. **Tomaino,** Michl T Jr. '90 (Sullivan & C LLP) -125 Broad -NY 10004
(716) 823-7189 .. **Tomaka,** D Donnalee '94 -701 Ridge Rd -Lackawanna 14218 **Fx:**662-7048
(518) 439-1007 .. **Tomakin,** Marco F G '06 -381 Delaware Av -Delmar 12054
(845) 265-9231 .. **Tomann,** Stephen G '86 -1705 Route 9D -Cold Spg 10516 **Fx:**265-9232
(516) 747-0400 .. **Tomao,** Jos L Jr. '84 (Tomao & M) -1225 Franklin Av -Gdn Cty 11530 **Fx:**248-8693
(516) 877-7015 .. **Tomao,** Peter J '77 -226 7th -Gdn Cty 11530 **Fx:**877-7021

(212) 986-6000 .. **Tomao,** Sharon M '97 (Kleinberg KW&C,PC) -551 5th Av -NY 10176
(212) 416-8553 .. **Tomari,** Anthony J '90 %Dept of Law -120 Bway -NY 10271
(631) 852-2500 .. **Tomaro,** Elena Luminita '94 %DA -200 Center Dr -Rvrhead 11901 **Fx:**852-1769
(212) 363-1380 .. **Tomasella,** Louis C '97 OfCnsl Herten BSCBL&H,LLC -747 3rd Av -NY 10017
(212) 644-6006 .. **Tomaselli,** Chas M '67 (Dickerson T&M) -600 Mad Av -NY 10022
(845) 735-4045 .. **Tomaselli,** Eugene A '53 -151 Fairvw Av -Pearl Rvr 10965 **Fx:**735-4045
(212) 262-0022 .. **Tomaselli,** John J '85 (Tomaselli & Co) -67 Wall -NY 10005 **Fx:**214-0318
(518) 689-2280 .. **Tomaselli,** Patrick J '77 -Bx97 -Poestenkill 12140 **Fx:**689-2280
(646) 414-6926 .. **Tomaselli,** Traci M '00 Cnsl Lowenstein S PC -1251 Av of Amer -NY 10020 **Fx:**(973) 422-6867
(212) 415-6684 .. **Tomasetti,** Nicholas R '05 Springbok Capital Mgmt -405 Park Av -NY 10022
(212) 799-9638 .. **Tomasini-Joshi,** Denise M '00 Columbia Univ-Tenant Asst Proj -647 Columbus Av -NY 10025
(914) 846-7000 .. **Tomasino,** Justin D '97 NY Life Ins -1 Rockwood Rd -Sleepy Hollow 10591 **Fx:**846-4755
(516) 328-1188 .. **Tomasone,** Fredk S '61 (Muscarella & T) -1040 Hempstd Tpk -Franklin Sq 11010
(585) 654-8924 .. **Tomasso,** Ellen Anderson '80 -141 Yarmouth Rd -Rchstr 14610
(212) 553-3200 .. **Tomaszewski,** John G '84 (Marulli LE&T,LLP) -5 Hanover Sq -NY 10004
(212) 382-6600 .. **Tomatore,** Suzanne M '01 %NYC Bar -42 W 44th -NY 10036 **Fx:**398-6634
(212) 735-3000 .. **Tomazos,** Anastasios '02 %Skadden ASM&F LLP -4 Times Sq -NY 10036
(212) 530-5000 .. **Tomback,** Andrew E '87 (Milbank TH&M LLP) -1 Chase Manh Plz -NY 10005
(914) 723-5678 .. **Tomback,** Peter A '59 -37 Church Ln -Scarsdale 10583 **Fx:**723-0753
(914) 592-3400 .. **Tombini,** Michele Mastandrea '86 (Pappalardo T&W LLP) -500 Mamaroneck Av -Harrison 10528
(212) 709-1642 .. **Tomczak,** Christine M '99 NYS Banking Dept -1 State -NY 10004
(212) 309-6000 .. **Tomczyk,** Anna '09 %Morgan L&B LLP -101 Park Av -NY 10178
(212) 233-9110 .. **Tomei,** Gary A '61 -20 Vesey -NY 10007 **Fx:**732-4545
(718) 815-0700 .. **Tomei,** Jeffrey E '88 Tomei & Assoc,PC -136 Bay -Staten Isl 10301 **Fx:**815-1872
(718) 448-7808 .. **Tomei,** Kimberly A '02 -136 Bay -Staten Isl 10301
(212) 474-1000 .. **Tomer,** Jasse S '07 %Cravath S&M LLP -825 8th Av -NY 10019
(212) 813-8800 .. **Tomer,** Kenneth Brent '06 %Goodwin P LLP -620 8th Av -NY 10018
(716) 373-0004 .. **Tomes,** Heather A '05 Pub Def -175 N Union -Olean 14760 **Fx:**373-3462
(516) 496-5822 .. **Tomforde,** Michl '07 %T Spina -170 Froehlich Farm Blvd -Woodbury 11797 **Fx:**496-5420
(212) 839-5300 .. **Tomiak,** Adam M '07 %Sidley A LLP -787 7th Av -NY 10019
(516) 228-8484 .. **Tomic,** Jaksha C '00 %Dilworth & B,LLP -1000 Woodbury Rd -Woodbury 11797
(516) 794-3500 .. **Tomich,** Philip L '75 (Brunetti A&T,PLLC) -170 Old Cntry Rd -Mineola 11501 **Fx:**794-3696
(212) 599-1001 .. **Tomkiel,** Matthew P '03 (Tomkiel & T) -60 E 42nd -NY 10165 **Fx:**599-1009
(212) 421-4100 .. **Tomkiel,** Melissa M '07 %Pryor C LLP -7 Times Sq -NY 10036
(212) 599-1001 .. **Tomkiel,** Stanley A Jr. '53 -60 E 42nd -NY 10165 **Fx:**599-1009
(212) 599-1001 .. **Tomkiel,** Stanley A III '79 (Tomkiel & T) -60 E 42nd -NY 10165 **Fx:**599-1009
(212) 373-3000 .. **Tomkins,** Judith W '10 %Paul WRW&G LLP -1285 Av of Amer -NY 10019
(607) 722-5840 .. **Tomkins,** Paul F '04 -57 Front -Bnghmtn 13905
(716) 645-2167 .. **Tomkins,** Suzanne E '93 -2342 Stony Pnt Rd -Grand Isl 14072 **Fx:**645-2900
(518) 474-6740 .. **Tomko,** Elisha S '02 Dept of State -41 State -Albany 12231 **Fx:**473-9211
(607) 723-5341 .. **Tomko,** Kenneth F '85 (Hinman H&K,LLP) -80 Exchange Bx5250 -Bnghmtn 13902
(518) 452-0802 .. **Tomko,** Sean A '02 %Taylor & Assoc -1 Columbia Cir -Albany 12203 **Fx:**452-1863
(212) 621-1796 .. **Tomlin,** David H '02 Associated Press -50 Rckfllr Plz -NY 10020
(845) 473-2555 .. **Tomlins,** Ronald R '87 -310 Mill -Poughkeepsie 12601 **Fx:**473-2633
(516) 625-9800 .. **Tomlinson,** Allison B '05 DY Consultants -1 Expwy Plz -Roslyn Hts 11577
(212) 790-9200 .. **Tomlinson,** Jill K '06 %Cowan L&L,PC -1133 Av of Amer -NY 10036
(212) 543-7726 .. **Tomlinson,** Krystina '04 Intralinks,Inc -150 E 42nd -NY 10017
(212) 336-2000 .. **Tomlinson,** Peter W '95 (Patterson BW&T LLP) -1133 Av of Amer -NY 10036
(212) 446-4800 .. **Tomlinson,** Stephen G '03 (Kirkland & E LLP) -153 E 53rd -NY 10022
(716) 882-5905 .. **Tommaney,** Elizabeth M '95 %Osmose Inc -980 Ellicott -Buffalo 14209
(518) 473-4217 .. **Tommaney,** Mary Anne '77 %State Comptroller -110 State -Albany 12236 **Fx:**473-9104
(518) 782-2511 .. **Tommaney,** Michl J '71 -1568 Central Av -Albany 12205 **Fx:**220-1444
(718) 261-1200 .. **Tommaso,** Peter E '66 -123-60 83rd Av -Kew Gdns 11415 **Fx:**261-2376
(718) 875-1300 .. **Tommer,** Karen E '87 %Appllt Div 2nd Dept -45 Monroe Pl -Brklyn 11201 **Fx:**858-2446
(716) 856-4000 .. **Tomovic,** Patrick M '90 (Hodgson R LLP) -140 Pearl -Buffalo 14202
(585) 344-2600 .. **Tompkins,** Allen C '90 %Tompkins Metal Finishing -6 Apollo Dr -Batavia 14020
(212) 962-5363 .. **Tompkins,** Christopher P '94 -225 Bway -NY 10007
(212) 944-6611 .. **Tompkins & Davidson,LLP** -5 Hanover Sq -NY 10004 **Fx:**944-9779
(516) 747-4301 .. **Tompkins,** Eva J '98 %Torino & B,PC -200 Old Cntry Rd -Mineola 11501
(212) 490-3000 .. **Tompkins,** George N Jr. '56 OfCnsl Wilson EME&D LLP -150 E 42nd -NY 10017
(212) 490-3000 .. **Tompkins,** George N III '86 (Wilson EME&D LLP) -150 E 42nd -NY 10017
(631) 324-3200 .. **Tompkins,** James R '60 -Bx899 -Sag Hbr 11963 **Fx:**725-8760
(845) 497-7265 .. **Tompkins,** Jeanne M '04 -11 E Main -Washingtnvll 10992 **Fx:**496-2882
(315) 266-4500 .. **Tompkins,** Jeffery G '93 Hon J Shkane - Family Ct -301 W Dominick -Rome 13440
(212) 848-4000 .. **Tompkins,** Jonathan J '09 %Shearman & S LLP -599 Lex Av -NY 10022
(718) 590-2000 .. **Tompkins,** Lisa '89 %DA -198 E 161st -Bronx 10451 **Fx:**590-6477
(212) 714-1720 .. **Tompkins McGuire Wachenfeld & Barry LLP** -140 Bway -NY 10005 **Fx:**785-3689
(212) 909-6000 .. **Tompkins,** Nicholas C '10 %Debevoise & P LLP -919 3rd Av -NY 10022
(518) 457-2070 .. **Tompkins,** Robt J '79 %Dept of Tax & Fin -Bldg 9 State Campus -Albany 12227 **Fx:**457-6131
(212) 428-2690 .. **Tompkins,** Sarah Dean '95 %OCA -25 Beaver -NY 10004 **Fx:**428-2819
(516) 488-3452 .. **Tompkins-Smith,** Isabel '93 %J Klein -276 Jericho Tpk Bx215 -Floral Pk 11002 **Fx:**437-9535
(585) 419-8800 .. **Tompsett,** Kevin W '01 (Harris B PLLC) -99 Garnsey Rd -Pittsfrd 14534
(212) 832-2700 .. **Toms,** Nicholas R H '82 %Edwardstone & Co Inc -154 Waverly Pl -NY 10014 **Fx:**832-3151
(212) 732-9000 .. **Tomsky,** John M '79 OfCnsl Sullivan PBM&C PC -120 Bway -NY 10271
(718) 286-6000 .. **Tomsky,** Michl E '08 %DA -125-01 Qns Blvd -Kew Gdns 11415
(212) 723-5707 .. **Tomson,** Danl C '93 Citigroup -390 Greenwich -NY 10013
(845) 469-4900 .. **Tomson,** Elizabeth C '82 %Greenwald Law Ofc -99 Brookside Av -Chester 10918 **Fx:**469-2022
(866) 866-2345 .. **Tona,** Thos '94 -872 Middle Cntry Rd St James 11780 **Fx:**(516) 224-7008
(212) 286-1666 .. **Tonachel & Lewis,PC** -276 5th Av -NY 10001 **Fx:**286-1616
(212) 509-2500 .. **Tonachio,** Nancy A '94 (Meyers M&T) -5 Hanover Sq -NY 10004 **Fx:**509-2424
(212) 761-1052 .. **Tonckens,** Jacob L '88 Morgan Stanley -1585 Bway -NY 10036
(212) 238-4800 .. **Tondel,** Kathryn C '07 %Landman CB&F,PC -120 Bway -NY 10271
(212) 839-5300 .. **Tondel,** Lawr C '72 (Sidley A LLP) -787 7th Av -NY 10019
(631) 261-8834 .. **Tondo,** Carrie-Ann '03 %Ingerman S LLP -150 Motor Pkwy -Hauppauge 11788
(212) 272-1842 .. **Tonelli,** John H '92 JP Morgan Chase -383 Mad Av -NY 10179
(212) 742-9700 .. **Toner,** Diane K '07 %Godosky & G,PC -61 Bway -NY 10006
(917) 778-6600 .. **Toner,** James E '86 %J Toomey -485 Lex Av -NY 10017 **Fx:**778-7048
(516) 294-1133 .. **Toner,** James E '93 -114 Old Cntry Rd -Mineola 11501
(212) 820-6227 .. **Toner,** Kathleen M '90 LaBranche & Co,Inc -33 Whitehall -NY 10004
(646) 557-5100 .. **Toner,** Kevin J '87 (Patton B LLP) -1185 Av of Amer -NY 10036
(631) 665-3636 .. **Toner,** Mary A '89 (Toner & T) -6 Niagara -Bay Shr 11706 **Fx:**665-3667
(518) 449-0044 .. **Toner,** Meghan Quigley '06 %Hoffman W&D LLC -75 State -Albany 12207 **Fx:**449-0047
(631) 755-0101 .. **Toner,** Patrick G '98 %Lewis JAA,LLP -425 Broad Hollow Rd -Melvll 11747
(212) 482-0001 .. **Toner,** Stephen B '86 (Russo K&T LLP) -33 Whitehall -NY 10004
(212) 318-3000 .. **Tonery,** Lisa M '01 (Fulbright & J LLP) -666 5th Av -NY 10103
(585) 399-7090 .. **Tones,** Jason R '06 Tones Law Firm,PLLC -155 Clinton Sq -Rchstr 14604 **Fx:**486-1772
(212) 801-6756 .. **Tonetti,** Gino G '07 %Greenberg T,LLP -200 Park Av -NY 10166
(631) 724-4233 .. **Tonetti,** Jos C '79 (Tonetti & A) -548 W Jericho Tpk -Smithtwn 11787 **Fx:**724-4776
(212) 756-2000 .. **Tong,** Brian C '08 %Schulte R&Z LLP -919 3rd Av -NY 10022
(212) 318-6000 .. **Tong,** Margaret '09 %Paul HJ&W LLP -75 E 55th -NY 10022
(212) 732-9000 .. **Tong,** Wendell Yuki '02 %Sullivan PBM&C PC -120 Bway -NY 10271
(212) 490-3000 .. **Tonorezos,** Ernest Anastasios '02 %Wilson EME&D LLP -150 E 42nd -NY 10017
(732) 855-6199 .. **Tonrey,** James E Jr. '95 Cnsl Wilentz G&S -110 William -NY 10038 **Fx:**726-6561
(518) 408-3976 .. **Tooher,** Meave M '86 %NYS Comm Pub Integrity -540 Bway -Albany 12207
(518) 584-1500 .. **Toohey,** Michl J '76 (Snyder KTC&C,LLP) -160 West Av Bx4367 -Saratoga Spgs 12866
(516) 536-6860 .. **Toohey,** Wm T '01 (W Toohey,PC) -2911 Fortesque Av -Oceanside 11572 **Fx:**764-0972
(212) 785-2929 .. **Toolan,** Michl J '70 (Conway FC&K,PC) -48 Wall -NY 10005
(315) 789-4618 .. **Toole,** Elisabeth A '90 Toole & T -4067 W Lake Rd -Geneva 14456 **Fx:**789-1938
(516) 747-0300 .. **Toole,** Kevin R '85 %Meltzer LG&B,LLP -190 Willis Av -Mineola 11501
(845) 291-2650 .. **Toole,** Stephen '86 %Cnty Atty -285 Main -Goshen 10924 **Fx:**291-3014
(212) 698-3500 .. **Tooley,** Ryan C '07 %Dechert LLP -1095 Av of Amer -NY 10036
(518) 688-2846 .. **Toombs,** Kathleen M '99 (Toombs & M,PLLC) -157 Barrett -Schnctdy 12305 **Fx:**688-2849
(212) 260-5027 .. **Toombs,** Nancy '89 -5 Peter Cooper Rd -NY 10010
(212) 984-8500 .. **Toomey,** David J '94 Gerson Lehrman Grp -850 3rd Av -NY 10022
(917) 778-6600 .. **Toomey,** James J Jr. '80 -485 Lex Av -NY 10017 **Fx:**778-7048
(212) 351-4000 .. **Toomey,** Melissa Torres '06 %Gibson D&C LLP -200 Park Av -NY 10166
(518) 743-9000 .. **Toomey,** Michl J '86 (Toomey & G) -1 South Wstrn Plz Bx2144 -Glens Fls 12801 **Fx:**743-9023
(212) 225-2000 .. **Toomey,** Neal E '10 %Cleary GS&H -1 Lbrty Plz -NY 10006
(518) 285-8799 .. **Toomey,** Paul G '90 OCA Judicial Inst -187 Wolf Rd -Albany 12205 **Fx:**438-3518
(212) 720-5026 .. **Toomey,** Robt B '88 %Fed Reserve Bk -33 Lbrty -NY 10045 **Fx:**785-5748
(516) 358-5690 .. **Toomey,** Vincent '86 -3000 Marcus Av -Lk Success 11042 **Fx:**775-0237
(518) 434-1197 .. **Toomey,** Wm A Jr. '55 -121 State -Albany 12207 **Fx:**434-0224
(518) 434-1197 .. **Toomey,** Wm A III '94 -121 State -Albany 12207
(212) 647-8100 .. **Toorock,** Michl S '68 (Toorock & R) -20 W 20th -NY 10011
(212) 647-8100 .. **Toorock & Rosen** -20 W 20th -NY 10011 **Fx:**647-8103

(914) 476-0600 .. **Toosie,** Maryam C '87 %Smith B&J,LLP -733 Ynkrs Av -Ynkrs 10704
(212) 916-2130 .. **Toothaker,** Thos R '71 UBS AG -101 Park Av -NY 10178
(212) 563-4300 .. **Topal,** Jack '53 (Topal & T) -225 W 34th -NY 10122
(212) 563-4300 .. **Topal,** Steven L '87 (Topal & T) -225 W 34th -NY 10122
(212) 918-3000 .. **Topaz,** Howard M '81 (Hogan L LLP) -875 3rd Av -NY 10022
(845) 732-8842 .. **Topazio,** Elizabeth A '96 %Active Media Srvcs -1 Blue Hill Plz -Pearl Rvr 10965 **Fx:**735-2342
(212) 351-4500 .. **Topel,** Eric B '04 %Epstein B&G,PC -250 Park Av -NY 10177
(212) 354-0498 .. **Topelsohn,** Lauren '92 -575 Mad Av -NY 10022 **Fx:**(866) 482-3171
(212) 277-6500 .. **Topic,** Courtney E '08 %Dickstein S LLP -1633 Bway -NY 10019
(212) 240-9077 .. **Topiel,** Abraham '85 -20 Vesey -NY 10007 **Fx:**619-6701
(718) 251-3333 .. **Topiel,** Fred N '82 -760 E 84th -Brklyn 11236 **Fx:**251-3833
(212) 986-6840 .. **Topiel,** Michl S '02 %N Brickman -317 Mad Av -NY 10017 **Fx:**986-7691
(646) 367-2020 .. **Topkins,** Keri B '03 Oberon Media Inc -1 World Fncl Ctr -NY 10281
(212) 373-3000 .. **Topkis,** Jay '49 OfCnsl Paul WRW&G LLP -1285 Av of Amer -NY 10019
(212) 480-7609 .. **Topman,** Bruce '67 Ins Dept -25 Beaver -NY 10004
(914) 682-6300 .. **Topman,** Jason S '99 -140 Grand -White Plns 10601
(212) 818-1110 .. **Topol,** Robin Levitt '80 OfCnsl Butzel L,PC -380 Mad Av -NY 10017
(212) 670-0135 .. **Topolosky,** Lindsay H '03 Merrill Lynch -222 Bway -NY 10038
(518) 437-8054 .. **Topolski,** Elissa R '98 %State Ins Fund -15 Computer Dr W -Albany 12205 **Fx:**485-8761
(212) 259-6233 .. **Topolski,** Jos P '96 (Dewey & L LLP) -1301 Av of Amer -NY 10019
(716) 674-4560 .. **Topp,** Joyce M '60 -5516 Seneca -W Seneca 14224
(212) 698-3500 .. **Topp,** Robt W '01 %Dechert LLP -1095 Av of Amer -NY 10036
(212) 980-0120 .. **Topper,** Bernard C Jr. '71 Cnsl Frankfurt KK&S,PC -488 Mad Av -NY 10022
(516) 889-6677 .. **Topper,** Brian '88 -84 E Park Av -Long Bch 11561 **Fx:**889-1703
(212) 619-5576 .. **Topper,** Elliot F '63 -225 Bway -NY 10007 **Fx:**406-3548
(212) 790-4500 .. **Topper,** Prana A '03 %Manatt P&P,LLP -7 Times Sq -NY 10036
(631) 423-5050 .. **Topper,** Robt '64 (R Topper,PC) -39 Fleets Cove Rd -Huntngtn 11743 **Fx:**423-5339
(516) 889-6677 .. **Topper,** Sharon '91 %Topper Realty -84 E Park Av -Long Bch 11561 **Fx:**889-1703
(518) 372-5401 .. **Toppeta,** Rita '47 Toppeta & T -1570 State -Schnctdy 12304
(212) 578-1030 .. **Toppeta,** Wm J '74 MetLife -1095 Av of Amer -NY 10036
(212) 819-8200 .. **Toppin,** Carlisle '99 %White & C LLP -1155 Av of Amer -NY 10036
(718) 740-7000 .. **Toppin,** Michelle C '94 -223-05 Hempstd Av -Qns Vllg 11429
(914) 323-7000 .. **Topping,** Joanna M '94 (Wilson EME&D LLP) -3 Gannett Dr -White Plns 10604
(212) 644-4420 .. **Toppo,** Christopher R '87 (Fabiani C&H,LLP) -570 Lex Av -NY 10022
(212) 699-8930 .. **Toptani,** Edw G '88 -127 E 59th -NY 10022 **Fx:**699-8939
(212) 536-3900 .. **Tor,** Loly Garcia '05 %K&L Gates LLP -599 Lex Av -NY 10022
(646) 808-0678 .. **Toraya,** Adam W '97 -1133 Bway -NY 10010 **Fx:**(866) 234-1798
(212) 554-0400 .. **Toraya,** David R '87 (Grubman I&S,PC) -152 W 57th -NY 10019
(516) 365-3890 .. **Torborg,** Gregory S '94 Columbia Sports Grp -22 Bayview Av -Manhsst 11030 **Fx:**365-3891
(716) 884-2000 .. **Torcello,** Michl L '00 %Doran & M -1234 Delaware Av -Buffalo 14209
(716) 854-4300 .. **Torcello,** Trevor M '08 %Gross SB&G,PC -465 Main -Buffalo 14203
(516) 678-1901 .. **Torchen,** Peter A '85 -113 Greystone Rd -Rockvll Ctr 11570
(213) 892-2105 .. **Torchia,** Claire E '06 %Chadbourne & P LLP -30 Rckfllr Plz -NY 10112 **Fx:**622-9865
(212) 310-8000 .. **Torchia,** Paul E '01 %Weil G&M LLP -767 5th Av -NY 10153
(212) 558-4000 .. **Torchiana,** Wm D '88 (Sullivan & C LLP) -125 Broad -NY 10004
(212) 856-9600 .. **Torchin,** Ariana J '07 %Morvillo AGIA&B,PC -565 5th Av -NY 10017
(718) 545-1433 .. **Torchin,** Jacqueline G '90 -37-08 28th Av -Astoria 11103
(212) 752-6977 .. **Torchio,** Danl S '88 -880 3rd Av -NY 10022 **Fx:**675-2237
(516) 355-9600 .. **Torczyner,** Neil S '96 %Friedman HK&P -3000 Marcus Av -Lk Success 11042
(212) 574-1200 .. **Tordesillas,** Angela C M '07 %Seward & K LLP -1 Bttry Pk Plz -NY 10004
(212) 838-7797 .. **Torell,** Catherine A '91 OfCnsl Cohen MS&T,PLLC -88 Pine -NY 10005
(518) 487-5460 .. **Torelli,** Christopher J '07 %DA -6 Lodge -Albany 12207 **Fx:**487-5093
(518) 449-0044 .. **Torelli,** Jayme M '08 %Hoffman W&D LLC -75 State -Albany 12207 **Fx:**449-0047
(212) 949-9022 .. **Toren,** David '60 OfCnsl Abelman F&S -666 3rd Av -NY 10017
(212) 506-1700 .. **Toren,** Peter J '88 (Kasowitz BT&F LLP) -1633 Bway -NY 10019
(917) 551-1300 .. **Torgalkar,** Manali S '09 %Koehler & I LLP -61 Bway -NY 10006
(212) 232-2500 .. **Torgan & Cooper,PC** -17 State -NY 10004 **Fx:**232-2509
(212) 232-2500 .. **Torgan,** Evan E '83 (Torgan & C,PC) -17 State -NY 10004
(212) 488-1598 .. **Torgerson,** Shanna R '06 %Havkins RR&V,LLP -11 Penn Plz -NY 10001
(212) 513-3200 .. **Toriello,** John M '78 (Holland & K LLP) -31 W 52nd -NY 10019
(516) 747-4301 .. **Torino & Bernstein,PC** -200 Old Cntry Rd -Mineola 11501 **Fx:**747-5956
(516) 747-4301 .. **Torino,** Bruce A '78 (Torino & B,PC) -200 Old Cntry Rd -Mineola 11501
(718) 260-2400 .. **Toritto,** James J '06 Hon V Pohorelsky -225 Cadman Plz E -Brklyn 11201
(914) 640-3622 .. **Torkelsen,** Steven M '02 Starwood Htls & Rsrts Wrldwide -1111 Wstchstr Av -White Plns 10604
(212) 375-2059 .. **Torkelson,** Eric J '96 ACA Capital Holdings -140 Bway -NY 10005 **Fx:**375-2302
(212) 848-4000 .. **Torkin,** Michl H '99 (Shearman & S LLP) -599 Lex Av -NY 10022
(914) 946-0400 .. **Tormay,** Anne Marie '86 %Schiavetti CDW&N,LLP -709 Wstchstr Av -White Plns 10604
(212) 808-7800 .. **Tormey,** Christine E '98 %Kelley D&W LLP -101 Park Av -NY 10178
(212) 768-6700 .. **Tormey,** Denise M '80 (Sonnenschein N&R LLP) -2 World Fncl Ctr -NY 10281
(212) 410-4142 .. **Tormey,** John J III '88 -217 E 86th PMB 221 -NY 10028 **Fx:**410-2380
(212) 480-3910 .. **Tormey,** Thos A Jr. '79 -140 Bway -NY 10005 **Fx:**480-5051
(212) 986-7070 .. **Torn,** Marsha '84 (Calabrese & T) -280 Mad Av -NY 10016 **Fx:**661-2876
(212) 644-1192 .. **Torna,** Vincent J '79 -101 E 52nd -NY 10022 **Fx:**644-1020
(212) 951-6560 .. **Tornabene,** Nina '85 %NYS Ed Dept-OLS -475 Park Av S -NY 10016 **Fx:**951-6573
(212) 931-7946 .. **Tornabene,** Paola R '05 MLB Properties -245 Park Av -NY 10167 **Fx:**949-5697
(212) 541-2000 .. **Tornay,** Chaeri K '08 %Bryan C LLP -1290 Av of Amer -NY 10104
(212) 770-7878 .. **Tornberg,** Jos E '02 %AIG -70 Pine -NY 10270
(518) 447-7150 .. **Torncello,** Peter M '92 %Pub Def -60 S Pearl -Albany 12207 **Fx:**447-5533
(212) 553-5516 .. **Torno,** Tania M '98 %Zurich NA -1 Lbrty Plz -NY 10006
(212) 598-5900 .. **Toro,** Joan '03 %Alonso A&K PC -920 Bway -NY 10010
(212) 259-8000 .. **Torpey,** Susannah Providence '05 %Dewey & L LLP -1301 Av of Amer -NY 10019
(212) 356-2914 .. **Torrado,** Laura L '94 %Knighthead Captl Mgmt -623 5th Av -NY 10022
(212) 637-2703 .. **Torrance,** Benjamin H '01 %US Atty -86 Chmbrs -NY 10007
(516) 868-8001 .. **Torre,** Jos E '64 -111 W Sunrise Hwy -Freeprt 11520 **Fx:**771-6862
(516) 240-8900 .. **Torre Lentz Gamell Gary & Rittmaster,LLP** -100 Jericho Quad -Jericho 11753 **Fx:**240-8950
(516) 240-8900 .. **Torre,** Michl '73 (Torre LGG&R,LLP) -100 Jericho Quad -Jericho 11753
(716) 854-2808 .. **Torre,** Nelson S '89 -438 Main -Buffalo 14202 **Fx:**854-1654
(718) 613-3500 .. **Torreggiani,** Dennis E '01 %UIA Bd -Bx29002 -Brklyn 11201 **Fx:**613-3566
(212) 425-3240 .. **Torregiano,** Vincent '07 %Marrinan & MM,PC -26 Bway -NY 10004
(718) 232-1250 .. **Torrellas,** Miguel A '93 %Polizzotto & P -6911 18th Av -Brklyn 11204 **Fx:**256-0966
(212) 264-3394 .. **Torrellas,** Nancy E '89 %DHS -26 Fed Plz -NY 10278
(212) 788-2738 .. **Torrent,** Carmen R '89 Comm on Womens Issues -100 Gold -NY 10038
(914) 993-4208 .. **Torrent,** Damaris E '93 Judicial Inst -84 N Bway -White Plns 10603
(212) 446-4800 .. **Torrente,** Christopher J '01 (Kirkland & E LLP) -153 E 53rd -NY 10022
(212) 382-0700 .. **Torrente,** David J '06 %Ostrolenk FG&S,LLP -1180 Av of Amer -NY 10036
(212) 790-9200 .. **Torrente,** John J '76 (Cowan L&L,PC) -1133 Av of Amer -NY 10036
(718) 332-7766 .. **Torrenzano,** Jay J '87 (Eaton & T,LLP) -1662 Sheepshead Bay Rd -Brklyn 11235 **Fx:**332-5898
(212) 506-1700 .. **Torres,** Aimee E '04 %Kasowitz BT&F LLP -1633 Bway -NY 10019
(718) 620-0106 .. **Torres,** Alberto '88 -629 Melrose Av -Bronx 10455 **Fx:**620-0107
(212) 371-1000 .. **Torres,** Ana D '96 Catholic Guardian Socy -1011 1st Av -NY 10022
(212) 335-4255 .. **Torres,** Andres F '10 DA -80 Centre -NY 10021
(516) 328-6300 .. **Torres,** Arturo '01 %Bridgeview Mortgage Corp -1200 Hempstd Tpk -Franklin Sq 11010
(212) 309-3132 .. **Torres,** Ausberto Jr. '98 %UBS PaineWebber -200 Park Av -NY 10166
(718) 654-6000 .. **Torres,** Austin '61 (Torres & T) -2705 Wllmsbrdg Rd -Bronx 10469 **Fx:**654-9875
(718) 237-2000 .. **Torres,** Azalia '88 %Leg Aid -111 Lvngstn -Brklyn 11201 **Fx:**237-8737
(718) 618-2500 .. **Torres,** Brenda L '01 %Civil Ct -851 Grnd Cncrs -Bronx 10451 **Fx:**590-7294
(631) 367-7100 .. **Torres,** Carolina C '07 %Coughlin SGR&R LLP -58 S Srvc Rd -Melvll 11747
(212) 209-3032 .. **Torres,** Chas E '96 (Reitler K&R LLC) -885 3rd Av -NY 10022
(212) 730-9009 .. **Torres,** Debra M '84 Kalorama Prtnrs LLC -570 Lex Av -NY 10022
(212) 374-6774 .. **Torres,** Dennisa A '99 %NYC Dept Educ-OLS -52 Chmbrs -NY 10007 **Fx:**374-5596
(212) 251-5374 .. **Torres,** Edna Y '97 %Segal Co -1 Park Av -NY 10016
(718) 365-0910 .. **Torres,** Eileen '00 Citizens Advice Bureau -2054 Morris Av -Bronx 10453
(718) 293-4700 .. **Torres,** Eric '01 -1000 Grnd Cncrs -Bronx 10451 **Fx:**293-4720
(631) 969-3100 .. **Torres,** Eun Jung '06 %Frenkel LWW&G,LLP -20 W Main -Bay Shr 11706
(516) 394-4200 .. **Torres,** Frank '84 %Duffy & D -1370 RXR Plz -Uniondale 11556
(212) 506-1700 .. **Torres,** Hector J '83 (Kasowitz BT&F LLP) -1633 Bway -NY 10019
(212) 964-7400 .. **Torres,** Ivan C '06 %Smith MDWY&Y,PC -111 John -NY 10038
(212) 765-5070 .. **Torres,** Jorge M '03 %Fish & R,PC -153 E 53rd -NY 10022
(917) 463-4616 .. **Torres,** Jose Luis '77 -202 Mamaroneck Av -White Plns 10601 **Fx:**546-0836
(212) 832-4540 .. **Torres,** Leslie '95 Roosevelt Island Operating Corp -591 Main -NY 10044 **Fx:**832-4582
(631) 224-1345 .. **Torres,** Lorraine '02 Threshold Land,Inc -584 Main -Islip 11751
(212) 872-1000 .. **Torres,** Lucas F '92 -One Bryant Park -NY 10036 **Fx:**872-1002
(718) 992-8500 .. **Torres,** Michl '75 (M Torres,PC) -903F Sheridan Av -Bronx 10451
(212) 728-8000 .. **Torres,** Michelle S '07 %Willkie F&G LLP -787 7th Av -NY 10019
(212) 264-0300 .. **Torres,** Olga C '95 %NLRB -26 Fed Plz -NY 10278 **Fx:**264-8427
(212) 264-8426 .. **Torres,** Olga Lucia '96 %NLRB -26 Fed Plz -NY 10278 **Fx:**264-8427
(917) 312-3169 .. **Torres,** Peter E '05 -112 E 23rd -NY 10010 **Fx:**(212) 473-7864
(212) 492-5991 .. **Torres,** Preeti '03 Kaplan,Inc -888 7th Av -NY 10106 **Fx:**489-2301
(212) 592-1400 .. **Torres,** Richd '97 %Herrick,F LLP -2 Park Av -NY 10016
(718) 237-2000 .. **Torres,** Richd J '04 Leg Aid -111 Lvngstn -Brklyn 11201 **Fx:**237-8737
(631) 968-2554 .. **Torres,** Robt A '98 Bay Shore Schl Dist -75 W Perkal -Bay Shr 11706
(917) 923-1302 .. **Torres,** Rosann '00 A&M Taxand,LLC -125 Park Av -NY 10017
(516) 560-7719 .. **Torres,** Roy A '88 %Workers Comp Bd -175 Fulton Av -Hempstd 11550
(212) 455-2000 .. **Torres,** Shannon P '08 %Simpson T&B LLP -425 Lex Av -NY 10017
(718) 654-6000 .. **Torres,** Sofia G '93 %Torres & T -2705 Wllmsbrdg Rd -Bronx 10469 **Fx:**654-9875
(646) 386-3025 .. **Torres,** Wm '86 %Supreme Ct-Law Dept -60 Centre -NY 10007
(212) 552-1395 .. **Torres,** Wm A '93 JP Morgan Chase -1 Chase Manh Plz -NY 10081
(212) 487-4421 .. **Torres-Lumsden,** Emilio A '06 %Dept Cnsmr Affrs -42 Bway -NY 10004 **Fx:**487-4197

(212) 998-6025 .. **Torres-Spelliscy,** Ciara C '02 Cnsl Brennan Ctr for Justice -161 Av of Amer -NY 10013 **Fx:**995-4550
(212) 715-1000 .. **Torres-Spelliscy,** Glynn K '02 %Arnold & P LLP -399 Park Av -NY 10022
(914) 941-4485 .. **Torrey,** David S '86 (Medina TSM&C PC) -31 Croton Av -Ossining 10562 **Fx:**941-4513
(631) 261-8834 .. **Torrey,** Julie Ann '96 %Ingerman S LLP -150 Motor Pkwy -Hauppauge 11788
(212) 804-4200 .. **Torrini,** Steven A '02 %Mound CW&G -One Bttry Pk Plz -NY 10004
(212) 563-4077 .. **Torrisi,** Naomi P '80 -1 Penn Plz -NY 10119 **Fx:**563-4079
(212) 821-3624 .. **Tortarolo,** Nicole M '04 UBS -299 Park Av -NY 10171
(516) 741-8198 .. **Torti,** Kenneth R '77 -1461 Franklin Av -Gdn Cty 11530
(631) 325-8185 .. **Torti,** Kenneth R '77 -167 Melody Ct -Eastport 11941 **Fx:**325-1385
(212) 532-5881 .. **Torto,** Thos A '79 -419 Park Av S -NY 10016 **Fx:**481-5851
(212) 294-1321 .. **Tortora,** Anthony A '05 Oasis Real Estate Partners -350 5th Av -NY 10118
(631) 864-6800 .. **Tortora,** Craig J '94 (Goldsmith & T) -2067 Jericho Tpk -Commack 11725
(516) 485-4221 .. **Tortora,** Lisa M '97 (Foley SO&W) -175 Fulton Av -Hempstd 11550
(212) 277-0478 .. **Tortora,** Marc R '01 Hartford Financial Products -2 Park Av -NY 10016
(315) 423-1104 .. **Tortora,** Ralph D III '81 %Medicaid Fraud Cntrl -615 Erie Blvd W -Syracuse 13204
(914) 421-1800 .. **Tortorella,** Geraldine N '88 (Hocherman T&W LLP) -1 N Bway -White Plns 10601
(212) 812-9511 .. **Tortorella,** Vincent '01 Guidepoint Global -730 3rd Av -NY 10017
(212) 207-4006 .. **Tortorelli,** Michele D '86 -444 Mad Av -NY 10022 **Fx:**308-2223
(718) 680-0471 .. **Tortorice,** Dominic A '61 -8118 13th Av -Brklyn 11228 **Fx:**921-3292
(718) 391-5666 .. **Tortorici,** Chas J '92 %Taxi & Limo Comm -32-02 Qns Blvd -LIC 11101 **Fx:**391-5695
(212) 225-2000 .. **Tortoriello,** Robt L '75 (Cleary GS&H) -1 Lbrty Plz -NY 10006
(212) 880-6000 .. **Torys LLP** -237 Park Av -NY 10017 **Fx:**682-0200
(917) 778-6600 .. **Tosca,** Eric P '86 %J Toomey -485 Lex Av -NY 10017 **Fx:**778-7048
(914) 666-2444 .. **Toscanini,** Marcela '99 (M Toscanini, PLLC) -125 Main -Mt Kisco 10549 **Fx:**666-3920
(212) 450-4000 .. **Toscano,** David B '93 Cnsl Davis P&W LLP -450 Lex Av -NY 10017
(718) 620-0084 .. **Toscano,** Ellyn M '82 Congressman J Serrano -788 Southrn Blvd -Bronx 10455 **Fx:**620-0658
(212) 685-7600 .. **Toscano,** Lawr J '70 (Heller H&F,PC) -292 Mad Av -NY 10017
(718) 478-7380 .. **Toscano,** Richd '89 -82-11 37th Av -Jcksn Hts 11372
(516) 571-3061 .. **Toscano,** Sondra M '01 Cnty Atty -1 West -Mineola 11501 **Fx:**571-6604
(516) 741-9300 .. **Toscano,** Thos A '88 (Toscano & Assoc,PC) -200 Old Cntry Rd -Mineola 11501 **Fx:**741-0345
(212) 848-4000 .. **Tosch,** K Mallory '08 %Shearman & S LLP -599 Lex Av -NY 10022
(718) 295-2002 .. **Toschi,** James P '75 %DMV Traffic Violations Bur -696 E Fordham Rd -Bronx 10458
(516) 931-1800 .. **Toss,** Raafat S '97 OfCnsl Catalano G&P LLP -100 Jericho Quadrangle -Jericho 11753
(516) 294-9797 .. **Tosti,** Vincent J '68 -400 Grdn City Plz -Gdn Cty 11530 **Fx:**294-5756
(914) 245-6060 .. **Tota,** Danl R '04 (Durante B&T,PLLC) -2000 Maple Hill -Yorktwn Hts 10598
(212) 648-0325 .. **Totah,** Michele L '05 JP Morgan Chase -245 Park Av -NY 10167
(718) 845-3100 .. **Totaram,** Kawal Persaud '87 -126-03 Lbrty Av -S Richmond Hll 11419
(212) 225-2000 .. **Toteja,** Ryan R '08 %Cleary GS&H -1 Lbrty Plz -NY 10006
(212) 964-6611 .. **Toth,** Jennifer L '02 %Lester SK&D -120 Bway -NY 10271
(718) 260-2653 .. **Toti,** Stephanie '04 %Hon N Gershon -225 Cadman Plz E -Brklyn 11201
(212) 468-4800 .. **Totino,** Angela Romina '06 %Davis & G LLP -1740 Bway -NY 10019
(212) 455-2000 .. **Totino,** Maryann '08 %Simpson T&B LLP -425 Lex Av -NY 10017
(973) 642-8841 .. **Toto,** Chas G '87 (Hawkins D&W LLP) -One Chase Manh Plz -NY 10005 **Fx:**642-6773
(212) 681-0117 .. **Toto,** Domenic D '88 OfCnsl Starr GD&R -530 5th Av -NY 10036
(212) 834-0600 .. **Toto,** John F '79 (Gordon & S,PC) -355 Lex Av -NY 10017
(212) 819-8200 .. **Toto,** Martin M '95 (White & C LLP) -1155 Av of Amer -NY 10036
(607) 754-5054 .. **Totolis,** Theodosis J '61 -6 Wshngtn Av -Endicott 13760 **Fx:**754-5307
(631) 591-1100 .. **Totten,** Annette M '04 -Bx1907 -Rvrhead 11901 **Fx:**591-1100
(212) 310-8000 .. **Toub,** Sherri L '04 %Weil G&M LLP -767 5th Av -NY 10153
(212) 859-8000 .. **Touchard,** Cyril J '08 %Fried FHS&J LLP -1 NY Plz -NY 10004
(212) 455-2000 .. **Touchstone,** Mary Beirne '89 %Simpson T&B LLP -425 Lex Av -NY 10017
(212) 506-2500 .. **Tougas,** Jeffrey G '05 Cnsl Mayer B LLP -1675 Bway -NY 10019
(212) 608-1234 .. **Touger,** David '85 (Peluso & T) -70 Lafayette -NY 10013
(212) 471-6211 .. **Touitou,** Philip '90 (Hinshaw & C LLP) -780 3rd Av -NY 10017
(516) 357-3700 .. **Toulas,** Wendy '01 %Cullen and D LLP -100 Q Roosevelt Blvd -Gdn Cty 11530
(212) 408-2500 .. **Toulouse,** Martin '98 SpclCnsl Baker B,LLP -30 Rckfllr Plz -NY 10112
(716) 282-3711 .. **Touma,** Craig N '85 -800 Main -Niagara Fls 14301
(917) 343-5390 .. **Touma,** Mona A '01 Goldman Sachs -1 NY Plz -NY 10004
(516) 869-8666 .. **Toumbekis,** Nicholas '95 Genatt Assoc,Inc -3333 New Hyde Pk Rd -New Hyde Pk 11042 **Fx:**869-8765
(718) 956-9558 .. **Toumbekis,** Peter '95 -34-58 32nd -LIC 11106 **Fx:**726-3348
(212) 558-4000 .. **Toumey,** Donald J '82 (Sullivan & C LLP) -125 Broad -NY 10004
(212) 907-0700 .. **Tountas,** Stephen W '04 %Labaton S LLP -140 Bway -NY 10005
(212) 335-4500 .. **Touray,** Sharif S '90 OfCnsl DLA Piper LLP -1251 Av of Amer -NY 10020
(212) 295-6423 .. **Tourikis,** Kiriaki '04 WilmerHale -399 Park Av -NY 10022
(646) 315-7428 .. **Toussaint,** Stacey M '02 %FINRA -14 Wall -NY 10005 **Fx:**315-7440
(212) 230-4500 .. **Toussi,** Sina '95 %One East Captl Advsrs -1 E 57th -NY 10022
(516) 535-1700 .. **Tovar,** Bryant F '06 %Horing W&R,PC -11 Hillside Av -Williston Pk 11596
(212) 701-3000 .. **Towbin,** Andrew J '06 %Cahill G&R LLP -80 Pine -NY 10005 **Fx:**269-5420
(212) 517-5500 .. **Towe,** Teri Noel '74 OfCnsl Ganz & H,PC -1394 3rd Av -NY 10075
(718) 990-7454 .. **Towers,** Chas G '92 St Johns Univ -8000 Utopia Pkwy -Jamaica 11439
(212) 546-3676 .. **Towers,** Julius Y '04 Bristol-Myers Squibb -345 Park Av -NY 10154 **Fx:**546-9562
(212) 408-5100 .. **Towers,** Meghan S '08 %Chadbourne & P LLP -30 Rckfllr Plz -NY 10112
(212) 468-4800 .. **Towers,** Tiffany A '01 %Davis & G LLP -1740 Bway -NY 10019
(518) 452-1800 .. **Towne,** James T Jr. '76 (Towne R & Prtnrs,PC) -450 New Karner Rd Bx15072 -Albany 12212
(212) 326-1000 .. **Towne,** L Stanton '77 Studley -300 Park Av -NY 10022 **Fx:**326-1034
(518) 452-1800 .. **Towne Ryan & Partners, PC** -450 New Karner Rd Bx15072 -Albany 12212 **Fx:**452-6435
(518) 587-7300 .. **Towne Ryan & Partners, PC** -137 Maple Av -Saratoga Spgs 12866 **Fx:**587-2734
(518) 296-8866 .. **Towne Ryan & Partners, PC** -2668 State Route 7 -Cobleskill 12043 **Fx:**296-8860
(845) 485-7525 .. **Towne Ryan & Partners, PC** -82 Wshngtn -Poughkeepsie 12601 **Fx:**485-7526
(631) 329-0400 .. **Towner,** Andrew T '87 (Caleca & T,PC) -257 Pantigo Rd -E Hampton 11937
(845) 228-2800 .. **Towner,** Devon D '07 %Dewbury & Assoc,PC -1787 Route 6 -Carmel 10512
(212) 669-8706 .. **Townes,** Jyll D '93 %Citywide Admin Srvcs EEO -1 Centre -NY 10007
(914) 834-6272 .. **Townley,** Rosemary A '92 -4 Coolidge -Larchmnt 10538 **Fx:**834-2992
(212) 450-4000 .. **Townley,** W Danforth '86 (Davis P&W LLP) -450 Lex Av -NY 10017
(718) 789-9390 .. **Towns,** Emanuel A '74 -1672 Bway -Brklyn 11207
(716) 200-5050 .. **Townsend,** Bradlee W '80 (Harris B PLLC) -726 Exchange -Buffalo 14210
(845) 778-2228 .. **Townsend,** Bruce D '85 -26 Albany Av -Walden 12586 **Fx:**778-2254
(212) 349-4540 .. **Townsend,** Clinton A '75 -170 Bway #1007 -NY 10038
(212) 687-3860 .. **Townsend,** Daniela A '03 Snow BK,PC -605 3rd Av -NY 10158
(585) 232-5225 .. **Townsend,** James T '72 (Remington GW&C,LLP) -183 E Main -Rchstr 14604
(716) 433-4022 .. **Townsend,** Jos F '90 -188 East Av -Lockprt 14094
(315) 685-4428 .. **Townsend,** Kimberly M '02 Welch Allyn,Inc -4341 State Street Rd -Skaneateles Fls 13153
(718) 595-4164 .. **Townsend,** Loretta J '90 DEP -59-17 Junction Blvd -Flushng 11373 **Fx:**595-4166
(585) 428-5293 .. **Townsend,** Maryanne H '83 %Supreme Ct -545 Hall of Justice -Rchstr 14614 **Fx:**425-2995
(585) 419-8800 .. **Townsend,** Michl J '83 (Harris B PLLC) -99 Garnsey Rd -Pittsfrd 14534
(212) 687-4385 .. **Townsend,** R Edw Jr. '71 (Townsend & V,LLP) -1212 Av of Amer -NY 10036
(212) 474-1000 .. **Townsend,** Robt I III '91 (Cravath S&M LLP) -825 8th Av -NY 10019
(716) 200-5179 .. **Townsend,** Stephen C '76 (S Townsend,PC) -726 Exchange -Buffalo 14210 **Fx:**200-5201
(212) 687-4385 .. **Townsend & Valente,LLP** -1212 Av of Amer -NY 10036 **Fx:**557-7894
(716) 847-8400 .. **Townson,** Alexandra E J '05 %Phillips L LLP -3400 HSBC Ctr -Buffalo 14203
(518) 436-7857 .. **Towse,** Seth '65 -8 Marian Ln -Albany 12211
(516) 739-0081 .. **Towsky,** Robt L '85 (Andrea & T) -320 Old Cntry Rd -Gdn Cty 11530
(518) 373-5064 .. **Towsley,** Darryll S '02 AYCO Co LP -1 Wall -Albany 12205
(212) 440-4400 .. **Toy,** Kelly A '02 %Buchanan I&R PC -620 8th Av -NY 10018
(347) 381-6192 .. **Toy,** Maria '00 -7725 250th -Bellerose 11426
(212) 508-6100 .. **Toy,** Timothy Michl '82 (Bracewell & G,LLP) -1251 Av of Amer -NY 10020
(585) 724-4026 .. **Toyer,** Judy A '84 %Eastman Kodak -343 State -Rchstr 14650
(212) 548-2100 .. **Tozaki,** Airi '06 %McGuire W LLP -1345 Av of Amer -NY 10105
(212) 720-5033 .. **Tozer,** Raleigh M '75 %Fed Reserve Bk -33 Lbrty -NY 10045 **Fx:**785-5748
(516) 571-2042 .. **Tozier,** Anne E '87 Surrogate's Ct -262 Old Cntry Rd -Mineola 11501 **Fx:**571-3864
(212) 754-5948 .. **Tozzi,** Piero A '97 %Catholic Fam & Human Rghts Inst -866 UN Plz -NY 10017 **Fx:**754-9291
(914) 995-3645 .. **Trabocchi,** Diane L '89 %Cnty Atty -148 Martine Av -White Plns 10601 **Fx:**995-5858
(516) 571-3800 .. **Trabold,** Gordon F '97 %DA -262 Old Cntry Rd -Mineola 11501 **Fx:**248-9479
(631) 475-0200 .. **Trabold,** Harold G '66 (Dranitzke LT&J) -73 N Ocean Av Bx510 -Patchogue 11772
(212) 548-2100 .. **Trabold,** Kathleen Marron '00 (McGuire W LLP) -1345 Av of Amer -NY 10105
(516) 478-5500 .. **Trabucchi,** Aldo A '62 -310 Old Cntry Rd -Gdn Cty 11530
(716) 692-6316 .. **Trabucco,** Ronald C '77 -535 Delaware -Tonawanda 14150 **Fx:**692-4409
(718) 250-2000 .. **Trabulsi,** Michl W '98 %DA -350 Jay -Brklyn 11201 **Fx:**250-2314
(212) 221-7811 .. **Trabulus,** Norman '75 -345 7th Av -NY 10001
(631) 724-8833 .. **Trace,** Stephan D '92 %Devitt SB,LLP -50 Route 111 -Smithtwn 11787
(315) 793-2225 .. **Trace,** Thos M '00 %Dept of Law -207 Genesee -Utica 13501 **Fx:**793-2228
(516) 488-3300 .. **Tracey,** Deirdre E '08 %Shaub AC&S,LLP -1983 Marcus Av -Lk Success 11042
(212) 918-3000 .. **Tracey,** Dennis H III '82 (Hogan L LLP) -875 3rd Av -NY 10022
(718) 741-3400 .. **Tracey,** Katherine '90 Childrens Law Ctr -2501 Grnd Cncrs -Bronx 10468
(845) 565-3999 .. **Trachte,** Kenyon C '07 %Trachte Law Ofc -26 West -Newburgh 12550 **Fx:**565-3997
(845) 565-3999 .. **Trachte,** Paul D '89 -26 West -Newburgh 12550 **Fx:**565-3997
(212) 868-1010 .. **Trachten,** Gary '85 (Kudman TA LLP) -350 5th Av -NY 10118
(718) 625-2200 .. **Trachtenberg,** Ben L W '06 %Bklyn Law Schl -250 Joralemon -Brklyn 11201 **Fx:**780-0393
(518) 382-7815 .. **Trachtenberg,** Bruce S '79 -2350 Barcelona Rd -Niskayuna 12309 **Fx:**382-7834
(212) 972-2929 .. **Trachtenberg,** David G '80 (Trachtenberg R&F LLP) -545 5th Av -NY 10017 **Fx:**972-7581

(212) 373-3000 .. **Trachtenberg,** Joanna L W '06 %Paul WRW&G LLP -1285 Av of Amer -NY 10019
(845) 359-3073 .. **Trachtenberg,** Jos '53 -323 Blauvelt Rd -Blauvelt 10913 **Fx:**620-1449
(212) 521-3500 .. **Trachtenberg,** Lawr '82 (Aronson M&S, LLP) -485 Lex Av -NY 10017
(631) 435-0700 .. **Trachtenberg,** Richd E '89 %M Silver,PC -330 Motor Pkwy -Hauppauge 11788 **Fx:**435-8253
(212) 952-6200 .. **Trachtman,** Alan C '69 OfCnsl Nourse & B,LLP -55 Bway -NY 10006
(212) 715-9100 .. **Trachtman,** Jeffrey S '85 (Kramer LN&F,LLP) -1177 Av of Amer -NY 10036
(917) 873-2232 .. **Tract,** Laurence T '03 O Positive,LLC -36 W 25th -NY 10010
(212) 940-8800 .. **Tract,** Marc M '85 (Katten MR LLP) -575 Mad Av -NY 10022
(212) 940-8800 .. **Tractenberg,** Beth D '88 (Katten MR LLP) -575 Mad Av -NY 10022
(212) 940-3722 .. **Tractenberg,** Craig R '08 (Nixon P LLP) -437 Mad Av -NY 10022
(914) 848-4800 .. **Tracy,** Adam W '05 Pernod Ricard USA -100 Manhattanvll Rd -Purchase 10577
(212) 218-2100 .. **Tracy,** Colleen '97 (Fitzpatrick CH&S) -1290 Av of Amer -NY 10104
(845) 634-6404 .. **Tracy,** Donald S '61 -317 Little Tor Rd S -New Cty 10956 **Fx:**634-6538
(315) 422-8191 .. **Tracy,** James P '74 %Leg Aid -351 S Warren -Syracuse 13202 **Fx:**472-2819
(212) 237-1000 .. **Tracy,** James P '07 %Windels ML&M,LLP -156 W 56th -NY 10019
(518) 457-9025 .. **Tracy,** Jerome '83 Dept of Labor -State Campus Bldg 12 -Albany 12240
(718) 442-1182 .. **Tracy,** John J '81 (Tracy & S,PC) -1688 Victory Blvd -Staten Isl 10314 **Fx:**442-0552
(516) 942-4233 .. **Tracy,** Leon H '63 -366 N Bway -Jericho 11753 **Fx:**935-2011
(212) 221-6900 .. **Tracy,** Matthew '92 (Winget S&S,LLP) -45 Bway -NY 10006
(516) 227-2300 .. **Tracy,** Nancy Ann '95 Wright Risk Mgmt -333 Earle Ovngton Blvd -Uniondale 11553
(212) 596-9000 .. **Tracy,** Philip A '10 %Ropes & G LLP -1211 Av of Amer -NY 10036
(212) 687-7410 .. **Tracy,** Robt J '86 (Clifton B&D,LLP) -420 Lex Av -NY 10170
(518) 473-5671 .. **Tracy,** Terrence X '84 %Div of Parole -97 Central Av -Albany 12206 **Fx:**473-6037
(212) 446-4800 .. **Tracy,** Thaddeus J '01 (Kirkland & E LLP) -153 E 53rd -NY 10022
(518) 388-4217 .. **Tracy-Ireland,** Laura H '89 %Cnty Ct -612 State -Schnctdy 12305
(718) 268-8700 .. **Tracz,** Brian M '93 -105-20 Metro Av -Frst Hlls 11375
(646) 871-7463 .. **Traeger,** Michele S '99 Equinox Fitness Clubs -895 Bway -NY 10003
(516) 873-2000 .. **Trafimow,** A Jonathan '93 (Moritt HH&H LLP) -400 Grdn City Plz -Gdn Cty 11530
(212) 244-6199 .. **Traflet & Fabian** -1001 Av of Amer -NY 10018
(212) 244-6199 .. **Traflet,** Stephen G '85 (Traflet & F) -1001 Av of Amer -NY 10018
(914) 375-0100 .. **Traganas,** Konstantine '08 %Novick ELRW&L,PC -733 Ynkrs Av -Ynkrs 10704
(516) 296-7000 .. **Traganas,** Kristen M '07 %Certilman BA&H,LLP -90 Merrick Av -E Meadow 11554
(212) 848-4000 .. **Trager,** Aaron D '09 %Shearman & S LLP -599 Lex Av -NY 10022
(212) 270-6000 .. **Trager,** Alan S '99 JP Morgan Sec -270 Park Av -NY 10017
(212) 688-1900 .. **Trager,** David A '60 (Greenberg T&H,LLP) -767 3rd Av -NY 10017
(516) 222-2333 .. **Trager,** Jordan E '95 %Barbara Law Firm -401 Franklin Av -Gdn Cty 11530 **Fx:**222-2935
(212) 837-6000 .. **Trager,** Josiah S '02 %Hughes H&R LLP -1 Bttry Pk Plz -NY 10004
(212) 782-8737 .. **Trager,** Katherine '75 Random House -7145 Bway -NY 10019 **Fx:**782-8499
(212) 721-1192 .. **Trager,** Leslie '63 -230 Park Av -NY 10169 **Fx:**557-7559
(212) 637-2799 .. **Trager,** Mara E '99 %US Atty -86 Chmbrs -NY 10007
(516) 571-3800 .. **Trager,** Marshall D '76 %DA -262 Old Cntry Rd -Mineola 11501 **Fx:**248-9479
(516) 292-9494 .. **Trager,** Seymour '50 -141 Willis Av -Mineola 11501
(315) 785-3001 .. **Trahan,** Diana D '92 Family Ct -163 Arsenal -Watertwn 13601 **Fx:**785-3143
(212) 659-8105 .. **Trahant,** Amelie P '05 Mt Sinai Med Ctr -1 Gustave L Levy Pl Bx 1099 -NY 10029 **Fx:**348-2230
(212) 752-1161 .. **Traiger,** Warren W '79 (Traiger & H LLP) -501 5th Av -NY 10017 **Fx:**937-5229
(718) 286-6000 .. **Traill,** Johnnette G A '93 %DA -125-01 Qns Blvd -Kew Gdns 11415
(718) 741-3400 .. **Traina,** Jara Renee '06 Childrens Law Ctr -2501 Grnd Cncrs -Bronx 10468
(212) 633-9779 .. **Traina,** Salvatore A '71 -99 Bank -NY 10014
(212) 593-1700 .. **Train-Gutierrez,** Patrick A '02 %Kaplan L LLP -1065 Av of Amer -NY 10018
(212) 317-8500 .. **Trainor,** Alison M '05 %Snitow KH&M,LLP -575 Lex Av -NY 10022
(631) 501-5700 .. **Trainor,** Christopher G '99 (Carter DF&S LLP) -445 Broadhallow Rd -Melvll 11747
(518) 457-4924 .. **Trainor,** Eamonn P '02 %Crime Victims Bd -1 Columbia Cir -Albany 12203 **Fx:**457-8658
(212) 425-1401 .. **Trainor,** James '05 %O'Hare P LLP -82 Wall -NY 10005 **Fx:**425-1421
(518) 899-9200 .. **Trainor,** James P '91 (Cutler T&C LLP) -2 Hemphill Pl -Malta 12020
(212) 819-8200 .. **Trainor,** James S Jr. '01 (White & C LLP) -1155 Av of Amer -NY 10036
(718) 318-3301 .. **Trainor,** Jos '96 (J Trainor & Assoc) -225 Beach 116th -Rckwy Pk 11694 **Fx:**318-3308
(518) 725-8555 .. **Trainor,** Matthew E '01 M Trainor,LLC -Bx1361 -Gloversvll 12078 **Fx:**725-2746
(516) 571-3742 .. **Trainor,** Michl J '67 %Supreme Ct -100 Supreme Ct Dr -Mineola 11501
(516) 465-8090 .. **Trainor,** Regina A '94 %North Shore-LIJ Hlth Systm -145 Community Dr -Gt Neck 11021 **Fx:**465-8013
(212) 474-1000 .. **Traister,** Jordan S '10 %Cravath S&M LLP -825 8th Av -NY 10019
(718) 721-7171 .. **Trakas,** Arthur G '83 -31-01 Bway -LIC 11106 **Fx:**204-2310
(212) 909-6000 .. **Trakht,** Tatyana '04 %Debevoise & P LLP -919 3rd Av -NY 10022
(212) 334-6858 .. **Trakinski,** Amy R '92 -165 W 91st -NY 10024 **Fx:**579-7315
(914) 631-6666 .. **Tramaglini,** Christopher S '06 %M Grossbach,PC -800 Wstchstr Av -Rye Brook 10573 **Fx:**524-7070
(212) 834-1073 .. **Tramantano,** Robt S '71 %GreenPoint Bk -90 Park Av -NY 10016 **Fx:**834-1402
(315) 422-8191 .. **Trammell,** Tara L '07 %Leg Aid -351 S Warren -Syracuse 13202 **Fx:**472-2819
(212) 713-9869 .. **Tramontana,** Janine M '01 UBS Securities LLC -1285 Av of Amer -NY 10019
(212) 513-3200 .. **Tramontano,** Christine '07 %Holland & K LLP -31 W 52nd -NY 10019
(516) 747-6700 .. **Tramontano,** Paul J '07 %Kirschenbaum & K -200 Grdn City Plz -Gdn Cty 11530 **Fx:**747-6781
(212) 596-9000 .. **Tramontine,** John O '60 OfCnsl Ropes & G LLP -1211 Av of Amer -NY 10036
(212) 822-9508 .. **Tran,** Dinh T '04 Advocates for Chldrn of NY -151 W 30th -NY 10001
(212) 669-2515 .. **Tran,** Serge Dang Hai '98 %Comptrollers Ofc -1 Centre -NY 10007
(212) 859-8000 .. **Tran,** Thao Ngoc '08 %Fried FHS&J LLP -1 NY Plz -NY 10004
(212) 607-2811 .. **Tran,** Trang Thi Thuy '05 %FTC -1 Bowling Grn -NY 10004 **Fx:**607-2822
(212) 381-5429 .. **Tran,** Yvonne K '96 Doubleclick Inc -111 8th Av -NY 10011
(516) 671-1295 .. **Tranchina,** Stacey '89 Cnsl D Rave -11 The Plz -Locust Vly 11560 **Fx:**671-1294
(212) 967-9998 .. **Trandafirescu,** Adriana '04 -350 5th Av -NY 10118 **Fx:**967-9997
(585) 781-5687 .. **Tranelli,** Kathleen Frensky '84 %Eastman Kodak -343 State -Rchstr 14650
(585) 641-8000 .. **Tranelli,** Steven J '84 (Fix SB&G,PC) -295 Woodcliff Dr -Fairprt 14450
(212) 551-8500 .. **Tranes,** Andrew P '00 %Israel Discount Bk -511 5th Av -NY 10017 **Fx:**551-8916
(212) 909-6000 .. **Tranetzki,** Kristen L '08 %Debevoise & P LLP -919 3rd Av -NY 10022
(212) 436-4580 .. **Trank,** Jos W '05 Deloitte & Touche LLP -2 World Fncl Ctr -NY 10281
(845) 255-2848 .. **Trank,** Lawr R '94 LR Trank,PLLC -124 Main Bx308 -New Paltz 12561 **Fx:**255-2849
(212) 454-6899 .. **Trapani,** Angelique Kournetas '00 %Deutsche Bank -60 Wall -NY 10005
(212) 788-1103 .. **Trapani,** Christina M '10 Law Dept -100 Church -NY 10007 **Fx:**788-0367
(212) 468-8000 .. **Trapani,** David A '99 OfCnsl Morrison & F LLP -1290 Av of Amer -NY 10104
(315) 727-5304 .. **Trapani,** Lawr P '86 -Bx555 -Manlius 13104
(212) 264-5420 .. **Trapani,** Ryan A '02 Hon J Barzilay -1 Fed Plz -NY 10278
(212) 758-0050 .. **Trapasso,** Barbara H '87 %Title Assoc -825 3rd Av -NY 10022 **Fx:**758-8223
(716) 856-1344 .. **Trapp,** Chris G '82 (Bouvier Prtnrshp,LLP) -350 Main -Buffalo 14202 **Fx:**856-1369
(516) 627-0267 .. **Trapp,** Louis A Jr. '57 -35 Central Dr -Plandome 11030
(518) 474-0871 .. **Traschen,** Ida L '88 %DMV -6 ESP -Albany 12228 **Fx:**486-4485
(718) 579-7956 .. **Trasen,** Jan L '96 Legal Aid -900 Sheridan Av -Bronx 10451
(716) 648-6700 .. **Trask,** Wm J '83 -3990 McKinley Pkwy -Blasdell 14219
(518) 402-0748 .. **Traskos,** Christine C '81 %Dept of Health -433 River -Troy 12180 **Fx:**402-0751
(212) 715-9100 .. **Trast,** Carissa R '08 %Kramer LN&F,LLP -1177 Av of Amer -NY 10036
(212) 701-3000 .. **Traster,** Jeremy M '07 %Cahill G&R LLP -80 Pine -NY 10005 **Fx:**269-5420
(845) 339-6600 .. **Trataros,** Ephie '94 -70 Maiden Ln -Kingston 12401 **Fx:**339-3574
(646) 695-7924 .. **Trataros,** Fanny '89 Kensington Vanguard National Land Srvcs -39 W 37th -NY 10018
(212) 867-1100 .. **Tratner,** Louis '81 (Tratner & M) -551 5th Av -NY 10176
(212) 867-1100 .. **Tratner & Molloy** -551 5th Av -NY 10176 **Fx:**972-1787
(212) 619-6700 .. **Trattler,** Stanley M '50 -20 Vesey -NY 10007
(212) 351-4500 .. **Traub,** Amy J '04 (Epstein B&G,PC) -250 Park Av -NY 10177
(845) 735-7351 .. **Traub,** Barry M '82 -1 Blue Hill Plz Bx1629 -Pearl Rvr 10965 **Fx:**735-7585
(212) 732-0208 .. **Traub,** Doris Ginsberg '81 (Traub & T) -39 Bway -NY 10006 **Fx:**571-0860
(212) 310-2000 .. **Traub,** Felicia G '94 %Colgate-Palmolive -300 Park Av -NY 10022 **Fx:**310-3406
(718) 250-0400 .. **Traub,** Jack J '90 %R Tusa -1 MetroTech Ctr -Brklyn 11201 **Fx:**250-0591
(212) 732-0208 .. **Traub,** Jeffrey '71 (Traub & T) -39 Bway -NY 10006 **Fx:**571-0860
(212) 877-0103 .. **Traub,** Joan '87 -2500 Johnson Av -Bronx 10463 **Fx:**(646) 330-5852
(914) 347-2600 .. **Traub Lieberman Straus & Shrewsberry LLP** -7 Skyline Dr -Hawthorne 10532 **Fx:**347-8898
(212) 541-6222 .. **Traub,** Lois M '79 %Kane K,PC -1350 Av of Amer -NY 10019
(212) 592-1400 .. **Traub,** M Darren '04 %Herrick,F LLP -2 Park Av -NY 10016
(212) 351-4500 .. **Traub,** Paul '78 (Epstein B&G,PC) -250 Park Av -NY 10177
(212) 966-7442 .. **Traub,** Peter P Jr. '83 -107 Grand -NY 10013 **Fx:**966-7448
(914) 347-2600 .. **Traub,** Richd K '76 (Traub LS&S LLP) -7 Skyline Dr -Hawthorne 10532
(212) 770-7000 .. **Traub,** Sandra A '92 %AIG -80 Pine -NY 10005 **Fx:**344-2286
(718) 435-5858 .. **Traube,** Leon '56 L Traube PC -4405 17th Av -Brklyn 11204 **Fx:**435-1386
(212) 837-6193 .. **Traube,** Michl J '08 %Hughes H&R LLP -1 Bttry Pk Plz -NY 10004 **Fx:**299-6193
(212) 263-3008 .. **Traube,** Morris '04 NYU Med Schl -550 1st Av -NY 10016
(212) 553-6886 .. **Traugot,** Diana Ganz '95 Moodys Investor Srvc -250 Greenwich -NY 10007
(516) 887-7739 .. **Traugot,** Wendy K '90 -106 Catlin Pl -Hewlett 11557
(212) 417-4327 .. **Traum,** David A '87 %OTDA Fair Hearings -330 W 34th -NY 10001
(212) 761-7006 .. **Traum,** Edw H '06 Morgan Stanley -1585 Bway -NY 10036
(718) 250-2000 .. **Traum,** Lauren Brooke '06 DA -350 Jay -Brklyn 11201 **Fx:**250-2314
(212) 954-5871 .. **Trauman,** Brian P '06 (KPMG LLP) -345 Park Av -NY 10154
(212) 277-5842 .. **Trauner,** Bruce E '66 (Beldock L&H LLP) -99 Park Av -NY 10016
(212) 391-8045 .. **Trauner,** Joshua S '07 %Slater & B LLP -61 Bway -NY 10006 **Fx:**391-8047
(212) 596-9000 .. **Traupman,** Matthew A '03 %Ropes & G LLP -1211 Av of Amer -NY 10036
(212) 594-5000 .. **Traurig,** Jeffrey M '97 %Togut S&S LLP -1 Penn Plz -NY 10119
(518) 370-5515 .. **Trauring,** James A '86 J Trauring & Assoc,LLC -705 Union -Schnctdy 12305
(212) 983-8500 .. **Trautmann,** Dean Cole Jr. '09 %Brown G&F LLP -355 Lex Av -NY 10017

(212) 474-1000 .. **Trautmann**, Joachim F '01 Cravath S&M LLP -825 8th Av -NY 10019
(518) 474-6400 .. **Trautwein**, Richd J '81 %Dept of Ed -89 Wshngtn Av -Albany 12234 **Fx**:473-2925
(212) 762-4000 .. **Travagliato**, Vincent C '94 Morgan Stanley -1221 Av of Amer -NY 10020
(914) 763-5393 .. **Travalino**, Dean S '80 -105 Spring -S Salem 10590 **Fx**:763-5402
(914) 739-5593 .. **Traver**, Carol '84 %Asimuth Multimedia Prod -23 N Division -Peekskill 10566
(718) 264-3340 .. **Traver**, Jos A '80 %MHLS -80-45 Wnchstr Blvd -Qns Vllg 11427 **Fx**:264-3329
(845) 454-3250 .. **Traver**, Kelly L '03 %Gellert & K,PC -75 Wshngtn -Poughkeepsie 12601
(212) 766-1411 .. **Travers**, Gordon K '80 -145 W Bway -NY 10013
(212) 551-4000 .. **Travers**, Martin J '98 Sanofi-Synthelabo -90 Park Av -NY 10016 **Fx**:551-4919
(212) 288-1100 .. **Travers-Frazier**, Jude '98 Regis High Schl -55 E 84th -NY 10028
(212) 677-7171 .. **Traverso**, Anthony A '96 Cnsl Trust for Public Land -666 Bway -NY 10012
(212) 292-4557 .. **Travieso**, Andre G '01 -521 5th Av -NY 10175
(212) 454-7052 .. **Travin**, David A '02 %Deutsche Bank -60 Wall -NY 10005
(518) 213-6000 .. **Travinski**, Michl S '98 %NYSUT -800 Troy-Schnctdy Rd -Latham 12110 **Fx**:213-6488
(212) 490-3000 .. **Travis**, Brooke '08 %Wilson EME&D LLP -150 E 42nd -NY 10017
(516) 542-5900 .. **Travis**, Francis A '80 (Congdon FORDT&F) -333 Earle Ovngton Blvd -Uniondale 11553
(516) 303-9220 .. **Travis**, Norton L '78 Radiation Theraoy Srvcs,Inc -1010 Nrthrn Blvd -Gt Neck 11021
(516) 571-2628 .. **Travis**, Ronald C '73 %Hon A Brandveen -262 Old Cntry Rd -Mineola 11501
(212) 819-8200 .. **Travis**, Sarah R '10 %White & C LLP -1155 Av of Amer -NY 10036
(212) 894-7200 .. **Travisano**, Robt M '00 (Entwistle & C LLP) -280 Park Av -NY 10017
(212) 617-6888 .. **Tray**, Cody R '05 %Bloomberg LP -731 Lex Av -NY 10022
(212) 521-5400 .. **Traymore**, Anthony S '03 %Reed S LLP -599 Lex Av -NY 10022
(914) 286-3400 .. **Traynor**, Eugene T '74 %Leg Aid -1 N Bway -White Plns 10601 **Fx**:682-4112
(212) 761-7452 .. **Traynor**, Gary F '98 %Morgan Stanley -1585 Bway -NY 10036
(315) 475-3127 .. **Traynor**, Mary E '99 %Leg Srvcs -472 S Salina -Syracuse 13202 **Fx**:475-2706
(518) 427-6613 .. **Traynor**, Michl R '83 -70 Salisbury Rd -Delmar 12054
(585) 232-3464 .. **Traynor Skehan & Marks** -45 Exchange -Rchstr 14614 **Fx**:232-5948
(518) 474-6740 .. **Treacy**, David M '97 %Dept of State -41 State -Albany 12231 **Fx**:473-9211
(212) 227-8150 .. **Treacy Schaffel Moore & Mueller** -111 Bway -NY 10006 **Fx**:285-1968
(516) 759-1212 .. **Treacy**, Stephen T '84 (Mohen & T LLP) -186 Birch Hill Rd -Locust Vly 11560
(516) 688-1700 .. **Treadway**, Todd L '09 IRS -1600 Stewart Av -Westbury 11590 **Fx**:688-1750
(212) 382-6777 .. **Treadwell**, Nathan M '10 NYC Bar Assn -42 W 44th -NY 10036
(212) 688-9112 .. **Treadwell**, Shawn L '98 EP Dine Inc -115 E 57th -NY 10022 **Fx**:755-8486
(914) 738-3173 .. **Treanor**, Michl R '66 OfCnsl Muldoon H&L -271 North Av -New Rchll 10801
(212) 771-1830 .. **Treanor**, Michl Ready Jr. '93 Fremont Rlty Capital -375 Park Av -NY 10152
(212) 839-5300 .. **Treanor**, Timothy J '97 (Sidley A LLP) -787 7th Av -NY 10019
(212) 371-5400 .. **Treanor**, Wm F '60 %Weisman CS&M PC -445 Park Av -NY 10022
(518) 473-7712 .. **Treasure**, Kathleen M '95 %Dept of Law -The Cptl -Albany 12224
(212) 465-6000 .. **Treat**, Lucinda Kinau '98 Madison Sq Grdn,LP -2 Penn Plz -NY 10121 **Fx**:465-6011
(718) 543-7174 .. **Trebach**, Bradford '94 Trebach Realty -3801 Greystone Av -Bronx 10463
(518) 474-6750 .. **Trebby**, Leslie W '77 %Liquor Auth -80 S Swan -Albany 12210 **Fx**:402-2304
(518) 473-2278 .. **Trechel**, Gary M '87 %Dept of State -41 State -Albany 12231 **Fx**:474-5173
(718) 994-2833 .. **Treco**, Arnold Jr. '99 -634 Nereid Av -Bronx 10470
(718) 994-2833 .. **Treco**, Erika E E '98 %A Treco Jr -634 Nereid Av -Bronx 10470
Tredici, Elisabetta '00 -18 The Hllws S -E Norwich 11732
(212) 351-4500 .. **Treece**, James M '03 %Epstein B&G,PC -250 Park Av -NY 10177
(631) 361-9494 .. **Trees**, Tammy A '96 %A Vardaro,PC -732 Smithtwn Bypass -Smithtwn 11787 **Fx**:361-8752
(212) 446-4800 .. **Treesh**, Kevin W '92 (Kirkland & E LLP) -153 E 53rd -NY 10022
(718) 599-3500 .. **Treff**, Jos '00 (Treff & L PLLC) -342 Bedford Av -Brklyn 11211 **Fx**:387-6282
(646) 386-3628 .. **Treff**, Leslie C '86 Supreme Ct Spcl Master -60 Centre -NY 10007
(718) 644-8586 .. **Treff**, Rivka Malkie '09 M Treff,PC -1023 Nielson -Far Rckwy 11691 **Fx**:(347) 752-9321
(518) 285-8300 .. **Treffiletti**, Regina K '89 NYS Unified Ct Sys -40 Steuben -Albany 12207 **Fx**:426-1604
(516) 357-3700 .. **Tregarthen**, Erin M '03 %Cullen and D LLP -100 Q Roosevelt Blvd -Gdn Cty 11530
(631) 737-8200 .. **Treglia**, Elisa '97 %T Campagna -4949 Express Dr N -Ronkonkoma 11779 **Fx**:737-8687
(212) 583-2000 .. **Treglia**, Kristine F '04 Baron Capital -767 5th Av -NY 10153
(516) 571-3800 .. **Treglia**, Stephen V '80 %DA -262 Old Cntry Rd -Mineola 11501 **Fx**:248-9479
(212) 506-2500 .. **Trehan**, Amit K '04 %Mayer B LLP -1675 Bway -NY 10019
(212) 558-4000 .. **Treichel**, Eric A '10 %Sullivan & C LLP -125 Broad -NY 10004
(607) 569-2114 .. **Treichler**, Rachel '82 -7988 Van Amburg Rd -Hammondsprt 14840
(212) 825-0365 .. **Treiman**, Dov '81 (AL Bailey,PC) -120 Bway -NY 10271 **Fx**:825-0999
(631) 715-7913 .. **Treinis Gatz**, Lara '96 %US Atty -610 Fed Plz -Central Islip 11722
(212) 984-2548 .. **Treisman**, Michl B '02 Tiger Mgmt LLC -101 Park Av -NY 10178
(212) 574-1200 .. **Treitmeier-McCarthy**, Monica A '89 %Seward & K LLP -1 Bttry Pk Plz -NY 10004
(212) 336-2838 .. **Treloar**, Irene Choi '05 %Patterson BW&T LLP -1133 Av of Amer -NY 10036
(212) 588-0800 .. **Treloar**, Jos W '05 %Frommer L&H LLP -745 5th Av -NY 10151
(518) 388-4364 .. **Tremante**, Christina N '07 %DA -612 State -Schnctdy 12305 **Fx**:388-4569
(845) 452-8267 .. **Tremarzo**, Nancy H '85 -23 Rosalind Rd -Poughkeepsie 12601
(212) 375-2047 .. **Tremblay**, Peter D '97 %Amer Capital Access -140 Bway -NY 10005
(518) 372-1208 .. **Tremblay**, Renee '97 Matrimonial & Family Law Firm -162 Lafayette -Schnctdy 12305 **Fx**:372-3601
(718) 948-8900 .. **Tremer**, Gary S '82 (Tremer & T,PC) -16 Driggs -Staten Isl 10308 **Fx**:317-8550
(718) 948-8900 .. **Tremer**, Joan L '82 (Tremer & T,PC) -16 Driggs -Staten Isl 10308 **Fx**:317-8550
(718) 447-1962 .. **Tremer**, Stephen A '10 %Hall & H,LLP -57 Beach -Staten Isl 10304 **Fx**:447-2761
(212) 859-5059 .. **Tremiti**, Jos F '91 Tremiti LLC -110 Wall -NY 10005
(315) 422-1152 .. **Tremont**, Michl A '79 (Costello C&F,PLLC) -500 Plum -Syracuse 13204
(718) 254-6389 .. **Tremonte**, Michl '99 US DOJ -271 Cadman Plz E -Brklyn 11201
(518) 794-8100 .. **Tremper**, Robt J '97 -3546 Cnty Route 9 -E Chatham 12060
(212) 267-2827 .. **Tremsky**, Walter '60 -20 Vesey -NY 10007
(212) 230-8867 .. **Trenchard**, Robt W '95 (WilmerHale) -399 Park Av -NY 10022
(212) 880-9505 .. **Trencher**, Barbara L '04 (Morvillo AGIA&B,PC) -565 5th Av -NY 10017
(212) 474-1000 .. **Trenda**, Erin C '09 %Cravath S&M LLP -825 8th Av -NY 10019
(914) 591-7222 .. **Trent**, Bruce L '75 -S Buckhout -Irvngtn 10533
(305) 613-9015 .. **Trent**, Sarah E '09 -19 W 8th -NY 10011
(914) 995-2839 .. **Trentacoste**, Linda M '89 %Cnty Atty -148 Martine Av -White Plns 10601 **Fx**:995-5858
(516) 592-6800 .. **Trentacoste**, Peter S '05 %Spellman RSGM&P,LLP -229 Seventh -Gdn Cty 11530
(718) 459-9000 .. **Trepel**, Mindy J '82 Cnsl Sweeney GR&B,LLP -95-25 Qns Blvd -Rego Pk 11374
(212) 514-5007 .. **Trepelkova**, Nathalie '10 Rosenbaum & R,PC -110 Wall -NY 10005 **Fx**:514-9178
(718) 625-1100 .. **Trepp**, Howard I '93 (Hoberman & T,PC) -2622 E Tremont Av -Bronx 10461
(212) 728-8000 .. **Trepper**, Myron '69 SrCnsl Willkie F&G LLP -787 7th Av -NY 10019
(718) 522-1786 .. **Trerotola**, Deborah A '88 %Bonina & B,PC -16 Court -Brklyn 11241 **Fx**:243-0414
(716) 852-5875 .. **Tresch**, Gordon D '77 (Feldman K LLP) -110 Pearl -Buffalo 14202
(315) 466-4444 .. **Trespasz**, Theo A Jr. '83 (Trespasz & M) -251 W Fayette -Syracuse 13202 **Fx**:466-5555
(646) 833-0900 .. **Tressler LLP** -One Penn Plz -NY 10119 **Fx**:(212) 971-6263
(516) 542-2000 .. **Treston**, Darlene T '01 %JP Joseph & Assoc -666 Old Cntry Rd -Gdn Cty 11530 **Fx**:542-2001
(718) 237-2483 .. **Tretin**, Marc '81 -16 Court -Brklyn 11241
(646) 312-4179 .. **Tretjak**, Kaja '06 Baruch Cllg Sociology & Anthropology -17 Lex Av #B4-260 -NY 10010 **Fx**:312-4461
(212) 252-0300 .. **Tretola**, Stephen M '02 %Kagan LLLG&C,LLP -200 Mad Av -NY 10016
(212) 226-2376 .. **Tretter**, Brian S '03 %Oved & O LLP -101 Av of Amer -NY 10013 **Fx**:226-7555
(212) 826-6426 .. **Tretter**, Elizabeth '96 %RZB Finance LLC -1133 Av of Amer -NY 10036
(914) 632-4700 .. **Tretter**, Franklin E '57 (McDonough Law Firm, LLP) -145 Huguenot -New Rchll 10801
(212) 918-3000 .. **Tretter**, Lyndon M '86 (Hogan L LLP) -875 3rd Av -NY 10022
(212) 508-6100 .. **Tretter**, Robb L '97 (Bracewell & G,LLP) -1251 Av of Amer -NY 10020
(212) 725-6418 .. **Treuhaft**, Ira '05 (Treuhaft & Z,LLP) -1011 Av of Amer -NY 10018
(212) 848-4000 .. **Treuhold**, Robt C '84 Shearman & S LLP -599 Lex Av -NY 10022
(716) 938-9111 .. **Treusdell**, John R '80 %Supreme Ct -303 Court -Little Vly 14755 **Fx**:938-6413
(585) 454-2181 .. **Trevett Cristo Salzer & Andolina,PC** -2 State -Rchstr 14614 **Fx**:454-4026
(585) 454-2181 .. **Trevett**, Thos N '67 (Trevett CS&A,PC) -2 State -Rchstr 14614
(212) 558-4000 .. **Trevino**, Marc R '95 (Sullivan & C LLP) -125 Broad -NY 10004
(585) 419-8800 .. **Trevvett**, Edw A '91 (Harris B PLLC) -99 Garnsey Rd -Pittsfrd 14534
(518) 445-8415 .. **Trexler**, Holly A '98 -100 State -Albany 12207 **Fx**:445-8416
(212) 566-8080 .. **Trexler**, Jonathan T '04 %Wong W & Assoc,PC -150 Bway -NY 10038 **Fx**:566-8960
(646) 471-4000 .. **Trey**, Jeffrey S '04 %PricewaterhouseCoopers LLP -300 Mad Av -NY 10017
(212) 897-5832 .. **Treyvus**, Kira '03 (Treyvus & K,PC) -305 Bway -NY 10007
(212) 483-2323 .. **Treyz**, Debra Beth '78 %JP Morgan Chase -345 Park Av -NY 10154
(212) 735-3000 .. **Triaca**, Hugo F '04 %Skadden ASM&F LLP -4 Times Sq -NY 10036
(718) 229-0100 .. **Triades**, Meri O '03 -214-05 39th Av -Bayside 11361
(718) 229-0100 .. **Triades**, Terry S '66 -214-05 39th Av -Bayside 11361 **Fx**:281-2531
(212) 872-9800 .. **Trialonas**, Lauren M '07 %Squire S&D LLP -30 Rckfllr Plz -NY 10112
(212) 689-4244 .. **Tribbitt**, Chas R '76 (Schaier T&S) -275 Mad Av -NY 10016
(914) 741-6100 .. **Tribble**, Julie Ann '05 %Kaufman B&R -200 Summit Lk Dr -Valhalla 10595
(518) 465-7581 .. **Tribble**, Phillip M '79 (Herzog Law Firm,PC) -7 Southwoods Blvd -Albany 12211
(718) 250-2000 .. **Tricardo**, Richd T '07 %DA -350 Jay -Brklyn 11201 **Fx**:250-2314
(212) 852-1000 .. **Tricarico**, Jos A '74 %US Trust Co,NA -114 W 47th -NY 10036 **Fx**:852-1310
(212) 269-4900 .. **Tricarico**, Michl J '92 (Ford MEW&G,LLP) -Wall Street Plz -NY 10005
(607) 734-3400 .. **Trice**, John R '85 (Proudfoot Law Firm) -150 Lk -Elmira 14901 **Fx**:733-0439
(212) 873-9570 .. **Trichter**, Nancy J '78 -285 Cntrl Pk W -NY 10024 **Fx**:874-4606
(212) 655-6000 .. **Tricomi**, Chas W '85 (Chapman & C LLP) -330 Mad Av -NY 10017
(212) 909-6000 .. **Tricot**, Dagmar '01 %Debevoise & P LLP -919 3rd Av -NY 10022
(212) 223-4000 .. **Tridgell**, Amy T '01 Cnsl Crowell & M LLP -590 Mad Av -NY 10022
(212) 777-5309 .. **Trieber**, Edw J '70 -55 W 16th -NY 10011
(845) 758-4113 .. **Triebwasser**, Jonah I '80 Vllg Justice Ct -7467 S Bway -Red Hook 12571 **Fx**:758-1695
(212) 221-5999 .. **Trief**, Frank '94 (Antin E&E,LLP) -49 W 37th -NY 10018
(212) 486-6060 .. **Trief & Olk** -150 E 58th -NY 10155 **Fx**:317-2946

(212) 486-6060 .. **Trief,** Ted E '77 (Trief & O) -150 E 58th -NY 10155
(212) 362-2173 .. **Trien,** Robt M '61 -90 Riverside Dr -NY 10024 **Fx:**787-8275
(212) 450-4000 .. **Trier,** Dana '75 (Davis P&W LLP) -450 Lex Av -NY 10017
(212) 483-9490 .. **Trif,** Greg '06 %McElroy DM&C,LLP -88 Pine -NY 10005
(212) 574-1200 .. **Trigg,** Erin E '08 %Seward & K LLP -1 Bttry Pk Plz -NY 10004
(212) 318-6000 .. **Trigg,** Stephen T '10 %Paul HJ&W LLP -75 E 55th -NY 10022
(516) 227-0700 .. **Trigger,** Jason '04 %Farrell F,PC -1320 RXR Plz -Uniondale 11556
(716) 854-4500 .. **Trigilio,** John L '83 -438 Main -Buffalo 14202 **Fx:**856-8628
(212) 326-2000 .. **Triller,** Todd R '98 (O'Melveny & M LLP) -7 Times Sq -NY 10036
(718) 478-3200 .. **Trillo,** Juan '82 -37-06 82nd -Jcksn Hts 11372 **Fx:**397-9061
(718) 829-7400 .. **Trimarchi,** Margaret C '93 %T Lavin Jr -2980 Bruckner Blvd -Bronx 10465 **Fx:**829-7356
(518) 487-7600 .. **Trimarchi,** Peter C '99 OfCnsl Whiteman O&H LLP -1 Commerce Plz -Albany 12260
(718) 643-4546 .. **Trimarchi,** Sadaf '98 Family Ct -283 Adams -Brklyn 11201
(212) 609-6800 .. **Trimarco,** Gina M '97 %McCarter & E,LLP -245 Park Av -NY 10167
(631) 543-3456 .. **Trimarco,** Vincent J '68 -1038 W Jericho Tpk -Smithtwn 11787
(631) 543-3456 .. **Trimarco,** Vincent J Jr. '97 %V Trimarco -1038 W Jericho Tpk -Smithtwn 11787
(212) 962-5757 .. **Trimming,** Sarah D '09 %Gaffin & M,PC -225 Bway -NY 10007
(716) 842-2150 .. **Trimper,** George J Jr. '78 %Workers Comp Bd -107 Delaware Av -Buffalo 14202
(315) 788-2010 .. **Trimper,** Paul D '79 (Weldon & T) -119-125 Sherman -Watertwn 13601
(212) 455-2000 .. **Tringali,** Jos F '81 (Simpson T&B LLP) -425 Lex Av -NY 10017
(914) 722-0422 .. **Tringali,** Jos J A '73 -670 Post Rd -Scarsdale 10583
(914) 328-0404 .. **Trinh,** Nadine T '07 %Jackson L LLP -1 N Bway -White Plns 10601
(212) 348-7449 .. **Trinidad,** Lenina C '01 %Legal Srvcs -1 W 125th -NY 10027 **Fx:**348-4093
(212) 351-4000 .. **Trinklein,** Jeffrey M '07 (Gibson D&C LLP) -200 Park Av -NY 10166
(212) 490-9550 .. **Trinko,** Curtis V '75 -16 W 46th -NY 10036 **Fx:**986-0158
(516) 465-8090 .. **Trinkoff,** Alexandra E '90 %North Shore-LIJ Hlth Systm -145 Community Dr -Gt Neck 11021 **Fx:**465-8013
(716) 842-1100 .. **Tripi,** Deanne M '96 (Palmer M&T) -288 Linwood Av -Buffalo 14209 **Fx:**842-1104
(716) 843-5700 .. **Tripi,** Jos M '04 %US Atty -138 Delaware Av -Buffalo 14202 **Fx:**551-3052
(212) 458-1174 .. **Tripodes,** Maria I '03 AIG -175 Water -NY 10038
(914) 962-0900 .. **Tripodi,** Anthony J '76 -40 Triangle Ctr -Yorktwn Hts 10598 **Fx:**962-4959
(212) 973-0572 .. **Tripodi,** Jos '98 (Wolff & S PC) -140 Bway -NY 10005
(212) 349-6775 .. **Tripodi,** Wendy C '92 %Peltz & W -222 Bway -NY 10038
(516) 316-2955 .. **Tripodianos,** Dimos C '08 -207 Mineola Av -Roslyn Hts 11577
(914) 428-2100 .. **Tripodianos,** Thos S '97 %Welby B&G,LLP -11 Martine Av -White Plns 10606
(212) 701-3000 .. **Tripodoro,** John A '90 (Cahill G&R LLP) -80 Pine -NY 10005 **Fx:**269-5420
(800) 521-1260 .. **Tripoli,** Louis J '88 %Petrone & P,PC -108 W Jffrsn -Syracuse 13202
(914) 749-8200 .. **Tripolitsiotis,** Matthew S '05 %Boies S&F LLP -333 Main -Armonk 10504
(315) 437-0661 .. **Tripolone,** Philip '68 -303 Leighton Av -Syracuse 13206
(212) 779-9910 .. **Tripp,** Alexander D '98 (Eaton & V LLP) -3 Park Av -NY 10016
(212) 505-2100 .. **Tripp,** James T B '67 %Envrnmntl Def Fund -257 Park Av S -NY 10010 **Fx:**505-2375
(631) 247-0404 .. **Tripp,** Noel P '07 %Jackson L LLP -58 S Srvc Rd -Melvll 11747
(212) 840-8334 .. **Trippett,** Lewis P '78 (Higgins & T LLP) -36 W 44th -NY 10036
(212) 261-8000 .. **Trismen,** Raymond R '84 (Mendes & M,LLP) -750 7th Av -NY 10019
(212) 701-3000 .. **Trisotto,** Robt S '10 %Cahill G&R LLP -80 Pine -NY 10005 **Fx:**269-5420
(212) 724-6289 .. **Tritter,** Danl F '84 -11 Riverside Dr -NY 10023
(212) 354-7700 .. **Tritto,** Sharyn A '87 %Penn PS&S -114 W 47th -NY 10036
(212) 697-2342 .. **Tritto,** Vincent B '88 Primus Asset Mgmt,Inc -360 Mad Av -NY 10017
(212) 964-0455 .. **Tritz,** Jerry L '72 -299 Bway -NY 10007 **Fx:**331-1044
(212) 558-4000 .. **Trivedi,** Harsh N '04 %Sullivan & C LLP -125 Broad -NY 10004
(718) 286-6000 .. **Trivedi,** Julie S '02 %DA -125-01 Qns Blvd -Kew Gdns 11415
(516) 470-1379 .. **Trivedi,** Nehal M '02 (DiCrescio & T,LLP) -400 Jericho Tpk -Jericho 11753 **Fx:**470-1382
(212) 969-3000 .. **Trivedi,** Paresh '02 %Proskauer R LLP -1585 Bway -NY 10036
(212) 230-8800 .. **Trivedi,** Somil B '10 %WilmerHale -399 Park Av -NY 10022
(212) 310-8000 .. **Trivedi,** Sujan H '08 %Weil G&M LLP -767 5th Av -NY 10153
(914) 949-9075 .. **Trivella,** Scott P '89 (Trivella & F LLP) -1311 Mamaroneck Av -White Plns 10605 **Fx:**949-4752
(212) 732-3200 .. **Trivigno,** Leonardo '06 %Carter L&M LLP -2 Wall -NY 10005
(718) 579-7900 .. **Trivikram,** Rekha '07 Leg Aid -900 Sheridan Av -Bronx 10451 **Fx:**293-8744
(212) 504-6000 .. **Troast,** Jean E '09 %Cadwalader W&T LLP -1 World Fncl Ctr -NY 10281
(516) 869-9000 .. **Trocchio,** Charlotte A '00 %Kimco Realty Corp -3333 New Hyde Pk Rd -New Hyde Pk 11042 **Fx:**869-7199
(646) 386-3041 .. **Trocchio,** Lisa M '03 Supreme Ct-Law Dept -60 Centre -NY 10007
(631) 382-7979 .. **Trodden,** Brian A '98 (Castro & T,LLC) -29 Bellemeade Av -Smithtwn 11787 **Fx:**382-7974
(516) 352-6677 .. **Trodden,** Pamela Giugliano '98 %F & F Roofing -311 Jericho Tpk -Floral Pk 11001 **Fx:**352-4440
(631) 462-0181 .. **Trodden,** Selena E '95 -22 Elton Dr -E Northprt 11731
(212) 201-2500 .. **Troetel,** Dana A '03 Aetos Capital -875 3rd Av -NY 10022
(914) 946-1875 .. **Troetti,** Thos J '81 -305 Old Tarrytown Rd -White Plns 10603 **Fx:**949-1342
(516) 877-5600 .. **Trogel,** Lawr J '94 %R Tusa -1225 Franklin Av -Gdn Cty 11530 **Fx:**877-5695
(212) 261-8000 .. **Troha,** Michl W '10 %Mendes & M,LLP -750 7th Av -NY 10019
(212) 233-9772 .. **Troia,** Andrew F '98 (Cullen & T,PC) -2 Rector -NY 10006
(212) 479-6000 .. **Troiano,** Anne Marie '00 SrCnsl Cooley LLP -1114 Av of Amer -NY 10036
(718) 541-0168 .. **Troiano,** Gabriele J '66 -105 W 46th -NY 10019
(718) 590-2000 .. **Troiano,** Jennifer C '04 %DA -198 E 161st -Bronx 10451 **Fx:**590-6477
(914) 779-2393 .. **Troiano,** Joy P '86 (Troiano & T) -81 Pondfld Rd -Bronxvll 10708 **Fx:**779-0161
(212) 735-3000 .. **Troiano,** Marissa E '10 %Skadden ASM&F LLP -4 Times Sq -NY 10036
(914) 779-2393 .. **Troiano,** Michl A '84 (Troiano & T) -81 Pondfld Rd -Bronxvll 10708 **Fx:**779-0161
(718) 858-7100 .. **Troiano,** Michl F '82 -26 Court -Brklyn 11242 **Fx:**522-2828
(212) 225-2000 .. **Troie,** Sergiu Z '08 %Cleary GS&H -1 Lbrty Plz -NY 10006
(212) 298-1826 .. **Troise,** Kenneth N '03 Bank of NY -101 Barclay -NY 10286
(631) 423-3800 .. **Troise,** Patrick A '73 -390 Wolf Hill Rd -Dix Hlls 11746 **Fx:**423-3819
(212) 553-5400 .. **Troisi,** Christopher J '94 %Zurich NA -1 Lbrty Plz -NY 10006
(212) 957-9600 .. **Troisi,** Filippo '92 %Gianni OG & Prtnrs -75 Rckfllr Plz -NY 10019
(516) 357-3000 .. **Troisi,** Michl A '86 (Rivkin R LLP) -926 RXR Plz -Uniondale 11556
(212) 353-0040 .. **Troisi,** Michl E '73 (Allen MT&S) -112 E 19th -NY 10003
(212) 872-1000 .. **Troitsky,** Roman V '01 -One Bryant Park -NY 10036 **Fx:**872-1002
(212) 687-0100 .. **Trokan,** Mark A '05 %Harris B PLLC -100 Wall -NY 10005
(212) 484-3900 .. **Trokenheim,** Matthew S '06 %Arent F LLP -1675 Bway -NY 10019
(212) 458-1563 .. **Trokenheim,** Michl S '97 %AIGTS -175 Water -NY 10038
(914) 694-9500 .. **Trokie,** Douglas S '84 (Trokie L LLP) -1133 Wstchstr Av -White Plns 10604
(914) 694-9500 .. **Trokie Landau LLP** -1133 Wstchstr Av -White Plns 10604 **Fx:**694-9550
(212) 964-1661 .. **Trokie Landau LLP** -225 Bway -NY 10007 **Fx:**(866) 822-5549
(212) 750-1200 .. **Trolman,** David S '60 (Trolman G&L,PC) -777 3rd Av -NY 10017
(212) 750-1200 .. **Trolman Glaser & Lichtman,PC** -777 3rd Av -NY 10017 **Fx:**980-4011
(518) 248-5023 .. **Trombadore,** Sarah J '95 -1426 Peaceable -Ballston Spa 12020
(518) 561-4400 .. **Trombley,** Edw John '59 Stafford OC&T,PLLC -1 Cumberland Av Bx2947 -Plattsbrgh 12901
(518) 429-4200 .. **Trombly,** Edw J '71 (Hiscock & B,LLP) -50 Beaver -Albany 12207
(631) 577-2400 .. **Tromello McDonnell & Kehoe** -25 Melvll Park Rd Bx9038 -Melvll 11747 **Fx:**577-2401
(631) 577-2400 .. **Tromello,** Michl C '83 (Tromello M&K) -25 Melvll Park Rd Bx9038 -Melvll 11747
(518) 402-6757 .. **Tromp,** Sharon K '95 %Workers Comp Bd -20 Park -Albany 12207
(212) 231-8094 .. **Troncoso,** Alberto J '94 %Macquarie Hldngs -125 W 55th -NY 10019
(716) 713-2199 .. **Tronolone,** Carl '56 -298 Main -Buffalo 14202 **Fx:**856-2629
(716) 856-2626 .. **Tronolone,** Danl G Sr. '70 (Tronolone & S,PC) -298 Main -Buffalo 14202
(716) 856-5140 .. **Tronolone,** Robt J '63 -42 Delaware Av -Buffalo 14202
(716) 856-2626 .. **Tronolone & Surgalla,PC** -298 Main -Buffalo 14202 **Fx:**856-2629
(845) 356-9340 .. **Troodler,** Meryl C '86 (Canetti & T,LLP) -3 Arcadian Dr -Spg Vly 10977
(845) 356-9340 .. **Troodler,** Nachman Aaron '00 (Canetti & T,LLP) -3 Arcadian Dr -Spg Vly 10977
(212) 504-6000 .. **Troop,** Andrew M '08 (Cadwalader W&T LLP) -1 World Fncl Ctr -NY 10281
(212) 852-1000 .. **Troost,** Glenn M '87 %US Trust Co,NA -114 W 47th -NY 10036 **Fx:**852-1310
(718) 357-4333 .. **Trop,** Gary M '78 (Trop & S) -19-02 Whitestone Expy -Whitestone 11357
(315) 445-8670 .. **Trop,** John V '88 %MA Bjork -5784 Widewaters Pkwy -DeWitt 13214 **Fx:**445-8688
(516) 785-2838 .. **Trop,** M Marc '91 -1414 Lbrty Av -N Bellmore 11710 **Fx:**781-9192
(516) 745-1800 .. **Trop,** Robt E '91 (Besen & T,LLP) -825 E Gate Blvd -Gdn Cty 11530
(718) 357-4333 .. **Trop & Spindler** -19-02 Whitestone Expy -Whitestone 11357
(212) 308-7558 .. **Trope,** Roland L '82 (Trope & T) -310 E 49th -NY 10017 **Fx:**980-1915
(914) 666-9309 .. **Tropp,** Arlene '85 (Tropp & T) -195 Croton Av -Mt Kisco 10549 **Fx:**666-4678
(718) 720-6060 .. **Tropp,** Chas R '68 -30 Bay -Staten Isl 10301 **Fx:**442-0923
(914) 666-9309 .. **Tropp,** Harvey '63 (Tropp & T) -195 Croton Av -Mt Kisco 10549 **Fx:**666-4678
(212) 902-4147 .. **Tropp,** Matthew E '95 %Goldman Sachs -1 NY Plz -NY 10004
(212) 859-8000 .. **Tropp,** Paul D '97 (Fried FHS&J LLP) -1 NY Plz -NY 10004
(212) 244-1717 .. **Tropper,** Martin David -445 Park Av Fifteenth Fl -NY 10022
(516) 576-1440 .. **Tropper,** Matthew B '93 Tropper Technologies -30 Southrn Pkwy -Plainvw 11803
(212) 592-1400 .. **Tross,** Scott T '82 (Herrick,F LLP) -2 Park Av -NY 10016
(607) 547-8500 .. **Trosset Group Attorneys** -31 Pioneer Bx28 -Cooperstwn 13326 **Fx:**547-8601
(607) 547-8500 .. **Trosset,** Michl E '99 (Trosset Grp) -31 Pioneer Bx28 -Cooperstwn 13326
(212) 237-0000 .. **Trost,** J Ronald '94 OfCnsl Vinson & E LLP -666 5th Av -NY 10103
(585) 586-8480 .. **Trost,** Jonathan H '66 OfCnsl Creary & C -18 N Main -Pittsfrd 14534
(718) 293-4300 .. **Trost,** Lonn A '72 (NY Yankees) -Yankee Stadium -Bronx 10451 **Fx:**681-1051
(212) 239-0300 .. **Trost,** Philip B '69 -330 W 42nd -NY 10036 **Fx:**239-4935
(866) 348-5819 .. **Trost,** Timothy '68 SSA-ODAR -50 Fountain Plz -Buffalo 14202 **Fx:**(716) 551-4078
(212) 891-1600 .. **Trostle,** Patrick J '93 (Jenner & B LLP) -919 3rd Av -NY 10022
(718) 346-9390 .. **Trotman,** Grace P '95 (G Trotman,PC) -5310 Church Av -Brklyn 11203 **Fx:**346-0274
(212) 225-2000 .. **Trotman,** Greta E M '10 %Cleary GS&H -1 Lbrty Plz -NY 10006
(212) 221-1500 .. **Trott,** Dennis C '74 -305 Bway -NY 10007 **Fx:**693-1410
(716) 849-0328 .. **Trott,** Emily P '97 -112 Franklin -Buffalo 14202
(914) 699-2991 .. **Trott,** Sophia L '92 S Trott,PC -9 W Prospect Av -Mt Vernon 10550
(212) 883-1700 .. **Trott,** Stacie E '07 %Duval & S LLP -101 Park Av -NY 10178
(212) 902-3854 .. **Trotta,** Louis '90 Goldman Sachs -85 Broad -NY 10004
(518) 789-3636 .. **Trotta,** Robt D '66 OfCnsl Davis & T -Millerton Plz Bx481 -Millerton 12546 **Fx:**789-6654
(212) 236-5924 .. **Trotta,** Stanley '94 Merrill Lynch Trust Co -Wrld Fncl Ctr -NY 10080
(212) 351-4500 .. **Trotter,** Amy M '07 %Epstein B&G,PC -250 Park Av -NY 10177
(716) 883-1900 .. **Trotter,** Joy C '95 Intl Inst of Buffalo -864 Delaware Av -Buffalo 14209
(516) 437-4385 .. **Trotti,** Jos '84 (Vishnick MM LLP) -3000 Marcus Av -Lk Success 11042
(631) 589-5000 .. **Trotto,** Janessa M '03 %Van Brunt J&R -140 Main -Sayvll 11782
(585) 453-0040 .. **Trotto,** Jonathan C '09 -1100 Long Pond Rd -Rchstr 14626
(518) 238-1345 .. **Troue,** Gary '84 %Troue -342 6th Av -Troy 12182 **Fx:**238-0143

(518) 238-1345 .. **Troue,** Sherry M '91 (Troue) -342 6th Av -Troy 12182 **Fx:**238-0143
(631) 853-4104 .. **Troulakis,** Maria A '09 %DA -400 Carleton Av Bx9082 -Central Islip 11722 **Fx:**853-7838
(212) 216-8000 .. **Troup,** Steven '81 (Tarter K&D LLP) -1350 Bway -NY 10018
(212) 714-1720 .. **Trousdale,** Wm H '87 (Tompkins MW&B LLP) -140 Bway -NY 10005
(212) 657-0628 .. **Trout,** Raquel U '04 Citigroup Global Mrkts -111 Wall -NY 10005
(212) 664-5511 .. **Troutman,** Rhonda D '96 %NBC -30 Rckfllr Plz -NY 10112
(212) 704-6000 .. **Troutman Sanders LLP** -405 Lex Av -NY 10174 **Fx:**704-6288
(631) 913-4444 .. **Trovato,** George C Jr. '96 (Dell LT&V LLP) -5 Orvll Dr -Bohemia 11716
(212) 578-5881 .. **Trovato,** Jos '82 %MetLife -27-01 Qns Plz N -LIC 11101
(716) 832-1118 .. **Trow,** W Clark '80 %N Saia -1925 Kensngtn Av -Buffalo 14215 **Fx:**832-7074
(212) 336-2000 .. **Trowbridge,** Caroline W '07 %Patterson BW&T LLP -1133 Av of Amer -NY 10036
(212) 486-0124 .. **Trowbridge & Sullivan** -515 Mad Av -NY 10022 **Fx:**486-0701
(212) 408-2500 .. **Trowbridge,** Thos R III '70 SpclCnsl Baker B,LLP -30 Rckfllr Plz -NY 10112
(212) 450-4000 .. **Trowel,** Kevin M '08 %Davis P&W LLP -450 Lex Av -NY 10017
(917) 551-1300 .. **Troxler,** Peter C '02 %Koehler & I LLP -61 Bway -NY 10006
(212) 557-2900 .. **Troy,** Bernard E '72 (Schwartzman GW&T,PC) -355 Lex Av -NY 10017
(212) 460-4600 .. **Troy,** Brian M '03 Con Ed -4 Irving Pl -NY 10003
(516) 677-9660 .. **Troy,** Catherine M '10 %Faber & T -180 Froehlich Farm Blvd -Woodbury 11797
(631) 239-6817 .. **Troy,** Edw J '88 -44 Bway -Greenlawn 11740 **Fx:**239-6816
(607) 722-6417 .. **Troy,** James J '81 -45 Chenango -Bnghmtn 13901 **Fx:**722-8019
(631) 738-1436 .. **Troy,** James J '88 (Troy & T,PC) -382 Rosevale Av -Lk Ronkonkoma 11779 **Fx:**738-1438
(212) 335-9000 .. **Troy,** Jessica R '04 %DA -1 Hogan Pl -NY 10013
(631) 738-1436 .. **Troy,** Jos B '95 Troy & T,PC -382 Rosevale Av -Lk Ronkonkoma 11779
(212) 728-8000 .. **Troy,** Joshua M '08 %Willkie F&G LLP -787 7th Av -NY 10019
(212) 538-1014 .. **Troy,** Kathryn J '90 CSFB -1 Mad Av -NY 10010
(718) 626-2765 .. **Troy,** Kevin F '05 Verizon -19-19 46th -Astoria 11105
(516) 677-9660 .. **Troy,** Matthew J III '88 %Faber & T -180 Froehlich Farm Blvd -Woodbury 11797
(631) 239-6817 .. **Troy,** Maureen S '92 %E Troy -44 Bway -Greenlawn 11740 **Fx:**239-6816
(718) 238-3599 .. **Troy,** Michl J '69 -6822 Colonial Rd -Brklyn 11220
(212) 806-5400 .. **Troy,** Pamela N '05 %Stroock &S&L LLP -180 Maiden Ln -NY 10038
(212) 839-5300 .. **Troy,** Patrick J '07 %Sidley A LLP -787 7th Av -NY 10019
(212) 773-6868 .. **Troy,** Patrisha S '09 Ernst & Young -5 Times Sq -NY 10036
(914) 468-0824 .. **Troy,** Richd L '95 -600 Mamaroneck Av -Harrison 10528
(914) 835-4789 .. **Troy,** Stuart '63 -Bx949 -Harrison 10528
(607) 277-6611 .. **Troy,** Wm J III '79 (Troy & T,PC) -120 E Buffalo -Ithaca 14850 **Fx:**277-3330
(212) 837-6000 .. **Troya,** Edmund B '03 %Hughes H&R LLP -1 Bttry Pk Plz -NY 10004
(212) 446-4800 .. **Troyer,** Travis M '08 %Kirkland & E LLP -153 E 53rd -NY 10022
(212) 447-6206 .. **Troyetsky,** A Mitchell '85 -185 Mad Av -NY 10016 **Fx:**447-6204
(212) 918-3000 .. **Trubin,** Andrew J '80 (Hogan L LLP) -875 3rd Av -NY 10022
(212) 732-7707 .. **Trubitsky,** Marina '99 M Trubitsky & Assoc,PLLC -11 Bway -NY 10004 **Fx:**732-7708
(845) 638-5001 .. **Trudell,** Robt H '07 %DA -1 S Main -New Cty 10956 **Fx:**638-5070
(212) 891-6100 .. **True,** Adam W '00 Capital Mrkts NA -9 W 57th -NY 10019
(607) 273-2301 .. **True,** Sally T '79 (True W&S,LLP) -950 Danby Rd -Ithaca 14850
(607) 273-2301 .. **True Walsh & Schubert,LLP** -950 Danby Rd -Ithaca 14850 **Fx:**272-1901
(212) 940-3027 .. **Trueheart,** Harry P III '70 (Nixon P LLP) -437 Mad Av -NY 10022
(585) 753-4500 .. **Truelove,** Alyssa M '06 DA -832 Watts Bldg -Rchstr 14614 **Fx:**753-4576
(516) 742-1460 .. **Trueman,** David L '97 -221 Mineola Blvd -Mineola 11501 **Fx:**294-5709
(212) 450-4000 .. **Truesdell,** Richd D Jr. '87 (Davis P&W LLP) -450 Lex Av -NY 10017
(716) 285-3475 .. **Truex,** Shelley Anne '93 (Quarantillo & T) -625 6th -Niagara Fls 14301 **Fx:**285-8162
(631) 734-6450 .. **Truglia,** Dunewood '77 %Dalton Environmental, Ltd -Bx222 -New Suffolk 11956 **Fx:**734-5152
(516) 342-2200 .. **Truhowsky,** Deborah N F '88 (Schwartzapfel Prtnrs) -300 Jericho Quad -Jericho 11753
(516) 489-3644 .. **Truicko,** Annalisa C '97 %Local 1298 Benefit Funds -681 Fulton Av Bx309 -Hempstd 11551 **Fx:**489-0639
(212) 672-1966 .. **Truitt,** Alan Brent '90 OfCnsl Hennigan B&D LLP -345 Park Av -NY 10154 **Fx:**672-1965
(516) 408-7030 .. **Truitt,** James P III '01 OfCnsl T Sherwood,LLC -300 Grdn City Plz -Gdn Cty 11530 **Fx:**408-7032
(212) 735-3000 .. **Trujillo,** Geralyn J '99 %Skadden ASM&F LLP -4 Times Sq -NY 10036
(212) 715-1000 .. **Trujillo,** Juan Manuel '99 (Arnold & P LLP) -399 Park Av -NY 10022
Trujillo, Luis R '04 -350 5th Av -NY 10118
(518) 235-0546 .. **Truland,** David W '84 -Bx367 -Waterfrd 12188
(212) 848-4000 .. **Trulock,** Sharon '89 Cnsl Shearman & S LLP -599 Lex Av -NY 10022
(212) 533-6300 .. **Truly,** Elizabeth A '77 %NYSUT -52 Bway -NY 10004 **Fx:**995-2347
(212) 294-6700 .. **Trum,** Sarah L '03 %Winston & S -200 Park Av -NY 10166
(212) 530-5000 .. **Truman,** Trevor K '07 %Milbank TH&M LLP -1 Chase Manh Plz -NY 10005
(212) 506-1700 .. **Trumbull,** Amber A '10 Kasowitz BT&F LLP -1633 Bway -NY 10019
(631) 423-6738 .. **Trumbull,** Wayne A '01 Greenholtz & Crocco -755 Park Av -Huntngtn 11743
(914) 997-6524 .. **Trummer-Napolitano,** Linda '83 -445 Hmltn Av -White Plns 10601 **Fx:**997-0199
(631) 689-8600 .. **Trump & Boutcher,LLP** -46 Route 25A Bx830 -E Setauket 11733 **Fx:**689-7412
(646) 213-0159 .. **Trump,** Denise M '05 IBM Business Consulting Srvcs -11 Mad Av -NY 10010
(631) 689-8600 .. **Trump,** James D '74 (Trump & B,LLP) -46 Route 25A Bx830 -E Setauket 11733
(716) 652-4263 .. **Trumpler,** Douglas R '87 -111 Kirkwood Dr -Elma 14059 **Fx:**652-1757
(516) 592-6800 .. **Truncale,** Benjamin J '00 (Spellman RSGM&P,LLP) -229 Seventh -Gdn Cty 11530
(212) 716-5800 .. **Truncellito,** Gene '83 %Amer Arbtrtn Assn -1633 Bway -NY 10019
(315) 435-2470 .. **Trunfio,** Domenic F '91 %DA -505 S State -Syracuse 13202 **Fx:**435-3969
(718) 622-4182 .. **Trunk,** Carl F Jr. '63 -153 Underhill Av -Brklyn 11238 **Fx:**622-7297
(212) 317-8500 .. **Trunkes,** Virginia K '98 %Snitow KH&M,LLP -575 Lex Av -NY 10022
(212) 733-6491 .. **Trunko,** Tiffany D '91 %Pfizer Inc -150 E 42nd -NY 10017
(212) 504-6000 .. **Trunzo,** Brian M '10 %Cadwalader W&T LLP -1 World Fncl Ctr -NY 10281
(631) 324-4999 .. **Trunzo,** Pat J III '85 -Bx5025 -E Hampton 11937 **Fx:**324-8904
(212) 859-8000 .. **Truong,** Sarah J T C '07 %Fried FHS&J LLP -1 NY Plz -NY 10004
(516) 364-7900 .. **Trupia,** Lee Ann R '90 Epstein F&G -45 Crsswys Park Dr W -Woodbury 11797
(212) 577-2523 .. **Trupp,** Claudia S '93 %Ctr for Appllt Litigation -74 Trinity Pl -NY 10006 **Fx:**577-2535
(718) 875-7325 .. **Truslow,** Sophia L '82 -212 Pacific -Brklyn 11201 **Fx:**488-7222
(212) 751-4300 .. **Trussell,** Jacquelyn R '05 %Hodgson R LLP -1540 Bway -NY 10036
(212) 506-2500 .. **Trust,** Brian '87 (Mayer B LLP) -1675 Bway -NY 10019
(212) 474-1000 .. **Trust,** Robt H '99 %Cravath S&M LLP -825 8th Av -NY 10019
(212) 986-7410 .. **Truyol,** Isabel '00 %Malina & Assoc -444 Mad Av -NY 10022 **Fx:**983-8421
(914) 789-2846 .. **Truzman,** Jose '02 Progenics Pharm -777 Old Saw Mill Rvr Rd -Tarrytwn 10591 **Fx:**789-2856
(212) 374-6888 .. **Trybulski,** Stanley F '95 %NYC Dept Educ-OLS -52 Chmbrs -NY 10007 **Fx:**374-5596
(716) 858-5000 .. **Trybus,** Janice R '79 Delaware North -40 Fountain Plz -Buffalo 14202 **Fx:**858-5056
(516) 571-3800 .. **Tryon,** Lora J '99 DA -262 Old Cntry Rd -Mineola 11501 **Fx:**248-9479
(212) 668-1900 .. **Trzaskoma,** Theresa M '99 (Brune & R LLP) -80 Broad -NY 10004
(888) 415-5382 .. **Tsadok,** Debra S '85 -16-79 E 3rd -Brklyn 11230 **Fx:**415-5383
(718) 993-5990 .. **Tsai,** Betsy C '02 %Sanctuary for Families -110 Wall -NY 10005 **Fx:**(212) 566-0344
(212) 732-2929 .. **Tsai,** Chang-Hui '07 %Dansker & A Assoc -30 Vesey -NY 10007 **Fx:**732-8795
Tsai, Daphne S '91 -5014 16th Av -Brklyn 11204
(212) 841-1000 .. **Tsai,** Edw '09 %Covington & B LLP -620 8th Av -NY 10018
(212) 538-3616 .. **Tsai,** Edw S '99 Credit Suisse -1 Mad Av -NY 10010
(212) 310-8000 .. **Tsai,** Jennifer C '07 %Weil G&M LLP -767 5th Av -NY 10153
(212) 259-8000 .. **Tsai,** Kelly Hsiao-I '00 %Dewey & L LLP -1301 Av of Amer -NY 10019
(212) 318-2000 .. **Tsai,** Rebecca L '05 Bloomberg LP -731 Lex Av -NY 10022
(646) 386-5700 .. **Tsai,** Richd A '00 %Civil Ct -111 Centre -NY 10013
(315) 475-3127 .. **Tsai,** Shelly P '09 %Leg Srvcs -472 S Salina -Syracuse 13202 **Fx:**475-2706
(212) 839-5300 .. **Tsai,** Susan '07 %Sidley A LLP -787 7th Av -NY 10019
(212) 625-9028 .. **Tsai,** Victor W '96 Tsai Law Firm -401 Bway -NY 10013 **Fx:**343-0908
(212) 593-2800 .. **Tsamblakos,** Isidoros I '03 %Ioannou & Assoc -414 E 59th -NY 10022 **Fx:**593-2933
(315) 218-8000 .. **Tsan,** Clifford G '04 %Bond S&K,PLLC -1 Lincoln Ctr -Syracuse 13202
(212) 704-5156 .. **Tsanas,** John A '86 OTB -1501 Bway -NY 10036 **Fx:**221-8025
(212) 450-4000 .. **Tsaneva,** Elena Roumenova '05 %Davis P&W LLP -450 Lex Av -NY 10017
(212) 384-1000 .. **Tsang,** George '01 %FBI -26 Fed Plz -NY 10278
(212) 788-5920 .. **Tsang,** Judy '08 Admin for Children Srvcs -220 Chruch -NY 10013 **Fx:**341-3888
(212) 925-3224 .. **Tsang,** Lisa Y '94 -191 Canal -NY 10013
(212) 383-1508 .. **Tsang,** Marjorie '86 %State Comptroller -59 Maiden Ln -NY 10038
(212) 227-2246 .. **Tsang,** Michl '97 -14 Wall -NY 10005
(631) 501-3100 .. **Tsantes,** Sophia M '02 %J Humphreys -3 Huntngtn Quad Bx9028 -Melvll 11747 **Fx:**501-3085
(212) 446-4800 .. **Tsao,** Peter '09 %Kirkland & E LLP -153 E 53rd -NY 10022
(212) 849-7000 .. **Tsapatsaris,** Peter N '04 %Quinn EU&S,LLP -51 Mad Av -NY 10010
(718) 627-2111 .. **Tsarnas,** Emanuel G '86 (E Tsarnas,PC) -1825 Coney Isl Av -Brklyn 11230 **Fx:**627-3349
(212) 999-5800 .. **Tsatalis,** Marina C '06 (Wilson SG&R) -1301 Av of Americas -NY 10019
(212) 425-7200 .. **Tsavaris,** John E II '88 Cnsl Kenyon & K,LLP -1 Bway -NY 10004
(212) 852-1000 .. **Tsavaris,** Loraine B '90 %US Trust Co,NA -114 W 47th -NY 10036 **Fx:**852-1310
(631) 424-6100 .. **Tschanz,** Felix F '93 %Advantage Title -410 NY Av -Huntngtn 11743 **Fx:**424-6049
(212) 756-2000 .. **Tschorke,** Alisa Hartman '10 %Schulte R&Z LLP -919 3rd Av -NY 10022
(408) 975-7983 .. **Tse,** Elizabeth Sukman '02 %Kenyon & K,LLP -1 Bway -NY 10004 **Fx:**975-7501
(212) 504-6000 .. **Tse,** Jane C W '81 SpclCnsl Cadwalader W&T LLP -1 World Fncl Ctr -NY 10281
(212) 348-7449 .. **Tse,** Lesley A '07 Legal Srvcs -1 W 125th -NY 10027 **Fx:**348-4093
(212) 796-8848 .. **Tsegaye,** Saml '04 %Klasko RS&S,LLP -317 Mad Av -NY 10017 **Fx:**297-1799
(212) 944-7434 .. **Tseitlin,** Alexandra V '88 -345 7th Av -NY 10001 **Fx:**398-8835
(212) 310-8218 .. **Tsekerides,** Theo E '94 (Weil G&M LLP) -767 5th Av -NY 10153
(212) 806-5400 .. **Tselnik,** Michl A '09 %Stroock &S&L LLP -180 Maiden Ln -NY 10038
(718) 267-8477 .. **Tsempelis,** James '05 -1008 150th -Whitestone 11357
(212) 310-8000 .. **Tseng,** Conray '07 %Weil G&M LLP -767 5th Av -NY 10153
(212) 455-2000 .. **Tseng,** L Danl '07 %Simpson T&B LLP -425 Lex Av -NY 10017
(347) 592-2200 .. **Tseng,** Vania M '03 %Leg Srvcs -89-00 Sutphin Blvd -Jamaica 11435 **Fx:**(718) 937-5350
(212) 506-2500 .. **Tsesmelis,** Christina H '06 %Mayer B LLP -1675 Bway -NY 10019
(516) 228-9350 .. **Tsevis,** Bill '97 %Solomon & S -50 Chas Lindbergh Blvd -Uniondale 11553
(212) 697-3434 .. **Tsevoukas,** Christina '04 %LISCR,LLC -99 Park Av -NY 10016 **Fx:**697-5655

(212) 225-2000 .. **Tseytkin,** Olga '09 %Cleary GS&H -1 Lbrty Plz -NY 10006
(212) 504-6000 .. **Tsin,** David L '10 Cadwalader W&T LLP -1 World Fncl Ctr -NY 10281
(914) 428-6565 .. **Tsiolis,** Mary '02 %Fentin & G,LLP -44 S Bway -White Plns 10601
(718) 438-1200 .. **Tsirelman,** Gary '01 -65 Jay -Brklyn 11201 **Fx:**438-8883
(212) 852-1000 .. **Tsirigotis,** Petros L '05 US Trust Co,NA -114 W 47th -NY 10036 **Fx:**852-1310
(718) 332-5600 .. **Tsiring,** Alexander Y '05 -1713 Sheepshead Bay Rd -Brklyn 11235
(212) 238-8900 .. **Tsiring,** Kira '08 %Melito & A,PC -233 Bway -NY 10279
(516) 328-3500 .. **Tsirkas,** Konstantinos '08 %McDonnell & A,PC -401 Franklin Av -Gdn Cty 11530
(718) 621-1568 .. **Tsirlina,** Anna '01 -1931 86th -Brklyn 11214 **Fx:**621-1572
(718) 375-9065 .. **Tsismenakis,** Georgia Artemios '95 -2086 E 19th -Brklyn 11229
(212) 298-5056 .. **Tso,** Andrew K '98 %Leg Aid -49 Thomas -NY 10013 **Fx:**298-5252
(718) 377-6600 .. **Tso,** Andy Y '92 -1777 Ocean Av -Brklyn 11230 **Fx:**951-1507
(212) 848-4000 .. **Tso,** Erica W '08 %Shearman & S LLP -599 Lex Av -NY 10022
(845) 647-4110 .. **Tso,** Jos '79 (Kooperman K&T) -47 N Main Bx511 -Ellenvll 12428
(212) 966-9812 .. **Tso,** Wendy '90 (W Tso,PC) -299 Bway -NY 10007 **Fx:**966-5909
(646) 536-3559 .. **Tsokos,** Sophia '00 Guinefort Grp,LLC -358 7th Av -Brklyn 11215
(516) 712-4000 .. **Tsonis,** Gregory A '06 %Milber MP&S LLP -1000 Woodbury Rd -Woodbury 11797
(718) 721-1250 .. **Tsoromokos,** Nick '03 (TCP Law Group) -3501 30th Av -Astoria 11103 **Fx:**721-1270
(212) 896-1926 .. **Tsou,** Jen-In '03 Buchbinder Tunick & Co -1 Penn Plz -NY 10119
(212) 446-4800 .. **Tsou,** Sarah K '07 %Kirkland & E LLP -153 E 53rd -NY 10022
(212) 837-6000 .. **Tsougarakis,** George A '87 (Hughes H&R LLP) -1 Bttry Pk Plz -NY 10004
(516) 248-1700 .. **Tsoukalas,** Andrea '01 %Forchelli CDSM&T,LLP -333 Earle Ovngton Blvd -Uniondale 11553
(516) 248-0885 .. **Tsoumpelis,** Bill '94 -200 Old Cntry Rd -Mineola 11501 **Fx:**739-3887
(212) 872-1000 .. **Tsourounis,** Emanuel II '04 -One Bryant Park -NY 10036 **Fx:**872-1002
(212) 854-2024 .. **Tsu,** Christina C '88 %Barnard College -3009 Bway -NY 10027 **Fx:**854-9470
(212) 918-3000 .. **Tsu,** Lillian '04 %Hogan L LLP -875 3rd Av -NY 10022
(212) 606-7175 .. **Tsubota,** Miori '91 %Sotheby's,Inc -1334 York Av -NY 10021 **Fx:**606-7574
(516) 746-8000 .. **Tsuei,** Yuhtyng '08 %Jaspan S LLP -300 Grdn City Plz -Gdn Cty 11530
(518) 474-0491 .. **Tsui,** Paul '97 Governors Appointments Ofc -The Cptl -Albany 12224
(212) 250-5189 .. **Tsui,** Tina M '05 Deutsche Bank AG -60 Wall -NY 10005
(212) 268-0900 .. **Tsui-Yip,** Gloria '97 (Miskin & T-Y) -1350 Bway -NY 10018 **Fx:**268-0904
(212) 782-4620 .. **Tsukamoto,** Kunio '08 Bk of Tokyo-Mitsubishi -1251 Av of Amer -NY 10020 **Fx:**782-6420
(631) 582-4000 .. **Tsunis Gasparis & Lustig, LLP** -2929 Express Dr N -Islandia 11749 **Fx:**582-4081
(631) 582-4000 .. **Tsunis,** John C '75 (Tsunis G&L,LLP) -2929 Express Dr N -Islandia 11749
(518) 533-3000 .. **Tsyn,** Jennifer L '04 %Bond S&K,PLLC -111 Wshngtn Av -Albany 12210
(518) 435-1919 .. **Tsyn,** Oleg '02 %Stockton B&M,LLP -2 Twr Pl -Albany 12203
(212) 337-9770 .. **Tsyngauz,** Yevgeny '01 (Tsyngauz & Assoc,PC) -18 W 21st -NY 10010 **Fx:**337-9773
(212) 446-4800 .. **Tu,** Karen Yu-Hsin '06 %Kirkland & E LLP -153 E 53rd -NY 10022
(212) 336-2000 .. **Tu,** Travis J '05 %Patterson BW&T LLP -1133 Av of Amer -NY 10036
(212) 233-8070 .. **Tua,** Judith '87 Callan & B -225 Bway -NY 10007
(212) 947-3330 .. **Tuan & Cho,LLP** -225 Bway -NY 10007 **Fx:**947-3366
(212) 809-5700 .. **Tuan,** Han-Hsien '89 (Adorno & Y LLP) -350 5th Av -NY 10118
(212) 735-3000 .. **Tubbs,** Adam C '10 %Skadden ASM&F LLP -4 Times Sq -NY 10036
(716) 853-3801 .. **Tuberdyck,** Amanda L '09 %Kenney SL&N,LLP -14 Lafayette Sq -Buffalo 14203
(585) 546-2434 .. **Tubiolo,** Richd S '82 (Hirsch & T PC) -1000 Rynlds Arcd Bldg -Rchstr 14614
(212) 943-0110 .. **Tublin,** Melvin J '54 (Poles TS&G, LLP) -46 Trinity Pl -NY 10006
(516) 781-4004 .. **Tubridy,** David J '51 -3330 Park Av -Wantagh 11793
(718) 286-6000 .. **Tubridy,** Jennifer A '08 %DA -125-01 Qns Blvd -Kew Gdns 11415
(631) 439-4200 .. **Tubridy,** Pauline A '92 %R Tusa -898 Vets Mem'l Hwy -Hauppauge 11788 **Fx:**439-4292
(718) 980-2373 .. **Tucci,** Anthony J '91 (A Tucci,PLLC) -575 Mdlnd Av -Staten Isl 10306
(631) 755-0101 .. **Tucci,** Karen H '99 %Lewis JAA,LLP -425 Broad Hollow Rd -Melvll 11747
(718) 254-0580 .. **Tucciarone,** John M '86 -161 Atl Av -Brklyn 11201 **Fx:**254-0019
(914) 769-6668 .. **Tucciarone,** John P '70 -390 Bedford Rd -Plsntvll 10570 **Fx:**741-2736
(516) 541-3162 .. **Tucciarone,** Peter M '06 -427 1st Av -Massapequa Pk 11762
(914) 439-4843 .. **Tuccillo,** Kenneth M '91 -Bx576 -Hastings-On-Hud 10706 **Fx:**478-4362
(212) 261-8000 .. **Tuccio,** Leigh A '09 %Mendes & M,LLP -750 7th Av -NY 10019
(516) 783-0062 .. **Tuch,** Kenneth R '94 (Pike & P,PC) -1921 Bellmore Av -Bellmore 11710 **Fx:**783-0082
(212) 455-2000 .. **Tuchinsky,** Jessica M '07 %Simpson T&B LLP -425 Lex Av -NY 10017
(516) 328-5634 .. **Tuchinsky,** Jos B '79 Canon USA,Inc -1 Canon Plz -New Hyde Pk 11042
(212) 687-3747 .. **Tuchman,** Bert '51 (Tuchman KWL&G,LLP) -6 E 45th -NY 10017
(212) 258-7500 .. **Tuchman,** Bruce G '90 %Nickelodeon -1515 Bway -NY 10036
(516) 364-5566 .. **Tuchman,** Chester '55 (Tuchman & T) -6800 Jericho Tpk -Syosset 11791 **Fx:**921-3824
(212) 735-3000 .. **Tuchman,** Deborah '81 Cnsl Skadden ASM&F LLP -4 Times Sq -NY 10036
(212) 728-8000 .. **Tuchman,** Deborah A '02 %Willkie F&G LLP -787 7th Av -NY 10019
(718) 544-1110 .. **Tuchman,** Ido '02 -82-70 Beverly Rd -Kew Gdns 11415 **Fx:**544-1110
(516) 338-1060 .. **Tuchman,** Isaac N '75 (Daniels & N,PC) -900 Merchants Cncrs -Westbury 11590 **Fx:**833-4932
(212) 687-3747 .. **Tuchman Korngold Weiss Lippman & Gelles,LLP** -6 E 45th -NY 10017 **Fx:**599-4459
(212) 836-8000 .. **Tuchman,** Louis H '85 (Kaye S LLP) -425 Park Av -NY 10022
(212) 213-8899 .. **Tuchman,** Morris '76 -134 Lex Av -NY 10016 **Fx:**213-6308
(212) 716-3937 .. **Tuchmann,** Eric P '95 %Amer Arbtrtn Assn -1633 Bway -NY 10019
(718) 254-7000 .. **Tuchmann,** Paul A '05 %US Atty -271 Cadman Plz E -Brklyn 11201 **Fx:**254-6479
(212) 563-4100 .. **Tuck,** Claire K '07 %Cohen W&S LLP -330 W 42nd -NY 10036
(212) 490-4100 .. **Tucker,** Bonnie A '03 %Storch A&M,PC -140 E 45th -NY 10017
(212) 840-0050 .. **Tucker,** Brian J '72 (Cohen & T) -1501 Bway -NY 10036
(914) 683-1800 .. **Tucker,** Corey B '97 (Luman H&T) -140 Grand -White Plns 10601
(212) 761-6041 .. **Tucker,** D Scott '95 Morgan Stanley -1585 Bway -NY 10036
(212) 857-8200 .. **Tucker,** Danl J '97 Amer Transit Ins Co -330 W 34th -NY 10001
(718) 529-7435 .. **Tucker,** Deron '96 -133-05 143rd -Jamaica 11436 **Fx:**529-4160
(718) 546-0950 .. **Tucker,** Donzell M '86 %Dept of Correction -75-20 Astoria Blvd -E Elmhrst 11370
(212) 732-0801 .. **Tucker,** Evelyn Tossas '92 -305 Bway -NY 10007
(516) 773-6216 .. **Tucker,** Henry R '78 -8 Old Farm Rd -Gt Neck 11020
(716) 858-2424 .. **Tucker,** Holly P '98 %DA -25 Delaware Av -Buffalo 14202 **Fx:**858-7425
(585) 722-9332 .. **Tucker,** James L '79 %Eastman Kodak -343 State -Rchstr 14650 **Fx:**477-1148
(631) 694-2300 .. **Tucker,** Jane Cantor '95 %Lamb & B,LLP -534 Broadhllw Rd Bx9034 -Melvll 11747
(212) 541-5800 .. **Tucker,** John E '94 Laurus Captl Mgmt -335 Mad Av -NY 10017 **Fx:**541-4434
(718) 875-4805 .. **Tucker,** Jordan W '90 (Reingold & T) -26 Court -Brklyn 11242
(646) 708-8088 .. **Tucker,** Jos P '93 Fidelity Natl Law Grp -350 5th Av -NY 10118 **Fx:**(212) 594-8378
(315) 946-7463 .. **Tucker,** Kathryn L '08 Leg Aid -9 Pearl -Lyons 14489 **Fx:**946-5964
(212) 227-1440 .. **Tucker,** Lenore W '78 -39 Bway -NY 10006 **Fx:**227-0747
(212) 715-9100 .. **Tucker,** Neil R '95 (Kramer LN&F,LLP) -1177 Av of Amer -NY 10036
(631) 665-6635 .. **Tucker,** Pamela Phillips '91 -65 Park Av -Bay Shr 11706
(212) 839-5300 .. **Tucker,** Peter G '08 %Sidley A LLP -787 7th Av -NY 10019
(718) 923-4206 .. **Tucker,** Raymond '92 %OTDA Fair Hearings -14 Boerum Pl -Brklyn 11201
(212) 805-0194 .. **Tucker,** Richd M '07 Hon NR Buchwald -500 Pearl -NY 10007
(585) 238-2000 .. **Tucker,** Richd T '07 %Phillips L LLP -1400 First Fed Plz -Rchstr 14614
(631) 493-0309 .. **Tucker,** Robt H '62 -16 Rosalie Pl Bx319 -Commack 11725 **Fx:**462-7925
(212) 472-6262 .. **Tucker,** Robt L '84 (Tucker & L,LLP) -160 E 84th -NY 10028 **Fx:**744-6509
(212) 422-0000 .. **Tucker,** Robt S '96 T&M Protection Resources -230 Park Av -NY 10169 **Fx:**422-3305
(212) 937-4000 .. **Tucker,** Stephen '81 (Fitzpatrick & HTCPA,LLP) -12 E 49th -NY 10017
(212) 558-4000 .. **Tucker,** Tiffany Jackson '10 %Sullivan & C LLP -125 Broad -NY 10004
(631) 351-1112 .. **Tucker,** Wm P '62 -775 Park Av -Huntngtn 11743
(212) 858-1000 .. **Tucker,** Winston C '04 %Pillsbury WSP LLP -1540 Bway -NY 10036
(845) 634-5799 .. **Tuckman,** Ellen Hope '83 -Bx532 -New Cty 10956 **Fx:**634-0222
(212) 766-9100 .. **Tuckner,** Jack B '88 (Tuckner SW&S) -120 Bway -NY 10271
(212) 408-5100 .. **Tucner,** Erez I '04 %Chadbourne & P LLP -30 Rckfllr Plz -NY 10112
(518) 463-3990 .. **Tuczinski Cavalier Gilchrist & Collura,PC** -54 State -Albany 12207 **Fx:**426-5067
(518) 463-3990 .. **Tuczinski,** Danl J '81 (Tuczinski CG&C,PC) -54 State -Albany 12207
(518) 486-4087 .. **Tuczinski,** Marlene O '80 %Dept of Law -The Cptl -Albany 12224
(212) 545-4783 .. **Tudisco,** Astra M '89 %Wolf HAF&H LLP -270 Mad Av -NY 10016
(212) 223-6700 .. **Tudor,** Louise I '91 (Zukerman GB&C,LLP) -875 3rd Av -NY 10022
(212) 577-1742 .. **Tudy-Jackson,** Janice '94 %Victim Srvcs Mediation Prog -346 Bway -NY 10013 **Fx:**577-1748
(212) 221-5700 .. **Tuero,** Sergio J '91 %Goldberg WFG LLP -1501 Bway -NY 10036
(212) 824-1120 .. **Tufano,** Richd J '75 %Enterprise Asset Mgmt -521 5th Av -NY 10175 **Fx:**824-1102
(631) 716-0091 .. **Tufariello,** Panagiota Betty '95 -8 Fountain Av -Selden 11784
(212) 986-4500 .. **Tufaro,** Gina M '03 %Horwitz H&P -405 Lex Av -NY 10174
(718) 590-2000 .. **Tuffarelli,** Nicholas S '06 %DA -198 E 161st -Bronx 10451 **Fx:**590-6477
(516) 365-6690 .. **Tuffin,** James W '85 Adm for the Prof -1800 Nrthrn Blvd -Roslyn 11576
(212) 506-2500 .. **Tuffin,** Paula A '89 (Mayer B LLP) -1675 Bway -NY 10019
(212) 947-4999 .. **Tuffy,** Jos O '05 %Camacho MM,LLP -350 5th Av -NY 10118
(631) 543-2100 .. **Tufo,** Danl A '83 (Rothstein & T,PC) -340 Vets Hwy -Commack 11725
(516) 249-1342 .. **Tufo,** Peter '00 %Grey & G,LLP -360 Main -Farmngdl 11735
(212) 373-8675 .. **Tufts,** Suzanne Israel '83 Friedman KS&A LLP -1633 Bway -NY 10019
(516) 357-3000 .. **Tugander,** Robt '93 (Rivkin R LLP) -926 RXR Plz -Uniondale 11556
(212) 264-0658 .. **Tugander,** Steven '90 %US DOJ Antitrust Div -26 Fed Plz Ste 3630 -NY 10278
(212) 219-0202 .. **Tugendrajch,** Lydia '78 -110 Greene -NY 10012 **Fx:**925-8443
(212) 935-7800 .. **Tuggle,** Thos M '85 %Babcock & Brown -600 Lex Av -NY 10022
(716) 852-5875 .. **Tuholski,** Jill M '96 (Feldman K LLP) -110 Pearl -Buffalo 14202
(212) 558-4000 .. **Tulchin,** David B '74 (Sullivan & C LLP) -125 Broad -NY 10004
(212) 813-8800 .. **Tulchin,** Matthew T '06 %Goodwin P LLP -620 8th Av -NY 10018
Tulchiner, Michl J '90 -2661 Rachel -Bellmore 11710
(212) 504-6000 .. **Tuliebitz,** Nicolas R '10 %Cadwalader W&T LLP -1 World Fncl Ctr -NY 10281
(718) 960-8559 .. **Tulier,** Esdras '79 %Lehman Cllg -250 Bedford Park Blvd W -Bronx 10468 **Fx:**960-6794
(212) 848-4000 .. **Tulimieri,** Christopher R '07 %Shearman & S LLP -599 Lex Av -NY 10022
(212) 735-3000 .. **Tulin,** Edw L '07 %Skadden ASM&F LLP -4 Times Sq -NY 10036
(212) 867-2600 .. **Tulin,** John '72 %Swank Inc -90 Park Av -NY 10016
(518) 306-0683 .. **Tulin,** Peter A '76 -Bx70 -Saratoga Spgs 12866
(718) 624-5521 .. **Tulip,** Mark E '75 -26 Court -Brklyn 11242 **Fx:**875-2811

(914) 422-3900 .. **Tulis,** Mark S '76 (Oxman TKW&G LLP) -120 Bloomingdale Rd -White Plns 10605
(646) 386-5891 .. **Tull,** David M '04 MHLS -41 Mad Av -NY 10010
(617) 570-1000 .. **Tulla-Isidro Vega,** Nilda M '08 %Goodwin P LLP -620 8th Av -NY 10018 **Fx:**523-1231
(646) 375-6187 .. **Tullar,** Kurt V '05 IQOR US Inc -335 Mad Av -NY 10017
(212) 807-2407 .. **Tuller,** Michl N '85 %The Foundation Ctr -79 5th Av -NY 10003 **Fx:**807-3677
(212) 578-2211 .. **Tuller,** Tammy E '81 %MetLife -27-01 Qns Plz N -LIC 11101
(212) 682-3025 .. **Tullman,** James E '92 %Weiss & L -551 5th Av -NY 10176
(212) 541-6222 .. **Tullman,** Jeffrey S '69 (Kane K,PC) -1350 Av of Amer -NY 10019
(845) 486-3048 .. **Tullo,** Janet V '84 %Cnty Atty -60 Market -Poughkeepsie 12601 **Fx:**486-2796
(718) 630-2900 .. **Tulloch,** Kathleen J '82 %VA -800 Poly Pl -Brklyn 11209 **Fx:**630-2917
(212) 416-6576 .. **Tully,** Amy '00 %Dept of Law -120 Bway -NY 10271
(914) 245-0044 .. **Tully,** Andrew W Jr. '68 -1830 Commerce -Yorktwn Hts 10598 **Fx:**245-3464
(212) 605-6200 .. **Tully,** Brendan J '06 %Levy P&K,LLP -800 3rd Av -NY 10022
(631) 424-2800 .. **Tully,** Brian A '98 -444 NY Av -Huntngtn 11743 **Fx:**424-2801
(518) 257-3000 .. **Tully,** Catherine M '86 %Dormitory Auth -515 Bway -Albany 12207 **Fx:**257-3101
(212) 931-7800 .. **Tully,** Christopher S '87 %Baseball Cmmssnr -245 Park Av -NY 10167
(212) 504-6000 .. **Tully,** Danielle V '05 %Cadwalader W&T LLP -1 World Fncl Ctr -NY 10281
(631) 424-2800 .. **Tully,** Diana '00 -82 Main -Huntngtn 11743 **Fx:**424-2801
(518) 266-3036 .. **Tully,** James H Jr. '61 %Tax Appls Tribunal -500 Fed -Troy 12180 **Fx:**271-0886
(845) 561-0550 .. **Tully,** Jeanne N '99 %Drake LHKGG&R PLLC -555 Hudson Valley Av -New Windsor 12553
(212) 318-3000 .. **Tully,** John F '71 OfCnsl Fulbright & J LLP -666 5th Av -NY 10103
(518) 486-7815 .. **Tully,** John M '06 Insurance Dept -99 Wshngtn Av -Albany 12257 **Fx:**473-4600
(212) 210-9493 .. **Tully,** Jos G '07 %Alston & B LLP -90 Park Av -NY 10016
(518) 402-3067 .. **Tully,** Karen M '02 %State Comptroller -110 State -Albany 12236 **Fx:**473-9104
(845) 255-0403 .. **Tully,** Martin F '67 (Tully & M) -176 Main Bx574 -New Paltz 12561 **Fx:**255-0858
(518) 218-7100 .. **Tully,** Mathew B '03 (Tully R,PLLC) -441 New Karner Rd -Albany 12205
(845) 639-7800 .. **Tully,** Michl H '05 %Mandel K&B,LLP -210 Route 303 -Vly Cottage 10989
(718) 446-7000 .. **Tully,** Peter K '86 %Tully Cnstr -127-50 Nrthrn Blvd -Flushng 11368 **Fx:**458-8150
(518) 218-7100 .. **Tully Rinckey,PLLC** -441 New Karner Rd -Albany 12205 **Fx:**218-0496
(631) 234-2376 .. **Tully,** Rosemarie '93 (R Tully,PC) -1 Suffolk Sq -Islandia 11749 **Fx:**234-8876
(518) 451-3019 .. **Tully,** Susan C '93 Aetna US Hlthcare -15 Columbia Cir -Albany 12203
(914) 245-0044 .. **Tully,** Tara A '05 Tully Law Ofc,PC -1830 Commerce -Yorktwn Hts 10598 **Fx:**245-3464
(212) 867-3600 .. **Tulman,** Scott B '84 -369 Lex Av -NY 10017 **Fx:**867-1914
(212) 669-4799 .. **Tumarkin,** Laurel A '04 Pub Advocates Ofc -1 Centre -NY 10007
(914) 323-7000 .. **Tumbarello,** Phillip A '80 (Wilson EME&D LLP) -3 Gannett Dr -White Plns 10604
(212) 612-4200 .. **Tumbleson,** Paul A '91 %Hoey KT&E -55 Water -NY 10041
(212) 566-4681 .. **Tumelty,** John P '87 (Tumelty & S,LLP) -160 Bway -NY 10038 **Fx:**566-4749
(212) 228-7727 .. **Tuminaro,** Amelia K '04 %Gladstein R&M,LLP -817 Bway -NY 10003
(631) 666-5766 .. **Tuminello,** Barry '71 (Long TBSWJ&S) -120 4th Av Bx5591 -Bay Shr 11706
(518) 374-3373 .. **Tumminelli,** Lisa M '89 (Silverman S&S) -527 State -Schnctdy 12305
(585) 427-0010 .. **Tumminelli,** Peter J '86 -2024 W Henrietta Rd -Rchstr 14623
(516) 873-7200 .. **Tumminello,** Julie E '09 %Saltzman C&R,LLP -300 Grdn City Plz -Gdn Cty 11530
(917) 454-1100 .. **Tumminia,** Frank J '98 %Police Dept -2 Lafayette -NY 10007
(212) 617-3515 .. **Tumminio,** Donna M '08 Bloomberg LP -731 Lex Av -NY 10022
(212) 819-8200 .. **Tumova,** Irena '01 %White & C LLP -1155 Av of Amer -NY 10036
(212) 687-5900 .. **Tumulty,** Christopher M '08 %Sullivan & G,LLP -475 Park Av S -NY 10016 **Fx:**687-4060
(212) 230-8800 .. **Tune,** Tara L '06 %WilmerHale -399 Park Av -NY 10022
(914) 428-0010 .. **Tung,** Andrew V '96 (Divney Tung Schwalbe,LLP) -One N Bway -White Plns 10601 **Fx:**428-0017
(914) 776-8063 .. **Tung,** Becky '03 WDF,Inc -30 N Macquesten Pkwy -Mt Vernon 10550
(212) 259-8000 .. **Tung,** Brandon K '10 %Dewey & L LLP -1301 Av of Amer -NY 10019
(716) 841-2315 .. **Tung,** Gea '84 %HSBC Bank -1 HSBC Ctr -Buffalo 14203 **Fx:**841-5087
(718) 758-0903 .. **Tung,** Jean '95 -1165 E 15th -Brklyn 11230
(585) 724-4000 .. **Tung,** Kenneth '88 Eastman Kodak Co -Bx92988 -Rchstr 14692
(718) 939-4633 .. **Tung,** Kevin K '99 (KK Tung PC) -38-21 Main -Flushng 11354 **Fx:**939-4468
(212) 468-8055 .. **Tung,** Ko-Yung '73 SrCnsl Morrison & F LLP -1290 Av of Amer -NY 10104
(212) 977-9700 .. **Tunick,** Andrew J '68 (Phillips N LLP) -666 5th Av -NY 10103
(914) 666-3600 .. **Tunick,** Jeffrey Pierce '89 -66 Main -Bedfrd Hlls 10507
(212) 841-2000 .. **Tunick,** Rebecca E '05 BNP Paribas -787 7th Av -NY 10019
(212) 770-1819 .. **Tunis,** Richd '88 %AIG -80 Pine -NY 10005 **Fx:**344-2286
(716) 278-4784 .. **Tunis-Manny,** Karen D '83 Memorial Medical Ctr -621 10th -Niagara Fls 14301
(516) 764-8786 .. **Tunkel,** Jacqueline '87 -3333 Balsam -Oceanside 11572 **Fx:**764-8786
(914) 328-7511 .. **Tunnell,** Norman D '73 T Square Properties -56 Lafayette Av -White Plns 10603 **Fx:**328-1416
(914) 946-7841 .. **Tunney,** Brian J '76 -5 Milford Dr -White Plns 10606
(607) 776-9631 .. **Tunney,** Christopher M '06 DA -3 E Pulteney Sq -Bath 14810 **Fx:**776-7052
(607) 776-9631 .. **Tunney,** John C '71 DA -3 E Pulteney Sq -Bath 14810 **Fx:**776-7052
(516) 822-4400 .. **Tunstead & Schechter** -500 N Bway -Jericho 11753 **Fx:**822-4462
(718) 298-8976 .. **Tuntigian,** Lisa E '02 %Leg Aid -153-01 Jamaica Av -Jamaica 11432 **Fx:**657-0537
(315) 701-0080 .. **Tuohey,** Melissa A '01 %Fed Pub Def -4 Clinton Sq -Syracuse 13202 **Fx:**701-0081
(585) 262-4280 .. **Tuohey,** Michl J '87 -144 Exchange Blvd -Rchstr 14614 **Fx:**546-6343
(516) 239-1600 .. **Tuohey,** P Richd '56 %John P Picone Inc -31 Grdn Ln Bx336 -Lawrence 11559 **Fx:**239-1757
(518) 402-9507 .. **Tuohy,** Dolores A '86 %DEC -625 Bway -Albany 12233 **Fx:**402-9018
(845) 469-4900 .. **Tuohy,** Marissa C '09 %Greenwald Law Ofc -99 Brookside Av -Chester 10918 **Fx:**469-2022
(631) 265-1051 .. **Tuohy,** Matthew B '99 (Palermo P&T) -1300 Vets Mem'l Hwy -Hauppauge 11788
(585) 232-6500 .. **Tuori,** Thos M '07 %Harter S&E LLP -1600 Bausch & Lomb Pl -Rchstr 14604
(212) 732-7810 .. **Tuozzo,** Edw C '79 -7 Dey -NY 10007 **Fx:**732-7896
(212) 696-6000 .. **Tupa,** Fernando A '08 %Curtis M-PC&M LLP -101 Park Av -NY 10178
(716) 856-5556 .. **Tupchik,** Lana V '05 -14 Lafayette Sq -Buffalo 14203
(718) 639-4437 .. **Turak,** Sadie B '33 -76-12 35th Av -Jcksn Hts 11372
(212) 657-1420 .. **Turan,** Edw G '74 Citigroup -77 Water -NY 10005
(516) 538-7474 .. **Turano,** John '70 -224 Nassau Blvd S -Gdn Cty 11530 **Fx:**538-7025
(718) 990-6632 .. **Turano,** Margaret V '78 %St John's Law Schl -8000 Utopia Pkwy -Jamaica 11439 **Fx:**591-1855
(212) 905-4900 .. **Turano,** Stephen '92 (Tacopina S&T,PC) -275 Mad Av -NY 10016 **Fx:**208-2981
(212) 262-2390 .. **Turano,** Stephen R '10 %Connell F LLP -888 7th Av -NY 10106
(212) 688-8555 .. **Turansick,** Michl F III '83 (Fragomen DB&L LLP) -7 Hanover Sq -NY 10004
(212) 558-4000 .. **Turbeville,** Ralston W Jr. '02 %Sullivan & C LLP -125 Broad -NY 10004
(212) 490-9100 .. **Turchetti,** Victoria A '04 %Condon & F LLP -7 Times Sq -NY 10036
(516) 296-1000 .. **Turchiano,** Jane D '84 %Miller & M,PC -100 Q Roosevelt Blvd -Gdn Cty 11530
(518) 785-3291 .. **Turchick,** Alexander '47 (Turchick & T) -457 Troy-Schnctdy Rd -Latham 12110 **Fx:**785-0833
(518) 785-3291 .. **Turchick,** Wm A '88 (Turchick & T) -457 Troy-Schnctdy Rd -Latham 12110 **Fx:**785-0833
(718) 252-1276 .. **Turchin & Hoffman** -976 E 19th -Brklyn 11230 **Fx:**(212) 949-8192
(718) 252-1276 .. **Turchin,** Morton J '63 (Turchin & H) -976 E 19th -Brklyn 11230
(212) 984-8364 .. **Turchin,** Peter C '98 CB Richard Ellis -200 Park Av -NY 10166 **Fx:**984-8040
(212) 765-6607 .. **Turchin,** R Leah '88 -170 West End Av -NY 10023 **Fx:**873-2109
(646) 746-9700 .. **Turcik,** Lara '02 CFTC -140 Bway -NY 10005 **Fx:**746-9938
(212) 227-2030 .. **Turck,** Shawn A '09 -225 Bway -NY 10007 **Fx:**766-2298
(212) 278-7091 .. **Turck-Avery,** Bettina M '06 %Societe Generale -1221 Av of Amer -NY 10020
(212) 964-7400 .. **Turco,** Jared A '05 Smith MDWY&Y,PC -111 John -NY 10038
(212) 935-6020 .. **Turco,** Jonathan E '01 Klein ZR LLP -485 Mad Av -NY 10022
(212) 937-8499 .. **Turcotte,** Christopher B '94 (CB Turcotte,PC) -575 Mad Av -NY 10022
(914) 946-4777 .. **Tureaud,** Andrew P '98 %Keane & B,PC -445 Hmltn Av -White Plns 10601
(212) 223-3562 .. **Turek,** Allen M '78 (Turek RM LLP) -377 5th Av -NY 10016
(212) 223-3562 .. **Turek Roth Mester LLP** -377 5th Av -NY 10016 **Fx:**223-3614
(212) 696-6000 .. **Turell,** Jeanine V '09 %Curtis M-PC&M LLP -101 Park Av -NY 10178
(518) 834-5240 .. **Turetsky,** Aaron '87 -1682 Front Bx367 -Keesevll 12944
(212) 757-0007 .. **Turetsky,** Brian A '03 %Scarola E LLP -888 7th Av -NY 10106
(212) 735-3000 .. **Turetsky,** David M '03 (Skadden ASM&F LLP) -4 Times Sq -NY 10036
(212) 521-5400 .. **Turetsky,** Debra S '07 %Reed S LLP -599 Lex Av -NY 10022
(516) 296-7000 .. **Turetsky,** Donna J '92 %Certilman BA&H,LLP -90 Merrick Av -E Meadow 11554
(212) 530-1800 .. **Turgeon,** Catherine M '01 %Richards K&O LLP -1 World Fncl Ctr -NY 10281
(212) 312-3000 .. **Turi,** A Edw III '86 %FGIC -125 Park Av -NY 10017 **Fx:**312-3221
(516) 327-2700 .. **Turi,** Albert J '93 BWD Grp LLC -BWD Plz Bx9050 -Jericho 11753 **Fx:**327-2800
(212) 355-5005 .. **Turi,** Andrew S '83 -48 W 48th -NY 10036 **Fx:**355-5009
(315) 734-2295 .. **Turi,** Bernard J '86 Utica Natl Ins -180 Genesee Bx530 -Utica 13502 **Fx:**734-2662
(518) 793-8581 .. **Turi,** John C '89 -25 May Bx131 -Glens Fls 12801 **Fx:**272-0540
(212) 425-9300 .. **Turiano,** Angela A '96 Cnsl Bressler A&R,PC -17 State -NY 10004
(516) 466-6464 .. **Turiel,** Bernard '59 -9 Park Pl -Gt Neck 11021
(845) 624-2727 .. **Turiel,** Lisa A '93 %L Goldheim -55 Old Tpk Rd -Nanuet 10954
(212) 728-8000 .. **Turina,** Alessandro '01 %Willkie F&G LLP -787 7th Av -NY 10019
(212) 335-9000 .. **Turino,** Samantha E '08 DA -1 Hogan Pl -NY 10013
(212) 506-1700 .. **Turinsky,** Danl E '01 SpclCnsl Kasowitz BT&F LLP -1633 Bway -NY 10019
(212) 576-4004 .. **Turitzin,** John N '82 Marvel Entertainmt -417 5th Av -NY 10016
(212) 265-4900 .. **Turk,** Adam S '09 (Turk & D PLLC) -250 W 57th -NY 10019 **Fx:**964-6600
(212) 715-0300 .. **Turk,** Bradley E '94 Cnsl Tishman Speyer Prop -45 Rckfllr Plz -NY 10111 **Fx:**332-6603
(212) 207-3825 .. **Turk,** Cheryl R '06 %Stern & Z LLP -110 E 59th -NY 10022 **Fx:**583-7464
(631) 853-4104 .. **Turk,** Christopher R '06 %DA -400 Carleton Av Bx9082 -Central Islip 11722 **Fx:**853-7838
(212) 732-9000 .. **Turk,** Hugh M '73 (Sullivan PBM&C PC) -120 Bway -NY 10271
(212) 837-6000 .. **Turk,** Jeremy '03 %Hughes H&R LLP -1 Bttry Pk Plz -NY 10004
(646) 386-3612 .. **Turk,** June T '82 %Supreme Ct-Law Dept -60 Centre -NY 10007
(631) 852-2500 .. **Turk,** Melissa J '03 %DA -200 Center Dr -Rvrhead 11901 **Fx:**852-1769
(718) 643-6810 .. **Turk,** Norman '50 -16 Court -Brklyn 11241 **Fx:**643-2690
(212) 834-3249 .. **Turk,** Peter J '96 JP Morgan Chase & Co -270 Park Av -NY 10017
(212) 687-3511 .. **Turk,** Stephen N '59 -300 E 40th -NY 10016
(212) 326-3939 .. **Turk,** Susan A '09 %Jones D -222 E 41st -NY 10017

(718) 220-6937 .. **Turk,** Susanne '89 Bronx Comm College -W 181st & Univ Av -Bronx 10453
(212) 906-1200 .. **Turke,** Bethany R '07 %Latham & W -885 3rd Av -NY 10022
(212) 687-1600 .. **Turkel,** Avram S '09 %Borstein & S -420 Lex Av -NY 10170
(212) 353-2200 .. **Turkel Forman & de la Vega LLP** -304 Park Av S -NY 10010 **Fx:**353-8828
(212) 867-6000 .. **Turkel,** Jeffrey '84 (Rosenberg & E,PC) -733 3rd Av -NY 10017
(212) 495-8271 .. **Turkel,** Jonathan D '81 DH Blair -44 Wall -NY 10005
(212) 353-2200 .. **Turkel,** Judith E '82 (Turkel F&D LLP) -304 Park Av S -NY 10010
(212) 619-4444 .. **Turkel,** Lauren R '08 %Marshall CW&B,PC -116 John -NY 10038
(212) 571-6546 .. **Turkel,** Simon G '99 -305 Bway -NY 10007
(212) 742-8700 .. **Turken,** Jason D '90 (Garson D&C LLP) -110 Wall -NY 10005
(212) 986-2340 .. **Turken,** Marvin '58 %Jordan & H -122 E 42nd -NY 10168
(212) 841-1000 .. **Turken,** Sara M '09 %Covington & B LLP -620 8th Av -NY 10018
(212) 983-5900 .. **Turkewitz,** Eric '86 Turkewitz Law Firm -228 E 45th -NY 10017
(646) 610-5400 .. **Turkin,** Gregg R '85 NYPD -1 Police Plz -NY 10038
(516) 802-0700 .. **Turkish,** Wm J '84 (Braunstein T LLP) -7600 Jericho Tpk -Woodbury 11797
(718) 222-2008 .. **Turkiya,** Vlad '03 %Law Dept -350 Jay -Brklyn 11201 **Fx:**222-2088
(212) 977-9700 .. **Turkle,** Bruce J '85 (Phillips N LLP) -666 5th Av -NY 10103
(212) 730-8133 .. **Turko,** Jessica L '02 %Gunderson DSVF&H,LLP -220 W 42nd -NY 10036
(212) 388-3600 .. **Turley,** Kathleen '87 %32B-J Leg Srvcs -101 Av of Amer -NY 10013 **Fx:**388-3061
(631) 582-3700 .. **Turley Redmond Rosaco & Rosasco, LLP** -3075 Vets Mem'l Hwy -Ronkonkoma 11779 **Fx:**580-3042
(631) 582-3700 .. **Turley,** Wm J '84 (Turley RR&R,LLP) -3075 Vets Mem'l Hwy -Ronkonkoma 11779
(718) 286-2000 .. **Turman,** Howard '72 %Leg Aid -120-46 Qns Blvd -Kew Gdns 11415 **Fx:**286-2286
(516) 208-8780 .. **Turman,** Jared P '06 J Turman,PLLC -1980 Broadcast Plz -Merrick 11566
(212) 735-3000 .. **Turman,** Rossie E III '99 (Skadden ASM&F LLP) -4 Times Sq -NY 10036
(516) 873-2000 .. **Turman,** Stephen E '00 %Moritt HH&H LLP -400 Grdn City Plz -Gdn Cty 11530
(212) 857-8230 .. **Turnacioglu,** Erdal A '07 %Baker MM&M,PC -330 W 34th -NY 10001
(212) 971-9725 .. **Turnamian,** Mark '87 -350 5th Av -NY 10118
(518) 449-3359 .. **Turnblom,** Laura K '04 %Malkin & R -80 State -Albany 12207 **Fx:**449-5788
(212) 559-3918 .. **Turnbull,** Douglas C '96 %Citigroup Inc -425 Park Av -NY 10043
(212) 309-6000 .. **Turnbull,** Kenneth J '92 (Morgan L&B LLP) -101 Park Av -NY 10178
(718) 993-9999 .. **Turnbull,** Steven W '08 OfCnsl J Oresky & Assoc,PLLC -155 E 149th -Bronx 10451 **Fx:**993-0142
(212) 455-2000 .. **Turner,** Alan C '01 (Simpson T&B LLP) -425 Lex Av -NY 10017
(212) 530-5000 .. **Turner,** Amy E '09 %Milbank TH&M LLP -1 Chase Manh Plz -NY 10005
(212) 679-1000 .. **Turner,** Barry S '68 -780 3rd Av -NY 10017 **Fx:**583-0072
(212) 269-8628 .. **Turner,** Bernard '68 (Grubin S&T) -60 Broad -NY 10004 **Fx:**809-6185
(914) 271-0713 .. **Turner,** Betsy H '92 (Turner & T) -35 Truesdale Dr -Croton-On-Hud 10520 **Fx:**271-3250
(212) 294-6700 .. **Turner,** Caleb M '07 %Winston & S -200 Park Av -NY 10166
(212) 588-5500 .. **Turner,** Candice M '97 %Davies WP&V LLP -625 Mad Av -NY 10022
(585) 753-1380 .. **Turner,** Chas S '67 %Cnty Atty -307 Cnty Ofc Bldg -Rchstr 14614 **Fx:**753-1331
(716) 852-6923 .. **Turner,** Christopher R '07 %Taylor & Santacrose -300 Pearl -Buffalo 14202 **Fx:**856-7417
(212) 306-4382 .. **Turner,** Corey M '98 %Housing Auth -250 Bway -NY 10007
(718) 565-2800 .. **Turner,** Ferris '77 -82-11 37th Av -Jcksn Hts 11372
(315) 487-0210 .. **Turner,** Francine G '83 %Adorante T & Assoc,PC -5111 W Genesee Bx600 -Camillus 13031 **Fx:**487-2990
(212) 839-7000 .. **Turner,** Francis W '82 (Hill B&N LLP) -200 Lbrty -NY 10281
(716) 854-2620 .. **Turner,** Fredk D '63 (Brown & K,LLP) -1500 Lbrty Bldg -Buffalo 14202
(914) 271-0713 .. **Turner,** Fredk W '81 (Turner & T) -35 Truesdale Dr -Croton-On-Hud 10520 **Fx:**271-3250
(914) 333-0700 .. **Turner,** Fredk W '81 Cnsl Snyder & S -94 Wht Plns Rd -Tarrytwn 10591 **Fx:**333-0659
(631) 853-4161 .. **Turner,** Jacob C '06 %DA -N Cnty Cmplx Bldg 77 -Hauppauge 11788 **Fx:**853-4192
(212) 930-9700 .. **Turner,** James M '08 %Sichenzia RFF LLP -61 Bway -NY 10006
(585) 454-6480 .. **Turner,** Jeffrey L '81 (Osborn R&B,LLP) -45 Exchange Blvd -Rchstr 14614
(212) 889-8569 .. **Turner,** Judith A '77 -245 E 25th -NY 10010
(212) 735-3000 .. **Turner,** Julie A '04 %Skadden ASM&F LLP -4 Times Sq -NY 10036
(212) 245-1000 .. **Turner,** Juno E '07 %Outten & G LLP -3 Park Av -NY 10016
(646) 497-4603 .. **Turner,** Kara J '06 Newberger Berman,LLC -605 3rd Av -NY 10158
(212) 270-5921 .. **Turner,** Karel Lee '87 Corp Human Resrcs -270 Park Av -NY 10017
(585) 454-5050 .. **Turner,** Karen Anne-Marie '97 %Brown & H -2 State -Rchstr 14614
(718) 250-2000 .. **Turner,** Karen P '00 %DA -350 Jay -Brklyn 11201 **Fx:**250-2314
(212) 756-2000 .. **Turner,** Kathryn L '99 SpclCnsl Schulte R&Z LLP -919 3rd Av -NY 10022
(212) 310-8000 .. **Turner,** Kim P E '09 %Weil G&M LLP -767 5th Av -NY 10153
(212) 270-0572 .. **Turner,** Kimberly L '02 JP Morgan Chase & Co -270 Park Av -NY 10017
(315) 353-6616 .. **Turner,** Lee H '56 -22 S Main Bx223 -Norwd 13668 **Fx:**353-6616
(716) 604-9069 .. **Turner,** Lorrie K '97 New Era Cap Co,Inc -160 Delaware Av -Buffalo 14202
(212) 838-3794 .. **Turner,** Mark N '06 Morse ZR&L LLP -405 Park Av -NY 10022
(212) 490-9100 .. **Turner,** Marshall S '73 (Condon & F LLP) -7 Times Sq -NY 10036
(518) 274-7252 .. **Turner,** Matthew J '91 M Turner,PC -54 2nd -Troy 12180 **Fx:**274-0348
(212) 903-9000 .. **Turner,** Maximilien Neuerburg '06 %Linklaters -1345 Av of Amer -NY 10105
(212) 403-1000 .. **Turner,** Meredith L '04 %Wachtell LR&K -51 W 52nd -NY 10019
(212) 425-7200 .. **Turner,** Michl S '08 %Kenyon & K,LLP -1 Bway -NY 10004
(212) 909-6000 .. **Turner,** Miranda H '08 %Debevoise & P LLP -919 3rd Av -NY 10022
(212) 334-1300 .. **Turner,** Nicholas R '01 %Vera Inst of Justice -233 Bway -NY 10279 **Fx:**941-9407
(212) 975-2993 .. **Turner,** Patrick '07 CBS Inc -51 W 52nd -NY 10019 **Fx:**975-3930
(212) 294-6700 .. **Turner,** Robt C '07 %Winston & S -200 Park Av -NY 10166
(516) 822-3550 .. **Turner,** Roderick S W '96 Hoffmann & B LLP -6900 Jericho Tpk -Syosset 11791 **Fx:**822-3582
(212) 474-1000 .. **Turner,** Roger D '77 (Cravath S&M LLP) -825 8th Av -NY 10019
(212) 490-3000 .. **Turner,** Ryan M '02 OfCnsl Wilson EME&D LLP -150 E 42nd -NY 10017
(212) 659-9593 .. **Turner,** Scott G '93 %Mt Sinai Med School -One Gustave Levy Plz -NY 10029
(585) 263-1000 .. **Turner,** Scott M '74 (Nixon P LLP) -1100 Clinton Sq -Rchstr 14604
(212) 820-9462 .. **Turner,** Steven I '73 (Hawkins D&W LLP) -One Chase Manh Plz -NY 10005
(646) 275-9408 .. **Turner,** Steven M '84 Turne & Assoc -135 W 16th -NY 10011
(212) 964-7556 .. **Turney,** Joel J '96 (J Turney,LLC) -30 Vesey -NY 10007 **Fx:**964-7441
(212) 642-5210 .. **Turnier,** Robt W '92 -244 Mad Av PMB 204 -NY 10016
(212) 222-3206 .. **Turnock,** Judith '76 -310 Riverside Dr -NY 10025
(518) 884-4795 .. **Turo,** Diane S '06 Pub Def -40 McMaster -Ballston Spa 12020 **Fx:**884-4789
(212) 541-2000 .. **Turoff,** Brian J '03 %Bryan C LLP -1290 Av of Amer -NY 10104
(917) 250-6988 .. **Turoff,** Jennifer B '03 (Tepper & T LLP) -1641 3rd Av -NY 10128 **Fx:**(973) 731-1829
(516) 606-2486 .. **Turofsky,** Deborah '00 -31 Arrandale Av -Gt Neck 11024 **Fx:**302-8447
(914) 606-9790 .. **Turpin,** Christopher J '87 (Cartafalsa ST&L) -560 Wht Plns Rd -Tarrytwn 10591
(212) 732-3665 .. **Turpin,** Lisa M '02 %Harmon L&R -42 Bway -NY 10004
(212) 962-1190 .. **Turret,** David B '78 (Sanocki N&T,LLP) -225 Bway -NY 10007
(631) 390-3100 .. **Turret,** Ira A '76 Turret & Assoc,PC -145 Pinelawn Rd -Melvll 11747 **Fx:**622-2084
(212) 837-6495 .. **Turrettini,** John P '09 %Hughes H&R LLP -1 Bttry Pk Plz -NY 10004
(585) 419-8800 .. **Turri,** Jos A '71 (Harris B PLLC) -99 Garnsey Rd -Pittsfrd 14534
(516) 741-6565 .. **Turro,** Andrew J '82 (Meyer SE&K,PC) -990 Stewart Av Bx9194 -Gdn Cty 11530
(212) 692-1000 .. **Turschmann,** Michl A '97 %Duane M LLP -1540 Bway -NY 10036
(212) 318-6000 .. **Turshen,** Benjamin '09 %Paul HJ&W LLP -75 E 55th -NY 10022
(212) 728-8000 .. **Turteltaub,** Adam M '99 (Willkie F&G LLP) -787 7th Av -NY 10019
(212) 482-0001 .. **Turturro,** Angela E '10 %Russo K&T LLP -33 Whitehall -NY 10004
(845) 256-3031 .. **Turturro,** Kelly Ruane '02 %DEC -21 S Putt Crnrs Rd -New Paltz 12561 **Fx:**255-4659
(212) 504-6000 .. **Turturro,** Walter '10 %Cadwalader W&T LLP -1 World Fncl Ctr -NY 10281
(212) 883-1700 .. **Turtz,** Beth '81 (Duval & S LLP) -101 Park Av -NY 10178
(212) 449-9609 .. **Turvey,** Saml A '84 %Merrill Lynch -220 Bway -NY 10038 **Fx:**449-2634
(212) 575-7900 .. **Turyn,** Richd '77 (Ballon SB&N,PC) -729 7th Av -NY 10019
(516) 327-2700 .. **Tusa,** Brian D '98 BWD Grp LLC -BWD Plz Bx9050 -Jericho 11753 **Fx:**327-2800
(212) 692-9666 .. **Tusa,** Chas S '70 (Gilbride TL&S LLC) -708 3rd Av -NY 10017
(212) 400-7100 .. **Tusa,** Jos S '96 (Whalen & T) -33 W 19th -NY 10011
(631) 724-0100 .. **Tusa,** Kathryn S '86 -Bx668 -St James 11780 **Fx:**724-0254
(631) 439-4200 .. **Tusa,** Robt P '85 R Tusa -898 Vets Mem'l Hwy -Hauppauge 11788 **Fx:**439-4292
(212) 698-3500 .. **Tusk,** Claude M '78 (Dechert LLP) -1095 Av of Amer -NY 10036
(212) 318-3000 .. **Tussing,** James D '82 (Fulbright & J LLP) -666 5th Av -NY 10103
(212) 885-5000 .. **Tuteur,** Robt I '03 (Blank R LLP) -405 Lex Av -NY 10174
(631) 369-1112 .. **Tuthill,** Lawr M Jr. '88 %Nassau/Sflk Law Srvc -313 W Main -Rvrhead 11901 **Fx:**369-1612
(631) 287-0018 .. **Tuths,** Paul G '87 (Tuths & T) -33 Flying Pnt Rd -Southampton 11968 **Fx:**287-7639
(631) 287-0018 .. **Tuths,** Susan Q '80 (Tuths & T) -33 Flying Pnt Rd -Southampton 11968 **Fx:**287-7639
(516) 741-2405 .. **Tutrone,** Ronald F '65 OfCnsl Geoghan C&B LLC -250 Mineola Blvd -Mineola 11501
(212) 935-4400 .. **Tuttle,** Alexander D '03 %LePatner & Assoc LLP -600 Lex Av -NY 10022 **Fx:**935-4404
(212) 248-3140 .. **Tuttle,** Helen E '99 (Drinker B&R LLP) -140 Bway -NY 10005
(518) 783-1001 .. **Tuttle,** James B '76 (Tuttle Law Firm) -10 Century Hill Dr -Latham 12110 **Fx:**783-1515
(845) 357-7156 .. **Tuttle,** Mary A '74 -56 Park Av Bx34 -Suffern 10901 **Fx:**(201) 252-2099
(212) 425-3100 .. **Tuttle,** Scott C '07 %McManus C&R,PC -48 Wall -NY 10005
(212) 508-0164 .. **Tuttle,** Stephen '83 Capital Properties -717 5th Av -NY 10022
(716) 372-3226 .. **Tuttle,** Wendy A '91 -3132 Route 417 Bx88 -Allegany 14706 **Fx:**373-3463
(718) 913-6890 .. **Tuttolomondo,** Giovanna M '06 (Toksoy & T PC) -15801 Crossbay Blvd -Howard Bch 11414
(516) 496-3868 .. **Tutunjian,** John G '94 (Keusey T&B,PC) -20 Crsswys Park Dr N -Woodbury 11797
(212) 483-9490 .. **Tuve,** Jessica M '08 %McElroy DM&C,LLP -88 Pine -NY 10005
(973) 596-4603 .. **Tuvel,** Jason R '05 %Gibbons PC -1 Penn Plz -NY 10119 **Fx:**639-8358
(212) 668-8888 .. **Tuy,** Salvador Jr. '89 (Prado & T,LLP) -305 Bway -NY 10007 **Fx:**668-8494
(212) 753-3468 .. **Tuychibaev,** Sherzod '06 %Wildes & W,PC -515 Mad Av -NY 10022
(212) 221-9610 .. **Tversky,** Saml A '05 -42 W 38th -NY 10018
(212) 768-6700 .. **Tvetenstrand,** Paul D '84 (Sonnenschein N&R LLP) -2 World Fncl Ctr -NY 10281
(718) 941-3962 .. **Tvrdy,** Linda Ann '91 -101 Marlboro Rd -Brklyn 11226
(212) 779-9910 .. **Tweedy,** Jeffrey C '66 (Eaton & V LLP) -3 Park Av -NY 10016
(212) 626-4100 .. **Tween,** Douglas M '90 (Baker & M LLP) -1114 Av of Amer -NY 10036
(718) 625-2200 .. **Twerski,** Aaron D '65 %Bklyn Law Schl -250 Joralemon -Brklyn 11201 **Fx:**780-0393
(212) 756-2000 .. **Twerski,** Shlomo C '84 (Schulte R&Z LLP) -919 3rd Av -NY 10022
(212) 422-8500 .. **Twersky,** Aaron '09 J Laufer PC -65 Bway -NY 10006 **Fx:**422-9038
(212) 201-1170 .. **Twersky,** Caryn L '00 Abrams GMB,LLP -237 W 35th -NY 10001
(212) 458-1104 .. **Twersky,** Danl A '07 AIG -175 Water -NY 10038 **Fx:**(866) 582-4844

(718) 852-8888 .. **Twersky,** Jonathan '86 %LSNYC-Brooklyn -180 Lvngstn -Brklyn 11201 **Fx:**858-1786
(212) 335-4500 .. **Twersky,** Michl J '99 %DLA Piper LLP -1251 Av of Amer -NY 10020
(212) 279-5050 .. **Twersky,** Mitchell M Z '92 (Abraham F&T LLP) -1 Penn Plz -NY 10119
(718) 250-2000 .. **Twersky,** Sholom J '84 %DA -350 Jay -Brklyn 11201 **Fx:**250-2314
(315) 424-7209 .. **Twichell,** P David '74 SrCnsl T Puleo -441 S Salina -Syracuse 13202 **Fx:**424-5553
(585) 295-4400 .. **Twietmeyer,** Don H '80 (Hiscock & B,LLP) -2000 HSBC Plz -Rchstr 14604
(212) 541-7800 .. **Twiggs,** Eileen Ann '98 %Planned Parenthood -434 W 33rd -NY 10001 **Fx:**868-4677
(518) 464-1300 .. **Twinam,** Amanda Davis '04 %Roemer WG&M LLP -13 Columbia Cir -Albany 12203
(212) 408-5100 .. **Twiste,** Eric '97 %Chadbourne & P LLP -30 Rckfllr Plz -NY 10112
(718) 748-9600 .. **Twohy,** John P '67 (Twohy & K) -477 86th -Brklyn 11209
(718) 748-9600 .. **Twohy & Kelleher** -477 86th -Brklyn 11209 **Fx:**748-0808
(212) 806-5400 .. **Twombly,** Jonathan D '98 %Stroock &S&L LLP -180 Maiden Ln -NY 10038
(315) 266-6100 .. **Twomey,** Angela M '09 Pub Def -235 Elizabeth -Utica 13501 **Fx:**266-6105
(718) 638-4075 .. **Twomey,** Bernard A '82 -209 Lincoln Pl -Brklyn 11217
(631) 777-7575 .. **Twomey,** Brendan P '82 -149 Intervale Av -Farmngdl 11735
(631) 727-2180 .. **Twomey Latham Shea Kelley Dubin & Quartararo,LLP** -33 W 2nd Bx9398 -Rvrhead 11901 **Fx:**727-1767
(212) 455-2000 .. **Twomey,** Laura M '98 (Simpson T&B LLP) -425 Lex Av -NY 10017
(516) 674-6100 .. **Twomey,** Liam I '79 -22 Pound Hllw Ct -Old Brookvll 11545 **Fx:**674-8717
(212) 682-8383 .. **Twomey,** Michl E '75 (Kantor DWMT&G,PC) -51 E 42nd -NY 10017
(631) 727-2180 .. **Twomey,** Thos A Jr. '72 (Twomey LSKD&Q,LLP) -33 W 2nd Bx9398 -Rvrhead 11901
(518) 455-4881 .. **Ty,** Sabrina M '90 %NYS Assembly -80 State -Albany 12248
(212) 348-7449 .. **Tyburec,** Lyda M '07 Legal Srvcs -1 W 125th -NY 10027 **Fx:**348-4093
(585) 227-7210 .. **Tydings,** Patrick E '80 -31 E Main -Rchstr 14614 **Fx:**227-7228
(212) 398-0055 .. **Tydniouk,** Anna '06 %Garwin G&F,LLP -1501 Bway -NY 10036
(718) 596-9000 .. **Tygar,** Howard H '94 %Cohen HEP&T -25 Chapel -Brklyn 11201
(315) 798-5870 .. **Tyksinski,** Adam P '08 %Pub Def -321 Main -Utica 13501 **Fx:**798-6419
(315) 361-3199 .. **Tyksinski,** Martin J '86 %Oneida Ltd -Kenwood Av -Oneida 13421 **Fx:**361-3700
(585) 263-6760 .. **Tyler,** Bradley E '79 %US Atty -620 Fed Bldg -Rchstr 14614 **Fx:**263-6226
(607) 273-4200 .. **Tyler,** David A '76 (Miller M,LLP) -202 E State -Ithaca 14850
(646) 708-8088 .. **Tyler,** David C '01 Fidelity Natl Law Grp -350 5th Av -NY 10118 **Fx:**(212) 594-8378
(607) 723-5341 .. **Tyler,** Gary C '02 %Hinman H&K,LLP -80 Exchange Bx5250 -Bnghmtn 13902
(212) 762-4836 .. **Tyler,** Jacob E IV '02 Morgan Stanley -1221 Av of Amer -NY 10020
(718) 237-5500 .. **Tyler,** Johnson M '90 %Leg Srvcs -105 Court -Brklyn 11201 **Fx:**855-0733
(212) 973-0572 .. **Tyler,** Jonathan A '95 %Wolff & S PC -140 Bway -NY 10005
(212) 261-8000 .. **Tyler,** Kate L '07 %Mendes & M,LLP -750 7th Av -NY 10019
(212) 480-7434 .. **Tyler,** Mark L '95 %DHCR -25 Beaver -NY 10004 **Fx:**480-7416
(516) 742-5201 .. **Tyler,** Milan K '88 (Phillips L LLP) -1100 Franklin Av -Gdn Cty 11530
(212) 759-4888 .. **Tyler,** Milan K '88 (Phillips L LLP) -437 Mad Av -NY 10022
(718) 934-4902 .. **Tylo,** Marina '96 -2807 Ocean Av -Brklyn 11229 **Fx:**934-4903
(518) 464-6770 .. **Tymann,** Jeffrey J '80 (Thorn GT&B,LLP) -5 Wembley Ct Bx15054 -Albany 12212
(212) 468-8000 .. **Tymann,** Lisa D '97 OfCnsl Morrison & F LLP -1290 Av of Amer -NY 10104
(516) 621-0007 .. **Tynan,** John P '90 -330 Willis Av -Roslyn Hts 11577
(212) 681-8313 .. **Tynan,** Luke M P '07 %Karaahmet L&G LLP -370 Lex Av -NY 10017 **Fx:**208-2917
(516) 379-9806 .. **Tynan,** Maureen '87 (Fishman & T) -2174 Hewlett Av -Merrick 11566
(212) 218-2100 .. **Tyndale,** Jamar W '08 %Fitzpatrick CH&S -1290 Av of Amer -NY 10104
(718) 250-2000 .. **Tyne,** Janine M '97 %DA -350 Jay -Brklyn 11201 **Fx:**250-2314
(518) 374-7411 .. **Tyner,** James E '03 %MJ Sacco -38 N Ferry -Schnctdy 12305 **Fx:**374-7475
(585) 289-4040 .. **Tyo,** John E '67 (Zimmerman & T) -6 E Main Bx7 -Shortsvll 14548 **Fx:**289-4043
(212) 956-8300 .. **Typermass,** David Arthur '98 %Bronstein Van V LLC -650 Mad Av -NY 10022
(212) 549-8328 .. **Tyras,** Jon C '99 Hyperion Brookfield Asset Mgmt -3 World Fncl Ctr -NY 10281
(914) 967-2114 .. **Tyre & DeThomas** -150 Purchase -Rye 10580 **Fx:**967-0574
(914) 967-2114 .. **Tyre,** Margaret H '79 (Tyre & D) -150 Purchase -Rye 10580
(212) 490-3000 .. **Tyrie,** James P '92 (Wilson EME&D LLP) -150 E 42nd -NY 10017
(646) 557-5100 .. **Tyrrell,** James E Jr. '76 (Patton B LLP) -1185 Av of Amer -NY 10036
(516) 248-5757 .. **Tyrrell,** Robin Young '99 %Colleran O&M,LLP -1225 Franklin Av -Gdn Cty 11530
(516) 221-5100 .. **Tyrrell,** Thos J '91 Quinn & T -3330 Park Av -Wantagh 11793 **Fx:**221-5173
(212) 859-8000 .. **Tyson,** Ann '77 %Fried FHS&J LLP -1 NY Plz -NY 10004
(212) 530-5000 .. **Tyson,** Blair M '98 %Milbank TH&M LLP -1 Chase Manh Plz -NY 10005
(718) 297-1717 .. **Tyson,** Craig K '90 %Viscardi B&B,PC -148-45 Hillside Av -Jamaica 11435
(518) 433-8800 .. **Tyson,** Danl J '75 (Lemery G LLC) -50 Beaver -Albany 12207
(917) 304-4040 .. **Tyson,** John K '03 -1636 3rd Av -NY 10128
(315) 218-8000 .. **Tyson,** Robt R '94 (Bond S&K,PLLC) -1 Lincoln Ctr -Syracuse 13202
(212) 375-2045 .. **Tyson,** Stacey L '01 %ACA Capital -140 Bway -NY 10005
(347) 338-0894 .. **Tyson-Phipps,** Jabari-Jason '09 -712 E 228th -Bronx 10466
(212) 841-1000 .. **Tytel,** Judith E '72 SpclCnsl Covington & B LLP -620 8th Av -NY 10018
(212) 669-8222 .. **Tyus,** Ethel E '99 %NYC Comptollers Ofc -1 Centre -NY 10007
(212) 289-5902 .. **Tzagoloff,** Helen '84 -152 E 94th -NY 10128
(646) 708-8088 .. **Tzakas,** Anna '08 Fidelity Natl Law Grp -350 5th Av -NY 10118 **Fx:**(212) 594-8378
(212) 909-6000 .. **Tzakas,** Eugenia P '09 %Debevoise & P LLP -919 3rd Av -NY 10022
(516) 742-0400 .. **Tzaneteas,** Nicholas E '99 %S Frankel -368 Willis Av -Mineola 11501 **Fx:**742-0499
(212) 883-0004 .. **Tzanides,** Kyriakos P '89 (Tzanides Law Firm,PLLC) -275 Mad Av -NY 10016 **Fx:**686-0252
(716) 854-1930 .. **Tzetzo,** Dimitri J '51 (Tzetzo & T,PLLC) -37 Franklin -Buffalo 14202
(716) 854-1930 .. **Tzetzo,** Nicholas B '99 (Tzetzo & T,PLLC) -37 Franklin -Buffalo 14202
(716) 856-0600 .. **Tzetzo,** Nicole R '99 (Jaeckle F&M,LLP) -12 Fountain Plz -Buffalo 14202
(212) 804-4200 .. **Tziavragos,** Paula M '99 (Mound CW&G) -One Bttry Pk Plz -NY 10004
(212) 557-5055 .. **Tzifas,** Constantine T '97 %Semetis Law Firm -286 Mad Av -NY 10017 **Fx:**557-5051
(212) 564-9800 .. **Tzimopoulos,** George '91 OfCnsl D'Agostino L&L,LLP -345 7th Av -NY 10001
(718) 725-3032 .. **Tzimorotas,** Rachel D '97 %Admin Children's Srvcs -151-20 Jamaica Av -Jamaica 11432
(212) 267-7600 .. **Tzokova-Natseva,** Maria M '03 %Solomon PBH&S LLP -40 Wall -NY 10005
(212) 557-7200 .. **Tzortzatos,** Dimitra '06 %Davidoff M&H,LLP -605 3rd Av -NY 10158
(718) 267-8471 .. **Tzortzatos,** Maria '02 -10-08 150th -Whitestone 11357 **Fx:**267-8470
(212) 267-6364 .. **Tzortzatos,** Olga '99 %Kossoff & U -217 Bway -NY 10007
(212) 846-3687 .. **Tzou,** Janet T '00 MTV Networks -1515 Bway -NY 10036
(716) 634-8300 .. **Uba,** Mark R '93 -5500 Main -Buffalo 14221
(212) 735-3000 .. **Ubani,** John Nnamaka '00 %Skadden ASM&F LLP -4 Times Sq -NY 10036
(516) 319-4043 .. **Ubert,** Wm A '86 -71 Exec Blvd -Farmngdl 11735 **Fx:**(877) 393-7760
(718) 722-3100 .. **Ubozoh,** Ferdinand I '89 %Leg Aid -111 Lvngstn -Brklyn 11201 **Fx:**722-3093
(212) 483-9490 .. **Uccello,** Louis A '05 %McElroy DM&C,LLP -88 Pine -NY 10005
(212) 850-2800 .. **Uchima,** Anju '84 OfCnsl Andrews K LLP -450 Lex Av -NY 10017
(212) 649-0389 .. **Uchimura,** Hiroya '98 Mizuho Corp Bk Ltd -1251 Av of Amer -NY 10020
(516) 625-9850 .. **Uchman,** Eileen A '88 (Shapiro U&M,PC) -Expwy Plz 1-#120 -Roslyn Hts 11577
(516) 832-3200 .. **Ucinski,** Annemarie '00 %1st Amer Title -333 Earle Ovngton Blvd -Uniondale 11553 **Fx:**832-3299
(516) 739-5100 .. **Ucinski,** Theo W '99 %Farber B&Z LLP -51 Charles -Mineola 11501
(212) 331-4478 .. **Udapi,** Guruprasad S '05 HRA -180 Water -NY 10038
(212) 756-2000 .. **Udashkin,** Joshua '10 %Schulte R&Z LLP -919 3rd Av -NY 10022
(212) 964-9282 .. **Uddin,** Hafiz '01 %N Weinrib & Assoc -305 Bway -NY 10007 **Fx:**964-9525
(718) 694-3802 .. **Uddoh,** Humphrey O '93 %Transit Auth -130 Lvngstn -Brklyn 11201 **Fx:**694-5726
(212) 809-8585 .. **Ude,** Thos W Jr. '08 Lambda LDEF, Inc -120 Wall -NY 10005 **Fx:**809-0055
(212) 506-2500 .. **Ude,** Ugochukwu O '07 %Mayer B LLP -1675 Bway -NY 10019
(718) 596-2410 .. **Udell,** Bernard '68 -26 Court -Brklyn 11242
(212) 998-6730 .. **Udell,** David S '83 %Brennan Ctr for Justice -161 Av of Amer -NY 10013
(212) 832-7900 .. **Udell,** Howard R '66 (Millard G&U) -15 E 62nd -NY 10065
(212) 451-2300 .. **Udell,** Jeffrey A '94 (Olshan GFR&W LLP) -65 E 55th -NY 10022
(212) 264-3650 .. **Udell,** Tracy L '05 %SSA Ofc Genl Cnsl -26 Fed Plz -NY 10278 **Fx:**264-6372
(646) 414-6974 .. **Udem,** Marianna '07 %Lowenstein S PC -1251 Av of Amer -NY 10020 **Fx:**(973) 422-6887
(718) 261-3047 .. **Uderitz,** Lori L '87 %Queens Law Assoc -118-21 Qns Blvd -Frst Hlls 11375 **Fx:**261-0798
(914) 225-7482 .. **Udeshi Crick,** Priya Jayendra '02 Morgan Stanley -2000 Wstchstr Av -Purchase 10577
(212) 484-3900 .. **Udin,** Andrew C '03 %Arent F LLP -1675 Bway -NY 10019
(212) 835-7845 .. **Udochi,** John F '95 %Dept of Labor -109 E 16th -NY 10003 **Fx:**529-3647
(212) 313-1200 .. **Udoff,** Michl D '70 %SIA -120 Bway -NY 10271 **Fx:**313-1301
(914) 824-5388 .. **Udoh,** Chinyelu O '01 %Hon L Martin -111 Dr Martin Luther King Jr Blvd -White Plns 10601
(212) 661-8888 .. **Udwadia,** Viraf A '84 -420 Lex Av -NY 10170 **Fx:**370-5637
(315) 798-5466 .. **Uebelhoer,** Gail N '79 NYS Supreme Ct -Ct Hse -Utica 13501 **Fx:**798-6431
(212) 238-3000 .. **Uehlinger,** John P '82 (Emmet M&M,LLP) -120 Bway -NY 10271
(212) 785-2929 .. **Uejio,** Jonathan T '89 (Conway FC&K,PC) -48 Wall -NY 10005
(212) 636-7328 .. **Uelmen,** Amelia J '96 %Fordham Univ Sch of Law -140 W 62nd -NY 10023 **Fx:**636-6899
(212) 326-3939 .. **Uelze,** Virginia T '10 %Jones D -222 E 41st -NY 10017
(212) 480-4800 .. **Ueno,** Chizuko '91 (Fox H&C LLP) -825 3rd Av -NY 10022
(212) 340-0400 .. **Ueno,** Takemi '94 %Appllt Div 1st Dept -27 Mad Av -NY 10010 **Fx:**889-4412
(212) 326-3939 .. **Uerkwitz,** Eri B '09 %Jones D -222 E 41st -NY 10017
(212) 918-3000 .. **Ufaeva,** Marina G '06 %Hogan L LLP -875 3rd Av -NY 10022
(212) 632-5500 .. **Uffleman,** Wayne R '10 %Salans LLP -620 5th Av -NY 10020
(718) 335-3300 .. **Uffner,** Gary H '78 %US Indust Products -96-12 43rd Av -Corona 11368
(212) 806-5400 .. **Uffner,** Jeffrey D '77 (Stroock &S&L LLP) -180 Maiden Ln -NY 10038
(212) 221-5700 .. **Uffner,** Steven '81 (Goldberg WFG LLP) -1501 Bway -NY 10036
(718) 275-3660 .. **Ugalde,** Francisco A '07 (Harris Law Grp,LLP) -96-14 63rd Dr -Rego Pk 11374 **Fx:**275-3405
(845) 639-5960 .. **Ugell,** Scott B '86 %Clarkstown Town Justice Ct -20 Maple Av -New Cty 10956 **Fx:**639-5910
(845) 639-7011 .. **Ugell,** Scott B '86 Ugell Law Firm,PC -24 S Main -New Cty 10956 **Fx:**639-7004
(718) 852-8641 .. **Ugelow,** Robt A '72 R Ugelow,PC -26 Court -Brklyn 11242 **Fx:**625-4176
(212) 751-6401 .. **Ugenyi,** Ihenji Buanya '97 NYS Ed Dept-Ofc Pro Discipline -475 Park Av S -NY 10016

(212) 859-8000 .. **Ughetta,** Edw F '97 (Fried FHS&J LLP) -1 NY Plz -NY 10004
(914) 417-3400 .. **Ughetta,** James C '82 (Littleton JUP&K LLP) -1 Manhattanvll Rd -Purchase 10577
(212) 504-6000 .. **Ughetta,** Robt L '94 (Cadwalader W&T LLP) -1 World Fncl Ctr -NY 10281
(718) 512-5448 .. **Ugokwe,** Ifeoma N '02 -337 Linden Blvd -Brklyn 11203
(212) 705-0105 .. **Ugurlayan,** Anahid M '01 Natl Advertising Div -70 W 36th -NY 10018
(212) 257-6800 .. **Uh,** Cindy E '08 %Thompson W&G LLP -85 5th Av -NY 10003
(516) 922-2083 .. **Uhl,** Virginia W '77 -353 Split Rock Rd -Syosset 11791
(212) 208-3369 .. **Uhlein,** John W III '82 Ambac Assurance Corp -1 State Street Plz -NY 10004 **Fx:**363-1459
(212) 839-5300 .. **Uhlir,** Clinton R '09 (Sidley A LLP) -787 7th Av -NY 10019
(212) 237-0000 .. **Uhrich,** Craig L '02 %Vinson & E LLP -666 5th Av -NY 10103
(631) 444-0345 .. **Ukeritis,** Jennifer M '03 DEC -SUNY Campus 50 Circle Rd -Stony Brk 11790 **Fx:**444-0348
(718) 554-0891 .. **Ukoha,** Ifeanyichukwu A '03 -255 Lvngstn -Brklyn 11217
(718) 250-2000 .. **Ukomadu,** Ugoeze N '03 %DA -350 Jay -Brklyn 11201 **Fx:**250-2314
(212) 732-8368 .. **Ulaner,** Marcelle K '78 (Caruso SLCU&S) -132 Nassau -NY 10038
(518) 587-9790 .. **Ulasewicz,** Patricia M '83 (Ulasewicz Law Firm,LLP) -112 Spring -Saratoga Spgs 12866 **Fx:**587-9706
(518) 587-9790 .. **Ulasewicz,** Thos A '77 (Ulasewicz Law Firm,LLP) -112 Spring -Saratoga Spgs 12866 **Fx:**587-9706
(716) 854-3400 .. **Ulatowski,** Jason G '08 %Rupp BPC&C LLC -1600 Lbrty Bldg -Buffalo 14202
(212) 437-9110 .. **Ule,** Carol '71 (Hartman UR&R,LLP) -305 Bway -NY 10007
(212) 237-3154 .. **Ulene,** Douglas E '92 Paramount Grp,Inc -1633 Bway -NY 10019
(212) 962-1020 .. **Ulezalka,** Tara M '06 %M Lamonsoff -80 Maiden Ln -NY 10038 **Fx:**962-3078
(516) 560-6400 .. **Ulgen,** Argun M '04 %Leg Aid -1 Helen Keller Way -Hempstd 11550 **Fx:**565-3694
(212) 963-8263 .. **Ulich,** Oliver '98 -UN -NY 10017
(212) 703-5060 .. **Ulicny,** Suzanne L '02 ICC Intl Ct of Arbitration -1212 Av of Amer -NY 10036 **Fx:**575-0327
(212) 404-5777 .. **Ulisse,** Rebecca L '03 %Littleton JUP&K LLP -39 Bway -NY 10006
(212) 728-2200 .. **Ulit,** Ithti Toy '06 Axinn V&H LLP -114 W 47th -NY 10036
(607) 721-8321 .. **Uljanov,** Kathleen M '92 %Workers Comp Bd -44 Hawley -Bnghmtn 13901
(212) 696-6000 .. **Ulke,** Guillermo '97 (Curtis M-PC&M LLP) -101 Park Av -NY 10178
(212) 632-5500 .. **Ullman,** Anthony B '85 (Salans LLP) -620 5th Av -NY 10020
(212) 351-4500 .. **Ullman,** Brian L '91 SrCnsl Epstein B&G,PC -250 Park Av -NY 10177
(516) 542-6356 .. **Ullman,** David '82 -600 Old Cntry Rd -Gdn Cty 11530 **Fx:**542-1088
(212) 480-4800 .. **Ullman,** Harold '89 (Fox H&C LLP) -825 3rd Av -NY 10022
(518) 474-2266 .. **Ullman,** Lisa '96 %Gov's Cnsls Ofc -242 State Cptl -Albany 12224
(212) 571-0068 .. **Ullman,** Marc S '86 (Ullman S&U,LLP) -299 Bway -NY 10007
(212) 867-6000 .. **Ullman,** Meredith A '04 %Rosenberg & E,PC -733 3rd Av -NY 10017
(212) 571-0068 .. **Ullman,** Robt '60 SrCnsl Ullman S&U,LLP -299 Bway -NY 10007
(212) 571-0068 .. **Ullman Shapiro & Ullman,LLP** -299 Bway -NY 10007 **Fx:**571-9424
(914) 834-0414 .. **Ullmann,** Gladys G '86 -1890 Palmer Av -Larchmnt 10538 **Fx:**834-4579
(516) 938-3100 .. **Ullmann,** Jonathan I '87 %P Roach & Assoc,PC -125 Michl Dr -Syosset 11791 **Fx:**931-4403
(212) 428-5502 .. **Ullo,** Christina M '04 %OCA -25 Beaver -NY 10004
(212) 323-7070 .. **Ullom,** Marc F '06 OfCnsl Rawle & H LLP -14 Wall -NY 10005
(845) 469-1277 .. **Ullrich,** Helen G '97 (Bergstein & U,LLP) -15 Railroad Av -Chester 10918
(516) 742-3470 .. **Ullrich,** John J '02 %Kral CRRP&G,LLP -538 Broadhllw Rd -Melvll 11747
(212) 307-5099 .. **Ulm,** Alice L '88 -17 W 54th -NY 10019 **Fx:**307-5099
(845) 354-6436 .. **Ulman,** Doris Friedman '58 -134 N Camp Hill Rd -Pomona 10970 **Fx:**354-3861
(845) 354-6436 .. **Ulman,** Jan '91 -134 N Camp Hill Rd -Pomona 10970 **Fx:**354-3861
(212) 995-8211 .. **Ulman,** Jan '91 -30 E 9th -NY 10003
(516) 676-4600 .. **Ulman,** Stephen V R '60 OfCnsl Humes & W -147 Forest Av Bx546 -Locust Vly 11560
(212) 596-9000 .. **Ulmer,** Merrill A '94 (Ropes & G LLP) -1211 Av of Amer -NY 10036
(212) 788-5882 .. **Ulrey,** Prescott D '95 Ofc of Mgmt & Budget -75 Park Pl -NY 10007 **Fx:**788-9197
(212) 909-6000 .. **Ulrich,** Amanda Jo Marsh '10 %Debevoise & P LLP -919 3rd Av -NY 10022
(631) 420-5000 .. **Ulrich,** Christopher P '95 Cydian Tech -445 Broadhllw Rd -Melvll 11747
(212) 425-7200 .. **Ulrich,** Clifford A '97 (Kenyon & K,LLP) -1 Bway -NY 10004
(585) 389-1210 .. **Ulrich,** Douglas E '85 -350 Linden Oaks -Rchstr 14625 **Fx:**389-1212
(212) 308-4411 .. **Ulrich,** Julia K '04 %Edwards AP&D LLP -750 Lex Av -NY 10022
(973) 596-4635 .. **Ulrich,** Peter J '87 (Gibbons PC) -1 Penn Plz -NY 10119 **Fx:**639-6323
(516) 739-0400 .. **Ulrich,** Susan M '05 %Kelly R&K,LLP -330 Old Cntry Rd -Mineola 11501
(585) 263-1000 .. **Ulterino,** Eugene D '66 (Nixon P LLP) -1100 Clinton Sq -Rchstr 14604
(516) 222-6200 .. **Ulto,** Christopher F '93 %Berkman HPP&F,PC -100 Grdn City Plz -Gdn Cty 11530
(212) 407-4000 .. **Um,** John T '97 %Loeb & L,LLP -345 Park Av -NY 10154
(914) 834-9648 .. **Uman,** Henry K '66 -53 Oak Av -Larchmnt 10538
(212) 223-0400 .. **Umane,** Frederic M '79 (Zeichner E&K LLP) -575 Lex Av -NY 10022
(516) 542-0200 .. **Umans,** Jay D '74 -90 Merrick Av -E Meadow 11554 **Fx:**542-9733
(212) 519-3000 .. **Umans-Gough,** Terry '78 PricewaterhouseCoopers LLP -11 Mad Av -NY 10010
(716) 712-0888 .. **Uminski,** Denis J '00 %W Piotrowski -3881 Seneca -W Seneca 14224 **Fx:**712-0622
(518) 860-7256 .. **Umlauf,** Ann Beck '09 Mechanical Dynamics & Analysis,Ltd -19 British Amer Blvd -Latham 12110
(718) 360-0527 .. **Umoh,** Nkereuwem Inyang '05 -255 Lvngstn -Brklyn 11217
(212) 575-1292 .. **Uncyk Borenkind & Nadler,LLP** -555 5th Av -NY 10017 **Fx:**768-4469
(212) 575-1292 .. **Uncyk,** Eli '70 (Uncyk B&N,LLP) -555 5th Av -NY 10017
(585) 258-2800 .. **Underberg & Kessler LLP** -300 Bausch & Lomb Pl -Rchstr 14604 **Fx:**258-2821
(585) 919-0009 .. **Underberg & Kessler LLP** -23 Sly -Canandaigua 14424 **Fx:**394-1614
(716) 848-9000 .. **Underberg & Kessler LLP** -1900 Main Pl Twr -Buffalo 14202 **Fx:**847-6004
(315) 331-4875 .. **Underberg & Kessler LLP** -634 S Main -Newark 14513 **Fx:**331-9336
(631) 271-5484 .. **Underberg,** Marc B '06 -33 Walt Whitman Rd -Huntngtn Sta 11746 **Fx:**271-5486
(212) 373-3000 .. **Underberg,** Mark A '82 (Paul WRW&G LLP) -1285 Av of Amer -NY 10019
(212) 294-6700 .. **Underberg,** Neil '52 (Winston & S) -200 Park Av -NY 10166
(585) 781-5824 .. **Underberg,** Sharon E '86 Eastman Kodak -343 State -Rchstr 14650 **Fx:**724-9448
(212) 770-7000 .. **Underhill,** Robt E '95 AIG -70 Pine -NY 10270
(212) 839-7000 .. **Underriner,** Eric M '97 SpclCnsl Hill B&N LLP -200 Lbrty -NY 10281
(914) 761-5628 .. **Underweiser,** Beatrice K '58 (Underweiser & U LLP) -1 Water -White Plns 10601 **Fx:**761-8927
(914) 761-5628 .. **Underweiser,** Irwin P '54 (Underweiser & U LLP) -1 Water -White Plns 10601 **Fx:**761-8927
(914) 761-5628 .. **Underweiser,** Jeffrey '93 (Underweiser & U LLP) -1 Water -White Plns 10601 **Fx:**761-8927
(914) 945-2756 .. **Underweiser,** Marian '98 IBM -Bx218 -Yorktwn Hts 10598
(212) 416-8000 .. **Underwood,** Barbara D '79 %Dept of Law -120 Bway -NY 10271
(212) 504-6000 .. **Underwood,** Colin A '90 (Cadwalader W&T LLP) -1 World Fncl Ctr -NY 10281
(315) 446-7084 .. **Underwood,** Derek S '01 (Colman & U) -7030 E Genesee -Fayettevll 13066
(212) 231-1728 .. **Underwood,** John Andrew '98 MacQuarie Securities -125 W 55th -NY 10019
(516) 624-6150 .. **Underwood,** Karen J '98 %Town Atty -Town Hall -Oyster Bay 11771 **Fx:**624-6196
(315) 446-7084 .. **Underwood,** Michl E '05 (Colman & U) -7030 E Genesee -Fayettevll 13066
(212) 806-5400 .. **Underwood,** Stephen E '09 %Stroock &S&L LLP -180 Maiden Ln -NY 10038
(716) 656-7676 .. **Underwood,** Stephen K '98 -1395 Union Rd -W Seneca 14224 **Fx:**674-2278
(212) 790-9200 .. **Underwood,** Steven D '99 %Cowan L&L,PC -1133 Av of Amer -NY 10036
(212) 766-1443 .. **Unegbu,** Obinna C '06 -225 Bway -NY 10007 **Fx:**766-0943
(212) 986-6000 .. **Ung,** Euchung '94 OfCnsl Kleinberg KW&C,PC -551 5th Av -NY 10176
(212) 669-7778 .. **Ung,** Sandra '02 %Comptroller -1 Centre -NY 10007 **Fx:**669-2884
(718) 623-0777 .. **Ungar,** Diane E '81 -10 Plz E -Brklyn 11238 **Fx:**623-0055
(212) 506-1700 .. **Ungar,** Dorit '04 %Kasowitz BT&F LLP -1633 Bway -NY 10019
(516) 227-2400 .. **Ungar,** Robt A '88 (R Ungar,PC) -200 Grdn City Plz -Gdn Cty 11530 **Fx:**227-2406
(212) 220-7123 .. **Ungar,** Stephen '88 Amtrust Financial Srvcs -59 Maiden Ln -NY 10038
(718) 222-2506 .. **Ungari,** Natalie A '05 Two Trees Mgmt Co,LLC -45 Main -Brklyn 11201
(212) 766-5800 .. **Ungaro & Cifuni** -291 Bway -NY 10007 **Fx:**766-6200
(212) 766-5800 .. **Ungaro,** Robt A '93 (Ungaro & C) -291 Bway -NY 10007
(212) 839-5300 .. **Unger,** Alan M '79 (Sidley A LLP) -787 7th Av -NY 10019
(212) 298-5188 .. **Unger,** Beth Ann '90 %Leg Aid -49 Thomas -NY 10013 **Fx:**298-5252
(718) 264-3340 .. **Unger,** Erik S '09 %MHLS -80-45 Wnchstr Blvd -Qns Vllg 11427 **Fx:**264-3559
(212) 755-4777 .. **Unger,** Harold M '71 -641 Lex Av -NY 10022
(212) 803-5100 .. **Unger,** Hilary D '89 %NY Cnty Defender Srvcs -225 Bway -NY 10007 **Fx:**571-6035
(212) 344-0410 .. **Unger,** Kimberly '84 %STANY -39 Bway -NY 10006
(212) 571-2255 .. **Unger,** Lawr P '88 -233 Bway -NY 10279
(718) 241-6012 .. **Unger,** Leonard N '80 -1002 E 59th -Brklyn 11234
(631) 499-1999 .. **Unger,** Marilyn '86 -93 Hamlet Dr -Commack 11725
(516) 296-7000 .. **Unger,** Martin P '64 (Certilman BA&H,LLP) -90 Merrick Av -E Meadow 11554
(516) 338-7520 .. **Unger,** Meredith E '02 %Daniels & N,PC -900 Merchants Cncrs -Westbury 11590
(212) 953-6000 .. **Unger,** Meryl Lynn '76 (Katsky K LLP) -605 3rd Av -NY 10158
(212) 425-1900 .. **Unger,** Michl E '92 (Freehill H&M LLP) -80 Pine -NY 10005
(718) 279-4500 .. **Unger,** Randall D '79 -42-40 Bell Blvd -Bayside 11361
(212) 335-4500 .. **Unger,** Robt M '79 (DLA Piper LLP) -1251 Av of Amer -NY 10020
(516) 829-3508 .. **Unger,** Robt M '80 (Kupillas & U) -11 Grace Av -Gt Neck 11021
(212) 788-7026 .. **Unger,** Russell B '02 NYC Council Govt Affrs Div -250 Bway -NY 10007
(212) 267-6364 .. **Unger,** Sally E '82 (Kossoff & U) -217 Bway -NY 10007
(212) 279-9090 .. **Unger,** Scott I '98 (Stark & S) -One Penn Plz -NY 10119 **Fx:**279-9113
(516) 741-0520 .. **Unger,** Susan J '90 X-Press Inc -734 Franklin Av -Gdn Cty 11530
(212) 836-8000 .. **Unger,** Sydney E '75 (Kaye S LLP) -425 Park Av -NY 10022
(716) 753-4356 .. **Ungerer,** Beverly D '84 Hon J Claire Family Ct -2 Academy -Mayvll 14757 **Fx:**753-4350
(212) 430-6040 .. **Ungerleider,** Robt M '67 OfCnsl Wasser & R LLP -80 Maiden Ln -NY 10038 **Fx:**430-6041
(212) 837-2420 .. **Ungerman,** Stephen M '85 JP Morgan Chase & Co -522 5th Av -NY 10036
(212) 986-2340 .. **Unikel,** Ricardo '03 %Jordan & H -122 E 42nd -NY 10168
(212) 850-2800 .. **Uniman,** Chas D '76 OfCnsl Andrews K LLP -450 Lex Av -NY 10017
(212) 850-2800 .. **Uniman,** Lynne M '80 (Andrews K LLP) -450 Lex Av -NY 10017
(315) 824-3605 .. **Uninsky,** Philip B '93 Youth Policy Inst -38 Payne -Hamilton 13346
(212) 704-6000 .. **Unis,** Eric L '02 %Troutman S LLP -405 Lex Av -NY 10174
(212) 812-7000 .. **Univer,** Scott M '77 Weiser LLP -135 W 50th -NY 10020 **Fx:**375-6888
(212) 306-7160 .. **Unkeless,** Elaine Rapp '82 %Ofc Cllctv Brgn -40 Rector -NY 10006 **Fx:**306-7167
(212) 496-9280 .. **Unroch,** Wm J '77 -140 West End Av -NY 10023 **Fx:**496-9330
(212) 541-8641 .. **Unter,** Jennifer L '99 %RLR Assoc Ltd -7 W 51st -NY 10019
(212) 449-1452 .. **Unterberg,** Andrew I '06 Merrill Lynch -4 World Fncl Ctr -NY 10080

(212) 659-7300 .. **Unterberg,** Craig S '09 (Haynes & B,LLP) -1221 Av of Amer -NY 10020
(212) 458-7044 .. **Unterlack,** Matthew E '98 %AIG -175 Water -NY 10038
(718) 643-4000 .. **Unterman,** Arthur M '77 -26 Court -Brklyn 11242 **Fx:**522-5434
(212) 899-4599 .. **Unterman,** Edan G '79 Kajima USA -1251 Av of Amer -NY 10020
(212) 867-9500 .. **Unterman,** Lee D '76 (Kurzman K&F,LLP) -230 Park Av -NY 10169
(585) 428-5755 .. **Unwin,** Robin P '03 Cnty Atty -50 W Main -Rchstr 14614 **Fx:**428-2031
(585) 295-5400 .. **Unwin,** S Philip '03 %Goldberg S LLP -2 State -Rchstr 14614
(516) 694-3000 .. **Unz,** Patricia A '95 %Guercio & G,LLP -77 Conklin -Farmngdl 11735 **Fx:**694-4738
(212) 661-5030 .. **Updike,** Chas B '67 (Schoeman U&K,LLP) -60 E 42nd -NY 10165
(212) 504-6000 .. **Updike,** Christopher J '07 %Cadwalader W&T LLP -1 World Fncl Ctr -NY 10281
(718) 923-4206 .. **Upshur,** Maryeta A '91 %OTDA Fair Hearings -14 Boerum Pl -Brklyn 11201
(212) 756-2000 .. **Uptegrove,** Wm M '10 %Schulte R&Z LLP -919 3rd Av -NY 10022
(212) 657-1422 .. **Upton,** Andrew M '81 Citigroup Global Mrkts -111 Wall -NY 10005 **Fx:**(646) 298-1472
(561) 441-8070 .. **Upton,** Arthur E '67 (A Upton,PC) -5 Buccaneer Ln -E Setauket 11733 **Fx:**362-0054
(212) 233-9300 .. **Upton,** John W '80 -70 Lafayette -NY 10013 **Fx:**233-9713
(212) 336-2000 .. **Upton,** Richd R '80 (Patterson BW&T LLP) -1133 Av of Amer -NY 10036
(212) 244-5553 .. **Upton,** Sean '93 %Turbochef Technologies -754 5th Av -NY 10019
(212) 828-6866 .. **Upton,** Susan H '95 -1125 Park Av -NY 10128
(631) 261-2622 .. **Upton,** Wm J '78 (WJ Upton PC) -52 Bway -Greenlawn 11740 **Fx:**754-7678
(212) 468-4800 .. **Uram,** Gerald R '67 (Davis & G LLP) -1740 Bway -NY 10019
(212) 867-9595 .. **Uram,** Jack '67 (Blindman & U) -630 3rd Av -NY 10017
(914) 328-3334 .. **Uram,** Susan Wanderer '88 -150 Stone Oaks Dr -Hartsdale 10530 **Fx:**328-3313
(212) 258-5389 .. **Urbach,** Rebecca M '08 Greater NY Hospital Assn -555 W 57th -NY 10019
(212) 468-4800 .. **Urbach,** Ronald R '77 (Davis & G LLP) -1740 Bway -NY 10019
(212) 307-1499 .. **Urbach Lissner,** Barbara '89 (Lissner & L LLP) -250 W 57th -NY 10107 **Fx:**757-1825
(212) 318-5675 .. **Urban,** Alexandra B '03 SrCnsl MeadWestvaco -299 Park Av -NY 10171 **Fx:**318-5035
(212) 788-0485 .. **Urban,** John R '69 %Law Dept -100 Church -NY 10007 **Fx:**788-0367
(212) 791-3900 .. **Urban,** Lisa Breier '91 (Breier DU&F PC) -111 Bway -NY 10006
(631) 968-0500 .. **Urban,** Richd C '81 (Urban & S) -130 Orinoco Dr -Brightwtrs 11718
(631) 968-0500 .. **Urban & Salatto** -130 Orinoco Dr -Brightwtrs 11718 **Fx:**968-0118
(631) 691-3303 .. **Urbano-DiSalvo,** Debra A '86 Justice Ct -16 Greene Av -Amityvll 11701 **Fx:**691-3304
(212) 506-3900 .. **Urbelis,** Alexander J '07 %Steptoe & J LLP -750 7th Av -NY 10019
(212) 849-7000 .. **Urbieta,** Olga M '08 %Quinn EU&S,LLP -51 Mad Av -NY 10010
(212) 916-5568 .. **Urbina,** Selina M '97 TIAA-CREF -730 3rd Av -NY 10017
(718) 482-4089 .. **Urda,** John K '99 %DEC -1 Hunters Pnt Plz -LIC 11101 **Fx:**482-4962
(607) 273-1204 .. **Urda,** Richd P '88 -408 N Tioga -Ithaca 14850
(212) 848-7969 .. **Urda Kassis,** Cynthia E '85 (Shearman & S LLP) -599 Lex Av -NY 10022
(631) 589-7242 .. **Urena De Checo,** Reinelda Elizabeth '03 Zabell & Assoc,LLP -4875 Sunrise Hwy -Bohemia 11716
(212) 571-1255 .. **Uretsky,** Jonathan C '00 (Phillipson & U,LLP) -111 Bway -NY 10006 **Fx:**571-1167
(518) 523-3389 .. **Urfirer,** Roland M '50 -75 Main -Lk Placid 12946 **Fx:**523-1495
(516) 304-5725 .. **Urfrig,** Courtney P '03 %H Kerker,PC -25 Kensngtn Cir -Manhsst 11030 **Fx:**304-5726
(718) 720-2292 .. **Urgo,** Thos '80 -40 Clinton -Brklyn 11201
(212) 228-9666 .. **Urias,** Peter D '07 Bantle & L LLP -817 Bway -NY 10003 **Fx:**228-7654
(212) 446-4800 .. **Urias,** Sergio A '08 %Kirkland & E LLP -153 E 53rd -NY 10022
(718) 250-2000 .. **Uriel,** Jacob '09 %DA -350 Jay -Brklyn 11201 **Fx:**250-2314
(718) 250-2000 .. **Uris,** Adam S '08 %DA -350 Jay -Brklyn 11201 **Fx:**250-2314
(212) 735-2212 .. **Uris,** Harvey R '80 (Skadden ASM&F LLP) -4 Times Sq -NY 10036 **Fx:**(917) 777-2212
(212) 855-3200 .. **Urist,** Carl H '70 %Depository Trust -55 Water -NY 10041 **Fx:**855-3279
(212) 521-5400 .. **Urist,** Joshua B '08 %Reed S LLP -599 Lex Av -NY 10022
(516) 486-7475 .. **Urist,** Leonard '91 Risk Mgmt Planning Grp -211 Station Rd -Mineola 11501
(212) 455-2000 .. **Urkevich,** Hayley M '09 %Simpson T&B LLP -425 Lex Av -NY 10017
(212) 508-6700 .. **Urman,** Lawr '79 %Tannenbaum HS&H LLP -900 3rd Av -NY 10022
(212) 558-4000 .. **Urowsky,** Richd J '73 (Sullivan & C LLP) -125 Broad -NY 10004
(212) 310-8000 .. **Urquhart,** Douglas R '90 (Weil G&M LLP) -767 5th Av -NY 10153
(212) 480-4800 .. **Urquia,** Rafael II '75 (Fox H&C LLP) -825 3rd Av -NY 10022
(718) 250-2000 .. **Urraca,** Yaniris '06 %DA -350 Jay -Brklyn 11201 **Fx:**250-2314
(914) 686-1700 .. **Urreta,** Peter L '93 %O'Connor R,LLP -200 Mamaroneck Av -White Plns 10601
(718) 590-2000 .. **Urrutia,** Eva M '93 %DA -198 E 161st -Bronx 10451 **Fx:**590-6477
(315) 453-3053 .. **Urrutia,** Julio E '85 (Finkelstein & Prtnrs,LLP) -716 7th N -Liverpool 13088
(212) 805-4616 .. **Urs,** Tara '09 Hon D Batts -500 Pearl -NY 10007
(212) 373-3000 .. **Urschel,** Michl L '08 %Paul WRW&G LLP -1285 Av of Amer -NY 10019
(516) 747-5757 .. **Urso,** Jos '92 (Colonna & U,LLP) -1551 Kellum Pl -Mineola 11501 **Fx:**747-2107
(718) 336-7000 .. **Ursulova,** Nadezhda '98 -31 West End Av -Brklyn 11235
(315) 424-9485 .. **Urtz,** Anastasia L '94 Cornell Univ Coop Extn of Onondaga Cnty -2 Clinton Sq -Syracuse 13202
(212) 554-1234 .. **Urueta,** Pamela '02 AXA Financial Inc -1290 Av of Amer -NY 10104 **Fx:**707-3963
(631) 734-5308 .. **Ury,** Arthur G Jr. '69 -3750 Stillwtr Av -Cutchogue 11935
(212) 325-3082 .. **Usami,** Yuko '85 Credit Suisse Securities -11 Mad Av -NY 10010
(212) 856-1214 .. **Uscher Quiat Uscher & Russo** -355 Lex Av -NY 10017 **Fx:**983-0772
(212) 597-1737 .. **Usdan,** Lynn E '85 %Donna Karan Co -550 7th Av -NY 10018 **Fx:**789-1688
(718) 965-9092 .. **Usdin,** Marvin '50 -374A 8th -Brklyn 11215 **Fx:**965-0071
(212) 545-4000 .. **Usenheimer,** Gena B '06 %Jackson L LLP -666 3rd Av -NY 10017
(212) 233-1433 .. **Ushan,** Marilyn F '94 (Schonfeld & U) -299 Bway -NY 10007 **Fx:**571-5340
(212) 558-4000 .. **Ushkow,** Michl J '07 %Sullivan & C LLP -125 Broad -NY 10004
(212) 508-6700 .. **Usiak,** Stacey A '01 (Tannenbaum HS&H LLP) -900 3rd Av -NY 10022
(585) 428-5753 .. **Usinger,** Edw J Jr. '77 %Hon E Frazee -433 Hall Of Justice -Rchstr 14614 **Fx:**428-2698
(516) 357-3700 .. **Usinger,** Elizabeth '08 %Cullen and D LLP -100 Q Roosevelt Blvd -Gdn Cty 11530
(212) 238-3000 .. **Usinger,** Eric D '05 %Emmet M&M,LLP -120 Bway -NY 10271
(212) 490-2020 .. **Uslaner,** Steven D '88 (Littman K LLP) -655 3rd Av -NY 10017
(212) 809-2663 .. **Usmani,** Farah Z '03 Bondholder Comm Grp -30 Broad -NY 10004
(518) 431-6700 .. **Ustin,** Mark R '97 Cnsl Manatt P&P,LLP -30 S Pearl -Albany 12207
(212) 922-9550 .. **Uswatte-Aratchi,** Kumudini '99 Clutch Grp LLC -370 Lex Av -NY 10017
(212) 308-6003 .. **Utevsky,** Michl D '79 -757 3rd Av -NY 10017 **Fx:**308-5862
(212) 878-8356 .. **Utley,** Fredk B III '75 (Clifford C LLP) -31 W 52nd -NY 10019
(212) 484-3900 .. **Utlik,** George V '08 %Arent F LLP -1675 Bway -NY 10019
(516) 539-6770 .. **Utrecht,** A Henry '63 (Nigro D&U) -215 Uniondale Av -Uniondale 11553
(212) 618-0532 .. **Utsey,** Keith J '97 Security Industries Assn -120 Bway -NY 10271
(585) 328-2550 .. **Uttaro,** Ralph A '82 %Wegmans Food Mrkts -1500 Brooks Av Bx30844 -Rchstr 14603 **Fx:**464-4636
(212) 742-0001 .. **Utz,** Joyce Morin '93 (Radna & A,LLP) -110 Wall -NY 10005 **Fx:**742-0005
(716) 773-2256 .. **Utz,** Karen M '86 -2286 Long Rd -Grand Isl 14072
(212) 421-8200 .. **Uva,** Anthony N '85 Simon Property Grp -747 3rd Av -NY 10017
(631) 473-1213 .. **Uveges,** Bruce A '92 -646-14 Main -Pt Jffrsn 11777 **Fx:**473-1337
(212) 471-8500 .. **Uvino,** Jos F '87 OfCnsl Herzfeld & R,PC -125 Broad -NY 10004
(718) 424-5560 .. **Uvino,** Louis J '93 (Uvino & B) -33-07 102nd -Corona 11368 **Fx:**424-5569
(718) 251-8110 .. **Uwechia,** Chukwuma K '99 -1151 E 101st -Brklyn 11236
(212) 966-3730 .. **Uysal,** Michl D '94 %Kelman W&V -2 Rector -NY 10006
(718) 409-3389 .. **Uzamere,** Osato Eugene '96 -1851 Watson Av -Bronx 10472
(212) 268-0900 .. **Uzar,** Wendi Opper '06 %Miskin & T-Y -1350 Bway -NY 10018 **Fx:**268-0904
(718) 874-6045 .. **Uzoh,** Ugochukwu '06 -255 Lvngstn -Brklyn 11217
(212) 592-9000 .. **Uzzi,** Francis A '03 -244 5th Av -NY 10001
(212) 819-8200 .. **Uzzi,** Gerard H '97 (White & C LLP) -1155 Av of Amer -NY 10036
(914) 699-0600 .. **Uzzo,** Mark F '89 (Scancarelli J&U,LLP) -22 W 1st -Mt Vernon 10550
(212) 440-4300 .. **Vaamonde,** Liliana K '92 Leg Aid-Civ Div -199 Water -NY 10038
(212) 768-1115 .. **Vacca,** Andrea '93 -245 5th Av -NY 10016 **Fx:**684-0646
(518) 374-0444 .. **Vacca,** Edw D '64 -514 State -Schnctdy 12305 **Fx:**370-1606
(585) 423-0110 .. **Vacca,** James P '85 -1 E Main -Rchstr 14614 **Fx:**546-2474
(585) 753-4500 .. **Vacca,** Meredith A '06 DA -832 Watts Bldg -Rchstr 14614 **Fx:**753-4576
(585) 325-3336 .. **Vacca,** Paul J Jr. '77 -1 E Main -Rchstr 14614
(212) 756-2000 .. **Vaccarello,** Steven M '10 %Schulte R&Z LLP -919 3rd Av -NY 10022
(212) 940-3108 .. **Vaccari,** Michl A '79 (Nixon P LLP) -437 Mad Av -NY 10022
(518) 270-5394 .. **Vaccariello,** Rebecca M '00 %Hon H Zwack -80 2nd -Troy 12180
(212) 309-8137 .. **Vaccarino,** Giselle A '02 Lexis/Nexis -125 Park Av -NY 10017
(718) 261-3047 .. **Vaccarino,** Jos A '70 (Queens Law Assoc) -118-21 Qns Blvd -Frst Hlls 11375 **Fx:**261-0798
(631) 273-7171 .. **Vaccaro,** Chas J '69 (Vaccaro & P) -325 Wireless Blvd -Hauppauge 11788
(212) 770-5133 .. **Vaccaro,** Jos D '99 %Alico -70 Pine -NY 10270
(516) 227-0700 .. **Vaccaro,** Lisa M '95 Cnsl Farrell F,PC -1320 RXR Plz -Uniondale 11556
(718) 250-2000 .. **Vaccaro,** Michl '03 %DA -350 Jay -Brklyn 11201 **Fx:**250-2314
(315) 422-1311 .. **Vaccaro,** Michl R '76 %Melvin & M,PLLC -217 S Salina -Syracuse 13202
(914) 328-0404 .. **Vaccaro,** Patrick L '66 (Jackson L LLP) -1 N Bway -White Plns 10601
(631) 273-7171 .. **Vaccaro & Prisco** -325 Wireless Blvd -Hauppauge 11788 **Fx:**273-9685
(212) 909-6000 .. **Vaccaro,** Stephen W '97 %Debevoise & P LLP -919 3rd Av -NY 10022
(212) 577-9100 .. **Vaccaro,** Steven R '98 (Vaccaro P,LLP) -225 W 14th -NY 10011 **Fx:**659-0760
(718) 390-5436 .. **Vaccarro-DiCarlo,** Patricia '89 %Supreme Ct -18 Richmond Ter -Staten Isl 10301
(716) 853-5100 .. **Vacco,** Dennis C '79 (Lippes MWF LLP) -665 Main -Buffalo 14203
(212) 487-4421 .. **Vachiraprapun,** Penney '06 Dept Cnsmr Affrs -42 Bway -NY 10004 **Fx:**487-4197
(212) 975-4467 .. **Vachris,** Michelle A '01 %CBS Inc -51 W 52nd -NY 10019 **Fx:**975-3930
(917) 806-2170 .. **Vachss,** Andrew H '76 -16 E 34th -NY 10016
(585) 342-4410 .. **Vackicev,** Alexi G '04 %Burke AH&R,LLP -1800 Hudson Av -Rchstr 14617
(212) 584-4171 .. **Vaczy,** Catherine M '89 Neostem, Inc -420 Lex Av -NY 10170 **Fx:**(646) 514-7787
(212) 244-4111 .. **Vadai,** Roi A '06 %Shiboleth YR&Z,LLP -1 Penn Plz -NY 10119
(607) 763-9200 .. **Vadala,** Caroline Ann '87 (Levene G&T,LLP) -BxF-1706 -Bnghmtn 13902
(718) 923-3368 .. **Vadala,** Steven J '89 OTDA Fair Hearings -14 Boerum Pl -Brklyn 11201
(718) 590-2000 .. **Vadasz,** Tammy M '04 %DA -198 E 161st -Bronx 10451 **Fx:**590-6477
(212) 357-3204 .. **Vaden,** Margaret E '01 %Goldman Sachs -1 NY Plz -NY 10004
(516) 741-2200 .. **Vadnais,** Robt '04 %Zisholtz & Z,LLP -170 Old Cntry Rd -Mineola 11501 **Fx:**746-1024
(716) 633-3700 .. **Vadnais,** Scott C '05 Hunt Mortgage -5400 Bway -Lancaster 14086 **Fx:**633-3718
(212) 436-4865 .. **Vaeth,** Karista N '09 Deloitte Tax LLP -2 World Fncl Ctr -NY 10281
(212) 909-6000 .. **Vagas,** Richd T '09 %Debevoise & P LLP -919 3rd Av -NY 10022

(718) 254-6182 .. **Vagelatos,** John '99 %US Atty -271 Cadman Plz E -Brklyn 11201 **Fx:**254-6479
(518) 452-0941 .. **Vagianelis,** John N '97 Segel GM&S,PC -9 Wshngtn Sq -Albany 12205
(212) 326-2000 .. **Vaglio,** Peter M '09 %O'Melveny & M LLP -7 Times Sq -NY 10036
(516) 203-7180 .. **Vagnini,** James A '99 (Valli K&V,LLP) -600 Old Cntry Rd -Gdn Cty 11530 **Fx:**706-0248
(631) 277-8425 .. **Vagra-Zanfardino,** Anne Marie N '90 -133 S Ocean Av -Islip 11751 **Fx:**277-2003
(212) 345-3853 .. **Vahdat,** Jeanne Marie '90 %Marsh USA -1166 Av of Amer -NY 10036 **Fx:**345-4808
(212) 578-2211 .. **Vahdat,** Lisa A '87 %MetLife -27-01 Qns Plz N -LIC 11101
(914) 287-8850 .. **Vahidi,** Maysa '01 Rockwood Capital,LLC -10 Bank -White Plns 10606
(609) 986-1300 .. **Vahidi,** Steven S '05 %Goldberg S LLP -1200 Av of Amer -NY 10036 **Fx:**986-1301
(212) 294-6700 .. **Vaiana,** Bradley C '01 (Winston & S) -200 Park Av -NY 10166
(518) 464-6400 .. **Vaida,** Elena C '80 (ECV Law Firm) -61 Columbia -Albany 12210
(212) 483-9490 .. **Vaida,** M Anthony '89 OfCnsl McElroy DM&C,LLP -88 Pine -NY 10005
(845) 485-2529 .. **Vaikness,** Stacee S '01 %J Spilbor,LLC -35 Main -Poughkeepsie 12601
(631) 287-3065 .. **Vail,** Elizabeth E '03 %Town Atty -116 Hmptn Rd -Southampton 11968 **Fx:**287-3662
(212) 431-1300 .. **Vail,** Gregory G '91 (Borah GAN&G PC) -377 Bway -NY 10013
(212) 697-0808 .. **Vail,** Jeffrey T '65 (Vail & S,PC) -275 Mad Av -NY 10016
(212) 728-8000 .. **Vail,** Jessica C '09 %Willkie F&G LLP -787 7th Av -NY 10019
(914) 276-3223 .. **Vail,** Mary E '93 %D Zwerner -Rts 100 & 202 -Somers 10589 **Fx:**276-2429
(212) 697-0808 .. **Vail & Schneider,PC** -275 Mad Av -NY 10016
(212) 859-8000 .. **Vaillant,** Danl P '09 %Fried FHS&J LLP -1 NY Plz -NY 10004
(212) 309-6000 .. **Vaillant,** Lynda Madera '09 %Morgan L&B LLP -101 Park Av -NY 10178
(212) 609-6800 .. **Vaillant,** Michele F '86 (McCarter & E,LLP) -245 Park Av -NY 10167
(718) 743-6611 .. **Vaiman,** Irina P '97 SrCnsl I Vaiman,PC -1322 Gravesend Neck Rd -Brklyn 11229 **Fx:**743-6211
(718) 336-5636 .. **Vaiman,** Julie J '07 -2955 Shell Rd -Brklyn 11224 **Fx:**336-5637
(212) 765-5070 .. **Vainberg,** Irina '07 %Fish & R,PC -153 E 53rd -NY 10022
(914) 276-0278 .. **Vairo,** Giulietta '86 -2450 Hering Av -Bronx 10469 **Fx:**276-0278
(212) 742-9700 .. **Vairo,** Pasquale V '93 %Godosky & G,PC -61 Bway -NY 10006
(212) 440-2350 .. **Vairo,** Peter E '91 %C Siegel -40 Wall -NY 10005 **Fx:**440-2385
(585) 227-2070 .. **Vaisey,** Jeffrey A '08 %Modica & Assoc -2430 Ridgeway Av -Rchstr 14626 **Fx:**368-1100
(718) 234-5353 .. **Vaisman,** Irene '05 OfCnsl Kleyman & Assoc,PC -2227 86th -Brklyn 11214
(718) 368-0690 .. **Vakarev,** Aleksandr '99 -2566 86th -Brklyn 11214 **Fx:**368-0692
(212) 373-3000 .. **Vakiener,** Jennifer K '09 %Paul WRW&G LLP -1285 Av of Amer -NY 10019
(781) 795-4709 .. **Vakili,** Lily Iran '93 %Faber D&R PC -110 E 59th -NY 10022
(516) 364-1095 .. **Vakser,** Regina '98 %McBreen & K -500 N Bway -Jericho 11753
(212) 587-3300 .. **Val,** Anna '02 -79 Pine -NY 10005 **Fx:**(877) 871-4412
(212) 848-4000 .. **Val,** Jennifer A '09 Shearman & S LLP -599 Lex Av -NY 10022
(718) 538-3344 .. **Valarezo,** Marlen B '09 NAICA -1075 Grnd Cncrs -Bronx 10452
(212) 779-8600 .. **Valassis,** Soulafreda '05 %Silverman SS&B PLLC -381 Park Av S -NY 10016
(212) 813-8800 .. **Valat,** Diana I '06 %Goodwin P LLP -620 8th Av -NY 10018
(212) 906-1200 .. **Valat,** Stephane '06 %Latham & W -885 3rd Av -NY 10022
(716) 853-4340 .. **Valauri,** Matthew D '09 %Getman & B -800 Rand Bldg -Buffalo 14203
(718) 320-3514 .. **Valbrune,** Mirande '03 Riverbay Corp -2049 Bartow Av -Bronx 10475
(212) 758-0299 .. **Valcic,** Susan J '87 -412 E 55th -NY 10022 **Fx:**758-0210
(516) 535-1100 .. **Valdebenito,** Cesar L '96 (Valdebenito & A) -1399 Franklin Av -Gdn Cty 11530 **Fx:**535-3936
(718) 435-1309 .. **Valdes,** Delvis '94 The Clarimar Group -4505 5th Av -Brklyn 11220 **Fx:**435-1353
(212) 999-5800 .. **Valdes,** Federico '10 %Wilson SG&R -1301 Av of Americas -NY 10019
(212) 576-6590 .. **Valdes,** Gilberto '88 NY Life Ins -51 Mad Av -NY 10010
(212) 474-1000 .. **Valdes,** Hector J '06 %Cravath S&M LLP -825 8th Av -NY 10019
(914) 332-6621 .. **Valdespino,** Andres J '79 -1 Neperan Rd -Tarrytwn 10591 **Fx:**332-6627
(212) 931-1125 .. **Valdez,** Estela M '99 Bowne & Co Inc -55 Water -NY 10041
(212) 841-1000 .. **Valdez,** Russell J '08 %Covington & B LLP -620 8th Av -NY 10018
(212) 819-8200 .. **Valdez,** Yvette D '05 %White & C LLP -1155 Av of Amer -NY 10036
(315) 253-1391 .. **Valdina,** Christopher T '98 %DA -95 Genesee -Auburn 13021 **Fx:**253-1521
(212) 956-0440 .. **Vale,** Eleanor P '02 -150 Cntrl Pk S -NY 10019 **Fx:**956-0007
(212) 732-8700 .. **Vale,** Ilana '03 %McAloon & F,PC -123 William -NY 10038
(607) 778-2403 .. **Valek,** Judith A '96 Pub Def -45 Hawley Bx1766 -Bnghmtn 13902 **Fx:**778-2432
(212) 688-4000 .. **Valella,** Alejandro '84 %NYS HFA -641 Lex Av -NY 10022 **Fx:**872-0362
(212) 745-3125 .. **Valencia,** Adrienne L '97 IBM Corp -590 Mad Av -NY 10022
(212) 436-6311 .. **Valencia,** John J '00 Deloitte & Touche LLP -2 World Fncl Ctr -NY 10281
(585) 753-4500 .. **Valencia,** Sara L '07 %DA -832 Watts Bldg -Rchstr 14614 **Fx:**753-4576
(212) 308-0888 .. **Valent,** Richd J '91 OfCnsl Widowski & S LLP -425 Mad Av -NY 10017
(718) 383-1400 .. **Valente,** Anthony F '94 Metro Fuel Oil Corp -500 Kngslnd Av -Brklyn 11222 **Fx:**383-9565
(631) 584-8000 .. **Valente,** Douglas '92 (Valente & K,PC) -112 Terry Rd -Smithtwn 11787 **Fx:**584-8808
(518) 626-9000 .. **Valente,** Edmond J '86 Cnsl Dewey & L LLP -99 Wshngtn Av -Albany 12210
(212) 687-4385 .. **Valente,** Francis L Jr. '59 (Townsend & V,LLP) -1212 Av of Amer -NY 10036
(518) 499-1272 .. **Valente,** John W '08 (Ryan S&C,PC) -134 Main Bx75 -Whitehall 12887
(718) 921-6601 .. **Valente,** Jos C '10 %T Beinert -155 Bay Ridge Av -Brklyn 11220 **Fx:**921-6609
(212) 593-3000 .. **Valente,** Lauren '06 %Platzer SKLG&J,LLP -1065 Av of Amer -NY 10018
(718) 935-2135 .. **Valente,** Michl J '93 NYC Dept of Ed -65 Court -Brklyn 11201
(212) 885-5000 .. **Valente,** Peter C '67 (Blank R LLP) -405 Lex Av -NY 10174
(212) 756-2000 .. **Valenti,** Danl J '10 %Schulte R&Z LLP -919 3rd Av -NY 10022
(585) 454-2181 .. **Valenti,** James A '78 (Trevett CS&A,PC) -2 State -Rchstr 14614
(585) 342-4410 .. **Valenti,** Jos A F '71 OfCnsl Burke AH&R,LLP -1800 Hudson Av -Rchstr 14617
(518) 485-2394 .. **Valenti,** Linda J '80 %NYS DPCA -80 Wolf Rd -Albany 12205 **Fx:**485-5140
(716) 481-0351 .. **Valenti,** Pamela Hastings '02 -9 Inwood Pl -Lancaster 14086
(212) 809-7600 .. **Valenti,** Robt J '94 %Cheven K&H -40 Wall -NY 10005
(315) 422-7000 .. **Valenti,** Thos J '78 %Pyramid -4 Clinton Sq -Syracuse 13202 **Fx:**422-2717
(914) 684-2100 .. **Valentin,** Elizabeth '02 %Littman K LLP -399 Knollwood Rd -White Plns 10603
(718) 618-2500 .. **Valentin,** Juana '91 %Civil Ct -851 Grnd Cncrs -Bronx 10451 **Fx:**590-7294
(718) 855-9000 .. **Valentin,** Lisann '06 %Cullen and D LLP -177 Montague -Brklyn 11201
(914) 721-2400 .. **Valentin,** Maria I '02 Scarsdale Bd of Ed -2 Brwstr Rd -Scarsdale 10583
(516) 802-5683 .. **Valentine,** Andrew '87 -9 Glenn Dr -Woodbury 11797 **Fx:**802-5682
(212) 863-8360 .. **Valentine,** Geneen F '90 Dept of Housing Preservation & Devpt -100 Gold -NY 10038
(845) 497-5010 .. **Valentine,** Jeanne M '00 J Valentine PLLC -5 Fairlawn Dr -Washingtnvll 10992
(516) 365-1910 .. **Valentine,** Jos B '77 OfCnsl Wheeler TK LLP -351 Abbey Rd -Manhsst 11030
(518) 455-2390 .. **Valentine,** Matthew O '07 NYS Senate Student Programs -1426 LOB -Albany 12247
(212) 785-8080 .. **Valentine,** Michl '95 SrCnsl PM Contracting Co -40 Exch Pl -NY 10005 **Fx:**785-2548
(212) 344-8000 .. **Valentine,** Michl A '95 Valentine Law Firm,PC -225 Bway -NY 10007
(212) 967-1800 .. **Valentine,** Nicole G '03 OfCnsl Bryant BJ&R LLP -140 Bway -NY 10005
(212) 689-1600 .. **Valentine,** Pamela S '84 (Marsh V&D LLP) -500 5th Av -NY 10110 **Fx:**689-0210
(914) 750-5933 .. **Valentine,** Paul W '10 %Kissel H&W LLP -580 Wht Plns Rd -Tarrytwn 10591
(716) 854-1389 .. **Valentine,** Richd P '82 (Hamsher & V) -300 Main -Buffalo 14202 **Fx:**854-1398
(315) 946-7472 .. **Valentine,** Ronald C '66 Pub Def -26 Church -Lyons 14489 **Fx:**946-7478
(212) 312-2315 .. **Valentine,** Sandrine A '02 %Leg Aid -60 Lafayette -NY 10013 **Fx:**349-0874
(718) 340-4219 .. **Valentine,** Sarah E '91 %CUNY Law Schl -65-21 Main -Flushng 11367 **Fx:**340-4482
(518) 474-6367 .. **Valentine,** Todd D '95 Bd of Elections -40 Steuben -Albany 12207
(585) 987-2800 .. **Valentino,** Christian N '01 %Woods OG LLP -2 State -Rchstr 14614
(631) 247-0404 .. **Valentino,** Christopher M '01 %Jackson L LLP -58 S Srvc Rd -Melvll 11747
(718) 643-5797 .. **Valentino,** James '87 %Surrogates Ct -2 Johnson -Brklyn 11201
(718) 250-2000 .. **Valentino,** James F '06 %DA -350 Jay -Brklyn 11201 **Fx:**250-2314
(315) 422-1391 .. **Valentino,** John L '88 (Green & S,PLLC) -One Lincoln Ctr #900 -Syracuse 13202
(585) 428-2991 .. **Valentino,** Jos J '00 %Hon P Marks -545 Hall of Justice -Rchstr 14614
(212) 704-2400 .. **Valentino,** Lisa '96 Volt Info Sciences -1065 Av of Amer -NY 10018 **Fx:**704-2417
(516) 873-6334 .. **Valentino,** Richd J '07 %Ohrenstein & B,LLP -1010 Franklin Av Bx9243 -Gdn Cty 11530
(212) 695-8100 .. **Valentino,** Rosalie C '07 %Goetz F,LLP -1 Penn Plz -NY 10119
(212) 380-4223 .. **Valentino,** Thos J '94 SpclCnsl The Counsel,PLLC -737 Park Av -NY 10021
(516) 333-3665 .. **Valenza,** Stacey M '98 (Iammarino & V PLLC) -2126 Stratford Dr -Westbury 11590 **Fx:**333-3275
(518) 447-3200 .. **Valenza,** Vincent L '91 (McNamee LT&W,PC) -677 Bway -Albany 12207
(607) 723-9511 .. **Valenzuela,** Reinaldo B '04 %Coughlin & G,LLP -19 Chenango Bx2039 -Bnghmtn 13902
(315) 471-1664 .. **Valerino,** Gary J '89 (Meggesto C&V,LLP) -313 E Willow -Syracuse 13203
(315) 476-0909 .. **Valerino,** Thos J '99 Valerino Law Ofc -307 S Clinton -Syracuse 13202 **Fx:**479-8847
(585) 442-1040 .. **Valerio & Kufta,PC** -400 Andrews -Rchstr 14604 **Fx:**442-3073
(914) 995-3497 .. **Valerio,** Lois Cullen '78 %DA -111 Martin Luther King Blvd -White Plns 10601 **Fx:**995-3363
(585) 442-1040 .. **Valerio,** Mark J '82 (Valerio & K,PC) -400 Andrews -Rchstr 14604
(718) 590-2000 .. **Valerio,** Raymond G '05 %DA -198 E 161st -Bronx 10451 **Fx:**590-6477
(212) 478-0762 .. **Valero,** Gerardo M C '07 DE Shaw & Co -120 W 45th -NY 10036
(212) 833-7991 .. **Valero,** Maria E '94 Sony BMG Music Entrtnmnt -550 Mad Av -NY 10022 **Fx:**833-4421
(212) 684-1880 .. **Valet,** Thos P '85 (Rheingold VRS&M LLP) -113 E 37th -NY 10016
(212) 264-9230 .. **Valetk,** Harry A '99 DOJ-Intl Trade Ofc -26 Fed Plz -NY 10278
(212) 441-2497 .. **Val-Hackett,** Pannonica A '02 Aon Grp,Inc -199 Water -NY 10038
(914) 961-1555 .. **Valicenti,** Alexandra '81 (Donovan & V) -80 Palmer Av -Bronxvll 10708
(212) 735-3000 .. **Valik,** Eva Neradova '98 Cnsl Skadden ASM&F LLP -4 Times Sq -NY 10036
(212) 805-3900 .. **Valinoti,** Danl S '07 %Clausen M PC -1 Chase Manh Plz -NY 10005
(718) 267-0300 .. **Valiotis,** Sophia E '05 Alma Realty -31-10 37th Av -LIC 11101
(212) 312-3201 .. **Valiquette,** Gabrielle N '98 FGIC -125 Park Av -NY 10017 **Fx:**312-3231
(212) 421-2111 .. **Valk,** Martin E '89 %Granoff W&F,PC -747 3rd Av -NY 10017
(845) 452-5900 .. **Valk,** Rebecca A '04 %Van DeWater & V,LLP -85 Civic Ctr Plz Bx112 -Poughkeepsie 12602
(607) 776-3306 .. **Valkenburgh,** Christine '91 (Cole & V,PC) -7 E Steuben Bx232 -Bath 14810 **Fx:**776-4189

(914) 368-0400 .. **Valkonen,** Sami J '06 Nokia Inc -102 Corp Park Dr -White Plns 10604
(518) 463-3990 .. **Valle,** Karen Martino '77 (Tuczinski CG&C,PC) -54 State -Albany 12207
(518) 432-1100 .. **Valle,** Susan L '85 %NYPTI -107 Columbia -Albany 12210 **Fx:**432-1180
(212) 576-4568 .. **Vallejo,** Norma '86 %NY Life Invstmt Asset Mgt LLC -51 Mad Av -NY 10010
(212) 401-0800 .. **Vallejo,** Raymond '88 %Disciplinary Comm -61 Bway -NY 10006 **Fx:**287-1045
(718) 588-3100 .. **Vallely,** John E '98 -934 Sheridan Av -Bronx 10451
(914) 779-0322 .. **Vallely,** Thos J '87 -107 Lk Av -Tuckahoe 10707 **Fx:**793-2114
(585) 428-5210 .. **Valleriani,** Sam L '09 %Pub Def -10 N Fitzhugh -Rchstr 14614 **Fx:**428-2234
(212) 977-9700 .. **Valletta,** Chryssa V '99 Cnsl Phillips N LLP -666 5th Av -NY 10103
(845) 228-5188 .. **Valletta,** Kathleen M '84 -70B Gleneida Av Bx820 -Carmel 10512 **Fx:**228-5185
(516) 938-2953 .. **Valley,** Douglas '89 -3 Bonnie Ct -Hicksvll 11801
(607) 962-2101 .. **Valley,** Joe M '06 -283½ S Hmltn Bx150 -Painted Post 14870 **Fx:**936-1503
(516) 203-7180 .. **Valli,** Robt J Jr. '91 (Valli K&V,LLP) -600 Old Cntry Rd -Gdn Cty 11530 **Fx:**706-0248
(212) 755-5200 .. **Valliere,** Timothy A '98 (Smith V PLLC) -509 Mad Av -NY 10022 **Fx:**755-5203
(212) 801-6903 .. **Vallo,** Jos A '85 OfCnsl Greenberg T,LLP -200 Park Av -NY 10166
(516) 874-8800 .. **Vallone,** Chas J '91 %FrankelLoughranStarrVallone -1475 Franklin Av -Gdn Cty 11530
(516) 228-6658 .. **Vallone,** David A '91 (Gervase & V,PC) -377 Oak -Gdn Cty 11530
(716) 206-0588 .. **Vallone,** Eric T '07 (Vallone Law Firm) -2560 Walden Av -Cheektowaga 14225
(716) 206-0588 .. **Vallone,** James M '83 (Vallone Law Firm) -2560 Walden Av -Cheektowaga 14225
(315) 425-9000 .. **Vallone,** Mark C '07 %Marjama MB&S LLP -250 S Clinton -Syracuse 13202
(212) 966-3730 .. **Vallone,** Patrick F '92 (Kelman W&V) -2 Rector -NY 10006
(718) 204-2929 .. **Vallone,** Paul A '92 (Vallone & V) -22-45 31st -Astoria 11105 **Fx:**274-8858
(716) 856-4000 .. **Vallone,** Paul J '95 (Hodgson R LLP) -140 Pearl -Buffalo 14202
(718) 204-2929 .. **Vallone,** Peter F '60 (Vallone & V) -22-45 31st -Astoria 11105 **Fx:**274-8858
(718) 204-2929 .. **Vallone,** Peter F Jr. '86 (Vallone & V) -22-45 31st -Astoria 11105 **Fx:**274-8858
(716) 681-3355 .. **Vallone,** Richd T Jr. '84 (Wojtan V&G) -2956 Union Rd -Cheektowaga 14227
(631) 881-0858 .. **Vallone-Heilmann,** Donna E '06 -445 Broadhllw Rd -Melvll 11747
(718) 761-5749 .. **Valloney,** Michl G '00 -Bx140582 -Staten Isl 10314 **Fx:**761-5749
(585) 396-4010 .. **Valone,** Kathleen Hart '90 DA -27 N Main -Canandaigua 14424 **Fx:**396-4860
(212) 335-6432 .. **Valouch,** Jacqueline '96 Fidelity Charitable Srvcs -640 5th Av -NY 10019
(212) 508-6100 .. **Valsamopoulos,** Danl F '09 %Bracewell & G,LLP -1251 Av of Amer -NY 10020
(212) 261-8000 .. **Valsangkar,** Neil '08 %Mendes & M,LLP -750 7th Av -NY 10019
(800) 518-7004 .. **Valvano,** James II '97 -75 S Bway -White Plns 10601 **Fx:**515-5388
(516) 357-3000 .. **Valverde,** Frank A '02 %Rivkin R LLP -926 RXR Plz -Uniondale 11556
(212) 450-4000 .. **Valverde,** Sam I '08 %Davis P&W LLP -450 Lex Av -NY 10017
(315) 266-6100 .. **Valvo,** Carmen J '68 Pub Def -235 Elizabeth -Utica 13501 **Fx:**266-6105
(716) 951-0813 .. **Valvo,** Janice R '93 -717 Central Av -Dunkirk 14048
(716) 882-3069 .. **Valvo,** Lisa Ann '90 -791 Columbus Pkwy -Buffalo 14213 **Fx:**882-3069
(212) 248-8800 .. **Valvo,** Louis E '88 (Callan KB&B LLP) -1 Whitehall -NY 10004
(716) 845-3650 .. **Valvo,** Vicky L '88 %MHLS -438 Main -Buffalo 14202 **Fx:**874-7794
(212) 385-9230 .. **Valz,** Norman M '98 (NM Valz,LLC) -305 Bway -NY 10007 **Fx:**385-9294
(212) 474-1000 .. **Van,** Austin P '10 %Cravath S&M LLP -825 8th Av -NY 10019
(212) 479-6000 .. **Van Aalten,** Seth '04 %Cooley LLP -1114 Av of Amer -NY 10036
(212) 484-3900 .. **Vanacore,** Jeffrey D '03 %Arent F LLP -1675 Bway -NY 10019
(518) 862-1386 .. **Van Aken,** Megan Bashford '00 %Burke SM&H,LLP -302 Wshngtn Av Ext Bx15085 -Albany 12212
(212) 306-1000 .. **Van Allen,** Eric P '00 %Amer Stock Exch -86 Trinity Pl -NY 10006
(585) 243-4320 .. **Van Allen,** Kevin '07 %Presutti Law Ofc,PC -32 Main Bx157 -Geneseo 14454 **Fx:**243-0420
(212) 504-6000 .. **Van Amburg,** John A '09 %Cadwalader W&T LLP -1 World Fncl Ctr -NY 10281
(212) 725-0200 .. **Van Arnam,** Frederic D Jr. '89 (Barnes R&C) -475 Park Av S -NY 10016
(585) 328-2550 .. **Van Arsdale,** Stephen R '85 %Wegmans Food Mrkts -1500 Brooks Av Bx30844 -Rchstr 14603 **Fx:**464-4636
(212) 393-1140 .. **Vanasek,** James T '00 VN Capital Mgmt,LLC -1133 Bway -NY 10010 **Fx:**393-1148
(212) 753-3468 .. **Vanasse,** Thos W '94 %Wildes & W,PC -515 Mad Av -NY 10022
(212) 450-4000 .. **Vanatko,** Nicole V '08 %Davis P&W LLP -450 Lex Av -NY 10017
(212) 785-3677 .. **Van Atten,** Carol Nicolina '84 Chas Hayden Fndtn -140 Bway -NY 10005 **Fx:**785-3689
(212) 294-6700 .. **Van Auken,** Lori J '87 (Winston & S) -200 Park Av -NY 10166
(518) 434-9807 .. **VanAuken,** Mia D '03 %D'Agostino KM&C,PC -16 Sage Estate -Menands 12204
(315) 793-8191 .. **Van Baalen,** Guy '83 %US Trustee -10 Broad -Utica 13501
(845) 340-3610 .. **Van Benschoten,** Christine F '83 %Family Ct -16 Lucas Av -Kingston 12401 **Fx:**340-3626
(845) 246-3655 .. **Van Benschoten,** David '76 Francello & V -34 W Brdg Bx359 -Saugerties 12477
(212) 909-6000 .. **Van Berg,** Jill '05 %Debevoise & P LLP -919 3rd Av -NY 10022
(315) 637-3663 .. **VanBeveren,** Matthew J '06 %Gale & D,LLC -Bx6527 -Syracuse 13217
(212) 548-5555 .. **VanBlaricum,** James R '10 Discovery Communications -850 3rd Av -NY 10022
(914) 925-2600 .. **Van Bomel,** John C '81 -49 Purchase -Rye 10580 **Fx:**925-0330
(518) 828-9444 .. **Van Bortel,** Sonya Smelyansky '07 %Rapport MWS&R,LLP -436 Union -Hudson 12534
(631) 589-5000 .. **Van Brunt Juzwiak & Russo** -140 Main -Sayvll 11782 **Fx:**589-5003
(518) 474-8266 .. **Van Buren,** Peter D '75 %Dept of Health -Corning Twr 24th Fl -Albany 12237 **Fx:**473-2430
(315) 252-3846 .. **Van Buskirk,** Adam H '07 %Camardo Law Firm,PC -127 Genesee -Auburn 13021 **Fx:**252-3508
(212) 509-3456 .. **VanBuskirk,** Paul A '96 (McGivney & K,PC) -80 Broad -NY 10004
(212) 536-3900 .. **Van Buskirk,** Tedd W '96 (K&L Gates LLP) -599 Lex Av -NY 10022
(718) 442-7301 .. **Van Caneghan,** Robt '79 -123 Radcliff Rd -Staten Isl 10305
(716) 362-0170 .. **Vance,** Cynthia E '94 Jensen ML&V LLC -360 Delaware Av -Buffalo 14202
(212) 335-9000 .. **Vance,** Cyrus R Jr. '83 (DA) -1 Hogan Pl -NY 10013
(212) 351-4000 .. **Vance,** Janet '88 (Gibson D&C LLP) -200 Park Av -NY 10166
(518) 474-6542 .. **Vance,** Lynn Homes '98 Ofc of Employee Relations -2 ESP -Albany 12223
(718) 262-7100 .. **Vance,** Maura Curtin '96 %Civil Ct -89-17 Sutphin Blvd -Jamaica 11435 **Fx:**262-7107
(716) 854-4474 .. **Vance,** Paul A '85 (Stiller & V) -300 Pearl -Buffalo 14202
(212) 513-3200 .. **Vance,** Tara L '98 %Holland & K LLP -31 W 52nd -NY 10019
(212) 832-0400 .. **Vance,** Thos R '09 Berdon LLP -360 Mad Av -NY 10017
(845) 342-0024 .. **Vance-Pauls,** Jacquelynn M '02 -28 Grand Av -Middletwn 10940 **Fx:**342-2492
(718) 259-4500 .. **Vanchieri & Ferrier** -1724 86th -Brklyn 11214 **Fx:**331-4750
(718) 259-4500 .. **Vanchieri,** Jack '59 (Vanchieri & F) -1724 86th -Brklyn 11214
(631) 757-5652 .. **Van Cleef,** Duncan '76 -10 Frazer Ct -Greenlawn 11740
(716) 847-2267 .. **Van Coevering,** Richd J '86 -65 Court -Buffalo 14202
(585) 352-2603 .. **Van Coske,** Lynda M '93 %BOCES -3599 Big Ridge Rd -Spencerprt 14559
(631) 727-2180 .. **Van Cott,** Bryan C '97 (Twomey LSKD&Q,LLP) -33 W 2nd Bx9398 -Rvrhead 11901
(518) 891-4050 .. **Van Cott,** Paul T '88 %Adirondack Pk Agncy -Bx99 -Ray Brk 12977 **Fx:**891-3938
(212) 715-9100 .. **Van Court,** Andrew Michl '06 %Kramer LN&F,LLP -1177 Av of Amer -NY 10036
(212) 487-9701 .. **Vandamme,** Hendrick '06 Robin HK&F -1 Bttry Pk Plz -NY 10014
(212) 344-9300 .. **Vandamme,** Hollis DeLeonardo '02 %S Golino -46 Trinity Pl -NY 10006 **Fx:**363-9444
(212) 576-7000 .. **Vandegrift,** Donald P '86 NY Life Ins -51 Mad Av -NY 10010 **Fx:**447-0569
(212) 728-8000 .. **Vandehaar,** Mark A '05 %Willkie F&G LLP -787 7th Av -NY 10019
(212) 584-0700 .. **Van De Kieft,** Christopher M '03 %Seeger W LLP -1 William -NY 10004
(212) 966-7193 .. **Van De Kieft,** Jennifer L '03 Lafayette Medical Mgmt -233 Lafayette -NY 10012
(212) 223-4000 .. **Van De Loo,** Kathleen S '05 %Crowell & M LLP -590 Mad Av -NY 10022
(607) 273-3339 .. **Van De Mark,** Allan C '94 (Williamson C&S) -317 N Tioga Bx126 -Ithaca 14850
(212) 907-7300 .. **VanDemark,** Carl D '99 %Golenbock EAB&P -437 Mad Av -NY 10022
(212) 803-5100 .. **Van De Mark,** Jos A '91 %NY Cnty Defender Srvcs -225 Bway -NY 10007 **Fx:**571-6035
(212) 889-2121 .. **Vandenabeele,** Thos P '06 %Kellner HG&F -470 Park Av S -NY 10016
(212) 763-6800 .. **Vandenberg & Feliu,LLP** -60 E 42nd -NY 10165 **Fx:**763-6810
(212) 763-6800 .. **Vandenberg,** Raymond L '76 (Vandenberg & F,LLP) -60 E 42nd -NY 10165
(518) 474-7751 .. **van den Broek,** Amy E '02 NYS Educ Dept -89 Wshngtn Av -Albany 12234 **Fx:**473-2042
(518) 862-9292 .. **Vandenburgh,** John W '88 (Napierski V&N,LLP) -296 Wshngtn Av Ext -Albany 12203
(631) 727-7731 .. **Vandenburgh,** Richd W '94 (Foster & V,LLP) -220 Roanoke Av -Rvrhead 11901
(212) 339-2579 .. **Vanden Heuvel,** Wm J '52 -711 5th Av -NY 10022 **Fx:**339-2657
(718) 356-6515 .. **van den Houten,** W F '86 -96 Lenevar Av -Staten Isl 10309
(845) 246-4623 .. **VanDerbeck,** Colette A '96 -19 VA Av -Saugerties 12477 **Fx:**246-4519
(212) 450-4000 .. **Van Der Berg,** Shanelle '09 %Davis P&W LLP -450 Lex Av -NY 10017
(518) 462-6765 .. **Vanderbles,** Robt C '10 %Leg Aid -55 Colvin Av -Albany 12206 **Fx:**427-8352
(585) 753-4500 .. **Vanderbrook,** Laura A '08 %DA -832 Watts Bldg -Rchstr 14614 **Fx:**753-4576
(315) 589-4500 .. **Vander Byl,** Wayne A '78 -3800 Railroad Av Bx937 -Williamson 14589 **Fx:**589-5154
(212) 733-1874 .. **Vandergrift,** Angel '08 Pfizer Inc -235 E 42nd -NY 10017
(516) 294-8844 .. **Vanderhall,** Cherice P '10 %L'Abbate BC&C,LLP -1001 Franklin Av -Gdn Cty 11530
(845) 638-5122 .. **Vanderhoef,** C Scott '82 %Cnty Exec -11 New Hempstd Rd -New Cty 10956 **Fx:**638-5856
(585) 396-4411 .. **Van Der Karr,** Philip A '64 %Cnty Atty -27 N Main -Canandaigua 14424 **Fx:**396-4481
(315) 474-2943 .. **Vanderlyke,** Amy M '08 %Sugarman Law Firm,LLP -211 W Jffrsn -Syracuse 13202
(516) 229-6000 .. **VanderMeer,** Melanie M '94 %R Lau & Assoc -300 Jericho Quad Bx9040 -Jericho 11753 **Fx:**229-6167
(718) 448-3100 .. **VanderNeut,** John '97 -1855 Victory Blvd -Staten Isl 10314 **Fx:**448-3112
(212) 398-1940 .. **Vanderpool,** David '77 %S Hurwitz -19 W 44th -NY 10036 **Fx:**764-5982
(212) 326-2000 .. **Van Derslice,** Kurt A '06 %O'Melveny & M LLP -7 Times Sq -NY 10036
(201) 390-0158 .. **vander Sterre,** Alexis P '04 -160 E 48th -NY 10017
(212) 848-4000 .. **Vander Stoep,** Stephen G '05 %Shearman & S LLP -599 Lex Av -NY 10022
(212) 609-6800 .. **Vanderstreet,** Michele McGuire '03 %McCarter & E,LLP -245 Park Av -NY 10167
(212) 246-2400 .. **Van Der Tuin,** John T '80 (Balber PM&VDT,PC) -1370 Av of Amer -NY 10019
(914) 995-3419 .. **Vandervelden,** Steven T '88 %DA -111 Martin Luther King Blvd -White Plns 10601 **Fx:**995-3363
(212) 355-4141 .. **Vandervoort,** Adam C '06 Independence Holding Co -485 Mad Av -NY 10022

(516) 294-9224 .. **Van der Waag,** Robt F '72 -62 Robbins Dr -Williston Pk 11596
(212) 589-4200 .. **Vanderwal,** Amy E '06 %Baker & H LLP -45 Rckfllr Plz -NY 10111
(585) 243-4222 .. **Vander Wal,** Elizabeth Dawson '05 (Dawson & VW,LLP) -129 Main Bx69 -Geneseo 14454 **Fx:**243-2387
(518) 388-3408 .. **Vanderwal,** Kent D '08 NYS Lottery -Bx7500 -Schnctdy 12301
(585) 263-1000 .. **Vander Wal,** Nathan E '04 %Nixon P LLP -1100 Clinton Sq -Rchstr 14604
(212) 264-0482 .. **Vanderweide,** Alexander J '05 US DOJ -26 Fed Plz -NY 10278
(646) 502-8066 .. **Van Der Zandt,** Carl M R '05 (Gusy V LLP) -500 5th Av -NY 10110 **Fx:**536-8154
(212) 334-6888 .. **Van Der Zee,** Avra C '08 Trespa NA Ltd -62 Greene -NY 10012 **Fx:**(866) 298-3499
(607) 272-4444 .. **Van Derzee,** Thos K '86 %CDL&M -401 E State -Ithaca 14850
(516) 746-4885 .. **Vande Stouwe,** Richd J '86 (Klemanowicz H&VS,LLP) -300 Old Cntry Rd -Mineola 11501 **Fx:**747-7292
(716) 849-1333 .. **Vandette,** James M '08 %Lipsitz GSC LLP -42 Delaware Av -Buffalo 14202
(212) 310-8000 .. **Van Deurzen,** Joshua F '09 %Weil G&M LLP -767 5th Av -NY 10153
(212) 559-0148 .. **Van Deventer,** Hugh IV '88 %Citibank -153 E 53rd -NY 10043
(212) 237-1000 .. **Vandever,** Delton L '00 %Windels ML&M,LLP -156 W 56th -NY 10019
(212) 416-8000 .. **Van De Water,** Christopher L '97 %Dept of Law -120 Bway -NY 10271
(845) 452-5900 .. **Van DeWater & Van DeWater,LLP** -85 Civic Ctr Plz Bx112 -Poughkeepsie 12602 **Fx:**452-5848
(212) 661-9100 .. **Van de Weghe,** Bart G '87 OfCnsl Otterbourg SH&R,PC -230 Park Av -NY 10169
(212) 248-3140 .. **Van Dillen,** Tracey A '05 %Drinker B&R LLP -140 Bway -NY 10005
(607) 756-0265 .. **Van Donsel,** Richd C '89 -1 N Main -Cortlnd 13045 **Fx:**753-7582
(212) 698-4570 .. **VanDoren,** A Reading Jr. '60 (Stapper & V) -10 Rckfllr Plz -NY 10020
(315) 435-2470 .. **Van Doren,** Beth J '83 %DA -505 S State -Syracuse 13202 **Fx:**435-3969
(212) 586-7895 .. **Van Doren,** Danl '87 -130 W 57th -NY 10019 **Fx:**586-8051
(212) 526-6698 .. **VanDoren,** James F '03 %Barclays Capital Inc -745 7th Av -NY 10019
(518) 474-5607 .. **Van Doren,** Noreen J '87 %Ofc Gnl Srvcs -Corning Twr ESP -Albany 12242 **Fx:**473-4973
(212) 768-6700 .. **Van Dorn,** Walter G Jr. '90 (Sonnenschein N&R LLP) -2 World Fncl Ctr -NY 10281
(516) 364-6514 .. **Van Dorn,** Wendy S '94 -12 Narcissus Dr -Syosset 11791
(718) 694-5785 .. **Vandoros,** Alexandra '99 %Transit Auth -130 Lvngstn -Brklyn 11201 **Fx:**694-0123
(212) 820-9307 .. **Van Dusen,** Bruce D '79 (Hawkins D&W LLP) -One Chase Manh Plz -NY 10005
(212) 805-3900 .. **VanDusen,** Matthew J '04 %Clausen M PC -1 Chase Manh Plz -NY 10005
(212) 277-4000 .. **Van Dusen,** Nicholas G W '01 %Freshfields BD LLP -520 Mad Av -NY 10022
(212) 820-9630 .. **Van Dusen,** Richd A '75 (Hawkins D&W LLP) -One Chase Manh Plz -NY 10005
(315) 474-2943 .. **Van Duser,** Kevin R '98 (Sugarman Law Firm,LLP) -211 W Jffrsn -Syracuse 13202
(518) 473-5671 .. **Van Dyk,** Bruce W '81 %Div of Parole -97 Central Av -Albany 12206 **Fx:**473-6037
(212) 735-3000 .. **VanDyke,** Brandon A '03 (Skadden ASM&F LLP) -4 Times Sq -NY 10036
(518) 395-4227 .. **Van Dyke,** Henry J '82 Naval Reactors Ofc Gen Cnsl -Bx1069 -Schnctdy 12301
(516) 484-4425 .. **Van Dyke,** Lawr H '81 -89 Jffrsn Av -Roslyn Hts 11577 **Fx:**209-4275
(315) 478-3074 .. **Van Dyke,** M Joanne '88 (Cote & V,LLP) -214 N State -Syracuse 13203 **Fx:**478-3094
(212) 546-9255 .. **Vanek,** Christine '99 Cnsl Scarinci H -107 Grand -NY 10013
(212) 225-2000 .. **Vanek,** Matthew J '08 %Cleary GS&H -1 Lbrty Plz -NY 10006
(212) 402-5472 .. **Vanel,** Kleindinst C '03 (Vanel Law Firm,PC) -234 5th Av -NY 10001
(212) 265-6888 .. **Van Elk,** Christopher F '02 %Porzio B&N,PC -156 W 56th -NY 10019
(631) 501-3100 .. **Vanella,** Linda M '98 J Humphreys -3 Huntngtn Quad Bx9028 -Melvll 11747 **Fx:**501-3085
(315) 471-2181 .. **Van Epps,** Dale L '66 -250 S Clinton -Syracuse 13202 **Fx:**471-1154
(718) 590-2000 .. **Van Epps,** Graham G '07 DA -198 E 161st -Bronx 10451 **Fx:**590-6477
(212) 753-1800 .. **Vaneria,** John S '74 (Vaneria & S) -52 Vndrblt Av -NY 10017
(212) 753-1800 .. **Vaneria & Spanos** -52 Vndrblt Av -NY 10017 **Fx:**223-0842
(212) 406-9710 .. **Van Etten,** Jeffrey '88 (Kral CRRP&G,LLP) -170 Bway -NY 10038
(716) 665-3024 .. **VanEvery,** Robt W '76 -19 N Work -Falconer 14733
(212) 735-3000 .. **Van Exel,** Devin E '06 %Skadden ASM&F LLP -4 Times Sq -NY 10036
(212) 788-0745 .. **Van Eysden,** Inga '90 %Law Dept -100 Church -NY 10007 **Fx:**788-0367
(212) 941-7744 .. **Van Gartenstein,** Adley '90 Film Movement -109 W 27th -NY 10001 **Fx:**941-7812
(212) 692-1000 .. **Van Gelder,** Christine Megna '94 SpclCnsl Duane M LLP -1540 Bway -NY 10036
(716) 566-5400 .. **Van Gelder,** Susan E '98 (Goldberg S LLP) -665 Main -Buffalo 14203
(212) 672-6000 .. **Van Gelderen,** Jody Cosgrove '82 %HYPO Vereinsbank -150 E 42nd -NY 10017
(212) 986-6840 .. **Van Gendt,** Nicole M '97 %N Brickman -317 Mad Av -NY 10017 **Fx:**986-7691
(585) 395-2457 .. **VanGraafeiland,** Anne '85 SUNY Brockport -350 New Campus Dr -Brockprt 14420
(585) 724-4332 .. **VanGraafeiland,** Gary '73 %Eastman Kodak -343 State -Rchstr 14650
(212) 574-1200 .. **Van Grover,** Robt B '84 (Seward & K LLP) -1 Bttry Pk Plz -NY 10004
(845) 675-7070 .. **Van Haaster,** Kimberly Canterino '92 (Mahon VH) -83 Main -Nyack 10960 **Fx:**675-7072
(212) 306-1822 .. **Van Hatten,** Scott G '96 %Amer Stock Exch -86 Trinity Pl -NY 10006 **Fx:**306-1802
(315) 422-7725 .. **Van Hee,** H Dana '00 %J McGraw -333 E Onondaga -Syracuse 13202 **Fx:**422-7741
(212) 297-0050 .. **Van Hemmen,** Jeanne-Marie D '91 (Betancourt VHG&K LLC) -46 Trinity Pl -NY 10006
(516) 489-0800 .. **Van Heyst,** Lonneke E '07 %T Restivo,PC -100 Q Roosevelt Blvd -Gdn Cty 11530 **Fx:**683-8732
(212) 474-1000 .. **Van Holewinckel,** Lisenka '07 %Cravath S&M LLP -825 8th Av -NY 10019
(585) 428-5210 .. **VanHooft,** Bronwen E '05 Pub Def -10 N Fitzhugh -Rchstr 14614 **Fx:**428-2234
(212) 972-5430 .. **Van Horn,** Alissa L '06 Rosin SM -801 2nd Av -NY 10017
(716) 856-0600 .. **Van Horn,** Ehret A '09 %Jaeckle F&M,LLP -12 Fountain Plz -Buffalo 14202
(212) 218-2100 .. **Van Horn,** Meghan M '10 %Fitzpatrick CH&S -1290 Av of Amer -NY 10104
(212) 448-1100 .. **Van Horn,** Paul E '95 (McLaughlin & S,LLP) -260 Mad Av -NY 10016
(315) 789-8511 .. **Van Horn,** Schuyler T '76 -33 Seneca Bx711 -Geneva 14456 **Fx:**781-1663
(212) 986-9500 .. **Van Horne,** John L III '80 -230 Park Av -NY 10169 **Fx:**568-1348
(516) 364-6006 .. **Van Houten,** Carol Anne '07 %Cohen & S,LLP -199 Crsswys Park Dr Bx9004 -Woodbury 11797
(607) 273-5475 .. **Van Houten,** L Matthew '96 (Holmberg GV&M) -200 E Buffalo -Ithaca 14850
(212) 227-1010 .. **van Hulsteyn,** Grace '84 %Berger & K -225 Bway -NY 10007
(718) 629-8715 .. **Vanier,** Beverley G '96 -245 7th -Brklyn 11215
(518) 483-1440 .. **Vanier,** Stephen A '93 (Poissant NG&V,PC) -367 W Main -Malone 12953
(718) 625-2200 .. **van Ingen,** Karen '81 Bklyn Law Schl -250 Joralemon -Brklyn 11201 **Fx:**780-0393
(212) 637-3151 .. **Van Itallie,** Michl J '92 %EPA -290 Bway -NY 10007 **Fx:**637-3096
(914) 323-7000 .. **Vanjak,** Petar K '07 %Wilson EME&D LLP -3 Gannett Dr -White Plns 10604
(607) 737-5674 .. **Van Keuren,** Robt F '95 %City Atty -317 E Church -Elmira 14901
(716) 983-8335 .. **VanKoughnet,** Rachel A '09 -Bx403 -Lk View 14085 **Fx:**624-3246
(212) 554-1400 .. **vanKwawegen,** Jeroen '04 %Bernstein LB&G LLP -1285 Av of Amer -NY 10019
(212) 450-4000 .. **Vanlandingham,** Kevin P '09 %Davis P&W LLP -450 Lex Av -NY 10017
(212) 608-1400 .. **Van-Lare,** Albert '01 -80 Wall -NY 10005 **Fx:**608-9347
(212) 225-2000 .. **VanLare,** Jane '08 %Cleary GS&H -1 Lbrty Plz -NY 10006
(212) 277-6500 .. **Van Leenen,** Stuart J '05 %Dickstein S LLP -1633 Bway -NY 10019
(212) 962-1596 .. **Van Leer,** Ivan L '79 (Van Leer V-G&G) -132 Nassau -NY 10038
(212) 962-1596 .. **Van Leer-Greenberg,** Valerie '77 (Van Leer V-G&G) -132 Nassau -NY 10038
(212) 317-9500 .. **Van Leeuwen,** David C '07 %Nadel & Assoc,PC -3 E 54th -NY 10022 **Fx:**317-9849
(607) 256-2000 .. **Van Leeuwen,** Meghan Anne '05 %Brown & M,PC -118 N Tioga -Ithaca 14850
(718) 855-9000 .. **van Lent,** Jean-Pierre D '79 OfCnsl Cullen and D LLP -177 Montague -Brklyn 11201
(212) 974-7474 .. **Van Lierop,** Robt F '68 OfCnsl Cowan DA&S LLP -41 Mad Av -NY 10010
(516) 624-6150 .. **Van Loan,** Arlene F '95 Town Atty -Town Hall -Oyster Bay 11771 **Fx:**624-6196
(845) 340-3315 .. **Van Loan,** Gerard '01 %DA -285 Wall -Kingston 12401 **Fx:**340-3185
(914) 358-0036 .. **Van Loggerenberg,** Conrad '10 %Gravett & G -100 S Bedford Rd -Mt Kisco 10549 **Fx:**358-0037
(212) 903-9000 .. **Van Loo,** Jonathan '08 %Linklaters -1345 Av of Amer -NY 10105
(585) 899-1414 .. **Van Loon,** Nathan A '00 (Harris COJW&L) -300 Linden Oaks -Rchstr 14625
(718) 601-2652 .. **Van Malden,** Stacey A '91 -6629 Bway -Bronx 10471 **Fx:**601-2652
(212) 473-3473 .. **vanMerkensteijn,** John H III '70 RA Investments -211 Cntrl Pk W -NY 10024
(212) 382-1700 .. **Vann,** Avrom R '68 -420 Lex Av -NY 10170 **Fx:**661-6976
(212) 693-0108 .. **Vann,** Guy Keith '82 (GK Vann,PC) -22 W 19th -NY 10011 **Fx:**267-7312
(212) 586-5800 .. **Vann,** Jos M '88 (Cohen TS&W PC) -420 Lex Av -NY 10170
(212) 401-5500 .. **Vann,** Nancy Sue '84 Reserve Fund -1250 Bway -NY 10001
(212) 351-4000 .. **Van Name,** John G '10 Gibson D&C LLP -200 Park Av -NY 10166
(914) 949-1070 .. **van Nes,** Hans A '67 (van N&M,LLP) -199 Main -White Plns 10601
(914) 949-1070 .. **van Nes & Marantis,LLP** -199 Main -White Plns 10601 **Fx:**997-1094
(917) 456-6918 .. **Van Ness,** Beverly M '79 -74 Trinity Pl -NY 10006
(518) 436-4781 .. **Van Nest,** Elizabeth Lynne '85 SrCnsl Comm Indp Cllg & Univ -17 Elk Bx7289 -Albany 12224 **Fx:**436-0417
(716) 848-9000 .. **Van Nest,** George S '95 SrCnsl Underberg & K LLP -1900 Main Pl Twr -Buffalo 14202
(585) 325-6880 .. **Van Nest,** Veronica Ann '96 Manning & Napier Advisors -290 Woodcliff Dr -Fairprt 14450 **Fx:**325-5617
(212) 930-0744 .. **Vanni,** Robt J '69 %NY Public Lib -5th Av & 42nd -NY 10018 **Fx:**391-2503
(518) 294-9964 .. **Van Niekerk,** Christiaan M '06 Lancaster Dvlpmnt -145 Podpadic Rd -Richmndvll 12149
(518) 382-5073 .. **Van Norden,** L John '88 %Law Dept -201 City Hall -Schnctdy 12305 **Fx:**382-5074
(212) 530-5000 .. **Van Norden,** Langdon Jr. '92 (Milbank TH&M LLP) -1 Chase Manh Plz -NY 10005
(315) 422-3300 .. **Van Norstrand,** Ronald L '84 -201 E Jffrsn -Syracuse 13202 **Fx:**474-0250
(631) 264-0303 .. **VanNostrand,** LeRoy Jr. '46 (VanNostrand & M) -53 Bway Bx307 -Amityvll 11701
(631) 264-0303 .. **VanNostrand & Martin** -53 Bway Bx307 -Amityvll 11701 **Fx:**264-0314
(212) 335-9000 .. **Van Noy,** Thos G '83 %DA -1 Hogan Pl -NY 10013
(212) 888-3033 .. **Van Nuys,** Peter '65 (Becker GM&M LLP) -299 Park Av -NY 10171
(518) 474-7072 .. **Van Ort,** David R '93 %Dept Pub Srvc -3 ESP -Albany 12223
(212) 779-9910 .. **Van Praag,** Alan '72 (Eaton & V LLP) -3 Park Av -NY 10016
(336) 785-9100 .. **Van-Riel,** Antoinette L '02 (A Van-Riel,PA) -305 Bway -NY 10007
(516) 922-3470 .. **Van Riper,** Jean M '77 -6 South Rd -Oyster Bay 11771
(845) 526-3568 .. **Van Ross,** Clement '71 -Bx134 -Putnam Vly 10579
(212) 826-5353 .. **Van Roy,** Jantra '96 (Zeichner E&K LLP) -575 Lex Av -NY 10022

(914) 249-5465 ..**Van Ryn,** Caroline Ann '97 MasterCard Intl -2000 Purchase -Purchase 10577
(315) 422-1311 ..**Van Ryn,** J Matthew '94 %Melvin & M,PLLC -217 S Salina -Syracuse 13202
(518) 474-6530 ..**Van Ryn,** Leonard J '83 %Dept Pub Srvc -3 ESP -Albany 12223
(518) 475-0016 ..**Van Ryn,** Paul W '81 (Maxwell & V) -2 Normanskill Blvd -Delmar 12054
(914) 422-1270 ..**Van Scoyoc,** Carol L '86 %Law Dept -255 Main -White Plns 10601 **Fx:**422-1231
(518) 473-0782 ..**Van Sickle,** Darlene '87 %Ofc for Technology -State Cptl ESP Bx2062 -Albany 12220
(718) 206-4688 ..**Van Slyck,** Peter W '92 %Law Dept -89-17 Sutphin Blvd -Jamaica 11435 **Fx:**206-4702
(585) 621-3499 ..**Van Son,** Gary W '78 -102 Kenilworth Terr -Rchstr 14605
(718) 520-3171 ..**Vanson,** Wm A '95 %Supreme Ct -125-01 Qns Blvd -Kew Gdns 11415 **Fx:**520-2494
(212) 973-0572 ..**Van Splinter,** James M '06 %Wolff & S PC -140 Bway -NY 10005
(716) 487-1142 ..**Vanstrom,** John D '92 (Spoto S&S) -112 Htl Jmstwn Ofc Bldg -Jamestwn 14701
(716) 845-7436 ..**Van Strydonck,** Sara S '05 %Hon S Troutman -25 Delaware Av -Buffalo 14202
(212) 455-2000 ..**Van Syoc,** Rhett A '07 %Simpson T&B LLP -425 Lex Av -NY 10017
(845) 452-5900 ..**VanTassell,** Amee C '06 %Van DeWater & V,LLP -85 Civic Ctr Plz Bx112 -Poughkeepsie 12602
(212) 521-5400 ..**Van Tassell,** Cameron G '10 %Reed S LLP -599 Lex Av -NY 10022
(718) 522-7870 ..**Vanterpool-Brown,** Ann Marie '91 -26 Court -Brklyn 11242
(212) 471-9354 ..**Van't Hooft,** Sietske K M '07 Loyens & L (USA) BV -555 Mad Av -NY 10022 **Fx:**489-0710
(212) 277-4000 ..**Vanto,** Jessica Bannon '02 %Freshfields BD LLP -520 Mad Av -NY 10022
(212) 918-3000 ..**Van Tol,** Pieter H B '95 (Hogan L LLP) -875 3rd Av -NY 10022
(212) 786-8219 ..**VanTuyl,** Erick W '03 Virgin Records -150 5th Av -NY 10011
(845) 896-2229 ..**Van Tuyl,** Jennifer L '71 (Cuddy & F LLP) -300 Westage Business Ctr -Fishkill 12524
(718) 748-2158 ..**van Tuyn,** Marcel M '88 -8917 Shore Ct -Brklyn 11209
(212) 326-3939 ..**Vantzos,** Zoe A '08 %Jones D -222 E 41st -NY 10017
(518) 783-4767 ..**Van Ullen,** Stephen J '79 (Wertime R&V,PC) -930 Albany Shaker Rd -Latham 12110
(212) 692-9666 ..**Van Valkenburgh,** Ashley M '06 %Gilbride TL&S LLC -708 3rd Av -NY 10017
(585) 428-5755 ..**Van Varick,** David '74 %Cnty Atty -50 W Main -Rchstr 14614 **Fx:**428-2031
(212) 728-8000 ..**Van Veldhuizen,** Ruth A '09 %Willkie F&G LLP -787 7th Av -NY 10019
(716) 566-5400 ..**Van Vessem,** Matthew C '98 (Goldberg S LLP) -665 Main -Buffalo 14203
(212) 564-9800 ..**VanVleet,** Jared B '03 %D'Agostino L&L,LLP -345 7th Av -NY 10001
(716) 731-4176 ..**Van Vleet,** Wayne M '95 %Orleans Niagara Boces -4232 Shelby Basin Rd -Medina 14103 **Fx:**798-4804
(212) 326-3939 ..**van Voorhees,** Alexander '07 %Jones D -222 E 41st -NY 10017
(585) 899-1414 ..**Van Voorhis,** Eugene '58 OfCnsl Harris COJW&L -300 Linden Oaks -Rchstr 14625
(212) 355-5575 ..**Van Voorhis,** Jennifer M '08 %Smith & N,LLP -363 7th Av -NY 10001 **Fx:**486-3150
(212) 318-2300 ..**Van Voris,** Robt M '95 Bloomberg Business News -499 Park Av -NY 10022
(516) 393-2200 ..**Van Vort,** Christina '94 (Garfunkel W,PC) -111 Grt Nck Rd -Gt Neck 11021
(518) 399-2588 ..**Van Vranken,** Robt E '75 -227-229 Kingsley Rd -Burnt Hlls 12027 **Fx:**399-2607
(607) 687-8643 ..**Van Wert,** John H '92 Cnty Atty Law Dept -20 Court -Owego 13827
(917) 664-3825 ..**VanWie,** Wendy '02 -1070 Cnty Route 25 -Kinderhook 12106
(914) 641-2065 ..**Van Winkle,** Peter H '92 %ITT Corp -1133 Wstchstr Av -White Plns 10604
(212) 660-3000 ..**VanWormer,** Matthew J '03 %Sullivan & W LLP -1290 Av of Amer -NY 10104
(212) 596-9000 ..**Van Wormer,** Nina I '08 %Ropes & G LLP -1211 Av of Amer -NY 10036
(212) 940-8800 ..**Vanyo,** Bruce G '08 (Katten MR LLP) -575 Mad Av -NY 10022
(845) 796-2100 ..**Van Zon,** Ingrid M '93 %Frontier Ins -Bx8000 -Rck Hll 12775
(212) 450-4000 ..**Van Zyl,** Hildegard '09 %Davis P&W LLP -450 Lex Av -NY 10017
(631) 501-5700 ..**Vapnyar,** Vadim '05 %Carter DF&S LLP -445 Broadhallow Rd -Melvll 11747
(845) 225-0574 ..**Vara,** Robt J '02 -18 Kent Acres Gypsy Trl Rd -Carmel 10512 **Fx:**225-9639
(914) 997-0905 ..**Varachi,** John P '72 (Tackel & V,LLP) -445 Hmltn Av -White Plns 10601 **Fx:**997-2021
(212) 578-2211 ..**Varady,** Andrew S Jr. '87 %MetLife -27-01 Qns Plz N -LIC 11101
(646) 855-4636 ..**Varah,** Harold S '99 Bank of America -1 Bryant Pk -NY 10036
(914) 528-1282 ..**Varble,** Michl R '97 -35 E Grassy Sprain Rd -Ynkrs 10710
(212) 436-1094 ..**Vardag-Muzaffar,** Faiza '86 IRS-Estate Tax -290 Bway -NY 10007
(845) 565-5656 ..**Vardan,** Swathi '99 -290 Bway -Newburgh 12550 **Fx:**565-2007
(631) 361-9494 ..**Vardaro,** Anthony P '77 -732 Smithtwn Bypass -Smithtwn 11787 **Fx:**361-8752
(212) 682-6800 ..**Vardaro,** Michl J '97 (Zetlin & D LLP) -801 2nd Av -NY 10017
(631) 361-9494 ..**Vardaro,** Prisco '94 -732 Smithtwn Bypass -Smithtwn 11787 **Fx:**361-8752
(212) 676-7908 ..**Vardaros,** Maria '02 ACS-Child Support Litgtn Unit -220 Church -NY 10013
(212) 474-1000 ..**Vardell,** James C III '81 (Cravath S&M LLP) -825 8th Av -NY 10019
(212) 819-8200 ..**Vardi,** Carolyn J '02 %White & C LLP -1155 Av of Amer -NY 10036
(585) 546-2500 ..**Varel,** Amy L '00 %McConville CC&M,PC -25 E Main -Rchstr 14614
(212) 285-0511 ..**Varela,** Carl D '87 -299 Bway -NY 10007
(212) 761-2392 ..**Varela,** Jorge W '96 Morgan Stanley -1585 Bway -NY 10036
(212) 474-1000 ..**Varellas,** James J III '09 %Cravath S&M LLP -825 8th Av -NY 10019
(212) 335-4500 ..**Varet,** Michl A '66 SrCnsl DLA Piper LLP -1251 Av of Amer -NY 10020
(212) 474-1000 ..**Varet,** Sarah Rosenwald '06 %Cravath S&M LLP -825 8th Av -NY 10019
(212) 371-6600 ..**Varga,** Edw M III '08 %Kirby M LLP -825 3rd Av -NY 10022
(212) 626-4206 ..**Varga,** Ildiko '91 (Nagy & T) -1114 Av of Amer -NY 10036
(212) 964-6611 ..**Varga,** Robt '03 %Lester SK&D -120 Bway -NY 10271
(212) 465-1110 ..**Vargas,** Christopher L '03 %Bader Y&N LLP -350 5th Av -NY 10118
(212) 225-2000 ..**Vargas,** Glorimari '06 %Cleary GS&H -1 Lbrty Plz -NY 10006
(646) 314-6330 ..**Vargas,** Howard R '00 -950 Gerard Av -Bronx 10452 **Fx:**201-4480
(212) 995-7496 ..**Vargas,** Ivanyla D '02 Cabrini Medical Ctr -227 E 19th -NY 10003
(718) 875-1300 ..**Vargas,** Javier Enrique '93 %Appllt Div 2nd Dept -45 Monroe Pl -Brklyn 11201 **Fx:**858-2446
(212) 637-2678 ..**Vargas,** Jeannette A '01 %US Atty -86 Chmbrs -NY 10007
(212) 725-6422 ..**Vargas,** Manuel D '85 SrCnsl Immigrant Defense Proj -3 W 29th -NY 10001 **Fx:**(800) 391-5713
(607) 778-2403 ..**Vargha,** Michl A '94 %Pub Def -45 Hawley Bx1766 -Bnghmtn 13902 **Fx:**778-2432
(212) 964-9282 ..**Varghese,** Ancy Sera '06 %N Weinrib & Assoc -305 Bway -NY 10007 **Fx:**964-9525
(914) 779-1100 ..**Varghese,** Cherian Gee '95 Veneruso CS&C,LLP -35 E Grassy Sprain Rd -Ynkrs 10710
(607) 739-3581 ..**Varghese,** Gloria '07 Cnsl GST BOCES -459 Philo Rd -Elmira 14903 **Fx:**795-5304
(914) 323-7000 ..**Varghese,** Jenson '04 %Wilson EME&D LLP -3 Gannett Dr -White Plns 10604
(212) 599-8200 ..**Varghese,** Lekha A '03 %Shaub AC&S,LLP -655 3rd Av -NY 10017
(212) 732-3200 ..**Varghese,** Libby B '02 %Carter L&M LLP -2 Wall -NY 10005
(212) 267-1900 ..**Varghese,** Maju '06 %Wade CM -111 Bway -NY 10006
(718) 990-6044 ..**Varghese,** Rena M '04 St Johns Univ Law Schl -8000 Utopia Pkwy -Jamaica 11439 **Fx:**990-1918
(212) 257-6800 ..**Varghese,** Renan F '08 %Thompson W&G LLP -85 5th Av -NY 10003
(516) 229-6000 ..**Varghese,** Sarah C '00 %R Lau & Assoc -300 Jericho Quad Bx9040 -Jericho 11753 **Fx:**229-6167
(212) 848-4000 ..**Varghese,** Tina M '08 %Shearman & S LLP -599 Lex Av -NY 10022
(212) 430-6469 ..**Varghese,** Vinoo P '01 -65 Bway -NY 10006
(516) 877-2900 ..**Vari,** Susan A '85 (Bartlett MB&M,LLP) -300 Old Cntry Rd -Mineola 11501
(212) 317-1717 ..**Varia,** Nita A '07 %Chemtob MF&T LLP -3 E 54th -NY 10022
(914) 632-0332 ..**Varian,** Gregory T '82 -270 North Av -New Rchll 10801 **Fx:**632-2022
(716) 824-7200 ..**Vario,** Robt R '83 -101 Slade Av -W Seneca 14224 **Fx:**824-8728
(212) 962-8020 ..**Varkoutas,** Christos '99 %Julien & S,PC -1 Whitehall -NY 10004
(212) 547-1534 ..**Varlack Betts,** Lisa O '02 Mizuho Capital Mrkts Corp -1440 Bway -NY 10018
(212) 506-5494 ..**Varlese,** Doris R '89 Grtr NY Hsptl Assn -555 W 57th -NY 10019 **Fx:**262-6350
(718) 312-4100 ..**Varlese,** Felicia M '86 %Empire Blue Cross -15 MetroTech Ctr -Brklyn 11201 **Fx:**312-6010
(718) 726-0694 ..**Varlese,** Rocco S '57 -2183 Steinway -Astoria 11105
(212) 788-3807 ..**Varley,** Alison M '04 %ACS -220 Church -NY 10013
(518) 458-8922 ..**Varley,** Kenneth G '78 (Donohue SV&H,LLP) -24 Aviation Rd -Albany 12205
(212) 252-0300 ..**Varley,** Myles P II '04 %Kagan LLLG&C,LLP -200 Mad Av -NY 10016
(718) 884-2152 ..**Varma,** Kanakatara '81 -2621 Palisade Av -Bronx 10463
(845) 562-9100 ..**Varma,** Vikas '08 %Rider W&F,PC -655 Little Britain Rd -New Windsor 12553
(718) 793-2874 ..**Varnai,** Oren '04 City Marshal -144-02 Jewel Av -Flushng 11367 **Fx:**793-2875
(212) 841-1000 ..**Varner,** Gretchen Hoff '08 %Covington & B LLP -620 8th Av -NY 10018
(516) 248-7000 ..**Varney,** Bruce B '94 %Albanese & A LLP -1050 Franklin Av -Gdn Cty 11530
(585) 428-2444 ..**Varney,** Joan E '88 City Court -6 Hall of Justice -Rchstr 14614
(315) 471-3151 ..**Varney,** John R '58 (Hancock & E,LLP) -1500 AXA Twr I Bx4976 -Syracuse 13221
(718) 391-1721 ..**Varoli,** David J '92 %Dept Design & Cnstrctn -30-30 Thomson Av -LIC 11101 **Fx:**391-1894
(212) 692-1000 ..**Varon,** Joanna R '04 %Duane M LLP -1540 Bway -NY 10036
(212) 732-8579 ..**Varon,** Michl L '95 %Sher HB&T,PC -277 Bway -NY 10007
(914) 666-5585 ..**Varona,** Danl R '78 %MBE Shipping -487 E Main -Mt Kisco 10549
(212) 513-7788 ..**Varrecchia,** Cindy '90 %Ahmuty D&M -123 William -NY 10038
(212) 488-1598 ..**Varriale,** Carla '93 (Havkins RR&V,LLP) -11 Penn Plz -NY 10001
(914) 741-6100 ..**Varriale,** David J '96 %Kaufman B&R -200 Summit Lk Dr -Valhalla 10595
(718) 876-6300 ..**Varriale,** Karen E '98 %DA -130 Styvsnt Pl -Staten Isl 10301
(516) 877-2900 ..**Varriale,** Paul R '96 %Bartlett MB&M,LLP -300 Old Cntry Rd -Mineola 11501
(718) 863-2897 ..**Varrichio,** Maria A '95 -3144 Wstchstr Av -Bronx 10461 **Fx:**863-3136
(718) 863-2897 ..**Varrichio,** Mark A Sr. '60 (M Varrichio & Assoc) -3144 Wstchstr Av -Bronx 10461 **Fx:**863-3136
(718) 863-2897 ..**Varrichio,** Mark A Jr. '93 -3144 Wstchstr Av -Bronx 10461 **Fx:**863-3136
(315) 786-7950 ..**Vars,** Addison F III '72 (Menter R&T,PC) -120 Wshngtn -Watertwn 13601
(212) 335-9000 ..**Varshavsky,** Vera '04 %DA -1 Hogan Pl -NY 10013
(718) 721-9667 ..**Varsos,** Norma Rhea '87 -28-47 37th -Astoria 11103 **Fx:**956-9474
(914) 962-3203 ..**Vartabedian,** Michl '70 -39 Wood -Katonah 10536 **Fx:**962-0267
(516) 572-2000 ..**Varughese,** Bena K '08 %DA -99 Main -Hempstd 11550 **Fx:**572-2606
(845) 371-4700 ..**Varughese,** Gini E '10 %Fein SK&S,PC -747 Chestnut Rdg Rd -Spg Vly 10977
(516) 466-6500 ..**Varughese,** Justin '04 %Parker WA LLP -6 Hrbr Park Dr S -Pt Wash 11050
(212) 323-2250 ..**Varughese,** Mathew C '06 %HHC-OLA-Medical Litigation -346 Bway -NY 10013 **Fx:**323-2251
(631) 852-2500 ..**Varuolo,** Raymond V '05 %DA -200 Center Dr -Rvrhead 11901 **Fx:**852-1769
(516) 745-8310 ..**Varvaro,** Jos '87 (Perez & V) -333 Earle Ovngton Blvd Bx9372 -Uniondale 11553
(212) 250-8383 ..**Vasady-Kovacs,** Julie R '89 Deutsche Bank -60 Wall -NY 10005
(212) 819-8200 ..**Vasandani,** Brian S '05 %White & C LLP -1155 Av of Amer -NY 10036

(212) 344-5680 .. **Vasantharam,** Sheila J '08 %Thompson H LLP -335 Mad Av -NY 10017
(212) 589-4200 .. **Vasel,** Denise D '10 %Baker & H LLP -45 Rckfllr Plz -NY 10111
(212) 407-4000 .. **Vasey,** Laura M '03 (Loeb & L,LLP) -345 Park Av -NY 10154
(212) 458-2162 .. **Vasic,** Gordana '08 AIG -175 Water -NY 10038
(718) 728-0555 .. **Vasilatos,** Andreas '04 (Benjamin & V LLC) -2809 Ditmars Blvd -Astoria 11105
(516) 746-8000 .. **Vasilatos,** Theodora D '08 %Jaspan S LLP -300 Grdn City Plz -Gdn Cty 11530
(212) 596-9000 .. **Vasilchenko,** Irina '08 %Ropes & G LLP -1211 Av of Amer -NY 10036
(585) 454-1660 .. **Vasile,** Gerald J '89 (Vasile Law Grp,PLLC) -1200 Jffrsn Rd -Rchstr 14623
(914) 632-9300 .. **Vasile,** John A '76 (McGovern C&D) -145 Huguenot -New Rchll 10801
(718) 927-4100 .. **Vasile,** Jos R '93 -5009 Av N -Brklyn 11234 **Fx:**927-1507
(516) 623-1111 .. **Vasile,** Roy W '79 -2174 Hewlett Av Bx801 -Merrick 11566 **Fx:**623-0758
(212) 336-0178 .. **Vasilescu,** Alexander M '89 %SEC -3 World Fncl Ctr -NY 10281 **Fx:**336-1323
(718) 274-6300 .. **Vasiliadis,** Bill '98 -32-07 Bway -Astoria 11106 **Fx:**274-9500
(914) 995-4206 .. **Vasilopoulos,** Agathy '89 %Supreme Ct -111 Martin Luther King Blvd -White Plns 10601
(631) 232-2400 .. **Vasiluth,** Carolyn '89 %Nassau/Sfflk Law Srv -1757 Vets Hwy -Islandia 11749 **Fx:**232-2489
(212) 909-6000 .. **Vasily,** John M '83 (Debevoise & P LLP) -919 3rd Av -NY 10022
(212) 513-3200 .. **Vasios,** H Barry '73 (Holland & K LLP) -31 W 52nd -NY 10019
(518) 474-2266 .. **Vasisht,** Gaurav '01 %Gov's Cnsls Ofc -242 State Cptl -Albany 12224
(718) 761-9300 .. **Vaslas,** Bill '86 (Vaslas LH&D LLP) -201 Edward Curry Av -Staten Isl 10314
(718) 761-9300 .. **Vaslas Lepowsky Hauss & Danke LLP** -201 Edward Curry Av -Staten Isl 10314 **Fx:**761-9090
(212) 374-9555 .. **Vaslas Lepowsky Hauss & Danke LLP** -630 3rd Av -NY 10017 **Fx:**983-9210
(212) 264-8000 .. **Vasquez,** Arlene C '95 %HUD -26 Fed Plz -NY 10278
(212) 964-6611 .. **Vasquez,** Carmen M '99 %Lester SK&D -120 Bway -NY 10271
(212) 686-7700 .. **Vasquez,** Consuelo A '98 %Mazur CR&S PC -1250 Bway -NY 10001
(212) 255-8833 .. **Vasquez,** Elsie C '05 %M Liu & Assoc PLLC -107 Grand -NY 10013 **Fx:**255-4981
(518) 482-5465 .. **Vasquez,** Jessica Frances '01 NYSCADV -350 New Scotland Av -Albany 12208 **Fx:**482-3807
(516) 775-2236 .. **Vasquez,** Julio J '99 %Santangelo B&S -1800 Nrthrn Blvd -Roslyn 11576
(212) 669-2609 .. **Vasquez,** Mario A '95 %Civil Srvc Comm -1 Centre -NY 10007
(212) 298-5118 .. **Vasquez,** Marlene '92 %Leg Aid -49 Thomas -NY 10013 **Fx:**298-5252
(718) 779-3701 .. **Vasquez,** Martin S '94 -38-08 Junction Blvd -Corona 11368
(212) 530-5000 .. **Vasquez,** Nicole A '09 %Milbank TH&M LLP -1 Chase Manh Plz -NY 10005
(212) 455-2000 .. **Vasquez,** Rafael '07 %Simpson T&B LLP -425 Lex Av -NY 10017
(212) 532-0500 .. **Vasquez,** Ricardo '01 %Heiberger & Assoc,PC -205 Lex Av -NY 10016 **Fx:**532-2040
(212) 290-1832 .. **Vass,** Michl A '79 %OTDA Fair Hearings -330 W 34th -NY 10001
(718) 855-9000 .. **Vassalle,** Andrew G '88 OfCnsl Cullen and D LLP -177 Montague -Brklyn 11201
(631) 756-2024 .. **Vassallo,** Christopher C '88 %Huenke & R -1 Huntngtn Quad -Melvll 11747
(631) 587-3004 .. **Vassallo,** Danl C '60 -510 Sunrise Hwy -W Babylon 11704 **Fx:**587-0209
(212) 218-2100 .. **Vassallo,** Edw E '74 (Fitzpatrick CH&S) -1290 Av of Amer -NY 10104
(212) 935-5500 .. **Vassallo,** John A '62 (Franklin WR&V) -488 Mad Av -NY 10022
(914) 935-2402 .. **Vassallo,** Stephen J '94 %Avon Products Inc -Avon Plz -Rye 10580
(516) 227-6300 .. **Vassalotti,** Julia '07 %Ettelman & H,PC -100 Q Roosevelt Blvd -Gdn Cty 11530
(516) 240-8030 .. **Vasselman,** Fredk W '05 (Vasselman & S) -1225 Franklin Av -Gdn Cty 11530
(212) 698-3500 .. **Vasser,** Shmuel '91 (Dechert LLP) -1095 Av of Amer -NY 10036
(212) 595-8009 .. **Vasserman,** Raquel M '10 Krol & O -320 W 81st -NY 10024 **Fx:**595-8149
(212) 417-4327 .. **Vassilakis,** Theo '85 %OTDA Fair Hearings -330 W 34th -NY 10001
(516) 741-8005 .. **Vassilas,** Christina '92 %Marshall & B -1305 Franklin Av -Gdn Cty 11530
(212) 603-5500 .. **Vassilev,** Peter P '06 Raine Grp LLC -1325 Av of Amer -NY 10019
(631) 499-6000 .. **Vassos,** Basilios '04 %J Prestiano,PC -631 Commack Rd -Commack 11725 **Fx:**499-6001
(212) 309-6000 .. **Vassos,** John M '86 (Morgan L&B LLP) -101 Park Av -NY 10178
(845) 635-8866 .. **Vasti,** Thos F III '92 (Vasti & V,PC) -1733 Main Bx656 -Plsnt Vlly 12569
(845) 635-8866 .. **Vasti & Vasti,PC** -1733 Main Bx656 -Plsnt Vlly 12569 **Fx:**635-8807
(212) 248-2694 .. **Vastola,** Joy L '86 -61 Bway -NY 10006
(212) 449-4175 .. **Vatel,** Serge '98 Merrill Lynch -4 World Fncl Ctr -NY 10080
(212) 218-2100 .. **Vathyam,** Sujatha '07 %Fitzpatrick CH&S -1290 Av of Amer -NY 10104
(212) 506-3900 .. **Vatis,** Michl A '89 (Steptoe & J LLP) -750 7th Av -NY 10019
(516) 746-8000 .. **Vatter,** Christopher E '02 (Jaspan S LLP) -300 Grdn City Plz -Gdn Cty 11530
(845) 569-7415 .. **Vatter,** Michl J '04 Fire Dept -22 Grand -Newburgh 12550
(607) 255-8994 .. **Vatti,** Hima '00 Cornell Univ -395 Pine Tree Rd -Ithaca 14850
(212) 695-0060 .. **Vaughan,** Glenda M '06 %Wilens & B,PC -450 7th Av -NY 10123
(212) 536-3900 .. **Vaughan,** John D '82 (K&L Gates LLP) -599 Lex Av -NY 10022
(631) 673-3222 .. **Vaughan,** Mark G '96 %J D'Elia -464 NY Av -Huntngtn 11743 **Fx:**673-4958
(631) 852-2157 .. **Vaughan,** Patricia A '81 Hon M Werner -235 Griffing Av -Rvrhead 11901
(212) 339-0575 .. **Vaughan,** Patricia C '85 %Population Council -1 Dag Hmmrskjld Plz -NY 10017
(212) 810-3001 .. **Vaughan,** Peter R '90 Blackrock,Inc -40 E 52nd -NY 10022
(212) 527-1000 .. **Vaughan,** Thos G '73 (Jones HC&B PC) -1 Bttry Pk Plz -NY 10004
(716) 674-6646 .. **Vaughan,** Thos J '75 -4211 Seneca Bx391 -W Seneca 14224 **Fx:**674-6672
(212) 422-9424 .. **Vaughn,** Anthony W Jr. '00 %Gogick B&O,LLP -11 Bway -NY 10004
(212) 909-6000 .. **Vaughn,** DePaul J '08 %Debevoise & P LLP -919 3rd Av -NY 10022
(212) 450-4000 .. **Vaughn,** Kyle M '08 %Davis P&W LLP -450 Lex Av -NY 10017
(212) 283-4870 .. **Vaughn,** Yasmin McFarlane '83 -345 W 145th -NY 10031 **Fx:**283-3746
(212) 588-0022 .. **Vaughn-Flam,** Eric '85 (Sanders OV&R) -501 Mad Av -NY 10022
(212) 667-1011 .. **Vavas,** John D '04 %Nomura Securities Intl -2 World Fncl Ctr -NY 10281
(716) 204-1055 .. **Vavonese,** Francis R '06 %Pfalzgraf B&M LLP -455 Cayuga Rd -Buffalo 14225 **Fx:**204-1080
(315) 422-1311 .. **Vavonese,** Frank J '75 (Melvin & M,PLLC) -217 S Salina -Syracuse 13202
(315) 471-0128 .. **Vavonese,** Michl J '84 -407 S Warren -Syracuse 13202 **Fx:**471-2056
(212) 753-1400 .. **Vavulitsky,** Irene M '02 %G Heinemann,PC -260 Mad Av -NY 10016 **Fx:**448-0066
(212) 952-6200 .. **Vayda,** John P '76 (Nourse & B,LLP) -55 Bway -NY 10006
(212) 332-3370 .. **Vayer,** M Scott '80 -620 5th Av -NY 10020
(718) 769-3639 .. **Vaygen,** Paul A '94 -2323 Brigham -Brklyn 11229
(718) 260-4711 .. **Vaynshenker,** Diana '08 Leg Aid -111 Lvngstn -Brklyn 11201
(212) 221-6900 .. **Vays,** Thos '01 (Winget S&S,LLP) -45 Bway -NY 10006
(212) 223-9395 .. **Vaysman,** Helen '04 -300 Park Av -NY 10022 **Fx:**(646) 478-9421
(212) 728-8000 .. **Vazirani,** Rina R '08 %Willkie F&G LLP -787 7th Av -NY 10019
(718) 237-5500 .. **Vazire,** Navid '07 %Leg Srvcs -105 Court -Brklyn 11201 **Fx:**855-0733
(212) 906-1200 .. **Vazova,** Lilia B '10 %Latham & W -885 3rd Av -NY 10022
(212) 318-3000 .. **Vazquez,** Alyssa M '04 %Fulbright & J LLP -666 5th Av -NY 10103
(718) 298-0602 .. **Vazquez,** Barbaro R '03 Cnty Clerk -88-11 Sutphin Blvd -Jamaica 11435
(212) 408-5100 .. **Vazquez,** Francisco '96 Cnsl Chadbourne & P LLP -30 Rckfllr Plz -NY 10112
(914) 390-4177 .. **Vazquez,** Gabrielle Y '08 Hon S Robinson -30 Quarropas -White Plns 10601
(212) 382-6600 .. **Vazquez,** Libby '05 NYC Bar -42 W 44th -NY 10036 **Fx:**398-6634
(212) 340-0400 .. **Vazquez,** Rosali '87 Appllt Div 1st Dept -27 Mad Av -NY 10010 **Fx:**889-4412
(212) 878-8000 .. **Vazquez,** Vanessa O '04 %Clifford C LLP -31 W 52nd -NY 10019
(585) 232-3730 .. **Vazzana,** James A '91 (Chamberlain D LLP) -1600 Crssrds Bldg -Rchstr 14614
(585) 454-5850 .. **Vazzana,** James G '71 (Wiedman VC&V,PC) -5 S Fitzhugh -Rchstr 14614
(585) 454-6040 .. **Vazzana,** Patricia O '69 -5 S Fitzhugh -Rchstr 14614
(516) 938-1118 .. **Vea,** Laura L '98 Healthpro Staffing -82 N Bway -Hicksvll 11801
(212) 804-4200 .. **Veach,** James D '75 (Mound CW&G) -One Bttry Pk Plz -NY 10004
(212) 407-7700 .. **Veber,** Jeffrey T '05 (Vedder P,PC) -1633 Bway -NY 10019
(212) 403-1000 .. **Veblen,** Mark F '06 %Wachtell LR&K -51 W 52nd -NY 10019
(212) 735-3000 .. **Vebman,** Jos '97 (Skadden ASM&F LLP) -4 Times Sq -NY 10036
(212) 279-3500 .. **Vecchi,** Sesto E '81 (Russin VB&B,LLP) -260 Mad Av -NY 10016
(212) 773-2088 .. **Vecchiariello,** Victor J '04 Ernst & Young LLP -5 Times Sq -NY 10036
(914) 835-1818 .. **Vecchio,** Eugenia M '87 (E Vecchio & Assoc) -550 Mamaroneck Av -Harrison 10528 **Fx:**835-1858
(212) 307-5500 .. **Vecchio,** Mark S '86 (Venable LLP) -1270 Av of Amer -NY 10020
(518) 857-2897 .. **Vecchio,** Philip J '82 P Vecchio,PC -24 Huntswood Ln -E Greenbush 12061 **Fx:**479-4335
(914) 686-3700 .. **Vecchio,** Richd S '86 (Worby GE LLP) -11 Martine Av -White Plns 10606
(917) 777-4200 .. **Vecchio,** Steven '07 %Bingham M LLP -1 Bttry Pk Plz -NY 10004
(516) 741-7575 .. **Vecchione,** Francis J '53 %Vecchione V&C LLP -147 Hrrcks Rd -Gdn Cty Pk 11040 **Fx:**294-4636
(718) 250-2000 .. **Vecchione,** Michl F '74 %DA -350 Jay -Brklyn 11201 **Fx:**250-2314
(516) 741-7575 .. **Vecchione,** Michl F '85 (Vecchione V&C LLP) -147 Hrrcks Rd -Gdn Cty Pk 11040 **Fx:**294-4636
(212) 449-2456 .. **Vecchione,** Phyllis T '94 Merrilly Lynch & Co Inc -250 Vesey -NY 10080
(516) 365-2000 .. **Vecchione,** Robt M '94 AAA Transportation -3333 New Hyde Pk Rd -New Hyde Pk 11042 **Fx:**365-9567
(631) 913-4444 .. **Vecere,** Andrew P '99 (Dell LT&V LLP) -5 Orvll Dr -Bohemia 11716
(315) 445-1086 .. **Vedder,** Karen A '88 -121 Marvelle Rd -Fayettevll 13066
(212) 407-7700 .. **Vedder Price,PC** -1633 Bway -NY 10019 **Fx:**407-7799
(212) 335-9000 .. **Vee,** Grace '93 %DA -1 Hogan Pl -NY 10013
(718) 298-7050 .. **Vee,** Harry '81 %Envrnmntl Cntrl Brd -144-06 94th Av -Jamaica 11435
(212) 761-4000 .. **Veech,** John V '84 (Morgan Stanley) -1585 Bway -NY 10036
(212) 264-8819 .. **Veen,** Jon E '03 SSA-Hearings & Appeals -26 Fed Plz -NY 10278
(212) 558-4000 .. **Veeraraghavan,** U Krishna '04 %Sullivan & C LLP -125 Broad -NY 10004
(212) 902-1000 .. **Veffer,** Barbra A '04 Goldman Sachs -1 NY Plz -NY 10004
(347) 581-5031 .. **Vega,** Aaron R '02 -65 Skyline Dr -Staten Isl 10304
(646) 471-6044 .. **Vega,** Alonso S '09 PricewaterhouseCoopers LP -300 Mad Av -NY 10017
(718) 665-8167 .. **Vega,** Bianka '01 -177 E 161st -Bronx 10451 **Fx:**588-1294
(212) 722-2000 .. **Vega,** Edwin '86 %Leg Aid -230 E 106th -NY 10029 **Fx:**876-5365
(212) 468-8000 .. **Vega,** Elisa N '10 %Morrison & F LLP -1290 Av of Amer -NY 10104
(212) 696-6000 .. **Vega,** Matias A '78 (Curtis M-PC&M LLP) -101 Park Av -NY 10178
(718) 742-6567 .. **Vega,** Myrna A '87 Bronx Student Suspension Hearings -501 Courtlandt Av -Bronx 10451
(212) 264-6113 .. **Vega,** Ricardo '97 DHS -26 Fed Plz -NY 10278 **Fx:**264-1641
(845) 794-3000 .. **Vegliante,** Steven E '94 Cnty Atty -100 North Bx5012 -Monticello 12701 **Fx:**794-4924
(212) 335-9945 .. **Veiga,** Jon '98 %DA -1 Hogan Pl -NY 10013 **Fx:**335-9288
(212) 536-3900 .. **Veilleux,** Marc J '89 (K&L Gates LLP) -599 Lex Av -NY 10022
(914) 703-6300 .. **Veilleux,** Neil T '86 %Pillinger MT,LLP -570 Taxter Rd -Elmsfrd 10523
(518) 408-1495 .. **Veino,** Robt A '78 %Dept of Health -Corning Twr 24th Fl -Albany 12237 **Fx:**473-2019
(212) 418-8600 .. **Veisz,** Howard S '75 (Kornstein VW&P,LLP) -757 3rd Av -NY 10017
(212) 455-2000 .. **Veit,** Andrew C R '10 %Simpson T&B LLP -425 Lex Av -NY 10017

(212) 558-4000 .. **Veit,** Ashlee Conley '10 %Sullivan & C LLP -125 Broad -NY 10004
(212) 310-8000 .. **Veit,** Cheri E '09 %Weil G&M LLP -767 5th Av -NY 10153
(845) 471-4440 .. **Veit,** Dawn R '07 %Quartararo & L PLLC -1399 Route 52 -Fishkill 12524 **Fx:**471-7318
(914) 762-8824 .. **Veit,** Fredk C '88 -21 Gordon Av -Briarclff Mnr 10510 **Fx:**923-1744
(212) 907-7300 .. **Veit,** Jacqueline G '90 (Golenbock EAB&P) -437 Mad Av -NY 10022
(516) 624-1235 .. **Veitch,** Meghan A '05 -60 Oak Dr -Syosset 11791
(914) 232-0100 .. **Veith,** Frank J Jr. '84 -135 Katonah Av -Katonah 10536 **Fx:**232-3250
(212) 922-1177 .. **Veith,** Richd C '82 (Stursberg & V) -1500 Bway -NY 10036
(212) 858-1000 .. **Vejvoda,** Chas H '57 (Pillsbury WSP LLP) -1540 Bway -NY 10036
(212) 259-8000 .. **Vekselman,** Irina A '09 %Dewey & L LLP -1301 Av of Amer -NY 10019
(212) 577-3908 .. **Vela,** Veronica '05 Leg Aid -199 Water -NY 10038
(212) 816-9741 .. **Vela-Montemayor,** Rodolfo '00 Citigroup Global Markets -388 Greenwich -NY 10013
(212) 637-1076 .. **Velamoor,** Niketh V '05 %US Atty -1 St Andrews Plz -NY 10007
(646) 855-3411 .. **Velamoor,** Priya A '02 Bank of Amer Securities LLC -1 Bryant Pk -NY 10036
(845) 279-4000 .. **Velardi,** Paul J '85 PJ Velardi,PLLC -609 Clock Twr Cmmns -Brewstr 10509 **Fx:**279-4236
(212) 434-0100 .. **Velardo,** Vincent J '97 Cnsl Litchfield C LLP -420 Lex Av -NY 10170
(212) 425-2200 .. **Velasco,** Michl Davis '01 %Claugus & M -110 Wall -NY 10005
(315) 671-1058 .. **Velasco,** Yvette '01 %Hon J Brunetti -505 S State -Syracuse 13202 **Fx:**671-1178
(212) 906-1200 .. **Velasquez,** Michelle D '08 %Latham & W -885 3rd Av -NY 10022
(212) 237-0000 .. **Velazquez,** Adorys '02 %Vinson & E LLP -666 5th Av -NY 10103
(212) 308-1550 .. **Velazquez,** Carlos M '75 (CM Velazquez & Assoc) -805 3rd Av -NY 10022
(212) 554-1234 .. **Velazquez,** Edw J '97 %AXA Financial Inc -1290 Av of Amer -NY 10104 **Fx:**707-3963
(718) 963-4430 .. **Velazquez,** Franklin '93 %Puerto Rican Family Inst -217 Havemeyerr -Brklyn 11211
(212) 373-3000 .. **Velazquez,** Liza M '97 (Paul WRW&G LLP) -1285 Av of Amer -NY 10019
(212) 809-7800 .. **Velazquez,** Roberto D '03 %Jaffe & K,LLP -40 Wall -NY 10005
(631) 852-1650 .. **Velazquez,** Victor '76 %Leg Aid -300 Center Dr -Rvrhead 11901 **Fx:**852-1655
(718) 248-1740 .. **Velella,** Benjamin D '86 %Citibank -1 Court Sq -LIC 11101
(212) 848-4000 .. **Velev,** Kalin S '04 %Shearman & S LLP -599 Lex Av -NY 10022
(212) 837-6309 .. **Velez,** Ana C '07 %Hughes H&R LLP -1 Bttry Pk Plz -NY 10004 **Fx:**299-6309
(212) 577-3001 .. **Velez,** Cristina M '04 %HIV Law Proj -15 Maiden Ln -NY 10038 **Fx:**577-3192
(914) 664-1667 .. **Velez,** Donato Jr. '03 Cnsl Mt Vernon Monetary Mgt Corp -403 E 3rd -Mt Vernon 10553 **Fx:**668-5715
(212) 446-4800 .. **Velez,** Manuel J '07 %Kirkland & E LLP -153 E 53rd -NY 10022
(718) 590-2083 .. **Velez,** Nelida '85 %DA -198 E 161st -Bronx 10451 **Fx:**590-6477
(718) 518-7380 .. **Velez,** Nicolas '78 %Bufete Juridico,PC -2010 Wllmsbrdg Rd -Bronx 10461
(212) 709-3554 .. **Velez,** Ricardo E '94 %Banking Dept -1 State -NY 10004 **Fx:**709-1655
(718) 299-1100 .. **Velez,** Roberto '90 Promesa Inc -1776 Clay Av -Bronx 10457 **Fx:**716-7822
(631) 224-1587 .. **Velez,** Rogerlyn '94 SpclCnsl R Cipriano -136 E Main -E Islip 11730 **Fx:**224-1643
(718) 993-3062 .. **Velez,** Rudy '85 -930 Grnd Cncrs -Bronx 10451
(212) 599-5799 .. **Velez,** Samantha '04 %Rutherford & C LLP -369 Lex Av -NY 10017
(212) 752-2100 .. **Velez-Camacho,** Mayra A '04 %SM Musa-Obregon -5521 69th -Maspeth 11378 **Fx:**752-8677
(212) 567-2778 .. **Velez-Lopez,** Maria I '93 -192 Lex Av -NY 10016 **Fx:**(201) 865-1127
(212) 660-3000 .. **Velie,** Franklin B '69 (Sullivan & W LLP) -1290 Av of Amer -NY 10104
(212) 773-0776 .. **Veliotis,** Stanley '90 Ernst & Young LLP -5 Times Sq -NY 10036
(212) 715-9100 .. **Vella,** Carly P '08 %Kramer LN&F,LLP -1177 Av of Amer -NY 10036
(716) 592-4914 .. **Vella,** Emily A '03 %G Vella -378 E Main -Sprngvll 14141 **Fx:**592-4915
(716) 592-4914 .. **Vella,** Gerald J '76 -378 E Main -Sprngvll 14141 **Fx:**592-4915
(518) 439-6001 .. **Vella,** Margaret A '95 Reed & V,LLP -203 Delaware Av -Delmar 12054 **Fx:**439-6108
(516) 873-8787 .. **Vella,** Robt M Jr. '90 (Pillari & V) -114 Old Cntry Rd -Mineola 11501
(315) 474-7541 .. **Vellano,** F Paul Jr. '78 (Menter R&T,PC) -308 Maltbie -Syracuse 13204
(212) 408-5100 .. **Vellucci,** Frank S '98 (Chadbourne & P LLP) -30 Rckfllr Plz -NY 10112
(718) 250-2000 .. **Vellucci,** Lisa M '06 DA -350 Jay -Brklyn 11201 **Fx:**250-2314
(212) 298-5113 .. **Vellucci,** Rosemary '98 %Leg Aid -49 Thomas -NY 10013 **Fx:**298-5252
(212) 715-9100 .. **Vellut,** Laetitia '05 %Kramer LN&F,LLP -1177 Av of Amer -NY 10036
(212) 248-3140 .. **Velocci,** Frank F '00 (Drinker B&R LLP) -140 Bway -NY 10005
(518) 862-3080 .. **Veloce,** Richd P '86 (Hanlon V&W) -94 New Karner Rd -Albany 12203
(212) 336-0180 .. **Velona,** Jess '89 %SEC -3 World Fncl Ctr -NY 10281 **Fx:**336-1323
(315) 472-7868 .. **Velonis,** Andrew T '85 %Weisberg & Z,PLLC -109 S Warren -Syracuse 13202 **Fx:**472-7070
(718) 746-1293 .. **Veloudios,** Stacy '92 -154-39 Powells Cove Blvd -Beechurst 11357 **Fx:**746-1398
(212) 238-3361 .. **Veltre,** Philip J '81 %Mncpl Crdt Union -22 Crtlandt -NY 10007 **Fx:**479-2975
(631) 234-5678 .. **Veltry,** Susan M '91 %Wallace WF&V,PC -600 Suffolk Av -Brentwd 11717
(718) 575-1218 .. **Vempaty,** Krishna M '76 -117-18 Qns Blvd -Frst Hlls 11375 **Fx:**865-4213
(212) 307-5500 .. **Venable LLP** -1270 Av of Amer -NY 10020 **Fx:**307-5598
(631) 287-3053 .. **Venables,** Dierdre S '92 -38 Nugent -Southampton 11968 **Fx:**287-2912
(212) 759-3300 .. **Venaglia,** Peter J '85 (Dornbush SS&V,LLP) -747 3rd Av -NY 10017
(631) 261-8834 .. **Venator,** Christopher '86 (Ingerman S LLP) -150 Motor Pkwy -Hauppauge 11788
(212) 698-3500 .. **Venderbush,** David R '98 (Dechert LLP) -1095 Av of Amer -NY 10036
(518) 373-5085 .. **Venditte,** Tara M '04 AYCO Co -855 Route 146 -Clifton Pk 12065
(212) 310-8000 .. **Venditti,** Danl J '05 %Weil G&M LLP -767 5th Av -NY 10153
(914) 288-9595 .. **Venditti,** David E '85 SrCnsl Gaines GP&N,LLP -1 N Bway -White Plns 10601
(212) 834-0600 .. **Venditto,** Anthony '91 (Gordon & S,PC) -355 Lex Av -NY 10017
(516) 624-6350 .. **Venditto,** John '76 Town Supervisor -54 Audrey Av -Oyster Bay 11771 **Fx:**624-6362
(212) 521-5400 .. **Venditto,** Michl '79 (Reed S LLP) -599 Lex Av -NY 10022
(516) 489-5000 .. **Venditto,** Michl '07 %Town Atty -Town Hall -Hempstd 11550 **Fx:**489-5150
(212) 530-5000 .. **Venditto,** Nicholas '09 %Milbank TH&M LLP -1 Chase Manh Plz -NY 10005
(212) 286-0044 .. **Venegas,** Alfonso '00 Lexcorp Abogados -405 Lex Av -NY 10174 **Fx:**286-0088
(212) 977-2400 .. **Vener,** Anastasia A '10 %JD Bachrach -55 Water -NY 10041
(845) 359-3560 .. **Vener,** Arthur S '96 -95 Dutch Hill Rd -Orangebrg 10962
(914) 779-1100 .. **Veneruso Curto Schwartz & Curto, LLP** -35 E Grassy Sprain Rd -Ynkrs 10710 **Fx:**793-0608
(914) 779-1100 .. **Veneruso,** James J '76 (Veneruso CS&C,LLP) -35 E Grassy Sprain Rd -Ynkrs 10710 **Fx:**793-0608
(914) 666-3354 .. **Venet,** Danl C '81 -195 Seven Brdgs Rd -Mt Kisco 10549 **Fx:**666-3516
(718) 934-1288 .. **Venetoklis,** George A '96 Emmons Enterprises Corp -1821 Emmons Av -Brklyn 11235
(718) 625-8940 .. **Venetsanos,** Angela '97 %B Lawrence -15 Metrotech Ctr N -Brklyn 11201 **Fx:**624-5756
(212) 902-5740 .. **Venezia,** Carmine A '94 %Goldman Sachs -1 NY Plz -NY 10004
(212) 541-2000 .. **Venezia,** Francesca Ann '90 %Bryan C LLP -1290 Av of Amer -NY 10104
(212) 425-1900 .. **Venezia,** Gina M '00 (Freehill H&M LLP) -80 Pine -NY 10005
(212) 267-7000 .. **Venezia,** Louis '75 -110-20 71st Rd -Frst Hlls 11375 **Fx:**(718) 268-5345
(315) 448-8400 .. **Venezia,** Michelle K '09 %Law Dept -233 E Wshngtn -Syracuse 13202 **Fx:**448-8381
(212) 310-8000 .. **Venezia,** Stefania Di Trolio '05 %Weil G&M LLP -767 5th Av -NY 10153
(212) 859-8000 .. **Venezia,** Teresa M '93 (Fried FHS&J LLP) -1 NY Plz -NY 10004
(914) 273-1300 .. **Veneziano,** Anthony F Jr. '84 (Veneziano & Assoc) -84 Business Park Dr -Armonk 10504 **Fx:**273-1303
(212) 344-7042 .. **Vengrow,** Stephen H '83 (Cichanowicz CKV&T,LLP) -61 Bway -NY 10006
(718) 838-7878 .. **Venhuizen,** Anne Marie '10 Bronx Defenders -860 Crtlandt Av -Bronx 10451 **Fx:**665-0100
(212) 335-4500 .. **Venick,** Jon D '10 %DLA Piper LLP -1251 Av of Amer -NY 10020
(212) 859-8000 .. **Venkatasamy,** Sri D '08 %Fried FHS&J LLP -1 NY Plz -NY 10004
(212) 242-4403 .. **Vennema,** Carey '58 -265 W 11th -NY 10014
(212) 744-2777 .. **Venner,** Stuart J '78 -229 E 79th -NY 10075
(718) 857-4646 .. **Venning,** Catina R '07 Bklyn Schl Career Dvlpmnt -510 Clermont Av -Brklyn 11238
(212) 204-8698 .. **Venokur,** Sherri '77 (Lowenstein S PC) -1251 Av of Amer -NY 10020 **Fx:**(973) 422-6811
(212) 724-4080 .. **Ventantonio,** James B '81 (Ventantonio & W) -570 Taxter Rd -Elmsfrd 10523
(212) 724-4080 .. **Ventantonio & Wildenhain** -570 Taxter Rd -Elmsfrd 10523 **Fx:**(914) 703-6688
(718) 783-4545 .. **Venterina,** Marilyn '84 (Sciretta & V, LLP) -26 Park Ct -Staten Isl 10301
(718) 783-4545 .. **Venterina,** Marilyn '84 (Sciretta & V, LLP) -753 Carroll -Brklyn 11215
(212) 962-0800 .. **Venti,** Artie W '10 %Estrin B&L -225 Bway -NY 10007 **Fx:**732-1408
(212) 541-6222 .. **Ventimiglia,** Jos J '98 %Kane K,PC -1350 Av of Amer -NY 10019
(516) 571-2373 .. **Ventra,** Jerome S '61 %Hon J DeMaro -100 Supreme Ct Dr -Mineola 11501
(315) 472-4313 .. **Ventre,** Frank Jr. '65 -5112 W Taft Rd -Liverpool 13088 **Fx:**472-4314
(315) 475-8461 .. **Ventre,** Robt D '64 (Coulter V&M,LLP) -636 Old Liverpool Rd -Liverpool 13088
(646) 428-8403 .. **Ventricelli,** Danl J '88 Protiviti,Inc -1290 Av of Amer -NY 10104
(315) 475-1202 .. **Ventrone,** Mark A '83 -103 E Water -Syracuse 13202 **Fx:**474-8867
(845) 567-1959 .. **Ventry,** Catherine V '79 -711 Bway -Newburgh 12550
(631) 293-4525 .. **Ventry-Kagan,** Amy L '98 (Littler M,PC) -290 Broadhllw Rd -Melvll 11747
(516) 328-9500 .. **Ventura,** Anthony J '80 (Bruno G&V) -99 Tulip Av -Floral Pk 11001 **Fx:**775-8326
(212) 298-5599 .. **Ventura,** Lourdes M '99 Cnsl NYS Senate Majority Leader -250 Bway -NY 10007 **Fx:**298-5605
(212) 348-7449 .. **Ventura,** Lynn Ibis '98 %Legal Srvcs -1 W 125th -NY 10027 **Fx:**348-4093
(516) 812-4500 .. **Ventura,** Melissa M '09 %Stagg TC&W LLP -401 Franklin Av -Gdn Cty 11530
(212) 673-6669 .. **Ventura Ribeiro & Smith** -280 Park Av S -NY 10010
(631) 395-5000 .. **Ventura,** Thos '95 -112 Pineway Av -Mastic Bch 11951
(212) 826-6800 .. **Venturini,** August C '90 (Venturini & Assoc) -230 Park Av -NY 10169 **Fx:**949-6162
(516) 933-4080 .. **Venturini,** Jean M '90 (Davis & V) -176 Woodbury Rd -Hicksvll 11801
(631) 234-0800 .. **Venturo,** Robt G '95 -1 Suffolk Sq -Islandia 11749 **Fx:**582-1737
(212) 762-6051 .. **Venugopal,** Balan '94 Morgan Stanley Trust -1221 Av of Americas -NY 10020
(315) 789-4549 .. **Venuti,** Mark A '86 (Heaton & V,LLP) -118 Genesee -Geneva 14456 **Fx:**781-2295
(607) 723-9324 .. **Venuti,** Michl D '83 %The Cook Bros Companies,Inc -76 Fredrck Bx2247 -Bnghmtn 13902 **Fx:**723-9307
(212) 267-1650 .. **Veny,** Jason R '07 %Fine O&A,LLP -39 Bway -NY 10006
(716) 854-7888 .. **Venzon,** Catharine M '83 (Venzon B,LLP) -300 Delaware Av -Buffalo 14202 **Fx:**854-0294
(212) 726-1252 .. **Vera,** Juan '05 -244 5th Av -NY 10001 **Fx:**726-3252
(516) 564-8000 .. **Vera,** Marcelo F '08 %J Hiebler & Assoc -901 Franklin Av -Gdn Cty 11530 **Fx:**564-1714

(212) 922-9300 .. **Veraja,** John Wesley '83 (Silversmith & V,LLP) -30 Broad -NY 10004
(631) 234-5558 .. **Veraldi,** Domenik Jr. '80 -1601 Vets Hwy -Islandia 11749 **Fx:**234-5080
(516) 571-5892 .. **Veras,** Mercedes '91 Supreme Ct -400 Cnty Seat Dr -Mineola 11501
(212) 406-9710 .. **Veras,** Michl J '89 %Kral CRRP&G,LLP -170 Bway -NY 10038
(516) 887-3650 .. **Verbesey,** Paul '78 -110 Johnson Av -Malverne 11565
(212) 733-6695 .. **Verbraska,** David H '97 %Pfizer Inc -235 E 42nd -NY 10017
(516) 571-3891 .. **Verby,** Christopher J '92 %Hon D Martin -100 Supreme Ct Dr -Mineola 11501 **Fx:**571-1095
(718) 485-0400 .. **Verchick,** Glenn '90 (Werbel W&V LLP) -1465 Rockaway Pkwy -Brklyn 11236 **Fx:**272-3242
(212) 274-9765 .. **Verchick,** Richd '77 -401 Bway -NY 10013 **Fx:**966-1801
(845) 278-8242 .. **Vercollone,** Richd W '80 -26 Red Fox Ln -Brewstr 10509 **Fx:**278-8242
(212) 996-0630 .. **Verde,** Louis J '87 (Verde S&P,LLC) -276 5th Av -NY 10001
(212) 940-8800 .. **Verde,** Michl I '89 (Katten MR LLP) -575 Mad Av -NY 10022
(212) 996-0630 .. **Verde Steinberg & Pontell,LLC** -276 5th Av -NY 10001 **Fx:**(201) 944-4562
(212) 940-3000 .. **Verdejo,** Desiree '09 %Nixon P LLP -437 Mad Av -NY 10022
(212) 807-2996 .. **Verderber,** Arlene R '93 %Thomson Reuters/RIA -195 Bway -NY 10007
(212) 310-8000 .. **Verdesca,** Jos T Jr. '99 (Weil G&M LLP) -767 5th Av -NY 10153
(631) 465-0042 .. **Verdi,** Raymond W Jr. '86 -48 S Srvc Rd -Melvll 11747
(646) 610-5400 .. **Verdi,** Vincent A '94 %NYPD -1 Police Plz -NY 10038
(212) 262-2390 .. **Verdibello,** Robt A '03 %Connell F LLP -888 7th Av -NY 10106
(718) 278-2518 .. **Verdieck,** Emma V '88 -9-29 27th Av -Astoria 11102 **Fx:**278-5027
(212) 683-7100 .. **Verdino,** Alida '03 %Gallo V&K,LLP -90 Broad -NY 10004
(718) 980-0454 .. **Verdirame,** Bart J '97 -166 Bancroft Av -Staten Isl 10306
(212) 504-6000 .. **Verdirame,** Bartholomew '76 (Cadwalader W&T LLP) -1 World Fncl Ctr -NY 10281
(212) 728-8000 .. **Verdirame,** Lauren T '10 %Willkie F&G LLP -787 7th Av -NY 10019
(516) 378-1700 .. **Verdirame,** Peter J '82 (Chesney & M) -2305 Grand Av -Baldwin 11510
(212) 450-4000 .. **Verdolini,** Mario J Jr. '92 (Davis P&W LLP) -450 Lex Av -NY 10017
(212) 464-1656 .. **Verdon,** Anne E '82 JP Morgan Chase & Co -345 Park Av -NY 10154
(212) 446-7599 .. **Verdon,** Jos P '94 McKinsey & Co -55 E 52nd -NY 10055 **Fx:**688-9521
(631) 273-8822 .. **Verdon,** Peter L '96 NYSUT -150 Vndrblt Motor Pkwy -Hauppauge 11788
(212) 578-0333 .. **Verebes,** Jos '92 %MetLife -27-01 Qns Plz N -LIC 11101 **Fx:**578-3916
(518) 785-1900 .. **Verga,** Rita J '06 %PEF -1168-70 Troy-Schnctdy Rd Bx12414 -Albany 12212 **Fx:**785-1323
(212) 250-6805 .. **Vergano,** Sandy K '97 %Deutsche Bk Mtg Cptl -60 Wall -NY 10005
(212) 244-9500 .. **Vergara,** Rafael '00 %White and W LLP -1 Penn Plz -NY 10119
(212) 344-3600 .. **Vergari,** Chase C '03 %Anderson & O,LLP -61 Bway -NY 10006 **Fx:**344-0970
(716) 693-2335 .. **Vergason,** Kendra Schamel '06 %Brick B&E,PC -91 Tremont Bx604 -N Tonawanda 14120
(718) 487-2300 .. **Vergata,** Patricia Murray '74 %Leg Srvcs Corp -256-260 Bway -Brklyn 11211 **Fx:**782-6790
(646) 313-4562 .. **Verghese,** Vinod P '06 Tata America Int'l Corp -101 Park Av -NY 10178
(845) 298-2000 .. **Vergilis,** Gerald A '72 (Vergilis SRD&D,LLP) -1136 Route 9 -Wappingers Fls 12590
(845) 298-2000 .. **Vergilis Stenger Roberts Davis & Diamond, LLP** -1136 Route 9 -Wappingers Fls 12590 **Fx:**298-2842
(716) 853-9555 .. **Vergos,** Chrysanthe E '88 %Leg Aid -237 Main -Buffalo 14203 **Fx:**853-3219
(212) 527-4880 .. **VerHaegen,** Dennis L '80 -625 Mad Av -NY 10022
(585) 546-1980 .. **Verhagen,** Jason P '05 %Fulton F&G LLP -28 E Main -Rchstr 14614
(585) 598-0900 .. **Verhelle,** Wm H '01 First Amer Bancorp -Bx96 -Fairprt 14450 **Fx:**598-0909
(516) 775-6800 .. **Verkowitz,** Charlene K '82 -561 Lakevll Rd -New Hyde Pk 11040
(212) 790-0200 .. **Verkuil,** Paul '68 Cnsl Benj N Cardozo Schl of Law -55 5th Av -NY 10003 **Fx:**790-0345
(212) 756-2000 .. **Verlenden,** Wm L IV '10 %Schulte R&Z LLP -919 3rd Av -NY 10022
(212) 418-4707 .. **Verlizzo,** David J '99 Icon Cptl Corp -100 5th Av -NY 10011
(212) 969-3000 .. **Vermal,** Ana '01 %Proskauer R LLP -1585 Bway -NY 10036
(212) 310-8992 .. **Vermes,** Ann M '92 Weil G&M LLP -767 5th Av -NY 10153
(212) 364-8517 .. **Vermeychuk,** Alexander G '03 Time Warner Cable -60 Columbus Av -NY 10023 **Fx:**364-8460
(914) 945-3158 .. **Verminski,** Brian P '03 IBM -1101 Kitchawan Rd Bx218 -Yorktwn Hts 10598
(212) 336-8000 .. **Vern,** Max '99 %Amster R&E -90 Park Av -NY 10016
(212) 736-0007 .. **Verna,** Anthony M III '06 (Weiss I PLLC) -462 7th Av -NY 10018
(315) 624-3217 .. **Verna,** Jessie M '98 Conmed Corp -525 French Rd -Utica 13502
(212) 455-2000 .. **Vernace,** Anthony F '06 %Simpson T&B LLP -425 Lex Av -NY 10017
(212) 480-1900 .. **Verne,** Maxine H '81 %SCOR US Corp -199 Water -NY 10038
(518) 459-2100 .. **Verner,** Kimberly Strauchon '00 %Pierro Law Grp,LLC -20 Corp Wds Blvd -Albany 12211 **Fx:**459-2200
(718) 250-2000 .. **Verner,** Natasha Kateral '02 %DA -350 Jay -Brklyn 11201 **Fx:**250-2314
(212) 631-8694 .. **Verner,** Richd B '85 (Laytin V LLP) -1 Penn Plz -NY 10119 **Fx:**273-4306
(518) 465-7581 .. **Verni,** Debra A '03 %Herzog Law Firm,PC -7 Southwoods Blvd -Albany 12211
(914) 948-4700 .. **Verni,** John A '88 (Kent HWCV&F,LLP) -111 Church -White Plns 10601
(212) 471-8474 .. **Vernick,** Kevin J '85 (Herzfeld & R,PC) -125 Broad -NY 10004
(212) 208-8832 .. **Vernier,** Michl K '89 %Standard & Poor's -55 Water -NY 10041
(212) 949-7300 .. **Vernon,** Darryl M '82 (Vernon & G,LLP) -261 Mad Av -NY 10016
(718) 206-2411 .. **Vernon,** Donald P '96 (Vernon & Assoc) -9004 161st -Jamaica 11432 **Fx:**297-4263
(212) 949-7300 .. **Vernon & Ginsburg,LLP** -261 Mad Av -NY 10016 **Fx:**697-4432
(914) 333-0610 .. **Vernon,** Jacqueline M '97 N Jain,PC -560 Wht Plns Rd -Tarrytwn 10591
(212) 474-1000 .. **Vernon,** Jeffrey G '09 %Cravath S&M LLP -825 8th Av -NY 10019
(518) 426-4600 .. **Vero,** John R '01 %Couch W,LLP -540 Bway Bx22222 -Albany 12201
(518) 533-3000 .. **Vero,** Sarah Delaney '05 %Bond S&K,PLLC -111 Wshngtn Av -Albany 12210
(212) 309-1000 .. **Veron,** Enid L '08 (Hunton & W) -200 Park Av -NY 10166
(315) 471-3151 .. **Verone,** Christina M '09 %Hancock & E,LLP -1500 AXA Twr I Bx4976 -Syracuse 13221
(212) 715-1000 .. **Veronick,** Alan C '07 %Arnold & P LLP -399 Park Av -NY 10022
(716) 854-1111 .. **Verrastro,** James P '75 (Spadafora & V) -2 Symphony Cir -Buffalo 14201
(718) 324-8900 .. **Verrelli,** Anthony L '95 (McMahon M&V) -147 E 233rd -Bronx 10470
(212) 504-6000 .. **Verrelli,** Megan B '06 %Cadwalader W&T LLP -1 World Fncl Ctr -NY 10281
(716) 852-1888 .. **Verrico,** James A '95 (Cantor LD&P,PC) -350 Main -Buffalo 14202
(212) 819-8200 .. **Verrier,** Hugh H '89 (White & C LLP) -1155 Av of Amer -NY 10036
(518) 399-3228 .. **Verrigni,** Alexandra '93 (AG Verrigni,PLLC) -865 Rivervw Rd -Rexfrd 12148 **Fx:**384-0795
(516) 681-9757 .. **Verrill,** Erika S '95 (Verill & G) -2 Robbins Ln -Jericho 11753 **Fx:**681-9766
(845) 359-5400 .. **Verrilli,** Gregg L '10 %Rogers M&H,PC -100 Dutch Hill Rd -Orangebrg 10962 **Fx:**359-5577
(585) 232-2640 .. **Verrillo,** Maurice J '87 -1 E Main -Rchstr 14614 **Fx:**262-2610
(646) 386-3170 .. **Versace,** Laurie I '96 Supreme Ct -60 Centre -NY 10007
(315) 339-8574 .. **Versace,** Meade H '00 -113 Rose Ln Bx408 -Rome 13442 **Fx:**339-2042
(315) 339-8574 .. **Versace,** Rocco L '69 -113 Rose Ln Bx408 -Rome 13442 **Fx:**339-2042
(518) 377-8321 .. **Versaci,** Romolo U '55 -831 Wright Av -Schnctdy 12309
(516) 803-2518 .. **Verscaj,** James P '81 %Cablevision Sys -1111 Stewart Av -Bethpage 11714
(212) 554-1234 .. **Verscaj,** Martha '85 AXA Financial Inc -1290 Av of Amer -NY 10104 **Fx:**707-3963
(212) 279-9200 .. **Verschell,** David T '95 %Abrams FFEGF&E,LLP -630 3rd Av -NY 10017
(631) 669-6941 .. **Verschuuren,** Chas L '56 -140 Vllg Line Rd -Babylon 11702 **Fx:**669-1483
(212) 536-3900 .. **Versfelt,** David S '77 (K&L Gates LLP) -599 Lex Av -NY 10022
(516) 357-3000 .. **Versichelli,** Michl P '94 (Rivkin R LLP) -926 RXR Plz -Uniondale 11556
(631) 249-6565 .. **Versocki,** James W '99 %Archer BG&L,LLP -425 Broadhllw Rd -Melvll 11747
(212) 326-3939 .. **Verstandig,** Adam S '07 %Jones D -222 E 41st -NY 10017
(518) 843-6000 .. **Vertucci,** Sherri L '90 S Vertucci,PC -177 Wallins Crnrs Rd -Amsterdam 12010 **Fx:**843-6540
(716) 439-7130 .. **Veruto,** Michl C '99 %Niagara County Surrogate's Ct -Niagara County Cthse -Lockprt 14094
(516) 741-7676 .. **Verveniotis,** Steven '86 (Miranda SSSV LLP) -240 Mineola Blvd -Mineola 11501
(212) 725-8900 .. **Verzani,** Marc E '03 -500 5th Av -NY 10110 **Fx:**725-8911
(516) 791-2846 .. **Vesely,** Thos '76 -18 Capts Rd -N Woodmere 11581
(516) 992-8060 .. **Vesnaver,** Paul G '84 -2016 Grand Av -Baldwin 11510 **Fx:**992-8059
(716) 882-2300 .. **Vesper,** Jessica L '07 %McCready & T -6 N Pearl -Buffalo 14202
(718) 855-9000 .. **Vespia,** Dina L '10 %Cullen and D LLP -177 Montague -Brklyn 11201
(845) 361-2800 .. **Vespo,** Jeffrey T '03 Vespo Mrktng Assoc,Inc -Bx60 -Thompson Rdg 10985
(516) 827-1160 .. **Vespoli,** Robt M '93 -28 Lincoln Av -Huntngtn Sta 11746 **Fx:**827-1171
(212) 835-1635 .. **Vessa,** Michl P '82 (Vessa & W,PC) -1 Penn Plz -NY 10119
(516) 248-8010 .. **Vessa,** Michl P '82 (Vessa & W,PC) -626 RXR Plz -Uniondale 11556 **Fx:**522-2831
(212) 835-1635 .. **Vessa,** Philip M '06 %Vessa & W,PC -1 Penn Plz -NY 10119
(516) 248-8010 .. **Vessa,** Philip M '06 %Vessa & W,PC -626 RXR Plz -Uniondale 11556 **Fx:**522-2831
(212) 715-9100 .. **Vessey,** Jonathan B '00 %Kramer LN&F,LLP -1177 Av of Amer -NY 10036
(212) 736-5300 .. **Vessup,** Kareem R '05 %Block O&M LLP -1 Penn Plz -NY 10119
(631) 283-4343 .. **Vest,** Darin K '04 Prudential Douglas Elliman -70 Jobs Ln -Southampton 11968
(518) 456-7002 .. **Vestal,** Erin P '06 Vestal Law,PLLC -1881 Wstrn Av -Albany 12203 **Fx:**456-7004
(631) 751-1464 .. **Vetere,** Laurie A '82 (Legakis & V,PC) -60 Route 25A -E Setauket 11733 **Fx:**751-2264
(845) 831-1405 .. **Vetrano,** Dennis R Jr. '99 (D Vetrano Jr,LLC) -492 Main -Beacon 12508 **Fx:**831-1407
(914) 738-0624 .. **Vetrano,** Patrick J '69 -1 Wolfs Ln -Pelham 10803 **Fx:**712-0951
(631) 472-6727 .. **Vetri,** Bruce P '87 -606-C Montauk Hwy -Bayport 11705 **Fx:**472-6726
(718) 238-9000 .. **Vetri,** Matthew J '60 -8910 3rd Av -Brklyn 11209
(212) 940-8800 .. **Vetri,** Scott M '00 (Katten MR LLP) -575 Mad Av -NY 10022
(631) 501-3100 .. **Vetro,** Christopher T '00 %J Humphreys -3 Huntngtn Quad Bx9028 -Melvll 11747 **Fx:**501-3085
(516) 742-2500 .. **Vetro,** Peter F '71 OfCnsl Gallagher & F -1050 Franklin Av -Gdn Cty 11530
(212) 788-7000 .. **Vetrone,** Louis J '92 %City Cncl Leg Div -250 Bway -NY 10007 **Fx:**788-7034
(212) 730-7750 .. **Vetter,** Christine M '05 %Nicoletti GS&O,LLP -555 5th Av -NY 10017
(212) 267-1900 .. **Vetter,** Gregory '90 (Wade CM) -111 Bway -NY 10006
(212) 661-8000 .. **Vetter,** Thos J '82 OfCnsl Lucas & M,LLP -475 Park Av S -NY 10016
(315) 733-0404 .. **Vetter,** Victor V '95 %WKTV -Smith Hill Rd Bx2 -Utica 13503 **Fx:**733-4893
(212) 819-8200 .. **Vetterli,** John R '99 (White & C LLP) -1155 Av of Amer -NY 10036
(212) 270-6000 .. **Veverka,** James P '08 JP Morgan Chase -270 Park Av -NY 10017
(914) 238-8431 .. **Vexler,** Robt I '83 -25 Hunting Ridge Rd Bx521 -Chappaqua 10514 **Fx:**238-8431
(212) 704-3100 .. **Vezeris,** David J '85 Anthos USA Inc -277 Park Av -NY 10172 **Fx:**768-2516
(212) 571-2640 .. **Vialet,** Theo A '96 -225 Bway -NY 10007 **Fx:**571-2302

(212) 848-9800 .. **Viana**, Sandra '00 %Withers B LLP -430 Park Av -NY 10022
(212) 463-2493 .. **Vianna**, Nicholas P '96 Saatchi & Saatchi -375 Hudson -NY 10014 **Fx**:691-0569
(212) 318-3000 .. **Vibbert**, Jami E M '08 %Fulbright & J LLP -666 5th Av -NY 10103
(212) 836-8000 .. **Vicari**, Angela R '05 %Kaye S LLP -425 Park Av -NY 10022
(914) 784-4982 .. **Vicari**, Dominick G '85 Momentive Performnc Materials Inc -769 Old Saw Mill Rvr Rd -Tarrytwn 10591
(718) 590-2000 .. **Vicario**, Michl A '10 %DA -198 E 161st -Bronx 10451 **Fx**:590-6477
(516) 620-8585 .. **Viceconte**, Roberto '94 %Schwartz & F,PC -3000 Marcus Av -Lk Success 11042 **Fx**:488-1238
(631) 543-3663 .. **Vicedomini**, Thos J '78 OfCnsl Migliore & I,PC -353 Vets Mem'l Hwy -Commack 11725
(212) 225-2000 .. **Vicens**, Elizabeth '06 %Cleary GS&H -1 Lbrty Plz -NY 10006
(212) 852-3621 .. **Vicenzino**, Santo S '96 US Trust Co,NA -114 W 47th -NY 10036 **Fx**:852-1310
(212) 963-5528 .. **Vicien-Milburn**, R Maria '80 United Nations -UN Secretariat 3294 -NY 10017 **Fx**:963-3685
(212) 880-6000 .. **Vicinanza**, Jos J '73 (Torys LLP) -237 Park Av -NY 10017
(585) 238-2000 .. **Vick**, Paul A '76 (Phillips L LLP) -1400 First Fed Plz -Rchstr 14614
(212) 336-2000 .. **Vickers**, A Leah '06 %Patterson BW&T LLP -1133 Av of Amer -NY 10036
(212) 628-2313 .. **Vickers**, Adam M '02 Vickers Realty -428 E 83rd -NY 10028
(212) 506-1700 .. **Vickers**, Jodi I '01 %Kasowitz BT&F LLP -1633 Bway -NY 10019
(212) 788-0891 .. **Vickers**, Judson K '90 %Law Dept -100 Church -NY 10007 **Fx**:788-0367
(212) 446-2300 .. **Vickery**, Alan B '84 (Boies S&F LLP) -575 Lex Av -NY 10022
(212) 446-2300 .. **Vickery**, Howard L '89 (Boies S&F LLP) -575 Lex Av -NY 10022
(212) 944-9112 .. **Vickery**, Kristin E '97 %Strategic Leg Solutions -110 E 42nd -NY 10017 **Fx**:944-8448
(518) 257-1854 .. **Vickey**, Allen J '06 %Hon D Homer US Magistrate -445 Bway -Albany 12207
(585) 425-5210 .. **Vick Lazenby**, Jennifer '98 Maximus Fed Srvcs -50 Square Dr -Victor 14564 **Fx**:425-5292
(518) 474-7330 .. **Vickrey**, Texanne '78 %Dept of Law -The Cptl -Albany 12224
(212) 720-5026 .. **Vicksman**, Sophia Rosner '96 %Fed Reserve Bk -33 Lbrty -NY 10045 **Fx**:785-5748
(516) 877-5700 .. **Vicory**, Anne L '90 %R Tusa -1225 Franklin Av -Gdn Cty 11530 **Fx**:877-5695
(212) 259-8000 .. **Victor**, A Paul '64 (Dewey & L LLP) -1301 Av of Amer -NY 10019
(212) 826-1756 .. **Victor**, Arthur H '73 -530 Park Av -NY 10065
(212) 875-6361 .. **Victor**, Danl J '80 Sesame Workshop -1 Lincoln Plz -NY 10023 **Fx**:875-6111
(718) 590-6312 .. **Victor**, David M '69 %Family Ct -900 Sheridan Av -Bronx 10451
(212) 994-8455 .. **Victor**, Diana P '96 %This Is That Corp -435 W 19th -NY 10011
(845) 298-0521 .. **Victor**, Jonathan M '09 %P Finn,PC -450 Piermont Av -Piermont 10968 **Fx**:(888) 874-5703
(516) 228-3553 .. **Victor**, Kim D '97 %Thaler & G,LLP -90 Merrick Av -E Meadow 11554
(212) 788-9779 .. **Victor**, Meredith S '09 %Law Dept -100 Church -NY 10007 **Fx**:788-0367
(212) 559-8224 .. **Victor**, Monique R '94 %Citibank -909 3rd Av -NY 10022 **Fx**:688-1117
(212) 977-9700 .. **Victor**, Paul A '59 SrCnsl Phillips N LLP -666 5th Av -NY 10103
(212) 310-8000 .. **Victor**, Ronald W '08 %Weil G&M LLP -767 5th Av -NY 10153
(315) 422-1152 .. **Victor**, Sabrina A '07 %Costello C&F,PLLC -500 Plum -Syracuse 13204
(212) 345-7894 .. **Victor**, Sanford L '81 %Marsh USA -1166 Av of Amer -NY 10036 **Fx**:345-4808
(212) 486-6000 .. **Victor**, Saul L '55 (Victor & B, PC) -18 E 41st -NY 10017 **Fx**:486-8668
(212) 709-8142 .. **Victori**, George E '00 G Victori,PC -110 Wall -NY 10005
(212) 971-9725 .. **Victoria**, Susan L '81 -350 5th Av PMB13M -NY 10118
(212) 325-2000 .. **Victoriano**, Jenna Moore '03 Credit Suisse -11 Mad Av -NY 10010
(212) 850-8500 .. **Victory**, Arjang '90 (Bruckmann & V,LLP) -420 Lex Av -NY 10170
(212) 837-6000 .. **Vidal**, Eduardo R '88 (Hughes H&R LLP) -1 Bttry Pk Plz -NY 10004
(518) 473-7051 .. **Vidal**, Maria T Rodriguez '89 %OTDA-Fair Hearings -40 N Pearl -Albany 12243 **Fx**:473-6735
(212) 788-8683 .. **Vidal**, Wm H '08 %Law Dept -100 Church -NY 10007 **Fx**:788-0367
(917) 538-5986 .. **Vidal-Montilla**, Denise '91 -Grnd Cncrs Station Bx1554 -Bronx 10451 **Fx**:(888) 284-7525
(516) 296-7000 .. **Vidas**, Misel '04 %Certilman BA&H,LLP -90 Merrick Av -E Meadow 11554
(718) 382-0011 .. **Vider**, Israel '90 -1507 Av M -Brklyn 11230 **Fx**:382-6574
(516) 742-1103 .. **Viders**, Elaine M '82 %J Viders,PLLC -1 Old Cntry Rd -Carle Pl 11514 **Fx**:747-6384
(516) 742-1103 .. **Viders**, Jay R '74 (J Viders,PLLC) -1 Old Cntry Rd -Carle Pl 11514 **Fx**:747-6384
(212) 371-8008 .. **Vidler**, Gregory P '03 %Guzov O,LLC -600 Mad Av -NY 10022
(516) 352-4353 .. **Vidoni**, Manlio L Jr. '72 -147 Sylvia Ln -New Hyde Pk 11040
(212) 682-4426 .. **Viducich**, Robt R '93 %O'Shea Prtnrs LLP -521 5th Av -NY 10175 **Fx**:682-4437
(212) 425-7200 .. **Vidugiris**, Gaudenis '10 %Kenyon & K,LLP -1 Bway -NY 10004
(718) 505-6650 .. **Vieira**, E Richd '87 %Kaplan & M -75-20 Astoria Blvd -E Elmhrst 11370
(212) 678-5992 .. **Vieira**, Monica Montenegro '00 -410 Cntrl Pk W -NY 10025
(212) 519-7862 .. **Vieland**, Eric J '08 %ACLU -125 Broad -NY 10004 **Fx**:549-2651
(585) 419-8075 .. **Viencek**, Mark F '89 -290 Linden Oaks -Rchstr 14625 **Fx**:(866) 818-9500
(212) 632-5511 .. **Viener**, John D '65 Cnsl Salans LLP -620 5th Av -NY 10020
(516) 741-5252 .. **Viener**, Jos B '93 (Sanders SBWV&G,PC) -100 Hrrcks Rd -Mineola 11501
(516) 741-5252 .. **Viener**, Meryl Sanders '93 (Sanders SBWV&G,PC) -100 Hrrcks Rd -Mineola 11501
(516) 342-2200 .. **Viera**, Theresa J '08 %Schwartzapfel Prtnrs -300 Jericho Quad -Jericho 11753
(212) 326-3939 .. **Vieta**, Amy E '04 (Jones D) -222 E 41st -NY 10017
(212) 259-8000 .. **Viets**, Heather A '07 %Dewey & L LLP -1301 Av of Amer -NY 10019
(212) 238-3000 .. **Viets**, Robt W '75 (Emmet M&M,LLP) -120 Bway -NY 10271
(212) 270-1268 .. **Viets**, Wm C '78 JP Morgan Chase -245 Park Av -NY 10167
(212) 259-8000 .. **Vig**, Vernon E '62 SpclCnsl Dewey & L LLP -1301 Av of Amer -NY 10019
(585) 232-5300 .. **Vigdor**, Justin L '51 (Boylan BCV&W,LLP) -2400 Chase Sq -Rchstr 14604
(585) 454-5650 .. **Vigdor**, Robt M '79 OfCnsl Lacy K LLP -130 E Main -Rchstr 14604
(212) 625-8030 .. **Vigdorchik**, Alla '09 %Sheindlin & S LLP -350 Bway -NY 10013 **Fx**:202-4378
(212) 230-8807 .. **Vigeland**, Peter Kristian '81 (WilmerHale) -399 Park Av -NY 10022
(212) 468-8000 .. **Viggiani**, Katie L '10 %Morrison & F LLP -1290 Av of Amer -NY 10104
(212) 705-7000 .. **Viggiano**, Jeanette M '01 Cnsl Bingham M LLP -399 Park Av -NY 10022
(212) 554-1234 .. **Viggiano**, John F '03 %AXA Financial Inc -1290 Av of Amer -NY 10104 **Fx**:707-3963
(212) 414-9161 .. **Vigil**, Marcos D '03 %Brody & B LLP -1 Penn Plz -NY 10119
(631) 654-7100 .. **Vigilante**, Cynthia C '03 Brookhaven Mem Hospital -101 Hsptl Rd -E Patchogue 11772
(212) 440-2745 .. **Vigliano**, Dean J '83 Colliau EMCK&M -40 Wall -NY 10005
(516) 935-9300 .. **Vigliarolo**, Frank S '85 -380 N Bway -Jericho 11753 **Fx**:932-8353
(631) 622-2080 .. **Vigliotta**, Michl G '10 %M Schulman & Assoc,PC -145 Pinelawn Rd -Melvll 11747 **Fx**:622-2084
(516) 385-2940 .. **Vigliotti**, Luigi '02 L Vigliotti PC -250 Mineola Blvd -Mineola 11501 **Fx**:248-7897
(212) 848-4000 .. **Vigman**, John P H '90 %Shearman & S LLP -599 Lex Av -NY 10022
(914) 287-2011 .. **Vigna**, Anthony P '89 -470 Mamaroneck Av -White Plns 10605 **Fx**:220-6127
(212) 735-3000 .. **Vigna**, Jason C '01 %Skadden ASM&F LLP -4 Times Sq -NY 10036
(212) 490-3000 .. **Vignali**, Rosario M '83 (Wilson EME&D LLP) -150 E 42nd -NY 10017
(914) 323-7000 .. **Vignali**, Rosario M '83 (Wilson EME&D LLP) -3 Gannett Dr -White Plns 10604
(716) 881-3010 .. **Vigneron**, Amy J '91 (Cohen & L,PC) -343 Elmwood Av Bx5204 -Buffalo 14213
(212) 645-5110 .. **Vignola**, Chad A '83 New Visions for Public Schls -320 W 13th -NY 10014
(718) 829-8080 .. **Vignola**, Rocco '71 -3111 E Tremont Av -Bronx 10461 **Fx**:829-9004
(212) 506-5000 .. **Vigod**, Michelle Y '09 %Orrick H&S LLP -51 W 52nd -NY 10019
(212) 857-8704 .. **Vigorita**, Howard A '83 %Ct of Appls -40 Foley Sq -NY 10007
(914) 448-0200 .. **Vigorito**, Alfred P '81 (Bartlett MB&M,LLP) -81 Main -White Plns 10601
(212) 227-3636 .. **Vijayan**, Bindhu '07 %Spar & B,PC -225 Bway -NY 10007
(212) 408-2500 .. **Vijaysankar**, Laxmi '06 %Baker B,LLP -30 Rckfllr Plz -NY 10112
(212) 318-6000 .. **Viklund**, David A '95 OfCnsl Paul HJ&W LLP -75 E 55th -NY 10022
(516) 357-3700 .. **Vikse**, Anna K '06 %Cullen and D LLP -100 Q Roosevelt Blvd -Gdn Cty 11530
(716) 856-1010 .. **Viksjo**, Thos M '76 -69 Delaware Av -Buffalo 14202 **Fx**:856-1008
(212) 298-9712 .. **Viktora**, Richd E '81 Cnsl Skidmore Owings & Merrill LLP -14 Wall -NY 10005 **Fx**:298-9400
(914) 214-8744 .. **Vila**, Gustavo L '99 -1820 Commerce -Yorktwn Hts 10598 **Fx**:214-8737
(718) 780-1776 .. **Vila**, Linda L '95 %Long Island Cllg Hospital -339 Hicks -Brklyn 11201
(607) 778-2403 .. **Vilani**, Regina M '06 %Pub Def -45 Hawley Bx1766 -Bnghmtn 13902 **Fx**:778-2432
(716) 852-5533 .. **Vilardo**, Lawr J '81 (Connors & V,LLP) -1000 Lbrty Bldg -Buffalo 14202
(585) 428-2152 .. **Vile**, Sherry E '89 Cnsl Hon T Stander -99 Exchange Blvd -Rchstr 14614
(212) 227-9755 .. **Vilella**, Dennis G '04 S Young,PC -225 Bway -NY 10007 **Fx**:732-4157
(212) 779-7070 .. **Vilensky**, Robt '80 (Ronemus & V) -112 Mad Av -NY 10016
(212) 474-1000 .. **Viles**, Thos C '88 Cravath S&M LLP -825 8th Av -NY 10019
(212) 259-8000 .. **Vilinsky**, Danielle B '08 %Dewey & L LLP -1301 Av of Amer -NY 10019
(718) 927-0100 .. **Vilinsky**, Edw '90 -1219 Av J -Brklyn 11230 **Fx**:927-0143
(212) 223-3300 .. **Vilkas**, Gil H '93 -211 E 46th -NY 10017 **Fx**:400-0902
(585) 325-6202 .. **Vilkhu**, Vikram S '07 %Relin G&C LLP -28 E Main -Rchstr 14614
(914) 793-1395 .. **Villa**, Leonard F '79 -32 Massitoa Rd -Ynkrs 10710
(518) 402-9003 .. **Villa**, Maria E '90 %DEC -625 Bway -Albany 12233 **Fx**:402-9018
(718) 667-9090 .. **Villa**, Mark A '84 (Menicucci V & Assoc) -2040 Victory Blvd -Staten Isl 10314 **Fx**:667-0700
(973) 342-8507 .. **Villa**, Suhlail C '10 -100 UN Plz -NY 10017
(631) 289-8012 .. **Villacara**, Victor F '73 -60 Medford Av Bx148 -Patchogue 11772 **Fx**:289-8293
(631) 231-1450 .. **Villacci**, Irene V '90 %Feldman K&M,PC -330 Vndrblt Motor Pkwy -Hauppauge 11788
(212) 450-2000 .. **Villafane**, Allison M '02 %NFL -280 Park Av -NY 10017 **Fx**:681-7599
(516) 671-5300 .. **Villafane**, Elena '84 (Polin P&V) -1 Schl -Glen Cove 11542
(631) 789-5210 .. **Villagran**, Ingrid J '02 Catholic Charities -143 Schleigel Blvd -Amityvll 11701
(718) 250-2000 .. **Villalona**, Bernarda A '06 %DA -350 Jay -Brklyn 11201 **Fx**:250-2314
(718) 466-3000 .. **Villa-Lugo**, Carmen J '92 %Civil Ct -1118 Grnd Cncrs -Bronx 10456 **Fx**:466-3006
(315) 946-9707 .. **Villani**, Anthony J '67 (A Villani,PC) -66 William -Lyons 14489 **Fx**:946-0373
(718) 590-2000 .. **Villani**, Cristina A '09 %DA -198 E 161st -Bronx 10451 **Fx**:590-6477
(718) 680-6008 .. **Villani**, James M '95 (Villani & G,PC) -8212 3rd Av -Brklyn 11209 **Fx**:238-8212
(212) 262-2390 .. **Villani**, Jos A '07 %Connell F LLP -888 7th Av -NY 10106
(212) 506-5000 .. **Villani**, Jos R '05 %Orrick H&S LLP -51 W 52nd -NY 10019
(315) 946-9707 .. **Villani**, Mary K '96 %A Villani,PC -66 William -Lyons 14489 **Fx**:946-0373
(315) 946-5445 .. **Villani**, Michele A '96 Wayne Cnty Hall of Justice -54 Broad -Lyons 14489
(516) 228-1300 .. **Villani**, Miriam E '85 (Sahn WC&B,PLLC) -333 Earle Ovngton Blvd -Uniondale 11553
(212) 878-8000 .. **Villani**, Robt A '90 (Clifford C LLP) -31 W 52nd -NY 10019
(516) 832-7423 .. **Villani**, Salvatore '99 Arbor Commercial Mrtge -333 Earle Ovngton Blvd -Uniondale 11553

(212) 482-0001 .. **Villani,** Theresa '81 %Russo K&T LLP -33 Whitehall -NY 10004
(518) 393-8011 .. **Villano,** Jos J '04 %Grasso R&G -751 State -Schnctdy 12307
(631) 265-5344 .. **Villanova,** Donna J '98 -1393 Vets Mem'l Hwy -Hauppauge 11788 **Fx:**549-1091
(212) 294-6700 .. **Villanti,** Christopher A '09 %Winston & S -200 Park Av -NY 10166
(718) 250-2000 .. **Villanueva,** Diana '94 %DA -350 Jay -Brklyn 11201 **Fx:**250-2314
(914) 723-7900 .. **Villanueva,** Jos P '98 (Villanueva & S,PLLC) -700 Wht Plns Rd -Scarsdale 10583 **Fx:**723-7922
(212) 806-5400 .. **Villanueva,** Lacy M '07 %Stroock &S&L LLP -180 Maiden Ln -NY 10038
(212) 977-7095 .. **Villanueva,** Raymond E '94 -119 W 57th -NY 10019 **Fx:**977-7085
(212) 964-0120 .. **Villanueva,** Rey O '06 %Golden RSLB&G,PC -111 John -NY 10038
(212) 256-8000 .. **Villanueva,** Rowena A '03 %Atticus Captl -767 5th Av -NY 10153
(212) 541-2000 .. **Villapol,** Jos J '90 (Bryan C LLP) -1290 Av of Amer -NY 10104
(631) 851-8700 .. **Villar,** Karyn A '99 %DA Courten -33 Kings Hwy -Hauppauge 11788 **Fx:**851-8703
(212) 648-0425 .. **Villar,** Patricia E '04 JP Morgan Chase -245 Park Av -NY 10167
(718) 492-3600 .. **Villar,** Richd '03 -471 54th -Brklyn 11220 **Fx:**492-3008
(718) 605-7050 .. **Villarin,** J Richd '86 -364 Wilson Av -Staten Isl 10312
(716) 648-0510 .. **Villarini,** Robt M '85 (Villarini & H,LLP) -16 Main -Hambrg 14075 **Fx:**648-1806
(212) 687-3860 .. **Villaronga,** Domingo J '04 %Snow BK,PC -605 3rd Av -NY 10158
(718) 222-2028 .. **Villarreal,** Clara '88 %Law Dept -350 Jay -Brklyn 11201 **Fx:**222-2088
(212) 310-8000 .. **Villarreal,** Kristopher S '07 %Weil G&M LLP -767 5th Av -NY 10153
(212) 318-2000 .. **Villarreal,** Miguel A '01 %Bloomberg LP -731 Lex Av -NY 10022
(212) 226-2376 .. **Villasana,** Dennis M '04 %Oved & O LLP -101 Av of Amer -NY 10013 **Fx:**226-7555
(212) 637-3248 .. **Villatora,** Liliana '98 %EPA -290 Bway -NY 10007 **Fx:**637-3104
(212) 455-2000 .. **Villaverde,** Mark D '04 %Simpson T&B LLP -425 Lex Av -NY 10017
(212) 370-5297 .. **Villaverde,** Sergio '97 (S Villaverde,PLLC) -295 Mad Av -NY 10017 **Fx:**370-0561
(718) 590-2000 .. **Villecco,** Thos R '08 %DA -198 E 161st -Bronx 10451 **Fx:**590-6477
(516) 357-3000 .. **Villeck,** Laura E '03 %Rivkin R LLP -926 RXR Plz -Uniondale 11556
(516) 741-5252 .. **Villeck,** Michl F '98 %Sanders SBWV&G,PC -100 Hrrcks Rd -Mineola 11501
(716) 855-0203 .. **Villeda,** Marisa '08 Western NY Law Ctr -237 Main -Buffalo 14203 **Fx:**270-4005
(212) 907-0700 .. **Villegas,** Carol C '03 %Labaton S LLP -140 Bway -NY 10005
(914) 347-2600 .. **Villegas-Ledbetter,** Viviana M '08 %Traub LS&S LLP -7 Skyline Dr -Hawthorne 10532
(718) 932-5465 .. **Villeta,** Adolfo '02 -30-87 46th -Astoria 11103 **Fx:**732-2945
(315) 369-3223 .. **Villiere,** George J '73 -2973 State Route 28 Bx1145 -Old Forge 13420 **Fx:**369-3204
(718) 990-6010 .. **Villiers,** Janice D '90 %St John's Law Schl -8000 Utopia Pkwy -Jamaica 11439 **Fx:**591-1855
(516) 270-5889 .. **Villoni,** Dominic A '69 -80 Brook -Gdn Cty 11530
(718) 293-2941 .. **Vilsaint,** Goetz L '97 -930 Grnd Cncrs -Bronx 10451 **Fx:**410-7776
(212) 521-5400 .. **Vilter,** Robt M '93 (Reed S LLP) -599 Lex Av -NY 10022
(716) 832-5900 .. **Vinal,** Gregory M '90 (Vinal & V) -335 LeBrun Rd -Buffalo 14226 **Fx:**832-6735
(716) 832-5900 .. **Vinal,** Jeanne M '90 (Vinal & V) -335 LeBrun Rd -Buffalo 14226 **Fx:**832-6735
(646) 610-5424 .. **Vinal,** Robt W '78 %NYPD -1 Police Plz -NY 10038
(845) 486-6800 .. **Vinall,** Jessica L '87 OfCnsl McCabe & M LLP -63 Wshngtn Bx509 -Poughkeepsie 12602
(718) 793-9226 .. **Vinar,** Benjamin '61 -144-15 77th Av -Flushng 11367 **Fx:**793-2742
(718) 499-4008 .. **Vinar,** Dov J '91 Ashokan Water Srvcs -515 3rd Av -Brklyn 11215
(212) 440-3312 .. **Vinar,** Jacqueline '89 CNA -40 Wall -NY 10005 **Fx:**440-7644
(718) 376-0216 .. **Vinbaytel,** Vinbaytel,Igor '05 (Bikhman & V,PC) -1909 E 17th -Brklyn 11229 **Fx:**228-6633
(518) 489-1098 .. **Vincelette,** Danl G '96 (D Vincelette,PC) -21 Everett Rd Ext -Albany 12205 **Fx:**489-3304
(718) 222-2114 .. **Vincent,** Dominique E '07 %Law Dept -350 Jay -Brklyn 11201 **Fx:**222-2393
(212) 937-4000 .. **Vincent,** Jason L '97 Fitzpatrick & HTCPA,LLP -12 E 49th -NY 10017
(585) 238-8300 .. **Vincent,** John S '91 %Workers Comp Bd -130 W Main -Rchstr 14614
(212) 239-9669 .. **Vincent,** Nadienne K '85 OfCnsl Catafago Law Firm -350 5th Av -NY 10118 **Fx:**239-9688
(518) 943-6621 .. **Vincent,** Oreste '50 -47 Austin Acres -Catskill 12414 **Fx:**943-3397
(716) 856-1300 .. **Vincent,** Pierre A '02 %Barth SB -43 Court -Buffalo 14202
(914) 249-0100 .. **Vincent,** Robt C Jr. '65 OfCnsl Gellert & K,PC -3010 Wstchstr Av -Purchase 10577
(212) 622-5767 .. **Vincent,** Robt C III '96 JP Morgan Chase & Co -270 Park Av -NY 10017
(212) 745-9754 .. **Vincent,** Steven P '84 Brigade Capital Mgmt -717 5th Av -NY 10022
(212) 509-4600 .. **Vincenti,** John V '94 (Vincenti & V,PC) -80 Broad -NY 10004 **Fx:**509-0406
(212) 509-4600 .. **Vincenti,** Paul J '96 %Vincenti & V,PC -80 Broad -NY 10004 **Fx:**509-0406
(212) 509-4600 .. **Vincenti,** Vito R '58 (Vincenti & V,PC) -80 Broad -NY 10004 **Fx:**509-0406
(212) 434-0100 .. **Vincenzi,** Victor A '88 OfCnsl Litchfield C LLP -420 Lex Av -NY 10170
(212) 692-1000 .. **Vincequerra,** James J '00 (Duane M LLP) -1540 Bway -NY 10036
(212) 758-0050 .. **Vinci,** Thos C '78 %Title Assoc -825 3rd Av -NY 10022 **Fx:**758-8223
(518) 431-0247 .. **Vinciguerra,** Joshua S '00 %US Atty -445 Bway -Albany 12207 **Fx:**431-0249
(212) 785-9100 .. **Vinciguerra,** Lori '86 SrCnsl Paduano & W LLP -1251 Av of Amer -NY 10020
(212) 526-0481 .. **Vinciguerra,** Marlisa '92 %Barclays Capital Inc -745 7th Av -NY 10019
(212) 805-3900 .. **Vinciguerra,** Matthew J '04 %Clausen M PC -1 Chase Manh Plz -NY 10005
(716) 854-3400 .. **Vincton,** Melissa L '10 %Rupp BPC&C LLC -1600 Lbrty Bldg -Buffalo 14202
(315) 363-3602 .. **Vindigni & Betro,PLLC** -146 Madison -Oneida 13421 **Fx:**363-2694
(315) 363-3602 .. **Vindigni,** Richd G '72 (Vindigni & B,PLLC) -146 Madison -Oneida 13421
(212) 872-1000 .. **Vine,** Stephen M '78 -One Bryant Park -NY 10036 **Fx:**872-1002
(212) 841-1000 .. **Vinegrad,** Alan '85 (Covington & B LLP) -620 8th Av -NY 10018
(212) 726-6194 .. **Vinelli,** Ryan L '10 Oxford Univ Press -198 Mad Av -NY 10016
(212) 210-9566 .. **Vines,** Michl E '05 %Alston & B LLP -90 Park Av -NY 10016
(631) 242-6300 .. **Vingan,** Howard F '85 %Heartland Mgmt Corp -1 Exec Dr -Edgewood 11717 **Fx:**242-2820
(845) 947-2727 .. **Vingiello,** J Richd '55 -87 E Lake Rd Bx351 -Tuxedo Pk 10987 **Fx:**947-2729
(212) 715-1000 .. **Vingoe,** D Grant '85 (Arnold & P LLP) -399 Park Av -NY 10022
(212) 594-5300 .. **Vinik,** Joshua H '88 (Milberg LLP) -1 Penn Plz -NY 10119
(518) 455-7500 .. **Vinikoff,** Jerald L '85 %Legis Bill Drftng Comm -310 The Cptl -Albany 12224 **Fx:**455-7598
(212) 269-4900 .. **Vinish,** Danl E '07 %Ford MEW&G,LLP -Wall Street Plz -NY 10005
(914) 948-4800 .. **Vink,** Paul T '87 A Greene & Assoc,PC -202 Mamaroneck Av -White Plns 10601 **Fx:**948-4936
(914) 949-6996 .. **Vinlander,** Vinai C '04 %Penino & M,LLP -180 E Post Rd -White Plns 10601
(212) 594-8292 .. **Vinluan,** Feliz B Q '98 (Vinluan & T) -224 W 35th -NY 10001 **Fx:**594-8296
(646) 761-5684 .. **Vinnitsky,** Oleg "Al" '04 SrCnsl DigiWorld Studios,Inc -540 Main -NY 10044 **Fx:**(530) 430-3467
(718) 790-0905 .. **Vino,** Salvatore J '99 -827 Hylan Blvd -Staten Isl 10305
(212) 474-1000 .. **Vinograd,** Ariane B '09 %Cravath S&M LLP -825 8th Av -NY 10019
(718) 339-4999 .. **Vinogradskaya,** Nataliya '09 ZE Ikhilov,PC -2357 Coney Isl Av -Brklyn 11223
(516) 897-0719 .. **Vinokur,** Nelson A '84 -100 W Park Av -Long Bch 11561 **Fx:**431-4219
(212) 863-6300 .. **Vinokur,** Robt D '02 HPD -100 Gold -NY 10038 **Fx:**863-8201
(718) 648-7700 .. **Vinokurov,** Bianca '98 Frayman Grp,Inc -128 Brighton Beach Av -Brklyn 11235 **Fx:**648-7702
(716) 822-9929 .. **Vinolus,** Athena M '01 %PA Vinolus -609 Ridge Rd -Lackawanna 14218 **Fx:**822-0925
(716) 822-9929 .. **Vinolus,** Peter A '55 -609 Ridge Rd -Lackawanna 14218 **Fx:**822-0925
(212) 237-0000 .. **Vinson & Elkins LLP** -666 5th Av -NY 10103 **Fx:**237-0100
(212) 547-5400 .. **Vint,** Mei-Li D S '07 %McDermott W&E LLP -340 Mad Av -NY 10173
(212) 969-3000 .. **Vinti,** Baldassare '99 SrCnsl Proskauer R LLP -1585 Bway -NY 10036
(212) 308-4411 .. **Viola,** Anthony J '88 (Edwards AP&D LLP) -750 Lex Av -NY 10022
(716) 285-9555 .. **Viola Cummings & Lindsay** -770 Main Bx948 -Niagara Fls 14302 **Fx:**284-0379
(212) 947-3793 .. **Viola,** Danl G '99 (Sadis & G LLP) -551 5th Av -NY 10176
(516) 627-5417 .. **Viola,** Jane Cava '90 OfCnsl R Eredics -103 Plandome Rd -Manhsst 11030 **Fx:**627-5852
(716) 285-9555 .. **Viola,** Robt '76 (Viola C&L) -770 Main Bx948 -Niagara Fls 14302
(518) 434-1022 .. **Violando,** Michl D '97 (Sullivan KO&V, LLP) -152 Central Av -Albany 12206
(716) 439-7085 .. **Violante,** Michl J '71 Niagara Cnty DA -175 Hawley -Lockprt 14094
(716) 843-5700 .. **Violanti,** Joel L '90 %US Atty -138 Delaware Av -Buffalo 14202 **Fx:**551-3052
(716) 662-2664 .. **Violanti,** Lawr J '83 OfCnsl A Hilton -4063 N Buffalo Rd -Orchard Pk 14127 **Fx:**662-2866
(716) 824-2221 .. **Violanti,** Louis P '00 -2221 Abbott Rd -Lackawanna 14218
(718) 448-8372 .. **Violette,** Timothy P '86 -79 Penbroke Av -Staten Isl 10301 **Fx:**442-8112
(718) 262-3407 .. **Violi,** Antoinette '02 Div Legal Srvcs -9231 Union Hall -Jamaica 11433
(914) 698-6200 .. **Violi,** Leonard '91 -910 E Bstn Post Rd -Mamaroneck 10543
(212) 335-9000 .. **Viorst,** Nicholas N '05 %DA -1 Hogan Pl -NY 10013
(212) 742-3390 .. **Vir,** Monica '04 %Lindabury ME&C,PC -26 Bway -NY 10004
(212) 766-5665 .. **Vira,** Anna E '02 %Lefkowicz & G -150 Bway -NY 10038 **Fx:**608-5201
(212) 294-6700 .. **Vira,** Bijal N '03 %Winston & S -200 Park Av -NY 10166
(212) 218-2100 .. **Vira,** Chandrika '08 %Fitzpatrick CH&S -1290 Av of Amer -NY 10104
(212) 872-1000 .. **Vira,** Danl Z '93 -One Bryant Park -NY 10036 **Fx:**872-1002
(212) 964-2160 .. **Virag,** Carol P '76 -160 Bway -NY 10038
(212) 478-7200 .. **Virani,** Zahir A '09 %Hahn & H LLP -488 Mad Av -NY 10022
(212) 929-6030 .. **Virant,** Adam C '04 (Karpf KV&S) -140 Bway -NY 10005 **Fx:**929-6123
(516) 570-3875 .. **Virdone,** John '95 (Seidner V LLP) -19 Park -Manhsst 11030 **Fx:**546-6880
(212) 637-2568 .. **Virella,** Federico E Jr. '73 %US Atty -1 St Andrews Plz -NY 10007
(212) 530-5000 .. **Virga,** Elizabeth M '07 %Milbank TH&M LLP -1 Chase Manh Plz -NY 10005
(212) 363-2500 .. **Virga,** Gerard '80 (Finkelstein & V PC) -90 Broad -NY 10004
(212) 735-3000 .. **Virgadamo,** Elena S '08 %Skadden ASM&F LLP -4 Times Sq -NY 10036
(212) 943-9080 .. **Virginia & Ambinder** -111 Bway -NY 10006
(212) 943-9080 .. **Virginia,** Chas R III '90 (Virginia & A) -111 Bway -NY 10006
(716) 773-5728 .. **Virk,** Kamaljit Kaur '05 OfCnsl S Virk -1561 W River Rd Bx751 -Grand Isl 14072 **Fx:**741-4879
(716) 773-5728 .. **Virk,** Surinder K '01 -1561 W River Rd Bx751 -Grand Isl 14072 **Fx:**741-4879
(315) 793-2225 .. **Virkler,** Sean B '04 %Dept of Law -207 Genesee -Utica 13501 **Fx:**793-2228
(315) 785-3019 .. **Virkler,** Timothy L '02 %Surrogate's Ct -163 Arsenal -Watertwn 13601
(212) 603-6300 .. **Virrill,** David C Jr. '85 %Robinson BLGG&G PC -875 3rd Av -NY 10022
(212) 474-1000 .. **Viruet,** John D '95 Cravath S&M LLP -825 8th Av -NY 10019
(718) 588-6400 .. **Viruet,** Saml '88 -859 Cncrs Vlg W -Bronx 10451
(631) 598-0337 .. **Virzera,** Diane L '94 OfCnsl Ansanelli K&S,LLP -92 Bway -Amityvll 11701 **Fx:**598-0352
(716) 851-2029 .. **Visano,** Ralph M '80 %State Ins Fund -225 Oak -Buffalo 14203

(718) 297-1717 .. **Viscardi Basner & Bigelow,PC** -148-45 Hillside Av -Jamaica 11435 **Fx:**297-1794
(518) 585-6737 .. **Viscardi,** Dominick J '50 (Viscardi H&R LLP) -15 Father Jogues Pl -Ticonderoga 12883 **Fx:**585-3572
(718) 680-5000 .. **Visci,** Jos J '87 JJ Visci -8302 13th Av -Brklyn 11228 **Fx:**833-2912
(607) 753-3019 .. **Visco,** Frank E Sr. '60 -1 Main -Cortlnd 13045 **Fx:**753-3010
(212) 998-8161 .. **Visconti,** Charlene '93 NYU -100 Wshngtn Sq E -NY 10003
(631) 543-7667 .. **Visconti,** Janna P '80 (Sarisohn Law Prtnrs LLP) -350 Vets Mem'l Hwy -Commack 11725 **Fx:**543-7901
(516) 639-5858 .. **Visconti,** Peter C '91 Homeland Sec -232 W Srvc Rd -Champlain 12919
(516) 739-0400 .. **Visconti,** Stephanie '05 %Kelly R&K,LLP -330 Old Cntry Rd -Mineola 11501
(718) 641-4700 .. **Viscusi,** Pasquale '02 NY Racing Assn -Bx90 -Ozone Pk 11417
(212) 382-0700 .. **Vishev,** Anna '99 %Ostrolenk FG&S,LLP -1180 Av of Amer -NY 10036
(516) 437-4385 .. **Vishnick,** Bernard '66 (Vishnick MM LLP) -3000 Marcus Av -Lk Success 11042
(516) 681-6666 .. **Vishnick,** Jason S '99 (Vishnick & V) -110 Wshngtn Av -Holtsvll 11742 **Fx:**681-1666
(516) 681-6666 .. **Vishnick,** Matthew S '97 (Vishnick & V) -110 Wshngtn Av -Holtsvll 11742 **Fx:**681-1666
(516) 437-4385 .. **Vishnick McGovern Milizio LLP** -3000 Marcus Av -Lk Success 11042 **Fx:**437-4395
(585) 419-8800 .. **Visingard,** Sara E '05 %Harris B PLLC -99 Garnsey Rd -Pittsfrd 14534
(315) 699-6214 .. **Visioni,** Guido J '75 -5455 Tourmaline Dr -Clay 13041
(646) 216-2400 .. **Viskovic,** Mauro '01 (Kranjac M&V LLP) -40 Wall -NY 10005 **Fx:**216-2373
(516) 294-1333 .. **Visnius,** Bryan S '02 (DeMartini & Y LLP) -264 Hillside Av -Williston Pk 11596
(347) 273-1356 .. **Visoky,** Neil M '93 -1110 South Av -Staten Isl 10314 **Fx:**273-1456
(716) 853-3700 .. **Vispi,** Jos C '52 -70 Niagara -Buffalo 14202 **Fx:**853-3710
(646) 260-6326 .. **Visser,** James '92 -3400 Paul Av -Bronx 10468
(516) 227-6363 .. **Vista,** Denise J '03 %Amato & Assoc,PC -666 Old Cntry Rd -Gdn Cty 11530 **Fx:**227-6367
(718) 250-2000 .. **Vista,** Michl S '03 %DA -350 Jay -Brklyn 11201 **Fx:**250-2314
(516) 328-2300 .. **Visvader,** Danielle M '06 %Abrams FFEGF&E,LLP -1111 Marcus Av -Lk Success 11042
(212) 264-7500 .. **Viswanath,** Dev B '06 Banad Law PC -291 Bway -NY 10007
(212) 474-1000 .. **Viswanatha,** Veena '10 %Cravath S&M LLP -825 8th Av -NY 10019
(212) 735-3000 .. **Viswanathan,** Anand R '06 %Skadden ASM&F LLP -4 Times Sq -NY 10036
(212) 735-3000 .. **Viswanathan,** Manoj '08 %Skadden ASM&F LLP -4 Times Sq -NY 10036
(212) 279-3230 .. **Viswanathan,** Nadi Ganesan '05 %P Patel,PC -1270 Bway -NY 10001 **Fx:**279-3280
(315) 443-2207 .. **Viswanathan,** Shruti A '05 SU-Cllg of Arts & Sciences -329 Hall of Languages -Syracuse 13244
(315) 218-8000 .. **Viswanathan,** Subhash '96 (Bond S&K,PLLC) -1 Lincoln Ctr -Syracuse 13202
(914) 939-5401 .. **Vita,** Jos A '77 -327 Irving Av -Pt Chester 10573 **Fx:**690-2007
(914) 747-5983 .. **Vita,** Loriann '97 L Vita,PC -Bx309 -Plsntvll 10570 **Fx:**747-1642
(315) 454-3263 .. **Vita,** Therese M '89 %City of Syracuse -Hancock Intl Airport -Syracuse 13212
(516) 622-9200 .. **Vita,** Wm E '84 (Westerman BEM&S,LLP) -1201 RXR Plz -Uniondale 11553
(718) 898-5060 .. **Vitacco,** Guy R '58 (Vitacco & V) -87-10 Qns Blvd -Elmhrst 11373 **Fx:**898-5110
(718) 898-5060 .. **Vitacco,** Guy R Jr. '89 (Vitacco & V) -87-10 Qns Blvd -Elmhrst 11373 **Fx:**898-5110
(914) 921-0333 .. **Vitagliano,** Aldo V '81 -150 Purchase -Rye 10580 **Fx:**921-0796
(212) 751-2288 .. **Vitagliano,** Maria T '80 -403 E 58th -NY 10022 **Fx:**207-9003
(585) 428-5210 .. **Vitale,** Andre A '95 Pub Def -10 N Fitzhugh -Rchstr 14614 **Fx:**428-2234
(631) 852-1650 .. **Vitale,** Edw J '74 %Leg Aid -300 Center Dr -Rvrhead 11901 **Fx:**852-1655
(212) 563-4100 .. **Vitale,** Jos J '90 (Cohen W&S LLP) -330 W 42nd -NY 10036
(631) 777-1700 .. **Vitale,** Jos M '69 (Vitale & L,PC) -445 Broad Hollow Rd -Melvll 11747
(212) 756-2000 .. **Vitale,** Jos P '98 (Schulte R&Z LLP) -919 3rd Av -NY 10022
(631) 777-1700 .. **Vitale & Levitt,PC** -445 Broad Hollow Rd -Melvll 11747 **Fx:**777-7732
(212) 225-2000 .. **Vitale,** Liana R '09 Cleary GS&H -1 Lbrty Plz -NY 10006
(718) 250-2000 .. **Vitale,** Paul W '09 %DA -350 Jay -Brklyn 11201 **Fx:**250-2314
(585) 325-2520 .. **Vitale,** Robt M '02 %Leg Assistance -1 W Main -Rchstr 14614 **Fx:**325-2559
(212) 506-2500 .. **Vitale,** Thos M '81 (Mayer B LLP) -1675 Bway -NY 10019
(845) 358-1069 .. **Vitale,** Victor S '83 -608 W Nyack Rd -W Nyack 10994 **Fx:**358-5817
(212) 801-6859 .. **Vitali,** Louis '89 (Greenberg T,LLP) -200 Park Av -NY 10166
(607) 334-9194 .. **Vitanza DiStefano & Dean,LLP** -15 Maple -Norwich 13815 **Fx:**336-1440
(212) 447-1111 .. **Vitanza,** Lynette N '96 %Ledy-Gurren B&S -475 Park Av S -NY 10016
(607) 723-5341 .. **Vitanza,** Matthew A '78 SpclCnsl Hinman H&K,LLP -80 Exchange Bx5250 -Bnghmtn 13902
(607) 334-9191 .. **Vitanza,** Thos A '58 (Vitanza D&D,LLP) -15 Maple -Norwich 13815
(718) 645-7770 .. **Vitarelli,** Jonathan R '96 %I Finkelshteyn -2305 65th -Brklyn 11204 **Fx:**382-6982
(212) 808-8100 .. **Vitayanon,** Jack Sudla '02 %Kostelanetz & F,LLP -7 Wrld Trd Ctr -NY 10007
(212) 282-5000 .. **Vitek,** Anna Maria '91 %Avon Products -1345 Av of Amer -NY 10105
(212) 537-6616 .. **Vitellio,** Gabrielle R '92 (Cassidy & V) -4315 Webster Av -Bronx 10470
(212) 605-6200 .. **Vitello,** Theresa A '05 %Levy P&K,LLP -800 3rd Av -NY 10022
(212) 902-5457 .. **Vitha,** John R II '92 %Goldman Sachs -1 NY Plz -NY 10004
(212) 417-4357 .. **Viti,** John Thos '87 %Dept of Health -90 Church -NY 10007 **Fx:**417-4392
(716) 856-4200 .. **Viti,** Norman B Jr. '90 (Gibson M&C,LLP) -69 Delaware Av -Buffalo 14202
(212) 262-2390 .. **Vitiello,** Anthony F '94 (Connell F LLP) -888 7th Av -NY 10106
(845) 225-1728 .. **Vitiello,** Frank E '56 -167 Fairway Dr -Carmel 10512
(315) 437-8453 .. **Vitiello,** Ralph J '75 %Hillsberg SC&V -346 N Midler Av Bx275 -Syracuse 13206
(212) 541-5800 .. **Vitiello,** Salvatore J '88 Laurus Captl Mgmt -335 Mad Av -NY 10017 **Fx:**541-4434
(212) 308-4411 .. **Vitkowsky,** Vincent J '81 (Edwards AP&D LLP) -750 Lex Av -NY 10022
(917) 566-7920 .. **Vitolo,** Todd C '01 -105 Duane -NY 10007
(212) 983-3100 .. **Vitti,** Irene C '91 %Enhance Fncl Srvcs -335 Mad Av -NY 10017
(212) 512-2564 .. **Vittor,** Kenneth M '75 %McGraw-Hill -1221 Av of Amer -NY 10020 **Fx:**512-4827
(212) 489-8104 .. **Vittoria & Purdy** -1 Rckfllr Plz -NY 10020 **Fx:**247-5202
(212) 489-8104 .. **Vittoria,** Theo J Jr. '65 (Vittoria & P) -1 Rckfllr Plz -NY 10020
(718) 833-8005 .. **Vittorioso,** Anthony M '84 -9201 4th Av -Brklyn 11209
(212) 513-7788 .. **Vitucci,** John '00 %Ahmuty D&M -123 William -NY 10038
(212) 683-7100 .. **Vitucci,** Matthew J '87 (Gallo V&K,LLP) -90 Broad -NY 10004
(212) 766-1888 .. **Viuker,** Barry M '75 (Morris DA&F) -2 Rector -NY 10006
(914) 798-5400 .. **Vivacharawongse,** Vacharaesorn '08 %Goldberg S LLP -11 Martine Av -White Plns 10606
(212) 564-5005 .. **Viverito,** Matthew K '00 %L Kucherovsky -212 W 35th -NY 10001 **Fx:**564-5121
(212) 530-5000 .. **Vivero,** Frank '96 OfCnsl Milbank TH&M LLP -1 Chase Manh Plz -NY 10005
(631) 486-7575 .. **Viviani,** Douglas D '88 -165 Continental Av -E Northprt 11731 **Fx:**486-7578
(315) 422-1152 .. **Viviani,** Louis J '92 (Costello C&F,PLLC) -500 Plum -Syracuse 13204
(914) 286-3400 .. **Viviano,** Richd A '83 %Leg Aid -1 N Bway -White Plns 10601 **Fx:**682-4112
(212) 756-2000 .. **Vivolo,** Assunta '04 %Schulte R&Z LLP -919 3rd Av -NY 10022
(212) 335-4500 .. **Vivona,** Alycia M '94 OfCnsl DLA Piper LLP -1251 Av of Amer -NY 10020
(607) 723-5341 .. **Vivona,** Peter J '70 (Hinman H&K,LLP) -80 Exchange Bx5250 -Bnghmtn 13902
(212) 732-3200 .. **Vizbaras,** Andris J '90 (Carter L&M LLP) -2 Wall -NY 10005
(212) 403-1000 .. **Vizcarrondo,** Paul Jr. '74 (Wachtell LR&K) -51 W 52nd -NY 10019
(516) 877-2900 .. **Vizza,** Robt G '91 %Bartlett MB&M,LLP -300 Old Cntry Rd -Mineola 11501
(716) 881-2447 .. **Vizzi,** Carl '74 -203 Jersey -Buffalo 14201
(631) 587-2300 .. **Vizzi,** John J '87 (Klein & V,LLP) -370 B Sunrise Hwy -W Babylon 11704
(718) 339-6686 .. **Vizzini,** Chas S '60 -1944 E 17th -Brklyn 11229
(212) 286-8585 .. **Vizzo,** Ana Maria '05 %Heidell PM&B,LLP -99 Park Av -NY 10016
(212) 514-9700 .. **Vlachos,** Dana '97 (Bowman & V) -575 Mad Av -NY 10022 **Fx:**202-4897
(631) 234-0055 .. **Vlachos,** George C '89 G Vlachos,PC -320 Carleton Av -Central Islip 11722 **Fx:**234-2282
(212) 403-7300 .. **Vladeck,** Anne C '79 (Vladeck WE&E,PC) -1501 Bway -NY 10036
(212) 403-7300 .. **Vladeck Waldman Elias & Engelhard,PC** -1501 Bway -NY 10036 **Fx:**221-3172
(631) 667-9666 .. **Vladimir,** Bert '59 OfCnsl Vladimir & Assoc -2137 Deer Prk Av -Deer Pk 11729 **Fx:**667-4710
(718) 261-3838 .. **Vladimir,** Paul '53 -83-19 141st -Jamaica 11435
(631) 667-9666 .. **Vladimir,** Peter L '98 (Vladimir & Assoc) -2137 Deer Prk Av -Deer Pk 11729 **Fx:**667-4710
(631) 667-9666 .. **Vladimir,** Richd M '96 (Vladimir & Assoc) -2137 Deer Prk Av -Deer Pk 11729 **Fx:**667-4710
(212) 506-1700 .. **Vladimirsky,** Michal J '08 %Kasowitz BT&F LLP -1633 Bway -NY 10019
(718) 680-8400 .. **Vlahakis,** Donna B '87 (Hanna & V) -7504 5th Av -Brklyn 11209
(212) 403-1000 .. **Vlahakis,** Patricia '82 (Wachtell LR&K) -51 W 52nd -NY 10019
(917) 534-4900 .. **Vlahoplus,** John C '90 %Zurich Capital Mrkts -105 E 17th -NY 10003
(516) 227-0700 .. **Vlahos,** Louis '88 (Farrell F,PC) -1320 RXR Plz -Uniondale 11556
(212) 964-7400 .. **Vlavianos,** Constantine Gus '87 Smith MDWY&Y,PC -111 John -NY 10038
(212) 557-0020 .. **Vlock,** Stephen '89 (Vlock & Assoc,PC) -230 Park Av -NY 10169 **Fx:**557-7283
(516) 877-5600 .. **Vlosky,** Michelle F '88 %R Tusa -1225 Franklin Av -Gdn Cty 11530 **Fx:**877-5695
(212) 768-6700 .. **Vo,** Stephanie Ha '02 %Sonnenschein N&R LLP -2 World Fncl Ctr -NY 10281
(516) 357-3000 .. **Vobis,** John J Jr. '08 %Rivkin R LLP -926 RXR Plz -Uniondale 11556
(212) 225-2000 .. **Vobis,** Kay-Mario '07 %Cleary GS&H -1 Lbrty Plz -NY 10006
(212) 801-6878 .. **Voce,** Mary F '70 (Greenberg T,LLP) -200 Park Av -NY 10166
(917) 612-0012 .. **Voce-Gardner,** Benjamin J '07 US Navy-JAG -40 Fifth Av -NY 10011
(212) 789-3100 .. **Voci,** Jennifer Batta '01 %Riemer & B LLP -7 Times Sq -NY 10036 **Fx:**719-0140
(914) 333-9627 .. **Vodopia,** John F '93 Philips Electronics -345 Scarborough Rd Bx3001 -Briarclff Mnr 10510 **Fx:**332-0615
(516) 822-3550 .. **Vodovozov,** Alexander G '01 %Hoffmann & B LLP -6900 Jericho Tpk -Syosset 11791 **Fx:**822-3582
(212) 408-5100 .. **Voelker,** Andrea L '10 %Chadbourne & P LLP -30 Rckfllr Plz -NY 10112
(646) 471-8307 .. **Voelker,** Karl E '05 %PricewaterhouseCoopers -300 Mad Av -NY 10017
(212) 824-5822 .. **Voelker,** Keith W '98 %Practising Law Inst -810 7th Av -NY 10019
(212) 816-9223 .. **Voelker,** Martin A '99 %Salomon Smith Barney -388 Greenwich -NY 10013
(716) 633-4030 .. **Voelkl,** Jeffrey F '93 %Robshaw & Assoc,PC -5672 Main -Williamsvll 14221 **Fx:**633-8154
(914) 739-9500 .. **Voelp,** John M '76 -8 John Walsh Blvd -Peekskill 10566 **Fx:**739-9593
(212) 435-3458 .. **Voetsch,** Allison C '07 Port Auth of NY/NJ -225 Park Av S -NY 10003 **Fx:**435-3555
(914) 835-0183 .. **Voetsch,** John M '73 -260 Harrison Av -Harrison 10528 **Fx:**835-1752
(212) 906-1200 .. **Voge,** Wm H '86 (Latham & W) -885 3rd Av -NY 10022

(516) 967-8996 .. **Vogel,** Andrew I '05 %R Dash -14 Valley Ln -Vly Stream 11581
(516) 877-7300 .. **Vogel,** Bernard H '66 (Seavey V & Assoc,LLP) -500 N Bway -Jericho 11753
(800) 553-9940 .. **Vogel,** Bryan J '01 (Robins KM&C LLP) -499 Park Av -NY 10022
(716) 858-2424 .. **Vogel,** Candace K '87 %DA -25 Delaware Av -Buffalo 14202 **Fx**:858-7425
(212) 412-1441 .. **Vogel,** Danl S '04 Barclay's Capital Inc -200 Park Av -NY 10166
(212) 361-8881 .. **Vogel,** David J '84 %Dept Probation -33 Beaver -NY 10004
(631) 499-4996 .. **Vogel,** Debra M L '92 (Levitt & V,LLP) -44 Hamlet Dr -Commack 11725 **Fx**:499-4997
(212) 484-3900 .. **Vogel,** Heike M '01 %Arent F LLP -1675 Bway -NY 10019
(917) 576-7840 .. **Vogel,** Ivan A '87 -110 Wall -NY 10005
(212) 775-8700 .. **Vogel,** Jason M '00 Cnsl Kilpatrick S,LLP -31 W 52nd -NY 10019
(585) 335-2238 .. **Vogel,** John W '76 -125 Main -Dansvll 14437 **Fx**:335-7337
(212) 997-7634 .. **Vogel,** Jos A '82 (Kravet & V,LLP) -1040 Av of Amer -NY 10018 **Fx**:997-7686
(516) 393-2200 .. **Vogel,** Justin M '03 %Garfunkel W,PC -111 Grt Nck Rd -Gt Neck 11021
(212) 837-6859 .. **Vogel,** Kathryn R '08 Hughes H&R LLP -1 Bttry Pk Plz -NY 10004
(212) 661-7100 .. **Vogel,** Liviu '85 (Salon MDN&B,LLP) -292 Mad Av -NY 10017
(212) 310-8000 .. **Vogel,** Mark A '63 (Weil G&M LLP) -767 5th Av -NY 10153
(212) 756-2000 .. **Vogel,** Michl '10 %Schulte R&Z LLP -919 3rd Av -NY 10022
(212) 571-0550 .. **Vogel,** Michl S '92 (Allegaert B&V LLP) -111 Bway -NY 10006
(212) 867-9595 .. **Vogel & Rosenberg** -630 Third Av -NY 10017 **Fx**:949-1857
(716) 947-9126 .. **Vogel,** Stasia Z '78 -6540 Old Lk Shr Rd -Derby 14047
(212) 335-4500 .. **Vogel,** Stephanie K '01 %DLA Piper LLP -1251 Av of Amer -NY 10020
(212) 728-8000 .. **Vogel,** Stephen B '04 %Willkie F&G LLP -787 7th Av -NY 10019
(212) 225-2000 .. **Vogele,** Matthew C '06 %Cleary GS&H -1 Lbrty Plz -NY 10006
(212) 816-2046 .. **Vogeli,** Angela G '02 Citigroup -388 Greenwich -NY 10013
(212) 889-5860 .. **Vogelman,** Donald H '77 -275 Mad Av -NY 10016 **Fx**:686-0252
(212) 761-5151 .. **Vogelsang,** Peter R '88 Morgan Stanley -1585 Bway -NY 10036
(347) 592-2500 .. **Vogelstein,** Lynn B '98 %Bklyn Fam Def Proj -177 Lvngstn -Brklyn 11201 **Fx**:(718) 596-4704
(212) 326-3939 .. **Vogl,** Peter D '88 (Jones D) -222 E 41st -NY 10017
(585) 338-7869 .. **Vogler,** Jennifer E '96 -4007 St Paul Blvd -Rchstr 14617 **Fx**:338-3657
(212) 513-1075 .. **Vogrin,** George J Jr. '00 (Stalker VB&F, LLP) -80 Broad -NY 10004
(212) 301-5324 .. **Vogt,** David M '03 Fox News Channel -1211 Av of Amer -NY 10036
(585) 232-7660 .. **Vogt,** Linda J '88 %R Vogt,PC -144 Exec Blvd -Rchstr 14614 **Fx**:232-5787
(212) 564-9090 .. **Vogt,** Philip P '81 (Altier & V,LLC) -450 7th Av -NY 10123
(585) 232-7660 .. **Vogt,** Richd G '59 (R Vogt,PC) -144 Exec Blvd -Rchstr 14614 **Fx**:232-5787
(315) 474-7447 .. **Vogt,** Thos J '85 -333 E Onondaga -Syracuse 13202
(718) 463-6340 .. **Vohra,** Shalini '95 S Vohra,PC -46-26 Robnsn -Flushng 11355
(212) 922-1920 .. **Vohra,** Vahida '93 %West Group -530 5th Av -NY 10036 **Fx**:867-2404
(212) 972-5430 .. **Voich,** JoAnn S '87 OfCnsl Rosin SM -801 2nd Av -NY 10017
(212) 788-0894 .. **Voigt,** Diana Goell '96 %Law Dept -100 Church -NY 10007 **Fx**:788-0367
(212) 804-4200 .. **Voigt,** Eric J '06 (Mound CW&G) -One Bttry Pk Plz -NY 10004
(212) 553-9137 .. **Vojtisek,** Edwin J '58 -233 Bway -NY 10279
(212) 351-4000 .. **Vojtisek,** John-Paul G '06 %Gibson D&C LLP -200 Park Av -NY 10166
(212) 382-0909 .. **Volack,** Richd R '99 (Peckar & A,PC) -41 Mad Av -NY 10154
(212) 645-7759 .. **Volan,** Douglas B '94 -321 W 24th -NY 10011 **Fx**:645-7759
(212) 969-3000 .. **Volchyok,** Leonid '09 %Proskauer R LLP -1585 Bway -NY 10036
(716) 853-8474 .. **Volcy,** Paul '77 %Dept of Law -350 Main Pl Twr -Buffalo 14202 **Fx**:853-8571
(212) 205-7000 .. **Voldstad,** Michl G '73 (Ashurst LLP) -7 Times Sq -NY 10036
(212) 279-9090 .. **Volet,** Melissa A '04 %Stark & S -One Penn Plz -NY 10119 **Fx**:279-9113
(212) 554-7800 .. **Volet,** Thos '75 (Moses & S LLP) -405 Lex Av -NY 10174
(212) 889-5915 .. **Voletsky,** Peter H '73 -250 W 57th -NY 10107
(516) 620-8433 .. **Volfman,** Boris '05 Weiser LLP -3000 Marcus Av -New Hyde Pk 11042
(518) 473-4596 .. **Volforte,** Michl N '97 %Gov Ofc Emply Rel -Agncy Bldg 2 ESP -Albany 12223
(212) 408-2500 .. **Volftsun,** Anna V '10 %Baker B,LLP -30 Rckfllr Plz -NY 10112
(212) 730-7700 .. **Volgina,** Lida '08 %Michelman & R,LLP -114 W 47th -NY 10036
(315) 479-3900 .. **Volhard,** Joachim J '81 %SSA-ODAR -300 S State -Syracuse 13202 **Fx**:479-3933
(631) 587-3325 .. **Voliano,** Jacqueline '90 -210 Young -W Babylon 11704
(212) 558-4000 .. **Volik,** Heather H '07 %Sullivan & C LLP -125 Broad -NY 10004
(212) 687-0100 .. **Volin,** Abby H '08 %Harris B PLLC -100 Wall -NY 10005
(212) 576-2670 .. **Volino,** Vincent '08 %J Osborn,PC -841 Bway -NY 10003 **Fx**:686-4023
(516) 233-1291 .. **Volitsky,** Aleksandra '09 %Best Deal Corp -1804 Plz Av -New Hyde Pk 11040
(518) 271-7000 .. **Volk,** Catherine M '97 %Kaleel Jamison Cnsltng Grp -297 River -Troy 12180 **Fx**:271-4400
(716) 847-3004 .. **Volk,** Katharine E '85 %OTDA -295 Main -Buffalo 14203 **Fx**:847-3699
(518) 457-2070 .. **Volk,** Mark F '85 %Dept of Tax & Fin -Bldg 9 State Campus -Albany 12227 **Fx**:457-6131
(845) 331-2525 .. **Volk,** Robt F '82 OfCnsl Ryan R&R,LLP -115 Green Bx3153 -Kingston 12402
(800) 285-3000 .. **Volk,** Stephen R '61 Citigroup -399 Park Av -NY 10022
(516) 771-0300 .. **Volkell,** Randolph Z '76 -14 Woodlnd Ter -Merrick 11566
(716) 685-4805 .. **Volker,** Dale M '67 %Senate -5441 Bway -Lancaster 14086 **Fx**:683-2736
(518) 429-4200 .. **Volkheimer,** Stephen H '86 Cnsl Hiscock & B,LLP -50 Beaver -Albany 12207
(212) 230-9115 .. **Volkman,** Brian P '99 Bayerische Landesbank -560 Lex Av -NY 10022
(845) 454-3250 .. **Volkman,** Scott L '86 (Gellert & K,PC) -75 Wshngtn -Poughkeepsie 12601
(631) 929-0900 .. **Volkmann,** Alfred A '65 -6302 Route 25A -Wading Rvr 11792
(212) 683-3560 .. **Volkmann,** Judith E '85 -7 Penn Plz -NY 10001
(718) 631-2346 .. **Volkomer,** Walter E '76 -269 Grnd Cntrl Pkwy -Floral Pk 11005
(212) 903-9000 .. **Volkova,** Elena Y '03 %Linklaters -1345 Av of Amer -NY 10105
(212) 225-2000 .. **Volkovitsch,** Michl J '97 (Cleary GS&H) -1 Lbrty Plz -NY 10006
(212) 351-4500 .. **Vollano,** Lauren R '08 %Epstein B&G,PC -250 Park Av -NY 10177
(212) 455-2000 .. **Vollbracht,** Jason R '07 %Simpson T&B LLP -425 Lex Av -NY 10017
(718) 286-6000 .. **Vollero,** Carly K '08 %DA -125-01 Qns Blvd -Kew Gdns 11415
(212) 648-0332 .. **Vollkommer,** John J '80 JP Morgan Chase -245 Park Av -NY 10167
(212) 458-1985 .. **Vollmer,** Melinda Hervey '92 AIG -175 Water -NY 10038
(516) 870-0335 .. **Vollmer,** Peter '86 (Vollmer & T) -500 N Bway -Jericho 11753 **Fx**:342-1551
(518) 388-2632 .. **Vollmer,** Shanon Dugan '05 MVP Hlth Care -625 State -Schnctdy 12305
(315) 218-8000 .. **Vollmer,** Stephen J '72 (Bond S&K,PLLC) -1 Lincoln Ctr -Syracuse 13202
(212) 670-0380 .. **Vollono,** Craig A '07 -222 Bway -NY 10038
(914) 347-2600 .. **Vollweiler,** Cheryl P '89 (Traub LS&S LLP) -7 Skyline Dr -Hawthorne 10532
(212) 837-1898 .. **Voloshin,** Ronen '02 JP Morgan Chase & Co -522 5th Av -NY 10036
(212) 792-4343 .. **Voloshin,** Victor '02 -245 Park Av -NY 10167
(212) 872-1000 .. **Volow,** Mark J '81 -One Bryant Park -NY 10036 **Fx**:872-1002
(212) 414-9558 .. **Volpe,** Azalia '05 -305 W 28th -NY 10001 **Fx**:414-9558
(212) 318-3000 .. **Volpe,** Dayna L '08 %Fulbright & J LLP -666 5th Av -NY 10103
(516) 877-7788 .. **Volpe,** Gregory J '88 -137 Willis Av -Mineola 11501
(212) 318-6000 .. **Volpe,** Jacquelyn E '06 %Paul HJ&W LLP -75 E 55th -NY 10022
(212) 302-8989 .. **Volpe,** John F '89 %Hedman & C,PC -1185 Av of Amer -NY 10036
(516) 829-0363 .. **Volpe,** Jos A '09 %Israel I&P,LLP -11 Grace Av -Gt Neck 11021 **Fx**:829-0366
(516) 746-4373 .. **Volpe,** Lisa R '92 %MHLS -170 Old Cntry Rd -Mineola 11501 **Fx**:746-0598
(212) 307-5500 .. **Volpe,** Michl J '91 (Venable LLP) -1270 Av of Amer -NY 10020
(914) 946-4777 .. **Volpe,** Suzanne E '08 %Keane & B,PC -445 Hmltn Av -White Plns 10601
(914) 286-3400 .. **Volper,** Raymond C '67 %Leg Aid -1 N Bway -White Plns 10601 **Fx**:682-4112
(212) 425-7200 .. **Volper,** Thos E '09 %Kenyon & K,LLP -1 Bway -NY 10004
(516) 471-1900 .. **Volpi,** Mark J '03 %Havkins RR&V,LLP -114 Old Cntry Rd -Mineola 11501
(718) 332-7700 .. **Volshteyn,** G Gabriella '01 (G Volshteyn,PLLC) -2470 E 16th -Brklyn 11235
(212) 595-6070 .. **Volsky,** Maxim '00 -5 Hanover Sq -NY 10004
(585) 454-5850 .. **Volta,** Sandra E '99 %Wiedman VC&V,PC -5 S Fitzhugh -Rchstr 14614
(585) 454-2020 .. **Voltz,** Robt L '91 %Cellino & B,PC -16 W Main -Rchstr 14614
(914) 761-2252 .. **Volynsky-Weisel,** Regina '02 %Boeggeman G&C,PC -1 Water -White Plns 10601
(631) 852-1745 .. **Volz,** Frank M '98 %Suffolk Cty Surrogate Ct -320 Center Dr -Rvrhead 11901
(914) 478-5129 .. **Volz,** Kristen L '97 %Quinlan & F -245 Saw Mill Rvr Rd -Hawthorne 10532 **Fx**:478-0817
(516) 694-3000 .. **Volz,** Thos M '91 (Guercio & G,LLP) -77 Conklin -Farmngdl 11735 **Fx**:694-4738
(212) 682-0700 .. **Vomvolakis,** George '00 -275 Mad Av -NY 10016 **Fx**:619-1028
(914) 779-1100 .. **Vomvolakis,** John '95 OfCnsl Veneruso CS&C,LLP -35 E Grassy Sprain Rd -Ynkrs 10710
(716) 849-0701 .. **Vona,** Keith R '06 %Lipsitz & P LLC -135 Delaware Av -Buffalo 14202
(716) 434-9177 .. **Vona,** P Andrew '86 (Muscato D&V) -107 East Av -Lockprt 14094
(518) 793-4204 .. **Von Ahn,** John F '99 WWARC -375 Bay Rd -Queensbury 12804 **Fx**:615-2134
(212) 848-9800 .. **Von Albertini,** Babetta Verena '98 %Withers B LLP -430 Park Av -NY 10022
(716) 845-2105 .. **von Arx,** Susan '87 Hon S Green -50 Delaware Av -Buffalo 14202 **Fx**:852-6367
(845) 424-3871 .. **von Bergen,** Camilla W '83 -11 Lewis Ln -Garrison 10524 **Fx**:424-4271
(212) 848-4000 .. **Von Bernuth,** J Mathias '05 %Shearman & S LLP -599 Lex Av -NY 10022
(518) 474-7793 .. **Von Bieberstein,** Gary '77 %Dept of Law -The Cptl -Albany 12224
(212) 225-2000 .. **Von Der Heyde,** Carlos E '08 %Cleary GS&H -1 Lbrty Plz -NY 10006
(212) 306-7160 .. **vonder Lieth,** Melissa A '99 %Ofc Cllctv Brgn -40 Rector -NY 10006 **Fx**:306-7167
(212) 885-4703 .. **Von Der Linden,** Kurt '98 CIBC -425 Lex Av -NY 10017
(212) 837-6887 .. **von der Weid,** Katherine A '05 %Hughes H&R LLP -1 Bttry Pk Plz -NY 10004 **Fx**:299-6887
(585) 225-3446 .. **Von Dohlen,** Wm L '65 (Darweesh LK&V,LLP) -1081 Long Pond Rd -Rchstr 14626
(718) 330-1200 .. **Von Dornum,** Deirdre D '01 %Fed Def of NY Inc -1 Pierrepont Plz -Brklyn 11201 **Fx**:855-0760
(518) 532-7324 .. **Vondrak,** Kitty '82 -Wood Thrush Way Bx475 -Schroon Lk 12870
(212) 977-9700 .. **von Eyb,** Florian A '08 %Phillips N LLP -666 5th Av -NY 10103
(212) 345-5019 .. **von Ferstel,** Alexandra '91 %Marsh USA -1166 Av of Amer -NY 10036 **Fx**:345-4808
(518) 271-1602 .. **Von Fricken Coonrad,** Anne L '06 City Ct -51 State -Troy 12180
(212) 456-7887 .. **Vonick,** Robt R Jr. '80 Walt Disney Co -77 W 66th -NY 10023 **Fx**:456-7834
(315) 435-2014 .. **Voninski,** John R '75 %Hon J Tormey III -Cnty Cthse -Syracuse 13202
(212) 969-3000 .. **Von Klemperer,** Benjamin S '06 %Proskauer R LLP -1585 Bway -NY 10036
(917) 797-6917 .. **Von Kreuzhof,** Adam L '04 -22 Jones -NY 10014
(212) 407-4000 .. **Von Latta,** Christa A '07 %Loeb & L,LLP -345 Park Av -NY 10154
(212) 661-1400 .. **Von Maltitz Derenberg Kunin Janssen & Giordano** -60 E 42nd -NY 10017 **Fx**:370-1819
(212) 940-8800 .. **Von Matthiessen,** Kathryn H '99 (Katten MR LLP) -575 Mad Av -NY 10022
(212) 858-7000 .. **von Maur,** Peter M '87 RBC Capital Markets -1 Lbrty Plz -NY 10006
(212) 626-4100 .. **von Mehren,** Philip T '91 (Baker & M LLP) -1114 Av of Amer -NY 10036
(212) 450-4000 .. **Vonnegut,** Eli J '08 %Davis P&W LLP -450 Lex Av -NY 10017
(212) 669-4166 .. **Von Nostitz,** Glenn F '78 NYSTLA -132 Nassau -NY 10038
(845) 735-6635 .. **von Ohlen,** Richd J '93 -3 1st Lt Ferris Ct -Pearl Rvr 10965

(516) 829-9378 .. **von Ohlen,** Susan '83 -25 W Woods Rd -Gt Neck 11020 **Fx:**773-4868
(631) 366-1010 .. **von Oiste,** Aida A '78 -199 E Main -Smithtwn 11787 **Fx:**265-2832
(212) 558-5500 .. **Von Oiste,** Douglas D '93 %Weitz & L,PC -700 Bway -NY 10003
(631) 473-7676 .. **von Oiste,** James J '59 -505 Main -Pt Jffrsn 11777 **Fx:**473-1020
(212) 783-4717 .. **VonPoblitz,** Adam R '00 Citi Trust -485 Lex Av -NY 10017
(518) 486-6612 .. **Von Reusner,** Susan C '09 %Dept of Law -The Cptl -Albany 12224
(718) 488-7765 .. **von Salis,** Andrew Mead '83 -26 Court -Brklyn 11242
(212) 514-8645 .. **Von Simson,** Chas B '96 (Von Simson & C) -62 William -NY 10005 **Fx:**514-8648
(212) 335-9000 .. **Vonsover,** Amir Jonah '06 %DA -1 Hogan Pl -NY 10013
(212) 464-1226 .. **Von Turk,** Philipp '73 JP Morgan Chase & Co -345 Park Av -NY 10154
(212) 687-4900 .. **von Turk,** Susanne Nienaber '88 (Wormser KG&J LLP) -825 3rd Av -NY 10022
(518) 402-9521 .. **von Wergers,** Mary R '89 %DEC -625 Bway -Albany 12233 **Fx:**402-9018
(212) 963-9741 .. **Von Willisen,** Alexandra J '02 UN-OLA -46th & 1st Av -NY 10017
(212) 751-7700 .. **von Ziegesar,** Petra '03 %Faust & O,LLP -488 Mad Av -NY 10022
(212) 902-1000 .. **Von Zuben,** Heather L '05 Goldman Sachs -1 NY Plz -NY 10004
(631) 324-0587 .. **Voorhees,** Danl G '69 (Dayton & V) -11 Muchmore Ln -E Hampton 11937 **Fx:**324-6593
(631) 852-1760 .. **Voorhees,** Oliver R III '94 %Hon P Mayer -1 Court -Rvrhead 11901
(716) 885-1300 .. **Voos,** Alan D '92 Maxwell & M -1230 Delaware Av -Buffalo 14209
(516) 804-3524 .. **Vopat,** Edw W '06 -14 Bell Ct -Bellmore 11710
(212) 902-2461 .. **Vora,** Parag M '03 Goldman Sachs & Co -85 Broad -NY 10004
(212) 546-4000 .. **Vora,** Sonia '98 %Bristol-Myers Squibb -345 Park Av -NY 10154 **Fx:**546-9562
(212) 218-5500 .. **Voreadis,** Evanthia M '01 %Seyfarth S LLP -620 8th Av -NY 10018
(212) 344-1600 .. **Vorhies,** Jennifer A '05 %Florio PS&F -80 Wall -NY 10005
(914) 995-2698 .. **Vorperian,** John M '88 %Cnty Atty -148 Martine Av -White Plns 10601 **Fx:**995-5858
(585) 720-9190 .. **Vorrasi,** John F '76 -Bx220 -N Greece 14515 **Fx:**720-9617
(212) 636-6000 .. **Vorspan,** Rachel '80 %Fordham Univ Sch of Law -140 W 62nd -NY 10023 **Fx:**636-6899
(518) 462-5814 .. **Vorwald,** Katherine J '10 %Becker & B -148 Central Av Bx575 -Albany 12201 **Fx:**462-6836
(212) 883-3900 .. **Vos,** John A '05 Spcl Funds Conservation Comm -205 E 42nd -NY 10017
(516) 889-5391 .. **Voses,** Courtney C '83 -603 W Olive -Long Bch 11561
(212) 308-4411 .. **Voses,** Marc S '99 %Edwards AP&D LLP -750 Lex Av -NY 10022
(646) 471-3000 .. **Voss,** David M '05 PricewaterhouseCoopers LLP -300 Mad Av -NY 10017
(212) 326-3939 .. **Voss,** Elena J '06 %Jones D -222 E 41st -NY 10017
(888) 332-6461 .. **Voss,** Marianne E '99 Fair Factories Clearinghouse -244 5th Av -NY 10001
(646) 386-4034 .. **Vossen,** Victoria A '88 %Hon W Wetzel -100 Centre -NY 10013
(212) 506-2500 .. **Vossler,** Andrea H '10 Mayer B LLP -1675 Bway -NY 10019
(212) 815-7474 .. **Vota,** James P '93 %Bk of NY -101 Barclay -NY 10007
(212) 318-6000 .. **Votano,** Bret C '04 %Paul HJ&W LLP -75 E 55th -NY 10022
(212) 599-7575 .. **Votava,** Christian '07 %Harnik & F LLP -645 5th Av -NY 10022 **Fx:**867-8120
(585) 203-1211 .. **Votava,** G Jos Jr. '81 (Seneca Financial Advisors) -400 Linden Oaks -Rchstr 14625 **Fx:**286-3858
(212) 715-1000 .. **Voth,** Wm H '81 OfCnsl Arnold & P LLP -399 Park Av -NY 10022
(718) 720-2877 .. **Votto & Cassata, LLP** -60 Bay -Staten Isl 10310 **Fx:**720-2999
(718) 720-2877 .. **Votto,** Jos '94 (Votto & C,LLP) -60 Bay -Staten Isl 10310
(516) 248-2047 .. **Voulo,** Raymond S '79 -145 Willis Av -Mineola 11501 **Fx:**746-4647
(212) 585-8101 .. **Vourakis,** Marie D '84 -401 Bway -NY 10013
(718) 250-2000 .. **Vourderis,** John '09 %DA -350 Jay -Brklyn 11201 **Fx:**250-2314
(646) 519-8728 .. **Vournas,** Elena C '03 The Claims Conference -535 8th Av -NY 10018
(914) 946-1400 .. **Vouté,** Arthur J Jr. '60 OfCnsl Vouté LM&C,LLP -170 Hmltn Av -White Plns 10601
(914) 946-1400 .. **Vouté Lohrfink Magro & Collins,LLP** -170 Hmltn Av -White Plns 10601 **Fx:**946-8024
(212) 867-9797 .. **Vouté Lohrfink Magro & Collins,LLP** -100 Park Av -NY 10017 **Fx:**867-5959
(315) 701-5722 .. **Voutsinas,** Elise M '05 -109 S Warren -Syracuse 13202 **Fx:**472-7070
(212) 980-0120 .. **Voutsinas,** Jean '94 Cnsl Frankfurt KK&S,PC -488 Mad Av -NY 10022
(914) 286-6426 .. **Vozza,** Antonio '89 Cnsl 1st Amer Title -1 Water -White Plns 10601 **Fx:**(646) 487-6932
(516) 294-5432 .. **Vozza,** David N '02 %Kern AC&S,PC -1325 Franklin Av -Gdn Cty 11530
(718) 654-3330 .. **Vozza,** F Frank '78 (Vozza & H) -2435 E Chester Rd -Bronx 10469 **Fx:**654-1374
(914) 381-9100 .. **Vozza,** Jos '00 -500 Mamaroneck Av -Harrison 10528 **Fx:**517-7580
(212) 661-2900 .. **Vozza,** Jos C '03 %Kriss & F LLP -360 Lex Av -NY 10017
(718) 863-2897 .. **Vozza,** Marjorie Varrichio '91 %M Varrichio & Assoc -3144 Wstchstr Av -Bronx 10461 **Fx:**863-3136
(914) 517-7570 .. **Vozza,** Rocco E '91 -500 Mamaroneck Av -Harrison 10528
(315) 472-6676 .. **Vozzo,** H Larry '81 Alario & Assoc,PC -500 S Salina -Syracuse 13202
(212) 964-6611 .. **Vozzo,** Michl D '06 %Lester SK&D -120 Bway -NY 10271
(212) 983-9330 .. **Vozzolo,** Antonio '99 Faruqi & F,LLP -369 Lex Av -NY 10017 **Fx:**983-9331
(212) 903-9000 .. **Vranka,** Lawr A Jr. '90 (Linklaters) -1345 Av of Amer -NY 10105
(212) 986-1200 .. **Vranum,** Peter J '90 Cnsl Gordon HR&C LLP -355 Lex Av -NY 10017
(718) 544-9400 .. **Vreeburg,** Elisabeth A '82 -125-10 Qns Blvd -Kew Gdns 11415 **Fx:**263-0134
(212) 566-7188 .. **Vreeland,** John R '01 Cnsl Genova B&G -115 Bway -NY 10006
(212) 458-1816 .. **Vreeland,** Wm G III '95 %AIG -175 Water -NY 10038
(212) 768-6700 .. **Vrettos,** Christine '02 %Sonnenschein N&R LLP -2 World Fncl Ctr -NY 10281
(212) 889-9362 .. **Vrionedes,** Leandros A '89 (L Vrionedes,PC) -381 Park Av S -NY 10016 **Fx:**202-6407
(212) 237-0000 .. **Vris,** Jane Lee '89 (Vinson & E LLP) -666 5th Av -NY 10103
(212) 318-6000 .. **Vrola,** Jean M '07 %Paul HJ&W LLP -75 E 55th -NY 10022
(212) 449-4823 .. **Vroman,** Ann Marie '90 Cnsl Merill Lynch -4 World Fncl Ctr -NY 10080
(212) 310-8078 .. **Vron,** Victoria '05 %Weil G&M LLP -767 5th Av -NY 10153
(516) 694-3000 .. **Vrona,** Maureen Halloran '80 %Guercio & G,LLP -77 Conklin -Farmngdl 11735 **Fx:**694-4738
(718) 522-1020 .. **Vrontos,** Kliopatra '98 %Rubenstein & R -16 Court -Brklyn 11241
(917) 237-2900 .. **Vrudhula,** Rajiv M '03 Axiom Legal -75 Spring -NY 10012
(212) 594-5300 .. **Vu,** Anne Marie '04 %Milberg LLP -1 Penn Plz -NY 10119
(212) 455-2000 .. **Vu,** Kim Thien '07 %Simpson T&B LLP -425 Lex Av -NY 10017
(212) 918-3000 .. **Vu,** Vi Tuong '08 %Hogan L LLP -875 3rd Av -NY 10022
(212) 403-1000 .. **Vucic,** Ante '01 (Wachtell LR&K) -51 W 52nd -NY 10019
(212) 940-8800 .. **Vujovic,** Jovana '06 %Katten MR LLP -575 Mad Av -NY 10022
(212) 446-4800 .. **Vuk,** Wm T '00 (Kirkland & E LLP) -153 E 53rd -NY 10022
(212) 335-4500 .. **Vukelj,** John '05 %DLA Piper LLP -1251 Av of Amer -NY 10020
(212) 819-8200 .. **Vukelj,** Stacey Leece '04 %White & C LLP -1155 Av of Amer -NY 10036
(914) 777-2500 .. **Vuksanaj,** Christine M '96 -274 Wht Plns Rd -Eastchstr 10709
(718) 515-0314 .. **Vuksanaj,** Pashko '91 -287 E Gun Hill Rd -Bronx 10467 **Fx:**515-6913
(516) 292-8100 .. **Vulcan,** Millicent J '88 %Nassau/Sfflk Law Srv -1 Helen Keller Way -Hempstd 11550 **Fx:**292-6529
(315) 474-2943 .. **Vulcano,** Saml '80 (Sugarman Law Firm,LLP) -211 W Jffrsn -Syracuse 13202
(212) 416-8521 .. **Vullo,** Maria T '88 %Dept of Law -120 Bway -NY 10271
(212) 998-2240 .. **Vullo,** Stephanie '95 %NYU Ofc Leg Cnsl -70 Wshngtn Sq S -NY 10012 **Fx:**995-3048
(212) 430-6400 .. **Vulpis,** Jessica M '06 %Carabba L LLP -100 William -NY 10038
(212) 935-3000 .. **Vuolo,** Ellen M '99 %Mintz LCFG&P,PC -666 3rd Av -NY 10017
(212) 259-8000 .. **Vuolo,** Matthew S '06 %Dewey & L LLP -1301 Av of Amer -NY 10019
(212) 819-8200 .. **Vuoso,** George '88 Cnsl White & C LLP -1155 Av of Amer -NY 10036
(718) 537-4958 .. **Vuotto,** Elizabeth Anne '05 %ODAR-SSA -226 E 161st -Bronx 10451 **Fx:**590-1673
(315) 435-2170 .. **Vural,** Elisabeth R '96 %Cnty Atty -421 Mntgmry -Syracuse 13202 **Fx:**435-5729
(585) 987-2800 .. **Vurraro,** Kristopher J '02 %Woods OG LLP -2 State -Rchstr 14614
(914) 995-3148 .. **Vutera,** David L '92 %Cnty Atty -148 Martine Av -White Plns 10601 **Fx:**995-5858
(212) 698-3500 .. **Vyas,** Ashish Sukh Dev '06 Dechert LLP -1095 Av of Amer -NY 10036
(212) 731-7731 .. **Vyas,** Hamel '97 Mt Sinai Med Ctr -1 Gustave L Levy Pl Bx1514 -NY 10029
(212) 237-0000 .. **Vydashenko,** Nikolay V '08 %Vinson & E LLP -666 5th Av -NY 10103
(212) 455-2000 .. **Vyskocil,** Mary K '84 (Simpson T&B LLP) -425 Lex Av -NY 10017
(718) 238-2021 .. **Vyzas,** Vincas M '89 (Vyzas & Assoc,PC) -250 93rd -Brklyn 11209 **Fx:**238-2099
(914) 997-0500 .. **Wable,** Kesav M '09 %Lowey DC&H,PC -1 N Bway -White Plns 10601
(516) 812-4500 .. **Wabnik,** Debra L '94 (Stagg TC&W LLP) -401 Franklin Av -Gdn Cty 11530
(212) 714-1720 .. **Wachenfeld,** Wm T '83 OfCnsl Tompkins MW&B LLP -140 Bway -NY 10005
(646) 386-3650 .. **Wachenheim,** Cynthia '96 %Supreme Ct-Law Dept -60 Centre -NY 10007
(718) 222-2314 .. **Wachs,** Melissa '07 %Law Dept -350 Jay -Brklyn 11201 **Fx:**222-2373
(212) 573-3986 .. **Wachs,** Mitchell '88 %Pfizer Inc -235 E 42nd -NY 10017
(212) 944-1580 .. **Wachs,** Stuart '84 (Fogel & W PC) -420 5th Av -NY 10018 **Fx:**944-1869
(212) 408-5100 .. **Wachsberger,** Chaim '77 (Chadbourne & P LLP) -30 Rckfllr Plz -NY 10112
(718) 692-9873 .. **Wachsman,** Bernard C '81 -26 Court -Brklyn 11242
(516) 624-2999 .. **Wachsman,** Harvey F '76 -55 Wall -NY 10005 **Fx:**(917) 591-1301
(516) 487-1212 .. **Wachsman,** Harvey F '76 -1010 Nrthrn Blvd -Gt Neck 11021
(516) 624-2999 .. **Wachsman,** Kathryn M '78 -55 Wall -NY 10005 **Fx:**(917) 591-1301
(212) 889-0686 .. **Wachsman,** Marea L '01 (Schreier & W,LLP) -240 Mad Av -NY 10016 **Fx:**889-0279
(718) 875-1300 .. **Wachspress,** Ruth J '02 %Appllt Div 2nd Dept -45 Monroe Pl -Brklyn 11201 **Fx:**858-2446
(212) 909-6000 .. **Wachsstock,** Chas E '99 Cnsl Debevoise & P LLP -919 3rd Av -NY 10022
(212) 640-8159 .. **Wachsstock,** Suzanne E '95 %Amer Exp -200 Vesey -NY 10285
(516) 482-6363 .. **Wachstock,** Jacob S '76 -185 Grt Nck Rd -Gt Neck 11021
(212) 490-1002 .. **Wacht,** James R '82 %Sierra Rlty -12 E 46th -NY 10017
(212) 754-4141 .. **Wacht,** Thos J '73 -445 Hmltn Av -White Plns 10601 **Fx:**593-7157
(212) 371-6500 .. **Wachtel,** Gary J '86 -14 E 60th -NY 10022 **Fx:**371-7722
(212) 529-0223 .. **Wachtel,** George D '99 %Kuby & P,LLP -119 W 23rd -NY 10011
(212) 953-6000 .. **Wachtel,** Marcy L '83 (Katsky K LLP) -605 3rd Av -NY 10158
(212) 909-9500 .. **Wachtel & Masyr,LLP** -885 2nd Av -NY 10017 **Fx:**371-0320
(845) 628-7577 .. **Wachtel,** Robt S '93 Capital Market Rsrcs -69 Wixon Pond Rd -Mahopac 10541
(212) 480-5284 .. **Wachtel,** Saml A '81 %Insurance Dept -25 Beaver -NY 10004 **Fx:**480-5272
(212) 344-7778 .. **Wachtel,** Steven J '05 %Bachner & Assoc -26 Bway -NY 10004
(212) 909-9500 .. **Wachtel,** Wm B '80 (Wachtel & M,LLP) -885 2nd Av -NY 10017
(212) 918-3000 .. **Wachtell,** Genevieve Treuille '09 %Hogan L LLP -875 3rd Av -NY 10022
(212) 403-1000 .. **Wachtell,** Herbert M '55 (Wachtell LR&K) -51 W 52nd -NY 10019
(212) 403-1000 .. **Wachtell Lipton Rosen & Katz** -51 W 52nd -NY 10019 **Fx:**403-2000
(914) 385-4100 .. **Wachtell,** Marc J '81 (Hoffman W&R,LLP) -399 Knollwood Rd -White Plns 10603
(212) 998-2240 .. **Wachter,** Hope A '01 %NYU Ofc Leg Cnsl -70 Wshngtn Sq S -NY 10012 **Fx:**995-3048
(718) 897-1044 .. **Wachter,** Howard C '68 -6625 103rd -Frst Hlls 11375
(212) 661-8000 .. **Wachter,** Jason R '09 %Lucas & M,LLP -475 Park Av S -NY 10016
(212) 564-9800 .. **Wachter,** Julia L '07 %D'Agostino L&L,LLP -345 7th Av -NY 10001
(212) 509-3900 .. **Wachtler,** Lauren J '79 (Mitchell S&K LLP) -12 E 49th -NY 10017
(631) 761-7000 .. **Wachtler,** Solomon '56 %Touro Cllg Law Ctr -225 Eastvw Dr -Central Islip 11722
(646) 290-9137 .. **Waciura,** Victoria Odette '99 AB Data Ltd -244 Mad Av -NY 10016

(212) 454-2580 .. **Wacker,** Allison Lee '05 Deutsche Bk Asset Mgmt -280 Park Av -NY 10017
(212) 836-8000 .. **Wacker,** Jeanna M '04 %Kaye S LLP -425 Park Av -NY 10022
(212) 755-5510 .. **Wacksman,** Jeffrey E '86 (Loeb B & Prtnrs) -505 Park Av -NY 10022
(212) 725-6100 .. **Wacksman,** Lee N '96 %Amsterdam & L -9 E 40th -NY 10016
(212) 755-5510 .. **Wacksman,** Leonard '51 Cnsl Loeb B & Prtnrs -505 Park Av -NY 10022
(212) 819-8200 .. **Wactlar,** Adam E '07 %White & C LLP -1155 Av of Amer -NY 10036
(516) 937-5900 .. **Wactlar,** Edw S '71 (Moomjian WW&C LLP) -100 Jericho Quad -Jericho 11753
(212) 407-4000 .. **Waddell,** Mark E '85 (Loeb & L,LLP) -345 Park Av -NY 10154
(212) 855-3260 .. **Waddle,** Jeffrey T '91 %Depository Trust -55 Water -NY 10041 **Fx:**855-3279
(212) 225-2000 .. **Wade,** Anthony E '06 %Cleary GS&H -1 Lbrty Plz -NY 10006
(518) 435-9000 .. **Wade & Burstein,PLLC** -250 Osborne Rd -Albany 12205 **Fx:**438-8700
(607) 734-2271 .. **Wade,** Caitlin E '02 %Sayles & E -1 W Church -Elmira 14901
(718) 990-6015 .. **Wade,** Cheryl L '89 %St John's Law Schl -8000 Utopia Pkwy -Jamaica 11439 **Fx:**591-1855
(212) 267-1900 .. **Wade Clark Mulcahy** -111 Bway -NY 10006 **Fx:**267-9470
(845) 897-1600 .. **Wade,** Danl B '04 %Rosicki R & Assoc,PC -2 Summit Ct -Fishkill 12524 **Fx:**897-2648
(607) 274-5461 .. **Wade,** David J '09 DA -320 N Tioga -Ithaca 14850 **Fx:**274-5429
(212) 267-1900 .. **Wade,** Dennis M '79 (Wade CM) -111 Bway -NY 10006
(646) 264-3650 .. **Wade,** Diane Z '74 %US Dept of Labor -201 Varick -NY 10014 **Fx:**264-3660
(518) 435-9000 .. **Wade,** Elizabeth A '96 Wade & B,PLLC -250 Osborne Rd -Albany 12205
(518) 453-9000 .. **Wade,** Elizabeth A '96 Gateway Title Agency,LLC -250 Osborne Rd -Albany 12205 **Fx:**438-8700
(347) 404-9133 .. **Wade,** George H '80 %Civil Ct -141 Lvngstn -Brklyn 11201 **Fx:**(718) 643-3733
(212) 848-4000 .. **Wade,** George J '63 OfCnsl Shearman & S LLP -599 Lex Av -NY 10022
(212) 490-1700 .. **Wade,** Jeffrey P '03 %Wiggin & D -450 Lex Av -NY 10017
(212) 728-8000 .. **Wade,** Jennifer E '09 %Willkie F&G LLP -787 7th Av -NY 10019
(718) 250-4269 .. **Wade,** Jill L '89 %Leg Aid -111 Lvngstn -Brklyn 11201 **Fx:**250-4243
(212) 415-9200 .. **Wade,** John B III '76 (Dorsey & W LLP) -250 Park Av -NY 10177
(845) 758-0096 .. **Wade,** Kevin T '94 -22 North Dr -Red Hook 12571 **Fx:**758-1297
(212) 220-3610 .. **Wade,** Locksley O '06 L Wade,LLC -110 Wall -NY 10005 **Fx:**253-4142
(718) 457-6727 .. **Wade,** Malachy J '49 -82-52 61st Rd -Middl Vllg 11379
(914) 793-7737 .. **Wade,** Peter J '66 -68 Main -Tuckahoe 10707 **Fx:**793-8936
(212) 318-6000 .. **Wade,** Susan M '00 %Paul HJ&W LLP -75 E 55th -NY 10022
(212) 558-4000 .. **Wade,** Wm H '09 %Sullivan & C LLP -125 Broad -NY 10004
(212) 468-8000 .. **Wade-Gery,** Wm R '98 (Morrison & F LLP) -1290 Av of Amer -NY 10104
(845) 986-1156 .. **Wadeson,** Jeanine Garritano '96 %Bonacic KCM&B,LLP -2 Bank Bx391 -Warwick 10990
(212) 336-0181 .. **Wadhwa,** Sanjay '97 %SEC -3 World Fncl Ctr -NY 10281 **Fx:**336-1323
(212) 440-2938 .. **Wadhwaney,** Manju Kotumal '93 CNA Ins -40 Wall -NY 10005
(212) 233-1212 .. **Wadia,** Darius '98 (D Wadia.LLC) -233 Bway -NY 10279 **Fx:**571-9149
(212) 687-5911 .. **Wadler,** Barry A '74 -711 3rd Av -NY 10017 **Fx:**(646) 658-0599
(845) 254-5508 .. **Wadler,** Lisa R '85 -47293 Route 28 Bx550 -Fleischmanns 12430 **Fx:**254-5020
(845) 331-4100 .. **Wadlin,** John J '70 (Rusk WH&M,LLP) -255 Fair Bx3356 -Kingston 12402
(716) 856-4000 .. **Wadsworth,** James M '65 (Hodgson R LLP) -140 Pearl -Buffalo 14202
(585) 232-6500 .. **Wadsworth,** Jeffrey A '07 %Harter S&E LLP -1600 Bausch & Lomb Pl -Rchstr 14604
(212) 227-3550 .. **Waesche Sheinbaum & O'Regan, PC** -111 Bway -NY 10006 **Fx:**267-5767
(607) 754-0184 .. **Wagar,** Dorothy B '73 -724 Pickwick Dr -Vestal 13850 **Fx:**757-0326
(212) 337-4208 .. **Wagenbrenner,** Anne E '00 Thomson Reuters -195 Bway -NY 10007
(212) 801-9363 .. **Wagener,** Jackson P '07 %Greenberg T,LLP -200 Park Av -NY 10166
(212) 558-4000 .. **Wagener,** Wm H '04 %Sullivan & C LLP -125 Broad -NY 10004
(516) 697-2947 .. **Wagenknecht,** Valerie T '95 -23 Johnstone Rd -Gt Neck 11021
(914) 472-3546 .. **Wager,** Lisa K '84 -19 Dickel Rd -Scarsdale 10583
(914) 995-3497 .. **Wager,** Maria I '92 %DA -111 Martin Luther King Blvd -White Plns 10601 **Fx:**995-3363
(914) 785-2000 .. **Wager,** Patricia '79 %Ciba Corp -540 Wht Plns Rd -Tarrytwn 10591 **Fx:**785-4831
(516) 240-8900 .. **Wager,** Patricia Anne '94 (Torre LGG&R,LLP) -100 Jericho Quad -Jericho 11753
(212) 714-3541 .. **Waggaman,** Parker P '95 -292 5th Av -NY 10001
(212) 326-2000 .. **Waglow,** Natasha L '10 %O'Melveny & M LLP -7 Times Sq -NY 10036
(518) 943-9184 .. **Wagman,** James M '84 -452 Main Bx488 -Catskill 12414 **Fx:**943-9186
(212) 592-1400 .. **Wagman,** Joel W '81 Cnsl Herrick,F LLP -2 Park Av -NY 10016
(212) 687-3860 .. **Wagman,** Leonard W '56 OfCnsl Snow BK,PC -605 3rd Av -NY 10158
(212) 878-8000 .. **Wagman,** Philip R '95 (Clifford C LLP) -31 W 52nd -NY 10019
(212) 637-3141 .. **Wagner,** Amelia M '89 %EPA -290 Bway -NY 10007 **Fx:**637-3096
(212) 298-5138 .. **Wagner,** Andrea L '04 Leg Aid -49 Thomas -NY 10013
(212) 687-7770 .. **Wagner,** Andrew J '95 %Rosen L&C LLP -275 Mad Av -NY 10016
(212) 415-3600 .. **Wagner,** Barry '67 %Omnicom Group -437 Mad Av -NY 10022 **Fx:**415-3530
(518) 474-8158 .. **Wagner,** Belinda A '86 %Dept of Law -The Cptl -Albany 12224
(718) 250-2000 .. **Wagner,** Brian M '10 %DA -350 Jay -Brklyn 11201 **Fx:**250-2314
(518) 447-3200 .. **Wagner,** Bruce J '86 (McNamee LT&W,PC) -677 Bway -Albany 12207
(845) 586-3065 .. **Wagner,** Carey '86 -555 Main Bx1213 -Margaretvll 12455 **Fx:**586-3066
(585) 241-2811 .. **Wagner,** Catherine M '97 NYS Dept Educ - OPD -85 Allen -Rchstr 14608
(212) 754-7000 .. **Wagner,** Chas H '79 Cnsl Danziger D&M -405 Park Av -NY 10022 **Fx:**758-0143
(212) 918-3000 .. **Wagner,** Christine M '07 %Hogan L LLP -875 3rd Av -NY 10022
(212) 790-4500 .. **Wagner,** Claudia '78 (Manatt P&P,LLP) -7 Times Sq -NY 10036
(516) 676-4600 .. **Wagner,** Colton P '50 (Humes & W) -147 Forest Av Bx546 -Locust Vly 11560
(212) 559-6463 .. **Wagner,** David J '81 %Citigroup -425 Park Av -NY 10022
(212) 909-5842 .. **Wagner,** David L '83 KPMG LLP -757 3rd Av -NY 10017
(845) 638-1400 .. **Wagner,** David M '65 (Freedman WT&W) -130 N Main -New Cty 10956
(212) 813-8800 .. **Wagner,** David R '05 %Goodwin P LLP -620 8th Av -NY 10018
(212) 481-9600 .. **Wagner Davis,PC** -99 Mad Av -NY 10016 **Fx:**481-8245
(516) 742-1444 .. **Wagner Doman & Leto,PC** -227 Mineola Blvd -Mineola 11501 **Fx:**742-1204
(631) 288-6550 .. **Wagner,** Dwayne S '95 D Wagner,PC -135 Main -Westhmptn Bch 11978 **Fx:**288-6553
(718) 667-7400 .. **Wagner,** Edw '91 (Wagner & W,LLP) -2508 Amboy Rd -Staten Isl 10306 **Fx:**667-3338
(716) 373-1600 .. **Wagner,** Edw J '73 (Wagner & H) -214 N Barry -Olean 14760
(212) 715-9100 .. **Wagner,** Elise '82 (Kramer LN&F,LLP) -1177 Av of Amer -NY 10036
(212) 661-1500 .. **Wagner,** Eric M '86 %S Kessler -122 E 42nd -NY 10168 **Fx:**297-0777
(212) 370-7602 .. **Wagner,** Eric M '00 UBS Financial Srvcs Inc -200 Park Av -NY 10166
(212) 986-6000 .. **Wagner,** Eric S '97 (Kleinberg KW&C,PC) -551 5th Av -NY 10176
(212) 686-7700 .. **Wagner,** Frank L '79 (Mazur CR&S PC) -1250 Bway -NY 10001
(516) 742-1444 .. **Wagner,** Gary A '78 (Wagner D&L,PC) -227 Mineola Blvd -Mineola 11501
(212) 500-2425 .. **Wagner,** Gretchen A '98 ARTstor,Inc -151 E 61st -NY 10065 **Fx:**500-2418
(631) 777-7774 .. **Wagner,** Harry '72 H Wagner,PC -445 Broadhllw Rd -Melvll 11747 **Fx:**777-7732
(716) 373-1600 .. **Wagner & Hart** -214 N Barry -Olean 14760 **Fx:**373-3246
(212) 385-1191 .. **Wagner,** Howard M '99 %Goodman & J LLP -75 Broad -NY 10004
(516) 280-2245 .. **Wagner,** Jacqueline R '92 -1055 Franklin Av -Gdn Cty 11530
(212) 225-2000 .. **Wagner,** Jade K '07 %Cleary GS&H -1 Lbrty Plz -NY 10006
(718) 921-6601 .. **Wagner,** Jimmy F '04 %T Beinert -155 Bay Ridge Av -Brklyn 11220 **Fx:**921-6609
(212) 889-4588 .. **Wagner,** Joan '80 -343 E 30th -NY 10016
(631) 979-3000 .. **Wagner,** John M '86 (Certilman BA&H,LLP) -1393 Vets Mem'l Hwy -Hauppauge 11788
(212) 481-9600 .. **Wagner,** John R '76 (Wagner D,PC) -99 Mad Av -NY 10016
(212) 715-9100 .. **Wagner,** Jonathan M '84 (Kramer LN&F,LLP) -1177 Av of Amer -NY 10036
(212) 771-9300 .. **Wagner,** Jorge S '01 CIT Grp -505 5th Av -NY 10017
(718) 667-7400 .. **Wagner,** Judy '86 (Wagner & W,LLP) -2508 Amboy Rd -Staten Isl 10306 **Fx:**667-3338
(716) 200-5050 .. **Wagner,** Judy Cuzzacrea '02 %Harris B PLLC -726 Exchange -Buffalo 14210
(212) 310-8000 .. **Wagner,** Justin '07 %Weil G&M LLP -767 5th Av -NY 10153
(212) 450-4000 .. **Wagner,** Karen E '77 (Davis P&W LLP) -450 Lex Av -NY 10017
(516) 496-5822 .. **Wagner,** Karen E '06 %T Spina -170 Froehlich Farm Blvd -Woodbury 11797 **Fx:**496-5420
(914) 997-0900 .. **Wagner,** Karen L '93 %Wormser KG&J LLP -399 Knollwood Rd -White Plns 10603
(212) 834-0178 .. **Wagner,** Kathryn E '96 National Music Publishers Assoc,Inc -601 W 26th -NY 10001
(315) 422-7111 .. **Wagner,** Kenneth L '91 (Blitman & K LLP) -443 N Franklin -Syracuse 13204
(212) 309-6000 .. **Wagner,** Kristy M '05 %Morgan L&B LLP -101 Park Av -NY 10178
(716) 439-7653 .. **Wagner,** Laura A '03 Dept of Social Srvcs -20 East Av Bx506 -Lockprt 14095 **Fx:**439-7794
(212) 474-1000 .. **Wagner,** Margot A '89 Cravath S&M LLP -825 8th Av -NY 10019
(914) 941-5668 .. **Wagner,** Matthew C '97 %Collen IP -80 S Highland Av -Ossining 10562 **Fx:**941-6091
(718) 802-2731 .. **Wagner,** Maureen F '04 ACS -330 Jay -Brklyn 11201 **Fx:**802-2798
(212) 738-6620 .. **Wagner,** Michl A '73 -1 North End Av -NY 10282
(212) 227-7200 .. **Wagner,** Michl G '75 (Klein W&M) -277 Bway -NY 10007
(212) 416-8000 .. **Wagner,** Monica Blong '08 %Dept of Law -120 Bway -NY 10271
(607) 257-5165 .. **Wagner,** Paul E '94 (Shea S,ALC) -1405 Hanshaw Rd -Ithaca 14850
(631) 482-1433 .. **Wagner,** Peter J '94 (Horan & W PC) -366 Vets Mem'l Hwy -Commack 11725 **Fx:**482-1436
(914) 273-5698 .. **Wagner,** Philip '46 -21 Meadow Hill Ln -Armonk 10504 **Fx:**273-3124
(212) 395-7022 .. **Wagner,** Richd H '82 %Verizon -140 West -NY 10007
(516) 627-7778 .. **Wagner,** Robt A '82 -1615 Nrthrn Blvd -Manhsst 11030 **Fx:**365-3164
(585) 223-2034 .. **Wagner,** Robt H '48 -150 Perinton Hills Ofc Park -Fairprt 14450
(212) 969-3000 .. **Wagner,** Robt P '02 %Proskauer R LLP -1585 Bway -NY 10036
(212) 576-5923 .. **Wagner,** Robin M '86 NY Life Ins Co -51 Mad Av -NY 10010
(212) 924-1220 .. **Wagner,** Sara N '97 %Teamsters Local 237 Legal Svcs -216 W 14th -NY 10011
(518) 455-5753 .. **Wagner,** Sarah L '05 Cnsl Asm R Brodsky -422 Lgsltv Ofc Bldg -Albany 12248
(212) 586-5800 .. **Wagner,** Stephen '85 (Cohen TS&W PC) -420 Lex Av -NY 10170
(212) 481-9600 .. **Wagner,** Steven R '78 (Wagner D,PC) -99 Mad Av -NY 10016
(212) 343-8000 .. **Wagner,** Stuart '88 (Morrison & W) -49 W 38th -NY 10018
(212) 644-4420 .. **Wagner,** Sue B '87 %Fabiani C&H,LLP -570 Lex Av -NY 10022
(212) 732-3200 .. **Wagner,** Theo R '68 (Carter L&M LLP) -2 Wall -NY 10005
(516) 208-8511 .. **Wagner,** Walter P '81 -510 Merrick Rd Bx369 -Rockvll Ctr 11571 **Fx:**208-8512
(212) 808-2700 .. **Wagner,** Wm R '94 (Pepper H LLP) -620 8th Av -NY 10018
(212) 243-1313 .. **Wagner-Goldstein,** Katherine A '07 Leg Action Ctr -225 Varick -NY 10014 **Fx:**675-0286
(845) 639-2060 .. **Wagner-Mele,** Amy B '95 Clarkstown Town Atty -10 Maple Av -New Cty 10956 **Fx:**639-2189
(212) 688-1900 .. **Wagowski,** Evan I '08 %Greenberg T&H,LLP -767 3rd Av -NY 10017
(212) 265-6888 .. **Wagstaff,** Anne M E '07 %Porzio B&N,PC -156 W 56th -NY 10019
(845) 306-1000 .. **Wah,** Carolyn R '85 %Watchtower -100 Watchtower Dr -Patterson 12563 **Fx:**306-0709

(212) 325-3039 ..**Wah,** David M '91 Credit Suisse -11 Mad Av -NY 10010
(212) 710-2643 ..**Wahab,** Kaiser '02 (Wahab & M,LLC) -1115 Bway -NY 10011 **Fx:**(646) 619-4195
(212) 451-2300 ..**Wahba,** Denise '07 %Olshan GFR&W LLP -65 E 55th -NY 10022
(212) 248-3140 ..**Wahba,** Monica '10 %Drinker B&R LLP -140 Bway -NY 10005
(212) 373-3000 ..**Wahbeh,** Ramy J '02 %Paul WRW&G LLP -1285 Av of Amer -NY 10019
(585) 227-2610 ..**Wahl,** Gerald F '81 (Bansbach Z&W,PC) -31 Erie Canal Dr -Rchstr 14626
(212) 373-3000 ..**Wahl,** Katharine R '09 %Paul WRW&G LLP -1285 Av of Amer -NY 10019
(518) 462-6765 ..**Wahlberg,** Wendy '81 %Leg Aid -55 Colvin Av -Albany 12206 **Fx:**427-8352
(212) 455-2000 ..**Wahlquist,** Andrea K '00 (Simpson T&B LLP) -425 Lex Av -NY 10017
(212) 302-3300 ..**Wahrman,** Harvey L '70 %Graf Repetti & Co -1114 Av of Amer -NY 10036
(212) 816-4803 ..**Wahrman,** Miriam Leah '89 Citibank NA -388 Greenwich -NY 10013
(212) 839-5300 ..**Waibsnaider,** Meital '08 %Sidley A LLP -787 7th Av -NY 10019
(212) 267-6700 ..**Waichman,** Herbert L '84 (Parker WA LLP) -111 John -NY 10038
(516) 466-6500 ..**Waichman,** Herbert L '84 (Parker WA LLP) -6 Hrbr Park Dr S -Pt Wash 11050
(212) 743-9244 ..**Waide,** Offer '03 -26 Bway -NY 10004 **Fx:**363-7703
(212) 984-1652 ..**Wailand,** Adele R '74 Case Pomeroy & Co -521 5th Av -NY 10175
(212) 701-3000 ..**Wailand,** George '73 SrCnsl Cahill G&R LLP -80 Pine -NY 10005 **Fx:**269-5420
(212) 574-1200 ..**Wain,** Royce L '93 -1 Bttry Pk Plz -NY 10004 **Fx:**480-8421
(212) 610-6300 ..**Wainer,** David K '99 (Allen & O) -1221 Av of Amer -NY 10020
(212) 458-1198 ..**Wainschtok,** Gabriela S '04 AIG -175 Water -NY 10038
(212) 755-1222 ..**Wainstein,** Michl '99 Private Capital Grp -1500 Bway -NY 10036
(212) 732-2000 ..**Waintraub,** Alan J '09 %Cullen and D LLP -44 Wall -NY 10005
(212) 504-6000 ..**Wainwright,** Jonathan M '68 (Cadwalader W&T LLP) -1 World Fncl Ctr -NY 10281
(212) 902-1831 ..**Wainwright,** Lauren L '01 Goldman Sachs -1 NY Plz -NY 10004
(212) 935-5300 ..**Wainwright,** Nanine J '05 (Seaman & W,LLP) -160 E 38th -NY 10016 **Fx:**935-5301
(631) 329-3777 ..**Wainwright,** Stuyvesant II '48 -Bx199 -Wainscott 11975 **Fx:**537-3777
(631) 324-2992 ..**Wainwright,** Stuyvesant '95 (S Wainwright IV,PC) -10 Pantigo Rd -E Hampton 11937 **Fx:**324-1424
(212) 918-3000 ..**Waisbrot,** Morris '76 (Hogan L LLP) -875 3rd Av -NY 10022
(212) 468-4800 ..**Waiser,** Lindsay M '06 %Davis & G LLP -1740 Bway -NY 10019
(646) 964-6257 ..**Waiser,** Melissa E '00 GloCap Search -156 W 56th -NY 10019
(212) 458-1534 ..**Waiser,** Neal N '96 %AIG Tech Srvcs -175 Water -NY 10038
(212) 809-1111 ..**Waisman,** Andrea E '93 OfCnsl Morgan MA -39 Bway -NY 10006
(212) 310-8000 ..**Waisman,** Shai Y '97 (Weil G&M LLP) -767 5th Av -NY 10153
(716) 856-4000 ..**Waiss,** Marla '03 %Hodgson R LLP -140 Pearl -Buffalo 14202
(518) 584-5844 ..**Wait,** Chas V Jr. '08 %Adirondack Trust Co -473 Bway -Saratoga Spgs 12866
(518) 869-5450 ..**Wait,** David A '57 -Bx38190 -Albany 12203 **Fx:**869-5450
(212) 878-7900 ..**Wait,** John A '06 (Fox R LLP) -100 Park Av -NY 10017
(518) 581-8800 ..**Wait,** Natalie I '08 %Lemery G LLC -60 Railroad Pl -Saratoga Spgs 12866
(516) 937-5900 ..**Waite,** Kevin W '97 (Moomjian WW&C LLP) -100 Jericho Quad -Jericho 11753
(718) 723-8122 ..**Waite,** Patricia Ann '98 -187-04A Linden Blvd -St Albans 11412 **Fx:**949-0411
(585) 258-2800 ..**Waite,** Stephen H '61 OfCnsl Underberg & K LLP -300 Bausch & Lomb Pl -Rchstr 14604
(518) 463-4257 ..**Waite,** Stephen J '79 (Waite & Assoc,PC) -2123 Wstrn Av -Guilderlnd 12084 **Fx:**463-4594
(212) 735-3000 ..**Waitman,** Adam G '96 Cnsl Skadden ASM&F LLP -4 Times Sq -NY 10036
(212) 949-9022 ..**Waitman,** Jennifer R '98 (Abelman F&S) -666 3rd Av -NY 10017
(212) 446-8141 ..**Waitman,** Robt M '96 %McKinsey & Co -55 E 52nd -NY 10055 **Fx:**688-9521
(718) 897-8924 ..**Waitzman,** Jay L '86 -102-20 67th Dr -Frst Hlls 11375
(212) 938-5000 ..**Waizer,** Harry '83 %Cantor Fitzgerald -110 E 59th -NY 10022
(212) 442-0421 ..**Wakefield,** Robin '00 %Law Dept -100 Church -NY 10007 **Fx:**788-0367
(518) 464-2022 ..**Wakefield Wells,** Theresa A '06 AYCO -1 Wall Bx15073 -Albany 12212
(212) 218-2100 ..**Wakeley,** John J '08 %Fitzpatrick CH&S -1290 Av of Amer -NY 10104
(518) 438-2000 ..**Wakeman,** Robt G '80 (Lombardi WWHA&D PC) -III Winners Cir -Albany 12205
(212) 836-8000 ..**Waks,** Jay W '72 (Kaye S LLP) -425 Park Av -NY 10022
(212) 577-3641 ..**Waksberg,** Judith D '83 %Leg Aid -199 Water -NY 10038 **Fx:**577-3520
(212) 310-8000 ..**Waksman,** Ted S '74 (Weil G&M LLP) -767 5th Av -NY 10153
(212) 421-6565 ..**Walaski,** Joni L '85 -52 Vndrblt Av -NY 10017
(716) 824-2559 ..**Walawender,** Norman F '58 -244 Martin Rd -Buffalo 14218 **Fx:**827-7884
(212) 547-5400 ..**Walbridge,** Morgan '05 %McDermott W&E LLP -340 Mad Av -NY 10173
(212) 506-5000 ..**Walcavich,** Sarah E '06 %Orrick H&S LLP -51 W 52nd -NY 10019
(212) 906-1200 ..**Walch,** Christeen N A '10 %Latham & W -885 3rd Av -NY 10022
(646) 252-1358 ..**Walcott,** Diana '04 MTA Civ Rights -2 Bway -NY 10004
(212) 227-6821 ..**Walcott,** Gavin L '98 %Roura & M -233 Bway -NY 10279
(212) 640-5941 ..**Walcott,** Wanji J '01 %Amer Exp -200 Vesey -NY 10285
(212) 326-3939 ..**Walcott-Edim,** Vicki R '02 %Jones D -222 E 41st -NY 10017
(315) 435-2170 ..**Walczyk,** Robt S Jr. '82 %Cnty Atty -421 Mntgmry -Syracuse 13202 **Fx:**435-5729
(212) 957-7600 ..**Wald,** Alexandra S '98 (Cohen & G LLP) -800 3rd Av -NY 10022
(212) 471-8475 ..**Wald,** Bernard J '55 (Herzfeld & R,PC) -125 Broad -NY 10004
(212) 446-3343 ..**Wald,** Michl J '96 %MSI Claims,Inc -560 Lex Av -NY 10022
(212) 940-8800 ..**Wald,** Wayne A '90 (Katten MR LLP) -575 Mad Av -NY 10022
(718) 522-3333 ..**Waldauer,** Jonathan '08 %Children's Law Ctr -44 Court -Brklyn 11201 **Fx:**522-7376
(315) 471-2129 ..**Waldauer,** Marc '74 -447 E Wshngtn -Syracuse 13202 **Fx:**478-4352
(212) 310-8706 ..**Waldbaum,** Brian A '00 Cnsl Weil G&M LLP -767 5th Av -NY 10153
(212) 753-5000 ..**Waldbaum,** Maxim H '71 (Schiff H LLP) -900 3rd Av -NY 10022
(212) 583-9700 ..**Waldbaum,** Scott I '99 Viscogliosi Bros LLC -505 Park Av -NY 10022 **Fx:**826-9509
(718) 618-2500 ..**Waldeier,** Valerie A '06 %Civil Ct -851 Grnd Cncrs -Bronx 10451 **Fx:**590-7294
(212) 541-2000 ..**Walden,** Alexander D '09 %Bryan C LLP -1290 Av of Amer -NY 10104
(212) 421-9630 ..**Walden,** David A '90 %Smythe Masterson & Judd -230 Park Av -NY 10169 **Fx:**421-9665
(212) 351-4000 ..**Walden,** James '92 (Gibson D&C LLP) -200 Park Av -NY 10166
(212) 259-8000 ..**Walden,** Katherine Huneke '04 %Dewey & L LLP -1301 Av of Amer -NY 10019
(212) 937-7215 ..**Walden,** S Calvin '97 (WilmerHale) -399 Park Av -NY 10022
(212) 756-2000 ..**Waldenberg,** Alan S '79 (Schulte R&Z LLP) -919 3rd Av -NY 10022
(212) 310-8000 ..**Walder,** Jessica N '09 %Weil G&M LLP -767 5th Av -NY 10153
(212) 530-5000 ..**Walder,** Jonathan M '10 %Milbank TH&M LLP -1 Chase Manh Plz -NY 10005
(716) 858-2424 ..**Walder,** Kristen M '06 %DA -25 Delaware Av -Buffalo 14202 **Fx:**858-7425
(212) 574-1200 ..**Walder,** Robt A '79 (Seward & K LLP) -1 Bttry Pk Plz -NY 10004
(212) 909-9500 ..**Walderman,** Richd A '85 OfCnsl Wachtel & M,LLP -885 2nd Av -NY 10017
(516) 802-5402 ..**Waldhauser,** Jay Ian '02 -485 Underhill Blvd -Syosset 11791
(212) 816-4228 ..**Waldhof,** Sharka Eva '89 Citibank NA -388 Greenwich -NY 10013
(212) 530-5000 ..**Waldie,** Justin J '10 %Milbank TH&M LLP -1 Chase Manh Plz -NY 10005
(212) 318-6000 ..**Walding,** Matthew W '05 %Paul HJ&W LLP -75 E 55th -NY 10022
(516) 535-4300 ..**Waldinger,** Jesse S '74 J Waldinger Assoc,PC -990 Stewart Av -Gdn Cty 11530 **Fx:**535-2930
(914) 666-8033 ..**Waldinger,** Steven E '88 (Banks SG&W,LLP) -118 N Bedford Rd Bx320 -Mt Kisco 10549
(212) 489-6789 ..**Waldman,** Benjamin J '90 HSBC Securities -666 5th Av -NY 10103
(845) 426-3210 ..**Waldman,** Boruch H '96 -36 Fairway Oval -Spg Vly 10977 **Fx:**426-3272
(212) 587-3434 ..**Waldman,** Bradley L '92 (Raskin & K LLP) -160 Bway -NY 10038
(212) 759-4600 ..**Waldman,** Chet B '86 (Wolf P LLP) -845 3rd Av -NY 10022
(212) 455-2000 ..**Waldman,** Craig S '05 %Simpson T&B LLP -425 Lex Av -NY 10017
(212) 829-7169 ..**Waldman,** Danl E '09 Cantor Fitzgerald -110 E 59th -NY 10022
(212) 571-4900 ..**Waldman,** David M '65 -5 Hanover Sq -NY 10004 **Fx:**571-0965
(212) 554-1234 ..**Waldman,** David S '76 %AXA Financial Inc -1290 Av of Amer -NY 10104 **Fx:**707-3963
(516) 877-0777 ..**Waldman,** Edw J '69 (Taub H&W,PLLC) -190 Willis Av -Mineola 11501
(914) 422-4096 ..**Waldman,** Emily Gold '03 Pace Law Schl -78 N Bway -White Plns 10603 **Fx:**422-4039
(212) 840-9300 ..**Waldman,** Eric S '08 %B Fischer LLC -550 5th Av -NY 10036 **Fx:**840-9323
(845) 794-7500 ..**Waldman,** Gary H '76 -504 Bway Bx1493 -Monticello 12701 **Fx:**791-1933
(212) 768-6700 ..**Waldman,** Ingrid M '06 %Sonnenschein N&R LLP -2 World Fncl Ctr -NY 10281
(212) 872-1000 ..**Waldman,** Jacob J '05 -One Bryant Park -NY 10036 **Fx:**872-1002
(212) 218-5500 ..**Waldman,** Jane Barouch '86 OfCnsl Seyfarth S LLP -620 8th Av -NY 10018
(516) 432-0302 ..**Waldman,** Larry '58 (Schwartz & W) -1839 Wilson Av -N Merrick 11566
(845) 331-0100 ..**Waldman,** Nathan J '61 OfCnsl Wapner K&F,PLLC -239 Wall Bx3268 -Kingston 12402
(845) 679-7207 ..**Waldman,** Nathan J '61 OfCnsl Wapner K&F,PLLC -45 Mill Hill Rd Bx572 -Woodstock 12498
(212) 403-7330 ..**Waldman,** Paul R '55 -1501 Bway -NY 10036 **Fx:**221-3172
(212) 947-9779 ..**Waldman,** Randee J '98 %Advocates for Chldrn of NY -151 W 30th -NY 10001
(212) 416-8208 ..**Waldman,** Roger L '65 %Dept of Law -120 Bway -NY 10271
(866) 931-4494 ..**Waldman,** Ronald L '84 %SSA-ODAR -375 N Bway -Jericho 11753
(212) 468-8000 ..**Waldmann,** Marian A '05 %Morrison & F LLP -1290 Av of Amer -NY 10104
(212) 354-4500 ..**Waldner,** Erinn Weeks '01 (Friedman & W) -1500 Bway -NY 10036
(212) 530-1800 ..**Waldner,** Robt J '01 %Richards K&O LLP -1 World Fncl Ctr -NY 10281
(212) 909-6000 ..**Waldoks,** Noam B '09 %Debevoise & P LLP -919 3rd Av -NY 10022
(212) 946-4737 ..**Waldon,** Ian P '95 (Waldon Law Grp,LLP) -11 Penn Plz -NY 10001 **Fx:**(646) 688-3674
(518) 869-9200 ..**Waldorf,** Jon B '04 %Rose Law Firm,PLLC -501 New Karner Rd -Albany 12205 **Fx:**869-3334
(585) 753-4500 ..**Waldorf,** Jos D '05 %DA -832 Watts Bldg -Rchstr 14614 **Fx:**753-4576
(212) 325-2067 ..**Waldorf,** Michl D '96 %Credit Suisse First Boston -11 Mad Av -NY 10010
(212) 227-0133 ..**Waldorf,** Thos F '86 (T Waldorf,PC) -277 Bway -NY 10007 **Fx:**227-0549
(516) 931-1800 ..**Waldren,** Rebecca J '06 %Catalano G&P LLP -100 Jericho Quadrangle -Jericho 11753
(212) 701-3000 ..**Waldrip,** Glenn J Jr. '87 (Cahill G&R LLP) -80 Pine -NY 10005 **Fx:**269-5420
(212) 448-1100 ..**Waldron,** Deanna R '92 (McLaughlin & S,LLP) -260 Mad Av -NY 10016
(516) 294-4014 ..**Waldron,** Michl K '82 (Waldron W&B) -49 Robin Rd -Westbury 11590
(212) 733-5086 ..**Waldron,** Roy F III '96 %Pfizer Inc -235 E 42nd -NY 10017
(516) 294-4014 ..**Waldron Waldron & Beyer** -49 Robin Rd -Westbury 11590 **Fx:**294-4016
(212) 448-1100 ..**Waldstein,** Mark B '89 (McLaughlin & S,LLP) -260 Mad Av -NY 10016
(631) 366-3555 ..**Waldvogel,** J Gary '76 -732 Smithtwn Bypass -Smithtwn 11787 **Fx:**366-3567
(631) 777-1313 ..**Walendowski,** Alfred S '97 (AS Walendowski,PC) -532 Broadhllw Rd -Melvll 11747 **Fx:**777-1919
(718) 549-3091 ..**Walerstein,** Robt J '91 -2115 Av U -Brklyn 11229 **Fx:**549-0510

(212) 554-1400 .. **Wales,** David L '87 (Bernstein LB&G LLP) -1285 Av of Amer -NY 10019
(212) 980-2160 .. **Wales,** H Elliot '55 -52 Riverside Dr -NY 10024 **Fx:**769-0054
(212) 558-4000 .. **Waleski,** Blaze D '93 SpclCnsl Sullivan & C LLP -125 Broad -NY 10004
(212) 659-7300 .. **Waley,** Tasmin B '05 %Haynes & B,LLP -1221 Av of Amer -NY 10020
(212) 336-0127 .. **Walfish,** Danl R '05 %SEC -3 World Fncl Ctr -NY 10281 **Fx:**336-1323
(212) 953-6000 .. **Walfish,** Mark '75 (Katsky K LLP) -605 3rd Av -NY 10158
(212) 455-2000 .. **Walgren,** Peter D '08 %Simpson T&B LLP -425 Lex Av -NY 10017
(212) 735-3000 .. **Walha,** Kulbir S '07 %Skadden ASM&F LLP -4 Times Sq -NY 10036
(212) 836-8000 .. **Walia,** Gurpreet S '10 %Kaye S LLP -425 Park Av -NY 10022
(212) 360-1484 .. **Walia,** Nayna '01 Dept of Parks & Rec -1234 5th Av -NY 10029
(716) 823-1000 .. **Walier,** Paul S '95 -1369 Abbott Rd -Lackawanna 14218
(212) 479-6090 .. **Walinsky,** Adam '62 -1114 Av of Amer -NY 10036
(212) 340-0400 .. **Walitt,** Pamela '07 %Appllt Div 1st Dept -27 Mad Av -NY 10010 **Fx:**889-4412
(212) 610-6300 .. **Walker,** Aaron T '09 %Allen & O -1221 Av of Amer -NY 10020
(631) 361-8737 .. **Walker,** Alfred M '77 -225 Old Cntry Rd -Melvll 11747 **Fx:**361-8792
(212) 530-5000 .. **Walker,** Andrew R '95 (Milbank TH&M LLP) -1 Chase Manh Plz -NY 10005
(585) 454-7350 .. **Walker,** April V '91 %Pre-Trial Srvcs Corp -80 W Main -Rchstr 14614
(212) 690-2990 .. **Walker,** Audrey C '92 %H Gordon -304 W 138th -NY 10030
(212) 558-4000 .. **Walker,** Benjamin R '06 %Sullivan & C LLP -125 Broad -NY 10004
(212) 857-8800 .. **Walker,** Bonnie H '04 US Ct Appls 2nd Circ -40 Foley Sq -NY 10007
(212) 403-1000 .. **Walker,** Brian M '09 %Wachtell LR&K -51 W 52nd -NY 10019
(845) 577-3284 .. **Walker,** Bruce J '01 -390 W Route 59 -Spg Vly 10977
(212) 228-2494 .. **Walker,** Chas L '79 -185 Bleecker -NY 10012
(914) 422-4128 .. **Walker,** Chauncey L '63 %Pace Law Schl -78 N Bway -White Plns 10603 **Fx:**422-4039
(718) 254-0700 .. **Walker,** Chauncey R '89 %Bklyn Defender Srvcs -177 Lvngstn -Brklyn 11201 **Fx:**254-0897
(212) 335-9905 .. **Walker,** Chevon N '08 DA -1 Hogan Pl -NY 10013
(212) 770-1764 .. **Walker,** Christopher T '89 %AIG -80 Pine -NY 10005 **Fx:**344-2286
(585) 428-4155 .. **Walker,** Connie Othella '82 Hon F Geraci Jr -545 Hall of Justice -Rchstr 14614
(347) 404-9133 .. **Walker,** Craig S '02 %Civil Ct -141 Lvngstn -Brklyn 11201 **Fx:**(718) 643-3733
(212) 299-2000 .. **Walker,** D Christopher '03 NYMEX -1 North End Av -NY 10282 **Fx:**301-4700
(518) 262-3828 .. **Walker,** Donald J '90 %Albany Med Ctr -43 New Scotland Av -Albany 12208 **Fx:**262-4184
(516) 229-4400 .. **Walker,** Donald S Jr. '01 Cnsl Kay & G -875 Merrick Av -Westbury 11590
(212) 557-2900 .. **Walker,** Edw N '61 (Schwartzman GW&T,PC) -355 Lex Av -NY 10017
(212) 849-7000 .. **Walker,** Elizabeth L '07 %Quinn EU&S,LLP -51 Mad Av -NY 10010
(212) 785-2929 .. **Walker,** Elizabeth M '08 %Conway FC&K,PC -48 Wall -NY 10005
(212) 421-2111 .. **Walker,** Ellen M '80 (Granoff W&F,PC) -747 3rd Av -NY 10017
(212) 628-2864 .. **Walker,** Frederic D '48 -220 E 67th -NY 10065 **Fx:**988-6673
(212) 833-6988 .. **Walker,** Gregg A '98 SONY -550 Mad Av -NY 10022
(212) 903-9000 .. **Walker,** Gregory C '07 %Linklaters -1345 Av of Amer -NY 10105
(212) 713-8501 .. **Walker,** Gregory D '89 UBS Securities LLC -1285 Av of Amer -NY 10019
(212) 758-8672 .. **Walker,** Herbert H '63 -321 E 54th -NY 10022 **Fx:**758-8672
(212) 450-4000 .. **Walker,** Ian K O '10 %Davis P&W LLP -450 Lex Av -NY 10017
(212) 530-1800 .. **Walker,** James Q '92 (Richards K&O LLP) -1 World Fncl Ctr -NY 10281
(212) 804-4200 .. **Walker,** Jan C '87 %Mound CW&G -One Bttry Pk Plz -NY 10004
(607) 273-2202 .. **Walker,** Jeffrey D '04 %Schlather SP&S -200 E Buffalo Bx353 -Ithaca 14851
(212) 704-6000 .. **Walker,** Jerome '86 (Troutman S LLP) -405 Lex Av -NY 10174
(718) 488-1256 .. **Walker,** Jerri E '03 Long Island Univ -1 Univ Plz -Brklyn 11201
(212) 558-4000 .. **Walker,** Jessica P '06 %Sullivan & C LLP -125 Broad -NY 10004
(212) 832-1930 .. **Walker,** Joel M '64 (Breslow & W,LLP) -767 3rd Av -NY 10017
(212) 455-2000 .. **Walker,** John L '80 (Simpson T&B LLP) -425 Lex Av -NY 10017
(212) 468-4800 .. **Walker,** Joshua W '03 %Davis & G LLP -1740 Bway -NY 10019
(973) 491-3522 .. **Walker,** Karol Corbin '87 (LeClairRyan,PC) -830 3rd Av -NY 10022 **Fx:**491-3555
(212) 773-5701 .. **Walker,** Karon S '85 Ernst & Young LLP -5 Times Sq -NY 10036
(212) 943-9080 .. **Walker,** Kellie T '99 %Virginia & A -111 Bway -NY 10006
(212) 728-8000 .. **Walker,** Kim A '92 SpclCnsl Willkie F&G LLP -787 7th Av -NY 10019
(315) 422-1152 .. **Walker,** Kristin L '09 %Costello C&F,PLLC -500 Plum -Syracuse 13204
(212) 878-8000 .. **Walker,** Kristyn Wittnauer '09 %Clifford C LLP -31 W 52nd -NY 10019
(718) 590-2000 .. **Walker,** Latrice V '09 %DA -198 E 161st -Bronx 10451 **Fx:**590-6477
(516) 481-7617 .. **Walker,** Lisa Y '99 -62 Nichols Ct -Hempstd 11550
(845) 348-2134 .. **Walker,** Marianne J '91 Nyack Hospital -160 N Mdlnd Av -Nyack 10960
(212) 225-2000 .. **Walker,** Mark A '67 (Cleary GS&H) -1 Lbrty Plz -NY 10006
(914) 241-2909 .. **Walker,** Maxine G '04 -107 Maple Av -Mt Kisco 10549
(516) 742-3470 .. **Walker,** Michl G '02 %Kral CRRP&G,LLP -538 Broadhllw Rd -Melvll 11747
(718) 680-9700 .. **Walker,** Michl L '07 -9052 Ft Hmltn Pkwy -Brklyn 11209 **Fx:**680-2025
(516) 248-2002 .. **Walker,** Michl R '05 %Gallagher WB&P -98 Willis Av -Mineola 11501
(212) 715-1000 .. **Walker,** Natalie L '08 %Arnold & P LLP -399 Park Av -NY 10022
(631) 261-8834 .. **Walker,** Noah '07 %Ingerman S LLP -150 Motor Pkwy -Hauppauge 11788
(646) 964-5749 .. **Walker,** Pamela A '03 (Walker GW&B,LLC) -1825 Park Av -NY 10035 **Fx:**(866) 422-4858
(212) 998-6687 .. **Walker,** Pascale Charlot '98 NYU Law Schl -245 Sullivan -NY 10012
(716) 852-4100 .. **Walker,** Patricia S '92 %D Coppola -37 Franklin -Buffalo 14202 **Fx:**852-0002
(212) 349-6775 .. **Walker,** Paul E '74 (Peltz & W) -222 Bway -NY 10038
(212) 218-5500 .. **Walker,** Peter A '78 (Seyfarth S LLP) -620 8th Av -NY 10018
(716) 856-7091 .. **Walker,** Regina A '96 %J Freedman -424 Main -Buffalo 14202 **Fx:**856-7097
(212) 250-8200 .. **Walker,** Richd H '77 %Deutsche Bank -60 Wall -NY 10005
(516) 248-2002 .. **Walker,** Robt J '79 (Gallagher WB&P) -98 Willis Av -Mineola 11501
(212) 335-9000 .. **Walker,** Robt M '92 %DA -1 Hogan Pl -NY 10013
(212) 318-6000 .. **Walker,** Robt W '10 %Paul HJ&W LLP -75 E 55th -NY 10022
(212) 407-4000 .. **Walker,** Rosa K '09 %Loeb & L,LLP -345 Park Av -NY 10154
(212) 885-5000 .. **Walker,** Saml M '00 (Blank R LLP) -405 Lex Av -NY 10174
(212) 980-9600 .. **Walker,** Sara K '05 %Kaufman B&R -120 Bway -NY 10271
(212) 228-4521 .. **Walker,** Scott A '86 -532 LaGuardia Pl -NY 10012 **Fx:**228-4525
(212) 318-6000 .. **Walker,** Shenade M '08 %Paul HJ&W LLP -75 E 55th -NY 10022
(518) 471-4831 .. **Walker,** Stanley G Jr. '75 %Appllt Div 3rd Dept -Capitol Station Bx7288 -Albany 12224 **Fx:**471-4750
(315) 471-8111 .. **Walker,** Steven A '09 %Scolaro SCF&B,PC -507 Plum -Syracuse 13204
(212) 576-7000 .. **Walker,** Stewart H '78 %NYLIM -51 Mad Av -NY 10010
(516) 334-4400 .. **Walker,** Taylor '67 T Walker -260 Jericho Tpk -Westbury 11590 **Fx:**333-3017
(631) 361-8737 .. **Walker,** Trudie Katz '77 -225 Old Cntry Rd -Melvll 11747
(212) 259-8000 .. **Walker,** Wendy A '06 %Dewey & L LLP -1301 Av of Amer -NY 10019
(212) 309-6000 .. **Walker,** Wendy Snowdon '91 (Morgan L&B LLP) -101 Park Av -NY 10178
(718) 858-3271 .. **Walker,** Wm A '93 -147 Congress -Brklyn 11201 **Fx:**858-3492
(585) 586-6280 .. **Walker,** Wm H Jr. '79 -349 W Cmmrcial -E Rchstr 14445 **Fx:**586-2023
(518) 473-8418 .. **Walker Bryce,** Karen '91 %OCFS -52 Wshngtn -Rensselaer 12144 **Fx:**486-6361
(716) 438-9091 .. **Walker-Dewitt,** Deborah Ann '90 -20 Market -Lockprt 14094
(212) 310-8000 .. **Walker-Fierce,** Naima K '02 Weil G&M LLP -767 5th Av -NY 10153
(914) 690-1010 .. **Walker Greenberg,** Alyse '89 Trayner Grp Ltd -66 Bowman Av -Rye Brook 10573
(718) 931-2078 .. **WalkerSantiago,** Doni M '97 -Bx149 -Bronx 10473 **Fx:**430-0943
(212) 309-6000 .. **Walkoff,** Judith Ann '93 (Morgan L&B LLP) -101 Park Av -NY 10178
(212) 558-4000 .. **Walkovik,** Donald C '74 (Sullivan & C LLP) -125 Broad -NY 10004
(212) 940-8800 .. **Walkup,** Jowita Januszewska '03 %Katten MR LLP -575 Mad Av -NY 10022
(212) 859-8000 .. **Wall,** Alexander J '07 Fried FHS&J LLP -1 NY Plz -NY 10004
(212) 762-8473 .. **Wall,** Ashley C '99 Morgan Stanley -1221 Av of Amer -NY 10020
(518) 399-7125 .. **Wall,** Carolyn B '89 -46 Garnsey Rd -Rexfrd 12148
(518) 457-3177 .. **Wall,** Danl E '92 %Dept Civil Srvc -Harriman Campus Bldg 1 -Albany 12239 **Fx:**457-6654
(212) 695-6008 .. **Wall,** Donald R '82 -10 Park Av -NY 10016 **Fx:**631-0910
(212) 819-8200 .. **Wall,** Duane D '69 (White & C LLP) -1155 Av of Amer -NY 10036
(718) 252-6096 .. **Wall,** Henry J Jr. '53 -2520 Av M -Brklyn 11210 **Fx:**252-6096
(716) 856-4000 .. **Wall,** Kathleen A '84 (Hodgson R LLP) -140 Pearl -Buffalo 14202
(212) 227-4210 .. **Wall,** Lisa N '96 %Weg & M,PC -52 Duane -NY 10007
(212) 709-1640 .. **Wall,** Lore E '92 %Banking Dept -1 State -NY 10004 **Fx:**709-1655
(315) 425-2700 .. **Wall,** Thos J '78 OfCnsl Hiscock & B,LLP -One Park Pl -Syracuse 13202
(212) 669-2568 .. **Walla,** Edw P '67 Comptrollers Ofc -1 Centre -NY 10007
(212) 231-1754 .. **Wallace,** Amanda L '00 MacQuarie Holdings,Inc -125 W 55th -NY 10019 **Fx:**231-1010
(212) 227-2197 .. **Wallace,** Andrew J '97 %NYC Cncl Finance Div -250 Bway -NY 10007 **Fx:**788-7061
(585) 295-4400 .. **Wallace,** Andrew J '98 %Hiscock & B,LLP -2000 HSBC Plz -Rchstr 14604
(646) 826-5793 .. **Wallace,** Blair H '08 OCH-Ziff Captl Mgmt -9 W 57th -NY 10019
(212) 848-4000 .. **Wallace,** Bradley J '09 %Shearman & S LLP -599 Lex Av -NY 10022
(631) 475-3100 .. **Wallace,** Bruce T '68 (Wruck & W LLP) -38 Church -Patchogue 11772 **Fx:**475-3154
(212) 306-1571 .. **Wallace,** Bryan C '02 FINRA-Amex Enforcement -65 Bway -NY 10006
(518) 434-3111 .. **Wallace,** Campbell H '06 %PIA Mgmt Srvcs -25 Chmbrlain Bx997 -Glenmont 12077 **Fx:**434-2342
(315) 735-4599 .. **Wallace,** Christopher B '92 -421 Broad -Utica 13501 **Fx:**735-4562
(845) 473-0900 .. **Wallace,** Craig M '92 (Wallace & W LLP) -299 Main -Poughkeepsie 12601 **Fx:**473-5548
(845) 557-0976 .. **Wallace,** David A '88 -774 Proctor Rd -Glen Spey 12737
(607) 776-4171 .. **Wallace,** David G '78 -108 E Steuben -Bath 14810 **Fx:**776-5591
(212) 408-5100 .. **Wallace,** David L '88 (Chadbourne & P LLP) -30 Rckfllr Plz -NY 10112
(212) 820-2557 .. **Wallace,** Dennis P '85 %AIG -160 Water -NY 10038
(212) 225-2000 .. **Wallace,** Derek E '09 %Cleary GS&H -1 Lbrty Plz -NY 10006
(212) 801-9299 .. **Wallace,** Edw C '77 (Greenberg T,LLP) -200 Park Av -NY 10166
(212) 226-5600 .. **Wallace,** Fred '66 (Minchenberg & W) -401 Bway -NY 10013 **Fx:**941-5963
(631) 281-4143 .. **Wallace,** Harry B '83 -207 Poospatuck Ln -Mastic 11950 **Fx:**281-5859
(914) 949-6996 .. **Wallace,** Heather Quigley '00 %Penino & M,LLP -180 E Post Rd -White Plns 10601
(845) 473-0900 .. **Wallace,** Herbert N '62 (Wallace & W LLP) -299 Main -Poughkeepsie 12601 **Fx:**473-5548
(212) 983-1221 .. **Wallace,** Holly A '02 %Ochs & G,LLP -60 E 42nd -NY 10165
(315) 422-1311 .. **Wallace,** Holly Salop '86 (Melvin & M,PLLC) -217 S Salina -Syracuse 13202
(212) 661-5306 .. **Wallace,** Ian F '01 -501 5th Av -NY 10017
(212) 506-2500 .. **Wallace,** Isabelle M C '00 %Mayer B LLP -1675 Bway -NY 10019
(315) 469-3246 .. **Wallace,** James J '87 (Scott & W) -4110 S Salina -Syracuse 13205 **Fx:**469-3249
(212) 841-1000 .. **Wallace,** Jenna R '09 %Covington & B LLP -620 8th Av -NY 10018
(716) 855-5710 .. **Wallace,** John '95 %J Quackenbush Jr -60 Lakefront Blvd -Buffalo 14202 **Fx:**855-5722
(212) 732-3200 .. **Wallace,** Judith M '06 %Carter L&M LLP -2 Wall -NY 10005
(212) 578-9034 .. **Wallace,** Kathleen M '83 MetLife -1 Met Life Plz -LIC 11101
(718) 720-1441 .. **Wallace,** Kathleen M '87 -67 New Dorp Plz -Staten Isl 10306 **Fx:**720-1441

(212) 259-8000 .. **Wallace,** Kevin C '01 %Dewey & L LLP -1301 Av of Amer -NY 10019
(212) 906-1200 .. **Wallace,** Kyle L '09 %Latham & W -885 3rd Av -NY 10022
(212) 308-1104 .. **Wallace,** Larry '84 (Wallace & Assoc) -50 Main -White Plns 10606
(212) 856-6059 .. **Wallace,** Linda A '81 %CIBC World Markets -425 Lex Av -NY 10017
(212) 416-6384 .. **Wallace,** Lisa C '96 %Dept of Law -120 Bway -NY 10271
(914) 636-8900 .. **Wallace,** Lisa L '01 (McCabe W&C,PC) -145 Huguenot -New Rchll 10801
(212) 635-1081 .. **Wallace,** Marcia '78 Bk of NY Mellon -1 Wall -NY 10286
(631) 234-5678 .. **Wallace,** Martin R '68 SrCnsl Wallace WF&V,PC -600 Suffolk Av -Brentwd 11717
(516) 394-4200 .. **Wallace,** Mary R '83 %Duffy & D -1370 RXR Plz -Uniondale 11556
(631) 547-9646 .. **Wallace,** Michl J '60 (Ferrari & W,LLP) -290 Broadhllw Rd -Melvll 11747
(716) 848-3063 .. **Wallace,** Michl P '76 %M & T Bk -1 Fountain Plz -Buffalo 14203
(716) 551-5626 .. **Wallace,** Monica Piga '95 Cnsl Hon R Arcara -68 Court -Buffalo 14202
(516) 692-8888 .. **Wallace,** Nathaniel T '01 (F Chau & Assoc,LLC) -130 Woodbury Rd -Woodbury 11797 **Fx:**692-8889
(212) 728-8000 .. **Wallace,** Nora Ann '77 (Willkie F&G LLP) -787 7th Av -NY 10019
(212) 351-4500 .. **Wallace,** Owen G '99 Epstein B&G,PC -250 Park Av -NY 10177
(212) 866-9519 .. **Wallace,** Richd L '74 -88 Morningside Dr -NY 10027
(607) 272-2102 .. **Wallace,** Richd M '90 (Guttman & W) -411 N Tioga -Ithaca 14850 **Fx:**272-2350
(518) 272-6565 .. **Wallace,** Richd P '67 (Martin SWD&J) -279 River Bx1530 -Troy 12181
(212) 262-2001 .. **Wallace,** Roy H '94 -233 Bway -NY 10279 **Fx:**246-7065
(212) 735-3000 .. **Wallace,** W Kirk '87 (Skadden ASM&F LLP) -4 Times Sq -NY 10036
(212) 836-8000 .. **Wallace,** W Stewart '03 %Kaye S LLP -425 Park Av -NY 10022
(212) 836-8000 .. **Wallace,** Wm E Jr. '80 (Kaye S LLP) -425 Park Av -NY 10022
(516) 742-9494 .. **Wallace,** Wm G '81 (Favata & W,LLP) -229 7th -Gdn Cty 11530
(516) 571-3800 .. **Wallace,** Wm J '86 %DA -262 Old Cntry Rd -Mineola 11501 **Fx:**248-9479
(631) 234-5678 .. **Wallace Witty Frampton & Veltry,PC** -600 Suffolk Av -Brentwd 11717 **Fx:**234-5751
(212) 360-4244 .. **Wallach,** Dana A '03 Guggenheim Fndtn -345 Hudson -NY 10014
(516) 292-0306 .. **Wallach,** Dennis R '83 -230 Hilton Av -Hempstd 11550
(212) 687-1811 .. **Wallach,** Edw S '61 %Walker Truesdell & Assoc -380 Lex Av -NY 10168 **Fx:**687-0994
(212) 506-1700 .. **Wallach,** Eric J '73 (Kasowitz BT&F LLP) -1633 Bway -NY 10019
(212) 826-0100 .. **Wallach,** Gail '88 FSA -31 W 52nd -NY 10019 **Fx:**893-2710
(516) 240-8900 .. **Wallach,** Henry J '60 OfCnsl Torre LGG&R,LLP -100 Jericho Quad -Jericho 11753
(212) 698-7037 .. **Wallach,** Jill F '94 %Simon & Schuster -1230 Av of Amer -NY 10020
(718) 739-6400 .. **Wallach,** Jonathan P '82 %DHCR -92-31 Union Hall -Jamaica 11433 **Fx:**262-7938
(212) 361-7996 .. **Wallach,** Keith M '05 Dept Homeless Srvcs -33 Beaver -NY 10004 **Fx:**361-8002
(212) 455-2000 .. **Wallach,** Kenneth B '94 (Simpson T&B LLP) -425 Lex Av -NY 10017
(212) 226-5054 .. **Wallach,** Margarita '00 OfCnsl Powley & G,PC -304 Hudson -NY 10013 **Fx:**266-5085
(716) 852-1835 .. **Wallach,** Mark S '74 -169 Delaware Av -Buffalo 14202 **Fx:**852-1857
(516) 747-1010 .. **Wallach,** Mindy '81 %Dollinger G&G -1 Old Cntry Rd -Carle Pl 11514
(914) 242-9494 .. **Wallach & Rendo,LLP** -239 Lex Av -Mt Kisco 10549 **Fx:**242-9899
(718) 252-4509 .. **Wallach,** Roberta Rose '94 -1106 E 19th -Brklyn 11230
(914) 242-9494 .. **Wallach,** Sherry Levin '96 (Wallach & R,LLP) -239 Lex Av -Mt Kisco 10549
(516) 887-7777 .. **Wallach,** Stephen C '96 -175 N Central Av -Vly Stream 11580
(516) 742-4343 .. **Wallach,** Steven I '89 (Scully SM&P PC) -400 Grdn City Plz -Gdn Cty 11530
(212) 303-9400 .. **Wallach,** Timothy N '79 %Halcyon Investments -477 Mad Av -NY 10022
(212) 221-6900 .. **Wallach,** Tracy M '08 %Winget S&S,LLP -45 Bway -NY 10006
(718) 237-6282 .. **Wallack,** Madeline R '86 %HRA -283 Adams -Brklyn 11201
(212) 753-3176 .. **Wallack,** Marc G '89 -18 E 64th -NY 10065
(212) 223-1300 .. **Wallack,** Robt M '01 (Wallack Firm,PC) -444 Mad Av -NY 10022 **Fx:**223-1301
(212) 885-5000 .. **Wallack,** Samantha '01 (Blank R LLP) -405 Lex Av -NY 10174
(212) 836-8000 .. **Wallance,** Gregory J '77 (Kaye S LLP) -425 Park Av -NY 10022
(718) 222-0033 .. **Walle,** Andrew F Jr. '81 -32 Court -Brklyn 11201 **Fx:**222-9865
(212) 661-9100 .. **Wallen,** Danl '74 (Otterbourg SH&R,PC) -230 Park Av -NY 10169
(585) 454-7660 .. **Wallen,** John C '75 -36 W Main -Rchstr 14614
(315) 343-6363 .. **Wallen,** Jos E III '80 (Amdursky PF&W,PC) -26 E Oneida -Oswego 13126
(212) 318-6000 .. **Wallen,** Nicole B '06 %Paul HJ&W LLP -75 E 55th -NY 10022
(718) 654-5788 .. **Wallen,** Wesley G '92 -3550 Wht Plns Rd -Bronx 10467
(518) 426-4600 .. **Wallender,** Michl T '76 (Couch W,LLP) -540 Bway Bx22222 -Albany 12201
(716) 858-2424 .. **Wallens,** Justin T '03 %DA -25 Delaware Av -Buffalo 14202 **Fx:**858-7425
(518) 464-1300 .. **Wallens,** Wm M '76 (Roemer WG&M LLP) -13 Columbia Cir -Albany 12203
(212) 227-7588 .. **Wallenstein,** Aaron M '02 -160 Bway -NY 10038
(516) 742-5600 .. **Wallenstein,** John S '75 -1100 Franklin Av -Gdn Cty 11530 **Fx:**742-5040
(212) 237-8364 .. **Wallenstein,** Martin A '91 John Jay Cllg of Crim Just -899 10th Av -NY 10019
(212) 693-0010 .. **Wallenstein,** Stanley H '60 SH Wallenstein,PC -41-43 Beekman -NY 10038 **Fx:**791-7547
(212) 332-8900 .. **Waller,** Brian D '94 (Simon & Prtnrs LLP) -551 5th Av -NY 10176 **Fx:**332-8909
(212) 465-2003 .. **Waller,** David S '92 Northern Funding LLC -132 W 31st -NY 10001
(212) 855-3200 .. **Waller,** Diane E '82 Depository Trust -55 Water -NY 10041 **Fx:**855-3279
(631) 851-0088 .. **Waller,** Jeffrey W '69 (Conforti & W) -140 Fell Ct -Hauppauge 11788 **Fx:**232-2380
(718) 590-2070 .. **Waller,** Lisa Jane '88 %DA -198 E 161st -Bronx 10451 **Fx:**590-6477
(212) 766-4411 .. **Waller,** Matthew B '05 %Ebanks & S,LLP -20 Vesey -NY 10007 **Fx:**766-5899
(212) 536-3900 .. **Waller,** Michl E '91 (K&L Gates LLP) -599 Lex Av -NY 10022
(212) 872-1000 .. **Wallick,** James L '04 -One Bryant Park -NY 10036 **Fx:**872-1002
(212) 351-4000 .. **Wallin,** J Ross '00 %Gibson D&C LLP -200 Park Av -NY 10166
(212) 762-6686 .. **Wallin,** James P '84 Morgan Stanley Invstmnt Mgmt -1221 Av of Amer -NY 10020
(518) 745-4257 .. **Walling,** G Scott '74 -13 Butternut Hill Dr -Queensbury 12804 **Fx:**(888) 860-8191
(716) 632-2782 .. **Walling,** Mark R '84 -6225 Sheridan Dr -Williamsvll 14221 **Fx:**631-2962
(516) 742-0707 .. **Walling,** Mary Anne W '88 %Sullivan PBM&C PC -55 Mineola Blvd -Mineola 11501
(718) 222-2023 .. **Wallisch,** Kira A '08 %Law Dept -350 Jay -Brklyn 11201 **Fx:**222-2088
(212) 682-7474 .. **Wallison,** Jeremy L '02 %Foley & L LLP -90 Park Av -NY 10016
(516) 393-2200 .. **Wallitt,** Caroline P '06 %Garfunkel W,PC -111 Grt Nck Rd -Gt Neck 11021
(212) 773-2405 .. **Wallner,** Beate '09 Ernst & Young LLP -5 Times Sq -NY 10036
(212) 594-5300 .. **Wallner,** Robt A '80 (Milberg LLP) -1 Penn Plz -NY 10119
(607) 723-9461 .. **Walls,** Donald G '54 -405 Press Bldg Bx507 -Bnghmtn 13902 **Fx:**723-9463
(518) 474-7856 .. **Walls,** Michele M '92 %Dept of Law -The Cptl -Albany 12224
(212) 474-1000 .. **Wall-Wolff,** Megan E '10 %Cravath S&M LLP -825 8th Av -NY 10019
(212) 277-6500 .. **Walmer,** Kira L '09 %Dickstein S LLP -1633 Bway -NY 10019
(212) 858-7475 .. **Walmsley,** John C '97 Cnsl RBC Capital Markets -165 Bway -NY 10006
(212) 554-4372 .. **Walner,** David R '93 %Paramount Capital -787 7th Av -NY 10019
(212) 536-3900 .. **Walpert,** Gary A '74 (K&L Gates LLP) -599 Lex Av -NY 10022
(212) 885-5000 .. **Walrath,** Margaret J '03 %Blank R LLP -405 Lex Av -NY 10174
(212) 446-8315 .. **Walrod,** David B '95 %McKinsey & Co -55 E 52nd -NY 10055 **Fx:**688-9521
(212) 683-1711 .. **Walsey,** David A '92 -9 E 37th -NY 10016 **Fx:**683-8845
(212) 986-6000 .. **Walsh,** Abbey K '00 (Kleinberg KW&C,PC) -551 5th Av -NY 10176
(631) 692-9743 .. **Walsh,** Amelia Tucker '92 -8 Beardsley Ln -Lloyd Hbr 11743
(914) 251-1115 .. **Walsh & Amicucci LLP** -2900 Wstchstr Av -Purchase 10577 **Fx:**251-0928
(212) 808-8100 .. **Walsh,** Amy '91 (Kostelanetz & F,LLP) -7 Wrld Trd Ctr -NY 10007
(212) 362-1776 .. **Walsh,** Aristea N '90 -65 W 85th -NY 10024 **Fx:**362-1626
(516) 741-1818 .. **Walsh,** Arthur T '88 (O'Reilly M&C,PC) -222 Old Cntry Rd -Mineola 11501
(914) 328-3661 .. **Walsh,** Brian P '87 -175 Main -White Plns 10601
(718) 448-9003 .. **Walsh,** Bruce H '79 -390 Manor Rd -Staten Isl 10314 **Fx:**816-6137
(518) 523-3304 .. **Walsh,** Chas E '73 -14 Saranac Av Bx 391 -Lk Placid 12946
(718) 286-6000 .. **Walsh,** Chas N '74 %DA -125-01 Qns Blvd -Kew Gdns 11415
(212) 820-7700 .. **Walsh,** Chelsea J '07 %Boundas SW&B,LLC -1 Bttry Pk Plz -NY 10004
(212) 449-6991 .. **Walsh,** Christine '85 %Merrill Lynch -220 Bway -NY 10038
(212) 506-2500 .. **Walsh,** Christine A '09 %Mayer B LLP -1675 Bway -NY 10019
(631) 584-8000 .. **Walsh,** Christine Healy '97 -112 Terry Rd -Smithtwn 11787 **Fx:**584-8808
(845) 353-2000 .. **Walsh,** Christopher J '87 %Feerick LM PLLC -96 S Bway -Nyack 10960
(973) 596-4883 .. **Walsh,** Christopher T '94 (Gibbons PC) -1 Penn Plz -NY 10119 **Fx:**639-6326
(914) 694-3300 .. **Walsh,** Colin M '03 %DiSciullo & Assoc -2975 Wstchstr Av -Purchase 10577 **Fx:**694-2244
(212) 335-9000 .. **Walsh,** Colleen S '06 %DA -1 Hogan Pl -NY 10013
(212) 709-5583 .. **Walsh,** Connie M '00 NYS Banking Dept -1 State -NY 10004 **Fx:**709-5592
(914) 681-0200 .. **Walsh,** Danl G '06 %DelBello DWW&W,LLP -1 N Lex Av -White Plns 10601
(800) 521-1260 .. **Walsh,** David H IV '80 %Petrone & P,PC -108 W Jffrsn -Syracuse 13202
(914) 437-9058 .. **Walsh,** Dennis M '92 (Fitzmaurice & W,LLP) -15 Chester Av -White Plns 10601
(212) 859-8000 .. **Walsh,** Dianna Lamb '06 %Fried FHS&J LLP -1 NY Plz -NY 10004
(315) 473-9495 .. **Walsh,** Donald J '85 %MHLS -224 Harrison -Syracuse 13202 **Fx:**473-9646
(212) 407-7700 .. **Walsh,** Edw J Jr. '58 OfCnsl Vedder P,PC -1633 Bway -NY 10019
(315) 473-0899 .. **Walsh,** Eileen D '02 %Anelli X,PC -441 S Salina -Syracuse 13202 **Fx:**473-0530
(518) 270-3761 .. **Walsh,** Elizabeth M '91 Rensselaer Cnty Fam Ct -1504 5th Av -Troy 12180
(516) 873-2000 .. **Walsh,** Elizabeth Moore '05 %Moritt HH&H LLP -400 Grdn City Plz -Gdn Cty 11530
(212) 715-1000 .. **Walsh,** Erik C '05 Arnold & P LLP -399 Park Av -NY 10022
(518) 462-0110 .. **Walsh,** Erin N '07 %Sheehan GCG&J LLP -54 State -Albany 12207
(518) 474-3197 .. **Walsh,** Frank K '81 %Dept of Law -The Cptl -Albany 12224
(212) 237-1000 .. **Walsh,** Gary E '78 (Windels ML&M,LLP) -156 W 56th -NY 10019
(212) 344-5680 .. **Walsh,** George J III '72 (Thompson H LLP) -335 Mad Av -NY 10017
(716) 855-3200 .. **Walsh,** Gerald T '87 (Zdarsky S&A) -298 Main -Buffalo 14202
(914) 824-5419 .. **Walsh,** Gretchen '88 Hon A Scheinkman -111 Dr ML King Jr Blvd -White Plns 10601
(518) 463-1269 .. **Walsh & Hacker** -18 Corp Wds Blvd -Albany 12211 **Fx:**432-1218
(212) 972-1000 .. **Walsh,** James '93 (London F LLP) -59 Maiden Ln -NY 10038
(212) 688-6310 .. **Walsh,** James C '66 -300 E 51st -NY 10022
(518) 527-9130 .. **Walsh,** James E '99 -514 State -Schnctdy 12305 **Fx:**370-4929
(518) 475-7727 .. **Walsh,** James P '61 -381 Delaware Av -Delmar 12054 **Fx:**439-4261
(716) 825-2203 .. **Walsh,** James R '56 -3819 S Park Av -Blasdell 14219 **Fx:**825-3433
(716) 856-1636 .. **Walsh,** James R '62 (Walsh R&G) -14 Lafayette Sq -Buffalo 14203
(518) 431-6700 .. **Walsh,** James S '97 Cnsl Manatt P&P,LLP -30 S Pearl -Albany 12207
(212) 838-3333 .. **Walsh,** Janet C '95 %Locks Law Firm,PLLC -747 3rd Av -NY 10017 **Fx:**838-3735
(516) 409-6200 .. **Walsh,** Jeffrey G '85 (Furey KWM&C,PC) -2174 Jackson Av -Seafrd 11783
(212) 237-1000 .. **Walsh,** Jerome K Jr. '58 Cnsl Windels ML&M,LLP -156 W 56th -NY 10019

(973) 438-4494 .. **Walsh,** Jillian '99 %Outside Cnsl Solutns LLP -1430 Bway -NY 10018 **Fx:**438-1225
(716) 684-8060 .. **Walsh,** John B '53 Ecology & Envrnmnt -368 Plsntvw Dr -Lancaster 14086 **Fx:**684-0844
(212) 753-0787 .. **Walsh,** John F '58 -400 E 55th -NY 10022 **Fx:**753-2630
(212) 541-2000 .. **Walsh,** John F Jr. '58 OfCnsl Bryan C LLP -1290 Av of Amer -NY 10104
(718) 646-2658 .. **Walsh,** John J '56 -2682 Gerritsen Av -Brklyn 11229 **Fx:**646-2724
(212) 732-3200 .. **Walsh,** John J '60 SrCnsl Carter L&M LLP -2 Wall -NY 10005
(212) 425-1900 .. **Walsh,** John J '78 (Freehill H&M LLP) -80 Pine -NY 10005
(914) 385-6000 .. **Walsh,** John J II '83 (Hodges W&S LLP) -55 Church -White Plns 10601 **Fx:**385-6060
(212) 227-7711 .. **Walsh,** John K Jr. '90 (Walsh & W) -277 Bway -NY 10007 **Fx:**227-8611
(631) 261-6400 .. **Walsh,** John L '63 (Rieger & W,LLP) -199 Main -Northprt 11768
(610) 213-4792 .. **Walsh,** John M '92 Compass Grp -27 Central Av -Hambrg 14075
(716) 847-3098 .. **Walsh,** John P '82 %Workers Comp Bd -107 Delaware Av -Buffalo 14202
(212) 696-6000 .. **Walsh,** Jonathan J '99 %Curtis M-PC&M LLP -101 Park Av -NY 10178
(914) 347-6360 .. **Walsh,** Jonathan R '86 %Epstein & R -565 Taxter Rd -Elmsfrd 10523
(212) 704-6000 .. **Walsh,** Jos '00 %Troutman S LLP -405 Lex Av -NY 10174
(212) 643-7000 .. **Walsh,** Jos C '06 %Sills C&G PC -One Rckfllr Plz -NY 10020
(518) 583-0171 .. **Walsh,** Jos M '81 (Walsh & W,LLP) -42 Long Alley -Saratoga Spgs 12866 **Fx:**583-1025
(516) 798-5363 .. **Walsh,** Jos P '82 (Kressel RW&R,LLC) -684 Bway -Massapequa 11758
(718) 694-9222 .. **Walsh,** Jos R '65 (Bergan & W) -26 Court -Brklyn 11242
(631) 852-2500 .. **Walsh,** Julie '02 %DA -200 Center Dr -Rvrhead 11901 **Fx:**852-1769
(212) 801-6774 .. **Walsh,** Kaitlin R '07 %Greenberg T,LLP -200 Park Av -NY 10166
(914) 251-1115 .. **Walsh,** Karen J '83 (Walsh & A LLP) -2900 Wstchstr Av -Purchase 10577
(516) 922-9100 .. **Walsh,** Karen J '92 %V McNamara -1045 Oyster Bay Rd -E Norwich 11732 **Fx:**922-9208
(212) 906-1200 .. **Walsh,** Kathleen Anne '90 (Latham & W) -885 3rd Av -NY 10022
(212) 834-0600 .. **Walsh,** Kathryn '07 %Gordon & S,PC -355 Lex Av -NY 10017
(212) 487-4072 .. **Walsh,** Keith T '06 %Dept Consumer Affrs -42 Bway -NY 10004
(914) 397-2400 .. **Walsh,** Kenneth G '74 %Ferguson C,LLP -1 N Lex Av -White Plns 10601 **Fx:**683-6956
(212) 371-6600 .. **Walsh,** Kenneth G '92 OfCnsl Kirby M LLP -825 3rd Av -NY 10022
(212) 259-8000 .. **Walsh,** Kevin '81 (Dewey & L LLP) -1301 Av of Amer -NY 10019
(845) 291-2454 .. **Walsh,** Kevin B '81 %Leg Aid -2 Court Ln Bx328 -Goshen 10924 **Fx:**294-2638
(516) 571-3056 .. **Walsh,** Kevin C '89 %Cnty Atty -1 West -Mineola 11501 **Fx:**571-6604
(716) 566-5400 .. **Walsh,** Kevin D '79 SpclCnsl Goldberg S LLP -665 Main -Buffalo 14203
(973) 596-4769 .. **Walsh,** Kevin G '99 (Gibbons PC) -1 Penn Plz -NY 10119 **Fx:**639-6470
(212) 415-8600 .. **Walsh,** Kevin J '75 (Locke LB&L LLP) -3 World Fncl Ctr -NY 10281
(718) 855-9000 .. **Walsh,** Kevin M '78 (Cullen and D LLP) -177 Montague -Brklyn 11201
(516) 408-9000 .. **Walsh,** Kevin M '83 (Walsh MM&D LLP) -229 Seventh -Gdn Cty 11530
(718) 222-9800 .. **Walsh,** Kevin P '80 (Brecher FPWT&Z,PC) -335 Adams -Brklyn 11201
(631) 979-3000 .. **Walsh,** Kevin P '07 %Certilman BA&H,LLP -1393 Vets Mem'l Hwy -Hauppauge 11788
(585) 263-1000 .. **Walsh,** Kristen M '98 %Nixon P LLP -1100 Clinton Sq -Rchstr 14604
(716) 839-8537 .. **Walsh,** Laurie A '91 %Daemen College -4380 Main -Amherst 14226
(518) 583-0171 .. **Walsh,** Marian Wait '85 (Walsh & W,LLP) -42 Long Alley -Saratoga Spgs 12866 **Fx:**583-1025
(631) 964-8312 .. **Walsh,** Maribeth '87 SpclCnsl Stewart Title Ins Co -125 Baylis Rd -Melvll 11747 **Fx:**964-8348
(212) 538-5797 .. **Walsh,** Marie E '04 Credit Suisse -1 Mad Av -NY 10010
(914) 777-1134 .. **Walsh,** Marion Mullen '90 %Ingerman S LLP -550 Mamaroneck Av -Harrison 10528
(212) 205-7000 .. **Walsh,** Mark G '99 Cnsl Ashurst LLP -7 Times Sq -NY 10036
(518) 432-7511 .. **Walsh,** Mark T '81 (Gleason DW&O) -40 Beaver -Albany 12207
(516) 408-9000 .. **Walsh Markus McDougal & DeBellis LLP** -229 Seventh -Gdn Cty 11530 **Fx:**747-0825
(607) 721-8771 .. **Walsh,** Mary A '83 %Dept of Law -44 Hawley -Bnghmtn 13901 **Fx:**721-8789
(315) 946-5438 .. **Walsh,** Mary Ellen '76 %Hon D Kehoe -54 Broad -Lyons 14489
(315) 356-1125 .. **Walsh,** Mary Pat '89 Hon J Shkane-Family Ct -201 W Dominick -Rome 13440 **Fx:**337-0480
(212) 351-4000 .. **Walsh,** Matthew C '05 %Gibson D&C LLP -200 Park Av -NY 10166
(212) 384-2763 .. **Walsh,** Matthew G '98 %FBI -26 Fed Plz -NY 10278
(718) 892-2600 .. **Walsh,** Matthew P '82 -1978 Wllmsbrdg Rd -Bronx 10461
(315) 421-1000 .. **Walsh,** Maureen K '85 -2 Clinton Sq -Syracuse 13202
(516) 571-3800 .. **Walsh,** Michl '88 %DA -262 Old Cntry Rd -Mineola 11501 **Fx:**248-9479
(716) 853-9555 .. **Walsh,** Michl C '80 %Leg Aid -237 Main -Buffalo 14203 **Fx:**853-3219
(315) 451-7575 .. **Walsh,** Michl E '01 -113 N Main -Syracuse 13212
(212) 310-8000 .. **Walsh,** Michl F '81 (Weil G&M LLP) -767 5th Av -NY 10153
(631) 726-5900 .. **Walsh,** Michl G '88 -860 Montauk Hwy -Water Mill 11976 **Fx:**726-4471
(212) 354-3800 .. **Walsh,** Michl J '83 %Burke & P -100 Park Av -NY 10017
(212) 310-8000 .. **Walsh,** Michl J '06 %Weil G&M LLP -767 5th Av -NY 10153
(718) 442-3900 .. **Walsh,** Michl M '83 -1688 Victory Blvd -Staten Isl 10314 **Fx:**876-4755
(516) 877-5600 .. **Walsh,** Michl P '94 %R Tusa -1225 Franklin Av -Gdn Cty 11530 **Fx:**877-5695
(631) 897-5500 .. **Walsh,** Michl P '02 -1040 W Jericho Tpke -Smithtwn 11787
(212) 820-7700 .. **Walsh,** Michl T '80 (Boundas SW&B,LLC) -1 Bttry Pk Plz -NY 10004
(212) 661-1100 .. **Walsh,** Murielle Steven '97 (Pomerantz HG&G LLP) -100 Park Av -NY 10017
(518) 463-1269 .. **Walsh,** Nancy E '88 (Walsh & H) -18 Corp Wds Blvd -Albany 12211
(516) 922-7300 .. **Walsh,** Owen B '58 -34 Audrey Av Bx102 -Oyster Bay 11771 **Fx:**922-5683
(212) 416-6197 .. **Walsh,** Patrick J '96 %Dept of Law -120 Bway -NY 10271
(212) 270-5792 .. **Walsh,** Paul R '92 JP Morgan Chase & Co -270 Park Av -NY 10017
(631) 821-3034 .. **Walsh,** Peter C '94 -15 Malba Dr -Sound Bch 11789 **Fx:**821-2150
(607) 273-2301 .. **Walsh,** Peter J '80 (True W&S,LLP) -950 Danby Rd -Ithaca 14850
(518) 463-1269 .. **Walsh,** Peter J '91 (Walsh & H) -18 Corp Wds Blvd -Albany 12211
(212) 471-6238 .. **Walsh,** Philip J '72 (Hinshaw & C LLP) -780 3rd Av -NY 10017
(212) 384-1000 .. **Walsh,** Richd M '93 %FBI -26 Fed Plz -NY 10278
(518) 438-2000 .. **Walsh,** Richd P Jr. '69 (Lombardi WWHA&D PC) -III Winners Cir -Albany 12205
(516) 535-1700 .. **Walsh,** Richd T '83 %Horing W&R,PC -11 Hillside Av -Williston Pk 11596
(631) 501-3100 .. **Walsh,** Richd W '81 %J Humphreys -3 Huntngtn Quad Bx9028 -Melvll 11747 **Fx:**501-3085
(716) 825-2203 .. **Walsh,** Robt G '83 -3819 S Park Av -Blasdell 14219 **Fx:**825-3433
(718) 250-2000 .. **Walsh,** Robt J '91 %DA -350 Jay -Brklyn 11201 **Fx:**250-2314
(716) 856-1636 .. **Walsh Roberts & Grace** -14 Lafayette Sq -Buffalo 14203 **Fx:**856-1610
(607) 753-9641 .. **Walsh,** Ronald T '00 -45 Church -Cortlnd 13045 **Fx:**758-8515
(718) 793-2488 .. **Walsh,** Ryan J '04 -70-50 Austin -Frst Hlls 11375 **Fx:**793-2247
(212) 701-3000 .. **Walsh,** Samantha M '09 %Cahill G&R LLP -80 Pine -NY 10005 **Fx:**269-5420
(212) 999-5800 .. **Walsh,** Sara Ciarelli '04 %Wilson SG&R -1301 Av of Americas -NY 10019
(718) 225-2807 .. **Walsh,** Sean M '74 (Walsh Assoc) -Bx238 -Douglastn 11363 **Fx:**225-2818
(718) 537-4958 .. **Walsh,** Sean P '76 ODAR-SSA -226 E 161st -Bronx 10451 **Fx:**590-1673
(212) 490-9100 .. **Walsh,** Stephen E '90 Condon & F LLP -7 Times Sq -NY 10036
(212) 221-7999 .. **Walsh,** Susan J '97 (Moskowitz B&W,LLP) -345 7th Av -NY 10001
(716) 681-7190 .. **Walsh,** Theresa M '99 %Brown C LLP -5775 Bway -Lancaster 14086
(518) 762-0011 .. **Walsh,** Thos C '74 (Russo W&W) -122 W Main -Johnstwn 12095
(585) 295-4400 .. **Walsh,** Thos F '86 (Hiscock & B,LLP) -2000 HSBC Plz -Rchstr 14604
(518) 463-1269 .. **Walsh,** Thos J '60 (Walsh & H) -18 Corp Wds Blvd -Albany 12211
(607) 773-2887 .. **Walsh,** Thos P '81 %US Atty -15 Henry -Bnghmtn 13901 **Fx:**773-2901
(914) 328-0404 .. **Walsh,** Thos V '87 (Jackson L LLP) -1 N Bway -White Plns 10601
(212) 558-4000 .. **Walsh,** Thos W '08 %Sullivan & C LLP -125 Broad -NY 10004
(716) 645-2943 .. **Walsh,** Tiffany R '01 Univ at Buffalo -111 Capen Hall -Buffalo 14260
(212) 233-8300 .. **Walsh,** Timothy C '90 %Epstein & C -7 Dey -NY 10007
(914) 576-0820 .. **Walsh,** Timothy J '57 -74 Oak Ln -Pelham Mnr 10803 **Fx:**738-3188
(212) 335-4500 .. **Walsh,** Timothy W '91 (DLA Piper LLP) -1251 Av of Amer -NY 10020
(212) 265-7200 .. **Walsh,** Tracey Spencer '95 SrCnsl Mayerson & Assoc -330 W 38th -NY 10018 **Fx:**265-1735
(845) 758-8893 .. **Walsh Wicks & Salisbury** -7405 S Bway -Red Hook 12571 **Fx:**758-2003
(845) 452-8200 .. **Walsh Wicks & Salisbury** -75 Wshngtn BxQ -Poughkeepsie 12602 **Fx:**473-8812
(212) 558-5500 .. **Walsh,** Wm A '90 %Weitz & L,PC -700 Bway -NY 10003
(212) 697-3242 .. **Walshe,** John W L '77 (J Walshe & Assoc) -144 E 44th -NY 10017 **Fx:**697-4828
(212) 806-5400 .. **Walsman,** Danielle A '04 %Stroock &S&L LLP -180 Maiden Ln -NY 10038
(914) 637-1319 .. **Walter,** Clark E '71 Sound Shore Med Ctr -16 Guion Pl -New Rchll 10801
(212) 715-9100 .. **Walter,** Erin A '98 %Kramer LN&F,LLP -1177 Av of Amer -NY 10036
(315) 474-2981 .. **Walter,** Francis I '75 (Tisdell M&W) -120 E Wshngtn -Syracuse 13202
(212) 566-3900 .. **Walter,** Joel S '70 (J Walter & Assoc,PC) -225 Bway -NY 10007 **Fx:**566-6699
(631) 659-3361 .. **Walter,** Karen Wallace '93 KW Walter,LLC -3 Pegs Ct -Cold Spg Hbr 11724
(518) 402-0205 .. **Walter,** Lanny E '71 UIA Bd -Troy Atrium Bx15126 -Albany 12212 **Fx:**402-6208
(516) 248-0810 .. **Walter,** Lauren J '88 (Barnett & W,LLP) -1205 Franklin Av -Gdn Cty 11530
(212) 687-1700 .. **Walter,** Maia M '94 %Kaufman FP&G,LLP -300 E 42nd -NY 10017
(718) 780-7921 .. **Walter,** Marilyn R '73 %Bklyn Law Schl -250 Joralemon -Brklyn 11201 **Fx:**780-0393
(212) 788-3300 .. **Walter,** Mark F '85 %Hlth & Hsptl Corp -125 Worth -NY 10013 **Fx:**267-6905
(631) 928-1110 .. **Walter,** Michl E '78 -407 E Main Bx95 -Pt Jffrsn 11777
(631) 451-6500 .. **Walter,** Michl E '78 %Brookhaven Law Dept -1 Indpndnc Hill -Farmngvll 11738 **Fx:**698-4489
(646) 312-3574 .. **Walter,** Paula G '78 Baruch College -17 Lex Av Bx 316 -NY 10010 **Fx:**312-3573
(716) 856-3500 .. **Walter,** Raymond W '08 %Magavern MG LLP -1100 Rand Bldg -Buffalo 14203
(631) 369-7858 .. **Walter,** Sean M '00 -Bx852 -Wading Rvr 11792
(518) 472-1224 .. **Walters,** Adam S '95 (Phillips L LLP) -30 S Pearl -Albany 12207
(716) 847-8400 .. **Walters,** Adam S '95 (Phillips L LLP) -3400 HSBC Ctr -Buffalo 14203
(212) 614-7664 .. **Walters,** Brent R '09 STV Inc -225 Park Av S -NY 10003 **Fx:**529-5237
(212) 573-7735 .. **Walters,** Debbie A '98 %Pfizer Inc -235 E 42nd -NY 10017
(212) 351-4000 .. **Walters,** Fredk A '95 %Gibson D&C LLP -200 Park Av -NY 10166
(516) 248-0339 .. **Walters,** Geralyn Ann '88 -45 Mulberry Av -Gdn Cty 11530
(212) 227-1666 .. **Walters,** Gerard A '70 -20 Vesey -NY 10007 **Fx:**571-4107
(212) 657-1423 .. **Walters,** Harry T '84 Citigroup -77 Water -NY 10005
(315) 443-9083 .. **Walters,** Jennifer A '00 Syracuse Univ -303 Univ Pl -Syracuse 13244 **Fx:**443-2805
(518) 486-3701 .. **Walters,** John M '01 %Consumer Protection Bd -5 ESP -Albany 12223 **Fx:**474-2474
(212) 735-3000 .. **Walters,** Khalilah '08 %Skadden ASM&F LLP -4 Times Sq -NY 10036
(212) 227-1666 .. **Walters,** Matthew J '07 %G Walters -20 Vesey -NY 10007 **Fx:**571-4107

(212) 326-3939 ..**Walters,** Meghan G '10 %Jones D -222 E 41st -NY 10017
(914) 686-4800 ..**Walters,** Melissa '99 (Harrington O&M,LLP) -81 Main -White Plns 10601
(718) 231-1043 ..**Walters,** Paul A '90 -3400 Tiemann Av -Bronx 10469 **Fx:**882-5950
(212) 474-1000 ..**Walters,** Randall D '07 %Cravath S&M LLP -825 8th Av -NY 10019
(212) 860-2680 ..**Walters,** Robt A '87 -1825 Park Av -NY 10035 **Fx:**860-2681
(212) 480-6794 ..**Walters,** Roderick J '83 %DHCR -25 Beaver -NY 10004 **Fx:**480-7416
(212) 513-7788 ..**Walters,** Rosalie S '06 %Ahmuty D&M -123 William -NY 10038
(716) 649-6111 ..**Walters,** Steven J '01 Town Supervisor -S6100 S Park Av -Hambrg 14075
(646) 486-5435 ..**Walters,** Yvonne A '95 %SBA -26 Fed Plz -NY 10278 **Fx:**(202) 481-6134
(212) 612-4200 ..**Walthall,** Gregory E '97 %Hoey KT&E -55 Water -NY 10041
(315) 724-3158 ..**Walthall,** Stephen L '75 (Kelly & W) -239 Genesee -Utica 13501
(212) 530-5000 ..**Walther-Meade,** Caroline V '97 %Milbank TH&M LLP -1 Chase Manh Plz -NY 10005
(212) 309-3056 ..**Waltman,** Guy S '66 UBS Fncl Srvcs -200 Park Av -NY 10166
(212) 636-2000 ..**Waltman,** Hartley B '88 Christie's -20 Rckfllr Plz -NY 10020
(212) 975-2552 ..**Waltman,** Naomi Brufsky '90 %CBS Inc -51 W 52nd -NY 10019 **Fx:**975-3930
(212) 246-7100 ..**Waltman,** Susan C '87 Grtr NY Hsptl Assn -555 W 57th -NY 10019
(212) 805-4737 ..**Walton,** Anne Ford '94 %Hon CS Haight Jr -500 Pearl -NY 10007
(718) 250-2000 ..**Walton,** Frank M '09 %DA -350 Jay -Brklyn 11201 **Fx:**250-2314
(212) 737-5850 ..**Walton,** Jonathan R '72 -530 E 88th -NY 10128
(315) 363-7777 ..**Walton,** Linus W '82 -233 Cedar -Oneida 13421 **Fx:**363-1330
(315) 685-7777 ..**Walton,** Linus W '82 -11 E Genesee -Skaneateles 13152 **Fx:**363-1330
(315) 788-5100 ..**Walton,** Peter L '93 (Conboy MB&K,LLP) -407 Sherman -Watertwn 13601
(212) 335-9000 ..**Walton,** Sherita M '03 DA -1 Hogan Pl -NY 10013
(212) 335-9000 ..**Walton,** Tiana L '02 %DA -1 Hogan Pl -NY 10013
(718) 646-1493 ..**Waltrous,** Evelyn F '80 -3046 Brighton 3rd -Brklyn 11235
(212) 580-3171 ..**Waltuch,** Barbara '81 -60 W 76th -NY 10023 **Fx:**580-7050
(212) 868-0880 ..**Waltzer,** David Sheridan '03 -99 Mamaroneck Av -White Plns 10601
(718) 469-6937 ..**Waltzman,** Renee I '62 -126 Stratford Rd -Brklyn 11218
(914) 995-5401 ..**Waluschka,** Katherine '98 Dept Socl Srvcs -112 E Post Rd -White Plns 10601
(212) 318-6000 ..**Walworth,** Carla R '09 (Paul HJ&W LLP) -75 E 55th -NY 10022
(212) 931-9988 ..**Walz,** Hermann P '93 -40 Exch Pl -NY 10005
(212) 652-4567 ..**Walz,** Richd A '98 Moon Capital Mgmt LP -499 Park Av -NY 10022 **Fx:**652-4501
(315) 475-1185 ..**Walzer,** Barbara T '76 -506 E Wshngtn -Syracuse 13202 **Fx:**701-4458
(212) 907-7357 ..**Walzer,** Martin J '50 -437 Mad Av -NY 10022 **Fx:**754-0330
(516) 484-1280 ..**Walzer,** Seymour B '51 -189 Pond Vw Dr -Pt Wash 11050 **Fx:**484-1280
(212) 907-9724 ..**Walzer,** Wm P '82 -250 Park Av -NY 10177 **Fx:**907-9800
(212) 220-3830 ..**Wamser,** Val E '00 %Nicoletti H&S -88 Pine -NY 10005
(718) 613-2403 ..**Wan,** Albert K '06 %Hon V Pohorelsky USDC -225 Cadman Plz E -Brklyn 11201
(718) 875-1300 ..**Wan,** Andrea V W '09 %Appllt Div 2nd Dept -45 Monroe Pl -Brklyn 11201 **Fx:**858-2446
(212) 608-3188 ..**Wan,** Dingding '07 %J Guttlein & Assoc,PC -291 Bway -NY 10007 **Fx:**385-0231
(212) 522-4910 ..**Wan,** Helen C '99 %Time Inc -1271 Av of Amer -NY 10020 **Fx:**522-0437
(212) 274-5102 ..**Wan,** Lillian '02 %ACS Leg Srvcs -220 Church -NY 10013
(718) 875-1300 ..**Wan,** Lourdes '84 %Appllt Div 2nd Dept -45 Monroe Pl -Brklyn 11201 **Fx:**858-2446
(631) 499-5400 ..**Wan,** Timothy C '01 (Smith CL PC) -5036 Jericho Tpk Bx49 -Commack 11725
(212) 756-2000 ..**Wanapha,** Watt '08 %Schulte R&Z LLP -919 3rd Av -NY 10022
(718) 250-2000 ..**Wancel,** Linda R '87 %DA -350 Jay -Brklyn 11201 **Fx:**250-2314
(631) 462-3434 ..**Wand,** Carl F '72 (Wand P&G) -1776 E Jericho Tpk -Huntngtn 11743 **Fx:**462-3939
(212) 557-7200 ..**Wander,** David H '85 Davidoff M&H,LLP -605 3rd Av -NY 10158
(518) 462-5601 ..**Wander,** Fred B '73 (O'Connell & A) -54 State -Albany 12207
(212) 880-6000 ..**Wanderer,** Joshua S '92 Cnsl Torys LLP -237 Park Av -NY 10017
(845) 357-0036 ..**Wanderman,** Carl L '58 OfCnsl Lexow B&A,PC -56 Park Av Bx239 -Suffern 10901
(845) 356-3334 ..**Wanderman,** Carl L '58 OfCnsl Greenberg W&F -150 Airport Exec Park -Nanuet 10954
(718) 248-9091 ..**Wanderman,** Susan M '71 %Citibank -1 Court Sq -LIC 11101
(716) 636-7600 ..**Wanemaker,** Jaclyn S '04 %HoganWillig -2410 N Forest Rd -Amherst 14068
(212) 551-9456 ..**Wanetik,** David L '75 %1st Amer Title -633 3rd Av -NY 10017 **Fx:**922-0881
(212) 530-5000 ..**Wang,** Alfred '07 %Milbank TH&M LLP -1 Chase Manh Plz -NY 10005
(516) 496-5822 ..**Wang,** Ann '04 %T Spina -170 Froehlich Farm Blvd -Woodbury 11797 **Fx:**496-5420
(212) 687-4900 ..**Wang,** Annie '89 (Wormser KG&J LLP) -825 3rd Av -NY 10022
(212) 478-7200 ..**Wang,** Anting J '06 %Hahn & H LLP -488 Mad Av -NY 10022
(212) 710-3900 ..**Wang,** Bin '09 %Clyde & Co US LLP -405 Lex Av -NY 10174 **Fx:**710-3950
(718) 353-9264 ..**Wang,** Chunyu J '06 -36-25 Main -Flushng 11354
(212) 232-1300 ..**Wang,** Danl D '99 %Lewis BB&S LLP -77 Water -NY 10005
(718) 445-3979 ..**Wang,** Danl J '91 -133-57 41st Rd -Flushng 11355 **Fx:**463-2869
(212) 558-4000 ..**Wang,** Davis J '04 %Sullivan & C LLP -125 Broad -NY 10004
(212) 906-1200 ..**Wang,** Elaine P '07 %Latham & W -885 3rd Av -NY 10022
(845) 486-0061 ..**Wang,** Elizabeth P '95 (Wang Law Firm,LLC) -11 Market Bx1871 -Poughkeepsie 12601 **Fx:**486-7782
(212) 455-2000 ..**Wang,** Elsa Y-H '08 %Simpson T&B LLP -425 Lex Av -NY 10017
(212) 450-4000 ..**Wang,** Eric D '09 %Davis P&W LLP -450 Lex Av -NY 10017
(718) 590-2000 ..**Wang,** Frances Y '03 %DA -198 E 161st -Bronx 10451 **Fx:**590-6477
(212) 479-6000 ..**Wang,** Franny Yu-Wen '06 %Cooley LLP -1114 Av of Amer -NY 10036
(212) 746-1426 ..**Wang,** Gary O '91 %NY Hospital -525 E 68th -NY 10065
(212) 506-5000 ..**Wang,** George H '79 (Orrick H&S LLP) -51 W 52nd -NY 10019
(212) 455-2000 ..**Wang,** George S '99 (Simpson T&B LLP) -425 Lex Av -NY 10017
(212) 836-8000 ..**Wang,** Gerald C '03 %Kaye S LLP -425 Park Av -NY 10022
(212) 577-2220 ..**Wang,** Hanbin '01 -277 Bway -NY 10007 **Fx:**577-2259
(212) 566-8080 ..**Wang,** Heng (Pierce) '08 %Wong W & Assoc,PC -150 Bway -NY 10038 **Fx:**566-8960
(212) 343-8884 ..**Wang,** I June Ophelia '09 IJO Wang,PC -401 Bway -NY 10013
(212) 969-3000 ..**Wang,** Jane Chih-Ying '04 %Proskauer R LLP -1585 Bway -NY 10036
(212) 833-1175 ..**Wang,** Jeffrey R '04 %Friedman KS&A LLP -1633 Bway -NY 10019 **Fx:**373-7975
(212) 474-1000 ..**Wang,** Jennifer Z '08 %Cravath S&M LLP -825 8th Av -NY 10019
(212) 530-5000 ..**Wang,** Jerry A '10 %Milbank TH&M LLP -1 Chase Manh Plz -NY 10005
(212) 418-4726 ..**Wang,** Jimmy A '03 Icon Capital Corp -100 5th Av -NY 10011
(212) 455-2000 ..**Wang,** John J '10 %Simpson T&B LLP -425 Lex Av -NY 10017
(212) 703-8484 ..**Wang,** Jonathan Chun '83 (Wang & S) -305 Mad Av -NY 10165 **Fx:**768-2766
(212) 239-8555 ..**Wang,** Jun '94 -1250 Bway -NY 10001
(718) 888-8880 ..**Wang,** Jun '08 %Dai & Assoc,PC -136-20 38th Av -Flushng 11354 **Fx:**888-9270
(212) 233-2988 ..**Wang,** Ke-En '05 %Hua Lian -39 E Bway -NY 10002
(973) 596-4579 ..**Wang,** Lisa H '03 %Gibbons PC -1 Penn Plz -NY 10119 **Fx:**639-6257
(212) 763-5000 ..**Wang,** Mariann Meier '97 (Emery CB&A LLP) -75 Rckfllr Plz -NY 10019
(212) 915-6100 ..**Wang,** Melinda '03 XL Capital Ltd -1540 Bway -NY 10036 **Fx:**287-0195
(212) 859-8000 ..**Wang,** Minyao '09 %Fried FHS&J LLP -1 NY Plz -NY 10004
(212) 589-4200 ..**Wang,** Ona Theresa '99 (Baker & H LLP) -45 Rckfllr Plz -NY 10111
(212) 246-7100 ..**Wang,** Patricia J '85 Grtr NY Hsptl Assn -555 W 57th -NY 10019
(212) 925-4884 ..**Wang,** Patrick '98 -325 Bway -NY 10007 **Fx:**925-6417
(212) 822-1486 ..**Wang,** Peter '70 -305 Bway -NY 10007
(212) 682-7474 ..**Wang,** Peter N '74 (Foley & L LLP) -90 Park Av -NY 10016
(212) 468-8000 ..**Wang,** Qian '09 %Morrison & F LLP -1290 Av of Amer -NY 10104
(212) 791-8400 ..**Wang,** Robt '55 OfCnsl Mait W&S -110 Wall -NY 10005
(212) 848-4000 ..**Wang,** Shirley A '08 %Shearman & S LLP -599 Lex Av -NY 10022
(212) 808-8300 ..**Wang,** Tong '00 SrCnsl Rosensteel Law -90 Park Av -NY 10016
(212) 452-7704 ..**Wang,** Tova A '97 Century Fndtn -41 E 70th -NY 10021
(212) 727-2700 ..**Wang,** Vivian H '10 %NRDC -40 W 20th -NY 10011 **Fx:**727-1773
(212) 425-7200 ..**Wang,** Weining '06 %Kenyon & K,LLP -1 Bway -NY 10004
(212) 227-8170 ..**Wang,** Weishan '05 -2 Mott -NY 10013
(212) 566-8080 ..**Wang,** Wendy W '08 %Wong W & Assoc,PC -150 Bway -NY 10038 **Fx:**566-8960
(212) 336-2000 ..**Wang,** Wm '05 %Patterson BW&T LLP -1133 Av of Amer -NY 10036
(212) 819-8200 ..**Wang,** Xiaogang Sean '01 %White & C LLP -1155 Av of Amer -NY 10036
(212) 558-4000 ..**Wang,** Xinghua Owen '10 %Sullivan & C LLP -125 Broad -NY 10004
(212) 608-6500 ..**Wang,** Xinsheng '08 %DeHeng C,LLC -225 Bway -NY 10007
(212) 735-3000 ..**Wang,** Yanjun '09 %Skadden ASM&F LLP -4 Times Sq -NY 10036
(212) 455-2000 ..**Wang,** Yi '08 %Simpson T&B LLP -425 Lex Av -NY 10017
(718) 939-4633 ..**Wang,** Yinan '06 %KK Tung PC -38-21 Main -Flushng 11354 **Fx:**939-4468
(212) 935-3101 ..**Wang,** Ying '05 Bank of China -410 Mad Av -NY 10017
(212) 455-2000 ..**Wang,** Ying '08 %Simpson T&B LLP -425 Lex Av -NY 10017
(212) 455-2000 ..**Wang,** Yu '08 %Simpson T&B LLP -425 Lex Av -NY 10017
(212) 343-3120 ..**Wang,** Yuming '03 -401 Bway -NY 10013
(212) 878-8000 ..**Wang,** Zhong '09 %Clifford C LLP -31 W 52nd -NY 10019
(212) 676-2400 ..**Wangel,** Jonathan C '04 Dept Hlth Emplymnt Law -2 Lafayette -NY 10007
(315) 478-6551 ..**Wangerman,** Laurence A '73 (Baldwin & W) -333 E Onondaga -Syracuse 13202
(631) 727-2180 ..**Wani,** Danl G '04 %Twomey LSKD&Q,LLP -33 W 2nd Bx9398 -Rvrhead 11901
(718) 206-2020 ..**Wani,** Zouhoor A '02 -16705 Hillside Av -Jamaica 11432 **Fx:**206-0505
(914) 681-0200 ..**Wank,** Bradley D '85 (DelBello DWW&W,LLP) -1 N Lex Av -White Plns 10601
(516) 739-0555 ..**Wank,** Jerald L '67 -114 Old Cntry Rd -Mineola 11501 **Fx:**739-2305
(212) 980-0120 ..**Wank,** Linda J '91 (Frankfurt KK&S,PC) -488 Mad Av -NY 10022
(631) 682-0231 ..**Wankel,** Richd E '03 -8 Damin Cir -St James 11780 **Fx:**980-3986
(718) 745-3835 ..**Wanker,** Robt E '85 -425 73rd -Brklyn 11209 **Fx:**836-2642
(212) 309-6000 ..**Wankmueller,** Donna L '09 %Morgan L&B LLP -101 Park Av -NY 10178
(212) 583-0700 ..**Wankoff,** David W '85 -767 3rd Av -NY 10017 **Fx:**583-9595
(212) 732-2000 ..**Wann,** Nancy '06 %Cullen and D LLP -44 Wall -NY 10005
(212) 701-3000 ..**Wann,** Robt Jr. '08 %Cahill G&R LLP -80 Pine -NY 10005 **Fx:**269-5420
(631) 360-7701 ..**Wannick,** Anthony R '61 -81 Ashland Dr -Kings Pk 11754 **Fx:**864-8542
(315) 483-8346 ..**Wanninger,** Gordon H '73 -8627 Greig Bx265 -Sodus Point 14555
(716) 858-2200 ..**Wannop,** Ruthanne '96 %Cnty Atty -95 Franklin -Buffalo 14202 **Fx:**858-2281
(845) 679-7207 ..**Wapner,** Gerald L '57 (Wapner K&F,PLLC) -45 Mill Hill Rd Bx572 -Woodstock 12498
(845) 331-0100 ..**Wapner,** Gerald L '57 (Wapner K&F,PLLC) -239 Wall Bx3268 -Kingston 12402
(845) 331-0100 ..**Wapner Koplovitz & Futerfas,PLLC** -239 Wall Bx3268 -Kingston 12402 **Fx:**331-0427
(845) 679-7207 ..**Wapner Koplovitz & Futerfas,PLLC** -45 Mill Hill Rd Bx572 -Woodstock 12498 **Fx:**679-4053
(518) 761-6207 ..**Wappett,** John P M '83 Pub Def -1340 State Route 9 -Lk George 12845
(212) 552-7024 ..**Warager,** David J '85 %JP Morgan Chase & Co -1 Chase Manh Plz -NY 10081 **Fx:**383-0250
(212) 715-4817 ..**Waranch,** Rachel A '06 Chanel Inc -9 W 57th -NY 10019 **Fx:**303-5979
(212) 218-5500 ..**Warburg,** David M '79 (Seyfarth S LLP) -620 8th Av -NY 10018
(212) 806-5400 ..**Warburg,** Tamar D '09 %Stroock &S&L LLP -180 Maiden Ln -NY 10038
(212) 363-6900 ..**Warcholak,** Adam T '01 %Faust GS&B LLP -2 Rector -NY 10006

(518) 385-7840 .. **Warczak,** James E '71 %GE -1 River Rd Bldg 36-3W -Schnctdy 12345 **Fx:**385-3345
(212) 370-1300 .. **Ward,** Adrienne M '95 Ellenoff G&S LLP -150 E 42nd -NY 10017
(212) 969-3000 .. **Ward,** Amber A '10 %Proskauer R LLP -1585 Bway -NY 10036
(212) 715-9100 .. **Ward,** Andrew I '03 %Kramer LN&F,LLP -1177 Av of Amer -NY 10036
(315) 797-7300 .. **Ward,** Andrew K '97 -23 Oxford Rd -New Hartfrd 13413 **Fx:**735-7924
(631) 249-0500 .. **Ward,** Anthony M '98 %CEP Consultants -1800 Walt Whitman Rd -Melvll 11747 **Fx:**694-6209
(917) 282-8685 .. **Ward,** Aubrey '09 -208 E 163rd -Bronx 10451
(716) 633-7860 .. **Ward Brenon & DiVita** -5500 Main -Williamsvll 14221 **Fx:**633-7142
(212) 885-5000 .. **Ward,** Brett S '01 %Blank R LLP -405 Lex Av -NY 10174
(718) 858-1900 .. **Ward,** Brian F '88 (BF Ward,LLC) -188 Montague -Brklyn 11201 **Fx:**522-2645
(212) 335-9559 .. **Ward,** Cassiah M '06 %DA -1 Hogan Pl -NY 10013
(716) 565-2000 .. **Ward,** Danl J '73 -5500 Main -Williamsvll 14221
(212) 335-4500 .. **Ward,** David J '05 %DLA Piper LLP -1251 Av of Amer -NY 10020
(631) 293-4525 .. **Ward,** Denise Barton '06 %Littler M,PC -290 Broadhllw Rd -Melvll 11747
(914) 937-2800 .. **Ward,** Denise P '84 (Grean & W) -222 Grace Church -Pt Chester 10573
(716) 633-7860 .. **Ward,** Dennis E '77 (Ward B&D) -5500 Main -Williamsvll 14221
(518) 438-9907 .. **Ward,** Douglas H '74 (Young SWRB&M,LLC) -5 Palisades Dr -Albany 12205
(212) 763-5070 .. **Ward,** Earl S '86 -75 Rckfllr Plz -NY 10019 **Fx:**763-5001
(585) 454-0700 .. **Ward,** Eric J '83 (Ward GH&R LLP) -300 State -Rchstr 14614
(718) 990-6017 .. **Ward,** Ettie '75 %St John's Law Schl -8000 Utopia Pkwy -Jamaica 11439 **Fx:**591-1855
(212) 244-2999 .. **Ward,** Eugene A '85 (Kopff N&D LLP) -440 9th Av -NY 10001
(315) 479-3900 .. **Ward,** Frank A '87 %SSA-ODAR -300 S State -Syracuse 13202 **Fx:**479-3933
(212) 632-4080 .. **Ward,** Gayllis Robinson '90 Fiduciary Trust Intl -600 5th Av -NY 10020
(212) 682-0020 .. **Ward,** Geoffrey H '78 (Putney TH&H LLP) -521 5th Av -NY 10175
(212) 264-5916 .. **Ward,** George J Jr. '93 %DHS -26 Fed Plz -NY 10278 **Fx:**264-9210
(585) 454-0700 .. **Ward Greenberg Heller & Reidy LLP** -300 State -Rchstr 14614 **Fx:**423-5910
(585) 492-1460 .. **Ward,** Hamilton Jr. '60 (Ward & K) -364 W Main Bx321 -Arcade 14009 **Fx:**492-1178
(212) 450-4000 .. **Ward,** Heather M '04 %Davis P&W LLP -450 Lex Av -NY 10017
(212) 909-5400 .. **Ward,** J Andrew '95 KPMG LLP -757 3rd Av -NY 10017
(212) 335-9000 .. **Ward,** Jaclyn Blake '04 %DA -1 Hogan Pl -NY 10013
(607) 722-0999 .. **Ward,** James D '97 -31 Lewis -Bnghmtn 13901 **Fx:**722-0989
(516) 741-2585 .. **Ward,** Janet C '05 %Rosicki R & Assoc,PC -51 E Bethpage Rd -Plainvw 11803 **Fx:**741-4748
(212) 661-9100 .. **Ward,** Jessica M '03 %Otterbourg SH&R,PC -230 Park Av -NY 10169
(607) 898-3190 .. **Ward,** John A '73 Ward & M -170 Main -Groton 13073
(212) 697-6262 .. **Ward,** John F '85 (Ward & O) -380 Mad Av -NY 10017
(212) 312-7929 .. **Ward,** John S '85 %State Ins Fund -199 Church -NY 10007 **Fx:**385-9199
(516) 228-1300 .. **Ward,** Jon A '92 (Sahn WC&B,PLLC) -333 Earle Ovngton Blvd -Uniondale 11553
(718) 520-4584 .. **Ward,** Kathleen S '80 %Hon R Buchter -125-01 Qns Blvd -Kew Gdns 11415
(718) 643-8052 .. **Ward,** Kerry J '89 %Hon A Gerges -360 Adams -Brklyn 11201 **Fx:**243-2542
(631) 853-4161 .. **Ward,** Kevin R '02 %DA -N Cnty Cmplx Bldg 77 -Hauppauge 11788 **Fx:**853-4192
(845) 855-5900 .. **Ward,** Lita Marie '03 %Daniels & P,LLP -517 Route 22 -Pawling 12564
(212) 732-2000 .. **Ward,** Margaret S '09 %Cullen and D LLP -44 Wall -NY 10005
(212) 708-3279 .. **Ward,** Michl L '83 %Showtime Networks Inc -1633 Bway -NY 10019 **Fx:**708-1391
(607) 898-3190 .. **Ward & Murphy** -170 Main -Groton 13073 **Fx:**898-3765
(212) 697-6262 .. **Ward & Olivo** -380 Mad Av -NY 10017 **Fx:**972-5866
(212) 408-5100 .. **Ward,** Peter M '51 OfCnsl Chadbourne & P LLP -30 Rckfllr Plz -NY 10112 **Fx:**974-0287
(516) 228-3908 .. **Ward,** Richd M '88 %UIA Bd -400 Oak -Gdn Cty 11530 **Fx:**794-1061
(212) 756-2000 .. **Ward,** Robt J '78 (Schulte R&Z LLP) -919 3rd Av -NY 10022
(212) 980-0120 .. **Ward,** S Jean '88 OfCnsl Frankfurt KK&S,PC -488 Mad Av -NY 10022
(212) 735-2126 .. **Ward,** Sarah M '87 (Skadden ASM&F LLP) -4 Times Sq -NY 10036
(212) 526-7216 .. **Ward,** Sean J '04 %Barclays Capital Inc -399 Park Av -NY 10022
(716) 876-4282 .. **Ward,** Thos M '66 -156 Devonshr Rd -Buffalo 14223
(212) 207-7000 .. **Ward,** Thos M '97 %HarperCollins Pub -10 E 53rd -NY 10022 **Fx:**207-7552
(212) 899-5560 .. **Ward,** Timothy M '02 Hercules USA,Inc -630 5th Av -NY 10111
(914) 995-4172 .. **Ward,** Timothy R '85 %DA -111 Martin Luther King Blvd -White Plns 10601 **Fx:**995-3363
(518) 393-5010 .. **Ward,** Wm '61 -1494 Wendell Av -Schnctdy 12308 **Fx:**374-6805
(516) 596-1602 .. **Ward,** Wm P '85 -81 Hempstd Av -Lynbrk 11563 **Fx:**596-1604
(518) 402-9184 .. **Ward,** Yvonne M '04 DEC -625 Bway -Albany 12233 **Fx:**402-9018
(212) 558-4000 .. **Warden,** John L '66 SrCnsl Sullivan & C LLP -125 Broad -NY 10004
(212) 336-2000 .. **Warder,** Fredk B III '91 (Patterson BW&T LLP) -1133 Av of Amer -NY 10036
(718) 824-6500 .. **Wardi,** Henry J '54 OfCnsl Coiro WC&S -1206 Castle Hill Av -Bronx 10462
(518) 587-7563 .. **Wardlaw,** Donna E '78 Wardlaw Assoc,PC -443 Bway -Saratoga Spgs 12866 **Fx:**587-2313
(315) 734-2000 .. **Wardley,** George '74 %Utica Natl Ins -180 Genesee Bx530 -Utica 13502 **Fx:**734-2662
(914) 946-4777 .. **Ward-Willis,** Nicholas M '94 (Keane & B,PC) -445 Hmltn Av -White Plns 10601
(212) 862-1196 .. **Ware,** Kenneth '90 -523 W 150th -NY 10031 **Fx:**862-1196
(212) 506-2500 .. **Ware,** Michl O '96 Cnsl Mayer B LLP -1675 Bway -NY 10019
(212) 980-0010 .. **Wareh,** Rashad '05 (Kozusko HVW LLP) -575 Mad Av -NY 10022 **Fx:**751-0084
(718) 230-5270 .. **Wareham,** Roger S '93 -394 Putnam Av -Brklyn 11216
(212) 880-2632 .. **Warfield,** Ronald J '90 -100 Park Av -NY 10017 **Fx:**880-6499
(718) 286-6000 .. **Warga,** Allison M '10 %DA -125-01 Qns Blvd -Kew Gdns 11415
(212) 801-3115 .. **Wargo,** Wm A '02 OfCnsl Greenberg T,LLP -200 Park Av -NY 10166
(716) 649-9561 .. **Wargula,** Michl A '80 -4819 South Park Av -Hambrg 14075
(212) 969-3000 .. **Warhaftig,** Solomon L '64 (Proskauer R LLP) -1585 Bway -NY 10036
(212) 794-1031 .. **Warhit,** George '52 -1365 York Av -NY 10021
(212) 883-4900 .. **Warin,** E Niki '98 OfCnsl Cozen O -277 Park Av -NY 10172
(212) 508-6100 .. **Warkol,** Craig S '00 (Bracewell & G,LLP) -1251 Av of Amer -NY 10020
(212) 402-9400 .. **Warlick,** Benjamin J '07 %McKool S,PC -1 Bryant Park -NY 10036
(212) 838-8400 .. **Warman,** Michele S '91 %Andrew W Mellon Fndtn -140 E 62nd -NY 10065
(212) 878-8000 .. **Warman,** Raymond E '74 SrCnsl Clifford C LLP -31 W 52nd -NY 10019
(631) 577-4077 .. **Warmbrand,** Abraham '79 -68 S Srvc Rd -Melvll 11747 **Fx:**293-4130
(212) 577-2800 .. **Warmflash,** David '65 (Sexter & W) -115 Bway -NY 10006
(718) 802-6644 .. **Warms,** Miggie '80 %Workers Comp Bd -111 Lvngstn -Brklyn 11201
(516) 512-8300 .. **Warmund,** Matthew J '61 (Gaylor & W LLP) -7 Atl Av -Lynbrk 11563 **Fx:**512-8301
(631) 732-2000 .. **Warmuth,** Glenn P '99 %Stim & W,PC -2 8th -Farmngvll 11738 **Fx:**732-2662
(631) 732-2000 .. **Warmuth,** Paula J '81 (Stim & W,PC) -2 8th -Farmngvll 11738 **Fx:**732-2662
(718) 590-2000 .. **Warne,** Sarah E '08 %DA -198 E 161st -Bronx 10451 **Fx:**590-6477
(212) 310-8000 .. **Warner,** A Millie '08 %Weil G&M LLP -767 5th Av -NY 10153
(716) 847-0662 .. **Warner,** Amanda M '06 %Volunteer Lwyrs Prjt -237 Main -Buffalo 14203 **Fx:**847-0307
(212) 969-3000 .. **Warner,** Barry E '94 %Proskauer R LLP -1585 Bway -NY 10036
(716) 843-4100 .. **Warner,** Burton E '91 %US SBA -130 S Elmwood Av -Buffalo 14202
(518) 487-5460 .. **Warner,** Carmen M '08 %DA -6 Lodge -Albany 12207 **Fx:**487-5093
(212) 460-4286 .. **Warner,** David P '94 Con Ed -4 Irving Pl -NY 10003
(212) 583-9600 .. **Warner,** David S '01 (Littler M,PC) -900 3rd Av -NY 10022
(212) 310-8000 .. **Warner,** Douglas P '87 (Weil G&M LLP) -767 5th Av -NY 10153
(212) 450-4000 .. **Warner,** E Waide '80 (Davis P&W LLP) -450 Lex Av -NY 10017
(212) 421-4100 .. **Warner,** Elizabeth S '09 %Pryor C LLP -7 Times Sq -NY 10036
(212) 878-7214 .. **Warner,** Eric J '71 MTA -347 Mad Av -NY 10017
(212) 509-3456 .. **Warner,** Eric J '07 %McGivney & K,PC -80 Broad -NY 10004
(212) 801-6886 .. **Warner,** G Ray '06 OfCnsl Greenberg T,LLP -200 Park Av -NY 10166
(914) 694-4102 .. **Warner,** Jacqueline J '00 SplCnsl Hinman H&K,LLP -106 Corp Park Dr -White Plns 10604
(631) 727-4153 .. **Warner,** James C '93 Warner Nursery -2669 Sound Av -Baiting Hollow 11933 **Fx:**727-4324
(212) 488-1598 .. **Warner,** Jarett L '02 Cnsl Havkins RR&V,LLP -11 Penn Plz -NY 10001
(716) 270-2431 .. **Warner,** Jerome F '80 %IRS -300 Pearl -Buffalo 14202
(212) 924-7111 .. **Warner,** Jonathon D '75 (Warner & S) -6 W 18th -NY 10011
(212) 272-3794 .. **Warner,** Kathleen DiGennaro '93 %JP Morgan Chase -383 Mad Av -NY 10179
(212) 593-8000 .. **Warner,** Kenneth E '70 (Warner Prtnrs,PC) -950 3rd Av -NY 10022 **Fx:**593-9058
(516) 336-2020 .. **Warner,** Kenneth P '92 -170 Old Cntry Rd -Mineola 11501
(212) 878-8000 .. **Warner,** Matthew K '10 %Clifford C LLP -31 W 52nd -NY 10019
(212) 593-8000 .. **Warner,** Rita Wasserstein '74 (Warner Prtnrs,PC) -950 3rd Av -NY 10022 **Fx:**593-9058
(212) 325-6893 .. **Warner,** Ross R '04 CSFB -11 Mad Av -NY 10010
(212) 924-7111 .. **Warner & Scheuerman** -6 W 18th -NY 10011 **Fx:**924-6111
(585) 425-0097 .. **Warner,** Stephen R '07 -7700 Pttsfrd Palmyra Rd -Fairpt 14450
(212) 259-8000 .. **Warner,** Stuart A '09 %Dewey & L LLP -1301 Av of Amer -NY 10019
(917) 692-5220 .. **Warner-Goldstein,** Jeannette '90 -Scarsdale 10583
(212) 455-2000 .. **Warnick,** Elizabeth A '09 %Simpson T&B LLP -425 Lex Av -NY 10017
(518) 449-0044 .. **Warnick,** Spencer K IV '98 (Hoffman W&D LLC) -75 State -Albany 12207 **Fx:**449-0047
(212) 458-3475 .. **Warnke,** Craig P '00 AIG -175 Water -NY 10038
(212) 259-8000 .. **Warnke,** Gordon E '84 (Dewey & L LLP) -1301 Av of Amer -NY 10019
(212) 596-9000 .. **Warnke,** Stephen A '88 (Ropes & G LLP) -1211 Av of Amer -NY 10036
(212) 687-4900 .. **Warnken,** Wayne L '74 (Wormser KG&J LLP) -825 3rd Av -NY 10022
(212) 750-3110 .. **Warnock,** Susan C '91 -880 3rd Av -NY 10022 **Fx:**750-9773
(212) 903-9000 .. **Warnot,** James R Jr. '91 (Linklaters) -1345 Av of Amer -NY 10105
(516) 794-7826 .. **Warokomski,** Henry A Jr. '67 -492 E Meadow Av -E Meadow 11554 **Fx:**542-0811
(631) 265-0010 .. **Warren,** Barry L '70 (Cohen & W,PC) -80 Maple Av Bx768 -Smithtwn 11787
(212) 705-7000 .. **Warren,** Brandyne S '06 %Bingham M LLP -399 Park Av -NY 10022
(212) 715-9100 .. **Warren,** Chas S '65 (Kramer LN&F,LLP) -1177 Av of Amer -NY 10036
(518) 392-2789 .. **Warren,** Christine L '98 %M Colton,PC -63 Norton Rd Bx65 -Austerlitz 12017 **Fx:**392-2754
(212) 454-2123 .. **Warren,** Christopher C '97 %DWS Scudder -345 Park Av -NY 10154
(716) 857-4688 .. **Warren,** Cynthia L '03 Univera Healthcare -205 Park Club Ln -Buffalo 14221
(212) 307-0023 .. **Warren,** Dara '96 Cnsl DeSimone AS&O LLP -145 Hudson -NY 10013
(845) 634-7010 .. **Warren,** David '96 (Montalbano C&F,PC) -67 N Main Bx1070 -New Cty 10956
(212) 479-6000 .. **Warren,** David M '76 (Cooley LLP) -1114 Av of Amer -NY 10036
(212) 578-3025 .. **Warren,** David R '01 %MetLife -1095 Av of Amer -NY 10036 **Fx:**578-3916
(914) 347-2600 .. **Warren,** Dawn M '02 %Traub LS&S LLP -7 Skyline Dr -Hawthorne 10532

(516) 223-5223 ..**Warren**, Dawn P '99 (Warren & W LLP) -11 W Sunrise Hwy -Freeprt 11520 **Fx:**223-5232
(516) 223-5223 ..**Warren**, Dennis E '88 (Warren & W LLP) -11 W Sunrise Hwy -Freeprt 11520 **Fx:**223-5232
(212) 837-6932 ..**Warren**, Deya M '08 %Hughes H&R LLP -1 Bttry Pk Plz -NY 10004
(212) 549-2607 ..**Warren**, E Vincent '94 %ACLU -125 Broad -NY 10004 **Fx:**549-2651
(212) 833-1447 ..**Warren**, Euphemia Brownell '97 Solera Capital,LLC -625 Mad Av -NY 10022
(718) 230-9790 ..**Warren**, Evelyn W '97 -580 Wshngtn Av -Brklyn 11238
(718) 875-9264 ..**Warren**, Harold '42 (Warren & W,PC) -185 Montague -Brklyn 11201 **Fx:**852-3069
(212) 310-8000 ..**Warren**, Irwin H '75 (Weil G&M LLP) -767 5th Av -NY 10153
(518) 731-7200 ..**Warren**, James W '79 -46 Reed -Coxsackie 12051 **Fx:**731-7222
(212) 541-2000 ..**Warren**, Jay P '78 (Bryan C LLP) -1290 Av of Amer -NY 10104
(716) 856-1010 ..**Warren**, Joan '82 -69 Delaware Av -Buffalo 14202 **Fx:**856-1008
(914) 833-1940 ..**Warren**, Jos '47 -2039 Palmer Av -Larchmnt 10538 **Fx:**834-6222
(212) 735-3000 ..**Warren**, Joshua B '09 %Skadden ASM&F LLP -4 Times Sq -NY 10036
(212) 492-1217 ..**Warren**, Joy A '03 EMI Music Pub -1290 Av of Amer -NY 10104
(212) 408-6095 ..**Warren**, Leslie K '03 ACE Guaranty -1325 Av of Amer -NY 10019
(646) 855-4077 ..**Warren**, Lewis M Jr. '88 Banc of Amer Securities -1 Bryant Pk -NY 10036
(212) 660-3000 ..**Warren**, Linda Lyons '89 (Sullivan & W LLP) -1290 Av of Amer -NY 10104
(716) 842-5667 ..**Warren**, Mark W '84 %M&T Bk -1 M & T Plz -Buffalo 14203 **Fx:**842-5376
(518) 457-2070 ..**Warren**, Marvis Ann '95 %Dept of Tax & Fin -Bldg 9 State Campus -Albany 12227 **Fx:**457-6131
(212) 728-8000 ..**Warren**, Mary K '93 (Willkie F&G LLP) -787 7th Av -NY 10019
(718) 254-7000 ..**Warren**, Michl H '78 %US Atty -271 Cadman Plz E -Brklyn 11201 **Fx:**254-6479
(212) 517-5498 ..**Warren**, Michl J '74 -10 East End Av -NY 10075
(718) 230-9790 ..**Warren**, Michl W '80 -580 Wshngtn Av -Brklyn 11238
(212) 335-9000 ..**Warren**, Michelle A '02 %DA -1 Hogan Pl -NY 10013
(914) 328-0404 ..**Warren**, Monique '07 %Jackson L LLP -1 N Bway -White Plns 10601
(516) 222-0200 ..**Warren**, Nicole A '08 %Keith S&F -666 Old Cntry Rd -Gdn Cty 11530
(315) 942-4117 ..**Warren**, Richd J '78 -105 Main Bx197 -Boonvll 13309 **Fx:**942-4117
(718) 875-9264 ..**Warren**, Richd J '78 (Warren & W,PC) -185 Montague -Brklyn 11201 **Fx:**852-3069
(212) 859-8000 ..**Warren**, Sarah F '02 %Fried FHS&J LLP -1 NY Plz -NY 10004
(212) 813-8800 ..**Warren**, Scott A '00 (Goodwin P LLP) -620 8th Av -NY 10018
(212) 397-5552 ..**Warren**, Sean C '87 %Soros Fund Mgmt LLC -888 7th Av -NY 10106 **Fx:**262-9637
(631) 390-0990 ..**Warren**, Susan '86 -1111 Route 110 -E Farmngdl 11735 **Fx:**390-0988
(212) 418-0500 ..**Warren**, Wm B '60 OfCnsl Morris & M LLP -767 3rd Av -NY 10017
(212) 578-2211 ..**Warrick**, Lance A '84 %MetLife -27-01 Qns Plz N -LIC 11101
(212) 468-8000 ..**Warrington**, Joan P '78 (Morrison & F LLP) -1290 Av of Amer -NY 10104
(212) 312-2296 ..**Warsaw**, Carla Yong Bok '09 %Leg Aid -60 Lafayette -NY 10013 **Fx:**349-0874
(718) 286-6000 ..**Warsawsky**, Jack '78 %DA -125-01 Qns Blvd -Kew Gdns 11415
(212) 687-4900 ..**Warshauer**, Alan M '66 Cnsl Wormser KG&J LLP -825 3rd Av -NY 10022
(631) 232-6130 ..**Warshauer**, Andrew M '95 %Weiner L LLP -888 Vets Mem'l Hwy -Hauppauge 11788
(212) 695-1004 ..**Warshauer**, Irene C '66 -60 E 42nd -NY 10165 **Fx:**213-0711
(212) 259-8000 ..**Warshauer**, Samantha Yael '06 %Dewey & L LLP -1301 Av of Amer -NY 10019
(212) 265-6530 ..**Warshavsky**, Lee '85 Settlement Housing Fund -247 W 37th -NY 10018
(212) 589-4200 ..**Warshavsky**, Oren J '98 (Baker & H LLP) -45 Rckfllr Plz -NY 10111
(212) 218-5500 ..**Warshaw** Aaron '08 %Seyfarth S LLP -620 8th Av -NY 10018
(212) 984-7700 ..**Warshaw Burstein Cohen Schlesinger & Kuh,LLP** -555 5th Av -NY 10017 **Fx:**972-9150
(845) 877-3737 ..**Warshaw**, David T '75 %MHLS -Taconic DDSO-Wassaic Campus -Wassaic 12592 **Fx:**877-9003
(212) 442-1736 ..**Warshaw**, Jason D '96 %Law Dept -100 Church -NY 10007 **Fx:**788-0367
(212) 966-4056 ..**Warshaw**, Jay E '95 %Warshaw Grp -540 Bway -NY 10012
(212) 722-2240 ..**Warshaw**, Jean '81 -450 E 78th -NY 10075 **Fx:**774-1999
(212) 987-9591 ..**Warshaw**, Laurence S '80 -1601 3rd Av -NY 10128
(212) 697-5369 ..**Warshaw**, Robt S '53 -501 5th Av -NY 10017
(212) 698-3000 ..**Warshawsky**, Sanford S '63 %Arnhold & Bleichroeder -1345 Av of Amer -NY 10105 **Fx:**299-4410
(718) 254-6060 ..**Warshawsky**, Steven M '03 %US Atty -271 Cadman Plz E -Brklyn 11201 **Fx:**254-6479
(516) 489-1295 ..**Wartel**, Powel F '42 -992 North Dr -N Merrick 11566 **Fx:**489-1295
(212) 349-3366 ..**Wartell**, Phillip L '04 %Rose & R -291 Bway -NY 10007 **Fx:**349-2292
(212) 326-3939 ..**Warter Sisitsky**, Aviva '98 (Jones D) -222 E 41st -NY 10017
(716) 854-1007 ..**Warth**, Patricia J '97 %Prisoners' Leg Srvcs -107 Delaware Av -Buffalo 14202 **Fx:**854-1008
(585) 295-4400 ..**Warth**, Thos J '91 (Hiscock & B,LLP) -2000 HSBC Plz -Rchstr 14604
(212) 566-7500 ..**Warywoda**, Nicholas E '01 Douglas & L -111 John -NY 10038
(585) 530-3153 ..**Washburn**, Andrew A '02 %Appllt Div 4th Dept -50 East Av Ste 200 -Rchstr 14604 **Fx:**530-3247
(212) 373-3000 ..**Washburn**, David T '56 OfCnsl Paul WRW&G LLP -1285 Av of Amer -NY 10019
(716) 692-0096 ..**Washburn**, Frederic C '55 -90 Greenwood Cir -N Tonawanda 14120 **Fx:**692-9430
(518) 746-2771 ..**Washburn**, John U '61 -158 Main Bx1236 -S Glens Fls 12803 **Fx:**792-2995
(516) 767-1255 ..**Washburn**, Kenneth G '86 -21 Pequot Av -Pt Wash 11050
(607) 547-2522 ..**Washburn**, Philip L '68 (Gozigian W&C) -103 Main Bx431 -Cooperstwn 13326
(212) 848-4000 ..**Washer**, Herbert S '92 (Shearman & S LLP) -599 Lex Av -NY 10022
(212) 825-1212 ..**Washienko**, Nicole M '09 %Morrison M LLP -17 State -NY 10004
(212) 455-2000 ..**Washington**, Alicia N '09 %Simpson T&B LLP -425 Lex Av -NY 10017
(212) 261-8000 ..**Washington**, Arthur J III '78 (Mendes & M,LLP) -750 7th Av -NY 10019
(716) 646-5530 ..**Washington**, Booker T '82 %UAW Ford Leg Srvcs -4819 S Park Av -Hambrg 14075 **Fx:**646-1519
(917) 546-6734 ..**Washington**, Corey A '08 -80 Broad -NY 10004
(212) 810-5723 ..**Washington**, Debrina L '06 BlackRock Inc -40 E 52nd -NY 10022
(212) 446-4800 ..**Washington**, Jason O '08 %Kirkland & E LLP -153 E 53rd -NY 10022
(212) 455-2000 ..**Washington**, Nicole L '09 %Simpson T&B LLP -425 Lex Av -NY 10017
(212) 484-8000 ..**Washington**, Paul F '97 %Time Warner -1 Time Warner Ctr -NY 10019
(718) 875-5799 ..**Washington**, Robt '86 -44 Court -Brklyn 11201 **Fx:**875-5398
(914) 683-6691 ..**Washington**, Roseanna H '78 -156 S Lex Av -White Plns 10606
(518) 402-2794 ..**Washington**, Val E '76 %DEC -625 Bway -Albany 12233 **Fx:**402-9016
(212) 406-1700 ..**Washor**, Barry A '81 (Queller FWF&K LLP) -233 Bway -NY 10279
(212) 697-5900 ..**Washor**, Michl S '59 -233 Bway -NY 10279 **Fx:**686-0252
(212) 918-3000 ..**Wasick**, Joanna F '07 %Hogan L LLP -875 3rd Av -NY 10022
(718) 875-1300 ..**Wasiewski**, Timothy '08 Appllt Div 2nd Dept -45 Monroe Pl -Brklyn 11201 **Fx:**858-2446
(315) 479-3900 ..**Wasileski**, Mark C '81 %SSA-ODAR -300 S State -Syracuse 13202 **Fx:**479-3933
(914) 941-5705 ..**Wasilko**, Peter J '93 -3 Mdwbrk Dr -Ossining 10562
(516) 681-1100 ..**Wasko**, Robt M '77 OfCnsl Kaufman DV&G,LLP -135 Crsswys Park Dr -Woodbury 11797
(212) 961-4408 ..**Wasko**, Sue Novick '77 %OCFS -163 W 125th -NY 10027
(212) 947-5262 ..**Waskover**, Donald S '82 -122 E 42nd -NY 10168 **Fx:**(201) 266-0503
(212) 902-7273 ..**Waskow**, Andrew V '00 Goldman Sachs -1 NY Plz -NY 10004
(212) 285-1200 ..**Wasmer**, Mark Conrad '00 %Mallin & Assoc,PC -132 Nassau -NY 10038 **Fx:**285-1202
(315) 474-7571 ..**Wasmund**, Mark W '86 (Mackenzie H LLP) -101 S Salina Bx4967 -Syracuse 13221
(212) 415-9200 ..**Wasnofski**, Robt M Jr. '97 (Dorsey & W LLP) -250 Park Av -NY 10177
(315) 448-7000 ..**Wason**, Jay W Jr. '82 %Unity Mutual Lifelns -507 Plum Bx5000 -Syracuse 13250 **Fx:**448-7203
(212) 486-1455 ..**Wason**, Patricia M '04 %Post PGM&S,PA -575 Mad Av -NY 10022
(212) 584-0700 ..**Wasp**, Danl R '99 %Seeger W LLP -1 William -NY 10004
(212) 318-2000 ..**Wass**, Erica F '03 Bloomberg LP -731 Lex Av -NY 10022
(914) 921-3365 ..**Wassall**, Donald A '76 -140 Forest Av -Rye 10580
(516) 357-3700 ..**Wassel**, Thos B '84 (Cullen and D LLP) -100 Q Roosevelt Blvd -Gdn Cty 11530
(516) 741-5614 ..**Wassem**, John M '92 -112 Lee Rd -Gdn Cty 11530
(212) 564-4010 ..**Wasser**, Brian F '83 %Mersel Klein & Wasser,LLP -450 7th Av -NY 10123 **Fx:**967-5040
(212) 935-5500 ..**Wasser**, Danl M '81 (Franklin WR&V) -488 Mad Av -NY 10022
(212) 430-6040 ..**Wasser**, Douglas F '81 (Wasser & R LLP) -80 Maiden Ln -NY 10038 **Fx:**430-6041
(212) 891-9100 ..**Wasser**, Marc E '98 (Goldfarb & F LLP) -345 Park Av -NY 10154
(212) 977-9700 ..**Wasser**, Martin B '74 (Phillips N LLP) -666 5th Av -NY 10103
(212) 962-6100 ..**Wasser**, Max '54 -132 Nassau -NY 10038 **Fx:**608-4176
(212) 788-0423 ..**Wasser**, Michl J '00 %Law Dept -100 Church -NY 10007 **Fx:**788-0367
(516) 295-3965 ..**Wasser**, Tina T '86 -871 Ivy Hill Rd -Woodmere 11598
(212) 810-8135 ..**Wasserman**, Aaron D '03 BlackRock -40 E 52nd -NY 10022
(212) 698-3500 ..**Wasserman**, Adam J '99 (Dechert LLP) -1095 Av of Amer -NY 10036
(212) 415-8600 ..**Wasserman**, Allen C '85 (Locke LB&L LLP) -3 World Fncl Ctr -NY 10281
(212) 344-8888 ..**Wasserman**, Andrew M '93 Willis NA -200 Lbrty -NY 10281
(516) 466-6050 ..**Wasserman**, Barry M '58 %Guardian Land Abstrct -1010 Nrthrn Blvd Bx385 -Gt Neck 11022 **Fx:**466-6011
(212) 432-9180 ..**Wasserman**, Bennett J '75 Cnsl Stryker T&D LLP -2 Penn Plz -NY 10121
(516) 763-1622 ..**Wasserman**, Blair M '85 (Pinsky & W PC) -Bx625 -Rockvll Ctr 11571 **Fx:**678-8332
(914) 375-0100 ..**Wasserman**, Chas D '96 (Novick ELRW&L,PC) -733 Ynkrs Av -Ynkrs 10704
(518) 220-5700 ..**Wasserman**, Cheryl Ann '93 %Blue Shield of NENY -30 Century Hill Dr -Latham 12110
(516) 741-5775 ..**Wasserman**, Clifford R '76 (C Wasserman,PC) -1 Old Cntry Rd -Carle Pl 11514 **Fx:**741-5779
(212) 506-1700 ..**Wasserman**, Danl A '09 %Kasowitz BT&F LLP -1633 Bway -NY 10019
(212) 732-8579 ..**Wasserman**, David M '91 %Sher HB&T,PC -277 Bway -NY 10007
(718) 454-4040 ..**Wasserman**, Drew B '80 %Campos & P,PC -186-09 Union Tpk -Flushng 11366
(908) 698-6326 ..**Wasserman**, Evan H '86 %Phillips-Van Heusen Corp -200 Mad Av -NY 10016 **Fx:**704-1022
(212) 581-3320 ..**Wasserman Grubin & Rogers,LLP** -1700 Bway -NY 10019 **Fx:**956-5255
(914) 835-1454 ..**Wasserman**, Harvey '71 -14 Glen Dr -Harrison 10528
(212) 566-4791 ..**Wasserman**, Howard I '70 -111 Bway -NY 10006 **Fx:**566-4795
(212) 403-7300 ..**Wasserman**, James I '81 (Vladeck WE&E,PC) -1501 Bway -NY 10036
(212) 508-6100 ..**Wasserman**, Jeffrey I '00 (Bracewell & G,LLP) -1251 Av of Amer -NY 10020
(516) 747-9300 ..**Wasserman**, Jeffrey S '81 (J Wasserman,PC) -1565 Franklin Av -Mineola 11501 **Fx:**747-9440
(718) 590-2000 ..**Wasserman**, Katie D '09 %DA -198 E 161st -Bronx 10451 **Fx:**590-6477
(212) 966-8663 ..**Wasserman**, Kenneth D '68 -401 Bway -NY 10013 **Fx:**219-9212
(212) 244-3399 ..**Wasserman**, Kenneth T '71 -350 5th Av -NY 10118 **Fx:**244-0980
(212) 834-0600 ..**Wasserman**, Lawr S '89 (Gordon & S,PC) -355 Lex Av -NY 10017
(212) 812-4252 ..**Wasserman**, Lee '84 %Rockefeller Family Fund -437 Mad Av -NY 10022
(212) 489-1600 ..**Wasserman**, Lee S '79 %Deloitte LLP -1633 Bway -NY 10019 **Fx:**492-4201

(212) 788-0641 .. **Wasserman,** Leonard M '73 %Law Dept -100 Church -NY 10007 **Fx:**788-0367
(718) 230-3100 .. **Wasserman,** M Chloe '94 %Brooklyn Public Library -1 Grand Army Plz -Brklyn 11238
(516) 228-3553 .. **Wasserman,** Marc '07 %Thaler & G,LLP -90 Merrick Av -E Meadow 11554
(631) 755-1234 .. **Wasserman,** Marc H '89 (M Wasserman,PC) -Bx718 -Mt Sinai 11766 **Fx:**331-4172
(212) 546-9255 .. **Wasserman,** Michl R '92 OfCnsl Scarinci H -107 Grand -NY 10013
(212) 270-8002 .. **Wasserman,** Peter J '81 JP Morgan Chase -270 Park Av -NY 10017
(212) 888-3033 .. **Wasserman,** Rachel Korn '79 (Becker GM&M LLP) -299 Park Av -NY 10171
(212) 581-3320 .. **Wasserman,** Richd '76 (Wasserman G&R,LLP) -1700 Bway -NY 10019
(718) 237-2000 .. **Wasserman,** Roy S '87 %Leg Aid -111 Lvngstn -Brklyn 11201 **Fx:**237-8737
(914) 375-0100 .. **Wasserman,** Sol M '75 (Novick ELRW&L,PC) -733 Ynkrs Av -Ynkrs 10704
(516) 843-9579 .. **Wasserman,** Stephen R '81 -5 Harrow Ln -Old Bethpage 11804 **Fx:**908-7853
(212) 577-3387 .. **Wasserman,** Steven B '81 %Leg Aid -199 Water -NY 10038 **Fx:**577-7964
(212) 209-4800 .. **Wasserman,** Steven F '84 (Brown R LLP) -7 Times Sq -NY 10036
(212) 335-4500 .. **Wasserman,** Steven L '79 DLA Piper LLP -1251 Av of Amer -NY 10020
(212) 877-1588 .. **Wasserman,** Steven M '88 (S Wasserman & Assoc) -328 W 77th -NY 10024 **Fx:**877-6249
(212) 874-6789 .. **Wasserman,** Susan K '76 -142 West End Av -NY 10023 **Fx:**874-6809
(914) 375-0100 .. **Wasserman-Dentz,** Amy R '04 Novick ELRW&L,PC -733 Ynkrs Av -Ynkrs 10704
(518) 436-6000 .. **Wassermann,** Edw H '81 (Marsh Wassmermann & McHugh,LLC) -677 Bway -Albany 12207 **Fx:**436-6009
(212) 735-3000 .. **Wasserstein,** Henry P '67 (Skadden ASM&F LLP) -4 Times Sq -NY 10036
(718) 260-2380 .. **Wasserstein,** Jeffrey N '97 %Hon A Ross -225 Cadman Plz E -Brklyn 11201
(516) 933-1515 .. **Wasserstein,** Lori J '93 (Santucci & W) -366 N Bway -Jericho 11753
(212) 822-0539 .. **Wasserstein,** Pamela Simone '06 Apollo Mgmt -9 W 57th -NY 10019
(212) 455-2000 .. **Wasserstrom,** Leigh A '10 %Simpson T&B LLP -425 Lex Av -NY 10017
(212) 553-3200 .. **Wassmuth,** Scott W '01 Marulli LE&T,LLP -5 Hanover Sq -NY 10004
(212) 259-8000 .. **Wassner,** Brien M '04 %Dewey & L LLP -1301 Av of Amer -NY 10019
(212) 588-0800 .. **Wasson,** Andrew S '06 %Frommer L&H LLP -745 5th Av -NY 10151
(518) 457-4380 .. **Wasyl,** Larissa C '07 %Dept of Labor -State Campus Bldg 12 -Albany 12240 **Fx:**457-1164
(718) 556-7114 .. **Waszak,** John D G '06 %DA -130 Styvsnt Pl -Staten Isl 10301
(212) 486-7005 .. **Watanabe,** Laura Ann '87 (Watanabe Law Firm,LLC) -444 Mad Av -NY 10022 **Fx:**486-6010
(212) 765-2100 .. **Watanabe,** Roy N '74 (Spivak L LLP) -1700 Bway -NY 10019
(212) 486-7005 .. **Watanabe,** Wm K '87 OfCnsl Watanabe Law Firm,LLC -444 Mad Av -NY 10022 **Fx:**486-6010
(212) 258-3333 .. **Watanabe,** Yasuhide '92 SpclCnsl Masuda Intl -152 W 57th -NY 10019 **Fx:**957-3939
(607) 698-4011 .. **Watches,** Chauncey J '85 -13 W Main -Canisteo 14823 **Fx:**698-4004
(718) 205-1010 .. **Waterbury,** David E '81 %E Ifraimoff & Assoc,PC -116-16 Qns Blvd -Frst Hlls 11375 **Fx:**205-2066
(212) 819-8212 .. **Waterfield,** Amy J '97 -1155 Av of Amer -NY 10036 **Fx:**354-8113
(212) 335-4500 .. **Waterhouse,** Melinda Harwood '07 %DLA Piper LLP -1251 Av of Amer -NY 10020
(212) 820-9339 .. **Waterman,** Christopher M '79 (Hawkins D&W LLP) -One Chase Manh Plz -NY 10005
(212) 610-6300 .. **Waterman,** Elizabeth '07 %Allen & O -1221 Av of Amer -NY 10020
(212) 532-0530 .. **Waterman,** Kathleen C '99 -419 Park Av S -NY 10016 **Fx:**684-3620
(631) 286-3344 .. **Waterman,** T Preston '57 Thornhedge,Ltd -13 N Howells Pnt Rd -Bellprt 11713 **Fx:**286-3970
(716) 854-2620 .. **Waterman,** Tara E '07 %Brown & K,LLP -1500 Lbrty Bldg -Buffalo 14202
(212) 872-1000 .. **Waters,** Ashley Ford '06 -One Bryant Park -NY 10036 **Fx:**872-1002
(315) 475-3127 .. **Waters,** Christine S '04 %Leg Srvcs -472 S Salina -Syracuse 13202 **Fx:**475-2706
(845) 638-5001 .. **Waters,** Christopher M '04 DA -1 S Main -New Cty 10956 **Fx:**638-5298
(212) 415-9200 .. **Waters,** Eric R '09 %Dorsey & W LLP -250 Park Av -NY 10177
(516) 741-7676 .. **Waters,** Gerald C Jr. '08 %Miranda SSSV LLP -240 Mineola Blvd -Mineola 11501
(212) 349-5300 .. **Waters,** Henrietta Davis '83 -44 Wall -NY 10005 **Fx:**530-4810
(214) 651-5366 .. **Waters,** James L '98 (Haynes & B,LLP) -1221 Av of Amer -NY 10020 **Fx:**200-0441
(516) 741-2585 .. **Waters,** Jean '97 %Rosicki R & Assoc,PC -51 E Bethpage Rd -Plainvw 11803 **Fx:**741-4748
(212) 227-7878 .. **Waters McPherson McNeill** -233 Bway -NY 10279 **Fx:**227-6534
(212) 277-6500 .. **Waters,** Michl J '88 Cnsl Dickstein S LLP -1633 Bway -NY 10019
(212) 336-2000 .. **Waters,** Timothy A '09 %Patterson BW&T LLP -1133 Av of Amer -NY 10036
(212) 788-0822 .. **Waters,** Virginia '75 %Law Dept -100 Church -NY 10007 **Fx:**788-0367
(212) 442-5924 .. **Waters,** Wm H '01 Dept Youth & Cmmnty Dvlpmnt -156 William -NY 10038
(718) 292-4500 .. **Waters,** Winston S '83 -840 Grnd Cncrs -Bronx 10451 **Fx:**292-0115
(212) 785-5840 .. **Watford,** Gregory J '95 -61 Bway -NY 10006
(212) 937-4281 .. **Watkins,** Adam F '08 Watkins B&C,LLP -228 Park Av S -NY 10003
(585) 442-7273 .. **Watkins,** Barry C '77 -399 Wstmnstr Rd -Rchstr 14607 **Fx:**324-1362
(845) 294-3991 .. **Watkins,** Christopher D '99 (Sussman & W) -40 Park Pl Bx1028 -Goshen 10924 **Fx:**294-1623
(212) 412-9500 .. **Watkins,** Cynthia R '93 %Flemming ZWZ LLP -1 Lbrty Plz -NY 10006
(518) 371-6125 .. **Watkins,** E Gray '78 -1745 Rt 9 -Clifton Pk 12065 **Fx:**371-6183
(518) 473-8418 .. **Watkins,** Edw G '78 %OCFS -52 Wshngtn -Rensselaer 12144 **Fx:**486-6361
(212) 722-6042 .. **Watkins,** Harvey K '80 -1185 Park Av -NY 10128
(914) 428-1292 .. **Watkins,** John E Jr. '69 (Watkins & W,LLP) -150 Grand -White Plns 10601 **Fx:**428-4104
(212) 259-8000 .. **Watkins,** John F '08 %Dewey & L LLP -1301 Av of Amer -NY 10019
(212) 209-3031 .. **Watkins,** John F F '96 (Reitler K&R LLC) -885 3rd Av -NY 10022
(212) 902-1000 .. **Watkins,** Kathryn R '07 Goldman Sachs & Co -200 West -NY 10282
(914) 428-1292 .. **Watkins,** Liane V '99 (Watkins & W,LLP) -150 Grand -White Plns 10601 **Fx:**428-4104
(845) 638-9868 .. **Watkins,** L'Tanya M '05 -120-126 N Main -New Cty 10956
(212) 837-6883 .. **Watkins,** Lucas P '10 %Hughes H&R LLP -1 Bttry Pk Plz -NY 10004 **Fx:**299-6883
(518) 449-3300 .. **Watkins,** Mark E '71 (Nolan & H,LLP) -39 N Pearl -Albany 12207
(212) 695-8871 .. **Watkins,** Martin '91 -500 W 43rd -NY 10036
(212) 336-0183 .. **Watkins,** Matthew J '03 SEC -3 World Fncl Ctr -NY 10281 **Fx:**336-1323
(518) 792-2117 .. **Watkins,** Patricia E '83 (Bartlett PS&R,PC) -1 Wshngtn Bx2168 -Glens Fls 12801
(212) 588-5500 .. **Watkins,** Paul R '09 %Davies WP&V LLP -625 Mad Av -NY 10022
(585) 477-8282 .. **Watkins,** Peyton C '98 %Eastman Kodak -343 State -Rchstr 14650
(212) 310-8000 .. **Watkins,** Robt P III '09 %Weil G&M LLP -767 5th Av -NY 10153
(914) 701-4000 .. **Watkins,** Sam R Jr. '73 (Watkins & C) -106 Corp Park Dr -White Plns 10604 **Fx:**701-4001
(212) 784-5800 .. **Watkins,** Saml C '88 (Hiscock & B,LLP) -7 Times Sq -NY 10036
(516) 483-1506 .. **Watkins,** Sandra C '89 %G Wright & Assoc -50 Clinton -Hempstd 11550
(917) 689-3180 .. **Watkins,** Zara K '05 -Bx627 -NY 10274
(202) 828-5851 .. **Watkiss,** Jeffrey D '05 (Bracewell & G,LLP) -1251 Av of Amer -NY 10020 **Fx:**857-2131
(516) 625-1531 .. **Watman,** Cindy F '80 -Bx1311 -Roslyn Hts 11577 **Fx:**625-6864
(212) 213-6886 .. **Watnick,** Donald E '89 -292 Mad Av -NY 10017 **Fx:**972-2245
(718) 289-5958 .. **Watnick,** Valerie J '89 %Bronx Comm College -Univ Av & W 181st -Bronx 10453
(646) 562-3405 .. **Watnik,** Ilissa L '02 %PLC -747 3rd Av -NY 10017
(212) 701-3000 .. **Watnik,** Scott J '04 %Cahill G&R LLP -80 Pine -NY 10005 **Fx:**269-5420
(914) 833-3812 .. **Watras,** Patricia A '82 -6 Howard -Larchmnt 10538 **Fx:**833-3812
(716) 852-3540 .. **Watson Bennett Colligan Johnson & Schechter** -12 Fountain Plz -Buffalo 14202 **Fx:**852-3546
(716) 683-3364 .. **Watson Bennett Colligan Johnson & Schechter** -3521 Union Rd -Cheektowaga 14225
(212) 683-7999 .. **Watson,** Carla D '03 Legal Srvcs for Children Inc -271 Mad Av -NY 10016 **Fx:**683-5544
(716) 852-1000 .. **Watson,** Craig R '88 %PW Beltz,PC -36 Church -Buffalo 14202 **Fx:**852-5887
(212) 863-6300 .. **Watson,** D Maria '90 %HPD -100 Gold -NY 10038 **Fx:**863-8201
(845) 452-2807 .. **Watson,** Denise M '89 -23 Alden Rd -Poughkeepsie 12603 **Fx:**462-8685
(212) 922-2200 .. **Watson Farley & Williams LLP** -1133 Av of Amer -NY 10036 **Fx:**922-1512
(917) 777-4200 .. **Watson,** Gail G '81 OfCnsl Bingham M LLP -1 Bttry Pk Plz -NY 10004
(212) 483-2323 .. **Watson,** James J '80 %JP Morgan Chase -345 Park Av -NY 10154
(212) 859-8000 .. **Watson,** Jenna L '09 %Fried FHS&J LLP -1 NY Plz -NY 10004
(516) 535-5223 .. **Watson,** Joanne C '84 Chicago Title Ins -330 Old Cntry Rd -Mineola 11501 **Fx:**742-5061
(518) 457-8066 .. **Watson,** John R M '98 %Crime Victims Bd -1 Columbia Cir -Albany 12203 **Fx:**457-8658
(516) 571-2883 .. **Watson,** Joy M '86 %Hon K Murphy -100 Supreme Ct Dr -Mineola 11501
(718) 250-2000 .. **Watson,** Karla D '00 %DA -350 Jay -Brklyn 11201 **Fx:**250-2314
(516) 571-9054 .. **Watson,** Kathleen '81 Family Ct -1200 Old Cntry Rd -Westbury 11590 **Fx:**571-9335
(631) 577-2400 .. **Watson,** Kathleen McDonald '86 %Tromello M&K -25 Melvll Park Rd Bx9038 -Melvll 11747
(718) 794-5907 .. **Watson,** Kevin '92 -2116 Wllmsbrdg Rd -Bronx 10461 **Fx:**792-7645
(212) 633-2225 .. **Watson,** Kipp E '82 %M Stumer & Assoc,PC -306 5th Av -NY 10001 **Fx:**691-3642
(212) 541-2000 .. **Watson,** Kira P '96 OfCnsl Bryan C LLP -1290 Av of Amer -NY 10104
(212) 483-9490 .. **Watson,** Margaret Larkin '91 OfCnsl McElroy DM&C,LLP -88 Pine -NY 10005
(212) 225-2000 .. **Watson,** Mary Perpetua '93 Cleary GS&H -1 Lbrty Plz -NY 10006
(212) 318-6000 .. **Watson,** Michl K '10 %Paul HJ&W LLP -75 E 55th -NY 10022
(212) 878-8000 .. **Watson,** Rebecca M '07 %Clifford C LLP -31 W 52nd -NY 10019
(212) 267-5353 .. **Watson,** Richd A '73 (Chamberlain WO&W) -575 8th Av -NY 10018
(516) 496-1919 .. **Watson,** Scott C '82 (Keller O&W,PC) -242 Crsswys Park Dr W -Woodbury 11797
(212) 556-7531 .. **Watson,** Solomon B IV '77 %The NY Times Co -620 8th Av -NY 10018 **Fx:**556-4634
(212) 708-9133 .. **Watson,** Stephen M '84 Bessemer Trst Co -630 5th Av -NY 10111 **Fx:**265-5826
(518) 474-6740 .. **Watson,** Susan L '88 %Dept of State -41 State -Albany 12231 **Fx:**473-9211
(212) 909-6000 .. **Watson,** Talik N '07 %Debevoise & P LLP -919 3rd Av -NY 10022
(631) 758-9666 .. **Watson,** Thos J '74 -22 W Main -Patchogue 11772 **Fx:**758-8106
(212) 841-1000 .. **Watson,** Victoria L '82 SpclCnsl Covington & B LLP -620 8th Av -NY 10018
(212) 230-8800 .. **Watson,** Violetta Guberman '07 %WilmerHale -399 Park Av -NY 10022
(914) 948-4500 .. **Watson,** Wm R '84 (O'Connor MCD&O) -1 Barker Av -White Plns 10601
(518) 587-8112 .. **Watt,** Christopher J '01 (Hamilton W PLLC) -480 Bway -Saratoga Spgs 12866 **Fx:**587-4140

(585) 258-4029 .. **Watt,** John H Jr. '85 %JP Morgan Chase -1 Chase Sq -Rchstr 14643 **Fx:**258-6458
(315) 477-9914 .. **Watt,** Jos C Jr. '69 OfCnsl Porter NH LLP -316 S Clinton -Syracuse 13202 **Fx:**477-9923
(716) 856-4000 .. **Watt,** Margot L '92 (Hodgson R LLP) -140 Pearl -Buffalo 14202
(212) 458-1637 .. **Watt,** Megan Clark '90 %AIG -175 Water -NY 10038
(212) 549-2500 .. **Watt,** Steven M '06 ACLU -125 Broad -NY 10004 **Fx:**549-2651
(718) 544-8998 .. **Wattenberg,** Marc R '91 -71-21 Austin -Frst Hlls 11375
(607) 776-4126 .. **Wattenberg,** Mark '74 %Leg Srvcs -104 E Steuben -Bath 14810 **Fx:**776-4029
(212) 603-8800 .. **Watters,** Connell J '90 %Sentinal Real Estate Grp -1251 Av of Amer -NY 10020
(516) 868-0660 .. **Watters,** Jacqueline Ann '93 -25 Merrick Av -Merrick 11566
(212) 679-8999 .. **Watters,** Kyle B '87 (Watters & S,LLP) -286 Mad Av -NY 10017 **Fx:**679-9791
(718) 273-2373 .. **Watters,** Laura J '91 -363 Bement Av -Staten Isl 10310
(516) 942-0244 .. **Watters,** Wm M '77 %Office oDA&R -375 N Bway -Jericho 11753 **Fx:**942-0353
(212) 756-2000 .. **Watterson,** Paul N Jr. '81 (Schulte R&Z LLP) -919 3rd Av -NY 10022
(212) 504-6000 .. **Wattman,** Malcolm P '69 (Cadwalader W&T LLP) -1 World Fncl Ctr -NY 10281
(212) 335-9000 .. **Watts,** Fredk J '83 %DA -1 Hogan Pl -NY 10013
(718) 875-5020 .. **Watts,** Gregory S '86 -26 Court -Brklyn 11242 **Fx:**237-0639
(212) 218-5500 .. **Watts,** Kyona A '04 Seyfarth S LLP -620 8th Av -NY 10018
(718) 741-3400 .. **Watts,** LaShonne R '03 Childrens Law Ctr -2501 Grnd Cncrs -Bronx 10468
(212) 906-1200 .. **Watts,** Lisa C '00 %Latham & W -885 3rd Av -NY 10022
(718) 681-0900 .. **Watts,** Patrick A H '81 -208 E 163rd -Bronx 10451
(631) 234-1500 .. **Watts,** Valerie E '08 %Rubin & R LLC -1787 Vets Hwy -Islandia 11749
(518) 965-1713 .. **Watz,** Christopher J '94 -169 Lk Rd -Pine Plns 12567
(716) 847-8400 .. **Watz,** James H '66 OfCnsl Phillips L LLP -3400 HSBC Ctr -Buffalo 14203
(212) 455-2000 .. **Watzman,** Alyssa R '08 %Simpson T&B LLP -425 Lex Av -NY 10017
(212) 225-2000 .. **Wauters,** Charles-Antoine '10 Cleary GS&H -1 Lbrty Plz -NY 10006
(212) 880-6000 .. **Wawro,** David W '78 (Torys LLP) -237 Park Av -NY 10017
(212) 935-6020 .. **Wawrynek,** Christine '05 %Klein ZR LLP -485 Mad Av -NY 10022
(212) 266-1221 .. **Wax,** Ari N '87 %Dept of Corrections -60 Hudson -NY 10013 **Fx:**266-1677
(212) 415-8600 .. **Wax,** David I '09 %Locke LB&L LLP -3 World Fncl Ctr -NY 10281
(718) 263-7758 .. **Wax,** Ronnie D '75 -98-20 Metro Av -Frst Hlls 11375
(212) 661-4400 .. **Waxenberg,** Cathy G '80 Laiken Assoc -56 W 45th -NY 10036 **Fx:**867-8209
(212) 969-3000 .. **Waxenberg,** Jay D '82 (Proskauer R LLP) -1585 Bway -NY 10036
(212) 364-8519 .. **Waxenberg,** Susan A '83 Time Warner Cable -60 Columbus Av -NY 10023 **Fx:**364-8460
(212) 584-0949 .. **Waxer,** Adam S '01 ProCure Treatment Ctrs,Inc -192 Lex Av -NY 10016
(914) 333-9608 .. **Waxler,** Aaron M '03 Philips Intellectual Prop -345 Scarborough Rd -Briarclff Mnr 10510
(212) 872-9831 .. **Waxman,** Alan N '84 (Squire S&D LLP) -30 Rckfllr Plz -NY 10112
(212) 836-8000 .. **Waxman,** Allen P '09 (Kaye S LLP) -425 Park Av -NY 10022
(212) 684-2200 .. **Waxman,** Danl E '09 %Waxman & W,PC -386 Park Av S -NY 10016
(212) 541-2000 .. **Waxman,** Danl P '93 (Bryan C LLP) -1290 Av of Amer -NY 10104
(516) 622-9200 .. **Waxman,** Eric G III '82 (Westerman BEM&S,LLP) -1201 RXR Plz -Uniondale 11553
(212) 684-2200 .. **Waxman,** Fran S '87 (Waxman & W,PC) -386 Park Av S -NY 10016
(212) 292-4872 .. **Waxman,** Gregg A '92 -2 Penn Plz -NY 10121
(212) 637-2200 .. **Waxman,** Hadassa R '01 %US Atty -1 St Andrews Plz -NY 10007
(212) 373-3000 .. **Waxman,** Ilana D '09 %Paul WRW&G LLP -1285 Av of Amer -NY 10019
(718) 875-3000 .. **Waxman,** Jay R '62 -625 Atl Av -Brklyn 11217
(212) 929-2562 .. **Waxman,** Jon M '73 -302 W 12th -NY 10014 **Fx:**229-1625
(718) 250-2000 .. **Waxman,** Joshua M '06 DA -350 Jay -Brklyn 11201 **Fx:**250-2314
(212) 806-5400 .. **Waxman,** Lauren J '08 %Stroock &S&L LLP -180 Maiden Ln -NY 10038
(212) 684-2200 .. **Waxman,** Lawr D '78 (Waxman & W,PC) -386 Park Av S -NY 10016
(212) 527-7375 .. **Waxman,** Leigh V '93 %Para Advisors LLC -520 Mad Av -NY 10022
(212) 535-1101 .. **Waxman,** Mark Z '69 -20 E 68th -NY 10065
(212) 213-2024 .. **Waxman,** Nathan '85 -404 Park Av S -NY 10016
(516) 374-3733 .. **Waxman,** Richd H '74 (RH Waxman,PC) -445 Central Av -Cedarhrst 11516 **Fx:**706-2911
(212) 369-9128 .. **Waxman,** Ronald B '89 -175 E 96th -NY 10128 **Fx:**348-7620
(212) 848-4000 .. **Waxman,** Saml A '01 (Shearman & S LLP) -599 Lex Av -NY 10022
(516) 622-0606 .. **Waxman,** Stanley R '63 OfCnsl P Rizzuto,PC -1 Old Cntry Rd -Carle Pl 11514 **Fx:**622-2112
(845) 592-7000 .. **Waxman,** Stuart S '93 (Donoghue TA&D LLP) -2517 Route 52 -Hopewell Junct 12533
(212) 684-2200 .. **Waxman & Waxman,PC** -386 Park Av S -NY 10016 **Fx:**679-5875
(631) 543-7667 .. **Waxner,** Marvin '64 OfCnsl Sarisohn Law Prtnrs LLP -350 Vets Mem'l Hwy -Commack 11725 **Fx:**543-7901
(212) 681-6000 .. **Way,** Barbara E '83 %Fed Home Loan Bk -101 Park Av -NY 10178 **Fx:**949-2007
(718) 488-1953 .. **Way,** Fred D III '85 (FD Way & Assoc) -44 Court -Brklyn 11201 **Fx:**624-4509
(516) 739-0400 .. **Way,** Kevin E '86 %Kelly R&K,LLP -330 Old Cntry Rd -Mineola 11501
(516) 333-4500 .. **Way,** Renny Wm '75 -7 Ferncote Ln -Glen Head 11545
(917) 494-4691 .. **Wayburn,** Robt F '72 -60 E 42nd -NY 10165 **Fx:**(212) 370-5206
(212) 425-9300 .. **Wayco,** Stefanie M '09 %Bressler A&R,PC -17 State -NY 10004
(212) 415-8600 .. **Wayda,** Andrea L '93 (Locke LB&L LLP) -3 World Fncl Ctr -NY 10281
(845) 469-4900 .. **Waye,** Judith A '89 %Greenwald Law Ofc -99 Brookside Av -Chester 10918 **Fx:**469-2022
(212) 455-2000 .. **Wayland,** Jos '84 (Simpson T&B LLP) -425 Lex Av -NY 10017
(607) 974-0463 .. **Wayland,** Randall S '06 %Corning -1 Rvrfrnt Plz -Corning 14831 **Fx:**974-6135
(315) 363-0585 .. **Wayland-Smith,** Tina M '91 (Campanie & W PLLC) -60 E State Bx70 -Sherrill 13461 **Fx:**363-1952
(914) 472-2300 .. **Wayne,** Deborah H '92 %Jones G,LLP -670 Wht Plns Rd -Scarsdale 10583
(212) 791-0285 .. **Wayne,** Eva Shanda '00 %Malaby & B,LLC -150 Bway -NY 10038 **Fx:**791-0286
(914) 723-3609 .. **Wayne,** Milton J '50 -23 Farragut Rd -Scarsdale 10583
(212) 306-7591 .. **Wayne,** Raymond V III '86 %Comm on Human Rights -40 Rector -NY 10006 **Fx:**306-7474
(973) 491-3312 .. **Wayne,** Robt A '81 (LeClairRyan,PC) -830 3rd Av -NY 10022 **Fx:**491-3555
(845) 778-8560 .. **Wayne,** Stanley M '01 (Wayne & W) -21 Valley Av -Walden 12586 **Fx:**778-3903
(845) 778-8560 .. **Wayne,** Suzanne K '03 (Wayne & W) -21 Valley Av -Walden 12586 **Fx:**778-3903
(212) 319-9300 .. **Wayner,** Linda M '02 Cnsl NYC Cmsn UN,Consular Corps & Protocol -2 UN Plz -NY 10017 **Fx:**319-3430
(212) 490-3000 .. **Wayner,** Veronica M '07 %Wilson EME&D LLP -150 E 42nd -NY 10017
(718) 286-2000 .. **Ways,** Meggan E '06 %Leg Aid -120-46 Qns Blvd -Kew Gdns 11415 **Fx:**286-2286
(212) 344-4700 .. **Waytowich,** Justin R '07 %DeOrchis & Prtnrs LLP -61 Bway -NY 10006
(518) 487-5460 .. **Weafer,** Kenneth C '08 %DA -6 Lodge -Albany 12207 **Fx:**487-5093
(212) 964-7400 .. **Weakland,** Shawn M '99 Smith MDWY&Y,PC -111 John -NY 10038
(845) 369-9000 .. **Wealcatch,** Wm W '56 -4 Exec Blvd -Suffern 10901 **Fx:**369-9006
(212) 594-5000 .. **Weall,** Katherine J '02 %Togut S&S LLP -1 Penn Plz -NY 10119
(315) 393-7924 .. **Wears,** Katherine Hannan '79 -731 Ford Bx213T -Ogdensbrg 13669 **Fx:**393-7941
(518) 487-7600 .. **Weatherby,** Danielle Day '06 %Whiteman O&H LLP -1 Commerce Plz -Albany 12260
(914) 345-3020 .. **Weathers,** Wendy M '97 Knuckles K&E,LLP -565 Taxter Rd -Elmsfrd 10523
(212) 806-5400 .. **Weathers-Lowin,** Benjamin '08 %Stroock &S&L LLP -180 Maiden Ln -NY 10038
(212) 225-2000 .. **Weaver,** Andrew W '03 %Cleary GS&H -1 Lbrty Plz -NY 10006
(845) 758-4400 .. **Weaver,** Ann '92 -7466 S Bway -Red Hook 12571 **Fx:**758-6220
(212) 649-2000 .. **Weaver,** Debra S '82 %Hearst Corp -300 W 57th -NY 10019 **Fx:**649-2035
(212) 553-0300 .. **Weaver,** Diana L '89 %Moody's Invstr Srvc -250 Greenwich -NY 10007
(631) 390-0010 .. **Weaver,** J Michl '95 %Bruno G&S,LLP -445 Broad Hollow Rd -Melvll 11747
(718) 286-6000 .. **Weaver,** Jessica Aerni '04 %DA -125-01 Qns Blvd -Kew Gdns 11415
(718) 596-8879 .. **Weaver,** Kecia J '98 -44 Court -Brklyn 11201 **Fx:**596-3140
(315) 218-8000 .. **Weaver,** Lisa M '07 %Bond S&K,PLLC -1 Lincoln Ctr -Syracuse 13202
(212) 425-7200 .. **Weaver,** Matthew R '10 %Kenyon & K,LLP -1 Bway -NY 10004
(212) 850-4859 .. **Weaver,** Robt P '91 %Emigrant Svngs Bk -5 E 42nd -NY 10017 **Fx:**850-4424
(212) 576-5879 .. **Weaver,** Robin D '86 NY Life Ins -51 Mad Av -NY 10010
(212) 869-3200 .. **Weaver,** Ross G '74 %Molod S&D,PC -104 W 40th -NY 10018
(212) 827-1400 .. **Weaver,** Sallie Campbell '98 %Screen Actors Guild -360 Mad Av -NY 10017 **Fx:**944-6774
(845) 639-1320 .. **Weaver,** Sandra L '84 (Samimi & M) -616 S Main -New Cty 10956 **Fx:**639-8069
(212) 735-3000 .. **Weavil,** Richd Scott '08 %Skadden ASM&F LLP -4 Times Sq -NY 10036
(732) 855-6162 .. **Webb,** Albertina '99 %Wilentz G&S -110 William -NY 10038 **Fx:**726-4707
(212) 319-1900 .. **Webb,** Chas S III '59 (Berger & W,LLP) -1633 Bway -NY 10019
(212) 310-8000 .. **Webb,** Claire L '08 %Weil G&M LLP -767 5th Av -NY 10153
(212) 754-6300 .. **Webb,** Cynthia '83 %Orenstein & O,LLC -425 Park Av -NY 10022 **Fx:**754-7141
(212) 225-2000 .. **Webb,** David E '87 Cnsl Cleary GS&H -1 Lbrty Plz -NY 10006
(212) 375-2000 .. **Webb,** David J '91 %American Capital Access -140 Bway -NY 10005
(212) 504-6000 .. **Webb,** Heather J '09 %Cadwalader W&T LLP -1 World Fncl Ctr -NY 10281
(212) 521-5400 .. **Webb,** John B '00 (Reed S LLP) -599 Lex Av -NY 10022
(212) 571-5970 .. **Webb,** Karen A '00 -233 Bway -NY 10279
(212) 556-2100 .. **Webb,** Lauren E '08 %King & S -1185 Av of Amer -NY 10036
(212) 395-2121 .. **Webb,** Morrison D '77 %Verizon -140 West -NY 10007
(585) 454-4460 .. **Webb,** Pamela B '79 (Petralia W&O,PC) -16 E Main -Rchstr 14614
(716) 488-1178 .. **Webb,** Paul V Jr. '73 (Erickson WS&H) -414 E Fairmount Av Bx414 -Lakewd 14750
(716) 488-1178 .. **Webb,** Paul V III '03 %Erickson WS&H -414 E Fairmount Av Bx414 -Lakewd 14750
(716) 694-2666 .. **Webb,** Thos E '64 -252 Fillmore Av -Tonawanda 14150
(716) 446-1189 .. **Webb,** Thos E Jr. '89 -Bx545 -Williamsvll 14231
(212) 715-9100 .. **Webber,** Amanda '08 Kramer LN&F,LLP -1177 Av of Amer -NY 10036
(585) 454-3377 .. **Webber,** Blake T '05 %Brown & T,LLC -19 Prince -Rchstr 14607
(212) 998-0373 .. **Webber,** David H '04 NYU Law Schl -44 W 4th -NY 10012
(212) 819-8200 .. **Webber,** Jason K '02 (White & C LLP) -1155 Av of Amer -NY 10036
(212) 815-1127 .. **Webber,** Karen A '00 DC 37 MELS -125 Barclay -NY 10007 **Fx:**815-1343
(212) 257-6800 .. **Webber,** Kathryn '99 (Thompson W&G LLP) -85 5th Av -NY 10003
(212) 583-9600 .. **Weber,** A Michl '73 (Littler M,PC) -900 3rd Av -NY 10022
(516) 229-4590 .. **Weber,** Andrew N '05 G Lauzon -875 Merrick Av -Westbury 11590
(845) 639-7800 .. **Weber,** Aron G '94 (Mandel K&B,LLP) -210 Route 303 -Vly Cottage 10989
(718) 972-4040 .. **Weber,** Aryeh '76 -220 Ditmas Av -Brklyn 11218
(212) 558-4000 .. **Weber,** Benjamin R '92 (Sullivan & C LLP) -125 Broad -NY 10004
(631) 549-2000 .. **Weber,** Bram D '01 (Weber Law Grp,LLP) -290 Broad Hollow Rd -Melvll 11747 **Fx:**549-2015
(212) 422-9424 .. **Weber,** Bryan R '05 %Gogick B&O,LLP -11 Bway -NY 10004
(212) 458-6008 .. **Weber,** Chas B '93 AIGTS -175 Water -NY 10038

(914) 694-4102 .. **Weber,** Clifford S '77 (Hinman H&K,LLP) -106 Corp Park Dr -White Plns 10604
(718) 446-2656 .. **Weber,** Dale R '87 -40-06 Warren -Elmhrst 11373 **Fx:**779-6984
(212) 735-3000 .. **Weber,** Daniela '09 %Skadden ASM&F LLP -4 Times Sq -NY 10036
(212) 245-4580 .. **Weber,** Dorothy M '82 (Shukat AHW&H,LLP) -111 W 57th -NY 10019
(212) 878-8000 .. **Weber,** Eli S '91 (Clifford C LLP) -31 W 52nd -NY 10019
(718) 815-1794 .. **Weber,** Elizabeth M '94 (E Weber & Assoc) -191 Catherine -Staten Isl 10302
(212) 626-4100 .. **Weber,** Eric J '08 %Baker & M LLP -1114 Av of Amer -NY 10036
(718) 815-1794 .. **Weber,** Frances H '81 %E Weber & Assoc -191 Catherine -Staten Isl 10302
(212) 858-4324 .. **Weber,** Frank M '94 FINRA -1 Lbrty Plz -NY 10006 **Fx:**858-4389
(516) 832-8002 .. **Weber,** Fred '89 Arbor Commercial Mortgage,LLC -333 Earle Ovngton Blvd -Uniondale 11553 **Fx:**832-8045
(212) 509-0999 .. **Weber,** Howard B '82 -61 Bway -NY 10006 **Fx:**509-1222
(631) 549-2000 .. **Weber,** Jaret S '04 %Weber Law Grp,LLP -290 Broad Hollow Rd -Melvll 11747 **Fx:**549-2015
(212) 940-8800 .. **Weber,** Jarrod N '06 %Katten MR LLP -575 Mad Av -NY 10022
(631) 321-6065 .. **Weber,** John '92 -400 W Main -Babylon 11702
(212) 407-3369 .. **Weber,** John R '04 Graphite Capital Intl Grp -126 E 56th -NY 10022
(212) 259-8000 .. **Weber,** John W Jr. '73 (Dewey & L LLP) -1301 Av of Amer -NY 10019
(315) 218-8000 .. **Weber,** Kathleen S '09 %Bond S&K,PLLC -1 Lincoln Ctr -Syracuse 13202
(973) 596-4895 .. **Weber,** Kevin W '09 %Gibbons PC -1 Penn Plz -NY 10119 **Fx:**639-8372
(212) 475-3673 .. **Weber,** Lindsay M '08 OfCnsl Tese & M -1 Minetta Ln -NY 10012
(718) 855-4076 .. **Weber,** Lindsey A '06 -161 Atl Av -Brklyn 11201 **Fx:**855-0030
(516) 227-2300 .. **Weber,** Lisa '92 %Wright Risk Mgmt -333 Earle Ovngton Blvd -Uniondale 11553 **Fx:**227-2352
(212) 888-8200 .. **Weber,** Marcel '61 (Feder K LLP) -845 3rd Av -NY 10022
(212) 804-4200 .. **Weber,** Mark J '93 (Mound CW&G) -One Bttry Pk Plz -NY 10004
(212) 395-6256 .. **Weber,** Mary Louise '87 %Verizon -140 West -NY 10007
(716) 285-3525 .. **Weber,** Matthew T '99 (Tisdale C&W) -800 Main -Niagara Fls 14302 **Fx:**285-8574
(585) 258-2133 .. **Weber,** Michl J '90 %State Ins Fund -100 Chestnut -Rchstr 14604 **Fx:**258-8143
(516) 327-7916 .. **Weber,** Michele M '94 %Astoria Fed Svngs & Loan -1 Astoria Fed Plz -Lk Success 11042 **Fx:**327-7988
(718) 250-2000 .. **Weber,** Michelle H '03 %DA -350 Jay -Brklyn 11201 **Fx:**250-2314
(631) 549-2000 .. **Weber,** Morton '68 (Weber Law Grp,LLP) -290 Broad Hollow Rd -Melvll 11747 **Fx:**549-2015
(212) 885-5000 .. **Weber,** Nichole R '04 %Blank R LLP -405 Lex Av -NY 10174
(212) 756-2000 .. **Weber,** Paul E '78 (Schulte R&Z LLP) -919 3rd Av -NY 10022
(212) 408-5100 .. **Weber,** Paul L '85 (Chadbourne & P LLP) -30 Rckfllr Plz -NY 10112
(212) 382-3300 .. **Weber,** Paul R '08 %Wollmuth M&D LLP -500 5th Av -NY 10110
(516) 364-7500 .. **Weber & Pullin,LLP** -7600 Jericho Tpk -Woodbury 11797 **Fx:**364-3456
(914) 592-1919 .. **Weber,** Richd E Jr. '92 %FG Cottrell -5 W Main -Elmsfrd 10523 **Fx:**592-2987
(315) 218-8000 .. **Weber,** Richd L '00 (Bond S&K,PLLC) -1 Lincoln Ctr -Syracuse 13202
(212) 335-9000 .. **Weber,** Richd M '92 %DA -1 Hogan Pl -NY 10013
(914) 499-6500 .. **Weber,** Robt C '06 IBM -1 New Orchrd Rd -Armonk 10504 **Fx:**499-7372
(212) 490-3000 .. **Weber,** Robt M '79 (Wilson EME&D LLP) -150 E 42nd -NY 10017
(516) 845-4900 .. **Weber,** Roger F '95 SpclCnsl Lavallee Law Ofc -4 W Gate Rd -Farmngdl 11735 **Fx:**756-4629
(212) 748-3355 .. **Weber,** Rose M '97 -225 Bway -NY 10007 **Fx:**233-5633
(631) 853-5212 .. **Weber,** Sharon '93 %Leg Aid -400 Carleton Av Bx9082 -Central Islip 11722 **Fx:**853-7798
(212) 788-0957 .. **Weber,** Steven D '07 %Law Dept -100 Church -NY 10007 **Fx:**788-0367
(518) 462-3247 .. **Weber,** Susan F '82 -14 Pepper Ln -Loudonvll 12211
(518) 285-5064 .. **Weber,** Todd W '79 %Hon J Plumadore (ret) -39 Main -Saranac Lk 12983
(212) 442-8703 .. **Weberg,** Arlene F '90 NYC HRA -220 Church -NY 10013 **Fx:**676-7956
(212) 735-3000 .. **Weberman,** Melissa L '09 %Skadden ASM&F LLP -4 Times Sq -NY 10036
(716) 876-1028 .. **Webster,** A Timothy '83 -98 Hiler Av -Kenmore 14217
(716) 842-2800 .. **Webster,** A Timothy '83 (Webster S LLP) -1400 Lbrty Bldg -Buffalo 14202
(718) 579-3000 .. **Webster,** Alison '85 %Leg Aid -1020 Grnd Cncrs -Bronx 10451 **Fx:**588-2611
(914) 366-5700 .. **Webster,** Annmarie E '79 %MA Bjork -660 Wht Plns Rd -Tarrytwn 10591 **Fx:**366-5759
(518) 257-1870 .. **Webster,** Cela D '00 Hon G Sharpe-USDC -445 Bway -Albany 12207
(716) 853-3087 .. **Webster,** Danl F '09 %Leg Srvcs -237 Main -Buffalo 14203 **Fx:**856-5317
(914) 286-3400 .. **Webster,** Diane T '84 %Leg Aid -1 N Bway -White Plns 10601 **Fx:**682-4112
(212) 918-3000 .. **Webster,** Edith F '02 (Hogan L LLP) -875 3rd Av -NY 10022
(607) 898-3190 .. **Webster,** Evan L '62 Ward & M -170 Main -Groton 13073
(585) 338-6800 .. **Webster,** Jon O '85 %Bausch & Lomb -One Bausch & Lomb Pl -Rchstr 14604 **Fx:**338-8706
(212) 360-1313 .. **Webster,** Lesley Douglass '76 %Dept of Parks & Rec -The Arsenal Cntrl Pk -NY 10065 **Fx:**360-1373
(718) 590-2000 .. **Webster,** Nicole M '08 %DA -198 E 161st -Bronx 10451 **Fx:**590-6477
(716) 842-2800 .. **Webster,** Paula Pope '83 (Webster S LLP) -1400 Lbrty Bldg -Buffalo 14202
(212) 858-1000 .. **Webster,** Robt D '63 SrCnsl Pillsbury WSP LLP -1540 Bway -NY 10036
(212) 903-9000 .. **Webster,** Stephanie E '02 %Linklaters -1345 Av of Amer -NY 10105
(212) 474-1000 .. **Webster,** Susan '85 (Cravath S&M LLP) -825 8th Av -NY 10019
(716) 842-2800 .. **Webster Szanyi LLP** -1400 Lbrty Bldg -Buffalo 14202 **Fx:**845-6709
(716) 842-2800 .. **Webster Szanyi LLP** -484 Main -E Aurora 14052 **Fx:**655-2637
(212) 847-7900 .. **Wechsler & Cohen,LLP** -17 State -NY 10004 **Fx:**847-7955
(212) 847-7900 .. **Wechsler,** David B '84 (Wechsler & C,LLP) -17 State -NY 10004
(516) 873-2000 .. **Wechsler,** David N '86 (Moritt HH&H LLP) -400 Grdn City Plz -Gdn Cty 11530
(212) 715-9100 .. **Wechsler,** Ernest S '91 (Kramer LN&F,LLP) -1177 Av of Amer -NY 10036
(646) 386-5891 .. **Wechsler,** Felice D '89 %MHLS -41 Mad Av -NY 10010
(718) 720-3900 .. **Wechsler,** Glenn S '94 OfCnsl Kuhn & O,LLP -1 Edgewtr Plz -Staten Isl 10305
(212) 869-3500 .. **Wechsler,** Jay A '02 %J Fuchsberg Law Firm,LLP -500 5th Av -NY 10110 **Fx:**398-1532
(212) 599-1900 .. **Wechsler,** Jeffrey L '98 -60 E 42nd -NY 10165 **Fx:**599-0535
(212) 815-0952 .. **Wechsler,** Justin K '07 DA -1 Hogan Pl -NY 10013
(516) 773-3565 .. **Wechsler,** Lawr I '80 (Wechsler & W) -1 Barstow Rd -Gt Neck 11021 **Fx:**466-3778
(212) 986-2340 .. **Wechsler,** Lawr I '80 OfCnsl Jordan & H -122 E 42nd -NY 10168
(212) 580-6630 .. **Wechsler,** Michl M '98 TheLaw.com -Bx237137 -NY 10023
(516) 773-3565 .. **Wechsler,** Robt E '80 (Wechsler & W) -1 Barstow Rd -Gt Neck 11021 **Fx:**466-3778
(212) 286-1666 .. **Wechsler,** Scott R '86 -276 5th Av -NY 10001 **Fx:**286-1616
(315) 443-3653 .. **Wechsler,** Steven '85 %Syracuse Univ Cllg of Law -Wht Hall -Syracuse 13244 **Fx:**443-4213
(212) 920-3072 .. **Wechsler,** Stuart D '58 OfCnsl KamberEdelson,LLC -11 Bway -NY 10004 **Fx:**202-6364
(212) 768-6700 .. **Wechter,** Kathleen A '86 OfCnsl Sonnenschein N&R LLP -2 World Fncl Ctr -NY 10281
(212) 558-6668 .. **Wecker,** David L '94 (Foley SO&W) -100 William -NY 10038
(718) 855-0200 .. **Wecker,** Marcy '98 %RD Herbert -26 Court -Brklyn 11242 **Fx:**855-3845
(718) 725-3044 .. **Wedderburn,** Wendy P '03 %Family Ct -151-20 Jamaica Av -Jamaica 11432
(718) 579-7900 .. **Weddle,** Jamien O '07 Leg Aid -900 Sheridan Av -Bronx 10451 **Fx:**293-8744
(212) 637-2627 .. **Weddle,** Justin S '96 %US Atty -1 St Andrews Plz -NY 10007
(646) 230-8266 .. **Wedeen,** Timothy D '96 (Wedeen & K) -137 5th Av -NY 10010 **Fx:**349-5888
(212) 446-4800 .. **Wedel,** Eric J '08 %Kirkland & E LLP -153 E 53rd -NY 10022
(212) 608-1900 .. **Wedgworth,** Peggy J '87 %Lovell SH LLP -61 Bway -NY 10006
(212) 313-3600 .. **Wedinger-Gyimesi,** Laurel '85 %Barry M&M -2 Rector -NY 10006
(607) 723-5341 .. **Wedlake,** Robt H '78 (Hinman H&K,LLP) -80 Exchange Bx5250 -Bnghmtn 13902
(212) 259-8000 .. **Wee,** Hian Hsin Sean '02 %Dewey & L LLP -1301 Av of Amer -NY 10019
(212) 373-3000 .. **Wee,** Lawr G '95 (Paul WRW&G LLP) -1285 Av of Amer -NY 10019
(315) 435-2470 .. **Weed,** Shawn '07 %DA -505 S State -Syracuse 13202 **Fx:**435-3969
(212) 819-8200 .. **Weedman,** Joshua D '05 %White & C LLP -1155 Av of Amer -NY 10036
(646) 264-3650 .. **Weekley,** Jennifer D '90 %US Dept of Labor -201 Varick -NY 10014 **Fx:**264-3660
(212) 916-2164 .. **Weeks,** Camila '04 UBS AG -101 Park Av -NY 10178
(718) 721-1236 .. **Weeks,** Gary W '83 -28-53 45th -Astoria 11103
(315) 637-2141 .. **Weeks,** James K '70 JK Weeks & Assoc -8025 Summervw Dr Bx707 -Fayettevll 13066 **Fx:**637-1835
(716) 483-0756 .. **Weeks,** Stanley A '39 %Hall & P -600 Htl Jmstwn Ofc Bldg -Jamestwn 14702 **Fx:**484-7352
(212) 909-6000 .. **Weeks,** Wm C '08 %Debevoise & P LLP -919 3rd Av -NY 10022
(212) 946-4781 .. **Weems Norris,** Kandance S '97 (Cumby + W LLP) -11 Penn Plz -NY 10001
(212) 964-1822 .. **Ween,** Jeffrey S '71 J Ween & Assoc -150 Bway -NY 10038 **Fx:**385-9827
(212) 490-3000 .. **Ween,** Martin M '71 (Wilson EME&D LLP) -150 E 42nd -NY 10017
(212) 848-7088 .. **Weerasinghe,** Rohan S '79 (Shearman & S LLP) -599 Lex Av -NY 10022
(212) 458-5692 .. **Weerth,** Julia A '03 AIG Domestic Claims,Inc -175 Water -NY 10038
(212) 227-0347 .. **Weerth,** Matthew E '02 %Weiss W&W,PC -25 Park Pl -NY 10007
(212) 679-4666 .. **Weg,** Moshe J '06 %Frenkel H&S LLP -16 E 34th -NY 10016
(212) 227-4210 .. **Weg & Myers,PC** -52 Duane -NY 10007 **Fx:**349-6702
(212) 697-3250 .. **Weg,** Steven A '08 %Goldberg & R PLLC -115 Bway -NY 10006 **Fx:**227-4533
(315) 676-3991 .. **Wegerski,** John P Jr. '72 (Wegerski Law Firm) -9663 Brewertn Rd Bx590 -Brewertn 13029 **Fx:**676-3971
(315) 676-3991 .. **Wegerski,** Mara J '09 %Wegerski Law Firm -9663 Brewertn Rd Bx590 -Brewertn 13029 **Fx:**676-3971
(631) 852-2339 .. **Weglein,** Gabrielle M '75 %Hon R Mazzei -235 Griffing Av -Rvrhead 11901
(585) 225-7370 .. **Wegman,** Philip R '70 -550 Latona Rd -Rchstr 14626
(212) 294-6700 .. **Wegrzyn,** Brian J '10 %Winston & S -200 Park Av -NY 10166
(212) 825-1212 .. **Wegrzyn,** Evan M '06 %Morrison M LLP -17 State -NY 10004
(212) 724-3397 .. **Wehle,** Jonathan F '83 -37 W 75th -NY 10023
(718) 335-0903 .. **Wehle,** Robt '53 -81-15 35th Av -Jcksn Hts 11372
(631) 913-4444 .. **Wehrheim,** Keri Ann '05 %Dell LT&V LLP -5 Orvll Dr -Bohemia 11716
(212) 474-1000 .. **Wei,** Edw S '06 %Cravath S&M LLP -825 8th Av -NY 10019
(888) 835-0006 .. **Wei,** Eric S '09 (Demba W,LLP) -1221 Av of Amer -NY 10020 **Fx:**835-1116
(516) 487-0100 .. **Wei,** James E '99 (Musso & W) -111 Grt Nck Rd -Gt Neck 11021 **Fx:**487-5524
(212) 756-2000 .. **Wei,** Jeanette S '10 %Schulte R&Z LLP -919 3rd Av -NY 10022
(212) 918-3000 .. **Wei,** Jun '93 (Hogan L LLP) -875 3rd Av -NY 10022
(718) 460-9393 .. **Wei,** Wen-Chi '84 -39-07 Prince -Flushng 11354 **Fx:**460-0961
(212) 756-2000 .. **Wei,** Yanjun '00 %Schulte R&Z LLP -919 3rd Av -NY 10022
(212) 610-6300 .. **Wei,** Yanmei '04 %Allen & O -1221 Av of Amer -NY 10020
(212) 756-2000 .. **Wei,** Ying Audrey '09 %Schulte R&Z LLP -919 3rd Av -NY 10022
(631) 653-6603 .. **Weichbrodt,** Randall C '00 -436-A Montauk Hwy Bx3042 -E Quogue 11942 **Fx:**653-6654
(212) 954-7905 .. **Weicher,** Michl B '90 KPMG -757 3rd Av -NY 10017
(212) 925-7881 .. **Weichsel,** John L '72 -225 Bway -NY 10007 **Fx:**966-8253
(212) 836-8000 .. **Weick,** Danl P '10 Kaye S LLP -425 Park Av -NY 10022
(212) 906-1200 .. **Weicker,** Lowell P '10 %Latham & W -885 3rd Av -NY 10022

(212) 801-6782 ..**Weidberg**, Jason L '06 %Greenberg T,LLP -200 Park Av -NY 10166
(631) 853-4104 ..**Weidenbaum**, Adina E '06 %DA -400 Carleton Av Bx9082 -Central Islip 11722 **Fx:**853-7838
(212) 832-7400 ..**Weidenbaum**, Barry J '94 (Weidenbaum & H,LLP) -708 3rd Av -NY 10017
(212) 832-7400 ..**Weidenbaum & Harari,LLP** -708 3rd Av -NY 10017 **Fx:**832-7761
(212) 695-8100 ..**Weidenbaum**, Paul M '79 (Goetz F,LLP) -1 Penn Plz -NY 10119
(212) 465-6350 ..**Weidenfeld**, Harold M '87 %Madison Sq Grdn,LP -2 Penn Plz -NY 10121 **Fx:**465-6011
(716) 853-1616 ..**Weider**, John R '72 (Harter S&E LLP) -12 Fountain Plz -Buffalo 14202
(585) 232-6500 ..**Weider**, John R '72 (Harter S&E LLP) -1600 Bausch & Lomb Pl -Rchstr 14604
(212) 813-8800 ..**Weidhaas**, Andrew J '01 (Goodwin P LLP) -620 8th Av -NY 10018
(585) 256-0020 ..**Weidman**, Andrew J '79 -80 Linden Oaks -Rchstr 14625
(212) 706-3041 ..**Weidman**, Edwin N '51 -150 E 69th -NY 10021 **Fx:**879-4554
(585) 427-7225 ..**Weidman**, James W '90 %G Reiber -3136 S Winton Rd -Rchstr 14623 **Fx:**427-7804
(212) 698-7142 ..**Weidman**, Jennifer K '90 %Simon & Schuster -1230 Av of Amer -NY 10020 **Fx:**698-7171
(631) 232-3288 ..**Weidman**, Keith H '86 -900 Old Nichols Rd -Islandia 11749
(212) 592-1400 ..**Weidman**, Richd '68 Cnsl Herrick,F LLP -2 Park Av -NY 10016
(716) 849-6500 ..**Weidner**, Brian J '85 (Brown & T,LLC) -14 Lafayette Sq -Buffalo 14203
(212) 878-8235 ..**Weidner**, James B '67 (Clifford C LLP) -31 W 52nd -NY 10019
(585) 232-6500 ..**Weidner**, Jennifer N '02 %Harter S&E LLP -1600 Bausch & Lomb Pl -Rchstr 14604
(212) 504-6000 ..**Weidner**, Neil J '92 (Cadwalader W&T LLP) -1 World Fncl Ctr -NY 10281
(607) 739-8763 ..**Weiermiller**, Mark A '87 (Cooper P&W,LLP) -2854 Wstnghse Rd -Horseheads 14845 **Fx:**739-9373
(716) 681-3289 ..**Weig**, Robt E '93 -2277 Como Park Blvd -Lancaster 14086 **Fx:**686-0233
(212) 525-0939 ..**Weigand**, Frank J '04 HSBC Securities,Inc -452 5th Av -NY 10018
(646) 471-4000 ..**Weigand**, Gregory M '04 PricewaterhouseCoopers LLP -300 Mad Av -NY 10017
(212) 885-5000 ..**Weigel**, Alan M '00 OfCnsl Blank R LLP -405 Lex Av -NY 10174
(212) 351-4000 ..**Weigel**, Robt L '82 (Gibson D&C LLP) -200 Park Av -NY 10166
(212) 450-4000 ..**Weigel**, Wm H '75 (Davis P&W LLP) -450 Lex Av -NY 10017
(212) 813-5900 ..**Weigell**, Chas T J '90 (Fross ZL&Z,PC) -866 UN Plz -NY 10017
(845) 454-3250 ..**Weigert**, Lillian S '77 (Gellert & K,PC) -75 Wshngtn -Poughkeepsie 12601
(212) 551-4000 ..**Weihe**, John A '85 %Sanofi-Synthelabo -90 Park Av -NY 10016 **Fx:**551-4919
(212) 225-2000 ..**Weiksner**, Sandra S '70 SrCnsl Cleary GS&H -1 Lbrty Plz -NY 10006
(212) 839-5300 ..**Weil**, Alan S '83 (Sidley A LLP) -787 7th Av -NY 10019
(516) 677-0300 ..**Weil**, C Fred '79 -35 Roosevelt Av -Syosset 11791 **Fx:**496-9047
Weil, Floyd S '60 -20 Birch Grove Dr -Armonk 10504
(212) 230-9801 ..**Weil**, Frank A '57 %Abacus & Assoc -147 E 48th -NY 10017
(718) 590-2000 ..**Weil**, Gary R '78 %DA -198 E 161st -Bronx 10451 **Fx:**590-6477
(212) 310-8000 ..**Weil Gotshal & Manges LLP** -767 5th Av -NY 10153 **Fx:**310-8007
(212) 732-3066 ..**Weil**, Henry I '82 -401 Bway -NY 10013
(212) 371-8008 ..**Weil**, Jay Howard '80 SrCnsl Guzov O,LLC -600 Mad Av -NY 10022
(212) 732-4888 ..**Weil**, Judith H '81 (Epstein & W) -225 Bway -NY 10007 **Fx:**732-6703
(212) 259-8000 ..**Weil**, Kristen B '09 %Dewey & L LLP -1301 Av of Amer -NY 10019
(718) 330-1200 ..**Weil**, Michl D '95 %Fed Def of NY Inc -1 Pierrepont Plz -Brklyn 11201 **Fx:**855-0760
(212) 431-7129 ..**Weil**, Teresa Kolb '01 (Purrington MW LLP) -320 W 13th -NY 10014
(212) 325-5480 ..**Weilamann**, Chas H '00 Credit Suisse -11 Mad Av -NY 10010
(516) 487-0175 ..**Weiland**, Elizabeth P '98 %E Schwartz -343 Grt Nck Rd -Gt Neck 11021 **Fx:**773-7706
(212) 308-4411 ..**Weild**, David III '60 (Edwards AP&D LLP) -750 Lex Av -NY 10022
(212) 869-9700 ..**Weiler**, Alan G '58 %Swig Weiler & Arnow -1114 Av of Amer -NY 10036 **Fx:**921-4967
(212) 788-1817 ..**Weiler**, Fred M '96 Law Dept -100 Church -NY 10007 **Fx:**788-0367
(516) 676-4600 ..**Weiler**, Peter M '66 (Humes & W) -147 Forest Av Bx546 -Locust Vly 11560
(315) 422-1391 ..**Weiler**, Robt K '78 (Green & S,PLLC) -One Lincoln Ctr #900 -Syracuse 13202
(212) 867-6000 ..**Weilgus**, Matthew R '07 %Rosenberg & E,PC -733 3rd Av -NY 10017
(631) 234-9240 ..**Weilhoefer**, Elizabeth K '06 %H Besunder -1 Suffolk Sq -Islandia 11749 **Fx:**234-9278
(212) 907-7300 ..**Weill**, Matthew T '07 %Golenbock EAB&P -437 Mad Av -NY 10022
(914) 749-8200 ..**Weill**, Richd E '80 Cnsl Boies S&F LLP -333 Main -Armonk 10504
(716) 854-3015 ..**Weimer**, Francis P '79 (Aaron DS&L,LLP) -43 Court -Buffalo 14202
(212) 552-4890 ..**Wein**, Aliza F '97 %JP Morgan Chase & Co -1 Chase Manh Plz -NY 10005
(212) 592-1400 ..**Wein**, Aviva Y '04 %Herrick,F LLP -2 Park Av -NY 10016
(212) 335-4500 ..**Wein**, Bruce J '70 (DLA Piper LLP) -1251 Av of Amer -NY 10020
(518) 869-9094 ..**Wein & Frament** -951 Albany Shaker Rd -Latham 12110 **Fx:**869-5142
(585) 256-3453 ..**Wein**, Gerald J '75 -130 Westland Av -Rchstr 14618
(212) 259-8000 ..**Wein**, Hershel '86 (Dewey & L LLP) -1301 Av of Amer -NY 10019
(718) 894-5501 ..**Wein**, Martin A '72 -65-12 69th Pl -Middl Vllg 11379 **Fx:**326-3781
(212) 721-7471 ..**Wein**, Nancy J '86 -150 West End Av -NY 10023
(518) 869-9094 ..**Wein**, Paul H '76 (Wein & F) -951 Albany Shaker Rd -Latham 12110
(516) 536-0900 ..**Wein**, Scott '79 %Jacobson & S -510 Merrick Rd Bx46 -Rockvll Ctr 11571
(212) 530-5000 ..**Weinacht**, Felix '02 %Milbank TH&M LLP -1 Chase Manh Plz -NY 10005
(516) 239-2386 ..**Weinbach Levy**, Aviva L '88 -33 Hrbrvw W -Lawrence 11559
(914) 948-0044 ..**Weinbaum**, George '72 -175 Main -White Plns 10601 **Fx:**686-4873
(212) 408-5100 ..**Weinbaum**, Matthew A '09 %Chadbourne & P LLP -30 Rckfllr Plz -NY 10112
(718) 984-2626 ..**Weinbaum**, Richd C '86 %Solomon & Assoc,PC -3309 Richmond Av -Staten Isl 10312 **Fx:**984-5820
(718) 237-0500 ..**Weinbaum**, Saml '55 -26 Court -Brklyn 11242 **Fx:**834-6064
(917) 320-2801 ..**Weinberg**, Alan M '79 FDIC -350 5th Av -NY 10118
(516) 829-3900 ..**Weinberg**, Amos '78 -49 Somerset Dr S -Gt Neck 11020
(212) 250-1851 ..**Weinberg**, Andrew L '95 Deutsche Bk Securities -60 Wall -NY 10005
(516) 466-2930 ..**Weinberg**, Andrew S '96 Silverstein Capital -185 Grt Nck Rd -Gt Neck 11021
(212) 232-1300 ..**Weinberg**, Beth L '04 %Lewis BB&S LLP -77 Water -NY 10005
(212) 335-9000 ..**Weinberg**, Brian P '06 %DA -1 Hogan Pl -NY 10013
(914) 946-0400 ..**Weinberg**, Carl D '83 (Schiavetti CDW&N,LLP) -709 Wstchstr Av -White Plns 10604
(845) 778-3793 ..**Weinberg**, David M '74 -110 Orange Av -Walden 12586 **Fx:**778-1839
(212) 949-7120 ..**Weinberg**, Diane L '88 %Meeks & S -330 Mad Av -NY 10017
(516) 466-0400 ..**Weinberg**, Edw H '55 -98 Cuttermill Rd -Gt Neck 11021 **Fx:**773-3673
(212) 643-7000 ..**Weinberg**, Edwin W '78 (Sills C&G PC) -One Rckfllr Plz -NY 10020
(212) 310-8000 ..**Weinberg**, Erika L '97 Cnsl Weil G&M LLP -767 5th Av -NY 10153
(212) 421-8495 ..**Weinberg**, Gale B '89 OfCnsl Pines & K -110 E 59th -NY 10022 **Fx:**421-8492
(718) 797-3950 ..**Weinberg**, Gary R '81 -26 Court -Brklyn 11242 **Fx:**522-4208
(516) 877-2424 ..**Weinberg Gross & Pergament LLP** -400 Grdn City Plz -Gdn Cty 11530 **Fx:**877-2460
(212) 863-6300 ..**Weinberg**, Harold P '82 %HPD -100 Gold -NY 10038 **Fx:**863-8201
(212) 989-2908 ..**Weinberg**, Harry M '85 -949 Allen Ln -Woodmere 11598
(212) 989-2908 ..**Weinberg**, Harry M '85 -11 Beach -NY 10013
(516) 877-2424 ..**Weinberg**, Harvey '70 (Weinberg G&P LLP) -400 Grdn City Plz -Gdn Cty 11530
(718) 286-3000 ..**Weinberg**, Hugh B '83 %Boro Pres Ofc -120-55 Qns Blvd -Kew Gdns 11424 **Fx:**286-2885
(212) 841-1000 ..**Weinberg**, J D '91 (Covington & B LLP) -620 8th Av -NY 10018
(212) 578-5883 ..**Weinberg**, Jane C '80 %MetLife -27-01 Qns Plz N -LIC 11101 **Fx:**578-3916
(212) 310-8000 ..**Weinberg**, Jeffrey J '74 SrCnsl Weil G&M LLP -767 5th Av -NY 10153
(516) 482-0962 ..**Weinberg**, Jenifer Ivy '97 %Kalin LW,LLC -185 Grt Nck Rd -Gt Neck 11021
(212) 408-5100 ..**Weinberg**, Jeremy O '04 %Chadbourne & P LLP -30 Rckfllr Plz -NY 10112
(212) 903-8750 ..**Weinberg**, Jessica G '03 %Roberts & H,LLP -825 8th Av -NY 10019
(212) 593-3000 ..**Weinberg**, Laurel J '79 %Platzer SKLG&J,LLP -1065 Av of Amer -NY 10018
(845) 246-7735 ..**Weinberg**, Lawr H '51 -559 W Saugerties/Woodstock Rd -Saugerties 12477
(212) 446-4800 ..**Weinberg**, Leah L '08 %Kirkland & E LLP -153 E 53rd -NY 10022
(718) 522-0366 ..**Weinberg**, Lysa M '91 %Superior Abstract -105 Court -Brklyn 11201 **Fx:**643-9054
(516) 484-1911 ..**Weinberg**, Martin R '55 -99 Powerhse Rd -Roslyn Hts 11577 **Fx:**484-5719
(212) 386-7629 ..**Weinberg**, Melissa A '97 (Weinberg & G,PC) -116 W 23rd -NY 10011
(212) 704-6418 ..**Weinberg**, Melvin '73 (Troutman S LLP) -405 Lex Av -NY 10174
(212) 596-9000 ..**Weinberg**, Michl E '08 %Ropes & G LLP -1211 Av of Amer -NY 10036
(718) 253-6300 ..**Weinberg**, Milton Robt '56 -1978 Flatbush Av -Brklyn 11234 **Fx:**252-3678
(212) 373-3000 ..**Weinberg**, Moira E '06 %Paul WRW&G LLP -1285 Av of Amer -NY 10019
(212) 596-9000 ..**Weinberg**, Morri H '95 (Ropes & G LLP) -1211 Av of Amer -NY 10036
(716) 626-1600 ..**Weinberg**, Neil '74 -5800 Main -Williamsvll 14221
(212) 916-5938 ..**Weinberg**, Peter A '82 %TIAA-CREF -730 3rd Av -NY 10017
(212) 880-9485 ..**Weinberg**, Richd D '73 (Morvillo AGIA&B,PC) -565 5th Av -NY 10017
(212) 335-4500 ..**Weinberg**, Scott A '89 (DLA Piper LLP) -1251 Av of Amer -NY 10020
(646) 356-0212 ..**Weinberg**, Seth B '01 Castle Brands Inc -122 E 42nd -NY 10168
(631) 755-0101 ..**Weinberg**, Seth M '09 %Lewis JAA,LLP -425 Broad Hollow Rd -Melvll 11747
(718) 286-3056 ..**Weinberg**, Shauna E '97 NY Dept of Probation -125-01 Qns Blvd -Kew Gdns 11415
(212) 977-9700 ..**Weinberg**, Stacey B '01 Cnsl Phillips N LLP -666 5th Av -NY 10103
(914) 289-2320 ..**Weinberg**, Stephen A '80 %Ct of Claims -140 Grand -White Plns 10601
(212) 495-0100 ..**Weinberg**, Steven '86 (Gottesman WMF&W,PC) -11 Hanover Sq -NY 10005
(212) 479-6000 ..**Weinberg**, Steven K '72 (Cooley LLP) -1114 Av of Amer -NY 10036
(212) 753-3468 ..**Weinberg**, Steven L '71 (Wildes & W,PC) -515 Mad Av -NY 10022
(212) 662-9064 ..**Weinberg**, Wm A '84 -310 W 94th -NY 10025
(212) 848-9800 ..**Weinberg-Brodt**, Chaya F '91 OfCnsl Withers B LLP -430 Park Av -NY 10022
(631) 727-9140 ..**Weinberg-Daly**, Jill D '03 (Schaub & D,LLP) -131 W Main -Rvrhead 11901
(212) 460-5757 ..**Weinberg Dieve**, Stacy '00 %Gellis & M,LLP -137 5th Av -NY 10010
(212) 753-2424 ..**Weinberger**, Audrey Ellen '05 %Reiss E LLP -425 Mad Av -NY 10017
(212) 728-8000 ..**Weinberger**, Brian J '07 %Willkie F&G LLP -787 7th Av -NY 10019
(212) 969-3000 ..**Weinberger**, David J '86 (Proskauer R LLP) -1585 Bway -NY 10036
(212) 279-5050 ..**Weinberger**, David M '04 %Abraham F&T LLP -1 Penn Plz -NY 10119
(212) 373-3000 ..**Weinberger**, Erica G '00 %Paul WRW&G LLP -1285 Av of Amer -NY 10019
(212) 715-9100 ..**Weinberger**, Harold P '71 (Kramer LN&F,LLP) -1177 Av of Amer -NY 10036
(212) 777-2060 ..**Weinberger**, Israel '02 %Coltown Prop LLC -95-04 Delancey -NY 10002
(212) 528-0844 ..**Weinberger**, Jack '54 -305 Bway -NY 10007 **Fx:**732-5486
(718) 222-8880 ..**Weinberger**, Jacqueline S '94 %Jones JO -45 Main -Brklyn 11201

(212) 813-5900 .. **Weinberger**, James D '00 (Fross ZL&Z,PC) -866 UN Plz -NY 10017

(845) 634-3350 .. **Weinberger**, Jeff A '82 -29 Third -New Cty 10956 **Fx**:634-3361

(914) 693-1629 .. **Weinberger**, Jeffry W '83 -51 Eastern Dr -Ardsley 10502

(212) 777-2060 .. **Weinberger**, Jonathan '06 Coltown Properties,LLC -9504 Delancey -NY 10002

(212) 752-3380 .. **Weinberger**, Jonathan D '82 -880 3rd Av -NY 10022

(212) 513-7788 .. **Weinberger**, Kristin L '07 %Ahmuty D&M -123 William -NY 10038

(516) 484-1234 .. **Weinberger**, Lawr W '77 -99 Mineola Av Bx1356 -Roslyn Hts 11577 **Fx**:484-2225

(212) 228-4404 .. **Weinberger**, Leo '80 -24 5th Av -NY 10011 **Fx**:228-4674

(718) 849-2000 .. **Weinberger**, Leonard A '54 -80-59 Lefferts Blvd -Kew Gdns 11415 **Fx**:805-1503

(516) 829-7270 .. **Weinberger**, Mark E '79 -50 Merrick Rd -Rockvll Ctr 11570 **Fx**:829-0102

(212) 736-2624 .. **Weinberger**, Michl '79 -236 W 26th -NY 10001 **Fx**:736-2604

(212) 225-2000 .. **Weinberger**, Michl D '93 (Cleary GS&H) -1 Lbrty Plz -NY 10006

(212) 768-6700 .. **Weinberger**, Michl J '59 (Sonnenschein N&R LLP) -1221 Av of Amer -NY 10020

(845) 849-1102 .. **Weinberger**, Paul I '89 -Bx527 -Poughkeepsie 12602

(212) 575-7900 .. **Weinberger**, Richd '63 OfCnsl Ballon SB&N,PC -729 7th Av -NY 10019

(212) 949-7600 .. **Weinberger Singer PC** -230 Park Av -NY 10169 **Fx**:949-6162

(212) 810-4943 .. **Weinberger**, Steven I '96 Broadway Prtnrs -1 Penn Plz -NY 10119

(212) 867-9595 .. **Weinberger**, Stuart A '83 (Goldberg and W) -630 3rd Av -NY 10017

(212) 806-5400 .. **Weinberger**, Thos R '95 (Stroock &S&L LLP) -180 Maiden Ln -NY 10038

(212) 788-0764 .. **Weinblatt**, Amy J '90 %Law Dept -100 Church -NY 10007 **Fx**:788-0367

(212) 597-3300 .. **Weinblatt**, Lawr S '85 PricewaterhouseCoopers LLP -1177 Av of Amer -NY 10036

(631) 582-5151 .. **Weinblatt**, Richd A '88 (Haley W&C,LLP) -1601 Vets Mem'l Hwy -Islandia 11749

(212) 657-0849 .. **Weindler**, John P '79 Citigroup -77 Water -NY 10005

(212) 218-5500 .. **Weindling**, Francesca Reah '07 Seyfarth S LLP -620 8th Av -NY 10018

(212) 575-0250 .. **Weindorf**, Sherry L '80 -1776 Bway -NY 10019 **Fx**:838-9534

(914) 378-2433 .. **Weine**, Kenneth N '96 Consumers Union -101 Truman Av -Ynkrs 10703

(631) 752-7400 .. **Weiner**, Alan E '69 SrCnsl Holtz Rubenstein Reminick LLP -125 Baylis Rd -Melvll 11747 **Fx**:752-1742

(212) 213-1220 .. **Weiner**, Alan S '82 (Weiner MM&B,LLC) -220 5th Av -NY 10001

(212) 269-2500 .. **Weiner**, Alice '82 %Gorlick K&L,PC -17 State -NY 10004

(212) 715-9100 .. **Weiner**, Amy '08 %Kramer LN&F,LLP -1177 Av of Amer -NY 10036

(212) 468-8000 .. **Weiner**, Andrew J '77 (Morrison & F LLP) -1290 Av of Amer -NY 10104

(212) 728-8000 .. **Weiner**, Andrew L '05 %Willkie F&G LLP -787 7th Av -NY 10019

(212) 877-0071 .. **Weiner**, Arthur S '86 -153 W 82nd -NY 10024

(518) 462-6831 .. **Weiner**, Barbara '82 %Empire Justice Ctr -119 Wshngtn Av -Albany 12210 **Fx**:462-6687

(212) 558-4000 .. **Weiner**, Benjamin H '10 %Sullivan & C LLP -125 Broad -NY 10004

(212) 730-5495 .. **Weiner**, Bennett I '81 -25 W 43rd -NY 10036 **Fx**:730-5450

(718) 855-6840 .. **Weiner**, Bruce '78 (Rosenberg M&W LLP) -26 Court -Brklyn 11242 **Fx**:625-1966

(845) 331-7330 .. **Weiner**, Cappy '88 (Miller W & Assoc,PC) -270 Fair Bx4030 -Kingston 12402 **Fx**:331-7596

(212) 944-0500 .. **Weiner**, Craig '92 Cnsl Hofheimer G&G,LLP -530 5th Av -NY 10036 **Fx**:897-4989

(212) 837-6000 .. **Weiner**, Danl H '85 (Hughes H&R LLP) -1 Bttry Pk Plz -NY 10004

(646) 471-2606 .. **Weiner**, David E '97 PricewaterhouseCoopers LLP -300 Mad Av -NY 10017

(212) 446-4800 .. **Weiner**, David J '08 %Kirkland & E LLP -153 E 53rd -NY 10022

(212) 351-4500 .. **Weiner**, Douglas J '85 SrCnsl Epstein B&G,PC -250 Park Av -NY 10177

(212) 558-4000 .. **Weiner**, Earl D '69 OfCnsl Sullivan & C LLP -125 Broad -NY 10004

(718) 283-7441 .. **Weiner**, Edw I '83 %Maimonides Med Ctr -4802 10th Av -Brklyn 11219 **Fx**:283-7180

(212) 468-4800 .. **Weiner**, Evan D '01 %Davis & G LLP -1740 Bway -NY 10019

(718) 250-2000 .. **Weiner**, Frances S '94 %DA -350 Jay -Brklyn 11201 **Fx**:250-2314

(310) 836-1400 .. **Weiner**, Gerald B '86 -21 Turn lane -Levittwn 11756 **Fx**:836-1420

(212) 859-8000 .. **Weiner**, Gregg L '92 (Fried FHS&J LLP) -1 NY Plz -NY 10004

(212) 909-5400 .. **Weiner**, Hadassah R '81 %KPMG LLP -280 Park Av -NY 10017

(212) 785-1100 .. **Weiner**, Howard S '99 -45 Bway -NY 10006 **Fx**:509-8403

(518) 392-2426 .. **Weiner**, Jack H '73 Interglobal Entertainment LLC -1488 Route 203 -Chatham 12037 **Fx**:392-0843

(718) 875-1300 .. **Weiner**, Jay L '85 %Appllt Div 2nd Dept -45 Monroe Pl -Brklyn 11201 **Fx**:858-2446

(212) 268-8888 .. **Weiner**, Jeffrey I '96 (Kresman & W) -7 Penn Plz -NY 10001

(212) 412-1072 .. **Weiner**, Jessica G '97 Barclays Capital Inc -200 Park Av -NY 10166

(718) 283-7441 .. **Weiner**, Joanna R '00 Maimonides Med Ctr -4802 10th Av -Brklyn 11219 **Fx**:283-7180

(212) 940-8800 .. **Weiner**, Jonathan D '05 %Katten MR LLP -575 Mad Av -NY 10022

(212) 848-4000 .. **Weiner**, Karin E '99 Cnsl Shearman & S LLP -599 Lex Av -NY 10022

(212) 286-8899 .. **Weiner**, Kristi R '10 Balsam J,LLP -315 Mad Av -NY 10017

(212) 269-0927 .. **Weiner**, Laura S '95 %D'Amato & L,LLP -2 World Fncl Ctr -NY 10281

(212) 909-6000 .. **Weiner**, Lauren M '08 %Debevoise & P LLP -919 3rd Av -NY 10022

(732) 855-6026 .. **Weiner**, Lawr C '97 (Wilentz G&S) -110 William -NY 10038 **Fx**:726-6639

(212) 482-0001 .. **Weiner**, Lee-David '06 %Russo K&T LLP -33 Whitehall -NY 10004

(212) 370-1660 .. **Weiner**, Leonard M '86 (L Weiner LLC) -206 E 38th -NY 10016 **Fx**:490-0354

(631) 232-6130 .. **Weiner Lesniak LLP** -888 Vets Mem'l Hwy -Hauppauge 11788 **Fx**:232-6184

(914) 682-3900 .. **Weiner**, Marc I '84 %Lawyers Title Ins -Ten Bank -White Plns 10606 **Fx**:682-3556

(914) 328-0404 .. **Weiner**, Margaret A '91 (Jackson L LLP) -1 N Bway -White Plns 10601

(845) 348-0443 .. **Weiner**, Mark C '83 -77 6th Av -Nyack 10960

(914) 244-0029 .. **Weiner**, Merryl '88 %Quaranta & Assoc -121 Smith Av -Mt Kisco 10549 **Fx**:244-0031

(212) 530-5000 .. **Weiner**, Michl B '08 %Milbank TH&M LLP -1 Chase Manh Plz -NY 10005

(516) 536-0900 .. **Weiner**, Michl C '76 %Jacobson & S -510 Merrick Rd Bx46 -Rockvll Ctr 11571

(516) 304-5858 .. **Weiner**, Michl J '95 (Glaser & W,LLP) -175 E Shore Rd -Gt Neck 11023 **Fx**:304-5855

(212) 779-8600 .. **Weiner**, Michl James '95 %Silverman SS&B PLLC -381 Park Av S -NY 10016

(212) 735-3000 .. **Weiner**, Michl L '81 (Skadden ASM&F LLP) -4 Times Sq -NY 10036

(212) 826-0808 .. **Weiner**, Michl S '87 %MLB Players Assn -12 E 49th -NY 10017 **Fx**:752-3649

(212) 213-1220 .. **Weiner Millo Morgan & Bonanno, LLC** -220 5th Av -NY 10001 **Fx**:889-5228

(718) 499-2976 .. **Weiner**, Morton J '59 -579A 6th -Brklyn 11215 **Fx**:499-1778

(516) 939-2930 .. **Weiner**, Nancy Rose '89 -734 Franklin Av -Gdn Cty 11530

(518) 348-7900 .. **Weiner**, Neil S '76 N Weiner,LLC -56 Clifton Country Rd -Clifton Pk 12065 **Fx**:348-7903

(845) 623-0090 .. **Weiner**, Neil S '98 OfCnsl Weiner & S -119 Rockland Ctr -Nanuet 10954

(646) 805-6443 .. **Weiner**, Rebecca Ulam '06 %NYPD -1 Police Plz -NY 10038

(518) 449-3300 .. **Weiner**, Richd H '75 (Nolan & H,LLP) -39 N Pearl -Albany 12207

(845) 623-0090 .. **Weiner**, Richd J '81 (Weiner & S) -119 Rockland Ctr -Nanuet 10954

(212) 547-5400 .. **Weiner**, Robt A '73 (McDermott W&E LLP) -340 Mad Av -NY 10173

(631) 226-2100 .. **Weiner**, Robt L '59 (Phillips WAC&M) -165 S Wellwood Av -Lindenhrst 11757

(914) 925-0000 .. **Weiner**, Robt M '01 %Elias Grp -411 Theo Fremd Av -Rye 10580 **Fx**:925-9344

(914) 761-4200 .. **Weiner**, Ronald W '84 %Steinberg & C,LLP -50 Main -White Plns 10606

(212) 980-4500 .. **Weiner**, Ryan '04 %Cohen L LLP -885 3rd Av -NY 10022

(212) 382-0700 .. **Weiner**, Saml H '62 (Ostrolenk FG&S,LLP) -1180 Av of Amer -NY 10036

(212) 961-8329 .. **Weiner**, Scott A '90 %NYS Liquor Auth -105 W 125th -NY 10027

(718) 630-2914 .. **Weiner**, Sharon J '93 %VA -800 Poly Pl -Brklyn 11209 **Fx**:630-2917

(866) 381-9100 .. **Weiner**, Shira D '03 Kurtzman Carson Cnsltnts -1230 Av of Amer -NY 10020

(845) 425-3363 .. **Weiner**, Stanley '74 -One S Mad Av -Spg Vly 10977 **Fx**:425-3368

(718) 222-9800 .. **Weiner**, Stephanie L '01 %Brecher FPWT&Z,PC -335 Adams -Brklyn 11201

(212) 858-1000 .. **Weiner**, Stephen A '58 SrCnsl Pillsbury WSP LLP -1540 Bway -NY 10036

(212) 566-4669 .. **Weiner**, Stephen H '85 -750 3rd Av -NY 10017 **Fx**:(646) 349-1679

(914) 741-6100 .. **Weiner**, Steven D '86 (Kaufman B&R) -200 Summit Lk Dr -Valhalla 10595

(718) 522-1743 .. **Weiner**, Steven M '90 (Reibman & W) -26 Court -Brklyn 11242 **Fx**:643-9297

(845) 623-0090 .. **Weiner & Strauss** -119 Rockland Ctr -Nanuet 10954

(212) 664-2806 .. **Weiner**, Susan E '80 %NBC -30 Rckfllr Plz -NY 10112

(914) 722-9111 .. **Weiner**, Valerie '93 -121 Brite Av -Scarsdale 10583 **Fx**:722-6866

(212) 551-0340 .. **Weinfeld**, Danl R '94 %GOI-MOD -800 2nd Av -NY 10017

(516) 742-4343 .. **Weinfeld**, Seth M '03 %Scully SM&P PC -400 Grdn City Plz -Gdn Cty 11530

(212) 556-2100 .. **Weingaertner**, Scott T '93 (King & S) -1185 Av of Amer -NY 10036

(212) 974-5200 .. **Weingard**, Laurence Jeffrey '65 -250 W 57th -NY 10107 **Fx**:977-7035

(516) 877-2424 .. **Weingard**, Marc J '91 (Weinberg G&P LLP) -400 Grdn City Plz -Gdn Cty 11530

(914) 686-4456 .. **Weingarden**, Mitchell I '84 (Marsh M&W PLLC) -81 Main -White Plns 10601 **Fx**:206-3998

(212) 655-3500 .. **Weingart**, Jeffrey P '90 (Meister S&F LLP) -140 E 45th -NY 10017

(212) 272-2251 .. **Weingarten**, Allen L '80 (JP Morgan Chase) -383 Mad Av -NY 10179

(315) 475-3127 .. **Weingarten**, Esther Gray '92 %Leg Srvcs -472 S Salina -Syracuse 13202 **Fx**:475-2706

(914) 225-5556 .. **Weingarten**, Ilan S '01 Morgan Stanley -2000 Wstchstr Av -Purchase 10577

(212) 756-2000 .. **Weingarten**, Marc '75 (Schulte R&Z LLP) -919 3rd Av -NY 10022

(914) 681-0200 .. **Weingarten**, Mark P '85 (DelBello DWW&W,LLP) -1 N Lex Av -White Plns 10601

(585) 232-5300 .. **Weingarten**, Martin S '61 OfCnsl Boylan BCV&W,LLP -2400 Chase Sq -Rchstr 14604

(212) 308-4411 .. **Weingarten**, Sandra Libeson '96 Edwards AP&D LLP -750 Lex Av -NY 10022

(516) 747-1010 .. **Weingarten**, Steven A '68 -1 Old Cntry Rd -Carle Pl 11514 **Fx**:747-2494

(518) 465-7330 .. **Weingarten**, Steven B '83 (Weingarten R&M,LLC) -1 Commerce Plz -Albany 12210 **Fx**:465-0273

(212) 909-6000 .. **Weingarten Nayman**, Yael S '05 %Debevoise & P LLP -919 3rd Av -NY 10022

(212) 254-1111 .. **Weinglass**, Leonard I '86 OfCnsl Rabinowitz BSK&L,PC -111 Bway -NY 10006

(212) 613-5000 .. **Weinglass**, Sandra '04 Leg Assist Grp -450 W 33rd -NY 10001 **Fx**:750-0820

(718) 403-1058 .. **Weingold**, Erik P '95 %National Grid -1 MetroTech Ctr -Brklyn 11201

(212) 715-9100 .. **Weingold**, Philip R '86 (Kramer LN&F,LLP) -1177 Av of Amer -NY 10036

(212) 468-4800 .. **Weingrad**, Howard R '88 (Davis & G LLP) -1740 Bway -NY 10019

(212) 244-4187 .. **Weingrad**, Stephen A '64 (Weingrad & W) -350 5th Av -NY 10118 **Fx**:594-2944

(518) 993-2313 .. **Weinheimer**, Richd P '91 R Weinheimer -4 Canal Bx228 -Ft Plain 13339 **Fx**:993-2036

(212) 440-4400 .. **Weinheimer**, Titus '98 Cnsl Buchanan I&R PC -620 8th Av -NY 10018

(716) 853-8100 .. **Weinholtz**, John J '88 (Nixon P LLP) -40 Fountain Plz -Buffalo 14202

(212) 640-8520 .. **Weinhouse**, Brett A '00 Amer Exp -3 World Fncl Ctr -NY 10285

(212) 588-0800 .. **Weinhouse**, Deena Levy '99 %Frommer L&H LLP -745 5th Av -NY 10151

(212) 661-9100 .. **Weinick**, Erik B '02 Otterbourg SH&R,PC -230 Park Av -NY 10169
(516) 248-5800 .. **Weinick**, Gary S '88 -1325 Franklin Av -Gdn Cty 11530 **Fx**:248-5839
(212) 973-0572 .. **Weinick**, Jeffrey M '92 (Wolff & S PC) -140 Bway -NY 10005
(516) 873-9550 .. **Weinick**, Matthew B '09 %Leeds M&B -1 Old Cntry Rd -Carle Pl 11514
(914) 997-0900 .. **Weinig**, Lynn E '90 %Wormser KG&J LLP -399 Knollwood Rd -White Plns 10603
(914) 921-5182 .. **Weininger**, Robt S '85 (R Weininger Assoc) -350 Theo Fremd Av -Rye 10580 **Fx**:921-0186
(914) 328-5900 .. **Weininger**, Wm P '78 -445 Hmltn Av -White Plns 10601 **Fx**:328-5953
(212) 661-7300 .. **Weinman**, Carol Ann '83 %Malapero & P LLP -295 Mad Av -NY 10017
(212) 947-3370 .. **Weinman**, J Bruce '72 -352 7th Av -NY 10001
(718) 707-7969 .. **Weinman**, Jeffrey P '97 Original Designs -44-40 11th -LIC 11101
(718) 250-2000 .. **Weinman**, Linda J '84 %DA -350 Jay -Brklyn 11201 **Fx**:250-2314
(718) 983-8800 .. **Weinman**, Peter J '01 %Lee & A,LLP -260 Christopher Ln -Staten Isl 10314
(718) 463-3700 .. **Weinman**, Victoria L '87 %H Katz,PC -61-25 Utopia Pkwy -Fresh Mdws 11365
(212) 689-1113 .. **Weinmann**, Kurt L '85 (Garbarini & S,PC) -432 Park Av S -NY 10016
(716) 855-0600 .. **Weinmann**, Peter A '88 (Wolfgang & W) -69 Delaware Av -Buffalo 14202 **Fx**:855-1016
(518) 297-3900 .. **Weinraub**, Alan Paul '76 -483 Route 11 Bx3335 -Champlain 12919 **Fx**:297-4530
(212) 732-0400 .. **Weinraub**, David '89 (Grad & W,LLP) -305 Bway -NY 10007 **Fx**:571-0831
(518) 427-7350 .. **Weinraub**, David N '85 (Brown & W PLLC) -79 Columbia -Albany 12210
(212) 735-3000 .. **Weinraub**, David S '99 Cnsl Skadden ASM&F LLP -4 Times Sq -NY 10036
(212) 682-2800 .. **Weinraub**, Martin '53 (Silverman & W) -50 E 42nd -NY 10017
(914) 834-0536 .. **Weinraub**, Sally '75 -12 Dimitri Pl -Larchmnt 10538
(631) 669-2255 .. **Weinreb**, Alan H '83 (Weinreb & Assoc,PLLC) -6800 Jericho Tpke -Syosset 11791 **Fx**:669-2577
(845) 369-1019 .. **Weinreb**, Bernard '85 -2 Pearlman Dr -Spg Vly 10977
(212) 271-7600 .. **Weinreb**, Elan E '03 %Katlowitz & Assoc -270 Mad Av -NY 10016 **Fx**:271-7601
(212) 267-2575 .. **Weinreb**, Elliot '96 -1375 Bway -NY 10018
(212) 865-5858 .. **Weinreb**, Jacob M '81 -276 Riverside Dr -NY 10025
(516) 682-8181 .. **Weinreb**, Robt '95 Sovereign Title Agency,LP -6851 Jericho Tpk -Syosset 11791 **Fx**:682-5970
(212) 264-0300 .. **Weinreb**, Ruth '88 %NLRB -26 Fed Plz -NY 10278 **Fx**:264-8427
Weinreb, Vivienne M '03 -85 Meadowfarm Rd -E Islip 11730
(212) 685-6500 .. **Weinreich**, Amy C '96 Dominion -200 Mad Av -NY 10016
(212) 704-2435 .. **Weinreich**, Howard B '67 Volt Info Sciences -1065 Av of Amer -NY 10018 **Fx**:704-2417
(212) 838-1177 .. **Weinreich**, Howard L '58 OfCnsl Morse ZR&L LLP -405 Park Av -NY 10022
(516) 584-7004 .. **Weinreich**, Lawr A '85 -1400 Old Cntry Rd -Westbury 11590 **Fx**:294-1954
(718) 496-2938 .. **Weinreich**, Marc E '98 -10819 65th Rd -Frst Hlls 11375
(718) 286-6000 .. **Weinrib**, Barry S '85 %DA -125-01 Qns Blvd -Kew Gdns 11415
(212) 935-5500 .. **Weinrib**, Kenneth M '84 (Franklin WR&V) -488 Mad Av -NY 10022
(212) 964-9282 .. **Weinrib**, Neil A '78 (N Weinrib & Assoc) -305 Bway -NY 10007 **Fx**:964-9525
(516) 747-6700 .. **Weinrib**, Rachel L '08 %Kirschenbaum & K -200 Grdn City Plz -Gdn Cty 11530 **Fx**:747-6781
(212) 506-1700 .. **Weinrib**, Russel C '08 Kasowitz BT&F LLP -1633 Bway -NY 10019
(212) 661-1100 .. **Weinrib**, Tamar A '05 %Pomerantz HG&G LLP -100 Park Av -NY 10017
(212) 344-8828 .. **Weinrich**, Johnathan E '78 -15 Maiden Ln -NY 10038 **Fx**:425-2539
(212) 806-5400 .. **Weinroth**, Lois L '68 (Stroock &S&L LLP) -180 Maiden Ln -NY 10038
(516) 799-4668 .. **Weinroth**, Margery '86 -75 Aster -Massapequa Pk 11762 **Fx**:541-1379
(516) 829-7000 .. **Weinroth**, Marvin J '74 -425 Nrthrn Blvd -Gt Neck 11021 **Fx**:829-7005
(212) 310-8000 .. **Weinschel**, Alan J '70 (Weil G&M LLP) -767 5th Av -NY 10153
(212) 719-5930 .. **Weinschenk**, Fritz '53 (Hamburger W&F) -36 W 44th -NY 10036
(631) 853-4049 .. **Weinschenk**, Richd H '09 %Cnty Atty -Dennison Bldg Bx6100 -Hauppauge 11788 **Fx**:853-5169
(718) 787-0288 .. **Weinschneider**, Devorah Sadowsky '93 -1357 E 29th -Brklyn 11210 **Fx**:787-0261
(212) 837-6000 .. **Weinsier**, Michl '87 (Hughes H&R LLP) -1 Bttry Pk Plz -NY 10004
(212) 688-4000 .. **Weinstat**, Michele L '82 NYS HFA -641 Lex Av -NY 10022 **Fx**:872-0362
(212) 872-1000 .. **Weinstein**, Adam K '95 -One Bryant Park -NY 10036 **Fx**:872-1002
(212) 799-9638 .. **Weinstein**, Adam N '96 %West Side SRO Lw Prj -647 Columbus Av -NY 10025 **Fx**:721-1514
(212) 873-3400 .. **Weinstein**, Amy A '84 NY Historical Society -2 W 77th -NY 10024
(212) 344-1600 .. **Weinstein**, Andrea I '91 (Schonfeld & W) -80 Wall -NY 10005 **Fx**:480-0717
(212) 582-8900 .. **Weinstein**, Andrew J '91 (Weinstein Law Firm PLLC) -521 5th Av -NY 10175 **Fx**:582-8989
(212) 407-4000 .. **Weinstein**, Andrew J '02 %Loeb & L,LLP -345 Park Av -NY 10154
(212) 969-1000 .. **Weinstein**, Andrew S '01 %Alliance Bernstein LP -1345 Av of Amer -NY 10105 **Fx**:554-4639
(718) 361-9191 .. **Weinstein**, Annie Vera '96 Hereford Ins Co -3601 43rd Av -LIC 11101
(212) 222-5034 .. **Weinstein**, Arthur I '67 -924 West End Av -NY 10025 **Fx**:222-5641
(212) 450-4000 .. **Weinstein**, Aryeh '09 %Davis P&W LLP -450 Lex Av -NY 10017
(718) 665-9000 .. **Weinstein**, Barry A '74 (Goldstein & W) -888 Grnd Cncrs -Bronx 10451 **Fx**:665-9147
(716) 634-7470 .. **Weinstein**, Barry A '77 -1445 Maple Rd -Williamsvll 14221
(212) 554-1400 .. **Weinstein**, Boaz A '03 %Bernstein LB&G LLP -1285 Av of Amer -NY 10019
(212) 450-4000 .. **Weinstein**, Brian S '99 (Davis P&W LLP) -450 Lex Av -NY 10017
(212) 777-7332 .. **Weinstein**, Charlene Magen '77 CM Weinstein,LLP -40 5th Av -NY 10011 **Fx**:777-2132
(718) 858-3100 .. **Weinstein Chase Messinger & Peters** -26 Court -Brklyn 11242 **Fx**:858-3190
(631) 952-6724 .. **Weinstein**, Chester J '68 NYS DMV -Vets Mem'l Hwy -Hauppauge 11788
(212) 968-0707 .. **Weinstein**, Claude '97 -100 William -NY 10038
(516) 482-7179 .. **Weinstein**, Cliff J '76 %Graphics LX Corp -11 Blue Sea Ln -Gt Neck 11024 **Fx**:482-7135
(212) 474-1000 .. **Weinstein**, Danl B '10 %Cravath S&M LLP -825 8th Av -NY 10019
(716) 845-9364 .. **Weinstein**, Danl J '70 %Supreme Ct -25 Delaware Av -Buffalo 14202 **Fx**:851-3293
(212) 980-1265 .. **Weinstein**, David A '90 -410 Park Av -NY 10022
(518) 474-8434 .. **Weinstein**, David A '95 %Gov's Cnsls Ofc -242 State Cptl -Albany 12224
(212) 902-1000 .. **Weinstein**, David L '95 %Goldman Sachs -1 NY Plz -NY 10004
(212) 805-9785 .. **Weinstein**, Dawn L '04 QBE the Americas -88 Pine -NY 10005
(212) 476-3298 .. **Weinstein**, Diane L '84 %Wellpoint -1 Lbrty Plz -NY 10006
(212) 909-6000 .. **Weinstein**, Dov M K '10 %Debevoise & P LLP -919 3rd Av -NY 10022
(212) 223-0200 .. **Weinstein**, Elizabeth S '06 %Stillman F&S,PC -425 Park Av -NY 10022
(315) 671-2108 .. **Weinstein**, Ellen S '91 Surrogates Ct -401 Mntgmry -Syracuse 13202 **Fx**:671-1162
(212) 869-7000 .. **Weinstein**, Eric S '90 (Feldman W&S LLP) -420 Lex Av -NY 10170
(607) 273-4200 .. **Weinstein**, Fred '68 -202 E State -Ithaca 14850 **Fx**:272-6694
(914) 285-9800 .. **Weinstein**, Fred D '80 (Kurzman EC&L,LLP) -1 N Bway -White Plns 10601
(212) 421-7850 .. **Weinstein**, Herschel S '81 Forest Labs Inc -909 3rd Av -NY 10022
(212) 696-9494 .. **Weinstein**, Howard M '88 (Park WC&N,LLP) -15 E 32nd -NY 10016 **Fx**:447-0968
(212) 636-6000 .. **Weinstein**, Ian S '88 %Fordham Univ Sch of Law -140 W 62nd -NY 10023 **Fx**:636-6899
(718) 241-2430 .. **Weinstein**, Ira N '77 -2200 Mill Av -Brklyn 11234 **Fx**:763-4950
(718) 858-3100 .. **Weinstein**, Irwin J '84 (Weinstein CM&P) -26 Court -Brklyn 11242
(516) 571-3800 .. **Weinstein**, Jason P '07 %DA -262 Old Cntry Rd -Mineola 11501 **Fx**:248-9479
(212) 859-8000 .. **Weinstein**, Jason S '07 %Fried FHS&J LLP -1 NY Plz -NY 10004
(516) 569-2146 .. **Weinstein**, Jay M '80 -503 Longacre Av -Woodmere 11598 **Fx**:569-2146
(212) 693-3737 .. **Weinstein**, Jeffrey L '91 -225 Bway -NY 10007 **Fx**:693-2020
(212) 804-4200 .. **Weinstein**, Jeffrey S '86 (Mound CW&G) -One Bttry Pk Plz -NY 10004
(631) 851-1090 .. **Weinstein**, Jennifer H '97 -10 Newton Pl -Hauppauge 11788
(212) 891-5736 .. **Weinstein**, Jill A '02 %Natixis Capital -9 W 57th -NY 10019
(212) 975-2832 .. **Weinstein**, Joel H '76 %Hewitt Grp -555 W 57th -NY 10019 **Fx**:975-2311
(212) 312-2260 .. **Weinstein**, Jordana S '08 Leg Aid -60 Lafayette -NY 10013 **Fx**:349-0874
(212) 787-2985 .. **Weinstein**, Judith S '86 -35 W 64th -NY 10023
(516) 877-2525 .. **Weinstein Kaplan & Cohen,PC** -1325 Franklin Av -Gdn Cty 11530 **Fx**:877-7760
(212) 705-7000 .. **Weinstein**, Katherine G '99 (Bingham M LLP) -399 Park Av -NY 10022
(516) 742-1400 .. **Weinstein**, Kenneth J '72 -100 Grdn City Plz -Gdn Cty 11530 **Fx**:741-3811
(212) 969-3000 .. **Weinstein**, Lawr I '80 (Proskauer R LLP) -1585 Bway -NY 10036
(631) 851-1090 .. **Weinstein**, Lloyd J '97 -10 Newton Pl -Hauppauge 11788
(973) 315-4538 .. **Weinstein**, Louis H '97 (Budd L) -140 Bway -NY 10005
(212) 837-6460 .. **Weinstein**, Marc A '94 (Hughes H&R LLP) -1 Bttry Pk Plz -NY 10004
(212) 922-9250 .. **Weinstein**, Margery N '85 (Ganfer & S LLP) -360 Lex Av -NY 10017
(212) 564-1250 .. **Weinstein**, Mark H '83 %Karp & K -370 7th Av -NY 10001
(212) 334-3355 .. **Weinstein**, Mark J '74 -100 Lafayette -NY 10013 **Fx**:226-6075
(212) 918-3000 .. **Weinstein**, Mark J '82 (Hogan L LLP) -875 3rd Av -NY 10022
(212) 973-9797 .. **Weinstein**, Marsha '83 (Saretsky KD&G,LLP) -475 Park Av S -NY 10016
(914) 725-2121 .. **Weinstein**, Martin A '65 -2 Sheridan Rd -Scarsdale 10583
(212) 687-4911 .. **Weinstein**, Marvin W '60 -360 Lex Av -NY 10017 **Fx**:983-6385
(212) 272-3245 .. **Weinstein**, Matthew L '05 %JP Morgan Chase -383 Mad Av -NY 10179
(718) 487-1300 .. **Weinstein**, Max McMeekin '06 %Leg Srvcs Corp A -80 Jamaica Av -Brklyn 11207 **Fx**:342-1780
(631) 271-6464 .. **Weinstein**, Maxwell D '62 MD Weinstein,PC -121 Beverly Rd -Huntngtn Sta 11746 **Fx**:421-3819
(631) 844-7800 .. **Weinstein**, Michl B '98 %Olsten Corp -175 Broadhllw Rd -Melvll 11747 **Fx**:844-7414
(212) 735-8600 .. **Weinstein**, Michl C '89 (Morrison C LLP) -909 3rd Av -NY 10022
(914) 332-8824 .. **Weinstein**, Michl D '85 -150 Wht Plns Rd -Tarrytwn 10591 **Fx**:332-1744
(631) 293-2310 .. **Weinstein**, Michl L '67 (M Weinstein & Assoc,LLP) -445 Broad Hollow Rd -Melvll 11747 **Fx**:293-2331
(212) 907-7300 .. **Weinstein**, Michl S '09 %Golenbock EAB&P -437 Mad Av -NY 10022
(718) 858-3100 .. **Weinstein**, Murray '52 (Weinstein CM&P) -26 Court -Brklyn 11242
(212) 891-9100 .. **Weinstein**, Neal A '82 (Goldfarb & F LLP) -345 Park Av -NY 10154
(212) 907-9600 .. **Weinstein**, Neal R '01 (Ingram YGC&B,LLP) -250 Park Av -NY 10177
(212) 238-3000 .. **Weinstein**, Paul T '86 (Emmet M&M,LLP) -120 Bway -NY 10271
(516) 571-3800 .. **Weinstein**, Peter A '78 %DA -262 Old Cntry Rd -Mineola 11501 **Fx**:248-9479
(212) 451-2300 .. **Weinstein**, Peter D '63 OfCnsl Olshan GFR&W LLP -65 E 55th -NY 10022
(212) 417-8700 .. **Weinstein**, Philip L '70 %Fed Def of NY Inc -52 Duane -NY 10007 **Fx**:571-0392
(212) 225-2000 .. **Weinstein**, Rebecca D '10 %Cleary GS&H -1 Lbrty Plz -NY 10006
(914) 725-5020 .. **Weinstein**, Rebecca L '82 -30 Vndrblt Rd -Scarsdale 10583
(212) 867-9090 .. **Weinstein**, Richd H '91 %Shenkman Cptl Mgmt Inc -461 5th Av -NY 10017
(212) 330-8257 .. **Weinstein**, Richd M '69 -1133 Bway -NY 10010
(212) 966-5333 .. **Weinstein**, Robt L '74 -350 Bway -NY 10013 **Fx**:966-0080
(212) 450-4000 .. **Weinstein**, Ronni T '10 %Davis P&W LLP -450 Lex Av -NY 10017
(212) 355-4175 .. **Weinstein**, Ruth A '75 (Rapaport Bros,PC) -18 E 48th -NY 10017
(516) 374-3525 .. **Weinstein**, Saul I '57 -965 South End -Woodmere 11598

(212) 576-3831 .. **Weinstein,** Scott W '96 NY Life Ins -51 Mad Av -NY 10010 **Fx:**447-0569
(585) 987-2800 .. **Weinstein,** Seth A '04 %Woods OG LLP -2 State -Rchstr 14614
(212) 964-6611 .. **Weinstein,** Seth I '95 (Lester SK&D) -120 Bway -NY 10271
(585) 248-3800 .. **Weinstein,** Seymour '52 SrCnsl WeinsteinMurphy -290 Linden Oaks -Rchstr 14625 **Fx:**248-4961
(212) 943-1200 .. **Weinstein,** Sheila '82 %Edelman & E,PC -61 Bway -NY 10006 **Fx:**943-0001
(585) 325-7440 .. **Weinstein,** Sherwin B '60 -135 Corp Woods -Rchstr 14623 **Fx:**454-3559
(212) 840-6543 .. **Weinstein Soybel & Kirwin** -36 W 44th -NY 10036 **Fx:**869-2817
(212) 267-4410 .. **Weinstein,** Stephen A '59 -18 Thornhedge Rd -Bellprt 11713
(212) 254-6068 .. **Weinstein,** Stephen J '76 -21 E 22nd -NY 10010
(212) 752-1000 .. **Weinstein,** Stephen L '87 (Eiseman LL&K,PC) -805 3rd Av -NY 10022
(212) 969-3000 .. **Weinstein,** Steven D '85 (Proskauer R LLP) -1585 Bway -NY 10036
(212) 977-7033 .. **Weinstein,** Steven M '85 %Perecman Firm PLLC -250 W 57th -NY 10107
(212) 521-4430 .. **Weinstein,** Steven R '80 (Becker M LLC) -590 Mad Av -NY 10022
(646) 723-2947 .. **Weinstein,** Wm R '85 (Sanford W&H,LLP) -1350 Av of Amer -NY 10019
(212) 953-6000 .. **Weinstock,** Ariel N '08 %Katsky K LLP -605 3rd Av -NY 10158
(212) 925-4430 .. **Weinstock,** Benjamin '52 -273 Church -NY 10013 **Fx:**925-5021
(516) 663-6600 .. **Weinstock,** Benjamin '79 (Ruskin MF,PC) -1425 RXR Plz -Uniondale 11556
(631) 367-3658 .. **Weinstock,** Bonnie Siber '79 -9 Cabriolet Ln -Melvll 11747
(516) 877-1020 .. **Weinstock,** Denis A '64 -200 Old Cntry Rd -Mineola 11501
(212) 689-1113 .. **Weinstock,** Gregg D '88 (Garbarini & S,PC) -432 Park Av S -NY 10016
(718) 698-8800 .. **Weinstock,** Jerome '80 %Golden Gate Hlthcare -191 Bradley Av -Staten Isl 10314 **Fx:**698-5536
(212) 770-2052 .. **Weinstock,** Jessica Lee '00 AIG Tech Srvcs -80 Pine -NY 10005
(212) 335-9000 .. **Weinstock,** Judith Ann '98 %DA -1 Hogan Pl -NY 10013
(718) 286-6000 .. **Weinstock,** Lauren P '08 %DA -125-01 Qns Blvd -Kew Gdns 11415
(212) 373-3000 .. **Weinstock,** Lindsey M '10 %Paul WRW&G LLP -1285 Av of Amer -NY 10019
(516) 327-2700 .. **Weinstock,** Risa H '86 BWD Grp LLC -BWD Plz Bx9050 -Jericho 11753 **Fx:**327-2800
(212) 373-3000 .. **Weinstock,** Robt A '10 %Paul WRW&G LLP -1285 Av of Amer -NY 10019
(516) 466-4400 .. **Weinstock,** Steve F '93 (Greenwald & W,LLP) -505 Nrthrn Blvd -Gt Neck 11021
(212) 859-8000 .. **Weinstock,** Y Dov '06 %Fried FHS&J LLP -1 NY Plz -NY 10004
(212) 648-0031 .. **Weintraub,** Alan M '83 JP Morgan Chase Bank,NA -245 Park Av -NY 10167
(212) 267-1900 .. **Weintraub,** Alison M '09 %Wade CM -111 Bway -NY 10006
(914) 347-8725 .. **Weintraub,** Allen L '87 -309 Mamaroneck Av -White Plns 10605 **Fx:**347-6607
(212) 607-2815 .. **Weintraub,** Ann F '95 Cnsl FTC -1 Bowling Grn -NY 10004 **Fx:**607-2822
(212) 558-5500 .. **Weintraub,** Bernard A '94 Weitz & L,PC -700 Bway -NY 10003
(516) 393-6142 .. **Weintraub,** Calvin A '80 %F Laurino -999 Stewart Av -Bethpage 11714 **Fx:**393-6130
(212) 968-7430 .. **Weintraub,** Chas H '67 -75 West -NY 10006
(718) 601-1100 .. **Weintraub,** Chas L '71 -6132 Riverdale Av -Bronx 10471 **Fx:**601-3786
(212) 272-6927 .. **Weintraub,** David A '96 %JP Morgan Chase -383 Mad Av -NY 10179
(516) 248-9042 .. **Weintraub,** David J '84 -120 Front Bx30 -Mineola 11501 **Fx:**348-9044
(212) 909-9519 .. **Weintraub,** Evan S '92 (Wachtel & M,LLP) -885 2nd Av -NY 10017
(516) 679-1379 .. **Weintraub,** Evelyn '85 -3431 Beltagh Av -Wantagh 11793 **Fx:**679-0878
(212) 688-8555 .. **Weintraub,** Freddi M '90 (Fragomen DB&L LLP) -7 Hanover Sq -NY 10004
(631) 421-2500 .. **Weintraub,** Gary N '67 (Caputi W&N) -50 Elm -Huntngtn 11743
(212) 944-1501 .. **Weintraub,** Harry H '77 (Glick & W) -1501 Bway -NY 10036 **Fx:**768-0785
(518) 474-8266 .. **Weintraub,** Henry S '75 %Dept of Health -Corning Twr 24th Fl -Albany 12237 **Fx:**473-2430
(718) 613-3500 .. **Weintraub,** Jacob Harris '88 %UIA Bd -Bx29002 -Brklyn 11201 **Fx:**613-3566
(212) 964-6611 .. **Weintraub,** Jay '98 %Lester SK&D -120 Bway -NY 10271
(718) 990-1833 .. **Weintraub,** Jeremy M '99 St John's Law Schl -8000 Utopia Pkwy -Jamaica 11439 **Fx:**591-1855
(917) 777-4200 .. **Weintraub,** Jill L '92 Cnsl Bingham M LLP -1 Bttry Pk Plz -NY 10004
(516) 241-0831 .. **Weintraub,** Joel '03 -164 Hempstd Av -Lynbrk 11563 **Fx:**764-5230
(518) 402-9184 .. **Weintraub,** Lawr H '87 DEC -625 Bway -Albany 12233 **Fx:**402-9018
(212) 785-9100 .. **Weintraub,** Leonard '88 (Paduano & W LLP) -1251 Av of Amer -NY 10020
(212) 644-3011 .. **Weintraub,** Leonard M '45 -110 E 59th -NY 10022
(212) 373-3000 .. **Weintraub,** Philip A '07 %Paul WRW&G LLP -1285 Av of Amer -NY 10019
(212) 655-3500 .. **Weintraub,** Racquel '96 SpclCnsl Meister S&F LLP -140 E 45th -NY 10017
(212) 545-4689 .. **Weintraub,** Robt B '78 OfCnsl Wolf HAF&H LLP -270 Mad Av -NY 10016
(212) 752-2555 .. **Weintraub,** Rosemary '88 -228 E 45th -NY 10017
(718) 380-1000 .. **Weintraub,** Stephen S '79 (S Weintraub,PC) -80-30 164th -Jamaica 11432 **Fx:**380-1750
(212) 833-1109 .. **Weintraub,** Wm P '80 (Friedman KS&A LLP) -1633 Bway -NY 10019 **Fx:**373-7909
(718) 285-4128 .. **Weintraub,** Yosef Y '01 Weintraub LLC -28 Dina Ct -Staten Isl 10306 **Fx:**(917) 210-3612
(212) 312-2260 .. **Weintrob,** Tracy Kaminetsky '08 Leg Aid -60 Lafayette -NY 10013 **Fx:**349-0874
(212) 776-5091 .. **Weinum,** Enid Malloy '88 %NYC Housing Auth -250 Bway -NY 10007 **Fx:**776-5039
(518) 392-4995 .. **Weir,** Carol '64 -185 Cnty Rd 61 -Chatham 12037 **Fx:**392-7920
(212) 270-4536 .. **Weir,** Claude V Jr. '81 JP Morgan Chase & Co -270 Park Av -NY 10017
(212) 530-5000 .. **Weir,** Dana Roitberg '06 %Milbank TH&M LLP -1 Chase Manh Plz -NY 10005
(212) 964-5570 .. **Weir,** Danl M '01 %Sacks & S -150 Bway -NY 10038 **Fx:**349-2141
(716) 636-8660 .. **Weir,** David C '99 %K Redding & Assoc -2420 Sweet Home Dr -Amherst 14228
(212) 878-8000 .. **Weir,** James M '07 %Clifford C LLP -31 W 52nd -NY 10019
(212) 572-6374 .. **Weir,** John K '72 J Weir LLC -300 Park Av -NY 10022 **Fx:**572-6449
(716) 854-3343 .. **Weir,** Jonathan D '98 (Weir Fncl) -424 Main -Buffalo 14202 **Fx:**854-4250
(212) 676-1347 .. **Weir,** Matthew C '09 %Law Dept -100 Church -NY 10007 **Fx:**788-0367
(212) 558-4000 .. **Weir,** Michl W '67 SrCnsl Sullivan & C LLP -125 Broad -NY 10004
(212) 360-6054 .. **Weir,** Peter F '59 -49 E 86th -NY 10028 **Fx:**831-3976
(347) 328-2680 .. **Weir,** Rhonda R '94 -26 Court -Brklyn 11242
(845) 291-2050 .. **Weir,** Seamus P '08 %DA -255-275 Main -Goshen 10924 **Fx:**291-2085
(585) 263-1000 .. **Weir,** Wm F '86 (Nixon P LLP) -1100 Clinton Sq -Rchstr 14604
(212) 558-4000 .. **Weir,** Wm H '09 %Sullivan & C LLP -125 Broad -NY 10004
(845) 565-1100 .. **Weires,** Rhett D '95 (Tarshis CLM&M,PLLC) -One Corwin Ct -Newburgh 12550
(845) 565-0999 .. **WeirMarek,** Tracy A '01 %E Harris -405 Robnsn Av-Rt 9W -Newburgh 12550 **Fx:**565-1281
(914) 686-9010 .. **Weis,** Claudine L '98 %Wilson BCC&C,PC -2 William -White Plns 10601
(914) 249-6055 .. **Weis,** Elene M '01 %MasterCard Intl -2000 Purchase -Purchase 10577
(516) 571-2878 .. **Weis,** Philip C '85 Hon D Palmieri -100 Supreme Ct Dr -Mineola 11501
(212) 733-4856 .. **Weis,** Philip I '88 %Pfizer Inc -235 E 42nd -NY 10017
(845) 228-4200 .. **Weis,** Robt A '91 %W Sayegh,PC -65 Gleneida Av -Carmel 10512 **Fx:**228-4832
(212) 391-8045 .. **Weisbard,** Neil M '06 %Slater & B LLP -61 Bway -NY 10006 **Fx:**391-8047
(716) 849-1333 .. **Weisbeck,** Richd P Jr. '83 (Lipsitz GSC LLP) -42 Delaware Av -Buffalo 14202
(585) 232-4090 .. **Weisbeck,** Stephen R '95 %Leg Aid -1 W Main -Rchstr 14614 **Fx:**232-2352
(212) 682-7474 .. **Weisbein,** Robt S '83 (Foley & L LLP) -90 Park Av -NY 10016
(212) 326-3939 .. **Weisberg,** Andrew H '04 %Jones D -222 E 41st -NY 10017
(212) 819-8200 .. **Weisberg,** Andrew N '09 %White & C LLP -1155 Av of Amer -NY 10036
(212) 492-4304 .. **Weisberg,** Anne C '87 Deloitte & Touche -1633 Bway -NY 10019
(718) 852-2816 .. **Weisberg,** Barry L '77 -134 State -Brklyn 11201
(212) 374-6592 .. **Weisberg,** Danl '99 NYC Dept of Ed -52 Chmbrs -NY 10007
(516) 466-2750 .. **Weisberg,** Danl J '95 (Weisberg & W) -98 Cutter Mill Rd -Gt Neck 11021 **Fx:**466-2799
(631) 476-6752 .. **Weisberg,** David C '62 Lawyers Equalizer -9 Mallard Path -Coram 11727 **Fx:**476-0375
(718) 875-6644 .. **Weisberg,** Eric J '91 %Packer Collegiate Inst -170 Joralemon -Brklyn 11201
(718) 246-4155 .. **Weisberg,** Erwin '61 -42 Willow -Brklyn 11201 **Fx:**246-4155
(212) 696-2666 .. **Weisberg Friedman & Klapisch** -261 5th Av -NY 10016 **Fx:**889-5697
(212) 787-7760 .. **Weisberg,** Harold H '62 (Weisberg & W) -2463 Bway -NY 10025 **Fx:**787-6237
(212) 687-1870 .. **Weisberg,** Joan L '76 (Weisberg & W) -475 Park Av S -NY 10016 **Fx:**687-1880
(518) 402-0552 .. **Weisberg,** Michl G '93 NYS Unmplymnt Ins Appls -Bx15126 -Albany 12212
(718) 237-5500 .. **Weisberg,** Michl L '03 %Leg Srvcs -105 Court -Brklyn 11201 **Fx:**855-0733
(212) 867-9500 .. **Weisberg,** Phyllis H '73 (Kurzman K&F,LLP) -230 Park Av -NY 10169
(212) 790-0299 .. **Weisberg,** Richd '76 %Benj N Cardozo Schl of Law -55 5th Av -NY 10003 **Fx:**790-0345
(212) 637-3223 .. **Weisberg,** Richd J '73 %EPA -290 Bway -NY 10007 **Fx:**637-3096
(212) 787-7760 .. **Weisberg,** S Michl '53 (Weisberg & W) -2463 Bway -NY 10025 **Fx:**787-6237
(516) 466-2750 .. **Weisberg,** Sidney A '65 (Weisberg & W) -98 Cutter Mill Rd -Gt Neck 11021 **Fx:**466-2799
(212) 687-1870 .. **Weisberg,** Wm I '61 (Weisberg & W) -475 Park Av S -NY 10016 **Fx:**687-1880
(212) 227-1777 .. **Weisberg,** Wm M '88 -217 Bway -NY 10007 **Fx:**619-7770
(212) 458-1218 .. **Weisblatt,** Stacey A '92 %AIG -175 Water -NY 10038
(914) 237-3348 .. **Weisblum,** Steven H '82 A Heilbraun,PC -1046 McLean Av -Ynkrs 10704
(212) 828-0424 .. **Weisbond,** Raymond D '54 -1165 5th Av -NY 10029 **Fx:**828-0424
(212) 493-7504 .. **Weisbrod,** Carl B '69 %NYC Partnership -1 Bttry Pk Plz -NY 10004
(212) 545-4000 .. **Weisbrod,** Dana Glick '07 %Jackson L LLP -666 3rd Av -NY 10017
(212) 977-9700 .. **Weisbrot,** N Ari '95 (Phillips N LLP) -666 5th Av -NY 10103
(212) 277-6500 .. **Weisburd,** Steven I '77 (Dickstein S LLP) -1633 Bway -NY 10019
(212) 848-4000 .. **Weisburg,** Henry '78 (Shearman & S LLP) -599 Lex Av -NY 10022
(212) 849-7000 .. **Weisburst,** Sanford I '01 OfCnsl Quinn EU&S,LLP -51 Mad Av -NY 10010
(718) 387-4000 .. **Weisel,** Abraham '02 %Levin & L PC -185 Marcy Av -Brklyn 11211
(516) 227-6363 .. **Weisel,** Benjamin T '07 %Amato & Assoc,PC -666 Old Cntry Rd -Gdn Cty 11530 **Fx:**227-6367
(516) 463-5655 .. **Weisel,** Martha S '82 Hofstra Univ -140 Weller Hall -Hempstd 11549
(212) 359-4233 .. **Weisel,** Nathaniel H '98 -122 W 27th -NY 10001
(212) 773-8257 .. **Weisel,** Nira '90 Ernst & Young LLP -5 Times Sq -NY 10036
(631) 981-6246 .. **Weiselberg,** Wm R '91 -196 Stanley Dr -Centereach 11720
(212) 479-6000 .. **Weisenberg,** Brent I '02 %Cooley LLP -1114 Av of Amer -NY 10036
(212) 233-8510 .. **Weisenberg,** Ronald B '00 -160 Bway -NY 10038 **Fx:**608-1659
(917) 658-5930 .. **Weisenfeld,** David J '82 -325 W End Av -NY 10023 **Fx:**(212) 873-7880
(646) 935-8277 .. **Weisenfeld,** J Jeffrey '65 -29 Mntgmry Pl -Brklyn 11215
(347) 404-9133 .. **Weisenfeld,** Lester I '85 %Civil Ct -141 Lvngstn -Brklyn 11201 **Fx:**(718) 643-3733

(914) 764-9202 ..**Weisenfreund,** Marc '72 -28 Twin Fawn Ln -Pound Rdg 10576
(212) 556-1234 ..**Weisenhaus,** Doreen G '84 %The NY Times Co -620 8th Av -NY 10018
(516) 741-6266 ..**Weisenreder,** Mark L '75 OfCnsl McCabe CM&F,LLP -346 Westbury Av Bx9000 -Carle Pl 11514
(914) 448-0200 ..**Weisensel,** Zoya '04 %Bartlett MB&M,LLP -81 Main -White Plns 10601
(718) 336-8886 ..**Weiser,** Chas '08 %H Skovronsky -1810 Av N -Brklyn 11230 **Fx:**336-8104
(212) 943-8940 ..**Weiser,** David '96 (Crisci W&H) -17 State -NY 10004 **Fx:**425-3428
(845) 639-7800 ..**Weiser,** Jonathan M '02 %Mandel K&B,LLP -210 Route 303 -Vly Cottage 10989
(212) 213-3111 ..**Weiser,** Martin J '67 (Weiser & Assoc) -150 E 58th -NY 10155 **Fx:**213-5939
(646) 888-4040 ..**Weiser,** Mary A '88 %Sloan-Kettering -1275 York Av -NY 10065 **Fx:**888-4047
(212) 254-9851 ..**Weiser,** Morris L '79 %Vistatech Entrprs Ltd -935 Bway -NY 10010 **Fx:**777-0805
(212) 213-3111 ..**Weiser,** Nicole S '97 (Weiser & Assoc) -150 E 58th -NY 10155 **Fx:**213-5939
(212) 589-4200 ..**Weiser,** Scott R '01 %Baker & H LLP -45 Rckfllr Plz -NY 10111
(718) 254-7000 ..**Weiser,** Steven E '96 %US Atty -271 Cadman Plz E -Brklyn 11201 **Fx:**254-6479
(212) 925-6635 ..**Weiser,** Wendy R '98 %Legal Momentum -395 Hudson -NY 10014 **Fx:**226-1066
(718) 422-0053 ..**Weiserbs,** Alena S '01 (Weiserbs & H) -270 Jay -Brklyn 11201 **Fx:**422-1459
(212) 209-4800 ..**Weisfelner,** Edw S '83 (Brown R LLP) -7 Times Sq -NY 10036
(212) 975-7030 ..**Weisfogel,** Amiel B '97 60 Minutes -555 W 57th -NY 10019
(914) 286-3400 ..**Weisfuse,** David B '74 %Leg Aid -1 N Bway -White Plns 10601 **Fx:**682-4112
(212) 983-3000 ..**Weisfuse,** Doreen K '80 (Weisfuse & W,LLP) -420 Lex Av -NY 10170 **Fx:**983-3006
(212) 983-3000 ..**Weisfuse,** Martin H '70 (Weisfuse & W,LLP) -420 Lex Av -NY 10170 **Fx:**983-3006
(212) 909-6000 ..**Weisgerber,** Erica S '09 %Debevoise & P LLP -919 3rd Av -NY 10022
(718) 613-2170 ..**Weisgerber,** Mary G '05 %Hon L Bloom USDC EDNY -225 Cadman Plz E -Brklyn 11201
(716) 845-6446 ..**Weishaar,** Michl A '05 %Gleichenhaus M&F,PC -43 Court -Buffalo 14202 **Fx:**845-6475
(585) 546-2500 ..**Weishaar,** Peter J '96 (McConville CC&M,PC) -25 E Main -Rchstr 14614
(845) 486-2300 ..**Weishaupt,** Matthew A III '88 %DA -236 Main -Poughkeepsie 12601 **Fx:**486-2324
(845) 340-3315 ..**Weishaupt,** Wm J Jr. '80 DA -285 Wall -Kingston 12401 **Fx:**340-3185
(516) 997-0700 ..**Weisinger,** Howard D '88 -25 Carle Rd -Westbury 11590
(212) 770-1650 ..**Weisinger,** Lynn A '92 %AIG -80 Pine -NY 10005
(646) 742-1100 ..**Weisinger,** Richd H '57 -675 3rd Av -NY 10017 **Fx:**(212) 599-0770
(212) 661-9100 ..**Weiskopf,** Alan R '71 (Otterbourg SH&R,PC) -230 Park Av -NY 10169
(212) 909-6000 ..**Weiskopf,** Danl M '09 %Debevoise & P LLP -919 3rd Av -NY 10022
(212) 541-2000 ..**Weiskopf,** Ian M '03 %Bryan C LLP -1290 Av of Amer -NY 10104
(212) 986-1200 ..**Weiskopf,** Nicholas R '69 SpclCnsl Gordon HR&C LLP -355 Lex Av -NY 10017
(718) 990-6008 ..**Weiskopf,** Nicholas R '69 %St John's Law Schl -8000 Utopia Pkwy -Jamaica 11439 **Fx:**591-1855
(518) 462-5601 ..**Weiskopf,** Richd H '75 OfCnsl O'Connell & A -54 State -Albany 12207
(315) 218-8000 ..**Weiskotten,** Natalie H '09 %Bond S&K,PLLC -1 Lincoln Ctr -Syracuse 13202
(212) 558-6668 ..**Weisman,** Allison J '04 %Foley SO&W -100 William -NY 10038
(914) 668-8900 ..**Weisman & Calderon LLP** -6 Gramatan Av -Mt Vernon 10550 **Fx:**668-8949
(212) 371-5400 ..**Weisman Celler Spett & Modlin PC** -445 Park Av -NY 10022 **Fx:**371-5407
(718) 390-5463 ..**Weisman,** Danl G '85 %Family Ct -100 Richmond Ter -Staten Isl 10301
(718) 447-8385 ..**Weisman,** Dea D '05 -84 Beverly Rd -Staten Isl 10305 **Fx:**815-4835
(646) 822-2281 ..**Weisman,** Hadas '99 Thomson Financial -195 Bway -NY 10007
(914) 668-8900 ..**Weisman,** Harold '58 (Weisman & C LLP) -6 Gramatan Av -Mt Vernon 10550
(212) 306-7100 ..**Weisman,** Hillary '85 %Campaign Finance Bd -40 Rector -NY 10006 **Fx:**306-7143
(718) 803-3782 ..**Weisman,** James J '78 %United Spinal Assn -75-20 Astoria Blvd -E Elmhrst 11370 **Fx:**803-0414
(212) 309-5452 ..**Weisman,** Marc R '00 Lexis/Nexis -125 Park Av -NY 10017 **Fx:**309-8187
(212) 968-9607 ..**Weisman,** Marcel '64 -45 Bway -NY 10006 **Fx:**968-0296
(212) 792-7600 ..**Weisman,** Max V '07 Peak Counsel -25 W 31st -NY 10001
(212) 535-7818 ..**Weisman,** Peter J '91 -444 E 82nd -NY 10028 **Fx:**535-7818
(516) 256-7737 ..**Weisman,** Rachel J '90 (Weisman Law Grp,PC) -140 Spruce -Cedarhrst 11516 **Fx:**256-7738
(914) 668-8900 ..**Weisman,** Richd S '83 (Weisman & C LLP) -6 Gramatan Av -Mt Vernon 10550
(631) 465-2064 ..**Weisman,** Robyn D '87 -68 S Srvc Rd -Melvll 11747 **Fx:**462-4273
(212) 558-6668 ..**Weisman,** Steven F '73 (Foley SO&W) -100 William -NY 10038
(212) 609-6800 ..**Weisman,** Steven H '95 (McCarter & E,LLP) -245 Park Av -NY 10167
(315) 682-1898 ..**Weisman,** Stewart '81 -8060 Shadow Rock Bx598 -Manlius 13104
(631) 969-7777 ..**Weisman,** Todd E '83 (Frenkel LWW&G,LLP) -20 W Main -Bay Shr 11706 **Fx:**206-0540
(212) 969-3000 ..**Weisman,** Wm H '07 %Proskauer R LLP -1585 Bway -NY 10036
(845) 291-1900 ..**Weisman-Estis,** Deborah I '85 (Cohen E & Assoc,LLP) -40 Matthews -Goshen 10924 **Fx:**291-8601
(917) 721-0067 ..**Weisner,** Scott A '98 -26 Court -Brklyn 11242
(212) 216-8000 ..**Weisner,** Wm W '85 (Tarter K&D LLP) -1350 Bway -NY 10018
(516) 328-8899 ..**Weiss,** Adam C '03 %Milman L Law Grp PLLC -3000 Marcus Av -Lk Success 11042 **Fx:**328-0082
(212) 308-6100 ..**Weiss,** Adam D '05 %Levi L&F LLP -1185 Av of Amer -NY 10036
(516) 794-1100 ..**Weiss,** Adam W '96 %Russo D&L -1975 Hempstd Tpk -E Meadow 11554
(718) 259-2100 ..**Weiss,** Alan '01 (Gutman W,PC) -2276 65th -Brklyn 11204 **Fx:**259-2105
(212) 681-3000 ..**Weiss,** Alan L '09 %Fischer Francis Trees & Watts -200 Park Av -NY 10166
(212) 909-9500 ..**Weiss,** Allan J '98 %Wachtel & M,LLP -885 2nd Av -NY 10017
(516) 622-2310 ..**Weiss,** Allen H '54 -3000 Marcus Av -New Hyde Pk 11042
(212) 259-8000 ..**Weiss,** Allison H '95 Cnsl Dewey & L LLP -1301 Av of Amer -NY 10019
(516) 873-8587 ..**Weiss,** Allison M '97 %Goldman & Assoc -100 Ring Rd W -Gdn Cty 11530 **Fx:**873-8535
(212) 407-4000 ..**Weiss,** Alyson M '90 (Loeb & L,LLP) -345 Park Av -NY 10154
(212) 841-1000 ..**Weiss,** Amanda L '08 %Covington & B LLP -620 8th Av -NY 10018
(212) 756-2000 ..**Weiss,** Andre '78 (Schulte R&Z LLP) -919 3rd Av -NY 10022
(212) 308-6100 ..**Weiss,** Andrea Likwornik '82 (Levi L&F LLP) -1185 Av of Amer -NY 10036
(914) 939-0616 ..**Weiss,** Andrew G '87 -315 King -Pt Chester 10573 **Fx:**(718) 504-7893
(516) 571-2733 ..**Weiss,** Andrew J '94 %DA -262 Old Cntry Rd -Mineola 11501 **Fx:**248-9479
(718) 557-6580 ..**Weiss,** Andrew S '81 OHA-SSA -155-10 Jamaica Av -Jamaica 11432 **Fx:**557-6554
(718) 457-0078 ..**Weiss,** Anita J '90 %J Blaha -87-02 Qns Blvd -Elmhrst 11373 **Fx:**458-0539
(646) 654-5096 ..**Weiss,** Anna B '96 VNU,Inc -770 Bway -NY 10003
(212) 922-9700 ..**Weiss,** Ari B '07 1st American Title Ins Co -633 3rd Av -NY 10017
(212) 319-4000 ..**Weiss,** Arnold M '58 (Weiss & H,PC) -600 Mad Av -NY 10022
(212) 564-6633 ..**Weiss,** Barbara '96 %White & M,PC -875 Av of Amer -NY 10001
(516) 228-8383 ..**Weiss,** Barry C '78 -50 Chas Lindbergh Blvd -Uniondale 11553 **Fx:**228-8390
(212) 366-6100 ..**Weiss,** Barry D '87 (Weiss & R,PC) -27 Union Sq W -NY 10003
(845) 638-0044 ..**Weiss,** Barry F '75 B Weiss,PC -20 S Main -New Cty 10956 **Fx:**638-3074
(845) 638-1400 ..**Weiss,** Barry I '77 (Freedman WT&W) -130 N Main -New Cty 10956
(220) 942-6819 ..**Weiss,** Baruch '82 (Arnold & P LLP) -399 Park Av -NY 10022 **Fx:**(202) 942-5999
(212) 922-9700 ..**Weiss,** Brian A '07 %1st Amer Title -633 3rd Av -NY 10017 **Fx:**922-0881
(212) 915-8393 ..**Weiss,** Brian J '02 Willis HRH -200 Lbrty -NY 10281
(212) 967-5710 ..**Weiss Buell & Bell** -11 Park Pl -NY 10007 **Fx:**967-1336
(914) 375-0431 ..**Weiss,** Carolyn L '92 (Weiss & W) -1250 Cntrl Pk Av -Ynkrs 10704 **Fx:**423-8964
(212) 425-7200 ..**Weiss,** Chas A '97 (Kenyon & K,LLP) -1 Bway -NY 10004
(212) 226-5454 ..**Weiss,** Chas W '77 (C Weiss,PC) -225 Old Cntry Rd -Melvll 11747
(914) 358-4934 ..**Weiss,** Christopher L '93 (Ferro L&Z LLC) -1025 Wstchstr Av -White Plns 10604
(212) 907-9600 ..**Weiss,** Cory L '83 (Ingram YGC&B,LLP) -250 Park Av -NY 10177
(212) 247-0848 ..**Weiss,** Danl A '01 %Bienstock & M,PC -250 W 57th -NY 10107
(212) 633-0124 ..**Weiss,** David H '85 -41 Mad Av -NY 10010 **Fx:**743-8120
(631) 737-6040 ..**Weiss,** David J '92 Dept of Law -2100 Middle Cntry Rd -Centereach 11720 **Fx:**737-6050
(718) 250-2000 ..**Weiss,** David J '06 DA -350 Jay -Brklyn 11201 **Fx:**250-2314
(516) 783-0330 ..**Weiss,** David Paul '77 -406 Bedford Av -Bellmore 11710 **Fx:**783-8739
(212) 809-5700 ..**Weiss,** Donald J '80 OfCnsl Adorno & Y LLP -350 5th Av -NY 10118
(212) 484-8000 ..**Weiss,** Edw J '93 %Time Warner -1 Time Warner Ctr -NY 10019
(516) 739-6200 ..**Weiss,** Edw J '07 (Azoulay W LLP) -864 Willis Av -Albertson 11507 **Fx:**739-6202
(212) 248-1010 ..**Weiss,** Eli '50 Oakwood Law Grp,LLP -40 Wall -NY 10005
(212) 859-8000 ..**Weiss,** Eli A '01 (Fried FHS&J LLP) -1 NY Plz -NY 10004
(212) 669-7503 ..**Weiss,** Eliezer S '04 Div of Real Estate Srvcs -1 Centre -NY 10007
(212) 848-5086 ..**Weiss,** Elizabeth R '02 %Shearman & S LLP -599 Lex Av -NY 10022
(631) 424-4882 ..**Weiss,** Ellen I '94 E Weiss,PC -Bx2309 -Halesite 11743 **Fx:**424-5273
(212) 225-2000 ..**Weiss,** Emily S '10 %Cleary GS&H -1 Lbrty Plz -NY 10006
(914) 375-0431 ..**Weiss,** Eric '91 (Weiss & W) -1250 Cntrl Pk Av -Ynkrs 10704 **Fx:**423-8964
(212) 688-9200 ..**Weiss,** Eric D '05 Empire Srch Prtnrs -445 Park Av -NY 10022 **Fx:**688-9212
(212) 530-5000 ..**Weiss,** Eric I '10 %Milbank TH&M LLP -1 Chase Manh Plz -NY 10005
(845) 735-1700 ..**Weiss,** Eric M '85 %Active Media Srvcs -1 Blue Hill Plz Bx1705 -Pearl Rvr 10965 **Fx:**735-2342
(212) 687-3747 ..**Weiss,** Eric S '82 (Tuchman KWL&G,LLP) -6 E 45th -NY 10017
(212) 227-0347 ..**Weiss,** Frank '69 (Weiss W&W,PC) -25 Park Pl -NY 10007
(718) 522-4200 ..**Weiss,** Frederic C '81 -105 Court -Brklyn 11201 **Fx:**852-4167
(212) 223-0555 ..**Weiss,** Frederic C '81 -124 E 55th -NY 10022 **Fx:**223-8338
(516) 938-5460 ..**Weiss,** Fredric '56 %Studebaker -100 Jericho Quad -Jericho 11753
(212) 259-8000 ..**Weiss,** George C '72 OfCnsl Dewey & L LLP -1301 Av of Amer -NY 10019
(212) 907-0600 ..**Weiss,** Gregg M '82 (Gardner W&R LLP) -270 Mad Av -NY 10016
(212) 455-2000 ..**Weiss,** Gregory A '74 OfCnsl Simpson T&B LLP -425 Lex Av -NY 10017
(212) 335-9000 ..**Weiss,** Gregory M '08 DA -1 Hogan Pl -NY 10013
(718) 250-1100 ..**Weiss,** Heidi M '84 %E Garfinkel -12 Metrotech Ctr -Brklyn 11201 **Fx:**250-1168
(212) 643-6400 ..**Weiss,** Herbert A '77 (Garganigo G&W) -14 Penn Plz -NY 10122
(212) 319-4000 ..**Weiss & Hiller,PC** -600 Mad Av -NY 10022 **Fx:**753-4530
(212) 756-2000 ..**Weiss,** Holly H '92 (Schulte R&Z LLP) -919 3rd Av -NY 10022
(212) 557-7200 ..**Weiss,** Howard S '82 (Davidoff M&H,LLP) -605 3rd Av -NY 10158
(212) 484-3900 ..**Weiss,** Jacqueline A '84 (Arent F LLP) -1675 Bway -NY 10019
(212) 997-4400 ..**Weiss,** Jaime L '93 Cnsl Teitler & T,LLP -1114 Av of Amer -NY 10036 **Fx:**997-4949
(212) 967-5710 ..**Weiss,** Jane C '78 -11 Park Pl -NY 10007 **Fx:**967-1336
(212) 351-4000 ..**Weiss,** Janet M '90 (Gibson D&C LLP) -200 Park Av -NY 10166
(212) 271-7600 ..**Weiss,** Jason Y '09 %Katlowitz & Assoc -270 Mad Av -NY 10016 **Fx:**271-7601

(212) 752-8000 .. **Weiss,** Jed M '03 %Cole SMF&L,PA -900 3rd Av -NY 10022
(516) 374-9000 .. **Weiss,** Jeff S '87 %Lawrence Woodmere Acad -336 Woodmere Blvd -Woodmere 11598 **Fx:**374-4707
(718) 409-7293 .. **Weiss,** Jeffrey A '88 %SUNY Maritime College -Ft Schuyler -Bronx 10465
(716) 200-5050 .. **Weiss,** Jeffrey J '97 (Harris B PLLC) -726 Exchange -Buffalo 14210
(845) 365-0955 .. **Weiss,** Jeffrey S '92 -500 Oak Tree Rd -Palisades 10964
(212) 639-2259 .. **Weiss,** Jerelyn P '94 %Sloan-Kettering -1275 York Av -NY 10065 **Fx:**717-3058
(518) 429-4200 .. **Weiss,** Jerry A '74 OfCnsl Hiscock & B,LLP -50 Beaver -Albany 12207
(212) 935-3131 .. **Weiss,** Jerry A '95 %Gallet D&B,LLP -845 3rd Av -NY 10022
(212) 474-1000 .. **Weiss,** Jesse M '09 %Cravath S&M LLP -825 8th Av -NY 10019
(212) 558-4000 .. **Weiss,** Jessica L '08 %Sullivan & C LLP -125 Broad -NY 10004
(212) 450-4000 .. **Weiss,** Joanna C '07 %Davis P&W LLP -450 Lex Av -NY 10017
(212) 788-3000 .. **Weiss,** Joanna G '01 %NYC Mayors Ofc -1 Centre -NY 10007
(845) 362-6100 .. **Weiss,** Joel '98 (Weiss & A LLP) -1540 Route 202 -Pomona 10970 **Fx:**362-6111
(516) 227-0700 .. **Weiss,** Joel R '78 Cnsl Farrell F,PC -1320 RXR Plz -Uniondale 11556
(212) 953-6000 .. **Weiss,** Joel S '82 (Katsky K LLP) -605 3rd Av -NY 10158
(718) 680-5717 .. **Weiss,** John B '89 -246 Bay Ridge Pkwy -Brklyn 11209
(212) 210-9412 .. **Weiss,** John W '04 (Alston & B LLP) -90 Park Av -NY 10016
(212) 421-2233 .. **Weiss,** Jonathan B '04 %Wilk A LLP -675 3rd Av -NY 10017
(212) 813-8800 .. **Weiss,** Jordan D '07 %Goodwin P LLP -620 8th Av -NY 10018
(212) 682-3025 .. **Weiss,** Jos H '73 (Weiss & L) -551 5th Av -NY 10176
(212) 530-5000 .. **Weiss,** Joshua D '10 %Milbank TH&M LLP -1 Chase Manh Plz -NY 10005
(212) 660-3000 .. **Weiss,** Joshua P '00 %Sullivan & W LLP -1290 Av of Amer -NY 10104
(212) 504-6000 .. **Weiss,** Joshua R '97 SpclCnsl Cadwalader W&T LLP -1 World Fncl Ctr -NY 10281
(212) 213-8899 .. **Weiss,** Judah A '01 %M Tuchman -134 Lex Av -NY 10016 **Fx:**213-6308
(212) 374-5110 .. **Weiss,** Julia M '79 %NYC Dept Educ -52 Chmbrs -NY 10007
(516) 248-9700 .. **Weiss,** Karen L Solomon '91 %S Levitt & Assoc,PC -2 Hillside Av -Williston Pk 11596 **Fx:**741-9224
(212) 558-4000 .. **Weiss,** Katherine M '08 %Sullivan & C LLP -125 Broad -NY 10004
(212) 560-4664 .. **Weiss,** Kenneth R '88 %MBL Fin Grp/Metlife Fin Srv -1 Penn Plz -NY 10119 **Fx:**560-4677
(516) 794-1800 .. **Weiss,** Larry H '74 -1900 Hempstd Tpk -E Meadow 11554 **Fx:**794-6535
(212) 209-4800 .. **Weiss,** Laura F '09 %Brown R LLP -7 Times Sq -NY 10036
(845) 920-0200 .. **Weiss,** Laura G '79 (L Weiss,PC) -1 Blue Hill Plz Bx1647 -Pearl Rvr 10965 **Fx:**920-0232
(631) 577-7770 .. **Weiss,** Laura R '04 %K Dodson -100 Baylis Rd -Melvll 11747 **Fx:**577-7199
(212) 909-9500 .. **Weiss,** Lee '07 %Wachtel & M,LLP -885 2nd Av -NY 10017
(212) 354-4901 .. **Weiss,** Lee A '92 (Browne WG LLP) -49 W 37th -NY 10018 **Fx:**354-4904
(518) 447-3200 .. **Weiss,** Leonard A '48 OfCnsl McNamee LT&W,PC -677 Bway -Albany 12207
(212) 598-8023 .. **Weiss,** Linda S '77 %Guardian Life -7 Hanover Sq -NY 10004
(212) 768-6700 .. **Weiss,** Lisa A '84 (Sonnenschein N&R LLP) -2 World Fncl Ctr -NY 10281
(212) 849-7000 .. **Weiss,** Lori E '05 %Quinn EU&S,LLP -51 Mad Av -NY 10010
(212) 682-3025 .. **Weiss & Lurie** -551 5th Av -NY 10176 **Fx:**682-3010
(516) 239-8126 .. **Weiss,** Mark B '82 -4 Beechwd Dr -Lawrence 11559
(631) 462-5577 .. **Weiss,** Mark H '74 (M Weiss,PC) -6165 Jericho Tpk -Commack 11725 **Fx:**462-1282
(212) 736-5588 .. **Weiss,** Marni E '03 (Weiss I PLLC) -462 7th Av -NY 10018
(845) 897-5199 .. **Weiss,** Marsha Solomon '79 OfCnsl Feldman K&C,LLP -995 Main BxA -Fishkill 12524
(718) 522-0366 .. **Weiss,** Martin '65 -105 Court -Brklyn 11201
(212) 683-7373 .. **Weiss,** Matthew J '88 (Weiss & Assoc,PC) -440 Park Av S -NY 10016 **Fx:**726-0135
(212) 323-0200 .. **Weiss,** Melissa L '96 OppenheimerFunds,Inc -225 Lbrty -NY 10281
(212) 756-2000 .. **Weiss,** Menachem Y '09 %Schulte R&Z LLP -919 3rd Av -NY 10022
(212) 223-1885 .. **Weiss,** Michl '87 -575 Lex Av -NY 10022 **Fx:**888-3182
(212) 297-5800 .. **Weiss,** Michl A '07 %Day P LLP -7 Times Sq -NY 10036
(212) 701-3000 .. **Weiss,** Michl B '91 (Cahill G&R LLP) -80 Pine -NY 10005 **Fx:**269-5420
(212) 554-4350 .. **Weiss,** Michl S '92 %Paramount Capital -787 7th Av -NY 10019
(845) 638-1400 .. **Weiss,** Michl S '04 Freedman WT&W -130 N Main -New Cty 10956
(212) 350-3725 .. **Weiss,** Michelle D '02 Wachovia Wlth Mgmt -12 E 49th -NY 10017
(800) 424-2233 .. **Weiss,** Miriam S '94 (M Weiss & Assoc,PC) -875 Av of Amer -NY 10001 **Fx:**(732) 418-9115
(212) 571-7171 .. **Weiss,** Mitchel E '86 -150 Bway #1307 -NY 10038 **Fx:**571-7174
(212) 902-3867 .. **Weiss,** Mitchell S '94 %Goldman Sachs -1 NY Plz -NY 10004
(212) 344-3100 .. **Weiss,** Monroe '73 (Frenkel LWW&G,LLP) -1 Whitehall -NY 10004
(212) 920-8395 .. **Weiss,** Neil L '07 Siesko Prtnrs -156 W 56th -NY 10019
(203) 254-2707 .. **Weiss,** Pamela L '93 Weiss & W,LLC -50 Main -White Plns 10606
(631) 725-4486 .. **Weiss,** Patricia Ann P '85 -Bx751 -Sag Hbr 11963
(716) 873-8833 .. **Weiss,** Paul D '91 (Bartlo H&W) -22 Victoria Blvd -Kenmore 14217
(212) 696-7161 .. **Weiss,** Peter B '86 %Walters & Samuels -419 Park Av S -NY 10016
(516) 739-1500 .. **Weiss,** Philip M '93 (Weiss & W) -300 Old Cntry Rd -Mineola 11501 **Fx:**739-2189
(718) 286-6000 .. **Weiss,** Phyllis C '82 %DA -125-01 Qns Blvd -Kew Gdns 11415
(212) 949-9022 .. **Weiss,** Rachel M '10 Abelman F&S -666 3rd Av -NY 10017
(212) 455-2000 .. **Weiss,** Rachel S '10 %Simpson T&B LLP -425 Lex Av -NY 10017
(212) 687-1736 .. **Weiss,** Randolph E '98 %R Schwartzberg & Assoc,PLLC -60 E 42nd -NY 10165
(914) 235-0833 .. **Weiss,** Richd '77 -481 Main -New Rchll 10801 **Fx:**235-0890
(212) 594-5300 .. **Weiss,** Richd H '84 (Milberg LLP) -1 Penn Plz -NY 10119
(516) 627-7000 .. **Weiss,** Richd J '83 (Weiss & Z,PC) -3333 New Hyde Pk Rd -New Hyde Pk 11042
(212) 809-5700 .. **Weiss,** Richd P '80 OfCnsl Adorno & Y LLP -350 5th Av -NY 10118
(212) 940-8800 .. **Weiss,** Robt '86 (Katten MR LLP) -575 Mad Av -NY 10022
(212) 233-0800 .. **Weiss,** Robt '96 -11 Bway -NY 10004
(212) 747-9100 .. **Weiss,** Robt A '94 Globe Tax Srvcs -90 Broad -NY 10004
(212) 878-8000 .. **Weiss,** Robt B '07 %Clifford C LLP -31 W 52nd -NY 10019
(516) 876-4213 .. **Weiss,** Robt H '85 (Hooper & W LLC) -50 Jericho Tpk -Jericho 11753 **Fx:**876-6906
(212) 448-1100 .. **Weiss,** Robt M '86 (McLaughlin & S,LLP) -260 Mad Av -NY 10016
(212) 351-4000 .. **Weiss,** Romina Field '92 (Gibson D&C LLP) -200 Park Av -NY 10166
(631) 271-3737 .. **Weiss,** Ronald D '89 (R Weiss,PC) -734 Walt Whitman Rd -Melvll 11747 **Fx:**271-3784
(585) 262-6390 .. **Weiss,** Ronald E '78 (Hamberger & W) -1 S Wshngtn -Rchstr 14614
(212) 735-3000 .. **Weiss,** Ronald J '81 (Skadden ASM&F LLP) -4 Times Sq -NY 10036
(212) 366-6100 .. **Weiss & Rosenbloom,PC** -27 Union Sq W -NY 10003 **Fx:**366-6254
(718) 430-0048 .. **Weiss,** Ruth C '90 -2155 Paulding Av -Bronx 10462
(917) 454-1100 .. **Weiss,** Scott M '98 %Police Dept -2 Lafayette -NY 10007
(516) 571-2660 .. **Weiss,** Seth D '98 Cnsl Cnty Clerks Ofc -240 Old Cntry Rd -Mineola 11501 **Fx:**742-4099
(212) 986-5309 .. **Weiss,** Sidney N '75 -675 3rd Av -NY 10017 **Fx:**986-5629
(212) 889-4440 .. **Weiss,** Stanley G '55 (Scolari G&W) -475 Park Av S -NY 10016
(646) 918-6023 .. **Weiss,** Stefanie J '08 -225 Rector Pl -NY 10280
(212) 751-4300 .. **Weiss,** Stephen A '66 (Hodgson R LLP) -1540 Bway -NY 10036
(212) 584-0700 .. **Weiss,** Stephen A '91 (Seeger W LLP) -1 William -NY 10004
(212) 683-6111 .. **Weiss,** Stephen J '65 OfCnsl Bell & Co LLP -350 5th Av -NY 10118 **Fx:**683-2911
(212) 554-7800 .. **Weiss,** Stephen N '75 (Moses & S LLP) -405 Lex Av -NY 10174
(212) 688-3200 .. **Weiss,** Steven E '68 Cnsl Scheichet & D,PC -767 3rd Av -NY 10017
(716) 856-1700 .. **Weiss,** Steven J '92 (Cannon H&W,LLP) -726 Exchange -Buffalo 14210
(646) 452-6712 .. **Weiss,** Steven K '97 Roosevelt Invtmnt Grp -317 Mad Av -NY 10017
(845) 691-3994 .. **Weiss,** Stuart A Jr. '94 -Bx707 -Highlnd 12528
(212) 843-8850 .. **Weiss,** Stuart L '86 -102 W 38th -NY 10018 **Fx:**843-8860
(212) 687-4900 .. **Weiss,** Tamara D '07 %Wormser KG&J LLP -825 3rd Av -NY 10022
(914) 761-0640 .. **Weiss,** Terri L '82 -162 Grand -White Plns 10601 **Fx:**761-1554
(516) 248-8131 .. **Weiss,** Thos '98 (T Weiss PC) -41 Hilton Av -Hempstd 11550 **Fx:**486-3700
(646) 290-5058 .. **Weiss,** Thos '98 (T Weiss,PC) -845 3rd Av -NY 10022 **Fx:**290-5001
(213) 268-5711 .. **Weiss,** Valerie S '07 Legal Care Unlmtd -204 W 80th -NY 10024
(845) 354-5500 .. **Weiss,** Victor '67 -441 Route 306 -Wesley Hills 10952 **Fx:**354-5978
(718) 263-5187 .. **Weiss,** Victor A '77 -141 Greenway S -Frst Hlls 11375
(212) 595-3839 .. **Weiss,** Warren A '57 -441 W End Av -NY 10024 **Fx:**595-3814
(212) 227-0347 .. **Weiss Wexler & Wornow, PC** -25 Park Pl -NY 10007 **Fx:**227-1549
(516) 627-7000 .. **Weiss & Zarett, PC** -3333 New Hyde Pk Rd -New Hyde Pk 11042 **Fx:**877-1172
(212) 833-1112 .. **Weissbard,** Harvey '82 Cnsl Friedman KS&A LLP -1633 Bway -NY 10019 **Fx:**373-7912
(631) 853-5761 .. **Weissbard,** Steven '90 %Cnty Atty -400 Carleton Av -Central Islip 11722 **Fx:**853-7788
(212) 336-2000 .. **Weissbart,** Sean Robt '08 %Patterson BW&T LLP -1133 Av of Amer -NY 10036
(212) 599-3303 .. **Weissberg,** Aaron '99 %Helfand & H -350 5th Av -NY 10118 **Fx:**599-3029
(718) 590-2000 .. **Weissberg,** Erica S '04 %DA -198 E 161st -Bronx 10451 **Fx:**590-6477
(646) 414-6872 .. **Weissberg,** Franklin R '57 OfCnsl Lowenstein S PC -1251 Av of Amer -NY 10020 **Fx:**(973) 422-6875
(212) 966-4414 .. **Weissberg,** Sheldon S '65 -401 Bway -NY 10013
(212) 326-3939 .. **Weissberger,** Alexis B '08 %Jones D -222 E 41st -NY 10017
(212) 552-9061 .. **Weiss-Blekht,** Yana '02 JP Morgan Chase -1 Chase Manh Plz -NY 10081
(914) 375-2900 .. **Weissblum,** George A '49 -570 Ynkrs Av -Ynkrs 10704 **Fx:**375-2901
(914) 933-6074 .. **Weisse,** Raymond J '97 Navigators Mgmt Co,Inc -6 Intl Dr -Rye Brook 10573
(212) 832-0400 .. **Weissenberg,** Kenneth A '83 Berdon LLP -360 Mad Av -NY 10017
(212) 351-4000 .. **Weisser,** Joshua P '06 Gibson D&C LLP -200 Park Av -NY 10166
(212) 310-8000 .. **Weisser,** Michl E '99 (Weil G&M LLP) -767 5th Av -NY 10153
(716) 853-1616 .. **Weissflach,** Robt C '93 (Harter S&E LLP) -12 Fountain Plz -Buffalo 14202
(516) 741-2585 .. **Weissinger,** George Jos '98 %Rosicki R & Assoc,PC -51 E Bethpage Rd -Plainvw 11803 **Fx:**741-4748
(212) 782-2137 .. **Weissler,** Harold J '79 %Bk Hapoalim -1177 Av of Amer -NY 10036 **Fx:**782-2141
(914) 682-6879 .. **Weissler,** Ronald '75 -50 Main -White Plns 10606 **Fx:**682-7784
(718) 855-5684 .. **Weissler,** Steven J '79 %Longo & D -26 Court -Brklyn 11242
(212) 302-2600 .. **Weissman,** Ahron '03 %Lauterbach GD&H LLP -22 W 38th -NY 10018
(914) 963-3200 .. **Weissman,** Alan L '93 %A Weissman Real Est -120 Old Post Rd -Rye 10580
(212) 619-4444 .. **Weissman,** Amy S '03 (Marshall CW&B,PC) -116 John -NY 10038
(212) 852-1000 .. **Weissman,** Andrew Seth '86 US Trust Co,NA -114 W 47th -NY 10036 **Fx:**852-1310
(212) 768-6700 .. **Weissman,** Barry L '92 (Sonnenschein N&R LLP) -1221 Av of Amer -NY 10020
(212) 669-4078 .. **Weissman,** Bruce B '75 %DCAS-DLS -1 Centre -NY 10007 **Fx:**669-2139
(212) 698-3500 .. **Weissman,** Chas I '83 (Dechert LLP) -1095 Av of Amer -NY 10036
(212) 973-0572 .. **Weissman,** Darryl '76 (Wolff & S PC) -140 Bway -NY 10005
(516) 228-5005 .. **Weissman,** David E '83 -58 Hilton Av -Hempstd 11550
(212) 521-5400 .. **Weissman,** David L '91 (Reed S LLP) -599 Lex Av -NY 10022
(631) 858-0456 .. **Weissman,** Dwayne '77 -2171 Jericho Tpk -Commack 11725 **Fx:**858-0458
(212) 937-1520 .. **Weissman,** Edw '79 -60 E 42nd -NY 10165 **Fx:**937-1529
(716) 856-4000 .. **Weissman,** Ellen V '77 (Hodgson R LLP) -140 Pearl -Buffalo 14202
(212) 668-5927 .. **Weissman,** Eric C '03 (Ropers MK&B) -17 State -NY 10004
(631) 393-5011 .. **Weissman,** Eric D '94 (Rubin & W,LLP) -200 Broadhllw Rd -Melvll 11747

(631) 979-7777 .. **Weissman,** Ira R '94 (Naiburg & W,LLP) -320 Carleton Av -Central Islip 11722
(516) 621-6327 .. **Weissman,** Janis '80 -22 Locust Ln -Roslyn Hts 11577 **Fx:**624-5451
(212) 833-5223 .. **Weissman,** Kenneth I '97 %Sony Corp of America -555 Mad Av -NY 10022
(516) 248-7844 .. **Weissman,** Marc H '00 (Cobert H&H) -1050 Franklin Av -Gdn Cty 11530
(212) 682-4426 .. **Weissman,** Mark A '98 %O'Shea Prtnrs LLP -521 5th Av -NY 10175 **Fx:**682-4437
(212) 968-9607 .. **Weissman,** Mark D '89 %M Weisman -45 Bway -NY 10006 **Fx:**968-0296
(732) 855-6048 .. **Weissman,** Matthew M '92 (Wilentz G&S) -110 William -NY 10038 **Fx:**726-6695
(212) 509-0918 .. **Weissman & Mintz LLC** -80 Pine -NY 10005 **Fx:**425-1588
(631) 231-1199 .. **Weissman,** Morton '52 OfCnsl Reynolds CGHL&Q,LLP -35 Arkay Dr -Hauppauge 11788
(516) 228-3200 .. **Weissman,** Neil Eric '92 -100 Twin Ln N -Wantagh 11793
(212) 541-2000 .. **Weissman,** Noah M '93 (Bryan C LLP) -1290 Av of Amer -NY 10104
(845) 354-5151 .. **Weissman,** Norbert '92 -6 Windsor Cir -New Cty 10956 **Fx:**354-5097
(845) 362-1490 .. **Weissman,** Robt '71 -4 Aspen Ct -Pomona 10970
(212) 973-9797 .. **Weissman,** Robt B '94 %Saretsky KD&G,LLP -475 Park Av S -NY 10016
(718) 776-3537 .. **Weissman,** Ronapam '87 -221-21 Union Tpk -Flushng 11364
(646) 415-8029 .. **Weissman,** Saml S '86 -44 Monroe -NY 10002
(516) 357-3000 .. **Weissman,** Stephen B '76 (Rivkin R LLP) -926 RXR Plz -Uniondale 11556
(212) 697-7444 .. **Weissman,** Steven '78 -150 E 39th -NY 10016 **Fx:**697-4914
(212) 522-3371 .. **Weissman,** Steven '80 %Time Inc -1271 Av of Amer -NY 10020 **Fx:**522-0437
(212) 949-5800 .. **Weissman,** Steven J '82 (Brady K&W,LLP) -501 5th Av -NY 10017
(212) 891-1600 .. **Weissmann,** Andrew A '85 (Jenner & B LLP) -919 3rd Av -NY 10022
(212) 504-6000 .. **Weissmann,** Jeffrey A '04 %Cadwalader W&T LLP -1 World Fncl Ctr -NY 10281
(914) 220-0110 .. **Weissmann,** Jeffrey E '83 (Weissmann A LLP) -445 Hmltn Av -White Plns 10601 **Fx:**(917) 368-6920
(845) 638-5001 .. **Weissmann,** Lawr A '87 %DA -1 S Main -New Cty 10956 **Fx:**638-5070
(212) 489-1600 .. **Weissmann,** Mara S '88 Deloitte & Touche LLP -1633 Bway -NY 10019
(516) 829-5000 .. **Weissmann,** Mark '85 OfCnsl R Whitehorn & Assoc,PC -98 Cuttermill Rd -Gt Neck 11021 **Fx:**829-5190
(212) 450-4000 .. **Weissmann,** Rachel J '01 %Davis P&W LLP -450 Lex Av -NY 10017
(212) 807-9042 .. **Weissmann,** Shlomo Z '02 Beth Din of America -305 7th Av -NY 10001 **Fx:**804-9183
(646) 386-5000 .. **Weissmeier,** Alicia A '94 Surrogates Ct -31 Chmbrs -NY 10007
(212) 756-2000 .. **Weist,** Cathy A '05 %Schulte R&Z LLP -919 3rd Av -NY 10022
(718) 590-2000 .. **Weiswasser,** Amy '03 %DA -198 E 161st -Bronx 10451 **Fx:**590-6477
(212) 310-8022 .. **Weiswasser,** Elizabeth S '95 (Weil G&M LLP) -767 5th Av -NY 10153
(212) 766-7600 .. **Weiswasser,** Howard H '67 H Weiswasser -225 Bway -NY 10007 **Fx:**766-7604
(212) 715-9100 .. **Weiswasser,** Julie M '06 %Kramer LN&F,LLP -1177 Av of Amer -NY 10036
(212) 661-1100 .. **Weiswasser,** Susan J '01 %Pomerantz HG&G LLP -100 Park Av -NY 10017
(212) 968-0120 .. **Weisz,** Danl '85 (Marans & W,LLC) -29 Bway -NY 10006 **Fx:**785-1618
(212) 687-2770 .. **Weisz,** Edw M '92 (Cohen PL&P) -551 5th Av -NY 10176
(212) 225-2000 .. **Weisz,** George '56 (Cleary GS&H) -1 Lbrty Plz -NY 10006
(212) 458-5663 .. **Weisz,** Jeffrey J '04 AIG -175 Water -NY 10038
(212) 309-1000 .. **Weisz,** Mason A '06 %Hunton & W -200 Park Av -NY 10166
(212) 385-2121 .. **Weisz,** Miriam J '91 (Gershbaum & W PC) -192 Lex Av -NY 10016 **Fx:**532-3801
(518) 465-2333 .. **Weisz,** Richd L '79 (Hodgson R LLP) -677 Bway -Albany 12207
(212) 684-3900 .. **Weisz,** Tiberiu '83 (Gottlieb R&R,PC) -270 Mad Av -NY 10016
(631) 952-6358 .. **Weit,** Lynn D '95 %Workers Comp Bd -220 Rabro Rd -Hauppauge 11788
(516) 826-9665 .. **Weit,** Victor A '73 -2460 Dogwood Av -E Meadow 11554
(212) 425-9300 .. **Weitberg,** Jordan S '83 (Bressler A&R,PC) -17 State -NY 10004
(212) 799-9638 .. **Weithman,** Martha A '01 %West Side SRO Lw Prj -647 Columbus Av -NY 10025 **Fx:**721-1514
(212) 834-0600 .. **Weitman,** Chas V '01 %Gordon & S,PC -355 Lex Av -NY 10017
(212) 574-1200 .. **Weitman,** Michl B '08 %Seward & K LLP -1 Bttry Pk Plz -NY 10004
(212) 829-9100 .. **Weitz,** Aaron '60 -200 W 86th -NY 10024 **Fx:**799-9199
(212) 553-9300 .. **Weitz,** Andrew L '98 (A Weitz & Assoc,PC) -233 Bway -NY 10279 **Fx:**553-9090
(212) 773-8809 .. **Weitz,** Auri L '01 Ernst & Young LLP -5 Times Sq -NY 10036
(718) 340-6837 .. **Weitz,** Bellanne Markizon '94 Cnsl FAMS -7520 Astoria Blvd -E Elmhrst 11370
(212) 428-2863 .. **Weitz,** Danl M '97 %OCA -25 Beaver -NY 10004 **Fx:**428-2696
(718) 243-3145 .. **Weitz,** Eugene I '74 NYC Transit Auth -370 Jay -Brklyn 11201
(718) 254-6148 .. **Weitz,** Evan S '02 %US Atty -271 Cadman Plz E -Brklyn 11201 **Fx:**254-6479
(212) 553-9000 .. **Weitz,** Harvey '54 (Weitz & Assoc,PC) -233 Bway -NY 10279 **Fx:**346-0876
(914) 723-6323 .. **Weitz,** Howard '60 (H Weitz,PC) -29 Lawrence Rd -Scarsdale 10583 **Fx:**723-4344
(212) 558-5500 .. **Weitz & Luxenberg,PC** -700 Bway -NY 10003 **Fx:**344-5461
(212) 636-6926 .. **Weitz,** Mitchell I '85 Fordham Law Schl -140 W 62nd -NY 10023
(212) 346-0045 .. **Weitz,** Paul B '84 (P Weitz & Assoc,PC) -233 Bway -NY 10279 **Fx:**346-0876
(718) 934-6904 .. **Weitz,** Paul M '75 -2716 Brown -Brklyn 11235
(212) 558-5500 .. **Weitz,** Perry '85 (Weitz & L,PC) -700 Bway -NY 10003
(212) 400-7177 .. **Weitz,** Sarit '06 %Garrity GMG&F -40 Wall -NY 10005
(212) 980-9595 .. **Weitz,** Seth S '82 -747 3rd Av -NY 10017 **Fx:**980-0729
(516) 357-9191 .. **Weitz,** Steven '02 (Lester & W,PC) -600 Old Cntry Rd -Gdn Cty 11530 **Fx:**357-9281
(914) 833-2681 .. **Weitz,** Theo M '72 (Halket & W LLP) -1214 W Bstn Post Rd -Mamaroneck 10543
(212) 592-1400 .. **Weitz,** Yael M '10 %Herrick,F LLP -2 Park Av -NY 10016
(212) 980-3500 .. **Weitzen,** Steven H '85 OfCnsl Pavia & H LLP -600 Mad Av -NY 10022
(212) 785-7887 .. **Weitzenberg,** Stanley J '79 -110 Wall -NY 10005
(212) 969-3000 .. **Weitzman,** Allan H '74 (Proskauer R LLP) -1585 Bway -NY 10036
(212) 637-1205 .. **Weitzman,** Avi '00 US Atty -1 St Andrews Plz -NY 10007
(212) 298-2472 .. **Weitzman,** Israel A '80 IRS-Appls Div -290 Bway -NY 10007 **Fx:**298-2410
(212) 536-3900 .. **Weitzman,** Jeffrey H '72 (K&L Gates LLP) -599 Lex Av -NY 10022
(212) 969-3000 .. **Weitzman,** Jessica M '09 %Proskauer R LLP -1585 Bway -NY 10036
(212) 687-7505 .. **Weitzman,** Jos M '69 -369 Lex Av -NY 10017 **Fx:**949-8194
(212) 248-5200 .. **Weitzman,** Raphael '95 -110 Wall -NY 10005
(914) 946-5469 .. **Weitzner,** Karen L '82 -Bx944 -Hartsdale 10530
(914) 285-9800 .. **Weitzner,** Michl J '78 OfCnsl Kurzman EC&L,LLP -1 N Bway -White Plns 10601
(718) 486-5300 .. **Weitzner,** Rephoel A '99 -134 Bway -Brklyn 11211 **Fx:**486-4998
(212) 417-3700 .. **Weizman,** Shelly R '09 %MFY Legal Srvcs -299 Bway -NY 10007 **Fx:**417-3890
(516) 487-0003 .. **Wekselblatt,** Steven M '84 -175 E Shore Rd -Gt Neck 11023
(914) 421-1800 .. **Wekstein,** Adam L '86 (Hocherman T&W LLP) -1 N Bway -White Plns 10601
(631) 261-7778 .. **Wekstein,** Joshua M '99 %Brody O&O -7 Bayview Av -Northprt 11768
(718) 422-2845 .. **Welber,** Susan E '99 Leg Aid -111 Lvngstn -Brklyn 11201
(914) 417-3400 .. **Welbourne,** Miranda J '07 %Littleton JUP&K LLP -1 Manhattanvll Rd -Purchase 10577
(212) 908-3914 .. **Welburn,** Stuart J '03 (Thompson H LLP) -335 Mad Av -NY 10017
(914) 428-2100 .. **Welby Brady & Greenblatt,LLP** -11 Martine Av -White Plns 10606 **Fx:**428-2172
(914) 633-1294 .. **Welby,** Lillian Krusz '82 %Family Ct -420 North Av -New Rchll 10801
(212) 728-8000 .. **Welby,** Monica '06 %Willkie F&G LLP -787 7th Av -NY 10019
(914) 428-2100 .. **Welby,** Thos H '86 (Welby B&G,LLP) -11 Martine Av -White Plns 10606
(212) 788-6760 .. **Welch,** Alicia H '08 %Law Dept -100 Church -NY 10007 **Fx:**788-0367
(585) 964-3950 .. **Welch,** Chas C '96 -1722 Lk Rd Bx165 -Hamlin 14464 **Fx:**964-2636
(585) 454-5650 .. **Welch,** Craig R '80 (Lacy K LLP) -130 E Main -Rchstr 14604
(585) 394-5220 .. **Welch,** Craig R '80 (Lacy K LLP) -23 North -Canandaigua 14424
(212) 468-8000 .. **Welch,** Edw M '06 %Morrison & F LLP -1290 Av of Amer -NY 10104
(585) 899-1414 .. **Welch,** Eugene '71 (Harris COJW&L) -300 Linden Oaks -Rchstr 14625
(607) 962-4641 .. **Welch,** George J '71 (Welch & Z) -19 E Market -Corning 14830
(607) 962-4641 .. **Welch,** George J Jr. '99 (Welch & Z) -19 E Market -Corning 14830
(718) 286-2145 .. **Welch,** George J III '07 %Leg Aid -120-46 Qns Blvd -Kew Gdns 11415 **Fx:**286-2286
(607) 936-8057 .. **Welch,** Jacob P '80 -8 Denison Pkwy E -Corning 14830 **Fx:**936-6815
(212) 428-2553 .. **Welch,** James P '90 %OCA -25 Beaver -NY 10004
(212) 325-4588 .. **Welch,** Jamie W '95 Credit Suisse -11 Mad Av -NY 10010
(212) 250-7980 .. **Welch,** Jeffrey T '90 %Deutsche Bank -60 Wall -NY 10005
(646) 610-5400 .. **Welch,** John S '04 NYPD -1 Police Plz -NY 10038
(315) 265-7533 .. **Welch,** Jos T '99 -8 Poplar -Potsdam 13676
(716) 634-2497 .. **Welch,** Justine M '92 %Kelly & S -5678 Main -Williamsvll 14221
(716) 847-0650 .. **Welch,** Karen M '91 %Leg Srvcs -237 Main -Buffalo 14203 **Fx:**847-0227
(914) 472-7700 .. **Welch,** Kelly M '00 %Bertine HHZD&D,LLP -700 Wht Plns Rd -Scarsdale 10583
(315) 435-2470 .. **Welch,** Margaret E '08 %DA -505 S State -Syracuse 13202 **Fx:**435-3969
(718) 933-3606 .. **Welch,** Mary Madeline '75 %Ursuline Convent -2885 Marion Av -Bronx 10458 **Fx:**561-4896
(212) 784-6400 .. **Welch,** Melissa Cronin '02 %Hanly CBSF&H LLP -112 Mad Av -NY 10016
(617) 678-8344 .. **Welch,** Melissa E '08 -251 W 76th -NY 10023
(315) 453-9426 .. **Welch,** Michl J '96 (Nicholas PSW&S) -219 1st Bx720 -Liverpool 13088
(516) 357-3000 .. **Welch,** Michl P '02 %Rivkin R LLP -926 RXR Plz -Uniondale 11556
(315) 488-2667 .. **Welch,** Michl S '91 (Welch & M LLP) -307 Kasson Rd Bx326 -Camillus 13031 **Fx:**488-6031
(646) 536-3024 .. **Welch,** Peter C '03 Take-Two Interactive Sftwr,Inc -622 Bway -NY 10012
(212) 238-4800 .. **Welch,** Rachel J '05 %Landman CB&F,PC -120 Bway -NY 10271
(718) 921-5277 .. **Welch,** Raymond E '94 %Brooklyn Cllg CUNY -2900 Bedford Av -Brklyn 11210
(212) 681-0117 .. **Welch,** Richd T '05 %Starr GD&R -530 5th Av -NY 10036
(212) 333-0200 .. **Welch,** Sara A '04 %Arkin KR LLP -590 Mad Av -NY 10022
(888) 909-4362 .. **Welch,** Thos P '94 %Fine O&A,LLP -537 James -Syracuse 13203
(315) 458-3331 .. **Welch,** Thos W '76 %Bertrand AW&P -107 S Main Bx277 -N Syracuse 13212
(585) 295-5400 .. **Welch,** Timothy P '01 %Goldberg S LLP -2 State -Rchstr 14614
(212) 506-1700 .. **Welch,** Trevor J '99 (Kasowitz BT&F LLP) -1633 Bway -NY 10019
(607) 962-4641 .. **Welch,** Vincent J '74 (Welch & Z) -19 E Market -Corning 14830
(585) 442-2551 .. **Welch,** Warren '70 OfCnsl Johnson M&B,PC -1399 Monroe Av -Rchstr 14618
(585) 396-4411 .. **Welch,** Wendy Ritz '99 Cnty Atty -27 N Main -Canandaigua 14424 **Fx:**396-4481
(607) 962-4641 .. **Welch & Zink** -19 E Market -Corning 14830 **Fx:**962-8401
(212) 839-5362 .. **Welcom,** Judith '79 (Sidley A LLP) -787 7th Av -NY 10019
(718) 284-6228 .. **Welcome,** Michele E '94 -426 E 35th -Brklyn 11203
(212) 848-8075 .. **Weld,** Jonathan M '67 OfCnsl Shearman & S LLP -599 Lex Av -NY 10022
(585) 671-0260 .. **Weld,** Parker L '70 -1674 Empire Blvd -Webster 14580
(212) 547-5400 .. **Weld,** Wm F '08 (McDermott W&E LLP) -340 Mad Av -NY 10173
(212) 937-8806 .. **Weldon,** Cherie L '03 SpclCnsl WilmerHale -399 Park Av -NY 10022
(914) 948-7000 .. **Weldon,** Christopher B '91 (Keidel W&C LLP) -925 Wstchstr Av -White Plns 10604

(212) 372-9500 .. **Weldon,** Julian '04 Garrison Invstmnt Grp LP -1350 Av of Amer -NY 10019 **Fx:**372-9525
(315) 788-2245 .. **Weldon,** Lisa '80 -247 Ten Eyck -Watertwn 13601 **Fx:**788-7167
(212) 446-7000 .. **Weldon,** Mark R '98 %McKinsey & Co -55 E 52nd -NY 10055 **Fx:**688-9521
(315) 788-2010 .. **Weldon,** Robt M Jr. '89 (Weldon & T) -119-125 Sherman -Watertwn 13601
(315) 788-2010 .. **Weldon & Trimper** -119-125 Sherman -Watertwn 13601 **Fx:**785-9264
(212) 577-2800 .. **Welfer,** Jeremy A '99 %Sexter & W -115 Bway -NY 10006
(212) 735-3000 .. **Welhouse,** Michl A '10 %Skadden ASM&F LLP -4 Times Sq -NY 10036
(518) 587-8326 .. **Weliczka,** Kenneth F '73 -15 Lonesome Pine Trl -Gansevoort 12831 **Fx:**587-8326
(212) 526-0546 .. **Welikson,** Jeffrey A '81 Lehman Bros -1271 Av of Amer -NY 10020
(516) 535-1700 .. **Welikson,** Niles C '75 (Horing W&R,PC) -11 Hillside Av -Williston Pk 11596
(212) 344-2515 .. **Weliky,** Mark '92 %CWA Dist 1 -80 Pine -NY 10005
(212) 667-1195 .. **Welker,** Colleen Sorrell '03 Nomura Securities Intl -2 World Fncl Ctr -NY 10281
(718) 286-2000 .. **Welkes,** Nathaniel D '72 %Leg Aid -120-46 Qns Blvd -Kew Gdns 11415 **Fx:**286-2286
(212) 806-5400 .. **Welkis,** Scott '97 (Stroock &S&L LLP) -180 Maiden Ln -NY 10038
(315) 218-8000 .. **Wellar,** Courtney A '01 (Bond S&K,PLLC) -1 Lincoln Ctr -Syracuse 13202
(212) 509-3900 .. **Weller,** Howard H '92 (Mitchell S&K LLP) -12 E 49th -NY 10017
(516) 832-7543 .. **Weller,** James W '89 (Nixon P LLP) -50 Jericho Quadrangle -Jericho 11753
(212) 882-5576 .. **Weller,** Keith A '92 UBS Glbl Asset Mgt -51 W 52nd -NY 10019
(646) 213-5174 .. **Weller,** Todd A '05 WTAS LLC -452 5th Av -NY 10018
(718) 253-8888 .. **Wellerstein,** Hedva '06 -2053 Flatbush Av -Brklyn 11234
(212) 762-4000 .. **Welles,** Dede W '99 Morgan Stanley -1221 Av of Amer -NY 10020
(212) 350-3925 .. **Welles,** Lauren B '94 Banco Santander Cntrl Hispano, SA -45 E 53rd -NY 10022
(212) 232-1300 .. **Wellikoff,** Scott M '05 %Lewis BB&S LLP -77 Water -NY 10005
(212) 922-0050 .. **Welling,** John F '80 %Stewart Title Ins -300 E 42nd -NY 10017 **Fx:**983-1133
(212) 455-2000 .. **Welling,** Thos J '08 %Simpson T&B LLP -425 Lex Av -NY 10017
(718) 264-3340 .. **Wellington,** Brian A '06 MHLS -80-45 Wnchstr Blvd -Qns Vllg 11427 **Fx:**264-3559
(212) 259-8000 .. **Wellington,** Paul J '08 %Dewey & L LLP -1301 Av of Amer -NY 10019
(212) 585-3425 .. **Wellman,** Ami '00 %B Kishner & Assoc -420 Lex Av -NY 10170 **Fx:**752-1810
(212) 527-1000 .. **Wellman,** Mark D '02 (Jones HC&B PC) -1 Bttry Pk Plz -NY 10004
(212) 833-1173 .. **Wellner,** Philip A '07 %Friedman KS&A LLP -1633 Bway -NY 10019 **Fx:**373-7973
(212) 841-1000 .. **Wells,** Albert L '88 (Covington & B LLP) -620 8th Av -NY 10018
(212) 759-4888 .. **Wells,** Andrew J '08 %Phillips L LLP -437 Mad Av -NY 10022
(212) 492-3932 .. **Wells,** Andrew N '80 %Deloitte LLP -1633 Bway -NY 10019 **Fx:**492-4201
(212) 309-6000 .. **Wells,** Annie C '04 %Morgan L&B LLP -101 Park Av -NY 10178
(212) 455-2000 .. **Wells,** Benjamin C '09 %Simpson T&B LLP -425 Lex Av -NY 10017
(212) 750-1200 .. **Wells,** Christina M '97 %Trolman G&L,PC -777 3rd Av -NY 10017
(212) 969-3000 .. **Wells,** Christopher M '82 (Proskauer R LLP) -1585 Bway -NY 10036
(212) 326-3939 .. **Wells,** Claire E '10 %Jones D -222 E 41st -NY 10017
(212) 270-5936 .. **Wells,** Elisabeth Montgomery '80 JP Morgan Chase -270 Park Av -NY 10017
(212) 788-0898 .. **Wells,** Elizabeth A '03 %Law Dept -100 Church -NY 10007 **Fx:**788-0367
(718) 774-2767 .. **Wells,** Helen L '77 -1467 Fulton -Brklyn 11216
(716) 373-3400 .. **Wells,** John M '09 %B O'Connell Jr,PLLC -122 N Barry -Olean 14760 **Fx:**373-2148
(212) 692-9666 .. **Wells,** Jonathan M '02 (Gilbride TL&S LLC) -708 3rd Av -NY 10017
(845) 566-5345 .. **Wells,** Kathleen V '01 %Larkin AI&T,LLP -356 Meadow Av -Newburgh 12550
(518) 743-0455 .. **Wells,** Kimberly M '05 %MK Purdue -5 Sagamore -Glens Fls 12801 **Fx:**743-1827
(518) 358-2530 .. **Wells,** Mark Flack '73 -Chateaugay Bx505 -Ft Covington 12937 **Fx:**358-9032
(315) 218-8000 .. **Wells,** Matthew N '99 (Bond S&K,PLLC) -1 Lincoln Ctr -Syracuse 13202
(212) 446-4800 .. **Wells,** Melody L '09 %Kirkland & E LLP -153 E 53rd -NY 10022
(212) 732-9000 .. **Wells,** Michl J '96 %Sullivan PBM&C PC -120 Bway -NY 10271
(212) 966-5959 .. **Wells,** Ozro T '59 -103 E 125th -NY 10035 **Fx:**722-4966
(716) 853-5100 .. **Wells,** Paul F '93 (Lippes MWF LLP) -665 Main -Buffalo 14203
(212) 836-8000 .. **Wells,** Peter B '06 %Kaye S LLP -425 Park Av -NY 10022
(212) 909-6000 .. **Wells,** Raymond G '79 Cnsl Debevoise & P LLP -919 3rd Av -NY 10022
(315) 472-4489 .. **Wells,** Robt G '78 -120 E Wshngtn -Syracuse 13202 **Fx:**472-1456
(212) 846-3922 .. **Wells,** Sandra Y '90 MTV Networks -1540 Bway -NY 10036
(516) 571-3056 .. **Wells,** Sara A '01 %Cnty Atty -1 West -Mineola 11501 **Fx:**571-6604
(212) 859-8000 .. **Wells,** Scott A '08 %Fried FHS&J LLP -1 NY Plz -NY 10004
(315) 435-2470 .. **Wells,** Scott E '05 %DA -505 S State -Syracuse 13202 **Fx:**435-3969
(516) 746-4373 .. **Wells,** Scott M '08 %MHLS -170 Old Cntry Rd -Mineola 11501 **Fx:**746-0598
(212) 476-5650 .. **Wells,** Stephen B '70 %Neuberger Berman Trust Co -605 3rd Av -NY 10158
(716) 856-4000 .. **Wells,** Steven W '04 %Hodgson R LLP -140 Pearl -Buffalo 14202
(212) 661-9100 .. **Wells,** Stuart J '99 %Otterbourg SH&R,PC -230 Park Av -NY 10169
(716) 366-0715 .. **Wells,** Susan L '95 Edgewood Investments -Bx635 -Dunkirk 14048
(518) 434-5050 .. **Wells,** Tara Brower '01 %Law Dept -106 City Hall -Albany 12207 **Fx:**434-5070
(212) 735-3000 .. **Wells,** Terry L Jr. '08 %Skadden ASM&F LLP -4 Times Sq -NY 10036
(212) 373-3000 .. **Wells,** Theo V Jr. '01 (Paul WRW&G LLP) -1285 Av of Amer -NY 10019
(914) 946-5700 .. **Wells,** W Whitfield '74 -925 Wstchstr Av -White Plns 10604
(212) 416-8000 .. **Wells Handy,** Edna '77 %Dept of Law -120 Bway -NY 10271
(212) 938-5000 .. **Wels,** Andrew C '86 Cantor Fitzgerald -110 E 59th -NY 10022
(917) 320-4573 .. **Welsch,** Andrea C N '06 Benfield Inc -199 Water -NY 10038
(716) 881-5800 .. **Welsh,** Brian R '84 Siegel K&K -426 Franklin -Buffalo 14202
(516) 741-8585 .. **Welsh,** Debra J '95 %Bondi & I -1055 Franklin Av -Gdn Cty 11530
(315) 824-3070 .. **Welsh,** Jane '85 -7676 McCormick Rd -Hamilton 13346
(212) 903-9000 .. **Welsh,** Matthew C '03 %Linklaters -1345 Av of Amer -NY 10105
(585) 768-2261 .. **Welsh,** Michl T '73 -41 Main Bx147 -Le Roy 14482 **Fx:**768-2261
(518) 431-4761 .. **Welsh,** Thos A '73 %IRS -1 Clinton Av -Albany 12207
(212) 577-3001 .. **Welsh,** Tracy L '92 (HIV Law Proj) -15 Maiden Ln -NY 10038 **Fx:**577-3192
(845) 548-4688 .. **Welsh,** Vernon J '79 -520 Wht Plns Rd -Tarrytwn 10591
(212) 455-2000 .. **Welshimer,** Courtney A '08 %Simpson T&B LLP -425 Lex Av -NY 10017
(212) 558-4000 .. **Welshimer,** Mark J '77 (Sullivan & C LLP) -125 Broad -NY 10004
(718) 339-4567 .. **Welsome,** Brian '90 -3029 Quentin Rd -Brklyn 11234
(518) 459-2667 .. **Welt Gabriels & Schunk LLP** -4 Exec Park Dr Bx3716 -Albany 12203 **Fx:**459-8927
(212) 792-6579 .. **Weltchek,** Andrew '86 -450 7th Av -NY 10123 **Fx:**(888) 338-5364
(716) 566-5400 .. **Welter,** Jos J '89 (Goldberg S LLP) -665 Main -Buffalo 14203
(914) 941-5785 .. **Weltman,** Barbara E '77 -50 Shingle Hse Rd -Millwd 10546
(212) 306-7653 .. **Weltman,** Dean S '98 NYCDCP -40 Rector -NY 10006
(212) 728-8000 .. **Weltman,** Laurence D '78 (Willkie F&G LLP) -787 7th Av -NY 10019
(212) 684-7800 .. **Weltman & Moskowitz,LLP** -270 Mad Av -NY 10016 **Fx:**684-7995
(516) 931-4088 .. **Weltman & Moskowitz,LLP** -575 Underhill Blvd -Syosset 11791 **Fx:**677-9405
(516) 931-4088 .. **Weltman,** Richd E '79 (Weltman & M,LLP) -575 Underhill Blvd -Syosset 11791
(212) 684-7800 .. **Weltman,** Richd E '79 (Weltman & M,LLP) -270 Mad Av -NY 10016
(516) 742-4343 .. **Weltsch,** Keith A '09 %Scully SM&P PC -400 Grdn City Plz -Gdn Cty 11530
(631) 331-3740 .. **Weltsek,** Barbara M '87 -55 Jesse Way -Mt Sinai 11766 **Fx:**331-7867
(212) 310-8000 .. **Welty,** Wm P III '04 %Weil G&M LLP -767 5th Av -NY 10153
(212) 370-1300 .. **Weltz,** Irwin '93 (Ellenoff G&S LLP) -150 E 42nd -NY 10017
(212) 726-0099 .. **Weltz,** Lisa B '95 (Weltz & W) -99 Mad Av -NY 10016 **Fx:**481-8425
(212) 726-0099 .. **Weltz,** Paul M '61 (Weltz & W) -99 Mad Av -NY 10016 **Fx:**481-8425
(212) 335-9000 .. **Welykyj,** Christina F '90 %DA -1 Hogan Pl -NY 10013
(718) 229-5390 .. **Welz,** Keith M '98 OfCnsl P Tischler -38-39 Bell Blvd -Bayside 11361 **Fx:**229-5759
(212) 223-6700 .. **Welzer,** Frank C '96 Zukerman GB&C,LLP -875 3rd Av -NY 10022
(212) 839-5300 .. **Wember,** Carolyn D '89 Sidley A LLP -787 7th Av -NY 10019
(212) 480-6538 .. **Wemegah,** Arthur '00 -40 Exch Pl -NY 10005
(518) 374-9125 .. **Wemple & Daly** -508 Union -Schnctdy 12305 **Fx:**374-4223
(631) 439-4200 .. **Wemyss,** Walter F '88 %R Tusa -898 Vets Mem'l Hwy -Hauppauge 11788 **Fx:**439-4292
(212) 416-6536 .. **Wen,** Fredk H '04 %Dept of Law -120 Bway -NY 10271
(212) 530-1800 .. **Wen,** Grace '08 %Richards K&O LLP -1 World Fncl Ctr -NY 10281
(212) 617-1779 .. **Wen,** Jean C '09 Bloomberg LP -731 Lex Av -NY 10022
(212) 258-8000 .. **Wen,** Pauline L '95 %MTV Networks -1515 Bway -NY 10036 **Fx:**258-8358
(607) 763-9200 .. **Wenban,** Carrie Ann '05 (Levene G&T,LLP) -BxF-1706 -Bnghmtn 13902
(212) 310-8000 .. **Wencelblat,** Patricia S '06 %Weil G&M LLP -767 5th Av -NY 10153
(212) 340-2203 .. **Wenchell,** Ioana '97 %Metro-North -347 Mad Av -NY 10017 **Fx:**697-9079
(212) 264-3650 .. **Wendel,** Dorothy A '94 %SSA Ofc Genl Cnsl -26 Fed Plz -NY 10278 **Fx:**264-6372
(212) 417-5300 .. **Wendel,** Heidi Ann '93 %Medicaid Fraud Cntrl -120 Bway -NY 10271 **Fx:**417-5274
(212) 696-6000 .. **Wendel,** Martin '79 OfCnsl Curtis M-PC&M LLP -101 Park Av -NY 10178
(212) 609-6800 .. **Wendell,** Adam R '01 %McCarter & E,LLP -245 Park Av -NY 10167
(212) 244-4111 .. **Wender,** Richd H '77 OfCnsl Shiboleth YR&Z,LLP -1 Penn Plz -NY 10119
(518) 885-2263 .. **Wendling,** Richd E '80 %DA -25 W High -Ballston Spa 12020 **Fx:**884-8627
(212) 678-2767 .. **Wendrovsky,** Gerry M '90 -2749 Bway -NY 10025 **Fx:**678-2772
(516) 488-3300 .. **Wendt,** Cheryl M '95 %Shaub AC&S,LLP -1983 Marcus Av -Lk Success 11042
(631) 423-5600 .. **Wendt,** Wm F '63 -10 Chichester Rd -Huntngtn Sta 11746
(212) 415-3322 .. **Wendy,** Howard '69 -437 Mad Av -NY 10022 **Fx:**415-3502
(212) 878-8000 .. **Wendy,** Jennifer L '98 %Clifford C LLP -31 W 52nd -NY 10019
(718) 590-8377 .. **Wenegrat,** Lauren E '03 ACS -900 Sheridan Av -Bronx 10451
(212) 788-1277 .. **Weng,** Jenny S-Y '07 %Law Dept -100 Church -NY 10007 **Fx:**788-0367
(212) 450-4000 .. **Weng,** Jinho Jean '03 Cnsl Davis P&W LLP -450 Lex Av -NY 10017
(212) 278-7284 .. **Weng,** Kevin '04 Societe Generale -1221 Av of Amer -NY 10020
(212) 566-6262 .. **Wenger & Arlia, Esqs LLP** -20 Vesey -NY 10007 **Fx:**608-6262
(845) 426-2727 .. **Wenger,** Barry Dov '01 -11 Harmony Rd -Spg Vly 10977 **Fx:**818-4131
(212) 566-6262 .. **Wenger,** Bruce L '94 (Wenger & A,LLP) -20 Vesey -NY 10007
(212) 335-4500 .. **Wenger,** David S '07 %DLA Piper LLP -1251 Av of Amer -NY 10020
(631) 247-0404 .. **Wenger,** Marc S '88 (Jackson L LLP) -58 S Srvc Rd -Melvll 11747
(212) 356-1400 .. **Wenger,** Michl B '02 %Rosenthal & Rosenthal -1370 Bway -NY 10018
(212) 598-1707 .. **Wengrofsky,** Lori D '94 %Time Warner NYC Cable Grp -120 E 23rd -NY 10010 **Fx:**420-4812
(646) 837-0100 .. **Wenick & Finger, PC** -28 E 28th -NY 10016 **Fx:**(212) 906-0417
(646) 837-0100 .. **Wenick,** Frank J '80 (Wenick & F,PC) -28 E 28th -NY 10016
(212) 374-9840 .. **Wenig,** Alan '87 (Wenig & W) -150 Bway -NY 10038 **Fx:**374-9844
(212) 515-3400 .. **Wenig,** Cindy L '92 AREA Property Prtnrs LP -60 Columbus Cir -NY 10023 **Fx:**515-3283
(212) 593-5550 .. **Wenig,** Devin N '92 %Reuters -3 Times Sq -NY 10036
(212) 867-4466 .. **Wenig,** Howard A '81 (Belkin BW&G,LLP) -270 Mad Av -NY 10016
(212) 831-6639 .. **Wenig,** Joanne R '80 -1172 Park Av -NY 10128
(212) 374-9840 .. **Wenig,** Larry '62 (Wenig & W) -150 Bway -NY 10038 **Fx:**374-9844
(718) 797-5700 .. **Wenig,** Meryl L '89 (Wenig S LLP) -26 Court -Brklyn 11242
(607) 721-8440 .. **Wenig,** Richd Jay '84 %MHLS -44 Hawley -Bnghmtn 13901 **Fx:**721-8447
(718) 797-5700 .. **Wenig Saltiel LLP** -26 Court -Brklyn 11242 **Fx:**522-0356
(315) 450-7131 .. **Wenk,** Joel L '95 -5977 Diffin Rd -Cicero 13039 **Fx:**454-8320

(212) 267-0011 .. **Wenk**, Timothy M '01 (Shafer G,LLP) -90 John -NY 10038
(631) 231-1450 .. **Wenkert**, Lynn Cosma '82 (Feldman K&M,PC) -330 Vndrblt Motor Pkwy -Hauppauge 11788
(212) 973-8000 .. **Wenner**, Scott J '85 (Schnader HS&L LLP) -140 Bway -NY 10005
(516) 432-8326 .. **Wenning**, Edw C '65 -524 E Harrison -Long Bch 11561
(315) 474-7571 .. **Wentlandt**, Arthur W '79 (Mackenzie H LLP) -101 S Salina Bx4967 -Syracuse 13221
(212) 756-2000 .. **Wentworth**, Jacob B '07 Schulte R&Z LLP -919 3rd Av -NY 10022
(212) 858-1480 .. **Wentzler**, Kimberly E '07 %Pillsbury WSP LLP -1540 Bway -NY 10036
(631) 751-1111 .. **Wenz**, Marilyn J '99 (Grobe & W,LP) -1344 Stony Brk Rd -Stony Brk 11790
(212) 883-4997 .. **Wenzel**, Abby M '89 (Cozen O) -277 Park Av -NY 10172 **Fx**:672-1197
(718) 286-6000 .. **Wenzel**, Andrew P '07 %DA -125-01 Qns Blvd -Kew Gdns 11415
(914) 995-2685 .. **Wenzel**, James J '01 %Cnty Atty -148 Martine Av -White Plns 10601 **Fx**:995-5858
(212) 903-9000 .. **Wenzel**, Talia K '10 %Linklaters -1345 Av of Amer -NY 10105
(914) 476-0600 .. **Wepman**, Yael J '02 %Smith B&J,LLP -733 Ynkrs Av -Ynkrs 10704
(212) 594-5300 .. **Weprin**, Barry A '79 (Milberg LLP) -1 Penn Plz -NY 10119
(212) 227-4848 .. **Weprin**, David I '81 (Ceccarelli W PLLC) -2 Wall -NY 10005
(718) 643-6748 .. **Weprin**, Earle F '81 -26 Court -Brklyn 11242 **Fx**:852-5360
(516) 222-6200 .. **Weprin**, Mark S '93 OfCnsl Berkman HPP&F,PC -100 Grdn City Plz -Gdn Cty 11530
(718) 981-3100 .. **Werb**, Lewis '52 -1 Edgewtr Plz -Staten Isl 10305 **Fx**:442-0406
(212) 553-0300 .. **Werbach**, Johanna L '99 %Moody's Invstr Srvc -250 Greenwich -NY 10007
(914) 683-1700 .. **Werbel**, Cherie Sherman '94 -12 E Post Rd -White Plns 10601 **Fx**:328-3047
(718) 489-5370 .. **Werbel**, Linda D '98 St Francis Cllg -180 Remsen -Brklyn 11201
(914) 683-1700 .. **Werbel**, Phillip A '75 -12 East Post Rd -White Plns 10601 **Fx**:328-3047
(917) 647-1740 .. **Werbel**, Robt H '63 R Werbel,PLLC -5 E 88th -NY 10128
(718) 485-0400 .. **Werbel**, Shelly Klausner '89 (Werbel W&V LLP) -1465 Rockaway Pkwy -Brklyn 11236 **Fx**:272-3242
(718) 260-4750 .. **Werber**, David A '86 %Leg Aid -111 Lvngstn -Brklyn 11201 **Fx**:260-4744
(212) 592-1400 .. **Werbin**, Barry A '82 (Herrick,F LLP) -2 Park Av -NY 10016
(516) 873-6300 .. **Werbin**, Stuart D '06 %J Lichtenstein,PC -131 Mineola Blvd -Mineola 11501 **Fx**:873-7986
(518) 369-7580 .. **Werblin**, Matthew J '07 -81 Molly Ct -Schnctdy 12309
(516) 627-7000 .. **Werblowsky**, Harvey Z '71 OfCnsl Weiss & Z,PC -3333 New Hyde Pk Rd -New Hyde Pk 11042
(718) 438-5579 .. **Wercberger**, Anton '82 -1205 47th -Brklyn 11219 **Fx**:436-7936
(212) 308-1999 .. **Werchen**, David '75 -845 3rd Av -NY 10022 **Fx**:593-1318
(212) 805-4253 .. **Werdell**, Jennifer M '02 Hon D Freeman -40 Centre -NY 10007
(212) 849-7000 .. **Werder**, Richd I Jr. '03 (Quinn EU&S,LLP) -51 Mad Av -NY 10010
(716) 849-1333 .. **Weremblewski**, Michl R '90 (Lipsitz GSC LLP) -42 Delaware Av -Buffalo 14202
(631) 582-3283 .. **Werfel**, Brian S '02 (Werfel & W,PLLC) -1 Rabro Dr -Hauppauge 11788 **Fx**:582-3387
(631) 582-3283 .. **Werfel**, David M '74 (Werfel & W,PLLC) -1 Rabro Dr -Hauppauge 11788 **Fx**:582-3387
(516) 327-3000 .. **Werfel**, Steven M '95 %Astoria Fed Svngs & Loan -1 Astoria Fed Plz -Lk Success 11042 **Fx**:327-7421
(212) 605-0303 .. **Werger Rosen**, Melissa '93 Rosen Law Grp -575 Mad Av -NY 10022
(212) 373-3000 .. **Werier**, Steven A '09 %Paul WRW&G LLP -1285 Av of Amer -NY 10019
(518) 499-1272 .. **Werle**, Mark F '90 (Ryan S&C,PC) -134 Main Bx75 -Whitehall 12887
(212) 803-6121 .. **Werley**, Elizabeth L '80 Transition Network -140 Bway -NY 10005
(718) 361-8080 .. **Werlin**, Jerald '72 -45-10 Court Sq -LIC 11101 **Fx**:361-0344
(518) 456-6439 .. **Werlin-Gorenstein**, Barbara '84 -3 Bonnie Dr -Guilderlnd 12084 **Fx**:456-6439
(212) 577-3530 .. **Werlwas**, Mary Lynne '95 %Leg Aid -199 Water -NY 10038 **Fx**:425-2465
(212) 813-1600 .. **Werner**, Andrew T '09 %Kalow & S -488 Mad Av -NY 10022
(212) 908-5028 .. **Werner**, Aviva '86 %Emerging Mkts Trdrs Assn -360 Mad Av -NY 10017
(585) 232-5300 .. **Werner**, Christopher K '76 (Boylan BCV&W,LLP) -2400 Chase Sq -Rchstr 14604
(516) 568-1850 .. **Werner**, Fred '60 (Werner ZSS&A) -360 Merrick Rd -Lynbrk 11563
(716) 270-0021 .. **Werner**, Harry E III '89 -1231 Delaware Av -Buffalo 14209 **Fx**:883-1592
(212) 381-3500 .. **Werner**, Hayley Wallis '96 %Phillips-Van Heusen Corp -200 Mad Av -NY 10016 **Fx**:381-3950
(718) 739-4100 .. **Werner**, Ivan L '92 Qns Cnty Bar Assn -90-35 148th -Jamaica 11435 **Fx**:657-1789
(212) 788-6298 .. **Werner**, Jeffrey M '01 Ofc of Mgmt & Budget -75 Park Pl -NY 10007
(845) 562-1154 .. **Werner**, Jeffrey Russell '82 -5020 Route 9W -Newburgh 12550 **Fx**:562-1159
(212) 582-1532 .. **Werner**, John D '01 -321 W 55th -NY 10019 **Fx**:963-3384
(646) 386-3001 .. **Werner**, John F '66 Supreme Ct -60 Centre -NY 10007 **Fx**:(212) 374-3326
(212) 594-2400 .. **Werner**, Jon '06 Lyons & F -65 W 36th -NY 10018
(212) 878-8526 .. **Werner**, Kathleen L '92 (Clifford C LLP) -31 W 52nd -NY 10019
(212) 530-1800 .. **Werner**, Kenneth E '05 (Richards K&O LLP) -1 World Fncl Ctr -NY 10281
(631) 666-5766 .. **Werner**, Kevin J '91 (Long TBSWJ&S) -120 4th Av Bx5591 -Bay Shr 11706
(212) 416-8424 .. **Werner**, Laura A '66 Dept of Law -120 Bway -NY 10271
(212) 859-8000 .. **Werner**, Michl J '06 %Fried FHS&J LLP -1 NY Plz -NY 10004
(845) 639-1658 .. **Werner**, Morris '88 -155 N Main -New Cty 10956 **Fx**:639-1767
(212) 541-2000 .. **Werner**, Patricia L '01 Cnsl Bryan C LLP -1290 Av of Amer -NY 10104
(516) 609-5137 .. **Werner**, Paul W '90 %Conner & C -15 Bryant Av -Roslyn 11576
(631) 261-1279 .. **Werner**, Peter R '68 -4 Dublin Ct -E Northprt 11731 **Fx**:757-7646
(212) 309-6000 .. **Werner**, Philip H '76 (Morgan L&B LLP) -101 Park Av -NY 10178
(212) 659-7300 .. **Werner**, Rick A '01 %Haynes & B,LLP -1221 Av of Amer -NY 10020
(212) 768-6700 .. **Werner**, Sara R '06 %Sonnenschein N&R LLP -2 World Fncl Ctr -NY 10281
(516) 568-1850 .. **Werner Zaroff Slotnick Stern & Ashkenazy** -360 Merrick Rd -Lynbrk 11563
(212) 725-3131 .. **Wernick**, Claudia N '93 OfCnsl Franklin G&C,PC -150 E 58th -NY 10155
(212) 701-3000 .. **Wernick**, Richd K '10 %Cahill G&R LLP -80 Pine -NY 10005 **Fx**:269-5420
(212) 701-3000 .. **Wernke**, Michl J '05 %Cahill G&R LLP -80 Pine -NY 10005 **Fx**:269-5420
(516) 877-7500 .. **Werring**, Thos F '75 %Franchina & G,PC -1100 Franklin Av -Gdn Cty 11530
(718) 701-0700 .. **Werschulz**, Patricia P '10 %Goldstein Law Ofc,PC -34 Dumont Av -Staten Isl 10305 **Fx**:(866) 243-8109
(212) 966-0854 .. **Wershaw**, Steven L '82 -401 Bway -NY 10013
(212) 674-0950 .. **Wertenteil**, Aaron J '90 (Matel Realty LLC) -303 E 6th -NY 10003 **Fx**:598-9821
(212) 732-4600 .. **Wertenteil**, Ephrem '89 -233 Bway -NY 10279 **Fx**:732-9167
(212) 906-1200 .. **Wertenteil**, Jack '10 %Latham & W -885 3rd Av -NY 10022
(631) 367-1485 .. **Werter**, Allen D '78 -215 E Main -Huntngtn 11743
(212) 685-5445 .. **Werth**, Robt D '90 -666 Greenwich -NY 10014
(212) 668-1700 .. **Wertheim**, Eric '88 OfCnsl V Mandel,PC -80 Wall -NY 10005 **Fx**:668-1701
(212) 558-4000 .. **Wertheim**, Fredk '88 (Sullivan & C LLP) -125 Broad -NY 10004
(212) 522-3505 .. **Wertheim**, Lewis Jon '00 Sports Illustrated -1271 Av of Amer -NY 10020
(914) 765-3945 .. **Wertheim**, Ram David '83 MBI Ins Corp -113 King -Armonk 10504
(212) 323-2250 .. **Wertheimer**, Chas '98 %HHC-OLA-Medical Litigation -346 Bway -NY 10013 **Fx**:323-2251
(212) 918-3000 .. **Wertheimer**, David F '85 (Hogan L LLP) -875 3rd Av -NY 10022
(212) 860-3086 .. **Wertheimer**, Elizabeth Adler '89 -124 E 93rd -NY 10128
(212) 964-1860 .. **Wertheimer**, Florrie L '54 (Wertheimer Assoc,PC) -225 Bway -NY 10007 **Fx**:349-2439
(212) 832-3600 .. **Wertheimer Fredman,LLC** -230 Park Av -NY 10169 **Fx**:832-5580
(212) 832-3600 .. **Wertheimer**, Jay W '60 (Wertheimer F,LLC) -230 Park Av -NY 10169
(212) 608-0900 .. **Wertheimer**, Lawr J '85 (LJ Wertheimer,PC) -225 Bway -NY 10007 **Fx**:962-0946
(212) 468-8000 .. **Wertheimer**, Rachel M '99 (Morrison & F LLP) -1290 Av of Amer -NY 10104
(212) 318-6000 .. **Wertheimer**, Robt J '80 (Paul HJ&W LLP) -75 E 55th -NY 10022
(212) 964-1860 .. **Wertheimer**, Robin M '99 %Wertheimer Assoc,PC -225 Bway -NY 10007 **Fx**:349-2439
(516) 471-1900 .. **Wertheimer**, Scott '07 %Havkins RR&V,LLP -114 Old Cntry Rd -Mineola 11501
(212) 335-9000 .. **Wertheimer**, Sylvia F '77 %DA -1 Hogan Pl -NY 10013
(212) 848-4000 .. **Werthenschlag**, Michel N '06 %Shearman & S LLP -599 Lex Av -NY 10022
(212) 695-6446 .. **Werther**, Ellen R '80 (Ressler & R) -48 Wall -NY 10005 **Fx**:268-0287
(518) 485-9374 .. **Werther**, Kathleen L '87 NYS Ed Dept -80 Wolf Rd -Albany 12205
(518) 783-4767 .. **Wertime Ries & Van Ullen,PC** -930 Albany Shaker Rd -Latham 12110 **Fx**:783-3077
(212) 309-6000 .. **Wertman**, Justin H '98 (Morgan L&B LLP) -101 Park Av -NY 10178
(646) 471-4000 .. **Wertz**, John W '83 %PricewaterhouseCoopers LLP -300 Mad Av -NY 10017
(212) 983-0044 .. **Werwaiss**, Gretchen N '96 Werwaiss & Co Inc -230 Park Av -NY 10169
(212) 237-0000 .. **Werzberger**, Tzvi '07 %Vinson & E LLP -666 5th Av -NY 10103
(212) 872-1000 .. **Wesch**, Kristina M '04 -One Bryant Park -NY 10036 **Fx**:872-1002
(212) 722-2000 .. **Weschler**, David W '69 %Leg Aid -230 E 106th -NY 10029 **Fx**:876-5365
(212) 323-7070 .. **Wescoe**, James A '04 (Rawle & H LLP) -14 Wall -NY 10005
(212) 858-1000 .. **Wesely**, Edwin J '54 SrCnsl Pillsbury WSP LLP -1540 Bway -NY 10036
(212) 455-2000 .. **Wesely**, Marissa C '81 (Simpson T&B LLP) -425 Lex Av -NY 10017
(718) 338-3000 .. **Weser**, Bonnie '87 (Weser & W,PC) -1392 Coney Isl Av -Brklyn 11230 **Fx**:377-6915
(718) 338-3000 .. **Weser**, Matthew '85 (Weser & W,PC) -1392 Coney Isl Av -Brklyn 11230 **Fx**:377-6915
(516) 932-4579 .. **Wesley**, Dane B '82 US Postal Inspctn Srvc -Bx160 -Hicksvll 11802 **Fx**:681-3402
(585) 753-4500 .. **Wesley**, Sarah E '07 %DA -832 Watts Bldg -Rchstr 14614 **Fx**:753-4576
(716) 852-2552 .. **Wesp**, Patrick W H '82 -2100 Rand Bldg -Buffalo 14203 **Fx**:852-8027
(212) 232-1300 .. **Wessel**, Mark D '08 %Lewis BB&S LLP -77 Water -NY 10005
(212) 530-5000 .. **Wessel**, Paul J '88 (Milbank TH&M LLP) -1 Chase Manh Plz -NY 10005
Wessel, Peter '81 -270 Mad Av -NY 10016
(212) 509-3456 .. **Wesselmann**, Nicole S '07 %McGivney & K,PC -80 Broad -NY 10004
(212) 210-9594 .. **Wessels**, Amber C '04 %Alston & B LLP -90 Park Av -NY 10016
(516) 239-1600 .. **Wessels**, Robt G '00 John Picone Inc -Bx9013 -Lawrence 11559
(212) 848-9800 .. **Wessely**, Robt P '76 (Withers B LLP) -430 Park Av -NY 10022
(718) 230-8080 .. **Wesser**, Marius C '95 M Wesser,PC -323 Wshngtn Av -Brklyn 11205 **Fx**:643-0845
(212) 349-5890 .. **Wesson**, Allister T '06 NYS Trial Lawyers Assn -132 Nassau -NY 10038
(914) 764-8314 .. **West**, Bernard '57 Westhaven Limited -131 Old Stone Hill Rd -Pound Rdg 10576
(212) 819-8200 .. **West**, Colin T '08 %White & C LLP -1155 Av of Amer -NY 10036
(607) 756-7542 .. **West**, Donna E '95 -55 Prospect Ter -Cortlnd 13045
(914) 769-0100 .. **West**, Eileen '75 -390 Bedford Rd -Plsntvll 10570 **Fx**:741-2736
(845) 565-0999 .. **West**, Gilbert J '01 %E Harris -405 Robnsn Av-Rt 9W -Newburgh 12550 **Fx**:565-1281
(315) 448-0672 .. **West**, Gregory A '77 %US Atty -100 S Clinton Bx7198 -Syracuse 13261 **Fx**:448-0689
(212) 815-7530 .. **West**, Hannah R '07 PELS -125 Barclay -NY 10007 **Fx**:815-7534
(518) 561-4400 .. **West**, Heather Deare '00 %Stafford OC&T,PLLC -1 Cumberland Av Bx2947 -Plattsbrgh 12901
(212) 343-1000 .. **West**, James B '81 (West & Assoc) -100 Lafayette -NY 10013 **Fx**:343-1375

(212) 692-0367 .. **West,** John T '90 (Hack POMW&M) -600 3rd Av -NY 10016
(212) 301-3150 .. **West,** Lesley A '04 Fox News Ntwrk -1211 Av of Amer -NY 10036
(212) 698-3500 .. **West,** M Holland '81 (Dechert LLP) -1095 Av of Amer -NY 10036
(212) 382-3300 .. **West,** Mathew B '97 Cnsl Wollmuth M&D LLP -500 5th Av -NY 10110
(607) 397-8062 .. **West,** Michl A '83 (Parshall & W) -153 Main Bx276 -Worcester 12197
(518) 296-8844 .. **West,** Michl A '83 (Parshall & W) -2668 State Route 7 -Cobleskill 12043
(212) 877-7319 .. **West,** Pamela G '88 -155 W 68th -NY 10023
(212) 672-1961 .. **West,** Richd L '00 -245 Park Av -NY 10167
(212) 530-5000 .. **West,** Ryan O '10 %Milbank TH&M LLP -1 Chase Manh Plz -NY 10005
(212) 558-4000 .. **West,** Stephen K '60 SrCnsl Sullivan & C LLP -125 Broad -NY 10004
(516) 741-2585 .. **West,** Susan A '04 %Rosicki R & Assoc,PC -51 E Bethpage Rd -Plainvw 11803 **Fx:**741-4748
(866) 353-3310 .. **West,** Teno A '94 (Pannone LD&W LLC) -81 Main -White Plns 10606
(518) 641-0500 .. **West,** Thos S '78 (West Firm,PLLC) -677 Bway -Albany 12207 **Fx:**615-1500
(607) 778-2403 .. **Westbrook,** Anthony J '93 %Pub Def -45 Hawley Bx1766 -Bnghmtn 13902 **Fx:**778-2432
(212) 574-1200 .. **Westbrook,** Christine M '03 %Seward & K LLP -1 Bttry Pk Plz -NY 10004
(716) 645-2490 .. **Westbrook,** David A '93 %SUNY Buffalo Lw Schl -O'Brian Hall -Buffalo 14260 **Fx:**645-5968
(845) 225-8404 .. **Westbrook,** Emily J '06 %Daniels & P,LLP -102 Gleneida Av -Carmel 10512
(212) 872-1000 .. **Westbrook,** Jessica M '05 -One Bryant Park -NY 10036 **Fx:**872-1002
(607) 797-7333 .. **Westbrook,** Martha E '95 %Rogers Srvc Group -245 Clinton -Bnghmtn 13905
(718) 694-3361 .. **Westcott,** Kimberly D '97 %Transit Auth -130 Lvngstn -Brklyn 11201 **Fx:**694-5726
(212) 735-3000 .. **Westenberg,** Erica L '07 %Skadden ASM&F LLP -4 Times Sq -NY 10036
(212) 980-0120 .. **Westerback,** Glen K '04 %Frankfurt KK&S,PC -488 Mad Av -NY 10022
(716) 664-5210 .. **Westerberg,** Ward W '73 (Price FM&W) -400 Key Bk Bldg Bx1219 -Jamestwn 14702
(212) 848-4000 .. **Westerfield,** Adrienne B '96 Shearman & S LLP -599 Lex Av -NY 10022
(212) 225-2000 .. **Westerfield,** Jennifer M '08 %Cleary GS&H -1 Lbrty Plz -NY 10006
(212) 586-0700 .. **Westergaard,** Steadman H '84 (Fulton R&H,LLP) -1 Rckfllr Plz -NY 10020
(212) 484-3900 .. **Westerlind,** James M '02 %Arent F LLP -1675 Bway -NY 10019
(516) 622-9200 .. **Westerman Ball Ederer Miller & Sharfstein,LLP** -1201 RXR Plz -Uniondale 11553 **Fx:**622-9212
(212) 310-8000 .. **Westerman,** Gavin '04 %Weil G&M LLP -767 5th Av -NY 10153
(914) 422-4252 .. **Westerman,** Gayl S '95 %Pace Law Schl -78 N Bway -White Plns 10603 **Fx:**422-4039
(516) 622-9200 .. **Westerman,** John E '83 (Westerman BEM&S,LLP) -1201 RXR Plz -Uniondale 11553
(914) 948-1200 .. **Westerman,** Kevin P '96 (Cerussi & S,PC) -1 N Lex Av -White Plns 10601
(315) 637-2731 .. **Westerman,** Leslie C '82 -7173 E Genesee -Fayettevll 13066 **Fx:**637-2770
(516) 794-7500 .. **Westermann,** David Jr. '81 (Westermann SKS&A,LLP) -333 Earle Ovngton Blvd -Uniondale 11553
(516) 794-7500 .. **Westermann Sheehy Keenan Samaan & Aydelott, LLP** -333 Earle Ovngton Blvd -Uniondale 11553 **Fx:**794-1277
(914) 946-7770 .. **Westermann Sheehy Keenan Samaan & Aydelott, LLP** -222 Bloomingdale Rd -White Plns 10605 **Fx:**946-4587
(631) 749-8944 .. **Westervelt,** Mary-Faith '93 -8 Shorewood Rd -Shelter Isl 11964
(585) 428-5890 .. **Westervelt,** Scott W '86 %Cnty Atty -300G Hall Of Justice -Rchstr 14614 **Fx:**428-2704
(607) 369-3811 .. **Westfall,** Beth E '87 (Coughlin & G,LLP) -176 Main Bx429 -Unadilla 13849
(607) 723-9511 .. **Westfall,** Beth E '87 (Coughlin & G,LLP) -19 Chenango Bx2039 -Bnghmtn 13902
(212) 556-2100 .. **Westfall,** Laura R '08 %King & S -1185 Av of Amer -NY 10036
(585) 546-8953 .. **Westfall,** Walter S '60 -1015 Union Trust Bldg -Rchstr 14614
(212) 532-6625 .. **Westfield,** Edw F '81 (E Westfield,PC) -274 Mad Av -NY 10016 **Fx:**532-6627
(518) 486-1098 .. **Westin,** Henrik N '09 State Comptroller -110 State -Albany 12236 **Fx:**473-9104
(315) 428-1221 .. **Westlake,** Marilyn A '80 (Westlake Law Firm,PC) -1390 Cloverleaf Rd -Locke 13092 **Fx:**497-1210
(212) 983-6900 .. **Westlake,** Susan E '86 OfCnsl Kaplan & L PC -630 3rd Av -NY 10017
(212) 530-5000 .. **Westland,** Chas W '74 OfCnsl Milbank TH&M LLP -1 Chase Manh Plz -NY 10005
(212) 885-5000 .. **Westle,** Thos R '81 (Blank R LLP) -405 Lex Av -NY 10174
(212) 658-6200 .. **Westlund,** Jon F '01 T-Systems NA -32 Av of Amer -NY 10013
(212) 953-2381 .. **Westlye,** Brad C '03 (Rubin F&F,LLP) -292 Mad Av -NY 10017
(716) 664-3223 .. **Westman,** James E '77 (Westman Law Firm) -300 E 6th -Jamestwn 14701
(716) 664-3223 .. **Westman,** John J '06 %Westman Law Firm -300 E 6th -Jamestwn 14701
(718) 783-6967 .. **Westmoreland,** James Ripley '86 -145 Lincoln -Brklyn 11217
(516) 393-2200 .. **Weston,** Burton S '77 (Garfunkel W,PC) -111 Grt Nck Rd -Gt Neck 11021
(212) 803-5100 .. **Weston,** Cori H '91 %NY Cnty Defender Srvcs -225 Bway -NY 10007 **Fx:**571-6035
(212) 858-1000 .. **Weston,** Gregory M '83 Cnsl Pillsbury WSP LLP -1540 Bway -NY 10036
(212) 833-8000 .. **Weston,** Ross L '91 Sony BMG Music Entrtnmnt -550 Mad Av -NY 10022 **Fx:**833-8406
(315) 218-8000 .. **Westover,** Caroline M '01 (Bond S&K,PLLC) -1 Lincoln Ctr -Syracuse 13202
(212) 530-5000 .. **Westover,** Melanie '05 %Milbank TH&M LLP -1 Chase Manh Plz -NY 10005
(212) 902-1000 .. **West-Pernica,** Ariane R '02 Goldman Sachs -85 Broad -NY 10004
(315) 253-1274 .. **Westphal,** Fredk R II '83 Cnty Atty -160 Genesee -Auburn 13021 **Fx:**253-1098
(212) 568-9881 .. **Westphal,** Jeanette M '96 -720 Ft Wshngtn Av -NY 10040 **Fx:**568-3947
(585) 473-9287 .. **Wetmore,** Kevin '83 -254 Culver Rd -Rchstr 14607
(607) 737-2944 .. **Wetmore,** Weeden A '79 %DA -226 Lk Bx588 -Elmira 14902 **Fx:**737-2965
(631) 475-4400 .. **Wetstein,** Paula '89 Cnsl Roe TT&P,LLP -One Corp Dr -Bohemia 11716
(718) 694-3869 .. **Wetstone,** Channon N '97 %Transit Auth -130 Lvngstn -Brklyn 11201 **Fx:**694-5726
(631) 423-0656 .. **Wetterer,** Chas M '57 -58 Conklin Ln -Huntngtn 11743
(212) 770-2436 .. **Wettick,** Brett E '88 %AIG Tech Srvcs -80 Pine -NY 10005
(518) 869-5552 .. **Wettig,** Sean M '04 Breakell PC -10 Airline Dr -Albany 12205 **Fx:**869-4222
(716) 566-1300 .. **Wettlaufer,** Catherine T '86 (Hiscock & B,LLP) -1100 M&T Ctr -Buffalo 14203
(718) 261-3047 .. **Wetzel,** Susan K '85 %Queens Law Assoc -118-21 Qns Blvd -Frst Hlls 11375 **Fx:**261-0798
(914) 683-1200 .. **Wetzel,** Wm A '66 OfCnsl Harris B PLLC -445 Hmltn Av -White Plns 10601
(516) 599-8822 .. **Wetzlar,** Leonard S '85 %Gellman & M -29 Bway -Lynbrk 11563
(212) 318-6000 .. **Wetzler,** Mor '08 Paul HJ&W LLP -75 E 55th -NY 10022
(212) 687-3860 .. **Wexelbaum,** Michl '72 (Snow BK,PC) -605 3rd Av -NY 10158
(212) 309-6000 .. **Wexler,** Adam S '06 %Morgan L&B LLP -101 Park Av -NY 10178
(716) 853-5100 .. **Wexler,** Alan S '71 (Lippes MWF LLP) -665 Main -Buffalo 14203
(718) 330-2844 .. **Wexler,** April M '88 %NLRB -2 Metrotech Ctr -Brklyn 11201 **Fx:**330-7579
(914) 835-1600 .. **Wexler,** Arlene Gold '82 -933 Mamaroneck Av -Mamaroneck 10543 **Fx:**835-1636
(212) 244-4630 .. **Wexler,** Brett A '09 %Katz & M,PC -1350 Av of Amer -NY 10019 **Fx:**(646) 219-5717
(212) 227-0347 .. **Wexler,** Bruce E '73 (Weiss W&W,PC) -25 Park Pl -NY 10007
(212) 407-4000 .. **Wexler,** Bruce J '80 (Loeb & L,LLP) -345 Park Av -NY 10154
(212) 318-6000 .. **Wexler,** Bruce M '93 (Paul HJ&W LLP) -75 E 55th -NY 10022
(914) 612-4388 .. **Wexler,** David J '99 Cadbury Schweppes -900 King -Rye Brook 10573 **Fx:**612-6302
(716) 881-0068 .. **Wexler,** David M '65 -88 Lex Av -Buffalo 14222
(212) 425-9300 .. **Wexler,** Emily J '07 %Bressler A&R,PC -17 State -NY 10004
(212) 758-6022 .. **Wexler,** Fran '81 Tourneau Inc -3 E 54th -NY 10022
(212) 983-8500 .. **Wexler,** Fred G '92 (Brown G&F LLP) -355 Lex Av -NY 10017
(914) 766-2747 .. **Wexler,** Gary D '96 IBM -294 Route 100 -Somers 10589
(212) 227-0347 .. **Wexler,** Gary M '04 %Weiss W&W,PC -25 Park Pl -NY 10007
(845) 369-4810 .. **Wexler,** Gene Lawr '81 Dress Barn,Inc -30 Dunnigan Dr -Suffern 10901
(212) 471-8480 .. **Wexler,** Howard L '78 (Herzfeld & R,PC) -125 Broad -NY 10004
(516) 267-6300 .. **Wexler,** Howard M '08 %Bond S&K,PLLC -1399 Franklin Av -Gdn Cty 11530
(212) 969-3000 .. **Wexler,** Jennifer B '01 %Proskauer R LLP -1585 Bway -NY 10036
(718) 780-7900 .. **Wexler,** Joan G '76 %Bklyn Law Schl -250 Joralemon -Brklyn 11201 **Fx:**780-0393
(516) 745-6830 .. **Wexler,** Joel G '72 (Golden W&B PC) -900 Merchants Cncrs -Westbury 11590
(212) 407-7700 .. **Wexler,** Jonathan A '89 %Vedder P,PC -1633 Bway -NY 10019
(212) 337-2228 .. **Wexler,** Karen Fern '95 %US Dept Labor -201 Varick -NY 10014
(212) 418-8600 .. **Wexler,** Marvin '76 (Kornstein VW&P,LLP) -757 3rd Av -NY 10017
(212) 351-4000 .. **Wexler,** Nili '09 Gibson D&C LLP -200 Park Av -NY 10166
(212) 308-5858 .. **Wexler,** Paul D '74 (Bragar WE&S,PC) -885 3rd Av -NY 10022
(212) 471-8500 .. **Wexler,** Shimshon '10 %Herzfeld & R,PC -125 Broad -NY 10004
(212) 686-4300 .. **Wexler,** Sidney D '67 -10 E 40th -NY 10016 **Fx:**689-2079
(516) 222-2230 .. **Wexler,** Stephen B '64 (Burkhart W&H,LLP) -585 Stewart Av -Gdn Cty 11530
(631) 422-2900 .. **Wexler,** Wm D '85 -816 Deer Prk Av -N Babylon 11703
(212) 735-3000 .. **Wexler,** Zev '07 %Skadden ASM&F LLP -4 Times Sq -NY 10036
(212) 692-1000 .. **Wexton,** Jane L '84 (Duane M LLP) -1540 Bway -NY 10036
(716) 532-3361 .. **Weyand,** Erich Sprague '94 %Weyand & W -113 W Main Bx26 -Gowanda 14070
(716) 532-3361 .. **Weyand,** Fredric F '80 (Weyand & W) -113 W Main Bx26 -Gowanda 14070
(914) 524-2741 .. **Weyand,** Karla M '95 Siemens Medical Solutions Diagnostics -511 Benedict Av -Tarrytwn 10591
(518) 471-4728 .. **Weyant,** Jeffrey L '82 %Appllt Div 3rd Dept -Capitol Station Bx7288 -Albany 12224 **Fx:**471-4750
(914) 962-6208 .. **Weyant,** Laura A '87 -2040 Crompond Rd -Yorktwn Hts 10598
(212) 521-5400 .. **Weyman,** Mark L '80 (Reed S LLP) -599 Lex Av -NY 10022
(845) 291-3150 .. **Whalan,** Susan L '99 %Cnty Atty -255 Main -Goshen 10924 **Fx:**291-3167
(516) 883-5432 .. **Whalen,** Annamaria A '99 %Publishers Clearing House -382 Channel Dr -Pt Wash 11050
(718) 725-3068 .. **Whalen,** Christina A '06 %Admin Childrens Srvcs -151-20 Jamaica Av -Jamaica 11432
(518) 238-4339 .. **Whalen,** David S '91 %OCA -187 Wolf Rd -Albany 12205 **Fx:**438-3518
(845) 877-9933 .. **Whalen,** George E '43 (Whalen & W) -Route 22 Bx 24 -Dover Plns 12522 **Fx:**877-6043
(518) 274-4800 .. **Whalen,** James M '04 Pioneer Savings Bk -21 2nd -Troy 12180
(914) 533-6544 .. **Whalen,** James T Jr. '79 OfCnsl Whalen & W -17 Col Ferris Rd -S Salem 10590
(212) 232-1300 .. **Whalen,** James T Jr. '79 (Lewis BB&S LLP) -77 Water -NY 10005
(212) 474-1000 .. **Whalen,** Jared R '09 %Cravath S&M LLP -825 8th Av -NY 10019
(518) 339-4238 .. **Whalen,** Jennifer A '92 OfCnsl Whalen Grp -96 Everett Rd -Albany 12205
(315) 472-7868 .. **Whalen,** Jerry W '87 %Weisberg & Z,PLLC -109 S Warren -Syracuse 13202 **Fx:**472-7070
(914) 948-7700 .. **Whalen,** Joanne C '88 OfCnsl E Campbell -2 Mad Av -Valhalla 10595 **Fx:**948-7795
(518) 432-1600 .. **Whalen,** Jonathan P '00 Meridian Captl Ptrns -20 Corp Wds Blvd -Albany 12211
(718) 237-2000 .. **Whalen,** Mark F '80 %Leg Aid -111 Lvngstn -Brklyn 11201 **Fx:**237-8737
(718) 330-1200 .. **Whalen,** Mildred M '93 %Fed Def of NY Inc -1 Pierrepont Plz -Brklyn 11201 **Fx:**855-0760
(212) 400-7100 .. **Whalen,** Paul C '96 (Whalen & T) -33 W 19th -NY 10011

(607) 754-0410 .. **Whalen**, Robt F '84 %Thomas C&M -1201 Monroe Bx329 -Endicott 13761
(212) 421-1845 .. **Whalen**, Ryan J '01 (Brown & W,PC) -711 3rd Av -NY 10017 **Fx:**421-8418
(914) 533-6544 .. **Whalen**, Suzanne T '87 %Whalen & W -17 Col Ferris Rd -S Salem 10590
(845) 877-9933 .. **Whalen**, Thos J '80 (Whalen & W) -Route 22 Bx 24 -Dover Plns 12522 **Fx:**877-6043
(212) 815-1818 .. **Whalen**, Wm '89 DC 37 MELS -125 Barclay -NY 10007 **Fx:**815-1343
(212) 909-3928 .. **Whaley**, Brian C '97 CIFG Svcs -825 3rd Av -NY 10022
(518) 408-0469 .. **Whaley**, Wm J II '91 %Workers Comp Bd -20 Park -Albany 12207
(212) 756-2000 .. **Whang**, Christine G '08 %Schulte R&Z LLP -919 3rd Av -NY 10022
(212) 515-7164 .. **Whang**, Edw '93 Dexia Global -445 Park Av -NY 10022
(212) 407-8439 .. **Whang**, Edw H '96 NBA Properties -645 5th Av -NY 10022
(212) 969-3000 .. **Whang**, Edw S '07 %Proskauer R LLP -1585 Bway -NY 10036
(212) 524-5000 .. **Whang**, Jun Chul '90 (Jacob M&F) -1270 Av of Amer -NY 10020
(212) 858-1000 .. **Whang**, Kenneth T '09 %Pillsbury WSP LLP -1540 Bway -NY 10036
(212) 528-1051 .. **Whang**, S Michl '88 Barclays Capital Inc -745 7th Av -NY 10019
(212) 239-2378 .. **Whang**, Tae Hyun '93 (Pak & W LLC) -16 W 32nd -NY 10001 **Fx:**239-8732
(718) 941-9094 .. **Wharton**, Frank A '87 -494 Flatbush Av -Brklyn 11225
(516) 571-2480 .. **Wharton**, Irina '02 Hon FD Winslow -100 Supreme Ct Dr -Mineola 11501
(518) 399-5400 .. **Wharton**, Jenifer M '95 (Gordon T&D,LLP) -113 Saratoga Rd -Glenvll 12302
(212) 771-7242 .. **Wharton**, Jennifer J '09 Tishman Speyer -11 W 42nd -NY 10036
(845) 569-9110 .. **Whateley**, Mary Jo '96 %Leg Srvcs -123 Grand -Newburgh 12550 **Fx:**569-9120
(212) 447-7070 .. **Whatley Drake & Kallas LLC** -1540 Bway -NY 10036 **Fx:**447-7077
(212) 447-7070 .. **Whatley**, Joe R Jr. '06 (Whatley D&K LLC) -1540 Bway -NY 10036
(914) 251-1115 .. **Whealan**, Maria B '95 %Walsh & A LLP -2900 Wstchstr Av -Purchase 10577
(914) 995-4728 .. **Whearty**, Richd F '77 %Supreme Ct -140 Grand -White Plns 10601 **Fx:**285-4396
(877) 847-6680 .. **Wheat**, Scott B '04 -305 Cayuga Rd -Buffalo 14224
(212) 906-1200 .. **Wheatley**, Adrienne Eason '99 (Latham & W) -885 3rd Av -NY 10022
(212) 596-9000 .. **Wheatley**, Christopher T '09 %Ropes & G LLP -1211 Av of Amer -NY 10036
(518) 464-1300 .. **Wheatley**, Dionne A '95 %Roemer WG&M LLP -13 Columbia Cir -Albany 12203
(845) 371-4700 .. **Wheatley-Liss**, Deirdre R '98 (Fein SK&S,PC) -747 Chestnut Rdg Rd -Spg Vly 10977
(212) 858-1000 .. **Wheaton**, James G '02 %Pillsbury WSP LLP -1540 Bway -NY 10036
(716) 858-2200 .. **Wheaton**, Kristin Klein '95 %Cnty Atty -95 Franklin -Buffalo 14202 **Fx:**858-2281
(718) 802-3111 .. **Wheeler**, Alan E '95 -Bx130211 -Laurelton 11413 **Fx:**802-3115
(212) 483-9490 .. **Wheeler**, Alfred '65 OfCnsl McElroy DM&C,LLP -88 Pine -NY 10005
(212) 685-3650 .. **Wheeler**, Amy C '06 -120 E 37th -NY 10016
(718) 855-9000 .. **Wheeler**, Dawn C '95 %Cullen and D LLP -177 Montague -Brklyn 11201
(212) 969-3000 .. **Wheeler**, Gail '92 %Proskauer R LLP -1585 Bway -NY 10036
(212) 558-4000 .. **Wheeler**, Isaac J '10 %Sullivan & C LLP -125 Broad -NY 10004
(212) 940-3734 .. **Wheeler**, Jennifer N '08 %Nixon P LLP -437 Mad Av -NY 10022
(607) 734-2271 .. **Wheeler**, Jos W '04 %Sayles & E -1 W Church -Elmira 14901
(212) 765-2100 .. **Wheeler**, Keren '09 %Spivak L LLP -1700 Bway -NY 10019
(212) 698-3500 .. **Wheeler**, Marisa N '03 Dechert LLP -1095 Av of Amer -NY 10036
(607) 273-6444 .. **Wheeler**, Mark B '80 (Harris B PLLC) -119 E Seneca -Ithaca 14850
(212) 906-1200 .. **Wheeler**, Patrick B '06 %Latham & W -885 3rd Av -NY 10022
(212) 506-2500 .. **Wheeler**, Reb D '00 (Mayer B LLP) -1675 Bway -NY 10019
(212) 509-9400 .. **Wheeler**, Russell G '03 %Cozen O -45 Bway Atrium -NY 10006
(718) 838-7878 .. **Wheeler**, S Isaac '05 %Bronx Defenders -860 Crtlandt Av -Bronx 10451 **Fx:**665-0100
(212) 558-4000 .. **Wheeler**, Stephanie G '94 (Sullivan & C LLP) -125 Broad -NY 10004
(315) 265-3216 .. **Wheeler**, Thos B '75 -63 Market Box 506 -Potsdam 13676
(973) 597-6248 .. **Wheeler**, Timothy R '03 Cnsl Lowenstein S PC -1251 Av of Amer -NY 10020 **Fx:**597-6249
(718) 558-7617 .. **Wheelwright**, Traci M '03 %LIRR -Jamaica Station -Jamaica 11435 **Fx:**558-8211
(212) 335-9000 .. **Whelan**, Anne-Marie '02 %DA -1 Hogan Pl -NY 10013
(732) 214-0300 .. **Whelan**, Chas D III '84 OfCnsl Wolff Law Ofc -147 W 80th -NY 10024
(914) 769-1025 .. **Whelan**, David J '61 -17 Stillman Ln -Plsntvll 10570 **Fx:**747-5216
(845) 357-0265 .. **Whelan**, Frank A '87 (Buckheit & W,PC) -49 N Airmont Rd -Suffern 10901 **Fx:**357-7192
(516) 571-3800 .. **Whelan**, Fredk J III '89 %DA -262 Old Cntry Rd -Mineola 11501 **Fx:**248-9479
(212) 773-2747 .. **Whelan**, Gerald E Jr. '01 Ernst & Young LLP -5 Times Sq -NY 10036 **Fx:**773-2794
(718) 263-3800 .. **Whelan**, James G '93 %Muss Dvlpmnt LLC -118-35 Qns Blvd -Frst Hlls 11375
(212) 841-7500 .. **Whelan**, Jeffrey R '86 %Cushman & Wakefield -1290 Av of Amer -NY 10104
(516) 466-2227 .. **Whelan**, John B '06 %D Reisman -98 Cutter Mill Rd -Gt Neck 11021 **Fx:**829-6219
(212) 732-3200 .. **Whelan**, John K '65 SrCnsl Carter L&M LLP -2 Wall -NY 10005
(631) 232-2400 .. **Whelan**, Kathleen '79 %Nassau/Sfflk Law Srv -1757 Vets Hwy -Islandia 11749 **Fx:**232-2489
(315) 488-5987 .. **Whelan**, Kevin '63 -2105 W Genesee -Syracuse 13219 **Fx:**468-1388
(631) 725-7844 .. **Whelan**, Mary M '91 -Bx2299 -Sag Hbr 11963 **Fx:**725-7847
(718) 321-1818 .. **Whelan**, Patrick J '05 Judlau Contracting,Inc -26-15 Ulmer -Flushng 11354
(212) 406-1855 .. **Whelan**, Richd Q '89 (Palmer B&H) -140 Bway -NY 10005
(212) 768-6700 .. **Whelan**, Stephen T '72 (Sonnenschein N&R LLP) -2 World Fncl Ctr -NY 10281
(315) 955-6700 .. **Whelan**, Terrence J '77 %Leg Aid -44 Pub Sq -Watertwn 13601 **Fx:**785-9118
(212) 746-1945 .. **Whelan**, Timothy P '90 %NY Presbyterian Hsptl -525 E 68th Bx88 -NY 10065 **Fx:**746-8603
(631) 957-0518 .. **Whelan**, Wm F '89 -361 15th -W Babylon 11704
(212) 474-1000 .. **Whelan**, Wm J III '84 (Cravath S&M LLP) -825 8th Av -NY 10019
(212) 336-1645 .. **Whelchel**, Betty A '86 Deutsche Bk AG -345 Park Av -NY 10154
(518) 859-4999 .. **Whelden**, John M '89 -27A Belvidere Av -Albany 12203 **Fx:**449-2903
(315) 788-6700 .. **Whelpley**, Dennis G '81 (Schwerzmann & W,PC) -215 Wshngtn Bx704 -Watertwn 13601
(212) 683-5320 .. **Whent**, Christopher R '85 -270 Mad Av -NY 10016 **Fx:**686-2182
(212) 909-6000 .. **Whetsell**, Jennifer F '03 %Debevoise & P LLP -919 3rd Av -NY 10022
(718) 590-2000 .. **Whetstone**, Kayonia L '06 DA -198 E 161st -Bronx 10451 **Fx:**590-6477
(845) 638-5180 .. **Whidbee-Jordan**, Venita D '98 Cnty Atty -Cnty Ofc Bldg -New Cty 10956 **Fx:**638-5676
(212) 632-5500 .. **Whidden**, Lee P '89 (Salans LLP) -620 5th Av -NY 10020
(845) 338-6500 .. **Whidden**, Stephanie M '87 -Bx249 -W Hurley 12491 **Fx:**338-8498
(518) 782-9100 .. **Whipple**, Barbara A '99 %Barbaruolo Law Firm PC -12 Cornell Rd -Latham 12110 **Fx:**782-9101
(212) 325-2000 .. **Whipple**, George C '81 Credit Suisse -1 Mad Av -NY 10010
(716) 673-1361 .. **Whipple**, Richd F Jr. '64 (Schaack WCN PC) -2 W Main Bx109 -Fredonia 14063
(315) 472-0496 .. **Whisenand**, Lucia B '82 (LB Whisenand,PC) -118 Julian Pl -Syracuse 13210 **Fx:**410-6010
(718) 707-3174 .. **Whisler**, Dorothy B '01 %G Schapira & Assoc,PLLC -4 Court Sq -LIC 11101
(518) 402-6757 .. **Whispell**, Russell S '93 %Workers Comp Bd -20 Park -Albany 12207
(716) 852-2025 .. **Whissel**, Thos '67 -80 W Huron -Buffalo 14202 **Fx:**852-8013
(212) 909-6000 .. **Whiston**, Elizabeth Woods '10 %Debevoise & P LLP -919 3rd Av -NY 10022
(516) 627-1892 .. **Whitaker**, Christina M '91 -156 Northwoods Rd -Manhsst 11030
(212) 297-5800 .. **Whitaker**, G Warren III '76 (Day P LLP) -7 Times Sq -NY 10036
(585) 419-8800 .. **Whitaker**, Janelle L '09 %Harris B PLLC -99 Garnsey Rd -Pittsfrd 14534
(212) 867-5800 .. **Whitaker**, Nathan J '08 %Osler H&H LLP -620 8th Av -NY 10018
(212) 218-5656 .. **Whitaker**, Ridley M '82 -570 Lex Av -NY 10022 **Fx:**218-5665
(315) 471-3151 .. **Whitaker**, Robt C '06 %Hancock & E,LLP -1500 AXA Twr I Bx4976 -Syracuse 13221
(518) 828-9444 .. **Whitbeck**, Carl G Jr. '75 (Rapport MWS&R,LLP) -436 Union -Hudson 12534
(585) 454-7545 .. **Whitbeck**, Paul M '76 -183 E Main -Rchstr 14604 **Fx:**232-7455
(716) 289-0548 .. **Whitbeck**, Scott J '04 -31 Edge Park Av -Buffalo 14216
(212) 699-8400 .. **Whitby**, Paul G '72 Van Wagner Comm,LLC -800 3rd Av -NY 10022 **Fx:**986-0927
(716) 856-1600 .. **Whitcher**, Michl J '86 (Hurwitz & D) -424 Main -Buffalo 14202
(716) 842-3911 .. **Whitchurch**, Phyllis R '97 P Whitchurch,PC -69 Delaware Av -Buffalo 14202 **Fx:**842-0203
(716) 847-8400 .. **Whitcomb**, James W '84 (Phillips L LLP) -3400 HSBC Ctr -Buffalo 14203
(914) 684-0090 .. **Whitcomb**, Jonathan P '91 (Diserio MO&C LLP) -50 Main -White Plns 10606
(212) 752-5258 .. **Whitcomb**, Philip B '86 Cnsl Schwartz SE&C LLC -845 3rd Av -NY 10022
(212) 577-9710 .. **White**, Adam D '91 (White M,PLLP) -225 Bway -NY 10007 **Fx:**577-9715
(914) 681-6200 .. **White**, Alice J '05 %NYPA -123 Main -White Plns 10601 **Fx:**390-8038
(212) 487-9700 .. **White**, Allan P '68 SrCnsl White F&F,LLP -61 Bway -NY 10006
(718) 579-7949 .. **White**, Amanda E '93 %Leg Aid -900 Sheridan Av -Bronx 10451 **Fx:**293-8744
(845) 220-2667 .. **White**, Andrew H '92 (McGillicuddy & S,PC) -233 Bway -Newburgh 12550
(212) 858-7280 .. **White**, Andrew S '00 %RBC Dominion -1 Lbrty Plz -NY 10006
(212) 530-4129 .. **White**, Ann O'Connor '85 %Risk Enterprise Mgmt -59 Maiden Ln -NY 10038
(718) 858-4500 .. **White**, Asher B '94 -26 Court -Brklyn 11242 **Fx:**596-2610
(212) 588-0800 .. **White**, Barry S '90 (Frommer L&H LLP) -745 5th Av -NY 10151
(845) 291-2050 .. **White**, Bradford H '08 %DA -255-275 Main -Goshen 10924 **Fx:**291-2085
(212) 821-3258 .. **White**, Bradley W '04 UBS -299 Park Av -NY 10171
(212) 709-8247 .. **White**, Brenda Farrow '85 -110 Wall -NY 10005
(212) 861-9850 .. **White**, Brendan M '96 (White & W) -148 E 78th -NY 10075 **Fx:**861-9870
(212) 696-6000 .. **White**, Brian M '09 %Curtis M-PC&M LLP -101 Park Av -NY 10178
(646) 720-9139 .. **White**, Brigitte M '01 DB Zwirn & Co -1345 Av of Amer -NY 10105
(718) 857-3721 .. **White**, Brooks '79 (Dube & W) -295 St Johns Pl -Brklyn 11238 **Fx:**857-3748
(212) 819-8200 .. **White & Case LLP** -1155 Av of Amer -NY 10036 **Fx:**354-8113
(718) 590-2000 .. **White**, Charlayne M '07 DA -198 E 161st -Bronx 10451 **Fx:**590-6477
(518) 842-0550 .. **White**, Chas N '62 -12 Summit Av -Amsterdam 12010
(646) 213-6761 .. **White**, Christian R '02 Grand Hyatt NY -109 E 42nd -NY 10017
(212) 788-0462 .. **White**, Christina M '97 SrCnsl Law Dept -100 Church -NY 10007 **Fx:**788-0367
(212) 223-4000 .. **White**, Christine L '02 (Crowell & M LLP) -590 Mad Av -NY 10022
(212) 564-6633 .. **White**, Christopher J '84 (White & M,PC) -875 Av of Amer -NY 10001
(914) 285-9770 .. **White**, Christopher J '88 -120 Caterson Ter -Hartsdale 10530
(516) 292-1818 .. **White Cirrito & Nally,LLP** -58 Hilton Av -Hempstd 11550 **Fx:**489-1940
(914) 251-4142 .. **White**, Claude E '86 IntegraMed America Inc -2 Manhattanvll Rd -Purchase 10577 **Fx:**253-8010
(516) 877-9653 .. **White**, Dana L '01 %Wolf Law Grp,PC -114 Old Cntry Rd -Mineola 11501 **Fx:**877-9660
(585) 889-2150 .. **White**, Danl H '73 -11 Maple -Scottsvll 14546
(212) 344-3100 .. **White**, Danl W '85 (Frenkel LWW&G,LLP) -1 Whitehall -NY 10004
(631) 424-2800 .. **White**, Danielle L '97 %B Tully -444 NY Av -Huntngtn 11743 **Fx:**424-2801

(914) 872-8804 .. **White,** Danielle M '03 Dannon Co,Inc -100 Hillside Av -White Plns 10603
(917) 592-1623 .. **White,** Dansby '89 Societe Generale -1221 Av of Amer -NY 10020
(716) 759-1500 .. **White,** David D '83 (Sheffer M&W) -10535 Main -Clarence 14031
(212) 233-0060 .. **White,** David M '03 White & Assoc,PC -233 Bway -NY 10279 **Fx:**233-0641
(212) 407-4000 .. **White,** Debra A '98 (Loeb & L,LLP) -345 Park Av -NY 10154
(212) 861-9850 .. **White,** Diarmuid M '85 (White & W) -148 E 78th -NY 10075 **Fx:**861-9870
(585) 546-6448 .. **White,** Donald A '82 %Davidson F LLP -28 E Main -Rchstr 14614
(212) 766-1888 .. **White,** Donna M '98 Morris DA&F -2 Rector -NY 10006
(212) 889-7990 .. **White,** Dru Saml '82 (Thomas & W) -104 W 27th -NY 10001
(212) 969-3000 .. **White,** Earl P '09 %Proskauer R LLP -1585 Bway -NY 10036
(914) 345-3701 .. **White,** Edgar R '10 %Marks OO&C,PC -530 Saw Mill Rvr Rd -Elmsfrd 10523
(212) 753-7500 .. **White,** Edw A '76 (Hartman & C LLP) -488 Mad Av -NY 10022
(212) 225-7700 .. **White,** Edw J '92 %Cartafalsa ST&L -165 Bway -NY 10006
(212) 371-1000 .. **White,** Eileen M '87 %Archdiocese of NY -1011 1st Av -NY 10022
(716) 847-0650 .. **White,** Elizabeth A '88 %Leg Srvcs -237 Main -Buffalo 14203 **Fx:**847-0227
(212) 868-6300 .. **White,** Elizabeth A '08 %Cary K LLP -1350 Bway -NY 10018
(212) 450-4000 .. **White,** Erika Diane '82 Cnsl Davis P&W LLP -450 Lex Av -NY 10017
(212) 373-3000 .. **White,** Erin E '10 %Paul WRW&G LLP -1285 Av of Amer -NY 10019
(212) 487-9700 .. **White Fleischner & Fino, LLP** -61 Bway -NY 10006 **Fx:**487-9777
(212) 466-8073 .. **White,** Fred B III '90 Sandler O'Neill + Partners,LP -919 3rd Av -NY 10022
(212) 735-3000 .. **White,** Gavin A '05 %Skadden ASM&F LLP -4 Times Sq -NY 10036
(718) 809-4055 .. **White,** Gerard J '00 -7617 Myrtle Av -Glendale 11385
(212) 669-0600 .. **White,** Gerard W '95 (Hill R LLP) -45 Bway -NY 10006
(212) 334-7025 .. **White,** H Roy II '87 -60 Horatio -NY 10014
(212) 530-5092 .. **White,** Harry E Jr. '65 -1 Chase Manh Plz -NY 10005 **Fx:**530-5219
(212) 309-6000 .. **White,** Ira '86 (Morgan L&B LLP) -101 Park Av -NY 10178
(716) 200-5050 .. **White,** J Ryan '04 %Harris B PLLC -726 Exchange -Buffalo 14210
(914) 499-4884 .. **White,** Jacquelyn G '05 IBM Corp -New Orchrd Rd -Armonk 10504
(585) 454-2060 .. **White,** James M '59 -341 Corwin Rd -Rchstr 14610
(212) 770-7000 .. **White,** James M '95 %AIG Tech Srvcs -80 Pine -NY 10005
(212) 412-4000 .. **White,** Jason D '02 Barclays Capital Inc -200 Park Av -NY 10166
(607) 778-2423 .. **White,** Jason W '09 DA -45 Hawley Bx1766 -Bnghmtn 13902 **Fx:**778-8870
(718) 260-2900 .. **White,** Jennifer A '99 Urban Womens Safe Haven -22 Chapel -Brklyn 11201
(212) 294-6700 .. **White,** Jennifer N '04 %Winston & S -200 Park Av -NY 10166
(212) 596-9000 .. **White,** Jesse J '10 %Ropes & G LLP -1211 Av of Amer -NY 10036
(518) 782-3484 .. **White,** Joanne M '89 J White -582 New Loudon Rd -Latham 12110 **Fx:**782-3478
(845) 331-2525 .. **White,** John D '89 %Ryan R&R,LLP -115 Green Bx3153 -Kingston 12402
(212) 530-5000 .. **White,** John K Jr. '06 %Milbank TH&M LLP -1 Chase Manh Plz -NY 10005
(212) 278-0400 .. **White,** John P '78 (Cooper & D LLP) -30 Rckfllr Plz -NY 10112
(516) 677-9660 .. **White,** John S '83 -180 Froehlich Farm Blvd -Woodbury 11797
(212) 474-1000 .. **White,** John W '74 (Cravath S&M LLP) -825 8th Av -NY 10019
(718) 204-7900 .. **White,** Jonathan D '89 %White Coffee Corp -18-35 38th -LIC 11105 **Fx:**956-8504
(212) 552-0795 .. **White,** Jos B '79 JP Morgan Chase -1 Chase Manh Plz -NY 10005
(212) 558-4000 .. **White,** Jos E '08 %Sullivan & C LLP -125 Broad -NY 10004
(212) 750-1333 .. **White,** Judith E '89 (I Garr,PC) -777 3rd Av -NY 10017 **Fx:**486-2978
(716) 631-9100 .. **White,** Justin S '83 (Shelby B&W) -5662 Main -Williamsvll 14221 **Fx:**631-7546
(212) 387-5619 .. **White,** Katherine P '72 %AT&T -32 Av of Amer -NY 10013
(212) 447-1111 .. **White,** Keela K '04 %Ledy-Gurren B&S -475 Park Av S -NY 10016
(646) 321-2594 .. **White,** Kenya S '04 -1275 E 51st -Brklyn 11234
(212) 816-8220 .. **White,** Kevin M '98 Citigroup Global Mrkts -388 Greenwich -NY 10013
(212) 574-1200 .. **White,** Kimberly E '05 %Seward & K LLP -1 Bttry Pk Plz -NY 10004
(716) 853-8400 .. **White,** Linda E '77 %Dept of Law -350 Main Pl Twr -Buffalo 14202 **Fx:**853-8571
(585) 272-1990 .. **White,** Lisa P '97 -2024 W Henrietta Rd -Rchstr 14623
(914) 528-9230 .. **White,** Lois A '76 -1299 Williams Dr -Shrub Oak 10588
(518) 358-2272 .. **White,** Lorraine M '06 St Regis Mohawk Tribe -412 State Route 37 -Hogansburg 13655
(212) 335-4500 .. **White,** Lucien D '87 OfCnsl DLA Piper LLP -1251 Av of Amer -NY 10020
(212) 909-6000 .. **White,** Mary Jo '75 (Debevoise & P LLP) -919 3rd Av -NY 10022
(516) 229-6000 .. **White,** Mary K '86 %R Lau & Assoc -300 Jericho Quad Bx9040 -Jericho 11753 **Fx:**229-6167
(212) 636-2638 .. **White,** Mary Lee '94 %Christies Inc -20 Rckfllr Plz -NY 10020
(518) 455-4191 .. **White,** Maryann Carroll '05 Ofc Cnsl to Majority -448M State Cptl -Albany 12248 **Fx:**455-4103
(516) 408-9000 .. **White,** Matthew G '02 %Walsh MM&D LLP -229 Seventh -Gdn Cty 11530
(212) 564-6633 .. **White & McSpedon,PC** -875 Av of Amer -NY 10001 **Fx:**564-9799
(212) 728-8000 .. **White,** Meghan E '07 %Willkie F&G LLP -787 7th Av -NY 10019
(212) 709-8354 .. **White,** Mendel '60 -110 Wall -NY 10005
(718) 834-6184 .. **White,** Michl D D '79 -62 Montague -Brklyn 11201 **Fx:**797-3193
(914) 824-5385 .. **White,** Michl J '86 -111 Martin Luther King Blvd -White Plns 10601 **Fx:**995-8654
(212) 458-1644 .. **White,** Michl J '90 %AIG -175 Water 4th Fl -NY 10038 **Fx:**458-1039
(646) 392-9250 .. **White,** Michl J '94 %M Klein & Assoc -200 Mad Av -NY 10016 **Fx:**(212) 779-1499
(212) 298-5386 .. **White,** Monyca '04 Leg Aid -49 Thomas -NY 10013 **Fx:**298-5252
(718) 306-1036 .. **White,** Norman K '02 Cmty Devpt Corp -120-20 Flatlands Av -Brklyn 11207
(212) 866-4541 .. **White,** Othia M '89 -382 Cntrl Pk W -NY 10025
(212) 556-2100 .. **White,** Pamela Caron '02 %King & S -1185 Av of Amer -NY 10036
(212) 830-6388 .. **White,** Peter B '89 AT&T Wireless -32 Av of Amer -NY 10013
(212) 335-4500 .. **White,** Peter C '85 (DLA Piper LLP) -1251 Av of Amer -NY 10020
(516) 222-2434 .. **White Quinlan & Staley** -377 Oak Bx9304 -Gdn Cty 11530 **Fx:**222-2508
(716) 852-5533 .. **White,** Randall D '87 (Connors & V,LLP) -1000 Lbrty Bldg -Buffalo 14202
(212) 770-0547 .. **White,** Rebecca Moffat '01 AIG Tech Srvcs -80 Pine -NY 10005
(518) 436-1100 .. **White,** Richd M '91 -18 Corp Wds Blvd -Albany 12211
(718) 546-0950 .. **White,** Richd R '91 Dept of Correction -75-20 Astoria Blvd -E Elmhrst 11370
(518) 891-4295 .. **White,** Robt E '74 -129 Main -Saranac Lk 12983 **Fx:**891-0615
(518) 239-6601 .. **White,** Robt J '90 -Bx11 -Cornwallville 12418 **Fx:**239-6602
(212) 468-8000 .. **White,** Ronald G '04 (Morrison & F LLP) -1290 Av of Amer -NY 10104
(212) 610-6300 .. **White,** Rowena M '09 %Allen & O -1221 Av of Amer -NY 10020
(212) 816-6342 .. **White,** Scott E '01 Citigroup -388 Greenwich -NY 10013
(212) 626-2067 .. **White,** Shawn R '02 Cnsl Prudential Fncl -1114 Av of Amer -NY 10036 **Fx:**626-2079
(518) 438-2000 .. **White,** Stephanie A '91 %Lombardi WWHA&D PC -III Winners Cir -Albany 12205
(212) 770-2465 .. **White,** Steven L '86 %AIG -80 Pine -NY 10005 **Fx:**425-2893
(212) 732-0707 .. **White,** Stuart A '08 %J Dratel,PC -2 Wall -NY 10005 **Fx:**571-3792
(212) 697-6555 .. **White,** Susan C '07 %Biedermann RH&R -570 Lex Av -NY 10022
(631) 952-6505 .. **White,** Tanya N '99 %UIA Bd -NYS Ofc Bldg -Hauppauge 11788 **Fx:**952-3385
(631) 851-0088 .. **White,** Teresa A '88 -140 Fell Ct -Hauppauge 11788 **Fx:**851-0820
(212) 558-4000 .. **White,** Thos C '08 %Sullivan & C LLP -125 Broad -NY 10004
(212) 571-1717 .. **White,** Thos D '75 -225 Bway -NY 10007 **Fx:**571-3124
(718) 639-1100 .. **White,** Thos J III '80 (Masone WP&C) -69-34 Grand Av -Maspeth 11378
(716) 753-4678 .. **White,** Thos W '83 -3 N Erie -Mayvll 14757
(585) 271-6780 .. **White,** Van Henri '90 -18 Grove Pl -Rchstr 14605
(315) 435-2470 .. **White,** Victoria M '86 %DA -505 S State -Syracuse 13202 **Fx:**435-3969
(516) 873-9550 .. **White,** Vincent P '09 %Leeds M&B -1 Old Cntry Rd -Carle Pl 11514
(718) 618-2500 .. **White,** Vivienne T '74 %Civil Ct -851 Grnd Cncrs -Bronx 10451 **Fx:**590-7294
(212) 504-6000 .. **White,** W Christopher '81 (Cadwalader W&T LLP) -1 World Fncl Ctr -NY 10281
(212) 926-8400 .. **White,** Wm Anderson '60 -740 St Nicholas Av -NY 10031 **Fx:**281-5925
(518) 793-3424 .. **White,** Wm J '89 (Brennan & W LLP) -163 Haviland Rd -Queensbury 12804 **Fx:**793-3422
(212) 345-5016 .. **White,** Wm J '92 %Marsh USA -1166 Av of Amer -NY 10036 **Fx:**345-4808
(516) 222-2434 .. **White,** Wm R '68 (White Q&S) -377 Oak Bx9304 -Gdn Cty 11530
(212) 244-9500 .. **White and Williams LLP** -1 Penn Plz -NY 10119 **Fx:**244-6200
(914) 487-7330 .. **White and Williams LLP** -427 Bedford Rd -Plsntvll 10570 **Fx:**487-7331
(212) 407-4000 .. **White-Hall,** Sandra J '09 %Loeb & L,LLP -345 Park Av -NY 10154
(718) 590-2000 .. **Whitehead,** Jason S '06 DA -198 E 161st -Bronx 10451 **Fx:**590-6477
(914) 949-6400 .. **Whitehead,** Linda B '87 (McCullough G&S,LLP) -1311 Mamaroneck Av -White Plns 10605
(646) 855-5992 .. **Whitehead,** Robt C '91 Bank of Amer -1 Bryant Pk -NY 10036
(212) 870-3216 .. **Whitehead,** Robin S '96 Morality Media -475 Riverside Dr -NY 10115
(212) 813-8800 .. **Whitehill,** Joshua A '10 Goodwin P LLP -620 8th Av -NY 10018
(212) 398-1110 .. **Whitehorn,** Jo-Ann H '73 -1407 Bway -NY 10018
(516) 829-5000 .. **Whitehorn,** Rex '96 (R Whitehorn & Assoc,PC) -98 Cuttermill Rd -Gt Neck 11021 **Fx:**829-5190
(914) 632-5416 .. **Whitehouse,** Maribeth P '96 -25 Shady Glen Ct -New Rchll 10805
(315) 472-7832 .. **Whitelaw,** Kenneth D '73 (Whitelaw & F) -247-259 W Fayette -Syracuse 13202 **Fx:**472-7816
(212) 964-6611 .. **Whiteley,** Darrell J '86 (Lester SK&D) -120 Bway -NY 10271
(516) 742-8111 .. **Whiteman,** John P III '06 %Fass & G,LLP -1225 Franklin Av -Gdn Cty 11530 **Fx:**742-8999
(518) 487-7600 .. **Whiteman,** Michl '64 (Whiteman O&H LLP) -1 Commerce Plz -Albany 12260
(518) 487-7600 .. **Whiteman Osterman & Hanna LLP** -1 Commerce Plz -Albany 12260 **Fx:**487-7777
(914) 949-2111 .. **Whiteman,** Robt G '77 (R Whiteman,PC) -51 Prospect -White Plns 10606
(212) 259-8000 .. **Whitener,** Jennifer O '05 %Dewey & L LLP -1301 Av of Amer -NY 10019
(212) 848-4000 .. **Whitener,** Robt L '08 %Shearman & S LLP -599 Lex Av -NY 10022
(212) 576-7000 .. **Whites,** Chas A '02 %NY Life Ins -51 Mad Av -NY 10010 **Fx:**447-0569
(845) 486-2300 .. **Whitesell,** Edw F '86 %DA -236 Main -Poughkeepsie 12601 **Fx:**486-2324
(212) 839-5300 .. **Whitesides,** Carol J '99 %Sidley A LLP -787 7th Av -NY 10019
(917) 517-3261 .. **Whitfield,** Dana M '01 -247 Ilyssa Way -Staten Isl 10312 **Fx:**(718) 605-0545
(516) 294-8844 .. **Whitfield,** Diane Peixoto '04 %L'Abbate BC&C,LLP -1001 Franklin Av -Gdn Cty 11530
(212) 848-4000 .. **Whitfield,** Kathryn V '06 %Shearman & S LLP -599 Lex Av -NY 10022
(585) 295-4400 .. **Whitford,** Mark T Jr. '06 %Hiscock & B,LLP -2000 HSBC Plz -Rchstr 14604
(917) 687-7530 .. **Whitford,** Thos C '89 -370 Riverside Dr -NY 10025
(607) 722-6417 .. **Whiting,** Chas E '02 %J Troy -45 Chenango -Bnghmtn 13901 **Fx:**722-8019
(212) 909-6000 .. **Whiting,** Corey S '08 %Debevoise & P LLP -919 3rd Av -NY 10022
(212) 243-1313 .. **Whiting,** Judith M '87 Leg Action Ctr -225 Varick -NY 10014 **Fx:**675-0286
(607) 722-0500 .. **Whiting,** Kenneth P III '78 -53 Chenango -Bnghmtn 13901 **Fx:**723-3671
(212) 360-4215 .. **Whiting,** Kristin B '00 Solomon R Guggenheim Fndtn -345 Hudson -NY 10014
(718) 448-9599 .. **Whiting,** Mary A '82 -214 Slosson Av -Staten Isl 10314 **Fx:**448-9599
(585) 768-6550 .. **Whiting,** Reid A '81 -31 W Main Bx100 -Le Roy 14482 **Fx:**768-9381
(518) 436-0751 .. **Whiting,** Saml R '65 (Hinman S PC) -121 State -Albany 12207
(716) 853-8400 .. **Whiting,** Wendy R '98 %Dept of Law -350 Main Pl Twr -Buffalo 14202 **Fx:**853-8571
(212) 210-9574 .. **Whitlock,** Sarah C '09 %Alston & B LLP -90 Park Av -NY 10016

(646) 602-5600 ..**Whitlow**, John B '04 %Urban Justice Ctr -123 William -NY 10038 **Fx:**(212) 533-4598
(212) 526-4123 ..**Whitman**, Bradley A '92 Barclays Capital Inc -745 7th Av -NY 10019
(212) 314-8000 ..**Whitman**, Brent C '89 Capgemini NA -623 5th Av -NY 10022
(212) 450-4000 ..**Whitman**, Chas S III '67 SrCnsl Davis P&W LLP -450 Lex Av -NY 10017
(212) 446-4800 ..**Whitman**, Devora '09 %Kirkland & E LLP -153 E 53rd -NY 10022
(212) 894-7200 ..**Whitman**, Johnston deForest Jr. '95 (Entwistle & C LLP) -280 Park Av -NY 10017
(631) 864-0910 ..**Whitman**, Kenneth F '99 -20 Hills Park Ln -Smithtwn 11787 **Fx:**979-5251
(212) 290-4700 ..**Whitman**, Lois '77 %Human Rights Watch -350 5th Av -NY 10118 **Fx:**736-1300
(914) 846-7000 ..**Whitman**, Paul B '02 %NY Life Ins -1 Rockwood Rd -Sleepy Hollow 10591 **Fx:**846-4755
(212) 556-2100 ..**Whitman**, Robt A '92 (King & S) -1185 Av of Amer -NY 10036
(212) 218-5500 ..**Whitman**, Robt S '98 (Seyfarth S LLP) -620 8th Av -NY 10018
(212) 744-8181 ..**Whitman**, Torrey L '77 %China Institute -125 E 65th -NY 10065
(631) 331-5272 ..**Whitman**, Wm A '83 -4400 Nesconset Hwy -Pt Jffrsn Sta 11776
(212) 775-8700 ..**Whitmer**, Fredk L '75 (Kilpatrick S,LLP) -31 W 52nd -NY 10019
(212) 468-8000 ..**Whitney**, Craig B '06 %Morrison & F LLP -1290 Av of Amer -NY 10104
(212) 790-9200 ..**Whitney**, Dorothy R '80 OfCnsl Cowan L&L,PC -1133 Av of Amer -NY 10036
(585) 223-2170 ..**Whitney**, Douglas W '67 -12 Plsnt -Fairprt 14450 **Fx:**223-9072
(212) 801-3153 ..**Whitney**, Eric N '08 (Greenberg T,LLP) -200 Park Av -NY 10166
(212) 637-3790 ..**Whitney**, Janice '82 %EPA -290 Bway -NY 10007 **Fx:**637-3772
(212) 858-1000 ..**Whitney**, Jonathan B '82 (Pillsbury WSP LLP) -1540 Bway -NY 10036
(212) 248-3140 ..**Whitney**, Jos J '06 %Drinker B&R LLP -140 Bway -NY 10005
(212) 902-0611 ..**Whitney**, Kevin N '88 %Goldman Sachs -1 NY Plz -NY 10004
(718) 286-6000 ..**Whitney**, Michl R '02 DA -125-01 Qns Blvd -Kew Gdns 11415
(212) 530-1800 ..**Whitney**, Nicholas A '99 Cnsl Richards K&O LLP -1 World Fncl Ctr -NY 10281
(516) 829-9490 ..**Whitney**, Richd A '67 -525 Nrthrn Blvd -Gt Neck 11021 **Fx:**466-6958
(518) 436-0751 ..**Whitney**, Samantha L '07 %Hinman S PC -121 State -Albany 12207
(212) 486-1455 ..**Whitney**, Thos J '05 %Post PGM&S,PA -575 Mad Av -NY 10022
(212) 701-3000 ..**Whitney**, Wm H '09 %Cahill G&R LLP -80 Pine -NY 10005 **Fx:**269-5420
(917) 603-8395 ..**Whitsett**, Clark A '06 -112-14 84th Av -Richmnd Hll 11418
(212) 290-4700 ..**Whitson**, Sarah Leah '92 %Human Rights Watch -350 5th Av -NY 10118 **Fx:**736-1300
(212) 335-9000 ..**Whitt**, Chas R '00 %DA -1 Hogan Pl -NY 10013
(212) 708-3355 ..**Whitt**, Sharon J '92 %Showtime Networks Inc -1633 Bway -NY 10019 **Fx:**708-1391
(212) 310-8000 ..**Whittaker**, Donald R '83 Cnsl Weil G&M LLP -767 5th Av -NY 10153
(212) 403-1000 ..**Whittaker**, Keola R '08 %Wachtell LR&K -51 W 52nd -NY 10019
(212) 576-7455 ..**Whittaker**, Lori S '97 %NY Life Ins -51 Mad Av -NY 10010 **Fx:**447-0569
(212) 756-2000 ..**Whittaker**, Megan Hayes '09 %Schulte R&Z LLP -919 3rd Av -NY 10022
(718) 590-3356 ..**Whittaker**, Patricia A '89 Family Ct -900 Sheridan Av -Bronx 10451
(212) 697-3122 ..**Whittaker**, Robt T '76 (Martin C&B LLP) -220 E 42nd -NY 10017
(212) 310-8000 ..**Whittaker**, Zillah K '08 %Weil G&M LLP -767 5th Av -NY 10153
(212) 318-6000 ..**Whittal**, Danl J '10 %Paul HJ&W LLP -75 E 55th -NY 10022
(212) 701-3000 ..**Whittemore**, Caroline Spindler '06 %Cahill G&R LLP -80 Pine -NY 10005 **Fx:**269-5420
(716) 652-9560 ..**Whittemore**, David S '94 %Bennett D&K,LLP -681 Main -E Aurora 14052
(516) 883-9500 ..**Whittemore**, Reed P '76 -14 Vanderventer Av -Pt Wash 11050 **Fx:**883-9508
(917) 225-4035 ..**Whitten**, Richd '96 -Bx231067 -NY 10023
(914) 741-6100 ..**Whittington**, Jeffrey S '98 %Kaufman B&R -200 Summit Lk Dr -Valhalla 10595
(212) 474-1000 ..**Whittington**, Saml J '09 %Cravath S&M LLP -825 8th Av -NY 10019
(914) 681-0444 ..**Whitton**, Christopher J '94 (Rende R&D,LLP) -202 Mamaroneck Av -White Plns 10601
(212) 902-1000 ..**Whitworth**, G Scott '03 %Goldman Sachs & Co -85 Broad -NY 10004
(212) 403-1000 ..**Whitworth**, J Bryan '69 OfCnsl Wachtell LR&K -51 W 52nd -NY 10019
(212) 294-6700 ..**Whitworth**, Paul J '09 %Winston & S -200 Park Av -NY 10166
(212) 922-9700 ..**Whooley**, Cornelius V '81 %1st Amer Title -633 3rd Av -NY 10017 **Fx:**922-0881
(212) 693-0085 ..**Whooley**, Kathleen E '09 Appellate Advocates -2 Rector -NY 10006 **Fx:**693-0878
(212) 225-2000 ..**Whoriskey**, Neil '92 (Cleary GS&H) -1 Lbrty Plz -NY 10006
(315) 472-1175 ..**Whritenour**, Matthew E '89 (Knych & W,LLC) -300 S State -Syracuse 13202
(914) 422-3900 ..**Whyatt**, Thos E '94 (Oxman TKW&G LLP) -120 Bloomingdale Rd -White Plns 10605
(315) 682-3850 ..**Whyland**, Christopher M '91 -4500 Brickyard Falls Rd -Manlius 13104 **Fx:**682-3851
(212) 284-2587 ..**Whyte**, Jeffrey R '97 Jefferies & Co -520 Mad Av -NY 10022
(516) 746-3500 ..**Whyte**, Marsha S '00 %Brand G&B,PC -600 Old Cntry Rd -Gdn Cty 11530
(212) 859-8000 ..**Whyte**, Megan K '06 %Fried FHS&J LLP -1 NY Plz -NY 10004
(212) 553-9145 ..**Whyte**, Rudyard F '86 Cochran Firm -233 Bway -NY 10279
(212) 446-4800 ..**Whyte**, Sara E '09 %Kirkland & E LLP -153 E 53rd -NY 10022
(585) 356-9304 ..**Wiater**, Mary Ann E '83 -1474 Indn Falls Rd -Corfu 14036
(212) 637-2307 ..**Wible**, Brent S '04 US Atty -1 St Andrews Plz -NY 10007
(212) 687-7410 ..**Wich**, Scott M '97 (Clifton B&D,LLP) -420 Lex Av -NY 10170
(716) 845-8948 ..**Wicher**, Camille P '89 %Roswell Park Cancer Inst -Elm & Carlton -Buffalo 14263
(845) 368-1710 ..**Wichler**, Ranan J '84 (Wichler & G,PC) -400 Rella Blvd -Suffern 10901 **Fx:**368-1470
(212) 323-8596 ..**Wichman**, Karin E '01 Creditex Grp Inc -875 3rd Av -NY 10022
(716) 683-3338 ..**Wick**, Edmund V '82 %Wick & W -5070 Bway -Depew 14043 **Fx:**681-2447
(716) 683-3338 ..**Wick**, Elaine Kupp '53 (Wick & W) -5070 Bway -Depew 14043 **Fx:**681-2447
(716) 683-3338 ..**Wick**, Henry S '51 (Wick & W) -5070 Bway -Depew 14043 **Fx:**681-2447
(212) 767-8731 ..**Wick**, Kelly L '01 Spike TV Ntwrk -345 Hudson -NY 10014
(716) 847-8400 ..**Wick**, Sharon L '85 (Phillips L LLP) -3400 HSBC Ctr -Buffalo 14203
(585) 343-0055 ..**Wicka**, Karen K '97 Genesee Community Cllg -1 Cllg Rd -Batavia 14020
(716) 849-6500 ..**Wicka**, Kevin P '97 (Brown & T,LLC) -14 Lafayette Sq -Buffalo 14203
(518) 372-5465 ..**Wickerham**, Richd D '76 -28 Jay Bx1167 -Schnctdy 12301 **Fx:**372-5525
(212) 239-4495 ..**Wickeri**, Elisabeth '05 Human Rts in China -350 5th Av -NY 10118
(212) 448-1100 ..**Wickersham**, Theo S '65 (McLaughlin & S,LLP) -260 Mad Av -NY 10016
(212) 230-1300 ..**Wickersham**, Thos M '00 (Beigelman F&F,PC) -100 Wall -NY 10005 **Fx:**230-1090
(518) 746-2216 ..**Wickes**, Roger A '93 Cnty Atty -383 Bway -Ft Edward 12828 **Fx:**746-2137
(631) 385-5051 ..**Wickesser**, Paul A '98 -502 Adams -Centerprt 11721 **Fx:**385-5052
(631) 232-2400 ..**Wickey**, Beth M '78 %Nassau/Sfflk Law Srv -1757 Vets Hwy -Islandia 11749 **Fx:**232-2489
(212) 733-3059 ..**Wick-Gilroy**, Esther S '01 Pfizer,Inc -235 E 42nd -NY 10017
(631) 298-8353 ..**Wickham**, Abigail A '77 (Wickham BG&G,PC) -13015 Main Rd Bx1424 -Mattituck 11952
(631) 298-8353 ..**Wickham Bressler Gordon & Geasa, PC** -13015 Main Rd Bx1424 -Mattituck 11952 **Fx:**298-8565
(631) 249-9480 ..**Wickham Bressler Gordon & Geasa, PC** -275 Broad Hollow Rd -Melvll 11747 **Fx:**249-9484
(718) 654-8988 ..**Wickham**, Carol M '79 %Koors & J -4234 Viero Av -Bronx 10470
(585) 381-2021 ..**Wickins & Ashnault** -1828 Penfld Rd -Penfld 14526 **Fx:**383-8423
(718) 858-1443 ..**Wickline**, Donovan L '99 (D Wickline,PC) -45 Pineapple -Brklyn 11201 **Fx:**625-6141
(212) 909-6000 ..**Wicklund**, David W '04 %Debevoise & P LLP -919 3rd Av -NY 10022
(212) 530-1800 ..**Wicklund**, Janine Ivanova '05 %Richards K&O LLP -1 World Fncl Ctr -NY 10281
(212) 785-9444 ..**Wickman**, Victoria '02 -7 Dey -NY 10007
(212) 248-3170 ..**Wickouski**, M Stephanie '00 %Drinker B&R LLP -140 Bway -NY 10005
(845) 758-8893 ..**Wicks**, Douglas F '67 (Walsh W&S) -7405 S Bway -Red Hook 12571
(516) 227-0700 ..**Wicks**, James M '89 (Farrell F,PC) -1320 RXR Plz -Uniondale 11556 **Fx:**336-2204
(631) 266-2820 ..**Wicks**, James R '86 -31 Cedar Rd -E Northprt 11731
(585) 325-6070 ..**Wicks**, Jeffrey '84 -36 W Main -Rchstr 14614
(212) 530-5000 ..**Wicks**, Ronan M '97 (Milbank TH&M LLP) -1 Chase Manh Plz -NY 10005
(914) 347-1292 ..**Wicks**, Stephanie C '10 %Rosenthal & M,LLP -45 Knollwood Rd -Elmsfrd 10523
(212) 606-7175 ..**Wickstrom**, Daryl S '94 %Sotheby's,Inc -1334 York Av -NY 10021 **Fx:**606-7574
(212) 406-4848 ..**Wickstrom**, Heidi L '08 %G Pillersdorf & Assoc,PC -225 Bway -NY 10007 **Fx:**406-5884
(718) 590-6213 ..**Wiczyk**, Dana J '07 %Law Dept -198 E 161st -Bronx 10451 **Fx:**590-2686
(718) 590-2000 ..**Wiczyk**, Omer '05 %DA -198 E 161st -Bronx 10451 **Fx:**590-6477
(212) 569-1555 ..**Widaen**, Eliot '00 -81 Seaman Av -NY 10034
(212) 489-1400 ..**Widell**, Alexander D '91 (Bickel & B) -767 5th Av -NY 10153
(718) 722-3100 ..**Wideman**, Jamila A '08 Leg Aid -111 Lvngstn -Brklyn 11201
(212) 326-2000 ..**Widen**, R Scott '90 Cnsl O'Melveny & M LLP -7 Times Sq -NY 10036
(212) 309-6000 ..**Wider**, Jedd H '93 (Morgan L&B LLP) -101 Park Av -NY 10178
(716) 938-9111 ..**Widger**, Jennifer A '94 OCA -303 Court -Little Vly 14755
(585) 263-1000 ..**Widger**, Stanley W Jr. '76 (Nixon P LLP) -1100 Clinton Sq -Rchstr 14604
(845) 634-3627 ..**Widholm**, Christopher T '96 %Leg Aid -2 Congers Rd -New Cty 10956 **Fx:**634-8505
(631) 853-5761 ..**Widirstky**, James A '84 %Cnty Atty -400 Carleton Av -Central Islip 11722 **Fx:**853-7788
(212) 925-6635 ..**Widiss**, Deborah A '00 Legal Momentum -395 Hudson -NY 10014
(212) 307-3169 ..**Widlitz**, Evan S '79 Weld Ltd -445 Park Av -NY 10022
(631) 427-3533 ..**Widlitz**, Stephen I '76 (Widlitz & S,PC) -700 NY Av -Huntngtn 11743
(631) 265-7200 ..**Widmaier**, Kurt P '93 (Russo KW&C) -400 Townline Rd -Hauppauge 11788
(212) 478-0618 ..**Widmann**, Douglas J '95 DE Shaw & Co,LP -120 W 45th -NY 10036
(212) 677-1900 ..**Widmann**, Miriam A '96 Rainforest Alliance -665 Bway -NY 10012 **Fx:**677-2187
(201) 401-3058 ..**Widmann**, Theresa L '00 -4 St Marks Pl -NY 10003 **Fx:**(419) 593-6161
(212) 308-0888 ..**Widowski**, Esther S '85 (Widowski & S LLP) -425 Mad Av -NY 10017
(212) 308-0888 ..**Widowski & Steinhart LLP** -425 Mad Av -NY 10017 **Fx:**308-7677
(212) 308-0888 ..**Widowski**, Stuart H '87 Cnsl Widowski & S LLP -425 Mad Av -NY 10017
(716) 753-4478 ..**Widrig**, Barbara L '92 %Dept Socl Srvcs -7 N Erie -Mayvll 14757 **Fx:**753-4444
(718) 888-9500 ..**Wie**, Jahyun '02 %Kim & C,LLP -158-14 Nrthrn Blvd -Flushng 11358
(212) 637-0206 ..**Wiebe**, Virgil O '95 %Hon JC Francis IV -500 Pearl -NY 10007
(212) 406-9606 ..**Wieber**, A Christopher '88 %M Scherzer -7 Dey -NY 10007 **Fx:**964-6903
(716) 692-3400 ..**Wiech**, Benjamin A '74 -15 Webster -N Tonawanda 14120 **Fx:**692-1996
(212) 715-9438 ..**Wieckowski**, Elizabeth M '96 Kramer LN&F LLP -1177 Av of Amer -NY 10036 **Fx:**715-8000
(716) 849-6500 ..**Wieczkowski**, Jeffrey A '94 (Brown & T,LLC) -14 Lafayette Sq -Buffalo 14203

(585) 344-2550 .. **Wieczorek,** Stephen D '81 %Ofc Ct Admin -1 W Main -Batavia 14020
(516) 742-7742 .. **Wieczorek,** Valerie A '86 V Wieczorek,PC -100 Grdn City Plz -Gdn Cty 11530 **Fx:**742-7740
(212) 809-7800 .. **Wiedemann,** Paul M '88 %Jaffe & K,LLP -40 Wall -NY 10005
(212) 264-5503 .. **Wiedemer,** Christopher L '10 US Ct of Intl Trade -1 Fed Plz -NY 10278
(212) 373-3000 .. **Wieder,** Allen M '81 Cnsl Paul WRW&G LLP -1285 Av of Amer -NY 10019
(212) 840-1181 .. **Wieder,** Howard '06 -580 5th Av -NY 10036 **Fx:**504-8334
(718) 298-1615 .. **Wieder,** Howard L '79 Supreme Ct -2510 Court Sq -LIC 11101
(646) 386-4076 .. **Wieder,** Janice S '87 %Hon J Sudolnik -111 Centre -NY 10013
(914) 377-9000 .. **Wieder,** John Arthur '93 (Wieder & W,PC) -35 E Grassy Sprain Rd -Ynkrs 10710 **Fx:**377-1007
(212) 637-3184 .. **Wieder,** Marla E '94 %EPA -290 Bway -NY 10007 **Fx:**637-3104
(212) 726-6500 .. **Wieder,** Mary F '91 %GT Interactive Software -417 5th Av -NY 10016 **Fx:**679-3424
(212) 508-7392 .. **Wieder,** Michl '01 Brown Harris Stevens -770 Lex Av -NY 10065
(212) 479-6000 .. **Wieder,** Stephen A '90 SpclCnsl Cooley LLP -1114 Av of Amer -NY 10036
(914) 377-9000 .. **Wieder,** Steven T '93 (Wieder & W,PC) -35 E Grassy Sprain Rd -Ynkrs 10710 **Fx:**377-1007
(718) 237-3100 .. **Wiederhorn,** Leah '07 Leg Aid -111 Lvngstn -Brklyn 11201 **Fx:**250-4243
(212) 363-6900 .. **Wiederhorn,** Steven J '97 (Faust GS&B LLP) -2 Rector -NY 10006
(914) 681-0200 .. **Wiederkehr,** Evan '99 %DelBello DWW&W,LLP -1 N Lex Av -White Plns 10601
(914) 681-0200 .. **Wiederkehr,** Lee S '69 (DelBello DWW&W,LLP) -1 N Lex Av -White Plns 10601
(212) 409-3581 .. **Wiedman,** Mark K '98 Black Rock -40 E 52nd -NY 10022
(585) 454-5850 .. **Wiedman Vazzana Corcoran & Volta,PC** -5 S Fitzhugh -Rchstr 14614 **Fx:**454-1273
(516) 357-3000 .. **Wiedmann,** Amy S '02 %Rivkin R LLP -926 RXR Plz -Uniondale 11556
(914) 636-1201 .. **Wiegand,** Jeffrey P '83 -54 Bon Air Av -New Rchll 10804
(212) 526-0026 .. **Wiegenfeld,** Yoav '01 %Barclays Capital Inc -745 7th Av -NY 10019
(914) 332-0222 .. **Wieghaus,** Brian J '87 %Philips Electronics -345 Scarborough Rd Bx3001 -Briarclff Mnr 10510 **Fx:**332-0615
(212) 997-8541 .. **Wiegley,** Roger '82 Winterthur -11 Mad Av -NY 10010
(212) 238-3000 .. **Wieland,** Matthew A '86 (Emmet M&M,LLP) -120 Bway -NY 10271
(212) 450-4000 .. **Wieman,** Lawr E '86 (Davis P&W LLP) -450 Lex Av -NY 10017
(212) 458-1221 .. **Wieman,** Marc E '82 %AIG -175 Water -NY 10038
(917) 551-1300 .. **Wien,** Howard G '95 %Koehler & I LLP -61 Bway -NY 10006
(212) 508-6700 .. **Wien,** Michl S '79 (Tannenbaum HS&H LLP) -900 3rd Av -NY 10022
(914) 907-9528 .. **Wien,** Robt W '77 -24 James Rd -Mt Kisco 10549 **Fx:**242-6221
(845) 634-7287 .. **Wienberg,** Christine K '98 C Wienberg,PC -37 Congers Rd -New Cty 10956
(716) 845-7465 .. **Wiencek,** John S '92 %Family Ct -1 Niagara Plz -Buffalo 14202 **Fx:**858-6293
(716) 841-2105 .. **Wiencek,** Mark A '84 %HSBC Bank -1 HSBC Ctr -Buffalo 14203 **Fx:**841-5087
(212) 836-1302 .. **Wiener,** Allison Merril '95 -130 E 59th -NY 10022 **Fx:**888-7538
(212) 644-4420 .. **Wiener,** Andrew '96 %Fabiani C&H,LLP -570 Lex Av -NY 10022
(718) 875-1552 .. **Wiener,** Arthur G '69 -166 Montague -Brklyn 11201
(212) 446-4752 .. **Wiener,** Beth T '95 Kirkland & E LLP -153 E 53rd -NY 10022
(212) 984-7878 .. **Wiener,** Bruce H '77 (Warshaw BCS&K,LLP) -555 5th Av -NY 10017
(914) 381-2066 .. **Wiener,** Cary R '80 %Pantaenius America Ltd -500 Mamaroneck Av -Harrison 10528 **Fx:**381-2052
(516) 599-3700 .. **Wiener,** Danl E '87 %41 Assoc -99 W Hawthorne Av -Vly Stream 11580
(516) 742-1212 .. **Wiener,** Edw A '92 (Stein W&R) -1 Old Cntry Rd -Carle Pl 11514
(212) 977-9700 .. **Wiener,** Elliot J '77 (Phillips N LLP) -666 5th Av -NY 10103
(212) 290-2800 .. **Wiener,** Fredk P '79 -1220 Bway -NY 10001 **Fx:**967-1112
(212) 962-1234 .. **Wiener,** Glen A '86 -1325 Av of Amer -NY 10019
(212) 848-4000 .. **Wiener,** Ira E '77 Shearman & S LLP -599 Lex Av -NY 10022
(212) 313-1200 .. **Wiener,** Jack R '87 SIFMA -120 Bway -NY 10271 **Fx:**313-1301
(212) 880-6000 .. **Wiener,** Jonathan B '02 (Torys LLP) -237 Park Av -NY 10017
(212) 655-4000 .. **Wiener,** Jos S '96 %M Gershweir -120 Bway -NY 10271 **Fx:**655-5039
(212) 442-6840 .. **Wiener,** Majorie D '73 %Law Dept -52 Duane -NY 10007 **Fx:**442-6868
(516) 248-7844 .. **Wiener,** Melanie I '07 %Cobert H&H -1050 Franklin Av -Gdn Cty 11530
(212) 940-8800 .. **Wiener,** Meryl E '74 (Katten MR LLP) -575 Mad Av -NY 10022
(914) 476-2346 .. **Wiener,** Michl A '71 -707 Ynkrs Av -Ynkrs 10704 **Fx:**476-2950
(516) 731-3770 .. **Wiener,** Mitchell S '96 %Bestcare,Inc -3000 Hempstd Tpk -Levittwn 11756 **Fx:**731-9271
(212) 577-3688 .. **Wiener,** Paul M '89 %Leg Aid -199 Water -NY 10038 **Fx:**509-8431
(212) 687-6900 .. **Wiener,** Paul R '79 (Connell & W) -555 5th Av -NY 10017 **Fx:**687-6999
(212) 751-8290 .. **Wiener,** Richd N '65 -460 Park Av -NY 10022
(212) 969-3000 .. **Wiener,** Susan L '85 %Proskauer R LLP -1585 Bway -NY 10036
(716) 847-0650 .. **Wiens,** Wallace W '04 Leg Srvcs -237 Main -Buffalo 14203 **Fx:**847-0227
(585) 232-6500 .. **Wier,** David A '66 Cnsl Harter S&E LLP -1600 Bausch & Lomb Pl -Rchstr 14604
(212) 944-6611 .. **Wierbicki,** Barbara Y '92 (Tompkins & D,LLP) -5 Hanover Sq -NY 10004
(212) 373-3000 .. **Wiersma,** Lindsey L '06 %Paul WRW&G LLP -1285 Av of Amer -NY 10019
(212) 593-3000 .. **Wierzbicka-Turner,** Anna E '06 %Platzer SKLG&J,LLP -1065 Av of Amer -NY 10018
(716) 894-0235 .. **Wierzbicki,** Richd J '56 -1332 Walden Av -Cheektowaga 14211 **Fx:**894-1817
(212) 554-1400 .. **Wierzbowski,** Adam H '04 %Bernstein LB&G LLP -1285 Av of Amer -NY 10019
(718) 351-3000 .. **Wierzbowski,** Anthony E '89 (Fiore & W,PC) -623 N Railroad Av -Staten Isl 10304 **Fx:**351-6513
(212) 788-1409 .. **Wies,** Peter E '87 %Law Dept -100 Church -NY 10007 **Fx:**788-0367
(718) 746-3440 .. **Wiese,** Andrew P '04 %Sacco & F,LLP -141-07 20th Av -Whitestone 11357
(718) 590-7344 .. **Wiese,** Hillard '73 %Hon R Hayes -851 Grnd Cncrs -Bronx 10451
(212) 728-8000 .. **Wiesel,** Allan A '09 %Willkie F&G LLP -787 7th Av -NY 10019
(212) 558-4000 .. **Wiesel,** Laurent S '02 %Sullivan & C LLP -125 Broad -NY 10004
(718) 357-6536 .. **Wieselthier,** Sol A '58 OHA-SSA -Bx319300 -Jamaica 11431 **Fx:**357-7931
(212) 381-8774 .. **Wiesen,** Irving L '81 -420 Lex Av -NY 10170
(516) 742-2212 .. **Wiesen,** Kenneth B '83 (K Wiesen,PLLC) -1 Old Cntry Rd -Carle Pl 11514 **Fx:**747-6384
(212) 687-7410 .. **Wiesen,** Robt A '77 (Clifton B&D,LLP) -420 Lex Av -NY 10170
(212) 471-8479 .. **Wiesenberg,** Anja '94 %Herzfeld & R,PC -125 Broad -NY 10004
(212) 940-3136 .. **Wiesenberg,** Lauren E '81 (Nixon P LLP) -437 Mad Av -NY 10022
(718) 923-4206 .. **Wiesenfeld,** Dulcie T '77 %OTDA Fair Hearings -14 Boerum Pl -Brklyn 11201
(718) 286-6000 .. **Wiesenfeld,** Michl A '02 %DA -125-01 Qns Blvd -Kew Gdns 11415
(212) 328-6180 .. **Wiesenthal,** Lauren M '85 %CMW Lgl Search -845 3rd Av -NY 10022 **Fx:**328-6181
(716) 636-0273 .. **Wieser,** John D '01 -2350 N Forest Rd -Getzvll 14068
(212) 351-4000 .. **Wiesner,** Andrew J '07 %Gibson D&C LLP -200 Park Av -NY 10166
(646) 471-4000 .. **Wiesner,** Angela D '03 %PricewaterhouseCoopers LLP -300 Mad Av -NY 10017
(212) 326-3939 .. **Wiesner,** Danl C '04 %Jones D -222 E 41st -NY 10017
(212) 629-7575 .. **Wiess,** John R '87 %KA Rigby PLLC -19 Fulton -NY 10038
(212) 848-4000 .. **Wiest,** Quentin W III '10 Shearman & S LLP -599 Lex Av -NY 10022
(718) 875-8580 .. **Wieziolowski,** Frank '87 (Halpern B&D) -26 Court -Brklyn 11242
(212) 257-6800 .. **Wigdor,** Douglas H '94 (Thompson W&G LLP) -85 5th Av -NY 10003
(212) 490-1700 .. **Wiggin & Dana** -450 Lex Av -NY 10017 **Fx:**490-0536
(212) 563-1234 .. **Wiggin,** Thos B '93 T Wiggin PC -1 Penn Plz -NY 10119 **Fx:**(917) 591-5475
(212) 578-0659 .. **Wiggins,** Brett E '01 MetLife -1 Met Life Plz -LIC 11101
(212) 310-8000 .. **Wiggins,** Erin A '09 %Weil G&M LLP -767 5th Av -NY 10153
(516) 229-6000 .. **Wiggins,** Gene W '74 %R Lau & Assoc -300 Jericho Quad Bx9040 -Jericho 11753 **Fx:**229-6167
(212) 986-6000 .. **Wiggins,** Kenneth R '07 %Kleinberg KW&C,PC -551 5th Av -NY 10176
(607) 272-0479 .. **Wiggins & Kopko, LLP** -308 N Tioga -Ithaca 14850 **Fx:**273-0502
(607) 272-0479 .. **Wiggins,** Walter J '51 (Wiggins & K,LLP) -308 N Tioga -Ithaca 14850
(212) 270-2962 .. **Wigginton,** Eric F '97 JP Morgan Chase & Co -270 Park Av -NY 10017
(212) 869-7000 .. **Wigg-Maxwell,** Paul D '87 SpclCnsl Feldman W&S LLP -420 Lex Av -NY 10170
(212) 836-8000 .. **Wiggum,** Kacy E '10 Kaye S LLP -425 Park Av -NY 10022
(516) 466-4767 .. **Wigler,** Andrew J '91 -98 Cuttermill Rd -Gt Neck 11021 **Fx:**466-2215
(516) 466-4767 .. **Wigler,** Nancy D '91 %A Wigler -98 Cuttermill Rd -Gt Neck 11021 **Fx:**466-2215
(718) 286-6000 .. **Wigle-Weiss,** Karen '80 %DA -125-01 Qns Blvd -Kew Gdns 11415
(212) 940-8800 .. **Wigness,** Kristin C '96 (Katten MR LLP) -575 Mad Av -NY 10022
(631) 232-2400 .. **Wigutow,** Michl S '87 %Nassau/Sfflk Law Srv -1757 Vets Hwy -Islandia 11749 **Fx:**232-2489
(212) 696-4848 .. **Wiig,** Danl K '07 Mintz & G LLP -470 Park Av S -NY 10016
(212) 751-1700 .. **Wikler,** Irwin I '79 %Jaffe R&L LLP -880 3rd Av -NY 10022
(212) 270-6080 .. **Wikman,** Kathryn '86 %JP Morgan Chase & Co -270 Park Av -NY 10017
(212) 983-2929 .. **Wikstrom,** David '81 -565 5th Av -NY 10017 **Fx:**856-9494
(212) 705-7000 .. **Wilamowsky,** Steven '95 (Bingham M LLP) -399 Park Av -NY 10022
(212) 578-2211 .. **Wiland,** Alison M '02 %MetLife -27-01 Qns Plz N -LIC 11101
(718) 432-0500 .. **Wilansky,** Wayne M '85 (Krieger W&H) -5602 Bway -Bronx 10463
(607) 778-2403 .. **Wilber,** Jay L '87 Pub Def -45 Hawley Bx1766 -Bnghmtn 13902 **Fx:**778-2432
(585) 325-5432 .. **Wilborn,** Derrick R '95 -16 E Main -Rchstr 14614
(212) 858-7575 .. **Wilbraham,** Edw J '00 (Wilbraham L&B PC) -140 Bway -NY 10005
(212) 858-7575 .. **Wilbraham Lawler & Buba PC** -140 Bway -NY 10005 **Fx:**943-9246
(518) 373-0333 .. **Wilcenski,** Edw V '96 (Jones W&P PLLC) -5 Emma Ln -Clifton Pk 12065
(516) 357-3000 .. **Wilck,** David S '94 %Rivkin R LLP -926 RXR Plz -Uniondale 11556
(212) 358-0358 .. **Wilcke,** Heinrich C '87 %Performing Assets Corp -250 Mercer -NY 10012 **Fx:**358-0084
(212) 832-2000 .. **Wilcke,** Nandini R '04 %Trump Orgn -725 5th Av -NY 10022 **Fx:**935-0141
(212) 460-3241 .. **Wilcken,** Michl A '79 Con Ed -4 Irving Pl -NY 10003
(212) 490-2277 .. **Wilcomes,** David R '97 %NY Land Srvcs -630 3rd Av -NY 10017 **Fx:**490-8012
(212) 609-6800 .. **Wilcomes,** Joanne M '01 %McCarter & E,LLP -245 Park Av -NY 10167
(518) 271-1001 .. **Wilcox,** Chas J '72 -251 River Bx1260 -Troy 12181
(516) 798-1043 .. **Wilcox,** Christina A '02 %Sapienza & F -5550 Merrick Rd -Massapequa 11758 **Fx:**798-3566
(585) 395-0424 .. **Wilcox,** Christopher T '04 -109 Main -Brockprt 14420 **Fx:**395-1235
(518) 489-3790 .. **Wilcox,** Galen D '01 -5 Wilson -Albany 12207
(212) 627-8100 .. **Wilcox,** Gwynne A '96 (Levy R,PC) -80 8th Av -NY 10011
(212) 898-7996 .. **Wilcox,** James F '90 %Americhoice -7 Hanover Sq -NY 10004
(718) 237-3100 .. **Wilcox,** Jessa M Desimone '08 Leg Aid -111 Lvngstn -Brklyn 11201 **Fx:**250-4243
(518) 285-8999 .. **Wilcox,** Jessica R '98 Hon J Egan Jr -50 Chapel -Albany 12207
(212) 805-7000 .. **Wilcox,** John C '74 Georgeson Shareholder Communications -17 State -NY 10004
(212) 345-6418 .. **Wilcox,** Neil H '95 %Marsh USA -1166 Av of Amer -NY 10036 **Fx:**345-4808
(212) 474-1000 .. **Wilcox,** Robt B Jr. '08 %Cravath S&M LLP -825 8th Av -NY 10019
(518) 884-4770 .. **Wilcox,** Robt D '79 Cnty Atty -Cnty Mncpl Ctr -Ballston Spa 12020 **Fx:**884-4720
(212) 715-9100 .. **Wilcox,** Robin M '98 (Kramer LN&F,LLP) -1177 Av of Amer -NY 10036
(716) 849-1333 .. **Wilcox,** Roger W Jr. '89 SpclCnsl Lipsitz GSC LLP -42 Delaware Av -Buffalo 14202

(212) 270-2243 .. **Wilcox,** Ronald A '86 Chase Manhattan Bk -270 Park Av -NY 10017
(607) 272-2102 .. **Wild,** Hilary E '06 %Guttman & W -411 N Tioga -Ithaca 14850 **Fx:**272-2350
(716) 856-4200 .. **Wild,** Katherine E '05 %Gibson M&C,LLP -69 Delaware Av -Buffalo 14202
(212) 480-4000 .. **Wild,** Matthew S '95 Cnsl Levitt & K -40 Fulton -NY 10038 **Fx:**480-4444
(845) 986-6931 .. **Wild,** Max '62 -98 Distillery Rd -Warwick 10990
(516) 393-2200 .. **Wild,** Robt A '68 (Garfunkel W,PC) -111 Grt Nck Rd -Gt Neck 11021
(716) 691-5400 .. **Wild,** Tracey A '90 %NCO Fncl Sys Inc -150 Crosspoint Pkwy -Getzvll 14068
(212) 238-3000 .. **Wilde,** Bruce R '91 OfCnsl Emmet M&M,LLP -120 Bway -NY 10271
(914) 422-4450 .. **Wilde,** Christopher M '02 Riverkeeper,Inc -78 N Bway -White Plns 10603
(212) 720-5277 .. **Wilde,** Valerie K '98 Fed Reserve Bk of NY -33 Lbrty -NY 10045
(518) 449-3300 .. **Wilder,** David H '80 (Nolan & H,LLP) -39 N Pearl -Albany 12207
(212) 490-3000 .. **Wilder,** Ellyn B '07 %Wilson EME&D LLP -150 E 42nd -NY 10017
(212) 649-8757 .. **Wilder,** Inga-Kerstin '97 %Dechert LLP -1095 Av of Amer -NY 10036
(716) 853-6001 .. **Wilder,** J Jos '84 (Wilder & L,LLP) -403 Main at Court -Buffalo 14203
(716) 853-6001 .. **Wilder & Linneball,LLP** -403 Main at Court -Buffalo 14203 **Fx:**853-6002
(917) 421-4669 .. **Wilder,** Michl D '85 IRS -33 Maiden Ln -NY 10038
(631) 247-0404 .. **Wilder,** Myra M '08 %Jackson L LLP -58 S Srvc Rd -Melvll 11747
(212) 804-4200 .. **Wilder,** Robt E '81 (Mound CW&G) -One Bttry Pk Plz -NY 10004
(212) 539-2207 .. **Wilder,** Sidnie '90 %Barnes & Noble -33 E 17th -NY 10003
(212) 490-3000 .. **Wildermuth,** Bruce R '80 OfCnsl Wilson EME&D LLP -150 E 42nd -NY 10017
(212) 753-3468 .. **Wildes,** Amy Messer '91 %Wildes & W,PC -515 Mad Av -NY 10022
(212) 806-5400 .. **Wildes,** Denise K '91 SpclCnsl Stroock &S&L LLP -180 Maiden Ln -NY 10038
(212) 468-4800 .. **Wildes,** Joy J '93 %Davis & G LLP -1740 Bway -NY 10019
(212) 753-3468 .. **Wildes,** Leon '58 (Wildes & W,PC) -515 Mad Av -NY 10022
(212) 753-3468 .. **Wildes,** Michl J '91 (Wildes & W,PC) -515 Mad Av -NY 10022
(646) 878-0800 .. **Wildes,** Morey B '91 Pearl CZL,LLP -1500 Bway -NY 10036
(212) 753-3468 .. **Wildes & Weinberg,PC** -515 Mad Av -NY 10022 **Fx:**753-3866
(518) 377-6700 .. **Wildgrube,** Michelle H '93 (Cioffi SW PC) -2310 Nott E -Niskayuna 12309
(518) 234-2545 .. **Wildove,** Edw '78 -558 Main Bx117 -Cobleskill 12043 **Fx:**234-4865
(585) 428-5200 .. **Wildrickcole,** Dawn A '99 %Surrogates Ct -541 Hall of Justice -Rchstr 14614
(914) 642-4694 .. **Wildstein,** Kenneth B '87 IBM -1133 Wstchstr Av -White Plns 10604
(516) 466-1790 .. **Wildstein,** Steven '83 (S Wildstein,PC) -98 Cuttermill Rd -Gt Neck 11021 **Fx:**466-1795
(716) 633-1320 .. **Wile,** Jonathan B '90 -5500 Main -Williamsvll 14221
(212) 927-1344 .. **Wilen,** Donald '79 -116 Pinehurst Av -NY 10033
(212) 715-9100 .. **Wilen,** Jennifer A '10 Kramer LN&F,LLP -1177 Av of Amer -NY 10036
(212) 695-0060 .. **Wilens & Baker,PC** -450 7th Av -NY 10123 **Fx:**643-0237
(212) 695-0060 .. **Wilens,** Lawr M '72 (Wilens & B,PC) -450 7th Av -NY 10123
(212) 695-0060 .. **Wilens,** Michl B '97 %Wilens & B,PC -450 7th Av -NY 10123
(718) 222-8880 .. **Wilensky,** Brian E '93 %Jones JO -45 Main -Brklyn 11201
Wilensky, Joel E '75 -75 Modular Av -Commack 11725
(516) 248-8010 .. **Wilensky,** Kenneth B '81 (Vessa & W,PC) -626 RXR Plz -Uniondale 11556 **Fx:**522-2831
(212) 835-1635 .. **Wilensky,** Kenneth B '81 (Vessa & W,PC) -1 Penn Plz -NY 10119
(212) 422-0202 .. **Wilensky,** Margot N '09 %Sedgwick DM&A LLP -125 Broad -NY 10004
(212) 903-8700 .. **Wilensky,** Mark E '02 %Roberts & H,LLP -825 8th Av -NY 10019
(212) 973-8000 .. **Wilensky,** Saul '67 (Schnader HS&L LLP) -140 Bway -NY 10005
(212) 267-3091 .. **Wilentz Goldman & Spitzer** -110 William -NY 10038 **Fx:**267-3828
(914) 723-0394 .. **Wilentz,** Thos M '01 -75 S Bway -White Plns 10601
(212) 733-4210 .. **Wilenzick,** Marc '98 %Pfizer Inc -235 E 42nd -NY 10017
(212) 906-1200 .. **Wiles,** Allegra C '08 %Latham & W -885 3rd Av -NY 10022
(518) 473-1149 .. **Wiles,** Ben '76 %Dept Pub Srvc -3 ESP -Albany 12223
(315) 448-4815 .. **Wiles,** Christopher '72 %Dept of Law -615 Erie Blvd W -Syracuse 13204 **Fx:**448-4853
(212) 354-6510 .. **Wiles,** Michl B '03 Snug Harbor -165 W 46th -NY 10036
(212) 909-6000 .. **Wiles,** Michl E '79 (Debevoise & P LLP) -919 3rd Av -NY 10022
(716) 854-2620 .. **Wiles,** Wm P '80 (Brown & K,LLP) -1500 Lbrty Bldg -Buffalo 14202
(516) 294-5433 .. **Wilewicz,** Agnieszka A '08 %Ahmuty D&M -200 IU Willets Rd -Albertson 11507
(516) 877-7000 .. **Wiley,** Dennis J '07 %McCoyd P&R,LLP -1100 Franklin Av -Gdn Cty 11530
(212) 310-8000 .. **Wiley,** Erin K M '10 %Weil G&M LLP -767 5th Av -NY 10153
(518) 436-0786 .. **Wiley,** Stephen J '75 (Featherstonhaugh W&C,LLP) -99 Pine -Albany 12207
(212) 351-4000 .. **Wilf,** David M '96 (Gibson D&C LLP) -200 Park Av -NY 10166
(212) 297-5800 .. **Wilfert,** Amy Kohler '84 (Day P LLP) -7 Times Sq -NY 10036
(212) 464-1437 .. **Wilfert,** David J '83 JP Morgan Chase -270 Park Av -NY 10017
(718) 884-6600 .. **Wilford,** Andrew M '76 (KF Ross,PC) -5683 Riverdale Av #203 Bx900 -Bronx 10471 **Fx:**601-1099
(212) 528-2741 .. **Wilford,** Edw D '82 -20 Vesey -NY 10007
(917) 778-6600 .. **Wilgard,** Mark A '88 %J Toomey -485 Lex Av -NY 10017 **Fx:**778-7048
(516) 433-1917 .. **Wilgard,** Sanford A '59 -49 Cntry Dr -Plainvw 11803
(212) 885-5000 .. **Wilgus,** Lauren B '09 %Blank R LLP -405 Lex Av -NY 10174
(718) 260-2420 .. **Wilhelm,** Danl F '98 %Hon F Block -225 Cadman Plz E -Brklyn 11201
(212) 545-7373 .. **Wilhelm,** Kenneth A '71 -445 Park Av -NY 10022 **Fx:**545-9093
(212) 819-8200 .. **Wilhelm,** Peter E '08 %White & C LLP -1155 Av of Amer -NY 10036
(518) 371-2075 .. **Wilhelm,** Robt O '71 (Wilhelm Law Firm,PLLC) -Park Nine Plz Bx869 -Clifton Pk 12065 **Fx:**371-2440
(518) 719-3590 .. **Wilhelm,** Terry J '81 %DA -411 Main -Catskill 12414 **Fx:**719-3792
(212) 225-2000 .. **Wilhelm,** Thos E '08 %Cleary GS&H -1 Lbrty Plz -NY 10006
(212) 661-1888 .. **Wilinsky,** Thos Bartlett '92 (Biancone & W,LLP) -230 Park Av -NY 10169
(212) 421-2233 .. **Wilk Auslander LLP** -675 3rd Av -NY 10017 **Fx:**752-6380
(212) 421-2233 .. **Wilk,** Jack '84 (Wilk A LLP) -675 3rd Av -NY 10017
(516) 829-8100 .. **Wilk,** Jarah S '06 1st Rehab Life Ins -600 Nrthrn Blvd -Gt Neck 11021
(212) 977-9700 .. **Wilk,** John F '94 SpclCnsl Phillips N LLP -666 5th Av -NY 10103
(315) 724-4741 .. **Wilk,** John S '84 -2635 Genesee -Utica 13501
(212) 237-1000 .. **Wilk,** Robt G '85 %Windels ML&M,LLP -156 W 56th -NY 10019
(516) 683-0225 .. **Wilk,** Stephen W '64 -1600 Stewart Av -Westbury 11590 **Fx:**683-0510
(518) 257-1443 .. **Wilke,** Eric E '06 CSEA,Inc -143 Wshngtn Av Bx7125 -Albany 12224 **Fx:**449-1525
(914) 225-5550 .. **Wilke,** Michelle Roanne '97 Morgan Stanley -2000 Wstchstr Av -Purchase 10577
(646) 386-3600 .. **Wilkenfeld,** Saml E '99 %Supreme Ct-Law Dept -60 Centre -NY 10007
(585) 419-8800 .. **Wilkens,** Beth E '75 (Harris B PLLC) -99 Garnsey Rd -Pittsfrd 14534
(516) 394-4200 .. **Wilkens,** James F '82 Cnsl Duffy & D -1370 RXR Plz -Uniondale 11556
(585) 454-6480 .. **Wilkens,** Jeffrey M '75 (Osborn R&B,LLP) -45 Exchange Blvd -Rchstr 14614
(716) 679-7200 .. **Wilkens,** Kimberly Ann '93 %Evans & E -131 Temple -Fredonia 14063
(518) 374-1800 .. **Wilkens,** Timothy F '89 %Capasso & M LLP -215 State Bx1088 -Schnctdy 12301
(212) 577-3530 .. **Wilker,** Dale A '85 %Leg Aid -199 Water -NY 10038 **Fx:**425-2465
(212) 361-8172 .. **Wilker,** P Jay '69 Ct of Claims -26 Bway -NY 10004 **Fx:**361-8103
(516) 365-9802 .. **Wilkes,** Caleb D '09 %Collard & R,PC -1077 Nrthrn Blvd -Roslyn 11576
(914) 631-1500 .. **Wilkes,** David C '93 (Huff W LLP) -200 Wht Plns Rd -Tarrytwn 10591 **Fx:**631-1501
(212) 695-1950 .. **Wilkes,** Traci D '05 Willinger Talent Agency -875 Av of Amer -NY 10001
(212) 553-6615 .. **Wilkey,** Alison '05 Youth Represent -346 Bway -NY 10013
(212) 513-3200 .. **Wilkie,** Austin T '88 (Holland & K LLP) -31 W 52nd -NY 10019
(516) 564-8301 .. **Wilkie,** Diane E '83 (Wilkie & W) -33 Hilton Av -Hempstd 11550 **Fx:**538-0161
(845) 338-4993 .. **Wilkie & Graff LLC** -78 Main Bx4148 -Kingston 12402 **Fx:**338-9358
(516) 564-8301 .. **Wilkie,** Robt A '82 (Wilkie & W) -33 Hilton Av -Hempstd 11550 **Fx:**538-0161
(212) 606-4114 .. **Wilkin,** Marissa A '06 Sothebys Intl Realty Inc -38 E 61st -NY 10065
(516) 327-6315 .. **Wilkins,** Brian T '09 BWD Grp LLC -113 S Srvc Rd -Jericho 11753
(716) 852-5875 .. **Wilkins,** Christopher E '89 (Feldman K LLP) -110 Pearl -Buffalo 14202
(212) 310-2231 .. **Wilkins,** Clifford E Jr. '95 %Colgate-Palmolive -300 Park Av -NY 10022 **Fx:**310-3230
(212) 809-0000 .. **Wilkins,** Jesse T '87 (Preston WM&E,PLLC) -65 Bway -NY 10006 **Fx:**809-4753
(518) 523-1409 .. **Wilkins,** John T '83 (Wilkins & G,PLLC) -2461 Main -Lk Placid 12946 **Fx:**523-1190
(212) 553-8300 .. **Wilkins,** Robt D '95 %Cohen K & Assoc -2 Park Av -NY 10016 **Fx:**553-8721
(212) 964-7400 .. **Wilkins,** Stanley '54 Smith MDWY&Y,PC -111 John -NY 10038
(212) 710-3900 .. **Wilkins,** Stephanie A '03 %Clyde & Co US LLP -405 Lex Av -NY 10174 **Fx:**710-3950
(212) 277-4000 .. **Wilkins,** Timothy A '94 (Freshfields BD LLP) -520 Mad Av -NY 10022
(212) 267-3091 .. **Wilkinson,** Anthony E '91 %Wilentz G&S -110 William -NY 10038 **Fx:**(732) 726-4734
(607) 274-5461 .. **Wilkinson,** Gwendolyn Parker '89 DA -320 N Tioga -Ithaca 14850 **Fx:**274-5429
(518) 449-8893 .. **Wilkinson,** Jacob R '08 %Wilson EME&D LLP -677 Bway -Albany 12207
(585) 591-1100 .. **Wilkinson,** Jennifer M '05 (Dadd N&W) -11 Exchange Bx238 -Attica 14011
(212) 751-2700 .. **Wilkinson,** John H '65 %JAMS -620 8th Av -NY 10018 **Fx:**751-4099
(631) 444-0260 .. **Wilkinson,** Kari E '05 %DEC -SUNY Campus 50 Circle Rd -Stony Brk 11790 **Fx:**444-0348
(212) 521-6467 .. **Wilkinson,** Lillian C '04 Centerline Captial Grp Inc -625 Mad Av -NY 10022
(518) 402-9185 .. **Wilkinson,** Lisa A '93 %DEC -625 Bway -Albany 12233 **Fx:**402-9018
(212) 408-5100 .. **Wilkinson,** Phoebe A '94 (Chadbourne & P LLP) -30 Rckfllr Plz -NY 10112
(516) 827-4900 .. **Wilkinson,** Robt E '96 Cameron Engineering -100 Sunnyside Blvd -Woodbury 11797
(516) 574-6144 .. **Wilkinson,** Terri J '97 %JP Morgan Chase -1985 Marcus Av -New Hyde Pk 11040
(518) 862-3080 .. **Wilkinson,** Thos J '84 (Hanlon V&W) -94 New Karner Rd -Albany 12203
(516) 479-6300 .. **Wilkinson,** Wade C '06 %Silverman A LLP -100 Jericho Quad -Jericho 11753
(212) 285-0510 .. **Wilkofsky Friedman Karel & Cummins** -299 Bway -NY 10007 **Fx:**285-0531
(212) 285-0510 .. **Wilkofsky,** Jonathan '82 (Wilkofsky FK&C) -299 Bway -NY 10007
(212) 640-5732 .. **Wilkov,** Marcy E '81 %Amer Exp -200 Vesey -NY 10285
(516) 876-0720 .. **Wilkow,** Mark H '92 -99 Jericho Tpk -Jericho 11753 **Fx:**908-4613
(718) 701-5450 .. **Wilks,** Franklin '84 -370 E 149th -Bronx 10455 **Fx:**255-5985
(845) 657-5882 .. **Wilks,** Kerri L '93 -75 Traver Hllw Rd -Boiceville 12412 **Fx:**657-5882
(516) 877-2225 .. **Will,** Alfred J '76 (Badiak & W,LLP) -106 3rd -Mineola 11501
(716) 852-3540 .. **Will,** Pauline Costanzo '97 (Watson BCJ&S) -12 Fountain Plz -Buffalo 14202
(212) 408-5100 .. **Willan,** Paige M '09 %Chadbourne & P LLP -30 Rckfllr Plz -NY 10112
(347) 404-9133 .. **Willard,** Elizabeth Anne '95 %Civil Ct -141 Lvngstn -Brklyn 11201 **Fx:**(718) 643-3733
(716) 884-5725 .. **Willbern,** Beaufort N '77 -381 Hudson -Buffalo 14201
(914) 285-9570 .. **Willcox,** Jon N '73 -1 N Bway -White Plns 10601 **Fx:**285-1501
(212) 808-8100 .. **Wille,** Brian C '87 (Kostelanetz & F,LLP) -7 Wrld Trd Ctr -NY 10007

(212) 885-5000 .. **Willecke,** Tara Jones '03 %Blank R LLP -405 Lex Av -NY 10174
(914) 238-5084 .. **Willemin,** Kathleen M '80 -76 Cross Ridge Rd -Chappaqua 10514 **Fx:**238-0184
(212) 306-1109 .. **Willen,** Marija '90 Amer Stock Exch -86 Trinity Pl -NY 10006
(212) 813-8800 .. **Willenbacher,** Eric C '06 %Goodwin P LLP -620 8th Av -NY 10018
(212) 449-9652 .. **Willenbucher,** Marguerite C '81 %Merrill Lynch -220 Bway -NY 10038
(212) 735-3000 .. **Willenken,** Karen E '00 Cnsl Skadden ASM&F LLP -4 Times Sq -NY 10036
(718) 768-6792 .. **Willens,** Jonathan A '87 (J Willens LLC) -449 5th -Brklyn 11215 **Fx:**(800) 879-7938
(914) 576-5874 .. **Willensky,** Beth A '80 -225 Overlook Rd -New Rchll 10804 **Fx:**632-3442
(212) 268-9445 .. **Willensky,** Kerri S '94 -224 W 35th -NY 10001 **Fx:**268-9441
(315) 379-2103 .. **Willer,** David D '90 %Dept Soc Srvcs -6 Judson -Canton 13617 **Fx:**386-2782
(212) 722-2000 .. **Willer,** Edlyn L '96 %Leg Aid -230 E 106th -NY 10029 **Fx:**876-5365
(212) 686-7533 .. **Willert,** Timothy F '79 -292 Mad Av -NY 10017 **Fx:**686-7602
(718) 875-8493 .. **Willett,** Beverly A '82 -414 Clinton -Brklyn 11231 **Fx:**875-8493
(716) 853-6529 .. **Willett,** Christopher C '92 1st Amer Title -110 Pearl -Buffalo 14202 **Fx:**856-9870
(212) 715-1001 .. **Willett,** John A '73 (Arnold & P LLP) -399 Park Av -NY 10022
(212) 735-3000 .. **Willett,** Kamali P '07 %Skadden ASM&F LLP -4 Times Sq -NY 10036
(716) 856-5500 .. **Willett,** Michl J '85 (Damon M LLP) -200 Delaware Av -Buffalo 14202
(585) 419-8800 .. **Willett,** Thos E '73 (Harris B PLLC) -99 Garnsey Rd -Pittsfrd 14534
(212) 940-8800 .. **Willey,** Jos V '84 (Katten MR LLP) -575 Mad Av -NY 10022
(212) 446-4800 .. **Willgoos,** Christine '02 (Kirkland & E LLP) -153 E 53rd -NY 10022
(212) 455-2000 .. **Williams,** Abigail W '09 %Simpson T&B LLP -425 Lex Av -NY 10017
(212) 374-3441 .. **Williams,** Adrienne D '84 %NYC Dept Educ-OLS -52 Chmbrs -NY 10007 **Fx:**374-5596
(718) 643-6246 .. **Williams,** Adrienne E '94 %Hon G Dabiri -360 Adams -Brklyn 11201
(716) 858-2424 .. **Williams,** Alan J '09 %DA -25 Delaware Av -Buffalo 14202 **Fx:**858-7425
(212) 969-3000 .. **Williams,** Allan R '76 (Proskauer R LLP) -1585 Bway -NY 10036
(212) 935-3000 .. **Williams,** Amy J '93 OfCnsl Mintz LCFG&P,PC -666 3rd Av -NY 10017
(212) 309-1000 .. **Williams,** Amy McDaniel '08 (Hunton & W) -200 Park Av -NY 10166
(212) 373-3000 .. **Williams,** Andre D '09 %Paul WRW&G LLP -1285 Av of Amer -NY 10019
(212) 246-7100 .. **Williams,** Andrea T '04 GNYHA Ventures Inc -555 W 57th -NY 10019 **Fx:**262-6350
(716) 829-6076 .. **Williams,** Ann Carol '94 SUNY Ofc Univ Cnsl -216 Harriaman Hall -Buffalo 14214
(585) 232-3051 .. **Williams,** Ann M '84 %Legal Srvcs -1 W Main -Rchstr 14614 **Fx:**232-5103
(607) 723-5341 .. **Williams,** Anne Samuelson '07 %Hinman H&K,LLP -80 Exchange Bx5250 -Bnghmtn 13902
(212) 335-4500 .. **Williams,** Anthony '74 (DLA Piper LLP) -1251 Av of Amer -NY 10020
(315) 331-1334 .. **Williams,** Arthur B '82 (Nesbitt & W) -180 E Union Bx226 -Newark 14513 **Fx:**331-1033
(212) 579-4625 .. **Williams,** Belinda L '89 Reese R LLP -875 6th Av 18th Fl -NY 10001 **Fx:**253-4272
(212) 883-6500 .. **Williams,** Benjamin M '09 %Podell SS&B,LLP -605 3rd Av -NY 10158
(718) 248-1358 .. **Williams,** Bernard Jr. '03 Citicorp Invstmnts Srvcs -1 Court Sq -LIC 11120
(212) 566-2424 .. **Williams,** Bryan R '82 (Pettus & W,PLLC) -150 Bway -NY 10038 **Fx:**566-2443
(212) 872-9800 .. **Williams,** Carine '09 %Squire S&D LLP -30 Rckfllr Plz -NY 10112
(212) 545-0546 .. **Williams,** Carman Y '02 -344 E 28th -NY 10016 **Fx:**545-0546
(718) 459-6000 .. **Williams,** Carolyn L '02 %Pennisi D&N LLP -97-77 Qns Blvd -Rego Pk 11374
(212) 336-2000 .. **Williams,** Catherine A '04 %Patterson BW&T LLP -1133 Av of Amer -NY 10036
(718) 528-0038 .. **Williams,** Cathleen E '97 -197-19 119th Av -St Albans 11412 **Fx:**528-0047
(718) 222-2331 .. **Williams,** Cecilia R '06 %Law Dept -350 Jay -Brklyn 11201 **Fx:**222-2373
(212) 837-6000 .. **Williams,** Cecily C '04 %Hughes H&R LLP -1 Bttry Pk Plz -NY 10004
(212) 610-6300 .. **Williams,** Chas D '99 (Allen & O) -1221 Av of Amer -NY 10020
(212) 382-0909 .. **Williams,** Chas E III '70 (Peckar & A,PC) -41 Mad Av -NY 10154
(718) 722-3100 .. **Williams,** Cheryl N '05 %Leg Aid -111 Lvngstn -Brklyn 11201 **Fx:**722-3093
(212) 577-3688 .. **Williams,** Cheryl P '94 %Leg Aid -199 Water -NY 10038 **Fx:**509-8431
(212) 895-6723 .. **Williams,** Christopher '81 Dresdner Bk -2 World Fncl Ctr -NY 10281
(212) 971-3645 .. **Williams,** Christopher R '89 -61 E 3rd -NY 10003
(212) 387-5158 .. **Williams,** Clifford K '88 AT&T -32 Av of Amer -NY 10013
(212) 310-3723 .. **Williams,** Courtney J '05 Colgate-Palmolive Co -300 Park Av -NY 10022
(212) 490-3000 .. **Williams,** Cruz M '05 %Wilson EME&D LLP -150 E 42nd -NY 10017
(212) 906-1200 .. **Williams,** Danica B '09 %Latham & W -885 3rd Av -NY 10022
(212) 436-1672 .. **Williams,** David A '94 %IRS-Crim Invstgtn Div -290 Bway -NY 10007
(914) 736-6648 .. **Williams,** David C '77 -8 Brook Ln -Cortlandt Manor 10567 **Fx:**737-8628
(212) 455-2000 .. **Williams,** David L '84 (Simpson T&B LLP) -425 Lex Av -NY 10017
(212) 653-8878 .. **Williams,** Dawanna L '95 -330 Mad Av -NY 10017 **Fx:**653-8879
(718) 298-8955 .. **Williams,** Deborah M '87 %Leg Aid -153-01 Jamaica Av -Jamaica 11432 **Fx:**657-0537
(716) 855-0203 .. **Williams,** Denetra D '08 Western NY Law Ctr -237 Main -Buffalo 14203 **Fx:**270-4005
(212) 980-9600 .. **Williams,** Dennis P '09 %Kaufman B&R -120 Bway -NY 10271
(212) 687-5464 .. **Williams,** Derek A '05 Cnsl JD Davis,PC -99 Park Av -NY 10016 **Fx:**557-0565
(518) 464-6770 .. **Williams,** Dina '08 %Thorn GT&B,LLP -5 Wembley Ct Bx15054 -Albany 12212
(212) 208-1469 .. **Williams,** Douglas '75 -140 Bway -NY 10005
(973) 491-3336 .. **Williams,** E Kenneth Jr. '84 (LeClairRyan,PC) -830 3rd Av -NY 10022 **Fx:**491-3555
(845) 291-2050 .. **Williams,** Eddie L '05 %DA -255-275 Main -Goshen 10924 **Fx:**291-2085
(212) 239-5500 .. **Williams,** Edw G '77 OfCnsl Stewart O,LLP -65 W 36th -NY 10018
(914) 846-3602 .. **Williams,** Elaine '82 NY Life Ins -1 Rockwood Rd -Sleepy Hollow 10591
(212) 408-2500 .. **Williams,** Eliot D '00 (Baker B,LLP) -30 Rckfllr Plz -NY 10112
(212) 839-5300 .. **Williams,** Elizabeth Poppe '08 %Sidley A LLP -787 7th Av -NY 10019
(718) 546-0347 .. **Williams,** Elvin V '90 NYC DOC -7520 Astoria Blvd -E Elmhrst 11370
(212) 298-5260 .. **Williams,** Eric S '01 Leg Aid -49 Thomas -NY 10013 **Fx:**298-5252
(516) 671-3207 .. **Williams,** Ernest J '52 -2 Eden Rock Dr -Locust Vly 11560
(631) 842-5931 .. **Williams,** Errol E '81 -2 Oak Rd -Amityvll 11701
(212) 808-8100 .. **Williams,** Esmonique '10 %Kostelanetz & F,LLP -7 Wrld Trd Ctr -NY 10007
(718) 254-6430 .. **Williams,** Evan C '97 %US Atty -271 Cadman Plz E -Brklyn 11201 **Fx:**254-6479
(518) 861-8560 .. **Williams,** Frank J Jr. '51 -160 Maple Av Bx477 -Altamont 12009
(518) 447-3200 .. **Williams,** G Kimball '81 (McNamee LT&W,PC) -677 Bway -Albany 12207
(315) 342-0162 .. **Williams,** Gay H '78 City Atty -13 W Oneida -Oswego 13126 **Fx:**342-8247
(718) 625-5860 .. **Williams & Geiger** -26 Court -Brklyn 11242
(212) 259-8000 .. **Williams,** George M Jr. '79 (Dewey & L LLP) -1301 Av of Amer -NY 10019
(585) 343-1486 .. **Williams,** Gerald O '55 (Williams Law Firm,LLP) -2 Court Street Plz Bx402 -Batavia 14021 **Fx:**343-1487
(315) 422-1391 .. **Williams,** Harrison V Jr. '59 (Green & S,PLLC) -One Lincoln Ctr #900 -Syracuse 13202
(516) 571-3140 .. **Williams,** Helena E '82 Ofc Cnty Exec -1 West -Mineola 11501
(585) 889-3000 .. **Williams,** Henry W Jr. '59 (Williams Law Ofc) -12 Rochester Bx8 -Scottsvll 14546 **Fx:**889-3044
(212) 468-8000 .. **Williams,** Hilary M '98 Morrison & F LLP -1290 Av of Amer -NY 10104
(646) 471-5087 .. **Williams,** J Martin '01 PricewaterhouseCoopers LLP -300 Mad Av -NY 10017
(518) 235-0827 .. **Williams,** J Richd '55 -130 Canvass -Cohoes 12047 **Fx:**235-2090
(212) 756-2000 .. **Williams,** James '03 %Schulte R&Z LLP -919 3rd Av -NY 10022
(718) 965-1979 .. **Williams,** James I '78 -363 6th Av -Brklyn 11215 **Fx:**965-1909
(315) 793-2225 .. **Williams,** James J '89 Dept of Law -207 Genesee -Utica 13501 **Fx:**793-2228
(315) 475-3127 .. **Williams,** James M '87 %Leg Srvcs -472 S Salina -Syracuse 13202 **Fx:**475-2706
(973) 538-6890 .. **Williams,** James R '71 (Jackson L LLP) -666 3rd Av -NY 10017
(646) 808-1559 .. **Williams,** James R III '06 Thumbplay,Inc -599 Bway -NY 10012
(212) 558-4000 .. **Williams,** James T '93 SpclCnsl Sullivan & C LLP -125 Broad -NY 10004
(518) 279-4730 .. **Williams,** Jane W '75 -132 Bellvw Rd -Troy 12180 **Fx:**279-4730
(212) 598-7536 .. **Williams,** Jared M '97 %Guardian Life Ins -7 Hanover Sq -NY 10004 **Fx:**677-4240
(212) 403-1000 .. **Williams,** Jason M '09 %Wachtell LR&K -51 W 52nd -NY 10019
(315) 853-4436 .. **Williams,** Jay G III '87 (Felt E,LLP) -4-6 N Park Row -Clinton 13323
(212) 889-2121 .. **Williams,** Jeanne-Marie '95 %Kellner HG&F -470 Park Av S -NY 10016
(212) 733-0744 .. **Williams,** Jeffery D '91 %Pfizer Inc -235 E 42nd -NY 10017
(212) 728-8000 .. **Williams,** Jeffrey A '08 %Willkie F&G LLP -787 7th Av -NY 10019
(516) 535-2882 .. **Williams,** Jeffrey G '87 TDK USA Corp -525 RXR Plz -Uniondale 11556
(212) 407-4000 .. **Williams,** Jennifer A '08 %Loeb & L,LLP -345 Park Av -NY 10154
(315) 474-7571 .. **Williams,** Jennifer Ploetz '00 %Mackenzie H LLP -101 S Salina Bx4967 -Syracuse 13221
(518) 862-1090 .. **Williams,** John G '92 %NYSERDA -17 Columbia Cir -Albany 12203 **Fx:**862-1091
(212) 610-6300 .. **Williams,** John R '01 (Allen & O) -1221 Av of Amer -NY 10020
(212) 558-5500 .. **Williams,** Jos P '93 %Weitz & L,PC -700 Bway -NY 10003
(212) 872-1000 .. **Williams,** Joshua R '04 -One Bryant Park -NY 10036 **Fx:**872-1002
(315) 448-8400 .. **Williams,** Juanita L '00 SpclCnsl Law Dept -233 E Wshngtn -Syracuse 13202 **Fx:**448-8381
(212) 310-8000 .. **Williams,** Julia S '06 %Weil G&M LLP -767 5th Av -NY 10153
(585) 352-2862 .. **Williams,** Karen J '04 Caldwell Manufctrng Co -2605 Manitou Rd -Rchstr 14624
(518) 585-2831 .. **Williams,** Karl G '92 %Moses Ludington Hsptl -2 Wickers -Ticonderoga 12883
(646) 833-0900 .. **Williams,** Kathleen Giles '05 %Tressler LLP -One Penn Plz -NY 10119
(716) 855-0203 .. **Williams,** Keisha A '09 Western NY Law Ctr -237 Main -Buffalo 14203 **Fx:**270-4005
(914) 995-4172 .. **Williams,** Kerrie N Roxroy '04 %DA -111 Martin Luther King Blvd -White Plns 10601 **Fx:**995-3363
(607) 763-9200 .. **Williams,** Kevin T '99 (Levene G&T,LLP) -BxF-1706 -Bnghmtn 13902
(212) 571-4235 .. **Williams,** Kim A '00 -30 Vesey -NY 10007
(845) 291-2670 .. **Williams,** Kimberly M '02 %Childrens Rts Society -213 W Main Bx1002 -Goshen 10924 **Fx:**291-2679
(212) 902-5915 .. **Williams,** Kyle R '02 %Goldman Sachs -1 NY Plz -NY 10004
(516) 298-9088 .. **Williams,** La Wanda J '01 -482 Pinebrook Av -W Hempstead 11552
(585) 385-7720 .. **Williams,** Leland T '82 -4030 East Av -Rchstr 14618
(516) 829-2940 .. **Williams,** Lisa M '04 %B Resnicoff -287 Nrthrn Blvd -Gt Neck 11021 **Fx:**829-0130
(914) 667-8338 .. **Williams,** Lyndon D '91 -10 Fiske Pl -Mt Vernon 10550
(607) 733-2105 .. **Williams,** Lynn C '02 Williams Capital Corp -215 W Water -Elmira 14901
(212) 732-6000 .. **Williams,** M Quentin '92 Cnsl McCarthy & K LLP -52 Duane -NY 10007

(212) 239-3680 .. **Williams,** Marc A '09 %Sim & P,LLP -450 7th Av -NY 10123 **Fx:**239-3683
(212) 909-6000 .. **Williams,** Marc A '10 %Debevoise & P LLP -919 3rd Av -NY 10022
(212) 450-4000 .. **Williams,** Marc O '99 (Davis P&W LLP) -450 Lex Av -NY 10017
(212) 940-8800 .. **Williams,** Margaret A '08 %Katten MR LLP -575 Mad Av -NY 10022
(631) 335-3749 .. **Williams,** Margarett M '06 -30 Eagle Cir -Bohemia 11716
(716) 373-0004 .. **Williams,** Mark S '87 (Pub Def) -175 N Union -Olean 14760 **Fx:**373-3462
(845) 291-2670 .. **Williams,** Marvin J '91 Childrens Rts Society -213 W Main Bx1002 -Goshen 10924 **Fx:**291-2679
(212) 335-9000 .. **Williams,** Matthew C '09 %DA -1 Hogan Pl -NY 10013
(212) 351-4000 .. **Williams,** Matthew J '99 (Gibson D&C LLP) -200 Park Av -NY 10166
(212) 657-0851 .. **Williams,** Melvin F Jr. '90 Citigroup -77 Water -NY 10005
(212) 558-4000 .. **Williams,** Meredith J '10 %Sullivan & C LLP -125 Broad -NY 10004
(716) 854-2020 .. **Williams,** Michl '05 (Cellino & B,PC) -350 Main -Buffalo 14202
(212) 941-9090 .. **Williams,** Michl G '87 %The Door -121 Av of Amer -NY 10013 **Fx:**941-0714
(516) 546-0390 .. **Williams,** Michl G '96 -22 Pine -Freeprt 11520 **Fx:**546-0392
(212) 577-7700 .. **Williams,** Michl H '94 %Safe Horizon -2 Lafayette -NY 10007 **Fx:**385-0331
(518) 464-0279 .. **Williams,** Michl P '96 AMRI -26 Corp Cir -Albany 12203 **Fx:**464-0289
(212) 980-0120 .. **Williams,** Michl R '93 (Frankfurt KK&S,PC) -488 Mad Av -NY 10022
(212) 653-8700 .. **Williams,** Michele E '04 (Sheppard MR&H LLP) -30 Rckfllr Plz -NY 10112
(585) 232-6551 .. **Williams,** Mitchell '49 Williams & W -28 E Main -Rchstr 14614 **Fx:**232-2381
(212) 768-6700 .. **Williams,** Mitchell G '86 (Sonnenschein N&R LLP) -2 World Fncl Ctr -NY 10281
(212) 474-1000 .. **Williams,** Morenike K '08 %Cravath S&M LLP -825 8th Av -NY 10019
(646) 722-8500 .. **Williams,** Natalia D '03 %Grant & E,PA -485 Lex Av -NY 10017
(212) 430-0800 .. **Williams,** Nathan T '07 Cnsl Kennedy LS&E -75 Maiden Ln -NY 10038
(212) 878-8000 .. **Williams,** Nicholas R '89 (Clifford C LLP) -31 W 52nd -NY 10019
(212) 766-2466 .. **Williams,** Nick Sondhi '99 (DiSanto LLP) -15 Maiden Ln -NY 10038 **Fx:**(866) 746-0504
(212) 596-9000 .. **Williams,** Nila W '04 %Ropes & G LLP -1211 Av of Amer -NY 10036
(914) 949-6996 .. **Williams,** Noel L C '88 %Penino & M,LLP -180 E Post Rd -White Plns 10601
(718) 625-5860 .. **Williams,** Norman '55 (Williams & G) -26 Court -Brklyn 11242
(212) 689-4769 .. **Williams,** Norman Jr. '96 Williams Law Ofc,PLLC -275 Mad Av -NY 10016 **Fx:**369-7105
(212) 310-8000 .. **Williams,** Olanrewaju A '07 %Weil G&M LLP -767 5th Av -NY 10153
(518) 443-5684 .. **Williams,** Pamela Miller '82 %SUNY Employee Relations -SUNY Plz -Albany 12246
(212) 220-3000 .. **Williams,** Pamela R '94 %Broadcast Music Inc -250 Greenwich -NY 10007
(212) 297-5800 .. **Williams,** Paul D '85 (Day P LLP) -7 Times Sq -NY 10036
(716) 858-2424 .. **Williams,** Paul J III '94 %DA -25 Delaware Av -Buffalo 14202 **Fx:**858-7425
(516) 742-0888 .. **Williams,** Paul R '82 (Schupbach W&P LLP) -1010 Franklin Av -Gdn Cty 11530
(518) 257-3000 .. **Williams,** Paul T Jr. '78 Dormitory Auth -515 Bway -Albany 12207 **Fx:**257-3101
(212) 504-6000 .. **Williams,** Penny M '07 %Cadwalader W&T LLP -1 World Fncl Ctr -NY 10281
(516) 747-7400 .. **Williams,** Peter J '96 %Rosenberg C&B LLP -100 Grdn City Plz -Gdn Cty 11530
(212) 504-6000 .. **Williams,** Peter J '00 SpclCnsl Cadwalader W&T LLP -1 World Fncl Ctr -NY 10281
(516) 571-3310 .. **Williams,** Peter S '76 %Hon P Collins -100 Supreme Ct Dr -Mineola 11501
(646) 361-5785 .. **Williams,** Peter W Jr. '97 PennantPark Invstmnt Advsrs -590 Mad Av -NY 10022
(862) 371-5656 .. **Williams,** Precious L '08 -493 Macon -Brklyn 11233
(212) 681-6500 .. **Williams,** Rachel E '04 %Stempel BC&H,PC -675 3rd Av -NY 10017
(212) 751-3001 .. **Williams,** Randy W '05 (Thompson & K LLP) -919 3rd Av -NY 10022
(718) 262-7100 .. **Williams,** Renee '09 Civil Ct -89-17 Sutphin Blvd -Jamaica 11435 **Fx:**262-7107
(718) 875-1300 .. **Williams,** Riad '96 %Appllt Div 2nd Dept -45 Monroe Pl -Brklyn 11201 **Fx:**858-2446
(212) 768-6700 .. **Williams,** Richd C '07 %Sonnenschein N&R LLP -2 World Fncl Ctr -NY 10281
(212) 435-3571 .. **Williams,** Richd D '84 %Port Auth of NY/NJ -225 Park Av S -NY 10003 **Fx:**435-3555
(585) 248-6216 .. **Williams,** Richd T II '77 Cnsl Town of Pittsford -11 S Main -Pittsfrd 14534 **Fx:**248-6247
(212) 530-5000 .. **Williams,** Robt B '84 (Milbank TH&M LLP) -1 Chase Manh Plz -NY 10005
(516) 536-5448 .. **Williams,** Robt C '67 -77 N Centre Av -Rockvll Ctr 11570 **Fx:**536-3201
(516) 429-0595 .. **Williams,** Robt H '87 -30 Lakeside Dr -Centerprt 11721 **Fx:**(631) 425-7137
(716) 886-0211 .. **Williams,** Robt J '98 %Benderson Dvlpmnt -570 Delaware Av -Buffalo 14202 **Fx:**886-2269
(518) 395-5400 .. **Williams,** Robt T '93 %Racing & Wagering Bd -1 Bway Ctr -Schnctdy 12305 **Fx:**347-1250
(315) 253-4050 .. **Williams,** Roberta G '84 (Williams HM&B) -11 Court -Auburn 13021 **Fx:**253-4223
(516) 357-3000 .. **Williams,** Roger V '03 %Rivkin R LLP -926 RXR Plz -Uniondale 11556
(718) 643-4422 .. **Williams,** Rubye J '87 Family Ct -283 Adams -Brklyn 11201
(212) 558-4000 .. **Williams,** Ryan C '03 %Sullivan & C LLP -125 Broad -NY 10004
(315) 472-7250 .. **Williams,** S Robt '82 -250 Harrison -Syracuse 13202 **Fx:**476-5350
(718) 596-9000 .. **Williams,** Sabrina M '09 Cohen HEP&T -25 Chapel -Brklyn 11201
(212) 506-2500 .. **Williams,** Sachanna E '08 %Mayer B LLP -1675 Bway -NY 10019
(914) 428-2323 .. **Williams,** Samantha C '02 %Galgano & Assoc -399 Knollwood Rd -White Plns 10603 **Fx:**428-3298
(845) 291-2650 .. **Williams,** Sandra Prezeau '90 %Cnty Atty -285 Main -Goshen 10924 **Fx:**291-3014
(212) 308-4411 .. **Williams,** Sani A '05 Cnsl Edwards AP&D LLP -750 Lex Av -NY 10022
(212) 370-1300 .. **Williams,** Sarah E '00 (Ellenoff G&S LLP) -150 E 42nd -NY 10017
(917) 940-0011 .. **Williams,** Sarah M '05 Cnsl SDSProcida -456 E 173rd -Bronx 10457 **Fx:**536-9797
(646) 458-6809 .. **Williams,** Scott J '07 Ace USA -140 Bway -NY 10005
(212) 815-6382 .. **Williams,** Shaquala R '09 %Bk of NY Mellon -101 Barclay -NY 10286
(212) 530-5000 .. **Williams,** Simon J C '08 %Milbank TH&M LLP -1 Chase Manh Plz -NY 10005
(718) 222-1637 .. **Williams,** Steve G '90 -26 Court -Brklyn 11242 **Fx:**643-2007
(212) 373-3000 .. **Williams,** Steven J '00 (Paul WRW&G LLP) -1285 Av of Amer -NY 10019
(212) 682-3198 .. **Williams,** Steven N '93 (Cotchett P&M) -100 Park Av -NY 10017
(315) 474-2911 .. **Williams,** Steven W '94 (Smith SK&S,PC) -250 S Clinton -Syracuse 13202
(716) 854-1112 .. **Williams,** Susan A '84 (Lovallo & W) -1088 Ellicott Sq Bldg -Buffalo 14203 **Fx:**854-1288
(516) 538-2500 .. **Williams,** Susan B '84 (Furey FLMW&D,PC) -600 Front -Hempstd 11550
(718) 368-5563 .. **Williams,** Tanisa '97 Kingsborough Comm Cllg -City Univ of NY -Brklyn 11235
(212) 218-5500 .. **Williams,** Tara Smith '04 %Seyfarth S LLP -620 8th Av -NY 10018
(212) 651-5409 .. **Williams,** Tatia L '91 %Oxygen Media LLC -75 9th Av -NY 10011
(315) 423-7100 .. **Williams,** Ted H '87 (Harris B PLLC) -300 S State -Syracuse 13202
(212) 770-0990 .. **Williams,** Terence D '08 AIG -80 Pine -NY 10005 **Fx:**770-0792
(516) 256-1100 .. **Williams,** Thos A '78 -164 Hendrickson Av -Vly Stream 11580
(585) 343-1486 .. **Williams,** Thos D '84 (Williams Law Firm,LLP) -2 Court Street Plz Bx402 -Batavia 14021 **Fx:**343-1487
(516) 512-6590 .. **Williams,** Thos P '76 %Pieret & Assoc -400 Grdn City Plz -Gdn Cty 11530 **Fx:**742-4116
(212) 735-3000 .. **Williams,** Thos W '07 %Skadden ASM&F LLP -4 Times Sq -NY 10036
(212) 974-0100 .. **Williams,** Timothy E '99 %Assured Guaranty -31 W 52nd -NY 10019 **Fx:**581-3268
(585) 385-6666 .. **Williams,** Toby J '01 Paychex Inc -911 Panorama Trl S -Rchstr 14625
(212) 735-3000 .. **Williams,** Vaughn C '77 (Skadden ASM&F LLP) -4 Times Sq -NY 10036
(718) 629-0004 .. **Williams,** Verbelle B '93 -471 E 56th -Brklyn 11203 **Fx:**629-0029
(212) 618-1791 .. **Williams,** Vivian Mortimer '04 (V Williams & Assoc) -14 Wall -NY 10005
(212) 530-5000 .. **Williams,** Wendy M '07 %Milbank TH&M LLP -1 Chase Manh Plz -NY 10005
(212) 558-4000 .. **Williams,** Wm J Jr. '61 OfCnsl Sullivan & C LLP -125 Broad -NY 10004
(212) 906-1200 .. **Williamson,** Bradd L '95 (Latham & W) -885 3rd Av -NY 10022
(212) 770-5052 .. **Williamson,** Chas E '97 %AIG -80 Pine -NY 10005
(607) 273-3339 .. **Williamson Clune & Stevens** -317 N Tioga Bx126 -Ithaca 14850 **Fx:**273-4164
(718) 250-2000 .. **Williamson,** Danl M '06 DA -350 Jay -Brklyn 11201 **Fx:**250-2314
(212) 278-1567 .. **Williamson,** Helen J '81 (Anderson K&O,PC) -1251 Av of Amer -NY 10020
(718) 855-9000 .. **Williamson,** Ian Todd '02 %Cullen and D LLP -177 Montague -Brklyn 11201
(212) 373-3000 .. **Williamson,** Jason D '09 %Paul WRW&G LLP -1285 Av of Amer -NY 10019
(212) 661-8900 .. **Williamson,** John F '67 (Rosenberg & W LLP) -100 Park Av -NY 10017
(716) 858-2424 .. **Williamson,** Lauren A '08 %DA -25 Delaware Av -Buffalo 14202 **Fx:**858-7425
(516) 222-7929 .. **Williamson,** Mitchell L '95 %Pressler & P LLP -305 Bway -NY 10007 **Fx:**(973) 753-5353
(914) 337-3434 .. **Williamson,** Peter W '63 (P Williamson,PC) -141 Pkwy Rd -Bronxvll 10708 **Fx:**337-3392
(212) 412-9500 .. **Williamson,** Richd A '70 (Flemming ZWZ LLP) -1 Lbrty Plz -NY 10006
(607) 273-3339 .. **Williamson,** Robt I '52 OfCnsl Williamson C&S -317 N Tioga Bx126 -Ithaca 14850
(212) 871-1300 .. **Williamson,** Stephen Z '01 (Schulman B&W,LLP) -980 Av of Amer -NY 10018 **Fx:**(646) 599-9320
(212) 708-9100 .. **Williamson,** Steven L '79 %Bessemer Trust Co -630 5th Av -NY 10111 **Fx:**265-5826
(212) 487-9700 .. **Williamson,** Walter '74 OfCnsl White F&F,LLP -61 Bway -NY 10006
(718) 590-1615 .. **Williams-Pulakos,** Charlene L '87 %Criminal Ct -265 E 161st -Bronx 10451
(716) 887-4664 .. **Williams Torres,** Stephanie '01 Kaleida Health -3 Gates Cir -Buffalo 14209 **Fx:**887-4668
(212) 972-2300 .. **Willick,** Nelson H '77 (Plotkin & W) -551 5th Av -NY 10176 **Fx:**972-2303
(718) 590-8586 .. **Willie,** Mara A '02 Admin Children's Srvcs -900 Sheridan Av -Bronx 10451
(212) 688-4000 .. **Willig,** Joy F '84 NYS HFA -641 Lex Av -NY 10022 **Fx:**872-0362
(212) 335-4500 .. **Willig,** Kenneth C H '81 (DLA Piper LLP) -1251 Av of Amer -NY 10020
(716) 636-7600 .. **Willig,** Ronald '66 OfCnsl HoganWillig -2410 N Forest Rd -Amherst 14068
(212) 269-0927 .. **Willig,** Stephen F '87 (D'Amato & L,LLP) -2 World Fncl Ctr -NY 10281
(518) 587-9215 .. **Willig,** Wm P '62 -65 Pepper Ln -Saratoga Spgs 12866 **Fx:**587-9522
(212) 303-1000 .. **Willinger,** Alan M '80 %RS Schaps & Co -757 3rd Av -NY 10017 **Fx:**755-5600
(212) 674-5190 .. **Willinger,** Lowell D '68 -369 1st Av -NY 10010 **Fx:**813-9838
(212) 943-1090 .. **Willinger,** Warren J '62 %Gair GCSMB&R -80 Pine -NY 10005
(212) 325-4475 .. **Willis,** Andrew S '98 %Credit Suisse First Boston -11 Mad Av -NY 10010

(585) 262-6390 ..**Willis,** Colleen L '02 %Hamberger & W -1 S Wshngtn -Rchstr 14614
(212) 969-2172 ..**Willis,** Dana L '00 Alliance Bernstein LP -1345 Av of Amer -NY 10105 **Fx:**554-4639
(212) 306-7701 ..**Willis,** Garfield R '02 %Comm on Human Rights -40 Rector -NY 10006 **Fx:**306-7414
(212) 639-9675 ..**Willis,** Juliet A '00 Dept of Finance-Parking -66 John -NY 10038
(716) 853-1887 ..**Willis,** Kathleen Tenney '87 %E Tenney -5 Niagara Sq -Buffalo 14202 **Fx:**853-1893
(212) 813-5900 ..**Willis,** Lisa M '06 %Fross ZL&Z,PC -866 UN Plz -NY 10017
(212) 302-6868 ..**Willis,** Lori '95 (Flaster & W,PC) -36 W 44th -NY 10036
(212) 449-1651 ..**Willis,** Mark L '95 Merril Lynch -4 World Fncl Ctr -NY 10080
(212) 556-2100 ..**Willis,** Michl A '08 %King & S -1185 Av of Amer -NY 10036
(518) 388-4364 ..**Willis,** Peter H '06 %DA -612 State -Schnctdy 12305 **Fx:**388-4569
(212) 558-4000 ..**Willis,** Wm E '52 SrCnsl Sullivan & C LLP -125 Broad -NY 10004
(212) 530-1800 ..**Willitt,** Troy E '99 %Richards K&O LLP -1 World Fncl Ctr -NY 10281
(585) 530-3050 ..**Willkens,** Mary M '03 %MHLS -50 East Av -Rchstr 14604 **Fx:**530-3079
(212) 728-8000 ..**Willkie Farr & Gallagher LLP** -787 7th Av -NY 10019 **Fx:**728-8111
(212) 688-5000 ..**Willkie,** Wendell L '79 %Westvaco -299 Park Av -NY 10171
(315) 622-2267 ..**Willmes,** Alan J '92 -8139 Oldbury Rd -Liverpool 13090
(212) 836-8000 ..**Willner,** Barry A '74 (Kaye S LLP) -425 Park Av -NY 10022
(212) 325-7198 ..**Willner,** Helena M '90 Credit Suisse -11 Mad Av -NY 10010
(212) 753-5599 ..**Willner,** Michl J '04 %Brill & M -845 3rd Av -NY 10022
(516) 739-0177 ..**Willoughby,** Ann '90 (Willoughby & G) -245 Hillside Av -Williston Pk 11596
(212) 880-6000 ..**Willoughby,** Richd G '02 (Torys LLP) -237 Park Av -NY 10017
(212) 526-7118 ..**Willoughby,** Scott E '89 Barclays Capital Inc -745 7th Av -NY 10019
(212) 669-0600 ..**Willoughby,** Thos E IV '78 (Hill R LLP) -45 Bway -NY 10006
(646) 428-3839 ..**Wills,** Randolph E '84 Ofc of Civil Rights-US Dept of Ed -32 Old Slip -NY 10005
(718) 703-2688 ..**Wills,** Yvette A H '94 -700 Linden Blvd -Brklyn 11203
(518) 462-6765 ..**Willsey,** Debra J '84 %Leg Aid -55 Colvin Av -Albany 12206 **Fx:**427-8352
(212) 345-7000 ..**Willsky,** Karen M '01 Mercer (US) Inc -1166 Av of Amer -NY 10036 **Fx:**345-7414
(914) 948-5656 ..**Willstatter,** Richd D '81 (Green & W) -200 Mamaroneck Av -White Plns 10601
(212) 408-2500 ..**Wilm,** Renee L '00 (Baker B,LLP) -30 Rckfllr Plz -NY 10112
(518) 402-4926 ..**Wilmarth,** Anthony M '03 State Comptroller -110 State -Albany 12236 **Fx:**473-9104
(212) 770-7659 ..**Wilmer,** Antje Westphal '92 %AIG -70 Pine -NY 10270 **Fx:**952-0129
(212) 230-8800 ..**Wilmer Cutler Pickering Hale and Dorr LLP** -399 Park Av -NY 10022 **Fx:**230-8888
(914) 750-5933 ..**Wilmer,** Fredk J '97 (Kissel H&W LLP) -580 Wht Plns Rd -Tarrytwn 10591
(212) 357-3284 ..**Wilmit,** Alan S '89 %Goldman Sachs -1 NY Plz -NY 10004
(845) 638-5687 ..**Wilmot,** Barbara M '88 Family Ct -1 S Main -New Cty 10956 **Fx:**638-5727
(585) 454-7145 ..**Wilmot,** Sandra G '85 (Gallo & I,LLP) -39 State -Rchstr 14614
(212) 953-2300 ..**Wilner,** Adam C '99 (Greenberg & W LLP) -232 Mad Av -NY 10016
(212) 680-5100 ..**Wilner,** Claudia E '04 NEDAP -176 Grand -NY 10013
(212) 319-7744 ..**Wilner,** Diane S '75 (Wilner & Assoc,PC) -110 E 59th -NY 10022 **Fx:**319-0354
(212) 248-8800 ..**Wilner,** Marc R '96 %Callan KB&B LLP -1 Whitehall -NY 10004
(917) 733-5932 ..**Wilner,** Peter A '84 -153-01 Jamaica Av -Jamaica 11432 **Fx:**(718) 479-2548
(212) 225-2000 ..**Wilner,** Steven L '89 (Cleary GS&H) -1 Lbrty Plz -NY 10006
(973) 438-4495 ..**Wilon,** Robt J '03 %Outside Cnsl Solutns LLP -1430 Bway -NY 10018 **Fx:**(212) 221-5343
(585) 232-3680 ..**Wilsey,** Karla Damico '82 %1st Amer Title -16 W Main -Rchstr 14614 **Fx:**423-8273
(212) 818-9600 ..**Wilsher,** Leslie J '80 (Greenfield S&S,LLP) -600 3rd Av -NY 10016
(212) 477-1723 ..**Wilshinsky,** Karen S '93 (McLaughlin & W,PC) -276 5th Av -NY 10001 **Fx:**477-1731
(212) 578-8743 ..**Wilson,** A Kaiper '85 %MetLife -27-01 Qns Plz N -LIC 11101
(212) 373-3000 ..**Wilson,** Alexander '07 %Paul WRW&G LLP -1285 Av of Amer -NY 10019
(516) 393-2200 ..**Wilson,** Alicia M '06 %Garfunkel W,PC -111 Grt Nck Rd -Gt Neck 11021
(716) 854-7525 ..**Wilson,** Andrew M '99 (Serotte R&W) -300 Delaware Av -Buffalo 14202
(518) 447-3200 ..**Wilson,** April M '02 %McNamee LT&W,PC -677 Bway -Albany 12207
(718) 547-5090 ..**Wilson,** Audrey M '00 (Wilson & W PC) -4460 Baychester Av -Bronx 10466 **Fx:**882-5950
(914) 686-9010 ..**Wilson Bave Conboy Cozza & Couzens,PC** -2 William -White Plns 10601 **Fx:**686-0873
(212) 513-3200 ..**Wilson,** Benjamin R '10 %Holland & K LLP -31 W 52nd -NY 10019
(212) 403-1000 ..**Wilson,** Bradley R '05 %Wachtell LR&K -51 W 52nd -NY 10019
(631) 261-4400 ..**Wilson,** Brian J '08 Vetrns Affrs Med Ctr -79 Middlevll Rd -Northprt 11768
(212) 803-5100 ..**Wilson,** Carolyn Parrott '81 %NY Cnty Defender Srvcs -225 Bway -NY 10007 **Fx:**571-6035
(212) 626-4100 ..**Wilson,** Christina M '05 %Baker & M LLP -1114 Av of Amer -NY 10036
(212) 676-1110 ..**Wilson,** Christopher C '87 %Taxi & Limo Comm -40 Rector -NY 10006
(607) 432-7410 ..**Wilson,** Christopher G '02 -48 Dietz -Oneonta 13820 **Fx:**433-2168
(212) 403-1000 ..**Wilson,** Christopher L '07 %Wachtell LR&K -51 W 52nd -NY 10019
(914) 225-5548 ..**Wilson,** Christopher M '95 Morgan Stanley & Co Inc -2000 Wstchstr Av -Purchase 10577 **Fx:**750-0330
(212) 308-8505 ..**Wilson,** Christopher S '05 %Akabas & S -488 Mad Av -NY 10022
(212) 705-0327 ..**Wilson,** Clay S '90 Needham & Co,Inc -445 Park Av -NY 10022
(212) 264-3895 ..**Wilson,** Darma A '95 %NLRB -26 Fed Plz -NY 10278 **Fx:**264-8427
(716) 852-6323 ..**Wilson,** David W '85 -434 Delaware Av -Buffalo 14202
(212) 230-8862 ..**Wilson,** Dawn M '96 SpclCnsl WilmerHale -399 Park Av -NY 10022
(716) 439-4860 ..**Wilson,** Debra D '85 -415 Bewley Bldg -Lockprt 14094
(212) 986-2233 ..**Wilson,** Derell D '08 %Early & S LLC -360 Lex Av Bx3601 -NY 10163
(212) 710-3900 ..**Wilson,** Diane Westwood '84 (Clyde & Co US LLP) -405 Lex Av -NY 10174 **Fx:**710-3950
(212) 227-4455 ..**Wilson,** Earl A '01 -65 Bway -NY 10006
(212) 924-1449 ..**Wilson,** Edw J '81 -525 W 22nd -NY 10011 **Fx:**255-2230
(718) 858-3442 ..**Wilson,** Edw N '64 -38 Grdn Pl -Brklyn 11201
(212) 490-3000 ..**Wilson Elser Moskowitz Edelman & Dicker LLP** -150 E 42nd -NY 10017 **Fx:**490-3038
(914) 323-7000 ..**Wilson Elser Moskowitz Edelman & Dicker LLP** -3 Gannett Dr -White Plns 10604 **Fx:**323-7001
(518) 449-8893 ..**Wilson Elser Moskowitz Edelman & Dicker LLP** -677 Bway -Albany 12207 **Fx:**449-8927
(315) 437-7600 ..**Wilson,** Eric J '92 (Ferrara FLB&R,PC) -5010 Campuswood Dr -E Syracuse 13057
(212) 808-7800 ..**Wilson,** Eric R '05 (Kelley D&W LLP) -101 Park Av -NY 10178
(718) 826-3060 ..**Wilson,** Ernest E '92 -111 Court -Brklyn 11201
(212) 474-1000 ..**Wilson,** Gabriel B '03 Cravath S&M LLP -825 8th Av -NY 10019
(212) 793-7601 ..**Wilson,** Gail S '83 Citigroup -425 Park Av -NY 10022 **Fx:**793-7600
(518) 272-3812 ..**Wilson,** Gary H '78 -287 N Greenbush Rd -Troy 12180 **Fx:**283-8060
(631) 727-0110 ..**Wilson,** George J '85 (Kelly R&K,LLP) -218 Griffing -Rvrhead 11901
(516) 739-0400 ..**Wilson,** George J '85 (Kelly R&K,LLP) -330 Old Cntry Rd -Mineola 11501
(212) 269-7308 ..**Wilson,** Gregory '94 (Leahey & J PC) -120 Wall -NY 10005
(212) 608-4400 ..**Wilson Grochow Druker & Nolet** -233 Bway -NY 10279 **Fx:**608-0746
(212) 969-3000 ..**Wilson,** Howard '65 (Proskauer R LLP) -1585 Bway -NY 10036
(914) 749-8200 ..**Wilson,** Jack A '06 %Boies S&F LLP -333 Main -Armonk 10504
(212) 777-7500 ..**Wilson,** James R '94 %United Fed of Teachers -260 Park Av S -NY 10010
(646) 278-6730 ..**Wilson,** Jeffrey L '06 -1375 Bway -NY 10018 **Fx:**253-1258
(212) 599-2085 ..**Wilson,** Jennifer H '99 %Braff H&S -305 Bway -NY 10007
(718) 250-2000 ..**Wilson,** Jessica '07 %DA -350 Jay -Brklyn 11201 **Fx:**250-2314
(212) 216-8000 ..**Wilson,** Joanne M '88 OfCnsl Tarter K&D LLP -1350 Bway -NY 10018
(585) 232-5300 ..**Wilson,** John M II '69 (Boylan BCV&W,LLP) -2400 Chase Sq -Rchstr 14604
(718) 788-6646 ..**Wilson,** John M '89 -332A 9th -Brklyn 11215
(716) 434-2010 ..**Wilson,** Jon L '76 -111 Ontario -Lockprt 14094 **Fx:**433-0502
(716) 434-2010 ..**Wilson,** Jon R R '09 %J Wilson -111 Ontario -Lockprt 14094 **Fx:**433-0502
(631) 957-3029 ..**Wilson,** Jos '07 %Babylon Town Atty -200 E Sunrise Hwy -Lindenhrst 11757 **Fx:**957-3146
(585) 295-4400 ..**Wilson,** Jos A '98 %Hiscock & B,LLP -2000 HSBC Plz -Rchstr 14604
(315) 233-8300 ..**Wilson,** Jos A '05 %Burr & B -101 S Salina -Syracuse 13202
(315) 798-5766 ..**Wilson,** Kara E '06 %DA -800 Park Av -Utica 13501 **Fx:**798-5582
(212) 613-5000 ..**Wilson,** Karline N '00 Leg Assist Grp -450 W 33rd -NY 10001 **Fx:**750-0820
(212) 891-0700 ..**Wilson,** Kathleen H '82 %FOJP Srvc Corp -28 E 28th -NY 10016 **Fx:**308-3911
(585) 530-3050 ..**Wilson,** Kevin D '98 %MHLS -50 East Av -Rchstr 14604 **Fx:**530-3079
(212) 335-9000 ..**Wilson,** Kevin J '04 %DA -1 Hogan Pl -NY 10013
(718) 590-3956 ..**Wilson,** Kim A '86 %Supreme Ct -851 Grnd Cncrs -Bronx 10451 **Fx:**590-8914
(914) 683-1200 ..**Wilson,** Kristen Kelley '04 SrCnsl Harris B PLLC -445 Hmltn Av -White Plns 10601
(315) 474-2911 ..**Wilson,** Kristen L '10 %Smith SK&S,PC -250 S Clinton -Syracuse 13202
(212) 214-5468 ..**Wilson,** Lance H '73 Wachovia Securities -375 Park Av -NY 10152
(585) 758-7615 ..**Wilson,** Laura Jane '92 %Univ of Rochester Med Ctr -Bx278979 -Rchstr 14627 **Fx:**272-9311
(212) 608-4400 ..**Wilson,** Lawr A II '92 (Wilson GD&N) -233 Bway -NY 10279
(212) 755-0100 ..**Wilson,** Leanne M '09 Grais & E LLP -40 E 52nd -NY 10022
(516) 792-1961 ..**Wilson,** Learie R '00 -282 N Central Av -Vly Stream 11580 **Fx:**792-1992
(914) 997-0825 ..**Wilson,** Leroy Jr. '69 (Wilson J,PC) -99 Court -White Plns 10601 **Fx:**997-0830
(212) 735-3000 ..**Wilson,** Lincoln D '09 %Skadden ASM&F LLP -4 Times Sq -NY 10036
(718) 298-1200 ..**Wilson,** Linda '92 Supreme Ct Law Dept -8811 Sutphin Blvd -Jamaica 11435
(516) 488-6700 ..**Wilson,** Lucy J '00 Canon USA -1 Canon Plz -Lk Success 11042
(212) 907-0803 ..**Wilson,** Marci B '98 Lasky & R,Ltd -140 Bway -NY 10005
(212) 547-5400 ..**Wilson,** Margaret C '95 (McDermott W&E LLP) -340 Mad Av -NY 10173
(646) 964-5749 ..**Wilson,** Maria '99 (Walker GW&B,LLC) -1825 Park Av -NY 10035 **Fx:**(866) 422-4858
(212) 306-7447 ..**Wilson,** Mark H '92 %Comm on Human Rights -40 Rector -NY 10006 **Fx:**306-7414
(585) 232-6500 ..**Wilson,** Mark R '97 (Harter S&E LLP) -1600 Bausch & Lomb Pl -Rchstr 14604
(631) 287-5720 ..**Wilson,** Mary C '99 Preservation Fund Mngr -116 Hmptn Rd -Southampton 11968
(718) 547-5090 ..**Wilson,** Maxine Petrona '99 (Wilson & W PC) -4460 Baychester Av -Bronx 10466 **Fx:**882-5950
(212) 902-1000 ..**Wilson,** Melanie J '96 Goldman Sachs & Co -85 Broad -NY 10004
(212) 450-2921 ..**Wilson,** Melissa Murray '95 %Cline Davis & Mann -220 E 42nd -NY 10017
(212) 669-0600 ..**Wilson,** Michl D '79 %Hill R LLP -45 Bway -NY 10006
(914) 779-7544 ..**Wilson,** Nancy J '84 -25 Parkvw Av -Bronxvll 10708
(845) 452-5714 ..**Wilson,** Neil A '91 -8 Morehouse Rd -Poughkeepsie 12603 **Fx:**452-5714
(212) 719-6358 ..**Wilson,** Neil M '94 %IRS -110 W 44th -NY 10036
(212) 763-5000 ..**Wilson,** O Andrew F '01 (Emery CB&A LLP) -75 Rckfllr Plz -NY 10019
(212) 909-6000 ..**Wilson,** Paul H Jr. '67 SrCnsl Debevoise & P LLP -919 3rd Av -NY 10022
(212) 371-9100 ..**Wilson,** Paul H III '98 PH Wilson Cnsltng -90 Broad -NY 10004
(212) 474-1000 ..**Wilson,** Peter S '80 (Cravath S&M LLP) -825 8th Av -NY 10019

(646) 230-0937 .. **Wilson**, Peter W '02 Alaric Compliance Srvcs,LLC -800 3rd Av -NY 10022
(212) 849-7000 .. **Wilson**, Robt B '97 (Quinn EU&S,LLP) -51 Mad Av -NY 10010
(914) 417-3400 .. **Wilson**, Robt D Jr. '82 OfCnsl Littleton JUP&K LLP -1 Manhattanvll Rd -Purchase 10577
(585) 724-4317 .. **Wilson**, Robt F '67 %ESL Fed Credit Union -225 Chestnut -Rchstr 14604 **Fx**:336-1014
(212) 474-1000 .. **Wilson**, Rowan D '87 (Cravath S&M LLP) -825 8th Av -NY 10019
(212) 446-2300 .. **Wilson**, Scott R '08 %Boies S&F LLP -575 Lex Av -NY 10022
(212) 735-3152 .. **Wilson**, Sharon L '01 Skadden ASM&F LLP -4 Times Sq -NY 10036 **Fx**:735-2000
(212) 282-2514 .. **Wilson**, Simone P '04 %Rockefeller Grp -1221 Av of Amer -NY 10020 **Fx**:282-2005
(212) 999-5800 .. **Wilson Sonsini Goodrich & Rosati** -1301 Av of Americas -NY 10019 **Fx**:999-5899
(518) 427-9700 .. **Wilson**, Steven D '01 %Harris B PLLC -677 Bway -Albany 12207
(212) 455-2000 .. **Wilson**, Steven M '05 -425 Lex Av -NY 10017 **Fx**:455-2502
(212) 490-3000 .. **Wilson**, Tammy A '06 %Wilson EME&D LLP -150 E 42nd -NY 10017
(518) 746-2150 .. **Wilson**, Ted M '91 %Hon S Pritzler - Cnty Ct -383 Bway -Ft Edward 12828
(718) 875-0021 .. **Wilson**, Thos D '73 -186 Montague -Brklyn 11201 **Fx**:246-0417
(212) 907-7300 .. **Wilson**, Thos J '90 (Golenbock EAB&P) -437 Mad Av -NY 10022
(212) 381-7000 .. **Wilson**, Thos M '93 %Sabin B&G LLP -4 Times Sq -NY 10036
(212) 490-3000 .. **Wilson**, Thos W '62 (Wilson EME&D LLP) -150 E 42nd -NY 10017
(914) 323-7000 .. **Wilson**, Thos W '62 (Wilson EME&D LLP) -3 Gannett Dr -White Plns 10604
(212) 490-3000 .. **Wilson**, Thos W Jr. '98 (Wilson EME&D LLP) -150 E 42nd -NY 10017
(212) 504-6000 .. **Wilson**, Trevor M '10 %Cadwalader W&T LLP -1 World Fncl Ctr -NY 10281
(718) 773-7442 .. **Wilson**, Victor M '91 -841 Park Pl -Brklyn 11216 **Fx**:773-8219
(718) 646-1955 .. **Wilson**, Wayne B '86 %J Giannakouros -120 Bay Ridge Av -Brklyn 11220 **Fx**:769-8264
(973) 494-0601 .. **Wilson**, Wm D '92 (Mound CW&G) -One Bttry Pk Plz -NY 10004
(585) 232-6500 .. **Wilson**, Wm Derek '04 %Harter S&E LLP -1600 Bausch & Lomb Pl -Rchstr 14604
(718) 658-0500 .. **Wilson-Campbell**, Theresa N '99 %Law Dept -151-20 Jamaica Av -Jamaica 11432 **Fx**:658-4025
(212) 837-6000 .. **Wiltenburg**, David W '75 (Hughes H&R LLP) -1 Bttry Pk Plz -NY 10004
(212) 686-0010 .. **Wilton**, Jane L '81 %NY Community Trst -909 3rd Av -NY 10022 **Fx**:532-8528
(716) 856-4000 .. **Wiltse**, Jessica S '05 %Hodgson R LLP -140 Pearl -Buffalo 14202
(716) 649-4423 .. **Wiltse**, Peter C '61 P Wiltse,PLLC -202 Main -Hambrg 14075 **Fx**:649-4429
(212) 683-2210 .. **Wiltsek**, Gena E '01 %Childrens Rts Inc -330 7th Av -NY 10001 **Fx**:683-4015
(212) 839-5300 .. **Wiltshire**, L Markus '82 (Sidley A LLP) -787 7th Av -NY 10019
(315) 349-3295 .. **Wiltsie**, Daryl A '83 Hon J Elliott -Cnty Cthse -Oswego 13126
(607) 272-3947 .. **Wiltsie**, George R '82 -302 Clinton Hse -Ithaca 14850 **Fx**:272-1685
(631) 501-5700 .. **Wiltzius**, James J '08 %Carter DF&S LLP -445 Broadhallow Rd -Melvll 11747
(631) 476-9873 .. **Wilutis**, Karen M '83 (Wilutis & W LLP) -Bx2021 -Miller Pl 11764 **Fx**:476-9876
(631) 476-9873 .. **Wilutis**, Steven J '70 (Wilutis & W LLP) -Bx2021 -Miller Pl 11764 **Fx**:476-9876
(212) 481-5858 .. **Wimer**, Chas H '73 %Fidelity Natl Title Ins -1 Park Av -NY 10016 **Fx**:481-8747
(516) 739-1462 .. **Wimmer**, Kevin J '06 %Brosnan & H -1325 Franklin Av -Gdn Cty 11530
(646) 328-0850 .. **Wimpfheimer**, Jan Steven '94 %Outside Cnsl Solutns LLP -1430 Bway -NY 10018 **Fx**:360-5000
(212) 247-8448 .. **Wimpfheimer**, Michl Clark '67 (Wimpfheimer & W) -330 W 58th -NY 10019 **Fx**:247-8196
(516) 504-8585 .. **Wimpfheimer**, Steven '66 -264-46 73rd Av -Floral Pk 11004 **Fx**:504-1003
(212) 310-8000 .. **Win**, Jacob Zaw '09 %Weil G&M LLP -767 5th Av -NY 10153
(518) 457-2411 .. **Winans**, David E '85 %DOT -50 Wolf Rd -Albany 12232 **Fx**:457-4021
(518) 943-4330 .. **Winans**, John W '79 Stiefel & W -331 Main -Catskill 12414
(212) 210-9435 .. **Winans**, Lloyd M '02 (Alston & B LLP) -90 Park Av -NY 10016
(212) 265-7200 .. **Wince**, Janna C '09 %Mayerson & Assoc -330 W 38th -NY 10018 **Fx**:265-1735
(212) 687-0100 .. **Winchester**, Alan M '90 Harris B PLLC -100 Wall -NY 10005
(845) 638-3902 .. **Winchester**, Lurlyn A '94 -120 N Main -New Cty 10956
(212) 575-8333 .. **Wincig**, Bernard '55 (Wincig & W) -137 5th Av -NY 10010 **Fx**:575-8525
(212) 575-8333 .. **Wincig**, Owen L '80 (Wincig & W) -137 5th Av -NY 10010 **Fx**:575-8525
(212) 918-3000 .. **Winckler**, J Christopher '98 %Hogan L LLP -875 3rd Av -NY 10022
(212) 318-6000 .. **Winckler**, Kristen C '99 (Paul HJ&W LLP) -75 E 55th -NY 10022
(716) 845-9442 .. **Wincott**, Therese Rahill '82 %Supreme Ct -92 Franklin -Buffalo 14202 **Fx**:851-3293
(914) 696-3400 .. **Wind**, David A '92 -108 Corp Park Dr -White Plns 10604
(914) 381-6177 .. **Wind**, Kelley D '00 Animal Welfare Trust -141 Halstead Av -Mamaroneck 10543
(212) 687-1492 .. **Wind**, Michl B '65 -1350 Bway -NY 10018 **Fx**:967-1711
(212) 450-4000 .. **Windels**, James H R '90 (Davis P&W LLP) -450 Lex Av -NY 10017
(212) 269-0927 .. **Windels**, Kevin '85 (D'Amato & L,LLP) -2 World Fncl Ctr -NY 10281
(212) 237-1000 .. **Windels Marx Lane & Mittendorf,LLP** -156 W 56th -NY 10019 **Fx**:262-1215
(212) 374-9260 .. **Windels**, Paul III '83 -187 Garth Rd -Scarsdale 10583
(212) 837-6128 .. **Windham**, Yusef Z '10 %Hughes H&R LLP -1 Bttry Pk Plz -NY 10004 **Fx**:299-6128
(212) 545-4000 .. **Windholz**, Diane '89 (Jackson L LLP) -666 3rd Av -NY 10017
(212) 788-1187 .. **Windholz**, Elaine '93 %Law Dept -100 Church -NY 10007 **Fx**:788-0367
(212) 788-5005 .. **Windholz**, Roslyn '90 %Dept Hlth -125 Worth CN-30 -NY 10013 **Fx**:788-4300
(212) 701-3000 .. **Windle**, S Penny '98 (Cahill G&R LLP) -80 Pine -NY 10005 **Fx**:269-5420
(917) 576-0127 .. **Windman**, Joel A '60 -14 N Chatsworth Av -Larchmnt 10538
(212) 264-7562 .. **Windrow**, Hayden E '06 %US Ct of Intl Trade -1 Fed Plz -NY 10278
(212) 258-8000 .. **Windt**, Heather J '01 %MTV Networks -1515 Bway -NY 10036 **Fx**:258-8358
(212) 457-9545 .. **Windwer**, Jill '86 %IncisiveMedia /NYLJ -120 Bway -NY 10271
(212) 906-1200 .. **Wine**, Jamie L '07 (Latham & W) -885 3rd Av -NY 10022
(212) 715-9100 .. **Winefsky**, Joshua S '10 %Kramer LN&F,LLP -1177 Av of Amer -NY 10036
(212) 373-3000 .. **Winegar**, Justin M '10 %Paul WRW&G LLP -1285 Av of Amer -NY 10019
(212) 233-6550 .. **Winer**, Harvey '68 (Salzman & W LLP) -305 Bway -NY 10007
(212) 310-8000 .. **Winer**, Jed P '05 %Weil G&M LLP -767 5th Av -NY 10153
(212) 230-8800 .. **Winer**, Jeremy S '04 Cnsl WilmerHale -399 Park Av -NY 10022
(516) 571-3800 .. **Winer**, Rebecca M '96 %DA -262 Old Cntry Rd -Mineola 11501 **Fx**:248-9479
(212) 272-9086 .. **Winer**, Stephen I '02 %JP Morgan Chase -383 Mad Av -NY 10179
(212) 756-2000 .. **Wines**, James M '97 SpclCnsl Schulte R&Z LLP -919 3rd Av -NY 10022
(212) 218-2100 .. **Wines**, Kelly L '07 %Fitzpatrick CH&S -1290 Av of Amer -NY 10104
(315) 425-2700 .. **Winfield**, Angela C '09 %Hiscock & B,LLP -One Park Pl -Syracuse 13202
(212) 921-8399 .. **Wing**, John R '64 (Lankler S&W LLP) -500 5th Av -NY 10110
(516) 931-8367 .. **Wing**, Jos B '91 -46 Locust Av -Bethpage 11714 **Fx**:931-8367
(718) 206-4083 .. **Wing**, Juanita E '99 J Wing,PC -89-31 161st -Jamaica 11432 **Fx**:206-4084
(845) 485-8529 .. **Wing**, Stephen J '73 -3 W Cllg Av -Poughkeepsie 12601 **Fx**:485-6626
(212) 421-8100 .. **Wingard**, Mary Katherine '07 %Wrobel & S LLP -1040 Av of Amer -NY 10018
(718) 852-5900 .. **Wingate Kearney & Cullen** -45 Main -Brklyn 11201 **Fx**:852-8168
(631) 694-5500 .. **Wingate Kearney & Cullen** -445 Broad Hollow Rd -Melvll 11747 **Fx**:694-5813
(212) 986-7353 .. **Wingate Russotti & Shapiro** -420 Lex Av -NY 10170 **Fx**:953-4308
(646) 414-6877 .. **Wingens**, Gary M '09 (Lowenstein S PC) -1251 Av of Amer -NY 10020 **Fx**:(973) 597-2559
(212) 841-1000 .. **Winger**, Michl '73 SpclCnsl Covington & B LLP -620 8th Av -NY 10018
(914) 323-7000 .. **Wingertzahn**, Wm M '93 (Wilson EME&D LLP) -3 Gannett Dr -White Plns 10604
(212) 221-6900 .. **Winget Spadafora & Schwartzberg,LLP** -45 Bway -NY 10006 **Fx**:221-6989
(212) 221-6900 .. **Winget**, Wm G '87 (Winget S&S,LLP) -45 Bway -NY 10006
(212) 813-8800 .. **Wingfield**, Calvin E Jr. '07 %Goodwin P LLP -620 8th Av -NY 10018
(212) 314-7376 .. **Winiarski**, Gregg J '98 IAC/InterActive Corp -555 W 18th -NY 10011
(212) 801-6885 .. **Winiarsky**, Myron '04 %Greenberg T,LLP -200 Park Av -NY 10166
(212) 869-5030 .. **Winiarsky**, Nativ '96 (Kucker & B,LLP) -747 3rd Av -NY 10017
(212) 653-8700 .. **Winick**, Alan C '56 SpclCnsl Sheppard MR&H LLP -30 Rckfllr Plz -NY 10112
(516) 746-8000 .. **Winick**, Allan L '50 OfCnsl Jaspan S LLP -300 Grdn City Plz -Gdn Cty 11530
(212) 878-8000 .. **Winick**, Danl M '04 %Clifford C LLP -31 W 52nd -NY 10019
(212) 687-6887 .. **Winick**, Eugene H '60 McIntosh & Otis,Inc -353 Lex Av -NY 10016 **Fx**:687-6894
(212) 765-5070 .. **Winick**, Jennifer D '06 %Fish & R,PC -153 E 53rd -NY 10022
(516) 625-9400 .. **Winick**, Steven J '76 (Topspin Prtnrs) -3 Expwy Plz -Roslyn Hts 11577
(212) 454-3272 .. **Winicour**, Sheldon B '89 %Deutsche Bank -60 Wall -NY 10005
(718) 590-2000 .. **Winik**, Jessica S '09 %DA -198 E 161st -Bronx 10451 **Fx**:590-6477
(212) 768-6700 .. **Winikoff**, Robt L '74 (Sonnenschein N&R LLP) -1221 Av of Amer -NY 10020
(212) 244-3333 .. **Winikow**, Scott K '94 (Donovan H LLP) -1350 Bway -NY 10018
(212) 872-1000 .. **Wininger**, Russell L '10 -One Bryant Park -NY 10036 **Fx**:872-1002
(212) 735-3000 .. **Wink**, Benton C '08 %Skadden ASM&F LLP -4 Times Sq -NY 10036
(518) 584-1991 .. **Wink**, Stephen P '92 (Cahill/Wink LLP) -60 Railroad Pl -Saratoga Spgs 12866
(516) 248-7000 .. **Wink**, Wayne H Jr. '97 OfCnsl Albanese & A LLP -1050 Franklin Av -Gdn Cty 11530
(212) 230-8808 .. **Winke**, Paul M '03 Cnsl WilmerHale -399 Park Av -NY 10022
(212) 837-6000 .. **Winkelman**, Jaime P '09 %Hughes H&R LLP -1 Bttry Pk Plz -NY 10004
(212) 382-0909 .. **Winkler**, Alan '83 (Peckar & A,PC) -41 Mad Av -NY 10154
(212) 947-3793 .. **Winkler**, Erika L '07 %Sadis & G LLP -551 5th Av -NY 10176
(212) 674-2779 .. **Winkler**, Fredk F '68 -301 E 21st -NY 10010
(631) 928-8000 .. **Winkler**, James R '77 (Winkler KW&K,LLP) -310 Hallock Av -Pt Jffrsn Sta 11776
(718) 590-3786 .. **Winkler**, Jeffrey M '82 Supreme Ct -851 Grnd Cncrs -Bronx 10451
(631) 928-8000 .. **Winkler Kurtz Winkler & Kuhn,LLP** -310 Hallock Av -Pt Jffrsn Sta 11776 **Fx**:928-8578
(631) 928-8000 .. **Winkler**, Richd D '83 (Winkler KW&K,LLP) -310 Hallock Av -Pt Jffrsn Sta 11776
(212) 226-1900 .. **Winkles**, Stephen P '01 (Tesser & C) -591 Bway -NY 10012
(212) 785-0900 .. **Winmill**, Thos B '88 %Bull & Bear Grp Inc -11 Hanover Sq -NY 10005
(800) 879-1805 .. **Winn**, Franshone '92 %BJ Barrett -26 Carroll -Amityvll 11701
(212) 422-0202 .. **Winn**, Jeffrey M '87 (Sedgwick DM&A LLP) -125 Broad -NY 10004
(518) 642-1365 .. **Winn**, John R '76 -13 North -Granvll 12832 **Fx**:642-1436
(516) 773-8525 .. **Winn**, Kim S '91 -9 N Clover Dr -Gt Neck 11021 **Fx**:482-7335
(516) 495-7907 .. **Winn**, Mitchell J '85 -1225 Franklin Av -Gdn Cty 11530 **Fx**:626-0565
(518) 746-7100 .. **Winn**, Robt M '81 -326 Bway -Ft Edward 12828
(516) 775-1414 .. **Winn**, Stephen G '64 (Monsour WK&W,LLP) -3000 Marcus Av -Lk Success 11042
(212) 644-1710 .. **Winne Banta Hetherington & Basralian,PC** -286 Mad Av -NY 10017 **Fx**:(201) 487-8529
(845) 876-3096 .. **Winne**, Robt F '50 -27 Mulberry -Rhinebeck 12572
(646) 386-5000 .. **Winner**, Ellen J '75 %Surrogates Ct -31 Chmbrs -NY 10007

(607) 734-0990 ..**Winner**, George H Jr. '77 (Keyser M&W LLP) -150 Lk -Elmira 14901
(212) 557-1004 ..**Winner**, Karen F '09 -233 5th Av -NY 10016
(212) 560-9020 ..**Winning**, Walter R '80 -350 5th Av -NY 10118
(212) 788-0959 ..**Winningham**, Katherine L '89 %Law Dept -100 Church -NY 10007 **Fx**:788-0367
(212) 436-1747 ..**Winningham**, Steven R '93 %IRS -290 Bway -NY 10007
(212) 268-6900 ..**Winograd**, Corey M '91 (Winograd & W PC) -450 7th Av -NY 10123 **Fx**:629-5825
(212) 788-0471 ..**Winograd**, Elliott C '64 %Law Dept -100 Church -NY 10007 **Fx**:788-0367
(212) 268-6900 ..**Winograd**, Joel '67 (Winograd & W PC) -450 7th Av -NY 10123 **Fx**:629-5825
(914) 682-5933 ..**Winograd**, Marc L '83 -11 Martine Av -White Plns 10606 **Fx**:(201) 947-3883
(212) 999-5800 ..**Winograd**, Michl S '01 OfCnsl Wilson SG&R -1301 Av of Americas -NY 10019
(212) 601-9700 ..**Winograd**, Richd M '81 (Ginarte OGG&W,LLP) -225 Bway -NY 10007
(718) 466-3000 ..**Winograd**, Susan R '98 %Civil Ct -1118 Grnd Cncrs -Bronx 10456 **Fx**:466-3006
(845) 623-6514 ..**Winoker**, Arthur '62 -15 Clearwtr Ct -Nanuet 10954 **Fx**:623-6514
(718) 263-5450 ..**Winokur**, Adrienne J '04 %M Winokur -18307 Union Tpk -Fresh Mdws 11366
(212) 698-3500 ..**Winokur**, Barton J '07 (Dechert LLP) -1095 Av of Amer -NY 10036
(212) 698-3500 ..**Winokur**, Derek M '98 (Dechert LLP) -1095 Av of Amer -NY 10036
(212) 693-1671 ..**Winokur**, Gil J '91 %H Kulefsky -111 John -NY 10038 **Fx**:385-4846
(718) 275-7475 ..**Winokur**, Michl S '68 -18307 Union Tpk -Fresh Mdws 11366
(212) 261-8000 ..**Winowiecki**, Jos J '81 (Mendes & M,LLP) -750 7th Av -NY 10019
(212) 277-6500 ..**Winsbro**, John P '88 Cnsl Dickstein S LLP -1633 Bway -NY 10019
(212) 636-6000 ..**Winship**, Verity E '01 %Fordham Univ Sch of Law -140 W 62nd -NY 10023 **Fx**:636-6899
(646) 688-5424 ..**Winslett**, Usher T '87 (Winslett SM&B LLP) -6 E 39th -NY 10016 **Fx**:(707) 549-4517
(914) 681-0200 ..**Winslow**, Heidi M '04 %DelBello DWW&W,LLP -1 N Lex Av -White Plns 10601
(845) 562-0500 ..**Winslow**, James W '81 -10 Little Britain Rd Bx2275 -Newburgh 12550 **Fx**:562-0839 ***[Criminal Law]***
(212) 595-1271 ..**Winslow**, Thos A '73 -57 W 68th -NY 10023
(212) 688-5151 ..**Winsor**, Christina L '07 %Gibney A&F,LLP -665 5th Av -NY 10022
(607) 965-6636 ..**Winsor**, Martin P '82 -36 South -Edmeston 13335 **Fx**:965-6636
(518) 465-5551 ..**Winsten**, Richd D '78 (Meyer SE&K,PC) -One Commerce Plz -Albany 12260
(631) 563-1188 ..**Winston**, Allan B '74 SpclCnsl J Miller III -213-1 Montauk Hwy -W Sayvll 11796 **Fx**:563-0896
(212) 532-2700 ..**Winston**, Arthur '49 (Winston & W,PC) -295 Mad Av -NY 10017 **Fx**:532-2722
(212) 770-5313 ..**Winston**, Blair Ann '95 AIG -70 Pine -NY 10270
(212) 966-3730 ..**Winston**, Diane I '88 (Kelman W&V) -2 Rector -NY 10006
(212) 686-4655 ..**Winston**, Frank P '94 (Abraham L&A LLP) -292 Mad Av -NY 10017
(212) 351-4000 ..**Winston**, Georgia K '01 %Gibson D&C LLP -200 Park Av -NY 10166
(516) 486-0732 ..**Winston**, Harold S '51 -670 Evergreen Dr -W Hempstead 11552
(718) 590-2000 ..**Winston**, Janelle L '05 %DA -198 E 161st -Bronx 10451 **Fx**:590-6477
(212) 532-2700 ..**Winston**, Jay M '95 (Winston & W,PC) -295 Mad Av -NY 10017 **Fx**:532-2722
(212) 317-8668 ..**Winston**, John '60 -30 E 62nd -NY 10065 **Fx**:758-1282
(212) 308-4411 ..**Winston**, Laura J '91 %Edwards AP&D LLP -750 Lex Av -NY 10022
(718) 881-5600 ..**Winston**, Marc A '76 (Lazarus L&W) -3699 Bainbrdg Av -Bronx 10467 **Fx**:881-5666
(212) 563-4100 ..**Winston**, Michl L '86 (Cohen W&S LLP) -330 W 42nd -NY 10036
(212) 368-2550 ..**Winston**, Michl R '80 -333 Convent Av -NY 10031
(212) 354-6000 ..**Winston**, Steven '72 %Daytop Vllg Inc -54 W 40th -NY 10018 **Fx**:382-3899
(212) 294-6700 ..**Winston & Strawn** -200 Park Av -NY 10166 **Fx**:294-4700
(212) 951-6401 ..**Winston-Day**, Jameione M '85 %Dept of Education -475 Park Av S -NY 10016 **Fx**:951-6465
(212) 909-6000 ..**Wint**, Cari A '09 %Debevoise & P LLP -919 3rd Av -NY 10022
(212) 310-8000 ..**Wint**, Damien T '09 %Weil G&M LLP -767 5th Av -NY 10153
(212) 468-4800 ..**Winter**, Alison H '07 %Davis & G LLP -1740 Bway -NY 10019
(212) 513-7788 ..**Winter**, Danl I '07 %Ahmuty D&M -123 William -NY 10038
(212) 769-9395 ..**Winter**, Dorothy '89 -165 West End Av -NY 10023 **Fx**:769-9395
(845) 358-1180 ..**Winter**, Ellen Eisenberg '83 -305 Highmount Ter -Upper Nyack 10960
(212) 361-7942 ..**Winter**, Fran S '83 %Dept Homeless Srvcs -33 Beaver -NY 10004 **Fx**:361-7977
(732) 577-0044 ..**Winter**, Frank S '64 -217 Bway -NY 10007
(212) 345-6000 ..**Winter**, Heather N '03 Marsh,Inc -1166 Av of Amer -NY 10036
(914) 448-0200 ..**Winter**, Janet C '83 (Bartlett MB&M,LLP) -81 Main -White Plns 10601
(516) 222-4900 ..**Winter**, Jerry '58 J Winter,PC -585 Stewart Av -Gdn Cty 11530 **Fx**:222-4515
(212) 336-2000 ..**Winter**, John D '82 (Patterson BW&T LLP) -1133 Av of Amer -NY 10036
(212) 408-2500 ..**Winter**, John M '02 SpclCnsl Baker B,LLP -30 Rckfllr Plz -NY 10112
(917) 903-8565 ..**Winter**, Jos '04 -60 E 42nd -NY 10165
(212) 382-0909 ..**Winter**, Laura E '09 %Peckar & A,PC -41 Mad Av -NY 10154
(212) 867-9500 ..**Winter**, Marissa Ann '87 %Kurzman K&F,LLP -230 Park Av -NY 10169
(212) 619-4350 ..**Winter**, Michl J '06 %Newman MKGH,PC -14 Wall -NY 10005
(716) 278-1800 ..**Winter**, Ronald J '82 %Supreme Ct -92 Franklin -Buffalo 14202 **Fx**:851-3293
(212) 750-5833 ..**Winter**, Scott S '03 Innisfree M&A Inc -501 Mad Av -NY 10022 **Fx**:750-5799
(212) 512-6801 ..**Winter**, Susan '80 %McGraw-Hill -1221 Av of Amer -NY 10020 **Fx**:512-4827
(914) 234-9759 ..**Winterbottom**, Edmund E '69 -33 Mt Hissarlik Way -Bedfrd 10506
(212) 558-4000 ..**Winterkorn-Meikle**, Margaret K '09 %Sullivan & C LLP -125 Broad -NY 10004
(212) 259-8000 ..**Winterode**, Robt P '10 %Dewey & L LLP -1301 Av of Amer -NY 10019
(212) 593-7979 ..**Winters**, Alan '81 (Ziegler S&W,PC) -575 Lex Av -NY 10022
(212) 521-5400 ..**Winters**, Danl K '95 (Reed S LLP) -599 Lex Av -NY 10022
(212) 416-6390 ..**Winters**, Diana R Hyman '04 Atty Gen -120 Bway -NY 10271
(212) 972-3000 ..**Winters**, Ian R '94 (Klestadt & W,LLP) -292 Mad Av -NY 10017
(212) 819-8200 ..**Winters**, Julia M '06 %White & C LLP -1155 Av of Amer -NY 10036
(516) 484-4700 ..**Winters**, Mark F '79 %Winters Landsearch -99 Powerhse Rd -Roslyn Hts 11577
(212) 450-4000 ..**Winters**, Rebecca L '96 Cnsl Davis P&W LLP -450 Lex Av -NY 10017
(845) 371-4700 ..**Winters**, Robt '85 OfCnsl Fein SK&S,PC -747 Chestnut Rdg Rd -Spg Vly 10977
(516) 802-0630 ..**Winterstein**, Paul J '06 %Simmons J,LLP -115 Eileen Way -Syosset 11791
(212) 473-5400 ..**Wintle**, Edwin J '94 Curtis Brown Ltd -10 Astor Pl -NY 10003
(212) 686-4401 ..**Wintner**, Howard A '81 Cnsl Abramson Law Grp PLLC -570 Lex Av -NY 10022 **Fx**:686-6515
(212) 403-1000 ..**Wintner**, Jeffrey M '90 (Wachtell LR&K) -51 W 52nd -NY 10019
(212) 578-4020 ..**Wintner**, Linda '87 %MetLife -27-01 Qns Plz N -LIC 11101 **Fx**:578-3916
(212) 806-5400 ..**Wintner**, Mark '73 (Stroock &S&L LLP) -180 Maiden Ln -NY 10038
(212) 335-4500 ..**Wintringham**, Drew M '83 (DLA Piper LLP) -1251 Av of Amer -NY 10020
(585) 428-5210 ..**Winward**, Thos M V '93 Pub Def -10 N Fitzhugh -Rchstr 14614 **Fx**:428-2234
(212) 867-5800 ..**Winzeler**, Heidi I '02 Cnsl Osler H&H LLP -620 8th Av -NY 10018
(631) 451-6500 ..**Wiplush**, Barbara M '93 %Brookhaven Law Dept -1 Indpndnc Hill -Farmngvll 11738 **Fx**:698-4489
(212) 226-2376 ..**Wipper**, Edw C '03 %Oved & O LLP -101 Av of Amer -NY 10013 **Fx**:226-7555
(917) 777-4200 ..**Wipperman**, Robt C '88 (Bingham M LLP) -1 Bttry Pk Plz -NY 10004
(212) 306-7160 ..**Wirenius**, John F '91 Cnsl Ofc Cllctv Brgn -40 Rector -NY 10006 **Fx**:306-7167
(212) 840-3555 ..**Wirfel**, Kenneth I '73 -500 5th Av -NY 10110 **Fx**:840-2144
(212) 839-5300 ..**Wirgin**, Michl K '05 %Sidley A LLP -787 7th Av -NY 10019
(585) 428-5210 ..**Wirley**, Brian J '94 %Pub Def -10 N Fitzhugh -Rchstr 14614 **Fx**:428-2234
(212) 788-7170 ..**Wirth**, Danl H '06 Admin Childrens Srvcs -220 Church -NY 10013
(914) 949-2700 ..**Wirth**, Mary Anne '79 OfCnsl Bleakley P&S,LLP -1 N Lex Av -White Plns 10601
(631) 864-0800 ..**Wirth**, Robt C '86 (Felberbaum H&W) -357 Vets Mem'l Hwy -Commack 11725
(212) 382-3300 ..**Wirth**, Steven R '99 Cnsl Wollmuth M&D LLP -500 5th Av -NY 10110
(212) 583-9600 ..**Wirtz**, David M '75 (Littler M,PC) -900 3rd Av -NY 10022
(212) 450-4000 ..**Wirtz**, Johannes '07 %Davis P&W LLP -450 Lex Av -NY 10017
(212) 837-6000 ..**Wirz**, Severin I '09 %Hughes H&R LLP -1 Bttry Pk Plz -NY 10004
(716) 845-6000 ..**Wisbaum**, Wayne D '60 (Kavinoky C LLP) -726 Exchange -Buffalo 14210
(212) 485-8490 ..**Wisch**, Lara K '99 MLB Advanced Media -75 9th Av -NY 10011
(212) 687-2770 ..**Wischhusen**, Carl B '01 Cnsl Cohen PL&P -551 5th Av -NY 10176
(516) 747-1990 ..**Wischhusen**, Gina M '09 %Cascone & K,LLP -1399 Franklin Av -Gdn Cty 11530
(212) 514-7400 ..**Wischmeyer**, Dereck A '09 %Buckley & C,PA -225 Bway -NY 10007
(212) 625-9949 ..**Wiscovitch**, Vincent J '95 Cnsl Joseph & S,LLC -2 Rector -NY 10006
(212) 891-8625 ..**Wisdom**, Debra M '97 OfCnsl E&E Cptl Advsrs LLC -160 W 87th -NY 10024
(212) 935-3131 ..**Wise**, Aaron N '65 (Gallet D&B,LLP) -845 3rd Av -NY 10022
(315) 788-6700 ..**Wise**, Anderson '63 (Schwerzmann & W,PC) -215 Wshngtn Bx704 -Watertwn 13601
(845) 291-7077 ..**Wise**, Carla Schuman '92 -60 Erie -Goshen 10924 **Fx**:294-3861
(718) 237-3100 ..**Wise**, Catherine S '08 Leg Aid -111 Lvngstn -Brklyn 11201 **Fx**:250-4243
(212) 450-4000 ..**Wise**, D Scott '78 (Davis P&W LLP) -450 Lex Av -NY 10017
(212) 545-6106 ..**Wise**, Danl J '73 American Lawyer Media/NYLJ -120 Bway -NY 10271
(845) 454-3250 ..**Wise**, David R '87 (Gellert & K,PC) -75 Wshngtn -Poughkeepsie 12601
(212) 617-1923 ..**Wise**, Desiree A '04 Bloomberg Finance -731 Lex Av -NY 10022
(585) 671-4473 ..**Wise**, Gregory W '84 (Murch & W,PC) -674 Ridge Rd -Webster 14580 **Fx**:671-1342
(212) 612-7000 ..**Wise**, H Lake '77 Daiwa Securities Amer -32 Old Slip -NY 10005
(212) 810-2430 ..**Wise**, Harry H III '76 -250 W 57th -NY 10107 **Fx**:810-2427
(212) 351-4000 ..**Wise**, J Eric '99 (Gibson D&C LLP) -200 Park Av -NY 10166
(212) 264-2800 ..**Wise**, Judith Ann '98 US Ct of Intl Trade -1 Fed Plz -NY 10278
(212) 756-2000 ..**Wise**, Julian M '93 (Schulte R&Z LLP) -919 3rd Av -NY 10022
(212) 249-9203 ..**Wise**, Linden H '80 -133 E 80th -NY 10075
(212) 335-4500 ..**Wise**, Mamie V J '09 %DLA Piper LLP -1251 Av of Amer -NY 10020
(914) 879-4642 ..**Wise**, Michl L '06 M Wise,LLC -260 Walsh -LaGrangevll 12540 **Fx**:(866) 747-1034
(212) 558-5500 ..**Wise**, Nicholas A '92 %Weitz & L,PC -700 Bway -NY 10003
(212) 759-8900 ..**Wise**, Norman '68 -251 E 51st -NY 10022
(914) 681-0200 ..**Wise**, Peter J '85 (DelBello DWW&W,LLP) -1 N Lex Av -White Plns 10601
(212) 450-4000 ..**Wise**, Robt F Jr. '73 (Davis P&W LLP) -450 Lex Av -NY 10017
(718) 639-2608 ..**Wisell**, Chas E '96 -37-06 82nd -Jcksn Hts 11372 **Fx**:639-0520
(718) 544-0041 ..**Wisell**, John T Jr. '91 -80-02 Kew Grdns Rd -Kew Gdns 11415 **Fx**:261-0316
(212) 335-9000 ..**Wiseman**, Alice A '93 %DA -1 Hogan Pl -NY 10013
(917) 779-9325 ..**Wiseman**, James P '00 %Cayuga Captl Mgmt LLC -331 W 57th -NY 10019 **Fx**:(212) 202-7967
(212) 558-4000 ..**Wiseman**, Michl M '79 (Sullivan & C LLP) -125 Broad -NY 10004
(716) 433-1991 ..**Wiseman**, Ruth R '84 UAW GM Leg Srvcs -90 Prof Pkwy -Lockprt 14094 **Fx**:433-4888
(212) 556-2100 ..**Wiseman**, Stephen M '86 (King & S) -1185 Av of Amer -NY 10036
(716) 881-5800 ..**Wiseman**, Steven G '77 Siegel K&K -426 Franklin -Buffalo 14202
(212) 679-0400 ..**Wiseman**, Wayne B '82 -450 7th Av -NY 10123 **Fx**:679-1080
(212) 822-1496 ..**Wisham**, Welton K '97 -305 Bway -NY 10007 **Fx**:822-1407

(212) 526-1305 .. **Wishengrad,** Cory '00 %Barclays Capital -745 7th Av -NY 10019
(212) 848-4000 .. **Wishengrad,** David I '06 %Shearman & S LLP -599 Lex Av -NY 10022
(585) 325-3427 .. **Wishengrad,** Marcia H '60 -264 Warren Av -Rchstr 14618 **Fx:**325-3456
(212) 732-8700 .. **Wishner,** Corey Lee '96 (McAloon & F,PC) -123 William -NY 10038
(516) 393-5555 .. **Wishnevski,** Hanita E '09 %Schneider M LLP -666 Old Cntry Rd -Gdn Cty 11530 **Fx:**393-5556
(212) 468-8000 .. **Wishnew,** Jordan A '03 %Morrison & F LLP -1290 Av of Amer -NY 10104
(212) 998-6430 .. **Wishnie,** Michl J '94 %NYU Law Schl -245 Sullivan -NY 10012 **Fx:**995-4031
(716) 847-8400 .. **Wishnoff,** Alan M '80 (Phillips L LLP) -3400 HSBC Ctr -Buffalo 14203
(631) 447-8100 .. **Wishod,** Eugene L '58 SrCnsl Egan & G,LLP -96 S Ocean Av -Patchogue 11772 **Fx:**447-8181
(212) 374-9300 .. **Wiskin,** Jerry P '75 (Simons & W) -45 Bway -NY 10006
(212) 788-1447 .. **Wisler,** Aubrey J '04 ACS -220 Church -NY 10013
(914) 345-3015 .. **Wislocki,** Stephan '90 -Bx129 -Hawthorne 10532
(585) 244-5600 .. **Wisner,** Donald J '66 (Wisner & W,LLP) -1209 East Av -Rchstr 14607 **Fx:**244-5601
(212) 878-8000 .. **Wisner,** Douglas L '79 (Clifford C LLP) -31 W 52nd -NY 10019
(585) 244-5600 .. **Wisner,** Todd J W '94 (Wisner & W,LLP) -1209 East Av -Rchstr 14607 **Fx:**244-5601
(212) 812-2626 .. **Wisnicki,** Robt '04 -1318 60th -Brklyn 11219
(212) 643-8203 .. **Wisniewski,** Bennett J '08 %Zhang & Assoc,PC -1350 Bway -NY 10018 **Fx:**643-5487
(716) 633-3313 .. **Wisniewski,** Brian '09 %Milber MP&S LLP -2809 Wehrle Dr -Williamsvll 14221
(914) 750-5933 .. **Wisniewski,** Christine A '09 %Kissel H&W LLP -580 Wht Plns Rd -Tarrytwn 10591
(716) 847-8120 .. **Wisniewski,** Danl E '80 -232 Delaware Av -Buffalo 14202 **Fx:**847-8122
(516) 432-9400 .. **Wisniewski,** Jacob J '07 %Peknic P&S LLC -1005 W Beech -Long Bch 11561 **Fx:**432-5396
(212) 788-0609 .. **Wisniewski,** Jessica '09 %Law Dept -100 Church -NY 10007 **Fx:**788-0367
(212) 267-2101 .. **Wisniewski,** Robt J '94 (RJ Wisniewski,PC) -225 Bway -NY 10007 **Fx:**587-8115
(212) 949-6900 .. **Wisnik,** Robt S '92 R Wisnik & Assoc -708 3rd Av -NY 10017 **Fx:**949-9449
(212) 282-5000 .. **Wisniowski,** Dorothy '04 Avon Products -1345 Av of Amer -NY 10105
(212) 685-7100 .. **Wisotsky,** Carl '75 C Wisotsky -112 Mad Av -NY 10016 **Fx:**689-9680
(845) 638-1415 .. **Wiss & Bouregy, PC** -222 N Main -New Cty 10956
(845) 638-1415 .. **Wiss,** Raymond R '81 (Wiss & B,PC) -222 N Main -New Cty 10956
(516) 747-3222 .. **Wiss,** Scott L '91 (Levine & W,PLLC) -259 Mineola Blvd -Mineola 11501
(845) 638-1415 .. **Wiss,** Timothy J '07 %Wiss & B,PC -222 N Main -New Cty 10956
(718) 786-5811 .. **Wissak,** Richd J '86 -45-16 Vernon Blvd -LIC 11101
(914) 666-3800 .. **Wissel,** Philip J '83 -45 Main -Bedfrd Hlls 10507 **Fx:**666-4303
(212) 848-4000 .. **Wissel,** Veronica M '08 %Shearman & S LLP -599 Lex Av -NY 10022
(516) 773-8300 .. **Wisselman,** Jerome A '72 (Wisselman H & Assoc,PC) -1010 Nrthrn Blvd -Gt Neck 11021 **Fx:**773-8304
(718) 670-1044 .. **Wissemann,** Wm P '89 NY Hospital of Queens -56-45 Main -Flushng 11355
(585) 777-2196 .. **Wisset,** Barry S '89 %Frontier & Citizens Communicatns -180 S Clinton Av -Rchstr 14646 **Fx:**263-9986
(212) 627-8100 .. **Wissinger,** G Micah '03 %Levy R,PC -80 8th Av -NY 10011
(518) 402-9003 .. **Wissler,** Richd R '80 %DEC -625 Bway -Albany 12233 **Fx:**402-9018
(212) 735-8600 .. **Wissman,** Sean D '03 %Morrison C LLP -909 3rd Av -NY 10022
(212) 406-9288 .. **Wissner,** Reid B '80 -325 Bway -NY 10007 **Fx:**571-2044
(212) 209-4800 .. **Wissner-Gross,** Sigmund S '83 (Brown R LLP) -7 Times Sq -NY 10036
(866) 348-5819 .. **Wistner,** Chas P '90 %SSA-ODAR -50 Fountain Plz -Buffalo 14202 **Fx:**(716) 551-4078
(212) 268-7474 .. **Wiswall,** Kyle S '06 Tri-State Transportn Cmpgn -350 W 31st -NY 10001 **Fx:**268-7333
(716) 847-8400 .. **Wiswall,** Thos S '75 (Phillips L LLP) -3400 HSBC Ctr -Buffalo 14203
(518) 477-9411 .. **Witbeck,** George H Jr. '42 -11 Troy Rd -E Greenbush 12061
(212) 840-2196 .. **Witchel,** Milton M '58 -36 W 44th -NY 10036 **Fx:**764-6795
(212) 627-2020 .. **Witcher,** Nicolette R '06 Hudson Rvr Prk Trst -Pier 40-W Houston at West -NY 10014
(585) 546-5530 .. **Witcher,** Tyesha M '00 %Thomson West -50 E Broad -Rchstr 14694
(212) 373-3000 .. **Witdorchic,** Lawr I '96 (Paul WRW&G LLP) -1285 Av of Amer -NY 10019
(518) 372-2827 .. **Witecki,** Glenn J '85 -8 S Church -Schnctdy 12305 **Fx:**372-2893
(212) 412-6707 .. **Witek,** Chas A III '91 Barclays Capital Inc -200 Park Av -NY 10166
(585) 272-0540 .. **Witenko,** Jessica L '09 Thomas & S LLP -693 East Av -Rchstr 14607
(716) 258-0590 .. **Witherby,** Fredk R H Jr. '76 -1076 Cayuga Dr -Niagara Fls 14304
(516) 571-3800 .. **Witherell,** Everett '07 %DA -262 Old Cntry Rd -Mineola 11501 **Fx:**248-9479
(212) 848-9800 .. **Withers Bergman LLP** -430 Park Av -NY 10022 **Fx:**848-9888
(212) 610-6300 .. **Withers,** Julie V A '04 %Allen & O -1221 Av of Amer -NY 10020
(212) 474-1000 .. **Withers,** Kathleen H '09 %Cravath S&M LLP -825 8th Av -NY 10019
(845) 486-2225 .. **Witherwax,** Wayne R '87 %Hon G Hayes -10 Market -Poughkeepsie 12601
(607) 277-3198 .. **Withiam,** Diane '79 Citzns Concrnd for Chldrn-Law Guardian Ofc -121 E Buffalo -Ithaca 14850 **Fx:**277-0246
(914) 421-3200 .. **Withiam,** Jack Jr. '75 Geo Little Mngmnt -1133 Wstchstr Av -West Harrison 10604 **Fx:**948-6388
(518) 587-5188 .. **Withington,** Mary M '82 %Leg Aid -112 Spring -Saratoga Spgs 12866 **Fx:**587-0959
(212) 408-2500 .. **Withstandley,** Peter '06 %Baker B,LLP -30 Rckfllr Plz -NY 10112
(212) 583-9600 .. **Witkin,** Eric D '73 Cnsl Littler M,PC -900 3rd Av -NY 10022
(718) 237-6290 .. **Witkin,** Joshua '82 %Div of Leg Srvcs -283 Adams -Brklyn 11201
(212) 855-3200 .. **Witkin,** Merrie Faye '80 %Depository Trust -55 Water -NY 10041 **Fx:**855-3279
(212) 885-5000 .. **Witkin,** Susan Peckett '82 (Blank R LLP) -405 Lex Av -NY 10174
(212) 672-4700 .. **Witkoff,** Steven C '85 %The Witkoff Group -220 E 42nd -NY 10017 **Fx:**672-4726
(516) 944-1710 .. **Witkoff,** Susan L '92 -65 Barkers Pnt Rd -Sands Pnt 11050
(585) 232-2225 .. **Witkowicz,** Steven M '80 (Handelman W&L) -410 Rynlds Arcd -Rchstr 14614
(518) 402-6757 .. **Witkowski,** Laura J '91 %Workers Comp Bd -20 Park -Albany 12207
(585) 263-1000 .. **Witmer,** G Robt Jr. '62 SrCnsl Nixon P LLP -1100 Clinton Sq -Rchstr 14604
(410) 212-0215 .. **Witmer,** Jonathan W '07 -415 Cobbs Hill Dr -Rchstr 14610
(212) 839-5300 .. **Witmer,** Michl J '07 %Sidley A LLP -787 7th Av -NY 10019
(585) 263-1000 .. **Witmeyer,** John D '71 (Nixon P LLP) -1100 Clinton Sq -Rchstr 14604
(212) 269-4900 .. **Witmeyer,** John J III '72 (Ford MEW&G,LLP) -Wall Street Plz -NY 10005
(212) 403-1000 .. **Witt,** Austin T '08 %Wachtell LR&K -51 W 52nd -NY 10019
(212) 854-0076 .. **Witt,** John F '00 Columbia Law Schl -435 W 116th -NY 10027 **Fx:**854-7946
(518) 462-5300 .. **Witt,** Robt Martin '08 DeGraff F&K LLP -90 State -Albany 12207
(212) 509-6300 .. **Witt,** Sheldon N '56 -17 Battery Pl -NY 10004 **Fx:**509-6996
(212) 840-8888 .. **Witt,** Sonya '97 %Tommy Hilfiger USA -25 W 39th -NY 10018
(212) 556-2100 .. **Witt,** Vanessa A '08 %King & S -1185 Av of Amer -NY 10036
(718) 665-0220 .. **Wittels,** Milton '51 (Irom WFB&S,PC) -349 E 149th -Bronx 10451
(646) 723-2947 .. **Wittels,** Steven L '85 (Sanford W&H,LLP) -1350 Av of Amer -NY 10019
(212) 553-6355 .. **Witten,** Elizabeth J '93 %CASES -346 Bway -NY 10013
(718) 286-6000 .. **Witten,** Michelle W '09 DA -125-01 Qns Blvd -Kew Gdns 11415
(212) 230-8850 .. **Witten,** Roger M '04 (WilmerHale) -399 Park Av -NY 10022
(212) 804-4200 .. **Witten,** Russell A '06 %Mound CW&G -One Bttry Pk Plz -NY 10004
(212) 691-4369 .. **Wittenberg,** Pauline '77 -302 W 12th -NY 10014
(315) 428-8100 .. **Wittenburg,** Richd A '66 (Wittenburg Law Firm,LLC) -920 Univ Bldg -Syracuse 13202 **Fx:**426-8102
(315) 428-8100 .. **Wittenburg,** Tracy M '92 (Wittenburg Law Firm,LLC) -920 Univ Bldg -Syracuse 13202 **Fx:**426-8102
(718) 261-8114 .. **Wittenstein,** Alyce B '99 (Wittenstein & W) -108-18 Qns Blvd -Frst Hlls 11375 **Fx:**263-4999
(212) 750-8700 .. **Wittenstein,** Andrew A '79 (Friedman & W,PC) -600 Lex Av -NY 10022
(718) 261-8114 .. **Wittenstein,** Fredk M '56 (Wittenstein & W) -108-18 Qns Blvd -Frst Hlls 11375 **Fx:**263-4999
(718) 449-5600 .. **Wittenstein,** Harlan A '88 Wittenstein & Assoc,PC -2502 86th -Brklyn 11214 **Fx:**449-9766
(212) 670-0420 .. **Witterschein,** Judith A '83 Merrill Lynch -222 Bway -NY 10038
(212) 788-0455 .. **Witterschein,** June A '79 %Law Dept -100 Church -NY 10007 **Fx:**788-0367
(212) 984-7824 .. **Wittes,** Robt P '64 (Warshaw BCS&K,LLP) -555 5th Av -NY 10017
(212) 556-2100 .. **Witthuhn,** Wilfried E '75 (King & S) -1185 Av of Amer -NY 10036
(585) 232-6500 .. **Wittlin,** Craig S '93 (Harter S&E LLP) -1600 Bausch & Lomb Pl -Rchstr 14604
(716) 853-1616 .. **Wittlin,** Craig S '93 (Harter S&E LLP) -12 Fountain Plz -Buffalo 14202
(212) 705-7000 .. **Wittlin,** Floyd I '83 (Bingham M LLP) -399 Park Av -NY 10022
(718) 243-6411 .. **Wittman,** Michl L '80 Legal Aid Society -111 Lvngstn -Brklyn 11201
(315) 366-2585 .. **Wittman,** Rebecca L '91 %Pub Def -Bx576 -Wampsville 13163 **Fx:**366-2816
(212) 785-0157 .. **Wittner,** Therese M '00 NYS Nurses Assn -120 Wall -NY 10005 **Fx:**785-0429
(212) 421-9630 .. **Wittstein,** Eric S '97 Smythe Masterson & Judd -230 Park Av -NY 10169 **Fx:**421-9665
(516) 328-8272 .. **Wittstruck,** Chris E '82 -33 Park Cir -New Hyde Pk 11040
(212) 331-3460 .. **Witty,** Elaine H '94 Ofc of Refugee & Immig Affrs -180 Water -NY 10038 **Fx:**331-4692
(631) 234-5678 .. **Witty,** Emanuel I '57 SrCnsl Wallace WF&V,PC -600 Suffolk Av -Brentwd 11717
(718) 579-3000 .. **Witty,** Frank P '92 %Leg Aid -1020 Grnd Cncrs -Bronx 10451 **Fx:**588-2611
(518) 449-8893 .. **Witz,** Thos M '98 (Wilson EME&D LLP) -677 Bway -Albany 12207
(212) 859-8000 .. **Witzel,** Steven M '84 (Fried FHS&J LLP) -1 NY Plz -NY 10004
(212) 308-8505 .. **Witztum,** Ruth J '78 OfCnsl Akabas & S -488 Mad Av -NY 10022
(212) 918-0635 .. **Wizenberg,** Darin B '01 -555 5th Av -NY 10017
(212) 813-8800 .. **Wizenfeld,** Chas '05 %Goodwin P LLP -620 8th Av -NY 10018
(212) 504-6000 .. **Wizenfeld,** Howard '03 %Cadwalader W&T LLP -1 World Fncl Ctr -NY 10281
(718) 896-2000 .. **Wizman,** Chaim Z '92 (Taller & W,PC) -118-35 Qns Blvd -Frst Hlls 11375
(212) 869-3850 .. **Wizmur,** Dina E I '09 Cnsl Medicare Rights Ctr -520 8th Av NW -NY 10018 **Fx:**869-3532
(315) 445-1700 .. **Wladis,** Mark N '90 (Wladis Law Firm,PC) -5795 Widewaters Pkwy -Syracuse 13214 **Fx:**251-1073
(914) 286-2900 .. **Wlazlo,** Artur M '05 %Greenberg T,LLP -445 Hmltn Av -White Plns 10601
(212) 326-2000 .. **Wlazlo,** Mark B '03 (O'Melveny & M LLP) -7 Times Sq -NY 10036
(212) 589-4200 .. **Wlodek,** Heather R '04 %Baker & H LLP -45 Rckfllr Plz -NY 10111
(212) 613-8900 .. **Wnek,** Linda A '95 77WABC & 95.5WPLJ -2 Penn Plz -NY 10121 **Fx:**613-3890
(914) 323-7000 .. **Wodarski,** Jos P III '00 %Wilson EME&D LLP -3 Gannett Dr -White Plns 10604
(212) 719-8347 .. **Woehlke,** James A '00 NYS Society of CPAs -530 5th Av -NY 10036
(585) 428-5738 .. **Woehrlen,** Patricia L '84 %Cnty Atty -50 W Main -Rchstr 14614 **Fx:**428-2031
(212) 596-9000 .. **Wofford,** Keith H '94 (Ropes & G LLP) -1211 Av of Amer -NY 10036
(212) 474-1000 .. **Wofford,** Travis J '10 %Cravath S&M LLP -825 8th Av -NY 10019
(516) 826-6500 .. **Wofse,** Adam P '95 OfCnsl LaMonica H&M LLP -3305 Jerusalem Av -Wantagh 11793
(212) 719-0200 .. **Wofse,** Ilyse Ara '96 Bar/Bri -1500 Bway -NY 10036
(212) 980-0120 .. **Wogan,** Maura J '80 (Frankfurt KK&S,PC) -488 Mad Av -NY 10022
(212) 596-9000 .. **Woglom,** Eric C '68 (Ropes & G LLP) -1211 Av of Amer -NY 10036

(212) 838-7380 .. **Wohabe,** Abdul W '62 (Wohabe) -405 Lex Av -NY 10174 **Fx:**838-7463
(212) 838-7380 .. **Wohabe,** David P '86 %Wohabe -405 Lex Av -NY 10174 **Fx:**838-7463
(212) 838-7380 .. **Wohabe,** Omar S '89 %Wohabe -405 Lex Av -NY 10174 **Fx:**838-7463
(607) 273-3666 .. **Wohl,** Betsy '91 %Leg Srvcs -215 N Cayuga -Ithaca 14850 **Fx:**273-5521
(212) 310-8000 .. **Wohl,** David E '96 (Weil G&M LLP) -767 5th Av -NY 10153
(212) 922-9250 .. **Wohl,** Eric M '06 %Ganfer & S LLP -360 Lex Av -NY 10017
(212) 907-0700 .. **Wohl,** Ethan D '94 %Labaton S LLP -140 Bway -NY 10005
(212) 921-8399 .. **Wohl,** Frank H '67 (Lankler S&W LLP) -500 5th Av -NY 10110
(212) 679-8080 .. **Wohl Loewe Stettner Fabricant & Deitz,PC** -9 E 40th -NY 10016 **Fx:**689-9436
(845) 291-2454 .. **Wohl,** Marc '74 %Leg Aid -2 Court Ln Bx328 -Goshen 10924 **Fx:**294-2638
(212) 331-5037 .. **Wohl,** Ronald M '86 %HRA -180 Water -NY 10038
(212) 336-2000 .. **Wohl,** Russell G '90 Cnsl Patterson BW&T LLP -1133 Av of Amer -NY 10036
(212) 370-5970 .. **Wohl,** Steven J '69 (Stern KP&W,LLP) -675 3rd Av -NY 10017
(914) 428-8800 .. **Wohl,** Steven J '69 (Stern KP&W,LLP) -1025 Wstchstr Av -White Plns 10604
(718) 252-1330 .. **Wohlberg,** Alan J '90 -2805 Av N -Brklyn 11210
(518) 673-2669 .. **Wohlberg,** Catherine F '93 -239 Groff Rd -Palatine Brdg 13428
(914) 375-0100 .. **Wohlberg,** Stephen I '86 %Novick ELRW&L,PC -733 Ynkrs Av -Ynkrs 10704
(212) 557-2900 .. **Wohlfarth,** Danl S '80 (Schwartzman GW&T,PC) -355 Lex Av -NY 10017
(212) 819-8200 .. **Wohlferd,** Clark A '07 %White & C LLP -1155 Av of Amer -NY 10036
(718) 579-3000 .. **Wohlford,** Jason C '90 %Leg Aid -1020 Grnd Cncrs -Bronx 10451 **Fx:**588-2611
(973) 596-4879 .. **Wohlforth,** E Evan Jr. '97 (Gibbons PC) -1 Penn Plz -NY 10119 **Fx:**639-6486
(212) 619-2457 .. **Wohlforth,** Karen Finkel '81 -299 Bway -NY 10007
(212) 265-6888 .. **Wohlgemuth,** Jerrold J '97 OfCnsl Porzio B&N,PC -156 W 56th -NY 10019
(845) 689-2400 .. **Wohlgemuth,** U Marc '03 (Kunstlinger & W PLLC) -235 N Main -Spg Vly 10977 **Fx:**689-2401
(718) 537-4958 .. **Wohlgemuth-Rothstein,** Elizabeth '01 SSA NY -226 E 161st -Bronx 10451
(516) 466-6100 .. **Wohlleber,** Alyssa M '98 %Swartz & S -80 Cutter Mill Rd -Gt Neck 11021 **Fx:**466-6104
(212) 361-1400 .. **Wohlstatter,** Rosalie '86 %Envrnmntl Cntrl Brd -66 John -NY 10038 **Fx:**361-1900
(518) 377-3046 .. **Woidzik,** Francis A '72 -4 Marshall Av -Schnctdy 12304
(718) 667-9421 .. **Woitkowski,** Matthew W '96 (Woitkowski & S) -159 Sand Ln -Staten Isl 10305 **Fx:**667-9422
(212) 692-1000 .. **Wojak,** John S Jr. '87 (Duane M LLP) -1540 Bway -NY 10036
(212) 610-6300 .. **Wojciechowski,** Mark S '81 (Allen & O) -1221 Av of Amer -NY 10020
(716) 856-1344 .. **Wojciechowski,** Thos J '71 (Bouvier Prtnrshp,LLP) -350 Main -Buffalo 14202 **Fx:**856-1369
(518) 408-2645 .. **Wojcik,** Martin J '06 %Insurance Dept -99 Wshngtn Av -Albany 12257 **Fx:**473-4600
(518) 402-9512 .. **Wojcik,** Mary E '06 %DEC -625 Bway -Albany 12233 **Fx:**402-9018
(716) 852-5200 .. **Wojcik,** Melanie M '03 %Hamberger & W -700 Main Pl Twr -Buffalo 14202
(212) 448-1800 .. **Wojcik,** Thaddeus P '05 SrCnsl Roberts RLSC&F LLP -235 Park Av S -NY 10003
(518) 812-9900 .. **Wojdyla,** Kara J '07 -15 Plum Ct -Gansevoort 12831
(914) 242-7861 .. **Wojewoda,** Anne C '03 -37 Radio Circle Dr -Mt Kisco 10549
(845) 433-1162 .. **Wojnicki,** Andrew J Jr. '00 IBM Corp -2455 South Rd MS/P386 -Poughkeepsie 12601
(212) 766-1386 .. **Wojszwilo,** Richd '70 -30 Vesey -NY 10007 **Fx:**571-0938
(212) 859-3492 .. **Wojtalik,** Iwona M '02 I Wojtalik,PC -110 Wall -NY 10005
(716) 681-3355 .. **Wojtan,** Gary J '82 (Wojtan V&G) -2956 Union Rd -Cheektowaga 14227
(716) 681-3355 .. **Wojtan Vallone & Gagola** -2956 Union Rd -Cheektowaga 14227 **Fx:**685-9844
(716) 439-7085 .. **Wojtaszek,** Caroline Ann '98 %DA -175 Hawley -Lockprt 14094 **Fx:**439-7102
(716) 285-1535 .. **Wojtaszek,** Henry F '88 (Harris B PLLC) -800 Main Bx712 -Niagara Fls 14302
(716) 845-9436 .. **Wojtaszek,** Paul B '91 %Supreme Ct -25 Delaware Av -Buffalo 14202 **Fx:**851-3293
(716) 693-8211 .. **Wojtaszek,** Thos E '57 -1438 Moll -N Tonawanda 14120
(718) 398-0869 .. **Wojtaszek,** Thos E '92 -695 Union -Brklyn 11215
(716) 278-1886 .. **Wojtaszek-Gariano,** Kathleen M '94 -775 3rd -Niagara Fls 14301
(212) 785-4100 .. **Wojtkowiak,** Matthew J '97 %Fensterstock & Prtnrs LLP -30 Wall -NY 10005
(518) 434-5050 .. **Wojton,** Michelina Capozzolo '03 Law Dept -106 City Hall -Albany 12207 **Fx:**434-5070
(718) 675-8630 .. **Wojtowicz,** Carol A '06 Hon J McMahon-Supreme Ct -18 Richmond Ter -Staten Isl 10301
(973) 596-4725 .. **Wolak,** John T '90 (Gibbons PC) -1 Penn Plz -NY 10119 **Fx:**639-6276
(607) 734-2271 .. **Wolan,** Conrad R '98 (Sayles & E) -1 W Church -Elmira 14901
(315) 724-3127 .. **Wolber,** Mark A '77 -239 Genesee -Utica 13501
(212) 773-4059 .. **Wolberg,** Allen J '01 Ernst & Young LLP -5 Times Sq -NY 10036
(212) 682-7474 .. **Wolchek,** Ellen C '94 SrCnsl Foley & L LLP -90 Park Av -NY 10016
(718) 701-6097 .. **Wolchok,** Stephanie S '04 Titledge -654 Sharrotts Rd -Staten Isl 10309
(315) 253-8401 .. **Wolczyk,** Jos M '84 NYS Dept of Corrections -164 State -Auburn 13021
(212) 421-4100 .. **Woldenberg,** Eric B '80 (Pryor C LLP) -7 Times Sq -NY 10036
(212) 351-4000 .. **Wolf,** Adam P '06 %Gibson D&C LLP -200 Park Av -NY 10166
(212) 353-4314 .. **Wolf,** Alan N '95 %Cooper Union -51 Astor Pl -NY 10003
(212) 605-0284 .. **Wolf,** Alexander Joel '05 Wolf & Assoc -575 Mad Av -NY 10022 **Fx:**591-6085
(212) 725-7111 .. **Wolf,** Alexis M '08 %Bender RI&R LLP -451 Park Av S -NY 10016
(212) 403-1000 .. **Wolf,** Amy R '80 OfCnsl Wachtell LR&K -51 W 52nd -NY 10019
(212) 679-4666 .. **Wolf,** Aron S '92 %Frenkel H&S LLP -16 E 34th -NY 10016
(212) 310-8209 .. **Wolf,** Barry M '85 (Weil G&M LLP) -767 5th Av -NY 10153
(212) 732-9000 .. **Wolf,** Benjamin J '05 %Sullivan PBM&C PC -120 Bway -NY 10271
(518) 383-0200 .. **Wolf,** Brendan R '06 %Fox & K,LLP -4 Old Route 146 Bx958 -Clifton Pk 12065
(914) 251-0716 .. **Wolf,** Carol S '86 -9 Westerleigh Rd -Purchase 10577
(516) 328-2300 .. **Wolf,** Carolyn Reinach '88 Abrams FFEGF&E,LLP -1111 Marcus Av -Lk Success 11042
(212) 446-4800 .. **Wolf,** Danl E '96 (Kirkland & E LLP) -153 E 53rd -NY 10022
(212) 974-7474 .. **Wolf,** David B '75 (Cowan DA&S LLP) -41 Mad Av -NY 10010
(212) 613-5000 .. **Wolf,** Debra J '85 Leg Assist Grp -450 W 33rd -NY 10001 **Fx:**750-0820
(212) 310-8000 .. **Wolf,** Dena L '79 Cnsl Weil G&M LLP -767 5th Av -NY 10153
(845) 339-8092 .. **Wolf,** Douglas C '95 -253 Wall Bx3101 -Kingston 12402 **Fx:**331-2948
(718) 410-0653 .. **Wolf,** Edw H '67 (Wolf & W,LLP) -910 Grnd Cncrs -Bronx 10451 **Fx:**588-8035
(631) 273-4400 .. **Wolf,** Edw L '63 E Wolf,PC -330 Motor Pkwy -Hauppauge 11788 **Fx:**273-4451
(718) 293-0980 .. **Wolf,** Eliot M '91 (Wolf & F) -1453 Webster Av -Bronx 10456
(845) 452-8300 .. **Wolf,** Elizabeth M '10 (Wolf & W) -577 North Av -Plsnt Vlly 12569
(212) 655-3500 .. **Wolf,** Emily B '03 %Meister S&F LLP -140 E 45th -NY 10017
(716) 856-5500 .. **Wolf,** Fredk A '67 SpclCnsl Damon M LLP -200 Delaware Av -Buffalo 14202
(718) 293-0980 .. **Wolf & Fuhrman** -1453 Webster Av -Bronx 10456 **Fx:**293-7507
(585) 223-2034 .. **Wolf,** George T '67 -150 Perinton Hills Pk -Fairprt 14450
(201) 894-1223 .. **Wolf,** Gerald A '62 -930 Grnd Cncrs -Bronx 10451 **Fx:**567-5222
(516) 877-9653 .. **Wolf,** Gerald P '73 (Wolf Law Grp,PC) -114 Old Cntry Rd -Mineola 11501 **Fx:**877-9660
(212) 545-4600 .. **Wolf Haldenstein Adler Freeman & Herz LLP** -270 Mad Av -NY 10016 **Fx:**686-0114
(716) 662-5901 .. **Wolf,** J Michl '73 -4529 Freeman Rd -Orchard Pk 14127
(212) 334-6022 .. **Wolf,** Jaime M '89 (Pelosi WE&S LLP) -233 Bway -NY 10279 **Fx:**965-1488
(718) 410-2323 .. **Wolf,** Jason M '02 (Wolf & W,LLP) -910 Grnd Cncrs -Bronx 10451 **Fx:**588-8035
(212) 788-1172 .. **Wolf,** Joshua M '09 %Law Dept -100 Church -NY 10007 **Fx:**788-0367
(718) 960-6502 .. **Wolf,** Keith D '94 %St Barnabas Hsptl -4422 3rd Av -Bronx 10457
(212) 883-1300 .. **Wolf,** Kenneth N '75 (Sandler T&R,PA) -551 5th Av -NY 10176
(716) 858-2424 .. **Wolf,** Kevin R '06 %DA -25 Delaware Av -Buffalo 14202 **Fx:**858-7425
(516) 747-1990 .. **Wolf,** Kimberly A '03 %Cascone & K,LLP -1399 Franklin Av -Gdn Cty 11530
(716) 847-0680 .. **Wolf,** Kristen M '92 %W Pacer Jr -298 Main -Buffalo 14202
(716) 858-4883 .. **Wolf,** Kristen Maricle '03 Erie Cnty Dept Soc Srvcs -95 Franklin -Buffalo 14202
(212) 903-8700 .. **Wolf,** Lary S '73 (Roberts & H,LLP) -825 8th Av -NY 10019
(914) 238-9242 .. **Wolf,** Lawr P '74 -6 Hemlock Hls -Chappaqua 10514
(212) 668-2870 .. **Wolf,** Lindsey E '07 Hon M Glenn -1 Bowling Grn -NY 10004
(212) 805-3900 .. **Wolf,** Mark S '89 %Clausen M PC -1 Chase Manh Plz -NY 10005
(212) 227-0640 .. **Wolf,** Martin '06 (Ginsberg & W,PC) -225 Bway -NY 10007
(914) 478-8000 .. **Wolf,** Peter D '74 -25 Main -Hastings-On-Hud 10706 **Fx:**478-0001
(718) 261-7580 .. **Wolf,** Peter M '76 -125-10 Qns Blvd -Kew Gdns 11415
(631) 265-2888 .. **Wolf,** Philip R '97 (Wolf Law Firm LLC) -20 Swallow Ln -Hauppauge 11788 **Fx:**265-2811
(212) 759-4600 .. **Wolf Popper LLP** -845 3rd Av -NY 10022 **Fx:**486-2093
(845) 454-1200 .. **Wolf,** Richd B '62 -510 Haight Av -Poughkeepsie 12603 **Fx:**454-3315
(212) 788-7845 .. **Wolf,** Richd T '73 Board Correction -51 Chmbrs -NY 10007
(212) 872-9800 .. **Wolf,** Robt A '77 (Squire S&D LLP) -30 Rckfllr Plz -NY 10112
(914) 948-4500 .. **Wolf,** Robt A '93 %O'Connor MCD&O -1 Barker Av -White Plns 10601
(212) 752-9700 .. **Wolf,** Robt S '83 (Gersten S LLP) -600 Lex Av -NY 10022
(212) 589-6339 .. **Wolf,** Ronald T '96 Cnsl MF Global Inc -717 5th Av -NY 10022 **Fx:**589-6277
(917) 751-4301 .. **Wolf,** Saml L '00 -67 Wall -NY 10005
(212) 909-6000 .. **Wolf,** Sarah H '09 %Debevoise & P LLP -919 3rd Av -NY 10022
(212) 468-8000 .. **Wolf,** Shiri Bilik '07 %Morrison & F LLP -1290 Av of Amer -NY 10104
(917) 232-4574 .. **Wolf,** Simy C '91 (S Wolf,PC) -24 Paerdegat 3rd -Brklyn 11236 **Fx:**(718) 251-8209
(212) 876-7700 .. **Wolf,** Stacy '86 %ASPCA -424 E 92nd -NY 10128 **Fx:**860-3560
(212) 449-0933 .. **Wolf,** Stephanie S '86 Merrill Lynch -4 World Fncl Ctr -NY 10080
(212) 357-6197 .. **Wolf,** Steven A '89 Goldman Sachs -1 NY Plz -NY 10004
(212) 691-2313 .. **Wolf,** Stewart A '04 Foster & W,PC -80 5th Av -NY 10011 **Fx:**691-2459
(212) 619-4444 .. **Wolf,** Tara L '03 %Marshall CW&B,PC -116 John -NY 10038
(212) 508-6700 .. **Wolf,** Timothy H '07 %Tannenbaum HS&H LLP -900 3rd Av -NY 10022
(585) 544-7944 .. **Wolf,** Wallace J Jr. '49 -164 Mt Airy Dr -Rchstr 14617
(212) 354-4500 .. **Wolf,** Wm K '89 (Friedman & W) -1500 Bway -NY 10036
(845) 362-3234 .. **Wolfberg,** Matisyahu '00 -25 Robt Pitt Dr -Monsey 10952 **Fx:**818-3905
(516) 367-6216 .. **Wolfbiss,** Denise R '82 -1 Magnolia Ln -Woodbury 11797
(845) 634-6760 .. **Wolfe,** Alden H '96 (A Wolfe,PC) -151 S Main -New Cty 10956
(315) 349-3286 .. **Wolfe,** Andrew T '92 %Cnty Ct -39 Churchill Rd -Oswego 13126 **Fx:**349-3457
(212) 526-0617 .. **Wolfe,** Bari Jane '84 Barclays Capital Inc -1301 Av of Amer -NY 10019
(212) 653-8700 .. **Wolfe,** Blanka K '08 %Sheppard MR&H LLP -30 Rckfllr Plz -NY 10112
(212) 979-9846 .. **Wolfe,** Brett I '88 -21 Styvsnt Oval -NY 10009
(212) 450-4000 .. **Wolfe,** Brian '08 %Davis P&W LLP -450 Lex Av -NY 10017
(212) 326-3939 .. **Wolfe,** Caryn L '08 %Jones D -222 E 41st -NY 10017
(212) 857-8500 .. **Wolfe,** Catherine O'Hagan '81 %US Ct of Appeals -40 Foley Sq -NY 10007 **Fx:**857-8710
(212) 788-0735 .. **Wolfe,** Christopher T '86 %Law Dept -100 Church -NY 10007 **Fx:**788-0367
(212) 278-6035 .. **Wolfe,** Cory A '93 %Societe Generale -1221 Av of Amer -NY 10020
(212) 808-7800 .. **Wolfe,** Craig A '06 (Kelley D&W LLP) -101 Park Av -NY 10178
(212) 692-8248 .. **Wolfe,** D Forest '01 Angelo Gordon & Co,LP -245 Park Av -NY 10167

(212) 918-3000 .. **Wolfe,** Deborah R '87 (Hogan L LLP) -875 3rd Av -NY 10022
(516) 224-6040 .. **Wolfe,** Douglas M '98 %ASM Capital -7600 Jericho Tpk -Woodbury 11797
(212) 592-1400 .. **Wolfe,** Eliyahu E '09 %Herrick,F LLP -2 Park Av -NY 10016
(718) 793-5000 .. **Wolfe,** Elysa B '97 %Tarshis & H,LLP -118-35 Qns Blvd -Frst Hlls 11375
(212) 480-5284 .. **Wolfe,** Ethan G '84 Insurance Dept -25 Beaver -NY 10004 **Fx:**480-5272
(212) 574-1200 .. **Wolfe,** Gary J '77 (Seward & K LLP) -1 Bttry Pk Plz -NY 10004
(716) 843-5700 .. **Wolfe,** Jane B '80 %US Atty -138 Delaware Av -Buffalo 14202 **Fx:**551-3052
(516) 747-9006 .. **Wolfe,** Jayson A '03 (Greco & W) -300 Grdn City Plz -Gdn Cty 11530
(212) 756-2000 .. **Wolfe,** Karin '02 %Schulte R&Z LLP -919 3rd Av -NY 10022
(315) 349-3276 .. **Wolfe,** Kathryn Greene '94 Hon N Seiter Jr -25 E Oneida -Oswego 13126 **Fx:**349-3299
(315) 687-7215 .. **Wolfe,** Keith R '78 %Baum & W -282 Genesee -Chittenango 13037
(315) 376-2331 .. **Wolfe,** Kenneth B '48 -7644 State Bx88 -Lowvll 13367
(718) 875-1300 .. **Wolfe,** Lara R '00 %Appllt Div 2nd Dept -45 Monroe Pl -Brklyn 11201 **Fx:**858-2446
(212) 218-2100 .. **Wolfe,** Lori A '01 %Fitzpatrick CH&S -1290 Av of Amer -NY 10104
(212) 371-8855 .. **Wolfe,** Marc-Andre '08 %Stikeman E LLP -445 Park Av -NY 10022
(212) 698-3500 .. **Wolfe,** Matthew A '08 %Dechert LLP -1095 Av of Amer -NY 10036
(212) 277-6500 .. **Wolfe,** Mauro M '06 (Dickstein S LLP) -1633 Bway -NY 10019
(845) 454-5586 .. **Wolfe,** Michl H '74 -4 Lbrty -Poughkeepsie 12601
(212) 492-3936 .. **Wolfe,** Mitchell J '91 %Deloitte LLP -1633 Bway -NY 10019 **Fx:**492-4201
(718) 722-6368 .. **Wolfe,** Patricia C '04 Appllt Div 2nd Dept -45 Monroe Pl -Brklyn 11201 **Fx:**858-2446
(212) 859-8000 .. **Wolfe,** Richd A '05 (Fried FHS&J LLP) -1 NY Plz -NY 10004
(315) 797-3550 .. **Wolfe,** Richd L '59 -2803 Genesee -Utica 13501 **Fx:**797-3551
(212) 746-1724 .. **Wolfe,** Robt L '68 NY Presbyterian Hsptl -525 E 68th Bx88 -NY 10065 **Fx:**746-8603
(212) 918-3000 .. **Wolfe,** Saml E '07 %Hogan L LLP -875 3rd Av -NY 10022
(212) 682-8383 .. **Wolfe,** Steven W '63 (Kantor DWMT&G,PC) -51 E 42nd -NY 10017
(212) 679-2900 .. **Wolfe,** Susan C '85 (Hoffman & P LLP) -260 Mad Av -NY 10016
(845) 497-3500 .. **Wolfe,** Wm J '01 Wolfe Law Firm,PC -100 Egbertson Rd -Campbell Hall 10916 **Fx:**497-3330
(516) 767-7100 .. **Wolfe & Yukelson PLLC** -14 Vanderventer Av -Pt Wash 11050 **Fx:**767-7115
(212) 974-0020 .. **Wolfensohn,** Naomi R '94 Jackson Hole Mgmt Inc -1350 Av of Amer -NY 10019
(212) 594-5367 .. **Wolfenson,** Carol B '77 -450 7th Av -NY 10123 **Fx:**947-8339
(845) 255-8400 .. **Wolfenson,** Carol B '77 -125 Dubois Rd -New Paltz 12561
(718) 613-3500 .. **Wolfermann,** Jos E '90 %UIA Bd -Bx29002 -Brklyn 11201 **Fx:**613-3566
(631) 324-5079 .. **Wolfersdorf,** Susan J '88 -Bx429 -E Quogue 11942
(914) 499-5686 .. **Wolfert,** Allan R '66 IBM -1 New Orchrd Rd -Armonk 10504
(914) 376-3757 .. **Wolfert,** Barbara Lee '91 %Leg Srvcs -30 S Bway -Ynkrs 10701 **Fx:**376-8739
(212) 218-5500 .. **Wolfert,** Jonathan P '81 (Seyfarth S LLP) -620 8th Av -NY 10018
(212) 506-1700 .. **Wolff,** Adam John '95 (Kasowitz BT&F LLP) -1633 Bway -NY 10019
(212) 451-2300 .. **Wolff,** Allen R '08 (Olshan GFR&W LLP) -65 E 55th -NY 10022
(718) 260-9696 .. **Wolff,** Andrea B '90 %M Lipman -32 Court -Brklyn 11201
(646) 772-6464 .. **Wolff,** Arnold J '62 (Steinberg & W) -95 Joralemon -Brklyn 11201
(212) 790-4500 .. **Wolff,** Benjamin E '04 (Manatt P&P,LLP) -7 Times Sq -NY 10036
(212) 735-3000 .. **Wolff,** Bert L '85 Cnsl Skadden ASM&F LLP -4 Times Sq -NY 10036
(212) 336-2000 .. **Wolff,** Bruce L '82 Cnsl Patterson BW&T LLP -1133 Av of Amer -NY 10036
(718) 260-2365 .. **Wolff,** Catherine A '99 %US Dist Ct -225 Cadman Plz E -Brklyn 11201
(518) 270-1911 .. **Wolff,** Elizabeth A '06 %Finkelstein & Prtnrs,LLP -759 Hoosick Rd -Troy 12180
(212) 701-3000 .. **Wolff,** Erica A '10 %Cahill G&R LLP -80 Pine -NY 10005 **Fx:**269-5420
(212) 644-6446 .. **Wolff,** Gary B '69 (G Wolff,PC) -488 Mad Av -NY 10022 **Fx:**644-6498
(212) 541-2000 .. **Wolff,** Gary W '90 (Bryan C LLP) -1290 Av of Amer -NY 10104
(315) 423-4400 .. **Wolff,** George R '68 OfCnsl Wolff G&G,LLP -217 Mntgmry -Syracuse 13202
(315) 423-4400 .. **Wolff Goodrich & Goldman, LLP** -217 Mntgmry -Syracuse 13202 **Fx:**424-1701
(212) 841-1000 .. **Wolff,** Jacqueline C '81 OfCnsl Covington & B LLP -620 8th Av -NY 10018
(212) 310-8000 .. **Wolff,** Jennifer M '04 %Weil G&M LLP -767 5th Av -NY 10153
(315) 539-3000 .. **Wolff,** Jerome B E '48 (Wolff W&W) -31 VA -Waterloo 13165
(212) 310-8000 .. **Wolff,** Jesse D '39 Cnsl Weil G&M LLP -767 5th Av -NY 10153
(212) 312-2260 .. **Wolff,** Jessee '08 Leg Aid -60 Lafayette -NY 10013 **Fx:**349-0874
(585) 336-7867 .. **Wolff,** Jocelyn Torres '05 Paychex,Inc -1175 John -W Henrietta 14586
(212) 757-1544 .. **Wolff,** John H '77 %CEW Prtnrs -780 3rd Av -NY 10017
(212) 848-4000 .. **Wolff,** Jordan D '07 %Shearman & S LLP -599 Lex Av -NY 10022
(212) 318-6000 .. **Wolff,** Justin S F '09 %Paul HJ&W LLP -75 E 55th -NY 10022
(212) 735-3000 .. **Wolff,** Kenneth M '00 (Skadden ASM&F LLP) -4 Times Sq -NY 10036
(212) 483-0105 .. **Wolff,** Kevin E '82 (Coughlin D LLP) -88 Pine-Wall St Plz -NY 10005
(212) 578-4461 .. **Wolff,** Lawr K '87 %MetLife -27-01 Qns Plz N -LIC 11101 **Fx:**251-1647
(516) 248-2222 .. **Wolff,** Liane R '88 %LI Advocacy Ctr -999 Hrrcks Rd -New Hyde Pk 11040 **Fx:**248-2290
(212) 688-4000 .. **Wolff,** Linda '76 %HFA -641 Lex Av -NY 10022 **Fx:**872-0388
(212) 735-3000 .. **Wolff,** Margaret L '80 OfCnsl Skadden ASM&F LLP -4 Times Sq -NY 10036
(516) 374-1691 .. **Wolff,** Melvin W '62 -941 Tee Ct -Woodmere 11598
(845) 292-4412 .. **Wolff,** Michl D '95 %Eisenberg & K -25 Darbee Ln Bx715 -Liberty 12754
(212) 974-7474 .. **Wolff,** Nancy E '82 (Cowan DA&S LLP) -41 Mad Av -NY 10010
(212) 986-6000 .. **Wolff,** Norris D '70 (Kleinberg KW&C,PC) -551 5th Av -NY 10176
(212) 246-8900 .. **Wolff,** Richd I '66 -551 5th Av -NY 10176
(212) 458-3383 .. **Wolff,** Richd M '88 AIG Domestic Claims Inc -175 Water -NY 10038
(212) 697-9280 .. **Wolff,** Robt H '82 (Rosenberg MF&W) -122 E 42nd -NY 10168
(518) 271-0801 .. **Wolff,** Robt L Jr. '76 -305 19th -Watervliet 12189 **Fx:**271-0797
(212) 973-0572 .. **Wolff & Samson PC** -140 Bway -NY 10005 **Fx:**858-7524
(315) 539-3000 .. **Wolff,** Thos J K '83 (Wolff W&W) -31 VA -Waterloo 13165
(315) 539-3000 .. **Wolff,** Vivian A '49 (Wolff W&W) -31 VA -Waterloo 13165
(212) 450-4000 .. **Wolffers,** Lorenz '05 %Davis P&W LLP -450 Lex Av -NY 10017
(716) 855-0600 .. **Wolfgang,** Michl G '55 (Wolfgang & W) -69 Delaware Av -Buffalo 14202 **Fx:**855-1016
(212) 752-3380 .. **Wolfman,** Valerie S '89 -880 3rd Av -NY 10022 **Fx:**826-7127
(585) 325-8000 .. **Wolford,** Elizabeth A '93 (Wolford Law LLP) -16 E Main -Rchstr 14614 **Fx:**325-8009
(585) 325-8000 .. **Wolford,** James S '97 %Wolford Law LLP -16 E Main -Rchstr 14614 **Fx:**325-8009
(585) 325-8000 .. **Wolford,** Michl R '68 (Wolford Law LLP) -16 E Main -Rchstr 14614 **Fx:**325-8009
(212) 808-7854 .. **Wolfram,** Peter '84 (Kelley D&W LLP) -101 Park Av -NY 10178
(917) 225-3950 .. **Wolfram,** Richd H '87 -410 Park Av -NY 10022
(516) 877-9653 .. **Wolf Rosenberg,** Debra L '09 %Wolf Law Grp,PC -114 Old Cntry Rd -Mineola 11501 **Fx:**877-9660
(914) 245-0900 .. **Wolfsie,** John L '89 -2000 Maple Hill -Yorktwn Hts 10598 **Fx:**962-2612
(212) 335-9000 .. **Wolfson,** Aaron T '04 %DA -1 Hogan Pl -NY 10013
(212) 859-3474 .. **Wolfson,** Alfred Jos '98 -110 Wall -NY 10005
(212) 506-1700 .. **Wolfson,** Allison S '04 %Kasowitz BT&F LLP -1633 Bway -NY 10019
(212) 855-3200 .. **Wolfson,** Anne R '99 %Depository Trust -55 Water -NY 10041 **Fx:**855-3279
(845) 454-2200 .. **Wolfson,** Carl S '65 OfCnsl Wolfson G&E PC -11 Market -Poughkeepsie 12601
(516) 741-2585 .. **Wolfson,** Craig J '97 %Rosicki R & Assoc,PC -51 E Bethpage Rd -Plainvw 11803 **Fx:**741-4748
(212) 530-5000 .. **Wolfson,** David J '94 (Milbank TH&M LLP) -1 Chase Manh Plz -NY 10005
(212) 687-4900 .. **Wolfson,** Donald Jay '77 (Wormser KG&J LLP) -825 3rd Av -NY 10022
(516) 745-8000 .. **Wolfson,** Donald M '75 (Wolfson & G LLP) -1600 Stewart Av -Westbury 11590
(212) 851-8418 .. **Wolfson,** Evan C '84 (Freedom to Marry) -116 W 23rd -NY 10011 **Fx:**(646) 375-2069
(212) 385-1422 .. **Wolfson,** Garth S '97 (Mahoney & K,LLP) -76 Beaver -NY 10005
(845) 454-2200 .. **Wolfson Greller & Egitto PC** -11 Market -Poughkeepsie 12601 **Fx:**454-4366
(516) 745-8000 .. **Wolfson & Grossman LLP** -1600 Stewart Av -Westbury 11590 **Fx:**745-8006
(212) 735-8600 .. **Wolfson,** Howard S '83 (Morrison C LLP) -909 3rd Av -NY 10022
(646) 855-1289 .. **Wolfson,** Joel R '08 Banc of Amer Securities -1 Bryant Park -NY 10036 **Fx:**855-5021
(212) 979-9464 .. **Wolfson,** Martin A '96 -385 Grand -NY 10002 **Fx:**979-1260
(212) 233-0314 .. **Wolfson,** Michl G '67 (Wolfson & C) -233 Bway -NY 10279 **Fx:**349-4911
(212) 768-6700 .. **Wolfson,** Peter D '78 (Sonnenschein N&R LLP) -1221 Av of Amer -NY 10020
(516) 220-1380 .. **Wolfson,** Richd B '88 RB Wolfson PC -100 Ring Rd -Gdn Cty 11530 **Fx:**693-9140
(212) 792-0198 .. **Wolfson,** Russell M '99 -233 Bway -NY 10279
(718) 479-8593 .. **Wolfson,** Sheldon '69 Leg Srvcs Plan Lcl 1500 -221-10 Jamaica Av -Qns Vllg 11428 **Fx:**479-6729
(516) 576-1060 .. **Wolfson,** Sheldon '69 -54 Sunnyside Blvd -Plainvw 11803 **Fx:**576-1039
(315) 471-3151 .. **Wolfson,** Warren D '75 (Hancock & E,LLP) -1500 AXA Twr I Bx4976 -Syracuse 13221
(212) 335-9000 .. **Wolfstaetter,** John P '89 %DA -1 Hogan Pl -NY 10013
(212) 495-0100 .. **Wolgel,** Harold H '43 (Gottesman WMF&W,PC) -11 Hanover Sq -NY 10005
(212) 720-6911 .. **Wolgemuth,** Jennifer Ann '96 Fed Reserve Bk -33 Lbrty -NY 10045 **Fx:**785-5748
(516) 938-1199 .. **Wolin,** Alan E '77 (Wolin & W) -420 Jericho Tpk -Jericho 11753 **Fx:**938-1178
(212) 735-3000 .. **Wolin,** David S '96 (Skadden ASM&F LLP) -4 Times Sq -NY 10036
(212) 872-1000 .. **Wolin,** Helena E '06 -One Bryant Park -NY 10036 **Fx:**872-1002
(516) 938-1199 .. **Wolin,** Jerold '75 (Wolin & W) -420 Jericho Tpk -Jericho 11753 **Fx:**938-1178
(845) 638-1943 .. **Wolin,** Matthew B '05 %Greenwald D LLP -30 Ramland Rd -Orangebrg 10962
(212) 766-1500 .. **Wolin,** Michl D '69 -225 Bway -NY 10007
(212) 962-1133 .. **Wolinetz,** Scott A '95 (S Wolinetz,PC) -233 Bway -NY 10279 **Fx:**962-1144
(516) 485-4221 .. **Wolinski,** Theresa E '80 (Foley SO&W) -175 Fulton Av -Hempstd 11550
(631) 588-2900 .. **Wolinsky,** Alan M '67 (Wolinsky P&M,LLP) -329 Hawkins Av -Lk Ronkonkoma 11779
(212) 865-0505 .. **Wolinsky,** Iris C '93 -227 Riverside Dr -NY 10025 **Fx:**865-0505
(845) 778-2121 .. **Wolinsky,** Larry '85 (Jacobowitz & G,LLP) -158 Orange Av Bx367 -Walden 12586
(212) 403-1000 .. **Wolinsky,** Marc '82 (Wachtell LR&K) -51 W 52nd -NY 10019
(631) 588-2900 .. **Wolinsky Parnell & Montgomery, LLP** -329 Hawkins Av -Lk Ronkonkoma 11779 **Fx:**588-2902
(212) 455-2000 .. **Wolitzer,** Michl W '90 (Simpson T&B LLP) -425 Lex Av -NY 10017
(212) 902-2866 .. **Wolitzer,** Neil E '03 Goldman Sachs -85 Broad -NY 10004
(212) 506-2500 .. **Wolk,** Adam C '08 %Mayer B LLP -1675 Bway -NY 10019
(845) 634-8179 .. **Wolk,** Allan '93 -96 3rd -New Cty 10956 **Fx:**634-2827
(631) 585-3600 .. **Wolk,** Andrew R '79 -3900 Vets Mem'l Hwy #120 -Bohemia 11716 **Fx:**588-7175
(212) 326-8646 .. **Wolk,** Brad M '03 %Studley,Inc -300 Park Av -NY 10022
(212) 752-5200 .. **Wolk,** Carol E '93 Greene Levin Snyder LLC -150 E 58th -NY 10155
(212) 818-0400 .. **Wolk,** Edmund F '56 -515 Mad Av -NY 10022 **Fx:**818-0440
(212) 412-4000 .. **Wolk,** Ivor C '89 Barclays Capital -200 Park Av -NY 10166
(212) 791-9730 .. **Wolk,** Jeffrey S '75 %PF Adams,PC -30 Vesey -NY 10007
(585) 263-1000 .. **Wolk,** Jeremy J '99 %Nixon P LLP -1100 Clinton Sq -Rchstr 14604
(212) 513-3200 .. **Wolk,** Lawr J '75 (Holland & K LLP) -31 W 52nd -NY 10019
(585) 295-5400 .. **Wolk,** Melanie A '99 SpclCnsl Goldberg S LLP -2 State -Rchstr 14614

(212) 818-0400 ..**Wolk,** Michl B '92 -515 Mad Av -NY 10022 **Fx:**818-0440
(212) 506-5000 ..**Wolk,** Neil T '87 (Orrick H&S LLP) -51 W 52nd -NY 10019
(212) 995-8757 ..**Wolk Neuman & Maziarz** -304 Park Av S -NY 10010 **Fx:**995-1351
(212) 803-5100 ..**Wolk,** Peter L '80 %NY Cnty Defender Srvcs -225 Bway -NY 10007 **Fx:**571-6035
(212) 995-8757 ..**Wolk,** Stuart R '61 (Wolk N&M) -304 Park Av S -NY 10010
(516) 431-4770 ..**Wolkenberg,** Alfred '51 -381 Lido Blvd -Long Bch 11561 **Fx:**431-0182
(518) 869-9500 ..**Wolkenbreit,** Jed B '73 (Ganz W&S,LLP) -1 Columbia Cir -Albany 12203
(212) 302-2600 ..**Wolkenstein,** David J '97 %Lauterbach GD&H LLP -22 W 38th -NY 10018
(212) 406-4252 ..**Wolkenstein,** Rachel H '74 -295 Greenwich -NY 10007
(212) 691-2313 ..**Wolkind,** Bryan E '98 (Foster & W,PC) -80 5th Av -NY 10011 **Fx:**691-2459
(212) 344-1013 ..**Wolkoff,** Eugene A '62 (Callahan & W) -88 Pine -NY 10005
(516) 248-0222 ..**Wolkofsky,** Michl B '82 -3000 Marcus Av -Lk Success 11042 **Fx:**354-4731
(845) 356-3919 ..**Wolkon,** Barry '61 %Ramapo Ice Rinks Inc -20 Cllg Rd -Monsey 10952 **Fx:**356-8811
(212) 953-2381 ..**Wolkow,** Lawr D '07 %Rubin F&F,LLP -292 Mad Av -NY 10017
(516) 536-3143 ..**Wolkow,** Michl C '86 -3167 Messick Av -Oceanside 11572 **Fx:**536-7410
(212) 335-9000 ..**Wolkowitz,** Jared S '02 %DA -1 Hogan Pl -NY 10013
(212) 635-6664 ..**Woll,** David C Jr. '08 Bank of NY Mellon -1 Wall -NY 10286
(212) 455-2000 ..**Woll,** David J '88 (Simpson T&B LLP) -425 Lex Av -NY 10017
(212) 340-0400 ..**Woll,** Deborah '82 %Appllt Div 1st Dept -27 Mad Av -NY 10010 **Fx:**889-4412
(212) 626-4100 ..**Woll,** Glenn H J '98 %Baker & M LLP -1114 Av of Amer -NY 10036
(212) 962-0360 ..**Woll,** Harvey L '79 OfCnsl Anes FL&B,PLLC -299 Bway -NY 10007
(212) 776-5186 ..**Woll,** Lois '85 %NYC Housing Auth -250 Bway -NY 10007 **Fx:**776-5039
(212) 593-6700 ..**Woll,** Natalie '04 %Aaronson RF&D,LLP -757 3rd Av -NY 10017
(212) 804-4200 ..**Wollan,** Eugene '50 SrCnsl Mound CW&G -One Bttry Pk Plz -NY 10004
(516) 535-1700 ..**Wollan,** Gary P '01 Horing W&R,PC -11 Hillside Av -Williston Pk 11596
(212) 717-8912 ..**Wolland,** Lisa Marlow '94 -1275 1st Av -NY 10065
(212) 949-1113 ..**Wollen,** Carolyn S '75 -551 5th Av -NY 10176
(212) 325-4078 ..**Wollen,** John R '94 Credit Suisse -11 Mad Av -NY 10010
(212) 446-4800 ..**Wollensack,** Amy F '08 %Kirkland & E LLP -153 E 53rd -NY 10022
(212) 474-1000 ..**Wollensack,** Rebecca S '08 %Cravath S&M LLP -825 8th Av -NY 10019
(212) 412-4750 ..**Wollerstein,** Alan J '67 (Wollerstein & F) -59 Maiden Ln -NY 10038
(212) 412-4750 ..**Wollerstein & Futoran** -59 Maiden Ln -NY 10038 **Fx:**363-1602
(212) 412-4750 ..**Wollerstein,** Neil D '99 %Wollerstein & F -59 Maiden Ln -NY 10038
(212) 351-4000 ..**Wollin,** Alison L '03 %Gibson D&C LLP -200 Park Av -NY 10166
(212) 371-9400 ..**Wollin,** Louis '82 %Newman & N,PC -460 Park Av -NY 10022 **Fx:**371-8022
(212) 715-9100 ..**Wollin,** Robt J '02 %Kramer LN&F,LLP -1177 Av of Amer -NY 10036
(212) 558-4000 ..**Wollman,** Diana L '94 (Sullivan & C LLP) -125 Broad -NY 10004
(212) 669-4766 ..**Wollman,** Eric '96 %Comptroller -1 Centre -NY 10007 **Fx:**669-3993
(518) 842-8213 ..**Wollman,** Jos D '90 (Wollman Law Firm) -41 Market -Amsterdam 12010 **Fx:**842-3420
(518) 842-8213 ..**Wollman,** Paul L '71 (Wollman Law Firm) -41 Market -Amsterdam 12010 **Fx:**842-3420
(212) 382-3300 ..**Wollmuth,** David H '89 (Wollmuth M&D LLP) -500 5th Av -NY 10110
(212) 382-3300 ..**Wollmuth Maher & Deutsch LLP** -500 5th Av -NY 10110 **Fx:**382-0050
(914) 235-2121 ..**Wolloch,** Richd D '79 -52 Gaby Ln -New Rchll 10804
(212) 557-7200 ..**Wolman,** Derek '84 Davidoff M&H,LLP -605 3rd Av -NY 10158
(212) 918-4940 ..**Wolman,** Karin '91 K Wolman,PLLC -48 Wall -NY 10005 **Fx:**918-4942
(718) 279-3142 ..**Wolman,** Mindy G '85 -221-59 59th Av -Oakland Gdns 11364 **Fx:**279-3146
(212) 309-6000 ..**Wolman,** Rachel B '06 %Morgan L&B LLP -101 Park Av -NY 10178
(212) 451-2300 ..**Wolnerman,** David Y '02 %Olshan GFR&W LLP -65 E 55th -NY 10022
(914) 833-7610 ..**Woloshin,** Stacey R '92 SRW Consulting -17 Maple Hill Dr -Larchmnt 10538
(212) 751-4300 ..**Wolosky,** Joel M '68 (Hodgson R LLP) -1540 Bway -NY 10036
(212) 446-2300 ..**Wolosky,** Lee S '96 (Boies S&F LLP) -575 Lex Av -NY 10022
(212) 451-2300 ..**Wolosky,** Steven '81 (Olshan GFR&W LLP) -65 E 55th -NY 10022
(212) 674-5151 ..**Wolosoff,** Amy J '95 %Macmillan -175 5th Av -NY 10010 **Fx:**529-0594
(516) 747-2000 ..**Wolosoff,** Kenneth D '77 Margolin Winer Evens,LLP -400 Grdn City Plz -Gdn Cty 11530 **Fx:**747-6707
(212) 436-4313 ..**Wolosoff,** Todd J '80 Deloitte & Touche,LLP -2 World Fncl Ctr -NY 10281
(607) 562-8802 ..**Woloson,** Kent R '63 -77 Canal Bx458 -Big Flats 14814 **Fx:**562-7536
(646) 252-7000 ..**Woloszyn,** Jeanette O '82 %TBTA -2 Bway -NY 10004
(212) 506-2500 ..**Wolowitz,** Steven '78 (Mayer B LLP) -1675 Bway -NY 10019
(914) 741-5050 ..**Wolper,** Robt W '84 Wolper Law Firm,PLLC -400 Columbus Av -Valhalla 10595 **Fx:**741-5850
(212) 788-0748 ..**Wolpert,** Carolyn M '00 %Law Dept -100 Church -NY 10007 **Fx:**788-0367
(212) 577-3688 ..**Wolpert,** Cynthia '90 %Leg Aid -199 Water -NY 10038 **Fx:**509-8431
(212) 698-3500 ..**Wolpert,** Stephen M '07 %Dechert LLP -1095 Av of Amer -NY 10036
(212) 373-3000 ..**Wolpin,** Alyssa F '97 Cnsl Paul WRW&G LLP -1285 Av of Amer -NY 10019
(212) 972-0592 ..**Wolpin,** Eric N '93 -60 E 42nd -NY 10165
(718) 859-9050 ..**Wolpoff,** Jerome '67 -1270 Flatbush Av -Brklyn 11226 **Fx:**421-5314
(718) 859-9050 ..**Wolpoff,** Lynn E '92 -1270 Flatbush Av -Brklyn 11226
(212) 696-6000 ..**Wolrich,** Peter '74 (Curtis M-PC&M LLP) -101 Park Av -NY 10178
(212) 463-9260 ..**Wolsk,** Paul M '63 -73 Perry -NY 10014 **Fx:**463-9258
(212) 406-2205 ..**Wolsky,** Arnie '86 -111 John -NY 10038
(212) 278-8600 ..**Wolson,** Milton M '68 OfCnsl Notaro M&Z PC -1270 Bway -NY 10001
(212) 637-2743 ..**Wolstein,** Elizabeth '94 %US Atty -86 Chmbrs -NY 10007
(516) 334-3500 ..**Wolstein,** Jeffrey S '05 %Malen & Assoc,PC -123 Frost -Westbury 11590
(585) 593-1090 ..**Woltag,** Marc I '75 (Embser & W,PC) -164 N Main -Wellsvll 14895
(646) 414-6966 ..**Wolter,** Richd C '09 %Lowenstein S PC -1251 Av of Amer -NY 10020 **Fx:**(973) 722-6787
(212) 489-1600 ..**Wolters,** Erin M '98 Deloitte LLP -1633 Bway -NY 10019 **Fx:**492-4201
(516) 338-1888 ..**Wolther,** Glen '82 %All Round Foods -437 Railroad Av -Westbury 11590
(212) 964-2120 ..**Wolther,** Glenn A '97 -305 Bway -NY 10007
(718) 459-9000 ..**Wolthoff,** John L '04 %Sweeney GR&B,LLP -95-25 Qns Blvd -Rego Pk 11374
(212) 530-5000 ..**Woltz,** Jennie D '08 %Milbank TH&M LLP -1 Chase Manh Plz -NY 10005
(718) 822-0707 ..**Woluewich,** Johnnie '05 -984 Morris Park Av -Bronx 10462 **Fx:**904-1030
(518) 462-0300 ..**Wolverton,** Kathy Ann '95 (Girvin & F,PC) -20 Corp Wds Blvd -Albany 12211
(516) 560-6400 ..**Womble,** Arthur K '06 %Leg Aid -1 Helen Keller Way -Hempstd 11550 **Fx:**565-3694
(585) 295-4400 ..**Womer,** Jason R '07 %Hiscock & B,LLP -2000 HSBC Plz -Rchstr 14604
(212) 685-4643 ..**Won,** Jos J '03 Young One Fashions -1201 Bway -NY 10001
(212) 479-6000 ..**Won,** Karen K '07 %Cooley LLP -1114 Av of Amer -NY 10036
(718) 590-2000 ..**Won,** Tae-Hoon C '01 %DA -198 E 161st -Bronx 10451 **Fx:**590-6477
(212) 858-7195 ..**Wong,** Albert '00 RBC Capital Mkts Corp -1 Lbrty Plz -NY 10006
(212) 808-8300 ..**Wong,** Alexandra Celine '98 %Rosensteel Law -90 Park Av -NY 10016
(212) 355-9500 ..**Wong,** Allen W '05 %Lieff CH&B,LLP -250 Hudson -NY 10013
(646) 471-4000 ..**Wong,** Allison S '01 %PricewaterhouseCoopers LLP -300 Mad Av -NY 10017
(212) 772-6285 ..**Wong,** Andrew M '95 -444 E 86th -NY 10028 **Fx:**772-3904
(212) 576-7000 ..**Wong,** Anna S '05 %NY Life Ins -51 Mad Av -NY 10010 **Fx:**447-0569
(212) 370-1300 ..**Wong,** Annie Yee '81 OfCnsl Ellenoff G&S LLP -150 E 42nd -NY 10017
(212) 701-3000 ..**Wong,** Boji '05 %Cahill G&R LLP -80 Pine -NY 10005 **Fx:**269-5420
(212) 848-4000 ..**Wong,** Carmen H '07 %Shearman & S LLP -599 Lex Av -NY 10022
(212) 815-1818 ..**Wong,** Carolyn M L '89 %DC 37 MELS -125 Barclay -NY 10007 **Fx:**815-1343
(212) 368-5529 ..**Wong,** Charmane A '93 %Graham-Windham -646 Lenox Av -NY 10037
(212) 558-4000 ..**Wong,** Cheryl Shu-Ling '07 %Sullivan & C LLP -125 Broad -NY 10004
(212) 451-2300 ..**Wong,** Christine Wing-Sei '03 %Olshan GFR&W LLP -65 E 55th -NY 10022
(212) 268-1188 ..**Wong,** Christopher A '99 %B Somerstein & Assoc,PC -370 7th Av -NY 10001 **Fx:**268-2688
(212) 226-5353 ..**Wong,** Chun W '91 -15 Division -NY 10002 **Fx:**226-8305
(212) 239-4495 ..**Wong,** Cynthia M '08 Human Rights in China -350 5th Av -NY 10118
(212) 773-0448 ..**Wong,** David '09 Ernst & Young LLP -5 Times Sq -NY 10036
(917) 778-6600 ..**Wong,** David L '82 %J Toomey -485 Lex Av -NY 10017 **Fx:**778-7048
(212) 371-7300 ..**Wong,** Denis '84 %Steinhardt Mgmt -650 Mad Av -NY 10022 **Fx:**421-0688
(212) 643-9668 ..**Wong Fleming,PC** -350 5th Av -NY 10118 **Fx:**643-9640
(212) 431-1996 ..**Wong,** George L '82 -244 Canal -NY 10013
(212) 218-2100 ..**Wong,** Ha Kung '00 (Fitzpatrick CH&S) -1290 Av of Amer -NY 10104
(212) 969-3000 ..**Wong,** Hoi-Ling '06 %Proskauer R LLP -1585 Bway -NY 10036
(212) 966-6668 ..**Wong,** Jaime Y '93 %Fong & W,PC -254 Canal -NY 10013
(212) 574-1200 ..**Wong,** James W C '08 %Seward & K LLP -1 Bttry Pk Plz -NY 10004
(212) 756-2000 ..**Wong,** Jared P B '09 %Schulte R&Z LLP -919 3rd Av -NY 10022
(718) 590-2000 ..**Wong,** Jason '07 %DA -198 E 161st -Bronx 10451 **Fx:**590-6477
(212) 808-7800 ..**Wong,** Jennifer L '03 %Kelley D&W LLP -101 Park Av -NY 10178
(212) 504-6000 ..**Wong,** Jessica '07 %Cadwalader W&T LLP -1 World Fncl Ctr -NY 10281
(212) 966-6699 ..**Wong,** Jos T '89 -100 Lafayette -NY 10013
(212) 962-7200 ..**Wong,** Juanita '88 -101 Lafayette -NY 10013
(212) 943-9080 ..**Wong,** Judy '99 %Virginia & A -111 Bway -NY 10006
(718) 298-8900 ..**Wong,** Kimberly R '09 %Leg Aid -153-01 Jamaica Av -Jamaica 11432 **Fx:**657-0537
(718) 990-7359 ..**Wong,** Kwokfai Matthew '98 St Johns Univ -8000 Utopia Pkwy -Jamaica 11439 **Fx:**990-1868
(212) 225-2000 ..**Wong,** Kyle C '06 %Hon S Sotomayor US Ct Appls -500 Pearl -NY 10007
(917) 838-9152 ..**Wong,** Laurence P '04 -7 E 8th -NY 10003
(631) 761-7157 ..**Wong,** Leslie '03 Touro Cllg Law Ctr -225 Eastvw Dr -Central Islip 11722
(212) 643-9668 ..**Wong,** Linda '00 (Wong F,PC) -350 5th Av -NY 10118
(212) 868-6710 ..**Wong,** Lydia Fan '00 -70 W 36th -NY 10018
(212) 687-8500 ..**Wong,** Maria W '09 %Liddle & R,LLP -800 3rd Av -NY 10022
(212) 834-5709 ..**Wong,** Matthew E '05 JP Morgan Chase & Co -270 Park Av -NY 10017
(845) 462-7321 ..**Wong,** Michl C '95 %US Army SJA -7 Thornberry Way -Poughkeepsie 12603
(212) 819-8200 ..**Wong,** Michl C '09 %White & C LLP -1155 Av of Amer -NY 10036
(212) 373-3000 ..**Wong,** Michl C W '08 %Paul WRW&G LLP -1285 Av of Amer -NY 10019
(212) 558-4000 ..**Wong,** Michl L '10 %Sullivan & C LLP -125 Broad -NY 10004
(212) 297-5148 ..**Wong,** Michelle M L '04 UN Population Fund -220 E 42nd -NY 10017
(917) 421-4750 ..**Wong,** Mimi M '00 IRS -33 Maiden Ln -NY 10038
(718) 242-7676 ..**Wong,** Nga '03 JP Morgan Chase -4 Metrotech Ctr -Brklyn 11201
(212) 587-4166 ..**Wong,** Paul K '87 -325 Bway -NY 10007 **Fx:**587-4135
(212) 250-4107 ..**Wong,** Pollyanna T '87 Deutsche Bk -60 Wall -NY 10005

(212) 566-8080 .. **Wong,** Raymond H '88 (Wong W & Assoc,PC) -150 Bway -NY 10038 **Fx:**566-8960
(212) 282-3241 .. **Wong,** Richd C '91 Mizuho Corp Bank Ltd -1251 Av of Amer -NY 10020
(212) 966-6668 .. **Wong,** Robt W '86 (Fong & W,PC) -254 Canal -NY 10013
(212) 373-3000 .. **Wong,** Sarah B '09 %Paul WRW&G LLP -1285 Av of Amer -NY 10019
(212) 820-9410 .. **Wong,** T Kam '81 (Hawkins D&W LLP) -One Chase Manh Plz -NY 10005
(718) 852-8888 .. **Wong,** Tanya E M '97 %LSNYC-Brooklyn -180 Lvngstn -Brklyn 11201 **Fx:**858-1786
(212) 966-8638 .. **Wong,** Timothy K '96 -33 Bowery -NY 10002 **Fx:**202-3631
(212) 566-8080 .. **Wong,** Valerie Y '05 (Wong W & Assoc,PC) -150 Bway -NY 10038 **Fx:**566-8960
(212) 888-0884 .. **Wong,** Vincent S '97 -246 5th Av -NY 10001
(212) 940-3028 .. **Wong,** Virginia O '94 (Nixon P LLP) -437 Mad Av -NY 10022
(212) 450-4000 .. **Wong,** Vivian Yin Mei '01 %Davis P&W LLP -450 Lex Av -NY 10017
(212) 858-1000 .. **Wong,** Wm '04 %Pillsbury WSP LLP -1540 Bway -NY 10036
(718) 461-8461 .. **Wong,** Xuejie '02 -136-20 38th Av -Flushng 11354 **Fx:**713-0292
(845) 291-3150 .. **Wong-Pan,** Laura '97 %Cnty Atty -255 Main -Goshen 10924 **Fx:**291-3167
(212) 788-0694 .. **Woo,** Betty C '90 %Law Dept -100 Church -NY 10007 **Fx:**788-0367
(212) 403-1000 .. **Woo,** Carmen '06 %Wachtell LR&K -51 W 52nd -NY 10019
(212) 813-5900 .. **Woo,** Giselle C '08 %Fross ZL&Z,PC -866 UN Plz -NY 10017
(718) 762-1380 .. **Woo,** Kailin '95 -55-10 Main -Flushng 11355
(212) 608-3899 .. **Woo,** Magdalen K '90 -225 Bway -NY 10007
(718) 256-8711 .. **Woo,** Sally S '03 -2127 64th -Brklyn 11204
(212) 521-5400 .. **Woo,** Shirley '07 %Reed S LLP -599 Lex Av -NY 10022
(212) 858-7424 .. **Woo,** Tina '01 Royal Bank of Canada -1 Lbrty Plz -NY 10006
(914) 666-5759 .. **Woocher,** Elliot D '67 -24 Peck Rd -Mt Kisco 10549
(212) 373-3000 .. **Wood,** Alastair '05 %Paul WRW&G LLP -1285 Av of Amer -NY 10019
(212) 318-6000 .. **Wood,** Alexander W '09 %Paul HJ&W LLP -75 E 55th -NY 10022
(518) 434-5050 .. **Wood,** Andrew H '06 %Law Dept -106 City Hall -Albany 12207 **Fx:**434-5070
(631) 962-2000 .. **Wood,** Barbara A '88 %OSI Pharm -41 Pinelawn Rd -Melvll 11747
(315) 423-0400 .. **Wood,** Bruce E '81 (Wood & S,PC) -110 W Fayette -Syracuse 13202 **Fx:**424-1011
(718) 579-3012 .. **Wood,** Carrie E '06 %Leg Aid -1020 Grnd Cncrs -Bronx 10451 **Fx:**588-2611
(518) 408-0469 .. **Wood,** Cheryl M '95 %Workers Comp Bd -20 Park -Albany 12207
(718) 630-2924 .. **Wood,** Christopher B '93 %VA -800 Poly Pl -Brklyn 11209 **Fx:**630-2917
(718) 636-8000 .. **Wood,** Claire O '84 (Wood R&W,LLP) -394-396 Waverly Av -Brklyn 11238 **Fx:**636-7442
(718) 636-8000 .. **Wood,** Curtis A Jr. '68 (Wood R&W,LLP) -394-396 Waverly Av -Brklyn 11238 **Fx:**857-5628
(914) 682-2004 .. **Wood,** Danna Morris '96 -50 Main -White Plns 10606 **Fx:**682-7784
(518) 565-4658 .. **Wood,** David L '77 %Family Ct -137 Margaret -Plattsbrgh 12901 **Fx:**565-4688
(212) 521-5400 .. **Wood,** Douglas J '77 (Reed S LLP) -599 Lex Av -NY 10022
(212) 837-3620 .. **Wood,** Edmund B '80 %JP Morgan Chase -530 5th Av -NY 10036
(212) 998-6730 .. **Wood,** Erika L '00 Brennan Ctr for Justice -161 Av of Americas -NY 10013
(607) 865-6575 .. **Wood,** Francis W '74 -28 Townsend Bx357 -Walton 13856 **Fx:**865-4405
(212) 833-3338 .. **Wood,** G Elaine '88 %Kroll Assoc -1166 Av of Amer -NY 10036 **Fx:**593-2631
(212) 906-9046 .. **Wood,** Greg V '04 -155 E 55th -NY 10022
(914) 663-9300 .. **Wood,** Gregory L '97 -630 Gramatan Av -Mt Vernon 10552 **Fx:**663-9398
(585) 295-4009 .. **Wood,** J Michl '95 (Chamberlain D LLP) -1600 Crssrds Bldg -Rchstr 14614
(518) 437-9864 .. **Wood,** James D '81 -16 Mohican Pl -Albany 12208
(212) 909-6000 .. **Wood,** Jeffrey S '73 SrCnsl Debevoise & P LLP -919 3rd Av -NY 10022
(518) 725-0653 .. **Wood,** Jeremiah '00 (Wood & S,LLP) -8 Fremont -Gloversvll 12078
(212) 751-3001 .. **Wood,** John Busey '79 (Thompson & K LLP) -919 3rd Av -NY 10022
(607) 274-5546 .. **Wood,** Jonathan '89 %Cnty Atty -125 E Court -Ithaca 14850 **Fx:**274-5547
(315) 782-3064 .. **Wood,** Kimberly A '96 -216 Central -Watertwn 13601 **Fx:**782-3064
(914) 736-0144 .. **Wood & Klarl** -2131 Albany Post Rd -Montrose 10548 **Fx:**736-9082
(212) 805-6387 .. **Wood,** Kyle O '03 Hon W Pauley III -500 Pearl -NY 10007
(212) 461-2323 .. **Wood,** Lisa C '00 (Saiber LLC) -44 Wall -NY 10005
(212) 973-0572 .. **Wood,** Margaret O'Rourke '02 %Wolff & S PC -140 Bway -NY 10005
(212) 627-0466 .. **Wood,** Mark R '07 -180 W 20th -NY 10011
(212) 916-6232 .. **Wood,** Martha Lee '90 %TIAA-CREF -730 3rd Av -NY 10017
(212) 216-8000 .. **Wood,** Michl R '07 %Tarter K&D LLP -1350 Bway -NY 10018
(518) 437-6961 .. **Wood,** Nancy E '91 %State Ins Fund -15 Computer Dr W -Albany 12205 **Fx:**485-8761
(212) 852-1000 .. **Wood,** Nancy Stanger '77 US Trust Co,NA -114 W 47th -NY 10036 **Fx:**852-1310
(212) 732-2000 .. **Wood,** Paul G '76 (Cullen and D LLP) -44 Wall -NY 10005
(718) 222-2360 .. **Wood,** Pia E '86 %Law Dept -350 Jay -Brklyn 11201 **Fx:**222-2373
(718) 636-8000 .. **Wood Rafalsky & Wood,LLP** -394-396 Waverly Av -Brklyn 11238 **Fx:**636-7442
(914) 761-8503 .. **Wood,** Ralph K '75 -399 Knollwood Rd -White Plns 10603 **Fx:**682-9128
(212) 574-1200 .. **Wood,** Robt E '02 %Seward & K LLP -1 Bttry Pk Plz -NY 10004
(585) 227-9830 .. **Wood,** Robt W '79 -2080 Ridge Rd W -Rchstr 14626 **Fx:**227-7985
(914) 328-5600 .. **Wood & Scher** -222 Bloomingdale Rd -White Plns 10605 **Fx:**328-5627
(518) 725-0653 .. **Wood & Seward,LLP** -8 Fremont -Gloversvll 12078 **Fx:**725-9875
(718) 222-2060 .. **Wood,** Shanel Spence '09 %Law Dept -350 Jay -Brklyn 11201 **Fx:**222-2088
(585) 428-5755 .. **Wood,** Sherri E '79 %Cnty Atty -50 W Main -Rchstr 14614 **Fx:**428-2031
(212) 259-8000 .. **Wood,** Spencer R '08 Cnsl Dewey & L LLP -1301 Av of Amer -NY 10019
(914) 499-4839 .. **Wood,** Teri Wilford '79 IBM -1 New Orchrd Rd -Armonk 10504 **Fx:**499-6085
(914) 736-0144 .. **Wood,** Thos F '79 (Wood & K) -2131 Albany Post Rd -Montrose 10548
(212) 735-3000 .. **Wood,** Thos F '09 %Skadden ASM&F LLP -4 Times Sq -NY 10036
(914) 328-5600 .. **Wood,** Wm L Jr. '69 (Wood & S) -222 Bloomingdale Rd -White Plns 10605
(646) 557-5100 .. **Woodall,** Kate S '08 %Patton B LLP -1185 Av of Amer -NY 10036
(212) 435-3940 .. **Woodall,** Shanelle D '05 Port Auth of NY/NJ -1 Mad Av -NY 10010
(212) 735-3000 .. **Woodard,** Andrew D '04 %Skadden ASM&F LLP -4 Times Sq -NY 10036
(212) 836-8000 .. **Woodard,** Arthur F '74 (Kaye S LLP) -425 Park Av -NY 10022
(212) 819-8200 .. **Woodard,** Brendan G '02 (White & C LLP) -1155 Av of Amer -NY 10036
(212) 605-6200 .. **Woodard,** Danl J '00 %Levy P&K,LLP -800 3rd Av -NY 10022
(212) 772-1198 .. **Woodard,** Harriet M '73 -535 E 86th -NY 10028 **Fx:**772-1309
(315) 423-7100 .. **Woodard,** Lee E '83 (Harris B PLLC) -300 S State -Syracuse 13202
(914) 328-0404 .. **Woodard,** Matthew H '04 %Jackson L LLP -1 N Bway -White Plns 10601
(631) 582-5757 .. **Woodard,** Terry R '83 -320 Carleton Av -Central Islip 11722 **Fx:**232-5343
(212) 512-1000 .. **Woodbury,** Thos M '78 %HBO -1100 Av of Amer -NY 10036 **Fx:**512-1986
(212) 297-5800 .. **Wooden,** Shawn T '07 (Day P LLP) -7 Times Sq -NY 10036
(212) 259-8000 .. **Woodeshick,** Keith W '08 %Dewey & L LLP -1301 Av of Amer -NY 10019
(212) 640-5774 .. **Woodfin,** Sarah L '84 %Amer Exp -200 Vesey -NY 10285
(607) 734-6191 .. **Woodhouse,** Richd P '70 (Moore & W,LLP) -150 Lk -Elmira 14901
(518) 444-8770 .. **Woodin,** David E '82 Greene Cnty Ct -320 Main -Catskill 12414 **Fx:**943-5995
(212) 751-2700 .. **Woodin,** Peter H '89 %JAMS -620 8th Av -NY 10018 **Fx:**751-4099
(718) 935-1010 .. **Woodland,** Rebecca '93 (Lonuzzi & W,LLP) -60 Sackett -Brklyn 11231 **Fx:**935-1935
(212) 259-8000 .. **Woodley,** Daphnee Saget '05 %Dewey & L LLP -1301 Av of Amer -NY 10019
(212) 765-5070 .. **Woodley,** Saml S III '03 Fish & R,PC -153 E 53rd -NY 10022
(212) 223-4000 .. **Woodley,** Stafford A Jr. '02 %Crowell & M LLP -590 Mad Av -NY 10022
(212) 310-8000 .. **Woodley,** Vaughn RaShawn '09 %Weil G&M LLP -767 5th Av -NY 10153
(315) 841-8021 .. **Woodman,** Richd S '38 (Woodman & G) -130 E Main -Waterville 13480 **Fx:**841-4472
(631) 439-4200 .. **Woodrick Chancellor,** Rosemarie G '90 %R Tusa -898 Vets Mem'l Hwy -Hauppauge 11788 **Fx:**439-4292
(212) 504-6000 .. **Woodrow,** Kate R '09 %Cadwalader W&T LLP -1 World Fncl Ctr -NY 10281
(716) 841-2334 .. **Woodrow,** Tracy Sendor '99 %HSBC Bank -1 HSBC Ctr -Buffalo 14203 **Fx:**841-5087
(718) 694-1054 .. **Woodruff,** John Y Jr. '86 %Transit Auth -130 Lvngstn -Brklyn 11201 **Fx:**694-5726
(212) 433-1480 .. **Woodruff,** Matthew W '90 OfCnsl Rich & I LLP -111 Bway -NY 10006 **Fx:**433-1481
(212) 248-3140 .. **Woodruff,** Michl C '00 (Drinker B&R LLP) -140 Bway -NY 10005
(212) 662-1984 .. **Woodruff,** Natalie L '93 Assured Guaranty Corp -1325 Av of Amer -NY 10019
(212) 775-8700 .. **Woods,** Christopher J '00 (Kilpatrick S,LLP) -31 W 52nd -NY 10019
(845) 641-5817 .. **Woods,** Ellen O'Hara '95 -Bx82 -Orangebrg 10962 **Fx:**359-0503
(518) 486-9730 .. **Woods,** James C '81 %Dept of Law -The Cptl -Albany 12224
(212) 684-2500 .. **Woods,** James F '89 -292 Mad Av -NY 10017 **Fx:**684-2512
(212) 529-5131 .. **Woods,** James J '99 OfCnsl Mauriel K&T LLP -151 1st -NY 10003 **Fx:**529-5132
(212) 710-3900 .. **Woods,** John M '81 (Clyde & Co US LLP) -405 Lex Av -NY 10174 **Fx:**710-3950
(212) 859-8000 .. **Woods,** Jordan B '04 %Fried FHS&J LLP -1 NY Plz -NY 10004
(212) 858-1000 .. **Woods,** Kent P '09 %Pillsbury WSP LLP -1540 Bway -NY 10036
(718) 448-1544 .. **Woods,** Laurie K '91 %Project Hospitality -100 Park Av -Staten Isl 10302 **Fx:**448-5129
(212) 975-2479 .. **Woods,** Mary C '00 CBS Inc -51 W 52nd -NY 10019 **Fx:**975-3930
(212) 239-4999 .. **Woods,** Melissa S '00 OfCnsl Meyer SE&K,PC -1350 Bway Bx822 -NY 10018
(585) 271-8321 .. **Woods,** Michl F '71 -530 Hillside Av -Rchstr 14610
(718) 928-3700 .. **Woods,** Nicole M '09 %LSNYC-Bronx -579 Courtlandt Av -Bronx 10451 **Fx:**402-7586
(518) 734-5245 .. **Woods,** Nuala Sheen '94 -122 Old Rd Bx1059 -Windham 12496
(585) 987-2800 .. **Woods Oviatt Gilman LLP** -2 State -Rchstr 14614 **Fx:**454-3968
(718) 520-7144 .. **Woods,** Patrick J '69 %Hon J Rosenzweig -125-01 Qns Blvd -Kew Gdns 11415
(585) 336-1000 .. **Woods,** Peter R '90 %ESL Fed Credit Union -225 Chestnut -Rchstr 14604 **Fx:**336-1014
(518) 427-7000 .. **Woods,** Roderick D '09 %O'Brien & Assoc -18 Corp Wds Blvd -Albany 12211 **Fx:**463-1721
(518) 462-6765 .. **Woods,** Shannon E '00 Leg Aid -55 Colvin Av -Albany 12206 **Fx:**427-8352
(212) 820-4603 .. **Woods,** Wm P '77 AIG -160 Water -NY 10038
(212) 340-0400 .. **Woodside,** Keith L '91 %Appllt Div 1st Dept -27 Mad Av -NY 10010 **Fx:**889-4412
(914) 967-8698 .. **Wood-Smith,** Lelia M '80 -2175 Wstchstr Av -Rye 10580 **Fx:**967-0193
(212) 872-1000 .. **Woodson,** Jennifer L '10 -One Bryant Park -NY 10036 **Fx:**872-1002
(212) 721-5167 .. **Woodson,** Odella C '04 -100 W 92nd -NY 10025
(212) 704-6000 .. **Woodson,** Summer M '09 %Troutman S LLP -405 Lex Av -NY 10174
(518) 485-1716 .. **Woodward,** Jamie '81 %Dept Tax & Fin -Bldg 9 State Campus -Albany 12227 **Fx:**457-0092
(716) 856-3500 .. **Woodward,** Laurence H '68 (Magavern MG LLP) -1100 Rand Bldg -Buffalo 14203
(212) 310-8000 .. **Woodworth,** Andrew J '05 %Weil G&M LLP -767 5th Av -NY 10153
(518) 668-4447 .. **Woodworth,** Neil F '79 Adirondack Mtn Club,Inc -RR 3 Bx 3055 -Lk George 12845

(212) 577-3500 ..**Woody,** Andrea Conarro '05 %Leg Aid -199 Water -NY 10038
(516) 822-0222 ..**Wool,** Alissa J '01 %NR Wool -475 S Oyster Bay Rd -Plainvw 11803 **Fx:**935-9417
(516) 496-7171 ..**Wool,** Frederic A '75 -7600 Jericho Tpk -Woodbury 11797 **Fx:**496-3450
(516) 393-2200 ..**Wool,** Hayden S '86 (Garfunkel W,PC) -111 Grt Nck Rd -Gt Neck 11021
(212) 717-5922 ..**Wool,** Ivan S '92 -345 E 81st -NY 10028
(212) 450-4000 ..**Wool,** Jeffrey I '02 %Davis P&W LLP -450 Lex Av -NY 10017
(518) 481-1536 ..**Wool,** Jonathan C '84 %Dept Soc Srvcs -422 Cnty Cthse -Malone 12953 **Fx:**483-7081
(516) 822-0222 ..**Wool,** N Richd '75 -475 S Oyster Bay Rd -Plainvw 11803 **Fx:**935-9417
(212) 446-4800 ..**Wool,** Stefanie Merry '06 %Kirkland & E LLP -153 E 53rd -NY 10022
(212) 496-8530 ..**Woolams,** Jack '78 -135 W 81st -NY 10024
(212) 875-5109 ..**Woolard,** Julie L '09 Lincoln Ctr for the Performing Arts -70 Lincoln Ctr Plz -NY 10023
(914) 949-3411 ..**Wooldridge,** Alexander J '06 %K Cohen,PC -30 Glenn -White Plns 10603 **Fx:**949-3444
(212) 474-1000 ..**Woolery,** James C '95 (Cravath S&M LLP) -825 8th Av -NY 10019
(212) 345-8646 ..**Wooley,** Tiffany D '00 Marsh & McLennan Cos -1166 Av of Amer -NY 10036
(516) 294-5775 ..**Woolf,** Andrew B '90 (Klee & W,LLP) -350 Willis Av -Mineola 11501
(212) 403-1000 ..**Woolf,** Andrew M '06 %Wachtell LR&K -51 W 52nd -NY 10019
(212) 848-4000 ..**Woolf,** Terence '03 %Shearman & S LLP -599 Lex Av -NY 10022
(914) 725-4406 ..**Woolfalk,** Harold B '83 (HB Woolfalk & Assoc,PC) -113 Walworth Av -Scarsdale 10583 **Fx:**725-4329
(917) 648-8407 ..**Woolfson,** Barry H '95 -295 Mad Av -NY 10017 **Fx:**(646) 304-8402
(516) 221-4894 ..**Woolley,** Megan E '94 -575 Jericho Tpk -Jericho 11753 **Fx:**221-4895
(212) 874-6482 ..**Woolman,** Alan D '72 -275 Cntrl Pk W -NY 10024
(518) 463-3109 ..**Woolsey,** James M Jr. '54 (Woolsey & W) -187 Wolf Rd -Albany 12205 **Fx:**463-3109
(212) 238-4800 ..**Woolsey,** James M III '87 (Landman CB&F,PC) -120 Bway -NY 10271
(518) 463-3109 ..**Woolsey,** John C '91 (Woolsey & W) -187 Wolf Rd -Albany 12205 **Fx:**463-3109
(516) 222-2262 ..**Wooster,** Allen '80 (Wooster & W LLP) -666 Old Cntry Rd -Gdn Cty 11530 **Fx:**745-1133
(516) 222-2262 ..**Wooster,** Scott '83 (Wooster & W LLP) -666 Old Cntry Rd -Gdn Cty 11530 **Fx:**745-1133
(518) 473-6188 ..**Wootan,** Brian S '90 %OTDA -40 N Pearl -Albany 12243 **Fx:**474-9389
(212) 627-6319 ..**Wooten,** Jeffrey M '99 (Wooten & W,PC) -307 W 38th -NY 10018
(914) 686-3700 ..**Worby,** David '77 (Worby GE LLP) -11 Martine Av -White Plns 10606
(914) 686-3700 ..**Worby Groner Edelman LLP** -11 Martine Av -White Plns 10606 **Fx:**686-8080
(212) 896-6500 ..**Worcester,** R Corey '03 %Howrey LLP -601 Lex Av -NY 10022
(212) 909-6000 ..**Worden,** Katherine Hill '07 %Debevoise & P LLP -919 3rd Av -NY 10022
(518) 457-3177 ..**Worden,** Mark F '81 %Dept Civil Srvc -Harriman Campus Bldg 1 -Albany 12239 **Fx:**457-6654
(631) 852-2378 ..**Worden,** Mary-Ellen '80 %Supreme Ct -Center Dr S -Rvrhead 11901 **Fx:**852-2020
(212) 269-4900 ..**Worden,** Rebecca L '09 %Ford MEW&G,LLP -Wall Street Plz -NY 10005
(631) 694-0033 ..**Worden,** Robt P Jr. '80 (Lawrence WR&B,PC) -425 Broadhllw Rd -Melvll 11747
(212) 557-7260 ..**Wordes,** Dana R '98 Alstrom Transportation Inc -353 Lex Av -NY 10016
(212) 705-7000 ..**Worenklein,** Jacob J '74 Bingham M LLP -399 Park Av -NY 10022
(718) 544-4026 ..**Worgan,** Andrew S '74 -125-10 Qns Blvd -Kew Gdns 11415
(212) 839-5300 ..**Work,** Clifford M '02 %Sidley A LLP -787 7th Av -NY 10019
(212) 373-3000 ..**Workman,** Gitanjali '03 %Paul WRW&G LLP -1285 Av of Amer -NY 10019
(212) 504-6000 ..**Workman,** Terence L '87 SpclCnsl Cadwalader W&T LLP -1 World Fncl Ctr -NY 10281
(212) 986-6181 ..**Workman,** Thos E '01 Life Ins Cncl of NY -551 5th Av -NY 10176 **Fx:**986-6549
(516) 551-7181 ..**Works,** Angela D '79 -40 Woods Ln -Locust Vly 11560 **Fx:**674-2350
(212) 644-5200 ..**Worley,** Maria G '05 %J Gutman -233 Bway -NY 10279
(585) 758-7600 ..**Wormer,** Susan L '08 Univ of Rochester Med Ctr -Bx278979 -Rchstr 14627 **Fx:**272-9311
(914) 965-1011 ..**Worms,** Margo R '07 %JG Dibbini -570 Ynkrs Av -Ynkrs 10704 **Fx:**965-0019
(718) 358-8787 ..**Worms,** Terrence J '01 -136-20 38th Av -Flushng 11354
(212) 374-9590 ..**Worms,** Victor A '89 (V Worms,PC) -65 Bway -NY 10006 **Fx:**591-6188
(212) 687-4900 ..**Wormser Kiely Galef & Jacobs LLP** -825 3rd Av -NY 10022 **Fx:**687-5703
(914) 997-0900 ..**Wormser Kiely Galef & Jacobs LLP** -399 Knollwood Rd -White Plns 10603 **Fx:**997-1039
(914) 949-4239 ..**Worner,** Matthew T '93 -90 Bryant Av -White Plns 10605 **Fx:**949-3567
(212) 335-9258 ..**Wornom,** Thos A '84 %DA -1 Hogan Pl -NY 10013
(212) 227-0347 ..**Wornow,** Darryl S '91 (Weiss W&W,PC) -25 Park Pl -NY 10007
(212) 408-2500 ..**Wornow,** Scott M '89 (Baker B,LLP) -30 Rckfllr Plz -NY 10112
(212) 245-7300 ..**Worob,** Jeffrey A '95 %Serling R&F,LLP -119 5th Av -NY 10003
(518) 783-0200 ..**Worona,** Jay '82 %NYS Schl Bds Assn -24 Century Hill Dr -Latham 12110
(315) 422-1311 ..**Woronov,** Howard J '65 (Melvin & M,PLLC) -217 S Salina -Syracuse 13202
(585) 419-8800 ..**Worrall,** Dale A '97 (Harris B PLLC) -99 Garnsey Rd -Pittsfrd 14534
(212) 640-3006 ..**Worrell,** Linda F '88 %Amer Exp -200 Vesey -NY 10285
(716) 849-0328 ..**Worrell,** Mark A '83 -112 Franklin -Buffalo 14202
(212) 692-1000 ..**Worrell,** Megan R '04 %Duane M LLP -1540 Bway -NY 10036
(212) 506-2500 ..**Worsley,** Maurice A '09 %Mayer B LLP -1675 Bway -NY 10019
(631) 289-6440 ..**Worsoe,** Tor Jacob Jr. '92 -997 Waverly Av -Holtsvll 11742 **Fx:**289-6040
(212) 345-5038 ..**Worth,** Douglas S '94 Marsh Finpro -1166 Av of Amer -NY 10036
(315) 366-2437 ..**Worth,** Elizabeth J '97 %Hon D McDermott -Bx607 -Wampsville 13163
(212) 964-8038 ..**Worth Longworth & London,LLP** -111 John -NY 10038 **Fx:**964-8164
(315) 798-5766 ..**Worth,** Matthew P '93 %DA -800 Park Av -Utica 13501 **Fx:**798-5582
(914) 472-7280 ..**Worth,** Sloane Merl '94 %W Hart -700 Wht Plns Rd -Scarsdale 10583 **Fx:**472-7285
(212) 964-8038 ..**Worth,** Stephen C '77 (Worth L&L,LLP) -111 John -NY 10038
(716) 684-8060 ..**Worthington,** Elizabeth R '03 Ecology & Envrnmnt -368 Plsntvw Dr -Lancaster 14086 **Fx:**684-0844
(212) 318-6000 ..**Worthington,** James B '04 %Paul HJ&W LLP -75 E 55th -NY 10022
(516) 877-5600 ..**Worthington,** Michl L '92 %R Tusa -1225 Franklin Av -Gdn Cty 11530 **Fx:**877-5695
(845) 291-3150 ..**Worthy-Spiegl,** Sharon '96 %Cnty Atty -255 Main -Goshen 10924 **Fx:**291-3167
(212) 571-4900 ..**Wortman,** Scott E '08 %M Harris & Assoc LLC -5 Hanover Sq -NY 10004 **Fx:**571-0965
(516) 742-9808 ..**Wortman,** Walter F '65 -114 Old Cntry Rd -Mineola 11501
(516) 357-3700 ..**Wortmann,** Erik J '97 %Cullen and D LLP -100 Q Roosevelt Blvd -Gdn Cty 11530
(212) 708-1800 ..**Wotherspoon,** Hugh R '02 %Ladas & P -26 W 61st -NY 10023
(516) 466-0300 ..**Wotman,** Danl R '82 (D Wotman & Assoc,LLC) -1010 Nrthrn Blvd -Gt Neck 11021 **Fx:**466-3999
(212) 836-8000 ..**Wound,** Lily J '01 %Kaye S LLP -425 Park Av -NY 10022
(646) 386-5891 ..**Woychuk,** Denis '85 %MHLS -41 Mad Av -NY 10010
(516) 741-5252 ..**Woycik,** E David Jr. '81 (Sanders SBWV&G,PC) -100 Hrrcks Rd -Mineola 11501
(212) 232-1300 ..**Wozman,** Jamie R '02 %Lewis BB&S LLP -77 Water -NY 10005
(585) 546-5530 ..**Wozniak,** Frank J '95 %Thomson West -50 E Broad -Rchstr 14694
(212) 578-2211 ..**Wozny,** Thaddeus G '84 %MetLife -27-01 Qns Plz N -LIC 11101
(212) 221-6900 ..**Wrann,** Phyllis M '94 %(Winget S&S,LLP) -45 Bway -NY 10006
(212) 969-2154 ..**Wrapp,** Emilie D '87 %Alliance Bernstein LP -1345 Av of Amer -NY 10105 **Fx:**554-4639
(212) 354-1920 ..**Wray,** David J '81 -9 E 40th -NY 10016
(716) 856-0400 ..**Wray,** Diane Y '84 (Hughes & W LLP) -63 Kenmore Av -Buffalo 14226 **Fx:**856-9255
(212) 361-8886 ..**Wray,** Michl B '89 %Dept Probation -33 Beaver -NY 10004
(914) 769-4000 ..**Wren,** John E '71 (Wren & M,LLP) -343 Manvll Rd -Plsntvll 10570 **Fx:**769-4153
(718) 966-0929 ..**Wren,** Kelly L '95 -885 Annadale Rd -Staten Isl 10312 **Fx:**966-1236
(516) 463-5858 ..**Wren,** Lauris P '94 %Hofstra Law Schl -121 Hofstra Univ -Hempstd 11549
(718) 852-9005 ..**Wrenn,** John J '59 -276 Hicks -Brklyn 11201 **Fx:**852-9005
(518) 459-4800 ..**Wrenn,** Joyce M '62 -1204 Central Av -Albany 12205
(718) 250-2000 ..**Wrenn-Myers,** Marie-Claude P '95 %DA -350 Jay -Brklyn 11201 **Fx:**250-2314
(212) 336-2000 ..**Wright,** Aaron J '06 %Patterson BW&T LLP -1133 Av of Amer -NY 10036
(212) 581-6405 ..**Wright,** Adam M '78 -250 W 57th -NY 10107
(718) 286-6000 ..**Wright,** Allison Patrinea '98 %DA -125-01 Qns Blvd -Kew Gdns 11415
(212) 446-4800 ..**Wright,** Andrew Lawson '00 (Kirkland & E LLP) -153 E 53rd -NY 10022
(212) 687-0100 ..**Wright,** B Michl '05 %Harris B PLLC -100 Wall -NY 10005
(516) 622-2263 ..**Wright,** Brian P '00 -1979 Marcus Av -Lk Success 11042
(607) 723-5341 ..**Wright,** Brian R '71 SpclCnsl Hinman H&K,LLP -80 Exchange Bx5250 -Bnghmtn 13902
(518) 295-8109 ..**Wright,** Chas M '62 -304 Main Bx100 -Schoharie 12157
(718) 243-6395 ..**Wright,** Christopher '00 Legal Aid Crim Def -111 Lvngstn -Brklyn 11201
(212) 848-4000 ..**Wright,** Cody L '09 %Shearman & S LLP -599 Lex Av -NY 10022
(212) 701-3000 ..**Wright,** Corey A '01 (Cahill G&R LLP) -80 Pine -NY 10005 **Fx:**269-5420
(212) 808-7800 ..**Wright,** Courtney M '07 %Kelley D&W LLP -101 Park Av -NY 10178
(716) 841-5361 ..**Wright,** Craig N '81 %HSBC Bank -1 HSBC Ctr -Buffalo 14203 **Fx:**841-5087
(716) 854-1400 ..**Wright,** David A '97 %HOME,Inc -700 Main -Buffalo 14202 **Fx:**854-1140
(914) 528-3981 ..**Wright,** David O '80 -2025 Crompond Rd -Yorktwn Hts 10598 **Fx:**245-5822
(646) 248-0811 ..**Wright,** David R '09 McKinsey & Co -485 Mad Av -NY 10022
(212) 298-5151 ..**Wright,** Deborah L '00 %Leg Aid -49 Thomas -NY 10013 **Fx:**298-5252
(917) 939-2624 ..**Wright,** Deborah P '01 -132 Greene Av -Brklyn 11238
(212) 735-3000 ..**Wright,** Delroy A '10 %Skadden ASM&F LLP -4 Times Sq -NY 10036
(716) 483-1122 ..**Wright,** Edw P '81 (Wright W&H) -525 Fairmount Av W E Bx1198 -Jamestwn 14702
(716) 362-1533 ..**Wright,** Elizabeth R '98 %Goldstein A&P,LLP -70 Niagara -Buffalo 14202
(718) 953-4419 ..**Wright,** Elizabeth V '90 (E Wright,PC) -1141 Eastern Pkwy -Brklyn 11213 **Fx:**953-2144
(518) 447-9664 ..**Wright,** F Elizabeth '86 %MHLS -75 New Scotland Av -Albany 12208 **Fx:**447-9697
(212) 619-4444 ..**Wright,** Frank H '72 OfCnsl Marshall CW&B,PC -116 John -NY 10038
(212) 483-8266 ..**Wright,** George W '80 (G Wright & Assoc,LLC) -88 Pine -NY 10005 **Fx:**483-0971
(516) 483-1506 ..**Wright,** Gerald G '84 (G Wright & Assoc) -50 Clinton -Hempstd 11550
(212) 619-1500 ..**Wright,** Glenn D '89 (The Wright Law Firm,PC) -306 5th Av -NY 10001 **Fx:**619-0394
(631) 907-3500 ..**Wright,** Heather A '99 Tarbet L&S -524 Montauk Hwy Bx2635 -Amagansett 11930 **Fx:**907-3501
(718) 336-8200 ..**Wright,** James M '76 -3029 Quentin Rd -Brklyn 11234
(315) 218-8000 ..**Wright,** James P Jr. '09 %Bond S&K,PLLC -1 Lincoln Ctr -Syracuse 13202
(585) 263-1000 ..**Wright,** Jeffrey G '82 (Nixon P LLP) -1100 Clinton Sq -Rchstr 14604

(845) 561-0550 .. **Wright,** Jennifer E '06 %Drake LHKGG&R PLLC -555 Hudson Valley Av -New Windsor 12553
(585) 232-6500 .. **Wright,** Jennifer L '06 %Harter S&E LLP -1600 Bausch & Lomb Pl -Rchstr 14604
(716) 471-3555 .. **Wright,** Jeri N '02 -Bx333 -Grand Isl 14072 **Fx:**773-4253
(212) 661-9100 .. **Wright,** John C '07 %Otterbourg SH&R,PC -230 Park Av -NY 10169
(518) 792-2117 .. **Wright,** John D '08 %Bartlett PS&R,PC -1 Wshngtn Bx2168 -Glens Fls 12801
(212) 619-4444 .. **Wright,** John R '77 (Marshall CW&B,PC) -116 John -NY 10038
(212) 450-4000 .. **Wright,** John T '82 Cnsl Davis P&W LLP -450 Lex Av -NY 10017
(718) 624-0154 .. **Wright,** Joylyn '09 Cnsl Katz & Assoc -26 Court -Brklyn 11242 **Fx:**624-4212
(315) 472-3434 .. **Wright,** Judith Rogers '95 %R Lahm,PLLC -711 E Genesee -Syracuse 13210 **Fx:**472-8214
(212) 558-4000 .. **Wright,** Julian '10 %Sullivan & C LLP -125 Broad -NY 10004
(585) 454-2020 .. **Wright,** K John '00 (Cellino & B,PC) -16 W Main -Rchstr 14614
(516) 571-5810 .. **Wright,** Kathleen '03 Hon E Stack -400 Cnty Seat Dr -Mineola 11501
(212) 490-4100 .. **Wright,** Kathleen E '94 Cnsl Storch A&M,PC -140 E 45th -NY 10017
(631) 724-8833 .. **Wright,** Kelly E '05 %Devitt SB,LLP -50 Route 111 -Smithtwn 11787
(212) 735-3000 .. **Wright,** Kenneth A Jr. '90 (Skadden ASM&F LLP) -4 Times Sq -NY 10036
(212) 265-6888 .. **Wright,** Kerri A '06 %Porzio B&N,PC -156 W 56th -NY 10019
(845) 803-0559 .. **Wright,** Kevin L '76 -Bx733 -Mahopac 10541
(718) 250-2000 .. **Wright,** Kia M '06 %DA -350 Jay -Brklyn 11201 **Fx:**250-2314
(212) 688-5151 .. **Wright,** Kristen '07 %Gibney A&F,LLP -665 5th Av -NY 10022
(716) 483-7774 .. **Wright,** Kristen M '92 %Ctr for Resolutn & Justice -Bx4 -Bemus Pnt 14712
(718) 263-3695 .. **Wright,** L Sean '03 -123-20 82nd Av -Kew Gdns 11415
(718) 643-6161 .. **Wright,** Lawr E '86 -32 Court -Brklyn 11201 **Fx:**625-6977
(631) 471-4888 .. **Wright,** Leigh Anne '01 Alpha Abstract -122 Remngtn Blvd -Ronkonkoma 11779
(212) 490-4100 .. **Wright,** Lita Beth '94 (Storch A&M,PC) -140 E 45th -NY 10017
(609) 895-6738 .. **Wright,** Luke P '06 %Fox R LLP -100 Park Av -NY 10017 **Fx:**896-1469
(845) 838-1699 .. **Wright,** Mark E '78 -Bx422 -Fishkill 12524 **Fx:**838-1701
(585) 781-5823 .. **Wright,** Mark R '86 %Eastman Kodak -343 State -Rchstr 14650
(718) 725-3088 .. **Wright,** Marsha M '04 ACS-DLS -151-20 Jamaica Av -Jamaica 11432
(845) 567-7776 .. **Wright,** Mary Ellen '94 (Finkelstein & Prtnrs,LLP) -103 Exec Dr -New Windsor 12553
(607) 763-9200 .. **Wright,** Michl R '78 (Levene G&T,LLP) -BxF-1706 -Bnghmtn 13902
(212) 490-3000 .. **Wright,** Nancy V '96 (Wilson EME&D LLP) -150 E 42nd -NY 10017
(212) 318-3000 .. **Wright,** Nicole K '08 %Fulbright & J LLP -666 5th Av -NY 10103
(212) 259-8000 .. **Wright,** P Bruce '71 (Dewey & L LLP) -1301 Av of Amer -NY 10019
(718) 590-2000 .. **Wright,** Patricia A '09 %DA -198 E 161st -Bronx 10451 **Fx:**590-6477
(516) 571-3800 .. **Wright,** Patricia P '94 %DA -262 Old Cntry Rd -Mineola 11501 **Fx:**248-9479
(212) 210-1421 .. **Wright,** R Chas '85 A & E Network -235 E 45th -NY 10017 **Fx:**210-1308
(212) 906-1200 .. **Wright,** Rebecca J '09 %Latham & W -885 3rd Av -NY 10022
(212) 408-5100 .. **Wright,** Richd J '99 %Chadbourne & P LLP -30 Rckfllr Plz -NY 10112
(212) 430-6000 .. **Wright,** Richd J '02 -80 Maiden Ln -NY 10038 **Fx:**430-6001
(518) 462-1015 .. **Wright,** Robt '74 %ODAR-SSA -74 N Pearl -Albany 12207
(212) 244-9500 .. **Wright,** Robt '99 (White and W LLP) -1 Penn Plz -NY 10119
(212) 664-4444 .. **Wright,** Robt C '69 %NBC -30 Rckfllr Plz -NY 10112
(212) 779-8600 .. **Wright,** Ryan L '09 %Silverman SS&B PLLC -381 Park Av S -NY 10016
(212) 319-5183 .. **Wright,** Scott W '97 -500 5th Av -NY 10110
(716) 483-1122 .. **Wright,** Stephen J '92 (Wright W&H) -525 Fairmount Av W E Bx1198 -Jamestwn 14702
(716) 373-6060 .. **Wright,** Steven A '84 -2656 W State -Olean 14760 **Fx:**373-6067
(212) 558-4000 .. **Wright,** T J '06 %Sullivan & C LLP -125 Broad -NY 10004
(212) 407-4000 .. **Wright,** Tahra T '00 (Loeb & L,LLP) -345 Park Av -NY 10154
(518) 295-8109 .. **Wright,** Therese Ann '84 %C Wright -304 Main Bx100 -Schoharie 12157
(212) 969-3000 .. **Wright,** Thos G '10 %Proskauer R LLP -1585 Bway -NY 10036
(212) 558-4000 .. **Wright,** Thos John '10 %Sullivan & C LLP -125 Broad -NY 10004
(212) 758-7687 .. **Wright,** Timothy S '82 Entec Works LLC -420 Lex Av -NY 10170
(716) 849-3500 .. **Wright,** Victor M '05 %Hagelin & K LLC -135 Delaware Av -Buffalo 14202 **Fx:**849-3501
(212) 264-5916 .. **Wright,** Virna A '94 %DHS -26 Fed Plz -NY 10278
(212) 373-3000 .. **Wright,** W Peter '06 %Paul WRW&G LLP -1285 Av of Amer -NY 10019
(800) 742-9696 .. **Wright,** Wanda L '96 %Binder & B,PC -33-00 Nrthrn Blvd -LIC 11101 **Fx:**(718) 512-2424
(212) 248-3140 .. **Wright,** Wm A '06 %Drinker B&R LLP -140 Bway -NY 10005
(716) 483-1122 .. **Wright,** Wm L Jr. '94 (Wright W&H) -525 Fairmount Av W E Bx1198 -Jamestwn 14702
(212) 307-9393 .. **Wright,** Wm R '82 -250 W 57th -NY 10107 **Fx:**247-0961
(716) 483-1122 .. **Wright Wright & Hampton** -525 Fairmount Av W E Bx1198 -Jamestwn 14702 **Fx:**483-2060
(315) 474-6448 .. **Wright,** Zea M '04 %Byrne C&P PC -100 Madison -Syracuse 13202
(212) 506-1700 .. **Wrightson,** Rachel M '04 %Kasowitz BT&F LLP -1633 Bway -NY 10019
(518) 677-8819 .. **Wrigley,** D Alan Jr. '77 (Wrigley & K) -27 W Main Bx255 -Cambrdg 12816
(518) 677-8819 .. **Wrigley & Kopec** -27 W Main Bx255 -Cambrdg 12816 **Fx:**677-8821
(212) 848-4642 .. **Wriston,** Kathryn D '64 -599 Lex Av -NY 10022 **Fx:**848-7179
(212) 421-8100 .. **Wrobel,** David C '84 (Wrobel & S LLP) -1040 Av of Amer -NY 10018
(212) 571-7100 .. **Wrobel,** Helen '95 O'Dwyer & B,LLP -52 Duane -NY 10007
(845) 473-5411 .. **Wrobel,** Lewis D '76 -12 Raymnd Av -Poughkeepsie 12603 **Fx:**473-3430
(914) 834-2520 .. **Wrobel,** Marcie Penn '84 -28 Colonial Av -Larchmnt 10538
(212) 421-8100 .. **Wrobel & Schatz LLP** -1040 Av of Amer -NY 10018 **Fx:**421-8170
(212) 524-5000 .. **Wrobleski,** Chester J '73 (Jacob M&F) -1270 Av of Amer -NY 10020
(716) 204-2400 .. **Wrona,** Michl J '94 %SJ Baum,PC -220 Nrthpnte Pkwy Bx1291 -Buffalo 14240 **Fx:**204-4600
(212) 821-0897 .. **Wrubel,** Austin S '93 NY Presbyterian Hospital -425 E 61st -NY 10065
(212) 735-3000 .. **Wrubel,** Barbara '82 OfCnsl Skadden ASM&F LLP -4 Times Sq -NY 10036
(212) 336-3500 .. **Wrubel,** David F '74 SrCnsl Miller & W,PC -570 Lex Av -NY 10022
(212) 448-1100 .. **Wrubel,** Eric I '96 (McLaughlin & S,LLP) -260 Mad Av -NY 10016
(631) 475-3100 .. **Wruck,** Ernest R '80 (Wruck & W LLP) -38 Church -Patchogue 11772 **Fx:**475-3154
(212) 508-6100 .. **Wry,** Jonathan D '98 (Bracewell & G,LLP) -1251 Av of Amer -NY 10020
(516) 773-9300 .. **Wrynn,** Brian G '86 McSam Hotel Grp LLC -420 Grt Nck Rd -Gt Neck 11021 **Fx:**733-9302
(914) 397-2400 .. **Wrynn,** Gerard M '89 (Ferguson C,LLP) -1 N Lex Av -White Plns 10601 **Fx:**683-6956
(718) 423-6800 .. **Wrynn,** James J '85 (MacKay W&B LLP) -40-26 235th -Douglastn 11363
(646) 654-7755 .. **Wrzesinski,** Heather R '05 Buzzmetrics,Inc -770 Bway -NY 10003
(212) 325-2850 .. **Wrzosek,** Robt A '98 Credit Suisse Securities LLC -11 Mad Av -NY 10010
(212) 755-8880 .. **Wu,** Allen '84 (Wu & K,PLLC) -747 3rd Av -NY 10017 **Fx:**755-8890
(212) 587-9641 .. **Wu,** Andrew C '00 Lower Dlvpmnt Mgmt Corp -1 Lbrty Plz -NY 10006
(212) 351-4000 .. **Wu,** Aric H '99 (Gibson D&C LLP) -200 Park Av -NY 10166
(212) 788-1332 .. **Wu,** Connie Y '01 %Law Dept -100 Church -NY 10007 **Fx:**788-0367
(212) 295-6436 .. **Wu,** Dino '98 (WilmerHale) -399 Park Av -NY 10022
(212) 310-8000 .. **Wu,** Edw D '09 %Weil G&M LLP -767 5th Av -NY 10153
(917) 797-9636 .. **Wu,** Faith '00 -979 Park Pl -Brklyn 11213
(212) 361-8050 .. **Wu,** Han-Wen Annie '05 %Dept Homeless Srvcs -33 Beaver -NY 10004 **Fx:**361-8002
(212) 848-4000 .. **Wu,** Horace Hao '08 %Shearman & S LLP -599 Lex Av -NY 10022
(212) 425-7200 .. **Wu,** Huiya '00 (Kenyon & K,LLP) -1 Bway -NY 10004
(718) 357-5073 .. **Wu,** Jenda '94 -142-05 Roosevelt Av -Flushng 11354 **Fx:**357-6506
(212) 238-4800 .. **Wu,** Jennifer '07 %Landman CB&F,PC -120 Bway -NY 10271
(212) 310-8000 .. **Wu,** Jennifer H '05 %Weil G&M LLP -767 5th Av -NY 10153
(212) 310-8000 .. **Wu,** Jenny C '09 %Weil G&M LLP -767 5th Av -NY 10153
(212) 916-7825 .. **Wu,** Jie '06 Rabobank Nederland -245 Park Av -NY 10167
(917) 443-8036 .. **Wu,** Jimmy C '90 -70-31 108th -Frst Hlls 11375
(212) 903-9000 .. **Wu,** John H '06 %Linklaters -1345 Av of Amer -NY 10105
(646) 822-4472 .. **Wu,** Judy '09 Signature Bk -565 5th Av -NY 10017
(212) 889-0575 .. **Wu,** Karen I '05 %Perlman & P -41 Mad Av -NY 10010 **Fx:**743-8120
(646) 386-4800 .. **Wu,** Kathy Giah-Yeh '03 %Comm Judicial Cndct -61 Bway -NY 10006 **Fx:**458-0037
(212) 684-4111 .. **Wu,** Kevin Chun '93 %Genetelli Consulting Grp -431 5th Av -NY 10016 **Fx:**213-1020
(212) 371-8008 .. **Wu,** Libing '07 %Guzov O,LLC -600 Mad Av -NY 10022
(212) 878-8000 .. **Wu,** MaryJean '10 %Clifford C LLP -31 W 52nd -NY 10019
(212) 267-0011 .. **Wu,** Melissa Y '09 %Shafer G,LLP -90 John -NY 10038
(212) 513-1799 .. **Wu,** Mitzi '94 Empire State Cptl Corp -170 Bway -NY 10038
(212) 839-5300 .. **Wu,** Patti T '82 (Sidley A LLP) -787 7th Av -NY 10019
(212) 752-9700 .. **Wu,** Qiong Joan '09 %Gersten S LLP -600 Lex Av -NY 10022
(212) 416-6312 .. **Wu,** Steven C '09 %Dept of Law -120 Bway -NY 10271
(212) 854-9808 .. **Wu,** Sylvia C '05 CU Initiative for Policy Dialogue -420 W 118th -NY 10027
(212) 854-2322 .. **Wu,** Timothy S '01 Columbia Law Schl -435 W 116th -NY 10027 **Fx:**854-7946
(212) 735-3000 .. **Wu,** Wen '04 %Skadden ASM&F LLP -4 Times Sq -NY 10036
(212) 455-2000 .. **Wu,** Wendy W '08 %Simpson T&B LLP -425 Lex Av -NY 10017
(212) 373-3000 .. **Wu,** Yin '06 %Paul WRW&G LLP -1285 Av of Amer -NY 10019
(212) 285-3038 .. **Wu,** Yolanda Sung '95 %Better Balance -75 Maiden Ln -NY 10038 **Fx:**724-3535
(212) 345-8744 .. **Wu-Dare,** Susie S '98 Marsh USA -1166 Av of Amer -NY 10036 **Fx:**345-5627
(212) 509-5050 .. **Wuersch,** Danl A '92 (Wuersch & G LLP) -100 Wall -NY 10005
(212) 509-5050 .. **Wuersch & Gering LLP** -100 Wall -NY 10005 **Fx:**509-9559
(212) 625-1570 .. **Wuestman,** Eric A '97 -401 Bway -NY 10013
(718) 585-7000 .. **Wughalter,** Eric A '83 (Rogers WKC&Z) -800 Grnd Cncrs -Bronx 10451 **Fx:**585-8969
(914) 332-1800 .. **Wugman,** Dan L '02 %Cherry E&K,LLP -150 Wht Plns Rd -Tarrytwn 10591
(212) 468-8000 .. **Wugmeister,** Miriam '93 (Morrison & F LLP) -1290 Av of Amer -NY 10104
(212) 325-2000 .. **Wui,** Yi Tung Rebecca '00 Credit Suisse Securities -1 Mad Av -NY 10010
(585) 591-1100 .. **Wujcik,** James M '06 %Dadd N&W -11 Exchange Bx238 -Attica 14011
(518) 447-3200 .. **Wukitsch,** David J '82 (McNamee LT&W,PC) -677 Bway -Albany 12207
(212) 698-3500 .. **Wukoson,** George P '09 %Dechert LLP -1095 Av of Amer -NY 10036
(845) 497-3220 .. **Wulfman,** Andrew S '87 (A Wulfman,LLC) -100 Egbertson Rd -Campbell Hall 10916 **Fx:**497-3279
(212) 732-6566 .. **Wulwick,** Alexander J '78 -233 Bway -NY 10279
(212) 509-8809 .. **Wun,** Herman H '02 -75 Maiden Ln -NY 10038
(315) 946-4844 .. **Wunder,** Richd C '74 -12 William Bx404 -Lyons 14489 **Fx:**946-9463
(631) 361-8081 .. **Wunderlich,** Howard J '87 -64 Smithtwn Blvd -Smithtwn 11787 **Fx:**360-8835
(212) 227-4000 .. **Wunderlich,** Scott W '01 %Mirman M&L,PC -291 Bway -NY 10007
(631) 207-5654 .. **Wurman & Hornberger,PC** -57 E Main -Patchogue 11772
(631) 207-5654 .. **Wurman,** Howard A '97 (Wurman & H,PC) -57 E Main -Patchogue 11772
(516) 498-2900 .. **Wurman,** Kenneth H '78 (Naidich WB&M,LLP) -80 Cuttermill Rd -Gt Neck 11021 **Fx:**466-3555
(212) 613-5038 .. **Wurmfeld,** Katherine Frazier '06 NY Leg Assistance Grp -450 W 33rd -NY 10001
(516) 663-6600 .. **Wurst,** Jeffrey '87 (Ruskin MF,PC) -1425 RXR Plz -Uniondale 11556

(718) 618-2500 .. **Wursthorn,** Eric J '08 %Civil Ct -851 Grnd Cncrs -Bronx 10451 **Fx:**590-7294
(585) 454-7145 .. **Wurtz,** Edw A '76 (Gallo & I,LLP) -39 State -Rchstr 14614
(516) 822-7866 .. **Wurtzel,** Elan '84 E Wurtzel,PC -527 Old Cntry Rd -Plainvw 11803 **Fx:**822-7889
(212) 766-4000 .. **Wurtzel,** Stewart E '84 (Deutsch TW&W,PC) -120 Bway -NY 10271
(212) 373-3000 .. **Wurzburger,** Andrew S '01 %Paul WRW&G LLP -1285 Av of Amer -NY 10019
(212) 883-2464 .. **Wurzel,** Marc A '89 %Grand Cntrl Prtnrshp -122 E 42nd -NY 10168
(518) 395-5005 .. **Wuttke,** Eric T '06 Siemens PTI -1482 Erie Blvd -Schnctdy 12305
(212) 774-7216 .. **Wyatt,** Brian M '99 %Hosp for Spcl Surgery -535 E 70th -NY 10021 **Fx:**517-8781
(212) 909-6000 .. **Wyatt,** Charity Brunson '10 %Debevoise & P LLP -919 3rd Av -NY 10022
(212) 681-0800 .. **Wyatt,** Douglas W '62 (Wyatt G&O,LLP) -99 Park Av -NY 10016
(212) 525-3170 .. **Wyatt,** Edna E '02 HSBC Bk -452 5th Av -NY 10018
(212) 681-0800 .. **Wyatt Gerber & O'Rourke,LLP** -99 Park Av -NY 10016 **Fx:**681-0810
(212) 557-2776 .. **Wyatt,** Justin R '01 (Ferraro & W,PLLC) -950 3rd Av -NY 10022 **Fx:**(646) 349-2776
(914) 273-5103 .. **Wyatt,** Richd T '75 %Wyatt & Co -22 Wrights Mill Rd -Armonk 10504 **Fx:**273-5106
(914) 273-5103 .. **Wyatt,** Rita Ann '71 %Wyatt & Co -22 Wrights Mill Rd -Armonk 10504 **Fx:**273-5106
(212) 682-1700 .. **Wybiral,** Leslie Scot '06 %L Burke,PC -460 Park Av -NY 10022 **Fx:**808-4280
(646) 486-9880 .. **Wyckoff,** E Lisk Jr. '61 -115 E 57th -NY 10022 **Fx:**486-9881
(212) 848-4000 .. **Wyckoff,** Gregory C '09 %Shearman & S LLP -599 Lex Av -NY 10022
(212) 940-8800 .. **Wyckoff,** Heather N '06 %Katten MR LLP -575 Mad Av -NY 10022
(585) 262-6390 .. **Wyder,** Stephen P Jr. '08 %Hamberger & W -1 S Wshngtn -Rchstr 14614
(716) 843-5700 .. **Wydysh,** Chas B '73 %US Atty -138 Delaware Av -Buffalo 14202 **Fx:**551-3052
(716) 566-5400 .. **Wydysh,** Mary Quinn '94 (Goldberg S LLP) -665 Main -Buffalo 14203
(212) 925-6665 .. **Wyetzner,** Leo '59 (Wyetzner & N) -401 Bway -NY 10013
(212) 925-6665 .. **Wyetzner & Needle** -401 Bway -NY 10013 **Fx:**941-7286
(716) 843-5700 .. **Wylegala,** Gretchen L '85 %US Atty -138 Delaware Av -Buffalo 14202 **Fx:**551-3052
(716) 826-9680 .. **Wylegala,** Raymond V '52 -4145 Chatham Dr -Hambrg 14075 **Fx:**826-9682
(212) 804-4200 .. **Wyles,** Gregory D '08 %Mound CW&G -One Bttry Pk Plz -NY 10004
(518) 565-4770 .. **Wylie,** Andrew J '88 (DA) -137 Margaret -Plattsbrgh 12901 **Fx:**565-4777
(212) 598-8000 .. **Wylie,** Gordon F '84 %Guardian Life Ins -7 Hanover Sq -NY 10004 **Fx:**919-2693
(718) 756-0237 .. **Wyllie,** Ingrid V '93 -4906 Church Av -Brklyn 11203 **Fx:**756-0983
(212) 820-6355 .. **Wylly,** J Douglas '83 %AIG -160 Water -NY 10038 **Fx:**425-6355
(631) 694-2300 .. **Wylly,** Virginia Medici '83 OfCnsl Lamb & B,LLP -534 Broadhllw Rd Bx9034 -Melvll 11747
(212) 455-2000 .. **Wyman,** Kenneth S '88 (Simpson T&B LLP) -425 Lex Av -NY 10017
(212) 848-4000 .. **Wyman,** Michl J '08 %Shearman & S LLP -599 Lex Av -NY 10022
(646) 386-4520 .. **Wyman,** Rosemarie A '82 %Criminal Ct -100 Centre -NY 10013
(212) 850-4312 .. **Wyman,** Russell T '93 Emigrant Svngs Bank -6 E 43rd -NY 10017
(315) 946-5842 .. **Wyner,** Danl M '70 (Cnty Atty) -26 Church -Lyons 14489 **Fx:**946-5942
(845) 876-2703 .. **Wyner,** Paul G '72 (Wyner & R) -42 E Market -Red Hook 12571 **Fx:**876-2703
(212) 497-8278 .. **Wyner,** Scott H '80 OfCnsl Storch A&M,PC -140 E 45th -NY 10017
(212) 450-4000 .. **Wynkoop,** Noah L '10 %Davis P&W LLP -450 Lex Av -NY 10017
(212) 402-6886 .. **Wynn,** Darryl L '88 -75 Maiden Ln -NY 10038
(212) 484-3900 .. **Wynn,** David N '81 (Arent F LLP) -1675 Bway -NY 10019
(212) 450-4000 .. **Wynn,** Javius C '10 %Davis P&W LLP -450 Lex Av -NY 10017
(516) 228-1505 .. **Wynne,** Anne T '00 Ivy Asset Mgmt -1 Jericho Plz -Jericho 11753
(914) 824-5070 .. **Wynne,** Anthony R '99 %Atty Grievance Comm -399 Knollwood Rd -White Plns 10603 **Fx:**949-0997
(516) 764-4331 .. **Wynne,** James D '77 -17 Loel Ct -Rockvll Ctr 11570
(516) 248-9700 .. **Wynne,** Jennifer A '02 %S Levitt & Assoc,PC -2 Hillside Av -Williston Pk 11596 **Fx:**741-9224
(212) 313-3600 .. **Wynne,** John V '87 (Barry M&M) -2 Rector -NY 10006
(212) 598-8000 .. **Wynne,** Kristin L '00 %Guardian Life Ins -7 Hanover Sq -NY 10004 **Fx:**919-2693
(718) 828-8270 .. **Wynne,** Patrick J '82 -3453 E Tremont Av -Bronx 10465 **Fx:**824-3355
(212) 819-8200 .. **Wynne,** Wm F Jr. '77 (White & C LLP) -1155 Av of Amer -NY 10036
(845) 896-3100 .. **Wynshaw,** Warren D '77 (W Wynshaw,PC) -1076 Main -Fishkill 12524 **Fx:**896-5387
(212) 878-8000 .. **Wypior,** Oda U '98 %Clifford C LLP -31 W 52nd -NY 10019
(212) 596-9000 .. **Wyrwoll,** Patricia Sales Teixeira '05 %Ropes & G LLP -1211 Av of Amer -NY 10036
(212) 445-3393 .. **Wyskoarko,** Nicole A '07 Island Def Jam Music Grp -825 8th Av -NY 10019
(212) 313-3600 .. **Wysnewski,** David L '90 %Barry M&M -2 Rector -NY 10006
(212) 612-9316 .. **Wysocki,** Henry V '81 %The Clearing House -450 W 33rd -NY 10001 **Fx:**612-9253
(716) 282-0001 .. **Wysocki,** Jacek A '70 %Niagara Falls Redevelopment -1625 Buffalo Av -Niagara Fls 14303
(212) 839-5300 .. **Wysocki,** Paul R '93 (Sidley A LLP) -787 7th Av -NY 10019
(212) 412-1310 .. **Wysoki,** David H '89 Barclays Bank PLC -222 Bway -NY 10038
(212) 438-2342 .. **Wyss,** Melissa P '99 Standard & Poor's -55 Water -NY 10041
(716) 882-2243 .. **Wyssling,** Richd H '69 -375 Linwood Av -Buffalo 14209 **Fx:**882-6113
(716) 674-9610 .. **Wyszynski,** Michl R '85 -950-A Union Rd -W Seneca 14224 **Fx:**674-9611
(212) 756-2000 .. **Wyttenbach,** Marc A '00 %Schulte R&Z LLP -919 3rd Av -NY 10022
(212) 349-5150 .. **Xanthakis,** Anthony C '89 (Galvano & X,PC) -150 Bway -NY 10038
(631) 342-5224 .. **Xanthos,** Anna Kampourakis '98 CA,Inc -1 CA Plz -Islandia 11749 **Fx:**342-4866
(212) 759-5800 .. **Xanthos,** Arthur P '91 (Gartner + B,PC) -801 2nd Av -NY 10017
(315) 473-0899 .. **Xavier,** Brent C '07 %Anelli X,PC -441 S Salina -Syracuse 13202 **Fx:**473-0530
(212) 940-8800 .. **Xethalis,** Gregory E '06 %Katten MR LLP -575 Mad Av -NY 10022
(212) 872-1000 .. **Xia,** Buxian '03 -One Bryant Park -NY 10036 **Fx:**872-1002
(212) 279-5442 .. **Xiang,** Lian '04 -45 W 34th -NY 10001
(718) 250-2000 .. **Xie,** Chow Yun '10 %DA -350 Jay -Brklyn 11201 **Fx:**250-2314
(212) 227-1018 .. **Xie,** Joan '99 -225 Bway -NY 10007 **Fx:**227-0452
(212) 608-6500 .. **Xie,** Rong '07 %DeHeng C,LLC -225 Bway -NY 10007
(212) 226-0188 .. **Xie,** Xiang '01 -401 Bway -NY 10013
(631) 444-3871 .. **Xikis,** James '07 %SUNY Stony Brook -L3-119 Health Sciences Ctr -Stony Brk 11794
(212) 596-9000 .. **Xiong,** Mark W '10 %Ropes & G LLP -1211 Av of Amer -NY 10036
(212) 578-3304 .. **Xiques,** Gladys '99 %MetLife -27-01 Qns Plz N -LIC 11101 **Fx:**743-0693
(212) 326-2000 .. **Xistris,** Demetrios G '86 SrCnsl O'Melveny & M LLP -7 Times Sq -NY 10036
(212) 464-2392 .. **Xistris,** Victor D '76 JP Morgan Chase & Co -345 Park Av -NY 10154
(212) 704-6000 .. **Xiu,** Jie '05 %Troutman S LLP -405 Lex Av -NY 10174
(607) 777-9601 .. **Xlander,** Fredk R '82 -520 Columbia Dr -Johnson Cty 13790 **Fx:**777-9609
(212) 218-2100 .. **Xu,** Feng '06 %Fitzpatrick CH&S -1290 Av of Amer -NY 10104
(212) 455-2000 .. **Xu,** Joyce Yusi '02 (Simpson T&B LLP) -425 Lex Av -NY 10017
(212) 610-6300 .. **Xu,** Zachary Weijia '05 %Allen & O -1221 Av of Amer -NY 10020
(212) 455-2000 .. **Xu,** Zhong Cheng '08 %Simpson T&B LLP -425 Lex Av -NY 10017
(212) 906-1200 .. **Xue,** Alfred Y '07 %Latham & W -885 3rd Av -NY 10022
(212) 219-2275 .. **Xue,** Benjamin B '02 (B Xue,PC) -401 Bway -NY 10013 **Fx:**219-2276
(718) 459-9000 .. **Xuereb,** Christopher '10 Sweeney GR&B,LLP -95-25 Qns Blvd -Rego Pk 11374
(203) 348-5433 .. **Xylas,** George M '85 (Xylas & Z,LLP) -240 E 86th -NY 10028 **Fx:**961-1183
(212) 201-1170 .. **Xylas,** Michl C '91 Abrams GMB,LLP -237 W 35th -NY 10001
(516) 490-4409 .. **Xylas,** Nikolaos '01 %Bookspan -501 Franklin Av -Gdn Cty 11530 **Fx:**490-4284
(212) 790-0333 .. **Yablon,** Chas M '76 %Benj N Cardozo Schl of Law -55 5th Av -NY 10003 **Fx:**790-0345
(718) 520-3732 .. **Yablon,** Elizabeth R '85 Supreme Ct -88-11 Sutphin Blvd -Jamaica 11435 **Fx:**262-7107
(212) 490-3000 .. **Yablon,** Heather D '96 OfCnsl Wilson EME&D LLP -150 E 42nd -NY 10017
(518) 377-6737 .. **Yablon,** Jay R '83 -910 Nrthmbrlnd Dr -Niskayuna 12309 **Fx:**377-6737
(212) 725-8566 .. **Yablon,** Lawr T '96 (Robinson & Y,PC) -232 Mad Av -NY 10016
(212) 259-8000 .. **Yablon,** Staci L '06 %Dewey & L LLP -1301 Av of Amer -NY 10019
(212) 884-7187 .. **Yablonowitz,** Scott R '69 -1290 Av of the Americas -NY 10104
(212) 969-3000 .. **Yablonski,** Elise A '91 SrCnsl Proskauer R LLP -1585 Bway -NY 10036
(212) 504-6000 .. **Yablonski,** Joshua J '99 SpclCnsl Cadwalader W&T LLP -1 World Fncl Ctr -NY 10281
(845) 371-4700 .. **Yablonsky,** Chad '05 %Fein SK&S,PC -747 Chestnut Rdg Rd -Spg Vly 10977
(212) 421-9630 .. **Yaccarino,** Scott D '04 Smythe Masterson & Judd -230 Park Av -NY 10169 **Fx:**421-9665
(212) 461-1809 .. **Yachbes,** Jack J '99 -110 Wall -NY 10005
(718) 725-3202 .. **Yacht,** Laura D '96 -151-20 Jamaica Av -Jamaica 11432
(212) 940-8800 .. **Yacker,** Allison C '03 (Katten MR LLP) -575 Mad Av -NY 10022
(212) 566-4060 .. **Yacker,** Jay B '90 (Dario YS&A) -44 Wall -NY 10005
(212) 836-8000 .. **Yacker,** Rhonda '86 Cnsl Kaye S LLP -425 Park Av -NY 10022
(516) 997-4040 .. **Yackow,** Jay L '83 -1400 Old Cntry Rd -Westbury 11590 **Fx:**997-4005
(212) 425-1999 .. **Yacos,** John G '90 Edelsteins F&B,LLP -61 Bway -NY 10006
(212) 373-3000 .. **Yacoub,** Alex R '10 %Paul WRW&G LLP -1285 Av of Amer -NY 10019
(212) 825-1212 .. **Yacoub,** John P '94 OfCnsl Morrison M LLP -17 State -NY 10004
(718) 590-2000 .. **Yacoub,** Pishoy B '06 DA -198 E 161st -Bronx 10451 **Fx:**590-6477
(914) 422-8755 .. **Yacyshyn,** Elaine Karassi '84 %Dept of Law -101 E Post Rd -White Plns 10601 **Fx:**422-8706
(212) 554-1234 .. **Yacyshyn,** Paul M '82 %AXA Financial Inc -1290 Av of Amer -NY 10104 **Fx:**707-3963
(212) 326-3939 .. **Yadava,** Nidhi '09 %Jones D -222 E 41st -NY 10017
(212) 326-5334 .. **Yadegari,** Steven A '99 Cramer Rosenthal McGlynn LLC -520 Mad Av -NY 10022
(212) 839-5300 .. **Yadgar,** Michl S '00 %Sidley A LLP -787 7th Av -NY 10019
(718) 866-5850 .. **Yadgarov,** Alex M '09 -1 Cross Isl Plz -Rosedale 11422
(212) 836-8000 .. **Yadlon,** Thos E '00 (Kaye S LLP) -425 Park Av -NY 10022
(212) 906-1200 .. **Yaecker,** Gregory P '10 %Latham & W -885 3rd Av -NY 10022
(212) 305-4794 .. **Yaeger,** Diane L '75 Columbia Univ Med Ctr -601 W 168th #22 -NY 10032
(716) 854-8705 .. **Yaeger,** Lisa M '91 Sen Antoine Thompson -65 Court -Buffalo 14202
(718) 254-7000 .. **Yaeger,** Michl L '04 %US Atty -271 Cadman Plz E -Brklyn 11201 **Fx:**254-6479
(631) 694-2400 .. **Yaffe,** David N '89 (Hamburger MYK&M,LLP) -225 Broadhllw Rd -Melvll 11747
(212) 294-6700 .. **Yaffe,** Evelyn B '08 %Winston & S -200 Park Av -NY 10166
(212) 742-3390 .. **Yaffe,** Scott M '84 OfCnsl Lindabury ME&C,PC -26 Bway -NY 10004
(212) 922-9700 .. **Yaffee,** Jared P '04 %1st Amer Title -633 3rd Av -NY 10017 **Fx:**922-0881
(212) 633-4400 .. **Yaged,** Jonathan R '96 %Disney Publishing -44 S Bway -White Plns 10601
(607) 753-7266 .. **Yager,** Donald Wm Jr. '67 (Yager Law Ofc) -15 Church -Cortlnd 13045 **Fx:**753-0986
(212) 489-1600 .. **Yager,** Martha R '84 %Deloitte LLP -1633 Bway -NY 10019 **Fx:**492-4201
(212) 964-7400 .. **Yagerman,** Evan D '08 Smith MDWY&Y,PC -111 John -NY 10038
(212) 681-6400 .. **Yagerman,** Howard W '78 (Burger Y&G LLP) -60 E 42nd -NY 10165 **Fx:**681-6999
(212) 964-7400 .. **Yagerman,** Mark S '80 Smith MDWY&Y,PC -111 John -NY 10038
(914) 422-4343 .. **Yaggi,** Marc A '00 %Riverkeeper Inc -78 N Bway -White Plns 10603
(212) 479-6000 .. **Yaghmaie,** Babak '00 (Cooley LLP) -1114 Av of Amer -NY 10036

(718) 706-2213 .. **Yagi**, Kanako '06 Kai Kai Kiki NY LLC -517 46th Rd -LIC 11101
(212) 317-8723 .. **Yahner**, David F '77 -570 Lex Av -NY 10022 **Fx:**317-8725
(212) 906-1200 .. **Yai**, Dennis K '07 %Latham & W -885 3rd Av -NY 10022
(212) 449-1000 .. **Yaish**, Yair '95 %Merrill Lynch -220 Bway -NY 10038
(212) 538-2313 .. **Yak**, Patricia '87 Credit Suisse -1 Mad Av -NY 10010
(631) 727-4100 .. **Yakaboski**, Francis J '66 (Smith FLI&Y) -456 Griffing Av Bx389 -Rvrhead 11901
(212) 294-6700 .. **Yakaboski**, Stacy A '96 (Winston & S) -200 Park Av -NY 10166
(212) 465-1110 .. **Yakaitis**, Paul A '80 (Bader Y&N LLP) -350 5th Av -NY 10118
(212) 326-3939 .. **Yakren**, Aviva '98 (Jones D) -222 E 41st -NY 10017
(212) 277-5823 .. **Yakren**, Sofia '05 %Beldock L&H LLP -99 Park Av -NY 10016
(212) 808-2700 .. **Yakulis**, Paul G '08 %Pepper H LLP -620 8th Av -NY 10018
(716) 856-4000 .. **Yalamanchili**, Sujata '99 (Hodgson R LLP) -140 Pearl -Buffalo 14202
(212) 559-0584 .. **Yalcinkaya**, Seda '99 Citigroup -425 Park Av -NY 10022
(212) 848-4000 .. **Yale**, Dorman T '06 %Shearman & S LLP -599 Lex Av -NY 10022
(212) 770-7000 .. **Yale**, Harris J '85 AIG -70 Pine -NY 10270
(212) 682-1220 .. **Yale**, Jerold S '71 -60 E 42nd -NY 10165 **Fx:**682-1822
(212) 906-1200 .. **Yale**, Nathanael B '06 %Latham & W -885 3rd Av -NY 10022
(607) 273-4200 .. **Yale-Loehr**, Stephen W '93 OfCnsl Miller M,LLP -202 E State -Ithaca 14850
(212) 637-2722 .. **Yalen**, Robt W '01 %US Atty -86 Chmbrs -NY 10007
(718) 292-2952 .. **Yalkut**, Arlen S '72 (Yalkut & I) -865B Walton Av -Bronx 10451
(718) 292-2952 .. **Yalkut & Israel** -865B Walton Av -Bronx 10451 **Fx:**993-1542
(212) 715-1000 .. **Yalowitz**, Kent A '88 (Arnold & P LLP) -399 Park Av -NY 10022
(631) 468-5851 .. **Yam**, John J '96 %Orange Business Svcs -4250 Vets Mem'l Hwy -Holbrook 11741
(212) 219-7783 .. **Yam**, Man C '99 -401 Bway -NY 10013
(212) 490-3000 .. **Yam**, Maria '08 %Wilson EME&D LLP -150 E 42nd -NY 10017
(212) 373-3000 .. **Yamada**, Karina '09 %Paul WRW&G LLP -1285 Av of Amer -NY 10019
(212) 782-4479 .. **Yamada**, Yoshisuke '97 %Bk of Tokyo-Mitsubishi -1251 Av of Amer -NY 10020
(718) 618-2500 .. **Yamagata**, Mary '91 %Civil Ct -851 Grnd Cncrs -Bronx 10451 **Fx:**590-7294
(212) 486-9494 .. **Yamaguchi**, Kenji '96 -488 Mad Av -NY 10022
(212) 969-3000 .. **Yamaguchi**, Shintaro '08 %Proskauer R LLP -1585 Bway -NY 10036
(516) 431-8546 .. **Yamall**, Jos A '90 -153 Jffrsn Av -Isl Pk 11558
(212) 402-7840 .. **Yamamoto**, Takako '02 %J Nolan -65 Bway -NY 10006
(212) 805-3900 .. **Yamamoto**, Yoko '02 %Clausen M PC -1 Chase Manh Plz -NY 10005
(212) 902-3261 .. **Yamamura**, Sylvia C '96 -85 Broad -NY 10004
(718) 361-1818 .. **Yamaner**, Jos N '84 -45-29 47th -Woodside 11377 **Fx:**729-0623
(718) 250-4525 .. **Yameogo-Warner**, Ivatchka '09 Leg Aid -111 Lvngstn -Brklyn 11201 **Fx:**250-4243
(212) 755-3100 .. **Yamin**, Michl G '59 (Kaufmann GR&O LLP) -777 3rd Av -NY 10017
(212) 343-1645 .. **Yamner**, David L '88 %Empire Entertainment -560 Bway -NY 10012 **Fx:**343-1646
(212) 506-5000 .. **Yan**, Barbara '08 %Orrick H&S LLP -51 W 52nd -NY 10019
(718) 888-7788 .. **Yan**, David '02 -13620 38th Av -Flushng 11354
(212) 788-6779 .. **Yan**, Jimmy S C '99 Mayors Ofc Immigrant Affrs -100 Gold -NY 10038
(212) 558-4000 .. **Yan**, Ran '06 %Sullivan & C LLP -125 Broad -NY 10004
(516) 227-0700 .. **Yan**, Robt C '02 %Farrell F,PC -1320 RXR Plz -Uniondale 11556
(212) 571-1160 .. **Yan**, Robt M '96 -120 E Bway -NY 10002
(917) 421-4721 .. **Yan**, Wendy C '98 IRS -33 Maiden Ln -NY 10038
(631) 473-2036 .. **Yanaros**, Wm D '76 Widder & Y -105 Route 112 -Pt Jffrsn Sta 11776
(518) 462-5300 .. **Yanas**, John J '54 (DeGraff F&K LLP) -90 State -Albany 12207
(212) 335-9000 .. **Yancey**, Felicia A '02 %DA -1 Hogan Pl -NY 10013
(917) 531-0028 .. **Yancey**, Trecarcia L '00 Yancey Consulting LLC -60 W Broad -Mt Vernon 10552
(516) 794-2800 .. **Yanega**, Thos '85 %M Devack,PLLC -90 Merrick Av -E Meadow 11554 **Fx:**794-2900
(212) 450-4000 .. **Yanes**, Raul F '93 (Davis P&W LLP) -450 Lex Av -NY 10017
(212) 728-8000 .. **Yanez**, Antonio Jr. '97 (Willkie F&G LLP) -787 7th Av -NY 10019
(212) 622-6976 .. **Yanez**, Fernando '03 JP Morgan -277 Park Av -NY 10172
(914) 235-2520 .. **Yanez**, Liliana C '99 -271 North Av -New Rchll 10801 **Fx:**235-2513
(212) 521-5400 .. **Yang**, Chau-Shin Yvonne '03 %Reed S LLP -599 Lex Av -NY 10022
(212) 756-2000 .. **Yang**, Chen Catherine '08 %Schulte R&Z LLP -919 3rd Av -NY 10022
(212) 274-9099 .. **Yang**, Chin-Ming '96 %Barst M&K LLP -168 Canal -NY 10013
(212) 277-6500 .. **Yang**, Cindy '03 %Dickstein S LLP -1633 Bway -NY 10019
(212) 506-5000 .. **Yang**, Cindy '06 Orrick H&S LLP -51 W 52nd -NY 10019
(212) 848-4000 .. **Yang**, Debra D '02 %Shearman & S LLP -599 Lex Av -NY 10022
(518) 473-3239 .. **Yang**, Diana '06 %Dept of Health -Corning Twr 24th Fl -Albany 12237 **Fx:**473-2019
(212) 556-1234 .. **Yang**, Eunice '02 %The NY Times Co -620 8th Av -NY 10018 **Fx:**556-4634
(646) 468-2971 .. **Yang**, Forrest D '09 PricewaterhouseCoopers -300 Mad Av -NY 10017
(212) 966-9076 .. **Yang**, Fuhao '07 -7 Mott -NY 10013 **Fx:**966-9078
(212) 326-3939 .. **Yang**, Grace '10 %Jones D -222 E 41st -NY 10017
(212) 732-9600 .. **Yang**, Jason Tsu-Hsin '05 %S Kartagener -225 Bway -NY 10007 **Fx:**732-6966
(718) 590-7834 .. **Yang**, Joan J '96 %Hon B Newman -851 Grnd Cncrs -Bronx 10451
(212) 556-2100 .. **Yang**, Kai-Ting '09 King & S -1185 Av of Amer -NY 10036
(718) 465-0996 .. **Yang**, Kangsun '02 %Zhongjian Law Firm -7344 196th -Fresh Mdws 11366
(212) 595-1250 .. **Yang**, Kathryn K '01 SJ Kim's Taekwon-Do LLC -2182 Bway -NY 10024
(212) 395-6584 .. **Yang**, Katie '97 %Verizon -140 West -NY 10007
(212) 605-2000 .. **Yang**, Lana Ting-Ya '00 %Mitsubishi Intl -655 3rd Av -NY 10017 **Fx:**605-2129
(212) 728-8000 .. **Yang**, Melissa '09 %Willkie F&G LLP -787 7th Av -NY 10019
(212) 969-3000 .. **Yang**, Michl L '05 %Proskauer R LLP -1585 Bway -NY 10036
(212) 318-6000 .. **Yang**, Michelle '09 %Paul HJ&W LLP -75 E 55th -NY 10022
(212) 601-9100 .. **Yang**, Ruth L '91 -805 3rd Av -NY 10022 **Fx:**202-6405
(212) 450-4000 .. **Yang**, Sharon S '05 %Davis P&W LLP -450 Lex Av -NY 10017
(718) 939-6066 .. **Yang**, Shengjin '00 -136-18 39th Av -Flushng 11354
(631) 715-7800 .. **Yang**, Stan Y '91 %US Trustees Ofc -560 Fed Plz -Central Islip 11722 **Fx:**715-7777
(212) 449-6353 .. **Yang**, Terrence C '92 Merrill Lynch -4 World Fncl Ctr -NY 10080
(315) 474-7541 .. **Yang-Patyi**, Josephine '99 (Menter R&T,PC) -308 Maltbie -Syracuse 13204
(585) 768-7030 .. **Yanik**, Mary Kay '93 -58 Main Bx7 -Le Roy 14482 **Fx:**768-8705
(212) 790-0200 .. **Yankah**, Ekow Nyansa '03 Benj N Cardozo Schl of Law -55 5th Av -NY 10003 **Fx:**790-0345
(716) 848-9000 .. **Yankelunas**, Edw P '83 (Underberg & K LLP) -1900 Main Pl Twr -Buffalo 14202
(718) 336-3031 .. **Yankilevich**, Gennady '05 -1909 E 17th -Brklyn 11229 **Fx:**228-6633
(516) 616-4440 .. **Yankowitz**, Arthur I '87 (Brea Y,PC) -35 N Tyson Av -Floral Pk 11001
(212) 446-4800 .. **Yankowitz**, Dana B '08 %Kirkland & E LLP -153 E 53rd -NY 10022
(516) 622-6200 .. **Yankowitz**, Jack A '79 Yankowitz Law Firm -175 E Shore Rd -Gt Neck 11023 **Fx:**829-4344
(631) 853-5212 .. **Yankus**, Patricia A '02 %Leg Aid -400 Carleton Av Bx9082 -Central Islip 11722 **Fx:**853-7798
(212) 872-9800 .. **Yankwitt**, George B '67 (Squire S&D LLP) -30 Rckfllr Plz -NY 10112
(914) 686-0024 .. **Yankwitt**, Ian J '95 (Tortoise Invstmnt Mgmt,LLC) -222 Mamarineck Av -White Plns 10605
(631) 475-0231 .. **Yannacone**, Victor John Jr. '59 Yannacone & Y -Bx109 -Patchogue 11772
(212) 226-2883 .. **Yannella**, Donald J '91 (D Yannella,PC) -7 Dey -NY 10007 **Fx:**226-2861
(516) 747-8600 .. **Yannelli**, Frank E '64 (Yannelli & Z) -100 Grdn City Plz -Gdn Cty 11530
(212) 909-6000 .. **Yannett**, Bruce B '86 (Debevoise & P LLP) -919 3rd Av -NY 10022
(212) 826-0100 .. **Yanney**, Margaret '95 FSA -31 W 52nd -NY 10019 **Fx:**893-2710
(212) 806-5400 .. **Yanney**, Pierre R '94 (Stroock &S&L LLP) -180 Maiden Ln -NY 10038
(518) 489-8668 .. **Yanni**, Chas J '69 -22 Fairway Ct -Albany 12208
(212) 232-1412 .. **Yannucci**, Cristina R '97 (Lewis BB&S LLP) -77 Water -NY 10005
(716) 849-3500 .. **Yannuzzi**, Lauren M '09 %Hagelin & K LLC -135 Delaware Av -Buffalo 14202 **Fx:**849-3501
(718) 268-2579 .. **Yanofsky**, Seymour I '63 -144-31 77th Av -Flushng 11367
(212) 277-4000 .. **Yanos**, Alexander A '95 OfCnsl Freshfields BD LLP -520 Mad Av -NY 10022
(516) 605-1666 .. **Yanover**, Adam C '92 (Yanover & Y) -300 Grdn City Plz -Gdn Cty 11530 **Fx:**605-1667
(516) 605-1666 .. **Yanover**, Jody A '92 (Yanover & Y) -300 Grdn City Plz -Gdn Cty 11530 **Fx:**605-1667
(212) 839-5300 .. **Yanowitch**, Michl H '85 (Sidley A LLP) -787 7th Av -NY 10019
(845) 638-3886 .. **Yanowitz**, Jeffrey B '98 (Loewenberg & Y,LLP) -155 N Main -New Cty 10956 **Fx:**638-3889
(516) 873-3932 .. **Yantsos**, Laura Ann '84 -34 Willis Av -Mineola 11501
(914) 703-6300 .. **Yanuck**, C Wm '79 %Pillinger MT,LLP -570 Taxter Rd -Elmsfrd 10523
(212) 697-3122 .. **Yao**, Arjay G '06 Cnsl Martin C&B LLP -220 E 42nd -NY 10017
(212) 357-7524 .. **Yao**, Suzzanne '03 %Goldman Sachs -1 NY Plz -NY 10004
(718) 782-5500 .. **Yap**, Beesian '04 %Kupfer & Assoc,PLLC -190 N 10th -Brklyn 11211 **Fx:**782-5577
(917) 343-8958 .. **Yap**, Caroline V '96 Goldman Sachs -1 NY Plz -NY 10004
(914) 358-0333 .. **Yap**, Eileen J H '04 My Sister's Place -487 S Bway -Ynkrs 10705
(212) 664-2527 .. **Yap**, Elisabeth Chiao '00 %NBC -30 Rckfllr Plz -NY 10112
(914) 798-5400 .. **Yapchanyk**, Christopher M '05 %Goldberg S LLP -11 Martine Av -White Plns 10606
(212) 365-2200 .. **Yapp**, Ken T '06 Transatlantic Reinsurance -80 Pine -NY 10005 **Fx:**365-2360
(516) 945-1900 .. **Yaraghi**, Arash M '87 Safavieh, Inc -40 Hrbr Park Dr -Pt Wash 11050 **Fx:**945-1938
(315) 536-3955 .. **Yarbrough**, C Denise '83 St Marks Church -179 Main -Penn Yan 14527
(212) 548-0120 .. **Yarbrough**, Robt '90 %Open Society Inst -400 W 59th -NY 10019
(516) 797-3427 .. **Yard**, Theresa I '88 -110 Adam Rd -Massapequa 11758 **Fx:**797-3427
(718) 444-2332 .. **Yarde**, Glenda S '94 -1794 Utica Av -Brklyn 11234 **Fx:**444-9617
(212) 354-0808 .. **Yarden**, Dalit A '92 %Moses P&Z,LLP -1065 Av of Amer -NY 10018
(212) 902-1000 .. **Yarden**, Linda '85 %Goldman Sachs -1 NY Plz -NY 10004
(212) 541-2000 .. **Yarden**, Nir D '91 Cnsl Bryan C LLP -1290 Av of Amer -NY 10104
(212) 735-3000 .. **Yardeni**, Sarah H '03 %Skadden ASM&F LLP -4 Times Sq -NY 10036
(212) 373-3000 .. **Yarett**, Jordan E '84 (Paul WRW&G LLP) -1285 Av of Amer -NY 10019
(516) 605-0024 .. **Yaris**, Craig E '96 Literacy Builders -11 Sarah Dr -Huntngtn Sta 11746
(516) 794-9566 .. **Yarkin**, Mark R '91 M Yarkin,CPA -173 Maple Av -E Meadow 11554 **Fx:**794-5137
(585) 232-6002 .. **Yarmel**, Richd T '87 (Abrams FFEGF&E,LLP) -45 Exchange Blvd -Rchstr 14614
(212) 407-4000 .. **Yarmish**, Danl M '00 %Loeb & L,LLP -345 Park Av -NY 10154
(212) 848-7037 .. **Yaro**, Wm M '77 (Shearman & S LLP) -599 Lex Av -NY 10022
(212) 619-4350 .. **Yaron**, Adrienne '04 %Newman MKGH,PC -14 Wall -NY 10005
(212) 790-0200 .. **Yaroshefsky**, Ellen C '83 Benj N Cardozo Schl of Law -55 5th Av -NY 10003 **Fx:**790-0345
(212) 697-2227 .. **Yaruss**, Howard S '84 Cnsl Primus Guaranty Ltd -360 Mad Av -NY 10017 **Fx:**697-3731
(212) 612-4000 .. **Yaryura**, Adriana M '96 %Chubb Grp -55 Water -NY 10041
(212) 264-8400 .. **Yasek**, John A '88 %USDA -26 Fed Plz -NY 10278
(845) 794-3000 .. **Yasgur**, Saml S '66 Cnty Atty -100 North Bx5012 -Monticello 12701 **Fx:**794-4924
(212) 859-8000 .. **Yashar**, Jennifer A '06 %Fried FHS&J LLP -1 NY Plz -NY 10004
(212) 274-5446 .. **Yashpan**, Ruth D '95 ACS-DLS -220 Church -NY 10013
(212) 629-9400 .. **Yaskhi Ishar Chow & Reddy LLP** -315 5th Av -NY 10016 **Fx:**629-7664
(718) 875-5200 .. **Yassky**, David '93 City Cncl -114 Court -Brklyn 11201
(845) 291-0011 .. **Yastion**, James G '02 %Blustein SR&B,LLP -10 Matthews -Goshen 10924
(212) 785-6600 .. **Yastremski**, Alex S '00 Linx Industries -35 E 21st -NY 10010 **Fx:**730-0892
(212) 297-5800 .. **Yasuda**, Hiroyuki '05 Cnsl Day P LLP -7 Times Sq -NY 10036

(212) 490-0810 .. **Yasuda,** Tsutomu '97 -350 5th Av -NY 10118
(212) 704-6517 .. **Yasunaga,** Koichiro '94 Sojitz Corp of Amer -1211 Av of Amer -NY 10036
(518) 583-4600 .. **Yates,** Allen L '93 (LeCours C&Y,LLP) -59 Church -Saratoga Spgs 12866 **Fx:**583-4642
(212) 768-6700 .. **Yates,** D Farrington '99 (Sonnenschein N&R LLP) -1221 Av of Amer -NY 10020
(315) 834-6621 .. **Yates,** Dale R '75 -8941 N Seneca -Weedsport 13166 **Fx:**834-6029
(212) 490-9100 .. **Yates,** David P '90 %Condon & F LLP -7 Times Sq -NY 10036
(212) 218-5500 .. **Yates,** Greg R '96 (Seyfarth S LLP) -620 8th Av -NY 10018
(212) 735-3000 .. **Yates,** Hope S '10 %Skadden ASM&F LLP -4 Times Sq -NY 10036
(212) 938-4848 .. **Yates,** Karen Manson '74 %Roosevelt Mgmt Co LLC -1540 Bway -NY 10036
(585) 325-6880 .. **Yates,** Richd B '93 Manning & Napier Advisors -290 Woodcliff Dr -Fairpt 14450
(212) 624-1895 .. **Yates,** Stacie L '01 Proctor Invstmt Mngrs -575 Lex Av -NY 10022
(212) 336-2000 .. **Yatrakis,** Christos G '03 %Patterson BW&T LLP -1133 Av of Amer -NY 10036
(212) 450-4000 .. **Yatter,** Douglas K '02 %Davis P&W LLP -450 Lex Av -NY 10017
(845) 562-0203 .. **Yatto,** Thos C '77 (Finkelstein & Prtnrs,LLP) -1279 Route 300 Bx1111 -Newburgh 12550
(212) 416-6136 .. **Yau,** Karen Kithan '98 %Dept of Law -120 Bway -NY 10271
(212) 867-9500 .. **Yavarkovsky,** David '67 OfCnsl Kurzman K&F,LLP -230 Park Av -NY 10169
(718) 590-2000 .. **Yavener,** Erin B '09 %DA -198 E 161st -Bronx 10451 **Fx:**590-6477
(212) 521-5400 .. **Yavitz,** Judith A '82 (Reed S LLP) -599 Lex Av -NY 10022
(718) 253-9181 .. **Yavne,** S Seth '85 -3407 Av K -Brklyn 11210 **Fx:**253-9176
(718) 434-1111 .. **Yavneh,** Avrohom M '89 -959 E 7th -Brklyn 11230
(845) 638-3310 .. **Yavner,** Stanley J '70 -5 Annabelle Ln -New Cty 10956 **Fx:**638-0546
(212) 682-4001 .. **Yavru-Sakuk,** Nadine '06 %Lynch R LLP -630 3rd Av -NY 10017
(716) 664-1112 .. **Yaw,** Gregory R '76 -408 W 5th -Jamestwn 14701 **Fx:**664-2772
(914) 253-2000 .. **Yawman,** David M '96 %Pepsico -700 Andrsn Hill Rd -Purchase 10577
(585) 546-5530 .. **Yaworsky,** Michl J '80 %Thomson West -50 E Broad -Rchstr 14694
(212) 442-6843 .. **Yazdian,** Pantea '10 Law Dept -100 Church -NY 10007 **Fx:**788-0367
(516) 746-8000 .. **Yazicioglu,** Hale '08 %Jaspan S LLP -300 Grdn City Plz -Gdn Cty 11530
(718) 250-4212 .. **Yazmajian,** Karen M '94 %Leg Aid -111 Lvngstn -Brklyn 11201 **Fx:**250-4243
(212) 269-1400 .. **Ye,** Chen '09 %Gusrae KB&N PLLC -120 Wall -NY 10005
(212) 753-3468 .. **Ye,** Min Hui '01 %Wildes & W,PC -515 Mad Av -NY 10022
(607) 724-3162 .. **Yeager,** Kevin H '86 -49 Court -Bnghmtn 13901 **Fx:**723-7970
(718) 492-9037 .. **Yeampierre,** Elizabeth C '91 -285 Wshngtn Av -Brklyn 11205 **Fx:**492-9030
(212) 850-2800 .. **Yearick,** Angelina M '07 %Andrews K LLP -450 Lex Av -NY 10017
(212) 752-5258 .. **Yearing,** Christine M '06 %Schwartz SE&C LLC -845 3rd Av -NY 10022
(718) 722-2060 .. **Yearwood,** Joyce C '93 NYS Div of Human Rights-OSHI -55 Hanson Pl -Brklyn 11217
(212) 349-6009 .. **Yeboah,** Angela Akua '06 %Sanctuary for Families -110 Wall -NY 10005 **Fx:**566-0344
(212) 813-8800 .. **Yecies,** Eric H '05 %Goodwin P LLP -620 8th Av -NY 10018
(212) 872-1000 .. **Yecies,** Jacqueline G '09 -One Bryant Park -NY 10036 **Fx:**872-1002
(212) 574-1200 .. **Yedid,** Isaac '04 %Seward & K LLP -1 Bttry Pk Plz -NY 10004
(631) 761-0800 .. **Yedid,** Saml '77 (Lazer AR&Y,PC) -225 Old Cntry Rd -Melvll 11747
(212) 446-4800 .. **Yee,** Clement K '09 %Kirkland & E LLP -153 E 53rd -NY 10022
(212) 387-5310 .. **Yee,** Edw L '98 %AT&T -32 Av of the Americas -NY 10013
(212) 449-6003 .. **Yee,** Eric M '96 Merrill Lynch & Co Inc -4 World Fncl Ctr -NY 10080 **Fx:**738-1513
(718) 636-8000 .. **Yee,** Kathleen '98 %Wood R&W,LLP -394-396 Waverly Av -Brklyn 11238 **Fx:**857-5628
(518) 474-8390 .. **Yee,** Lai-Sun M '91 %Governors Ofc -State Cptl -Albany 12224
(212) 863-6300 .. **Yee,** Lisa S '78 %HPD -100 Gold -NY 10038
(914) 785-2000 .. **Yee,** Margaret G '86 %Ciba Corp -540 Wht Plns Rd -Tarrytwn 10591 **Fx:**785-4831
(212) 455-2000 .. **Yee,** Marsha W '04 %Simpson T&B LLP -425 Lex Av -NY 10017
(646) 375-2073 .. **Yee,** Robt T '00 Cnsl Diamond Select Toys & Collectibles,LLC -116 W 23rd -NY 10011
(212) 720-2740 .. **Yee,** Rosalie '99 Fed Reserve Bk -33 Maiden Ln -NY 10045
(212) 417-5300 .. **Yee,** Saml A '06 %Medicaid Fraud Cntrl -120 Bway -NY 10271 **Fx:**417-5274
(212) 748-3335 .. **Yee,** Tsui H '99 (Yee & D,LLP) -74 Trinity Pl -NY 10006 **Fx:**748-3336
(212) 264-6425 .. **Yee,** Victor '95 DHS -26 Fed Plz -NY 10278 **Fx:**264-1645
(516) 678-2500 .. **Yegelwel,** Chad F '84 (Sakofsky & Y,PC) -100 N Centre Av -Rockvll Ctr 11570
(212) 909-9500 .. **Yeger,** David '05 %Wachtel & M,LLP -885 2nd Av -NY 10017 **Fx:**909-9462
(718) 875-1900 .. **Yeger,** Eli '78 -16 Court -Brklyn 11241 **Fx:**802-0276
(718) 969-4888 .. **Yeger,** Itamar J '95 -16 Court -Brklyn 11241 **Fx:**380-2305
(212) 351-4000 .. **Yeger,** Yeeta '09 %Gibson D&C LLP -200 Park Av -NY 10166
(718) 387-0800 .. **Yegnukian,** Garo '90 Erebuni Corp -158 Roebling -Brklyn 11211
(212) 552-2019 .. **Yeh,** Charlie '05 JP Morgan Chase Bk NA -1 Chase Manh Plz -NY 10005
(212) 558-4000 .. **Yeh,** Chieh-Ting '10 %Sullivan & C LLP -125 Broad -NY 10004
(212) 610-6300 .. **Yeh,** Danl I '06 %Allen & O -1221 Av of Amer -NY 10020
(212) 407-4000 .. **Yeh,** Jack S '02 %Loeb & L,LLP -345 Park Av -NY 10154
(212) 578-3175 .. **Yeh,** Jennifer Jer-Fen '05 %MetLife -27-01 Qns Plz N -LIC 11101
(516) 572-2000 .. **Yeh,** Jenny '08 %DA -99 Main -Hempstd 11550 **Fx:**572-2606
(212) 765-5070 .. **Yeh,** Karen '09 %Fish & R,PC -153 E 53rd -NY 10022
(212) 250-8237 .. **Yeh,** Lincoln P L '06 Deutsche Bk -60 Wall -NY 10005
(716) 626-3420 .. **Yeh,** Steven I '01 -300 Intl Dr -Williamsvll 14221
(718) 741-8428 .. **Yeh,** Tang-Chi '93 Div of Human Rights -1 Fordham Plz -Bronx 10458 **Fx:**741-8102
(212) 446-4800 .. **Yehezkel,** Ariel '04 %Kirkland & E LLP -153 E 53rd -NY 10022
(607) 275-6521 .. **Yehl,** Michl A '95 -417 N Cayuga -Ithaca 14850 **Fx:**(888) 241-6496
(516) 625-5585 .. **Yehuda,** Anita Nissan '94 -99 Powerhse Rd -Roslyn Hts 11577 **Fx:**484-5719
(212) 309-6000 .. **Yel,** Leon A '08 %Morgan L&B LLP -101 Park Av -NY 10178
(212) 408-5100 .. **Yelenick,** Mary T '82 (Chadbourne & P LLP) -30 Rckfllr Plz -NY 10112
(212) 391-4755 .. **Yellen,** Barry J '75 -261 Mad Av -NY 10016 **Fx:**697-4432
(212) 728-8000 .. **Yellen,** Cindy Ann '91 %Willkie F&G LLP -787 7th Av -NY 10019
(212) 575-7900 .. **Yellen,** Dwight '80 (Ballon SB&N,PC) -729 7th Av -NY 10019
(716) 856-5500 .. **Yellen,** Richd D '63 SpclCnsl Damon M LLP -200 Delaware Av -Buffalo 14202
(212) 404-6988 .. **Yellen,** Richd L '93 (R Yellen & Assoc LLP) -111 Bway -NY 10006 **Fx:**404-7857
(212) 458-2253 .. **Yellen,** Robt M '90 %AIG -175 Water -NY 10038
(845) 735-7000 .. **Yellen,** Susan G '91 %Johnson & C,LLP -1 Blue Hill Plz -Pearl Rvr 10965
(516) 967-1753 .. **Yellin,** Jordan R '10 -4 Governors Ct -Gt Neck 11023
(646) 775-6646 .. **Yellin,** Susan Denburg '77 -104 W 29th -NY 10001 **Fx:**775-6602
(631) 232-4430 .. **Yellon,** Herman '38 -300 Rabro Dr -Hauppauge 11788 **Fx:**232-9188
(718) 802-6644 .. **Yellon,** Laura P '97 %Workers Comp Bd -111 Lvngstn -Brklyn 11201
(212) 403-1000 .. **Yemm,** Kristin M '09 %Wachtell LR&K -51 W 52nd -NY 10019
(212) 713-1261 .. **Yen,** Karen L '03 UBS -1285 Av of Amer -NY 10019
(914) 225-5569 .. **Yen,** Marianne '93 Morgan Stanley -2000 Wstchstr Av -Purchase 10577
(212) 218-2100 .. **Yen,** Vanessa Y '10 %Fitzpatrick CH&S -1290 Av of Amer -NY 10104
(212) 940-3011 .. **Yenal,** Ali '01 %Nixon P LLP -437 Mad Av -NY 10022
(212) 596-9000 .. **Yeo,** Jeehyun Jesse '02 %Ropes & G LLP -1211 Av of Amer -NY 10036
(212) 327-8071 .. **Yeoh,** Deborah '86 Rockefeller Univ -1230 York Av Bx 81 -NY 10065 **Fx:**327-7688
(631) 342-2678 .. **Yeomans,** Bonnie L '88 %CA,Inc -1 CA Plz -Islandia 11749 **Fx:**342-4866
(212) 576-6881 .. **Yeomans,** Gayle A '75 NY Life Ins -51 Mad Av -NY 10010
(315) 476-2812 .. **Yeomans,** Wm B '77 Yeomans,PC -221 Walton -Syracuse 13202 **Fx:**476-3408
(315) 476-2935 .. **Yeomans,** Wm B Jr. '06 Brookline Dvlpmnt Co,LLC -221 Walton -Syracuse 13202
(212) 779-1828 .. **Yeon,** Bong W '01 -1261 Bway -NY 10001 **Fx:**779-0820
(212) 688-6262 .. **Yepez,** Yajaira '04 Sen HR Clinton -780 3rd Av -NY 10017
(518) 435-1919 .. **Yerdon,** Shawn W '01 %Stockton B&M,LLP -2 Twr Pl -Albany 12203
(914) 251-1525 .. **Yeres,** Alexander G '08 %Pollock & M,LLP -106 Corp Park Dr -White Plns 10604
(212) 878-8075 .. **Yeres,** David J '74 (Clifford C LLP) -31 W 52nd -NY 10019
(718) 544-5967 .. **Yeretzian,** Richd C '83 -111-15 Qns Blvd -Frst Hlls 11375
(646) 613-0290 .. **Yerman,** Bruce A '93 -350 Bway -NY 10013
(212) 836-8000 .. **Yerman,** Fredric W '67 (Kaye S LLP) -425 Park Av -NY 10022
(212) 219-0288 .. **Yerman,** Gary J '03 (Yerman & Assoc) -401 Bway -NY 10013
(631) 738-9100 .. **Yermash,** Arthur '09 %Campolo M&M,LLP -3340 Vets Mem'l Hwy -Bohemia 11716 **Fx:**738-0659
(212) 940-3000 .. **Yeroushalmi,** Sherli '10 %Nixon P LLP -437 Mad Av -NY 10022
(631) 764-8660 .. **Yerrakadu,** Andrew A '92 -123-35 82nd Rd -Kew Gdns 11415
(212) 715-9100 .. **Yerramalli,** Anupama '08 %Kramer LN&F,LLP -1177 Av of Amer -NY 10036
(212) 891-1600 .. **Yerramalli,** Prashant '08 %Jenner & B LLP -919 3rd Av -NY 10022
(516) 466-0090 .. **Yerushalmi,** Jos '76 (Yerushalmi & Assoc) -17 Barstow Rd -Gt Neck 11021 **Fx:**466-8988
(585) 419-8800 .. **Yesawich,** Paul J III '75 (Harris B PLLC) -99 Garnsey Rd -Pittsfrd 14534
(212) 225-2000 .. **Yeshaya,** Asaf J '08 %Cleary GS&H -1 Lbrty Plz -NY 10006
(212) 675-1140 .. **Yesko,** Thos A '51 -200 E 36th -NY 10016
(212) 983-0900 .. **Yeskoo Hogan & Tamlyn LLP** -909 3rd Av -NY 10022 **Fx:**983-0907
(212) 983-0900 .. **Yeskoo,** Richd C '79 (Yeskoo H&T LLP) -909 3rd Av -NY 10022
(516) 766-7500 .. **Yesnowitz,** Gilbert '60 -20 E Sunrise Hwy -Vly Stream 11581 **Fx:**766-8186
(212) 689-4386 .. **Yessel,** Barbara L '75 -55 Park Av -NY 10016
(212) 610-6300 .. **Yessios,** Dorina '00 SrCnsl Allen & O -1221 Av of Amer -NY 10020
(212) 558-4000 .. **Yestrumskas,** Alexandra H '10 %Sullivan & C LLP -125 Broad -NY 10004
(516) 408-9000 .. **Yetman,** John R '09 %Walsh MM&D LLP -229 Seventh -Gdn Cty 11530
(212) 277-5828 .. **Yetzer,** Jody L '98 %Beldock L&H LLP -99 Park Av -NY 10016
(973) 597-2498 .. **Yeu,** Susan '95 Cnsl Lowenstein S PC -1251 Av of Amer -NY 10020 **Fx:**597-2499
(212) 626-4100 .. **Yeum,** Jung Hye June '00 (Baker & M LLP) -1114 Av of Amer -NY 10036
(212) 526-4584 .. **Yeung,** Andrew M W '01 %Barclays Capital Inc -1271 Av of Amer -NY 10020
(212) 310-2000 .. **Yeung,** Anita K '88 %Colgate-Palmolive -300 Park Av -NY 10022 **Fx:**310-3406
(212) 841-1000 .. **Yeung,** Christopher Y L '08 %Covington & B LLP -620 8th Av -NY 10018
(212) 385-2122 .. **Yeung,** Grace Y '04 %N Cheng -11 E Bway -NY 10038 **Fx:**385-2022
(212) 338-5429 .. **Yeung,** Janet '92 %Loral Space & Comm Inc -600 3rd Av -NY 10016 **Fx:**338-5320
(718) 238-6960 .. **Yeung-Ha,** Pauline '00 (Grimaldi & Y LLP) -9201 4th Av -Brklyn 11209
(212) 819-8200 .. **Yevmenenko,** Irina '07 %White & C LLP -1155 Av of Amer -NY 10036
(212) 250-0981 .. **Yew,** Andrew Y W '03 %Deutsche Bank -60 Wall -NY 10005
(516) 294-5059 .. **Yezzo,** Dominick '91 -7 12th -Gdn Cty 11530 **Fx:**294-1490
(718) 423-8681 .. **Yhun,** Sukhan '02 -251-11 Nrthrn Blvd -Little Neck 11362 **Fx:**423-8916
(212) 269-7444 .. **Yi,** Jos H '03 %Cilmi & Assoc PLLC -39 Bway -NY 10006 **Fx:**269-3958
(212) 310-8000 .. **Yi,** Justin D '10 %Weil G&M LLP -767 5th Av -NY 10153
(516) 294-1333 .. **Yi,** Kyun '98 (DeMartini & Y LLP) -264 Hillside Av -Williston Pk 11596
(212) 271-0664 .. **Yi,** Michl M '89 (Lee AC LLP) -350 5th Av -NY 10118
(212) 859-8000 .. **Yi,** Mildred M '09 %Fried FHS&J LLP -1 NY Plz -NY 10004
(718) 286-6000 .. **Yi,** Myongjae M '08 %DA -125-01 Qns Blvd -Kew Gdns 11415
(212) 640-1449 .. **Yi,** Po '98 Amer Exp -200 Vesey -NY 10285

(212) 538-6711 .. **Yi,** Scott H '98 CSFB -1 Mad Av -NY 10010
(212) 303-0077 .. **Yi,** Suyon '99 -302 5th Av -NY 10001
(212) 836-8000 .. **Yiannopoulos,** Konstantinos II '08 %Kaye S LLP -425 Park Av -NY 10022
(212) 682-6800 .. **Yick,** Jeffrey T '03 %Zetlin & D LLP -801 2nd Av -NY 10017
(212) 997-7595 .. **Yildiz,** Isil '08 %Hafetz N&R -500 5th Av -NY 10110
(718) 843-6464 .. **Yilmaz,** Kenan M '96 Bachu & Assoc -127-21 Lbrty Av -Richmnd Hll 11419 **Fx:**843-2192
(212) 858-1000 .. **Yim,** Jinho '00 %Pillsbury WSP LLP -1540 Bway -NY 10036
(212) 859-8000 .. **Yim,** Maxwell P '09 %Fried FHS&J LLP -1 NY Plz -NY 10004
(212) 561-5522 .. **Yim,** Michl D '06 (Gil Y&C) -636 Bway -NY 10012
(212) 610-6300 .. **Yim,** Saml '09 %Allen & O -1221 Av of Amer -NY 10020
(212) 659-7300 .. **Yim,** Sascha S W '08 %Haynes & B,LLP -1221 Av of Amer -NY 10020
(212) 232-0710 .. **Yin,** David H '93 %Dept Probation -33 Beaver -NY 10004 **Fx:**232-0718
(212) 328-2100 .. **Yin,** Jeffrey J '99 Medallion Fncl Corp -437 Mad Av -NY 10022 **Fx:**328-2121
(212) 592-1400 .. **Ying,** Christina '93 Cnsl Herrick,F LLP -2 Park Av -NY 10016
(212) 446-7994 .. **Ying,** Ray '97 %McKinsey & Co -55 E 52nd -NY 10055 **Fx:**421-3875
(212) 969-3000 .. **Yip,** Donna Lee '06 %Proskauer R LLP -1585 Bway -NY 10036
(212) 225-2000 .. **Yip-Williams,** Julie L '03 %Cleary GS&H -1 Lbrty Plz -NY 10006
(212) 244-4111 .. **Yisraeli,** Yaacov '80 (Shiboleth YR&Z,LLP) -1 Penn Plz -NY 10119
(212) 945-8174 .. **Yitzhak,** Erica T '02 -1979 Marcus Av -New Hyde Pk 11042
(212) 297-5800 .. **Ylitalo,** Susan Wall '07 %Day P LLP -7 Times Sq -NY 10036
(814) 459-2800 .. **Yoars,** Peter W Jr. '99 %Knox MG&S,PC -509 N Main -Jamestwn 14701 **Fx:**453-4530
(212) 558-4000 .. **Yoder,** Bryce J '09 %Sullivan & C LLP -125 Broad -NY 10004
(212) 902-0328 .. **Yoder,** Jon C '00 %Goldman Sachs -1 NY Plz -NY 10004
(718) 558-8352 .. **Yodice,** Christopher P '91 %LIRR -Jamaica Station -Jamaica 11435 **Fx:**558-8211
(631) 451-6500 .. **Yodice,** Julie L '07 Town of Brookhaven-Dept of Law -1 Indpndnc Hl -Farmngvll 11738
(212) 735-3000 .. **Yodowitz,** Edw J '72 OfCnsl Skadden ASM&F LLP -4 Times Sq -NY 10036
(212) 973-9797 .. **Yodowitz,** Robt '83 OfCnsl Saretsky KD&G,LLP -475 Park Av S -NY 10016
(845) 398-3030 .. **Yodowitz,** Sheri A '83 OfCnsl Saretsky KD&G,LLP -450 Piermont Av -Piermont 10968
(212) 472-7270 .. **Yoeli Gottlieb & Etra LLP** -260 Mad Av -NY 10016 **Fx:**579-0814
(718) 222-5441 .. **Yoeli,** Matthew E '10 DA -350 Jay -Brklyn 11201
(212) 472-7270 .. **Yoeli,** Michl '78 (Yoeli G&E LLP) -260 Mad Av -NY 10016
(212) 981-4500 .. **Yoel Newman,** Rachel E '01 PeterSan Grp -1450 Bway -NY 10018 **Fx:**981-4560
(516) 466-5700 .. **Yoh,** James S '93 -525 Nrthrn Blvd -Gt Neck 11021 **Fx:**466-6958
(212) 310-8000 .. **Yohai,** David L '95 (Weil G&M LLP) -767 5th Av -NY 10153
(718) 292-0030 .. **Yohanan,** Yotvat '05 Infinity Moving & Storage -175 Walnut Av -Bronx 10454
(212) 250-5022 .. **Yohe,** Kathleen A '98 %Deutsche Bank -60 Wall -NY 10005
(518) 449-8893 .. **Yohey,** Alissa M '02 %Wilson EME&D LLP -677 Bway -Albany 12207
(212) 468-7769 .. **Yohn,** Chad M '97 BNY ConvergEx -1633 Bway -NY 10019
(914) 345-7912 .. **Yokoyama,** Izumi '04 Regeneron Pharmaceuticals -777 Old Saw Mill Rvr Rd -Tarrytwn 10591
(212) 735-3000 .. **Yokozuka,** Noriko '06 %Skadden ASM&F LLP -4 Times Sq -NY 10036
(212) 935-3000 .. **Yolin,** Nili Schipper '02 %Mintz LCFG&P,PC -666 3rd Av -NY 10017
(212) 310-8000 .. **Yolkut,** David E '06 %Weil G&M LLP -767 5th Av -NY 10153
(212) 594-3656 .. **Yom,** Sang C '90 -38 W 32nd -NY 10001 **Fx:**594-3621
(212) 969-3000 .. **Yon,** Sanghyok '07 %Proskauer R LLP -1585 Bway -NY 10036
(212) 596-9000 .. **Yonas,** Hadas '09 %Ropes & G LLP -1211 Av of Amer -NY 10036
(716) 856-1700 .. **Yonaty,** Stephen L '95 (Cannon H&W,LLP) -726 Exchange -Buffalo 14210
(646) 878-0800 .. **Yonay,** Guy '97 (Pearl CZL,LLP) -1500 Bway -NY 10036
(516) 739-0000 .. **Yong,** Jeffrey P '06 %Martyn T&M -330 Old Cntry Rd -Mineola 11501
(212) 233-6855 .. **Yong,** John S '83 -11 E Bway -NY 10038 **Fx:**233-6530
(718) 465-0996 .. **Yong,** Kangsun '02 %Zhongjian Law Firm -7344 196th -Fresh Mdws 11366
(646) 912-8461 .. **Yonker,** Michl T '99 -225 Bway -NY 10007 **Fx:**304-5665
(716) 856-4000 .. **Yonkers,** Jill L '00 (Hodgson R LLP) -140 Pearl -Buffalo 14202
(212) 227-3333 .. **Yontef,** Sharon C '90 %Smith & L,LLP -291 Bway -NY 10007
(212) 735-3000 .. **Yoo,** Dwight Sukwon '01 Cnsl Skadden ASM&F LLP -4 Times Sq -NY 10036
(212) 973-0572 .. **Yoo,** Elizabeth C '07 %Wolff & S PC -140 Bway -NY 10005
(212) 812-8420 .. **Yoo,** Eric S '08 Vendome Grp LLC -149 5th Av -NY 10010
(914) 366-7557 .. **Yoo,** Eunsung '02 -520 Wht Plns Rd -Tarrytwn 10591
(212) 594-6616 .. **Yoo,** Ik Dong '93 -358 5th Av -NY 10001 **Fx:**594-6614
(212) 909-6000 .. **Yoo,** Jaesuk '08 %Debevoise & P LLP -919 3rd Av -NY 10022
(212) 806-5400 .. **Yoo,** Jane J '09 %Stroock &S&L LLP -180 Maiden Ln -NY 10038
(212) 687-4900 .. **Yoo,** Jos M '98 %Wormser KG&J LLP -825 3rd Av -NY 10022
(212) 258-7500 .. **Yoo,** Julie '97 %Nickelodeon -1515 Bway -NY 10036
(212) 762-5206 .. **Yoo,** Julien H '97 Morgan Stanley Invstmnt Mgmt -1221 Av of Amer -NY 10020
(646) 595-7005 .. **Yoo,** Maria H '08 %Stavitsky & Assoc LLC -5 Penn Plz -NY 10001
(212) 244-4664 .. **Yoo,** Pauline Hyun-Soo '96 %NY Lawyers Pub Intrst -151 W 30th -NY 10001 **Fx:**244-4570
(212) 325-2912 .. **Yoo,** Saml S '97 Credit Suisse -1 Mad Av -NY 10010
(718) 224-7070 .. **Yoo,** Youn Tae '97 (Yoo & K,PC) -194-02 Nrthrn Blvd -Flushng 11358 **Fx:**224-7775
(212) 408-5100 .. **Yoo,** Young '09 %Chadbourne & P LLP -30 Rckfllr Plz -NY 10112
(212) 310-8000 .. **Yoon,** Andrew J '00 (Weil G&M LLP) -767 5th Av -NY 10153
(212) 839-6500 .. **Yoon,** Brian '03 NY DOT - Legal Affairs -55 Water -NY 10041
(212) 756-2000 .. **Yoon,** Catherine '08 %Schulte R&Z LLP -919 3rd Av -NY 10022
(212) 584-0058 .. **Yoon,** Chas M '90 (Yoon & K LLP) -11 E 44th -NY 10017
(212) 576-7443 .. **Yoon,** Cordelia Mi-Ra '95 %NY Life Intl,Inc -51 Mad Av -NY 10010 **Fx:**576-4291
(212) 422-4034 .. **Yoon,** Dana M '04 Hon J Restani -1 Fed Plz -NY 10278
(718) 321-2244 .. **Yoon,** Doug Jin '99 -164-10 Nrthrn Blvd -Flushng 11358
(212) 474-1000 .. **Yoon,** Eugene Y '09 %Cravath S&M LLP -825 8th Av -NY 10019
(646) 459-3003 .. **Yoon,** Haeyoung '01 %Urban Justice Ctr -123 William -NY 10038 **Fx:**(212) 533-4598
(212) 225-2000 .. **Yoon,** Jaewon '08 %Cleary GS&H -1 Lbrty Plz -NY 10006
(212) 450-4000 .. **Yoon,** Jane H '03 %Davis P&W LLP -450 Lex Av -NY 10017
(585) 428-5210 .. **Yoon,** Jane Inyoung '02 %Pub Def -10 N Fitzhugh -Rchstr 14614 **Fx:**428-2234
(212) 935-5700 .. **Yoon,** Janice Koh-un '05 %Colucci & U -218 E 50th -NY 10022
(516) 775-2236 .. **Yoon,** John F '10 %Santangelo B&S -1800 Nrthrn Blvd -Roslyn 11576
(212) 969-3000 .. **Yoon,** Joon Ro '07 %Proskauer R LLP -1585 Bway -NY 10036
(212) 609-6800 .. **Yoon,** Kenneth K '94 (McCarter & E,LLP) -245 Park Av -NY 10167
(212) 565-2583 .. **Yoon,** Keum A '98 Google Inc -76 9th Av -NY 10011
(212) 584-0058 .. **Yoon & Kim LLP** -11 E 44th -NY 10017 **Fx:**584-0059
(212) 455-2000 .. **Yoon,** Lauren S '10 %Simpson T&B LLP -425 Lex Av -NY 10017
(212) 735-8600 .. **Yoon,** Lisa Jiah '06 %Morrison C LLP -909 3rd Av -NY 10022
(212) 768-6700 .. **Yoon,** Matthew Seok Buom '00 Cnsl Sonnenschein N&R LLP -2 World Fncl Ctr -NY 10281
(212) 889-7200 .. **Yoon,** Richd S J '92 -404 Park Av S -NY 10016 **Fx:**889-8357
(212) 935-3000 .. **Yoon,** Seok-Ho Bryan '06 %Mintz LCFG&P,PC -666 3rd Av -NY 10017
(212) 770-1910 .. **Yoon,** Simon '97 %AIG Tech Srvcs -80 Pine -NY 10005
(212) 808-7800 .. **Yoon,** Sojin '09 %Kelley D&W LLP -101 Park Av -NY 10178
(212) 878-8000 .. **Yoon,** Yeon Hoo '10 %Clifford C LLP -31 W 52nd -NY 10019
(718) 533-1111 .. **Yoon,** Youngik '94 (Yoon & H) -75-21 Bway -Elmhrst 11373 **Fx:**429-6786
(212) 389-5000 .. **Yopp,** Mark W '08 %Sutherland A&B LLP -1114 Av of Amer -NY 10036
(518) 465-3484 .. **Yoquinto,** Wm D '80 (Carter CCBM&L,PC) -20 Corp Wds Blvd -Albany 12211
(212) 335-9000 .. **Yoran,** Dafna '94 %DA -1 Hogan Pl -NY 10013
(212) 776-5000 .. **Yordan,** A Joaquin '77 %NYC Housing Auth -250 Bway -NY 10007 **Fx:**776-5039
(914) 250-2400 .. **Yorio,** Albert E '69 Benchmark Ttle LLC -222 Bloomingdale Rd -White Plns 10605 **Fx:**422-1500
(646) 728-4520 .. **Yorio,** Michl J '04 OASAS -501 7th Av -NY 10018
(607) 962-3194 .. **Yorio & Roche** -145 W High -Painted Post 14870 **Fx:**962-3197
(607) 776-9631 .. **Yorio,** Ronald A '70 %DA -3 E Pulteney Sq -Bath 14810 **Fx:**776-7052
(607) 962-3194 .. **Yorio,** Ronald A '70 (Yorio & R) -145 W High -Painted Post 14870
(716) 664-1140 .. **York,** Brian C '76 -106 Forest Av -Jamestwn 14701 **Fx:**483-3671
(212) 310-8000 .. **York,** Bryant S '06 %Weil G&M LLP -767 5th Av -NY 10153
(845) 225-3641 .. **York,** Christopher '84 %DA -40 Gleneida Av -Carmel 10512
(212) 732-8700 .. **York,** Stephen S '78 (McAloon & F,PC) -123 William -NY 10038
(315) 762-2942 .. **York,** Terri Conti '88 OfCnsl DePerno & K -Bx83 -Sylvan Bch 13157 **Fx:**762-2946
(212) 325-2000 .. **Yorke,** Edw M '85 Credit Suisse Grp -11 Mad Av -NY 10010
(718) 613-3500 .. **Yorke,** Paula S '86 %UIA Bd -Bx29002 -Brklyn 11201 **Fx:**613-3566
(212) 293-9400 .. **Yormak,** Jonathon K '97 (Ruben Cos) -600 Mad Av -NY 10022 **Fx:**293-9401
(212) 446-4000 .. **Yoseloff,** Anthony A '02 %Davidson Kempner Cptl Mgmt -65 E 55th -NY 10022
(212) 442-2054 .. **Yosha,** Andrew '85 %Dept Bldgs -11 Park Pl -NY 10007
(716) 842-5464 .. **Yoshida,** Brian R '98 M&T Bk -1 M & T Plz -Buffalo 14203 **Fx:**842-5376
(212) 751-3001 .. **Yoshida,** Toshiyuki '06 OfCnsl Thompson & K LLP -919 3rd Av -NY 10022
(212) 574-1200 .. **Yoskowitz,** Jack '93 (Seward & K LLP) -1 Bttry Pk Plz -NY 10004
(212) 878-8000 .. **Yoskowitz,** Rachel S '04 %Clifford C LLP -31 W 52nd -NY 10019
(212) 558-4000 .. **Yoslov,** Zena M '02 (Sullivan & C LLP) -125 Broad -NY 10004
(212) 688-8555 .. **Yost,** Ellen Ginsberg '84 (Fragomen DB&L LLP) -7 Hanover Sq -NY 10004
(718) 767-6400 .. **Yost,** Karen M '75 (Yost & O) -24-44 F Lewis Blvd -Whitestone 11357 **Fx:**767-1824
(212) 326-3939 .. **Yost,** Kristina A '09 %Jones D -222 E 41st -NY 10017
(212) 596-9000 .. **Yothers,** Stuart W '05 %Ropes & G LLP -1211 Av of Amer -NY 10036
(212) 756-2000 .. **You,** Jihye '08 %Schulte R&Z LLP -919 3rd Av -NY 10022
(212) 630-2608 .. **You,** Justin J '04 You & Assoc -130 W 42nd -NY 10036 **Fx:**504-8249
(212) 931-5500 .. **Youbi,** Mathias A '03 %McCue S&Z,PC -521 5th Av -NY 10175
(212) 575-8500 .. **Youdelman,** Robt '59 R Youdelman,PC -113 Univ Pl -NY 10003 **Fx:**937-2067
(212) 766-1888 .. **Youkilis,** Paul B '06 %Morris DA&F -2 Rector -NY 10006
(516) 742-8058 .. **Youllar,** Thos J '02 %Abamont & Assoc -200 Grdn City Plz Bx9250 -Gdn Cty 11530 **Fx:**742-7308
(212) 812-5943 .. **Youm,** Gary '04 Jones Lang LaSalle -153 E 53rd -NY 10022
(212) 530-5000 .. **Youn,** Brian '10 %Milbank TH&M LLP -1 Chase Manh Plz -NY 10005
(212) 998-6741 .. **Youn,** Monica Y '00 Brennan Ctr for Justice -161 Av of Amer -NY 10013 **Fx:**995-4550
(212) 735-3000 .. **Youn,** Sooryun '94 Cnsl Skadden ASM&F LLP -4 Times Sq -NY 10036
(212) 848-4000 .. **Younai,** Kevin '08 %Shearman & S LLP -599 Lex Av -NY 10022
(212) 981-4500 .. **Youner Musman,** Melissa B '93 PeterSan Grp -1450 Bway -NY 10018 **Fx:**981-4560
(212) 521-5400 .. **Young,** Aaron M '03 (Reed S LLP) -599 Lex Av -NY 10022
(212) 651-2000 .. **Young,** Abigail B '97 %Oxygen Media LLC -75 9th Av -NY 10011
(212) 684-4777 .. **Young,** Adam J '99 A Young,LLC -475 Park Av S -NY 10016 **Fx:**684-7303
(212) 836-8000 .. **Young,** Alice '75 (Kaye S LLP) -425 Park Av -NY 10022
(212) 265-6888 .. **Young,** Allan I '86 Cnsl Porzio B&N,PC -156 W 56th -NY 10019
(212) 506-5000 .. **Young,** Allison '06 %Orrick H&S LLP -51 W 52nd -NY 10019
(212) 506-2500 .. **Young,** Allison A '07 %Mayer B LLP -1675 Bway -NY 10019
(212) 419-1550 .. **Young,** Amy S '92 CWA Legal Dept -350 7th Av -NY 10001 **Fx:**419-1555
(914) 723-4300 .. **Young,** Andrew F '99 %Lackenbach S LLP -1 Chase Rd -Scarsdale 10583
(212) 530-5000 .. **Young,** Andrew J '06 Milbank TH&M LLP -1 Chase Manh Plz -NY 10005
(212) 318-6000 .. **Young,** Bradford E '05 %Paul HJ&W LLP -75 E 55th -NY 10022
(212) 965-0050 .. **Young,** Bruce A '81 -181 Hudson -NY 10013 **Fx:**(646) 405-0169

(914) 470-0001 .. **Young,** Bruce M '85 (Babchik & Y,LLP) -200 E Post Rd -White Plns 10601
(212) 594-8870 .. **Young,** Carl S '65 (C Young & Assoc) -104 W 40th -NY 10018
(212) 771-1444 .. **Young,** Caryn R '99 Finl Srvcs Volunteer Corps -800 3rd Av -NY 10022
(212) 558-4000 .. **Young,** Christina C '06 %Sullivan & C LLP -125 Broad -NY 10004
(518) 859-4363 .. **Young,** Christine E '06 -55 Pine Trl Bx204 -Sand Lake 12153
(212) 351-4000 .. **Young,** Colin R '05 %Gibson D&C LLP -200 Park Av -NY 10166
(585) 442-0540 .. **Young,** D Scott '87 (Ashcraft FY&P,LLP) -150 Allens Crk Rd -Rchstr 14618
(716) 532-5765 .. **Young,** Danl M '93 -12140 Main -Perrysburg 14129
(212) 902-4012 .. **Young,** Danl M '00 Goldman Sachs -1 NY Plz -NY 10004
(518) 786-9069 .. **Young,** Danl N '09 Schiller & K LLP -950 New Loudon Rd -Latham 12110
(518) 373-1500 .. **Young,** David E '09 %R Beebe LLC -514 Vischers Ferry Rd -Clifton Pk 12065 **Fx:**373-0030
(585) 258-5403 .. **Young,** Deborah Schwind '80 %JP Morgan Chase -1 Chase Sq -Rchstr 14643 **Fx:**258-6458
(914) 769-6301 .. **Young,** Debra E '87 -56 Brook Manor -Plsntvll 10570
(518) 455-9952 .. **Young,** Debra J '97 (Thuillez FGB&Y,LLP) -20 Corp Wds Blvd -Albany 12211
(212) 361-7996 .. **Young,** Dennis A '73 %Dept Homeless Srvcs -33 Beaver -NY 10004 **Fx:**361-8002
(212) 931-7300 .. **Young,** Dennison Jr. '69 %Giuliani Prtnrs -5 Times Sq -NY 10036
(212) 530-5000 .. **Young,** Diane R '08 %Milbank TH&M LLP -1 Chase Manh Plz -NY 10005
(585) 232-5300 .. **Young,** Donald A '08 %Boylan BCV&W,LLP -2400 Chase Sq -Rchstr 14604
(212) 878-7900 .. **Young,** Donald R '61 (Fox R LLP) -100 Park Av -NY 10017
(518) 445-2311 .. **Young,** Donna E '93 %Albany Law Schl -80 New Scotland Av -Albany 12208 **Fx:**445-2315
(212) 335-4500 .. **Young,** Drew M III '08 %DLA Piper LLP -1251 Av of Amer -NY 10020
(631) 661-0006 .. **Young,** Edw R '76 E Young & Assoc -112 Route 109 -W Babylon 11704 **Fx:**661-0226
(212) 872-1000 .. **Young,** Elizabeth J '07 -One Bryant Park -NY 10036 **Fx:**872-1002
(212) 593-6700 .. **Young,** Elizabeth M '88 OfCnsl Aaronson RF&D,LLP -757 3rd Av -NY 10017
(212) 735-8600 .. **Young,** Eric D '92 Morrison C LLP -909 3rd Av -NY 10022
(315) 479-1769 .. **Young,** Eugene B '76 (Davidson & Y) -333 E Onondaga -Syracuse 13202 **Fx:**474-4575
(212) 431-1300 .. **Young,** Eva '07 %Borah GAN&G PC -377 Bway -NY 10013
(518) 456-6767 .. **Young Fenton Kelsey & Brown, PC** -1881 Wstrn Av -Albany 12203
(914) 285-1500 .. **Young,** Francis X '84 (Young & B,LLP) -81 Main -White Plns 10601 **Fx:**285-0055
(516) 826-8938 .. **Young,** Gary J '98 %R Young & Assoc -1321 Bellmore Av -Bellmore 11710 **Fx:**826-8932
(212) 592-1400 .. **Young,** Gary S '75 (Herrick,F LLP) -2 Park Av -NY 10016
(212) 521-5400 .. **Young,** Geoffrey G '07 %Reed S LLP -599 Lex Av -NY 10022
(631) 421-5500 .. **Young,** Gordon W '70 (G Young,LLC) -155 W Carver -Huntngtn 11743 **Fx:**421-5509
(646) 227-5620 .. **Young,** Gregg A '79 Argent Trading -521 5th Av -NY 10175
(914) 935-3950 .. **Young,** Gregory P '72 306 Fayette Rlty -566 Wstchstr Av -Rye Brook 10573
(212) 225-2000 .. **Young,** Hailey H '10 %Cleary GS&H -1 Lbrty Plz -NY 10006
(516) 764-5772 .. **Young,** Harold '51 -3423 1st -Oceanside 11572
(212) 766-1200 .. **Young,** Hayes '85 (Shestack & Y,LLP) -233 Bway -NY 10279
(212) 210-6957 .. **Young,** Heidi R '86 %J Walter Thompson -466 Lex Av -NY 10017
(914) 995-2660 .. **Young,** Holly C '05 %Cnty Atty -148 Martine Av -White Plns 10601 **Fx:**995-5858
(631) 852-4570 .. **Young,** Ivan E '06 Cnty Bd of Elections -Bx700 -Yaphank 11980
(212) 964-7400 .. **Young,** J Jay '81 Smith MDWY&Y,LLP -111 John -NY 10038
(607) 535-5400 .. **Young,** James D '95 %Welliver McGuire Inc -250 N Genesee -Montour Fls 14865
(607) 734-2271 .. **Young,** James F '71 (Sayles & E) -1 W Church -Elmira 14901
(212) 878-8000 .. **Young,** Jason P '00 (Clifford C LLP) -31 W 52nd -NY 10019
(212) 594-5300 .. **Young,** Jennifer L '04 (Milberg LLP) -1 Penn Plz -NY 10119
(718) 772-4903 .. **Young,** Jesse A '87 -790 Wshngtn Av -Brklyn 11238
(516) 746-8000 .. **Young,** Jesse H '04 %Jaspan S LLP -300 Grdn City Plz -Gdn Cty 11530
(212) 252-0004 .. **Young,** Joanna L '02 %Carroll M&K LLC -570 Lex Av -NY 10022
(212) 474-1000 .. **Young,** John E '61 SrCnsl Cravath S&M LLP -825 8th Av -NY 10019
(607) 257-6533 .. **Young,** John F '83 -410 Triphammer Rd -Ithaca 14850
(212) 479-6000 .. **Young,** John F '07 (Cooley LLP) -1114 Av of Amer -NY 10036
(607) 722-3426 .. **Young,** John W '63 (Young & Y) -22 Riverside Dr -Bnghmtn 13905 **Fx:**722-5175
(631) 698-6565 .. **Young,** Jonathan M '67 -479 Middle Cntry Rd -Coram 11727 **Fx:**698-2067
(845) 695-2600 .. **Young,** Jos E '79 MediaCom LLC -100 Crystal Run Rd -Middletwn 10941
(212) 310-8000 .. **Young,** Josephine '09 %Weil G&M LLP -767 5th Av -NY 10153
(914) 945-3593 .. **Young,** Karen '96 IBM -Bx218 -Yorktwn Hts 10598 **Fx:**241-4038
(212) 264-8400 .. **Young,** Kathleen M '96 %US Dept of Agriculture -26 Fed Plz -NY 10278
(518) 438-9907 .. **Young,** Kevin M '82 (Young SWRB&M,LLC) -5 Palisades Dr -Albany 12205
(718) 793-5100 .. **Young Klein & Lontos,PC** -86-25 Lefferts Blvd -Richmnd Hll 11418 **Fx:**793-5105
(315) 422-8191 .. **Young,** Lawr J '64 Leg Aid -351 S Warren -Syracuse 13202 **Fx:**472-2819
(212) 325-1866 .. **Young,** Lawr M '94 Credit Suisse -11 Mad Av -NY 10010
(607) 724-2472 .. **Young,** Lisa M '85 Columbian Mutual Life Ins Co -4704 Vestal Pkwy E Bx1381 -Bnghmtn 13902 **Fx:**724-2801
(212) 258-4160 .. **Young,** Llewellyn P Jr. '85 %Siemens Corp -153 E 53rd -NY 10022 **Fx:**767-0580
(607) 962-6876 .. **Young,** Marianne Wilder '92 Market St Trust Co -80 E Market -Corning 14830 **Fx:**962-6709
(585) 232-4240 .. **Young,** Mark A '94 -45 Exchange Blvd -Rchstr 14614 **Fx:**232-4247
(212) 336-2000 .. **Young,** Mark G '03 %Patterson BW&T LLP -1133 Av of Amer -NY 10036
(607) 722-3426 .. **Young,** Mark H '93 (Young & Y) -22 Riverside Dr -Bnghmtn 13905 **Fx:**722-5175
(212) 768-6700 .. **Young,** Marlo A '98 (Sonnenschein N&R LLP) -2 World Fncl Ctr -NY 10281
(212) 373-3000 .. **Young,** Martin '99 Paul WRW&G LLP -1285 Av of Amer -NY 10019
(607) 772-1442 .. **Young,** Marya '92 %R Benjamin -126 Riverside Dr Bx607 -Bnghmtn 13902 **Fx:**772-1678
(518) 533-3000 .. **Young,** Matthew A '06 %Bond S&K,PLLC -111 Wshngtn Av -Albany 12210
(212) 421-4100 .. **Young,** Matthew O '02 %Pryor C LLP -7 Times Sq -NY 10036
(518) 385-4486 .. **Young,** Maureen W '92 GE Energy -1 River Rd -Schnctdy 12345
(212) 242-4336 .. **Young,** Michl A '71 -165 Christopher -NY 10014
(212) 751-2700 .. **Young,** Michl D '82 %JAMS -620 8th Av -NY 10018 **Fx:**751-4099
(315) 376-7543 .. **Young,** Michl F '78 -7659 N State -Lowvll 13367 **Fx:**376-8766
(212) 728-8000 .. **Young,** Michl R '82 (Willkie F&G LLP) -787 7th Av -NY 10019
(212) 705-7000 .. **Young,** Nancy '81 OfCnsl Bingham M LLP -399 Park Av -NY 10022
(716) 845-9327 .. **Young,** Oliver C '81 %Supreme Ct -92 Franklin -Buffalo 14202 **Fx:**856-4670
(212) 310-8000 .. **Young,** Patricia '06 %Weil G&M LLP -767 5th Av -NY 10153
(631) 224-7500 .. **Young,** Patrick F '00 (Young & Y,LLP) -863 Islip Av -Central Islip 11722 **Fx:**224-9400
(516) 489-8330 .. **Young,** Patrick J '86 %Carecen -91 N Franklin -Hempstd 11550 **Fx:**489-8308
(212) 560-3541 .. **Young,** R Cooper '07 EBC -450 W 33rd -NY 10001 **Fx:**560-3191
(315) 785-2404 .. **Young,** Randall C '92 %DEC -317 Wshngtn -Watertwn 13601 **Fx:**785-2242
(212) 428-5254 .. **Young,** Richd L '05 Smith Barney -1 NY Plz -NY 10004
(631) 224-7500 .. **Young,** Richd W '93 (Young & Y,LLP) -863 Islip Av -Central Islip 11722 **Fx:**224-9400
(518) 584-7180 .. **Young,** Rita M '05 RM Young & Assoc,PLLC -18 Division -Saratoga Spgs 12866 **Fx:**584-7161
(518) 573-7595 .. **Young,** Robt '04 -10 Utica Av -Latham 12110 **Fx:**785-1265
(516) 826-8938 .. **Young,** Robt K '68 (R Young & Assoc) -1321 Bellmore Av -Bellmore 11710 **Fx:**826-8932
(845) 221-4720 .. **Young,** Robt K '91 -Bx62 -Hopewell Junct 12533 **Fx:**226-2818
(212) 653-8700 .. **Young,** Robyn E '05 %Sheppard MR&H LLP -30 Rckfllr Plz -NY 10112
(212) 489-1600 .. **Young,** Roland S '95 %Deloitte LLP -1633 Bway -NY 10019 **Fx:**492-4201
(212) 475-6416 .. **Young,** Roy Traywick '69 -16 E 23rd -NY 10010
(212) 486-2400 .. **Young,** S Alyssa '98 (Leader & B LLP) -630 3rd Av -NY 10017
(315) 475-3127 .. **Young,** Saml C '94 Leg Srvcs -472 S Salina -Syracuse 13202 **Fx:**475-2706
(212) 227-9755 .. **Young,** Sanford F '77 -225 Bway -NY 10007 **Fx:**732-4157
(212) 735-3000 .. **Young,** Sean '07 %Skadden ASM&F LLP -4 Times Sq -NY 10036
(518) 438-9907 .. **Young Sommer Ward Ritzenberg Baker & Moore,LLC** -5 Palisades Dr -Albany 12205 **Fx:**438-9914
(212) 697-3122 .. **Young,** Stacie L '88 (Martin C&B LLP) -220 E 42nd -NY 10017
(516) 512-8904 .. **Young,** Stanley N '64 SN Young,PC -1225 Franklin Av -Gdn Cty 11530 **Fx:**248-7736
(212) 770-5049 .. **Young,** Stanton A '76 %AIG -70 Pine -NY 10270 **Fx:**785-1468
(212) 259-8000 .. **Young,** Steven J '88 Cnsl Dewey & L LLP -1301 Av of Amer -NY 10019
(914) 323-7000 .. **Young,** Steven L '79 (Wilson EME&D LLP) -3 Gannett Dr -White Plns 10604
(212) 947-0600 .. **Young,** Sun W '90 -38 W 32nd -NY 10001 **Fx:**563-2567
(315) 475-3127 .. **Young,** Susan M '87 %Leg Srvcs -472 S Salina -Syracuse 13202 **Fx:**475-2706
(212) 474-1000 .. **Young,** Tamir M '00 %Cravath S&M LLP -825 8th Av -NY 10019
(631) 853-4049 .. **Young,** Thos C '69 %Cnty Atty -Dennison Bldg Bx6100 -Hauppauge 11788 **Fx:**853-5169
(585) 232-6500 .. **Young,** Thos P '81 Cnsl Harter S&E LLP -1600 Bausch & Lomb Pl -Rchstr 14604
(646) 386-3363 .. **Young,** Tracy W '84 Hon SW Kornreich-Supreme Ct -60 Centre -NY 10007
(845) 634-3627 .. **Young,** Veronica Jo '87 %Leg Aid -2 Congers Rd -New Cty 10956 **Fx:**634-8505
(718) 254-6057 .. **Young,** Wm B '87 %US Atty -271 Cadman Plz E -Brklyn 11201 **Fx:**254-6479
(518) 456-6767 .. **Young,** Wm N Jr. '73 (Young FK&B,PC) -1881 Wstrn Av -Albany 12203
(212) 450-4000 .. **Young-Anglim,** James A '08 %Davis P&W LLP -450 Lex Av -NY 10017
(212) 972-6161 .. **Youngbar,** Alice M '03 %Cassin & C LLP -711 3rd Av -NY 10017
(212) 895-3100 .. **Youngberg,** Kim '94 Wind Up Ent -79 Mad Av -NY 10016
(518) 438-5364 .. **Youngblood,** Chas G '87 (Sullivan H&Y,PC) -4 Exec Park Dr -Albany 12203
(212) 803-5100 .. **Youngblood,** John M '81 %NY Cnty Defender Srvcs -225 Bway -NY 10007 **Fx:**571-6035
(212) 373-8081 .. **Youngblood,** Valerie J '83 Ctr for Ct Inonovation -520 8th Av -NY 10018
(212) 788-9394 .. **Youngclaus,** Elisabeth Corliss '94 Mayors Ofc-Crim Justice -1 Centre -NY 10007
(212) 610-6300 .. **Younger,** Meredith D '00 %Allen & O -1221 Av of Amer -NY 10020
(212) 336-2000 .. **Younger,** Stephen P '83 (Patterson BW&T LLP) -1133 Av of Amer -NY 10036
(860) 424-4325 .. **Youngling,** Megan M '08 %Pullman & C,LLC -50 Main -White Plns 10606
(212) 547-5400 .. **Youngman,** Douglas I '97 OfCnsl McDermott W&E LLP -340 Mad Av -NY 10173
(516) 505-0600 .. **Youngman,** Joshua R '07 %J McCormack,PC -1035 Stewart Av -Gdn Cty 11530 **Fx:**505-0632
(315) 946-7472 .. **Youngman,** Richd W '75 %Pub Def -26 Church -Lyons 14489 **Fx:**946-7478
(315) 471-3151 .. **Youngs,** James P '08 %Hancock & E,LLP -1500 AXA Twr I Bx4976 -Syracuse 13221
(212) 373-3000 .. **Youngwood,** Alfred D '62 OfCnsl Paul WRW&G LLP -1285 Av of Amer -NY 10019
(212) 455-2000 .. **Youngwood,** Jonathan K '95 (Simpson T&B LLP) -425 Lex Av -NY 10017

(315) 422-8191 .. **Younis,** Michl J '01 %Leg Aid -351 S Warren -Syracuse 13202 **Fx:**472-2819
(212) 286-0040 .. **Younkins,** Kathy A '85 (Younkins & S LLP) -420 Lex Av -NY 10170 **Fx:**949-1920
(212) 428-2120 .. **Younkins,** Ronald P '80 %OCA -25 Beaver -NY 10004 **Fx:**428-2190
(212) 751-3001 .. **Youree,** Shelly A '06 (Thompson & K LLP) -919 3rd Av -NY 10022
(212) 622-7879 .. **Yourous,** Mark B '01 Healthcor Mgmt -152 W 57th -NY 10019
(516) 794-7780 .. **Youshah,** Lawr S '95 %B Mirotznik -2115 Hempstd Tpk -E Meadow 11554
(917) 709-5884 .. **Youssef,** Michl M '02 -920 59th -Brklyn 11219 **Fx:**(718) 305-4008
(516) 393-5555 .. **Youssef,** Suzanne '89 %Schneider M LLP -666 Old Cntry Rd -Gdn Cty 11530 **Fx:**393-5556
(347) 436-8320 .. **Youssef,** Wassim '09 -1515 Bway -NY 10036
(212) 541-6222 .. **Yousuf,** Sarah Bawany '05 %Kane K,PC -1350 Av of Amer -NY 10019
(516) 294-9292 .. **Yovino,** Anthony F '84 (Tabat CB&Y,LLP) -1205 Franklin Av -Gdn Cty 11530
(212) 455-2000 .. **Yowell,** Aaron J '08 %Simpson T&B LLP -425 Lex Av -NY 10017
(718) 941-3990 .. **Yu,** Alexander Jia-Yo '95 (Yu & Y LLP) -903 Ocean Av -Brklyn 11226 **Fx:**941-3990
(212) 965-1888 .. **Yu,** Alexander K '94 (A Yu,PC) -401 Bway -NY 10013 **Fx:**965-9588
(212) 808-7800 .. **Yu,** Benjamin '04 %Kelley D&W LLP -101 Park Av -NY 10178
(212) 918-3000 .. **Yu,** Catherine J '07 %Hogan L LLP -875 3rd Av -NY 10022
(212) 683-7100 .. **Yu,** Cindy M '03 %Gallo V&K,LLP -90 Broad -NY 10004
(212) 969-3000 .. **Yu,** Diane '08 %Proskauer R LLP -1585 Bway -NY 10036
(212) 806-5400 .. **Yu,** Hannah '10 %Stroock &S&L LLP -180 Maiden Ln -NY 10038
(212) 335-4500 .. **Yu,** Hualiang '05 %DLA Piper LLP -1251 Av of Amer -NY 10020
(718) 941-3990 .. **Yu,** Hui Hui '92 (Yu & Y LLP) -903 Ocean Av -Brklyn 11226 **Fx:**941-3990
(212) 218-5500 .. **Yu,** James S '04 (Seyfarth S LLP) -620 8th Av -NY 10018
(212) 637-3178 .. **Yu,** Jeannie M '96 %EPA -290 Bway -NY 10007 **Fx:**637-3096
(212) 735-3000 .. **Yu,** Jennifer S '08 %Skadden ASM&F LLP -4 Times Sq -NY 10036
(718) 260-8728 .. **Yu,** Jenny '03 ACS -345 Adams -Brklyn 11201
(914) 941-1500 .. **Yu,** John T '79 -10 Palisade Av -Ynkrs 10701
(212) 230-8800 .. **Yu,** Jos J '10 %WilmerHale -399 Park Av -NY 10022
(212) 695-1008 .. **Yu,** Junmo Jeffrey '94 (Yu & Assoc) -11 Penn Plz -NY 10001 **Fx:**(201) 567-1277
(212) 637-2734 .. **Yu,** Li '03 US Atty -86 Chmbrs -NY 10007
(212) 325-2000 .. **Yu,** Lin '04 Credit Suisse -1 Mad Av -NY 10010
(646) 210-9615 .. **Yu,** Liu '01 -52 E Bway -NY 10002
(718) 286-6000 .. **Yu,** Milton '06 %DA -125-01 Qns Blvd -Kew Gdns 11415
(212) 325-1634 .. **Yu,** Mina K '98 CSFB -11 Mad Av -NY 10010
(212) 219-0096 .. **Yu,** Patrick K '95 -401 Bway -NY 10013
(212) 461-6363 .. **Yu,** Peter M '92 (Cartesian Capital Grp) -505 5th Av -NY 10017 **Fx:**461-6366
(212) 815-0581 .. **Yu,** Rosemary '06 %Ofc of Special Narc -80 Centre -NY 10013
(212) 761-4000 .. **Yu,** Sherman M '95 Morgan Stanley -1585 Bway -NY 10036
(212) 468-8000 .. **Yu,** Shouhua Helen '05 %Morrison & F LLP -1290 Av of Amer -NY 10104
(212) 833-5629 .. **Yu,** Stephanie '03 Sony BMG Music Entrtnmnt -550 Mad Av -NY 10022 **Fx:**833-8406
(212) 553-0300 .. **Yu,** Wai-Yin Alice '04 %Moody's Invstr Srvc -250 Greenwich -NY 10007
(212) 450-4000 .. **Yu,** Xin '09 %Davis P&W LLP -450 Lex Av -NY 10017
(718) 461-1778 .. **Yuan,** Alexander W '03 1st County Capital -4048 Main -Flushng 11354
(212) 446-4800 .. **Yuan,** Cheryl '09 %Kirkland & E LLP -153 E 53rd -NY 10022
(212) 930-9700 .. **Yuan,** Jessica S '08 %Sichenzia RFF LLP -61 Bway -NY 10006
(212) 310-8000 .. **Yuan,** Jie '07 %Weil G&M LLP -767 5th Av -NY 10153
(212) 373-3000 .. **Yuan,** Jun Marshall '09 %Paul WRW&G LLP -1285 Av of Amer -NY 10019
(212) 446-2300 .. **Yuan,** Kelly '99 Cnsl Boies S&F LLP -575 Lex Av -NY 10022
(212) 480-3030 .. **Yuan,** Nancy Y '93 %M Pressman -125 Maiden Ln -NY 10038 **Fx:**480-2590
(212) 233-5525 .. **Yuan,** Paul K '85 -8 Chatham Sq -NY 10038 **Fx:**233-9069
(212) 603-5000 .. **Yuan,** Roberta '05 CASAM Advisers -1301 Av of Amer -NY 10019 **Fx:**603-5001
(212) 225-2000 .. **Yuan,** Shubing '05 %Cleary GS&H -1 Lbrty Plz -NY 10006
(212) 878-8000 .. **Yuan,** Yan '08 %Clifford C LLP -31 W 52nd -NY 10019
(212) 373-3707 .. **Yuan-Garg,** Xiang Pearl '04 %Paul WRW&G LLP -1285 Av of Amer -NY 10019 **Fx:**492-0707
(212) 373-3000 .. **Yuasa,** Mashiho '06 %Paul WRW&G LLP -1285 Av of Amer -NY 10019
(212) 822-1461 .. **Yucevicius,** Michl S '85 -305 Bway -NY 10007
(212) 755-6000 .. **Yudell,** Kenneth S '93 (Aronauer R&Y,LLP) -444 Mad Av -NY 10022
(212) 421-2150 .. **Yudelson,** David S '92 (Sive P&R,PC) -460 Park Av -NY 10022
(212) 334-9900 .. **Yudenfriend,** Vicki '82 -335 Bway -NY 10013
(212) 922-2200 .. **Yudes,** Alfred E Jr. '84 (Watson F&W LLP) -1133 Av of Amer -NY 10036
(718) 380-1122 .. **Yudilovich,** Ron Y '09 %Levi & M,LLP -15916 Union Tpk -Fresh Mdws 11366 **Fx:**380-1124
(212) 225-2000 .. **Yudin,** David W S '02 %Cleary GS&H -1 Lbrty Plz -NY 10006
(212) 949-7979 .. **Yudin,** Ronald M '91 (Yudin & Y) -7 Penn Plz -NY 10001 **Fx:**949-8094
(212) 949-7979 .. **Yudin,** Steven G '86 (Yudin & Y) -7 Penn Plz -NY 10001 **Fx:**949-8094
(212) 691-0950 .. **Yudkoff,** Dari M '09 %Ctr for Family Representation -116 John -NY 10038
(212) 776-5058 .. **Yudkovitz,** Robin A '07 %NYC Housing Auth -250 Bway -NY 10007 **Fx:**776-5039
(212) 664-2961 .. **Yudkowitz,** Martin J '80 %NBC -30 Rckfllr Plz -NY 10112
(212) 336-2000 .. **Yue,** Herman H '08 %Patterson BW&T LLP -1133 Av of Amer -NY 10036
(718) 675-9297 .. **Yue,** Shiqing '00 -36-09 Main -Flushng 11354 **Fx:**799-0412
(718) 884-9330 .. **Yuelys,** Nicholas D '52 -3240 Tibbett Av -Bronx 10463
(212) 609-6800 .. **Yuen,** Chas Allen '88 SpclCnsl McCarter & E,LLP -245 Park Av -NY 10167
(718) 546-0348 .. **Yuen,** Eric Kok-Mun '00 DOC -7520 Astoria Blvd -E Elmhrst 11370
(212) 351-4000 .. **Yuen,** Eric W '09 %Gibson D&C LLP -200 Park Av -NY 10166
(212) 286-8585 .. **Yuen,** Jennifer W '08 %Heidell PM&B,LLP -99 Park Av -NY 10016
(212) 964-6611 .. **Yuen,** Michelle '09 %Lester SK&D -120 Bway -NY 10271
(212) 353-4152 .. **Yuen,** Milton '94 %Cooper Union -30 Cooper Sq -NY 10003
(212) 608-1178 .. **Yuen,** Po-Wang '77 (Yuen RS&S PC) -132 Nassau -NY 10038 **Fx:**608-2913
(212) 571-7150 .. **Yuen,** Sean C '94 (Au & Y,PC) -401 Bway -NY 10013 **Fx:**571-7153
(212) 468-8000 .. **Yuen,** Sunni June '09 %Morrison & F LLP -1290 Av of Amer -NY 10104
(212) 820-7700 .. **Yuen,** Tammy '04 %Boundas SW&B,LLC -1 Bttry Pk Plz -NY 10004
(212) 608-1178 .. **Yuen,** Veronica Chan '83 (Yuen RS&S PC) -132 Nassau -NY 10038 **Fx:**608-2913
(212) 809-7800 .. **Yufa,** Svetlana '02 %Jaffe & K,LLP -40 Wall -NY 10005
(212) 586-1870 .. **Yuh,** Kyuhong '85 Gale Intl -11 W 42nd -NY 10036
(212) 649-2000 .. **Yuhan,** Stephen H '05 Hearst Corp -300 W 57th -NY 10019 **Fx:**649-2035
(315) 391-0640 .. **Yuhas,** John Jr. '79 -1868 Willowdale Rd -Skaneateles 13152
(212) 351-4000 .. **Yuhas,** Kimberly A '10 Gibson D&C LLP -200 Park Av -NY 10166
(212) 225-2000 .. **Yuille,** Lua K '06 %Cleary GS&H -1 Lbrty Plz -NY 10006
(212) 218-2100 .. **Yu Jahnes,** Lock See '99 (Fitzpatrick CH&S) -1290 Av of Amer -NY 10104
(516) 227-6300 .. **Yuk,** John '96 %Ettelman & H,PC -100 Q Roosevelt Blvd -Gdn Cty 11530
(212) 688-5151 .. **Yukawa,** Trisha K '02 (Gibney A&F,LLP) -665 5th Av -NY 10022
(516) 767-7100 .. **Yukelson,** Bruce '74 (Wolfe & Y PLLC) -14 Vanderventer Av -Pt Wash 11050
(718) 590-2000 .. **Yukelson,** Caryn Fae '05 DA -198 E 161st -Bronx 10451 **Fx:**590-6477
(212) 408-5100 .. **Yuksel,** Ayse '96 (Chadbourne & P LLP) -30 Rckfllr Plz -NY 10112
(631) 754-8500 .. **Yule,** Edw J '91 -46 Woodbine Av -Northprt 11768 **Fx:**262-1906
(212) 239-1515 .. **Yun,** Chang H '93 -350 5th Av -NY 10118 **Fx:**239-6879
(973) 228-5700 .. **Yun,** Edw J '96 %Brach E LLC -100 Park Av -NY 10017 **Fx:**228-7852
(212) 973-0572 .. **Yun,** Eric I '08 %Wolff & S PC -140 Bway -NY 10005
(917) 379-5567 .. **Yun,** Ni '09 -29-24 148th -Flushng 11354
(212) 756-2000 .. **Yun,** Rosa Min Hye '09 %Schulte R&Z LLP -919 3rd Av -NY 10022
(212) 902-9958 .. **Yun,** Wendy '99 Goldman Sachs -1 NY Plz -NY 10004
(718) 670-0028 .. **Yung,** Keith Ngan-Kit '97 -136-20 38th Av -Flushng 11354
(212) 310-8000 .. **Yung,** Kevin K '09 %Weil G&M LLP -767 5th Av -NY 10153
(716) 759-9759 .. **Yungbluth,** Gregory C '75 (Damon M LLP) -9276 Main -Clarence 14031
(212) 715-9100 .. **Yungwirth,** Christian J '10 %Kramer LN&F,LLP -1177 Av of Amer -NY 10036
(315) 428-4000 .. **Yunis,** Bebette E '92 %Dept of State -333 E Wshngtn -Syracuse 13202
(607) 737-5233 .. **Yunis,** Jeffery N '76 -1020 Ctr -Horseheads 14845 **Fx:**732-4667
(212) 940-8666 .. **Yunis,** Joel A '67 (Katten MR LLP) -575 Mad Av -NY 10022
(646) 378-7885 .. **Yurasov-Lichtenberg,** Michl A '09 (Havens & L,PLLC) -1115 Bway -NY 10010
(212) 205-7000 .. **Yurke,** Alice F '88 (Ashurst LLP) -7 Times Sq -NY 10036
(212) 580-7473 .. **Yurkofsky,** David E '88 -125 Riverside Dr -NY 10024 **Fx:**580-7473
(212) 863-8944 .. **Yurnet-Thomas,** Mirta '04 HPD -100 Gold -NY 10038
(212) 436-4583 .. **Yurowitz,** Aaron '05 Deloitte & Touche LLP -2 World Fncl Ctr -NY 10281
(212) 909-6000 .. **Yurowitz,** Alan J '10 %Debevoise & P LLP -919 3rd Av -NY 10022
(212) 308-7900 .. **Yurowitz,** Steven Y '97 (Newman & G) -950 3rd Av -NY 10022
(631) 423-4390 .. **Yurus,** Wm '95 %Mincone & M,PC -110 Walt Whitman Rd -South Huntington 11746 **Fx:**423-4408
(718) 850-6990 .. **Yusaf,** A Ali '96 -114-08 101st Av -Richmnd Hll 11419 **Fx:**850-6999
(914) 968-7619 .. **Yuscak,** Paul R '98 -Bx1013 -Ynkrs 10703
(716) 200-5050 .. **Yusick,** Andrew D Jr. '74 (Harris B PLLC) -726 Exchange -Buffalo 14210
(716) 362-9350 .. **Yusick,** Matthew D '02 %Hon J McCarthy-US Magistrate -424 US Cthse -Buffalo 14202
(516) 536-7171 .. **Yuskevich,** Edw W '81 -14 Rockvll Av -Rockvll Ctr 11570
(914) 345-3020 .. **Yusko,** Robt T '09 Knuckles K&E,LLP -565 Taxter Rd -Elmsfrd 10523
(646) 240-4872 .. **Yuson,** Restituto (Rusty) '96 (Bortstein & I LLC) -275 Mad Av -NY 10016 **Fx:**(866) 955-9403
(212) 986-6000 .. **Yustein,** Ross L '95 (Kleinberg KW&C,PC) -551 5th Av -NY 10176
(718) 243-6454 .. **Yuster,** Dawn L '03 %Leg Aid -111 Lvngstn -Brklyn 11201 **Fx:**237-8737
(212) 484-3900 .. **Yusuf,** Temitope K '09 %Arent F LLP -1675 Bway -NY 10019
(914) 762-0111 .. **Yuter,** Seymour C '61 -407 Cedar Dr W -Briarcliff Mnr 10510
(212) 431-1188 .. **Yutkin,** Stephanie H '90 S Yutkin -401 Bway -NY 10013 **Fx:**294-1832
(212) 417-9643 .. **Yuvienco,** Marie E '98 %Medsite,Inc -370 7th Av -NY 10001 **Fx:**369-8916
(212) 907-9600 .. **Yuzek,** Dean G '76 (Ingram YGC&B,LLP) -250 Park Av -NY 10177
(212) 230-8800 .. **Yvon,** Anne-Marie C '08 %WilmerHale -399 Park Av -NY 10022
(212) 223-4000 .. **Zabarauskas,** Bruce J '88 Cnsl Crowell & M LLP -590 Mad Av -NY 10022
(212) 909-2548 .. **Zabel,** Laurel A '05 Unison Site Mgmt -340 Mad Av -NY 10173
(212) 637-2627 .. **Zabel,** Richd B '88 US Atty -1 St Andrews Plz -NY 10007
(212) 756-2000 .. **Zabel,** Wm D '61 (Schulte R&Z LLP) -919 3rd Av -NY 10022
(212) 455-2000 .. **Zabell,** David E '07 %Simpson T&B LLP -425 Lex Av -NY 10017
(631) 589-7242 .. **Zabell,** Saul D '96 (Zabell & Assoc,LLP) -4875 Sunrise Hwy -Bohemia 11716
(212) 695-6000 .. **Zabicki,** Eric C '02 (Pick & Z LLP) -369 Lex Av -NY 10017 **Fx:**695-6007
(212) 298-5298 .. **Zablocki,** Yossi M '00 %Leg Aid -49 Thomas -NY 10013 **Fx:**298-5252
(212) 446-4800 .. **Zablotney,** Sara Barron '03 (Kirkland & E LLP) -153 E 53rd -NY 10022
(716) 819-0891 .. **Zablotski,** Jos M '96 -14 Lafayette Sq -Buffalo 14203 **Fx:**819-0893
(914) 225-5544 .. **Zabrocki,** Edw J '00 Morgan Stanley -2000 Wstchstr Av -Purchase 10577
(212) 265-2800 .. **Zabrowsky,** Solomon '88 %Expansion Grp -250 W 57th -NY 10107 **Fx:**262-9457
(716) 648-3020 .. **Zaccagnino,** Leonard D '84 (Shaw & S) -4819 S Park Av -Hambrg 14075 **Fx:**648-3730
(914) 921-5222 .. **Zaccagnino,** Robt J '90 -14 Elm Pl -Rye 10580 **Fx:**921-6333

(212) 609-6800 ..**Zaccaria,** Anthony '94 (McCarter & E,LLP) -245 Park Av -NY 10167
(516) 228-5500 ..**Zaccaria,** Dayva B '95 (Gewurz & Z,PC) -50 Chas Lindbergh Blvd -Uniondale 11553 **Fx:**228-8390
(518) 457-3815 ..**Zaccaria,** James M '77 %Dept Tax & Fin -State Ofc Bldg Campus Bldg 8 -Albany 12227 **Fx:**457-8609
(845) 359-7700 ..**Zaccaria,** John '95 (Notaro M&Z PC) -100 Dutch Hill Rd -Orangebrg 10962
(516) 487-1602 ..**Zaccaria & Sasson** -175 E Shore Rd -Gt Neck 11023 **Fx:**487-0552
(516) 487-1602 ..**Zaccaria,** Wm J '78 (Zaccaria & S) -175 E Shore Rd -Gt Neck 11023
(212) 226-1212 ..**Zaccaro,** John A Jr. '94 -218 Lafayette -NY 10012
(315) 218-8000 ..**Zaccheo,** Philip J '93 (Bond S&K,PLLC) -1 Lincoln Ctr -Syracuse 13202
(845) 255-5667 ..**Zaccheo,** Robt J Jr. '02 -379 State Route 208 -New Paltz 12561 **Fx:**255-1415
(646) 472-1893 ..**Zacchia,** Carlo '00 -441 Lex -NY 10017 **Fx:**224-8512
(718) 351-3900 ..**Zaccone,** John W '88 -2141 Richmond Rd -Staten Isl 10306 **Fx:**227-9354
(212) 373-3000 ..**Zaccone,** Tracey Anne '98 (Paul WRW&G LLP) -1285 Av of Amer -NY 10019
(212) 637-2410 ..**Zach,** John T '02 US Atty -1 St Andrews Plz -NY 10007
(212) 336-0455 ..**Zach,** Olivia J '02 SEC -3 World Fncl Ctr -NY 10281 **Fx:**336-1323
(212) 803-5100 ..**Zach,** Susan J '87 %NY Cnty Defender Srvcs -225 Bway -NY 10007 **Fx:**571-6035
(212) 714-1720 ..**Zacharda,** Andrew P '05 (Tompkins MW&B LLP) -140 Bway -NY 10005
(212) 446-4800 ..**Zachariah,** Joshua M '06 %Kirkland & E LLP -153 E 53rd -NY 10022
(212) 737-8851 ..**Zacharias,** Anthony M '96 Auto Care East,Inc -243 E 94th -NY 10128
(212) 326-2000 ..**Zacharias,** Jasmine '10 %O'Melveny & M LLP -7 Times Sq -NY 10036
(877) 722-3332 ..**Zacharisen,** David K '89 -303 Park Av S -NY 10010
(212) 698-1171 ..**Zacharopoulos,** Melina '99 %WS Beslow -620 5th Av -NY 10020 **Fx:**698-1182
(718) 442-2828 ..**Zachary,** Deborah C '83 (Zachary & Z,PC) -75 Little Clove Rd -Staten Isl 10301 **Fx:**720-5935
(212) 446-4800 ..**Zachary,** Jason K '08 (Kirkland & E LLP) -153 E 53rd -NY 10022
(212) 857-8800 ..**Zachary,** Michl S '85 %2nd Circ Ct of Appls -40 Foley Sq -NY 10007
(212) 318-6000 ..**Zachary,** Seth M '77 (Paul HJ&W LLP) -75 E 55th -NY 10022
(212) 384-1000 ..**Zacher,** Erin P '01 FBI -26 Fed Plz -NY 10278
(212) 855-7158 ..**Zachman,** Sheila M '01 RBC Capital Mrkts Corp -165 Bway -NY 10006
(212) 446-4800 ..**Zachman,** Susan J '03 (Kirkland & E LLP) -153 E 53rd -NY 10022
(914) 642-4972 ..**Zachmann,** Jeffrey T '87 IBM -1133 Wstchstr Av -White Plns 10604
(718) 746-3440 ..**Zachry,** Christopher G '00 %Sacco & F,LLP -141-07 20th Av -Whitestone 11357
(212) 236-6104 ..**Zachter,** Debra L '99 Merrill Lynch -2 World Fncl Ctr -NY 10281
(212) 687-3000 ..**Zachter,** Jeffrey S '03 %Jaffe & A,LLP -600 3rd Av -NY 10016
(212) 839-5300 ..**Zack,** David '02 %Sidley A LLP -787 7th Av -NY 10019
(212) 336-2000 ..**Zack,** Jason S '09 %Patterson BW&T LLP -1133 Av of Amer -NY 10036
(212) 754-4050 ..**Zack,** Leonard '87 (L Zack & Assoc) -405 Park Av -NY 10022 **Fx:**759-8890
(716) 855-2800 ..**Zack,** Marianne C '03 %Mura & S,PLLC -14 Lafayette Sq #930 -Buffalo 14203
(212) 323-0200 ..**Zack,** Robt G '76 OppenheimerFunds,Inc -225 Lbrty -NY 10281
(716) 204-2400 ..**Zackem,** Ronald W '70 %SJ Baum,PC -220 Nrthpnte Pkwy Bx1291 -Buffalo 14240 **Fx:**204-4600
(212) 788-1299 ..**Zacker,** Brooke Birnbaum '04 Law Dept -100 Church -NY 10007 **Fx:**788-0367
(516) 674-2261 ..**Zacker,** John '87 -64 Weir Ln Bx644 -Locust Vly 11560 **Fx:**(877) 812-7348
(212) 586-8806 ..**Zackon,** Richd B '95 -676A 9th Av -NY 10036
(718) 847-4000 ..**Zadek,** Peter S '85 (Stein & Z) -86-52 Woodhvn Blvd -Woodhvn 11421
(718) 286-6000 ..**Zadnoff,** David S '78 %DA -125-01 Qns Blvd -Kew Gdns 11415
(718) 250-2000 ..**Zador,** Natalie '04 %DA -350 Jay -Brklyn 11201 **Fx:**250-2314
(212) 294-8531 ..**Zadourian,** Kevin S '05 Ionic Capital Mgmt LLC -366 Mad Av -NY 10017
(718) 319-8070 ..**Zadrima,** Alexander J '00 -1841 Wllmsbrdg Rd -Bronx 10461
(516) 747-8877 ..**Zaferiou,** George C '84 %Spizz & C,LLP -114 Old Cntry Rd -Mineola 11501
(914) 422-8755 ..**Zaffrann,** Rachel C '99 %Dept of Law -101 E Post Rd -White Plns 10601 **Fx:**422-8706
(516) 505-7001 ..**Zafonte,** Albert Jr. '86 A Zafonte & Assoc -215 Uniondale Av -Uniondale 11553 **Fx:**505-5120
(631) 501-3100 ..**Zafonte,** Dominic P '01 %J Humphreys -3 Huntngtn Quad Bx9028 -Melvll 11747 **Fx:**501-3085
(516) 545-5160 ..**Zafonte,** Lisa M '90 Natl Grid -175 E Old Cntry Rd -Hicksvll 11801 **Fx:**545-5029
(212) 408-5100 ..**Zafran,** Kimberly N '09 %Chadbourne & P LLP -30 Rckfllr Plz -NY 10112
(212) 730-7700 ..**Zafrin,** Mark H '81 (Michelman & R,LLP) -114 W 47th -NY 10036
(212) 878-1038 ..**Zagajeski,** Edw F '76 %MTA -347 Mad Av -NY 10017
(212) 250-8188 ..**Zagalis,** Penny '95 Deutsche Bk -60 Wall -NY 10005
(212) 547-5400 ..**Zagar,** Paul M '03 (McDermott W&E LLP) -340 Mad Av -NY 10173
(212) 977-6000 ..**Zagat,** Nina S '67 -4 Columbus Cir -NY 10019 **Fx:**977-6488
(718) 252-4200 ..**Zagelbaum,** Yoel A '04 %Riverside Abstract LLC -3839 Flatlands Av -Brklyn 11234 **Fx:**252-4226
(845) 794-3660 ..**Zager,** Michl L '73 (ML Zager,PC) -543 Bway Bx948 -Monticello 12701 **Fx:**794-3919
(212) 872-1000 ..**Zager,** Steven M '08 -One Bryant Park -NY 10036 **Fx:**872-1002
(845) 897-5199 ..**Zagon,** David R '96 %Feldman K&C,LLP -995 Main BxA -Fishkill 12524
(212) 941-1666 ..**Zagoory,** Jodi '87 -377 Bway -NY 10013 **Fx:**431-4460
(212) 216-8000 ..**Zagorsky,** Arthur '96 (Tarter K&D LLP) -1350 Bway -NY 10018
(315) 218-8000 ..**Zagraniczny,** Jos '79 (Bond S&K,PLLC) -1 Lincoln Ctr -Syracuse 13202
(914) 833-9785 ..**Zagreda,** Angela '07 %Tilem & C,LLP -188 E Post Rd -White Plns 10601 **Fx:**833-9788
(212) 278-1000 ..**Zagroba,** Dennis A '76 (Anderson K&O,PC) -1251 Av of Amer -NY 10020
(212) 264-5916 ..**Zagzoug,** Randa '91 %DHS -26 Fed Plz -NY 10278
(718) 276-7676 ..**Zahakos,** Peter J '82 -1 Cross Isl Plz -Rosedale 11422 **Fx:**276-7968
(212) 969-3000 ..**Zahedani,** Leila '08 %Proskauer R LLP -1585 Bway -NY 10036
(631) 207-1057 ..**Zaher,** John C '99 J Zaher,PC -156 N Ocean Av -Patchogue 11772
(845) 634-1420 ..**Zahl,** Adam S '92 (A Zahl,PC) -254 S Main -New Cty 10956 **Fx:**634-0943
(212) 734-3619 ..**Zahler,** Karen Gantz '80 -860 5th Av -NY 10065 **Fx:**734-0057
(516) 352-6600 ..**Zahler,** Melvin B '80 (M Zahler,PC) -3000 Marcus Av -Lk Success 11042 **Fx:**437-3791
(212) 428-2120 ..**Zahler-Gringer,** Barbara '77 %OCA -25 Beaver -NY 10004 **Fx:**428-2190
(866) 348-5819 ..**Zahm,** Marilyn Dixon '73 %SSA-ODAR -50 Fountain Plz -Buffalo 14202 **Fx:**(716) 551-4078
(718) 884-5600 ..**Zahm,** Maryann B '90 -3611 H Hdsn Pkwy -Bronx 10463 **Fx:**884-2615
(212) 836-8000 ..**Zahn,** Bari S '96 %Kaye S LLP -425 Park Av -NY 10022
(631) 471-3851 ..**Zahn,** Danl A '85 -1597 Grundy Av -Holbrook 11741
(212) 789-2000 ..**Zahnd,** Richd H '72 %NHL Enterprises,LP -1185 Av of Amer -NY 10036 **Fx:**789-2020
(212) 768-6700 ..**Zahner,** Brendan E '02 %Sonnenschein N&R LLP -1221 Av of Amer -NY 10020
(212) 635-0202 ..**Zahner,** Celia A '88 %Investigators Ofc -17 Battery Pl -NY 10004 **Fx:**363-1935
(518) 374-9818 ..**Zahnleuter,** Linda S '93 -7 Crimson Oak Ct -Niskayuna 12309 **Fx:**374-2290
(518) 473-4282 ..**Zahnleuter,** Richd J '82 %Dept of Health -Corning Twr 24th Fl -Albany 12237 **Fx:**473-2430
(212) 578-2211 ..**Zahs,** Gregory D '96 %MetLife -27-01 Qns Plz N -LIC 11101
(212) 878-8000 ..**Zaidi,** Ali H '09 %Clifford C LLP -31 W 52nd -NY 10019
(585) 428-5210 ..**Zaidi,** Azra B '08 Pub Def -10 N Fitzhugh -Rchstr 14614 **Fx:**428-2234
(646) 315-7300 ..**Zaidi,** Naveen '03 %FINRA -14 Wall -NY 10005 **Fx:**315-7440
(718) 779-8900 ..**Zaidi,** Syed H '88 -37-52 72nd -Jcksn Hts 11372
(212) 335-4500 ..**Zaidi,** Zahra F '07 DLA Piper LLP -1251 Av of Amer -NY 10020
(646) 644-7433 ..**Zaidi,** Zeeshan Hussain '01 LimeWire LLC -45 Howard -NY 10013
(212) 407-1200 ..**Zaiger,** Jeffrey H '08 %Joseph Law Ofcs LLC -485 Lex Av -NY 10017 **Fx:**407-1299
(212) 231-1000 ..**Zaino,** Michl '02 %Macquarie Grp -125 W 55th -NY 10019
(516) 747-1400 ..**Zaino,** Stephen E '85 (Bonchonsky & Z,LLP) -226 7th -Gdn Cty 11530
(212) 872-1000 ..**Zaiss,** Rolf '93 -One Bryant Park -NY 10036 **Fx:**872-1002
(212) 696-9190 ..**Zaitz,** Michl M '89 (Guararra & Z) -100 Park Av -NY 10017 **Fx:**696-9189
(212) 735-3000 ..**Zaitzeff,** Lara M '00 %Skadden ASM&F LLP -4 Times Sq -NY 10036
(212) 653-8700 ..**Zaitzeff,** Roger M '70 (Sheppard MR&H LLP) -30 Rckfllr Plz -NY 10112
(516) 822-8900 ..**Zajac,** Andrew J '81 Fiedelman & M -2 Jericho Plz -Jericho 11753
(212) 894-1547 ..**Zajac,** Ellen M '07 Sotheby's -1334 York Av -NY 10021
(212) 547-5400 ..**Zajac,** Jared D '09 %McDermott W&E LLP -340 Mad Av -NY 10173
(716) 549-5150 ..**Zajas,** J Grant '71 -8193 Erie Rd -Angola 14006
(917) 637-3600 ..**Zajkowski,** Julia A '03 %Ctr for Reproductive Rts -120 Wall -NY 10005 **Fx:**637-3666
(212) 558-4000 ..**Zak,** Ari M '07 %Sullivan & C LLP -125 Broad -NY 10004
(716) 646-6441 ..**Zak,** Cheryl McFadden '94 -12 Norwood Av -Hambrg 14075
(716) 856-4000 ..**Zak,** John J '86 (Hodgson R LLP) -140 Pearl -Buffalo 14202
(212) 721-0015 ..**Zak,** Oshrie '92 -165 West End Av -NY 10023 **Fx:**(914) 238-8192
(212) 837-6135 ..**Zakai,** Jason E '09 %Hughes H&R LLP -1 Bttry Pk Plz -NY 10004
(212) 421-4100 ..**Zakarin,** Donald S '76 (Pryor C LLP) -7 Times Sq -NY 10036
(516) 357-3000 ..**Zakarin,** Harris J '96 (Rivkin R LLP) -926 RXR Plz -Uniondale 11556
(212) 725-6418 ..**Zakarin,** Miriam E '05 (Treuhaft & Z,LLP) -1011 Av of Amer -NY 10018
(212) 891-6137 ..**Zakes,** Albert P '00 CDC Ixis NA -9 W 57th -NY 10019 **Fx:**891-1922
(212) 839-5300 ..**Zakharova,** Tatiana V '07 %Sidley A LLP -787 7th Av -NY 10019
(212) 595-8009 ..**Zakhary,** Leana '04 %Krol & O -320 W 81st -NY 10024 **Fx:**595-8149
(718) 947-4035 ..**Zakhary,** Mariam Y '08 NY Ctr for Interpersonal Dvlpmnt -130 Styvsnt Pl -Staten Isl 10301 **Fx:**876-6068
(516) 515-1191 ..**Zakheim,** Fawn H '05 -968 E End -Woodmere 11598 **Fx:**570-3530
(212) 554-7800 ..**Zakheim,** Joshua H '80 OfCnsl Moses & S LLP -405 Lex Av -NY 10174
(716) 636-7600 ..**Zakia,** Nelson F Jr. '74 %HoganWillig -2410 N Forest Rd -Amherst 14068
(212) 984-8129 ..**Zakin,** Kenneth L '74 %Insignia/ESG Cptl Advisors -200 Park Av -NY 10166 **Fx:**984-6688
(212) 824-1510 ..**Zakin,** Richd J '81 Solomon-Page Grp LLC -260 Mad Av -NY 10016
(631) 859-0300 ..**Zaklukiewicz Puzo & Morrissey,LLP** -2701 Sunrise Hwy Bx389 -Islip Terr 11752 **Fx:**859-5284
(212) 736-2624 ..**Zaklukiewicz Puzo & Morrissey,LLP** -236 W 26th -NY 10001 **Fx:**981-0528
(631) 859-0300 ..**Zaklukiewicz,** Stephen F '95 %Zaklukiewicz P&M,LLP -2701 Sunrise Hwy Bx389 -Islip Terr 11752
(212) 770-8612 ..**Zakow,** Patti A '93 %AIG -160 Water -NY 10038
(212) 635-1183 ..**Zakrocki,** Andrew A '01 %Bk of NY Mellon -1 Wall -NY 10286
(212) 277-6300 ..**Zakrzewski,** Karen M '06 %Schindler C&H LLP -100 Wall -NY 10005
(212) 340-0400 ..**Zalaman,** Bruce M '76 %Appllt Div 1st Dept -27 Mad Av -NY 10010 **Fx:**889-4412
(914) 682-0707 ..**Zalantis,** Katherine H '96 (Silverberg Z LLP) -220 Wht Plns Rd -Tarrytwn 10591
(212) 418-5122 ..**Zalasin,** Andrew L '92 -126 E 56th -NY 10022
(607) 763-9200 ..**Zalbowitz,** Alan M '64 OfCnsl Levene G&T,LLP -BxF-1706 -Bnghmtn 13902
(914) 422-4082 ..**Zalcman,** Fred '97 Pace Law Schl -78 N Bway -White Plns 10603 **Fx:**422-4039

(718) 222-9800 ..**Zalduondo**, Jose J '09 Brecher FPWT&Z,PC -335 Adams -Brklyn 11201
(631) 732-7789 ..**Zale**, Larry C '66 -290 Main -E Setauket 11733
(212) 865-1616 ..**Zalel**, Melvin J '53 -840 W End Av -NY 10025 **Fx:**865-5108
(518) 474-2063 ..**Zalen**, Stanley L '73 Bd of Elections -40 Steuben -Albany 12207
(212) 310-8000 ..**Zalenski**, Walter E '10 (Weil G&M LLP) -767 5th Av -NY 10153
(212) 788-1020 ..**Zaleon**, Janet L '84 %Law Dept -100 Church -NY 10007 **Fx:**788-0367
(212) 336-2000 ..**Zalesin**, Steven A '86 (Patterson BW&T LLP) -1133 Av of Amer -NY 10036
(212) 506-5000 ..**Zaleskas**, Donna M '05 %Orrick H&S LLP -51 W 52nd -NY 10019
(212) 336-0189 ..**Zaleskas**, Kristine M '98 %SEC -3 World Fncl Ctr -NY 10281 **Fx:**336-1323
(631) 852-1764 ..**Zaleski**, H Alexander '75 %Hon HE Seidell -210 Center Dr -Rvrhead 11901 **Fx:**852-2700
(845) 788-5070 ..**Zaleski**, Terence M '85 -437 Old Albany Post Rd -Garrison 10524
(212) 335-9000 ..**Zaleta**, James M '04 %DA -1 Hogan Pl -NY 10013
(718) 263-6800 ..**Zalewski**, Steven '87 (S Zalewski & Assoc,PC) -125-10 Qns Blvd -Kew Gdns 11415 **Fx:**520-9401
(212) 980-8490 ..**Zalk**, Richd '69 -110 E 59th -NY 10022 **Fx:**980-8495
(212) 310-8000 ..**Zalka**, Caroline '04 %Weil G&M LLP -767 5th Av -NY 10153
(212) 688-4000 ..**Zalka**, Stuart '82 %NYS HFA -641 Lex Av -NY 10022 **Fx:**872-0362
(212) 430-8020 ..**Zalkin**, Jeffrey M '80 (LeClairRyan,PC) -830 3rd Av -NY 10022
(212) 541-6222 ..**Zalkin**, Jonathan A '97 %Kane K,PC -1350 Av of Amer -NY 10019
(212) 633-1399 ..**Zalkin**, Seth R '98 -303 Park Av S -NY 10010
(212) 608-4704 ..**Zalkin**, Steven O '79 (S Zalkin,PC) -15 Maiden Ln -NY 10038 **Fx:**385-4661
(845) 357-6800 ..**Zall**, Michl E '74 -2 Yorkshire Dr -Suffern 10901
(212) 969-3000 ..**Zall**, Richd J '81 (Proskauer R LLP) -1585 Bway -NY 10036
(212) 668-0059 ..**Zalman**, Benjamin '59 (Zalman & S) -61 Bway -NY 10006
(212) 808-7800 ..**Zalman**, David '01 (Kelley D&W LLP) -101 Park Av -NY 10178
(212) 668-0059 ..**Zalman & Schnurman** -61 Bway -NY 10006 **Fx:**514-7072
(718) 261-3000 ..**Zaloba**, Edw '84 -118-21 Qns Blvd -Frst Hlls 11375 **Fx:**793-0385
(973) 324-2444 ..**Zalon**, Jules D '63 -3 Spruce Hllw -Armonk 10504 **Fx:**324-2180
(212) 346-0045 ..**Zaloudek**, Steven J '02 %P Weitz & Assoc,PC -233 Bway -NY 10279 **Fx:**346-0876
(212) 361-7735 ..**Zalph**, Diana '87 %Dept Consumer Affrs -66 John -NY 10038
(212) 560-9100 ..**Zalta**, Marcos '86 -350 5th Av -NY 10118
(631) 661-7132 ..**Zalud-Crawford**, Joanne '03 J Zalud-Crawford,PLLC -199 E Main -Babylon 11702 **Fx:**661-7134
(212) 558-4000 ..**Zaluski**, Oded '09 %Sullivan & C LLP -125 Broad -NY 10004
(212) 538-3613 ..**Zam**, Morgan '99 Credit Suisse -1 Mad Av -NY 10010
(212) 403-1000 ..**Zamacona**, Yelena '04 %Wachtell LR&K -51 W 52nd -NY 10019
(212) 742-1414 ..**Zamansky**, Jacob H '82 Zamansky & Assoc LLC -50 Bway -NY 10005 **Fx:**742-1177
(585) 352-5556 ..**Zambito**, Chas N '78 (Foster F&Z) -5500 W Ridge Rd -Spencerprt 14559
(212) 889-2300 ..**Zambito**, Peter J '61 (Dougherty RGZ&H) -131 E 38th -NY 10016
(631) 852-2163 ..**Zambito**, Vincent '81 Hon A Crecca -210 Center Dr -Rvrhead 11901 **Fx:**852-3043
(585) 258-2800 ..**Zamboni**, Helen A '78 SrCnsl Underberg & K LLP -300 Bausch & Lomb Pl -Rchstr 14604
(518) 429-4200 ..**Zambri**, Melissa M '99 (Hiscock & B,LLP) -50 Beaver -Albany 12207
(212) 223-4000 ..**Zambrzycki**, Jacob Z '10 %Crowell & M LLP -590 Mad Av -NY 10022
(631) 851-4466 ..**Zamek**, Scott '87 -3124 Expwy Dr S -Islandia 11749 **Fx:**851-0412
(315) 682-0724 ..**Zamelis**, Douglas H '90 -8363 Vassar Dr -Manlius 13104
(845) 561-0550 ..**Zamenick**, Amy L '10 %Drake LHKGG&R PLLC -555 Hudson Valley Av -New Windsor 12553
(212) 969-3000 ..**Zametto**, Marc A '00 %Proskauer R LLP -1585 Bway -NY 10036
(212) 979-8600 ..**Zamfotis**, Gregory J '09 Gregorys Coffee -327 Park Av S -NY 10010
(631) 501-1000 ..**Zamir**, Amy J '97 %Balfe & H,PC -135 Pinelawn Rd -Melvll 11747
(585) 327-6247 ..**Zammiello**, David F '02 %Thomson West -50 E Broad -Rchstr 14694
(212) 318-3000 ..**Zammit**, Jos P '72 (Fulbright & J LLP) -666 5th Av -NY 10103
(212) 640-7581 ..**Zammit**, Michl J '06 %Am Ex -200 Vesey -NY 10285
(800) 281-1515 ..**Zammitti**, Valerie K '08 %Power Law Firm LLP -590 Mad Av -NY 10022 **Fx:**903-1993
(212) 883-8833 ..**Zammitti Shaw**, Natalie A '99 %Tacopina & A -275 Mad Av -NY 10016
(212) 513-7501 ..**Zamora**, Herman '84 -139 Fulton -NY 10038
(718) 537-4958 ..**Zamora**, Louis '79 %ODAR-SSA -226 E 161st -Bronx 10451 **Fx:**590-1673
(212) 490-9000 ..**Zamora**, Oscar A '95 %TIAA-CREF -730 3rd Av -NY 10017
(212) 538-0269 ..**Zamore**, Eric A '99 Credit Suisse -11 Mad Av -NY 10010
(315) 737-8697 ..**Zamorski**, Jerome F '67 -3805 Oneida -New Hartfrd 13413 **Fx:**737-8698
(212) 725-4500 ..**Zamorsky**, Tania '97 GS Schwartz & Co -470 Park Av S -NY 10016 **Fx:**725-9188
(212) 848-9800 ..**Zamparelli**, Justin M '00 (Withers B LLP) -430 Park Av -NY 10022
(917) 637-3600 ..**Zampas**, Christina '96 %Ctr for Reproductive Rts -120 Wall -NY 10005 **Fx:**637-3666
(212) 808-4600 ..**Zampino**, Ana L '08 %J Zampino,PC -405 Lex Av -NY 10174
(212) 808-4600 ..**Zampino**, John P '71 (J Zampino,PC) -405 Lex Av -NY 10174
(516) 571-2480 ..**Zampino**, Rachel Schechter '02 NYS Supreme Ct -100 Supreme Ct Dr -Mineola 11501 **Fx:**571-0213
(212) 808-4600 ..**Zampino**, Sarah Tribit '04 J Zampino,PC -405 Lex Av -NY 10174
(212) 883-6500 ..**Zampino**, Thos '86 (Podell SS&B,LLP) -605 3rd Av -NY 10158
(212) 788-3159 ..**Zamudio**, Raul S '09 %Law Dept -60 Lafayette -NY 10013 **Fx:**442-6865
(631) 249-6644 ..**Zamurs**, Karl E '83 (Garcia & S) -2076 Deer Prk Av -Deer Pk 11729
(212) 846-4429 ..**Zan**, Koethi '97 MTV Networks -1515 Bway -NY 10036
(646) 278-0888 ..**Zanani**, Doron '85 -11 Bway -NY 10004 **Fx:**(212) 943-1238
(914) 946-5100 ..**Zanazzi**, Anthony L '69 OfCnsl Bashian & F,LLP -235 Main -White Plns 10601
(212) 732-3200 ..**Zancolli**, Mark R '99 Cnsl Carter L&M LLP -2 Wall -NY 10005
(845) 255-1556 ..**Zand**, J Philip '66 -153 Main Bx55 -New Paltz 12561 **Fx:**255-1582
(212) 962-2800 ..**Zand**, Richd V '62 Schwartz G&C,LLP -90 Broad -NY 10004
(718) 758-2200 ..**Zand**, Saml T '09 %Lowenthal & K,PC -2001 Flatbush Av -Brklyn 11234
(516) 482-5758 ..**Zander**, Lester P '54 -228 Clent Rd -Gt Neck 11021
(212) 825-5900 ..**Zander**, Louis Stephan '92 %Dept of Invstgtn -80 Maiden Ln -NY 10038 **Fx:**825-2860
(516) 739-5100 ..**Zane**, Audra S '96 (Farber B&Z LLP) -51 Charles -Mineola 11501
(212) 697-3476 ..**Zane**, Danl M '49 -60 E 42nd -NY 10165 **Fx:**697-0877
(212) 483-9600 ..**Zane**, David N '88 (Costello S&G LLP) -44 Wall -NY 10005
(212) 245-2222 ..**Zane and Rudofsky** -601 W 26th -NY 10001 **Fx:**541-5555
(516) 365-9191 ..**Zanelotti**, Christopher J '97 %S Friedman -1 Hllw Ln -New Hyde Pk 11042 **Fx:**365-6138
(212) 233-3330 ..**Zanetti**, Robt '02 %Hanley & G LLP -233 Bway -NY 10279
(212) 541-2000 ..**Zang**, Jihong '06 %Bryan C LLP -1290 Av of Amer -NY 10104
(212) 571-7600 ..**Zang**, Neil M '66 -225 Bway -NY 10007 **Fx:**571-4352
(212) 607-2816 ..**Zang**, Theo '88 SrCnsl FTC -1 Bowling Grn -NY 10004 **Fx:**607-2822
(212) 309-8206 ..**Zangara**, Chas J '00 ING Grp -230 Park Av -NY 10169
(212) 415-3707 ..**Zangara**, Deborah E '97 Omnicom Group -437 Mad Av -NY 10022 **Fx:**415-3530
(212) 735-8600 ..**Zangara**, Henry A '96 (Morrison C LLP) -909 3rd Av -NY 10022
(315) 457-2129 ..**Zangari**, David P '88 -209 2nd -Liverpool 13088
(212) 247-2603 ..**Zanger**, Hugh M '96 %Orsidrealty Corp -1740 Bway -NY 10019
(212) 859-8000 ..**Zanger**, Jonathan J '09 %Fried FHS&J LLP -1 NY Plz -NY 10004
(212) 578-2211 ..**Zanghi**, Phyllis J '98 %MetLife -27-01 Qns Plz N -LIC 11101
(716) 753-3900 ..**Zanghi**, Stephen P '86 %Young Title Agency -13 S Erie -Mayvll 14757 **Fx:**753-3325
(845) 794-3344 ..**Zangla**, Robt L '98 %DA -414 Bway -Monticello 12701 **Fx:**794-3646
(516) 741-7676 ..**Zangos**, Anne K '08 %Miranda SSSV LLP -240 Mineola Blvd -Mineola 11501
(212) 893-4345 ..**Zangri**, Jos A '94 %Bloomberg LP -499 Park Av -NY 10022
(516) 663-6600 ..**Zangwill**, Matthew J '06 %Ruskin MF,PC -1425 RXR Plz -Uniondale 11556
(212) 768-6700 ..**Zanias**, Eleni '08 %Sonnenschein N&R LLP -2 World Fncl Ctr -NY 10281
(516) 229-6000 ..**Zanickrowsky**, John W '76 %R Lau & Assoc -300 Jericho Quad Bx9040 -Jericho 11753 **Fx:**229-6167
(516) 466-6050 ..**Zankel**, Ira L '70 %N Shore Abstrct -1010 Nrthrn Blvd -Gt Neck 11021 **Fx:**466-6011
(631) 694-2300 ..**Zankel**, Jeffrey A '78 (Lamb & B,LLP) -534 Broadhllw Rd Bx9034 -Melvll 11747
(212) 259-8000 ..**Zanko**, Jennifer M '05 %Dewey & L LLP -1301 Av of Amer -NY 10019
(716) 849-8900 ..**Zanner**, Kevin J '97 (Hurwitz & F,PC) -1300 Lbrty Bldg -Buffalo 14202
(212) 825-0635 ..**Zanolin**, Peter L '01 Dept of Invstgtn -80 Maiden Ln -NY 10038 **Fx:**825-2860
(631) 981-2512 ..**Zanoni**, Elio D '93 -15 Babcock Av -Ronkonkoma 11779 **Fx:**981-2512
(212) 834-0600 ..**Zanoni**, Marc H '98 %Gordon & S,PC -355 Lex Av -NY 10017
(631) 271-6363 ..**Zanzalari**, Loretta '00 %Cannon & A,LLP -1923 NY Av -Huntngtn Sta 11746 **Fx:**271-7128
(516) 229-4300 ..**Zapantis**, Chrisanthy N '99 %J Bilello & Assoc -875 Merrick Av -Westbury 11590
(212) 267-3700 ..**Zapantis**, Marina '06 %Napoli BR LLP -350 5th Av -NY 10118
(212) 766-9870 ..**Zapata**, Fausto E Jr. '02 -277 Bway -NY 10007
(516) 625-1700 ..**Zapata**, Louis W '98 %Salamon GB&S,PC -97 Powerhse Rd -Roslyn Hts 11577
(212) 918-3000 ..**Zapata**, Roberto '01 %Hogan L LLP -875 3rd Av -NY 10022
(585) 295-7610 ..**Zapesochny**, Alexander '98 iCardiac Technologies -150 Allens Crk Rd -Rchstr 14618 **Fx:**295-7609
(212) 931-5500 ..**Zapfel**, Elaine B '82 (McCue S&Z,PC) -521 5th Av -NY 10175
(718) 698-6026 ..**Zapin**, Michl E '92 -2222 Richmond Av -Staten Isl 10314 **Fx:**698-6054
(212) 977-9700 ..**Zapotocky**, Meagan A '04 %Phillips N LLP -666 5th Av -NY 10103
(212) 410-3351 ..**Zapp**, Johanna S '03 -550 Grand -NY 10002 **Fx:**(917) 492-1879
(516) 512-8946 ..**Zappa**, Joann M '94 (J Zappa,PC) -1225 Franklin Av -Gdn Cty 11530
(518) 566-7211 ..**Zappala**, Frank G '91 -Bx2886 -Plattsbrgh 12901
(518) 431-0401 ..**Zappen**, Matthew J '04 %Hon R Miner-US Ct Appls -445 Bway -Albany 12207 **Fx:**431-0400
(585) 263-1000 ..**Zappia**, Andrew P '96 (Nixon P LLP) -1100 Clinton Sq -Rchstr 14604
(518) 238-3231 ..**Zappia**, Graig F '03 -5205 Admirals Walk Dr -Cohoes 12047
(518) 783-2600 ..**Zappone**, Jos W '94 (Zappone & F) -6 Century Hill Dr -Latham 12110 **Fx:**783-2607
(516) 248-6400 ..**Zapson**, Michl G '86 OfCnsl Davidoff M&H,LLP -200 Grdn City Plz -Gdn Cty 11530
(212) 619-4500 ..**Zara**, Maurice Robt '89 -111 John -NY 10038 **Fx:**619-4520
(516) 822-3550 ..**Zaradic**, Sandy '04 %Hoffmann & B LLP -6900 Jericho Tpk -Syosset 11791 **Fx:**822-3582
(718) 222-2112 ..**Zaragoza**, Paul M '10 %Law Dept -350 Jay -Brklyn 11201 **Fx:**222-2393
(516) 741-6601 ..**Zaransky**, Michl B '99 (Chapman Z LLP) -114 Old Cntry Rd -Mineola 11501 **Fx:**741-6602
(516) 228-1300 ..**Zaratin**, Erik '07 %Sahn WC&B,PLLC -333 Earle Ovngton Blvd -Uniondale 11553
(212) 839-5300 ..**Zarchan**, Aryeh H '00 (Sidley A LLP) -787 7th Av -NY 10019
(845) 528-8882 ..**Zarcone**, John M Jr. '94 -11 Peekskill Hllw Rd Bx642 -Putnam Vly 10579 **Fx:**526-4992
(716) 854-8002 ..**Zarcone**, Kelly V '98 Zarcone Assoc,PLLC -2350 N Forest Rd -Getzvll 14068 **Fx:**693-5775
(518) 436-1408 ..**Zarcone**, Michl A '89 %MetLife -111 Wshngtn Av -Albany 12210
(516) 621-6364 ..**Zareh**, Batia Mojdeh '96 %Zamilco Intl -1163 Willis Av -Albertson 11507
(212) 400-7224 ..**Zaremba**, John D '03 (Zaremba B&B PLLC) -40 Wall -NY 10005 **Fx:**(646) 512-5607
(212) 586-5330 ..**Zaremski**, Jack '89 Hanover Leg Personnel Srvcs,Inc -124 W 60th -NY 10023 **Fx:**265-6542
(585) 262-4140 ..**Zaretsky**, Allen J '84 -11 Arnold Park -Rchstr 14607 **Fx:**262-2605
(212) 319-3737 ..**Zaretsky**, Donn B '91 (J Silberman Assoc,PC) -145 E 57th -NY 10022 **Fx:**319-8188
(212) 578-5441 ..**Zaretsky**, Jamie R '05 MetLife -1095 Av of Amer -NY 10036 **Fx:**578-3916
(212) 869-2147 ..**Zaretsky**, Michl J '76 (Carlet GK&Z) -645 5th Av -NY 10022

(516) 627-7000 ..**Zarett,** David A '86 (Weiss & Z,PC) -3333 New Hyde Pk Rd -New Hyde Pk 11042
(646) 386-5700 ..**Zarfati,** Ariella S '01 %Civil Ct -111 Centre -NY 10013
(212) 490-2277 ..**Zarfati,** Yossi '02 NY Land Srvcs -630 3rd Av -NY 10017
(212) 506-5000 ..**Zarfes,** Marlene '81 OfCnsl Orrick H&S LLP -51 W 52nd -NY 10019
(212) 373-3000 ..**Zargar,** Ehsan '09 %Paul WRW&G LLP -1285 Av of Amer -NY 10019
(212) 309-6000 ..**Zargari,** Jos D '06 %Morgan L&B LLP -101 Park Av -NY 10178
(212) 592-1400 ..**Zargari,** Michl '07 %Herrick,F LLP -2 Park Av -NY 10016
(914) 945-3701 ..**Zarick,** Gail H '99 IBM -Bx218 -Yorktwn Hts 10598
(212) 521-2000 ..**Zarin,** Glenn P '94 %Loews Corp -667 Mad Av -NY 10065 **Fx:**521-2997
(212) 538-5296 ..**Zarin,** Heath B '99 CSFB -11 Mad Av -NY 10010
(718) 643-5624 ..**Zarin,** Lenore '80 %Hon L Elkins -283 Adams -Brklyn 11201
(914) 682-7800 ..**Zarin,** Michl D '86 (Zarin & S) -81 Main -White Plns 10601
(516) 487-7450 ..**Zarin,** Michl S '56 Wellfleet Invstmnts LLC -40 Cutter Mill Rd Bx222142 -Gt Neck 11022 **Fx:**487-7480
(212) 309-6000 ..**Zarin,** Richd S '86 (Morgan L&B LLP) -101 Park Av -NY 10178
(914) 682-7800 ..**Zarin & Steinmetz** -81 Main -White Plns 10601 **Fx:**683-5490
(212) 297-5800 ..**Zarin,** Todd B '96 Cnsl Day P LLP -7 Times Sq -NY 10036
(631) 471-5887 ..**Zarkadas,** Paraskevi '91 (P Zarkadas,PC) -82 Eastwood Blvd -Centereach 11720
(212) 521-5400 ..**Zarkin,** Sloan J '04 %Reed S LLP -599 Lex Av -NY 10022
(914) 378-3900 ..**Zarkower,** Michl A '95 %Kaplan & M -1 Exec Blvd -Ynkrs 10701
(212) 225-5628 ..**Zarkowski,** Thos M '99 Scotia Capital -1 Lbrty Plz -NY 10006
(212) 759-4888 ..**Zarlock,** Preston L '93 (Phillips L LLP) -437 Mad Av -NY 10022
(716) 847-8400 ..**Zarlock,** Preston L '93 (Phillips L LLP) -3400 HSBC Ctr -Buffalo 14203
(516) 358-5555 ..**Zarnowski,** Lucien '62 -1 Holland Av -Floral Pk 11001 **Fx:**775-2085
(212) 643-7000 ..**Zaro,** Jerold L '89 OfCnsl Sills C&G PC -One Rckfllr Plz -NY 10020
(212) 425-1401 ..**Zarocostas,** Michl G '97 SpclCnsl O'Hare P LLP -82 Wall -NY 10005 **Fx:**425-1421
(516) 568-1850 ..**Zaroff,** Allan R '68 (Werner ZSS&A) -360 Merrick Rd -Lynbrk 11563
(516) 280-5590 ..**Zaroff,** Caren H '01 %Zaroff & Z LLP -300 Grdn City Plz -Gdn Cty 11530
(516) 280-5590 ..**Zaroff,** Ira S '01 (Zaroff & Z LLP) -300 Grdn City Plz -Gdn Cty 11530
(516) 280-5590 ..**Zaroff,** Richd M '69 (Zaroff & Z LLP) -300 Grdn City Plz -Gdn Cty 11530
(718) 351-4199 ..**Zarou,** George R '86 -35 E Franklin Ln -Staten Isl 10306
(718) 398-2532 ..**Zarowin,** Marc D '91 -47 Plz W -Brklyn 11217 **Fx:**398-2329
(212) 220-3000 ..**Zarr,** Michelle L '03 %Broadcast Music Inc -250 Greenwich -NY 10007
(212) 312-2260 ..**Zarrabi,** Azadeh Z '09 Leg Aid -60 Lafayette -NY 10013 **Fx:**349-0874
(973) 539-6500 ..**Zarrella,** Maria L '97 %Bubb G&C,LLP -65 W 36th -NY 10018 **Fx:**539-6409
(212) 944-8450 ..**Zarrello,** Marilyn L '87 -1501 Bway -NY 10036 **Fx:**944-7803
(212) 373-5850 ..**Zarro,** Jos N '98 Kenneth Cole Prdctns -603 W 50th -NY 10019
(212) 417-8700 ..**Zas,** Edw S '91 %Fed Def of NY Inc -52 Duane -NY 10007 **Fx:**571-0392
(212) 969-3000 ..**Zasky,** Aliza '03 %Proskauer R LLP -1585 Bway -NY 10036
(212) 289-4324 ..**Zaslav,** H Gary '58 Zaslav & A,PC -1825 Park Av -NY 10035 **Fx:**289-4894
(845) 348-0033 ..**Zaslav,** Steven L '93 -119 Rockland Ctr -Nanuet 10954
(212) 222-5223 ..**Zaslav,** Steven L '93 Cnsl Zaslav Law Grp -1825 Park Av -NY 10035 **Fx:**289-4894
(718) 237-2000 ..**Zaslofsky,** Mary '86 %Leg Aid -111 Lvngstn -Brklyn 11201 **Fx:**237-8737
(212) 219-2600 ..**Zaslowsky,** Danl N '54 (Kulak & Z) -401 Bway -NY 10013
(212) 626-4100 ..**Zaslowsky,** David '85 (Baker & M LLP) -1114 Av of Amer -NY 10036
(585) 256-0090 ..**Zatkowsky,** Miles P '82 (Dutcher & Z) -1399 Monroe Av -Rchstr 14618
(212) 819-8200 ..**Zatz,** Andrew T '08 %White & C LLP -1155 Av of Amer -NY 10036
(212) 259-4325 ..**Zauderer,** Howard J '90 Longacre Fund Mgmt,LLC -810 7th Av -NY 10019
(212) 564-5900 ..**Zauderer,** Louis '83 -120 W 31st -NY 10001
(212) 412-9500 ..**Zauderer,** Mark C '72 (Flemming ZWZ LLP) -1 Lbrty Plz -NY 10006
(212) 474-1000 ..**Zaur,** Isaac B '08 %Cravath S&M LLP -825 8th Av -NY 10019
(516) 741-6565 ..**Zausmer,** Robt N '74 (Meyer SE&K,PC) -990 Stewart Av Bx9194 -Gdn Cty 11530
(212) 909-6604 ..**Zausmer,** Sara M '05 %DA -1 Hogan Pl -NY 10013
(212) 474-1000 ..**Zavaglia,** Jos D '05 %Cravath S&M LLP -825 8th Av -NY 10019
(315) 430-3311 ..**Zavaglia,** Jos J '02 -307 S Clinton -Syracuse 13202
(212) 344-5680 ..**Zavarella,** Marisa F A '08 %Thompson H LLP -335 Mad Av -NY 10017
(516) 921-1200 ..**Zavatsky Mendelsohn & Levy,LLP** -33 Qns Bx510 -Syosset 11791 **Fx:**921-1670
(516) 921-1200 ..**Zavatsky,** Peter G '77 (Zavatsky M&L,LLP) -33 Qns Bx510 -Syosset 11791
(212) 407-4000 ..**Zavin,** Jonathan '73 (Loeb & L,LLP) -345 Park Av -NY 10154
(212) 759-7810 ..**Zawadzka,** Margaret A '02 -575 Mad Av -NY 10022 **Fx:**(646) 619-4830
(212) 980-9600 ..**Zawadzki,** Deborah M '06 %Kaufman B&R -120 Bway -NY 10271
(212) 478-7200 ..**Zawadzki,** Jeffrey '04 %Hahn & H LLP -488 Mad Av -NY 10022
(718) 388-3330 ..**Zawisny,** Mark T '92 (Zawisny & Z,PC) -578 Driggs Av -Brklyn 11211 **Fx:**338-3877
(718) 388-3330 ..**Zawisny,** Yolanda J '97 (Zawisny & Z,PC) -578 Driggs Av -Brklyn 11211 **Fx:**338-3877
(631) 852-1684 ..**Zawyrucha,** Thos S '81 Supreme Ct -210 Center Dr -Rvrhead 11901 **Fx:**852-2020
(845) 659-4112 ..**Zayas,** Richd R '82 -Bx596 -Stony Pnt 10980
(518) 474-8816 ..**Zayas,** Steven D '93 %Comm Prof Standrds -40 Steuben -Albany 12207 **Fx:**474-0389
(212) 878-8000 ..**Zaychik,** Inna '07 %Clifford C LLP -31 W 52nd -NY 10019
(212) 451-2300 ..**Zaytsev,** Renée M '08 %Olshan GFR&W LLP -65 E 55th -NY 10022
(212) 609-6800 ..**Zazzali,** Danl P '03 %McCarter & E,LLP -245 Park Av -NY 10167
(973) 623-1822 ..**Zazzali Fagella Nowak Kleinbaum & Friedman** -15 W 72nd -NY 10023 **Fx:**(212) 875-8275
(973) 596-4723 ..**Zazzali-Hogan,** Mara E '00 (Gibbons PC) -1 Penn Plz -NY 10119 **Fx:**639-8331
(718) 987-2700 ..**Zazzera,** Kevin B '95 -182 Rose Av -Staten Isl 10306 **Fx:**987-7282
(917) 237-4801 ..**Zbar,** Jordana R '07 RGL Forensics -5 Hanover Sq -NY 10004 **Fx:**237-4802
(212) 310-8000 ..**Zborovsky,** Evgeny '09 %Weil G&M LLP -767 5th Av -NY 10153
(845) 356-0855 ..**Zdanis,** Karen '01 -55 Old Tpk Rd -Nanuet 10954
(716) 855-3200 ..**Zdarsky,** Jos E '72 (Zdarsky S&A) -298 Main -Buffalo 14202
(716) 855-3200 ..**Zdarsky Sawicki & Agostinelli** -298 Main -Buffalo 14202 **Fx:**855-3101
(585) 262-2667 ..**Zea,** Danl E '99 OfCnsl Connors & F,LLP -3445 Winton Pl -Rchstr 14623
(212) 204-4200 ..**Zealand,** Elise S '00 Penton Media,Inc -249 W 17th -NY 10011
(845) 331-6198 ..**Zeayter,** Saraa '07 Absolute Connections -39 W Chestnut -Kingston 12401
(212) 589-4200 ..**Zeballos,** Gonzalo S '01 (Baker & H LLP) -45 Rckfllr Plz -NY 10111
(212) 759-2500 ..**Zebicoff,** Christian G '94 (Jones G,LLP) -60 E 42nd -NY 10165
(212) 637-2710 ..**Zebrowski,** Kathleen A '87 %US Atty -86 Chmbrs -NY 10007
(845) 634-7701 ..**Zebrowski,** Kenneth P '06 OfCnsl Braunfotel & F LLC -49 Maple Av -New Cty 10956 **Fx:**634-7710
(607) 562-8770 ..**Zebrowski,** Walter S '59 -28 Wynnwd Dr -Big Flats 14814
(716) 694-6622 ..**Zebulske,** Edw A III '95 -150 Payne Av Bx159 -N Tonawanda 14120
(914) 681-6060 ..**Zecca,** Jos M '82 %S Owens -140 Grand -White Plns 10601
(845) 294-2544 ..**Zeccola,** Frank J '73 (Zeccola & S) -45 Webster Av -Goshen 10924
(845) 294-2544 ..**Zeccola & Selinger** -45 Webster Av -Goshen 10924 **Fx:**294-3507
(212) 986-3361 ..**Zeche,** Stephen '67 S Zeche,PC -800 3rd Av -NY 10022
(212) 687-7070 ..**Zeche,** Stephen '67 OfCnsl Rand RR&G LLP -800 3rd Av -NY 10022
(212) 848-4000 ..**Zecher,** Robt A '10 Shearman & S LLP -599 Lex Av -NY 10022
(518) 561-4400 ..**Zedick,** Meghan E '07 %Stafford OC&T,PLLC -1 Cumberland Av Bx2947 -Plattsbrgh 12901
(518) 489-9423 ..**Zee,** Donald '79 (D Zee,PC) -1 Winners Cir -Albany 12205 **Fx:**489-9429
(212) 450-4000 ..**Zeehandelaar,** Rachel S '09 %Davis P&W LLP -450 Lex Av -NY 10017
(212) 949-8700 ..**Zeff,** Lawr S '70 %Eisner LLP -750 3rd Av -NY 10017 **Fx:**891-4100
(212) 889-2498 ..**Zeffiro,** Michl P '82 %Fager & A,LLP -2 Park Av -NY 10016
(212) 949-8700 ..**Zefi,** Jon J '99 Eisner LLP -750 3rd Av -NY 10017 **Fx:**891-4100
(716) 381-9141 ..**Zeftel,** Bruce S '78 -69 Delaware Av -Buffalo 14202
(973) 848-5600 ..**Zefutie,** John J Jr. '05 %Patton B LLP -1185 Av of Amer -NY 10036 **Fx:**848-5601
(914) 681-8700 ..**Zegarelli,** David C '01 %Milber MP&S LLP -3 Barker Av -White Plns 10601
(518) 465-6420 ..**Zegarelli,** Jennifer C '04 %DerOhannesian & D -677 Bway -Albany 12207 **Fx:**427-0614
(212) 986-4848 ..**Zegen,** Jeffrey H '69 (Zegen & F) -261 Mad Av -NY 10016 **Fx:**808-9808
(212) 858-7700 ..**Zeglarski,** Lori J '06 %Budd L -140 Bway -NY 10005
(212) 588-0022 ..**Zeglarski,** Robt L '05 %Sanders OV&R -501 Mad Av -NY 10022
(631) 249-4939 ..**Zeh,** Christopher W '99 (McNamara & Z PC) -560 Broadhllw Rd -Melvll 11747 **Fx:**249-4943
(315) 445-8670 ..**Zehe,** Theresa M '89 %MA Bjork -5784 Widewaters Pkwy -DeWitt 13214 **Fx:**445-8688
(212) 297-6155 ..**Zehner,** Nancy D '90 The Artemis Grp Ltd -420 Lex Av -NY 10170
(212) 223-0400 ..**Zeichner Ellman & Krause LLP** -575 Lex Av -NY 10022 **Fx:**753-0396
(212) 794-3885 ..**Zeichner,** Harvey '82 -304 E 65th -NY 10065
(212) 244-4431 ..**Zeichner,** Ira '73 -3 W 35th -NY 10001 **Fx:**594-0019
(718) 538-6100 ..**Zeichner,** Jeffrey '99 R Neiger -895 Sheridan Av -Bronx 10451 **Fx:**538-5101
(212) 223-0400 ..**Zeichner,** Mark '75 (Zeichner E&K LLP) -575 Lex Av -NY 10022
(718) 590-2000 ..**Zeidan,** Najah '09 %DA -198 E 161st -Bronx 10451 **Fx:**590-6477
(212) 541-2000 ..**Zeidel,** Adam E '09 %Bryan C LLP -1290 Av of Amer -NY 10104
(212) 735-3000 ..**Zeidel,** Michl J '96 (Skadden ASM&F LLP) -4 Times Sq -NY 10036
(914) 640-5250 ..**Zeidel,** Robin L '98 Starwood Hotels & Resorts -1111 Wstchstr Av -White Plns 10604
(845) 735-7000 ..**Zeiderman,** Lisa '05 %Johnson & C,LLP -1 Blue Hill Plz -Pearl Rvr 10965
(516) 921-4898 ..**Zeidman,** David S '75 -16 Donald Dr -Syosset 11791
(718) 340-4357 ..**Zeidman,** Steven M '82 %CUNY Law Schl -65-21 Main -Flushng 11367 **Fx:**340-4482
(516) 249-3450 ..**Zeidner,** Jennifer L '07 %Carman C&I,LLP -266 Main -Farmngdl 11735
(212) 805-0546 ..**Zeidner,** Lisa E '06 %Hon RC Casey USDC -500 Pearl -NY 10007
(212) 530-1800 ..**Zeif,** Doron E '03 %Richards K&O LLP -1 World Fncl Ctr -NY 10281
(212) 532-4000 ..**Zeif,** Robt S '68 (Dobrish ZG LLP) -757 3rd Av -NY 10017
(212) 222-1560 ..**Zeifer,** F Ellen '80 -322 Cntrl Pk W -NY 10025 **Fx:**662-7620
(845) 434-4777 ..**Zeiger,** Jay L '78 (Kalter KZ&F) -6166 State Rte 42 Bx30 -Woodbourne 12788
(845) 647-4110 ..**Zeiger,** Jay L '78 (Kalter KZ&F) -47 N Main Bx186 -Ellenvll 12428
(212) 431-2824 ..**Zeigler,** Donald H '72 %NY Law Schl -185 W Bway -NY 10013 **Fx:**431-9205
(212) 728-8000 ..**Zeigler,** Emily M '81 OfCnsl Willkie F&G LLP -787 7th Av -NY 10019
(315) 410-1389 ..**Zeigler,** Jason B '06 -333 E Onondaga -Syracuse 13202 **Fx:**410-1364
(518) 465-2333 ..**Zeigler,** Nadene E '95 (Hodgson R LLP) -677 Bway -Albany 12207
(646) 610-5330 ..**Zeigler,** Neldra Major '80 %Police Dept -1 Police Plz -NY 10038
(631) 727-0600 ..**Zeikowitz,** Steven E '95 %Fidelity Natl Title Ins -20 Commerce Dr -Rvrhead 11901 **Fx:**727-0606
(212) 818-9200 ..**Zeisler,** Aaron M '00 (Satterlee SB&B LLP) -230 Park Av -NY 10169
(212) 526-7599 ..**Zeisler,** Gwen J '04 %Lehman Bros -1271 Av of Amer -NY 10020
(212) 605-1658 ..**Zeiss,** Michl G '75 BMO Nesbitt Burns -3 Times Sq -NY 10036
(212) 907-0867 ..**Zeiss,** Nicole M '96 OfCnsl Labaton S LLP -140 Bway -NY 10005
(516) 365-6366 ..**Zeitlan,** Marilyn Labb '79 -37 Laurel Ln -Roslyn Hts 11577
(212) 697-3122 ..**Zeitler,** John G '09 %Martin C&B LLP -220 E 42nd -NY 10017
(518) 966-5500 ..**Zeitler,** Joyce Rice '87 -Route 32 N Bx425 -Greenvll 12083 **Fx:**966-5501
(718) 987-8444 ..**Zeitler,** Richd J '01 %Chelli & B -149 New Dorp Ln -Staten Isl 10306

(718) 596-6815 ..**Zeitlin**, David A '99 -50 Court -Brklyn 11201 **Fx**:522-5644
(212) 408-5100 ..**Zeitlin**, George E '54 (Chadbourne & P LLP) -30 Rckfllr Plz -NY 10112
(212) 940-8800 ..**Zeitlin**, Janeen Franki '03 Katten MR LLP -575 Mad Av -NY 10022
(212) 973-0325 ..**Zeitlin**, June H '74 Womens Environment & Devlpmnt -355 Lex Av -NY 10017
(718) 596-6815 ..**Zeitlin**, Stephen M '70 S Zeitlin,PC -50 Court -Brklyn 11201 **Fx**:522-5644
(212) 270-5551 ..**Zeitlin-Siegel**, Rhonda D '76 JP Morgan Chase -270 Park Av -NY 10017
(212) 370-4220 ..**Zeitoune**, Raymond '08 %CR Clark,PLLC -570 Lex Av -NY 10022 **Fx**:370-4270
(585) 419-8800 ..**Zeitounzian**, Kareen Vahe '06 %Harris B PLLC -99 Garnsey Rd -Pittsfrd 14534
(212) 373-3000 ..**Zeituni**, Karen R '10 %Paul WRW&G LLP -1285 Av of Amer -NY 10019
(212) 906-1200 ..**Zeitzer**, Taurie M '99 (Latham & W) -885 3rd Av -NY 10022
(212) 571-4080 ..**Zekaria**, Daphna '97 (Sokolski & Z,PC) -305 Bway -NY 10007 **Fx**:571-4079
(516) 466-6500 ..**Zekowski**, Brett A '00 %Parker WA LLP -6 Hrbr Park Dr S -Pt Wash 11050
(718) 658-9795 ..**Zelaya**, Ivette M '00 -9050 Parsons Blvd -Jamaica 11432 **Fx**:206-2291
(845) 855-1555 ..**Zelazny**, Gayle K '90 OfCnsl Marvin & M PLLC -3 W Main Bx420 -Pawling 12564 **Fx**:855-9526
(212) 225-2000 ..**Zelbo**, Howard S '88 (Cleary GS&H) -1 Lbrty Plz -NY 10006
(212) 302-2600 ..**Zelcer**, Harry '84 -22 W 38th -NY 10018 **Fx**:764-3269
(516) 742-7600 ..**Zeldin**, Lee M '04 %Raiser & K,PC -1517 Franklin Av -Mineola 11501
(212) 967-8500 ..**Zelen**, Clifford F '85 (Ross LRZ&F,LLP) -450 7th Av -NY 10123
(212) 964-7400 ..**Zelenetsky**, Ava L '00 Smith MDWY&Y,PC -111 John -NY 10038
(914) 725-4800 ..**Zelenetz**, Debora '98 %S Cooper & Assoc,PC -455 S Central Av -Scarsdale 10583 **Fx**:725-3217
(516) 944-3376 ..**Zeleniak**, Martha A '79 -7 Andvr -Pt Wash 11050
(718) 523-1111 ..**Zelenitz**, Bradley M '96 (Gildin Z&S,PC) -138-44 Qns Blvd -Briarwd 11435
(718) 590-2000 ..**Zelenka**, Wm '87 %DA -198 E 161st -Bronx 10451 **Fx**:590-6477
(212) 223-4000 ..**Zelenko**, Danl L '98 (Crowell & M LLP) -590 Mad Av -NY 10022
(212) 940-8800 ..**Zelensky**, Natalya S '10 %Katten MR LLP -575 Mad Av -NY 10022
(914) 761-4200 ..**Zelermyer**, Benjamin '71 Cnsl Steinberg & C,LLP -50 Main -White Plns 10606
(212) 577-3530 ..**Zelermyer**, Milton '90 %Leg Aid -199 Water -NY 10038 **Fx**:425-2465
(212) 986-6000 ..**Zelezen**, Kelly A '03 %Kleinberg KW&C,PC -551 5th Av -NY 10176
(212) 417-3700 ..**Zelhof**, Jeanette '86 %MFY Legal Srvcs -299 Bway -NY 10007 **Fx**:417-3890
(212) 701-3000 ..**Zelig**, Joshua M '07 %Cahill G&R LLP -80 Pine -NY 10005 **Fx**:269-5420
(212) 455-2000 ..**Zelig**, Peri L '08 %Simpson T&B LLP -425 Lex Av -NY 10017
(212) 867-5800 ..**Zeliger**, Benjamin A '05 %Osler H&H LLP -620 8th Av -NY 10018
(518) 285-8791 ..**Zeliger**, Jeremy A K '96 %OCA -187 Wolf Rd -Albany 12205
(212) 414-1250 ..**Zeligson**, Laurie '85 -96 5th Av -NY 10011
(212) 303-8043 ..**Zeligson**, Sheryl '89 Hadassah -50 W 58th -NY 10019 **Fx**:303-7436
(212) 454-3064 ..**Zelikoff**, Lina Gelfer '02 Deutsche Asset Mgmt -345 Park Av -NY 10154
(212) 558-5500 ..**Zelikovic**, Allan '82 %Weitz & L,PC -700 Bway -NY 10003
(212) 848-4000 ..**Zelin**, Brenda L '07 %Shearman & S LLP -599 Lex Av -NY 10022
(516) 997-6900 ..**Zelin**, Randy Scott '88 (RS Zelin,PC) -675 Old Cntry Rd -Westbury 11590 **Fx**:333-7333
(212) 558-4000 ..**Zelinger**, Chaim A '06 %Sullivan & C LLP -125 Broad -NY 10004
(718) 261-1226 ..**Zelinger**, Philip '93 -144-21 68th Av -Flushng 11367 **Fx**:261-6834
(212) 790-0200 ..**Zelinsky**, Edw A '88 Benj N Cardozo Schl of Law -55 5th Av -NY 10003 **Fx**:790-0345
(212) 728-8000 ..**Zelinsky**, Marina I '09 %Willkie F&G LLP -787 7th Av -NY 10019
(212) 354-7700 ..**Zelko**, Mark I '96 OfCnsl Penn PS&S -114 W 47th -NY 10036
(212) 836-8000 ..**Zelkowitz**, Joshua '10 %Kaye S LLP -425 Park Av -NY 10022
(212) 478-7200 ..**Zelkowitz**, Joshua E '06 %Hahn & H LLP -488 Mad Av -NY 10022
(516) 357-3700 ..**Zelkowitz**, Steven L '79 OfCnsl Cullen and D LLP -100 Q Roosevelt Blvd -Gdn Cty 11530
(315) 432-9171 ..**Zell**, Amy Maloney '01 POMCO -2425 James -Syracuse 13206
(212) 504-6000 ..**Zell**, Ariel I '08 %Cadwalader W&T LLP -1 World Fncl Ctr -NY 10281
(212) 223-0400 ..**Zell**, James N '99 OfCnsl Zeichner E&K LLP -575 Lex Av -NY 10022
(212) 750-7800 ..**Zellan**, Andrea L '97 %Brafman & Assoc -767 3rd Av -NY 10017 **Fx**:750-3906
(212) 341-6632 ..**Zellan**, Jeffrey S '96 NY Liquidation Bureau -123 William -NY 10038
(845) 369-2000 ..**Zeller**, Chas J '78 Avon Products -Avon Pl -Suffern 10901
(914) 699-6230 ..**Zeller**, Gabrielle H '98 %Zelco Industries -65 Haven Av -Mt Vernon 10553
(718) 263-9591 ..**Zeller**, Justin A '03 %H Dalton & Assoc,PC -69-12 Austin -Frst Hlls 11375 **Fx**:263-9598
(585) 232-6500 ..**Zeller**, M Stephanie '72 Cnsl Harter S&E LLP -1600 Bausch & Lomb Pl -Rchstr 14604
(212) 785-0090 ..**Zeller**, Paul W '73 Lambert Dvlpmnt LLC -5 Hanover Sq -NY 10004
(212) 446-8048 ..**Zeller**, Randi E '83 %McKinsey & Co -55 E 52nd -NY 10055 **Fx**:688-9521
(914) 273-3232 ..**Zellinger**, James A '77 -92 Round Hill Rd -Armonk 10504
(718) 286-6000 ..**Zellner**, Jessica L '01 %DA -125-01 Qns Blvd -Kew Gdns 11415
(212) 247-4650 ..**Zelma**, George P '69 -888 7th Av -NY 10106
(212) 869-5030 ..**Zelman**, Abner T '80 Cnsl Kucker & B,LLP -747 3rd Av -NY 10017
(212) 935-6020 ..**Zelman**, Andrew E '70 (Klein ZR LLP) -485 Mad Av -NY 10022
(716) 566-1300 ..**Zelman**, Arnold N '58 OfCnsl Hiscock & B,LLP -1100 M&T Ctr -Buffalo 14203
(516) 616-0707 ..**Zelman**, Bonita E '76 -2001 Marcus Av -Lk Success 11042 **Fx**:616-0761
(718) 604-3072 ..**Zelman**, David A '99 -612 Eastern Pkwy -Brklyn 11225 **Fx**:604-3074
(516) 433-0733 ..**Zelman**, Harriette G '78 -100 Jericho Quad -Jericho 11753
(212) 245-6100 ..**Zelman**, Stephen M '74 -888 7th Av -NY 10106 **Fx**:245-1231
(212) 337-4266 ..**Zelman**, Steven A '76 %Thomson Reuters/RIA -195 Bway -NY 10007 **Fx**:337-4213
(914) 245-0600 ..**Zelman Friedman**, Elizabeth '85 -1940 Commerce -Yorktwn Hts 10598
(212) 686-1515 ..**Zelmanovitch**, Yitzhak '04 Roran Capital -30 E 29th -NY 10016
(914) 765-6059 ..**Zelmanovitz**, Abraham I '02 IBM -1 N Castle Dr -Armonk 10504
(516) 569-1108 ..**Zelmanovitz**, Esther Schwartz '02 -4 Park Cir -Cedarhrst 11516
(212) 757-5000 ..**Zelmanovitz**, Jacob '02 %Sklover D&F,LLC -10 Rckfllr Plz -NY 10020 **Fx**:757-5002
(212) 826-6422 ..**Zelmanovitz**, Jos '81 (Stahl & Z) -747 3rd Av -NY 10017 **Fx**:826-6402
(718) 753-7279 ..**Zelmanovitz**, Judah A '06 -1734 E 31st -Brklyn 11234
(212) 309-6000 ..**Zelmanovitz**, Menachem O '78 (Morgan L&B LLP) -101 Park Av -NY 10178
(845) 426-5790 ..**Zelmanow**, Peter J '74 -11 N Airmont Rd -Suffern 10901 **Fx**:426-5793
(212) 953-6633 ..**Zelner**, Martin '64 SrCnsl Cox PS&S LLP -630 3rd Av -NY 10017
(212) 874-4026 ..**Zelnick**, Irene '63 -173 Riverside Dr -NY 10024 **Fx**:595-6907
(212) 735-8600 ..**Zelnick**, Jeanne '07 %Morrison C LLP -909 3rd Av -NY 10022
(212) 277-4000 ..**Zelnick**, Kimberly H '04 %Freshfields BD LLP -520 Mad Av -NY 10022
(212) 838-1177 ..**Zelnick**, Stephen '61 (Morse ZR&L LLP) -405 Park Av -NY 10022
(212) 733-6344 ..**Zelson**, Cindy M '87 Pfizer Inc -150 E 42nd -NY 10017
(212) 409-2800 ..**Zelson**, Steve T '83 Vector Tobacco -712 5th Av -NY 10019
(212) 310-8000 ..**Zeltner**, David E '78 (Weil G&M LLP) -767 5th Av -NY 10153
(914) 472-7700 ..**Zeltner**, Peter P '72 (Bertine HHZD&D,LLP) -700 Wht Plns Rd -Scarsdale 10583
(914) 472-7700 ..**Zeltner**, Wm R '01 (Bertine HHZD&D,LLP) -700 Wht Plns Rd -Scarsdale 10583
(212) 596-9000 ..**Zeltser**, Alexander '02 %Ropes & G LLP -1211 Av of Amer -NY 10036
(646) 205-7880 ..**Zeltser**, Alexander D '09 %Cruz & G & Assoc -110 William -NY 10038 **Fx**:(212) 233-9848
(212) 643-0105 ..**Zeltser**, Emanuel E '90 -2 Penn Plz -NY 10121 **Fx**:643-8254
(631) 755-0100 ..**Zeman-Bonnett**, Nicolle Y '98 (Smith & D,PA) -145 Pinelawn Rd -Melvll 11747
(212) 972-1000 ..**Zemann**, Danl Jr. '88 (London F LLP) -59 Maiden Ln -NY 10038
(718) 595-6533 ..**Zemble**, Karen S '98 DEP -59-17 Junction Blvd -Flushng 11373 **Fx**:595-6543
(212) 318-3000 ..**Zembrzuski**, James A '02 %Fulbright & J LLP -666 5th Av -NY 10103
(631) 577-7507 ..**Zemcik**, Mark S '90 %K Dodson -100 Baylis Rd -Melvll 11747 **Fx**:577-7199
(212) 546-9255 ..**Zemel**, Fred D '93 (Scarinci H) -107 Grand -NY 10013
(212) 819-8200 ..**Zemser**, Scott M '91 (White & C LLP) -1155 Av of Amer -NY 10036
(516) 485-3800 ..**Zemsky**, David E '85 (Zemsky & S,PC) -95 Front -Hempstd 11550 **Fx**:485-3280
(212) 490-3000 ..**Zemsky**, Jessica '07 %Wilson EME&D LLP -150 E 42nd -NY 10017
(212) 735-3000 ..**Zen**, Kevin L '09 %Skadden ASM&F LLP -4 Times Sq -NY 10036
(212) 708-1800 ..**Zendel**, Danl F '73 (Ladas & P) -26 W 61st -NY 10023
(845) 348-8074 ..**Zeng**, Ling '01 Barr Labs -2 Quaker Rd -Pomona 10970
(212) 839-5300 ..**Zeng**, Mingzhang '10 %Sidley A LLP -787 7th Av -NY 10019
(212) 373-3000 ..**Zeng**, Xun '08 %Paul WRW&G LLP -1285 Av of Amer -NY 10019
(516) 746-0180 ..**Zenir**, John M '89 (J Zenir,PC) -114 Old Cntry Rd -Mineola 11501 **Fx**:741-7853
(631) 723-2341 ..**Zenk**, Carolyn '89 -143 W Montauk Hwy -Hampton Bays 11946 **Fx**:723-2341
(212) 833-1110 ..**Zenkel**, Danl R '85 -875 3rd Av -NY 10022 **Fx**:355-6401
(212) 435-3571 ..**Zenkel**, Elliot L '72 %Port Auth of NY/NJ -225 Park Av S -NY 10003 **Fx**:435-3555
(212) 664-7200 ..**Zenkel**, Gary Burton '88 NBC Sports -30 Rckfllr Plz -NY 10112 **Fx**:664-5835
(212) 699-7084 ..**Zenker**, Jennifer A '06 Charmer Sunbelt Grp -60 E 42nd -NY 10165
(212) 587-5875 ..**Zenkewich**, John A '84 %State Ins Fund -199 Church -NY 10007 **Fx**:385-9199
(718) 636-1600 ..**Zeno**, Jesus M '86 -53 5th Av -Brklyn 11217
(212) 577-2523 ..**Zeno**, Mark W '87 %Ctr for Appllt Litigation -74 Trinity Pl -NY 10006 **Fx**:577-2535
(212) 380-8582 ..**Zenon**, Gregory W '99 -110 Wall -NY 10005 **Fx**:(440) 794-6686
(212) 872-1000 ..**Zensky**, David M '88 -One Bryant Park -NY 10036 **Fx**:872-1002
(212) 571-7000 ..**Zentner**, Michl D '01 %Petrocelli & C -217 Bway -NY 10007 **Fx**:571-6454
(315) 701-1115 ..**Zenzel**, Carol A '89 C Zenzel,PLLC -2507 James -Syracuse 13206 **Fx**:431-9771
(914) 937-2168 ..**Zepf**, Jos R '52 -2 Brower Pl -Pt Chester 10573
(631) 563-0133 ..**Zepf**, Thos P '99 -205 Greeley Av -Sayvll 11782 **Fx**:563-0130
(212) 964-9595 ..**Zepnick**, Jon A '02 OfCnsl S Zepnick,PC -61 Bway -NY 10006 **Fx**:732-0554
(212) 964-9595 ..**Zepnick**, Sol '53 -61 Bway -NY 10006 **Fx**:732-0554
(212) 602-1059 ..**Zeppieri**, Laurie '90 Deutsche Bk -60 Wall -NY 10005
(914) 835-7100 ..**Zeppieri**, Lisa Ann '05 %NY Title Rsch Corp -550 Mamaroneck Av -Harrison 10528
(516) 739-0400 ..**Zeppieri**, Loris '98 (Kelly R&K,LLP) -330 Old Cntry Rd -Mineola 11501
(631) 727-0110 ..**Zeppieri**, Loris '98 (Kelly R&K,LLP) -218 Griffing -Rvrhead 11901
(914) 287-0100 ..**Zerafa**, James D '97 %P Belefant -2 William -White Plns 10601 **Fx**:287-0500
(914) 946-5100 ..**Zerafa**, Michele J '97 %Bashian & F,LLP -235 Main -White Plns 10601
(212) 208-8758 ..**Zerarka**, Sabine '92 %Standard & Poor's -55 Water -NY 10041
(212) 223-4000 ..**Zerbe**, Rodney M '86 Cnsl Crowell & M LLP -590 Mad Av -NY 10022
(917) 604-1684 ..**Zerbib**, Frederic '09 -204 W 111th -NY 10026
(914) 285-9800 ..**Zerden**, Judith C '78 OfCnsl Kurzman EC&L,LLP -1 N Bway -White Plns 10601
(914) 961-3330 ..**Zerilli**, Robt F '99 -35 E Grassy Sprain Rd -Ynkrs 10710
(212) 490-3000 ..**Zerilli**, Tina '07 %Wilson EME&D LLP -150 E 42nd -NY 10017
(212) 968-8300 ..**Zeris**, James N '91 (Mintzer SZL&M LLP) -39 Bway -NY 10006
(212) 998-7494 ..**Zerkin**, Allen J '77 %NYU Negotn & Cnflct Rsolutn Prgm -4 Wshngtn Sq N -NY 10003 **Fx**:995-3890
(914) 428-0494 ..**Zern**, Martin H '67 -175 Main -White Plns 10601 **Fx**:949-6810

(212) 457-8598 ..**Zern,** Tova R '03 %J Sussman,PC -132 W 31st -NY 10001 **Fx:**457-8599
(516) 732-0008 ..**Zerner,** Scott B '94 -400 Post Av -Westbury 11590
(718) 326-3434 ..**Zero-Matuszewski,** Joelle '04 (Sabani R&Z-M,PC) -65-17 Grand Av -Maspeth 11378
(518) 449-5152 ..**Zeronda,** Francis J '79 -7 Crumitie Rd -Loudonvll 12211
(914) 225-5510 ..**Zervas,** Amy '02 Morgan Stanley -2000 Wstchstr Av -Purchase 10577
(212) 383-2672 ..**Zervas,** Katerina '06 State Comptroller -59 Maiden Ln -NY 10038 **Fx:**383-3901
(718) 298-1079 ..**Zervopoulos,** Alexandra '93 %Hon J Rios -88-11 Sutphin Blvd -Jamaica 11435
(212) 267-1950 ..**Zervopoulos,** John '01 %Salenger SSK&B,LLP -233 Bway -NY 10279
(212) 439-6995 ..**Zervos,** Joanne A '87 -144 E 84th -NY 10028 **Fx:**772-3324
(516) 773-3516 ..**Zervos,** Mitra Kavoussi '92 (Zervos & K) -505 Nrthrn Blvd -Gt Neck 11021 **Fx:**759-6120
(212) 508-6700 ..**Zervoudakis,** Christina '08 %Tannenbaum HS&H LLP -900 3rd Av -NY 10022
(516) 227-0700 ..**Zerykier,** Aaron E '03 %Farrell F,PC -1320 RXR Plz -Uniondale 11556
(718) 357-5898 ..**Zessimopoulos,** Mona '89 M Zessimopoulos,PC -42-40 Bell Blvd -Bayside 11361 **Fx:**357-3127
(212) 850-4852 ..**Zetes,** Maria J '88 %Emigrant Svngs Bk -5 E 42nd -NY 10017 **Fx:**850-4424
(212) 682-6800 ..**Zetlin & De Chiara LLP** -801 2nd Av -NY 10017 **Fx:**682-6861
(212) 682-6800 ..**Zetlin,** Michl S '86 (Zetlin & D LLP) -801 2nd Av -NY 10017
(212) 230-8800 ..**Zetlin-Jones,** J David '07 %WilmerHale -399 Park Av -NY 10022
(212) 416-8882 ..**Zeve,** Oren L '93 %Dept of Law -120 Bway -NY 10271
(212) 732-3320 ..**Zevgaras,** Ioanna O '04 %Short & B,PC -217 Bway -NY 10007
(516) 747-8600 ..**Zevin,** Marvin '66 (Yannelli & Z) -100 Grdn City Plz -Gdn Cty 11530
(914) 633-5600 ..**Zezima,** Ronald V '83 -271 North Av -New Rchll 10801 **Fx:**633-8998
(914) 422-4034 ..**Zezula,** Tiffany B '04 Land Use Law Ctr -78 N Bway -White Plns 10603
(212) 336-2000 ..**Zgliniec,** Sarah E '98 (Patterson BW&T LLP) -1133 Av of Amer -NY 10036
(212) 450-4000 ..**Zha,** James Z Y '07 %Davis P&W LLP -450 Lex Av -NY 10017
(212) 790-9200 ..**Zhadina,** Anastasia '03 %Cowan L&L,PC -1133 Av of Amer -NY 10036
(212) 909-0422 ..**Zhai,** Jin '01 CIFG Assurance NA -825 3rd Av -NY 10022
(212) 450-4000 ..**Zhang,** Daying '09 %Davis P&W LLP -450 Lex Av -NY 10017
(718) 463-1111 ..**Zhang,** Dehai '01 -136-20 38th Av -Flushng 11354 **Fx:**463-1378
(212) 736-0007 ..**Zhang,** Guohui '06 Weiss I PLLC -462 7th Av -NY 10018
(212) 267-0608 ..**Zhang,** Henry '01 Zhang & Assoc,PC -325 Bway -NY 10007
(212) 909-6000 ..**Zhang,** Huyue Angela '09 %Debevoise & P LLP -919 3rd Av -NY 10022
(212) 474-1000 ..**Zhang,** Jenny X '10 %Cravath S&M LLP -825 8th Av -NY 10019
(212) 839-5300 ..**Zhang,** Jinfei '06 %Sidley A LLP -787 7th Av -NY 10019
(212) 903-9000 ..**Zhang,** Jingsong Jeffrey '06 %Linklaters -1345 Av of Amer -NY 10105
(212) 903-8700 ..**Zhang,** Libin '09 %Roberts & H,LLP -825 8th Av -NY 10019
(212) 326-3939 ..**Zhang,** Lulu '09 %Jones D -222 E 41st -NY 10017
(718) 939-4633 ..**Zhang,** Mengxi '09 KK Tung PC -38-21 Main -Flushng 11354 **Fx:**939-4468
(212) 343-0730 ..**Zhang,** Michl Y '09 -401 Bway -NY 10013 **Fx:**343-0782
(212) 308-2608 ..**Zhang,** Philip Xuan '02 -305 Bway -NY 10007
(212) 765-5070 ..**Zhang,** T Tony '08 %Fish & R,PC -153 E 53rd -NY 10022
(212) 326-3939 ..**Zhang,** Wei '07 %Jones D -222 E 41st -NY 10017
(212) 474-1000 ..**Zhang,** Wenying '10 %Cravath S&M LLP -825 8th Av -NY 10019
(607) 723-5341 ..**Zhang,** Xiaoqin '03 %Hinman H&K,LLP -80 Exchange Bx5250 -Bnghmtn 13902
(212) 446-4800 ..**Zhang,** Xiaoyan '08 %Kirkland & E LLP -153 E 53rd -NY 10022
(212) 450-4000 ..**Zhang,** Yan '05 %Davis P&W LLP -450 Lex Av -NY 10017
(212) 326-2000 ..**Zhang,** Yan '07 %O'Melveny & M LLP -7 Times Sq -NY 10036
(212) 373-3000 ..**Zhang,** Yun '04 %Paul WRW&G LLP -1285 Av of Amer -NY 10019
(212) 530-5000 ..**Zhang,** Zen Zhen '10 %Milbank TH&M LLP -1 Chase Manh Plz -NY 10005
(212) 625-0511 ..**Zhang,** Zhong Yue '98 Zhang & Assoc,LLC -401 Bway -NY 10013 **Fx:**625-0516
(212) 836-8000 ..**Zhang-Whitaker,** Pang '01 %Kaye S LLP -425 Park Av -NY 10022
(212) 867-3600 ..**Zhao,** Jenny J '05 OfCnsl S Tulman -369 Lex Av -NY 10017 **Fx:**867-1914
(718) 837-1048 ..**Zhao,** Jianbo K '04 -6626 Cameron Ct -Brklyn 11204 **Fx:**837-1048
(718) 939-4633 ..**Zhao,** Kun '06 %KK Tung PC -38-21 Main -Flushng 11354 **Fx:**939-4468
(212) 326-2000 ..**Zhao,** Lucy R '09 %O'Melveny & M LLP -7 Times Sq -NY 10036
(212) 236-6031 ..**Zheng,** Jen '02 Merrill Lynch -2 World Fncl Ctr -NY 10281
(718) 766-5242 ..**Zheng,** Qiteng '09 (Milner & Z) -8302 Bway -Elmhrst 11373
(718) 544-3635 ..**Zheng,** T Justin '09 %J Siegel & Assoc,PLLC -108-18 Qns Blvd -Frst Hlls 11375 **Fx:**544-7812
(212) 558-4000 ..**Zheng,** Yeqing '10 %Sullivan & C LLP -125 Broad -NY 10004
(212) 343-2168 ..**Zheng,** Yi '02 -401 Bway -NY 10013
(718) 888-8880 ..**Zheng,** Yuan '06 %Dai & Assoc,PC -136-20 38th Av -Flushng 11354 **Fx:**888-9270
(212) 425-7200 ..**Zhong,** Jialin '08 %Kenyon & K,LLP -1 Bway -NY 10004
(718) 888-9961 ..**Zhong,** Jianhua '04 -39-01 Main -Flushng 11354
(718) 939-4633 ..**Zhong,** Quantang '06 %KK Tung PC -38-21 Main -Flushng 11354 **Fx:**939-4468
(212) 406-0108 ..**Zhou,** Gang '98 -277 Bway -NY 10007
(212) 225-2000 ..**Zhou,** Jason '09 %Cleary GS&H -1 Lbrty Plz -NY 10006
(212) 530-5000 ..**Zhou,** Jenny H '10 %Milbank TH&M LLP -1 Chase Manh Plz -NY 10005
(212) 643-8203 ..**Zhou,** Jian '00 (Zhang & Assoc,PC) -1350 Bway -NY 10018 **Fx:**643-5487
(718) 539-7098 ..**Zhou,** Joe Zhenghong '99 -136-20 38th Av -Flushng 11354 **Fx:**539-7177
(212) 537-9000 ..**Zhou,** Lanlan Linda '07 %Cohen G&S,LLP -850 3rd Av -NY 10022
(212) 226-9442 ..**Zhou,** Oliver G '96 -41 Elizabeth -NY 10013
(212) 703-8702 ..**Zhou,** Xiao Lin '93 -630 5th Av -NY 10111 **Fx:**703-8720
(212) 530-5000 ..**Zhou,** Yeping '07 %Milbank TH&M LLP -1 Chase Manh Plz -NY 10005
(212) 225-2000 ..**Zhou,** Zheng '08 %Cleary GS&H -1 Lbrty Plz -NY 10006
(212) 318-6000 ..**Zhu,** B Chen '08 %Paul HJ&W LLP -75 E 55th -NY 10022
(212) 227-2245 ..**Zhu,** Michl H '95 -14 Wall -NY 10005
(212) 530-5000 ..**Zhu,** Victoria L '08 %Milbank TH&M LLP -1 Chase Manh Plz -NY 10005
(718) 353-8380 ..**Zhu,** Wei '06 -36-40 Main -Flushng 11354
(516) 742-4343 ..**Zhu,** Xiaochun '03 (Scully SM&P PC) -400 Grdn City Plz -Gdn Cty 11530
(212) 883-1700 ..**Zhu,** Xin Liang '09 %Duval & S LLP -101 Park Av -NY 10178
(718) 888-0963 ..**Zhu,** Yiming '93 -136-56 39th Av -Flushng 11354
(212) 704-6000 ..**Zhuang,** Yuan '09 %Troutman S LLP -405 Lex Av -NY 10174
(212) 779-8600 ..**Zia,** Adam D '05 %Silverman SS&B PLLC -381 Park Av S -NY 10016
(718) 645-3111 ..**Ziabkin,** Andrei V '01 %Leg Aid Society Ofc for the Aging -111 Lvngstn -Brklyn 11201 **Fx:**260-4722
(212) 302-6574 ..**Ziabkina,** Natasha G '99 (Riker DSH&P LLP) -500 5th Av -NY 10110
(718) 238-6110 ..**Ziade,** Richd '96 -241 87th -Brklyn 11209
(212) 290-4700 ..**Ziai,** Fatemeh '91 %Human Rights Watch -350 5th Av -NY 10118 **Fx:**736-1300
(585) 678-7100 ..**Ziakas,** Helen E '95 %Constellation Brands -207 Hgh Pnt Dr -Victor 14564
(212) 308-3999 ..**Ziavras,** Katherine H '89 %Akst & A -150 E 58th -NY 10155 **Fx:**317-2946
(212) 232-1300 ..**Zibas,** Jura Christine '95 (Lewis BB&S LLP) -77 Water -NY 10005
(518) 474-7700 ..**Zibell,** Eileen '83 %NYS OPWDD -44 Holland Av -Albany 12229 **Fx:**474-7382
(914) 699-0700 ..**Zibelli,** Jos R '49 -22 W 1st -Mt Vernon 10550 **Fx:**667-2872
(212) 355-4149 ..**Zibkow,** Jill L '94 Goldweber E LLP -635 Mad Av -NY 10022
(585) 232-6500 ..**Zicari,** Craig J '75 (Harter S&E LLP) -1600 Bausch & Lomb Pl -Rchstr 14604
(914) 328-2810 ..**Ziccardi,** Matthew A Jr. '99 (Ziccardi & R,PC) -237 Mamaroneck Av -White Plns 10605 **Fx:**328-2812
(203) 348-5433 ..**Ziccardi,** Richd M '77 (Xylas & Z,LLP) -240 E 86th -NY 10028 **Fx:**961-1183
(212) 792-4214 ..**Zich,** Jonathan '78 Glastonbury Capital LLC -245 Park Av -NY 10167
(212) 972-5560 ..**Zichello & McIntyre,LLP** -60 E 42nd -NY 10165 **Fx:**972-5569
(212) 972-5560 ..**Zichello,** Vincent J '65 (Zichello & M,LLP) -60 E 42nd -NY 10165
(212) 382-0909 ..**Zicherman,** Michl S '93 (Peckar & A,PC) -41 Mad Av -NY 10154
(212) 474-1000 ..**Zicherman,** Sharon S '09 %Cravath S&M LLP -825 8th Av -NY 10019
(212) 742-9280 ..**Zick,** Kimberly M '07 Waterfront Comm -39 Bway -NY 10006 **Fx:**480-0587
(585) 343-0811 ..**Zickl,** Randolph P '65 -81 Main -Batavia 14020 **Fx:**343-0880
(585) 344-2550 ..**Zickl,** Robt R '84 %DA -1 W Main -Batavia 14020 **Fx:**344-8544
(585) 344-2550 ..**Zickl,** Wm G '87 %DA -1 W Main -Batavia 14020 **Fx:**344-8544
(212) 715-9100 ..**Zide,** Stephen D '05 %Kramer LN&F,LLP -1177 Av of Amer -NY 10036
(212) 629-0454 ..**Ziedalski,** Bozena '00 -350 5th Av -NY 10118
(212) 968-2300 ..**Zieden-Weber,** Wm G '93 Chartwell Law Ofc,LLP -39 Bway -NY 10006 **Fx:**968-2400
(212) 474-1000 ..**Ziefert,** Jon S '95 %Cravath S&M LLP -825 8th Av -NY 10019
(212) 354-0808 ..**Ziegelman,** Andrea R '90 (Moses P&Z,LLP) -1065 Av of Amer -NY 10018
(212) 596-9000 ..**Ziegler,** Alyssa '10 %Ropes & G LLP -1211 Av of Amer -NY 10036
(716) 845-9469 ..**Ziegler,** Amy J '88 %Supreme Ct -25 Delaware Av -Buffalo 14202 **Fx:**851-3293
(516) 296-7000 ..**Ziegler,** Andrea C '82 %Certilman BA&H,LLP -90 Merrick Av -E Meadow 11554
(518) 477-7951 ..**Ziegler,** April A '00 (Maney M&L) -77 Troy Rd -E Greenbush 12061
(516) 296-7000 ..**Ziegler,** Brian K '81 (Certilman BA&H,LLP) -90 Merrick Av -E Meadow 11554
(212) 947-6441 ..**Ziegler,** Catherine A '84 Henegan Construction -250 W 30th -NY 10001 **Fx:**736-0696
(212) 213-0030 ..**Ziegler,** George P '61 (Ziegler & R) -25 W 43rd -NY 10036 **Fx:**696-9417
(718) 370-7030 ..**Ziegler,** Irene '90 (Amabile & E,PC) -1000 South Av -Staten Isl 10314
(631) 265-2550 ..**Ziegler,** Joel J '68 (Greshin Z&A) -199 E Main Bx829 -Smithtwn 11787
(716) 851-3404 ..**Ziegler,** John A '83 %Hon R Sconiers -77 W Eagle -Buffalo 14202 **Fx:**851-3328
(516) 742-3773 ..**Ziegler,** Jordan A '92 (Brecher FPWT&Z,PC) -1325 Franklin Av -Gdn Cty 11530
(516) 688-1700 ..**Ziegler,** Laurence D '71 %IRS -1600 Stewart Av -Westbury 11590 **Fx:**688-1750
(718) 264-9162 ..**Ziegler,** Leonard H '82 -139-69 73rd Ter -Flushng 11367 **Fx:**264-9167
(212) 692-1000 ..**Ziegler,** Michl L '76 (Duane M LLP) -1540 Bway -NY 10036
(516) 367-7610 ..**Ziegler,** Noel Mary '85 -Bx336 -Woodbury 11797 **Fx:**692-4501
(212) 891-1600 ..**Ziegler,** Richd F '76 (Jenner & B LLP) -919 3rd Av -NY 10022
(212) 584-5100 ..**Ziegler,** Ruth Ann '96 Sirius Satellite Radio -1221 Av of Amer -NY 10020
(212) 593-7979 ..**Ziegler Sagal & Winters,PC** -575 Lex Av -NY 10022
(212) 319-7600 ..**Ziegler,** Scott A '86 (Ziegler Z & Assoc LLP) -570 Lex Av -NY 10022 **Fx:**319-7605
(212) 593-7979 ..**Ziegler,** Stephen S '59 (Ziegler S&W,PC) -575 Lex Av -NY 10022
(212) 425-9300 ..**Ziegler,** Tobias F '09 %Bressler A&R,PC -17 State -NY 10004
(212) 310-8000 ..**Ziegler,** Venera E '03 %Weil G&M LLP -767 5th Av -NY 10153
(212) 558-4000 ..**Ziegler,** Wm A '49 SrCnsl Sullivan & C LLP -125 Broad -NY 10004
(212) 818-9200 ..**Ziegler,** Wm R '68 OfCnsl Satterlee SB&B LLP -230 Park Av -NY 10169
(212) 561-7700 ..**Ziehl,** Dean A '03 (Pachulski SZ&J) -780 3rd Av -NY 10017
(212) 704-6000 ..**Zielaznicki,** Karl M '88 OfCnsl Troutman S LLP -405 Lex Av -NY 10174
(315) 724-3158 ..**Zielenski-McGahey,** Anne M '01 %Kelly & W -239 Genesee -Utica 13501
(212) 691-0950 ..**Zielinski,** Christine E '07 Ctr for Family Representation -116 John -NY 10038
(212) 483-9490 ..**Zielinski,** Joshua A '00 (McElroy DM&C,LLP) -88 Pine -NY 10005
(585) 335-6031 ..**Zielinski,** Wm S Jr. '49 -15 Clara Barton -Dansvll 14437 **Fx:**335-3654

(585) 263-1000 ..**Ziemba**, Leah V '07 %Nixon P LLP -1100 Clinton Sq -Rchstr 14604
(212) 918-4496 ..**Ziemba**, Peter M '83 WisdomTree Invstmnts -48 Wall -NY 10005 **Fx**:918-4582
(845) 294-9432 ..**Ziemelis**, Hugh Scott '92 -51 Greenwich Av Bx954 -Goshen 10924 **Fx**:691-1512
(212) 761-6102 ..**Ziemer**, Elayna M '94 %Morgan Stanley -1585 Bway -NY 10036
(212) 773-2393 ..**Zieminski**, Stephen E '09 Ernst & Young -5 Times Sq -NY 10036
(212) 298-5040 ..**Zien**, Marnie L '04 Leg Aid -49 Thomas -NY 10013 **Fx**:298-5252
(212) 270-2435 ..**Zients**, Michl R '83 JP Morgan Chase -245 Park Av -NY 10167
(718) 260-4501 ..**Zier**, Jill Hanekamp '92 USDC-EDNY -225 Cadman Plz E -Brklyn 11201
(212) 259-8000 ..**Ziering**, Zhanna A '08 %Dewey & L LLP -1301 Av of Amer -NY 10019
(212) 403-1000 ..**Zieske**, Alison M '07 %Wachtell LR&K -51 W 52nd -NY 10019
(212) 735-3000 ..**Ziessler**, Martin '96 Cnsl Skadden ASM&F LLP -4 Times Sq -NY 10036
(212) 836-8000 ..**Zifchak**, Wm C '74 (Kaye S LLP) -425 Park Av -NY 10022
(212) 735-3000 ..**Ziff**, Elaine D '83 Cnsl Skadden ASM&F LLP -4 Times Sq -NY 10036
(212) 728-8000 ..**Ziff**, Eric S '10 %Willkie F&G LLP -787 7th Av -NY 10019
(718) 265-2211 ..**Ziff**, Jeffrey '75 -2875 W 8th -Brklyn 11224 **Fx**:265-2252
(212) 292-6503 ..**Ziff**, Robt D '99 Ziff Brothers Invstmnts -153 E 53rd -NY 10022
(516) 571-3800 ..**Ziff**, Wm H '07 %DA -262 Old Cntry Rd -Mineola 11501 **Fx**:248-9479
(212) 506-1700 ..**Ziffer**, Adam S '96 (Kasowitz BT&F LLP) -1633 Bway -NY 10019
(212) 925-9100 ..**Ziffer**, Jay H '86 (Reddy L&Z,PC) -85 Worth -NY 10013
(212) 957-2525 ..**Ziffer**, Matthew J '97 %1 William St Capital -1271 Av of Amer -NY 10020
(516) 681-1100 ..**Zigelman**, Michl L '99 %Kaufman DV&G,LLP -135 Crsswys Park Dr -Woodbury 11797
(212) 310-8000 ..**Zigman**, Abigail L '07 %Weil G&M LLP -767 5th Av -NY 10153
(516) 294-6410 ..**Zigman**, Alan S '93 S Cohn -1 Old Cntry Rd -Carle Pl 11514 **Fx**:294-0094
(212) 373-2480 ..**Zigman**, Anita J '85 Paul WRW&G LLP -1285 Av of Amer -NY 10019
(516) 827-1441 ..**Zigman**, David B '88 -103 Forest Dr -Jericho 11753
(718) 520-3740 ..**Zigman**, Gail S '78 %Supr Ct -88-11 Qns Blvd -Jamaica 11435
(212) 310-8000 ..**Zigmund**, Jesse B '05 %Weil G&M LLP -767 5th Av -NY 10153
(212) 885-5000 ..**Zikas**, Jonas S '08 %Blank R LLP -405 Lex Av -NY 10174
(212) 909-6000 ..**Zilanawala**, Munir '09 %Debevoise & P LLP -919 3rd Av -NY 10022
(212) 859-8000 ..**Zilberberg**, David A '99 %Fried FHS&J LLP -1 NY Plz -NY 10004
(212) 558-4000 ..**Zilberberg**, Eduardo '10 %Sullivan & C LLP -125 Broad -NY 10004
(718) 256-2000 ..**Zilberberg**, Mendel '95 (M Zilberberg & Assoc,PC) -6619 13th Av -Brklyn 11219 **Fx**:256-7900
(914) 720-7532 ..**Zilberfein**, Paul S '94 -78 Old Orchrd Rd -New Rchll 10804 **Fx**:297-6444
(212) 687-7800 ..**Zilberg**, Michl '98 (Certain & Z,PLLC) -909 3rd Av -NY 10017 **Fx**:687-7801
(212) 608-2629 ..**Zilbergeld**, Benjamin H '10 %Gregory & R,PC -111 Bway -NY 10006
(518) 466-9600 ..**Zilgme**, Arnis '85 -29 New Shaker Rd -Albany 12205
(646) 722-8500 ..**Zilka**, Diane '86 SrCnsl Grant & E,PA -485 Lex Av -NY 10017
(212) 819-8200 ..**Zilkha**, Nazim '91 (White & C LLP) -1155 Av of Amer -NY 10036
(716) 636-7600 ..**Ziller**, Arthur J '79 OfCnsl HoganWillig -2410 N Forest Rd -Amherst 14068
(212) 983-6900 ..**Ziluck**, Scott A '95 %Kaplan & L PC -630 3rd Av -NY 10017
(212) 344-5400 ..**Zilz**, Hillary S '95 OfCnsl Schlam S&D LLP -26 Bway -NY 10004
(914) 375-0100 ..**Zim**, Craig D '90 (Novick ELRW&L,PC) -733 Ynkrs Av -Ynkrs 10704
(212) 644-1857 ..**Zim**, Eric M '90 (Horwitz & Z,PC) -250 W 57th -NY 10107 **Fx**:644-6553
(212) 735-3000 ..**Ziman**, Kenneth S '92 (Skadden ASM&F LLP) -4 Times Sq -NY 10036
(212) 808-7800 ..**Zimand**, Harvey F '57 (Kelley D&W LLP) -101 Park Av -NY 10178
(914) 681-7175 ..**Zimbalist**, Lisa B '95 %Bartels & F LLP -925 Wstchstr Av -White Plns 10604
(914) 366-7210 ..**Zimbardo**, Ralph J '73 %Stinnes Corp -120 Wht Plns Rd -Tarrytwn 10591 **Fx**:366-8226
(347) 404-9133 ..**Zimberg**, Joyce S '84 %Civil Ct -141 Lvngstn -Brklyn 11201 **Fx**:(718) 643-3733
(646) 610-8404 ..**Zimberg**, Stephanie L '81 NYPD - Legal Bureau -1 Police Plz -NY 10038
(607) 776-9631 ..**Zimberlin**, John F '04 Pub Def -3 E Pulteney Sq -Bath 14810 **Fx**:664-2496
(914) 238-1377 ..**Zimet**, Barbara T R '75 (Grimes & Z) -16 S Bedford Rd -Chappaqua 10514
(212) 570-6375 ..**Zimet**, Barbara T R '75 (Grimes & Z) -33 E 70th -NY 10021
(212) 748-0919 ..**Zimet**, Jonathan D '82 Supreme Ct -100 Centre -NY 10013
(212) 436-2317 ..**Zimet**, Lee G '85 Deloitte & Touche,LLP -2 World Fncl Ctr -NY 10281
(212) 735-3000 ..**Zimet**, Robt E '75 (Skadden ASM&F LLP) -4 Times Sq -NY 10036
(718) 940-9365 ..**Zimet**, Sidney '32 -400 Rugby -Brklyn 11226
(212) 554-2600 ..**Zimiles**, Ellen Silverman '84 Daylight Forensic -1 Rckfllr Plz -NY 10020
(631) 913-4444 ..**Zimler**, Michl D '80 -5 Orvll Dr -Bohemia 11716
(631) 852-2339 ..**Zimmer**, Cheryl M '80 %Hon HP Leis III -235 Griffing Av -Rvrhead 11901
(516) 785-5246 ..**Zimmer**, Donald J '52 -3470 Homestead Av -Wantagh 11793
(212) 858-1000 ..**Zimmer**, Elizabeth '03 Cnsl Pillsbury WSP LLP -1540 Bway -NY 10036
(212) 831-6554 ..**Zimmer**, Emanuel '54 -11 E 86th -NY 10028 **Fx**:534-6826
(212) 755-5200 ..**Zimmer**, Gregory '00 SpclCnsl Smith V PLLC -509 Mad Av -NY 10022 **Fx**:755-5203
(315) 422-9909 ..**Zimmer**, Kimberly M '89 (Zimmer Law Ofc,PLLC) -333 E Onondaga -Syracuse 13202 **Fx**:422-7741
(212) 744-7410 ..**Zimmer**, Mary Ann '76 -401 E 74th -NY 10021
(631) 470-4872 ..**Zimmer**, Ronald S '00 -6080 Jericho Tpk -Commack 11725 **Fx**:499-1549
(212) 944-0500 ..**Zimmer**, Sharon M '74 (Hofheimer G&G,LLP) -530 5th Av -NY 10036 **Fx**:897-4986
(631) 979-1111 ..**Zimmer**, Steven R '78 -400 Townline Rd -Hauppauge 11788 **Fx**:979-1695
(631) 493-0278 ..**Zimmer**, Todd J '93 -6080 Jericho Tpk -Commack 11725 **Fx**:499-1549
(845) 371-7680 ..**Zimmerer Murray Conyngham & Kunzier** -10 Esquire Rd -New Cty 10956
(212) 308-0210 ..**Zimmerli**, Cheryl '01 -110 E 59th -NY 10022 **Fx**:308-0213
(315) 475-7777 ..**Zimmerman**, Aaron M '77 -117 S State -Syracuse 13202 **Fx**:475-4225
(718) 990-6624 ..**Zimmerman**, Adam S '04 St John's Law Schl -8000 Utopia Pkwy -Jamaica 11439 **Fx**:591-1855
(718) 613-2170 ..**Zimmerman**, Aron M '07 %Hon L Bloom US Magistrate -225 Cadman Plz E -Brklyn 11201
(212) 869-3500 ..**Zimmerman**, Bradley S '92 (J Fuchsberg Law Firm,LLP) -500 5th Av -NY 10110 **Fx**:398-1532
(718) 855-6413 ..**Zimmerman**, Brian J '86 -44 Court -Brklyn 11201
(212) 289-5756 ..**Zimmerman**, Carol P '77 -49 E 96th -NY 10128 **Fx**:831-0495
(212) 227-0347 ..**Zimmerman**, Cory I '93 %Weiss W&W,PC -25 Park Pl -NY 10007
(212) 481-3818 ..**Zimmerman**, Dana B '95 Fidelity Natl Title Ins -1 Park Av -NY 10016 **Fx**:481-8747
(212) 701-3000 ..**Zimmerman**, Danl F '02 %Cahill G&R LLP -80 Pine -NY 10005 **Fx**:269-5420
(212) 789-2000 ..**Zimmerman**, David '87 %NHL -1251 Av of Amer -NY 10020 **Fx**:789-2050
(716) 849-1333 ..**Zimmerman**, David C '95 (Lipsitz GSC LLP) -42 Delaware Av -Buffalo 14202
(917) 703-4849 ..**Zimmerman**, Derryl '00 -930 E 223rd -Bronx 10466 **Fx**:(718) 654-2114
(212) 998-6250 ..**Zimmerman**, Diane L '77 %NYU Law Schl -40 Wshngtn Sq S -NY 10012 **Fx**:995-4881
(212) 728-8000 ..**Zimmerman**, Drew J '05 %Willkie F&G LLP -787 7th Av -NY 10019
(212) 389-5000 ..**Zimmerman**, Earl S '93 (Sutherland A&B LLP) -1114 Av of Amer -NY 10036
(716) 652-0056 ..**Zimmerman**, Edw M '64 -358 North -E Aurora 14052
(518) 736-2900 ..**Zimmerman**, Eleanor M '93 %Hodgson R LLP -55 E Main -Johnstwn 12095
(212) 836-1312 ..**Zimmerman**, Ellen R '81 UJA-Federation -130 E 59th -NY 10022 **Fx**:836-1779
(212) 705-7000 ..**Zimmerman**, Emily '08 %Bingham M LLP -399 Park Av -NY 10022
(212) 735-3000 ..**Zimmerman**, George '80 (Skadden ASM&F LLP) -4 Times Sq -NY 10036
(315) 475-3322 ..**Zimmerman**, Golda '84 G Zimmerman,PC -711 E Genesee -Syracuse 13210 **Fx**:475-7727
(516) 764-7745 ..**Zimmerman**, Harvey '56 -540 Rebecca Ln -Oceanside 11572 **Fx**:764-2702
(212) 949-9696 ..**Zimmerman**, Ira Brandt '51 -60 E 42nd -NY 10165 **Fx**:949-6241
(646) 829-4368 ..**Zimmerman**, Ivan '85 WNYC -160 Varick -NY 10013
(631) 231-1450 ..**Zimmerman**, Jason F '90 %Feldman K&M,PC -330 Vndrblt Motor Pkwy -Hauppauge 11788
(212) 705-7000 ..**Zimmerman**, Jay S '81 (Bingham M LLP) -399 Park Av -NY 10022
(866) 261-5656 ..**Zimmerman**, Jean '80 Arrowsight,Inc -45 Kensico Dr -Mt Kisco 10549
(914) 750-5933 ..**Zimmerman**, Jean E '89 %Kissel H&W LLP -580 Wht Plns Rd -Tarrytwn 10591
(212) 334-3543 ..**Zimmerman**, Jeffrey I '03 DMA -446 Bway -NY 10013
(212) 364-8536 ..**Zimmerman**, Jeffrey M '85 Time Warner Cable -60 Columbus Av -NY 10023 **Fx**:364-8460
(212) 537-2450 ..**Zimmerman**, Jennifer H '89 Morgan Stanley -1633 Bway -NY 10019
(516) 228-3355 ..**Zimmerman**, Jodi B '08 %L Edelstein -300 Grdn City Plz -Gdn Cty 11530 **Fx**:228-3356
(212) 408-4276 ..**Zimmerman**, Jory B '86 Bk of NY -1290 Av of Amer -NY 10104
(212) 966-8533 ..**Zimmerman**, K Steven '00 -305 Bway -NY 10007 **Fx**:693-1410
(716) 853-9555 ..**Zimmerman**, Karla J '98 %Leg Aid -237 Main -Buffalo 14203 **Fx**:853-3219
(212) 232-1300 ..**Zimmerman**, Kevin '07 %Lewis BB&S LLP -77 Water -NY 10005
(518) 429-4200 ..**Zimmerman**, Lawr A '76 (Hiscock & B,LLP) -50 Beaver -Albany 12207
(212) 977-9700 ..**Zimmerman**, Marc B '95 (Phillips N LLP) -666 5th Av -NY 10103
(212) 689-0931 ..**Zimmerman**, Mark E '70 (Zimmerman & M) -333 E 30th -NY 10016 **Fx**:689-0934
(212) 247-7272 ..**Zimmerman**, Michl A '75 OfCnsl Kane K,PC -1350 Av of Amer -NY 10019
(212) 907-7300 ..**Zimmerman**, Pamela B '07 %Golenbock EAB&P -437 Mad Av -NY 10022
(212) 554-7800 ..**Zimmerman**, Philippe A '92 (Moses & S LLP) -405 Lex Av -NY 10174
(212) 962-1818 ..**Zimmerman**, Richd A '84 -233 Bway -NY 10279 **Fx**:(240) 218-6456
(212) 907-7300 ..**Zimmerman**, Robt B '76 (Golenbock EAB&P) -437 Mad Av -NY 10022
(212) 891-9100 ..**Zimmerman**, Robt M '99 (Goldfarb & F LLP) -345 Park Av -NY 10154
(585) 289-4040 ..**Zimmerman**, Robt W '82 (Zimmerman & T) -6 E Main Bx7 -Shortsvll 14548 **Fx**:289-4043
(212) 698-3500 ..**Zimmerman**, Scott M '85 (Dechert LLP) -1095 Av of Amer -NY 10036
(212) 286-8585 ..**Zimmerman**, Scott M '95 (Heidell PM&B,LLP) -99 Park Av -NY 10016
(212) 759-4433 ..**Zimmerman**, Scott M '06 %Alvarez & Marsal -600 Lex Av -NY 10022
(212) 325-7093 ..**Zimmerman**, Taryn R '05 %Credit Suisse -1 Mad Av -NY 10010
(212) 349-3873 ..**Zimmerman**, Theo J '59 -40 Harrison -NY 10013
(585) 454-2181 ..**Zimmermann**, Clark J Jr. '92 (Trevett CS&A,PC) -2 State -Rchstr 14614
(212) 227-7878 ..**Zimmermann**, E Neal '83 (Waters MM) -233 Bway -NY 10279
(914) 693-3322 ..**Zimmermann**, Evan S '94 (E Zimmermann,PC) -9A Spruce Hill Ct -Plsntvll 10570 **Fx**:478-0832
(716) 853-8400 ..**Zimmermann**, George M '89 %Dept of Law -350 Main Pl Twr -Buffalo 14202 **Fx**:853-8571
(716) 853-9555 ..**Zimmermann**, Helen W '82 %Leg Aid -237 Main -Buffalo 14203 **Fx**:853-3219
(315) 443-8943 ..**Zimmermann**, Molly C '84 Syracuse Univ Cllg of Law -Wht Hall -Syracuse 13244 **Fx**:443-4213
(212) 696-6000 ..**Zimmermann**, Victor L '78 (Curtis M-PC&M LLP) -101 Park Av -NY 10178

(212) 922-1330 ..**Zimmet Bieber LLP** -437 Mad Av -NY 10022 **Fx:**922-0815
(212) 922-1330 ..**Zimmet**, Brian J '92 (Zimmet B LLP) -437 Mad Av -NY 10022
(212) 755-0808 ..**Zimmett**, Mark P '76 -126 E 56th -NY 10022 **Fx:**755-0888
(631) 789-1200 ..**Zimnoch**, Bernard J '08 -1909 Grt Nck Rd -Copiague 11726 **Fx:**789-1332
(516) 731-4358 ..**Zimny**, Max '50 -3688 Regent Ln -Wantagh 11793 **Fx:**520-5018
(315) 671-1091 ..**Zimpel**, Robin C '04 Onondaga Cnty -401 Mntgmry -Syracuse 13202
(716) 856-4200 ..**Zimpfer**, Rochelle K '09 %Gibson M&C,LLP -69 Delaware Av -Buffalo 14202
(212) 964-6611 ..**Zimring**, Joshua C '00 OfCnsl Lester SK&D -120 Bway -NY 10271
(212) 715-1000 ..**Zimroth**, Peter L '75 (Arnold & P LLP) -399 Park Av -NY 10022
(212) 788-0887 ..**Zinaman**, Jamie '07 %Law Dept -100 Church -NY 10007 **Fx:**788-0367
(212) 679-6500 ..**Zinbarg**, Eugene D '60 (Rosenberg & Z) -515 Mad Av -NY 10022 **Fx:**679-5888
(212) 907-9600 ..**Zinberg**, David J '79 (Ingram YGC&B,LLP) -250 Park Av -NY 10177
(718) 222-2027 ..**Zincke**, Mary Ellen '74 %Law Dept -350 Jay -Brklyn 11201 **Fx:**222-2088
(212) 225-7700 ..**Zincke**, Patricia '80 %Cartafalsa ST&L -165 Bway -NY 10006
(212) 728-8000 ..**Zinder**, Michl I '79 (Willkie F&G LLP) -787 7th Av -NY 10019
(212) 355-3400 ..**Zingale**, Mark '00 NaviSite, Inc -654 Mad Av -NY 10065
(212) 521-2000 ..**Zinghini**, Kenneth J '89 %Loews Corp -667 Mad Av -NY 10065 **Fx:**521-2997
(212) 207-3825 ..**Zingman**, Mitchell S '81 (Stern & Z LLP) -110 E 59th -NY 10022 **Fx:**583-7464
(212) 878-8000 ..**Zingraff**, Owen S '09 %Clifford C LLP -31 W 52nd -NY 10019
(716) 856-5500 ..**Zini**, Gregory R J '98 (Damon M LLP) -200 Delaware Av -Buffalo 14202
(607) 962-4641 ..**Zink**, Colleen G '95 (Welch & Z) -19 E Market -Corning 14830
(212) 408-5100 ..**Zink**, N Theo Jr. '96 (Chadbourne & P LLP) -30 Rckfllr Plz -NY 10112
(212) 664-5489 ..**Zink**, Sharon A '00 %NBC -30 Rckfllr Plz -NY 10112
(631) 265-2133 ..**Zinker**, Edw '66 (Zinker & H,LLP) -278 E Main Bx866 -Smithtwn 11787
(631) 265-2133 ..**Zinker & Herzberg,LLP** -278 E Main Bx866 -Smithtwn 11787 **Fx:**265-4233
(212) 898-4383 ..**Zinkevitch**, Ellada '05 %Liberty Intl -55 Water -NY 10041
(917) 263-2111 ..**Zinkin**, Ephraim Z '97 Ecko Complex,LLC -40 W 23rd -NY 10010 **Fx:**263-2112
(212) 696-6000 ..**Zinman**, Andrew B '96 %Curtis M-PC&M LLP -101 Park Av -NY 10178
(212) 530-1800 ..**Zinman**, Danl C '94 %Richards K&O LLP -1 World Fncl Ctr -NY 10281
(212) 506-1700 ..**Zinman**, Danl N '98 SpclCnsl Kasowitz BT&F LLP -1633 Bway -NY 10019
(212) 446-4800 ..**Zinman**, Jonathan S '08 %Kirkland & E LLP -153 E 53rd -NY 10022
(914) 693-0400 ..**Zinman**, Peter E '93 -466 Saw Mill Rd -Ardsley 10502 **Fx:**693-3824
(718) 990-6646 ..**Zinman**, Robt M '61 %St John's Law Schl -8000 Utopia Pkwy -Jamaica 11439 **Fx:**591-1855
(914) 220-1900 ..**Zinn**, Danl M '07 (Nelson Law Firm,LLC) -1 N Bway -White Plns 10601
(516) 746-8000 ..**Zinn**, Marci S '91 (Jaspan S LLP) -300 Grdn City Plz -Gdn Cty 11530
(631) 588-6400 ..**Zinn**, Richd A '71 -1919 Middle Cntry Rd -Centereach 11720
(212) 558-6668 ..**Zinn**, Richd C '77 (Foley SO&W) -100 William -NY 10038
(212) 536-3900 ..**Zinn**, Robt P '83 K&L Gates LLP -599 Lex Av -NY 10022
(212) 551-8500 ..**Zinna**, Jennifer A '03 IDB Bank -511 5th Av -NY 10017
(212) 697-6262 ..**Zinna**, Michl J '01 %Ward & O -380 Mad Av -NY 10017
(212) 680-5100 ..**Zinner**, Joshua '96 %NEDAP -176 Grand -NY 10013 **Fx:**680-5104
(212) 521-5400 ..**Zinner**, Kerren B '02 %Reed S LLP -599 Lex Av -NY 10022
(718) 464-2700 ..**Zinner**, Ronald P '94 -205-07 Hillside Av -Hollis 11423 **Fx:**464-7941
(631) 414-7730 ..**Zinner**, Stanley S '71 -58 S Srvc Rd -Melvll 11747 **Fx:**414-7732
(585) 343-3037 ..**Zinni**, Frank V '76 -206 E Main Bx406 -Batavia 14021 **Fx:**343-7125
(585) 343-3037 ..**Zinni**, Nicholas '51 -Bx406 -Batavia 14021
(718) 585-7000 ..**Zinno**, Andrea '93 (Rogers WKC&Z) -800 Grnd Cncrs -Bronx 10451 **Fx:**585-8969
(212) 297-5800 ..**Zinser**, Amy E '08 %Day P LLP -7 Times Sq -NY 10036
(718) 273-4046 ..**Zinsley**, Keith H '90 %Bosco B&M -857 Forest Av -Staten Isl 10310
(716) 858-2200 ..**Ziobro**, Eric R '99 %Cnty Atty -95 Franklin -Buffalo 14202 **Fx:**858-2281
(845) 986-1136 ..**Ziobro**, John E '95 (Stage N&Z,LLP) -23 West -Warwick 10990
(516) 712-4000 ..**Ziolkowski**, Sarah M '06 %Milber MP&S LLP -1000 Woodbury Rd -Woodbury 11797
(212) 619-4444 ..**Ziolkowski**, Steven M '95 %Marshall CW&B,PC -116 John -NY 10038
(718) 250-2000 ..**Zion**, Adam I '93 %DA -350 Jay -Brklyn 11201 **Fx:**250-2314
(212) 557-1616 ..**Zion**, Adina '97 %Herbst & Assoc -230 Park Av -NY 10169 **Fx:**661-2153
(212) 205-7000 ..**Zion**, Isaac '98 %Ashurst LLP -7 Times Sq -NY 10036
(646) 878-0848 ..**Zion**, Jacqueline '01 %Pearl CZL,LLP -1500 Bway -NY 10036
(718) 741-8413 ..**Zions**, Neil L '91 %Div of Human Rights -1 Fordham Plz -Bronx 10458 **Fx:**741-8102
(716) 631-2700 ..**Zionts**, H A Terri '82 -110 Indn Trl Rd -Williamsvll 14221 **Fx:**631-3700
(845) 357-2215 ..**Zipern**, Martin S '62 (Reiter & Z) -75 Montebello Rd -Suffern 10901 **Fx:**357-4437
(212) 510-0500 ..**Zipes**, Greg M '92 %US Trustees Ofc -33 Whitehall -NY 10004 **Fx:**668-2255
(914) 766-4840 ..**Zipkin**, Baba M '80 %IBM -294 Route 100 -Somers 10589
(516) 222-7929 ..**Zipkin**, Mitchell E '09 %Pressler & P LLP -305 Bway -NY 10007 **Fx:**(973) 753-5353
(212) 336-8000 ..**Zipkin**, Neil M '74 (Amster R&E) -90 Park Av -NY 10016
(212) 216-8000 ..**Zipkowitz**, Eric M '90 (Tarter K&D LLP) -1350 Bway -NY 10018
(212) 974-0100 ..**Zipper**, Michl E '94 Capital RE -1325 Av Of The Americas -NY 10019
(212) 880-3800 ..**Zipser**, Howard A '71 (Akerman S) -335 Mad Av -NY 10017
(212) 636-6000 ..**Zipursky**, Benjamin C '92 %Fordham Univ Sch of Law -140 W 62nd -NY 10023 **Fx:**636-6899
(718) 268-8800 ..**Zirbes**, Peter M '91 (PM Zirbes & Assoc) -108-18 Qns Blvd -Frst Hlls 11375 **Fx:**268-4502
(212) 839-5300 ..**Zirin**, James D '65 SrCnsl Sidley A LLP -787 7th Av -NY 10019
(212) 558-4000 ..**Zirinis**, Basil P III '86 (Sullivan & C LLP) -125 Broad -NY 10004
(212) 801-9222 ..**Zirinsky**, Bruce R '73 (Greenberg T,LLP) -200 Park Av -NY 10166
(212) 758-4801 ..**Zirinsky**, John '77 -60 E 42nd -NY 10165 **Fx:**490-6991
(212) 751-4625 ..**Zirinsky**, Robt A '79 -60 E 56th -NY 10022 **Fx:**751-3636
(914) 249-6015 ..**Zirkel**, Timothy Z '95 MasterCard Intl -2000 Purchase -Purchase 10577
(315) 424-0513 ..**Zirkman**, Jos A '87 %Carrols Corp -968 James Bx6969 -Syracuse 13217 **Fx:**475-9619
(212) 909-6000 ..**Zirlin**, Harry '90 %Debevoise & P LLP -919 3rd Av -NY 10022
(212) 766-1177 ..**Zirlin**, Neil A '93 %J Mullen Jr -30 Vesey -NY 10007 **Fx:**766-1131
(212) 770-7000 ..**Zirogiannis**, Lewis D '03 %AIG -70 Pine -NY 10270
(845) 794-5928 ..**Zirt**, Richd S '94 -Bx1315 -Monticello 12701 **Fx:**794-5961
(212) 806-5400 ..**Ziser**, Boris '95 (Stroock &S&L LLP) -180 Maiden Ln -NY 10038
(845) 357-0444 ..**Zisgen**, Robt P '85 (Banks & Z LLC) -56 Park Av Bx501 -Suffern 10901 **Fx:**(201) 512-0633
(212) 373-3000 ..**Zisholtz**, Evan R '10 %Paul WRW&G LLP -1285 Av of Amer -NY 10019
(516) 741-2200 ..**Zisholtz**, Gerald '54 (Zisholtz & Z,LLP) -170 Old Cntry Rd -Mineola 11501 **Fx:**746-1024
(516) 741-2200 ..**Zisholtz**, Stuart S '93 (Zisholtz & Z,LLP) -170 Old Cntry Rd -Mineola 11501 **Fx:**746-1024
(212) 735-3000 ..**Zisk**, Matthew B '98 Cnsl Skadden ASM&F LLP -4 Times Sq -NY 10036
(716) 849-1333 ..**Ziske**, Robt E '80 (Lipsitz GSC LLP) -42 Delaware Av -Buffalo 14202
(631) 462-1417 ..**Ziskin**, Richd B '98 %Ziskin Law Firm LLP -6268 Jericho Tpk -Commack 11725 **Fx:**462-1486
(631) 462-1417 ..**Ziskin**, Robt M '64 (Ziskin Law Firm LLP) -6268 Jericho Tpk -Commack 11725 **Fx:**462-1486
(631) 462-1417 ..**Ziskin**, Stacey E '95 (Ziskin Law Firm LLP) -6268 Jericho Tpk -Commack 11725 **Fx:**462-1486
(631) 462-1417 ..**Ziskin**, Suzanne Harmon '98 %Ziskin Law Firm LLP -6268 Jericho Tpk -Commack 11725 **Fx:**462-1486
(212) 494-9063 ..**Ziskind**, Nachman Y '01 Econmc Grp Pension Srvcs -333 7th Av -NY 10001 **Fx:**760-0172
(212) 244-4111 ..**Zisman**, Itzhak '91 (Shiboleth YR&Z,LLP) -1 Penn Plz -NY 10119
(914) 377-6100 ..**Zisman**, Philip A '87 (Inspector Gen) -City Hall -Ynkrs 10701
(212) 851-9168 ..**Zisowitz**, Terry S '72 Cardiovascular Research Fndtn -111 E 59th -NY 10022
(516) 423-1928 ..**Ziss**, Dafna '01 -123 Birchwood Dr -New Hyde Pk 11040
(516) 466-2972 ..**Zisselman**, Marc D '96 -475 Nrthrn Blvd -Gt Neck 11021 **Fx:**466-7995
(212) 872-9800 ..**Zisser**, Peter A '91 OfCnsl Squire S&D LLP -30 Rckfllr Plz -NY 10112
(718) 279-4500 ..**Zissou**, Steve '83 -42-40 Bell Blvd -Bayside 11361 **Fx:**281-0850
(212) 223-0200 ..**Zissu**, Erik M '03 %Stillman F&S,PC -425 Park Av -NY 10022
(212) 805-3900 ..**Zissu**, Jacob R '04 %Clausen M PC -1 Chase Manh Plz -NY 10005
(914) 286-5600 ..**Zissu**, John N '04 Cybersettle,Inc -44 S Bway -White Plns 10601
(212) 222-7277 ..**Zissu**, Michl J '64 (Murphy & Z) -375 Riverside Dr -NY 10025
(212) 813-5900 ..**Zissu**, Roger L '63 (Fross ZL&Z,PC) -866 UN Plz -NY 10017
(212) 839-5300 ..**Zito**, Elizabeth M '00 %Sidley A LLP -787 7th Av -NY 10019
(212) 335-9000 ..**Zito**, Lisa '03 %DA -1 Hogan Pl -NY 10013
(212) 732-3200 ..**Zito**, Robt J A '83 (Carter L&M LLP) -2 Wall -NY 10005
(845) 786-7740 ..**Zitofsky**, Eric W '00 -206 Samsondale Prof Bldg -W Haverstraw 10993 **Fx:**786-7749
(718) 459-6200 ..**Zitofsky**, Michelle D '83 (Simon & G) -91-31 Qns Blvd -Elmhrst 11373
(212) 408-7166 ..**Zitrin**, Anthony '91 %Bank of NY -1290 Av of Amer -NY 10104
(914) 347-2600 ..**Zitrin**, Ariel S '05 %Traub LS&S LLP -7 Skyline Dr -Hawthorne 10532
(716) 856-4200 ..**Zittel**, Melissa L '01 %Gibson M&C,LLP -69 Delaware Av -Buffalo 14202
(212) 819-8200 ..**Zitter**, Adam S '06 %White & C LLP -1155 Av of Amer -NY 10036
(212) 532-8000 ..**Zitter**, Kenneth A '71 -260 Mad Av -NY 10016 **Fx:**679-8998
(914) 323-7000 ..**Zitzmann**, Chas C '08 %Wilson EME&D LLP -3 Gannett Dr -White Plns 10604
(212) 450-4000 ..**Ziurys**, Lina E '04 %Davis P&W LLP -450 Lex Av -NY 10017
(212) 278-0400 ..**Zivin**, Norman H '68 (Cooper & D LLP) -30 Rckfllr Plz -NY 10112
(212) 872-1000 ..**Zivot**, Louis J '02 -One Bryant Park -NY 10036 **Fx:**872-1002
(718) 833-7333 ..**Zivotov**, Boris '95 B Zivotov,PC -457 77th -Brklyn 11209 **Fx:**836-0277
(516) 352-0300 ..**Ziwot**, Susan M '04 %Campbell & Assoc -99 Tulip Av -Floral Pk 11001 **Fx:**775-0352
(212) 661-6800 ..**Zizmor**, Andrew S '88 (Cyruli SH&Z LLP) -420 Lex Av -NY 10170
(718) 881-2912 ..**Zizmor**, Edw S '72 -881 Gerard Av -Bronx 10452 **Fx:**(201) 342-6172
(646) 840-5734 ..**Zizza**, Emio F '97 J Records -745 5th Av -NY 10151
(212) 530-3900 ..**Zizzamia**, Matthew J '02 %Hannum FP&M, LLC -55 Bway -NY 10006
(212) 504-6000 ..**Zizzo**, John M '73 (Cadwalader W&T LLP) -1 World Fncl Ctr -NY 10281
(212) 677-1900 ..**Zlatarski**, Vera Vassileva '01 Rainforest Alliance -665 Bway -NY 10012
(212) 608-2600 ..**Zlobinsky**, Vladimir I '86 V Zlobinsky,LLC -530 Bway -NY 10012 **Fx:**608-6388
(212) 225-2000 ..**Zloczower**, Dina '08 %Cleary GS&H -1 Lbrty Plz -NY 10006
(212) 659-7300 ..**Zlotchew**, David M '97 OfCnsl Haynes & B,LLP -1221 Av of Amer -NY 10020
(212) 416-8000 ..**Zlotchew**, Ethan Granoff '98 %Dept of Law -120 Bway -NY 10271
(212) 220-9945 ..**Zlotnick**, Andrew '88 Cnsl Taconic Invstmnt Prtnrs LLC -111 8th Av -NY 10011 **Fx:**220-9949
(516) 294-0250 ..**Zlotnick**, Brandon M '03 %M Haskel -167 Willis Av -Mineola 11501 **Fx:**294-0854
(212) 661-9100 ..**Zlotnick**, Craig D '87 %Otterbourg SH&R,PC -230 Park Av -NY 10169
(212) 554-7800 ..**Zlotnick**, Ira W '96 (Moses & S LLP) -405 Lex Av -NY 10174
(212) 935-3000 ..**Zlotnick**, Peter B '91 (Mintz LCFG&P,PC) -666 3rd Av -NY 10017
(212) 223-9188 ..**Zlotogura**, Mindy R '84 %Newman & S,LLP -845 3rd Av -NY 10022
(631) 564-0055 ..**Zlotolow**, Scott '92 -270 W Main -Sayvll 11782

(212) 688-5640 ..**Zobel,** Amy L '01 %Joseph & H LLP -757 3rd Av -NY 10017
(212) 474-1000 ..**Zobitz,** George E '96 (Cravath S&M LLP) -825 8th Av -NY 10019
(212) 525-5107 ..**Zobkiw,** Richd N Jr. '08 %HSBC Bank -452 5th Av -NY 10018
(516) 781-7486 ..**Zobler,** Ludwik H '62 -2175 Wantagh Av -Wantagh 11793
(212) 626-4100 ..**Zoccolillo,** Alan F Jr. '00 (Baker & M LLP) -1114 Av of Amer -NY 10036
(212) 373-3000 ..**Zochowski,** T Robt Jr. '90 (Paul WRW&G LLP) -1285 Av of Amer -NY 10019
(914) 345-3020 ..**Zodda,** Jos R '01 %Knuckles K&E,LLP -565 Taxter Rd -Elmsfrd 10523
(631) 563-3222 ..**Zodda,** Richd V '86 -50 Harp Ln -Sayvll 11782 **Fx:**563-3432
(845) 624-8661 ..**Zodda,** Rudolph O III '96 %C Johns -154 S Mddltwn Rd -Nanuet 10954 **Fx:**624-3586
(212) 556-4097 ..**Zoellner,** Alison C M '91 %The NY Times Co -620 8th Av -NY 10018 **Fx:**556-4634
(212) 237-1000 ..**Zoffinger,** Richd G '01 %Windels ML&M,LLP -156 W 56th -NY 10019
(631) 694-5500 ..**Zogas,** Peter N '75 (Wingate K&C) -445 Broad Hollow Rd -Melvll 11747
(585) 238-2000 ..**Zogas,** Robt F '79 (Phillips L LLP) -1400 First Fed Plz -Rchstr 14614
(212) 504-6000 ..**Zogby,** Benjamin P '10 %Cadwalader W&T LLP -1 World Fncl Ctr -NY 10281
(585) 227-2610 ..**Zoghlin,** Mindy L '84 (Bansbach Z&W,PC) -31 Erie Canal Dr -Rchstr 14626
(585) 428-5210 ..**Zoghlin,** Sonya A '88 Pub Def -10 N Fitzhugh -Rchstr 14614 **Fx:**428-2234
(212) 571-1112 ..**Zohar,** Gil '98 (Zohar L&P,LLP) -42 Bway -NY 10004 **Fx:**571-1113
(212) 586-5100 ..**Zohn,** Eric S '93 %Wm Morris Agency -1325 Av of Amer -NY 10019 **Fx:**903-1473
(212) 603-6300 ..**Zohny,** Danl I '07 %Robinson BLGG&G PC -875 3rd Av -NY 10022
(212) 333-6400 ..**Zoia,** Adam D '97 (Glocap Ptnrs) -156 W 56th -NY 10019 **Fx:**333-6401
(212) 277-6500 ..**Zola,** Jared '04 %Dickstein S LLP -1633 Bway -NY 10019
(631) 470-5000 ..**Zola,** Neil L '91 Garden City Grp Inc -105 Maxess Rd -Melvll 11747 **Fx:**470-5100
(212) 810-5140 ..**Zolan,** Craig R '96 Black Rock -55 E 52nd -NY 10055
(646) 610-5336 ..**Zoland,** Deborah L '80 %NYPD -1 Police Plz -NY 10038
(212) 240-9100 ..**Zoldan-Leite,** Melissa B '98 (Schuchman S&Z-L,LLP) -225 Bway -NY 10007 **Fx:**732-4580
(212) 673-9394 ..**Zoldessy,** Adam V '93 (A Zoldessy,PC) -227 W 11th -NY 10014 **Fx:**673-7934
(212) 545-4000 ..**Zoldessy,** Jason A '04 %Jackson L LLP -666 3rd Av -NY 10017
(914) 576-2688 ..**Zoldessy,** Marc L '75 -2 Saldo Cir -New Rchll 10804
(646) 365-1604 ..**Zoler,** Amelia J '91 Tigris Fncl Grp Ltd -1370 Av of Amer -NY 10019
(212) 916-4260 ..**Zoler,** Shelley M '75 %TIAA-CREF -730 3rd Av -NY 10017
(315) 479-3900 ..**Zolezzi,** Thos P '66 %SSA-ODAR -300 S State -Syracuse 13202 **Fx:**479-3933
(212) 813-8800 ..**Zoli,** Elise N '94 (Goodwin P LLP) -620 8th Av -NY 10018
(212) 742-9200 ..**Zolin,** Donald M '73 -61 Bway -NY 10006 **Fx:**742-7033
(718) 261-3047 ..**Zoll,** John F Jr. '92 %Queens Law Assoc -118-21 Qns Blvd -Frst Hlls 11375 **Fx:**261-0798
(212) 752-5258 ..**Zoller,** Beth P '00 %Schwartz SE&C LLC -845 3rd Av -NY 10022
(212) 449-0572 ..**Zoller,** Eric N '02 Merrill Lynch -4 World Fncl Ctr -NY 10080
(315) 823-3360 ..**Zoller,** John J '36 -553 Grdn Bx635 -Little Fls 13365
(212) 574-1200 ..**Zoller,** Lacey M '09 %Seward & K LLP -1 Bttry Pk Plz -NY 10004
(631) 543-3456 ..**Zollo,** John B '85 -1038 W Jericho Tpk -Smithtwn 11787
(631) 361-6767 ..**Zollo,** Zoe '86 -870 Middle Cntry Rd -St James 11780 **Fx:**361-6794
(315) 446-5362 ..**Zolna,** Fredrick '76 -101 Enfield Pl -Syracuse 13214
(212) 506-2500 ..**Zolot,** Allison J '10 %Mayer B LLP -1675 Bway -NY 10019
(212) 577-2523 ..**Zolot,** Barbara '86 %Ctr for Appllt Litigation -74 Trinity Pl -NY 10006 **Fx:**577-2535
(718) 779-6545 ..**Zolot,** Chas '82 -37-06 82nd -Jcksn Hts 11372 **Fx:**639-0520
(646) 525-2157 ..**Zolotova,** Irena '10 -295 Dover -Brklyn 11235
(212) 756-2000 ..**Zolty,** Elie '09 %Schulte R&Z LLP -919 3rd Av -NY 10022
(516) 374-9040 ..**Zomick,** Nomi N '81 -824 Fiske -Woodmere 11598 **Fx:**569-6928
(212) 210-6339 ..**Zomper,** Jeffrey B '87 %Daily News,LP -450 W 33rd -NY 10001 **Fx:**643-7855
(716) 881-1202 ..**Zona,** Christine Wojcik '83 -329 Elmwood Av -Buffalo 14222
(518) 346-3850 ..**Zonderman,** Paul S '77 -Bx9073 -Schnctdy 12309 **Fx:**346-3850
(212) 752-9700 ..**Zone,** Barry S '93 (Gersten S LLP) -600 Lex Av -NY 10022
(347) 277-6419 ..**Zonenshein,** Robt '00 -1136 E 31st -Brklyn 11210
(212) 422-6111 ..**Zonghetti,** Gino A '86 (Kenny S&Z) -26 Bway -NY 10004
(518) 758-9664 ..**Zoni,** Shane A '03 -Bx653 -Kinderhook 12106
(212) 791-2911 ..**Zonies,** Deborah '90 Immtech Intl -1 N End Av -NY 10282
(516) 227-6363 ..**Zonin,** Craig R '93 %Amato & Assoc,PC -666 Old Cntry Rd -Gdn Cty 11530 **Fx:**227-6367
(212) 878-8000 ..**Zonis,** Jonathan '92 (Clifford C LLP) -31 W 52nd -NY 10019
(585) 343-5450 ..**Zonitch,** John M '81 %Leg Srvcs -5073 Clinton St Rd -Batavia 14020 **Fx:**343-5503
(212) 617-3531 ..**Zoob,** Kimberly L '06 Bloomberg LP -731 Lex Av -NY 10022
(212) 277-6500 ..**Zoogman,** Nicholas J '74 (Dickstein S LLP) -1633 Bway -NY 10019
(914) 286-3430 ..**Zoppo,** Darien Jay '80 %Leg Aid -1 N Bway -White Plns 10601 **Fx:**682-4112
(212) 765-5070 ..**Zoppo,** Michl T '05 %Fish & R,PC -153 E 53rd -NY 10022
(212) 530-5000 ..**Zoracki,** Seth M '07 %Milbank TH&M LLP -1 Chase Manh Plz -NY 10005
(516) 466-6500 ..**Zore-Smrek,** Jacqueline M '04 Parker WA LLP -6 Hrbr Park Dr S -Pt Wash 11050
(212) 306-7160 ..**Zorgniotti,** Alessandra F '95 %Ofc Cllctv Brgn -40 Rector -NY 10006 **Fx:**306-7167
(585) 325-5150 ..**Zorn,** Brian M '78 (Faraci L,LLP) -28 E Main -Rchstr 14614
(212) 685-7474 ..**Zorn,** Stephen A '87 SpclCnsl Mayerson SA LLP -292 Mad Av -NY 10017
(212) 637-2720 ..**Zornberg,** Lisa R '95 %US Atty -1 St Andrews Plz -NY 10007
(585) 815-0288 ..**Zornek,** Anna M '10 %Rosicki R & Assoc,PC -26 Harvester Av -Batavia 14020 **Fx:**815-0299
(631) 723-1010 ..**Zornes,** Walter W '92 -107 W Montauk Hwy -Hampton Bays 11946
(212) 578-2211 ..**Zornik,** Todd E '02 MetLife -2701 Qns Plz N -LIC 11101
(212) 735-3000 ..**Zornow,** David M '81 (Skadden ASM&F LLP) -4 Times Sq -NY 10036
(718) 590-2000 ..**Zortman,** Brenna K '09 %DA -198 E 161st -Bronx 10451 **Fx:**590-6477
(212) 381-7000 ..**Zorzi,** Christine A '00 (Sabin B&G LLP) -4 Times Sq -NY 10036
(716) 542-5413 ..**Zosh,** Michl R '98 (Nicholas PSB&Z) -12364 Main Rd Bx176 -Akron 14001
(646) 261-8012 ..**Zotinis,** Christine V '98 -404 W 15th -NY 10011
(212) 818-9200 ..**Zotos,** Nicholas A '08 %Satterlee SB&B LLP -230 Park Av -NY 10169
(212) 819-8200 ..**Zou,** Francis Yijun '00 (White & C LLP) -1155 Av of Amer -NY 10036
(212) 455-2000 ..**Zou,** Jinghua '06 %Simpson T&B LLP -425 Lex Av -NY 10017
(718) 661-9562 ..**Zou,** Xianfeng '98 -136-20 38th Av -Flushng 11354
(212) 474-1000 ..**Zoubek,** Damien R '00 (Cravath S&M LLP) -825 8th Av -NY 10019
(212) 326-3939 ..**Zoubek,** Nancy A '90 Cnsl Jones D -222 E 41st -NY 10017
(212) 794-0160 ..**Zoughi,** Laleh '03 Zoughi Law Grp,LLC -401 E 77th -NY 10075 **Fx:**(888) 854-3419
(631) 549-4677 ..**Zouros,** Maria '96 %Sobel K&S,PC -464 NY Av -Huntngtn 11743
(212) 686-0855 ..**Zraick Nahas & Rich** -303 5th Av -NY 10016 **Fx:**779-9548
(631) 385-1864 ..**Zrake,** Anthony P '94 -267 Cook -Huntngtn Sta 11746
(212) 670-0200 ..**Zrike,** Katherine A '85 Merrill Lynch -222 Bway -NY 10038
(516) 873-6200 ..**Zryb,** Matthew S '08 %R Macchia & Assoc -98 Front -Mineola 11501 **Fx:**873-1611
(516) 349-8181 ..**Zsuffa,** Paul '71 -255 Exec Dr -Plainvw 11803 **Fx:**349-1980
(212) 968-8600 ..**Zu,** Min '05 %Manchanda Law Ofc,PLLC -80 Wall -NY 10005 **Fx:**968-8601
(212) 632-1496 ..**Zuba,** Jeremy E '02 Lazard Asset Mgmt -30 Rckfllr Plz -NY 10112
(212) 757-0007 ..**Zubatov,** Alexander '01 %Scarola E LLP -888 7th Av -NY 10106
(212) 373-3000 ..**Zubaty,** Rebecca R '08 %Paul WRW&G LLP -1285 Av of Amer -NY 10019
(607) 722-8823 ..**Zube,** L David '76 -59 Court -Bnghmtn 13901 **Fx:**722-8824
(212) 558-4000 ..**Zuber,** Aryeh '07 %Sullivan & C LLP -125 Broad -NY 10004
(212) 836-8711 ..**Zubick,** Marc N '08 %Kaye S LLP -425 Park Av -NY 10022
(212) 446-4800 ..**Zubkis,** David '09 %Kirkland & E LLP -153 E 53rd -NY 10022
(212) 701-3000 ..**Zubkoff,** Danl J '83 (Cahill G&R LLP) -80 Pine -NY 10005 **Fx:**269-5420
(716) 885-1150 ..**Zubler,** Jill M '97 %US Trustees Ofc -42 Delaware Av -Buffalo 14202 **Fx:**551-5560
(516) 487-5777 ..**Zubli,** Harry '96 -1010 Nrthrn Blvd -Gt Neck 11021 **Fx:**487-4834
(212) 813-8800 ..**Zubok,** Maryana '06 %Goodwin P LLP -620 8th Av -NY 10018
(212) 349-0900 ..**Zuccardy,** Jill M '91 OfCnsl Lansner KS&Z -325 Bway -NY 10007
(716) 854-7525 ..**Zuccaro,** Brian D '04 %Serotte R&W -300 Delaware Av -Buffalo 14202
(212) 906-1200 ..**Zuccaro,** Robt A '83 (Latham & W) -885 3rd Av -NY 10022
(646) 315-7637 ..**Zucco,** Massiel E '09 Steps to End Family Violence -Bx287326 -NY 10128
(716) 439-7085 ..**Zucco,** Robt A '79 %DA -175 Hawley -Lockprt 14094 **Fx:**439-7102
(212) 310-8000 ..**Zuccotti,** John E '66 Cnsl Weil G&M LLP -767 5th Av -NY 10153
(212) 869-4646 ..**Zuchlewski,** Pearl '80 (Kraus & Z LLP) -500 5th Av -NY 10110
(518) 432-7861 ..**Zucker,** Cliff '84 %Disability Advocates,Inc -5 Clinton Sq -Albany 12207 **Fx:**427-6561
(516) 621-0052 ..**Zucker,** Danl A '50 -105 Poplar Dr -Roslyn 11576
(212) 833-5454 ..**Zucker,** Danl B '86 Zomba Records -550 Mad Av -NY 10022
(516) 747-5900 ..**Zucker,** Danl M '02 %Kaye & L -220 Mineola Blvd -Mineola 11501
(718) 263-7676 ..**Zucker,** David G '75 (Schwed & Z) -125-10 Qns Blvd -Kew Gdns 11415
(212) 593-6700 ..**Zucker,** Elliott J '90 (Aaronson RF&D,LLP) -757 3rd Av -NY 10017
(718) 624-1211 ..**Zucker,** Gary A '77 (Zucker & B,PC) -186 Joralemon -Brklyn 11201 **Fx:**624-6037
(516) 622-9200 ..**Zucker,** Greg S '98 (Westerman BEM&S,LLP) -1201 RXR Plz -Uniondale 11553
(212) 820-9362 ..**Zucker,** Howard '78 (Hawkins D&W LLP) -One Chase Manh Plz -NY 10005
(516) 385-6699 ..**Zucker,** Isaac M '89 -600 Old Cntry Rd -Gdn Cty 11530
(212) 272-7333 ..**Zucker,** Jacqueline Abramson '90 %JP Morgan Chase -383 Mad Av -NY 10179
(212) 918-3000 ..**Zucker,** James S '98 %Hogan L LLP -875 3rd Av -NY 10022
(201) 227-4530 ..**Zucker,** Jay B '90 (Zucker & K,LLP) -2307 Eastchstr Rd -Bronx 10469 **Fx:**227-4531
(518) 474-1331 ..**Zucker,** Jay L '81 %Ofc Mntl Health -44 Holland Av -Albany 12229 **Fx:**473-7863
(516) 496-5822 ..**Zucker,** Keith S '07 %T Spina -170 Froehlich Farm Blvd -Woodbury 11797 **Fx:**496-5420
(800) 499-2610 ..**Zucker & Kwestel, LLP** -77 Spruce -Cedarhrst 11516 **Fx:**(877) 761-7245
(800) 499-2610 ..**Zucker & Kwestel, LLP** -56 Harrison -New Rchll 10801 **Fx:**(877) 761-7245
(800) 499-2610 ..**Zucker & Kwestel, LLP** -2307 Eastchstr Rd -Bronx 10469 **Fx:**(877) 761-7245
(914) 302-2460 ..**Zucker,** Leo '75 -Bx1177 -Yorktwn Hts 10598 **Fx:**302-2459
(212) 761-4000 ..**Zucker,** Margaret R '02 Morgan Stanley -1221 Av of Amer -NY 10020
(212) 808-7800 ..**Zucker,** Matthew '08 %Kelley D&W LLP -101 Park Av -NY 10178
(212) 891-5700 ..**Zucker,** Scott B '88 CDC Mortg Capital -9 W 57th -NY 10019
(914) 762-5815 ..**Zuckerberg,** Joel '77 -2 Rivervw Ct -Ossining 10562 **Fx:**945-7158
(212) 421-4100 ..**Zuckerberg,** Joshua '98 (Pryor C LLP) -7 Times Sq -NY 10036
(718) 641-2300 ..**Zuckerberg,** Marvin '54 -110-22 Lbrty Av -S Richmond Hll 11419
(212) 421-2233 ..**Zuckerbrod,** Alan D '84 (Wilk A LLP) -675 3rd Av -NY 10017
(516) 374-3133 ..**Zuckerbrod,** Martin '56 (Zuckerbrod & T) -575 Chestnut Bx488 -Cedarhrst 11516
(516) 374-3133 ..**Zuckerbrod & Taubenfeld** -575 Chestnut Bx488 -Cedarhrst 11516 **Fx:**374-3490
(212) 801-6820 ..**Zuckerbrot,** Kenneth '68 (Greenberg T,LLP) -200 Park Av -NY 10166
(212) 351-4500 ..**Zuckerman,** Adrian '84 (Epstein B&G,PC) -250 Park Av -NY 10177
(212) 704-1368 ..**Zuckerman,** Andrew D '95 Interpublic Grp -1114 Av of Amer -NY 10036 **Fx:**704-1201
(718) 576-1632 ..**Zuckerman,** Andrew J '78 -125-10 Qns Blvd -Kew Gdns 11415
(646) 885-4790 ..**Zuckerman,** Barbara J '85 Dept of Sanitation -125 Worth -NY 10013 **Fx:**(212) 442-9090
(212) 776-5000 ..**Zuckerman,** Barbara L '79 %NYC Housing Auth -250 Bway -NY 10007 **Fx:**776-5039

(631) 724-5251 ..**Zuckerman,** Bryan A '08 %A Arpino -155 E Main Bx830 -Smithtwn 11787 **Fx:**724-5527
(718) 270-3780 ..**Zuckerman,** Connie A '86 %Humanities In Med -SUNY Bx116 -Brklyn 11203
(914) 666-6700 ..**Zuckerman,** David S '83 (Zuckerman & C) -121 Smith Av -Mt Kisco 10549 **Fx:**666-0605
(718) 681-1111 ..**Zuckerman,** David S '83 (Zuckerman & C) -910 Sheridan Av -Bronx 10451
(212) 953-6000 ..**Zuckerman,** Elias M '78 (Katsky K LLP) -605 3rd Av -NY 10158
(212) 753-7500 ..**Zuckerman,** Eliot H '77 (Hartman & C LLP) -488 Mad Av -NY 10022
(631) 852-3160 ..**Zuckerman,** Evan M '04 %Supreme Ct -210 Center Dr -Rvrhead 11901 **Fx:**852-3161
(212) 685-5968 ..**Zuckerman,** Gary J '70 -10 E 40th -NY 10016
(631) 666-4700 ..**Zuckerman,** George R '52 (Zuckerman & Z) -320 Carleton Av -Central Islip 11722 **Fx:**666-1325
(914) 762-3660 ..**Zuckerman,** Gerald '61 -175 Main -Ossining 10562
(914) 997-6220 ..**Zuckerman,** Glenda '83 (Braunstein & Z) -123 Main -White Plns 10601 **Fx:**328-0916
(212) 558-5500 ..**Zuckerman,** Glenn A '97 %Weitz & L,PC -700 Bway -NY 10003
(212) 479-9014 ..**Zuckerman,** Heather P '97 %Neuberger Berman Grp -605 3rd Av -NY 10158
(212) 972-3600 ..**Zuckerman,** Howard J '69 Meridian Cptl Grp -1 Bttry Pk Plz -NY 10004
(212) 595-9337 ..**Zuckerman,** Howard R '86 -205 West End Av -NY 10023
(212) 334-9699 ..**Zuckerman,** Ira H '72 %M Leifer,PC -214 Sullivan -NY 10012 **Fx:**966-9544
(516) 482-3886 ..**Zuckerman,** James R '56 -100 Lndng Rd -Roslyn 11576 **Fx:**482-3886
(212) 696-6000 ..**Zuckerman,** Jeffrey I '73 (Curtis M-PC&M LLP) -101 Park Av -NY 10178
(212) 661-0036 ..**Zuckerman,** Jeffrey R '81 J Zuckerman PC -60 E 42nd -NY 10165
(212) 940-8550 ..**Zuckerman,** Jos '63 Cnsl Katten MR LLP -575 Mad Av -NY 10022
(631) 231-7500 ..**Zuckerman,** Landon R '49 (Zuckerman & P) -1622 Brentwood Rd -Bay Shr 11706 **Fx:**231-7561
(212) 407-7700 ..**Zuckerman,** Lyle S '97 (Vedder P,PC) -1633 Bway -NY 10019
(631) 666-4700 ..**Zuckerman,** Marjorie E '89 (Zuckerman & Z) -320 Carleton Av -Central Islip 11722 **Fx:**666-1325
(516) 791-3200 ..**Zuckerman,** Mark '85 -79 Fieldstone Ln -Vly Stream 11581
(212) 442-8248 ..**Zuckerman,** Mark D '97 %Law Dept -100 Church -NY 10007 **Fx:**788-0367
(607) 763-9200 ..**Zuckerman,** Michl H '64 (Levene G&T,LLP) -BxF-1706 -Bnghmtn 13902
(212) 606-7077 ..**Zuckerman,** Mitchell '75 %Sotheby's,Inc -1334 York Av -NY 10021 **Fx:**606-7574
(212) 480-5284 ..**Zuckerman,** Paul A '79 %Insurance Dept -25 Beaver -NY 10004 **Fx:**480-5272
(212) 367-1900 ..**Zuckerman,** Paul H '68 -226 W 26th -NY 10001 **Fx:**255-6562
(516) 390-4644 ..**Zuckerman,** Peter J '94 (P Zuckerman,PC) -50 Chas Lindbergh Blvd -Uniondale 11553 **Fx:**390-4645
(631) 694-2300 ..**Zuckerman,** Richd K '85 (Lamb & B,LLP) -534 Broadhllw Rd Bx9034 -Melvll 11747
(212) 398-5213 ..**Zuckerman,** Richd M '76 (Sonnenschein N&R LLP) -1221 Av of Amer -NY 10020
(516) 829-7808 ..**Zuckerman,** Robin Heidi '97 -7 Hllcrst Dr -Gt Neck 11021 **Fx:**829-7808
(212) 460-2159 ..**Zuckerman,** Rosalie G '97 Con Ed -4 Irving Pl -NY 10003
(212) 839-5300 ..**Zuckerman,** Russell B '10 %Sidley A LLP -787 7th Av -NY 10019
(718) 250-2000 ..**Zuckerman,** Seth J '09 %DA -350 Jay -Brklyn 11201 **Fx:**250-2314
(212) 704-9600 ..**Zuckerman Spaeder,LLP** -1540 Bway -NY 10036 **Fx:**704-4256
(212) 716-3973 ..**Zuckerman,** Susan C '82 Amer Arbitration Assn -1633 Bway -NY 10019
(212) 644-1010 ..**Zuckerman,** Wm E '92 (Kauff M&M LLP) -950 3rd Av -NY 10022
(516) 357-3000 ..**Zuckermann,** Steven M '97 (Rivkin R LLP) -926 RXR Plz -Uniondale 11556
(212) 559-0615 ..**Zuckert,** Michl S '84 Citigroup -399 Park Av -NY 10022
(212) 877-0971 ..**Zucker-Zarett,** Barbara '89 -160 W 66th -NY 10023
(518) 678-9086 ..**Zuckoff,** Eugene V '79 -1213 Route 23A -Catskill 12414
(516) 869-7600 ..**Zuech,** Linda B '96 %Town Atty -220 Plandome Rd -Manhsst 11030 **Fx:**869-7605
(212) 909-5400 ..**Zuffante,** Mark '88 KPMG LLP -757 3rd Av -NY 10017
(716) 856-4000 ..**Zuffranieri,** Benjamin M Jr. '84 (Hodgson R LLP) -140 Pearl -Buffalo 14202
(716) 875-5000 ..**Zuffranieri,** Martin J '88 -6024 Main -Buffalo 14221 **Fx:**875-8359
(718) 250-2000 ..**Zuflacht,** Lindsay A '09 %DA -350 Jay -Brklyn 11201 **Fx:**250-2314
(631) 465-7530 ..**Zuflacht,** Michele M '93 -445 Broad Hollow Rd -Melvll 11747 **Fx:**293-7886
(516) 742-1343 ..**Zuflacht,** Robt A '76 -1 Old Cntry Rd -Carle Pl 11514
(845) 638-5180 ..**Zugibe,** Patricia '88 %Cnty Atty -Cnty Ofc Bldg -New Cty 10956 **Fx:**638-5676
(845) 638-5001 ..**Zugibe,** Thos Patrick '80 (DA) -1 S Main -New Cty 10956 **Fx:**638-5070
(212) 238-3000 ..**Zujkowski,** Edw P '79 (Emmet M&M,LLP) -120 Bway -NY 10271
(212) 244-9500 ..**Zujkowski,** Frances R '79 Cnsl White and W LLP -1 Penn Plz -NY 10119
(212) 504-6000 ..**Zujkowski,** Jos V '08 %Cadwalader W&T LLP -1 World Fncl Ctr -NY 10281
(607) 962-6876 ..**Zuk,** Marianne R P '91 %Market St Trust Co -80 E Market -Corning 14830
(516) 364-6006 ..**Zukaitis,** Lynda M '01 %Cohen & S,LLP -199 Crsswys Park Dr Bx9004 -Woodbury 11797
(212) 223-6700 ..**Zukerman Gore Brandeis & Crossman,LLP** -875 3rd Av -NY 10022 **Fx:**223-6433
(212) 223-6700 ..**Zukerman,** Jeffrey D '83 (Zukerman GB&C,LLP) -875 3rd Av -NY 10022
(212) 984-7836 ..**Zukerman,** Michl '65 OfCnsl Warshaw BCS&K,LLP -555 5th Av -NY 10017
(315) 472-7868 ..**Zukher,** David E '00 (Weisberg & Z,PLLC) -109 S Warren -Syracuse 13202 **Fx:**472-7070
(212) 732-0040 ..**Zukoff,** Seth D '84 -60 E 42nd -NY 10165 **Fx:**732-4302
(212) 532-0500 ..**Zukofsky,** Joshua '07 %Heiberger & Assoc,PC -205 Lex Av -NY 10016 **Fx:**532-2040
(212) 701-3000 ..**Zukowski,** Charlotte A '08 %Cahill G&R LLP -80 Pine -NY 10005 **Fx:**269-5420
(631) 714-5470 ..**Zukowski,** Christine A '94 (Zukowski & Z,PC) -45 Rsrch Way -E Setauket 11733
(631) 714-5470 ..**Zukowski,** John A '94 (Zukowski & Z,PC) -45 Rsrch Way -E Setauket 11733
(212) 412-9500 ..**Zulack,** John F '70 (Flemming ZWZ LLP) -1 Lbrty Plz -NY 10006
(212) 279-8833 ..**Zuller & Bondy** -42 W 38th -NY 10018 **Fx:**279-2633
(212) 279-8833 ..**Zuller,** Michl E '79 (Zuller & B) -42 W 38th -NY 10018
(914) 923-0721 ..**Zullig,** Walter E Jr. '64 -77 Mystic Dr -Ossining 10562 **Fx:**923-0735
(631) 293-2300 ..**Zullo,** Matthew J '87 %Rappaport GG&L LLP -1355 Motor Pkwy -Hauppauge 11749
(718) 261-6604 ..**Zullo,** Peter F '67 (Casil P&Z) -118-21 Qns Blvd -Frst Hlls 11375 **Fx:**261-6609
(212) 530-5000 ..**Zullow,** Fredrick M '88 (Milbank TH&M LLP) -1 Chase Manh Plz -NY 10005
(212) 813-8800 ..**Zullow,** Keith A '95 (Goodwin P LLP) -620 8th Av -NY 10018
(212) 683-8464 ..**Zulu,** Motisola E '99 M Zulu,PC -303 5th Av -NY 10016 **Fx:**213-8826
(516) 734-2636 ..**Zumaran,** Melody C '01 -1 Hllw Ln -New Hyde Pk 11042
(518) 442-5654 ..**Zumbo,** Jos D '84 Student Lgl Srvcs -1400 Wshngtn Av -Albany 12222
(212) 474-1000 ..**Zumbro,** Paul H '98 (Cravath S&M LLP) -825 8th Av -NY 10019
(631) 422-4900 ..**Zumbrunn,** Werner J '72 (Zumbrunn & H) -1801 Argyle Sq -Babylon 11702 **Fx:**422-4994
(718) 520-3363 ..**Zummo,** Michl A '87 %Criminal Ct -125-01 Qns Blvd -Kew Gdns 11415
(716) 553-3306 ..**Zummo,** Peter G '96 -95 New Rd -E Amherst 14051
(315) 793-3622 ..**Zumpano,** David J '93 (Estate Planning Law Ctr) -555 French Rd -New Hartfrd 13413
(718) 267-2666 ..**Zunic,** John '91 -32-66 Steinway -Astoria 11103
(914) 993-0936 ..**Zunich,** Jeanne E '83 OfCnsl R Bowler -10 Bank -White Plns 10606 **Fx:**683-1369
(718) 701-5894 ..**Zuniga,** Cesar '04 (Zuniga Firm,LLC) -555 Kappock -Bronx 10463
(212) 805-9860 ..**Zuniga-Dominach,** Narda M '96 Cnsl QBE Specialty Ins Co -88 Pine -NY 10005
(212) 259-8000 ..**Zuñiga Parkinson,** Sara Childs '08 %Dewey & L LLP -1301 Av of Amer -NY 10019
(585) 392-6882 ..**Zunno,** Harriet L '92 -35 Heinz Bx624 -Hilton 14468 **Fx:**392-6364
(212) 589-4200 ..**Zunno,** Kathryn M '08 %Baker & H LLP -45 Rckfllr Plz -NY 10111
(614) 477-2089 ..**Zunshine,** Zach '06 -Bx231398 -NY 10023
(718) 442-2232 ..**Zuntag,** Matthew S '97 (Zuntag & Z) -1688 Victory Blvd -Staten Isl 10314 **Fx:**442-3308
(718) 442-2232 ..**Zuntag,** Steven F '73 (Zuntag & Z) -1688 Victory Blvd -Staten Isl 10314 **Fx:**442-3308
(212) 885-5000 ..**Zunz,** Lyonel E '45 SrCnsl Blank R LLP -405 Lex Av -NY 10174
(631) 765-6112 ..**Zupa,** Victor J '72 -4565 Paradise Pnt Rd -Southold 11971
(212) 218-2100 ..**Zupcic,** Anthony M '75 (Fitzpatrick CH&S) -1290 Av of Amer -NY 10104
(212) 318-6000 ..**Zuppone,** Michl L '89 (Paul HJ&W LLP) -75 E 55th -NY 10022
(212) 552-2569 ..**Zur,** Talee S '01 JP Morgan Chase -1 Chase Manh Plz -NY 10081
(607) 778-2117 ..**Zurenda-Cruz,** Holly M '04 Cnty Atty -Cnty Ofc Bldg Bx1766 -Bnghmtn 13902 **Fx:**778-6122
(845) 526-8589 ..**Zurhellen,** J Owen III '68 -Bx333 -Putnam Vly 10579
(917) 538-3670 ..**Zurica,** Anthony '06 -101 Tyrellan Av -Staten Isl 10309 **Fx:**(718) 984-7770
(518) 792-1880 ..**Zurlo,** George J '64 -16 Pearl -Glens Fls 12801 **Fx:**743-8204
(212) 969-3000 ..**Zurndorfer,** M David '72 (Proskauer R LLP) -1585 Bway -NY 10036
(212) 572-7008 ..**Zuro,** Brian A '02 %Vivendi,SA -800 3rd Av -NY 10022 **Fx:**572-7496
(212) 701-3000 ..**Zurofsky,** Adam N '98 (Cahill G&R LLP) -80 Pine -NY 10005 **Fx:**269-5420
(716) 753-4241 ..**Zuroski,** John C '88 %DA -Cnty Cthse -Mayvll 14757 **Fx:**753-4628
(516) 822-3550 ..**Zuschlag,** Steven T '98 Hoffmann & B LLP -6900 Jericho Tpk -Syosset 11791 **Fx:**822-3582
(585) 454-5050 ..**Zusman,** Ronit '95 %Brown & H -2 State -Rchstr 14614
(212) 421-4300 ..**Zussman,** Michl J '08 %Kent B&G,LLP -425 Park Av -NY 10022
(718) 324-2500 ..**Zutell,** Raymond '58 -4348 Katonah Av -Bronx 10470 **Fx:**994-0101
(212) 225-2000 ..**Zutshi,** Rishi N '09 %Cleary GS&H -1 Lbrty Plz -NY 10006
(845) 528-4410 ..**Zutt,** Wm A '71 (Bolger H&Z) -Bx8 -Putnam Vly 10579
(716) 847-8400 ..**Zuydhoek,** Paul B '69 (Phillips L LLP) -3400 HSBC Ctr -Buffalo 14203
(212) 661-9100 ..**Zuzolo,** Kevin '09 %Otterbourg SH&R,PC -230 Park Av -NY 10169
(212) 483-9490 ..**Zviti,** Ben '07 %McElroy DM&C,LLP -88 Pine -NY 10005
(212) 872-1000 ..**Zvonkovic,** Mark '92 -One Bryant Park -NY 10036 **Fx:**872-1002
(212) 619-5400 ..**Zwaig,** Brian J '05 %Newman F LLP -1250 Bway -NY 10001
(631) 588-4040 ..**Zwaik,** Mitchell C '80 (M Zwaik & Assoc,PC) -3900 Vets Mem'l Hwy -Bohemia 11716 **Fx:**588-7175
(212) 608-8840 ..**Zwal,** Michl C '85 (Bamundo Z&S,LLP) -111 John -NY 10038
(212) 588-0800 ..**Zwally,** David A '01 (Frommer L&H LLP) -745 5th Av -NY 10151
(718) 254-7000 ..**Zwany,** Deborah B '80 %US Atty -271 Cadman Plz E -Brklyn 11201 **Fx:**254-6479
(845) 338-8900 ..**Zweben,** Andrew P '73 A Zweben -12 John -Kingston 12401 **Fx:**338-8947
(212) 735-3000 ..**Zweben,** Danl I '09 %Skadden ASM&F LLP -4 Times Sq -NY 10036
(212) 351-4000 ..**Zweifach,** Lawr J '74 (Gibson D&C LLP) -200 Park Av -NY 10166
(516) 294-3300 ..**Zweig,** Ellen P '88 %N Moldovan,PC -1 Old Cntry Rd -Carle Pl 11514 **Fx:**294-4019
(212) 308-6100 ..**Zweig,** Gail R '90 OfCnsl Levi L&F LLP -1185 Av of Amer -NY 10036
(212) 687-1980 ..**Zweig,** Jason A '99 (Kaplan F&K LLP) -850 3rd Av -NY 10022
(718) 722-6462 ..**Zweig,** Marie L '98 %Appllt Div 2nd Dept -45 Monroe Pl -Brklyn 11201 **Fx:**858-2446
(212) 450-8064 ..**Zweig,** Matthew J '01 Intrepid Captl Mgt -360 Mad Av -NY 10017
(212) 407-4000 ..**Zweig,** Michl P '78 (Loeb & L,LLP) -345 Park Av -NY 10154
(212) 385-0111 ..**Zweig,** Richd H '84 -325 Bway -NY 10007 **Fx:**571-7476
(212) 453-5900 ..**Zweig,** Stephen E '76 (Ford & H LLP) -100 Park Av -NY 10017
(716) 856-5500 ..**Zweig,** Steven M '86 %Damon M LLP -200 Delaware Av -Buffalo 14202

(212) 221-5700 ..**Zweigbaum,** Barry E '87 (Goldberg WFG LLP) -1501 Bway -NY 10036
(718) 330-7713 ..**Zweighaft,** Rachel Mead '98 %NLRB -2 Metrotech Ctr -Brklyn 11201 **Fx:**330-7579
(212) 554-2391 ..**Zweiman,** Ari J '01 -595 Mad Av -NY 10022
(212) 374-9840 ..**Zwerin,** David S '07 %Wenig & W -150 Bway -NY 10038 **Fx:**374-9844
(212) 506-5000 ..**Zwerin,** Russell I '09 %Orrick H&S LLP -51 W 52nd -NY 10019
(516) 393-2200 ..**Zwerling,** Andrew L '83 (Garfunkel W,PC) -111 Grt Nck Rd -Gt Neck 11021
(516) 374-3605 ..**Zwerling,** Andrew S '78 -128 Finucane Pl -Woodmere 11598
(212) 407-7700 ..**Zwerling,** Jay S '96 (Vedder P,PC) -1633 Bway -NY 10019
(516) 832-9600 ..**Zwerling,** Jeffrey C '72 (Zwerling S&Z,LLP) -990 Stewart Av -Gdn Cty 11530
(212) 705-0116 ..**Zwerling,** Martin S '95 Cncl of Better Business Bureaus -70 W 36th -NY 10018
(212) 223-3900 ..**Zwerling,** Robin F '76 (Zwerling S&Z,LLP) -41 Mad Av -NY 10010
(212) 223-3900 ..**Zwerling Schachter & Zwerling,LLP** -41 Mad Av -NY 10010 **Fx:**371-5969
(516) 832-9600 ..**Zwerling Schachter & Zwerling,LLP** -990 Stewart Av -Gdn Cty 11530 **Fx:**832-9605
(212) 436-4348 ..**Zwerling,** Stuart H '86 Deloitte & Touche,LLP -2 World Fncl Ctr -NY 10281
(212) 321-8120 ..**Zwerling,** Susanna M '91 %Verizon -140 West -NY 10007
(914) 276-3223 ..**Zwerner,** Danl P '81 -Rts 100 & 202 -Somers 10589 **Fx:**276-2429
(914) 276-3040 ..**Zwerner,** Jane M '82 -352 Route 202 -Somers 10589 **Fx:**276-2429
(631) 852-1648 ..**Zweroff,** Burt '78 %Hon R Oliver -210 Center Dr -Rvrhead 11901
(718) 438-2525 ..**Zwick,** Jeffrey B '07 NC Caller,PC -4309 13th Av -Brklyn 11219 **Fx:**972-4154
(212) 682-3025 ..**Zwick,** Yaacov Y '94 %Weiss & L -551 5th Av -NY 10176
(518) 943-1111 ..**Zwickel,** Chas '79 (Brown K&Z,LLP) -370 Main -Catskill 12414
(518) 474-5988 ..**Zwickel,** Howard L '76 Ofc Gnl Srvcs -Corning Twr ESP -Albany 12242 **Fx:**473-4973
(212) 354-1252 ..**Zwiebach,** Peter L '97 Professional Staff Congress -61 Bway -NY 10006 **Fx:**302-7815
(845) 338-0510 ..**Zwiebel,** Alan S '74 (Zwiebel & F,LLP) -72 Maiden Ln Bx3907 -Kingston 12402
(212) 797-9000 ..**Zwiebel,** David '80 Agudath Israel -42 Bway -NY 10004 **Fx:**(646) 254-1650
(845) 338-0510 ..**Zwiebel & Fairbanks, LLP** -72 Maiden Ln Bx3907 -Kingston 12402 **Fx:**338-6007
(212) 506-1700 ..**Zwiebel,** Megan K '07 %Kasowitz BT&F LLP -1633 Bway -NY 10019
(518) 745-1400 ..**Zwijacz,** Ellen K '08 FitzGerald MBF -16 Pearl Bx2017 -Glens Fls 12801
(631) 853-4049 ..**Zwilling,** Arlene S '85 %Cnty Atty -Dennison Bldg Bx6100 -Hauppauge 11788 **Fx:**853-5169
(845) 639-6666 ..**Zwillinger,** Stanley '64 %Kleinman S&B,PC -151 N Main Bx947 -New Cty 10956
(732) 855-6150 ..**Zwillman,** Blair R '83 (Wilentz G&S) -110 William -NY 10038 **Fx:**726-6578
(516) 432-0160 ..**Zwirn,** Gerard '60 -366 E Penn -Long Bch 11561
(315) 497-0363 ..**Zwirn,** Richd J '75 Zwirn & Z -157 Main Bx631 -Moravia 13118 **Fx:**497-0409
(718) 615-7400 ..**Zwirn,** Warren A '96 (Zwirn & S) -2606 E 15th -Brklyn 11235
(516) 571-0186 ..**Zwirn-Turkin,** Jane N '86 %DA -262 Old Cntry Rd -Mineola 11501 **Fx:**248-9479
(518) 884-4795 ..**Zwisohn,** Van '84 %Pub Def -40 McMaster -Ballston Spa 12020 **Fx:**884-4789
(212) 225-2000 ..**Zwitter-Tehovnik,** Mirna '02 %Cleary GS&H -1 Lbrty Plz -NY 10006
(212) 839-5300 ..**Zwitter-Tehovnik,** Mirt '06 %Sidley A LLP -787 7th Av -NY 10019
(718) 741-8411 ..**Zwyer,** Arlyne R '83 %Div of Human Rights -1 Fordham Plz -Bronx 10458 **Fx:**741-8102
(212) 416-8000 ..**Zybert,** Ann P '83 %Dept of Law -120 Bway -NY 10271
(516) 433-6450 ..**Zychick,** Joel D '85 Z Cnsl,LLC -326 Bway -Bethpage 11714
(716) 855-4428 ..**Zygaj,** David S '90 Niagara Frontier -1 Seymour H Knox III Plz -Buffalo 14203 **Fx:**855-4121
(212) 819-8200 ..**Zylberberg,** Abraham L '74 (White & C LLP) -1155 Av of Amer -NY 10036
(845) 635-3399 ..**Zylberberg,** Marc P '84 -39 Gretna Rd -Plsnt Vlly 12569
(212) 310-8000 ..**Zylberberg,** Saml M '88 (Weil G&M LLP) -767 5th Av -NY 10153
(212) 848-4000 ..**Zylberg,** Barbara '06 %Shearman & S LLP -599 Lex Av -NY 10022
(212) 421-4100 ..**Zylberg,** Philippe '02 %Pryor C LLP -7 Times Sq -NY 10036
(212) 310-8000 ..**Zynda,** Tarra L '06 %Weil G&M LLP -767 5th Av -NY 10153
(518) 474-2705 ..**Zyra,** Lawr J '88 %NYS Div Human Rghts -Bx2049 -Albany 12220
(518) 474-4567 ..**Zyra,** Thos C '85 %Insurance Dept -99 Wshngtn Av -Albany 12257 **Fx:**473-4600
(631) 289-3745 ..**Zysk,** Robt J '74 -629 Rt 112 -Patchogue 11772 **Fx:**289-3747
(212) 660-5000 ..**Zysman Aharoni & Gayer LLP** -1290 Av of Amer -NY 10104 **Fx:**660-5010
(315) 724-2293 ..**Zywiak,** Louis J '53 -435 Sunlit Ter -Utica 13502

CORPORATION COUNSEL AND CITY ATTORNEYS

Albany
Corporation Counsel: John J. Reilly
106 City Hall, 24 Eagle St., Albany 12207
(518) 434-5050; Fax: (518) 434-5070
Deputy Corporation Counsel: Tara B. Wells
106 City Hall, 24 Eagle St., Albany 12207
(518) 434-5050; Fax: (518) 434-5070

Amsterdam
Corporation Counsel: Gerard DeCusatis
61 Church St., Amsterdam 12010 (518) 842-1414

Auburn
Corporation Counsel: John C. Rossi
Memorial City Hall, 24 South St., Auburn 13021
(315) 255-4176; Fax: (315) 255-4735
E-mail: jrossi@ci.auburn.ny.us

Batavia
City Atty.: George VanNest
1900 Main Pl. Tower, Buffalo 14202
(716) 848-9000; Fax: (716) 847-6004
E-mail: gvannest@underbergkessler.com

Beacon
City Atty.: Nicholas M. Ward-Willis
Keane & Beane, P.C.,
200 Westage Business Ctr., Suite 120, Fishkill 12524
(845) 896-0120
E-mail: nward-willis@kblaw.com

Binghamton
Corporation Counsel: Kenneth J. Frank
City Hall, 38 Hawley St., Binghamton 13901
(607) 772-7013; Fax: (607) 723-6164

Buffalo
Corporation Counsel (Acting): David Rodriguez
1100 City Hall, 65 Niagara Sq., Buffalo 14202
(716) 851-4333; Fax: (716) 851-4105
E-mail: drodriguez@city-buffalo.com

Canandaigua
Corporation Counsel: Michele O. Smith
2 N. Main St., Canandaigua 14424
(585) 613-1999; Fax: (585) 396-5016
E-mail: micheleosmith@nysbar.com

Cohoes
Corporation Counsel: Gregory J. Teresi
City Hall, Room 16, 97 Mohawk St., Cohoes 12047
(518) 233-2114; Fax: (518) 233-2160
E-mail: gteresi@ci.cohoes.ny.us

Corning
City Atty.: Pamela Doyle Gee
c/o Davidson O'Mara, 243 Lake St., Elmira 14901-3192
(607) 733-4635; Fax: (607) 732-1033
E-mail: pdgee@omaralaw.com

Cortland
Corporation Counsel: Ronald Walsh
City Hall, 25 Court St., Cortland 13045
(607) 753-0872; Fax: (607) 753-0385
E-mail: corpcounsel@cortland.org

Dunkirk
City Atty.: Michael Robert Cerrie
City Hall, 342 Central Ave., Dunkirk 14048
(716) 366-9866; Fax: (716) 366-1329

Elmira
Corporation Counsel: John J. Ryan, Jr.
City Hall, 317 E. Church St., Elmira 14901
(607) 737-5674; Fax: (607) 737-5995

Fulton
City Atty.: Vacancy at Press Time
141 S. 1st St., Fulton 13069
(315) 592-7330; Fax: (315) 598-7051

Geneva
City Atty.: David Lee Foster
438 Exchange St., P.O. Box 143, Geneva 14456
(315) 781-0138; Fax: (315) 781-0138

Glen Cove
City Atty.: Vincent P. Taranto
3 School St., Suite 208, Glen Cove 11542
(516) 759-1111; Fax: (516) 676-3969; E-mail: vptpc@aol.com

Glens Falls
City Atty.: Ronald Newell
16 Maple St., P.O. Box 2152, Glens Falls 12801
(518) 798-1758; Fax: (518) 798-0740

Gloversville
City Atty.: Matthew E. Trainor
3 Frontage Rd., Gloversville 12078
(518) 773-4554; Fax: (518) 773-4581

Hornell
City Atty.: Joseph G. Pelych
211 Main St., Hornell 14843
(607) 324-6111; Fax: (607) 324-6255

Hudson
City Atty.: John G. Connor
76 Green St., P.O. Box 427, Hudson 12534
(518) 828-2712; Fax: (518) 822-8442

Ithaca
City Atty.: Daniel L. Hoffman
403 City Hall, 108 E. Green St., Ithaca 14850
(607) 274-6504; Fax: (607) 274-6507
E-mail: attorney@cityofithaca.org

Jamestown
Corporation Counsel: Marilyn Fiore-Lehman
City Hall, 200 E. Third St., Jamestown 14701
(716) 483-7540; Fax: (716) 483-7591

Johnstown
City Atty.: Susan Palmer Johnson
33-41 E. Main St., P.O. Box 160, Johnstown 12095
(518) 736-4018; Fax: (518) 762-4939
E-mail: susan.johnson@cityofjohnstown-ny.com

Kingston
Corporation Counsel: MaryLou Christiana
420 Broadway, Kingston 12401
(845) 334-3947; Fax: (845) 334-3959
Asst. Corporation Counsel: Shayne R. Gallo
420 Broadway, Kingston 12401
(845) 334-3947; Fax: (845) 334-3959

Lackawanna
City Atty.: Arc Petricca
714 Ridge Rd., Room 313, Lackawanna 14218
(716) 827-6479; Fax: (716) 827-6480

Little Falls
City Atty.: Edward J. Rose
31 N. Ann St., Little Falls 13365
(315) 823-0835; Fax: (315) 823-3826

Lockport
Corporation Counsel: John J. Ottaviano
1 Locks Plaza, Lockport 14094
(716) 439-6670; Fax: (716) 439-6668
E-mail: jottaviano@elockport.com

Long Beach
Asst. Corporation Counsel: Noreen O. Costello
1 West Chester St., Room 402, Long Beach 11561
(516) 431-1000; Fax: (516) 431-1016
Corporation Counsel: Corey E. Klein
1 West Chester St., Room 402, Long Beach 11561
(516) 431-1000, Ext. 1003; Fax: (516) 431-1016

Mechanicville
City Atty.: Val M. Serbalik
100 N. Main St., Mechanicville 12118
(518) 664-7342; Fax: (518) 664-2315
E-mail: vserbalik@verizon.net

Middletown

Corporation Counsel: Richard J. Guertin
16 James St., Middletown 10940
(845) 346-4140; Fax: (845) 346-4146

Asst. Corporation Counsel: Alex Smith
16 James St., Middletown 10940
(845) 346-4140; Fax: (845) 346-4146

Mount Vernon

Corporation Counsel: Loretta J. Hottinger
Department of Law, City Hall, One Roosevelt Sq., Mount Vernon 10550
(914) 665-2366; Fax: (914) 665-9142

New Rochelle

Corporation Counsel: Kathleen Gill
515 North Ave., New Rochelle 10801
(914) 654-2120; Fax: (914) 654-2345

New York City

Corporation Counsel: Michael A. Cardozo
100 Church St., 6th Floor, N.Y.C. 10007
(212) 788-0800; Fax: (212) 227-5641;
Law Dept.: (212) 788-0303; Law Dept. Fax: (212) 788-0367
E-mail: mcardozo@law.nyc.gov

Newburgh

Corporation Counsel: Bernis E. Nelson
City Hall, 83 Broadway, Newburgh 12550
(845) 569-7335; Fax: (845) 569-7338

Asst. Corporation Counsel: Michelle Kelson
City Hall, 83 Broadway, Newburgh 12550
(845) 569-7335; Fax: (845) 569-7338
E-mail: mkelson@cityofnewburgh-ny.gov

Niagara Falls

Corporation Counsel: Craig H. Johnson
745 Main St., Niagara Falls 14302
(716) 286-4422; Fax: (716) 286-4424
E-mail: craig.johnson@niagarafallsny.gov

First Deputy Corporation Counsel: Thomas O'Donnell
745 Main St., Niagara Falls 14302
(716) 286-4409; Fax: (716) 286-4424
E-mail: thomas.odonnell@niagarafallsny.gov

Deputy Corporation Counsel: Christopher Mazur
745 Main St., Niagara Falls 14302
(716) 286-4423; Fax: (716) 286-4424
E-mail: christopher.mazur@niagarafallsny.gov

Asst. Corporation Counsel: Douglas A. Janese
745 Main St., Niagara Falls 14302 (716) 286-4379
E-mail: douglas.janese@niagarafallsny.gov

North Tonawanda

City Atty.: Shawn P. Nickerson
216 Payne Ave., North Tonawanda 14120
(716) 695-8590; Fax: (716) 695-8592

324 Wheatfield St., North Tonawanda 14120

Ogdensburg

City Atty.: Andy Silver
330 Ford St., Ogdensburg 13669
(315) 393-6100; Fax: (315) 393-1136

Olean

City Atty.: Wendy G. Peterson
Municipal Bldg., 101 E. State St., P.O. Box 668, Olean 14760-0668 (716) 376-5682; Fax: (716) 373-4906
E-mail: wpeterson@cityofolean.org

Oneida

City Atty.: Justin R. Murphy
248 Main St., P.O. Box 673, Oneida 13421
(315) 363-5285

Oneonta

City Atty.: David S. Merzig
City Hall, 258 Main St., Oneonta 13820
(607) 432-4242; Fax: (607) 433-3420

8-12 Dietz St., Suite 202, Oneonta 13820

Oswego

City Atty.: Gay H. Williams
City Hall, 13 W. Oneida St., Oswego 13126
(315) 342-0162; Fax: (315) 342-8247

Peekskill

Corporation Counsel: Paul E. Schwerman
City Hall, 840 Main St., Peekskill 10566
(914) 734-4180; Fax: (914) 734-4183

Plattsburgh

Corporation Counsel: John E. Clute, Jr.
121 Bridge St., P.O. Box 2885, Plattsburgh 12901
(518) 563-4884; Fax: (518) 563-5845
E-mail: john@cctlaw.com

Port Jervis

Corporation Counsel: Damian Brady
Bonacic, Krahulik, Cuddeback, McMahon & Brady, L.L.P., 17 E. Main St., P.O. Box 1114, Port Jervis 12771
(845) 856-5178; Fax: (845) 856-5515
E-mail: dbrady@hvlaw.net

Poughkeepsie

Corporation Counsel: G. Brian Morgan
P.O. Box 300, Poughkeepsie 12602
(845) 451-4065; Fax: (845) 451-4070
E-mail: bmorgan@cityofpoughkeepsie.com

Rensselaer

Corporation Counsel: John P. Hicks
City Hall, 62 Washington St., Rensselaer 12144
(518) 462-6606; Fax: (518) 462-9895
E-mail: jve1984@aol.com

60 Loudonville Rd., Albany 12204 (518) 463-4441

Rochester

Corporation Counsel: Thomas S. Richards
30 Church St., Room 400A, Rochester 14614
(585) 428-6986; Fax: (585) 428-6950
E-mail: thomas.richards@cityofrochester.gov

Rome

City Atty.: Diane Martin-Grande
City Hall, 198 N. Washington St., Rome 13440
(315) 339-7670; Fax: (315) 838-1166
E-mail: dmgrande@romegov.com

Rye

Corporation Counsel (Acting): Kristen K. Wilson
City Hall, 1051 Boston Post Rd., Rye 10580
(914) 967-7074; Fax: (914) 967-4604

Saratoga Springs

City Atty.: Joseph C. Scala
474 Broadway, Saratoga Springs 12866
(518) 587-3550, Ext. 2414; Fax: (518) 587-1688
E-mail: joe.scala@saratoga-springs.org

Schenectady

Corporation Counsel: L. John Van Norden
City Hall, Room 201, 105 Jay St., Schenectady 12305
(518) 382-5073; Fax: (518) 382-5074
E-mail: ljvannorden@schenectadyny.gov

Sherrill

City Atty.: S. John Campanie
60 E. State St., P.O. Box 70, Sherrill 13461
(315) 363-0585; Fax: (315) 363-1952
E-mail: sjclaw@twcny.rr.com

Syracuse

Corporation Counsel: Juanita Perez Williams
300 City Hall, 233 E. Washington St., Syracuse 13202
(315) 448-8400; Fax: (315) 448-8381
E-mail: law@ci.syracuse.ny.us

Tonawanda

City Atty.: Ronald C. Trabucco
200 Niagara St., Tonawanda 14150
(716) 692-6316; Fax: (716) 692-4409

Young Bros. Bldg., 535 Delaware St., Tonawanda 14150
(716) 692-6316; Fax: (716) 692-4409

Troy
Corporation Counsel: Charles A. Sarris
1776 6th Ave., Troy 12180
(518) 270-4606; Fax: (518) 270-4609

Utica
Corporation Counsel: Linda Sullivan Fatata
1 Kennedy Plaza, Utica 13502
(315) 792-0171; Fax: (315) 792-0175
E-mail: lfatata@cityofutica.com

Watervliet
Corporation Counsel: Yorden C. Huban
City Hall, Room 5, 2 Fifteenth St., Watervliet 12189
(518) 270-3800, Ext. 120; Fax: (518) 270-3832

White Plains
Corporation Counsel: John G. Callahan
255 Main St., Room 204, White Plains 10601
(914) 422-1244; Fax: (914) 422-1231
E-mail: jcallahan@whiteplainsny.gov

Yonkers
Corporation Counsel: Mark W. Blanchard
City Hall, Room 300, 40 S. Broadway, Yonkers 10701
(914) 377-6240; Fax: (914) 964-0563

NEW YORK LEGAL AID, PUBLIC DEFENDER AND LEGAL SERVICES OFFICES

STATEWIDE

Center for Constitutional Rights
666 Broadway, 7th Floor, N.Y.C. 10012
(212) 614-6464; Fax: (212) 614-6499
E-mail: info@ccrjustice
Internet: http://ccrjustice.org

Exec. Dir.: Vincent Warren

Assoc. Exec. Dir.: Carolyn Chambers

Sr. Staff Atty.: Maria Lahood

Civil Rights, Human Rights

Center for Judicial Accountability, Inc.
P.O. Box 3002, Southampton 11969
(631) 377-3583; Fax: (631) 377-3582
E-mail: cja@judgewatch.org
Internet: www.judgewatch.org

Administrative/Corporate Office, 283 Soundview Ave., White Plains 10606 (914) 421-1200

Director: Elena Ruth Sassower
E-mail: elena@judgewatch.org

Administrator: Doris L. Sassower
E-mail: doris@judgewatch.org

Special Counsel: Eli Vigliano

Serves litigant and lawyer victims of judicial misconduct.

Empire Justice Center
119 Washington Ave., 2nd Floor, Albany 12210
(518) 462-6831; Fax: (518) 462-6687;
Toll Free: (800) 635-0355
Internet: www.empirejustice.org

President/C.E.O.: Anne Erickson, Ext. 103
E-mail: aerickson@empirejustice.org

Senior Attys.:
Susan Antos, Ext. 105
E-mail: santos@empirejustice.org
Louise M. Tarantino, Ext. 102
E-mail: ltarantino@empirejustice.org
Barbara Weiner, Ext. 104
E-mail: bweiner@empirejustice.org

Staff Attys.:
Saima Akhtar, Ext. 116
E-mail: sakhtar@empirejustice.org
Kristen Keefe, Ext. 109
E-mail: kkeefe@empirejustice.org

Public Interest Law
Serves all of New York state except N.Y.C.; Formerly Greater Upstate Law Project; formed as a result of the merger between the Greater Upstate Law Project and the Public Interest Law Office of Rochester

Empire Justice Center
Telesca Center for Justice, Suite 200,
1 W. Main St., Rochester 14614
(585) 454-4060; Fax: (585) 454-2518;
Toll-Free: (800) 724-0490

Chief Counsel: Bryan Hetherington (585) 295-5809
E-mail: bhetherington@empirejustice.org

Senior Attys.:
Kate Callery (585) 295-5727
E-mail: kcallery@empirejustice.org
Trilby de Jung (585) 295-5722
E-mail: tdejung@empirejustice.org
Peter Dellinger (585) 295-5811
E-mail: pdellinger@empirejustice.org
Jonathan Feldman (585) 295-5813
E-mail: jfeldman@empirejustice.org
L. J. Fisher (585) 295-5804
E-mail: lfisher@empirejustice.org
Michael Hanley (585) 295-5723
E-mail: mhanley@empirejustice.org
Ruhi Maker (585) 295-5808
E-mail: rmaker@empirejustice.org
Amy Schwartz (585) 295-5726
E-mail: aschwartz@empirejustice.org

Staff Attys.:
Katie Courtney (585) 295-5802
E-mail: kcourtney@empirejustice.org
Jane Gabriele (585) 295-5806
E-mail: jgabriele@empirejustice.org
Rebecca Case Grammatico (585) 295-5725
E-mail: rcase@empirejustice.org
Alexander Karsten (585) 295-5816
E-mail: akarsten@empirejustice.org
Michael Mule (585) 295-5724
E-mail: mmule@empirejustice.org
Kevin Purcell (585) 295-5820
E-mail: kpurcell@empirejustice.org
Persis Yu (585) 295-5630
E-mail: psyu@empirejustice.org

Training Dir.: Jerry Wein (585) 295-5721
E-mail: jwein@empirejustice.org

Public Benefits (Welfare, Medicaid, S.S.I. / S.S.A.), Housing, Consumer Law, Employment, Domestic Violence, Civil Rights, Health, HIV / AIDS, Education, Foreclosure Prevention, Disability
Serves all of New York state except N.Y.C.; Formerly the Greater Upstate Law Project

Empire Justice Center
80 N. Broadway, White Plains 10603
(914) 422-4333; Fax: (914) 422-4391
E-mail: info@empirejustice.org
Internet: www.empirejustice.org

Staff Attys.:
Linda Bennett-Rodriguez
E-mail: lbennett@empirejustice.org
Rob Cisneros (914) 422-4329
E-mail: rcisneros@empirejustice.org

Civil Law, Immigration, HIV / AIDS
Formerly Hudson Valley Poverty Law Center—Greater Upstate Law Project; serves all of New York State except N.Y.C.

Empire Justice Center
Public Advocacy Center, Touro Law Center, Room 222,
225 Eastview Dr., Central Islip 11722
(631) 650-2306; Fax: (631) 348-3571

Managing Atty.: Don Friedman (631) 650-2316

Staff Atty.: Linda Hassberg (631) 650-2305

Paralegal: Cheryl Keshner (631) 650-2317

Public Benefits and Immigrants
Serves all of New York state except N.Y.C.

Farmworker Law Project
Legal Aid Society of Mid-New York
52 S. Manheim Blvd., New Paltz 12561
(845) 256-9096, (800) 804-8575; Fax: (845) 256-0494

Managing Atty.: Charlotte Sibley
E-mail: csibley@wnylc.com

Statewide Migrant Farmworker Program

Farmworker Legal Services of New York, Inc.
1187 Culver Rd., Rochester 14609
(585) 325-3050; Fax: (585) 325-7614
Internet: www.flsny.org

Director: Lewis Papenfuse; E-mail: lpapenfuse@wnylc.com

Attys.:
David Irving
Amee Sampat

Provides legal services to migrant and seasonal farm workers

N.Y. State Defenders Association, Inc.
194 Washington Ave., Suite 500, Albany 12210-2314
(518) 465-3524; Fax: (518) 465-3249
E-mail: info@nysda.org
Internet: www.nysda.org

Exec. Dir.: Jonathan E. Gradess; E-mail: jgradess@nysda.org

Managing Atty.: Charles F. O'Brien
E-mail: cobrien@nysda.org

Criminal Law and Immigration Law

Statewide—Cont'd

N.Y. State Defenders Association Immigrant Defense Project (NYSDA)
3 W. 29th St., Suite 803, N.Y.C. 10001
(212) 725-6422; Fax: (800) 391-5713
Internet: www.immigrantdefenseproject.org
Co-Directors:
Michelle Fei (212) 725-6486
E-mail: mfei@immigrantdefenseproject.org
Benita Jain (212) 725-6485
E-mail: bjain@immigrantdefenseproject.org
Senior Counsel: Manuel D. Vargas (212) 725-6485
E-mail: mvargas@immigrantdefenseproject.org

NYS Mental Hygiene Legal Service
Third Department
40 Steuben St., Suite 501, Albany 12207
(518) 451-8710; Fax: (518) 473-5849
Director: Sheila E. Shea
Deputy Dir.: David M. LeVine

Prisoners' Legal Services of New York
Central Office, 41 State St., Suite M112, Albany 12207
(518) 445-6050; Fax: (518) 445-6053

114 Prospect St., Ithaca 14850
(607) 273-2283; Fax: (518) 272-9122

237 Main St., Suite 1535, Buffalo 14203
(716) 854-1007; Fax: (716) 854-1008

121 Bridge St., Suite 202, Plattsburgh 12901
(518) 561-3088; Fax: (518) 561-3262
Exec. Dir., Central Office: Karen Murtagh-Monks, Ext. 116
Managing Attys.:
Jim Bogin (Albany Office)
Michael Cassidy (Plattsburgh Office)
Betsy Hutchings (Ithaca Offices)
Maria Pagano (Buffalo Offices)

Public Utility Law Project (PULP)
194 Washington Ave., Suite 420, Albany 12210-2314
(518) 449-3375; Fax: (518) 449-1769
E-mail: info@pulp.tc
Internet: www.pulp.tc
Exec. Dir.: Gerald A. Norlander, Ext. 113
Senior Atty.: Lou Manuta, Ext. 118
Staff Atty.: Geraldine Gauthier, Ext. 114
Utility Law

ALBANY COUNTY

Albany County Conflict Defender
112 State St., Suite 1220, Albany 12207
(518) 447-5532; Fax: (518) 447-7416
Director: Thomas N. Dulin
Criminal Defense

Legal Aid Society of Northeastern New York, Inc.
55 Colvin Ave., Albany 12206
(518) 462-6765, (800) 462-2922; Fax: (518) 427-8352
Internet: www.lasnny.org
Exec. Dir.: Lillian M. Moy (518) 689-6304
E-mail: lmoy@lasnny.org
Also serves counties of Columbia, Greene, Rensselaer, Schenectady
Civil matters only

The Legal Project, Capital District Women's Bar Assn.
Stuyvesant Plaza, 1475 Western Ave., Albany 12203
(518) 435-1770; Fax: (518) 435-1773
E-mail: info@legalproject.org
Internet: www.legalproject.org
Exec. Dir.: Lisa A. Frisch
Supervising Atty.: Ellen C. Schell
Also serves counties of Rensselaer, Saratoga, Schenectady
Affordable Housing, Bankruptcy, Domestic Violence, Small Business, Military Domestic Violence, Foreclosure

Public Defender Albany County
60 S. Pearl St., Albany 12207
(518) 447-7150; Fax: (518) 447-5533
Internet: www.albanycounty.com
Public Defender: Peter M. Torncello
E-mail: ptorncello@albanycounty.com
Criminal, Family Court

ALLEGANY COUNTY

Assigned Counsel Plan of Allegany County
Embser & Woltag, P.C., 164 N. Main St., Wellsville 14895-1152
(585) 593-1090; Fax: (585) 593-6540
Administrator: J. Timothy Embser
Real Estate and Estate Matters

NYS Mental Hygiene Legal Service Fourth Dept., Eighth Judicial District Office
See Erie County

Public Defender Allegany County
7 Court St., Belmont 14813
(585) 268-9246; Fax: (585) 268-5888
Public Defender: Barbara J. Kelley
E-mail: kelleybj@alleganyco.com

Rural Law Center of New York
See Clinton County

Southern Tier Legal Services
See Steuben County

BRONX COUNTY

Office of the Appellate Defender First Dept. Assigned Counsel Corp.
See New York County

Asian American Legal Defense and Education Fund
See New York County

Assigned Counsel Plan for the City of New York
See New York County

Center for Appellate Litigation
See New York County

Lawyer Referral Service Queens County Bar Assn.
See Queens County

Lawyers Alliance for New York
See New York County

Legal Action Center of the City of New York, Inc.
See New York County

The Legal Aid Society—Bronx County
Civil Division
953 Southern Blvd., Bronx 10459
(718) 991-4600; Fax: (718) 842-2867
Internet: www.legal-aid.org
Supervising Atty.: Marshall Green
E-mail: mwgreen@legal-aid.org

Criminal Practice Division
1020 Grand Concourse, Bronx 10451
(718) 579-3000; Fax: (718) 588-2611
Atty.-in-Charge: David Clarke

Juvenile Rights Division
900 Sheridan Ave., Room 6-C12, Bronx 10451
(718) 579-7900; Fax: (718) 293-8744
Atty.-in-Charge: Amanda White
E-mail: aewhite@legal-aid.org

Legal Services NYC—Bronx
579 Courtlandt Ave., Bronx 10451
(718) 928-3700; Fax: (718) 402-7586
Internet: www.bronx.legalservicesnyc.org
Exec. Dir.: Vacancy at Press Time (718) 928-3736
Dir. of Litigation: Jill Siegel (718) 928-3744
General Practice, Elder Law, Poverty Law
Formerly Bronx Legal Services

Bronx County—Cont'd

MFY Legal Services, Inc.
See New York County

NYS Mental Hygiene Legal Service First Dept.
See New York County

Sanctuary for Families
Center for Battered Women's Legal Services
See New York County

BROOME COUNTY

Lawyer Referral Service
Broome County Bar Association
19 Chenango St., Suite 308, Binghamton 13901
(607) 723-6331; Fax: (607) 724-4085
Exec. Dir.: Sindy L. Garey
Also serves counties of Chenango, Tioga

Legal Aid Society of Mid-New York
30 Fayette St., Binghamton 13901
(607) 231-5900; Fax: (607) 724-7211
Managing Atty.: Alice Decker
Attys.:

Charlotte Bunzey	Lauren Praske
Suzanne Myette	Raymond Recchia
Susan Oakes	Arlene Sanders
Willa Payne	Christopher Smith

Also serves county of Chenango
Concentration in Civil Law

Public Defender Broome County
George Harvey Justice Bldg., 6th Floor,
45 Hawley St., Binghamton 13901
Mailing Address: P.O. Box 1766, Binghamton 13902
(607) 778-2403; Fax: (607) 778-2432
Public Defender: Jay L. Wilber
Criminal Law

CATTARAUGUS COUNTY

Assigned Counsel Plan of Cattaraugus County
4 S. Main St., Franklinville 14737
(716) 676-5524; Fax: (716) 676-3541
Administrator: James I. McAuley
Criminal, Family

NYS Mental Hygiene Legal Service Fourth Dept., Eighth Judicial District Office
See Erie County

Rural Law Center of New York
See Clinton County

Southern Tier Legal Services
See Steuben County

CAYUGA COUNTY

Assigned Counsel Plan of Cayuga County
Cayuga County Court House, 152 Genesee St.,
Auburn 13021
(315) 253-1402; Fax: (315) 253-1544
Internet: www.cayugacounty.us/counsel/index.html
Administrator: Lloyd E. Hoskins
E-mail: defender@co.cayuga.ny.us
Criminal, Family, Appellate

Legal Aid Society of Mid-New York, Inc.
See Onondaga County

Legal Aid Society of Mid-New York, Inc.
See Oswego County

NYS Mental Hygiene Legal Service Fourth Dept., Fifth Judicial District Office
See Onondaga County

Rural Law Center of New York
See Clinton County

CHAUTAUQUA COUNTY

Legal Aid of Chautauqua Region, Inc.
Chautauqua County Legal Services
111 W. 2nd St., Suite 250, Jamestown 14701
(716) 483-2116; Fax: (716) 664-9590

Dunkirk Office, 314 Central Ave., Dunkirk 14048
Director: Clyde W. Card
Legal Dir.: Sally A. Jaroszynski
Staff Atty.: Robert W. Schnizler
Civil

NYS Mental Hygiene Legal Service Fourth Dept., Eighth Judicial District Office
See Erie County

Public Defender Chautauqua County
Hall R. Clothier Bldg., Room 106, 7 N. Erie St.,
Mayville 14757-1027
(716) 753-4376; Fax: (716) 753-4751
Public Defender: William F. Coughlin
Criminal & Family Court Matters

Rural Law Center of New York
See Clinton County

CHEMUNG COUNTY

Chemung County Neighborhood Legal Services
215 E. Church St., Suite 301, Elmira 14901-2889
(607) 734-1647; Fax: (607) 734-1018
Atty.: Thomas S. Dubel
Also serves county of Schuyler
Welfare, Eviction, S.S.I.

Public Defender Chemung County
163 Lake St., P.O. Box 588, Elmira 14902-0588
(607) 737-2969; Fax: (607) 737-2853
Public Defender: Scott N. Fierro
E-mail: sfierro@co.chemung.ny.us
Criminal Law

Rural Law Center of New York
See Clinton County

CHENANGO COUNTY

Chenango County Public Defender
5 Court St., Room 212, Norwich 13815
(607) 337-1870; Fax: (607) 337-1489
E-mail: publicdefender@co.chenango.ny.us
Public Defender: Alan E. Gordon (607) 843-8955
Criminal and Family Court

Lawyer Referral Service Broome County Bar Assn.
See Broome County

Legal Aid Society of Mid-New York
See Broome County

Legal Aid Society of Mid-New York, Inc.
27 W. Main St., Norwich 13815
(607) 336-8256; Fax: (607) 334-8004
Managing Atty.: Alice Decker; E-mail: adecer@wnylc.com

Rural Law Center of New York
See Clinton County

CLINTON COUNTY

Assigned Counsel Plan of Clinton County
178 Broad St., Plattsburgh 12901-2524
(518) 561-9251; Fax: (518) 561-9254
Administrator: Richard E. Cantwell
E-mail: firm@cantwelllaw.com

Clinton County—Cont'd

Legal Aid Society of Northeastern New York, Inc.
100 Court St., P.O. Box 989, Plattsburgh 12901
(518) 563-4022, (800) 722-7380; Fax: (518) 563-4058
Internet: www.lasnny.org/
Deputy Dir.: Peter Racette, Ext. 18
E-mail: pracette@lasnny.org
Attys.:
Daniel Alley, Ext. 13
E-mail: dalley@lasnny.org
Stephen Baker, Ext. 19
E-mail: sbaker@lasnny.org
Gerry Schafer, Ext. 14
E-mail: gschafer@lasnny.org
Brenna Sharp, Ext. 20
E-mail: bsharp@lasnny.org
Also serves counties of Essex, Franklin, Hamilton
Formerly North Country Legal Services, Inc.

Rural Law Center of New York
22 U.S. Oval, Suite 203, Plattsburgh 12903
(518) 561-5460; Fax: (518) 561-5468
Internet: http://rurallawcenter.org
Exec. Dir.: Susan L. Patnode
Also serves counties of Allegany, Cattaraugus, Cayuga, Chautauqua, Chemung, Chenango, Columbia, Cortland, Delaware, Essex, Franklin, Fulton, Genesee, Greene, Hamilton, Herkimer, Jefferson, Lewis, Livingston, Madison, Montgomery, Ontario, Orleans, Oswego, Otsego, Putnam, Rensselaer, St. Lawrence, Saratoga, Schenectady, Schoharie, Schuyler, Seneca, Steuben, Sullivan, Tioga, Tompkins, Ulster, Warren, Washington, Wayne, Wyoming, Yates
Civil Law

COLUMBIA COUNTY

Legal Aid Society of Northeastern New York, Inc.
See Albany County

Public Defender Columbia County
610 State St., Hudson 12534
(518) 828-3410; Fax: (518) 828-4076
Public Defender: Arlene Levinson
Criminal, Appellate, Family

Rural Law Center of New York
See Clinton County

Workers' Rights Law Center of New York, Inc.
See Ulster County

CORTLAND COUNTY

Legal Aid Society of Mid-New York, Inc.
111 Port Watson St., Cortland 13045
(607) 428-8400; Fax: (607) 753-7257
Senior Managing Atty.: Dan Altwarg
E-mail: daltwarg@wnylc.com

Public Defender Cortland County
60 Central Ave., Cortland 13045-5590
(607) 753-5046; Fax: (607) 753-0781
E-mail: lmanning@Cortland-co.org
Public Defender: Keith D. Dayton

Rural Law Center of New York
See Clinton County

DELAWARE COUNTY

Assigned Counsel Plan of Delaware County
P.O. Box 204, Harpersfield 13786
Administrator: Teresa C. Mulliken (607) 652-9790
Criminal, Family

Legal Aid Society of Mid-New York, Inc.
See Otsego County

Rural Law Center of New York
See Clinton County

DUTCHESS COUNTY

Legal Services of the Hudson Valley
See Westchester County

NYS Mental Hygiene Legal Service
Second Judicial Department
See Nassau County

NYS Mental Hygiene Legal Service Second Dept., Ninth Judicial District Office
See Rockland County

Public Defender Dutchess County
22 Market St., Poughkeepsie 12601
(845) 486-2280; Fax: (845) 486-2266
Public Defender: David Goodman
E-mail: dgoodman@co.dutchess.ny.us

Workers' Rights Law Center of New York, Inc.
See Ulster County

ERIE COUNTY

Erie County Bar Association
Aid to Indigent Prisoners Society, Inc.
Assigned Counsel Progam, 170 Franklin St., Suite 400, Buffalo 14202
(716) 856-8804; Fax: (716) 856-0424
Internet: http://assigned.org
Administrator: Robert D. Lonski
E-mail: rlonski@assigned.org
Criminal, Family Law

The Legal Aid Bureau of Buffalo, Inc.
237 Main St., Suite 1602, Buffalo 14203-2723
(716) 853-9555; Fax: (716) 853-3219
Internet: www.legalaidbuffalo.org
Executive Dir.: David C. Schopp, Ext. 450
Public Interest Law, Criminal Defense, Juvenile Rights, Law Guardian representation, Domestic Relations, Consumer and Housing matters, Mortgage Foreclosure Prevention.

Public Defender Unit
50 Delaware Ave., 4th Floor, Buffalo 14202
(716) 855-1553; Fax: (716) 856-3951
Chief Atty. of Criminal Services:
Helen W. Zimmermann, Ext. 43

Neighborhood Legal Services, Inc.
237 Main St., 4th Floor, Buffalo 14203
(716) 847-0650; Fax: (716) 847-0227
Internet: www.nls.org
Exec. Dir.: William J. Hawkes
E-mail: whawkes@nls.org
Supervising Attys.:
Grace Andriette (Housing)
Keith Morgenheim (Family)
James Sheldon (Disability)
Elizabeth White (Public Benefits)
Civil Legal Services to low-income people

NYS Mental Hygiene Legal Service
Fourth Department, Eighth Judicial District Office
438 Main St., Suite 400, Buffalo 14202-3211
(716) 845-3650; Fax: (716) 874-7794
Principal Atty. in Charge: Keith M. Fehrer
Also serves counties of Allegany, Cattaraugus, Chautauqua, Genesee, Niagara, Orleans

ESSEX COUNTY

Legal Aid Society of Northeastern New York, Inc.
See Clinton County

Rural Law Center of New York
See Clinton County

FRANKLIN COUNTY

Legal Aid Society of Northeastern New York, Inc.
See Clinton County

Legal Aid Society of Northeastern New York, Inc.
See Saint Lawrence County

Public Defender Franklin County
355 W. Main St., Suite 237, Malone 12953
(518) 481-1624; Fax: (518) 483-4690
Public Defender: Thomas G. Soucia (518) 481-1627
Assigned Counsel Coordinator: Shawn Fournier (518) 481-1423; Fax: (518) 481-1425

Rural Law Center of New York
See Clinton County

FULTON COUNTY

Legal Aid Society of Northeastern New York, Inc.
See Montgomery County

Public Defender Fulton County
55 E. Main St., Suite 20, Johnstown 12095
(518) 736-5820; Fax: (518) 762-0122
Public Defender: J. Gerard McAuliffe, Jr.

Rural Law Center of New York
See Clinton County

GENESEE COUNTY

Genesee County Legal Assistance Corp.
81 Main St., Suite 1, Batavia 14020
(585) 343-0811; Fax: (585) 343-0880
Administrator: Randolph Zickl

Legal Aid Society of Rochester
See Monroe County

NYS Mental Hygiene Legal Service Fourth Dept., Eighth Judicial District Office
See Erie County

Oak Orchard Legal Services
Division of Neighborhood Legal Services, Inc.
5073 Clinton Street Rd., Batavia 14020-1126
(585) 343-5450, (800) 724-7544; Fax: (585) 343-5503
Managing Atty.: John M. Zonitch
Also serves counties of Orleans, Wyoming
Civil

Public Defender Genesee County
Genesee County Courts Facility, 1 W. Main St., Batavia 14020
(585) 344-2550, Ext. 2280; Fax: (585) 344-8553
Public Defender: Gary A. Horton
E-mail: ghorton@co.genesee.ny.us

Rural Law Center of New York
See Clinton County

GREENE COUNTY

Legal Aid Society of Northeastern New York, Inc.
See Albany County

Public Defender Greene County
Greene County Office Bldg., 2nd Floor, 411 Main St., P.O. Box 413, Catskill 12414
(518) 719-3220; Fax: (518) 719-3785
E-mail: publicdefender@discovergreene.com
Public Defender: Dominic J. Cornelius

Rural Law Center of New York
See Clinton County

Workers' Rights Law Center of New York, Inc.
See Ulster County

HAMILTON COUNTY

Hamilton County Public Defense Program
County Courthouse, Rte. 8, P.O. Box 205, Lake Pleasant 12108-0205
(518) 548-6651; Fax: (518) 548-7608
Coordinator: William Farber
Formerly Indigent Defendant Program

Legal Aid Society of Northeastern New York, Inc.
See Clinton County

Rural Law Center of New York
See Clinton County

HERKIMER COUNTY

Assigned Counsel Program of Herkimer County
209 N. Washington St., Herkimer 13350
(315) 866-0006; Fax: (315) 866-0689
Administrator: Keith D. Bowers
Criminal, Family Court

Legal Aid Society of Mid-New York, Inc. Main Office
See Oneida County

NYS Mental Hygiene Legal Service Fourth Dept., Fifth Judicial District
See Oneida County

Rural Law Center of New York
See Clinton County

JEFFERSON COUNTY

Assigned Counsel Plan of Jefferson County
255 State St., Carthage 13619
(315) 493-0311; Fax: (315) 493-1097
E-mail: tpg@twcny.rr.com
Administrator: Thomas P. Goodwin

Legal Aid Society of Mid-New York, Inc.
44 Public Sq., Watertown 13601
(315) 955-6700; Fax: (315) 785-9118
Managing Atty.: Terrence J. Whelan
E-mail: twhelan@wnylc.com
Staff Attys.:
Catherine Palermo Robert Peace
Also serves county of Lewis
Public Assistance/Landlord & Tenant

NYS Mental Hygiene Legal Service Fourth Dept., Fifth Judicial District Office
See Onondaga and Oneida Counties

Public Defender Jefferson County
County Office Bldg., 4th Floor, 175 Arsenal St., Watertown 13601
(315) 785-3152; Fax: (315) 785-5060
E-mail: joannem@co.jefferson.ny.us
Public Defender: Julie M. Hutchins

Rural Law Center of New York
See Clinton County

KINGS COUNTY

Appellate Advocates
See New York County

Asian American Legal Defense and Education Fund
See New York County

Assigned Counsel Plan for the City of New York
See New York County

Bedford-Stuyvesant Community Legal Services Corp.
1360 Fulton St., Suite 301, Brooklyn 11216-2674
(718) 636-1155; Fax: (718) 398-6414
E-mail: bed-stuy-legal-services@bsls.org
Managing Dir./General Counsel: Victor Olds
Civil cases only

Kings County—Cont'd

Brooklyn Defender Services
177 Livingston St., 5th Floor, Brooklyn 11201
(718) 254-0700; Fax: (718) 254-0897
Internet: www.bds.org
Exec. Dir.: Lisa Schreibersdorf
Criminal, Family Court

Brooklyn Legal Services Corp. A
Williamsburg Office
256-260 Broadway, Brooklyn 11211 (718) 487-2300
Internet: www.bka.org
Project Dir. and Chief Counsel: Martin S. Needelman
E-mail: mneedelman@bka.org
Civil cases only

Bushwick Office
1455 Myrtle Ave., Brooklyn 11237
(718) 487-1300; Fax: (718) 326-2944
Managing Atty.: David J. Bryan (718) 487-0856
E-mail: dbryan@bka.org
Landlord / Tenant, Family, Benefits, Poverty Law, Foreclosure Prevention

East Brooklyn Office
80 Jamaica Ave., 2nd Floor, Brooklyn 11207
(718) 487-1300; Fax: (718) 342-1780
General Counsel: Paul J. Acinapura
(718) 487-1338; Fax: (718) 345-2810
E-mail: pacinapura@bka.org
Civil, including Housing, HIV, SSI, Group Housing, Community Economic Development

Lawyer Referral Service Queens County Bar Assn.
See Queens County

Lawyers Alliance for New York
See New York County

Legal Action Center of the City of New York, Inc.
See New York County

The Legal Aid Society—Kings County

Brooklyn Civil Neighborhood Office
111 Livingston St., 7th Floor, Brooklyn 11201
(718) 722-3100; Fax: (718) 722-3093
Internet: www.legal-aid.org
Atty.-in-Charge: Emily Ruben

Criminal Defense Division
111 Livingston St., 9th Floor, Brooklyn 11201
(718) 237-2000; Fax: (718) 237-8737
Atty.-in-Charge: Dawn C. Ryan
E-mail: dryan@legal-aid.org

Brooklyn Office for the Aging
111 Livingston St., 6th Floor, Brooklyn 11201
(718) 645-3111; Fax: (718) 260-4722
Atty.-in-Charge: Diane E. Lutwak
E-mail: delutwak@legal-aid.org
Civil Legal Services for the elderly poor

Juvenile Rights Division
111 Livingston St., 8th Floor, Brooklyn 11201
(718) 237-3100; Fax: (718) 250-4243
Atty.-in-Charge: Martin Feinman (718) 250-4238

Federal Defender Division
See U.S. District Court, Eastern District of New York under Federal Defenders of New York, Inc.

Legal Services NYC—Brooklyn
180 Livingston St., Brooklyn 11201
(718) 852-8888; Fax: (718) 858-1786
Internet: www.lsnybb.org
Brighton Branch, 3049 Brighton 6th St., Brooklyn 11235
32 Penn St., Brooklyn 11211 (718) 643-9700
Project Dir.: Jennifer Levy; E-mail: jlevy@sbls.org
Poverty Law
Formerly Comm. Action for Legal Services, Inc.

MFY Legal Services, Inc.
See New York County

NYS Mental Hygiene Legal Service Second Judicial Department
See Nassau County

NYS Mental Hygiene Legal Service Second Dept., Second, Eleventh & Thirteenth Judicial District Office
See Queens County

Sanctuary for Families Center for Battered Women's Legal Services
See New York County

South Brooklyn Legal Services
105 Court St., 3rd Floor, Brooklyn 11201
(718) 237-5500; Fax: (718) 855-0733
Internet: www.sbls.org
Project Dir.: John C. Gray
Dir. of Litigation: Edward Josephson
Formerly Brooklyn Legal Services Corp. B—South Brooklyn Office.

LEWIS COUNTY

Legal Aid Society of Mid-New York, Inc.
See Jefferson County

Lewis Defenders, P.L.L.C.
7659 N. State St., Suite 301, Lowville 13367
(315) 874-4201; Fax: (315) 376-8766
Public Defender: Michael F. Young

NYS Mental Hygiene Legal Service Fourth Dept., Fifth Judicial District
See Oneida County

Rural Law Center of New York
See Clinton County

LIVINGSTON COUNTY

Legal Aid Society of Rochester
See Monroe County

Legal Assistance of Western New York, Inc.
See Ontario County

NYS Mental Hygiene Legal Service Fourth Dept.
See Monroe County

Public Defender Livingston County
Livingston County Govt. Center, Room 109, 6 Court St., Geneseo 14454 (585) 243-7028; Fax: (585) 243-7193
Public Defender: Marcea Clark Tetamore
E-mail: mctetamore@co.livingston.ny.us

Rural Law Center of New York
See Clinton County

MADISON COUNTY

Legal Aid Society of Mid-New York, Inc. Main Office
See Oneida County

Public Defender Madison County
Madison County Office Bldg., North Court St.,
P.O. Box 576, Wampsville 13163
(315) 366-2585; Fax: (315) 366-2816
Director: Paul H. Hadley
First Asst.: Rebecca L. Wittman
Second Asst.: Peter R. Bereskin
Third Asst.: William M. Roth
Criminal Defense

Rural Law Center of New York
See Clinton County

MONROE COUNTY

Legal Aid Society of Rochester
1 W. Main St., Suite 800, Rochester 14614
(585) 232-4090; Fax: (585) 232-2352
Internet: www.lasroc.org
Exec. Dir.: Alan S. Harris; E-mail: aharris@lasroc.org
Also serves counties of Genesee, Livingston, Orleans
Housing, Family, Immigration, Education

Monroe County Legal Assistance Center
1 W. Main St., 4th Floor, Rochester 14614
(585) 325-2520; Fax: (585) 325-2559
Internet: www.lawny.org
Exec. Dir.: C. Kenneth Perri
Legal Assistance of Western New York, Inc.,
361 S. Main St., Geneva 14456
(315) 781-1465, Ext. 1713
Managing Atty.: Louis Prieto
Poverty Law

NYS Mental Hygiene Legal Service
Fourth Department
M. Dolores Denman Cthse., Suite 402, 50 East Ave., Rochester 14604
(585) 530-3050; Fax: (585) 530-3079
Director: Emmett J. Creahan
Deputy Dir.: Neil J. Rowe
Principal Atty. in Charge: Walter F. Martin
Also serves counties of Livingston, Ontario, Seneca, Steuben, Wayne, Wyoming, Yates

Public Defender Monroe County
10 N. Fitzhugh St., Rochester 14614
(585) 753-4210; Fax: (585) 753-4234
Public Defender: Timothy P. Donaher
E-mail: tdonaher@monroecounty.gov

MONTGOMERY COUNTY

Legal Aid Society of Northeastern New York, Inc.
1 Kimball St., Amsterdam 12010
(518) 842-9466, (800) 821-8347; Fax: (518) 843-1792
Atty.-in-Charge: Wendy Wahlberg (Deputy Director)
Staff Attys.:
Melissa Johnson Robert Romaker
Also serves counties of Fulton, Schoharie
Civil Law
Formerly an office of Legal Aid Society Mid-New York, Inc.

Rural Law Center of New York
See Clinton County

NASSAU COUNTY

Community Legal Assistance Corp.
School of Law, 108 Hofstra Univ., Hempstead 11549-1080
(516) 463-5934; Fax: (516) 463-5937
Dir. of Clinical Programs: Theo S. Liebmann
(516) 463-6078; Fax: (516) 463-5937
Also serves county of Queens
Criminal Misdemeanors, Housing Rights, Child Advocacy, Mediation, Political Asylum and Securities Arbitration, Community and Economic Development

Lawyer Referral Information Service
Bar Association of Nassau County, NY, Inc.
15th & West Sts., Mineola 11501
Clients: (516) 747-4832; Attorneys: (516) 747-4070;
Fax: (516) 747-4147

Lawyer Referral Service Queens County Bar Assn.
See Queens County

Legal Aid Society of Nassau County, N.Y.
1 Helen Keller Way, 3rd Floor, Hempstead 11550
(516) 560-6400; Fax: (516) 565-3694
Internet: www.nclas.org
President: N. Scott Banks
Atty.-in-Chief: Kent V. Moston, Ext. 412
Criminal, Family

Nassau County Bar Association Assigned Counsel Defender Plan, Inc.
15th and West Sts., Mineola 11501
(516) 747-8448; Fax: (516) 873-8032
E-mail: acdp@optonline.net
Internet: www.nassau18b.org
Administrator: Patrick L. McCloskey (516) 747-8448
Criminal Law

Nassau/Suffolk Law Services Committee, Inc.
1 Helen Keller Way, 5th Floor, Hempstead 11550-3903
(516) 292-8100; Fax: (516) 292-6529;
Elder Law: (516) 292-8088;
Volunteer Lawyers Project: (516) 292-8299
Internet: www.nslawservices.org
Exec. Dir.: Jeffrey A. Seigel; E-mail: jseigel@wnylc.com
Poverty Law, Civil Matters, Elder Law

NYS Mental Hygiene Legal Service
Second Judicial Department
170 Old Country Rd., Suite 500, Mineola 11501
(516) 746-4545; Fax: (516) 746-4372
Director: Sidney Hirschfeld
Deputy Dir.: Lesley DeLia
Also serves counties of Dutchess, Kings, Orange, Putnam, Queens, Richmond, Rockland, Suffolk, Westchester
Limited to representing the mentally disabled.

NYS Mental Hygiene Legal Service Second Dept., Tenth Judicial District Office
See Suffolk County

NEW YORK COUNTY

Appellate Advocates
2 Rector St., 10th Floor, N.Y.C. 10006
(212) 693-0085; Fax: (212) 693-0878
Internet: www.appad.org
Atty.-in-Charge: Lynn W.L. Fahey
E-mail: lfahey@appad.org
Asst. Atty. in Charge: Barry Stendig
Also serves counties of Kings, Queens, Richmond
Criminal Appeals

Office of the Appellate Defender
First Department Assigned Counsel Corp.
11 Park Pl., Suite 1601, N.Y.C. 10007
(212) 402-4100; Fax: (212) 402-4199
E-mail: info@appellatedefender.org
Internet: www.appellatedefender.org
Atty.-in-Charge: Richard M. Greenberg
E-mail: rgreenberg@appellatedefender.org
Also serves county of Bronx
Criminal Appeals

Asian American Legal Defense and Education Fund
99 Hudson St., 12th Floor, N.Y.C. 10013-2869
(212) 966-5932; Fax: (212) 966-4303
E-mail: info@aaldef.org
Internet: www.aaldef.org
Exec. Dir.: Margaret Fung
Also serves counties of Bronx, Kings, Queens, Richmond
Civil Rights, Immigration, Employment, Labor, Education

Assigned Counsel Plan for the City of New York
253 Broadway, Room 200, N.Y.C. 10007
(212) 676-0066; Fax: (212) 676-0088
Co-Directors:
Larry Parkins (212) 676-0093
Mimi Shui-Han (212) 676-0057
Administrators:
Barbara DiFiore
(2nd Dept. (Brooklyn, Queens, Staten Island))
(212) 676-0055; Fax: (212) 676-0089
Jacqueline P. Flug (1st Dept. (Manhattan & Bronx))
(212) 676-0061; Fax: (212) 676-0089
Also serves counties of Bronx, Kings, Queens, Richmond
Criminal, Appeals

New York County—Cont'd

Capital Defender Office
Kevin Doyle, Arnold & Porter, L.L.P., 35th Floor,
399 Park Ave., N.Y.C. 10022
(212) 715-1000; Fax: (212) 715-1399

Capital Defender Office has ceased operations due to abolition of the death penalty in New York. Information on former cases available at above address.

Center for Appellate Litigation
74 Trinity Pl., 11th Floor, N.Y.C. 10006
(212) 577-2523; Fax: (212) 577-2535
Internet: www.appellate-litigation.org

Attorney-in-Charge: Robert S. Dean
E-mail: rdean@cfal.org

Also serves county of Bronx

Criminal Appeals

LatinoJustice PRLDEF
99 Hudson St., 14th Floor, N.Y.C. 10013
(212) 219-3360, (800) 328-2322; Fax: (212) 431-4276
E-mail: info@latinojustice.org
Internet: www.latinojustice.org

President/General Counsel: Cesar A. Perales

Class Action Civil Rights cases, Human Rights, Voting Rights, Language Access and Immigrant Rights

Lawyer Referral Service Queens County Bar Assn.
See Queens County

Lawyers Alliance for New York
171 Madison Ave., 6th Floor, N.Y.C. 10016
(212) 219-1800; Fax: (212) 941-7458
E-mail: info@lawyersalliance.org
Internet: www.lawyersalliance.org

Exec. Dir.: Sean C. Delany, Ext. 227
E-mail: sdelany@lawyersalliance.org

Deputy Exec. Dir.: Elizabeth Guggenheimer, Ext. 231
E-mail: eguggenheimer@lawyersalliance.org

Legal Dir.: Linda S. Manley, Ext. 239
E-mail: lmanley@lawyersalliance.org

Pro Bono Mgr.: Jolynda Burton, Ext. 242
E-mail: jburton@lawyersalliance.org

Also serves counties of Bronx, Kings, Queens, Richmond

Provides non-litigation legal services to non-profit organizations throughout New York City.

Legal Action Center of the City of New York, Inc.
225 Varick St., 4th Floor, N.Y.C. 10014
(212) 243-1313; Fax: (212) 675-0286
Internet: http://lac.org

Director/President: Paul N. Samuels

Legal Dir.: Sally Friedman

Also serves counties of Bronx, Kings, Queens, Richmond

The Legal Aid Society
Administrative Offices
199 Water St., N.Y.C. 10038
(212) 577-3300; Fax: (212) 509-8761
Internet: www.legal-aid.org

President: Blaine (Fin) V. Fogg

Atty-in-Chief: Steven Banks
E-mail: sbanks@legal-aid.org

Civil Practice—Administration
199 Water St., N.Y.C. 10038
(212) 577-3300; Fax: (212) 509-8753
Internet: www.legal-aid.org

Harlem Community Law Office,
230 E. 106th St., N.Y.C. 10029
(212) 426-3000; Fax: (212) 876-5365

Bronx Neighborhood Office, 953 Southern Blvd.,
Bronx 10459 (718) 991-4600; Fax: (718) 842-2867

Queens Neighborhood Office,
120-46 Queens Blvd., 2nd Floor, Kew Gardens 11415
(718) 286-2450; Fax: (718) 263-4234

Lower Manhattan Neighborhood Office,
199 Water St., N.Y.C. 10038
(212) 577-3300; Fax: (212) 509-8761

Staten Island Neighborhood Office, 60 Bay St., 3rd Floor,
Staten Island 10301 (347) 422-5333

Brooklyn Neighborhood Office,
111 Livingston St., 7th Floor, Brooklyn 11201
(718) 722-3100; Fax: (718) 722-3093

Brooklyn Office for the Aging, 7th Floor,
111 Livingston St., Brooklyn 11201
(718) 645-3111; Fax: (718) 260-4722

Attys.-in-Charge:
Marshall Green (Bronx Office)
E-mail: mwgreen@legal-aid.org
Elizabeth Hay
(Lower Manhattan & Harlem Community Offices)
E-mail: eahay@legal-aid.org
Adriene Holder (Civil Practice)
E-mail: aholder@legal-aid.org
Christopher Lamb (Staten Island)
E-mail: clamb@legal-aid.org
Diane Lutwak (Brooklyn Office for the Aging)
E-mail: delutwak@legal-aid.org
April Newbauer (Queens Office)
E-mail: anewbauer@legal-aid.org
Scott Rosenberg (Homeless Rights/Law Reform)
E-mail: srosenberg@legal-aid.org
Emily Ruben (Brooklyn Office)
E-mail: epruben@legal-aid.org

Supervising Attys.:
Jojo Annobil (Immigration Unit)
E-mail: jannobil@legal-aid.org
Anne Callagy (Disability Advocacy Project)
E-mail: acallagy@legal-aid.org
Jocelyne Martinez (Disability Advocacy Project)
E-mail: jgmartinez@legal-aid.org
Emily Ruben (Family Law Unit)
E-mail: epruben@legal-aid.org
Lisa Sbrana (Health Law Unit)
E-mail: lbsbrana@legal-aid.org

Criminal Practice—Administration
199 Water St., 6th Floor, N.Y.C. 10038
(212) 577-3300; Fax: (212) 809-2942
Internet: www.legal-aid.org

49 Thomas St., N.Y.C. 10013
(212) 732-5000; Fax: (212) 298-5252

111 Livingston St., 7th Floor, Brooklyn 11201
(718) 237-2000; Fax: (718) 237-8737

1020 Grand Concourse, Bronx 10451
(718) 579-3000; Fax: (718) 588-2611

120-46 Queens Blvd., Kew Gardens 11415
(718) 286-2000; Fax: (718) 286-2486

Atty.-in-Charge: Seymour W. James, Jr.
E-mail: swjames@legal-aid.org

Federal Defender Division

See U.S. District Court, Eastern and Southern Districts of New York under Federal Defenders of New York, Inc.

Juvenile Rights Practice
199 Water St., 3rd Floor, N.Y.C. 10038
(212) 577-3300; Fax: (212) 577-3521
Internet: www.legal-aid.org

60 Lafayette St., Room 9A, N.Y.C. 10013
(212) 312-2260; Fax: (212) 349-0874

111 Livingston St., 8th Floor, Brooklyn 11201
(718) 237-3100; Fax: (718) 250-4243

900 Sheridan Ave., Room 6-C12, Bronx 10451
(718) 579-7900; Fax: (718) 293-8744

153-01 Jamaica Ave., Jamaica 11432
(718) 298-8900; Fax: (718) 657-0537

60 Bay St., 2nd Floor, Staten Island 10301
(718) 981-0219; Fax: (718) 981-6623

Atty.-in-Charge: Tamara Steckler
E-mail: tasteckler@legal-aid.org

New York County—Cont'd

Legal Services NYC
350 Broadway, 6th Floor, N.Y.C. 10013
(212) 431-7200, 646-3600; Fax: (212) 966-9571
Internet: www.legalservicesnyc.org
Exec. Dir./President: Andrew Scherer
E-mail: ascherer@ls-nyc.org
Also serves counties of Bronx, Kings, Queens, Richmond
Civil Law
Formerly Comm. Action for Legal Services, Inc.

Manhattan Legal Services, Inc.
1 West 125th St., 2nd Floor, N.Y.C. 10027
(646) 442-3100; Fax: (212) 348-4093

90 John St., Suite 301, N.Y.C. 10038
(646) 442-3100; Fax: (212) 227-9798
Exec. Dir.: Peggy Earisman
Housing Law, Public Entitlement Law, Family Law, Domestic Violence and HIV Project, Social Security Law, Employment & Immigration

MFY Legal Services, Inc.
299 Broadway, N.Y.C. 10007
(212) 417-3700; Fax: (212) 417-3890
Internet: www.mfy.org
Exec. Dir.: Christopher D. Lamb
Deputy Dir.: Jeanette Zelhof
Supervising Attys.:
Elise Brown
Ramonita Cordero
Sara J. Fulton
Andrew Goldberg
Kenneth Lau
Christopher Schwartz
Also serves counties of Bronx, Kings, Queens, Richmond
Civil, Poverty Law, Employment Law, Housing Law, Mental Health, Consumer

New York Civil Liberties Union
125 Broad St., 19th Floor, N.Y.C. 10004
(212) 607-3300; Fax: (212) 607-3318, 29
Internet: www.nyclu.org
Exec. Dir.: Donna Lieberman
Legal Dir.: Arthur Eisenberg
Civil Liberties cases only

NYS Mental Hygiene Legal Service
First Department
41 Madison Ave., 26th Floor, N.Y.C. 10010
(646) 386-5891; Fax: (212) 779-1894
Director: Marvin Bernstein
Deputy Dir.: Stephen Harkavy
Also serves county of Bronx

Puerto Rican Legal Defense and Education Fund
See LatinoJustice PRLDEF

Sanctuary for Families
Center for Battered Women's Legal Services
Wall St. Station, P.O. Box 1406, N.Y.C. 10268
(212) 349-6009; Fax: (212) 566-0344
Internet: www.sanctuaryforfamilies.org
Exec. Dir.: Laurel W. Eisner
Director: Dorchen A. Leidholdt
Also serves counties of Bronx, Kings, Queens, Richmond
Family, Criminal, Immigration

Volunteer Lawyers for the Arts
The Paley Bldg., 6th Floor, 1 E. 53rd St., N.Y.C. 10022
(212) 319-2787, Ext. 1; Fax: (212) 752-6575
Internet: www.vlany.org
Exec. Dir.: Elena M. Paul, Ext. 17
E-mail: epaul@vlany.org
Chairman: David Leichtman
Intellectual Property; Entertainment Law; Art Law; Help for Arts Non-Profits; Corporate Law.

Volunteers of Legal Service, Inc.
54 Greene St., N.Y.C. 10013
(212) 966-4400; Fax: (212) 219-8943
E-mail: info@volsprobono.org
Exec. Dir.: William J. Dean; E-mail: wdean@volsprobono.org
Civil Law

NIAGARA COUNTY

Niagara County Legal Aid Society
775 Third St., P.O. Box 844, Niagara Falls 14302-0844
(716) 284-8831; Fax: (716) 284-8040
Managing Atty.: Mary Ann Oliver
Civil Law

NYS Mental Hygiene Legal Service Fourth Dept., Eighth Judicial District Office
See Erie County

Public Defender Niagara County
139 Niagara St., Lockport 14094
Mailing Address: Niagara County Courthouse, 175 Hawley St., Lockport 14094-2740
(716) 439-7071

1925 Main St., Niagara Falls 14305
(716) 286-4706
Public Defender: David J. Farrugia

ONEIDA COUNTY

Assigned Counsel Plan of Oneida County
800 Park Ave., Utica 13501
(315) 793-6042; Fax: (315) 798-4042
Administrator: Chad D. DeFina

Legal Aid Society of Mid-New York, Inc.
Main Office
255 Genesee St., 2nd Floor, Utica 13501
(315) 793-7000; Toll-free: (877) 203-1062;
Fax: (315) 732-3202
Internet: www.lasmny.org
Exec. Dir.: Paul J. Lupia (315) 793-7077
E-mail: plupia@wnylc.com
Managing Atty.: Cindy Domingue-Hendrickson
(315) 793-7033; E-mail: cdh@wnylc.com
Staff Attys.:
Olli Baker (315) 793-7029
E-mail: obaker@wnylc.com
Gregory J. Dziwis (315) 793-7037
E-mail: gdziwis@wnylc.com
Brian Ehrhard (315) 793-7089
E-mail: behrhard@whylc.com
Danielle Mustard (315) 793-7049
E-mail: dmustard@wnylc.com
Christina Reilly (315) 793-7081
E-mail: creilly@wnylc.com
Ellen Sekreta (315) 793-7045
E-mail: esekreta@wnylc.com
Also serves counties of Herkimer, Madison
Civil Legal Services

NYS Mental Hygiene Legal Service
Fourth Department, Fifth Judicial District
207 Genesee St., Suite 1601, Utica 13501-2876
(315) 793-2370; Fax: (315) 793-2371
Director: Emmett J. Creahan
(585) 530-3050; Fax: (585) 530-3079
Deputy Chief Atty.: Michael J. Hungerford
Also serves counties of Herkimer, Jefferson, Lewis

Public Defender Oneida County
Civil Division
235 Elizabeth St., 2nd Floor, Utica 13501
(315) 266-6100; Fax: (315) 266-6105

301 W. Dominick St., Rome 13440 (315) 266-4528
Public Defender: Frank J. Furno; E-mail: ffurno@ocgov.net
Family

Public Defender Oneida County
Criminal Division
250 Boehlert Center, 321 Main St., Utica 13501
(315) 798-5870; Fax: (315) 734-0364
E-mail: pubdef@ocgov.net
Internet: www.onediacounty.org
Public Defender: Frank J. Nebush, Jr.

ONONDAGA COUNTY

Assigned Counsel Program Inc.
Onondaga County Bar Association
State Tower Bldg., Suite 6, 109 S. Warren St., Syracuse 13202
(315) 476-2921; Fax: (315) 476-0576

Exec. Dir.: Renee S. Captor

Frank H. Hiscock Legal Aid Society
351 S. Warren St., Syracuse 13202-2057
(315) 422-8191; Fax: (315) 472-2819

President/C.E.O.: Susan R. Horn
E-mail: srhorn@wnylc.com

Civil, Family, Appeals

Legal Aid Society of Mid-New York, Inc.
472 S. Salina St., Suite 400, Syracuse 13202-2498
(315) 703-6600; Fax: (315) 671-0062

Senior Managing Atty.: Dan Altwarg
E-mail: daltwarg@wnylc.com

Attys.:
William Bodwitch
Maureen Kieffer
Lewis Liebler
Gigi Meyers

Also serves county of Cayuga

Civil Law

NYS Mental Hygiene Legal Service
Fourth Department, Fifth Judicial District Office
The Syracuse Bldg., Suite 502, 224 Harrison St., Syracuse 13202
(315) 473-9495; Fax: (315) 473-9646

Deputy Chief Atty.: Michael J. Hungerford

Principal Atty. In Charge: Donald Walsh
Also serves counties of Cayuga, Jefferson, Oswego

Syracuse University College of Law
Office of Clinical Legal Education
306 MacNaughton Hall, Syracuse 13244-1030
Mailing Address: P.O. Box 6543, Syracuse 13217-6543
(315) 443-4582; Fax: (315) 443-3636

Director: Mary Helen McNeal

Clinic Administrator: Sue E. Davie

Family Law, Disability Rights, Indigent Criminal Defense, Community Development, Securities, Consumer, Low Income Taxpayer Issues and Elder Law.

ONTARIO COUNTY

Assigned Counsel Plan of Ontario County
66 N. Main St., Canandaigua 14424
(585) 396-2852; Fax: (585) 396-9409
E-mail: acpdefenders@yahoo.com

Administrator: Alexandra Burkett

Criminal, Family Court

Legal Assistance of Western New York, Inc.
361 S. Main St., Geneva 14456
(315) 781-1465; Fax: (315) 781-2565;
Toll-Free: (866) 781-5235
E-mail: lafl@lafl.org
Internet: www.lawny.org

Exec. Dir.: C. Kenneth Perri, Ext. 1713

Managing Atty.: Keith McCafferty
Also serves counties of Livingston, Seneca, Wayne, Yates

Civil including: Housing, Government Benefits, Domestic Violence, Seniors, Pro Se Divorce Clinics

NYS Mental Hygiene Legal Service Fourth Dept.
See Monroe County

Rural Law Center of New York
See Clinton County

ORANGE COUNTY

Assigned Counsel Plan of Orange County
Orange County Government Center, 255-275 Main St., Goshen 10924
(845) 294-7990; Fax: (845) 294-9233

Administrator: Mark D. Stern

Legal Aid Society of Orange County, Inc.
2 Court Ln., P.O. Box 328, Goshen 10924
(845) 291-2454; Fax: (845) 294-2638

Chief Atty.: Gary Abramson

Criminal and Family Court

Legal Services of the Hudson Valley
See Westchester County

NYS Mental Hygiene Legal Service
Second Judicial Department
See Nassau County

NYS Mental Hygiene Legal Service Second Dept., Ninth Judicial District Office
See Rockland County

Workers' Rights Law Center of New York, Inc.
See Ulster County

ORLEANS COUNTY

Legal Aid Society of Rochester
See Monroe County

NYS Mental Hygiene Legal Service Fourth Dept., Eighth Judicial District Office
See Erie County

Oak Orchard Legal Services Division of Neighborhood Legal Services, Inc.
See Genesee County

Public Defender Orleans County
Courthouse, Suite 5, 1 S. Main St., Albion 14411
(585) 589-7335; Fax: (585) 589-2592

Public Defender: Sanford A. Church

Rural Law Center of New York
See Clinton County

OSWEGO COUNTY

Assigned Counsel Plan of Oswego County
46 E. Bridge St., Oswego 13126
(315) 349-8575; Fax: (315) 349-8298

Administrator: Stephen C. Greene, Jr.

Criminal indigent defendants and other assignments of counsel authorized by the New York State County Law 722.

Legal Aid Society of Mid-New York, Inc.
108 W. Bridge St., Oswego 13126
(315) 532-6900; Fax: (315) 342-1891

Staff Atty.: Susan M. Faust
E-mail: sfaust@wnylc.com
Also serves county of Cayuga

NYS Mental Hygiene Legal Service Fourth Dept., Fifth Judicial District Office
See Onondaga County

Rural Law Center of New York
See Clinton County

OTSEGO COUNTY

Legal Aid Society of Mid-New York, Inc.
189 Main St., Suite 401, P.O. Box 887, Oneonta 13820
(607) 433-2220; Toll-Free: (800) 821-9895;
Fax: (607) 433-1433
Internet: www.lasmny.org

Supervising Atty.: Alice D. Decker
E-mail: adecker@wnylc.com
Also serves county of Delaware

Civil and Social Services

Otsego County—Cont'd

Public Defender Otsego County
48 Dietz St., Suite E, Oneonta 13820
(607) 432-7410; Fax: (607) 433-2168
Public Defender: Richard A. Rothermel

Rural Law Center of New York
See Clinton County

PUTNAM COUNTY

Legal Services of the Hudson Valley
See Westchester County

NYS Mental Hygiene Legal Service
Second Judicial Department
See Nassau County

NYS Mental Hygiene Legal Service Second Dept., Ninth Judicial District Office
See Rockland County

Putnam County Legal Aid Society, Inc.
20 Fair Street, Carmel 10512
(845) 225-8466; Fax: (845) 225-0517
Atty.-in-Charge: Patrick J. Brophy
Criminal and Family Court Cases

Rural Law Center of New York
See Clinton County

Workers' Rights Law Center of New York, Inc.
See Ulster County

QUEENS COUNTY

Appellate Advocates
See New York County

Asian American Legal Defense and Education Fund
See New York County

Assigned Counsel Plan for the City of New York
See New York County

Community Legal Assistance Corp.
See Nassau County

Community Legal Resource Network
CUNY School of Law, 65-21 Main St., Room 200B, Flushing 11367
(718) 340-4451; Fax: (718) 340-4404
E-mail: clrnoffice@mail.law.cuny.edu
Internet: www.law.cuny.edu
Director: Frederick P. Rooney
E-mail: rooney@mail.law.cuny.edu
Assoc. Dir.: Lisa Reiner
E-mail: lisa.reiner@mail.law.cuny.edu
Program operated by CUNY Alumni Network

Lawyer Referral Service
Queens County Bar Association
90-35 148th St., Jamaica 11435-4097
(718) 291-4500; Fax: (718) 657-1789
E-mail: info@qcba.org
Exec. Dir.: Arthur N. Terranova
Also serves counties of Bronx, Kings, Nassau, New York, Suffolk
All areas except Education, Environmental, International, Military, and Veteran's Affairs.
Serves N.Y.C. and Long Island

Lawyers Alliance for New York
See New York County

Legal Action Center of the City of New York, Inc.
See New York County

The Legal Aid Society—Queens County
Civil Division
Queens Neighborhood Office, 120-46 Queens Blvd., 3rd Floor, Kew Gardens 11415
(718) 286-2450; Fax: (718) 263-4234
Internet: www.legal-aid.org
Atty.-in-Charge: April A. Newbauer
Supervising Atty.: Susan E. Gibson-O'Gara
Housing, Public Benefits, Family Law, Consumer Law

Criminal Defense Practice
120-46 Queens Blvd., Kew Gardens 11415
(718) 286-2000; Fax: (718) 286-2486
Atty.-in-Charge: Timothy B. Rountree
E-mail: trountree@legal-aid.org

Juvenile Rights Division
153-01 Jamaica Ave., 3rd Floor, Jamaica 11432
(718) 298-8900; Fax: (718) 657-0537
Atty.-in-Charge: Dodd Terry

Legal Services NYC
See New York County

MFY Legal Services, Inc.
See New York County

NYS Mental Hygiene Legal Service
Second Judicial Department
See Nassau County

NYS Mental Hygiene Legal Service
Second Department, Second, Eleventh & Thirteenth Judicial District Office
Creedmoor Psychiatric Center, Bldg. 73 CBU #25, 80-45 Winchester Blvd., Queens Village 11427
(718) 264-3480; Fax: (718) 264-3329
Director: Sidney Hirschfeld
Deputy Chief: Joseph Traver
Also serves counties of Kings, Richmond

Queens Law Associates
118-21 Queens Blvd., Suite 212, Forest Hills 11375
(718) 261-3047; Fax: (718) 261-0798
Exec. Dir.: Joseph Vaccarino
Deputy Dir.: Lori Zeno
Criminal Law

Queens Legal Services Corporation
Long Island City Office
89-00 Sutphin Blvd., Suite 206, Jamaica 11435
(347) 592-2200
Internet: www.queenslegalservices.org

42-15 Crescent St., 9th Floor, Long Island City 11101
Director: Jennifer Ching
Deputy Dir.: Ann Biddle (Long Island City)

Sanctuary for Families
Center for Battered Women's Legal Services
See New York County

RENSSELAER COUNTY

Assigned Counsel Plan of Rensselaer County
Ned Pattison Government Center, 1600 7th Ave., Troy 12180
(518) 270-2950; Fax: (518) 270-2954
County Atty.: Stephen A. Pechenik
E-mail: spechenik@rensco.com

Legal Aid Society of Northeastern New York, Inc.
See Albany County

The Legal Project, Capital District Women's Bar Assn.
See Albany County

Public Defender Rensselaer County
Courthouse, 80 Second St., Troy 12180
(518) 270-4030; Fax: (518) 270-4033
Public Defender: Jerome K. Frost

Rural Law Center of New York
See Clinton County

RICHMOND COUNTY

Appellate Advocates
See New York County

Asian American Legal Defense and Education Fund
See New York County

Assigned Counsel Plan for the City of New York
See New York County

Lawyers Alliance for New York
See New York County

Legal Action Center of the City of New York, Inc.
See New York County

The Legal Aid Society—Staten Island
Civil & Juvenile Rights Division
60 Bay St., Staten Island 10301
(347) 422-5333; Fax: (347) 442-6193, (718) 981-6623
Attys.-in-Charge:
Teresa DeFonso (Civil)
Lou Sartori (Juvenile Rights)
Housing, Public Benefits, Family Law, Consumer Law, Juvenile Rights

Legal Referral Panel
Richmond County Bar Assn.
152 Stuyvesant Pl., Suite 203, Staten Island 10301
Mailing Address: P.O. Box 140593, Staten Island 10314
(718) 442-4500; Fax: (718) 442-2019
E-mail: rcbaweb@gmail.com
Internet: www.richmondcountybar.org
Admin. Asst.: Elisa Lefkowitz

Legal Services NYC
See New York County

MFY Legal Services, Inc.
See New York County

NYS Mental Hygiene Legal Service
Second Judicial Department
See Nassau County

NYS Mental Hygiene Legal Service Second Dept., Second, Eleventh & Thirteenth Judicial Dist. Office
See Queens County

Sanctuary for Families Center for Battered Women's Legal Services
See New York County

ROCKLAND COUNTY

Assigned Counsel Plan of Rockland County
120 N. Main St., New City 10956
(845) 634-7701; Fax: (845) 634-7710
Administrator: Keith Braunfotel
E-mail: keith@braunfotelandfrendel.com

Legal Aid Society of Rockland County, Inc.
2 Congers Rd., New City 10956
(845) 634-3627; Fax: (845) 634-8505
Exec. Dir.: Alexander Bursztein; E-mail: alexb@wnylc.org
Civil; Family

Legal Services of the Hudson Valley
See Westchester County

NYS Mental Hygiene Legal Service
Second Judicial Department
See Nassau County

NYS Mental Hygiene Legal Service
Second Department, Ninth Judicial District Office
3 Wilbur Rd., Room 57, P.O. Box 470, Thiells 10984-0400
(845) 947-6401; Fax: (845) 947-6391
Director: Sidney Hirschfeld (516) 746-4545
Deputy Chief Atty.: Vacancy at Press Time
Also serves counties of Dutchess, Orange, Putnam, Westchester

Public Defender Rockland County
11 New Hempstead Rd., New City 10956
(845) 638-5660; Fax: (845) 638-5667
Public Defender: James D. Licata
E-mail: licataj@co.rockland.ny.us

SAINT LAWRENCE COUNTY

Assigned Counsel Plan of St. Lawrence County
48 Court St., Canton 13617
(315) 379-2401; Fax: (315) 379-0401
Administrator: Francis Cappello
Coordinator: Lisa M. Vecchio
E-mail: lvecchio@co.st-lawrence.ny.us
Criminal & Family; Appeals

Legal Aid Society of Northeastern New York, Inc.
17 Hodskin St., P.O. Box 648, Canton 13617
(315) 386-4586, (800) 822-8283; Fax: (315) 386-2868
Exec. Dir.: Lillian Moy
Deputy Dirs.:
Peter Racette   Wendy Wahlberg
Staff Attys.:
Cynthia A. Eyler; E-mail: ceyler@lasnny.org
Susan E. Griskonis; E-mail: sgriskonis@lasnny.org
Jennifer K. Karr; E-mail: jkarr@lasnny.org
Also serves county of Franklin; also Saint Regis Indian Reservation
Civil
Formerly North Country Legal Services, Inc.

Rural Law Center of New York
See Clinton County

SARATOGA COUNTY

Assigned Counsel Plan of Saratoga County Bar Assn.
Counsel to Indigent Defendants
40 McMaster St., Ballston Spa 12020
(518) 884-4795; Fax: (518) 884-4789
Administrator: John H. Ciulla, Jr.
E-mail: publicdefender@saratogacountyny.gov
Family Court, Criminal, Vehicle & Traffic Law

Legal Aid Society of Northeastern New York, Inc.
112 Spring St., Suite 109, Saratoga Springs 12866
(518) 587-5188, (800) 870-8343; Fax: (518) 587-0959
Supervising Atty.: Mary M. Withington
E-mail: mwithington@lasnny.org
Also serves counties of Warren, Washington

The Legal Project, Capital District Women's Bar Assn.
See Albany County

Public Defender Saratoga County
40 McMaster St., Ballston Spa 12020
(518) 884-4795; Fax: (518) 884-4789
E-mail: publicdefender@saratogacountyny.gov
Public Defender: John H. Ciulla, Jr.
Family Court, Criminal Law, Vehicle & Traffic Law

Rural Law Center of New York
See Clinton County

SCHENECTADY COUNTY

Assigned Counsel Plan of Schenectady
620 State St., Schenectady 12307
(518) 388-4276; Fax: (518) 388-4493
Administrator: Howard G. Carpenter, Jr.
E-mail: howard.carpenter@schenectadycounty.com

Legal Aid Society of Northeastern New York, Inc.
See Albany County

The Legal Project, Capital District Women's Bar Assn.
See Albany County

Public Defender Schenectady County
519 State St., Schenectady 12305
(518) 386-2266; Fax: (518) 386-2814
Public Defender: Mark J. Caruso

Rural Law Center of New York
See Clinton County

SCHOHARIE COUNTY

Assigned Counsel Plan of Schoharie County
283 Main St., P.O. Box 490, Schoharie 12157-0490
(518) 295-7515
Administrator: Raynor Duncombe

Legal Aid Society of Northeastern New York, Inc.
See Montgomery County

Rural Law Center of New York
See Clinton County

SCHUYLER COUNTY

Chemung County Neighborhood Legal Services
See Chemung County

Public Defender Schuyler County
105 9th St., Unit 7, Watkins Glen 14891
(607) 535-6400
Public Defender: Holly Mosher
Asst. Public Defender: Wesley A. Roe

Rural Law Center of New York
See Clinton County

SENECA COUNTY

Legal Assistance of Western New York, Inc.
See Ontario County

NYS Mental Hygiene Legal Service Fourth Dept.
See Monroe County

Public Defender Seneca County
P.O. Box 702, Seneca Falls 13148
(315) 568-4975; Fax: (315) 568-2324
Public Defender: Michael J. Mirras
Asst. Public Defenders:
Matthew D. Conlon (315) 789-2795
John J. Nabinger (315) 422-1464
Stephen R. Ricci (315) 568-1345
Criminal Law / Family Law

Rural Law Center of New York
See Clinton County

STEUBEN COUNTY

NYS Mental Hygiene Legal Service Fourth Dept.
See Monroe County

Public Defender Steuben County
3 E. Pulteney Sq., Bath 14810
(607) 776-9631, Ext. 2410; Fax: (607) 664-2496
Public Defender: Byrum Cooper

Rural Law Center of New York
See Clinton County

Southern Tier Legal Services
104 E. Steuben St., Bath 14810
(607) 776-4126; Fax: (607) 776-4029

103 S. Barry St., Olean 14760
(716) 373-4701; Fax: (716) 373-7771

Hotel Jamestown Bldg., Suite 507, 110 W. 3rd St., Jamestown 14701 (716) 664-4535; Fax: (716) 664-7179
Deputy Dir.: Amy L. Christensen
Also serves counties of Allegany, Cattaraugus
Civil
Formerly Legal Aid of Western New York, Inc.

SUFFOLK COUNTY

Assigned Counsel Defender Plan of Suffolk County
120 Fourth Ave., P.O. Box 5591, Bay Shore 11706
(631) 666-5766, Ext. 225; Fax: (631) 666-8401
E-mail: suffolk18b@optonline.net
Internet: www.suffolk18b.org
Administrator: David H. Besso
Indigent Defense Services

Lawyer Referral Service Queens County Bar Assn.
See Queens County

Legal Aid Society of Suffolk County
Administrative Office
John P. Cohalan, Jr. Court Complex, 4th Floor, 400 Carlton Ave., P.O. Box 9082, Central Islip 11722-9082
(631) 853-7770; Fax: (631) 853-4336
Atty.-in-Charge: Robert C. Mitchell

Criminal Office
Arthur M. Cromarty Court Complex, 300 Center Dr., Riverhead 11901 (631) 852-1650; Fax: (631) 852-1655
Chief Atty., Felony Bureau: Edward Vitale
Chief Atty., Appeals Bureau: James H. Miller III
Chief Atty., East End Bureau: Sabato Caponi

District Court Office
John P. Cohalan, Jr. Court Complex, 4th Floor, 400 Carleton Ave., P.O. Box 9082, Central Islip 11722-9082
(631) 853-5212; Fax: (631) 853-7798
Bureau Chief: Sabato Caponi (631) 853-5220
Chief Atty., Family Court Bureau: Thomas Sartain (631) 853-4343
Chief Atty., Law Guardian Office: Jayne Ann McPartlin (631) 853-4336

Nassau/Suffolk Law Services Committee, Inc.
313 W. Main St., Riverhead 11901-2480
(631) 369-1112; Fax: (631) 369-1612
Internet: www.nslawservices.org
Exec. Dir.: Jeffrey Seigel
Sr. Staff Atty.: Beth Wickey
Public Benefits, S.S.I., Housing

Islandia Office
1757 Veterans Hwy., Suite 50, Islandia 11722
(631) 232-2400; Fax: (631) 232-2489
Supervising Atty.: Victoria Osk
Civil, Welfare, Domestic Violence, Pro Bono

NYS Mental Hygiene Legal Service
Second Department, Tenth Judicial District Office
Supreme Court Bldg., One Court St., Riverhead 11901
(631) 852-2325; Fax: (631) 852-2392
Director: Sidney Hirschfeld
Deputy Chief Atty.: Mary D'Andrea
Also serves county of Nassau

Workers' Rights Law Center of New York, Inc.
See Ulster County

SULLIVAN COUNTY

Legal Services of the Hudson Valley
See Westchester County

Rural Law Center of New York
See Clinton County

Sullivan Legal Aid Panel, Inc.
11 Bank St., Monticello 12701-1701
(845) 794-4094; Fax: (845) 794-0119
Exec. Dir.: Stephan Schick
E-mail: schickhavas@hotmail.com
Criminal, Family Law

Workers' Rights Law Center of New York, Inc.
See Ulster County

TIOGA COUNTY

Lawyer Referral Service Broome County Bar Assn.
See Broome County

Legal Assistance of Western New York, Inc.
Tompkins/Tioga Neighborhood Legal Services
See Tompkins County

Public Defender Tioga County
171 Main St., P.O. Box 507, Owego 13827
(607) 687-1000; Fax: (607) 687-6075
Public Defender: George C. Awad, Jr.

Rural Law Center of New York
See Clinton County

TOMPKINS COUNTY

Assigned Counsel Program of Tompkins County
171 E. State St., Suite 227, Ithaca 14850
(607) 272-7487; Fax: (607) 272-7489
Administrator: Wesley E. McDermott (Acting)
Coordinator: Julia P. Hughes
E-mail: jhughes@tompkins-co.org

Cornell Legal Aid Clinic
G40 Myron Taylor Hall, Cornell Univ., Ithaca 14853-4901
(607) 255-4196; Fax: (607) 255-3269
Co-Directors:
Glenn Galbreath   Barry Strom
Clinical Administrator: Deborah Schaaf
Social Security, Disability Benefits, Unemployment, Insurance Benefits

Legal Assistance of Western New York, Inc.
Tompkins/Tioga Neighborhood Legal Services
DeWitt Bldg., 215 N. Cayuga St., Ithaca 14850-4901
(607) 273-3666; Fax: (607) 273-5521
Managing Atty.: Gregg A. Thomas
E-mail: gthomas@baka.com
Also serves county of Tioga
Public Benefits (Public Assistance, Food stamps, Medicaid, SSI) and Housing

Rural Law Center of New York
See Clinton County

ULSTER COUNTY

Legal Services of the Hudson Valley
See Westchester County

Public Defender Ulster County
18 Lucas Ave., P.O. Box 1800, Kingston 12402
(845) 340-3232; Fax: (845) 340-3744
Internet: www.co.ulster.ny.us/resources/publicdefender
Public Defender: Andrew Kossover
E-mail: akos@co.ulster.ny.us

Rural Law Center of New York
See Clinton County

Workers' Rights Law Center of New York, Inc.
101 Hurley Ave., Suite 5, Kingston 12401
(845) 331-6615; Fax: (845) 331-6617
E-mail: info@workersrightsny.org
Internet: www.workersrightsny.org
Exec. Dir.: Milan Bhatt
Also serves counties of Columbia, Dutchess, Greene, Orange, Putnam, Suffolk, Sullivan
Serves low wage workers in employment & civil rights matters.

WARREN COUNTY

Assigned Counsel Plan of Warren County
Warren County Municipal Center, 1340 State Route 9, Lake George 12845
(518) 761-6460; Fax: (518) 761-6443
Administrator: Joy A. LaFountain
E-mail: lafountainj@co.warren.ny.us
Criminal, Family Court

Legal Aid Society of Northeastern New York, Inc.
See Saratoga County

Public Defender Warren County
Warren County Municipal Center, 1340 State Route 9, Lake George 12845 (518) 761-6207
Public Defender: John P.M. Wappett
E-mail: wappettj@co.warren.ny.us

Rural Law Center of New York
See Clinton County

WASHINGTON COUNTY

Legal Aid Society of Northeastern New York, Inc.
See Saratoga County

Rural Law Center of New York
See Clinton County

WAYNE COUNTY

The Legal Aid Society of Wayne County, Inc.
9 Pearl St., Lyons 14489
(315) 946-7463; Fax: (315) 946-5964
E-mail: legalaid@waynelegalaid.com
President: Ronald Valentine
Executive Atty.: David Lee Foster
E-mail: davidlee@davidleefoster.com
Staff Attys.:
Chelsea B. Carter   Kathryn L. Tucker
Family Law, Domestic Relations and Divorces

Legal Assistance of Western New York, Inc.
See Ontario County

NYS Mental Hygiene Legal Service Fourth Dept.
See Monroe County

Public Defender Wayne County
26 Church St., 2nd Floor, Lyons 14489
(315) 946-7472; Fax: (315) 946-7478
Public Defender: Ronald C. Valentine
E-mail: rvalentine@co.wayne.ny.us

Rural Law Center of New York
See Clinton County

WESTCHESTER COUNTY

The Legal Aid Society of Westchester County
1 N. Broadway, 9th Floor, White Plains 10601
(914) 286-3400; Fax: (914) 682-4112
Exec. Dir./Chief Counsel: Stephen J. Pittari
(914) 286-3472

Legal Services of the Hudson Valley
90 Maple Ave., White Plains 10601
(914) 949-1305; Fax: (914) 949-6213;
TDD: (914) 949-1305, Ext. 149
Internet: www.lshv.org

29 N. Hamilton St., Poughkeepsie 12601
(845) 471-0058; Fax: (845) 471-0244

30 S. Broadway, Yonkers 10701
(914) 376-3757; Fax: (914) 376-8739

123 Grand St., Newburgh 12550
(845) 569-9110; Fax: (845) 569-9120;
Toll Free intake: (877) 574-8529

101 Hurley Ave., Kingston 12401
(845) 331-9373; Fax: (845) 331-4813

100 E. First St., 8th Fl., Suite 810, Mount Vernon 10550
(914) 813-6880; Fax: (914) 813-6890
Exec. Dir.: Barbara Finkelstein
E-mail: bfinkelstein@lshv.org
Deputy Dir.: Lewis Creekmore (Newburgh Office)
E-mail: lcreekmore@lshv.org
Managing Attys.:
Jill Bradshaw-Soto (Mt. Vernon Office)
E-mail: jbradshaw@lshv.org
Mary Grace Ferone (White Plains Office)
E-mail: mferone@lshv.org
William Flynn (Newburgh Office)
E-mail: wflynn@lshv.org
Kathleen Healey (Poughkeepsie & Kingston Offices)
E-mail: khealey@lshv.org
Robin Stiebel (Yonkers Office)
E-mail: rstiebel@lshv.org
Dir. of Finance and Administration: George Christatos
E-mail: gchristatos@lshv.org
Also serves counties of Dutchess, Orange, Putnam, Rockland, Sullivan, Ulster
Civil Law
Formerly known as Westchester/Putnam Legal Services

Westchester County—Cont'd

NYS Mental Hygiene Legal Service
Second Judicial Department
See Nassau County

NYS Mental Hygiene Legal Service Second Dept., Ninth Judicial District Office
See Rockland County

Pro Bono Partnership
237 Mamaroneck Ave., Suite 300, White Plains 10605
(914) 328-0674; Fax: (914) 328-0538
E-mail: information@probonopartner.org
Internet: www.probonopartner.org

160 Littleton Rd., Suite 205, Parsippany, NJ 07054
(973) 968-7043; Fax: (973) 394-7943

Exec. Dir.: Richard S. Hobish

Dir., New York & Fairfield County: Maurice K. Segall

A coordination and resource center that matches volunteer attorneys with nonprofit organizations requesting legal assistance; serves organizations only. Does not serve prisoners or individuals.

WYOMING COUNTY

Assigned Counsel Plan of Wyoming County Bar Assn.
11 Exchange St., P.O. Box 238, Attica 14011
(585) 591-1724; Fax: (585) 591-1722

Managing Atty.: Eric T. Dadd
E-mail: edadd@daddandnelson.com

Attica Legal Aid Bureau, Inc. & Public Defender Wyoming County
18 Linwood Ave., Warsaw 14569
(585) 786-8450; Fax: (585) 786-8478
E-mail: attlegal@yahoo.com

Exec. Dir./Public Defender: Norman Effman

Attica Legal Aid Bureau, Inc. Serves Inmates only

NYS Mental Hygiene Legal Service Fourth Dept.
See Monroe County

Oak Orchard Legal Services
Division of Neighborhood Legal Services, Inc.
See Genesee County

Rural Law Center of New York
See Clinton County

YATES COUNTY

Assigned Counsel Program of Yates County
126 Main St., P.O. Box 412, Penn Yan 14527
(315) 531-3441; Fax: (315) 531-3442

Administrator: Dianne S. Lovejoy

Criminal and Family Court

Legal Assistance of Western New York, Inc.
See Ontario County

NYS Mental Hygiene Legal Service Fourth Dept.
See Monroe County

Public Defender Yates County
See Ontario County

Rural Law Center of New York
See Clinton County

MARRIAGE LAWS

Revised by Gary N. Skoloff and Jonathan W. Wolfe of the New Jersey Bar

State or other jurisdiction	Age at which marriage can be contracted with parental consent: Male	Age at which marriage can be contracted with parental consent: Female	Age below which parental consent is required: Male	Age below which parental consent is required: Female	Common-law marriage recognized	Physical examination and blood test for male and female: Maximum period between examination and issuance of license	Physical examination and blood test for male and female: Scope of medical examination	Waiting period: Before issuance of license	Waiting period: After issuance of license (Expiration)
Alabama	16(1)(33)	16(1)(33)	18	18	*(33)			(33)	30 da.
Alaska	14(65)	14(65)	18	18	recognized before 1/2/64			3 da.(25)	90 da.
Arizona †	16(14)(33)	16(14)(33)	18	18	(30)				1 yr.
Arkansas †	17(6)(33)	16(6)(33)	18	18	(30)			(24)	1 yr.(24)
California (23)(48)	(2)(14)(27)	(2)(14)(27)	18	18	(30)		(60)		60 da.
Colorado (22)(48)	16(29)	16(29)	18	18	*(7)				30 da.
Connecticut (48)	16(29)(44)	16(29)(44)	18	18				4 da.(25)	65 da.
Delaware	18(6)(29)(46)	16(6)(29)(45)(46)	18	18	(30)			24 hrs.(9)(26)	30 da.(59)
Florida	16(1)(6)(49)	16(1)(6)(49)	18	18	recognized before 1/2/1968			3 da.(25)(50)	60 da.
Georgia	16	16	18	18	recognized before 1/2/1996(30)		(41)	3 da.	30 da.
Hawaii (48)	15(14)	15(14)	18	18	(30)		(11)		30 da.
Idaho	16(14)	16(14)	18	18	recognized before 1/1/1997 (30)		(11)		
Illinois	16(43)	16(43)	18	18	recognized before 7/1/1905		(51)	1 da.(12)	60 da.
Indiana	17(6)(29)(33)	17(6)(29)(33)	18	18	recognized before 1/2/1958		(41)		60 da.
Iowa (48)	16(14)	16(14)	18	18	*(30)			3 da.(25)	
Kansas	16(14)	16(14)	18	18	*			3 da.(25)	180 da.
Kentucky	16(6)(33)	16(6)(33)	18	18	*(30)				30 da.
Louisiana †	16(29)(52)	16(29)(52)	18	18		10 da.	(3)	3 da.	30 da.
Maine (48)	16(14)	16(14)	18	18				3 da.(25)	90 da.
Maryland (48)	16(6)(10)	16(6)(10)	18	18	(30)			48 hrs.(25)	180 da.
Massachusetts (48)	14(14)	12(14)	18	18				3 da.(24)(25)	6 mo.
Michigan	16	16	18	18	recognized before 1/1/1957(30)			3 da.(25)	33 da.
Minnesota	16	16	18	18	recognized before 4/26/1941(30)			5 da.(25)	180 da.
Mississippi	17(2)(29)(53)	15(2)(29)(53)	21	21	recognized before 4/5/1956(30)	30 da.	(3)	3 da.(25)	
Missouri	15(8)	15(8)	18	18	recognized before 3/31/1921(30)		(61)		30 da.
Montana (23)	16(33)	16(33)	18	18	*(30)(33)		(34)(57)		180 da.
Nebraska (23)	17(29)	17(29)	19	19	recognized before 1/1/1923(30)		(35)		1 yr.
Nevada (48)	16(8)	16(8)	18	18	recognized before 3/12/1943(55)				1 yr.
New Hampshire (48)	14(15)	13(15)	18	18	(30)(63)		(61)		90 da.
New Jersey (48)	16(6)(29)	16(6)(29)	18	18	recognized before 12/1/1939		(64)	72 hrs.(25)	30 da.
New Mexico (37)	16(6)(8)	16(6)(8)	18	18	(30)	30 da.	(3)		
New York (38)	16(15)(29)	16(15)(29)	18	18	recognized before 4/29/1933(30)		(19)	24 hrs. (12)	60 da.
North Carolina	16(6)(8)	16(6)(8)	18	18	(30)(55)				60 da.
North Dakota	16	16	18	18					60 da.
Ohio	18(17)	16(17)	18(17)	18(17)	recognized before 10/10/1991(30)			5 da.	60 da.
Oklahoma	16(6)(29)	16(6)(29)	18	18	recognized before 11/1/1998 (30)(55)	30 da.(25)	(3)	(20)	30 da.
Oregon (48)	17(21)	17(21)	18	18	(30)			3 da.(25)	60 da.
Pennsylvania	16(8)(29)	16(8)(29)	18	18	*(62)			3 da.(25)	60 da.
Puerto Rico (22)(39)	18(6)(8)	16(6)(8)	21(6)	21(6)			(3)(33)		
Rhode Island (58)	18(8)(29)(33)	16(8)(29)(33)	18	18	*(13)		(61)		90 da.

MARRIAGE LAWS

Revised by Gary N. Skoloff and Jonathan W. Wolfe of the New Jersey Bar

State or other jurisdiction		Age at which marriage can be contracted with parental consent		Age below which parental consent is required		Common-law marriage recognized	Physical examination and blood test for male and female		Waiting period	
		Male	*Female*	*Male*	*Female*		*Maximum period between examination and issuance of license*	*Scope of medical examination*	*Before issuance of license*	*After issuance of license (Expiration)*
South Carolina		16(6)(29)	14(6)(29)	18	18	*			1 da.	
South Dakota		16(6)(29)	16(6)(29)	18	18	recognized before 7/1/1959(13)		(41)		20 da.
Tennessee		16(8)(29)	16(8)(29)	18	18	(30)		(41)	3 da.(7)(25)	30 da.
Texas	(22)(23)	16(43)	16(43)	18(27)	18(27)	*(30)		(41)	72 hrs.(25)(33)	30 da.
Utah		15(1)(14)(33)	15(1)(14)(33)	18(27)(1)	18(27)(1)	(40)				30 da.
Vermont	(48)	16(29)	16(29)	18	18		30 da.(25)	(3)	1 da.(25)	60 da.
Virginia		16(1)(6)	16(1)(6)	18(1)	18(1)	(30)		(61)		60 da.
Washington	(48)	17(8)(29)	17(8)(29)	18	18	(30)		(5)	3 da.	60 da.
West Virginia		18(6)	18(6)	18	18	(30)		(3)	3 da.(25)	60 da.
Wisconsin		16	16	18	18			(11)(32)	5 da.(25)	30 da.
Wyoming		16(8)(29)(33)	16(8)(29)(33)	16	16	(30)				1 yr.
Dist. of Columbia	(48)	16(1)	16(1)	18(1)	18(1)	*			3 da.(26)	
Virgin Islands		16(1)	14(1)	18(1)	18(1)	(30)			8 da.(25)	

Footnotes

* Indicates common-law marriage recognized.
† Indicates covenant marriage recognized.
(1) Parental consent not required if minor was previously married.
(2) No age limits.
(3) Venereal diseases. In West Virginia and Oklahoma, Circuit Court judge may waive requirement. In Mississippi, Oklahoma, Pennsylvania and West Virginia, applicant must be free of syphilis. In Puerto Rico, applicant must be free from mental illness or idiocy.
(4) Venereal diseases and Rubella (for female). In some states Rubella test requirements may be waived. In Connecticut, rubella only.
(5) No exam required, but parties must file affidavit of non-affliction of contagious sexually-transmitted disease.
(6) Younger parties may obtain licence in case of pregnancy or birth of child.
(7) Unless parties are over 18 years of age.
(8) Statute establishes procedure whereby younger parties may obtain license in special circumstances.
(9) Residents, 24-hr. waiting period; non-residents, 96-hr. waiting period.
(10) If parties are at least 16 years of age, proof of age and the consent of parents in person required. If a parent is ill, an affidavit by the incapacitated parent and a physician's affidavit to that effect required.
(11) Applicants must receive AIDS information pamphlet and certify having read it.
(12) License effective 1 day after issuance, unless court orders otherwise, valid for 60 days only.
(13) No case law or statutes as to recognition of out-of-state common law marriages.
(14) Parental consent and/or permission of judge required.
(15) Judge can grant marriage to anyone under 18, no younger than 14 year old male and 13 year old female. In New York, female must be at least 14.
(16) Doctor's certificate must be filed 30 days prior to notice of intention.
(17) Applicants under age 18 must state that they have had marriage counseling.
(18) Venereal diseases; test for sickle cell anemia given at request of examining physician.
(19) Test for sickle cell anemia may be requested for certain applicants.
(20) If one or both parties are below the age for marriage without parental consent (3 day waiting period).
(21) If a party has no parent residing within state, and one party has residence within state for six months, no permission required.
(22) Marriages by proxy are valid.
(23) Statute authorizes proxy marriage under certain conditions.
(24) Parties must file notice of intention to marry with local clerk.
(25) Statute establishes procedure whereby waiting period may be avoided.
(26) Time may be shortened. In West Virginia, requirement may be waived by a Circuit Court judge.
(27) Counties may require premarital counseling for persons under 19 or previously divorced.
(28) Not generally valid except for limited purpose of recovery in Workers Compensation cases.
(29) Younger parties may marry with parental consent and/or permission of judge. In Connecticut, judicial approval.
(30) Common law marriage, if valid where contracted, recognized. In New York, including post-1933 good faith relationships started in New York if sojourn in common-law jurisdiction. In Georgia, for there to be a common law marriage, the parties must be able to contract, agree to live together as husband and wife, and consummate the agreement.
(31) When unmarried man and unmarried woman, not minors, have been living together as man and wife, they may, without health certificate, be married upon issuance of appropriate authorization.
(32) Application shall contain such information as directed by Dept. of Health & Social Services.
(33) Other statutory requirements apply.
(34) Rubella for female, but there are certain exceptions. In some states, District judge may waive medical examination on proof that emergency exists.
(35) Any unsterilized female under 50 must submit with application for license a medical report stating whether she has immunological response to rubella, or written record that rubella vaccine was administered on or after her first birthday. Judge may by order dispense with these requirements.
(36) Parties must sign affidavit affirming that they have received and discussed brochure prepared by Division of Public Health Services, Department of Health and Human Services.
(37) No statutory authorization for proxy marriage, but May 11, 1943 opinion of Attorney General that such marriage is valid, but new ceremony when possible recommended.
(38) Proxy marriages are not explicitly authorized by statute but are not contrary to public policy if valid in state where contracted.
(39) Proxy marriage between a person present in Puerto Rico and one absent is permitted.
(40) Unsolemnized marriage arising out of contract is valid if court or administrative order finds two parties: (i) capable of consent; (ii) legally capable of solemnized marriage; (iii) have cohabitated; (iv) mutually assume marital rights, duties and obligations; and (v) contend and are believed to be husband and wife. Determination must be made during or within 1 year of termination of relationship.
(41) Must be provided with information on AIDS and tests available.
(42) Medical exam requirement repealed; applicant must show certificate of HIV counseling, transmission/prevention of venerial diseases.
(43) Judicial consent may be given when parents refuse to consent.
(44) If under age party is under care of guardian or conservator, written consent signed in presence of witness and notarized must be filed with the registrar.
(45) Physician's certificate stating the underage female is pregnant is required.
(46) Consent forms shall be signed in the presence of two reputable witnesses unless signed by a judge.
(47) If individual cannot afford services of physician or other authorized for tests or required statement, a medical officer of the Dept. of Human Services may conduct tests and provide statement at no cost. Medical exam may be waived at discretion of Superior Court Judge in case of public policy or emergency.

(48) In DC, two unmarried individuals may register themselves as a "Domestic Partnership" and obtain certain benefits. In CT, IA, MA, ME, NH, and VT, same-sex couples may obtain legal marriage. In CA, CO, HI, MD, NV, NJ, OR, and WA, same-sex couples are eligible for certain benefits under state law.
(49) No consent required if both parents are deceased.
(50) Both parties must file a statement specifying completion of a premarital preparatory course and both parties have read or accessed information from the Family Law Handbook. Failure to do so will delay effective date of marriage.
(51) All parties shall be provided a brochure concerning sexually transmitted diseases and inherited metabolic diseases. A judge in county where license is to be issued may waive medical exam for religious reasons.
(52) In certain circumstances, marriage between two minors is not void or voidable merely because it was contracted without parental consent.
(53) If either party is not of legal age to marry, parental consent as well as written waiver of minimum age requirements is necessary.
(54) No pre-trial serological tests required. However, test will be required on the woman; however, tests will be required on the woman or on the umbilical cord upon birth of the child.
(55) Marriages according to Native American customs are recognized.
(56) Certificate of genetic counseling from physician must be filed with notice of marriage intention between a man and a daughter of his father's brother or sister, or corresponding marriage by a woman.
(57) Each female applicant for license, unless exempted for medical reasons, must present pre-marital certification of physician on official form stating she has had standard seriological tests.
(58) Marriages between Jews within degrees of consanguinity permitted by their religion are valid.
(59) Clerk of Peace has discretion to lengthen time period, up to 180 days.
(60) Parties must be provided state-prepared brochure covering genetic defects, AIDS and domestic violence.
(61) Parties must be provided state-prepared brochure covering effects of drugs and alcohol on fetus.
(62) Common law marriage valid if entered into prior to 9/17/2003 (see *PNC Bank Corp.v. WCAB*, 831 A.2d 1269 (Pa. Cmwlth.), possibly 1/2/2005 (see 2004 House Bill No. 2719).
(63) Only recognized for the purposes of probate (see N.H. R.S.A. § 457.39).
(64) Parties must be provided with information concerning where they may be tested for genetic diseases including Cooley's Anemia, Sickle Cell Anemia, and Tay-Sachs Disease.
(65) Age 16 if have parental consent. If Age 14, Superior Court judge may grant permission to wed if parents give consent or parents absent, disagree to marriage, are unfit, or withholding consent.

Note: All states prohibit marriage between persons of varying degrees of consanguinity.

DIVORCE LAWS

There are presently pending, in most states, proposed divorce reform laws. The data set forth herein is correct as of June 2010. It is suggested that the attorney utilizing this chart consult amendments to local statutes.

State or other jurisdiction	Residence required before filing suit of divorce	Grounds for absolute divorce						
		Adultery	*Mental and/or physical cruelty*	*Abandonment*	*Alcoholism*	*Impotency*	*Non-support*	*Insanity*
Alabama	6 mos. (82)	*	*	1 yr.	*		2 yrs.	5 yrs.(66)
Alaska	6 mos. (1)	*	*	1 yr.	1 yr.	*		18 mos.(66)
Arizona	90 da.	‡	‡	‡1 yr.	‡			
Arkansas	60 da. (83)	*†‡	*‡		*†1 yr.	*	*	*3 yrs.
California	6 mos. (13)							(66)
Colorado	90 da.							
Connecticut	1 yr. (16)	*	*	1 yr.(14)	*		*	5 yrs.
Delaware	6 mos.	*	*	*	*	(29)		*
Florida	6 mos.							3 yrs.
Georgia	6 mos.	*	*	1 yr.	*	*		2 yrs.(66)
Hawaii	6 mos.							
Idaho	6 wks.	*(110)	*1 yr.		*1 yr.			3 yrs.(66)
Illinois	90 da.	*	*	1 yr.	2 yrs.	*		
Indiana	6 mos. (13)					*		2 yrs.(66)
Iowa	1 yr. (28)					(29)		(4)
Kansas	60 da.							2 yrs.
Kentucky	180 da.					(29)		
Louisiana	6 mos. (84)	*†‡	‡	‡				
Maine	6 mos.(31)	*	*	3 yrs.	*	*	(100)	7 yrs. (4)
Maryland	(38)	*	*	1 yr.†			(100)	3 yrs.(66)
Massachusetts	1 yr. (41)	*	*	1 yr.	*	*	*	(4)
Michigan	180 da. (42) (43)							
Minnesota	180 da.							
Mississippi	6 mos. (60)	*	*	1 yr.	*	*(4)	†	3 yrs.(4)(46)(66)
Missouri	90 da.	†		6 mos. †				
Montana	90 da.					(29)		

DIVORCE LAWS

There are presently pending, in most states, proposed divorce reform laws. The data set forth herein is correct as of June 2010. It is suggested that the attorney utilizing this chart consult amendments to local statutes.

State or other jurisdiction	Residence required before filing suit of divorce	*Grounds for absolute divorce* Adultery	Mental and/or physical cruelty	Abandonment	Alcoholism	Impotency	Non-support	Insanity
Nebraska	1 yr. (50)					(29)		(4)
Nevada	6 wks.			90 da.†				2 yrs.†
New Hampshire	1 yr. (51)	*†	*†	2 yrs.†	2 yrs.†	*†	2 yrs.†	
New Jersey	1 yr. (57)	*†	*†	1 yr.†	†	(29)		2 yrs.†
New Mexico	6 mos.	*	*	*				
New York	1 yr. (59)	*†	1 yr.†	1 yr.†			†	(4)
North Carolina	6 mos.	(3)	(3)	(3)	(3)	(29)		3 yrs.(66)
North Dakota	6 mos.	*	*	*	*			5 yrs.(66)
Ohio	6 mos.	*†	*†	1 yr.†	*†		*	
Oklahoma	6 mos. (87)	*†	*†	1 yr.†	*	*†	*	5 yrs.(66)†
Oregon	6 mos. (41)							
Pennsylvania	6 mos.	*	*	1 yr.				*18 mos.
Rhode Island	1 yr.	*	*	5 yrs. (71)	*	*	1 yr.	
South Carolina	1 yr. (11)	*		1 yr. (22)	*			
South Dakota	(68)	*†	*†	†	1 yr. †		1 yr.†	
Tennessee	6 mos.(41)	*†	*†	1 yr.†	*†	*†	*†	
Texas	6 mos.(13)	*	*	1 yr.		(29)		3 yrs.
Utah	3 mos.(13)(106)	*	*	1 yr.†	*	(29)	*	(66)
Vermont	6 mos.(73)(74)	*†	*†	7 yrs.†			*†	5 yrs.†(45)(66)
Virginia	6 mos.	*	*†(3)	1 yr.† (37)(3)		(29)		(4)
Washington	bona fide resid. (79)							
West Virginia	1 yr. (41)(86)	*†	*†	6 mo.†	*†	(29)		3 yrs.(66)
Wisconsin	6 mos.(87)					(29)		
Wyoming	2 mos.(76)							2 yrs. †(66)
District of Columbia	6 mos.							(4)
Virgin Islands	6 wks.							(4)
Puerto Rico	1 yr.(41)	*	*	1 yr.	*	*		7 yrs.(66)

DIVORCE LAWS

There are presently pending, in most states, proposed divorce reform laws. The data set forth herein is correct as of June 2010. It is suggested that the attorney utilizing this chart consult amendments to local statutes.

	Grounds for absolute divorce					*Grounds for "no-fault" divorce*					*Other Grounds*	*Period before parties may remarry after final decree*	
State or other jurisdiction	*Bigamy*	*Felony Conviction or imprisonment*	*Drug Addiction*	*Fraud, force or duress*	*Prior decree of limited divorce*	*Irreconcilable Differences or Irretrievable Breakdown*	*Incompatibility*	*Living Separate and Apart*	*Judicial Separation or Maintenance*	*Mutual Consent*	*Other*	*Plaintiff*	*Defendant*
Alabama	(4)	(9)	*	(4)	(12)	*†	*	2 yrs.	2 yrs.(25)		(7)(17)(23)(89)(103)	60 da.	60 da.
Alaska	(4)	*	*	(4)			*(98)				(23)(90)		
Arizona		‡	‡	(4)		*		‡(109)		†‡	(23)		
Arkansas		*†‡		(4)				*18 mos, ‡2yrs..		*	(5)(7)(15)(23)(90)(94)		
California	(4)			(4)		*				†	(5)(7)(23)		
Colorado	(4)			(4)	(12)	*†				(7)(23)(69)	(70)(90)	(70)	
Connecticut	(4)	(15)		*	(12)	*	*	18 mos.			(23)(30)(91)		
Delaware	*	(108)		(4)		(2)(18)	*	6 mos.			(7)(23)(29)(101)		
Florida						*					(7)(23)(24)		
Georgia	(4)	(21)	*	*		*(107)					(5)(7)(20)(23)(44)		
Hawaii	(4)			(4)	(12)	*		*(35)	2 yrs. (25)		(7)(23)(88)		
Idaho	(4)	*(110)		(4)		*		5 yrs.			(5)(7)(20)(23)(30)(100)(101)		
Illinois	*(4)	*	2 yrs.			(64)		†(64)		(64)	(7)(23)(27)(90)		
Indiana		*		(4)		*					(5)(7)(23)(102)		
Iowa	(4)					*†					(7)(23)		
Kansas	(4)			(4)			*†				(5)(23)(30)(90)		
Kentucky	(4)			(4)		*†					(5)(7)(23)(90)		
Louisiana	(4)	*(32)†‡		(4)				*†(33), ‡2 yrs.			(6)(23)		
Maine	(4)		*			*		†(8)		†	(5)(23)		
Maryland	(4)	*(36)			(12)			†(35)		(37)	(23)		
Massachusetts	(4)	(39)	*			*					(23)		
Michigan						*†					(5)(7)(23)		
Minnesota						*		180 da.			(5)(7)(23)		
Mississippi	*	*	*	(4)		*				(65)	(5)(7)(17)(23)(44)(99)	(85)	(85)
Missouri	(4)			(4)	*	*		†(35)		†	(7)(23)		
Montana	(4)			(4)		*	†	180 da.			(5)(7)(23)(90)		

DIVORCE LAWS

There are presently pending, in most states, proposed divorce reform laws. The data set forth herein is correct as of June 2010. It is suggested that the attorney utilizing this chart consult amendments to local statutes.

State or other jurisdiction	*Grounds for absolute divorce* Bigamy	Felony Conviction or imprisonment	Drug Addiction	Fraud, force or duress	Prior decree of limited divorce	*Grounds for "no-fault" divorce* Irreconcilable Differences or Irretrievable Breakdown	Incompatibility	Living Separate and Apart	Judicial Separation or Maintenance	Mutual Consent	*Other Grounds* Other	*Period before parties may remarry after final decree* Plaintiff	Defendant
Nebraska	(4)			(4)		*					(5)(23)	30 da. (67)	30 da. (67)
Nevada	(4)			(4)			*†	1 yr.†			(7)(23)		
New Hampshire	(4)	(52)†				*†		2 yrs.†			(23)(49)(54)(55)(56)(101)		
New Jersey	(4)	18 mos.†	†	(4)				18 mos.†		*	(5)(7)(23)(58)		
New Mexico							*				(7)(23)		
New York	(4)	3 yrs.†		(4)	1 yr.			1 yr.	1 yr.	(65)	(5)(7)(23)		
North Carolina	(4)		(3)	(4)				1 yr.			(5)(7)(23)		
North Dakota	(4)	*		(4)		*					(5)(7)(23)(100)	(62)	(62)
Ohio	*	*†		*(4)(91)			*†	1 yr.†(40)		(65)	(5)(7)(23)(63)(90)(100)		
Oklahoma	(4)	*		(91)†			*				(7)(23)(44)(63)(100)	6 mos. (67)	6 mos. (67)
Oregon	(4)			*(4)		*†		*1 yr.†		*	(5)(7)(23)		
Pennsylvania	*	2 yr.				*(69)		2 yr.		(69)	(5)(7)(23)(94)		
Rhode Island	*	*	*			*		3 yrs.			(7)(23)(100)(104)		
South Carolina	*		*			*		1 yr. (37)			(7)(22)(23)		
South Dakota	(4)	*		(4)		*(34)			†		(5)(7)(23)(100)		
Tennessee	*†	*†	*†	(4)	2 yrs.	*(60)†		2 yrs.†			(5)(15)(22)(23)(26)(44)(61)(93)(100)(101)		
Texas	*	1 yr.		(4)		*	*	3 yrs.			(7)(23)	30 da. (71)	30 da. (71)
Utah	(4)	*			*	*		3 yrs.†(105)	*3 yrs.		(7)(23)(27)(75)(100)	(70)	(70)
Vermont	(4)	3 yrs.†		(4)				6 mos.†			(5)(7)(23)(78)(90)(100)		
Virginia	(4)	1 yr.†		(4)				1 yr.† (77)			(5)(7)(23)(44)(96)(101)	(70)	(70)
Washington	(4)			(4)		*†					(7)(23)	(70)	(70)
West Virginia	(4)	*†	*†			*†		1 yr.			(5)(7)(15)(19)(23)(27)(44)(95)(101)		
Wisconsin	(4)			(4)		*†				*	(7)(23)	6 mos.	6 mos.
Wyoming	(4)			(4)		*†			†		(5)(7)(20)(23)		
Dist. of Columbia	(4)			(4)	(92)			6 mos. (10)†		*	(7)(23)		
Virgin Islands	(4)			(4)†		*					(5)(7)(23)		
Puerto Rico	(4)	*	*					2 yrs.		*	(5)(23)(27)(80)(81)		

Footnotes

* Indicates ground for absolute divorce.
† Indicates ground for limited divorce or legal separation.
‡ Indicates ground for dissolution of covenant marriage.
(1) No residency requirement where plaintiff a resident and marriage solemnized in state. If marriage not solemnized in state, suit may be filed regardless of residency.
(2) Irreconcilable differences or irretrievable breakdown must be accompanied by one of the "traditional" grounds.
(3) Ground for separation from bed and board.
(4) Ground for annulment. In Hawaii, lack of mental capacity. In California, bigamy renders the later marriage either void or voidable, depending on the circumstances.
(5) Personal indignities, unsound mind, mental incapacity at time of marriage.
(6) Effective July 15, 1997, statute provides for an optional, voluntary form of marriage that is more difficult to dissolve through divorce. The covenant marriage requires pre-marriage counseling and limits grounds for divorce to such issues as spousal or child abuse, imprisonment, adultery or abandonment of the matrimonial domicile for one year.
(7) Lacked capacity to consent to marriage at time of marriage.
(8) Where one party has deserted the other or is living apart from the other for justifiable cause for at least 60 days.
(9) Imprisonment for 2 years of a 7 year (or longer) sentence.
(10) 6 months by voluntary separation, one year living separate and apart.
(11) Three months (plaintiff) if both parties reside in state.
(12) Legal separation that may be enlarged into an absolute divorce; Colorado, 6 months after decree of separation; Hawaii, after decree for separation from bed and board (issued by any court of competent juridiction) has expired or 2 years after decree of separate maintenance.
(13) 3 months in county.
(14) Also seven years absence.
(15) Infamous crime; in Connecticut, life imprisonment or crime involving violation of conjugal duty punishable by imprisonment of excess of one year.
(16) For certain circumstances a lesser period of time may be required; one party may be domiciled in state at time of marriage and returned to state before filing of complaint with intention of permanently residing in state, or cause of dissolution arose after either party moved into the state.
(17) Pregnancy at time of marriage.
(18) A marriage is irretrievably broken down when it is characterized by (i) voluntary separation or (ii) separation caused by respondent's misconduct or (iii) separation caused by respondent's mental illness or (iv) separation caused by incompatibility where reconciliation is impossible.
(19) Ground for annulment if, before marriage, husband was a notorious, licentious person without the wife's knowledge.
(20) Mental incompetence.
(21) Conviction of offense involving moral turpitude and under which party is sentenced to two year term.
(22) Abandonment by one party for five years without the abandonee knowing where the abandoner is living creates a presumption of abandoner's death, and remarriage is possible. In South Carolina, seven years.
(23) Intermarriage by persons within the prohibited degrees of consanguinity or affinity. Ground for divorce or annulment. In Georgia, such marriages may be voidable, not void.
(24) If there are minor children, or if claim of irretrievable breakdown is denied, court may order counseling, continue the proceeding for up to three months to enable the parties to effect a reconciliation, or take such other actions as may be in the best interest of the parties and minor children of the marriage.
(25) In addition to living separate and apart for two years after decree of separation or execution of a properly filed and executed separation agreement, or where terms of court ordered separation has expired.
(26) Attempted murder of other spouse by poison or other means showing malice.
(27) Infected the other spouse with venereal disease and/or AIDS. Ground for divorce or annulment.
(28) None if both parties are residents.
(29) Annulment due to impotency at time of marriage.
(30) Failure to perform marital duty or obligations.
(31) 3 months for member of Armed Forces stationed in Maine, or spouse.
(32) Felony conviction plus sentence to death or imprisonment at hard labor.
(33) 6 months for living separate and apart; also, divorce shall be granted upon rule to show cause filed by spouse when either spouse has filed petition for divorce and upon proof that 180 days have elapsed from service of petition and that spouses have lived separate and apart continously since filing of petition.
(34) "Irreconcilable differences" is defined as "those grounds which are determined to be substantial reasons for not continuing the marriage, and which make it appear that the marriage should be dissolved." Both parties are required to consent to the no-fault divorce unless one party has not made a general appearance.
(35) Living apart voluntarily twelve months or uninterrupted separation for two years.
(36) At least 12 months of 3 year sentence have been served prior to filing complaint.
(37) Without cohabitation, for 12 consecutive months, prior to filing with no reasonable expectation of reconciliation.
(38) No specific period required, except one year if cause occurred out of state and two years if on ground of insanity.
(39) Confinement for life or five years or more in a state or federal institution. A later pardon does not restore conjugal rights.
(40) Joint Bill—parties must execute separation agreement and reaffirm agreement in court.
(41) None if libellant domiciled in state and cause accrued within state.
(42) One year residency where cause of action occurred out of state.
(43) Ten days in the county, unless the defendant was born in or is a citizen in another country and the parties have a child who is at risk of being taken out of the U.S. and retained in another country by the defendant.
(44) Pregnancy of wife, at time of marriage, by another than husband, is ground for divorce; in Tennessee, without husband's knowledge.
(45) Cause of divorce must have occurred or existed within five years before commencement of suit.
(46) Or at time of the marriage.
(47) Mutual consent divorce for irreconcilable differences upon joint bill or where defendant personally served and no contest or denial.
(48) If contested, petitioner must show adultery, incompatibility, six month's abandonment, living apart by mutual consent for one year, or two year's living separate and apart.
(49) Serious injury to health or endangerment to reason.
(50) No requirement if marriage solemnized in state and continued residency in state until filing of petition.

(51) None except where defendant is non-resident; then one year continued residency, or defendant personally served with process within state. Cause must have arisen in state.
(52) One year sentence or longer and actual imprisonment under such sentence.
(53) 90-day waiting period between date of service and hearing, unless court waives this requirement on grounds of emergency or necessity.
(54) Either party joins a religious sect or society which professes to believe the relation of husband and wife is unlawful and has refused cohabitation for six months or more.
(55) Where wife residing outside of state for two years without his consent and without returning to claim marital rights.
(56) Where wife is alien or citizen of another state who resides in New Hampshire for two years, left the U.S. with intention of becoming citizen of another country and not having come into the state to claim marital rights nor provide suitable support.
(57) Except adultery if cause of action arose in state.
(58) Deviant sexual conduct.
(59) No residence requirement when cause occurred in state and both parties are residents at time of commencement. One year residence requirement in all other cases except when neither the marriage nor the cause of action occurred within the state, then two years.
(60) 60-day waiting period if there are minor children; 90-day period if no minor children.
(61) Refusing to live in same state with the spouse.
(62) In court's discretion.
(63) Defendant obtained divorce from plaintiff in another state.
(64) Irretrievable breakdown and two years living separate and apart required; if both parties consent the period becomes 6 months.
(65) Mutual consent divorce—Mississippi, irreconciliable differences upon joint bill or where defendant personally served and no contest or denial (although joint application filed to revoke divorce and former wife provided sufficient evidence of reconciliation prior to former husband's death, former husband's death made it impossible to resume status of marriage); Ohio, petition by both spouses, and execution of separation agreement; New York, legal separation is implied consent to a divorce one year later.
(66) If incurable.
(67) Longer if appeal taken.
(68) Plaintiff must be resident when action begun but need not maintain residency to be entitled to entry of a decree or judgment of divorce or separate maintenance.
(69) Mutual consent divorce for irretrievable breakdown if both parties have filed affidavits of consent and 90 days have elapsed.
(70) Remarriage of either party (except to each other) is prohibited during period allowed for appeal or pending appeal.
(71) Or lesser time in court's discretion.
(72) Condonation is defense only if there is finding of reasonable expectation of reconciliation.
(73) No divorce is granted unless the plaintiff has resided in state for one year next preceding the date of the final hearing.
(74) No divorce is granted where the grounds for divorce are insanity, unless the plaintiff has resided in the state for two years.
(75) Decree becomes absolute on date signed by court and entered by clerk if both parties who have a child or children have completed attendance at mandatory course for divorcing parents, unless court waives that requirement, or at expiration of court-designated time period.
(76) Unless marriage solemnized in state and plaintiff resided in state from time of marriage to filing of petition.
(77) Separate and apart for one year is sufficient, six months if there is a separation agreement and there are no children.
(78) Decree issued is a divorce nisi in first instance; becomes absolute in three months; court has discretion to fix earlier date.
(79) Petitioner must be state resident or married to a resident. 90-day cooling-off period after filing required.
(80) Attempt of husband or wife to corrupt their sons or to prostitute their daughters and connivance in their corruption or prostitution.
(81) Proposal of husband to prostitute his wife.
(82) None if plaintiff is domiciled in state and defendant submits to jurisdiction. If nonsupport, two years of separation.
(83) Statute does not require 3 months residence immediately before entry of divorce.
(84) 6 months, creates rebuttable presumption of domicile in state and parish of such residence.
(85) Judge may remove prohibition after 1 year upon petition and evidence of reformation.
(86) Where cause is adultery, one party must be a bona fide resident of West Virginia.
(87) Action may be brought in county in which plaintiff has resided for 30 days immediately preceding filing, or in county in which plaintiff resides.
(88) One party suffered from leprosy or loathsome disease, and this fact was concealed from or unknown by party seeking annulment.
(89) Crime against nature before or after marriage is ground for divorce.
(90) Failure to consummate at time of marriage and continuing at commencement of action is ground for divorce.
(91) Fraudulent contract is ground for divorce.
(92) Decree of legal separation may be enlarged to absolute divorce if court finds that no reconciliation has taken place or is probable and separation has continued voluntarily and without interruption for 6 month period or without interruption for 1 year.
(93) Grounds for divorce from bed and board: (i) abandonment; (ii) malicously turning other out of doors, (iii) cruel and barbarous treatment endangering life; (iv) indignities to person, rendering life burdensome and conditions intolerable; (v) rendering life unbearable by excessive use of alcohol or drugs (except in Tennessee); (vi) adultery (except in Tennessee).
(94) Indignities rendering condition intolerable and life burdensome is ground for divorce.
(95) Abuse, neglect of child is ground for divorce.
(96) Annulment for prostitution of a party before marriage without knowledge of other party.
(97) If parties were married in state, and at least one of parties is a resident at the time action is commenced, no length of residency is required.
(98) Husband and wife may together petition court if they have agreed on custody, support and property rights. Either spouse may petition court if other spouse's whereabouts are unknown and spouse cannot be served personally within or without the state.
(99) Failure to procure a valid license; grounds for annulment.
(100) Gross neglect of duty.
(101) Homosexuality.
(102) Marriages entered into after Sept. 1, 1977 between first cousins 65 or older not void.
(103) Fraudulent intent not to perform marriage vows is grounds for annulment.
(104) Gross misbehavior and wickedness, in either of parties, repugnant to and in violation of marriage covenant.
(105) Under decree of separation from any state for 3 consecutive years without cohabitation.
(106) 6 months if children residing in state.
(107) Court will not grant a divorce on these grounds until at least 30 days after date of service on respondent.
(108) Conviction of crime the sentence of which may be 1 or more years incarceration.
(109) Continuous without reconciliation for 1 year from date that decree of legal separation was entered or 2 years before filing for dissolution of marriage.
(110) Action must be commenced within 2 years of act of adultery, 1 year from pardon or termination of sentence in the case of imprisonment and within a reasonable time in all other cases.

MOTOR VEHICLE LAWS

State or other jusrisdiction	Age for Driver's license: Regular	Learner's	Restrictive	License renewal (years)	Liability laws	Minimum Financial Responsibility Limits†	Vehicle inspection	Transfer of plates to new owner
Alabama	17 + 6 mos.	15(d)	14(e), 16(r)	4	S	25/50/25	spot (f)	. . .
Alaska	18	14(g,i)	16(r)	5	S	50/100/25	spot (h)	*
Arizona	16 + 6 mos.	15 + 6 mo.(g,i)	16(g,r)	until 65th birthday	S	15/30/10	spot (l)	. . .
Arkansas	18	14(d)	14 + 6 mo.(g,i,t)	4	S,N	25/50/25	spot	. . .
California	17	15 + 6 mo.(i,j)	16(j,r)	5	(k)	15/30/5(aa)	(l)	*
Colorado	17	15(j), 15 + 6 mo.(d,i), 16	16(r)	5	S,C,N	25/50/15	spot (l)	. . .
Connecticut	18	16(d,i,r)	16 + 6 mo.(j,r)	2 or 6(n)	C	20/40/10	*	. . .
Delaware	17	16(d,i,j)	16 + 6 mo.(j,r)	5	S,N	15/30/10	*	*
Florida	18	15(d,i,r)	16(g,r)	6 or 8 (n)	C,N	10/20/10	spot	. . .
Georgia	18	15(i)	17(g,r)	5	C	25/50/25	spot (l)	. . .
Hawaii	17	15 + 6 mo. (d,j)	16(g,j,r)	2 or 4 or 8(n)	C	20/40/10	spot	. . .
Idaho	17	14 + 6 mo. (d,i)	15(j,r,t)	4 or 8 (n)	S,C	25/50/15	(l)	. . .
Illinois	18	15(d,p,r)	16(g,j,r)	2 or 4(n)	S,C	20/40/15	(l)	. . .
Indiana	18	15 + 6 mo. (p), 16	16+6mo.(g,j,r,t)	2 or 3 or 6(n)	C	25/50/10	spot (l)	*
Iowa	17	14(i)	16(j,r)	2 or 5(n)	S,C	20/40/15	spot	. . .
Kansas	16 + 6 mo.	14(g,i)	14(a), 15(g,j)	4 or 6 (n)	C,N	25/50/10	spot	. . .
Kentucky	18	16(d,i,r)	16 + 6 mo.(g,j,r,t)	4	C,N	25/50/10	(l)	*
Louisiana	17	15(i,j)	16(j,r)	4	C	10/20/10	*	. . .
Maine	18	15(d,i)	16(j,r)	4 or 6 or 8 (n)	S,C,U	50/100/25	*	. . .
Maryland	17 + 9 mo.	15 + 9 mo.(d,i,j)	16 + 6 mo.(g,j,r)	5	C,N,U	20/40/15	*	. . .
Massachusetts	18	16(d,i)	16 + 6 mo.(g,j,r)	5	C,N	20/40/5	*	. . .
Michigan	17	14 + 9 mo.(d,j)	16(g,j,r)	4	C,N	20/40/10	spot	. . .
Minnesota	18	15(d,j)	15 + 6 mo.(j,r)	4	C,N	30/60/10	(f)	*
Mississippi	16 + 6 mo.	15(d,i)	16(r)	1 or 4(n)	S,F	25/50/25	*	. . .
Missouri	18	15(i)	16(r)	3 or 6(n)	C	25/50/10	*	. . .
Montana	16	14 + 6 mo.	15(g,j,r)	4 or 6 or 8(n)	C	25/50/10	spot	. . .
Nebraska	17	15(d,i)	14(m), 16 (j,r)	5	F,C	25/50/25	. . .	. . .
Nevada	18	15 + 6 mo.(d,i)	16(g,j,r)	4	F,C	15/30/10	spot (q,l)	. . .
New Hampshire	18	15 + 6 mo.(i)	16(g,j,r)	5	S,F	25/50/25	*	. . .
New Jersey	18	16(i,j)	16(a), 17(r)	4	S,C,N,J,U	15/30/5	*	. . .
New Mexico	16 + 6 mo.	15(i,j)	15 + 6 mo.(j,r)	4 or 8	C	25/50/10	(h)	. . .
New York	18	16(i,c,r)	16(g,c,r)	8	S,C,N	25/50/10(x)	*	. . .
North Carolina	16 + 6 mo.	15(i,j,r)	16(r)	5 or 8(n)	C,U	30/60/25	*	. . .
North Dakota	16	14(d,g,i)	14 + 6 mo.(g)	4	S,C,N,U,J	25/50/25	spot	. . .
Ohio	18	15 + 6 mo.(i,r)	16(j,r)	4	C,F	12.5/25/7.5	spot (l)	. . .
Oklahoma	16 + 6 mo.(j), 17	15 + 6 mo.(i,p), 16 (i)	16(r)	4	S,C	25/50/25	spot	. . .
Oregon	18	15(i)	16(r)	8	F,C,N	25/50/20 (bb)	spot (l)	. . .
Pennsylvania	17 + 6 mo.(j)	16(d,i)	16 + 6 mo.(g,r)	4	C	15/30/5	*	. . .
Puerto Rico	18	16(d,i)	16(g)	6	(v)	. . .	*	. . .
Rhode Island	17 + 6 mo.	16(d,i,j)	16 + 6 mo.(j,r)	2 or 5(n)	S	25/50/25	*	. . .

MOTOR VEHICLE LAWS

State or other jusrisdiction	Age for Driver's license: Regular	Learner's	Restrictive	License renewal (years)	Liability laws	Minimum Financial Responsibility Limits†	Vehicle inspection	Transfer of plates to new owner
South Carolina	17	15(d,i,r)	15 + 6 mo.(j,r,t)	5 or 10 (n)	C	25/50/25	...	...
South Dakota	18	14(i)	14+3 mo.(g,j,r), 14+6 mo.(g,r)	5	C,F,U	25/50/25	...	...
Tennessee	17	15(i,r)	16(w,r)	5	S,F	25/50/10	(l)	...
Texas	17	15(i,j,t)	16(r)	2 or 6 (n)	S,C,F,U	30/60/25	*	*
Utah	17	15(i,g)	16(j,r)	5	S,N,U	25/65/15	*	...
Vermont	18	15(i,j)	16(i,j)	2 or 4	C	25/50/10	*	...
Virginia	18	15 + 6 mo.(g,i)	16 + 3 mo.(g,r)	8	S,U	25/50/20	*	...
Washington	18	15(p), 15 + 6 mo.(d)	16(j,r)	5	S,C,F	25/50/10	(l)	...
West Virginia	17	15(d,g,i,r)	16(g,r)	5	S,C	20/40/10	*	...
Wisconsin	18	15 + 6 mo.(d,i)	16(j,r,t)	8(z)	S	50/100/15	spot (l)	*
Wyoming	16 + 6 mo.(j),17	15(g,i)	16(g,r)	4	S,C	25/50/20	...	...
District of Columbia	18	16(d,i,r)	16+6 mo.(g,r)	8	C	25/50/10	*	...
Virgin Islands	18	16(g,j)	...	3	C	10/20/10	*	...

The following are present in all jurisdictions: Chemical test for intoxication; Implied consent doctrine; Child restraint law; Non-resident service of process law (except Hawaii & Puerto Rico)

* Indicates provision is present in this jurisdiction
† Denotes (in thousands of dollars) minimum amounts for injury to one person, injury to more than one person, and property damage
(a) Agricultural use only
(b) Student permit issued under special conditions
(c) Driving prohibited in New York City by drivers with restrictive licenses; also restricted driving hours in Nassau and Suffolk Counties
(d) Permit required. In Arkansas, for six months prior to 18th birthday
(e) Restricted to mopeds
(f) Cities have authority to maintain inspection stations
(g) Guardian or parental consent required
(h) Emission inspection required in certain municipalities
(i) Driver must be accompanied by licensed operator; in some states must be parent or guardian
(j) Must have completed approved driver education course
(k) Financial responsibility required of every driver/owner of motor vehicle at all times
(l) Mandatory annual emissions test in certain counties
(m) Special school license in certain circumstances
(n) Depending upon age of driver; in Florida, also depends upon driving record
(o) Trucks and buses only
(p) Must be enrolled in driver education course.
(q) Mandatory inspection only under certain circumstances
(r) Driving hours restricted
(s) Required for motorcyclists only. Otherwise, unlicensed persons who are being taught to drive must be accompanied by licensed operator 25 years or older; minimum age 15 + 6 mo.
(t) Must be a high school graduate or a student; subject to license suspension for violation of certain school regulations
(u) Upon proof of hardship
(v) Compulsory insurance system administered by the Commonwealth; limited coverage
(w) Persons under 18 must have held learner's permit, or out-of-state license at least six months
(x) If accident results in death, minimum limits are 50/100/10
(y) Commercial vehicles only
(z) Initial license only for 2 years
(aa) Special policies for low-income motorists have limits of 20/10/3
(bb) If convicted of driving under the influence, limits of 50/100/20

KEY TO LIABILITY LAWS

S Security-type law (following accident, must show ability to pay damages resulting from accident, including results of legal actions)
C Compulsory Insurance law (motorist must show proof of liability insurance, usually as a condition of vehicle registration)
F Future-proof type law (persons convicted of certain driving offenses or failing to pay accident damages judgment must make a showing of financial responsibility)
N No-fault insurance law (owner reimbursed for accident damages by own insurance company, rather than having to prove fault in court)
J Unsatisfied judgment funds law (financed with fees from motorists unable to prove evidence of insurance or by assessments on insurance companies to cover pedestrians and others without no-fault insurance)
U Uninsured motorist law (mandatory coverage against potential damage from uninsured motorists)

NEW YORK LAW SCHOOLS

ALBANY LAW SCHOOL
80 New Scotland Ave., Albany 12208 (518) 445-2311
Internet: www.albanylaw.edu
Dean: Thomas F. Guernsey
(518) 445-2321; Fax: (518) 472-5865
Assoc. Dean of Academic Affairs: Connie Mayer
(518) 445-2393; E-mail: cmaye@albanylaw.edu
Asst. Dean of Career Center: Sandra Mans
(518) 445-2377; E-mail: smans@albanylaw.edu
V.P. for Institutional Advancement: Helen Adams Keane
(518) 445-3206; E-mail: hadam@albanylaw.edu
Dir. of Admissions: Gail Bensen
(518) 445-2326; E-mail: gbens@albanylaw.edu
Registrar: Joann Fitzsimmons
(518) 445-2330; E-mail: registrar@albanylaw.edu
Dir., Law Library: Robert T. Begg (Assoc. Dean)
(518) 445-2336; E-mail: rbegg@albanylaw.edu

BROOKLYN LAW SCHOOL
250 Joralemon St., Brooklyn 11201 (718) 625-2200
Internet: www.brooklaw.edu
President: Joan G. Wexler (718) 780-7900; Fax: (718) 780-0393
E-mail: joan.wexler@brooklaw.edu
Dean: Michael A. Gerber (Acting) (718) 780-7923
E-mail: michael.gerber@brooklaw.edu
Dean of Admissions & Financial Aid:
Henry W. Haverstick III (718) 780-7906; Fax: (718) 780-0395
E-mail: henry.haverstick@brooklaw.edu
Assoc. Dean for Academic Affairs: Lawrence M. Solan
(718) 780-0357; Fax: (718) 780-0393
E-mail: larry.solan@brooklaw.edu
Assoc. Dean for Student Affairs: Beryl R. Jones-Woodin
(718) 780-7957; Fax: (718) 780-0393
E-mail: beryl.jones@brooklaw.edu
Asst. Dean for External Affairs: Linda Harvey
(718) 780-0382; Fax: (718) 625-5245
E-mail: linda.harvey@brooklaw.edu
Dir., Alumni Affairs: Caitlin Monck-Marcellino
(718) 780-0322; Fax: (718) 643-4726
Dir., Career Svces.: Camile Chin Kee-Fatt
(718) 780-7963; Fax: (718) 780-0374
E-mail: camille.chinkeefatt@brooklaw.edu
Dir., Residence Life: Jennifer Lang
(718) 780-0383; Fax: (718) 780-4518
E-mail: jennifer.lang@brooklaw.edu
Registrar: Suzanne M. Dennis (718) 780-7913
E-mail: suzanne.dennis@brooklaw.edu
Dir., Law Library: Victoria J. Szymczak
(718) 780-7973; Fax: (718) 780-0369
E-mail: victoria.szymczak@brooklaw.edu

BENJAMIN N. CARDOZO SCHOOL OF LAW
Yeshiva University, 55 Fifth Ave., N.Y.C. 10003-4391
(212) 790-0200; Fax: (212) 790-0203
Internet: www.cardozo.yu.edu
Dean: Matthew Diller (212) 790-0310
Vice Dean: Edward Stein, 10th Floor (212) 790-0310
Assoc. Dean for Student Services and Minority Students: Judy Mender, 10th Floor
(212) 790-0313; E-mail: mender@yu.edu
Assoc. Dean for Admissions: David Martinidez
11th Floor (212) 790-0329; E-mail: martinidez@yu.edu
Assoc. Dean for Career Services: Arthur Fama
11th Floor (212) 790-0374; E-mail: fama@yu.edu
Dir. of Externships: Becky Rosenfeld, 11th Floor
(212) 790-0894; E-mail: becky.rosenfeld@yu.edu
Asst. Dean for Graduate & International Programs:
Amy Sugin, 10th Floor (212) 790-0361
E-mail: sugin@yu.edu
Dir. of Alumni Affairs: Kristen Worrell, 10th Floor
(212) 790-0298; E-mail: worrell@yu.edu
Dir. of Institutional Advancement: Patricia Weiss
10th Floor (212) 790-0270; E-mail: pweiss@yu.edu
Assoc. Dean for Library Services: Lynn Wishart
7th Floor (212) 790-0222; E-mail: wishart@yu.edu

CITY UNIVERSITY OF NEW YORK
School of Law at Queens College
65-21 Main St., Flushing 11367-1300
(718) 340-4200; Fax: (718) 340-4275, 340-4482
Internet: www.law.cuny.edu
Dean: Michelle J. Anderson (718) 340-4202
Assoc. Dean for Academic Affairs:
Natalie Gomez-Velez (718) 340-4340
E-mail: gomez-velez@mail.law.cuny.edu
Assoc. Dean for Administration & Finance:
Gregory Koster (718) 340-4264
E-mail: koster@mail.law.cuny.edu
Asst. Dean for Student Affairs: Angela Burton (Acting)
(718) 340-4179; E-mail: burton@mail.law.cuny.edu
Asst. Dean for Enrollment Mgmt.:
Yvonne Cherena-Pacheco (Dir. of Admissions)
(718) 340-4291; E-mail: cherena-pacheco@mail.law.cuny.edu
Dir., Development: Laura Kotkin (718) 340-4483
E-mail: laura.kotkin@mail.law.cuny.edu
Dir. of Career Planning: Sam Sue (718) 340-4233
E-mail: sue@mail.law.cuny.edu
Dir., Law Library: Prof. Julie Lim (718) 340-4259
E-mail: lim@mail.law.cuny.edu

COLUMBIA UNIVERSITY SCHOOL OF LAW
435 W. 116th St., N.Y.C. 10027
(212) 854-2640; Fax: (212) 854-9740
Internet: www.law.columbia.edu
Dean: David M. Schizer, Box B-12
(212) 854-2675; E-mail: dschiz@law.columbia.edu
Dean of Students: Michelle Greenberg-Kobrin
Box B-25, (212) 854-7420
E-mail: michelle.greenberg-kobrin@law.columbia.edu
Dean of Admissions: E. Nkonye Iwerebon
1125 Amsterdam Ave., 5th Floor, N.Y.C. 10027
Mailing Address: Mail Code 4004,
435 W. 116th St., N.Y.C. 10027
(212) 854-2670; Fax: (212) 854-1109
Dean of Career Services: Petal N. Modeste, Box A-5
(212) 854-1664; E-mail: petal.modeste@law.columbia.edu
Assoc. Dean for Administration and Finance:
Edward Moroni (212) 854-1375; Fax: (512) 212-7944
E-mail: emoroni@law.columbia.edu
Assoc. Dean for Development and Alumnae/i Relations: Bruno Santoncito
1125 Amsterdam Ave., 7th Floor, N.Y.C. 10025
Mailing Address: 435 W. 116th St., Box A-2, N.Y.C. 10027
(212) 854-1387; E-mail: bsanto@law.columbia.edu
Law Librarian: Kent McKeever (212) 854-4228
E-mail: mckeever@law.columbia.edu

CORNELL LAW SCHOOL
Cornell University
Myron Taylor Hall, 524 College Ave., Ithaca 14853-4901
(607) 255-3527; Fax: (607) 255-7193
Internet: www.lawschool.cornell.edu/
Dean: Stewart J. Schwab (607) 255-3527
Vice Dean: Barbara Holden Smith (607) 255-8577
Assoc. Dean Academic Affairs: Stephen P. Garvey
(607) 255-8589
Assoc. Dean & Dean of Student Affairs: Anne Lukingbeal
Room 165 (607) 255-5839
Assoc. Dean of Enrollment & Communications:
Richard D. Geiger (607) 255-5141
Assoc. Dean for Alumni Affairs & Development:
Peter Cronin (607) 255-3370
Asst. Dean for Student & Career Services:
John DeRosa (607) 255-9982
Asst. Dean for Public Service: Karen V. Comstock
(607) 255-3597
Registrar: Nan A. Colvin (607) 255-7190
Edward Cornell Law Librarian: Prof. Claire M. Germain
(Dir., Dual Degree Programs, Paris & Berlin)
(607) 255-5857

FORDHAM UNIVERSITY SCHOOL OF LAW
140 W. 62nd St., N.Y.C. 10023 (212) 636-6000
Internet: http://law.fordham.edu

Dean: Michael M. Marin (Acting) (212) 636-6875

Assoc. Dean for Academic Affairs: Sheila Foster (212) 636-7771; E-mail: sfoster@law.fordham.edu

Assoc. Dean for Administration: Nicola Lee (212) 636-7692; E-mail: nlee@law.fordham.edu

Asst. Dean for Administration: Darin Neely (212) 636-7289; E-mail: dneely@law.fordham.edu

Asst. Dean for Student Affairs: Nitza Milagros Escalera (212) 636-6818; E-mail: nescalera@law.fordham.edu

Asst. Dean for Financial Aid: Judith McNatt (212) 636-6872; E-mail: jmcnatt@law.fordham.edu

Asst. Dean for Career Planning and Placement: Suzanne Endrizzi (212) 636-7157 E-mail: sendrizzi@law.fordham.edu

Asst. Dean for Alumni Affairs: Michael Schiumo (212) 636-7293; E-mail: mschiumo@law.fordham.edu

Dir. of Admissions: Kathryn Espiritu (212) 636-6811

Assoc. Dir. of Finance: Laura Gibney (212) 636-6893 E-mail: lgibney@law.fordham.edu

Dir., Law Library: Prof. Robert J. Nissenbaum (212) 636-7609; E-mail: rnissenbaum@law.fordham.edu

HOFSTRA UNIVERSITY SCHOOL OF LAW
121 Hofstra University, Hempstead 11549-1210
(516) 463-6340; Internet: http://law.hofstra.edu

Dean: Nora V. Demleitner (516) 463-5854; Fax: (516) 463-6091 E-mail: lawnvd@hofstra.edu

Vice Dean for Academic Affairs: Jennifer Gundlach (516) 463-4190; Fax: (516) 463-6091 E-mail: lawjzg@hofstra.edu

Assoc. Dean of Information Services and Dir., Law Library: Michelle M. Wu (516) 463-5901; Fax: (516) 463-5129 E-mail: lawmmw@hofstra.edu

Assoc. Dean and Dean for Professional Development: Victoria Roberts (516) 463-5865; Fax: (516) 463-1017 E-mail: victoria.roberts@hofstra.edu

Asst. Dean for Administration and Operations: Jeffrey A. Dodge (Dir., CLE Programs) (516) 463-0417; Fax: (516) 463-6091 E-mail: lawjad@hofstra.edu

Asst. Dean for Career Services: Michael Ende 108 Hofstra University, Hempstead 11549-1210 (516) 463-5871; Fax: (516) 463-7351 E-mail: lawmje@hofstra.edu

Dir., Career Services: Vernadette Horne (516) 463-5387; Fax: (516) 463-7351 E-mail: lawvhh@hofstra.edu

Asst. Dean for Enrollment Mgmt.: John Chalmers 108 Hofstra University, Hempstead 11549-1210 (516) 463-5916; Fax: (516) 463-6264 E-mail: lawjwc@hofstra.edu

Dir., Enrollment Mgmt.: Shawn McShay 108 Hofstra University, Hempstead 11549-1210 (516) 463-5916; Fax: (516) 463-6264 E-mail: lawsdm@hofstra.edu

Dir. of Financial Aid: Gerard Anderson 108 Hofstra University, Hempstead 11549-1210 (516) 463-5929; Fax: (516) 463-6264 E-mail: lawgna@hofstra.edu

Asst. Dean for External Relations: Lisa Berman (516) 463-4758; E-mail: lawlhb@hofstra.edu

Dir., Alumni Relations: Kelley Spencer (516) 463-5188; Fax: (516) 463-1017 E-mail: lawkms@hofstra.edu

Dirs., Student Affairs:
Lisa McCluskey (516) 463-4809; Fax: (516) 463-4710 E-mail: lisa.mccluskey@hofstra.edu
Claire O'Keefe (516) 463-5270; Fax: (516) 463-4710 E-mail: lawcto@hofstra.edu

NEW YORK LAW SCHOOL
185 W. Broadway, N.Y.C. 10013-2921
(212) 431-2100; Fax: (212) 406-0103
Internet: www.nyls.edu

Dean/President: Richard A. Matasar (212) 431-2840; Fax: (212) 219-3752 E-mail: rmatasar@nyls.edu

V.P. for Finance and Administration: Fred DeJohn (212) 431-2881

V.P. for Academic Publishing: Jethro Lieberman (212) 431-2842

V.P. for Marketing & Communications: Nancy Guida (212) 431-2325

Assoc. Dean for Academic Affairs: Carol Buckler (212) 431-2182

Assoc. Dean and V.P. for Development & Alumni Relations: Suzanne J.S. Davidson (212) 431-2808

Assoc. Dean for Faculty Development and Collaborative Learning: Stephen Ellmann (212) 431-2392

Assoc. Dean for Professional Dev.: Mariana Hogan (212) 431-2345

Asst. Dean for Admissions and Financial Aid: William Perez (212) 431-2888 E-mail: admissions@nyls.edu

Asst. Dean for Career Planning: Margaret Reuter (212) 431-2158

Asst. Dean for Student Services: Helena Prigal (212) 431-2851

Asst. Dean/Registrar: Oral C. Hope (212) 431-0302 E-mail: ohope@nyls.edu

Assoc. Dean for Information Services & Dir., Law Library: Camille Broussard 57 Worth St., N.Y.C. 10016-2960 (212) 431-2354

NEW YORK UNIVERSITY SCHOOL OF LAW
40 Washington Square S., N.Y.C. 10012
(212) 998-6000
Internet: www.law.nyu.edu

Dean: Richard Revesz, Room 406 (212) 998-6000

Vice Deans:
Barry Friedman, Room 317 (212) 998-6293; E-mail: barry.friedman@nyu.edu
Liam Murphy, Room 337 (212) 998-6160; E-mail: liam.murphy@nyu.edu

Assoc. Dean for Planning: Brookes Billman, Room 430-E (212) 998-6158; E-mail: brookes.billman@nyu.edu

Assoc. Dean for Development and Alumni Relations: Jeannie Forrest, 161 Sixth Ave., 5th Floor, N.Y.C. 10013 (212) 998-6424; E-mail: jeannie.forrest@nyu.edu

Assoc. Dean for Financial Mgmt. & Chief Financial Officer: Barbara Timpano 161 Sixth Ave., 5th Floor, N.Y.C. 10013 (212) 998-6245; E-mail: barbara.timpano@nyu.edu

Asst. Dean for Student Affairs: Pascale Walker 245 Sullivan St., Room 413, N.Y.C. 10012 (212) 998-6188; E-mail: pascale.walker@nyu.edu

Asst. Dean for Admissions: Kenneth R. Kleinrock 161 Sixth Ave., 5th Floor, N.Y.C. 10013 (212) 998-6063; E-mail: ken.kleinrock@nyu.edu

Asst. Dean for Career Services: Irene Dorzback 245 Sullivan St., Room 444, N.Y.C. 10012 (212) 998-6721; E-mail: irene.dorzback@nyu.edu

Dir., Law Library: Radu Popa, Room 102 (212) 998-6320; E-mail: radu.popa@nyu.edu

PACE UNIVERSITY SCHOOL OF LAW
78 N. Broadway, White Plains 10603-3796
(914) 422-4205
Internet: www.law.pace.edu

Dean: Michelle S. Simon (914) 422-4407; Fax: (914) 422-4426 E-mail: msimon@law.pace.edu

Dean for Students: Angela M. D'Agostino (914) 422-4146; Fax: (914) 422-4015 E-mail: adagostino@law.pace.edu

Pace University School of Law—Cont'd

Vice Dean of Academic Affairs: Jeffrey Miller (914) 422-4014; Fax: (914) 422-4229 E-mail: jmiller@law.pace.edu

Asst. Dean for Admissions: Cathy Alexander (914) 422-4212; Fax: (914) 989-8714 E-mail: calexander@law.pace.edu

Asst. Dean/Registrar: Nilda Rodriguez (914) 422-4018; Fax: (914) 422-4248 E-mail: nrodriguez@law.pace.edu

Asst. Dean for Career Development and External Relations: Rachel Littman (914) 422-4218; Fax: (914) 422-4243 E-mail: rlittman@law.pace.edu

Dir., of Philanthropy and Alumni Relations: David Bernhardt (914) 422-4072; Fax: (914) 422-4039 E-mail: dbernhardt@law.pace.edu

Dir., Law Library: Marie Newman (914) 422-4169; Fax: (914) 422-4139 E-mail: mnewman@law.pace.edu

ST. JOHN'S UNIVERSITY SCHOOL OF LAW
8000 Utopia Pkwy., Queens 11439
(718) 990-6600; Fax: (718) 591-1855
Internet: www.law.stjohns.edu

Dean: Michael A. Simons (718) 990-6601 E-mail: simonsm@stjohns.edu

Vice Dean Emeritus: Andrew J. Simons (718) 990-6098 E-mail: simonsa@stjohns.edu

Associate Academic Dean: Margaret V. Turano (718) 990-6632; E-mail: turanom@stjohns.edu

Assoc. Dean for Faculty Scholarship: Paul F. Kirgis 8000 Utopia Pkwy., Queens 11439 (718) 990-6610 E-mail: kirgisp@stjohns.edu

Sr. Asst. Dean for Students: Katherine G. Sullivan (718) 990-6045; E-mail: sullivak@stjohns.edu

Asst. Dean for Alumni Relations and CLE: Claire C. McKeever (718) 990-6028 E-mail: mckeevec@stjohns.edu

Asst. Dean for Admissions: Robert M. Harrison (718) 990-2310; E-mail: harrisor@stjohns.edu

Asst. Dean for Career Services: Dawne M. Smith (718) 990-2337; E-mail: smithd1@stjohns.edu

Registrar: Ann M. Hurt (718) 990-8350 E-mail: hurta@stjohns.edu

Dir., Rittenberg Law Library and Research Professor of Law: Barbara G. Traub (Acting) (718) 990-1668; E-mail: traubb@stjohns.edu

STATE UNIVERSITY OF NEW YORK AT BUFFALO LAW SCHOOL
John Lord O'Brian Hall, Buffalo 14260-1100
(716) 645-2052; Fax: (716) 645-5968
Internet: www.law.buffalo.edu

Dean: Makua W. Mutua, Room 319

Vice Dean: Alan S. Carrel, Room 311 (716) 645-6222

Vice Dean for Academic Affairs: James A. Gardner Room 514 (716) 645-3607

Vice Dean for Student Affairs: Melinda R. Saran Room 313 (716) 645-6223

Vice Dean for Alumni, Public Relations and Communications: Ilene R. Fleischmann (Exec. Dir. of Alumni Assoc.), Room 310 (716) 645-2107; Fax: (716) 645-5940

Vice Dean for Admissions and Financial Aid: Lillie Wiley-Upshaw, Room 309 (716) 645-2907; Fax: (716) 645-6676

Vice Dean for Administration: James R. Newton Room 318 (716) 645-5997

Assoc. Dean for Career Services: Lisa M. Patterson Room 609 (716) 645-2056; Fax: (716) 645-7336

Assoc. Dean for Development: Karen Kaczmarski (716) 645-6429

Registrar: BobbyJo LaDelfa (Dir. of Records & Registration) Room 304 (716) 645-2060

Vice Dean for Legal Information Services & Dir. of Law Library: James A. Wooten Room 713 (716) 645-2318

SYRACUSE UNIVERSITY COLLEGE OF LAW
E.I. White Hall, Syracuse 13244-1030
(315) 443-2524; Fax: (315) 443-4213
Internet: www.law.syr.edu

Dean: Hannah R. Arterian, Suite 440 (315) 443-9580

Assoc. Dean for Academic Affairs: Christian C. Day Suite 182 (315) 443-3650; Fax: (315) 443-4213

Assoc. Dean for Enrollment Mgmt. and Chief Financial Officer: Cheryl A. Ficarra Suite 440 (315) 443-2540; Fax: (315) 443-4213

Sr. Asst. Dean of Student Life: Tomas A. Gonzalez Suite 444 (315) 443-1146; Fax: (315) 443-9719

Asst. Dean of Developmental & Institutional Advancement: Alexandra C. Epsilanty Suite 425 (315) 443-4536; Fax: (315) 443-4585

Dir. of Admissions: Anikka S. Laubenstein Suite 340 (315) 443-1962; Fax: (315) 442-9568

Dir. of Financial Aid: Gina M. Soliz Suite 340 (315) 443-1963; Fax: (315) 443-9568

Dir. of Professional & Career Development: Kimberly Wolf Price, Suite 344 (315) 443-1941; Fax: (315) 443-3086

Registrar: Jo Ann Larkin, Suite 542 (315) 443-2036; Fax: (315) 443-5103

Assoc. Dean, H. Douglas Barclay Law Library: Thomas R. French, Suite 530 (315) 443-1221; Fax: (315) 443-9567

TOURO COLLEGE
Jacob D. Fuchsberg Law Center
225 Eastview Dr., Central Islip 11722
(631) 761-7100; Fax: (631) 761-7109
Internet: www.tourolaw.edu

Dean: Lawrence Raful (631) 761-7100 E-mail: lraful@tourolaw.edu

Assoc. Dean Academic Affairs and Faculty Development: Louise Harmon (631) 761-7102 E-mail: louiseh@tourolaw.edu

Assoc. Dean for Administration: Kenneth A. Rosenblum (631) 761-7001; E-mail: kenr@tourolaw.edu

Asst. Dean for Student Affairs: Charlotte Taylor (631) 761-7050; E-mail: ctaylor@tourolaw.edu

Asst. Dean for Admissions: George Justice (631) 761-7010; E-mail: gjustice@tourolaw.edu

Asst. Dean for Institutional Advancement: Linda Howard Weissman (631) 761-7061; E-mail: lindah@tourolaw.edu

Asst. Dean for Career Services: Margarett Williams (631) 761-7030; E-mail: margarettw@tourolaw.edu

Dir. of Enrollment: Susan Thompson (631) 761-7012; E-mail: susant@tourolaw.edu

Dir. of Development & Alumni Relations: Kristin Matthews (631) 761-7063; E-mail: kmatthews@tourolaw.edu

Registrar: Paula Klutch (631) 761-7040; E-mail: paulak@tourolaw.edu

Dir., Law Library: April Schwartz (631) 761-7151; E-mail: aschwartz@tourolaw.edu

CITIES, VILLAGES AND UNINCORPORATED COMMUNITIES WITH THEIR RESPECTIVE COUNTIES, JUDICIAL DISTRICTS, AREA CODES AND ZIP CODES

Note: The Zip Code precedes the community. Where communities have more than one Zip Code, the sectional center is indicated and the zones are indicated with ##

Accord (Ulster) (3rd) (845) 12404
Acra (Greene) (3rd) (518) 12405
Adams (Jefferson) (5th) (315) 13605
Adams Basin (Monroe) (7th) (585) 14410
Adams Center (Jefferson) (5th) (315) 13606
Adams Corners (Putnam) (9th) (845) 10579
Adams Cove (Jefferson) (5th) (315) 13634
Addisleigh Park (Queens) (11th) (718) 11433, 11434
Addison (Steuben) (7th) (607) 14801
Adelphi (Kings) (2nd) (718) 11238
Adirondack (Warren) (4th) (518) 12808
Afton (Chenango) (6th) (607) 13730
Airmont (Rockland) (9th) (845) 10901, 10952
Akron (Erie) (8th) (716) 14001
Akwesasne (Franklin) (4th) (518) 13655
Alabama (Genesee) (8th) (585) 14013
Albany (Albany) (3rd) (518) 122##
Albertson (Nassau) (10th) (516) 11507
Albia (Rensselaer) (3rd) (518) 12180
Albion (Orleans) (8th) (585) 14411
Albion (Oswego) (5th) (315) 13302
Alburgh (Franklin) (4th) (518) 12916
Alcove (Albany) (3rd) (518) 12007
Alden (Erie) (8th) (716) 14004
Alden Manor (Nassau) (10th) (516) 11003
Alder Bend (Clinton) (3rd) (518) 12910
Alder Creek (Oneida) (5th) (315) 13301
Alexander (Genesee) (8th) (585) 14005
Alexandria (Jefferson) (5th) (315) 13607
Alexandria Bay (Jefferson) (5th) (315) 13607
Alfred (Allegany) (8th) (607) 14802
Alfred Station (Allegany) (8th) (607) 14803
Allaben (Ulster) (3rd) (845) 12480
Allegany (Cattaraugus) (8th) (716) 14706
Allegany Indian Reservation (Cattagaugus) (716) 14719
Allen (Allegany) (8th) (585) 14735
Allens Point (Cayuga) (7th) (315) 13160
Allentown (Allegany) (8th) (585) 14707
Allenwood (Nassau) (10th) (516) 11021
Allerton (Bronx) (12th) (718) 10467
Alligerville (Ulster) (3rd) (845) 12440
Alma (Allegany) (8th) (585) 14708, 14715
Almond (Allegany) (8th) (585) 14804
Almond (Steuben) (7th) (607) 14804
Alpine (Schuyler) (6th) (607) 14805
Alplaus (Schenectady) (4th) (518) 12008
Alps (Rensselaer) (3rd) (518) 12018
Altamont (Albany) (3rd) (518) 12009
Altamont (Franklin) (4th) (518) 12986
Altmar (Oswego) (5th) (315) 13302
Alton (Wayne) (7th) (315) 14413
Altona (Clinton) (4th) (518) 12910
Amagansett (Suffolk) (10th) (631) 11930
Amawalk (Westchester) (9th) (914) 10501
Amber (Onondaga) (5th) (315) 13110
Ambierville (Chenango) (6th) (607) 13843
Amboy (Oswego) (5th) (315) 13493
Amenia (Dutchess) (9th) (845) 12501
Ames (Montgomery) (4th) (518) 13317
Amherst (Erie) (8th) (716) 14051, 142##
Amity (Allegany) (8th) (585) 14813
Amity Harbor (Suffolk) (10th) (631) 11701
Amityville (Suffolk) (10th) (631) 11701
Amsterdam (Montgomery) (4th) (518) 12010
Ancram (Columbia) (3rd) (518) 12502
Ancramdale (Columbia) (3rd) (518) 12503
Andes (Delaware) (6th) (845) 13731
Andover (Allegany) (8th) (607) 14806
Angelica (Allegany) (8th) (585) 14709
Angola (Erie) (8th) (716) 14006
Angola on the Lake (Erie) (8th) (716) 14006
Annandale-on-Hudson (Dutchess) (9th) (845) 12504
Annsville (Oneida) (5th) (315) 13471
Antwerp (Jefferson) (5th) (315) 13608, 13671
Apalachin (Tioga) (6th) (607) 13732
Apex (Delaware) (6th) (607) 13783
Appleton (Niagara) (8th) (716) 14008
Apulia Station (Onondaga) (5th) (315) 13020
Aquebogue (Suffolk) (10th) (631) 11931
Arcade (Wyoming) (8th) (585) 14009
Arcadia (Wayne) (7th) (315) 14513
Arden (Orange) (9th) (845) 10910
Ardonia (Ulster) (3rd) (845) 12505
Ardsley (Westchester) (9th) (914) 10502
Ardsley-on-Hudson (Westchester) (9th) (914) 10503
Argo Village (Nassau) (10th) (518) 11003
Argusville (Schoharie) (3rd) (518) 13459
Argyle (Washington) (4th) (518) 12809
Arietta (Hamilton) (4th) (518) 12030
Arkport (Steuben) (7th) (607) 14807
Arkville (Delaware) (6th) (845) 12406
Arkwright (Chautauqua) (8th) (716) 14063
Arlington (Dutchess) (9th) (845) 12603
Armonk (Westchester) (9th) (914) 10504
Arverne (Queens) (11th) (718) 11692
Asharoken (Suffolk) (10th) (631) 11768
Ashford (Cattaraugus) (8th) (716) 14731
Ashland (Chemung) (6th) (607) 14894
Ashland (Greene) (3rd) (518) 12407
Ashokan (Ulster) (3rd) (845) 12481
Ashville (Chautauqua) (8th) (716) 14710
Assembly Point (Warren) (4th) (518) 12845
Astoria (Queens) (11th) (718) 1110#
Athens (Greene) (3rd) (518) 12015
Athol (Warren) (4th) (518) 12810
Athol Springs (Erie) (8th) (716) 14010
Atlanta (Steuben) (7th) (585) 14808
Atlantic Beach (Nassau) (10th) (516) 11509
Attica (Genesee) (8th) (585) 14011
Attica (Wyoming) (8th) (585) 14011
Atwater (Cayuga) (7th) (315) 13081
Atwell (Herkimer) (5th) (315) 13338
Au Sable Chasm (Clinton) (4th) (518) 12911
Au Sable Forks (Clinton, Essex) (4th) (518) 12912
Auburn (Cayuga) (7th) (315) 1302#
Augusta (Oneida) (5th) (315) 13425
Aurelius (Cayuga) (7th) (315) 13021
Auriesville (Montgomery) (4th) (518) 12016
Aurora (Cayuga) (7th) (315) 13026
Aurora (Erie) (8th) (716) 14052
Ausable (Clinton) (4th) (518) 12944
Austerlitz (Columbia) (3rd) (518) 12017
Ava (Oneida) (5th) (315) 13303
Averill Park (Rensselaer) (3rd) (518) 12018
Avoca (Steuben) (7th) (607) 14809
Avon (Livingston) (7th) (585) 14414
Babylon (Suffolk) (10th) (631) 1170#
Bacon Hill (Saratoga) (4th) (518) 12871
Bainbridge (Chenango) (6th) (607) 13733
Baiting Hollow (Suffolk) (10th) (631) 11933
Bakers Mills (Warren) (4th) (518) 12811
Bald Mountain (Washington) (4th) (518) 12834
Baldwin (Chemung) (6th) (607) 14861
Baldwin (Nassau) (10th) (516) 11510
Baldwin Harbor (Nassau) (10th) (516) 11510
Baldwin Place (Westchester) (9th) (914) 10505
Baldwinsville (Onondaga) (5th) (315) 13027
Ballston (Saratoga) (4th) (518) 12019
Ballston Center (Saratoga) (4th) (518) 12020
Ballston Lake (Saratoga) (4th) (518) 12019
Ballston Spa (Saratoga) (4th) (518) 12020
Balmat (St. Lawrence) (4th) (315) 13609
Balmville (Orange) (9th) (845) 12550
Bangall (Dutchess) (9th) (845) 12506
Bangor (Franklin) (4th) (518) 12966
Banksville (Westchester) (9th) (914) 10506
Bar Harbor (Nassau) (10th) (516) 11762
Barbourville (Broome) (6th) (607) 13754
Bardonia (Rockland) (9th) (845) 10954
Barker (Broome) (6th) (607) 13746
Barker (Niagara) (8th) (716) 14012
Barkersville (Saratoga) (4th) (518) 12850
Barnerville (Schoharie) (3rd) (518) 12092
Barnes Corners (Lewis) (5th) (315) 13626
Barneveld (Oneida) (5th) (315) 13304
Barnum Island (Nassau) (10th) (516) 11558
Barre (Orleans) (8th) (585) 14411
Barrington (Yates) (7th) (607) 14837
Barrytown (Dutchess) (9th) (845) 12507
Barryville (Sullivan) (3rd) (845) 12719
Bartlett (Oneida) (5th) (315) 13440
Bartlett Hollow (Delaware) (6th) (607) 13775
Barton (Tioga) (6th) (607) 13734
Basom (Genesee) (8th) (585) 14013
Batavia (Genesee) (8th) (585) 14020, 14021
Bath (Steuben) (7th) (607) 14810
Battenville (Washington) (4th) (518) 12834
Baxter Estates (Nassau) (10th) (516) 11050
Bay Hills (Suffolk) (10th) (631) 11743
Bay Point (Suffolk) (10th) (631) 11963
Bay Port (Suffolk) (10th) (631) 11705
Bay Ridge (Kings) (2nd) (718) 11220
Bay Shore (Suffolk) (10th) (631) 11706
Bay Terrace (Queens) (11th) (718) 11360
Bayberry (Onondaga) (5th) (315) 13089
Bayberry Point (Suffolk) (10th) (631) 11751
Baychester (Bronx) (12th) (718) 10469
Baycrest (Suffolk) (10th) (631) 11743
Bayport (Suffolk) (10th) (631) 11705
Bayside (Queens) (11th) (718) 11359, 11360, 11361
Bayside Hills (Queens) (11th) (718) 11364
Bayville (Nassau) (10th) (516) 11709
Beach Hampton (Suffolk) (10th) (631) 11930
Beacon (Dutchess) (9th) (845) 12508
Bear Mountain (Rockland) (9th) (845) 10911
Bearsville (Ulster) (3rd) (845) 12409
Beaver Dams (Schuyler) (6th) (607) 14812
Beaver Falls (Lewis) (5th) (315) 13305
Beaver Meadow (Chenango) (6th) (315) 13832
Beaver River (Lewis) (5th) (315) 13367
Beckers Corners (Albany) (3rd) (518) 12158
Bedell (Delaware) (6th) (845) 12430
Bedford (Westchester) (9th) (914) 10506
Bedford Corners (Westchester) (9th) (914) 10549
Bedford Hills (Westchester) (9th) (914) 10507
Bedford Village (Westchester) (9th) (914) 10506
Beech Croft (Suffolk) (10th) (631) 11743
Beechhurst (Queens) (10th) (718) 11357
Beekman (Dutchess) (9th) (845) 12533
Beekmantown (Clinton) (4th) (518) 12901
Beerston (Delaware) (6th) (607) 13856
Belcher (Washington) (4th) (518) 12865
Belden (Broome) (6th) (607) 13787
Belfast (Allegany) (8th) (585) 14711
Belfort (Lewis) (5th) (315) 13327
Belgium (Onondaga) (5th) (315) 13027
Bellaire (Queens) (11th) (718) 11423
Belle Harbor (Queens) (11th) (718) 11694
Belle Terre (Suffolk) (10th) (631) 11777
Bellerose (Nassau) (10th) (516) 11426
Bellerose Manor (Queens) (11th) (718) 11427, 11428
Bellerose Village (Nassau) (10th) (516) 11001
Belleville (Jefferson) (5th) (315) 13611
Bellevue (Schenectady) (4th) (518) 12306
Bellevue-Homewood Park (Erie) (8th) (716) 14225
Bellmont (Franklin) (4th) (518) 12953
Bellmore (Nassau) (10th) (516) 11710
Bellona (Yates) (7th) (315) 14415
Bellport (Suffolk) (10th) (631) 11713
Bellvale (Orange) (9th) (845) 10912
Belmont (Allegany) (8th) (585) 14813
Bemis Heights (Saratoga) (4th) (518) 12170
Bemus Point (Chautauqua) (8th) (716) 14712
Bennettsville (Chenango) (6th) (607) 13733
Benson Mines (Saint Lawrence) (4th) (315) 13690
Bennington (Wyoming) (8th) (585) 14011
Benson (Hamilton) (4th) (518) 12134
Benton (Yates) (7th) (315) 14527
Bergen (Genesee) (8th) (585) 14416
Berkshire (Tioga) (6th) (607) 13736
Berlin (Rensselaer) (3rd) (518) 12022
Berne (Albany) (3rd) (518) 12023
Bernhards Bay (Oswego) (5th) (315) 13028
Berwyn (Onondaga) (5th) (315) 13084
Bethany (Genesee) (8th) (585) 14054
Bethel (Sullivan) (3rd) (845) 12720
Bethlehem (Albany) (3rd) (518) 12054
Bethlehem Center (Albany) (3rd) (518) 12077
Bethpage (Nassau) (10th) (516) 11714
Bible School Park (Broome) (6th) (607) 13737
Big Brook (Oneida) (5th) (315) 13486
Big Flats (Chemung) (6th) (607) 14814
Big Indian (Ulster) (3rd) (845) 12410
Big Moose (Herkimer) (5th) (315) 13331
Bigelow (St. Lawrence) (4th) (315) 13681
Billings (Dutchess) (9th) (845) 12510
Billington Bay (Madison) (6th) (315) 13030
Binghamton (Broome) (6th) (607) 1390#
Binnewater (Ulster) (3rd) (845) 12401
Birdsall (Allegany) (8th) (607) 14722
Black Brook (Clinton) (4th) (518) 12912
Black Creek (Allegany) (8th) (585) 14714
Black River (Jefferson) (5th) (315) 13612
Blasdell (Erie) (8th) (716) 14219
Blauvelt (Rockland) (9th) (845) 10913
Bleecker (Fulton) (4th) (518) 12078
Blenheim (Schoharie) (3rd) (518) 12131
Bliss (Wyoming) (8th) (585) 14024
Blodgett Mills (Cortland) (6th) (607) 13738
Bloomfield (Ontario) (7th) (315) 14469
Blooming Grove (Orange) (9th) (845) 10914
Bloomingburg (Sullivan) (3rd) (845) 12721
Bloomingdale (Essex) (4th) (518) 12913
Bloomington (Ulster) (3rd) (845) 12411
Bloomville (Delaware) (6th) (607) 13739
Blossvale (Oneida) (5th) (315) 13308, 13401
Blue Mountain Lake (Hamilton) (4th) (518) 12812

Blue Point (Suffolk) (10th) (631) 11715
Blue Ridge (Essex) (4th) (518) 12870
Bluff Point (Yates) (7th) (315) 14478
Blythebourne (Kings) (2nd) (718) 11219
Boght Corners (Albany) (3rd) (518) 12047
Bohemia (Suffolk) (10th) (631) 11716
Boiceville (Ulster) (3rd) (845) 12412
Bolivar (Allegany) (8th) (585) 14715
Bolton (Warren) (4th) (518) 12824
Bolton Landing (Warren) (4th) (518) 12814
Bombay (Franklin) (4th) (518) 12914, 13655
Bonney (Chenango) (6th) (607) 13464
Boonville (Oneida) (5th) (315) 13309
Boston (Erie) (8th) (716) 14025
Boston Corner (Columbia) (3rd) (518) 12546
Bouckville (Madison) (6th) (315) 13310
Boulton's Beach (Jefferson) (5th) (315) 13685
Bovina (Delaware) (6th) (607) 13740
Bovina Center (Delaware) (6th) (607) 13740
Bowens Corners (Oswego) (5th) (315) 13069
Bowmansville (Erie) (8th) (716) 14026
Box Hill (Suffolk) (10th) (631) 11780
Boylston (Oswego) (5th) (315) 13083
Boyntonville (Rensselaer) (3rd) (518) 12090
Bradford (Steuben) (7th) (607) 14815
Brainard (Rensselaer) (3rd) (518) 12024
Brainardsville (Franklin) (4th) (518) 12915
Braman Corners (Schenectady) (4th) (518) 12053
Bramanville (Schoharie) (3rd) (518) 12092
Branchport (Yates) (7th) (315) 14418
Brandon (Franklin) (4th) (518) 12966
Brandreth (Hamilton) (4th) (518) 12847
Brandywine (Schenectady) (4th) (518) 12304
Brant (Erie) (8th) (716) 14027
Brant Lake (Warren) (4th) (518) 12815
Brantingham (Lewis) (5th) (315) 13312
Brasher (St. Lawrence) (4th) (315) 13613
Brasher Falls (St. Lawrence) (4th) (315) 13613
Brasie Corners (Saint Lawrence) (4th) (315) 13642
Breakabeen (Schoharie) (3rd) (518) 12122
Breesport (Chemung) (6th) (607) 14816
Breezy Point (Queens) (11th) (718) 11697
Brentwood (Suffolk) (10th) (631) 11717
Brewerton (Onondaga) (5th) (315) 13029
Brewster (Putnam) (9th) (845) 10509
Brewster Station (Putnam) (9th) (845) 10509
Briar Park (Nassau) (10th) (516) 11793
Briarcliff (Westchester) (9th) (914) 10510
Briarcliff Manor (Westchester) (9th) (914) 10510
Briarwood (Queens) (11th) (718) 11435
Bridgehampton (Suffolk) (10th) (631) 11932
Bridgeport (Madison) (6th) (315) 13030
Bridgewater (Oneida) (5th) (315) 13313
Brier Hill (St. Lawrence) (4th) (315) 13614
Brighton (Franklin) (4th) (518) 12970
Brighton (Monroe) (7th) (585) 14610, 14620
Brightside (Hamilton) (4th) (518) 13436
Brightwaters (Suffolk) (10th) (631) 11718
Brisben (Chenango) (6th) (607) 13830
Bristol (Ontario) (7th) (585) 14469
Bristol Center (Ontario) (7th) (315) 14419
Broad Channel (Queens) (11th) (718) 11693
Broadacres (Broome) (6th) (607) 13905
Broadalbin (Fulton) (4th) (518) 12025
Brockport (Monroe) (7th) (585) 14420
Brocton (Chautauqua) (8th) (716) 14716
Bronx (Bronx) (12th) (718) 104##
Bronxville (Westchester) (9th) (914) 10708
Brookfield (Madison) (6th) (315) 13314, 13318
Brookhaven (Suffolk) (10th) (631) 11719
Brooklyn (Kings) (2nd) (718) 112##
Brooktondale (Tompkins) (6th) (607) 14817
Brookview (Rensselaer) (3rd) (518) 12033
Brookville (Nassau) (10th) (516) 11545, 11548
Broome (Schoharie) (3rd) (518) 12076
Brown's Hollow (Montgomery) (4th) (518) 13317
Brownville (Jefferson) (5th) (315) 13615
Brunswick (Rensselaer) (3rd) (518) 12180
Brushton (Franklin) (4th) (518) 12916
Brutus (Cayuga) (7th) (315) 13166
Buchanan (Westchester) (9th) (914) 10511
Buck's Bridge (Saint Lawrence) (4th) (315) 13617
Buel (Montgomery) (4th) (518) 13317
Buffalo (Erie) (8th) (716) 142##
Bullshead (Monroe) (7th) (585) 146##
Bullville (Orange) (9th) (845) 10915
Bundyville (Oswego) (5th) (315) 13126
Burden Lake (Rensselaer) (3rd) (518) 12018
Burdett (Schuyler) (6th) (607) 14818
Burke (Franklin) (4th) (518) 12917
Burlingham (Sullivan) (3rd) (845) 12722
Burlington (Otsego) (6th) (607) 13315
Burlington Flats (Otsego) (6th) (607) 13315
Burns (Allegany) (8th) (607) 14807
Burnt Hills (Saratoga) (4th) (518) 12019, 12027
Burnwood (Delaware) (6th) (607) 13756
Burt (Niagara) (8th) (716) 14028
Burtonsville (Montgomery) (4th) (518) 12066
Bushville (Genesee) (8th) (585) 14020
Bushville (Sullivan) (3rd) (845) 12701
Buskirk (Rensselaer) (3rd) (518) 12028
Busti (Chautauqua) (8th) (716) 14701
Butler (Wayne) (7th) (315) 14590
Butternuts (Otsego) (6th) (315) 13776
Byron (Genesee) (8th) (585) 14422
Cabinhill (Delaware) (6th) (607) 13752
Cadosia (Delaware) (6th) (607) 13783
Cadyville (Clinton) (4th) (518) 12918
Cairo (Greene) (3rd) (518) 12413
Calcium (Jefferson) (5th) (315) 13616
Caldwell (Warren) (4th) (518) 12845
Caledonia (Livingston) (7th) (585) 14423
Callicoon (Sullivan) (3rd) (845) 12723
Callicoon Center (Sullivan) (3rd) (845) 12724
Calverton (Suffolk) (10th) (631) 11933
Cambria (Niagara) (8th) (716) 14094
Cambria Heights (Queens) (11th) (718) 11411
Cambridge (Washington) (4th) (518) 12816
Camden (Oneida) (5th) (315) 13316
Cameron (Steuben) (7th) (607) 14819
Cameron Mills (Steuben) (7th) (607) 14819, 14820
Camillus (Onondaga) (5th) (315) 13031
Campbell (Steuben) (7th) (607) 14821
Campbell Hall (Orange) (9th) (845) 10916
Campville (Broome) (6th) (607) 13760
Camroden (Oneida) (5th) (315) 13440
Canaan (Columbia) (3rd) (518) 12029
Canaan Lake (Suffolk) (10th) (631) 11772
Canada Lake (Fulton) (4th) (516) 12030
Canadice (Ontario) (7th) (585) 14560
Canajoharie (Montgomery) (4th) (518) 13317
Canandaigua (Ontario) (7th) (585) 14424, 14425
Canaseraga (Allegany) (8th) (607) 14822
Canastota (Madison) (6th) (315) 13032
Candor (Tioga) (6th) (607) 13743
Caneadea (Allegany) (8th) (585) 14717
Canisteo (Steuben) (7th) (607) 14823
Canoga (Seneca) (7th) (315) 13148
Canton (St. Lawrence) (4th) (315) 13617
Cape Vincent (Jefferson) (5th) (315) 13618
Captree Island (Suffolk) (10th) (516) 11702
Cardiff (Onondaga) (5th) (315) 13084
Carle Place (Nassau) (10th) (516) 11514
Carlisle (Schoharie) (3rd) (518) 12031
Carlton (Orleans) (8th) (585) 14411
Carmel (Putnam) (9th) (845) 10512
Caroga Lake (Fulton) (4th) (518) 12032
Caroline (Tompkins) (6th) (607) 14817
Caroline Depot (Tompkins) (6th) (607) 14817
Carroll (Chautauqua) (8th) (716) 14738
Carrolton (Cattaraugus) (8th) (716) 14748
Carthage (Jefferson) (5th) (315) 13619
Carver Park (Suffolk) (10th) (631) 11980
Cassadaga (Chautauqua) (8th) (716) 14718
Cassville (Oneida) (5th) (315) 13318
Castile (Wyoming) (8th) (585) 14427
Castle Creek (Broome) (6th) (607) 13744
Castle Point (Dutchess) (9th) (845) 12511
Castleton-on-Hudson (Rensselaer) (3rd) (518) 12033
Castorland (Lewis) (5th) (315) 13620
Catatonk (Tioga) (6th) (607) 13827
Catharine (Schuyler) (6th) (607) 14869
Catlin (Chemung) (6th) (607) 14845
Cato (Cayuga) (7th) (315) 13033
Caton (Steuben) (7th) (607) 14830
Catskill (Greene) (3rd) (518) 12414
Cattaraugus (Cattaraugus) (8th) (716) 14719
Cattaraugus Indian Reservation (Cattaraugus) (8th) (716) 14719
Cattaraugus Indian Reservation (Chautauqua) (8th) (716) 14719
Cattaraugus Indian Reservation (Erie) (8th) (716) 14719
Cattown (Otsego) (6th) (607) 13337
Cayuga Lake Park (Seneca) (7th) (315) 13148
Cayuga (Cayuga) (7th) (315) 13034
Cayuga Heights (Tompkins) (6th) (607) 14850
Cayuta (Schuyler) (6th) (607) 14824
Caywood (Seneca) (7th) (607) 14860
Cazenovia (Madison) (6th) (315) 13035
Cedarhurst (Nassau) (10th) (516) 11516
Cedarville (Herkimer) (5th) (315) 13357
Celoron (Chautauqua) (8th) (716) 14720
Cementon (Greene) (3rd) (845) 12414
Center Berlin (Rensselaer) (3rd) (518) 12022
Center Brunswick (Rensselaer) (3rd) (518) 12180
Center Cambridge (Washington) (4th) (518) 12816
Center Moriches (Suffolk) (10th) (631) 11934
Centereach (Suffolk) (10th) (631) 11720
Centerlisle (Broome) (6th) (607) 13797
Centerport (Suffolk) (10th) (631) 11721
Centerville (Allegany) (8th) (585) 14029
Central Bridge (Schoharie) (3rd) (518) 12035
Central Islip (Suffolk) (10th) (631) 11722, 11749, 11760
Central Nyack (Rockland) (9th) (845) 10960
Central Square (Oswego) (5th) (315) 13036
Central Valley (Orange) (9th) (845) 10917
Centre Island (Nassau) (10th) (516) 11771
Centre Village (Broome) (6th) (607) 13787
Centuck (Westchester) (9th) (914) 10710
Ceres (Allegany) (8th) (585) 14721
Chadwick Bay (Chautauqua) (8th) (716) 14048
Chadwicks (Oneida) (5th) (315) 13319
Chaffee (Erie) (8th) (716) 14030
Champion (Jefferson) (5th) (315) 13619
Champlain (Clinton) (4th) (518) 12919
Chapin (Ontario) (7th) (315) 14424
Chappaqua (Westchester) (9th) (914) 10514
Charleston (Montgomery) (4th) (518) 12166
Charleston Four Corners (Montgomery) (4th) (518) 12166
Charlotte (Chautauqua) (8th) (716) 14612
Charlotteville (Schoharie) (3rd) (607) 12036
Charlton (Saratoga) (4th) (518) 12019
Chase Lake (Lewis) (5th) (315) 13343
Chase Mills (St. Lawrence) (4th) (315) 13621
Chaseville (Otsego) (6th) (607) 12116
Chateaugay (Franklin) (4th) (518) 12920
Chatham (Columbia) (3rd) (518) 12037
Chatham Center (Columbia) (3th) (518) 12184
Chaumont (Jefferson) (5th) (315) 13622
Chauncey (Westchester) (9th) (914) 10522
Chautauqua (Chautauqua) (8th) (716) 14722
Chazy (Clinton) (4th) (518) 12921
Chazy Landing (Clinton) (4th) (518) 12921
Cheektowaga (Erie) (8th) (716) 142##
Chelsea (Dutchess) (9th) (845) 12512
Chemung (Chemung) (6th) (607) 14825
Chenango (Broome) (6th) (607) 13745
Chenango Bridge (Broome) (6th) (607) 13745
Chenango Forks (Broome) (6th) (607) 13746
Chenango Lake (Chenango) (6th) (607) 13815
Chepachet (Herkimer) (5th) (315) 13491
Cherry Creek (Chautauqua) (8th) (716) 14723
Cherry Grove (Suffolk) (10th) (631) 11782
Cherry Plain (Rensselaer) (3rd) (518) 12040
Cherry Valley (Montgomery) (4th) (518) 13320
Cherry Valley (Otsego) (6th) (607) 13320, 13450
Cherrytown (Ulster) (3rd) (845) 12446
Chester (Orange) (9th) (845) 10918
Chester (Warren) (4th) (518) 12860
Chesterfield (Essex) (4th) (518) 12944
Chestertown (Warren) (4th) (518) 12817
Chestnut Ridge (Rockland) (9th) (845) 10952, 10965, 10977
Cheviot (Columbia) (3th) (518) 12526
Chichester (Ulster) (3rd) (845) 12416
Childwold (St. Lawrence) (4th) (518) 12922
Chili (Monroe) (7th) (585) 14514
Chilson (Essex) (4th) (518) 12883
China (Broome) (6th) (607) 13754
Chinatown (New York) (1st) (212) 10013
Chippewa Bay (St. Lawrence) (4th) (315) 13623
Chittenango (Madison) (6th) (315) 13037
Chittenango Station (Madison) (6th) (315) 13038
Choconut Center (Broome) (6th) (607) 13905
Churchville (Monroe) (7th) (585) 14428
Churubusco (Clinton) (4th) (518) 12923
Cicero (Onondaga) (5th) (315) 13039
Cincinnatus (Cortland) (6th) (607) 13040
Circleville (Orange) (9th) (845) 10919
Clare (St. Lawrence) (4th) (315) 13684
Clarence (Erie) (8th) (716) 14031, 14221
Clarence Center (Erie) (8th) (716) 14032
Clarendon (Orleans) (8th) (585) 14429
Clark Mills (Oneida) (5th) (315) 13321
Clarks Mills (Washington) (4th) (518) 12834
Clarkson (Monroe) (7th) (585) 14430
Clarkstown (Rockland) (9th) (845) 10956
Clarksville (Albany) (3rd) (518) 12041
Clarksville (Allegany) (8th) (585) 14786
Claryville (Sullivan) (3rd) (845) 12725
Claverack (Columbia) (3rd) (518) 12513
Clay (Onondaga) (5th) (315) 13041
Clayburg (Clinton) (4th) (518) 12981
Clayton (Jefferson) (5th) (315) 13624
Clayville (Oneida) (5th) (315) 13322
Cleaver (Delaware) (6th) (607) 13856
Clemons (Washington) (4th) (518) 12819
Clermont (Columbia) (3rd) (518) 12526
Cleveland (Oswego) (5th) (315) 13042
Cleverdale (Warren) (4th) (518) 12820
Clifton (Monroe) (7th) (585) 14428
Clifton (Richmond) (13th) (718) 10304
Clifton (St. Lawrence) (4th) (315) 13666
Clifton Park (Saratoga) (4th) (518) 12065
Clifton Springs (Ontario) (7th) (315) 14432
Climax (Greene) (3rd) (518) 12042
Clinton (Clinton) (4th) (518) 12923
Clinton (Dutchess) (9th) (845) 12514
Clinton (Oneida) (5th) (315) 13323
Clinton Corners (Dutchess) (9th) (845) 12514
Clintondale (Ulster) (3rd) (845) 12515
Clintonville (Clinton) (4th) (518) 12924
Clockville (Madison) (6th) (315) 13043
Clough Corners (Broome) (6th) (607) 13862
Clove (Orange) (9th) (845) 10914
Clyde (Wayne) (7th) (315) 14433
Clymer (Chautauqua) (8th) (716) 14724
Cobleskill (Schoharie) (3rd) (518) 12043
Cochecton (Sullivan) (3rd) (845) 12726
Cochecton Center (Sullivan) (3rd) (845) 12727
Coeymans (Albany) (3rd) (518) 12045
Coeymans Hollow (Albany) (3rd) (518) 12046
Cohocton (Steuben) (7th) (585) 14826

Cohoes (Albany) (3rd) (518) 12047
Coila (Washington) (4th) (518) 12816
Colchester (Delaware) (6th) (607) 13856
Cold Brook (Herkimer) (5th) (315) 13324
Cold Spring (Cattaraugus) (8th) (716) 14783
Cold Spring (Putnam) (9th) (845) 10516
Cold Spring Harbor (Suffolk) (10th) (631) 11724
Cold Spring Hills (Suffolk) (10th) (631) 11743
Cold Water (Monroe) (7th) (585) 14624
Colden (Erie) (8th) (716) 14033
Colesville (Broome) (6th) (607) 13787
College Point (Queens) (11th) (718) 11356
Colliersville (Otsego) (6th) (607) 13747
Collins (Erie) (8th) (716) 14034
Collins Center (Erie) (8th) (716) 14035
Collins Landing (Jefferson) (5th) (315) 13607
Collinsville (Lewis) (5th) (315) 13433
Colonie (Albany) (3rd) (518) 12205
Colosse (Oswego) (5th) (315) 13131
Colton (St. Lawrence) (4th) (315) 13625
Columbia (Herkimer) (5th) (315) 13357
Columbiaville (Columbia) (3rd) (518) 12050
Columbus (Chenango) (6th) (607) 13411
Colvin (Onondaga) (5th) (315) 13205
Commack (Suffolk) (10th) (631) 11725
Comstock (Washington) (4th) (518) 12821
Concord (Erie) (8th) (718) 14055
Conesus (Livingston) (7th) (585) 14435
Conesville (Schoharie) (3rd) (518) 12076
Conewango (Cattaraugus) (8th) (716) 14726
Conewango Valley (Chautauqua) (8th) (716) 14726
Conger Corners (Oneida) (5th) (315) 13480
Congers (Rockland) (9th) (845) 10920
Conifer (St. Lawrence) (4th) (315) 12986
Conklin (Broome) (6th) (607) 13748
Conklin Forks (Broome) (6th) (607) 13903
Conklingville (Saratoga) (4th) (518) 12835
Connelly (Ulster) (3rd) (845) 12417
Conquest (Cayuga) (7th) (315) 13140
Constable (Franklin) (4th) (518) 12926
Constableville (Lewis) (5th) (315) 13325
Constantia (Oswego) (5th) (315) 13044
Cooksburg (Albany) (3rd) (518) 12469
Cooks Corners (Franklin) (4th) (518) 12916
Cooks Falls (Delaware) (6th) (845) 12728
Coonrod (Oneida) (5th) (315) 13440
Coopers Plains (Steuben) (7th) (607) 14827
Cooperstown (Otsego) (6th) (607) 13326
Cooperstown Junction (Otsego) (6th) (607) 12116
Coopersville (Clinton) (4th) (518) 12919
Copake (Columbia) (3rd) (518) 12516, 12593
Copake Falls (Columbia) (3rd) (518) 12517
Copenhagen (Lewis) (5th) (315) 13626
Copiague (Suffolk) (10th) (631) 11726
Coram (Suffolk) (10th) (631) 11727
Corbett (Delaware) (6th) (607) 13755
Corbettsville (Broome) (6th) (607) 13749
Coreys (Franklin) (4th) (518) 12986
Corfu (Genesee) (8th) (585) 14036
Corinth (Saratoga) (4th) (518) 12822
Corneil Estates (Suffolk) (10th) (631) 11770
Corning (Steuben) (7th) (607) 14830, 14831
Cornwall (Orange) (9th) (845) 12518
Cornwall Southwest (Orange) (9th) (845) 12518
Cornwall Landing (Orange) (9th) (845) 12520
Cornwall-on-the-Hudson (Orange) (9th) (845) 12520
Cornwallville (Greene) (3rd) (518) 12418
Corona (Queens) (11th) (718) 11368
Cortland (Cortland) (6th) (607) 13045
Cortlandt Manor (Westchester) (9th) (914) 10567
Cortlandville (Cortland) (6th) (607) 13045
Cossayuna (Washington) (4th) (518) 12823
Cottekill (Ulster) (3rd) (845) 12419
Cove Neck (Nassau) (10th) (516) 11771
Coventry (Chenango) (6th) (607) 13778
Coventryville (Chenango) (6th) (607) 13733
Covert (Seneca) (7th) (607) 14847
Covington (Wyoming) (8th) (585) 14525
Cowlesville (Wyoming) (8th) (585) 14011, 14037
Coxsackie (Greene) (3rd) (518) 12051, 12192
Crab Meadow (Suffolk) (10th) (631) 11768
Cragsmoor (Ulster) (3rd) (845) 12420
Cranberry Lake (St. Lawrence) (4th) (315) 12927
Crary Mills (St. Lawrence) (4th) (315) 13617
Craryville (Columbia) (3rd) (518) 12521
Crestview Heights (Broome) (6th) (607) 13760
Craterclub (Essex) (4th) (518) 12936
Crawford (Orange) (9th) (845) 12566
Creek Locks (Ulster) (3rd) (845) 12472
Crittenden (Erie) (8th) (716) 14038
Crofts Corners (Putnam) (9th) (845) 10579
Croghan (Lewis) (5th) (315) 13327
Crompond (Westchester) (9th) (914) 10517
Cropseyville (Rensselaer) (3rd) (518) 12052
Cross Lake (Onondaga) (5th) (315) 13080
Cross River (Westchester) (9th) (914) 10518
Croton Falls (Westchester) (9th) (914) 10519
Croton-on-Hudson (Westchester) (9th) (914) 10520, 10521
Crotona Park (Bronx) (12th) (718) 10460
Crotonville (Westchester) (9th) (914) 10562
Crown Point (Essex) (4th) (518) 12928
Crown Point Center (Essex) (4th) (518) 12928
Crugers (Westchester) (9th) (914) 10521
Crum Creek (Montgomery) (4th) (518) 13452
Cuba (Allegany) (8th) (585) 14727
Cuddebackville (Orange) (9th) (845) 12729
Cullen (Otsego) (6th) (315) 13439
Curry (Sullivan) (3rd) (845) 12765
Cutchogue (Suffolk) (10th) (631) 11935
Cuyler (Cortland) (6th) (607) 13158
Cuylerville (Livingston) (7th) (585) 14481
Dadville (Lewis) (5th) (315) 13367
Dale (Wyoming) (8th) (585) 14039
Dalton (Livingston) (7th) (585) 14836
Danby (Tompkins) (6th) (607) 14850
Dannemora (Clinton) (4th) (518) 12929
Dansville (Livingston) (7th) (585) 14437
Dansville (Steuben) (7th) (607) 14807
Danube (Herkimer) (5th) (315) 13365
Darien (Genesee) (8th) (585) 14040
Darien Center (Genesee) (8th) (585) 14040
Darts (Herkimer) (5th) (315) 13307
Davenport (Delaware) (6th) (607) 13750
Davenport Center (Delaware) (6th) (607) 13751
Davis Park (Suffolk) (10th) (631) 11772
Day (Saratoga) (4th) (518) 12835
Dayton (Cattaraugus) (8th) (716) 14041
Daytonville (Oneida) (5th) (315) 13480
De Kalb (St. Lawrence) (4th) (315) 13630
De Kalb Junction (St. Lawrence) (4th) (315) 13630
De Lancey (Delaware) (6th) (607) 13752
De Peyster (St. Lawrence) (4th) (315) 13633
De Ruyter (Madison) (6th) (315) 13052
De Witt (Onondaga) (5th) (315) 13214
Deansboro (Oneida) (5th) (315) 13328
Decatur (Otsego) (6th) (607) 12197
Deer Park (Suffolk) (10th) (631) 11729
Deer River (Lewis) (5th) (315) 13627
Deer Wells (Suffolk) (10th) (631) 11780
Deerfield (Oneida) (5th) (516) 13502
Deerland (Hamilton) (4th) (518) 12847
Deerpark (Orange) (9th) (845) 12729
Deferiet (Jefferson) (5th) (315) 13628
Defreestville (Rensselaer) (3rd) (518) 12144
Degrasse (St. Lawrence) (4th) (315) 13684
Delancey (Delaware) (6th) (607) 13752
Delanson (Schenectady) (4th) (518) 12053
Delaware (Sullivan) (3rd) (845) 12723
Delevan (Cattaraugus) (8th) (716) 14042
Delhi (Delaware) (6th) (607) 13753
Delmar (Albany) (3rd) (518) 12054
Delphi Falls (Onondaga) (5th) (315) 13051
Demster (Oswego) (5th) (315) 13126
Denmark (Lewis) (5th) (315) 13631
Denning (Ulster) (3rd) (845) 12725
Dennison Corners (Herkimer) (5th) (315) 13407
Denver (Delaware) (6th) (518) 12421
Depauville (Jefferson) (5th) (315) 13632
Depew (Erie) (8th) (716) 14043
Deposit (Broome) (6th) (607) 13754
Deposit (Delaware) (6th) (607) 13754
Derby (Erie) (8th) (716) 14047
Dering Harbor (Suffolk) (10th) (631) 11964
Dewittville (Chautauqua) (8th) (716) 14728, 14756
Dexter (Jefferson) (5th) (315) 13634, 13657
Diamond (Jefferson) (5th) (315) 13659
Diamond Point (Warren) (4th) (518) 12824
Diana (Lewis) (5th) (315) 13648
Dickinson (Broome) (6th) (607) 13905
Dickinson (Franklin) (4th) (518) 12930
Dickinson Center (Franklin) (4th) (518) 12930
Divine Corners (Sullivan) (3rd) (845) 12759
Dix (Schuyler) (6th) (607) 14891
Dix Hills (Suffolk) (10th) (631) 11746, 11747
Dobbs Ferry (Westchester) (9th) (914) 10522
Dolgeville (Fulton) (4th) (315) 13329
Dolgeville (Herkimer) (5th) (315) 13329
Dominion Park (Onondaga) (5th) (315) 13090
Dongan Hills (Richmond) (13th) (718) 10304
Doonan Corners (Delaware) (6th) (607) 13739
Doraville (Broome) (6th) (607) 13813
Dorloo (Schoharie) (3rd) (518) 12043
Dormansville (Albany) (3rd) (518) 12055
Douglaston (Queens) (11th) (718) 11362, 11363
Dover (Dutchess) (9th) (845) 12522
Dover Plains (Dutchess) (9th) (845) 12522
Downsville (Delaware) (6th) (607) 13755
Doyle (Erie) (8th) (716) 14225
Doyle Dresden (Washington) (4th) (518) 12887
Dresden (Yates) (7th) (315) 14441
Dresden Station (Washington) (4th) (518) 12887
Dryden (Tompkins) (6th) (607) 13053
Duane (Franklin) (4th) (518) 12953
Duanesburg (Schenectady) (4th) (518) 12056
Dundee (Yates) (7th) (607) 14837
Dunham Hollow (Rensselaer) (3rd) (518) 12018
Dunkirk (Chautauqua) (8th) (716) 14048, 14166
Dunsbach Ferry (Albany) (3rd) (518) 12047
Durham (Greene) (3rd) (518) 12422
Durhamville (Oneida) (5th) (315) 13054
Eagle (Wyoming) (8th) (585) 14024
Eagle Bay (Herkimer) (5th) (315) 13331
Eagle Bridge (Rensselaer) (3rd) (518) 12057
Eagle Harbor (Orleans) (8th) (585) 14411
Eagle Lake (Essex) (4th) (518) 12883
Eagle Mills (Rensselaer) (3rd) (518) 12180
Eagle Nest (Hamilton) (4th) (518) 12812
Eagleville (Washington) (4th) (518) 12873
Earlton (Greene) (3rd) (518) 12058
Earlville (Chenango) (6th) (607) 13332
Earlville (Madison) (6th) (315) 13332
East Amherst (Erie) (8th) (716) 14051
East Atlantic Beach (Nassau) (10th) (516) 11561
East Aurora (Erie) (8th) (716) 14052
East Berkshire (Tioga) (6th) (607) 13736
East Berne (Albany) (3rd) (518) 12059
East Bethany (Genesee) (8th) (585) 14054
East Bloomfield (Ontario) (7th) (315) 14443, 14469
East Branch (Delaware) (6th) (607) 13756
East Chatham (Columbia) (3rd) (518) 12060
East Concord (Erie) (8th) (716) 14055
East Dickinson (Franklin) (4th) (518) 12930
East Durham (Greene) (3rd) (518) 12423
East Elmhurst (Queens) (11th) (718) 11369, 11370, 11371
East Farmingdale (Nassau) (10th) (516) 11735
East Fishkill (Dutchess) (9th) (845) 12533
East Floyd (Oneida) (5th) (315) 13354
East Freetown (Cortland) (6th) (607) 13040
East Genoa (Cayuga) (7th) (315) 13092
East Glenville (Schenectady) (4th) (518) 12302
East Greenbush (Rensselaer) (3rd) (518) 12061
East Greenwich (Washington) (4th) (518) 12865
East Hampton (Suffolk) (10th) (631) 11937
East Hebron (Washington) (4th) (518) 12865
East Hempstead (Nassau) (10th) (516) 11553
East Herkimer (Herkimer) (5th) (315) 13350
East Hills (Nassau) (10th) (516) 11548, 11576, 11577
East Homer (Cortland) (6th) (607) 13056, 13158
East Irvington (Westchester) (9th) (914) 10533
East Islip (Suffolk) (10th) (631) 11730
East Jefferson (Schoharie) (3rd) (518) 12093
East Jewett (Greene) (3rd) (518) 12424
East Kingston (Ulster) (3rd) (845) 12401
East Line (Saratoga) (4th) (518) 12020
East Maine (Broome) (6th) (607) 13790
East Marion (Suffolk) (10th) (631) 11939
East Masonville (Delaware) (6th) (607) 13839
East Massapequa (Nassau) (10th) (516) 11758
East McDonough (Chenango) (6th) (607) 13830
East Meadow (Nassau) (10th) (516) 11554
East Meredith (Delaware) (6th) (607) 13757
East Middletown (Orange) (9th) (845) 10940
East Moriches (Suffolk) (10th) (631) 11940
East Nassau (Rensselaer) (3rd) (518) 12062
East Neck (Suffolk) (10th) (631) 11721
East Nichols (Tioga) (6th) (607) 13812
East Northport (Suffolk) (10th) (631) 11731
East Norwich (Nassau) (10th) (516) 11732
East Oakfield (Genesee) (8th) (585) 14125
East Otto (Cattaraugus) (8th) (716) 14729
East Palmyra (Wayne) (7th) (315) 14513
East Patchogue (Suffolk) (10th) (631) 11772
East Pembroke (Genesee) (8th) (585) 14056
East Pharsalia (Chenango) (6th) (607) 13758
East Pitcairn (Lewis) (5th) (315) 13648
East Poestenkill (Rensselaer) (3rd) (518) 12018
East Quogue (Suffolk) (10th) (631) 11942
East Randolph (Cattaraugus) (8th) (716) 14730
East Rochester (Monroe) (7th) (585) 14445
East Rockaway (Nassau) (10th) (516) 11518
East Rodman (Jefferson) (5th) (315) 13682
East Schodack (Rensselaer) (3rd) (518) 12063
East Setauket (Suffolk) (10th) (631) 11733
East Sidney (Delaware) (6th) (607) 13775
East Springfield (Otsego) (6th) (607) 13333
East Syracuse (Onondaga) (5th) (315) 13057
East Vestal (Broome) (6th) (607) 13903
East View (Westchester) (9th) (914) 10595
East White Plains (Westchester) (9th) (914) 10604
East Williamson (Wayne) (7th) (315) 14449
East Williston (Nassau) (10th) (516) 11596
East Windham (Greene) (3rd) (518) 12439
East Winfield (Herkimer) (5th) (315) 13491
East Windsor (Broome) (6th) (607) 13865
East Worcester (Otsego) (6th) (607) 12064
East Yaphank (Suffolk) (10th) (631) 11967
Eastchester (Westchester) (9th) (914) 10707, 10709
Easthampton (Suffolk) (10th) (631) 11937
Easton (Washington) (4th) (518) 12154
Eastport (Suffolk) (10th) (631) 11941
Eastport-Spoenk (Suffolk) (10th) (631) 11941
Eastview (Westchester) (9th) (914) 10595
Eastwood (Onondaga) (5th) (315) 13206
Eaton (Madison) (6th) (315) 13334
Eaton's Neck (Suffolk) (10th) (631) 11768
Eben (St. Lawrence) (4th) (315) 13676
Ebenezer (Erie) (8th) (716) 14224
Eddy (St. Lawrence) (4th) (315) 13617
Eddyville (Ulster) (3rd) (845) 12401
Eden (Erie) (8th) (716) 14057

Edgemere (Queens) (11th) (718) . . . 11690
Edgemont (Westchester) (9th) (914) . . . 10583
Edgewood (Suffolk) (10th) (631) . . . 11717
Edgewood Park (Jefferson) (5th) (315) . . . 13607
Edinburg (Saratoga) (4th) (518) . . . 12134
Edmeston (Otsego) (6th) (607) . . . 13335
Edwards (St. Lawrence) (4th) (315) . . . 13635
Edwardsville (St. Lawrence) (4th) (315) . . . 13646
Eggertsville (Erie) (8th) (716) . . . 14226
Elba (Genesee) (8th) (585) . . . 14058
Elbridge (Onondaga) (5th) (315) . . . 13060
Eldred (Sullivan) (3rd) (845) . . . 12732
Elizabethtown (Essex) (4th) (518) . . . 12932
Elizaville (Columbia) (3rd) (845) . . . 12523
Elk Creek (Otsego) (6th) (607) . . . 12155
Elka Park (Greene) (3rd) (518) . . . 12427
Elko (Cattaraugus) (8th) (716) . . . 14779
Ellenburg (Clinton) (4th) (518) . . . 12933
Ellenburg Center (Clinton) (4th) (518) . . . 12934
Ellenburg Depot (Clinton) (4th) (518) . . . 12935
Ellenville (Ulster) (3rd) (845) . . . 12428
Ellery (Chautauqua) (8th) (716) . . . 14712
Ellicott (Chautauqua) (8th) (716) . . . 14733
Ellicottville (Cattaraugus) (8th) (716) . . . 14731
Ellington (Chautauqua) (8th) (716) . . . 14732
Ellisburg (Jefferson) (5th) (315) . . . 13636
Elm Grove (Otsego) (6th) (607) . . . 13808
Elma (Erie) (8th) (716) . . . 14059
Elmdale (St. Lawrence) (4th) (315) . . . 13642
Elmhurst (Queens) (11th) (718) . . . 11373, 11379, 11380
Elmira (Chemung) (6th) (607) . . . 1490#, 14925
Elmira Heights (Chemung) (6th) (607) . . . 14903
Elmont (Nassau) (10th) (516) . . . 11003
Elmsford (Westchester) (9th) (914) . . . 10523
Elmwood (Onondaga) (5th) (315) . . . 13207
Elnora (Saratoga) (4th) (518) . . . 12065
Elsmere (Albany) (3rd) (518) . . . 12054
Elton (Cattaraugus) (8th) (716) . . . 14042
Elwood (Suffolk) (10th) (631) . . . 11731
Emeryville (St. Lawrence) (4th) (315) . . . 13642
Emmons (Otsego) (6th) (607) . . . 13820
Empeyville (Oneida) (5th) (315) . . . 13316
Endicott (Broome) (6th) (607) . . . 13760, 13761, 13763
Endwell (Broome) (6th) (607) . . . 13760, 13762
Enfield (Tompkins) (6th) (607) . . . 14850
Ephratah (Fulton) (4th) (518) . . . 13339
Erieville (Madison) (6th) (315) . . . 13061
Erin (Chemung) (6th) (607) . . . 14838
Erwin (Steuben) (7th) (607) . . . 14870
Esopus (Ulster) (3rd) (845) . . . 12429
Esperance (Schoharie) (3rd) (518) . . . 12066
Esplanade (Bronx) (12th) (718) . . . 10469
Essex (Essex) (4th) (518) . . . 12936
Etna (Tompkins) (6th) (607) . . . 13062
Evans (Erie) (8th) (716) . . . 14006
Evans Mills (Jefferson) (5th) (315) . . . 13637
Exeter (Otsego) (6th) (607) . . . 13315
Fabius (Onondaga) (5th) (315) . . . 13063
Factory Village (Saratoga) (4th) (518) . . . 12020
Factoryville (Essex) (4th) (518) . . . 12928
Fair Harbor (Suffolk) (10th) (631) . . . 11706
Fair Haven (Cayuga) (7th) (315) . . . 13064
Fairdale (Oswego) (5th) (315) . . . 13074
Fairfield (Herkimer) (5th) (315) . . . 13406
Fairmount (Onondaga) (5th) (315) . . . 13219
Fairport (Monroe) (7th) (585) . . . 14450
Fairview (Dutchess) (9th) (845) . . . 12601
Falconer (Chautauqua) (8th) (716) . . . 14733
Fallsburg (Sullivan) (3rd) (845) . . . 12733
Fancher (Orleans) (8th) (585) . . . 14452
Far Rockaway (Queens) (11th) (718) . . . 11096, 1169#
Farleys Point (Cayuga) (7th) (315) . . . 13160
Farmersville (Cattaraugus) (8th) (716) . . . 14060
Farmersville Station (Cattaraugus) (8th) (716) . . . 14060
Farmingdale (Nassau) (10th) (516) . . . 1173#, 11774
Farmington (Ontario) (7th) (585) . . . 14425
Farmingville (Suffolk) (10th) (631) . . . 11738
Farnham (Erie) (8th) (716) . . . 14061
Faust (Franklin) (4th) (518) . . . 12986
Fayette (Seneca) (7th) (315) . . . 13065
Fayetteville (Onondaga) (5th) (315) . . . 13066
Felts Mills (Jefferson) (5th) (315) . . . 13638
Fenner (Madison) (6th) (315) . . . 13035
Fenton (Broome) (6th) (607) . . . 13833
Fergusonville (Otsego) (6th) (607) . . . 12155
Ferndale (Sullivan) (3rd) (845) . . . 12734
Fernwood (Oswego) (5th) (315) . . . 13142
Feura Bush (Albany) (3rd) (518) . . . 12067
Filer Corners (Otsego) (6th) (607) . . . 13808
Fillmore (Allegany) (8th) (585) . . . 14735
Findley Lake (Chautauqua) (8th) (716) . . . 14736
Fine (St. Lawrence) (4th) (315) . . . 13639
Fineview (Jefferson) (5th) (315) . . . 13640
Fire Island (Suffolk) (10th) (631) . . . 11770
Fire Island Pines (Suffolk) (10th) (631) . . . 11782
Firms (Onondaga) (5th) (315) . . . 13251
Firthcliffe (Orange) (9th) (845) . . . 12518
Fish Creek (Lewis) (5th) (315) . . . 13325
Fish House (Fulton) (4th) (518) . . . 12025
Fishers (Ontario) (7th) (585) . . . 14453
Fishers Island (Suffolk) (10th) (631) . . . 06390
Fishers Landing (Jefferson) (5th) (315) . . . 13641
Fishkill (Dutchess) (9th) (845) . . . 12524
Fishs Eddy (Delaware) (6th) (607) . . . 13774
Fivemile Point (Broome) (6th) (607) . . . 13795
Flanders (Suffolk) (10th) (631) . . . 11901
Flat Creek (Montgomery) (4th) (518) . . . 13317
Fleetwood (Westchester) (9th) (914) . . . 10552
Fleischmanns (Delaware) (6th) (845) . . . 12430
Fleming (Cayuga) (7th) (315) . . . 13021
Flemingville (Tioga) (6th) (607) . . . 13827
Floral Park (Nassau) (10th) (516) . . . 1100#
Florence (Oneida) (5th) (315) . . . 13316
Florida (Montgomery) (4th) (518) . . . 12010
Florida (Orange) (9th) (845) . . . 10921
Flower Hill (Nassau) (10th) (516) . . . 11###
Flowerfield (Suffolk) (10th) (631) . . . 11780
Floyd (Oneida) (5th) (315) . . . 13440
Fluvanna (Chautauqua) (8th) (716) . . . 14701
Flushing (Queens) (11th) (718) . . . 113##
Flushing Meadows (Queens) (11th) (718) . . . 113##
Fly Creek (Otsego) (6th) (607) . . . 13337
Fonda (Montgomery) (4th) (518) . . . 12068
Fordham (Bronx) (12th) (718) . . . 10458
Forest (Clinton) (4th) (518) . . . 12935
Forest Hills (Queens) (11th) (718) . . . 11375
Forestburgh (Sullivan) (3rd) (845) . . . 12777
Forestport (Oneida) (5th) (315) . . . 13338
Forestville (Chautauqua) (8th) (716) . . . 14062
Forks (Erie) (8th) (716) . . . 14225
Forsyth (Chautauqua) (8th) (716) . . . 14775
Fort Ann (Washington) (4th) (518) . . . 12827
Fort Covington (Franklin) (4th) (518) . . . 12937
Fort Drum (Jefferson) (5th) (315) . . . 13602, 13603
Fort Edward (Washington) (4th) (518) . . . 12828
Fort Hamilton (Kings) (2nd) (718) . . . 11252
Fort Herkimer (Herkimer) (5th) (315) . . . 13407
Fort Hunter (Montgomery) (4th) (518) . . . 12069
Fort Jackson (St. Lawrence) (4th) (315) . . . 12965
Fort Johnson (Montgomery) (4th) (518) . . . 12070
Fort Miller (Washington) (4th) (518) . . . 12828
Fort Montgomery (Orange) (9th) (845) . . . 10922
Fort Plain (Montgomery) (4th) (518) . . . 13339
Fort Salonga (Suffolk) (10th) (631) . . . 11768
Fort Ticonderoga (Essex) (4th) (518) . . . 12883
Fort Tilden (Queens) (11th) (718) . . . 11695
Fort Totten (Queens) (11th) (718) . . . 11359
Fort Washington (New York) (1st) (212) . . . 10032
Fortsville (Saratoga) (4th) (518) . . . 12831
Foster (Tioga) (6th) (607) . . . 13827
Fosterdale (Sullivan) (3rd) (845) . . . 12726
Fosterville (Cayuga) (7th) (315) . . . 13021
Fowler (St. Lawrence) (4th) (315) . . . 13642
Fowlersville (Lewis) (5th) (315) . . . 13433
Frankfort (Herkimer) (5th) (315) . . . 13340
Franklin (Delaware) (6th) (607) . . . 13775, 13846
Franklin (Franklin) (4th) (518) . . . 12913
Franklin Depot (Delaware) (6th) (607) . . . 13839
Franklin Springs (Oneida) (5th) (315) . . . 13341
Franklin Square (Nassau) (10th) (516) . . . 11010
Franklinville (Cattaraugus) (8th) (716) . . . 14737
Fraser (Delaware) (6th) (607) . . . 13753
Fredonia (Chautauqua) (8th) (716) . . . 14063
Freedom (Cattaraugus) (8th) (716) . . . 14065
Freehold (Greene) (3rd) (518) . . . 12431
Freeport (Nassau) (10th) (516) . . . 11520
Freetown (Cortland) (6th) (607) . . . 13803
Freetown (Suffolk) (10th) (631) . . . 11937
Freetown Corners (Cortland) (6th) (607) . . . 13803
Freeville (Tompkins) (6th) (607) . . . 13068
Fremont (Steuben) (7th) (607) . . . 14807
Fremont (Sullivan) (3rd) (845) . . . 12736
Fremont Center (Sullivan) (3rd) (845) . . . 12736
French Creek (Chautauqua) (8th) (716) . . . 14724
French Woods (Delaware) (6th) (607) . . . 13783
Frenchville (Oneida) (5th) (315) . . . 13486
Fresh Meadows (Queens) (11th) (718) . . . 11365, 11366
Fresh Pond (Queens) (11th) (718) . . . 11385
Frewsburg (Chautauqua) (8th) (716) . . . 14738
Friendship (Allegany) (8th) (585) . . . 14739
Frontenac (Jefferson) (5th) (315) . . . 13624
Frontier (Monroe) (7th) (585) . . . 14646
Fruit Valley (Oswego) (5th) (315) . . . 13126
Fulfillment (Nassau) (10th) (516) . . . 11774
Fullerville (St. Lawrence) (4th) (315) . . . 13642
Fulton (Oswego) (5th) (315) . . . 13069
Fulton (Schoharie) (3rd) (518) . . . 12122
Fultonham (Schoharie) (3rd) (518) . . . 12071
Fultonville (Montgomery) (4th) (518) . . . 12016, 12072
Furniss (Oswego) (5th) (315) . . . 13126
Gabriels (Franklin) (4th) (518) . . . 12939
Gage (Yates) (7th) (315) . . . 14415
Gaines (Orleans) (8th) (585) . . . 14411
Gainesville (Wyoming) (8th) (585) . . . 14066
Galatia (Cortland) (6th) (607) . . . 13803
Galen (Wayne) (7th) (315) . . . 14433
Galeville (Onondaga) (5th) (315) . . . 13088
Gallatin (Columbia) (3rd) (518) . . . 12567
Gallupville (Schoharie) (3rd) (518) . . . 12073
Galway (Saratoga) (4th) (518) . . . 12074
Galway Lake (Fulton) (4th) (518) . . . 12025
Gansevoort (Saratoga) (4th) (518) . . . 12831
Garden City (Nassau) (10th) (516) . . . 1153#, 11599
Garden City Park (Nassau) (10th) (516) . . . 11040
Gardenville (Erie) (8th) (716) . . . 14224
Gardiner (Ulster) (3rd) (845) . . . 12525
Gardnertown (Orange) (9th) (845) . . . 12550
Garnerville (Rockland) (9th) (845) . . . 10923
Garnet Lake (Warren) (4th) (518) . . . 12843
Garoga (Fulton) (4th) (518) . . . 12095
Garrattsville (Otsego) (6th) (607) . . . 13342
Garrison (Putnam) (9th) (845) . . . 10524
Gaskill (Tioga) (6th) (607) . . . 13827
Gasport (Niagara) (8th) (716) . . . 14067
Gates (Monroe) (7th) (585) . . . 14606, 14624
Gates Center (Monroe) (7th) (585) . . . 14611
Gayhead (Greene) (3rd) (518) . . . 12451
Gayville (Oswego) (5th) (315) . . . 13044
Geddes (Onondaga) (5th) (315) . . . 13209
Gedney (Westchester) (9th) (914) . . . 10605
Geers Corners (Lewis) (5th) (315) . . . 13648
Genegantslet (Chenango) (6th) (607) . . . 13778
Genesee (Allegany) (8th) (585) . . . 14754
Genesee Falls (Wyoming) (8th) (585) . . . 14536
Geneseo (Livingston) (7th) (585) . . . 14454
Geneva (Ontario) (7th) (315) . . . 14456
Genoa (Cayuga) (7th) (315) . . . 13071
Georgetown (Chenango) (6th) (607) . . . 13129
Georgetown (Madison) (6th) (315) . . . 13072
Georgetown Station (Madison) (6th) (315) . . . 13334
German (Chenango) (6th) (607) . . . 13801
German Flatts (Herkimer) (5th) (315) . . . 13407
Germantown (Columbia) (3rd) (518) . . . 12526
Gerry (Chautauqua) (8th) (716) . . . 14740
Getzville (Erie) (8th) (716) . . . 14068
Ghent (Columbia) (3rd) (518) . . . 12075
Gilbertsville (Otsego) (6th) (607) . . . 13776
Gilboa (Schoharie) (3rd) (518) . . . 12076
Gilgo Beach (Suffolk) (10th) (631) . . . 11702
Gilmantown (Hamilton) (4th) (518) . . . 12190
Glasco (Ulster) (3rd) (845) . . . 12432
Glass Lake (Rensselaer) (3rd) (518) . . . 12018
Glen (Montgomery) (4th) (518) . . . 12072
Glen Aubrey (Broome) (6th) (607) . . . 13777
Glen Castle (Broome) (6th) (607) . . . 13901
Glen Cove (Nassau) (10th) (516) . . . 11542
Glen Head (Nassau) (10th) (516) . . . 11545
Glen Island (Warren) (4th) (518) . . . 12814
Glen Oaks (Queens) (11th) (718) . . . 11004
Glen Park (Jefferson) (5th) (315) . . . 13601
Glen Spey (Sullivan) (3rd) (845) . . . 12737
Glen Wild (Sullivan) (3rd) (845) . . . 12738
Glenburnie (Washington) (4th) (518) . . . 12861
Glendale (Queens) (11th) (718) . . . 11385
Glenfield (Lewis) (5th) (315) . . . 13312, 13343, 13345
Glenford (Ulster) (3rd) (845) . . . 12433
Glenham (Dutchess) (9th) (845) . . . 12527
Glenmont (Albany) (3rd) (518) . . . 12077
Glens Falls (Warren) (4th) (518) . . . 12801, 12803, 12804
Glenville (Schenectady) (4th) (518) . . . 12302, 12325
Glenwood (Erie) (8th) (716) . . . 14069
Glenwood Landing (Nassau) (10th) (516) . . . 11547
Glenwood Park (Orange) (9th) (845) . . . 12550
Gloversville (Fulton) (4th) (518) . . . 12078
Godeffroy (Orange) (9th) (845) . . . 12739
Goldens Bridge (Westchester) (9th) (914) . . . 10526
Goodyears Corners (Cayuga) (7th) (315) . . . 13081
Gordon Heights (Suffolk) (10th) (631) . . . 11763
Gorham (Ontario) (7th) (315) . . . 14461
Goshen (Orange) (9th) (845) . . . 10924
Goulds Mill (Lewis) (5th) (315) . . . 13368
Gouverneur (St. Lawrence) (4th) (315) . . . 13642
Gowanda (Cattaraugus) (8th) (716) . . . 14070
Gowanda (Erie) (8th) (716) . . . 14070
Gracie (New York) (1st) (212) . . . 10130
Grafton (Rensselaer) (3rd) (518) . . . 12082
Grahamsville (Sullivan) (3rd) (845) . . . 12740
Granby (Oswego) (5th) (315) . . . 13069
Grand Gorge (Delaware) (6th) (518) . . . 12434
Grand Island (Erie) (8th) (716) . . . 14072
Grand View-on-Hudson (Rockland) (9th) (845) . . . 10960
Granger (Allegany) (8th) (585) . . . 14735
Grangerville (Saratoga) (4th) (518) . . . 12871
Granite Springs (Westchester) (9th) (914) . . . 10527
Grant (Herkimer) (5th) (315) . . . 13324
Grantville (St. Lawrence) (4th) (315) . . . 13667
Granville (Washington) (4th) (518) . . . 12832
Graphite (Warren) (4th) (518) . . . 12836
Grassy Point (Rockland) (9th) (845) . . . 10980
Gravesville (Herkimer) (5th) (315) . . . 13431
Gray (Herkimer) (5th) (315) . . . 13324
Great Bend (Jefferson) (5th) (315) . . . 13643
Great Kills (Richmond) (13th) (718) . . . 10308
Great Neck (Nassau) (10th) (516) . . . 1102#
Great Neck Estates (Nassau) (10th) (516) . . . 11021
Great Neck Plaza (Nassau) (10th) (516) . . . 1102#
Great River (Suffolk) (10th) (631) . . . 11739
Great Valley (Cattaraugus) (8th) (716) . . . 14741
Greece (Monroe) (7th) (585) . . . 1461#, 14626
Green Island (Albany) (3rd) (518) . . . 12183

Greenburgh (Westchester) (9th) (914) ... 10607
Greene (Chanango) (6th) (607) ... 13778
Greenfield (Saratoga) (4th) (518) ... 12833
Greenfield Center (Saratoga) (4th) (518) ... 12833
Greenfield Park (Ulster) (3rd) (845) ... 12435
Greenhurst (Chautauqua) (8th) (716) ... 14742
Greenlawn (Suffolk) (10th) (631) ... 11740
Greenport (Columbia) (3rd) (518) ... 12534
Greenport (Suffolk) (10th) (631) ... 11944
Greenport Center (Columbia) (3rd) (518) ... 12534
Greenvale (Nassau) (10th) (516) ... 11548
Greenville (Greene) (3rd) (518) ... 12083
Greenville (Orange) (9th) (845) ... 12771
Greenville (Westchester) (9th) (914) ... 10583
Greenville Center (Greene) (3rd) (518) ... 12083
Greenway (Oneida) (5th) (315) ... 13440
Greenwich (Washington) (4th) (518) ... 12834
Greenwood (Steuben) (7th) (607) ... 14839
Greenwood Lake (Orange) (9th) (845) ... 10925
Gregorytown (Delaware) (6th) (607) ... 13755
Greig (Lewis) (5th) (315) ... 13345
Grenell (Jefferson) (5th) (315) ... 13624
Gridleyville (Tioga) (6th) (607) ... 13864
Griffis AFB (Madison) (6th) (315) ... 13440
Grindstone (Jefferson) (5th) (315) ... 13624
Groton (Tompkins) (6th) (607) ... 13073
Grove (Allegany) (8th) (607) ... 14884
Groveland (Livingston) (7th) (585) ... 14462, 14545
Grover Hills (Essex) (4th) (518) ... 12956
Guffin Bay (Jefferson) (5th) (315) ... 13634
Guilderland (Albany) (3rd) (518) ... 12084
Guilderland Center (Albany) (3rd) (518) ... 12085
Guilford (Chenango) (6th) (607) ... 13780
Gulf Summit (Broome) (6th) (607) ... 13865
Gurn Spring (Saratoga) (4th) (518) ... 12831
Hadley (Saratoga) (4th) (518) ... 12835
Hagaman (Montgomery) (4th) (518) ... 12086
Hagedorns Mills (Saratoga) (4th) (518) ... 12074
Hagerman-North Bellport (Suffolk) (10th) (631) ... 11772
Hague (Warren) (4th) (518) ... 12836
Hailesboro (St. Lawrence) (4th) (315) ... 13645
Haines Falls (Greene) (3rd) (518) ... 12436
Halcott (Greene) (3rd) (845) ... 12437
Halcott Center (Greene) (3rd) (845) ... 12430
Halcottsville (Delaware) (6th) (518) ... 12438
Hale Eddy (Delaware) (6th) (607) ... 13783
Halesite (Suffolk) (10th) (631) ... 11743
Halfmoon (Saratoga) (4th) (518) ... 12065
Hall (Ontario) (7th) (315) ... 14463
Hallsville (Montgomery) (4th) (518) ... 13339
Halsey Valley (Tioga) (6th) (607) ... 14883
Hambletville (Broome) (6th) (607) ... 13754
Hamburg (Erie) (8th) (716) ... 14075, 14219
Hamburg-Lake Shore (Erie) (8th) (716) ... 14075
Hamden (Delaware) (6th) (607) ... 13782
Hamilton (Madison) (6th) (315) ... 13346
Hamlet (Chautauqua) (8th) (716) ... 14138
Hamlin (Monroe) (7th) (585) ... 14464
Hammond (St. Lawrence) (4th) (315) ... 13646
Hammondsport (Steuben) (7th) (607) ... 14840
Hampton (Rensselaer) (3rd) (518) ... 12144
Hampton (Washington) (4th) (518) ... 12837
Hampton Bays (Suffolk) (10th) (631) ... 11946
Hamptonburg (Orange) (9th) (845) ... 10916
Hancock (Delaware) (6th) (607) ... 13783
Hankins (Sullivan) (3rd) (845) ... 12741
Hannacroix (Greene) (3rd) (518) ... 12087
Hannawa Falls (St. Lawrence) (4th) (315) ... 13647
Hannibal (Oswego) (5th) (315) ... 13074
Hanover (Chautauqua) (8th) (716) ... 14136
Harbor Acres (Nassau) (10th) (516) ... 11050
Harbor Heights (Suffolk) (10th) (631) ... 11743
Harbor Hills (Nassau) (10th) (516) ... 11023
Harbor Island (Nassau) (10th) (516) ... 11558
Hardenburgh (Ulster) (3rd) (845) ... 12455
Harford (Cortland) (6th) (607) ... 13784
Harford Mills (Tioga) (6th) (607) ... 13835
Harkness (Clinton) (4th) (518) ... 12972
Harmon-on-Hudson (Westchester) (9th) (914) ... 10520
Harmony (Chautauqua) (8th) (716) ... 14767
Harmony Corners (Saratoga) (4th) (518) ... 12020
Harpersfield (Delaware) (6th) (518) ... 13786
Harpursville (Broome) (6th) (607) ... 13787, 13826
Harrietstown (Franklin) (4th) (518) ... 12983
Harriman (Orange) (9th) (845) ... 10926
Harris (Sullivan) (3rd) (845) ... 12742
Harrisburg (Lewis) (5th) (315) ... 13367
Harris Hill (Erie) (8th) (716) ... 14221
Harrison (Westchester) (9th) (914) ... 10528
Harrisville (Lewis) (5th) (315) ... 13648
Hart Lot (Onondaga) (5th) (315) ... 13060
Hartford (Washington) (4th) (518) ... 12838
Hartland (Niagara) (8th) (716) ... 14067
Hartsdale (Westchester) (9th) (914) ... 10530
Hartsville (Steuben) (7th) (607) ... 14843
Hartwick (Otsego) (6th) (607) ... 13348
Hartwick Seminary (Otsego) (6th) (607) ... 13326
Hartwood (Sullivan) (3rd) (845) ... 12729
Harvard (Delaware) (6th) (607) ... 13756
Hastings (Oswego) (5th) (315) ... 13076
Hastings-on-Hudson (Westchester) (9th) (914) ... 10706
Hatchs Corner (St. Lawrence) (4th) (315) ... 13684
Hauppauge (Suffolk) (10th) (631) ... 11749, 11788
Haverstraw (Rockland) (9th) (845) ... 10927
Hawkeye (Clinton) (4th) (518) ... 12912
Hawkinsville (Oneida) (5th) (315) ... 13309
Hawleys (Delaware) (6th) (607) ... 13856
Hawleyton (Broome) (6th) (607) ... 13903
Hawthorne (Westchester) (9th) (914) ... 10532
Hayt Corners (Seneca) (7th) (607) ... 14521
Head of the Harbor (Suffolk) (10th) (631) ... 11780, 11790
Heathcote (Weschester) (9th) (914) ... 10583
Hebron (Washington) (4th) (518) ... 12832
Hecla (Oneida) (5th) (315) ... 13490
Hector (Schuyler) (6th) (607) ... 14841
Heer Park (Suffolk) (10th) (631) ... 11757
Helena (St. Lawrence) (4th) (315) ... 13649
Helmuth (Erie) (8th) (716) ... 14034
Hemlock (Livingston) (7th) (585) ... 14466
Hempstead (Nassau) (10th) (516) ... 11549, 11550, 11551
Hempstead Gardens (Nassau) (10th) (516) ... 11552
Henderson (Jefferson) (5th) (315) ... 13650
Henderson Harbor (Jefferson) (5th) (315) ... 13651
Henrietta (Monroe) (7th) (585) ... 14467
Hensonville (Greene) (3rd) (518) ... 12439
Herkimer (Herkimer) (5th) (315) ... 13350
Hermon (St. Lawrence) (4th) (315) ... 13652
Herricks (Nassau) (10th) (516) ... 11040
Herrings (Jefferson) (5th) (315) ... 13619
Hessville (Montgomery) (4th) (518) ... 13339
Heuvelton (St. Lawrence) (4th) (315) ... 13654
Hewittville (St. Lawrence) (4th) (315) ... 13668
Hewlett (Nassau) (10th) (516) ... 11557
Hewlett Bay Park (Nassau) (10th) (516) ... 11557
Hewlett Harbor (Nassau) (10th) (516) ... 11557
Hewlett Neck (Nassau) (10th) (516) ... 11598
Hicksville (Nassau) (10th) (516) ... 118##
Higgins Bay (Hamilton) (4th) (518) ... 12108
Higginsville (Oneida) (5th) (315) ... 13054
High Falls (Ulster) (3rd) (845) ... 12440
Highbridge (Bronx) (12th) (718) ... 10452
Highland (Sullivan) (3rd) (845) ... 12732
Highland (Ulster) (3rd) (845) ... 12528
Highland Falls (Orange) (9th) (845) ... 10928
Highland Lake (Sullivan) (3rd) (845) ... 12743
Highland Mills (Orange) (9th) (845) ... 10930
Highland on the Lake (Erie) (8th) (716) ... 14047
Highlands (Orange) (9th) (845) ... 10928
High Market (Lewis) (5th) (315) ... 13325
Highmount (Ulster) (3rd) (845) ... 12441
Highview (Sullivan) (3rd) (845) ... 12721
Hiler (Erie) (8th) (716) ... 14223
Hillburn (Rockland) (9th) (845) ... 10931
Hillcrest (Broome) (6th) (607) ... 13901
Hillsboro (Oneida) (5th) (315) ... 13316
Hillsdale (Columbia) (3rd) (518) ... 12529
Hillside (Bronx) (12th) (718) ... 10469
Hillside Manor (Nassau) (10th) (516) ... 11040
Hilton (Monroe) (7th) (585) ... 14468
Himrod (Yates) (7th) (607) ... 14842
Hinckley (Oneida) (5th) (315) ... 13352
Hinman's Corners (Broome) (6th) (607) ... 13905
Hinmansville (Oswego) (5th) (315) ... 13135
Hinsdale (Cattaraugus) (8th) (716) ... 14743
Hither Plains (Suffolk) (10th) (631) ... 11954
Hoag Corners (Rensselaer) (3rd) (518) ... 12062
Hobart (Delaware) (6th) (607) ... 13788
Hoboken (Chenango) (6th) (607) ... 13411
Hoffmans (Schenectady) (4th) (518) ... 12088
Hoffmeister (Hamilton) (4th) (315) ... 13353
Hoffmeister (Nassau) (10th) (516) ... 11549
Hogansburg (Franklin) (4th) (518) ... 13655
Holbrook (Suffolk) (10th) (631) ... 11741
Holcomb (Ontario) (7th) (315) ... 14469
Holcombville (Warren) (4th) (518) ... 12853
Holland (Erie) (8th) (716) ... 14080
Holland Patent (Oneida) (5th) (315) ... 13354
Holley (Orleans) (8th) (585) ... 14470
Hollis (Queens) (11th) (718) ... 11423
Hollis Hills (Queens) (11th) (718) ... 11364, 11427
Hollowville (Columbia) (3rd) (518) ... 12530
Holmes (Dutchess) (9th) (845) ... 12531
Holmesville (Chenango) (6th) (607) ... 13843
Holtsville (Suffolk) (10th) (631) ... 00501, 00544, 11742
Homer (Cortland) (6th) (607) ... 13077
Honeoye (Ontario) (7th) (585) ... 14471
Honeoye Falls (Monroe) (7th) (585) ... 14472
Honeywell Corners (Fulton) (4th) (518) ... 12025
Honnedaga Lake (Oneida) (5th) (315) ... 13338
Hoopers Valley (Tioga) (6th) (607) ... 13812
Hoosick (Rensselaer) (3rd) (518) ... 12089
Hoosick Falls (Renssselaer) (3rd) (518) ... 12090
Hoosick Junction (Rensselaer) (3rd) (518) ... 12133
Hope (Hamilton) (4th) (518) ... 12134
Hope Farm (Dutchess) (9th) (845) ... 12532
Hopewell (Dutchess) (9th) (845) ... 12533
Hopewell (Ontario) (7th) (315) ... 14424
Hopewell Junction (Dutchess) (9th) (845) ... 12533
Hopkinton (St. Lawrence) (4th) (315) ... 12965
Horace Harding (Queens) (11th) (718) ... 11362
Horicon (Warren) (4th) (518) ... 12815
Hornby (Steuben) (7th) (607) ... 14812
Hornell (Steuben) (7th) (607) ... 14843
Hornellsville (Steuben) (7th) (607) ... 14807
Horseheads (Chemung) (6th) (607) ... 14845
Horseshoe (St. Lawrence) (4th) (518) ... 12986
Horton (Delaware) (6th) (845) ... 12776
Hortonville (Sullivan) (3rd) (845) ... 12745
Houghton (Allegany) (8th) (585) ... 14744
Hounsfield (Jefferson) (5th) (315) ... 13685
Houseville (Lewis) (5th) (315) ... 13473
Howard (Steuben) (7th) (607) ... 14843
Howard Beach (Queens) (11th) (718) ... 11414
Howardville (Oswego) (5th) (315) ... 13302
Howells (Orange) (9th) (845) ... 10932
Howes Cave (Schoharie) (3rd) (518) ... 12092
Howlett Hill (Onondaga) (5th) (315) ... 13031
Hubbardsville (Madison) (6th) (315) ... 13355
Hubbardtown (Tioga) (6th) (607) ... 13743
Hubbell Cors (Delaware) (4th) (607) ... 12474
Hudson (Columbia) (3rd) (518) ... 12534
Hudson Falls (Washington) (4th) (518) ... 12839
Hughsonville (Dutchess) (9th) (845) ... 12537
Huguenot (Orange) (9th) (845) ... 12746
Hulberton (Orleans) (8th) (585) ... 14470
Huletts Landing (Washington) (4th) (518) ... 12841
Hullsville (Tioga) (6th) (607) ... 13827
Hume (Allegany) (8th) (585) ... 14745
Humphrey (Cattaraugus) (8th) (716) ... 14741
Hunt (Livingston) (7th) (585) ... 14846
Hunter (Greene) (3rd) (518) ... 12442
Hunter Lake (Sullivan) (3rd) (845) ... 12768
Huntersland (Schoharie) (3th) (518) ... 12122
Huntington (Suffolk) (10th) (631) ... 11743
Huntington Bay (Suffolk) (10th) (631) ... 11743
Huntington Station (Suffolk) (10th) (631) ... 11746, 11747
Hunts Corners (Cortland) (6th) (607) ... 13803
Hurley (Ulster) (3rd) (845) ... 12443
Hurleyville (Sullivan) (3rd) (845) ... 12747
Huron (Wayne) (7th) (315) ... 14590
Hyde Park (Dutchess) (9th) (845) ... 12538
Hyndsville (Schoharie) (3rd) (518) ... 12043
Igerna (Warren) (4th) (518) ... 12853
Ilion (Herkimer) (5th) (315) ... 13357
Independence (Allegany) (8th) (607) ... 14806
Indian Lake (Hamilton) (4th) (518) ... 12842
Indian River (Lewis) (5th) (315) ... 13327
Indian Village (Onondaga) (5th) (315) ... 13120
Industry (Monroe) (7th) (585) ... 14543
Ingraham (Clinton) (4th) (518) ... 12992
Inlet (Hamilton) (4th) (518) ... 13360
Interlaken (Seneca) (7th) (607) ... 14847
Inwood (Nassau) (10th) (516) ... 11096
Ionia (Ontario) (7th) (315) ... 14475
Ira (Cayuga) (7th) (315) ... 13033
Irish Corners (Franklin) (4th) (518) ... 12916
Irona (Clinton) (4th) (518) ... 12910
Irondequoit (Monroe) (7th) (585) ... 14609, 14617, 14621, 14622
Ironville (Essex) (4th) (518) ... 12928
Irving (Chautauqua) (8th) (716) ... 14081
Irvington (Westchester) (9th) (914) ... 10533
Ischua (Cattaraugus) (8th) (716) ... 14743
Island Park (Nassau) (10th) (516) ... 11558
Island Trees (Nassau) (10th) (516) ... 11756
Islandia (Suffolk) (10th) (631) ... 11749, 11760
Islip (Suffolk) (10th) (631) ... 11751
Islip Manor (Suffolk) (10th) (631) ... 11751
Islip Terrace (Suffolk) (10th) (631) ... 11752
Italy (Yates) (7th) (315) ... 14512
Itaska (Broome) (6th) (607) ... 13862
Ithaca (Tompkins) (6th) (607) ... 1485#, 14882
Ivanhoe (Delaware) (6th) (607) ... 13839
Jackson (Washington) (4th) (518) ... 12816
Jackson Heights (Queens) (11th) (718) ... 11372
Jacksonville (Tompkins) (6th) (607) ... 14854
Jamaica (Queens) (11th) (718) ... 114##
Jamaica Square (Nassau) (10th) (516) ... 11003
Jamesport (Suffolk) (10th) (631) ... 11947
Jamestown (Chautauqua) (8th) (716) ... 14701, 14702
Jamesville (Onondaga) (5th) (315) ... 13078
Janesville (Schoharie) (3rd) (518) ... 12043
Jasper (Steuben) (7th) (607) ... 14855
Java (Wyoming) (8th) (585) ... 14082
Java Center (Wyoming) (8th) (585) ... 14082
Java Village (Wyoming) (8th) (585) ... 14083
Jay (Essex) (4th) (518) ... 12941
Jefferson (Schoharie) (3rd) (518) ... 12093
Jefferson Park (Jefferson) (5th) (315) ... 13650
Jefferson Valley (Westchester) (9th) (914) ... 10535
Jeffersonville (Sullivan) (3rd) (845) ... 12748
Jenksville (Tioga) (6th) (607) ... 13736
Jericho (Nassau) (10th) (516) ... 11753, 11853
Jerome (Bronx) (12th) (718) ... 10468
Jerusalem (Yates) (7th) (315) ... 14418
Jewell (Oneida) (5th) (315) ... 13042
Jewell Manor (Onondaga) (5th) (315) ... 13088
Jewett (Greene) (3rd) (518) ... 12444
Jingo (Erie) (8th) (716) ... 14233
Johnsburg (Warren) (4th) (518) ... 12843
Johnson (Orange) (9th) (845) ... 10933

Johnson City (Broome) (6th) (607) . . . 13790
Johnsonburg (Wyoming) (8th) (585) . . . 14084
Johnsonville (Rensselaer) (3rd) (518) . . . 12094
Johnstown (Fulton) (4th) (518) . . . 12095
Johnsville (Montgomery) (4th) (518) . . . 13452
Jonesville (Saratoga) (4th) (518) . . . 12065
Jordan (Onondaga) (5th) (315) . . . 13080
Jordanville (Herkimer) (5th) (315) . . . 13361
Junius (Seneca) (7th) (315) . . . 13165
Kanona (Steuben) (7th) (607) . . . 14856
Kasoag (Oswego) (5th) (315) . . . 13302
Katonah (Westchester) (9th) (914) . . . 10536
Kattelville (Broome) (6th) (607) . . . 13901
Kattskill Bay (Warren) (4th) (518) . . . 12844
Kauneonga Lake (Sullivan) (3rd) (845) . . . 12749
Kayuta Lake (Oneida) (5th) (315) . . . 13338
Keene (Essex) (4th) (518) . . . 12942
Keene Valley (Essex) (4th) (518) . . . 12943
Keeseville (Essex) (4th) (518) . . . 12911, 12924, 12944
Keeseville (Clinton) (4th) (518) . . . 12911, 12924, 12944
Kelly Corners (Delaware) (6th) (845) . . . 12455
Kelsey (Delaware) (6th) (607) . . . 13783
Kendall (Orleans) (8th) (585) . . . 14476
Kenilworth (Nassau) (10th) (516) . . . 11024
Kenmore (Erie) (8th) (716) . . . 14217, 14223
Kennedy (Chautauqua) (8th) (716) . . . 14747
Kenoza Lake (Sullivan) (3rd) (845) . . . 12750
Kensington (Nassau) (10th) (516) . . . 11201
Kent (Orleans) (8th) (585) . . . 14477
Kent (Putnam) (9th) (845) . . . 10512
Kent Lakes (Putnam) (9th) (845) . . . 10512
Kenwood (Madison) (6th) (315) . . . 13421
Kerhonkson (Ulster) (3rd) (845) . . . 12446
Ketchumville (Tioga) (6th) (607) . . . 13736
Keuka (Steuben) (7th) (607) . . . 14837, 14840
Keuka Park (Yates) (7th) (315) . . . 14478
Kew Gardens (Queens) (11th) (718) . . . 11415, 11418, 11424
Kew Gardens Hills (Queens) (11th) (718) . . . 11367
Kiamesha Lake (Sullivan) (3rd) (845) . . . 12751
Kiantone (Chautauqua) (8th) (716) . . . 14701
Kill Buck (Cattaraugus) (8th) (716) . . . 14748
Killawog (Broome) (6th) (607) . . . 13794
Kinderhook (Columbia) (3rd) (518) . . . 12106
Kings Ferry (Cayuga) (7th) (315) . . . 13081
Kings Park (Suffolk) (10th) (631) . . . 11754
Kings Point (Nassau) (10th) (631) . . . 11024
Kings Settlement (Chenango) (6th) (607) . . . 13815
Kings Station (Saratoga) (4th) (518) . . . 12831
Kingsbury (Washington) (4th) (518) . . . 12839
Kingston (Ulster) (3rd) (845) . . . 12401, 12402
Kirk (Chenango) (6th) (607) . . . 13844
Kirkland (Oneida) (5th) (315) . . . 13323
Kirkville (Onondaga) (5th) (315) . . . 13082
Kirkwood (Broome) (6th) (607) . . . 13795
Kirschnerville (Lewis) (5th) (315) . . . 13327
Kiryas Joel (Orange) (9th) (845) . . . 10950
Kismet (Suffolk) (10th) (631) . . . 11706
Kitchawan (Westchester) (9th) (914) . . . 10562
Knapp Creek (Cattaraugus) (8th) (716) . . . 14760
Knapps Station (St. Lawrence) (4th) (315) . . . 13668
Knollwood Beach (Suffolk) (10th) (631) . . . 11743
Knowlesville (Orleans) (8th) (585) . . . 14479
Knowsville (Jefferson) (5th) (315) . . . 13601
Knox (Albany) (3rd) (518) . . . 12107
Knoxboro (Oneida) (5th) (315) . . . 13362
Kortright (Delaware) (6th) (607) . . . 13739
Kringsbush (Montgomery) (4th) (518) . . . 13452
Krumville (Ulster) (3rd) (845) . . . 12461
Kyserike (Ulster) (3rd) (845) . . . 12440
La Fargeville (Jefferson) (5th) (315) . . . 13656
La Fayette (Onondaga) (5th) (315) . . . 13084
La Grange (Dutchess) (9th) (845) . . . 12540
La Grangeville (Dutchess) (9th) (845) . . . 12540
La Salle (Niagara) (8th) (716) . . . 14304
Lackawack (Ulster) (3rd) (845) . . . 12740
Lackawanna (Erie) (8th) (716) . . . 14218
Lacona (Oswego) (5th) (315) . . . 13083
Ladleton (Ulster) (3rd) (845) . . . 12725
Lairdsville (Oneida) (5th) (315) . . . 13323
Lake Bonaparte (Lewis) (5th) (315) . . . 13648
Lake Carmel (Putnam) (9th) (845) . . . 10512
Lake Clear (Franklin) (4th) (518) . . . 12945
Lake Clear Junction (Franklin) (4th) (518) . . . 12945
Lake Colby (Franklin) (4th) (518) . . . 12983
Lake Delaware (Delaware) (6th) (607) . . . 13753
Lake Delta (Oneida) (5th) (315) . . . 13440
Lake Desolation (Saratoga) (4th) (518) . . . 12850
Lake Erie Beach (Erie) (8th) (716) . . . 14006
Lake Gardens (Nassau) (10th) (516) . . . 11022
Lake George (Warren) (4th) (518) . . . 12845
Lake Grove (Suffolk) (10th) (631) . . . 11755
Lake Hill (Ulster) (3rd) (845) . . . 12448
Lake Huntington (Sullivan) (3rd) (845) . . . 12752
Lake Katonah (Westchester) (9th) (914) . . . 10536
Lake Katrine (Ulster) (3rd) (845) . . . 12449
Lake Kitchawan (Westchester) (9th) (914) . . . 10590
Lake Lincolndale (Westchester) (9th) (914) . . . 10541
Lake Luzerne (Warren) (4th) (518) . . . 12846
Lake Mahopac (Putnam) (9th) (845) . . . 10541
Lake Minnewaska (Ulster) (3rd) (845) . . . 12561
Lake Mohegan (Westchester) (9th) (914) . . . 10547
Lake Panamoka (Suffolk) (10th) (631) . . . 11961
Lake Peekskill (Putnam) (9th) (845) . . . 10537
Lake Placid (Essex) (4th) (518) . . . 12946
Lake Placid Club (Essex) (4th) (518) . . . 12946
Lake Pleasant (Hamilton) (4th) (518) . . . 12108
Lake Ronkonkoma (Suffolk) (10th) (631) . . . 11779
Lake Ronkonkoma Heights (Suffolk) (10th) (631) . . . 11779
Lake Secor (Putnam) (9th) (845) . . . 10541
Lake Shenorock (Westchester) (9th) (914) . . . 10587
Lake Success (Nassau) (10th) (516) . . . 11020, 11040, 11042
Lake View (Erie) (8th) (716) . . . 14085
Lake View (Nassau) (10th) (516) . . . 11552, 11570
Lakemont (Yates) (7th) (607) . . . 14857
Lakeport (Madison) (6th) (315) . . . 13037
Lakeview (Nassau) (10th) (516) . . . 11552, 11570
Lakeville (Livingston) (7th) (585) . . . 14480
Lakeville Estates (Nassau) (10th) (516) . . . 11040
Lakewood (Chautauqua) (8th) (716) . . . 14750
Lancaster (Erie) (8th) (716) . . . 14043, 14086
Lanesville (Greene) (3rd) (845) . . . 12450
Langdon (Broome) (6th) (607) . . . 13795
Langdon Corners (St. Lawrence) (4th) (315) . . . 13617
Lansing (Tompkins) (6th) (607) . . . 14882
Lansingburg (Rensselaer) (3rd) (518) . . . 12182
Lapeer (Cortland) (6th) (607) . . . 13803
Larchmont (Westchester) (9th) (914) . . . 10538
Lassellsville (Montgomery) (4th) (518) . . . 13452
Latham (Albany) (3rd) (518) . . . 12110, 12128
Lathams Corners (Chenango) (6th) (607) . . . 13843
Lattingtown (Nassau) (10th) (516) . . . 11560
Laurel (Suffolk) (10th) (631) . . . 11948
Laurel Hill (Queens) (11th) (718) . . . 11378
Laurel Hollow (Nassau) (10th) (516) . . . 11771, 11791
Laurelton (Queens) (11th) (718) . . . 11413
Laurens (Otsego) (6th) (607) . . . 13796
Lawrence (Nassau) (10th) (516) . . . 11559
Lawrence (St. Lawrence) (4th) (315) . . . 12965
Lawrenceville (St. Lawrence) (4th) (315) . . . 12949
Lawtons (Erie) (8th) (716) . . . 14091
Lawyersville (Schoharie) (3rd) (518) . . . 12043
Le Ray (Jefferson) (5th) (315) . . . 13637
Le Roy (Genesee) (8th) (585) . . . 14482
Lebanon (Madison) (6th) (315) . . . 13332
Lebanon Springs (Columbia) (3rd) (518) . . . 12125
Ledyard (Cayuga) (7th) (315) . . . 13026
Lee (Oneida) (5th) (315) . . . 13440
Lee Center (Oneida) (5th) (315) . . . 13363
Leeds (Greene) (3rd) (518) . . . 12451
Leibhardt (Ulster) (3rd) (845) . . . 12404
Leicester (Livingston) (7th) (585) . . . 14481
Lenox (Madison) (6th) (315) . . . 13032
Leon (Cattaraugus) (8th) (716) . . . 14751
Leonardsville (Madison) (6th) (315) . . . 13364
Leonta (Delaware) (6th) (607) . . . 13775
Levanna (Cayuga) (7th) (315) . . . 13086
Levittown (Nassau) (10th) (516) . . . 11756
Lew Beach (Sullivan) (3rd) (845) . . . 12758
Lewis (Essex) (4th) (518) . . . 12950
Lewis (Lewis) (5th) (315) . . . 13489
Lewisboro (Westchester) (9th) (914) . . . 10590
Lewiston (Niagara) (8th) (716) . . . 14092
Lexington (Greene) (3rd) (518) . . . 12452
Leyden (Lewis) (5th) (315) . . . 13433
Liberty (Sullivan) (3rd) (845) . . . 12754
Lido Beach (Nassau) (10th) (516) . . . 11561
Lily Dale (Chautauqua) (8th) (716) . . . 14752
Lima (Livingston) (7th) (585) . . . 14485
Limerick (Jefferson) (5th) (315) . . . 13657
Limestone (Cattaraugus) (8th) (716) . . . 14753
Lincklaen (Chenango) (6th) (315) . . . 13052
Lincoln (Madison) (6th) (315) . . . 13043
Lincoln Park (Ulster) (3rd) (845) . . . 12401
Lincolndale (Westchester) (9th) (914) . . . 10540
Lincolnton (New York) (1st) (212) . . . 10037
Linden Hill (Queens) (11th) (718) . . . 11354
Lindenhurst (Suffolk) (10th) (631) . . . 11757
Lindley (Steuben) (7th) (607) . . . 14858
Linlithgo (Columbia) (3rd) (518) . . . 12526
Linwood (Genesee) (7th) (585) . . . 14486
Linwood (Livingston) (7th) (585) . . . 14486
Lisbon (St. Lawrence) (4th) (315) . . . 13658
Lisle (Broome) (6th) (607) . . . 13797
Litchfield (Herkimer) (5th) (315) . . . 13456
Little Falls (Herkimer) (5th) (315) . . . 13365
Little Genesee (Allegany) (8th) (585) . . . 14754
Little Neck (Queens) (11th) (718) . . . 11362, 11363
Little Valley (Cattaraugus) (8th) (716) . . . 14755
Little York (Cortland) (6th) (607) . . . 13087
Liverpool (Onondaga) (5th) (315) . . . 13088, 13089, 13090
Livingston (Columbia) (3rd) (518) . . . 12541
Livingston Manor (Sullivan) (3rd) (845) . . . 12758
Livingstonville (Schoharie) (3rd) (518) . . . 12122
Livonia (Livingston) (7th) (585) . . . 14487
Livonia Center (Livingston) (7th) (585) . . . 14488
Lloyd (Ulster) (3rd) (845) . . . 12528
Lloyd Harbor (Suffolk) (10th) (631) . . . 11743
Lloyd Neck (Suffolk) (10th) (631) . . . 11743
Loch Sheldrake (Sullivan) (3rd) (845) . . . 12759
Locke (Cayuga) (7th) (315) . . . 13092
Lockport (Niagara) (8th) (716) . . . 14094, 14095
Lockwood (Tioga) (6th) (607) . . . 14859
Locust Grove (Nassau) (10th) (516) . . . 11791
Locust Valley (Nassau) (10th) (516) . . . 11560
Locustwood (Nassau) (10th) (516) . . . 11003
Lodi (Seneca) (7th) (607) . . . 14860
Long Beach (Nassau) (10th) (516) . . . 11561
Long Eddy (Sullivan) (3rd) (845) . . . 12760
Long Island City (Queens) (11th) (718) . . . 1110#, 11120
Long Lake (Hamilton) (4th) (518) . . . 12847
Longwood (Bronx) (12th) (718) . . . 10459
Loon Lake (Franklin) (4th) (518) . . . 12989
Lordville (Delaware) (6th) (607) . . . 13783
Lorraine (Jefferson) (5th) (315) . . . 13659
Loudonville (Albany) (3rd) (518) . . . 12211
Louisville (St. Lawrence) (4th) (315) . . . 13678
Lounsberry (Tioga) (6th) (607) . . . 13812
Low Hampton (Washington) (4th) (518) . . . 12887
Lower Genegantslet Corner (Chenango) (6th) (607) . . . 13778
Lower Oswegatchie (St. Lawrence) (4th) (315) . . . 13670
Lower Rotterdam (Schenectady) (4th) (518) . . . 12306
Lowman (Chemung) (6th) (607) . . . 14861
Lowville (Lewis) (5th) (315) . . . 13367
Ludlowville (Tompkins) (6th) (607) . . . 14862
Lumberland (Sullivan) (3rd) (845) . . . 12770
Luzerne (Warren) (4th) (518) . . . 12846
Lycoming (Oswego) (5th) (315) . . . 13093
Lyell (Monroe) (7th) (585) . . . 14606
Lykers (Montgomery) (4th) (518) . . . 12166
Lyme (Jefferson) (5th) (315) . . . 13693
Lynbrook (Nassau) (10th) (516) . . . 11563
Lyncourt (Onondaga) (5th) (315) . . . 13208
Lyndon (Cattaraugus) (8th) (315) . . . 14737
Lyndonville (Orleans) (8th) (585) . . . 14098
Lyon Mountain (Clinton) (4th) (518) . . . 12952, 12955
Lyons (Wayne) (7th) (315) . . . 14489
Lyons Falls (Lewis) (5th) (315) . . . 13368
Lyonsdale (Lewis) (5th) (315) . . . 13368
Lyonsville (Ulster) (3rd) (845) . . . 12404
Lysander (Onondaga) (5th) (315) . . . 13027
MacDougall (Seneca) (7th) (315) . . . 14541
Macedon (Wayne) (7th) (315) . . . 14502
Macedon Center (Wayne) (7th) (315) . . . 14502
Machias (Cattaraugus) (8th) (716) . . . 14101
Macomb (St. Lawrence) (4th) (315) . . . 13642
Madison (Madison) (6th) (315) . . . 13402
Madrid (St. Lawrence) (4th) (315) . . . 13660
Madrid Springs (St. Lawrence) (4th) (315) . . . 13660
Mahopac (Putnam) (9th) (845) . . . 10541
Mahopac Falls (Putnam) (9th) (845) . . . 10542
Maine (Broome) (6th) (607) . . . 13802
Malba (Queens) (11th) (718) . . . 11357
Malden (Ulster) (3rd) (845) . . . 12453
Malden Bridge (Columbia) (3rd) (518) . . . 12115
Malden-on-Hudson (Ulster) (3rd) (845) . . . 12453
Mallory (Oswego) (5th) (315) . . . 13103
Malone (Franklin) (4th) (518) . . . 12953
Malta (Saratoga) (4th) (518) . . . 12919, 12020, 12118, 12151
Malta Ridge (Saratoga) (4th) (518) . . . 12020
Maltaville (Saratoga) (4th) (518) . . . 12020
Malverne (Nassau) (10th) (516) . . . 11565
Mamakating (Sullivan) (3rd) (845) . . . 12790
Mamaroneck (Westchester) (9th) (914) . . . 10543
Manchester (Ontario) (7th) (315) . . . 14504
Mandana (Onondaga) (5th) (315) . . . 13152
Manhasset (Nassau) (10th) (516) . . . 11030
Manhasset Hills (Nassau) (10th) (516) . . . 11040
Manheim (Herkimer) (5th) (315) . . . 13329
Manitou (Putnam) (9th) (845) . . . 10524
Manlius (Onondaga) (5th) (315) . . . 13104
Mannsville (Jefferson) (5th) (315) . . . 13661
Mannville (Albany) (3rd) (518) . . . 12189
Manor Park (Suffolk) (10th) (631) . . . 11950
Manorhaven (Nassau) (10th) (516) . . . 11050
Manorville (Suffolk) (10th) (631) . . . 11949
Mansfield (Cattaraugus) (8th) (716) . . . 14755
Maple Grove (Otsego) (6th) (607) . . . 13808
Maple Springs (Chautauqua) (8th) (716) . . . 14756
Maple Valley (Otsego) (6th) (607) . . . 13488
Maple View (Oswego) (5th) (315) . . . 13107
Maplecrest (Greene) (3rd) (518) . . . 12454
Mapletown (Montgomery) (4th) (518) . . . 13317
Maplewood (Albany) (3rd) (518) . . . 12189
Marathon (Cortland) (6th) (607) . . . 13803
Marbletown (Ulster) (3rd) (845) . . . 12401
Marcellus (Onondaga) (5th) (315) . . . 13108
Marcellus Falls (Onondaga) (5th) (315) . . . 13108
Marconiville (Suffolk) (10th) (631) . . . 11726
Marcy (Oneida) (5th) (315) . . . 13403
Margaretville (Delaware) (6th) (845) . . . 12455
Mariaville (Schenectady) (4th) (518) . . . 12137
Marietta (Onondaga) (5th) (315) . . . 13110
Marilla (Erie) (8th) (716) . . . 14102
Marion (Wayne) (7th) (315) . . . 14505
Marlborough (Ulster) (3rd) (845) . . . 12542
Marshall (Oneida) (5th) (315) . . . 13328
Marshville (Montgomery) (4th) (518) . . . 13317
Martindale Depot (Columbia) (3rd) (518) . . . 12521
Martinsburg (Lewis) (5th) (315) . . . 13404
Martisco (Onondaga) (5th) (315) . . . 13108

Martville (Cayuga) (7th) (315) ... 13111
Maryknoll (Westchester) (9th) (914) ... 10545
Maryland (Otsego) (6th) (607) ... 12116
Marymount (Westchester) (9th) (914) ... 10591
Masonville (Delaware) (6th) (607) ... 13804
Maspeth (Queens) (11th) (718) ... 11378
Massapequa (Nassau) (10th) (516) ... 11758
Massapequa Park (Nassau) (10th) (516) ... 11762
Massawepie (Franklin) (4th) (518) ... 12986
Massena (St. Lawrence) (4th) (315) ... 13662
Massena Center (St. Lawrence) (4th) (315) ... 13662
Massena Springs (St. Lawrence) (4th) (315) ... 13662
Mastic (Suffolk) (10th) (631) ... 11950
Mastic Beach (Suffolk) (10th) (631) ... 11951
Matinecock (Nassau) (10th) (516) ... 11560
Mattituck (Suffolk) (10th) (631) ... 11952
Mattydale (Onondaga) (5th) (315) ... 13211
Maybrook (Orange) (9th) (845) ... 12543
Mayfair (Schenectady) (4th) (518) ... 12302
Mayfield (Fulton) (4th) (518) ... 12117
Mayville (Chautauqua) (8th) (716) ... 14757
Maywood (Albany) (3rd) (518) ... 12205
McClure (Broome) (6th) (607) ... 13754
McConnellsville (Oneida) (5th) (315) ... 13401
McDonough (Chenango) (6th) (607) ... 13801
McGraw (Cortland) (6th) (607) ... 13101
McKeever (Herkimer) (5th) (315) ... 13427
McKeever (Oneida) (5th) (315) ... 13338
McKownville (Albany) (3rd) (518) ... 12203
McLean (Tompkins) (6th) (607) ... 13102
Meacham (Nassau) (10th) (516) ... 11003
Meadowmere Park (Nassau) (10th) (516) ... 11559
Mechanicville (Saratoga) (4th) (518) ... 12118
Mecklenburg (Schuyler) (6th) (607) ... 14863
Meco (Fulton) (4th) (518) ... 12078
Medford (Suffolk) (10th) (631) ... 11763
Medford Station (Suffolk) (10th) (631) ... 11763
Medina (Orleans) (8th) (585) ... 14103
Medusa (Albany) (3rd) (518) ... 12120
Mellenville (Columbia) (3rd) (518) ... 12544
Melrose (Rensselaer) (3rd) (518) ... 12121
Melrose Park (Cayuga) (7th) (315) ... 13021
Melville (Suffolk) (10th) (631) ... 11747, 11750, 11775
Memphis (Onondaga) (5th) (315) ... 13112
Menands (Albany) (3rd) (518) ... 12204
Mendon (Monroe) (7th) (585) ... 14506
Mentz (Cayuga) (7th) (315) ... 13140
Meredith (Delaware) (6th) (607) ... 13753
Meridale (Delaware) (6th) (607) ... 13806
Meridian (Cayuga) (7th) (315) ... 13113
Merrick (Nassau) (10th) (516) ... 11566
Merrickville (Delaware) (6th) (607) ... 13839
Merriewold (Sullivan) (3rd) (845) ... 12701
Merrifield (Cayuga) (7th) (315) ... 13147
Merrill (Clinton) (4th) (518) ... 12955
Merrillsville (Madison) (6th) (315) ... 13421
Messengerville (Cortland) (6th) (607) ... 13803
Mettacahonts (Ulster) (3rd) (845) ... 12404
Mexico (Oswego) (5th) (315) ... 13114
Mid Hudson (Orange) (9th) (845) ... 12555
Mid Island (Suffolk) (10th) (631) ... 11805
Middle Falls (Washington) (4th) (518) ... 12848
Middle Granville (Washington) (4th) (518) ... 12849
Middle Grove (Saratoga) (4th) (518) ... 12850
Middle Hope (Orange) (9th) (845) ... 12550
Middle Island (Suffolk) (10th) (631) ... 11953
Middle Village (Queens) (11th) (718) ... 11379
Middleburgh (Schoharie) (3rd) (518) ... 12122
Middlebury (Wyoming) (8th) (585) ... 14591
Middlefield (Otsego) (6th) (315) ... 13405
Middleport (Niagara) (8th) (716) ... 14105
Middlesex (Yates) (7th) (315) ... 14507
Middletown (Delaware) (6th) (607) ... 12455
Middletown (Orange) (9th) (845) ... 10940, 10941, 10943
Middleville (Herkimer) (5th) (315) ... 13406
Midwood (Kings) (2nd) (718) ... 11230
Milan (Dutchess) (9th) (845) ... 12571
Mileses (Sullivan) (3rd) (845) ... 12741
Milford (Otsego) (6th) (607) ... 13807
Milford Center (Otsego) (6th) (607) ... 13820
Mill Neck (Nassau) (10th) (516) ... 11765
Millbrook (Dutchess) (9th) (845) ... 12545
Miller Place (Suffolk) (10th) (631) ... 11764
Millers Mills (Herkimer) (5th) (315) ... 13491
Millerton (Dutchess) (9th) (518) ... 12546
Millport (Chemung) (6th) (607) ... 14864
Millwood (Westchester) (9th) (914) ... 10546
Milo (Yates) (7th) (315) ... 14527
Milton (Saratoga) (4th) (518) ... 12020
Milton (Ulster) (3rd) (845) ... 12547
Milton Center (Saratoga) (4th) (518) ... 12020
Mina (Chautauqua) (8th) (716) ... 14781
Minden (Montgomery) (4th) (518) ... 13339
Mindenville (Montgomery) (4th) (518) ... 13339
Mineola (Nassau) (10th) (516) ... 11501
Mineral Springs (Schoharie) (3rd) (518) ... 12043
Minerva (Essex) (4th) (518) ... 12851
Minetto (Oswego) (5th) (315) ... 13115
Mineville (Essex) (4th) (518) ... 12956
Minisink (Orange) (9th) (845) ... 10998
Minoa (Onondaga) (5th) (315) ... 13116
Mitchell Field (Nassau) (10th) (516) ... 11530, 11533
Model City (Niagara) (8th) (716) ... 14107
Modena (Ulster) (3rd) (845) ... 12548
Mohawk (Herkimer) (5th) (315) ... 13407
Mohawk (Montgomery) (4th) (518) ... 12068
Mohawk Hill (Oneida) (3rd) (315) ... 13309
Mohegan Lake (Westchester) (9th) (914) ... 10547
Mohonk Lake (Ulster) (3rd) (845) ... 12561
Moira (Franklin) (4th) (518) ... 12957
Mongaup Valley (Sullivan) (3rd) (845) ... 12762
Monroe (Orange) (9th) (845) ... 10949, 10950
Monsey (Rockland) (9th) (845) ... 10952
Montague (Lewis) (5th) (315) ... 13367
Montauk (Suffolk) (10th) (631) ... 11954
Montebello (Rockland) (9th) (845) ... 10901
Montezuma (Cayuga) (7th) (315) ... 13117
Montgomery (Orange) (9th) (845) ... 12549
Monticello (Sullivan) (3rd) (845) ... 12701, 12777
Montour (Schuyler) (6th) (607) ... 14865
Montour Falls (Schuyler) (6th) (607) ... 14865
Montrose (Westchester) (9th) (914) ... 10548
Montville (Cayuga) (7th) (315) ... 13118
Moody (Franklin) (4th) (518) ... 12986
Mooers (Clinton) (4th) (518) ... 12958
Mooers Forks (Clinton) (4th) (518) ... 12959
Moose River (Lewis) (5th) (315) ... 13433
Moravia (Cayuga) (7th) (315) ... 13118
Moreau (Saratoga) (4th) (518) ... 12801
Morehouse (Herkimer) (5th) (315) ... 13324
Morehouseville (Herkimer) (5th) (518) ... 13324
Moriah (Essex) (4th) (518) ... 12960
Moriah Center (Essex) (4th) (518) ... 12961
Moriah Corners (Essex) (4th) (518) ... 12960
Moriches (Suffolk) (10th) (631) ... 11955
Morley (St. Lawrence) (4th) (315) ... 13617
Morris (Otsego) (6th) (607) ... 13808
Morris Heights (Bronx) (12th) (718) ... 10453
Morris Park (Bronx) (12th) (718) ... 10461
Morrisania (Bronx) (12th) (718) ... 10456
Morrisonville (Clinton) (4th) (518) ... 12962
Morristown (St. Lawrence) (4th) (315) ... 13664
Morrisville (Madison) (6th) (315) ... 13408
Morrisville Station (Madison) (6th) (315) ... 13408
Morton (Orleans) (8th) (585) ... 14508
Mosherville (Saratoga) (4th) (518) ... 12074
Mosholu (Bronx) (12th) (718) ... 10467
Mott Haven (Bronx) (12th) (718) ... 10454
Mottville (Onondaga) (5th) (315) ... 13119
Mount Hope (Orange) (9th) (845) ... 10940
Mount Ivy (Rockland) (9th) (845) ... 10970
Mount Kisco (Westchester) (9th) (914) ... 10549
Mount Marion (Ulster) (3rd) (845) ... 12456
Mount McGregor (Saratoga) (4th) (518) ... 12866
Mount Merion Park (Ulster) (3rd) (845) ... 12456
Mount Morris (Livingston) (7th) (585) ... 14510
Mount Pleasant (Ulster) (3rd) (845) ... 12457
Mount Pleasant (Westchester) (9th) (914) ... 10582
Mount Ross (Dutchess) (9th) (518) ... 12567
Mount Sinai (Suffolk) (10th) (631) ... 11766
Mount Tremper (Ulster) (3rd) (845) ... 12457
Mount Upton (Chenango) (6th) (607) ... 13809
Mount Vernon (Westchester) (9th) (914) ... 1055#
Mount Vision (Otsego) (6th) (607) ... 13810
Mountain Dale (Sullivan) (3rd) (845) ... 12763
Mountain View (Franklin) (4th) (518) ... 12969
Mountainville (Orange) (9th) (845) ... 10953
Mumford (Monroe) (7th) (585) ... 14511
Munnsville (Madison) (6th) (315) ... 13409
Munsons Corners (Cortland) (6th) (607) ... 13045
Munsey Park (Nassau) (10th) (516) ... 11030
Munson (Nassau) (10th) (516) ... 11512
Murray (Orleans) (8th) (585) ... 14470
Murray Isle (Jefferson) (5th) (315) ... 13624
Muskalounge (Jefferson) (5th) (315) ... 13634
Muttontown (Nassau) (10th) (516) ... 11545, 117##
Myers (Tompkins) (6th) (607) ... 14866
Nanticoke (Broome) (6th) (607) ... 13802
Nanuet (Rockland) (9th) (845) ... 10954
Napanock (Ulster) (3rd) (845) ... 12458
Naples (Ontario) (7th) (585) ... 14512
Napoli (Cattaraugus) (8th) (716) ... 14755
Narrowsburg (Sullivan) (3rd) (845) ... 12764
Nassau (Rensselaer) (3rd) (518) ... 12123
Nassau Point (Suffolk) (10th) (631) ... 11935
Natural Bridge (Jefferson) (5th) (315) ... 13665
Natural Dam (St. Lawrence) (4th) (315) ... 13642
Navarino (Onondaga) (5th) (315) ... 13108
Nedrow (Onondaga) (5th) (315) ... 13120
Nehasane (Hamilton) (4th) (518) ... 12889
Nelliston (Montgomery) (4th) (518) ... 13410
Nelson (Madison) (6th) (315) ... 13035
Nelsonville (Putnam) (9th) (845) ... 10516
Neponsit (Queens) (11th) (718) ... 11694
Nesconset (Suffolk) (10th) (631) ... 11767
Neversink (Sullivan) (3rd) (845) ... 12765
Nevis (Dutchess) (9th) (845) ... 12583
New Albion (Cattaraugus) (8th) (716) ... 14719
New Baltimore (Greene) (3rd) (518) ... 12124
New Berlin (Chenango) (6th) (607) ... 13411
New Berlin Junction (Chenango) (6th) (607) ... 13733
New Bremen (Lewis) (5th) (315) ... 13367
New Brighton (Richmond) (13th) (718) ... 10310
New Castle (Westchester) (9th) (914) ... 10514
New Cassel (Nassau) (10th) (516) ... 11590
New City (Rockland) (9th) (845) ... 10956
New Dorp (Richmond) (13th) (718) ... 10306
New Hamburg (Dutchess) (9th) (845) ... 12590
New Hampton (Orange) (9th) (845) ... 10958
New Hartford (Oneida) (5th) (315) ... 13413
New Haven (Oswego) (5th) (315) ... 13121
New Hempstead (Rockland) (9th) (845) ... 10977
New Hudson (Allegany) (8th) (585) ... 14714
New Hyde Park (Nassau) (10th) (516) ... 11040, 11042
New Kingston (Delaware) (6th) (845) ... 12459
New Lebanon (Columbia) (3rd) (518) ... 12125
New Lebanon Center (Columbia) (3rd) (518) ... 12125
New Lisbon (Otsego) (6th) (607) ... 13415
New Lots (Kings) (2nd) (718) ... 11208
New Market (Niagara) (8th) (716) ... 14301
New Milford (Orange) (9th) (845) ... 10959
New Paltz (Ulster) (3rd) (845) ... 12561
New Rochelle (Westchester) (9th) (914) ... 1080#
New Russia (Essex) (4th) (518) ... 12964
New Scotland (Albany) (3rd) (518) ... 12127
New Square (Rockland) (9th) (845) ... 10977
New Suffolk (Suffolk) (10th) (631) ... 11956
New Windsor (Orange) (9th) (845) ... 12553
New Woodstock (Madison) (6th) (315) ... 13122
New York (New York) (1st) (212) ... 10###
New York City (Bronx) (12th) (212) ... 104##
New York City (Kings) (2nd) (718) ... 112##
New York City (New York) (1st) (212) ... 100##
New York City (Queens) (11th) (718) ... 11###
New York City (Richmond) (13th) (718) ... 103##
New York Mills (Oneida) (315) ... 13417
Newark (Wayne) (7th) (315) ... 14513
Newark Valley (Tioga) (6th) (607) ... 13811
Newburgh (Orange) (9th) (845) ... 1255#
Newcomb (Essex) (4th) (518) ... 12852, 12879
Newfane (Niagara) (8th) (716) ... 14108
Newfield (Tompkins) (6th) (607) ... 14867
Newport (Herkimer) (5th) (315) ... 13416
Newstead (Erie) (8th) (716) ... 14001
Newton Falls (St. Lawrence) (4th) (315) ... 13666
Newton Hook (Columbia) (3rd) (518) ... 12173
Newtonville (Albany) (3rd) (518) ... 12110, 12128
Niagara Falls (Niagara) (8th) (716) ... 1430#
Niagara University (Niagara) (8th) (716) ... 14109
Nichols (Tioga) (6th) (607) ... 13812
Nicholville (St. Lawrence) (4th) (315) ... 12965
Nile (Allegany) (8th) (585) ... 14739
Niles (Onondaga) (5th) (315) ... 13152
Nimmonsburg (Broome) (6th) (607) ... 13901
Nineveh (Broome) (6th) (607) ... 13813
Nineveh Junction (Chenango) (6th) (607) ... 13730
Niobe (Chautauqua) (8th) (716) ... 14758
Niskayuna (Schenectady) (4th) (518) ... 12309
Nissequogue (Suffolk) (10th) (631) ... 11780
Niverville (Columbia) (3rd) (518) ... 12130
Noblesboro (Herkimer) (5th) (315) ... 13324
Norfolk (St. Lawrence) (4th) (315) ... 13667
North Afton (Chenango) (6th) (607) ... 13730
North Amityville (Suffolk) (10th) (631) ... 11701
North Argyle (Washington) (4th) (518) ... 12809
North Babylon (Suffolk) (10th) (631) ... 11703
North Baldwin (Nassau) (10th) (516) ... 11510
North Bangor (Franklin) (4th) (518) ... 12966
North Bay (Oneida) (5th) (315) ... 13123
North Bay Shore (Suffolk) (10th) (631) ... 11706
North Bellmore (Nassau) (10th) (516) ... 11710
North Bellport (Suffolk) (10th) (631) ... 11713
North Blenheim (Schoharie) (3rd) (518) ... 12131
North Boston (Erie) (8th) (716) ... 14110
North Branch (Sullivan) (3rd) (845) ... 12766
North Bridgewater (Oneida) (5th) (315) ... 13318
North Broadalbin (Fulton) (4th) (518) ... 12025
North Brookfield (Madison) (6th) (315) ... 13418
North Castle (Westchester) (9th) (914) ... 10504
North Chatham (Columbia) (3rd) (518) ... 12132
North Chili (Monroe) (7th) (585) ... 14514
North Chittenango (Madison) (6th) (315) ... 13037
North Clymer (Chautauqua) (8th) (716) ... 14767
North Cohocton (Steuben) (585) ... 14808
North Collins (Erie) (8th) (716) ... 14111
North Columbia (Herkimer) (5th) (315) ... 13357
North Creek (Warren) (4th) (518) ... 12853
North Dansville (Livingston) (7th) (585) ... 14437
North East (Dutchess) (9th) (845) ... 12546
North Elba (Essex) (4th) (518) ... 12946
North Evans (Erie) (8th) (716) ... 14112
North Fenton (Broome) (6th) (607) ... 13746
North Franklin (Otsego) (6th) (607) ... 13820
North Granville (Washington) (4th) (518) ... 12854
North Greece (Monroe) (7th) (585) ... 14515
North Greenbush (Rensselaer) (3rd) (518) ... 12198
North Hannibal (Oswego) (5th) (315) ... 13126
North Harmony (Chautauqua) (8th) (716) ... 14785
North Harpersfield (Schoharie) (3rd) (518) ... 12093
North Haven (Suffolk) (10th) (631) ... 11963

North Hebron (Washington) (4th) (518) 12832
North Hempstead (Nassau) (10th) (516) 11040
North Highland (Putnam) (9th) (845) 10516
North Hills (Nassau) (10th) (516) 11040
North Hoosick (Rensselaer) (3rd) (518) 12133
North Hornell (Steuben) (7th) (607) 14843
North Hudson (Essex) (4th) (518) 12855
North Ilion (Herkimer) (5th) (315) 13340
North Java (Wyoming) (8th) (585) 14113
North Kortright (Delaware) (6th) (607) 13750
North Lawrence (St. Lawrence) (4th) (315) 12967
North Lindenhurst (Suffolk) (10th) (631) 11757
North Massapequa (Nassau) (10th) (516) 11758
North Merrick (Nassau) (10th) (516) 11566
North New Hyde Park (Nassau) (10th) (516) 11040, 11042
North Norwich (Chenango) (6th) (607) 13814
North Patchogue (Suffolk) (10th) (631) 11772
North Pelham (Westchester) (9th) (914) 10803
North Petersburg (Rensselaer) (3rd) (518) 12138
North Pharsalia (Chenango) (6th) (607) 13844
North Pitcher (Chenango) (6th) (607) 13124
North Pole (Essex) (4th) (518) 12946
North River (Warren) (4th) (518) 12856
North Rose (Wayne) (7th) (518) 14516
North Russell (St. Lawrence) (4th) (315) 13617
North Salem (Westchester) (9th) (914) 10560
North Sanford (Broome) (6th) (607) 13754
North Stockholm (St. Lawrence) (4th) (315) 13668
North Syracuse (Onondaga) (5th) (315) 13212
North Tarrytown (Westchester) (9th) (914) 10591
North Tonawanda (Niagara) (8th) (716) 14120
North Valley Stream (Nassau) (10th) (516) 11580
North Wantagh (Nassau) (10th) (516) 11793
North Western (Oneida) (5th) (315) 13419
North White Plains (Westchester) (9th) (914) 10603
North Wilmurt (Oneida) (5th) (315) 13438
North Winfield (Herkimer) (5th) (315) 13491
North Woodmere (Nassau) (10th) (516) 11581
Northampton (Fulton) (4th) (518) 12025
Northampton (Suffolk) (10th) (631) 11901
Northbush (Fulton) (4th) (518) 12095
Northfield (Delaware) (6th) (607) 13856
Northport (Suffolk) (10th) (631) 11768
Northside (Steuben) (7th) (607) 14830
Northumberland (Saratoga) (4th) (518) 12871
Northville (Fulton) (4th) (518) 12134
Northville (Suffolk) (10th) (631) 11091
Norton Hill (Greene) (3rd) (518) 12083
Norway (Herkimer) (5th) (315) 13416
Norwich (Chenango) (6th) (607) 13815
Norwood (St. Lawrence) (4th) (315) 13668
Nunda (Livingston) (7th) (585) 14517
Nyack (Rockland) (9th) (845) 10960
Oak Beach (Suffolk) (10th) (631) 11702
Oak Hill (Greene) (3rd) (518) 12460
Oak Island (Suffolk) (10th) (631) 11702
Oakdale (Suffolk) (10th) (631) 11769
Oakfield (Genesee) (8th) (585) 14125
Oakland Gardens (Queens) (11th) (718) 11364
Oaks Corners (Ontario) (7th) (315) 14518
Oaksville (Otsego) (6th) (607) 13337
Obernburg (Sullivan) (3rd) (845) 12767
Ocean Bay Park (Suffolk) (10th) (631) 11770
Ocean Beach (Suffolk) (10th) (631) 11770
Oceanside (Nassau) (10th) (516) 11572
Odessa (Schuyler) (6th) (607) 14869
Ogden (Monroe) (7th) (585) 14559
Ogdensburg (St. Lawrence) (4th) (315) 13669
Ohio (Herkimer) (5th) (315) 13324
Olcott (Niagara) (8th) (716) 14126
Old Bethpage (Nassau) (10th) (516) 11804
Old Brookville (Nassau) (10th) (516) 11545, 11548
Old Chatham (Columbia) (3rd) (518) 12136
Old Field (Suffolk) (10th) (631) 11733
Old Forge (Herkimer) (5th) (315) 13420
Old Mastic (Suffolk) (10th) (631) 11951
Old Village (Nassau) (10th) (516) 11023
Old Westbury (Nassau) (10th) (516) 11568
Old Westfield (Suffolk) (10th) (631) 11784
Olean (Cattaraugus) (8th) (716) 14760
Olive (Ulster) (3rd) (845) 12461
Olivebridge (Ulster) (3rd) (845) 12461
Oliverea (Ulster) (3rd) (845) 12410
Olmstedville (Essex) (4th) (518) 12857
Omar (Jefferson) (5th) (315) 13656
Onchiota (Franklin) (4th) (518) 12989
Oneida (Madison) (6th) (315) 13421
Oneida Castle (Madison) (6th) (315) 13421
Oneonta (Otsego) (6th) (607) 13820
Onondaga (Onondaga) (5th) (315) 13215
Onondaga Indian Reservation (Onondaga) (5th) (315) 12120
Onoville (Cattaraugus) (8th) (716) 14779
Ontario (Wayne) (7th) (315) 14519
Ontario Center (Wayne) (7th) (315) 14520
Oppenheim (Herkimer) (5th) (315) 13329
Oquaga Lake (Broome) (6th) (607) 13754
Oramel (Allegany) (8th) (585) 14765
Oran (Onondaga) (5th) (315) 13104
Orange (Schuyler) (6th) (607) 14812
Orangeburg (Rockland) (9th) (845) 10962
Orangetown (Rockland) (9th) (845) 10960
Orangeville (Wyoming) (8th) (585) 14569
Orchard Park (Erie) (8th) (716) 14127
Orient (Suffolk) (10th) (631) 11957
Orient Point (Suffolk) (10th) (631) 11957
Oriskany (Oneida) (5th) (315) 13424
Oriskany Falls (Oneida) (5th) (315) 13425
Orleans (Ontario) (7th) (585) 14432
Orwell (Oswego) (5th) (315) 13426
Oscawana (Westchester) (9th) (914) 10521
Oscawana Lake (Putnam) (9th) (854) 10579
Osceola (Lewis) (5th) (315) 13316
Ossian (Livingston) (7th) (585) 14437
Ossining (Westchester) (9th) (914) 10562
Oswegatchie (St. Lawrence) (4th) (315) 13670, 13691
Oswego (Oswego) (5th) (315) 13126
Oswego Center (Oswego) (5th) (315) 13126
Otego (Otsego) (6th) (607) 13825
Otisco (Onondaga) (5th) (315) 13159
Otisco Valley (Onondaga) (5th) (315) 13110
Otisville (Orange) (9th) (845) 10963
Otsdawa (Otsego) (6th) (607) 13825
Otsego (Otsego) (6th) (607) 13337
Otselic (Chenango) (6th) (315) 13072
Otter Creek (Lewis) (5th) (315) 13343
Otter Lake (Oneida) (5th) (315) 13338
Otto (Cattaraugus) (8th) (716) 14766
Ouaquaga (Broome) (6th) (607) 13826
Ovid (Seneca) (7th) (607) 14521
Owasco (Cayuga) (7th) (315) 13021
Owego (Tioga) (6th) (607) 13827
Owls Head (Franklin) (4th) (518) 12969
Oxbow (Jefferson) (5th) (315) 13608, 13671
Oxford (Chenango) (6th) (607) 13830
Oyster Bay (Nassau) (10th) (516) 11771
Oyster Bay Cove (Nassau) (10th) (516) 11771, 11791
Ozone Park (Queens) (11th) (718) 11416, 11417
Paddy Hill (Jefferson) (5th) (315) 13615
Paines Hollow (Herkimer) (5th) (315) 13407
Painted Post (Steuben) (7th) (607) 14870
Palatine (Montgomery) (4th) (518) 13428
Palatine Bridge (Montgomery) (4th) (518) 13428
Palenville (Greene) (3rd) (518) 12463
Palermo (Oswego) (5th) (315) 13069
Palisades (Rockland) (9th) (845) 10964
Palmer (Saratoga) (4th) (518) 12822
Palmyra (Wayne) (7th) (315) 14522
Pamelia (Jefferson) (5th) (315) 13637
Panama (Chautauqua) (8th) (716) 14767
Panamoka (Suffolk) (10th) (631) 11961
Panorama (Monroe) (7th) (585) 14625
Paradox (Essex) (4th) (518) 12858
Paris (Oneida) (5th) (315) 13456
Parish (Oswego) (5th) (315) 13107, 13131
Parishville (St. Lawrence) (4th) (315) 13672
Parishville Center (St. Lawrence) (4th) (315) 13676
Paris Station (Oneida) (5th) (315) 13430
Parma (Monroe) (7th) (585) 14468
Park Terrace (Broome) (6th) (607) 13903
Parkside (Queens) (11th) (718) 11375
Parksville (Sullivan) (3rd) (845) 12768
Patchogue (Suffolk) (10th) (631) 11772
Patchogue Highlands (Suffolk) (10th) (631) 11772
Patent (Otsego) (6th) (607) 13348
Patria (Schoharie) (3rd) (518) 12187
Patterson (Putnam) (9th) (845) 12563
Pattersonville (Schenectady) (4th) (518) 12137
Paul Smiths (Franklin) (4th) (518) 12970
Pavilion (Genesee) (8th) (585) 14525
Pawling (Dutchess) (9th) (845) 12564
Peakville (Delaware) (6th) (607) 13756
Pearl River (Rockland) (9th) (845) 10965
Peasleeville (Clinton) (4th) (518) 12985
Peconic (Suffolk) (10th) (631) 11958
Peekskill (Westchester) (9th) (914) 10566
Pelham (Westchester) (9th) (914) 10803
Pelham Manor (Westchester) (9th) (914) 10803
Pembroke (Genesee) (8th) (585) 14036
Pendleton (Niagara) (8th) (716) 14094, 14120, 14132
Penfield (Monroe) (7th) (585) 14526
Penn Yan (Yates) (7th) (315) 14527
Pennellville (Oswego) (5th) (315) 13132
Pepacton (Delaware) (6th) (607) 12776
Perch River (Jefferson) (5th) (315) 13634
Perinton (Monroe) (7th) (585) 14450
Perkinsville (Steuben) (7th) (585) 14529
Perry (Wyoming) (8th) (585) 14530
Perrys Mills (Clinton) (4th) (518) 12919
Perrysburg (Cattaraugus) (8th) (716) 14129
Perryville (Madison) (6th) (315) 13032
Persia (Cattaraugus) (8th) (716) 14070
Perth (Montgomery) (4th) (518) 12010
Peru (Clinton) (4th) (518) 12972
Peterboro (Madison) (6th) (315) 13134
Petersburgh (Rensselaer) (3rd) (518) 12138
Pharsalia (Chenango) (6th) (607) 13758
Phelps (Ontario) (7th) (315) 14532
Philadelphia (Jefferson) (5th) (315) 13673
Philipse Manor (Westchester) (9th) (914) 10591
Philipstown (Putnam) (9th) (845) 10516
Phillipsport (Sullivan) (3rd) (845) 12769
Philmont (Columbia) (3rd) (518) 12565
Phoenicia (Ulster) (3rd) (845) 12464
Phoenix (Oswego) (5th) (315) 13135
Piercefield (St. Lawrence) (4th) (518) 12973
Pierces Corner (St. Lawrence) (4th) (315) 13642
Pierceville (Madison) (6th) (315) 13334
Piermont (Rockland) (9th) (845) 10968
Pierrepont (St. Lawrence) (4th) (315) 13617
Pierrepont Manor (Jefferson) (5th) (315) 13674
Piffard (Livingston) (7th) (585) 14533
Pike (Wyoming) (8th) (585) 14130
Pilgrim (Bronx) (12th) (718) 10461
Pillar Point (Jefferson) (5th) (315) 13634
Pilot Knob (Washington) (4th) (518) 12844
Pinckney (Lewis) (5th) (315) 13610
Pine (Albany) (3rd) (518) 12203
Pine Air (Suffolk) (10th) (631) 11717
Pine Bush (Orange) (9th) (845) 12566
Pine City (Chemung) (6th) (607) 14871
Pine Grove (Lewis) (5th) (315) 13343
Pine Hill (Ulster) (3rd) (845) 12465
Pine Island (Orange) (9th) (845) 10969
Pine Lake (Fulton) (4th) (518) 12032
Pine Meadows (Oswego) (5th) (315) 13302
Pine Neck (Suffolk) (10th) (631) 11963
Pine Plains (Dutchess) (9th) (518) 12567
Pine Valley (Chemung) (6th) (607) 14872
Pine Woods (Madison) (5th) (315) 13310
Pineville (Delaware) (6th) (607) 13856
Pioneer (Saratoga) (4th) (518) 12020
Piseco (Hamilton) (4th) (518) 12139
Pitcairn (St. Lawrence) (4th) (315) 13648
Pitcher (Chenango) (6th) (607) 13136
Pittsfield (Chenango) (6th) (607) 13411
Pittsford (Monroe) (7th) (716) 14534
Pittstown (Rensselaer) (3rd) (518) 12094
Plainedge (Nassau) (10th) (516) 11756
Plainfield (Herkimer) (5th) (315) 13491
Plainview (Nassau) (10th) (516) 11803
Plainville (Onondaga) (5th) (315) 13137
Plandome (Nassau) (10th) (516) 11030
Plandome Heights (Nassau) (10th) (516) 11030
Plandome Manor (Nassau) (10th) (516) 11030
Plattekill (Ulster) (3rd) (845) 12568
Plattsburgh (Clinton) (4th) (518) 12901, 12903
Pleasant Valley (Dutchess) (9th) (845) 12569
Pleasantdale (Rensselaer) (3rd) (518) 12182
Pleasantville (Westchester) (9th) (914) 10570
Plessis (Jefferson) (5th) (315) 13675
Plymouth (Chenango) (6th) (607) 13832
Pocantico Hills (Westchester) (9th) (914) 10591
Poestenkill (Rensselaer) (3rd) (518) 12140
Point Chautauqua (Chautauqua) (8th) (585) 14728
Point Lookout (Nassau) (10th) (516) 11569
Point O Woods (Suffolk) (10th) (631) 11706
Point Pleasant (Monroe) (7th) (716) 14622
Point Richmond (Richmond) (13th) (718) 10302
Point Rock (Oneida) (5th) (315) 13471
Point Vivian (Jefferson) (5th) (315) 13607
Poland (Chautauqua) (8th) (716) 14747
Poland (Herkimer) (5th) (315) 13431
Pomfret (Chautauqua) (8th) (716) 14065
Pomona (Rockland) (9th) (845) 10970
Pomonok (Queens) (11th) (718) 11365
Pompey (Onondaga) (5th) (315) 13138
Pond Eddy (Sullivan) (3rd) (845) 12770
Poolville (Chenango) (6th) (607) 13332
Pope Mills (St. Lawrence) (4th) (315) 13654
Poplar Ridge (Cayuga) (7th) (315) 13139
Poquott (Suffolk) (10th) (631) 11733
Port Byron (Cayuga) (7th) (315) 13140
Port Chester (Westchester) (9th) (914) 10573
Port Crane (Broome) (6th) (607) 13833
Port Dickinson (Broome) (6th) (607) 13901
Port Ewen (Ulster) (3rd) (845) 12466
Port Gibson (Ontario) (7th) (315) 14537
Port Henry (Essex) (4th) (518) 12974
Port Jefferson (Suffolk) (10th) (631) 11777
Port Jefferson Station (Suffolk) (10th) (631) 11776, 11777
Port Jervis (Orange) (9th) (845) 12771, 12785
Port Kent (Essex) (4th) (518) 12975
Port Leyden (Lewis) (5th) (315) 13433
Port Ontario (Oswego) (5th) (315) 13142
Port Washington (Nassau) (10th) (516) 1105#
Portage (Livingston) (7th) (585) 14846
Portageville (Wyoming) (8th) (585) 14536
Porter (Niagara) (8th) (716) 14131
Porter Corners (Saratoga) (4th) (518) 12859
Porterville (Erie) (8th) (716) 14052
Portland (Chautauqua) (8th) (716) 14769
Portlandville (Otsego) (6th) (607) 13834
Portville (Cattaraugus) (8th) (716) 14770
Potsdam (St. Lawrence) (4th) (315) 13676, 13699
Potter (Yates) (7th) (315) 14527
Potter Hollow (Albany) (3rd) (518) 12467
Pottersville (Warren) (4th) (518) 12860
Poughkeepsie (Dutchess) (9th) (845) 1260#
Poughquag (Dutchess) (9th) (845) 12570
Pound Ridge (Westchester) (9th) (914) 10576

Pratts Hollow (Madison) (6th) (315) . . . 13409
Prattsburgh (Steuben) (7th) (607) . . . 14873
Prattsville (Greene) (3rd) (518) . . . 12468
Preble (Cortland) (6th) (607) . . . 13141
Preston (Chenango) (6th) (607) . . . 13830
Preston Hollow (Albany) (3rd) (518) . . . 12469
Prince (New York) (1st) (212) . . . 10012
Prince Bay (Richmond) (13th) (718) . . . 10309
Princetown (Schenectady) (4th) (518) . . . 12056
Promised Land (Suffolk) (10th) (631) . . . 11930
Prospect (Oneida) (5th) (315) . . . 13435
Providence (Saratoga) (4th) (518) . . . 12850
Pulaski (Oswego) (5th) (315) . . . 13142
Pulteney (Steuben) (7th) (607) . . . 14874
Pultneyville (Wayne) (7th) (315) . . . 14538
Purchase (Westchester) (9th) (914) . . . 10577
Purdy Station (Westchester) (9th) (914) . . . 10578
Purdys (Westchester) (9th) (914) . . . 10578
Purdys Mills (Clinton) (4th) (518) . . . 12910
Purling (Greene) (3rd) (518) . . . 12470
Putnam Lake (Putnam) (9th) (845) . . . 10509
Putnam Station (Washington) (4th) (518) . . . 12861
Putnam Valley (Putnam) (9th) (845) . . . 10579
Pyrites (St. Lawrence) (4th) (315) . . . 13677
Quaker Bridge (Cattaraugus) (8th) (716) . . . 14779
Quaker Springs (Saratoga) (4th) (518) . . . 12871
Quaker Street (Schenectady) (4th) (518) . . . 12141
Queens Village (Queens) (11th) (718) . . . 1142#
Queensbury (Warren) (4th) (518) . . . 12801, 12804
Quinneville (Broome) (6th) (607) . . . 13746
Quioque (Suffolk) (10th) (631) . . . 11978
Quogue (Suffolk) (10th) (631) . . . 11959
Radisson (Onondaga) (5th) (315) . . . 13027
Rainbow Lake (Franklin) (4th) (518) . . . 12976
Ramapo (Rockland) (9th) (845) . . . 10931
Randall (Montgomery) (4th) (518) . . . 12142
Randall's Island (New York) (1st) (212) . . . 10035
Randallsville (Madison) (6th) (315) . . . 13346
Randolph (Cattaraugus) (8th) (716) . . . 14772
Ransomville (Niagara) (8th) (716) . . . 14131
Raquette Lake (Hamilton) (4th) (518) . . . 13436
Rathbone (Steuben) (7th) (607) . . . 14801
Ravena (Albany) (3rd) (518) . . . 12143
Ray Brook (Essex) (4th) (518) . . . 12977
Raymertown (Rensselaer) (3rd) (518) . . . 12180
Raymondville (St. Lawrence) (4th) (315) . . . 13678
Readburn (Delaware) (6th) (607) . . . 13856
Reading (Schuyler) (6th) (607) . . . 14876
Reading Center (Schuyler) (6th) (607) . . . 14876
Reber (Essex) (4th) (518) . . . 12996
Red Creek (Wayne) (7th) (315) . . . 13143
Red Falls (Greene) (3rd) (518) . . . 12468
Red Hook (Dutchess) (9th) (845) . . . 12504, 12507, 12571
Red House (Cattaraugus) (8th) (716) . . . 14779
Red Mills (St. Lawrence) (4th) (315) . . . 13669
Red Rock (Columbia) (3rd) (518) . . . 12060
Redfield (Oswego) (5th) (315) . . . 13437
Redford (Clinton) (4th) (518) . . . 12978
Redwood (Jefferson) (5th) (315) . . . 13679
Rego Park (Queens) (11th) (718) . . . 11374
Reidsville (Albany) (3rd) (518) . . . 12186
Remsen (Oneida) (5th) (315) . . . 13438
Remsenburg (Suffolk) (10th) (631) . . . 11960
Rensselaer (Rensselaer) (3rd) (518) . . . 12144
Rensselaer Falls (St. Lawrence) (4th) (315) . . . 13680
Rensselaerville (Albany) (3rd) (518) . . . 12147
Retsof (Livingston) (7th) (585) . . . 14539
Rexford (Saratoga) (4th) (518) . . . 12008, 12148
Rexville (Steuben) (7th) (607) . . . 14877
Rhinebeck (Dutchess) (9th) (845) . . . 12572
Rhinecliff (Dutchess) (9th) (845) . . . 12574
Ricard (Oswego) (5th) (315) . . . 13302
Riceville (Fulton) (4th) (518) . . . 12078
Richburg (Allegany) (8th) (585) . . . 14774
Richfield (Otsego) (6th) (315) . . . 13439
Richfield Junction (Oneida) (5th) (315) . . . 13439
Richfield Springs (Otsego) (6th) (315) . . . 13439
Richford (Cortland) (6th) (315) . . . 13784
Richford (Tioga) (6th) (607) . . . 13835
Richland (Oswego) (5th) (315) . . . 13144
Richmond (Ontario) (7th) (585) . . . 14471
Richmond (Richmond) (13th) (718) . . . 103##
Richmond Hill (Queens) (11th) (718) . . . 11418
Richmondville (Schoharie) (3rd) (518) . . . 12149
Richville (St. Lawrence) (4th) (315) . . . 13681
Ridge (Suffolk) (10th) (631) . . . 11961
Ridge Mills (Oneida) (5th) (315) . . . 13440
Ridgebury (Orange) (9th) (845) . . . 10973
Ridgemont (Monroe) (7th) (585) . . . 14626
Ridgeway (Orleans) (8th) (585) . . . 14013
Ridgewood (Queens) (11th) (718) . . . 11385, 11386
Rifton (Ulster) (3rd) (845) . . . 12471
Riga (Monroe) (7th) (585) . . . 14428
Riley Cove (Saratoga) (4th) (518) . . . 12020
Rio (Orange) (9th) (845) . . . 12780
Riparius (Warren) (4th) (518) . . . 12862
Ripley (Chautauqua) (8th) (716) . . . 14775
Riverbank (Warren) (4th) (518) . . . 12885
Riverdale (Bronx) (12th) (718) . . . 10463, 10471
Riverhead (Suffolk) (10th) (631) . . . 11901
Rivers Edge (Suffolk) (10th) (631) . . . 11950
Riverside (Steuben) (7th) (607) . . . 14830, 14870
Riverview (Clinton) (4th) (518) . . . 12981
Rochdale (Dutchess) (9th) (845) . . . 12603
Rochdale (Queens) (11th) (718) . . . 11434
Rochester (Monroe) (7th) (585) . . . 146##
Rochester (Ulster) (3rd) (845) . . . 12404
Rochester Junction (Monroe) (7th) (585) . . . 14472
Rock City Falls (Saratoga) (4th) (518) . . . 12863
Rock Glen (Wyoming) (8th) (585) . . . 14550
Rock Hill (Sullivan) (3rd) (845) . . . 12775
Rock Stream (Schuyler) (7th) (607) . . . 14878
Rock Tavern (Orange) (9th) (845) . . . 12575
Rockaway Beach (Queens) (11th) (718) . . . 11693
Rockaway Park (Queens) (11th) (718) . . . 11694
Rockaway Point (Queens) (11th) (516) . . . 11697
Rockdale (Chenango) (6th) (607) . . . 13809
Rockhurst (Warren) (4th) (518) . . . 12820
Rockland (Rockland) (9th) (845) . . . 10962
Rockland (Sullivan) (3rd) (845) . . . 12776
Rockland Lake (Rockland) (9th) (845) . . . 10989
Rockroyal (Delaware) (6th) (607) . . . 13856
Rockville Centre (Nassau) (10th) (516) . . . 1157#
Rockwell Springs (Onondaga) (5th) (315) . . . 13120
Rockwells Mills (Chenango) (6th) (607) . . . 13843
Rockwood (Fulton) (4th) (518) . . . 12095
Rocky Point (Suffolk) (10th) (631) . . . 11778
Rodman (Jefferson) (5th) (315) . . . 13682
Rodman (Lewis) (5th) (315) . . . 13610
Roe Park (Westchester) (9th) (914) . . . 10566
Roessleville (Albany) (3rd) (518) . . . 12205
Rome (Oneida) (5th) (315) . . . 1344#
Romulus (Seneca) (7th) (607) . . . 14541
Ronkonkoma (Suffolk) (10th) (631) . . . 11749, 11779
Ronkonkoma West (Suffolk) (10th) (631) . . . 11779
Roosa Gap (Sullivan) (3rd) (845) . . . 12721
Roosevelt (Nassau) (10th) (516) . . . 11575
Roosevelt Field (Nassau) (10th) (516) . . . 11530, 11531
Roosevelt Island (New York) (1st) (212) . . . 10044
Rooseveltown (St. Lawrence) (4th) (315) . . . 13683
Root (Montgomery) (4th) (518) . . . 12166
Roscoe (Sullivan) (3rd) (607) . . . 12776
Rose (Wayne) (7th) (315) . . . 14542
Rosebank (Richmond) (13th) (718) . . . 10305
Roseboom (Otsego) (6th) (607) . . . 13450
Rosedale (Queens) (11th) (718) . . . 11422
Rose Hill (Onondaga) (5th) (315) . . . 13110
Rosendale (Ulster) (3rd) (845) . . . 12472
Roseton (Orange) (9th) (845) . . . 12576
Rosiere (Jefferson) (5th) (315) . . . 13618
Roslyn (Nassau) (10th) (516) . . . 11576
Roslyn Estates (Nassau) (10th) (516) . . . 11576
Roslyn Harbor (Nassau) (10th) (516) . . . 11545, 11548, 11576
Roslyn Heights (Nassau) (10th) (516) . . . 11577
Ross Corners (Broome) (6th) (607) . . . 13850
Rossburg (Allegany) (8th) (585) . . . 14776
Rossburg (Wyoming) (8th) (585) . . . 14536
Rossie (St. Lawrence) (4th) (315) . . . 13646
Rotterdam (Schenectady) (4th) (518) . . . 12303
Rotterdam Junction (Schenectady) (4th) (518) . . . 12150
Round Lake (Saratoga) (4th) (518) . . . 12151
Round Top (Greene) (3rd) (518) . . . 12473
Rouses Point (Clinton) (4th) (518) . . . 12979
Roxbury (Delaware) (6th) (607) . . . 12474
Royalton (Niagara) (8th) (716) . . . 14105
Ruby (Ulster) (3rd) (845) . . . 12475
Ruby Corner (St. Lawrence) (4th) (315) . . . 13646
Rural Grove (Montgomery) (4th) (518) . . . 12166
Rural Hill (Jefferson) (5th) (315) . . . 13650
Rush (Monroe) (7th) (585) . . . 14543
Rushford (Allegany) (8th) (585) . . . 14777
Rushville (Ontario) (7th) (315) . . . 14544
Rushville (Yates) (7th) (315) . . . 14544
Russell (St. Lawrence) (4th) (315) . . . 13684
Russell Gardens (Nassau) (10th) (516) . . . 11021
Russia (Herkimer) (5th) (315) . . . 13431
Rutland (Jefferson) (5th) (315) . . . 13638
Rye (Westchester) (9th) (914) . . . 10580
Rye Brook (Westchester) (9th) (914) . . . 10573
Sabael (Hamilton) (4th) (518) . . . 12864
Sabattis (Hamilton) (4th) (518) . . . 12847
Sabbath Day Point (Warren) (4th) (518) . . . 12874
Sacandaga (Fulton) (4th) (518) . . . 12134
Sackets Harbor (Jefferson) (5th) (315) . . . 13685
Saddle Rock (Nassau) (10th) (516) . . . 11023
Saddle Rock Estates (Nassau) (10th) (516) . . . 11021
Sag Harbor (Suffolk) (10th) (631) . . . 11963
Sagaponack (Suffolk) (10th) (631) . . . 11962
Saint Albans (Queens) (11th) (718) . . . 11412
Saint Armand (Essex) (4th) (518) . . . 12913
Saint Bonaventure (Cattaraugus) (8th) (716) . . . 14778
Saint George (Richmond) (13th) (718) . . . 10301
Saint Huberts (Essex) (4th) (518) . . . 12943
Saint James (Suffolk) (10th) (631) . . . 11780
Saint Johnsville (Montgomery) (4th) (518) . . . 13452
Saint Josephs (Sullivan) (3rd) (845) . . . 12777
Saint Lawrence Park (Jefferson) (5th) (315) . . . 13607
Saint Regis Falls (Franklin) (4th) (518) . . . 12980
Saint Regis Indian Reservation (Franklin) (4th) (518)
Saint Remy (Ulster) (3rd) (845) . . . 12401
Salamanca (Cattaraugus) (8th) (716) . . . 14779
Salem (Washington) (4th) (518) . . . 12865
Salem Center (Westchester) (9th) (914) . . . 10578
Salina (Onondaga) (5th) (315) . . . 13088
Salisbury (Herkimer) (5th) (315) . . . 13365
Salisbury Center (Herkimer) (5th) (315) . . . 13454
Salisbury Mills (Orange) (9th) (845) . . . 12577
Salt Point (Dutchess) (9th) (845) . . . 12578
Salt Springville (Otsego) (6th) (518) . . . 13320
Saltaire (Suffolk) (10th) (631) . . . 11706
Sammonsville (Montomery) (4th) (518) . . . 12068
Samsonville (Ulster) (3rd) (845) . . . 12461
San Remo (Suffolk) (10th) (631) . . . 11754
Sanborn (Niagara) (8th) (716) . . . 14132
Sand Hill (Montgomery) (4th) (518) . . . 13339
Sand Lake (Rensselaer) (3rd) (518) . . . 12153
Sandfordville (St. Lawrence) (4th) (315) . . . 13676
Sands Point (Nassau) (10th) (516) . . . 11050
Sandusky (Cattaraugus) (8th) (716) . . . 14065, 14133
Sandy Beach (Erie) (8th) (716) . . . 14072
Sandy Creek (Oswego) (5th) (315) . . . 13145
Sandy Hill (Washington) (4th) (518) . . . 12839
Sanford (Broome) (6th) (607) . . . 13754
Sangerfield (Oneida) (5th) (315) . . . 13455
Sanitaria Springs (Broome) (6th) (607) . . . 13833
Santa Clara (Franklin) (4th) (518) . . . 12980
Saranac (Clinton) (4th) (518) . . . 12981
Saranac Inn (Franklin) (4th) (518) . . . 12982
Saranac Lake (Essex) (4th) (518) . . . 12983
Saranac Lake (Franklin) (4th) (518) . . . 12983
Saratoga (Saratoga) (4th) (518) . . . 12866
Saratoga Springs (Saratoga) (4th) (518) . . . 12866
Sardinia (Erie) (8th) (716) . . . 14134
Saugerties (Ulster) (3rd) (845) . . . 12477
Sauquoit (Oneida) (5th) (315) . . . 13456
Savannah (Wayne) (7th) (315) . . . 13146
Savona (Steuben) (7th) (607) . . . 14879
Sayville (Suffolk) (10th) (631) . . . 11782
Scarborough (Westchester) (9th) (914) . . . 10510
Scarsdale (Westchester) (9th) (914) . . . 10583
Scarsdale Park (Westchester) (9th) (914) . . . 10583
Schaghticoke (Rensselaer) (3rd) (518) . . . 12154
Schenectady (Schenectady) (4th) (518) . . . 1230#, 12325, 12345
Schenevus (Otsego) (6th) (607) . . . 12155
Schodack (Rensselaer) (3rd) (518) . . . 12033
Schodack Landing (Rensselaer) (3rd) (518) . . . 12156
Schoharie (Schoharie) (3rd) (518) . . . 12157
Schroeppel (Oswego) (5th) (315) . . . 12135
Schroon (Essex) (4th) (518) . . . 12870
Schroon Lake (Essex) (4th) (518) . . . 12870
Schuyler (Herkimer) (5th) (315) . . . 13340, 13502
Schuyler Falls (Clinton) (4th) (518) . . . 12985
Schuyler Lake (Otsego) (6th) (315) . . . 13457
Schuylerville (Saratoga) (4th) (518) . . . 12871
Scio (Allegany) (8th) (585) . . . 14880
Sciota (Clinton) (4th) (518) . . . 12992
Scipio (Cayuga) (7th) (315) . . . 13147
Scipio Center (Cayuga) (7th) (315) . . . 13147
Scipioville (Cayuga) (7th) (315) . . . 13147
Scoreball (Erie) (8th) (716) . . . 14276
Scotchbush (Montgomery) (4th) (518) . . . 13452
Scotchtown (Orange) (9th) (845) . . . 10940, 10941
Scotia (Schenectady) (4th) (518) . . . 12302
Scott (Cortland) (6th) (607) . . . 13077
Scotts Beach (Suffolk) (10th) (631) . . . 11789
Scotts Corners (Westchester) (9th) (914) . . . 10576
Scottsburg (Livingston) (7th) (585) . . . 14545
Scottsville (Monroe) (7th) (585) . . . 14546
Scranton (Erie) (8th) (716) . . . 14075
Scriba (Oswego) (5th) (315) . . . 13126
Scriba Center (Oswego) (5th) (315) . . . 13126
Scribner Corners (Madison) (6th) (315) . . . 13421
Sea Breeze (Monroe) (7th) (585) . . . 14617
Sea Cliff (Nassau) (10th) (516) . . . 11579
Seaford (Nassau) (10th) (516) . . . 11783
Seager (Ulster) (3rd) (845) . . . 12406
Sears Corners (Putnam) (9th) (845) . . . 10509
Seaview (Suffolk) (10th) (631) . . . 11770
Seifert Corners (Oneida) (5th) (315) . . . 13440
Selden (Suffolk) (10th) (631) . . . 11784
Selkirk (Albany) (3rd) (518) . . . 12158
Sempronius (Cayuga) (7th) (315) . . . 13118
Seneca (Ontario) (7th) (315) . . . 14561
Seneca Castle (Ontario) (7th) (315) . . . 14547
Seneca Falls (Seneca) (7th) (315) . . . 13148
Seneca Hill (Oswego) (5th) (315) . . . 13126
Sennett (Cayuga) (7th) (315) . . . 13021
Sentinel Heights (Onondaga) (5th) (315) . . . 13078
Setauket (Suffolk) (10th) (631) . . . 11733
Severance (Essex) (4th) (518) . . . 12872
Seward (Schoharie) (3rd) (518) . . . 12043
Shackport (Delaware) (6th) (607) . . . 13757
Shady (Ulster) (3rd) (845) . . . 12409
Shandaken (Ulster) (3rd) (845) . . . 12480
Sharon (Schoharie) (3rd) (518) . . . 13459
Sharon Springs (Schoharie) (3rd) (518) . . . 13459
Shavertown (Delaware) (6th) (845)
Shawangunk (Ulster) (3rd) (845) . . . 12589
Sheds (Madison) (6th) (315) . . . 13122
Shekomeko (Dutchess) (9th) (518) . . . 12567

Shelby (Orleans) (8th) (585) 14105
Sheldon (Wyoming) (8th) (585) 14145
Shelter Island (Suffolk) (10th) (631) 11964
Shelter Island Heights (Suffolk) (10th) (631) 11965
Shenorock (Westchester) (9th) (914) 10587
Sherburne (Chenango) (6th) (607) 13460
Sheridan (Chautauqua) (8th) (716) 14135
Sherman (Chautauqua) (8th) (716) 14781
Sherrill (Oneida) (5th) (315) 13461
Sherwin Bay (Jefferson) (5th) (315) 13634
Shinhopple (Delaware) (6th) (607) 13837
Shinnecock Hills (Suffolk) (10th) (631) 11968
Shinnecock Indian Reservation (Suffolk) (10th) (631)
Shirley (Suffolk) (10th) (631) 11967
Shokan (Ulster) (3rd) (845) 12481
Shoreham (Suffolk) (10th) (631) 11786
Shortsville (Ontario) (7th) (585) 14548
Shrub Oak (Westchester) (9th) (914) 10588
Shushan (Washington) (4th) (518) 12873
Sidney (Delaware) (6th) (607) 13838
Sidney Center (Delaware) (6th) (607) 13839
Siena (Albany) (3rd) (518) 12211
Silver Bay (Warren) (4th) (518) 12874
Silver Creek (Chautauqua) (8th) (716) 14136
Silver Lake (Orange) (9th) (845) 10940
Silver Lake (Wyoming) (8th) (585) 14549
Silver Springs (Wyoming) (8th) (585) 14550
Simpsonville (Otsego) (6th) (607) 12155
Sinclairville (Chautauqua) (8th) (716) 14782
Sissonville (St. Lawrence) (4th) (315) 13676
Skaneateles (Onondaga) (5th) (315) 13152
Skaneateles Falls (Onondaga) (5th) (315) 13119, 13153
Slab City (St. Lawrence) (4th) (315) 13676
Slate Hill (Orange) (9th) (845) 10973
Slaterville Springs (Tompkins) (6th) (607) 14881
Slateville (Washington) (4th) (518) 12832
Sleepy Hollow (Westchester) (9th) (914) 10591
Slingerlands (Albany) (3rd) (518) 12159
Sloan (Erie) (8th) (716) 14212
Sloansville (Schoharie) (3rd) (518) 12160
Sloatsburg (Rockland) (9th) (845) 10974
Smallwood (Sullivan) (3rd) (845) 12778
Smartville (Oswego) (5th) (315) 13083
Smithboro (Tioga) (6th) (607) 13840
Smithfield (Madison) (6th) (315) 13134
Smiths Basin (Washington) (4th) (518) 12839
Smiths Point (Suffolk) (10th) (631) 11967
Smithtown (Suffolk) (10th) (631) 11787, 11788
Smithtown Branch (Suffolk) (10th) (631) 11787
Smithville (Chenango) (6th) (607) 13778
Smithville (Jefferson) (5th) (315) 13605
Smithville Flats (Chenango) (6th) (607) 13841
Smyrna (Chenango) (6th) (607) 13464
Snowden (Otsego) (6th) (607) 13348
Snyder (Erie) (8th) (716) 14215, 14226
Snyder Square (Erie) (8th) (716) 14226
Snyders Corners (Rensselaer) (3rd) (518) 12180
Snyders Lake (Rensselaer) (3rd) (518) 12180
Sodus (Wayne) (7th) (315) 14551
Sodus Center (Wayne) (7th) (315) 14551
Sodus Point (Wayne) (7th) (315) 14555
Solon (Cortland) (6th) (607) 13055
Solsville (Madison) (6th) (315) 13465
Solvay (Onondaga) (5th) (315) 13209
Somers (Westchester) (9th) (914) 10589
Somerset (Niagara) (8th) (716) 14012
Somerville (St. Lawrence) (4th) (315) 13642
Sonyea (Livingston) (7th) (585) 14556
Sound Avenue (Suffolk) (10th) (631) 11901
Sound Beach (Suffolk) (10th) (631) 11789
South Albion (Oswego) (5th) (315) 13302
South Apalachin (Tioga) (6th) (607) 13732
South Argyle (Washington) (4th) (518) 12809
South Bay (Madison) (6th) (315) 13302
South Bay Village (Washington) (4th) (518) 12827
South Berne (Albany) (3rd) (518) 12023
South Bethlehem (Albany) (3rd) (518) 12161
South Bolivar (Allegany) (8th) (585) 14715
South Bombay (Franklin) (4th) (518) 12957
South Bristol (Ontario) (7th) (315) 14512
South Brookfield (Madison) (6th) (315) 13485
South Butler (Wayne) (7th) (315) 13154
South Byron (Genesee) (8th) (585) 14557
South Cairo (Greene) (3rd) (518) 12482
South Cheektowaga (Erie) (8th) (716) 14227
South Colton (St. Lawrence) (4th) (315) 13687
South Columbia (Otsego) (6th) (315) 13439
South Corning (Steuben) (7th) (607) 14830
South Danby (Tioga) (6th) (607) 13864
South Dayton (Cattaraugus) (8th) (716) 14138
South Durham (Greene) (3rd) (518) 12405
South Edmeston (Chenango) (6th) (607) 13411
South Edwards (St. Lawrence) (4th) (315) 13635
South Fallsburg (Sullivan) (3rd) (845) 12779
South Farmingdale (Nassau) (10th) (516) 11735
South Floral Park (Nassau) (10th) (516) 11001
South Gilboa (Schoharie) (3rd) (518) 12167
South Glens Falls (Saratoga) (4th) (518) 12803
South Granville (Washington) (4th) (518) 12832
South Hamilton (Chenango) (6th) (607) 13332
South Hammond (St. Lawrence) (4th) (315) 13646
South Hannibal (Oswego) (5th) (315) 13074
South Hartford (Washington) (4th) (518) 12838
South Hauppauge (Suffolk) (10th) (631) 11722
South Haven (Suffolk) (10th) (631) 11719
South Hempstead (Nassau) (10th) (516) 11550
South Huntington (Suffolk) (10th) (631) 11746
South Ilion (Herkimer) (5th) (315) 13357
South Jamesport (Suffolk) (10th) (631) 11970
South Kortright (Delaware) (6th) (607) 13842
South Lansing (Tompkins) (6th) (607) 14882
South Lebanon (Chenango) (6th) (607) 13332
South Lima (Livingston) (7th) (585) 14558
South Millbrook (Dutchess) (9th) (845)
South New Berlin (Chenango) (6th) (607) 13843
South Ninevah (Broome) (6th) (607) 13787
South Nyack (Rockland) (9th) (845) 10960
South Onondaga (Onondaga) (5th) (315) 13120
South Otselic (Chenango) (6th) (315) 13155
South Owego (Tioga) (6th) (607) 13827
Souht Oxford (Chenango) (6th) (607) 13830
South Ozone Park (Queens) (11th) (718) 11420, 11436
South Plattsburgh (Clinton) (4th) (518) 12901
South Plymouth (Chenango) (6th) (607) 13844
South Richmond Hill (Queens) (11th) (718) 11419
South Russell (St. Lawrence) (4th) (315) 13684
South Rutland (Jefferson) (5th) (315) 13626
South Salem (Westchester) (9th) (914) 10590
South Schenectady (Schenectady) (4th) (518) 12303
South Schodack (Rensselaer) (3rd) (518) 12033
South Schroon (Essex) (4th) (518) 12877
South Setauket (Suffolk) (10th) (631) 11720
South Trenton (Oneida) (5th) (315) 13304
South Valley (Cattaraugus) (8th) (716) 14779
South Valley (Otsego) (6th) (607) 13320
South Vestal (Broome) (6th) (607) 13850
South Wales (Erie) (8th) (716) 14139
South Westbury (Nassau) (10th) (516) 11590
South Westerlo (Greene) (3rd) (518) 12083
South Worcester (Otsego) (6th) (607) 12197
Southampton (Suffolk) (10th) (631) 11968, 11969
Southeast (Putnam) (9th) (845) 10509
Southfields (Orange) (9th) (845) 10975
Southold (Suffolk) (10th) (631) 11971
Southport (Chemung) (6th) (607) 14904
Southwest Oswego (Oswego) (5th) (315) 13126
Spafford (Onondaga) (5th) (607) 13077
Sparkill (Rockland) (9th) (845) 10976
Sparrow Bush (Orange) (9th) (845) 12780
Sparta (Livingston) (7th) (585) 10562
Speculator (Hamilton) (4th) (518) 12164
Speedsville (Tioga) (6th) (607) 13736
Speigletown (Rensselaer) (3rd) (518) 12180, 12182
Spencer (Tioga) (6th) (607) 14883
Spencer Settlement (Oneida) (5th) (315) 13440
Spencerport (Monroe) (7th) (585) 14559
Spencertown (Columbia) (3rd) (518) 12165
Speonk (Suffolk) (10th) (631) 11972
Spinnerville (Herkimer) (5th) (315) 13357
Split Rock (Onondaga) (5th) (315) 13031
Sprague ville (St. Lawrence) (4th) (315) 13689
Sprakers (Montgomery) (4th) (518) 12166
Spring Brook (Erie) (8th) (716) 14140
Spring Glen (Ulster) (3rd) (845) 12483
Spring Valley (Rockland) (9th) (845) 10977
Springfield (Otsego) (6th) (607) 13468
Springfield Center (Otsego) (6th) (315) 13468
Springfield Gardens (Queens) (11th) (718) 11413
Springport (Cayuga) (7th) (315) 13160
Springvale (Chenango) (6th) (607) 13815
Springville (Erie) (8th) (716) 14141
Springwater (Livingston) (7th) (585) 14560
Sprout Brook (Montgomery) (4th) (518) 13317
Spruceton (Greene) (3rd) (518) 12492
Spuyten Duyvil (Bronx) (12th) (718) 10463
Staatsburgh (Dutchess) (9th) (845) 12580
Stacy Basin (Oneida) (5th) (315) 13054
Stafford (Genesee) (8th) (585) 14143
Stamford (Delaware) (6th) (607) 12167
Standish (Clinton) (4th) (518) 12952
Stanford (Dutchess) (9th) (845) 12581
Stanfordville (Dutchess) (9th) (845) 12581
Stanley (Ontario) (7th) (585) 14561
Stanwix (Oneida) (5th) (315) 13440
Stanwix Heights (Oneida) (5th) (315) 13440
Stapleton (Richmond) (13th) (718) 10304
Star Lake (St. Lawrence) (4th) (315) 13690
Stark (Herkimer) (5th) (315) 13339
Starkey (Yates) (7th) (607) 14837
Starkville (Montgomery) (4th) (518) 13339
Staten Island (Richmond) (13th) (718) 1030#, 1031#
State School (Orange) (9th) (845) 10990
Steamburg (Cattaraugus) (8th) (716) 14783
Stella (Broome) (6th) (607) 13905, 13790
Stella Niagara (Niagara) (8th) (716) 14092, 14144
Stephentown (Rensselaer) (3rd) (518) 12168, 12169
Stephentown Center (Renssalaer) (518) 12168
Sterling (Cayuga) (7th) (315) 13156
Sterling Forest (Orange) (9th) (845) 10979
Sterlington (Orange) (9th) (845) 10974
Stetsonville (Otsego) (6th) (607) 13415
Steuben (Oneida) (5th) (315) 13354
Steuben Valley (Oneida) (5th) (315) 13354
Stevers Mills (Fulton) (4th) (518) 12025
Stewart Manor (Nassau) (10th) (516) 11530
Stilesville (Broome) (6th) (607) 13754
Stillwater (Saratoga) (4th) (518) 12170
Stittville (Oneida) (5th) (315) 13469
Stockbridge (Madison) (6th) (315) 13409
Stockholm (St. Lawrence) (4th) (315) 13697
Stockport (Columbia) (3rd) (518) 12171
Stockton (Chautauqua) (8th) (716) 14784
Stockwell (Oneida) (5th) (315) 13480
Stokes (Oneida) (5th) (315) 13363
Stone Arabia (Montgomery) (4th) (518) 13339
Stone Mills (Jefferson) (5th) (315) 13656
Stone Ridge (Ulster) (3rd) (845) 12484
Stony Brook (Suffolk) (10th) (631) 11790, 11794
Stony Creek (Warren) (4th) (518) 12878
Stony Point (Rockland) (9th) (845) 10980
Stony Wold (Franklin) (4th) (518) 12968
Stoodley Corners (Schenectady) (4th) (518) 12302
Stormville (Dutchess) (9th) (845) 12582
Stottville (Columbia) (3rd) (518) 12172
Stow (Chautauqua) (8th) (716) 14785
Straits Corners (Tioga) (6th) (607) 13827
Stratford (Fulton) (4th) (315) 13470
Strathmore (Nassau) (10th) (516) 11030
Streetroad (Essex) (4th) (518) 12883
Strongs Neck (Suffolk) (10th) (631) 11733
Strykersville (Wyoming) (8th) (585) 14145
Sturges Corner (Delaware) (6th) (607) 13750
Stuyvesant (Columbia) (3rd) (518) 12173
Stuyvesant Falls (Columbia) (3rd) (518) 12174
Suffern (Rockland) (9th) (845) 10901, 10952
Sugar Loaf (Orange) (9th) (845) 10981
Sullivan (Madison) (6th) (315) 13037
Summerhill (Cayuga) (7th) (315) 13092
Summit (Schoharie) (3rd) (518) 12175
Summitville (Sullivan) (3rd) (845) 12781
Sundown (Sullivan) (3rd) (845) 12740
Sundown (Ulster) (3rd) (845) 12782
Sunken Meadow (Suffolk) (10th) (631) 11768
Sunmount (Franklin) (4th) (518) 12986
Sunnyside (Queens) (11th) (718) 11104
Sunset Bay (Chautauqua) (8th) (716) 14712
Surprise (Greene) (3rd) (518) 12176
Swain (Allegany) (8th) (585) 14884
Swan Lake (Sullivan) (3rd) (845) 12783
Swastika (Clinton) (4th) (518) 12985
Sweden (Monroe) (7th) (585) 14420
Swormville (Erie) (8th) (716) 14051
Sycaway (Rensselaer) (3rd) (518) 12180
Sylvan Beach (Oneida) (5th) (315) 13157
Syosset (Nassau) (10th) (516) 11773, 11791
Syracuse (Onondaga) (5th) (315) 132##
Taberg (Oneida) (5th) (315) 13471
Taborton (Rensselaer) (3rd) (518) 12153
Taconic Lake (Rensselaer) (3rd) (518) 12138
Taghkanic (Columbia) (3rd) (518) 12523
Tahawus (Essex) (4th) (518) 12879
Talcottville (Oneida) (5th) (315) 13309
Tallman (Rockland) (9th) (845) 10982
Tannersville (Greene) (3rd) (518) 12424, 12485
Tappan (Rockland) (9th) (845) 10983
Tarrytown (Westchester) (9th) (914) 10591
Taunton (Onondaga) (5th) (315) 13219
Taylor (Cortland) (6th) (607) 13040
Ten Mile River (Sullivan) (3rd) (845) 12764
Terryville (Suffolk) (10th) (631) 11776
Texas Valley (Cortland) (6th) (607) 13803
The Glen (Warren) (4th) (518) 12885
The Terrace (Nassau) (10th) (516) 11050
The Vly (Ulster) (3rd) (845) 12484
Thendara (Herkimer) (5th) (315) 13472
Theresa (Jefferson) (5th) (315) 13691
Thiells (Rockland) (9th) (845) 10984
Thomaston (Nassau) (10th) (516) 11021
Thompson (Sullivan) (3rd) (845) 12701
Thompson Ridge (Orange) (9th) (845) 10985
Thompsons Lake (Albany) (3rd) (518) 12009
Thompsonville (Sullivan) (3rd) (845) 12784
Thomson (Washington) (4th) (518) 12834
Thornwood (Westchester) (9th) (914) 10594
Thousand Island Park (Jefferson) (5th) (315) 13692
Three Mile Bay (Jefferson) (5th) (315) 13693
Throggs Neck (Bronx) (12th) (718) 10465
Throop (Cayuga) (7th) (315) 13021
Thurman (Warren) (4th) (518) 12885
Thurston (Steuben) (7th) (607) 14821
Ticonderoga (Essex) (4th) (518) 12858, 12883
Tillson (Ulster) (3rd) (845) 12486
Tilly Forster (Putnam) (9th) (845) 10509
Tioga (Tioga) (6th) (607) 13845
Tioga Center (Tioga) (6th) (607) 13845
Tiona (Tioga) (6th) (607) 13811
Tivoli (Dutchess) (9th) (845) 12583
Tomkins Cove (Rockland) (9th) (845) 10986
Tompkins (Broome) (6th) (607) 13754
Tompkins Corners (Putnam) (9th) (845) 10579

Tonawanda (Erie) (8th) (716) ... 1415#, 142##
Tonawanda Indian Reservation (Erie) (8th) (716)
Tonawanda Indian Reservation (Genesee) (8th) (585)
Tonawanda Indian Reservation (Niagara) (8th) (716)
Torrey (Yates) (7th) (315) ... 14441
Tottenville (Richmond) (13th) (718) ... 10307
Towners (Putnam) (9th) (845) ... 12563
Town Branch (Orange) (9th) (845) ... 12550
Town Line (Erie) (8th) (716) ... 14165
Townline (Erie) (8th) (716) ... 14004
Tracy Creek (Broome) (6th) (607) ... 13850
Trainsmeadow (Queens) (11th) (718) ... 11370
Treadwell (Delaware) (6th) (607) ... 13846
Trenton (Oneida) (5th) (315) ... 13304
Triangle (Chenango) (6th) (607) ... 13778
Tribes Hill (Montgomery) (4th) (518) ... 12177
Troupsburg (Steuben) (7th) (607) ... 14885
Trout Creek (Delaware) (6th) (607) ... 13847
Trout Lake (Warren) (4th) (518) ... 12824
Trout River (Franklin) (4th) (518) ... 12926
Troy (Rensselaer) (3rd) (518) ... 1218#
Trumansburg (Tompkins) (6th) (607) ... 14886
Truthville (Washington) (4th) (518) ... 12832
Truxton (Cortland) (6th) (607) ... 13056, 13158
Tuckahoe (Westchester) (9th) (914) ... 10707
Tully (Onondaga) (5th) (315) ... 13159
Tunnel (Broome) (6th) (607) ... 13848
Tupper Lake (Franklin) (4th) (518) ... 12986
Turin (Lewis) (5th) (315) ... 13473
Turnwood (Ulster) (3rd) (845) ... 12758
Tuscarora (Livingston) (7th) (585) ... 14510
Tuscarora (Steuben) (7th) (607) ... 14801
Tuscarora Indian Reservation (Niagara) (8th) (716)
Tusten (Sullivan) (3rd) (845) ... 12764
Tuxedo (Orange) (9th) (845) ... 10987
Tuxedo Park (Orange) (9th) (845) ... 10987
Twin Orchards (Broome) (6th) (607) ... 13850
Tyner (Chenango) (6th) (607) ... 13830
Tyre (Seneca) (7th) (315) ... 13148
Tyrone (Schuyler) (6th) (607) ... 14887
Ulster (Ulster) (3rd) (845) ... 12401
Ulster Park (Ulster) (3rd) (845) ... 12487
Ulysses (Tompkins) (6th) (607) ... 14886
Unadilla (Otsego) (6th) (607) ... 13849
Unadilla Forks (Herkimer) (5th) (315) ... 13491
Union (Broome) (6th) (607) ... 13763
Union Center (Broome) (6th) (607) ... 13760
Union Hill (Wayne) (7th) (585) ... 14563
Union Mills (Fulton) (4th) (518) ... 12025
Union Springs (Cayuga) (7th) (315) ... 13160
Union Vale (Dutchess) (9th) (845) ... 12585
Uniondale (Nassau) (10th) (516) ... 11553, 11555, 11556
Unionville (Orange) (9th) (845) ... 10988
University Gardens (Nassau) (10th) (516) ... 11020
University Heights (Bronx) (12th) (718) ... 10452
Upper Brookville (Nassau) (10th) (516) ... 11545, 11732, 11771
Upper Grandview (Rockland) (9th) (845) ... 10960
Upper Jay (Essex) (4th) (518) ... 12987
Upper Lisle (Broome) (6th) (607) ... 13862
Upper Nyack (Rockland) (9th) (845) ... 10960
Upper Saint Regis (Franklin) (4th) (518) ... 12945
Upper Union (Schenectady) (4th) (518) ... 12309
Upperville (Chenango) (6th) (607) ... 13464
Upton (Suffolk) (10th) (631) ... 11973
Urbana (Steuben) (7th) (607) ... 14840
Ushers (Saratoga) (4th) (518) ... 12151
Utica (Oneida) (5th) (315) ... 1350#, 13599
Utopia (Queens) (11th) (718) ... 11366
Vail Mills (Fulton) (4th) (518) ... 12025
Vails Gate (Orange) (9th) (845) ... 12584
Valatie (Columbia) (3rd) (518) ... 12184
Valcour (Clinton) (4th) (518) ... 12972
Valhalla (Westchester) (9th) (914) ... 10595
Valley Cottage (Rockland) (9th) (845) ... 10989
Valley Falls (Rensselaer) (3rd) (518) ... 12185
Valley Mills (Madison) (6th) (315) ... 13409
Valley Stream (Nassau) (10th) (516) ... 11580, 11581, 11582
Vallonia Springs (Broome) (6th) (607) ... 13813
Valois (Schuyler) (6th) (607) ... 14841
Van Buren (Onondaga) (5th) (315) ... 13027
Van Buren Bay (Chautauqua) (8th) (716) ... 14048, 14166
Van Buren Point (Chautauqua) (8th) (716) ... 14166
Van Cott (Bronx) (12th) (718) ... 10467
Van Deusenville (Montgomery) (4th) (518) ... 13317
Van Etten (Chemung) (6th) (607) ... 14889
Van Hornesville (Herkimer) (5th) (315) ... 13475
Varick (Seneca) (7th) (315) ... 14541
Varysburg (Wyoming) (8th) (585) ... 14167
Vega (Delaware) (6th) (518) ... 12445
Venice (Cayuga) (7th) (315) ... 13147
Venice Center (Cayuga) (7th) (315) ... 13147
Verbank (Dutchess) (9th) (845) ... 12585
Verdoy (Albany) (3rd) (518) ... 12110
Vermontville (Franklin) (4th) (518) ... 12989
Vernon (Oneida) (5th) (315) ... 13476
Vernon Center (Oneida) (5th) (315) ... 13477
Vernon Valley (Suffolk) (10th) (631) ... 11731
Verona (Oneida) (5th) (315) ... 13478
Verona Beach (Oneida) (5th) (315) ... 13162
Verplanck (Westchester) (9th) (914) ... 10596
Versailles (Cattaraugus) (8th) (716) ... 14168
Vesper (Onondaga) (5th) (315) ... 13159
Vestal (Broome) (6th) (607) ... 13850, 13851
Vestal Center (Broome) (6th) (607) ... 13850
Vestal Gardens (Broome) (6th) (607) ... 13850
Veteran (Chemung) (6th) (607) ... 12477
Victor (Ontario) (7th) (585) ... 14564
Victory (Cayuga) (7th) (315) ... 13033
Victory (Saratoga) (4th) (518) ... 12884
Victory Heights (Chemung) (6th) (607) ... 14903
Victory Mills (Saratoga) (4th) (518) ... 12884
Vienna (Oneida) (5th) (315) ... 13308
Village of the Branch (Suffolk) (10th) (631) ... 11787
Villenova (Chautauqua) (8th) (716) ... 14138
Virgil (Cortland) (6th) (607) ... 13045
Vischer Ferry (Saratoga) (4th) (518) ... 12148
Volney (Oswego) (5th) (315) ... 13069
Voorheesville (Albany) (3rd) (518) ... 12186
Waccabuc (Westchester) (9th) (914) ... 10597
Waddington (St. Lawrence) (4th) (315) ... 13694
Wadhams (Essex) (4th) (518) ... 12993
Wading River (Suffolk) (10th) (631) ... 11792
Wadsworth (Livingston) (7th) (585) ... 14533
Wainscott (Suffolk) (10th) (631) ... 11975
Waits (Tioga) (6th) (607) ... 13827
Wakefield (Bronx) (12th) (718) ... 10466
Walden (Orange) (9th) (845) ... 12586
Wales (Erie) (8th) (716) ... 14138
Wales Center (Erie) (8th) (716) ... 14169
Walesville (Oneida) (5th) (315) ... 13492
Walker (Monroe) (7th) (585) ... 14566
Walker Valley (Ulster) (3rd) (845) ... 12588
Wallace (Steuben) (7th) (607) ... 14809
Wallington (Wayne) (7th) (315) ... 14551
Wallkill (Orange) (9th) (845) ... 10919
Wallkill (Ulster) (3rd) (845) ... 12589
Walloomsac (Rensselaer) (3rd) (518) ... 12090
Walton (Delaware) (6th) (607) ... 13856
Walworth (Wayne) (7th) (315) ... 14568
Wampsville (Madison) (6th) (315) ... 13163
Wanakena (St. Lawrence) (4th) (315) ... 13695
Wantagh (Nassau) (10th) (516) ... 11793
Wappinger (Dutchess) (9th) (845) ... 12590
Wappingers Falls (Dutchess) (9th) (845) ... 12590
Ward (Allegany) (8th) (585) ... 14880
Wards Island (New York) (1st) (212) ... 10035
Warners (Onondaga) (5th) (315) ... 13164
Warnerville (Schoharie) (3rd) (518) ... 12187
Warren (Otsego) (5th) (315) ... 13439
Warrensburg (Warren) (4th) (518) ... 12885
Warsaw (Wyoming) (8th) (585) ... 14569
Warwick (Orange) (9th) (845) ... 10990
Washington (Dutchess) (9th) (845) ... 12545
Washington Heights (New York) (1st) (212) ... 100XX
Washington Heights (Orange) (9th) (845) ... 10940
Washington Mills (Oneida) (5th) (315) ... 13479
Washingtonville (Orange) (9th) (845) ... 10992
Wassaic (Dutchess) (9th) (845) ... 12592
Water Mill (Suffolk) (10th) (631) ... 11976
Waterford (Saratoga) (4th) (518) ... 12188
Waterloo (Seneca) (7th) (315) ... 13165
Waterport (Orleans) (8th) (585) ... 14571
Watertown (Jefferson) (5th) (315) ... 13601, 13602, 13603
Waterville (Oneida) (5th) (315) ... 13480
Watervliet (Albany) (3rd) (518) ... 12189
Watkins Glen (Schuyler) (6th) (607) ... 14891
Watson (Lewis) (5th) (315) ... 13367
Wave Crest (Queens) (11th) (718) ... 11690
Waverly (Franklin) (4th) (518) ... 12980
Waverly (Tioga) (6th) (607) ... 14892
Wawarsing (Ulster) (3rd) (845) ... 12489
Wawayanda (Orange) (9th) (845) ... 10973
Wayland (Steuben) (7th) (585) ... 14572
Wayne (Schuyler) (6th) (607) ... 14893
Webb (Herkimer) (5th) (315) ... 13420
Webster (Monroe) (7th) (585) ... 14580
Webster Crossing (Livingston) (7th) (585) ... 14560
Weedsport (Cayuga) (7th) (315) ... 13166
Wegatchie (Jefferson) (5th) (315) ... 13608
Welcome (Otsego) (6th) (607) ... 13810
Wellesley (Jefferson) (5th) (315) ... 13640
Wellesley Island (Jefferson) (5th) (315) ... 13640
Wells (Hamilton) (4th) (518) ... 12190
Wells Bridge (Otsego) (6th) (607) ... 13859
Wellsburg (Chemung) (6th) (607) ... 14894
Wellsville (Allegany) (8th) (585) ... 14895
Weltonville (Tioga) (6th) (607) ... 13811
Wesley Hills (Rockland) (9th) (845) ... 10952, 10977
West Albany (Albany) (3rd) (518) ... 122##
West Almond (Allegany) (8th) (607) ... 14304
West Amherst (Erie) (8th) (716) ... 14228
West Amityville (Nassau) (10th) (516) ... 11701
West Babylon (Suffolk) (10th) (631) ... 11704, 11707
West Bainbridge (Chenango) (6th) (607) ... 13733
West Bangor (Franklin) (4th) (518) ... 12966
West Bay Shore (Suffolk) (10th) (631) ... 11706
West Berne (Albany) (3rd) (518) ... 12023
West Bloomfield (Ontario) (7th) (585) ... 14585
West Branch (Oneida) (5th) (315) ... 13303
West Brentwood (Suffolk) (10th) (631) ... 11717
West Burlington (Otsego) (6th) (607) ... 13482
West Bush (Fulton) (4th) (518) ... 12078
West Camp (Ulster) (3rd) (845) ... 12490
West Candor (Tioga) (6th) (607) ... 13743
West Carthage (Jefferson) (5th) (315) ... 13619
West Charlton (Montgomery) (4th) (518) ... 12010
West Chazy (Clinton) (4th) (518) ... 12992
West Chenango (Broome) (6th) (607) ... 13905
West Clarksville (Allegany) (8th) (585) ... 14786
West Colesville (Broome) (6th) (607) ... 13904
West Copake (Columbia) (3rd) (518) ... 12593
West Corners (Broome) (6th) (607) ... 13760
West Coxsackie (Greene) (3rd) (518) ... 12192
West Danby (Tioga) (6th) (607) ... 14883
West Danby (Tompkins) (6th) (607) ... 14896
West Davenport (Delaware) (6th) (607) ... 13860
West Delhi (Delaware) (6th) (607) ... 13753
West Durham (Greene) (3rd) (518) ... 12422
West Eaton (Madison) (6th) (315) ... 13484
West Edmeston (Madison) (6th) (315) ... 13485
West Ellicott (Chautauqua) (8th) (716) ... 14701
West Elmira (Chemung) (6th) (607) ... 14905
West End (Otsego) (6th) (315) ... 13820
West Endicott (Broome) (6th) (607) ... 13760
West Exeter (Herkimer) (5th) (315) ... 13491
West Falls (Erie) (8th) (716) ... 14170
West Farms (Bronx) (12th) (718) ... 10460
West Fort Ann (Washington) (4th) (518) ... 12827
West Fulton (Schoharie) (3rd) (518) ... 12194
West Gilgo Beach (Suffolk) (10th) (631) ... 11702
West Glens Falls (Warren) (4th) (518) ... 12801
West Glenville (Montgomery) (4th) (518) ... 12010
West Granville Corners (Washington) (4th) (518) ... 12832
West Groton (Tompkins) (6th) (607) ... 13073
West Harpersfield (Delaware) (6th) (607) ... 13786
West Harrison (Westchester) (9th) (914) ... 10604
West Haverstraw (Rockland) (9th) (845) ... 10993
West Hebron (Washington) (4th) (518) ... 12865
West Hempstead (Nassau) (10th) (516) ... 11552
West Henrietta (Monroe) (7th) (585) ... 14586
West Hills (Suffolk) (10th) (631) ... 11743
West Hurley (Ulster) (3rd) (845) ... 12491
West Islip (Suffolk) (10th) (631) ... 11795
West Junius (Ontario) (7th) (315) ... 14532
West Kill (Greene) (518) ... 12492
West Latham (Albany) (3rd) (518) ... 12110
West Laurens (Otsego) (6th) (607) ... 13796
West Lebanon (Columbia) (3rd) (518) ... 12195
West Lee (Oneida) (5th) (315) ... 13363
West Leyden (Lewis) (5th) (315) ... 13489
West Lowville (Lewis) (5th) (315) ... 13367
West Meredith (Delaware) (6th) (607) ... 13757
West Milton (Saratoga) (4th) (518) ... 12020
West Monroe (Oswego) (5th) (315) ... 13167
West New Brighton (Richmond) (13th) (718) ... 10310
West Newark (Tioga) (6th) (607) ... 13811
West Nyack (Rockland) (9th) (845) ... 10994
West Oneonta (Otsego) (6th) (607) ... 13861
West Parishville (St. Lawrence) (4th) (315) ... 13676
West Park (Ulster) (3rd) (845) ... 12493
West Pierrepont (St. Lawrence) (4th) (315) ... 13617
West Plattsburgh (Clinton) (4th) (518) ... 12962
West Point (Orange) (9th) (845) ... 10996, 10997
West Potsdam (St. Lawrence) (4th) (315) ... 13676
West Richmondville (Schoharie) (3rd) (518) ... 12149
West Rush (Monroe) (7th) (585) ... 14543
West Sand Lake (Rensselaer) (3rd) (518) ... 12196
West Saugerties (Ulster) (3rd) (845) ... 12477
West Sayville (Suffolk) (10th) (631) ... 11796
West Seneca (Erie) (8th) (716) ... 1421#, 1422#
West Shokan (Ulster) (3rd) (845) ... 12494
West Sparta (Livingston) (7th) (585) ... 14437
West Stephentown (Rensselaer) (3rd) (518) ... 12169
West Stockholm (St. Lawrence) (4th) (315) ... 13696
West Turin (Lewis) (5th) (315) ... 13325
West Union (Steuben) (7th) (607) ... 14877
West Valley (Cattaraugus) (8th) (716) ... 14171
West Valley Falls (Rensselaer) (3rd) (518) ... 12185
West Webster (Monroe) (7th) (585) ... 14580
West Windsor (Broome) (6th) (607) ... 13865
West Winfield (Herkimer) (5th) (315) ... 13491
Westbrookville (Sullivan) (3rd) (845) ... 12785
Westbury (Nassau) (10th) (516) ... 11568, 11590
Westchester (Bronx) (12th) (718) ... 10461
Westdale (Oneida) (5th) (315) ... 13483
Westerlo (Albany) (3rd) (518) ... 12055, 12193
Western (Oneida) (5th) (315) ... 13419
Westernville (Oneida) (5th) (315) ... 13486
Westfield (Chautauqua) (8th) (716) ... 14787
Westford (Otsego) (6th) (607) ... 13488
Westgate (Monroe) (7th) (585) ... 14624
Westhampton (Suffolk) (10th) (631) ... 11977
Westhampton Beach (Suffolk) (10th) (631) ... 11978
Westhampton Dunes (Suffolk) (10th) (631) ... 11978
Westmere (Albany) (3rd) (518) ... 12203
Westminster Park (Jefferson) (3rd) (315) ... 13607
Westmoreland (Oneida) (5th) (315) ... 13490
Westons Mills (Cattaraugus) (8th) (716) ... 14788
Westover (Broome) (6th) (607) ... 13790
Westport (Essex) (4th) (518) ... 12993

Westtown (Orange) (9th) (845) 10998
Westvale (Onondaga) (5th) (315) 13219
Westview (Broome) (6th) (607) 13905
Westville (Otsego) (6th) (607) 12155
Westville Center (Franklin) (4th) (518) 12926
Wethersfield (Wyoming) (8th) (585) 14569
Wevertown (Warren) (4th) (518) 12886
Whaley Lake (Dutchess) (9th) (845) 12531
Whallonsburg (Essex) (4th) (518) 12936
Wheatfield (Niagara) (8th) (716) 14120, 14304
Wheatland (Monroe) (7th) (585) 14546
Wheatley Heights (Suffolk) (10th) (631) 11798
Wheeler (Steuben) (7th) (607) 14810
Wheelerville (Fulton) (4th) (518) 12032
Whippleville (Franklin) (4th) (518) 12995
White Creek (Rensselaer) (3rd) (518) 12057
White Lake (Sullivan) (3rd) (845) 12786
White Plains (Westchester) (9th) (914) 1060#, 10610
White Sulphur Springs (Sullivan) (3rd) (845) 12787
Whiteface (Essex) (4th) (518) 12946
Whiteface Mountain (Essex) (4th) (518) 12997
Whitehall (Washington) (4th) (518) 12887
Whitelaw (Madison) (6th) (315) 13032
Whites Store (Chenango) (6th) (607) 13843
Whitesboro (Oneida) (5th) (315) 13492
Whitestone (Queens) (11th) (718) 11357
Whitestown (Oneida) (5th) (315) 13492
Whitesville (Allegany) (8th) (607) 14897
Whitfield (Ulster) (3rd) (845) 12404
Whitman (Delaware) (6th) (607) 13804
Whitney Point (Broome) (6th) (607) 13862
Wiccopee (Dutchess) (9th) (845) 12533
Wildwood (Suffolk) (10th) (631) 11792
Willard (Seneca) (7th) (607) 14588
Willet (Cortland) (6th) (607) 13863
Williamsbridge (Bronx) (12th) (718) 10467
Williamson (Wayne) (7th) (315) 14589
Williamstown (Oswego) (5th) (315) 13493
Williamsville (Erie) (8th) (716) 14221, 14231
Willing (Allegany) (8th) (585) 14895
Williston Park (Nassau) (10th) (516) 11596
Willow (Ulster) (3rd) (845) 12495
Willow Point (Broome) (6th) (607) 13850
Willowvale (Oneida) (5th) (315) 13319
Willsboro (Essex) (4th) (518) 12996
Willsboro Point (Essex) (4th) (518) 12996
Willseyville (Tioga) (6th) (607) 13864
Willwood (Suffolk) (10th) (631) 11792
Wilmington (Essex) (4th) (518) 12997
Wilna (Jefferson) (5th) (315) 13619
Wilson (Niagara) (8th) (716) 14172
Wilton (Saratoga) (4th) (518) 12831
Winchester (Erie) (8th) (716) 14224
Wincoma (Suffolk) (10th) (631) 11743
Windham (Greene) (3rd) (518) 12496
Windsor (Broome) (6th) (607) 13865
Winfield (Herkimer) (5th) (315) 13491
Wingdale (Dutchess) (9th) (845) 12594
Winona Lakes (Orange) (9th) (845) 12550
Winterton (Sullivan) (3rd) (845) 12721
Winthrop (St. Lawrence) (4th) (315) 13697
Wirt (Allegany) (8th) (585) 14774
Wiscoy (Allegany) (8th) (585) 14536
Witherbee (Essex) (4th) (518) 12998
Wittenberg (Ulster) (3rd) (845) 12457
Wolcott (Wayne) (7th) (315) 14590
Woodbourne (Sullivan) (3rd) (845) 12788
Woodbury (Nassau) (10th) (516) 11797
Woodbury (Orange) (9th) (845) 10930
Woodgate (Oneida) (5th) (315) 13494
Woodhaven (Queens) (11th) (718) 11421
Woodhull (Steuben) (7th) (607) 14898
Woodland (Ulster) (3rd) (845) 12464
Woodlawn (Erie) (8th) (716) 14219
Woodlawn Beach (Erie) (716) 14219
Woodmere (Nassau) (10th) (516) 11598
Woodridge (Sullivan) (3rd) (845) 12789
Woods Corners (Chenango) (6th) (607) 13815
Woodsburgh (Nassau) (10th) (516) 11598
Woodside (Queens) (11th) (718) 11377
Woodstock (Ulster) (3rd) (845) 12498
Woodville (Jefferson) (5th) (315) 13650
Worcester (Otsego) (607) 12197
Worth (Jefferson) (5th) (315) 13659
Wright (Schoharie) (3rd) (518) 12661
Wurtsboro (Sullivan) (3rd) (845) 12790
Wurtsboro Hills (Sullivan) (3rd) (845) 12790
Wyandanch (Suffolk) (10th) (631) 11798
Wykagyl (Westchester) (9th) (914) 10804
Wynantskill (Rensselaer) (3rd) (518) 12198
Wyoming (Wyoming) (8th) (585) 14591
Yaleville (St. Lawrence) (4th) (518) 13668
Yaphank (Suffolk) (10th) (631) 11980
Yates (Orleans) (8th) (585) 14098
Yonkers (Westchester) (9th) (914) 1070#, 10710
York (Livingston) (7th) (585) 14592
Yorkshire (Cattaragus) (716) 14173
Yorktown (Westchester) (9th) (914) 10598
Yorktown Heights (Westchester) (9th) (914) 10598
Yorkville (Oneida) (5th) (315) 13495
Youngs (Otsego) (6th) (607) 13849
Youngstown (Niagara) (8th) (716) 14174
Youngsville (Sullivan) (3rd) (845) 12791
Yulan (Sullivan) (3rd) (845) 12792

NEWSPAPERS IN NEW YORK

NEWSPAPERS

ADIRONDACK DAILY ENTERPRISE
54 Broadway, Saranac Lake 12983
(518) 891-2600; Fax: (518) 891-2756
E-mail: adenews@adirondackdailyenterprise.com
Internet: www.adirondackdailyenterprise.com

Managing Editor: Peter Crowley
E-mail: pcrowley@adirondackdailyenterprise.com

Publisher/Advertising Mgr.: Cathy Moore
E-mail: cmoore@adirondackdailyenterprise.com

Legal Notices: Connie Amell
E-mail: classifieds@adirondackdailyenterprise.com

ADVANCE-NEWS
See The Ogdensburg Journal

AMERICAN BANKER
1 State St. Plaza, 27th Floor, N.Y.C. 10004
(212) 803-8200; Fax: (212) 843-9600
Internet: www.americanbanker.com

Editor-in-Chief: Barbara A. Rehm (571) 403-3852

V.P./Group Publisher: John DelMauro

Advertising Dir.: Chris Driscoll

AMERICAN METAL MARKET
230 Park Ave. S., 6th Floor, N.Y.C. 10003-1528
(212) 213-6202; Fax: (212) 213-6617
Internet: www.amm.com

Editors: (646) 274-6230
Jo Isenberg-O'Loughlin Josephine Mason

Publisher: Raju Daswani

Classified Sales: Dianne McLarty (646) 274-6242
Daily Newspaper covering metals industries and markets

THE BUFFALO NEWS
One News Plaza, Washington & Scott Sts., Buffalo 14203
Mailing Address: P.O. Box 100, Buffalo 14240
(716) 856-5555; Classifieds: (800) 777-8653;
Fax: (716) 849-3455
Internet: www.buffalonews.com

Editor: Margaret M. Sullivan

Publisher: Stanford Lipsey

Advertising Mgr.: Warren T. Colville

THE CITIZEN
25 Dill St., Auburn 13021
(315) 253-5311; Fax: (315) 253-6031;
Classified: (315) 255-2241; Classified Fax: (315) 255-3874
Internet: www.auburnpub.com

Exec. Editor: Jeremy Boyer

Publisher: Michael Rifanburg

Advertising Mgr.: Tom Kirkwood

Legal Notices: Kathy Weldon

THE CORNING LEADER
34 W. Pulteney St., Corning 14830
(607) 936-4651; Legal Notices Fax: (607) 962-0782
Internet: www.the-leader.com

Managing Editor: Joe Dunning

Publisher: Dennis Bruen

Classifieds Mgr.: Kurt Bartenstein

CORTLAND STANDARD
110 Main St., Cortland 13045
(607) 756-5665; Fax: (607) 756-5665
E-mail: news@cortlandstandard.net
Internet: www.cortlandstandard.net

Editor: Kevin Conlon

Publisher: Kevin R. Howe

Advertising Mgr.: Michael Anderson

Legal Notices: Stephen Clark

DAILY & SUNDAY FREEMAN
79 Hurley Ave., Kingston 12401
(845) 331-5000; Advertising Fax: (845) 338-0672
E-mail: classified@freemanonline.com
Internet: www.dailyfreeman.com

Managing Editor: Tony Adamis, Ext. 514

Publisher: Ira Fusfeld, Ext. 550

Classifieds Mgr.: Penny Ducker, Ext. 456

DAILY CHALLENGE
1195 Atlantic Ave., Brooklyn 11216
(718) 636-9500; Legal Notices Fax: (718) 636-8421
E-mail: challengegroup@yahoo.com

Editor: Gareth Brown

Publisher: Tom Watkins, Jr.

Advertising Mgr./Legal Notices: Arianna Perez
Ext. 15; E-mail: challengegroup@gmail.com

THE DAILY COURIER OBSERVER
1 Harrowgate Commons, P.O. Box 300, Massena 13662
(315) 769-2451; Legal Notices Fax: (315) 764-0337

Editor: Ryne Martin

Publisher: Charles Kelly

Legal Notices: Jackie Mitchell

THE DAILY GAZETTE
2345 Maxon Rd. Ext., P.O. Box 1090, Schenectady 12301-1090
(518) 374-4141; Legal Notices: (518) 395-3048
E-mail: gazette@dailygazette.net
Internet: www.dailygazette.com

Editor: Judy Patrick

Publisher: John E. N. Hume III

Legal Notices: Lynn Thomas

DAILY MAIL
414 Main St., Catskill 12414
(518) 943-2100; Fax: (518) 943-2063;
Legal Notices: (518) 828-1616, Ext. 2223;
Legal Notices Fax: (518) 828-9437
E-mail: editorial@thedailymail.net
Internet: www.thedailymail.net

Exec. Editor: Theresa E. Hyland (518) 828-1616, Ext. 2257

Publisher: Roger F. Coleman (518) 828-1616, Ext. 2249

Advertising Dir.: Pamela Geskie (518) 828-1616, Ext. 2233

Classified Dir.: Bobbi-Jo Race

THE DAILY MESSENGER
73 Buffalo St., Canandaigua 14424
(585) 394-0770; Legal Notices Fax: (585) 394-6837
Internet: www.mpnnow.com

Managing Editors:
Kevin Frisch Margaret Poe

Publisher/Exec. Editor: Rick Jensen

Advertising Dir.: Ken Henry

Legal Notices: Sally Brozell
E-mail: messengerlegals@mpnewspapers.com

DAILY NEWS
2 Apollo Dr., Batavia 14020
(585) 343-8000; Fax: (585) 343-2623;
Classifieds: (585) 343-8068
E-mail: news@batavianews.com

Managing Editor: Mark Graczyk

Publisher: Tom Turnbull

Advertising Dir.: Sheila Mitchell

DAILY SENTINEL
333 W. Dominick St., P.O. Box 471, Rome 13440
(315) 337-4000; Fax: (315) 337-4704
Internet: http://romesentinel.com

Managing Editor: David Swanson

Publisher/Advertising Mgr.: Stephen B. Waters

THE DAILY STAR
102 Chestnut St., P.O. Box 250, Oneonta 13820
(607) 432-1000; Fax: (607) 432-5847
Internet: www.thedailystar.com
Editor: Sam Pollak
Publisher: Armand Nardi
Advertising Mgr.: Bob Evans
Legal Notices: Terry LaPointe

DEMOCRAT AND CHRONICLE
55 Exchange Blvd., Rochester 14614-2001
(585) 232-7100; Legal Notices: (585) 546-7000;
Legal Notices Fax: (585) 258-2329
Internet: www.democratandchronicle.com
Editor: Karen Magnuson
Publisher: Ali M. Zoibi
Advertising Dir.: Jo Ann Geiger

EL DIARIO/LA PRENSA
1 Metro Tech Ctr., 18th Floor, Brooklyn 11201
(212) 807-4600; Fax: (212) 807-4705;
Legal Notices: (212) 807-4601;
Legal Notice Fax: (212) 807-4617
Editor: Alberto Vourvoulias-Bush
Publisher: Rossana Rosado
Advertising Mgr.: Jorge Ayala

THE EVENING SUN
29 Lackawanna Ave., P.O. Box 151, Norwich 13815
(607) 334-3276; Fax: (607) 334-8273
E-mail: news@evesun.com
Internet: www.evesun.com
Editor: Jeff Genung
Publisher: Richard Snyder
Advertising Mgr.: Russ Foote
Legal Notices: Jan Rowe

THE EVENING TELEGRAM
111 Green St., Herkimer 13350
(315) 866-2220; Fax: (315) 866-5913
Internet: www.herkimertelegram.com
Editor: Lorraine Heath
Publisher/Advertising Dir.: Beth A. Brewer
Legal Notices: Michea Supry

THE EVENING TIMES
347 S. Second St., Little Falls 13365
(315) 823-3680; Fax: (315) 823-4086
Internet: www.littlefallstimes.com
Editor: Todd Dewan
Publisher: Beth Brewer
Legal Notices: Kathy Kelly; Fax: (315) 823-0789

THE EVENING TRIBUNE
85 Canisteo St., Hornell 14843
(607) 324-1425; Legal Notices Fax: (607) 324-1753
E-mail: eveningtribune@infoblvd.net
Internet: www.eveningtribune.com
Managing Editor: Andy Thompson
Publisher: Tom Connors
Legal Notices: Beth Hultz

FINGER LAKES TIMES
218 Genesee St., P.O. Box 393, Geneva 14456
(315) 789-3333; Legal Notices Fax: (315) 789-3376
E-mail: fltimes@fltimes.com
Internet: www.fltimes.com
Managing Editor: Chuck Schading
Publisher: Wayne Hemstreet
Advertising Dir.: Diane Lahr Smith
Legal Notices: Sandy Erbmann

THE ITEM
1 Gannett Dr., White Plains 10604
(914) 696-8274; Fax: (914) 696-8228
E-mail: theitemnews@hotmail.com
See The Journal News

THE ITHACA JOURNAL
123-127 W. State St., Ithaca 14850
(607) 272-2321; Legal Notices: (800) 642-3186;
Legal Notices Fax: (607) 798-0261
Internet: www.theithacajournal.com
Managing Editor/General Mgr.: Bruce Estes (607) 274-9242
Publisher: Sherman Bodner (607) 798-1112
Advertising Dir.: Carol Becker (607) 274-9255
Legal Notices: Becky Lockett (607) 798-1326

THE JOURNAL NEWS
1 Gannett Dr., White Plains 10604
(914) 694-9300; Legal Notices: (914) 694-5123;
Legal Notices Fax: (914) 696-8403
Internet: www.lohud.com
Managing Editor: CynDee Royle
Publisher: Michael Fisch
Legal Notices: Bonnie Christain

THE JOURNAL-REGISTER
541-543 Main St., Medina 14103
(585) 798-1400; Fax: (585) 798-0290
Internet: www.journal-register.com
Editor: Holly Toal, Ext. 8225
Publisher: Diane Crowe
Legal Notices: Sharon Wood, Ext. 8236

LAKE PLACID NEWS
6179 Sentinel Rd., P.O. Box 319, Lake Placid 12946
(518) 523-4401; Fax: (518) 523-1351;
Classifieds: (518) 891-2600
News E-mail: news@lakeplacidnews.com
Internet: www.lakeplacidnews.com
Editor: Richard Rosentreter
Publisher/Advertising Mgr.: Cathy Moore
Legal Notices: Connie Amell

THE LEADER-HERALD
8 E. Fulton St., Gloversville 12078
(518) 725-8616; Fax: (518) 773-3384
Internet: www.leaderherald.com
Managing Editor: Tim Fonda
Publisher: Patricia Beck
Advertising Dir.: Dale Webb
Classified Ads:
Sonny Duross   Scott Murphy

LOCKPORT UNION-SUN AND JOURNAL
170 East Ave., Lockport 14094
(716) 439-9222; Legal Notices: (716) 282-2311;
Fax: (716) 282-1643
Internet: www.lockportjournal.com
Editor: Tim Marren, Ext. 6238
Publisher: Diane Crowe, Ext. 6233
Legal Notices: Peggy Villont

MAMARONECK DAILY TIMES
See The Journal News

MOUNT VERNON DAILY ARGUS
See The Journal News

NEW RUSSIAN WORD
350 5th Ave., Suite 5301, N.Y.C. 10118
(646) 218-6900; Fax: (646) 218-6951
E-mail: redaktor@nrs.com
Editor/Publisher: Lawrence Weinberg
Advertising Mgr.: Lina Barskaya

NEW YORK DAILY NEWS
450 W. 33rd St., 3rd Floor, N.Y.C. 10001
(212) 210-2100; Classified Advertising: (212) 949-2000;
Fax: (212) 643-7831
Internet: www.nydailynews.com
Editor-in-Chief: Kevin Convey
Publisher: Mortimer Zuckerman

THE NEW YORK POST
1211 Ave. of the Americas, N.Y.C. 10036
(212) 930-8000; Legal Notices Fax: (212) 930-8121
Internet: www.nypost.com
Editor: Col Allan
Publisher: Rupert Murdoch
Legal Notices:
Maranda Greene Byron Stevens

THE NEW YORK TIMES
229 W. 43rd St., N.Y.C. 10036
(212) 556-1234; Legal Notices: (800) 421-4572;
Legal Notices Fax: (212) 556-8829
Internet: www.nytimes.com
Exec. Editor: Bill Keller
Publisher: Arthur Ochs Sulzberger, Jr.
Legal Notices: Maria Roche

NEWSDAY
235 Pinelawn Rd., Melville 11747-4250
(631) 843-2700; Fax: (631) 843-2953;
Legal Notices Fax: (631) 843-3033
Internet: www.newsday.com
Editor: Debby Krenek; E-mail: editor@newsday.com
Publisher: Terry Jimenez; E-mail: publisher@newsday.com
Sr. V.P., Advertising: Ray McCutcheon
E-mail: advertising@newsday.com

NIAGARA GAZETTE
310 Niagara St., P.O. Box 549, Niagara Falls 14302-0549
(716) 282-2311; Legal Notices Fax: (716) 282-1643
Internet: www.niagra-gazette.com
Managing Editor: Matt Winterhalter
Publisher: Peter Mio
Legal Notices: Peggy Villont

OBSERVER
10 E. 2nd St., P.O. Box 391, Dunkirk 14048
(716) 366-3000; Fax: (716) 366-3005
Internet: www.observertoday.com
Editor: Gregory Bacon
Publisher: John D'Agostino
Advertising Dir.: Meredith V. Patton
Legal Notices: Joyce Klawon

OBSERVER-DISPATCH
221 Oriskany Plaza, Utica 13501
(315) 792-5000; Classified Advertising Fax: (315) 792-5085;
Legal Notices Fax: (888) 707-6840, (315) 798-0261
Internet: www.uticaod.com
Editor: Vacancy at Press Time
Publisher: Donna M. Donovan
Legal Notices: Carol English

THE OGDENSBURG JOURNAL
308 Isabella St., P.O. Box 409, Ogdensburg 13669
(315) 393-1000; Legal Notices Fax: (315) 393-5108
E-mail: parknews@mail.tsf.com
Internet: www.ogd.com
Editor/Publisher: Charles W. Kelly
Legal Notices: Lisa Decker

THE ONEIDA DAILY DISPATCH
130 Broad St., Oneida 13421
(315) 363-5100; Fax: (315) 363-9832
Internet: www.oneidadispatch.com
Managing Editor: Kurt W. Wanfried
Publisher: Phillip R. Austin
Advertising Dir.: Karen Alvord
Legal Notices:
Donna Bouchard Jennifer Howe

THE PALLADIUM-TIMES
140 W. First St., Oswego 13126
(315) 343-3800; Fax: (315) 343-0273
Internet: http://palltimes.com
Editor: Sarah McCrobie
Publisher: Jon Spaulding
Legal Notices: Heather Cripp

THE POST-JOURNAL
15 W. 2nd. St., P.O. Box 3386, Jamestown 14702
(716) 487-1111; Fax: (716) 664-3119;
Legal Notices Fax: (716) 488-9190
Internet: www.post-journal.com
Editor: Cristie Herbst
Publisher: Michael Bird
Advertising Dir.: Debra Brunner

THE POST-STANDARD
1 Clinton Sq., Syracuse 13202
Mailing Address: P.O. Box 4915, Syracuse 13221
(315) 470-0011; Legal Notices Fax: (315) 470-2050
Internet: www.syracuse.com
Editor/Publisher: Stephen A. Rogers
Advertising Dir.: Bill Allison
Legal Notices: Catherine Tobin (315) 470-2051

THE POST-STAR
76 Lawrence St., P.O. Box 2157, Glens Falls 12801
(518) 792-3131; Legal Notices Fax: (518) 798-5738
Internet: www.poststar.com
Editor: Ken Tingley
Publisher: Rick Emanuel (518) 742-3211
Advertising/Classified Mgr.: Jim Murphy
(518) 742-3243

POUGHKEEPSIE JOURNAL
85 Civic Center Plaza, Poughkeepsie 12601
Mailing Address: P.O. Box 1231, Poughkeepsie 12602
(845) 454-2000; Legal Notices Fax: (845) 437-4903
Internet: www.poughkeepsiejournal.com
Exec. Editor: Stuart Shinske
Publisher: Barry Rothfeld
Advertising Dir.: Jan Dewey
Legal Notices: Cheryl Fowx

PRESS & SUN-BULLETIN
33 Lewis Rd., Binghamton 13905-1044
Mailing Address: P.O. Box 1270, Binghamton 13902
(607) 798-1234; Legal Notices Fax: (607) 798-0261
Internet: www.pressconnects.com
Exec. Editor: Calvin Stovall
Publisher: Sherman Bodner
Advertising Mgr.: Jodie Reisbeck
Legal Notices: Denise Royko
E-mail: legals@pressconnects.com

PRESS-REPUBLICAN
170 Margaret St., P.O. Box 459, Plattsburgh 12901
(518) 561-2300; Fax: (518) 561-3362;
Legal Notices: (518) 565-4178
E-mail: news@pressrepublican.com
Internet: www.pressrepublican.com
Editor: Bob Grady
Publisher: Robert Parks
Advertising Mgr.: George Rock
Legal Notices: Brenda Uptown

THE RECORD
501 Broadway, Troy 12180
(518) 270-1200; Legal Notices Fax: (518) 270-1203
Internet: www.troyrecord.com
Editor: Lisa Robert Lewis
Publisher: John Murphy
Advertising Dir.: Heather DeForge

THE RECORDER
1 Venner Rd., Amsterdam 12010
(518) 843-1100; Legal Notices Fax: (518) 843-1338
Internet: www.recordernews.com
Managing Editor: J'Lyn Wimple
Publisher: Kevin McClary
Advertising/Marketing Dir.: Brian Krohn
Legal Notices: Audie DiCaprio

REGISTER-STAR
364 Warren St., Hudson 12534
(518) 828-1616; Fax: (518) 828-9437
Internet: www.registerstar.com
Editor: Theresa E. Hyland, Ext. 2257
Publisher: Roger F. Coleman, Ext. 2249
Legal Notices: Bobbi Jo Race

SALAMANCA PRESS
36 River St., Salamanca 14779
(716) 945-1644; Legal Notices Fax: (716) 945-4285
Internet: www.salamancapress.com
Managing Editor: Kip Doyle
Publisher: Chris Chapman
Advertising Mgr.: Kasey Stockman
Legal Notices: Heather Skeels

THE SARATOGIAN
20 Lake Ave., Saratoga Springs 12866
(518) 584-4242; Classified Fax: (518) 583-8014
Internet: www.saratogian.com
Managing Editor: Barbara Lombardo
Publisher: Michael F. O'Sullivan
Advertising Dir.: Lauren Rose
Legal Notices: Sara Coville

STAR-GAZETTE
201 Baldwin St., P.O. Box 285, Elmira 14902-0285
(607) 734-5151; Fax: (607) 733-4408;
Legal Notices Fax: (607) 798-0261
Internet: www.star-gazette.com
Managing Editor: Lois Wilson
Publisher: Monte I. Trammer
Advertising Dir.: Jon Spaulding
Legal Notices: Denise Royko

STATEN ISLAND ADVANCE
950 Fingerboard Rd., Staten Island 10305
(718) 981-1234; Fax: (718) 981-5679
Internet: www.silive.com
Editor: Brian J. Laline
Publisher: Caroline D. Harrison
Advertising Dir.: Gary Cognetta
Classifieds Mgr.: Tony Mulholland; Fax: (718) 981-1415

TARRYTOWN NEWS
See The Journal News

TIMES HERALD-RECORD
40 Mulberry St., Middletown 10940
(845) 341-1100; Legal Notices Fax: (845) 343-2934
E-mail: legalads@th-record.com
Internet: www.recordonline.com
Executive Editor: Derek Osenenko
Publisher: Joe Vanderhoof
Legal Notices: Patricia Foddrill, Ext. 3601

THE TIMES UNION
News Plaza, Box 15000, Albany 12212
(518) 454-5694; Legal Notices: (518) 454-5543
Internet: www.timesunion.com
V.P. Editor: Rex Smith (518) 454-5040
Publisher & C.E.O.: George R. Hearst III (518) 454-5406
V.P., Advertising: Kathleen Hallion (518) 454-5568
Legal Notices: Tim Dollard
E-mail: tulegals@timesunion.com

THE TIMES-HERALD
639 Norton Dr., Olean 14760
(716) 372-3121; Legal Notices Fax: (716) 372-0740
E-mail: news@oleantimesherald.com
Internet: www.oleantimesherald.com
Editor: Jim Eckstrom, Ext. 223
Publisher: Jim Bonn, Ext. 210
Advertising Mgr.: Debbie Perry, Ext. 261
Legal Notices: Cathy Powley, Ext. 248

TONAWANDA NEWS
435 River Rd., North Tonawanda 14120
(716) 693-1000; Fax: (716) 693-0124
Internet: www.tonawanda-news.com
Managing Editor: Eric DuVall
Publisher: Pete Mio
Advertising Dir.: John Brundo
Legal Notices: Peggy Villont
(716) 282-2311, Ext. 2305; Fax: (716) 282-1643

USA TODAY
See The Journal News

THE WALL STREET JOURNAL
1211 Ave. of the Americas, N.Y.C. 10036
(212) 416-2000; Fax: (212) 640-7900;
Legal Notices: (212) 640-7939
Internet: www.wsj.com
Exec. Editor: Alan Murray
Managing Editor: Almar Latour
Publisher: Les Linton
V.P., Global Advertising: Judy Barry
1155 Avenue of the Americas, N.Y.C. 10036
(212) 597-6045

WATERTOWN DAILY TIMES
Times Bldg., 260 Washington St., Watertown 13601
(315) 782-1000; Legal Notices Fax: (315) 661-2521
Internet: www.wdt.net
Managing Editor: Bob Gorman
Co-Publishers:
Harold B. Johnson John B. Johnson, Jr.
Advertising Mgr.: John B. Johnson
Classified Advertising Mgr.: Barbara Peck
Legal Notices: Kayla Burke

THE WELLSVILLE DAILY REPORTER
159 N. Main St., Wellsville 14895-0602
(585) 593-5300; Fax: (585) 593-5303
Internet: www.wellsvilledaily.com
Managing Editor: John Anderson
Publisher/Advertising Mgr.: Oak Duke
Classified Advertising Mgr.: Jody Wood

WHITE PLAINS REPORTER DISPATCH
See The Journal News

NEWSPAPERS, LEGAL

THE BROOKLYN DAILY EAGLE
30 Henry St., Brooklyn 11201
(718) 422-7400; Fax: (718) 858-4483;
Legal Notices Fax: (718) 237-5115
Internet: www.brooklyneagle.com
Editor: Raanan Geberer
Publisher: J. Dozier Hasty
Advertising Mgr./Classifieds: Patricia Higgins
Legal Notices: Jessie Leon

THE DAILY RECORD
16 W. Main St., Rochester 14614
(585) 232-6920; Fax: (585) 232-2740
Internet: www.nydailyrecord.com
Editor: Tara Buck; E-mail: tara.buck@nydailyrecord.com
Publisher: Kevin Momot
E-mail: kevin.momot@nydailyrecord.com
Advertising Representative: Elizabeth Roach
E-mail: elizabeth.roach@nydailyrecord.com
Public Notices: Elayna Malley
E-mail: elayna.malley@nydailyrecord.com

THE JOURNAL OF COMMERCE
33 Washington St., 13th Floor, Newark, NJ 07102
(973) 848-7000; Legal Notices: (973) 848-7166;
Legal Notices Fax: (973) 848-7045
Internet: www.joc.com
Managing Editor: Chris Brooks (973) 848-7156
Publisher: Liam Power (973) 776-7804
Legal Notices: Craig Wilson (973) 848-7166

NEW YORK LAW JOURNAL
120 Broadway, 5th Floor, N.Y.C. 10271
(212) 457-9545; Legal Notices Fax: (212) 437-7361
Internet: www.nylj.com
Chief Editor: Kris Fischer (212) 457-9544
Publisher: George M. Dillehay (212) 457-9403
Legal Notices: Cynthia Byrd (866) 305-3058

ALABAMA
67 Counties

Autauga
Baldwin
Barbour
Bibb
Blount
Bullock
Butler
Calhoun
Chambers
Cherokee
Chilton
Choctaw
Clarke
Clay
Cleburne
Coffee
Colbert
Conecuh
Coosa
Covington
Crenshaw
Cullman
Dale
Dallas
DeKalb
Elmore
Escambia
Etowah
Fayette
Franklin
Geneva
Greene
Hale
Henry
Houston
Jackson
Jefferson
Lamar
Lauderdale
Lawrence
Lee
Limestone
Lowndes
Macon
Madison
Marengo
Marion
Marshall
Mobile
Monroe
Montgomery
Morgan
Perry
Pickens
Pike
Randolph
Russell
Saint Clair
Shelby
Sumter
Talladega
Tallapoosa
Tuscaloosa
Walker
Washington
Wilcox
Winston

ALASKA
27 Census Div.

Aleutians East Borough
Aleutians West
Anchorage Municipality
Bethel
Bristol Bay Borough
Denali Borough
Dillingham
Fairbanks North Star Borough
Haines Borough
Juneau Borough
Kenai Peninsula Borough
Ketchikan Gateway Borough
Kodiak Island Borough
Lake and Peninsula Borough
Matanuska-Susitna Borough
Nome
North Slope Borough

ALASKA
(Continued)

Northwest Arctic Borough
Prince of Wales-Outer Ketchikan
Sitka City and Borough
Skagway-Hoonah-Angoon
Southeast Fairbanks
Valdez-Cordova
Wade Hampton
Wrangell- Petersburg
Yakutat City and Borough
Yukon-Koyukuk

ARIZONA
15 Counties

Apache
Cochise
Coconino
Gila
Graham
Greenlee
La Paz
Maricopa
Mohave
Navajo
Pima
Pinal
Santa Cruz
Yavapai
Yuma

ARKANSAS
75 Counties

Arkansas
Ashley
Baxter
Benton
Boone
Bradley
Calhoun
Carroll
Chicot
Clark
Clay
Cleburne
Cleveland
Columbia
Conway
Craighead
Crawford
Crittenden
Cross
Dallas
Desha
Drew
Faulkner
Franklin
Fulton
Garland
Grant
Greene
Hempstead
Hot Spring
Howard
Independence
Izard
Jackson
Jefferson
Johnson
Lafayette
Lawrence
Lee
Lincoln
Little River
Logan
Lonoke
Madison
Marion
Miller
Mississippi
Monroe
Montgomery
Nevada
Newton
Ouachita
Perry
Phillips
Pike
Poinsett
Polk
Pope
Prairie
Pulaski
Randolph

ARKANSAS
(Continued)

Saint Francis
Saline
Scott
Searcy
Sebastian
Sevier
Sharp
Stone
Union
Van Buren
Washington
White
Woodruff
Yell

CALIFORNIA
58 Counties

Alameda
Alpine
Amador
Butte
Calaveras
Colusa
Contra Costa
Del Norte
El Dorado
Fresno
Glenn
Humboldt
Imperial
Inyo
Kern
Kings
Lake
Lassen
Los Angeles
Madera
Marin
Mariposa
Mendocino
Merced
Modoc
Mono
Monterey
Napa
Nevada
Orange
Placer
Plumas
Riverside
Sacramento
San Benito
San Bernardino
San Diego
San Francisco
San Joaquin
San Luis Obispo
San Mateo
Santa Barbara
Santa Clara
Santa Cruz
Shasta
Sierra
Siskiyou
Solano
Sonoma
Stanislaus
Sutter
Tehama
Trinity
Tulare
Tuolumne
Ventura
Yolo
Yuba

COLORADO
64 Counties

Adams
Alamosa
Arapahoe
Archuleta
Baca
Bent
Boulder
Broomfield
Chaffee
Cheyenne
Clear Creek
Conejos
Costilla
Crowley
Custer
Delta
Denver
Dolores
Douglas
Eagle

COLORADO
(Continued)

Elbert
El Paso
Fremont
Garfield
Gilpin
Grand
Gunnison
Hinsdale
Huerfano
Jackson
Jefferson
Kiowa
Kit Carson
Lake
La Plata
Larimer
Las Animas
Lincoln
Logan
Mesa
Mineral
Moffat
Montezuma
Montrose
Morgan
Otero
Ouray
Park
Phillips
Pitkin
Prowers
Pueblo
Rio Blanco
Rio Grande
Routt
Saguache
San Juan
San Miguel
Sedgwick
Summit
Teller
Washington
Weld
Yuma

CONNECTICUT
8 Counties

Fairfield
Hartford
Litchfield
Middlesex
New Haven
New London
Tolland
Windham

DELAWARE
3 Counties

Kent
New Castle
Sussex

DISTRICT OF COLUMBIA
1 District

DC

FLORIDA
67 Counties

Alachua
Baker
Bay
Bradford
Brevard
Broward
Calhoun
Charlotte
Citrus
Clay
Collier
Columbia
De Soto
Dixie
Duval
Escambia
Flagler
Franklin
Gadsden
Gilchrist
Glades
Gulf
Hamilton
Hardee
Hendry
Hernando
Highlands

FLORIDA
(Continued)

Hillsborough
Holmes
Indian River
Jackson
Jefferson
Lafayette
Lake
Lee
Leon
Levy
Liberty
Madison
Manatee
Marion
Martin
Miami-Dade
Monroe
Nassau
Okaloosa
Okeechobee
Orange
Osceola
Palm Beach
Pasco
Pinellas
Polk
Putnam
Saint Johns
Saint Lucie
Santa Rosa
Sarasota
Seminole
Sumter
Suwannee
Taylor
Union
Volusia
Wakulla
Walton
Washington

GEORGIA
159 Counties

Appling
Atkinson
Bacon
Baker
Baldwin
Banks
Barrow
Bartow
Ben Hill
Berrien
Bibb
Bleckley
Brantley
Brooks
Bryan
Bulloch
Burke
Butts
Calhoun
Camden
Candler
Carroll
Catoosa
Charlton
Chatham
Chattahoochee
Chattooga
Cherokee
Clarke
Clay
Clayton
Clinch
Cobb
Coffee
Colquitt
Columbia
Cook
Coweta
Crawford
Crisp
Dade
Dawson
Decatur
De Kalb
Dodge
Dooly
Dougherty
Douglas
Early
Echols
Effingham
Elbert
Emanuel
Evans

GEORGIA
(Continued)

Fannin
Fayette
Floyd
Forsyth
Franklin
Fulton
Gilmer
Glascock
Glynn
Gordon
Grady
Greene
Gwinnett
Habersham
Hall
Hancock
Haralson
Harris
Hart
Heard
Henry
Houston
Irwin
Jackson
Jasper
Jeff Davis
Jefferson
Jenkins
Johnson
Jones
Lamar
Lanier
Laurens
Lee
Liberty
Lincoln
Long
Lowndes
Lumpkin
McDuffie
McIntosh
Macon
Madison
Marion
Meriwether
Miller
Mitchell
Monroe
Montgomery
Morgan
Murray
Muscogee
Newton
Oconee
Oglethorpe
Paulding
Peach
Pickens
Pierce
Pike
Polk
Pulaski
Putnam
Quitman
Rabun
Randolph
Richmond
Rockdale
Schley
Screven
Seminole
Spalding
Stephens
Stewart
Sumter
Talbot
Taliaferro
Tattnall
Taylor
Telfair
Terrell
Thomas
Tift
Toombs
Towns
Treutlen
Troup
Turner
Twiggs
Union
Upson
Walker
Walton
Ware
Warren
Washington
Wayne
Webster
Wheeler
White
Whitfield
Wilcox
Wilkes
Wilkinson
Worth

HAWAII
5 Counties

Hawaii
Honolulu
Kalawao*
Kauai
Maui
*Administered by State Govt.

IDAHO
44 Counties

Ada
Adams
Bannock
Bear Lake
Benewah
Bingham
Blaine
Boise
Bonner
Bonneville
Boundary
Butte
Camas
Canyon
Caribou
Cassia
Clark
Clearwater
Custer
Elmore
Franklin
Fremont
Gem
Gooding
Idaho
Jefferson
Jerome
Kootenai
Latah
Lemhi
Lewis
Lincoln
Madison
Minidoka
Nez Perce
Oneida
Owyhee
Payette
Power
Shoshone
Teton
Twin Falls
Valley
Washington

ILLINOIS
102 Counties

Adams
Alexander
Bond
Boone
Brown
Bureau
Calhoun
Carroll
Cass
Champaign
Christian
Clark
Clay
Clinton
Coles
Cook
Crawford
Cumberland
DeKalb
De Witt
Douglas
DuPage
Edgar
Edwards
Effingham
Fayette
Ford
Franklin
Fulton
Gallatin
Greene
Grundy

ILLINOIS
(Continued)

Hamilton
Hancock
Hardin
Henderson
Henry
Iroquois
Jackson
Jasper
Jefferson
Jersey
Jo Daviess
Johnson
Kane
Kankakee
Kendall
Knox
Lake
La Salle
Lawrence
Lee
Livingston
Logan
McDonough
McHenry
McLean
Macon
Macoupin
Madison
Marion
Marshall
Mason
Massac
Menard
Mercer
Monroe
Montgomery
Morgan
Moultrie
Ogle
Peoria
Perry
Piatt
Pike
Pope
Pulaski
Putnam
Randolph
Richland
Rock Island
Saint Clair
Saline
Sangamon
Schuyler
Scott
Shelby
Stark
Stephenson
Tazewell
Union
Vermilion
Wabash
Warren
Washington
Wayne
White
Whiteside
Will
Williamson
Winnebago
Woodford

INDIANA
92 Counties

Adams
Allen
Bartholomew
Benton
Blackford
Boone
Brown
Carroll
Cass
Clark
Clay
Clinton
Crawford
Daviess
Dearborn
Decatur
DeKalb
Delaware
Dubois
Elkhart
Fayette
Floyd
Fountain
Franklin
Fulton
Gibson
Grant
Greene
Hamilton
Hancock

INDIANA
(Continued)

Harrison
Hendricks
Henry
Howard
Huntington
Jackson
Jasper
Jay
Jefferson
Jennings
Johnson
Knox
Kosciusko
LaGrange
Lake
LaPorte
Lawrence
Madison
Marion
Marshall
Martin
Miami
Monroe
Montgomery
Morgan
Newton
Noble
Ohio
Orange
Owen
Parke
Perry
Pike
Porter
Posey
Pulaski
Putnam
Randolph
Ripley
Rush
Saint Joseph
Scott
Shelby
Spencer
Starke
Steuben
Sullivan
Switzerland
Tippecanoe
Tipton
Union
Vanderburgh
Vermilion
Vigo
Wabash
Warren
Warrick
Washington
Wayne
Wells
White
Whitley

IOWA
99 Counties

Adair
Adams
Allamakee
Appanoose
Audubon
Benton
Black Hawk
Boone
Bremer
Buchanan
Buena Vista
Butler
Calhoun
Carroll
Cass
Cedar
Cerro Gordo
Cherokee
Chickasaw
Clarke
Clay
Clayton
Clinton
Crawford
Dallas
Davis
Decatur
Delaware
Des Moines
Dickinson
Dubuque
Emmet
Fayette
Floyd
Franklin
Fremont

IOWA
(Continued)

Greene
Grundy
Guthrie
Hamilton
Hancock
Hardin
Harrison
Henry
Howard
Humboldt
Ida
Iowa
Jackson
Jasper
Jefferson
Johnson
Jones
Keokuk
Kossuth
Lee
Linn
Louisa
Lucas
Lyon
Madison
Mahaska
Marion
Marshall
Mills
Mitchell
Monona
Monroe
Montgomery
Muscatine
O'Brien
Osceola
Page
Palo Alto
Plymouth
Pocahontas
Polk
Pottawattamie
Poweshiek
Ringgold
Sac
Scott
Shelby
Sioux
Story
Tama
Taylor
Union
Van Buren
Wapello
Warren
Washington
Wayne
Webster
Winnebago
Winneshiek
Woodbury
Worth
Wright

KANSAS
105 Counties

Allen
Anderson
Atchison
Barber
Barton
Bourbon
Brown
Butler
Chase
Chautauqua
Cherokee
Cheyenne
Clark
Clay
Cloud
Coffey
Comanche
Cowley
Crawford
Decatur
Dickinson
Doniphan
Douglas
Edwards
Elk
Ellis
Ellsworth
Finney
Ford
Franklin
Geary
Gove
Graham

KANSAS
(Continued)

Grant
Gray
Greeley
Greenwood
Hamilton
Harper
Harvey
Haskell
Hodgeman
Jackson
Jefferson
Jewell
Johnson
Kearny
Kingman
Kiowa
Labette
Lane
Leavenworth
Lincoln
Linn
Logan
Lyon
McPherson
Marion
Marshall
Meade
Miami
Mitchell
Montgomery
Morris
Morton
Nemaha
Neosho
Ness
Norton
Osage
Osborne
Ottawa
Pawnee
Phillips
Pottawatomie
Pratt
Rawlins
Reno
Republic
Rice
Riley
Rooks
Rush
Russell
Saline
Scott
Sedgwick
Seward
Shawnee
Sheridan
Sherman
Smith
Stafford
Stanton
Stevens
Sumner
Thomas
Trego
Wabaunsee
Wallace
Washington
Wichita
Wilson
Woodson
Wyandotte

KENTUCKY
120 Counties

Adair
Allen
Anderson
Ballard
Barren
Bath
Bell
Boone
Bourbon
Boyd
Boyle
Bracken
Breathitt
Breckinridge
Bullitt
Butler
Caldwell
Calloway
Campbell
Carlisle
Carroll
Carter
Casey
Christian
Clark
Clay

KENTUCKY
(Continued)

Clinton
Crittenden
Cumberland
Daviess
Edmonson
Elliott
Estill
Fayette
Fleming
Floyd
Franklin
Fulton
Gallatin
Garrard
Grant
Graves
Grayson
Green
Greenup
Hancock
Hardin
Harlan
Harrison
Hart
Henderson
Henry
Hickman
Hopkins
Jackson
Jefferson
Jessamine
Johnson
Kenton
Knott
Knox
Larue
Laurel
Lawrence
Lee
Leslie
Letcher
Lewis
Lincoln
Livingston
Logan
Lyon
McCracken
McCreary
McLean
Madison
Magoffin
Marion
Marshall
Martin
Mason
Meade
Menifee
Mercer
Metcalfe
Monroe
Montgomery
Morgan
Muhlenberg
Nelson
Nicholas
Ohio
Oldham
Owen
Owsley
Pendleton
Perry
Pike
Powell
Pulaski
Robertson
Rockcastle
Rowan
Russell
Scott
Shelby
Simpson
Spencer
Taylor
Todd
Trigg
Trimble
Union
Warren
Washington
Wayne
Webster
Whitley
Wolfe
Woodford

LOUISIANA
64 Parishes

Acadia
Allen
Ascension
Assumption
Avoyelles
Beauregard

LOUISIANA
(Continued)

Bienville
Bossier
Caddo
Calcasieu
Caldwell
Cameron
Catahoula
Claiborne
Concordia
De Soto
East Baton Rouge
East Carroll
East Feliciana
Evangeline
Franklin
Grant
Iberia
Iberville
Jackson
Jefferson
Jefferson Davis
Lafayette
Lafourche
La Salle
Lincoln
Livingston
Madison
Morehouse
Natchitoches
Orleans
Ouachita
Plaquemines
Pointe Coupee
Rapides
Red River
Richland
Sabine
Saint Bernard
Saint Charles
Saint Helena
Saint James
Saint John the Baptist
Saint Landry
Saint Martin
Saint Mary
Saint Tammany
Tangipahoa
Tensas
Terrebonne
Union
Vermilion
Vernon
Washington
Webster
West Baton Rouge
West Carroll
West Feliciana
Winn

MAINE
16 Counties

Androscoggin
Aroostook
Cumberland
Franklin
Hancock
Kennebec
Knox
Lincoln
Oxford
Penobscot
Piscataquis
Sagadahoc
Somerset
Waldo
Washington
York

MARYLAND
23 Counties
1 Ind. City

Allegany
Anne Arundel
Baltimore City
Baltimore County
Calvert
Caroline
Carroll
Cecil
Charles
Dorchester
Frederick
Garrett
Harford
Howard

MARYLAND
(Continued)

Kent
Montgomery
Prince George's
Queen Anne's
Saint Mary's
Somerset
Talbot
Washington
Wicomico
Worcester

MASSACHUSETTS
14 Counties

Barnstable
Berkshire
Bristol
Dukes
Essex
Franklin
Hampden
Hampshire
Middlesex
Nantucket
Norfolk
Plymouth
Suffolk
Worcester

MICHIGAN
83 Counties

Alcona
Alger
Allegan
Alpena
Antrim
Arenac
Baraga
Barry
Bay
Benzie
Berrien
Branch
Calhoun
Cass
Charlevoix
Cheboygan
Chippewa
Clare
Clinton
Crawford
Delta
Dickinson
Eaton
Emmet
Genesee
Gladwin
Gogebic
Grand Traverse
Gratiot
Hillsdale
Houghton
Huron
Ingham
Ionia
Iosco
Iron
Isabella
Jackson
Kalamazoo
Kalkaska
Kent
Keweenaw
Lake
Lapeer
Leelanau
Lenawee
Livingston
Luce
Mackinac
Macomb
Manistee
Marquette
Mason
Mecosta
Menominee
Midland
Missaukee
Monroe
Montcalm
Montmorency
Muskegon
Newaygo
Oakland
Oceana
Ogemaw
Ontonagon
Osceola
Oscoda
Otsego

MICHIGAN
(Continued)

Ottawa
Presque Isle
Roscommon
Saginaw
Saint Clair
Saint Joseph
Sanilac
Schoolcraft
Shiawassee
Tuscola
Van Buren
Washtenaw
Wayne
Wexford

MINNESOTA
87 Counties

Aitkin
Anoka
Becker
Beltrami
Benton
Big Stone
Blue Earth
Brown
Carlton
Carver
Cass
Chippewa
Chisago
Clay
Clearwater
Cook
Cottonwood
Crow Wing
Dakota
Dodge
Douglas
Faribault
Fillmore
Freeborn
Goodhue
Grant
Hennepin
Houston
Hubbard
Isanti
Itasca
Jackson
Kanabec
Kandiyohi
Kittson
Koochiching
Lac qui Parle
Lake
Lake of the Woods
Le Sueur
Lincoln
Lyon
McLeod
Mahnomen
Marshall
Martin
Meeker
Mille Lacs
Morrison
Mower
Murray
Nicollet
Nobles
Norman
Olmsted
Otter Tail
Pennington
Pine
Pipestone
Polk
Pope
Ramsey
Red Lake
Redwood
Renville
Rice
Rock
Roseau
Saint Louis
Scott
Sherburne
Sibley
Stearns
Steele
Stevens
Swift
Todd
Traverse
Wabasha
Wadena
Waseca
Washington
Watonwan
Wilkin
Winona
Wright
Yellow Medicine

MISSISSIPPI
82 Counties

Adams
Alcorn
Amite
Attala
Benton
Bolivar
Calhoun
Carroll
Chickasaw
Choctaw
Claiborne
Clarke
Clay
Coahoma
Copiah
Covington
De Soto
Forrest
Franklin
George
Greene
Grenada
Hancock
Harrison
Hinds
Holmes
Humphreys
Issaquena
Itawamba
Jackson
Jasper
Jefferson
Jefferson Davis
Jones
Kemper
Lafayette
Lamar
Lauderdale
Lawrence
Leake
Lee
Leflore
Lincoln
Lowndes
Madison
Marion
Marshall
Monroe
Montgomery
Neshoba
Newton
Noxubee
Oktibbeha
Panola
Pearl River
Perry
Pike
Pontotoc
Prentiss
Quitman
Rankin
Scott
Sharkey
Simpson
Smith
Stone
Sunflower
Tallahatchie
Tate
Tippah
Tishomingo
Tunica
Union
Walthall
Warren
Washington
Wayne
Webster
Wilkinson
Winston
Yalobusha
Yazoo

MISSOURI
114 Counties
1 Ind. City

Adair
Andrew
Atchison
Audrain
Barry
Barton
Bates
Benton
Bollinger
Boone
Buchanan
Butler
Caldwell
Callaway
Camden

MISSOURI
(Continued)

Cape Girardeau
Carroll
Carter
Cass
Cedar
Chariton
Christian
Clark
Clay
Clinton
Cole
Cooper
Crawford
Dade
Dallas
Daviess
De Kalb
Dent
Douglas
Dunklin
Franklin
Gasconade
Gentry
Greene
Grundy
Harrison
Henry
Hickory
Holt
Howard
Howell
Iron
Jackson
Jasper
Jefferson
Johnson
Knox
Laclede
Lafayette
Lawrence
Lewis
Lincoln
Linn
Livingston
McDonald
Macon
Madison
Maries
Marion
Mercer
Miller
Mississippi
Moniteau
Monroe
Montgomery
Morgan
New Madrid
Newton
Nodaway
Oregon
Osage
Ozark
Pemiscot
Perry
Pettis
Phelps
Pike
Platte
Polk
Pulaski
Putnam
Ralls
Randolph
Ray
Reynolds
Ripley
Saint Charles
Saint Clair
Saint Francois
Saint Louis City
Saint Louis County
Sainte Genevieve
Saline
Schuyler
Scotland
Scott
Shannon
Shelby
Stoddard
Stone
Sullivan
Taney
Texas
Vernon
Warren
Washington
Wayne
Webster
Worth
Wright

MONTANA
56 Counties

Beaverhead
Big Horn
Blaine
Broadwater
Carbon
Carter
Cascade
Chouteau
Custer
Daniels
Dawson
Deer Lodge
Fallon
Fergus
Flathead
Gallatin
Garfield
Glacier
Golden Valley
Granite
Hill
Jefferson
Judith Basin
Lake
Lewis & Clark
Liberty
Lincoln
McCone
Madison
Meagher
Mineral
Missoula
Musselshell
Park
Petroleum
Phillips
Pondera
Powder River
Powell
Prairie
Ravalli
Richland
Roosevelt
Rosebud
Sanders
Sheridan
Silver Bow
Stillwater
Sweet Grass
Teton
Toole
Treasure
Valley
Wheatland
Wibaux
Yellowstone

NEBRASKA
93 Counties

Adams
Antelope
Arthur
Banner
Blaine
Boone
Box Butte
Boyd
Brown
Buffalo
Burt
Butler
Cass
Cedar
Chase
Cherry
Cheyenne
Clay
Colfax
Cuming
Custer
Dakota
Dawes
Dawson
Deuel
Dixon
Dodge
Douglas
Dundy
Fillmore
Franklin
Frontier
Furnas
Gage
Garden
Garfield
Gosper
Grant
Greeley
Hall
Hamilton
Harlan

NEBRASKA
(Continued)

Hayes
Hitchcock
Holt
Hooker
Howard
Jefferson
Johnson
Kearney
Keith
Keya Paha
Kimball
Knox
Lancaster
Lincoln
Logan
Loup
McPherson
Madison
Merrick
Morrill
Nance
Nemaha
Nuckolls
Otoe
Pawnee
Perkins
Phelps
Pierce
Platte
Polk
Red Willow
Richardson
Rock
Saline
Sarpy
Saunders
Scotts Bluff
Seward
Sheridan
Sherman
Sioux
Stanton
Thayer
Thomas
Thurston
Valley
Washington
Wayne
Webster
Wheeler
York

NEVADA
16 Counties
1 Ind. City

Carson City
Churchill
Clark
Douglas
Elko
Esmeralda
Eureka
Humboldt
Lander
Lincoln
Lyon
Mineral
Nye
Pershing
Storey
Washoe
White Pine

NEW HAMPSHIRE
10 Counties

Belknap
Carroll
Cheshire
Coos
Grafton
Hillsborough
Merrimack
Rockingham
Strafford
Sullivan

NEW JERSEY
21 Counties

Atlantic
Bergen
Burlington
Camden
Cape May
Cumberland
Essex
Gloucester
Hudson
Hunterdon
Mercer
Middlesex

NEW JERSEY
(Continued)

Monmouth
Morris
Ocean
Passaic
Salem
Somerset
Sussex
Union
Warren

NEW MEXICO
33 Counties

Bernalillo
Catron
Chaves
Cibola
Colfax
Curry
DeBaca
Dona Ana
Eddy
Grant
Guadalupe
Harding
Hidalgo
Lea
Lincoln
Los Alamos
Luna
McKinley
Mora
Otero
Quay
Rio Arriba
Roosevelt
Sandoval
San Juan
San Miguel
Santa Fe
Sierra
Socorro
Taos
Torrance
Union
Valencia

NEW YORK
62 Counties

Albany
Allegany
Bronx
Broome
Cattaraugus
Cayuga
Chautauqua
Chemung
Chenango
Clinton
Columbia
Cortland
Delaware
Dutchess
Erie
Essex
Franklin
Fulton
Genesee
Greene
Hamilton
Herkimer
Jefferson
Kings
Lewis
Livingston
Madison
Monroe
Montgomery
Nassau
New York
Niagara
Oneida
Onondaga
Ontario
Orange
Orleans
Oswego
Otsego
Putnam
Queens
Rensselaer
Richmond
Rockland
Saint Lawrence
Saratoga
Schenectady
Schoharie
Schuyler
Seneca
Steuben
Suffolk

NEW YORK
(Continued)

Sullivan
Tioga
Tompkins
Ulster
Warren
Washington
Wayne
Westchester
Wyoming
Yates

NORTH CAROLINA
100 Counties

Alamance
Alexander
Alleghany
Anson
Ashe
Avery
Beaufort
Bertie
Bladen
Brunswick
Buncombe
Burke
Cabarrus
Caldwell
Camden
Carteret
Caswell
Catawba
Chatham
Cherokee
Chowan
Clay
Cleveland
Columbus
Craven
Cumberland
Currituck
Dare
Davidson
Davie
Duplin
Durham
Edgecombe
Forsyth
Franklin
Gaston
Gates
Graham
Granville
Greene
Guilford
Halifax
Harnett
Haywood
Henderson
Hertford
Hoke
Hyde
Iredell
Jackson
Johnston
Jones
Lee
Lenoir
Lincoln
McDowell
Macon
Madison
Martin
Mecklenburg
Mitchell
Montgomery
Moore
Nash
New Hanover
Northampton
Onslow
Orange
Pamlico
Pasquotank
Pender
Perquimans
Person
Pitt
Polk
Randolph
Richmond
Robeson
Rockingham
Rowan
Rutherford
Sampson
Scotland
Stanly
Stokes

NORTH CAROLINA
(Continued)

Surry
Swain
Transylvania
Tyrrell
Union
Vance
Wake
Warren
Washington
Watauga
Wayne
Wilkes
Wilson
Yadkin
Yancey

NORTH DAKOTA
53 Counties

Adams
Barnes
Benson
Billings
Bottineau
Bowman
Burke
Burleigh
Cass
Cavalier
Dickey
Divide
Dunn
Eddy
Emmons
Foster
Golden Valley
Grand Forks
Grant
Griggs
Hettinger
Kidder
La Moure
Logan
McHenry
McIntosh
McKenzie
McLean
Mercer
Morton
Mountrail
Nelson
Oliver
Pembina
Pierce
Ramsey
Ransom
Renville
Richland
Rolette
Sargent
Sheridan
Sioux
Slope
Stark
Steele
Stutsman
Towner
Traill
Walsh
Ward
Wells
Williams

OHIO
88 Counties

Adams
Allen
Ashland
Ashtabula
Athens
Auglaize
Belmont
Brown
Butler
Carroll
Champaign
Clark
Clermont
Clinton
Columbiana
Coshocton
Crawford
Cuyahoga
Darke
Defiance
Delaware
Erie
Fairfield
Fayette
Franklin
Fulton
Gallia
Geauga

OHIO
(Continued)

Greene
Guernsey
Hamilton
Hancock
Hardin
Harrison
Henry
Highland
Hocking
Holmes
Huron
Jackson
Jefferson
Knox
Lake
Lawrence
Licking
Logan
Lorain
Lucas
Madison
Mahoning
Marion
Medina
Meigs
Mercer
Miami
Monroe
Montgomery
Morgan
Morrow
Muskingum
Noble
Ottawa
Paulding
Perry
Pickaway
Pike
Portage
Preble
Putnam
Richland
Ross
Sandusky
Scioto
Seneca
Shelby
Stark
Summit
Trumbull
Tuscarawas
Union
Van Wert
Vinton
Warren
Washington
Wayne
Williams
Wood
Wyandot

OKLAHOMA
77 Counties

Adair
Alfalfa
Atoka
Beaver
Beckham
Blaine
Bryan
Caddo
Canadian
Carter
Cherokee
Choctaw
Cimarron
Cleveland
Coal
Comanche
Cotton
Craig
Creek
Custer
Delaware
Dewey
Ellis
Garfield
Garvin
Grady
Grant
Greer
Harmon
Harper
Haskell
Hughes
Jackson
Jefferson
Johnston
Kay
Kingfisher
Kiowa
Latimer
Le Flore
Lincoln
Logan

OKLAHOMA
(Continued)

Love
McClain
McCurtain
McIntosh
Major
Marshall
Mayes
Murray
Muskogee
Noble
Nowata
Okfuskee
Oklahoma
Okmulgee
Osage
Ottawa
Pawnee
Payne
Pittsburg
Pontotoc
Pottawatomie
Pushmataha
Roger Mills
Rogers
Seminole
Sequoyah
Stephens
Texas
Tillman
Tulsa
Wagoner
Washington
Washita
Woods
Woodward

OREGON
36 Counties

Baker
Benton
Clackamas
Clatsop
Columbia
Coos
Crook
Curry
Deschutes
Douglas
Gilliam
Grant
Harney
Hood River
Jackson
Jefferson
Josephine
Klamath
Lake
Lane
Lincoln
Linn
Malheur
Marion
Morrow
Multnomah
Polk
Sherman
Tillamook
Umatilla
Union
Wallowa
Wasco
Washington
Wheeler
Yamhill

PENNSYLVANIA
67 Counties

Adams
Allegheny
Armstrong
Beaver
Bedford
Berks
Blair
Bradford
Bucks
Butler
Cambria
Cameron
Carbon
Centre
Chester
Clarion
Clearfield
Clinton
Columbia
Crawford
Cumberland
Dauphin
Delaware
Elk
Erie
Fayette
Forest

PENNSYLVANIA
(Continued)

Franklin
Fulton
Greene
Huntingdon
Indiana
Jefferson
Juniata
Lackawanna
Lancaster
Lawrence
Lebanon
Lehigh
Luzerne
Lycoming
McKean
Mercer
Mifflin
Monroe
Montgomery
Montour
Northampton
Northumberland
Perry
Philadelphia
Pike
Potter
Schuylkill
Snyder
Somerset
Sullivan
Susquehanna
Tioga
Union
Venango
Warren
Washington
Wayne
Westmoreland
Wyoming
York

RHODE ISLAND
5 Counties

Bristol
Kent
Newport
Providence
Washington

SOUTH CAROLINA
46 Counties

Abbeville
Aiken
Allendale
Anderson
Bamberg
Barnwell
Beaufort
Berkeley
Calhoun
Charleston
Cherokee
Chester
Chesterfield
Clarendon
Colleton
Darlington
Dillon
Dorchester
Edgefield
Fairfield
Florence
Georgetown
Greenville
Greenwood
Hampton
Horry
Jasper
Kershaw
Lancaster
Laurens
Lee
Lexington
McCormick
Marion
Marlboro
Newberry
Oconee
Orangeburg
Pickens
Richland
Saluda
Spartanburg
Sumter
Union
Williamsburg
York

SOUTH DAKOTA
66 Counties

Aurora
Beadle
Bennett
Bon Homme
Brookings
Brown
Brule
Buffalo
Butte
Campbell
Charles Mix
Clark
Clay
Codington
Corson
Custer
Davison
Day
Deuel
Dewey
Douglas
Edmunds
Fall River
Faulk
Grant
Gregory
Haakon
Hamlin
Hand
Hanson
Harding
Hughes
Hutchinson
Hyde
Jackson
Jerauld
Jones
Kingsbury
Lake
Lawrence
Lincoln
Lyman
McCook
McPherson
Marshall
Meade
Mellette
Miner
Minnehaha
Moody
Pennington
Perkins
Potter
Roberts
Sanborn
Shannon
Spink
Stanley
Sully
Todd
Tripp
Turner
Union
Walworth
Yankton
Ziebach

TENNESSEE
95 Counties

Anderson
Bedford
Benton
Bledsoe
Blount
Bradley
Campbell
Cannon
Carroll
Carter
Cheatham
Chester
Claiborne
Clay
Cocke
Coffee
Crockett
Cumberland
Davidson
Decatur
De Kalb
Dickson
Dyer
Fayette
Fentress
Franklin
Gibson
Giles
Grainger
Greene
Grundy
Hamblen
Hamilton
Hancock
Hardeman

TENNESSEE
(Continued)

Hardin
Hawkins
Haywood
Henderson
Henry
Hickman
Houston
Humphreys
Jackson
Jefferson
Johnson
Knox
Lake
Lauderdale
Lawrence
Lewis
Lincoln
Loudon
McMinn
McNairy
Macon
Madison
Marion
Marshall
Maury
Meigs
Monroe
Montgomery
Moore
Morgan
Obion
Overton
Perry
Pickett
Polk
Putnam
Rhea
Roane
Robertson
Rutherford
Scott
Sequatchie
Sevier
Shelby
Smith
Stewart
Sullivan
Sumner
Tipton
Trousdale
Unicoi
Union
Van Buren
Warren
Washington
Wayne
Weakley
White
Williamson
Wilson

TEXAS
254 Counties

Anderson
Andrews
Angelina
Aransas
Archer
Armstrong
Atascosa
Austin
Bailey
Bandera
Bastrop
Baylor
Bee
Bell
Bexar
Blanco
Borden
Bosque
Bowie
Brazoria
Brazos
Brewster
Briscoe
Brooks
Brown
Burleson
Burnet
Caldwell
Calhoun
Callahan
Cameron
Camp
Carson
Cass
Castro
Chambers
Cherokee

TEXAS
(Continued)

Childress
Clay
Cochran
Coke
Coleman
Collin
Collingsworth
Colorado
Comal
Comanche
Concho
Cooke
Coryell
Cottle
Crane
Crockett
Crosby
Culberson
Dallam
Dallas
Dawson
Deaf Smith
Delta
Denton
DeWitt
Dickens
Dimmit
Donley
Duval
Eastland
Ector
Edwards
Ellis
El Paso
Erath
Falls
Fannin
Fayette
Fisher
Floyd
Foard
Fort Bend
Franklin
Freestone
Frio
Gaines
Galveston
Garza
Gillespie
Glasscock
Goliad
Gonzales
Gray
Grayson
Gregg
Grimes
Guadalupe
Hale
Hall
Hamilton
Hansford
Hardeman
Hardin
Harris
Harrison
Hartley
Haskell
Hays
Hemphill
Henderson
Hidalgo
Hill
Hockley
Hood
Hopkins
Houston
Howard
Hudspeth
Hunt
Hutchinson
Irion
Jack
Jackson
Jasper
Jeff Davis
Jefferson
Jim Hogg
Jim Wells
Johnson
Jones
Karnes
Kaufman
Kendall
Kenedy
Kent
Kerr
Kimble
King
Kinney
Kleberg
Knox
Lamar
Lamb

TEXAS
(Continued)

Lampasas
La Salle
Lavaca
Lee
Leon
Liberty
Limestone
Lipscomb
Live Oak
Llano
Loving
Lubbock
Lynn
McCulloch
McLennan
McMullen
Madison
Marion
Martin
Mason
Matagorda
Maverick
Medina
Menard
Midland
Milam
Mills
Mitchell
Montague
Montgomery
Moore
Morris
Motley
Nacogdoches
Navarro
Newton
Nolan
Nueces
Ochiltree
Oldham
Orange
Palo Pinto
Panola
Parker
Parmer
Pecos
Polk
Potter
Presidio
Rains
Randall
Reagan
Real
Red River
Reeves
Refugio
Roberts
Robertson
Rockwall
Runnels
Rusk
Sabine
San Augustine
San Jacinto
San Patricio
San Saba
Schleicher
Scurry
Shackelford
Shelby
Sherman
Smith
Somervell
Starr
Stephens
Sterling
Stonewall
Sutton
Swisher
Tarrant
Taylor
Terrell
Terry
Throckmorton
Titus
Tom Green
Travis
Trinity
Tyler
Upshur
Upton
Uvalde
Val Verde
Van Zandt
Victoria
Walker
Waller
Ward
Washington
Webb
Wharton
Wheeler

TEXAS
(Continued)

Wichita
Wilbarger
Willacy
Williamson
Wilson
Winkler
Wise
Wood
Yoakum
Young
Zapata
Zavala

UTAH
29 Counties

Beaver
Box Elder
Cache
Carbon
Daggett
Davis
Duchesne
Emery
Garfield
Grand
Iron
Juab
Kane
Millard
Morgan
Piute
Rich
Salt Lake
San Juan
Sanpete
Sevier
Summit
Tooele
Uintah
Utah
Wasatch
Washington
Wayne
Weber

VERMONT
14 Counties

Addison
Bennington
Caledonia
Chittenden
Essex
Franklin
Grand Isle
Lamoille
Orange
Orleans
Rutland
Washington
Windham
Windsor

VIRGINIA
95 Counties
39 Ind. Cities

Accomack
Albermarle
Alleghany
Amelia
Amherst
Appomattox
Arlington
Augusta
Bath
Bedford
Bland
Botetourt
Brunswick
Buchanan
Buckingham
Campbell
Caroline
Carroll
Charles City
Charlotte
Chesterfield
Clarke
Craig
Culpeper
Cumberland
Dickenson
Dinwiddie
Essex
Fairfax
Fauquier
Floyd
Fluvanna
Franklin
Frederick
Giles

VIRGINIA
(Continued)

Gloucester
Goochland
Grayson
Greene
Greensville
Halifax
Hanover
Henrico
Henry
Highland
Isle of Wight
James City
King & Queen
King George
King William
Lancaster
Lee
Loudoun
Louisa
Lunenburg
Madison
Mathews
Mecklenburg
Middlesex
Montgomery
Nelson
New Kent
Northampton
Northumberland
Nottoway
Orange
Page
Patrick
Pittsylvania
Powhatan
Prince Edward
Prince George
Prince William
Pulaski
Rappahannock
Richmond
Roanoke
Rockbridge
Rockingham
Russell
Scott
Shenandoah
Smyth
Southampton
Spotsylvania
Stafford
Surry
Sussex
Tazewell
Warren
Washington
Westmoreland
Wise
Wythe
York

Ind. Cities

Alexandria
Bedford
Bristol
Buena Vista
Charlottesville
Chesapeake
Colonial Heights
Covington
Danville
Emporia
Fairfax
Falls Church
Franklin
Fredericksburg
Galax
Hampton
Harrisonburg
Hopewell
Lexington
Lynchburg
Manassas
Manassas Park
Martinsville
Newport News
Norfolk
Norton
Petersburg
Poquoson
Portsmouth
Radford
Richmond
Roanoke
Salem
Staunton
Suffolk
Virginia Beach
Waynesboro
Williamsburg
Winchester

WASHINGTON
39 Counties

Adams
Asotin
Benton
Chelan
Clallam
Clark
Columbia
Cowlitz
Douglas
Ferry
Franklin
Garfield
Grant
Grays Harbor
Island
Jefferson
King
Kitsap
Kittitas
Klickitat
Lewis
Lincoln
Mason
Okanogan
Pacific
Pend Oreille
Pierce
San Juan
Skagit
Skamania
Snohomish
Spokane
Stevens
Thurston
Wahkiakum
Walla Walla
Whatcom
Whitman
Yakima

WEST VIRGINIA
55 Counties

Barbour
Berkeley
Boone
Braxton
Brooke
Cabell
Calhoun
Clay
Doddridge
Fayette
Gilmer
Grant
Greenbrier
Hampshire
Hancock
Hardy
Harrison
Jackson
Jefferson
Kanawha
Lewis
Lincoln
Logan
McDowell
Marion
Marshall
Mason
Mercer
Mineral
Mingo
Monongalia
Monroe
Morgan
Nicholas
Ohio
Pendleton
Pleasants
Pocahontas
Preston
Putnam
Raleigh
Randolph
Ritchie
Roane
Summers
Taylor
Tucker
Tyler
Upshur
Wayne
Webster
Wetzel
Wirt
Wood
Wyoming

WISCONSIN
72 Counties

Adams
Ashland
Barron
Bayfield
Brown
Buffalo
Burnett
Calumet
Chippewa
Clark
Columbia
Crawford
Dane
Dodge
Door
Douglas
Dunn
Eau Claire
Florence
Fond du Lac

WISCONSIN
(Continued)

Forest
Grant
Green
Green Lake
Iowa
Iron
Jackson
Jefferson
Juneau
Kenosha
Kewaunee
La Crosse
Lafayette
Langlade
Lincoln
Manitowoc
Marathon
Marinette
Marquette
Menominee

WISCONSIN
(Continued)

Milwaukee
Monroe
Oconto
Oneida
Outagamie
Ozaukee
Pepin
Pierce
Polk
Portage
Price
Racine
Richland
Rock
Rusk
Saint Croix
Sauk
Sawyer
Shawano
Sheboygan

WISCONSIN
(Continued)

Taylor
Trempealeau
Vernon
Vilas
Walworth
Washburn
Washington
Waukesha
Waupaca
Waushara
Winnebago
Wood

WYOMING
23 Counties

Albany
Big Horn
Campbell
Carbon
Converse

WYOMING
(Continued)

Crook
Fremont
Goshen
Hot Springs
Johnson
Laramie
Lincoln
Natrona
Niobrara
Park
Platte
Sheridan
Sublette
Sweetwater
Teton
Unita
Washakie
Weston

Expectation Of Life and Expected Deaths, by Race, Sex, and Age: 2006

AGE (years)	EXPECTATION OF LIFE IN YEARS					EXPECTED DEATHS PER 1,000 ALIVE AT SPECIFIED AGE [2]				
	Total[1]	White		Black		Total[1]	White		Black	
		Male	Female	Male	Female		Male	Female	Male	Female
At birth	77.7	75.7	80.6	69.7	76.5	6.71	6.12	5.01	14.48	12.23
1	77.2	75.1	80.0	69.7	76.5	0.44	0.40	0.39	0.76	0.60
2	76.3	74.2	79.0	68.7	75.5	0.30	0.29	0.23	0.46	0.48
3	75.3	73.2	78.0	67.8	74.6	0.21	0.22	0.17	0.37	0.24
4	74.3	72.2	77.1	66.8	73.6	0.18	0.18	0.15	0.27	0.24
5	73.3	71.2	76.1	65.8	72.6	0.17	0.17	0.13	0.27	0.21
6	72.3	70.2	75.1	54.8	71.6	0.15	0.16	0.12	0.26	0.18
7	71.3	69.2	74.1	63.9	70.6	0.14	0.15	0.11	0.24	0.16
8	70.4	68.2	73.1	62.9	69.6	0.12	0.13	0.10	0.20	0.14
9	69.4	67.3	72.1	61.9	68.6	0.10	0.10	0.09	0.15	0.13
10	68.4	66.3	71.1	60.9	67.7	0.09	0.08	0.08	0.10	0.14
11	67.4	65.3	70.1	59.9	66.7	0.09	0.08	0.08	0.10	0.15
12	66.4	64.3	69.1	58.9	65.7	0.12	0.13	0.10	0.17	0.17
13	65.4	63.3	68.1	57.9	54.7	0.20	0.24	0.15	0.34	0.20
14	64.4	62.3	67.1	56.9	63.7	0.31	0.39	0.21	0.58	0.23
15	63.4	61.3	66.1	56.0	62.7	0.43	0.54	0.27	0.84	0.27
16	62.4	60.4	65.2	55.0	61.7	0.55	0.69	0.33	1.09	0.32
17	61.5	59.4	54.2	54.1	60.8	0.65	0.84	0.38	1.31	0.36
18	60.5	58.4	63.2	53.1	59.8	0.74	0.98	0.41	1.50	0.42
19	59.6	57.5	62.2	52.2	58.8	0.82	1.10	0.43	1.67	0.47
20	58.6	56.6	61.3	51.3	57.8	0.89	1.23	0.44	1.84	0.54
21	57.7	55.6	60.3	50.4	56.9	0.97	1.35	0.45	2.01	0.60
22	56.7	54.7	59.3	49.5	55.9	1.02	1.43	0.46	2.15	0.67
23	55.8	53.8	58.3	48.6	54.9	1.03	1.44	0.47	2.23	0.71
24	54.8	52.9	57.4	47.7	54.0	1.02	1.40	0.48	2.26	0.75
25	53.9	51.9	56.4	46.8	53.0	1.00	1.35	0.49	2.28	0.79
26	53.0	51.0	55.4	46.0	52.1	0.99	1.31	0.50	2.30	0.83
27	52.0	50.1	54.5	45.1	51.1	0.98	1.27	0.51	2.31	0.87
28	51.1	49.1	53.5	44.2	50.1	0.98	1.26	0.53	2.34	0.92
29	50.1	48.2	52.5	43.3	49.2	1.00	1.27	0.55	2.38	0.90
30	49.2	47.3	51.5	42.4	48.2	1.02	1.29	0.57	2.43	1.04
31	48.2	46.3	50.6	41.5	47.3	1.05	1.31	0.60	2.47	1.12
32	47.3	45.4	49.6	40.6	46.3	1.09	1.34	0.64	2.58	1.21
33	46.3	44.5	48.6	39.7	45.4	1.13	1.37	0.69	2.59	1.30
34	45.4	43.5	47.7	38.8	44.5	1.18	1.42	0.74	2.66	1.40
35	44.4	42.6	46.7	37.9	43.5	1.24	1.48	0.80	2.75	1.51
36	43.5	41.6	45.7	37.0	42.6	1.32	1.55	0.86	2.86	1.63
37	42.5	40.7	44.8	36.1	41.7	1.14	1.66	0.94	2.99	1.78
38	41.6	39.8	43.8	35.3	40.7	1.53	1.80	1.04	3.16	1.96
39	40.7	38.9	42.9	34.4	39.8	1.68	1.97	1.15	3.36	2.17
40	39.7	37.9	41.9	33.5	38.9	1.84	2.15	1.27	3.58	2.37
41	38.8	37.0	41.0	32.6	38.0	2.00	2.34	1.39	3.83	2.59
42	37.9	36.1	40.0	31.8	37.1	2.18	2.55	1.52	4.12	2.82
43	37.0	35.2	39.1	30.9	36.2	2.38	2.77	1.66	4.48	3.08
44	36.1	34.3	38.2	30.1	35.3	2.59	3.01	1.81	4.89	3.36
45	35.2	33.4	37.2	29.2	34.5	2.81	3.26	1.98	5.31	3.66
46	34.3	32.5	36.3	28.4	33.6	3.03	3.52	2.14	5.76	3.95
47	33.4	31.6	35.4	27.6	32.7	3.27	3.80	2.31	6.28	4.26
48	32.5	30.8	34.5	26.8	31.9	3.53	4.11	2.48	6.92	4.57
49	31.6	29.9	33.6	26.0	31.0	3.82	4.45	2.65	7.65	4.90
50	30.7	29.0	32.6	25.2	30.2	4.13	4.83	2.85	8.47	5.25
51	29.9	28.2	31.7	24.4	29.4	4.46	5.22	3.06	9.32	5.63
52	29.0	27.4	30.8	23.7	28.5	4.80	5.62	3.30	10.10	6.01
53	28.2	26.5	29.9	23.0	27.7	5.13	6.01	3.57	10.76	6.39
54	27.3	25.7	29.1	22.3	26.9	5.46	6.37	3.84	11.29	6.76
55	26.5	24.9	28.2	21.6	26.1	5.79	6.73	4.13	11.80	7.14
56	25.6	24.1	27.3	20.9	25.3	6.14	7.11	4.44	12.34	7.54
57	24.8	23.2	26.4	20.2	24.5	6.52	7.54	4.78	12.88	7.96
58	24.0	22.4	25.6	19.5	23.8	6.98	8.05	5.20	13.48	8.43
59	23.2	21.6	24.7	18.8	23.0	7.52	8.67	5.69	14.16	8.96
60	22.4	20.9	23.8	18.2	22.2	8.17	9.40	6.29	14.97	9.58
61	21.6	20.9	23.0	17.5	21.5	8.90	10.22	6.96	15.88	10.30
62	20.8	20.1	22.2	16.9	20.7	9.65	11.07	7.64	16.79	11.06
63	20.0	19.3	21.4	16.3	20.0	10.35	11.86	8.25	17.55	11.78
64	19.2	18.6	20.6	15.7	19.3	10.99	12.59	8.80	18.12	12.41
65	18.5	17.1	19.8	15.1	18.6	11.65	13.36	9.40	18.57	13.01
70	14.9	13.6	15.9	12.3	15.1	16.01	18.25	13.65	22.05	16.72
75	11.6	10.5	12.3	9.8	12.0	23.15	25.77	21.02	25.72	22.66
80	8.7	7.8	9.3	7.7	9.3	30.69	32.57	30.17	26.22	28.04
85	6.4	5.7	6.7	5.9	7.1	34.73	34.06	37.36	22.77	30.41
90	4.6	4.0	4.7	4.5	5.3	30.44	26.27	36.07	15.76	26.97
95	3.2	2.8	3.3	3.5	3.9	17.84	12.62	23.12	7.97	17.71
100	2.3	2.0	2.2	2.6	2.8	17.37	8.04	23.73	9.12	28.48

[1]Includes other races not shown separately. [2]Based on the proportion of the cohort who are alive at the beginning of an indicated age who will die before reaching the age shown plus 1. For example, out of every 1,000 people alive and exactly 50 years old at the beginning of the period, between 4 and 5 (4.13) will die before reaching their 51st birthdays.

Source: U.S. National Center for Health Statistics. Unpublished data.

Statistical Abstract of the United States, 2010

DEGREES OF KINDRED

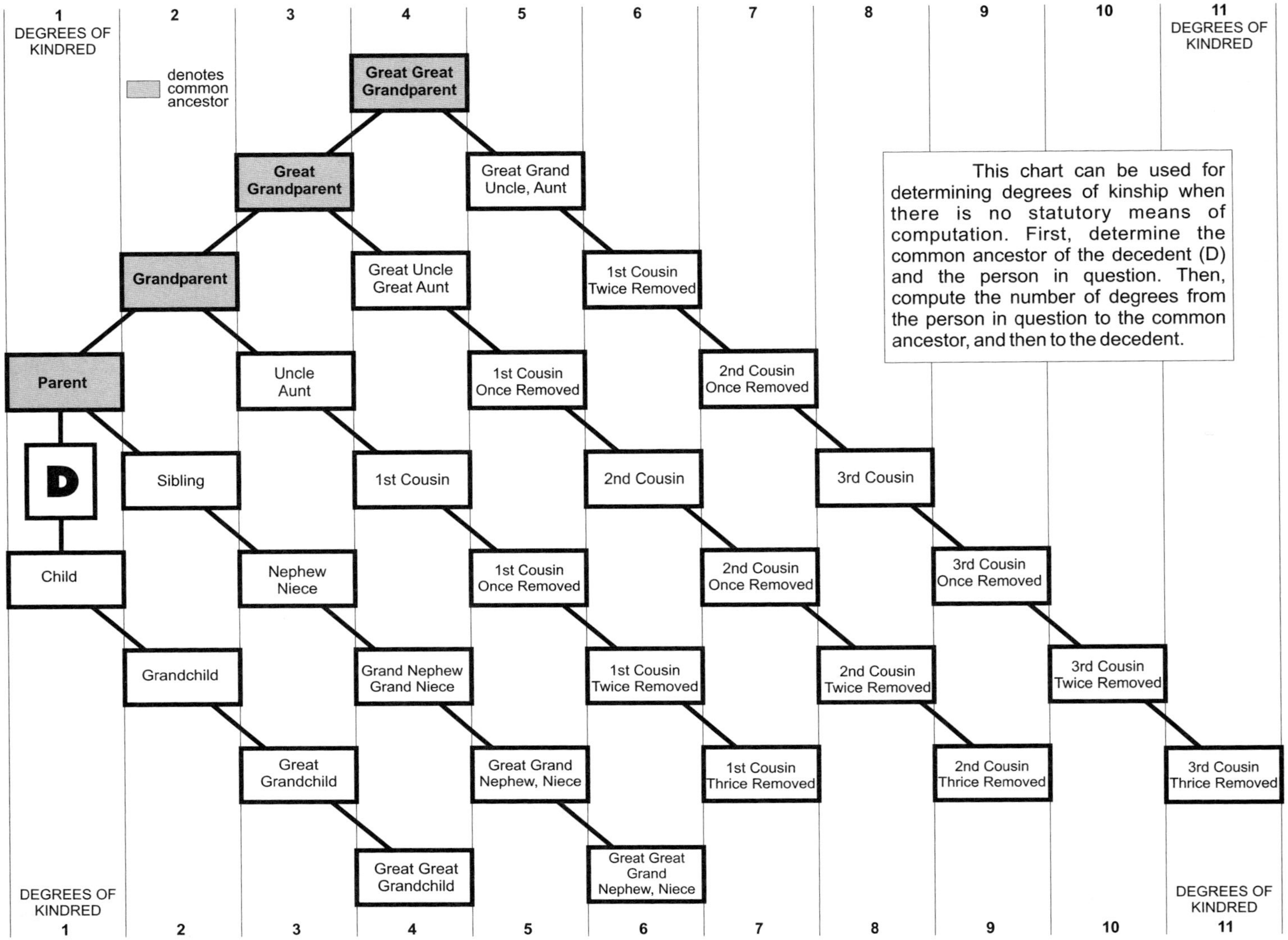

This chart can be used for determining degrees of kinship when there is no statutory means of computation. First, determine the common ancestor of the decedent (D) and the person in question. Then, compute the number of degrees from the person in question to the common ancestor, and then to the decedent.

SECTION OF LAND SHOWING ACREAGE AND DISTANCES

SECTION = One Square Mile = 640 Acres

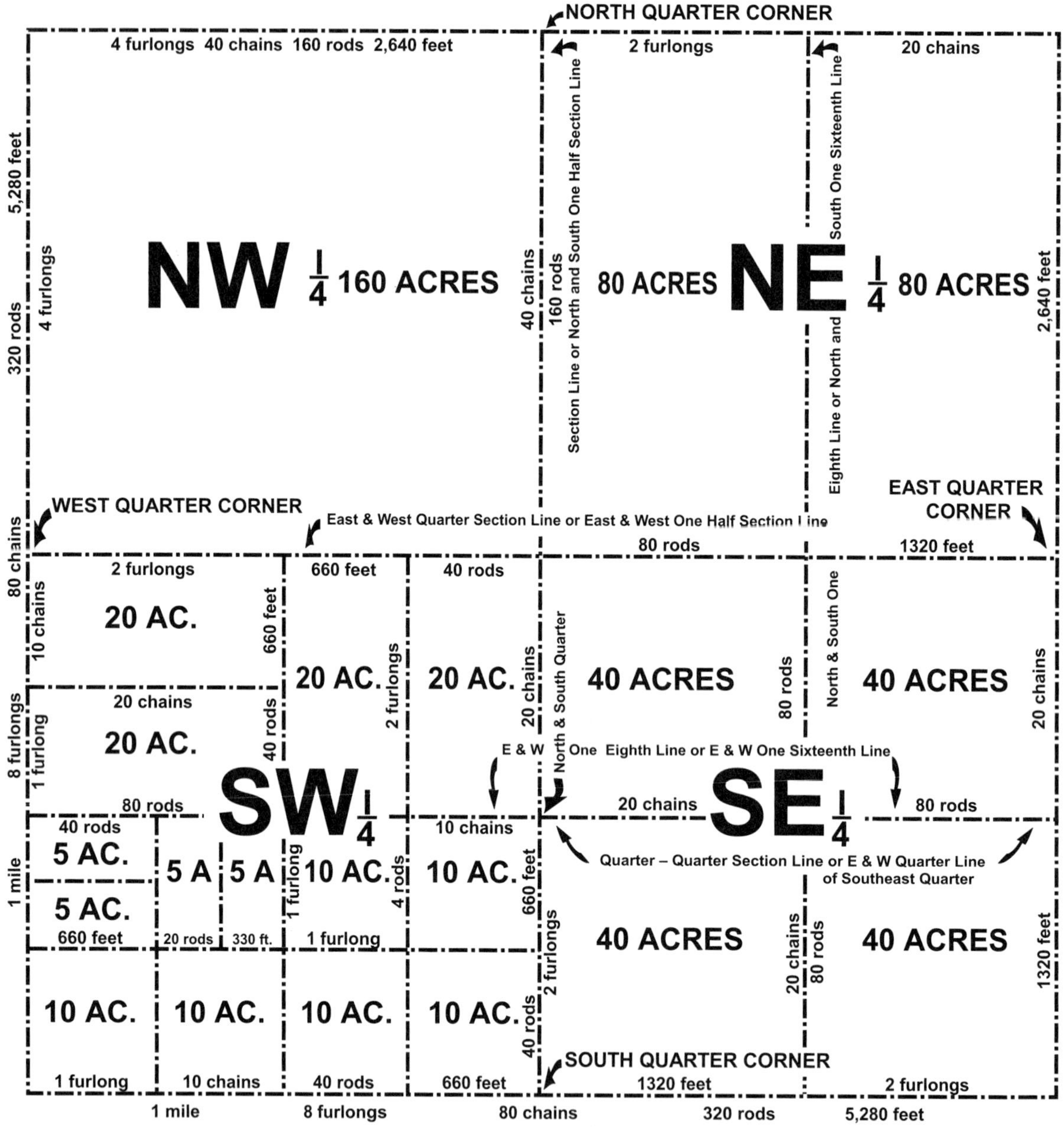

1 link — 7.92 inches
1 rod — 16½ feet
1 chain — 4 rods or 66 feet or 100 links
1 furlong — 660 feet or 40 rods
1 mile — 8 furlongs or 320 rods or 80 chains or 5,280 feet
1 sq. rod — 272¼ sq. feet or 30¼ sq. yards
1 acre — 43,560 sq. feet or 160 sq. rods
1 acre is 132 feet x 330 feet (or any two numbers of feet whose product is 43,560)
1 acre is 8 rods x 20 rods (or any two numbers of rods whose product is 160)
1 section — 1 square mile or 640 acres

PRO-RATING TABLE FOR RENTS, TAXES AND INSURANCE

Number of years, months and days	RENTS One Month		TAXES & INS.		INSURANCE						Number of years, months and days
	Days to Month		One Year		Three Years			Five Years			
	30	31	Months	Days	Years	Months	Days	Years	Months	Days	
1	.0333	.0323	.0833	.0028	.3333	.0278	.0009	.2000	.0167	.0006	1
2	.0667	.0645	.1667	.0056	.6667	.0556	.0019	.4000	.0333	.0011	2
3	.1000	.0968	.2500	.0083	1.0000	.0833	.0028	.6000	.0500	.0017	3
4	.1333	.1290	.3333	.0111		.1111	.0037	.8000	.0667	.0022	4
5	.1667	.1613	.4167	.0139		.1389	.0046	1.0000	.0833	.0028	5
6	.2000	.1935	.5000	.0167		.1667	.0056		.1000	.0033	6
7	.2333	.2258	.5833	.0194		.1944	.0065		.1167	.0039	7
8	.2667	.2581	.6667	.0222		.2222	.0074		.1333	.0044	8
9	.3000	.2903	.7500	.0250		.2500	.0083		.1500	.0050	9
10	.3333	.3226	.8333	.0278		.2778	.0093		.1667	.0056	10
11	.3667	.3548	.9167	.0306		.3056	.0102		.1833	.0061	11
12	.4000	.3871	1.0000	.0333		.3333	.0111		.2000	.0067	12
13	.4333	.4194		.0361			.0120			.0072	13
14	.4667	.4516		.0389			.0130			.0078	14
15	.5000	.4839		.0417			.0139			.0083	15
16	.5333	.5161		.0444			.0148			.0089	16
17	.5667	.5484		.0472			.0157			.0094	17
18	.6000	.5806		.0500			.0167			.0100	18
19	.6333	.6129		.0528			.0176			.0106	19
20	.6667	.6452		.0556			.0185			.0111	20
21	.7000	.6774		.0583			.0194			.0117	21
22	.7333	.7097		.0611			.0204			.0122	22
23	.7667	.7419		.0639			.0213			.0128	23
24	.8000	.7742		.0667			.0222			.0133	24
25	.8333	.8065		.0694			.0231			.0139	25
26	.8667	.8387		.0722			.0241			.0144	26
27	.9000	.8710		.0750			.0250			.0150	27
28	.9333	.9032		.0778			.0259			.0156	28
29	.9667	.9355		.0806			.0269			.0161	29
30	1.0000	.9677		.0833			.0278			.0167	30
31		1.0000									31

Example:
Rent $135.00 per mo.
To find value of 23 days of a 31 day mo.
From table: —
23 days = .7419
.7419 x 135.00 = $100.16

Example:
Taxes = $1215.12.
To find value of 7 mos. and 19 days
From Table: —
7 mos. = .5833
19 days = .0528

7 mos. 19 days = .6361
.6361 x 1215.12 = 772.95

Example:
3 Year Policy Premium = 58.75
To find the value of 1 yr. 3 mos. 11 days
From table: —
1 yr. = .3333
3 mos. = .0833
11 days = .0102

1 yr. 3 mos. 11 days = .4268
.4268 x 58.75 = 25.07

Example:
5 Year Policy Premium = 312.82
To find the value of 3 yrs. 4 mos. 13 days
From table: —
3 yrs. = .6000
4 mos. = .0667
13 days = .0072

3 yrs. 4 mos. 13 days = .6739
.6739 x 312.82 = 210.81

Robert Kratovil, **REAL ESTATE LAW**, 3rd edition (c) 1958. Prentice-Hall, Englewood Cliffs, N.J.

The Law Firm of Joffe & Joffe, P.A.

Attorneys at Law

Florida Federal Criminal Defense Law Firm focusing on white collar crime.

Florida Federal Criminal Defense Attorney, David J. Joffe

- Focuses on representing clients whose professional reputations, assets and social status would be at risk if convicted of a serious white collar crime. This includes, but is not limited to, stockbrokers, bank officers, CEO's, attorneys, physicians, entrepreneurs and other trade professionals.
- Since 1989, has represented people and businesses charged with serious crimes in both U.S. federal and state courts. He is admitted to practice before the United States Supreme Court, and all lower Federal Courts, including U.S. Tax Court.
- Has personally handled over 300 federal criminal cases.
- His experienced staff are fully equipped to defend you in any serious state or federal criminal case.

Referral Fees Paid per Florida Bar Rules.

Types of Cases

Antitrust Violations
Asset Forfeiture
Bank Fraud
Bankruptcy Fraud
Bribery
Business Fraud and Theft
Child Pornography
Computer Fraud
Conspiracy Cases
Counterfeiting
Credit Card Fraud
Cyberstalking
Drug Charges
Drug Trafficking
DUI/DWI
Economic Espionage
Embezzlement
Environmental Law Violations
Expunging Criminal Records
Federal Criminal Appeals
Federal Criminal Trials
Financial Fraud
Government Fraud
Grand Jury Representation
Healthcare Fraud
Insider Trading
Insurance Fraud
International Crimes
International Extradition
Internet Fraud
IRS Violations
Kickbacks
Mail Fraud
Money Laundering
Public Corruption
RICO Cases
Security Violations
Sex Crimes
State Felony Appeals
State Felony Trials
Tax Evasion
Tax Fraud
Telemarketing Fraud
Trade Secret Theft
White Collar Crimes

Main Office
Wachovia Bank Building
One East Broward Blvd.
Suite 700
Fort Lauderdale, FL 33301
T: 954-723-0007
F: 954-723-0033

The White Building
One Northeast Second Avenue
Suite 200
Miami, FL 33132
T: 305-579-0048
F: 305-358-2503

The Regions Bank Building
1100 Fifth Avenue South
Suite 201
Naples, FL 34102
T: 239-263-6161
F: 239-261-6877

www.joffelaw.com

ATTORNEYS GROUPED BY AREAS OF PRACTICE

The following attorneys have listed themselves under various fields of law. These listings do not imply special abilities or competency, merely that they are available to consult or associate with other attorneys under the particular field of law. Attorneys who limit their practice to a particular field of law, or who are admitted in other jurisdictions, or who are certified, may have these facts indicated in italics.

ABC MATTERS

(732) 727-5030 FAX 727-5028
SKENE LAW FIRM, P.C.
(Robert D. Skene)
2614 Route 516, 2nd Floor, Old Bridge, NJ 08857
Website: www.skenelawfirm.com E-Mail: rdskene@skenelawfirm.com

ADMIRALTY & MARITIME LAW

(212) 233-9385
FRIEDMAN, JAMES & BUCHSBAUM L.L.P.
(Bernard Friedman, John James, Andrew Buchsbaum)
132 Nassau Street, Suite 900, New York, NY 10038
Website: www.friedmanjames.com
Seamen, Pleasure Boats, Cruise Passengers, Fishermen, Longshoremen and Other Maritime Personal Injury, NY & NJ.

ADVERTISING LAW

(212) 683-9180 FAX 683-9181
THE LUSTIGMAN FIRM, P.C.
149 Madison Avenue, Suite 805, New York, NY 10016
Website: www.lustigmanfirm.com
Advertising Review, Sweepstakes, Internet Law, Regulatory Defense and Related Litigation.

APPELLATE PRACTICE

(212) 972-1355 FAX 972-1356
THOMAS S. FLEISHELL & ASSOCIATES, P.C.
561 7th Avenue, 19th Floor, New York, NY 10018

(718) 575-8588
NOREEN M. GIUSTI
123-35 82nd Road, Kew Gardens, NY 11415

(914) 533-3049 FAX 533-3051
ANNETTE G. HASAPIDIS
450 Oak Ridge Commons, South Salem, NY 10590
Website: www.nyappellateattorneys.com E-Mail: ahasapidis@appellatelaw.biz

(212) 682-0707
STEPHEN R. KRAWITZ
271 Madison Avenue, New York, NY 10016
Website: www.injuryappeals.com
Specializing in Personal Injury Appeals

(212) 732-0522
LEONARD J. LEVENSON
225 Broadway, New York, NY 10007
Criminal, Post Appellate and Parole Appeals Practice - Federal and State

(631) 499-3015 (877) USNYLAW
SUSAN R. NUDELMAN
92 Stonehurst Lane, Dix Hills, NY 11746-7934
Website: www.newyorkappeal.com E-Mail: srnesq@gmail.com
Civil Appeals, Memos, Motions, Research; J.D. Columbia '79

(718) 793-9226 FAX 793-2742
BENJAMIN VINAR
144-15 77th Avenue, Flushing, NY 11367
E-Mail: vinar@verizon.net

ARBITRATION

(212) 608-0919 FAX 791-6927
LEONA BEANE
11 Park Place, Suite 1100, New York, NY 10007
Available for Service as Arbitrator in Business Transactions and All Types of Proceedings.

(973) 252-7151 FAX 927-5684
MELISSA H. BIREN
4 Cramer Drive, Chester, NJ 07930
E-Mail: mhbiren@aol.com

(718) 793-9226 FAX 793-2742
BENJAMIN VINAR
144-15 77th Avenue, Flushing, NY 11367
E-Mail: vinar@verizon.net
Commercial Arbitration / as Arbitrator or Attorney

ATTORNEYS GROUPED BY AREAS OF PRACTICE

The following attorneys have listed themselves under various fields of law. These listings do not imply special abilities or competency, merely that they are available to consult or associate with other attorneys under the particular field of law. Attorneys who limit their practice to a particular field of law, or who are admitted in other jurisdictions, or who are certified, may have these facts indicated in italics.

ASBESTOS LITIGATION

(212) 558-5782 **WEITZ & LUXENBERG, P.C.**
FAX 558-5692 700 Broadway, New York, NY 10003
Website: www.weitzlux.com
Accepting referrals of all NY State asbestos cases

BANKRUPTCY LAW

(516) 228-4280 **STUART P. GELBERG**
FAX 228-4278 600 Old Country Road - Ste. 410, Garden City, NY 11530-2009
20 Years AV Rated. 30 Years Bankruptcy Experience.

(914) 946-1444 **DANIEL GRAUBART**
34 South Broadway, White Plains, NY 10601

(212) 684-7800 **WELTMAN & MOSKOWITZ, L.L.P.**
FAX 684-7995 (Richard E. Weltman, Michael L. Moskowitz, Michele K. Jaspan)
270 Madison Avenue, Suite 1400, New York, NY 10016
Website: www.weltmosk.com E-Mail: info@weltmosk.com
Bankruptcy & creditor-debtor litigation, incl. workouts & reorganizations, throughout NY & NJ

CIVIL RIGHTS LAW

(718) 852-8300 **OFODILE & ASSOCIATES, P.C.**
498 Atlantic Avenue, Brooklyn, NY 11217
False Arrests / Imprisonment, Police Brutality / Misconduct, Correction Brutality, Prisoners' Rights Including Medical Malpractice (civil cases only).
Prisoners Note: No Original Documents. Will Only Return Documents Requested by My Office. Will Respond to Your Letter if Interested in Your Case.

COLLECTION LAW

(631) 427-1140 **TODD E. HOUSLANGER, ESQ.**
FAX 427-1143 (Houslanger and Associates, P.L.L.C.)
372 New York Avenue, Huntington, NY 11743
(800) 431-1140 45 Kensico Drive, Mount Kisco, NY 10549
All Collections, Post Judgment Recovery, Bank Restraints, Asset Search and Liquidation. Entire State of New York.

(212) 736-2624 **THE LAW OFFICE OF MANUEL B. MOSES**
FAX 981-0528 236 West 26th Street, Suite 303, New York, NY 10001

(516) 795-7808 **ANNE ROSENBACH, P.C.**
FAX 795-9584 3 Delta Road, Massapequa, NY 11758

(212) 599-0971 **ERIC STREICH, P.C.**
FAX 599-0972 51 East 42nd Street, Suite 310, New York, NY 10017-5404
Website: www.ericstreichpc.com E-Mail: espc@ericstreichpc.com

COMMERCIAL LITIGATION

(516) 229-2360 **DAVID J. ABESHOUSE**
FAX 229-2361 626 RXR Plaza, Uniondale, NY 11556

CONSTRUCTION LAW

(856) 751-1860 **STEVEN A. BERKOWITZ & ASSOCIATES, P.C.**
FAX 751-1677 One Greentree Center, Suite 201, Marlton, NJ 08053
Website: www.ContractorLawOffices.com
NY, NJ, PA, Consultation in Construction matters

ATTORNEYS GROUPED BY AREAS OF PRACTICE

The following attorneys have listed themselves under various fields of law. These listings do not imply special abilities or competency, merely that they are available to consult or associate with other attorneys under the particular field of law. Attorneys who limit their practice to a particular field of law, or who are admitted in other jurisdictions, or who are certified, may have these facts indicated in italics.

CONTEST & GAMING LAW

(212) 683-9180 — **THE LUSTIGMAN FIRM, P.C.**
FAX 683-9181 — 149 Madison Avenue, Suite 805, New York, NY 10016
Website: www.lustigmanfirm.com; www.sweepstakeslaw.com
Advertising Review, Sweepstakes, Internet Law, Regulatory Defense and Related Litigation.

CRIMINAL LAW

(212) 939-9539 — **DAWN M. FLORIO LAW FIRM, P.L.L.C.**
FAX 939-9533 — 3604 Broadway, New York, NY 10031
Former prosecutor with 21 years experience specializing in all state and federal cases.

(954) 723-0007 — **THE LAW FIRM OF JOFFE & JOFFE, P.A.**
FAX 723-0033 — The Wachovia Bank Building, 1 East Broward Boulevard, Suite 700, Fort Lauderdale, FL 33301
(754) 423-6057 — The White Building, 1 NE 2nd Avenue, Suite 200, Miami, FL 33132
(866) 226-9596 — The Regions Bank Building, 1100 5th Avenue South, Suite 201, Naples, FL 34102
Website: www.joffelaw.com
Florida AV Rated Criminal Defense Attorney; Referral Fee Paid Pursuant to Court Rules.
Listed in the Registry of Preeminent Attorneys for Martindale-Hubbell.
See Display Ad on Page 1620

(845) 562-0500 — **THE LAW OFFICE OF JAMES W. WINSLOW, P.C.**
FAX 562-0839 — 10 Little Britain Road, Suite 201, P.O. Box 2275, Newburgh, NY 12550
Website: www.winslowlawoffice.com E-Mail: butwin@hvc.rr.com
Serving all NY State & Federal courts from the Mid-Hudson Valley. Traffic tickets to murder.

CUSTOMS LAW

(212) 973-7728 — **PETER W. KLESTADT**
FAX 557-4415 — (Grunfeld, Desiderio, Lebowitz, Silverman & Klestadt, L.L.P.)
399 Park Avenue, 25th Floor, New York, NY 10022-4877
Website: www.gdlsk.com E-Mail: pklestadt@gdlsk.com
Customs and International Trade

DISCRIMINATION LAW

(718) 852-8300 — **OFODILE & ASSOCIATES, P.C.**
498 Atlantic Avenue, Brooklyn, NY 11217
Employment Discrimination Based on Race, Color, National Origin, Age, Sex or Religion.
Housing Discrimination, Sexual Harassment, Equal Pay, Wage/Hour Law.

DOMESTIC RELATIONS LAW

(718) 366-6418 — **ALAN H. JOSEPH**
69-38 Myrtle Avenue, Glendale, NY 11385

DRUG & MEDICAL DEVICE LITIGATION

(212) 558-5782 — **WEITZ & LUXENBERG, P.C.**
FAX 558-5692 — 700 Broadway, New York, NY 10003
Website: www.weitzlux.com
Accepting referrals of all drug & medical device cases

ATTORNEYS GROUPED BY AREAS OF PRACTICE

The following attorneys have listed themselves under various fields of law. These listings do not imply special abilities or competency, merely that they are available to consult or associate with other attorneys under the particular field of law. Attorneys who limit their practice to a particular field of law, or who are admitted in other jurisdictions, or who are certified, may have these facts indicated in italics.

EDUCATION LAW

(212) 644-4414 **LAW OFFICES OF LAUREN A. BAUM, P.C.**
FAX 644-8470 (Lauren A. Baum, Richard A. Liese, Scott M. Cohen)
307 East 53rd Street, Suite 501, New York, NY 10022
Website: www.nyspecialedlaw.com

(212) 732-9450 **LAW OFFICES OF NEAL H. ROSENBERG**
FAX 571-9893 (Neal H. Rosenberg, Alex Hindes, Karen Newman, Nate Kuzma, Jenna Pantel)
9 Murray Street, Suite 4W, New York, NY 10007

(212) 532-9736 **LAW OFFICES OF REGINA SKYER & ASSOCIATES**
FAX 532-9846 (Regina P. Skyer, Jesse C. Cutler, Samantha Bernstein, Gregory Cangiano, Sonia M. Castro, Jaime Chlupsa, Lara Damashek, Diana K. Gersten)
276 Fifth Avenue, New York, NY 10001
E-Mail: skyerlaw@aol.com

ELDER LAW

(516) 829-9595 **BUSELL & STIER, P.L.L.C.**
(Sandra N. Busell, Eileen D. Stier)
98 Cuttermill Road, Suite 395N, Great Neck, NY 11021
Member, National Academy of Elder Law Attorneys, NYSBA Elder Law Section

(516) 466-4422 **RONALD FATOULLAH & ASSOCIATES**
(Ronald A. Fatoullah, Stacey Meshnick, Debby Rosenfeld, Carol M. Adams)
425 Northern Boulevard, Suite 20, Great Neck, NY 11021
(212) 751-7600 475 Park Avenue South, 18th Floor, New York, NY 10016
(718) 261-1700 100-15 Queens Boulevard, Suite 1, Forest Hills, NY 11375
(718) 621-5300 1861 86th Street, Brooklyn, NY 11214
(516) 466-3300 466 Central Avenue, 2nd Floor, Cedarhurst, NY 11516

(212) 387-8400 **GOLDFARB ABRANDT SALZMAN & KUTZIN L.L.P.**
FAX 387-8404 The Empire State Building, 350 5th Avenue, #1100, New York, NY 10118

(212) 490-2020 **LITTMAN KROOKS L.L.P.**
FAX 490-2990 655 Third Avenue, New York, NY 10017
(914) 684-2100 399 Knollwood Road, White Plains, NY 10603
(845) 896-1106 300 Westage Business Center Drive, Fishkill, NY 12524
Website: www.littmankrooks.com E-Mail: info@littmankrooks.com

(516) 683-1717 **VINCENT J. RUSSO & ASSOCIATES, P.C.**
FAX 683-9393 1600 Stewart Avenue, Suite 300, Westbury, NY 11590
(631) 582-1919 3740 Expressway Drive South, Islandia, NY 11749
(516) 897-7100 250 Lido Boulevard, Lido Beach, NY 11561
(516) 682-8282 7600 Jericho Turnpike, Suite 110, Woodbury, NY 11797
Website: www.vjrussolaw.com E-Mail: info@vjrussolaw.com

EMPLOYMENT LAW

(516) 248-2121 **LAW OFFICE OF RAYMOND NARDO**
129 Third Street, Mineola, NY 11501
Website: www.raynardo.com E-Mail: raymondnardo@gmail.com
Representing Employees in all Areas of Employment Law

(718) 852-8300 **OFODILE & ASSOCIATES, P.C.**
498 Atlantic Avenue, Brooklyn, NY 11217
Represents Labor in Discrimination Cases, Including Sexual Harassment. Accepts Atty. Referrals.

ATTORNEYS GROUPED BY AREAS OF PRACTICE

The following attorneys have listed themselves under various fields of law. These listings do not imply special abilities or competency, merely that they are available to consult or associate with other attorneys under the particular field of law. Attorneys who limit their practice to a particular field of law, or who are admitted in other jurisdictions, or who are certified, may have these facts indicated in italics.

ENTERTAINMENT LAW

(212) 725-1818 **FURGANG & ADWAR, L.L.P.**
FAX 941-9711 1325 Avenue of the Americas, 28th Floor, New York, NY 10019
(914) 428-5300 11 Martine Avenue, Penthouse, White Plains, NY 10606
(845) 353-1818 Centerock East, 2 Crosfield Avenue, Suite 210, West Nyack, NY 10994
Fax numbers: (914) 428-0226 (845) 353-1996
Languages spoken: English & Spanish

(516) 987-2104 **THE JACOBSON FIRM, P.C.**
FAX 374-4127 (Jeffrey E. Jacobson)
60 Madison Avenue, Suite 1026, New York, NY 10010
1208 West Broadway, P.O. Box 425, Hewlett, NY 11557
Website: www.jacobsonfirm.com E-Mail: jejesq@aol.com

ENVIRONMENTAL LAW

(516) 845-8087 **THEODORE W. FIRETOG**
111 Thomas Powell Boulevard, Farmingdale, NY 11735

(212) 558-5782 **WEITZ & LUXENBERG, P.C.**
FAX 558-5692 700 Broadway, New York, NY 10003
Website: www.weitzlux.com
Accepting referrals of all environmental toxic tort cases

ESTATE PLANNING & ADMINISTRATION

(516) 829-9595 **BUSELL & STIER, P.L.L.C.**
(Sandra N. Busell, Eileen D. Stier)
98 Cuttermill Road, Suite 395N, Great Neck, NY 11021
Member, National Academy of Elder Law Attorneys, NYSBA Elder Law Section

(516) 466-4422 **RONALD FATOULLAH & ASSOCIATES**
(Ronald A. Fatoullah, Stacey Meshnick, Debby Rosenfeld, Carol M. Adams)
425 Northern Boulevard, Suite 20, Great Neck, NY 11021
(212) 751-7600 475 Park Avenue South, 18th Floor, New York, NY 10016
(718) 261-1700 100-15 Queens Boulevard, Suite 1, Forest Hills, NY 11375
(718) 621-5300 1861 86th Street, Brooklyn, NY 11214
(516) 466-3300 466 Central Avenue, 2nd Floor, Cedarhurst, NY 11516

FRANCHISE LAW

(212) 725-1818 **FURGANG & ADWAR, L.L.P.**
FAX 941-9711 1325 Avenue of the Americas, 28th Floor, New York, NY 10019
(914) 428-5300 11 Martine Avenue, Penthouse, White Plains, NY 10606
(845) 353-1818 Centerock East, 2 Crosfield Avenue, Suite 210, West Nyack, NY 10994
Fax numbers: (914) 428-0226 (845) 353-1996
Languages spoken: English & Spanish

GRIEVANCES LAW

(516) 294-8000 **EDWIN J. MULHERN**
FAX 877-1195 One Old Country Road, Carle Place, NY 11514
Accepting Referrals Relating to Grievance & Ethical Matters

ATTORNEYS GROUPED BY AREAS OF PRACTICE

The following attorneys have listed themselves under various fields of law. These listings do not imply special abilities or competency, merely that they are available to consult or associate with other attorneys under the particular field of law. Attorneys who limit their practice to a particular field of law, or who are admitted in other jurisdictions, or who are certified, may have these facts indicated in italics.

IMMIGRATION & NATURALIZATION LAW

(212) 695-2877 FAX 213-2393
LAW OFFICES OF JEFFREY GABEL
286 Madison Avenue, Suite 502, New York, NY 10017

(877) 846-4111
PANKAJ MALIK
75-35 31st Avenue, Suite 207A, East Elmhurst, NY 11370
Website: www.virtualimmigration.com E-Mail: palavimalik@malikpc.com
Immigration Litigation and CLE

(201) 670-0006 FAX 670-0009
NACHMAN & ASSOCIATES, P.C.
(David H. Nachman, Ludka Zimovcak, Véronique Malka and Victoria Donoghue)
7 West 36th Street, 14th Floor, New York, NY 10018
Website: www.visaserve.com
Special Emphasis on Corporate, Employment and Business Related Immigration Matters.
Languages Spoken: Spanish, Russian, Korean, Chinese, Polish, Hindi, Slovak, French & Japanese.

INSURANCE LAW

(212) 834-0600 FAX 490-0035
GORDON & SILBER, P.C.
355 Lexington Avenue, 7th Floor, New York, NY 10017
E-Mail: acohen@gordon-silber.com

(718) 793-9226 FAX 793-2742
BENJAMIN VINAR
144-15 77th Avenue, Flushing, NY 11367
E-Mail: vinar@verizon.net

LANDLORD & TENANT LAW

(212) 972-1355 FAX 972-1356
THOMAS S. FLEISHELL & ASSOCIATES, P.C.
561 7th Avenue, 19th Floor, New York, NY 10018

(212) 349-3000 FAX 587-0744
HIMMELSTEIN, MCCONNELL, GRIBBEN, DONOGHUE & JOSEPH
15 Maiden Lane, 17th Floor, New York, NY 10038

(212) 869-5030 FAX 944-5818
KUCKER & BRUH, L.L.P.
(Saul D. Bruh, Alan D. Kucker, Patrick K. Munson, James R. Marino, Nativ Winiarsky, Andrew B. Bittens, John Churneftsky, William Hummell, Louis L. Nock, Catherine A. Helwig)
747 Third Avenue, New York, NY 10017

(718) 852-5769 FAX 858-4861
ALAN J. REDNER
26 Court Street, Suite 2410, Brooklyn, NY 11242

(212) 397-6661 FAX 307-5197
BARRY S. SCHWARTZ
119 West 57th Street, New York, NY 10019
Website: www.barrysschwartz.com
Martindale-Hubbell rated AV

LEGAL MALPRACTICE

(718) 793-9226 FAX 793-2742
BENJAMIN VINAR
144-15 77th Avenue, Flushing, NY 11367
E-Mail: vinar@verizon.net

MALPRACTICE LITIGATION

(212) 752-3380 FAX 593-3807
ROBERT D. BECKER
880 Third Avenue, New York, NY 10022

(212) 661-9000
DAVID B. GOLOMB
230 Park Avenue, Suite 527, New York, NY 10169
Accepting Referrals Relating to Medical and Professional Malpractice & all Personal Injury Matters

ATTORNEYS GROUPED BY AREAS OF PRACTICE

The following attorneys have listed themselves under various fields of law. These listings do not imply special abilities or competency, merely that they are available to consult or associate with other attorneys under the particular field of law. Attorneys who limit their practice to a particular field of law, or who are admitted in other jurisdictions, or who are certified, may have these facts indicated in italics.

MALPRACTICE LITIGATION (Cont'd)

(212) 244-2999
KOPFF, NARDELLI & DOPF, L.L.P.
440 Ninth Avenue, New York, NY 10001
Practice Centered Around Defense of Personal Injury and Wrongful Death Actions.
Also Concentrate in Defending Professional Liability Actions Including: Medical Malpractice, Legal Malpractice, Accountant Malpractice, Construction Liability and General Liability Defense

(212) 684-1880
FAX 689-8156
RHEINGOLD, VALET, RHEINGOLD, SHKOLNIK & MCCARTNEY L.L.P.
113 E. 37th Street, New York, NY 10016
Erb's Palsy and All Other Areas of Malpractice

MEDIATION

(516) 229-2360
FAX 229-2361
DAVID J. ABESHOUSE
626 RXR Plaza, Uniondale, NY 11556
Business & Commercial ADR (contracts, corporations, partnerships, LLCs, entrepreneurs, etc.)

(212) 608-0919
FAX 791-6927
LEONA BEANE
11 Park Place, Suite 1100, New York, NY 10007
Available for Service as Mediator in Corporate, Partnership & Contract Disputes, Trusts & Estates and All Other Types of Disputes.

MEDICAL MALPRACTICE

(973) 403-9200
FAX 226-0031
AMOS GERN
(Starr, Gern, Davison & Rubin, P.C.)
105 Eisenhower Parkway, Roseland, NJ 07068
See Display Ad on Page 1621

(212) 736-2624
FAX 981-0528
THE LAW OFFICE OF MANUEL B. MOSES
236 West 26th Street, Suite 303, New York, NY 10001

(212) 558-5555
FAX 558-5788
WEITZ & LUXENBERG, P.C.
(Gary R. Klein)
700 Broadway, New York, NY 10003
Website: www.weitzlux.com
Accepting referrals of all Medical Malpractice cases

NEGLIGENCE LAW

(212) 661-9000
DAVID B. GOLOMB
230 Park Avenue, Suite 527, New York, NY 10169
Accepting Referrals Relating to Medical and Professional Malpractice & all Personal Injury Matters

(718) 366-6418
ALAN H. JOSEPH
69-38 Myrtle Avenue, Glendale, NY 11385

OIL & GAS LAW

(315) 446-2384
ROY D. PINSKY
5790 Widewaters Parkway, Suite 250, Syracuse, NY 13214

PAROLE REVOCATION DEFENSE

(631) 427-1140
FAX 427-1143
TODD E. HOUSLANGER, ESQ.
(Houslanger and Associates, P.L.L.C.)
372 New York Avenue, Huntington, NY 11743

ATTORNEYS GROUPED BY AREAS OF PRACTICE

The following attorneys have listed themselves under various fields of law. These listings do not imply special abilities or competency, merely that they are available to consult or associate with other attorneys under the particular field of law. Attorneys who limit their practice to a particular field of law, or who are admitted in other jurisdictions, or who are certified, may have these facts indicated in italics.

PATENT, COPYRIGHT & TRADEMARK LAW

(212) 725-1818 **FURGANG & ADWAR, L.L.P.**
FAX 941-9711 1325 Avenue of the Americas, 28th Floor, New York, NY 10019
(914) 428-5300 11 Martine Avenue, Penthouse, White Plains, NY 10606
(845) 353-1818 Centerock East, 2 Crosfield Avenue, Suite 210, West Nyack, NY 10994
Fax numbers: (914) 428-0226 (845) 353-1996
Languages spoken: English & Spanish

(516) 987-2104 **THE JACOBSON FIRM, P.C.**
FAX 374-4127 (Jeffrey E. Jacobson)
60 Madison Avenue, Suite 1026, New York, NY 10010
1208 West Broadway, P.O. Box 425, Hewlett, NY 11557
Website: www.jacobsonfirm.com E-Mail: jejesq@aol.com

PER DIEM SERVICES

(212) 631-7436 **BRONFELD & SCHIFF, ESQS.**
352 Seventh Avenue, Suite 905, New York, NY 10001
See Display Ad on Page 1621

(516) 621-6689 **ILENE H. COHEN, ESQ.**
FAX 621-0259 P.O. Box 221, Roslyn, NY 11576
Website: www.PerDiemAttorneys.com
Coverage provided in 62 NY State counties.

(516) 795-7808 **ANNE ROSENBACH, P.C.**
FAX 795-9584 3 Delta Road, Massapequa, NY 11758

PERSONAL INJURY LITIGATION

(212) 661-9000 **DAVID B. GOLOMB**
230 Park Avenue, Suite 527, New York, NY 10169
Accepting Referrals Relating to Medical and Professional Malpractice & all Personal Injury Matters

(212) 736-2624 **THE LAW OFFICE OF MANUEL B. MOSES**
FAX 981-0528 236 West 26th Street, Suite 303, New York, NY 10001

(718) 793-9226 **BENJAMIN VINAR**
FAX 793-2742 144-15 77th Avenue, Flushing, NY 11367
E-Mail: vinar@verizon.net

(212) 558-5555 **WEITZ & LUXENBERG, P.C.**
FAX 558-5788 (Gary R. Klein)
700 Broadway, New York, NY 10003
Website: www.weitzlux.com
Accepting referrals of all Personal Injury cases

PROBATE & SURROGATE'S COURT PROCEEDINGS

(212) 608-0919 **LEONA BEANE**
FAX 791-6927 11 Park Place, Suite 1100, New York, NY 10007

(914) 375-2900 **GEORGE A. WEISSBLUM, ESQ.**
FAX 375-2901 570 Yonkers Avenue, Yonkers, NY 10704

PRODUCTS LIABILITY LAW

(212) 684-1880 **RHEINGOLD, VALET, RHEINGOLD, SHKOLNIK & MCCARTNEY L.L.P.**
FAX 689-8156 113 E. 37th Street, New York, NY 10016
Drugs, Vehicles and All Other Products.

(212) 558-5782 **WEITZ & LUXENBERG, P.C.**
FAX 558-5692 700 Broadway, New York, NY 10003
Website: www.weitzlux.com
Accepting referrals of certain product liability cases

ATTORNEYS GROUPED BY AREAS OF PRACTICE

The following attorneys have listed themselves under various fields of law. These listings do not imply special abilities or competency, merely that they are available to consult or associate with other attorneys under the particular field of law. Attorneys who limit their practice to a particular field of law, or who are admitted in other jurisdictions, or who are certified, may have these facts indicated in italics.

REAL ESTATE LAW

(646) 709-8120 FAX 403-4753
TALIYA A. BASHANI, ESQ.
(TAB Law Firm, P.C.)
65 Broadway, Suite 829, New York, NY 10006

(212) 679-6240 FAX 481-9569
DRESNER & DRESNER
(Byron Dresner, Cheryl Dresner)
276 Fifth Avenue, Suite 403, New York, NY 10001
Website: www.dresnerlaw.com E-Mail: bdr@dresnerlaw.com

(212) 972-1355 FAX 972-1356
THOMAS S. FLEISHELL & ASSOCIATES, P.C.
561 7th Avenue, 19th Floor, New York, NY 10018

(212) 349-3000 FAX 587-0744
HIMMELSTEIN, MCCONNELL, GRIBBEN, DONOGHUE & JOSEPH
15 Maiden Lane, 17th Floor, New York, NY 10038

SECURITIES ARBITRATION LAW

(212) 826-1500 FAX 688-6457
(631) 261-0250 FAX 261-0395
TIMOTHY J. DENNIN, P.C.
270 Madison Avenue, 13th Floor, New York, NY 10016
316 Main Street, Northport, NY 11768
Website: www.denninlaw.com

(718) 638-2383 FAX 857-9339
LAWRENCE R. GELBER
The Vanderbilt Plaza, 34 Plaza Street, Suite 1107, Brooklyn, NY 11238
Website: www.gelberlaw.net E-Mail: gelberlaw@aol.com

(212) 943-1233 FAX 943-1238
MALECKI LAW
11 Broadway, Suite 715, New York, NY 10004
Website: www.aboutsecuritieslaw.com

(212) 764-3100 FAX (646) 843-4964
STUART D. MEISSNER, L.L.C.
450 Seventh Avenue, Suite 2205, New York, NY 10123
Website: www.stockesq.com

(212) 308-3456 FAX 879-6806
THE NOLAN LAW FIRM
444 E. 75th Street, Apt. 15D, New York, NY 10021
E-Mail: wpn@attorneysnewyork.com
Recognized in Martindale-Hubbell's 2010 Register of Preeminent Lawyers

(212) 742-1414 FAX 742-1177
ZAMANSKY & ASSOCIATES
50 Broadway, 32nd Floor, New York, NY 10004

SECURITIES LAW

(212) 826-1500 FAX 688-6457
(631) 261-0250 FAX 261-0395
TIMOTHY J. DENNIN, P.C.
270 Madison Avenue, 13th Floor, New York, NY 10016
316 Main Street, Northport, NY 11768
Website: www.denninlaw.com

(212) 943-1233 FAX 943-1238
MALECKI LAW
11 Broadway, Suite 715, New York, NY 10004
Website: www.aboutsecuritieslaw.com

SOCIAL SECURITY DISABILITY

(877) 527-5529
KAZMIERCZAK & KAZMIERCZAK, L.L.P.
5 Penn Plaza, 250 West 34th Street, New York, NY 10119
Website: www.karlkaz.com E-Mail: kazmierczak@verizon.net
Board Certified Social Security Disability Specialist; Veterans Disability Law

ATTORNEYS GROUPED BY AREAS OF PRACTICE

The following attorneys have listed themselves under various fields of law. These listings do not imply special abilities or competency, merely that they are available to consult or associate with other attorneys under the particular field of law. Attorneys who limit their practice to a particular field of law, or who are admitted in other jurisdictions, or who are certified, may have these facts indicated in italics.

SOCIAL SECURITY LAW

(212) 608-4100 **WENDY BRILL**
9 Murray Street, 4th Floor, New York, NY 10007
(631) 726-5435 P.O. Box 205, Watermill, NY 11976
E-Mail: wbrillatty@optonline.net
Accepting Referrals Relating to Social Security Disability Claims in the five Boroughs of NY, Nassau, Suffolk, Westchester and NJ. Clients do not need to travel.
Thirty Years Experience.

TAXATION

(212) 227-2424 **RICHARD C. ANTONELLI**
(732) 390-9898 225 Broadway, Suite 1200, New York, NY 10007
Accepting Referrals in Civil & Criminal Tax Matters
Admitted to Practice in NJ and NY
Former IRS Tax Court Trial Attorney and Appellate Conferee

(516) 579-7700 **LEON LEBENSBAUM**
FAX 579-7945 3601 Hempstead Turnpike, Levittown, NY 11756
CPA and Attorney at Law. Retired Special Agent; Certified Fraud Examiner; DABFA; Accepting Referrals on Tax Fraud Matters; Criminal Tax Matters; Non-Filers; Audits; Appeals; Payroll Tax Matters; Financial Investigations.

TRAFFIC LAW

(914) 271-5383 **CASEY W. RASKOB, III**
FAX 271-4548 34 Lounsbury Road, Croton, NY 10520
Website: www.speedlaw.net E-Mail: info@speedlaw.net
Accepting Referrals of all Motor Vehicle Violations Statewide, Commercial & Non-Commercial
Your Speed Trap Solution

TRANSPORTATION LAW

(315) 446-2384 **PINSKY & SKANDALIS**
5790 Widewaters Parkway, Suite 250, Syracuse, NY 13214

VETERANS DISABILITY LAW

(877) 527-5529 **KAZMIERCZAK & KAZMIERCZAK, L.L.P.**
5 Penn Plaza, 250 West 34th Street, New York, NY 10119
Website: www.karlkaz.com E-Mail: kazmierczak@verizon.net
Veterans Disability Law; Board Certified Social Security Disability Specialist

WILLS, ESTATES & TRUSTS

(212) 608-0919 **LEONA BEANE**
FAX 791-6927 11 Park Place, Suite 1100, New York, NY 10007

(212) 387-8400 **GOLDFARB ABRANDT SALZMAN & KUTZIN L.L.P.**
FAX 387-8404 The Empire State Building, 350 5th Avenue, #1100, New York, NY 10118

ATTORNEYS GROUPED BY AREAS OF PRACTICE

The following attorneys have listed themselves under various fields of law. These listings do not imply special abilities or competency, merely that they are available to consult or associate with other attorneys under the particular field of law. Attorneys who limit their practice to a particular field of law, or who are admitted in other jurisdictions, or who are certified, may have these facts indicated in italics.

WORKERS' COMPENSATION LAW

(718) 446-4400
FAX 446-6537

BANGEL & COHEN, L.L.P.
(David J. Bangel, Stephen H. Cohen)
91-31 Queens Boulevard, Suite 212, Elmhurst, NY 11373
Accepting Referrals in all Matters Relating to New York Workers' Compensation

(631) 367-1362
FAX 367-1363

THE LAW OFFICES OF THOMAS S. HARKINS, P.C.
24 Glen Way, Cold Spring Harbor, NY 11724
Accepting Referrals Relating to Federal Workers' Compensation Matters

(516) 294-5775
FAX 228-0044

KLEE & WOOLF, L.L.P.
(Jonathan Klee, Andrew Woolf)
350 Willis Avenue, Mineola, NY 11501
(718) 229-9002 — 26 Court Street, Suite 2606, Brooklyn, NY 11242
(516) 294-5775 — 116 Spruce Street, Cedarhurst, NY 11516
Website: www.kleewoolflaw.com E-Mail: info@kleewoolflaw.com
Accepting Referrals in all Matters Relating to New York Workers' Compensation

ZONING, PLANNING & LAND USE

(845) 294-7944

FABRICANT LIPMAN & FRISHBERG, P.L.L.C.
(Alan S. Lipman)
One Harriman Square, P.O. Box 60, Goshen, NY 10924

WEIGHTS AND MEASURES

APOTHECARIES' WEIGHT

20 grains............... 1 scruple — 8 drams.................. 1 ounce
3 scruples............... 1 dram — 12 ounces.............. 1 pound

Ounce and pound are the same as in Troy Weight

AVOIRDUPOIS WEIGHT

27 11/32 grains......... 1 dram — 25 pounds............ 1 quarter
16 drams................ 1 ounce — 4 quarters................ 1 cwt.
16 ounces............... 1 pound — 2,000 lbs............ 1 short ton
2,240 pounds.. 1 long ton

TROY WEIGHT

24 grains.. 1 pwt.
20 pwt.................. 1 ounce — 12 ounces.............. 1 pound

Used for weighing gold, silver and jewels

CLOTH MEASURE

2 1/4 inches.............. 1 nail — 4 nails................ 1 quarter
4 quarters.. 1 yard

CUBIC MEASURE

1,728 cubic inches.................................. 1 cubic foot
27 cubic feet.. 1 cubic yard
128 cubic feet...................................... 1 cord (wood)
40 cubic feet...................................... 1 ton (shipping)
2,150.42 cubic inches.............................. 1 standard bushel
231 cubic inches............................... 1 U.S. standard gallon
1 cubic foot.................................... about 4/5 of a bushel

DRY MEASURE

2 pints.................. 1 quart — 4 pecks.................. 1 bushel
8 quarts.................. 1 peck — 36 bushels.......... 1 chaldron

LIQUID MEASURE

4 gills...................... 1 pint — 4 quarts................ 1 gallon
2 pints.................. 1 quart — 31 1/2 gallons.......... 1 barrel
2 barrels.. 1 hogshead

LONG MEASURE

12 inches.................. 1 foot — 40 rods................ 1 furlong
3 feet...................... 1 yard — 8 furlongs....... 1 statute mile
5 1/2 yards................ 1 rod — 3 miles................ 1 league

MARINERS' MEASURE

6 feet.. 1 fathom
120 fathoms.................................. 1 cable length
7 1/2 cable lengths.............................. 1 mile
5,280 feet.................................... 1 statute mile
6,080.2 feet.................................. 1 nautical mile

PAPER MEASURE

24 sheets................ 1 quire — 20 quires, 1 ream (480 sheets)
2 reams................ 1 bundle — 5 bundles.................. 1 bale

SQUARE MEASURE

144 sq. inches........... 1 sq. ft. — 40 sq. rods................ 1 rood
9 sq. ft.................. 1 sq. yard — 4 roods...................... 1 acre
30 1/4 sq. yards....... 1 sq. rod — 640 acres.............. 1 sq. mile

SURVEYORS' MEASURE

7.92 inches.. 1 link
25 links.. 1 rod
4 rods.. 1 chain
10 sq. chains or 160 sq. rods.......................... 1 acre
43,560 sq. feet.. 1 acre
640 acres.. 1 sq. mile
36 sq. miles (6 miles sq.)............................ 1 township

TIME MEASURE

60 seconds............. 1 minute — 60 minutes.............. 1 hour
24 hours..................... 1 day — 7 days...................... 1 week
28, 29, 30 or 31 days............................ 1 calendar month
30 days.................. 1 month — .... in computing interest
365 days.................. 1 year — 366 days............ 1 leap year

MISCELLANEOUS

3 inches.................. 1 palm — 4 inches.................. 1 hand
6 inches.................... 1 span — 18 inches................ 1 cubit
21.8 inches.. 1 Bible cubit
2 1/2 feet.. 1 military pace

METRIC EQUIVALENTS—Linear Measure

1 centimeter.. 0.3937 inch
1 inch.. 2.54 centimeters
1 decimeter....... 3.937 inches .... 0.328 foot
1 foot.. 3.048 decimeters
1 meter........... 39.37 inches .... 1.0936 yards
1 yard.. 0.9144 meter
1 dekameter.. 1.9884 rods
1 rod.. 0.5029 dekameter
1 kilometer.. 0.62137 mile
1 mile.. 1.6093 kilometers

Square Measure

1 square centimeter.............................. 0.1550 square inch
1 square inch.............................. 6.452 square centimeters
1 square decimeter.............................. 0.1076 square foot
1 square foot.............................. 9.2903 square decimeters
1 square meter.............................. 1.196 square yards
1 square yard.............................. 0.8361 square meter
1 acre.. 160 square rods
1 square rod.. 0.00625 acre
1 hectare.. 2.47 acres
1 acre.. 0.4047 hectare
1 square kilometer.............................. 0.386 square mile
1 square mile.............................. 2.59 square kilometers

Measure of Volume

1 cubic centimeter.............................. 0.061 cubic inch
1 cubic inch.............................. 16.39 cubic centimeters
1 cubic decimeter.............................. 0.0353 cubic foot
1 cubic foot.............................. 28.317 cubic decimeters
1 cubic meter.............................. 1.308 cubic yards
1 cubic yard.............................. 0.7646 cubic meter
1 stere.. 0.2759 cord
1 cord.. 3.624 steres
1 liter.......... 0.908 quart dry .... 1.0567 quarts liquid
1 quart dry.. 1.101 liters
1 quart liquid.. 0.9463 liter
1 dekaliter..... 2.6417 gallons .... 1.135 pecks
1 gallon.. 0.3785 dekaliter
1 peck.. 0.881 dekaliter
1 hektoliter.. 2.8375 bushels
1 bushel.. 0.3524 hektoliter

Weights

1 gram.. 0.03527 ounce
1 ounce.. 28.35 grams
1 kilogram.. 2.2046 pounds
1 pound.. 0.4536 kilogram
1 metric ton.............................. 0.98421 English ton
1 English ton.............................. 1.016 metric tons

APPROXIMATE METRIC EQUIVALENTS

1 decimeter.. 4 inches
1 liter.............................. 1.06 quarts liquid, 0.9 quart dry
1 meter.. 1.1 yards
1 kilometer.. 5/8 of a mile
1 hektoliter.. 2 5/8 bushels
1 hectare.. 2 1/2 acres
1 kilogram.. 2 1/5 pounds
1 stere, or cubic meter.............................. 1/4 of a cord
1 metric ton.. 2,200 pounds

TEMPERATURES

Fahrenheit

Milk.............................. Freezes 30° above Zero
Water.............................. Freezes 32° above Zero
Olive Oil.............................. Freezes 36° above Zero
Wine.............................. Freezes 20° above Zero
Vinegar.............................. Freezes 28° above Zero
Alcohol.............................. Boils at 173° above Zero
Water.............................. Boils at 212° above Zero
Petroleum.................. (average) Boils at 306° above Zero
Blood Heat.............................. 98.4° above Zero
Eggs Hatch.............................. 104° above Zero

CALENDARS — 1800 TO 2050

INDEX

1800 4	1828 ...10	1856 ...10	1884 ...10	1912 9	1940 9	1968 9	1996 9	2024 9
1801 5	1829 5	1857 5	1885 5	1913 4	1941 4	1969 4	1997 4	2025 4
1802 6	1830 6	1858 6	1886 6	1914 5	1942 5	1970 5	1998 5	2026 5
1803 7	1831 7	1859 7	1887 7	1915 6	1943 6	1971 6	1999 6	2027 6
1804 8	1832 8	1860 8	1888 8	1916 ...14	1944 ...14	1972 ...14	2000 ...14	2028 14
1805 3	1833 3	1861 3	1889 3	1917 2	1945 2	1973 2	2001 2	2029 2
1806 4	1834 4	1862 4	1890 4	1918 3	1946 3	1974 3	2002 3	2030 3
1807 5	1835 5	1863 5	1891 5	1919 4	1947 4	1975 4	2003 4	2031 4
1808 13	1836 ...13	1864 ...13	1892 ...13	1920 ...12	1948 ...12	1976 ...12	2004 ...12	2032 12
1809 1	1837 1	1865 1	1893 1	1921 7	1949 7	1977 7	2005 7	2033 7
1810 2	1838 2	1866 2	1894 2	1922 1	1950 1	1978 1	2006 1	2034 1
1811 3	1839 3	1867 3	1895 3	1923 2	1951 2	1979 2	2007 2	2035 2
1812 11	1840 ...11	1868 ...11	1896 ...11	1924 ...10	1952 ...10	1980 ...10	2008 ...10	2036 10
1813 6	1841 6	1869 6	1897 6	1925 5	1953 5	1981 5	2009 5	2037 5
1814 7	1842 7	1870 7	1898 7	1926 6	1954 6	1982 6	2010 6	2038 6
1815 1	1843 1	1871 1	1899 1	1927 7	1955 7	1983 7	2011 7	2039 7
1816 9	1844 9	1872 9	1900 2	1928 8	1956 8	1984 8	2012 8	2040 8
1817 4	1845 4	1873 4	1901 3	1929 3	1957 3	1985 3	2013 3	2041 3
1818 5	1846 5	1874 5	1902 4	1930 4	1958 4	1986 4	2014 4	2042 4
1819 6	1847 6	1875 6	1903 5	1931 5	1959 5	1987 5	2015 5	2043 5
1820 14	1848 ...14	1876 ...14	1904 ...13	1932 ...13	1960 ...13	1988 ...13	2016 ...13	2044 13
1821 2	1849 2	1877 2	1905 1	1933 1	1961 1	1989 1	2017 1	2045 1
1822 3	1850 3	1878 3	1906 2	1934 2	1962 2	1990 2	2018 2	2046 2
1823 4	1851 4	1879 4	1907 3	1935 3	1963 3	1991 3	2019 3	2047 3
1824 12	1852 ...12	1880 ...12	1908 ...11	1936 ...11	1964 ...11	1992 ...11	2020 ...11	2048 11
1825 7	1853 7	1881 7	1909 6	1937 6	1965 6	1993 6	2021 6	2049 6
1826 1	1854 1	1882 1	1910 7	1938 7	1966 7	1994 7	2022 7	2050 7
1827 2	1855 2	1883 2	1911 1	1939 1	1967 1	1995 1	2023 1	

DIRECTIONS FOR USE

Look for the year you want in the index at left. The number opposite each year is the number of the calendar to use for that year.

1

JANUARY							MAY							SEPTEMBER						
S	M	T	W	T	F	S	S	M	T	W	T	F	S	S	M	T	W	T	F	S
1	2	3	4	5	6	7		1	2	3	4	5	6						1	2
8	9	10	11	12	13	14	7	8	9	10	11	12	13	3	4	5	6	7	8	9
15	16	17	18	19	20	21	14	15	16	17	18	19	20	10	11	12	13	14	15	16
22	23	24	25	26	27	28	21	22	23	24	25	26	27	17	18	19	20	21	22	23
29	30	31					28	29	30	31				24	25	26	27	28	29	30
FEBRUARY							JUNE							OCTOBER						
S	M	T	W	T	F	S	S	M	T	W	T	F	S	S	M	T	W	T	F	S
			1	2	3	4					1	2	3	1	2	3	4	5	6	7
5	6	7	8	9	10	11	4	5	6	7	8	9	10	8	9	10	11	12	13	14
12	13	14	15	16	17	18	11	12	13	14	15	16	17	15	16	17	18	19	20	21
19	20	21	22	23	24	25	18	19	20	21	22	23	24	22	23	24	25	26	27	28
26	27	28					25	26	27	28	29	30		29	30	31				
MARCH							JULY							NOVEMBER						
S	M	T	W	T	F	S	S	M	T	W	T	F	S	S	M	T	W	T	F	S
			1	2	3	4							1				1	2	3	4
5	6	7	8	9	10	11	2	3	4	5	6	7	8	5	6	7	8	9	10	11
12	13	14	15	16	17	18	9	10	11	12	13	14	15	12	13	14	15	16	17	18
19	20	21	22	23	24	25	16	17	18	19	20	21	22	19	20	21	22	23	24	25
26	27	28	29	30	31		23	24	25	26	27	28	29	26	27	28	29	30		
							30	31												
APRIL							AUGUST							DECEMBER						
S	M	T	W	T	F	S	S	M	T	W	T	F	S	S	M	T	W	T	F	S
						1			1	2	3	4	5						1	2
2	3	4	5	6	7	8	6	7	8	9	10	11	12	3	4	5	6	7	8	9
9	10	11	12	13	14	15	13	14	15	16	17	18	19	10	11	12	13	14	15	16
16	17	18	19	20	21	22	20	21	22	23	24	25	26	17	18	19	20	21	22	23
23	24	25	26	27	28	29	27	28	29	30	31			24	25	26	27	28	29	30
30														31						

2

JANUARY							MAY							SEPTEMBER						
S	M	T	W	T	F	S	S	M	T	W	T	F	S	S	M	T	W	T	F	S
	1	2	3	4	5	6			1	2	3	4	5							1
7	8	9	10	11	12	13	6	7	8	9	10	11	12	2	3	4	5	6	7	8
14	15	16	17	18	19	20	13	14	15	16	17	18	19	9	10	11	12	13	14	15
21	22	23	24	25	26	27	20	21	22	23	24	25	26	16	17	18	19	20	21	22
28	29	30	31				27	28	29	30	31			23	24	25	26	27	28	29
														30						
FEBRUARY							JUNE							OCTOBER						
S	M	T	W	T	F	S	S	M	T	W	T	F	S	S	M	T	W	T	F	S
				1	2	3						1	2		1	2	3	4	5	6
4	5	6	7	8	9	10	3	4	5	6	7	8	9	7	8	9	10	11	12	13
11	12	13	14	15	16	17	10	11	12	13	14	15	16	14	15	16	17	18	19	20
18	19	20	21	22	23	24	17	18	19	20	21	22	23	21	22	23	24	25	26	27
25	26	27	28				24	25	26	27	28	29	30	28	29	30	31			
MARCH							JULY							NOVEMBER						
S	M	T	W	T	F	S	S	M	T	W	T	F	S	S	M	T	W	T	F	S
				1	2	3	1	2	3	4	5	6	7					1	2	3
4	5	6	7	8	9	10	8	9	10	11	12	13	14	4	5	6	7	8	9	10
11	12	13	14	15	16	17	15	16	17	18	19	20	21	11	12	13	14	15	16	17
18	19	20	21	22	23	24	22	23	24	25	26	27	28	18	19	20	21	22	23	24
25	26	27	28	29	30	31	29	30	31					25	26	27	28	29	30	
APRIL							AUGUST							DECEMBER						
S	M	T	W	T	F	S	S	M	T	W	T	F	S	S	M	T	W	T	F	S
1	2	3	4	5	6	7				1	2	3	4							1
8	9	10	11	12	13	14	5	6	7	8	9	10	11	2	3	4	5	6	7	8
15	16	17	18	19	20	21	12	13	14	15	16	17	18	9	10	11	12	13	14	15
22	23	24	25	26	27	28	19	20	21	22	23	24	25	16	17	18	19	20	21	22
29	30						26	27	28	29	30	31		23	24	25	26	27	28	29
														30	31					

3

JANUARY							MAY							SEPTEMBER						
S	M	T	W	T	F	S	S	M	T	W	T	F	S	S	M	T	W	T	F	S
		1	2	3	4	5				1	2	3	4	1	2	3	4	5	6	7
6	7	8	9	10	11	12	5	6	7	8	9	10	11	8	9	10	11	12	13	14
13	14	15	16	17	18	19	12	13	14	15	16	17	18	15	16	17	18	19	20	21
20	21	22	23	24	25	26	19	20	21	22	23	24	25	22	23	24	25	26	27	28
27	28	29	30	31			26	27	28	29	30	31		29	30					
FEBRUARY							JUNE							OCTOBER						
S	M	T	W	T	F	S	S	M	T	W	T	F	S	S	M	T	W	T	F	S
					1	2							1			1	2	3	4	5
3	4	5	6	7	8	9	2	3	4	5	6	7	8	6	7	8	9	10	11	12
10	11	12	13	14	15	16	9	10	11	12	13	14	15	13	14	15	16	17	18	19
17	18	19	20	21	22	23	16	17	18	19	20	21	22	20	21	22	23	24	25	26
24	25	26	27	28			23	24	25	26	27	28	29	27	28	29	30	31		
							30													
MARCH							JULY							NOVEMBER						
S	M	T	W	T	F	S	S	M	T	W	T	F	S	S	M	T	W	T	F	S
					1	2		1	2	3	4	5	6						1	2
3	4	5	6	7	8	9	7	8	9	10	11	12	13	3	4	5	6	7	8	9
10	11	12	13	14	15	16	14	15	16	17	18	19	20	10	11	12	13	14	15	16
17	18	19	20	21	22	23	21	22	23	24	25	26	27	17	18	19	20	21	22	23
24	25	26	27	28	29	30	28	29	30	31				24	25	26	27	28	29	30
31																				
APRIL							AUGUST							DECEMBER						
S	M	T	W	T	F	S	S	M	T	W	T	F	S	S	M	T	W	T	F	S
	1	2	3	4	5	6					1	2	3	1	2	3	4	5	6	7
7	8	9	10	11	12	13	4	5	6	7	8	9	10	8	9	10	11	12	13	14
14	15	16	17	18	19	20	11	12	13	14	15	16	17	15	16	17	18	19	20	21
21	22	23	24	25	26	27	18	19	20	21	22	23	24	22	23	24	25	26	27	28
28	29	30					25	26	27	28	29	30	31	29	30	31				

4

JANUARY							MAY							SEPTEMBER						
S	M	T	W	T	F	S	S	M	T	W	T	F	S	S	M	T	W	T	F	S
			1	2	3	4					1	2	3		1	2	3	4	5	6
5	6	7	8	9	10	11	4	5	6	7	8	9	10	7	8	9	10	11	12	13
12	13	14	15	16	17	18	11	12	13	14	15	16	17	14	15	16	17	18	19	20
19	20	21	22	23	24	25	18	19	20	21	22	23	24	21	22	23	24	25	26	27
26	27	28	29	30	31		25	26	27	28	29	30	31	28	29	30				
FEBRUARY							JUNE							OCTOBER						
S	M	T	W	T	F	S	S	M	T	W	T	F	S	S	M	T	W	T	F	S
						1	1	2	3	4	5	6	7				1	2	3	4
2	3	4	5	6	7	8	8	9	10	11	12	13	14	5	6	7	8	9	10	11
9	10	11	12	13	14	15	15	16	17	18	19	20	21	12	13	14	15	16	17	18
16	17	18	19	20	21	22	22	23	24	25	26	27	28	19	20	21	22	23	24	25
23	24	25	26	27	28		29	30						26	27	28	29	30	31	
MARCH							JULY							NOVEMBER						
S	M	T	W	T	F	S	S	M	T	W	T	F	S	S	M	T	W	T	F	S
						1			1	2	3	4	5							1
2	3	4	5	6	7	8	6	7	8	9	10	11	12	2	3	4	5	6	7	8
9	10	11	12	13	14	15	13	14	15	16	17	18	19	9	10	11	12	13	14	15
16	17	18	19	20	21	22	20	21	22	23	24	25	26	16	17	18	19	20	21	22
23	24	25	26	27	28	29	27	28	29	30	31			23	24	25	26	27	28	29
30	31													30						
APRIL							AUGUST							DECEMBER						
S	M	T	W	T	F	S	S	M	T	W	T	F	S	S	M	T	W	T	F	S
		1	2	3	4	5						1	2		1	2	3	4	5	6
6	7	8	9	10	11	12	3	4	5	6	7	8	9	7	8	9	10	11	12	13
13	14	15	16	17	18	19	10	11	12	13	14	15	16	14	15	16	17	18	19	20
20	21	22	23	24	25	26	17	18	19	20	21	22	23	21	22	23	24	25	26	27
27	28	29	30				24	25	26	27	28	29	30	28	29	30	31			
							31													

5

JANUARY							MAY							SEPTEMBER						
S	M	T	W	T	F	S	S	M	T	W	T	F	S	S	M	T	W	T	F	S
				1	2	3						1	2			1	2	3	4	5
4	5	6	7	8	9	10	3	4	5	6	7	8	9	6	7	8	9	10	11	12
11	12	13	14	15	16	17	10	11	12	13	14	15	16	13	14	15	16	17	18	19
18	19	20	21	22	23	24	17	18	19	20	21	22	23	20	21	22	23	24	25	26
25	26	27	28	29	30	31	24	25	26	27	28	29	30	27	28	29	30			
							31													
FEBRUARY							JUNE							OCTOBER						
S	M	T	W	T	F	S	S	M	T	W	T	F	S	S	M	T	W	T	F	S
1	2	3	4	5	6	7		1	2	3	4	5	6					1	2	3
8	9	10	11	12	13	14	7	8	9	10	11	12	13	4	5	6	7	8	9	10
15	16	17	18	19	20	21	14	15	16	17	18	19	20	11	12	13	14	15	16	17
22	23	24	25	26	27	28	21	22	23	24	25	26	27	18	19	20	21	22	23	24
							28	29	30					25	26	27	28	29	30	31
MARCH							JULY							NOVEMBER						
S	M	T	W	T	F	S	S	M	T	W	T	F	S	S	M	T	W	T	F	S
1	2	3	4	5	6	7				1	2	3	4	1	2	3	4	5	6	7
8	9	10	11	12	13	14	5	6	7	8	9	10	11	8	9	10	11	12	13	14
15	16	17	18	19	20	21	12	13	14	15	16	17	18	15	16	17	18	19	20	21
22	23	24	25	26	27	28	19	20	21	22	23	24	25	22	23	24	25	26	27	28
29	30	31					26	27	28	29	30	31		29	30					
APRIL							AUGUST							DECEMBER						
S	M	T	W	T	F	S	S	M	T	W	T	F	S	S	M	T	W	T	F	S
			1	2	3	4							1			1	2	3	4	5
5	6	7	8	9	10	11	2	3	4	5	6	7	8	6	7	8	9	10	11	12
12	13	14	15	16	17	18	9	10	11	12	13	14	15	13	14	15	16	17	18	19
19	20	21	22	23	24	25	16	17	18	19	20	21	22	20	21	22	23	24	25	26
26	27	28	29	30			23	24	25	26	27	28	29	27	28	29	30	31		
							30	31												

6

JANUARY							MAY							SEPTEMBER						
S	M	T	W	T	F	S	S	M	T	W	T	F	S	S	M	T	W	T	F	S
					1	2							1				1	2	3	4
3	4	5	6	7	8	9	2	3	4	5	6	7	8	5	6	7	8	9	10	11
10	11	12	13	14	15	16	9	10	11	12	13	14	15	12	13	14	15	16	17	18
17	18	19	20	21	22	23	16	17	18	19	20	21	22	19	20	21	22	23	24	25
24	25	26	27	28	29	30	23	24	25	26	27	28	29	26	27	28	29	30		
31							30	31												
FEBRUARY							JUNE							OCTOBER						
S	M	T	W	T	F	S	S	M	T	W	T	F	S	S	M	T	W	T	F	S
	1	2	3	4	5	6			1	2	3	4	5						1	2
7	8	9	10	11	12	13	6	7	8	9	10	11	12	3	4	5	6	7	8	9
14	15	16	17	18	19	20	13	14	15	16	17	18	19	10	11	12	13	14	15	16
21	22	23	24	25	26	27	20	21	22	23	24	25	26	17	18	19	20	21	22	23
28							27	28	29	30				24	25	26	27	28	29	30
														31						
MARCH							JULY							NOVEMBER						
S	M	T	W	T	F	S	S	M	T	W	T	F	S	S	M	T	W	T	F	S
	1	2	3	4	5	6					1	2	3		1	2	3	4	5	6
7	8	9	10	11	12	13	4	5	6	7	8	9	10	7	8	9	10	11	12	13
14	15	16	17	18	19	20	11	12	13	14	15	16	17	14	15	16	17	18	19	20
21	22	23	24	25	26	27	18	19	20	21	22	23	24	21	22	23	24	25	26	27
28	29	30	31				25	26	27	28	29	30	31	28	29	30				
APRIL							AUGUST							DECEMBER						
S	M	T	W	T	F	S	S	M	T	W	T	F	S	S	M	T	W	T	F	S
				1	2	3	1	2	3	4	5	6	7				1	2	3	4
4	5	6	7	8	9	10	8	9	10	11	12	13	14	5	6	7	8	9	10	11
11	12	13	14	15	16	17	15	16	17	18	19	20	21	12	13	14	15	16	17	18
18	19	20	21	22	23	24	22	23	24	25	26	27	28	19	20	21	22	23	24	25
25	26	27	28	29	30		29	30	31					26	27	28	29	30	31	